PETERSON'S®
GRADUATE PROGRAMS IN ENGINEERING & APPLIED SCIENCES

2016

About Peterson's®

Peterson's® is excited to be celebrating 50 years of trusted educational publishing. It's a milestone we're quite proud of, as we continue to provide the most accurate, dependable, high-quality education content in the field, providing you with everything you need to succeed. No matter where you are on your academic or professional path, you can rely on Peterson's publications and its online information at **www.petersons.com** for the most up-to-date education exploration data, expert test-prep tools, and the highest quality career success resources—everything you need to achieve your educational goals.

For more information, contact Peterson's, 3 Columbia Circle, Suite 205, Albany, NY 12203-5158; 800-338-3282 Ext. 54229; or find us online at **www.petersons.com.**

ISSN 1093-8443
ISBN: 978-0-7689-3968-2

Printed in the United States of America

10 9 8 7 6 5 4 3 2 1   18 17 16

Fiftieth Edition

By producing this book on recycled paper (10% post-consumer waste) 44 trees were saved.

CONTENTS

A Note from the Peterson's Editors

The six volumes of Peterson's *Graduate and Professional Programs*, the only annually updated reference work of its kind, provide wide-ranging information on the graduate and professional programs offered by accredited colleges and universities in the United States, U.S. territories, and Canada and by those institutions outside the United States that are accredited by U.S. accrediting bodies. More than 44,000 individual academic and professional programs at more than 2,300 institutions are listed. Peterson's *Graduate and Professional Programs* have been used for more than fifty years by prospective graduate and professional students, placement counselors, faculty advisers, and all others interested in postbaccalaureate education.

Graduate & Professional Programs: An Overview contains information on institutions as a whole, while the other books in the series are devoted to specific academic and professional fields:

- ***Graduate Programs in the Biological/Biomedical Sciences & Health-Related Medical Professions***

- ***Graduate Programs in Business, Education, Information Studies, Law & Social Work***

- ***Graduate Programs in Engineering & Applied Sciences***

- ***Graduate Programs in the Humanities, Arts & Social Sciences***

- ***Graduate Programs in the Physical Sciences, Mathematics, Agricultural Sciences, the Environment & Natural Resources***

The books may be used individually or as a set. For example, if you have chosen a field of study but do not know what institution you want to attend or if you have a college or university in mind but have not chosen an academic field of study, it is best to begin with the Overview guide.

Graduate & Professional Programs: An Overview presents several directories to help you identify programs of study that might interest you; you can then research those programs further in the other books in the series by using the Directory of Graduate and Professional Programs by Field, which lists 500 fields and gives the names of those institutions that offer graduate degree programs in each.

For geographical or financial reasons, you may be interested in attending a particular institution and will want to know what it has to offer. You should turn to the Directory of Institutions and Their Offerings, which lists the degree programs available at each institution. As in the Directory of Graduate and Professional Programs by Field, the level of degrees offered is also indicated.

All books in the series include advice on graduate education, including topics such as admissions tests, financial aid, and accreditation. **The Graduate Adviser** includes two essays and information about accreditation. The first essay, "The Admissions Process," discusses general admission requirements, admission tests, factors to consider when selecting a graduate school or program, when and how to apply, and how admission decisions are made. Special information for international students and tips for minority students are also included. The second essay, "Financial Support," is an overview of the broad range of support available at the graduate level. Fellowships, scholarships, and grants; assistantships and internships; federal and private loan programs, as well as Federal Work-Study; and the GI bill are detailed. This essay concludes with advice on applying for need-based financial aid. "Accreditation and Accrediting Agencies" gives information on accreditation and its purpose and lists institutional accrediting agencies first and then specialized accrediting agencies relevant to each volume's specific fields of study.

With information on more than 40,000 graduate programs in more than 500 disciplines, Peterson's *Graduate and Professional Programs* give you all the information you need about the programs that are of interest to you in three formats: **Profiles** (capsule summaries of basic information), **Displays** (information that an institution or program wants to emphasize), and **Close-Ups** (written by administrators, with more expansive information than the **Profiles**, emphasizing different aspects of the programs). By using these various formats of program information, coupled with **Appendixes** and **Indexes** covering directories and subject areas for all six books, you will find that these guides provide the most comprehensive, accurate, and up-to-date graduate study information available.

Peterson's publishes a full line of resources with information you need to guide you through the graduate admissions process. Peterson's publications can be found at college libraries and career centers and your local bookstore or library—or visit us on the Web at www.petersons.com.

Colleges and universities will be pleased to know that Peterson's helped you in your selection. Admissions staff members are more than happy to answer questions, address specific problems, and help in any way they can. The editors at Peterson's wish you great success in your graduate program search!

THE GRADUATE ADVISER

The Admissions Process

Generalizations about graduate admissions practices are not always helpful because each institution has its own set of guidelines and procedures. Nevertheless, some broad statements can be made about the admissions process that may help you plan your strategy.

Factors Involved in Selecting a Graduate School or Program

Selecting a graduate school and a specific program of study is a complex matter. Quality of the faculty; program and course offerings; the nature, size, and location of the institution; admission requirements; cost; and the availability of financial assistance are among the many factors that affect one's choice of institution. Other considerations are job placement and achievements of the program's graduates and the institution's resources, such as libraries, laboratories, and computer facilities. If you are to make the best possible choice, you need to learn as much as you can about the schools and programs you are considering before you apply.

The following steps may help you narrow your choices.

- Talk to alumni of the programs or institutions you are considering to get their impressions of how well they were prepared for work in their fields of study.
- Remember that graduate school requirements change, so be sure to get the most up-to-date information possible.
- Talk to department faculty members and the graduate adviser at your undergraduate institution. They often have information about programs of study at other institutions.
- Visit the websites of the graduate schools in which you are interested to request a graduate catalog. Contact the department chair in your chosen field of study for additional information about the department and the field.
- Visit as many campuses as possible. Call ahead for an appointment with the graduate adviser in your field of interest and be sure to check out the facilities and talk to students.

General Requirements

Graduate schools and departments have requirements that applicants for admission must meet. Typically, these requirements include undergraduate transcripts (which provide information about undergraduate grade point average and course work applied toward a major), admission test scores, and letters of recommendation. Most graduate programs also ask for an essay or personal statement that describes your personal reasons for seeking graduate study. In some fields, such as art and music, portfolios or auditions may be required in addition to other evidence of talent. Some institutions require that the applicant have an undergraduate degree in the same subject as the intended graduate major.

Most institutions evaluate each applicant on the basis of the applicant's total record, and the weight accorded any given factor varies widely from institution to institution and from program to program.

The Application Process

You should begin the application process at least one year before you expect to begin your graduate study. Find out the application deadline for each institution (many are provided in the **Profile** section of this guide). Go to the institution's website and find out if you can apply online. If not, request a paper application form. Fill out this form thoroughly and neatly. Assume that the school needs all the information it is requesting and that the admissions officer will be sensitive to the

neatness and overall quality of what you submit. Do not supply more information than the school requires.

The institution may ask at least one question that will require a three- or four-paragraph answer. Compose your response on the assumption that the admissions officer is interested in both what you think and how you express yourself. Keep your statement brief and to the point, but, at the same time, include all pertinent information about your past experiences and your educational goals. Individual statements vary greatly in style and content, which helps admissions officers differentiate among applicants. Many graduate departments give considerable weight to the statement in making their admissions decisions, so be sure to take the time to prepare a thoughtful and concise statement.

If recommendations are a part of the admissions requirements, carefully choose the individuals you ask to write them. It is generally best to ask current or former professors to write the recommendations, provided they are able to attest to your intellectual ability and motivation for doing the work required of a graduate student. It is advisable to provide stamped, preaddressed envelopes to people being asked to submit recommendations on your behalf.

Completed applications, including references, transcripts, and admission test scores, should be received at the institution by the specified date.

Be advised that institutions do not usually make admissions decisions until all materials have been received. Enclose a self-addressed postcard with your application, requesting confirmation of receipt. Allow at least ten days for the return of the postcard before making further inquiries.

If you plan to apply for financial support, it is imperative that you file your application early.

ADMISSION TESTS

The major testing program used in graduate admissions is the Graduate Record Examinations (GRE®) testing program, sponsored by the GRE Board and administered by Educational Testing Service, Princeton, New Jersey.

The Graduate Record Examinations testing program consists of a General Test and eight Subject Tests. The General Test measures critical thinking, verbal reasoning, quantitative reasoning, and analytical writing skills. It is offered as an Internet-based test (iBT) in the United States, Canada, and many other countries.

The GRE® revised General Test's questions were designed to reflect the kind of thinking that students need to do in graduate or business school and demonstrate that students are indeed ready for graduate-level work.

- **Verbal Reasoning**—Measures ability to analyze and evaluate written material and synthesize information obtained from it, analyze relationships among component parts of sentences, and recognize relationships among words and concepts.
- **Quantitative Reasoning**—Measures problem-solving ability, focusing on basic concepts of arithmetic, algebra, geometry, and data analysis.
- **Analytical Writing**—Measures critical thinking and analytical writing skills, specifically the ability to articulate and support complex ideas clearly and effectively.

The computer-delivered GRE® revised General Test is offered year-round at Prometric™ test centers and on specific dates at testing locations outside of the Prometric test center network. Appointments are scheduled on a first-come, first-served basis. The GRE® revised General Test is also offered as a paper-based test three times a year in areas where computer-based testing is not available.

You can take the computer-delivered GRE® revised General Test once every twenty-one days, up to five times within any continuous rolling twelve-month period (365 days)—even if you canceled your scores on a previously taken test. You may take the paper-delivered GRE® revised General Test as often as it is offered.

Three scores are reported on the revised General Test:

1. A **Verbal Reasoning score** is reported on a 130–170 score scale, in 1-point increments.
2. A **Quantitative Reasoning score** is reported on a 130–170 score scale, in 1-point increments.
3. An **Analytical Writing score** is reported on a 0–6 score level, in half-point increments.

The GRE® Subject Tests measure achievement and assume undergraduate majors or extensive background in the following eight disciplines:

- Biochemistry, Cell and Molecular Biology
- Biology
- Chemistry
- Computer Science
- Literature in English
- Mathematics
- Physics
- Psychology

The Subject Tests are available three times per year as paper-based administrations around the world. Testing time is approximately 2 hours and 50 minutes. You can obtain more information about the GRE® by visiting the ETS website at www.ets.org or consulting the *GRE® Information and Registration Bulletin*. The *Bulletin* can be obtained at many undergraduate colleges. You can also download it from the ETS website or obtain it by contacting Graduate Record Examinations, Educational Testing Service, P.O. Box 6000, Princeton, NJ 08541-6000; phone: 609-771-7670.

If you expect to apply for admission to a program that requires any of the GRE® tests, you should select a test date well in advance of the application deadline. Scores on the computer-based General Test are reported within ten to fifteen days; scores on the paper-based Subject Tests are reported within six weeks.

Another testing program, the Miller Analogies Test® (MAT®), is administered at more than 500 Controlled Testing Centers, licensed by Harcourt Assessment, Inc., in the United States, Canada, and other countries. The MAT® computer-based test is now available. Testing time is 60 minutes. The test consists of 120 partial analogies. You can obtain the *Candidate Information Booklet*, which contains a list of test centers and instructions for taking the test, from http://www.milleranalogies.com or by calling 800-328-5999 (toll-free).

Check the specific requirements of the programs to which you are applying.

How Admission Decisions Are Made

The program you apply to is directly involved in the admissions process. Although the final decision is usually made by the graduate dean (or an associate) or the faculty admissions committee, recommendations from faculty members in your intended field are important. At some institutions, an interview is incorporated into the decision process.

A Special Note for International Students

In addition to the steps already described, there are some special considerations for international students who intend to apply for graduate study in the United States. All graduate schools require an indication of competence in English. The purpose of the Test of English as a Foreign Language (TOEFL®) is to evaluate the English proficiency of people who are nonnative speakers of English and want to study at colleges and universities where English is the language of instruction. The TOEFL® is administered by Educational Testing Service (ETS) under the general direction of a policy board established by the College Board and the Graduate Record Examinations Board.

The TOEFL® iBT assesses the four basic language skills: listening, reading, writing, and speaking. It was administered for the first time in September 2005, and ETS continues to introduce the TOEFL® iBT in selected cities. The Internet-based test is administered at secure, official test centers. The testing time is approximately 4 hours. Because the TOEFL® iBT includes a speaking section, the Test of Spoken English (TSE) is no longer needed.

The TOEFL® is also offered in the paper-based format in areas of the world where Internet-based testing is not available. The paper-based TOEFL® consists of three sections—listening comprehension, structure and written expression, and reading comprehension. The testing time is approximately 3 hours. The Test of Written English (TWE®) is also given. The TWE® is a 30-minute essay that measures the examinee's ability to compose in English. Examinees receive a TWE® score separate from their TOEFL® score. The *Information Bulletin* contains information on local fees and registration procedures.

The TOEFL® paper-based test (TOEFL® PBT) began being phased out in mid-2012. For those who may have taken the TOEFL® PBT, scores remain valid for two years after the test date. The Test of Written English (TWE®) is also given. The TWE® is a 30-minute essay that measures the examinee's ability to compose in English. Examinees receive a TWE® score separate from their TOEFL® score. The Information Bulletin contains information on local fees and registration procedures.

Additional information and registration materials are available from TOEFL® Services, Educational Testing Service, P.O. Box 6151, Princeton, New Jersey 08541-6151. Phone: 609-771-7100. Website: www.toefl.org.

International students should apply especially early because of the number of steps required to complete the admissions process. Furthermore, many United States graduate schools have a limited number of spaces for international students, and many more students apply than the schools can accommodate.

International students may find financial assistance from institutions very limited. The U.S. government requires international applicants to submit a certification of support, which is a statement attesting to the applicant's financial resources. In addition, international students *must* have health insurance coverage.

Tips for Minority Students

Indicators of a university's values in terms of diversity are found both in its recruitment programs and its resources directed to student success. Important questions: Does the institution vigorously recruit minorities for its graduate programs? Is there funding available to help with the costs associated with visiting the school? Are minorities represented in the institution's brochures or website or on their faculty rolls? What campus-based resources or services (including assistance in locating housing or career counseling and placement) are available? Is funding available to members of underrepresented groups?

At the program level, it is particularly important for minority students to investigate the "climate" of a program under consideration. How many minority students are enrolled and how many have graduated? What opportunities are there to work with diverse faculty and mentors whose research interests match yours? How are conflicts resolved or concerns addressed? How interested are faculty in building strong and supportive relations with students? "Climate" concerns should be addressed by posing questions to various individuals, including faculty members, current students, and alumni.

Information is also available through various organizations, such as the Hispanic Association of Colleges & Universities (HACU), and publications such as *Diverse Issues in Higher Education* and *Hispanic Outlook* magazine. There are also books devoted to this topic, such as *The Multicultural Student's Guide to Colleges* by Robert Mitchell.

Financial Support

The range of financial support at the graduate level is very broad. The following descriptions will give you a general idea of what you might expect and what will be expected of you as a financial support recipient.

Fellowships, Scholarships, and Grants

These are usually outright awards of a few hundred to many thousands of dollars with no service to the institution required in return. Fellowships and scholarships are usually awarded on the basis of merit and are highly competitive. Grants are made on the basis of financial need or special talent in a field of study. Many fellowships, scholarships, and grants not only cover tuition, fees, and supplies but also include stipends for living expenses with allowances for dependents. However, the terms of each should be examined because some do not permit recipients to supplement their income with outside work. Fellowships, scholarships, and grants may vary in the number of years for which they are awarded.

In addition to the availability of these funds at the university or program level, many excellent fellowship programs are available at the national level and may be applied for before and during enrollment in a graduate program. A listing of many of these programs can be found at the Council of Graduate Schools' website: http://www. cgsnet.org. There is a wealth of information in the "Programs" and "Awards" sections.

Assistantships and Internships

Many graduate students receive financial support through assistantships, particularly involving teaching or research duties. It is important to recognize that such appointments should not be viewed simply as employment relationships but rather should constitute an integral and important part of a student's graduate education. As such, the appointments should be accompanied by strong faculty mentoring and increasingly responsible apprenticeship experiences. The specific nature of these appointments in a given program should be considered in selecting that graduate program.

TEACHING ASSISTANTSHIPS

These usually provide a salary and full or partial tuition remission and may also provide health benefits. Unlike fellowships, scholarships, and grants, which require no service to the institution, teaching assistantships require recipients to provide the institution with a specific amount of undergraduate teaching, ideally related to the student's field of study. Some teaching assistants are limited to grading papers, compiling bibliographies, taking notes, or monitoring laboratories. At some graduate schools, teaching assistants must carry lighter course loads than regular full-time students.

RESEARCH ASSISTANTSHIPS

These are very similar to teaching assistantships in the manner in which financial assistance is provided. The difference is that recipients are given basic research assignments in their disciplines rather than teaching responsibilities. The work required is normally related to the student's field of study; in most instances, the assistantship supports the student's thesis or dissertation research.

ADMINISTRATIVE INTERNSHIPS

These are similar to assistantships in application of financial assistance funds, but the student is given an assignment on a part-time basis, usually as a special assistant with one of the university's administrative offices. The assignment may not necessarily be directly related to the recipient's discipline.

RESIDENCE HALL AND COUNSELING ASSISTANTSHIPS

These assistantships are frequently assigned to graduate students in psychology, counseling, and social work, but they may be offered to students in other disciplines, especially if the student has worked in this capacity during his or her undergraduate years. Duties can vary from being available in a dean's office for a specific number of hours for consultation with undergraduates to living in campus residences and being responsible for both counseling and administrative tasks or advising student activity groups. Residence hall assistantships often include a room and board allowance and, in some cases, tuition assistance and stipends. Contact the Housing and Student Life Office for more information.

Health Insurance

The availability and affordability of health insurance is an important issue and one that should be considered in an applicant's choice of institution and program. While often included with assistantships and fellowships, this is not always the case and, even if provided, the benefits may be limited. It is important to note that the U.S. government requires international students to have health insurance.

The GI Bill

This provides financial assistance for students who are veterans of the United States armed forces. If you are a veteran, contact your local Veterans Administration office to determine your eligibility and to get full details about benefits. There are a number of programs that offer educational benefits to current military enlistees. Some states have tuition assistance programs for members of the National Guard. Contact the VA office at the college for more information.

Federal Work-Study Program (FWS)

Employment is another way some students finance their graduate studies. The federally funded Federal Work-Study Program provides eligible students with employment opportunities, usually in public and private nonprofit organizations. Federal funds pay up to 75 percent of the wages, with the remainder paid by the employing agency. FWS is available to graduate students who demonstrate financial need. Not all schools have these funds, and some only award them to undergraduates. Each school sets its application deadline and workstudy earnings limits. Wages vary and are related to the type of work done. You must file the Free Application for Federal Student Aid (FAFSA) to be eligible for this program.

Loans

Many graduate students borrow to finance their graduate programs when other sources of assistance (which do not have to be repaid) prove insufficient. You should always read and understand the terms of any loan program before submitting your application.

FEDERAL DIRECT LOANS

Federal Direct Stafford Loans. The Federal Direct Stafford Loan Program offers a variable-fixed interest rate loan to graduate students with the Department of Education acting as the lender. Students receive a new rate with each new loan, but that rate is fixed for the life of the loan. Beginning with loans made on or after July 1, 2013, the interest rate for loans made each July 1st to June 30th period are determined based on the last 10-year Treasury note auction prior to June 1st of that year, plus an added percentage. The interest rate can be no higher than 9.5%.

Beginning July 1, 2012, the Federal Direct Stafford Loan for graduate students is an unsubsidized loan. Under the unsubsidized program, the grad borrower pays the interest on the loan from the day proceeds are issued and is responsible for paying interest during all periods. If the borrower chooses not to pay the interest while in school, or during the grace periods, deferment, or forbearance, the interest accrues and will be capitalized.

Graduate students may borrow up to $20,500 per year through the Direct Stafford Loan Program, up to a cumulative maximum of $138,500, including undergraduate borrowing. No more than $65,000 of the $138,500 can be from subsidized loans that the grad borrower may have received for periods of enrollment that began before July 1, 2012, or for prior undergraduate borrowing. You may borrow up to the cost of attendance at the school in which you are enrolled or will attend, minus estimated financial assistance from other federal, state, and private sources, up to a maximum of $20,500. Grad borrowers who reach the aggregate loan limit over the course of their education cannot receive additional loans; however, if they repay some of their loans to bring the outstanding balance below the aggregate limit, they could be eligible to borrow again, up to that limit.

For Unsubsidized loans first disbursed on or after July 1, 2015, and before July 1, 2016, the interest rate is 5.84%. For those first disbursed on or after July 1, 2014, and before July 1, 2015, the interest rate was 6.21%.

A fee is deducted from the loan proceeds upon disbursement. Loans with a first disbursement on or after July 1, 2010 but before July 1, 2012, have a borrower origination fee of 1 percent. For loans disbursed after July 1, 2012, these fee deductions no longer apply. The Budget Control Act of 2011, signed into law on August 2, 2011, eliminated Direct Subsidized Loan eligibility for graduate and professional students for periods of enrollment beginning on or after July 1, 2012 and terminated the authority of the Department of Education to offer most repayment incentives to Direct Loan borrowers for loans disbursed on or after July 1, 2012.

Under the *subsidized* Federal Direct Stafford Loan Program, repayment begins six months after your last date of enrollment on at least a half-time basis. Under the *unsubsidized* program, repayment of interest begins within thirty days from disbursement of the loan proceeds, and repayment of the principal begins six months after your last enrollment on at least a half-time basis. Some borrowers may choose to defer interest payments while they are in school. The accrued interest is added to the loan balance when the borrower begins repayment. There are several repayment options.

Federal Perkins Loans. The Federal Perkins Loan is available to students demonstrating financial need and is administered directly by the school. Not all schools have these funds, and some may award them to undergraduates only. Eligibility is determined from the information you provide on the FAFSA. The school will notify you of your eligibility.

Eligible graduate students may borrow up to $8,000 per year, up to a maximum of $60,000, including undergraduate borrowing (even if your previous Perkins Loans have been repaid). The interest rate for Federal Perkins Loans is 5 percent, and no interest accrues while you remain in school at least half-time. Students who are attending less than half-time need to check with their school to determine the length of their grace period. There are no guarantee, loan, or disbursement fees. Repayment begins nine months after your last date of enrollment on at least a half-time basis and may extend over a maximum of ten years with no prepayment penalty.

Federal Direct Graduate PLUS Loans. Effective July 1, 2006, graduate and professional students are eligible for Graduate PLUS loans. This program allows students to borrow up to the cost of attendance, less any other aid received. These loans have a fixed interest rate, and interest begins to accrue at the time of disbursement. Beginning with loans made on or after July 1, 2013, the interest rate for loans made each July 1st to June 30th period are determined based on the last 10-year Treasury note auction prior to June 1st of that year. The interest rate can be no higher than 10.5%. The PLUS loans do involve a credit check; a PLUS borrower may obtain a loan with a cosigner if his or her credit is not good enough. Grad PLUS loans may be deferred while a student is in school and for the six months following a drop below half-time

enrollment. For more information, you should contact a representative in your college's financial aid office.

Deferring Your Federal Loan Repayments. If you borrowed under the Federal Direct Stafford Loan Program, Federal Direct PLUS Loan Program, or the Federal Perkins Loan Program for previous undergraduate or graduate study, your payments may be deferred when you return to graduate school, depending on when you borrowed and under which program.

There are other deferment options available if you are temporarily unable to repay your loan. Information about these deferments is provided at your entrance and exit interviews. If you believe you are eligible for a deferment of your loan payments, you must contact your lender or loan servicer to request a deferment. The deferment must be filed prior to the time your payment is due, and it must be re-filed when it expires if you remain eligible for deferment at that time.

SUPPLEMENTAL (PRIVATE) LOANS

Many lending institutions offer supplemental loan programs and other financing plans, such as the ones described here, to students seeking additional assistance in meeting their education expenses. Some loan programs target all types of graduate students; others are designed specifically for business, law, or medical students. In addition, you can use private loans not specifically designed for education to help finance your graduate degree.

If you are considering borrowing through a supplemental or private loan program, you should carefully consider the terms and be sure to read the fine print. Check with the program sponsor for the most current terms that will be applicable to the amounts you intend to borrow for graduate study. Most supplemental loan programs for graduate study offer unsubsidized, credit-based loans. In general, a credit-ready borrower is one who has a satisfactory credit history or no credit history at all. A creditworthy borrower generally must pass a credit test to be eligible to borrow or act as a cosigner for the loan funds.

Many supplemental loan programs have minimum and maximum annual loan limits. Some offer amounts equal to the cost of attendance minus any other aid you will receive for graduate study. If you are planning to borrow for several years of graduate study, consider whether there is a cumulative or aggregate limit on the amount you may borrow. Often this cumulative or aggregate limit will include any amounts you borrowed and have not repaid for undergraduate or previous graduate study.

The combination of the annual interest rate, loan fees, and the repayment terms you choose will determine how much you will repay over time. Compare these features in combination before you decide which loan program to use. Some loans offer interest rates that are adjusted monthly, quarterly, or annually. Some offer interest rates that are lower during the in-school, grace, and deferment periods and then increase when you begin repayment. Some programs include a loan origination fee, which is usually deducted from the principal amount you receive when the loan is disbursed and must be repaid along with the interest and other principal when you graduate, withdraw from school, or drop below half-time study. Sometimes the loan fees are reduced if you borrow with a qualified cosigner. Some programs allow you to defer interest and/or principal payments while you are enrolled in graduate school. Many programs allow you to capitalize your interest payments; the interest due on your loan is added to the outstanding balance of your loan, so you don't have to repay immediately, but this increases the amount you owe. Other programs allow you to pay the interest as you go, which reduces the amount you later have to repay. The private loan market is very competitive, and your financial aid office can help you evaluate these programs.

Applying for Need-Based Financial Aid

Schools that award federal and institutional financial assistance based on need will require you to complete the FAFSA and, in some cases, an institutional financial aid application.

If you are applying for federal student assistance, you **must** complete the FAFSA. A service of the U.S. Department of Education, the FAFSA is free to all applicants. Most applicants apply online at www.fafsa.ed.gov. Paper applications are available at the financial aid office of your local college.

After your FAFSA information has been processed, you will receive a Student Aid Report (SAR). If you provided an e-mail address on the FAFSA, this will be sent to you electronically; otherwise, it will be mailed to your home address.

Follow the instructions on the SAR if you need to correct information reported on your original application. If your situation changes after you file your FAFSA, contact your financial aid officer to discuss amending your information. You can also appeal your financial aid award if you have extenuating circumstances.

If you would like more information on federal student financial aid, visit the FAFSA website or download the most recent version of *Funding Education Beyond High School: The Guide to Federal Student Aid* at http://studentaid.ed.gov/students/publications/student_guide/index.html. This guide is also available in Spanish.

The U.S. Department of Education also has a toll-free number for questions concerning federal student aid programs. The number is 1-800-4-FED AID (1-800-433-3243). If you are hearing impaired, call toll-free, 1-800-730-8913.

Summary

Remember that these are generalized statements about financial assistance at the graduate level. Because each institution allots its aid differently, you should communicate directly with the school and the specific department of interest to you. It is not unusual, for example, to find that an endowment vested within a specific department supports one or more fellowships. You may fit its requirements and specifications precisely.

Accreditation and Accrediting Agencies

Colleges and universities in the United States, and their individual academic and professional programs, are accredited by nongovernmental agencies concerned with monitoring the quality of education in this country. Agencies with both regional and national jurisdictions grant accreditation to institutions as a whole, while specialized bodies acting on a nationwide basis—often national professional associations—grant accreditation to departments and programs in specific fields.

Institutional and specialized accrediting agencies share the same basic concerns: the purpose an academic unit—whether university or program—has set for itself and how well it fulfills that purpose, the adequacy of its financial and other resources, the quality of its academic offerings, and the level of services it provides. Agencies that grant institutional accreditation take a broader view, of course, and examine university-wide or college-wide services with which a specialized agency may not concern itself.

Both types of agencies follow the same general procedures when considering an application for accreditation. The academic unit prepares a self-evaluation, focusing on the concerns mentioned above and usually including an assessment of both its strengths and weaknesses; a team of representatives of the accrediting body reviews this evaluation, visits the campus, and makes its own report; and finally, the accrediting body makes a decision on the application. Often, even when accreditation is granted, the agency makes a recommendation regarding how the institution or program can improve. All institutions and programs are also reviewed every few years to determine whether they continue to meet established standards; if they do not, they may lose their accreditation.

Accrediting agencies themselves are reviewed and evaluated periodically by the U.S. Department of Education and the Council for Higher Education Accreditation (CHEA). Recognized agencies adhere to certain standards and practices, and their authority in matters of accreditation is widely accepted in the educational community.

This does not mean, however, that accreditation is a simple matter, either for schools wishing to become accredited or for students deciding where to apply. Indeed, in certain fields the very meaning and methods of accreditation are the subject of a good deal of debate. For their part, those applying to graduate school should be aware of the safeguards provided by regional accreditation, especially in terms of degree acceptance and institutional longevity. Beyond this, applicants should understand the role that specialized accreditation plays in their field, as this varies considerably from one discipline to another. In certain professional fields, it is necessary to have graduated from a program that is accredited in order to be eligible for a license to practice, and in some fields the federal government also makes this a hiring requirement. In other disciplines, however, accreditation is not as essential, and there can be excellent programs that are not accredited. In fact, some programs choose not to seek accreditation, although most do.

Institutions and programs that present themselves for accreditation are sometimes granted the status of candidate for accreditation, or what is known as "preaccreditation." This may happen, for example, when an academic unit is too new to have met all the requirements for accreditation. Such status signifies initial recognition and indicates that the school or program in question is working to fulfill all requirements; it does not, however, guarantee that accreditation will be granted.

Institutional Accrediting Agencies—Regional

MIDDLE STATES ASSOCIATION OF COLLEGES AND SCHOOLS
Accredits institutions in Delaware, District of Columbia, Maryland, New Jersey, New York, Pennsylvania, Puerto Rico, and the Virgin Islands.
Dr. Elizabeth Sibolski, President
Middle States Commission on Higher Education
3624 Market Street, Second Floor West
Philadelphia, Pennsylvania 19104
Phone: 267-284-5000
Fax: 215-662-5501
E-mail: info@msche.org
Website: www.msche.org

NEW ENGLAND ASSOCIATION OF SCHOOLS AND COLLEGES
Accredits institutions in Connecticut, Maine, Massachusetts, New Hampshire, Rhode Island, and Vermont.
Dr. Barbara E. Brittingham, President/Director
Commission on Institutions of Higher Education
3 Burlington Woods Drive, Suite 100
Burlington, Massachusetts 01803-4531
Phone: 855-886-3272 or 781-425-7714
Fax: 781-425-1001
E-mail: cihe@neasc.org
Website: http://cihe.neasc.org

THE HIGHER LEARNING COMMISSION
Accredits institutions in Arizona, Arkansas, Colorado, Illinois, Indiana, Iowa, Kansas, Michigan, Minnesota, Missouri, Nebraska, New Mexico, North Dakota, Ohio, Oklahoma, South Dakota, West Virginia, Wisconsin, and Wyoming.
Dr. Barbara Gellman-Danley, President
The Higher Learning Commission
230 South LaSalle Street, Suite 7-500
Chicago, Illinois 60604-1413
Phone: 800-621-7440 or 312-263-0456
Fax: 312-263-7462
E-mail: info@hlcommission.org
Website: www.hlcommission.org

NORTHWEST COMMISSION ON COLLEGES AND UNIVERSITIES
Accredits institutions in Alaska, Idaho, Montana, Nevada, Oregon, Utah, and Washington.
Dr. Sandra E. Elman, President
8060 165th Avenue, NE, Suite 100
Redmond, Washington 98052
Phone: 425-558-4224
Fax: 425-376-0596
E-mail: selman@nwccu.org
Website: www.nwccu.org

SOUTHERN ASSOCIATION OF COLLEGES AND SCHOOLS
Accredits institutions in Alabama, Florida, Georgia, Kentucky, Louisiana, Mississippi, North Carolina, South Carolina, Tennessee, Texas, and Virginia.
Dr. Belle S. Wheelan, President
Commission on Colleges
1866 Southern Lane
Decatur, Georgia 30033-4097
Phone: 404-679-4500 Ext. 4504
Fax: 404-679-4558
E-mail: questions@sacscoc.org
Website: www.sacscoc.org

WESTERN ASSOCIATION OF SCHOOLS AND COLLEGES
Accredits institutions in California, Guam, and Hawaii.
Dr. Mary Ellen Petrisko, President
Accrediting Commission for Senior Colleges and Universities
985 Atlantic Avenue, Suite 100
Alameda, California 94501
Phone: 510-748-9001
Fax: 510-748-9797
E-mail: wasc@wascsenior.org
Website: http://www.wascsenior.org/

Institutional Accrediting Agencies—Other

ACCREDITING COUNCIL FOR INDEPENDENT COLLEGES AND SCHOOLS
Albert C. Gray, Ph.D., Executive Director and CEO
750 First Street, NE, Suite 980
Washington, DC 20002-4241
Phone: 202-336-6780
Fax: 202-842-2593
E-mail: info@acics.org
Website: www.acics.org

DISTANCE EDUCATION AND ACCREDITING COMMISSION (DEAC)
Accrediting Commission
Leah Matthews, Executive Director
1101 17th Street, NW, Suite 808
Washington, DC 20036-4704
Phone: 202-234-5100
Fax: 202-332-1386
E-mail: info@deac.org
Website: www.deac.org

Specialized Accrediting Agencies

ACUPUNCTURE AND ORIENTAL MEDICINE
Mark S. McKenzie, LAc MsOM DiplOM, Executive Director
Accreditation Commission for Acupuncture and Oriental Medicine
8941 Aztec Drive
Eden Prairie, Minnesota 55347
Phone: 952-212-2434
Fax: 301-313-0912
E-mail: coordinator@acaom.org
Website: www.acaom.org

ART AND DESIGN
Karen P. Moynahan, Executive Director
National Association of Schools of Art and Design (NASAD)
Commission on Accreditation
11250 Roger Bacon Drive, Suite 21
Reston, Virginia 20190-5248
Phone: 703-437-0700
Fax: 703-437-6312
E-mail: info@arts-accredit.org
Website: http://nasad.arts-accredit.org

ATHLETIC TRAINING EDUCATION
Micki Cuppett, Executive Director
Commission on Accreditation of Athletic Training Education (CAATE)
6850 Austin Center Blvd., Suite 100
Austin, Texas 78731-3184
Phone: 512-733-9700
E-mail: micki@caate.net
Website: www.caate.net

AUDIOLOGY EDUCATION
Doris Gordon, Executive Director
Accreditation Commission for Audiology Education (ACAE)
1718 M Street, NW #297
Washington, DC 20036
Phone: 202-986-9550
Fax: 202-986-9500
E-mail: info@acaeaccred.org
Website: www.acaeaccred.org

AVIATION
Gary J. Northam, Executive Director
Aviation Accreditation Board International (AABI)
3410 Skyway Drive
Auburn, Alabama 36830
Phone: 334-844-2431
Fax: 334-844-2432
E-mail: bayenva@auburn.edu
Website: www.aabi.aero

BUSINESS
Robert D. Reid, Executive Vice President and Chief Accreditation Officer
AACSB International—The Association to Advance Collegiate Schools of Business
777 South Harbour Island Boulevard, Suite 750
Tampa, Florida 33602
Phone: 813-769-6500
Fax: 813-769-6559
E-mail: bob@aacsb.edu
Website: www.aacsb.edu

BUSINESS EDUCATION
Dennis N. Gash, President and Chief Accreditation Officer
International Assembly for Collegiate Business Education (IACBE)
11257 Strang Line Road
Lenexa, KS 66215
Phone: 913-631-3009
Fax: 913-631-9154
E-mail:iacbe@iacbe.org
Website: www.iacbe.org

CHIROPRACTIC
Craig S. Little, President
Council on Chiropractic Education (CCE)
Commission on Accreditation
8049 North 85th Way
Scottsdale, Arizona 85258-4321
Phone: 480-443-8877 or 888-443-3506
Fax: 480-483-7333
E-mail: cce@cce-usa.org
Website: www.cce-usa.org

CLINICAL LABORATORY SCIENCES
Dianne M. Cearlock, Ph.D., Chief Executive Officer
National Accrediting Agency for Clinical Laboratory Sciences
5600 North River Road, Suite 720
Rosemont, Illinois 60018-5119
Phone: 773-714-8880 or 847-939-3597
Fax: 773-714-8886
E-mail: info@naacls.org
Website: www.naacls.org

CLINICAL PASTORAL EDUCATION
Trace Haythorn, Executive Director
Association for Clinical Pastoral Education, Inc.
1549 Clairmont Road, Suite 103
Decatur, Georgia 30033-4611
Phone: 404-320-1472
Fax: 404-320-0849
E-mail: acpe@acpe.edu
Website: www.acpe.edu

DANCE
Karen P. Moynahan, Executive Director
National Association of Schools of Dance (NASD)
Commission on Accreditation
11250 Roger Bacon Drive, Suite 21
Reston, Virginia 20190-5248
Phone: 703-437-0700
Fax: 703-437-6312
E-mail: info@arts-accredit.org
Website: http://nasd.arts-accredit.org

DENTISTRY
Dr. Sherin Tooks, Director
Commission on Dental Accreditation
American Dental Association
211 East Chicago Avenue, Suite 1900
Chicago, Illinois 60611
Phone: 312-440-4643 or 800-621-8099
E-mail: accreditation@ada.org
Website: www.ada.org

DIETETICS AND NUTRITION
Mary B. Gregoire, Ph.D., Executive Director; RD, FADA, FAND
Academy of Nutrition and Dietetics
Accreditation Council for Education in Nutrition and Dietetics (ACEND)
120 South Riverside Plaza, Suite 2000
Chicago, Illinois 60606-6995
Phone: 800-877-1600 Ext. 5400 or 312-899-0040
Fax: 312-899-4817
E-mail: acend@eatright.org
Website: www.eatright.org/ACEND

EDUCATION PREPARATION
Christopher Koch, Interim President
Council for the Accreditation of Education Preparation (CAEP)
1140 19th Street NW, Suite 400
Washington, DC 20036
Phone: 202-223-0077
E-mail: christopher.koch@caepnet.org
Website: www.caepnet.org

ENGINEERING
Michael Milligan, Ph.D., PE, Executive Director
Accreditation Board for Engineering and Technology, Inc. (ABET)
415 North Charles Street
Baltimore, Maryland 21201
Phone: 410-347-7700
E-mail: accreditation@abet.org
Website: www.abet.org

FORENSIC SCIENCES
Nancy J. Jackson, Director of Development and Accreditation
American Academy of Forensic Sciences (AAFS)
Forensic Science Education Program Accreditation Commission (FEPAC)
410 North 21st Street
Colorado Springs, Colorado 80904
Phone: 719-636-1100
Fax: 719-636-1993
E-mail: njackson@aafs.org
Website: www.fepac-edu.org

FORESTRY
Carol L. Redelsheimer
Director of Science and Education
Society of American Foresters
5400 Grosvenor Lane
Bethesda, Maryland 20814-2198
Phone: 301-897-8720 or 866-897-8720
Fax: 301-897-3690
E-mail: redelsheimerc@safnet.org
Website: www.safnet.org

HEALTHCARE MANAGEMENT
Commission on Accreditation of Healthcare Management Education (CAHME)
Margaret Schulte, President and CEO
1700 Rockville Pike
Suite 400
Rockville, Maryland 20852
Phone: 301-998-6101
E-mail: info@cahme.org
Website: www.cahme.org

HEALTH INFORMATICS AND HEALTH MANAGEMENT
Claire Dixon-Lee, Executive Director
Commission on Accreditation for Health Informatics and Information Management Education (CAHIIM)
233 North Michigan Avenue, 21st Floor
Chicago, Illinois 60601-5800
Phone: 312-233-1100
Fax: 312-233-1948
E-mail:E-mail: claire.dixon-lee@cahiim.org
Website: www.cahiim.org

HUMAN SERVICE EDUCATION
Dr. Elaine Green, President
Council for Standards in Human Service Education (CSHSE)
3337 Duke Street
Alexandria, VA 22314
Phone: 571-257-3959
E-mail: info@cshse.org
Web: http://www.cshse.org

INTERIOR DESIGN
Holly Mattson, Executive Director
Council for Interior Design Accreditation
206 Grandview Avenue, Suite 350
Grand Rapids, Michigan 49503-4014
Phone: 616-458-0400
Fax: 616-458-0460
E-mail: info@accredit-id.org
Website: www.accredit-id.org

JOURNALISM AND MASS COMMUNICATIONS
Susanne Shaw, Executive Director
Accrediting Council on Education in Journalism and Mass Communications (ACEJMC)
School of Journalism
Stauffer-Flint Hall
University of Kansas
1435 Jayhawk Boulevard
Lawrence, Kansas 66045-7575
Phone: 785-864-3973
Fax: 785-864-5225
E-mail: sshaw@ku.edu
Website: http://www2.ku.edu/~acejmc/

LANDSCAPE ARCHITECTURE
Ronald C. Leighton, Executive Director
Landscape Architectural Accreditation Board (LAAB)
American Society of Landscape Architects (ASLA)
636 Eye Street, NW
Washington, DC 20001-3736
Phone: 202-898-2444 or 888-999-2752
Fax: 202-898-1185
E-mail: info@asla.org
Website: www.asla.org

LAW
Barry Currier, Managing Director of Accreditation & Legal Education
American Bar Association
321 North Clark Street, 21st Floor
Chicago, Illinois 60654
Phone: 312-988-6738
Fax: 312-988-5681
E-mail: legaled@americanbar.org
Website: http://www.americanbar.org/groups/legal_education/resources/accreditation.html

LIBRARY
Karen O'Brien, Director
Office for Accreditation
American Library Association
50 East Huron Street
Chicago, Illinois 60611-2795
Phone: 312-280-2432
Fax: 312-280-2433
E-mail: accred@ala.org
Website: www.ala.org/accreditation/

MARRIAGE AND FAMILY THERAPY
Tanya A. Tamarkin, Director of Educational Affairs
Commission on Accreditation for Marriage and Family Therapy
     Education (COAMFTE)
American Association for Marriage and Family Therapy
112 South Alfred Street
Alexandria, Virginia 22314-3061
Phone: 703-838-9808
Fax: 703-838-9805
E-mail: coa@aamft.org
Website: www.aamft.org

MEDICAL ILLUSTRATION
Kathleen Megivern, Executive Director
Commission on Accreditation of Allied Health Education Programs
     (CAAHEP)
1361 Park Street
Clearwater, Florida 33756
Phone: 727-210-2350
Fax: 727-210-2354
E-mail: mail@caahep.org
Website: www.caahep.org

MEDICINE
Liaison Committee on Medical Education (LCME)
Robert B. Hash, M.D., LCME Secretary
American Medical Association
Council on Medical Education
330 North Wabash Avenue, Suite 39300
Chicago, Illinois 60611-5885
Phone: 312-464-4933
E-mail: lcme@aamc.org
Website: www.ama-assn.org

Liaison Committee on Medical Education (LCME)
Heather Lent, M.A., Director
Accreditation Services
Association of American Medical Colleges
655 K Street, NW
Washington, DC 20001-2399
Phone: 202-828-0596
E-mail: lcme@aamc.org
Website: www.lcme.org

MUSIC
Karen P. Moynahan, Executive Director
National Association of Schools of Music (NASM)
Commission on Accreditation
11250 Roger Bacon Drive, Suite 21
Reston, Virginia 20190-5248
Phone: 703-437-0700
Fax: 703-437-6312
E-mail: info@arts-accredit.org
Website: http://nasm.arts-accredit.org/

NATUROPATHIC MEDICINE
Daniel Seitz, J.D., Ed.D., Executive Director
Council on Naturopathic Medical Education
P.O. Box 178
Great Barrington, Massachusetts 01230
Phone: 413-528-8877
E-mail: www.cnme.org/contact.html
Website: www.cnme.org

NURSE ANESTHESIA
Francis R.Gerbasi, Ph.D., CRNA, COA Executive Director
Council on Accreditation of Nurse Anesthesia Educational Programs
     (CoA-NAEP)
American Association of Nurse Anesthetists
222 South Prospect Avenue, Suite 304
Park Ridge, Illinois 60068-4001
Phone: 847-692-7050, Ext. 1154
Fax: 847-692-7137

E-mail: accreditation@coa.us.com
Website: http://home.coa.us.com

NURSE EDUCATION
Jennifer L. Butlin, Executive Director
Commission on Collegiate Nursing Education (CCNE)
One Dupont Circle, NW, Suite 530
Washington, DC 20036-1120
Phone: 202-887-6791
Fax: 202-887-8476
E-mail: jbutlin@aacn.nche.edu
Website: www.aacn.nche.edu/accreditation

NURSE MIDWIFERY
Heather L. Maurer, M.A., Executive Director
Accreditation Commission for Midwifery Education (ACME)
American College of Nurse-Midwives
8403 Colesville Road, Suite 1550
Silver Spring, Maryland 20910
Phone: 240-485-1800
Fax: 240-485-1818
E-mail: info@acnm.org
Website: www.midwife.org/Program-Accreditation

NURSE PRACTITIONER
Gay Johnson, CEO
National Association of Nurse Practitioners in Women's Health
Council on Accreditation
505 C Street, NE
Washington, DC 20002
Phone: 202-543-9693 Ext. 1
Fax: 202-543-9858
E-mail: info@npwh.org
Website: www.npwh.org

NURSING
Marsal P. Stoll, Chief Executive Director
Accreditation Commission for Education in Nursing (ACEN)
3343 Peachtree Road, NE, Suite 850
Atlanta, Georgia 30326
Phone: 404-975-5000
Fax: 404-975-5020
E-mail: info@acenursing.org
Website: www.acenursing.org

OCCUPATIONAL THERAPY
Heather Stagliano, DHSc, OTR/L, Director of Accreditation
The American Occupational Therapy Association, Inc.
4720 Montgomery Lane, Suite 200
Bethesda, Maryland 20814-3449
Phone: 301-652-6611 Ext. 2914
TDD: 800-377-8555
Fax: 240-762-5150
E-mail: accred@aota.org
Website: www.aoteonline.org

OPTOMETRY
Joyce L. Urbeck, Administrative Director
Accreditation Council on Optometric Education (ACOE)
American Optometric Association
243 North Lindbergh Boulevard
St. Louis, Missouri 63141-7881
Phone: 314-991-4100, Ext. 4246
Fax: 314-991-4101
E-mail: accredit@aoa.org
Website: www.theacoe.org

OSTEOPATHIC MEDICINE
Konrad C. Miskowicz-Retz, Ph.D., CAE
Director, Department of Accreditation
Commission on Osteopathic College Accreditation (COCA)
American Osteopathic Association
142 East Ontario Street

Chicago, Illinois 60611
Phone: 312-202-8097
Fax: 312-202-8397
E-mail: predoc@osteopathic.org
Website: www.osteopathic.org

PHARMACY
Peter H. Vlasses, PharmD, Executive Director
Accreditation Council for Pharmacy Education
135 South LaSalle Street, Suite 4100
Chicago, Illinois 60603-4810
Phone: 312-664-3575
Fax: 312-664-4652
E-mail: csinfo@acpe-accredit.org
Website: www.acpe-accredit.org

PHYSICAL THERAPY
Sandra Wise, Senior Director
Commission on Accreditation in Physical Therapy Education (CAPTE)
American Physical Therapy Association (APTA)
1111 North Fairfax Street
Alexandria, Virginia 22314-1488
Phone: 703-706-3240
Fax: 703-706-3387
E-mail: accreditation@apta.org
Website: www.capteonline.org

PHYSICIAN ASSISTANT STUDIES
John E. McCarty, Executive Director
Accredittion Review Commission on Education for the Physician Assistant, Inc. (ARC-PA)
12000 Findley Road, Suite 150
Johns Creek, Georgia 30097
Phone: 770-476-1224
Fax: 770-476-1738
E-mail: arc-pa@arc-pa.org
Website: www.arc-pa.org

PLANNING
Ms. Shonagh Merits, Executive Director
American Institute of Certified Planners/Association of Collegiate Schools of Planning/American Planning Association
Planning Accreditation Board (PAB)
2334 West Lawrence Avenue, Suite 209
Chicago, Illinois 60625
Phone: 773-334-7200
E-mail: smerits@planningaccreditationboard.org
Website: www.planningaccreditationboard.org

PODIATRIC MEDICINE
Alan R. Tinkleman, M.P.A., Executive Director
Council on Podiatric Medical Education (CPME)
American Podiatric Medical Association (APMA)
9312 Old Georgetown Road
Bethesda, Maryland 20814-1621
Phone: 301-581-9200
Fax: 301-571-4903
Website: www.cpme.org

PSYCHOLOGY AND COUNSELING
Jacqueline Remondet Wall, Director, Office of Program Consultation and Accreditation and Associate Executive Director
Education Directorate
American Psychological Association
750 First Street, NE
Washington, DC 20002-4202
Phone: 202-336-5979 or 800-374-2721
TDD/TTY: 202-336-6123
Fax: 202-336-5978
E-mail: apaaccred@apa.org
Website: www.apa.org/ed/accreditation

Carol L. Bobby, Ph.D., Executive Director
Council for Accreditation of Counseling and Related Educational Programs (CACREP)
1001 North Fairfax Street, Suite 510
Alexandria, Virginia 22314
Phone: 703-535-5990
Fax: 703-739-6209
E-mail: cacrep@cacrep.org
Website: www.cacrep.org
Richard M. McFall, Executive Director
Psychological Clinical Science Accreditation System (PCSAS)
1101 East Tenth Street
IU Psychology Building
Bloomington, Indiana 47405-7007
Phone: 812-856-2570
Fax: 812-322-5545
E-mail: rmmcfall@pcsas.org
Website: www.pcsas.org

PUBLIC HEALTH
Laura Rasar King, M.P.H., MCHES, Executive Director
Council on Education for Public Health
1010 Wayne Avenue, Suite 220
Silver Spring, Maryland 20910
Phone: 202-789-1050
Fax: 202-789-1895
E-mail: Lking@ceph.org
Website: www.ceph.org

PUBLIC POLICY, AFFAIRS AND ADMINISTRATION
Crystal Calarusse, Chief Accreditation Officer
Commission on Peer Review and Accreditation
Network of Schools of Public Policy, Affairs, and Administration (NASPAA-COPRA)
1029 Vermont Avenue, NW, Suite 1100
Washington, DC 20005
Phone: 202-628-8965
Fax: 202-626-4978
E-mail: copra@naspaa.org
Website: www.naspaa.org

REHABILITATION EDUCATION
Frank Lane, Ph.D., Executive Director
Council on Rehabilitation Education (CORE)
Commission on Standards and Accreditation
1699 Woodfield Road, Suite 300
Schaumburg, Illinois 60173
Phone: 847-944-1345
Fax: 847-944-1346
E-mail: flane@core-rehab.org
Website: www.core-rehab.org

RESPIRATORY CARE
Thomas Smalling, Executive Director
Commission on Accreditation for Respiratory Care (CoARC)
1248 Harwood Road
Bedford, TX 76021-4244
Phone: 817-283-2835
Fax: 817-354-8519
E-mail: tom@coarc.com
Website: www.coarc.com

SOCIAL WORK
Jo Ann Regan, Ph.D., Director
Office of Social Work Accreditation
Council on Social Work Education
1701 Duke Street, Suite 200
Alexandria, Virginia 22314
Phone: 703-683-8080
Fax: 703-683-8099
E-mail: info@cswe.org
Website: www.cswe.org

SPEECH-LANGUAGE PATHOLOGY AND AUDIOLOGY
Patrima L. Tice, Director of Accreditation
American Speech-Language-Hearing Association
Council on Academic Accreditation in Audiology and Speech-Language
     Pathology
2200 Research Boulevard
Rockville, Maryland 20850-3289
Phone: 301-296-5796
Fax: 301-296-8750
E-mail: ptice@asha.org
Website: www.asha.org/academic/accreditation/default.htm

TEACHER EDUCATION
Mark LaCelle-Peterson, President
Council for the Accreditation of Educator Preparation
1140 19th Street, NW, Suite 400
Washington, DC 20036
Phone: 202-223-0077
E-mail: caep@caepnet.org
Website: www.teac.org

TECHNOLOGY
Michale S. McComis, Ed.D., Executive Director
Accrediting Commission of Career Schools and Colleges
2101 Wilson Boulevard, Suite 302
Arlington, Virginia 22201
Phone: 703-247-4212
Fax: 703-247-4533
E-mail: mccomis@accsc.org
Website: www.accsc.org

TECHNOLOGY, MANAGEMENT, AND APPLIED ENGINEERING
Michele Anderson, Director of Accreditation
The Association of Technology, Management, and Applied Engineering
(ATMAE)
275 N. York Street, Suite 401
Elmhurst, Illinois 60126
Phone: 630-433-4514
Fax: 630-563-9181
E-mail: Michele@atmae.org
Website: www.atmae.org

THEATER
Karen P. Moynahan, Executive Director
National Association of Schools of Theatre Commission on
     Accreditation
11250 Roger Bacon Drive, Suite 21
Reston, Virginia 20190
Phone: 703-437-0700
Fax: 703-437-6312
E-mail: info@arts-accredit.org
Website: http://nast.arts-accredit.org/

THEOLOGY
Keith Sharfman, Director
Association of Advanced Rabbinical and Talmudic Schools (AARTS)
Accreditation Commission
11 Broadway, Suite 405
New York, New York 10004
Phone: 212-363-1991
Fax: 212-533-5335
E-mail: k.sharfman.aarts@gmail.com

Daniel O. Aleshire, Executive Director
Association of Theological Schools in the United States and Canada
     (ATS)
Commission on Accrediting
10 Summit Park Drive
Pittsburgh, Pennsylvania 15275
Phone: 412-788-6505
Fax: 412-788-6510
E-mail: ats@ats.edu
Website: www.ats.edu

Paul Boatner, President
Transnational Association of Christian Colleges and Schools (TRACS)
Accreditation Commission
15935 Forest Road
Forest, Virginia 24551
Phone: 434-525-9539
Fax: 434-525-9538
E-mail: info@tracs.org
Website: www.tracs.org

VETERINARY MEDICINE
Dr. Karen Brandt, Director of Education and Research
American Veterinary Medical Association (AVMA)
Council on Education
1931 North Meacham Road, Suite 100
Schaumburg, Illinois 60173-4360
Phone: 847-925-8070 Ext. 6674
Fax: 847-285-5732
E-mail: info@avma.org
Website: www.avma.org

How to Use These Guides

As you identify the particular programs and institutions that interest you, you can use both the *Graduate & Professional Programs: An Overview* volume and the specialized volumes in the series to obtain detailed information.

- *Graduate Programs in the Biological/Biomedical Sciences & Health-Related Professions*
- *Graduate Programs in Business, Education, Information Studies, Law & Social Work*
- *Graduate Programs in Engineering & Applied Sciences*
- *Graduate Programs the Humanities, Arts & Social Sciences*
- *Graduate Programs in the Physical Sciences, Mathematics, Agricultural Sciences, the Environment & Natural Resources*

Each of the specialized volumes in the series is divided into sections that contain one or more directories devoted to programs in a particular field. If you do not find a directory devoted to your field of interest in a specific volume, consult "Directories and Subject Areas" (located at the end of each volume). After you have identified the correct volume, consult the "Directories and Subject Areas in This Book" index, which shows (as does the more general directory) what directories cover subjects not specifically named in a directory or section title.

Each of the specialized volumes in the series has a number of general directories. These directories have entries for the largest unit at an institution granting graduate degrees in that field. For example, the general Engineering and Applied Sciences directory in the *Graduate Programs in Engineering & Applied Sciences* volume consists of **Profiles** for colleges, schools, and departments of engineering and applied sciences.

General directories are followed by other directories, or sections, that give more detailed information about programs in particular areas of the general field that has been covered. The general Engineering and Applied Sciences directory, in the previous example, is followed by nineteen sections with directories in specific areas of engineering, such as Chemical Engineering, Industrial/Management Engineering, and Mechanical Engineering.

Because of the broad nature of many fields, any system of organization is bound to involve a certain amount of overlap. Environmental studies, for example, is a field whose various aspects are studied in several types of departments and schools. Readers interested in such studies will find information on relevant programs in the *Graduate Programs in the Biological/Biomedical Sciences & Health-Related Professions* volume under Ecology and Environmental Biology and Environmental and Occupational Health; in the *Graduate Programs in the Physical Sciences, Mathematics, Agricultural Sciences, the Environment & Natural Resources* volume under Environmental Management and Policy and Natural Resources; and in the *Graduate Programs in Engineering & Applied Sciences* volume under Energy Management and Policy and Environmental Engineering. To help you find all of the programs of interest to you, the introduction to each section within the specialized volumes includes, if applicable, a paragraph suggesting other sections and directories with information on related areas of study.

Directory of Institutions with Programs in Engineering and Applied Sciences

This directory lists institutions in alphabetical order and includes beneath each name the academic fields in which each institution offers graduate programs. The degree level in each field is also indicated, provided that the institution has supplied that information in response to Peterson's Annual Survey of Graduate and Professional Institutions.

An M indicates that a master's degree program is offered; a D indicates that a doctoral degree program is offered; a P indicates that the first professional degree is offered; an O signifies that other advanced degrees (e.g., certificates or specialist degrees) are offered; and an * (asterisk) indicates that a **Close-Up** and/or **Display** is located in this volume. See the index, "Close-Ups and Displays," for the specific page number.

Profiles of Academic and Professional Programs in the Specialized Volumes

Each section of **Profiles** has a table of contents that lists the Program Directories, **Displays**, and **Close-Ups**. Program Directories consist of the **Profiles** of programs in the relevant fields, with **Displays** following if programs have chosen to include them. **Close-Ups,** which are more individualized statements, are also listed for those graduate schools or programs that have chosen to submit them.

The **Profiles** found in the 500 directories in the specialized volumes provide basic data about the graduate units in capsule form for quick reference. To make these directories as useful as possible, **Profiles** are generally listed for an institution's smallest academic unit within a subject area. In other words, if an institution has a College of Liberal Arts that administers many related programs, the **Profile** for the individual program (e.g., Program in History), not the entire College, appears in the directory.

There are some programs that do not fit into any current directory and are not given individual **Profiles**. The directory structure is reviewed annually in order to keep this number to a minimum and to accommodate major trends in graduate education.

The following outline describes the **Profile** information found in the guides and explains how best to use that information. Any item that does not apply to or was not provided by a graduate unit is omitted from its listing. The format of the **Profiles** is constant, making it easy to compare one institution with another and one program with another.

A ★ graphic next to the school's name indicates the institution has additional detailed information in a "Premium Profile" on Petersons.com. After reading their information here, you can learn more about the school by visiting www.petersons.com and searching for that particular college or university's graduate program.

Identifying Information. The institution's name, in boldface type, is followed by a complete listing of the administrative structure for that field of study. (For example, University of Akron, Buchtel College of Arts and Sciences, Department of Theoretical and Applied Mathematics, Program in Mathematics.) The last unit listed is the one to which all information in the **Profile** pertains. The institution's city, state, and zip code follow.

Offerings. Each field of study offered by the unit is listed with all postbaccalaureate degrees awarded. Degrees that are not preceded by a specific concentration are awarded in the general field listed in the unit name. Frequently, fields of study are broken down into subspecializations, and those appear following the degrees awarded; for example, "Offerings in secondary education (M.Ed.), including English education, mathematics education, science education." Students enrolled in the M.Ed. program would be able to specialize in any of the three fields mentioned.

Professional Accreditation. Some **Profiles** indicate whether a program is professionally accredited. Because it is possible for a program to receive or lose professional accreditation at any time, students entering fields in which accreditation is important to a career should verify the status of programs by contacting either the chairperson or the appropriate accrediting association.

Jointly Offered Degrees. Explanatory statements concerning programs that are offered in cooperation with other institutions are included in the list of degrees offered. This occurs most commonly on a regional basis (for example, two state universities offering a cooperative Ph.D. in special education) or where the specialized nature of the institutions encourages joint efforts (a J.D./M.B.A. offered by a law school at an institution with no formal business programs and an institution with a business school but lacking a law school). Only programs that are truly cooperative are listed; those involving only limited course work at another institution are not. Interested students should contact the heads of such units for further information.

Part-Time and Evening/Weekend Programs. When information regarding the availability of part-time or evening/weekend study appears in the **Profile**, it means that students are able to earn a degree exclusively through such study.

Postbaccalaureate Distance Learning Degrees. A postbaccalaureate distance learning degree program signifies that course requirements can be fulfilled with minimal or no on-campus study.

Faculty. Figures on the number of faculty members actively involved with graduate students through teaching or research are separated into full- and part-time as well as men and women whenever the information has been supplied.

Students. Figures for the number of students enrolled in graduate and professional programs pertain to the semester of highest enrollment from the 2014–15 academic year. These figures are broken down into full- and part-time and men and women whenever the data have been supplied. Information on the number of matriculated students enrolled in the unit who are members of a minority group or are international students appears here. The average age of the matriculated students is followed by the number of applicants, the percentage accepted, and the number enrolled for fall 2014.

Degrees Awarded. The number of degrees awarded in the calendar year is listed. Many doctoral programs offer a terminal master's degree if students leave the program after completing only part of the requirements for a doctoral degree; that is indicated here. All degrees are classified into one of four types: master's, doctoral, first professional, and other advanced degrees. A unit may award one or several degrees at a given level; however, the data are only collected by type and may therefore represent several different degree programs.

Degree Requirements. The information in this section is also broken down by type of degree, and all information for a degree level pertains to all degrees of that type unless otherwise specified. Degree requirements are collected in a simplified form to provide some very basic information on the nature of the program and on foreign language, thesis or dissertation, comprehensive exam, and registration requirements. Many units also provide a short list of additional requirements, such as fieldwork or an internship. For complete information on graduation requirements, contact the graduate school or program directly.

Entrance Requirements. Entrance requirements are broken down into the four degree levels of master's, doctoral, first professional, and other advanced degrees. Within each level, information may be provided in two basic categories: entrance exams and other requirements. The entrance exams are identified by the standard acronyms used by the testing agencies, unless they are not well known. Other entrance requirements are quite varied, but they often contain an undergraduate or graduate grade point average (GPA). Unless otherwise stated, the GPA is calculated on a 4.0 scale and is listed as a minimum required for admission. Additional exam requirements/recommendations for international students may be listed here. Application deadlines for domestic and international students, the application fee, and whether electronic applications are accepted may be listed here. Note that the deadline should be used for reference only; these dates are subject to change, and students interested in applying should always contact the graduate unit directly about application procedures and deadlines.

Expenses. The typical cost of study for the 2015–2016 academic year (2014–15 if 2015–16 figures were not available) is given in two basic categories: tuition and fees. Cost of study may be quite complex at a graduate institution. There are often sliding scales for part-time study, a different cost for first-year students, and other variables that make it impossible to completely cover the cost of study for each graduate program. To provide the most usable information, figures are given for full-time study for a full year where available and for part-time study in terms of a per-unit rate (per credit, per semester hour, etc.). Occasionally, variances may be noted in tuition and fees for reasons such as the type of program, whether courses are taken during the day or evening, whether courses are at the master's or doctoral level, or other institution-specific reasons. Respondents were also given the opportunity to provide more specific and detailed tuition and fees infor-

mation at the unit level. When provided, this information will appear in place of any typical costs entered elsewhere on the university-level survey. Expenses are usually subject to change; for exact costs at any given time, contact your chosen schools and programs directly. Keep in mind that the tuition of Canadian institutions is usually given in Canadian dollars.

Financial Support. This section contains data on the number of awards administered by the institution and given to graduate students during the 2014–15 academic year. The first figure given represents the total number of students receiving financial support enrolled in that unit. If the unit has provided information on graduate appointments, these are broken down into three major categories: fellowships give money to graduate students to cover the cost of study and living expenses and are not based on a work obligation or research commitment, research assistantships provide stipends to graduate students for assistance in a formal research project with a faculty member, and teaching assistantships provide stipends to graduate students for teaching or for assisting faculty members in teaching undergraduate classes. Within each category, figures are given for the total number of awards, the average yearly amount per award, and whether full or partial tuition reimbursements are awarded. In addition to graduate appointments, the availability of several other financial aid sources is covered in this section. Tuition waivers are routinely part of a graduate appointment, but units sometimes waive part or all of a student's tuition even if a graduate appointment is not available. Federal WorkStudy is made available to students who demonstrate need and meet the federal guidelines; this form of aid normally includes 10 or more hours of work per week in an office of the institution. Institutionally sponsored loans are low-interest loans available to graduate students to cover both educational and living expenses. Career-related internships or fieldwork offer money to students who are participating in a formal off-campus research project or practicum. Grants, scholarships, traineeships, unspecified assistantships, and other awards may also be noted. The availability of financial support to part-time students is also indicated here.

Some programs list the financial aid application deadline and the forms that need to be completed for students to be eligible for financial awards. There are two forms: FAFSA, the Free Application for Federal Student Aid, which is required for federal aid, and the CSS PROFILE®.

Faculty Research. Each unit has the opportunity to list several keyword phrases describing the current research involving faculty members and graduate students. Space limitations prevent the unit from listing complete information on all research programs. The total expenditure for funded research from the previous academic year may also be included.

Unit Head and Application Contact. The head of the graduate program for each unit may be listed with academic title, phone and fax numbers, and e-mail address. In addition to the unit head's contact information, many graduate programs also list a separate contact for application and admission information, followed by the graduate school, program, or department's website. If no unit head or application contact is given, you should contact the overall institution for information on graduate admissions.

Displays and Close-Ups

The **Displays** and **Close-Ups** are supplementary insertions submitted by deans, chairs, and other administrators who wish to offer an additional, more individualized statement to readers. A number of graduate school and program administrators have attached a **Display** ad near the **Profile** listing. Here you will find information that an institution or program wants to emphasize. The **Close-Ups** are by their very nature more expansive and flexible than the **Profiles**, and the administrators who have written them may emphasize different aspects of their programs. All of the **Close-Ups** are organized in the same way (with the exception of a few that describe research and training opportunities instead of degree programs), and in each one you will find information on the same basic topics, such as programs of study, research facilities, tuition and fees, financial aid, and application procedures. If an institution or program has submitted a **Close-Up**, a boldface cross-reference appears below its **Profile**. As with the **Displays**, all of the **Close-Ups** in the guides have been submitted by choice; the absence of a **Display** or **Close-Up** does not reflect any type of editorial judgment on the part of Peterson's, and their presence in the guides should not be taken as an indication of status, quality, or approval. Statements regarding a university's objectives and accomplishments are a reflection of its own beliefs and are not the opinions of the Peterson's editors.

Appendixes

This section contains two appendixes. The first, "Institutional Changes Since the 2015 Edition," lists institutions that have closed, merged, or changed their name or status since the last edition of the guides. The second, "Abbreviations Used in the Guides," gives abbreviations of degree names, along with what those abbreviations stand for. These appendixes are identical in all six volumes of *Peterson's Graduate and Professional Programs*.

Indexes

There are three indexes presented here. The first index, "Close-Ups and Displays," gives page references for all programs that have chosen to place **Close-Ups** and **Displays** in this volume. It is arranged alphabetically by institution; within institutions, the arrangement is alphabetical by subject area. It is not an index to all programs in the book's directories of **Profiles**; readers must refer to the directories themselves for **Profile** information on programs that have not submitted the additional, more individualized statements. The second index, "Directories and Subject Areas in Other Books in This Series", gives book references for the directories in the specialized volumes and also includes cross-references for subject area names not used in the directory structure, for example, "Computing Technology (see Computer Science)." The third index, "Directories and Subject Areas in This Book," gives page references for the directories in this volume and cross-references for subject area names not used in this volume's directory structure.

Data Collection Procedures

The information published in the directories and Profiles of all the books is collected through Peterson's Annual Survey of Graduate and Professional Institutions. The survey is sent each spring to nearly 2,300 institutions offering postbaccalaureate degree programs, including accredited institutions in the United States, U.S. territories, and Canada and those institutions outside the United States that are accredited by U.S. accrediting bodies. Deans and other administrators complete these surveys, providing information on programs in the 500 academic and professional fields covered in the guides as well as overall institutional information. While every effort has been made to ensure the accuracy and completeness of the data, information is sometimes unavailable or changes occur after publication deadlines. All usable information received in time for publication has been included. The omission of any particular item from a directory or Profile signifies either that the item is not applicable to the institution or program or that information was not available. Profiles of programs scheduled to begin during the 2015–16 academic year cannot, obviously, include statistics on enrollment or, in many cases, the number of faculty members. If no usable data were submitted by an institution, its name, address, and program name appear in order to indicate the availability of graduate work.

Criteria for Inclusion in This Guide

To be included in this guide, an institution must have full accreditation or be a candidate for accreditation (preaccreditation) status by an institutional or specialized accrediting body recognized by the U.S. Department of Education or the Council for Higher Education Accreditation (CHEA). Institutional accrediting bodies, which review each institution as a whole, include the six regional associations of schools and colleges (Middle States, New England, North Central, Northwest, Southern, and Western), each of which is responsible for a specified portion of the United States and its territories. Other institutional accrediting bodies are national in scope and accredit specific kinds of institutions (e.g., Bible colleges, independent colleges, and rabbinical and Talmudic schools). Program registration by the New York State Board of Regents is considered to be the equivalent of institutional accreditation, since the board requires that all programs offered by an institution meet its standards before recognition is granted. A Canadian institution must be chartered and authorized to grant degrees by the provincial government, affiliated with a chartered institution, or accredited by a recognized U.S. accrediting body. This guide also includes institutions outside the United States that are accredited by these U.S. accrediting bodies. There are recognized specialized or professional accrediting bodies in more than fifty different fields, each of which is authorized to accredit institutions or specific programs in its particular field. For specialized institutions that offer programs in one field only, we designate this to be the equivalent of institutional accreditation. A full explanation of the accrediting process and complete information on recognized institutional (regional and national) and specialized accrediting bodies can be found online at www.chea.org or at www.ed.gov/admins/finaid/accred/index.html.

DIRECTORY OF INSTITUTIONS AND THEIR OFFERINGS

ACADEMY OF ART UNIVERSITY
Game Design and
    Development   M
Modeling and Simulation   M

ACADIA UNIVERSITY
Computer Science   M

ADELPHI UNIVERSITY
Health Informatics   M,O

AIR FORCE INSTITUTE OF TECHNOLOGY
Aerospace/Aeronautical
    Engineering   M,D
Computer Engineering   M,D
Computer Science   M,D
Electrical Engineering   M,D
Engineering and Applied
    Sciences—General   M,D
Engineering Management   M
Engineering Physics   M,D
Environmental Engineering   M
Management of Technology   M,D
Materials Sciences   M,D
Nuclear Engineering   M,D
Operations Research   M,D
Systems Engineering   M,D

ALABAMA AGRICULTURAL AND MECHANICAL UNIVERSITY
Computer Science   M
Engineering and Applied
    Sciences—General   M
Materials Sciences   M,D

ALASKA PACIFIC UNIVERSITY
Telecommunications
    Management   M

ALCORN STATE UNIVERSITY
Computer Science   M
Information Science   M

ALFRED UNIVERSITY
Bioengineering   M,D
Ceramic Sciences and
    Engineering   M,D
Electrical Engineering   M,D
Engineering and Applied
    Sciences—General   M,D
Materials Sciences   M,D
Mechanical Engineering   M,D

AMERICAN INTERCONTINENTAL UNIVERSITY ATLANTA
Information Science   M

AMERICAN INTERCONTINENTAL UNIVERSITY ONLINE
Computer and Information
    Systems Security   M
Information Science   M

AMERICAN PUBLIC UNIVERSITY SYSTEM
Aerospace/Aeronautical
    Engineering   M
Computer and Information
    Systems Security   M
Software Engineering   M

AMERICAN SENTINEL UNIVERSITY
Computer Science   M
Health Informatics   M

THE AMERICAN UNIVERSITY IN CAIRO
Computer Science   M,O
Construction Engineering   M
Engineering and Applied
    Sciences—General   M,D,O
Mechanical Engineering   M

THE AMERICAN UNIVERSITY IN DUBAI
Construction Management   M

AMERICAN UNIVERSITY OF ARMENIA
Computer Science   M
Energy Management
    and Policy   M
Industrial/Management
    Engineering   M
Information Science   M
Manufacturing Engineering   M

AMERICAN UNIVERSITY OF BEIRUT
Civil Engineering   M,D
Computer Engineering   M,D
Computer Science   M,D
Electrical Engineering   M,D
Engineering and Applied
    Sciences—General   M,D
Engineering Management   M,D
Mechanical Engineering   M,D
Water Resources Engineering   M,D

AMERICAN UNIVERSITY OF SHARJAH
Chemical Engineering   M
Civil Engineering   M
Computer Engineering   M
Electrical Engineering   M
Engineering Management   M
Mechanical Engineering   M

ANNA MARIA COLLEGE
Fire Protection Engineering   M

APPALACHIAN STATE UNIVERSITY
Computer Science   M
Energy and Power
    Engineering   M
Engineering Physics   M

ARIZONA STATE UNIVERSITY AT THE TEMPE CAMPUS
Aerospace/Aeronautical
    Engineering   M,D
Bioinformatics   M,D
Biomedical Engineering   M,D
Biotechnology   M,D
Chemical Engineering   M,D
Civil Engineering   M,D
Computer Engineering   M,D
Computer Science   M,D
Construction Engineering   M,D
Construction Management   M,D
Electrical Engineering   M,D,O
Energy and Power
    Engineering   M,D
Engineering and Applied
    Sciences—General   M,D
Environmental Engineering   M,D
Ergonomics and Human
    Factors   M
Geological Engineering   M,D
Industrial/Management
    Engineering   M,D
Information Science   M
Management of Technology   M
Manufacturing Engineering   M
Materials Engineering   M,D
Materials Sciences   M,D

Mechanical Engineering   M,D
Medical Informatics   M,D
Modeling and Simulation   M,D
Nanotechnology   M,D
Nuclear Engineering   M,D,O
Reliability Engineering   M
Software Engineering   M,D
Systems Engineering   M
Systems Science   M,D
Technology and Public Policy   M
Transportation and Highway
    Engineering   M,D,O

ARKANSAS STATE UNIVERSITY
Biotechnology   M,O
Computer Science   M
Engineering and Applied
    Sciences—General   M
Engineering Management   M

ARKANSAS TECH UNIVERSITY
Engineering and Applied
    Sciences—General   M
Health Informatics   M
Information Science   M

ARMSTRONG STATE UNIVERSITY
Computer and Information
    Systems Security   M,O
Computer Science   M
Information Science   M
Medical Informatics   M,O

ART CENTER COLLEGE OF DESIGN
Transportation and Highway
    Engineering   M

ASPEN UNIVERSITY
Information Science   M,O

ATHABASCA UNIVERSITY
Information Science   M
Management of Technology   M,O

AUBURN UNIVERSITY
Aerospace/Aeronautical
    Engineering   M,D
Biosystems Engineering   M,D
Chemical Engineering   M,D
Civil Engineering   M,D
Computer Engineering   M,D
Computer Science   M,D
Construction Engineering   M,D
Construction Management   M
Electrical Engineering   M,D
Engineering and Applied
    Sciences—General   M,D,O
Environmental Engineering   M,D
Geotechnical Engineering   M,D
Hydraulics   M,D
Industrial/Management
    Engineering   M,D,O
Materials Engineering   M,D
Mechanical Engineering   M,D
Polymer Science and
    Engineering   M,D
Software Engineering   M,D
Structural Engineering   M,D
Systems Engineering   M,D,O
Transportation and Highway
    Engineering   M,D

AUBURN UNIVERSITY AT MONTGOMERY
Computer and Information
    Systems Security   M
Information Science   M

AUSTIN PEAY STATE UNIVERSITY
Database Systems   M
Engineering and Applied
    Sciences—General   M

BALL STATE UNIVERSITY
Computer Science   M
Information Science   M
Telecommunications   M

BARRY UNIVERSITY
Health Informatics   O
Information Science   M

BARUCH COLLEGE OF THE CITY UNIVERSITY OF NEW YORK
Financial Engineering   M

BAYLOR COLLEGE OF MEDICINE
Bioengineering   D
Biomedical Engineering   D

BAYLOR UNIVERSITY
Biomedical Engineering   M
Computer Engineering   M,D
Computer Science   M
Electrical Engineering   M,D
Mechanical Engineering   M

BAY PATH UNIVERSITY
Computer and Information
    Systems Security   M

BELLEVUE UNIVERSITY
Information Science   M

BENEDICTINE UNIVERSITY
Computer and Information
    Systems Security   M
Health Informatics   M

BENTLEY UNIVERSITY
Ergonomics and Human
    Factors   M
Information Science   M

BINGHAMTON UNIVERSITY, STATE UNIVERSITY OF NEW YORK
Biomedical Engineering   M,D
Computer Science   M,D
Electrical Engineering   M,D
Engineering and Applied
    Sciences—General   M,D
Industrial/Management
    Engineering   M,D
Materials Engineering   M,D
Materials Sciences   M,D
Mechanical Engineering   M,D
Systems Science   M,D

BOISE STATE UNIVERSITY
Civil Engineering   M
Computer Engineering   M,D
Computer Science   M
Electrical Engineering   M,D
Engineering and Applied
    Sciences—General   M,D,O
Materials Engineering   M,D
Mechanical Engineering   M

BOSTON UNIVERSITY
Bioinformatics   M,D
Biomedical Engineering   M,D
Computer and Information
    Systems Security   M,O
Computer Engineering   M,D,O
Computer Science   M,O

Database Systems	M,O
Electrical Engineering	M,D
Energy Management and Policy	M,D
Engineering and Applied Sciences—General	M,D
Health Informatics	M,O
Management of Technology	M
Manufacturing Engineering	M,D
Materials Engineering	M,D
Materials Sciences	M,D
Mechanical Engineering	M,D
Systems Engineering	M,D
Telecommunications Management	M,O
Telecommunications	M,O

BOWIE STATE UNIVERSITY

Computer Science	M,D

BOWLING GREEN STATE UNIVERSITY

Computer Science	M
Construction Management	M
Manufacturing Engineering	M
Operations Research	M
Software Engineering	M

BRADLEY UNIVERSITY

Civil Engineering	M
Computer Science	M
Construction Engineering	M
Electrical Engineering	M
Engineering and Applied Sciences—General	M
Industrial/Management Engineering	M
Information Science	M
Manufacturing Engineering	M
Mechanical Engineering	M

BRANDEIS UNIVERSITY

Bioinformatics	M
Biotechnology	M
Computer and Information Systems Security	M
Computer Science	M
Health Informatics	M
Medical Informatics	M
Software Engineering	M

BRIDGEWATER STATE UNIVERSITY

Computer Science	M

BRIGHAM YOUNG UNIVERSITY

Biotechnology	M,D
Chemical Engineering	M,D
Civil Engineering	M,D
Computer Engineering	M,D
Computer Science	M,D
Construction Management	M
Electrical Engineering	M,D
Engineering and Applied Sciences—General	M,D
Information Science	M
Mechanical Engineering	M,D

BROCK UNIVERSITY

Biotechnology	M,D
Computer Science	M

BROOKLYN COLLEGE OF THE CITY UNIVERSITY OF NEW YORK

Computer Science	M,O
Health Informatics	M,O
Information Science	M,O

BROWN UNIVERSITY

Biochemical Engineering	M,D
Biomedical Engineering	M,D
Biotechnology	M,D
Chemical Engineering	M,D
Computer Engineering	M,D
Computer Science	M,D
Electrical Engineering	M,D
Engineering and Applied Sciences—General	M,D
Materials Sciences	M,D
Mechanical Engineering	M,D
Mechanics	M,D

BUCKNELL UNIVERSITY

Chemical Engineering	M
Civil Engineering	M
Electrical Engineering	M
Engineering and Applied Sciences—General	M
Mechanical Engineering	M

BUFFALO STATE COLLEGE, STATE UNIVERSITY OF NEW YORK

Industrial/Management Engineering	M

CALIFORNIA BAPTIST UNIVERSITY

Construction Management	M

CALIFORNIA INSTITUTE OF TECHNOLOGY

Aerospace/Aeronautical Engineering	M,D,O
Bioengineering	M,D
Chemical Engineering	M,D
Civil Engineering	M,D,O
Computer Science	M,D
Electrical Engineering	M,D,O
Engineering and Applied Sciences—General	M,D,O
Environmental Engineering	M,D
Materials Sciences	M,D
Mechanical Engineering	M,D,O
Mechanics	M,D
Systems Engineering	M,D

CALIFORNIA LUTHERAN UNIVERSITY

Management of Technology	M,O

CALIFORNIA MARITIME ACADEMY

Engineering Management	M

CALIFORNIA MIRAMAR UNIVERSITY

Telecommunications Management	M
Telecommunications	M

CALIFORNIA NATIONAL UNIVERSITY FOR ADVANCED STUDIES

Engineering and Applied Sciences—General	M
Engineering Management	M

CALIFORNIA POLYTECHNIC STATE UNIVERSITY, SAN LUIS OBISPO

Aerospace/Aeronautical Engineering	M
Civil Engineering	M
Computer Science	M
Electrical Engineering	M

Engineering and Applied Sciences—General	M
Environmental Engineering	M
Industrial/Management Engineering	M
Mechanical Engineering	M
Polymer Science and Engineering	M

CALIFORNIA STATE POLYTECHNIC UNIVERSITY, POMONA

Aerospace/Aeronautical Engineering	M
Biotechnology	M
Civil Engineering	M
Computer Science	M
Electrical Engineering	M
Engineering Management	M
Mechanical Engineering	M

CALIFORNIA STATE UNIVERSITY CHANNEL ISLANDS

Bioinformatics	M
Biotechnology	M
Computer Science	M

CALIFORNIA STATE UNIVERSITY, CHICO

Computer Engineering	M
Computer Science	M
Electrical Engineering	M
Engineering and Applied Sciences—General	M

CALIFORNIA STATE UNIVERSITY, DOMINGUEZ HILLS

Bioinformatics	M
Computer Science	M

CALIFORNIA STATE UNIVERSITY, EAST BAY

Computer Science	M
Construction Management	M
Engineering and Applied Sciences—General	M
Engineering Management	M
Industrial/Management Engineering	M

CALIFORNIA STATE UNIVERSITY, FRESNO

Civil Engineering	M
Computer Science	M
Electrical Engineering	M
Engineering and Applied Sciences—General	M
Industrial/Management Engineering	M
Mechanical Engineering	M

CALIFORNIA STATE UNIVERSITY, FULLERTON

Biotechnology	M
Civil Engineering	M
Computer Science	M
Electrical Engineering	M
Engineering and Applied Sciences—General	M
Environmental Engineering	M
Information Science	M
Mechanical Engineering	M
Software Engineering	M
Systems Engineering	M

CALIFORNIA STATE UNIVERSITY, LONG BEACH

Aerospace/Aeronautical Engineering	M

Chemical Engineering	M
Civil Engineering	M
Computer Engineering	M
Computer Science	M
Electrical Engineering	M
Engineering Management	M,D
Ergonomics and Human Factors	M
Mechanical Engineering	M,D

CALIFORNIA STATE UNIVERSITY, LOS ANGELES

Civil Engineering	M
Computer Science	M
Electrical Engineering	M
Engineering and Applied Sciences—General	M
Management of Technology	M
Mechanical Engineering	M

CALIFORNIA STATE UNIVERSITY, NORTHRIDGE

Artificial Intelligence/Robotics	M
Civil Engineering	M
Computer Science	M
Electrical Engineering	M
Engineering and Applied Sciences—General	M
Engineering Management	M
Ergonomics and Human Factors	M
Industrial/Management Engineering	M
Manufacturing Engineering	M
Materials Engineering	M
Mechanical Engineering	M
Software Engineering	M
Structural Engineering	M
Systems Engineering	M

CALIFORNIA STATE UNIVERSITY, SACRAMENTO

Civil Engineering	M
Computer Science	M
Electrical Engineering	M
Engineering and Applied Sciences—General	M
Mechanical Engineering	M
Software Engineering	M

CALIFORNIA STATE UNIVERSITY, SAN BERNARDINO

Computer and Information Systems Security	M
Computer Science	M

CALIFORNIA STATE UNIVERSITY, SAN MARCOS

Computer Science	M

CAMBRIDGE COLLEGE

Management of Technology	M
Medical Informatics	M

CANISIUS COLLEGE

Health Informatics	M,O

CAPELLA UNIVERSITY

Computer and Information Systems Security	M,D
Health Informatics	M
Management of Technology	M,D
Operations Research	M

CAPITOL TECHNOLOGY UNIVERSITY

Computer and Information Systems Security	M

M—masters degree; D—doctorate; O—other advanced degree; *—Close-Up and/or Display

Computer Science	M
Electrical Engineering	M
Information Science	M
Telecommunications Management	M

CARLETON UNIVERSITY

Aerospace/Aeronautical Engineering	M,D
Biomedical Engineering	M
Civil Engineering	M,D
Computer Science	M,D
Electrical Engineering	M,D
Engineering and Applied Sciences—General	M,D
Environmental Engineering	M,D
Information Science	M,D
Management of Technology	M
Materials Engineering	M,D
Mechanical Engineering	M,D
Systems Engineering	M,D
Systems Science	M,D

CARLOW UNIVERSITY

Computer and Information Systems Security	M

CARNEGIE MELLON UNIVERSITY

Architectural Engineering	M,D
Artificial Intelligence/Robotics	M,D
Bioengineering	M,D
Biomedical Engineering	M,D
Biotechnology	M
Chemical Engineering	M,D
Civil Engineering	M,D
Computer and Information Systems Security	M
Computer Engineering	M,D
Computer Science	M,D
Construction Management	M,D
Electrical Engineering	M,D
Energy and Power Engineering	M,D
Environmental Engineering	M,D
Human-Computer Interaction	M,D
Information Science	M,D
Materials Engineering	M,D
Materials Sciences	M,D
Mechanical Engineering	M,D
Mechanics	M,D
Modeling and Simulation	M,D
Nanotechnology	D
Operations Research	D
Polymer Science and Engineering	M
Software Engineering	M,D
Systems Engineering	M
Technology and Public Policy	M,D
Telecommunications Management	M
Water Resources Engineering	M,D

CARROLL UNIVERSITY

Software Engineering	M

CASE WESTERN RESERVE UNIVERSITY

Aerospace/Aeronautical Engineering	M,D
Biomedical Engineering	M,D*
Chemical Engineering	M,D
Civil Engineering	M,D
Computer Engineering	M,D
Computer Science	M,D
Electrical Engineering	M,D
Engineering and Applied Sciences—General	M,D
Engineering Management	M
Information Science	M,D
Materials Engineering	M,D
Materials Sciences	M,D
Mechanical Engineering	M,D
Operations Research	M,D

Polymer Science and Engineering	M,D
Systems Engineering	M,D

THE CATHOLIC UNIVERSITY OF AMERICA

Biomedical Engineering	M,D
Civil Engineering	M,D
Computer Science	M,D
Electrical Engineering	M,D
Engineering and Applied Sciences—General	M,D,O
Engineering Management	M,O
Environmental Engineering	M,D
Ergonomics and Human Factors	M,D
Materials Engineering	M
Materials Sciences	M
Mechanical Engineering	M,D
Operations Research	M

CENTRAL CONNECTICUT STATE UNIVERSITY

Computer Science	M,O
Construction Management	M,O
Engineering and Applied Sciences—General	M,O
Management of Technology	M,O

CENTRAL MICHIGAN UNIVERSITY

Computer and Information Systems Security	O
Computer Science	M
Engineering and Applied Sciences—General	M
Engineering Management	M,O
Materials Sciences	D

CENTRAL WASHINGTON UNIVERSITY

Engineering and Applied Sciences—General	M
Industrial/Management Engineering	M

CHAMPLAIN COLLEGE

Management of Technology	M

CHICAGO STATE UNIVERSITY

Computer Science	M

CHRISTIAN BROTHERS UNIVERSITY

Engineering and Applied Sciences—General	M

CHRISTOPHER NEWPORT UNIVERSITY

Computer Science	M

THE CITADEL, THE MILITARY COLLEGE OF SOUTH CAROLINA

Civil Engineering	M
Computer Science	M
Engineering Management	M
Information Science	M

CITY COLLEGE OF THE CITY UNIVERSITY OF NEW YORK

Biomedical Engineering	M,D
Chemical Engineering	M,D
Civil Engineering	M,D
Computer Science	M,D
Electrical Engineering	M,D
Engineering and Applied Sciences—General	M,D
Mechanical Engineering	M,D

CITY UNIVERSITY OF SEATTLE

Computer and Information Systems Security	M,O
Computer Science	M,O
Management of Technology	M,O

CLAFLIN UNIVERSITY

Biotechnology	M

CLAREMONT GRADUATE UNIVERSITY

Financial Engineering	M
Health Informatics	M,D,O
Information Science	M,D,O
Operations Research	M,D
Systems Science	M,D,O
Telecommunications	M,D,O

CLARION UNIVERSITY OF PENNSYLVANIA

Database Systems	M

CLARK ATLANTA UNIVERSITY

Computer Science	M
Information Science	M

CLARKSON UNIVERSITY

Biotechnology	D
Chemical Engineering	M,D
Civil Engineering	M,D
Computer Engineering	M,D
Computer Science	M,D
Electrical Engineering	M,D
Engineering and Applied Sciences—General	M,D*
Engineering Management	M
Environmental Engineering	M,D
Information Science	M*
Materials Engineering	D
Materials Sciences	D
Mechanical Engineering	M,D

CLARK UNIVERSITY

Information Science	M

CLEMSON UNIVERSITY

Automotive Engineering	M,D
Bioengineering	M,D,O
Biosystems Engineering	M,D
Chemical Engineering	M,D
Civil Engineering	M,D
Computer Engineering	M,D
Computer Science	M,D
Construction Management	M
Electrical Engineering	M,D
Engineering and Applied Sciences—General	M,D,O
Environmental Engineering	M,D
Ergonomics and Human Factors	D
Human-Computer Interaction	D
Industrial/Management Engineering	M,D
Manufacturing Engineering	M
Materials Engineering	M,D
Materials Sciences	M,D
Mechanical Engineering	M,D
Operations Research	M,D

CLEVELAND STATE UNIVERSITY

Biomedical Engineering	D
Chemical Engineering	M,D
Civil Engineering	M,D
Computer Science	M,D
Electrical Engineering	M,D
Engineering and Applied Sciences—General	M,D
Environmental Engineering	M,D
Industrial/Management Engineering	M,D
Information Science	M,D

Mechanical Engineering	M,D
Software Engineering	M,D

COASTAL CAROLINA UNIVERSITY

Computer Science	M,D,O

COLEMAN UNIVERSITY

Information Science	M
Management of Technology	M

COLLEGE FOR CREATIVE STUDIES

Automotive Engineering	M
Transportation and Highway Engineering	M

COLLEGE OF CHARLESTON

Computer Science	M

THE COLLEGE OF SAINT ROSE

Computer Science	M
Information Science	M

THE COLLEGE OF ST. SCHOLASTICA

Health Informatics	M,O

COLLEGE OF STATEN ISLAND OF THE CITY UNIVERSITY OF NEW YORK

Computer Science	M

THE COLLEGE OF WILLIAM AND MARY

Applied Science and Technology	M,D
Artificial Intelligence/Robotics	M,D
Computer Science	M,D
Nanotechnology	M,D
Operations Research	M
Polymer Science and Engineering	M,D

COLORADO CHRISTIAN UNIVERSITY

Computer and Information Systems Security	M

COLORADO SCHOOL OF MINES

Bioengineering	M,D
Chemical Engineering	M,D
Civil Engineering	M,D
Computer Science	M,D
Construction Engineering	M,D
Electrical Engineering	M,D
Electronic Materials	M,D
Engineering and Applied Sciences—General	M,D,O
Engineering Management	M,D
Environmental Engineering	M,D
Geological Engineering	M,D
Management of Technology	M,D
Materials Engineering	M,D
Materials Sciences	M,D
Mechanical Engineering	M,D
Metallurgical Engineering and Metallurgy	M,D
Mineral/Mining Engineering	M,D
Nuclear Engineering	M,D
Operations Research	M,D
Petroleum Engineering	M,D

COLORADO STATE UNIVERSITY

Biomedical Engineering	M,D
Chemical Engineering	M,D
Civil Engineering	M,D
Computer Science	M,D
Construction Management	M
Electrical Engineering	M,D

Engineering and Applied
   Sciences—General   M,D
Mechanical Engineering   M,D

**COLORADO STATE
UNIVERSITY–PUEBLO**
Applied Science and
   Technology   M
Engineering and Applied
   Sciences—General   M
Industrial/Management
   Engineering   M
Systems Engineering   M

**COLORADO TECHNICAL
UNIVERSITY COLORADO
SPRINGS**
Computer and Information
   Systems Security   M,D
Computer Engineering   M
Computer Science   M,D
Database Systems   M,D
Electrical Engineering   M
Management of Technology   M,D
Software Engineering   M,D
Systems Engineering   M

**COLORADO TECHNICAL
UNIVERSITY DENVER SOUTH**
Computer and Information
   Systems Security   M
Computer Engineering   M
Computer Science   M
Database Systems   M
Electrical Engineering   M
Management of Technology   M
Software Engineering   M
Systems Engineering   M

COLUMBIA UNIVERSITY
Biomedical Engineering   M,D
Biotechnology   M,D
Chemical Engineering   M,D
Civil Engineering   M,D
Computer Engineering   M,D
Computer Science   M,D*
Construction Engineering   M,D
Construction Management   M,D
Database Systems   M
Electrical Engineering   M,D
Engineering and Applied
   Sciences—General   M,D
Environmental Engineering   M,D
Financial Engineering   M,D
Industrial/Management
   Engineering   M,D
Management of Technology   M
Materials Engineering   M,D
Materials Sciences   M,D
Mechanical Engineering   M,D
Mechanics   M,D
Medical Informatics   M,D,O
Operations Research   M,D

COLUMBUS STATE UNIVERSITY
Computer and Information
   Systems Security   M,O
Computer Science   M,O
Modeling and Simulation   M,O

**CONCORDIA UNIVERSITY
(CANADA)**
Aerospace/Aeronautical
   Engineering   M
Biotechnology   M,D,O
Civil Engineering   M,D,O
Computer and Information
   Systems Security   M,O
Computer Engineering   M,D
Computer Science   M,D,O

Construction Engineering   M,D,O
Electrical Engineering   M,D
Engineering and Applied
   Sciences—General   M,D,O
Environmental Engineering   M,D,O
Game Design and
   Development   M,O
Industrial/Management
   Engineering   M,D,O
Mechanical Engineering   M,D,O
Software Engineering   M,D,O
Systems Engineering   M,O
Telecommunications
   Management   M,O

**CONCORDIA UNIVERSITY
COLLEGE OF ALBERTA**
Computer and Information
   Systems Security   M

**COOPER UNION FOR
THE ADVANCEMENT OF
SCIENCE AND ART**
Chemical Engineering   M
Civil Engineering   M
Electrical Engineering   M
Engineering and Applied
   Sciences—General   M
Mechanical Engineering   M

CORNELL UNIVERSITY
Aerospace/Aeronautical
   Engineering   M,D
Agricultural Engineering   M,D
Artificial Intelligence/Robotics   M,D
Biochemical Engineering   M,D
Bioengineering   M,D
Biomedical Engineering   M,D
Biotechnology   M,D
Chemical Engineering   M,D
Civil Engineering   M,D
Computer Engineering   M,D
Computer Science   M,D
Electrical Engineering   M,D
Energy and Power
   Engineering   M,D
Engineering and Applied
   Sciences—General   M,D
Engineering Management   M,D
Engineering Physics   M,D
Environmental Engineering   M,D
Ergonomics and Human
   Factors   M
Geotechnical Engineering   M,D
Human-Computer Interaction   M,D
Industrial/Management
   Engineering   M,D
Information Science   D
Manufacturing Engineering   M,D
Materials Engineering   M,D
Materials Sciences   M,D
Mechanical Engineering   M,D
Mechanics   M,D
Nanotechnology   M,D
Operations Research   M,D
Polymer Science and
   Engineering   M,D
Structural Engineering   M,D
Systems Engineering   M
Textile Sciences and
   Engineering   M,D
Transportation and Highway
   Engineering   M,D
Water Resources Engineering   M,D

DAKOTA STATE UNIVERSITY
Computer Science   M,D,O
Health Informatics   M,D,O
Information Science   M,D,O

DALHOUSIE UNIVERSITY
Agricultural Engineering   M,D
Bioengineering   M,D
Bioinformatics   M,D
Biomedical Engineering   M,D
Chemical Engineering   M,D
Civil Engineering   M,D
Computer Engineering   M,D
Computer Science   M,D
Electrical Engineering   M,D
Engineering and Applied
   Sciences—General   M,D
Environmental Engineering   M,D
Human-Computer Interaction   M
Industrial/Management
   Engineering   M,D
Materials Engineering   M,D
Mechanical Engineering   M,D
Medical Informatics   M,D
Mineral/Mining Engineering   M,D

DALLAS BAPTIST UNIVERSITY
Engineering Management   M
Management of Technology   M

DARTMOUTH COLLEGE
Biochemical Engineering   M,D
Biomedical Engineering   M,D
Biotechnology   M,D
Computer Engineering   M,D
Computer Science   M,D
Engineering and Applied
   Sciences—General   M,D
Engineering Management   M
Environmental Engineering   M,D
Materials Engineering   M,D
Materials Sciences   M,D
Mechanical Engineering   M,D

DAVENPORT UNIVERSITY
Computer and Information
   Systems Security   M

DEPAUL UNIVERSITY
Computer and Information
   Systems Security   M,D
Computer Science   M,D
Game Design and
   Development   M,D
Health Informatics   M,D
Human-Computer Interaction   M,D
Information Science   M,D
Management of Technology   M,D
Software Engineering   M,D

DESALES UNIVERSITY
Information Science   M

DEVRY UNIVERSITY
Electrical Engineering   M

**DIGIPEN INSTITUTE OF
TECHNOLOGY**
Computer Science   M

DREXEL UNIVERSITY
Architectural Engineering   M,D
Biochemical Engineering   M
Biomedical Engineering   M,D
Chemical Engineering   M,D
Civil Engineering   M,D
Computer Engineering   M
Computer Science   M,D
Construction Management   M
Electrical Engineering   M
Engineering and Applied
   Sciences—General   M,D,O
Engineering Management   M,O
Environmental Engineering   M,D

Geotechnical Engineering   M,D
Health Informatics   M
Hydraulics   M,D
Information Science   M,D
Materials Engineering   M,D
Mechanical Engineering   M,D
Mechanics   M,D
Software Engineering   M
Structural Engineering   M,D
Telecommunications   M

DUKE UNIVERSITY
Bioinformatics   D,O
Biomedical Engineering   M,D
Civil Engineering   M,D
Computer Engineering   M,D
Computer Science   M,D
Electrical Engineering   M,D*
Energy Management
   and Policy   M,O
Engineering and Applied
   Sciences—General   M
Engineering Management   M
Environmental Engineering   M,D
Materials Engineering   M
Materials Sciences   M,D
Mechanical Engineering   M,D

DUQUESNE UNIVERSITY
Biotechnology   M

EAST CAROLINA UNIVERSITY
Biomedical Engineering   M
Biotechnology   M
Computer and Information
   Systems Security   M,D,O
Computer Engineering   M,D,O
Computer Science   M,D,O
Construction Management   M
Health Informatics   M
Management of Technology   M,D,O
Software Engineering   M
Telecommunications
   Management   M,D,O

EASTERN ILLINOIS UNIVERSITY
Computer and Information
   Systems Security   M,O
Computer Science   M
Energy Management
   and Policy   M
Engineering and Applied
   Sciences—General   M,O
Systems Science   M,O

**EASTERN KENTUCKY
UNIVERSITY**
Industrial/Management
   Engineering   M
Manufacturing Engineering   M

**EASTERN MICHIGAN
UNIVERSITY**
Artificial Intelligence/Robotics   M,O
Computer and Information
   Systems Security   O
Computer Science   M,O
Construction Management   M
Engineering and Applied
   Sciences—General   M
Engineering Management   M
Management of Technology   D
Polymer Science and
   Engineering   M
Technology and Public Policy   M

**EASTERN VIRGINIA
MEDICAL SCHOOL**
Biotechnology   M

*M—masters degree; D—doctorate; O—other advanced degree; *—Close-Up and/or Display*

EASTERN WASHINGTON UNIVERSITY
Computer Science — M

EAST STROUDSBURG UNIVERSITY OF PENNSYLVANIA
Computer Science — M

EAST TENNESSEE STATE UNIVERSITY
Computer Science — M,O
Information Science — M,O
Manufacturing Engineering — M,O

ÉCOLE POLYTECHNIQUE DE MONTRÉAL
Aerospace/Aeronautical Engineering — M,D,O
Biomedical Engineering — M,D,O
Chemical Engineering — M,D,O
Civil Engineering — M,D,O
Computer Engineering — M,D,O
Computer Science — M,D,O
Electrical Engineering — M,D,O
Engineering and Applied Sciences—General — M,D,O
Engineering Physics — M,D,O
Environmental Engineering — M,D,O
Geotechnical Engineering — M,D,O
Hydraulics — M,D,O
Industrial/Management Engineering — M,D,O
Management of Technology — M,D,O
Mechanical Engineering — M,D,O
Mechanics — M,D,O
Nuclear Engineering — M,D,O
Operations Research — M,D,O
Structural Engineering — M,D,O
Transportation and Highway Engineering — M,D,O

ELMHURST COLLEGE
Database Systems — M

EMBRY-RIDDLE AERONAUTICAL UNIVERSITY–DAYTONA
Aerospace/Aeronautical Engineering — M,D
Computer and Information Systems Security — M
Computer Engineering — M
Electrical Engineering — M
Engineering Physics — M,D
Ergonomics and Human Factors — M,D
Mechanical Engineering — M,D
Software Engineering — M
Systems Engineering — M,D

EMBRY-RIDDLE AERONAUTICAL UNIVERSITY–PRESCOTT
Safety Engineering — M

EMBRY-RIDDLE AERONAUTICAL UNIVERSITY–WORLDWIDE
Aerospace/Aeronautical Engineering — M
Engineering Management — M
Systems Engineering — M

EMORY UNIVERSITY
Bioinformatics — M,D
Computer Science — M,D
Health Informatics — M,D

EVERGLADES UNIVERSITY
Aviation — M
Information Science — M

EXCELSIOR COLLEGE
Management of Technology — M,O
Medical Informatics — M,O

FAIRFIELD UNIVERSITY
Computer and Information Systems Security — M,O
Computer Engineering — M,O
Database Systems — M,O
Electrical Engineering — M,O
Engineering and Applied Sciences—General — M,O
Management of Technology — M,O
Manufacturing Engineering — M,O
Mechanical Engineering — M,O
Software Engineering — M,O
Telecommunications — M,O

FAIRLEIGH DICKINSON UNIVERSITY, COLLEGE AT FLORHAM
Chemical Engineering — M,O
Computer Science — M
Management of Technology — M,O

FAIRLEIGH DICKINSON UNIVERSITY, METROPOLITAN CAMPUS
Computer Engineering — M
Computer Science — M
Electrical Engineering — M
Engineering and Applied Sciences—General — M
Systems Science — M

FERRIS STATE UNIVERSITY
Computer and Information Systems Security — M
Database Systems — M

FITCHBURG STATE UNIVERSITY
Computer Science — M

FLORIDA AGRICULTURAL AND MECHANICAL UNIVERSITY
Biomedical Engineering — M,D
Chemical Engineering — M,D
Civil Engineering — M,D
Electrical Engineering — M,D
Engineering and Applied Sciences—General — M,D
Industrial/Management Engineering — M,D
Mechanical Engineering — M,D
Software Engineering — M

FLORIDA ATLANTIC UNIVERSITY
Bioengineering — M,D
Biotechnology — M,D
Civil Engineering — M
Computer Engineering — M,D
Computer Science — M,D
Electrical Engineering — M,D
Engineering and Applied Sciences—General — M,D
Environmental Engineering — M
Mechanical Engineering — M,D
Ocean Engineering — M,D

FLORIDA GULF COAST UNIVERSITY
Computer Science — M
Information Science — M

FLORIDA INSTITUTE OF TECHNOLOGY
Aerospace/Aeronautical Engineering — M,D
Aviation — M,D
Biomedical Engineering — M,D
Biotechnology — M,D

Chemical Engineering — M,D
Civil Engineering — M,D
Computer and Information Systems Security — M
Computer Science — M,D
Electrical Engineering — M,D
Engineering and Applied Sciences—General — M,D
Engineering Management — M,D
Ergonomics and Human Factors — M,D
Human-Computer Interaction — M
Management of Technology — M,D
Mechanical Engineering — M,D
Ocean Engineering — M,D
Operations Research — M,D
Safety Engineering — M
Software Engineering — M,D
Systems Engineering — M,D

FLORIDA INTERNATIONAL UNIVERSITY
Biomedical Engineering — M,D
Civil Engineering — M,D
Computer Engineering — M
Computer Science — M,D
Construction Management — M
Electrical Engineering — M,D
Engineering and Applied Sciences—General — M,D
Environmental Engineering — M
Information Science — M,D
Materials Engineering — M,D
Materials Sciences — M,D
Mechanical Engineering — M,D
Telecommunications — M

FLORIDA STATE UNIVERSITY
Bioinformatics — M,D
Biomedical Engineering — M,D
Chemical Engineering — M,D
Civil Engineering — M,D
Computer and Information Systems Security — M,D
Computer Science — M,D
Electrical Engineering — M,D
Energy and Power Engineering — M,D
Engineering and Applied Sciences—General — M,D
Environmental Engineering — M,D
Industrial/Management Engineering — M,D
Manufacturing Engineering — M,D
Materials Engineering — M,D
Materials Sciences — M,D
Mechanical Engineering — M,D

FORDHAM UNIVERSITY
Computer Science — M,O

FRANKLIN PIERCE UNIVERSITY
Energy Management and Policy — M,D,O
Telecommunications — M,D,O

FRANKLIN UNIVERSITY
Computer Science — M

FROSTBURG STATE UNIVERSITY
Computer Science — M

FULL SAIL UNIVERSITY
Game Design and Development — M

GANNON UNIVERSITY
Computer Science — M
Electrical Engineering — M
Engineering Management — M
Environmental Engineering — M

Information Science — M
Mechanical Engineering — M
Software Engineering — M

GEORGE MASON UNIVERSITY
Bioengineering — D
Bioinformatics — M,D,O
Civil Engineering — M,D
Computer and Information Systems Security — M,D,O
Computer Engineering — M,D,O
Computer Science — M,D,O
Construction Engineering — M,D
Electrical Engineering — M,D,O
Energy Management and Policy — M
Engineering and Applied Sciences—General — M,D,O
Engineering Physics — M,D,O
Environmental Engineering — M,D
Health Informatics — M,D
Information Science — M,D,O
Management of Technology — M
Operations Research — M,D,O
Software Engineering — M,D,O
Structural Engineering — M,D
Systems Engineering — M,D,O
Telecommunications — M,D,O
Transportation and Highway Engineering — M,D
Water Resources Engineering — M,D

GEORGETOWN UNIVERSITY
Bioinformatics — M,O
Computer Science — M,D
Management of Technology — M,D
Materials Sciences — D
Systems Engineering — M,D

THE GEORGE WASHINGTON UNIVERSITY
Aerospace/Aeronautical Engineering — M,D,O
Bioinformatics — M
Biotechnology — M,D,O
Civil Engineering — M,D,O
Computer and Information Systems Security — M,D,O
Computer Engineering — M,D,O
Computer Science — M,D,O
Electrical Engineering — M,D,O
Engineering and Applied Sciences—General — M,D,O*
Engineering Management — M,D,O
Environmental Engineering — M,D,O
Management of Technology — M,D
Materials Sciences — M,D
Mechanical Engineering — M,D,O
Systems Engineering — M,D,O
Technology and Public Policy — M,O
Telecommunications — M,D,O

GEORGIA INSTITUTE OF TECHNOLOGY
Aerospace/Aeronautical Engineering — M,D
Artificial Intelligence/Robotics — D
Bioengineering — M,D
Bioinformatics — M,D
Biomedical Engineering — M,D
Chemical Engineering — M,D
Civil Engineering — M,D
Computer and Information Systems Security — M
Computer Engineering — M,D
Computer Science — M,D
Electrical Engineering — M,D
Engineering and Applied Sciences—General — M,D
Environmental Engineering — M,D
Ergonomics and Human Factors — D
Human-Computer Interaction — M

Industrial/Management
  Engineering — M,D
Materials Engineering — M,D
Mechanical Engineering — M,D
Mechanics — M,D
Nuclear Engineering — M,D
Operations Research — M,D
Systems Engineering — M

GEORGIA REGENTS UNIVERSITY
Health Informatics — M

GEORGIA SOUTHERN UNIVERSITY
Computer Science — M
Electrical Engineering — M
Energy and Power
  Engineering — M
Engineering and Applied
  Sciences—General — M,O
Engineering Management — M
Manufacturing Engineering — O
Mechanical Engineering — M
Systems Engineering — M

GEORGIA SOUTHWESTERN STATE UNIVERSITY
Computer Science — M,O

GEORGIA STATE UNIVERSITY
Bioinformatics — M,D
Computer Science — M,D
Health Informatics — M,D,O
Information Science — M,D,O
Operations Research — M,D

GOLDEN GATE UNIVERSITY
Health Informatics — M,D,O
Management of Technology — M,D,O

GOVERNORS STATE UNIVERSITY
Computer Science — M

THE GRADUATE CENTER, CITY UNIVERSITY OF NEW YORK
Biomedical Engineering — D
Chemical Engineering — D
Civil Engineering — D
Computer Science — D
Electrical Engineering — D
Engineering and Applied
  Sciences—General — D
Mechanical Engineering — D

GRAND CANYON UNIVERSITY
Health Informatics — M

GRAND VALLEY STATE UNIVERSITY
Bioinformatics — M
Computer Engineering — M
Computer Science — M
Electrical Engineering — M
Engineering and Applied
  Sciences—General — M
Information Science — M
Manufacturing Engineering — M
Mechanical Engineering — M
Medical Informatics — M
Software Engineering — M

HAMPTON UNIVERSITY
Computer and Information
  Systems Security — M
Computer Science — M

HARDING UNIVERSITY
Management of Technology — M

HARRISBURG UNIVERSITY OF SCIENCE AND TECHNOLOGY
Construction Management — M
Management of Technology — M
Systems Engineering — M

HARVARD UNIVERSITY
Applied Science and
  Technology — M,O
Biomedical Engineering — D
Biotechnology — M,O
Computer Science — M,D
Engineering and Applied
  Sciences—General — M,D
Information Science — M,D,O
Management of Technology — D

HEC MONTREAL
Financial Engineering — M
Operations Research — M

HERZING UNIVERSITY ONLINE
Management of Technology — M

HOFSTRA UNIVERSITY
Computer and Information
  Systems Security — M
Engineering and Applied
  Sciences—General — M
Internet Engineering — M

HOLY NAMES UNIVERSITY
Energy Management
  and Policy — M

HOOD COLLEGE
Biotechnology — M,O
Computer and Information
  Systems Security — M,O
Computer Science — M,O
Information Science — M,O
Systems Science — M

HOWARD UNIVERSITY
Biotechnology — M,D
Chemical Engineering — M
Civil Engineering — M
Computer Science — M
Electrical Engineering — M,D
Engineering and Applied
  Sciences—General — M,D
Mechanical Engineering — M,D

HUMBOLDT STATE UNIVERSITY
Hazardous Materials
  Management — M

IDAHO STATE UNIVERSITY
Civil Engineering — M
Engineering and Applied
  Sciences—General — M,D,O
Environmental Engineering — M
Hazardous Materials
  Management — M
Management of Technology — M
Mechanical Engineering — M
Nuclear Engineering — M,D
Operations Research — M

ILLINOIS INSTITUTE OF TECHNOLOGY
Aerospace/Aeronautical
  Engineering — M,D
Agricultural Engineering — M

Architectural Engineering — M,D
Artificial Intelligence/Robotics — M,D
Bioengineering — M,D
Biomedical Engineering — M,D
Chemical Engineering — M,D
Civil Engineering — M,D
Computer and Information
  Systems Security — M,D
Computer Engineering — M,D
Computer Science — M,D
Construction Engineering — M,D
Construction Management — M,D
Database Systems — M,D
Electrical Engineering — M,D
Engineering and Applied
  Sciences—General — M,D
Environmental Engineering — M,D
Geotechnical Engineering — M,D
Manufacturing Engineering — M,D
Materials Engineering — M,D
Materials Sciences — M,D
Mechanical Engineering — M,D
Software Engineering — M,D
Structural Engineering — M,D
Telecommunications — M,D
Transportation and Highway
  Engineering — M,D

ILLINOIS STATE UNIVERSITY
Biotechnology — M
Industrial/Management
  Engineering — M
Management of Technology — M

INDIANA STATE UNIVERSITY
Computer Engineering — M
Computer Science — M
Engineering and Applied
  Sciences—General — M
Industrial/Management
  Engineering — M
Management of Technology — D

INDIANA UNIVERSITY BLOOMINGTON
Artificial Intelligence/Robotics — M,D
Bioinformatics — M,D
Biotechnology — M,D
Computer and Information
  Systems Security — M,D
Computer Science — M,D
Energy Management
  and Policy — M,D,O
Ergonomics and Human
  Factors — M,D
Health Informatics — M,D
Human-Computer Interaction — M,D
Information Science — M,D,O
Materials Sciences — M,D
Safety Engineering — M,D
Telecommunications — M
Water Resources Engineering — M,D,O

INDIANA UNIVERSITY OF PENNSYLVANIA
Nanotechnology — M

INDIANA UNIVERSITY–PURDUE UNIVERSITY FORT WAYNE
Civil Engineering — M
Computer Engineering — M
Computer Science — M
Electrical Engineering — M
Engineering and Applied
  Sciences—General — M,O
Industrial/Management
  Engineering — M
Information Science — M
Mechanical Engineering — M

Operations Research — M,O
Systems Engineering — M

INDIANA UNIVERSITY–PURDUE UNIVERSITY INDIANAPOLIS
Bioinformatics — M,D
Biomedical Engineering — M,D,O
Computer Engineering — M,D
Computer Science — M,D,O
Electrical Engineering — M,D
Health Informatics — M,D
Human-Computer Interaction — M,D
Information Science — M
Mechanical Engineering — M,D,O

INDIANA UNIVERSITY SOUTH BEND
Computer Science — M

INSTITUTO CENTROAMERICANO DE ADMINISTRACIÓN DE EMPRESAS
Management of Technology — M

INSTITUTO TECNOLOGICO DE SANTO DOMINGO
Construction Management — M,O
Energy and Power
  Engineering — M,D,O
Energy Management
  and Policy — M,D,O
Engineering and Applied
  Sciences—General — M,O
Environmental Engineering — M,O
Industrial/Management
  Engineering — M,O
Information Science — M,O
Software Engineering — M,O
Structural Engineering — M,O
Telecommunications — M,O

INSTITUTO TECNOLÓGICO Y DE ESTUDIOS SUPERIORES DE MONTERREY, CAMPUS CENTRAL DE VERACRUZ
Computer Science — M

INSTITUTO TECNOLÓGICO Y DE ESTUDIOS SUPERIORES DE MONTERREY, CAMPUS CHIHUAHUA
Computer Engineering — M,O
Electrical Engineering — M,O
Engineering Management — M,O
Industrial/Management
  Engineering — M,O
Mechanical Engineering — M,O
Systems Engineering — M,O

INSTITUTO TECNOLÓGICO Y DE ESTUDIOS SUPERIORES DE MONTERREY, CAMPUS CIUDAD DE MÉXICO
Computer Science — M,D
Environmental Engineering — M,D
Industrial/Management
  Engineering — M,D
Telecommunications
  Management — M

INSTITUTO TECNOLÓGICO Y DE ESTUDIOS SUPERIORES DE MONTERREY, CAMPUS CIUDAD OBREGÓN
Engineering and Applied
  Sciences—General — M
Telecommunications
  Management — M

*M—masters degree; D—doctorate; O—other advanced degree; *—Close-Up and/or Display*

INSTITUTO TECNOLÓGICO Y DE ESTUDIOS SUPERIORES DE MONTERREY, CAMPUS CUERNAVACA
Computer Science — M,D
Information Science — M,D
Management of Technology — M,D

INSTITUTO TECNOLÓGICO Y DE ESTUDIOS SUPERIORES DE MONTERREY, CAMPUS ESTADO DE MÉXICO
Computer Science — M,D
Information Science — M,D
Materials Engineering — M,D
Materials Sciences — M,D
Telecommunications Management — M,D

INSTITUTO TECNOLÓGICO Y DE ESTUDIOS SUPERIORES DE MONTERREY, CAMPUS IRAPUATO
Computer Science — M,D
Information Science — M,D
Management of Technology — M,D
Telecommunications Management — M,D

INSTITUTO TECNOLÓGICO Y DE ESTUDIOS SUPERIORES DE MONTERREY, CAMPUS LAGUNA
Industrial/Management Engineering — M

INSTITUTO TECNOLÓGICO Y DE ESTUDIOS SUPERIORES DE MONTERREY, CAMPUS MONTERREY
Agricultural Engineering — M,D
Artificial Intelligence/Robotics — M,D
Biotechnology — M,D
Chemical Engineering — M,D
Civil Engineering — M,D
Computer Science — M,D
Electrical Engineering — M,D
Engineering and Applied Sciences—General — M,D
Environmental Engineering — M,D
Industrial/Management Engineering — M,D
Information Science — M,D
Manufacturing Engineering — M,D
Mechanical Engineering — M,D
Systems Engineering — M,D

INSTITUTO TECNOLÓGICO Y DE ESTUDIOS SUPERIORES DE MONTERREY, CAMPUS SONORA NORTE
Information Science — M

INTER AMERICAN UNIVERSITY OF PUERTO RICO, BAYAMÓN CAMPUS
Biotechnology — M

INTER AMERICAN UNIVERSITY OF PUERTO RICO, FAJARDO CAMPUS
Computer Science — M

INTER AMERICAN UNIVERSITY OF PUERTO RICO, GUAYAMA CAMPUS
Computer and Information Systems Security — M
Computer Science — M

INTER AMERICAN UNIVERSITY OF PUERTO RICO, METROPOLITAN CAMPUS
Computer Science — M

INTERNATIONAL TECHNOLOGICAL UNIVERSITY
Computer Engineering — M
Electrical Engineering — M,D
Engineering Management — M
Software Engineering — M

THE INTERNATIONAL UNIVERSITY OF MONACO
Financial Engineering — M

IONA COLLEGE
Computer and Information Systems Security — M
Computer Science — M
Management of Technology — M,O

IOWA STATE UNIVERSITY OF SCIENCE AND TECHNOLOGY
Aerospace/Aeronautical Engineering — M,D
Agricultural Engineering — M,D
Bioinformatics — M,D
Chemical Engineering — M,D
Civil Engineering — M,D
Computer Engineering — M,D
Computer Science — M,D
Construction Engineering — M,D
Electrical Engineering — M,D
Environmental Engineering — M,D
Geotechnical Engineering — M,D
Human-Computer Interaction — M,D
Industrial/Management Engineering — M,D
Information Science — M
Materials Engineering — M,D
Materials Sciences — M,D
Mechanical Engineering — M,D
Mechanics — M,D
Operations Research — M,D
Structural Engineering — M,D
Systems Engineering — M
Transportation and Highway Engineering — M,D

JACKSON STATE UNIVERSITY
Computer Science — M
Materials Sciences — M

JACKSONVILLE STATE UNIVERSITY
Computer Science — M
Software Engineering — M

JAMES MADISON UNIVERSITY
Applied Science and Technology — M
Computer Science — M

JOHN MARSHALL LAW SCHOOL
Computer and Information Systems Security — M,D

JOHNS HOPKINS UNIVERSITY
Aerospace/Aeronautical Engineering — M,O
Artificial Intelligence/Robotics — M
Bioengineering — M,D
Bioinformatics — M,D,O
Biomedical Engineering — M,D,O
Biotechnology — M
Chemical Engineering — M,D
Civil Engineering — M,D
Computer and Information Systems Security — M,O
Computer Engineering — M,D,O

Computer Science — M,D,O
Electrical Engineering — M,D,O
Energy Management and Policy — M,O
Engineering and Applied Sciences—General — M,D,O
Engineering Management — M
Environmental Engineering — M,D,O
Health Informatics — M,D,O
Information Science — M
Management of Technology — M,O
Materials Engineering — M,D
Materials Sciences — M,D
Mechanical Engineering — M,D
Mechanics — M
Medical Informatics — M,D,O
Nanotechnology — M
Operations Research — M,D
Systems Engineering — M,O
Telecommunications — M,O

KANSAS STATE UNIVERSITY
Agricultural Engineering — M,D
Architectural Engineering — M
Bioengineering — M,D
Chemical Engineering — M,D,O
Civil Engineering — M,D
Computer Engineering — M,D
Computer Science — M,D
Electrical Engineering — M,D
Energy and Power Engineering — M,D
Energy Management and Policy — M,D
Engineering and Applied Sciences—General — M,D,O
Engineering Management — M,D
Environmental Engineering — M,D
Geotechnical Engineering — M,D
Industrial/Management Engineering — M,D
Information Science — M,D
Management of Technology — M
Manufacturing Engineering — M,D
Mechanical Engineering — M,D
Nuclear Engineering — M,D
Operations Research — M,D
Structural Engineering — M,D
Transportation and Highway Engineering — M,D
Water Resources Engineering — M,D

KAPLAN UNIVERSITY, DAVENPORT CAMPUS
Computer and Information Systems Security — M

KEAN UNIVERSITY
Biotechnology — M

KEISER UNIVERSITY
Computer and Information Systems Security — M

KENNESAW STATE UNIVERSITY
Computer Science — M
Information Science — M

KENT STATE UNIVERSITY
Computer and Information Systems Security — M,O
Computer Science — M,D
Engineering and Applied Sciences—General — M
Information Science — M,O

KENTUCKY STATE UNIVERSITY
Computer Science — M

KETTERING UNIVERSITY
Electrical Engineering — M
Engineering Management — M
Manufacturing Engineering — M
Mechanical Engineering — M

KNOWLEDGE SYSTEMS INSTITUTE
Computer Science — M
Information Science — M

KUTZTOWN UNIVERSITY OF PENNSYLVANIA
Computer Science — M

LAKEHEAD UNIVERSITY
Computer Engineering — M
Computer Science — M
Electrical Engineering — M
Engineering and Applied Sciences—General — M
Environmental Engineering — M

LAMAR UNIVERSITY
Chemical Engineering — D
Computer Science — M
Electrical Engineering — M,D
Engineering and Applied Sciences—General — M,D
Engineering Management — M,D
Environmental Engineering — M
Industrial/Management Engineering — M,D
Mechanical Engineering — M,D

LA SALLE UNIVERSITY
Computer Science — M,O
Management of Technology — M,O

LAURENTIAN UNIVERSITY
Engineering and Applied Sciences—General — M,D
Mineral/Mining Engineering — M,D

LAWRENCE TECHNOLOGICAL UNIVERSITY
Architectural Engineering — M,D
Automotive Engineering — M,D
Civil Engineering — M,D
Computer Engineering — M,D
Computer Science — M
Construction Engineering — M,D
Electrical Engineering — M,D
Engineering and Applied Sciences—General — M,D
Engineering Management — M,D
Industrial/Management Engineering — M,D
Manufacturing Engineering — M,D
Mechanical Engineering — M,D

LEBANESE AMERICAN UNIVERSITY
Computer Science — M

LEHIGH UNIVERSITY
Bioengineering — M,D
Chemical Engineering — M,D
Civil Engineering — M,D
Computer Engineering — M,D
Computer Science — M,D
Electrical Engineering — M,D
Energy and Power Engineering — M
Engineering and Applied Sciences—General — M,D
Engineering Management — M,D
Environmental Engineering — M,D
Industrial/Management Engineering — M,D
Information Science — M

Manufacturing Engineering	M
Materials Engineering	M,D
Materials Sciences	M,D
Mechanical Engineering	M,D
Mechanics	M,D
Polymer Science and Engineering	M,D
Systems Engineering	M,D

LEHMAN COLLEGE OF THE CITY UNIVERSITY OF NEW YORK
Computer Science	M

LETOURNEAU UNIVERSITY
Engineering and Applied Sciences—General	M
Engineering Management	M

LEWIS UNIVERSITY
Aviation	M
Computer and Information Systems Security	M
Database Systems	M
Management of Technology	M

LIBERTY UNIVERSITY
Computer and Information Systems Security	M,D,O
Engineering and Applied Sciences—General	M
Management of Technology	M,D,O

LIPSCOMB UNIVERSITY
Computer and Information Systems Security	M,O
Database Systems	M,O
Engineering Management	M
Health Informatics	M,O
Management of Technology	M,O

LOGAN UNIVERSITY
Health Informatics	M,D

LONG ISLAND UNIVERSITY–LIU BROOKLYN
Computer Science	M

LONG ISLAND UNIVERSITY–LIU POST
Information Science	M,D,O

LOUISIANA STATE UNIVERSITY AND AGRICULTURAL & MECHANICAL COLLEGE
Agricultural Engineering	M,D
Applied Science and Technology	M
Bioengineering	M,D
Chemical Engineering	M,D
Civil Engineering	M,D
Computer Engineering	M,D
Computer Science	M,D
Construction Management	M,D
Electrical Engineering	M,D
Engineering and Applied Sciences—General	M,D
Environmental Engineering	M,D
Geotechnical Engineering	M,D
Mechanical Engineering	M,D
Mechanics	M,D
Petroleum Engineering	M,D
Structural Engineering	M,D
Systems Science	M,D
Transportation and Highway Engineering	M,D
Water Resources Engineering	M,D

LOUISIANA STATE UNIVERSITY IN SHREVEPORT
Computer Science	M
Systems Science	M

LOUISIANA TECH UNIVERSITY
Biomedical Engineering	D
Chemical Engineering	M,D
Civil Engineering	M,D
Computer Science	M
Electrical Engineering	M,D
Engineering and Applied Sciences—General	M,D
Engineering Management	M
Engineering Physics	M,D
Health Informatics	M
Industrial/Management Engineering	M
Mechanical Engineering	M,D
Modeling and Simulation	M,D

LOYOLA MARYMOUNT UNIVERSITY
Civil Engineering	M
Engineering Management	M
Mechanical Engineering	M
Systems Engineering	M

LOYOLA UNIVERSITY CHICAGO
Computer Science	M
Information Science	M
Software Engineering	M

LOYOLA UNIVERSITY MARYLAND
Computer and Information Systems Security	O
Computer Science	M
Software Engineering	M

MAHARISHI UNIVERSITY OF MANAGEMENT
Computer Science	M

MANHATTAN COLLEGE
Chemical Engineering	M
Civil Engineering	M
Computer Engineering	M
Electrical Engineering	M
Engineering and Applied Sciences—General	M
Environmental Engineering	M
Mechanical Engineering	M

MARIST COLLEGE
Computer Science	M,O
Management of Technology	M,O
Software Engineering	M,O

MARLBORO COLLEGE
Information Science	M,O

MARQUETTE UNIVERSITY
Bioinformatics	M,D
Biomedical Engineering	M,D
Civil Engineering	M,D,O
Computer Engineering	M,D,O
Computer Science	M,D
Construction Engineering	M,D,O
Construction Management	M,D,O
Electrical Engineering	M,D,O
Engineering and Applied Sciences—General	M,D,O
Engineering Management	M,D,O
Environmental Engineering	M,D,O
Hazardous Materials Management	M,D,O
Management of Technology	M,D
Mechanical Engineering	M,D,O

Structural Engineering	M,D,O
Transportation and Highway Engineering	M,D,O
Water Resources Engineering	M,D,O

MARSHALL UNIVERSITY
Computer Science	M
Engineering and Applied Sciences—General	M
Engineering Management	M
Environmental Engineering	M
Health Informatics	M
Information Science	M
Management of Technology	M
Mechanical Engineering	M
Transportation and Highway Engineering	M

MARYMOUNT UNIVERSITY
Computer and Information Systems Security	M,O
Medical Informatics	M,O

MARYWOOD UNIVERSITY
Biotechnology	M
Computer and Information Systems Security	M

MASSACHUSETTS INSTITUTE OF TECHNOLOGY
Aerospace/Aeronautical Engineering	M,D,O
Bioengineering	M,D
Bioinformatics	M,D
Biomedical Engineering	M,D
Chemical Engineering	M,D
Civil Engineering	M,D,O
Computer Engineering	M,D,O
Computer Science	M,D,O
Construction Engineering	M,D,O
Electrical Engineering	M,D,O
Engineering and Applied Sciences—General	M,D,O
Engineering Management	M,D
Environmental Engineering	M,D,O
Geotechnical Engineering	M,D,O
Information Science	M,D,O
Manufacturing Engineering	M,D,O
Materials Engineering	M,D,O
Materials Sciences	M,D,O
Mechanical Engineering	M,D,O
Nuclear Engineering	M,D,O
Ocean Engineering	M,D,O
Operations Research	M,D
Structural Engineering	M,D,O
Systems Engineering	M,D
Technology and Public Policy	M,D
Transportation and Highway Engineering	M,D,O

MAYO GRADUATE SCHOOL
Biomedical Engineering	D

MCGILL UNIVERSITY
Aerospace/Aeronautical Engineering	M,D
Agricultural Engineering	M,D
Bioengineering	M,D
Bioinformatics	M,D
Biomedical Engineering	M,D
Biotechnology	M,D,O
Chemical Engineering	M,D
Civil Engineering	M,D
Computer Engineering	M,D
Computer Science	M,D
Electrical Engineering	M,D
Engineering and Applied Sciences—General	M,D,O
Environmental Engineering	M,D
Geotechnical Engineering	M,D

Hydraulics	M,D
Materials Engineering	M,D,O
Mechanical Engineering	M,D
Mechanics	M,D
Mineral/Mining Engineering	M,D,O
Structural Engineering	M,D
Water Resources Engineering	M,D

MCMASTER UNIVERSITY
Chemical Engineering	M,D
Civil Engineering	M,D
Computer Science	M,D
Electrical Engineering	M,D
Engineering and Applied Sciences—General	M,D
Engineering Physics	M,D
Materials Engineering	M,D
Materials Sciences	M,D
Mechanical Engineering	M,D
Nuclear Engineering	M,D
Software Engineering	M,D

MCNEESE STATE UNIVERSITY
Chemical Engineering	M
Civil Engineering	M
Computer Science	M
Electrical Engineering	M
Engineering and Applied Sciences—General	M,O
Engineering Management	M
Mechanical Engineering	M,O

MEDICAL COLLEGE OF WISCONSIN
Bioinformatics	M
Medical Informatics	M

MEMORIAL UNIVERSITY OF NEWFOUNDLAND
Civil Engineering	M,D
Computer Engineering	M,D
Computer Science	M,D
Electrical Engineering	M,D
Engineering and Applied Sciences—General	M,D
Environmental Engineering	M
Mechanical Engineering	M,D
Ocean Engineering	M,D

MERCER UNIVERSITY
Biomedical Engineering	M
Computer Engineering	M
Electrical Engineering	M
Engineering and Applied Sciences—General	M
Engineering Management	M
Environmental Engineering	M
Management of Technology	M
Mechanical Engineering	M
Software Engineering	M

MERCY COLLEGE
Computer and Information Systems Security	M

MERRIMACK COLLEGE
Engineering and Applied Sciences—General	M
Engineering Management	M
Mechanical Engineering	M

METROPOLITAN STATE UNIVERSITY
Computer and Information Systems Security	M,D,O
Computer Science	M
Database Systems	M,D,O
Health Informatics	M,D,O

*M—masters degree; D—doctorate; O—other advanced degree; *—Close-Up and/or Display*

MIAMI UNIVERSITY
Chemical Engineering	M
Engineering and Applied Sciences—General	M
Systems Science	M

MICHIGAN STATE UNIVERSITY
Biosystems Engineering	M,D
Chemical Engineering	M,D
Civil Engineering	M,D
Computer Science	M,D
Construction Management	M,D
Electrical Engineering	M,D
Engineering and Applied Sciences—General	M,D
Environmental Engineering	M,D
Game Design and Development	M
Manufacturing Engineering	M,D
Materials Engineering	M,D
Materials Sciences	M,D
Mechanical Engineering	M,D
Mechanics	M,D
Telecommunications	M

MICHIGAN TECHNOLOGICAL UNIVERSITY
Automotive Engineering	M,D,O
Biomedical Engineering	M,D
Chemical Engineering	M,D
Civil Engineering	M,D
Computer Engineering	M,D,O
Computer Science	M,D
Electrical Engineering	M,D,O
Energy Management and Policy	M,D
Engineering and Applied Sciences—General	M,D,O
Engineering Physics	M,D
Environmental Engineering	M,D,O
Ergonomics and Human Factors	M,D
Geological Engineering	M,D
Materials Engineering	M,D
Mechanical Engineering	M,D,O
Mechanics	M,D,O
Metallurgical Engineering and Metallurgy	M,D
Mineral/Mining Engineering	M,D

MIDDLE TENNESSEE STATE UNIVERSITY
Aerospace/Aeronautical Engineering	M
Biotechnology	M
Computer Science	M
Engineering Management	M
Medical Informatics	M

MIDWESTERN STATE UNIVERSITY
Computer Science	M
Health Informatics	M,O

MILLENNIA ATLANTIC UNIVERSITY
Health Informatics	M

MILLS COLLEGE
Computer Science	M,O

MILWAUKEE SCHOOL OF ENGINEERING
Architectural Engineering	M
Civil Engineering	M
Construction Management	M
Engineering and Applied Sciences—General	M*
Engineering Management	M
Medical Informatics	M

MINNESOTA STATE UNIVERSITY MANKATO
Automotive Engineering	M
Database Systems	M,O
Electrical Engineering	M
Manufacturing Engineering	M

MISSISSIPPI COLLEGE
Computer Science	M

MISSISSIPPI STATE UNIVERSITY
Aerospace/Aeronautical Engineering	M,D
Bioengineering	M,D
Chemical Engineering	M,D
Civil Engineering	M,D
Computer Engineering	M,D
Computer Science	M,D
Electrical Engineering	M,D
Engineering and Applied Sciences—General	M,D
Industrial/Management Engineering	M,D
Mechanical Engineering	M,D
Systems Engineering	M,D

MISSISSIPPI VALLEY STATE UNIVERSITY
Bioinformatics	M

MISSOURI STATE UNIVERSITY
Applied Science and Technology	M
Computer Science	M
Construction Management	M
Materials Sciences	M

MISSOURI UNIVERSITY OF SCIENCE AND TECHNOLOGY
Aerospace/Aeronautical Engineering	M,D
Ceramic Sciences and Engineering	M,D
Chemical Engineering	M,D
Civil Engineering	M,D
Computer Engineering	M,D
Computer Science	M,D
Construction Engineering	M,D
Electrical Engineering	M,D
Engineering and Applied Sciences—General	M,D
Engineering Management	M,D
Environmental Engineering	M,D
Geological Engineering	M,D
Geotechnical Engineering	M,D
Hydraulics	M,D
Information Science	M
Manufacturing Engineering	M,D
Mechanical Engineering	M,D
Mechanics	M,D
Metallurgical Engineering and Metallurgy	M,D
Mineral/Mining Engineering	M,D
Nuclear Engineering	M,D
Petroleum Engineering	M,D
Systems Engineering	M,D

MISSOURI WESTERN STATE UNIVERSITY
Computer and Information Systems Security	M
Engineering and Applied Sciences—General	M
Ergonomics and Human Factors	M

MOLLOY COLLEGE
Health Informatics	M,D,O

MONMOUTH UNIVERSITY
Computer Science	M,O
Software Engineering	M,O

MONTANA STATE UNIVERSITY
Chemical Engineering	M,D
Civil Engineering	M,D
Computer Engineering	M,D
Computer Science	M,D
Construction Engineering	M,D
Electrical Engineering	M,D
Engineering and Applied Sciences—General	M,D
Environmental Engineering	M,D
Industrial/Management Engineering	M,D
Mechanical Engineering	M,D
Mechanics	M,D

MONTANA TECH OF THE UNIVERSITY OF MONTANA
Electrical Engineering	M
Engineering and Applied Sciences—General	M
Environmental Engineering	M
Geological Engineering	M
Health Informatics	O
Industrial/Management Engineering	M
Materials Sciences	D
Metallurgical Engineering and Metallurgy	M
Mineral/Mining Engineering	M
Petroleum Engineering	M

MONTCLAIR STATE UNIVERSITY
Computer Science	M,O
Database Systems	O

MOREHEAD STATE UNIVERSITY
Industrial/Management Engineering	M

MORGAN STATE UNIVERSITY
Bioinformatics	M
Civil Engineering	M,D
Electrical Engineering	M,D
Engineering and Applied Sciences—General	M,D
Industrial/Management Engineering	M,D
Transportation and Highway Engineering	M

MOUNT ST. MARY'S UNIVERSITY (MD)
Biotechnology	M

MURRAY STATE UNIVERSITY
Management of Technology	M
Safety Engineering	M
Telecommunications Management	M

NATIONAL UNIVERSITY
Computer and Information Systems Security	M,O
Computer Science	M,O
Database Systems	M,O
Engineering Management	M,O
Environmental Engineering	M,O
Health Informatics	M,D,O
Management of Technology	M,O
Medical Informatics	M,D,O
Software Engineering	M,O
Systems Engineering	M,O
Telecommunications	M,O

NAVAL POSTGRADUATE SCHOOL
Aerospace/Aeronautical Engineering	M,D,O

Applied Science and Technology	M,D
Computer and Information Systems Security	M,D
Computer Engineering	M,D,O
Computer Science	M,D,O
Electrical Engineering	M,D,O
Engineering Management	M,D,O
Information Science	M,D,O
Mechanical Engineering	M,D,O
Modeling and Simulation	M,D
Operations Research	M,D
Software Engineering	M,D
Systems Engineering	M,D,O

NEW ENGLAND INSTITUTE OF TECHNOLOGY
Construction Management	M

NEW JERSEY CITY UNIVERSITY
Computer and Information Systems Security	M,D

NEW JERSEY INSTITUTE OF TECHNOLOGY
Bioinformatics	M,D
Biomedical Engineering	M,D
Chemical Engineering	M,D
Computer and Information Systems Security	M,D
Computer Engineering	M,D
Computer Science	M,D
Electrical Engineering	M,D
Energy and Power Engineering	M,D
Engineering and Applied Sciences—General	M,D
Engineering Management	M,D
Industrial/Management Engineering	M,D
Information Science	M,D
Internet Engineering	M,D
Manufacturing Engineering	M,D
Materials Engineering	M,D
Materials Sciences	M,D
Mechanical Engineering	M,D
Pharmaceutical Engineering	M,D
Safety Engineering	M,D
Software Engineering	M,D
Systems Science	M,D
Telecommunications	M,D
Transportation and Highway Engineering	M,D

NEW MEXICO HIGHLANDS UNIVERSITY
Computer Science	M

NEW MEXICO INSTITUTE OF MINING AND TECHNOLOGY
Computer Science	M,D
Electrical Engineering	M
Engineering Management	M
Environmental Engineering	M
Hazardous Materials Management	M
Materials Engineering	M,D
Mechanical Engineering	M
Mechanics	M
Mineral/Mining Engineering	M
Operations Research	M,D
Petroleum Engineering	M,D
Systems Engineering	M
Water Resources Engineering	M

NEW MEXICO STATE UNIVERSITY
Aerospace/Aeronautical Engineering	M,D
Bioinformatics	M,D
Biotechnology	M,D
Chemical Engineering	M,D
Civil Engineering	M,D

Computer Engineering	M,D,O
Computer Science	M,D
Electrical Engineering	M,D,O
Engineering and Applied Sciences—General	M,D,O
Geological Engineering	M,D
Industrial/Management Engineering	M,D,O
Mechanical Engineering	M,D
Systems Engineering	M,D,O

NEWSCHOOL OF ARCHITECTURE AND DESIGN

Construction Management	M

NEW YORK INSTITUTE OF TECHNOLOGY

Computer and Information Systems Security	M
Computer Engineering	M
Computer Science	M
Electrical Engineering	M
Energy and Power Engineering	M,O
Energy Management and Policy	M,O
Engineering and Applied Sciences—General	M,O
Environmental Engineering	M

NEW YORK UNIVERSITY

Agricultural Engineering	M,D
Bioinformatics	M,D
Biomedical Engineering	M,D
Biotechnology	M
Chemical Engineering	M,D
Civil Engineering	M,D
Computer and Information Systems Security	O
Computer Engineering	M,O
Computer Science	M,D
Construction Management	M,D,O
Database Systems	M,O
Electrical Engineering	M,D
Energy Management and Policy	M,O
Engineering and Applied Sciences—General	M,D,O
Environmental Engineering	M
Ergonomics and Human Factors	M,D
Financial Engineering	M,O
Game Design and Development	M
Industrial/Management Engineering	M
Management of Technology	M,D,O
Manufacturing Engineering	M
Mechanical Engineering	M,D
Software Engineering	O
Systems Engineering	M
Telecommunications Management	M,D,O
Transportation and Highway Engineering	M,D

NICHOLLS STATE UNIVERSITY

Computer Science	M

NORFOLK STATE UNIVERSITY

Computer Engineering	M
Computer Science	M
Electrical Engineering	M
Materials Sciences	M

NORTH CAROLINA AGRICULTURAL AND TECHNICAL STATE UNIVERSITY

Bioengineering	M
Chemical Engineering	M

Civil Engineering	M
Computer Engineering	M,D
Computer Science	M
Construction Management	M
Electrical Engineering	M,D
Energy and Power Engineering	M,D
Engineering and Applied Sciences—General	M,D
Industrial/Management Engineering	M,D
Management of Technology	M
Mechanical Engineering	M,D
Systems Engineering	M,D

NORTH CAROLINA STATE UNIVERSITY

Aerospace/Aeronautical Engineering	M,D
Agricultural Engineering	M,D,O
Bioengineering	M,D,O
Bioinformatics	M,D
Biomedical Engineering	M,D
Biotechnology	M
Chemical Engineering	M,D
Civil Engineering	M,D
Computer Engineering	M,D
Computer Science	M,D
Electrical Engineering	M,D
Engineering and Applied Sciences—General	M,D
Ergonomics and Human Factors	D
Financial Engineering	M
Industrial/Management Engineering	M,D
Management of Technology	D
Manufacturing Engineering	M
Materials Engineering	M,D
Materials Sciences	M,D
Mechanical Engineering	M,D
Nuclear Engineering	M,D
Operations Research	M,D
Paper and Pulp Engineering	M,D
Polymer Science and Engineering	D
Textile Sciences and Engineering	M,D

NORTH CENTRAL COLLEGE

Computer Science	M

NORTH DAKOTA STATE UNIVERSITY

Agricultural Engineering	M,D
Bioinformatics	M,D
Biosystems Engineering	M,D
Civil Engineering	M,D
Computer Engineering	M,D
Computer Science	M,D,O
Construction Management	M
Electrical Engineering	M,D
Engineering and Applied Sciences—General	M,D*
Environmental Engineering	M,D
Industrial/Management Engineering	M,D
Manufacturing Engineering	M,D
Materials Sciences	M,D
Mechanical Engineering	M,D
Mechanics	M,D
Nanotechnology	M,D
Operations Research	M,D,O
Polymer Science and Engineering	M,D
Software Engineering	M,D,O

NORTHEASTERN ILLINOIS UNIVERSITY

Computer Science	M

NORTHEASTERN UNIVERSITY

Bioengineering	M,D,O
Bioinformatics	M
Biotechnology	M,D,O
Chemical Engineering	M,D,O
Civil Engineering	M,D,O
Computer and Information Systems Security	M,D,O
Computer Engineering	M,D,O
Computer Science	M,D
Electrical Engineering	M,D,O
Energy and Power Engineering	M,D,O
Engineering and Applied Sciences—General	M,D,O
Engineering Management	M,D,O
Health Informatics	M,D,O
Industrial/Management Engineering	M,D,O
Information Science	M,D,O
Mechanical Engineering	M,D,O
Operations Research	M,D,O
Systems Engineering	M,D,O
Telecommunications	M,D,O

NORTHERN ARIZONA UNIVERSITY

Civil Engineering	M
Computer Science	M
Electrical Engineering	M
Engineering and Applied Sciences—General	M,D,O
Environmental Engineering	M
Mechanical Engineering	M

NORTHERN ILLINOIS UNIVERSITY

Computer Science	M
Electrical Engineering	M
Engineering and Applied Sciences—General	M
Industrial/Management Engineering	M
Mechanical Engineering	M

NORTHERN KENTUCKY UNIVERSITY

Computer and Information Systems Security	M,O
Computer Science	M,O
Health Informatics	M,O
Information Science	M,O
Management of Technology	M
Software Engineering	M,O

NORTHWESTERN POLYTECHNIC UNIVERSITY

Computer Engineering	M
Computer Science	M
Electrical Engineering	M
Engineering and Applied Sciences—General	M

NORTHWESTERN UNIVERSITY

Bioengineering	D
Biomedical Engineering	M,D
Biotechnology	M,D
Chemical Engineering	M,D
Civil Engineering	M,D
Computer and Information Systems Security	M
Computer Engineering	M,D
Computer Science	M,D
Database Systems	M
Electrical Engineering	M,D
Engineering and Applied Sciences—General	M,D,O
Engineering Design	M
Engineering Management	M
Environmental Engineering	M,D
Geotechnical Engineering	M,D
Health Informatics	D

Industrial/Management Engineering	M,D
Information Science	M
Materials Engineering	M,D,O
Materials Sciences	M,D,O
Mechanical Engineering	M,D
Mechanics	M,D
Medical Informatics	M,D
Software Engineering	M
Structural Engineering	M,D
Transportation and Highway Engineering	M,D

NORTHWEST MISSOURI STATE UNIVERSITY

Computer Science	M

NORWICH UNIVERSITY

Civil Engineering	M
Computer and Information Systems Security	M
Construction Management	M
Environmental Engineering	M
Geotechnical Engineering	M
Structural Engineering	M
Water Resources Engineering	M

NOTRE DAME COLLEGE (OH)

Computer Science	M,O

NOTRE DAME DE NAMUR UNIVERSITY

Computer Science	M
Information Science	M
Management of Technology	M

NOVA SOUTHEASTERN UNIVERSITY

Bioinformatics	M,D,O
Computer and Information Systems Security	M,D
Computer Science	M,D
Health Informatics	M,D,O
Information Science	M,D
Medical Informatics	M,D,O
Software Engineering	M,D

OAKLAND UNIVERSITY

Computer Engineering	M
Computer Science	M
Electrical Engineering	M
Engineering and Applied Sciences—General	M,D
Engineering Management	M
Mechanical Engineering	M,D
Software Engineering	M
Systems Engineering	M,D
Systems Science	M

THE OHIO STATE UNIVERSITY

Aerospace/Aeronautical Engineering	M,D
Agricultural Engineering	M,D
Bioengineering	M,D
Biomedical Engineering	M,D
Chemical Engineering	M,D
Civil Engineering	M,D
Computer Engineering	M,D
Computer Science	M,D
Electrical Engineering	M,D
Engineering and Applied Sciences—General	M,D
Industrial/Management Engineering	M,D
Materials Engineering	M,D
Materials Sciences	M,D
Mechanical Engineering	M,D
Metallurgical Engineering and Metallurgy	M,D

*M—masters degree; D—doctorate; O—other advanced degree, *—Close-Up and/or Display*

Nuclear Engineering	M,D
Operations Research	M
Systems Engineering	M,D

OHIO UNIVERSITY

Biomedical Engineering	M
Chemical Engineering	M,D
Civil Engineering	M,D
Computer Science	M,D
Construction Engineering	M,D
Electrical Engineering	M,D
Engineering and Applied Sciences—General	M,D
Environmental Engineering	M,D
Geotechnical Engineering	M,D
Industrial/Management Engineering	M,D
Mechanical Engineering	M,D
Mechanics	M,D
Structural Engineering	M,D
Systems Engineering	M
Telecommunications	M
Transportation and Highway Engineering	M,D
Water Resources Engineering	M,D

OKLAHOMA BAPTIST UNIVERSITY

Energy Management and Policy	M

OKLAHOMA CHRISTIAN UNIVERSITY

Engineering and Applied Sciences—General	M

OKLAHOMA CITY UNIVERSITY

Computer Science	M
Energy Management and Policy	M

OKLAHOMA STATE UNIVERSITY

Agricultural Engineering	M,D
Bioengineering	M,D
Chemical Engineering	M,D
Civil Engineering	M,D
Computer Engineering	M,D
Computer Science	M,D
Electrical Engineering	M,D
Engineering and Applied Sciences—General	M,D
Environmental Engineering	M,D
Fire Protection Engineering	M,D
Industrial/Management Engineering	M,D
Information Science	M,D
Mechanical Engineering	M,D
Telecommunications Management	M,D,O

OLD DOMINION UNIVERSITY

Aerospace/Aeronautical Engineering	M,D
Biomedical Engineering	D
Civil Engineering	M,D
Computer Engineering	M,D
Computer Science	M,D
Electrical Engineering	M,D
Engineering and Applied Sciences—General	M,D
Engineering Management	M,D
Environmental Engineering	M,D
Ergonomics and Human Factors	D
Information Science	D
Management of Technology	M
Mechanical Engineering	M,D
Modeling and Simulation	M,D
Systems Engineering	M,D

OREGON HEALTH & SCIENCE UNIVERSITY

Biomedical Engineering	M,D
Computer Engineering	M,D
Computer Science	M,D
Electrical Engineering	M,D
Environmental Engineering	M,D
Health Informatics	M,D,O
Medical Informatics	M,D,O

OREGON INSTITUTE OF TECHNOLOGY

Manufacturing Engineering	M

OREGON STATE UNIVERSITY

Artificial Intelligence/Robotics	M,D
Bioengineering	M,D
Biotechnology	M
Chemical Engineering	M,D
Civil Engineering	M,D
Computer Engineering	M,D
Computer Science	M,D
Electrical Engineering	M,D
Engineering and Applied Sciences—General	M,D
Environmental Engineering	M,D
Industrial/Management Engineering	M,D
Materials Sciences	M,D
Mechanical Engineering	M,D
Nuclear Engineering	M,D
Water Resources Engineering	M,D

OUR LADY OF THE LAKE UNIVERSITY OF SAN ANTONIO

Computer and Information Systems Security	M

PACE UNIVERSITY

Computer and Information Systems Security	M,D,O
Computer Science	M,D,O
Information Science	M,D,O
Software Engineering	M,D,O
Telecommunications	M,D,O

PACIFIC STATES UNIVERSITY

Computer Science	M
Management of Technology	M,D

PENN STATE ERIE, THE BEHREND COLLEGE

Engineering and Applied Sciences—General	M

PENN STATE GREAT VALLEY

Engineering and Applied Sciences—General	M,O
Engineering Management	M,O
Software Engineering	M,O
Systems Engineering	M,O

PENN STATE HARRISBURG

Computer Science	M,O
Electrical Engineering	M,O
Engineering and Applied Sciences—General	M,O
Engineering Management	M,O
Environmental Engineering	M,O
Structural Engineering	M,O

PENN STATE UNIVERSITY PARK

Aerospace/Aeronautical Engineering	M,D
Agricultural Engineering	M,D
Architectural Engineering	M,D
Bioengineering	M,D
Biotechnology	M,D
Chemical Engineering	M,D
Civil Engineering	M,D
Computer Engineering	M,D

Computer Science	M,D
Electrical Engineering	M,D
Engineering and Applied Sciences—General	M,D
Engineering Design	M
Environmental Engineering	M,D
Geotechnical Engineering	M,D
Industrial/Management Engineering	M,D
Information Science	M,D
Materials Engineering	M,D
Materials Sciences	M,D
Mechanical Engineering	M,D
Mechanics	M,D
Mineral/Mining Engineering	M,D
Nuclear Engineering	M,D

PHILADELPHIA UNIVERSITY

Construction Management	M
Modeling and Simulation	M
Textile Sciences and Engineering	M,D

PITTSBURG STATE UNIVERSITY

Construction Engineering	M
Engineering and Applied Sciences—General	M
Polymer Science and Engineering	M

POINT PARK UNIVERSITY

Engineering Management	M

POLYTECHNIC UNIVERSITY OF PUERTO RICO

Civil Engineering	M
Computer Engineering	M
Computer Science	M
Electrical Engineering	M
Engineering Management	M
Management of Technology	M
Manufacturing Engineering	M
Mechanical Engineering	M

POLYTECHNIC UNIVERSITY OF PUERTO RICO, MIAMI CAMPUS

Construction Management	M
Environmental Engineering	M

POLYTECHNIC UNIVERSITY OF PUERTO RICO, ORLANDO CAMPUS

Construction Management	M
Engineering Management	M
Environmental Engineering	M
Management of Technology	M

PONTIFICIA UNIVERSIDAD CATOLICA MADRE Y MAESTRA

Engineering and Applied Sciences—General	M
Structural Engineering	M

PORTLAND STATE UNIVERSITY

Artificial Intelligence/Robotics	M,D,O
Civil Engineering	M,D,O
Computer Engineering	M,D
Computer Science	M,D
Electrical Engineering	M,D
Engineering and Applied Sciences—General	M,D,O
Engineering Management	M,D,O
Environmental Engineering	M,D
Management of Technology	M,D
Manufacturing Engineering	M,D
Mechanical Engineering	M,D,O
Modeling and Simulation	M,D,O
Software Engineering	M,D
Systems Science	M,D,O

PRAIRIE VIEW A&M UNIVERSITY

Computer Science	M,D
Electrical Engineering	M,D
Engineering and Applied Sciences—General	M,D

PRINCETON UNIVERSITY

Aerospace/Aeronautical Engineering	M,D
Chemical Engineering	M,D
Civil Engineering	M,D
Computer Science	M,D
Electrical Engineering	M,D
Electronic Materials	D
Engineering and Applied Sciences—General	M,D
Environmental Engineering	M,D
Financial Engineering	M,D
Materials Sciences	D
Mechanical Engineering	M,D
Ocean Engineering	D
Operations Research	M,D

PURDUE UNIVERSITY

Aerospace/Aeronautical Engineering	M,D
Agricultural Engineering	M,D
Biomedical Engineering	M,D
Biotechnology	D
Chemical Engineering	M,D
Civil Engineering	M,D
Computer and Information Systems Security	M
Computer Engineering	M,D
Computer Science	M,D
Construction Management	M
Electrical Engineering	M,D
Engineering and Applied Sciences—General	M,D,O
Ergonomics and Human Factors	M,D
Industrial/Management Engineering	M,D
Management of Technology	M,D
Materials Engineering	M,D
Mechanical Engineering	M,D,O
Nuclear Engineering	M,D

PURDUE UNIVERSITY CALUMET

Biotechnology	M
Computer Engineering	M
Computer Science	M
Electrical Engineering	M
Engineering and Applied Sciences—General	M
Mechanical Engineering	M

QUEENS COLLEGE OF THE CITY UNIVERSITY OF NEW YORK

Computer Science	M

QUEEN'S UNIVERSITY AT KINGSTON

Chemical Engineering	M,D
Civil Engineering	M,D
Computer Engineering	M,D
Computer Science	M,D
Electrical Engineering	M,D
Engineering and Applied Sciences—General	M,D
Mechanical Engineering	M,D
Mineral/Mining Engineering	M,D

REGIS COLLEGE (MA)

Biotechnology	M

REGIS UNIVERSITY

Computer and Information Systems Security	M,O
Computer Science	M,O
Database Systems	M,O
Health Informatics	M,O

Information Science M,O
Software Engineering M,O
Systems Engineering M,O

RENSSELAER AT HARTFORD
Computer Engineering M
Computer Science M
Electrical Engineering M
Engineering and Applied
    Sciences—General M
Information Science M
Mechanical Engineering M
Systems Science M

RENSSELAER POLYTECHNIC INSTITUTE
Aerospace/Aeronautical
    Engineering M,D
Bioengineering M,D
Biomedical Engineering M,D
Chemical Engineering M,D
Civil Engineering M,D
Computer Engineering M,D
Computer Science M,D
Electrical Engineering M,D
Engineering and Applied
    Sciences—General M,D
Engineering Management M,D
Engineering Physics M,D
Environmental Engineering M,D
Financial Engineering M
Human-Computer Interaction M
Industrial/Management
    Engineering M,D
Information Science M
Management of Technology M,D
Materials Engineering M,D
Materials Sciences M,D
Mechanical Engineering M,D
Nuclear Engineering M,D
Systems Engineering M,D
Technology and Public Policy M,D
Transportation and Highway
    Engineering M,D

RICE UNIVERSITY
Bioengineering M,D
Bioinformatics M,D
Biomedical Engineering M,D
Chemical Engineering M,D
Civil Engineering M,D
Computer Engineering M,D
Computer Science M,D
Electrical Engineering M,D
Engineering and Applied
    Sciences—General M,D
Environmental Engineering M,D
Materials Sciences M,D
Mechanical Engineering M,D

RIVIER UNIVERSITY
Computer Science M

ROBERT MORRIS UNIVERSITY
Computer and Information
    Systems Security M,D
Engineering and Applied
    Sciences—General M
Engineering Management M
Information Science M,D

ROBERT MORRIS UNIVERSITY ILLINOIS
Computer and Information
    Systems Security M

ROBERTS WESLEYAN COLLEGE
Health Informatics M

ROCHESTER INSTITUTE OF TECHNOLOGY
Bioinformatics M
Computer and Information
    Systems Security M,O
Computer Engineering M
Computer Science M,D
Database Systems O
Electrical Engineering M
Engineering and Applied
    Sciences—General M,D,O
Engineering Management M
Game Design and
    Development M
Human-Computer Interaction M
Industrial/Management
    Engineering M
Information Science M,D
Manufacturing Engineering M
Materials Engineering M
Materials Sciences M
Mechanical Engineering M
Medical Informatics M
Safety Engineering M
Software Engineering M
Systems Engineering M,D
Technology and Public Policy M

ROGER WILLIAMS UNIVERSITY
Computer and Information
    Systems Security M
Construction Management M

ROLLINS COLLEGE
Management of Technology M,D

ROOSEVELT UNIVERSITY
Biotechnology M
Computer Science M
Telecommunications M

ROSE-HULMAN INSTITUTE OF TECHNOLOGY
Biomedical Engineering M
Chemical Engineering M
Civil Engineering M
Computer Engineering M
Electrical Engineering M
Engineering and Applied
    Sciences—General M
Engineering Management M
Environmental Engineering M
Mechanical Engineering M
Software Engineering M
Systems Engineering M

ROWAN UNIVERSITY
Bioinformatics M
Chemical Engineering M
Civil Engineering M
Computer Science M
Electrical Engineering M
Engineering and Applied
    Sciences—General M
Mechanical Engineering M

ROYAL MILITARY COLLEGE OF CANADA
Chemical Engineering M,D
Civil Engineering M,D
Computer Engineering M,D
Computer Science M
Electrical Engineering M,D
Engineering and Applied
    Sciences—General M,D
Environmental Engineering M,D
Materials Sciences M,D
Mechanical Engineering M,D
Nuclear Engineering M,D
Software Engineering M,D

RUTGERS, THE STATE UNIVERSITY OF NEW JERSEY, CAMDEN
Computer Science M

RUTGERS, THE STATE UNIVERSITY OF NEW JERSEY, NEWARK
Bioinformatics M,D
Biomedical Engineering O
Management of Technology D
Medical Informatics M,D,O

RUTGERS, THE STATE UNIVERSITY OF NEW JERSEY, NEW BRUNSWICK
Aerospace/Aeronautical
    Engineering M,D
Biochemical Engineering M,D
Biomedical Engineering M,D
Chemical Engineering M,D
Civil Engineering M,D
Computer Engineering M,D
Computer Science M,D
Electrical Engineering M,D
Environmental Engineering M,D
Hazardous Materials
    Management M,D
Industrial/Management
    Engineering M,D
Materials Engineering M,D
Materials Sciences M,D
Mechanical Engineering M,D
Mechanics M,D
Operations Research D
Systems Engineering M,D

SACRED HEART UNIVERSITY
Computer and Information
    Systems Security M,O
Computer Science M,O
Database Systems M,O
Game Design and
    Development M,O
Health Informatics M
Information Science M,O

SAGINAW VALLEY STATE UNIVERSITY
Energy and Power
    Engineering M
Engineering and Applied
    Sciences—General M
Materials Engineering M

ST. AMBROSE UNIVERSITY
Management of Technology M

ST. CLOUD STATE UNIVERSITY
Biomedical Engineering M
Computer and Information
    Systems Security M
Computer Science M
Electrical Engineering M
Engineering and Applied
    Sciences—General M
Engineering Management M
Mechanical Engineering M
Technology and Public Policy M

ST. FRANCIS XAVIER UNIVERSITY
Computer Science M

ST. JOHN'S UNIVERSITY (NY)
Biotechnology M
Database Systems M
Information Science

SAINT JOSEPH'S UNIVERSITY
Computer Science M,O

SAINT LEO UNIVERSITY
Computer and Information
    Systems Security M

SAINT LOUIS UNIVERSITY
Biomedical Engineering M,D

SAINT MARTIN'S UNIVERSITY
Civil Engineering M
Engineering Management M
Mechanical Engineering M

SAINT MARY'S UNIVERSITY (CANADA)
Applied Science and
    Technology M

ST. MARY'S UNIVERSITY (UNITED STATES)
Computer Engineering M
Computer Science M
Electrical Engineering M
Engineering and Applied
    Sciences—General M
Engineering Management M
Industrial/Management
    Engineering M
Information Science M
Software Engineering M

SAINT MARY'S UNIVERSITY OF MINNESOTA
Telecommunications M

SAINT PETER'S UNIVERSITY
Database Systems M

SAINT XAVIER UNIVERSITY
Computer Science M

SALEM INTERNATIONAL UNIVERSITY
Computer and Information
    Systems Security M

SALVE REGINA UNIVERSITY
Computer and Information
    Systems Security M,O

SAMFORD UNIVERSITY
Energy Management
    and Policy M

SM HOUSTON STATE UNIVERSITY
Computer and Information
    Systems Security M,D
Computer Science M,D
Information Science M,D

SAN DIEGO STATE UNIVERSITY
Aerospace/Aeronautical
    Engineering M,D
Civil Engineering M
Computer Science M
Electrical Engineering M
Engineering and Applied
    Sciences—General M,D
Engineering Design M,D
Mechanical Engineering M,D
Mechanics M,D
Telecommunications
    Management M

M—masters degree; D—doctorate; O—other advanced degree; *—Close-Up and/or Display

SAN FRANCISCO STATE UNIVERSITY

Biotechnology	M
Computer Science	M
Energy and Power Engineering	M
Engineering and Applied Sciences—General	M

SAN JOSE STATE UNIVERSITY

Aerospace/Aeronautical Engineering	M
Chemical Engineering	M
Civil Engineering	M
Computer Engineering	M
Computer Science	M
Electrical Engineering	M
Engineering and Applied Sciences—General	M
Industrial/Management Engineering	M
Materials Engineering	M
Mechanical Engineering	M
Software Engineering	M
Systems Engineering	M

SANTA CLARA UNIVERSITY

Bioengineering	M,D,O
Civil Engineering	M,D,O
Computer and Information Systems Security	M,D,O
Computer Engineering	M,D,O
Computer Science	M,D,O
Electrical Engineering	M,D,O
Energy and Power Engineering	M,D,O
Energy Management and Policy	M,D,O
Engineering and Applied Sciences—General	M,D,O
Engineering Design	M,D,O
Engineering Management	M,D,O
Materials Engineering	M,D,O
Mechanical Engineering	M,D,O
Software Engineering	M,D,O

SAVANNAH COLLEGE OF ART AND DESIGN

Game Design and Development	M,O

SCHOOL OF THE ART INSTITUTE OF CHICAGO

Materials Sciences	M

SEATTLE UNIVERSITY

Computer Science	M
Engineering and Applied Sciences—General	M
Software Engineering	M

SETON HALL UNIVERSITY

Management of Technology	M

SHENANDOAH UNIVERSITY

Health Informatics	M,D,O

SHEPHERD UNIVERSITY (CA)

Game Design and Development	M

SHIPPENSBURG UNIVERSITY OF PENNSYLVANIA

Computer Science	M

SILICON VALLEY UNIVERSITY

Computer Engineering	M
Computer Science	M

SIMMONS COLLEGE

Information Science	M,D,O

SIMON FRASER UNIVERSITY

Bioinformatics	M,D,O
Biotechnology	M,D,O
Computer Science	M,D
Engineering and Applied Sciences—General	M,D
Management of Technology	M,D,O
Mechanical Engineering	M,D
Operations Research	M,D
Systems Engineering	M,D

SOUTH CAROLINA STATE UNIVERSITY

Civil Engineering	M
Mechanical Engineering	M

SOUTH DAKOTA SCHOOL OF MINES AND TECHNOLOGY

Artificial Intelligence/Robotics	M
Bioengineering	D
Biomedical Engineering	M,D
Chemical Engineering	M,D
Civil Engineering	M
Construction Management	M
Electrical Engineering	M
Engineering and Applied Sciences—General	M,D
Engineering Management	M
Geological Engineering	M,D
Management of Technology	M
Materials Engineering	M,D
Materials Sciences	M,D
Mechanical Engineering	M,D
Mineral/Mining Engineering	M
Nanotechnology	D

SOUTH DAKOTA STATE UNIVERSITY

Agricultural Engineering	M,D
Biosystems Engineering	M,D
Civil Engineering	M
Electrical Engineering	M,D
Engineering and Applied Sciences—General	M,D
Industrial/Management Engineering	M
Mechanical Engineering	M,D

SOUTHEASTERN LOUISIANA UNIVERSITY

Applied Science and Technology	M

SOUTHEASTERN OKLAHOMA STATE UNIVERSITY

Aviation	M
Biotechnology	M

SOUTHEAST MISSOURI STATE UNIVERSITY

Management of Technology	M

SOUTHERN ARKANSAS UNIVERSITY–MAGNOLIA

Computer Science	M

SOUTHERN CONNECTICUT STATE UNIVERSITY

Computer Science	M

SOUTHERN ILLINOIS UNIVERSITY CARBONDALE

Biomedical Engineering	M
Civil Engineering	M
Computer Engineering	M,D
Computer Science	M,D
Electrical Engineering	M,D
Engineering and Applied Sciences—General	M,D
Engineering Management	M
Mechanical Engineering	M
Mechanics	M
Mineral/Mining Engineering	M

SOUTHERN ILLINOIS UNIVERSITY EDWARDSVILLE

Civil Engineering	M
Computer Science	M
Electrical Engineering	M
Engineering and Applied Sciences—General	M
Environmental Engineering	M
Geotechnical Engineering	M
Health Informatics	M
Industrial/Management Engineering	M
Mechanical Engineering	M
Operations Research	M
Structural Engineering	M
Transportation and Highway Engineering	M

SOUTHERN METHODIST UNIVERSITY

Applied Science and Technology	M,D
Civil Engineering	M,D
Computer Engineering	M,D
Computer Science	M,D
Database Systems	M
Electrical Engineering	M,D
Engineering and Applied Sciences—General	M,D
Engineering Management	M,D
Environmental Engineering	M,D
Information Science	M,D
Manufacturing Engineering	M,D
Materials Engineering	M,D
Materials Sciences	M,D
Mechanical Engineering	M,D
Operations Research	M,D
Software Engineering	M,D
Structural Engineering	M,D
Systems Engineering	M,D
Systems Science	M,D
Telecommunications	M,D
Water Resources Engineering	M,D

SOUTHERN NEW HAMPSHIRE UNIVERSITY

Health Informatics	M,O

SOUTHERN OREGON UNIVERSITY

Computer Science	M

SOUTHERN POLYTECHNIC STATE UNIVERSITY

Computer and Information Systems Security	M,O
Computer Engineering	M
Computer Science	M,O
Construction Management	M
Electrical Engineering	M
Engineering and Applied Sciences—General	M,O
Health Informatics	M,O
Industrial/Management Engineering	M,O
Information Science	M,O
Management of Technology	M,O
Software Engineering	M,O
Systems Engineering	M,O

SOUTHERN UNIVERSITY AND AGRICULTURAL AND MECHANICAL COLLEGE

Computer Science	M
Engineering and Applied Sciences—General	M

STANFORD UNIVERSITY

Aerospace/Aeronautical Engineering	M,D,O
Bioengineering	M,D
Biomedical Engineering	M
Chemical Engineering	M,D
Civil Engineering	M,D,O
Computer Science	M,D
Construction Engineering	M,D,O
Electrical Engineering	M,D
Energy and Power Engineering	M,D,O
Engineering and Applied Sciences—General	M,D,O
Engineering Design	M
Engineering Management	M,D
Environmental Engineering	M,D,O
Geotechnical Engineering	M,D,O
Industrial/Management Engineering	M,D
Materials Engineering	M,D
Materials Sciences	M,D
Mechanical Engineering	M,D,O
Mechanics	M,D,O
Medical Informatics	M,D
Petroleum Engineering	M,D,O
Structural Engineering	M,D,O

STATE UNIVERSITY OF NEW YORK AT NEW PALTZ

Computer Science	M
Electrical Engineering	M

STATE UNIVERSITY OF NEW YORK AT OSWEGO

Human-Computer Interaction	M

STATE UNIVERSITY OF NEW YORK COLLEGE OF ENVIRONMENTAL SCIENCE AND FORESTRY

Construction Management	M,D
Environmental Engineering	M,D
Materials Sciences	M,D,O
Paper and Pulp Engineering	M,D,O
Water Resources Engineering	M,D

STATE UNIVERSITY OF NEW YORK DOWNSTATE MEDICAL CENTER

Biomedical Engineering	M,D

STATE UNIVERSITY OF NEW YORK POLYTECHNIC INSTITUTE

Computer and Information Systems Security	M
Computer Science	M
Information Science	M
Management of Technology	M
Telecommunications	M

STEPHEN F. AUSTIN STATE UNIVERSITY

Biotechnology	M
Computer Science	M

STEPHENS COLLEGE

Health Informatics	M,O

STEVENS INSTITUTE OF TECHNOLOGY

Aerospace/Aeronautical Engineering	M,O
Bioinformatics	M,D,O
Biomedical Engineering	M,O
Chemical Engineering	M,D,O
Civil Engineering	M,D,O
Computer and Information Systems Security	M,D,O
Computer Engineering	M,D,O
Computer Science	M,D,O

Construction Engineering	M,O
Construction Management	M,O
Database Systems	M,D,O
Electrical Engineering	M,D,O
Engineering and Applied Sciences—General	M,D,O
Engineering Design	M
Engineering Management	M,D
Engineering Physics	M,D,O
Environmental Engineering	M,D,O
Financial Engineering	M
Health Informatics	M,D,O
Information Science	M,O
Management of Technology	M,D,O
Manufacturing Engineering	M
Materials Engineering	M,D
Mechanical Engineering	M,D,O
Modeling and Simulation	M,D,O
Ocean Engineering	M,D
Polymer Science and Engineering	M,D,O
Software Engineering	M,D,O
Structural Engineering	M,D,O
Systems Engineering	M,D,O
Systems Science	M,D
Telecommunications Management	M,D,O
Telecommunications	M,D,O
Water Resources Engineering	M,D,O

STEVENSON UNIVERSITY

Computer and Information Systems Security	M
Management of Technology	M

STONY BROOK UNIVERSITY, STATE UNIVERSITY OF NEW YORK

Bioinformatics	M,D
Biomedical Engineering	M,D,O
Computer Engineering	M,D
Computer Science	M,D,O
Electrical Engineering	M,D
Engineering and Applied Sciences—General	M,D,O
Management of Technology	M
Materials Engineering	M,D
Materials Sciences	M,D
Mechanical Engineering	M,D
Software Engineering	M,D,O
Systems Engineering	M
Technology and Public Policy	D

STRATFORD UNIVERSITY (VA)

Computer and Information Systems Security	M
Software Engineering	M
Telecommunications	M

STRAYER UNIVERSITY

Computer and Information Systems Security	M
Information Science	M
Software Engineering	M
Systems Science	M
Telecommunications Management	M

SYRACUSE UNIVERSITY

Aerospace/Aeronautical Engineering	M,D
Bioengineering	M,D
Chemical Engineering	M,D
Civil Engineering	M,D
Computer and Information Systems Security	M,O
Computer Engineering	M,D,O
Computer Science	M
Electrical Engineering	M,D,O

Energy and Power Engineering	M
Engineering and Applied Sciences—General	M,D,O
Engineering Management	M
Environmental Engineering	M
Information Science	D
Mechanical Engineering	M,D
Systems Engineering	O
Telecommunications Management	M,O
Telecommunications	M

TARLETON STATE UNIVERSITY

Engineering Management	M

TÉLÉ-UNIVERSITÉ

Computer Science	M,D

TEMPLE UNIVERSITY

Bioengineering	M,D
Biotechnology	M,D
Civil Engineering	M,D,O
Computer Science	M,D
Electrical Engineering	M,D
Engineering and Applied Sciences—General	D
Engineering Management	M,O
Environmental Engineering	M,D,O
Financial Engineering	M
Health Informatics	M
Information Science	M,D
Mechanical Engineering	M,D

TENNESSEE STATE UNIVERSITY

Biomedical Engineering	M,D
Biotechnology	M,D
Civil Engineering	M,D
Computer Engineering	M,D
Electrical Engineering	M,D
Engineering and Applied Sciences—General	M,D
Environmental Engineering	M,D
Manufacturing Engineering	M,D
Mechanical Engineering	M,D
Systems Engineering	M,D

TENNESSEE TECHNOLOGICAL UNIVERSITY

Chemical Engineering	M
Civil Engineering	M
Computer Science	M
Electrical Engineering	M
Engineering and Applied Sciences—General	M,D
Mechanical Engineering	M
Software Engineering	M

TEXAS A&M UNIVERSITY

Aerospace/Aeronautical Engineering	M,D
Agricultural Engineering	M,D
Bioengineering	M,D
Biomedical Engineering	M,D
Chemical Engineering	M,D
Civil Engineering	M,D
Computer Engineering	M,D
Computer Science	M,D
Construction Management	M
Electrical Engineering	M,D
Industrial/Management Engineering	M,D
Manufacturing Engineering	M
Materials Engineering	M,D
Materials Sciences	M,D
Mechanical Engineering	M,D
Nuclear Engineering	M,D
Ocean Engineering	M,D
Petroleum Engineering	M,D

TEXAS A&M UNIVERSITY–CORPUS CHRISTI

Computer Science	M

TEXAS A&M UNIVERSITY–KINGSVILLE

Chemical Engineering	M
Civil Engineering	M
Computer Science	M
Electrical Engineering	M
Energy and Power Engineering	D
Engineering and Applied Sciences—General	M,D
Environmental Engineering	M,D
Industrial/Management Engineering	M
Mechanical Engineering	M
Petroleum Engineering	M
Systems Engineering	D

TEXAS A&M UNIVERSITY–SAN ANTONIO

Computer and Information Systems Security	M

TEXAS CHRISTIAN UNIVERSITY

Energy Management and Policy	M

TEXAS SOUTHERN UNIVERSITY

Computer Science	M
Industrial/Management Engineering	M
Transportation and Highway Engineering	M

TEXAS STATE UNIVERSITY

Computer Science	M
Engineering and Applied Sciences—General	M
Industrial/Management Engineering	M
Management of Technology	M
Manufacturing Engineering	M
Materials Engineering	D
Materials Sciences	M,D
Software Engineering	M

TEXAS TECH UNIVERSITY

Bioengineering	M
Biotechnology	M,D
Chemical Engineering	M,D
Civil Engineering	M,D
Computer Science	M,D
Electrical Engineering	M,D
Energy and Power Engineering	M,D
Engineering and Applied Sciences—General	M,D
Engineering Management	M,D
Environmental Engineering	M,D
Industrial/Management Engineering	M,D
Mechanical Engineering	M,D
Operations Research	M,D
Petroleum Engineering	M,D
Software Engineering	M,D
Systems Engineering	M,D

TEXAS TECH UNIVERSITY HEALTH SCIENCES CENTER

Biotechnology	M

THOMAS EDISON STATE COLLEGE

Applied Science and Technology	O

THOMAS JEFFERSON UNIVERSITY

Biomedical Engineering	D
Biotechnology	D

TOWSON UNIVERSITY

Computer and Information Systems Security	M,D,O
Computer Science	M
Database Systems	M,D,O
Information Science	M,D,O
Management of Technology	M,O
Software Engineering	M,D,O

TOYOTA TECHNOLOGICAL INSTITUTE OF CHICAGO

Computer Science	D

TRENT UNIVERSITY

Computer Science	M
Materials Sciences	M
Modeling and Simulation	M,D

TREVECCA NAZARENE UNIVERSITY

Information Science	M,D
Management of Technology	M,O

TRIDENT UNIVERSITY INTERNATIONAL

Computer and Information Systems Security	M,D
Health Informatics	M,D,O

TRINE UNIVERSITY

Civil Engineering	M
Engineering and Applied Sciences—General	M
Engineering Management	M

TROY UNIVERSITY

Computer Science	M

TUFTS UNIVERSITY

Bioengineering	M,D,O
Bioinformatics	M,D
Biomedical Engineering	M,D
Biotechnology	M,D,O
Chemical Engineering	M,D
Civil Engineering	M,D
Computer Science	M,D,O
Electrical Engineering	M,D,O
Engineering and Applied Sciences—General	M,D
Engineering Management	M
Environmental Engineering	M,D
Ergonomics and Human Factors	M,D
Geotechnical Engineering	M,D
Hazardous Materials Management	M,D
Human-Computer Interaction	O
Manufacturing Engineering	O
Mechanical Engineering	M,D
Structural Engineering	M,D
Water Resources Engineering	M,D

TULANE UNIVERSITY

Biomedical Engineering	M,D
Chemical Engineering	D
Energy Management and Policy	M,D

TUSKEGEE UNIVERSITY

Computer and Information Systems Security	M
Electrical Engineering	M

*M—masters degree; D—doctorate; O—other advanced degree, *—Close-Up and/or Display*

Engineering and Applied
   Sciences—General   M,D
Materials Engineering   D
Mechanical Engineering   M

UNION GRADUATE COLLEGE
Computer Science   M
Electrical Engineering   M
Engineering and Applied
   Sciences—General   M
Engineering Management   M
Mechanical Engineering   M

**UNITED STATES MERCHANT
MARINE ACADEMY**
Civil Engineering   M

**UNIVERSIDAD AUTONOMA DE
GUADALAJARA**
Computer Science   M,D
Energy and Power
   Engineering   M,D
Manufacturing Engineering   M,D
Systems Science   M,D

**UNIVERSIDAD CENTRAL DEL
ESTE**
Environmental Engineering   M

**UNIVERSIDAD DE LAS
AMÉRICAS PUEBLA**
Biotechnology   M
Chemical Engineering   M
Computer Science   M,D
Construction Management   M
Electrical Engineering   M
Engineering and Applied
   Sciences—General   M,D
Industrial/Management
   Engineering   M
Manufacturing Engineering   M

UNIVERSIDAD DEL ESTE
Computer and Information
   Systems Security   M

UNIVERSIDAD DEL TURABO
Telecommunications   M

**UNIVERSIDAD NACIONAL
PEDRO HENRIQUEZ URENA**
Environmental Engineering   M

UNIVERSITÉ DE MONCTON
Civil Engineering   M
Computer Science   M,O
Electrical Engineering   M
Engineering and Applied
   Sciences—General   M
Industrial/Management
   Engineering   M
Mechanical Engineering   M

UNIVERSITÉ DE MONTRÉAL
Bioinformatics   M,D
Biomedical Engineering   M,D,O
Computer Science   M,D
Ergonomics and Human
   Factors   O

UNIVERSITÉ DE SHERBROOKE
Chemical Engineering   M,D
Civil Engineering   M,D
Computer and Information
   Systems Security   M
Electrical Engineering   M,D
Engineering and Applied
   Sciences—General   M,D,O
Engineering Management   M,O
Environmental Engineering   M

Information Science   M,D
Mechanical Engineering   M,D

**UNIVERSITÉ DU QUÉBEC
À CHICOUTIMI**
Engineering and Applied
   Sciences—General   M,D

**UNIVERSITÉ DU QUÉBEC
À MONTRÉAL**
Ergonomics and Human
   Factors   O

**UNIVERSITÉ DU QUÉBEC
À RIMOUSKI**
Engineering and Applied
   Sciences—General   M

**UNIVERSITÉ DU QUÉBEC
À TROIS-RIVIÈRES**
Computer Science   M
Electrical Engineering   M,D
Industrial/Management
   Engineering   M,O

**UNIVERSITÉ DU QUÉBEC, ÉCOLE
DE TECHNOLOGIE SUPÉRIEURE**
Engineering and Applied
   Sciences—General   M,D,O

**UNIVERSITÉ DU QUÉBEC EN
ABITIBI-TÉMISCAMINGUE**
Engineering and Applied
   Sciences—General   M,O
Mineral/Mining Engineering   M,O

**UNIVERSITÉ DU QUÉBEC
EN OUTAOUAIS**
Computer Science   M,D,O

**UNIVERSITÉ DU QUÉBEC,
INSTITUT NATIONAL DE LA
RECHERCHE SCIENTIFIQUE**
Energy Management
   and Policy   M,D
Materials Sciences   M,D
Telecommunications   M,D

UNIVERSITÉ LAVAL
Aerospace/Aeronautical
   Engineering   M
Agricultural Engineering   M
Chemical Engineering   M,D
Civil Engineering   M,D,O
Computer Science   M,D
Electrical Engineering   M,D
Engineering and Applied
   Sciences—General   M,D,O
Environmental Engineering   M,D
Industrial/Management
   Engineering   O
Mechanical Engineering   M,D
Metallurgical Engineering and
   Metallurgy   M,D
Mineral/Mining Engineering   M,D
Modeling and Simulation   M,O
Software Engineering   O

**UNIVERSITY AT ALBANY, STATE
UNIVERSITY OF NEW YORK**
Computer Science   M,D
Information Science   M,D,O
Management of Technology   M
Nanotechnology   M,D

**UNIVERSITY AT BUFFALO, THE
STATE UNIVERSITY OF NEW
YORK**
Aerospace/Aeronautical
   Engineering   M,D

Bioengineering   M,D
Bioinformatics   M,D
Biomedical Engineering   M,D
Biotechnology   M
Chemical Engineering   M,D
Civil Engineering   M,D
Computer Science   M,D,O
Electrical Engineering   M,D
Engineering and Applied
   Sciences—General   M,D,O*
Environmental Engineering   M,D
Health Informatics   O
Industrial/Management
   Engineering   M,D
Mechanical Engineering   M,D
Medical Informatics   O
Modeling and Simulation   M,D,O
Structural Engineering   M,D

**UNIVERSITY OF
ADVANCING TECHNOLOGY**
Computer and Information
   Systems Security   M
Computer Science   M
Game Design and
   Development   M
Management of Technology   M

THE UNIVERSITY OF AKRON
Biomedical Engineering   M,D
Chemical Engineering   M,D
Civil Engineering   M,D
Computer Engineering   M,D
Computer Science   M
Electrical Engineering   M,D
Engineering and Applied
   Sciences—General   M,D
Geological Engineering   M
Management of Technology   M
Mechanical Engineering   M,D
Polymer Science and
   Engineering   M,D

THE UNIVERSITY OF ALABAMA
Aerospace/Aeronautical
   Engineering   M,D
Chemical Engineering   M,D
Civil Engineering   M,D
Computer Engineering   M,D
Computer Science   M,D
Construction Engineering   M,D
Electrical Engineering   M,D
Engineering and Applied
   Sciences—General   M,D
Environmental Engineering   M,D
Ergonomics and Human
   Factors   M
Materials Engineering   M,D
Materials Sciences   D
Mechanical Engineering   M,D
Mechanics   M,D
Metallurgical Engineering and
   Metallurgy   M,D

**THE UNIVERSITY OF ALABAMA
AT BIRMINGHAM**
Bioinformatics   D
Biomedical Engineering   M,D
Biotechnology   M
Civil Engineering   M,D
Computer and Information
   Systems Security   M
Computer Engineering   D
Computer Science   M,D
Construction Engineering   M
Electrical Engineering   M
Engineering and Applied
   Sciences—General   M,D
Engineering Design   M
Engineering Management   M,D
Environmental Engineering   D
Health Informatics   M
Information Science   M,D

Materials Engineering   M,D
Materials Sciences   D
Mechanical Engineering   M
Safety Engineering   M

**THE UNIVERSITY OF
ALABAMA IN HUNTSVILLE**
Aerospace/Aeronautical
   Engineering   M,D
Biotechnology   M,D
Chemical Engineering   M,D
Civil Engineering   M,D
Computer and Information
   Systems Security   M,D,O
Computer Engineering   M,D,O
Computer Science   M,D,O
Electrical Engineering   M,D
Engineering and Applied
   Sciences—General   M,D
Environmental Engineering   M,D
Geotechnical Engineering   M,D
Industrial/Management
   Engineering   M,D
Management of Technology   M,O
Materials Sciences   M,D
Mechanical Engineering   M,D
Modeling and Simulation   M,D,O
Operations Research   M,D
Software Engineering   M,D,O
Structural Engineering   M,D
Systems Engineering   M,D
Transportation and Highway
   Engineering   M,D
Water Resources Engineering   M,D

**UNIVERSITY OF ALASKA
ANCHORAGE**
Civil Engineering   M,O
Engineering and Applied
   Sciences—General   M,O
Engineering Management   M
Environmental Engineering   M
Geological Engineering   M
Ocean Engineering   M,O

**UNIVERSITY OF ALASKA
FAIRBANKS**
Civil Engineering   M,D,O
Computer Science   M
Construction Management   M,D,O
Electrical Engineering   M
Engineering and Applied
   Sciences—General   D
Engineering Management   M
Environmental Engineering   M,D
Geological Engineering   M
Hazardous Materials
   Management   M,D,O
Mechanical Engineering   M
Mineral/Mining Engineering   M
Petroleum Engineering   M

UNIVERSITY OF ALBERTA
Biomedical Engineering   M,D
Biotechnology   M,D
Chemical Engineering   M,D
Civil Engineering   M,D
Computer Engineering   M,D
Computer Science   M,D
Construction Engineering   M,D
Electrical Engineering   M,D
Energy and Power
   Engineering   M,D
Engineering Management   M,D
Environmental Engineering   M,D
Geotechnical Engineering   M,D
Materials Engineering   M,D
Mechanical Engineering   M,D
Mineral/Mining Engineering   M,D
Nanotechnology   M,D
Petroleum Engineering   M,D
Structural Engineering   M,D
Systems Engineering   M,D

Telecommunications	M,D
Water Resources Engineering	M,D

THE UNIVERSITY OF ARIZONA

Aerospace/Aeronautical Engineering	M,D
Agricultural Engineering	M,D
Biomedical Engineering	M,D
Biosystems Engineering	M,D
Chemical Engineering	M,D
Computer Engineering	M,D
Computer Science	M,D
Electrical Engineering	M,D
Engineering and Applied Sciences—General	M,D,O
Environmental Engineering	M,D
Geological Engineering	M,D,O
Industrial/Management Engineering	M,D
Materials Engineering	M,D
Materials Sciences	M,D
Mechanical Engineering	M,D
Medical Informatics	M,D,O
Mineral/Mining Engineering	M,D,O
Systems Engineering	M,D

UNIVERSITY OF ARKANSAS

Agricultural Engineering	M,D
Bioengineering	M
Biomedical Engineering	M
Chemical Engineering	M,D
Civil Engineering	M,D
Computer Engineering	M,D
Computer Science	M,D
Electrical Engineering	M,D
Electronic Materials	M,D
Engineering and Applied Sciences—General	M,D
Environmental Engineering	M
Industrial/Management Engineering	M,D
Mechanical Engineering	M,D
Operations Research	M,D
Telecommunications	M,D
Transportation and Highway Engineering	M,D

UNIVERSITY OF ARKANSAS AT LITTLE ROCK

Applied Science and Technology	M,D
Bioinformatics	M,D
Computer Science	M,D
Construction Management	M
Information Science	M,D,O
Systems Engineering	M,D,O

UNIVERSITY OF ARKANSAS FOR MEDICAL SCIENCES

Bioinformatics	M,D,O

UNIVERSITY OF BALTIMORE

Human-Computer Interaction	M

UNIVERSITY OF BRIDGEPORT

Biomedical Engineering	M
Computer Engineering	M,D
Computer Science	M,D
Electrical Engineering	M
Engineering and Applied Sciences—General	M,D
Management of Technology	M
Mechanical Engineering	M

THE UNIVERSITY OF BRITISH COLUMBIA

Chemical Engineering	M,D
Civil Engineering	M,D
Computer Engineering	M,D
Computer Science	M,D
Electrical Engineering	M,D
Engineering and Applied Sciences—General	M,D
Geological Engineering	M,D
Materials Engineering	M,D
Materials Sciences	M,D
Mechanical Engineering	M,D
Metallurgical Engineering and Metallurgy	M,D
Mineral/Mining Engineering	M,D
Operations Research	M
Software Engineering	M

UNIVERSITY OF CALGARY

Biomedical Engineering	M,D
Biotechnology	M
Chemical Engineering	M,D
Civil Engineering	M,D
Computer Engineering	M,D
Computer Science	M,D
Electrical Engineering	M,D
Energy and Power Engineering	M,D
Energy Management and Policy	M,D
Engineering and Applied Sciences—General	M,D
Environmental Engineering	M,D
Geotechnical Engineering	M,D
Manufacturing Engineering	M,D
Materials Sciences	M,D
Mechanical Engineering	M,D
Mechanics	M,D
Petroleum Engineering	M,D
Software Engineering	M,D
Structural Engineering	M,D
Transportation and Highway Engineering	M,D

UNIVERSITY OF CALIFORNIA, BERKELEY

Applied Science and Technology	D
Bioengineering	D
Chemical Engineering	M,D
Civil Engineering	M,D
Computer Science	M,D
Construction Management	O
Electrical Engineering	M,D
Energy Management and Policy	M,D
Engineering and Applied Sciences—General	M,D,O
Engineering Management	M,D
Environmental Engineering	M,D
Financial Engineering	M
Geotechnical Engineering	M,D
Industrial/Management Engineering	M,D
Materials Engineering	M,D
Materials Sciences	M,D
Mechanical Engineering	M,D
Mechanics	M,D
Nuclear Engineering	M,D
Operations Research	M,D
Structural Engineering	M,D
Transportation and Highway Engineering	M,D
Water Resources Engineering	M,D

UNIVERSITY OF CALIFORNIA, DAVIS

Aerospace/Aeronautical Engineering	M,D,O
Applied Science and Technology	M,D
Bioengineering	M,D
Biomedical Engineering	M,D
Chemical Engineering	M,D
Civil Engineering	M,D,O

Computer Science	M,D
Electrical Engineering	M,D
Engineering and Applied Sciences—General	M,D
Geological Engineering	M,D
Materials Engineering	M,D
Materials Sciences	M,D
Mechanical Engineering	M,D
Metallurgical Engineering and Metallurgy	M,D
Mineral/Mining Engineering	M,D
Operations Research	M
Software Engineering	M

UNIVERSITY OF CALIFORNIA, IRVINE

Aerospace/Aeronautical Engineering	M,D
Biochemical Engineering	M,D
Biomedical Engineering	M,D
Biotechnology	M
Chemical Engineering	M,D
Civil Engineering	M,D
Computer Science	M,D
Electrical Engineering	M,D
Engineering and Applied Sciences—General	M,D
Engineering Management	M
Environmental Engineering	M,D
Information Science	M,D
Manufacturing Engineering	M,D
Materials Engineering	M,D
Materials Sciences	M,D
Mechanical Engineering	M,D
Transportation and Highway Engineering	M,D

UNIVERSITY OF CALIFORNIA, LOS ANGELES

Aerospace/Aeronautical Engineering	M,D
Bioengineering	M,D
Bioinformatics	M,D
Biomedical Engineering	M,D
Chemical Engineering	M,D
Civil Engineering	M,D
Computer Science	M,D
Electrical Engineering	M,D
Engineering and Applied Sciences—General	M,D
Environmental Engineering	M,D
Financial Engineering	M,D
Manufacturing Engineering	M
Materials Engineering	M,D
Materials Sciences	M,D
Mechanical Engineering	M,D

UNIVERSITY OF CALIFORNIA, MERCED

Bioengineering	M,D
Computer Science	M,D
Electrical Engineering	M,D
Engineering and Applied Sciences—General	M,D
Environmental Engineering	M,D
Information Science	M,D
Mechanical Engineering	M,D
Mechanics	M,D
Systems Engineering	M,D

UNIVERSITY OF CALIFORNIA, RIVERSIDE

Artificial Intelligence/Robotics	M,D
Bioengineering	M,D
Bioinformatics	D
Chemical Engineering	M,D
Computer Engineering	M
Computer Science	M,D
Electrical Engineering	M,D
Environmental Engineering	M,D
Materials Engineering	M,D
Materials Sciences	M,D

Computer Engineering	M,D
Computer Science	M,D
Electrical Engineering	M,D
Engineering and Applied Sciences—General	M,D,O
Environmental Engineering	M,D,O
Materials Engineering	M,D
Materials Sciences	M,D
Mechanical Engineering	M,D,O
Medical Informatics	M
Transportation and Highway Engineering	M,D

UNIVERSITY OF CALIFORNIA, SAN DIEGO

Aerospace/Aeronautical Engineering	M,D
Architectural Engineering	M
Artificial Intelligence/Robotics	M,D
Bioengineering	M,D
Bioinformatics	M,D
Chemical Engineering	M,D
Computer Engineering	M,D
Computer Science	M,D
Electrical Engineering	M,D
Engineering Physics	M,D
Materials Sciences	M,D
Mechanical Engineering	M,D
Mechanics	M,D
Modeling and Simulation	M,D
Nanotechnology	M,D
Ocean Engineering	M,D
Structural Engineering	M,D
Telecommunications	M,D

UNIVERSITY OF CALIFORNIA, SAN FRANCISCO

Bioengineering	D
Bioinformatics	D

UNIVERSITY OF CALIFORNIA, SANTA BARBARA

Bioengineering	M,D
Biotechnology	M,D
Chemical Engineering	M,D
Computer Engineering	M,D
Computer Science	M,D
Electrical Engineering	M,D
Engineering and Applied Sciences—General	M,D
Management of Technology	M
Materials Engineering	M,D
Materials Sciences	M,D
Mechanical Engineering	M,D

UNIVERSITY OF CALIFORNIA, SANTA CRUZ

Bioinformatics	M,D
Computer Engineering	M,D
Computer Science	M,D
Electrical Engineering	M,D
Engineering and Applied Sciences—General	M,D
Management of Technology	M,D
Telecommunications	M,D

UNIVERSITY OF CENTRAL ARKANSAS

Computer Science	M

UNIVERSITY OF CENTRAL FLORIDA

Aerospace/Aeronautical Engineering	M
Biotechnology	M,D
Civil Engineering	M,D,O
Computer Engineering	M,D,O
Computer Science	M,D
Construction Engineering	M,D,O
Electrical Engineering	M,D,O
Engineering and Applied Sciences—General	M,D,O
Environmental Engineering	M,D
Game Design and Development	M
Health Informatics	M,O
Industrial/Management Engineering	M,D,O
Materials Engineering	M,D
Materials Sciences	M,D

Mechanical Engineering	M,D
Nanotechnology	M,D

*M—masters degree; D—doctorate; O—other advanced degree; *—Close-Up and/or Display*

Mechanical Engineering M,D
Modeling and Simulation M,D,O
Structural Engineering M,D;O
Transportation and Highway
   Engineering M,D,O

UNIVERSITY OF CENTRAL MISSOURI
Aerospace/Aeronautical
   Engineering M,D,O
Computer Science M,D,O
Information Science M,D,O
Management of Technology M,D,O

UNIVERSITY OF CENTRAL OKLAHOMA
Biomedical Engineering M
Computer Science M
Electrical Engineering M
Engineering and Applied
   Sciences—General M
Engineering Physics M
Mechanical Engineering M

UNIVERSITY OF CHICAGO
Bioengineering D
Computer Science M,D

UNIVERSITY OF CINCINNATI
Aerospace/Aeronautical
   Engineering M,D
Bioinformatics D
Biomedical Engineering D
Chemical Engineering M,D
Civil Engineering M,D
Computer Engineering M,D
Computer Science M,D
Electrical Engineering M,D
Engineering and Applied
   Sciences—General M,D
Environmental Engineering M,D
Ergonomics and Human
   Factors M,D
Industrial/Management
   Engineering M,D
Materials Engineering M,D
Materials Sciences M,D
Mechanical Engineering M,D
Mechanics M,D
Nuclear Engineering M,D

UNIVERSITY OF COLORADO BOULDER
Aerospace/Aeronautical
   Engineering M,D
Architectural Engineering M,D
Chemical Engineering M,D
Civil Engineering M,D
Computer Engineering M,D
Computer Science M,D
Construction Engineering M,D
Electrical Engineering M,D
Engineering and Applied
   Sciences—General M,D
Engineering Management M
Environmental Engineering M,D
Geotechnical Engineering M,D
Mechanical Engineering M,D
Operations Research M
Structural Engineering M,D
Telecommunications
   Management M
Telecommunications M
Water Resources Engineering M,D

UNIVERSITY OF COLORADO COLORADO SPRINGS
Aerospace/Aeronautical
   Engineering M,D
Computer and Information
   Systems Security M,D
Computer Science M

Electrical Engineering M
Energy and Power
   Engineering M,D
Engineering and Applied
   Sciences—General M,D
Engineering Management M,D
Mechanical Engineering M
Software Engineering M,D
Systems Engineering M,D

UNIVERSITY OF COLORADO DENVER
Applied Science and
   Technology M
Bioengineering M,D
Bioinformatics D
Civil Engineering M,D
Computer Science M,D
Electrical Engineering M,D
Energy Management
   and Policy M
Engineering and Applied
   Sciences—General M,D
Environmental Engineering M,D
Geotechnical Engineering M,D
Hazardous Materials
   Management M
Hydraulics M,D
Information Science M,D
Management of Technology M
Mechanical Engineering M,D
Mechanics M
Medical Informatics M,D
Operations Research M,D
Structural Engineering M,D
Transportation and Highway
   Engineering M,D

UNIVERSITY OF CONNECTICUT
Biomedical Engineering M,D
Chemical Engineering M,D
Civil Engineering M,D
Computer Science M,D
Electrical Engineering M,D
Engineering and Applied
   Sciences—General M,D
Environmental Engineering M,D
Materials Engineering M,D
Materials Sciences M,D
Mechanical Engineering M,D
Metallurgical Engineering and
   Metallurgy M,D
Polymer Science and
   Engineering M,D
Software Engineering M,D

UNIVERSITY OF DALLAS
Management of Technology M

UNIVERSITY OF DAYTON
Aerospace/Aeronautical
   Engineering M,D
Bioengineering M
Chemical Engineering M
Civil Engineering M
Computer and Information
   Systems Security M
Computer Engineering M,D
Computer Science M
Electrical Engineering M,D
Engineering Management M
Environmental Engineering M
Geotechnical Engineering M
Materials Engineering M
Mechanical Engineering M,D
Mechanics M
Structural Engineering M
Transportation and Highway
   Engineering M
Water Resources Engineering M

UNIVERSITY OF DELAWARE
Biotechnology M,D

Chemical Engineering M,D
Civil Engineering M,D
Computer Engineering M,D
Computer Science M,D
Electrical Engineering M,D
Energy Management
   and Policy M,D
Engineering and Applied
   Sciences—General M,D
Environmental Engineering M,D
Geotechnical Engineering M,D
Information Science M,D
Management of Technology M
Materials Engineering M,D
Materials Sciences M,D
Mechanical Engineering M,D
Ocean Engineering M,D
Operations Research M
Structural Engineering M,D
Transportation and Highway
   Engineering M,D
Water Resources Engineering M,D

UNIVERSITY OF DENVER
Bioengineering M,D
Computer and Information
   Systems Security M,O
Computer Engineering M,D
Computer Science M,D
Construction Management M
Electrical Engineering M,D
Engineering and Applied
   Sciences—General M,D
Engineering Management M,D
Internet Engineering M,O
Management of Technology M,O
Materials Engineering M,D
Materials Sciences M,D
Mechanical Engineering M,D
Software Engineering M,O
Telecommunications M,O

UNIVERSITY OF DETROIT MERCY
Architectural Engineering M
Civil Engineering M,D
Computer Engineering M,D
Computer Science M
Electrical Engineering M,D
Engineering and Applied
   Sciences—General M,D
Engineering Management M
Environmental Engineering M,D
Information Science M
Mechanical Engineering M,D
Software Engineering M

THE UNIVERSITY OF FINDLAY
Health Informatics M,D

UNIVERSITY OF FLORIDA
Aerospace/Aeronautical
   Engineering M,D
Agricultural Engineering M,D,O
Bioengineering M,D,O
Biomedical Engineering M,D,O
Chemical Engineering M,D,O
Civil Engineering M,D
Computer Engineering M,D
Computer Science M,D
Construction Management M,D
Electrical Engineering M,D
Engineering and Applied
   Sciences—General M,D,O
Environmental Engineering M,D,O
Industrial/Management
   Engineering M,D,O
Information Science M,D
Materials Engineering M,D,O
Materials Sciences M,D,O
Mechanical Engineering M,D
Nuclear Engineering M,D
Ocean Engineering M,D
Systems Engineering M,D,O

UNIVERSITY OF GEORGIA
Agricultural Engineering M,D
Artificial Intelligence/Robotics M
Biochemical Engineering M
Bioengineering M
Bioinformatics M,D,O
Computer Science M,D
Environmental Engineering M
Internet Engineering M

UNIVERSITY OF GUELPH
Bioengineering M,D
Biotechnology M,D
Computer Science M,D
Engineering and Applied
   Sciences—General M,D
Environmental Engineering M,D
Water Resources Engineering M,D

UNIVERSITY OF HARTFORD
Engineering and Applied
   Sciences—General M

UNIVERSITY OF HAWAII AT MANOA
Bioengineering M
Civil Engineering M,D
Computer Science M,D,O
Electrical Engineering M,D
Engineering and Applied
   Sciences—General M,D
Environmental Engineering M,D
Financial Engineering M
Geological Engineering M,D
Information Science M,D
Mechanical Engineering M,D
Ocean Engineering M,D
Telecommunications O

UNIVERSITY OF HOUSTON
Biomedical Engineering D
Chemical Engineering M,D
Civil Engineering M,D
Computer and Information
   Systems Security M
Computer Science M,D
Construction Management M
Electrical Engineering M,D
Engineering and Applied
   Sciences—General M,D
Industrial/Management
   Engineering M,D
Information Science M,D
Mechanical Engineering M,D
Petroleum Engineering M,D
Telecommunications M

UNIVERSITY OF HOUSTON–CLEAR LAKE
Biotechnology M
Computer Engineering M
Computer Science M
Information Science M
Software Engineering M
Systems Engineering M

UNIVERSITY OF HOUSTON–VICTORIA
Computer Science M

UNIVERSITY OF IDAHO
Agricultural Engineering M,D
Bioengineering M,D
Bioinformatics M,D
Chemical Engineering M,D
Civil Engineering M,D
Computer Engineering M,D
Computer Science M,D
Electrical Engineering M,D
Engineering and Applied
   Sciences—General M,D
Engineering Management M,D

Environmental Engineering	M,D
Geological Engineering	M,D
Management of Technology	M,D
Materials Sciences	M,D
Mechanical Engineering	M,D
Nuclear Engineering	M,D
Water Resources Engineering	M,D

UNIVERSITY OF ILLINOIS AT CHICAGO

Bioengineering	M,D
Bioinformatics	M,D
Biotechnology	M,D
Chemical Engineering	M,D
Civil Engineering	M,D
Computer Science	M,D
Engineering and Applied Sciences—General	M,D
Health Informatics	M,O
Industrial/Management Engineering	M,D
Materials Engineering	M,D
Mechanical Engineering	M,D
Operations Research	M,D

UNIVERSITY OF ILLINOIS AT SPRINGFIELD

Computer Science	M

UNIVERSITY OF ILLINOIS AT URBANA–CHAMPAIGN

Aerospace/Aeronautical Engineering	M,D
Agricultural Engineering	M,D
Bioengineering	M,D
Bioinformatics	M,D,O
Chemical Engineering	M,D
Civil Engineering	M,D
Computer Engineering	M,D
Computer Science	M,D
Electrical Engineering	M,D
Energy and Power Engineering	M,D
Energy Management and Policy	M
Engineering and Applied Sciences—General	M,D
Environmental Engineering	M,D
Financial Engineering	M
Health Informatics	M,D,O
Human-Computer Interaction	M,D,O
Industrial/Management Engineering	M,D
Information Science	M,D,O
Management of Technology	M,D
Materials Engineering	M,D
Materials Sciences	M,D
Mechanical Engineering	M,D
Mechanics	M,D
Medical Informatics	M,D,O
Nuclear Engineering	M,D
Systems Engineering	M,D

THE UNIVERSITY OF IOWA

Biochemical Engineering	M,D
Bioinformatics	M,D,O
Biomedical Engineering	M,D
Chemical Engineering	M,D
Civil Engineering	M,D
Computer Engineering	M,D
Computer Science	M,D
Electrical Engineering	M,D
Energy and Power Engineering	M,D
Engineering and Applied Sciences—General	M,D*
Environmental Engineering	M,D
Ergonomics and Human Factors	M,D,O
Health Informatics	M,D,O

Industrial/Management Engineering	M,D
Information Science	M,D,O
Manufacturing Engineering	M,D
Materials Engineering	M,D
Mechanical Engineering	M,D
Operations Research	M,D

THE UNIVERSITY OF KANSAS

Aerospace/Aeronautical Engineering	M,D
Architectural Engineering	M
Bioengineering	M,D
Bioinformatics	D
Biotechnology	M
Chemical Engineering	M,D
Civil Engineering	M,D
Computer Engineering	M
Computer Science	M,D
Construction Management	M
Electrical Engineering	M,D
Engineering and Applied Sciences—General	M,D
Engineering Management	M
Environmental Engineering	M,D
Health Informatics	M
Mechanical Engineering	M,D
Medical Informatics	M,D,O
Petroleum Engineering	M,D

UNIVERSITY OF KENTUCKY

Agricultural Engineering	M,D
Biomedical Engineering	M,D
Chemical Engineering	M,D
Civil Engineering	M,D
Computer Science	M,D
Electrical Engineering	M,D
Engineering and Applied Sciences—General	M,D
Information Science	M
Manufacturing Engineering	M
Materials Engineering	M,D
Materials Sciences	M,D
Mechanical Engineering	M,D
Mineral/Mining Engineering	M,D

UNIVERSITY OF LETHBRIDGE

Computer Science	M,D

UNIVERSITY OF LOUISIANA AT LAFAYETTE

Architectural Engineering	M
Chemical Engineering	M
Civil Engineering	M
Computer Engineering	M,D
Computer Science	M,D
Engineering Management	M
Mechanical Engineering	M
Petroleum Engineering	M
Telecommunications	M

UNIVERSITY OF LOUISVILLE

Bioengineering	M
Chemical Engineering	M,D
Civil Engineering	M,D,O
Computer and Information Systems Security	M,D,O
Computer Engineering	M,D,O
Computer Science	M,D,O
Electrical Engineering	M,D
Engineering and Applied Sciences—General	M,D,O
Engineering Management	M,D,O
Environmental Engineering	M,D,O
Industrial/Management Engineering	M,D,O
Mechanical Engineering	M,D

UNIVERSITY OF MAINE

Bioinformatics	M,D

Biomedical Engineering	M,D
Chemical Engineering	M,D
Civil Engineering	M,D
Computer Engineering	M,D
Computer Science	M,D,O
Electrical Engineering	M,D
Engineering and Applied Sciences—General	M,D
Engineering Physics	M,D
Information Science	M,D,O
Mechanical Engineering	M,D

UNIVERSITY OF MANAGEMENT AND TECHNOLOGY

Computer Science	M,O
Engineering Management	M
Software Engineering	M,O

THE UNIVERSITY OF MANCHESTER

Aerospace/Aeronautical Engineering	M,D
Biochemical Engineering	M,D
Bioinformatics	M,D
Biotechnology	M,D
Chemical Engineering	M,D
Civil Engineering	M,D
Computer Science	M,D
Electrical Engineering	M,D
Engineering Management	M,D
Environmental Engineering	M,D
Hazardous Materials Management	M,D
Materials Sciences	M,D
Mechanical Engineering	M,D
Metallurgical Engineering and Metallurgy	M,D
Modeling and Simulation	M,D
Nuclear Engineering	M,D
Paper and Pulp Engineering	M,D
Polymer Science and Engineering	M,D
Structural Engineering	M,D

UNIVERSITY OF MANITOBA

Biosystems Engineering	M,D
Civil Engineering	M,D
Computer Engineering	M,D
Computer Science	M,D
Electrical Engineering	M,D
Engineering and Applied Sciences—General	M,D
Industrial/Management Engineering	M,D
Manufacturing Engineering	M,D
Mechanical Engineering	M,D

UNIVERSITY OF MARY

Energy Management and Policy	M

UNIVERSITY OF MARYLAND, BALTIMORE COUNTY

Biochemical Engineering	M,D,O
Biotechnology	M,O
Chemical Engineering	M,D
Computer and Information Systems Security	M,O
Computer Engineering	M,D
Computer Science	M,D
Electrical Engineering	M,D
Engineering and Applied Sciences—General	M,D,O
Engineering Management	M,O
Environmental Engineering	M,D
Health Informatics	M
Information Science	M,D
Mechanical Engineering	M,D,O
Systems Engineering	M,O

UNIVERSITY OF MARYLAND, COLLEGE PARK

Aerospace/Aeronautical Engineering	M,D
Bioengineering	M,D
Bioinformatics	D
Chemical Engineering	M,D
Civil Engineering	M,D
Computer Engineering	M,D
Computer Science	M,D
Electrical Engineering	M,D
Engineering and Applied Sciences—General	M
Environmental Engineering	M,D
Fire Protection Engineering	M
Manufacturing Engineering	M,D
Materials Engineering	M,D
Materials Sciences	M,D
Mechanical Engineering	M,D
Mechanics	M,D
Nuclear Engineering	M,D
Reliability Engineering	M,D
Systems Engineering	M
Telecommunications	M

UNIVERSITY OF MARYLAND EASTERN SHORE

Computer Science	M

UNIVERSITY OF MARYLAND UNIVERSITY COLLEGE

Biotechnology	M,O
Computer and Information Systems Security	M,O
Database Systems	M,O
Health Informatics	M,O
Information Science	M,O
Management of Technology	M,O

UNIVERSITY OF MASSACHUSETTS AMHERST

Architectural Engineering	M,D
Biotechnology	M,D
Chemical Engineering	M,D
Civil Engineering	M,D
Computer Engineering	M,D
Computer Science	M,D
Electrical Engineering	M,D
Engineering and Applied Sciences—General	M,D
Environmental Engineering	M,D
Geotechnical Engineering	M,D
Industrial/Management Engineering	M,D
Mechanical Engineering	M,D
Mechanics	M,D
Operations Research	M,D
Polymer Science and Engineering	M,D
Structural Engineering	M,D
Transportation and Highway Engineering	M,D
Water Resources Engineering	M,D

UNIVERSITY OF MASSACHUSETTS BOSTON

Biomedical Engineering	D
Biotechnology	M,D
Computer Science	M,D

UNIVERSITY OF MASSACHUSETTS DARTMOUTH

Biomedical Engineering	M,D
Biotechnology	M,D
Civil Engineering	M
Computer Engineering	M,D,O
Computer Science	M,D,O
Electrical Engineering	M,D,O
Engineering and Applied Sciences—General	D

*M—masters degree; D—doctorate; O—other advanced degree; *—Close-Up and/or Display*

Industrial/Management
   Engineering — M,D
Information Science — D
Mechanical Engineering — M
Mechanics — D
Systems Engineering — M,D
Telecommunications — M,D,O
Textile Sciences and
   Engineering — M

UNIVERSITY OF MASSACHUSETTS LOWELL
Biotechnology — M,D
Chemical Engineering — M,D
Civil Engineering — M,D,O
Computer Engineering — M
Computer Science — M,D
Electrical Engineering — M,D
Energy and Power
   Engineering — M,D
Engineering and Applied
   Sciences—General — M,D,O
Environmental Engineering — M,D,O
Ergonomics and Human
   Factors — M,D,O
Health Informatics — M,O
Industrial/Management
   Engineering — M,D,O
Materials Engineering — M,D,O
Mechanical Engineering — M,D
Nuclear Engineering — M,D
Polymer Science and
   Engineering — M,D,O

UNIVERSITY OF MASSACHUSETTS WORCESTER
Bioinformatics — M,D

UNIVERSITY OF MEMPHIS
Biomedical Engineering — M,D
Civil Engineering — M,D
Computer Engineering — M,D
Computer Science — M,D
Electrical Engineering — M,D
Energy and Power
   Engineering — M,D
Engineering and Applied
   Sciences—General — M,D
Environmental Engineering — M,D
Industrial/Management
   Engineering — M,D
Mechanical Engineering — M,D
Structural Engineering — M,D
Transportation and Highway
   Engineering — M,D
Water Resources Engineering — M,D

UNIVERSITY OF MIAMI
Aerospace/Aeronautical
   Engineering — M,D
Architectural Engineering — M,D
Biomedical Engineering — M,D
Civil Engineering — M,D
Computer Engineering — M,D
Computer Science — M,D
Electrical Engineering — M,D
Engineering and Applied
   Sciences—General — M,D
Ergonomics and Human
   Factors — M
Industrial/Management
   Engineering — M,D
Management of Technology — M,D
Mechanical Engineering — M,D

UNIVERSITY OF MICHIGAN
Aerospace/Aeronautical
   Engineering — M,D
Artificial Intelligence/Robotics — M,D
Automotive Engineering — M,D
Bioinformatics — M,D
Biomedical Engineering — M,D
Chemical Engineering — M,D,O

Civil Engineering — M,D,O
Computer Engineering — M,D
Computer Science — M,D
Construction Engineering — M,D,O
Electrical Engineering — M,D
Energy and Power
   Engineering — M,D
Engineering and Applied
   Sciences—General — M,D,O
Environmental Engineering — M,D,O
Financial Engineering — M,D
Health Informatics — M,D
Industrial/Management
   Engineering — M,D
Information Science — M,D*
Manufacturing Engineering — M,D
Materials Engineering — M,D
Materials Sciences — M,D
Mechanical Engineering — M,D
Nuclear Engineering — M,D,O
Ocean Engineering — M,D,O
Operations Research — M,D
Pharmaceutical Engineering — M,D
Structural Engineering — M,D,O

UNIVERSITY OF MICHIGAN–DEARBORN
Automotive Engineering — M,D
Computer Engineering — M
Database Systems — M
Electrical Engineering — M
Energy and Power
   Engineering — M
Engineering and Applied
   Sciences—General — M,D
Engineering Management — M
Health Informatics — M
Industrial/Management
   Engineering — M
Information Science — M
Manufacturing Engineering — M
Mechanical Engineering — M
Software Engineering — M
Systems Engineering — M,D

UNIVERSITY OF MICHIGAN–FLINT
Computer Science — M
Information Science — M

UNIVERSITY OF MINNESOTA, DULUTH
Computer Engineering — M
Computer Science — M
Electrical Engineering — M
Engineering Management — M
Safety Engineering — M

UNIVERSITY OF MINNESOTA, TWIN CITIES CAMPUS
Aerospace/Aeronautical
   Engineering — M,D
Biomedical Engineering — M,D
Biosystems Engineering — M,D
Biotechnology — M
Chemical Engineering — M,D
Civil Engineering — M,D,O
Computer and Information
   Systems Security — M
Computer Engineering — M,D
Computer Science — M,D
Database Systems — M
Electrical Engineering — M,D
Engineering and Applied
   Sciences—General — M,D,O
Geological Engineering — M,D,O
Health Informatics — M,D
Industrial/Management
   Engineering — M,D
Management of Technology — M
Materials Engineering — M,D
Materials Sciences — M,D
Mechanical Engineering — M,D
Mechanics — M,D

Paper and Pulp Engineering — M,D
Software Engineering — M
Technology and Public Policy — M

UNIVERSITY OF MISSISSIPPI
Applied Science and
   Technology — M,D
Engineering and Applied
   Sciences—General — M,D

UNIVERSITY OF MISSISSIPPI MEDICAL CENTER
Materials Sciences — M,D

UNIVERSITY OF MISSOURI
Aerospace/Aeronautical
   Engineering — M,D
Agricultural Engineering — M,D
Bioengineering — M,D
Bioinformatics — D
Chemical Engineering — M,D
Civil Engineering — M,D
Computer Science — M,D
Electrical Engineering — M,D
Engineering and Applied
   Sciences—General — M,D,O
Environmental Engineering — M,D
Geotechnical Engineering — M,D
Health Informatics — M,D,O
Industrial/Management
   Engineering — M,D
Manufacturing Engineering — M,D
Mechanical Engineering — M,D
Nuclear Engineering — M,D,O
Structural Engineering — M,D
Transportation and Highway
   Engineering — M,D
Water Resources Engineering — M,D

UNIVERSITY OF MISSOURI–KANSAS CITY
Bioinformatics — M,D,O
Civil Engineering — M,D,O
Computer Engineering — M,D,O
Computer Science — M,D,O
Construction Engineering — M,D,O
Electrical Engineering — M,D,O
Engineering and Applied
   Sciences—General — M,D,O
Engineering Management — M,D,O
Mechanical Engineering — M,D,O
Polymer Science and
   Engineering — M,D
Software Engineering — M,D,O
Telecommunications — M,D,O

UNIVERSITY OF MISSOURI–ST. LOUIS
Computer Science — M,D

THE UNIVERSITY OF MONTANA
Computer Science — M

UNIVERSITY OF NEBRASKA AT OMAHA
Artificial Intelligence/Robotics — M,O
Bioinformatics — M,D,O
Computer and Information
   Systems Security — M,D,O
Computer Science — M,O
Information Science — M,D,O
Medical Informatics — M,D,O
Software Engineering — M,O
Systems Engineering — M,O

UNIVERSITY OF NEBRASKA–LINCOLN
Agricultural Engineering — M,D
Architectural Engineering — M,D
Bioengineering — M,D
Bioinformatics — M,D

Biomedical Engineering — M,D
Chemical Engineering — M,D
Civil Engineering — M,D
Computer Engineering — M,D
Computer Science — M,D
Electrical Engineering — M,D
Engineering and Applied
   Sciences—General — M,D
Engineering Management — M,D
Environmental Engineering — M,D
Industrial/Management
   Engineering — M,D
Information Science — M,D
Manufacturing Engineering — M,D
Materials Engineering — M,D
Materials Sciences — M,D
Mechanical Engineering — M,D
Mechanics — M,D
Metallurgical Engineering and
   Metallurgy — M,D

UNIVERSITY OF NEBRASKA MEDICAL CENTER
Bioinformatics — M,D

UNIVERSITY OF NEVADA, LAS VEGAS
Biomedical Engineering — M,D,O
Civil Engineering — M,D
Computer Engineering — M,D
Computer Science — M,D
Electrical Engineering — M,D
Engineering and Applied
   Sciences—General — M,D,O
Environmental Engineering — M,D
Materials Engineering — M,D,O
Mechanical Engineering — M,D,O
Nuclear Engineering — M,D,O
Transportation and Highway
   Engineering — M,D

UNIVERSITY OF NEVADA, RENO
Biomedical Engineering — M,D
Biotechnology — M
Chemical Engineering — M,D
Civil Engineering — M,D
Computer Engineering — M,D
Computer Science — M,D
Electrical Engineering — M,D
Engineering and Applied
   Sciences—General — M,D
Geological Engineering — M,D
Materials Engineering — M,D
Mechanical Engineering — M,D
Metallurgical Engineering and
   Metallurgy — M,D
Mineral/Mining Engineering — M

UNIVERSITY OF NEW BRUNSWICK FREDERICTON
Chemical Engineering — M,D
Civil Engineering — M,D
Computer Engineering — M,D
Computer Science — M,D
Construction Engineering — M,D
Electrical Engineering — M,D
Engineering and Applied
   Sciences—General — M,D,O
Engineering Management — M
Environmental Engineering — M,D
Geotechnical Engineering — M,D
Materials Sciences — M,D
Mechanical Engineering — M,D
Mechanics — M,D
Structural Engineering — M,D
Surveying Science and
   Engineering — M,D
Transportation and Highway
   Engineering — M,D

UNIVERSITY OF NEW HAMPSHIRE
Chemical Engineering — M,D
Civil Engineering — M,D

Computer Science	M,D,O		
Electrical Engineering	M,D		
Materials Sciences	M,D		
Mechanical Engineering	M,D		
Ocean Engineering	M,D,O		
Software Engineering	M,O		

UNIVERSITY OF NEW HAVEN

Computer and Information Systems Security	M,D,O
Computer Engineering	M
Computer Science	M,D,O
Database Systems	M,O
Electrical Engineering	M
Engineering and Applied Sciences—General	M,O
Engineering Management	M,O
Environmental Engineering	M
Fire Protection Engineering	M,O
Hazardous Materials Management	M
Industrial/Management Engineering	M,O
Information Science	M,O
Mechanical Engineering	M
Software Engineering	M,O
Systems Engineering	M,O
Water Resources Engineering	M

UNIVERSITY OF NEW MEXICO

Biomedical Engineering	M,D
Chemical Engineering	M,D
Civil Engineering	M,D
Computer and Information Systems Security	M
Computer Engineering	M,D
Computer Science	M,D
Construction Management	M,D
Electrical Engineering	M,D
Engineering and Applied Sciences—General	M,D,O
Management of Technology	M
Manufacturing Engineering	M
Mechanical Engineering	M,D
Nanotechnology	M,D
Nuclear Engineering	M,D
Systems Engineering	M,D

UNIVERSITY OF NEW ORLEANS

Computer Science	M
Engineering and Applied Sciences—General	M,D
Engineering Management	M
Mechanical Engineering	M

THE UNIVERSITY OF NORTH CAROLINA AT CHAPEL HILL

Bioinformatics	D
Biomedical Engineering	M,D
Computer Science	M,D
Environmental Engineering	M,D
Materials Sciences	M,D
Operations Research	M,D
Telecommunications	M,D

THE UNIVERSITY OF NORTH CAROLINA AT CHARLOTTE

Bioinformatics	M,D,O
Civil Engineering	M,D
Computer and Information Systems Security	M,D,O
Computer Engineering	M,D
Computer Science	M,O
Construction Management	M
Database Systems	M,O
Electrical Engineering	M,D
Energy and Power Engineering	M,D,O

Engineering and Applied Sciences—General	M,D,O
Engineering Management	M,D,O
Environmental Engineering	M,D,O
Fire Protection Engineering	M
Game Design and Development	M,O
Health Informatics	M,O
Information Science	M,D,O
Mechanical Engineering	M,D
Systems Engineering	M,D,O

THE UNIVERSITY OF NORTH CAROLINA AT GREENSBORO

Computer Science	M

THE UNIVERSITY OF NORTH CAROLINA WILMINGTON

Computer Science	M

UNIVERSITY OF NORTH DAKOTA

Aviation	M
Chemical Engineering	M
Civil Engineering	M
Computer Science	M,D
Electrical Engineering	M
Engineering and Applied Sciences—General	D
Environmental Engineering	M
Geological Engineering	M
Management of Technology	M
Mechanical Engineering	M
Mineral/Mining Engineering	M
Structural Engineering	M

UNIVERSITY OF NORTHERN BRITISH COLUMBIA

Computer Science	M,D,O

UNIVERSITY OF NORTH FLORIDA

Civil Engineering	M
Computer Science	M
Construction Management	M
Electrical Engineering	M
Mechanical Engineering	M
Software Engineering	M

UNIVERSITY OF NORTH TEXAS

Biomedical Engineering	M,D,O
Computer Engineering	M,D,O
Computer Science	M,D,O
Electrical Engineering	M,D,O
Energy and Power Engineering	M,D,O
Engineering and Applied Sciences—General	M,D,O
Information Science	M,D,O
Mechanical Engineering	M,D,O

UNIVERSITY OF NORTH TEXAS HEALTH SCIENCE CENTER AT FORT WORTH

Biotechnology	M,D

UNIVERSITY OF NOTRE DAME

Aerospace/Aeronautical Engineering	M,D
Bioengineering	M,D
Chemical Engineering	M,D
Civil Engineering	M,D
Computer Engineering	M,D
Computer Science	M,D
Database Systems	M
Electrical Engineering	M,D
Engineering and Applied Sciences—General	M,D
Environmental Engineering	M,D
Mechanical Engineering	M,D

UNIVERSITY OF OKLAHOMA

Aerospace/Aeronautical Engineering	M,D
Bioengineering	M,D
Bioinformatics	M,D
Chemical Engineering	M,D
Civil Engineering	M,D
Computer Engineering	M,D
Computer Science	M,D
Construction Management	M
Electrical Engineering	M,D
Engineering and Applied Sciences—General	M,D
Engineering Physics	M,D
Environmental Engineering	M,D
Geological Engineering	M,D
Industrial/Management Engineering	M,D
Mechanical Engineering	M,D
Petroleum Engineering	M,D
Telecommunications	M

UNIVERSITY OF OREGON

Computer Science	M,D
Information Science	M,D

UNIVERSITY OF OTTAWA

Aerospace/Aeronautical Engineering	M,D
Bioengineering	M,D
Biomedical Engineering	M
Chemical Engineering	M,D
Civil Engineering	M,D
Computer Engineering	M,D
Computer Science	M,D
Electrical Engineering	M,D
Engineering and Applied Sciences—General	M,D,O
Engineering Management	M,O
Information Science	M,O
Mechanical Engineering	M,D
Systems Science	M,D,O

UNIVERSITY OF PENNSYLVANIA

Bioengineering	M,D
Biotechnology	M
Chemical Engineering	M,D
Computer Science	M,D
Electrical Engineering	M,D
Engineering and Applied Sciences—General	M,D,O*
Information Science	M,D
Management of Technology	M
Materials Engineering	M,D
Materials Sciences	M,D
Mechanical Engineering	M,D
Mechanics	M,D
Systems Engineering	M,D
Telecommunications Management	M
Telecommunications	M

UNIVERSITY OF PHOENIX –ATLANTA CAMPUS

Management of Technology	M

UNIVERSITY OF PHOENIX –AUGUSTA CAMPUS

Management of Technology	M

UNIVERSITY OF PHOENIX –AUSTIN CAMPUS

Management of Technology	M

UNIVERSITY OF PHOENIX–BAY AREA CAMPUS

Energy Management and Policy	M,D

Management of Technology	M,D

UNIVERSITY OF PHOENIX –BIRMINGHAM CAMPUS

Health Informatics	M
Management of Technology	M

UNIVERSITY OF PHOENIX –BOSTON CAMPUS

Management of Technology	M

UNIVERSITY OF PHOENIX –CENTRAL VALLEY CAMPUS

Management of Technology	M

UNIVERSITY OF PHOENIX –CHARLOTTE CAMPUS

Health Informatics	M
Management of Technology	M

UNIVERSITY OF PHOENIX –CHICAGO CAMPUS

Management of Technology	M

UNIVERSITY OF PHOENIX –CLEVELAND CAMPUS

Management of Technology	M

UNIVERSITY OF PHOENIX –COLORADO CAMPUS

Management of Technology	M

UNIVERSITY OF PHOENIX –COLORADO SPRINGS DOWNTOWN CAMPUS

Management of Technology	M

UNIVERSITY OF PHOENIX –COLUMBIA CAMPUS

Management of Technology	M

UNIVERSITY OF PHOENIX –COLUMBUS GEORGIA CAMPUS

Management of Technology	M

UNIVERSITY OF PHOENIX –DALLAS CAMPUS

Management of Technology	M

UNIVERSITY OF PHOENIX –DES MOINES CAMPUS

Health Informatics	M,D
Management of Technology	M

UNIVERSITY OF PHOENIX –HAWAII CAMPUS

Management of Technology	M

UNIVERSITY OF PHOENIX –HOUSTON CAMPUS

Management of Technology	M

UNIVERSITY OF PHOENIX –IDAHO CAMPUS

Management of Technology	M

UNIVERSITY OF PHOENIX –INDIANAPOLIS CAMPUS

Management of Technology	M

UNIVERSITY OF PHOENIX –JERSEY CITY CAMPUS

Management of Technology	M

*M—masters degree; D—doctorate; O—other advanced degree; *—Close-Up and/or Display*

**UNIVERSITY OF PHOENIX
–KANSAS CITY CAMPUS**
Management of Technology   M

**UNIVERSITY OF PHOENIX
–LAS VEGAS CAMPUS**
Management of Technology   M

**UNIVERSITY OF PHOENIX
–MARYLAND CAMPUS**
Management of Technology   M

**UNIVERSITY OF PHOENIX
–MEMPHIS CAMPUS**
Management of Technology   M

**UNIVERSITY OF PHOENIX
–MILWAUKEE CAMPUS**
Energy Management
    and Policy   M

**UNIVERSITY OF PHOENIX
–MINNEAPOLIS/ST. PAUL
CAMPUS**
Management of Technology   M

**UNIVERSITY OF PHOENIX
–NASHVILLE CAMPUS**
Management of Technology   M

**UNIVERSITY OF PHOENIX
–NEW MEXICO CAMPUS**
Management of Technology   M

**UNIVERSITY OF PHOENIX
–OKLAHOMA CITY CAMPUS**
Management of Technology   M

**UNIVERSITY OF PHOENIX
–ONLINE CAMPUS**
Energy Management
    and Policy   M,O
Health Informatics   M,O
Management of Technology   M,O

**UNIVERSITY OF PHOENIX
–OREGON CAMPUS**
Management of Technology   M

**UNIVERSITY OF
PHOENIX–PHILADELPHIA
CAMPUS**
Management of Technology   M

**UNIVERSITY OF
PHOENIX–PHOENIX CAMPUS**
Energy Management
    and Policy   M,O
Management of Technology   M,O
Medical Informatics   M,O

**UNIVERSITY OF
PHOENIX–PUERTO RICO CAMPUS**
Energy Management
    and Policy
Management of Technology   M

**UNIVERSITY OF
PHOENIX–RICHMOND-VIRGINIA
BEACH CAMPUS**
Management of Technology   M

**UNIVERSITY OF PHOENIX
–SACRAMENTO VALLEY CAMPUS**
Management of Technology   M

**UNIVERSITY OF PHOENIX
–SAN ANTONIO CAMPUS**
Management of Technology   M

**UNIVERSITY OF PHOENIX
–SAN DIEGO CAMPUS**
Management of Technology   M

**UNIVERSITY OF PHOENIX
–SAVANNAH CAMPUS**
Management of Technology   M

**UNIVERSITY OF PHOENIX
–SOUTHERN ARIZONA CAMPUS**
Management of Technology   M

**UNIVERSITY OF PHOENIX
–SOUTHERN CALIFORNIA
CAMPUS**
Energy Management
    and Policy   M
Management of Technology   M

**UNIVERSITY OF PHOENIX
–UTAH CAMPUS**
Management of Technology   M

**UNIVERSITY OF PHOENIX
–WASHINGTON D.C. CAMPUS**
Health Informatics   M,D

UNIVERSITY OF PITTSBURGH
Artificial Intelligence/Robotics   M,D
Bioengineering   M,D
Bioinformatics   M,D,O
Chemical Engineering   M,D
Civil Engineering   M,D
Computer and Information
    Systems Security   M,D,O
Computer Engineering   M,D
Computer Science   M,D
Electrical Engineering   M,D
Energy Management
    and Policy   M
Engineering and Applied
    Sciences—General   M,D
Environmental Engineering   M,D
Industrial/Management
    Engineering   M,D
Information Science   M,D,O
Materials Sciences   M,D
Mechanical Engineering   M,D
Modeling and Simulation   D
Petroleum Engineering   M,D
Telecommunications   M,D,O

UNIVERSITY OF PORTLAND
Biomedical Engineering   M
Civil Engineering   M
Computer Science   M
Electrical Engineering   M
Engineering and Applied
    Sciences—General   M
Management of Technology   M
Mechanical Engineering   M

**UNIVERSITY OF PUERTO RICO,
MAYAGÜEZ CAMPUS**
Chemical Engineering   M,D
Civil Engineering   M,D
Computer Engineering   M,D
Computer Science   M,D
Electrical Engineering   M,D
Engineering and Applied
    Sciences—General   M,D
Industrial/Management
    Engineering   M
Information Science   M,D
Mechanical Engineering   M

**UNIVERSITY OF PUERTO RICO,
MEDICAL SCIENCES CAMPUS**
Health Informatics   M

**UNIVERSITY OF PUERTO RICO,
RÍO PIEDRAS CAMPUS**
Information Science   M,O

UNIVERSITY OF REGINA
Computer Engineering   M,D
Computer Science   M,D
Engineering and Applied
    Sciences—General   M,D
Engineering Management   M,O
Environmental Engineering   M,D
Industrial/Management
    Engineering   M,D
Petroleum Engineering   M,D
Software Engineering   M
Systems Engineering   M,D

UNIVERSITY OF RHODE ISLAND
Biomedical Engineering   M,D,O
Biotechnology   M,D
Chemical Engineering   M,D
Civil Engineering   M,D
Computer Engineering   M,D,O
Computer Science   M,D,O
Electrical Engineering   M,D,O
Engineering and Applied
    Sciences—General   M,D,O
Environmental Engineering   M,D
Ocean Engineering   M,D

UNIVERSITY OF ROCHESTER
Biomedical Engineering   M,D
Chemical Engineering   M,D*
Computer Engineering   M,D
Computer Science   M,D
Electrical Engineering   M,D
Energy and Power
    Engineering   M
Energy Management
    and Policy   M
Engineering and Applied
    Sciences—General   M,D
Materials Sciences   M,D
Mechanical Engineering   M,D

UNIVERSITY OF ST. THOMAS (MN)
Computer and Information
    Systems Security   M,O
Electrical Engineering   M,O
Engineering and Applied
    Sciences—General   M,O
Engineering Management   M,O
Management of Technology   M,O
Manufacturing Engineering   M,O
Mechanical Engineering   M,O
Software Engineering   M,O
Systems Engineering   M,O

UNIVERSITY OF SAN DIEGO
Health Informatics   M,D

UNIVERSITY OF SAN FRANCISCO
Biotechnology   M
Computer Science   M
Database Systems   M
Internet Engineering   M

UNIVERSITY OF SASKATCHEWAN
Bioengineering   M,D
Biomedical Engineering   M,D
Biotechnology   M
Chemical Engineering   M,D
Civil Engineering   M,D
Computer Science   M,D
Electrical Engineering   M,D,O
Engineering and Applied
    Sciences—General   M,D,O

Engineering Physics   M,D
Geological Engineering   M,D
Mechanical Engineering   M,D

THE UNIVERSITY OF SCRANTON
Software Engineering   M

UNIVERSITY OF SOUTH AFRICA
Chemical Engineering   M
Engineering and Applied
    Sciences—General   M
Information Science   M,D
Technology and Public Policy   M,D
Telecommunications
    Management   M,D

UNIVERSITY OF SOUTH ALABAMA
Chemical Engineering   M
Civil Engineering   M
Computer Science   M,D
Engineering and Applied
    Sciences—General   M,D
Mechanical Engineering   M
Systems Engineering   D

**UNIVERSITY OF SOUTH
CAROLINA**
Chemical Engineering   M,D
Civil Engineering   M,D
Computer Engineering   M,D
Computer Science   M,D
Electrical Engineering   M,D
Engineering and Applied
    Sciences—General   M,D
Hazardous Materials
    Management   M,D
Mechanical Engineering   M,D
Nuclear Engineering   M,D
Software Engineering   M,D

**UNIVERSITY OF SOUTH
CAROLINA UPSTATE**
Health Informatics   M
Information Science   M

**THE UNIVERSITY OF SOUTH
DAKOTA**
Computer Science   M

**UNIVERSITY OF SOUTHERN
CALIFORNIA**
Aerospace/Aeronautical
    Engineering   M,D,O
Artificial Intelligence/Robotics   M,D
Bioinformatics   D
Biomedical Engineering   M,D
Chemical Engineering   M,D,O
Civil Engineering   M,D,O
Computer and Information
    Systems Security   M,D
Computer Engineering   M,D,O
Computer Science   M,D
Construction Management   M,D,O
Electrical Engineering   M,D,O
Engineering and Applied
    Sciences—General   M,D,O
Engineering Management   M,D,O
Environmental Engineering   M,D,O
Game Design and
    Development   M,D
Geotechnical Engineering   M,D,O
Hazardous Materials
    Management   M,D,O
Industrial/Management
    Engineering   M,D,O
Manufacturing Engineering   M,D,O
Materials Engineering   M,D,O
Materials Sciences   M,D,O
Mechanical Engineering   M,D,O
Mechanics   M,D,O
Modeling and Simulation   M,D
Operations Research   M,D,O

Petroleum Engineering	M,D,O
Safety Engineering	M,D,O
Software Engineering	M,D
Systems Engineering	M,D,O
Telecommunications	M,D,O
Transportation and Highway Engineering	M,D,O

UNIVERSITY OF SOUTHERN INDIANA

Engineering and Applied Sciences—General	M

UNIVERSITY OF SOUTHERN MAINE

Computer Science	M,O
Software Engineering	M,O

UNIVERSITY OF SOUTHERN MISSISSIPPI

Computer Science	M,D
Construction Engineering	M
Polymer Science and Engineering	M,D
Transportation and Highway Engineering	M

UNIVERSITY OF SOUTH FLORIDA

Bioinformatics	M,D,O
Biomedical Engineering	M,D,O
Biotechnology	M,D,O
Chemical Engineering	M,D,O
Civil Engineering	M,D,O
Computer Engineering	M,D
Computer Science	M,D
Electrical Engineering	M,D,O
Engineering and Applied Sciences—General	M,D
Engineering Management	M,D
Environmental Engineering	M,D
Geotechnical Engineering	M,D
Health Informatics	M,D,O
Industrial/Management Engineering	M,D,O
Information Science	M
Management of Technology	O
Materials Engineering	M,D,O
Materials Sciences	M,D,O
Mechanical Engineering	M,D
Structural Engineering	M,D
Systems Engineering	O
Transportation and Highway Engineering	M,D,O
Water Resources Engineering	M,D,O

THE UNIVERSITY OF TENNESSEE

Aerospace/Aeronautical Engineering	M,D
Agricultural Engineering	M
Aviation	M
Biomedical Engineering	M,D
Biosystems Engineering	M,D
Chemical Engineering	M,D
Civil Engineering	M,D
Computer Engineering	M,D
Computer Science	M,D
Electrical Engineering	M,D
Energy and Power Engineering	D
Engineering and Applied Sciences—General	M,D
Engineering Management	M,D
Environmental Engineering	M
Industrial/Management Engineering	M,D
Information Science	M,D
Materials Engineering	M,D
Materials Sciences	M,D
Mechanical Engineering	M,D
Nuclear Engineering	M,D

Polymer Science and Engineering	M,D
Reliability Engineering	M,D

THE UNIVERSITY OF TENNESSEE AT CHATTANOOGA

Chemical Engineering	M
Civil Engineering	M
Computer Science	M,O
Electrical Engineering	M
Energy and Power Engineering	M,O
Engineering Management	M,O
Industrial/Management Engineering	M
Mechanical Engineering	M
Medical Informatics	M,D,O
Nuclear Engineering	M,O

THE UNIVERSITY OF TENNESSEE HEALTH SCIENCE CENTER

Biomedical Engineering	M,D
Health Informatics	M,D

THE UNIVERSITY OF TEXAS AT ARLINGTON

Aerospace/Aeronautical Engineering	M,D
Bioengineering	M,D
Civil Engineering	M,D
Computer Engineering	M,D
Computer Science	M,D
Construction Management	M,D
Electrical Engineering	M,D
Engineering and Applied Sciences—General	M,D
Engineering Management	M
Industrial/Management Engineering	M,D
Materials Engineering	M,D
Materials Sciences	M,D
Mechanical Engineering	M,D
Software Engineering	M,D
Systems Engineering	M

THE UNIVERSITY OF TEXAS AT AUSTIN

Aerospace/Aeronautical Engineering	M,D
Architectural Engineering	M
Biomedical Engineering	M,D
Chemical Engineering	M,D
Civil Engineering	M,D
Computer Engineering	M,D
Computer Science	M,D
Electrical Engineering	M,D
Engineering and Applied Sciences—General	M,D
Environmental Engineering	M,D
Geotechnical Engineering	M,D
Industrial/Management Engineering	M,D
Materials Engineering	M,D
Materials Sciences	M,D
Mechanical Engineering	M,D
Mechanics	M,D
Mineral/Mining Engineering	M
Operations Research	M,D
Petroleum Engineering	M,D
Technology and Public Policy	M
Textile Sciences and Engineering	M
Water Resources Engineering	M,D

THE UNIVERSITY OF TEXAS AT BROWNSVILLE

Computer Science	M

THE UNIVERSITY OF TEXAS AT DALLAS

Biomedical Engineering	M,D
Biotechnology	M,D
Computer Engineering	M,D
Computer Science	M,D
Electrical Engineering	M,D
Engineering and Applied Sciences—General	M,D
Management of Technology	M
Materials Engineering	M,D
Materials Sciences	M,D
Mechanical Engineering	M,D
Software Engineering	M,D
Systems Engineering	M,D
Telecommunications	M,D

THE UNIVERSITY OF TEXAS AT EL PASO

Bioinformatics	M,D
Biomedical Engineering	M,D,O
Civil Engineering	M,D,O
Computer Engineering	M,D
Computer Science	M,D
Construction Management	M,D,O
Electrical Engineering	M,D
Engineering and Applied Sciences—General	M,D,O
Environmental Engineering	M,D,O
Industrial/Management Engineering	M,O
Information Science	M,D
Manufacturing Engineering	M,O
Materials Engineering	M,D
Materials Sciences	M,D
Mechanical Engineering	M,D
Metallurgical Engineering and Metallurgy	M,D
Software Engineering	M,D,O
Systems Engineering	M,O

THE UNIVERSITY OF TEXAS AT SAN ANTONIO

Biomedical Engineering	M,D
Biotechnology	M,D
Civil Engineering	M,D
Computer and Information Systems Security	M,D,O
Computer Engineering	M,D
Computer Science	M,D
Electrical Engineering	M,D
Engineering and Applied Sciences—General	M,D
Environmental Engineering	M,D
Information Science	M,D,O
Management of Technology	M,D,O
Manufacturing Engineering	M,D
Materials Engineering	M,D
Mechanical Engineering	M,D

THE UNIVERSITY OF TEXAS AT TYLER

Civil Engineering	M
Computer Science	M
Electrical Engineering	M
Environmental Engineering	M
Mechanical Engineering	M
Structural Engineering	M
Transportation and Highway Engineering	M
Water Resources Engineering	M

THE UNIVERSITY OF TEXAS HEALTH SCIENCE CENTER AT HOUSTON

Health Informatics	M,D,O

THE UNIVERSITY OF TEXAS HEALTH SCIENCE CENTER AT SAN ANTONIO

Biomedical Engineering	M,D

THE UNIVERSITY OF TEXAS MEDICAL BRANCH

Bioinformatics	D

THE UNIVERSITY OF TEXAS OF THE PERMIAN BASIN

Computer Science	M

THE UNIVERSITY OF TEXAS–PAN AMERICAN

Computer Science	M
Electrical Engineering	M
Engineering Management	M
Manufacturing Engineering	M
Mechanical Engineering	M
Systems Engineering	M

THE UNIVERSITY OF TEXAS SOUTHWESTERN MEDICAL CENTER

Biomedical Engineering	M,D

UNIVERSITY OF THE DISTRICT OF COLUMBIA

Computer Science	M
Electrical Engineering	M
Engineering and Applied Sciences—General	M

UNIVERSITY OF THE PACIFIC

Engineering and Applied Sciences—General	M

UNIVERSITY OF THE SACRED HEART

Information Science	O

UNIVERSITY OF THE SCIENCES

Bioinformatics	M
Biotechnology	M,D

THE UNIVERSITY OF TOLEDO

Bioengineering	M,D
Bioinformatics	M,O
Biomedical Engineering	D
Chemical Engineering	M,D
Civil Engineering	M,D
Computer Science	M,D
Electrical Engineering	M,D
Engineering and Applied Sciences—General	M
Industrial/Management Engineering	M,D
Materials Sciences	M,D
Mechanical Engineering	M,D

UNIVERSITY OF TORONTO

Aerospace/Aeronautical Engineering	M,D
Biomedical Engineering	M,D
Biotechnology	M
Chemical Engineering	M,D
Civil Engineering	M,D
Computer Engineering	M,D
Computer Science	M,D
Electrical Engineering	M,D
Engineering and Applied Sciences—General	M,D
Health Informatics	M
Industrial/Management Engineering	M,D
Management of Technology	M
Manufacturing Engineering	M

*M—masters degree; D—doctorate; O—other advanced degree; *—Close-Up and/or Display*

Materials Engineering	M,D
Materials Sciences	M,D
Mechanical Engineering	M,D

THE UNIVERSITY OF TULSA

Chemical Engineering	M,D
Computer Engineering	D
Computer Science	M,D
Electrical Engineering	M,D
Energy Management and Policy	M
Engineering and Applied Sciences—General	M,D
Engineering Physics	M
Financial Engineering	M
Mechanical Engineering	M,D
Petroleum Engineering	M,D

UNIVERSITY OF UTAH

Bioengineering	M,D*
Bioinformatics	M,D,O
Biotechnology	M
Chemical Engineering	M,D
Civil Engineering	M,D
Computer and Information Systems Security	M,O
Computer Science	M,D
Electrical Engineering	M,D
Engineering and Applied Sciences—General	M,D
Environmental Engineering	M,D
Game Design and Development	M
Geological Engineering	M,D
Materials Engineering	M,D
Materials Sciences	M,D
Mechanical Engineering	M,D
Metallurgical Engineering and Metallurgy	M,D
Mineral/Mining Engineering	M,D
Nuclear Engineering	M,D
Petroleum Engineering	M,D
Software Engineering	M,O
Systems Engineering	M,O

UNIVERSITY OF VERMONT

Biomedical Engineering	D
Civil Engineering	M,D
Computer Science	M,D
Electrical Engineering	M,D
Engineering and Applied Sciences—General	M,D
Environmental Engineering	M,D
Materials Sciences	M,D
Mechanical Engineering	M,D

UNIVERSITY OF VICTORIA

Computer Engineering	M,D
Computer Science	M,D
Electrical Engineering	M,D
Engineering and Applied Sciences—General	M,D
Health Informatics	M
Mechanical Engineering	M,D

UNIVERSITY OF VIRGINIA

Aerospace/Aeronautical Engineering	M,D
Biomedical Engineering	M,D
Chemical Engineering	M,D
Civil Engineering	M,D
Computer Engineering	M,D
Computer Science	M,D
Construction Engineering	D
Database Systems	M
Electrical Engineering	M,D
Engineering and Applied Sciences—General	M,D
Engineering Physics	M,D
Health Informatics	M
Materials Sciences	M,D
Mechanical Engineering	M,D
Systems Engineering	M,D

UNIVERSITY OF WASHINGTON

Aerospace/Aeronautical Engineering	M,D
Bioengineering	M,D
Bioinformatics	M,D
Biotechnology	D
Chemical Engineering	M,D
Civil Engineering	M,D
Computer Science	M,D
Construction Engineering	M,D
Construction Management	M
Electrical Engineering	M,D
Engineering and Applied Sciences—General	M,D
Environmental Engineering	M,D
Geotechnical Engineering	M,D
Health Informatics	M,D
Industrial/Management Engineering	M,D
Information Science	M,D
Management of Technology	M,D
Materials Engineering	M,D
Materials Sciences	M,D
Mechanical Engineering	M,D
Medical Informatics	M,D
Nanotechnology	M,D
Structural Engineering	M,D
Transportation and Highway Engineering	M,D
Water Resources Engineering	M,D

UNIVERSITY OF WASHINGTON, BOTHELL

Computer Engineering	M
Software Engineering	M

UNIVERSITY OF WASHINGTON, TACOMA

Computer Engineering	M
Software Engineering	M

UNIVERSITY OF WATERLOO

Chemical Engineering	M,D
Civil Engineering	M,D
Computer Engineering	M,D
Computer Science	M,D
Electrical Engineering	M,D
Engineering and Applied Sciences—General	M,D
Engineering Management	M,D
Environmental Engineering	M,D
Information Science	M,D
Management of Technology	M,D
Mechanical Engineering	M,D
Operations Research	M,D
Software Engineering	M,D
Systems Engineering	M,D

THE UNIVERSITY OF WESTERN ONTARIO

Biochemical Engineering	M,D
Chemical Engineering	M,D
Civil Engineering	M,D
Computer Engineering	M,D
Computer Science	M,D
Electrical Engineering	M,D
Engineering and Applied Sciences—General	M,D
Environmental Engineering	M,D
Materials Engineering	M,D
Mechanical Engineering	M,D

UNIVERSITY OF WEST FLORIDA

Biotechnology	M
Computer Science	M
Database Systems	M,O
Software Engineering	M,O

UNIVERSITY OF WEST GEORGIA

Computer Science	M

UNIVERSITY OF WINDSOR

Civil Engineering	M,D
Computer Science	M,D
Electrical Engineering	M,D
Engineering and Applied Sciences—General	M,D
Environmental Engineering	M,D
Industrial/Management Engineering	M,D
Manufacturing Engineering	M,D
Materials Engineering	M,D
Mechanical Engineering	M,D

UNIVERSITY OF WISCONSIN–LA CROSSE

Software Engineering	M

UNIVERSITY OF WISCONSIN–MADISON

Agricultural Engineering	M,D
Biomedical Engineering	M,D
Chemical Engineering	D
Civil Engineering	M,D
Computer and Information Systems Security	M
Computer Science	M,D
Electrical Engineering	M,D
Engineering and Applied Sciences—General	M,D
Engineering Physics	M,D
Environmental Engineering	M,D
Geological Engineering	M,D
Industrial/Management Engineering	M,D
Management of Technology	M
Manufacturing Engineering	M
Materials Engineering	M,D
Materials Sciences	M,D
Mechanical Engineering	M,D
Mechanics	M,D
Nuclear Engineering	M,D
Polymer Science and Engineering	M,D
Systems Engineering	M,D

UNIVERSITY OF WISCONSIN–MILWAUKEE

Civil Engineering	M,D,O
Computer Engineering	M,D,O
Computer Science	M
Electrical Engineering	M,D,O
Engineering and Applied Sciences—General	M,D,O
Engineering Management	M,D,O
Ergonomics and Human Factors	M,D,O
Health Informatics	M,O
Industrial/Management Engineering	M,D,O
Manufacturing Engineering	M,D,O
Materials Engineering	M,D,O
Mechanical Engineering	M,D,O
Mechanics	M,D,O
Medical Informatics	D

UNIVERSITY OF WISCONSIN–PARKSIDE

Computer Science	M
Information Science	M

UNIVERSITY OF WISCONSIN–PLATTEVILLE

Computer Science	M
Engineering and Applied Sciences—General	M

UNIVERSITY OF WISCONSIN–STOUT

Industrial/Management Engineering	M
Information Science	M
Management of Technology	M

Manufacturing Engineering	M
Telecommunications Management	M

UNIVERSITY OF WISCONSIN–WHITEWATER

Management of Technology	M

UNIVERSITY OF WYOMING

Biotechnology	D
Chemical Engineering	M,D
Civil Engineering	M,D
Computer Science	M,D
Electrical Engineering	M,D
Engineering and Applied Sciences—General	M,D
Environmental Engineering	M
Mechanical Engineering	M,D
Petroleum Engineering	M,D

UTAH STATE UNIVERSITY

Aerospace/Aeronautical Engineering	M,D
Agricultural Engineering	M,D
Civil Engineering	M,D,O
Computer Science	M,D
Electrical Engineering	M,D
Engineering and Applied Sciences—General	M,D,O
Environmental Engineering	M,D,O
Mechanical Engineering	M,D
Water Resources Engineering	M,D

UTICA COLLEGE

Computer and Information Systems Security	M

VALPARAISO UNIVERSITY

Computer and Information Systems Security	M
Engineering Management	M,O

VANDERBILT UNIVERSITY

Bioinformatics	M,D
Biomedical Engineering	M,D
Chemical Engineering	M,D
Civil Engineering	M,D
Computer Science	M,D
Electrical Engineering	M,D
Engineering and Applied Sciences—General	M,D
Environmental Engineering	M,D
Materials Sciences	M,D
Mechanical Engineering	M,D

VERMONT LAW SCHOOL

Energy Management and Policy	M

VILLANOVA UNIVERSITY

Artificial Intelligence/Robotics	M,O
Biochemical Engineering	M,O
Chemical Engineering	M,O
Civil Engineering	M
Computer Engineering	M,O
Computer Science	M,O
Database Systems	M
Electrical Engineering	M,O
Engineering and Applied Sciences—General	M,D,O
Environmental Engineering	M,O
Manufacturing Engineering	M,O
Mechanical Engineering	M,O
Software Engineering	M
Water Resources Engineering	M,O

VIRGINIA COMMONWEALTH UNIVERSITY

Bioengineering	M,D
Bioinformatics	M,D
Biomedical Engineering	M,D

Chemical Engineering	M,D
Computer Science	M,D
Electrical Engineering	M,D
Engineering and Applied Sciences—General	M,D
Mechanical Engineering	M,D
Modeling and Simulation	M,D
Nanotechnology	M,D
Nuclear Engineering	M,D
Operations Research	M,D

VIRGINIA INTERNATIONAL UNIVERSITY

Computer Science	M

VIRGINIA POLYTECHNIC INSTITUTE AND STATE UNIVERSITY

Aerospace/Aeronautical Engineering	M,D,O
Agricultural Engineering	M,D
Bioengineering	M,D
Bioinformatics	M,D
Biomedical Engineering	M,D
Biotechnology	M,D
Chemical Engineering	M,D
Civil Engineering	M,D,O
Computer and Information Systems Security	M,O
Computer Engineering	M,D,O
Computer Science	M,D,O
Construction Engineering	M,D,O
Construction Management	M,D,O
Electrical Engineering	M,D,O
Engineering and Applied Sciences—General	M,D
Engineering Management	M,O
Environmental Engineering	M,D,O
Industrial/Management Engineering	M,D,O
Materials Engineering	M,D
Materials Sciences	M,D
Mechanical Engineering	M,D
Mechanics	M,D
Mineral/Mining Engineering	M,D
Nuclear Engineering	M,D
Ocean Engineering	M,D,O
Software Engineering	M,O
Systems Engineering	M,D,O
Transportation and Highway Engineering	M,O

VIRGINIA STATE UNIVERSITY

Computer Science	M

WAKE FOREST UNIVERSITY

Biomedical Engineering	M,D
Computer Science	M

WALDEN UNIVERSITY

Computer and Information Systems Security	M,D,O
Health Informatics	M,D,O

WASHINGTON STATE UNIVERSITY

Agricultural Engineering	M,D
Bioengineering	M,D
Chemical Engineering	M,D
Civil Engineering	M,D
Computer Engineering	M,D
Computer Science	M,D
Electrical Engineering	M,D
Energy and Power Engineering	M,D
Engineering and Applied Sciences—General	M,D,O
Engineering Management	M,O
Environmental Engineering	M,D
Management of Technology	M,O
Materials Engineering	M,D

Materials Sciences	M,D
Mechanical Engineering	M,D

WASHINGTON UNIVERSITY IN ST. LOUIS

Aerospace/Aeronautical Engineering	M,D
Biomedical Engineering	M,D
Chemical Engineering	M,D
Computer Engineering	M,D
Computer Science	M,D
Database Systems	M
Engineering and Applied Sciences—General	M,D
Environmental Engineering	M,D
Materials Sciences	M,D
Mechanical Engineering	M,D

WAYNESBURG UNIVERSITY

Energy Management and Policy	M,D

WAYNE STATE UNIVERSITY

Automotive Engineering	M,O
Bioinformatics	M,D,O
Biomedical Engineering	M,D,O
Biotechnology	M,D
Chemical Engineering	M,D
Civil Engineering	M,D
Computer Engineering	M,D
Computer Science	M,D,O
Electrical Engineering	M,D
Energy and Power Engineering	M,O
Engineering and Applied Sciences—General	M,D,O
Engineering Management	M,O
Industrial/Management Engineering	M,D
Manufacturing Engineering	M
Materials Sciences	M,D,O
Mechanical Engineering	M,D
Polymer Science and Engineering	M,D,O
Systems Engineering	M,D,O

WEBSTER UNIVERSITY

Aerospace/Aeronautical Engineering	M
Computer Science	M
Engineering Management	M

WEILL CORNELL MEDICAL COLLEGE

Health Informatics	M

WENTWORTH INSTITUTE OF TECHNOLOGY

Construction Management	M
Management of Technology	M

WESLEYAN UNIVERSITY

Computer Science	M,D

WEST CHESTER UNIVERSITY OF PENNSYLVANIA

Computer and Information Systems Security	M,O
Computer Science	M,O

WESTERN CAROLINA UNIVERSITY

Computer Science	M
Construction Management	M
Industrial/Management Engineering	M

WESTERN GOVERNORS UNIVERSITY

Computer and Information Systems Security	M
Information Science	M

WESTERN ILLINOIS UNIVERSITY

Computer Science	M
Manufacturing Engineering	M

WESTERN INTERNATIONAL UNIVERSITY

Systems Engineering	M

WESTERN KENTUCKY UNIVERSITY

Computer Science	M
Management of Technology	M

WESTERN MICHIGAN UNIVERSITY

Aerospace/Aeronautical Engineering	M,D
Chemical Engineering	M,D
Civil Engineering	M
Computer Engineering	M,D
Computer Science	M,D
Electrical Engineering	M,D
Engineering and Applied Sciences—General	M,D
Engineering Management	M,D
Industrial/Management Engineering	M,D
Manufacturing Engineering	M
Mechanical Engineering	M,D
Paper and Pulp Engineering	M,D

WESTERN NEW ENGLAND UNIVERSITY

Electrical Engineering	M
Engineering and Applied Sciences—General	M,D
Engineering Management	M,D
Manufacturing Engineering	M
Mechanical Engineering	M

WESTERN WASHINGTON UNIVERSITY

Computer Science	M

WESTMINSTER COLLEGE (UT)

Management of Technology	M,O

WEST TEXAS A&M UNIVERSITY

Engineering and Applied Sciences—General	M

WEST VIRGINIA STATE UNIVERSITY

Biotechnology	M

WEST VIRGINIA UNIVERSITY

Aerospace/Aeronautical Engineering	M,D
Chemical Engineering	M,D
Civil Engineering	M,D
Computer Engineering	D
Computer Science	M,D
Electrical Engineering	M,D
Engineering and Applied Sciences—General	M,D,O
Environmental Engineering	M,D
Game Design and Development	O
Industrial/Management Engineering	M,D
Mechanical Engineering	M,D
Mineral/Mining Engineering	M,D
Petroleum Engineering	M,D

Safety Engineering	M
Software Engineering	M

WICHITA STATE UNIVERSITY

Aerospace/Aeronautical Engineering	M,D
Computer Engineering	M,D
Computer Science	M,D
Electrical Engineering	M,D
Engineering and Applied Sciences—General	M,D
Engineering Management	M,D
Industrial/Management Engineering	M,D
Manufacturing Engineering	M,D
Mechanical Engineering	M,D

WIDENER UNIVERSITY

Biomedical Engineering	M
Chemical Engineering	M
Civil Engineering	M
Computer Engineering	M
Engineering and Applied Sciences—General	M
Engineering Management	M
Mechanical Engineering	M
Software Engineering	M
Telecommunications	M

WILFRID LAURIER UNIVERSITY

Management of Technology	M,D

WILKES UNIVERSITY

Bioengineering	M
Electrical Engineering	M
Engineering and Applied Sciences—General	M
Engineering Management	M
Mechanical Engineering	M

WILLIAM PATERSON UNIVERSITY OF NEW JERSEY

Biotechnology	M,D

WILMINGTON UNIVERSITY

Computer and Information Systems Security	M
Internet Engineering	M

WINSTON-SALEM STATE UNIVERSITY

Computer Science	M

WINTHROP UNIVERSITY

Software Engineering	M,O

WOODS HOLE OCEANOGRAPHIC INSTITUTION

Ocean Engineering	D

WORCESTER POLYTECHNIC INSTITUTE

Artificial Intelligence/Robotics	M,D
Bioinformatics	M,D
Biomedical Engineering	M,D,O
Biotechnology	M,D
Chemical Engineering	M,D
Civil Engineering	M,D,O
Computer Engineering	M,D,O
Computer Science	M,D,O
Construction Management	M,D,O
Database Systems	M,O
Electrical Engineering	M,D,O
Energy and Power Engineering	M,D
Engineering and Applied Sciences—General	M,D,O
Engineering Design	M,D,O

*M—masters degree; D—doctorate; O—other advanced degree; *—Close-Up and/or Display*

Environmental Engineering	M,D,O		
Fire Protection Engineering	M,D,O		
Game Design and Development	M		
Manufacturing Engineering	M,D		
Materials Engineering	M,D		
Materials Sciences	M,D		
Mechanical Engineering	M,D,O		
Modeling and Simulation	M,D		
Systems Engineering	M,O		
Systems Science	M,D,O		

WORCESTER STATE UNIVERSITY

Biotechnology	M

WRIGHT STATE UNIVERSITY

Biomedical Engineering	M
Computer Engineering	M,D
Computer Science	M,D
Electrical Engineering	M
Engineering and Applied Sciences—General	M,D
Ergonomics and Human Factors	M,D
Materials Engineering	M
Materials Sciences	M
Mechanical Engineering	M

YALE UNIVERSITY

Bioinformatics	D
Biomedical Engineering	M,D
Chemical Engineering	M,D
Computer Science	M,D
Electrical Engineering	M,D
Engineering and Applied Sciences—General	M,D*
Engineering Physics	M,D
Environmental Engineering	M,D
Mechanical Engineering	M,D

YORK UNIVERSITY

Computer Science	M,D

YOUNGSTOWN STATE UNIVERSITY

Civil Engineering	M
Computer Engineering	M
Computer Science	M
Electrical Engineering	M
Engineering and Applied Sciences—General	M
Environmental Engineering	M
Industrial/Management Engineering	M
Information Science	M
Mechanical Engineering	M

ACADEMIC AND PROFESSIONAL PROGRAMS IN ENGINEERING & APPLIED SCIENCES

Section 1
Engineering and Applied Sciences

This section contains a directory of institutions offering graduate work in engineering and applied sciences, followed by in-depth entries submitted by institutions that chose to prepare detailed program descriptions. Additional information about programs listed in the directory but not augmented by an in-depth entry may be obtained by writing directly to the dean of a graduate school or chair of a department at the address given in the directory.

For programs in specific areas of engineering, see all other sections in this book. In the other guides in this series:

Graduate Programs in the Humanities, Arts & Social Sciences
See *Applied Arts and Design (Industrial Design)* and *Architecture (Environmental Design)*

Graduate Programs in the Biological/Biomedical Sciences & Health-Related Medical Professions
See *Ecology, Environmental Biology,* and *Evolutionary Biology*

Graduate Programs in the Physical Sciences, Mathematics, Agricultural Sciences, the Environment & Natural Resources
See *Agricultural and Food Sciences* and *Natural Resources*

CONTENTS

Engineering and Applied Sciences—General

Air Force Institute of Technology, Graduate School of Engineering and Management, Dayton, OH 45433-7765. Offers MS, PhD. *Accreditation:* ABET (one or more programs are accredited). Part-time programs available. *Degree requirements:* For master's, thesis; for doctorate, thesis/dissertation. *Entrance requirements:* For master's, GRE General Test, minimum GPA of 3.0; for doctorate, GRE General Test.

Alabama Agricultural and Mechanical University, School of Graduate Studies, School of Engineering and Technology, Huntsville, AL 35811. Offers M Ed, MS. Part-time and evening/weekend programs available. *Degree requirements:* For master's, comprehensive exam, thesis optional. *Entrance requirements:* For master's, GRE General Test. Additional exam requirements/recommendations for international students: Required—TOEFL (minimum score 500 paper-based; 61 iBT). Electronic applications accepted. *Faculty research:* Ionized gases, hypersonic flow phenomenology, robotics systems development.

Alfred University, Graduate School, New York State College of Ceramics, Kazuo Inamori School of Engineering, Alfred, NY 14802. Offers biomaterials engineering (MS); ceramic engineering (MS); ceramics (PhD); electrical engineering (MS); glass science (MS, PhD); materials science and engineering (MS, PhD); mechanical engineering (MS). Part-time programs available. *Degree requirements:* For master's, thesis; for doctorate, thesis/dissertation. *Entrance requirements:* Additional exam requirements/recommendations for international students: Required—TOEFL (minimum score 590 paper-based; 90 iBT), IELTS (minimum score 6.5). Electronic applications accepted. *Expenses:* Contact institution. *Faculty research:* X-ray diffraction, biomaterials and polymers, thin-film processing, electronic and optical ceramics, solid-state chemistry.

The American University in Cairo, School of Sciences and Engineering, New Cairo, Egypt. Offers M Chem, M Comp, M Eng, MS, PhD, Graduate Diploma. Part-time programs available. *Faculty:* 36 full-time (6 women), 12 part-time/adjunct (1 woman). *Students:* 57 full-time (24 women), 299 part-time (151 women), 11 international. 308 applicants, 65% accepted, 72 enrolled. In 2014, 77 master's, 4 doctorates awarded. *Degree requirements:* For master's, comprehensive exam (for some programs), thesis (for some programs); for doctorate, comprehensive exam (for some programs), thesis/dissertation. *Entrance requirements:* Additional exam requirements/recommendations for international students: Required—TOEFL (minimum score 450 paper-based; 45 iBT), IELTS (minimum score 5). *Application deadline:* For fall admission, 2/1 priority date for domestic students, 1/30 priority date for international students; for spring admission, 10/1 priority date for domestic students, 11/1 priority date for international students. Applications are processed on a rolling basis. Application fee: $52. Electronic applications accepted. Tuition and fees vary according to course load and program. *Financial support:* Fellowships with partial tuition reimbursements, scholarships/grants, and unspecified assistantships available. Financial award application deadline: 7/1. *Faculty research:* Construction, mechanical and electronics engineering, physics, computer science, biotechnology and nanotechnology. *Unit head:* Dr. Tarek Shawki, Dean, 20-2615-2926, E-mail: tshawki@aucegypt.edu. *Application contact:* Maha Hegazi, Assistant Director for Graduate Admissions, 20-22615-1462, E-mail: mahahegazi@aucegypt.edu.
Website: http://www.aucegypt.edu/sse/Pages/default.aspx.

American University of Beirut, Graduate Programs, Faculty of Engineering and Architecture, Beirut, Lebanon. Offers applied energy (ME); civil engineering (PhD); electrical and computer engineering (PhD); engineering management (MEM); environmental and water resources (ME); environmental technology (MSES); mechanical engineering (ME, PhD); urban design (MUD); urban planning and policy (MUPP). Part-time programs available. *Faculty:* 93 full-time (18 women), 3 part-time/adjunct (1 woman). *Students:* 268 full-time (111 women), 58 part-time (27 women). Average age 26. 225 applicants, 68% accepted, 79 enrolled. In 2014, 114 master's, 9 doctorates awarded. Terminal master's awarded for partial completion of doctoral program. *Degree requirements:* For master's, one foreign language, comprehensive exam, thesis (for some programs); for doctorate, one foreign language, comprehensive exam, thesis/dissertation, publications. *Entrance requirements:* For master's, letters of recommendation; for doctorate, GRE, letters of recommendation, master's degree, transcripts, curriculum vitae, interview. Additional exam requirements/recommendations for international students: Required—TOEFL (minimum score 600 paper-based; 100 iBT), IELTS (minimum score 7.5). *Application deadline:* For fall admission, 2/5 priority date for domestic and international students; for spring admission, 11/1 priority date for domestic students, 11/1 for international students. Application fee: $50. Electronic applications accepted. *Expenses: Tuition:* Full-time $15,462; part-time $859 per credit. *Required fees:* $692. Tuition and fees vary according to course load and program. *Financial support:* In 2014–15, 190 students received support, including 2 fellowships with full tuition reimbursements available (averaging $24,800 per year), 64 research assistantships with full tuition reimbursements available (averaging $24,800 per year), 124 teaching assistantships with full tuition reimbursements available (averaging $9,800 per year); career-related internships or fieldwork, institutionally sponsored loans, scholarships/grants, health care benefits, and unspecified assistantships also available. *Total annual research expenditures:* $1.5 million. *Unit head:* Prof. Makram T. Suidan, Dean, 961-1350000 Ext. 3400, Fax: 961-1744462, E-mail: msuidan@aub.edu.lb. *Application contact:* Dr. Salim Kanaan, Director, Admissions Office, 961-1350000 Ext. 2594, Fax: 961-1750775, E-mail: sk00@aub.edu.lb.
Website: http://staff.aub.edu.lb/~webfea.

Arizona State University at the Tempe campus, Ira A. Fulton Schools of Engineering, The Polytechnic School, Mesa, AZ 85212. Offers MS, PhD. Part-time and evening/weekend programs available. *Degree requirements:* For master's, thesis, interactive Program of Study (iPOS) submitted before completing 50 percent of required credit hours. *Entrance requirements:* For master's, GRE, minimum GPA of 3.0 or equivalent in last 2 years of work leading to bachelor's degree. Additional exam requirements/recommendations for international students: Required—TOEFL, IELTS, or PTE. Electronic applications accepted. *Expenses:* Contact institution.

Arkansas State University, Graduate School, College of Engineering, State University, AR 72467. Offers MEM, MS Eng. Part-time programs available. *Faculty:* 7 full-time (0 women). *Students:* 22 full-time (6 women), 9 part-time (0 women); includes 1 minority (Black or African American, non-Hispanic/Latino), 28 international. Average age 25. 91 applicants, 49% accepted, 25 enrolled. In 2014, 7 master's awarded. *Degree requirements:* For master's, comprehensive exam. *Entrance requirements:* For master's, GRE, appropriate bachelor's degree, official transcript, letters of recommendation, resume, immunization records. Additional exam requirements/recommendations for international students: Required—TOEFL (minimum score 550 paper-based; 79 iBT), IELTS (minimum score 6), PTE (minimum score 56). *Application deadline:* For fall admission, 6/1 for domestic and international students; for spring admission, 10/15 for domestic and international students. Applications are processed on a rolling basis. Application fee: $30 ($40 for international students). Electronic applications accepted. *Expenses:* Expenses: Contact institution. *Financial support:* In 2014–15, 7 students received support. Career-related internships or fieldwork, scholarships/grants, and unspecified assistantships available. Financial award application deadline: 7/1; financial award applicants required to submit FAFSA. *Unit head:* Dr. Paul Mixon, Interim Dean, 870-972-2088, Fax: 870-972-3539, E-mail: pmixon@astate.edu. *Application contact:* Vickey Ring, Graduate Admissions Coordinator, 870-972-3029, Fax: 870-972-3857, E-mail: vickeyring@astate.edu.
Website: http://www.astate.edu/college/engineering/index.dot.

Arkansas Tech University, College of Engineering and Applied Sciences, Russellville, AR 72801. Offers emergency management (MS); engineering (M Engr); information technology (MS). Part-time programs available. Postbaccalaureate distance learning degree programs offered (no on-campus study). *Students:* 83 full-time (31 women), 48 part-time (16 women); includes 14 minority (5 Black or African American, non-Hispanic/Latino; 1 American Indian or Alaska Native, non-Hispanic/Latino; 1 Asian, non-Hispanic/Latino; 3 Hispanic/Latino; 4 Two or more races, non-Hispanic/Latino), 60 international. Average age 28. In 2014, 39 master's awarded. *Degree requirements:* For master's, comprehensive exam (for some programs), thesis (for some programs), internship. *Entrance requirements:* For master's, GRE General Test. Additional exam requirements/recommendations for international students: Required—TOEFL (minimum score 550 paper-based; 79 iBT), IELTS (minimum score 6). *Application deadline:* For fall admission, 3/1 priority date for domestic students, 5/1 priority date for international students; for spring admission, 10/1 priority date for domestic and international students. Applications are processed on a rolling basis. Application fee: $25 ($75 for international students). Electronic applications accepted. *Expenses:* Tuition, state resident: full-time $6264; part-time $261 per credit hour. Tuition, nonresident: full-time $12,528; part-time $522 per credit hour. *Required fees:* $423 per semester. Tuition and fees vary according to course load. *Financial support:* In 2014–15, research assistantships with full tuition reimbursements (averaging $4,800 per year), teaching assistantships with full tuition reimbursements (averaging $4,800 per year) were awarded; career-related internships or fieldwork, Federal Work-Study, scholarships/grants, health care benefits, and unspecified assistantships also available. Support available to part-time students. Financial award application deadline: 4/15; financial award applicants required to submit FAFSA. *Unit head:* Dr. William Hoefler, Dean, 479-968-0353, E-mail: whoeflerjr@atu.edu. *Application contact:* Dr. Mary B. Gunter, Dean of Graduate College, 479-968-0398, Fax: 479-964-0542, E-mail: gradcollege@atu.edu.
Website: http://www.atu.edu/appliedsci/.

Auburn University, Graduate School, Ginn College of Engineering, Auburn University, AL 36849. Offers M Ch E, M Mtl E, MAE, MCE, MEE, MISE, MME, MS, MSWE, PhD, Graduate Certificate. Part-time programs available. *Faculty:* 146 full-time (14 women), 16 part-time/adjunct (1 woman). *Students:* 588 full-time (136 women), 297 part-time (57 women); includes 57 minority (22 Black or African American, non-Hispanic/Latino; 2 American Indian or Alaska Native, non-Hispanic/Latino; 21 Asian, non-Hispanic/Latino; 12 Hispanic/Latino), 500 international. Average age 27. 1,418 applicants, 49% accepted, 216 enrolled. In 2014, 179 master's, 62 doctorates, 12 other advanced degrees awarded. *Degree requirements:* For master's, thesis (for some programs); for doctorate, thesis/dissertation. *Entrance requirements:* For master's and doctorate, GRE General Test. *Application deadline:* For fall admission, 7/7 for domestic students; for spring admission, 11/24 for domestic students. Applications are processed on a rolling basis. Application fee: $50 ($60 for international students). Electronic applications accepted. *Expenses:* Tuition, state resident: full-time $8586; part-time $477 per credit hour. Tuition, nonresident: full-time $25,758; part-time $1431 per credit hour. *Required fees:* $804 per semester. Tuition and fees vary according to degree level and program. *Financial support:* Fellowships, research assistantships, teaching assistantships, and Federal Work-Study available. Support available to part-time students. Financial award application deadline: 3/15; financial award applicants required to submit FAFSA. *Unit head:* Dr. Chris Roberts, Dean, 334-844-2308. *Application contact:* Dr. George Flowers, Dean of the Graduate School, 334-844-2125.
Website: http://www.eng.auburn.edu/.

Austin Peay State University, College of Graduate Studies, The Austin Peay Center at Ft. Campbell, Department of Engineering Technology, Clarksville, TN 37044. Offers MS.

Binghamton University, State University of New York, Graduate School, Thomas J. Watson School of Engineering and Applied Science, Vestal, NY 13850. Offers M Eng, MS, PhD. Part-time and evening/weekend programs available. Postbaccalaureate distance learning degree programs offered. *Faculty:* 92 full-time (13 women), 30 part-time/adjunct (7 women). *Students:* 679 full-time (158 women), 342 part-time (66 women); includes 89 minority (16 Black or African American, non-Hispanic/Latino; 43 Asian, non-Hispanic/Latino; 24 Hispanic/Latino; 6 Native Hawaiian or other Pacific Islander, non-Hispanic/Latino), 733 international. Average age 26. 1,965 applicants, 64% accepted, 406 enrolled. In 2014, 226 master's, 44 doctorates awarded. Terminal master's awarded for partial completion of doctoral program. *Degree requirements:* For master's, comprehensive exam (for some programs), thesis (for some programs); for doctorate, comprehensive exam (for some programs), thesis/dissertation. *Entrance requirements:* For master's and doctorate, GRE General Test. Additional exam requirements/recommendations for international students: Required—TOEFL (minimum score 550 paper-based; 80 iBT). *Application deadline:* Applications are processed on a rolling basis. Application fee: $75. Electronic applications accepted. *Expenses:* Expenses: $5,435 resident; $11,105 non-resident. *Financial support:* In 2014–15, 276 students received support, including 2 fellowships with full tuition reimbursements available (averaging $10,000 per year), 138 research assistantships with full tuition reimbursements available (averaging $16,500 per year), 94 teaching assistantships with full tuition reimbursements available (averaging $16,500 per year); career-related internships or fieldwork, Federal Work-Study, institutionally sponsored loans, scholarships/grants, health care benefits, tuition waivers (full and partial), and unspecified assistantships also available. Financial award application deadline: 2/15; financial award applicants required to submit FAFSA. *Unit head:* Ellen Tilden, Coordinator of Graduate Programs, The Watson School, 607-777-2873, E-mail: etilden@binghamton.edu. *Application contact:* Kishan Zuber, Recruiting and Admissions Coordinator, 607-777-2151, Fax: 607-777-2501, E-mail: kzuber@binghamton.edu.
Website: http://watson.binghamton.edu.

Boise State University, College of Engineering, Boise, ID 83725-0399. Offers M Engr, MS, PhD, Graduate Certificate. Part-time programs available. Postbaccalaureate distance learning degree programs offered (no on-campus study). *Faculty:* 64 full-time, 35 part-time/adjunct. *Students:* 96 full-time (26 women), 245 part-time (121 women); includes 42 minority (13 Black or African American, non-Hispanic/Latino; 1 American Indian or Alaska Native, non-Hispanic/Latino; 14 Asian, non-Hispanic/Latino; 8 Hispanic/Latino; 6 Two or more races, non-Hispanic/Latino), 35 international. 428 applicants, 94% accepted, 214 enrolled. In 2014, 86 master's, 1 doctorate, 25 other advanced degrees awarded. *Entrance requirements:* For master's, minimum GPA of 3.0. *Application deadline:* For fall admission, 3/1 priority date for domestic students; for spring admission, 10/1 priority date for domestic students. Applications are processed on a rolling basis. Application fee: $55. Electronic applications accepted. *Expenses:* Tuition, state resident: part-time $331 per credit hour. Tuition, nonresident: part-time $531 per credit hour. *Financial support:* In 2014–15, 68 students received support, including 49 research assistantships with full and partial tuition reimbursements available (averaging $10,900 per year), 8 teaching assistantships with partial tuition reimbursements available (averaging $6,800 per year); career-related internships or fieldwork, Federal Work-Study, institutionally sponsored loans, tuition waivers (full), and unspecified assistantships also available. Support available to part-time students. Financial award application deadline: 3/1. *Unit head:* Dr. Amy Moll, Dean, 208-426-5719. *Application contact:* Linda Platt, Office Services Supervisor, Graduate Admission and Degree Services, 208-426-1074, Fax: 208-426-2789, E-mail: lplatt@boisestate.edu. Website: http://coen.boisestate.edu/.

Boston University, College of Engineering, Boston, MA 02215. Offers M Eng, MS, PhD, MD/PhD, MS/MBA. Part-time programs available. Postbaccalaureate distance learning degree programs offered (no on-campus study). *Faculty:* 112 full-time (12 women), 9 part-time/adjunct (1 woman). *Students:* 685 full-time (194 women), 123 part-time (33 women); includes 122 minority (8 Black or African American, non-Hispanic/Latino; 1 American Indian or Alaska Native, non-Hispanic/Latino; 72 Asian, non-Hispanic/Latino; 26 Hispanic/Latino; 1 Native Hawaiian or other Pacific Islander, non-Hispanic/Latino; 14 Two or more races, non-Hispanic/Latino), 410 international. Average age 25. 1,931 applicants, 25% accepted, 245 enrolled. In 2014, 226 master's, 53 doctorates awarded. Terminal master's awarded for partial completion of doctoral program. *Degree requirements:* For master's, thesis (for some programs); for doctorate, comprehensive exam, thesis/dissertation. *Entrance requirements:* For master's and doctorate, GRE General Test. Additional exam requirements/recommendations for international students: Required—TOEFL (minimum score 550 paper-based; 84 iBT) or IELTS (minimum score 6.5). *Application deadline:* For fall admission, 3/15 for domestic and international students; for spring admission, 10/1 for domestic and international students. Application fee: $70. Electronic applications accepted. *Expenses: Tuition:* Full-time $45,686; part-time $1428 per credit hour. *Required fees:* $660; $60 per semester. Tuition and fees vary according to program. *Financial support:* In 2014–15, 458 students received support, including 70 fellowships with full tuition reimbursements available (averaging $28,950 per year), 241 research assistantships with full tuition reimbursements available (averaging $19,300 per year), 62 teaching assistantships with full tuition reimbursements available (averaging $19,300 per year); career-related internships or fieldwork, Federal Work-Study, institutionally sponsored loans, scholarships/grants, traineeships, health care benefits, and tuition waivers (full and partial) also available. Financial award application deadline: 1/15; financial award applicants required to submit FAFSA. *Faculty research:* Photonics, bioengineering, computer and information systems, nanotechnology, materials science and engineering. *Unit head:* Dr. Kenneth R. Lutchen, Dean, 617-353-2800, Fax: 617-358-3468, E-mail: klutch@bu.edu. *Application contact:* Director of Graduate Programs, 617-353-9760, Fax: 617-353-0259, E-mail: enggrad@bu.edu. Website: http://www.bu.edu/eng/.

Bradley University, Graduate School, College of Engineering and Technology, Peoria, IL 61625-0002. Offers MS, MSCE, MSEE, MSME. Part-time and evening/weekend programs available. *Faculty:* 38 full-time (4 women), 2 part-time/adjunct (0 women). *Students:* 133 full-time (27 women), 92 part-time (16 women); includes 2 minority (1 Black or African American, non-Hispanic/Latino; 1 Hispanic/Latino), 191 international. 560 applicants, 41% accepted, 108 enrolled. *Degree requirements:* For master's, comprehensive exam, thesis optional. *Entrance requirements:* Additional exam requirements/recommendations for international students: Required—TOEFL (minimum score 550 paper-based; 79 iBT), IELTS (minimum score 6.5). *Application deadline:* For fall admission, 5/15 priority date for domestic and international students; for spring admission, 10/15 priority date for domestic and international students. Applications are processed on a rolling basis. Application fee: $40 ($50 for international students). Electronic applications accepted. *Expenses:* Expenses: Contact institution. *Financial support:* Research assistantships with full and partial tuition reimbursements, teaching assistantships, institutionally sponsored loans, scholarships/grants, tuition waivers (partial), and unspecified assistantships available. Support available to part-time students. Financial award application deadline: 4/1. *Unit head:* Lex Akers, Dean, 309-677-2721, E-mail: lakers@bradley.edu. *Application contact:* Kayla Carroll, Director of International Admissions and Student Services, 309-677-2375, E-mail: klcarroll@fsmail.bradley.edu.

Brigham Young University, Graduate Studies, Ira A. Fulton College of Engineering and Technology, Provo, UT 84602. Offers MS, PhD. *Faculty:* 108 full-time (1 woman). *Students:* 341 full-time (38 women); includes 23 minority (1 Black or African American, non-Hispanic/Latino; 12 Asian, non-Hispanic/Latino; 5 Hispanic/Latino; 1 Native Hawaiian or other Pacific Islander, non-Hispanic/Latino; 4 Two or more races, non-Hispanic/Latino), 59 international. Average age 27. 186 applicants, 70% accepted, 93 enrolled. In 2014, 113 master's, 13 doctorates awarded. *Degree requirements:* For master's, comprehensive exam (for some programs), thesis (for some programs); for doctorate, comprehensive exam (for some programs), thesis/dissertation (for some programs). *Entrance requirements:* For master's and doctorate, GRE, at least 3 letters of recommendation, transcripts from each institution attended, ecclesiastical endorsement, minimum cumulative GPA of 3.0 in last 60 hours of coursework. Additional exam requirements/recommendations for international students: Required—TOEFL (minimum score 580 paper-based; 85 iBT), IELTS (minimum score 7). *Application deadline:* For fall admission, 1/15 for domestic and international students; for winter admission, 6/15 for domestic and international students; for spring admission, 10/15 for domestic and international students; for summer admission, 2/15 for domestic and international students. Application fee: $50. Electronic applications accepted. *Expenses: Tuition:* Full-time $6310; part-time $371 per credit hour. Tuition and fees vary according to program and student's religious affiliation. *Financial support:* In 2014–15, 124 students received support, including 25 fellowships with full and partial tuition reimbursements available (averaging $8,157 per year), 238 research assistantships with full and partial tuition reimbursements available (averaging $16,039 per year), 124 teaching assistantships with full and partial tuition reimbursements available (averaging $10,710 per year); scholarships/grants and health care benefits also available. Financial award application deadline: 3/1; financial award applicants required to submit FAFSA. *Faculty research:* Combustion, microwave remote sensing, structural optimization, biomedical engineering, networking. *Total annual research expenditures:* $12.5 million. *Unit head:* Dr. Alan R. Parkinson, Dean, 801-422-4327, Fax: 801-422-0218, E-mail: college@et.byu.edu. *Application contact:* Claire A. DeWitt, Adviser, 801-422-4541, Fax: 801-422-0270, E-mail: gradstudies@byu.edu. Website: http://www.et.byu.edu/.

Brown University, Graduate School, School of Engineering, Providence, RI 02912. Offers biomedical engineering (Sc M, PhD); chemical and biochemical engineering (Sc M, PhD); electrical sciences and computer engineering (Sc M, PhD); fluid and thermal sciences (Sc M, PhD); materials science and engineering (Sc M, PhD); mechanics of solids and structures (Sc M, PhD). *Degree requirements:* For doctorate, thesis/dissertation, preliminary exam.

Bucknell University, Graduate Studies, College of Engineering, Lewisburg, PA 17837. Offers MS Ch E, MSCE, MSEE, MSEV, MSME. Part-time programs available. *Degree requirements:* For master's, thesis. *Entrance requirements:* For master's, GRE General Test, minimum GPA of 3.0. Additional exam requirements/recommendations for international students: Required—TOEFL (minimum score 600 paper-based).

California Institute of Technology, Division of Engineering and Applied Science, Pasadena, CA 91125. Offers aeronautics (MS, PhD, Engr); applied and computational mathematics (MS, PhD); applied mechanics (MS, PhD); applied physics (MS, PhD); bioengineering (MS, PhD); civil engineering (MS, PhD, Engr); computation and neural systems (MS, PhD); computer science (MS, PhD); control and dynamical systems (MS, PhD); electrical engineering (MS, PhD, Engr); environmental science and engineering (MS, PhD); materials science (MS, PhD); mechanical engineering (MS, PhD, Engr). Terminal master's awarded for partial completion of doctoral program. *Degree requirements:* For doctorate, thesis/dissertation. *Entrance requirements:* For master's and doctorate, GRE (strongly recommended), minimum GPA of 3.5. Additional exam requirements/recommendations for international students: Required—TOEFL; Recommended—TWE (minimum score 5). Electronic applications accepted.

California National University for Advanced Studies, College of Engineering, Northridge, CA 91325. Offers MS Eng. Part-time programs available. Postbaccalaureate distance learning degree programs offered (no on-campus study). *Degree requirements:* For master's, thesis or alternative, project. *Entrance requirements:* For master's, minimum GPA of 3.0. Electronic applications accepted.

California Polytechnic State University, San Luis Obispo, College of Engineering, Department of Biomedical and General Engineering, San Luis Obispo, CA 93407. Offers MS, MBA/MS, MCRP/MS. Part-time programs available. *Faculty:* 9 full-time (2 women). *Students:* 80 full-time (27 women), 20 part-time (8 women); includes 25 minority (1 Black or African American, non-Hispanic/Latino; 12 Asian, non-Hispanic/Latino; 8 Hispanic/Latino; 4 Two or more races, non-Hispanic/Latino), 5 international. Average age 24. 81 applicants, 60% accepted, 37 enrolled. In 2014, 85 master's awarded. *Degree requirements:* For master's, comprehensive exam (for some programs), thesis (for some programs). *Application deadline:* For fall admission, 2/1 for domestic and international students; for winter admission, 11/1 for domestic students, 6/30 for international students; for spring admission, 2/1 for domestic students. Applications are processed on a rolling basis. Application fee: $55. Electronic applications accepted. *Expenses:* Tuition, state resident: full-time $6738; part-time $3906 per year. Tuition, nonresident: full-time $15,666; part-time $8370 per year. *Required fees:* $3447; $1001 per quarter. One-time fee: $3447 full-time; $3003 part-time. *Financial support:* Fellowships, research assistantships, teaching assistantships, Federal Work-Study, and scholarships/grants available. Support available to part-time students. Financial award application deadline: 3/2; financial award applicants required to submit FAFSA. *Faculty research:* Biomedical engineering, materials engineering, water engineering, stem cell research. *Unit head:* Dr. David Clague, Graduate Coordinator, 805-756-5145, Fax: 805-756-6424, E-mail: dclague@calpoly.edu. *Application contact:* Dr. James Maraviglia, Associate Vice Provost for Marketing and Enrollment Development, 805-756-2311, Fax: 805-756-5400, E-mail: admissions@calpoly.edu. Website: http://bmegene.calpoly.edu/.

California State University, Chico, Office of Graduate Studies, College of Engineering, Computer Science, and Technology, Chico, CA 95929-0722. Offers MS. Part-time programs available. Postbaccalaureate distance learning degree programs offered. *Faculty:* 7 full-time (1 woman), 1 part-time/adjunct (0 women). *Students:* 74 full-time (14 women), 16 part-time (1 woman); includes 2 minority (1 Black or African American, non-Hispanic/Latino; 1 Hispanic/Latino), 83 international. Average age 24. 266 applicants, 65% accepted, 63 enrolled. In 2014, 22 master's awarded. *Degree requirements:* For master's, thesis or project. *Entrance requirements:* For master's, GRE. Additional exam requirements/recommendations for international students: Required—TOEFL (minimum score 550 paper-based; 80 iBT), IELTS (minimum score 6.5), PTE (minimum score 59). *Application deadline:* For fall admission, 3/1 priority date for domestic students, 3/1 for international students; for spring admission, 9/15 priority date for domestic students, 9/15 for international students. Application fee: $55. Electronic applications accepted. *Expenses:* Tuition, state resident: full-time $7002. Tuition, nonresident: full-time $18,162. *Required fees:* $1530. Tuition and fees vary according to program. *Financial support:* Fellowships, research assistantships, teaching assistantships, career-related internships or fieldwork, Federal Work-Study, scholarships/grants, and traineeships available. Support available to part-time students. Financial award application deadline: 3/1; financial award applicants required to submit FAFSA. *Unit head:* Dr. Ben Juliano, Interim Dean, 530-898-5963, Fax: 530-898-4070, E-mail: ecc@csuchico.edu. *Application contact:* Judy L. Rice, Graduate Admissions Counselor, 530-898-5416, Fax: 530-898-3342, E-mail: jlrice@csuchico.edu. Website: http://www.ecst.csuchico.edu.

California State University, East Bay, Office of Academic Programs and Graduate Studies, College of Science, School of Engineering, Hayward, CA 94542-3000. Offers construction management (MS); engineering management (MS). *Degree requirements:* For master's, comprehensive exam (for some programs), research project or exam. *Entrance requirements:* For master's, GRE or GMAT, minimum GPA of 2.5; personal statement; 2 letters of recommendation; resume; college algebra/trigonometry or equivalent. Additional exam requirements/recommendations for international students: Required—TOEFL (minimum score 550 paper-based). *Application deadline:* For fall admission, 6/30 for domestic and international students. Application fee: $55. Electronic applications accepted. *Expenses:* Tuition, state resident: full-time $7830; part-time $1302 per credit hour. Tuition, nonresident: full-time $16,368. *Required fees:* $327 per quarter. Tuition and fees vary according to course load and program. *Financial support:* Federal Work-Study and institutionally sponsored loans available. Support available to part-time students. Financial award application deadline: 3/2; financial award applicants required to submit FAFSA. *Faculty research:* Operations research, production planning, simulation, human factors/ergonomics, quality assurance, sustainability. *Unit head:* Dr. Saeid Motavalli, Chair/Graduate Advisor, 510-885-4481, E-mail: saeid.motavalli@csueastbay.edu. *Application contact:* Dr. Donna Wiley, Interim Associate Vice President for Academic Programs and Graduate Studies, 510-885-3716, Fax: 510-885-4777, E-mail: donna.wiley@csueastbay.edu. Website: http://www20.csueastbay.edu/csci/departments/engineering/.

California State University, Fresno, Division of Graduate Studies, College of Engineering and Computer Science, Fresno, CA 93740-8027. Offers MS. Part-time and evening/weekend programs available. *Degree requirements:* For master's, thesis or alternative. *Entrance requirements:* For master's, GRE General Test, minimum GPA of 2.7. Additional exam requirements/recommendations for international students: Required—TOEFL. Electronic applications accepted. *Faculty research:* Exhaust emission, blended fuel testing, waste management.

California State University, Fullerton, Graduate Studies, College of Engineering and Computer Science, Fullerton, CA 92834-9480. Offers MS. Part-time programs available. *Students:* 406 full-time (98 women), 825 part-time (187 women); includes 321 minority (29 Black or African American, non-Hispanic/Latino; 177 Asian, non-Hispanic/Latino; 96 Hispanic/Latino; 2 Native Hawaiian or other Pacific Islander, non-Hispanic/Latino; 17

Engineering and Applied Sciences—General

Two or more races, non-Hispanic/Latino), 725 international. Average age 29. 2,098 applicants, 56% accepted, 562 enrolled. In 2014, 274 master's awarded. *Degree requirements:* For master's, comprehensive exam, project or thesis. *Entrance requirements:* For master's, minimum undergraduate GPA of 2.5. Application fee: $55. *Financial support:* Career-related internships or fieldwork, Federal Work-Study, institutionally sponsored loans, and scholarships/grants available. Support available to part-time students. Financial award application deadline: 3/1; financial award applicants required to submit FAFSA. *Unit head:* Dr. Raman Unnikrishnan, Dean, 657-278-3362. *Application contact:* Admissions/Applications, 657-278-2371.

California State University, Los Angeles, Graduate Studies, College of Engineering, Computer Science, and Technology, Los Angeles, CA 90032-8530. Offers MA, MS. Part-time and evening/weekend programs available. *Entrance requirements:* Additional exam requirements/recommendations for international students: Required—TOEFL (minimum score 550 paper-based). Electronic applications accepted. *Expenses:* Tuition, state resident: full-time $6738; part-time $3609 per year. Tuition, nonresident: full-time $15,666; part-time $8073 per year. Tuition and fees vary according to course load, degree level and program.

California State University, Northridge, Graduate Studies, College of Engineering and Computer Science, Northridge, CA 91330. Offers MS. Part-time and evening/weekend programs available. *Students:* 411 full-time (77 women), 255 part-time (55 women); includes 110 minority (1 Black or African American, non-Hispanic/Latino; 1 American Indian or Alaska Native, non-Hispanic/Latino; 39 Asian, non-Hispanic/Latino; 50 Hispanic/Latino; 3 Native Hawaiian or other Pacific Islander, non-Hispanic/Latino; 16 Two or more races, non-Hispanic/Latino), 362 international. Average age 27. *Entrance requirements:* For master's, GRE General Test, minimum GPA of 2.5. Additional exam requirements/recommendations for international students: Required—TOEFL. *Application deadline:* For fall admission, 11/30 for domestic students. Application fee: $55. *Expenses: Required fees:* $12,402. *Financial support:* Teaching assistantships, career-related internships or fieldwork, and Federal Work-Study available. Support available to part-time students. Financial award application deadline: 3/1. *Unit head:* Dr. S. K. Ramesh, Dean, 818-677-4501, E-mail: s.ramesh@csun.edu. Website: http://www.ecs.csun.edu/ecsdean/index.html.

California State University, Sacramento, Office of Graduate Studies, College of Engineering and Computer Science, Sacramento, CA 95819. Offers MS. Part-time and evening/weekend programs available. *Degree requirements:* For master's, writing proficiency exam. *Entrance requirements:* Additional exam requirements/recommendations for international students: Required—TOEFL. Electronic applications accepted.

Carleton University, Faculty of Graduate Studies, Faculty of Engineering and Design, Ottawa, ON K1S 5B6, Canada. Offers M Arch, M Des, M Eng, M Sc, MA Sc, PhD. *Degree requirements:* For doctorate, thesis/dissertation. *Entrance requirements:* For master's, honors degree; for doctorate, MA Sc or M Eng. Additional exam requirements/recommendations for international students: Required—TOEFL.

Case Western Reserve University, School of Graduate Studies, Case School of Engineering, Cleveland, OH 44106. Offers ME, MEM, MS, PhD, MD/MS, MD/PhD. Part-time and evening/weekend programs available. Postbaccalaureate distance learning degree programs offered (minimal on-campus study). *Faculty:* 114 full-time (14 women). *Students:* 544 full-time (158 women), 73 part-time (21 women); includes 73 minority (12 Black or African American, non-Hispanic/Latino; 45 Asian, non-Hispanic/Latino; 12 Hispanic/Latino; 4 Two or more races, non-Hispanic/Latino), 343 international. 1,360 applicants, 21% accepted, 100 enrolled. In 2014, 133 master's, 59 doctorates awarded. Terminal master's awarded for partial completion of doctoral program. *Degree requirements:* For master's, thesis (for some programs); for doctorate, thesis/dissertation, qualifying exam, teaching experience. *Entrance requirements:* For master's and doctorate, GRE General Test. Additional exam requirements/recommendations for international students: Required—TOEFL (minimum score 577 paper-based; 90 iBT), IELTS (minimum score 7). *Application deadline:* Applications are processed on a rolling basis. Application fee: $50. Electronic applications accepted. *Financial support:* In 2014–15, 344 students received support, including 50 fellowships with full and partial tuition reimbursements available, 235 research assistantships with full and partial tuition reimbursements available, 24 teaching assistantships; career-related internships or fieldwork, Federal Work-Study, and institutionally sponsored loans also available. Support available to part-time students. Financial award applicants required to submit FAFSA. *Faculty research:* Advanced materials, biomedical engineering and human health, electrical engineering and computer science, civil engineering, engineering management. *Total annual research expenditures:* $43.4 million. *Unit head:* Jeffrey L. Duerk, Dean/Professor, 216-368-4436, Fax: 216-368-6939, E-mail: duerk@case.edu. *Application contact:* Dr. Gary Wnek, Associate Dean, Academics, 216-368-3116, Fax: 216-368-6939, E-mail: cseinfo@case.edu. Website: http://www.engineering.case.edu.

The Catholic University of America, School of Engineering, Washington, DC 20064. Offers MBE, MCE, MEE, MME, MS, MSCS, MSE, PhD, Certificate. Part-time programs available. *Faculty:* 35 full-time (3 women), 32 part-time/adjunct (4 women). *Students:* 83 full-time (28 women), 115 part-time (33 women); includes 43 minority (20 Black or African American, non-Hispanic/Latino; 7 Asian, non-Hispanic/Latino; 8 Hispanic/Latino; 8 Two or more races, non-Hispanic/Latino), 101 international. Average age 32. 219 applicants, 71% accepted, 72 enrolled. In 2014, 65 master's, 10 doctorates awarded. *Degree requirements:* For master's, thesis optional; for doctorate, comprehensive exam, thesis/dissertation. *Entrance requirements:* For master's and doctorate, statement of purpose, official copies of academic transcripts, three letters of recommendation. Additional exam requirements/recommendations for international students: Required—TOEFL (minimum score 580 paper-based). *Application deadline:* For fall admission, 7/15 priority date for domestic students, 7/1 for international students; for spring admission, 11/15 priority date for domestic students, 11/1 for international students. Applications are processed on a rolling basis. Application fee: $55. Electronic applications accepted. *Expenses:* Expenses: Contact institution. *Financial support:* Fellowships, research assistantships, teaching assistantships, Federal Work-Study, scholarships/grants, tuition waivers (full and partial), and unspecified assistantships available. Financial award application deadline: 2/1; financial award applicants required to submit FAFSA. *Faculty research:* Rehabilitation engineering, cardiopulmonary biomechanics, geotechnical engineering, signal and image processing, fluid mechanics. *Total annual research expenditures:* $1.3 million. *Unit head:* Dr. Charles C. Nguyen, Dean, 202-319-5160, Fax: 202-319-4499, E-mail: nguyen@cua.edu. *Application contact:* Director of Graduate Admissions, 202-319-5057, Fax: 202-319-6533, E-mail: cua-admissions@cua.edu. Website: http://engineering.cua.edu/.

Central Connecticut State University, School of Graduate Studies, School of Engineering, Science and Technology, Department of Engineering, New Britain, CT 06050-4010. Offers MS. Part-time and evening/weekend programs available. *Faculty:* 5 full-time (1 woman). *Students:* 1 (woman) full-time, 9 part-time (1 woman); includes 4 minority (1 Black or African American, non-Hispanic/Latino; 1 Asian, non-Hispanic/Latino; 1 Hispanic/Latino; 1 Two or more races, non-Hispanic/Latino). Average age 33.

13 applicants, 38% accepted, 3 enrolled. In 2014, 7 master's awarded. *Degree requirements:* For master's, comprehensive exam, thesis or alternative. *Entrance requirements:* For master's, minimum undergraduate GPA of 2.7; four-year BS program in engineering technology, engineering or other programs with specific courses. Additional exam requirements/recommendations for international students: Required—TOEFL (minimum score 550 paper-based; 79 iBT). *Application deadline:* For fall admission, 6/1 for domestic students, 5/1 for international students; for spring admission, 11/1 for domestic and international students. Applications are processed on a rolling basis. Application fee: $50. Electronic applications accepted. *Expenses: Tuition, area resident:* Full-time $5730; part-time $534 per credit. Tuition, state resident: full-time $8596; part-time $534 per credit. Tuition, nonresident: full-time $15,964; part-time $548 per credit. *Required fees:* $4211; $215 per credit. *Financial support:* Application deadline: 3/1. *Unit head:* Dr. Peter Baumann, Chair, 860-832-1815, E-mail: baumannp@ccsu.edu. *Application contact:* Patricia Gardner, Associate Director of Graduate Studies, 860-832-2350, Fax: 860-832-2362, E-mail: graduateadmissions@ccsu.edu. Website: http://web.ccsu.edu/set/academics/programs/engineering/.

Central Connecticut State University, School of Graduate Studies, School of Engineering, Science and Technology, Department of Technology and Engineering Education, New Britain, CT 06050-4010. Offers MS, Certificate. Part-time and evening/weekend programs available. *Faculty:* 2 full-time (0 women). *Students:* 1 full-time (0 women), 30 part-time (9 women). Average age 36. 23 applicants, 87% accepted, 16 enrolled. In 2014, 5 master's awarded. *Degree requirements:* For master's, comprehensive exam, thesis or alternative; for Certificate, qualifying exam. *Entrance requirements:* For master's, minimum undergraduate GPA of 2.7. Additional exam requirements/recommendations for international students: Required—TOEFL (minimum score 550 paper-based; 79 iBT). *Application deadline:* For fall admission, 6/1 for domestic students, 5/1 for international students; for spring admission, 11/1 for domestic and international students. Applications are processed on a rolling basis. Application fee: $50. Electronic applications accepted. *Expenses: Tuition, area resident:* Full-time $5730; part-time $534 per credit. Tuition, state resident: full-time $8596; part-time $534 per credit. Tuition, nonresident: full-time $15,964; part-time $548 per credit. *Required fees:* $4211; $215 per credit. *Financial support:* In 2014–15, 2 students received support. Application deadline: 3/1; applicants required to submit FAFSA. *Faculty research:* Instruction, curriculum development, administration, occupational training. *Unit head:* Dr. James DeLaura, Chair, 860-832-1850, E-mail: delaura@ccsu.edu. *Application contact:* Patricia Gardner, Associate Director of Graduate Studies, 860-832-2350, Fax: 860-832-2362, E-mail: graduateadmissions@ccsu.edu. Website: http://web.ccsu.edu/set/academics/programs/techEducation/.

Central Michigan University, College of Graduate Studies, College of Science and Technology, School of Engineering and Technology, Mount Pleasant, MI 48859. Offers industrial management and technology (MA). Part-time programs available. *Degree requirements:* For master's, thesis or alternative. Electronic applications accepted. *Faculty research:* Computer applications, manufacturing process control, mechanical engineering automation, industrial technology.

Central Washington University, Graduate Studies and Research, College of Education and Professional Studies, Department of Industrial and Engineering Technology, Ellensburg, WA 98926. Offers engineering technology (MS). Part-time programs available. *Degree requirements:* For master's, thesis or alternative. *Entrance requirements:* For master's, minimum GPA of 3.0. Additional exam requirements/recommendations for international students: Required—TOEFL (minimum score 550 paper-based; 79 iBT), IELTS (minimum score 6.5). Electronic applications accepted.

Christian Brothers University, School of Engineering, Memphis, TN 38104-5581. Offers MEM, MSEM. Part-time and evening/weekend programs available. Postbaccalaureate distance learning degree programs offered (no on-campus study). *Degree requirements:* For master's, engineering management project. *Entrance requirements:* For master's, GRE. Additional exam requirements/recommendations for international students: Required—TOEFL.

City College of the City University of New York, Graduate School, Grove School of Engineering, New York, NY 10031-9198. Offers ME, MS, PhD. Part-time programs available. Terminal master's awarded for partial completion of doctoral program. *Degree requirements:* For master's, thesis optional; for doctorate, one foreign language, comprehensive exam, thesis/dissertation. *Entrance requirements:* For master's, GRE General Test, minimum B average in undergraduate coursework; for doctorate, GRE General Test, minimum GPA of 3.5. Additional exam requirements/recommendations for international students: Required—TOEFL (minimum score 500 paper-based; 61 iBT). *Faculty research:* Robotics, network systems, structures.

★ **Clarkson University,** Graduate School, Wallace H. Coulter School of Engineering, Potsdam, NY 13699. Offers ME, MS, PhD. Part-time programs available. *Faculty:* 107 full-time (23 women), 19 part-time/adjunct (5 women). *Students:* 161 full-time (30 women), 5 part-time (1 woman); includes 9 minority (3 Black or African American, non-Hispanic/Latino; 2 Asian, non-Hispanic/Latino; 3 Hispanic/Latino; 1 Two or more races, non-Hispanic/Latino), 95 international. Average age 28. 231 applicants, 67% accepted, 42 enrolled. In 2014, 38 master's, 17 doctorates awarded. Terminal master's awarded for partial completion of doctoral program. *Degree requirements:* For master's, thesis; for doctorate, comprehensive exam, thesis/dissertation, departmental qualifying exam. *Entrance requirements:* For master's and doctorate, GRE, transcripts of all college coursework, resume, personal statement, three letters of recommendation. Additional exam requirements/recommendations for international students: Required—TOEFL (minimum score 550 paper-based; 80 iBT), IELTS (minimum score 6.5). *Application deadline:* For fall admission, 1/30 priority date for domestic and international students; for spring admission, 9/1 priority date for domestic and international students. Applications are processed on a rolling basis. Application fee: $25 ($35 for international students). Electronic applications accepted. *Expenses: Tuition:* Full-time $16,680; part-time $1390 per credit. *Required fees:* $295 per semester. *Financial support:* In 2014–15, 142 students received support, including 11 fellowships with full tuition reimbursements available (averaging $24,029 per year), 55 research assistantships with full tuition reimbursements available (averaging $24,029 per year), 43 teaching assistantships with full tuition reimbursements available (averaging $24,029 per year); scholarships/grants, tuition waivers (partial), and unspecified assistantships also available. *Faculty research:* Advanced materials processing, renewable energy rehabilitation, environmental issues. *Unit head:* Dr. William Jemison, Dean, 315-268-6446, Fax: 315-268-4494, E-mail: wjemison@clarkson.edu. *Application contact:* Kelly Sharlow, Assistant to the Dean, 315-268-7929, Fax: 315-268-4494, E-mail: ksharlow@clarkson.edu. Website: http://www.clarkson.edu/engineering/.

See Display on next page and Close-Up on page 79.

Clemson University, Graduate School, College of Engineering and Science, Clemson, SC 29634. Offers M Eng, M Engr, MFA, MS, PhD, Certificate. Part-time programs available. Postbaccalaureate distance learning degree programs offered. *Faculty:* 379 full-time (86 women), 43 part-time/adjunct (15 women). *Students:* 1,525 full-time (407 women), 269 part-time (62 women); includes 117 minority (46 Black or African American, non-Hispanic/Latino; 3 American Indian or Alaska Native, non-Hispanic/

Latino; 26 Asian, non-Hispanic/Latino; 19 Hispanic/Latino; 1 Native Hawaiian or other Pacific Islander, non-Hispanic/Latino; 22 Two or more races, non-Hispanic/Latino), 1,033 international. Average age 27. 4,331 applicants, 33% accepted, 748 enrolled. In 2014, 417 master's, 125 doctorates awarded. Terminal master's awarded for partial completion of doctoral program. *Degree requirements:* For master's, comprehensive exam (for some programs), thesis (for some programs); for doctorate, comprehensive exam (for some programs), thesis/dissertation. *Entrance requirements:* For master's and doctorate, GRE General Test. Additional exam requirements/recommendations for international students: Required—TOEFL. Application fee: $70 ($80 for international students). Electronic applications accepted. *Financial support:* In 2014–15, 774 students received support, including 125 fellowships with full and partial tuition reimbursements available (averaging $5,788 per year), 397 research assistantships with partial tuition reimbursements available (averaging $19,940 per year), 344 teaching assistantships with partial tuition reimbursements available (averaging $21,926 per year); career-related internships or fieldwork, institutionally sponsored loans, scholarships/grants, health care benefits, and unspecified assistantships also available. Support available to part-time students. Financial award applicants required to submit FAFSA. *Total annual research expenditures:* $38 million. *Unit head:* Dr. Anand Gramopadhye, Dean, 864-656-3202, E-mail: agrampo@clemson.edu. *Application contact:* Dr. Tanju Karanfil, Associate Dean for Research and Graduate Studies, 864-656-3201, Fax: 864-656-4513, E-mail: tkaranf@clemson.edu. Website: http://www.clemson.edu/ces/.

Cleveland State University, College of Graduate Studies, Fenn College of Engineering, Cleveland, OH 44115. Offers MS, D Eng. Part-time and evening/weekend programs available. *Faculty:* 54 full-time (5 women), 12 part-time/adjunct (1 woman). *Students:* 130 full-time (19 women), 413 part-time (87 women); includes 35 minority (11 Black or African American, non-Hispanic/Latino; 13 Asian, non-Hispanic/Latino; 6 Hispanic/Latino; 5 Two or more races, non-Hispanic/Latino), 344 international. Average age 26. 1,037 applicants, 48% accepted, 143 enrolled. In 2014, 131 master's, 9 doctorates awarded. *Degree requirements:* For master's, thesis or alternative; for doctorate, thesis/dissertation, candidacy and qualifying exams. *Entrance requirements:* For master's, GRE General Test, BS in engineering, minimum GPA of 3.0 (2.75 for students from ABET-/EAC-accredited programs from the U.S. and Canada); for doctorate, GRE General Test, MS in engineering, minimum GPA of 3.25. Additional exam requirements/recommendations for international students: Required—TOEFL (minimum score 525 paper-based). *Application deadline:* For fall admission, 7/15 for domestic students, 5/15 for international students; for spring admission, 12/5 for domestic students, 11/1 for international students. Applications are processed on a rolling basis. Application fee: $30. Electronic applications accepted. *Expenses:* Tuition, state resident: full-time $9566; part-time $531 per credit hour. Tuition, nonresident: full-time $17,980; part-time $999 per credit hour. *Required fees:* $25 per semester. Tuition and fees vary according to degree level and program. *Financial support:* In 2014–15, 93 students received support, including 1 fellowship with full tuition reimbursement available, 120 research assistantships with full and partial tuition reimbursements available (averaging $8,694 per year), 20 teaching assistantships with full and partial tuition reimbursements available (averaging $8,082 per year); career-related internships or fieldwork, institutionally sponsored loans, scholarships/grants, tuition waivers (full and partial), and unspecified assistantships also available. Support available to part-time students. Financial award application deadline: 3/30. *Faculty research:* Structural analysis and design, dynamic system and controls, applied biomedical engineering, transportation, water resources, telecommunication, power electronics, computer engineering, industrial automation, engineering management, mechanical design, thermodynamics and fluid mechanics, material engineering, tribology. *Total annual research expenditures:* $7.2 million. *Unit head:* Dr. Paul P. Lin, Associate Dean, 216-

687-2556, Fax: 216-687-9280, E-mail: p.lin@csuohio.edu. *Application contact:* Deborah L. Brown, Interim Assistant Director, Graduate Admissions, 216-523-7572, Fax: 216-687-9214, E-mail: d.l.brown@csuohio.edu. Website: http://www.csuohio.edu/engineering/.

Colorado School of Mines, Graduate School, Golden, CO 80401. Offers ME, MS, PMS, PhD, Graduate Certificate. Part-time programs available. *Faculty:* 363 full-time (103 women), 190 part-time/adjunct (58 women). *Students:* 1,093 full-time (283 women), 180 part-time (43 women); includes 121 minority (12 Black or African American, non-Hispanic/Latino; 4 American Indian or Alaska Native, non-Hispanic/Latino; 30 Asian, non-Hispanic/Latino; 61 Hispanic/Latino; 14 Two or more races, non-Hispanic/Latino), 385 international. Average age 29. 2,112 applicants, 38% accepted, 406 enrolled. In 2014, 426 master's, 83 doctorates awarded. *Degree requirements:* For master's, thesis (for some programs); for doctorate, comprehensive exam, thesis/dissertation. *Entrance requirements:* For master's, doctorate, and Graduate Certificate, GRE General Test. Additional exam requirements/recommendations for international students: Required—TOEFL (minimum score 550 paper-based; 80 iBT). *Application deadline:* For fall admission, 12/15 priority date for domestic and international students; for spring admission, 9/1 priority date for domestic and international students. Application fee: $50 ($70 for international students). Electronic applications accepted. *Financial support:* In 2014–15, 723 students received support, including 73 fellowships with full tuition reimbursements available (averaging $21,120 per year), 513 research assistantships with full tuition reimbursements available (averaging $21,220 per year), 171 teaching assistantships with full tuition reimbursements available (averaging $21,120 per year); career-related internships or fieldwork, Federal Work-Study, institutionally sponsored loans, scholarships/grants, health care benefits, and unspecified assistantships also available. Financial award application deadline: 12/15; financial award applicants required to submit FAFSA. *Faculty research:* Energy, environment, materials, minerals, engineering systems. *Total annual research expenditures:* $55.2 million. *Unit head:* Dr. Tom M. Boyd, Dean of Graduate Studies, 303-273-3020, Fax: 303-273-3244, E-mail: tboyd@mines.edu. *Application contact:* Angel Dotson, Graduate Admissions Coordinator, 303-273-3348, Fax: 303-273-3247, E-mail: grad-app@mines.edu. Website: http://mines.edu/graduate_admissions.

Colorado State University, Graduate School, College of Engineering, Fort Collins, CO 80523-1301. Offers ME, MEE, MS, PhD. *Accreditation:* ABET. Part-time programs available. *Faculty:* 102 full-time (16 women), 5 part-time/adjunct (0 women). *Students:* 359 full-time (95 women), 572 part-time (138 women); includes 91 minority (14 Black or African American, non-Hispanic/Latino; 28 Asian, non-Hispanic/Latino; 35 Hispanic/Latino; 14 Two or more races, non-Hispanic/Latino), 354 international. Average age 30. 1,162 applicants, 50% accepted, 225 enrolled. In 2014, 151 master's, 33 doctorates awarded. *Degree requirements:* For doctorate, thesis/dissertation. *Entrance requirements:* For master's, GRE General Test, minimum GPA of 3.0, 3 letters of recommendation; for doctorate, GRE General Test, minimum GPA of 3.0, transcripts, 3 letters of recommendation, statement of purpose with interests. Additional exam requirements/recommendations for international students: Required—TOEFL (minimum score 550 paper-based; 80 iBT), IELTS (minimum score 6.5). *Application deadline:* For fall admission, 2/1 priority date for domestic and international students; for spring admission, 9/1 priority date for domestic and international students. Applications are processed on a rolling basis. Application fee: $50. Electronic applications accepted. *Expenses:* Tuition, state resident: full-time $9348; part-time $519 per credit. Tuition, nonresident: full-time $22,916; part-time $1273 per credit. *Required fees:* $1584. *Financial support:* In 2014–15, 291 students received support, including 33 fellowships with full tuition reimbursements available (averaging $36,809 per year), 206 research assistantships with full tuition reimbursements available (averaging $17,853 per year), 52 teaching assistantships with full tuition reimbursements available (averaging $10,487

per year); career-related internships or fieldwork, Federal Work-Study, institutionally sponsored loans, scholarships/grants, traineeships, health care benefits, and unspecified assistantships also available. Financial award application deadline: 1/15; financial award applicants required to submit FAFSA. *Faculty research:* Atmospheric science, biological engineering, civil and environmental engineering, electrical and computer engineering, mechanical and biomedical engineering. *Total annual research expenditures:* $104.4 million. *Unit head:* Dr. David McLean, Dean, 970-491-3366, E-mail: david.mclean@colostate.edu. *Application contact:* Dr. Tom Siller, Associate Dean, 970-491-6220, Fax: 970-491-3429, E-mail: thomas.siller@colostate.edu.
Website: http://www.engr.colostate.edu/.

Colorado State University–Pueblo, College of Education, Engineering and Professional Studies, Pueblo, CO 81001-4901. Offers M Ed, MS. Part-time and evening/weekend programs available. *Degree requirements:* For master's, thesis optional. *Entrance requirements:* For master's, GRE General Test. Additional exam requirements/recommendations for international students: Required—TOEFL (minimum score 500 paper-based). Electronic applications accepted. *Expenses:* Contact institution. *Faculty research:* Nanotechnology, applied operations, research transportation, decision analysis.

Columbia University, Fu Foundation School of Engineering and Applied Science, New York, NY 10027. Offers MS, Eng Sc D, PhD, MS/MBA. Part-time programs available. Postbaccalaureate distance learning degree programs offered (no on-campus study). *Faculty:* 417 full-time (74 women), 240 part-time/adjunct (19 women). *Students:* 1,824 full-time (551 women), 989 part-time (293 women); includes 274 minority (17 Black or African American, non-Hispanic/Latino; 193 Asian, non-Hispanic/Latino; 40 Hispanic/Latino; 24 Two or more races, non-Hispanic/Latino), 2,170 international. 8,868 applicants, 29% accepted, 1231 enrolled. In 2014, 1,068 master's, 109 doctorates awarded. Terminal master's awarded for partial completion of doctoral program. *Degree requirements:* For master's, comprehensive exam (for some programs), thesis (for some programs); for doctorate, comprehensive exam (for some programs), thesis/dissertation, qualifying exam. *Entrance requirements:* For master's, GRE General Test; for doctorate, GRE General Test, GRE Subject Test (applied physics program only). Additional exam requirements/recommendations for international students: Required—TOEFL (minimum score 590 paper-based; 96 iBT), IELTS (minimum score 6.5), PTE. *Application deadline:* For fall admission, 12/15 priority date for domestic and international students; for spring admission, 10/1 priority date for domestic and international students. Application fee: $85. Electronic applications accepted. *Financial support:* In 2014–15, 718 students received support, including 95 fellowships with full and partial tuition reimbursements available (averaging $27,630 per year), 486 research assistantships with full and partial tuition reimbursements available (averaging $29,703 per year), 161 teaching assistantships with full and partial tuition reimbursements available (averaging $25,041 per year); career-related internships or fieldwork, traineeships, health care benefits, and unspecified assistantships also available. Financial award application deadline: 12/15; financial award applicants required to submit FAFSA. *Total annual research expenditures:* $154.1 million. *Unit head:* Dr. Mary Cunningham Boyce, Dean, 212-854-1123, Fax: 212-864-0104, E-mail: seasdean@columbia.edu. *Application contact:* Jocelyn Morales, Associate Director, 212-854-6901, Fax: 212-854-5900, E-mail: seasgradmit@columbia.edu.
Website: http://www.engineering.columbia.edu/.

Concordia University, School of Graduate Studies, Faculty of Engineering and Computer Science, Montréal, QC H3G 1M8, Canada. Offers M App Comp Sc, M Comp Sc, M Eng, MA Sc, PhD, Certificate, Diploma. *Degree requirements:* For doctorate, comprehensive exam, thesis/dissertation. *Expenses:* Contact institution.

Cooper Union for the Advancement of Science and Art, Albert Nerken School of Engineering, New York, NY 10003-7120. Offers chemical engineering (ME); civil engineering (ME); electrical engineering (ME); mechanical engineering (ME). Part-time programs available. *Faculty:* 27 full-time (1 woman), 15 part-time/adjunct (2 women). *Students:* 45 full-time (10 women), 20 part-time (4 women); includes 24 minority (3 Black or African American, non-Hispanic/Latino; 15 Asian, non-Hispanic/Latino; 4 Hispanic/Latino; 2 Two or more races, non-Hispanic/Latino), 4 international. Average age 23. 86 applicants, 71% accepted, 44 enrolled. In 2014, 22 master's awarded. *Degree requirements:* For master's, thesis (for some programs). *Entrance requirements:* For master's, BE or BS in engineering discipline, high school and college transcripts, two letters of recommendation, resume. Additional exam requirements/recommendations for international students: Required—TOEFL (minimum score 600 paper-based; 100 iBT). *Application deadline:* For fall admission, 4/1 for domestic and international students. Application fee: $70. Electronic applications accepted. *Expenses: Tuition:* Full-time $39,600; part-time $1173 per credit. *Required fees:* $925 per semester. One-time fee: $250. *Financial support:* In 2014–15, 65 students received support, including 4 fellowships with full and partial tuition reimbursements available (averaging $11,000 per year); career-related internships or fieldwork, Federal Work-Study, tuition waivers (full and partial), and tuition scholarships offered to exceptional students also available. Support available to part-time students. Financial award application deadline: 5/1; financial award applicants required to submit FAFSA. *Faculty research:* Civil infrastructure, imaging and sensing technology, biomedical engineering, encryption technology, process engineering. *Unit head:* Dr. Teresa Dahlberg, Dean of Engineering, 212-353-4285, E-mail: dahlberg@cooper.edu. *Application contact:* Student Contact, 212-353-4120, E-mail: admissions@cooper.edu.
Website: http://cooper.edu/engineering.

Cornell University, Graduate School, Graduate Fields of Engineering, Ithaca, NY 14853-0001. Offers M Eng, MPS, MS, PhD, M Eng/MBA. *Degree requirements:* For doctorate, comprehensive exam, thesis/dissertation. *Entrance requirements:* Additional exam requirements/recommendations for international students: Required—TOEFL. Electronic applications accepted.

Dalhousie University, Faculty of Engineering, Halifax, NS B3H 4R2, Canada. Offers M Eng, M Sc, MA Sc, PhD, M Eng/M Plan, MA Sc/M Plan, MBA/M Eng. *Entrance requirements:* Additional exam requirements/recommendations for international students: Required—1 of 5 approved tests: TOEFL, IELTS, CANTEST, CAEL, Michigan English Language Assessment Battery.

Dartmouth College, Thayer School of Engineering, Hanover, NH 03755. Offers MEM, MS, PhD, MD/MS, MD/PhD. *Faculty:* 49 full-time (9 women), 42 part-time/adjunct (3 women). *Students:* 189 full-time (55 women), 1 part-time (0 women); includes 28 minority (4 Black or African American, non-Hispanic/Latino; 1 American Indian or Alaska Native, non-Hispanic/Latino; 16 Asian, non-Hispanic/Latino; 5 Hispanic/Latino; 2 Two or more races, non-Hispanic/Latino), 95 international. Average age 24. 680 applicants, 20% accepted, 68 enrolled. In 2014, 58 master's, 18 doctorates awarded. *Degree requirements:* For doctorate, thesis/dissertation, candidacy oral exam. *Entrance requirements:* For master's and doctorate, GRE General Test. Additional exam requirements/recommendations for international students: Required—TOEFL. *Application deadline:* For fall admission, 1/1 priority date for domestic and international students. Applications are processed on a rolling basis. Application fee: $45. Electronic applications accepted. *Financial support:* In 2014–15, 199 students received support, including 26 fellowships with full tuition reimbursements available (averaging $25,320 per year), 75 research assistantships with full tuition reimbursements available (averaging $25,320 per year), 9 teaching assistantships with partial tuition reimbursements available (averaging $7,500 per year); career-related internships or fieldwork, institutionally sponsored loans, scholarships/grants, and tuition waivers (full and partial) also available. Financial award application deadline: 2/15; financial award applicants required to submit CSS PROFILE. *Faculty research:* Biomedical engineering, biotechnology and biochemical engineering, electrical and computer engineering, engineering physics, environmental engineering, materials science and engineering, mechanical systems engineering. *Unit head:* Dr. Joseph J. Helbie, Dean, 603-646-2238, Fax: 603-646-2580, E-mail: joseph.j.helbie@dartmouth.edu. *Application contact:* Candace S. Potter, Graduate Admissions & Financial Aid Administrator, 603-646-3844, Fax: 603-646-1620, E-mail: candace.s.potter@dartmouth.edu.
Website: http://engineering.dartmouth.edu/.

Drexel University, College of Engineering, Philadelphia, PA 19104-2875. Offers MS, MSEE, MSSE, PhD, Certificate. Part-time and evening/weekend programs available. *Degree requirements:* For doctorate, thesis/dissertation. *Entrance requirements:* Additional exam requirements/recommendations for international students: Required—TOEFL. Electronic applications accepted.

Drexel University, Goodwin College of Professional Studies, School of Technology and Professional Studies, Philadelphia, PA 19104-2875. Offers construction management (MS); creativity and innovation (MS); engineering technology (MS); food science (MS); hospitality management (MS); professional studies: creativity studies (MS); professional studies: e-learning leadership (MS); professional studies: homeland security management (MS); project management (MS); property management (MS); sport management (MS). Part-time and evening/weekend programs available. *Entrance requirements:* Additional exam requirements/recommendations for international students: Required—TOEFL, IELTS. Electronic applications accepted. Application fee is waived when completed online.

Duke University, Graduate School, Pratt School of Engineering, Master of Engineering Program, Durham, NC 27708-0271. Offers biomedical engineering (M Eng); civil engineering (M Eng); electrical and computer engineering (M Eng); environmental engineering (M Eng); materials science and engineering (M Eng); mechanical engineering (M Eng); photonics and optical sciences (M Eng). Part-time programs available. *Students:* 45 full-time (17 women); includes 5 minority (1 Black or African American, non-Hispanic/Latino; 2 Asian, non-Hispanic/Latino; 2 Hispanic/Latino), 23 international. Average age 24. 285 applicants, 43% accepted, 45 enrolled. In 2014, 45 master's awarded. *Entrance requirements:* For master's, GRE General Test, resume, 3 letters of recommendation, statement of purpose, transcripts. Additional exam requirements/recommendations for international students: Required—TOEFL. *Application deadline:* For fall admission, 6/15 for domestic students, 2/15 for international students; for spring admission, 11/1 for domestic students, 9/1 for international students. Application fee: $75. *Expenses: Tuition:* Full-time $45,760; part-time $2765 per credit. *Required fees:* $978. Full-time tuition and fees vary according to program. *Financial support:* Merit scholarships/grants available. *Unit head:* Dr. Bradley A. Fox, Executive Director, 919-660-5455, Fax: 919-660-5456. *Application contact:* Susan Brown, Assistant Director of Admissions, 919-660-8451, Fax: 919-660-5456, E-mail: susan.brown@duke.edu.
Website: http://meng.pratt.duke.edu/.

Eastern Illinois University, Graduate School, Lumpkin College of Business and Applied Sciences, School of Technology, Charleston, IL 61920. Offers computer technology (Certificate); quality systems (Certificate); technology (MS); technology security (Certificate); work performance improvement (Certificate); MS/MBA; MS/MS. Part-time and evening/weekend programs available. *Faculty:* 28. *Students:* 133 full-time (43 women), 68 part-time (39 women); includes 17 minority (11 Black or African American, non-Hispanic/Latino; 2 Asian, non-Hispanic/Latino; 2 Hispanic/Latino; 2 Two or more races, non-Hispanic/Latino), 124 international. Average age 28. 449 applicants, 31% accepted, 58 enrolled. In 2014, 61 master's awarded. *Application deadline:* For fall admission, 3/31 priority date for domestic students. Applications are processed on a rolling basis. Application fee: $30. *Expenses:* Tuition, state resident: full-time $3113; part-time $283 per credit hour. Tuition, nonresident: full-time $7469; part-time $679 per credit hour. *Required fees:* $2287; $96 per credit hour. Tuition and fees vary according to course load. *Financial support:* In 2014–15, 107 students received support, including 7 research assistantships with tuition reimbursements available, 6 teaching assistantships with tuition reimbursements available. *Unit head:* Austin Cheney, Chair, 217-581-3226, Fax: 217-581-6607, E-mail: acheney@eiu.edu. *Application contact:* Peter Ping Liu, Coordinator, 217-581-6267, Fax: 217-581-6607, E-mail: pliu@eiu.edu.
Website: http://www.eiu.edu/tech/.

Eastern Michigan University, Graduate School, College of Technology, School of Engineering Technology, Programs in Computer Aided Engineering, Ypsilanti, MI 48197. Offers CAD/CAM (MS); computer-aided technology (MS). Part-time and evening/weekend programs available. Postbaccalaureate distance learning degree programs offered (minimal on-campus study). *Students:* 2 full-time (1 woman), 23 part-time (4 women); includes 7 minority (2 Black or African American, non-Hispanic/Latino; 5 Asian, non-Hispanic/Latino), 9 international. Average age 33. 22 applicants, 73% accepted, 9 enrolled. In 2014, 3 master's awarded. *Entrance requirements:* Additional exam requirements/recommendations for international students: Required—TOEFL. *Application deadline:* Applications are processed on a rolling basis. Application fee: $45. *Financial support:* Fellowships, research assistantships with full tuition reimbursements, teaching assistantships with full tuition reimbursements, and tuition waivers (partial) available. Financial award applicants required to submit FAFSA. *Application contact:* Dr. Tony Shay, Program Coordinator, 734-487-2040, Fax: 734-487-8755, E-mail: tony.shay@emich.edu.

École Polytechnique de Montréal, Graduate Programs, Montréal, QC H3C 3A7, Canada. Offers M Eng, M Sc A, PhD, DESS. Part-time and evening/weekend programs available. Terminal master's awarded for partial completion of doctoral program. *Degree requirements:* For master's, one foreign language, thesis; for doctorate, one foreign language, thesis/dissertation. *Entrance requirements:* For master's, minimum GPA of 2.75; for doctorate, minimum GPA of 3.0. Electronic applications accepted. *Faculty research:* Chemical engineering, environmental engineering, microelectronics and communications, biomedical engineering, engineering physics.

Fairfield University, School of Engineering, Fairfield, CT 06824. Offers automated manufacturing (CAS); database management (CAS); electrical and computer engineering (MS); information security (CAS); management of technology (MS); mechanical engineering (MS); network technology (CAS); software engineering (MS); Web application development (CAS). Part-time and evening/weekend programs available. *Faculty:* 4 full-time (1 woman), 18 part-time/adjunct (5 women). *Students:* 193 full-time (50 women), 69 part-time (11 women); includes 20 minority (4 Black or African American, non-Hispanic/Latino; 6 Asian, non-Hispanic/Latino; 10 Hispanic/Latino), 199 international. Average age 27. 516 applicants, 64% accepted, 124 enrolled. In 2014, 38 master's awarded. *Degree requirements:* For master's, thesis, capstone course. *Entrance requirements:* For master's, interview, minimum GPA of 2.8, resume, 2 recommendations. Additional exam requirements/recommendations for international

students: Required—TOEFL (minimum score 550 paper-based; 80 iBT) or IELTS (minimum score 6.5). *Application deadline:* For fall admission, 5/15 for international students; for spring admission, 10/15 for international students. Applications are processed on a rolling basis. Application fee: $60. Electronic applications accepted. *Expenses:* Expenses: $750 per credit hour. *Financial support:* In 2014–15, 30 students received support. Scholarships/grants and unspecified assistantships available. Financial award applicants required to submit FAFSA. *Faculty research:* Ocean dynamics modeling, thermo fluids, Web/mobile software applications, microwaves/electromagnetics, micro/nano manufacturing. *Unit head:* Dr. Bruce Berdanier, Dean, 203-254-4147, Fax: 203-254-4013, E-mail: bberdanier@fairfield.edu. *Application contact:* Marianne Gumpper, Director of Graduate and Continuing Studies Admission, 203-254-4184, Fax: 203-254-4073, E-mail: gradadmis@fairfield.edu.
Website: http://www.fairfield.edu/academicsschoolscollegescenters/schoolofengineering/graduateprograms/.

Fairleigh Dickinson University, Metropolitan Campus, University College: Arts, Sciences, and Professional Studies, School of Computer Sciences and Engineering, Teaneck, NJ 07666-1914. Offers computer engineering (MS); computer science (MS); e-commerce (MS); electrical engineering (MSEE); management information systems (MS); mathematical foundation (MS).

Florida Agricultural and Mechanical University, Division of Graduate Studies, Research, and Continuing Education, FAMU-FSU College of Engineering, Tallahassee, FL 32307-3200. Offers M Eng, MS, PhD. College administered jointly by Florida State University. *Entrance requirements:* For master's, GRE General Test, minimum GPA of 3.0. Additional exam requirements/recommendations for international students: Required—TOEFL (minimum score 550 paper-based).

Florida Atlantic University, College of Engineering and Computer Science, Boca Raton, FL 33431-0991. Offers MS, PhD. Part-time and evening/weekend programs available. Postbaccalaureate distance learning degree programs offered (minimal on-campus study). Terminal master's awarded for partial completion of doctoral program. *Degree requirements:* For master's, thesis optional; for doctorate, thesis/dissertation, qualifying exam. *Entrance requirements:* For master's, GRE General Test, minimum GPA of 3.0; for doctorate, GRE General Test. Additional exam requirements/recommendations for international students: Required—TOEFL (minimum score 500 paper-based; 61 iBT), IELTS (minimum score 6). *Expenses:* Tuition, state resident: full-time $7396; part-time $369.82 per credit hour. Tuition, nonresident: full-time $19,392; part-time $1024.81 per credit hour. Tuition and fees vary according to course load. *Faculty research:* Automated underwater vehicles, communication systems, computer networks, materials, neural networks.

Florida Institute of Technology, Graduate Programs, College of Engineering, Melbourne, FL 32901-6975. Offers MS, PhD. Part-time and evening/weekend programs available. *Faculty:* 84 full-time (8 women), 19 part-time/adjunct (3 women). *Students:* 656 full-time (148 women), 240 part-time (52 women); includes 59 minority (12 Black or African American, non-Hispanic/Latino; 1 American Indian or Alaska Native, non-Hispanic/Latino; 23 Asian, non-Hispanic/Latino; 17 Hispanic/Latino; 6 Two or more races, non-Hispanic/Latino), 670 international. Average age 30. 2,791 applicants, 51% accepted, 280 enrolled. In 2014, 190 master's, 16 doctorates awarded. Terminal master's awarded for partial completion of doctoral program. *Degree requirements:* For master's, comprehensive exam (for some programs), thesis or final exam; for doctorate, comprehensive exam, thesis/dissertation. *Entrance requirements:* For master's, GRE, minimum GPA of 3.0, 3 letters of recommendation, resume, statement of objectives; for doctorate, GRE, minimum GPA of 3.2, 3 letters of recommendation, resume, statement of objectives. Additional exam requirements/recommendations for international students: Required—TOEFL (minimum score 550 paper-based; 79 iBT). *Application deadline:* For fall admission, 4/1 for international students; for spring admission, 9/30 for international students. Applications are processed on a rolling basis. Electronic applications accepted. *Expenses: Tuition:* Part-time $1179 per credit hour. Tuition and fees vary according to campus/location. *Financial support:* In 2014–15, 1 fellowship with full and partial tuition reimbursement, 32 research assistantships with full and partial tuition reimbursements (averaging $6,263 per year), 46 teaching assistantships with full and partial tuition reimbursements (averaging $6,976 per year) were awarded; career-related internships or fieldwork, institutionally sponsored loans, unspecified assistantships, and tuition remissions also available. Support available to part-time students. Financial award application deadline: 3/1; financial award applicants required to submit FAFSA. *Faculty research:* Electrical and computer science and engineering; aerospace, chemical, civil, mechanical, and ocean engineering; environmental science and oceanography. *Total annual research expenditures:* $6.1 million. *Unit head:* Dr. Martin Glicksman, Interim Dean, 321-674-8020, Fax: 321-674-7270, E-mail: mglicksman@fit.edu. *Application contact:* Cheryl A. Brown, Associate Director of Graduate Admissions, 321-674-7581, Fax: 321-723-9468, E-mail: cbrown@fit.edu.
Website: http://coe.fit.edu.

Florida International University, College of Engineering and Computing, Miami, FL 33175. Offers MS, PMS, PhD. Part-time and evening/weekend programs available. Postbaccalaureate distance learning degree programs offered. Terminal master's awarded for partial completion of doctoral program. *Degree requirements:* For master's, thesis (for some programs); for doctorate, comprehensive exam, thesis/dissertation. *Entrance requirements:* For master's, GRE (depending on program), minimum GPA of 3.0; for doctorate, GRE General Test, minimum GPA of 3.0. Additional exam requirements/recommendations for international students: Required—TOEFL (minimum score 550 paper-based; 80 iBT). Electronic applications accepted. *Faculty research:* Databases, informatics, computing systems, software engineering, security, biosensors, imaging, tissue engineering, biomaterials and bionanotechnology, transportation, wind engineering, hydrology, environmental engineering, engineering management, sustainability and green construction, risk management and decision systems, infrastructure systems, digital signal processing, power systems, nanophotonics, embedded systems, image processing, nanotechnology.

Florida State University, The Graduate School, FAMU-FSU College of Engineering, Tallahassee, FL 32310-6046. Offers M Eng, MS, PhD. Part-time programs available. *Degree requirements:* For master's, thesis (for some programs); for doctorate, comprehensive exam, thesis/dissertation, preliminary exam, qualifying exam. *Entrance requirements:* For master's and doctorate, GRE General Test. Additional exam requirements/recommendations for international students: Required—TOEFL (minimum score 550 paper-based; 80 iBT). *Expenses:* Tuition, state resident: part-time $403.51 per credit hour. Tuition, nonresident: part-time $1004.85 per credit hour. *Required fees:* $75.81 per credit hour. One-time fee: $20 part-time. Tuition and fees vary according to campus/location.

George Mason University, Volgenau School of Engineering, Fairfax, VA 22030. Offers M Eng, MS, PhD, Certificate. Part-time and evening/weekend programs available. Postbaccalaureate distance learning degree programs offered. *Faculty:* 165 full-time (36 women), 156 part-time/adjunct (24 women). *Students:* 691 full-time (204 women), 873 part-time (184 women); includes 358 minority (81 Black or African American, non-Hispanic/Latino; 194 Asian, non-Hispanic/Latino; 59 Hispanic/Latino; 3 Native Hawaiian or other Pacific Islander, non-Hispanic/Latino; 21 Two or more races, non-Hispanic/Latino), 567 International. Average age 30. 1,891 applicants, 55% accepted, 421 enrolled. In 2014, 496 master's, 44 doctorates, 68 other advanced degrees awarded. *Degree requirements:* For master's, thesis optional; for doctorate, thesis/dissertation, comprehensive oral and written exams. *Entrance requirements:* For master's, minimum GPA of 3.0 in last 60 hours of course work; for doctorate, GRE General Test, minimum graduate GPA of 3.5. Additional exam requirements/recommendations for international students: Required—TOEFL (minimum score 575 paper-based; 80 iBT), IELTS (minimum score 6.5), PTE. Application fee: $65 ($80 for international students). Electronic applications accepted. *Expenses:* Expenses: Contact institution. *Financial support:* In 2014–15, 260 students received support, including 4 fellowships (averaging $8,915 per year), 106 research assistantships with full and partial tuition reimbursements available (averaging $19,415 per year), 157 teaching assistantships with full and partial tuition reimbursements available (averaging $14,216 per year); career-related internships or fieldwork, Federal Work-Study, scholarships/grants, unspecified assistantships, and health care benefits (for full-time research or teaching assistantship recipients) also available. Support available to part-time students. Financial award application deadline: 3/1; financial award applicants required to submit FAFSA. *Faculty research:* Systems management, quality assurance, decision support systems, cognitive ergonomics. *Total annual research expenditures:* $16.3 million. *Unit head:* Kenneth S. Ball, Dean, 703-993-1498, Fax: 703-993-1734, E-mail: vsdean@gmu.edu. *Application contact:* Jade T. Perez, Director, Graduate Services, 703-993-2426, E-mail: jperezc@gmu.edu.
Website: http://volgenau.gmu.edu.

The George Washington University, School of Engineering and Applied Science, Washington, DC 20052. Offers MS, D Sc, PhD, App Sc, Engr, Graduate Certificate. Part-time and evening/weekend programs available. *Faculty:* 99 full-time (18 women), 183 part-time/adjunct (15 women). *Students:* 576 full-time (161 women), 1,115 part-time (287 women); includes 379 minority (179 Black or African American, non-Hispanic/Latino; 4 American Indian or Alaska Native, non-Hispanic/Latino; 128 Asian, non-Hispanic/Latino; 52 Hispanic/Latino; 7 Native Hawaiian or other Pacific Islander, non-Hispanic/Latino; 9 Two or more races, non-Hispanic/Latino), 615 international. Average age 32. 2,089 applicants, 61% accepted, 435 enrolled. In 2014, 757 master's, 43 doctorates, 162 other advanced degrees awarded. *Degree requirements:* For master's, thesis optional; for doctorate, thesis/dissertation, qualifying exam. *Entrance requirements:* For master's, appropriate bachelor's degree; for doctorate, GRE (if highest earned degree is BS), appropriate bachelor's or master's degree; for other advanced degree, appropriate master's degree. Additional exam requirements/recommendations for international students: Required—TOEFL or The George Washington University English as a Foreign Language Test. *Application deadline:* For fall admission, 3/1 for domestic students; for spring admission, 10/1 for domestic students. Applications are processed on a rolling basis. Application fee: $75. *Financial support:* In 2014–15, 216 students received support. Fellowships with full and partial tuition reimbursements available, research assistantships with full and partial tuition reimbursements available, teaching assistantships with full and partial tuition reimbursements available, career-related internships or fieldwork, Federal Work-Study, institutionally sponsored loans, and tuition waivers (full and partial) available. Financial award application deadline: 3/1; financial award applicants required to submit FAFSA. *Faculty research:* Fatigue fracture and structural reliability, computer-integrated manufacturing, materials engineering, artificial intelligence and expert systems, quality assurance. *Total annual research expenditures:* $6.3 million. *Unit head:* David S. Dolling, Dean, 202-994-6080, E-mail: dolling@gwu.edu. *Application contact:* Adina Lav, Marketing, Recruiting and Admissions, 202-994-5827, Fax: 202-994-0909, E-mail: engineering@gwu.edu.
Website: http://www.seas.gwu.edu/.

See Display on next page and Close-Up on page 81.

Georgia Institute of Technology, Graduate Studies, College of Engineering, Atlanta, GA 30332-0001. Offers MBID, MS, PMS, PhD. Part-time programs available. Postbaccalaureate distance learning degree programs offered. *Faculty:* 400 full-time (65 women), 19 part-time/adjunct (4 women). *Students:* 3,295 full-time (717 women), 807 part-time (145 women); includes 659 minority (91 Black or African American, non-Hispanic/Latino; 4 American Indian or Alaska Native, non-Hispanic/Latino; 335 Asian, non-Hispanic/Latino; 156 Hispanic/Latino; 3 Native Hawaiian or other Pacific Islander, non-Hispanic/Latino; 70 Two or more races, non-Hispanic/Latino), 2,045 international. Average age 25. 8,147 applicants, 32% accepted, 1181 enrolled. In 2014, 1,103 master's, 378 doctorates awarded. Terminal master's awarded for partial completion of doctoral program. *Degree requirements:* For doctorate, thesis/dissertation. *Entrance requirements:* For master's and doctorate, GRE. Additional exam requirements/recommendations for international students: Required—TOEFL (minimum score 550 paper-based; 79 iBT). *Application deadline:* Applications are processed on a rolling basis. Application fee: $75. Electronic applications accepted. *Expenses:* Tuition, state resident: full-time $12,344; part-time $515 per credit hour. Tuition, nonresident: full-time $27,600; part-time $1150 per credit hour. *Required fees:* $1196 per term. Part-time tuition and fees vary according to course load. *Financial support:* Fellowships, research assistantships, teaching assistantships, career-related internships or fieldwork, Federal Work-Study, institutionally sponsored loans, tuition waivers (partial), and unspecified assistantships available. Support available to part-time students. Financial award application deadline: 5/1. *Total annual research expenditures:* $151 million. *Unit head:* David Bamburowski, Director, Graduate Studies, 404-894-1610, E-mail: david.bamburowski@grad.gatech.edu. *Application contact:* Graduate Coordinator, 404-894-1610, E-mail: gradinfo@mail.gatech.edu.
Website: http://www.coe.gatech.edu.

Georgia Southern University, Jack N. Averitt College of Graduate Studies, Allen E. Paulson College of Engineering and Information Technology, Statesboro, GA 30460. Offers MS, MSAE, Graduate Certificate. Part-time programs available. Postbaccalaureate distance learning degree programs offered (no on-campus study). *Faculty:* 46 full-time (4 women), 1 part-time/adjunct (0 women). *Students:* 39 full-time (4 women), 71 part-time (10 women); includes 38 minority (17 Black or African American, non-Hispanic/Latino; 2 Asian, non-Hispanic/Latino; 17 Hispanic/Latino; 2 Two or more races, non-Hispanic/Latino), 21 international. Average age 30. 70 applicants, 60% accepted, 24 enrolled. In 2014, 25 master's awarded. *Degree requirements:* For master's, comprehensive exam, thesis (for some programs). *Entrance requirements:* For master's, GRE, undergraduate major or equivalent in proposed study area. Additional exam requirements/recommendations for international students: Recommended—TOEFL (minimum score 80 iBT). Application fee: $50. *Expenses:* Tuition, state resident: full-time $7236; part-time $277 per semester hour. Tuition, nonresident: full-time $27,118; part-time $1105 per semester hour. *Required fees:* $2092. *Financial support:* In 2014–15, 39 students received support, including research assistantships (averaging $7,200 per year), teaching assistantships (averaging $7,200 per year); Federal Work-Study, scholarships/grants, tuition waivers (partial), and unspecified assistantships also available. Financial award applicants required to submit FAFSA. *Faculty research:* Electromagnetics, biomechatronics, cyber physical systems, big data, nanocomposite material science, renewable energy and engines, robotics. *Total annual research*

Engineering and Applied Sciences—General

expenditures: $178,285. *Unit head:* Dr. Mohammad S. Davoud, Dean, 912-478-8046, E-mail: mdavoud@georgiasouthern.edu.
Website: http://ceit.georgiasouthern.edu/.

The Graduate Center, City University of New York, Graduate Studies, Program in Engineering, New York, NY 10016-4039. Offers biomedical engineering (PhD); chemical engineering (PhD); civil engineering (PhD); electrical engineering (PhD); mechanical engineering (PhD). *Degree requirements:* For doctorate, thesis/dissertation. *Entrance requirements:* For doctorate, GRE General Test. Additional exam requirements/recommendations for international students: Required—TOEFL. Electronic applications accepted.

Grand Valley State University, Padnos College of Engineering and Computing, School of Engineering, Allendale, MI 49401-9403. Offers electrical and computer engineering (MSE); manufacturing operations (MSE); mechanical engineering (MSE); product design and manufacturing engineering (MSE). Part-time and evening/weekend programs available. *Faculty:* 15 full-time (2 women). *Students:* 29 full-time (6 women), 30 part-time (5 women); includes 4 minority (1 Asian, non-Hispanic/Latino; 3 Hispanic/Latino), 23 international. Average age 28. 66 applicants, 73% accepted, 23 enrolled. In 2014, 14 master's awarded. *Degree requirements:* For master's, project or thesis. *Entrance requirements:* For master's, engineering degree, minimum GPA of 3.0. Additional exam requirements/recommendations for international students: Required—TOEFL. *Application deadline:* Applications are processed on a rolling basis. Application fee: $30. Electronic applications accepted. *Expenses:* Tuition, state resident: full-time $10,602; part-time $589 per credit hour. Tuition, nonresident: full-time $14,022; part-time $779 per credit hour. Tuition and fees vary according to degree level and program. *Financial support:* In 2014–15, 31 students received support, including 10 fellowships (averaging $3,049 per year), 25 research assistantships with full tuition reimbursements available (averaging $10,237 per year); career-related internships or fieldwork, Federal Work-Study, institutionally sponsored loans, scholarships/grants, and unspecified assistantships also available. *Faculty research:* Digital signal processing, computer aided design, computer aided manufacturing, manufacturing simulation, biomechanics, product design. *Total annual research expenditures:* $300,000. *Unit head:* Dr. Charles Standridge, Acting Director, 616-331-6750, Fax: 616-331-7215, E-mail: standric@gvsu.edu. *Application contact:* Dr. Pranod Chaphalkar, Graduate Director, 616-331-6843, Fax: 616-331-7215, E-mail: chaphalp@gvsu.edu.
Website: http://www.engineer.gvsu.edu/.

Harvard University, Graduate School of Arts and Sciences, School of Engineering and Applied Sciences, Cambridge, MA 02138. Offers applied mathematics (ME, SM, PhD); applied physics (ME, SM, PhD); computer science (ME, SM, PhD); engineering science (ME); engineering sciences (SM, PhD). Part-time programs available. Terminal master's awarded for partial completion of doctoral program. *Degree requirements:* For master's, thesis optional; for doctorate, comprehensive exam, thesis/dissertation. *Entrance requirements:* For master's and doctorate, GRE General Test, GRE Subject Test (recommended), 3 letters of recommendation. Additional exam requirements/recommendations for international students: Required—TOEFL (minimum score 80 iBT). Electronic applications accepted. *Faculty research:* Applied mathematics, applied physics, computer science and electrical engineering, environmental engineering, mechanical and biomedical engineering.

Hofstra University, School of Engineering and Applied Science, Hempstead, NY 11549. Offers computer science (MS), including cybersecurity, Web engineering. Part-time and evening/weekend programs available. Postbaccalaureate distance learning degree programs offered (no on-campus study). *Faculty:* 7 full-time (2 women), 3 part-time/adjunct. *Students:* 13 full-time (3 women), 17 part-time (3 women); includes 4 minority (all Asian, non-Hispanic/Latino), 8 international. Average age 30. 27 applicants, 59% accepted, 12 enrolled. In 2014, 6 master's awarded. *Degree requirements:* For master's, thesis optional, 30 credits, 3.0 GPA. *Entrance requirements:* For master's, GRE, Minimum GPA of 3.0. Additional exam requirements/recommendations for international students: Required—TOEFL (minimum score 550 paper-based; 80 iBT). *Application deadline:* Applications are processed on a rolling basis. Application fee: $70 ($75 for international students). Electronic applications accepted. *Expenses: Tuition:* Full-time $20,610; part-time $1145 per credit hour. *Required fees:* $970; $165 per term. Tuition and fees vary according to program. *Financial support:* In 2014–15, 10 students received support, including 4 fellowships with full and partial tuition reimbursements available (averaging $4,300 per year), 1 research assistantship with full and partial tuition reimbursement available (averaging $8,147 per year); Federal Work-Study, institutionally sponsored loans, scholarships/grants, tuition waivers (full and partial), and unspecified assistantships also available. Support available to part-time students. Financial award applicants required to submit FAFSA. *Faculty research:* Semantic web, software engineering, data mining and machine learning, programming languages, cybersecurity. *Unit head:* Dr. Sina Rabbany, Acting Dean, 516-463-6672, E-mail: eggsyr@hofstra.edu. *Application contact:* Sunil Samuel, Assistant Vice President of Admissions, 516-463-4723, Fax: 516-463-4664, E-mail: graduateadmission@hofstra.edu.
Website: http://www.hofstra.edu/academics/colleges/seas/.

Howard University, College of Engineering, Architecture, and Computer Sciences, School of Engineering and Computer Science, Washington, DC 20059. Offers M Eng, MCS, MS, PhD. Part-time programs available. Terminal master's awarded for partial completion of doctoral program. *Degree requirements:* For doctorate, one foreign language, thesis/dissertation, preliminary exam. *Entrance requirements:* For master's and doctorate, GRE General Test, minimum GPA of 3.0. Additional exam requirements/recommendations for international students: Required—TOEFL. Electronic applications accepted. *Faculty research:* Environmental engineering, solid-state electronics, dynamics and control of large flexible space structures, power systems, reaction kinetics.

Idaho State University, Office of Graduate Studies, College of Science and Engineering, Pocatello, ID 83209-8060. Offers MA, MNS, MS, DA, PhD, Postbaccalaureate Certificate. *Accreditation:* ABET. Part-time programs available. *Degree requirements:* For master's, comprehensive exam (for some programs), thesis, thesis project, 2 semesters of seminar; for doctorate, comprehensive exam, thesis/dissertation, oral presentation and defense of research, oral examination; for Postbaccalaureate Certificate, comprehensive exam (for some programs), thesis optional, oral exam or thesis defense. *Entrance requirements:* For master's, GRE General Test, minimum GPA of 3.0 in upper-division undergraduate classes; for doctorate, GRE General Test, master's degree in engineering or physics, 1-page statement of research interests, resume, 3 letters of reference, 1-page statement of career interests; for Postbaccalaureate Certificate, GRE (if GPA between 2.0 and 3.0), bachelor's degree, minimum GPA of 3.0 in upper-division courses. Additional exam requirements/recommendations for international students: Required—TOEFL (minimum score 550 paper-based; 80 iBT). Electronic applications accepted. *Faculty research:* Nuclear engineering, biomedical engineering, robotics, measurement and control, structural systems.

Illinois Institute of Technology, Graduate College, Armour College of Engineering, Chicago, IL 60616. Offers M Arch E, M Env E, M Geoenv E, M Trans E, MAS, MCEM, MGE, MPW, MS, MSE, PhD, MS/MAS, MS/MS. Part-time and evening/weekend programs available. Postbaccalaureate distance learning degree programs offered (no on-campus study). *Faculty:* 101 full-time (15 women), 32 part-time/adjunct (4 women). *Students:* 964 full-time (227 women), 191 part-time (33 women); includes 48 minority (6 Black or African American, non-Hispanic/Latino; 29 Asian, non-Hispanic/Latino; 11

Hispanic/Latino; 1 Native Hawaiian or other Pacific Islander, non-Hispanic/Latino; 1 Two or more races, non-Hispanic/Latino), 954 international. Average age 27. 5,930 applicants, 37% accepted, 425 enrolled. In 2014, 365 master's, 36 doctorates awarded. Terminal master's awarded for partial completion of doctoral program. *Degree requirements:* For master's, comprehensive exam (for some programs), thesis (for some programs); for doctorate, comprehensive exam, thesis/dissertation. *Entrance requirements:* For master's and doctorate, GRE General Test, minimum undergraduate GPA of 3.0. Additional exam requirements/recommendations for international students: Required—TOEFL (minimum score 550 paper-based; 80 iBT); Recommended—IELTS (minimum score 5.5). *Application deadline:* For fall admission, 5/1 for domestic and international students; for spring admission, 10/15 for domestic and international students. Applications are processed on a rolling basis. Application fee: $50. Electronic applications accepted. *Expenses: Tuition:* Full-time $22,500; part-time $1250 per credit hour. *Required fees:* $30 per course. $260 per semester. One-time fee: $235. Tuition and fees vary according to course load and program. *Financial support:* Fellowships with tuition reimbursements, research assistantships with tuition reimbursements, teaching assistantships with tuition reimbursements, career-related internships or fieldwork, Federal Work-Study, institutionally sponsored loans, scholarships/grants, health care benefits, tuition waivers (full and partial), and unspecified assistantships available. Support available to part-time students. Financial award applicants required to submit FAFSA. *Unit head:* Dr. Natacha DePaola, Dean, 312-567-3009, Fax: 312-567-7961, E-mail: engineering@iit.edu. *Application contact:* Rishab Malhotra, Director, Graduate Admission, 866-472-3448, Fax: 312-567-3138, E-mail: inquiry.grad@iit.edu.
Website: http://www.iit.edu/engineering/.

Indiana State University, College of Graduate and Professional Studies, College of Technology, Terre Haute, IN 47809. Offers MS, MA/MS. *Entrance requirements:* For master's, bachelor's degree in industrial technology or related field. Additional exam requirements/recommendations for international students: Required—TOEFL. Electronic applications accepted.

Indiana University–Purdue University Fort Wayne, College of Engineering, Technology, and Computer Science, Fort Wayne, IN 46805-1499. Offers MS, MSE, Certificate. Part-time programs available. *Faculty:* 43 full-time (8 women), 1 part-time/adjunct (0 women). *Students:* 27 full-time (15 women), 60 part-time (20 women); includes 14 minority (8 Black or African American, non-Hispanic/Latino; 1 American Indian or Alaska Native, non-Hispanic/Latino; 3 Asian, non-Hispanic/Latino; 2 Hispanic/Latino), 17 international. Average age 33. 46 applicants, 100% accepted, 36 enrolled. In 2014, 56 master's awarded. *Entrance requirements:* For master's, GRE General Test, minimum GPA of 3.0. Additional exam requirements/recommendations for international students: Required—TOEFL (minimum score 550 paper-based; 79 iBT); Recommended—TWE. *Application deadline:* For fall admission, 7/15 for domestic students, 5/15 for international students; for spring admission, 12/1 for domestic students, 10/15 for international students. Applications are processed on a rolling basis. Application fee: $55 ($60 for international students). Electronic applications accepted. *Financial support:* In 2014–15, 3 research assistantships with partial tuition reimbursements (averaging $13,522 per year), 5 teaching assistantships with partial tuition reimbursements (averaging $13,522 per year) were awarded; career-related internships or fieldwork, scholarships/grants, and unspecified assistantships also available. Support available to part-time students. Financial award application deadline: 3/1; financial award applicants required to submit FAFSA. *Faculty research:* Software-defined radios, embedded system software, wireless cloud architecture. *Total annual research expenditures:* $841,333. *Unit head:* Dr. Max Yen, Dean, 260-481-6839, Fax: 260-481-5734, E-mail: yens@ipfw.edu.
Website: http://www.ipfw.edu/etcs.

Instituto Tecnologico de Santo Domingo, Graduate School, Area of Engineering, Santo Domingo, Dominican Republic. Offers construction administration (MS, Certificate); data telecommunications (M Eng, MS, Certificate); industrial engineering (M Eng, Certificate); industrial management (M Mgmt); information technology (Certificate); maintenance engineering (M Eng); occupational hazard prevention (M Mgmt); production management (Certificate); quantitative methods (Certificate); sanitary and environmental engineering (M Eng); structural engineering (M Eng); systems engineering and electronic data processing (Certificate); transportation (Certificate).

Instituto Tecnológico y de Estudios Superiores de Monterrey, Campus Ciudad Obregón, Program in Engineering, Ciudad Obregón, Mexico. Offers ME.

Instituto Tecnológico y de Estudios Superiores de Monterrey, Campus Monterrey, Graduate and Research Division, Programs in Engineering, Monterrey, Mexico. Offers applied statistics (M Eng); artificial intelligence (PhD); automation engineering (M Eng); chemical engineering (M Eng); civil engineering (M Eng); electrical engineering (M Eng); electronic engineering (M Eng); environmental engineering (M Eng); industrial engineering (M Eng, PhD); manufacturing engineering (M Eng); mechanical engineering (M Eng); systems and quality engineering (M Eng). M Eng program offered jointly with University of Waterloo; PhD in industrial engineering with Texas A&M University. Part-time and evening/weekend programs available. Terminal master's awarded for partial completion of doctoral program. *Degree requirements:* For master's, one foreign language, thesis; for doctorate, one foreign language, thesis/dissertation. *Entrance requirements:* For master's, EXADEP; for doctorate, GRE, master's degree in related field. Additional exam requirements/recommendations for international students: Required—TOEFL. *Faculty research:* Flexible manufacturing cells, materials, statistical methods, environmental prevention, control and evaluation.

Johns Hopkins University, Engineering Program for Professionals, Elkridge, MD 21075. Offers M Ch E, M Mat SE, MCE, MEE, MME, MS, MSE, Graduate Certificate, Post-Master's Certificate. Part-time and evening/weekend programs available. Electronic applications accepted.

Johns Hopkins University, G. W. C. Whiting School of Engineering, Baltimore, MD 21218-2699. Offers M Ch E, M Mat SE, MA, MEE, MME, MS, MSE, MSEM, MSSI, PhD, Certificate, Post-Master's Certificate. Terminal master's awarded for partial completion of doctoral program. *Degree requirements:* For master's, comprehensive exam (for some programs), thesis (for some programs); for doctorate, comprehensive exam, thesis/dissertation, oral exam. *Entrance requirements:* For master's, GRE General Test, letters of recommendation, transcripts; for doctorate, GRE General Test, letters of recommendation. Additional exam requirements/recommendations for international students: Required—TOEFL (minimum score 600 paper-based; 100 iBT) or IELTS (minimum score 7). Electronic applications accepted. *Faculty research:* Biomedical engineering, environmental systems and engineering, materials science and engineering, signal and image processing, structural dynamics and geomechanics.

Kansas State University, Graduate School, College of Engineering, Manhattan, KS 66506. Offers MEM, MS, MSE, PhD, Graduate Certificate. Part-time programs available. Postbaccalaureate distance learning degree programs offered (minimal on-campus study). *Faculty:* 123 full-time (20 women), 24 part-time/adjunct (4 women). *Students:* 259 full-time (75 women), 204 part-time (36 women); includes 53 minority (18 Black or African American, non-Hispanic/Latino; 1 American Indian or Alaska Native, non-Hispanic/Latino; 18 Asian, non-Hispanic/Latino; 9 Hispanic/Latino; 1 Native Hawaiian or other Pacific Islander, non-Hispanic/Latino; 6 Two or more races, non-Hispanic/Latino), 181 international. Average age 29. 614 applicants, 32% accepted, 91 enrolled. In 2014, 112 master's, 26 doctorates, 2 other advanced degrees awarded. *Degree requirements:* For doctorate, thesis/dissertation. *Entrance requirements:* For master's and doctorate, GRE. Additional exam requirements/recommendations for international students: Required—TOEFL. *Application deadline:* For fall admission, 2/1 priority date for domestic students, 1/1 priority date for international students; for spring admission, 8/1 priority date for domestic and international students. Applications are processed on a rolling basis. Application fee: $50 ($75 for international students). Electronic applications accepted. *Financial support:* In 2014–15, 126 research assistantships (averaging $16,448 per year), 83 teaching assistantships (averaging $14,697 per year) were awarded; career-related internships or fieldwork, Federal Work-Study, institutionally sponsored loans, and scholarships/grants also available. Support available to part-time students. Financial award application deadline: 3/1; financial award applicants required to submit FAFSA. *Total annual research expenditures:* $20.3 million. *Unit head:* Dr. Darren Dawson, Dean, 785-532-5590, Fax: 785-532-7810, E-mail: dmdawson@k-state.edu. *Application contact:* Maureen Lockhart, Administrative Assistant to the Dean, 785-532-5441, Fax: 785-532-7810, E-mail: maureen@k-state.edu.
Website: http://www.engg.k-state.edu/.

Kent State University, College of Applied Engineering, Sustainability and Technology, Kent, OH 44242-0001. Offers MT. Part-time programs available. Postbaccalaureate distance learning degree programs offered. *Faculty:* 19 full-time (0 women). *Students:* 14 full-time (8 women), 47 part-time (12 women); includes 5 minority (2 Black or African American, non-Hispanic/Latino; 3 Hispanic/Latino), 13 international. Average age 34. 95 applicants, 68% accepted, 38 enrolled. In 2014, 18 master's awarded. *Degree requirements:* For master's, thesis optional. *Entrance requirements:* For master's, minimum GPA of 3.0, transcript, goal statement, resume, 3 letters of recommendation. Additional exam requirements/recommendations for international students: Required—TOEFL (minimum score: paper-based 525, iBT 71), Michigan English Language Assessment Battery (minimum score of 75), IELTS (minimum score of 6.0), PTE Academic (minimum score of 48), or completion of ELS level 112 Intensive Program. *Application deadline:* For fall admission, 7/12 for domestic students, 5/15 for international students; for spring admission, 11/29 for domestic students, 10/15 for international students. Applications are processed on a rolling basis. Application fee: $45 ($70 for international students). Electronic applications accepted. *Expenses:* Tuition, state resident: full-time $8730; part-time $485 per credit hour. Tuition, nonresident: full-time $14,886; part-time $827 per credit hour. Tuition and fees vary according to campus/location and program. *Financial support:* Research assistantships with full tuition reimbursements, teaching assistantships with full tuition reimbursements, career-related internships or fieldwork, Federal Work-Study, and unspecified assistantships available. Financial award application deadline: 2/1. *Unit head:* Robert Sines, Jr., Interim Dean, 330-672-0790, E-mail: rsines@kent.edu. *Application contact:* Dr. John Duncan, Assistant Professor/Coordinator, Graduate Program, 330-672-2892, E-mail: caest@kent.edu.
Website: http://www.kent.edu/caest.

Lakehead University, Graduate Studies, Faculty of Engineering, Thunder Bay, ON P7B 5E1, Canada. Offers control engineering (M Sc Engr); electrical/computer engineering (M Sc Engr); environmental engineering (M Sc Engr). Part-time programs available. *Degree requirements:* For master's, thesis. *Entrance requirements:* For master's, bachelor's degree in chemical, electrical or mechanical engineering, minimum B average. Additional exam requirements/recommendations for international students: Required—TOEFL. *Faculty research:* Pulp and paper, adaptive/process control, robust/interactive learning control, vibration control.

Lamar University, College of Graduate Studies, College of Engineering, Beaumont, TX 77710. Offers ME, MEM, MES, MS, DE, PhD. Part-time and evening/weekend programs available. *Faculty:* 38 full-time (4 women), 2 part-time/adjunct (0 women). *Students:* 527 full-time (82 women), 115 part-time (23 women); includes 26 minority (9 Black or African American, non-Hispanic/Latino; 11 Asian, non-Hispanic/Latino; 5 Hispanic/Latino; 1 Two or more races, non-Hispanic/Latino), 593 international. Average age 24. 923 applicants, 59% accepted, 265 enrolled. In 2014, 60 master's, 14 doctorates awarded. Terminal master's awarded for partial completion of doctoral program. *Degree requirements:* For doctorate, thesis/dissertation. *Entrance requirements:* For master's and doctorate, GRE General Test. Additional exam requirements/recommendations for international students: Required—TOEFL (minimum score 550 paper-based; 79 iBT), IELTS (minimum score 6.5). *Application deadline:* For fall admission, 8/1 for domestic students, 7/1 for international students; for spring admission, 1/5 for domestic students, 12/1 for international students. Applications are processed on a rolling basis. Application fee: $25 ($50 for international students). *Expenses:* Tuition, state resident: full-time $5724; part-time $1908 per semester. Tuition, nonresident: full-time $12,240; part-time $4080 per semester. *Required fees:* $1940; $318 per credit hour. *Financial support:* In 2014–15, fellowships with partial tuition reimbursements (averaging $6,000 per year), research assistantships with partial tuition reimbursements (averaging $7,500 per year), teaching assistantships with partial tuition reimbursements (averaging $7,500 per year) were awarded; career-related internships or fieldwork, Federal Work-Study, institutionally sponsored loans, scholarships/grants, tuition waivers (full and partial), and laboratory assistantships also available. Support available to part-time students. Financial award application deadline: 4/1. *Faculty research:* Energy alternatives; process analysis, design, and control; pollution prevention. *Unit head:* Dr. Srinivas Palanki, Dean, 409-880-8784, Fax: 409-880-2197. *Application contact:* Melissa Gallien, Director, Admissions and Academic Services, 409-880-8888, Fax: 409-880-7419, E-mail: gradmissions@lamar.edu.
Website: http://engineering.lamar.edu.

Laurentian University, School of Graduate Studies and Research, School of Engineering, Sudbury, ON P3E 2C6, Canada. Offers mineral resources engineering (M Eng, MA Sc); natural resources engineering (PhD). Part-time programs available. *Faculty research:* Mining engineering, rock mechanics (tunneling, rockbursts, rock support), metallurgy (mineral processing, hydro and pyrometallurgy), simulations and remote mining, simulations and scheduling.

Lawrence Technological University, College of Engineering, Southfield, MI 48075-1058. Offers architectural engineering (MS); automotive engineering (MS); civil engineering (MA, MS, PhD); construction engineering management (MA); electrical and computer engineering (MS); engineering management (MEM); industrial engineering (MS); manufacturing systems (ME, DE); mechanical engineering (MS, DE); mechatronic systems engineering (MS). Part-time and evening/weekend programs available. *Faculty:* 24 full-time (5 women), 15 part-time/adjunct (0 women). *Students:* 16 full-time (6 women), 478 part-time (71 women); includes 295 minority (15 Black or African American, non-Hispanic/Latino; 271 Asian, non-Hispanic/Latino; 7 Hispanic/Latino; 2 Two or more races, non-Hispanic/Latino), 38 international. Average age 27. 1,786 applicants, 40% accepted, 218 enrolled. In 2014, 106 master's awarded. *Degree requirements:* For master's, thesis (for some programs). *Entrance requirements:* Additional exam requirements/recommendations for international students: Required—TOEFL (minimum score 550 paper-based; 79 iBT). *Application deadline:* For fall admission, 8/1 priority date for domestic students, 5/29 for international students; for

spring admission, 12/1 priority date for domestic students, 10/15 for international students. Applications are processed on a rolling basis. Application fee: $50. Electronic applications accepted. *Expenses: Tuition:* Full-time $14,700; part-time $1050 per credit hour. *Required fees:* $150. One-time fee: $150 part-time. *Financial support:* In 2014–15, 31 students received support, including 8 research assistantships (averaging $9,338 per year); Federal Work-Study and institutionally sponsored loans also available. Support available to part-time students. Financial award application deadline: 4/1; financial award applicants required to submit FAFSA. *Faculty research:* Advanced composite materials in bridges, strengthening existing bridges with carbon and glass fiber sheets, development of drive shafts using composite materials. *Unit head:* Dr. Nabil Grace, Dean, 248-204-2500, Fax: 248-204-2509, E-mail: engrdean@ltu.edu. *Application contact:* Jane Rohrback, Director of Admissions, 248-204-3160, Fax: 248-204-2228, E-mail: admissions@ltu.edu.
Website: http://www.ltu.edu/engineering/index.asp.

Lehigh University, P.C. Rossin College of Engineering and Applied Science, Bethlehem, PA 18015. Offers M Eng, MS, PhD, MBA/E. Part-time programs available. Postbaccalaureate distance learning degree programs offered (no on-campus study). *Faculty:* 131 full-time (20 women), 13 part-time/adjunct (3 women). *Students:* 548 full-time (121 women), 169 part-time (43 women); includes 62 minority (15 Black or African American, non-Hispanic/Latino; 29 Asian, non-Hispanic/Latino; 14 Hispanic/Latino; 4 Two or more races, non-Hispanic/Latino), 394 international. Average age 26. 2,701 applicants, 20% accepted, 182 enrolled. In 2014, 249 master's, 35 doctorates awarded. Terminal master's awarded for partial completion of doctoral program. *Degree requirements:* For master's, comprehensive exam (for some programs), thesis (for some programs); for doctorate, comprehensive exam (for some programs), thesis/dissertation. *Entrance requirements:* For master's and doctorate, GRE General Test, BS. Additional exam requirements/recommendations for international students: Required—TOEFL (minimum score 550 paper-based; 79 iBT). *Application deadline:* For fall admission, 7/15 for domestic and international students; for spring admission, 12/1 for domestic and international students. Applications are processed on a rolling basis. Application fee: $75. Electronic applications accepted. *Expenses:* Expenses: $1,380 per credit. *Financial support:* In 2014–15, 379 students received support, including 32 fellowships with full and partial tuition reimbursements available (averaging $19,920 per year), 203 research assistantships with full and partial tuition reimbursements available (averaging $26,560 per year), 82 teaching assistantships with full and partial tuition reimbursements available (averaging $20,490 per year); career-related internships or fieldwork, institutionally sponsored loans, scholarships/grants, health care benefits, tuition waivers (full and partial), and unspecified assistantships also available. Financial award application deadline: 1/15. *Faculty research:* Energy and the environment, health and healthcare, infrastructure, nanotechnology and high performance computing. *Unit head:* Dr. John P. Coulter, Associate Dean of Graduate Studies and Research, 610-758-6310, Fax: 610-758-5623, E-mail: john.coulter@lehigh.edu. *Application contact:* Brianne Lisk, Manager of Graduate Programs, 610-758-6310, Fax: 610-758-5623, E-mail: brie.lisk@lehigh.edu.
Website: http://www.lehigh.edu/engineering/.

LeTourneau University, Graduate Programs, Longview, TX 75607-7001. Offers business administration (MBA); counseling (MA); curriculum and instruction (M Ed); education administration (M Ed); engineering (ME, MS); engineering management (MEM); health care administration (MS); marriage and family therapy (MA); psychology (MA); strategic leadership (MSL); teacher leadership (M Ed); teaching and learning (M Ed). Part-time programs available. Postbaccalaureate distance learning degree programs offered (no on-campus study). *Faculty:* 14 full-time (4 women), 41 part-time/adjunct (18 women). *Students:* 58 full-time (37 women), 359 part-time (289 women); includes 140 minority (78 Black or African American, non-Hispanic/Latino; 2 American Indian or Alaska Native, non-Hispanic/Latino; 4 Asian, non-Hispanic/Latino; 40 Hispanic/Latino; 16 Two or more races, non-Hispanic/Latino), 11 international. Average age 38. 199 applicants, 73% accepted, 130 enrolled. In 2014, 139 master's awarded. *Degree requirements:* For master's, thesis (for some programs). *Entrance requirements:* For master's, GRE (for engineering and psychology programs). Additional exam requirements/recommendations for international students: Required—TOEFL. *Application deadline:* For fall admission, 8/22 for domestic students, 8/29 for international students; for winter admission, 10/10 for domestic students; for spring admission, 1/2 for domestic students, 1/10 for international students; for summer admission, 5/1 for domestic and international students. Applications are processed on a rolling basis. Electronic applications accepted. Application fee is waived when completed online. *Financial support:* In 2014–15, 11 students received support, including 16 research assistantships (averaging $11,621 per year); institutionally sponsored loans and unspecified assistantships also available. Financial award applicants required to submit FAFSA. *Application contact:* Chris Fontaine, Assistant Vice President for Global Campus Admissions, 903-233-4312, E-mail: chrisfontaine@letu.edu.
Website: http://www.letu.edu.

Liberty University, School of Engineering and Computational Sciences, Lynchburg, VA 24515. Offers cyber security (MS). Part-time programs available. Postbaccalaureate distance learning degree programs offered (no on-campus study). *Students:* 26 full-time (4 women), 44 part-time (10 women); includes 18 minority (14 Black or African American, non-Hispanic/Latino; 1 American Indian or Alaska Native, non-Hispanic/Latino; 1 Asian, non-Hispanic/Latino; 2 Two or more races, non-Hispanic/Latino). Average age 37. 258 applicants, 41% accepted, 58 enrolled. *Entrance requirements:* For master's, baccalaureate degree or its equivalent in computer science, information technology, or other technical degree, or baccalaureate degree in any field along with significant technical work experience. *Application deadline:* Applications are processed on a rolling basis. Application fee: $50. Electronic applications accepted. *Unit head:* David Donahoo, Dean, 434-592-7150. *Application contact:* Jay Bridge, Director of Admissions, 800-424-9595, Fax: 800-628-7977, E-mail: gradadmissions@liberty.edu.

Louisiana State University and Agricultural & Mechanical College, Graduate School, College of Engineering, Department of Biological and Agricultural Engineering, Baton Rouge, LA 70803. Offers biological and agricultural engineering (MSBAE); engineering science (MS, PhD). Part-time programs available. *Faculty:* 12 full-time (3 women). *Students:* 12 full-time (3 women), 2 part-time (0 women); includes 1 minority (Black or African American, non-Hispanic/Latino), 5 international. Average age 25. 8 applicants, 38% accepted, 3 enrolled. In 2014, 7 master's awarded. Terminal master's awarded for partial completion of doctoral program. *Degree requirements:* For master's, thesis; for doctorate, thesis/dissertation. *Entrance requirements:* For master's and doctorate, GRE General Test, minimum GPA of 3.0. Additional exam requirements/recommendations for international students: Required—TOEFL (minimum score 550 paper-based; 79 IBT), IELTS (minimum score 6.5), or PTE (minimum score 59). *Application deadline:* For fall admission, 1/1 priority date for domestic students, 5/15 for international students; for spring admission, 10/15 for domestic and international students; for summer admission, 5/15 for domestic and international students. Applications are processed on a rolling basis. Application fee: $50 ($70 for international students). Electronic applications accepted. *Financial support:* In 2014–15, 13 students received support, including 1 fellowship (averaging $18,139 per year), 8 research assistantships with partial tuition reimbursements available (averaging $18,125 per year); teaching assistantships with partial tuition reimbursements available, career-related internships or fieldwork, Federal Work-Study, institutionally sponsored loans, scholarships/grants, health care benefits, and unspecified assistantships also available. Financial award application deadline: 7/1; financial award applicants required to submit FAFSA. *Faculty research:* Bioenergy, bioprocess engineering, cellular and molecular engineering, drug delivery using nanotechnology, environmental engineering. *Total annual research expenditures:* $229,597. *Unit head:* Dr. David Constant, Head, 225-578-3153, Fax: 225-578-3492, E-mail: dconstant@agcenter.lsu.edu. *Application contact:* Dr. Steven Hall, Graduate Coordinator, 225-578-1049, Fax: 225-578-3492, E-mail: sghall@agcenter.lsu.edu.
Website: http://www.bae.lsu.edu/.

Louisiana State University and Agricultural & Mechanical College, Graduate School, College of Engineering, Interdepartmental Program in Engineering Science, Baton Rouge, LA 70803. Offers engineering science (MSES, PhD). Part-time and evening/weekend programs available. *Students:* 51 full-time (23 women), 13 part-time (2 women); includes 7 minority (6 Black or African American, non-Hispanic/Latino; 1 Hispanic/Latino), 43 international. Average age 31. 35 applicants, 57% accepted, 8 enrolled. In 2014, 3 master's, 2 doctorates awarded. Terminal master's awarded for partial completion of doctoral program. *Degree requirements:* For master's, thesis optional; for doctorate, thesis/dissertation. *Entrance requirements:* For master's and doctorate, GRE General Test, minimum GPA of 3.0. Additional exam requirements/recommendations for international students: Required—TOEFL (minimum score 550 paper-based; 79 IBT), IELTS (minimum score 6.5), or PTE (minimum score 59). *Application deadline:* For fall admission, 1/1 priority date for domestic students, 5/15 for international students; for spring admission, 10/15 for domestic and international students; for summer admission, 5/15 for domestic and international students. Applications are processed on a rolling basis. Application fee: $50 ($70 for international students). *Financial support:* In 2014–15, 56 students received support, including 5 fellowships (averaging $24,530 per year), 29 research assistantships with full and partial tuition reimbursements available (averaging $18,097 per year), 12 teaching assistantships with full and partial tuition reimbursements available (averaging $12,358 per year); Federal Work-Study, scholarships/grants, health care benefits, tuition waivers (full and partial), and unspecified assistantships also available. Support available to part-time students. Financial award application deadline: 3/1; financial award applicants required to submit FAFSA. *Faculty research:* Environmental engineering, transportation engineering, enhanced oil recovery, microelectrical-mechanical systems, manufacturing. *Total annual research expenditures:* $671,168. *Unit head:* Dr. Warren Waggenspack, Associate Dean for Academic Programs, 225-578-5731, Fax: 225-578-4845, E-mail: mewagg@me.lsu.edu. *Application contact:* Vicki Hannan, Coordinator, 225-578-5704, Fax: 225-578-4548, E-mail: eghann@eng.lsu.edu.
Website: http://www.eng.lsu.edu/academics/gradprogs/engrsci/overview.

Louisiana Tech University, Graduate School, College of Engineering and Science, Ruston, LA 71272. Offers MS, PhD. Part-time programs available. Terminal master's awarded for partial completion of doctoral program. *Degree requirements:* For doctorate, thesis/dissertation. *Entrance requirements:* For master's, GRE General Test, minimum GPA of 3.0 in last 60 hours. Additional exam requirements/recommendations for international students: Required—TOEFL. *Faculty research:* Trenchless technology, micromanufacturing, radionuclide transport, microbial liquefaction, hazardous waste treatment.

Manhattan College, Graduate Programs, School of Engineering, Riverdale, NY 10471. Offers chemical engineering (MS), including chemical engineering, cosmetic engineering; civil engineering (MS); computer engineering (MS); electrical engineering (MS); environmental engineering (ME, MS); mechanical engineering (MS). Part-time and evening/weekend programs available. *Faculty:* 28 full-time (6 women), 20 part-time/adjunct (4 women). *Students:* 76 full-time (18 women), 126 part-time (32 women); includes 17 minority (11 Asian, non-Hispanic/Latino; 4 Hispanic/Latino; 2 Two or more races, non-Hispanic/Latino). Average age 24. 127 applicants, 80% accepted, 69 enrolled. In 2014, 67 master's awarded. *Degree requirements:* For master's, thesis or alternative. *Entrance requirements:* For master's, GRE (recommended), minimum GPA of 3.0. Additional exam requirements/recommendations for international students: Required—TOEFL (minimum score 550 paper-based; 80 iBT), IELTS (minimum score 6). *Application deadline:* For fall admission, 8/10 priority date for domestic students, 8/10 for international students; for spring admission, 1/7 for domestic and international students. Applications are processed on a rolling basis. Application fee: $60. *Expenses:* Expenses: Contact institution. *Financial support:* In 2014–15, 31 students received support, including 3 fellowships with full tuition reimbursements available (averaging $15,000 per year), 6 research assistantships with full tuition reimbursements available (averaging $18,000 per year), 25 teaching assistantships with partial tuition reimbursements available (averaging $7,700 per year); career-related internships or fieldwork, Federal Work-Study, scholarships/grants, unspecified assistantships, and laboratory assistantships also available. Support available to part-time students. Financial award application deadline: 2/1. *Faculty research:* Environmental/water, nucleation, environmental/management, heat transfer. *Total annual research expenditures:* $400,000. *Unit head:* Dr. Tim J. Ward, Dean, 718-862-7281, Fax: 718-862-8015, E-mail: deanengr@manhattan.edu. *Application contact:* Sheila M. Halpin, Information Contact, 718-862-7281, Fax: 718-862-8015, E-mail: deanengr@manhattan.edu.
Website: http://www.manhattan.edu/academics/engineering/.

Marquette University, Graduate School, Opus College of Engineering, Milwaukee, WI 53201-1881. Offers ME, MS, MSEM, PhD, Certificate. Part-time and evening/weekend programs available. *Degree requirements:* For doctorate, thesis/dissertation. *Entrance requirements:* For master's, minimum GPA of 3.0; for doctorate, GRE General Test, minimum GPA of 3.0. Additional exam requirements/recommendations for international students: Required—TOEFL (minimum score 530 paper-based). Electronic applications accepted. *Faculty research:* Urban watershed management, microsensors for environmental pollutants, orthopedic rehabilitation engineering, telemedicine, ergonomics.

Marshall University, Academic Affairs Division, College of Information Technology and Engineering, Huntington, WV 25755. Offers MS, MSE. Part-time and evening/weekend programs available. *Faculty:* 12 full-time (1 woman), 7 part-time/adjunct (1 woman). *Students:* 81 full-time (16 women), 66 part-time (12 women); includes 6 minority (all Black or African American, non-Hispanic/Latino), 45 international. Average age 30. In 2014, 44 master's awarded. *Degree requirements:* For master's, final project, oral exam. Application fee: $40. *Expenses:* Expenses: Contact institution. *Financial support:* Fellowships and tuition waivers (full) available. Support available to part-time students. Financial award application deadline: 8/1; financial award applicants required to submit FAFSA. *Unit head:* Dr. Wael Zatar, Interim Dean, 304-696-6043, E-mail: zatar@marshall.edu. *Application contact:* Information Contact, 304-746-1900, Fax: 304-746-1902, E-mail: services@marshall.edu.
Website: http://www.marshall.edu/cite/.

Massachusetts Institute of Technology, School of Engineering, Cambridge, MA 02139. Offers M Eng, SM, PhD, Sc D, CE, EAA, ECS, EE, Mat E, Mech E, NE, Naval E,

SM/MBA. *Faculty:* 376 full-time (68 women), 2 part-time/adjunct (0 women). *Students:* 3,088 full-time (868 women), 55 part-time (16 women); includes 651 minority (40 Black or African American, non-Hispanic/Latino; 5 American Indian or Alaska Native, non-Hispanic/Latino; 388 Asian, non-Hispanic/Latino; 143 Hispanic/Latino; 75 Two or more races, non-Hispanic/Latino), 1,347 international. Average age 27. 8,692 applicants, 18% accepted, 1081 enrolled. In 2014, 760 master's, 355 doctorates, 14 other advanced degrees awarded. Terminal master's awarded for partial completion of doctoral program. *Degree requirements:* For master's, thesis (for some programs); for doctorate, comprehensive exam, thesis/dissertation; for other advanced degree, thesis. Application fee: $75. Electronic applications accepted. *Expenses: Tuition:* Full-time $44,720; part-time $699 per unit. *Required fees:* $296. *Financial support:* In 2014–15, 2,582 students received support, including 655 fellowships (averaging $36,300 per year), 1,686 research assistantships (averaging $34,100 per year), 284 teaching assistantships (averaging $35,200 per year); Federal Work-Study, institutionally sponsored loans, scholarships/grants, health care benefits, and unspecified assistantships also available. Financial award application deadline: 4/15; financial award applicants required to submit FAFSA. *Total annual research expenditures:* $391.2 million. *Unit head:* Prof. Ian A. Waitz, Dean, 617-253-3291, Fax: 617-253-8549. *Application contact:* Graduate Admissions, E-mail: mitgrad@mit.edu.
Website: http://engineering.mit.edu/.

McGill University, Faculty of Graduate and Postdoctoral Studies, Faculty of Engineering, Montréal, QC H3A 2T5, Canada. Offers M Arch I, M Arch II, M Eng, M Sc, MMM, MUP, PhD, Diploma.

McGill University, Faculty of Graduate and Postdoctoral Studies, Faculty of Science, Department of Mathematics and Statistics, Montréal, QC H3A 2T5, Canada. Offers computational science and engineering (M Sc); mathematics and statistics (M Sc, MA, PhD), including applied mathematics (M Sc, MA), pure mathematics (M Sc, MA), statistics (M Sc, MA).

McMaster University, School of Graduate Studies, Faculty of Engineering, Hamilton, ON L8S 4M2, Canada. Offers M Eng, M Sc, MA Sc, PhD. Part-time programs available. *Degree requirements:* For doctorate, comprehensive exam, thesis/dissertation. *Entrance requirements:* Additional exam requirements/recommendations for international students: Required—TOEFL (minimum score 550 paper-based). *Faculty research:* Computer process control, water resources engineering, elasticity, flow induced vibrations, microelectronics.

McNeese State University, Doré School of Graduate Studies, College of Engineering and Engineering Technology, Lake Charles, LA 70609. Offers M Eng, Graduate Certificate, Postbaccalaureate Certificate. Part-time and evening/weekend programs available. *Degree requirements:* For master's, thesis or alternative. *Entrance requirements:* For master's, GRE, minimum undergraduate GPA of 3.0. Additional exam requirements/recommendations for international students: Required—TOEFL (minimum score 560 paper-based; 83 iBT).

Memorial University of Newfoundland, School of Graduate Studies, Faculty of Engineering and Applied Science, St. John's, NL A1C 5S7, Canada. Offers civil engineering (M Eng, PhD); electrical and computer engineering (M Eng, PhD); mechanical engineering (M Eng, PhD); ocean and naval architecture engineering (M Eng, PhD). Part-time programs available. *Degree requirements:* For master's, thesis; for doctorate, comprehensive exam, thesis/dissertation, oral thesis defense. *Entrance requirements:* For master's, 2nd class degree; for doctorate, master's degree in engineering. Electronic applications accepted. *Faculty research:* Engineering analysis, environmental and hydrotechnical studies, manufacturing and robotics, mechanics, structures and materials.

Mercer University, Graduate Studies, Macon Campus, School of Engineering, Macon, GA 31207. Offers biomedical engineering (MSE); computer engineering (MSE); electrical engineering (MSE); engineering management (MSE); environmental engineering (MSE); environmental systems (MS); mechanical engineering (MSE); software engineering (MSE); software systems (MS); technical communications management (MS); technical management (MS). Part-time and evening/weekend programs available. Postbaccalaureate distance learning degree programs offered (no on-campus study). *Faculty:* 20 full-time (6 women), 2 part-time/adjunct (0 women). *Students:* 10 full-time (4 women), 75 part-time (16 women); includes 10 minority (5 Black or African American, non-Hispanic/Latino; 4 Asian, non-Hispanic/Latino; 1 Hispanic/Latino), 4 international. Average age 42. In 2014, 70 master's awarded. *Degree requirements:* For master's, thesis or alternative. *Entrance requirements:* For master's, minimum undergraduate GPA of 3.0. Additional exam requirements/recommendations for international students: Required—TOEFL (minimum score 550 paper-based; 80 iBT). *Application deadline:* For fall admission, 4/1 priority date for domestic and international students; for spring admission, 11/1 priority date for domestic and international students. Applications are processed on a rolling basis. Application fee: $75. *Expenses:* Expenses: Contact institution. *Financial support:* Federal Work-Study available. *Unit head:* Dr. Wade H. Shaw, Dean, 478-301-2459, Fax: 478-301-5593, E-mail: shaw_wh@mercer.edu. *Application contact:* Dr. Richard O. Mines, Program Director, 478-301-2347, Fax: 478-301-5433, E-mail: mines_ro@mercer.edu.
Website: http://engineering.mercer.edu/.

Merrimack College, School of Science and Engineering, North Andover, MA 01845-5800. Offers mechanical engineering (MS), including engineering management. Part-time programs available. *Faculty:* 4 full-time (0 women), 1 part-time/adjunct (0 women). *Students:* 13 full-time (3 women), 3 part-time (0 women); includes 1 minority (Two or more races, non-Hispanic/Latino), 1 international. Average age 27. 22 applicants, 59% accepted, 8 enrolled. In 2014, 5 master's awarded. *Degree requirements:* For master's, variable foreign language requirement, comprehensive exam, thesis optional. *Entrance requirements:* For master's, official college transcripts, resume, personal statement, 2 recommendations. Additional exam requirements/recommendations for international students: Required—TOEFL (minimum score 84 iBT), IELTS (minimum score 6.5), PTE (minimum score 56). *Application deadline:* For fall admission, 8/15 for domestic and international students; for winter admission, 12/1 for domestic students, 11/15 for international students; for spring admission, 1/10 for domestic and international students. Applications are processed on a rolling basis. Application fee: $0. Electronic applications accepted. *Expenses:* Expenses: Contact institution. *Financial support:* Career-related internships or fieldwork, scholarships/grants, and health care benefits available. Support available to part-time students. Financial award application deadline: 5/1; financial award applicants required to submit FAFSA. *Application contact:* Rachael Tampone, Graduate Admission Counselor, 978-837-5196, E-mail: tamponer@merrimack.edu.
Website: http://www.merrimack.edu/academics/graduate/engineering/.

Miami University, College of Engineering and Computing, Oxford, OH 45056. Offers MCS, MS. *Expenses:* Tuition, state resident: full-time $12,887; part-time $537 per credit hour. Tuition, nonresident: full-time $28,449; part-time $1186 per credit hour. *Required fees:* $530; $24 per credit hour. $30 per quarter. Part-time tuition and fees vary according to course load and program. *Unit head:* Dr. Marek Dollar, Dean, 513-529-

0700, E-mail: cec@miamioh.edu. *Application contact:* Graduate Admission Coordinator, 513-529-3734, E-mail: applygrad@miamioh.edu.
Website: http://miamioh.edu/cec/.

Michigan State University, The Graduate School, College of Engineering, East Lansing, MI 48824. Offers MS, PhD. Part-time programs available. Electronic applications accepted.

Michigan Technological University, Graduate School, College of Engineering, Houghton, MI 49931. Offers M Eng, MS, PhD, Graduate Certificate. Part-time programs available. Postbaccalaureate distance learning degree programs offered (no on-campus study). *Faculty:* 205 full-time, 100 part-time/adjunct. *Students:* 717 full-time (167 women), 196 part-time (38 women); includes 44 minority (12 Black or African American, non-Hispanic/Latino; 11 Asian, non-Hispanic/Latino; 14 Hispanic/Latino; 1 Native Hawaiian or other Pacific Islander, non-Hispanic/Latino; 6 Two or more races, non-Hispanic/Latino), 618 international. Average age 27. 3,674 applicants, 32% accepted, 275 enrolled. In 2014, 238 master's, 42 doctorates, 29 other advanced degrees awarded. Terminal master's awarded for partial completion of doctoral program. *Degree requirements:* For master's, comprehensive exam (for some programs), thesis (for some programs); for doctorate, comprehensive exam, thesis/dissertation. *Entrance requirements:* For master's and doctorate, GRE, statement of purpose, official transcripts, 2-3 letters of recommendation; for Graduate Certificate, statement of purpose, official transcripts. Additional exam requirements/recommendations for international students: Required—TOEFL or IELTS. *Application deadline:* Applications are processed on a rolling basis. Electronic applications accepted. *Expenses:* Tuition, state resident: full-time $14,769; part-time $820.50 per credit. Tuition, nonresident: full-time $14,769; part-time $820.50 per credit. *Required fees:* $248; $248 per year. Tuition and fees vary according to course load and program. *Financial support:* In 2014–15, 560 students received support, including 44 fellowships with full and partial tuition reimbursements available (averaging $13,824 per year), 136 research assistantships with full and partial tuition reimbursements available (averaging $13,824 per year), 80 teaching assistantships with full and partial tuition reimbursements available (averaging $13,824 per year); career-related internships or fieldwork, Federal Work-Study, scholarships/grants, health care benefits, unspecified assistantships, and cooperative program also available. Financial award applicants required to submit FAFSA. *Faculty research:* Engineering, sustainability, energy systems, transportation, health technologies. *Total annual research expenditures:* $12.9 million. *Unit head:* Dr. Wayne Pennington, Dean, 906-487-2005, Fax: 906-487-2782, E-mail: wayne@mtu.edu. *Application contact:* Carol T. Wingerson, Administrative Aide, 906-487-2328, Fax: 906-487-2284, E-mail: gradadms@mtu.edu.
Website: http://www.mtu.edu/engineering/.

Milwaukee School of Engineering, Department of Electrical Engineering and Computer Science, Program in Engineering, Milwaukee, WI 53202-3109. Offers MS. Part-time and evening/weekend programs available. *Faculty:* 1 full-time (0 women), 7 part-time/adjunct (3 women). *Students:* 18 full-time (3 women), 30 part-time (3 women); includes 3 minority (1 Black or African American, non-Hispanic/Latino; 2 Asian, non-Hispanic/Latino), 18 international. Average age 28. 41 applicants, 44% accepted, 15 enrolled. In 2014, 14 master's awarded. *Degree requirements:* For master's, thesis, design project or capstone. *Entrance requirements:* For master's, GRE General Test or GMAT if undergraduate GPA less than 2.8, BS in engineering, 2 letters of recommendation. Additional exam requirements/recommendations for international students: Required—TOEFL (minimum score 79 iBT), IELTS (minimum score 6.5). *Application deadline:* Applications are processed on a rolling basis. Application fee: $0. Electronic applications accepted. *Expenses: Tuition:* Part-time $732 per credit. *Financial support:* In 2014–15, 10 students received support, including 3 research assistantships (averaging $8,043 per year); career-related internships or fieldwork, institutionally sponsored loans, scholarships/grants, and tuition waivers (partial) also available. Financial award application deadline: 3/15; financial award applicants required to submit FAFSA. *Faculty research:* Microprocessors, materials, thermodynamics, artificial intelligence, fluid power/hydraulics. *Unit head:* Dr. Subha Kumpaty, Director, 414-277-7466, Fax: 414-277-2222, E-mail: kumpaty@msoe.edu. *Application contact:* Ian Dahlinghaus, Graduate Admissions Counselor, 414-277-7208, E-mail: dahlinghaus@msoe.edu.
Website: http://www.msoe.edu/community/academics/engineering/page/1277/mse overview.

See Display on next page and Close-Up on page 83.

Mississippi State University, Bagley College of Engineering, Mississippi State, MS 39762. Offers M Eng, MS, PhD. Part-time programs available. Postbaccalaureate distance learning degree programs offered (no on-campus study). *Faculty:* 118 full-time (15 women), 9 part-time/adjunct (2 women). *Students:* 337 full-time (72 women), 251 part-time (54 women); includes 99 minority (35 Black or African American, non-Hispanic/Latino; 24 Asian, non-Hispanic/Latino; 32 Hispanic/Latino; 1 Native Hawaiian or other Pacific Islander, non-Hispanic/Latino; 7 Two or more races, non-Hispanic/Latino), 194 international. Average age 31. 698 applicants, 38% accepted, 137 enrolled. In 2014, 98 master's, 42 doctorates awarded. *Degree requirements:* For master's, comprehensive exam (for some programs), thesis; for doctorate, comprehensive exam (for some programs), thesis/dissertation. *Entrance requirements:* For master's, GRE, minimum GPA of 2.75; for doctorate, GRE. Additional exam requirements/recommendations for international students: Required—TOEFL (minimum score 477 paper-based; 53 iBT); Recommended—IELTS (minimum score 4.5). *Application deadline:* For fall admission, 7/1 for domestic students, 5/1 for international students; for spring admission, 11/1 for domestic students, 9/1 for international students. Applications are processed on a rolling basis. Application fee: $60. Electronic applications accepted. *Expenses:* Tuition, state resident: full-time $7140; part-time $783 per credit hour. Tuition, nonresident: full-time $18,478; part-time $2043 per credit hour. *Financial support:* In 2014–15, 92 research assistantships with full tuition reimbursements (averaging $15,282 per year), 20 teaching assistantships with full tuition reimbursements (averaging $8,980 per year) were awarded; Federal Work-Study, institutionally sponsored loans, scholarships/grants, and unspecified assistantships also available. Financial award application deadline: 4/1; financial award applicants required to submit FAFSA. *Faculty research:* Fluid dynamics, combustion, composite materials, computer design, high-voltage phenomena. *Total annual research expenditures:* $37.6 million. *Unit head:* Dr. Jason Keith, Interim Dean, 662-325-2270, Fax: 662-325-8573, E-mail: rburrell@bagley.msstate.edu. *Application contact:* Rita Burrell, Manager, Graduate and Distance Education, 662-325-5923, Fax 662-325-8573, E-mail: rburrell@bagley.msstate.edu.
Website: http://www.engr.msstate.edu/.

Missouri University of Science and Technology, Graduate School, School of Engineering, Rolla, MO 65409. Offers M Eng, MS, DE, PhD. Part-time and evening/weekend programs available. Electronic applications accepted.

Missouri Western State University, Program in Applied Science, St. Joseph, MO 64507-2294. Offers chemistry (MAS); engineering technology management (MAS); human factors and usability testing (MAS); industrial life science (MAS); information technology management (MAS); sport and fitness management (MAS). Part-time programs available. *Students:* 42 full-time (14 women), 34 part-time (10 women);

includes 6 minority (5 Black or African American, non-Hispanic/Latino; 1 Asian, non-Hispanic/Latino), 25 international. Average age 28. 40 applicants, 100% accepted, 26 enrolled. In 2014, 16 master's awarded. *Entrance requirements:* Additional exam requirements/recommendations for international students: Recommended—TOEFL (minimum score 70 iBT), IELTS (minimum score 6). *Application deadline:* For fall admission, 7/15 for domestic and international students; for spring admission, 11/1 for domestic students, 10/15 for international students; for summer admission, 4/29 for domestic students. Applications are processed on a rolling basis. Application fee: $45 ($50 for international students). Electronic applications accepted. *Expenses:* Tuition, state resident: full-time $5506; part-time $305.91 per credit hour. Tuition, nonresident: full-time $10,075; part-time $559.71 per credit hour. *Required fees:* $504; $99 per credit hour. $176 per semester. Tuition and fees vary according to course load and program. *Financial support:* Scholarships/grants and unspecified assistantships available. Support available to part-time students. *Unit head:* Dr. Benjamin D. Caldwell, Dean of the Graduate School, 816-271-4394, Fax: 816-271-4525, E-mail: graduate@missouriwestern.edu.

Montana State University, The Graduate School, College of Engineering, Department of Chemical and Biological Engineering, Bozeman, MT 59717. Offers chemical engineering (MS); engineering (PhD), including chemical engineering option, environmental engineering option; environmental engineering (MS). Part-time programs available. *Degree requirements:* For master's, comprehensive exam, thesis (for some programs); for doctorate, comprehensive exam, thesis/dissertation. *Entrance requirements:* For master's and doctorate, GRE General Test. Additional exam requirements/recommendations for international students: Required—TOEFL (minimum score 550 paper-based). Electronic applications accepted. *Faculty research:* Biofuels, extremophilic bioprocessing, and situ biocatalyzed heavy metal transformations; metabolic network analysis and engineering; magnetic resonance microscopy; modeling of biological systems; the development of protective coatings on planar solid oxide fuel cell (SOFC) metallic interconnects; characterizing corrosion mechanisms of materials in precisely-controlled exposures; testing materials in poly-crystalline silicon production environments; environmental biotechnology and bioremediation.

Montana State University, The Graduate School, College of Engineering, Department of Civil Engineering, Bozeman, MT 59717. Offers civil engineering (MS); construction engineering management (MCEM); engineering (PhD), including applied mechanics option, civil engineering option. Part-time programs available. *Degree requirements:* For master's, comprehensive exam, thesis (for some programs); for doctorate, comprehensive exam, thesis/dissertation. *Entrance requirements:* For master's and doctorate, GRE General Test. Additional exam requirements/recommendations for international students: Required—TOEFL (minimum score 550 paper-based). Electronic applications accepted. *Faculty research:* Snow and ice mechanics, biofilm engineering, transportation, structural and geo materials, water resources.

Montana State University, The Graduate School, College of Engineering, Department of Mechanical and Industrial Engineering, Bozeman, MT 59717. Offers engineering (PhD), including industrial engineering, mechanical engineering; industrial and management engineering (MS); mechanical engineering (MS). Part-time programs available. *Degree requirements:* For master's, comprehensive exam, thesis, oral exams; for doctorate, comprehensive exam, thesis/dissertation, qualifying exam. *Entrance requirements:* For master's, GRE, official transcript, minimum GPA of 3.0, demonstrated potential for success, statement of goals, three letters of recommendation, proof of funds affidavit; for doctorate, minimum undergraduate GPA of 3.0, 3.2 graduate; three letters of recommendation; statement of objectives. Additional exam requirements/recommendations for international students: Required—TOEFL or IELTS. Electronic applications accepted. *Faculty research:* Human factors engineering, energy, design and manufacture, systems modeling, materials and structures, measurement systems.

Montana Tech of The University of Montana, Graduate School, Department of General Engineering, Butte, MT 59701-8997. Offers MS. Part-time programs available. *Degree requirements:* For master's, comprehensive exam (for some programs), thesis optional. *Entrance requirements:* For master's, minimum GPA of 3.0. Additional exam requirements/recommendations for international students: Required—TOEFL (minimum score 525 paper-based; 71 iBT). Electronic applications accepted. *Expenses:* Tuition, state resident: full-time $5802; part-time $241 per credit. Tuition, nonresident: full-time $15,895; part-time $662 per credit. *Required fees:* $1516; $414 per credit. $207 per semester. One-time fee: $30. *Faculty research:* Wind energy and power controls, robotics, concurrent engineering, remotely piloted aircraft, composite materials.

Morgan State University, School of Graduate Studies, Clarence M. Mitchell, Jr. School of Engineering, Baltimore, MD 21251. Offers civil engineering (M Eng, D Eng); electrical and computer engineering (M Eng, MS, D Eng); industrial and systems engineering (M Eng, D Eng); transportation (MS). Part-time and evening/weekend programs available. *Degree requirements:* For master's, thesis, comprehensive exam or equivalent; for doctorate, thesis/dissertation, comprehensive exam or equivalent. *Entrance requirements:* For master's, GRE, minimum undergraduate GPA of 2.5; for doctorate, GRE, minimum GPA of 3.0. Additional exam requirements/recommendations for international students: Required—TOEFL (minimum score 550 paper-based).

New Jersey Institute of Technology, Newark College of Engineering, Newark, NJ 07102. Offers biomedical engineering (MS, PhD); chemical engineering (MS, PhD); computer engineering (MS, PhD); electrical engineering (MS, PhD); engineering management (MS); healthcare systems management (MS); industrial engineering (MS, PhD); Internet engineering (MS); manufacturing engineering (MS); mechanical engineering (MS, PhD); occupational safety and health engineering (MS); pharmaceutical bioprocessing (MS); pharmaceutical engineering (MS); pharmaceutical systems management (MS); power and energy systems (MS); telecommunications (MS); transportation (MS, PhD). Part-time and evening/weekend programs available. Terminal master's awarded for partial completion of doctoral program. *Degree requirements:* For master's, thesis optional; for doctorate, thesis/dissertation. *Entrance requirements:* For master's, GRE General Test; for doctorate, GRE General Test, minimum graduate GPA of 3.5. Additional exam requirements/recommendations for international students: Required—TOEFL (minimum score 550 paper-based; 79 iBT). Electronic applications accepted.

New Mexico State University, College of Engineering, Las Cruces, NM 88003-8001. Offers MS Ch E, MS Env E, MSAE, MSCE, MSEE, MSIE, MSME, PhD, Graduate Certificate. Part-time programs available. *Faculty:* 64 full-time (10 women), 2 part-time/adjunct (0 women). *Students:* 272 full-time (58 women), 187 part-time (32 women); includes 123 minority (12 Black or African American, non-Hispanic/Latino; 6 American Indian or Alaska Native, non-Hispanic/Latino; 10 Asian, non-Hispanic/Latino; 88 Hispanic/Latino; 7 Two or more races, non-Hispanic/Latino), 206 international. Average age 30. 474 applicants, 49% accepted, 94 enrolled. In 2014, 121 master's, 20 doctorates, 5 other advanced degrees awarded. *Degree requirements:* For doctorate, thesis/dissertation. *Entrance requirements:* Additional exam requirements/recommendations for international students: Required—TOEFL (minimum score 550 paper-based; 79 iBT), IELTS (minimum score 6.5). *Application deadline:* For fall admission, 7/1 priority date for domestic students; for spring admission, 11/1 for domestic students. Applications are processed on a rolling basis. Application fee: $40 ($50 for international students). Electronic applications accepted. *Expenses:* Tuition,

state resident: full-time $3969; part-time $220.50 per credit hour. Tuition, nonresident: full-time $13,838; part-time $768.80 per credit hour. *Required fees:* $853; $47.40 per credit hour. *Financial support:* In 2014–15, 259 students received support, including 11 fellowships (averaging $2,908 per year), 88 research assistantships (averaging $13,838 per year), 95 teaching assistantships (averaging $11,806 per year); career-related internships or fieldwork, Federal Work-Study, scholarships/grants, traineeships, health care benefits, and unspecified assistantships also available. Support available to part-time students. Financial award application deadline: 3/1. *Faculty research:* Structures and nondestructive testing, environmental science and engineering, telecommunication theory and systems, manufacturing methods and systems, high performance computing and software engineering. *Total annual research expenditures:* $7.2 million. *Unit head:* Dr. Ricardo Jacquez, Dean, 575-646-7234, Fax: 575-646-3549, E-mail: rjaquez@nmsu.edu. *Application contact:* Graduate Admissions, 575-646-3121, E-mail: admissions@nmsu.edu.
Website: http://engr.nmsu.edu/.

New York Institute of Technology, School of Engineering and Computing Sciences, Old Westbury, NY 11568-8000. Offers MS, Advanced Certificate. Part-time and evening/weekend programs available. Postbaccalaureate distance learning degree programs offered (minimal on-campus study). *Degree requirements:* For master's, thesis. *Entrance requirements:* Additional exam requirements/recommendations for international students: Required—TOEFL (minimum score 550 paper-based; 79 iBT), IELTS (minimum score 6). Electronic applications accepted. *Faculty research:* Entrepreneurship and technology innovation center, electric vehicle support equipment, image procession, multimedia CD-ROMs, prototype modules of digital television application environment, computer networks, control theory, light waves and optics, robotics, signal processing, development and testing of methodology to assess health risks and environmental impacts from separate sanitary sewage, introduction of technology innovation.

New York University, Polytechnic School of Engineering, Brooklyn, NY 11201. Offers MS, PhD, Advanced Certificate, Certificate, Graduate Certificate. *Faculty:* 117 full-time (19 women), 141 part-time/adjunct (15 women). *Students:* 2,130 full-time (580 women), 608 part-time (165 women); includes 310 minority (54 Black or African American, non-Hispanic/Latino; 1 American Indian or Alaska Native, non-Hispanic/Latino; 174 Asian, non-Hispanic/Latino; 66 Hispanic/Latino; 15 Two or more races, non-Hispanic/Latino), 2,051 international. Average age 27. 7,379 applicants, 36% accepted, 1151 enrolled. In 2014, 1,036 master's, 47 doctorates awarded. *Entrance requirements:* Additional exam requirements/recommendations for international students: Required—TOEFL (minimum score 550 paper-based; 80 iBT). *Application deadline:* For fall admission, 2/15 for domestic and international students; for spring admission, 11/1 for domestic and international students. Applications are processed on a rolling basis. Application fee: $75. Electronic applications accepted. *Total annual research expenditures:* $24.3 million. *Application contact:* New York University Information, 212-998-1212.
Website: http://engineering.nyu.edu/.

North Carolina Agricultural and Technical State University, School of Graduate Studies, College of Engineering, Greensboro, NC 27411. Offers MS, MSCE, MSCS, MSE, MSEE, MSIE, MSME, PhD. Part-time programs available.

North Carolina State University, Graduate School, College of Engineering, Raleigh, NC 27695. Offers M Ch E, M Eng, MC Sc, MCE, MIE, MIMS, MMSE, MNE, MOR, MS, PhD. Part-time programs available. Terminal master's awarded for partial completion of doctoral program. *Degree requirements:* For doctorate, thesis/dissertation. Electronic applications accepted.

North Dakota State University, College of Graduate and Interdisciplinary Studies, College of Engineering and Architecture, Fargo, ND 58108. Offers M Arch, MS, PhD. Part-time programs available. Terminal master's awarded for partial completion of doctoral program. *Degree requirements:* For master's, thesis; for doctorate, comprehensive exam, thesis/dissertation. *Entrance requirements:* For master's and doctorate, minimum GPA of 3.0. Additional exam requirements/recommendations for international students: Required—TOEFL. Electronic applications accepted. *Expenses:* Contact institution. *Faculty research:* Theoretical mechanics, robotics, automation, environmental engineering, man-made materials.
See Display below and Close-Up on page 85.

Northeastern University, College of Engineering, Boston, MA 02115-5096. Offers bioengineering (PhD); chemical engineering (MS, PhD); civil engineering (MS, PhD); computer engineering (PhD); computer systems engineering (MS); electrical and computer engineering (MS); electrical and engineering leadership (MS); electrical engineering (PhD); energy systems (MS); engineering leadership (Certificate); engineering management (MRTP); industrial engineering (MS, PhD); information assurance (PhD); information systems (MS); interdisciplinary (PhD); mechanical engineering (MS, PhD); operations research (MS); telecommunication systems management (MS). Part-time programs available. *Expenses:* Contact institution.

Northern Arizona University, Graduate College, College of Engineering, Forestry and Natural Sciences, Flagstaff, AZ 86011. Offers M Eng, MAST, MAT, MF, MS, MSE, MSF, PhD, Certificate. *Entrance requirements:* For master's, minimum GPA of 3.0 in final 60 hours of undergraduate course work.

Northern Illinois University, Graduate School, College of Engineering and Engineering Technology, De Kalb, IL 60115-2854. Offers MS. Part-time and evening/weekend programs available. *Faculty:* 36 full-time (2 women), 2 part-time/adjunct (0 women). *Students:* 117 full-time (23 women), 104 part-time (19 women); includes 21 minority (4 Black or African American, non-Hispanic/Latino; 14 Asian, non-Hispanic/Latino; 3 Hispanic/Latino), 142 international. Average age 27. 585 applicants, 42% accepted, 74 enrolled. In 2014, 59 master's awarded. *Degree requirements:* For master's, comprehensive exam, thesis optional. *Entrance requirements:* For master's, GRE General Test, minimum GPA of 2.75. Additional exam requirements/recommendations for international students: Required—TOEFL (minimum score 550 paper-based). *Application deadline:* For fall admission, 6/1 for domestic students, 5/1 for international students; for spring admission, 11/1 for domestic students, 10/1 for international students. Applications are processed on a rolling basis. Application fee: $40. Electronic applications accepted. *Financial support:* In 2014–15, 16 research assistantships with full tuition reimbursements, 17 teaching assistantships with full tuition reimbursements were awarded; fellowships with full tuition reimbursements, career-related internships or fieldwork, Federal Work-Study, scholarships/grants, tuition waivers (full), and unspecified assistantships also available. Support available to part-time students. Financial award applicants required to submit FAFSA. *Unit head:* Dr. Promod Vohra, Dean, 815-753-1281, Fax: 815-753-1310, E-mail: pvohra@niu.edu. *Application contact:* Graduate School Office, 815-753-0395, E-mail: gradsch@niu.edu.
Website: http://www.niu.edu/CEET/.

Northwestern Polytechnic University, School of Engineering, Fremont, CA 94539-7482. Offers computer science (MS); computer systems engineering (MS); electrical engineering (MS). Part-time and evening/weekend programs available. *Degree requirements:* For master's, thesis optional. *Entrance requirements:* For master's, minimum GPA of 3.0. Additional exam requirements/recommendations for international students: Required—TOEFL (minimum score 550 paper-based; 79 iBT). *Faculty research:* Computer networking, database design, Internet technology, software engineering, digital signal processing.

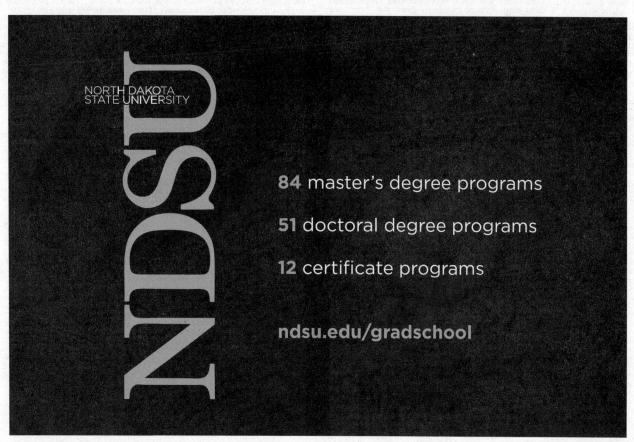

Engineering and Applied Sciences—General

Northwestern University, McCormick School of Engineering and Applied Science, Evanston, IL 60208. Offers MEM, MIT, MME, MMM, MPD, MS, PhD, Certificate, MBA/MEM. MS and PhD admissions and degrees offered through The Graduate School. Part-time and evening/weekend programs available. *Faculty:* 187 full-time (29 women). *Students:* 1,560 full-time (488 women), 297 part-time (81 women); includes 308 minority (39 Black or African American, non-Hispanic/Latino; 3 American Indian or Alaska Native, non-Hispanic/Latino; 170 Asian, non-Hispanic/Latino; 71 Hispanic/Latino; 3 Native Hawaiian or other Pacific Islander, non-Hispanic/Latino; 22 Two or more races, non-Hispanic/Latino), 933 international. Average age 26. 5,639 applicants, 22% accepted, 584 enrolled. In 2014, 357 master's, 129 doctorates awarded. Terminal master's awarded for partial completion of doctoral program. *Degree requirements:* For master's, comprehensive exam (for some programs), thesis (for some programs); for doctorate, comprehensive exam, thesis/dissertation. *Entrance requirements:* For master's and doctorate, GRE General Test. Additional exam requirements/recommendations for international students: Required—TOEFL (minimum score 577 paper-based; 90 iBT) or IELTS (minimum score 7). *Application deadline:* For fall admission, 12/31 for domestic and international students; for winter admission, 11/15 for domestic students, 11/1 for international students; for spring admission, 2/15 for domestic students, 2/1 for international students. Application fee: $75. Electronic applications accepted. *Financial support:* In 2014–15, 50 students received support. Fellowships with tuition reimbursements available, research assistantships with tuition reimbursements available, teaching assistantships with tuition reimbursements available, career-related internships or fieldwork, Federal Work-Study, institutionally sponsored loans, traineeships, health care benefits, and unspecified assistantships available. Financial award application deadline: 1/15; financial award applicants required to submit FAFSA. *Total annual research expenditures:* $117 million. *Unit head:* Dr. Julio Ottino, Dean, 847-491-3558, Fax: 847-491-5220, E-mail: jm-ottino@northwestern.edu. *Application contact:* Dr. Bruce Alan Lindvall, Assistant Dean for Graduate Studies, 847-491-4547, Fax: 847-491-5341, E-mail: b-lindvall@northwestern.edu.
Website: http://www.mccormick.northwestern.edu/.

Oakland University, Graduate Study and Lifelong Learning, School of Engineering and Computer Science, Rochester, MI 48309-4401. Offers MS, PhD. Part-time and evening/weekend programs available. *Degree requirements:* For doctorate, thesis/dissertation. *Entrance requirements:* For master's and doctorate, minimum GPA of 3.0. Additional exam requirements/recommendations for international students: Required—TOEFL (minimum score 550 paper-based). Electronic applications accepted. *Expenses:* Contact institution.

The Ohio State University, Graduate School, College of Engineering, Columbus, OH 43210. Offers M Arch, M Land Arch, MCRP, MS, PhD. Part-time and evening/weekend programs available. *Faculty:* 309. *Students:* 1,721 full-time (393 women), 126 part-time (26 women); includes 138 minority (27 Black or African American, non-Hispanic/Latino; 3 American Indian or Alaska Native, non-Hispanic/Latino; 63 Asian, non-Hispanic/Latino; 32 Hispanic/Latino; 13 Two or more races, non-Hispanic/Latino), 1,031 international. Average age 26. In 2014, 491 master's, 136 doctorates awarded. *Degree requirements:* For doctorate, thesis/dissertation. *Entrance requirements:* For master's and doctorate, GRE. Additional exam requirements/recommendations for international students: Required—TOEFL (minimum score 600 paper-based; 100 iBT), Michigan English Language Assessment Battery (minimum score 86); Recommended—IELTS (minimum score 8). *Application deadline:* For fall admission, 1/7 for domestic students, 11/30 for international students; for winter admission, 12/1 for domestic students, 11/1 for international students; for spring admission, 12/1 for domestic students, 11/30 for international students. Applications are processed on a rolling basis. Application fee: $60 ($70 for international students). Electronic applications accepted. *Financial support:* Fellowships with tuition reimbursements, research assistantships with tuition reimbursements, teaching assistantships with tuition reimbursements, career-related internships or fieldwork, Federal Work-Study, institutionally sponsored loans, and unspecified assistantships available. Support available to part-time students. *Total annual research expenditures:* $119 million. *Unit head:* Dr. David B. Williams, Dean, 614-292-2836, Fax: 614-292-9615, E-mail: williams.4219@osu.edu. *Application contact:* Graduate and Professional Admissions, 614-292-9444, Fax: 614-292-3895, E-mail: gpadmissions@osu.edu.
Website: http://engineering.osu.edu/.

Ohio University, Graduate College, Russ College of Engineering and Technology, Athens, OH 45701-2979. Offers M Eng Mgt, MS, PhD. Part-time programs available. *Degree requirements:* For master's, comprehensive exam (for some programs), thesis (for some programs); for doctorate, comprehensive exam, thesis/dissertation. *Entrance requirements:* For master's, GRE General Test, BS in engineering or related field; for doctorate, GRE General Test, MS in engineering or related field. Additional exam requirements/recommendations for international students: Required—TOEFL or IELTS. Electronic applications accepted. *Expenses:* Contact institution. *Faculty research:* Avionics engineering, coal research, transportation engineering, software systems integration, materials processing.

Oklahoma Christian University, Graduate School of Engineering, Oklahoma City, OK 73136-1100. Offers MSE. Electronic applications accepted.

Oklahoma State University, College of Engineering, Architecture and Technology, Stillwater, OK 74078. Offers MS, PhD. Postbaccalaureate distance learning degree programs offered. *Faculty:* 114 full-time (11 women), 14 part-time/adjunct (3 women). *Students:* 334 full-time (86 women), 414 part-time (74 women); includes 77 minority (12 Black or African American, non-Hispanic/Latino; 8 American Indian or Alaska Native, non-Hispanic/Latino; 10 Asian, non-Hispanic/Latino; 19 Hispanic/Latino; 1 Native Hawaiian or other Pacific Islander, non-Hispanic/Latino; 27 Two or more races, non-Hispanic/Latino), 439 international. Average age 28. 1,569 applicants, 21% accepted, 166 enrolled. In 2014, 213 master's, 33 doctorates awarded. *Degree requirements:* For master's, thesis (for some programs); for doctorate, comprehensive exam, thesis/dissertation. *Entrance requirements:* For master's and doctorate, GRE or GMAT. Additional exam requirements/recommendations for international students: Required—TOEFL (minimum score 550 paper-based; 79 iBT). *Application deadline:* For fall admission, 3/1 priority date for international students; for spring admission, 8/1 priority date for international students. Applications are processed on a rolling basis. Application fee: $40 ($75 for international students). Electronic applications accepted. *Expenses:* Tuition, state resident: full-time $4488; part-time $187 per credit hour. Tuition, nonresident: full-time $18,360; part-time $765 per credit hour. *Required fees:* $2413; $100.55 per credit hour. Tuition and fees vary according to campus/location. *Financial support:* In 2014–15, 191 research assistantships (averaging $16,935 per year), 144 teaching assistantships (averaging $15,127 per year) were awarded; career-related internships or fieldwork, Federal Work-Study, scholarships/grants, health care benefits, tuition waivers (partial), and unspecified assistantships also available. Support available to part-time students. Financial award application deadline: 3/1; financial award applicants required to submit FAFSA. *Unit head:* Dr. Paul Tikalsky, Dean, 405-744-5140, E-mail: paul.tikalsky@okstate.edu.
Website: http://www.ceat.okstate.edu.

Old Dominion University, Frank Batten College of Engineering and Technology, Norfolk, VA 23529. Offers ME, MEM, MS, D Eng, PhD. Part-time and evening/weekend programs available. Postbaccalaureate distance learning degree programs offered. *Faculty:* 93 full-time (12 women), 32 part-time/adjunct (5 women). *Students:* 169 full-time (46 women), 592 part-time (113 women); includes 152 minority (57 Black or African American, non-Hispanic/Latino; 3 American Indian or Alaska Native, non-Hispanic/Latino; 32 Asian, non-Hispanic/Latino; 37 Hispanic/Latino; 4 Native Hawaiian or other Pacific Islander, non-Hispanic/Latino; 19 Two or more races, non-Hispanic/Latino), 188 international. Average age 32. 558 applicants, 63% accepted, 144 enrolled. In 2014, 239 master's, 29 doctorates awarded. *Degree requirements:* For master's, comprehensive exam, thesis (for some programs); for doctorate, thesis/dissertation, candidacy exam. *Entrance requirements:* For master's, GRE, minimum GPA of 3.0; for doctorate, GRE, minimum GPA of 3.5. Additional exam requirements/recommendations for international students: Required—TOEFL (minimum score 550 paper-based). *Application deadline:* For fall admission, 6/1 for domestic students, 2/15 priority date for international students; for spring admission, 11/1 for domestic students, 10/1 for international students. Applications are processed on a rolling basis. Application fee: $50. Electronic applications accepted. *Expenses:* Tuition, state resident: full-time $10,488; part-time $437 per credit. Tuition, nonresident: full-time $26,136; part-time $1089 per credit. *Required fees:* $64 per semester. One-time fee: $50. *Financial support:* In 2014–15, 168 students received support, including 8 fellowships with full and partial tuition reimbursements available (averaging $15,000 per year), 92 research assistantships with full and partial tuition reimbursements available (averaging $15,000 per year), 68 teaching assistantships with full and partial tuition reimbursements available (averaging $15,000 per year); career-related internships or fieldwork, Federal Work-Study, institutionally sponsored loans, scholarships/grants, and unspecified assistantships also available. Support available to part-time students. Financial award applicants required to submit FAFSA. *Faculty research:* Physical electronics, computational applied mechanics, structural dynamics, computational fluid dynamics, coastal engineering of water resources, modeling and simulation. *Total annual research expenditures:* $31.8 million. *Unit head:* Dr. Oktay Baysal, Dean, 757-683-3789, Fax: 757-683-4898, E-mail: obaysal@odu.edu. *Application contact:* Dr. Linda Vahala, Associate Dean, 757-683-3789, Fax: 757-683-4898, E-mail: lvahala@odu.edu.
Website: https://www.odu.edu/eng.

Oregon State University, College of Engineering, Corvallis, OR 97331. Offers M Eng, MHP, MMP, MS, PhD. Part-time programs available. Postbaccalaureate distance learning degree programs offered (no on-campus study). *Faculty:* 171 full-time (24 women), 12 part-time/adjunct (5 women). *Students:* 886 full-time (181 women), 160 part-time (35 women); includes 76 minority (3 Black or African American, non-Hispanic/Latino; 31 Asian, non-Hispanic/Latino; 24 Hispanic/Latino; 18 Two or more races, non-Hispanic/Latino), 545 international. Average age 28. In 2014, 235 master's, 71 doctorates awarded. Terminal master's awarded for partial completion of doctoral program. *Degree requirements:* For doctorate, thesis/dissertation. *Application deadline:* Applications are processed on a rolling basis. Application fee: $60. *Expenses:* Expenses: $15,359 full-time resident tuition and fees; $23,405 non-resident. *Financial support:* Fellowships with full tuition reimbursements, research assistantships with full tuition reimbursements, teaching assistantships with full tuition reimbursements, and instructorships available. Financial award application deadline: 2/1. *Faculty research:* Molecular beam epitaxy, wave-structure interaction, pavement materials, toxic wastes, mechanical design methodology. *Total annual research expenditures:* $32 million. *Unit head:* Scott Ashford, Dean, 541-737-5232. *Application contact:* Dr. Christine Kelly, Associate Dean, Academic and Student Affairs, 541-737-6755, Fax: 541-737-1805, E-mail: christine.kelly@oregonstate.edu.
Website: http://engineering.oregonstate.edu/.

Penn State Erie, The Behrend College, Graduate School, Erie, PA 16563-0001. Offers business administration (MBA); project management (MPM); quality and manufacturing management (MMM). *Accreditation:* AACSB. Part-time programs available. *Students:* 26 full-time (11 women), 111 part-time (33 women). Average age 31. 59 applicants, 90% accepted, 34 enrolled. In 2014, 35 master's awarded. *Entrance requirements:* Additional exam requirements/recommendations for international students: Required—TOEFL (minimum score 550 paper-based; 80 iBT), IELTS. *Application deadline:* Applications are processed on a rolling basis. Application fee: $65. Electronic applications accepted. *Financial support:* Federal Work-Study available. Financial award application deadline: 3/1; financial award applicants required to submit FAFSA. *Unit head:* Dr. Donald L. Birx, Chancellor, 814-898-6160, Fax: 814-898-6461, E-mail: dlb69@psu.edu. *Application contact:* Ann M. Burbules, Assistant Director, Graduate Admissions, 866-374-3378, Fax: 814-898-6053, E-mail: psbehrendmba@psu.edu.
Website: http://psbehrend.psu.edu/.

Penn State Great Valley, Graduate Studies, Engineering Division, Malvern, PA 19355-1488. Offers engineering management (MEM); software engineering (MSE); systems engineering (M Eng). *Unit head:* Dr. Craig S. Edelbrock, Chancellor, 610-648-3202 Ext. 610, Fax: 610-889-1334, E-mail: cse1@psu.edu. *Application contact:* JoAnn Kelly, Director of Admissions, 610-648-3315, Fax: 610-725-5296, E-mail: jek2@psu.edu.
Website: http://www.sgps.psu.edu/Academics/Degrees/31884.htm.

Penn State Harrisburg, Graduate School, School of Science, Engineering and Technology, Middletown, PA 17057-4898. Offers computer science (MS); electrical engineering (M Eng, MS); engineering management (MPS); engineering science (M Eng); environmental engineering (M Eng); structural engineering (Certificate). Part-time and evening/weekend programs available. *Unit head:* Dr. Mukund S. Kulkarni, Chancellor, 717-948-6105, Fax: 717-948-6452, E-mail: msk5@psu.edu. *Application contact:* Robert W. Coffman, Jr., Director of Enrollment Management, Admissions, 717-948-6250, Fax: 717-948-6325, E-mail: ric1@psu.edu.
Website: http://harrisburg.psu.edu/science-engineering-technology.

Penn State University Park, Graduate School, College of Engineering, University Park, PA 16802. Offers M Eng, MAE, MS, PhD. Part-time and evening/weekend programs available. Postbaccalaureate distance learning degree programs offered. *Students:* 1,276 full-time (280 women), 112 part-time (29 women). Average age 27. 4,489 applicants, 21% accepted, 347 enrolled. *Entrance requirements:* Additional exam requirements/recommendations for international students: Required—TOEFL (minimum score 550 paper-based; 80 iBT), IELTS. *Application deadline:* Applications are processed on a rolling basis. Application fee: $65. Electronic applications accepted. *Financial support:* Fellowships, research assistantships, teaching assistantships, Federal Work-Study, scholarships/grants, traineeships, health care benefits, and unspecified assistantships available. Support available to part-time students. Financial award application deadline: 3/1; financial award applicants required to submit FAFSA. *Unit head:* Dr. Amr S. Elnashai, Dean, 814-865-7537, Fax: 814-863-4749, E-mail: ase2@psu.edu. *Application contact:* Lori A. Stania, Director, Graduate Student Services, 814-867-5278, Fax: 814-863-4627, E-mail: gswww@psu.edu.
Website: http://www.engr.psu.edu/.

Pittsburg State University, Graduate School, College of Technology, Department of Engineering Technology, Pittsburg, KS 66762. Offers MET. *Degree requirements:* For master's, thesis or alternative.

Pontificia Universidad Catolica Madre y Maestra, Graduate School, Faculty of Engineering Sciences, Santiago, Dominican Republic. Offers earthquake engineering (ME); logistics management (ME).

Portland State University, Graduate Studies, Maseeh College of Engineering and Computer Science, Portland, OR 97207-0751. Offers M Eng, ME, MS, MSE, PhD, Certificate, MS/MBA, MS/MS. Part-time and evening/weekend programs available. *Faculty:* 85 full-time (13 women), 24 part-time/adjunct (4 women). *Students:* 480 full-time (132 women), 303 part-time (66 women); includes 92 minority (16 Black or African American, non-Hispanic/Latino; 2 American Indian or Alaska Native, non-Hispanic/Latino; 49 Asian, non-Hispanic/Latino; 15 Hispanic/Latino; 1 Native Hawaiian or other Pacific Islander, non-Hispanic/Latino; 9 Two or more races, non-Hispanic/Latino), 418 international. Average age 31. 1,043 applicants, 42% accepted, 244 enrolled. In 2014, 210 master's, 13 doctorates awarded. *Degree requirements:* For doctorate, one foreign language, thesis/dissertation. *Entrance requirements:* For master's, doctorate, and Certificate, Varies by Dept. Additional exam requirements/recommendations for international students: Required—TOEFL (minimum score 550 paper-based; 80 iBT). *Application deadline:* For fall admission, 4/1 for domestic students, 3/1 for international students; for winter admission, 9/1 for domestic and international students; for spring admission, 2/1 for domestic and international students. Application fee: $50. *Expenses:* Tuition, state resident: part-time $222 per credit. Tuition, nonresident: part-time $527 per credit. *Required fees:* $22 per contact hour. $100 per quarter. Tuition and fees vary according to program. *Financial support:* In 2014–15, 65 research assistantships with full and partial tuition reimbursements (averaging $7,925 per year), 71 teaching assistantships with full and partial tuition reimbursements (averaging $3,421 per year) were awarded; career-related internships or fieldwork, Federal Work-Study, scholarships/grants, and unspecified assistantships also available. Support available to part-time students. Financial award application deadline: 3/1; financial award applicants required to submit FAFSA. *Total annual research expenditures:* $8.6 million. *Unit head:* Dr. Renjeng Su, Dean, 503-725-8393, Fax: 503-725-2825, E-mail: renjengs@pdx.edu. *Application contact:* Yeruwelle de Rouen, Outreach and Recruitment Manager, 503-725-5030, Fax: 503-725-2825, E-mail: derouen@pdx.edu.
Website: http://www.pdx.edu/cecs/.

Prairie View A&M University, College of Engineering, Prairie View, TX 77446-0519. Offers computer information systems (MSCIS); computer science (MSCS); electrical engineering (MSEE, PhDEE); engineering (MS Engr). Part-time and evening/weekend programs available. *Faculty:* 29 full-time (5 women), 1 (woman) part-time/adjunct. *Students:* 113 full-time (46 women), 55 part-time (23 women); includes 72 minority (49 Black or African American, non-Hispanic/Latino; 1 American Indian or Alaska Native, non-Hispanic/Latino; 18 Asian, non-Hispanic/Latino; 3 Hispanic/Latino; 1 Two or more races, non-Hispanic/Latino), 73 international. Average age 32. 106 applicants, 98% accepted, 64 enrolled. In 2014, 37 master's, 5 doctorates awarded. *Degree requirements:* For master's, thesis (for some programs); for doctorate, comprehensive exam, thesis/dissertation. *Entrance requirements:* For master's, GRE General Test (minimum score of 900), bachelor's degree in engineering from ABET-accredited institution; for doctorate, minimum GPA of 3.0. Additional exam requirements/recommendations for international students: Required—TOEFL (minimum score 550 paper-based; 79 iBT). *Application deadline:* For fall admission, 7/1 priority date for domestic students, 6/1 priority date for international students; for spring admission, 11/1 priority date for domestic students, 10/1 priority date for international students; for summer admission, 3/1 priority date for domestic students, 2/1 priority date for international students. Application fee: $50. Electronic applications accepted. *Expenses:* Expenses: $6,686 tuition and fees. *Financial support:* In 2014–15, 14 research assistantships with partial tuition reimbursements (averaging $8,000 per year), 14 teaching assistantships with partial tuition reimbursements (averaging $7,500 per year) were awarded; career-related internships or fieldwork, institutionally sponsored loans, scholarships/grants, health care benefits, tuition waivers (partial), and unspecified assistantships also available. Financial award application deadline: 3/1; financial award applicants required to submit FAFSA. *Faculty research:* Applied radiation research, thermal science, computational fluid dynamics, analog mixed signal, aerial space battlefield. *Unit head:* Dr. Kendall T. Harris, Dean, 936-261-9956, Fax: 936-261-9869, E-mail: tharris@pvamu.edu. *Application contact:* Pauline Walker, Administrative Assistant II, Research and Graduate Studies, 936-261-3521, Fax: 936-261-3529, E-mail: pmwalker@pvamu.edu.

Princeton University, Graduate School, School of Engineering and Applied Science, Princeton, NJ 08544-1019. Offers M Eng, MSE, PhD. Terminal master's awarded for partial completion of doctoral program. *Degree requirements:* For master's, thesis (for some programs); for doctorate, thesis/dissertation, research, teaching, general exam. *Entrance requirements:* For master's and doctorate, GRE General Test, official transcript(s), 3 letters of recommendation, personal statement. Additional exam requirements/recommendations for international students: Required—TOEFL. Electronic applications accepted.

Purdue University, College of Engineering, West Lafayette, IN 47907-2045. Offers MS, MSAAE, MSABE, MSBME, MSCE, MSChE, MSE, MSECE, MSIE, MSME, MSMSE, MSNE, PhD, Certificate, MD/PhD. *Accreditation:* ABET. Part-time programs available. Postbaccalaureate distance learning degree programs offered (no on-campus study). Terminal master's awarded for partial completion of doctoral program. *Degree requirements:* For master's, thesis (for some programs); for doctorate, comprehensive exam, thesis/dissertation. *Entrance requirements:* Additional exam requirements/recommendations for international students: Required—TOEFL (minimum score 550 paper-based) or IELTS (minimum score 6.5); Recommended—TWE. Electronic applications accepted. *Expenses:* Contact institution. *Faculty research:* Nanotechnology, advanced materials manufacturing, tissue and cell engineering, intelligent infrastructures, global sustainable industrial systems.

Purdue University Calumet, Graduate Studies Office, School of Engineering, Mathematics, and Science, Department of Engineering, Hammond, IN 46323-2094. Offers computer engineering (MSE); electrical engineering (MSE); engineering (MS); mechanical engineering (MSE). Evening/weekend programs available. *Entrance requirements:* Additional exam requirements/recommendations for international students: Required—TOEFL.

Purdue University Calumet, Graduate Studies Office, School of Technology, Hammond, IN 46323-2094. Offers MS.

Queen's University at Kingston, School of Graduate Studies, Faculty of Applied Science, Kingston, ON K7L 3N6, Canada. Offers M Eng, M Sc, M Sc Eng, PhD. Part-time programs available. *Degree requirements:* For doctorate, comprehensive exam, thesis/dissertation. *Entrance requirements:* Additional exam requirements/recommendations for international students: Required—TOEFL. Electronic applications accepted.

Rensselaer at Hartford, Department of Engineering, Hartford, CT 06120-2991. Offers ME, MS. Part-time and evening/weekend programs available. *Entrance requirements:* For master's, GRE. Additional exam requirements/recommendations for international students: Required—TOEFL (minimum score 600 paper-based; 100 iBT). Electronic applications accepted.

Rensselaer Polytechnic Institute, Graduate School, School of Engineering, Troy, NY 12180-3590. Offers M Eng, MS, D Eng, PhD. Part-time programs available. *Faculty:* 370 full-time (71 women), 50 part-time/adjunct (12 women). *Students:* 478 full-time (114 women), 44 part-time (7 women); includes 55 minority (8 Black or African American, non-Hispanic/Latino; 29 Asian, non-Hispanic/Latino; 12 Hispanic/Latino; 6 Two or more races, non-Hispanic/Latino), 279 international. Average age 27. 1,617 applicants, 24% accepted, 166 enrolled. In 2014, 106 master's, 78 doctorates awarded. Terminal master's awarded for partial completion of doctoral program. *Degree requirements:* For master's, comprehensive exam (for some programs), thesis (for some programs); for doctorate, comprehensive exam (for some programs), thesis/dissertation. *Entrance requirements:* For master's and doctorate, GRE. Additional exam requirements/recommendations for international students: Required—TOEFL (minimum score 570 paper-based; 88 iBT), IELTS (minimum score 6.5), PTE (minimum score 60). *Application deadline:* For fall admission, 1/1 priority date for domestic and international students; for spring admission, 8/15 priority date for domestic and international students. Applications are processed on a rolling basis. Application fee: $75. Electronic applications accepted. *Expenses: Tuition:* Full-time $46,700; part-time $1945 per credit. Tuition and fees vary according to course load. *Financial support:* In 2014–15, 364 students received support, including research assistantships (averaging $18,500 per year), teaching assistantships (averaging $18,500 per year); fellowships also available. Financial award application deadline: 1/1. *Faculty research:* Aeronautical, biomedical, chemical, civil, computer and systems, engineering physics, environmental, industrial and management, materials science, mechanical, nuclear, systems engineering and technology management, transportation. *Total annual research expenditures:* $37.5 million. *Unit head:* Dr. Tarek Abdoun, Associate Dean, School of Engineering, 518-276-6544, E-mail: abdout@rpi.edu. *Application contact:* Office of Graduate Admissions, 518-276-6216, E-mail: gradadmissions@rpi.edu.
Website: http://www.eng.rpi.edu/.

Rice University, Graduate Programs, George R. Brown School of Engineering, Houston, TX 77251-1892. Offers M Ch E, M Stat, MA, MBE, MCAM, MCE, MCS, MEE, MEE, MES, MME, MMS, MS, PhD, MBA/M Stat, MBA/ME, MBA/MEE, MD/PhD. MD/PhD offered jointly with Baylor College of Medicine, The University of Texas Health Science Center at Houston. Part-time programs available. Terminal master's awarded for partial completion of doctoral program. *Degree requirements:* For master's, comprehensive exam (for some programs), thesis (for some programs); for doctorate, comprehensive exam (for some programs), thesis/dissertation. *Entrance requirements:* For master's and doctorate, GRE General Test. Additional exam requirements/recommendations for international students: Required—TOEFL (minimum score 600 paper-based). Electronic applications accepted. *Faculty research:* Digital signal processing, tissue engineering, groundwater remediation, computational engineering and high performance computing, nanoscale science and technology.

Robert Morris University, Graduate Studies, School of Engineering, Mathematics and Science, Moon Township, PA 15108-1189. Offers engineering management (MS). Part-time and evening/weekend programs available. *Faculty:* 7 full-time (0 women). *Students:* 42 part-time (4 women); includes 4 minority (all Black or African American, non-Hispanic/Latino), 9 international. Average age 30. 45 applicants, 38% accepted, 15 enrolled. In 2014, 32 master's awarded. *Entrance requirements:* For master's, letters of recommendation. Additional exam requirements/recommendations for international students: Required—TOEFL (minimum score 550 paper-based; 79 iBT). *Application deadline:* For fall admission, 7/1 priority date for domestic and international students; for spring admission, 11/1 priority date for domestic and international students. Applications are processed on a rolling basis. Application fee: $35. Electronic applications accepted. *Expenses:* Expenses: Contact institution. *Financial support:* Federal Work-Study, institutionally sponsored loans, and unspecified assistantships available. Financial award application deadline: 5/1; financial award applicants required to submit FAFSA. *Unit head:* Dr. Maria V. Kalevitch, Dean, 412-397-4020, Fax: 412-397-2472, E-mail: kalevitch@rmu.edu.
Website: http://www.rmu.edu/web/cms/schools/sems/.

Rochester Institute of Technology, Graduate Enrollment Services, Kate Gleason College of Engineering, Rochester, NY 14623-5603. Offers ME, MS, PhD, Advanced Certificate. Part-time and evening/weekend programs available. Postbaccalaureate distance learning degree programs offered (no on-campus study). *Students:* 460 full-time (101 women), 261 part-time (55 women); includes 47 minority (11 Black or African American, non-Hispanic/Latino; 22 Asian, non-Hispanic/Latino; 12 Hispanic/Latino; 2 Two or more races, non-Hispanic/Latino), 417 international. Average age 26. 1,764 applicants, 43% accepted, 278 enrolled. In 2014, 248 master's, 9 doctorates, 5 other advanced degrees awarded. Terminal master's awarded for partial completion of doctoral program. *Degree requirements:* For master's, thesis (for some programs); for doctorate, thesis/dissertation. *Entrance requirements:* For master's and doctorate, GRE, TOEFL, IELTS, or PTE for non-native English speakers, Recommended minimum GPA of 3.0; for Advanced Certificate, TOEFL, IELTS, or PTE for non-native English speakers, Recommended minimum GPA of 3.0. Additional exam requirements/recommendations for international students: Required—PTE (minimum score 58), TOEFL (minimum score 550 paper-based; 79 iBT) or IELTS (minimum score 6.5). *Application deadline:* For fall admission, 2/15 priority date for domestic and international students. Applications are processed on a rolling basis. Application fee: $60. Electronic applications accepted. *Expenses:* Expenses: $1,673 per credit hour. *Financial support:* Fellowships with full and partial tuition reimbursements, research assistantships with full and partial tuition reimbursements, teaching assistantships with full and partial tuition reimbursements, career-related internships or fieldwork, Federal Work-Study, institutionally sponsored loans, scholarships/grants, health care benefits, tuition waivers (full and partial), and unspecified assistantships available. Support available to part-time students. Financial award applicants required to submit FAFSA. *Faculty research:* Advanced materials, computer vision, embedded systems and control, high performance computing, operations, photonics, semiconductor processing, supply chain and logistics, sustainability. *Unit head:* Dr. Harvey Palmer, Dean, 585-475-2145, Fax: 585-475-6879, E-mail: coe@rit.edu. *Application contact:* Diane Ellison, Associate Vice President, Graduate Enrollment Services, 585-475-2229, Fax: 585-475-7164, E-mail: gradinfo@rit.edu.
Website: http://www.rit.edu/kgcoe/.

Rose-Hulman Institute of Technology, Faculty of Engineering and Applied Sciences, Terre Haute, IN 47803-3999. Offers M Eng, MS, MD/MS. Part-time and evening/weekend programs available. Postbaccalaureate distance learning degree programs offered (minimal on-campus study). *Faculty:* 116 full-time (20 women), 8 part-time/adjunct (2 women). *Students:* 80 full-time (24 women), 28 part-time (8 women); includes 9 minority (2 Black or African American, non-Hispanic/Latino; 2 American Indian or Alaska Native, non-Hispanic/Latino; 2 Asian, non-Hispanic/Latino; 3 Two or more races, non-Hispanic/Latino), 52 international. Average age 25. 132 applicants, 82% accepted, 59 enrolled. In 2014, 46 master's awarded. *Degree requirements:* For master's, thesis (for some programs). *Entrance requirements:* For master's, GRE, minimum GPA of 3.0. Additional exam requirements/recommendations for international students: Required—TOEFL (minimum score 580 paper-based; 92 iBT). *Application deadline:* For fall admission, 2/1 priority date for domestic students. Applications are processed on a

rolling basis. Application fee: $0. *Expenses: Tuition:* Full-time $40,449. *Financial support:* In 2014–15, 89 students received support. Fellowships with full and partial tuition reimbursements available, research assistantships with full and partial tuition reimbursements available, institutionally sponsored loans, scholarships/grants, and tuition waivers (full and partial) available. *Faculty research:* Optical instrument design and prototypes, biomaterials, adsorption and adsorption-based separations, image and speech processing, groundwater, solid and hazardous waste. *Total annual research expenditures:* $411,652. *Application contact:* Dr. Azad Siahmakoun, Associate Dean of the Faculty, 812-877-8400, Fax: 812-877-8061, E-mail: siahmako@rose-hulman.edu.
Website: http://www.rose-hulman.edu.

Rowan University, Graduate School, College of Engineering, Program in Engineering, Glassboro, NJ 08028-1701. Offers MSE. Part-time and evening/weekend programs available. *Faculty:* 3 full-time (0 women), 3 part-time/adjunct (0 women). *Students:* 3 full-time (1 woman), 28 part-time (5 women); includes 8 minority (3 Black or African American, non-Hispanic/Latino; 2 Asian, non-Hispanic/Latino; 3 Hispanic/Latino). Average age 30. 20 applicants, 80% accepted, 11 enrolled. In 2014, 12 master's awarded. *Degree requirements:* For master's, thesis (for some programs). *Entrance requirements:* For master's, GRE General Test. Additional exam requirements/recommendations for international students: Required—TOEFL. *Application deadline:* For fall admission, 8/1 for domestic students; for spring admission, 11/1 for domestic students; for summer admission, 4/1 for domestic students. Applications are processed on a rolling basis. Application fee: $65. Electronic applications accepted. *Expenses: Tuition, area resident:* Part-time $648 per credit. Tuition, state resident: part-time $648 per credit. Tuition, nonresident: part-time $648 per credit. *Required fees:* $145 per credit. Tuition and fees vary according to degree level, campus/location, program and student level. *Financial support:* Career-related internships or fieldwork, scholarships/grants, health care benefits, and unspecified assistantships available. *Unit head:* Dr. Horacio Sosa, Dean, College of Graduate and Continuing Education, 856-256-4747, Fax: 856-256-5638, E-mail: sosa@rowan.edu. *Application contact:* Admissions and Enrollment Services, 856-256-5145, Fax: 856-256-5637, E-mail: cgceadmissions@rowan.edu.

Royal Military College of Canada, Division of Graduate Studies and Research, Engineering Division, Kingston, ON K7K 7B4, Canada. Offers M Eng, M Sc, MA Sc, PhD. *Degree requirements:* For master's, thesis; for doctorate, comprehensive exam, thesis/dissertation. *Entrance requirements:* For master's, honours degree with second-class standing; for doctorate, master's degree. Electronic applications accepted.

Saginaw Valley State University, College of Science, Engineering, and Technology, University Center, MI 48710. Offers energy and materials (MS). Part-time and evening/weekend programs available. *Faculty:* 2 full-time (0 women), 3 part-time/adjunct (1 woman). *Students:* 2 full-time (0 women), 5 part-time (1 woman); includes 1 minority (Black or African American, non-Hispanic/Latino), 3 international. Average age 30. 12 applicants, 58% accepted, 4 enrolled. In 2014, 1 master's awarded. *Degree requirements:* For master's, field project or thesis work. *Entrance requirements:* For master's, minimum GPA of 3.0. Additional exam requirements/recommendations for international students: Required—TOEFL (minimum score 550 paper-based; 79 iBT). *Application deadline:* For fall admission, 7/15 for international students; for winter admission, 11/15 for international students; for spring admission, 4/15 for international students. Applications are processed on a rolling basis. Application fee: $30 ($90 for international students). Electronic applications accepted. *Expenses:* Tuition, state resident: full-time $8957; part-time $497.60 per credit hour. Tuition, nonresident: full-time $17,081; part-time $948.95 per credit hour. *Required fees:* $263; $14.60 per credit hour. Tuition and fees vary according to degree level. *Financial support:* Federal Work-Study and scholarships/grants available. Support available to part-time students. Financial award application deadline: 4/1; financial award applicants required to submit FAFSA. *Unit head:* Dr. Robert Tuttle, Program Coordinator, 989-964-4144, Fax: 989-964-2717. *Application contact:* Jenna Briggs, Director, Graduate and International Admissions, 989-964-6096, Fax: 989-964-2788, E-mail: gradadm@svsu.edu.
Website: http://www.svsu.edu/collegeofscienceengineeringtechnology/.

St. Cloud State University, School of Graduate Studies, College of Science and Engineering, St. Cloud, MN 56301-4498. Offers MA, MEM, MS. *Degree requirements:* For master's, thesis or alternative. *Entrance requirements:* For master's, GRE General Test, minimum GPA of 2.75. Additional exam requirements/recommendations for international students: Required—TOEFL (minimum score 550 paper-based). Electronic applications accepted.

St. Mary's University, Graduate School, Department of Engineering, San Antonio, TX 78228-8507. Offers computer engineering (MS); electrical engineering (MS); engineering systems management (MS); industrial engineering (MS); software engineering (MS). Part-time programs available. *Students:* 23 full-time (5 women), 29 part-time (8 women); includes 16 minority (1 Black or African American, non-Hispanic/Latino; 15 Hispanic/Latino), 26 international. Average age 30. 77 applicants, 29% accepted, 8 enrolled. In 2014, 40 master's awarded. *Degree requirements:* For master's, comprehensive exam. *Entrance requirements:* For master's, GRE, Bachelor's Degree in engineering or related field. Minimum GPA of 3.00. Additional exam requirements/recommendations for international students: Required—TOEFL (minimum score 550 paper-based; 80 iBT), IELTS (minimum score 6). *Application deadline:* Applications are processed on a rolling basis. Application fee: $0. Electronic applications accepted. *Expenses: Tuition:* Full-time $15,070; part-time $800 per credit hour. *Required fees:* $156 per semester. *Financial support:* Career-related internships or fieldwork, Federal Work-Study, institutionally sponsored loans, scholarships/grants, and health care benefits available. Financial award application deadline: 3/31; financial award applicants required to submit FAFSA. *Faculty research:* Digital signal processing, image processing, wireless communication, neural networks, pattern recognition, computer architecture, parallel processing, computer security, computer networking.

San Diego State University, Graduate and Research Affairs, College of Engineering, San Diego, CA 92182. Offers MS, PhD. Part-time and evening/weekend programs available. Terminal master's awarded for partial completion of doctoral program. *Degree requirements:* For master's, thesis optional; for doctorate, thesis/dissertation. *Entrance requirements:* For master's, GRE General Test; for doctorate, GRE, 3 letters of recommendation. Additional exam requirements/recommendations for international students: Required—TOEFL. Electronic applications accepted.

San Francisco State University, Division of Graduate Studies, College of Science and Engineering, School of Engineering, San Francisco, CA 94132-1722. Offers energy systems (MS); structural/earthquake engineering (MS). Part-time programs available. *Application deadline:* Applications are processed on a rolling basis. Electronic applications accepted. *Expenses:* Tuition, state resident: full-time $6738. Tuition, nonresident: full-time $17,898; part-time $372 per credit hour. *Required fees:* $498 per semester. *Unit head:* Dr. Wenshen Pong, Director, 415-338-7738, Fax: 415-338-0525, E-mail: wspong@sfsu.edu. *Application contact:* Dr. Hamid Shahnasser, Graduate Coordinator, 415-338-2124, Fax: 415-338-0525, E-mail: hamid@sfsu.edu.
Website: http://engineering.sfsu.edu/.

San Jose State University, Graduate Studies and Research, Charles W. Davidson College of Engineering, Department of General Engineering, San Jose, CA 95192-0001. Offers MS. Electronic applications accepted.

Santa Clara University, School of Engineering, Santa Clara, CA 95053. Offers analog circuit design (Certificate); applied mathematics (MS); ASIC design and test (Certificate); bioengineering (MS); civil engineering (MS); computer science and engineering (MS, PhD); controls (Certificate); digital signal processing (Certificate); dynamics (Certificate); electrical engineering (MS, PhD); engineering (Engineer); engineering management (MS); fundamentals of electrical engineering (Certificate); information assurance (Certificate); materials engineering (Certificate); mechanical design analysis (Certificate); mechanical engineering (MS, PhD); mechatronics systems engineering (Certificate); microwave and antennas (Certificate); networking (Certificate); renewable energy (Certificate); software engineering (Certificate); sustainable energy (MS); technology jump-start (Certificate); thermofluids (Certificate). Part-time and evening/weekend programs available. *Faculty:* 59 full-time (23 women), 80 part-time/adjunct (14 women). *Students:* 584 full-time (239 women), 353 part-time (102 women); includes 224 minority (7 Black or African American, non-Hispanic/Latino; 144 Asian, non-Hispanic/Latino; 50 Hispanic/Latino; 2 Native Hawaiian or other Pacific Islander, non-Hispanic/Latino; 21 Two or more races, non-Hispanic/Latino), 548 international. Average age 27. 1,248 applicants, 51% accepted, 375 enrolled. In 2014, 283 master's, 5 doctorates, 1 other advanced degree awarded. *Degree requirements:* For master's, thesis (for some programs); for doctorate, thesis/dissertation; for other advanced degree, thesis. *Entrance requirements:* For master's, GRE, transcript; for doctorate, GRE, master's degree or equivalent; for other advanced degree, master's degree, published paper. Additional exam requirements/recommendations for international students: Required—TOEFL (minimum score 550 paper-based; 79 iBT). *Application deadline:* For fall admission, 8/1 for domestic students, 7/15 for international students; for winter admission, 10/28 for domestic students, 9/23 for international students; for spring admission, 2/25 for domestic students, 1/21 for international students. Applications are processed on a rolling basis. Application fee: $60. Electronic applications accepted. *Expenses:* Expenses: Contact institution. *Financial support:* In 2014–15, 94 students received support. Fellowships with full and partial tuition reimbursements available, research assistantships with full and partial tuition reimbursements available, teaching assistantships with full tuition reimbursements available, career-related internships or fieldwork, Federal Work-Study, institutionally sponsored loans, and scholarships/grants available. Support available to part-time students. Financial award application deadline: 3/2; financial award applicants required to submit FAFSA. *Faculty research:* Video encoding, nanostructures, robotics, microfluidics, water resources. *Total annual research expenditures:* $1.6 million. *Unit head:* Dr. Alex Zecevic, Associate Dean for Graduate Studies, 408-554-2394, E-mail: azecevic@scu.edu. *Application contact:* Stacey Tinker, Director of Enrollment Management, 408-554-4748, Fax: 408-554-4323, E-mail: stinker@scu.edu.
Website: http://www.scu.edu/engineering/graduate/.

Seattle University, College of Science and Engineering, Seattle, WA 98122-1090. Offers MSCS, MSE. Part-time and evening/weekend programs available. *Faculty:* 8 full-time (3 women), 2 part-time/adjunct (0 women). *Students:* 27 full-time (21 women), 43 part-time (16 women); includes 20 minority (1 Black or African American, non-Hispanic/Latino; 14 Asian, non-Hispanic/Latino; 3 Hispanic/Latino; 2 Two or more races, non-Hispanic/Latino), 24 international. Average age 29. 80 applicants, 36% accepted, 18 enrolled. In 2014, 24 master's awarded. *Degree requirements:* For master's, thesis. *Entrance requirements:* For master's, GRE General Test, 2 years of related work experience. *Application deadline:* For fall admission, 7/1 for domestic students. Application fee: $55. *Expenses:* Expenses: Contact institution. *Financial support:* In 2014–15, 9 students received support. Career-related internships or fieldwork and Federal Work-Study available. Support available to part-time students. Financial award applicants required to submit FAFSA. *Unit head:* Dr. Michael Quinn, Dean, 206-296-5500, Fax: 206-296-2071. *Application contact:* Janet Shandley, Director of Graduate Admissions, 206-296-5900, Fax: 206-298-5656, E-mail: grad_admissions@seattleu.edu.
Website: https://www.seattleu.edu/scieng/.

Simon Fraser University, Office of Graduate Studies, Faculty of Applied Sciences, School of Engineering Science, Burnaby, BC V5A 1S6, Canada. Offers M Eng, MA Sc, PhD. Part-time programs available. *Degree requirements:* For master's, thesis (for some programs); for doctorate, thesis/dissertation, qualifying exam, seminar presentations. *Entrance requirements:* For master's, minimum GPA of 3.0 (on scale of 4.33), or 3.33 based on last 60 credits of undergraduate courses; for doctorate, minimum GPA of 3.5 (on scale of 4.33). Additional exam requirements/recommendations for international students: Recommended—TOEFL (minimum score 580 paper-based; 93 iBT), IELTS (minimum score 7), TWE (minimum score 5). Electronic applications accepted. *Faculty research:* Biomedical engineering, communications, microelectronics, systems and robotics.

South Dakota School of Mines and Technology, Graduate Division, College of Engineering, Rapid City, SD 57701-3995. Offers MS, PhD. Part-time programs available. Postbaccalaureate distance learning degree programs offered (no on-campus study). *Faculty:* 80 full-time (16 women), 15 part-time/adjunct (3 women). *Students:* 163 full-time (44 women), 86 part-time (17 women); includes 15 minority (3 Black or African American, non-Hispanic/Latino; 2 American Indian or Alaska Native, non-Hispanic/Latino; 4 Asian, non-Hispanic/Latino; 5 Hispanic/Latino; 1 Two or more races, non-Hispanic/Latino), 79 international. Average age 28. 269 applicants, 45% accepted, 81 enrolled. In 2014, 57 master's, 18 doctorates awarded. *Degree requirements:* For doctorate, thesis/dissertation. *Entrance requirements:* For doctorate, minimum graduate GPA of 3.0. Additional exam requirements/recommendations for international students: Required—TOEFL (minimum score 520 paper-based; 68 iBT), TWE. *Application deadline:* For fall admission, 7/1 priority date for domestic students, 4/1 for international students; for spring admission, 11/1 for domestic students, 9/1 for international students. Applications are processed on a rolling basis. Application fee: $35. Electronic applications accepted. *Expenses:* Tuition, state resident: full-time $5050; part-time $210.40 per credit hour. Tuition, nonresident: full-time $11,290; part-time $470.30 per credit hour. *Required fees:* $4680. *Financial support:* In 2014–15, 29 fellowships (averaging $3,982 per year), 172 research assistantships with partial tuition reimbursements (averaging $8,132 per year), 101 teaching assistantships with partial tuition reimbursements (averaging $3,989 per year) were awarded; Federal Work-Study and institutionally sponsored loans also available. Support available to part-time students. Financial award application deadline: 5/15. *Faculty research:* Contaminants in soil, nitrate leaching, environmental changes, fracture formations, greenhouse effect. *Total annual research expenditures:* $5.3 million. *Unit head:* Dr. Douglas Wells, Dean, 605-394-1763, E-mail: douglas.wells@sdsmt.edu. *Application contact:* Rachel Howard, Office of Graduate Education, 605-355-3468, Fax: 605-394-1767, E-mail: rachel.howard@sdsmt.edu.

South Dakota State University, Graduate School, College of Engineering, Brookings, SD 57007. Offers MS, PhD. Part-time programs available. *Degree requirements:* For master's, thesis, oral exam; for doctorate, thesis/dissertation, preliminary oral and written exams. *Entrance requirements:* Additional exam requirements/

recommendations for international students: Required—TOEFL. *Faculty research:* Process control and management, ground source heat pumps, water quality, heat transfer, power systems.

Southern Illinois University Carbondale, Graduate School, College of Engineering, Carbondale, IL 62901-4701. Offers ME, MS, PhD. *Faculty:* 55 full-time (3 women), 3 part-time/adjunct (0 women). *Students:* 336 full-time (71 women), 153 part-time (24 women); includes 29 minority (14 Black or African American, non-Hispanic/Latino; 1 American Indian or Alaska Native, non-Hispanic/Latino; 6 Asian, non-Hispanic/Latino; 8 Hispanic/Latino), 356 international. 818 applicants, 40% accepted, 104 enrolled. In 2014, 97 master's, 18 doctorates awarded. *Degree requirements:* For master's, comprehensive exam; for doctorate, thesis/dissertation. *Entrance requirements:* For master's, minimum GPA of 2.7; for doctorate, GRE General Test, minimum GPA of 3.5. Additional exam requirements/recommendations for international students: Required—TOEFL. *Application deadline:* Applications are processed on a rolling basis. Application fee: $50. *Expenses:* Tuition, state resident: full-time $10,176; part-time $1153 per credit. Tuition, nonresident: full-time $20,814; part-time $1744 per credit. *Required fees:* $7092; $394 per credit. $2364 per semester. *Financial support:* In 2014–15, 1 fellowship, 58 research assistantships, 95 teaching assistantships were awarded; Federal Work-Study, institutionally sponsored loans, and tuition waivers (full) also available. Support available to part-time students. *Faculty research:* Electrical systems, all facets of fossil energy, mechanics. *Unit head:* Dr. John J. Warwick, Dean, 618-453-4321, E-mail: warwick@siu.edu. *Application contact:* Toni Baker, Student Contact, 618-453-4321, Fax: 618-453-4235, E-mail: toni@engr.siu.edu.

Southern Illinois University Edwardsville, Graduate School, School of Engineering, Edwardsville, IL 62026. Offers MS. Part-time and evening/weekend programs available. *Faculty:* 52 full-time (5 women). *Students:* 144 full-time (40 women), 138 part-time (22 women); includes 19 minority (7 Black or African American, non-Hispanic/Latino; 7 Asian, non-Hispanic/Latino; 4 Hispanic/Latino; 1 Two or more races, non-Hispanic/Latino), 182 international. 685 applicants, 40% accepted. In 2014, 78 master's awarded. *Degree requirements:* For master's, thesis (for some programs), research paper, final exam. *Entrance requirements:* Additional exam requirements/recommendations for international students: Required—TOEFL (minimum score 550 paper-based; 79 iBT), IELTS (minimum score 6.5). *Application deadline:* For fall admission, 7/24 for domestic students, 7/15 for international students; for spring admission, 12/11 for domestic students, 11/15 for international students; for summer admission, 4/29 for domestic students, 4/15 for international students. Applications are processed on a rolling basis. Application fee: $30. Electronic applications accepted. *Expenses:* Tuition, state resident: full-time $5026. Tuition, nonresident: full-time $12,566. *International tuition:* $25,136 full-time. *Required fees:* $1682. Tuition and fees vary according to course load, campus/location and program. *Financial support:* In 2014–15, 133 students received support, including 6 fellowships with full tuition reimbursements available (averaging $8,370 per year), 60 research assistantships with full tuition reimbursements available, 67 teaching assistantships with full tuition reimbursements available; institutionally sponsored loans, scholarships/grants, and unspecified assistantships also available. Financial award application deadline: 3/1; financial award applicants required to submit FAFSA. *Unit head:* Dr. Hasan Sevim, Dean, 618-650-2541, E-mail: hsevim@siue.edu. *Application contact:* Melissa K. Mace, Assistant Director of Admissions and Graduate and International Recruitment, 618-650-2756, Fax: 618-650-3618, E-mail: mmace@siue.edu.
Website: http://www.siue.edu/engineering.

Southern Methodist University, Bobby B. Lyle School of Engineering, Dallas, TX 75275. Offers MA, MS, MS Cp E, MSEE, MSEM, MSIEM, MSME, DE, PhD. Part-time and evening/weekend programs available. Postbaccalaureate distance learning degree programs offered (no on-campus study). Terminal master's awarded for partial completion of doctoral program. *Degree requirements:* For master's, thesis optional; for doctorate, thesis/dissertation, oral and written qualifying exams. *Entrance requirements:* For master's, GRE General Test, minimum GPA of 3.0 in last 2 years; bachelor's degree in engineering, mathematics, or sciences; for doctorate, bachelor's degree in related field. Additional exam requirements/recommendations for international students: Required—TOEFL (minimum score 550 paper-based). *Expenses:* Contact institution. *Faculty research:* Mobile and fault-tolerant computing, manufacturing systems, telecommunications, solid state devices and materials, fluid and thermal sciences.

Southern Polytechnic State University, School of Engineering, Marietta, GA 30060-2896. Offers MS, Graduate Certificate. Part-time and evening/weekend programs available. Postbaccalaureate distance learning degree programs offered (no on-campus study). *Degree requirements:* For master's, thesis optional. *Entrance requirements:* For master's, GRE. Additional exam requirements/recommendations for international students: Required—TOEFL (minimum score 550 paper-based; 79 iBT), IELTS (minimum score 6.5). Electronic applications accepted. *Faculty research:* Supply chain and logistics reliability, maintainability system analysis, design optimization, engineering education.

Southern Polytechnic State University, School of Engineering Technology and Management, Marietta, GA 30060-2896. Offers MBA, MS, MSA, Graduate Certificate, Graduate Transition Certificate. Part-time and evening/weekend programs available. Postbaccalaureate distance learning degree programs offered (no on-campus study). *Degree requirements:* For master's, comprehensive exam (for some programs), thesis. *Entrance requirements:* For master's, GMAT, GRE, references, statement of purpose. Additional exam requirements/recommendations for international students: Required—TOEFL (minimum score 550 paper-based; 79 iBT), IELTS (minimum score 6.5). Electronic applications accepted. *Faculty research:* Ethics, virtual reality, sustainability, management of technology, quality management, capacity planning, human-computer interaction/interface, enterprise integration planning, economic impact of educational institutions, behavioral accounting, accounting ethics, taxation, information security, visualization simulation, human-computer interaction, supply chain, logistics, economics, analog and digital communications, computer networking, analog and low power electronics design.

Southern University and Agricultural and Mechanical College, Graduate School, College of Engineering, Baton Rouge, LA 70813. Offers ME. *Degree requirements:* For master's, thesis. *Entrance requirements:* For master's, GRE General Test. Additional exam requirements/recommendations for international students: Required—TOEFL (minimum score 525 paper-based).

Stanford University, School of Engineering, Stanford, CA 94305-9991. Offers MS, PhD, Eng. *Degree requirements:* For doctorate, thesis/dissertation; for Eng, thesis. *Entrance requirements:* For master's, doctorate, and Eng, GRE General Test. Additional exam requirements/recommendations for international students: Required—TOEFL. Electronic applications accepted. *Expenses:* Contact institution.

Stevens Institute of Technology, Graduate School, Charles V. Schaefer Jr. School of Engineering, Hoboken, NJ 07030. Offers M Eng, MS, PhD, Certificate, Engr. Part-time and evening/weekend programs available. Postbaccalaureate distance learning degree programs offered. Terminal master's awarded for partial completion of doctoral program. *Degree requirements:* For doctorate, thesis/dissertation. *Entrance requirements:*

Additional exam requirements/recommendations for international students: Required—TOEFL. Electronic applications accepted.

Stony Brook University, State University of New York, Graduate School, College of Engineering and Applied Sciences, Stony Brook, NY 11794. Offers MS, PhD, Advanced Certificate, Certificate. Part-time and evening/weekend programs available. *Faculty:* 170 full-time (36 women), 43 part-time/adjunct (9 women). *Students:* 1,285 full-time (336 women), 227 part-time (61 women); includes 133 minority (19 Black or African American, non-Hispanic/Latino; 89 Asian, non-Hispanic/Latino; 21 Hispanic/Latino; 4 Two or more races, non-Hispanic/Latino), 1,153 international. 4,884 applicants, 32% accepted, 562 enrolled. In 2014, 499 master's, 71 doctorates, 2 other advanced degrees awarded. *Degree requirements:* For doctorate, comprehensive exam, thesis/ dissertation. *Entrance requirements:* For doctorate, GRE General Test. Additional exam requirements/recommendations for international students: Required—TOEFL. *Application deadline:* For fall admission, 1/15 for domestic students; for spring admission, 10/1 for domestic students. Application fee: $100. *Expenses:* Tuition, state resident: full-time $10,370; part-time $432 per credit. Tuition, nonresident: full-time $20,190; part-time $841 per credit. *Required fees:* $1431. *Financial support:* In 2014–15, 37 fellowships, 286 research assistantships, 155 teaching assistantships were awarded; career-related internships or fieldwork also available. *Total annual research expenditures:* $28.3 million. *Unit head:* Dr. Yacov Shamash, Dean, 631-632-8380. *Application contact:* Melissa Jordan, Assistant Dean for Records and Admission, 631-632-9712, Fax: 631-632-7243, E-mail: gradadmissions@stonybrook.edu.
Website: http://www.ceas.sunysb.edu/.

Syracuse University, L. C. Smith College of Engineering and Computer Science, Syracuse, NY 13244. Offers MS, PhD, CAS, CE, EE. Part-time and evening/weekend programs available. *Faculty:* 80 full-time (14 women), 24 part-time/adjunct (3 women). *Students:* 1,053 full-time (276 women), 121 part-time (24 women); includes 53 minority (19 Black or African American, non-Hispanic/Latino; 1 American Indian or Alaska Native, non-Hispanic/Latino; 21 Asian, non-Hispanic/Latino; 6 Hispanic/Latino; 1 Native Hawaiian or other Pacific Islander, non-Hispanic/Latino; 5 Two or more races, non-Hispanic/Latino), 983 international. Average age 25. 3,254 applicants, 40% accepted, 399 enrolled. In 2014, 324 master's, 34 doctorates, 1 other advanced degree awarded. *Degree requirements:* For master's, comprehensive exam (for some programs), thesis (for some programs); for doctorate, comprehensive exam, thesis/dissertation. *Entrance requirements:* For master's and doctorate, GRE General Test. Additional exam requirements/recommendations for international students: Required—TOEFL (minimum score 100 iBT). *Application deadline:* For fall admission, 7/1 priority date for domestic students, 6/1 priority date for international students; for spring admission, 11/15 priority date for domestic students, 10/15 priority date for international students. Applications are processed on a rolling basis. Application fee: $75. Electronic applications accepted. *Expenses:* Tuition: Part-time $1341 per credit. *Required fees:* $1341 per credit. *Financial support:* Fellowships with full tuition reimbursements, research assistantships with full and partial tuition reimbursements, teaching assistantships with full and partial tuition reimbursements, scholarships/grants, and tuition waivers (partial) available. Financial award application deadline: 1/1; financial award applicants required to submit FAFSA. *Faculty research:* Environmental systems, information assurance, biomechanics, solid mechanics and materials, software engineering. *Unit head:* Dr. Teresa A. J. Dahlberg, Dean. *Application contact:* Kathleen Joyce, Assistant Dean, 314-443-2219, E-mail: topgrads@syr.edu.
Website: http://lcs.syr.edu/.

Temple University, College of Engineering, PhD in Engineering Program, Philadelphia, PA 19122-6096. Offers PhD. Part-time and evening/weekend programs available. *Faculty:* 59 full-time (13 women). *Students:* 62 full-time (22 women), 10 part-time (3 women); includes 7 minority (2 Black or African American, non-Hispanic/Latino; 3 Asian, non-Hispanic/Latino; 2 Hispanic/Latino), 41 international. 103 applicants, 73% accepted, 16 enrolled. In 2014, 11 doctorates awarded. *Degree requirements:* For doctorate, thesis/dissertation, preliminary exam, dissertation proposal and defense. *Entrance requirements:* For doctorate, GRE, minimum undergraduate GPA of 3.0; MS in engineering from ABET-accredited or equivalent institution (preferred); resume; goals statement; three letters of reference; official transcripts. Additional exam requirements/ recommendations for international students: Required—TOEFL (minimum score 550 paper-based; 79 iBT), IELTS (minimum score 6.5). *Application deadline:* For fall admission, 1/15 priority date for domestic and international students; for spring admission, 11/1 priority date for domestic students, 8/1 priority date for international students. Applications are processed on a rolling basis. Application fee: $60. Electronic applications accepted. *Expenses:* Expenses: $913 per credit hour in-state; $1,210 per credit hour out-of-state. *Financial support:* Fellowships with full and partial tuition reimbursements, research assistantships with full and partial tuition reimbursements, teaching assistantships with full and partial tuition reimbursements, Federal Work-Study, scholarships/grants, health care benefits, and unspecified assistantships available. Financial award application deadline: 3/1; financial award applicants required to submit FAFSA. *Faculty research:* Advanced/computer-aided manufacturing and advanced materials processing; bioengineering; computer engineering; construction engineering and management; dynamics, controls, and systems; energy and environmental science; engineering physics and engineering mathematics; green engineering; signal processing and communication; transportation engineering; water resources, hydrology, and environmental engineering. *Unit head:* Dr. Keya Sadeghipour, Dean, College of Engineering, 215-204-5285. *Application contact:* Mojan Arshad, Assistant Coordinator, Graduate Studies, 215-204-7800, Fax: 215-204-6936, E-mail: gradengr@temple.edu.
Website: http://engineering.temple.edu/additional-programs/phd-engineering.

Tennessee State University, The School of Graduate Studies and Research, College of Engineering, Nashville, TN 37209-1561. Offers biomedical engineering (ME); civil engineering (ME); computer and information systems engineering (MS, PhD); electrical engineering (ME); environmental engineering (ME); manufacturing engineering (ME); mathematical sciences (MS); mechanical engineering (ME). Part-time and evening/ weekend programs available. *Degree requirements:* For master's, project; for doctorate, comprehensive exam, thesis/dissertation. *Entrance requirements:* For doctorate, minimum GPA of 3.3. *Faculty research:* Robotics, intelligent systems, human-computer interaction software systems, biomedical engineering, signal/image processing, probabilistic design, intelligent manufacturing, cooperative mobile robots, condition based maintenance, sensor fusion.

Tennessee Technological University, College of Graduate Studies, College of Engineering, Cookeville, TN 38505. Offers MS, PhD. Part-time programs available. *Faculty:* 76 full-time (2 women). *Students:* 112 full-time (21 women), 63 part-time (14 women); includes 6 minority (2 Black or African American, non-Hispanic/Latino; 2 Asian, non-Hispanic/Latino; 2 Two or more races, non-Hispanic/Latino), 104 international. Average age 28. 584 applicants, 41% accepted, 67 enrolled. In 2014, 31 master's, 13 doctorates awarded. *Degree requirements:* For master's, comprehensive exam, thesis; for doctorate, comprehensive exam, thesis/dissertation. *Entrance requirements:* For master's, GRE General Test; for doctorate, GRE, minimum GPA of 3.5. Additional exam requirements/recommendations for international students: Required—TOEFL (minimum score 550 paper-based; 79 iBT), IELTS (minimum score 5.5), PTE (minimum score 53), or TOEIC (Test of English as an International Communication). *Application deadline:* For fall admission, 8/1 for domestic students, 5/1 for international students; for spring admission, 12/1 for domestic students, 10/1 for international students. Applications are processed on a rolling basis. Application fee: $35 ($40 for international students). Electronic applications accepted. *Expenses:* Tuition, state resident: full-time $9783; part-time $492 per credit hour. Tuition, nonresident: full-time $24,071; part-time $1179 per credit hour. *Financial support:* In 2014–15, 3 fellowships (averaging $8,000 per year), 71 research assistantships (averaging $9,293 per year), 41 teaching assistantships (averaging $7,223 per year) were awarded; career-related internships or fieldwork also available. Support available to part-time students. Financial award application deadline: 4/1. *Unit head:* Dr. Joseph Rencis, Dean, 931-372-3172, Fax: 931-372-6172, E-mail: jjrencis@tntech.edu. *Application contact:* Shelia K. Kendrick, Coordinator of Graduate Studies, 931-372-3808, Fax: 931-372-3497, E-mail: skendrick@tntech.edu.

Texas A&M University–Kingsville, College of Graduate Studies, College of Engineering, Kingsville, TX 78363. Offers ME, MS, PhD. *Faculty:* 44 full-time (6 women), 6 part-time/adjunct (1 woman). *Students:* 1,253 full-time (243 women), 284 part-time (68 women); includes 70 minority (18 Black or African American, non-Hispanic/Latino; 8 Asian, non-Hispanic/Latino; 42 Hispanic/Latino; 2 Two or more races, non-Hispanic/Latino), 1,439 international. Average age 25. 2,660 applicants, 78% accepted, 674 enrolled. In 2014, 285 master's, 4 doctorates awarded. *Degree requirements:* For master's, variable foreign language requirement, comprehensive exam, thesis (for some programs); for doctorate, variable foreign language requirement, comprehensive exam, thesis/dissertation (for some programs). *Entrance requirements:* For master's and doctorate, GRE, MAT, GMAT. Additional exam requirements/recommendations for international students: Required—TOEFL (minimum score 550 paper-based; 79 iBT). *Application deadline:* For fall admission, 8/15 for domestic students, 6/1 for international students; for spring admission, 12/15 for domestic students, 11/1 for international students; for summer admission, 5/15 for domestic students, 4/1 for international students. Applications are processed on a rolling basis. Application fee: $35 ($50 for international students). Electronic applications accepted. *Financial support:* In 2014–15, 379 students received support, including 42 research assistantships (averaging $4,968 per year), 78 teaching assistantships (averaging $2,510 per year); career-related internships or fieldwork, Federal Work-Study, institutionally sponsored loans, scholarships/grants, health care benefits, tuition waivers (full and partial), and unspecified assistantships also available. Support available to part-time students. Financial award application deadline: 5/15; financial award applicants required to submit FAFSA. *Unit head:* Dr. Stephan Nix, Dean, 361-593-2001, Fax: 361-593-2106, E-mail: stephan.nix@tamuk.edu. *Application contact:* Dr. Mohamed Abdelrahman, Dean of Graduate Studies, 361-593-2809, E-mail: mohamed.abdelrahman@tamuk.edu.

Texas State University, The Graduate College, College of Science and Engineering, Program in Engineering, San Marcos, TX 78666. Offers manufacturing engineering (MS). *Faculty:* 15 full-time (2 women), 1 part-time/adjunct (0 women). *Degree requirements:* For master's, comprehensive exam, thesis (for some programs). *Entrance requirements:* For master's, GRE (minimum preferred scores of 285 overall, 135 verbal, 150 quantitative), baccalaureate degree from regionally-accredited university in engineering, computer science, physics, technology, or closely-related field with minimum GPA of 3.0 on last 60 undergraduate semester hours. Additional exam requirements/recommendations for international students: Required—TOEFL (minimum score 78 iBT), IELTS (minimum score 6.5). *Application deadline:* For fall admission, 2/15 priority date for domestic students, 2/1 priority date for international students. Electronic applications accepted. *Unit head:* Dr. Vishu Viswanathan, Graduate Advisor, 512-245-1826, E-mail: v_v42@txstate.edu. *Application contact:* Dr. Andrea Golato, Dean of Graduate School, 512-245-2581, Fax: 512-245-8365, E-mail: gradcollege@txstate.edu. Website: http://www.engineering.txstate.edu/.

Texas Tech University, Graduate School, Edward E. Whitacre Jr. College of Engineering, Lubbock, TX 79409-3103. Offers M Engr, MENVEGR, MS, MS Ch E, MSCE, MSEE, MSIE, MSME, MSPE, MSSEM, PhD, JD/M Engr. Part-time and evening/weekend programs available. Postbaccalaureate distance learning degree programs offered (no on-campus study). *Faculty:* 153 full-time (25 women), 11 part-time/adjunct (1 woman). *Students:* 697 full-time (167 women), 175 part-time (28 women); includes 85 minority (13 Black or African American, non-Hispanic/Latino; 1 American Indian or Alaska Native, non-Hispanic/Latino; 19 Asian, non-Hispanic/Latino; 45 Hispanic/Latino; 7 Two or more races, non-Hispanic/Latino), 572 international. Average age 28. 2,300 applicants, 33% accepted, 299 enrolled. In 2014, 169 master's, 58 doctorates awarded. *Degree requirements:* For master's, comprehensive exam, thesis (for some programs); for doctorate, comprehensive exam, thesis/dissertation. *Entrance requirements:* For master's, GRE (Verbal and Quantitative), minimum GPA of 3.0. Additional exam requirements/recommendations for international students: Required—TOEFL (minimum score 550 paper-based; 79 iBT), IELTS (minimum score 6.5). *Application deadline:* For fall admission, 6/1 priority date for domestic students, 1/15 priority date for international students; for spring admission, 9/1 priority date for domestic students, 6/15 priority date for international students. Applications are processed on a rolling basis. Application fee: $60. Electronic applications accepted. *Expenses:* Expenses: Contact institution. *Financial support:* In 2014–15, 601 students received support, including 587 fellowships (averaging $2,279 per year), 95 research assistantships (averaging $26,582 per year), 145 teaching assistantships (averaging $19,700 per year). Financial award application deadline: 4/15; financial award applicants required to submit FAFSA. *Faculty research:* Bioengineering, interdisciplinary studies, health care engineering, intellectual property, law and engineering. *Total annual research expenditures:* $17.1 million. *Unit head:* Dr. Albert Sacco, Jr., Dean, Edward E. Whitacre Jr. College of Engineering, 806-742-3451, Fax: 806-742-3493, E-mail: al.sacco-jr@ttu.edu. *Application contact:* Dr. Stephen Ekwaro-Osire, Associate Dean of Research and Graduate Programs, Edward E. Whitacre Jr. College of Engineering, 806-742-3451, Fax: 806-742-3493, E-mail: stephen.ekwaro-osire@ttu.edu.
Website: http://www.depts.ttu.edu/coe/.

Trine University, Allen School of Engineering and Technology, Angola, IN 46703-1764. Offers civil engineering (ME); engineering management (MS). Part-time and evening/weekend programs available. *Students:* 2 full-time (0 women). In 2014, 4 master's awarded. *Degree requirements:* For master's, comprehensive exam, thesis. *Entrance requirements:* Additional exam requirements/recommendations for international students: Required—TOEFL. *Application deadline:* For fall admission, 6/30 for domestic students. Application fee: $100. *Expenses: Tuition:* Full-time $12,000; part-time $670 per credit hour. Tuition and fees vary according to degree level, campus/location, program and student level. *Financial support:* Career-related internships or fieldwork and traineeships available. Financial award application deadline: 3/1; financial award applicants required to submit FAFSA. *Faculty research:* CAD, computer numerical control, parametric modeling, megatronics. *Unit head:* Dr. VK Sharma, Dean, Allen School of Engineering and Technology, 260-665-4432, E-mail: sharmavk@trine.edu. *Application contact:* Dr. Earl D. Brooks, II, President, 260-665-4101, E-mail: brookse@trine.edu.

Tufts University, School of Engineering, Medford, MA 02155. Offers ME, MS, MSEM, PhD. Part-time programs available. *Faculty:* 74 full-time, 22 part-time/adjunct. *Students:* 442 full-time (149 women), 153 part-time (44 women); includes 93 minority (11 Black or African American, non-Hispanic/Latino; 47 Asian, non-Hispanic/Latino; 17 Hispanic/Latino; 18 Two or more races, non-Hispanic/Latino), 177 international. Average age 29. 1,286 applicants, 35% accepted, 217 enrolled. In 2014, 164 master's, 32 doctorates awarded. Terminal master's awarded for partial completion of doctoral program. *Degree requirements:* For master's, thesis (for some programs); for doctorate, thesis/dissertation. *Entrance requirements:* For master's and doctorate, GRE General Test. Additional exam requirements/recommendations for international students: Required—TOEFL (minimum score 550 paper-based; 80 iBT), IELTS (minimum score 6.5). *Application deadline:* For fall admission, 1/15 priority date for domestic students, 1/15 for international students; for spring admission, 9/15 for domestic and international students. Applications are processed on a rolling basis. Application fee: $75. Electronic applications accepted. *Expenses: Tuition:* Full-time $45,590; part-time $1161 per credit hour. *Required fees:* $782. Full-time tuition and fees vary according to degree level, program and student level. Part-time tuition and fees vary according to course load. *Financial support:* Fellowships with full tuition reimbursements, research assistantships with full and partial tuition reimbursements, teaching assistantships with full and partial tuition reimbursements, Federal Work-Study, scholarships/grants, tuition waivers (partial), and unspecified assistantships available. Financial award application deadline: 5/15; financial award applicants required to submit FAFSA. *Unit head:* Dr. Karen Panetta, Graduate Program Director. *Application contact:* Office of Graduate Admissions, 617-627-3395, E-mail: gradadmissions@tufts.edu.
Website: http://www.ase.tufts.edu/engineering/.

Tuskegee University, Graduate Programs, College of Engineering, Tuskegee, AL 36088. Offers MSEE, MSME, PhD. *Degree requirements:* For master's, thesis or alternative. *Entrance requirements:* For master's, GRE General Test, GRE Subject Test. Additional exam requirements/recommendations for international students: Required—TOEFL (minimum score 500 paper-based). *Expenses: Tuition:* Full-time $18,560; part-time $1542 per credit hour. *Required fees:* $2910; $1455 per semester.

Union Graduate College, School of Engineering and Computer Science, Schenectady, NY 12308-3107. Offers computer science (MS); electrical engineering (MS); engineering and management systems (MS); mechanical engineering (MS). Part-time and evening/weekend programs available. *Degree requirements:* For master's, capstone course. *Entrance requirements:* For master's, minimum GPA of 3.0, letters of recommendation. Additional exam requirements/recommendations for international students: Required—TOEFL (minimum score 550 paper-based). Electronic applications accepted. *Expenses:* Contact institution.

Universidad de las Américas Puebla, Division of Graduate Studies, School of Engineering, Puebla, Mexico. Offers M Adm, MS, PhD. Part-time and evening/weekend programs available. *Degree requirements:* For master's, one foreign language, thesis. *Faculty research:* Artificial intelligence, food technology, construction, telecommunications, computers in education, operations research.

Université de Moncton, Faculty of Engineering, Moncton, NB E1A 3E9, Canada. Offers civil engineering (M Sc A); electrical engineering (M Sc A); industrial engineering (M Sc A); mechanical engineering (M Sc A). *Degree requirements:* For master's, thesis, proficiency in French. *Faculty research:* Structures, energy, composite materials, quality control, geo-environment, telecommunications, instrumentation, analog and digital electronics.

Université de Sherbrooke, Faculty of Engineering, Sherbrooke, QC J1K 2R1, Canada. Offers M Eng, M Env, M Sc A, PhD, Diploma. Part-time programs available. *Degree requirements:* For master's, one foreign language, thesis; for doctorate, comprehensive exam, thesis/dissertation. *Entrance requirements:* For master's, bachelor's degree in engineering or equivalent. Electronic applications accepted.

Université du Québec à Chicoutimi, Graduate Programs, Program in Engineering, Chicoutimi, QC G7H 2B1, Canada. Offers M Sc A, PhD. Part-time programs available. *Degree requirements:* For master's, thesis; for doctorate, thesis/dissertation. *Entrance requirements:* For master's, appropriate bachelor's degree, proficiency in French.

Université du Québec à Rimouski, Graduate Programs, Program in Engineering, Rimouski, QC G5L 3A1, Canada. Offers M Sc A. Program offered jointly with Université du Québec à Chicoutimi.

Université du Québec, École de technologie supérieure, Graduate Programs, Montréal, QC H3C 1K3, Canada. Offers M Eng, PhD, Diploma. Postbaccalaureate distance learning degree programs offered (minimal on-campus study). *Entrance requirements:* For master's and Diploma, appropriate bachelor's degree, proficiency in French; for doctorate, appropriate master's degree, proficiency in French.

Université du Québec en Abitibi-Témiscamingue, Graduate Programs, Program in Engineering, Rouyn-Noranda, QC J9X 5E4, Canada. Offers engineering (ME); mineral engineering (ME); mining engineering (DESS).

Université Laval, Faculty of Sciences and Engineering, Québec, QC G1K 7P4, Canada. Offers M Sc, PhD, Diploma. Part-time programs available. *Degree requirements:* For doctorate, thesis/dissertation. Electronic applications accepted.

★ **University at Buffalo, the State University of New York,** Graduate School, School of Engineering and Applied Sciences, Buffalo, NY 14260. Offers ME, MS, PhD, Certificate. Part-time and evening/weekend programs available. Postbaccalaureate distance learning degree programs offered (minimal on-campus study). *Faculty:* 170 full-time (23 women), 24 part-time/adjunct (3 women). *Students:* 1,835 full-time (393 women), 88 part-time (11 women); includes 68 minority (17 Black or African American, non-Hispanic/Latino; 3 American Indian or Alaska Native, non-Hispanic/Latino; 29 Asian, non-Hispanic/Latino; 11 Hispanic/Latino; 8 Two or more races, non-Hispanic/Latino), 1,608 international. Average age 25. 8,247 applicants, 24% accepted, 621 enrolled. In 2014, 503 master's, 84 doctorates awarded. Terminal master's awarded for partial completion of doctoral program. *Degree requirements:* For doctorate, thesis/dissertation. *Entrance requirements:* For master's and doctorate, GRE General Test. Additional exam requirements/recommendations for international students: Required—TOEFL (minimum score 550 paper-based; 79 iBT). *Application deadline:* For fall admission, 2/1 priority date for domestic and international students; for spring admission, 10/1 priority date for domestic students, 10/1 for international students. Applications are processed on a rolling basis. Application fee: $75. Electronic applications accepted. *Financial support:* In 2014–15, 520 students received support, including 38 fellowships with full and partial tuition reimbursements available (averaging $26,734 per year), 215 research assistantships with full and partial tuition reimbursements available (averaging $21,800 per year), 185 teaching assistantships with full and partial tuition reimbursements available (averaging $21,875 per year); career-related internships or fieldwork, Federal Work-Study, institutionally sponsored loans, scholarships/grants, tuition waivers (full and partial), and unspecified assistantships also available. Support available to part-time students. Financial award applicants required to submit FAFSA. *Faculty research:* Bioengineering, infrastructure and environmental engineering, electronic and photonic materials, simulation and

visualization, information technology and computing. *Total annual research expenditures:* $59.2 million. *Unit head:* Dr. Liesl Folks, Dean, 716-645-2771, Fax: 716-645-2495, E-mail: lfolks@buffalo.edu. *Application contact:* Dr. Gary Dargush, Associate Dean for Graduate Education and Research, 716-645-1470, Fax: 716-645-2495, E-mail: gdargush@buffalo.edu.
Website: http://www.eng.buffalo.edu/.

See Display below and Close-Up on page 87.

The University of Akron, Graduate School, College of Engineering, Akron, OH 44325. Offers MS, PhD, MD/PhD. Part-time and evening/weekend programs available. *Faculty:* 89 full-time (11 women), 24 part-time/adjunct (1 woman). *Students:* 350 full-time (79 women), 71 part-time (11 women); includes 13 minority (1 Black or African American, non-Hispanic/Latino; 6 Asian, non-Hispanic/Latino; 4 Hispanic/Latino; 2 Two or more races, non-Hispanic/Latino), 283 international. Average age 28. 470 applicants, 50% accepted, 77 enrolled. In 2014, 70 master's, 30 doctorates awarded. Terminal master's awarded for partial completion of doctoral program. *Degree requirements:* For master's, thesis optional; for doctorate, one foreign language, thesis/dissertation, candidacy exam, qualifying exam. *Entrance requirements:* For master's, GRE, minimum GPA of 2.75, letters of recommendation, statement of purpose, resume; for doctorate, GRE, minimum GPA of 3.0 with bachelor's degree, 3.5 with master's degree; letters of recommendation; statement of purpose, resume. Additional exam requirements/recommendations for international students: Required—TOEFL (minimum score 550 paper-based; 79 iBT), IELTS (minimum score 6.5). *Application deadline:* Applications are processed on a rolling basis. Application fee: $45 ($70 for international students). Electronic applications accepted. *Expenses:* Tuition, state resident: full-time $7578; part-time $421 per credit hour. Tuition, nonresident: full-time $12,977; part-time $721 per credit hour. *Required fees:* $1388; $35 per credit hour. Tuition and fees vary according to course load. *Financial support:* In 2014–15, 1 fellowship with full tuition reimbursement, 160 research assistantships with full tuition reimbursements, 132 teaching assistantships with full tuition reimbursements were awarded; career-related internships or fieldwork and Federal Work-Study also available. *Faculty research:* Engineering materials, energy research, nano and microelectromechanical systems (NEMS and MEMS), bio-engineering, computational methods. *Total annual research expenditures:* $12.5 million. *Unit head:* Dr. George Haritos, Dean, 330-972-6978, E-mail: haritos@uakron.edu. *Application contact:* Dr. Craig Menzemer, Associate Dean, 330-972-5536, E-mail: ccmenze@uakron.edu.
Website: http://www.uakron.edu/engineering/.

The University of Alabama, Graduate School, College of Engineering, Tuscaloosa, AL 35487. Offers MS, MS Ch E, MS Met E, MSAEM, MSCE, PhD. Part-time programs available. Postbaccalaureate distance learning degree programs offered (no on-campus study). *Faculty:* 115 full-time (16 women), 1 part-time/adjunct (0 women). *Students:* 236 full-time (48 women), 43 part-time (1 woman); includes 23 minority (8 Black or African American, non-Hispanic/Latino; 7 Asian, non-Hispanic/Latino; 5 Hispanic/Latino; 3 Two or more races, non-Hispanic/Latino), 131 international. Average age 28. 350 applicants, 44% accepted, 67 enrolled. In 2014, 77 master's, 30 doctorates awarded. Terminal master's awarded for partial completion of doctoral program. *Degree requirements:* For master's, comprehensive exam; for doctorate, thesis/dissertation. *Entrance requirements:* For master's and doctorate, minimum GPA of 3.0. Additional exam requirements/recommendations for international students: Required—TOEFL (minimum score 550 paper-based). *Application deadline:* For fall admission, 7/1 for domestic students, 4/15 for international students; for spring admission, 11/15 for domestic students, 9/1 for international students. Applications are processed on a rolling basis. Application fee: $50 ($60 for international students). Electronic applications accepted. *Expenses:* Tuition, state resident: full-time $9826. Tuition, nonresident: full-time

$24,950. *Financial support:* In 2014–15, 188 students received support, including 23 fellowships with full tuition reimbursements available (averaging $16,022 per year), 85 research assistantships with full tuition reimbursements available (averaging $16,022 per year), 73 teaching assistantships with full tuition reimbursements available (averaging $16,022 per year); career-related internships or fieldwork, Federal Work-Study, and institutionally sponsored loans also available. Financial award application deadline: 2/15. *Faculty research:* Materials and biomaterials networks and sensors, transportation, energy. *Total annual research expenditures:* $23.7 million. *Unit head:* Dr. Charles Karr, Dean, 205-348-6405, Fax: 205-348-8573. *Application contact:* Dr. David A. Francko, Dean, 205-348-8280, Fax: 205-348-0400, E-mail: dfrancko@ua.edu.
Website: http://coeweb.eng.ua.edu/.

The University of Alabama at Birmingham, School of Engineering, Birmingham, AL 35294. Offers M Eng, MS Mt E, MSBME, MSCE, MSEE, MSME, PhD. Part-time and evening/weekend programs available. Postbaccalaureate distance learning degree programs offered (no on-campus study). *Students:* 131 full-time (25 women), 341 part-time (63 women); includes 132 minority (92 Black or African American, non-Hispanic/Latino; 1 American Indian or Alaska Native, non-Hispanic/Latino; 13 Asian, non-Hispanic/Latino; 13 Hispanic/Latino; 13 Two or more races, non-Hispanic/Latino), 93 international. Average age 33. In 2014, 120 master's, 14 doctorates awarded. *Degree requirements:* For doctorate, thesis/dissertation. *Entrance requirements:* For master's, GRE General Test. *Application deadline:* Applications are processed on a rolling basis. Electronic applications accepted. *Expenses:* Tuition, state resident: full-time $7090; part-time $370 per credit hour. Tuition, nonresident: full-time $16,072; part-time $869 per credit hour. Full-time tuition and fees vary according to course load and program. *Financial support:* Fellowships with full tuition reimbursements, research assistantships with full tuition reimbursements, career-related internships or fieldwork, Federal Work-Study, institutionally sponsored loans, and tuition waivers (full and partial) available. Support available to part-time students. *Faculty research:* High performance computing/modeling and simulation, sustainable engineering design and construction, composite materials applications and development, metals processing and research, tissue engineering, cardiac rhythm management, biomedical imaging. *Unit head:* Dr. J. Iwan Alexander, Dean, 205-934-8400, Fax: 205-934-8437, E-mail: ialex@uab.edu. *Application contact:* Susan Noblitt Banks, Director of Graduate School Operations, 205-934-8227, Fax: 205-934-8413, E-mail: gradschool@uab.edu.
Website: http://www.uab.edu/engineering/.

The University of Alabama in Huntsville, School of Graduate Studies, College of Engineering, Huntsville, AL 35899. Offers MS, MSE, MSOR, MSSE, PhD. Part-time and evening/weekend programs available. Postbaccalaureate distance learning degree programs offered (minimal on-campus study). *Degree requirements:* For master's, comprehensive exam, thesis or alternative, oral and written exams; for doctorate, comprehensive exam, thesis/dissertation, oral and written exams. *Entrance requirements:* For master's and doctorate, GRE General Test, minimum GPA of 3.0. Additional exam requirements/recommendations for international students: Required—TOEFL (minimum score 500 paper-based; 80 iBT), IELTS (minimum score 6.5). Electronic applications accepted. *Faculty research:* Transport technology, biotechnology, advanced computer architecture and systems, systems and engineering process, rocket propulsion and plasma engineering.

University of Alaska Anchorage, School of Engineering, Anchorage, AK 99508. Offers M AEST, MCE, MS, Certificate. Part-time and evening/weekend programs available. *Degree requirements:* For master's, comprehensive exam (for some programs), thesis (for some programs). *Entrance requirements:* For master's, GRE General Test. Additional exam requirements/recommendations for international students: Required—TOEFL (minimum score 550 paper-based).

Engineering and Applied Sciences—General

University of Alaska Fairbanks, College of Engineering and Mines, PhD Programs in Engineering, Fairbanks, AK 99775-5960. Offers PhD. Part-time programs available. *Students:* 20 full-time (6 women), 11 part-time (1 woman); includes 3 minority (2 American Indian or Alaska Native, non-Hispanic/Latino; 1 Two or more races, non-Hispanic/Latino), 12 international. Average age 35. 15 applicants, 20% accepted, 1 enrolled. In 2014, 4 doctorates awarded. *Degree requirements:* For doctorate, comprehensive exam, thesis/dissertation, oral defense of dissertation. *Entrance requirements:* For doctorate, GRE General Test, minimum cumulative GPA of 3.0. Additional exam requirements/recommendations for international students: Required—TOEFL (minimum score 550 paper-based, 79 iBT) or IELTS (minimum score 6.5). *Application deadline:* For fall admission, 6/1 for domestic students, 3/1 for international students; for spring admission, 10/15 for domestic students, 9/1 for international students. Applications are processed on a rolling basis. Application fee: $60. Electronic applications accepted. *Expenses:* Tuition, state resident: full-time $7614; part-time $423 per credit. Tuition, nonresident: full-time $15,552; part-time $864 per credit. Tuition and fees vary according to course level, course load and reciprocity agreements. *Financial support:* In 2014–15, 10 research assistantships (averaging $10,453 per year), 4 teaching assistantships (averaging $6,493 per year) were awarded; career-related internships or fieldwork, Federal Work-Study, scholarships/grants, health care benefits, and unspecified assistantships also available. Support available to part-time students. Financial award application deadline: 7/1; financial award applicants required to submit FAFSA. *Faculty research:* Transportation, energy, housing, and climate change. *Unit head:* Dr. Douglas J. Goering, Dean, 907-474-7730, Fax: 907-474-6994, E-mail: fycem@uaf.edu. *Application contact:* Mary Kreta, Director of Admissions, 907-474-7500, Fax: 907-474-7097, E-mail: admissions@uaf.edu.
Website: http://cem.uaf.edu/.

The University of Arizona, College of Engineering, Tucson, AZ 85721. Offers M Eng, ME, MS, PhD, Certificate. Part-time programs available. Postbaccalaureate distance learning degree programs offered (no on-campus study). *Degree requirements:* For doctorate, thesis/dissertation. *Entrance requirements:* Additional exam requirements/recommendations for international students: Required—TOEFL (minimum score 550 paper-based; 79 iBT). Electronic applications accepted.

University of Arkansas, Graduate School, College of Engineering, Fayetteville, AR 72701-1201. Offers MS, MS Cmp E, MS Ch E, MS En E, MS Tc E, MSBE, MSBME, MSCE, MSE, MSEE, MSIE, MSME, MSOR, MSTE, PhD. *Degree requirements:* For doctorate, one foreign language, thesis/dissertation. Electronic applications accepted.

University of Bridgeport, School of Engineering, Bridgeport, CT 06604. Offers MS, PhD. Part-time and evening/weekend programs available. Postbaccalaureate distance learning degree programs offered (no on-campus study). *Degree requirements:* For master's, thesis optional; for doctorate, thesis/dissertation. *Entrance requirements:* Additional exam requirements/recommendations for international students: Recommended—TOEFL (minimum score 550 paper-based; 80 iBT), IELTS (minimum score 6.5). Electronic applications accepted. *Expenses:* Contact institution. *Faculty research:* Atmospheric chemistry, minicomputers, heat transfer.

The University of British Columbia, Faculty of Applied Science, Vancouver, BC V6T 1Z1, Canada. Offers M Arch, M Eng, M Sc, MA Sc, MASA, MASLA, MLA, MSN, MSS, PhD. Part-time programs available. *Degree requirements:* For master's, comprehensive exam (for some programs), thesis (for some programs); for doctorate, comprehensive exam, thesis/dissertation. *Entrance requirements:* Additional exam requirements/recommendations for international students: Required—TOEFL (minimum score 550 paper-based). Electronic applications accepted. *Faculty research:* Architecture, nursing, engineering, landscape architecture.

University of Calgary, Faculty of Graduate Studies, Schulich School of Engineering, Calgary, AB T2N 1N4, Canada. Offers M Eng, M Sc, MPM, PhD. Part-time and evening/weekend programs available. *Degree requirements:* For doctorate, comprehensive exam, thesis/dissertation. *Entrance requirements:* Additional exam requirements/recommendations for international students: Required—TOEFL, IELTS. Electronic applications accepted. *Faculty research:* Chemical and petroleum engineering, civil engineering, electrical and computer engineering, geomatics engineering, mechanical engineering and computer-integrated manufacturing.

University of California, Berkeley, Graduate Division, College of Engineering, Berkeley, CA 94720-1500. Offers M Eng, MS, D Eng, PhD, M Arch/MS, MCP/MS, MPP/MS. *Degree requirements:* For doctorate, thesis/dissertation, exam. *Entrance requirements:* For master's and doctorate, GRE General Test, minimum GPA of 3.0, 3 letters of recommendation.

University of California, Berkeley, UC Berkeley Extension, Certificate Programs in Engineering, Construction and Facilities Management, Berkeley, CA 94720-1500. Offers construction management (Certificate); HVAC (Certificate); integrated circuit design and techniques (online) (Certificate). Postbaccalaureate distance learning degree programs offered.

University of California, Davis, College of Engineering, Davis, CA 95616. Offers M Engr, MS, D Engr, PhD, Certificate, M Engr/MBA. Part-time programs available. Terminal master's awarded for partial completion of doctoral program. *Degree requirements:* For master's, comprehensive exam (for some programs), thesis (for some programs); for doctorate, comprehensive exam, thesis/dissertation. *Entrance requirements:* For doctorate, GRE. Additional exam requirements/recommendations for international students: Required—TOEFL (minimum score 550 paper-based). Electronic applications accepted.

University of California, Irvine, Henry Samueli School of Engineering, Irvine, CA 92697. Offers MS, PhD. Part-time programs available. *Students:* 965 full-time (287 women), 84 part-time (19 women); includes 220 minority (7 Black or African American, non-Hispanic/Latino; 2 American Indian or Alaska Native, non-Hispanic/Latino; 142 Asian, non-Hispanic/Latino; 52 Hispanic/Latino; 1 Native Hawaiian or other Pacific Islander, non-Hispanic/Latino; 16 Two or more races, non-Hispanic/Latino), 603 international. Average age 26. 4,811 applicants, 24% accepted, 420 enrolled. In 2014, 219 master's, 83 doctorates awarded. Terminal master's awarded for partial completion of doctoral program. *Degree requirements:* For doctorate, thesis/dissertation. *Entrance requirements:* For master's and doctorate, GRE General Test, minimum GPA of 3.0, 3 letters of recommendation. Additional exam requirements/recommendations for international students: Required—TOEFL (minimum score 550 paper-based). *Application deadline:* For fall admission, 1/15 priority date for domestic students, 1/15 for international students. Applications are processed on a rolling basis. Application fee: $90 ($110 for international students). Electronic applications accepted. *Financial support:* Fellowships with tuition reimbursements, research assistantships with full tuition reimbursements, teaching assistantships with tuition reimbursements, institutionally sponsored loans, traineeships, health care benefits, and unspecified assistantships available. Financial award application deadline: 3/1; financial award applicants required to submit FAFSA. *Faculty research:* Biomedical, chemical and biochemical, civil and environmental, electrical and computer, mechanical and aerospace engineering. *Unit head:* Gregory N. Washington, Dean, 949-824-4333, Fax: 949-824-8200, E-mail: engineering@uci.edu. *Application contact:* Jean Bennett, Director of Graduate Student Affairs, 949-824-6475, Fax: 949-824-8200, E-mail: jean.bennett@uci.edu.
Website: http://www.eng.uci.edu/.

University of California, Los Angeles, Graduate Division, Henry Samueli School of Engineering and Applied Science, Los Angeles, CA 90095-1601. Offers MS, PhD, MBA/MS. Evening/weekend programs available. Postbaccalaureate distance learning degree programs offered (no on-campus study). *Faculty:* 157 full-time (21 women), 24 part-time/adjunct (1 woman). *Students:* 1,928 full-time (424 women); includes 488 minority (15 Black or African American, non-Hispanic/Latino; 1 American Indian or Alaska Native, non-Hispanic/Latino; 348 Asian, non-Hispanic/Latino; 93 Hispanic/Latino; 1 Native Hawaiian or other Pacific Islander, non-Hispanic/Latino; 30 Two or more races, non-Hispanic/Latino), 1,033 international. 6,162 applicants, 29% accepted, 767 enrolled. In 2014, 586 master's, 177 doctorates awarded. Terminal master's awarded for partial completion of doctoral program. *Degree requirements:* For master's, comprehensive exam or thesis; for doctorate, thesis/dissertation, qualifying exams. *Entrance requirements:* For master's, GRE General Test, minimum GPA of 3.0; for doctorate, GRE General Test, minimum GPA of 3.25. Additional exam requirements/recommendations for international students: Required—TOEFL (minimum score 560 paper-based; 87 iBT), IELTS (minimum score 7). *Application deadline:* For fall admission, 12/1 for domestic and international students. Application fee: $80 ($100 for international students). Electronic applications accepted. *Financial support:* In 2014–15, 618 fellowships, 1,508 research assistantships, 576 teaching assistantships were awarded; career-related internships or fieldwork, Federal Work-Study, institutionally sponsored loans, and tuition waivers (full and partial) also available. Financial award application deadline: 3/2; financial award applicants required to submit FAFSA. *Total annual research expenditures:* $101.7 million. *Unit head:* Dr. Richard D. Wesel, Associate Dean, Academic and Student Affairs, 310-825-2942, E-mail: wesel@ee.ucla.edu. *Application contact:* Jan LaBuda, Director, Office of Academic and Student Affairs, 310-825-2514, Fax: 310-825-2473, E-mail: jan@seas.ucla.edu.
Website: http://www.engineer.ucla.edu/.

University of California, Merced, Graduate Division, School of Engineering, Merced, CA 95343. Offers biological engineering and small scale technologies (MS, PhD); electrical engineering and computer science (MS, PhD); environmental systems (MS, PhD); mechanical engineering (MS); mechanical engineering and applied mechanics (PhD). *Faculty:* 38 full-time (6 women), 1 part-time/adjunct (0 women). *Students:* 128 full-time (36 women), 2 part-time (0 women); includes 21 minority (1 Black or African American, non-Hispanic/Latino; 11 Asian, non-Hispanic/Latino; 6 Hispanic/Latino; 3 Two or more races, non-Hispanic/Latino), 72 international. Average age 28. 230 applicants, 39% accepted, 38 enrolled. In 2014, 5 master's, 18 doctorates awarded. *Degree requirements:* For master's, variable foreign language requirement, comprehensive exam, thesis (for some programs); for doctorate, variable foreign language requirement, comprehensive exam, thesis/dissertation. *Entrance requirements:* For master's and doctorate, GRE. Additional exam requirements/recommendations for international students: Required—TOEFL (minimum score 550 paper-based; 68 iBT); Recommended—IELTS. Application fee: $80 ($100 for international students). *Expenses:* Tuition, state resident: full-time $11,220; part-time $2805 per semester. *Required fees:* $1940; $970 per semester hour. *Financial support:* In 2014–15, 19 fellowships with full and partial tuition reimbursements (averaging $6,683 per year) were awarded; scholarships/grants also available. *Faculty research:* Artificial intelligence, biomedical imaging, thermal science, ecology, nanotechnology. *Unit head:* Dr. Erik Rolland, Interim Dean, 209-228-4296, Fax: 209-228-4047, E-mail: erolland@ucmerced.edu. *Application contact:* Tsu Ya, Graduate Admissions and Academic Services Manager, 209-228-4521, Fax: 209-228-6906, E-mail: tya@ucmerced.edu.

University of California, Santa Barbara, Graduate Division, College of Engineering, Santa Barbara, CA 93106-5130. Offers MS, MTM, PhD, MS/PhD. Terminal master's awarded for partial completion of doctoral program. *Degree requirements:* For doctorate, thesis/dissertation. *Entrance requirements:* For master's, GRE, 3 letters of recommendation, resume/curriculum vitae; for doctorate, GRE, 3 letters of recommendation, statement of purpose, personal achievements/contributions statement, resume/curriculum vitae, transcripts for post-secondary institutions attended. Additional exam requirements/recommendations for international students: Required—TOEFL, IELTS. Electronic applications accepted.

University of California, Santa Cruz, Division of Graduate Studies, Jack Baskin School of Engineering, Santa Cruz, CA 95064. Offers MS, PhD. *Entrance requirements:* For master's and doctorate, GRE General Test. Additional exam requirements/recommendations for international students: Required—TOEFL (minimum score 570 paper-based; 89 iBT); Recommended—IELTS (minimum score 8). Electronic applications accepted.

University of Central Florida, College of Engineering and Computer Science, Orlando, FL 32816. Offers MS, MS Cp E, MS Env E, MSAE, MSCE, MSEE, MSIE, MSME, MSMSE, PhD, Certificate. Part-time and evening/weekend programs available. *Faculty:* 158 full-time (23 women), 38 part-time/adjunct (0 women). *Students:* 754 full-time (166 women), 537 part-time (114 women); includes 259 minority (43 Black or African American, non-Hispanic/Latino; 1 American Indian or Alaska Native, non-Hispanic/Latino; 61 Asian, non-Hispanic/Latino; 133 Hispanic/Latino; 21 Two or more races, non-Hispanic/Latino), 523 international. Average age 30. 1,391 applicants, 65% accepted, 383 enrolled. In 2014, 362 master's, 78 doctorates, 26 other advanced degrees awarded. *Degree requirements:* For doctorate, thesis/dissertation, candidacy exam, departmental qualifying exam. *Entrance requirements:* For master's, GRE General Test, minimum GPA of 3.0 in last 60 hours; for doctorate, minimum GPA of 3.5 in last 60 hours, resume. Additional exam requirements/recommendations for international students: Required—TOEFL. *Application deadline:* For fall admission, 7/15 for domestic students; for spring admission, 12/1 for domestic students. Application fee: $30. Electronic applications accepted. *Expenses:* Tuition, state resident: part-time $288.16 per credit hour. Tuition, nonresident: part-time $1073.31 per credit hour. *Financial support:* In 2014–15, 365 students received support, including 117 fellowships with partial tuition reimbursements available (averaging $4,900 per year), 247 research assistantships with partial tuition reimbursements available (averaging $10,300 per year), 140 teaching assistantships with partial tuition reimbursements available (averaging $10,400 per year); career-related internships or fieldwork, Federal Work-Study, institutionally sponsored loans, tuition waivers (partial), and unspecified assistantships also available. Financial award application deadline: 3/1; financial award applicants required to submit FAFSA. *Faculty research:* Electro-optics, lasers, materials, simulation, microelectronics. *Unit head:* Dr. Michael Georgiopoulos, Dean, 407-823-2156, E-mail: michaelg@ucf.edu. *Application contact:* Barbara Rodriguez Lamas, Director, Admissions and Student Services, 407-823-2766, Fax: 407-823-6442, E-mail: gradadmissions@ucf.edu.
Website: http://www.cecs.ucf.edu/.

University of Central Oklahoma, The Jackson College of Graduate Studies, College of Mathematics and Science, Department of Engineering and Physics, Edmond, OK 73034-5209. Offers biomedical engineering (MS); electrical engineering (MS); mechanical systems (MS); physics (MS). Part-time programs available. *Degree requirements:* For master's, thesis optional. *Entrance requirements:* For master's, GRE,

24 hours of course work in physics or equivalent, mathematics through differential equations, minimum GPA of 2.75 overall and 3.0 in last 60 hours attempted. Additional exam requirements/recommendations for international students: Required—TOEFL (minimum score 550 paper-based). Electronic applications accepted.

University of Cincinnati, Graduate School, College of Engineering and Applied Science, Cincinnati, OH 45221. Offers MS, PhD, MBA/MS. *Accreditation:* ABET (one or more programs are accredited). Part-time and evening/weekend programs available. Terminal master's awarded for partial completion of doctoral program. *Degree requirements:* For master's, thesis or alternative; for doctorate, comprehensive exam, thesis/dissertation. *Entrance requirements:* For master's and doctorate, GRE General Test. Additional exam requirements/recommendations for international students: Required—TOEFL (minimum score 520 paper-based).

University of Colorado Boulder, Graduate School, College of Engineering and Applied Science, Boulder, CO 80309. Offers ME, MS, PhD, JD/MS, MBA/MS. *Faculty:* 175 full-time (30 women). *Students:* 1,303 full-time (328 women), 426 part-time (86 women); includes 210 minority (18 Black or African American, non-Hispanic/Latino; 9 American Indian or Alaska Native, non-Hispanic/Latino; 78 Asian, non-Hispanic/Latino; 69 Hispanic/Latino; 36 Two or more races, non-Hispanic/Latino), 558 international. Average age 28. 3,413 applicants, 40% accepted, 499 enrolled. In 2014, 423 master's, 116 doctorates awarded. *Degree requirements:* For doctorate, thesis/dissertation. *Entrance requirements:* For master's, minimum undergraduate GPA of 2.75. Application fee: $50 ($70 for international students). Electronic applications accepted. *Expenses:* Expenses: Contact institution. *Financial support:* In 2014–15, 2,299 students received support, including 376 fellowships (averaging $12,022 per year), 504 research assistantships with full and partial tuition reimbursements available (averaging $35,164 per year), 155 teaching assistantships with full and partial tuition reimbursements available (averaging $31,144 per year); institutionally sponsored loans, scholarships/grants, health care benefits, and unspecified assistantships also available. Financial award applicants required to submit FAFSA. *Faculty research:* Chemical engineering, civil engineering, mechanical engineering, materials engineering, transport phenomena. *Total annual research expenditures:* $66 million.
Website: http://engineering.colorado.edu.

University of Colorado Colorado Springs, College of Engineering and Applied Science, Colorado Springs, CO 80933-7150. Offers ME, MS, PhD. Part-time and evening/weekend programs available. *Faculty:* 41 full-time (6 women), 32 part-time/adjunct (6 women). *Students:* 35 full-time (7 women), 289 part-time (51 women); includes 45 minority (3 Black or African American, non-Hispanic/Latino; 3 American Indian or Alaska Native, non-Hispanic/Latino; 14 Asian, non-Hispanic/Latino; 22 Hispanic/Latino; 3 Two or more races, non-Hispanic/Latino), 120 international. Average age 33. 251 applicants, 65% accepted, 68 enrolled. In 2014, 72 master's, 6 doctorates awarded. *Degree requirements:* For master's, comprehensive exam (for some programs), thesis or alternative; for doctorate, comprehensive exam, thesis/dissertation. *Entrance requirements:* For master's, GRE General Test, minimum GPA of 3.0; for doctorate, GRE General Test, minimum GPA of 3.3. Additional exam requirements/recommendations for international students: Required—TOEFL (minimum score 550 paper-based; 80 iBT). *Application deadline:* For fall admission, 6/15 for domestic students, 4/1 for international students; for spring admission, 10/1 for domestic and international students. Applications are processed on a rolling basis. Application fee: $60 ($100 for international students). *Expenses:* Expenses: Contact institution. *Financial support:* In 2014–15, 32 students received support, including 2 fellowships (averaging $6,000 per year), 16 research assistantships (averaging $11,500 per year); teaching assistantships, career-related internships or fieldwork, Federal Work-Study, and scholarships/grants also available. Support available to part-time students. Financial award application deadline: 3/1; financial award applicants required to submit FAFSA. *Faculty research:* Synthesis and modeling of digital systems, microelectronics, superconductive thin films, sol-gel processes, linear and nonlinear adaptive filtering, wireless communications networks, computer architecture. *Total annual research expenditures:* $2 million. *Unit head:* Dr. Ramaswami Dandapani, Dean, 719-255-3543, Fax: 719-255-3542, E-mail: rdan@cas.uccs.edu. *Application contact:* Dawn House, Office of Student Support, 719-255-3246, E-mail: dhouse@uccs.edu.
Website: http://eas.uccs.edu/.

University of Colorado Denver, College of Engineering and Applied Science, Denver, CO 80217. Offers M Eng, MS, EASPh D, PhD. Part-time and evening/weekend programs available. *Faculty:* 62 full-time (16 women), 20 part-time/adjunct (4 women). *Students:* 396 full-time (118 women), 159 part-time (28 women); includes 57 minority (16 Black or African American, non-Hispanic/Latino; 14 Asian, non-Hispanic/Latino; 19 Hispanic/Latino; 1 Native Hawaiian or other Pacific Islander, non-Hispanic/Latino; 7 Two or more races, non-Hispanic/Latino), 286 international. Average age 28. 1,146 applicants, 53% accepted, 209 enrolled. In 2014, 128 master's, 11 doctorates awarded. *Degree requirements:* For master's, comprehensive exam, thesis; for doctorate, comprehensive exam, thesis/dissertation. *Entrance requirements:* For master's, GRE, minimum undergraduate GPA of 2.75; for doctorate, GRE, minimum cumulative GPA of 3.0. Additional exam requirements/recommendations for international students: Required—TOEFL (minimum score 550 paper-based; 79 iBT); Recommended—IELTS (minimum score 6.8). Application fee: $50 ($75 for international students). Electronic applications accepted. *Expenses:* Expenses: Contact institution. *Financial support:* In 2014–15, 82 students received support. Fellowships, research assistantships, teaching assistantships, Federal Work-Study, institutionally sponsored loans, scholarships/grants, and traineeships available. Financial award application deadline: 4/1; financial award applicants required to submit FAFSA. *Faculty research:* Civil engineering, bioengineering, mechanical engineering, electrical engineering, computer science. *Total annual research expenditures:* $2.5 million. *Unit head:* Dr. Mark Ingber, Dean, 303-556-2870, Fax: 303-556-2511, E-mail: marc.ingber@ucdenver.edu. *Application contact:* Graduate School Admissions, 303-556-2704, E-mail: admissions@ucdenver.edu.
Website: http://www.ucdenver.edu/academics/colleges/Engineering/Pages/EngineeringAppliedScience.aspx.

University of Connecticut, Graduate School, School of Engineering, Storrs, CT 06269. Offers M Eng, MS, PhD. Terminal master's awarded for partial completion of doctoral program. *Degree requirements:* For master's, comprehensive exam; for doctorate, thesis/dissertation. *Entrance requirements:* For master's and doctorate, GRE General Test. Additional exam requirements/recommendations for international students: Required—TOEFL (minimum score 550 paper-based). Electronic applications accepted.

University of Delaware, College of Engineering, Newark, DE 19716. Offers M Ch E, MAS, MCE, MEM, MMSE, MS, MSECE, MSME, PhD. Part-time and evening/weekend programs available. Postbaccalaureate distance learning degree programs offered (minimal on-campus study). Terminal master's awarded for partial completion of doctoral program. *Degree requirements:* For master's, thesis (for some programs); for doctorate, thesis/dissertation. *Entrance requirements:* For master's and doctorate, GRE General Test. Additional exam requirements/recommendations for international students: Required—TOEFL (minimum score 550 paper-based). Electronic applications accepted. *Faculty research:* Biotechnology, photonics, transportation, composite materials, materials science.

University of Denver, Daniel Felix Ritchie School of Engineering and Computer Science, Denver, CO 80208. Offers MS, PhD. *Faculty:* 33 full-time (4 women), 7 part-time/adjunct (2 women). *Students:* 11 full-time (4 women), 180 part-time (33 women); includes 22 minority (3 Black or African American, non-Hispanic/Latino; 7 Asian, non-Hispanic/Latino; 7 Hispanic/Latino; 5 Two or more races, non-Hispanic/Latino), 82 international. Average age 29. 259 applicants, 42% accepted, 51 enrolled. In 2014, 50 master's, 15 doctorates awarded. *Degree requirements:* For master's, thesis (for some programs); for doctorate, variable foreign language requirement, comprehensive exam, thesis/dissertation. *Entrance requirements:* For master's, GRE General Test, bachelor's degree, transcripts, three letters of recommendation, personal statement; for doctorate, GRE General Test, master's degree, transcripts, three letters of recommendation, personal statement. Additional exam requirements/recommendations for international students: Required—TOEFL (minimum score 550 paper-based; 80 iBT). *Application deadline:* Applications are processed on a rolling basis. Application fee: $65. Electronic applications accepted. *Expenses:* Expenses: $1,199 per credit hour. *Financial support:* In 2014–15, 77 students received support, including 30 research assistantships with full and partial tuition reimbursements available (averaging $12,429 per year), 43 teaching assistantships with full and partial tuition reimbursements available (averaging $11,724 per year); Federal Work-Study, institutionally sponsored loans, scholarships/grants, health care benefits, and unspecified assistantships also available. Support available to part-time students. Financial award application deadline: 2/15; financial award applicants required to submit FAFSA. *Unit head:* Dr. Michael Keables, Interim Dean, 303-871-2621, Fax: 303-871-2716, E-mail: mkeables@du.edu. *Application contact:* Information Contact, 303-871-3787, E-mail: ritchieschool@du.edu.
Website: http://www.du.edu/rsecs/index.html.

University of Detroit Mercy, College of Engineering and Science, Detroit, MI 48221. Offers M Eng Mgt, MATM, ME, MS, MSCS, DE. Part-time and evening/weekend programs available. *Degree requirements:* For doctorate, thesis/dissertation. *Expenses:* Contact institution.

University of Florida, Graduate School, College of Engineering, Gainesville, FL 32611. Offers ME, MS, PhD, Certificate, Engr, JD/MS, MD/PhD, MSM/MS. Part-time programs available. Postbaccalaureate distance learning degree programs offered (no on-campus study). *Faculty:* 31 full-time, 162 part-time/adjunct (28 women). *Students:* 1,907 full-time (448 women), 543 part-time (120 women); includes 338 minority (71 Black or African American, non-Hispanic/Latino; 6 American Indian or Alaska Native, non-Hispanic/Latino; 114 Asian, non-Hispanic/Latino; 147 Hispanic/Latino), 1,357 international. 5,188 applicants, 42% accepted, 787 enrolled. In 2014, 1,175 master's, 219 doctorates awarded. *Degree requirements:* For doctorate, thesis/dissertation. *Entrance requirements:* For master's and doctorate, minimum GPA of 3.0; for other advanced degree, GRE General Test. Additional exam requirements/recommendations for international students: Required—TOEFL (minimum score 550 paper-based; 80 iBT), IELTS (minimum score 6). *Application deadline:* Applications are processed on a rolling basis. Application fee: $30. Electronic applications accepted. *Financial support:* Career-related internships or fieldwork, Federal Work-Study, institutionally sponsored loans, and unspecified assistantships available. Support available to part-time students. Financial award applicants required to submit FAFSA. *Unit head:* Cammy R. Abernathy, PhD, Dean, 352-392-6000, E-mail: caber@eng.ufl.edu. *Application contact:* Mark E. Law, PhD, Associate Dean, 352-392-0943, E-mail: mlaw@eng.ufl.edu.
Website: http://www.eng.ufl.edu/.

University of Guelph, Graduate Studies, College of Physical and Engineering Science, School of Engineering, Guelph, ON N1G 2W1, Canada. Offers biological engineering (M Eng, M Sc, MA Sc, PhD); engineering systems and computing (M Eng, M Sc, MA Sc, PhD); environmental engineering (M Eng, M Sc, MA Sc, PhD); water resources engineering (M Eng, M Sc, MA Sc, PhD). Part-time programs available. *Degree requirements:* For master's, thesis (for some programs); for doctorate, comprehensive exam, thesis/dissertation. *Entrance requirements:* For master's, minimum B- average during previous 2 years of course work; for doctorate, minimum B average. Additional exam requirements/recommendations for international students: Required—TOEFL (minimum score 550 paper-based; 89 iBT), IELTS (minimum score 6.5). Electronic applications accepted. *Faculty research:* Water and food safety, environmental contaminant fates and mechanisms, computer systems, robotics and mechatronics, waste treatment.

University of Hartford, College of Engineering, Technology and Architecture, Program in Engineering, West Hartford, CT 06117-1599. Offers M Eng. *Entrance requirements:* Additional exam requirements/recommendations for international students: Required—TOEFL.

University of Hawaii at Manoa, Graduate Division, College of Engineering, Honolulu, HI 96822. Offers MS, PhD. *Accreditation:* ABET (one or more programs are accredited). Part-time programs available. *Entrance requirements:* Additional exam requirements/recommendations for international students: Required—TOEFL or IELTS.

University of Houston, Cullen College of Engineering, Houston, TX 77204. Offers M Pet E, MCE, MCHE, MEE, MIE, MME, MSEE, MSME, PhD. Part-time programs available. Terminal master's awarded for partial completion of doctoral program. *Degree requirements:* For master's, thesis (for some programs); for doctorate, thesis/dissertation, departmental qualifying exam. *Entrance requirements:* For master's and doctorate, GRE General Test. *Faculty research:* Superconducting materials, microantennas for space packs, direct numerical simulation of pairing vortices.

University of Idaho, College of Graduate Studies, College of Engineering, Moscow, ID 83844-1011. Offers M Engr, MS, PhD. *Faculty:* 62 full-time, 7 part-time/adjunct. *Students:* 106 full-time (12 women), 254 part-time (40 women). Average age 35. In 2014, 110 master's, 21 doctorates awarded. *Degree requirements:* For doctorate, thesis/dissertation. *Entrance requirements:* For doctorate, minimum undergraduate GPA of 2.8, graduate 3.0. Additional exam requirements/recommendations for international students: Required—TOEFL (minimum score 550 paper-based). *Application deadline:* For fall admission, 8/1 for domestic students; for spring admission, 12/15 for domestic students. Applications are processed on a rolling basis. Application fee: $60. Electronic applications accepted. *Expenses:* Tuition, state resident: full-time $4784; part-time $280.50 per credit hour. Tuition, nonresident: full-time $18,314; part-time $957.50 per credit hour. *Required fees:* $2000; $58.50 per credit hour. Tuition and fees vary according to program. *Financial support:* Fellowships, research assistantships, teaching assistantships, career-related internships or fieldwork, and Federal Work-Study available. Support available to part-time students. Financial award applicants required to submit FAFSA. *Faculty research:* Robotics, micro-electronic packaging, water resources engineering and science, oscillating flows in macro- and micro-scale methods of mechanical separation, nuclear energy. *Unit head:* Dr. Larry Stauffer, Dean, 208-885-6470, E-mail: deanengr@uidaho.edu. *Application contact:* Sean Scoggin, Graduate Recruitment Coordinator, 208-885-4001, Fax: 208-885-4406, E-mail: graduateadmissions@uidaho.edu.
Website: http://www.uidaho.edu/engr/.

University of Illinois at Chicago, Graduate College, College of Engineering, Chicago, IL 60607-7128. Offers M Eng, MEE, MS, PhD. Part-time and evening/weekend programs available. *Faculty:* 125 full-time (25 women), 53 part-time/adjunct (10 women). *Students:* 976

Engineering and Applied Sciences—General

full-time (264 women), 227 part-time (53 women); includes 146 minority (18 Black or African American, non-Hispanic/Latino; 2 American Indian or Alaska Native, non-Hispanic/Latino; 81 Asian, non-Hispanic/Latino; 40 Hispanic/Latino; 5 Two or more races, non-Hispanic/Latino), 841 international. Average age 27. 4,010 applicants, 42% accepted, 422 enrolled. In 2014, 337 master's, 62 doctorates awarded. Terminal master's awarded for partial completion of doctoral program. *Degree requirements:* For doctorate, thesis/dissertation. *Entrance requirements:* For doctorate, GRE. Additional exam requirements/recommendations for international students: Required—TOEFL. *Application deadline:* For fall admission, 5/15 for domestic students, 1/9 for international students; for spring admission, 11/1 for domestic students. Applications are processed on a rolling basis. Application fee: $60. Electronic applications accepted. *Expenses:* Expenses: $21,236 in-state, $33,234 out-of-state (for engineering); $17,602 in-state, $29,600 out-of-state (for all other programs). *Financial support:* In 2014–15, 19 fellowships with full tuition reimbursements were awarded; research assistantships with full tuition reimbursements, teaching assistantships with full tuition reimbursements, career-related internships or fieldwork, Federal Work-Study, scholarships/grants, traineeships, tuition waivers (full), and unspecified assistantships also available. Financial award application deadline: 3/1; financial award applicants required to submit FAFSA. *Total annual research expenditures:* $21.3 million. *Unit head:* Prof. Peter C. Nelson, Dean, 312-996-2400. *Application contact:* Receptionist, 312-413-2550, E-mail: gradcoll@uic.edu.
Website: http://www.uic.edu/depts/enga/.

University of Illinois at Urbana–Champaign, Graduate College, College of Engineering, Champaign, IL 61820. Offers M Eng, MCS, MS, PhD, M Arch/MS, MBA/MS, MCS/JD, MCS/M Arch, MCS/MBA, MS/MBA, PhD/MBA. Part-time and evening/weekend programs available. Postbaccalaureate distance learning degree programs offered. *Students:* 3,097. Application fee: $70 ($90 for international students). *Expenses:* Expenses: Contact institution. *Unit head:* Dr. Andreas C. Cangellaris, Dean, 217-333-6037, Fax: 217-244-7705, E-mail: cangella@illinois.edu. *Application contact:* Gregory S. Harman, Admissions Support Staff, 217-244-4637.
Website: http://engineering.illinois.edu/.

The University of Iowa, Graduate College, College of Engineering, Iowa City, IA 52242-1527. Offers MS, PhD. *Faculty:* 79 full-time (12 women), 14 part-time/adjunct (1 woman). *Students:* 316 full-time (77 women); includes 31 minority (8 Black or African American, non-Hispanic/Latino; 12 Asian, non-Hispanic/Latino; 9 Hispanic/Latino; 2 Two or more races, non-Hispanic/Latino), 147 international. Average age 27. 478 applicants, 18% accepted, 33 enrolled. In 2014, 52 master's, 38 doctorates awarded. *Degree requirements:* For master's, comprehensive exam (for some programs), oral exam and/or thesis; for doctorate, comprehensive exam, thesis/dissertation. *Entrance requirements:* For master's and doctorate, GRE, official academic records/transcripts, 3 letters of recommendation, resume, statement of purpose. Additional exam requirements/recommendations for international students: Required—TOEFL (minimum score 550 paper-based; 81 iBT). *Application deadline:* For fall admission, 1/15 priority date for domestic and international students; for spring admission, 8/1 priority date for domestic and international students; for summer admission, 1/1 for domestic and international students. Applications are processed on a rolling basis. Application fee: $60 ($100 for international students). Electronic applications accepted. *Expenses:* Expenses: $9,901 in-state; $26,783 out-of-state; out-of-state engineering students with appointment are assessed at an in-state rate. *Financial support:* In 2014–15, 27 fellowships with full and partial tuition reimbursements (averaging $21,493 per year), 205 research assistantships with full and partial tuition reimbursements (averaging $20,430 per year), 47 teaching assistantships with full and partial tuition reimbursements (averaging $18,080 per year) were awarded; career-related internships or fieldwork, Federal Work-Study, scholarships/grants, traineeships, health care benefits, and unspecified assistantships also available.

Financial award application deadline: 1/15; financial award applicants required to submit FAFSA. *Total annual research expenditures:* $51.4 million. *Unit head:* Dr. Alec Scranton, Dean, 319-335-5766, Fax: 319-335-6086, E-mail: alec-scranton@uiowa.edu. *Application contact:* Dr. Brent Gage, Associate Vice President for Enrollment Management, 319-335-1525, Fax: 319-335-1535, E-mail: gradmail@uiowa.edu.
Website: http://www.engineering.uiowa.edu/.

See Display below and Close-Up on page 89.

The University of Kansas, Graduate Studies, School of Engineering, Lawrence, KS 66045. Offers MCE, MCM, ME, MS, DE, PhD. Part-time and evening/weekend programs available. Postbaccalaureate distance learning degree programs offered (no on-campus study). *Faculty:* 131. *Students:* 437 full-time (125 women), 244 part-time (50 women); includes 55 minority (15 Black or African American, non-Hispanic/Latino; 2 American Indian or Alaska Native, non-Hispanic/Latino; 18 Asian, non-Hispanic/Latino; 7 Hispanic/Latino; 13 Two or more races, non-Hispanic/Latino), 305 international. Average age 28. 903 applicants, 53% accepted, 195 enrolled. In 2014, 126 master's, 33 doctorates awarded. Terminal master's awarded for partial completion of doctoral program. *Degree requirements:* For master's, 30-33 credit hours; for doctorate, comprehensive exam, thesis/dissertation, 45-60 credit hours. *Entrance requirements:* For master's and doctorate, GRE, minimum GPA of 3.0. Additional exam requirements/recommendations for international students: Required—TOEFL. *Application deadline:* Applications are processed on a rolling basis. Application fee: $55 ($65 for international students). Electronic applications accepted. *Expenses:* Expenses: Contact institution. *Financial support:* Fellowships, research assistantships with full and partial tuition reimbursements, teaching assistantships with full and partial tuition reimbursements, career-related internships or fieldwork, Federal Work-Study, scholarships/grants, and unspecified assistantships available. *Faculty research:* Global change, transportation, water, energy, healthcare, information technology, sustainable infrastructure, remote sensing, environmental sustainability, telecommunications, oil recovery, airplane design, structured materials, robotics, sustainable fuels and chemicals, radar systems, composite materials and structures, precision particles, tissue engineering, chemoenzymatic catalysis, communication systems and networks, intelligent systems, data mining, fuel cells, imaging. *Total annual research expenditures:* $17 million. *Unit head:* Dr. Michael S. Branicky, Dean, 785-864-2930, E-mail: msb@ku.edu. *Application contact:* Amy Wierman, Assistant to the Dean, 785-864-2930, E-mail: awierman@ku.edu.
Website: http://www.engr.ku.edu/.

University of Kentucky, Graduate School, College of Engineering, Lexington, KY 40506-0032. Offers M Eng, MCE, MME, MS, MS Ch E, MS Min, MSCE, MSEE, MSEM, MSMAE, MSME, MSMSE, PhD. Part-time programs available. *Degree requirements:* For master's, comprehensive exam; for doctorate, comprehensive exam, thesis/dissertation. *Entrance requirements:* For master's, GRE General Test, minimum undergraduate GPA of 2.75; for doctorate, GRE General Test, minimum undergraduate GPA of 3.0. Additional exam requirements/recommendations for international students: Required—TOEFL (minimum score 550 paper-based). Electronic applications accepted.

University of Louisville, J. B. Speed School of Engineering, Louisville, KY 40292-0001. Offers M Eng, MS, PhD, Certificate, Graduate Certificate, M Eng/MBA. *Accreditation:* ABET (one or more programs are accredited). Part-time programs available. Postbaccalaureate distance learning degree programs offered (no on-campus study). *Students:* 382 full-time (84 women), 295 part-time (58 women); includes 83 minority (23 Black or African American, non-Hispanic/Latino; 23 Asian, non-Hispanic/Latino; 20 Hispanic/Latino; 17 Two or more races, non-Hispanic/Latino), 221 international. Average age 28. 350 applicants, 59% accepted, 99 enrolled. In 2014, 94 master's, 23 doctorates, 11 other advanced degrees awarded. Terminal master's

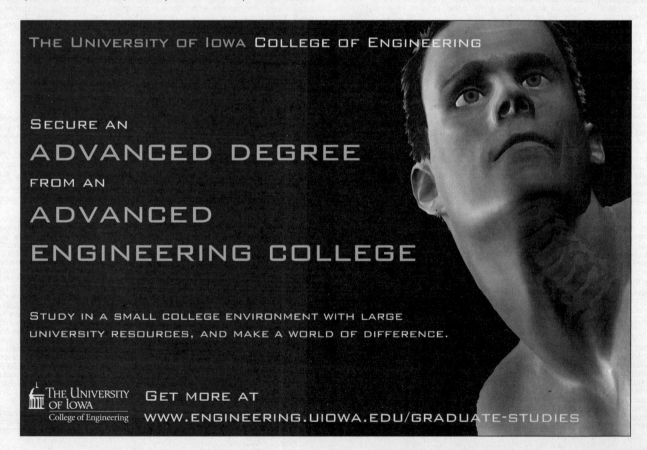

awarded for partial completion of doctoral program. *Degree requirements:* For master's, comprehensive exam (for some programs), thesis optional, minimum GPA of 3.0; for doctorate, comprehensive exam, thesis/dissertation, minimum GPA of 3.0. *Entrance requirements:* For master's and doctorate, GRE, letters of recommendation, final official transcripts; for other advanced degree, undergraduate degree. Additional exam requirements/recommendations for international students: Required—TOEFL (minimum score 80 iBT) or IELTS. *Application deadline:* For fall admission, 6/15 for domestic students, 5/1 priority date for international students; for spring admission, 11/22 for domestic students, 11/1 priority date for international students; for summer admission, 3/31 for domestic students, 4/1 priority date for international students. Application fee: $60. Electronic applications accepted. *Expenses:* Tuition, state resident: full-time $11,326; part-time $630 per credit hour. Tuition, nonresident: full-time $23,568; part-time $1311 per credit hour. *Required fees:* $196. Tuition and fees vary according to program and reciprocity agreements. *Financial support:* In 2014–15, 12 students received support, including 12 fellowships with full tuition reimbursements available (averaging $22,000 per year); research assistantships with full tuition reimbursements available, teaching assistantships with full tuition reimbursements available, and scholarships/grants also available. Financial award application deadline: 2/3. *Faculty research:* Energy and sustainability; advanced manufacturing and logistics; engineering human health; materials science and engineering, including nanoscience, cyber-enabled discovery. *Total annual research expenditures:* $21.4 million. *Unit head:* Dr. Neville G. Pinto, Dean, 502-852-6281, Fax: 502-852-7033, E-mail: neville.degouveapinto@louisville.edu. *Application contact:* Dr. Michael Harris, Director of Academic Programs, J. B. Speed School of Engineering, 502-852-6278, Fax: 502-852-7294, E-mail: mharris@louisville.edu.
Website: http://louisville.edu/speed/.

University of Maine, Graduate School, College of Engineering, Orono, ME 04469. Offers ME, MS, PSM, PhD. Part-time programs available. *Faculty:* 64 full-time (5 women), 52 part-time/adjunct (6 women). *Students:* 104 full-time (28 women), 17 part-time (6 women); includes 8 minority (1 Black or African American, non-Hispanic/Latino; 2 American Indian or Alaska Native, non-Hispanic/Latino; 2 Asian, non-Hispanic/Latino; 1 Hispanic/Latino; 1 Native Hawaiian or other Pacific Islander, non-Hispanic/Latino; 1 Two or more races, non-Hispanic/Latino), 41 international. Average age 31. 153 applicants, 65% accepted, 32 enrolled. In 2014, 16 master's, 6 doctorates awarded. Terminal master's awarded for partial completion of doctoral program. *Degree requirements:* For master's, thesis (for some programs); for doctorate, comprehensive exam, thesis/dissertation. *Entrance requirements:* For master's and doctorate, GRE General Test. Additional exam requirements/recommendations for international students: Required—TOEFL. *Application deadline:* For fall admission, 2/1 priority date for domestic students. Applications are processed on a rolling basis. Application fee: $65. Electronic applications accepted. *Expenses:* Tuition, state resident: part-time $658 per credit hour. Tuition, nonresident: part-time $1550 per credit hour. *Financial support:* In 2014–15, 76 students received support, including 6 fellowships (averaging $23,100 per year), 41 research assistantships (averaging $14,600 per year), 22 teaching assistantships (averaging $14,600 per year); Federal Work-Study, institutionally sponsored loans, scholarships/grants, tuition waivers (full and partial), and unspecified assistantships also available. Financial award application deadline: 3/1. *Unit head:* Dr. Dana Humphrey, Interim Dean, 207-581-2217, Fax: 207-581-2220, E-mail: dana.humphrey@umit.maine.edu. *Application contact:* Scott G. Delcourt, Assistant Vice President for Graduate Studies and Senior Associate Dean, 207-581-3291, Fax: 207-581-3232, E-mail: graduate@maine.edu.
Website: http://engineering.umaine.edu.

University of Manitoba, Faculty of Graduate Studies, Faculty of Engineering, Winnipeg, MB R3T 2N2, Canada. Offers M Eng, M Sc, PhD.

University of Maryland, Baltimore County, The Graduate School, College of Engineering and Information Technology, Baltimore, MD 21250. Offers MPS, MS, PhD, Postbaccalaureate Certificate. Part-time and evening/weekend programs available. Postbaccalaureate distance learning degree programs offered (no on-campus study). *Faculty:* 102 full-time (29 women), 47 part-time/adjunct (8 women). *Students:* 505 full-time (167 women), 637 part-time (180 women); includes 278 minority (127 Black or African American, non-Hispanic/Latino; 3 American Indian or Alaska Native, non-Hispanic/Latino; 99 Asian, non-Hispanic/Latino; 36 Hispanic/Latino; 1 Native Hawaiian or other Pacific Islander, non-Hispanic/Latino; 12 Two or more races, non-Hispanic/Latino), 384 international. Average age 31. 1,446 applicants, 46% accepted, 350 enrolled. In 2014, 239 master's, 36 doctorates, 53 other advanced degrees awarded. *Degree requirements:* For master's, comprehensive exam (for some programs), thesis (for some programs); for doctorate, comprehensive exam, thesis/dissertation. *Entrance requirements:* Additional exam requirements/recommendations for international students: Required—TOEFL (minimum score 550 paper-based; 80 iBT). *Application deadline:* For fall admission, 6/1 for domestic students, 1/1 for international students; for spring admission, 11/1 for domestic students, 6/1 for international students. Applications are processed on a rolling basis. Application fee: $70. Electronic applications accepted. *Expenses:* Tuition, state resident: part-time $557. Tuition, nonresident: part-time $922. *Required fees:* $122 per semester. One-time fee: $200 part-time. *Financial support:* In 2014–15, 9 fellowships with full tuition reimbursements (averaging $21,750 per year), 103 research assistantships with full tuition reimbursements (averaging $19,250 per year), 105 teaching assistantships with full tuition reimbursements (averaging $16,750 per year) were awarded; career-related internships or fieldwork, Federal Work-Study, scholarships/grants, health care benefits, tuition waivers (partial), and unspecified assistantships also available. Support available to part-time students. Financial award application deadline: 6/30; financial award applicants required to submit FAFSA. *Faculty research:* Biomaterials engineering, water resources engineering, security and information assurance, human-centered computing, design and manufacturing. *Total annual research expenditures:* $12.2 million. *Unit head:* Dr. Julia M. Ross, Dean and Professor, 410-455-3270, Fax: 410-455-3559, E-mail: jross@umbc.edu. *Application contact:* Graduate School, 410-455-2537, E-mail: umbcgrad@umbc.edu.
Website: http://www.coeit.umbc.edu.

University of Maryland, College Park, Academic Affairs, A. James Clark School of Engineering and School of Public Policy, Program in Engineering and Public Policy, College Park, MD 20742. Offers MS.

University of Massachusetts Amherst, Graduate School, College of Engineering, Amherst, MA 01003. Offers MS, MS Env E, MSCE, MSChE, MSECE, MSEM, MSIE, MSME, PhD. Part-time programs available. *Faculty:* 132 full-time (20 women). *Students:* 482 full-time (148 women), 57 part-time (18 women); includes 40 minority (7 Black or African American, non-Hispanic/Latino; 1 American Indian or Alaska Native, non-Hispanic/Latino; 15 Asian, non-Hispanic/Latino; 11 Hispanic/Latino; 6 Two or more races, non-Hispanic/Latino), 351 international. Average age 26. 1,996 applicants, 28% accepted, 164 enrolled. In 2014, 135 master's, 32 doctorates awarded. Terminal master's awarded for partial completion of doctoral program. *Degree requirements:* For master's, thesis (for some programs); for doctorate, comprehensive exam, thesis/dissertation. *Entrance requirements:* For master's and doctorate, GRE General Test. Additional exam requirements/recommendations for international students: Required—TOEFL (minimum score 550 paper-based; 80 iBT), IELTS (minimum score 6.5).

Application deadline: For fall admission, 1/15 for domestic and international students; for spring admission, 10/1 for domestic and international students. Applications are processed on a rolling basis. Application fee: $75. Electronic applications accepted. *Expenses:* Tuition, state resident: full-time $1980; part-time $110 per credit. Tuition, nonresident: full-time $14,644; part-time $414 per credit. *Required fees:* $11,417. One-time fee: $357. *Financial support:* Fellowships with full and partial tuition reimbursements, research assistantships with full and partial tuition reimbursements, teaching assistantships with full and partial tuition reimbursements, career-related internships or fieldwork, Federal Work-Study, scholarships/grants, traineeships, health care benefits, tuition waivers (full and partial), and unspecified assistantships available. Support available to part-time students. Financial award application deadline: 1/15. *Unit head:* Dr. Timothy Anderson, Dean, 413-545-6388. *Application contact:* Lindsay DeSantis, Supervisor of Admissions, 413-545-0722, Fax: 413-577-0010, E-mail: gradadm@grad.umass.edu.
Website: http://www.engineering.umass.edu/.

University of Massachusetts Dartmouth, Graduate School, College of Engineering, Program in Engineering and Applied Science, North Dartmouth, MA 02747-2300. Offers applied mechanics and materials (PhD); computational science and engineering (PhD); computer science and information systems (PhD); industrial and systems engineering (PhD). Part-time programs available. *Students:* 21 full-time (6 women), 1 (woman) part-time; includes 2 minority (1 Black or African American, non-Hispanic/Latino; 1 Two or more races, non-Hispanic/Latino), 12 international. Average age 30. 23 applicants, 65% accepted, 5 enrolled. In 2014, 1 doctorate awarded. *Degree requirements:* For doctorate, comprehensive exam, thesis/dissertation. *Entrance requirements:* For doctorate, GRE, statement of purpose (minimum of 300 words), resume, 3 letters of recommendation, official transcripts. Additional exam requirements/recommendations for international students: Required—TOEFL (minimum score 550 paper-based; 79 iBT). *Application deadline:* For fall admission, 2/15 priority date for domestic students, 1/15 priority date for international students; for spring admission, 11/15 priority date for domestic students, 10/15 priority date for international students. Applications are processed on a rolling basis. Application fee: $60. Electronic applications accepted. *Expenses:* Tuition, state resident: full-time $2071; part-time $86.29 per credit. Tuition, nonresident: full-time $8099; part-time $337.46 per credit. *Required fees:* $16,520; $712.33 per credit. Tuition and fees vary according to course load and reciprocity agreements. *Financial support:* In 2014–15, 8 fellowships with full tuition reimbursements (averaging $16,577 per year), 8 research assistantships with full tuition reimbursements (averaging $13,627 per year), 5 teaching assistantships with full tuition reimbursements (averaging $12,400 per year) were awarded; Federal Work-Study and unspecified assistantships also available. Support available to part-time students. Financial award application deadline: 3/1; financial award applicants required to submit FAFSA. *Faculty research:* Tissue/cell engineering, biotransport sensors/networks, marine systems biomimetic materials, composite/polymeric materials, resilient infrastructure robotics, renewable energy. *Total annual research expenditures:* $1.7 million. *Unit head:* Gaurav Khanna, Graduate Program Director, 508-910-6605, Fax: 508-999-9115, E-mail: gkhanna@umassd.edu. *Application contact:* Steven Briggs, Director of Marketing and Recruitment for Graduate Studies, 508-999-8604, Fax: 508-999-8183, E-mail: graduate@umassd.edu.
Website: http://www.umassd.edu/engineering/graduate/doctoraldegreeprograms/egrandappliedsciencephd/.

University of Massachusetts Lowell, Francis College of Engineering, Lowell, MA 01854. Offers MS Eng, MSES, D Eng, PhD, Certificate, Graduate Certificate. Part-time and evening/weekend programs available. Terminal master's awarded for partial completion of doctoral program. *Degree requirements:* For doctorate, thesis/dissertation. *Entrance requirements:* For master's and doctorate, GRE General Test.

University of Memphis, Graduate School, Herff College of Engineering, Memphis, TN 38152. Offers MS, PhD. Part-time programs available. *Faculty:* 35 full-time (4 women), 2 part-time/adjunct (0 women). *Students:* 116 full-time (37 women), 50 part-time (9 women); includes 35 minority (21 Black or African American, non-Hispanic/Latino; 8 Asian, non-Hispanic/Latino; 2 Hispanic/Latino; 4 Two or more races, non-Hispanic/Latino), 78 international. Average age 28. 98 applicants, 82% accepted, 29 enrolled. In 2014, 49 master's, 2 doctorates awarded. *Degree requirements:* For master's, comprehensive exam, thesis optional, 30-36 hours of course work, completion of course work within 6 years, continuous enrollment; for doctorate, comprehensive exam, thesis/dissertation, completion of degree within 12 years, residency, continuous enrollment. *Entrance requirements:* For master's, GRE, MAT, GMAT or PRAXIS; for doctorate, GRE, MAT, GMAT. Additional exam requirements/recommendations for international students: Required—TOEFL (minimum score 550 paper-based; 79 iBT). *Application deadline:* For fall admission, 7/1 for domestic students, 5/1 for international students; for spring admission, 12/1 for domestic students, 9/15 for international students. Application fee: $35 ($60 for international students). Electronic applications accepted. *Financial support:* In 2014–15, 29 students received support. Fellowships with full tuition reimbursements available, research assistantships with full tuition reimbursements available, teaching assistantships with full tuition reimbursements available, career-related internships or fieldwork, Federal Work-Study, scholarships/grants, tuition waivers (full and partial), and unspecified assistantships available. Financial award application deadline: 2/15; financial award applicants required to submit FAFSA. *Faculty research:* Medical and biological applications of engineering; infrastructure, including transportation, ground water and GPS studies; computational intelligence and modeling; sensors. *Unit head:* Dr. Richard Joseph Sweigard, Dean, 901-678-4306, Fax: 901-678-4180, E-mail: rjswgard@memphis.edu. *Application contact:* Dr. Deborah Hochstein, Associate Dean for Academic Affairs and Administration, 901-678-3258, Fax: 901-678-5030, E-mail: dhochstn@memphis.edu.
Website: http://www.memphis.edu/herff/index.php.

University of Miami, Graduate School, College of Engineering, Coral Gables, FL 33124. Offers MS, MSAE, MSBE, MSCE, MSECE, MSIE, MSME, MSOES, PhD, MBA/MSIE. Part-time and evening/weekend programs available. *Degree requirements:* For master's, thesis (for some programs); for doctorate, comprehensive exam, thesis/dissertation. *Entrance requirements:* For master's and doctorate, GRE General Test, minimum GPA of 3.0. Additional exam requirements/recommendations for international students: Required—TOEFL (minimum score 550 paper-based; 59 iBT). Electronic applications accepted.

University of Michigan, College of Engineering, Ann Arbor, MI 48109. Offers M Eng, MS, MSE, D Eng, PhD, CE, Certificate, Ch E, Mar Eng, Nav Arch, Nuc E, M Arch/M Eng, M Arch/MSE, MBA/M Eng, MBA/MS, MBA/MSE, MSE/MS. Part-time programs available. Postbaccalaureate distance learning degree programs offered (no on-campus study). *Faculty:* 358 full-time (72 women). *Students:* 2,895 full-time (651 women), 317 part-time (54 women). 9,225 applicants, 25% accepted, 1009 enrolled. In 2014, 1,020 master's, 291 doctorates awarded. *Application deadline:* Applications are processed on a rolling basis. Electronic applications accepted. *Expenses:* Expenses: Contact institution. *Financial support:* Fellowships, research assistantships, teaching assistantships, career-related internships or fieldwork, Federal Work-Study, institutionally sponsored loans, scholarships/grants, traineeships, health care benefits, tuition waivers (full and partial), and unspecified assistantships available. Support

available to part-time students. Financial award applicants required to submit FAFSA. *Total annual research expenditures:* $251.6 million. *Unit head:* Prof. David C. Munson, Chair, 734-647-7008, Fax: 734-647-7009, E-mail: munson@umich.edu. *Application contact:* Andria Rose, Recruiting Contact, 734-647-7030, Fax: 734-647-7045, E-mail: ajrose@umich.edu.
Website: http://www.engin.umich.edu/.

University of Michigan–Dearborn, College of Engineering and Computer Science, Dearborn, MI 48126. Offers MS, MSE, PhD, MBA/MSE. Part-time and evening/weekend programs available. Postbaccalaureate distance learning degree programs offered (no on-campus study). *Faculty:* 72 full-time (6 women), 29 part-time/adjunct (3 women). *Students:* 273 full-time (67 women), 603 part-time (135 women); includes 119 minority (23 Black or African American, non-Hispanic/Latino; 1 American Indian or Alaska Native, non-Hispanic/Latino; 65 Asian, non-Hispanic/Latino; 23 Hispanic/Latino; 1 Native Hawaiian or other Pacific Islander, non-Hispanic/Latino; 6 Two or more races, non-Hispanic/Latino), 429 international. 914 applicants, 57% accepted, 299 enrolled. In 2014, 199 master's, 2 doctorates awarded. *Degree requirements:* For master's, thesis optional; for doctorate, thesis/dissertation. *Entrance requirements:* For doctorate, GRE. Additional exam requirements/recommendations for international students: Required—TOEFL (minimum score 560 paper-based, 84 iBT), IELTS (minimum score 6.5), or Michigan English Language Assessment Battery (minimum score 80). *Application deadline:* For fall admission, 8/1 priority date for domestic students, 5/1 priority date for international students; for winter admission, 12/1 priority date for domestic students, 9/1 priority date for international students; for spring admission, 4/1 priority date for domestic students, 1/1 priority date for international students. Applications are processed on a rolling basis. Application fee: $60. Electronic applications accepted. *Expenses:* Tuition, state resident: full-time $12,202; part-time $707 per credit hour. Tuition, nonresident: full-time $20,980; part-time $1209 per credit hour. *Required fees:* $798; $302 per term. Tuition and fees vary according to course level, course load, degree level and program. *Financial support:* In 2014–15, 313 students received support, including 49 research assistantships with full and partial tuition reimbursements available (averaging $12,597 per year), 6 teaching assistantships (averaging $6,258 per year); fellowships, career-related internships or fieldwork, Federal Work-Study, health care benefits, unspecified assistantships, and non-residential student scholarships also available. Financial award application deadline: 4/1; financial award applicants required to submit FAFSA. *Faculty research:* Data science and machine learning, connected vehicles, power electronics and energy systems, operations research, integrated design and manufacturing, materials processing and additive manufacturing. *Total annual research expenditures:* $4.1 million. *Unit head:* Dr. Anthony England, Dean, 313-593-5290, Fax: 313-593-9967, E-mail: england@umich.edu. *Application contact:* Office of Graduate Studies Staff, 313-583-6321, E-mail: umdgrad@umd.umich.edu.
Website: http://umdearborn.edu/cecs/.

University of Minnesota, Twin Cities Campus, College of Science and Engineering, Minneapolis, MN 55455. Offers M Ch E, M Geo E, M Mat SE, MA, MCE, MCS, MFM, MS, MS Ch E, MS Mat SE, MSEE, MSME, MSMOT, MSSE, MSST, PhD, Certificate, MD/PhD. Part-time and evening/weekend programs available. Postbaccalaureate distance learning degree programs offered (minimal on-campus study). Terminal master's awarded for partial completion of doctoral program. *Degree requirements:* For master's, thesis (for some programs); for doctorate, thesis/dissertation. *Entrance requirements:* Additional exam requirements/recommendations for international students: Required—TOEFL (minimum score 550 paper-based; 79 iBT). Electronic applications accepted.

University of Mississippi, Graduate School, School of Engineering, University, MS 38677. Offers engineering science (MS, PhD). *Degree requirements:* For master's, thesis (for some programs); for doctorate, thesis/dissertation. *Entrance requirements:* For master's, GRE General Test, minimum GPA of 3.0; for doctorate, GRE General Test. Additional exam requirements/recommendations for international students: Required—TOEFL. Electronic applications accepted.

University of Missouri, Office of Research and Graduate Studies, College of Engineering, Columbia, MO 65211. Offers ME, MS, PhD, Certificate. Part-time programs available. *Faculty:* 125 full-time (15 women), 6 part-time/adjunct (0 women). *Students:* 355 full-time (88 women), 279 part-time (60 women); includes 22 minority (4 Black or African American, non-Hispanic/Latino; 7 Asian, non-Hispanic/Latino; 7 Hispanic/Latino; 4 Two or more races, non-Hispanic/Latino), 464 international. Average age 27. 888 applicants, 34% accepted, 153 enrolled. In 2014, 109 master's, 25 doctorates awarded. *Degree requirements:* For doctorate, thesis/dissertation. *Entrance requirements:* For master's and doctorate, GRE General Test. Additional exam requirements/recommendations for international students: Required—TOEFL. *Application deadline:* Applications are processed on a rolling basis. Application fee: $55 ($75 for international students). *Financial support:* Fellowships, research assistantships, teaching assistantships, institutionally sponsored loans, scholarships/grants, traineeships, health care benefits, and unspecified assistantships available. Support available to part-time students. *Unit head:* Dr. James E. Thompson, Dean, 573-882-4378, E-mail: thompsonje@missouri.edu. *Application contact:* Robert Tzou, Associate Dean for Academic Programs, 573-882-4060, E-mail: tzour@missouri.edu.
Website: http://engineering.missouri.edu/.

University of Missouri–Kansas City, School of Computing and Engineering, Kansas City, MO 64110-2499. Offers civil engineering (MS); computer and electrical engineering (PhD); computer science (MS), including bioinformatics, software engineering, telecommunications networking; computer science and informatics (PhD); computing (PhD); electrical engineering (MS); engineering (PhD); engineering and construction management (Graduate Certificate); mechanical engineering (MS); telecommunications and computer networking (PhD). PhD (interdisciplinary) offered through the School of Graduate Studies. Part-time programs available. *Faculty:* 39 full-time (5 women), 26 part-time/adjunct (3 women). *Students:* 500 full-time (143 women), 136 part-time (28 women); includes 18 minority (5 Black or African American, non-Hispanic/Latino; 8 Asian, non-Hispanic/Latino; 4 Hispanic/Latino; 1 Two or more races, non-Hispanic/Latino), 551 international. Average age 24. 1,924 applicants, 39% accepted, 200 enrolled. In 2014, 124 master's, 1 other advanced degree awarded. *Degree requirements:* For doctorate, thesis/dissertation. *Entrance requirements:* For master's, GRE General Test, minimum GPA of 3.0, 3 letters of recommendation from professors; for doctorate, GRE General Test, minimum GPA of 3.5. Additional exam requirements/recommendations for international students: Required—TOEFL (minimum score 550 paper-based; 80 iBT). *Application deadline:* For fall admission, 1/15 priority date for domestic students, 1/15 for international students. Applications are processed on a rolling basis. Application fee: $45 ($50 for international students). *Financial support:* In 2014–15, 34 research assistantships with partial tuition reimbursements (averaging $15,602 per year), 24 teaching assistantships with partial tuition reimbursements (averaging $15,090 per year) were awarded; career-related internships or fieldwork, Federal Work-Study, scholarships/grants, tuition waivers (partial), and unspecified assistantships also available. Support available to part-time students. Financial award application deadline: 3/1; financial award applicants required to submit FAFSA. *Faculty research:* Algorithms, bioinformatics and medical informatics, biomechanics/biomaterials, civil engineering materials, networking and telecommunications, thermal science. *Unit head:* Dr. Kevin Z. Truman, Dean, 816-235-2399, Fax: 816-235-5159. *Application contact:* 816-235-2399, Fax: 816-235-5159.
Website: http://sce.umkc.edu/.

University of Nebraska–Lincoln, Graduate College, College of Engineering, Lincoln, NE 68588. Offers M Eng, MAE, MEE, MS, PhD. *Degree requirements:* For doctorate, comprehensive exam, thesis/dissertation. *Entrance requirements:* For master's and doctorate, GRE General Test. Additional exam requirements/recommendations for international students: Required—TOEFL. Electronic applications accepted.

University of Nevada, Las Vegas, Graduate College, Howard R. Hughes College of Engineering, Las Vegas, NV 89154-4005. Offers MS, MSCS, PhD, Certificate, MS/MS, MS/PhD. Part-time programs available. *Faculty:* 55 full-time (5 women), 5 part-time/adjunct (2 women). *Students:* 155 full-time (41 women), 71 part-time (22 women); includes 43 minority (7 Black or African American, non-Hispanic/Latino; 10 Asian, non-Hispanic/Latino; 13 Hispanic/Latino; 13 Two or more races, non-Hispanic/Latino), 109 international. Average age 30. 185 applicants, 61% accepted, 61 enrolled. In 2014, 57 master's, 13 doctorates, 5 other advanced degrees awarded. *Degree requirements:* For master's, comprehensive exam (for some programs), thesis (for some programs), final project; for doctorate, comprehensive exam, thesis/dissertation. *Entrance requirements:* Additional exam requirements/recommendations for international students: Required—TOEFL (minimum score 550 paper-based; 80 iBT), IELTS (minimum score 7). *Application deadline:* For fall admission, 5/1 for international students; for spring admission, 10/1 for international students. Application fee: $60 ($95 for international students). Electronic applications accepted. *Financial support:* In 2014–15, 155 students received support, including 53 research assistantships with partial tuition reimbursements available (averaging $14,368 per year), 102 teaching assistantships with partial tuition reimbursements available (averaging $13,370 per year); institutionally sponsored loans, scholarships/grants, health care benefits, and unspecified assistantships also available. Financial award application deadline: 3/1. *Total annual research expenditures:* $5 million. *Unit head:* Dr. Rama Venkat, Dean, 702-895-1094, Fax: 702-895-4059, E-mail: venkat@ee.unlv.edu. *Application contact:* Graduate College Admissions Evaluator, 702-895-3320, Fax: 702-895-4180, E-mail: gradcollege@unlv.edu.
Website: http://engineering.unlv.edu/.

University of Nevada, Reno, Graduate School, College of Engineering, Reno, NV 89557. Offers MS, PhD. Terminal master's awarded for partial completion of doctoral program. *Degree requirements:* For master's, thesis optional; for doctorate, thesis/dissertation. *Entrance requirements:* For master's, GRE General Test, minimum GPA of 2.75; for doctorate, GRE General Test, minimum GPA of 3.0. Additional exam requirements/recommendations for international students: Required—TOEFL (minimum score 500 paper-based; 61 iBT), IELTS (minimum score 6). Electronic applications accepted. *Faculty research:* Fabrication, development of new materials, structural and earthquake engineering, computer vision/virtual reality, acoustics, smart materials.

University of New Brunswick Fredericton, School of Graduate Studies, Faculty of Engineering, Fredericton, NB E3B 5A3, Canada. Offers M Eng, M Sc E, PhD, Certificate. Part-time programs available. *Faculty:* 63 full-time (9 women), 55 part-time/adjunct (8 women). *Students:* 203 full-time (40 women), 51 part-time (13 women). In 2014, 63 master's, 17 doctorates awarded. *Degree requirements:* For master's, thesis; for doctorate, comprehensive exam, thesis/dissertation, qualifying exam. *Entrance requirements:* For master's, minimum GPA of 3.0. Additional exam requirements/recommendations for international students: Required—TOEFL, TWE. *Application deadline:* For fall admission, 3/1 priority date for domestic students. Applications are processed on a rolling basis. Application fee: $50 Canadian dollars. Electronic applications accepted. *Financial support:* In 2014–15, 278 fellowships, 298 research assistantships, 247 teaching assistantships were awarded; career-related internships or fieldwork also available. *Unit head:* Dr. David Coleman, Dean, 506-453-4570, Fax: 506-453-4943, E-mail: dcoleman@unb.ca. *Application contact:* Dr. John Kershaw, Dean of Graduate Studies, 506-447-3065, Fax: 506-453-4817, E-mail: kershaw@unb.ca.
Website: http://www.unbf.ca/eng/.

University of New Haven, Graduate School, Tagliatela College of Engineering, West Haven, CT 06516-1916. Offers EMS, MS, MSIE, Certificate, MBA/MSIE. Part-time and evening/weekend programs available. *Degree requirements:* For master's, thesis or alternative. *Entrance requirements:* Additional exam requirements/recommendations for international students: Required—TOEFL (minimum score 75 iBT), IELTS, PTE (minimum score 50). Electronic applications accepted. Application fee is waived when completed online.

University of New Mexico, Graduate School, School of Engineering, Albuquerque, NM 87131. Offers M Eng, MCM, MEME, MS, MSCE, PhD, Post-Doctoral Certificate, MBA/MEME. Part-time programs available. *Faculty:* 96 full-time (16 women), 22 part-time/adjunct (4 women). *Students:* 361 full-time (78 women), 234 part-time (50 women); includes 141 minority (6 Black or African American, non-Hispanic/Latino; 2 American Indian or Alaska Native, non-Hispanic/Latino; 13 Asian, non-Hispanic/Latino; 110 Hispanic/Latino; 10 Two or more races, non-Hispanic/Latino), 187 international. Average age 29. 867 applicants, 36% accepted, 202 enrolled. In 2014, 142 master's, 53 doctorates, 1 other advanced degree awarded. Terminal master's awarded for partial completion of doctoral program. *Degree requirements:* For master's, comprehensive exam, thesis or alternative; for doctorate, comprehensive exam, thesis/dissertation. *Entrance requirements:* For master's, GRE, GMAT, letters of recommendation; letter of intent; for doctorate, GRE, letters of recommendation; letter of intent. Additional exam requirements/recommendations for international students: Required—TOEFL (minimum score 550 paper-based). *Application deadline:* For fall admission, 1/15 priority date for domestic and international students; for spring admission, 7/14 priority date for domestic and international students. Applications are processed on a rolling basis. Application fee: $50. Electronic applications accepted. *Financial support:* Federal Work-Study, scholarships/grants, health care benefits, and unspecified assistantships available. Financial award application deadline: 3/1; financial award applicants required to submit FAFSA. *Faculty research:* Emerging energy technologies, biomedical engineering and biocomputing, water resources and environmental engineering, optical engineering and optoelectronic materials, graphics and digital imaging. *Unit head:* Prof. Gruia-Catalin Roman, Dean, 505-277-5522, Fax: 505-277-1422, E-mail: gcroman@unm.edu. *Application contact:* Deborah Kieltyka, Associate Director, Admissions, 505-277-3140, Fax: 505-277-6686, E-mail: deborahk@unm.edu.
Website: http://soe.unm.edu/.

University of New Orleans, Graduate School, College of Engineering, New Orleans, LA 70148. Offers MS, PhD. Part-time programs available. Terminal master's awarded for partial completion of doctoral program. *Degree requirements:* For master's, comprehensive exam, thesis optional; for doctorate, comprehensive exam, thesis/dissertation. *Entrance requirements:* For master's, GRE General Test, minimum GPA of 3.0; for doctorate, GRE General Test. Additional exam requirements/recommendations for international students: Required—TOEFL (minimum score 550 paper-based; 79 iBT). Electronic applications accepted. *Faculty research:* Electrical, civil, environmental, mechanical, naval architecture, and marine engineering.

The University of North Carolina at Charlotte, The William States Lee College of Engineering, Charlotte, NC 28223-0001. Offers ME, MS, MSCE, MSE, MSEE, MSEM, MSME, PhD, Graduate Certificate. Part-time and evening/weekend programs available. Postbaccalaureate distance learning degree programs offered (no on-campus study). *Faculty:* 122 full-time (17 women), 2 part-time/adjunct (0 women). *Students:* 421 full-time (83 women), 191 part-time (47 women); includes 58 minority (30 Black or African American, non-Hispanic/Latino; 1 American Indian or Alaska Native, non-Hispanic/Latino; 10 Asian, non-Hispanic/Latino; 14 Hispanic/Latino; 3 Two or more races, non-Hispanic/Latino), 379 international. Average age 27. 1,544 applicants, 45% accepted, 236 enrolled. In 2014, 136 master's, 26 doctorates awarded. Terminal master's awarded for partial completion of doctoral program. *Degree requirements:* For master's, thesis or alternative, project; for doctorate, thesis/dissertation, project. *Entrance requirements:* For master's and doctorate, GRE General Test, letters of recommendation. Additional exam requirements/recommendations for international students: Required—TOEFL (minimum score 557 paper-based; 83 iBT). *Application deadline:* For fall admission, 5/1 priority date for domestic students, 5/1 for international students; for spring admission, 10/1 priority date for domestic students, 10/1 for international students. Applications are processed on a rolling basis. Application fee: $75. Electronic applications accepted. *Expenses:* Tuition, state resident: full-time $4008. Tuition, nonresident: full-time $16,295. *Required fees:* $2755. Tuition and fees vary according to course load and program. *Financial support:* In 2014–15, 234 students received support, including 7 fellowships (averaging $38,510 per year), 146 research assistantships (averaging $9,117 per year), 81 teaching assistantships (averaging $6,376 per year); career-related internships or fieldwork, institutionally sponsored loans, scholarships/grants, and unspecified assistantships also available. Support available to part-time students. Financial award application deadline: 4/1; financial award applicants required to submit FAFSA. *Faculty research:* Environmental engineering, structures and geotechnical engineering, precision engineering and precision metrology, optoelectronics and microelectronics, communications. *Total annual research expenditures:* $6.8 million. *Unit head:* Dr. Robert E. Johnson, Dean, 704-687-8242, Fax: 704-687-2352, E-mail: robejohn@uncc.edu. *Application contact:* Kathy B. Giddings, Director of Graduate Admissions, 704-687-5503, Fax: 704-687-1668, E-mail: gradadm@uncc.edu. Website: http://www.coe.uncc.edu/.

University of North Dakota, Graduate School, School of Engineering and Mines, Program in Engineering, Grand Forks, ND 58202. Offers PhD. *Degree requirements:* For doctorate, comprehensive exam, thesis/dissertation, final exam. *Entrance requirements:* For doctorate, minimum GPA of 3.0. Additional exam requirements/recommendations for international students: Required—TOEFL (minimum score 550 paper-based; 79 iBT), IELTS (minimum score 6.5). Electronic applications accepted. *Faculty research:* Combustion science, energy conversion, power transmission, environmental engineering.

University of North Texas, Robert B. Toulouse School of Graduate Studies, Denton, TX 76203-5459. Offers accounting (MS); applied anthropology (MA, MS); applied behavior analysis (Certificate); applied geography (MA); applied technology and performance improvement (M Ed, MS); art education (MA); art history (MA); art museum education (Certificate); arts leadership (Certificate); audiology (Au D); behavior analysis (MS); behavioral science (PhD); biochemistry and molecular biology (MS); biology (MA, MS); biomedical engineering (MS); business analysis (MS); chemistry (MS); clinical health psychology (PhD); communication studies (MA, MS); computer engineering (MS); computer science (MS); counseling (M Ed, MS), including clinical mental health counseling (MS), college and university counseling, elementary school counseling, secondary school counseling; creative writing (MA); criminal justice (MS); curriculum and instruction (M Ed); decision sciences (MBA); design (MA, MFA), including fashion design (MFA), innovation studies, interior design (MFA); early childhood studies (MS); economics (MS); educational leadership (M Ed, Ed D); educational psychology (MS, PhD), including family studies (MS), gifted and talented (MS), human development (MS), learning and cognition (MS), research, measurement and evaluation (MS); electrical engineering (MS); emergency management (MPA); engineering technology (MS); English (MA); English as a second language (MA); environmental science (MS); finance (MBA, MS); financial management (MPA); French (MA); health services management (MBA); higher education (M Ed, Ed D); history (MA, MS); hospitality management (MS); human resources management (MPA); information science (MS); information systems (PhD); information technologies (MBA); interdisciplinary studies (MA, MS); international studies (MA); international sustainable tourism (MS); jazz studies (MM); journalism (MA, MJ, Graduate Certificate), including interactive and virtual digital communication (Graduate Certificate), narrative journalism (Graduate Certificate), public relations (Graduate Certificate); kinesiology (MS); linguistics (MA); local government management (MPA); logistics (PhD); logistics and supply chain management (MBA); long-term care, senior housing, and aging services (MA); management (PhD); marketing (MBA); mathematics (MA, MS); mechanical and energy engineering (MS, PhD); music (MA), including ethnomusicology, music theory, musicology, performance; music composition (PhD); music education (MM Ed, PhD); nonprofit management (MPA); operations and supply chain management (MBA); performance (MM, DMA); philosophy (MA); political science (MA); professional and technical communication (MA); radio, television and film (MA, MFA); rehabilitation counseling (Certificate); sociology (MA); Spanish (MA); special education (M Ed); speech-language pathology (MA); strategic management (MBA); studio art (MFA); teaching (M Ed); MBA/MS. Part-time and evening/weekend programs available. Postbaccalaureate distance learning degree programs offered. *Faculty:* 651 full-time (215 women), 233 part-time/adjunct (139 women). *Students:* 3,040 full-time (1,598 women), 3,401 part-time (2,097 women); includes 1,740 minority (533 Black or African American, non-Hispanic/Latino; 15 American Indian or Alaska Native, non-Hispanic/Latino; 286 Asian, non-Hispanic/Latino; 746 Hispanic/Latino; 3 Native Hawaiian or other Pacific Islander, non-Hispanic/Latino; 157 Two or more races, non-Hispanic/Latino), 1,145 international. Terminal master's awarded for partial completion of doctoral program. *Degree requirements:* For master's, variable foreign language requirement, comprehensive exam (for some programs), thesis (for some programs); for doctorate, variable foreign language requirement, comprehensive exam (for some programs), thesis/dissertation; for other advanced degree, variable foreign language requirement, comprehensive exam (for some programs). *Entrance requirements:* For master's and doctorate, GRE, GMAT. Additional exam requirements/recommendations for international students: Required—TOEFL (minimum score 550 paper-based; 79 iBT). *Application deadline:* For fall admission, 7/15 for domestic students, 3/15 for international students; for spring admission, 11/15 for domestic students, 9/15 for international students; for summer admission, 5/1 for domestic students. Applications are processed on a rolling basis. Application fee: $60. Electronic applications accepted. *Expenses:* Tuition, state resident: full-time $5450; part-time $3633 per year. Tuition, nonresident: full-time $11,966; part-time $7977 per year. *Required fees:* $1301; $398 per credit hour. $685 per semester. Tuition and fees vary according to program and reciprocity agreements. *Financial support:* Fellowships with partial tuition reimbursements, research assistantships with partial tuition reimbursements, teaching assistantships, career-related internships or fieldwork, Federal Work-Study, institutionally sponsored loans, scholarships/grants, health care benefits, and library assistantships available. Support available to part-time students. Financial award applicants required to submit FAFSA. *Unit head:* Mark Wardell, Dean, 940-565-2383, E-mail: mark.wardell@unt.edu. *Application contact:* Toulouse School of Graduate Studies, 940-565-2383, Fax: 940-565-2141, E-mail: gradsch@unt.edu. Website: http://tsgs.unt.edu/.

University of Notre Dame, Graduate School, College of Engineering, Notre Dame, IN 46556. Offers M Eng, MEME, MS, MS Aero E, MS Bio E, MS Ch E, MS Env E, MSCE, MSCSE, MSEE, MSME, PhD. Terminal master's awarded for partial completion of doctoral program. *Degree requirements:* For master's, comprehensive exam; for doctorate, thesis/dissertation. *Entrance requirements:* For master's and doctorate, GRE General Test. Additional exam requirements/recommendations for international students: Required—TOEFL. Electronic applications accepted.

University of Oklahoma, Gallogly College of Engineering, Department of General Engineering, Norman, OK 73019. Offers MS, PhD. Part-time and evening/weekend programs available. Postbaccalaureate distance learning degree programs offered (minimal on-campus study). *Faculty:* 3 full-time (2 women), 1 part-time/adjunct (0 women). *Students:* 5 full-time (2 women), 9 part-time (4 women); includes 2 minority (both American Indian or Alaska Native, non-Hispanic/Latino), 7 international. Average age 34. Terminal master's awarded for partial completion of doctoral program. *Degree requirements:* For master's, thesis (for some programs); for doctorate, comprehensive exam, thesis/dissertation. *Entrance requirements:* For master's and doctorate, GRE, minimum GPA of 3.0. Additional exam requirements/recommendations for international students: Required—TOEFL (minimum score 79 iBT). *Application deadline:* For fall admission, 6/1 for domestic students, 3/1 for international students; for spring admission, 11/1 for domestic students, 9/1 for international students. Applications are processed on a rolling basis. Application fee: $50 ($100 for international students). Electronic applications accepted. *Expenses:* Tuition, state resident: full-time $4394; part-time $183.10 per credit hour. Tuition, nonresident: full-time $16,970; part-time $707.10 per credit hour. *Required fees:* $2892; $109.95 per credit hour. $126.50 per semester. *Financial support:* Career-related internships or fieldwork, scholarships/grants, and unspecified assistantships available. Financial award application deadline: 6/1; financial award applicants required to submit FAFSA. *Faculty research:* Interdisciplinary engineering topics, engineering education, data science and analytics. *Unit head:* Dr. James J. Sluss, Senior Associate Dean, 405-325-2621, Fax: 405-325-7508, E-mail: sluss@ou.edu. *Application contact:* Cerry Leffler, Assistant to the Senior Associate Dean, 405-325-4536, Fax: 405-325-7508, E-mail: cerry@ou.edu. Website: http://www.ou.edu/coe.

University of Ottawa, Faculty of Graduate and Postdoctoral Studies, Faculty of Engineering, Ottawa, ON K1N 6N5, Canada. Offers M Eng, MA Sc, MCS, PhD, Certificate. *Degree requirements:* For master's, thesis or alternative; for doctorate, thesis/dissertation. *Entrance requirements:* For master's, honors degree or equivalent, minimum B average. Electronic applications accepted.

University of Pennsylvania, School of Engineering and Applied Science, Philadelphia, PA 19104. Offers EMBA, MCIT, ME, MIPD, MS, MSE, PhD, AC, MArch/MSE, MD/PhD, MSE/MBA, MSE/MCP, VMD/PhD. Part-time and evening/weekend programs available. *Faculty:* 115 full-time (18 women), 26 part-time/adjunct (3 women). *Students:* 1,159 full-time (364 women), 221 part-time (81 women); includes 167 minority (13 Black or African American, non-Hispanic/Latino; 121 Asian, non-Hispanic/Latino; 24 Hispanic/Latino; 9 Two or more races, non-Hispanic/Latino), 850 international. 5,810 applicants, 22% accepted, 624 enrolled. In 2014, 688 master's, 69 doctorates awarded. *Degree requirements:* For doctorate, thesis/dissertation. *Entrance requirements:* Additional exam requirements/recommendations for international students: Required—TOEFL. *Application deadline:* For fall admission, 6/1 priority date for domestic students, 5/1 priority date for international students; for spring admission, 11/1 priority date for domestic students, 10/1 priority date for international students. Applications are processed on a rolling basis. Application fee: $70. Electronic applications accepted. *Financial support:* In 2014–15, 393 students received support. Fellowships, research assistantships, teaching assistantships, institutionally sponsored loans, scholarships/grants, traineeships, health care benefits, and unspecified assistantships available. Financial award application deadline: 12/15. *Unit head:* Eduardo D. Glandt, Dean, 215-898-7244, E-mail: seasdean@seas.upenn.edu. *Application contact:* School of Engineering and Applied Science Graduate Admissions, 215-898-4542, E-mail: gradstudies@seas.upenn.edu. Website: http://www.seas.upenn.edu.

See Display on next page and Close-Up on page 91.

University of Pittsburgh, Katz Graduate School of Business, MBA/Master of Science in Engineering Joint Degree Program, Pittsburgh, PA 15260. Offers MBA/MSE. *Accreditation:* AACSB. Part-time and evening/weekend programs available. *Faculty:* 53 full-time (12 women), 31 part-time/adjunct (9 women). *Students:* 11 full-time (3 women), 27 part-time (1 woman); includes 10 minority (2 Black or African American, non-Hispanic/Latino; 1 American Indian or Alaska Native, non-Hispanic/Latino; 3 Asian, non-Hispanic/Latino; 3 Hispanic/Latino; 1 Two or more races, non-Hispanic/Latino). Average age 33. 14 applicants, 57% accepted, 7 enrolled. *Entrance requirements:* Additional exam requirements/recommendations for international students: Required—TOEFL or IELTS. *Application deadline:* For fall admission, 4/1 priority date for domestic students, 2/1 priority date for international students. Application fee: $50. Electronic applications accepted. *Expenses:* Tuition, state resident: full-time $20,742; part-time $838 per credit. Tuition, nonresident: full-time $33,960; part-time $1389 per credit. *Required fees:* $800; $205 per term. Tuition and fees vary according to program. *Financial support:* In 2014–15, 6 students received support. Scholarships/grants available. Financial award application deadline: 6/1; financial award applicants required to submit FAFSA. *Faculty research:* Accounting systems/financial reporting, corporate finance, shopper marketing/consumer behavior, management information systems, organizational behavior and entrepreneurship. *Unit head:* William Valenta, Jr., Assistant Dean, MBA and Executive Programs, 412-648-1694, Fax: 412-648-1659, E-mail: valenta@pitt.edu. *Application contact:* Thomas Keller, Director of MBA Admissions, 412-648-1700, Fax: 412-648-1659, E-mail: mba@katz.pitt.edu. Website: http://business.pitt.edu/katz/mba/academics/programs/mba-msengineering.php.

University of Pittsburgh, Swanson School of Engineering, Pittsburgh, PA 15260. Offers MS, MS Ch E, MSBENG, MSCEE, MSEE, MSIE, MSME, MSNE, MSPE, PhD, MD/PhD, MS Ch E/MSPE. Part-time programs available. *Faculty:* 121 full-time (16 women), 156 part-time/adjunct (23 women). *Students:* 709 full-time (193 women), 279 part-time (43 women); includes 89 minority (24 Black or African American, non-Hispanic/Latino; 37 Asian, non-Hispanic/Latino; 16 Hispanic/Latino; 12 Two or more races, non-Hispanic/Latino), 490 international. 3,051 applicants, 30% accepted, 278 enrolled. In 2014, 241 master's, 69 doctorates awarded. Terminal master's awarded for partial completion of doctoral program. *Degree requirements:* For doctorate, comprehensive exam, thesis/dissertation, final oral exams. *Entrance requirements:* For master's and doctorate, minimum GPA of 3.0. Additional exam requirements/recommendations for international students: Required—TOEFL (minimum score 550 paper-based; 80 iBT). *Application deadline:* For fall admission, 3/1 priority date for domestic and international students; for spring admission, 7/1 priority date for domestic and international students. Applications are processed on a rolling basis. Application fee: $50. Electronic applications accepted. *Expenses:* Expenses: Contact institution. *Financial support:* In

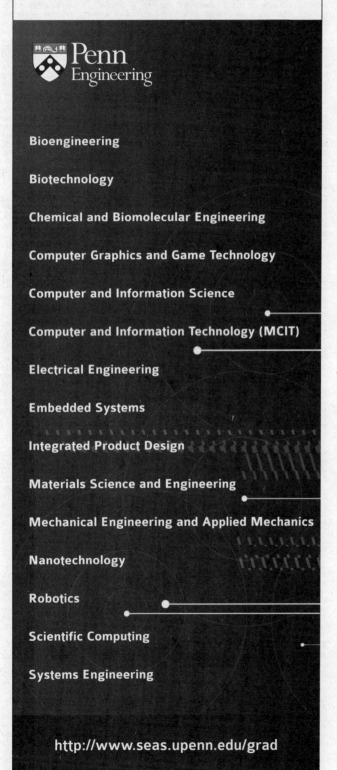

UNIVERSITY OF PENNSYLVANIA

Master's Degree Programs in Engineering

Penn Engineering

- Bioengineering
- Biotechnology
- Chemical and Biomolecular Engineering
- Computer Graphics and Game Technology
- Computer and Information Science
- Computer and Information Technology (MCIT)
- Electrical Engineering
- Embedded Systems
- Integrated Product Design
- Materials Science and Engineering
- Mechanical Engineering and Applied Mechanics
- Nanotechnology
- Robotics
- Scientific Computing
- Systems Engineering

http://www.seas.upenn.edu/grad

2014–15, 412 students received support, including 61 fellowships with full tuition reimbursements available (averaging $29,376 per year), 220 research assistantships with full tuition reimbursements available (averaging $25,756 per year), 131 teaching assistantships with full tuition reimbursements available (averaging $26,094 per year); scholarships/grants, traineeships, and tuition waivers (full and partial) also available. Financial award application deadline: 4/15. *Faculty research:* Artificial organs, biotechnology, signal processing, construction management, fluid dynamics. *Total annual research expenditures:* $91 million. *Unit head:* Dr. Gerald D. Holder, Dean, 412-624-9811, Fax: 412-624-0412, E-mail: holder@engrng.pitt.edu. *Application contact:* 412-624-9800, Fax: 412-624-9808, E-mail: ssoeadm@pitt.edu. Website: http://www.engineering.pitt.edu/.

University of Portland, School of Engineering, Portland, OR 97203-5798. Offers biomedical engineering (MBME); civil engineering (ME); computer science (ME); electrical engineering (ME); mechanical engineering (ME). Part-time and evening/weekend programs available. *Faculty:* 10 full-time (2 women), 1 part-time/adjunct (0 women). *Students:* 4 full-time (1 woman), 2 part-time (0 women); includes 1 minority (Two or more races, non-Hispanic/Latino), 1 international. Average age 27. In 2014, 2 master's awarded. *Degree requirements:* For master's, thesis optional. *Entrance requirements:* For master's, GRE General Test, minimum GPA of 3.0, 3 letters of recommendation, resume, statement of goals, official transcripts. Additional exam requirements/recommendations for international students: Required—TOEFL (minimum score 550 paper-based; 80 iBT), IELTS (minimum score 7). *Application deadline:* For fall admission, 7/15 priority date for domestic and international students; for spring admission, 12/15 priority date for domestic and international students. Applications are processed on a rolling basis. Application fee: $50. *Expenses:* Expenses: Contact institution. *Financial support:* Career-related internships or fieldwork, Federal Work-Study, and scholarships/grants available. Support available to part-time students. Financial award application deadline: 3/1; financial award applicants required to submit FAFSA. *Unit head:* Dr. Sharon Jones, Dean, 503-943-8169, E-mail: joness@up.edu. *Application contact:* Allison Able, Graduate Program Coordinator, 503-943-7107, Fax: 503-943-7315, E-mail: able@up.edu. Website: http://engineering.up.edu/default.aspx?cid-6464&pid-2432.

University of Puerto Rico, Mayagüez Campus, Graduate Studies, College of Engineering, Mayagüez, PR 00681-9000. Offers ME, MS, PhD. Part-time programs available. *Faculty:* 155 full-time (33 women), 8 part-time/adjunct (5 women). *Students:* 321 full-time (91 women), 35 part-time (5 women). 138 applicants, 83% accepted, 80 enrolled. In 2014, 67 master's, 10 doctorates awarded. *Degree requirements:* For master's, comprehensive exam, thesis; for doctorate, one foreign language, thesis/dissertation. *Entrance requirements:* For doctorate, GRE. Additional exam requirements/recommendations for international students: Required—TOEFL or IELTS. *Application deadline:* For fall admission, 2/15 for domestic and international students; for spring admission, 9/15 for domestic and international students. Applications are processed on a rolling basis. Application fee: $25. *Expenses:* Tuition, area resident: Full-time $2466; part-time $822 per credit. *International tuition:* $6371 full-time. *Required fees:* $1095; $1095 per year. Tuition and fees vary according to course level, course load and reciprocity agreements. *Financial support:* In 2014–15, 260 students received support, including 160 research assistantships (averaging $7,874 per year), 144 teaching assistantships (averaging $6,016 per year); fellowships with full tuition reimbursements available, Federal Work-Study, institutionally sponsored loans, and unspecified assistantships also available. *Unit head:* Dr. Manuel Jimenez, Dean, 787-265-3823, Fax: 787-833-6965. Website: http://ing.uprm.edu/.

University of Regina, Faculty of Graduate Studies and Research, Faculty of Engineering and Applied Science, Regina, SK S4S 0A2, Canada. Offers M Eng, MA Sc, PhD. Part-time programs available. *Faculty:* 39 full-time (7 women), 24 part-time/adjunct (0 women). *Students:* 250 full-time (73 women), 19 part-time (5 women). 683 applicants, 24% accepted. In 2014, 75 master's, 14 doctorates awarded. *Degree requirements:* For master's, thesis, project, report; for doctorate, comprehensive exam, thesis/dissertation. *Entrance requirements:* Additional exam requirements/recommendations for international students: Required—TOEFL (minimum score 550 paper-based; 80 iBT), IELTS (minimum score 6.5), PTE (minimum score 59). *Application deadline:* For fall admission, 3/31 for domestic and international students; for winter admission, 7/31 for domestic and international students; for spring admission, 11/30 for domestic and international students. Application fee: $100. Electronic applications accepted. *Expenses:* Expenses: $2,588.85 per semester of full time study (M Eng); $1,633.35 (for MA Sc); $1,755.60 (for PhD). *Financial support:* In 2014–15, 42 fellowships (averaging $6,405 per year), 55 teaching assistantships (averaging $2,477 per year) were awarded; research assistantships, career-related internships or fieldwork, and scholarships/grants also available. Financial award application deadline: 6/15. *Unit head:* Dr. Esam Hussein, Dean, 306-585-4160, Fax: 306-585-4556, E-mail: esam.hussein@uregina.ca. *Application contact:* Dr. Raphael Idem, Associate Dean, Graduate Studies and Research, 306-585-4470, Fax: 306-585-4855, E-mail: raphael.idem@uregina.ca. Website: http://www.uregina.ca/engineering/.

University of Rhode Island, Graduate School, College of Engineering, Kingston, RI 02881. Offers MS, PhD, Graduate Certificate. Part-time programs available. *Faculty:* 64 full-time (12 women), 3 part-time/adjunct (0 women). *Students:* 121 full-time (26 women), 97 part-time (18 women); includes 15 minority (4 Black or African American, non-Hispanic/Latino; 4 Asian, non-Hispanic/Latino; 7 Hispanic/Latino), 83 international. In 2014, 61 master's, 13 doctorates awarded. *Entrance requirements:* Additional exam requirements/recommendations for international students: Required—TOEFL (minimum score 550 paper-based). Application fee: $65. Electronic applications accepted. *Expenses:* Tuition, state resident: full-time $11,532; part-time $641 per credit. Tuition, nonresident: full-time $23,606; part-time $1311 per credit. *Required fees:* $1442; $39 per credit. $35 per semester. One-time fee: $155. *Financial support:* In 2014–15, 22 research assistantships with full and partial tuition reimbursements (averaging $9,421 per year), 16 teaching assistantships with full and partial tuition reimbursements (averaging $9,236 per year) were awarded. Financial award applicants required to submit FAFSA. *Total annual research expenditures:* $6.6 million. *Unit head:* Dr. Raymond Wright, Dean, 401-874-2186, Fax: 401-782-1066, E-mail: dean@egr.uri.edu. *Application contact:* Graduate Admission, 401-874-2872, E-mail: gradadm@etal.uri.edu. Website: http://www.egr.uri.edu/.

University of Rochester, Hajim School of Engineering and Applied Sciences, Rochester, NY 14627. Offers MS, PhD. Part-time programs available. *Faculty:* 91 full-time (10 women). *Students:* 553 full-time (152 women), 27 part-time (5 women); includes 39 minority (5 Black or African American, non-Hispanic/Latino; 1 American Indian or Alaska Native, non-Hispanic/Latino; 16 Asian, non-Hispanic/Latino; 15 Hispanic/Latino; 2 Two or more races, non-Hispanic/Latino), 345 international. 1,929 applicants, 36% accepted, 185 enrolled. In 2014, 187 master's, 56 doctorates awarded. Terminal master's awarded for partial completion of doctoral program. *Degree requirements:* For master's, comprehensive exam, thesis optional; for doctorate, thesis/dissertation, preliminary and oral exams. *Entrance requirements:* For master's and doctorate, GRE. Additional exam requirements/recommendations for international students: Required—TOEFL. *Application deadline:* For fall admission, 1/1 priority date for domestic students. Application fee: $60. *Expenses:* Tuition: Full-time $46,150; part-time $1442 per credit hour. *Required fees:* $504. *Financial support:* Fellowships, research assistantships, teaching assistantships, and tuition waivers (full and partial) available. Financial award application deadline: 2/1. *Unit head:* Rob Clark, Dean, 585-275-4151. *Application contact:* Dr. Margaret Kearney, Dean of Graduate Studies, 585-275-3540. Website: http://www.hajim.rochester.edu/.

University of St. Thomas, Graduate Studies, School of Engineering, St. Paul, MN 55105-1096. Offers electrical engineering (MS); manufacturing engineering and operations (MS); manufacturing systems (Certificate); mechanical engineering (MS); medical device development (Certificate); regulatory science (MS); software engineering (MS); software management (MS); systems engineering (MS); technology leadership (Certificate); technology management (MS). *Accreditation:* ABET (one or more programs are accredited). *Entrance requirements:* For master's, resume, official transcripts. Additional exam requirements/recommendations for international students: Required—TOEFL (minimum score 550 paper-based). Electronic applications accepted. *Expenses:* Contact institution.

University of Saskatchewan, College of Graduate Studies and Research, College of Engineering, Saskatoon, SK S7N 5A9, Canada. Offers M Eng, M Sc, PhD, PGD. Part-time programs available. *Degree requirements:* For master's, 30 credits (for M Eng); thesis and 12 credits (for MS); for doctorate, comprehensive exam, thesis/dissertation, qualifying exam, 18 credits. *Entrance requirements:* For master's and doctorate, GRE. Additional exam requirements/recommendations for international students: Required—TOEFL, TOEFL (minimum iBT score of 80), IELTS (6.5), CanTEST (4.5), or PTE (59). Electronic applications accepted.

University of South Africa, College of Science, Engineering and Technology, Pretoria, South Africa. Offers chemical engineering (M Tech); information technology (M Tech).

University of South Alabama, College of Engineering, Mobile, AL 36688. Offers MS Ch E, MSCE, MSEE, MSME, D Sc. Part-time programs available. *Faculty:* 26 full-time (2 women), 2 part-time/adjunct (0 women). *Students:* 155 full-time (23 women), 14 part-time (4 women); includes 14 minority (6 Black or African American, non-Hispanic/Latino; 2 Asian, non-Hispanic/Latino; 5 Hispanic/Latino; 1 Two or more races, non-Hispanic/Latino), 114 international. Average age 25. 435 applicants, 55% accepted, 78 enrolled. In 2014, 34 master's awarded. *Degree requirements:* For master's, comprehensive exam, project or thesis; for doctorate, comprehensive exam, thesis/dissertation. *Entrance requirements:* For master's, GRE General Test, BS in engineering, minimum GPA of 3.0; for doctorate, GRE, MS in engineering, minimum graduate GPA of 3.0. Additional exam requirements/recommendations for international students: Required—TOEFL (minimum score 575 paper-based; 71 iBT). *Application deadline:* For fall admission, 7/15 priority date for domestic students, 6/15 priority date for international students; for spring admission, 12/1 priority date for domestic students, 11/1 priority date for international students. Applications are processed on a rolling basis. Application fee: $35. Electronic applications accepted. *Expenses:* Tuition, state resident: full-time $9288; part-time $387 per credit hour. Tuition, nonresident: full-time $18,576; part-time $774 per credit hour. Part-time tuition and fees vary according to course load and program. *Financial support:* Fellowships, research assistantships, teaching assistantships, career-related internships or fieldwork, Federal Work-Study, institutionally sponsored loans, scholarships/grants, and unspecified assistantships available. Support available to part-time students. Financial award application deadline: 5/31; financial award applicants required to submit FAFSA. *Unit head:* Dr. John Steadman, Dean, College of Engineering, 251-460-6140, Fax: 251-460-6343, E-mail: engineering@southalabama.edu. *Application contact:* Dr. Thomas G. Thomas, Jr., Graduate Studies, College of Engineering, 251-460-6140, Fax: 251-460-6343, E-mail: engineering@southalabama.edu.
Website: http://www.southalabama.edu/colleges/engineering.

University of South Carolina, The Graduate School, College of Engineering and Computing, Columbia, SC 29208. Offers ME, MS, PhD. Part-time and evening/weekend programs available. Postbaccalaureate distance learning degree programs offered (minimal on-campus study). *Degree requirements:* For master's, thesis (for some programs); for doctorate, thesis/dissertation. *Entrance requirements:* For master's and doctorate, GRE General Test. Additional exam requirements/recommendations for international students: Required—TOEFL. Electronic applications accepted. *Faculty research:* Electrochemical engineering/fuel cell technology, fracture mechanics and nondestructive evaluation, virtual prototyping for electric power systems, wideband-gap electronics materials behavior/composites and smart materials.

University of Southern California, Graduate School, Viterbi School of Engineering, Los Angeles, CA 90089. Offers MCM, ME, MS, PhD, Engr, Graduate Certificate, MS/MBA. Part-time programs available. Postbaccalaureate distance learning degree programs offered (no on-campus study). Terminal master's awarded for partial completion of doctoral program. *Degree requirements:* For doctorate, comprehensive exam, thesis/dissertation. *Entrance requirements:* For master's and doctorate, GRE. Additional exam requirements/recommendations for international students: Recommended—TOEFL. Electronic applications accepted. *Expenses:* Contact institution. *Faculty research:* Mechanics and materials, aerodynamics of air/ground vehicles, gas dynamics, aerosols, astronautics and space science, geophysical and microgravity flows, planetary physics, power MEMs and MEMS vacuum pumps, heat transfer and combustion, health systems, transportation and logistics, manufacturing and automation, engineering systems design, risk and economic analysis, electromagnetic devices circuits and VLSI, MEMS and nanotechnology, electromagnetics and plasmas.

University of Southern Indiana, Graduate Studies, Pott College of Science, Engineering, and Education, Evansville, IN 47712-3590. Offers MS, MSE. Part-time and evening/weekend programs available. *Faculty:* 19 full-time (8 women), 4 part-time/adjunct (2 women). *Students:* 7 full-time (all women), 47 part-time (29 women); includes 2 minority (both Black or African American, non-Hispanic/Latino), 11 international. Average age 33. In 2014, 64 master's awarded. *Degree requirements:* For master's, project. *Entrance requirements:* For master's, GRE General Test, NTE, PRAXIS I, minimum GPA of 2.5 and BS in engineering or engineering technology (MSIM); minimum GPA of 3.0 and teaching license (MSE). Additional exam requirements/recommendations for international students: Required—TOEFL (minimum score 550 paper-based; 79 iBT), IELTS (minimum score 6). *Application deadline:* For fall admission, 8/15 priority date for domestic students, 3/1 priority date for international students. Applications are processed on a rolling basis. Application fee: $40. Electronic applications accepted. *Financial support:* In 2014–15, 12 students received support. Federal Work-Study, scholarships/grants, tuition waivers (full and partial), and unspecified assistantships available. Financial award application deadline: 3/1; financial award applicants required to submit FAFSA. *Unit head:* Dr. Scott A. Gordon, Dean, 812-465-7137, E-mail: sgordon@usi.edu. *Application contact:* Dr. Mayola Rowser, Director, Graduate Studies, 812-465-7016, Fax: 812-464-1956, E-mail: mrowser@usi.edu.
Website: http://www.usi.edu/science/.

University of South Florida, College of Engineering, Tampa, FL 33620-9951. Offers M Ch E, MCE, MEVE, MME, MSBE, MSBE, MSCE, MSCH, MSCP, MSCS, MSEE, MSEM, MSES, MSEV, MSIE, MSIT, MSME, MSMSE, PhD, MSBE/MS, PhD/MD. Part-time and evening/weekend programs available. *Faculty:* 108 full-time (18 women), 2 part-time/adjunct (0 women). *Students:* 677 full-time (188 women), 320 part-time (72 women); includes 172 minority (36 Black or African American, non-Hispanic/Latino; 1 American Indian or Alaska Native, non-Hispanic/Latino; 33 Asian, non-Hispanic/Latino; 86 Hispanic/Latino; 1 Native Hawaiian or other Pacific Islander, non-Hispanic/Latino; 15 Two or more races, non-Hispanic/Latino), 519 international. Average age 28. 1,862 applicants, 46% accepted, 277 enrolled. In 2014, 268 master's, 49 doctorates awarded. Terminal master's awarded for partial completion of doctoral program. *Degree requirements:* For master's, comprehensive exam, thesis (for some programs); for doctorate, comprehensive exam, thesis/dissertation. *Entrance requirements:* For master's, GRE General Test, minimum GPA of 3.0 in last 60 hours of coursework; for doctorate, GRE General Test, minimum GPA of 3.3 in last 60 hours of coursework. Additional exam requirements/recommendations for international students: Required—TOEFL (minimum score 550 paper-based; 79 iBT). *Application deadline:* For fall admission, 2/15 for domestic students, 1/2 priority date for international students; for spring admission, 10/15 for domestic students, 6/1 priority date for international students. Applications are processed on a rolling basis. Application fee: $30. Electronic applications accepted. *Financial support:* Career-related internships or fieldwork, Federal Work-Study, scholarships/grants, health care benefits, and unspecified assistantships available. Financial award application deadline: 3/1. *Faculty research:* Biomedical engineering and sustainability, particularly in water resources and energy; electrical engineering; civil/environmental engineering; industrial/management systems engineering; chemical engineering; computer science and engineering; mechanical engineering. *Total annual research expenditures:* $990. *Unit head:* Dr. Robert Bishop, Dean, 813-974-3864, Fax: 813-974-5094, E-mail: robertbishop@usf.edu. *Application contact:* Dr. Rafael Perez, Associate Dean for Academic Affairs, 813-974-3934, Fax: 813-974-5094, E-mail: perez@usf.edu.
Website: http://www2.eng.usf.edu/.

The University of Tennessee, Graduate School, College of Engineering, Knoxville, TN 37966. Offers MS, PhD, MS/MBA, MS/PhD. Part-time programs available. Postbaccalaureate distance learning degree programs offered (minimal on-campus study). *Faculty:* 263 full-time (30 women), 71 part-time/adjunct (9 women). *Students:* 732 full-time (157 women), 238 part-time (30 women); includes 85 minority (23 Black or African American, non-Hispanic/Latino; 2 American Indian or Alaska Native, non-Hispanic/Latino; 28 Asian, non-Hispanic/Latino; 10 Hispanic/Latino; 22 Two or more races, non-Hispanic/Latino), 352 international. Average age 30. 1,767 applicants, 31% accepted, 335 enrolled. In 2014, 230 master's, 100 doctorates awarded. *Degree requirements:* For master's, thesis or alternative; for doctorate, comprehensive exam, thesis/dissertation. *Entrance requirements:* For master's, GRE General Test (for MS students pursuing research thesis), minimum GPA of 2.7 (for U.S. degree holders), 3.0 (for international degree holders); 3 references; statement of purpose; for doctorate, GRE General Test, minimum GPA of 3.0 on previous graduate course work; 3 references; statement of purpose. Additional exam requirements/recommendations for international students: Required—TOEFL (minimum score 550 paper-based). *Application deadline:* For fall admission, 2/1 priority date for domestic and international students; for spring admission, 6/15 for domestic and international students. Applications are processed on a rolling basis. Application fee: $35. Electronic applications accepted. *Financial support:* In 2014–15, 624 students received support, including 114 fellowships with full tuition reimbursements available (averaging $19,690 per year), 304 research assistantships with full tuition reimbursements available (averaging $22,188 per year), 199 teaching assistantships with full tuition reimbursements available (averaging $19,949 per year); career-related internships or fieldwork, Federal Work-Study, institutionally sponsored loans, health care benefits, and unspecified assistantships also available. Financial award application deadline: 2/1; financial award applicants required to submit FAFSA. *Faculty research:* Chemical and biomolecular engineering; civil and environmental engineering; electrical engineering and computer science; nuclear engineering; materials science and engineering; mechanical, aerospace, and biomedical engineering; industrial and information engineering. *Total annual research expenditures:* $54.8 million. *Unit head:* Dr. Wayne T. Davis, Dean, 865-974-5321, Fax: 865-974-8890, E-mail: wtdavis@utk.edu. *Application contact:* Dr. Masood Parang, Associate Dean of Student Affairs, 865-974-2454, Fax: 865-974-9871, E-mail: mparang@utk.edu.
Website: http://www.engr.utk.edu/.

The University of Texas at Arlington, Graduate School, College of Engineering, Arlington, TX 76019. Offers M Engr, MCM, MS, PhD. Part-time and evening/weekend programs available. Postbaccalaureate distance learning degree programs offered (minimal on-campus study). Terminal master's awarded for partial completion of doctoral program. *Degree requirements:* For master's, thesis optional; for doctorate, thesis/dissertation. *Entrance requirements:* For master's, GRE General Test, minimum GPA of 3.0 in last 60 hours of coursework; for doctorate, GRE General Test. Additional exam requirements/recommendations for international students: Required—TOEFL (minimum score 550 paper-based). *Faculty research:* Nanotechnology, mobile pervasive computing, bioinformatics intelligent systems.

The University of Texas at Austin, Graduate School, Cockrell School of Engineering, Austin, TX 78712-1111. Offers MA, MS, MSE, PhD, MBA/MSE, MD/PhD, MP Aff/MSE. Part-time and evening/weekend programs available. *Entrance requirements:* For master's and doctorate, GRE General Test. Additional exam requirements/recommendations for international students: Required—TOEFL (minimum score 550 paper-based). Electronic applications accepted.

The University of Texas at Dallas, Erik Jonsson School of Engineering and Computer Science, Richardson, TX 75080. Offers MS, MSEE, MSME, MSTE, PhD. Part-time and evening/weekend programs available. *Faculty:* 141 full-time (20 women), 18 part-time/adjunct (3 women). *Students:* 2,009 full-time (517 women), 591 part-time (167 women); includes 182 minority (27 Black or African American, non-Hispanic/Latino; 93 Asian, non-Hispanic/Latino; 49 Hispanic/Latino; 13 Two or more races, non-Hispanic/Latino), 2,178 international. Average age 26. 6,741 applicants, 35% accepted, 995 enrolled. In 2014, 614 master's, 70 doctorates awarded. *Degree requirements:* For master's, thesis optional; for doctorate, thesis/dissertation. *Entrance requirements:* For master's, GRE General Test, minimum GPA of 3.0 in related bachelor's course work; for doctorate, GRE General Test, minimum GPA of 3.5. Additional exam requirements/recommendations for international students: Required—TOEFL (minimum score 550 paper-based). *Application deadline:* For fall admission, 7/15 for domestic students, 5/1 priority date for international students; for spring admission, 11/15 for domestic students, 9/1 priority date for international students. Applications are processed on a rolling basis. Application fee: $50 ($100 for international students). Electronic applications accepted. *Expenses:* Tuition, state resident: full-time $11,940; part-time $663 per credit. Tuition, nonresident: full-time $22,282; part-time $1238 per credit. *Financial support:* In 2014–15, 679 students received support, including 35 fellowships with partial tuition reimbursements available (averaging $8,688 per year), 298 research assistantships with partial tuition reimbursements available (averaging $17,938 per year), 190 teaching assistantships with partial tuition reimbursements available (averaging $17,280 per year); career-related internships or fieldwork, Federal Work-Study, institutionally sponsored loans, scholarships/grants, and unspecified assistantships also available. Support available to part-time students. Financial award application deadline: 4/30;

financial award applicants required to submit FAFSA. *Faculty research:* Semiconducting materials, nano-fabrication and bio-nanotechnology, biomedical devices and organic electronics, signal processing and language technology, cloud computing and IT security. *Total annual research expenditures:* $38.3 million. *Unit head:* Dr. Mark W. Spong, Dean, 972-883-2974, Fax: 972-883-2813, E-mail: ecsdean@utdallas.edu. Website: http://ecs.utdallas.edu/.

The University of Texas at El Paso, Graduate School, College of Engineering, El Paso, TX 79968-0001. Offers biomedical engineering (PhD); civil engineering (MEENE, MS, MSENE, PhD, Certificate), including civil engineering (MS), civil engineering (PhD), construction management (MS, Certificate), environmental engineering (MEENE, MSENE); computer science (MS, MSIT, PhD), including computer science (MS, PhD), information technology (MSIT); education engineering (M Eng); electrical and computer engineering (MS, PhD), including computer engineering (MS), electrical and computer engineering (PhD), electrical engineering (MS); industrial engineering (MS, Certificate), including industrial engineering (MS), manufacturing engineering (MS); systems engineering; mechanical engineering (MS, PhD), including environmental science and engineering (PhD), mechanical engineering (MS); metallurgical and materials engineering (MS, PhD), including materials science and engineering (PhD), metallurgical and materials engineering (MS); software engineering (M Eng). Part-time and evening/weekend programs available. *Degree requirements:* For master's, thesis optional; for doctorate, thesis/dissertation. *Entrance requirements:* For master's, GRE, minimum GPA of 3.0, letters of reference; for doctorate, GRE, statement of purpose, letters of reference. Additional exam requirements/recommendations for international students: Required—TOEFL; Recommended—IELTS. Electronic applications accepted. *Expenses:* Contact institution.

The University of Texas at San Antonio, College of Engineering, San Antonio, TX 78249-0617. Offers MCE, MS, MSCE, MSEE, PhD. Part-time and evening/weekend programs available. *Faculty:* 57 full-time (7 women), 7 part-time/adjunct (0 women). *Students:* 358 full-time (100 women), 198 part-time (43 women); includes 123 minority (13 Black or African American, non-Hispanic/Latino; 28 Asian, non-Hispanic/Latino; 70 Hispanic/Latino; 12 Two or more races, non-Hispanic/Latino), 320 international. Average age 27. 756 applicants, 77% accepted, 216 enrolled. In 2014, 91 master's, 17 doctorates awarded. Terminal master's awarded for partial completion of doctoral program. *Degree requirements:* For master's, variable foreign language requirement, comprehensive exam, thesis optional, completion of all course work requirements within six-year time limit; no courses with grade of less than C; minimum GPA of 3.0; for doctorate, variable foreign language requirement, comprehensive exam, thesis/dissertation, continuous enrollment until time of graduation; all completed coursework included in the final program of study must have been taken within the preceding eight years to include successful completion and defense of the dissertation. *Entrance requirements:* For master's, GRE, baccalaureate degree in related field from regionally-accredited college or university in the U.S. or proof of equivalent training at foreign institution; minimum GPA of 3.0 in last 60 semester credit hours or foreign institution equivalent of coursework taken; for doctorate, GRE, baccalaureate degree or MS in related field from regionally-accredited college or university in the U.S. or proof of equivalent training at foreign institution; minimum GPA of 3.0, 3.3 in upper-division/graduate courses. Additional exam requirements/recommendations for international students: Required—TOEFL (minimum score 550 paper-based; 79 iBT), IELTS (minimum score 6.5). *Application deadline:* For fall admission, 7/1 for domestic students, 4/1 for international students; for spring admission, 11/1 for domestic students, 9/1 for international students. Application fee: $45 ($80 for international students). *Expenses:* Expenses: $3,297.80 full-time state resident per semester; $9,973.10 full-time non-resident. *Financial support:* In 2014–15, 120 students received support. Career-related internships or fieldwork, Federal Work-Study, institutionally sponsored loans, scholarships/grants, health care benefits, unspecified assistantships, and Valero Research Scholar awards available. Financial award application deadline: 9/15. *Faculty research:* Biomedical engineering, civil and environmental science engineering, electrical and computer engineering, advanced materials engineering, mechanical engineering. *Total annual research expenditures:* $6.7 million. *Unit head:* Dr. JoAnn Browning, Dean of Engineering, 210-458-5526, Fax: 210-458-5515, E-mail: joann.browning@utsa.edu. *Application contact:* Monica Rodriguez, Director of Graduate Admissions, 210-458-4331, Fax: 210-458-4332, E-mail: graduateadmissions@utsa.edu. Website: http://engineering2.utsa.edu/.

University of the District of Columbia, School of Engineering and Applied Science, Washington, DC 20008-1175. Offers MS.

University of the Pacific, School of Engineering and Computer Science, Stockton, CA 95211-0197. Offers engineering science (MS). *Students:* 23 full-time (5 women), 13 part-time (2 women); includes 14 minority (2 Black or African American, non-Hispanic/Latino; 1 American Indian or Alaska Native, non-Hispanic/Latino; 5 Asian, non-Hispanic/Latino; 4 Hispanic/Latino; 2 Two or more races, non-Hispanic/Latino), 5 international. 30 applicants, 47% accepted, 9 enrolled. In 2014, 60 master's awarded. *Entrance requirements:* For master's, GRE, three references; official transcripts; personal statement; bachelor's degree in engineering, computer science, or a closely related discipline. Additional exam requirements/recommendations for international students: Required—TOEFL (minimum score 550 paper-based; 80 iBT). *Application deadline:* For fall admission, 3/1 for domestic students; for spring admission, 10/1 for domestic students. Electronic applications accepted. *Financial support:* Teaching assistantships available. *Unit head:* Dr. Steven Howell, Dean, 209-946-3905, E-mail: erafanan@pacific.edu. *Application contact:* Office of Graduate Admissions, 209-946-2011.

The University of Toledo, College of Graduate Studies, College of Engineering, Program in Engineering, Toledo, OH 43606-3390. Offers general engineering (MS). *Entrance requirements:* For master's, GRE General Test, minimum GPA of 2.7, industrial experience.

University of Toronto, School of Graduate Studies, Faculty of Applied Science and Engineering, Toronto, ON M5S 2J7, Canada. Offers M Eng, MA Sc, MH Sc, PhD. Part-time programs available. *Degree requirements:* For doctorate, thesis/dissertation. *Expenses:* Contact institution.

The University of Tulsa, Graduate School, College of Engineering and Natural Sciences, Tulsa, OK 74104-3189. Offers ME, MS, MSE, MTA, PhD, JD/MS, MBA/MS, MSF/MSAM. Part-time programs available. *Faculty:* 102 full-time (11 women), 2 part-time/adjunct (1 woman). *Students:* 280 full-time (77 women), 60 part-time (17 women); includes 15 minority (2 Black or African American, non-Hispanic/Latino; 7 American Indian or Alaska Native, non-Hispanic/Latino; 1 Asian, non-Hispanic/Latino; 4 Hispanic/Latino; 1 Two or more races, non-Hispanic/Latino), 252 international. Average age 28. 751 applicants, 32% accepted, 106 enrolled. In 2014, 83 master's, 19 doctorates awarded. Terminal master's awarded for partial completion of doctoral program. *Degree requirements:* For master's, thesis (for some programs); for doctorate, comprehensive exam, thesis/dissertation. *Entrance requirements:* For master's and doctorate, GRE General Test. Additional exam requirements/recommendations for international students: Required—TOEFL (minimum score 550 paper-based), IELTS (minimum score 6). *Application deadline:* Applications are processed on a rolling basis. Application fee: $55. Electronic applications accepted. *Expenses: Tuition:* Full-time $20,160; part-time

$1120 per credit hour. *Required fees:* $6 per credit hour. Tuition and fees vary according to course level and course load. *Financial support:* In 2014–15, 281 students received support, including 56 fellowships with full and partial tuition reimbursements available (averaging $4,638 per year), 142 research assistantships with full and partial tuition reimbursements available (averaging $10,129 per year), 83 teaching assistantships with full and partial tuition reimbursements available (averaging $10,905 per year); career-related internships or fieldwork, Federal Work-Study, scholarships/grants, health care benefits, tuition waivers (full and partial), and unspecified assistantships also available. Support available to part-time students. Financial award application deadline: 2/1; financial award applicants required to submit FAFSA. *Total annual research expenditures:* $15.7 million. *Unit head:* Dr. James Sorem, Dean, 918-631-2288, E-mail: james-sorem@utulsa.edu. *Application contact:* Graduate School, 918-631-2336, Fax: 918-631-2156, E-mail: grad@utulsa.edu. Website: http://engineering.utulsa.edu/.

University of Utah, Graduate School, College of Engineering, Salt Lake City, UT 84112. Offers ME, MEAE, MS, PhD, MS/MBA. *Accreditation:* ABET. Part-time and evening/weekend programs available. *Faculty:* 144 full-time (22 women), 71 part-time/adjunct (9 women). *Students:* 861 full-time (167 women), 277 part-time (35 women); includes 81 minority (8 Black or African American, non-Hispanic/Latino; 41 Asian, non-Hispanic/Latino; 16 Hispanic/Latino; 2 Native Hawaiian or other Pacific Islander, non-Hispanic/Latino; 14 Two or more races, non-Hispanic/Latino), 505 international. Average age 29. 1,944 applicants, 35% accepted, 344 enrolled. In 2014, 219 master's, 75 doctorates awarded. *Degree requirements:* For master's, comprehensive exam (for some programs), thesis (for some programs); for doctorate, comprehensive exam (for some programs), thesis/dissertation (for some programs). *Entrance requirements:* For master's and doctorate, GRE, minimum GPA of 3.0. Additional exam requirements/recommendations for international students: Required—TOEFL (minimum score 550 paper-based; 80 iBT), IELTS (minimum score 6.5). Electronic applications accepted. *Expenses:* Expenses: Contact institution. *Financial support:* Fellowships with full tuition reimbursements, research assistantships with full and partial tuition reimbursements, teaching assistantships with full and partial tuition reimbursements, career-related internships or fieldwork, Federal Work-Study, institutionally sponsored loans, scholarships/grants, traineeships, health care benefits, tuition waivers (full and partial), and unspecified assistantships available. Support available to part-time students. Financial award applicants required to submit FAFSA. *Faculty research:* Biomaterials, wastewater treatment, computer-aided graphics design, semiconductors, polymers. *Total annual research expenditures:* $22.5 million. *Unit head:* Dr. Richard B. Brown, Dean, 801-585-7498, E-mail: brown@utah.edu. *Application contact:* Dianne Leonard, Academic Program Manager, 801-585-7769, Fax: 801-581-8692, E-mail: dleonard@coe.utah.edu. Website: http://www.coe.utah.edu/.

University of Vermont, Graduate College, College of Engineering and Mathematics, Burlington, VT 05405. Offers MS, MST, PhD. Part-time programs available. *Degree requirements:* For doctorate, thesis/dissertation. *Entrance requirements:* Additional exam requirements/recommendations for international students: Required—TOEFL (minimum score 550 paper-based; 80 iBT). Electronic applications accepted.

University of Victoria, Faculty of Graduate Studies, Faculty of Engineering, Victoria, BC V8W 2Y2, Canada. Offers M Eng, M Sc, MA Sc, PhD.

University of Virginia, School of Engineering and Applied Science, Charlottesville, VA 22903. Offers MCS, ME, MEP, MMSE, MS, PhD, ME/MBA. Part-time programs available. Postbaccalaureate distance learning degree programs offered (no on-campus study). *Faculty:* 148 full-time (16 women), 2 part-time/adjunct (0 women). *Students:* 565 full-time (148 women), 27 part-time (4 women); includes 65 minority (9 Black or African American, non-Hispanic/Latino; 36 Asian, non-Hispanic/Latino; 14 Hispanic/Latino; 6 Two or more races, non-Hispanic/Latino), 270 international. Average age 26. 1,840 applicants, 18% accepted, 144 enrolled. In 2014, 126 master's, 96 doctorates awarded. Terminal master's awarded for partial completion of doctoral program. *Degree requirements:* For doctorate, comprehensive exam, thesis/dissertation. *Entrance requirements:* For master's, GRE General Test, 3 letters of recommendation; for doctorate, GRE General Test, 3 letters of recommendation, essay. Additional exam requirements/recommendations for international students: Required—TOEFL (minimum score 600 paper-based; 90 iBT), IELTS (minimum score 7). *Application deadline:* For fall admission, 8/1 for domestic students, 4/1 for international students; for winter admission, 12/1 for domestic students, 8/1 for international students; for spring admission, 5/1 for domestic students, 1/1 for international students. Applications are processed on a rolling basis. Electronic applications accepted. *Expenses:* Tuition, state resident: full-time $14,164; part-time $349 per credit hour. Tuition, nonresident: full-time $23,722; part-time $1300 per credit hour. *Required fees:* $2514. *Financial support:* Fellowships with full tuition reimbursements, research assistantships with full tuition reimbursements, teaching assistantships with full tuition reimbursements, and career-related internships or fieldwork available. Financial award application deadline: 1/15; financial award applicants required to submit FAFSA. *Unit head:* James H. Aylor, Dean, 434-924-3072, Fax: 434-243-2083. *Application contact:* Pamela M. Morris, Associate Dean for Research and Graduate Programs, 434-243-7683, Fax: 434-982-3044, E-mail: pamela@virginia.edu. Website: http://www.seas.virginia.edu/.

University of Washington, Graduate School, College of Engineering, Seattle, WA 98195-2180. Offers MAE, MISE, MS, MSAA, MSCE, MSE, MSME, PhD. Part-time programs available. Postbaccalaureate distance learning degree programs offered. *Faculty:* 246 full-time (55 women). *Students:* 1,441 full-time (434 women), 747 part-time (191 women); includes 429 minority (29 Black or African American, non-Hispanic/Latino; 2 American Indian or Alaska Native, non-Hispanic/Latino; 255 Asian, non-Hispanic/Latino; 90 Hispanic/Latino; 53 Two or more races, non-Hispanic/Latino), 715 international. Average age 27. 6,539 applicants, 28% accepted, 819 enrolled. In 2014, 509 master's, 134 doctorates awarded. *Degree requirements:* For master's, comprehensive exam (for some programs), thesis optional; for doctorate, comprehensive exam, thesis/dissertation. *Entrance requirements:* Additional exam requirements/recommendations for international students: Required—TOEFL; Recommended—IELTS. *Application deadline:* For fall admission, 12/1 for domestic and international students. Application fee: $85. Electronic applications accepted. *Expenses:* Expenses: Contact institution. *Financial support:* In 2014–15, 1,109 students received support, including 200 fellowships with full tuition reimbursements available, 649 research assistantships with full tuition reimbursements available, 245 teaching assistantships with full tuition reimbursements available; career-related internships or fieldwork, Federal Work-Study, institutionally sponsored loans, scholarships/grants, traineeships, health care benefits, tuition waivers (full), unspecified assistantships, and stipend supplements also available. Financial award application deadline: 2/28; financial award applicants required to submit FAFSA. *Total annual research expenditures:* $133.7 million. *Unit head:* Dr. Michael B. Bragg, Dean of Engineering, 206-543-0340, Fax: 206-685-0666, E-mail: mbragg@uw.edu. *Application contact:* Scott Winter, Director, Academic Affairs, 206-685-4074, Fax: 206-685-0666, E-mail: swinter@uw.edu. Website: http://www.engr.washington.edu/.

University of Waterloo, Graduate Studies, Faculty of Engineering, Waterloo, ON N2L 3G1, Canada. Offers M Arch, M Eng, MA Sc, MBET, MMS, PhD. Part-time and evening/weekend programs available. Postbaccalaureate distance learning degree programs offered (no on-campus study). *Degree requirements:* For master's, research paper or thesis; for doctorate, comprehensive exam, thesis/dissertation. *Entrance requirements:* For master's, honors degree; for doctorate, master's degree, minimum A- average. Additional exam requirements/recommendations for international students: Required—TOEFL, TWE. Electronic applications accepted.

The University of Western Ontario, Faculty of Graduate Studies, Physical Sciences Division, Faculty of Engineering, London, ON N6A 5B8, Canada. Offers chemical and biochemical engineering (ME Sc, PhD); civil and environmental engineering (M Eng, ME Sc, PhD); electrical and computer engineering (M Eng, ME Sc, PhD); mechanical and materials engineering (M Eng, ME Sc, PhD). Part-time programs available. Terminal master's awarded for partial completion of doctoral program. *Degree requirements:* For master's, thesis; for doctorate, thesis/dissertation. *Entrance requirements:* For master's, minimum B average; for doctorate, minimum B+ average. *Faculty research:* Wind, geotechnical, chemical reactor engineering, applied electrostatics, biochemical engineering.

University of Windsor, Faculty of Graduate Studies, Faculty of Engineering, Windsor, ON N9B 3P4, Canada. Offers M Eng, MA Sc, PhD. Part-time programs available. *Degree requirements:* For doctorate, comprehensive exam, thesis/dissertation. *Entrance requirements:* For master's, minimum B average; for doctorate, master's degree. Additional exam requirements/recommendations for international students: Required—TOEFL. Electronic applications accepted.

University of Wisconsin–Madison, Graduate School, College of Engineering, Madison, WI 53706-1380. Offers ME, MS, PhD. Part-time programs available. Postbaccalaureate distance learning degree programs offered (minimal on-campus study). *Degree requirements:* For doctorate, thesis/dissertation. Electronic applications accepted. *Expenses:* Tuition, state resident: full-time $10,723; part-time $745 per credit. Tuition, nonresident: full-time $24,054; part-time $1578 per credit. *Required fees:* $374 per semester. Tuition and fees vary according to course load, program and reciprocity agreements.

University of Wisconsin–Milwaukee, Graduate School, College of Engineering and Applied Science, Milwaukee, WI 53211. Offers MS, PhD, Certificate, MUP/MS. Part-time programs available. *Students:* 209 full-time (51 women), 212 part-time (50 women); includes 38 minority (3 Black or African American, non-Hispanic/Latino; 26 Asian, non-Hispanic/Latino; 2 Hispanic/Latino; 7 Two or more races, non-Hispanic/Latino), 245 international. Average age 31. 494 applicants, 58% accepted, 114 enrolled. In 2014, 82 master's, 32 doctorates awarded. *Degree requirements:* For master's, comprehensive exam (for some programs), thesis or alternative; for doctorate, thesis/dissertation, internship. *Entrance requirements:* For master's, GRE, minimum GPA of 2.75; for doctorate, GRE, minimum GPA of 3.5. Additional exam requirements/recommendations for international students: Required—TOEFL (minimum score 550 paper-based; 79 iBT), IELTS (minimum score 6.5). *Application deadline:* For fall admission, 1/1 for domestic students; for spring admission, 9/1 for domestic students. Applications are processed on a rolling basis. Application fee: $56 ($96 for international students). Electronic applications accepted. *Financial support:* In 2014–15, 31 research assistantships, 82 teaching assistantships were awarded; fellowships, career-related internships or fieldwork, Federal Work-Study, and unspecified assistantships also available. Support available to part-time students. Financial award application deadline: 4/15. *Unit head:* Dr. Brett Peters, Dean, 414-229-4126, E-mail: petersba@uwm.edu. *Application contact:* Betty Warras, General Information Contact, 414-229-6169, Fax: 414-229-6958, E-mail: ceas-graduate@uwm.edu.
Website: http://uwm.edu/engineering/.

University of Wisconsin–Platteville, School of Graduate Studies, Distance Learning Center, Online Master of Science in Engineering Program, Platteville, WI 53818-3099. Offers MS. Part-time and evening/weekend programs available. Postbaccalaureate distance learning degree programs offered (no on-campus study). *Degree requirements:* For master's, thesis or alternative. *Entrance requirements:* Additional exam requirements/recommendations for international students: Required—TOEFL (minimum score 500 paper-based; 61 iBT), IELTS (minimum score 6). Electronic applications accepted. *Expenses:* Contact institution.

University of Wyoming, College of Engineering and Applied Sciences, Laramie, WY 82071. Offers MS, PhD. Part-time programs available. *Entrance requirements:* For master's and doctorate, GRE General Test, minimum GPA of 3.0. Additional exam requirements/recommendations for international students: Required—TOEFL. Electronic applications accepted.

Utah State University, School of Graduate Studies, College of Engineering, Logan, UT 84322. Offers ME, MS, PhD, CE. Part-time and evening/weekend programs available. Terminal master's awarded for partial completion of doctoral program. *Degree requirements:* For master's, thesis (for some programs); for doctorate, thesis/dissertation. *Entrance requirements:* For master's and doctorate, GRE General Test, minimum GPA of 3.0. Additional exam requirements/recommendations for international students: Required—TOEFL. Electronic applications accepted. *Faculty research:* Crop-yield modeling, earthquake engineering, digital signal processing, technology and the public school, cryogenic cooling.

Vanderbilt University, School of Engineering, Nashville, TN 37235. Offers M Eng, MS, PhD, MD/PhD. MS and PhD offered through the Graduate School. Part-time programs available. Terminal master's awarded for partial completion of doctoral program. *Degree requirements:* For master's, comprehensive exam (for some programs), thesis (for some programs); for doctorate, comprehensive exam (for some programs), thesis/dissertation. *Entrance requirements:* For master's and doctorate, GRE General Test. Additional exam requirements/recommendations for international students: Required—TOEFL. Electronic applications accepted. Application fee is waived when completed online. *Expenses: Tuition:* Full-time $42,768; part-time $1782 per credit hour. *Required fees:* $422. One-time fee: $30 full-time. *Faculty research:* Robotics, microelectronics, reliability in design, software engineering, medical imaging.

Villanova University, College of Engineering, Villanova, PA 19085-1699. Offers MSCPE, MSChE, MSEE, MSME, MSWREE, PhD, Certificate. Part-time and evening/weekend programs available. Postbaccalaureate distance learning degree programs offered (minimal on-campus study). Terminal master's awarded for partial completion of doctoral program. *Degree requirements:* For master's, thesis optional; for doctorate, thesis/dissertation. *Entrance requirements:* For master's, GRE General Test (for applicants with degrees from foreign universities), minimum GPA of 3.0; for doctorate, GRE General Test. Additional exam requirements/recommendations for international students: Required—TOEFL (minimum score 600 paper-based; 100 iBT). Electronic applications accepted. *Expenses:* Contact institution. *Faculty research:* Composite materials, economy and risk, heat transfer, signal detection.

Virginia Commonwealth University, Graduate School, School of Engineering, Richmond, VA 23284-9005. Offers MS, PhD, MD/PhD. *Degree requirements:* For doctorate, thesis/dissertation, comprehensive oral and written exams. *Entrance requirements:* For master's and doctorate, GRE General Test. Additional exam requirements/recommendations for international students: Required—TOEFL (minimum score 600 paper-based; 100 iBT). Electronic applications accepted. *Faculty research:* Artificial hearts, orthopedic implants, medical imaging, medical instrumentation and sensors, cardiac monitoring.

Virginia Polytechnic Institute and State University, Graduate School, College of Engineering, Blacksburg, VA 24061. Offers aerospace engineering (ME, MS, PhD); biological systems engineering (ME, MS, PhD); biomedical engineering (MS, PhD); chemical engineering (ME, MS, PhD); civil engineering (ME, MS, PhD); computer engineering (ME, MS, PhD); computer science (MS, PhD); electrical engineering (ME, PhD); engineering education (PhD); engineering mechanics (ME, MS, PhD); environmental engineering (MS); environmental science and engineering (MS); industrial and systems engineering (ME, MS, PhD); materials science and engineering (ME, MS, PhD); mechanical engineering (ME, MS, PhD); mining and minerals engineering (PhD); mining engineering (ME, MS); nuclear engineering (MS, PhD); ocean engineering (MS); systems engineering (ME, MS). *Accreditation:* ABET (one or more programs are accredited). *Faculty:* 356 full-time (60 women), 3 part-time/adjunct (1 woman). *Students:* 1,700 full-time (398 women), 345 part-time (58 women); includes 213 minority (43 Black or African American, non-Hispanic/Latino; 1 American Indian or Alaska Native, non-Hispanic/Latino; 87 Asian, non-Hispanic/Latino; 58 Hispanic/Latino; 1 Native Hawaiian or other Pacific Islander, non-Hispanic/Latino; 23 Two or more races, non-Hispanic/Latino), 1,079 international. Average age 27. 5,228 applicants, 18% accepted, 471 enrolled. In 2014, 438 master's, 211 doctorates awarded. *Degree requirements:* For master's, comprehensive exam (for some programs), thesis (for some programs); for doctorate, comprehensive exam (for some programs), thesis/dissertation (for some programs). *Entrance requirements:* For master's and doctorate, GRE/GMAT (may vary by department). Additional exam requirements/recommendations for international students: Required—TOEFL (minimum score 550 paper-based). *Application deadline:* For fall admission, 8/1 for domestic students, 4/1 for international students; for spring admission, 1/1 for domestic students, 9/1 for international students. Applications are processed on a rolling basis. Application fee: $75. Electronic applications accepted. *Expenses:* Tuition, state resident: full-time $11,656; part-time $647.50 per credit hour. Tuition, nonresident: full-time $23,351; part-time $1297.25 per credit hour. *Required fees:* $2533; $465.75 per semester. Tuition and fees vary according to course load, campus/location and program. *Financial support:* In 2014–15, 148 fellowships with full tuition reimbursements (averaging $8,031 per year), 855 research assistantships with full tuition reimbursements (averaging $22,855 per year), 288 teaching assistantships with full tuition reimbursements (averaging $20,291 per year) were awarded. Financial award application deadline: 3/1; financial award applicants required to submit FAFSA. *Total annual research expenditures:* $90.5 million. *Unit head:* Dr. Richard C. Benson, Dean, 540-231-9752, Fax: 540-231-3031, E-mail: deaneng@vt.edu. *Application contact:* Linda Perkins, Executive Assistant, 540-231-9752, Fax: 540-231-3031, E-mail: lperkins@vt.edu.
Website: http://www.eng.vt.edu/.

Washington State University, Voiland College of Engineering and Architecture, Pullman, WA 99164-2714. Offers M Arch, METM, MS, PhD, Certificate. *Students:* 22 full-time (7 women), 10 part-time (3 women); includes 3 minority (1 Asian, non-Hispanic/Latino; 2 Two or more races, non-Hispanic/Latino), 18 international. Average age 32. 10 applicants, 20% accepted, 2 enrolled. In 2014, 2 master's, 7 doctorates awarded. Terminal master's awarded for partial completion of doctoral program. *Degree requirements:* For master's, comprehensive exam (for some programs), thesis (for some programs), oral exam; for doctorate, comprehensive exam, thesis/dissertation, oral exam. *Entrance requirements:* For master's, GRE, minimum GPA of 3.0, 3 letters of recommendation; for doctorate, GRE, minimum GPA of 3.4, 3 letters of recommendation. Additional exam requirements/recommendations for international students: Required—TOEFL (minimum score 520 paper-based). *Application deadline:* For fall admission, 3/1 priority date for domestic students, 3/1 for international students; for spring admission, 7/1 priority date for domestic students, 7/1 for international students. Applications are processed on a rolling basis. Application fee: $75. *Expenses:* Tuition, state resident: full-time $11,768. Tuition, nonresident: full-time $25,200. *Required fees:* $960. Tuition and fees vary according to program. *Financial support:* In 2014–15, 14 research assistantships with full and partial tuition reimbursements (averaging $14,880 per year), 4 teaching assistantships with full and partial tuition reimbursements (averaging $16,982 per year) were awarded; career-related internships or fieldwork, Federal Work-Study, institutionally sponsored loans, tuition waivers (partial), and teaching associateships also available. Financial award application deadline: 4/1; financial award applicants required to submit FAFSA. *Unit head:* Dr. Candis Claiborn, Dean, 509-335-5593, Fax: 509-335-7632, E-mail: claiborn@wsu.edu. *Application contact:* Graduate School Admissions, 800-GRADWSU, Fax: 509-335-1949, E-mail: gradsch@wsu.edu.
Website: http://vcea.wsu.edu/.

Washington University in St. Louis, School of Engineering and Applied Science, Saint Louis, MO 63130-4899. Offers M Eng, MCE, MCM, MEM, MIM, MPM, MS, MSEE, MSEE, MSI, D Sc, PhD. Part-time and evening/weekend programs available. Terminal master's awarded for partial completion of doctoral program. *Degree requirements:* For master's, comprehensive exam (for some programs), thesis (for some programs); for doctorate, comprehensive exam, thesis/dissertation. *Entrance requirements:* For master's and doctorate, GRE. Additional exam requirements/recommendations for international students: Required—TOEFL (minimum score 550 paper-based; 90 iBT), IELTS (minimum score 6.5) or TWE. Electronic applications accepted.

Wayne State University, College of Engineering, Detroit, MI 48202. Offers MS, MSET, PhD, Certificate, Graduate Certificate, Postbaccalaureate Certificate. Part-time and evening/weekend programs available. *Faculty:* 103 full-time (11 women). *Students:* 841 full-time (173 women), 355 part-time (80 women); includes 149 minority (35 Black or African American, non-Hispanic/Latino; 96 Asian, non-Hispanic/Latino; 10 Hispanic/Latino; 8 Two or more races, non-Hispanic/Latino), 763 international. Average age 28. 2,912 applicants, 45% accepted, 396 enrolled. In 2014, 237 master's, 56 doctorates, 2 other advanced degrees awarded. Terminal master's awarded for partial completion of doctoral program. *Degree requirements:* For master's, thesis optional; for doctorate, thesis/dissertation. *Entrance requirements:* For master's, minimum GPA of 2.8 from ABET-accredited institution and in all upper-division courses; for doctorate, minimum overall GPA of 3.2, 3.5 in last two years as undergraduate student if being admitted directly from a bachelor's program. Additional exam requirements/recommendations for international students: Required—TOEFL (minimum score 550 paper-based; 79 iBT), TWE (minimum score 5.5), Michigan English Language Assessment Battery (minimum score 85); Recommended—IELTS (minimum score 6.5). *Application deadline:* For fall admission, 6/1 priority date for domestic students, 5/1 priority date for international students; for winter admission, 10/1 priority date for domestic students, 9/1 priority date for international students; for spring admission, 2/1 priority date for domestic students, 1/1 priority date for international students. Applications are processed on a rolling basis. Application fee: $0. Electronic applications accepted. *Expenses:* Expenses: Contact institution. *Financial support:* In 2014–15, 499 students received support, including 25 fellowships with tuition reimbursements available (averaging $16,127 per year), 86 research assistantships with tuition reimbursements available (averaging $19,201 per

year), 84 teaching assistantships with tuition reimbursements available (averaging $18,769 per year); Federal Work-Study, scholarships/grants, health care benefits, tuition waivers (full and partial), and unspecified assistantships also available. Support available to part-time students. Financial award application deadline: 3/31; financial award applicants required to submit FAFSA. *Faculty research:* Biomedical research, integrated automotive safety, energy solutions, advanced manufacturing and materials, big data and business analytics. *Total annual research expenditures:* $18.2 million. *Unit head:* Dr. Farshad Fotouhi, Dean, 313-577-3776, E-mail: fotouhi@wayne.edu. *Application contact:* Jameshia Granberry, Director, Office of Graduate Admissions, 313-577-4723, E-mail: gradadmissions@wayne.edu.
Website: http://engineering.wayne.edu/.

Western Michigan University, Graduate College, College of Engineering and Applied Sciences, Kalamazoo, MI 49008. Offers MS, MSE, PhD. Part-time programs available. *Degree requirements:* For doctorate, thesis/dissertation. *Application deadline:* For fall admission, 2/15 for domestic students. *Financial support:* Application deadline: 2/15. *Application contact:* Admissions and Orientation, 269-387-2000, Fax: 269-387-2096.

Western New England University, College of Engineering, Springfield, MA 01119. Offers MSEE, MSEM, MSME, PhD, MSEM/MBA. Part-time and evening/weekend programs available. Postbaccalaureate distance learning degree programs offered. *Faculty:* 32 full-time (5 women). *Students:* 97 part-time (14 women); includes 13 minority (4 Black or African American, non-Hispanic/Latino; 3 Asian, non-Hispanic/Latino; 2 Hispanic/Latino; 4 Two or more races, non-Hispanic/Latino), 19 international. Average age 30. In 2014, 35 master's awarded. *Degree requirements:* For master's, comprehensive exam (for some programs), thesis optional; for doctorate, comprehensive exam, thesis/dissertation. *Entrance requirements:* For master's, bachelor's degree in engineering or related field, official transcript, two letters of recommendation, resume; for doctorate, GRE, official transcript, master's or bachelor's degree in engineering or closely-related discipline, two letters of recommendation. Additional exam requirements/recommendations for international students: Required—TOEFL (minimum score 79 iBT). *Application deadline:* For fall admission, 1/15 priority date for domestic students. Applications are processed on a rolling basis. Application fee: $30. Electronic applications accepted. *Financial support:* Fellowships with full and partial tuition reimbursements available. Financial award application deadline: 4/15; financial award applicants required to submit FAFSA. *Faculty research:* Fluid mechanics, control systems. *Unit head:* Dr. S. Hossein Cheraghi, Dean, 413-782-1285, E-mail: cheraghi@wne.edu. *Application contact:* Matthew Fox, Director of Admissions for Graduate Students and Adult Learners, 413-782-1517, Fax: 413-782-1777, E-mail: study@wne.edu.
Website: http://www1.wne.edu/adultlearning/index.cfm?selection-doc.6281.

West Texas A&M University, College of Agriculture, Science and Engineering, Department of Mathematics, Physical Sciences and Engineering Technology, Canyon, TX 79016-0001. Offers chemistry (MS); engineering technology (MS); mathematics (MS). Part-time and evening/weekend programs available. *Degree requirements:* For master's, comprehensive exam, thesis optional. *Entrance requirements:* For master's, GRE General Test. Additional exam requirements/recommendations for international students: Required—TOEFL (minimum score 550 paper-based). Electronic applications accepted. *Faculty research:* Stochastic temporal series, fuzzy network, computer-assisted/introductory physics classes, development of photorefractive polymers, central nervous system.

West Texas A&M University, College of Agriculture, Science and Engineering, School of Engineering and Computer Science, Canyon, TX 79016-0001. Offers engineering technology (MS). Part-time programs available. *Degree requirements:* For master's, comprehensive exam, thesis optional. *Entrance requirements:* For master's, GRE General Test. Additional exam requirements/recommendations for international students: Required—TOEFL (minimum score 550 paper-based). Electronic applications accepted. *Faculty research:* Composites, firearms technology, small arms research and development.

West Virginia University, College of Engineering and Mineral Resources, Morgantown, WV 26506. Offers MS, MS Ch E, MS Min E, MSAE, MSCE, MSCS, MSE, MSEE, MSIE, MSME, MSPNGE, MSSE, PhD, Graduate Certificate. *Accreditation:* ABET (one or more programs are accredited). Part-time programs available. Terminal master's awarded for partial completion of doctoral program. *Degree requirements:* For master's, thesis optional; for doctorate, comprehensive exam, thesis/dissertation. *Entrance requirements:* Additional exam requirements/recommendations for international students: Required—TOEFL (minimum score 550 paper-based). *Expenses:* Contact institution. *Faculty research:* Composite materials, software engineering, information systems, aerodynamics, vehicle propulsion and emission.

Wichita State University, Graduate School, College of Engineering, Wichita, KS 67260. Offers MEM, MS, PhD. Part-time and evening/weekend programs available. *Unit head:* Dr. Royce O. Bowden, Dean, 316-978-3400, Fax: 316-978-3853, E-mail: royce.bowden@wichita.edu. *Application contact:* Jordan Oleson, Admissions Coordinator, 316-978-3095, Fax: 316-978-3253, E-mail: jordan.oleson@wichita.edu.
Website: http://www.wichita.edu/engineering.

Widener University, Graduate Programs in Engineering, Chester, PA 19013-5792. Offers M Eng, MSMT, ME/MBA. Part-time and evening/weekend programs available. *Degree requirements:* For master's, thesis optional. *Entrance requirements:* Additional exam requirements/recommendations for international students: Required—TOEFL (minimum score 550 paper-based). *Expenses:* Contact institution. *Faculty research:* Collagen, geosynthetics, mobile computing, image and signal processing.

Wilkes University, College of Graduate and Professional Studies, College of Science and Engineering, Wilkes-Barre, PA 18766-0002. Offers MS, MSEE. Part-time programs available. *Students:* 33 full-time (7 women), 26 part-time (5 women); includes 8 minority (2 Black or African American, non-Hispanic/Latino; 3 Asian, non-Hispanic/Latino; 2 Hispanic/Latino; 1 Two or more races, non-Hispanic/Latino), 21 international. Average age 29. In 2014, 24 master's awarded. *Entrance requirements:* Additional exam requirements/recommendations for international students: Required—TOEFL (minimum score 550 paper-based; 79 iBT). *Application deadline:* Applications are processed on a rolling basis. Application fee: $45 ($65 for international students). Electronic applications accepted. *Financial support:* Federal Work-Study and unspecified assistantships available. Financial award application deadline: 3/1; financial award applicants required to submit FAFSA. *Unit head:* Dr. Terese Wignot, Interim Dean, 570-408-4600, Fax: 570-408-7860, E-mail: terese.wignot@wilkes.edu. *Application contact:* Joanne Thomas, Director of Graduate Enrollment, 570-408-4234, Fax: 570-408-7846, E-mail: joanne.thomas1@wilkes.edu.
Website: http://www.wilkes.edu/academics/colleges/science-and-engineering/index.aspx.

Worcester Polytechnic Institute, Graduate Studies and Research, Worcester, MA 01609-2280. Offers M Eng, MBA, ME, MME, MS, PhD, Advanced Certificate, Graduate Certificate. Part-time and evening/weekend programs available. Postbaccalaureate distance learning degree programs offered (no on-campus study). *Faculty:* 166 full-time (36 women), 79 part-time/adjunct (9 women). *Students:* 1,081 full-time (376 women), 853 part-time (181 women); includes 194 minority (22 Black or African American, non-Hispanic/Latino; 1 American Indian or Alaska Native, non-Hispanic/Latino; 79 Asian, non-Hispanic/Latino; 55 Hispanic/Latino; 37 Two or more races, non-Hispanic/Latino), 774 international. Average age 28. 3,752 applicants, 51% accepted, 664 enrolled. In 2014, 661 master's, 31 doctorates awarded. Terminal master's awarded for partial completion of doctoral program. *Degree requirements:* For master's, thesis (for some programs); for doctorate, thesis/dissertation. *Entrance requirements:* For master's and doctorate, 3 letters of recommendation. Additional exam requirements/recommendations for international students: Required—TOEFL (minimum score 563 paper-based; 84 iBT), IELTS (minimum score 7). *Application deadline:* For fall admission, 1/1 priority date for domestic and international students; for spring admission, 10/1 priority date for domestic and international students. Applications are processed on a rolling basis. Application fee: $70. Electronic applications accepted. *Financial support:* Research assistantships, teaching assistantships, institutionally sponsored loans, scholarships/grants, tuition waivers, and unspecified assistantships available. Financial award application deadline: 1/1; financial award applicants required to submit FAFSA. *Unit head:* Dr. Terri Camesano, Dean, 508-831-5380, E-mail: grad@wpi.edu. *Application contact:* Lynne Dougherty, Administrative Assistant, 508-831-5301, Fax: 508-831-5717, E-mail: grad@wpi.edu.
Website: http://grad.wpi.edu/.

Wright State University, School of Graduate Studies, College of Engineering and Computer Science, Dayton, OH 45435. Offers MS, MSCE, MSE, PhD. Part-time and evening/weekend programs available. *Degree requirements:* For master's, thesis optional; for doctorate, thesis/dissertation, candidacy and general exams. *Entrance requirements:* For doctorate, GRE General Test, minimum GPA of 3.3. Additional exam requirements/recommendations for international students: Required—TOEFL. *Faculty research:* Robotics, heat transfer, fluid dynamics, microprocessors, mechanical vibrations.

Yale University, Graduate School of Arts and Sciences, School of Engineering and Applied Science, New Haven, CT 06520. Offers MS, PhD. Part-time programs available. Terminal master's awarded for partial completion of doctoral program. *Degree requirements:* For doctorate, thesis/dissertation, exam. *Entrance requirements:* For master's and doctorate, GRE General Test. Additional exam requirements/recommendations for international students: Required—TOEFL.

See Display on next page and Close-Up on page 93.

Youngstown State University, Graduate School, College of Science, Technology, Engineering and Mathematics, Youngstown, OH 44555-0001. Offers MCIS, MSE. Part-time and evening/weekend programs available. *Degree requirements:* For master's, thesis optional. *Entrance requirements:* For master's, minimum GPA of 2.75 in field. Additional exam requirements/recommendations for international students: Required—TOEFL. *Faculty research:* Structural mechanics, water quality, wetlands engineering, control systems, power systems, heat transfer, kinematics and dynamics.

Applied Science and Technology

The College of William and Mary, Faculty of Arts and Sciences, Department of Applied Science, Williamsburg, VA 23187-8795. Offers accelerator science (PhD); applied mathematics (PhD); applied mechanics (PhD); applied robotics (PhD); applied science (MS); interface, thin film and surface science (PhD); lasers and optics (PhD); magnetic resonance (PhD); nanotechnology (PhD); non-destructive evaluation (PhD); polymer chemistry (PhD); remote sensing (PhD). Part-time programs available. *Faculty:* 8 full-time (2 women), 2 part-time/adjunct (0 women). *Students:* 28 full-time (11 women), 5 part-time (2 women); includes 5 minority (2 Black or African American, non-Hispanic/Latino; 2 Asian, non-Hispanic/Latino; 1 Hispanic/Latino), 13 international. Average age 28. 32 applicants, 38% accepted, 7 enrolled. In 2014, 6 master's, 4 doctorates awarded. Terminal master's awarded for partial completion of doctoral program. *Degree requirements:* For master's, comprehensive exam, thesis; for doctorate, comprehensive exam, thesis/dissertation, 4 core courses. *Entrance requirements:* For master's and doctorate, GRE General Test, GRE Subject Test. Additional exam requirements/recommendations for international students: Required—TOEFL, TWE. *Application deadline:* For fall admission, 2/3 priority date for domestic students, 2/3 for international students; for spring admission, 10/15 priority date for domestic students, 10/14 for international students. Applications are processed on a rolling basis. Application fee: $45. Electronic applications accepted. *Financial support:* Fellowships, research assistantships, teaching assistantships, Federal Work-Study, health care benefits, tuition waivers (full), and unspecified assistantships available. Financial award application deadline: 4/15; financial award applicants required to submit FAFSA. *Faculty research:* Computational biology, non-destructive evaluation, neurophysiology, lasers and optics. *Total annual research expenditures:* $1.7 million. *Unit head:* Dr. Christopher Del Negro, Chair, 757-221-7808, Fax: 757-221-2050, E-mail: cadeln@wm.edu. *Application contact:* Lianne Rios Ashburne, Graduate Program Coordinator, 757-221-2563, Fax: 757-221-2050, E-mail: lrashburne@wm.edu.
Website: http://www.wm.edu/as/appliedscience.

Colorado State University–Pueblo, College of Science and Mathematics, Pueblo, CO 81001-4901. Offers applied natural science (MS), including biochemistry, biology, chemistry. Part-time and evening/weekend programs available. *Degree requirements:* For master's, comprehensive exam (for some programs), thesis (for some programs), internship report (if non-thesis). *Entrance requirements:* For master's, GRE General Test (minimum score 1000), 2 letters of reference, minimum GPA of 3.0. Additional exam requirements/recommendations for international students: Required—TOEFL (minimum score 500 paper-based), IELTS (minimum score 5). *Faculty research:* Fungal cell walls, molecular biology, bioactive materials synthesis, atomic force microscopy-surface chemistry, nanoscience.

Applied Science and Technology

Harvard University, Extension School, Cambridge, MA 02138-3722. Offers applied sciences (CAS); biotechnology (ALM); educational technologies (ALM); educational technology (CET); English for graduate and professional studies (DGP); environmental management (ALM, CEM); information technology (ALM); journalism (ALM); liberal arts (ALM); management (ALM, CM); mathematics for teaching (ALM); museum studies (ALM); premedical studies (Diploma); publication and communication (CPC). Part-time and evening/weekend programs available. *Degree requirements:* For master's, thesis. *Entrance requirements:* For master's, 3 completed graduate courses with grade of B or higher. Additional exam requirements/recommendations for international students: Required—TOEFL (minimum score 600 paper-based), TWE (minimum score 5). *Expenses:* Contact institution.

James Madison University, The Graduate School, College of Integrated Science and Technology, Department of Integrated Science and Technology, Harrisonburg, VA 22807. Offers MS. *Degree requirements:* For master's, thesis or alternative. *Entrance requirements:* For master's, GRE General Test. Additional exam requirements/recommendations for international students: Required—TOEFL. Electronic applications accepted.

Louisiana State University and Agricultural & Mechanical College, Graduate School, College of Science, Master of Natural Sciences Program, Baton Rouge, LA 70803. Offers MNS. Part-time programs available. *Students:* 11 full-time (7 women), 10 part-time (8 women); includes 6 minority (4 Black or African American, non-Hispanic/Latino; 2 Asian, non-Hispanic/Latino), 2 international. Average age 36. 3 applicants, 67% accepted. In 2014, 28 master's awarded. *Degree requirements:* For master's, comprehensive exam. *Entrance requirements:* For master's, GRE General Test, minimum GPA of 3.0. Additional exam requirements/recommendations for international students: Required—TOEFL (minimum score 550 paper-based; 79 iBT), IELTS (minimum score 6.5), or PTE (minimum score 59). *Application deadline:* For fall admission, 1/1 priority date for domestic students, 5/15 for international students; for spring admission, 10/15 for domestic and international students. Applications are processed on a rolling basis. Application fee: $50 ($70 for international students). Electronic applications accepted. *Financial support:* In 2014–15, 19 students received support, including 7 fellowships (averaging $11,225 per year), 9 research assistantships (averaging $33,333 per year), 1 teaching assistantship with partial tuition reimbursement available (averaging $19,500 per year); Federal Work-Study, institutionally sponsored loans, and health care benefits also available. Financial award applicants required to submit FAFSA. *Total annual research expenditures:* $130,151. *Unit head:* Dr. Guillermo Ferreyra, Director, 225-578-7677, Fax: 225-578-8826, E-mail: dnferr@lsu.edu. *Application contact:* Dr. John Lynn, Associate Dean, 225-578-4205, Fax: 225-578-8826, E-mail: zolynn@lsu.edu.
Website: http://science.lsu.edu/Student-Resources/Degree-Program-Choices/MNS/item39871.html.

Missouri State University, Graduate College, College of Natural and Applied Sciences, Department of Biology, Springfield, MO 65897. Offers biology (MS); natural and applied science (MNAS), including biology (MNAS, MS Ed); secondary education (MS Ed); including biology (MNAS, MS Ed). *Faculty:* 18 full-time (3 women), 7 part-time/adjunct (2 women). *Students:* 17 full-time (9 women), 34 part-time (23 women); includes 2 minority (1 Asian, non-Hispanic/Latino; 1 Two or more races, non-Hispanic/Latino), 5 international. Average age 26. 29 applicants, 52% accepted, 13 enrolled. In 2014, 20 master's awarded. *Degree requirements:* For master's, comprehensive exam, thesis or alternative. *Entrance requirements:* For master's, GRE (MS, MNAS), 24 hours of course work in biology (MS); minimum GPA of 3.0 (MS, MNAS), 9-12 teacher certification (MS Ed). Additional exam requirements/recommendations for international students: Required—TOEFL (minimum score 550 paper-based; 79 iBT). *Application deadline:* For fall admission, 7/20 priority date for domestic students, 5/1 for international students; for

spring admission, 12/20 priority date for domestic students, 9/1 for international students. Applications are processed on a rolling basis. Application fee: $35 ($50 for international students). Electronic applications accepted. *Expenses:* Tuition, state resident: full-time $2250; part-time $250 per credit hour. Tuition, nonresident: full-time $4509; part-time $501 per credit hour. Tuition and fees vary according to course level, course load and program. *Financial support:* In 2014–15, 7 research assistantships with full tuition reimbursements (averaging $10,573 per year), 24 teaching assistantships with full tuition reimbursements (averaging $9,746 per year) were awarded; Federal Work-Study, institutionally sponsored loans, scholarships/grants, and unspecified assistantships also available. Financial award application deadline: 3/31; financial award applicants required to submit FAFSA. *Faculty research:* Hibernation physiology of bats, behavioral ecology of salamanders, mussel conservation, plant evolution and systematics, cellular/molecular mechanisms involved in migraine pathology. *Unit head:* Dr. S. Alicia Mathis, Head, 417-836-5126, Fax: 417-836-6934, E-mail: biology@missouristate.edu. *Application contact:* Misty Stewart, Coordinator of Graduate Recruitment, 417-836-6079, Fax: 417-836-6200, E-mail: mistystewart@missouristate.edu.
Website: http://biology.missouristate.edu/.

Missouri State University, Graduate College, College of Natural and Applied Sciences, Department of Computer Science, Springfield, MO 65897. Offers MNAS. Part-time programs available. *Faculty:* 6 full-time (1 woman). *Students:* 2 full-time (0 women), both international. Average age 26. 10 applicants, 30% accepted, 1 enrolled. *Degree requirements:* For master's, comprehensive exam, thesis or alternative. *Entrance requirements:* For master's, GRE, minimum GPA of 3.0. Additional exam requirements/recommendations for international students: Required—TOEFL (minimum score 550 paper-based; 79 iBT). *Application deadline:* For fall admission, 7/20 priority date for domestic students, 5/1 for international students; for spring admission, 12/20 priority date for domestic students, 9/1 for international students. Applications are processed on a rolling basis. Application fee: $35 ($50 for international students). Electronic applications accepted. *Expenses:* Tuition, state resident: full-time $2250; part-time $250 per credit hour. Tuition, nonresident: full-time $4509; part-time $501 per credit hour. Tuition and fees vary according to course level, course load and program. *Financial support:* Federal Work-Study, institutionally sponsored loans, scholarships/grants, and unspecified assistantships available. Financial award application deadline: 3/31; financial award applicants required to submit FAFSA. *Faculty research:* Floating point numbers, data compression, graph theory. *Unit head:* Dr. Kenneth Vollmar, Head, 417-836-4157, Fax: 417-836-6659, E-mail: computerscience@missouristate.edu. *Application contact:* Misty Stewart, Coordinator of Graduate Recruitment, 417-836-6079, Fax: 417-836-6200, E-mail: mistystewart@missouristate.edu.
Website: http://computerscience.missouristate.edu/.

Missouri State University, Graduate College, College of Natural and Applied Sciences, Department of Geography, Geology, and Planning, Springfield, MO 65897. Offers geography, geology and planning (MNAS); secondary education (MS Ed), including earth science, physical geography. *Accreditation:* ACSP. Part-time and evening/weekend programs available. *Faculty:* 18 full-time (4 women), 1 part-time/adjunct (0 women). *Students:* 12 full-time (5 women), 12 part-time (8 women); includes 1 minority (Asian, non-Hispanic/Latino), 3 international. Average age 30. 16 applicants, 100% accepted, 9 enrolled. In 2014, 11 master's awarded. *Degree requirements:* For master's, comprehensive exam, thesis (for some programs). *Entrance requirements:* For master's, GRE General Test (MS, MNAS), minimum undergraduate GPA of 3.0 (MS, MNAS), 9-12 teacher certification (MS Ed). Additional exam requirements/recommendations for international students: Required—TOEFL (minimum score 550 paper-based; 79 iBT). *Application deadline:* For fall admission, 7/20 priority date for domestic students, 5/1 for international students; for spring admission, 12/20 priority date for domestic students, 9/

Applied Science and Technology

1 for international students. Applications are processed on a rolling basis. Application fee: $35 ($50 for international students). Electronic applications accepted. *Expenses:* Tuition, state resident: full-time $2250; part-time $250 per credit hour. Tuition, nonresident: full-time $4509; part-time $501 per credit hour. Tuition and fees vary according to course level, course load and program. *Financial support:* In 2014–15, 3 research assistantships with full tuition reimbursements (averaging $11,574 per year), 12 teaching assistantships with full tuition reimbursements (averaging $9,365 per year) were awarded; career-related internships or fieldwork, Federal Work-Study, institutionally sponsored loans, scholarships/grants, and unspecified assistantships also available. Financial award application deadline: 3/31; financial award applicants required to submit FAFSA. *Faculty research:* Stratigraphy and ancient meteorite impacts, environmental geochemistry of karst, hyperspectral image processing, water quality, small town planning. *Unit head:* Dr. Thomas Plymate, Head, 417-836-5800, Fax: 417-836-6934, E-mail: tomplymate@missouristate.edu. *Application contact:* Misty Stewart, Coordinator of Graduate Recruitment, 417-836-6079, Fax: 417-836-6200, E-mail: mistystewart@missouristate.edu.
Website: http://geosciences.missouristate.edu/.

Missouri State University, Graduate College, College of Natural and Applied Sciences, Department of Mathematics, Springfield, MO 65897. Offers mathematics (MNAS, MS); secondary education (MS Ed), including mathematics. Part-time programs available. *Faculty:* 21 full-time (4 women). *Students:* 17 full-time (3 women), 19 part-time (11 women), 9 international. Average age 27. 22 applicants, 86% accepted, 13 enrolled. In 2014, 12 master's awarded. *Degree requirements:* For master's, comprehensive exam, thesis or alternative. *Entrance requirements:* For master's, GRE (MS, MNAS), minimum undergraduate GPA of 3.0 (MS, MNAS), 9-12 teacher certification (MS Ed). Additional exam requirements/recommendations for international students: Required—TOEFL (minimum score 550 paper-based; 79 iBT). *Application deadline:* For fall admission, 7/20 priority date for domestic students, 5/1 for international students; for spring admission, 12/20 priority date for domestic students, 9/1 for international students. Applications are processed on a rolling basis. Application fee: $35 ($50 for international students). Electronic applications accepted. *Expenses:* Tuition, state resident: full-time $2250; part-time $250 per credit hour. Tuition, nonresident: full-time $4509; part-time $501 per credit hour. Tuition and fees vary according to course level, course load and program. *Financial support:* In 2014–15, 9 teaching assistantships with full tuition reimbursements (averaging $9,060 per year) were awarded; Federal Work-Study, institutionally sponsored loans, scholarships/grants, and unspecified assistantships also available. Financial award application deadline: 3/31; financial award applicants required to submit FAFSA. *Faculty research:* Harmonic analysis, commutative algebra, number theory, K-theory, probability. *Unit head:* Dr. William Bray, Department Head, 417-836-5112, Fax: 417-836-6966, E-mail: mathematics@missouristate.edu. *Application contact:* Misty Stewart, Coordinator of Graduate Recruitment, 417-836-6079, Fax: 417-836-6200, E-mail: mistystewart@missouristate.edu.
Website: http://math.missouristate.edu/.

Missouri State University, Graduate College, College of Natural and Applied Sciences, Department of Physics, Astronomy, and Materials Science, Springfield, MO 65897. Offers materials science (MS); physics (MNAS), including physics (MNAS, MS Ed); secondary education (MS Ed), including physics (MNAS, MS Ed). Part-time programs available. *Faculty:* 9 full-time (0 women). *Students:* 12 full-time (2 women), 5 part-time (0 women), 11 international. Average age 26. 8 applicants, 88% accepted, 5 enrolled. In 2014, 10 master's awarded. *Degree requirements:* For master's, comprehensive exam, thesis. *Entrance requirements:* For master's, GRE (MS, MNAS), minimum undergraduate GPA of 3.0 (MS and MNAS), 9-12 teaching certification (MS Ed). Additional exam requirements/recommendations for international students: Required—TOEFL (minimum score 550 paper-based; 79 iBT). *Application deadline:* For fall admission, 7/20 priority date for domestic students, 5/1 for international students; for spring admission, 12/20 priority date for domestic students, 9/1 for international students. Applications are processed on a rolling basis. Application fee: $35 ($50 for international students). Electronic applications accepted. *Expenses:* Tuition, state resident: full-time $2250; part-time $250 per credit hour. Tuition, nonresident: full-time $4509; part-time $501 per credit hour. Tuition and fees vary according to course level, course load and program. *Financial support:* In 2014–15, 3 research assistantships with full tuition reimbursements (averaging $10,280 per year), 9 teaching assistantships with full tuition reimbursements (averaging $10,280 per year) were awarded; Federal Work-Study, institutionally sponsored loans, scholarships/grants, and unspecified assistantships also available. Financial award application deadline: 3/31; financial award applicants required to submit FAFSA. *Faculty research:* Nanocomposites, ferroelectricity, infrared focal plane array sensors, biosensors, pulsating stars. *Unit head:* Dr. David Cornelison, Department Head, 417-836-4467, Fax: 417-836-6226, E-mail: physics@missouristate.edu. *Application contact:* Misty Stewart, Coordinator of Graduate Recruitment, 417-836-6079, Fax: 417-836-6200, E-mail: mistystewart@missouristate.edu.
Website: http://physics.missouristate.edu/.

Naval Postgraduate School, Departments and Academic Groups, Department of Operations Research, Monterey, CA 93943. Offers applied science (MS), including operations research; cost estimating analysis (MS); human systems integration (MS); operations research (MS, PhD); systems analysis (MS). Program only open to commissioned officers of the United States and friendly nations and selected United States federal civilian employees. Part-time programs available. *Degree requirements:* For master's, thesis (for some programs); for doctorate, thesis/dissertation. *Faculty research:* Next generation network science, performance analysis of ground solider mobile ad-hoc networks, irregular warfare methods and tools, human social cultural behavior modeling, large-scale optimization.

Naval Postgraduate School, Departments and Academic Groups, Undersea Warfare Academic Group, Monterey, CA 93943. Offers applied mathematics (MS); applied physics (MS); applied science (MS), including acoustics, operations research, physical oceanography, signal processing; electrical engineering (MS); engineering acoustics (MS, PhD); engineering science (MS), including electrical engineering, mechanical engineering; mechanical engineer (ME); mechanical engineering (MS, MSME); meteorology (MS); operations research (MS); physical oceanography (MS). Program only open to commissioned officers of the United States and friendly nations and selected United States federal civilian employees. Part-time programs available. *Degree requirements:* For master's, thesis. *Faculty research:* Unmanned/autonomous vehicles, sea mines and countermeasures, submarine warfare in the twentieth and twenty-first centuries.

Saint Mary's University, Faculty of Science, Interdisciplinary Program in Applied Science, Halifax, NS B3H 3C3, Canada. Offers M Sc.

Southeastern Louisiana University, College of Science and Technology, Program in Integrated Science and Technology, Hammond, LA 70402. Offers MS. Part-time and evening/weekend programs available. *Faculty:* 16 full-time (4 women). *Students:* 12 full-time (8 women), 5 part-time (2 women); includes 4 minority (all Black or African American, non-Hispanic/Latino), 7 international. Average age 26. *Degree requirements:* For master's, thesis (for some programs), 33-36 hours. *Entrance requirements:* For master's, GRE (minimum combined score 850), undergraduate degree; minimum GPA of 2.75; 30 semester hours in any combination of chemistry, computer science, industrial technology, mathematics, or physics; two letters of recommendation; transcripts of previous undergraduate or graduate work. Additional exam requirements/recommendations for international students: Required—TOEFL (minimum score 500 paper-based; 61 iBT). *Application deadline:* For fall admission, 7/15 priority date for domestic students, 6/1 priority date for international students; for spring admission, 12/1 priority date for domestic students, 10/1 priority date for international students. Applications are processed on a rolling basis. Application fee: $20 ($30 for international students). Electronic applications accepted. *Financial support:* In 2014–15, 8 research assistantships (averaging $8,112 per year), 1 teaching assistantship (averaging $10,100 per year) were awarded; career-related internships or fieldwork, Federal Work-Study, institutionally sponsored loans, scholarships/grants, and unspecified assistantships also available. Support available to part-time students. Financial award application deadline: 5/1; financial award applicants required to submit FAFSA. *Faculty research:* Remote sensing of magnetospheric dynamics, molecular modeling, CAD solid modeling, research statistical computational methods, artificial intelligence. *Total annual expenditures:* $357,958. *Unit head:* Dr. Ken S. Li, Graduate Coordinator, 985-549-3822, E-mail: kli@selu.edu. *Application contact:* Sandra Meyers, Graduate Admissions Analyst, 985-549-5620, Fax: 985-549-5632, E-mail: admissions@selu.edu.
Website: http://www.southeastern.edu/acad_research/programs/isat/index.html.

Southern Methodist University, Bobby B. Lyle School of Engineering, Department of Electrical Engineering, Dallas, TX 75275-0338. Offers applied science (MS); electrical engineering (MSEE, PhD); telecommunications (MS). Part-time and evening/weekend programs available. Postbaccalaureate distance learning degree programs offered (no on-campus study). Terminal master's awarded for partial completion of doctoral program. *Degree requirements:* For master's, thesis optional; for doctorate, thesis/dissertation, oral and written qualifying exams, oral final exam. *Entrance requirements:* For master's, GRE General Test, minimum GPA of 3.0 in last 2 years; bachelor's degree in engineering, mathematics, or sciences; for doctorate, preliminary counseling exam, minimum GPA of 3.0, bachelor's degree in related field. Additional exam requirements/recommendations for international students: Required—TOEFL. Electronic applications accepted. *Faculty research:* Mobile communications, optical communications, digital signal processing, photonics.

Thomas Edison State College, School of Applied Science and Technology, Trenton, NJ 08608-1176. Offers Graduate Certificate. Part-time programs available. Postbaccalaureate distance learning degree programs offered (no on-campus study). *Entrance requirements:* Additional exam requirements/recommendations for international students: Required—TOEFL (minimum score 550 paper-based; 79 iBT). Electronic applications accepted.

University of Arkansas at Little Rock, Graduate School, George W. Donughey College of Engineering and Information Technology, Department of Applied Science, Little Rock, AR 72204-1099. Offers MS, PhD. Part-time programs available. *Degree requirements:* For master's, comprehensive exam, thesis optional, oral exams; for doctorate, thesis/dissertation, 2 semesters of residency, candidacy exams. *Entrance requirements:* For master's, GRE General Test, interview, minimum GPA of 3.0; for doctorate, GRE General Test, interview, minimum graduate GPA of 3.5. Additional exam requirements/recommendations for international students: Required—TOEFL. *Application deadline:* Applications are processed on a rolling basis. *Expenses:* Tuition, state resident: full-time $6000; part-time $300 per credit hour. Tuition, nonresident: full-time $13,800; part-time $690 per credit hour. *Required fees:* $1126; $603 per term. One-time fee: $40 full-time. *Financial support:* Fellowships, research assistantships with tuition reimbursements, teaching assistantships with tuition reimbursements, Federal Work-Study, tuition waivers (full), and unspecified assistantships available. *Faculty research:* Particle and powder science and technology, optical sensors, process control and automation, signal and image processing, biomedical measurement systems. *Unit head:* Dr. Thomas McMillan, Chair, 501-569-8102, E-mail: tcmcmillan@ualr.edu. *Application contact:* Dr. Brian Berry, Graduate Coordinator, 501-569-8000, E-mail: bcberry@ualr.edu.
Website: http://ualr.edu/appliedscience/.

University of California, Berkeley, Graduate Division, College of Engineering, Group in Applied Science and Technology, Berkeley, CA 94720-1500. Offers PhD. *Degree requirements:* For doctorate, thesis/dissertation, preliminary exam, qualifying exam. *Entrance requirements:* For doctorate, GRE General Test, BA or BS in engineering, physics, mathematics, chemistry, or related field; minimum GPA of 3.0, 3 letters of recommendation.

University of California, Davis, College of Engineering, Program in Applied Science, Davis, CA 95616. Offers MS, PhD. Terminal master's awarded for partial completion of doctoral program. *Degree requirements:* For master's, comprehensive exam (for some programs), thesis (for some programs); for doctorate, thesis/dissertation. *Entrance requirements:* For master's and doctorate, GRE General Test, minimum GPA of 3.3. Additional exam requirements/recommendations for international students: Required—TOEFL (minimum score 550 paper-based). Electronic applications accepted. *Faculty research:* Plasma physics, scientific computing, fusion technology, laser physics and nonlinear optics.

University of Colorado Denver, College of Liberal Arts and Sciences, Program in Integrated Sciences, Denver, CO 80217. Offers applied science (MIS); computer science (MIS); mathematics (MIS). Part-time and evening/weekend programs available. *Faculty:* 1 (woman) full-time. *Students:* 6 full-time (2 women), 4 part-time (2 women); includes 2 minority (both Asian, non-Hispanic/Latino). Average age 33. 7 applicants, 57% accepted, 3 enrolled. In 2014, 2 master's awarded. *Degree requirements:* For master's, 30 credit hours; thesis or project. *Entrance requirements:* For master's, GRE if undergraduate GPA is 3.0 or less, minimum of 40 semester hours in mathematics, computer science, physics, biology, chemistry and/or geology; essay; three letters of recommendation. Additional exam requirements/recommendations for international students: Required—TOEFL (minimum score 537 paper-based; 75 iBT); Recommended—IELTS (minimum score 6.5). *Application deadline:* For fall admission, 4/15 for domestic students, 4/15 priority date for international students; for spring admission, 10/15 for domestic students, 10/15 priority date for international students. Application fee: $50 ($75 for international students). Electronic applications accepted. *Financial support:* In 2014–15, 4 students received support. Fellowships, research assistantships, teaching assistantships, Federal Work-Study, institutionally sponsored loans, scholarships/grants, and traineeships available. Financial award application deadline: 4/1; financial award applicants required to submit FAFSA. *Faculty research:* Computer science, applied science, mathematics. *Unit head:* Dr. Martin Huber, Director of Integrated Sciences, 303-556-3561, E-mail: martin.huber@ucdenver.edu. *Application contact:* Marissa Tornatore, Graduate School Application Specialist, 303-315-0049, E-mail: marissa.tornatore@ucdenver.edu.
Website: http://www.ucdenver.edu/academics/colleges/CLAS/Programs/MastersofIntegratedSciences/Pages/ProgramOverview.aspx.

University of Mississippi, Graduate School, School of Applied Sciences, University, MS 38677. Offers MA, MS, MSW, PhD. *Entrance requirements:* For master's, GRE General Test, minimum GPA of 3.0. Additional exam requirements/recommendations for international students: Required—TOEFL. Electronic applications accepted.

CLARKSON UNIVERSITY
Coulter School of Engineering

 For more information, visit http://petersons.to/clarksonengineering

Programs of Study

The Coulter School of Engineering, comprising departments of chemical and biomolecular, civil and environmental, electrical and computer, and mechanical and aeronautical engineering, offers programs of study leading to the Doctor of Philosophy (Ph.D.), Master of Science (M.S.), and Master of Engineering (M.E.) degrees. Interdisciplinary programs allow the student to specialize in such areas as materials processing, information technology, computer science, and environmental science and engineering. Descriptions of these programs can be found at http://www.clarkson.edu/engineering/graduate.

The Master of Science degree is awarded upon completion of 30 credit hours of graduate work, including a thesis. The Master of Engineering degree can be obtained in one calendar year; it includes the completion of a design-oriented project. In addition, Clarkson has initiated a two-year, two-degree program whereby students may obtain an M.E. degree in one year and continue on for an additional year to obtain an M.B.A.

The Ph.D. is awarded upon completion of a minimum of 90 credit hours of graduate work, corresponding to a minimum of three academic years of full-time study beyond the bachelor's degree. The candidacy procedure for the Ph.D. requires the presentation and defense of a proposal for the Ph.D. research. Candidates for the Ph.D. are required to prepare an original dissertation in an advanced research area and defend it in an oral examination.

The academic year consists of two semesters of fifteen weeks each. There is no formal summer session for graduate classes; graduate students and faculty members devote the summer entirely to research.

Research Facilities

The Department of Chemical and Biomolecular Engineering houses research labs for chemical-mechanical planarization (CMP); bioengineering; nucleation; chemical metallurgy; chemical kinetics; process design; electrochemistry and electrochemical engineering; materials synthesis and characterization; experimental and computational fluid mechanics, including two research-grade wind tunnels; heat and mass transfer; and interfacial fluid mechanics, including a bubble column equipped with a motorized camera platform. The Department has facilities for conducting research on thin films and coatings, alternative energy sources, nonthermal plasma, and access to a 150 kW high-efficiency, low-emissions word pellet boiler. In addition, excellent facilities are available for aerosol generation, chamber studies, and ambient and indoor air pollution sampling and chemical analysis, as well as tools for advanced data analysis.

The Department of Civil and Environmental Engineering has well-equipped environmental engineering laboratories with pilot plant facilities, walk-in constant-temperature rooms, and modern research instrumentation for organic and inorganic analyses; a hydraulics laboratory with a large automated tilting flume; temperature-controlled cold rooms and ice mechanics laboratories; a geomechanics laboratory with a wide array of laboratory and field testing equipment for geotechnical problems, including a number of specialized sensors, and a variety of loading systems, such as 200-kip closed-loop controlled stepping motor system and a 20-kip hydraulic closed-loop controlled servo-valve controlled axial-torsional system; structural and materials testing laboratories, including a unique strong floor and strong wall testing facility and an Instron 220-kip UTM; a blade test facility (BTF) for wind turbine blades and other structural components and accommodating test specimens with lengths up to 15 meters; and soil mechanics and materials laboratories including sieves and hydrometers, consolidation test, direct shear test, and triaxial test systems, as well as nondestructive test systems for material imaging at various scales from millimeters to hundreds of meters for soil/rock/concrete.

The Department of Electrical and Computer Engineering has laboratories for distributed computing networks, intelligent information processing, microelectronics, motion control, robotics, software engineering, power electronics, microwave photonics, electric machines and drives, embedded systems, liquid dielectric breakdown, biomedical signal and image processing, advanced visualization and networked multimedia and networked systems, and a 1-million-volt high-voltage measurement laboratory.

The Department of Mechanical and Aeronautical Engineering houses three wind tunnels, a clean room for microcontamination and nanotechnology research, and labs for fluid mechanics, heat transfer, aerosol and multiphase flow, CAD, image processing, energy conversion, vibrations, combustion, materials processing, manufacturing, and welding.

Much of the research work is conducted in conjunction with the University's interdisciplinary research centers: the New York State Center for Advanced Materials Processing (CAMP), Institute for the Sustainable Environment (ISE), Center for Sustainable Energy Systems (CRES), Center for Rehabilitation Engineering Science and Technology (CREST), and Center for Air Resources Engineering and Science (CARES). Computing facilities within the School of Engineering include an IBM series and a variety of Sun and IBM workstations, all interconnected to each office and laboratory by a high-speed wide-band network. Clarkson's Campus Information Services houses modern information storage and retrieval facilities, the computing center, and the library.

Financial Aid

Several forms of financial assistance are available, which permit a full-time program of study and provide a stipend plus tuition. Instructional assistantships involve an obligation of 12 hours per week of assistance in courses or laboratories. Research assistantships require research activity that is also used to satisfy thesis requirements. Partial-tuition scholarships are available for all degree programs.

Cost of Study

Tuition for graduate work is $1,457 per credit hour in 2015–16. Fees are about $590 per year.

Living and Housing Costs

Graduate students can find rooms or apartments near the campus. The University maintains single and married student housing units. Off-campus apartments for 2 students rent for approximately $500 per month and up.

Student Group

There are approximately 200 students on campus pursuing graduate work in engineering. The total Graduate School enrollment is 400, and the undergraduate enrollment is 2,600.

Location

Potsdam, New York, is an attractive village located along the banks of the Raquette River on a rolling plain between the Adirondack Mountains and the St. Lawrence River. Three other colleges (one in Potsdam) provide a total college student body of 11,000 within a 12-mile radius. Potsdam is 100 miles from Montreal, 80 miles from Ottawa and Lake Placid, and 140 miles from Syracuse. The St. Lawrence Seaway, the Thousand Islands, and Adirondack resort areas are within a short drive. Opportunities for fishing, hiking, boating, golfing, camping, swimming, and skiing abound throughout the area.

The University

Clarkson University is a privately endowed school of science, engineering, and business. Master's degrees are offered in the engineering departments and in business administration, chemistry, computer science, mathematics, management systems, and physics; Ph.D. degrees are offered in chemical engineering, chemistry, civil and environmental engineering, electrical and computer engineering, engineering science, environmental science and engineering, materials science and engineering, mathematics, mechanical engineering, and physics.

Applying

It is recommended that applications be submitted by January 30 for the fall semester and September 15 for the spring semester to allow for full financial aid consideration. Study may begin in August, January, or June. Scores on the General Test of the GRE are required for all applications except those of Clarkson students. TOEFL scores of at least 550 (paper-based test), 213 (computer-based test), 6.5 (IELTS), or 80 (Internet-based test) are required for all international applications.

Correspondence and Information

Wallace H. Coulter School of Engineering
Graduate Studies Office
Box 5700
Clarkson University
Potsdam, New York 13699-5700
Phone: 315-268-7929
Fax: 315-268-4494
E-mail: enggrad@clarkson.edu
Website: http://www.clarkson.edu/engineering/graduate

THE FACULTY AND THEIR RESEARCH

Department of Chemical and Biomolecular Engineering

S. V. Babu, Professor; Ph.D., SUNY at Stony Brook. Chemical-mechanical planarization of metal and dielectric films and thin films for photovoltaic applications.

Ruth E. Baltus, Professor; Ph.D., Carnegie Mellon. Transport in porous media, membrane separations, membrane characterization, room temperature ionic liquids and biosensors.

Philip K. Hopke, Professor; Ph.D., Princeton. Multivariate statistical methods for data analysis; characterization of source/receptor relationships for ambient air pollutants; sampling, chemical, and physical characterization of airborne particles; experimental studies of homogeneous, heterogeneous, and ion-induced nucleation; indoor air quality; exposure and risk assessment.

Sitaraman Krishnan, Associate Professor; Ph.D., Lehigh. Nanostructured material design using self-assembly, polymers and nanocomposites, colloids and interfaces, thermal and transport properties of complex fluids, X-ray techniques for nanoscale materials characterization, multiphase reaction kinetics.

Richard J. McCluskey, Associate Professor; Ph.D., Minnesota. Reaction kinetics and thermodynamics.

John B. McLaughlin, Professor; Ph.D., Harvard. Fluid mechanics, modeling of the flow of air and suspended particles, development of a grid electrostatic filter, modeling of polymers.

David Mitlin, Professor and GE Chair in Oil and Gas Systems; Ph.D., Berkeley. Corrosion-fouling of surfaces, supercapacitors and lithium batteries, oxygen reduction reaction electrodes, hydrogen storage in thin films and multilayers, metallic MEMS, corrosion in supercritical water.

Shunsuke Nakao, Assistant Professor; Ph.D., California, Riverside. Aerosol-cloud-climate interaction, air quality, atmospheric chemistry, aerosol physics.

Don H. Rasmussen, Professor; Ph.D., Wisconsin–Madison. Nucleation and phase transformations, metal reduction, colloidal and interfacial phenomena.

Marco Satyro, Assistant Professor; Ph.D., Calgary. New equation of state development, error propagation in flowsheet computations, natural gas dehydration and sweetening, heavy hydrocarbon phase modeling, process simulation.

R. Shankar Subramanian, Professor; Ph.D., Clarkson. Transport phenomena; colloidal and interfacial phenomena, especially the motion of bubbles and drops.

Ross Taylor, Professor; Ph.D., Manchester. Multicomponent mass transfer, separation process simulation, engineering applications of computer algebra.

Selma Mededovic Thagard, Assistant Professor; Ph.D., Florida State. Nonthermal plasma for air and wastewater treatment, plasma-assisted material synthesis, plasma chemistry, mathematical modeling of electrical discharges in gases and liquids.

William R. Wilcox, Professor; Ph.D., Berkeley. Materials processing, crystal growth.

Department of Civil and Environmental Engineering

Norbert L. Ackermann, Professor Emeritus; Ph.D., Carnegie Tech. Mechanics of granular flow, river hydraulics.

Gordon Batson, Professor Emeritus; Ph.D., Carnegie Mellon. Structural applications: fracture mechanics.

Clarkson University

James S. Bonner, Professor and Chief Research and Education Officer of the Beacon Institute; Ph.D., Clarkson. Water quality and spill monitoring.

John P. Dempsey, Professor and Shipley Center for Innovation Fellow; Ph.D., Auckland (New Zealand). Fracture mechanics, tribology, ice-structure interaction.

Andrea Ferro, Professor; Ph.D., Stanford. Air pollution, indoor air quality.

Stefan J. Grimberg, Professor and Chair; Ph.D., North Carolina at Chapel Hill. Bioremediation, bioavailability of organic environmental pollutants.

Thomas M. Holsen, Professor; Ph.D., Berkeley. Fate and transport of chemicals in the environment.

Kerop Janoyan, Professor; Ph.D., UCLA. Geotechnical and structural engineering, soil-structural interactions, structural health monitoring.

Ian M. Knack, Assistant Professor; Ph.D., Clarkson. River ice processes.

Feng-Bor Lin, Professor; Ph.D., Carnegie Mellon. Modeling traffic operations, systems analysis.

Levon Minnetyan, Professor; Ph.D., Duke. Structural analysis and design.

Narutoshi Nakata, Associate Professor, Ph.D., Illinois at Urbana-Champaign. Experimental methods in structural engineering, earthquake engineering and bridge engineering, smart structures, structural dynamics.

Sulapha Peethamparan, Associate Professor; Ph.D., Purdue. Characterization and control of cement and concrete materials.

Susan E. Powers, Professor and Associate Director for Sustainability; Ph.D., Michigan. Multiphase fluid flow, hazardous-waste management.

Shane Rogers, Associate Professor; Ph.D., Iowa State. Fate and transport of etiological agents and anthropogenic compounds.

Hayley H. Shen, Research Professor; Ph.D., Clarkson; Ph.D., Iowa. Granular flow, sea ice processes.

Hung Tao Shen, Research Professor; Ph.D., Iowa. River hydraulics, river ice processes, mathematical modeling.

Tyler J. Smith, Assistant Professor, Ph.D., Montana State. Water resources, water quality.

Khiem Tran, Assistant Professor, Ph.D., Florida. Nondestructive Testing and evaluation, foundation design, and capacity verification.

Steven F. Wojtkiewicz, Jr., Associate Professor, Ph.D., Illinois at Urbana-Champaign. Uncertainty quantification and validation of computational models; dynamics, optimization, and control of structures; real-time hybrid simulation.

Poojitha Yapa, Professor; Ph.D., Clarkson. Mathematical modeling of oil spills.

Department of Electrical and Computer Engineering

Mahesh Banavar, Assistant Professor; Ph.D., Arizona State. Distributed sensing for cyber-physical systems, distributed localization, distributed inference with realistic power amplifier models, distributed nonlinear average consensus, robustness to noise and outliers.

James J. Carroll, Associate Professor; Ph.D., Clemson. High-performance motion control, nonlinear control, control strategies.

Ming-Cheng Cheng, Professor; Ph.D., Polytechnic. Device physics and modeling and simulation of electronic and thermal characteristics for advanced solid state devices.

Susan E. Conry, Professor Emeritus; Ph.D., Rice. Multiagent systems, distributed problem solving, design of coordination strategies.

Daqing Hou, Associate Professor; Ph.D., Alberta. Software design, program analysis, semantics of programming languages, software development environments and tools, software reuse, documentation, software evolution, formal methods.

William Jemison, Professor and Chair; Ph.D. Drexel. Microwave photonic systems, microwave/mm-wave antenna design and measurement, radar systems, wireless and optical communications systems, lidar systems, biological applications of microwaves and photonics.

Baruk Kantarci, Assistant Professor; Ph.D., Instanbul Tech. Cloud computing and communications, big data analytics in the cloud, energy-efficient communications and computing, heterogeneous wireless sensor networks, next generation broadband and access networks.

Melike Erol Kantarci, Assistant Professor; Ph.D., Istanbul Tech. Smart grid security and big data, sensing in cyber-physical systems and critical infrastructures, sustainable wireless sensor networks for smart grid and electric vehicle applications, underwater sensor networks.

Abul N. Khondker, Associate Professor; Ph.D., Rice. Digital design using FPGA embedded systems.

Jack Koplowitz, Associate Professor; Ph.D., Colorado. Image and signal processing, computer vision, pattern recognition.

Chen Liu, Assistant Professor; Ph.D., California, Irvine. Embedded systems, processor architectures, power-aware many-core computing, interaction between operating systems and micro-architectures.

Paul B. McGrath, Professor and Executive Officer; Ph.D., Queen Mary College, London University. Dielectric materials and high-voltage engineering, insulation problems.

Robert A. Meyer, Professor Emeritus; Ph.D., Rice. Artificial intelligence and distributed problem solving, verification of hardware designs, software engineering.

Thomas H. Ortmeyer, Professor; Ph.D., Iowa State. Power electronics, power quality, power system operation.

Vladimir Privman, Professor; D.Sci., Technion (Israel). Quantum devices: quantum computing, spintronics, nanoscale electronics; colloids and nanoparticles; synthesis and properties.

Liya L. Regel, Research Professor and Director, International Center for Gravity Materials Science and Applications; Ph.D., Irkutsk State (Russia); Doctorat, Ioffe Institute (Russia). Materials science and its influence on properties and device performance.

Charles J. Robinson, Founding Director, Center for Rehabilitation Engineering, Science, and Technology (CREST), and Herman L. Shulman Chair Professor; D.Sc., Washington (St. Louis). Combining the development of microdevices and nanodevices capable of measuring stroke sequences with fundamental research that characterizes the behavior of the nervous system, quantification of tremor through signal processing analysis of graphical drawings, and determining and describing the control systems employed in health and disease to permit upright standing in humans.

Stephanie Schuckers, Professor; Ph.D., Michigan. Biomedical signal processing, medical devices, pattern recognition, large datasets.

James A. Svoboda, Associate Professor; Ph.D., Wisconsin. Circuit theory, system theory, electronics, digital signal processing.

Lei Wu, Assistant Professor, Ph.D., IIT. Stochastic modeling and optimization of large-scale power systems, smart grid, high-penetration renewable energy applications, power systems reliability and economics, market power analysis and risk management.

Department of Mechanical and Aeronautical Engineering

Ajit Achuthan, Assistant Professor; Ph.D., Purdue. Solid mechanics, ferroelectrics, nanomechanics and smart structures and materials, fiber-optic sensors.

Goodarz Ahmadi, Clarkson Distinguished Professor and Robert R. Hill '48 Professor; Ph.D., Purdue. Fluid mechanics, solid mechanics, multiphase flows, aerosols, microcontamination, surface cleaning.

Daryush Aidun, Professor; Ph.D., Rensselaer. Welding metallurgy and automation, corrosion, materials processing and solidification, reliability analysis of engineering components/systems.

Douglas Bohl, Associate Professor; Ph.D., Michigan State. Experimental fluid mechanics and thermal science.

Frederick Carlson, Professor Emeritus; Ph.D., Connecticut. Heat transfer, crystal growth.

Cetin Cetinkaya, Professor; Ph.D., Illinois at Urbana-Champaign. Solid mechanics, stress wave propagation, surface cleaning and nanotechnology.

Suresh Dhaniyala, Professor; Ph.D., Minnesota. Aerosols, nanoparticles, particle instrumentation, atmospheric aerosols, aircraft and ground-based sampling, fluid mechanics.

Bryon Erath, Assistant Professor; Ph.D., Purdue. Fluid mechanics, focus on laryngeal aerodynamics of voiced speech, experimental investigations and computational modeling of the speech process.

Kevin Fite, Associate Professor and Executive Officer; Ph.D., Vanderbilt. Dynamic systems and controls, robotics and mechatronics.

James Gilbert, Assistant Professor; Ph.D., Clemson. Nonlinear dynamics, vibrations, smart materials, optimization, additive manufacturing, energy harvesting.

Brian Helenbrook, Professor; Ph.D., Princeton. Computational fluid dynamics and combustion.

Kathleen Issen, Associate Professor; Ph.D., Northwestern. Solid mechanics, inelastic behavior and failure of geomaterials.

James Kane, Associate Professor; Ph.D., Connecticut. Solid mechanics, boundary-element methods.

Laurel Kuxhaus, Assistant Professor; Ph.D., Pittsburgh. Biomechanics; mechanics and control of the upper extremity, especially the elbow; elbow joint stiffness and its application to arthritis; prosthetic upper limb control and the diagnosis of Parkinson's disease; mathematical modeling of ligaments; mechanical properties of vertebral bone.

Ronald LaFleur, Associate Professor; Ph.D., Connecticut. Fluid mechanics, thermofluid design.

Sung P. Lin, Professor Emeritus; Ph.D., Michigan. Fluid mechanics, fluid dynamic stability.

Pier Marzocca, Professor; Ph.D., Virginia Tech. Solid mechanics, nonlinear systems control.

Ioannis Mastorakos, Assistant Professor; Ph.D., Aristotle of Thessaloniki. Materials.

Arthur Michaleh, Assistant Professor; Ph.D., Vermont. Bioengineering.

Parisa Mirbod, Assistant Professor; Ph.D., CUNY, City College. Fluid and solid mechanics, flow through porous media, non-Newtonian fluid mechanics, suspensions and technology development.

John Moosbrugger, Professor and Associate Dean; Ph.D., Georgia Tech. Solid mechanics, plasticity.

David Morrison, Associate Professor; Ph.D., Michigan. Materials science, fracture mechanics.

Eric Thacher, Professor Emeritus and Senior Research Professor; Ph.D., New Mexico State. Thermal sciences, solar energy.

Daniel Valentine, Professor and Chair; Ph.D., Catholic University. Fluid mechanics, hydrodynamics.

Kenneth Visser, Associate Professor; Ph.D., Notre Dame. Experimental aerodynamics.

Kenneth Willmert, Professor; Ph.D., Case Western Reserve. Solid mechanics, optimal design.

Steven W. Yurgartis, Associate Professor; Ph.D., Rensselaer. Solid mechanics, composite materials.

Philip A. Yuya, Assistant Professor; Ph.D., Nebraska-Lincoln. Constitutive modeling and experimental mechanics of materials with special emphasis on biomaterials, nanofibers and polymers.

Materials Science and Engineering Ph.D. program

Director, Marilyn Miller Freeman, Ph.D., Texas at Austin. Materials science and engineering with applications to electronic materials, dielectrics, thin-film storage devices, and power and energy.

About 30 Clarkson faculty members participate in the interdisciplinary Ph.D. program in Materials Science and Engineering, with a goal of understanding the structure, properties, processing, and performance of advanced materials. This multidisciplinary approach is required given the complex nature of advanced materials. Applications of advanced materials to the fields of energy, biotechnology, microelectronic devices, and the environment are at the forefront of current materials research. Further information is available online at http://www.clarkson.edu/engineering/graduate/mat_sci_eng_phd/index.html.

Topics covered in the program include:

Advanced materials for alternative energy:
- Polymers that absorb visible light and form anti-reflective coatings on photovoltaic cells.
- Colloidal methods for creating electrical contacts to photovoltaic cells.
- Phase change materials for solar thermal applications.
- Thin film deposition of semiconductor materials that absorb visible light.

Biomaterials:
- Materials for enzymatic biosensors, antibody biosensors, and enzymatic biocomputing.
- Biopolymers and stimuli-responsive polymers.
- Fluid mechanics of inhalable drugs.
- New polymer materials for protein immobilization, and to prevent biofouling.
- Acoustic methods for monitoring drug tablets.

Colloid science and technology:
- Colloidal methods for creating electrical contacts to photovoltaic cells, microelectronic devices, fuel cells, and other electrical devices.
- Creation of catalyst materials for fuel cells, reduction of environmentally harmful emissions, and other applications.
- Mechanical properties of metals with nano-sized grains.
- Particle removal using acoustic methods.

Materials processing for microelectronic devices:
- Chemical mechanical planarization (CMP)
- Fluid mechanics and particle mechanics during CMP.
- Nanoparticle removal using laser-induced plasmas.
- Thin film deposition using colloidal methods and electrochemical methods.

Materials of construction:
- Metallurgy
- Concrete
- Fatigue and fracture of construction materials.

THE GEORGE WASHINGTON UNIVERSITY
School of Engineering and Applied Science

School of Engineering & Applied Science
THE GEORGE WASHINGTON UNIVERSITY

Programs of Study

The School of Engineering and Applied Science (SEAS) at the George Washington University (GW) offers the graduate degrees of Master of Science, Applied Scientist, Engineer, and Doctor of Philosophy as well as graduate-level certificate programs. The ten fields of study include biomedical engineering, civil and environmental engineering, computer engineering, computer science, cybersecurity in computer science, electrical engineering, engineering management, mechanical and aerospace engineering, systems engineering, and telecommunications engineering. Interdisciplinary study is encouraged, especially at the doctoral level. Within most fields, students may design their degree programs to pursue their own professional goals and academic interests, following curricular guidelines of the School and in consultation with their academic adviser. The minimum master's program consists of 24 credit hours plus a 6-credit-hour thesis; the nonthesis option consists of 30 to 36 credit hours, depending on the field of study. The professional degree programs (Applied Scientist and Engineer) require a minimum of 30 hours of courses beyond the master's degree. A technical project may be required. Course work done for the professional degree may be transferred to the Doctor of Philosophy, and vice versa, under certain conditions. The Doctor of Philosophy program requires a minimum of 30 hours of course work beyond the master's degree or 54 hours beyond the bachelor's degree, followed by a doctoral qualifying examination. The dissertation, requiring a minimum of 24 credit hours of work under the guidance of an adviser, is also presented orally in the final examination. The School's dissertations have been used in industry, such as an evaluation model of an oil spill contingency plan or an analysis of red blood cell flow; in government, for example, in projecting risks associated with nuclear reactors; and in higher education, through refined theoretical formulations of traditional problems.

Areas of Research

Biomedical Engineering: This program is designed to prepare students to apply engineering principles to problems in medicine and biology, to understand and model multiple attributes of living systems, and to synthesize biomedical systems and devices. Students choose between two areas of focus: medical imaging and medical instrumentation.

Civil and Environmental Engineering: Students choose from a variety of areas of focus for their research: engineering mechanics, environmental engineering, geotechnical engineering, structural engineering, water resources engineering, and transportation safety engineering. Those studying environmental and water resources engineering use one of the world's largest wastewater treatment plants as a real-world laboratory to improve the water quality of the Potomac River and the Chesapeake Bay Watershed. Structural and geotechnical engineering students study earthquake engineering and extreme event design of structures, bridges, and geostructures on a state-of-the-art, six-degree-of-freedom earthquake simulator at the Earth Engineering and Structures Laboratory. Transportation engineering students learn from faculty and experts at GW's National Crash Analysis Center, the Federal Outdoor Impact Laboratory, Center for Intelligent Transportation Research, and more.

Computer Engineering: This program offers up-to-date knowledge and skills in the advances of computer systems architecture and networking and in the rapidly growing use of superscalar microprocessors, real-time embedded systems, VLSI and ASIC design modules, digital signal processors, and networked computing platforms. Students learn sophisticated computer architecture and integrated circuit design techniques using industry-standard computer-aided design tools and choose from two areas of focus, either computer architecture and high-performance computing or MEMS, electronics, and photonics.

Computer Science: Students choose from numerous focus areas, including algorithms and theory; computer security and information assurance; systems, networks, cloud computing, mobile computing, and parallel and distributed computing; artificial intelligence, including machine learning, natural language processing, and robotics; computer graphics, human computer interaction, and multimedia; database and information systems; software engineering; and bioinformatics and biomedical engineering.

Cybersecurity in Computer Science: The M.S. in Cybersecurity is the first such degree program in the nation's capital, and one of the few graduate degrees in cybersecurity in the U.S. and the world. Coursework covers the design and analysis of algorithms, computer architectures, and advanced software paradigms. Students may also take courses in cryptography, network security, and information policy.

Electrical Engineering: Students learn to understand and apply the principles of electrical engineering to diverse areas such as communications, power and energy, and micro- and nano-electronics. Students choose from six areas of focus: communications and networks; electrical power and energy; electromagnetics, radiation systems, and microwave engineering; electronics, photonics, and MEMS; and signal and image processing, systems, and controls.

Engineering Management: Students in engineering management learn techniques for managing technical and scientific organizations, choosing from five areas of focus: crisis, emergency, and risk management; economics, finance, and cost engineering; engineering and technology management; environmental and energy management; and knowledge and information management.

Mechanical and Aerospace Engineering: Faculty and students in mechanical and aerospace engineering conduct research that aims to control adult stem cell differentiation to treat human disease, develop autonomous mobile robots that can be used in search and rescue and other high-risk missions, enhance nuclear reactor safety, develop a plasma scalpel that can minimize the need for blood transfusions during surgery, and more. Research areas include aerospace engineering; design of mechanical engineering systems; fluid mechanics, thermal sciences, and energy; robotics, mechatronics, and controls; and solid mechanics and materials science.

Systems Engineering: This program provides broad knowledge of the "systems approach" for designing and managing large-scale engineering systems throughout the lifecycle, with faculty and students exploring case studies and methodologies from NASA, the U.S. Department of Defense, and U.S. corporations. Students can pursue research in one of three areas of focus: operations research and management science, systems engineering and integration, or enterprise information assurance.

Telecommunications Engineering: Students in telecommunications engineering develop a foundation in the fundamentals of the field, covering topics in their coursework such as transmission systems, computer networking, network architectures and protocols, and telecommunications security protocols. Students may also conduct research in optical networking, wireless networking, cloud computing, and other topics.

Research Facilities

In January 2015, the University unveiled the Science and Engineering Hall, a state-of-the-art facility with eight floors of teaching labs, study rooms, and specialized labs for studying aerospace structures, nanotechnology, and more.

The Science and Engineering Hall includes three core lab facilities. The first is the high bay, an expansive, three-story lab featuring a reinforced "strong wall" and a "strong floor" to test the strength of enormous objects, like bridge beams, and is made for studying civil engineering. The high bay lab also includes a 20-ton crane, a dedicated loading bay, and a machine shop. The second core lab facility is the Class 100 nanofabrication clean room, where each cubic foot of air contains no more than 100 particles larger than 0.5 microns to facilitate the creation of devices that measure mere billionths of a meter. The third core lab facility is the microscopy suite, which is composed of five rooms housing high-resolution microscopy equipment, allowing researchers to study nanometer-sized samples in ultra-fine detail and create 3-D reconstructions of specimens.

Research centers, institutes, and special programs include the following:

Biofluid Dynamics Laboratory	Computational Aero and Hydrodynamics Laboratory
Bioengineering Laboratory for Nanomedicine and Tissue Engineering	Computational Materials Science and Molecular Modeling Group
Cardiac Ischemia Research Laboratory	Cooperative Vehicle Systems Laboratory
Center for Biomimetics and Bioinspired Engineering (COBRE)	Cyber Security Policy and Research Institute
Center for Intelligent Systems Research	Earthquake Engineering and Structures Laboratory

The George Washington University

Environmental Engineering Laboratory

Flight Dynamics and Control Lab

Fluid Mechanics and Hydraulics Lab

George Washington University Institute for Nanotechnology (GWin)

High-Performance Computing Laboratory

Institute for Biomedical Engineering

Institute for Computer Graphics

Institute for Crisis, Disaster and Risk Management

Institute for Massively Parallel Applications and Computing Technologies (IMPACT)

Institute for Magnetics Research

Institute for MEMS and VLSI Technology

Laboratory for Advanced Computer Applications in Medicine

Laboratory for Medical Imaging and Applications of MEMS in Medicine

Magnetic Material Testing Laboratory

Magnetic Refrigeration Research Laboratory

Magneto-Optics Laboratory

Medical Image Analysis Laboratory

Micro-propulsion and Nanotechnology Laboratory

Microwave Laboratory

Motion Capture and Analysis Laboratory (MOCA)

Multiscale Computational Mechanics Laboratory

National Crash Analysis Center

National Science Foundation Center for High-Performance Reconfigurable Computing

Optofluidics Laboratory

Robotics and Mechatronics Laboratory

Smart Systems Laboratory

Soil Mechanics Laboratory

Structural Testing/Materials Science Laboratory

Therapeutic Ultrasound Lab

VLSI and MEMS Systems Design and Testing

Financial Aid

Scholarships and fellowships are available for eligible students. Consideration for scholarships and fellowships is included in the application for admission and will require the applicant to submit a minimum of three letters of recommendation. Teaching and research assistantships may be offered to eligible full-time students and may be augmented by up to 18 semester hours of tuition credit.

Cost of Study

Tuition is charged at the rate of $1,585 per credit hour for the 2015–16 academic year. Information on all other fees and charges is available on the GW website at http://studentaccounts.gwu.edu/fees-charges.

Living and Housing Costs

The University has limited on-campus housing for graduate students. Therefore, it is highly encouraged for students to seek housing in one of the many neighborhoods surrounding the Foggy Bottom campus, including Dupont, Georgetown, Columbia Heights, or Arlington, Virginia. As of March 2015, the average cost of apartment rent was $1,500 per month.

Student Group

SEAS students include graduates from the majority of U.S. colleges and universities and from seventy countries around the world. Approximately 900 students are working on master's degrees, 25 on professional degrees, and 400 on doctorates. Approximately 70 percent of SEAS students are international, and 30 percent are women.

Location

SEAS offers most programs at the main campus in the Foggy Bottom neighborhood of Washington, D.C., as well as select programs at off-campus sites and the Virginia campus near Washington Dulles International Airport. Cultural activities in Washington, D.C., include the prestigious Smithsonian museums and galleries (many of which are free of charge), as well as other museums; performing arts in numerous local and national theaters such as Wolf Trap Farm Park and the Kennedy Center for the Performing Arts; seasonal events and athletics along the Potomac River and the C&O Canal; and scores of restaurants featuring ethnic-American and international foods.

Within a couple of hours' drive east of the University lie the beaches of Virginia, Maryland, and Delaware, and west to the mountains are U.S. national forests and parks, where recreation includes skiing, fishing, hiking, and camping.

The University and The School

The George Washington University was chartered as a private university in 1821, in response to President George Washington's hope that a national university would be established in the federal city. GW has two colleges and six schools in addition to the School of Engineering and Applied Science. The others, which offer collaborative opportunities for engineering students, include arts and sciences, business, education, international affairs, law, medicine, and public health and health services. Organized at GW in 1884, the School of Engineering and Applied Science is one of the oldest engineering schools in America and was one of the first to admit women as part of its student body.

Applying

For all graduate programs, applications are due January 15 for fall semester entry; September 1 for spring semester entry; and March 1 for summer semester entry. Please note that international applicants are not eligible to apply in the summer. International applicants who do not hold a bachelor's, master's, or doctoral degree from a college or university in the U.S., or who do not hold a degree from a country where the language of instruction was English, must submit TOEFL, IELTS, or PTE scores.

For the TOEFL, a score of 550 on the paper-based test (80 on the Internet-based test) is the minimum for admission. Applicants to the engineering management or systems engineering programs are required to have a minimum of 100 on the Internet-based exam. Applicants who would like to be considered for funding opportunities must have a 600 on the paper-based exam or 100 on the Internet-based exam.

SEAS also accepts the IELTS test with an overall minimum band score of 6.0, with no individual band score below 5.0. Applicants to the engineering management or systems engineering programs are required to have a minimum score of 7.0. Applicants who would like to be considered for funding opportunities must have an overall band score of 7.0 with no individual score below 6.0.

For international applicants, SEAS accepts the PTE Academic exam with a minimum score of 53. Applicants who would like to be considered for funding opportunities must have a 68 or higher.

Submission of Graduate Record Examinations scores is required for admission to a doctoral program and/or when an assistantship or fellowship is desired. It is recommended for all other applicants, but not required.

Correspondence and Information

Office of Graduate Admissions and Student Services
School of Engineering and Applied Science
Science and Engineering Hall
The George Washington University
800 22nd Street NW, Suite 2885
Washington, D.C. 20052
United States
Phone: 202-994-1802
E-mail: engineering@gwu.edu
Website: http://www.graduate.seas.gwu.edu

The Science and Engineering Hall on GW's main campus in the Foggy Bottom neighborhood of Washington, D.C., opened in January 2015. At approximately 500,000 square feet, the building features teaching labs, faculty office space, and three specialized labs for civil engineering, nanotechnology production, and high-resolution imaging.

MILWAUKEE SCHOOL OF ENGINEERING
Graduate Programs in Engineering

Programs of Study

Milwaukee School of Engineering (MSOE) offers thirteen master's degree programs.

The Master of Science in Engineering (MSE) is an interdisciplinary engineering program with primary emphases in the areas of electrical engineering (EE) and mechanical engineering (ME). A key benefit of the MSE program is the breadth of engineering skills and knowledge that graduates attain in areas of systems engineering, EE, and ME. This program is offered in face-to-face and 100 percent–online formats.

The Master of Science in Engineering Management (MSEM) program is best described as a master's degree in general management with a technological orientation. The MSEM program is based on the philosophy that, in order for American companies to grow and compete domestically and internationally, their technical personnel must have the tools to effectively manage and participate in the decision-making process. This program is offered in blended and 100 percent online formats.

The Master of Science in Construction and Business Management program was created in conjunction with MSOE's Rader School of Business and the Civil and Architectural Engineering and Construction Management Department. This degree targets professionals who are working or have experience in the construction industry. It offers students the leadership tools necessary to compete in the ever-changing and highly competitive construction management environment. This program is offered in a blended format.

The Master of Science in Architectural Engineering (MSAE) program allows specialization in the analysis and design of building structural systems or in building mechanical, electrical, and plumbing systems (MEP). Attainment of degree requirements enables architectural engineers to apply advanced knowledge and skill sets to design structural or MEP systems for modern buildings. This program is offered in a face-to-face format.

The Master of Science in Civil Engineering (MSCVE) program is designed to equip students with the advanced knowledge and skills necessary for professional practice. Students are able to specialize in one of the following three areas: (1) construction management, (2) environmental and water resources engineering, and (3) structural engineering. This program is offered in a face-to-face format.

Research Facilities

The Applied Technology Center™ (ATC) is the research arm of MSOE. It conducts applied (strategic) research in conjunction with the university's various academic programs, utilizing faculty and student expertise as well as industrial-size laboratories to solve technological problems confronting business and industry. The close association between MSOE and the business and industrial community has long been one of the university's strengths. The ATC is heavily involved in the transferring of new technologies into real business practice through the Rapid Prototyping Center, the Fluid Power Institute™, the Photonics and Applied Optics Center, the Construction Science and Engineering Center, the NanoEngineering Laboratory, and the Center for BioMolecular Modeling. MSOE is the only university in the world to possess five leading rapid prototyping technologies, and America's first fluid power research facility university. The ATC deals in research operations that include advanced manufacturing technologies, motion control and ultrafast videography, engineering and manufacturing consultation, and environmental areas. Both graduate and undergraduate students pursue research opportunities in the ATC.

Financial Aid

Most graduate students receive some type of tuition reimbursement from their employers. For those students who do not have this benefit, several loan options may be available. Nonimmigrant alien graduate students are not eligible for federal or state financial assistance or MSOE loan money. MSOE offers a limited number of graduate research assistantships.

Cost of Study

The 2015–16 tuition for all graduate programs is $732 per credit hour.

Living and Housing Costs

MSOE operates three on-campus residence halls. Although undergraduate students compose the largest segment of the resident population, the residence halls offer an on-campus option to the graduate student. The Housing Department can provide more information on what is available and how personal needs might be accommodated. Alternative off-campus housing is available from the many independently owned rental units near the university.

Student Group

In fall 2014, MSOE had 2,810 full- and part-time students. Of these, 214 were graduate students. The majority of graduate students at MSOE have prior professional experience in their field.

Location

MSOE is located just a few blocks from Lake Michigan on the east side of downtown Milwaukee, which is approximately 90 miles north of Chicago. MSOE is in a vibrant downtown neighborhood in Milwaukee called East Town. There are countless activities within walking distance from campus including shopping, theaters, restaurants, professional sporting venues, and more.

The University

Milwaukee School of Engineering is an independent, nonprofit university with about 2,800 students that was founded in 1903. MSOE offers bachelor's and master's degrees in engineering, business, mathematics, and nursing. The university has a national academic reputation, longstanding ties to business and industry, dedicated professors with real-world experience, a 96 percent undergraduate placement rate, and the highest ROI and average starting and midcareer salaries of any Wisconsin university according to PayScale Inc. MSOE graduates are well-rounded, technologically experienced, and highly productive professionals and leaders.

Applying

Applicants can submit an application online for no cost at http://msoe.edu/apply.

General application requirements include an official transcript of all undergraduate and graduate course work, two or three letters of recommendation (depending on the program), and GMAT/GRE test scores, depending upon the program and/or undergraduate cumulative grade point average.

International students will be required to submit additional documentation. Some programs may have additional requirements; program-specific details are available on MSOE's website.

Correspondence and Information

Graduate and Professional Education
Milwaukee School of Engineering
1025 North Broadway
Milwaukee, Wisconsin 53202-3109
United States
Phone: 800-321-6763 (toll-free)
E-mail: gpe@msoe.edu
Website: http://www.msoe.edu/graduate
 http://facebook.com/msoegpe (Facebook)
 http://twitter.com/msoegpe (Twitter)

THE FACULTY AND THEIR RESEARCH

MSOE's faculty focus is on teaching, both in the classroom and in its world-class research facilities. Unlike many educational institutions, MSOE does not utilize teaching assistants. MSOE has more than 200 full- and part-time faculty members. Small classes, a low 12:1 student-faculty ratio for undergraduate courses, and a 7:1 student-faculty ratio for graduate courses ensures that students receive personal attention.

The Applied Technology Center™ (ATC) is the research arm of the university. It serves as a technology transfer catalyst among academia, business and industry, and governmental agencies. The close association

Milwaukee School of Engineering

between MSOE and the business and industrial community has long been one of the university's strengths; applied research serves as a renewable resource in this linkage. The ATC undertakes more than 250 company-sponsored projects per year that involve faculty, staff members, and students. Interdisciplinary capabilities provide a major advantage and can span fields such as engineering, science, health care, business, computers, and technical communication. Modes of interaction include applied research and consulting by faculty members with industrial experience, often with graduate and undergraduate research assistants; projects in engineering and business disciplines, which are coordinated by company and faculty advisers; and referrals, which serve as an initial contact point for networking with others to optimize expertise and facilities for technology transfer.

The ATC is organized into several areas:

The Rapid Prototyping Center (RPC) is a joint effort of industry, government, and MSOE that is dedicated to the application of proven technologies to novel challenges. MSOE is the only university that has a laboratory devoted to all five commercially available rapid prototyping systems—stereolithography (SLA), laminated object manufacturing (LOM), selective laser sintering (SLS), fused deposition modeling (FDM), and Z-Corp processing. A rapid scanning system has recently been acquired, which allows the automatic preparation of 3-D databases from laser scanning of any object, thereby making it possible to reproduce the object using rapid prototyping systems. Rapid prototyping historically has been a tool for reducing product development cycle times. The RPC continues to advance the state-of-the-art in this area, using computer-based manufacturing techniques and complementary processes to reduce the time and cost of industrial products ranging from functional models to full-scale production.

Established in 1991, the Rapid Prototyping Consortium continues MSOE's tradition of building strong ties to business and industry. The consortium includes industrial companies and educational institutions that cooperate in understanding the consortium's vitality and success in a high level of industrial parts design and fabrication activity. Companies that take advantage of the facilities and expertise within the consortium become stronger and more competitive.

The RPC also is extending the use of rapid prototyping through research projects as diverse as biomolecular and biomedical modeling, architectural modeling, and manufacturing tooling. Rapid prototyping research is involved in several biomolecular technology development programs, including nanomagnetics, liquid crystals, and digital manufacturing. There is significant activity in novel internally structured solid objects and advanced high-resolution metal casting processes.

The Center for BioMolecular Modeling (CBMM) is established within MSOE's RPC. The center creates unique physical models of molecular structures using rapid prototyping technologies and works with research scientists to create custom models of the proteins whose structures they are investigating. The center also works closely with educators at both the secondary and postsecondary levels to create innovative products that make the molecular world real for students. The center is unique in the world, bringing together the disciplines of engineering, structural biology, and computer visualization.

The Fluid Power Institute™ (FPI) was established in 1962 as one of the first research facilities of its kind in the country and has remained a pioneer in motion control and fluid power education. Through its state-of-the-art facilities, it conducts a variety of performance, endurance, and environmental evaluations of components and systems. FPI also performs component and system design, modeling and simulation, contamination, and various education programs. A $5-million endowment from the estate of Otto J. Maha provides resources to ensure continued advancement of fluid power education. FPI uses an interdisciplinary workforce comprised of faculty and staff members from various academic departments and undergraduate and graduate students to conduct fluid power, motion control, and related industry projects. FPI's approach uses mechanical, electrical, computer, and software engineering along with MSOE's Rapid Prototyping Center. MSOE is a member of the National Fluid Power Association and supports the activities of the Fluid Power Society and the Fluid Power Educational Foundation. It has expanded into electrohydraulic interface studies and currently has active programs in fluid power systems design, applications of fluid power to manufacturing, computerized fluid dynamics (CFD), electromagnetic actuators and sensors, component evaluation, and filtration and contamination testing.

The NanoEngineering Laboratory allows research and education at the nanoscale, which is becoming more critical each year as research and development focuses on nanoscale phenomena, ultrafine structures, and interfaces between matters. Atomic Force Microscopy (AFM) allows the force between a small tip and a chosen sample surface to be measured with atomic-scale resolution. Initially, lateral forces between the tip and the sample can also be measured to better understand the origins of

friction at the molecular scale. Other types of AFM surface measurement models include plastic deformations, electrical conductivity, and thermal conductivity. All these capabilities make the AFM an indispensable tool for characterization and manipulation in all areas of the emerging field of technology called nanotechnology. Leveraging the state-of-the-art AFM capabilities, research is conducted in the areas of wear reduction and surface enhancement. Other areas include Solid Freeform Fabrication (SFF) of metal matrix composites and numerous projects for biological and industrial applications (e.g., MEMS).

The High-Speed Video Analysis system has the ability to digitally capture—and immediately play back—events in the 1,000 to 12,000 frames per second range. Powerful motion analysis software is used to track and graph up to nine points in the visual field.

The Photonics and Applied Optics Center features state-of-the-art optical sensor, laser, fiber-optic, and other photonic instrumentation. The center includes six 4-by-8-foot optical tables and a collection of optical instruments and apparatus that includes picowatt optical power meters, computer-controlled monochromators, and a broad array of optical sources, including an optical time-domain reflectometer. The center focuses on sensing, holography, spectral analysis, and communication applied research.

The Construction Science and Engineering Center promotes innovation in the building design and construction industries by conducting applied research in structural materials and systems as well as construction methods. The lab has multiple computerized data acquisition capabilities and an extensive array of transducers for measuring force, displacement, and strain.

MSOE's new Grohmann Tower apartments, which opened in the fall of 2014.

NORTH DAKOTA STATE UNIVERSITY
College of Engineering

NDSU GRADUATE SCHOOL

Programs of Study

Fargo-based North Dakota State University (NDSU) is a public research university with a graduate student enrollment of about 2,200 out of a total enrollment of 14,700 students. NDSU has earned a place on *U.S. News & World Report*'s Best National Universities and Top Public Schools lists. *U.S. News & World Report* also ranks the College of Engineering at North Dakota State among the Best Engineering Schools, with recognized programs in agricultural and biological, civil, computer, electrical, industrial and manufacturing, and mechanical engineering. NDSU also offers graduate programs in environmental engineering and construction management and engineering.

The College of Engineering (CoE) is the largest college at North Dakota State. It offers a broad range of graduate-level degree programs, most with both Master of Science and Ph.D. options.

Agricultural and Biosystems Engineering: Students interested in high-level careers in agribusiness, biorenewable energy development, and related fields may choose to earn the M.S. or the Ph.D. in Agricultural and Biosystems Engineering. The master's degree program consists of 30 credits, with up to 24 credit hours earned in the classroom and the remainder in thesis research and writing. The Ph.D. program requires an additional 60 credit hours beyond the M.S., including dissertation research and research publication.

Civil and Environmental Engineering: The Department of Civil and Environmental Engineering at NDSU administers four graduate-degree programs. The M.S. in Civil Engineering is intended for students who want to work as planners, consultants, designers, or managers for public and private enterprises. Course work covers the civil engineering sub-fields of environmental, geotechnical, water resource, transportation, and structural engineering.

Course work is also offered in engineering mechanics. The Ph.D. in Civil Engineering gives students the opportunity to delve into a particular sub-field or to develop an interdisciplinary path of study. The M.S. in Environmental Engineering program covers air pollution, wastewater and water quality management, hazardous waste management, and related topics.

Construction Management and Engineering: NDSU offers two master's degree programs in construction management and engineering. The M.S. in Construction Management is a research-oriented program that requires 31 credit hours of work, including a thesis. The Master of Construction Management (M.Cons.M.) program is administered entirely online and is designed for working professionals. This program requires 30 credit hours of course work without a thesis to prepare students for the Associate Constructor and Certified Professional Constructor national exams.

Working students who want a graduate certificate in construction management may apply to NDSU's 9-credit online program, which covers construction cost estimating, construction management, and scheduling and project control. The department also offers supervision for doctoral students in civil engineering who specialize in construction management and engineering.

Industrial and Manufacturing (IME): There are two industrial and manufacturing (IME) master's degree programs at North Dakota State University: the M.S. in Manufacturing Engineering and the M.S. in Industrial Engineering and Management. Each degree program is available with a thesis option or, for working engineers, a project option. The programs are available full- or part-time to accommodate working students. Both the thesis and the project option total 30 credit hours of work, with course topics including engineering economics, logistics and systems engineering and management, quality assurance and control, and supply chain management.

The Ph.D. in Industrial and Manufacturing Engineering requires an additional 60 credit hours; 30 hours of course work and 30 hours of dissertation work.

Mechanical Engineering: Mechanical engineering is critical to a number of industries, and the graduate programs at NDSU are designed to prepare students for engineering and management careers in the public and private sectors. NDSU offers both the M.S. in Mechanical Engineering and the Ph.D. in Mechanical Engineering. The master's program is available with a thesis or a comprehensive study option. Students who hope to obtain an assistantship with the mechanical engineering department must choose the thesis option.

The Ph.D. in Mechanical Engineering may be pursued after completion of the M.S. program or as part of a combined M.S./Ph.D. program for bachelor's degree holders.

Electrical and Computer Engineering (ECE): Students seeking a graduate degree in electrical and computer engineering have three options at NDSU. The M.S. in Electrical and Computer Engineering requires a thesis and is the choice for students seeking an assistantship. The Master of Engineering (M.Engr.) in ECE is a course-only program for students who are not interested in an assistantship position. The Ph.D. in ECE requires a dissertation. Specialized areas of graduate study within the ECE department include: biomedical engineering, communications and signal processing, computer architecture, cyber physical and embedded systems, electromagnetics and optics, power and energy, and very-large scale integration. Prospective students are encouraged to contact NDSU ECE faculty members directly for detailed information on specialized study topics.

Interdisciplinary Graduate Degree Programs: The College of Engineering supports several interdisciplinary graduate degree programs in collaboration with other North Dakota State University colleges. The programs include the M.S. and Ph.D. in Environmental and Conservation Science, the M.S. and Ph.D. in Natural Resources Management, and Ph.D. programs in Materials and Nanotechnology, Transportation and Logistics, and STEM (science, technology, engineering and mathematics) Education.

Research

North Dakota State spends more than $135 million each year on research conducted through government and industry grants and partnerships. Some examples of research topics studied by departments within the College of Engineering include the following:

- the role of precision agricultural technology in reducing energy usage
- the use of nanoparticles for remediation of contaminated soil and water
- the role of RFID technology in leadless cardiac pacemaker electrodes
- ergonomic design

North Dakota State University

NDSU's Bison Ventures and Bison Microventures elective programs are project-based research efforts that bring together small teams of students and faculty for problem-solving and entrepreneurial development of lab research. Other participants in the Bison Ventures program are NDSU's Department of Architecture and Landscape Architecture, College of Business, and Center for Technical Enterprise.

Financial Aid

Applicants are automatically considered for financial support, such as assistantships that include a full tuition waiver and a stipend. Research and teaching assistantship availability varies by department. Master's degree students should be aware that most programs require them to select the thesis option in order to qualify for an assistantship.

North Dakota State University funds a number of general and departmental scholarships that may be open to graduate engineering students. NDSU also supports educational benefit programs for military veterans and their families, including the Yellow Ribbon program and the G.I. Bill.

Cost of Study

Up-to-date information on costs can be found online at https://www.ndsu.edu/bisonconnection/accounts/tuition.

Living and Housing Costs

Information about on-campus housing for graduate students can be found at www.ndsu.edu/reslife/general_apartment_information. There is not a specific residence hall for graduate students, but they can live in the University apartments. In addition, there are numerous housing options in the Fargo-Moorhead community.

The Faculty

Faculty members in the College of Engineering at NDSU have won numerous awards for teaching and research. For example, Dr. Eakalak Khan, Professor and Director of the Environmental and Conservation Sciences graduate program, has won two teaching awards while at NDSU, along with a Career Award from the National Science Foundation. His research on water quality improvement and water management has been underwritten by the National Science Foundation, the U.S. Department of Agriculture, and the New York State Department of Transportation.

Assistant Professor Na Gong, Ph.D., teaches in the ECE department and conducts research on energy efficient very-large scale integration and computer architecture. She has served as an associate editor for *Mobile Computing, Microelectronics Journal*, and other publications.

Location

NDSU is located on the eastern edge of North Dakota in Fargo, the state's largest community. With its sister city, Moorhead, Minnesota, directly across the Red River, Fargo is one of the largest metropolitan centers between Minneapolis and Seattle and offers a family friendly environment with excellent schools, safe neighborhoods, and a low crime rate; an active arts and cultural scene, including a symphony, civic opera company, art museums, and community theater; and many places to shop and eat, including numerous restaurants, coffee shops, and a newly refurbished downtown district.

Applying

Students interested in applying for admission are advised to communicate with the Graduate Program Coordinator(s) and the faculty member(s) with whom they wish to work in the specific department(s) within the College of Engineering. Applicants should visit the NDSU Graduate School website at https://www.ndsu.edu/gradschool/. More information can be obtained from individual CoE academic units.

Correspondence and Information

College of Engineering
North Dakota State University
Graduate School
Dept. 2820, P.O. Box 6050
Fargo, North Dakota 58108-6050
Phone: 701-231-7033
        800-608-6378 (toll-free)
E-mail: ndsu.grad.school@ndsu.edu
Website: www.ndsu.edu/gradschool
        facebook.com/ndsugradschool (Facebook)
        @NDSUGradSchool (Twitter)

NDSU's Agricultural and Biosystems Engineering program strives to generate new knowledge in engineering and allied technologies for production agriculture, the food system, and related environmental resources.

NDSU's Electrical and Computer Engineering program offers graduate students the broad education necessary to understand the impact of engineering solutions in a global, economic, environmental, and societal context.

UNIVERSITY AT BUFFALO, THE STATE UNIVERSITY OF NEW YORK

School of Engineering and Applied Sciences

School of Engineering and Applied Sciences
University at Buffalo *The State University of New York*

 For more information, visit http://petersons.to/buffaloengineering

Programs of Study

The University at Buffalo (SUNY) offers degrees in all major fields of engineering through the School of Engineering and Applied Sciences. Students may pursue master's and doctoral degrees in the departments of biomedical engineering; chemical and biological engineering; civil, structural, and environmental engineering; computer science and engineering; electrical engineering; industrial and systems engineering; and mechanical and aerospace engineering. In the top 15 percent of the nation's 300 engineering schools, the School of Engineering and Applied Sciences offers a wide variety of excellent instruction, research opportunities, resources, and facilities to its students.

Research Facilities

Center for Biomedical Engineering (CBE): The Center for Biomedical Engineering conducts research in biomedical engineering, sponsors a seminar series, and publishes brochures and reports on biomedical engineering. It also serves as a resource for students seeking information about biomedical engineering programs, for companies seeking to hire engineers or become involved in collaborative projects, and for other outside agencies.

Center of Excellence for Document Analysis and Recognition (CEDAR): Research at CEDAR focuses on the theory and applications of pattern recognition, machine learning, and information retrieval. Over the years, the applications explored have included document analysis and recognition, object recognition in images in three-dimensional scenes, forensic document examination, textual information retrieval, biometrics, and bioinformatics.

Center for Excellence in Global Enterprise Management (GEM): The Center for Excellence in Global Enterprise Management was established in 1998 to deliver leading edge research driven by industrial need with results that have immediate practical impact.

Center of Hybrid Nanodevices and Systems (CoHNS): The mission of the Center on Hybrid Nanodevices and Systems (CoHNS) is to integrate device concepts and systems principles in the design, development and implementation of new nano/micro/macro hybrid and complex systems with engineering solutions for domain-specific applications. Bringing together complex engineering multiscale systems and information technologies, CoHNS promotes new directions in the UB research and generates original engineering values and design technologies. Finally, CoHNS optimizes and integrates distributed systems within the broader environment of society and nature.

Center for Unified Biometrics (CUBS): CUBS is focused on advancing the fundamental science of biometrics and providing key enabling technologies to build engineered systems. For the very first time anywhere, UB researchers are taking a unified view of biometric technologies by integrating software algorithms for accurate identification of various biometrics and data analysis (informatics) with hardware acquisition devices.

Center of Excellence in Information Systems Assurance Research and Education (CEISARE): The goals of CEISARE are graduate education and coordinated research in computer security and information assurance by faculty members from several schools and departments at the University at Buffalo.

Center for Integrated Waste Management (CIWM): Founded in 1987 as the New York State Center for Hazardous Waste Management, the Center was established by New York State legislation to initiate and coordinate research and technology development in the areas of toxic substances and hazardous wastes.

Center for Multisource Information Fusion (CMIF): CMIF serves as one focal point for the conduct of research and development in information fusion, and serves as an incubation center for small businesses, professorial, and individual entrepreneurial activities.

Energy Systems Institute (ESI): The research focus of the ESI is the development of mechanisms to predict failure in electronic systems.

Great Lakes Program (GLP): The mission of the Great Lakes Program is to develop, evaluate, and synthesize scientific and technical knowledge on the Great Lakes ecosystem in support of public education and policy formation.

Multidisciplinary Center for Earthquake Engineering to Extreme Events (MCEER): MCEER's overall goal is to enhance the seismic resiliency of communities through improved engineering and management tools for critical infrastructure systems (water supply, electric power, hospitals, transportation systems).

New York State Center for Engineering Design and Industrial Innovation (NYSCEDII): NYSCEDII's mission is to provide state-of-the-art technologies and expertise that will enable New York State industry to achieve a greater degree of competitiveness.

Research Institute for Safety and Security in Transportation (RISST): RISST, established jointly by the University at Buffalo and the Transportation Security Administration (TSA), is a resource to the aviation community for improving human factors aspects of security and maintenance system performance.

The Center for Industrial Effectiveness (TCIE): The Center for Industrial Effectiveness (TCIE) forges a link between the University at Buffalo's technical resources and the business community. TCIE fosters partnerships and manages diverse projects.

Financial Aid

For highly qualified applicants, a variety of research appointments are available, as are University-supported assistantships and fellowships. Tuition scholarships are also available. Summer support is available for most research appointments. Work done as a research assistant is generally applicable to the student's thesis or dissertation.

Cost of Study

Tuition and fees for in-state residents total $12,985 per academic year for full-time study. Out-of-state tuition and fees total $24,325 per academic year. Detailed cost of attendance data is available at: http://financialaid.buffalo.edu/costs/gradcost.php.

Living and Housing Costs

The University at Buffalo offers students residence hall accommodations as well as apartments at several complexes surrounding the campus. Housing costs vary, depending upon location.

Student Group

More than 1,800 graduate students are enrolled in degree programs through the School of Engineering and Applied Sciences. Approximately 525 students are enrolled in doctoral programs, while the remaining students are enrolled as master's degree candidates.

Location

The city of Buffalo, New York, is located on the banks of Lake Erie, within an hour's drive of Lake Ontario and just minutes from the majestic scenery of Niagara Falls. It is within easy driving distance of Toronto and lies directly in the middle of the Northeastern trade corridor that runs from Chicago to Boston. With more than 9 million residents, it is the third-largest trade market in North America and is home to several professional sports franchises, museums, art galleries, and numerous areas for outdoor recreation throughout the year.

The University and The School

The School of Engineering and Applied Sciences is part of the State University of New York (SUNY) at Buffalo, the largest comprehensive public university in the state of New York, and is located on the North Campus in Amherst, New York.

Applying

To apply, interested students should visit their department of interest at http://www.eng.buffalo.edu/academics/depts/. The deadline for application materials varies by each department. The academic year begins in August. Applicants must hold a bachelor's degree in a science or engineering-related field. All international applicants must be able to document their ability to meet all educational and living expenses for their entire length of study.

Additional admissions information may be obtained via e-mail: seasgrad@buffalo.edu.

Correspondence and Information

University at Buffalo (SUNY)
School of Engineering and Applied Sciences
412 Bonner Hall
Buffalo, New York 14260-1900
Phone: 716-645-0956
E-mail: seasgrad@buffalo.edu
Website: http://www.eng.buffalo.edu

University at Buffalo, The State University of New York

FACULTY HEADS AND AREAS OF RESEARCH

Biomedical Engineering
Dr. Debanjan Sarkar, Director of Graduate Study.

The Department of Biomedical Engineering combines expertise from the School of Engineering and the School of Medicine and Biomedical Sciences to engage in cutting-edge research for improvement of overall quality of life. Examples of research include photoacoustic imaging, nanomedicine, regenerative therapeutics, orthopedic prostheses, sensors, and imaging. Funding for this research comes from federal agencies such as the National Science Foundation, the National Institutes of Health, and the Department of Defense as well as from industry. (Website: http://www.bme.buffalo.edu)

Chemical and Biological Engineering
Dr. Paschalis Alexandridis, Director of Graduate Study.

The Department of Chemical and Biological Engineering has attained international recognition for its excellence in research and teaching. Cutting-edge research projects span the areas of advanced materials and nanotechnology; molecular and multiscale modeling and simulation; and biochemical, biomolecular, and biomedical engineering. These projects are supported by federal agencies such as the National Science Foundation and the National Institutes of Health, and by industry. (Website: http://www.cbe.buffalo.edu)

Civil, Structural, and Environmental Engineering
Dr. Joseph Atkinson, Director of Graduate Study.

Current research in the Department of Civil, Structural, and Environmental Engineering focuses on five key areas including computational mechanics; environmental and hydrosystems engineering (biological process analysis, bioremediation, drinking water, ecosystem restoration, groundwater, toxic substances fate, volatile organics, and wastewater treatment); geomechanics and geotechnical engineering (soil dynamics); structural and earthquake engineering (active and passive control of structures, blast-resistant design, bridge engineering, fiber-reinforced polymeric structures, nuclear structures, nonstructural systems, and steel and reinforced concrete structures); and transportation systems engineering (artificial intelligence applications, dynamic network modeling and control, freight modeling, integrated transportation and land-use modeling, intelligent transportation systems, traffic simulation, and traveler behavior modeling). The department is home to the Multidisciplinary Center for Earthquake Engineering Research (MCEER), the Great Lakes Program, and the Structural Engineering and Earthquake Simulation Laboratory, among others. (Website: http://www.csee.buffalo.edu/)

Computer Science and Engineering
Dr. Hung Ngo, Director of Graduate Study.

The Department of Computer Science and Engineering conducts research in algorithms and theory of computing, augmentative technology for the handicapped, bioinformatics and computational biology, biometrics, computational linguistics and cognitive science, computer networks and distributed systems, computer science education, computer security and information assurance, computer vision, cyberinfrastructure and computational science, databases, data fusion, data mining, data-intensive computing, embedded systems and computer architecture, high-performance computing, grid and cloud computing, information visualization, knowledge representation and reasoning, medical image processing and applications, multimedia databases and information retrieval, pattern recognition and machine learning, pervasive computing, programming languages and software systems, VLSI circuits and systems, and wireless and sensor networks. (Website: http://www.cse.buffalo.edu/)

Electrical Engineering
Dr. Leslie Ying, Director of Graduate Study.

The Department of Electrical Engineering conducts research in the following areas:

• signal processing, communications, and networking (adaptive signal processing, detection and estimation, coding and sequences, radar systems, communication theory and systems, secure communications, multimedia systems and video communications, digital data hiding, MIMO communications, cooperative communications, wireless networks, cognitive cross-layer networking, underwater communications, and networks);

• electronics, optics, and photonics (bio-MEMS, computational and applied magnetics, computational electromagnetics/photonics, computational fluid dynamics, electromagnetic compatibility, MEMS, metamaterials, microfluidics, micromachined microwave systems, MIR and THz devices, molecular beam epitaxy, nanotechnology, optoelectronics, photonics, photovoltaics, plasmonics, superconductivity, and TFTs); and

• energy systems (batteries, clean and renewable energy, electrochemical power, energy distribution and generation, energy storage, power electronics, power packaging, plasma processing, and smart grid power systems). (Website: http://www.ee.buffalo.edu)

Industrial and Systems Engineering
Dr. Li Lin, Director of Graduate Study.

The Department of Industrial and Systems Engineering offers three areas of specialization for the Ph.D.: human factors (applications of engineering, psychology, computer science, and physical ergonomics to the modeling, analysis, and design of various environments and other systems), operations research (applies math and engineering principles to formulate models and solve problems in long range planning, energy and urban systems, and manufacturing), and production systems (focuses on production planning and scheduling, computer-integrated manufacturing, quality assurance, and related topics). In addition to the three areas of specialization mentioned above, there are two other programs (for a total of five) at the master's level: service systems engineering (applies industrial engineering principles to the growing service sector) and engineering management (focuses on leadership practices for a variety of engineering areas). (Website: http://www.ise.buffalo.edu/index.shtml)

Mechanical and Aerospace Engineering
Dr. Puneet Singla, Director of Graduate Study.

Faculty members and students in the Department of Mechanical and Aerospace Engineering are involved in a wide range of research activities in the fluid and thermal sciences, dynamic systems and control, design, materials engineering, biomedical engineering, and applied mechanics. Faculty interests include computer and mathematical modeling as well as laboratory and experimental efforts in both basic and applied research. (Website: http://www.mae.buffalo.edu/)

THE UNIVERSITY OF IOWA

College of Engineering

★ For more information, visit http://petersons.to/iowaengineering

THE UNIVERSITY OF IOWA
College of Engineering

Programs of Study

The College of Engineering (http://www.engineering.uiowa.edu) at the University of Iowa (http://www.uiowa.edu) offers M.S. and Ph.D. programs in biomedical engineering, chemical and biochemical engineering, civil and environmental engineering, electrical and computer engineering, industrial engineering, and mechanical engineering. The College excels nationally and internationally in several specialty and interdisciplinary research areas, including computer-aided design and simulation, human factors, environmental health solutions, biotechnology, bioinformatics, medical imaging, photopolymerization, hydraulics and water/air resources, and nanotechnology. Master's candidates must maintain at least a 3.0 grade point average and may choose either a thesis or nonthesis program. Students must also successfully complete a minimum of 30 semester hours, 24 of which must be taken at the University of Iowa. Doctoral candidates must complete three years beyond the bachelor's degree, with a minimum of 72 semester hours. One academic year must be in residence. Research tools may be required as specified by the individual program. Those interested should contact the specific department for additional requirements. Graduate students often do interdisciplinary research work in a variety of programs and facilities noted in this description.

Research Facilities

The College of Engineering has twenty research locations in eastern Iowa, covering its six academic programs, four research centers reporting to the College, and interdisciplinary research efforts. IIHR–Hydroscience & Engineering (http://www.iihr.uiowa.edu) is unique for its state-of-the-art in-house capabilities in both computational simulations and laboratory modeling and for field observational research. IIHR pioneers high-speed computational analysis and simulation of complex flow phenomena while maintaining exceptional experimental laboratory capabilities and facilities. Observational facilities include a Mississippi River environmental research station (http://www.iihr.uiowa.edu/lacmrers) and a wide range of remote sensing equipment. Experimental facilities include hydraulic flumes, a hydraulic wave basin, air- and water-flow units, sediment labs, and advanced instruments for laboratory and field measurements. Engineers in IIHR's mechanical and electronic shops provide in-house expertise for construction of models and instruments. Active academic and research programs at IIHR are supported by a diverse set of computing resources and facilities. For high-performance computing (HPC) IIHR operates two parallel, distributed-memory computer clusters (Helium, Neon) comprised of more than 6,300 Intel Xeon cores, 45 TB memory, and 3 PB of scratch space running Linux, MPI, OpenMP, and the Intel and GNU compiler and tool suites. The computing nodes feature an InfiniBand quad data rate (fully unblocked at DDR) interconnect for high-speed, low-latency message passing. Three log-in nodes provide access to the cluster for compiling and launching jobs.

The Center for Computer-Aided Design (http://www.ccad.uiowa.edu) is housed in the Engineering Research Facility and in two buildings located off site, at the Iowa City Regional Airport and the University of Iowa Research Park. The Engineering Research Facility has 7,500 square feet of office space for staff researchers, student assistants, and program administration. Eight on-site laboratories house research facilities for two state-of-the-art motion capture research laboratories, one of which includes a 6-DOF shaker table motion platform, a fully immersive virtual reality environment, robotic systems, materials testing fixtures, and equipment for individual student research in various engineering disciplines. The off-site facility at the Iowa City Regional Airport that includes three flight simulation capabilities (a high-performance, functional Boeing 737-800 mockup for high-workload simulation and analysis as well as functional Boeing 777 and F-15 mock-ups). CCAD's Iowa City airport facility also houses six dedicated research aircraft, including a single-engine Beechcraft A-36 Bonanza aircraft, outfitted to create the CCAD Computerized Airborne Research Platform (CARP) in support of airborne human factors research for advanced flight deck technology; two single-engine tandem seat L-29 jet trainer aircraft, to provide flight testing for additional avionics systems research programs; two Czechoslovakian L-29s; and an MI-2 helicopter. The Iowa City Airport facility also houses a fully instrumented automotive test platform and a recently acquired HMMWV vehicle platform supporting cognitive assessment testing related to ground vehicle human-machine interaction and operation activities at the Operator Performance Laboratory. The center's computer infrastructure incorporates high-performance workstations, servers, and PC network in support of intensive computation, geometric modeling and analysis, software development, and visualization and simulation. The National Advanced Driving Simulator (NADS) is located at the University of Iowa Research Park (http://enterprise.uiowa.edu/researchpark). The advent of automated vehicle and connected vehicle technologies is set to globally change the face of transportation in the coming years. The NADS is a self-sustained transportation safety research center that provides research and development services to the private and public sectors (http://www.nads-sc.uiowa.edu/). Services include running research studies on a world-class suite of driving simulators and on-road vehicles. NADS also sells driving simulators and provides expertise to support other universities, companies, and research labs around the world. NADS employs 18 students and 21 full-time staff members whose expertise include automated vehicles, effects of drugs/drowsiness/distraction on driving, connected vehicle technologies, human factors, vehicle safety systems, data collection technologies, and simulation science. Development and research conducted at the NADS saves lives, improves quality of life for motorists, and improves the efficiency and productivity of the automotive and supporting industries.

Other engineering research-related facilities include the Engineering Research Facility; Iowa Advanced Technology Laboratories; Iowa Injury Prevention Research Center (http://www.public-health.uiowa.edu/IPRC); University of Iowa Hospitals and Clinics (http://www.uihealthcare.com/uihospitalsandclinics/index.html); National Advanced Driving Simulator (http://www.nads-sc.uiowa.edu); Center for Biocatalysis and Bioprocessing (http:/www.uiowa.edu/~biocat); and the chemistry building, which supports laboratories devoted to such areas as biomechanics, biotechnology, molecular and computational biology, bioinformatics, environmental contamination, and remote sensing.

Engineering Computer Services (http://www.engineering.uiowa.edu/ecs) provides the curricular and research computing needs of the College through state-of-the-art hardware, the same commercial software used by engineers in the industry, and a dedicated professional support staff. All engineering students receive computer accounts and maintain those accounts throughout their college careers. Full Internet and Web access complement local educational resources, which include enhanced classroom instruction, online classes, engineering design and simulation packages, programming languages, and productivity software. There are 32 physical Linux and 220 physical Windows workstations located in five drop-in labs as well as over 400 virtual computers available to students remotely, supported by more than $10 million worth of professional software dedicated for student use 24 hours a day.

The H. William Lichtenberger Engineering Library provides Internet access to indexes and abstracts, more than 125,000 volumes, ANSI standards, and electronic access to thousands of engineering and science journals.

Financial Aid

Financial aid is available to graduate students in the form of research and teaching assistantships as well as fellowships from federal agencies and industry. Support includes a competitive stipend reduction in tuition and partial payment of tuition. Specific information is available from individual departments.

Cost of Study

The estimated annual tuition and fee expenses based on 2015–16 for U.S. citizen and permanent resident graduate engineering students enrolled for 9 or more semester hours in the fall and spring semesters (academic year) is $10,094 for Iowa residents and $27,272 for nonresidents. This includes fees for technology, arts and cultural events, student activity, student services, student union, building, recreation, professional enhancement, and health. For international students with 1/4-time or greater graduate assistantships, the estimated annual tuition is $8,396 plus fees. For international students without assistantships, the estimated annual tuition is $25,574 plus fees. Book fees for graduate students are estimated at $1,240. The latest information on engineering cost of study can be found at http://grad.admissions.uiowa.edu/engineering-estimated-costs.

Living and Housing Costs

Housing is available in apartments or private homes within walking distance of the campus. Estimated costs for living and housing can be found online at http://grad.admissions.uiowa.edu/engineering-estimated-costs.

Student Group

Total enrollment at the University for fall 2014 was 31,387 students. Students come from all fifty states, two U.S. possessions, and 114 other countries. Engineering enrollment for fall 2014 was 2,120 undergraduate students and 302 graduate students.

Student Outcomes

Nearly half of the graduates accept positions in Iowa and Illinois, though companies and academic institutions from across the country present offers. Recent graduates have taken positions with companies such as 3M, Accenture, Cargill, Caterpillar, Deere & Company, General Mills, Hewlett-Packard, HNI, Monsanto, Motorola, Pella, and Rockwell Collins.

Location

The University is located in Iowa City, known as the "Athens of the Midwest" because of the many cultural, intellectual, and diverse opportunities available. The Iowa City metropolitan area is a community of 152,586 people, approximately 25 miles from Cedar Rapids, Iowa's second-largest city, with nearly 255,452 people.

The University

The University of Iowa, established in 1847, comprises eleven colleges. The University was the first state university to admit women on an equal basis with men. The University founded the first law school west of the Mississippi River, established one of the first university-based medical centers in the Midwest, and was the first state university in the nation to establish an interfaith school of religion. It was an innovator in accepting creative work—fine art, musical compositions, poetry, drama, and fiction—for academic credit. The University established Iowa City as a national college-prospect testing center. It was a leader in the development of actuarial science as an essential tool of business administration. As a pioneering participant in space exploration, it has become a center for education and research in astrophysical science.

Applying

The application fee is $60 ($100 for international students). Admission requirements differ in each department; students should contact the department in which they are interested for additional requirements.

Correspondence and Information

Admissions
107 Calvin Hall
The University of Iowa
Iowa City, Iowa 52242
Website: http://www.grad.uiowa.edu/ (Graduate College)
http://www.engineering.uiowa.edu/research (College of Engineering)
http://www.engineering.uiowa.edu/graduate-studies (College of Engineering)

The University of Iowa

DEPARTMENTS, CHAIRS, AND AREAS OF FACULTY RESEARCH

STUDIES BY ENGINEERING DISCIPLINE

Biomedical Engineering (http://www.engineering.uiowa.edu/bme).

Joseph M. Reinhardt, Departmental Executive Officer. Biomechanics of the spine, low back pain and scoliosis, upper-extremity biomechanics, articular joint contact mechanics, total joint replacement, computational simulation of artificial heart valve dynamics, hemodynamics of arterial disease, mechanical properties of diseased arteries, biomechanics and rupture predication of abdominal aorta aneurysms, mechanobiology, control and coordination of the cardiovascular and respiratory systems, controlled drug delivery, medical image acquisition, processing and quantitative analysis, models of cellular processes based on nonequilibrium thermodynamics, tissue-engineered vascular grafts, bioinformatics and computational biology, drug/target discovery, gene therapy, development of genomic resources.

Chemical and Biochemical Engineering (http://www.cbe.engineering.uiowa.edu). Allan Guymon, Departmental Executive Officer. Air pollution engineering, atmospheric aerosol particles, atmospheric chemistry, biocatalysis, biochemical engineering, biofilms, biofuels, biomaterials, biotechnological applications of extremophiles, controlled release, drug delivery, engineering education, fermentation, high-speed computing, insect and mammalian cell culture, medical aerosols, microlithography, nanotechnology, oxidative stress in cell culture, photopolymerization, polymer reaction engineering, polymer science, polymer/liquid crystal composites, process scale protein purification, protein crystallography, reversible emulsifiers, spectroscopy, supercritical fluids, surface science, vaccines, virus infection, chemicals from biomass, green chemistry, and sustainable energy.

Civil and Environmental Engineering (http://www.cee.engineering.uiowa.edu). Michelle M. Scherer, Departmental Executive Officer. Water sustainability, water quality, flood prediction and mitigation, hydroclimatology, river networks, environmental remediation, air pollution, drinking water quality, bioremediation, biogeochemistry, computational solid mechanics, digital human modeling, design of hydraulics structures, design simulation, hydropower, optimal control of nonlinear systems, optimal design of nonlinear structures, diverse aspects of water resources engineering, rainfall and flood forecasting, wind energy, transportation-infrastructure modeling, highway pavements, winter highway maintenance.

Electrical and Computer Engineering (http://www.ece.engineering.uiowa.edu). Er-wei Bai, Departmental Executive Officer. Big data analytics, sustainable energy, quantitative medical image processing, Imaging processing and Inverse problems, communication systems and computer networks, sensors and sensor networks, wireless communication, controls, compressive sensing and optimization, information and coding theory, signal processing, networks, parallel and distributed computing systems, large-scale intelligent systems, database management systems, bioinformatics, large scale-heterogeneous-multi-site data collections using modern HPC resources, photonics, algorithm design-analysis-implementation, software engineering, design and testing of very-large-scale integrated circuits, nanotechnology, materials, and devices.

Industrial Engineering (http://www.mie.engineering.uiowa.edu/IEProgram/IEMain.php). Ching-Long Lin, Departmental Executive Officer. Computational intelligence, data analytics, informatics, reliability and quality control, health-care systems, human factors and ergonomics, human-computer interfaces, digital human modeling, engineering design and manufacturing, operations research and applied statistics, renewable energy, engineering management, and financial engineering.

Mechanical Engineering (http://www.mie.engineering.uiowa.edu/MEProgram/MEMain.php). Ching-Long Lin, Departmental Executive Officer. Biomechanics and biofluids, biology-based design, biorenewable and alternative fuels, bioengineering, casting and solidification, cloud computation, combustion, chemically reactive flows, computational mechanics, computer-aided analysis and design, dynamics, fatigue and fracture mechanics, fluid mechanics and ship hydrodynamics, fluid mechanics, human organ modeling, heat transfer, manufacturing, materials processing and behavior, multiscale modeling and simulation, reliability-based design, robotics, composite materials, nanotechnology, renewable energy, structural mechanics, system simulation, thermal systems, vehicle dynamics and simulation, virtual prototyping, and wind energy.

COLLEGE RESEARCH CENTERS, INSTITUTES, AND LABORATORIES

Center for Bioinformatics and Computational Biology (http://genome.uiowa.edu). Thomas L. Casavant, Director. Catalyzes the development of new areas of study and expanded research opportunities in informatics areas related to the basic biological sciences and applied medical research. Founded in 2002 as a joint enterprise spanning the Colleges of Engineering and Medicine and Science, the center involves faculty from seven colleges, and more than twenty-two departments. It serves as a coordinating home for interdisciplinary research, undergraduate, pre-, and post-doctoral training, as well as faculty recruiting and professional development. At the hub of an inherently interdisciplinary field, the goal of the center is to assist in overcoming traditional disciplinary hurdles to collaboration and assist in utilizing state-of-the-art instrumentation and analysis methods needed by twenty-first century biomedical and basic science research. State-of-the-art practice of bioinformatics involves collection, QC, analysis, archive, and searching of molecular and clinical data. The center has extensive data storage and processing capabilities, as well as a wealth of installed and maintained software analysis tools to enable research and experiment execution at the leading edge of modern biomedical research.

Center for Computer-Aided Design (http://www.ccad.uiowa.edu). Karim Abdel-Malek, Director. National Advanced Driving Simulator (highway safety and transportation efficiency, equipment product development effectiveness enhancement via virtual prototyping, vehicle dynamics and simulation, simulator technology and virtual reality environment and human factors); Virtual Soldier Research (musculoskeletal model, whole body vibration, validation, motion capture, intuitive interface, immersive virtual reality, physiology, standard ergonomic assessments, zone differentiation, posture and motion prediction, hand model, spine modeling, gait: walking and running, predictive dynamics, dynamic strength and fatigue, modeling of clothing, human performance, armor and soldier performance); Operator Performance Laboratory (OPL) [flight test, jet aircraft, turbine helicopter, Opt LiDAR, RADAR, Airborne surveillance, aircraft instrumentation, rotorcraft, Unmanned Aircraft Systems (UAS), Ground Control Station (GCS), GPS Denied Operations, Airborne Data Link, Aerial Combat Training Systems, Live Virtual Constructive, Close Air Support, flight simulation, task analysis, warning-system effectiveness, physiological based workload assessment, cognitive modeling]; Advanced Manufacturing Technology (AMTech) next-generation manufacturing technologies, model-based manufacturing, electrical engineering, optimization, electronics, digital human modeling, digital manufacturing, product manufacturing information (PMI) and development of standards, system integration, modeling, and simulation for electromechanical systems. The Musculoskeletal Imaging, Modeling, and EXperimentation (MIMX) Division is a collaborative effort directed at computational modeling of anatomic structures. A primary objective is to automate the development of patient-/ subject- specific models using a combination of imaging and modeling techniques, with an emphasis on finite element modeling. Surgical interventions, namely orthopaedic and neurosurgical, are of particular interest. Reliability and Sensor Prognostic Systems (mesh-free methods for structural analysis and design-sensitivity analysis, composite materials, probabilistic mechanics and reliability, reliability-based design optimization, topology optimization, multidisciplinary design optimization, sensor technologies, sensor-based process monitoring optimization). BioMechanics of Soft Tissues (BioMOST) (Tools for diagnosis and treatment of diseases, modeling of soft tissue structures, biomechanical experimentation, mathematical modeling, computational simulations.

IIHR–Hydroscience and Engineering (http://www.iihr.uiowa.edu). Larry J. Weber, Director. IIHR is one of the world's leading institutes in fundamental and applied fluids-related research. Cutting-edge research activities incorporate computational fluid dynamics with laboratory modeling and field observational studies. Research areas at IIHR include: fluid dynamics (ship hydrodynamics, turbulent flows, biological fluid flow); environmental hydraulics (structures, river and dam hydraulics, fish passage at dams, sediment management, heat dispersal in water bodies, water-quality monitoring); water and air resources (atmospheric boundary layer, hydrology, hydrometeorology, remote sensing); environmental engineering and science (air pollution, water-quality modeling, chemical contamination of aquatic environments, organic contaminant cycling, environmental biotechnology); and water sustainability (actinide chemistry, nanotubes, pollutant fate and transport, water treatment, wastewater nutrient removal, environmental toxicology, human impact on aquatic environments, social vulnerability, catchment science, solute transport and fate). IIHR is also home to the Iowa Flood Center (www.iowafloodcenter.org) and the Iowa Geological Survey. Today IIHR pioneers high-speed computational analysis and simulation of complex flow phenomena while maintaining exceptional experimental laboratory capabilities and facilities. Academic and research programs at IIHR are supported by diverse computing resources and facilities. Observational facilities include a Mississippi River environmental research station (www.iihr.uiowa.edu/lacmrers) and a wide range of remote-sensing equipment. Experimental facilities include flumes, a wave basin, sediment labs, and advanced instruments for laboratory and field measurements. Engineers in IIHR's mechanical and electronic shops provide in-house model construction expertise. In addition, IIHR houses the Water Sustainability Initiative (http://www.iihr.uiowa.edu/research/water-sustainability-initiative/). The University of Iowa has expanded its existing strength in interdisciplinary research on water including its availability, quality, reuse, health impact, and its relationship to a changing climate. Economics, policy, and communications, as well as the natural sciences and engineering, are all engaged to solve the problems of water. The faculty alliance on water sustainability encompasses the Colleges of Liberal Arts and Sciences, Public Health, Engineering, the Graduate College, and the Public Policy Center. Among the various resources already developed to advance the initiative are the Iowa Flood Center and the University of Iowa Office of Sustainability.

Iowa Institute for Biomedical Imaging (http://www.biomed-imaging.uiowa.edu). Milan Sonka, Director. Medical image acquisition (MR, CT, ultrasound, X-ray, OCT, and MR spectroscopy). Knowledge-based analysis of biomedical images from a variety of imaging modalities (e.g., X-ray, CT, MR, OCT, IVUS, and ultrasound). Current focus areas include development of computer-aided and automated techniques for quantitative analysis of human, animal, and cellular image data with applications to translational applications in radiology, radiation oncology, cardiology, pulmonology, ophthalmology, and orthopedics, as well as in clinical and epidemiologic trials. Healthcare big data analytics and medical imaging informatics. Development of novel image acquisition approaches with focus on 7T-3T imaging translation, MR-based pH and T1rho imaging, MR spectroscopy, physiologic X-ray CT, and high-value image acquisition strategies.

INTERDISCIPLINARY RESEARCH CENTERS AND INSTITUTES

Medicine and Bioengineering

The Center for Biocatalysis and Bioprocessing (CBB) (http://www.uiowa.edu/~biocat). Mark Arnold, Director. CBB is a microbial pilot plant facility for production of products ranging from ethanol to proteins. Most of the work is focused on therapeutic protein production. CBB also operates a GMP facility for production of therapeutic proteins for human Phase I trials. In addition, CBB also takes on projects such as enzyme/microbe-based production of chemicals from feedstocks, bioprocessing, new biocatalyst discovery, novel biocatalyst applications for chemicals and fuels, biosensing technology, and gene/protein expression and production. Typically CBB operates 10–14 projects on a biweekly basis for biotechnology companies, including several Iowa-based companies.

Center for International Rural and Environmental Health (http://www.public-health.uiowa.edu/cireh). Laurence Fuortes, MD, Director. Rural and environmental health, with special emphasis on adverse health effects that threaten agricultural and other rural populations; promotes greater understanding and awareness of the causes, consequences, and prevention of communicable, chronic, environmental, and occupational diseases in all regions of the globe, focusing on nations with substantial agrarian economies.

Iowa Injury Prevention Research Center (http://www.public-health.uiowa.edu/IPRC). Corinne Peek-Asa, Director. Established in 1990, the University of Iowa Injury Prevention Center (IPRC) aims to use interdisciplinary research to control and prevent injuries, especially in rural communities. The center's activities constitute a broad multidisciplinary and collaborative program in research, training, and outreach. The IPRC has grown to include 66 researchers from twenty-three departments in five colleges, as well as a wide network of community and government collaborators. Six expert research teams are organized around priority research topics: road traffic safety; interpersonal violence; intervention and translation science; rural acute care; global injury and violence, and sports and recreational injury prevention. Teams promote the growth of research within their topic areas by linking researchers to IPRC core services, mentoring students and junior faculty, and engaging with community partners.

Orthopaedic Biomechanics Laboratory (http://poppy.obrl.uiowa.edu). Thomas D. Brown, Director. Application of advanced innovative computational formulations and novel experimental approaches to clinically-oriented problems across the diverse spectrum of musculoskeletal biomechanical research; total joint replacement (hip, spine, knee, ankle), posttraumatic arthritis, osteonecrosis of the hip, high-energy limb trauma, carpal tunnel syndrome, and articular contact stresses as they relate to joint degeneration.

Environmental and Hydroscience

NSF Center for Environmentally Beneficial Catalysis (http://www.uiowa.edu/~biocat/edu_CEBC.html). Tonya Peeples, University of Iowa faculty representative. A multidisciplinary, multi-university research center. Catalyst design, synthesis, and characterization; biocatalyst preparation and characterization; synthesis of catalyst supports with controlled pore structure; benign media, including carbon dioxide–based solvents and ionic liquids; probing reaction mechanisms with advanced analytical tools; advanced molecular modeling of chemical, physical, and thermodynamic properties involving reactions and media; multiphase reactor design and analysis; economic and environmental impact analysis; computational fluid dynamics.

Center for Global and Regional Environmental Research (http://www.cgrer.uiowa.edu). Gregory R. Carmichael and Jerald L. Schnoor, Co-directors. Multiple aspects of global environmental change, including the regional effects on natural ecosystems, environments, and resources and on human health, culture, and social systems.

Center for Health Effects of Environmental Contamination (http://www.cheec.uiowa.edu). Gene F. Parkin, Director. Conducts and supports research on the identification and measurement of environmental toxins, particularly water contaminants, and possible associations between exposure to environmental contaminants and adverse health effects. Provides environmental database design and development and systems support for environmental health research.

Environmental Health Sciences Research Center (http://www.ehsrc.uiowa.edu). Peter S. Thorne, Director. Agricultural and rural environmental exposures and health effects, agricultural chemical exposures and health effects.

Science and Technology

Iowa Alliance for Wind Innovation and Novel Development (http://www.iawind.org). P. Barry Butler, Principal Investigator. The Iowa Alliance for Wind Innovation and Novel Development (IAWIND) is a partnership with state and local governments, community colleges, Regents Universities, independent Iowa colleges, the private sector, and the federal government. It is designed to serve as a catalyst for the growth of wind energy and to support and to facilitate the research and training needs of wind energy companies.

Nanoscience and Nanotechnology Institute (http://research.uiowa.edu/nniui). Vicki Grassian, Director. Environment and health (air quality, natural environment, workplace environment, human and animal toxicity, environmental health, drug delivery, disease detection, imaging, bioanalytical assays, environmental remediation and decontamination, green chemistry, fuel cells, energy, sustainability, sensors); nanomaterials (quantum theory, understanding condensed-phase matter at the nanoscale, synthesis and characterization of nanomaterials, defense-related applications).

Optical Science and Technology Center (http://www.ostc.uiowa.edu). Michael Flatté, Director. Laser spectroscopy and photochemistry, photonics and optoelectronics, ultrafast laser development, condensed-matter physics, materials growth techniques, device physics/engineering, surface chemistry, chemical sensors, environmental chemistry, polymer science, plasma physics, nonlinear optics.

NSF IUCRC Photopolymerization Center (http://css.engineering.uiowa.edu/~cfap). Allan Guymon, Director. Kinetics and mechanisms of photopolymerizations and their impact on the structure and properties of photopolymerized materials.

Public Policy Center (http://ppc.uiowa.edu). Peter C. Damiano, Director. Transportation, environmental quality, health care, economic growth and development.

UNIVERSITY OF PENNSYLVANIA
School of Engineering and Applied Science

 For more information, visit http://petersons.to/pennengineering

Programs of Study

Penn Engineering's collaborative research and learning environment truly distinguish the School from its peers, as research and education form its dynamic, creative graduate mission. The excitement and discovery of research is open to all students and is the keystone of the School's world-renowned doctoral programs. These programs are augmented by a diverse array of master's degree offerings.

Students work with and learn from faculty mentors within the core disciplinary programs as well as through scholarly interactions involving the School of Medicine, the School of Arts and Sciences, and the Wharton School, to note a few. This environment is further enriched by Penn's many institutes, centers, and laboratories. For more than 100 years, Penn Engineering has been at the forefront of innovation, just like the University's founder was in his day: Benjamin Franklin, America's first scientist and engineer.

The six Doctor of Philosophy (Ph.D.) programs are research-oriented degree programs for students of superior caliber who will make original contributions to theory and practice in their fields of interest. The programs prepare them for a research career in academe, government, or industry. Curricula are purposely designed to develop the intellectual skills essential for the rapidly changing character of research.

Penn Engineering's fifteen master's programs serve a wide range of highly qualified students such as those expanding on their undergraduate training for professional engineering practice, preparing for doctoral studies, or working toward greater expertise to advance their careers. The School's constantly evolving curricula are grounded in up-to-the-minute research findings and industrial priorities that focus on practical applications of knowledge and responses to career and professional interests, as well as to the needs of today's high-tech society and economy.

Research Facilities

Shared research laboratories and facilities are an integral part of research and education at Penn Engineering. The School's collection of labs and facilities share a physical connectivity that enables collaborations with faculty, students, and postdoctoral scholars across Penn. It includes interdisciplinary research centers and institutes, such as the Singh Center for Nanotechnology, GRASP Lab, Nano/Bio Interface Center (NBIC), SIG Center for Computer Graphics, and PRECISE Lab (http://www.seasupenn.edu/research/centers-institutes.php).

Cost of Study

The cost for four courses in the academic year 2015–16 is $38,344. This includes tuition and general and technology fees. Students are charged per course unit registered for. Additional information can be found at http://www.seas.upenn.edu/prospective-students/graduate/admissions/pay.php.

Living and Housing Costs

On-campus housing is available for both single and married students. There are also numerous privately-owned apartments for rent in the immediate area. More information can be found on the Graduate Housing website at http://cms.business-services.upenn.edu/residential-services/applications-a-assignments/graduate-students.html.

Student Population

There are approximately 21,000 students at the University, around 11,000 of whom are enrolled in graduate and professional schools. Of these, approximately 1,400 are in graduate engineering programs.

Location

The University of Pennsylvania is located in West Philadelphia, just a few blocks from the heart of the city. Philadelphia is a twenty-first-century city with seventeenth-century origins, a patchwork of distinctive neighborhoods ranging from Society Hill to Chinatown. Renowned museums, concert halls, theaters, and sports arenas provide cultural and recreational outlets for students. Fairmount Park, the largest urban park network in the country, extends through large sections of Philadelphia. Not far away are the Jersey shore to the east, Pennsylvania Dutch country to the west, and the Pocono Mountains to the north. The city is also less than a 3-hour drive from New York City and Washington D.C.

The School

The School of Engineering and Applied Science has a distinguished reputation for the quality of its programs. The School's alumni have achieved international distinction in research, higher education, management, entrepreneurship and industrial development, and government service.

Research is led by faculty members at the forefront of modern technology and makes major contributions in a wide variety of fields.

The University of Pennsylvania was founded in 1740 by Benjamin Franklin. A member of the Ivy League and one of the world's leading universities, Penn is renowned for its graduate schools, faculty, research centers, and institutes. Conveniently situated on a compact and attractive campus, Penn offers an abundance of multidisciplinary educational programs with exceptional opportunities for individually tailored graduate education.

Applying

Candidates may apply directly to the School of Engineering through an online application system. Applicants should visit the admissions website for detailed application requirements and access to the online application system. Ph.D. applications for fall admission must be received by December 15 or January 2 (depending on the program). Master's applications must be received by November 15 or March 15. Admission is based on the student's academic record, research, test scores, and letters of recommendation. Scores on the Graduate Record Examinations (GRE) are required. All students whose native language is not English must arrange to take either the Test of English as a Foreign Language (TOEFL) or International English Language Testing System (IELTS) test prior to the application process. The admissions website can be found at http://www.seas.upenn.edu/prospective-students/graduate/admissions.php.

Correspondence and Information

Graduate Admissions
School of Engineering and Applied Science
111 Towne Building
University of Pennsylvania
220 South 33rd Street
Philadelphia, Pennsylvania 19104-6391
Phone: 215-898-4542
E-mail: gradstudies@seas.upenn.edu
Website: http://www.seas.upenn.edu/grad
PennEngGradAdm (Twitter)

AREAS OF RESEARCH

Bioengineering: The Bioengineering master's program has an inter-disciplinary focus on scientific and engineering fundamentals, specifically new developments in bioengineering. The bioengineering Ph.D. program is designed to train individuals for academic, government, or industrial research careers. Research interests for these programs include: tissue engineering, cellular engineering, molecular engineering, theoretical and computational bioengineering, biomaterials, cardiovascular and pulmonary bioengineering, cardiovascular cell and tissue mechanics, cell mechanics, cellular and molecular imaging, medical imaging and imagining instrumentation, imaging theory and analysis, computational neuroscience and engineering, experimental neuroscience and engineering, drug and gene delivery, injury biomechanics, and orthopaedic biomechanics (http://www.be.seas.upenn.edu/).

Biotechnology: The Master of Biotechnology (M.B.) program prepares students for leadership in the critically important and dynamic industries of biotechnology and pharmaceuticals. Strongly interdisciplinary, this program draws its faculty and courses from the Schools of Engineering, Arts and Sciences, and Medicine. Research interests are: molecular biology, biopharmaceutical/engineering biotechnology, and biomedical technologies (http://www.upenn.edu/biotech/).

Chemical and Biomolecular Engineering: The Master of Science in Engineering program in Chemical and Biomolecular Engineering (CBE) provides students with the firm theoretical foundation and interdisciplinary skills that are essential in the rapidly-changing field of chemical and biomolecular engineering. The Ph.D. CBE program is a research-oriented degree for students showing exceptional promise for original contributions to the theory and practice of chemical and biomolecular engineering. Research interests are: biochemical and biomolecular engineering, catalysis and reaction engineering, polymer science and engineering, process design and control, thermodynamics and statistical mechanics, and transport phenomena (http://www.cbe.seas.upenn.edu).

Computer Graphics and Game Technology: The master's program in Computer Graphics and Game Technology is nationally recognized for preparing students for leadership careers as designers, technical animators, directors, and game programmers. Students receive first-hand experience in the latest graphics and animation technologies, interactive media design principles, product development methodologies, and entrepreneurship. Courses utilize Penn's Center for Human Modeling and Simulation,

University of Pennsylvania

internationally recognized for cutting-edge research in 3-D computer graphics, human simulation, and the behavioral animation of embodied intelligent agents (http://www.cis.upenn.edu/grad/cggt/cggt-overview.shtml).

Computer and Information Science: The M.S.E. program in Computer and Information Science (CIS) is one of the nation's top programs, preparing students to be innovators, leaders, and visionaries. M.S.E. students develop their own advanced study focus and arrange interdisciplinary programs such as CIS and telecommunications, CIS and computational linguistics, CIS and biomedical computation. The Ph.D. CIS program is designed for candidates with strong training in disciplines related to modern information processing, with an emphasis on computer science and mathematics. The curriculum is intended to develop intellectual skills essential for the rapidly changing character of research and to meet the demands of academe and industry. Research interests include: architecture and compilers, artificial intelligence, bioinformatics and computational biology, computational linguistics, databases and data management, embedded and real-time systems, formal methods and software engineering, graphics, machine learning, networks and distributed systems, programming languages, robotics, security and information assurance, theory, and vision. There are also interdisciplinary collaborations with fields such as biology, genetics, linguistics, mathematics, and electrical engineering (http://www.cis.upenn.edu/grad/).

Computer and Information Technology: The master's program in Computer and Information Technology (MCIT) is specifically designed for students and professionals with minimal or no prior computing experience or formal training in computer science. This program gives students the expertise needed to understand and succeed in today's highly innovative and competitive workplace. It benefits students and industry professionals who want to begin or advance a career in information technology or prepare for doctoral studies in computer science (http://www.cis.upenn.edu/grad/mcit/).

Electrical and Systems Engineering: The graduate group in electrical and systems engineering offers a Ph.D. in Electrical and Systems Engineering (ESE), an M.S.E. in Electrical Engineering (EE), and an M.S.E. in Systems Engineering (SE). The EE program enables students to tailor their own interests and goals, from electromagnetics and photonics, sensors and MEMS, to VLSI and nanotechnology. It gives students the theoretical foundation and interdisciplinary skills needed to deal with the new ideas and new applications that are the hallmarks of modern electroscience. The SE program, grounded in the intersection of electrical and systems engineering, gives students in-depth theoretical foundation and interdisciplinary skills required by the growing complexity of technological systems. In addition, students are also able to complete a Certificate in Engineering Entrepreneurship, where they take cross degree courses at Wharton, including leadership and Fundamentals of High-Tech Ventures.

The Ph.D. program focuses on the development of research skills to prepare the student for scholarship in their field of interest. These research themes are: circuits and computer engineering, nanodevices and nanosystems, and information and decision systems (http://www.ese.upenn.edu/about-ese/index.php).

Embedded Systems: The Master of Science in Engineering in Embedded Systems (EMBS) is an innovative degree program offered jointly by the departments of Computer and Information Science and Electrical and Systems Engineering and is integrated with the PRECISE Center for Research in Embedded Systems. The program is best for students with either computer science or electrical engineering academic backgrounds who wish to pursue industrial jobs within automotive, aerospace, defense, and consumer electronics, as well as for practicing engineers in the embedded systems industry who want to gain knowledge of state-of-the-art tools and theories. Research interests are: embedded controls, real-time operating systems, model-based design and verification, and implementation of embedded systems (http://www.cis.upenn.edu/grad/embedded.shtml).

Integrated Product Design: Two integrated product design degree programs are offered: the Master of Integrated Product Design (M:IPD) and the Master of Engineering in Integrated Product Design (M.S.E. in IPD). The M:IPD is intended for students with a non-engineering background or students with an engineering background who wish to build their skills in other disciplines. Students gain an interdisciplinary perspective of product design, building skills in conceptualization, ideation, manufacturing, marketing, and business planning. The M.S.E. in IPD is intended for students who have an undergraduate degree in engineering. The degree emphasizes technology and manufacturing processes, including coursework in advanced CAD/CAM and mechatronics (http://ipd.me.upenn.edu).

Materials Science and Engineering: The master's and doctoral programs in Materials Science and Engineering prepare students to be leaders, innovators, and visionaries in the materials revolution. Students have access to a broad range of state-of-the-art instrumentation in the department and the Laboratory for Research on the Structure of Matter (LRSM). Research interests include: biomaterials, carbon nanotube materials, ceramics, chemistry of materials, electron microscopy, electronic and optical properties, energy, materials theory and modeling, mechanical behavior, metals, nanostructured materials, polymers, scanning probe microscopies, semiconductors, surfaces and interfaces, X-ray and neutron scattering (http://www.mse.seas.upenn.edu/).

Mechanical Engineering and Applied Mechanics: The master's in Mechanical Engineering and Applied Mechanics (MEAM) is nationally recognized for its excellence. Research interests are: design and manufacturing, micro/nano systems, mechatronic and robotic systems, heat transfer, and fluid mechanics with applications in energy production, and mechanics of materials. The MEAM Ph.D. is an interdisciplinary, hands-on, research-focused program that collaborates with material sciences, computer sciences, electrical and systems engineering, chemical and biomolecular engineering, and the School of Medicine. Research interests are: biorobotics, thermal sciences, fluid mechanics, design and manufacturing, mechanics of materials, mechanics of biomaterials, computational mechanics, micro and nano mechanics, micro and nano systems, energy conversion, and robotics (http://www.me.upenn.edu).

Nanotechnology: The master's degree in Nanotechnology prepares students for leadership roles in emerging high-tech industries as well as traditional industries that utilize nanoscale phenomena. Nanotechnology is a highly interdisciplinary field and students are able to take courses from the Schools of Engineering, Arts and Sciences, and Wharton. Technical courses are organized into three research interests: synthesis, materials, and nanofabrication; devices and fundamental properties; and biotechnology (http://www.masters.nano.upenn.edu/).

Robotics: The master's program in Robotics is a unique program administered by Penn's General Robotics, Automation, Sensing and Perception (GRASP) Laboratory, recognized as one of the nation's premier research centers. Multidisciplinary in scope, it provides an ideal foundation for what today's experts in robotics and intelligent systems need to know. Research interests are: artificial intelligence, computer vision, control systems, dynamics and machine learning, design, programming, and prototyping of robotic systems (https://www.grasp.upenn.edu/education/masters).

Scientific Computing: The master's program in Scientific Computing will debut in 2015. It encompasses multifaceted graduate training in the fundamentals and applications of computational science and data analytics. The program provides a rigorous computational foundation for applications to a broad range of scientific disciplines, combining a comprehensive set of core courses centered on numerical methods, algorithm development for high-performance computational platforms, and the analysis of large data. In addition, it offers flexibility to specialize in different computational science application areas. Students may elect to pursue a thesis in computationally oriented research within the School of Engineering and Applied Science (http://www.seas.upenn.edu/prospective-students/graduate/programs/masters/).

Smith Walk in the Penn Engineering Quad.

Dr. George J. Pappas, Joseph Moore Professor and Chair of the Department of Electrical and Systems Engineering, with students.

YALE UNIVERSITY
School of Engineering & Applied Science

Programs of Study

All research and instructional programs in engineering and applied science are coordinated by the School of Engineering & Applied Science (SEAS), which consists of the Departments of Biomedical Engineering, Chemical & Environmental Engineering, Computer Science, Electrical Engineering, and Mechanical Engineering & Materials Science. These five units have autonomous faculty appointments and instructional programs, and students may obtain degrees designated according to different disciplines. A Director of Graduate Studies in each department oversees all graduate student matters. Students have considerable freedom in selecting programs to suit their interests and may choose programs of study that draw upon the resources of departments that are not within the School of Engineering & Applied Science, including the Departments of Applied Physics, Physics, Chemistry, Mathematics, Statistics, Astronomy, Geology and Geophysics, and Molecular Biophysics and Biochemistry, and departments of the School of Medicine and the School of Management.

In most departments within SEAS, the student plans his or her course of study in consultation with faculty advisers (the student's advisory committee). A minimum of ten term courses is required and they must be completed in the first two years. Mastery of the topics is expected, and the core courses, as identified by each department/program, should be taken in the first year. No more than two courses should be Special Investigations, and at least two should be outside the area of the dissertation. Periodically, the faculty reviews the overall performance of the student to determine whether he or she may continue working toward the Ph.D. degree. At the end of the first year, a faculty member typically agrees to accept the student as a research assistant. By December 5 of the third year, an area examination must be passed and a written prospectus submitted before dissertation research is begun. These events result in the student's admission to candidacy. Subsequently, students report orally each year to the full advisory committee on their progress. When the research is nearing completion, but before the thesis writing has commenced, the full advisory committee advises the student on the thesis plan. A final oral presentation of the dissertation research is required during term time. There is no foreign language requirement.

In the Computer Science department, to be admitted to candidacy, a student must (1) pass ten courses (including CPSC 690 and CPSC 691) with at least two grades of honors, the remainder at least high pass, including three advanced courses in an area of specialization; (2) take six advanced courses in areas of general computer science; (3) successfully complete a research project in CPSC 690, 691, and submit a written report on it to the faculty; (4) pass a qualifying examination in an area of specialization; (5) be accepted as a thesis student by a regular department faculty member; (6) serve as a teaching assistant for two terms (four TF units); and (7) submit a written dissertation prospectus, with a tentative title for the dissertation. To satisfy the distribution requirement (item 2 above), the student must take one course in programming languages or systems, one programming-intensive course, two theory courses, and two in application areas. In order to gain teaching experience, all graduate students are required to serve as teaching assistants for two terms during their first three years of study. All requirements for admission to candidacy must be completed prior to the end of the third year. In addition to all other requirements, students must successfully complete CPSC 991, Ethical Conduct of Research, prior to the end of their first year of study. This requirement must be met prior to registering for a second year of study.

M.S. degrees are offered and require the successful completion of at least eight term courses, two of which may be special projects. Although this program can normally be completed in one year of full-time study, a part-time M.S. program is available for practicing engineers and others. Its requirements are the successful completion of eight term courses in a time period not to exceed four calendar years.

Research Facilities

Department facilities are equipped with state-of-the-art experimental and computational equipment in support of the research activity described above. They are centrally located on campus in Mason, Dunham, and Becton Laboratories; the Malone Engineering Center; and the Arthur K. Watson Hall, adjacent to the Department of Mathematics and near the complex of facilities for physics, chemistry, and the biological sciences. The Center for Engineering Innovation and Design is a new 8,500-square-foot area for students to learn, practice, and share engineering design principles in courses, extracurricular activities, and workshops. The School of Engineering & Applied Science has a rich computing environment, including servers, workstations, and personal computers. High-speed data wired and wireless networks interconnect engineering and extends to the campus network. In addition, advanced instrumentation, computing, and networking are combined in a number of laboratories.

Financial Aid

Almost all first-year Ph.D. students receive a University fellowship paying full tuition and an adjusted stipend. Support thereafter is generally provided by research assistantships, which pay $32,400 plus full tuition in 2015–16. Prize fellowships are available to exceptional students. Fellowship support is not available for master's degree students.

Cost of Study

Tuition is $38,700 for the 2015–16 academic year.

Living and Housing Costs

On-campus graduate dormitory housing units range from $4,722 to $8,064 per academic year. Graduate apartment units range from $497 to $1,226 per month. Additional housing details can be found at http://housing.yale.edu/graduate-housing.

Student Group

Yale has 11,800 students—5,300 are undergraduates and the remainder are graduate and professional students. About 250 graduate students are in engineering, most of them working toward the Ph.D.

Location

Situated on Long Island Sound, among the scenic attractions of southern New England, New Haven provides outstanding cultural and recreational opportunities. The greater New Haven area has a population of more than 350,000 and is only 1½ hours from New York by train or car.

The University

Yale is the third-oldest university in the United States, and its engineering program is also one of the oldest. All programs at the University, including those in the School of Engineering & Applied Science, are structured to give students a high degree of flexibility in arranging their programs, with close interaction between individual students and faculty members.

Applying

Students with a bachelor's degree in any field of engineering or in mathematics, physics, or chemistry may apply for admission to graduate study, as may other students prepared to do graduate-level work in any of the study areas of the chosen department, regardless of their specific undergraduate field. Students are admitted only for the beginning of the fall term. Application should be initiated about a year in advance of desired admission, and the application should be submitted before December 25; the file, including letters of reference, should be completed before January 2. Notifications of admission and award of financial aid are sent by April 1. Applicants must take the General Test of the Graduate Record Examinations; the exam should be taken in October. International applicants must submit scores on the TOEFL unless the undergraduate degree is from an institution in which English is the primary language of instruction.

Correspondence and Information

Office of Graduate Studies
School of Engineering & Applied Science
Yale University
P.O. Box 208267
New Haven, Connecticut 06520-8267
United States
Phone: 203-432-4252
Fax: 203-432-7736
Website: http://www.seas.yale.edu/

THE FACULTY AND AREAS OF RESEARCH

APPLIED MECHANICS/MECHANICAL ENGINEERING/MATERIALS SCIENCE: C. Ahn, E. Brown, J. Cha, A. Dollar, E. Dufresne, J. Fernández de la Mora, A. Gomez, M. B Long, C. S. O'Hern, J. Schroers, U. D. Schwarz, M. D. Smooke, M. Venkadesan. Joint appointments (with primary appointment in another department): D. Bercovici, S. Ismail-Beigi, S.-I. Karato, B. Scassellati. Emeritus faculty: I. B. Bernstein.

Fluids and Thermal Sciences: Wetting; macroscopic and particle-scale dynamics of emulsions, foams, and colloidal suspensions; electrospray theory and applications; electrical propulsion applications; studies of clusters and nanoparticles in the gas phase; turbulence; magnetohydrodynamic dynamos; combustion and flames; computational methods for fluid dynamics and reacting flows; laser diagnostics of reacting and nonreacting flows.

Materials Science: Hard and Soft Matter: Studies of thin films; material properties in reduced dimensions; renewable energy nanomaterials; atomic-scale investigations of surface structure, interactions, and properties; nanotribology; combinatorial strategies in materials discovery and characterization; characterization of crystallization and other phase transformations; jamming and slow dynamics in glasses and granular materials; mechanical properties of soft and biological materials; self assembly; dynamics of macromolecules; nano-imprinting.

Robotics/Mechatronics: Machine and mechanism design; dynamics and control; robotic grasping and manipulation; human-machine interface; rehabilitation robotics; haptics; electromechanical energy conversion; biomechanics of human movement; human powered vehicles.

BIOMEDICAL ENGINEERING: S. Campbell, R. E. Carson, R. T. Constable, J. Duncan, T. Fahmy, R. Fan, A. Gonzalez, J. Humphrey, F. Hyder, T. Kyriakides, A. Levchenko, K. Miller-Jensen, M. Murrell, D. Rothman, M. Saltzman, L. Staib, S. Zucker. Joint appointments (with primary appointment in another department): J. Bewersdorf, M. Choma, N. Christakis, R. de Graaf, E. Dufresne, K. Hirschi, E. Morris, C Liu, L. Niklason, X. Papademetris, M. Schwartz, F. Sigworth, B. Smith, S. Tommasini, H. Tagare, P. Van Tassel, C. Wilson, J. Zhou.

Biomedical Imaging and Biosignals: Formation of anatomical and functional medical images; magnetic resonance spectroscopy; analysis and processing of medical image data, including functional MRI (fMRI); diffusion tensor imaging; imaging of brain biochemical processes; image-guided neurosurgery; using biomechanical models to guide recovery of left ventricular strain from medical images; biomedical signal processing; relating EEG and fMRI information.

Biomechanics: Simulation and loading of the lumbar spine in regard to tissue loads during heavy lifting, low-back pain and mechanical instability of the spine, muscle mechanics and electromyography, mechanical performance of implants, microcirculation in skeletal muscle, mechanisms of blood-flow control, cell-to-cell communication in vascular resistance networks.

Biomolecular Engineering and Biotechnology: Drug delivery and tissue engineering, drug delivery systems, polymers as biomaterials, tissue engineering, spinal cord regeneration, drug delivery and repair in retina and optic nerve, new biomaterials for drug delivery and tissue engineering, bioseparations, chromatography and electrophoresis, electrical recording (patch clamp) and signal processing of ion channel currents, studies of structure and function of ion channel proteins, cryoelectron microscopy methods for macromolecular structure determination.

COMPUTER SCIENCE: D. Abadi, D. Angluin, J. Aspnes, M. Balakrishnan, J. Dorsey, S. Eisenstat, J. Feigenbaum, M. Fischer, D. Gelernter, D. McDermott, R. Piskac, V. Rokhlin, H. Rushmeier, B. Scassellati, Z. Shao, A. Silberschatz, D. Spielman, Y. R. Yang, S. Zucker. Joint appointments (with primary appointment in another department): D. Bergeman, R. Coifman, M. Gerstein, W. Hu, A. Karbasi, S. Negahban, F. Shic, J. Szefer. Emeritus faculty: M. Schultz.

Artificial intelligence (vision, robotics, planning, computational neuroscience, knowledge representation, neural networks); programming languages (functional programming, parallel languages and architectures, programming environments, formal semantics, compilation techniques, modern computer architecture, type theory/systems, metaprogramming); systems (databases, operating systems, networks, software engineering); scientific computing (numerical linear algebra, numerical solution of partial differential equations, mathematical software, parallel algorithms); theory of computation (algorithms and data structures, complexity, distributed systems, learning, online algorithms, graph algorithms, geometric algorithms, fault tolerance, reliable communication, cryptography, security, electronic commerce); topics of discrete mathematics with application to computer science (combinatorics, graph theory, combinatorial optimization).

CHEMICAL & ENVIRONMENTAL ENGINEERING: E. I. Altman, M. Elimelech, D. Gentner, J. Kim, M. Loewenberg, C. Osuji, J. Peccia, L. D. Pfefferle, D. Plata, M. Saltzman, A. D. Taylor, P. Van Tassel, T. K. Vanderlick, C. Wilson, J. Zimmerman. Adjunct faculty: A. Firoozabadi, Y. Khalil, R. McGraw, J. Pignatello. Joint appointments (with primary appointment in another department): M. Bell, G. Benoit, R. Blake, E. Dufresne, T. Fahmy,

T. E. Graedel, E. Kaplan, A. Miranker, J. Saiers, U. D. Schwarz, K. W. Zilm. Emeritus faculty: G. L. Haller, D. E. Rosner.

Nanomaterials: Carbon and inorganic nanotubes, nanoscale polymer films, nanoscale devices, nanomaterials and biomolecules in engineered and natural aquatic systems.

Soft Matter and Interfacial Phenomena: Colloidal and interfacial phenomena, surface science, physics of synthetic and biological macromolecules, microfluidic biosensors, self-assembled soft materials for biomedical applications.

Biomolecular Engineering: Biomolecules at interfaces, nanofilm biomaterials, bioaerosol detection and source tracking, microarrays and other high throughput measurements, production of functional binding biomolecules, biological production of sustainable fuels, transport and fate of microbial pathogens in aquatic environments, membrane separations for desalination and water quality control.

Energy: Biofuels, energy extraction from waste materials, efficient water treatment and delivery, integration of science and engineering with economics and policy.

Water: Sustainable and culturally appropriate technologies for low-quality-source water reclamation in the developing world.

Sustainability: Green solvents, bio-based materials, safer nanotechnology and systems optimization for reduced environmental impact and enhanced economic competitiveness.

ELECTRICAL ENGINEERING: J. Han, W. Hu, A. Karbasi, R. Kuc, M. Lee, T. P. Ma, A. S. Morse, K. S. Narendra, M. A. Reed, J. Szefer, H. Tang, L. Tassiulas, S. Tatikonda, J. R. Vaisnys, F. Xia. Joint appointments (with primary appointment in another department): J. Duncan, L. Staib, H. D. Tagare, R. Yang. Adjunct faculty: R. Lethin. Emeritus faculty: R. C. Barker, P. M. Schultheiss.

Signal, Systems, and Networks: Linear system models, automatic control systems, representation of information in signals, transmission and storage of information, processing information by computers, networking and communication theory. Applications include bioengineering, digital signal processing, image processing, neural networks, robotics, sensors, and telecommunication systems.

Computer Engineering, Sensor Networks, Circuits and Systems: Study and design of digital circuits and computer systems; computer architecture; sensor networks; very-large-scale integrated (VLSI) circuit design, implementation, and testing. Applications include computing networks, computer design, biomedical instrumentation, bio-inspired circuits and systems.

Electronics, Photonics, and Nanodevices: Design, fabrication, and characterization of novel electronic, photonic, and nano devices; study of structure-property relationships in electronic and photonic materials. Applications include chem/bio-sensing, solid-state lighting, solar cells, micro/nano-electromechanical systems, non-volatile memory, and ultrafast devices.

Malone Engineering Center

Section 2
Aerospace/Aeronautical Engineering

This section contains a directory of institutions offering graduate work in aerospace/aeronautical engineering. Additional information about programs listed in the directory may be obtained by writing directly to the dean of a graduate school or chair of a department at the address given in the directory.

For programs offering related work, see also in this book *Engineering and Applied Sciences* and *Mechanical Engineering and Mechanics.* In another guide in this series:

Graduate Programs in the Physical Sciences, Mathematics, Agricultural Sciences, the Environment & Natural Resources
See *Geosciences* and *Physics*

CONTENTS

Program Directories

Aerospace/Aeronautical Engineering

Air Force Institute of Technology, Graduate School of Engineering and Management, Department of Aeronautics and Astronautics, Dayton, OH 45433-7765. Offers aeronautical engineering (MS, PhD); astronautical engineering (MS, PhD); materials science (MS, PhD); space operations (MS); systems engineering (MS, PhD). *Accreditation:* ABET (one or more programs are accredited). Part-time programs available. *Degree requirements:* For master's, thesis; for doctorate, thesis/dissertation. *Entrance requirements:* For master's and doctorate, GRE General Test, minimum GPA of 3.0, U.S. citizenship. *Faculty research:* Computational fluid dynamics, experimental aerodynamics, computational structural mechanics, experimental structural mechanics, aircraft and spacecraft stability and control.

American Public University System, AMU/APU Graduate Programs, Charles Town, WV 25414. Offers accounting (MBA, MS); criminal justice (MA), including business administration, emergency and disaster management, general (MA, MS); educational leadership (M Ed); emergency and disaster management (MA); entrepreneurship (MBA); environmental policy and management (MS), including environmental planning, environmental sustainability, fish and wildlife management, general (MA, MS), global environmental management; finance (MBA); general (MBA); global business management (MBA); history (MA), including American history, ancient and classical history, European history, global history, public history; homeland security (MA), including business administration, counter-terrorism studies, criminal justice, cyber, emergency management and public health, intelligence studies, transportation security; homeland security resource allocation (MBA); humanities (MA); information technology (MS), including digital forensics, enterprise software development, information assurance and security, IT project management; information technology management (MBA); intelligence studies (MA), including criminal intelligence, cyber, general (MA, MS), homeland security, intelligence analysis, intelligence collection, intelligence management, intelligence operations, terrorism studies; international relations and conflict resolution (MA), including comparative and security issues, conflict resolution, international and transnational security issues, peacekeeping; legal studies (MA); management (MA), including defense management, general (MA, MS), human resource management, organizational leadership, public administration; marketing (MBA); military history (MA), including American military history, American Revolution, civil war, war since 1945, World War II; military studies (MA), including joint warfare, strategic leadership; national security studies (MA), including general (MA, MS), homeland security, regional security studies, security and intelligence analysis, terrorism studies; nonprofit management (MBA); political science (MA), including American politics and government, comparative government and development, general (MA, MS), international relations, public policy; psychology (MA); public administration (MPA), including disaster management, environmental policy, health policy, human resources, national security, organizational management, security management; public health (MPH); reverse logistics management (MA); school counseling (M Ed); security management (MA); space studies (MS), including aerospace science, general (MA, MS), planetary science; sports and health sciences (MS); teaching (M Ed), including curriculum and instruction for elementary teachers, elementary reading, English language learners, instructional leadership, online learning, special education; transportation and logistics management (MA), including general (MA, MS), maritime engineering management, reverse logistics management. Programs offered via distance learning only. Part-time and evening/weekend programs available. Postbaccalaureate distance learning degree programs offered (no on-campus study). *Faculty:* 426 full-time (236 women), 1,864 part-time/adjunct (880 women). *Students:* 475 full-time (215 women), 10,067 part-time (4,085 women); includes 3,462 minority (1,863 Black or African American, non-Hispanic/Latino; 74 American Indian or Alaska Native, non-Hispanic/Latino; 273 Asian, non-Hispanic/Latino; 831 Hispanic/Latino; 78 Native Hawaiian or other Pacific Islander, non-Hispanic/Latino; 343 Two or more races, non-Hispanic/Latino), 131 international. Average age 36. In 2014, 3,740 master's awarded. *Degree requirements:* For master's, comprehensive exam or practicum. *Entrance requirements:* For master's, official transcript showing earned bachelor's degree from institution accredited by recognized accrediting body. Additional exam requirements/recommendations for international students: Required—TOEFL (minimum score 550 paper-based), IELTS (minimum score 6.5). *Application deadline:* Applications are processed on a rolling basis. Application fee: $0. Electronic applications accepted. *Financial support:* Applicants required to submit FAFSA. *Faculty research:* Military history, criminal justice, management performance, national security. *Unit head:* Dr. Karan Powell, Executive Vice President and Provost, 877-468-6268, Fax: 304-724-3780. *Application contact:* Terry Grant, Vice President of Enrollment Management, 877-468-6268, Fax: 304-724-3780, E-mail: info@apus.edu.
Website: http://www.apus.edu.

Arizona State University at the Tempe campus, Ira A. Fulton Schools of Engineering, School for Engineering of Matter, Transport and Energy, Tempe, AZ 85281. Offers aerospace engineering (MS, PhD); chemical engineering (MS, PhD); materials science and engineering (MS, PhD); mechanical engineering (MS, PhD); solar energy engineering and commercialization (PSM). Part-time and evening/weekend programs available. Postbaccalaureate distance learning degree programs offered (minimal on-campus study). Terminal master's awarded for partial completion of doctoral program. *Degree requirements:* For master's, thesis and oral defense (MS); applied project or comprehensive exam (MSE); interactive Program of Study (iPOS) submitted before completing 50 percent of required credit hours; for doctorate, comprehensive exam, thesis/dissertation, interactive Program of Study (iPOS) submitted before completing 50 percent of required credit hours. *Entrance requirements:* For master's, GRE, minimum GPA of 3.0 or equivalent in last 2 years of work leading to bachelor's degree; for doctorate, GRE, minimum GPA of 3.0 in last 2 years of work leading to bachelor's degree. Additional exam requirements/recommendations for international students: Required—TOEFL, IELTS, or PTE. Electronic applications accepted. *Expenses:* Contact institution. *Faculty research:* Electronic materials and packaging, materials for energy (batteries), adaptive/intelligent materials and structures, multiscale fluid mechanics, membranes, therapeutics and bioseparations, flexible structures, nanostructured materials, and micro/nano transport.

Auburn University, Graduate School, Ginn College of Engineering, Department of Aerospace Engineering, Auburn University, AL 36849. Offers MAE, MS, PhD. Part-time programs available. *Faculty:* 9 full-time (0 women), 5 part-time/adjunct (0 women). *Students:* 24 full-time (2 women), 24 part-time (6 women); includes 5 minority (3 Asian, non-Hispanic/Latino; 2 Hispanic/Latino), 8 international. Average age 26. 48 applicants, 44% accepted, 13 enrolled. In 2014, 15 master's, 1 doctorate awarded. *Degree requirements:* For master's, thesis (MS), exam; for doctorate, thesis/dissertation, exams. *Entrance requirements:* For master's and doctorate, GRE General Test. *Application deadline:* For fall admission, 7/7 for domestic students; for spring admission, 11/24 for domestic students. Applications are processed on a rolling basis. Application fee: $50 ($60 for international students). Electronic applications accepted. *Expenses:* Tuition,

state resident: full-time $8586; part-time $477 per credit hour. Tuition, nonresident: full-time $25,758; part-time $1431 per credit hour. *Required fees:* $804 per semester. Tuition and fees vary according to degree level and program. *Financial support:* Fellowships, research assistantships, teaching assistantships, and Federal Work-Study available. Support available to part-time students. Financial award application deadline: 3/15; financial award applicants required to submit FAFSA. *Faculty research:* Aerodynamics, flight dynamics and simulation, propulsion, structures and aeroelasticity, aerospace smart structures. *Unit head:* Dr. Joe Majdalani, Head, 334-844-6800. *Application contact:* Dr. George Flowers, Dean of the Graduate School, 334-844-2125. Website: http://www.eng.auburn.edu/department/ae/.

California Institute of Technology, Division of Engineering and Applied Science, Option in Aeronautics, Pasadena, CA 91125-0001. Offers MS, PhD, Engr. Terminal master's awarded for partial completion of doctoral program. *Degree requirements:* For doctorate, thesis/dissertation. *Faculty research:* Computational fluid dynamics, technical fluid dynamics, structural mechanics, mechanics of fracture, aeronautical engineering and propulsion.

California Polytechnic State University, San Luis Obispo, College of Engineering, Department of Aerospace Engineering, San Luis Obispo, CA 93407. Offers MS. Part-time programs available. *Faculty:* 7 full-time (2 women), 2 part-time/adjunct (0 women). *Students:* 15 full-time (4 women), 20 part-time (3 women); includes 13 minority (3 Asian, non-Hispanic/Latino; 9 Hispanic/Latino; 1 Two or more races, non-Hispanic/Latino), 3 international. Average age 25. 47 applicants, 62% accepted, 21 enrolled. In 2014, 24 master's awarded. *Degree requirements:* For master's, thesis. *Application deadline:* For fall admission, 1/1 for domestic and international students; for winter admission, 11/1 for domestic students, 6/30 for international students; for spring admission, 2/1 for domestic students. Applications are processed on a rolling basis. Application fee: $55. Electronic applications accepted. *Expenses:* Tuition, state resident: full-time $6738; part-time $3906 per year. Tuition, nonresident: full-time $15,666; part-time $8370 per year. *Required fees:* $3447; $1001 per quarter. One-time fee: $3447 full-time; $3003 part-time. *Financial support:* Fellowships, research assistantships, teaching assistantships, career-related internships or fieldwork, Federal Work-Study, scholarships/grants, and unspecified assistantships available. Support available to part-time students. Financial award application deadline: 3/2; financial award applicants required to submit FAFSA. *Faculty research:* Space systems engineering, space vehicle design, aerodynamics, aerospace propulsion, dynamics and control. *Unit head:* Dr. David Marshall, Graduate Coordinator, 805-756-6849, Fax: 805-756-2376, E-mail: ddmarsha@calpoly.edu. *Application contact:* Dr. James Maraviglia, Associate Vice Provost for Marketing and Enrollment Development, 805-756-2311, Fax: 805-756-5400, E-mail: admissions@calpoly.edu.
Website: http://aero.calpoly.edu.

California State Polytechnic University, Pomona, Program in Engineering, Pomona, CA 91768-2557. Offers MSE. *Students:* 3 full-time (2 women), 17 part-time (2 women); includes 10 minority (1 Black or African American, non-Hispanic/Latino; 5 Asian, non-Hispanic/Latino; 3 Hispanic/Latino; 1 Native Hawaiian or other Pacific Islander, non-Hispanic/Latino). Average age 28. 23 applicants, 26% accepted, 3 enrolled. In 2014, 4 master's awarded. *Application deadline:* Applications are processed on a rolling basis. Application fee: $55. Electronic applications accepted. *Expenses:* Tuition, state resident: full-time $6738. Tuition, nonresident: full-time $12,300. *Required fees:* $1400. *Unit head:* Dr. Ali R. Ahmadi, Department Chair, 909-869-2470, Fax: 909-869-6920, E-mail: arahmadi@cpp.edu.
Website: http://www.cpp.edu/~engineering.

California State University, Long Beach, Graduate Studies, College of Engineering, Department of Mechanical and Aerospace Engineering, Program in Aerospace Engineering, Long Beach, CA 90840. Offers MSAE. Part-time programs available. *Degree requirements:* For master's, thesis or alternative. *Entrance requirements:* Additional exam requirements/recommendations for international students: Required—TOEFL. Electronic applications accepted. *Faculty research:* Aerodynamic flows, ice accretion, stability and transition.

Carleton University, Faculty of Graduate Studies, Faculty of Engineering and Design, Department of Mechanical and Aerospace Engineering, Ottawa, ON K1S 5B6, Canada. Offers aerospace engineering (M Eng, MA Sc, PhD); materials engineering (M Eng, MA Sc); mechanical engineering (M Eng, MA Sc, PhD). *Degree requirements:* For master's, thesis optional; for doctorate, thesis/dissertation. *Entrance requirements:* For master's, honors degree; for doctorate, MA Sc or M Eng. Additional exam requirements/recommendations for international students: Required—TOEFL. *Faculty research:* Thermal fluids engineering, heat transfer, vehicle engineering.

Case Western Reserve University, School of Graduate Studies, Case School of Engineering, Department of Mechanical and Aerospace Engineering, Cleveland, OH 44106. Offers MS, PhD, MD/PhD. Part-time programs available. Postbaccalaureate distance learning degree programs offered (no on-campus study). *Faculty:* 14 full-time (3 women). *Students:* 84 full-time (11 women), 12 part-time (3 women); includes 10 minority (2 Black or African American, non-Hispanic/Latino; 5 Asian, non-Hispanic/Latino; 2 Hispanic/Latino; 1 Two or more races, non-Hispanic/Latino), 53 international. In 2014, 11 master's, 7 doctorates awarded. *Degree requirements:* For master's, thesis (for some programs); for doctorate, thesis/dissertation, qualifying exam, teaching experience. *Entrance requirements:* For master's and doctorate, GRE General Test. Additional exam requirements/recommendations for international students: Required—TOEFL. *Application deadline:* For fall admission, 7/1 priority date for domestic students. Applications are processed on a rolling basis. Application fee: $50. *Financial support:* In 2014–15, 5 fellowships with full and partial tuition reimbursements, 21 research assistantships with full and partial tuition reimbursements, 9 teaching assistantships were awarded; institutionally sponsored loans and tuition waivers (full and partial) also available. Financial award application deadline: 3/1; financial award applicants required to submit FAFSA. *Faculty research:* Musculoskeletal biomechanics, combustion diagnostics and computation, mechanical behavior of advanced materials and nanostructures, biorobotics. *Total annual research expenditures:* $4.1 million. *Unit head:* Dr. Robert Gao, Department Chair, 216-368-6045, Fax: 216-368-6445, E-mail: robert.gao@case.edu. *Application contact:* Carla Wilson, Student Affairs Coordinator, 216-368-4580, Fax: 216-368-3007, E-mail: cxw75@case.edu.
Website: http://www.engineering.case.edu/emae.

Concordia University, School of Graduate Studies, Faculty of Engineering and Computer Science, Program in Aerospace Engineering, Montréal, QC H3G 1M8, Canada. Offers M Eng. Program offered jointly with École Polytechnique de Montréal and McGill University. *Degree requirements:* For master's, thesis or alternative. *Faculty research:* Aeronautics and propulsion avionics and control, structures and materials, space engineering.

Cornell University, Graduate School, Graduate Fields of Engineering, Field of Aerospace Engineering, Ithaca, NY 14853-0001. Offers M Eng, MS, PhD. Terminal master's awarded for partial completion of doctoral program. *Degree requirements:* For master's, thesis (MS); for doctorate, one foreign language, comprehensive exam, thesis/ dissertation. *Entrance requirements:* For master's and doctorate, GRE General Test, 3 letters of recommendation. Additional exam requirements/recommendations for international students: Required—TOEFL (minimum score 550 paper-based; 77 iBT). Electronic applications accepted. *Faculty research:* Aerodynamics, fluid mechanics, turbulence, combustion/propulsion, aeroacoustics.

École Polytechnique de Montréal, Graduate Programs, Department of Mechanical Engineering, Montréal, QC H3C 3A7, Canada. Offers aerothermics (M Eng, M Sc A, PhD); applied mechanics (M Eng, M Sc A, PhD); tool design (M Eng, M Sc A, PhD). Part-time and evening/weekend programs available. *Degree requirements:* For master's, one foreign language, thesis; for doctorate, one foreign language, thesis/ dissertation. *Entrance requirements:* For master's, minimum GPA of 2.75; for doctorate, minimum GPA of 3.0. *Faculty research:* Noise control and vibration, fatigue and creep, aerodynamics, composite materials, biomechanics, robotics.

Embry-Riddle Aeronautical University–Daytona, Department of Aerospace Engineering, Daytona Beach, FL 32114-3900. Offers aerospace engineering (MAE, MSAE, PhD); unmanned and autonomous systems engineering (MS). Part-time programs available. *Faculty:* 20 full-time (2 women), 3 part-time/adjunct (0 women). *Students:* 146 full-time (24 women), 15 part-time (3 women); includes 11 minority (1 Black or African American, non-Hispanic/Latino; 4 Asian, non-Hispanic/Latino; 4 Hispanic/Latino; 2 Two or more races, non-Hispanic/Latino), 114 international. Average age 24. 174 applicants, 47% accepted, 47 enrolled. In 2014, 37 master's awarded. *Degree requirements:* For master's, thesis; for doctorate, comprehensive exam, thesis/ dissertation. *Entrance requirements:* For master's, BS in Aeronautical or Aerospace Engineering, or equivalent; minimum CGPA of 3.0; for doctorate, Graduate Record Examination (GRE), a Masters or Bachelor degree in aerospace engineering or closely related engineering discipline; minimum Masters cumulative grade point average (CGPA) of 3.5. Additional exam requirements/recommendations for international students: Required—TOEFL (minimum score 550 paper-based; 79 iBT). *Application deadline:* For fall admission, 1/15 priority date for domestic students, 12/15 priority date for international students; for spring admission, 6/15 priority date for domestic and international students. Applications are processed on a rolling basis. Application fee: $50. Electronic applications accepted. *Expenses: Tuition:* Full-time $15,360; part-time $1280 per credit hour. *Required fees:* $1334. *Financial support:* In 2014–15, 44 students received support, including research assistantships with full and partial tuition reimbursements available (averaging $7,500 per year); career-related internships or fieldwork and unspecified assistantships also available. Financial award application deadline: 1/15. *Faculty research:* Aeroacoustic modeling, rotorcraft aerodynamics, flow control, airbreathing hypersonic and rocket propulsion, autonomous unpiloted air and ground vehicles, aircraft and spacecraft guidance, navigation and control, aeroelasticity, composites, nanomaterials, smart materials, structural health monitoring, computational structural mechanics and design optimization. *Unit head:* Dr. Anastasios Lyrintzis, Distinguished Professor and Chair, Aerospace Engineering, 386-226-7007, Fax: 386-226-6747, E-mail: lyrintzi@erau.edu. *Application contact:* International and Graduate Admissions, 386-226-6176, E-mail: graduate.admissions@erau.edu.
Website: http://daytonabeach.erau.edu/college-engineering/aerospace/index.html.

Embry-Riddle Aeronautical University–Daytona, Department of Applied Aviation Sciences, Daytona Beach, FL 32114-3900. Offers MSA. Part-time and evening/ weekend programs available. *Faculty:* 14 full-time (1 woman), 1 part-time/adjunct (0 women). *Students:* 51 full-time (7 women), 17 part-time (6 women); includes 6 minority (2 Black or African American, non-Hispanic/Latino; 1 Asian, non-Hispanic/Latino; 3 Two or more races, non-Hispanic/Latino), 28 international. Average age 28. 73 applicants, 68% accepted, 19 enrolled. In 2014, 44 master's awarded. *Degree requirements:* For master's, thesis optional, either a Thesis (6 credits), or a Graduate Capstone Project (GCP) (3 credits). *Entrance requirements:* For master's, minimum CGPA of 3.0; prerequisite knowledge in the areas of Behavioral Science, Economics, Computer Applications, Mathematics (including Statistics). Additional exam requirements/ recommendations for international students: Required—TOEFL (minimum score 550 paper-based; 79 iBT). *Application deadline:* For fall admission, 7/1 priority date for domestic students, 6/1 priority date for international students; for spring admission, 11/1 priority date for domestic students, 10/1 priority date for international students. Applications are processed on a rolling basis. Application fee: $50. Electronic applications accepted. *Expenses: Tuition:* Full-time $15,360; part-time $1280 per credit hour. *Required fees:* $1334. *Financial support:* In 2014–15, 17 students received support, including research assistantships with full and partial tuition reimbursements available (averaging $12,000 per year); career-related internships or fieldwork and unspecified assistantships also available. Financial award application deadline: 4/15. *Faculty research:* Air traffic controller turnover, accident rates, interplanetary navigation trajectories, fire whirls, flight data monitoring. *Unit head:* Antonio I. Cortes, PhD, Department Chair, Applied Aviation Sciences, 386-226-7560, E-mail: Antonio.Cortes@erau.edu. *Application contact:* International and Graduate Admissions, 386-226-6176, Fax: 386-226-7070, E-mail: graduate.admissions@erau.edu.
Website: http://daytonabeach.erau.edu/college-aviation/applied-aviation-sciences /index.html.

Embry-Riddle Aeronautical University–Worldwide, College of Aeronautics, Daytona Beach, FL 32114-3900. Offers aeronautical science (MAS); human factors (MS); occupational safety management (MS); systems engineering (M Sys E); unmanned systems (MS). Part-time and evening/weekend programs available. Postbaccalaureate distance learning degree programs offered (no on-campus study). *Faculty:* 34 full-time (4 women), 189 part-time/adjunct (23 women). *Students:* 1,151 full-time (188 women), 1,227 part-time (191 women); includes 498 minority (198 Black or African American, non-Hispanic/Latino; 7 American Indian or Alaska Native, non-Hispanic/Latino; 66 Asian, non-Hispanic/Latino; 92 Hispanic/Latino; 4 Native Hawaiian or other Pacific Islander, non-Hispanic/Latino; 131 Two or more races, non-Hispanic/Latino), 109 international. Average age 37. In 2014, 882 master's awarded. *Degree requirements:* For master's, comprehensive exam (for some programs), thesis or alternative, thesis or capstone project. *Entrance requirements:* Additional exam requirements/ recommendations for international students: Recommended—TOEFL (minimum score 550 paper-based; 79 iBT). *Application deadline:* Applications are processed on a rolling basis. Application fee: $50. Electronic applications accepted. *Expenses: Tuition:* Full-time $6720; part-time $560 per credit hour. *Financial support:* In 2014–15, 385 students received support. Career-related internships or fieldwork available. *Faculty research:* Aerodynamics statistical design and educational development. *Unit head:* Dr. Ian McAndrew, Department Chair, Department of Aeronautics, Graduate Studies, E-mail: ian.mcandrew@erau.edu. *Application contact:* Admissions, 800-522-6787, E-mail: worldwide@erau.edu.
Website: http://worldwide.erau.edu/degrees-programs/colleges/aeronautics /department-of-graduate-studies/index.html.

Florida Institute of Technology, Graduate Programs, College of Aeronautics, Melbourne, FL 32901-6975. Offers airport development and management (MSA); applied aviation safety (MSA); aviation human factors (MS); aviation safety (MSA); aviation sciences (PhD); human factors in aeronautics (MS). Part-time and evening/ weekend programs available. Postbaccalaureate distance learning degree programs offered (no on-campus study). *Faculty:* 8 full-time (3 women), 2 part-time/adjunct (0 women). *Students:* 37 full-time (10 women), 8 part-time (1 woman); includes 5 minority (3 Black or African American, non-Hispanic/Latino; 1 Asian, non-Hispanic/Latino; 1 Hispanic/Latino), 23 international. Average age 32. 78 applicants, 47% accepted, 15 enrolled. In 2014, 38 master's awarded. *Degree requirements:* For master's, thesis or capstone project; for doctorate, thesis/dissertation or alternative. *Entrance requirements:* For master's, GRE, minimum GPA of 3.0, 3 letters of recommendation, resume, statement of objectives; for doctorate, GRE, minimum GPA of 3.2; master's degree in an aviation field (for international applicants). Additional exam requirements/ recommendations for international students: Required—TOEFL (minimum score 550 paper-based; 79 iBT). *Application deadline:* For fall admission, 4/1 for international students; for spring admission, 9/30 for international students. Applications are processed on a rolling basis. Electronic applications accepted. *Expenses: Tuition:* Part-time $1179 per credit hour. Tuition and fees vary according to campus/location. *Financial support:* Career-related internships or fieldwork, institutionally sponsored loans, tuition waivers (partial), and tuition remissions available. Support available to part-time students. Financial award application deadline: 3/1; financial award applicants required to submit FAFSA. *Faculty research:* Aircraft cockpit design, medical human factors, operating room human factors, hypobaric chamber operations and effects, aviation professional education. *Total annual research expenditures:* $138,016. *Unit head:* Dr. Korhan Oyman, Dean, 321-674-8971, Fax: 321-674-7368, E-mail: koyman@fit.edu. *Application contact:* Cheryl A. Brown, Associate Director of Graduate Admissions, 321-674-7581, Fax: 321-723-9468, E-mail: cbrown@fit.edu.
Website: http://coa.fit.edu.

Florida Institute of Technology, Graduate Programs, College of Engineering, Program in Flight Test Engineering, Melbourne, FL 32901-6975. Offers MS. *Degree requirements:* For master's, comprehensive exam. *Entrance requirements:* For master's, GRE General Test, 1 year of undergraduate work in mechanical engineering, resume, letters of recommendation. *Application deadline:* Applications are processed on a rolling basis. Electronic applications accepted. *Expenses: Tuition:* Part-time $1179 per credit hour. Tuition and fees vary according to campus/location. *Unit head:* Dr. Hamid Hefazi, Department Head, 321-674-7255, E-mail: hhefazi@fit.edu. *Application contact:* Cheryl A. Brown, Associate Director of Graduate Admissions, 321-674-7581, Fax: 321-723-9468, E-mail: cbrown@fit.edu.
Website: http://www.fit.edu/programs/8233/ms-flight-test-engineering#.VT_kvE10ypo.

Florida Institute of Technology, Graduate Programs, Extended Studies Division, Melbourne, FL 32901-6975. Offers acquisition and contract management (MS); aerospace engineering (MS); business administration (MBA, DBA); computer information systems (MS); computer science (MS); electrical engineering (MS); engineering management (MS); human resources management (MS); logistics management (MS), including humanitarian and disaster relief logistics; management (MS), including acquisition and contract management, e-business, human resources management, information systems, logistics management, management, transportation management; material acquisition management (MS); mechanical engineering (MS); operations research (MS); project management (MS), including information systems, operations research; public administration (MPA); quality management (MS); software engineering (MS); space systems (MS); space systems management (MS); supply chain management (MS); systems management (MS), including information systems, operations research; technology management (MS). Part-time and evening/weekend programs available. Postbaccalaureate distance learning degree programs offered (no on-campus study). *Faculty:* 7 full-time (1 woman), 112 part-time/adjunct (29 women). *Students:* 98 full-time (45 women), 975 part-time (396 women); includes 440 minority (292 Black or African American, non-Hispanic/Latino; 13 American Indian or Alaska Native, non-Hispanic/Latino; 32 Asian, non-Hispanic/Latino; 79 Hispanic/Latino; 1 Native Hawaiian or other Pacific Islander, non-Hispanic/Latino; 23 Two or more races, non-Hispanic/Latino), 4 international. Average age 37. 807 applicants, 56% accepted, 258 enrolled. In 2014, 457 master's awarded. *Degree requirements:* For master's, comprehensive exam (for some programs), capstone course. *Entrance requirements:* For master's, GMAT or resume showing 8 years of supervised experience, minimum GPA of 3.0, 2 letters of recommendation, resume. Additional exam requirements/ recommendations for international students: Required—TOEFL (minimum score 550 paper-based; 79 iBT). *Application deadline:* For fall admission, 4/1 for international students; for spring admission, 9/30 for international students. Applications are processed on a rolling basis. Electronic applications accepted. *Expenses:* Expenses: Contact institution. *Financial support:* Application deadline: 3/1; applicants required to submit FAFSA. *Unit head:* Dr. Theodore R. Richardson, III, Senior Associate Dean, 321-674-8123, Fax: 321-674-7597, E-mail: trichardson@fit.edu. *Application contact:* Carolyn Farrior, Director of Graduate Admissions, Online Learning and Off-Campus Programs, 321-674-7118, Fax: 321-674-8216, E-mail: cfarrior@fit.edu.
Website: http://es.fit.edu.

The George Washington University, School of Engineering and Applied Science, Department of Mechanical and Aerospace Engineering, Washington, DC 20052. Offers mechanical and aerospace engineering (Engr). Part-time and evening/weekend programs available. *Faculty:* 22 full-time (4 women), 15 part-time/adjunct (0 women). *Students:* 70 full-time (10 women), 64 part-time (11 women); includes 17 minority (1 Black or African American, non-Hispanic/Latino; 6 Asian, non-Hispanic/Latino; 5 Hispanic/Latino; 1 Native Hawaiian or other Pacific Islander, non-Hispanic/Latino; 4 Two or more races, non-Hispanic/Latino), 71 international. Average age 28. 265 applicants, 63% accepted, 44 enrolled. In 2014, 33 master's, 6 doctorates, 1 other advanced degree awarded. *Degree requirements:* For master's, thesis optional; for doctorate, thesis/ dissertation, final and qualifying exams. *Entrance requirements:* For master's, appropriate bachelor's degree, minimum GPA of 3.0; for doctorate, GRE (if highest earned degree is BS), appropriate bachelor's or master's degree, minimum GPA of 3.4; for other advanced degree, appropriate master's degree, minimum GPA of 3.0. Additional exam requirements/recommendations for international students: Required—TOEFL or The George Washington University English as a Foreign Language Test. *Application deadline:* For fall admission, 3/1 priority date for domestic students; for spring admission, 10/1 for domestic students. Applications are processed on a rolling basis. Application fee: $75. *Financial support:* In 2014–15, 51 students received support. Fellowships with tuition reimbursements available, research assistantships, teaching assistantships with tuition reimbursements available, career-related internships or fieldwork, and institutionally sponsored loans available. Financial award application deadline: 3/1; financial award applicants required to submit FAFSA. *Unit head:* Dr. Michael Plesniak, Chairman, 202-994-6749, E-mail: maeng@gwu.edu. *Application contact:* Adina Lav, Marketing, Recruiting and Admissions, 202-994-5827, Fax: 202-994-0909, E-mail: engineering@gwu.edu.
Website: http://www.gwu.edu/graduate-programs/mechanical-and-aerospace -engineering.

Aerospace/Aeronautical Engineering

Georgia Institute of Technology, Graduate Studies, College of Engineering, School of Aerospace Engineering, Atlanta, GA 30332-0001. Offers MS, PhD. Part-time programs available. *Students:* 424 full-time (65 women), 79 part-time (16 women); includes 74 minority (8 Black or African American, non-Hispanic/Latino; 33 Asian, non-Hispanic/Latino; 26 Hispanic/Latino; 7 Two or more races, non-Hispanic/Latino), 188 international. Average age 25. 597 applicants, 39% accepted, 120 enrolled. In 2014, 147 master's, 47 doctorates awarded. Terminal master's awarded for partial completion of doctoral program. *Degree requirements:* For master's, thesis optional; for doctorate, thesis/dissertation. *Entrance requirements:* For master's and doctorate, GRE, http://www.grad.gatech.edu/ae. Additional exam requirements/recommendations for international students: Required—TOEFL (minimum score 550 paper-based; 79 iBT). *Application deadline:* For fall admission, 12/15 for domestic students, 6/1 for international students; for spring admission, 10/1 for domestic and international students; for summer admission, 12/15 for domestic students, 3/1 for international students. Applications are processed on a rolling basis. Application fee: $75. Electronic applications accepted. *Expenses:* Tuition, state resident: full-time $12,344; part-time $515 per credit hour. Tuition, nonresident: full-time $27,600; part-time $1150 per credit hour. *Required fees:* $1196 per term. Part-time tuition and fees vary according to course load. *Financial support:* Fellowships, research assistantships, teaching assistantships, career-related internships or fieldwork, Federal Work-Study, institutionally sponsored loans, tuition waivers (partial), and unspecified assistantships available. Support available to part-time students. Financial award application deadline: 5/1. *Faculty research:* Structural mechanics and dynamics, fluid mechanics, flight mechanics and controls, combustion and propulsion, system design and optimization. *Total annual research expenditures:* $14.3 million. *Unit head:* Jeff Jagoda, Director, 404-894-3060, E-mail: jeff.jagoda@aerospace.gatech.edu. *Application contact:* Daurette Joseph, Graduate Coordinator, 404-385-1595, E-mail: daurette.joseph@aerospace.gatech.edu.
Website: http://www.ae.gatech.edu.

Illinois Institute of Technology, Graduate College, Armour College of Engineering, Department of Mechanical, Materials and Aerospace Engineering, Chicago, IL 60616. Offers manufacturing engineering (MAS, MS); materials science and engineering (MAS, MS, PhD); mechanical and aerospace engineering (MAS, MS, PhD), including economics (MS), energy (MS), environment (MS). Part-time and evening/weekend programs available. Postbaccalaureate distance learning degree programs offered (minimal on-campus study). *Faculty:* 29 full-time (3 women), 10 part-time/adjunct (2 women). *Students:* 187 full-time (35 women), 27 part-time (3 women); includes 8 minority (2 Black or African American, non-Hispanic/Latino; 4 Asian, non-Hispanic/Latino; 2 Hispanic/Latino), 168 international. Average age 26. 1,562 applicants, 31% accepted, 76 enrolled. In 2014, 74 master's, 7 doctorates awarded. Terminal master's awarded for partial completion of doctoral program. *Degree requirements:* For master's, comprehensive exam (for some programs), thesis (for some programs); for doctorate, comprehensive exam, thesis/dissertation. *Entrance requirements:* For master's and doctorate, GRE General Test (minimum score 1000 Quantitative and Verbal, 3.0 Analytical Writing), minimum undergraduate GPA of 3.0. Additional exam requirements/recommendations for international students: Required—TOEFL (minimum score 550 paper-based; 80 iBT). *Application deadline:* For fall admission, 5/1 for domestic and international students; for spring admission, 10/15 for domestic and international students. Applications are processed on a rolling basis. Application fee: $50. Electronic applications accepted. *Expenses: Tuition:* Full-time $22,500; part-time $1250 per credit hour. *Required fees:* $30 per course. $260 per semester. One-time fee: $235. Tuition and fees vary according to course load and program. *Financial support:* Fellowships with full and partial tuition reimbursements, research assistantships with full and partial tuition reimbursements, teaching assistantships with full and partial tuition reimbursements, Federal Work-Study, institutionally sponsored loans, scholarships/grants, health care benefits, tuition waivers, and unspecified assistantships available. Support available to part-time students. Financial award applicants required to submit FAFSA. *Faculty research:* Fluid dynamics, metallurgical and materials engineering, solids and structures, computational mechanics, computer added design and manufacturing, thermal sciences, dynamic analysis and control of complex systems. *Unit head:* Dr. Keith Bowman, Chair of the Department of Mechanical, Materials and Aerospace Engineering & Duchossois Leadership Professor of Materials Engineering, 312-567-3175, Fax: 312-567-7230, E-mail: keith.bowman@iit.edu. *Application contact:* Rishab Malhotra, Director, Graduate Admission, 866-472-3448, Fax: 312-567-3138, E-mail: inquiry.grad@iit.edu.
Website: http://www.mmae.iit.edu.

Iowa State University of Science and Technology, Department of Aerospace Engineering and Engineering Mechanics, Ames, IA 50011. Offers aerospace engineering (M Eng, MS, PhD); engineering mechanics (M Eng, MS, PhD). *Degree requirements:* For master's, thesis (for some programs); for doctorate, thesis/dissertation. *Entrance requirements:* For master's and doctorate, GRE General Test, resume. Additional exam requirements/recommendations for international students: Required—TOEFL (minimum score 550 paper-based; 80 iBT), IELTS (minimum score 6.5). Electronic applications accepted.

Johns Hopkins University, Engineering Program for Professionals, Part-time Program in Space Systems Engineering, Baltimore, MD 21218-2699. Offers MS, Post-Master's Certificate. Postbaccalaureate distance learning degree programs offered. *Entrance requirements:* For master's, undergraduate degree in a technical discipline; at least two years of experience in the space technology or space science field; minimum of two years of relevant work experience; resume; official transcripts from all college studies. Electronic applications accepted.

Massachusetts Institute of Technology, School of Engineering, Department of Aeronautics and Astronautics, Cambridge, MA 02139. Offers aeronautics and astronautics (SM, PhD, Sc D, EAA); aerospace computational engineering (PhD, Sc D); air transportation systems (PhD, Sc D); air-breathing propulsion (PhD, Sc D); aircraft systems engineering (PhD, Sc D); autonomous systems (PhD, Sc D); communications and networks (PhD, Sc D); controls (PhD, Sc D); humans in aerospace (PhD, Sc D); materials and structures (PhD, Sc D); space propulsion (PhD, Sc D); space systems (PhD, Sc D); SM/MBA. *Faculty:* 34 full-time (8 women). *Students:* 233 full-time (51 women); includes 49 minority (1 Black or African American, non-Hispanic/Latino; 21 Asian, non-Hispanic/Latino; 17 Hispanic/Latino; 10 Two or more races, non-Hispanic/Latino), 83 international. Average age 26. 534 applicants, 19% accepted, 77 enrolled. In 2014, 70 master's, 34 doctorates, 1 other advanced degree awarded. *Degree requirements:* For master's and EAA, thesis; for doctorate, comprehensive exam, thesis/dissertation, Minimum cumulative 4.4/5.0 grade point average. *Entrance requirements:* For master's and doctorate, GRE General Test. Additional exam requirements/recommendations for international students: Required—TOEFL (minimum score 600 paper-based; 100 iBT), IELTS (minimum score 7). *Application deadline:* For fall admission, 12/15 for domestic and international students. Application fee: $75. Electronic applications accepted. *Expenses: Tuition:* Full-time $44,720; part-time $699 per unit. *Required fees:* $296. *Financial support:* In 2014–15, 195 students received support, including 59 fellowships (averaging $40,600 per year), 145 research assistantships (averaging $32,600 per year), 16 teaching assistantships (averaging $37,900 per year); Federal Work-Study, institutionally sponsored loans, scholarships/grants, health care benefits, and unspecified assistantships also available. Financial award application deadline: 4/15; financial award applicants required to submit FAFSA. *Faculty research:* Space exploration; autonomous humans-in-the-loop systems; aviation, energy, environment; aerospace communications networks; aerospace computation design and simulation; air transportation; fielding large-scale complex systems; advancing engineering education. *Total annual research expenditures:* $30.9 million. *Unit head:* Prof. Jaime Peraire, Department Head, 617-258-7537, E-mail: aeroastro-info@mit.edu. *Application contact:* Graduate Administrator, 617-253-0043, Fax: 617-253-0823, E-mail: aagradinfo@mit.edu.
Website: http://aeroastro.mit.edu/.

McGill University, Faculty of Graduate and Postdoctoral Studies, Faculty of Engineering, Department of Mechanical Engineering, Montréal, QC H3A 2T5, Canada. Offers aerospace (M Eng); manufacturing management (MMM); mechanical engineering (M Eng, M Sc, PhD).

Middle Tennessee State University, College of Graduate Studies, College of Basic and Applied Sciences, Department of Aerospace, Murfreesboro, TN 37132. Offers aerospace education (M Ed); aviation administration (MS). Part-time and evening/weekend programs available. Postbaccalaureate distance learning degree programs offered. *Degree requirements:* For master's, comprehensive exam, thesis optional. *Entrance requirements:* For master's, GRE General Test or MAT. Additional exam requirements/recommendations for international students: Required—TOEFL (minimum score 525 paper-based; 71 iBT) or IELTS (minimum score 6). Electronic applications accepted. *Faculty research:* Unmanned vehicles, air traffic control.

Mississippi State University, Bagley College of Engineering, Department of Aerospace Engineering, Mississippi State, MS 39762. Offers aerospace engineering (MS); engineering (PhD), including aerospace engineering. Part-time programs available. *Faculty:* 17 full-time (2 women), 2 part-time/adjunct (1 woman). *Students:* 24 full-time (3 women), 11 part-time (1 woman); includes 1 minority (Black or African American, non-Hispanic/Latino), 8 international. Average age 28. 40 applicants, 48% accepted, 9 enrolled. In 2014, 14 master's, 1 doctorate awarded. *Degree requirements:* For master's, comprehensive exam, thesis optional, oral exam; for doctorate, comprehensive exam, thesis/dissertation. *Entrance requirements:* For master's, GRE (for graduates from program not accredited by EAC/ABET), bachelor's degree in engineering with minimum GPA of 3.0 from junior and senior years; for doctorate, GRE, bachelor's or master's degree in aerospace engineering or closely-related field. Additional exam requirements/recommendations for international students: Required—TOEFL (minimum score 550 paper-based; 79 iBT); Recommended—IELTS (minimum score 6.5). *Application deadline:* For fall admission, 7/1 for domestic students, 5/1 for international students; for spring admission, 11/1 for domestic students, 9/1 for international students. Applications are processed on a rolling basis. Application fee: $60. Electronic applications accepted. *Expenses:* Tuition, state resident: full-time $7140; part-time $783 per credit hour. Tuition, nonresident: full-time $18,478; part-time $2043 per credit hour. *Financial support:* In 2014–15, 4 research assistantships with partial tuition reimbursements (averaging $15,215 per year), 6 teaching assistantships with partial tuition reimbursements (averaging $12,831 per year) were awarded; Federal Work-Study, institutionally sponsored loans, and unspecified assistantships also available. Financial award application deadline: 4/1; financial award applicants required to submit FAFSA. *Faculty research:* Computational fluid dynamics, flight mechanics, aerodynamics, composite structures, prototype development. *Total annual research expenditures:* $3.7 million. *Unit head:* Dr. Thomas E. Lacy, Interim Department Head, 662-325-3623, Fax: 662-325-7730, E-mail: lacy@ae.msstate.edu. *Application contact:* Dr. Mark Janus, Professor and Graduate Coordinator, 662-325-2463, Fax: 662-325-7730, E-mail: mark@hpc.msstate.edu.
Website: http://www.ae.msstate.edu/.

Missouri University of Science and Technology, Graduate School, Department of Mechanical and Aerospace Engineering, Rolla, MO 65409. Offers aerospace engineering (MS, PhD); mechanical engineering (MS, DE, PhD). Part-time and evening/weekend programs available. Terminal master's awarded for partial completion of doctoral program. *Degree requirements:* For master's, thesis optional; for doctorate, comprehensive exam, thesis/dissertation. *Entrance requirements:* For master's, GRE General Test (minimum score 1100 verbal and quantitative, writing 3.5), minimum GPA of 3.0; for doctorate, GRE General Test (minimum score: verbal and quantitative 1100, writing 3.5), minimum GPA of 3.5. Additional exam requirements/recommendations for international students: Required—TOEFL. Electronic applications accepted. *Faculty research:* Dynamics and controls, acoustics, computational fluid dynamics, space mechanics, hypersonics.

Naval Postgraduate School, Departments and Academic Groups, Department of Defense Analysis, Monterey, CA 93943. Offers command and control (MS); communications (MS); defense analysis (MS), including astronautics; financial management (MS); information operations (MS); irregular warfare (MS); national security affairs (MS); operations analysis (MS); special operations (MA, MS), including command and control (MS), communications (MS), financial management (MS), information operations (MS), irregular warfare (MS), national security affairs, operations analysis (MS), tactile missiles (MS), terrorist operations and financing (MS); tactile missiles (MS); terrorist operations and financing (MS). Program only open to commissioned officers of the United States and friendly nations and selected United States federal civilian employees. Part-time programs available. *Degree requirements:* For master's, thesis. *Faculty research:* CTF Global Ecco Project, Afghanistan endgames, core lab Philippines project, Defense Manpower Data Center (DMDC) data vulnerability.

Naval Postgraduate School, Departments and Academic Groups, Department of Mechanical and Aerospace Engineering, Monterey, CA 93943. Offers astronautical engineer (AstE); astronautical engineering (MS); engineering science (MS), including astronautical engineering, mechanical engineering; mechanical and aerospace engineering (PhD); mechanical engineering (MS). Program only open to commissioned officers of the United States and friendly nations and selected United States federal civilian employees. *Accreditation:* ABET (one or more programs are accredited). Part-time programs available. Postbaccalaureate distance learning degree programs offered. *Degree requirements:* For master's, thesis (for some programs), capstone or research/dissertation paper (for some programs); for doctorate, thesis/dissertation; for AstE, thesis. *Faculty research:* Sensors and actuators, new materials and methods, mechanics of materials, laser and material interaction, energy harvesting and storage.

Naval Postgraduate School, Departments and Academic Groups, Space Systems Academic Group, Monterey, CA 93943. Offers applied physics (MS); astronautical engineering (MS); computer science (MS); electrical engineering (MS); mechanical engineering (MS); space systems (Engr); space systems operations (MS). Program only open to commissioned officers of the United States and friendly nations and selected United States federal civilian employees. Part-time programs available. *Degree requirements:* For master's and Engr, thesis; for doctorate, thesis/dissertation. *Faculty research:* Military applications for space; space reconnaissance and remote sensing; radiation-hardened electronics for space; design, construction and operations of small satellites; satellite communications systems.

New Mexico State University, College of Engineering, Department of Mechanical Engineering, Las Cruces, NM 88003-8001. Offers MSAE, MSME, PhD. Part-time programs available. Postbaccalaureate distance learning degree programs offered (no on-campus study). *Faculty:* 18 full-time (1 woman), 1 part-time/adjunct (0 women). *Students:* 38 full-time (8 women), 15 part-time (1 woman); includes 12 minority (1 Black or African American, non-Hispanic/Latino; 1 Asian, non-Hispanic/Latino; 9 Hispanic/Latino; 1 Two or more races, non-Hispanic/Latino), 29 international. Average age 27. 89 applicants, 40% accepted, 12 enrolled. In 2014, 10 master's, 3 doctorates awarded. *Degree requirements:* For master's, thesis (for some programs); for doctorate, comprehensive exam, thesis/dissertation, 2 research tools, qualifying exam. *Entrance requirements:* For master's and doctorate, GRE, minimum GPA of 3.0. Additional exam requirements/recommendations for international students: Required—TOEFL (minimum score 550 paper-based; 79 iBT), IELTS (minimum score 6.5). *Application deadline:* For fall admission, 7/1 priority date for domestic students; for spring admission, 11/1 for domestic students. Applications are processed on a rolling basis. Application fee: $40 ($50 for international students). Electronic applications accepted. *Expenses:* Tuition, state resident: full-time $3969; part-time $220.50 per credit hour. Tuition, nonresident: full-time $13,838; part-time $768.80 per credit hour. *Required fees:* $853; $47.40 per credit hour. *Financial support:* In 2014–15, 38 students received support, including 12 research assistantships (averaging $14,176 per year), 21 teaching assistantships (averaging $14,534 per year); career-related internships or fieldwork, Federal Work-Study, scholarships/grants, traineeships, health care benefits, and unspecified assistantships also available. Support available to part-time students. Financial award application deadline: 3/1. *Faculty research:* Computational mechanics and micromechanics; robotics and mechatronics; control, dynamics, and nonlinear vibrations; composites; experimental and computational fluid dynamics; aeroelasticity and flutter. *Total annual research expenditures:* $1.3 million. *Unit head:* Dr. Ian Leslie, Academic Department Head, 575-646-1945, Fax: 575-646-6111, E-mail: ileslie@nmsu.edu. *Application contact:* 575-646-3502, Fax: 575-646-6111. Website: http://mae.nmsu.edu/.

North Carolina State University, Graduate School, College of Engineering, Department of Mechanical and Aerospace Engineering, Program in Aerospace Engineering, Raleigh, NC 27695. Offers MS, PhD. Postbaccalaureate distance learning degree programs offered (no on-campus study). *Degree requirements:* For master's, thesis (for some programs), oral exam; for doctorate, thesis/dissertation, oral and preliminary exams. *Entrance requirements:* For master's and doctorate, GRE General Test. Additional exam requirements/recommendations for international students: Required—TOEFL (minimum score 550 paper-based). Electronic applications accepted. *Faculty research:* Aerodynamics, computational fluid dynamics, flight research, smart structures, propulsion.

The Ohio State University, Graduate School, College of Engineering, Department of Mechanical and Aerospace Engineering, Columbus, OH 43210. Offers aerospace engineering (MS, PhD); mechanical engineering (MS, PhD); nuclear engineering (MS, PhD). *Faculty:* 63. *Students:* 312 full-time (47 women), 10 part-time (1 woman); includes 20 minority (3 Black or African American, non-Hispanic/Latino; 1 American Indian or Alaska Native, non-Hispanic/Latino; 10 Asian, non-Hispanic/Latino; 3 Hispanic/Latino; 3 Two or more races, non-Hispanic/Latino), 115 international. Average age 25. In 2014, 122 master's, 33 doctorates awarded. *Degree requirements:* For doctorate, thesis/dissertation. *Entrance requirements:* For master's and doctorate, GRE. Additional exam requirements/recommendations for international students: Required—TOEFL (minimum score 550 paper-based; 79 iBT), Michigan English Language Assessment Battery (minimum score 82); Recommended—IELTS (minimum score 7). *Application deadline:* For fall admission, 11/30 priority date for domestic and international students; for winter admission, 12/1 for domestic students, 11/1 for international students; for spring admission, 10/1 for domestic and international students. Applications are processed on a rolling basis. Application fee: $60 ($70 for international students). Electronic applications accepted. *Financial support:* Fellowships, research assistantships, teaching assistantships, career-related internships or fieldwork, Federal Work-Study, institutionally sponsored loans, and unspecified assistantships available. Support available to part-time students. *Unit head:* Dr. Ahmet Selamet, Chair, 614-292-4143, E-mail: selamet.1@osu.edu. *Application contact:* Janeen Sands, Graduate Program Administrator, 614-247-6605, Fax: 614-292-3656, E-mail: maegradadmissions@osu.edu. Website: http://mae.osu.edu/.

Old Dominion University, Frank Batten College of Engineering and Technology, Programs in Aerospace Engineering, Norfolk, VA 23529. Offers ME, MS, D Eng, PhD. Part-time and evening/weekend programs available. Postbaccalaureate distance learning degree programs offered (no on-campus study). *Faculty:* 22 full-time (2 women). *Students:* 9 full-time (1 woman), 28 part-time (2 women); includes 2 minority (1 Asian, non-Hispanic/Latino; 1 Hispanic/Latino), 6 international. Average age 29. 50 applicants, 60% accepted, 10 enrolled. In 2014, 13 master's, 3 doctorates awarded. *Degree requirements:* For master's, comprehensive exam, thesis (MS), exam/project (ME); for doctorate, thesis/dissertation, candidacy exam, proposal, exam. *Entrance requirements:* For master's, GRE, minimum GPA of 3.0; for doctorate, GRE, minimum GPA of 3.5. Additional exam requirements/recommendations for international students: Required—TOEFL (minimum score 550 paper-based; 79 iBT). *Application deadline:* For fall admission, 7/1 priority date for domestic students, 5/1 priority date for international students; for spring admission, 10/1 priority date for domestic students, 9/1 priority date for international students. Applications are processed on a rolling basis. Application fee: $50. Electronic applications accepted. *Expenses:* Tuition, state resident: full-time $10,488; part-time $437 per credit. Tuition, nonresident: full-time $26,136; part-time $1089 per credit. *Required fees:* $64 per semester. One-time fee: $50. *Financial support:* In 2014–15, 4 students received support, including 3 fellowships with full and partial tuition reimbursements available (averaging $16,000 per year), 30 research assistantships with full and partial tuition reimbursements available (averaging $16,000 per year); career-related internships or fieldwork, scholarships/grants, and unspecified assistantships also available. Financial award application deadline: 2/15; financial award applicants required to submit FAFSA. *Faculty research:* Computational fluid dynamics, experimental fluid dynamics, structural mechanics, dynamics and control, maglev, microfluidics. *Total annual research expenditures:* $1.8 million. *Unit head:* Dr. Sebastian Bawab, Chair, 757-683-5637, Fax: 757-683-5344, E-mail: sbawab@odu.edu. *Application contact:* Dr. Han Bao, Graduate Program Director, 757-683-4922, Fax: 757-683-3200, E-mail: hbao@aero.odu.edu. Website: http://www.eng.odu.edu/mae.

Penn State University Park, Graduate School, College of Engineering, Department of Aerospace Engineering, University Park, PA 16802. Offers M Eng, MS, PhD. *Unit head:* Dr. Amr S. Elnashai, Dean, 814-865-7537, Fax: 814-863-4749, E-mail: ase2@psu.edu. *Application contact:* Lori A. Stania, Director, Graduate Student Services, 814-867-5278, Fax: 814-863-4627, E-mail: gswww@psu.edu. Website: http://www.aero.psu.edu/.

Princeton University, Graduate School, School of Engineering and Applied Science, Department of Mechanical and Aerospace Engineering, Princeton, NJ 08544. Offers M Eng, MSE, PhD. Terminal master's awarded for partial completion of doctoral program. *Degree requirements:* For master's, thesis (MSE); for doctorate, thesis/dissertation, general exam. *Entrance requirements:* For master's, GRE General Test, 3 letters of recommendation; for doctorate, GRE General Test, official transcript(s), 3 letters of recommendation, personal statement. Additional exam requirements/recommendations for international students: Required—TOEFL. Electronic applications accepted. *Faculty research:* Bioengineering and bio-mechanics; combustion, energy conversion, and climate; fluid mechanics, dynamics, and control systems; lasers and applied physics; materials and mechanical systems.

Purdue University, College of Engineering, School of Aeronautics and Astronautics Engineering, West Lafayette, IN 47907. Offers MS, MSAAE, MSE, PhD. Part-time programs available. Postbaccalaureate distance learning degree programs offered (no on-campus study). Terminal master's awarded for partial completion of doctoral program. *Entrance requirements:* For master's, GRE General Test, minimum GPA of 3.2; for doctorate, GRE General Test, minimum GPA of 3.5. Additional exam requirements/recommendations for international students: Required—TOEFL (minimum score 550 paper-based; 77 iBT), IELTS (minimum score 6.5); Recommended—TWE. Electronic applications accepted. *Faculty research:* Structures and materials, propulsion, aerodynamics, dynamics and control.

Rensselaer Polytechnic Institute, Graduate School, School of Engineering, Program in Aerospace Engineering, Troy, NY 12180. Offers M Eng, MS, D Eng, PhD. *Faculty:* 29 full-time (5 women), 2 part-time/adjunct (1 woman). *Students:* 30 full-time (6 women), 3 part-time (1 woman); includes 8 minority (6 Asian, non-Hispanic/Latino; 2 Hispanic/Latino), 8 international. Average age 26. 69 applicants, 51% accepted, 13 enrolled. In 2014, 7 master's, 6 doctorates awarded. *Degree requirements:* For master's, thesis (for some programs); for doctorate, thesis/dissertation. *Entrance requirements:* For master's and doctorate, GRE. Additional exam requirements/recommendations for international students: Required—TOEFL (minimum score 600 paper-based; 100 iBT), IELTS (minimum score 7), PTE (minimum score 68). *Application deadline:* For fall admission, 1/1 priority date for domestic and international students; for spring admission, 8/15 priority date for domestic and international students. Applications are processed on a rolling basis. Application fee: $75. Electronic applications accepted. *Expenses: Tuition:* Full-time $46,700; part-time $1945 per credit. Tuition and fees vary according to course load. *Financial support:* In 2014–15, 27 students received support, including research assistantships with full tuition reimbursements available (averaging $18,500 per year), teaching assistantships with full tuition reimbursements available (averaging $18,500 per year); fellowships also available. Financial award application deadline: 1/1. *Faculty research:* Advanced nuclear materials, aerodynamics, design, dynamics and vibrations, fission systems and radiation transport, fluid mechanics (computational, theoretical, and experimental), heat transfer and energy conversion, manufacturing, medical imaging, health physics, multiscale/computational modeling, nanostructured materials and properties, nuclear physics/nuclear reactor, propulsion. *Total annual research expenditures:* $1.7 million. *Unit head:* Dr. Theo Borca-Tasciuc, Graduate Program Director, 518-276-2627, E-mail: borcat@rpi.edu. *Application contact:* Office of Graduate Admissions, 518-276-6216, E-mail: gradadmissions@rpi.edu. Website: http://mane.rpi.edu/aerospace.

Rutgers, The State University of New Jersey, New Brunswick, Graduate School-New Brunswick, Program in Mechanical and Aerospace Engineering, Piscataway, NJ 08854-8097. Offers design and control (MS, PhD); fluid mechanics (MS, PhD); solid mechanics (MS, PhD); thermal sciences (MS, PhD). Part-time and evening/weekend programs available. *Degree requirements:* For master's, thesis (for some programs); for doctorate, thesis/dissertation. *Entrance requirements:* For master's, GRE General Test, BS in mechanical/aerospace engineering or related field; for doctorate, GRE General Test, MS in mechanical/aerospace engineering or related field. Additional exam requirements/recommendations for international students: Required—TOEFL. Electronic applications accepted. *Faculty research:* Combustion, propulsion, thermal transport, crystal plasticity, optimization, fabrication, nanoidentation.

San Diego State University, Graduate and Research Affairs, College of Engineering, Department of Aerospace Engineering and Engineering Mechanics, San Diego, CA 92182. Offers aerospace engineering (MS); engineering mechanics (MS); engineering sciences and applied mechanics (PhD); flight dynamics (MS); fluid dynamics (MS). PhD offered jointly with University of California, San Diego and Department of Mechanical Engineering. Terminal master's awarded for partial completion of doctoral program. *Degree requirements:* For master's, comprehensive exam (for some programs), thesis (for some programs); for doctorate, thesis/dissertation. *Entrance requirements:* For master's, GRE General Test; for doctorate, GRE, 3 letters of recommendation. Additional exam requirements/recommendations for international students: Required—TOEFL. Electronic applications accepted. *Faculty research:* Organized structures in post-stall flow over wings/three dimensional separated flow, airfoil growth effect, probabilities, structural mechanics.

San Jose State University, Graduate Studies and Research, Charles W. Davidson College of Engineering, Department of Mechanical and Aerospace Engineering, Program in Aerospace Engineering, San Jose, CA 95192-0001. Offers MS. *Entrance requirements:* For master's, GRE. Electronic applications accepted.

Stanford University, School of Engineering, Department of Aeronautics and Astronautics, Stanford, CA 94305-9991. Offers MS, PhD, Eng. Terminal master's awarded for partial completion of doctoral program. *Degree requirements:* For doctorate, thesis/dissertation; for Eng, thesis. *Entrance requirements:* For master's and Eng, GRE General Test, GRE Subject Test; for doctorate, GRE General Test, GRE Engineering Subject Test. Additional exam requirements/recommendations for international students: Required—TOEFL. Electronic applications accepted. *Expenses: Tuition:* Full-time $44,184; part-time $982 per credit hour. *Required fees:* $191.

Stevens Institute of Technology, Graduate School, School of Systems and Enterprises, Program in Space Systems Engineering, Hoboken, NJ 07030. Offers M Eng, Certificate.

Syracuse University, L. C. Smith College of Engineering and Computer Science, Program in Mechanical and Aerospace Engineering, Syracuse, NY 13244. Offers MS, PhD. Part-time programs available. *Students:* 171 full-time (23 women), 22 part-time (2 women); includes 9 minority (4 Black or African American, non-Hispanic/Latino; 2 Asian, non-Hispanic/Latino; 1 Hispanic/Latino; 2 Two or more races, non-Hispanic/Latino), 159 international. Average age 25. 358 applicants, 60% accepted, 74 enrolled. In 2014, 55 master's, 8 doctorates awarded. *Degree requirements:* For master's, project or thesis; for doctorate, comprehensive exam, thesis/dissertation. *Entrance requirements:* For master's and doctorate, GRE General Test. Additional exam requirements/recommendations for international students: Required—TOEFL (minimum score 100 iBT). *Application deadline:* For fall admission, 7/1 priority date for domestic students, 6/1 priority date for international students. Applications are processed on a rolling basis. Application fee: $75. Electronic applications accepted. *Expenses: Tuition:* Part-time $1341 per credit. *Required fees:* $1341 per credit. *Financial support:* Fellowships with full tuition reimbursements, research assistantships with full and partial tuition reimbursements, teaching assistantships with full and partial tuition reimbursements, scholarships/grants, and tuition waivers (partial) available. Financial award application

deadline: 1/1. *Faculty research:* Solid mechanics and materials, fluid mechanics, thermal sciences, controls and robotics. *Unit head:* Dr. H. Ezzat Khalifa, Department Chair, 315-443-2341, Fax: 315-443-9099, E-mail: gradinfo@syr.edu. *Application contact:* Kathy Datthyn-Madigan, Information Contact, 315-443-4367, E-mail: kjdatthy@syr.edu.
Website: http://lcs.syr.edu/our-departments/mechanical-and-aerospace-engineering.

Texas A&M University, College of Engineering, Department of Aerospace Engineering, College Station, TX 77843. Offers M Eng, MS, PhD. *Faculty:* 28. *Students:* 103 full-time (13 women), 9 part-time (1 woman); includes 10 minority (1 Black or African American, non-Hispanic/Latino; 1 American Indian or Alaska Native, non-Hispanic/Latino; 2 Asian, non-Hispanic/Latino; 5 Hispanic/Latino; 1 Two or more races, non-Hispanic/Latino), 37 international. Average age 27. 276 applicants, 12% accepted, 23 enrolled. In 2014, 11 master's, 18 doctorates awarded. *Degree requirements:* For master's, thesis (MS); for doctorate, thesis/dissertation. *Entrance requirements:* For master's and doctorate, GRE General Test. Additional exam requirements/recommendations for international students: Required—TOEFL. *Application deadline:* For fall admission, 1/1 priority date for domestic students; for spring admission, 7/1 priority date for domestic students; for summer admission, 12/1 priority date for domestic students. Applications are processed on a rolling basis. Application fee: $50 ($90 for international students). Electronic applications accepted. *Expenses:* Tuition, state resident: full-time $4078; part-time $226.55 per credit hour. Tuition, nonresident: full-time $10,594; part-time $577.55 per credit hour. *Required fees:* $2813; $237.70 per credit hour. $278.50 per semester. Tuition and fees vary according to degree level and student level. *Financial support:* In 2014–15, 107 students received support, including 6 fellowships with full and partial tuition reimbursements available (averaging $27,042 per year), 88 research assistantships with full and partial tuition reimbursements available (averaging $8,356 per year), 1 teaching assistantship with full and partial tuition reimbursement available (averaging $7,000 per year); career-related internships or fieldwork, institutionally sponsored loans, scholarships/grants, traineeships, health care benefits, tuition waivers (full and partial), and unspecified assistantships also available. Support available to part-time students. Financial award application deadline: 3/1; financial award applicants required to submit FAFSA. *Faculty research:* Materials and structures, aerodynamics and computational fluid dynamics (CFD), flight dynamics and control. *Unit head:* Dr. Rodney Bowersox, Department Head, 979-854-4184, E-mail: bowersox@tamu.edu. *Application contact:* Karen Knabe, Administrative Coordinator, Graduate Programs, 979-845-5520, Fax: 979-845-6051, E-mail: k-knabe@tamu.edu.
Website: http://engineering.tamu.edu/aerospace.

Université Laval, Faculty of Sciences and Engineering, Department of Mechanical Engineering, Program in Aerospace Engineering, Québec, QC G1K 7P4, Canada. Offers M Sc. Program offered jointly with Concordia University, École Polytechnique de Montréal, McGill University, and Université de Sherbrooke. Part-time programs available. *Entrance requirements:* For master's, knowledge of French and English. Electronic applications accepted.

University at Buffalo, the State University of New York, Graduate School, School of Engineering and Applied Sciences, Department of Mechanical and Aerospace Engineering, Buffalo, NY 14260. Offers aerospace engineering (MS, PhD); mechanical engineering (MS, PhD). Part-time programs available. *Faculty:* 35 full-time (5 women), 8 part-time/adjunct (1 woman). *Students:* 212 full-time (32 women), 28 part-time (2 women); includes 10 minority (4 Black or African American, non-Hispanic/Latino; 5 Asian, non-Hispanic/Latino; 1 Hispanic/Latino), 167 international. Average age 25. 1,216 applicants, 14% accepted, 55 enrolled. In 2014, 67 master's, 6 doctorates awarded. Terminal master's awarded for partial completion of doctoral program. *Degree requirements:* For master's, comprehensive exam, project or thesis; for doctorate, thesis/dissertation. *Entrance requirements:* For master's and doctorate, GRE General Test, GRE Subject Test. Additional exam requirements/recommendations for international students: Required—TOEFL (minimum score 79 iBT). *Application deadline:* For fall admission, 2/1 priority date for domestic and international students; for spring admission, 10/1 priority date for domestic and international students. Applications are processed on a rolling basis. Application fee: $75. Electronic applications accepted. *Financial support:* In 2014–15, 85 students received support, including 11 fellowships with full and partial tuition reimbursements available (averaging $30,000 per year), 16 research assistantships with full and partial tuition reimbursements available (averaging $27,660 per year), 32 teaching assistantships with full and partial tuition reimbursements available (averaging $21,775 per year); career-related internships or fieldwork, Federal Work-Study, institutionally sponsored loans, scholarships/grants, health care benefits, tuition waivers (full and partial), and unspecified assistantships also available. Support available to part-time students. Financial award application deadline: 2/1; financial award applicants required to submit FAFSA. *Faculty research:* Fluid and thermal sciences, systems and design, mechanics and materials. *Total annual research expenditures:* $7.8 million. *Unit head:* Dr. Kemper Lewis, Chair, 716-645-2682, Fax: 716-645-2883, E-mail: kelewis@buffalo.edu. *Application contact:* Dr. Pineet Singla, Director of Graduate Studies, 716-645-1429, Fax: 716-645-3875, E-mail: psingla@buffalo.edu.
Website: http://www.mae.buffalo.edu/.

The University of Alabama, Graduate School, College of Engineering, Department of Aerospace Engineering and Mechanics, Tuscaloosa, AL 35487. Offers aerospace engineering (MSAEM); engineering science and mechanics (PhD). Part-time programs available. Postbaccalaureate distance learning degree programs offered (no on-campus study). *Faculty:* 16 full-time (1 woman), 1 part-time/adjunct (0 women). *Students:* 22 full-time (1 woman), 27 part-time (3 women); includes 1 minority (Black or African American, non-Hispanic/Latino), 15 international. Average age 28. 45 applicants, 58% accepted, 11 enrolled. In 2014, 10 master's, 2 doctorates awarded. Terminal master's awarded for partial completion of doctoral program. *Degree requirements:* For master's, comprehensive exam (for some programs), thesis (for some programs); for doctorate, comprehensive exam, thesis/dissertation, 1-year residency. *Entrance requirements:* For master's and doctorate, GRE (minimum score of 300), minimum undergraduate GPA of 3.0. Additional exam requirements/recommendations for international students: Required—TOEFL (minimum score 550 paper-based; 79 iBT). *Application deadline:* For fall admission, 1/1 priority date for domestic students, 5/15 priority date for international students; for spring admission, 1/1 priority date for domestic students, 6/1 priority date for international students. Applications are processed on a rolling basis. Application fee: $50 ($60 for international students). Electronic applications accepted. *Expenses:* Tuition, state resident: full-time $9826. Tuition, nonresident: full-time $24,950. *Financial support:* In 2014–15, 18 students received support, including fellowships with full tuition reimbursements available (averaging $15,000 per year), research assistantships with full tuition reimbursements available (averaging $20,000 per year), teaching assistantships with full tuition reimbursements available (averaging $14,025 per year); Federal Work-Study, institutionally sponsored loans, scholarships/grants, health care benefits, and unspecified assistantships also available. Financial award application deadline: 2/15. *Faculty research:* Aeronautics, astronautics, solid mechanics, fluid mechanics, computational modeling. *Total annual research expenditures:* $1.2 million. *Unit head:* Dr. John Baker, Professor/Department Head, 205-348-4997, Fax: 205-348-7240, E-mail: john.baker@eng.ua.edu. *Application contact:* Dr. James Paul Hubner, Associate Professor, 205-348-1617, Fax: 208-348-7240, E-mail: phubner@eng.ua.edu.
Website: http://aem.eng.ua.edu/.

The University of Alabama in Huntsville, School of Graduate Studies, College of Engineering, Department of Mechanical and Aerospace Engineering, Huntsville, AL 35899. Offers aerospace engineering (MSE), including aerospace engineering, missile systems engineering, rotorcraft systems engineering; aerospace systems engineering (MS, PhD); mechanical engineering (MSE, PhD). Part-time and evening/weekend programs available. *Degree requirements:* For master's, comprehensive exam, thesis or alternative, oral and written exams; for doctorate, comprehensive exam, thesis/dissertation, oral and written exams. *Entrance requirements:* For master's, GRE General Test, BSE, minimum GPA of 3.0; for doctorate, GRE General Test, minimum GPA of 3.0. Additional exam requirements/recommendations for international students: Required—TOEFL (minimum score 500 paper-based; 80 iBT), IELTS (minimum score 6.5). Electronic applications accepted. *Faculty research:* Rocket propulsion and plasma engineering, materials engineering and solid mechanics, energy conversion, transport, and storage.

The University of Arizona, College of Engineering, Department of Aerospace and Mechanical Engineering, Program in Aerospace Engineering, Tucson, AZ 85721. Offers MS, PhD. Part-time programs available. *Degree requirements:* For master's, thesis or alternative; for doctorate, thesis/dissertation. *Entrance requirements:* For master's and doctorate, GRE General Test, minimum GPA of 3.25. Additional exam requirements/recommendations for international students: Required—TOEFL (minimum score 550 paper-based; 79 iBT). Electronic applications accepted. *Faculty research:* Fluid mechanics, structures, computer-aided design, stability and control, combustion.

University of California, Davis, College of Engineering, Program in Mechanical and Aeronautical Engineering, Davis, CA 95616. Offers aeronautical engineering (M Engr, MS, D Engr, PhD, Certificate); mechanical engineering (M Engr, MS, D Engr, PhD, Certificate); M Engr/MBA. *Degree requirements:* For master's, comprehensive exam (for some programs), thesis (for some programs); for doctorate, thesis/dissertation. *Entrance requirements:* For master's and doctorate, GRE General Test, minimum GPA of 3.0. Additional exam requirements/recommendations for international students: Required—TOEFL (minimum score 550 paper-based). Electronic applications accepted.

University of California, Irvine, Henry Samueli School of Engineering, Department of Mechanical and Aerospace Engineering, Irvine, CA 92697. Offers MS, PhD. Part-time programs available. *Students:* 164 full-time (32 women), 7 part-time (1 woman); includes 40 minority (1 Black or African American, non-Hispanic/Latino; 1 American Indian or Alaska Native, non-Hispanic/Latino; 18 Asian, non-Hispanic/Latino; 17 Hispanic/Latino; 3 Two or more races, non-Hispanic/Latino), 83 international. Average age 26. 724 applicants, 22% accepted, 75 enrolled. In 2014, 44 master's, 18 doctorates awarded. Terminal master's awarded for partial completion of doctoral program. *Degree requirements:* For doctorate, thesis/dissertation. *Entrance requirements:* For master's and doctorate, GRE General Test, minimum GPA of 3.0, 3 letters of recommendation. Additional exam requirements/recommendations for international students: Required—TOEFL (minimum score 550 paper-based). *Application deadline:* For fall admission, 1/15 priority date for domestic students, 1/15 for international students. Applications are processed on a rolling basis. Application fee: $90 ($110 for international students). Electronic applications accepted. *Financial support:* Fellowships with tuition reimbursements, research assistantships with full tuition reimbursements, teaching assistantships with tuition reimbursements, institutionally sponsored loans, traineeships, health care benefits, and unspecified assistantships available. Financial award application deadline: 3/1; financial award applicants required to submit FAFSA. *Faculty research:* Thermal and fluid sciences, combustion and propulsion, control systems, robotics, lightweight structures. *Unit head:* Prof. Derek Dunn-Rankin, Chair, 949-824-8745, Fax: 949-824-8585, E-mail: ddunnran@uci.edu. *Application contact:* Prof. Timothy Rupert, Graduate Admissions Advisor, 949-824-4937, Fax: 949-824-8585, E-mail: trupert@uci.edu.
Website: http://mae.eng.uci.edu/.

University of California, Los Angeles, Graduate Division, Henry Samueli School of Engineering and Applied Science, Department of Mechanical and Aerospace Engineering, Program in Aerospace Engineering, Los Angeles, CA 90095-1597. Offers MS, PhD. *Faculty:* 31 full-time (2 women), 6 part-time/adjunct (0 women). *Students:* 52 full-time (3 women); includes 22 minority (2 Black or African American, non-Hispanic/Latino; 12 Asian, non-Hispanic/Latino; 6 Hispanic/Latino; 2 Two or more races, non-Hispanic/Latino), 13 international. 176 applicants, 38% accepted, 19 enrolled. In 2014, 18 master's, 4 doctorates awarded. *Degree requirements:* For master's, comprehensive exam or thesis; for doctorate, thesis/dissertation, qualifying exams. *Entrance requirements:* For master's, GRE General Test, minimum GPA of 3.0; for doctorate, GRE General Test, minimum GPA of 3.25. Additional exam requirements/recommendations for international students: Required—TOEFL (minimum score 560 paper-based; 87 iBT), IELTS (minimum score 7). *Application deadline:* For fall admission, 12/15 for domestic and international students; for winter admission, 10/1 for domestic students; for spring admission, 12/31 for domestic students. Application fee: $80 ($100 for international students). Electronic applications accepted. *Financial support:* In 2014–15, 105 fellowships, 194 research assistantships, 89 teaching assistantships were awarded; Federal Work-Study, institutionally sponsored loans, and tuition waivers (full and partial) also available. Financial award application deadline: 12/15; financial award applicants required to submit FAFSA. *Faculty research:* Applied mathematics, applied plasma physics, dynamics, fluid mechanics, heat and mass transfer, design, robotics and manufacturing, nanoelectromechanical/microelectromechanical systems (NEMS/MEMS), structural and solid mechanics, systems and control. *Total annual research expenditures:* $12.6 million. *Unit head:* Dr. Tsu-Chin Tsao, Chair, 310-206-2819, E-mail: ttsao@seas.ucla.edu. *Application contact:* Angie Castillo, Student Affairs Officer, 310-825-7793, Fax: 310-206-4830, E-mail: angie@seas.ucla.edu.
Website: http://www.mae.ucla.edu/.

University of California, San Diego, Graduate Division, Department of Mechanical and Aerospace Engineering, Program in Aerospace Engineering, La Jolla, CA 92093. Offers MS, PhD. *Students:* 21 full-time (3 women), 4 part-time (0 women); includes 7 minority (1 Black or African American, non-Hispanic/Latino; 4 Asian, non-Hispanic/Latino; 2 Hispanic/Latino), 6 international. 114 applicants, 29% accepted, 12 enrolled. In 2014, 2 master's awarded. *Degree requirements:* For master's, comprehensive exam or thesis; for doctorate, comprehensive exam, thesis/dissertation. *Entrance requirements:* For master's and doctorate, GRE General Test, minimum GPA of 3.0. Additional exam requirements/recommendations for international students: Required—TOEFL (minimum score 550 paper-based; 80 iBT), IELTS (minimum score 7). *Application deadline:* For fall admission, 12/15 for domestic students, 1/2 for international students. Application fee: $90 ($110 for international students). Electronic applications accepted. *Expenses:* Tuition, state resident: full-time $11,220; part-time $5610 per quarter. Tuition, nonresident: full-time $26,322; part-time $13,161 per quarter. *Required fees:* $570 per quarter. Tuition and fees vary according to program. *Financial support:* Fellowships, research assistantships, teaching assistantships, scholarships/grants, and unspecified

assistantships available. Financial award application deadline: 1/2; financial award applicants required to submit FAFSA. *Faculty research:* Aerodynamics, turbulence and fluid mechanics. *Unit head:* Vitali Nesterenko, Chair, 858-534-0113, E-mail: mae-chair-l@ucsd.edu. *Application contact:* Linda McKamey, Graduate Coordinator, 858-534-4065, E-mail: mae-gradadm-l@ucsd.edu.
Website: http://maeweb.ucsd.edu/.

University of Central Florida, College of Engineering and Computer Science, Department of Mechanical and Aerospace Engineering, Program in Aerospace Engineering, Orlando, FL 32816. Offers MSAE. *Students:* 15 full-time (2 women), 11 part-time (0 women); includes 8 minority (2 Black or African American, non-Hispanic/Latino; 1 American Indian or Alaska Native, non-Hispanic/Latino; 4 Hispanic/Latino; 1 Two or more races, non-Hispanic/Latino). Average age 25. 37 applicants, 62% accepted, 13 enrolled. In 2014, 17 master's awarded. *Degree requirements:* For master's, thesis or alternative. *Application deadline:* For fall admission, 7/15 priority date for domestic students; for spring admission, 12/1 priority date for domestic students. Application fee: $30. Electronic applications accepted. *Expenses:* Tuition, state resident: part-time $288.16 per credit hour. Tuition, nonresident: part-time $1073.31 per credit hour. *Financial support:* In 2014–15, 6 students received support, including fellowships with partial tuition reimbursements available (averaging $2,000 per year), 6 research assistantships with partial tuition reimbursements available (averaging $8,600 per year), 2 teaching assistantships with partial tuition reimbursements available (averaging $10,700 per year); career-related internships or fieldwork, institutionally sponsored loans, scholarships/grants, tuition waivers (partial), and unspecified assistantships also available. *Unit head:* Dr. Challapalli Suryanarayana, Interim Chair, 407-823-6662, Fax: 407-823-0208, E-mail: surya@ucf.edu. *Application contact:* Barbara Rodriguez Lamas, Director, Admissions and Student Services, 407-823-2766, Fax: 407-823-6442, E-mail: gradadmissions@ucf.edu.
Website: http://mae.ucf.edu/academics/graduate/.

University of Central Missouri, The Graduate School, Warrensburg, MO 64093. Offers accountancy (MA); accounting (MBA); applied mathematics (MS); aviation safety (MA); biology (MS); business administration (MBA); career and technical education leadership (MS); college student personnel administration (MS); communication (MA); computer science (MS); counseling (MS); criminal justice (MS); educational leadership (Ed D); educational technology (MS); elementary and early childhood education (MSE); English (MA); environmental studies (MA); finance (MBA); history (MA); human services/educational technology (Ed S); human services/learning resources (Ed S); human services/professional counseling (Ed S); industrial hygiene (MS); industrial management (MS); information systems (MBA); information technology (MS); kinesiology (MS); library science and information services (MS); literacy education (MSE); marketing (MBA); mathematics (MS); music (MA); occupational safety management (MS); psychology (MS); rural family nursing (MS); school administration (MSE); social gerontology (MS); sociology (MA); special education (MSE); speech language pathology (MS); superintendency (Ed S); teaching (MAT); teaching English as a second language (MA); technology (MS); technology management (PhD); theatre (MA). Part-time programs available. *Faculty:* 314 full-time (137 women), 24 part-time/adjunct (14 women). *Students:* 1,624 full-time (542 women), 1,773 part-time (1,055 women); includes 194 minority (104 Black or African American, non-Hispanic/Latino; 6 American Indian or Alaska Native, non-Hispanic/Latino; 23 Asian, non-Hispanic/Latino; 41 Hispanic/Latino; 3 Native Hawaiian or other Pacific Islander, non-Hispanic/Latino; 17 Two or more races, non-Hispanic/Latino), 1,592 international. Average age 31. 2,800 applicants, 63% accepted, 1223 enrolled. In 2014, 796 master's, 81 other advanced degrees awarded. *Degree requirements:* For master's and Ed S, comprehensive exam (for some programs), thesis (for some programs). *Entrance requirements:* Additional exam requirements/recommendations for international students: Required—TOEFL (minimum score 550 paper-based; 79 iBT). *Application deadline:* For fall admission, 6/1 for domestic students; for spring admission, 10/1 for domestic and international students. Applications are processed on a rolling basis. Application fee: $30 ($75 for international students). Electronic applications accepted. *Expenses:* Tuition, state resident: full-time $6630; part-time $276.25 per credit hour. Tuition, nonresident: full-time $13,260; part-time $552.50 per credit hour. *Required fees:* $29 per credit hour. Tuition and fees vary according to campus/location. *Financial support:* In 2014–15, 118 students received support, including 271 research assistantships with full and partial tuition reimbursements available (averaging $7,500 per year), 109 teaching assistantships with full and partial tuition reimbursements available (averaging $7,500 per year); career-related internships or fieldwork, Federal Work-Study, scholarships/grants, and administrative and laboratory assistantships also available. Support available to part-time students. Financial award application deadline: 3/1; financial award applicants required to submit FAFSA. *Unit head:* Tina Church-Hockett, Director of Graduate School and International Admissions, 660-543-4621, Fax: 660-543-4778, E-mail: church@ucmo.edu. *Application contact:* Brittany Lawrence, Graduate Student Services Coordinator, 660-543-4621, Fax: 660-543-4778, E-mail: gradinfo@ucmo.edu.
Website: http://www.ucmo.edu/graduate/.

University of Cincinnati, Graduate School, College of Engineering and Applied Science, Department of Aerospace Engineering and Engineering Mechanics, Cincinnati, OH 45221. Offers MS, PhD. Part-time programs available. Terminal master's awarded for partial completion of doctoral program. *Degree requirements:* For master's, project or thesis; for doctorate, thesis/dissertation. *Entrance requirements:* For master's and doctorate, GRE General Test. Additional exam requirements/recommendations for international students: Required—TOEFL (minimum score 550 paper-based). Electronic applications accepted. *Faculty research:* Computational fluid mechanics/propulsion, large space structures, dynamics and guidance of VTOL vehicles.

University of Colorado Boulder, Graduate School, College of Engineering and Applied Science, Department of Aerospace Engineering Sciences, Boulder, CO 80309. Offers MS, PhD. *Faculty:* 31 full-time (3 women). *Students:* 234 full-time (46 women), 32 part-time (7 women); includes 38 minority (1 Black or African American, non-Hispanic/Latino; 14 Asian, non-Hispanic/Latino; 12 Hispanic/Latino; 11 Two or more races, non-Hispanic/Latino), 34 international. Average age 26. 217 applicants, 55% accepted, 75 enrolled. In 2014, 78 master's, 18 doctorates awarded. Terminal master's awarded for partial completion of doctoral program. *Degree requirements:* For master's, comprehensive exam, thesis or alternative; for doctorate, comprehensive exam, thesis/dissertation. *Entrance requirements:* For master's, GRE General Test, minimum undergraduate GPA of 3.0; for doctorate, minimum undergraduate GPA of 3.25. *Application deadline:* For fall admission, 1/5 for domestic students, 12/1 for international students; for spring admission, 10/1 for domestic students, 8/1 for international students. Applications are processed on a rolling basis. Application fee: $50 ($70 for international students). Electronic applications accepted. *Financial support:* In 2014–15, 393 students received support, including 92 fellowships (averaging $15,208 per year), 92 research assistantships with full and partial tuition reimbursements available (averaging $35,989 per year), 27 teaching assistantships with full and partial tuition reimbursements available (averaging $32,677 per year); institutionally sponsored loans, scholarships/grants, health care benefits, and unspecified assistantships also available. Financial award application deadline: 2/1; financial award applicants required to submit FAFSA. *Faculty research:* Aeronautical/astronautical engineering, atmospheric sciences, aerodynamics, computational mechanics. *Total annual research expenditures:* $15.6 million.
Website: http://www.colorado.edu/aerospace/.

University of Colorado Colorado Springs, College of Engineering and Applied Science, Program in General Engineering, Colorado Springs, CO 80933-7150. Offers energy engineering (ME); engineering management (ME); information assurance (ME); software engineering (ME); space operations (ME); systems engineering (ME). Part-time and evening/weekend programs available. Postbaccalaureate distance learning degree programs offered (minimal on-campus study). *Faculty:* 2 full-time (0 women), 8 part-time/adjunct (2 women). *Students:* 15 full-time (2 women), 159 part-time (30 women); includes 29 minority (3 Black or African American, non-Hispanic/Latino; 1 American Indian or Alaska Native, non-Hispanic/Latino; 10 Asian, non-Hispanic/Latino; 12 Hispanic/Latino; 3 Two or more races, non-Hispanic/Latino), 63 international. Average age 36. 113 applicants, 65% accepted, 39 enrolled. In 2014, 29 master's, 6 doctorates awarded. *Degree requirements:* For master's, thesis, portfolio, or project; for doctorate, comprehensive exam, thesis/dissertation. *Entrance requirements:* For master's, GRE (minimum score of 148 new grading scale on quantitative portion if GPA is less than 3.0); for doctorate, GRE (minimum score of 148 new grading scale on the quantitative portion if the applicant has not graduated from a program of recognized standing), minimum GPA of 3.3 in the bachelor or master degree program attempted. Additional exam requirements/recommendations for international students: Required—TOEFL (minimum score 80 iBT), IELTS (minimum score 6). *Application deadline:* For fall admission, 6/1 for domestic and international students; for spring admission, 11/1 for domestic and international students; for summer admission, 4/15 for domestic and international students. Application fee: $60 ($100 for international students). Electronic applications accepted. *Expenses:* Expenses: Contact institution. *Financial support:* In 2014–15, 10 students received support, including 2 fellowships (averaging $6,000 per year), 16 research assistantships (averaging $11,600 per year); teaching assistantships, Federal Work-Study, and scholarships/grants also available. Support available to part-time students. Financial award application deadline: 3/1; financial award applicants required to submit FAFSA. *Total annual research expenditures:* $91,458. *Unit head:* Dr. Ramaswami Dandapani, Dean, 719-255-3543, Fax: 719-255-3542, E-mail: rdan@cas.uccs.edu. *Application contact:* Dawn House, Coordinator, 719-255-3246, E-mail: dhouse@uccs.edu.

University of Dayton, Department of Mechanical and Aerospace Engineering, Dayton, OH 45469. Offers aerospace engineering (MSAE, DE, PhD); mechanical engineering (MSME, DE, PhD); renewable and clean energy (MS). Part-time programs available. Postbaccalaureate distance learning degree programs offered (no on-campus study). *Faculty:* 15 full-time (3 women), 10 part-time/adjunct (1 woman). *Students:* 197 full-time (43 women), 37 part-time (6 women); includes 11 minority (7 Black or African American, non-Hispanic/Latino; 2 Asian, non-Hispanic/Latino; 2 Hispanic/Latino), 156 international. Average age 27. 340 applicants, 44% accepted, 58 enrolled. In 2014, 69 master's, 2 doctorates awarded. Terminal master's awarded for partial completion of doctoral program. *Degree requirements:* For master's, thesis optional; for doctorate, variable foreign language requirement, thesis/dissertation, departmental qualifying exam. *Entrance requirements:* For master's, BS in engineering, math, or physics. Additional exam requirements/recommendations for international students: Required—TOEFL (minimum score 550 paper-based; 80 iBT), IELTS (minimum score 6.5). *Application deadline:* For fall admission, 8/1 priority date for domestic students, 5/1 priority date for international students; for winter admission, 9/1 for international students; for spring admission, 12/1 for domestic students, 9/1 priority date for international students; for summer admission, 4/1 for domestic students, 3/1 priority date for international students. Applications are processed on a rolling basis. Application fee: $0 ($50 for international students). Electronic applications accepted. *Expenses: Tuition:* Full-time $10,176; part-time $848 per credit. *Required fees:* $25; $25 per course. Part-time tuition and fees vary according to course level, course load, degree level and program. *Financial support:* In 2014–15, 3 fellowships with full tuition reimbursements (averaging $25,000 per year), 16 research assistantships with full tuition reimbursements (averaging $12,000 per year), 4 teaching assistantships with full tuition reimbursements (averaging $8,000 per year) were awarded; institutionally sponsored loans, health care benefits, and unspecified assistantships also available. Financial award application deadline: 3/1; financial award applicants required to submit FAFSA. *Faculty research:* Jet engine combustion, surface coating friction and wear, aircraft thermal management, aerospace fuels, energy efficient buildings, energy efficient manufacturing, renewable energy. *Total annual research expenditures:* $1.2 million. *Unit head:* Dr. Kelly Kissock, Chair, 937-229-2999, Fax: 937-229-4766, E-mail: jkissock1@udayton.edu. *Application contact:* Dr. Vinod Jain, Graduate Program Director, 937-229-2992, Fax: 937-229-4766, E-mail: vjain1@udayton.edu.
Website: https://www.udayton.edu/engineering/departments-mechanical_and_aerospace/index.php.

University of Florida, Graduate School, College of Engineering, Department of Mechanical and Aerospace Engineering, Gainesville, FL 32611. Offers aerospace engineering (ME, MS, PhD); mechanical engineering (ME, MS, PhD). Part-time programs available. Postbaccalaureate distance learning degree programs offered. *Faculty:* 50 full-time (4 women), 30 part-time/adjunct (5 women). *Students:* 386 full-time (38 women), 92 part-time (11 women); includes 61 minority (11 Black or African American, non-Hispanic/Latino; 24 Asian, non-Hispanic/Latino; 26 Hispanic/Latino), 259 international. 739 applicants, 59% accepted, 192 enrolled. In 2014, 186 master's, 37 doctorates awarded. *Degree requirements:* For master's, thesis (for some programs); for doctorate, comprehensive exam, thesis/dissertation. *Entrance requirements:* For master's and doctorate, minimum GPA of 3.0. Additional exam requirements/recommendations for international students: Required—TOEFL (minimum score 550 paper-based; 80 iBT), IELTS (minimum score 6). *Application deadline:* Applications are processed on a rolling basis. Application fee: $30. Electronic applications accepted. *Financial support:* Institutionally sponsored loans and unspecified assistantships available. Support available to part-time students. Financial award applicants required to submit FAFSA. *Faculty research:* Thermal sciences, design, controls and robotics, manufacturing, energy transport and utilization. *Unit head:* David W. Hahn, PhD, Chair, 352-392-0807, Fax: 352-392-1071, E-mail: dwhahn@ufl.edu. *Application contact:* David W. Mikolaitis, PhD, Graduate Coordinator, 352-392-7632, Fax: 352-392-7303, E-mail: mollusk@ufl.edu.
Website: http://www.mae.ufl.edu/.

University of Illinois at Urbana–Champaign, Graduate College, College of Engineering, Department of Aerospace Engineering, Champaign, IL 61820. Offers MS, PhD. Part-time programs available. Postbaccalaureate distance learning degree programs offered (no on-campus study). *Students:* 137 (17 women). Application fee: $70 ($90 for international students). *Unit head:* Dr. Philippe H. Geubelle, Head, 217-244-7648, Fax: 217-244-0720, E-mail: geubelle@illinois.edu. *Application contact:* Staci L. Tankersley, Program Coordinator, 217-333-3674, Fax: 217-244-0720, E-mail: tank@illinois.edu.
Website: http://www.ae.illinois.edu/.

Aerospace/Aeronautical Engineering

The University of Kansas, Graduate Studies, School of Engineering, Program in Aerospace Engineering, Lawrence, KS 66045. Offers ME, MS, DE, PhD. *Faculty:* 11 full-time. *Students:* 39 full-time (7 women), 8 part-time (0 women); includes 4 minority (3 Asian, non-Hispanic/Latino; 1 Hispanic/Latino), 23 international. Average age 27. 70 applicants, 73% accepted, 15 enrolled. In 2014, 8 master's, 5 doctorates awarded. *Degree requirements:* For master's, comprehensive exam, thesis; for doctorate, comprehensive exam, thesis/dissertation, research and responsible scholarship skills, qualifying exam. *Entrance requirements:* For master's, GRE, minimum GPA of 3.0; for doctorate, GRE, minimum GPA of 3.5. Additional exam requirements/recommendations for international students: Required—TOEFL (minimum score 570 paper-based; 80 iBT). *Application deadline:* For fall admission, 1/1 priority date for domestic and international students; for spring admission, 12/1 priority date for domestic and international students. Applications are processed on a rolling basis. Application fee: $55 ($65 for international students). Electronic applications accepted. *Financial support:* Fellowships with full and partial tuition reimbursements, research assistantships with full and partial tuition reimbursements, teaching assistantships with full and partial tuition reimbursements, career-related internships or fieldwork, scholarships/grants, tuition waivers (full and partial), and unspecified assistantships available. Financial award application deadline: 1/1. *Faculty research:* Artificial intelligence, composite materials and structures, computational fluid dynamics and computational aeroacoustics, structural vibrations of high performance structures, flight test engineering. *Unit head:* ZJ Wang, Chair, 785-864-2440, E-mail: zjw@ku.edu. *Application contact:* Lesslee Smithhisler, Administrative Assistant, 785-864-2960, E-mail: lksmithh@ku.edu.
Website: http://www.ae.engr.ku.edu/.

The University of Manchester, School of Materials, Manchester, United Kingdom. Offers advanced aerospace materials engineering (M Sc); advanced metallic systems (PhD); biomedical materials (M Phil, M Sc, PhD); ceramics and glass (M Phil, M Sc, PhD); composite materials (M Sc, PhD); corrosion and protection (M Phil, M Sc, PhD); materials (M Phil, PhD); metallic materials (M Phil, M Sc, PhD); nanostructural materials (M Phil, M Sc, PhD); paper science (M Phil, M Sc, PhD); polymer science and engineering (M Phil, M Sc, PhD); technical textiles (M Sc); textile design, fashion and management (M Phil, M Sc, PhD); textile science and technology (M Phil, M Sc, PhD); textiles (M Phil, PhD); textiles and fashion (M Ent).

The University of Manchester, School of Mechanical, Aerospace and Civil Engineering, Manchester, United Kingdom. Offers advanced manufacturing technology (M Ent); aerospace engineering (M Phil, M Sc, PhD); civil engineering (M Phil, M Sc, PhD); environmental engineering (M Phil, PhD); management of projects (M Phil, M Sc, PhD); mechanical engineering (M Phil, M Sc, PhD); mechanical engineering design (M Ent); nuclear engineering (M Phil, D Eng, PhD).

University of Maryland, College Park, Academic Affairs, A. James Clark School of Engineering, Department of Aerospace Engineering, College Park, MD 20742. Offers M Eng, MS, PhD. Part-time and evening/weekend programs available. Postbaccalaureate distance learning degree programs offered. *Degree requirements:* For master's, thesis optional; for doctorate, thesis/dissertation. *Entrance requirements:* For master's and doctorate, GRE General Test (recommended), 3 letters of recommendation. Electronic applications accepted. *Faculty research:* Aerodynamics and propulsion, structural mechanics, flight dynamics, rotor craft, space robotics.

University of Miami, Graduate School, College of Engineering, Department of Mechanical and Aerospace Engineering, Coral Gables, FL 33124. Offers MSME, PhD. Part-time programs available. *Degree requirements:* For master's, thesis (for some programs); for doctorate, comprehensive exam, thesis/dissertation. *Entrance requirements:* For master's and doctorate, GRE General Test, minimum GPA of 3.0. Additional exam requirements/recommendations for international students: Required—TOEFL (minimum score 550 paper-based). Electronic applications accepted. *Faculty research:* Internal combustion engines, heat transfer, hydrogen energy, controls, fuel cells.

University of Michigan, College of Engineering, Department of Aerospace Engineering, Ann Arbor, MI 48109. Offers M Eng, MS, MSE, PhD. Part-time programs available. *Students:* 187 full-time (31 women), 11 part-time (1 woman). 511 applicants, 27% accepted, 68 enrolled. In 2014, 68 master's, 24 doctorates awarded. *Degree requirements:* For doctorate, thesis/dissertation, oral defense of dissertation, preliminary exams. *Entrance requirements:* For master's, GRE General Test; for doctorate, GRE General Test, master's degree. *Application deadline:* Applications are processed on a rolling basis. Electronic applications accepted. *Financial support:* Fellowships, research assistantships, teaching assistantships, Federal Work-Study, and tuition waivers (full and partial) available. *Faculty research:* Turbulent flows and combustion, advanced spacecraft control, helicopter aeroelasticity, experimental fluid dynamics, space propulsion, optimal structural design, interactive materials, computational fluid and solid dynamics. *Total annual research expenditures:* $11.5 million. *Unit head:* Dr. Daniel Inman, Department Chair, 734-764-7320, Fax: 734-763-0578, E-mail: daninman@umich.edu. *Application contact:* Denise Phelps, Graduate Admissions Coordinator, 734-615-4406, Fax: 734-763-0578, E-mail: dphelps@umich.edu.
Website: http://www.engin.umich.edu/dept/aero/.

University of Michigan, College of Engineering, Department of Atmospheric, Oceanic, and Space Sciences, Ann Arbor, MI 48109. Offers atmospheric and space sciences (MS, PhD); geoscience and remote sensing (PhD); space and planetary sciences (PhD); space engineering (M Eng). Part-time programs available. *Students:* 95 full-time (33 women), 2 part-time (1 woman). 143 applicants, 25% accepted, 16 enrolled. In 2014, 45 master's, 6 doctorates awarded. Terminal master's awarded for partial completion of doctoral program. *Degree requirements:* For master's, thesis (for some programs); for doctorate, thesis/dissertation, oral defense of dissertation, preliminary exams. *Entrance requirements:* For master's and doctorate, GRE General Test. Additional exam requirements/recommendations for international students: Required—TOEFL. *Application deadline:* Applications are processed on a rolling basis. Electronic applications accepted. *Financial support:* Fellowships, research assistantships, teaching assistantships, career-related internships or fieldwork, Federal Work-Study, institutionally sponsored loans, and health care benefits available. Support available to part-time students. Financial award applicants required to submit FAFSA. *Faculty research:* Planetary environments, space instrumentation, air pollution meteorology, global climate change, sun-earth connection, space weather. *Total annual research expenditures:* $40.9 million. *Unit head:* Dr. James Slavin, Chair, 734-764-7221, Fax: 734-615-4645, E-mail: jaslavin@umich.edu. *Application contact:* Sandra Pytlinski, Graduate Student Services Coordinator, 734-936-0482, Fax: 734-763-0437, E-mail: aoss.um@umich.edu.
Website: http://aoss.engin.umich.edu/.

University of Minnesota, Twin Cities Campus, College of Science and Engineering, Department of Aerospace Engineering and Mechanics, Minneapolis, MN 55455-0213. Offers MS, PhD. Part-time programs available. *Degree requirements:* For doctorate, thesis/dissertation. *Entrance requirements:* Additional exam requirements/recommendations for international students: Required—TOEFL (minimum score 550 paper-based). Electronic applications accepted. *Faculty research:* Fluid mechanics, solid mechanics and materials, aerospace systems, nanotechnology.

University of Missouri, Office of Research and Graduate Studies, College of Engineering, Department of Mechanical and Aerospace Engineering, Columbia, MO 65211. Offers MS, PhD. *Faculty:* 22 full-time (0 women), 1 part-time/adjunct (0 women). *Students:* 57 full-time (8 women), 45 part-time (8 women); includes 4 minority (1 Black or African American, non-Hispanic/Latino; 1 Asian, non-Hispanic/Latino; 2 Hispanic/Latino), 73 international. Average age 26. 167 applicants, 23% accepted, 22 enrolled. In 2014, 21 master's, 6 doctorates awarded. *Degree requirements:* For master's, thesis; for doctorate, one foreign language, thesis/dissertation. *Entrance requirements:* For master's and doctorate, GRE General Test, minimum GPA of 3.0. Additional exam requirements/recommendations for international students: Required—TOEFL (minimum score 500 paper-based; 61 iBT). *Application deadline:* For fall admission, 5/31 priority date for domestic and international students; for winter admission, 10/31 priority date for domestic and international students; for spring admission, 4/30 priority date for domestic and international students. Applications are processed on a rolling basis. Application fee: $55 ($75 for international students). Electronic applications accepted. *Financial support:* Fellowships, research assistantships, teaching assistantships, institutionally sponsored loans, scholarships/grants, health care benefits, and unspecified assistantships available. Support available to part-time students. *Faculty research:* Dynamics and control, design and manufacturing, materials and solids and thermal and fluid science engineering. *Unit head:* Dr. Yuwen Zhang, Interim Department Chair, 573-882-6936, E-mail: zhangyu@missouri.edu. *Application contact:* Marilyn Nevels, Graduate Administrative Assistant, 573-884-8610, E-mail: nevelsma@missouri.edu.
Website: http://engineering.missouri.edu/mae/degree-programs/.

University of Notre Dame, Graduate School, College of Engineering, Department of Aerospace and Mechanical Engineering, Notre Dame, IN 46556. Offers aerospace and mechanical engineering (M Eng, PhD); aerospace engineering (MS Aero E); mechanical engineering (MEME, MSME). Terminal master's awarded for partial completion of doctoral program. *Degree requirements:* For master's, comprehensive exam, thesis or alternative; for doctorate, thesis/dissertation, candidacy exam. *Entrance requirements:* For master's and doctorate, GRE General Test. Additional exam requirements/recommendations for international students: Required—TOEFL (minimum score 600 paper-based; 80 iBT). Electronic applications accepted. *Faculty research:* Aerodynamics/fluid dynamics, design and manufacturing, controls/robotics, solid mechanics or biomechanics/biomaterials.

University of Oklahoma, Gallogly College of Engineering, School of Aerospace and Mechanical Engineering, Program in Aerospace Engineering, Norman, OK 73019. Offers composites (MS); structures (PhD). Part-time programs available. *Students:* 2 full-time (0 women), 11 part-time (1 woman); includes 1 minority (Black or African American, non-Hispanic/Latino), 5 international. Average age 31. 8 applicants, 38% accepted, 2 enrolled. In 2014, 4 master's awarded. *Degree requirements:* For master's, comprehensive exam (for some programs), thesis (for some programs); for doctorate, comprehensive exam, thesis/dissertation. *Entrance requirements:* For master's and doctorate, GRE, letters of reference, resume, statement of purpose. Additional exam requirements/recommendations for international students: Required—TOEFL (minimum score 79 iBT). *Application deadline:* For fall admission, 1/15 for domestic and international students; for spring admission, 9/1 for domestic and international students. Application fee: $50 ($100 for international students). Electronic applications accepted. *Expenses:* Tuition, state resident: full-time $4394; part-time $183.10 per credit hour. Tuition, nonresident: full-time $16,970; part-time $707.10 per credit hour. *Required fees:* $2892; $109.95 per credit hour. $126.50 per semester. *Financial support:* In 2014–15, 5 students received support. Scholarships/grants and unspecified assistantships available. Financial award application deadline: 6/1; financial award applicants required to submit FAFSA. *Faculty research:* Composite materials, nanomechanics, robotics, biomechanics/soft tissues, multi-phase flows. *Unit head:* Dr. Cengiz Altan, Director, 405-325-1744, Fax: 405-325-1088, E-mail: altan@ou.edu. *Application contact:* Kate O'Brien-Hamoush, Student Services Coordinator, 405-325-5013, Fax: 405-325-1088, E-mail: kobrien@ou.edu.
Website: http://www.ou.edu/content/coe/ame.html.

University of Ottawa, Faculty of Graduate and Postdoctoral Studies, Faculty of Engineering, Ottawa-Carleton Institute for Mechanical and Aerospace Engineering, Ottawa, ON K1N 6N5, Canada. Offers M Eng, MA Sc, PhD. MA Sc, M Eng, PhD offered jointly with Carleton University. *Degree requirements:* For master's, thesis or alternative; for doctorate, thesis/dissertation, seminar series, qualifying exam. *Entrance requirements:* For master's, honors degree or equivalent, minimum B average; for doctorate, master's degree, minimum B+ average. Electronic applications accepted. *Faculty research:* Fluid mechanics-heat transfer, solid mechanics, design, manufacturing and control.

University of Southern California, Graduate School, Viterbi School of Engineering, Department of Aerospace and Mechanical Engineering, Los Angeles, CA 90089. Offers aerospace and mechanical engineering: computational fluid and solid mechanics (MS); aerospace and mechanical engineering: dynamics and control (MS); aerospace engineering (MS, PhD, Engr), including aerospace engineering (PhD, Engr); green technologies (MS); mechanical engineering (MS, PhD, Engr), including energy conversion (MS), mechanical engineering (PhD, Engr), nuclear power (MS); product development engineering (MS). Part-time and evening/weekend programs available. Postbaccalaureate distance learning degree programs offered (no on-campus study). Terminal master's awarded for partial completion of doctoral program. *Degree requirements:* For master's, thesis optional; for doctorate, thesis/dissertation. *Entrance requirements:* For master's, doctorate, and Engr, GRE General Test. Additional exam requirements/recommendations for international students: Recommended—TOEFL. Electronic applications accepted. *Faculty research:* Mechanics and materials, aerodynamics of air/ground vehicles, gas dynamics, aerosols, astronautics and space science, geophysical and microgravity flows, planetary physics, power MEMs and MEMS vacuum pumps, heat transfer and combustion.

University of Southern California, Graduate School, Viterbi School of Engineering, Division of Astronautics and Space Technology, Los Angeles, CA 90089. Offers astronautical engineering (MS, PhD, Engr, Graduate Certificate). Part-time and evening/weekend programs available. Postbaccalaureate distance learning degree programs offered (no on-campus study). Terminal master's awarded for partial completion of doctoral program. *Degree requirements:* For master's, thesis optional; for doctorate, thesis/dissertation; for other advanced degree, comprehensive exam (for some programs). *Entrance requirements:* For master's, doctorate, and other advanced degree, GRE General Test. Additional exam requirements/recommendations for international students: Recommended—TOEFL. Electronic applications accepted. *Faculty research:* Space technology, space science and applications, space instrumentation, advanced propulsion, fundamental processes in gases and plasmas.

The University of Tennessee, Graduate School, College of Engineering, Department of Mechanical, Aerospace and Biomedical Engineering, Program in Aerospace Engineering, Knoxville, TN 37996. Offers MS, PhD, MS/MBA. Part-time programs available. Postbaccalaureate distance learning degree programs offered (minimal on-campus study). *Faculty:* 6 full-time (1 woman). *Students:* 12 full-time (2 women), 11 part-time (0 women); includes 1 minority (Black or African American, non-Hispanic/Latino), 5

international. Average age 28. 42 applicants, 43% accepted, 5 enrolled. In 2014, 7 master's, 4 doctorates awarded. *Degree requirements:* For master's, thesis or alternative; for doctorate, comprehensive exam, thesis/dissertation. *Entrance requirements:* For master's, GRE General Test (for MS students pursuing research thesis), minimum GPA of 2.7 (for U.S. degree holders), 3.0 (for international degree holders); 3 references; statement of purpose; for doctorate, GRE General Test (for all PhD candidates), minimum GPA of 3.0 on previous graduate course work; 3 references; statement of purpose. Additional exam requirements/recommendations for international students: Required—TOEFL (minimum score 550 paper-based). *Application deadline:* For fall admission, 2/1 priority date for domestic and international students; for spring admission, 6/15 for domestic and international students. Applications are processed on a rolling basis. Application fee: $35. Electronic applications accepted. *Financial support:* In 2014–15, 5 students received support, including 5 teaching assistantships with full tuition reimbursements available (averaging $15,560 per year); fellowships with full tuition reimbursements available, research assistantships with full tuition reimbursements available, career-related internships or fieldwork, Federal Work-Study, institutionally sponsored loans, health care benefits, and unspecified assistantships also available. Financial award application deadline: 2/1; financial award applicants required to submit FAFSA. *Faculty research:* Atmospheric re-entry mechanics, hybrid rocket propulsion, laser-induced plasma spectroscopy, unsteady aerodynamics and aeroelasticity. *Unit head:* Dr. Matthew Mench, Head, 865-974-5115, Fax: 865-974-5274, E-mail: mmench@utk.edu. *Application contact:* Dr. Gary V. Smith, Associate Head, 865-974-5271, Fax: 865-974-5274, E-mail: gvsmith@utk.edu.
Website: http://www.engr.utk.edu/mabe/.

The University of Tennessee, The University of Tennessee Space Institute, Tullahoma, TN 37388. Offers aerospace engineering (MS, PhD); biomedical engineering (MS, PhD); engineering science (MS, PhD); industrial and systems engineering/engineering management (MS, PhD); mechanical engineering (MS, PhD); physics (MS, PhD). Part-time programs available. Postbaccalaureate distance learning degree programs offered. *Faculty:* 19 full-time (3 women), 4 part-time/adjunct. *Students:* 31 full-time (6 women), 82 part-time (11 women); includes 10 minority (6 Black or African American, non-Hispanic/Latino; 1 American Indian or Alaska Native, non-Hispanic/Latino; 2 Asian, non-Hispanic/Latino; 1 Hispanic/Latino), 11 international. 60 applicants, 55% accepted, 22 enrolled. In 2014, 25 master's, 5 doctorates awarded. Terminal master's awarded for partial completion of doctoral program. *Degree requirements:* For doctorate, one foreign language, thesis/dissertation. *Entrance requirements:* Additional exam requirements/recommendations for international students: Required—TOEFL (minimum score 550 paper-based; 80 iBT), IELTS (minimum score 6.5). *Application deadline:* For fall admission, 2/1 for international students; for spring admission, 6/15 for international students. Applications are processed on a rolling basis. Application fee: $60. Electronic applications accepted. *Financial support:* In 2014–15, 6 fellowships with full tuition reimbursements (averaging $2,451 per year), 24 research assistantships with full tuition reimbursements (averaging $20,244 per year) were awarded; career-related internships or fieldwork, Federal Work-Study, institutionally sponsored loans, health care benefits, and unspecified assistantships also available. *Faculty research:* Fluid mechanics/aerodynamics, chemical and electric propulsion and laser diagnostics, computational mechanics and simulations, carbon fiber production and composite materials. *Total annual research expenditures:* $1.8 million. *Unit head:* Dr. Charles Johnson, Associate Executive Director, 931-393-7318, Fax: 931-393-7211, E-mail: cjohnson@utsi.edu. *Application contact:* Dee Merriman, Director, 931-393-7213, Fax: 931-393-7211, E-mail: dmerrima@utsi.edu.
Website: http://www.utsi.edu/.

The University of Texas at Arlington, Graduate School, College of Engineering, Department of Mechanical and Aerospace Engineering, Program in Aerospace Engineering, Arlington, TX 76019. Offers M Engr, MS, PhD. Part-time and evening/weekend programs available. Postbaccalaureate distance learning degree programs offered (minimal on-campus study). Terminal master's awarded for partial completion of doctoral program. *Degree requirements:* For master's, thesis optional; for doctorate, comprehensive exam, thesis/dissertation. *Entrance requirements:* For master's and doctorate, GRE General Test, minimum GPA of 3.0. Additional exam requirements/recommendations for international students: Required—TOEFL (minimum score 550 paper-based).

The University of Texas at Austin, Graduate School, Cockrell School of Engineering, Department of Aerospace Engineering and Engineering Mechanics, Program in Aerospace Engineering, Austin, TX 78712-1111. Offers MSE, PhD. *Entrance requirements:* For master's and doctorate, GRE General Test. Electronic applications accepted.

University of Toronto, School of Graduate Studies, Faculty of Applied Science and Engineering, Institute for Aerospace Studies, Toronto, ON M5S 2J7, Canada. Offers M Eng, MA Sc, PhD. Part-time programs available. *Degree requirements:* For master's, thesis (for some programs); for doctorate, thesis/dissertation, formal manuscript for publication. *Entrance requirements:* For master's, BA Sc or equivalent in engineering (M Eng); bachelor's degree in physics, mathematics, engineering or chemistry (MA Sc); 2 letters of reference; for doctorate, master's degree in applied science, engineering, mathematics, physics, or chemistry; demonstrated ability to perform advanced research, 2 letters of reference. Additional exam requirements/recommendations for international students: Required—TOEFL (minimum score 580 paper-based), TWE (minimum score 5). Electronic applications accepted.

University of Virginia, School of Engineering and Applied Science, Department of Mechanical and Aerospace Engineering, Charlottesville, VA 22903. Offers ME, MS, PhD. Postbaccalaureate distance learning degree programs offered (no on-campus study). *Faculty:* 24 full-time (3 women). *Students:* 79 full-time (12 women), 7 part-time (1 woman); includes 7 minority (5 Asian, non-Hispanic/Latino; 2 Hispanic/Latino), 36 international. Average age 26. 217 applicants, 22% accepted, 25 enrolled. In 2014, 15 master's, 9 doctorates awarded. *Degree requirements:* For master's, thesis (MS); for doctorate, comprehensive exam, thesis/dissertation. *Entrance requirements:* For master's and doctorate, GRE General Test, 3 letters of recommendation. Additional exam requirements/recommendations for international students: Required—TOEFL (minimum score 650 paper-based; 90 iBT), IELTS (minimum score 7). *Application deadline:* For fall admission, 8/1 for domestic students, 4/1 for international students; for winter admission, 12/1 for domestic students, 8/1 for international students; for spring admission, 5/1 for domestic students, 1/1 for international students. Applications are processed on a rolling basis. Application fee: $60. Electronic applications accepted. *Expenses:* Tuition, state resident: full-time $14,164; part-time $349 per credit hour. Tuition, nonresident: full-time $23,722; part-time $1300 per credit hour. *Required fees:* $2514. *Financial support:* Fellowships, research assistantships, and teaching assistantships available. Financial award application deadline: 1/15; financial award applicants required to submit FAFSA. *Faculty research:* Solid mechanics, dynamical systems and control, thermofluids. *Unit head:* Hossein Haj-Hariri, Chair, 434-924-7424, Fax: 434-982-2037, E-mail: mae-adm@virginia.edu. *Application contact:* Graduate Secretary, 434-924-7425, Fax: 434-982-2037, E-mail: mae-adm@virginia.edu.
Website: http://www.mae.virginia.edu/NewMAE/.

University of Washington, Graduate School, College of Engineering, William E. Boeing Department of Aeronautics and Astronautics, Seattle, WA 98195-2400. Offers MAE, MSAA, PhD. Part-time programs available. Postbaccalaureate distance learning degree programs offered (minimal on-campus study). *Faculty:* 20 full-time (2 women). *Students:* 110 full-time (17 women), 87 part-time (21 women); includes 46 minority (4 Black or African American, non-Hispanic/Latino; 27 Asian, non-Hispanic/Latino; 15 Hispanic/Latino), 26 international. Average age 27. 334 applicants, 46% accepted, 79 enrolled. In 2014, 40 master's, 7 doctorates awarded. Terminal master's awarded for partial completion of doctoral program. *Degree requirements:* For master's, thesis optional, completion of all work within 6 years; for doctorate, comprehensive exam, thesis/dissertation, qualifying, general and final exams; completion of all work toward within 10 years. *Entrance requirements:* For master's and doctorate, GRE General Test, minimum GPA of 3.0, letters of recommendation, statement of objectives, undergraduate degree in aerospace or mechanical engineering. Additional exam requirements/recommendations for international students: Required—TOEFL (minimum score 580 paper-based; 92 iBT); Recommended—IELTS (minimum score 7). *Application deadline:* For fall admission, 12/15 for domestic and international students. Application fee: $85. Electronic applications accepted. *Expenses:* Expenses: Contact institution. *Financial support:* In 2014–15, 58 students received support, including 11 fellowships (averaging $19,000 per year), 28 research assistantships with full tuition reimbursements available (averaging $26,703 per year), 18 teaching assistantships with full tuition reimbursements available (averaging $17,523 per year); career-related internships or fieldwork, Federal Work-Study, health care benefits, tuition waivers (full), and unspecified assistantships also available. Financial award application deadline: 1/15; financial award applicants required to submit FAFSA. *Faculty research:* Space systems, aircraft systems, energy systems, aerospace control systems, advanced composite materials and structures, fluid mechanics. *Total annual research expenditures:* $7.9 million. *Unit head:* Dr. Anthony Waas, Professor and Chair, 206-543-1950, Fax: 206-543-0217, E-mail: awass@aa.washington.edu. *Application contact:* Ed Connery, Advisor and Admissions Coordinator, 206-543-6725, Fax: 206-543-0217, E-mail: econnery@aa.washington.edu.
Website: http://www.aa.washington.edu/.

Utah State University, School of Graduate Studies, College of Engineering, Department of Mechanical and Aerospace Engineering, Logan, UT 84322. Offers aerospace engineering (MS, PhD); mechanical engineering (ME, MS, PhD). Terminal master's awarded for partial completion of doctoral program. *Degree requirements:* For master's, thesis (for some programs); for doctorate, thesis/dissertation. *Entrance requirements:* For master's, GRE General Test, minimum GPA of 3.0; for doctorate, GRE General Test, minimum GPA of 3.3. Additional exam requirements/recommendations for international students: Required—TOEFL. *Faculty research:* In-space instruments, cryogenic cooling, thermal science, space structures, composite materials.

Virginia Polytechnic Institute and State University, Graduate School, College of Engineering, Blacksburg, VA 24061. Offers aerospace engineering (ME, MS, PhD); biological systems engineering (ME, MS, PhD); biomedical engineering (MS, PhD); chemical engineering (ME, MS, PhD); civil engineering (ME, MS, PhD); computer engineering (ME, MS, PhD); computer science (MS, PhD); electrical engineering (ME, PhD); engineering education (PhD); engineering mechanics (ME, MS, PhD); environmental engineering (MS); environmental science and engineering (MS); industrial and systems engineering (ME, MS, PhD); materials science and engineering (ME, MS, PhD); mechanical engineering (ME, MS, PhD); mining and minerals engineering (PhD); mining engineering (ME, MS); nuclear engineering (MS, PhD); ocean engineering (MS); systems engineering (ME, MS). *Accreditation:* ABET (one or more programs are accredited). *Faculty:* 356 full-time (60 women), 3 part-time/adjunct (1 woman). *Students:* 1,700 full-time (398 women), 345 part-time (58 women); includes 213 minority (43 Black or African American, non-Hispanic/Latino; 1 American Indian or Alaska Native, non-Hispanic/Latino; 87 Asian, non-Hispanic/Latino; 58 Hispanic/Latino; 1 Native Hawaiian or other Pacific Islander, non-Hispanic/Latino; 23 Two or more races, non-Hispanic/Latino), 1,079 international. Average age 27. 5,228 applicants, 18% accepted, 471 enrolled. In 2014, 438 master's, 211 doctorates awarded. *Degree requirements:* For master's, comprehensive exam (for some programs), thesis (for some programs); for doctorate, comprehensive exam (for some programs), thesis/dissertation (for some programs). *Entrance requirements:* For master's and doctorate, GRE/GMAT (may vary by department). Additional exam requirements/recommendations for international students: Required—TOEFL (minimum score 550 paper-based). *Application deadline:* For fall admission, 8/1 for domestic students, 4/1 for international students; for spring admission, 1/1 for domestic students, 9/1 for international students. Applications are processed on a rolling basis. Application fee: $75. Electronic applications accepted. *Expenses:* Tuition, state resident: full-time $11,656; part-time $647.50 per credit hour. Tuition, nonresident: full-time $23,351; part-time $1297.25 per credit hour. *Required fees:* $2533; $465.75 per semester. Tuition and fees vary according to course load, campus/location and program. *Financial support:* In 2014–15, 148 fellowships with full tuition reimbursements (averaging $8,031 per year), 855 research assistantships with full tuition reimbursements (averaging $22,855 per year), 288 teaching assistantships with full tuition reimbursements (averaging $20,291 per year) were awarded. Financial award application deadline: 3/1; financial award applicants required to submit FAFSA. *Total annual research expenditures:* $90.5 million. *Unit head:* Dr. Richard C. Benson, Dean, 540-231-9752, Fax: 540-231-3031, E-mail: deaneng@vt.edu. *Application contact:* Linda Perkins, Executive Assistant, 540-231-9752, Fax: 540-231-3031, E-mail: lperkins@vt.edu.
Website: http://www.eng.vt.edu/.

Virginia Polytechnic Institute and State University, VT Online, Blacksburg, VA 24061. Offers advanced transportation systems (Certificate); aerospace engineering (MS); agricultural and life sciences (MSLFS); business information systems (Graduate Certificate); career and technical education (MS); civil engineering (MS); computer engineering (M Eng, MS); decision support systems (Graduate Certificate); eLearning leadership (MA); electrical engineering (M Eng, MS); engineering administration (MEA); environmental engineering (Certificate); environmental politics and policy (Graduate Certificate); environmental sciences and engineering (MS); foundations of political analysis (Graduate Certificate); health product risk management (Graduate Certificate); industrial and systems engineering (MS); information policy and society (Graduate Certificate); information security (Graduate Certificate); information technology (MIT); instructional technology (MA); integrative STEM education (MA Ed); liberal arts (Graduate Certificate); life sciences: health product risk management (MS); natural resources (MNR, Graduate Certificate); networking (Graduate Certificate); nonprofit and nongovernmental organization management (Graduate Certificate); ocean engineering (MS); political science (MA); security studies (Graduate Certificate); software development (Graduate Certificate). *Expenses:* Tuition, state resident: full-time $11,656; part-time $647.50 per credit hour. Tuition, nonresident: full-time $23,351; part-time $1297.25 per credit hour. *Required fees:* $2533; $465.75 per semester. Tuition and fees vary according to course load, campus/location and program.

Washington University in St. Louis, School of Engineering and Applied Science, Department of Mechanical Engineering and Materials Science, St. Louis, MO 63130-

Aerospace/Aeronautical Engineering

4899. Offers aerospace engineering (MS, PhD); materials science (MS); mechanical engineering (M Eng, MS, PhD). Part-time programs available. Terminal master's awarded for partial completion of doctoral program. *Degree requirements:* For master's, thesis optional; for doctorate, thesis/dissertation optional. *Entrance requirements:* For master's, GRE; for doctorate, GRE General Test, departmental qualifying exam. *Faculty research:* Aerosols science and technology, applied mechanics, biomechanics and biomedical engineering, design, dynamic systems, combustion science, composite materials, materials science.

Webster University, George Herbert Walker School of Business and Technology, Department of Management, St. Louis, MO 63119-3194. Offers business and organizational security management (MA); health administration (MHA); health care management (MA); health services management (MA); human resources development (MA); human resources management (MA); information technology management (MS); management and leadership (MA); marketing (MA); nonprofit leadership (MA); procurement and acquisitions management (MA); public administration (MPA); space systems operations management (MS). Part-time and evening/weekend programs available. Postbaccalaureate distance learning degree programs offered (no on-campus study). *Degree requirements:* For master's, thesis (for some programs). *Entrance requirements:* Additional exam requirements/recommendations for international students: Required—TOEFL.

Western Michigan University, Graduate College, College of Engineering and Applied Sciences, Department of Mechanical and Aerospace Engineering, Kalamazoo, MI

49008. Offers mechanical engineering (MSE, PhD). Part-time programs available. *Degree requirements:* For master's, thesis optional; for doctorate, thesis/dissertation. *Application deadline:* For fall admission, 2/15 for domestic students. *Financial support:* Application deadline: 2/15. *Application contact:* Admissions and Orientation, 269-387-2000, Fax: 269-387-2096.

West Virginia University, College of Engineering and Mineral Resources, Department of Mechanical and Aerospace Engineering, Program in Aerospace Engineering, Morgantown, WV 26506. Offers MSAE, PhD. Part-time programs available. Terminal master's awarded for partial completion of doctoral program. *Degree requirements:* For master's, thesis; for doctorate, comprehensive exam, thesis/dissertation, qualifying exams, proposal defense. *Entrance requirements:* For master's and doctorate, GRE General Test, minimum GPA of 3.0, 3 reference letters. Additional exam requirements/recommendations for international students: Required—TOEFL (minimum score 550 paper-based; 79 iBT). *Faculty research:* Transonic flight controls and simulations, thermal science, composite materials, aerospace design.

Wichita State University, Graduate School, College of Engineering, Department of Aerospace Engineering, Wichita, KS 67260. Offers MS, PhD. Part-time programs available. *Unit head:* Dr. L. Scott Miller, Chairperson, 316-978-3410, E-mail: scott.miller@wichita.edu. *Application contact:* Jordan Oleson, Admission Coordinator, 316-978-3095, E-mail: jordan.oleson@wichita.edu. Website: http://www.wichita.edu/ae.

Aviation

Everglades University, Graduate Programs, Program in Aviation Science, Boca Raton, FL 33431. Offers MSA. *Entrance requirements:* Additional exam requirements/recommendations for international students: Recommended—TOEFL (minimum score 500 paper-based). Electronic applications accepted.

Florida Institute of Technology, Graduate Programs, College of Aeronautics, Program in Applied Aviation Safety, Melbourne, FL 32901-6975. Offers MSA. *Students:* 7 full-time (0 women); includes 2 minority (1 Black or African American, non-Hispanic/Latino; 1 Hispanic/Latino), 4 international. Average age 26. 15 applicants, 53% accepted, 1 enrolled. In 2014, 5 master's awarded. *Degree requirements:* For master's, comprehensive exam (for some programs), thesis or alternative, capstone, 30 credit hours. *Entrance requirements:* For master's, letter of recommendation, resume, statement of objectives. *Expenses: Tuition:* Part-time $1179 per credit hour. Tuition and fees vary according to campus/location. *Unit head:* Dr. Korhan Oyman, Dean, 321-674-8971, E-mail: koyman@fit.edu. *Application contact:* Cheryl A. Brown, Associate Director of Graduate Admissions, 321-674-7581, Fax: 321-723-9468, E-mail: cbrown@fit.edu. Website: http://www.fit.edu/programs/8205/msa-aviation-applied-aviation-safety#.VUDm_k10ypo.

Florida Institute of Technology, Graduate Programs, College of Aeronautics, Program in Aviation Safety, Melbourne, FL 32901-6975. Offers MSA. Postbaccalaureate distance learning degree programs offered (no on-campus study). In 2014, 8 master's awarded. *Degree requirements:* For master's, comprehensive exam (for some programs), thesis or alternative, capstone course, 36 credit hours. *Entrance requirements:* For master's, letter of recommendation, resume, statement of objectives. *Expenses: Tuition:* Part-time $1179 per credit hour. Tuition and fees vary according to campus/location. *Unit head:* Dr. Korhan Oyman, Dean, 321-674-8971, E-mail: koyman@fit.edu. *Application contact:* Cheryl A. Brown, Associate Director of Graduate Admissions, 321-674-7581, Fax: 321-723-9468, E-mail: cbrown@fit.edu. Website: http://coa.fit.edu/programs/aviation-safety.php.

Florida Institute of Technology, Graduate Programs, College of Aeronautics, Program in Aviation Sciences, Melbourne, FL 32901-6975. Offers PhD. *Students:* 5 full-time (2 women), 6 part-time (1 woman); includes 1 minority (Black or African American, non-Hispanic/Latino), 3 international. Average age 40. 18 applicants, 67% accepted, 3 enrolled. *Degree requirements:* For doctorate, thesis/dissertation, alternative, 51 semester hours. *Entrance requirements:* For doctorate, 3 letters of recommendation, resume, statement of objectives, minimum GPA of 3.2. *Expenses: Tuition:* Part-time $1179 per credit hour. Tuition and fees vary according to campus/location. *Unit head:* Dr. Korhan Oyman, Dean, 321-674-8971, E-mail: koyman@fit.edu. *Application contact:*

Cheryl A. Brown, Associate Director of Graduate Admissions, 321-674-7581, Fax: 321-723-9468, E-mail: cbrown@fit.edu. Website: http://www.fit.edu/programs/9103/phd-aviation-sciences#.VT_V4E10ypo.

Lewis University, College of Arts and Sciences, Program in Aviation and Transportation, Romeoville, IL 60446. Offers administration (MS); safety and security (MS). Part-time and evening/weekend programs available. Postbaccalaureate distance learning degree programs offered (no on-campus study). *Students:* 18 full-time (5 women), 20 part-time (6 women); includes 11 minority (7 Black or African American, non-Hispanic/Latino; 2 Asian, non-Hispanic/Latino; 1 Hispanic/Latino; 1 Two or more races, non-Hispanic/Latino), 8 international. Average age 33. *Entrance requirements:* For master's, bachelor's degree, minimum GPA of 3.0, personal statement, 3 letters of recommendation. Additional exam requirements/recommendations for international students: Required—TOEFL (minimum score 550 paper-based; 80 iBT). *Application deadline:* For fall admission, 5/1 priority date for international students; for spring admission, 11/15 priority date for international students. Applications are processed on a rolling basis. Application fee: $40. Electronic applications accepted. *Financial support:* Application deadline: 5/1; applicants required to submit FAFSA. *Unit head:* Dr. Randal DeMik, Program Chair, 815-838-0500 Ext. 5559, E-mail: demikra@lewisu.edu. *Application contact:* Julie Branchaw, Assistant Director, Graduate and Adult Admission, 815-836-5574, E-mail: branchju@lewisu.edu.

Southeastern Oklahoma State University, Department of Aviation Science, Durant, OK 74701-0609. Offers aerospace administration and logistics (MS). Part-time and evening/weekend programs available. *Entrance requirements:* For master's, minimum GPA of 3.0 in last 60 hours or 2.75 overall. Additional exam requirements/recommendations for international students: Required—TOEFL (minimum score 550 paper-based; 79 iBT). Electronic applications accepted.

University of North Dakota, Graduate School, John D. Odegard School of Aerospace Sciences, Department of Aviation, Grand Forks, ND 58202. Offers MS. Part-time programs available. Postbaccalaureate distance learning degree programs offered (minimal on-campus study). *Degree requirements:* For master's, comprehensive exam. *Entrance requirements:* For master's, GRE General Test, FAA private pilot certificate or foreign equivalent. Additional exam requirements/recommendations for international students: Required—TOEFL (minimum score 550 paper-based; 79 iBT), IELTS (minimum score 6.5). Electronic applications accepted.

The University of Tennessee, Graduate School, Intercollegiate Programs, Program in Aviation Systems, Knoxville, TN 37996. Offers MS. Part-time programs available. Postbaccalaureate distance learning degree programs offered (no on-campus study). *Degree requirements:* For master's, thesis optional. *Entrance requirements:* For master's, minimum GPA of 2.7. Additional exam requirements/recommendations for international students: Required—TOEFL. Electronic applications accepted.

Section 3
Agricultural Engineering and Bioengineering

This section contains a directory of institutions offering graduate work in agricultural engineering and bioengineering, followed by an in-depth entry submitted by an institution that chose to prepare a detailed program description. Additional information about programs listed in the directory but not augmented by an in-depth entry may be obtained by writing directly to the dean of a graduate school or chair of a department at the address given in the directory.

For programs offering related work, see also in this book *Biomedical Engineering and Biotechnology; Civil and Environmental Engineering; Engineering and Applied Sciences;* and *Management of Engineering and Technology.* In the other guides in this series:

Graduate Programs in the Biological/Biomedical Sciences & Health-Related Medical Professions
See *Biological and Biomedical Sciences; Ecology, Environmental Biology, and Evolutionary Biology; Marine Biology; Nutrition;* and *Zoology*

Graduate Programs in the Physical Sciences, Mathematics, Agricultural Sciences, the Environment & Natural Resources
See *Agricultural and Food Sciences* and *Natural Resources*

CONTENTS

Agricultural Engineering

Cornell University, Graduate School, Graduate Fields of Agriculture and Life Sciences and Graduate Fields of Engineering, Field of Biological and Environmental Engineering, Ithaca, NY 14853-0001. Offers bioenergy and integrated energy systems (M Eng, MPS, MS, PhD); biological engineering (M Eng, MPS, MS, PhD); bioprocess engineering (M Eng, MPS, MS, PhD); ecohydrology (M Eng, MPS, MS, PhD); environmental engineering (M Eng, MPS, MS, PhD); environmental management (MPS); food engineering (M Eng, MPS, MS, PhD); industrial biotechnology (M Eng, MPS, MS, PhD); nanobiotechnology (M Eng, MPS, MS, PhD); sustainable systems (M Eng, MPS, MS, PhD); synthetic biology (MS); syntheticbiology (M Eng, MPS, PhD). Terminal master's awarded for partial completion of doctoral program. *Degree requirements:* For master's, thesis (MS); for doctorate, comprehensive exam, thesis/dissertation. *Entrance requirements:* For master's, letters of recommendation (3 for MS, 2 for M Eng and MPS); for doctorate, GRE General Test, 3 letters of recommendation. Additional exam requirements/recommendations for international students: Required—TOEFL (minimum score 550 paper-based; 77 iBT). Electronic applications accepted. *Faculty research:* Biological and food engineering, environmental, soil and water engineering, international agricultural engineering, structures and controlled environments, machine systems and energy.

Dalhousie University, Faculty of Engineering, Department of Biological Engineering, Halifax, NS B3J 2X4, Canada. Offers M Eng, MA Sc, PhD. *Degree requirements:* For master's, thesis; for doctorate, thesis/dissertation. *Entrance requirements:* Additional exam requirements/recommendations for international students: Required—TOEFL, IELTS, CANTEST, CAEL, or Michigan English Language Assessment Battery. *Faculty research:* Waste management, energy and environment, bio-machinery and robotics, soil and water, aquacultural and food engineering.

Illinois Institute of Technology, Graduate College, School of Applied Technology, Institute for Food Safety and Health, Bedford Park, IL 60501-1957. Offers food process engineering (MFPE, MS); food safety and technology (MFST, MS). Part-time programs available. *Faculty:* 6 full-time (2 women). *Students:* 89 full-time (51 women), 71 part-time (46 women); includes 5 minority (4 Asian, non-Hispanic/Latino; 1 Hispanic/Latino), 137 international. Average age 25. 236 applicants, 46% accepted, 59 enrolled. In 2014, 42 master's awarded. *Degree requirements:* For master's, comprehensive exam (for some programs), thesis (for some programs). *Entrance requirements:* For master's, MS FST or FPE w/thesis: GRE minimum score 304; MAS FST or MAS FST w/specialization in business: GRE minimum score 295, minimum undergraduate GPA of 3.0. Additional exam requirements/recommendations for international students: Required—TOEFL (minimum score 550 paper-based; 80 iBT). *Application deadline:* For fall admission, 5/1 for domestic and international students; for spring admission, 10/15 for domestic and international students. Applications are processed on a rolling basis. Application fee: $50. Electronic applications accepted. *Expenses: Tuition:* Full-time $22,500; part-time $1250 per credit hour. *Required fees:* $30 per course. $260 per semester. One-time fee: $235. Tuition and fees vary according to course load and program. *Financial support:* Fellowships with partial tuition reimbursements, research assistantships with full and partial tuition reimbursements, Federal Work-Study, institutionally sponsored loans, scholarships/grants, health care benefits, and unspecified assistantships available. Support available to part-time students. Financial award applicants required to submit FAFSA. *Faculty research:* Microbial food safety and security, food virology, interfacial colloidial phenomena, development of DNA-based methods for detection, differentiation and tracking of food borne pathogens in food systems and environment, appetite and obesity management and vascular disease. *Unit head:* Dr. Robert E. Brackett, Vice President and Director, 708-563-1533, E-mail: rbrackett@iit.edu. *Application contact:* Rishab Malhotra, Director, Graduate Admission, 866-472-3448, Fax: 312-567-3138, E-mail: inquiry.grad@iit.edu.
Website: http://www.iit.edu/ifsh/.

Instituto Tecnológico y de Estudios Superiores de Monterrey, Campus Monterrey, Graduate and Research Division, Program in Agriculture, Monterrey, Mexico. Offers agricultural parasitology (PhD); agricultural sciences (MS); farming productivity (MS); food processing engineering (MS); phytopathology (MS). Part-time programs available. *Degree requirements:* For master's, one foreign language, thesis; for doctorate, one foreign language, thesis/dissertation. *Entrance requirements:* For master's, EXADEP; for doctorate, GMAT or GRE, master's degree in related field. Additional exam requirements/recommendations for international students: Required—TOEFL. *Faculty research:* Animal embryos and reproduction, crop entomology, tropical agriculture, agricultural productivity, induced mutation in oleaginous plants.

Iowa State University of Science and Technology, Program in Agricultural and Biosystems Engineering, Ames, IA 50011. Offers M En, MS, PhD. *Degree requirements:* For master's, thesis (for some programs); for doctorate, thesis/dissertation. *Entrance requirements:* For master's and doctorate, GRE. Additional exam requirements/recommendations for international students: Required—TOEFL (minimum score 550 paper-based; 79 iBT), IELTS (minimum score 6.5). Electronic applications accepted. *Faculty research:* Grain processing and quality, tillage systems, simulation and controls, water management, environmental quality.

Kansas State University, Graduate School, College of Agriculture, Department of Grain Science and Industry, Manhattan, KS 66506. Offers MS, PhD. Part-time programs available. *Faculty:* 19 full-time (5 women), 7 part-time/adjunct (2 women). *Students:* 40 full-time (20 women), 16 part-time (8 women); includes 5 minority (1 Black or African American, non-Hispanic/Latino; 2 Asian, non-Hispanic/Latino; 2 Hispanic/Latino), 27 international. Average age 28. 17 applicants, 59% accepted, 10 enrolled. In 2014, 7 master's, 5 doctorates awarded. Terminal master's awarded for partial completion of doctoral program. *Degree requirements:* For master's, thesis, oral exam; for doctorate, thesis/dissertation, preliminary exam. *Entrance requirements:* For master's and doctorate, GRE General Test, minimum undergraduate GPA of 3.0. Additional exam requirements/recommendations for international students: Required—TOEFL (minimum score 550 paper-based; 79 iBT), IELTS (minimum score 7). *Application deadline:* For fall admission, 5/1 priority date for domestic students, 2/1 priority date for international students; for spring admission, 10/1 priority date for domestic students, 8/1 priority date for international students. Applications are processed on a rolling basis. Application fee: $50 ($75 for international students). Electronic applications accepted. *Financial support:* In 2014–15, fellowships (averaging $25,000 per year), 35 research assistantships (averaging $20,192 per year), 2 teaching assistantships with partial tuition reimbursements (averaging $16,150 per year) were awarded; Federal Work-Study, institutionally sponsored loans, and scholarships/grants also available. Support available to part-time students. Financial award application deadline: 3/1; financial award applicants required to submit FAFSA. *Faculty research:* Cereal science, bakery science and management, feed science and management, milling science and management. *Total annual research expenditures:* $4.4 million. *Unit head:* Gordon Smith, Head, 785-532-6161, Fax: 785-532-7010, E-mail: glsmith@ksu.edu. *Application*

contact: Jon Faubion, Chair, Graduate Admissions, 785-532-5320, Fax: 785-532-7010, E-mail: jfaubion@ksu.edu.
Website: http://www.grains.k-state.edu/.

Kansas State University, Graduate School, College of Engineering, Department of Biological and Agricultural Engineering, Manhattan, KS 66506. Offers MS, PhD. *Faculty:* 15 full-time (4 women), 6 part-time/adjunct (0 women). *Students:* 24 full-time (14 women), 9 part-time (2 women); includes 5 minority (3 Black or African American, non-Hispanic/Latino; 1 Asian, non-Hispanic/Latino; 1 Two or more races, non-Hispanic/Latino), 17 international. Average age 31. 23 applicants, 48% accepted, 10 enrolled. In 2014, 7 master's, 3 doctorates awarded. Terminal master's awarded for partial completion of doctoral program. *Degree requirements:* For master's, thesis; for doctorate, thesis/dissertation, preliminary exam. *Entrance requirements:* For master's, GRE, bachelor's degree in biological and agricultural engineering; for doctorate, GRE. Additional exam requirements/recommendations for international students: Required—TOEFL (minimum score 550 paper-based; 79 iBT). *Application deadline:* For fall admission, 2/1 priority date for domestic students, 1/1 priority date for international students; for spring admission, 8/1 priority date for domestic and international students. Applications are processed on a rolling basis. Application fee: $50 ($75 for international students). Electronic applications accepted. *Financial support:* In 2014–15, 2 students received support, including 21 research assistantships (averaging $20,114 per year); fellowships, teaching assistantships, Federal Work-Study, institutionally sponsored loans, and scholarships/grants also available. Support available to part-time students. Financial award application deadline: 3/1; financial award applicants required to submit FAFSA. *Faculty research:* Ecological engineering, watershed modeling, air quality, bioprocessing, bio-fuel, sensors and controls, 3D engineered biomaterials and biomedical devices, mobile health, point-of-care diagnosis, protein biomarker discovery, cancer early detection. *Total annual research expenditures:* $1.1 million. *Unit head:* Dr. Joseph Harner, Head, 785-532-5580, Fax: 785-532-5825, E-mail: jharner@k-state.edu. *Application contact:* Dr. Naiqian Zhang, Graduate Coordinator, 785-532-2910, Fax: 785-532-5825, E-mail: zhangn@k-state.edu.
Website: http://www.bae.ksu.edu/.

Louisiana State University and Agricultural & Mechanical College, Graduate School, College of Engineering, Department of Biological and Agricultural Engineering, Baton Rouge, LA 70803. Offers biological and agricultural engineering (MSBAE); engineering science (MS, PhD). Part-time programs available. *Faculty:* 12 full-time (3 women). *Students:* 12 full-time (3 women), 2 part-time (0 women); includes 1 minority (Black or African American, non-Hispanic/Latino), 5 international. Average age 25. 8 applicants, 38% accepted, 3 enrolled. In 2014, 7 master's awarded. Terminal master's awarded for partial completion of doctoral program. *Degree requirements:* For master's, thesis; for doctorate, thesis/dissertation. *Entrance requirements:* For master's and doctorate, GRE General Test, minimum GPA of 3.0. Additional exam requirements/recommendations for international students: Required—TOEFL (minimum score 550 paper-based; 79 iBT), IELTS (minimum score 6.5), or PTE (minimum score 59). *Application deadline:* For fall admission, 1/1 priority date for domestic students, 5/15 for international students; for spring admission, 10/15 for domestic and international students; for summer admission, 5/15 for domestic and international students. Applications are processed on a rolling basis. Application fee: $50 ($70 for international students). Electronic applications accepted. *Financial support:* In 2014–15, 13 students received support, including 1 fellowship (averaging $18,139 per year), 8 research assistantships with partial tuition reimbursements available (averaging $18,125 per year); teaching assistantships with partial tuition reimbursements available, career-related internships or fieldwork, Federal Work-Study, institutionally sponsored loans, scholarships/grants, health care benefits, and unspecified assistantships also available. Financial award application deadline: 7/1; financial award applicants required to submit FAFSA. *Faculty research:* Bioenergy, bioprocess engineering, cellular and molecular engineering, drug delivery using nanotechnology, environmental engineering. *Total annual research expenditures:* $229,597. *Unit head:* Dr. David Constant, Head, 225-578-3153, Fax: 225-578-3492, E-mail: dconstant@agcenter.lsu.edu. *Application contact:* Dr. Steven Hall, Graduate Coordinator, 225-578-1049, Fax: 225-578-3492, E-mail: sghall@agcenter.lsu.edu.
Website: http://www.bae.lsu.edu/.

McGill University, Faculty of Graduate and Postdoctoral Studies, Faculty of Agricultural and Environmental Sciences, Department of Bioresource Engineering, Montréal, QC H3A 2T5, Canada. Offers computer applications (M Sc, M Sc A, PhD); food engineering (M Sc, M Sc A, PhD); grain drying (M Sc, M Sc A, PhD); irrigation and drainage (M Sc, M Sc A, PhD); machinery (M Sc, M Sc A, PhD); pollution control (M Sc, M Sc A, PhD); post-harvest technology (M Sc, M Sc A, PhD); soil dynamics (M Sc, M Sc A, PhD); structure and environment (M Sc, M Sc A, PhD); vegetable and fruit storage (M Sc, M Sc A, PhD).

New York University, Graduate School of Arts and Science, Department of Environmental Medicine, New York, NY 10012-1019. Offers environmental health sciences (MS, PhD), including biostatistics (PhD), environmental hygiene (MS), epidemiology (PhD), ergonomics and biomechanics (PhD), exposure assessment and health effects (PhD), molecular toxicology/carcinogenesis (PhD), toxicology. Part-time programs available. *Faculty:* 26 full-time (7 women). *Students:* 65 full-time (35 women), 9 part-time (5 women); includes 18 minority (1 Black or African American, non-Hispanic/Latino; 8 Asian, non-Hispanic/Latino; 8 Hispanic/Latino; 1 Two or more races, non-Hispanic/Latino), 27 international. Average age 30. 79 applicants, 44% accepted, 20 enrolled. In 2014, 8 master's, 6 doctorates awarded. Terminal master's awarded for partial completion of doctoral program. *Degree requirements:* For master's, thesis or alternative; for doctorate, one foreign language, thesis/dissertation, oral and written exams. *Entrance requirements:* For master's and doctorate, GRE General Test, minimum GPA of 3.0; bachelor's degree in biological, physical, or engineering science. Additional exam requirements/recommendations for international students: Required—TOEFL. *Application deadline:* For fall admission, 12/18 for domestic and international students. Application fee: $100. *Financial support:* Fellowships with tuition reimbursements, teaching assistantships with tuition reimbursements, career-related internships or fieldwork, Federal Work-Study, institutionally sponsored loans, and health care benefits available. Financial award application deadline: 12/18; financial award applicants required to submit FAFSA. *Unit head:* Dr. Max Costa, Chair, 845-731-3661, Fax: 845-351-4510, E-mail: ehs@env.med.nyu.edu. *Application contact:* Dr. Jerome J. Solomon, Director of Graduate Studies, 845-731-3661, Fax: 845-351-4510, E-mail: ehs@env.med.nyu.edu.
Website: http://environmental-medicine.med.nyu.edu/.

North Carolina State University, Graduate School, College of Agriculture and Life Sciences, Department of Biological and Agricultural Engineering, Raleigh, NC 27695. Offers MBAE, MS, PhD, Certificate. Part-time programs available. Postbaccalaureate distance learning degree programs offered. *Degree requirements:* For master's, thesis (for some programs); for doctorate, thesis/dissertation. *Entrance requirements:* For master's and doctorate, GRE. Additional exam requirements/recommendations for international students: Required—TOEFL. Electronic applications accepted. *Faculty research:* Bioinstrumentation, animal waste management, water quality engineering, machine systems, controlled environment agriculture.

North Dakota State University, College of Graduate and Interdisciplinary Studies, College of Engineering and Architecture, Department of Agricultural and Biosystems Engineering, Fargo, ND 58108. Offers agricultural and biosystems engineering (MS, PhD); engineering (PhD); natural resource management (MS); natural resources management (PhD). Part-time programs available. *Degree requirements:* For master's, thesis; for doctorate, thesis/dissertation. *Entrance requirements:* For master's and doctorate, BS in engineering or the equivalent, minimum undergraduate GPA of 3.0. Additional exam requirements/recommendations for international students: Required—TOEFL (minimum score 550 paper-based; 79 iBT). Electronic applications accepted. *Faculty research:* Irrigation, crop processing, food engineering, environmental resources, sensors and instrumentation.

The Ohio State University, Graduate School, College of Food, Agricultural, and Environmental Sciences, Department of Food, Agricultural, and Biological Engineering, Columbus, OH 43210. Offers MS, PhD. Program offered jointly with College of Engineering. *Faculty:* 23. *Students:* 45 full-time (22 women), 6 part-time (1 woman); includes 4 minority (1 Black or African American, non-Hispanic/Latino; 2 Hispanic/Latino; 1 Two or more races, non-Hispanic/Latino), 24 international. Average age 27. In 2014, 10 master's, 5 doctorates awarded. *Degree requirements:* For master's, thesis optional; for doctorate, thesis/dissertation. *Entrance requirements:* For master's and doctorate, GRE General Test, GRE Subject Test in engineering (recommended). Additional exam requirements/recommendations for international students: Required—TOEFL (minimum score 550 paper-based; 79 iBT), Michigan English Language Assessment Battery (minimum score 82); Recommended—IELTS (minimum score 7). *Application deadline:* For fall admission, 12/13 priority date for domestic students, 11/30 priority date for international students; for spring admission, 12/14 for domestic students, 11/12 for international students; for summer admission, 5/15 for domestic students, 4/14 for international students. Applications are processed on a rolling basis. Application fee: $60 ($70 for international students). Electronic applications accepted. *Financial support:* Fellowships with tuition reimbursements, research assistantships with tuition reimbursements, teaching assistantships with tuition reimbursements, career-related internships or fieldwork, Federal Work-Study, and institutionally sponsored loans available. Support available to part-time students. *Unit head:* Dr. Scott Shearer, Chair, 614-292-7284, E-mail: shearer.95@osu.edu. *Application contact:* Graduate and Professional Admissions, 614-292-9444, Fax: 614-292-3895, E-mail: gpadmissions@osu.edu.
Website: http://fabe.osu.edu/.

Oklahoma State University, College of Agricultural Science and Natural Resources, Department of Biosystems and Agricultural Engineering, Stillwater, OK 74078. Offers biosystems engineering (MS, PhD); environmental and natural resources (MS, PhD). *Faculty:* 26 full-time (3 women). *Students:* 19 full-time (13 women), 23 part-time (5 women); includes 5 minority (2 American Indian or Alaska Native, non-Hispanic/Latino; 2 Hispanic/Latino; 1 Two or more races, non-Hispanic/Latino), 19 international. Average age 29. 43 applicants, 30% accepted, 8 enrolled. In 2014, 4 master's, 6 doctorates awarded. *Degree requirements:* For master's, thesis; for doctorate, comprehensive exam, thesis/dissertation. *Entrance requirements:* For master's and doctorate, GRE or GMAT. Additional exam requirements/recommendations for international students: Required—TOEFL (minimum score 550 paper-based; 79 iBT). *Application deadline:* For fall admission, 3/1 priority date for international students; for spring admission, 8/1 priority date for international students. Applications are processed on a rolling basis. Application fee: $40 ($75 for international students). Electronic applications accepted. *Expenses:* Tuition, state resident: full-time $4488; part-time $187 per credit hour. Tuition, nonresident: full-time $18,360; part-time $765 per credit hour. *Required fees:* $2413; $100.55 per credit hour. Tuition and fees vary according to campus/location. *Financial support:* In 2014–15, 33 research assistantships (averaging $17,683 per year), 2 teaching assistantships (averaging $14,100 per year) were awarded; career-related internships or fieldwork, Federal Work-Study, scholarships/grants, health care benefits, tuition waivers (partial), and unspecified assistantships also available. Support available to part-time students. Financial award application deadline: 3/1; financial award applicants required to submit FAFSA. *Unit head:* Dr. Daniel Thomas, Department Head, 405-744-5431, Fax: 405-744-6059, E-mail: daniel.thomas@okstate.edu. *Application contact:* Glenn Brown, Professor/Graduate Coordinator, 405-744-8425, E-mail: gbrown@okstate.edu.
Website: http://bae.okstate.edu/.

Penn State University Park, Graduate School, College of Agricultural Sciences, Department of Agricultural and Biological Engineering, University Park, PA 16802. Offers agricultural and biological engineering (MS, PhD); biorenewable systems (MS, PhD). *Unit head:* Dr. Richard T. Roush, Dean, 814-865-2541, Fax: 814-865-3103, E-mail: rtr10@psu.edu. *Application contact:* Lori A. Stania, Director, Graduate Student Services, 814-867-5278, Fax: 814-863-4627, E-mail: gswww@psu.edu.
Website: http://abe.psu.edu/.

Purdue University, College of Engineering, Department of Agricultural and Biological Engineering, West Lafayette, IN 47907-2093. Offers MS, MSABE, MSE, PhD. Part-time programs available. Terminal master's awarded for partial completion of doctoral program. *Degree requirements:* For master's, thesis (for some programs); for doctorate, thesis/dissertation. *Entrance requirements:* For master's and doctorate, GRE General Test. Additional exam requirements/recommendations for international students: Required—TOEFL (minimum score 550 paper-based; 77 iBT). Electronic applications accepted. *Faculty research:* Food and biological engineering, environmental engineering, machine systems, biotechnology, machine intelligence.

South Dakota State University, Graduate School, College of Engineering, Department of Agricultural and Biosystems Engineering, Brookings, SD 57007. Offers biological sciences (MS, PhD); engineering (MS). PhD offered jointly with Iowa State University of Science and Technology. Part-time programs available. *Degree requirements:* For master's, thesis (for some programs), oral exam; for doctorate, thesis/dissertation, preliminary oral and written exams. *Entrance requirements:* For master's and doctorate, engineering degree. Additional exam requirements/recommendations for international students: Required—TOEFL (minimum score 550 paper-based; 79 iBT). *Faculty research:* Water resources, food engineering, natural resources engineering, machine design, bioprocess engineering.

Texas A&M University, College of Agriculture and Life Sciences and College of Engineering, Department of Biological and Agricultural Engineering, College Station, TX 77843. Offers agricultural systems management (MS); biological and agricultural engineering (MS, PhD). Part-time programs available. *Faculty:* 18. *Students:* 59 full-time (26 women), 23 part-time (7 women); includes 17 minority (5 Black or African American, non-Hispanic/Latino; 2 Asian, non-Hispanic/Latino; 9 Hispanic/Latino; 1 Two or more races, non-Hispanic/Latino), 45 international. Average age 29. 45 applicants, 53% accepted, 11 enrolled. In 2014, 19 master's, 7 doctorates awarded. *Degree requirements:* For master's, thesis (MS), preliminary and final exams; for doctorate, thesis/dissertation, preliminary and final exams. *Entrance requirements:* For master's and doctorate, GRE General Test. Additional exam requirements/recommendations for international students: Required—TOEFL (minimum score 550 paper-based). *Application deadline:* For fall admission, 2/1 priority date for domestic students; for spring admission, 10/1 for domestic students. Applications are processed on a rolling basis. Application fee: $50 ($90 for international students). Electronic applications accepted. *Expenses:* Tuition, state resident: full-time $4078; part-time $226.55 per credit hour. Tuition, nonresident: full-time $10,594; part-time $577.55 per credit hour. *Required fees:* $2813; $237.70 per credit hour. $278.50 per semester. Tuition and fees vary according to degree level and student level. *Financial support:* In 2014–15, 69 students received support, including 7 fellowships with full and partial tuition reimbursements available (averaging $18,786 per year), 22 research assistantships with full and partial tuition reimbursements available (averaging $5,829 per year), 13 teaching assistantships with full and partial tuition reimbursements available (averaging $6,283 per year); career-related internships or fieldwork, institutionally sponsored loans, scholarships/grants, traineeships, health care benefits, tuition waivers (full and partial), and unspecified assistantships also available. Support available to part-time students. Financial award application deadline: 3/1; financial award applicants required to submit FAFSA. *Faculty research:* Water quality and quantity; air quality; biological, food, ecological engineering; off-road equipment; mechatronics. *Unit head:* Dr. Steve Searcy, Professor and Head, 979-845-3940, Fax: 979-862-3442, E-mail: s-searcy@tamu.edu. *Application contact:* Dr. Sandun Fernando, Graduate Coordinator, 979-845-9793, E-mail: sfernando@tamu.edu.
Website: http://baen.tamu.edu.

Université Laval, Faculty of Agricultural and Food Sciences, Department of Soils and Agricultural Engineering, Programs in Agri-Food Engineering, Québec, QC G1K 7P4, Canada. Offers agri-food engineering (M Sc); environmental technology (M Sc). *Degree requirements:* For master's, thesis (for some programs). *Entrance requirements:* For master's, knowledge of French. Electronic applications accepted.

The University of Arizona, College of Agriculture and Life Sciences, Department of Agricultural and Biosystems Engineering, Tucson, AZ 85721. Offers MS, PhD. Terminal master's awarded for partial completion of doctoral program. *Degree requirements:* For master's, thesis; for doctorate, thesis/dissertation. *Entrance requirements:* For master's, minimum GPA of 3.0 in last 2 years of undergraduate study, 3 letters of recommendation; for doctorate, minimum GPA of 3.0 in last 2 years of undergraduate study, 3 letters of recommendation, statement of purpose. Additional exam requirements/recommendations for international students: Required—TOEFL (minimum score 550 paper-based; 79 iBT). Electronic applications accepted. *Faculty research:* Irrigation system design, energy-use management, equipment for alternative crops, food properties enhancement.

University of Arkansas, Graduate School, College of Engineering, Department of Biological and Agricultural Engineering, Fayetteville, AR 72701-1201. Offers biological and agricultural engineering (MSE, PhD); biological engineering (MSBE); biomedical engineering (MSBME). *Degree requirements:* For master's, thesis; for doctorate, one foreign language, thesis/dissertation. Electronic applications accepted.

University of Florida, Graduate School, College of Engineering and College of Agricultural and Life Sciences, Department of Agricultural and Biological Engineering, Gainesville, FL 32611. Offers agricultural and biological engineering (ME, MS, PhD); biological systems modeling (Certificate). Part-time programs available. *Faculty:* 29 full-time (5 women), 3 part-time/adjunct (1 woman). *Students:* 65 full-time (36 women), 15 part-time (7 women); includes 15 minority (3 Black or African American, non-Hispanic/Latino; 1 American Indian or Alaska Native, non-Hispanic/Latino; 6 Asian, non-Hispanic/Latino; 5 Hispanic/Latino), 45 international. 38 applicants, 45% accepted, 9 enrolled. In 2014, 15 master's, 15 doctorates awarded. Terminal master's awarded for partial completion of doctoral program. *Degree requirements:* For master's, comprehensive exam, thesis (for some programs); for doctorate, comprehensive exam, thesis/dissertation. *Entrance requirements:* For master's and doctorate, minimum GPA of 3.0, 3 letters of recommendation, statement of purpose. Additional exam requirements/recommendations for international students: Required—TOEFL (minimum score 550 paper-based; 80 iBT), IELTS (minimum score 6). *Application deadline:* For fall admission, 12/15 for domestic and international students; for spring admission, 7/15 for domestic and international students. Applications are processed on a rolling basis. Application fee: $30. Electronic applications accepted. *Financial support:* Unspecified assistantships available. Financial award application deadline: 2/15; financial award applicants required to submit FAFSA. *Faculty research:* Bioenergy and bioprocessing; hydrological, biological and agricultural modeling; biosensors; precision agriculture and robotics; food packaging and food security. *Total annual research expenditures:* $5.1 million. *Unit head:* Dorota Z. Haman, PhD, Professor and Chair, 352-392-1864 Ext. 120, Fax: 352-392-4092, E-mail: dhaman@ufl.edu. *Application contact:* Ray A. Bucklin, PhD, Graduate Coordinator, 352-392-1864 Ext. 169, Fax: 352-392-4092, E-mail: bucklin@ufl.edu.
Website: http://www.abe.ufl.edu/.

University of Georgia, College of Agricultural and Environmental Sciences, Department of Biological and Agricultural Engineering, Athens, GA 30602. Offers agricultural engineering (MS); biological and agricultural engineering (PhD); biological engineering (MS). *Degree requirements:* For master's, thesis; for doctorate, one foreign language, thesis/dissertation. *Entrance requirements:* For master's and doctorate, GRE General Test. Electronic applications accepted.

University of Idaho, College of Graduate Studies, College of Engineering, Department of Biological and Agricultural Engineering, Moscow, ID 83844-0904. Offers M Engr, MS, PhD. Program offered jointly with College of Agricultural and Life Sciences. *Faculty:* 8 full-time. *Students:* 3 full-time, 8 part-time. Average age 36. In 2014, 3 master's awarded. *Degree requirements:* For master's, thesis or alternative; for doctorate, one foreign language, thesis/dissertation. *Entrance requirements:* For master's, minimum GPA of 2.8; for doctorate, minimum undergraduate GPA of 2.8, 3.0 graduate. *Application deadline:* For fall admission, 8/1 for domestic students; for spring admission, 12/15 for domestic students. Applications are processed on a rolling basis. Application fee: $60. Electronic applications accepted. *Expenses:* Tuition, state resident: full-time $4784; part-time $280.50 per credit hour. Tuition, nonresident: full-time $18,314; part-time $957.50 per credit hour. *Required fees:* $2000; $58.50 per credit hour. Tuition and fees vary according to program. *Financial support:* Research assistantships, teaching assistantships, and career-related internships or fieldwork available. Financial award applicants required to submit FAFSA. *Faculty research:* Water and environmental research, alternative fuels/biodiesel, agricultural safety health, biological processes for agricultural/food waste. *Unit head:* Dr. Jon Van Gerpen, Interim Department Head, 208-885-6182, E-mail: baengr@uidaho.edu. *Application contact:* Sean Scoggin, Graduate Recruitment Coordinator, 208-885-4001, Fax: 208-885-4406, E-mail: graduateadmissions@uidaho.edu.
Website: http://www.uidaho.edu/cals/bae/.

Agricultural Engineering

University of Illinois at Urbana–Champaign, Graduate College, College of Agricultural, Consumer and Environmental Sciences, Department of Agricultural and Biological Engineering, Champaign, IL 61820. Offers agricultural and biological engineering (MS, PhD); technical systems management (MS, PSM). *Students:* 75 full-time (23 women). Application fee: $70 ($90 for international students). *Unit head:* Kuan Chong Ting, Head, 217-333-3570, Fax: 217-244-0323, E-mail: kcting@illinois.edu. *Application contact:* Jana R. Lenz, Office Administrator, 217-324-1654, Fax: 217-244-0323, E-mail: janalenz@illinois.edu.
Website: http://abe.illinois.edu.

University of Kentucky, Graduate School, College of Agriculture, Food and Environment, Program in Biosystems and Agricultural Engineering, Lexington, KY 40506-0032. Offers MS, PhD. Part-time programs available. *Degree requirements:* For master's, comprehensive exam, thesis optional; for doctorate, comprehensive exam, thesis/dissertation. *Entrance requirements:* For master's, GRE General Test, minimum undergraduate GPA of 2.75; for doctorate, GRE General Test, minimum graduate GPA of 3.0. Additional exam requirements/recommendations for international students: Required—TOEFL (minimum score 550 paper-based). Electronic applications accepted. *Faculty research:* Machine systems, food engineering, fermentation, hydrology, water quality.

University of Missouri, Office of Research and Graduate Studies, College of Engineering, Department of Biological Engineering, Columbia, MO 65211. Offers agricultural engineering (MS); biological engineering (MS, PhD). *Faculty:* 20 full-time (2 women). *Students:* 24 full-time (14 women), 30 part-time (7 women); includes 3 minority (1 Black or African American, non-Hispanic/Latino; 1 Hispanic/Latino; 1 Two or more races, non-Hispanic/Latino), 35 international. Average age 28. 32 applicants, 50% accepted, 13 enrolled. In 2014, 7 master's, 3 doctorates awarded. *Degree requirements:* For master's, thesis; for doctorate, thesis/dissertation. *Entrance requirements:* For master's and doctorate, GRE General Test, minimum GPA of 3.0. Additional exam requirements/recommendations for international students: Required—TOEFL (minimum score 550 paper-based; 80 iBT). *Application deadline:* For fall admission, 4/1 for domestic students. Applications are processed on a rolling basis. Application fee: $55 ($75 for international students). Electronic applications accepted. *Financial support:* Fellowships, research assistantships, teaching assistantships, institutionally sponsored loans, scholarships/grants, traineeships, health care benefits, and unspecified assistantships available. Support available to part-time students. *Faculty research:* Biomedical engineering: biophotonics and biosensing, membrane transport and signaling; bioprocess engineering: biomass-based products and food engineering; bioenvironmental engineering: water quality, precision agriculture, cropping systems. *Unit head:* Dr. Jinglu Tan, Division Director, 573-882-2369, E-mail: tanj@missouri.edu. *Application contact:* Jean Gruenewald, Advising and Scholarship Coordinator, 573-882-1114 Ext. 311, E-mail: gruenewaldj@missouri.edu.
Website: http://bioengineering.missouri.edu/graduate/.

University of Nebraska–Lincoln, Graduate College, College of Engineering, Department of Biological Systems Engineering, Interdepartmental Area of Agricultural and Biological Systems Engineering, Lincoln, NE 68588. Offers MS, PhD. *Degree requirements:* For master's, thesis optional. *Entrance requirements:* Additional exam requirements/recommendations for international students: Required—TOEFL (minimum score 550 paper-based). Electronic applications accepted. *Faculty research:* Hydrological engineering, tractive performance, biomedical engineering, irrigation systems.

The University of Tennessee, Graduate School, College of Agricultural Sciences and Natural Resources, Department of Biosystems Engineering and Environmental Science, Program in Biosystems Engineering Technology, Knoxville, TN 37996. Offers MS. *Degree requirements:* For master's, thesis or alternative. *Entrance requirements:* For master's, GRE General Test, minimum GPA of 2.7. Additional exam requirements/recommendations for international students: Required—TOEFL. Electronic applications accepted.

University of Wisconsin–Madison, Graduate School, College of Agricultural and Life Sciences, Department of Biological Systems Engineering, Madison, WI 53706. Offers MS, PhD. Part-time programs available. Terminal master's awarded for partial completion of doctoral program. *Degree requirements:* For master's, thesis; for doctorate, thesis/dissertation. *Entrance requirements:* Additional exam requirements/recommendations for international students: Required—TOEFL. Electronic applications accepted. *Expenses:* Tuition, state resident: full-time $10,723; part-time $745 per credit. Tuition, nonresident: full-time $24,054; part-time $1578 per credit. *Required fees:* $374 per semester. Tuition and fees vary according to course load, program and reciprocity agreements. *Faculty research:* Biomaterials, biosensors, food safety, food engineering, bioprocessing, machinery systems, natural resources and environment, structures engineering.

Utah State University, School of Graduate Studies, College of Engineering, Department of Biological and Irrigation Engineering, Logan, UT 84322. Offers biological and agricultural engineering (MS, PhD); irrigation engineering (MS, PhD). Part-time programs available. Terminal master's awarded for partial completion of doctoral program. *Degree requirements:* For master's, thesis (for some programs); for doctorate, thesis/dissertation. *Entrance requirements:* For master's and doctorate, GRE General Test, minimum GPA of 3.0. Additional exam requirements/recommendations for international students: Required—TOEFL. *Faculty research:* On-farm water management, crop-water yield modeling, irrigation, biosensors, biological engineering.

Virginia Polytechnic Institute and State University, Graduate School, College of Engineering, Blacksburg, VA 24061. Offers aerospace engineering (ME, MS, PhD); biological systems engineering (ME, MS, PhD); biomedical engineering (MS, PhD); chemical engineering (ME, MS, PhD); civil engineering (ME, MS, PhD); computer engineering (ME, MS, PhD); computer science (MS, PhD); electrical engineering (ME, PhD); engineering education (PhD); engineering mechanics (ME, MS, PhD); environmental engineering (MS); environmental science and engineering (MS); industrial and systems engineering (ME, MS, PhD); materials science and engineering (ME, MS, PhD); mechanical engineering (ME, MS, PhD); mining and minerals engineering (PhD); mining engineering (ME, MS); nuclear engineering (MS, PhD); ocean engineering (MS); systems engineering (ME, MS). *Accreditation:* ABET (one or more programs are accredited). *Faculty:* 356 full-time (60 women), 3 part-time/adjunct (1 woman). *Students:* 1,700 full-time (398 women), 345 part-time (58 women); includes 213 minority (43 Black or African American, non-Hispanic/Latino; 1 American Indian or Alaska Native, non-Hispanic/Latino; 87 Asian, non-Hispanic/Latino; 58 Hispanic/Latino; 1 Native Hawaiian or other Pacific Islander, non-Hispanic/Latino; 23 Two or more races, non-Hispanic/Latino), 1,079 international. Average age 27. 5,228 applicants, 18% accepted, 471 enrolled. In 2014, 438 master's, 211 doctorates awarded. *Degree requirements:* For master's, comprehensive exam (for some programs), thesis (for some programs); for doctorate, comprehensive exam (for some programs), thesis/dissertation (for some programs). *Entrance requirements:* For master's and doctorate, GRE/GMAT (may vary by department). Additional exam requirements/recommendations for international students: Required—TOEFL (minimum score 550 paper-based). *Application deadline:* For fall admission, 8/1 for domestic students, 4/1 for international students; for spring admission, 1/1 for domestic students, 9/1 for international students. Applications are processed on a rolling basis. Application fee: $75. Electronic applications accepted. *Expenses:* Tuition, state resident: full-time $11,656; part-time $647.50 per credit hour. Tuition, nonresident: full-time $23,351; part-time $1297.25 per credit hour. *Required fees:* $2533; $465.75 per semester. Tuition and fees vary according to course load, campus/location and program. *Financial support:* In 2014–15, 148 fellowships with full tuition reimbursements (averaging $8,031 per year), 855 research assistantships with full tuition reimbursements (averaging $22,855 per year), 288 teaching assistantships with full tuition reimbursements (averaging $20,291 per year) were awarded. Financial award application deadline: 3/1; financial award applicants required to submit FAFSA. *Total annual research expenditures:* $90.5 million. *Unit head:* Dr. Richard C. Benson, Dean, 540-231-9752, Fax: 540-231-3031, E-mail: deaneng@vt.edu. *Application contact:* Linda Perkins, Executive Assistant, 540-231-9752, Fax: 540-231-3031, E-mail: lperkins@vt.edu.
Website: http://www.eng.vt.edu/.

Washington State University, College of Agricultural, Human, and Natural Resource Sciences, Department of Biological Systems Engineering, Pullman, WA 99164-6120. Offers biological and agricultural engineering (MS, PhD). Program applications must be made through the Pullman campus. *Students:* 61 full-time (25 women), 6 part-time (1 woman); includes 2 minority (1 Asian, non-Hispanic/Latino; 1 Hispanic/Latino), 57 international. Average age 30. 66 applicants, 29% accepted, 10 enrolled. In 2014, 2 master's, 15 doctorates awarded. *Degree requirements:* For master's, comprehensive exam, thesis (for some programs), written and oral exam; for doctorate, comprehensive exam, thesis/dissertation, written and oral exam. *Entrance requirements:* For master's and doctorate, minimum GPA of 3.0, bachelor's degree in engineering or closely-related subject. Additional exam requirements/recommendations for international students: Required—TOEFL. *Application deadline:* For fall admission, 1/31 priority date for domestic and international students; for spring admission, 7/1 priority date for domestic and international students. Applications are processed on a rolling basis. Application fee: $75. Electronic applications accepted. *Expenses:* Tuition, state resident: full-time $11,768. Tuition, nonresident: full-time $25,200. *Required fees:* $960. Tuition and fees vary according to program. *Financial support:* In 2014–15, 30 research assistantships (averaging $14,162 per year) were awarded; tuition waivers also available. *Faculty research:* Agricultural automation engineering; bioenergy and bioproducts engineering; food engineering; land, air, and water resources and environmental engineering. *Total annual research expenditures:* $4 million. *Unit head:* Dr. Claudio Stockle, Chair, 509-335-1578, Fax: 509-335-2722, E-mail: stockle@wsu.edu. *Application contact:* WSU Graduate School, 800-GRADWSU, Fax: 509-335-1949, E-mail: gradsch@wsu.edu.
Website: http://www.bsyse.wsu.edu.

Bioengineering

Alfred University, Graduate School, New York State College of Ceramics, Kazuo Inamori School of Engineering, Alfred, NY 14802. Offers biomaterials engineering (MS); ceramic engineering (MS); ceramics (PhD); electrical engineering (MS); glass science (MS, PhD); materials science and engineering (MS, PhD); mechanical engineering (MS). Part-time programs available. *Degree requirements:* For master's, thesis; for doctorate, thesis/dissertation. *Entrance requirements:* Additional exam requirements/recommendations for international students: Required—TOEFL (minimum score 590 paper-based; 90 iBT), IELTS (minimum score 6.5). Electronic applications accepted. *Expenses:* Contact institution. *Faculty research:* X-ray diffraction, biomaterials and polymers, thin-film processing, electronic and optical ceramics, solid-state chemistry.

Baylor College of Medicine, Graduate School of Biomedical Sciences, Program in Translational Biology and Molecular Medicine, Houston, TX 77030-3498. Offers PhD. *Degree requirements:* For doctorate, thesis/dissertation, public defense. *Entrance requirements:* For doctorate, GRE, minimum GPA of 3.0. Additional exam requirements/recommendations for international students: Required—TOEFL. Electronic applications accepted. *Faculty research:* Molecular medicine, translational biology, human disease biology and therapy.

California Institute of Technology, Division of Engineering and Applied Science, Option in Bioengineering, Pasadena, CA 91125-0001. Offers MS, PhD. *Degree requirements:* For master's, thesis; for doctorate, thesis/dissertation. *Faculty research:* Biosynthesis and analysis, biometrics.

Carnegie Mellon University, Carnegie Institute of Technology, Biomedical and Health Engineering Program, Pittsburgh, PA 15213-3891. Offers bioengineering (MS, PhD); MD/PhD. *Degree requirements:* For master's, thesis; for doctorate, thesis/dissertation, qualifying exam. *Entrance requirements:* For master's and doctorate, GRE General Test. Additional exam requirements/recommendations for international students: Required—TOEFL. Electronic applications accepted. *Faculty research:* Cellular and molecular systematics, signal and image processing, materials and mechanics.

Clemson University, Graduate School, College of Engineering and Science, Department of Bioengineering, Clemson, SC 29634-0905. Offers M Eng, MS, PhD, Certificate. Part-time programs available. *Faculty:* 22 full-time (7 women), 5 part-time/adjunct (1 woman). *Students:* 114 full-time (47 women), 12 part-time (1 woman); includes 10 minority (2 Black or African American, non-Hispanic/Latino; 1 American Indian or Alaska Native, non-Hispanic/Latino; 3 Asian, non-Hispanic/Latino; 2 Hispanic/Latino; 2 Two or more races, non-Hispanic/Latino), 38 international. Average age 26. 162 applicants, 40% accepted, 38 enrolled. In 2014, 23 master's, 15 doctorates awarded. *Degree requirements:* For master's, thesis optional; for doctorate, thesis/dissertation. *Entrance requirements:* For master's and doctorate, GRE General Test. Additional exam requirements/recommendations for international students: Required—TOEFL. *Application deadline:* For fall admission, 6/1 for domestic students, 4/15 for international students; for spring admission, 11/1 for domestic students, 9/15 for international students. Applications are processed on a rolling basis. Application fee: $70 ($80 for international students). Electronic applications accepted. *Expenses:* Expenses: $4,033 full-time resident, $8,429 full-time non-resident. *Financial support:* In

2014–15, 72 students received support, including 6 fellowships with full and partial tuition reimbursements available (averaging $8,615 per year), 43 research assistantships with partial tuition reimbursements available (averaging $18,116 per year), 26 teaching assistantships with partial tuition reimbursements available (averaging $21,183 per year); career-related internships or fieldwork, institutionally sponsored loans, scholarships/grants, health care benefits, and unspecified assistantships also available. Support available to part-time students. Financial award application deadline: 2/15; financial award applicants required to submit FAFSA. *Faculty research:* Biomaterials, biomechanics, bioimaging, tissue engineering. *Total annual research expenditures:* $5.1 million. *Unit head:* Dr. Martine LaBerge, Interim Chair, 864-656-5556, Fax: 864-656-4466, E-mail: laberge@eng.clemson.edu. *Application contact:* Maria Torres, Graduate Student Services Coordinator, 864-656-7276, Fax: 864-656-4466, E-mail: mariam@clemson.edu.
Website: http://www.clemson.edu/ces/bioe/.

Colorado School of Mines, Graduate School, Department of Chemical and Biological Engineering, Golden, CO 80401. Offers MS, PhD. Part-time programs available. *Faculty:* 34 full-time (12 women), 10 part-time/adjunct (1 woman). *Students:* 77 full-time (17 women), 4 part-time (1 woman); includes 5 minority (1 Asian, non-Hispanic/Latino; 1 Hispanic/Latino; 3 Two or more races, non-Hispanic/Latino), 33 international. Average age 29. 162 applicants, 36% accepted, 27 enrolled. In 2014, 7 master's, 3 doctorates awarded. Terminal master's awarded for partial completion of doctoral program. *Degree requirements:* For master's, thesis (for some programs); for doctorate, comprehensive exam, thesis/dissertation. *Entrance requirements:* For master's and doctorate, GRE General Test. Additional exam requirements/recommendations for international students: Required—TOEFL (minimum score 550 paper-based; 80 iBT). *Application deadline:* For fall admission, 12/15 priority date for domestic and international students; for spring admission, 10/15 for domestic and international students. Application fee: $50 ($70 for international students). Electronic applications accepted. *Financial support:* In 2014–15, 69 students received support, including fellowships with full tuition reimbursements available (averaging $21,120 per year), 45 research assistantships with full tuition reimbursements available (averaging $21,120 per year), 20 teaching assistantships with full tuition reimbursements available (averaging $21,120 per year); scholarships/grants, health care benefits, and unspecified assistantships also available. Financial award application deadline: 12/15; financial award applicants required to submit FAFSA. *Faculty research:* Liquid fuels for the future, responsible management of hazardous substances, surface and interfacial engineering, advanced computational methods and process control, gas hydrates. *Total annual research expenditures:* $6.3 million. *Unit head:* Dr. David Marr, Head, 303-273-3008, E-mail: dmarr@mines.edu. *Application contact:* Dr. Deanna Jacobs, Program Assistant, 303-273-3720, E-mail: Djacobs@mines.edu.
Website: http://chemeng.mines.edu/.

Cornell University, Graduate School, Graduate Fields of Agriculture and Life Sciences and Graduate Fields of Engineering, Field of Biological and Environmental Engineering, Ithaca, NY 14853-0001. Offers bioenergy and integrated energy systems (M Eng, MPS, MS, PhD); biological engineering (M Eng, MPS, MS, PhD); bioprocess engineering (M Eng, MPS, MS, PhD); ecohydrology (M Eng, MPS, MS, PhD); environmental engineering (M Eng, MPS, MS, PhD); environmental management (MPS); food engineering (M Eng, MPS, MS, PhD); industrial biotechnology (M Eng, MPS, MS, PhD); nanobiotechnology (M Eng, MPS, MS, PhD); sustainable systems (M Eng, MPS, MS, PhD); synthetic biology (MS); syntheticbiology (M Eng, MPS, PhD). Terminal master's awarded for partial completion of doctoral program. *Degree requirements:* For master's, thesis (MS); for doctorate, comprehensive exam, thesis/dissertation. *Entrance requirements:* For master's, letters of recommendation (3 for MS, 2 for M Eng and MPS); for doctorate, GRE General Test, 3 letters of recommendation. Additional exam requirements/recommendations for international students: Required—TOEFL (minimum score 550 paper-based; 77 iBT). Electronic applications accepted. *Faculty research:* Biological and food engineering, environmental, soil and water engineering, international agricultural engineering, structures and controlled environments, machine systems and energy.

Dalhousie University, Faculty of Engineering, Department of Biological Engineering, Halifax, NS B3J 2X4, Canada. Offers M Eng, MA Sc, PhD. *Degree requirements:* For master's, thesis; for doctorate, thesis/dissertation. *Entrance requirements:* Additional exam requirements/recommendations for international students: Required—TOEFL, IELTS, CANTEST, CAEL, or Michigan English Language Assessment Battery. *Faculty research:* Waste management, energy and environment, bio-machinery and robotics, soil and water, aquacultural and food engineering.

Florida Atlantic University, College of Engineering and Computer Science, Department of Computer and Electrical Engineering and Computer Science, Boca Raton, FL 33431-0991. Offers bioengineering (MS); computer engineering (MS, PhD); computer science (MS, PhD); electrical engineering (MS, PhD); information technology and management (MS). Part-time and evening/weekend programs available. Terminal master's awarded for partial completion of doctoral program. *Degree requirements:* For master's, thesis optional; for doctorate, thesis/dissertation, qualifying exam. *Entrance requirements:* For master's, GRE General Test, minimum GPA of 3.0; for doctorate, GRE General Test, master's degree, minimum GPA of 3.5. Additional exam requirements/recommendations for international students: Required—TOEFL (minimum score 500 paper-based; 61 iBT), IELTS (minimum score 6). *Expenses:* Tuition, state resident: full-time $7396; part-time $369.82 per credit hour. Tuition, nonresident: full-time $19,392; part-time $1024.81 per credit hour. Tuition and fees vary according to course load. *Faculty research:* VLSI and neural networks, communication networks, software engineering, computer architecture, multimedia and video processing.

George Mason University, Volgenau School of Engineering, Department of Bioengineering, Fairfax, VA 22030. Offers PhD. *Expenses:* Tuition, state resident: full-time $9794; part-time $408 per credit hour. Tuition, nonresident: full-time $26,978; part-time $1124 per credit hour. *Required fees:* $2820; $118 per credit hour. Tuition and fees vary according to course load and program. *Unit head:* Kenneth S. Ball, Dean, 703-993-1498, Fax: 703-993-1734, E-mail: vsdean@gmu.edu. *Application contact:* Jade T. Perez, Director, Graduate Services, 703-993-2426, E-mail: jperezc@gmu.edu.

Georgia Institute of Technology, Graduate Studies, College of Engineering, Wallace H. Coulter Department of Biomedical Engineering, Atlanta, GA 30332-0001. Offers biomedical engineering (PhD); biomedical innovation and development (MBID); PhD offered jointly with Emory University (Georgia) and Peking University (China). Part-time programs available. *Students:* 174 full-time (74 women), 4 part-time (2 women); includes 50 minority (8 Black or African American, non-Hispanic/Latino; 25 Asian, non-Hispanic/Latino; 8 Hispanic/Latino; 1 Native Hawaiian or other Pacific Islander, non-Hispanic/Latino; 8 Two or more races, non-Hispanic/Latino), 46 international. Average age 25. 285 applicants, 40% accepted, 52 enrolled. *Degree requirements:* For master's, thesis; for doctorate, thesis/dissertation. *Entrance requirements:* For master's, GRE, https://bioid.gatech.edu/bioid7/admissions; for doctorate, GRE, http://www.grad.gatech.edu/bmed. Additional exam requirements/recommendations for international students: Required—TOEFL (minimum score 600 paper-based; 100 iBT). *Application deadline:* For fall admission, 12/1 for domestic and international students. Applications are

processed on a rolling basis. Application fee: $75. Electronic applications accepted. *Expenses:* Expenses: $8,203 per term in-state, $21,390 out-of-state plus fees of $1,196 per term (for PhD); $13,522 per term in-state, $18,493 out-of-state plus fees of $1,196 per term (for MBID). *Financial support:* Fellowships, research assistantships, teaching assistantships, career-related internships or fieldwork, Federal Work-Study, institutionally sponsored loans, tuition waivers (partial), and unspecified assistantships available. Support available to part-time students. Financial award application deadline: 5/1. *Faculty research:* Biomechanics and tissue engineering, bioinstrumentation and medical imaging. *Total annual research expenditures:* $20.8 million. *Unit head:* Garrett Stanley, Director, 404-385-5037, E-mail: garrett.stanley@bme.gatech.edu. *Application contact:* Shannon Sullivan, Graduate Coordinator, 404-385-2557, E-mail: shannon.sullivan@bme.gatech.edu.
Website: http://www.bme.gatech.edu/.

Georgia Institute of Technology, Graduate Studies, Multidisciplinary Program in Bioengineering, Atlanta, GA 30332-0001. Offers MS, PhD. Program offered jointly with College of Computing, School of Aerospace Engineering, Wallace H. Coulter Department of Biomedical Engineering, School of Civil and Environmental Engineering, School of Chemical and Biomolecular Engineering, School of Electrical and Computer Engineering, School of Materials Science and Engineering, and George W. Woodruff School of Mechanical Engineering. Part-time programs available. *Students:* 90 full-time (34 women), 5 part-time; includes 36 minority (3 Black or African American, non-Hispanic/Latino; 18 Asian, non-Hispanic/Latino; 10 Hispanic/Latino; 5 Two or more races, non-Hispanic/Latino), 20 international. Average age 25. 323 applicants, 17% accepted, 14 enrolled. In 2014, 7 master's, 23 doctorates awarded. *Degree requirements:* For master's, thesis; for doctorate, thesis/dissertation. *Entrance requirements:* For master's, GRE General Test, http://www.grad.gatech.edu/bioe; for doctorate, GRE General Test, http://www.grad.gatech.edu/bioe. Additional exam requirements/recommendations for international students: Required—TOEFL (minimum score 620 paper-based; 105 iBT). *Application deadline:* For fall admission, 1/10 priority date for domestic and international students. Applications are processed on a rolling basis. Application fee: $75. Electronic applications accepted. *Expenses:* Tuition, state resident: full-time $12,344; part-time $515 per credit hour. Tuition, nonresident: full-time $27,600; part-time $1150 per credit hour. *Required fees:* $1196 per term. Part-time tuition and fees vary according to course load. *Financial support:* Fellowships, research assistantships, teaching assistantships, career-related internships or fieldwork, Federal Work-Study, institutionally sponsored loans, tuition waivers (partial), and unspecified assistantships available. Support available to part-time students. Financial award application deadline: 5/1. *Unit head:* Andres Garcia, Director, E-mail: andres.garcia@me.gatech.edu. *Application contact:* Laura Paige, Graduate Coordinator, 404-385-6655, E-mail: laura.paige@bioengineering.gatech.edu.
Website: http://bioengineering.gatech.edu.

Illinois Institute of Technology, Graduate College, Armour College of Engineering, Department of Chemical and Biological Engineering, Chicago, IL 60616. Offers biological engineering (MAS); chemical engineering (MAS, MS, PhD); MS/MAS. Part-time and evening/weekend programs available. Postbaccalaureate distance learning degree programs offered (minimal on-campus study). *Faculty:* 18 full-time (2 women), 1 part-time/adjunct (0 women). *Students:* 128 full-time (42 women), 20 part-time (8 women); includes 5 minority (1 Black or African American, non-Hispanic/Latino; 4 Asian, non-Hispanic/Latino), 127 international. Average age 26. 618 applicants, 40% accepted, 42 enrolled. In 2014, 42 master's, 11 doctorates awarded. Terminal master's awarded for partial completion of doctoral program. *Degree requirements:* For master's, comprehensive exam (for some programs), thesis (for some programs); for doctorate, comprehensive exam, thesis/dissertation. *Entrance requirements:* For master's, GRE General Test with minimum score of 950 Quantitative and Verbal, 2.5 Analytical Writing (for MAS); GRE General Test with minimum score of 1100 Quantitative and Verbal, 3.0 Analytical Writing (for MS), minimum undergraduate GPA of 3.0; for doctorate, GRE General Test (minimum score 1100 Quantitative and Verbal, 3.0 Analytical Writing), minimum undergraduate GPA of 3.0. Additional exam requirements/recommendations for international students: Required—TOEFL (minimum score 550 paper-based; 80 iBT). *Application deadline:* For fall admission, 5/1 for domestic and international students; for spring admission, 10/15 for domestic and international students. Applications are processed on a rolling basis. Application fee: $50. Electronic applications accepted. *Expenses:* Tuition: Full-time $22,500; part-time $1250 per credit hour. *Required fees:* $30 per course. $260 per semester. One-time fee: $235. Tuition and fees vary according to course load and program. *Financial support:* Fellowships with partial tuition reimbursements, research assistantships with full and partial tuition reimbursements, teaching assistantships with full tuition reimbursements, Federal Work-Study, institutionally sponsored loans, scholarships/grants, health care benefits, and unspecified assistantships available. Support available to part-time students. Financial award applicants required to submit FAFSA. *Faculty research:* Energy and sustainability, biological engineering, advanced materials, systems engineering. *Unit head:* Dr. Sohail Murad, Chair and Professor of Chemical Engineering, 312-567-3867, Fax: 312-567-8874, E-mail: smurad1@iit.edu. *Application contact:* Rishab Malhotra, Director, Graduate Admission, 866-472-3448, Fax: 312-567-3138, E-mail: inquiry.grad@iit.edu.
Website: http://engineering.iit.edu/chbe.

Johns Hopkins University, G. W. C. Whiting School of Engineering and School of Medicine, Department of Biomedical Engineering, Baltimore, MD 21205. Offers bioengineering innovation and design (MSE); biomedical engineering (MSE, PhD). Terminal master's awarded for partial completion of doctoral program. *Degree requirements:* For master's, thesis; for doctorate, comprehensive exam, thesis/dissertation. *Entrance requirements:* For master's and doctorate, GRE General Test. Additional exam requirements/recommendations for international students: Required—TOEFL or IELTS. Electronic applications accepted. *Faculty research:* Cell and tissue engineering, systems neuroscience, imaging, cardiovascular systems physiology, theoretical and computational biology.

Johns Hopkins University, G. W. C. Whiting School of Engineering, Department of Chemical and Biomolecular Engineering, Baltimore, MD 21218. Offers MSE, PhD. Part-time programs available. Terminal master's awarded for partial completion of doctoral program. *Degree requirements:* For master's, essay presentation; for doctorate, thesis/dissertation, oral exam; thesis presentation. *Entrance requirements:* For master's and doctorate, GRE General Test. Additional exam requirements/recommendations for international students: Required—TOEFL (minimum score 600 paper-based; 100 iBT). Electronic applications accepted. *Faculty research:* Nanotechnology, materials by design, alternative energy, smart molecules and devices, biomolecular design and engineering, physics of cancer.

Kansas State University, Graduate School, College of Engineering, Department of Biological and Agricultural Engineering, Manhattan, KS 66506. Offers MS, PhD. *Faculty:* 15 full-time (4 women), 6 part-time/adjunct (0 women). *Students:* 24 full-time (14 women), 9 part-time (2 women); includes 5 minority (3 Black or African American, non-Hispanic/Latino; 1 Asian, non-Hispanic/Latino; 1 Two or more races, non-Hispanic/Latino), 17 international. Average age 31. 23 applicants, 48% accepted, 10 enrolled. In 2014, 7 master's, 3 doctorates awarded. Terminal master's awarded for partial

completion of doctoral program. *Degree requirements:* For master's, thesis; for doctorate, thesis/dissertation, preliminary exam. *Entrance requirements:* For master's, GRE, bachelor's degree in biological and agricultural engineering; for doctorate, GRE. Additional exam requirements/recommendations for international students: Required—TOEFL (minimum score 550 paper-based; 79 iBT). *Application deadline:* For fall admission, 2/1 priority date for domestic students, 1/1 priority date for international students; for spring admission, 8/1 priority date for domestic and international students. Applications are processed on a rolling basis. Application fee: $50 ($75 for international students). Electronic applications accepted. *Financial support:* In 2014–15, 2 students received support, including 21 research assistantships (averaging $20,114 per year); fellowships, teaching assistantships, Federal Work-Study, institutionally sponsored loans, and scholarships/grants also available. Support available to part-time students. Financial award application deadline: 3/1; financial award applicants required to submit FAFSA. *Faculty research:* Ecological engineering, watershed modeling, air quality, bioprocessing, bio-fuel, sensors and controls, 3D engineered biomaterials and biomedical devices, mobile health, point-of-care diagnosis, protein biomarker discovery, cancer early detection. *Total annual research expenditures:* $1.1 million. *Unit head:* Dr. Joseph Harner, Head, 785-532-5580, Fax: 785-532-5825, E-mail: jharner@k-state.edu. *Application contact:* Dr. Naiqian Zhang, Graduate Coordinator, 785-532-2910, Fax: 785-532-5825, E-mail: zhangn@k-state.edu.
Website: http://www.bae.ksu.edu/.

Kansas State University, Graduate School, College of Engineering, Department of Electrical and Computer Engineering, Manhattan, KS 66506. Offers electrical engineering (MS), including bioengineering, communication systems, design of computer systems, electrical engineering, energy and power systems, integrated circuits and devices, real time embedded systems, renewable energy, signal processing. Part-time and evening/weekend programs available. Postbaccalaureate distance learning degree programs offered (no on-campus study). *Faculty:* 21 full-time (4 women), 1 (woman) part-time/adjunct. *Students:* 38 full-time (8 women), 45 part-time (6 women); includes 13 minority (4 Black or African American, non-Hispanic/Latino; 8 Asian, non-Hispanic/Latino; 1 Hispanic/Latino), 37 international. Average age 28. 126 applicants, 29% accepted, 14 enrolled. In 2014, 22 master's, 5 doctorates awarded. *Degree requirements:* For master's, thesis or alternative, final exam; for doctorate, thesis/dissertation, final exam, preliminary exams. *Entrance requirements:* For master's, GRE General Test, bachelor's degree in electrical engineering or computer science, minimum GPA of 3.0; for doctorate, GRE General Test. Additional exam requirements/recommendations for international students: Required—TOEFL (minimum score 600 paper-based; 85 iBT). *Application deadline:* For fall admission, 1/1 priority date for domestic and international students; for spring admission, 8/1 priority date for domestic and international students. Applications are processed on a rolling basis. Application fee: $50 ($75 for international students). Electronic applications accepted. *Financial support:* In 2014–15, 40 students received support, including 22 research assistantships with tuition reimbursements available (averaging $12,100 per year), 18 teaching assistantships with full tuition reimbursements available (averaging $12,220 per year); career-related internships or fieldwork, institutionally sponsored loans, and scholarships/grants also available. Support available to part-time students. Financial award application deadline: 3/1; financial award applicants required to submit FAFSA. *Faculty research:* Energy systems and renewable energy, computer systems and real time embedded systems, communication systems and signal processing, integrated circuits and devices, bioengineering. *Total annual research expenditures:* $1.3 million. *Unit head:* Dr. Don Gruenbacher, Head, 785-532-5600, Fax: 785-532-1188, E-mail: grue@k-state.edu. *Application contact:* Dr. Andrew Rys, Graduate Program Director, 785-532-4665, Fax: 785-532-1188, E-mail: andrys@k-state.edu.
Website: http://www.ece.k-state.edu/.

Lehigh University, P.C. Rossin College of Engineering and Applied Science, Program in Bioengineering, Bethlehem, PA 18015. Offers MS, PhD. *Faculty:* 12 full-time (4 women). *Students:* 12 full-time (3 women), 8 international. Average age 27. 27 applicants, 44% accepted, 3 enrolled. In 2014, 2 master's awarded. Terminal master's awarded for partial completion of doctoral program. *Degree requirements:* For master's, thesis; for doctorate, comprehensive exam, thesis/dissertation. *Entrance requirements:* For master's and doctorate, GRE. Additional exam requirements/recommendations for international students: Required—TOEFL (minimum score 79 iBT). *Application deadline:* For fall admission, 7/15 for domestic and international students. Applications are processed on a rolling basis. Application fee: $75. Electronic applications accepted. *Financial support:* In 2014–15, 17 students received support, including 7 research assistantships (averaging $25,100 per year), 7 teaching assistantships (averaging $26,000 per year); health care benefits also available. Financial award application deadline: 1/15. *Faculty research:* Biomaterials, biomechanics (biomolecular, cellular, fluid and solid mechanics), BioMEMS Biosensors, bioelectronics/biophotonics, biopharmaceutical engineering. *Unit head:* Dr. Susan Perry, Faculty Graduate Coordinator in Bioengineering, 610-758-4330, E-mail: sup3@lehigh.edu. *Application contact:* Brianne Lisk, Administrative Coordinator of Graduate Studies and Research, 610-758-6310, Fax: 610-758-5623, E-mail: brc3@lehigh.edu.
Website: http://www.lehigh.edu/~inbioe/graduate/index.html.

Louisiana State University and Agricultural & Mechanical College, Graduate School, College of Engineering, Department of Biological and Agricultural Engineering, Baton Rouge, LA 70803. Offers biological and agricultural engineering (MSBAE); engineering science (MS, PhD). Part-time programs available. *Faculty:* 12 full-time (3 women). *Students:* 12 full-time (3 women), 2 part-time (0 women); includes 1 minority (Black or African American, non-Hispanic/Latino), 5 international. Average age 25. 8 applicants, 38% accepted, 3 enrolled. In 2014, 7 master's awarded. Terminal master's awarded for partial completion of doctoral program. *Degree requirements:* For master's, thesis; for doctorate, thesis/dissertation. *Entrance requirements:* For master's and doctorate, GRE General Test, minimum GPA of 3.0. Additional exam requirements/recommendations for international students: Required—TOEFL (minimum score 550 paper-based; 79 IBT), IELTS (minimum score 6.5), or PTE (minimum score 59). *Application deadline:* For fall admission, 1/1 priority date for domestic students, 5/15 for international students; for spring admission, 10/15 for domestic and international students; for summer admission, 5/15 for domestic and international students. Applications are processed on a rolling basis. Application fee: $50 ($70 for international students). Electronic applications accepted. *Financial support:* In 2014–15, 13 students received support, including 1 fellowship (averaging $18,139 per year), 8 research assistantships with partial tuition reimbursements available (averaging $18,125 per year); teaching assistantships with partial tuition reimbursements available, career-related internships or fieldwork, Federal Work-Study, institutionally sponsored loans, scholarships/grants, health care benefits, and unspecified assistantships also available. Financial award application deadline: 7/1; financial award applicants required to submit FAFSA. *Faculty research:* Bioenergy, bioprocess engineering, cellular and molecular engineering, drug delivery using nanotechnology, environmental engineering. *Total annual research expenditures:* $229,597. *Unit head:* Dr. David Constant, Head, 225-578-3153, Fax: 225-578-3492, E-mail: dconstant@agcenter.lsu.edu. *Application contact:* Dr. Steven Hall, Graduate Coordinator, 225-578-1049, Fax: 225-578-3492, E-mail: sghall@agcenter.lsu.edu.
Website: http://www.bae.lsu.edu/.

Massachusetts Institute of Technology, School of Engineering, Department of Biological Engineering, Cambridge, MA 02139. Offers applied biosciences (PhD, Sc D); bioengineering (PhD, Sc D); biological engineering (PhD, Sc D); biomedical engineering (M Eng); toxicology (SM); SM/MBA. *Faculty:* 34 full-time (7 women). *Students:* 134 full-time (52 women); includes 50 minority (3 Black or African American, non-Hispanic/Latino; 33 Asian, non-Hispanic/Latino; 8 Hispanic/Latino; 6 Two or more races, non-Hispanic/Latino), 32 international. Average age 26. 483 applicants, 8% accepted, 26 enrolled. In 2014, 2 master's, 18 doctorates awarded. Terminal master's awarded for partial completion of doctoral program. *Degree requirements:* For master's, thesis; for doctorate, comprehensive exam, thesis/dissertation. *Entrance requirements:* For master's and doctorate, GRE General Test. Additional exam requirements/recommendations for international students: Required—IELTS (minimum score 7). *Application deadline:* For fall admission, 12/15 for domestic and international students. Application fee: $75. Electronic applications accepted. *Expenses: Tuition:* Full-time $44,720; part-time $699 per unit. *Required fees:* $296. *Financial support:* In 2014–15, 129 students received support, including 63 fellowships (averaging $41,400 per year), 67 research assistantships (averaging $36,500 per year); teaching assistantships, Federal Work-Study, institutionally sponsored loans, scholarships/grants, traineeships, health care benefits, and unspecified assistantships also available. Financial award application deadline: 4/15; financial award applicants required to submit FAFSA. *Faculty research:* Biomaterials; biophysics; cell and tissue engineering; computational modeling of biological and physiological systems; discovery and delivery of molecular therapeutics; new tools for genomics; functional genomics; proteomics and glycomics; macromolecular biochemistry and biophysics; molecular, cell and tissue biomechanics; synthetic biology; systems biology. *Total annual research expenditures:* $49.1 million. *Unit head:* Prof. Douglas A. Lauffenburger, Department Head, 617-253-1712, E-mail: be-acad@mit.edu. *Application contact:* Graduate Admissions, 617-253-1712, Fax: 617-258-8676, E-mail: be-acad@mit.edu.
Website: http://web.mit.edu/be/.

McGill University, Faculty of Graduate and Postdoctoral Studies, Faculty of Agricultural and Environmental Sciences, Department of Bioresource Engineering, Montréal, QC H3A 2T5, Canada. Offers computer applications (M Sc, M Sc A, PhD); food engineering (M Sc, M Sc A, PhD); grain drying (M Sc, M Sc A, PhD); irrigation and drainage (M Sc, M Sc A, PhD); machinery (M Sc, M Sc A, PhD); pollution control (M Sc, M Sc A, PhD); post-harvest technology (M Sc, M Sc A, PhD); soil dynamics (M Sc, M Sc A, PhD); structure and environment (M Sc, M Sc A, PhD); vegetable and fruit storage (M Sc, M Sc A, PhD).

Mississippi State University, College of Agriculture and Life Sciences, Department of Agricultural and Biological Engineering, Mississippi State, MS 39762. Offers agricultural sciences (PhD), including engineering technology (MS, PhD); agriculture (MS), including engineering technology (MS, PhD); biological engineering (MS); engineering (PhD), including biological engineering. *Faculty:* 15 full-time (3 women). *Students:* 29 full-time (11 women), 8 part-time (2 women); includes 6 minority (1 Black or African American, non-Hispanic/Latino; 3 Asian, non-Hispanic/Latino; 2 Two or more races, non-Hispanic/Latino), 14 international. Average age 29. 32 applicants, 34% accepted, 10 enrolled. In 2014, 7 master's, 3 doctorates awarded. *Degree requirements:* For master's, thesis (for some programs); for doctorate, thesis/dissertation, preliminary exam. *Entrance requirements:* For master's, GRE General Test, minimum undergraduate GPA of 2.75 (3.0 for biomedical engineering); for doctorate, GRE General Test, minimum GPA of 3.0 (biomedical engineering). Additional exam requirements/recommendations for international students: Required—TOEFL (minimum score 550 paper-based; 79 iBT); Recommended—IELTS (minimum score 6.5). *Application deadline:* For fall admission, 7/1 for domestic students, 5/1 for international students; for spring admission, 11/1 for domestic students, 9/1 for international students. Applications are processed on a rolling basis. Application fee: $60. Electronic applications accepted. *Expenses:* Tuition, state resident: full-time $7140; part-time $783 per credit hour. Tuition, nonresident: full-time $18,478; part-time $2043 per credit hour. *Financial support:* In 2014–15, 17 research assistantships with partial tuition reimbursements (averaging $15,375 per year) were awarded; Federal Work-Study, institutionally sponsored loans, and unspecified assistantships also available. Financial award application deadline: 4/1; financial award applicants required to submit FAFSA. *Faculty research:* Bioenvironmental engineering, bioinstrumentation, biomechanics/biomaterials, precision agriculture, tissue engineering, ergonomics human factors, biosimulation and modeling. *Total annual research expenditures:* $473,000. *Unit head:* Dr. Jonathan Pote, Department Head and Professor, 662-325-3282, Fax: 662-325-3853, E-mail: abe_head@abe.msstate.edu. *Application contact:* Dr. Rajkumar Prabhu, Professor and Graduate Coordinator, 662-325-7351, Fax: 662-325-3853, E-mail: pr66@msstate.edu.
Website: http://www.abe.msstate.edu/.

North Carolina Agricultural and Technical State University, School of Graduate Studies, College of Engineering, Department of Chemical and Bioengineering, Greensboro, NC 27411. Offers bioengineering (MS); biological engineering (MS); chemical engineering (MS).

North Carolina State University, Graduate School, College of Agriculture and Life Sciences, Department of Biological and Agricultural Engineering, Raleigh, NC 27695. Offers MBAE, MS, PhD, Certificate. Part-time programs available. Postbaccalaureate distance learning degree programs offered. *Degree requirements:* For master's, thesis (for some programs); for doctorate, thesis/dissertation. *Entrance requirements:* For master's and doctorate, GRE. Additional exam requirements/recommendations for international students: Required—TOEFL. Electronic applications accepted. *Faculty research:* Bioinstrumentation, animal waste management, water quality engineering, machine systems, controlled environment agriculture.

Northeastern University, College of Engineering, Boston, MA 02115-5096. Offers bioengineering (PhD); chemical engineering (MS, PhD); civil engineering (MS, PhD); computer engineering (PhD); computer systems engineering (MS); electrical and computer engineering (MS); electrical and engineering leadership (MS); electrical engineering (PhD); energy systems (MS); engineering leadership (Certificate); engineering management (MRTP); industrial engineering (MS, PhD); information assurance (PhD); information systems (MS); interdisciplinary (PhD); mechanical engineering (MS, PhD); operations research (MS); telecommunication systems management (MS). Part-time programs available. *Expenses:* Contact institution.

Northwestern University, The Graduate School, Interdisciplinary Biological Sciences Program (IBiS), Evanston, IL 60208. Offers biochemistry (PhD); bioengineering and biotechnology (PhD); biotechnology (PhD); cell and molecular biology (PhD); developmental and systems biology (PhD); nanotechnology (PhD); neurobiology (PhD); structural biology and biophysics (PhD). *Degree requirements:* For doctorate, thesis/dissertation, qualifying exam. *Entrance requirements:* For doctorate, GRE General Test. Additional exam requirements/recommendations for international students: Required—TOEFL (minimum score 600 paper-based). Electronic applications accepted. *Faculty* *research:* Biophysics/structural biology, cell/molecular biology, synthetic biology, developmental systems biology, chemical biology/nanotechnology.

The Ohio State University, Graduate School, College of Food, Agricultural, and Environmental Sciences, Department of Food, Agricultural, and Biological Engineering, Columbus, OH 43210. Offers MS, PhD. Program offered jointly with College of Engineering. *Faculty:* 23. *Students:* 45 full-time (22 women), 6 part-time (1 woman); includes 4 minority (1 Black or African American, non-Hispanic/Latino; 2 Hispanic/Latino; 1 Two or more races, non-Hispanic/Latino), 24 international. Average age 27. In 2014, 10 master's, 5 doctorates awarded. *Degree requirements:* For master's, thesis optional; for doctorate, thesis/dissertation. *Entrance requirements:* For master's and doctorate, GRE General Test, GRE Subject Test in engineering (recommended). Additional exam requirements/recommendations for international students: Required—TOEFL (minimum score 550 paper-based; 79 iBT), Michigan English Language Assessment Battery (minimum score 82); Recommended—IELTS (minimum score 7). *Application deadline:* For fall admission, 12/13 priority date for domestic students, 11/30 priority date for international students; for spring admission, 12/14 for domestic students, 11/12 for international students; for summer admission, 5/15 for domestic students, 4/14 for international students. Applications are processed on a rolling basis. Application fee: $60 ($70 for international students). Electronic applications accepted. *Financial support:* Fellowships with tuition reimbursements, research assistantships with tuition reimbursements, teaching assistantships with tuition reimbursements, career-related internships or fieldwork, Federal Work-Study, and institutionally sponsored loans available. Support available to part-time students. *Unit head:* Dr. Scott Shearer, Chair, 614-292-7284, E-mail: shearer.95@osu.edu. *Application contact:* Graduate and Professional Admissions, 614-292-9444, Fax: 614-292-3895, E-mail: gpadmissions@osu.edu.
Website: http://fabe.osu.edu/.

Oklahoma State University, College of Agricultural Science and Natural Resources, Department of Biosystems and Agricultural Engineering, Stillwater, OK 74078. Offers biosystems engineering (MS, PhD); environmental and natural resources (MS, PhD). *Faculty:* 26 full-time (3 women). *Students:* 19 full-time (13 women), 23 part-time (5 women); includes 5 minority (2 American Indian or Alaska Native, non-Hispanic/Latino; 2 Hispanic/Latino; 1 Two or more races, non-Hispanic/Latino), 19 international. Average age 29. 43 applicants, 30% accepted, 8 enrolled. In 2014, 4 master's, 6 doctorates awarded. *Degree requirements:* For master's, thesis; for doctorate, comprehensive exam, thesis/dissertation. *Entrance requirements:* For master's and doctorate, GRE or GMAT. Additional exam requirements/recommendations for international students: Required—TOEFL (minimum score 550 paper-based; 79 iBT). *Application deadline:* For fall admission, 3/1 priority date for international students; for spring admission, 8/1 priority date for international students. Applications are processed on a rolling basis. Application fee: $40 ($75 for international students). Electronic applications accepted. *Expenses:* Tuition, state resident: full-time $4488; part-time $187 per credit hour. Tuition, nonresident: full-time $18,360; part-time $765 per credit hour. *Required fees:* $2413; $100.55 per credit hour. Tuition and fees vary according to campus/location. *Financial support:* In 2014–15, 33 research assistantships (averaging $17,683 per year), 2 teaching assistantships (averaging $14,100 per year) were awarded; career-related internships or fieldwork, Federal Work-Study, scholarships/grants, health care benefits, tuition waivers (partial), and unspecified assistantships also available. Support available to part-time students. Financial award application deadline: 3/1; financial award applicants required to submit FAFSA. *Unit head:* Dr. Daniel Thomas, Department Head, 405-744-5431, Fax: 405-744-6059, E-mail: daniel.thomas@okstate.edu. *Application contact:* Glenn Brown, Professor/Graduate Coordinator, 405-744-8425, E-mail: gbrown@okstate.edu.
Website: http://bae.okstate.edu/.

Oregon State University, College of Engineering, Program in Biological and Ecological Engineering, Corvallis, OR 97331. Offers M Eng, MS, PhD. Part-time programs available. *Faculty:* 8 full-time (2 women), 4 part-time/adjunct (0 women). *Students:* 12 full-time (2 women), 1 part-time (0 women), 8 international. Average age 30. 21 applicants, 14% accepted, 1 enrolled. In 2014, 1 master's, 3 doctorates awarded. Terminal master's awarded for partial completion of doctoral program. *Degree requirements:* For master's, thesis or alternative; for doctorate, thesis/dissertation. *Entrance requirements:* For master's and doctorate, GRE, minimum GPA of 3.0 in last 90 hours. Additional exam requirements/recommendations for international students: Required—TOEFL (minimum score 80 iBT), IELTS (minimum score 6.5). *Application deadline:* For fall admission, 8/1 for domestic students, 4/1 for international students; for winter admission, 12/1 for domestic students, 7/1 for international students; for spring admission, 2/1 for domestic students, 10/1 for international students; for summer admission, 5/1 for domestic students, 1/1 for international students. Application fee: $60. *Expenses:* Expenses: $15,359 full-time resident tuition and fees; $23,405 non-resident. *Financial support:* Fellowships with full tuition reimbursements, research assistantships with full tuition reimbursements, teaching assistantships, Federal Work-Study, and institutionally sponsored loans available. Support available to part-time students. Financial award application deadline: 2/1. *Faculty research:* Bioengineering, water resources engineering, food engineering, cell culture and fermentation, vadose zone transport. *Unit head:* Dr. John P. Bolte, Head, 541-737-6303, Fax: 541-737-2082, E-mail: info-bee@engr.orst.edu. *Application contact:* Ganti Murthy, Biological and Ecological Engineering Advisor, 541-737-6291, E-mail: info-bee@engr.orst.edu.
Website: http://bee.oregonstate.edu/programs/graduate.

Penn State University Park, Graduate School, College of Agricultural Sciences, Department of Agricultural and Biological Engineering, University Park, PA 16802. Offers agricultural and biological engineering (MS, PhD); biorenewable systems (MS, PhD). *Unit head:* Dr. Richard T. Roush, Dean, 814-865-2541, Fax: 814-865-3103, E-mail: rtr10@psu.edu. *Application contact:* Lori A. Stania, Director, Graduate Student Services, 814-867-5278, Fax: 814-863-4627, E-mail: gswww@psu.edu.
Website: http://abe.psu.edu/.

Penn State University Park, Graduate School, Intercollege Graduate Programs, Intercollege Graduate Program in Bioengineering, University Park, PA 16802. Offers MS, PhD. *Unit head:* Dr. Regina Vasilatos-Younken, Interim Dean, 814-865-2516, Fax: 814-863-4627, E-mail: rxv@psu.edu. *Application contact:* Lori A. Stania, Director, Graduate Student Services, 814-867-5278, Fax: 814-863-4627, E-mail: gswww@psu.edu.

Rensselaer Polytechnic Institute, Graduate School, School of Engineering, Program in Chemical Engineering, Troy, NY 12180-3590. Offers M Eng, MS, D Eng, PhD. *Faculty:* 34 full-time (4 women), 2 part-time/adjunct (1 woman). *Students:* 69 full-time (20 women), 4 part-time (0 women); includes 9 minority (8 Asian, non-Hispanic/Latino; 1 Two or more races, non-Hispanic/Latino), 36 international. Average age 26. 182 applicants, 19% accepted, 10 enrolled. In 2014, 3 master's, 13 doctorates awarded. Terminal master's awarded for partial completion of doctoral program. *Entrance requirements:* For master's, GRE; for doctorate, GRE. Additional exam requirements/recommendations for international students: Required—TOEFL (minimum score 570 paper-based; 88 iBT), IELTS (minimum score 6.5), PTE (minimum score 60). *Application deadline:* For fall admission, 1/1 priority date for domestic and international

students; for spring admission, 8/15 priority date for domestic and international students. Applications are processed on a rolling basis. Electronic applications accepted. *Expenses: Tuition:* Full-time $46,700; part-time $1945 per credit. Tuition and fees vary according to course load. *Financial support:* In 2014–15, 33 students received support, including research assistantships with full tuition reimbursements available (averaging $18,500 per year), teaching assistantships with full tuition reimbursements available (averaging $18,500 per year); fellowships also available. Financial award application deadline: 1/1. *Faculty research:* Advanced materials, biochemical engineering; biomedical engineering; biotechnology; drug delivery; energy; fluid mechanics; interfacial phenomena; mass transport; molecular simulations; molecular thermodynamics; nanotechnology; polymers; process control, design, and optimization; separation and bioseparation processes; systems biology; systems engineering; transport phenomena. *Total annual research expenditures:* $5.5 million. *Unit head:* Dr. Ravi Kane, Graduate Program Director, 518-276-2536, E-mail: kaner@rpi.edu. *Application contact:* Office of Graduate Admissions, 518-276-6216, E-mail: gradadmissions@rpi.edu.
Website: http://cbe.rpi.edu/graduate.

Rice University, Graduate Programs, George R. Brown School of Engineering, Department of Bioengineering, Houston, TX 77251-1892. Offers MBE, MS, PhD, MD/PhD. Terminal master's awarded for partial completion of doctoral program. *Degree requirements:* For master's, thesis; for doctorate, thesis/dissertation, qualifying exam, internship. *Entrance requirements:* For master's and doctorate, GRE General Test. Additional exam requirements/recommendations for international students: Required—TOEFL (minimum score 600 paper-based; 90 iBT). Electronic applications accepted. *Faculty research:* Biomaterials, tissue engineering, laser-tissue interactions, biochemical engineering, gene therapy.

Rice University, Graduate Programs, George R. Brown School of Engineering, Department of Electrical and Computer Engineering, Houston, TX 77251-1892. Offers bioengineering (MS, PhD); circuits, controls, and communication systems (MS, PhD); computer science and engineering (MS, PhD); electrical engineering (MEE); lasers, microwaves, and solid-state electronics (MS, PhD); MBA/MEE. Part-time programs available. *Degree requirements:* For master's, thesis (for some programs); for doctorate, thesis/dissertation. *Entrance requirements:* For master's and doctorate, GRE General Test, GRE Subject Test, minimum GPA of 3.0. Additional exam requirements/recommendations for international students: Required—TOEFL (minimum score 600 paper-based; 90 iBT). Electronic applications accepted. *Faculty research:* Physical electronics, systems, computer engineering, bioengineering.

Santa Clara University, School of Engineering, Santa Clara, CA 95053. Offers analog circuit design (Certificate); applied mathematics (MS); ASIC design and test (Certificate); bioengineering (MS); civil engineering (MS); computer science and engineering (MS, PhD); controls (Certificate); digital signal processing (Certificate); dynamics (Certificate); electrical engineering (MS, PhD); engineering (Engineer); engineering management (MS); fundamentals of electrical engineering (Certificate); information assurance (Certificate); materials engineering (Certificate); mechanical design analysis (Certificate); mechanical engineering (MS, PhD); mechatronics systems engineering (Certificate); microwave and antennas (Certificate); networking (Certificate); renewable energy (Certificate); software engineering (Certificate); sustainable energy (MS); technology jump-start (Certificate); thermofluids (Certificate). Part-time and evening/weekend programs available. *Faculty:* 59 full-time (23 women), 80 part-time/adjunct (14 women). *Students:* 584 full-time (239 women), 353 part-time (102 women); includes 224 minority (7 Black or African American, non-Hispanic/Latino; 144 Asian, non-Hispanic/Latino; 50 Hispanic/Latino; 2 Native Hawaiian or other Pacific Islander, non-Hispanic/Latino; 21 Two or more races, non-Hispanic/Latino), 548 international. Average age 27. 1,248 applicants, 51% accepted, 375 enrolled. In 2014, 283 master's, 5 doctorates, 1 other advanced degree awarded. *Degree requirements:* For master's, thesis (for some programs); for doctorate, thesis/dissertation; for other advanced degree, thesis. *Entrance requirements:* For master's, GRE, transcript; for doctorate, GRE, master's degree or equivalent; for other advanced degree, master's degree, published paper. Additional exam requirements/recommendations for international students: Required—TOEFL (minimum score 550 paper-based; 79 iBT). *Application deadline:* For fall admission, 8/1 for domestic students, 7/15 for international students; for winter admission, 10/28 for domestic students, 9/23 for international students; for spring admission, 2/25 for domestic students, 1/21 for international students. Applications are processed on a rolling basis. Application fee: $60. Electronic applications accepted. *Expenses:* Expenses: Contact institution. *Financial support:* In 2014–15, 94 students received support. Fellowships with full and partial tuition reimbursements available, research assistantships with full and partial tuition reimbursements available, teaching assistantships with full tuition reimbursements available, career-related internships or fieldwork, Federal Work-Study, institutionally sponsored loans, and scholarships/grants available. Support available to part-time students. Financial award application deadline: 3/2; financial award applicants required to submit FAFSA. *Faculty research:* Video encoding, nanostructures, robotics, microfluidics, water resources. *Total annual research expenditures:* $1.6 million. *Unit head:* Dr. Alex Zecevic, Associate Dean for Graduate Studies, 408-554-2394, E-mail: azecevic@scu.edu. *Application contact:* Stacey Tinker, Director of Enrollment Management, 408-554-4748, Fax: 408-554-4323, E-mail: stinker@scu.edu.
Website: http://www.scu.edu/engineering/graduate/.

South Dakota School of Mines and Technology, Graduate Division, Program in Chemical and Biological Engineering, Rapid City, SD 57701-3995. Offers PhD. Part-time programs available. *Faculty:* 13 full-time (6 women). *Students:* 16 full-time (3 women), 2 part-time (0 women); includes 2 minority (both Black or African American, non-Hispanic/Latino), 9 international. Average age 31. 8 applicants, 13% accepted, 1 enrolled. In 2014, 7 doctorates awarded. *Degree requirements:* For doctorate, thesis/dissertation. *Entrance requirements:* Additional exam requirements/recommendations for international students: Required—TOEFL (minimum score 520 paper-based; 68 iBT). *Application deadline:* For fall admission, 7/1 priority date for domestic students, 4/1 for international students; for spring admission, 11/1 for domestic students, 9/1 for international students. Applications are processed on a rolling basis. Application fee: $35. Electronic applications accepted. *Expenses:* Tuition, state resident: full-time $5050; part-time $210.40 per credit hour. Tuition, nonresident: full-time $11,290; part-time $470.30 per credit hour. *Required fees:* $4680. *Financial support:* In 2014–15, 3 fellowships (averaging $5,138 per year), 30 research assistantships with partial tuition reimbursements (averaging $9,284 per year) were awarded; teaching assistantships with partial tuition reimbursements also available. Financial award application deadline: 5/15. *Faculty research:* Polymer synthesis, processing, and characterization; composite material processing; characterization and prototyping. *Total annual research expenditures:* $408,983. *Unit head:* Dr. Robb Winter, Department Head, 605-394-1237, E-mail: robb.winter@sdsmt.edu. *Application contact:* Rachel Howard, Office of Graduate Education, 605-355-3468, Fax: 605-394-1767, E-mail: rachel.howard@sdsmt.edu.
Website: http://www.sdsmt.edu/Academics/Departments/Chemical-and-Biological-Engineering/Graduate-Education/Chemical-and-Biological-Engineering—PhD/.

Bioengineering

Stanford University, School of Engineering, Department of Bioengineering, Stanford, CA 94305-9991. Offers MS, PhD. *Expenses: Tuition:* Full-time $44,184; part-time $982 per credit hour. *Required fees:* $191.

Stanford University, School of Medicine, Department of Bioengineering, Stanford, CA 94305-9991. Offers MS, PhD. *Degree requirements:* For master's, thesis optional; for doctorate, comprehensive exam, thesis/dissertation. *Entrance requirements:* For master's and doctorate, GRE General Test. Additional exam requirements/recommendations for international students: Required—TOEFL. Electronic applications accepted. *Expenses: Tuition:* Full-time $44,184; part-time $982 per credit hour. *Required fees:* $191. *Faculty research:* Biomedical computation, regenerative medicine/tissue engineering, molecular and cell bioengineering, biomedical imaging, biomedical devices.

Syracuse University, L. C. Smith College of Engineering and Computer Science, Program in Bioengineering, Syracuse, NY 13244. Offers MS, PhD. Part-time programs available. *Students:* 70 full-time (30 women), 8 part-time (5 women); includes 9 minority (3 Black or African American, non-Hispanic/Latino; 3 Asian, non-Hispanic/Latino; 2 Hispanic/Latino; 1 Two or more races, non-Hispanic/Latino), 48 international. Average age 25. 103 applicants, 51% accepted, 18 enrolled. In 2014, 12 master's, 2 doctorates awarded. *Degree requirements:* For master's, thesis (for some programs); for doctorate, comprehensive exam, thesis/dissertation. *Entrance requirements:* For master's and doctorate, GRE General Test. Additional exam requirements/recommendations for international students: Required—TOEFL (minimum score 100 iBT). *Application deadline:* For fall admission, 7/1 priority date for domestic students, 6/1 priority date for international students; for spring admission, 10/15 for domestic students, 11/15 priority date for international students. Applications are processed on a rolling basis. Application fee: $75. Electronic applications accepted. *Expenses: Tuition:* Part-time $1341 per credit. *Required fees:* $1341 per credit. *Financial support:* Fellowships with full tuition reimbursements, research assistantships with full and partial tuition reimbursements, teaching assistantships with full and partial tuition reimbursements, and tuition waivers (partial) available. Financial award application deadline: 1/1; financial award applicants required to submit FAFSA. *Unit head:* Dr. Radhakrishna Sureshkumar, Department Chair, 315-443-1931, Fax: 315-443-9175, E-mail: topgrads@syr.edu. *Application contact:* Kathleen Joyce, Assistant Dean, 314-443-2219, E-mail: topgrads@syr.edu.

Temple University, College of Engineering, Department of Bioengineering, Philadelphia, PA 19122-6096. Offers bioengineering (MS); engineering (PhD). Part-time and evening/weekend programs available. *Faculty:* 11 full-time (4 women). *Students:* 18 full-time (7 women), 1 (woman) part-time; includes 5 minority (all Asian, non-Hispanic/Latino), 9 international. Average age 26. 38 applicants, 71% accepted, 7 enrolled. In 2014, 9 master's awarded. Terminal master's awarded for partial completion of doctoral program. *Degree requirements:* For master's, thesis optional; for doctorate, thesis/dissertation, preliminary exam, dissertation proposal and defense. *Entrance requirements:* For master's, GRE General Test, minimum undergraduate GPA of 3.0; BS in engineering from ABET-accredited or equivalent institution; resume; goals statement; three letters of reference; official transcripts; for doctorate, GRE General Test, minimum undergraduate GPA of 3.0; MS in engineering from ABET-accredited or equivalent institution (preferred); resume; goals statement; three letters of reference; official transcripts. Additional exam requirements/recommendations for international students: Required—TOEFL (minimum score 550 paper-based; 79 iBT), IELTS (minimum score 6.5). *Application deadline:* For fall admission, 3/1 priority date for domestic and international students; for spring admission, 11/1 priority date for domestic students, 8/1 priority date for international students. Applications are processed on a rolling basis. Application fee: $60. Electronic applications accepted. *Expenses:* Expenses: $913 per credit hour in-state; $1,210 per credit hour out-of-state. *Financial support:* Fellowships with full and partial tuition reimbursements, research assistantships with full and partial tuition reimbursements, teaching assistantships with full and partial tuition reimbursements, Federal Work-Study, scholarships/grants, health care benefits, and unspecified assistantships available. Financial award application deadline: 3/1; financial award applicants required to submit FAFSA. *Faculty research:* Soft tissue mechanics, injury biomechanics, targeted drug delivery, brain-computer interface, regenerative medicine, smart nanotechnology-based biomaterials, tissue spectroscopy. *Unit head:* Dr. Peter Lelkes, Chair, Department of Bioengineering, 215-204-3307, Fax: 215-204-6936, E-mail: pilelkes@temple.edu. *Application contact:* Mojan Arshad, Assistant Coordinator, Graduate Studies, 215-204-7800, Fax: 215-204-6936, E-mail: gradengr@temple.edu.
Website: http://engineering.temple.edu/bioengineering.

Texas A&M University, College of Agriculture and Life Sciences and College of Engineering, Department of Biological and Agricultural Engineering, College Station, TX 77843. Offers agricultural systems management (MS); biological and agricultural engineering (MS, PhD). Part-time programs available. *Faculty:* 18. *Students:* 59 full-time (26 women), 23 part-time (7 women); includes 17 minority (5 Black or African American, non-Hispanic/Latino; 2 Asian, non-Hispanic/Latino; 9 Hispanic/Latino; 1 Two or more races, non-Hispanic/Latino), 45 international. Average age 29. 45 applicants, 53% accepted, 11 enrolled. In 2014, 19 master's, 7 doctorates awarded. *Degree requirements:* For master's, thesis (MS), preliminary and final exams; for doctorate, thesis/dissertation, preliminary and final exams. *Entrance requirements:* For master's and doctorate, GRE General Test. Additional exam requirements/recommendations for international students: Required—TOEFL (minimum score 550 paper-based). *Application deadline:* For fall admission, 2/1 priority date for domestic students; for spring admission, 10/1 for domestic students. Applications are processed on a rolling basis. Application fee: $50 ($90 for international students). Electronic applications accepted. *Expenses:* Tuition, state resident: full-time $4078; part-time $226.55 per credit hour. Tuition, nonresident: full-time $10,594; part-time $577.55 per credit hour. *Required fees:* $2813; $237.70 per credit hour. $278.50 per semester. Tuition and fees vary according to degree level and student level. *Financial support:* In 2014–15, 69 students received support, including 7 fellowships with full and partial tuition reimbursements available (averaging $18,786 per year), 22 research assistantships with full and partial tuition reimbursements available (averaging $5,829 per year), 13 teaching assistantships with full and partial tuition reimbursements available (averaging $6,283 per year); career-related internships or fieldwork, institutionally sponsored loans, scholarships/grants, traineeships, health care benefits, tuition waivers (full and partial), and unspecified assistantships also available. Support available to part-time students. Financial award application deadline: 3/1; financial award applicants required to submit FAFSA. *Faculty research:* Water quality and quantity; air quality; biological, food, ecological engineering; off-road equipment; mechatronics. *Unit head:* Dr. Steve Searcy, Professor and Head, 979-845-3940, Fax: 979-862-3442, E-mail: s-searcy@tamu.edu. *Application contact:* Dr. Sandun Fernando, Graduate Coordinator, 979-845-9793, E-mail: sfernando@tamu.edu.
Website: http://baen.tamu.edu.

Texas Tech University, Graduate School, Edward E. Whitacre Jr. College of Engineering, Interdisciplinary Program in Bioengineering, Lubbock, TX 79409-3103. Offers MS. *Students:* 10 full-time (3 women); includes 2 minority (1 Black or African American, non-Hispanic/Latino; 1 Asian, non-Hispanic/Latino), 5 international. Average age 24. 24 applicants, 54% accepted, 5 enrolled. In 2014, 1 master's awarded. *Degree requirements:* For master's, comprehensive exam, thesis (for some programs). *Entrance requirements:* For master's, GRE (Verbal and Quantitative). Additional exam requirements/recommendations for international students: Required—TOEFL (minimum score 550 paper-based; 79 iBT). Application fee: $60. *Expenses:* Tuition, state resident: full-time $6310; part-time $262.92 per credit hour. Tuition, nonresident: full-time $14,998; part-time $624.92 per credit hour. *Required fees:* $2701; $36.50 per credit. $912.50 per semester. Tuition and fees vary according to course load. *Financial support:* In 2014–15, 5 students received support, including 3 fellowships (averaging $1,000 per year), 1 research assistantship (averaging $27,500 per year), 1 teaching assistantship (averaging $10,000 per year); scholarships/grants, tuition waivers (partial), and unspecified assistantships also available. Financial award application deadline: 4/15; financial award applicants required to submit FAFSA. *Faculty research:* Bioengineering, biomaterials, drug and vaccine delivery, cellular signal transduction, cancer detection and drug screening. *Unit head:* Dr. Mary Baker, Director, 806-834-0065, Fax: 806-742-1245, E-mail: mary.baker@ttu.edu.
Website: http://www.depts.ttu.edu/coe/bioengineering/.

Tufts University, Graduate School of Arts and Sciences, Graduate Certificate Programs, Program in Bioengineering, Medford, MA 02155. Offers Certificate. Part-time and evening/weekend programs available. Electronic applications accepted. *Expenses: Tuition:* Full-time $45,590; part-time $1161 per credit hour. *Required fees:* $782. Full-time tuition and fees vary according to degree level, program and student level. Part-time tuition and fees vary according to course load.

Tufts University, School of Engineering, Department of Biomedical Engineering, Medford, MA 02155. Offers bioengineering (ME, MS), including biomaterials; biomedical engineering (PhD). Part-time programs available. *Faculty:* 10 full-time (2 women), 5 part-time/adjunct (2 women). *Students:* 51 full-time (25 women), 13 part-time (3 women); includes 12 minority (1 Black or African American, non-Hispanic/Latino; 7 Asian, non-Hispanic/Latino; 2 Hispanic/Latino; 2 Two or more races, non-Hispanic/Latino), 19 international. Average age 26. 226 applicants, 18% accepted, 11 enrolled. In 2014, 12 master's, 9 doctorates awarded. Terminal master's awarded for partial completion of doctoral program. *Degree requirements:* For master's, thesis (for some programs); for doctorate, thesis/dissertation. *Entrance requirements:* For master's and doctorate, GRE General Test. Additional exam requirements/recommendations for international students: Required—TOEFL (minimum score 550 paper-based; 80 iBT), IELTS (minimum score 6.5). *Application deadline:* For fall admission, 1/15 priority date for domestic students, 1/15 for international students; for spring admission, 9/15 for domestic and international students. Applications are processed on a rolling basis. Application fee: $75. Electronic applications accepted. *Expenses: Tuition:* Full-time $45,590; part-time $1161 per credit hour. *Required fees:* $782. Full-time tuition and fees vary according to degree level, program and student level. Part-time tuition and fees vary according to course load. *Financial support:* Fellowships with full tuition reimbursements, research assistantships with full and partial tuition reimbursements, teaching assistantships with full tuition reimbursements, Federal Work-Study, scholarships/grants, tuition waivers (partial), and unspecified assistantships available. Financial award application deadline: 1/15; financial award applicants required to submit FAFSA. *Faculty research:* Regenerative medicine with biomaterials and tissue engineering, diffuse optical imaging and spectroscopy, optics in the development of biomedical devices, ultrafast nonlinear optics and biophotonics, optical diagnostics for diseased and engineered tissues. *Unit head:* Dr. Irene Georgakoudi, Graduate Program Director. *Application contact:* Office of Graduate Admissions, 617-627-3395, E-mail: gradadmissions@tufts.edu.
Website: http://engineering.tufts.edu/bme.

Tufts University, School of Engineering, Department of Chemical and Biological Engineering, Medford, MA 02155. Offers bioengineering (ME, MS), including cell and bioprocess engineering; biotechnology engineering (PhD); chemical and biological engineering (ME, MS, PhD). Part-time programs available. *Faculty:* 10 full-time (2 women), 1 part-time/adjunct (0 women). *Students:* 35 full-time (11 women), 12 part-time (7 women); includes 6 minority (5 Asian, non-Hispanic/Latino; 1 Hispanic/Latino), 23 international. Average age 27. 152 applicants, 22% accepted, 18 enrolled. In 2014, 5 master's, 1 doctorate awarded. Terminal master's awarded for partial completion of doctoral program. *Degree requirements:* For master's, thesis (for some programs); for doctorate, thesis/dissertation. *Entrance requirements:* For master's and doctorate, GRE General Test. Additional exam requirements/recommendations for international students: Required—TOEFL (minimum score 550 paper-based; 80 iBT), IELTS (minimum score 6.5). *Application deadline:* For fall admission, 1/15 priority date for domestic students, 1/15 for international students; for spring admission, 9/15 for domestic and international students. Applications are processed on a rolling basis. Application fee: $75. Electronic applications accepted. *Expenses: Tuition:* Full-time $45,590; part-time $1161 per credit hour. *Required fees:* $782. Full-time tuition and fees vary according to degree level, program and student level. Part-time tuition and fees vary according to course load. *Financial support:* Fellowships with full tuition reimbursements, research assistantships with full and partial tuition reimbursements, teaching assistantships with full and partial tuition reimbursements, Federal Work-Study, scholarships/grants, tuition waivers (partial), and unspecified assistantships available. Financial award application deadline: 1/15; financial award applicants required to submit FAFSA. *Faculty research:* Clean energy with materials, biomaterials, colloids; metabolic engineering, biotechnology; process control; reaction kinetics, catalysis; transport phenomena. *Unit head:* Dr. Matt Panzer, Graduate Program Director. *Application contact:* Office of Graduate Admissions, 617-627-3395, E-mail: gradadmissions@tufts.edu.
Website: http://engineering.tufts.edu/chbe/.

Tufts University, School of Engineering, Department of Civil and Environmental Engineering, Medford, MA 02155. Offers bioengineering (ME, MS), including environmental technology; civil engineering (ME, MS, PhD), including geotechnical engineering, structural engineering, water diplomacy (PhD); environmental engineering (ME, MS, PhD), including environmental engineering and environmental sciences, environmental geotechnology, environmental health, environmental science and management, hazardous materials management, water diplomacy (PhD), water resources engineering. Part-time programs available. *Faculty:* 24 full-time (5 women), 6 part-time/adjunct (1 woman). *Students:* 66 full-time (29 women), 19 part-time (6 women); includes 5 minority (1 Black or African American, non-Hispanic/Latino; 2 Asian, non-Hispanic/Latino; 1 Hispanic/Latino; 1 Two or more races, non-Hispanic/Latino), 25 international. Average age 29. 166 applicants, 42% accepted, 27 enrolled. In 2014, 21 master's, 6 doctorates awarded. Terminal master's awarded for partial completion of doctoral program. *Degree requirements:* For master's, thesis or alternative; for doctorate, thesis/dissertation. *Entrance requirements:* For master's and doctorate, GRE General Test. Additional exam requirements/recommendations for international students: Required—TOEFL (minimum score 550 paper-based; 80 iBT), IELTS (minimum score 6.5). *Application deadline:* For fall admission, 1/15 priority date for domestic students, 1/15 for international students; for spring admission, 9/15 for domestic and international students. Applications are processed on a rolling basis. Application fee: $75. Electronic applications accepted. *Expenses: Tuition:* Full-time $45,590; part-time $1161 per credit hour. *Required fees:* $782. Full-time tuition and fees

vary according to degree level, program and student level. Part-time tuition and fees vary according to course load. *Financial support:* Fellowships with full tuition reimbursements, research assistantships with full and partial tuition reimbursements, teaching assistantships with full and partial tuition reimbursements, Federal Work-Study, scholarships/grants, tuition waivers (partial), and unspecified assistantships available. Financial award application deadline: 5/15; financial award applicants required to submit FAFSA. *Faculty research:* Environmental and water resources engineering, environmental health, geotechnical and geoenvironmental engineering, structural engineering and mechanics, water diplomacy. *Unit head:* Dr. Kurt Pennell, Graduate Program Director. *Application contact:* Office of Graduate Admissions, 617-627-3395, E-mail: gradadmissions@tufts.edu.
Website: http://www.ase.tufts.edu/cee/.

Tufts University, School of Engineering, Department of Computer Science, Medford, MA 02155. Offers bioengineering (ME, MS), including bioinformatics; cognitive science (PhD); computer science (MS, PhD). Part-time programs available. *Students:* 57 full-time (17 women), 19 part-time (4 women); includes 13 minority (1 Black or African American, non-Hispanic/Latino; 4 Asian, non-Hispanic/Latino; 2 Hispanic/Latino; 6 Two or more races, non-Hispanic/Latino), 25 international. Average age 29. 218 applicants, 24% accepted, 23 enrolled. In 2014, 18 master's, 4 doctorates awarded. Terminal master's awarded for partial completion of doctoral program. *Degree requirements:* For master's, thesis (for some programs); for doctorate, thesis/dissertation. *Entrance requirements:* For master's and doctorate, GRE General Test. Additional exam requirements/recommendations for international students: Required—TOEFL (minimum score 550 paper-based; 80 iBT), IELTS (minimum score 6.5). *Application deadline:* For fall admission, 1/15 for domestic and international students; for spring admission, 9/15 for domestic and international students. Applications are processed on a rolling basis. Application fee: $75. Electronic applications accepted. *Expenses: Tuition:* Full-time $45,590; part-time $1161 per credit hour. *Required fees:* $782. Full-time tuition and fees vary according to degree level, program and student level. Part-time tuition and fees vary according to course load. *Financial support:* Fellowships with full tuition reimbursements, research assistantships with full and partial tuition reimbursements, teaching assistantships with full and partial tuition reimbursements, Federal Work-Study, scholarships/grants, tuition waivers (partial), and unspecified assistantships available. Financial award application deadline: 4/15; financial award applicants required to submit FAFSA. *Faculty research:* Computational biology, computational geometry, and computational systems biology; cognitive sciences, human-computer interaction, and human-robotic interaction; visualization and graphics, educational technologies; machine learning and data mining; programming languages and systems. *Unit head:* Dr. Samuel Guyer, Graduate Program Director. *Application contact:* Office of Graduate Admissions, 617-623-3395, E-mail: gradadmissions@cs.tufts.edu.
Website: http://www.cs.tufts.edu/.

Tufts University, School of Engineering, Department of Electrical and Computer Engineering, Medford, MA 02155. Offers bioengineering (ME, MS), including signals and systems; electrical engineering (MS, PhD). Part-time programs available. *Faculty:* 17 full-time (3 women), 3 part-time/adjunct. *Students:* 64 full-time (20 women), 11 part-time (3 women); includes 7 minority (4 Asian, non-Hispanic/Latino; 1 Hispanic/Latino; 2 Two or more races, non-Hispanic/Latino), 53 international. Average age 27. 203 applicants, 33% accepted, 21 enrolled. In 2014, 16 master's, 6 doctorates awarded. Terminal master's awarded for partial completion of doctoral program. *Degree requirements:* For master's, thesis or alternative; for doctorate, thesis/dissertation. *Entrance requirements:* For master's and doctorate, GRE General Test. Additional exam requirements/recommendations for international students: Required—TOEFL (minimum score 550 paper-based; 80 iBT), IELTS (minimum score 6.5). *Application deadline:* For fall admission, 1/15 priority date for domestic students, 1/15 for international students; for spring admission, 9/15 for domestic and international students. Applications are processed on a rolling basis. Application fee: $75. Electronic applications accepted. *Expenses: Tuition:* Full-time $45,590; part-time $1161 per credit hour. *Required fees:* $782. Full-time tuition and fees vary according to degree level, program and student level. Part-time tuition and fees vary according to course load. *Financial support:* Fellowships with full tuition reimbursements, research assistantships with full and partial tuition reimbursements, teaching assistantships with full and partial tuition reimbursements, Federal Work-Study, scholarships/grants, tuition waivers (partial), and unspecified assistantships available. Financial award application deadline: 5/15; financial award applicants required to submit FAFSA. *Faculty research:* Communication theory, networks, protocol, and transmission technology; simulation and modeling; digital processing technology; image and signal processing for security and medical applications; integrated circuits and VLSI. *Unit head:* Dr. Eric Miller, Graduate Program Director. *Application contact:* Office of Graduate Admissions, 617-627-3395, E-mail: gradadmissions@tufts.edu.
Website: http://engineering.tufts.edu/ece/.

Tufts University, School of Engineering, Department of Mechanical Engineering, Medford, MA 02155. Offers bioengineering (ME, MS), including bioinformatics, biomechanical systems and devices, signals and systems; bioinformatics (MS); human factors (MS); mechanical engineering (ME, MS, PhD). Part-time programs available. *Faculty:* 15 full-time (1 woman), 7 part-time/adjunct (1 woman). *Students:* 35 full-time (12 women), 23 part-time (11 women); includes 11 minority (3 Black or African American, non-Hispanic/Latino; 1 American Indian or Alaska Native, non-Hispanic/Latino; 3 Asian, non-Hispanic/Latino; 2 Hispanic/Latino; 2 Two or more races, non-Hispanic/Latino), 14 international. Average age 27. 112 applicants, 47% accepted, 16 enrolled. In 2014, 18 master's, 6 doctorates awarded. Terminal master's awarded for partial completion of doctoral program. *Degree requirements:* For master's, thesis; for doctorate, thesis/dissertation. *Entrance requirements:* For master's and doctorate, GRE General Test. Additional exam requirements/recommendations for international students: Required—TOEFL (minimum score 550 paper-based; 80 iBT), IELTS (minimum score 6.5). *Application deadline:* For fall admission, 1/15 priority date for domestic students, 1/15 for international students; for spring admission, 9/15 for domestic and international students. Applications are processed on a rolling basis. Application fee: $75. Electronic applications accepted. *Expenses: Tuition:* Full-time $45,590; part-time $1161 per credit hour. *Required fees:* $782. Full-time tuition and fees vary according to degree level, program and student level. Part-time tuition and fees vary according to course load. *Financial support:* Fellowships with full tuition reimbursements, research assistantships with full and partial tuition reimbursements, teaching assistantships with full and partial tuition reimbursements, Federal Work-Study, scholarships/grants, tuition waivers (partial), and unspecified assistantships available. Financial award application deadline: 5/15; financial award applicants required to submit FAFSA. *Faculty research:* Applied mechanics, biomaterials, controls/robotics, design/ systems, human factors. *Unit head:* Dr. Robert C. White, Graduate Program Director. *Application contact:* Office of Graduate Admissions, 617-627-3395, E-mail: gradadmissions@tufts.edu.
Website: http://engineering.tufts.edu/me.

University at Buffalo, the State University of New York, Graduate School, School of Engineering and Applied Sciences, Department of Chemical and Biological Engineering, Buffalo, NY 14260. Offers ME, MS, PhD. Part-time programs available. *Faculty:* 17 full-time (1 woman), 5 part-time/adjunct (1 woman). *Students:* 109 full-time (32 women), 4 part-time (2 women); includes 4 minority (1 Black or African American, non-Hispanic/ Latino; 2 Asian, non-Hispanic/Latino; 1 Two or more races, non-Hispanic/Latino), 89 international. Average age 26. 411 applicants, 29% accepted, 20 enrolled. In 2014, 27 master's, 15 doctorates awarded. *Degree requirements:* For master's, thesis (for some programs); for doctorate, comprehensive exam, thesis/dissertation. *Entrance requirements:* For master's and doctorate, GRE General Test. Additional exam requirements/recommendations for international students: Required—TOEFL (minimum score 550 paper-based; 79 iBT). *Application deadline:* For fall admission, 2/1 priority date for domestic and international students; for spring admission, 10/1 priority date for domestic and international students. Applications are processed on a rolling basis. Application fee: $75. Electronic applications accepted. *Financial support:* In 2014–15, 55 students received support, including 3 fellowships with full and partial tuition reimbursements available (averaging $25,000 per year), 40 research assistantships with full and partial tuition reimbursements available (averaging $21,120 per year); teaching assistantships with full and partial tuition reimbursements available, institutionally sponsored loans, scholarships/grants, health care benefits, tuition waivers (full and partial), and unspecified assistantships also available. Support available to part-time students. Financial award application deadline: 2/28; financial award applicants required to submit FAFSA. *Faculty research:* Transport, polymers, nanomaterials, biochemical engineering, catalysis. *Total annual research expenditures:* $7.8 million. *Unit head:* Dr. Stylianos Andreadis, Chairman, 716-645-2911, Fax: 716-645-3822, E-mail: sandread@buffalo.edu. *Application contact:* Dr. Paschalis Alexandridis, Director of Graduate Studies, 716-645-1183, Fax: 716-645-3822, E-mail: cegrad@buffalo.edu.
Website: http://www.cbe.buffalo.edu/.

University of Arkansas, Graduate School, College of Engineering, Department of Biological and Agricultural Engineering, Program in Biological Engineering, Fayetteville, AR 72701-1201. Offers MSBE. *Accreditation:* ABET. Electronic applications accepted.

University of California, Berkeley, Graduate Division, Bioengineering Graduate Program Berkeley/UCSF, Berkeley, CA 94720-1762. Offers PhD. Program offered jointly with University of California, San Francisco. *Degree requirements:* For doctorate, comprehensive exam, thesis/dissertation. *Entrance requirements:* For doctorate, GRE General Test, minimum GPA of 3.0. Additional exam requirements/recommendations for international students: Required—TOEFL (minimum score 570 paper-based; 68 iBT). Electronic applications accepted. *Faculty research:* Biomaterials, biomechanics, biomedical imaging and instrumentation, computational biology, drug delivery systems and pharmacogenomics, neural systems engineering and vision science, systems and synthetic biology, tissue engineering and regenerative medicine.

University of California, Davis, College of Engineering, Program in Biological Systems Engineering, Davis, CA 95616. Offers M Engr, MS, D Engr, PhD, M Engr/MBA. Terminal master's awarded for partial completion of doctoral program. *Degree requirements:* For master's, thesis; for doctorate, thesis/dissertation. *Entrance requirements:* For master's, minimum GPA of 3.0; for doctorate, GRE, minimum graduate GPA of 3.25. Additional exam requirements/recommendations for international students: Required—TOEFL (minimum score 550 paper-based). Electronic applications accepted. *Faculty research:* Forestry, irrigation and drainage, power and machinery, structures and environment, information and energy technologies.

University of California, Los Angeles, Graduate Division, Henry Samueli School of Engineering and Applied Science, Department of Chemical and Biomolecular Engineering, Los Angeles, CA 90095-1592. Offers MS, PhD. *Faculty:* 13 full-time (2 women), 5 part-time/adjunct (0 women). *Students:* 100 full-time (29 women); includes 31 minority (1 Black or African American, non-Hispanic/Latino; 1 American Indian or Alaska Native, non-Hispanic/Latino; 23 Asian, non-Hispanic/Latino; 5 Hispanic/Latino; 1 Two or more races, non-Hispanic/Latino), 46 international. 410 applicants, 11% accepted, 23 enrolled. In 2014, 6 master's, 6 doctorates awarded. *Degree requirements:* For master's, comprehensive exam (for some programs), thesis (for some programs); for doctorate, thesis/dissertation, qualifying exams. *Entrance requirements:* For master's, GRE General Test, minimum GPA of 3.0; for doctorate, GRE General Test, minimum GPA of 3.25. Additional exam requirements/recommendations for international students: Required—TOEFL (minimum score 560 paper-based; 87 iBT), IELTS (minimum score 7). *Application deadline:* For fall admission, 1/15 for domestic and international students; for winter admission, 10/1 for domestic and international students; for spring admission, 12/31 for domestic and international students. Application fee: $80 ($100 for international students). Electronic applications accepted. *Financial support:* In 2014–15, 73 fellowships, 177 research assistantships, 62 teaching assistantships were awarded; Federal Work-Study, institutionally sponsored loans, and tuition waivers (full and partial) also available. Financial award application deadline: 1/15; financial award applicants required to submit FAFSA. *Faculty research:* Biomolecular engineering, renewable energy, water technology, advanced materials processing, process systems engineering. *Total annual research expenditures:* $11.2 million. *Unit head:* Dr. James C. Liao, Chair, 310-825-1656, E-mail: liaoj@ucla.edu. *Application contact:* John Berger, Student Affairs Officer, 310-825-9063, Fax: 310-206-4107, E-mail: jpberger@ea.ucla.edu.
Website: http://www.chemeng.ucla.edu/.

University of California, Merced, Graduate Division, School of Engineering, Merced, CA 95343. Offers biological engineering and small scale technologies (MS, PhD); electrical engineering and computer science (MS, PhD); environmental systems (MS, PhD); mechanical engineering (MS); mechanical engineering and applied mechanics (PhD). *Faculty:* 38 full-time (6 women), 1 part-time/adjunct (0 women). *Students:* 128 full-time (36 women), 2 part-time (0 women); includes 21 minority (1 Black or African American, non-Hispanic/Latino; 11 Asian, non-Hispanic/Latino; 6 Hispanic/Latino; 3 Two or more races, non-Hispanic/Latino), 72 international. Average age 28. 230 applicants, 39% accepted, 38 enrolled. In 2014, 5 master's, 18 doctorates awarded. *Degree requirements:* For master's, variable foreign language requirement, comprehensive exam, thesis (for some programs); for doctorate, variable foreign language requirement, comprehensive exam, thesis/dissertation. *Entrance requirements:* For master's and doctorate, GRE. Additional exam requirements/recommendations for international students: Required—TOEFL (minimum score 550 paper-based; 68 iBT); Recommended—IELTS. Application fee: $80 ($100 for international students). *Expenses:* Tuition, state resident: full-time $11,220; part-time $2805 per semester. *Required fees:* $1940; $970 per semester hour. *Financial support:* In 2014–15, 19 fellowships with full and partial tuition reimbursements (averaging $6,683 per year) were awarded; scholarships/grants also available. *Faculty research:* Artificial intelligence, biomedical imaging, thermal science, ecology, nanotechnology. *Unit head:* Dr. Erik Rolland, Interim Dean, 209-228-4296, Fax: 209-228-4047, E-mail: erolland@ucmerced.edu. *Application contact:* Tsu Ya, Graduate Admissions and Academic Services Manager, 209-228-4521, Fax: 209-228-6906, E-mail: tya@ucmerced.edu.

University of California, Riverside, Graduate Division, Department of Bioengineering, Riverside, CA 92521-0102. Offers MS, PhD. Part-time programs available. *Degree requirements:* For doctorate, thesis/dissertation, qualifying exams. *Entrance requirements:* Additional exam requirements/recommendations for international students: Required—TOEFL (minimum score 550 paper-based; 80 iBT). *Expenses:* Tuition, state resident: full-time $5399. Tuition, nonresident: full-time $10,433.

University of California, San Diego, Graduate Division, Department of Bioengineering, La Jolla, CA 92093. Offers M Eng, MS, PhD. *Students:* 175 full-time (57 women), 15 part-time (6 women); includes 83 minority (5 Black or African American, non-Hispanic/Latino; 2 American Indian or Alaska Native, non-Hispanic/Latino; 57 Asian, non-Hispanic/Latino; 19 Hispanic/Latino), 44 international. 691 applicants, 20% accepted, 54 enrolled. In 2014, 24 master's, 17 doctorates awarded. *Degree requirements:* For doctorate, comprehensive exam, thesis/dissertation. *Entrance requirements:* For master's, GRE General Test, minimum GPA of 3.0 (for M Eng), 3.4 (for MS); for doctorate, GRE General Test, minimum GPA of 3.4. Additional exam requirements/recommendations for international students: Required—TOEFL (minimum score 550 paper-based; 80 iBT), IELTS. *Application deadline:* For fall admission, 12/14 for domestic students. Application fee: $90 ($110 for international students). Electronic applications accepted. *Expenses:* Tuition, state resident: full-time $11,220; part-time $5610 per quarter. Tuition, nonresident: full-time $26,322; part-time $13,161 per quarter. *Required fees:* $570 per quarter. Tuition and fees vary according to program. *Financial support:* Fellowships, research assistantships, teaching assistantships, scholarships/grants, traineeships, and unspecified assistantships available. Financial award applicants required to submit FAFSA. *Faculty research:* Bioinformatics, multi-scale biology, quantitative biology. *Unit head:* Geert W. Schmid-Schoenbein, Chair, 858-534-3852, E-mail: be-chair@eng.ucsd.edu. *Application contact:* Jan Lenington, Graduate Coordinator, 858-822-1604, E-mail: jlenington@ucsd.edu.
Website: http://www.be.ucsd.edu/graduate_prospective_students_admissions_faq.

University of California, San Francisco, Graduate Division, Program in Bioengineering, Berkeley, CA 94720-1762. Offers PhD. Program offered jointly with University of California, Berkeley. *Degree requirements:* For doctorate, thesis/dissertation, qualifying exam. *Entrance requirements:* For doctorate, GRE General Test, minimum GPA of 3.0. Additional exam requirements/recommendations for international students: Required—TOEFL (minimum score 570 paper-based). Electronic applications accepted. *Faculty research:* Bioengineering, biomaterials, biomedical imaging and instrumentation, biomechanics, microfluidics, computational biology, systems biology, drug delivery systems and pharmacogenomics, neural systems engineering and vision science, synthetic biology, tissue engineering, regenerative medicine.

University of California, Santa Barbara, Graduate Division, College of Letters and Sciences, Division of Mathematics, Life, and Physical Sciences, Department of Statistics and Applied Probability, Santa Barbara, CA 93106-3110. Offers bioengineering (PhD); financial mathematics and statistics (PhD); quantitative methods in the social sciences (PhD); statistics (MA), including applied statistics, mathematical statistics; statistics and applied probability (PhD); MA/PhD. Terminal master's awarded for partial completion of doctoral program. *Degree requirements:* For master's, comprehensive exam, thesis optional; for doctorate, comprehensive exam, thesis/dissertation. *Entrance requirements:* For master's and doctorate, GRE General Test. Additional exam requirements/recommendations for international students: Required—TOEFL (minimum score 550 paper-based; 80 iBT), IELTS (minimum score 7). Electronic applications accepted. *Faculty research:* Bayesian inference, financial mathematics, stochastic processes, environmental statistics, biostatistical modeling.

University of California, Santa Barbara, Graduate Division, College of Letters and Sciences, Division of Mathematics, Life, and Physical Sciences, Interdepartmental Graduate Program in Biomolecular Science and Engineering, Santa Barbara, CA 93106-2014. Offers biochemistry and molecular biology (PhD), including biochemistry and molecular biology, biophysics and bioengineering. Terminal master's awarded for partial completion of doctoral program. *Degree requirements:* For doctorate, thesis/dissertation. *Entrance requirements:* For doctorate, GRE General Test. Additional exam requirements/recommendations for international students: Required—TOEFL (minimum score 630 paper-based; 109 iBT), IELTS (minimum score 7). Electronic applications accepted. *Faculty research:* Biochemistry and molecular biology, biophysics, biomaterials, bioengineering, systems biology.

University of Chicago, Institute for Molecular Engineering, Chicago, IL 60637. Offers PhD. *Faculty:* 11 full-time (3 women). *Students:* 36 full-time (9 women); includes 5 minority (3 Asian, non-Hispanic/Latino; 1 Hispanic/Latino; 1 Two or more races, non-Hispanic/Latino), 14 international. Average age 27. 121 applicants, 36% accepted, 21 enrolled. In 2014, 1 doctorate awarded. *Degree requirements:* For doctorate, thesis/dissertation, qualifying research presentation and teaching. *Entrance requirements:* For doctorate, GRE General Test. Additional exam requirements/recommendations for international students: Required—TOEFL (minimum score 90 iBT), IELTS (minimum score 7). *Application deadline:* For fall admission, 1/5 for domestic and international students. Application fee: $0. Electronic applications accepted. *Expenses: Tuition:* Full-time $46,899. *Required fees:* $347. *Financial support:* In 2014–15, 45 students received support, including 7 fellowships (averaging $4,000 per year), 45 research assistantships with full tuition reimbursements available (averaging $31,362 per year); career-related internships or fieldwork, scholarships/grants, traineeships, health care benefits, and unspecified assistantships also available. *Faculty research:* Bimolecular engineering, spintronics, nanotechnology, quantum computing, protein folding and aggregation, liquid crystals, theoretical and computational modeling of materials, immunology, nanolithography, directed self-assembly, cancer research. *Total annual research expenditures:* $2.9 million. *Unit head:* Dr. Sharon Feng, Senior Associate Dean. *Application contact:* Dr. Novia Pagone, Associate Dean of Students, 773-834-1437, E-mail: ime@uchicago.edu.
Website: http://ime.uchicago.edu/.

University of Colorado Denver, College of Engineering and Applied Science, Department of Bioengineering, Aurora, CO 80045-2560. Offers assistive technology and rehabilitation engineering (MS, PhD); device design and entrepreneurship (MS, PhD); research (MS, PhD); translational bioengineering (MS, PhD). Part-time programs available. *Faculty:* 18 full-time (9 women), 5 part-time/adjunct (1 woman). *Students:* 43 full-time (20 women), 15 part-time (4 women); includes 12 minority (4 Black or African American, non-Hispanic/Latino; 3 Asian, non-Hispanic/Latino; 3 Hispanic/Latino; 2 Two or more races, non-Hispanic/Latino), 4 international. Average age 27. 88 applicants, 55% accepted, 18 enrolled. In 2014, 8 master's, 2 doctorates awarded. Terminal master's awarded for partial completion of doctoral program. *Degree requirements:* For master's, thesis or alternative, 30 credit hours; for doctorate, comprehensive exam, 36 credit hours of classwork (18 core, 18 elective), additional 30 hours of thesis work, three formal examinations, approval of dissertations. *Entrance requirements:* For master's and doctorate, GRE, transcripts, three letters of recommendation, resume, statement of purpose. Additional exam requirements/recommendations for international students: Required—TOEFL (minimum score 550 paper-based; 79 iBT), TOEFL (minimum score 600 paper-based; 100 iBT) for PhD. *Application deadline:* For fall admission, 1/15 priority date for domestic students, 1/1 priority date for international students. Application fee: $50 ($75 for international students). Electronic applications accepted. *Expenses:* Expenses: Contact institution. *Financial support:* In 2014–15, 13 students received support. Fellowships, research assistantships, teaching assistantships, Federal Work-Study, institutionally sponsored loans, scholarships/grants, and traineeships available. Financial award application deadline: 4/1; financial award applicants required to submit FAFSA. *Faculty research:* Imaging and biophotonics, cardiovascular biomechanics and hemodynamics, orthopedic biomechanics, ophthalmology, neuroscience engineering, diabetes, surgery and urological sciences. *Unit head:* Dr. Robin Shandas, Chair, 303-724-4196, E-mail: robin.shandas@ucdenver.edu. *Application contact:* Shawna McMahon, Graduate School Admissions, 303-724-5893, E-mail: shawna.mcmahon@ucdenver.edu.
Website: http://www.ucdenver.edu/academics/colleges/Engineering/Programs/bioengineering/Pages/Bioengineering.aspx.

University of Dayton, Department of Chemical Engineering, Dayton, OH 45469. Offers bioengineering (MS); chemical engineering (MS Ch E). Part-time and evening/weekend programs available. *Faculty:* 9 full-time (2 women), 5 part-time/adjunct (1 woman). *Students:* 42 full-time (13 women), 6 part-time (2 women); includes 1 minority (Black or African American, non-Hispanic/Latino), 36 international. Average age 26. 91 applicants, 54% accepted, 16 enrolled. In 2014, 42 master's awarded. *Degree requirements:* For master's, comprehensive exam (for some programs), thesis optional. *Entrance requirements:* For master's, GRE (for bioengineering). Additional exam requirements/recommendations for international students: Required—TOEFL (minimum score 550 paper-based; 80 iBT). *Application deadline:* For fall admission, 8/1 for domestic students, 5/1 for international students; for spring admission, 11/1 for international students. Applications are processed on a rolling basis. Application fee: $0 ($50 for international students). Electronic applications accepted. *Expenses: Tuition:* Full-time $10,176; part-time $848 per credit. *Required fees:* $25; $25 per course. Part-time tuition and fees vary according to course level, course load, degree level and program. *Financial support:* In 2014–15, 4 research assistantships with full tuition reimbursements (averaging $12,329 per year) were awarded; institutionally sponsored loans, health care benefits, and unspecified assistantships also available. Financial award application deadline: 3/1; financial award applicants required to submit FAFSA. *Faculty research:* Vertically-aligned carbon nanotubes infiltrated with temperature-responsive polymers: smart nanocomposite films for self-cleaning and controlled release, bilayer and bulk heterojunction solar cells using liquid crystalline porphyrins as donors by solution processing, DNA damage induced by multiwalled carbon nanotubes in mouse embryonic stem cells. *Unit head:* Dr. Charles Browning, Chair, 937-229-2627, E-mail: cbrowning1@udayton.edu. *Application contact:* Dr. Kevin Myers, Graduate Program Director, 937-229-2627, E-mail: kmyers1@udayton.edu.
Website: https://www.udayton.edu/engineering/departments/chemical_and_materials/index.php.

University of Denver, Daniel Felix Ritchie School of Engineering and Computer Science, Department of Mechanical and Materials Engineering, Denver, CO 80208. Offers bioengineering (MS); engineering (MS, PhD); engineering/management (MS); materials science (MS, PhD); mechanical engineering (MS, PhD); nanoscale science and engineering (MS, PhD). Part-time programs available. *Faculty:* 10 full-time (1 woman), 1 (woman) part-time/adjunct. *Students:* 4 full-time (2 women), 44 part-time (12 women); includes 6 minority (1 Black or African American, non-Hispanic/Latino; 3 Asian, non-Hispanic/Latino; 1 Hispanic/Latino; 1 Two or more races, non-Hispanic/Latino), 20 international. Average age 29. 67 applicants, 88% accepted, 16 enrolled. In 2014, 7 master's, 1 doctorate awarded. Terminal master's awarded for partial completion of doctoral program. *Degree requirements:* For master's, thesis optional; for doctorate, comprehensive exam, thesis/dissertation. *Entrance requirements:* For master's, GRE General Test, bachelor's degree, transcripts, personal statement, resume or curriculum vitae, two letters of recommendation; for doctorate, GRE General Test, master's degree, transcripts, personal statement, resume or curriculum vitae, two letters of recommendation. Additional exam requirements/recommendations for international students: Required—TOEFL (minimum score 550 paper-based; 80 iBT). *Application deadline:* For fall admission, 2/1 priority date for domestic and international students. Applications are processed on a rolling basis. Application fee: $65. Electronic applications accepted. *Expenses:* Expenses: $1,199 per credit hour. *Financial support:* In 2014–15, 24 students received support, including 17 research assistantships with full and partial tuition reimbursements available (averaging $12,842 per year), 17 teaching assistantships with full and partial tuition reimbursements available (averaging $9,975 per year); Federal Work-Study, institutionally sponsored loans, scholarships/grants, health care benefits, and unspecified assistantships also available. Financial award application deadline: 2/15; financial award applicants required to submit FAFSA. *Faculty research:* Aerosols, biomechanics, composite materials, photo optics, drug delivery. *Unit head:* Dr. Matt Gordon, Chair, 303-871-3580, Fax: 303-871-4450, E-mail: matthew.gordon@du.edu. *Application contact:* Yvonne Petitt, Assistant to the Chair, 303-871-2107, Fax: 303-871-4450, E-mail: yvonne.petitt@du.edu.
Website: http://www.du.edu/rsecs/departments/mme/index.html.

University of Florida, Graduate School, College of Engineering and College of Agricultural and Life Sciences, Department of Agricultural and Biological Engineering, Gainesville, FL 32611. Offers agricultural and biological engineering (ME, MS, PhD); biological systems modeling (Certificate). Part-time programs available. *Faculty:* 29 full-time (5 women), 3 part-time/adjunct (1 woman). *Students:* 65 full-time (36 women), 15 part-time (7 women); includes 15 minority (3 Black or African American, non-Hispanic/Latino; 1 American Indian or Alaska Native, non-Hispanic/Latino; 6 Asian, non-Hispanic/Latino; 5 Hispanic/Latino), 45 international. 38 applicants, 45% accepted, 9 enrolled. In 2014, 15 master's, 15 doctorates awarded. Terminal master's awarded for partial completion of doctoral program. *Degree requirements:* For master's, comprehensive exam, thesis (for some programs); for doctorate, comprehensive exam, thesis/dissertation. *Entrance requirements:* For master's and doctorate, minimum GPA of 3.0, 3 letters of recommendation, statement of purpose. Additional exam requirements/recommendations for international students: Required—TOEFL (minimum score 550 paper-based; 80 iBT), IELTS (minimum score 6). *Application deadline:* For fall admission, 12/15 for domestic and international students; for spring admission, 7/15 for domestic and international students. Applications are processed on a rolling basis. Application fee: $30. Electronic applications accepted. *Financial support:* Unspecified assistantships available. Financial award application deadline: 2/15; financial award applicants required to submit FAFSA. *Faculty research:* Bioenergy and bioprocessing; hydrological, biological and agricultural modeling; biosensors; precision agriculture and robotics; food packaging and food security. *Total annual research expenditures:* $5.1 million. *Unit head:* Dorota Z. Haman, PhD, Professor and Chair, 352-392-1864 Ext. 120, Fax: 352-392-4092, E-mail: dhaman@ufl.edu. *Application contact:* Ray A. Bucklin, PhD, Graduate Coordinator, 352-392-1864 Ext. 169, Fax: 352-392-4092, E-mail: bucklin@ufl.edu.
Website: http://www.abe.ufl.edu/.

University of Georgia, College of Agricultural and Environmental Sciences, Department of Biological and Agricultural Engineering, Athens, GA 30602. Offers agricultural engineering (MS); biological and agricultural engineering (PhD); biological engineering (MS). *Degree requirements:* For master's, thesis; for doctorate, one foreign language, thesis/dissertation. *Entrance requirements:* For master's and doctorate, GRE General Test. Electronic applications accepted.

University of Guelph, Graduate Studies, College of Physical and Engineering Science, School of Engineering, Guelph, ON N1G 2W1, Canada. Offers biological engineering (M Eng, M Sc, MA Sc, PhD); engineering systems and computing (M Eng, M Sc, MA Sc, PhD); environmental engineering (M Eng, M Sc, MA Sc, PhD); water resources engineering (M Eng, M Sc, MA Sc, PhD). Part-time programs available. *Degree requirements:* For master's, thesis (for some programs); for doctorate, comprehensive exam, thesis/dissertation. *Entrance requirements:* For master's, minimum B- average during previous 2 years of course work; for doctorate, minimum B average. Additional exam requirements/recommendations for international students: Required—TOEFL (minimum score 550 paper-based; 89 iBT), IELTS (minimum score 6.5). Electronic applications accepted. *Faculty research:* Water and food safety, environmental contaminant fates and mechanisms, computer systems, robotics and mechatronics, waste treatment.

University of Hawaii at Manoa, Graduate Division, College of Tropical Agriculture and Human Resources, Department of Molecular Biosciences and Bioengineering, Program in Bioengineering, Honolulu, HI 96822. Offers MS. Part-time programs available. *Degree requirements:* For master's, thesis optional. *Entrance requirements:* For master's, GRE General Test. Additional exam requirements/recommendations for international students: Required—TOEFL (minimum score 500 paper-based; 61 iBT), IELTS (minimum score 5).

University of Idaho, College of Graduate Studies, College of Engineering, Department of Biological and Agricultural Engineering, Moscow, ID 83844-0904. Offers M Engr, MS, PhD. Program offered jointly with College of Agricultural and Life Sciences. *Faculty:* 8 full-time. *Students:* 3 full-time, 8 part-time. Average age 36. In 2014, 3 master's awarded. *Degree requirements:* For master's, thesis or alternative; for doctorate, one foreign language, thesis/dissertation. *Entrance requirements:* For master's, minimum GPA of 2.8; for doctorate, minimum undergraduate GPA of 2.8, 3.0 graduate. *Application deadline:* For fall admission, 8/1 for domestic students; for spring admission, 12/15 for domestic students. Applications are processed on a rolling basis. Application fee: $60. Electronic applications accepted. *Expenses:* Tuition, state resident: full-time $4784; part-time $280.50 per credit hour. Tuition, nonresident: full-time $18,314; part-time $957.50 per credit hour. *Required fees:* $2000; $58.50 per credit hour. Tuition and fees vary according to program. *Financial support:* Research assistantships, teaching assistantships, and career-related internships or fieldwork available. Financial award applicants required to submit FAFSA. *Faculty research:* Water and environmental research, alternative fuels/biodiesel, agricultural safety health, biological processes for agricultural/food waste. *Unit head:* Dr. Jon Van Gerpen, Interim Department Head, 208-885-6182, E-mail: baengr@uidaho.edu. *Application contact:* Sean Scoggin, Graduate Recruitment Coordinator, 208-885-4001, Fax: 208-885-4406, E-mail: graduateadmissions@uidaho.edu.
Website: http://www.uidaho.edu/cals/bae/.

University of Illinois at Chicago, Graduate College, College of Engineering, Department of Bioengineering, Chicago, IL 60607-7128. Offers MS, PhD. *Faculty:* 21 full-time (5 women), 10 part-time/adjunct (4 women). *Students:* 125 full-time (52 women), 16 part-time (6 women); includes 42 minority (2 Black or African American, non-Hispanic/Latino; 1 American Indian or Alaska Native, non-Hispanic/Latino; 28 Asian, non-Hispanic/Latino; 9 Hispanic/Latino; 2 Two or more races, non-Hispanic/Latino), 67 international. Average age 27. 225 applicants, 36% accepted, 28 enrolled. In 2014, 14 master's, 10 doctorates awarded. Terminal master's awarded for partial completion of doctoral program. *Degree requirements:* For master's, thesis; for doctorate, thesis/dissertation. *Entrance requirements:* For master's and doctorate, GRE Subject Test, minimum GPA of 3.0. Additional exam requirements/recommendations for international students: Required—TOEFL. *Application deadline:* For fall admission, 3/15 for domestic students, 1/1 for international students; for spring admission, 10/1 for domestic students. Applications are processed on a rolling basis. Application fee: $60. Electronic applications accepted. *Expenses:* Expenses: $17,602 in-state; $29,600 out-of-state. *Financial support:* In 2014–15, 3 fellowships with full tuition reimbursements were awarded; research assistantships with full tuition reimbursements, teaching assistantships with full tuition reimbursements, career-related internships or fieldwork, Federal Work-Study, scholarships/grants, traineeships, tuition waivers (full), and unspecified assistantships also available. Financial award application deadline: 3/1; financial award applicants required to submit FAFSA. *Faculty research:* Imaging systems, bioinstrumentation, electrophysiology, biological control, laser scattering. *Total annual research expenditures:* $3.6 million. *Unit head:* Dr. Thomas J. Royston, Head, 312-996-2335, E-mail: troyston@uic.edu. *Application contact:* Receptionist, 312-413-2550, E-mail: gradcoll@uic.edu.
Website: http://www.bioe.uic.edu/BIOE/WebHome.

University of Illinois at Urbana–Champaign, Graduate College, College of Agricultural, Consumer and Environmental Sciences, Department of Agricultural and Biological Engineering, Champaign, IL 61820. Offers agricultural and biological engineering (MS, PhD); technical systems management (MS, PSM). *Students:* 75 full-time (23 women). Application fee: $70 ($90 for international students). *Unit head:* Kuan Chong Ting, Head, 217-333-3570, Fax: 217-244-0323, E-mail: kcting@illinois.edu. *Application contact:* Jana R. Lenz, Office Administrator, 217-324-1654, Fax: 217-244-0323, E-mail: janalenz@illinois.edu.
Website: http://abe.illinois.edu.

University of Illinois at Urbana–Champaign, Graduate College, College of Engineering, Department of Bioengineering, Champaign, IL 61820. Offers MS, PhD. *Students:* 78 (38 women). Application fee: $70 ($90 for international students). *Unit head:* Rashid Bashir, Interim Head, 217-333-1867, Fax: 217-265-0246, E-mail: rbashir@illinois.edu. *Application contact:* Krista Smith, Academic Programs Specialist, 217-300-4474, Fax: 217-265-0246, E-mail: kristasm@illinois.edu.
Website: http://bioengineering.illinois.edu/.

University of Illinois at Urbana–Champaign, Graduate College, College of Liberal Arts and Sciences, School of Chemical Sciences, Department of Chemical and Biomolecular Engineering, Champaign, IL 61820. Offers bioinformatics: chemical and biomolecular engineering (MS); chemical engineering (MS, PhD). *Students:* 84 (29 women). *Entrance requirements:* For master's, minimum GPA of 3.0. Application fee: $70 ($90 for international students). *Unit head:* Paul Kenis, Head, 217-244-9214, Fax: 217-333-5052, E-mail: kenis@illinois.edu. *Application contact:* Christine M. Bowser, Office Manager, 217-244-9214, Fax: 217-333-5052, E-mail: cbowser@illinois.edu.
Website: http://chbe.illinois.edu/.

The University of Kansas, Graduate Studies, School of Engineering, Program in Bioengineering, Lawrence, KS 66045. Offers MS, PhD. *Students:* 51 full-time (27 women), 2 part-time (1 woman); includes 5 minority (1 American Indian or Alaska Native, non-Hispanic/Latino; 2 Asian, non-Hispanic/Latino; 2 Two or more races, non-Hispanic/Latino), 11 international. Average age 26. 33 applicants, 61% accepted, 13 enrolled. In 2014, 4 master's, 7 doctorates awarded. Terminal master's awarded for partial completion of doctoral program. *Degree requirements:* For master's, thesis; for doctorate, comprehensive exam, thesis/dissertation. *Entrance requirements:* For master's and doctorate, GRE. Additional exam requirements/recommendations for international students: Required—TOEFL. *Application deadline:* For fall admission, 12/13 priority date for domestic and international students; for spring admission, 10/25 priority date for domestic students, 9/27 priority date for international students. Application fee: $55 ($65 for international students). Electronic applications accepted. *Financial support:* Fellowships, research assistantships with full and partial tuition reimbursements, and teaching assistantships available. Financial award application deadline: 12/15. *Faculty research:* Biomaterials and tissue engineering, biomechanics and neural engineering, biomedical product design and development, biomolecular engineering, bioimaging and bioinformatics. *Unit head:* Dr. Stevin Gehrke, Graduate Studies Director, E-mail: shgehrke@ku.edu. *Application contact:* Denise Bridwell, Program Assistant, 785-864-5258, E-mail: dbridwell@ku.edu.
Website: http://bio.engr.ku.edu/.

University of Louisville, J. B. Speed School of Engineering, Department of Bioengineering, Louisville, KY 40292-0001. Offers M Eng. Part-time programs available. Postbaccalaureate distance learning degree programs offered (no on-campus study). *Students:* 13 full-time (3 women), 7 part-time (3 women); includes 5 minority (2 Asian, non-Hispanic/Latino; 1 Hispanic/Latino; 2 Two or more races, non-Hispanic/Latino). Average age 23. 1 applicant, 1 enrolled. In 2014, 9 master's awarded. *Degree requirements:* For master's, thesis optional, minimum GPA of 3.0. *Entrance requirements:* For master's, GRE, letters of recommendation, final official transcripts. Additional exam requirements/recommendations for international students: Required—PTE (minimum score 550), TOEFL (minimum score 80 iBT) or IELTS. *Application deadline:* For fall admission, 6/15 for domestic students, 5/1 priority date for international students; for spring admission, 11/22 for domestic students, 11/1 priority date for international students; for summer admission, 3/31 for domestic students, 4/1 priority date for international students. Electronic applications accepted. *Expenses:* Tuition, state resident: full-time $11,326; part-time $630 per credit hour. Tuition, nonresident: full-time $23,568; part-time $1311 per credit hour. *Required fees:* $196. Tuition and fees vary according to program and reciprocity agreements. *Financial support:* Fellowships with full tuition reimbursements, research assistantships with full tuition reimbursements, and teaching assistantships with full tuition reimbursements available. Financial award application deadline: 2/3. *Unit head:* Dr. Robert S. Keynton, Chair, 502-852-6356, Fax: 502-852-6806. *Application contact:* Dr. Michael Harris, Director of Academic Programs, J. B. Speed School of Engineering, 502-852-6278, Fax: 502-852-7294, E-mail: mharris@louisville.edu.
Website: https://louisville.edu/speed/bioengineering/.

University of Maryland, College Park, Academic Affairs, A. James Clark School of Engineering, Department of Chemical and Biomolecular Engineering, College Park, MD 20742. Offers bioengineering (MS, PhD); chemical engineering (M Eng, MS, PhD). Part-time and evening/weekend programs available. *Degree requirements:* For master's, thesis optional; for doctorate, variable foreign language requirement, thesis/dissertation, exam, oral presentation. *Entrance requirements:* For master's and doctorate, GRE General Test, 3 letters of recommendation. Additional exam requirements/recommendations for international students: Required—TOEFL. Electronic applications accepted. *Faculty research:* Applied polymer science, biochemical engineering, thermal properties, bioprocess monitoring.

University of Maryland, College Park, Academic Affairs, A. James Clark School of Engineering, Fischell Department of Bioengineering, College Park, MD 20742. Offers MS, PhD. *Degree requirements:* For master's, thesis optional; for doctorate, thesis/dissertation. *Entrance requirements:* For master's, GRE General Test, minimum GPA of 3.0, 3 letters of recommendation. Electronic applications accepted. *Faculty research:* Bioengineering, bioenvironmental and water resources engineering, natural resources management.

University of Missouri, Office of Research and Graduate Studies, College of Engineering, Department of Biological Engineering, Columbia, MO 65211. Offers agricultural engineering (MS); biological engineering (MS, PhD). *Faculty:* 20 full-time (2 women). *Students:* 24 full-time (14 women), 30 part-time (7 women); includes 3 minority (1 Black or African American, non-Hispanic/Latino; 1 Hispanic/Latino; 1 Two or more races, non-Hispanic/Latino), 35 international. Average age 28. 32 applicants, 50% accepted, 13 enrolled. In 2014, 7 master's, 3 doctorates awarded. *Degree requirements:* For master's, thesis; for doctorate, thesis/dissertation. *Entrance requirements:* For master's and doctorate, GRE General Test, minimum GPA of 3.0. Additional exam requirements/recommendations for international students: Required—TOEFL (minimum score 550 paper-based; 80 iBT). *Application deadline:* For fall admission, 4/1 for domestic students. Applications are processed on a rolling basis. Application fee: $55 ($75 for international students). Electronic applications accepted. *Financial support:* Fellowships, research assistantships, teaching assistantships, institutionally sponsored loans, scholarships/grants, traineeships, health care benefits, and unspecified assistantships available. Support available to part-time students. *Faculty research:* Biomedical engineering: biophotonics and biosensing, membrane transport and signaling; bioprocess engineering: biomass-based products and food engineering; bioenvironmental engineering: water quality, precision agriculture, cropping systems. *Unit head:* Dr. Jinglu Tan, Division Director, 573-882-2369, E-mail: tanj@missouri.edu. *Application contact:* Jean Gruenewald, Advising and Scholarship Coordinator, 573-882-1114 Ext. 311, E-mail: gruenewaldj@missouri.edu.
Website: http://bioengineering.missouri.edu/graduate/.

University of Nebraska–Lincoln, Graduate College, College of Engineering, Department of Biological Systems Engineering, Interdepartmental Area of Agricultural and Biological Systems Engineering, Lincoln, NE 68588. Offers MS, PhD. *Degree requirements:* For master's, thesis optional. *Entrance requirements:* Additional exam requirements/recommendations for international students: Required—TOEFL (minimum score 550 paper-based). Electronic applications accepted. *Faculty research:* Hydrological engineering, tractive performance, biomedical engineering, irrigation systems.

University of Nebraska–Lincoln, Graduate College, College of Engineering, Department of Chemical and Biomolecular Engineering, Lincoln, NE 68588. Offers MS, PhD. *Degree requirements:* For master's, thesis; for doctorate, comprehensive exam, thesis/dissertation. *Entrance requirements:* For master's and doctorate, GRE. Additional exam requirements/recommendations for international students: Required—TOEFL (minimum score 550 paper-based). Electronic applications accepted. *Faculty research:* Fermentation, radioactive waste remediation, chemical fuels from renewable feedstocks.

University of Notre Dame, Graduate School, College of Engineering, Department of Civil Engineering and Geological Sciences, Notre Dame, IN 46556. Offers bioengineering (MS Bio E); civil engineering (MSCE); civil engineering and geological sciences (PhD); environmental engineering (MS Env E); geological sciences (MS). Terminal master's awarded for partial completion of doctoral program. *Degree requirements:* For master's, comprehensive exam; for doctorate, thesis/dissertation, candidacy exam. *Entrance requirements:* For master's and doctorate, GRE General Test. Additional exam requirements/recommendations for international students: Required—TOEFL (minimum score 600 paper-based; 80 iBT). Electronic applications accepted. *Faculty research:* Environmental modeling, biological-waste treatment, petrology, environmental geology, geochemistry.

University of Oklahoma, Gallogly College of Engineering, Center for Bioengineering, Norman, OK 73019. Offers MS, PhD. *Students:* 11 full-time (3 women), 3 part-time (0 women); includes 1 minority (Black or African American, non-Hispanic/Latino), 6 international. Average age 29. 16 applicants, 25% accepted, 4 enrolled. In 2014, 4 master's, 3 doctorates awarded. Terminal master's awarded for partial completion of doctoral program. *Degree requirements:* For master's, thesis; for doctorate, comprehensive exam, thesis/dissertation. *Entrance requirements:* For master's and doctorate, GRE (recommended), minimum GPA of 3.0. Additional exam requirements/recommendations for international students: Required—TOEFL (minimum score 550 paper-based; 100 iBT). *Application deadline:* For fall admission, 4/1 for domestic students, 3/1 for international students; for spring admission, 11/1 for domestic students, 9/1 for international students. Application fee: $50 ($100 for international students). Electronic applications accepted. *Expenses:* Tuition, state resident: full-time $4394; part-time $183.10 per credit hour. Tuition, nonresident: full-time $16,970; part-time $707.10 per credit hour. *Required fees:* $2892; $109.95 per credit hour. $126.50 per semester. *Financial support:* In 2014–15, 12 students received support, including 1 fellowship with full tuition reimbursement available (averaging $2,500 per year); scholarships/grants, health care benefits, tuition waivers (partial), and unspecified assistantships also available. Financial award application deadline: 6/1; financial award applicants required to submit FAFSA. *Faculty research:* Nanomedicine, neuroengineering, medical imaging, biomechanics/biotransport, molecular, cellular and tissue. *Unit head:* Dr. Roger Harrison, Interim Director, 405-325-4367, E-mail: rharrison@ou.edu. *Application contact:* PJ Meek, Assistant to the Director, 405-325-5453, E-mail: ojmeek@ou.edu.
Website: http://ou.edu/coe/biomedeng.

University of Ottawa, Faculty of Graduate and Postdoctoral Studies, Faculty of Engineering, Department of Chemical and Biological Engineering, Ottawa, ON K1N 6N5, Canada. Offers M Eng, MA Sc, PhD. *Degree requirements:* For master's, thesis or alternative; for doctorate, comprehensive exam, thesis/dissertation. *Entrance requirements:* For master's, honors degree or equivalent, minimum B average; for doctorate, master's degree, minimum B+ average. Electronic applications accepted. *Faculty research:* Material development, process engineering, clean technologies.

University of Pennsylvania, School of Engineering and Applied Science, Department of Bioengineering, Philadelphia, PA 19104. Offers MSE, PhD, MD/PhD, VMD/PhD. *Faculty:* 36 full-time (6 women), 15 part-time/adjunct (0 women). *Students:* 136 full-time (54 women), 18 part-time (10 women); includes 51 minority (2 Black or African American, non-Hispanic/Latino; 37 Asian, non-Hispanic/Latino; 9 Hispanic/Latino; 3 Two or more races, non-Hispanic/Latino), 32 international. 551 applicants, 17% accepted, 48 enrolled. In 2014, 56 master's, 23 doctorates awarded. Terminal master's awarded for partial completion of doctoral program. *Degree requirements:* For master's, thesis optional; for doctorate, thesis/dissertation. *Entrance requirements:* For master's and doctorate, GRE General Test. Additional exam requirements/recommendations for international students: Required—TOEFL. *Application deadline:* For fall admission, 6/1 priority date for domestic students, 5/1 priority date for international students. Applications are processed on a rolling basis. Application fee: $70. Electronic applications accepted. *Financial support:* Fellowships, research assistantships, teaching assistantships, institutionally sponsored loans, scholarships/grants, traineeships, health care benefits, and unspecified assistantships available. *Faculty research:* Biomaterials and biomechanics, biofluid mechanics and transport, bioelectric phenomena, computational neuroscience. *Unit head:* Eduardo D. Glandt, Dean, 215-898-7244, E-mail: seasdean@seas.upenn.edu. *Application contact:* School of Engineering and Applied Science Graduate Admissions, 215-898-4542, E-mail: gradstudies@seas.upenn.edu.
Website: http://www.be.seas.upenn.edu.

University of Pittsburgh, Dietrich School of Arts and Sciences, Program in Computational Modeling and Simulation, Pittsburgh, PA 15260. Offers bioengineering (PhD); biological science (PhD); civil and environmental engineering (PhD); computer science (PhD); economics (PhD); industrial engineering (PhD); mathematics (PhD); mechanical engineering and materials science (PhD); physics and astronomy (PhD); psychology (PhD); statistics (PhD). Part-time programs available. *Faculty:* 4 full-time (0 women). *Students:* 5 full-time (2 women), 1 part-time (0 women), 5 international. Average age 22. 14 applicants, 14% accepted, 2 enrolled. *Degree requirements:* For doctorate, comprehensive exam, thesis/dissertation, preliminary exam. *Entrance requirements:* For doctorate, GRE, statement of purpose, transcripts for all college-level institutions attended, three letters of reference. Additional exam requirements/recommendations for international students: Required—TOEFL (minimum score 90 iBT), IELTS (minimum score 7). *Application deadline:* For fall admission, 2/21 for domestic and international students. Applications are processed on a rolling basis. Application fee: $0 ($50 for international students). Electronic applications accepted. *Expenses:* Tuition, state resident: full-time $20,742; part-time $838 per credit. Tuition, nonresident: full-time $33,960; part-time $1389 per credit. *Required fees:* $800; $205 per term. Tuition and fees vary according to program. *Financial support:* In 2014–15, 5 students received support, including 3 fellowships with tuition reimbursements available (averaging $25,500 per year), 2 research assistantships with tuition reimbursements available (averaging $26,000 per year). *Unit head:* Kathleen Blee, Associate Dean, Graduate Studies and Research, 412-624-3939, Fax: 412-624-6855. *Application contact:* Dave R. Carmen, Administrative Secretary, 412-624-6094, Fax: 412-624-6855, E-mail: drc41@pitt.edu.
Website: http://cmsp.pitt.edu/.

University of Pittsburgh, Swanson School of Engineering, Department of Bioengineering, Pittsburgh, PA 15260. Offers MSBENG, PhD, MD/PhD. Part-time programs available. *Faculty:* 22 full-time (3 women), 58 part-time/adjunct (14 women). *Students:* 167 full-time (62 women), 11 part-time (2 women); includes 43 minority (8 Black or African American, non-Hispanic/Latino; 23 Asian, non-Hispanic/Latino; 5 Hispanic/Latino; 7 Two or more races, non-Hispanic/Latino), 46 international. 316 applicants, 24% accepted, 48 enrolled. In 2014, 9 master's, 19 doctorates awarded. Terminal master's awarded for partial completion of doctoral program. *Degree requirements:* For master's, thesis; for doctorate, comprehensive exam, thesis/dissertation, final oral exams. *Entrance requirements:* For master's and doctorate, GRE General Test, minimum GPA of 3.0. Additional exam requirements/recommendations for international students: Required—TOEFL (minimum score 550 paper-based; 80 iBT). *Application deadline:* For fall admission, 3/1 priority date for domestic and international students; for spring admission, 7/1 priority date for domestic and international students. Applications are processed on a rolling basis. Application fee: $50. Electronic applications accepted. *Expenses:* Tuition, state resident: full-time $20,742; part-time $838 per credit. Tuition, nonresident: full-time $33,960; part-time $1389 per credit. *Required fees:* $800; $205 per term. Tuition and fees vary according to program. *Financial support:* In 2014–15, 100 students received support, including 31 fellowships with full tuition reimbursements available (averaging $29,376 per year), 53 research assistantships with full tuition reimbursements available (averaging $27,000 per year), 16 teaching assistantships with full tuition reimbursements available (averaging $27,000 per year); scholarships/grants and traineeships also available. Financial award application deadline: 4/15. *Faculty research:* Artificial organs, biomechanics, biomaterials, signal processing, biotechnology. *Total annual research expenditures:* $56.2 million. *Unit head:* Sanjeev G. Shroff, Chairman, 412-383-9713, Fax: 412-383-8788, E-mail: sshroff@pitt.edu. *Application contact:* 412-624-9800, Fax: 412-624-9808, E-mail: ssoeadm@pitt.edu.
Website: http://www.engineering.pitt.edu/Bioengineering/.

University of Saskatchewan, College of Graduate Studies and Research, College of Engineering, Biological Engineering Program, Saskatoon, SK S7N 5A9, Canada. Offers M Eng, M Sc, PhD. Part-time programs available. *Degree requirements:* For master's, thesis (for some programs), 30 credits (for M Eng); thesis and 12 credits (for MS); for doctorate, comprehensive exam, thesis/dissertation, qualifying exam, 18 credits. *Entrance requirements:* For master's and doctorate, GRE. Additional exam requirements/recommendations for international students: Required—TOEFL, TOEFL (minimum iBT score of 80), IELTS (6.5), CanTEST (4.5), or PTE (59). Electronic applications accepted. *Faculty research:* Agricultural machinery systems, animal welfare, biomechanical engineering, feed processing, food and bioprocess engineering, irrigation, livestock odor control, post-harvest technologies, soil and water conservation.

The University of Texas at Arlington, Graduate School, College of Engineering, Bioengineering Department, Arlington, TX 76019. Offers MS, PhD. Programs offered jointly with The University of Texas Southwestern Medical Center at Dallas. Part-time programs available. Terminal master's awarded for partial completion of doctoral program. *Degree requirements:* For master's, comprehensive exam (for some programs), thesis (for some programs); for doctorate, comprehensive exam, thesis/dissertation, qualifying exam. *Entrance requirements:* For master's, GRE General Test (minimum total of 1100 with minimum verbal score of 400), minimum GPA of 3.0 in last 60 hours of course work, 3 letters of recommendation; for doctorate, GRE General Test (minimum total of 1175 with minimum verbal score of 400), minimum GPA of 3.4 in last 60 hours of course work, 3 letters of recommendation. Additional exam requirements/recommendations for international students: Required—TOEFL. *Faculty research:* Instrumentation, mechanics, materials.

The University of Toledo, College of Graduate Studies, College of Engineering, Department of Bioengineering, Toledo, OH 43606-3390. Offers MS, PhD. Terminal master's awarded for partial completion of doctoral program. *Degree requirements:* For master's, thesis optional; for doctorate, thesis/dissertation, qualifying exam. *Entrance requirements:* For master's, GRE General Test, minimum GPA of 3.0; for doctorate, GRE General Test, minimum GPA of 3.3. Additional exam requirements/recommendations for international students: Required—TOEFL (minimum score 550 paper-based; 80 iBT). Electronic applications accepted. *Faculty research:* Artificial organs, biochemical engineering, bioelectrical systems, biomechanics, cellular engineering.

★ **University of Utah,** Graduate School, College of Engineering, Department of Bioengineering, Salt Lake City, UT 84112-9202. Offers MS, PhD, MS/MBA. *Faculty:* 25 full-time (3 women), 12 part-time/adjunct (2 women). *Students:* 109 full-time (19 women), 25 part-time (4 women); includes 21 minority (19 Asian, non-Hispanic/Latino; 2 Hispanic/Latino), 6 international. Average age 28. 281 applicants, 15% accepted, 30 enrolled. In 2014, 16 master's, 11 doctorates awarded. Terminal master's awarded for partial completion of doctoral program. *Degree requirements:* For master's, comprehensive exam, thesis, written project, oral presentation; for doctorate, thesis/dissertation. *Entrance requirements:* For master's and doctorate, GRE General Test, minimum GPA of 3.0. Additional exam requirements/recommendations for international students: Required—TOEFL (minimum score 500 paper-based; 80 iBT). *Application deadline:* For fall admission, 4/1 for domestic and international students. Application fee: $0 ($15 for international students). Electronic applications accepted. *Expenses:* Expenses: Contact institution. *Financial support:* In 2014–15, 10 fellowships with full tuition reimbursements (averaging $25,000 per year), 95 research assistantships with full tuition reimbursements (averaging $24,000 per year), 4 teaching assistantships with full tuition reimbursements (averaging $24,000 per year) were awarded; traineeships, health care benefits, tuition waivers (full), and unspecified assistantships also available. Financial award application deadline: 3/2; financial award applicants required to submit FAFSA. *Faculty research:* Ultrasonic bioinstrumentation, medical imaging, neuroprosthesis, biomaterials and tissue engineering, biomechanical biomedical computing/modeling, cardiac electrophysiology and biophysics and bioinnovation. *Total annual research expenditures:* $16.4 million. *Unit head:* Dr. Patrick A. Tresco, Chair, 801-587-9263, Fax: 801-585-5361, E-mail: patrick.tresco@utah.edu. *Application contact:* Karen Lynn Terry, Graduate Program Advisor and Coordinator, 801-581-8559, Fax: 801-585-5361, E-mail: karen.terry@utah.edu.
Website: http://www.bioen.utah.edu/.

See Display on next page and Close-Up on page 119.

University of Washington, Graduate School, College of Engineering and School of Medicine, Department of Bioengineering, Seattle, WA 98195-5061. Offers bioengineering (MS, PhD); bioengineering and nanotechnology (PhD); pharmaceutical bioengineering (MS). Evening/weekend programs available. *Faculty:* 23 full-time (7 women). *Students:* 130 full-time (46 women), 23 part-time (14 women). Average age 26. 536 applicants, 12% accepted, 28 enrolled. In 2014, 29 master's, 16 doctorates awarded. *Degree requirements:* For master's, comprehensive exam, thesis; for doctorate, comprehensive exam, thesis/dissertation, qualifying exam, general exam, thesis defense. *Entrance requirements:* For master's and doctorate, GRE General Test, minimum GPA of 3.0, transcripts, statement of purpose, letters of recommendation. Additional exam requirements/recommendations for international students: Required—TOEFL (minimum score 580 paper-based; 92 iBT); Recommended—IELTS (minimum score 7). *Application deadline:* For fall admission, 12/1 for domestic and international students. Application fee: $85. Electronic applications accepted. *Expenses:* Expenses: Contact institution. *Financial support:* In 2014–15, 136 students received support, including 22 fellowships with full tuition reimbursements available, 97 research assistantships with full tuition reimbursements available, 7 teaching assistantships with full tuition reimbursements available; Federal Work-Study, institutionally sponsored loans, traineeships, health care benefits, and tuition waivers (full) also available. Support available to part-time students. Financial award application deadline: 12/1; financial award applicants required to submit FAFSA. *Faculty research:* Imaging and image guided therapy, molecular and cellular engineering, biomaterials and regenerative medicine, technology for expanding access to healthcare, synthetic and quantitative biology. *Total annual research expenditures:* $24 million. *Unit head:* Dr. Cecilia Giachelli, Professor/Chair, 206-685-2000, Fax: 206-685-3300, E-mail: ceci@uw.edu. *Application contact:* Senior Academic Counselor, 206-685-3494, Fax: 206-685-3300, E-mail: bioeng@uw.edu.
Website: http://depts.washington.edu/bioe/.

Virginia Commonwealth University, Graduate School, School of Engineering, Department of Chemical and Life Science Engineering, Richmond, VA 23284-9005. Offers MS, PhD. *Entrance requirements:* For master's and doctorate, GRE. Additional exam requirements/recommendations for international students: Required—TOEFL (minimum score 600 paper-based; 100 iBT). Electronic applications accepted. *Faculty research:* Advanced polymers, including biopolymers and polymers in medicine; chemical and biochemical reactor analysis; the study of supercritical fluids for environmentally favorable processes; systems biological engineering; stem cell engineering; biosensors and biochips; computational bioinformatics and rational drug design.

Virginia Polytechnic Institute and State University, Graduate School, College of Engineering, Blacksburg, VA 24061. Offers aerospace engineering (ME, MS, PhD); biological systems engineering (ME, MS, PhD); biomedical engineering (ME, MS, PhD); chemical engineering (ME, MS, PhD); civil engineering (ME, MS, PhD); computer engineering (ME, MS, PhD); computer science (MS, PhD); electrical engineering (ME, PhD); engineering education (PhD); engineering mechanics (ME, MS, PhD); environmental engineering (MS); environmental science and engineering (MS); industrial and systems engineering (ME, MS, PhD); materials science and engineering (ME, MS, PhD); mechanical engineering (ME, MS, PhD); mining and minerals engineering (PhD); mining engineering (ME, MS); nuclear engineering (MS, PhD); ocean engineering (MS); systems engineering (ME, MS). *Accreditation:* ABET (one or more programs are accredited). *Faculty:* 356 full-time (60 women), 3 part-time/adjunct (1 woman). *Students:* 1,700 full-time (398 women), 345 part-time (58 women); includes 213 minority (43 Black or African American, non-Hispanic/Latino; 1 American Indian or Alaska Native, non-Hispanic/Latino; 87 Asian, non-Hispanic/Latino; 58 Hispanic/Latino; 1 Native Hawaiian or other Pacific Islander, non-Hispanic/Latino; 23 Two or more races, non-Hispanic/Latino), 1,079 international. Average age 27. 5,228 applicants, 18% accepted, 471 enrolled. In 2014, 438 master's, 211 doctorates awarded. *Degree requirements:* For master's, comprehensive exam (for some programs), thesis (for some programs); for doctorate, comprehensive exam (for some programs), thesis/dissertation (for some programs). *Entrance requirements:* For master's and doctorate, GRE/GMAT (may vary by department). Additional exam requirements/recommendations for international students: Required—TOEFL (minimum score 550 paper-based). *Application deadline:* For fall admission, 8/1 for domestic students, 4/1 for international students; for spring admission, 1/1 for domestic students, 9/1 for international students. Applications are processed on a rolling basis. Application fee: $75. Electronic applications accepted. *Expenses:* Tuition, state resident: full-time $11,656; part-time $647.50 per credit hour. Tuition, nonresident: full-time $23,351; part-time $1297.25 per credit hour. *Required fees:* $2533; $465.75 per semester. Tuition and fees vary according to course load, campus/location and program. *Financial support:* In 2014–15, 148 fellowships with full tuition reimbursements (averaging $8,031 per year), 855 research assistantships with full tuition reimbursements (averaging $22,855 per year), 288 teaching assistantships with full tuition reimbursements (averaging $20,291 per year) were awarded. Financial award application deadline: 3/1; financial award applicants required to submit FAFSA. *Total annual research expenditures:* $90.5 million. *Unit head:* Dr. Richard C. Benson, Dean, 540-231-9752, Fax: 540-231-3031, E-mail: deaneng@vt.edu. *Application contact:* Linda Perkins, Executive Assistant, 540-231-9752, Fax: 540-231-3031, E-mail: lperkins@vt.edu. Website: http://www.eng.vt.edu/.

Washington State University, College of Agricultural, Human, and Natural Resource Sciences, Department of Biological Systems Engineering, Pullman, WA 99164-6120. Offers biological and agricultural engineering (MS, PhD). Program applications must be made through the Pullman campus. *Students:* 61 full-time (25 women), 6 part-time (1 woman); includes 2 minority (1 Asian, non-Hispanic/Latino; 1 Hispanic/Latino), 57 international. Average age 30. 66 applicants, 29% accepted, 10 enrolled. In 2014, 2 master's, 15 doctorates awarded. *Degree requirements:* For master's, comprehensive exam, thesis (for some programs), written and oral exam; for doctorate, comprehensive exam, thesis/dissertation, written and oral exam. *Entrance requirements:* For master's and doctorate, minimum GPA of 3.0, bachelor's degree in engineering or closely-related subject. Additional exam requirements/recommendations for international students: Required—TOEFL. *Application deadline:* For fall admission, 1/31 priority date for domestic and international students; for spring admission, 7/1 priority date for domestic and international students. Applications are processed on a rolling basis. Application fee: $75. Electronic applications accepted. *Expenses:* Tuition, state resident: full-time $11,768. Tuition, nonresident: full-time $25,200. *Required fees:* $960. Tuition and fees vary according to program. *Financial support:* In 2014–15, 30 research assistantships (averaging $14,162 per year) were awarded; tuition waivers also available. *Faculty research:* Agricultural automation engineering; bioenergy and bioproducts engineering; food engineering; land, air, and water resources and environmental engineering. *Total annual research expenditures:* $4 million. *Unit head:* Dr. Claudio Stockle, Chair, 509-335-1578, Fax: 509-335-2722, E-mail: stockle@wsu.edu. *Application contact:* WSU Graduate School, 800-GRADWSU, Fax: 509-335-1949, E-mail: gradsch@wsu.edu. Website: http://www.bsyse.wsu.edu.

Wilkes University, College of Graduate and Professional Studies, College of Science and Engineering, Department of Electrical Engineering and Physics, Wilkes-Barre, PA 18766-0002. Offers bioengineering (MS); electrical engineering (MSEE). Part-time programs available. *Students:* 18 full-time (6 women), 10 part-time (4 women); includes 4 minority (1 Black or African American, non-Hispanic/Latino; 2 Asian, non-Hispanic/Latino; 1 Hispanic/Latino), 7 international. Average age 26. In 2014, 2 master's awarded. *Entrance requirements:* For master's, GRE General Test. Additional exam requirements/recommendations for international students: Required—TOEFL (minimum score 550 paper-based; 79 iBT). *Application deadline:* Applications are processed on a rolling basis. Application fee: $45 ($65 for international students). Electronic applications accepted. *Financial support:* Federal Work-Study and unspecified assistantships available. Financial award application deadline: 3/1; financial award applicants required to submit FAFSA. *Unit head:* Dr. Terese Wignot, Interim Dean, 570-408-4600, Fax: 570-408-7846, E-mail: terese.wignot@wilkes.edu. *Application contact:* Joanne Thomas, Director of Graduate Enrollment, 570-408-4234, Fax: 570-408-7846, E-mail: joanne.thomas1@wilkes.edu. Website: http://www.wilkes.edu/academics/colleges/science-and-engineering /engineering-physics/electrical-engineering-physics/index.aspx.

Department of Bioengineering
UNIVERSITY OF UTAH

The Department of Bioengineering at the University of Utah, established in 1974, is an internationally renowned center of interdisciplinary basic and applied medically related research. It has a rich history in artificial organs, including the heart-lung machine, the intra-aortic balloon pump heart assist device, the artificial eye, the artificial heart and the dialysis machine—the first of which was engineered out of sausage casing and part of a Ford automobile water pump during WWII by Willem Kolff. In addition, the Department has a history of developments in biomaterials, drug delivery, and entrepreneurial activity.

Current research activities of the Department include biobased engineering, biosensors, medical imaging, biomaterials, biomechanics, computation/modeling, drug/gene delivery, neural interfaces, computational bioengineering, tissue engineering, and other specialty areas. Among these strong areas of research, five current initiatives are particularly noteworthy: Neural Engineering; Cardiovascular Engineering; Biomedical Imaging; Cell, Molecular, and Tissue Therapeutics; BioDesign.

For more information, contact:
Karen L. Terry, Academic Advisor & Coordinator
Department of Bioengineering
University of Utah
Salt Lake City, Utah 84112

karen.terry@utah.edu   http://www.bioen.utah.edu/

Biosystems Engineering

Auburn University, Graduate School, Ginn College of Engineering, Department of Biosystems Engineering, Auburn University, AL 36849. Offers MS, PhD. *Faculty:* 9 full-time (0 women). *Students:* 25 full-time (9 women), 4 part-time (1 woman); includes 1 minority (Asian, non-Hispanic/Latino), 24 international. Average age 26. 24 applicants, 50% accepted, 10 enrolled. In 2014, 2 master's awarded. *Expenses:* Tuition, state resident: full-time $8586; part-time $477 per credit hour. Tuition, nonresident: full-time $25,758; part-time $1431 per credit hour. *Required fees:* $804 per semester. Tuition and fees vary according to degree level and program. *Unit head:* Steven Taylor, Head, 334-844-4180. *Application contact:* Dr. George Flowers, Dean of the Graduate School, 334-844-2125.
Website: http://www.eng.auburn.edu/programs/bsen/programs/graduate/index.html.

Clemson University, Graduate School, College of Engineering and Science, Department of Environmental Engineering and Earth Sciences and College of Engineering and Science, Program in Biosystems Engineering, Clemson, SC 29634. Offers MS, PhD. Part-time programs available. *Students:* 4 full-time (3 women), 1 part-time (0 women), 3 international. Average age 30. 8 applicants, 38% accepted, 2 enrolled. In 2014, 5 master's, 2 doctorates awarded. *Degree requirements:* For master's, thesis; for doctorate, comprehensive exam, thesis/dissertation. *Entrance requirements:* For master's and doctorate, GRE General Test, minimum GPA of 3.0. Additional exam requirements/recommendations for international students: Required—TOEFL. *Application deadline:* For fall admission, 6/1 for domestic students, 4/15 for international students; for spring admission, 9/15 for international students. Applications are processed on a rolling basis. Application fee: $70 ($80 for international students). Electronic applications accepted. *Financial support:* In 2014–15, 2 students received support, including 1 research assistantship with partial tuition reimbursement available (averaging $16,000 per year), 1 teaching assistantship with partial tuition reimbursement available (averaging $17,784 per year); fellowships with full and partial tuition reimbursements available, career-related internships or fieldwork, institutionally sponsored loans, scholarships/grants, health care benefits, and unspecified assistantships also available. Support available to part-time students. Financial award application deadline: 2/15. *Faculty research:* Sustainable bioprocessing, biofuels and bioenergy, ecological engineering. *Unit head:* Dr. Tanju Karanfil, Chair, 864-653-3278, Fax: 864-656-0672, E-mail: tkaranf@clemson.edu. *Application contact:* Dr. Terry Walker, Graduate Coordinator, 864-656-0351, Fax: 864-656-0672, E-mail: walker4@clemson.edu.
Website: http://www.clemson.edu/cafls/departments/agbioeng/be/.

Michigan State University, The Graduate School, College of Agriculture and Natural Resources and College of Engineering, Department of Biosystems and Agricultural Engineering, East Lansing, MI 48824. Offers biosystems engineering (MS, PhD). *Entrance requirements:* Additional exam requirements/recommendations for international students: Required—TOEFL. Electronic applications accepted.

North Dakota State University, College of Graduate and Interdisciplinary Studies, College of Engineering and Architecture, Department of Agricultural and Biosystems Engineering, Fargo, ND 58108. Offers agricultural and biosystems engineering (MS, PhD); engineering (PhD); natural resource management (MS); natural resources management (PhD). Part-time programs available. *Degree requirements:* For master's, thesis; for doctorate, thesis/dissertation. *Entrance requirements:* For master's and doctorate, BS in engineering or the equivalent, minimum undergraduate GPA of 3.0. Additional exam requirements/recommendations for international students: Required—TOEFL (minimum score 550 paper-based; 79 iBT). Electronic applications accepted. *Faculty research:* Irrigation, crop processing, food engineering, environmental resources, sensors and instrumentation.

South Dakota State University, Graduate School, College of Agriculture and Biological Sciences, Department of Agricultural and Biosystems Engineering, Brookings, SD 57007. Offers MS, PhD. Part-time programs available. *Degree requirements:* For master's, thesis; for doctorate, comprehensive exam, thesis/dissertation, preliminary oral and written exams. *Entrance requirements:* Additional exam requirements/recommendations for international students: Required—TOEFL (minimum score 525 paper-based; 71 iBT).

South Dakota State University, Graduate School, College of Engineering, Department of Agricultural and Biosystems Engineering, Brookings, SD 57007. Offers biological sciences (MS, PhD); engineering (MS). PhD offered jointly with Iowa State University of Science and Technology. Part-time programs available. *Degree requirements:* For master's, thesis (for some programs), oral exam; for doctorate, thesis/dissertation, preliminary oral and written exams. *Entrance requirements:* For master's and doctorate, engineering degree. Additional exam requirements/recommendations for international students: Required—TOEFL (minimum score 550 paper-based; 79 iBT). *Faculty research:* Water resources, food engineering, natural resources engineering, machine design, bioprocess engineering.

The University of Arizona, College of Agriculture and Life Sciences, Department of Agricultural and Biosystems Engineering, Tucson, AZ 85721. Offers MS, PhD. Terminal master's awarded for partial completion of doctoral program. *Degree requirements:* For master's, thesis; for doctorate, thesis/dissertation. *Entrance requirements:* For master's, minimum GPA of 3.0 in last 2 years of undergraduate study, 3 letters of recommendation; for doctorate, minimum GPA of 3.0 in last 2 years of undergraduate study, 3 letters of recommendation, statement of purpose. Additional exam requirements/recommendations for international students: Required—TOEFL (minimum score 550 paper-based; 79 iBT). Electronic applications accepted. *Faculty research:* Irrigation system design, energy-use management, equipment for alternative crops, food properties enhancement.

University of Manitoba, Faculty of Graduate Studies, Faculty of Engineering, Department of Biosystems Engineering, Winnipeg, MB R3T 2N2, Canada. Offers M Eng, M Sc, PhD.

University of Minnesota, Twin Cities Campus, Graduate School, College of Food, Agricultural and Natural Resource Sciences, Bioproducts and Biosystems Science, Engineering and Management Graduate Program, Saint Paul, MN 55108. Offers MS, PhD. Part-time programs available. Terminal master's awarded for partial completion of doctoral program. *Degree requirements:* For master's, comprehensive exam, thesis, written and oral preliminary exams; for doctorate, comprehensive exam, thesis/dissertation, written and oral preliminary exams. *Entrance requirements:* For master's and doctorate, GRE, BS in engineering, mathematics, physical or biological sciences, or related field. Additional exam requirements/recommendations for international students: Required—TOEFL (minimum score 550 paper-based; 79 iBT), IELTS (minimum score 6.5). Electronic applications accepted. *Faculty research:* Water quality, bioprocessing, food engineering, terramechanics, process and machine control.

The University of Tennessee, Graduate School, College of Agricultural Sciences and Natural Resources, Department of Biosystems Engineering and Environmental Science, Program in Biosystems Engineering, Knoxville, TN 37996. Offers MS, PhD. *Degree requirements:* For master's, thesis; for doctorate, thesis/dissertation. *Entrance requirements:* For master's and doctorate, GRE General Test, minimum GPA of 2.7. Additional exam requirements/recommendations for international students: Required—TOEFL. Electronic applications accepted.

The University of Tennessee, Graduate School, College of Agricultural Sciences and Natural Resources, Department of Biosystems Engineering and Environmental Science, Program in Biosystems Engineering Technology, Knoxville, TN 37996. Offers MS. *Degree requirements:* For master's, thesis or alternative. *Entrance requirements:* For master's, GRE General Test, minimum GPA of 2.7. Additional exam requirements/recommendations for international students: Required—TOEFL. Electronic applications accepted.

UNIVERSITY OF UTAH
Department of Bioengineering

 For more information, visit http://petersons.to/utahbioengineering

Programs of Study

The Department of Bioengineering at the University of Utah prepares graduates to be leaders in the integration of engineering, biology, and medicine to detect and treat human disease and disability. The Department's programs are consistently ranked among the highest in the United States. The students are among the highest achieving students entering any interdepartmental program on campus. Graduate instruction leads to the Master of Science (M.S.) (thesis and course options) and Doctor of Philosophy (Ph.D.) degrees. Research programs include biomechanics, biomaterials, biosensors, computation and modeling, drug and gene delivery, medical imaging, neural interfaces, tissue engineering, and other specialty areas. The graduate program draws more than 140 faculty members from over thirty departments across four colleges.

Students in the M.S. program must complete the master's-level core curriculum and elective courses in one of the following areas: bioInnovate, biomaterials and therapeutics, bioinstrumentation, biomechanics, cardiac electrophysiology and biophysics, neural interfaces or imaging. In addition, all M.S. thesis students are required to defend their thesis in a public forum. The Department also offers an M.S./Course Option program.

Students may be admitted directly to the Ph.D. program at the time of admission, depending upon the decision of the Graduate Admissions Committee. Ph.D. students must successfully complete the bioengineering graduate core curriculum or its equivalent and take additional advanced graduate courses. Students must also pass a written qualifying exam, write a research proposal on their dissertation topic, and publicly defend their dissertation.

The Ph.D. degree program typically takes a minimum of five years to complete. It is strongly recommended that all graduate students select a research direction and begin thesis research as soon as they begin their studies. In addition, the program is individually tailored to meet the specific objectives of each candidate and may involve collaboration with faculty members in other departments.

Research Facilities

The Department of Bioengineering at the University of Utah is an internationally renowned center of interdisciplinary basic and applied medically related research. It has a rich history in artificial organs, biomaterials, and drug delivery. Research laboratories and Department offices are located in the new state-of-the-art Sorenson Molecular Biotechnology Building (SMBB). Additional labs are located across campus in locations including: Merrill Engineering Building, Warnock Engineering Building, Biomedical Polymers Research Building, University Hospital, Huntsman Cancer Institute, Primary Children's and Orthopedic Specialty Hospitals, the School of Medicine, and the College of Pharmacy. Centers and institutes include: Scientific Computing and Imaging Institute (SCI), Cardiovascular Research and Training Institute (CVRTI), Huntsman Cancer Institute (HCI), Utah Center for Advanced Imaging Research (UCAIR), Center for Controlled Chemical Delivery (CCCD), Keck Center for Tissue Engineering (KCTE), Center for Neural Interfaces, and Nano Institute.

The University has excellent libraries and state-of-the-art computing centers.

Financial Aid

Ph.D. students making satisfactory progress in the Department typically receive support and tuition waivers throughout their graduate studies, typically through their graduate advisor. A limited number of University and Department fellowships are offered on a competitive basis to exceptionally well-qualified applicants.

Cost of Study

Bioengineering graduate students may receive full-time scholarships, fellowships, or assistantships. In addition, graduate students receiving financial support through the University of Utah are given full tuition waivers. Tuition and fees for 2015–16 for 11 credit hours are $4,700 for state residents and $11,970 for nonresidents per semester.

Living and Housing Costs

Housing for unmarried graduate students begins at approximately $385 (double room) per month. Unfurnished apartments for married students range from $594 to $2,113 per month in the University Village, Medical Plaza, and historic Fort Douglas. Off-campus housing near the University is also available. For more specific information, students should visit http://www.apartments.utah.edu or http://www.housing.utah.edu.

Student Group

The University of Utah has a student population of more than 30,000, representing all fifty states and fifty other countries. The Department of Bioengineering welcomes approximately 35 to 40 new students each year and maintains an average total graduate enrollment of 130 students. Graduates are successful in industry, academics, medicine, government, and entrepreneurial pursuits.

Location

Salt Lake City is the center of a metropolitan area of nearly a million people. It lies in a valley with an elevation varying between 4,200 and 5,500 feet and is surrounded by mountain peaks reaching nearly 12,000 feet in elevation. The city is the cultural center of the intermountain area, with world-class ballet and modern dance companies, theater and opera companies, and a symphony orchestra. It also supports professional basketball, hockey, soccer, arena football, and baseball. Salt Lake City was the proud host of the 2002 Winter Olympics and is within 30 minutes of several world-class ski resorts. A major wilderness area is less than 2 hours away, and ten national parks are within a short drive of the city.

The University

The 1,500-acre University campus is nestled in the foothills of the Wasatch Mountains and is characterized by its modern buildings and attractive landscaping. Within a few minutes' walk of the University is Red Butte Gardens, which is a large, established garden and ecological center with an area of more than 400 miles, with display gardens and hiking trails. An international faculty of 3,600 members provides comprehensive instruction and research in disciplines ranging from medicine and law to fine arts and business.

Applying

Instructions for applying to the program can be obtained by writing to the Department of Bioengineering or from the Department's home page at http://www.bioen.utah.edu. In addition to the application form and fee, students must submit three letters of recommendation, scores on the General Test of the Graduate Record Examinations, university transcripts, and a written statement of interests and goals.

Detailed information on the various aspects of the Department of Bioengineering at the University of Utah can be obtained by accessing the Department's home page.

Correspondence and Information

Chair, Graduate Admissions Committee
Department of Bioengineering
University of Utah
Sorenson Molecular Biotechnology Building
36 S. Wasatch Drive, Room 3223
Salt Lake City, Utah 84112
United States
Website: http://www.bioen.utah.edu

THE FACULTY AND THEIR RESEARCH

[**Bold** *indicates primary faculty (tenure and career line);* **Adjunct faculty;* **Emeritus faculty]

Orly Alter, Ph.D., Stanford. Genomic signal processing and systems biology.
*Marcus Aman, Ph.D.
*B. Ambati, Ph.D.
**J. D. Andrade, Ph.D., Denver. Interfacial biochemistry, biochemical sensors, proteins engineering, integrated science education, bioluminescence.
*Andrew E. Anderson, Ph.D., Utah. Computational modeling, tissue experimental biomechanics.
*Jeffrey Anderson, Ph.D.
*A. Angelucci, M.D., Rome (Italy); Ph.D., MIT. Mammalian visual system.
*K. N. Bachus, Ph.D., Utah. Bone biomechanics, fracture analysis, implant failure mechanisms.
*You Han Bae, Ph.D., Korea. Pharmaceutical chemistry.
*K. Balagurunathan, Ph.D., Iowa. Biomaterials, chemical biology.
*Stacy Bamberg, Ph.D., Harvard-MIT. Bioinstrumentation, gait analysis, aging.
*Helen Barkan, Ph.D. Neurology.
*Andrea Bild, Ph.D.
*S. M. Blair, Ph.D., Colorado. Integrated-optics resonance biosensors.
*R. D. Bloebaum, Ph.D., Western Australia. Orthopedic implants.
*D. Bloswick, Ph.D., Michigan. Biomechanics, ergonomics.
S. C. Bock, Ph.D., California, Irvine. Antithrombin III heparin cofactor, medically useful serpins, glycoprotein N-glycosylation.

University of Utah

Robert Bowles, Ph.D., Duke.
*Lara Brewer, Ph.D. Anesthesiology.
*D. W. Britt, Ph.D., Utah. High-resolution microscopy, thin films, protein-surface interactions.
K. Broadhead, Ph.D., Utah. Tissue engineering.
*M. B. Bromberg, Ph.D., Vermont; M.D., Michigan. Bioelectric signals from nerve/muscle, neurophysiology.
*R. B. Brown, Ph.D., Utah. Medical applications for sensors, bioinstrumentation, implantable electronics.
*J. B. Bunnell, Sc.D., MIT. Medical device development.
Christopher Buston, Ph.D., Utah.
**K. D. Caldwell, Ph.D., Uppsala (Sweden). Separation and characterization of biopolymers, subcellular particles, and cells.
*T. E. Cheatham, Ph.D., California, San Francisco. Computer simulation of biological macromolecules.
*Elena Cherkaev, Ph.D., St. Petersburg (Russia). Mathematics.
D. A. Christensen, Ph.D., Utah. Optical/ultrasonic bioinstrumentation.
*Edward B. Clark, Ph.D.
G. A. Clark, Ph.D., California, Irvine. Neurobiology, basis of behavior, cell neurophysiology and learning mechanisms, computational neuroscience.
*Brittany Coats, Ph.D., Pennsylvania. Head and eye injury biomechanics.
Tara Deans, Ph.D., Johns Hopkins. Synthetic biology, tissue engineering.
*E. V. R. DiBella, Ph.D., Georgia Tech. Medical imaging, dynamic cardiac SPECT.
A. D. Dorval, Ph.D. Boston. Neural engineering and interfaces.
Derek Dosdall, Ph.D., Arizona State. Cardiac mapping and electrophyusiology.
*Adam Douglass, Ph.D.
**Carl Durney, Ph.D.
*Talmage D. Egan, M.D., Utah. Anesthesiology.
Benjamin Ellis, Ph.D., Utah. Musculoskeletal research.
*Colleen Farmer, Ph.D. Brown, Pulmonary fluid dynamics.
*Peter Fitzgerald, Ph.D. Tissue remodeling.
*A. L. Fogelson, Ph.D., NYU. Physiological systems modeling.
*B. K. Gale, Ph.D., Utah. MEMS devices and their applications to biology and medicine.
*Guido Gerig, Ph.D., ETH Zurich. Medical imaging analysis.
*J. M. Gerton, Ph.D., Rice. Bioimaging techniques, biophysics.
H. Ghandehari, Ph.D., Utah. Pharmaceutics, drug/gene delivery.
D. W. Grainger, Ph.D., Utah. Biomaterials, drug delivery, biotechnology, fluorinated surface chemistry.
*J. M. Harris, Ph.D., Purdue. Laser-based bioinstrumentation, interfacial spectroscopy.
*T. G. Henderson, Ph.D., Texas at Austin. Artificial intelligence, computer vision, robotics.
*Heath B. Henninger, Ph.D., Utah, Orthopaedics.
*J. N. Herron, Ph.D., Illinois. Protein engineering, molecular graphics, biosensors.
R. W. Hitchcock, Ph.D., Utah. Medical product development.
V. Hlady, Ph.D., Zagreb (Croatia). Biochemistry/biophysics at interfaces, solid-liquid interface of biomaterials, proteins as engineering.
**K. W. Horch, D.Sc., Yale. Neuroprostheses, biomedical instrumentation, information processing in the somatosensory system, tactile aids.
*Harriet Hopf, Ph.D., Dartmouth. Genetics of health-care associated infection.
*Eric Hunter, Ph.D., Iowa. Vibration, exposure, acoustics.
E. W. Hsu, Ph.D., Johns Hopkins. Magnetic resonance imaging and applications to bioengineering.
*D. T. Hutchinson, M.D., Jefferson Medical. Orthopedics implants for the hand.
*Margit Maria Janat Amsbury, Ph.D.
**Jaramila Janatova, Ph.D., Utah.
Sujeevini Jeyapalina, Ph.D.
*C. R. Johnson, Ph.D., Utah. Theoretical/computational electrophysiology, inverse electrocardiography, dynamical systems theory.
*Kenward Johnson, M.D., Tulane. Anesthesiology.
*E. M. Jorgensen, Ph.D., Washington (Seattle). Molecular biology, genetics, cellular neurophysiology.
S. C. Joshi, D.Sc., Washington (St. Louis). Computational anatomy, statistical shape analysis in medical imaging.
*D. J. Kadrmas, Ph.D., North Carolina. Molecular imaging, positron emission tomography (PET) of cancerous tissues.
Aditya Kaza, Ph.D.
*J. P. Keener, Ph.D., Caltech. Applied mathematics, nonlinear differential equations, chemical/biological dynamics.
*P. S. Khanwilkar, Ph.D., Utah. Artificial heart/assist devices, design, control, surgical implantation/physiologic interfaces.
*Daniel Kim, Ph.D.
*Hanseup Kim, Ph.D., Michigan. Bionano-micro systems in moving fluids.
S. W. Kim, Ph.D., Utah. Blood compatibility, drug-delivery systems.
*Richard Daniel King, Ph.D., Harvard. Alzheimer's image analysis.
*Michael Kirby, Ph.D., Brown. Large-scale scientific computation and visualization.
*Patrick Kiser, Ph.D.
**Willem Kolff, Ph.D., Leiden (The Netherlands). Late Distinguished Professor of bioengineering, surgery, and medicine.
J. Kopecek, Ph.D., Czechoslovak Academy of Sciences. Biomaterials, chemistry/biochemistry of macromolecules, drug-delivery systems.
*Erik Kubiak, M.D., Washington (Seattle). Scientific computing and visualization, modeling, stimulation of ECG drug diffusion.
*Kai Kuck, Ph.D. Anesthesiology.
*Thomas Lane, Ph.D.
*John T. Langell, M.D., Ph.D., Drexel. Surgery.
*Paul LaStayo, Ph.D. Northern Arizona. Physical therapy
*Gianluca Lazzi, Ph.D., Utah. Computation, electromagnetics.
*Dean Li, Ph.D. Molecular medicine.
**Donald Lyman, Ph.D.
R. S. MacLeod, Ph.D., Dalhousie. Cardiac bioelectric modeling, body surface potential mapping, cardiac electrophysiology, scientific visualization.
*B. A. MacWilliams, Ph.D., Worcester Polytechnic. Vascular fluid dynamics, kinematic/kinetic biomechanics.
*B. Mann, Ph.D., Iowa State. Tissue engineering.

*Carlos Mastrangelo, Ph.D., Berkeley. Microfabricated systems, bioMEMS.
*Tyler McCabe, Ph.D., Utah. Research Scientist.
*Daniel McDonnall, Ph.D. Medical devices.
*J. C. McRea, Ph.D., Utah. Medical device development.
*S. G. Meek, Ph.D., Utah. Prosthetic design and control, EMG signal processing, biomechanics.
*Rajesh Menon, Ph.D. Electrical and computer engineering.
*Ken Monson, Ph.D., Berkeley, Traumatic brain injury, biomechanics.
*Alonso P. Moreno, Ph.D., IPN (Mexico). Molecular and biophysical properties of gap junctions, intercellular heterologous communication.
*C. J. Myers, Ph.D., Stanford. Modeling/analysis of biological networks.
*J. R. Nelson, Ph.D., Utah. Microbiology, immunology.
*F. Noo, Ph.D., Liege (Belgium). 3-D tomographic reconstruction.
**R. A. Normann, Ph.D., Berkeley. Cell physiology, bioinstrumentation, neuroprosthetics.
**D. B. Olsen, D.V.M., Colorado State. Artificial heart/assist devices, design, control, surgical implantation/physiologic interfaces.
*Joseph A. Orr, Ph.D., Utah.
*Agnes E. Ostafin, Ph.D., Minnesota. Nanobiotechnology.
*D. L. Parker, Ph.D., Utah. Medical imaging, applications of physics in medicine.
*Amit Patel, Ph.D.
*Allison Payne, Ph.D. Radiology.
T. J. Petelenz, Ph.D., Utah. Medical instrumentation.
*Christopher Peters, M.D., Ph.D. Orthopedic surgery.
*John Phillips, Ph.D. Hematology.
*W. G. Pitt, Ph.D., Wisconsin–Madison. Polymers and composite materials for biomedical applications, surface chemistry.
*Mark Porter, Ph.D., Ohio State. Discovery, rapid screening therapeutic compounds.
*G. D. Prestwich, Ph.D., Stanford. Bioorganic chemistry.
*A. Pungor, Ph.D., Technical University (Hungary). Scanning-force microscopy, near-field optical microscopy, bioinstrumentation.
R. D. Rabbitt, Ph.D., Rensselaer. Biomechanics, hearing/vestibular mechanisms, computational mechanics, computational neuroscience.
*Ravi Ranjan, Ph.D., John's Hopkins. Cardiac electrophysiology.
**N. Rapoport, Ph.D., Moscow State; D.Sc., Academy of Sciences (USSR). Polymeric materials, biological magnetic resonance.
*R. B. Roemer, Ph.D., Stanford. Heat transfer, thermodynamics, design, optimization to biomedical problems.
*Jody Rosenblatt, Ph.D.
F. B. Sachse, Dr.-Ing., Karlsruhe (Germany). Computational cardiac electrophysiology, cardiac electromechanics.
*Derek Sakata, Ph.D.
*Charles Saltzman, Ph.D., North Carolina. Orthopaedics.
*Sujatha Sampath, Ph.D.
*C. Shelton, M.D., Texas Southwestern Medical Center at Dallas. Hearing systems physiology.
*M. E. Smith, M.D., Illinois. Otolaryngology, neural interfaces.
*F. Solzbacher, Ph.D., Technical University (Germany). MEMS, micromachining.
*K. W. Spitzer, Ph.D., Buffalo, SUNY. Cardiac cellular electrophysiology, intracellular pH regulation.
R. J. Stewart, Ph.D., California, Santa Barbara. Protein engineering, energy transduction, protein structure-activities, molecular motors.
*Ami Stuart, Ph.D. Orthopedics.
*Masood Tabib-Azar, Ph.D., Rensselaer. Advanced metrology and nano-device applications.
*Christi M. Terry, Ph.D.
Ning Tian, M.D., Ph.D. Ophthalmology and visual science.
*Ingo Titze, Ph.D.
P. A. Tresco, Ph.D., Brown. Molecular delivery systems, synthetic membrane fabrication, neurodegenerative/neuroendocrine/endocrine disorders.
*P. Triolo, Ph.D., Utah. Development/regulatory approval of biomaterials/diagnostic devices, tissue-engineered products.
David Warren, Ph.D., Utah. Applied peripheral nervous system neuroscience.
Mark Warren, Ph.D., Universitat Autonoma De Barcelona.
J. A. Weiss, Ph.D., Utah. Biomechanics, mechanics of normal/healing soft tissues, evaluation of injury mechanics/treatment regimens.
**D. R. Westenskow, Ph.D., Utah. Bioinstrumentation, microprocessor applications in medicine.
*Ross Whitaker, Ph.D., North Carolina. Image processing, computer vision, visualization.
*J. White, Ph.D., Johns Hopkins. Neural engineering and interfaces.
*Barbara Wirostko, Ph.D.
*Carl Thomas Wittwer, Ph.D., Michigan. Real-time PCR and DNA analysis.
*M. Yoshigi, M.D., Kyoto (Japan); Ph.D., Tokyo Women's Medical College. Cardiovascular physiology and embryology.
*Darrin Young, Ph.D., Berkeley. Wireless micro-nano-system.
Michael Yu, Ph.D., Massachusetts. Polymer science and engineering.
A. V. Zaitsev, Ph.D., Moscow State (Russia). Cardioelectrophysiology.
*G. L. Zeng, Ph.D., New Mexico. Biomedical imaging.
*Lei Jeffrey Zhang, Ph.D.

Section 4
Architectural Engineering

This section contains a directory of institutions offering graduate work in architectural engineering. Additional information about programs listed in the directory may be obtained by writing directly to the dean of a graduate school or chair of a department at the address given in the directory.

For programs offering related work, see also in this book *Engineering and Applied Sciences* and *Management of Engineering and Technology*. In the other guides in this series:

Graduate Programs in the Humanities, Arts & Social Sciences
See *Applied Arts and Design (Industrial Design and Interior Design), Architecture (Environmental Design), Political Science and International Affairs,* and *Public, Regional, and Industrial Affairs (Urban and Regional Planning and Urban Studies)*

Graduate Programs in the Physical Sciences, Mathematics, Agricultural Sciences, the Environment & Natural Resources
See *Environmental Sciences and Management*

CONTENTS

Architectural Engineering

Carnegie Mellon University, College of Fine Arts, School of Architecture, Pittsburgh, PA 15213-3891. Offers architecture (MSA); architecture, engineering, and construction management (PhD); building performance and diagnostics (MS, PhD); computational design (MS, PhD); engineering construction management (MSA); tangible interaction design (MTID); urban design (MUD). Terminal master's awarded for partial completion of doctoral program. *Degree requirements:* For doctorate, thesis/dissertation. *Entrance requirements:* For master's and doctorate, GRE General Test. Additional exam requirements/recommendations for international students: Required—TOEFL.

Drexel University, College of Engineering, Department of Civil, Architectural, and Environmental Engineering, Philadelphia, PA 19104-2875. Offers architectural / building systems engineering (PhD); architectural/building systems engineering (MS); civil engineering (MS, PhD); environmental engineering (MS, PhD); geotechnical, geoenvironmental and geosynthetics engineering (MS, PhD); hydraulics, hydrology and water resources engineering (MS, PhD); structures (MS). Part-time and evening/weekend programs available. *Degree requirements:* For master's, thesis optional; for doctorate, thesis/dissertation. *Entrance requirements:* For master's, minimum GPA of 3.0; for doctorate, minimum GPA of 3.5, MS in civil engineering. Additional exam requirements/recommendations for international students: Required—TOEFL. Electronic applications accepted. *Faculty research:* Structural dynamics, hazardous wastes, water resources, pavement materials, groundwater.

Illinois Institute of Technology, Graduate College, Armour College of Engineering, Department of Civil, Architectural and Environmental Engineering, Chicago, IL 60616. Offers architectural engineering (M Arch E); civil engineering (MS, PhD), including architectural engineering (MS), construction engineering and management (MS), geoenvironmental engineering (MS), geotechnical engineering (MS), structural engineering (MS), transportation engineering (MS); construction engineering and management (MCEM); environmental engineering (M Env E, MS, PhD); geoenvironmental engineering (M Geoenv E); geotechnical engineering (MGE); infrastructure engineering and management (MPW); structural engineering (MSE); transportation engineering (M Trans E). Part-time and evening/weekend programs available. Postbaccalaureate distance learning degree programs offered (minimal on-campus study). *Faculty:* 12 full-time (1 woman), 15 part-time/adjunct (1 woman). *Students:* 165 full-time (48 women), 54 part-time (11 women); includes 31 minority (2 Black or African American, non-Hispanic/Latino; 21 Asian, non-Hispanic/Latino; 7 Hispanic/Latino; 1 Native Hawaiian or other Pacific Islander, non-Hispanic/Latino), 157 international. Average age 29. 1,039 applicants, 42% accepted, 82 enrolled. In 2014, 94 master's, 7 doctorates awarded. Terminal master's awarded for partial completion of doctoral program. *Degree requirements:* For master's, thesis (for some programs); for doctorate, comprehensive exam, thesis/dissertation. *Entrance requirements:* For master's, GRE General Test (minimum score 900 Quantitative and Verbal, 2.5 Analytical Writing), minimum undergraduate GPA of 3.0; for doctorate, GRE General Test (minimum score 1000 Quantitative and Verbal, 3.0 Analytical Writing), minimum undergraduate GPA of 3.0. Additional exam requirements/recommendations for international students: Required—TOEFL (minimum score 550 paper-based; 80 iBT). *Application deadline:* For fall admission, 5/1 for domestic and international students; for spring admission, 10/15 for domestic and international students. Applications are processed on a rolling basis. Application fee: $50. Electronic applications accepted. *Expenses: Tuition:* Full-time $22,500; part-time $1250 per credit hour. *Required fees:* $30 per course. $260 per semester. One-time fee: $235. Tuition and fees vary according to course load and program. *Financial support:* Fellowships with full and partial tuition reimbursements, research assistantships with full and partial tuition reimbursements, teaching assistantships with full and partial tuition reimbursements, Federal Work-Study, institutionally sponsored loans, scholarships/grants, health care benefits, tuition waivers (partial), and unspecified assistantships available. Support available to part-time students. Financial award applicants required to submit FAFSA. *Faculty research:* Structural, architectural, geotechnical and geoenvironmental engineering; construction engineering and management; transportation engineering; environmental engineering and public works. *Unit head:* Dr. Gongkang Fu, Professor and Chairman, 312-567-3540, Fax: 312-567-3519, E-mail: gfu2@iit.edu. *Application contact:* Rishab Malhotra, Director, Graduate Admission, 866-472-3448, Fax: 312-567-3138, E-mail: inquiry.grad@iit.edu.
Website: http://engineering.iit.edu/caee.

Kansas State University, Graduate School, College of Engineering, Department of Architectural Engineering and Construction Science, Manhattan, KS 66506. Offers MS. *Faculty:* 15 full-time (2 women), 3 part-time/adjunct (0 women). *Students:* 2 full-time (1 woman), 7 part-time (2 women); includes 3 minority (all Asian, non-Hispanic/Latino), 2 international. Average age 23. 9 applicants, 33% accepted. In 2014, 5 master's awarded. *Degree requirements:* For master's, thesis or alternative. *Entrance requirements:* For master's, GRE, minimum GPA of 3.0, undergraduate degree (BS) from ABET-accredited engineering program. Additional exam requirements/recommendations for international students: Required—TOEFL. *Application deadline:* For fall admission, 2/1 priority date for domestic students, 1/1 priority date for international students; for spring admission, 8/1 priority date for domestic and international students. Applications are processed on a rolling basis. Application fee: $50 ($75 for international students). Electronic applications accepted. *Financial support:* Fellowships, research assistantships, teaching assistantships, career-related internships or fieldwork, institutionally sponsored loans, and scholarships/grants available. Support available to part-time students. Financial award application deadline: 3/1; financial award applicants required to submit FAFSA. *Faculty research:* Structural systems design and analysis, building electrical and lighting systems, building HVAC and plumbing systems, sustainable engineering. *Unit head:* Raphael Yunk, Head, 785-532-5964, Fax: 785-532-3556, E-mail: yunk@k-state.edu. *Application contact:* Dr. Kimberly Kramer, Director of Graduate Studies, 785-532-5964, Fax: 785-532-3556, E-mail: arecns@k-state.edu.
Website: http://www.k-state.edu/are-cns/.

Lawrence Technological University, College of Engineering, Southfield, MI 48075-1058. Offers architectural engineering (MS); automotive engineering (MS); civil engineering (MA, MS, PhD); construction engineering management (MS); electrical and computer engineering (MS); engineering management (MEM); industrial engineering (MS); manufacturing systems (ME, DE); mechanical engineering (MS, DE); mechatronic systems engineering (MS). Part-time and evening/weekend programs available. *Faculty:* 24 full-time (5 women), 15 part-time/adjunct (0 women). *Students:* 16 full-time (6 women), 478 part-time (71 women); includes 295 minority (15 Black or African American, non-Hispanic/Latino; 271 Asian, non-Hispanic/Latino; 7 Hispanic/Latino; 2 Two or more races, non-Hispanic/Latino), 38 international. Average age 27. 1,786 applicants, 40% accepted, 218 enrolled. In 2014, 106 master's awarded. *Degree requirements:* For master's, thesis (for some programs). *Entrance requirements:* Additional exam requirements/recommendations for international students: Required—TOEFL (minimum score 550 paper-based; 79 iBT). *Application deadline:* For fall admission, 8/1 priority date for domestic students, 5/29 for international students; for spring admission, 12/1 priority date for domestic students, 10/15 for international students. Applications are processed on a rolling basis. Application fee: $50. Electronic applications accepted. *Expenses: Tuition:* Full-time $14,700; part-time $1050 per credit hour. *Required fees:* $150. One-time fee: $150 part-time. *Financial support:* In 2014–15, 31 students received support, including 8 research assistantships (averaging $9,338 per year); Federal Work-Study and institutionally sponsored loans also available. Support available to part-time students. Financial award application deadline: 4/1; financial award applicants required to submit FAFSA. *Faculty research:* Advanced composite materials in bridges, strengthening existing bridges with carbon and glass fiber sheets, development of drive shafts using composite materials. *Unit head:* Dr. Nabil Grace, Dean, 248-204-2500, Fax: 248-204-2509, E-mail: engrdean@ltu.edu. *Application contact:* Jane Rohrback, Director of Admissions, 248-204-3160, Fax: 248-204-2228, E-mail: admissions@ltu.edu.
Website: http://www.ltu.edu/engineering/index.asp.

Milwaukee School of Engineering, Civil and Architectural Engineering and Construction Management Department, Program in Architectural Engineering, Milwaukee, WI 53202-3109. Offers MSAE. Part-time and evening/weekend programs available. *Faculty:* 1 full-time (0 women), 2 part-time/adjunct (0 women). *Students:* 2 full-time (0 women), 6 part-time (2 women), 1 international. Average age 26. 16 applicants, 56% accepted, 7 enrolled. In 2014, 14 master's awarded. *Degree requirements:* For master's, thesis, design project. *Entrance requirements:* For master's, GRE General Test or GMAT if undergraduate GPA less than 3.0, 2 letters of recommendation; BS in architectural, structural, or civil engineering or a related field. Additional exam requirements/recommendations for international students: Required—TOEFL (minimum score 90 iBT), IELTS (minimum score 6.5). *Application deadline:* Applications are processed on a rolling basis. Application fee: $0. Electronic applications accepted. *Expenses: Tuition:* Part-time $732 per credit. *Financial support:* Research assistantships, career-related internships or fieldwork, institutionally sponsored loans, and scholarships/grants available. Financial award application deadline: 3/15; financial award applicants required to submit FAFSA. *Faculty research:* Steel, materials. *Unit head:* Dr. Richard DeVries, Director, 414-277-7596, E-mail: devries@msoe.edu. *Application contact:* Ian Dahlinghaus, Graduate Program Associate, 414-277-7208, E-mail: dahlinghaus@msoe.edu.
Website: http://www.msoe.edu/community/academics/engineering/page/1290/structural-engineering-overview.

See Display on page 58 and Close-Up on page 83.

Penn State University Park, Graduate School, College of Engineering, Department of Architectural Engineering, University Park, PA 16802. Offers M Eng, MAE, MS, PhD. *Unit head:* Dr. Amr S. Elnashai, Dean, 814-865-7537, Fax: 814-863-4749, E-mail: ase2@psu.edu. *Application contact:* Lori A. Stania, Director, Graduate Student Services, 814-867-5278, Fax: 814-863-4627, E-mail: gswww@psu.edu.
Website: http://www.engr.psu.edu/ae/.

University of California, San Diego, Graduate Division, Program in Architecture-based Enterprise Systems Engineering, La Jolla, CA 92093. Offers MAS. Part-time programs available. *Students:* 25 full-time (6 women); includes 7 minority (1 Black or African American, non-Hispanic/Latino; 5 Asian, non-Hispanic/Latino; 1 Hispanic/Latino), 2 international. 30 applicants, 90% accepted, 25 enrolled. In 2014, 29 master's awarded. *Degree requirements:* For master's, capstone project. *Entrance requirements:* For master's, 3 letters of recommendation, statement of purpose, resume or curriculum vitae. Additional exam requirements/recommendations for international students: Required—TOEFL, IELTS. *Application deadline:* For fall admission, 6/30 for domestic students. Application fee: $90 ($110 for international students). Electronic applications accepted. *Expenses:* Expenses: Contact institution. *Financial support:* Applicants required to submit FAFSA. *Unit head:* Ingolf Krueger, Director, 858-822-5116, E-mail: ikrueger@ucsd.edu. *Application contact:* Lydia Ramirez, Coordinator, 858-534-1069, E-mail: lpramirez@ucsd.edu.
Website: http://maseng.ucsd.edu/aese/.

University of Colorado Boulder, Graduate School, College of Engineering and Applied Science, Department of Civil, Environmental, and Architectural Engineering, Boulder, CO 80309. Offers building systems engineering (MS, PhD); construction engineering management (MS, PhD); environmental engineering (MS, PhD); geotechnical engineering and geomechanics (MS, PhD); hydrology, water resources and environmental fluid mechanics (MS, PhD); structural engineering and structural mechanics (MS, PhD). *Faculty:* 37 full-time (8 women). *Students:* 235 full-time (81 women), 36 part-time (9 women); includes 24 minority (9 Asian, non-Hispanic/Latino; 6 Hispanic/Latino; 9 Two or more races, non-Hispanic/Latino), 83 international. Average age 28. 391 applicants, 63% accepted, 68 enrolled. In 2014, 76 master's, 30 doctorates awarded. Terminal master's awarded for partial completion of doctoral program. *Degree requirements:* For master's, comprehensive exam, thesis or alternative; for doctorate, thesis/dissertation. *Entrance requirements:* For master's, GRE General Test, minimum undergraduate GPA of 3.0. *Application deadline:* For fall admission, 1/31 for domestic and international students; for spring admission, 10/1 for domestic and international students. Application fee: $50 ($70 for international students). Electronic applications accepted. *Financial support:* In 2014–15, 387 students received support, including 75 fellowships (averaging $11,889 per year), 92 research assistantships with full and partial tuition reimbursements available (averaging $34,669 per year), 17 teaching assistantships with full and partial tuition reimbursements available (averaging $28,513 per year); institutionally sponsored loans, scholarships/grants, health care benefits, and unspecified assistantships also available. Financial award application deadline: 1/15; financial award applicants required to submit FAFSA. *Faculty research:* Civil engineering, environmental engineering, architectural engineering, geotechnical engineering, hydrology. *Total annual research expenditures:* $13 million.
Website: http://civil.colorado.edu/.

University of Detroit Mercy, School of Architecture, Detroit, MI 48221. Offers M Arch. *Entrance requirements:* For master's, BS in architecture, minimum GPA of 3.0, portfolio.

The University of Kansas, Graduate Studies, School of Engineering, Program in Architectural Engineering, Lawrence, KS 66045. Offers MS. Part-time programs available. *Faculty:* 25 full-time, 8 part-time/adjunct. *Students:* 7 full-time (3 women), 3 part-time (2 women), 2 international. Average age 23. 10 applicants, 80% accepted, 4 enrolled. In 2014, 1 master's awarded. *Degree requirements:* For master's, thesis or alternative, exam. *Entrance requirements:* For master's, GRE, BS in engineering. Additional exam requirements/recommendations for international students: Required—TOEFL. *Application deadline:* For fall admission, 7/1 priority date for domestic students, 3/1 priority date for international students; for spring admission, 12/1 priority date for domestic students, 8/15 priority date for international students. Applications are processed on a rolling basis. Application fee: $55 ($65 for international students). Electronic applications accepted. *Financial support:* Fellowships with full tuition reimbursements, research assistantships with full tuition reimbursements, teaching assistantships with full tuition reimbursements, and career-related internships or fieldwork available. Financial award application deadline: 2/7. *Faculty research:* Structural engineering, construction engineering, building mechanical systems, energy management. *Unit head:* David Darwin, Chair, 785-864-3827, E-mail: daved@ku.edu. *Application contact:* Susan Scott, Senior Administrative Associate, 785-864-3826, Fax: 785-864-5631, E-mail: sbscott@ku.edu. Website: http://www.ceae.ku.edu/.

University of Louisiana at Lafayette, College of the Arts, School of Architecture, Lafayette, LA 70504. Offers M Arch. *Degree requirements:* For master's, thesis. *Entrance requirements:* For master's, GRE General Test. Additional exam requirements/recommendations for international students: Required—TOEFL (minimum score 550 paper-based). Electronic applications accepted.

University of Massachusetts Amherst, Graduate School, College of Natural Sciences, Department of Environmental Conservation, Amherst, MA 01003. Offers building systems (MS, PhD); environmental policy and human dimensions (MS, PhD); forest resources (MS, PhD); sustainability science (MS); water, wetlands and watersheds (MS, PhD); wildlife and fisheries conservation (MS, PhD). Part-time programs available. *Faculty:* 45 full-time (10 women). *Students:* 68 full-time (34 women), 34 part-time (14 women); includes 3 minority (1 Black or African American, non-Hispanic/Latino; 1 Hispanic/Latino; 1 Two or more races, non-Hispanic/Latino), 17 international. Average age 31. 97 applicants, 45% accepted, 30 enrolled. In 2014, 31 master's, 5 doctorates awarded. Terminal master's awarded for partial completion of doctoral program. *Degree requirements:* For master's, thesis or alternative; for doctorate, comprehensive exam, thesis/dissertation. *Entrance requirements:* For master's and doctorate, GRE General Test. Additional exam requirements/recommendations for international students: Required—TOEFL (minimum score 550 paper-based; 80 iBT), IELTS (minimum score 6.5). *Application deadline:* For fall admission, 2/1 for domestic and international students; for spring admission, 10/1 for domestic and international students. Applications are processed on a rolling basis. Application fee: $75. Electronic applications accepted. *Expenses:* Tuition, state resident: full-time $1980; part-time $110 per credit. Tuition, nonresident: full-time $14,644; part-time $414 per credit. *Required fees:* $11,417. One-time fee: $357. *Financial support:* Fellowships with full and partial tuition reimbursements, research assistantships with full and partial tuition reimbursements, teaching assistantships with full and partial tuition reimbursements, career-related internships or fieldwork, Federal Work-Study, scholarships/grants, traineeships, health care benefits, tuition waivers (full and partial), and unspecified assistantships available. Support available to part-time students. Financial award application deadline: 2/1. *Unit head:* Dr. Curtice R. Griffin, Head, 413-545-2640, Fax: 413-545-4358. *Application contact:* Lindsay DeSantis, Supervisor of Admissions, 413-545-0721, Fax: 413-577-0100, E-mail: gradadm@grad.umass.edu. Website: http://eco.umass.edu/.

University of Miami, Graduate School, College of Engineering, Department of Civil, Architectural, and Environmental Engineering, Coral Gables, FL 33124. Offers architectural engineering (MSAE); civil engineering (MSCE, PhD). Part-time programs available. Terminal master's awarded for partial completion of doctoral program. *Degree requirements:* For master's, thesis (for some programs); for doctorate, comprehensive exam, thesis/dissertation. *Entrance requirements:* For master's, GRE General Test (minimum score 1000 verbal and quantitative), minimum GPA of 3.0; for doctorate, GRE General Test, minimum GPA of 3.5 in preceding degree. Additional exam requirements/recommendations for international students: Required—TOEFL (minimum score 550 paper-based). Electronic applications accepted. *Faculty research:* Structural assessment and wind engineering, sustainable construction and materials, moisture transport and management, wastewater and waste engineering, water management and risk analysis.

University of Nebraska–Lincoln, Graduate College, College of Engineering, Program in Architectural Engineering, Lincoln, NE 68588. Offers M Eng, MAE, MS, PhD. *Accreditation:* ABET. *Entrance requirements:* Additional exam requirements/recommendations for international students: Required—TOEFL (minimum score 550 paper-based).

The University of Texas at Austin, Graduate School, Cockrell School of Engineering, Department of Civil, Architectural and Environmental Engineering, Program in Architectural Engineering, Austin, TX 78712-1111. Offers MSE. Part-time programs available. *Degree requirements:* For master's, thesis. *Entrance requirements:* For master's, GRE General Test. Additional exam requirements/recommendations for international students: Required—TOEFL. Electronic applications accepted. *Faculty research:* Materials engineering, structural engineering, construction engineering, project management.

Section 5
Biomedical Engineering and Biotechnology

This section contains a directory of institutions offering graduate work in biomedical engineering and biotechnology, followed by an in-depth entry submitted by an institution that chose to prepare a detailed program description. Additional information about programs listed in the directory but not augmented by an in-depth entry may be obtained by writing directly to the dean of a graduate school or chair of a department at the address given in the directory.

For programs offering related work, see also in this book *Aerospace/Aeronautical Engineering, Engineering and Applied Sciences, Engineering Design, Engineering Physics, Management of Engineering and Technology,* and *Mechanical Engineering and Mechanics.* In the other guides in this series:

Graduate Programs in the Biological/Biomedical Sciences & Health-Related Medical Professions
See *Allied Health, Biological and Biomedical Sciences,* and *Physiology.*

Graduate Programs in the Physical Sciences, Mathematics, Agricultural Sciences, the Environment & Natural Resources
See *Mathematical Sciences (Biometrics and Biostatistics)*

CONTENTS

Biomedical Engineering

Arizona State University at the Tempe campus, Ira A. Fulton Schools of Engineering, School of Biological and Health Systems Engineering, Tempe, AZ 85287-9709. Offers biological design (PhD); biomedical engineering (MS, PhD). Part-time and evening/weekend programs available. Terminal master's awarded for partial completion of doctoral program. *Degree requirements:* For master's, thesis and oral defense or applied project; interactive Program of Study (iPOS) submitted before completing 50 percent of required credit hours; for doctorate, comprehensive exam, thesis/dissertation, interactive Program of Study (iPOS) submitted before completing 50 percent of required credit hours. *Entrance requirements:* For master's and doctorate, GRE General Test, minimum GPA of 3.0 or equivalent in last 2 years of work leading to bachelor's degree, 3 letters of recommendation, one-page personal statement. Additional exam requirements/recommendations for international students: Required—TOEFL (minimum score 580 paper-based; 92 iBT). Electronic applications accepted. *Expenses:* Contact institution. *Faculty research:* Cardiovascular engineering; synthetic/computational biology; medical devices and diagnostics; neuroengineering; rehabilitation; regenerative medicine; imaging; molecular, cellular and tissue engineering; virtual reality healthcare delivery systems.

Baylor College of Medicine, Graduate School of Biomedical Sciences, Program in Translational Biology and Molecular Medicine, Houston, TX 77030-3498. Offers PhD. *Degree requirements:* For doctorate, thesis/dissertation, public defense. *Entrance requirements:* For doctorate, GRE, minimum GPA of 3.0. Additional exam requirements/recommendations for international students: Required—TOEFL. Electronic applications accepted. *Faculty research:* Molecular medicine, translational biology, human disease biology and therapy.

Baylor University, Graduate School, School of Engineering and Computer Science, Department of Mechanical Engineering, Waco, TX 76798. Offers biomedical engineering (MSBME); engineering (ME); mechanical engineering (MS). Part-time programs available. *Degree requirements:* For master's, thesis (for some programs). *Entrance requirements:* For master's, GRE. Additional exam requirements/recommendations for international students: Required—TOEFL (minimum score 550 paper-based; 80 iBT), IELTS (minimum score 6.5), PTE (minimum score 58). Electronic applications accepted.

Binghamton University, State University of New York, Graduate School, Thomas J. Watson School of Engineering and Applied Science, Department of Bioengineering, Vestal, NY 13850. Offers biomedical engineering (MS, PhD). *Faculty:* 11 full-time (4 women), 2 part-time/adjunct (1 woman). *Students:* 37 full-time (12 women), 12 part-time (5 women); includes 5 minority (1 Black or African American, non-Hispanic/Latino; 1 Asian, non-Hispanic/Latino; 3 Hispanic/Latino), 31 international. Average age 26. 54 applicants, 91% accepted, 22 enrolled. In 2014, 4 master's, 2 doctorates awarded. *Degree requirements:* For master's, thesis; for doctorate, comprehensive exam, thesis/dissertation. *Entrance requirements:* For master's and doctorate, GRE General Test. Additional exam requirements/recommendations for international students: Required—TOEFL (minimum score 550 paper-based; 80 iBT). Application fee: $75. *Expenses:* Expenses: $5,435 resident; $11,105 non-resident. *Financial support:* In 2014–15, 18 students received support, including 7 research assistantships (averaging $16,500 per year), 8 teaching assistantships with full tuition reimbursements available (averaging $16,500 per year); career-related internships or fieldwork, Federal Work-Study, institutionally sponsored loans, scholarships/grants, health care benefits, tuition waivers (full and partial), and unspecified assistantships also available. Financial award application deadline: 2/15; financial award applicants required to submit FAFSA. *Unit head:* Ellen Tilden, Coordinator of Graduate Studies, 607-777-2873, Fax: 607-777-5349, E-mail: etilden@binghamton.edu. *Application contact:* Kishan Zuber, Recruiting and Admissions Coordinator, 607-777-2151, Fax: 607-777-2501, E-mail: kzuber@binghamton.edu.
Website: http://www2.binghamton.edu/watson/programs/academic-departments/bioengineering/.

Boston University, College of Engineering, Department of Biomedical Engineering, Boston, MA 02215. Offers M Eng, MS, PhD, MD/PhD. Part-time programs available. *Faculty:* 34 full-time (4 women), 3 part-time/adjunct (1 woman). *Students:* 147 full-time (58 women), 7 part-time (2 women); includes 33 minority (2 Black or African American, non-Hispanic/Latino; 24 Asian, non-Hispanic/Latino; 5 Hispanic/Latino; 2 Two or more races, non-Hispanic/Latino), 50 international. Average age 25. 652 applicants, 24% accepted, 47 enrolled. In 2014, 39 master's, 20 doctorates awarded. Terminal master's awarded for partial completion of doctoral program. *Degree requirements:* For master's, thesis (for some programs); for doctorate, comprehensive exam, thesis/dissertation. *Entrance requirements:* For master's and doctorate, GRE General Test. Additional exam requirements/recommendations for international students: Required—TOEFL (minimum score 550 paper-based; 84 iBT), IELTS (minimum score 7). *Application deadline:* For fall admission, 1/15 for domestic and international students; for spring admission, 10/1 for domestic and international students. Applications are processed on a rolling basis. Application fee: $80. Electronic applications accepted. *Expenses:* Tuition: Full-time $45,686; part-time $1428 per credit hour. *Required fees:* $660; $60 per semester. Tuition and fees vary according to program. *Financial support:* In 2014–15, 125 students received support, including 40 fellowships with full tuition reimbursements available (averaging $28,950 per year), 86 research assistantships with full tuition reimbursements available (averaging $19,300 per year), 18 teaching assistantships with full tuition reimbursements available (averaging $19,300 per year); career-related internships or fieldwork, Federal Work-Study, scholarships/grants, and tuition waivers (partial) also available. Financial award application deadline: 1/15; financial award applicants required to submit FAFSA. *Faculty research:* Biomaterials, tissue engineering and drug delivery; modeling of biological systems; molecular bioengineering and biophysics; neuroscience and neural disease; synthetic biology and systems biology. *Total annual research expenditures:* $18.7 million. *Unit head:* Dr. John White, Chairman, 617-353-2805, Fax: 617-353-6766. *Application contact:* Dr. Solomon Eisenberg, Senior Associate Dean of Academic Programs, 617-353-9760, Fax: 617-353-0259, E-mail: enggrad@bu.edu.
Website: http://www.bu.edu/bme/.

Brown University, Graduate School, Division of Biology and Medicine, Department of Molecular Pharmacology, Physiology and Biotechnology, Providence, RI 02912. Offers biomedical engineering (Sc M, PhD); biotechnology (PhD); molecular pharmacology and physiology (PhD); MD/PhD. *Degree requirements:* For doctorate, thesis/dissertation, preliminary exam. *Entrance requirements:* For master's and doctorate, GRE General Test, GRE Subject Test. Additional exam requirements/recommendations for international students: Required—TOEFL. Electronic applications accepted. *Faculty research:* Structural biology, antiplatelet drugs, nicotinic receptor structure/function.

Brown University, Graduate School, Division of Biology and Medicine and School of Engineering, Program in Biomedical Engineering, Providence, RI 02912. Offers Sc M, PhD. *Entrance requirements:* For master's and doctorate, GRE General Test, interview.

Additional exam requirements/recommendations for international students: Required—TOEFL.

Brown University, Graduate School, School of Engineering and Division of Biology and Medicine, Center for Biomedical Engineering, Providence, RI 02912. Offers Sc M, PhD. *Degree requirements:* For master's, thesis.

Carleton University, Faculty of Graduate Studies, Faculty of Engineering and Design, Ottawa-Carleton Institute for Biomedical Engineering, Ottawa, ON K1S 5B6, Canada. Offers MA Sc. *Degree requirements:* For master's, thesis optional. *Entrance requirements:* For master's, honours degree. Additional exam requirements/recommendations for international students: Required—TOEFL.

Carnegie Mellon University, Carnegie Institute of Technology, Biomedical and Health Engineering Program, Pittsburgh, PA 15213-3891. Offers bioengineering (MS, PhD); MD/PhD. *Degree requirements:* For master's, thesis; for doctorate, thesis/dissertation, qualifying exam. *Entrance requirements:* For master's and doctorate, GRE General Test. Additional exam requirements/recommendations for international students: Required—TOEFL. Electronic applications accepted. *Faculty research:* Cellular and molecular systematics, signal and image processing, materials and mechanics.

Case Western Reserve University, School of Graduate Studies, Case School of Engineering, Department of Biomedical Engineering, Cleveland, OH 44106. Offers MS, PhD, MD/MS, MD/PhD. *Faculty:* 22 full-time (3 women). *Students:* 104 full-time (50 women), 22 part-time (6 women); includes 33 minority (1 Black or African American, non-Hispanic/Latino; 26 Asian, non-Hispanic/Latino; 5 Hispanic/Latino; 1 Two or more races, non-Hispanic/Latino), 41 international. In 2014, 11 master's, 22 doctorates awarded. Terminal master's awarded for partial completion of doctoral program. *Degree requirements:* For master's, thesis (for some programs); for doctorate, thesis/dissertation, qualifying exam, teaching experience. *Entrance requirements:* For master's and doctorate, GRE General Test. Additional exam requirements/recommendations for international students: Required—TOEFL. *Application deadline:* For fall admission, 4/1 priority date for domestic students; for spring admission, 10/1 priority date for domestic students. Applications are processed on a rolling basis. Application fee: $50. *Financial support:* In 2014–15, 41 fellowships with full tuition reimbursements, 52 research assistantships with full and partial tuition reimbursements were awarded; traineeships also available. Financial award application deadline: 2/15; financial award applicants required to submit FAFSA. *Faculty research:* Neuroengineering, biomaterials/tissue engineering, drug delivery, biomedical imaging, biomedical sensors/systems. *Total annual research expenditures:* $12.2 million. *Unit head:* Dr. Robert Kirsch, Department Chair, 216-368-3158, Fax: 216-368-4969, E-mail: robert.kirsch@case.edu. *Application contact:* Carol Adrine, Academic Operations Coordinator, 216-368-4094, Fax: 216-368-4969, E-mail: caa7@case.edu.
Website: http://bme.case.edu.

See Display on next page and Close-Up on page 147.

The Catholic University of America, School of Engineering, Department of Biomedical Engineering, Washington, DC 20064. Offers MBE, PhD. Part-time programs available. *Faculty:* 7 full-time (1 woman), 1 part-time/adjunct (0 women). *Students:* 10 full-time (7 women), 16 part-time (7 women); includes 7 minority (3 Black or African American, non-Hispanic/Latino; 2 Hispanic/Latino; 2 Two or more races, non-Hispanic/Latino), 13 international. Average age 30. 33 applicants, 76% accepted, 9 enrolled. In 2014, 9 master's, 2 doctorates awarded. *Degree requirements:* For master's, thesis or alternative; for doctorate, comprehensive exam, thesis/dissertation, oral exams. *Entrance requirements:* For master's, GRE (minimum score: 1250), minimum GPA of 3.0, statement of purpose, official copies of academic transcripts, three letters of recommendation; for doctorate, GRE (minimum score: 1300), minimum GPA of 3.4, statement of purpose, official copies of academic transcripts, three letters of recommendation. Additional exam requirements/recommendations for international students: Required—TOEFL (minimum score 580 paper-based). *Application deadline:* For fall admission, 7/15 priority date for domestic students, 7/1 for international students; for spring admission, 11/15 priority date for domestic students, 11/1 for international students. Applications are processed on a rolling basis. Application fee: $55. Electronic applications accepted. *Expenses:* Expenses: Contact institution. *Financial support:* Fellowships, research assistantships, teaching assistantships, Federal Work-Study, scholarships/grants, tuition waivers (full and partial), and unspecified assistantships available. Financial award application deadline: 2/1; financial award applicants required to submit FAFSA. *Faculty research:* Cardiopulmonary biomechanics, robotics and human motor control, cell and tissue engineering, biomechanics, rehabilitation engineering. *Total annual research expenditures:* $268,287. *Unit head:* Dr. Peter S. Lum, Chair, 202-319-5181, Fax: 202-319-4287, E-mail: tran@cua.edu. *Application contact:* Director of Graduate Admissions, 202-319-5057, Fax: 202-319-6533, E-mail: cua-admissions@cua.edu.
Website: http://biomedical.cua.edu/.

City College of the City University of New York, Graduate School, Grove School of Engineering, Department of Biomedical Engineering, New York, NY 10031-9198. Offers ME, PhD. *Entrance requirements:* For master's, GRE. Additional exam requirements/recommendations for international students: Required—TOEFL (minimum score 550 paper-based).

Cleveland State University, College of Graduate Studies, Fenn College of Engineering, Department of Chemical and Biomedical Engineering, Program in Applied Biomedical Engineering, Cleveland, OH 44115. Offers D Eng. Part-time and evening/weekend programs available. *Faculty:* 8 full-time (1 woman), 1 part-time/adjunct (0 women). *Students:* 5 full-time (1 woman), 26 part-time (8 women); includes 2 minority (both Black or African American, non-Hispanic/Latino), 18 international. Average age 29. 5 applicants, 80% accepted, 2 enrolled. *Degree requirements:* For doctorate, thesis/dissertation. *Entrance requirements:* For doctorate, GRE, minimum undergraduate GPA of 2.75, MS or MD 3.25; degree in engineering. Additional exam requirements/recommendations for international students: Required—TOEFL (minimum score 525 paper-based). *Application deadline:* For fall admission, 4/15 for domestic and international students; for spring admission, 11/15 for domestic and international students. Applications are processed on a rolling basis. Application fee: $30. *Expenses:* Tuition, state resident: full-time $9566; part-time $531 per credit hour. Tuition, nonresident: full-time $17,980; part-time $999 per credit hour. *Required fees:* $25 per semester. Tuition and fees vary according to degree level and program. *Financial support:* In 2014–15, research assistantships with full and partial tuition reimbursements (averaging $5,696 per year) were awarded; career-related internships or fieldwork, scholarships/grants, and tuition waivers (full) also available. Financial award application deadline: 3/30. *Faculty research:* Biomechanics, drug delivery systems, medical imaging, tissue engineering, artificial heart valves. *Unit head:* Dr. Dhananjai B. Shah, Director, 216-687-3569, Fax: 216-687-9220, E-mail: d.shah@csuohio.edu. *Application* *contact:* Becky Laird, Administrative Coordinator, 216-687-2571, Fax: 216-687-9220, E-mail: b.laird@csuohio.edu. Website: http://www.csuohio.edu/engineering/chemical/ABE/index.html.

Colorado State University, Graduate School, School of Biomedical Engineering, Fort Collins, CO 80523-1376. Offers ME, MS, PhD. Part-time and evening/weekend programs available. Postbaccalaureate distance learning degree programs offered (no on-campus study). *Students:* 13 full-time (7 women), 19 part-time (7 women); includes 3 minority (2 Asian, non-Hispanic/Latino; 1 Hispanic/Latino), 1 international. Average age 28. 79 applicants, 9% accepted, 6 enrolled. In 2014, 2 master's awarded. Terminal master's awarded for partial completion of doctoral program. *Degree requirements:* For master's, thesis (for some programs); for doctorate, comprehensive exam, thesis/dissertation, qualifying process (minimum B average in core classes); preliminary exam. *Entrance requirements:* For master's and doctorate, GRE General Test, minimum GPA of 3.0. Additional exam requirements/recommendations for international students: Required—TOEFL (minimum score 550 paper-based; 95 iBT). *Application deadline:* For fall admission, 1/15 priority date for domestic and international students; for spring admission, 9/1 priority date for domestic and international students. Application fee: $50. Electronic applications accepted. *Expenses:* Tuition, state resident: full-time $9348; part-time $519 per credit. Tuition, nonresident: full-time $22,916; part-time $1273 per credit. *Required fees:* $1584. *Financial support:* In 2014–15, 20 students received support, including 13 research assistantships with full tuition reimbursements available (averaging $14,620 per year), 7 teaching assistantships with full tuition reimbursements available (averaging $7,996 per year); fellowships and unspecified assistantships also available. Financial award application deadline: 6/1; financial award applicants required to submit FAFSA. *Faculty research:* Regenerative and rehabilitative medicine, imaging and diagnostics, medical devices and therapeutics. *Unit head:* Dr. Kevin Lear, Director, School of Biomedical Engineering, 970-491-0718, Fax: 970-491-3827, E-mail: kevin.lear@colostate.edu. *Application contact:* Sara Neys, Academic Advisor, 970-491-7157, E-mail: sara.neys@colostate.edu. Website: http://www.engr.colostate.edu/sbme/.

Columbia University, Fu Foundation School of Engineering and Applied Science, Department of Biomedical Engineering, New York, NY 10027. Offers MS, Eng Sc D, PhD. Part-time programs available. Postbaccalaureate distance learning degree programs offered (no on-campus study). *Faculty:* 19 full-time (5 women), 22 part-time/adjunct (1 woman). *Students:* 123 full-time (59 women), 19 part-time (7 women); includes 40 minority (33 Asian, non-Hispanic/Latino; 3 Hispanic/Latino; 4 Two or more races, non-Hispanic/Latino), 59 international. 410 applicants, 24% accepted, 51 enrolled. In 2014, 28 master's, 20 doctorates awarded. *Degree requirements:* For doctorate, thesis/dissertation, qualifying exam. *Entrance requirements:* For master's and doctorate, GRE General Test. Additional exam requirements/recommendations for international students: Required—TOEFL, IELTS, PTE. *Application deadline:* For fall admission, 12/15 priority date for domestic and international students; for spring admission, 10/1 priority date for domestic and international students. Application fee: $85. Electronic applications accepted. *Financial support:* In 2014–15, 109 students received support, including 19 fellowships with full and partial tuition reimbursements available (averaging $31,667 per year), 74 research assistantships with full and partial tuition reimbursements available (averaging $31,667 per year), 16 teaching assistantships with full and partial tuition reimbursements available (averaging $31,667 per year); health care benefits also available. Financial award application deadline: 12/15; financial award applicants required to submit FAFSA. *Faculty research:* Biomechanics, biosignal and biomedical imaging, cellular and tissue engineering. *Unit head:* Dr. Andrew Laine, Professor and Chair, Biomedical Engineering, 212-854-4460, E-mail: laine@columbia.edu. Website: http://www.bme.columbia.edu.

Cornell University, Graduate School, Graduate Fields of Engineering, Field of Biomedical Engineering, Ithaca, NY 14853-0001. Offers M Eng, MS, PhD. *Degree requirements:* For master's, thesis; for doctorate, comprehensive exam, thesis/dissertation. *Entrance requirements:* For master's and doctorate, GRE General Test, GRE Subject Test (engineering), 3 letters of recommendation. Additional exam requirements/recommendations for international students: Required—TOEFL (minimum score 77 iBT). Electronic applications accepted. *Faculty research:* Biomaterials; biomedical instrumentation and diagnostics; biomedical mechanics; drug delivery, design, and metabolism.

Dalhousie University, Faculty of Engineering and Faculty of Medicine, Department of Biomedical Engineering, Halifax, NS B3H3J5, Canada. Offers MA Sc, PhD. *Entrance requirements:* Additional exam requirements/recommendations for international students: Required—TOEFL, IELTS, CANTEST, CAEL, or Michigan English Language Assessment Battery. Electronic applications accepted.

Dartmouth College, Thayer School of Engineering, Program in Biomedical Engineering, Hanover, NH 03755. Offers MS, PhD. *Faculty research:* Imaging, physiological modeling, cancer hyperthermia and radiation therapy, bioelectromagnetics, biomedical optics and lasers. *Total annual research expenditures:* $6.6 million. *Unit head:* Dr. Joseph J. Helbie, Dean, 603-646-2238, Fax: 603-646-2580, E-mail: joseph.j.helbie@dartmouth.edu. *Application contact:* Candace S. Potter, Graduate Admissions Administrator, 603-646-3844, Fax: 603-646-1620, E-mail: candace.s.potter@dartmouth.edu.

Drexel University, School of Biomedical Engineering, Science and Health Systems, Program in Biomedical Engineering, Philadelphia, PA 19104-2875. Offers MS, PhD. *Degree requirements:* For master's, thesis (for some programs); for doctorate, thesis/dissertation. Electronic applications accepted.

Duke University, Graduate School, Pratt School of Engineering, Department of Biomedical Engineering, Durham, NC 27708. Offers MS, PhD. *Faculty:* 28 full-time. *Students:* 217 full-time (91 women); includes 59 minority (6 Black or African American, non-Hispanic/Latino; 1 American Indian or Alaska Native, non-Hispanic/Latino; 42 Asian, non-Hispanic/Latino; 10 Hispanic/Latino), 64 international. 567 applicants, 14% accepted, 36 enrolled. In 2014, 41 master's, 21 doctorates awarded. *Degree requirements:* For doctorate, thesis/dissertation. *Entrance requirements:* For master's and doctorate, GRE General Test. Additional exam requirements/recommendations for international students: Required—TOEFL (minimum score 90 iBT), IELTS (minimum score 7). *Application deadline:* For fall admission, 12/8 priority date for domestic and international students; for spring admission, 10/15 for domestic and international students. Application fee: $80. *Expenses: Tuition:* Full-time $45,760; part-time $2765 per credit. *Required fees:* $978. Full-time tuition and fees vary according to program. *Financial support:* Fellowships, research assistantships, teaching assistantships, and Federal Work-Study available. Financial award application deadline: 12/8. *Unit head:* Dr. Adam Wax, Director of Graduate Studies, 919-660-5143, Fax: 919-681-7432, E-mail: a.wax@duke.edu. *Application contact:* Kristen Rivers, Program Coordinator, 919-660-5590, Fax: 919-613-0716, E-mail: kristen.rivers@duke.edu. Website: http://www.bme.duke.edu/grad.

Duke University, Graduate School, Pratt School of Engineering, Master of Engineering Program, Durham, NC 27708-0271. Offers biomedical engineering (M Eng); civil engineering (M Eng); electrical and computer engineering (M Eng); environmental engineering (M Eng); materials science and engineering (M Eng); mechanical engineering (M Eng); photonics and optical sciences (M Eng). Part-time programs available. *Students:* 45 full-time (17 women); includes 5 minority (1 Black or African American, non-Hispanic/Latino; 2 Asian, non-Hispanic/Latino; 2 Hispanic/Latino), 23

international. Average age 24. 285 applicants, 43% accepted, 45 enrolled. In 2014, 45 master's awarded. *Entrance requirements:* For master's, GRE General Test, resume, 3 letters of recommendation, statement of purpose, transcripts. Additional exam requirements/recommendations for international students: Required—TOEFL. *Application deadline:* For fall admission, 6/15 for domestic students, 2/15 for international students; for spring admission, 11/1 for domestic students, 9/1 for international students. Application fee: $75. *Expenses: Tuition:* Full-time $45,760; part-time $2765 per credit. *Required fees:* $978. Full-time tuition and fees vary according to program. *Financial support:* Merit scholarships/grants available. *Unit head:* Dr. Bradley A. Fox, Executive Director, 919-660-5455, Fax: 919-660-5456. *Application contact:* Susan Brown, Assistant Director of Admissions, 919-660-8451, Fax: 919-660-5456, E-mail: susan.brown@duke.edu.
Website: http://meng.pratt.duke.edu/.

East Carolina University, Graduate School, College of Engineering and Technology, Department of Engineering, Greenville, NC 27858-4353. Offers biomedical engineering (MS). *Expenses:* Tuition, state resident: full-time $4223. Tuition, nonresident: full-time $16,540. *Required fees:* $2184.

École Polytechnique de Montréal, Graduate Programs, Institute of Biomedical Engineering, Montréal, QC H3C 3A7, Canada. Offers M Sc A, PhD, DESS. M Sc A and PhD programs offered jointly with Université de Montréal. Part-time programs available. *Degree requirements:* For master's, one foreign language, thesis; for doctorate, one foreign language, thesis/dissertation. *Entrance requirements:* For master's, minimum GPA of 2.75; for doctorate, minimum GPA of 3.0. *Faculty research:* Cardiac electrophysiology, biomedical instrumentation, biomechanics, biomaterials, medical imagery.

Florida Agricultural and Mechanical University, Division of Graduate Studies, Research, and Continuing Education, FAMU-FSU College of Engineering, Department of Chemical and Biomedical Engineering, Tallahassee, FL 32307-3200. Offers biomedical engineering (MS, PhD); chemical engineering (MS, PhD). *Degree requirements:* For master's, thesis optional; for doctorate, thesis/dissertation, paper presentation at professional meeting. *Entrance requirements:* For master's, GRE General Test, minimum GPA of 3.3, letters of recommendation (3); for doctorate, minimum GPA of 3.3. Additional exam requirements/recommendations for international students: Required—TOEFL (minimum score 550 paper-based). *Faculty research:* Cellular signaling, cancer therapy, drug delivery, cellular and tissue engineering, brain physiology.

Florida Institute of Technology, Graduate Programs, College of Engineering, Program in Biomedical Engineering, Melbourne, FL 32901-6975. Offers MS, PhD. Part-time programs available. *Students:* 27 full-time (11 women), 4 part-time (2 women); includes 3 minority (1 Asian, non-Hispanic/Latino; 2 Hispanic/Latino), 23 international. Average age 26. 86 applicants, 59% accepted, 13 enrolled. In 2014, 4 master's awarded. Terminal master's awarded for partial completion of doctoral program. *Degree requirements:* For master's, comprehensive exam (for some programs), thesis or final exam; for doctorate, comprehensive exam, thesis/dissertation. *Entrance requirements:* For master's, GRE, minimum GPA of 3.0, 3 letters of recommendation, resume, statement of objectives; for doctorate, GRE, minimum GPA of 3.2, 3 letters of recommendation, resume, statement of objectives. Additional exam requirements/recommendations for international students: Required—TOEFL (minimum score 550 paper-based; 79 iBT). *Application deadline:* For fall admission, 4/1 priority date for international students; for spring admission, 9/30 for international students. Applications are processed on a rolling basis. Electronic applications accepted. *Expenses: Tuition:* Part-time $1179 per credit hour. Tuition and fees vary according to campus/location. *Financial support:* In 2014–15, 9 research assistantships with full and partial tuition reimbursements, 6 teaching assistantships with full and partial tuition reimbursements were awarded; career-related internships or fieldwork, institutionally sponsored loans, tuition waivers (partial), unspecified assistantships, and tuition remissions also available. Support available to part-time students. Financial award application deadline: 3/1; financial award applicants required to submit FAFSA. *Faculty research:* Biosensors, biomechanics, short pulse lasers, bioactive materials, medical photonics. *Total annual research expenditures:* $23,662. *Unit head:* Dr. Ted Conway, Department Head, 321-674-8491, Fax: 321-674-7270, E-mail: tconway@fit.edu. *Application contact:* Cheryl A. Brown, Associate Director of Graduate Admissions, 321-674-7581, Fax: 321-723-9468, E-mail: cbrown@fit.edu.
Website: http://coe.fit.edu/biomedical-engineering/.

Florida International University, College of Engineering and Computing, Department of Biomedical Engineering, Miami, FL 33175. Offers MS, PhD. Part-time and evening/weekend programs available. *Degree requirements:* For master's, thesis; for doctorate, comprehensive exam, thesis/dissertation. *Entrance requirements:* For master's, GRE General Test (minimum combined score 1000, verbal 350, quantitative 650), minimum GPA of 3.0; for doctorate, GRE General Test (minimum combined score 1150, verbal 450, quantitative 700), minimum GPA of 3.0, letter of intent, letters of recommendation. Additional exam requirements/recommendations for international students: Required—TOEFL (minimum score 550 paper-based; 80 iBT). Electronic applications accepted. *Faculty research:* Bio-imaging and bio-signal processing, bio-instrumentation, devices and sensors, biomaterials and bio-nano technology, cellular and tissue engineering.

Florida State University, The Graduate School, FAMU-FSU College of Engineering, Department of Chemical and Biomedical Engineering, Tallahassee, FL 32310-6046. Offers biomedical engineering (MS, PhD); chemical engineering (MS, PhD). Part-time programs available. Terminal master's awarded for partial completion of doctoral program. *Degree requirements:* For master's, thesis (for some programs); for doctorate, comprehensive exam, thesis/dissertation, qualifying exam. *Entrance requirements:* For master's, GRE General Test (recommended minimum scores: verbal 151/8th percentile; quantitative: 158/75th percentile), BS in chemical engineering or other physical science/engineering, minimum GPA of 3.0; for doctorate, GRE General Test (recommended minimum scores: verbal 151/8th percentile; quantitative: 158/75th percentile), BS in chemical engineering or other physical science/engineering, minimum GPA of 3.0, or MS in chemical or biomedical engineering. Additional exam requirements/recommendations for international students: Required—TOEFL (minimum score 550 paper-based; 80 iBT), Michigan English Language Assessment Battery (minimum score 77); Recommended—IELTS (minimum score 6.5). Electronic applications accepted. *Expenses:* Contact institution. *Faculty research:* Macromolecular transport and reaction; polymer characterization and processing; solid NMR-MRI for solid state spectroscopy and cell microscopy; protein, cell, and tissue engineering; electrochemical and fuel cell engineering.

Georgia Institute of Technology, Graduate Studies, College of Engineering, Wallace H. Coulter Department of Biomedical Engineering, Atlanta, GA 30332-0001. Offers biomedical engineering (PhD); biomedical innovation and development (MBID). PhD offered jointly with Emory University (Georgia) and Peking University (China). Part-time programs available. *Students:* 174 full-time (74 women), 4 part-time (2 women); includes 50 minority (8 Black or African American, non-Hispanic/Latino; 25 Asian, non-Hispanic/Latino; 8 Hispanic/Latino; 1 Native Hawaiian or other Pacific Islander, non-Hispanic/Latino; 8 Two or more races, non-Hispanic/Latino), 46 international. Average age 25. 285 applicants, 40% accepted, 52 enrolled. *Degree requirements:* For master's, thesis; for doctorate, thesis/dissertation. *Entrance requirements:* For master's, GRE, https://bioid.gatech.edu/bioid7/admissions; for doctorate, GRE, http://www.grad.gatech.edu/bmed. Additional exam requirements/recommendations for international students: Required—TOEFL (minimum score 600 paper-based; 100 iBT). *Application deadline:* For fall admission, 12/1 for domestic and international students. Applications are processed on a rolling basis. Application fee: $75. Electronic applications accepted. *Expenses:* Expenses: $8,203 per term in-state, $21,390 out-of-state plus fees of $1,196 per term (for PhD); $13,522 per term in-state, $18,493 out-of-state plus fees of $1,196 per term (for MBID). *Financial support:* Fellowships, research assistantships, teaching assistantships, career-related internships or fieldwork, Federal Work-Study, institutionally sponsored loans, tuition waivers (partial), and unspecified assistantships available. Support available to part-time students. Financial award application deadline: 5/1. *Faculty research:* Biomechanics and tissue engineering, bioinstrumentation and medical imaging. *Total annual research expenditures:* $20.8 million. *Unit head:* Garrett Stanley, Director, 404-385-5037, E-mail: garrett.stanley@bme.gatech.edu. *Application contact:* Shannon Sullivan, Graduate Coordinator, 404-385-2557, E-mail: shannon.sullivan@bme.gatech.edu.
Website: http://www.bme.gatech.edu/.

The Graduate Center, City University of New York, Graduate Studies, Program in Engineering, New York, NY 10016-4039. Offers biomedical engineering (PhD); chemical engineering (PhD); civil engineering (PhD); electrical engineering (PhD); mechanical engineering (PhD). *Degree requirements:* For doctorate, thesis/dissertation. *Entrance requirements:* For doctorate, GRE General Test. Additional exam requirements/recommendations for international students: Required—TOEFL. Electronic applications accepted.

Harvard University, Graduate School of Arts and Sciences, Department of Physics, Cambridge, MA 02138. Offers experimental physics (PhD); medical engineering/medical physics (PhD), including applied physics, engineering sciences, physics; theoretical physics (PhD). *Degree requirements:* For doctorate, thesis/dissertation, final exams, laboratory experience. *Entrance requirements:* For doctorate, GRE General Test, GRE Subject Test. Additional exam requirements/recommendations for international students: Required—TOEFL. *Faculty research:* Particle physics, condensed matter physics, atomic physics.

Illinois Institute of Technology, Graduate College, Armour College of Engineering, Department of Biomedical Engineering, Chicago, IL 60616. Offers MAS, MS, PhD. Part-time programs available. *Faculty:* 11 full-time (4 women). *Students:* 45 full-time (18 women); includes 4 minority (1 Black or African American, non-Hispanic/Latino; 2 Asian, non-Hispanic/Latino; 1 Two or more races, non-Hispanic/Latino), 26 international. Average age 26. 250 applicants, 33% accepted, 19 enrolled. In 2014, 4 doctorates awarded. *Degree requirements:* For doctorate, comprehensive exam, thesis/dissertation. *Entrance requirements:* For master's and doctorate, GRE (minimum 1800 combined; 1200 quantitative + verbal; 3.0 analytical writing), minimum cumulative undergraduate GPA of 3.2. *Application deadline:* For fall admission, 5/1 for domestic and international students; for spring admission, 10/15 for domestic and international students. Applications are processed on a rolling basis. Application fee: $60. Electronic applications accepted. *Expenses: Tuition:* Full-time $22,500; part-time $1250 per credit hour. *Required fees:* $30 per course. $260 per semester. One-time fee: $235. Tuition and fees vary according to course load and program. *Financial support:* Fellowships with full tuition reimbursements, research assistantships with partial tuition reimbursements, teaching assistantships with full and partial tuition reimbursements, Federal Work-Study, institutionally sponsored loans, scholarships/grants, health care benefits, and unspecified assistantships available. Support available to part-time students. Financial award applicants required to submit FAFSA. *Faculty research:* Cell and tissue engineering, medical imaging, neural engineering. *Unit head:* John Georgiadis, Chair, 312-567-5790, Fax: 312-567-5770, E-mail: jgeorgia@iit.edu. *Application contact:* Rishab Malhotra, Director, Graduate Admission, 866-472-3448, Fax: 312-567-3138, E-mail: inquiry.grad@iit.edu.
Website: http://www.iit.edu/engineering/bme/.

Indiana University–Purdue University Indianapolis, School of Engineering and Technology, Department of Electrical Engineering, Indianapolis, IN 46202. Offers biomedical engineering (MS, PhD); electrical and computer engineering (MS, PhD); engineering (interdisciplinary) (MSE). *Students:* 64 full-time (15 women), 74 part-time (14 women); includes 13 minority (2 Black or African American, non-Hispanic/Latino; 9 Asian, non-Hispanic/Latino; 2 Hispanic/Latino), 95 international. Average age 27. 147 applicants, 63% accepted, 41 enrolled. In 2014, 27 master's awarded. Application fee: $55 ($65 for international students). *Unit head:* Brian King, Acting Chair, 317-274-9723. *Application contact:* Valerie Diemer, Graduate Program, 317-278-4960, Fax: 317-278-1671, E-mail: grad@engr.iupui.edu.
Website: http://www.engr.iupui.edu/departments/ece/.

Indiana University–Purdue University Indianapolis, School of Engineering and Technology, Department of Mechanical Engineering, Indianapolis, IN 46202. Offers biomedical engineering (MS Bm E); computer-aided mechanical engineering (Certificate); mechanical engineering (MSME, PhD). Part-time programs available. *Students:* 57 full-time (4 women), 59 part-time (7 women); includes 7 minority (1 Black or African American, non-Hispanic/Latino; 3 Asian, non-Hispanic/Latino; 2 Hispanic/Latino; 1 Two or more races, non-Hispanic/Latino), 72 international. Average age 28. 177 applicants, 56% accepted, 47 enrolled. In 2014, 29 master's, 1 other advanced degree awarded. *Degree requirements:* For master's, thesis optional. *Entrance requirements:* For master's, GRE. Additional exam requirements/recommendations for international students: Required—TOEFL. *Application deadline:* For fall admission, 7/1 for domestic students. Application fee: $55 ($65 for international students). *Financial support:* Fellowships with tuition reimbursements, research assistantships with full and partial tuition reimbursements, and tuition waivers (full and partial) available. Financial award application deadline: 3/1. *Faculty research:* Computational fluid dynamics, heat transfer, finite-element methods, composites, biomechanics. *Unit head:* Dr. Jie Chen, Chairman, 317-274-9717. *Application contact:* Valerie Diemer, Graduate Program, 317-278-4960, Fax: 317-278-1671, E-mail: grad@engr.iupui.edu.
Website: http://www.engr.iupui.edu/me/.

Johns Hopkins University, Engineering Program for Professionals, Part-time Program in Applied Biomedical Engineering, Baltimore, MD 21218-2699. Offers MS, Post-Master's Certificate. Part-time and evening/weekend programs available. Electronic applications accepted.

Johns Hopkins University, G. W. C. Whiting School of Engineering and School of Medicine, Department of Biomedical Engineering, Baltimore, MD 21205. Offers bioengineering innovation and design (MSE); biomedical engineering (MSE, PhD). Terminal master's awarded for partial completion of doctoral program. *Degree requirements:* For master's, thesis; for doctorate, comprehensive exam, thesis/dissertation. *Entrance requirements:* For master's and doctorate, GRE General Test. Additional exam requirements/recommendations for international students: Required—TOEFL or IELTS. Electronic applications accepted. *Faculty research:* Cell and tissue engineering, systems neuroscience, imaging, cardiovascular systems physiology, theoretical and computational biology.

Louisiana Tech University, Graduate School, College of Engineering and Science, Department of Biomedical Engineering, Ruston, LA 71272. Offers PhD. Part-time programs available. Terminal master's awarded for partial completion of doctoral program. *Degree requirements:* For doctorate, thesis/dissertation. *Entrance requirements:* For doctorate, minimum graduate GPA of 3.25 (with MS) or GRE General Test. Additional exam requirements/recommendations for international students: Required—TOEFL. *Faculty research:* Microbiosensors and microcirculatory transport, speech recognition, artificial intelligence, rehabilitation engineering, bioelectromagnetics.

Marquette University, Graduate School, Opus College of Engineering, Department of Biomedical Engineering, Milwaukee, WI 53201-1881. Offers biocomputing (ME); bioimaging (ME); bioinstrumentation (ME); bioinstrumentation/computers (MS, PhD); biomechanics (ME); biomechanics/biomaterials (MS, PhD); biorehabilitation (ME); functional imaging (PhD); healthcare technologies management (MS); rehabilitation bioengineering (PhD); systems physiology (MS, PhD). Part-time and evening/weekend programs available. Terminal master's awarded for partial completion of doctoral program. *Degree requirements:* For master's, comprehensive exam, thesis; for doctorate, comprehensive exam, thesis/dissertation, dissertation defense, qualifying exam. *Entrance requirements:* For master's, GRE General Test, minimum GPA of 3.0, official transcripts from all current and previous colleges/universities except Marquette, three letters of recommendation, brief statement of purpose that includes proposed area of research specialization, interview with program director (for ME), one year of post-baccalaureate professional work experience; for doctorate, GRE General Test, minimum GPA of 3.0, official transcripts from all current and previous colleges/universities except Marquette, three letters of recommendation, brief statement of purpose that includes proposed area of research specialization. Additional exam requirements/recommendations for international students: Required—TOEFL (minimum score 530 paper-based). Electronic applications accepted. *Faculty research:* Cell and organ physiology, signal processing, gait analysis, orthopedic rehabilitation engineering, telemedicine.

Massachusetts Institute of Technology, School of Engineering, Department of Biological Engineering, Cambridge, MA 02139. Offers applied biosciences (PhD, Sc D); bioengineering (PhD, Sc D); biological engineering (PhD, Sc D); biomedical engineering (M Eng); toxicology (SM); SM/MBA. *Faculty:* 34 full-time (7 women). *Students:* 134 full-time (52 women); includes 50 minority (3 Black or African American, non-Hispanic/Latino; 33 Asian, non-Hispanic/Latino; 8 Hispanic/Latino; 6 Two or more races, non-Hispanic/Latino), 32 international. Average age 26. 483 applicants, 8% accepted, 26 enrolled. In 2014, 2 master's, 18 doctorates awarded. Terminal master's awarded for partial completion of doctoral program. *Degree requirements:* For master's, thesis; for doctorate, comprehensive exam, thesis/dissertation. *Entrance requirements:* For master's and doctorate, GRE General Test. Additional exam requirements/recommendations for international students: Required—IELTS (minimum score 7). *Application deadline:* For fall admission, 12/15 for domestic and international students. Application fee: $75. Electronic applications accepted. *Expenses: Tuition:* Full-time $44,720; part-time $699 per unit. *Required fees:* $296. *Financial support:* In 2014–15, 129 students received support, including 63 fellowships (averaging $41,400 per year), 67 research assistantships (averaging $36,500 per year); teaching assistantships, Federal Work-Study, institutionally sponsored loans, scholarships/grants, traineeships, health care benefits, and unspecified assistantships also available. Financial award application deadline: 4/15; financial award applicants required to submit FAFSA. *Faculty research:* Biomaterials; biophysics; cell and tissue engineering; computational modeling of biological and physiological systems; discovery and delivery of molecular therapeutics; new tools for genomics; functional genomics; proteomics and glycomics; macromolecular biochemistry and biophysics; molecular, cell and tissue biomechanics; synthetic biology; systems biology. *Total annual research expenditures:* $49.1 million. *Unit head:* Prof. Douglas A. Lauffenburger, Department Head, 617-253-1712, E-mail: be-acad@mit.edu. *Application contact:* Graduate Admissions, 617-253-1712, Fax: 617-258-8676, E-mail: be-acad@mit.edu.
Website: http://web.mit.edu/be/.

Massachusetts Institute of Technology, School of Engineering, Harvard-MIT Health Sciences and Technology Program, Cambridge, MA 02139. Offers health sciences and technology (SM, PhD, Sc D), including bioastronautics (PhD, Sc D), bioinformatics and integrative genomics (PhD, Sc D), medical engineering and medical physics (PhD, Sc D), speech and hearing bioscience and technology (PhD, Sc D). *Faculty:* 131 full-time (23 women). *Students:* 231 full-time (87 women), 51 part-time (16 women); includes 80 minority (2 Black or African American, non-Hispanic/Latino; 1 American Indian or Alaska Native, non-Hispanic/Latino; 64 Asian, non-Hispanic/Latino; 9 Hispanic/Latino; 4 Two or more races, non-Hispanic/Latino), 52 international. Average age 26. 213 applicants, 16% accepted, 23 enrolled. In 2014, 2 master's, 19 doctorates awarded. Terminal master's awarded for partial completion of doctoral program. *Degree requirements:* For master's, thesis; for doctorate, comprehensive exam, thesis/dissertation. *Entrance requirements:* For doctorate, GRE General Test (for medical engineering and medical physics). Additional exam requirements/recommendations for international students: Required—TOEFL (minimum score 600 paper-based; 100 iBT), IELTS (minimum score 7). *Application deadline:* For fall admission, 12/15 for domestic and international students. Application fee: $75. Electronic applications accepted. *Expenses: Tuition:* Full-time $44,720; part-time $699 per unit. *Required fees:* $296. *Financial support:* In 2014–15, 127 students received support, including 41 fellowships (averaging $34,000 per year), 65 research assistantships (averaging $34,100 per year), 3 teaching assistantships (averaging $29,400 per year); Federal Work-Study, institutionally sponsored loans, scholarships/grants, traineeships, health care benefits, and unspecified assistantships also available. Financial award application deadline: 4/15; financial award applicants required to submit FAFSA. *Faculty research:* Signal processing, biomedical imaging, drug delivery, medical devices, medical diagnostics, regenerative biomedical technologies. *Unit head:* Emery N. Brown, Director, 617-452-4091. *Application contact:* Emery N. Brown, Director, 617-452-4091.
Website: http://hst.mit.edu/.

Mayo Graduate School, Graduate Programs in Biomedical Sciences, Program in Biomedical Engineering, Rochester, MN 55905. Offers PhD. *Degree requirements:* For doctorate, oral defense of dissertation, qualifying oral and written exam. *Entrance requirements:* For doctorate, GRE, 1 year of chemistry, biology, calculus, and physics. Additional exam requirements/recommendations for international students: Required—TOEFL. Electronic applications accepted.

McGill University, Faculty of Graduate and Postdoctoral Studies, Faculty of Medicine, Department of Biomedical Engineering, Montréal, QC H3A 2T5, Canada. Offers M Eng, PhD.

Mercer University, Graduate Studies, Macon Campus, School of Engineering, Macon, GA 31207. Offers biomedical engineering (MSE); computer engineering (MSE); electrical engineering (MSE); engineering management (MSE); environmental engineering (MSE); environmental systems (MS); mechanical engineering (MSE); software engineering (MSE); software systems (MS); technical communications management (MS); technical management (MS). Part-time and evening/weekend programs available. Postbaccalaureate distance learning degree programs offered (no on-campus study). *Faculty:* 20 full-time (6 women), 2 part-time/adjunct (0 women). *Students:* 10 full-time (4 women), 75 part-time (16 women); includes 10 minority (5 Black or African American, non-Hispanic/Latino; 4 Asian, non-Hispanic/Latino; 1 Hispanic/Latino), 4 international. Average age 42. In 2014, 70 master's awarded. *Degree requirements:* For master's, thesis or alternative. *Entrance requirements:* For master's, minimum undergraduate GPA of 3.0. Additional exam requirements/recommendations for international students: Required—TOEFL (minimum score 550 paper-based; 80 iBT). *Application deadline:* For fall admission, 4/1 priority date for domestic and international students; for spring admission, 11/1 priority date for domestic and international students. Applications are processed on a rolling basis. Application fee: $75. *Expenses:* Expenses: Contact institution. *Financial support:* Federal Work-Study available. *Unit head:* Dr. Wade H. Shaw, Dean, 478-301-2459, Fax: 478-301-5593, E-mail: shaw_wh@mercer.edu. *Application contact:* Dr. Richard O. Mines, Program Director, 478-301-2347, Fax: 478-301-5433, E-mail: mines_ro@mercer.edu.
Website: http://engineering.mercer.edu/.

Michigan Technological University, Graduate School, College of Engineering, Department of Biomedical Engineering, Houghton, MI 49931. Offers MS, PhD. Part-time programs available. *Faculty:* 10 full-time, 3 part-time/adjunct. *Students:* 27 full-time, 3 part-time; includes 1 minority (Black or African American, non-Hispanic/Latino), 16 international. Average age 26. 109 applicants, 55% accepted, 10 enrolled. In 2014, 4 master's, 1 doctorate awarded. *Degree requirements:* For master's, comprehensive exam (for some programs), thesis (for some programs); for doctorate, comprehensive exam, thesis/dissertation. *Entrance requirements:* For master's, GRE (recommended for students with a Michigan Tech degree), statement of purpose, official transcripts, 3 letters of recommendation, resume/curriculum vitae; for doctorate, GRE, statement of purpose, official transcripts, 3 letters of recommendation, resume/curriculum vitae. Additional exam requirements/recommendations for international students: Required—TOEFL (recommended score 100 iBT) or IELTS. *Application deadline:* Applications are processed on a rolling basis. Electronic applications accepted. *Expenses:* Expenses: Contact institution. *Financial support:* In 2014–15, 22 students received support, including 1 fellowship with full and partial tuition reimbursement available (averaging $13,824 per year), 8 research assistantships with full and partial tuition reimbursements available (averaging $13,824 per year), 3 teaching assistantships with full and partial tuition reimbursements available (averaging $13,824 per year); career-related internships or fieldwork, Federal Work-Study, scholarships/grants, health care benefits, unspecified assistantships, and cooperative program also available. Financial award applicants required to submit FAFSA. *Faculty research:* Biomaterials/tissue engineering, physiology measurement and biosensors, biomechanics, mechanotransduction, biomedical optics. *Total annual research expenditures:* $651,214. *Unit head:* Dr. Sean J. Kirkpatrick, Chair, 906-487-2167, Fax: 906-487-1717, E-mail: sjkirkpa@mtu.edu. *Application contact:* Stacey L. Sedar, Department Coordinator, 906-487-2772, Fax: 906-487-1717, E-mail: slsedar@mtu.edu.
Website: http://www.mtu.edu/biomedical/.

New Jersey Institute of Technology, Newark College of Engineering, Newark, NJ 07102. Offers biomedical engineering (MS, PhD); chemical engineering (MS, PhD); computer engineering (MS, PhD); electrical engineering (MS, PhD); engineering management (MS); healthcare systems management (MS); industrial engineering (MS, PhD); Internet engineering (MS); manufacturing engineering (MS); mechanical engineering (MS, PhD); occupational safety and health engineering (MS); pharmaceutical bioprocessing (MS); pharmaceutical engineering (MS); pharmaceutical systems management (MS); power and energy systems (MS); telecommunications (MS); transportation (MS, PhD). Part-time and evening/weekend programs available. Terminal master's awarded for partial completion of doctoral program. *Degree requirements:* For master's, thesis optional; for doctorate, thesis/dissertation. *Entrance requirements:* For master's, GRE General Test; for doctorate, GRE General Test, minimum graduate GPA of 3.5. Additional exam requirements/recommendations for international students: Required—TOEFL (minimum score 550 paper-based; 79 iBT). Electronic applications accepted.

New York University, Polytechnic School of Engineering, Department of Chemical and Biomolecular Engineering, Major in Biomedical Engineering, New York, NY 10012-1019. Offers MS, PhD. *Students:* 36 full-time (16 women), 11 part-time (6 women); includes 12 minority (7 Asian, non-Hispanic/Latino; 4 Hispanic/Latino; 1 Two or more races, non-Hispanic/Latino), 18 international. Average age 25. 222 applicants, 33% accepted, 22 enrolled. In 2014, 13 master's, 2 doctorates awarded. *Degree requirements:* For master's, comprehensive exam (for some programs), thesis (for some programs); for doctorate, comprehensive exam, thesis/dissertation. *Entrance requirements:* Additional exam requirements/recommendations for international students: Required—TOEFL (minimum score 550 paper-based; 80 iBT); Recommended—IELTS (minimum score 6.5). *Application deadline:* For fall admission, 2/15 priority date for domestic and international students; for spring admission, 11/1 priority date for domestic and international students. Applications are processed on a rolling basis. Application fee: $75. Electronic applications accepted. *Unit head:* Dr. Gene R. DiResta, Academic Director, 718-260-3269, E-mail: grdiresta@nyu.edu. *Application contact:* Raymond Lutzky, Director, Graduate Enrollment Management, 718-637-5984, Fax: 718-260-3624, E-mail: rlutzky@poly.edu.

North Carolina State University, Graduate School, College of Engineering, Joint Department of Biomedical Engineering UNC-Chapel Hill and NC State, Raleigh, NC 27695. Offers MS, PhD. Programs offered jointly with the University of North Carolina at Chapel Hill. Terminal master's awarded for partial completion of doctoral program. *Degree requirements:* For master's, comprehensive exam, thesis, research laboratory experience; for doctorate, one foreign language, comprehensive exam, thesis/dissertation, written and oral examinations, dissertation defense, teaching experience, research laboratory experience. *Entrance requirements:* For master's and doctorate, GRE General Test. Additional exam requirements/recommendations for international students: Required—TOEFL. Electronic applications accepted.

Northwestern University, McCormick School of Engineering and Applied Science, Department of Biomedical Engineering, Evanston, IL 60208. Offers MS, PhD. Admissions and degrees offered through The Graduate School. Part-time programs available. *Faculty:* 21 full-time (2 women). *Students:* 126 full-time (48 women), 14 part-time (6 women); includes 36 minority (8 Black or African American, non-Hispanic/Latino; 20 Asian, non-Hispanic/Latino; 6 Hispanic/Latino; 2 Two or more races, non-Hispanic/Latino), 38 international. Average age 26. 427 applicants, 22% accepted, 36 enrolled. In 2014, 33 master's, 16 doctorates awarded. Terminal master's awarded for partial completion of doctoral program. *Degree requirements:* For master's, comprehensive exam, thesis (for some programs); for doctorate, comprehensive exam, thesis/dissertation. *Entrance requirements:* For master's and doctorate, GRE General Test. Additional exam requirements/recommendations for international students: Required—TOEFL (minimum score 577 paper-based; 90 iBT), IELTS (minimum score 7). *Application deadline:* For fall admission, 12/31 for domestic and international students; for winter admission, 11/15 for domestic students, 11/1 for international students; for spring admission, 2/15 for domestic students, 2/1 for international students. Application fee: $95. Electronic applications accepted. *Financial support:* Fellowships with full tuition reimbursements, research assistantships with full tuition reimbursements,

teaching assistantships with full tuition reimbursements, career-related internships or fieldwork, institutionally sponsored loans, traineeships, health care benefits, and unspecified assistantships available. Support available to part-time students. Financial award application deadline: 1/15; financial award applicants required to submit FAFSA. *Faculty research:* Neural engineering and rehabilitation; cardiovascular engineering; materials, cells, and tissues; imaging and biophotonics; vision research. *Total annual research expenditures:* $32.3 million. *Unit head:* Dr. John B. Troy, Chair, 847-491-3822, Fax: 847-491-4928, E-mail: j-troy@northwestern.edu. *Application contact:* Dr. Matthew Tresch, Director of Graduate Admissions, 312-503-1373, Fax: 847-491-4928, E-mail: m-tresch@northwestern.edu.
Website: http://www.bme.northwestern.edu/.

The Ohio State University, Graduate School, College of Engineering, Department of Biomedical Engineering, Columbus, OH 43210. Offers MS, PhD. Evening/weekend programs available. *Faculty:* 19. *Students:* 76 full-time (23 women), 4 part-time (1 woman); includes 20 minority (5 Black or African American, non-Hispanic/Latino; 10 Asian, non-Hispanic/Latino; 4 Hispanic/Latino; 1 Two or more races, non-Hispanic/Latino), 19 international. Average age 26. In 2014, 16 master's, 5 doctorates awarded. *Degree requirements:* For master's, thesis optional; for doctorate, thesis/dissertation. *Entrance requirements:* For master's and doctorate, GRE General Test. Additional exam requirements/recommendations for international students: Required—TOEFL (minimum score 550 paper-based; 79 iBT), Michigan English Language Assessment Battery (minimum score 82); Recommended—IELTS (minimum score 7). *Application deadline:* For fall admission, 12/13 priority date for domestic students, 11/29 priority date for international students; for winter admission, 12/1 for domestic students, 11/1 for international students; for spring admission, 11/1 for domestic and international students. Applications are processed on a rolling basis. Application fee: $60 ($70 for international students). Electronic applications accepted. *Financial support:* Fellowships with tuition reimbursements, research assistantships with tuition reimbursements, career-related internships or fieldwork, Federal Work-Study, and institutionally sponsored loans available. Support available to part-time students. *Unit head:* Dr. Richard T. Hart, Chair, 614-292-1285, E-mail: hart.322@osu.edu. *Application contact:* Graduate and Professional Admissions, 614-292-9444, Fax: 614-292-3895, E-mail: gpadmissions@osu.edu.
Website: http://bme.osu.edu.

Ohio University, Graduate College, Russ College of Engineering and Technology, Department of Chemical and Biomolecular Engineering, Program in Biomedical Engineering, Athens, OH 45701-2979. Offers MS. Part-time programs available. *Degree requirements:* For master's, thesis. *Entrance requirements:* For master's, GRE General Test. Additional exam requirements/recommendations for international students: Required—TOEFL (minimum score 590 paper-based; 96 iBT), IELTS (minimum score 7). Electronic applications accepted. *Faculty research:* Molecular mechanisms of human disease, molecular therapeutics, biomedical information analysis and management, image analysis, biomechanics.

Ohio University, Graduate College, Russ College of Engineering and Technology, Department of Mechanical Engineering, Athens, OH 45701-2979. Offers biomedical engineering (MS); mechanical engineering (MS), including CAD/CAM, design, energy, manufacturing, materials, robotics, thermofluids. Part-time programs available. *Degree requirements:* For master's, comprehensive exam (for some programs), thesis. *Entrance requirements:* For master's, GRE, BS in engineering or science, minimum GPA of 2.8. Additional exam requirements/recommendations for international students: Required—TOEFL (minimum score 550 paper-based; 80 iBT) or IELTS (minimum score 6.5). Electronic applications accepted. *Faculty research:* Biomedical, energy and the environment, materials and manufacturing, bioengineering.

Old Dominion University, Frank Batten College of Engineering and Technology, Program in Biomedical Engineering, Norfolk, VA 23529. Offers PhD. Part-time and evening/weekend programs available. *Faculty:* 3 full-time (0 women). *Students:* 6 full-time (3 women), 5 part-time (1 woman); includes 1 minority (Two or more races, non-Hispanic/Latino), 4 international. Average age 28. 4 applicants, 50% accepted, 2 enrolled. *Degree requirements:* For doctorate, thesis/dissertation, candidacy exam. *Entrance requirements:* For doctorate, GRE, master's degree, minimum graduate GPA of 3.5, three letters of recommendation, statement of purpose. Additional exam requirements/recommendations for international students: Required—TOEFL (minimum score 550 paper-based). *Application deadline:* For fall admission, 6/1 for domestic students, 2/15 priority date for international students; for spring admission, 11/1 for domestic students, 10/1 for international students. Applications are processed on a rolling basis. Application fee: $50. Electronic applications accepted. *Expenses:* Tuition, state resident: full-time $10,488; part-time $437 per credit. Tuition, nonresident: full-time $26,136; part-time $1089 per credit. *Required fees:* $64 per semester. One-time fee: $50. *Financial support:* In 2014–15, 2 students received support. Applicants required to submit FAFSA. *Faculty research:* Brain-computer interface, cardiac electrophysiology, medical devices. *Unit head:* Dr. Dean Krusienski, Director, 757-683-3752, Fax: 757-683-3220, E-mail: dkrusien@odu.edu. *Application contact:* Dr. Linda Vahala, Associate Dean, 757-683-3789, Fax: 757-683-4898, E-mail: lvahala@odu.edu.
Website: http://www.eng.odu.edu/bme/academics/PhD.shtml.

Oregon Health & Science University, School of Medicine, Graduate Programs in Medicine, Department of Biomedical Engineering, Portland, OR 97239-3098. Offers MS, PhD. Part-time programs available. *Faculty:* 28 full-time (13 women), 5 part-time/adjunct (0 women). *Students:* 26 full-time (14 women); includes 6 minority (4 Asian, non-Hispanic/Latino; 1 Hispanic/Latino; 1 Two or more races, non-Hispanic/Latino), 6 international. Average age 28. 32 applicants, 25% accepted, 8 enrolled. In 2014, 4 doctorates awarded. Terminal master's awarded for partial completion of doctoral program. *Degree requirements:* For master's, thesis optional, does not admit Master Students; for doctorate, comprehensive exam, thesis/dissertation, qualifying exam. *Entrance requirements:* For doctorate, GRE General Test (minimum scores: 153 Verbal/148 Quantitative/4.5 Analytical). Additional exam requirements/recommendations for international students: Required—IELTS or TOEFL. *Application deadline:* For fall admission, 1/15 for domestic students, 1/15 priority date for international students; for winter admission, 10/15 for domestic students, 9/15 for international students; for spring admission, 1/15 for domestic students, 12/15 for international students. Applications are processed on a rolling basis. Application fee: $70. Electronic applications accepted. *Financial support:* Health care benefits, tuition waivers, and full tuition and stipends (for PhD students) available. *Faculty research:* Blood cells in cancer and cancer biology, smart homes and machine learning, computational mechanics and multiscale modeling, tissue optics and biophotonics, nanomedicine and nanobiotechnology. *Unit head:* Dr. Peter Heeman, Program Director, 503-418-9316, E-mail: info@bme.ogi.edu. *Application contact:* Janet Itami, Administrative Coordinator, 503-418-9304, E-mail: itamij@ohsu.edu.

Purdue University, College of Engineering, Weldon School of Biomedical Engineering, West Lafayette, IN 47907-2032. Offers MSBME, PhD, MD/PhD. Degree programs offered jointly with School of Mechanical Engineering, School of Electrical and Computer Engineering, and School of Chemical Engineering. *Entrance requirements:* For master's and doctorate, GRE General Test, minimum GPA of 3.25. Additional exam requirements/recommendations for international students: Required—TOEFL (minimum score 550 paper-based; 77 iBT); Recommended—TWE. Electronic applications accepted. *Faculty research:* Biomaterials, biomechanics, medical image and signal processing, medical instrumentation, tissue engineering.

Rensselaer Polytechnic Institute, Graduate School, School of Engineering, Program in Biomedical Engineering, Troy, NY 12180-3590. Offers MS, D Eng, PhD. *Faculty:* 29 full-time (9 women), 3 part-time/adjunct (0 women). *Students:* 53 full-time (17 women), 5 part-time (2 women); includes 10 minority (1 Black or African American, non-Hispanic/Latino; 7 Asian, non-Hispanic/Latino; 2 Hispanic/Latino), 13 international. Average age 26. 170 applicants, 29% accepted, 17 enrolled. In 2014, 14 master's, 6 doctorates awarded. Terminal master's awarded for partial completion of doctoral program. *Degree requirements:* For master's, thesis optional; for doctorate, thesis/dissertation. *Entrance requirements:* For master's and doctorate, GRE. Additional exam requirements/recommendations for international students: Required—TOEFL (minimum score 570 paper-based; 88 iBT), IELTS (minimum score 6.5), PTE (minimum score 60). *Application deadline:* For fall admission, 1/1 priority date for domestic and international students; for spring admission, 8/15 priority date for domestic and international students. Applications are processed on a rolling basis. Electronic applications accepted. *Expenses: Tuition:* Full-time $46,700; part-time $1945 per credit. Tuition and fees vary according to course load. *Financial support:* In 2014–15, 45 students received support, including research assistantships with full tuition reimbursements available (averaging $18,500 per year), teaching assistantships with full tuition reimbursements available (averaging $18,500 per year); fellowships also available. Financial award application deadline: 2/1. *Faculty research:* Biomolecular science and engineering, biomedical imaging, musculoskeletal engineering, neural engineering, systems biology and biocomputation, vascular engineering. *Total annual research expenditures:* $2.4 million. *Unit head:* Dr. Ryan Gilbert, Graduate Program Director, 518-276-2032, E-mail: gilber2@rpi.edu. *Application contact:* Office of Graduate Admissions, 518-276-6216, E-mail: gradadmissions@rpi.edu.
Website: http://www.bme.rpi.edu/.

Rice University, Graduate Programs, George R. Brown School of Engineering, Department of Chemical and Biomolecular Engineering, Houston, TX 77251-1892. Offers chemical and biomolecular engineering (MS, PhD); chemical engineering (M Ch E). Part-time programs available. *Degree requirements:* For master's, thesis (for some programs); for doctorate, thesis/dissertation. *Entrance requirements:* For master's and doctorate, GRE General Test, minimum GPA of 3.0. Additional exam requirements/recommendations for international students: Required—TOEFL (minimum score 600 paper-based; 90 iBT). Electronic applications accepted. *Faculty research:* Thermodynamics, phase equilibria, rheology, fluid mechanics, polymers, biomedical engineering, interfacial phenomena, process control, petroleum engineering, reaction engineering and catalysis, biomaterials, metabolic engineering.

Rose-Hulman Institute of Technology, Faculty of Engineering and Applied Sciences, Department of Biology and Biomedical Engineering, Terre Haute, IN 47803-3999. Offers MS, MD/MS. Part-time programs available. *Faculty:* 13 full-time (6 women). *Students:* 3 full-time (2 women). Average age 23. 7 applicants, 71% accepted, 1 enrolled. In 2014, 1 master's awarded. *Degree requirements:* For master's, thesis. *Entrance requirements:* For master's, GRE, minimum GPA of 3.0. Additional exam requirements/recommendations for international students: Required—TOEFL (minimum score 580 paper-based; 92 iBT). *Application deadline:* For fall admission, 2/1 priority date for domestic students. Applications are processed on a rolling basis. Application fee: $0. *Expenses: Tuition:* Full-time $40,449. *Financial support:* In 2014–15, 2 students received support. Fellowships with full and partial tuition reimbursements available, research assistantships with full and partial tuition reimbursements available, institutionally sponsored loans, scholarships/grants, and tuition waivers (full and partial) available. *Faculty research:* Biomedical instrumentation, biomechanics, biomedical fluid mechanics, biomedical materials, quantitative physiology, soft tissue biomechanics, tissue-biomaterial interaction, biomaterials, biomedical instrumentation, biomedical fluid mechanics. *Total annual research expenditures:* $105,185. *Unit head:* Dr. Jameel Ahmed, Chairman, 812-872-6033, Fax: 812-877-8545, E-mail: jameel.ahmed@rose-hulman.edu. *Application contact:* Dr. Azad Siahmakoun, Associate Dean of the Faculty, 812-877-8400, Fax: 812-877-8061, E-mail: siahmako@rose-hulman.edu.
Website: http://www.rose-hulman.edu/abbe/.

Rutgers, The State University of New Jersey, Newark, Graduate School of Biomedical Sciences, Department of Biomedical Engineering, Newark, NJ 07107. Offers Certificate. *Entrance requirements:* Additional exam requirements/recommendations for international students: Required—TOEFL. Electronic applications accepted.

Rutgers, The State University of New Jersey, New Brunswick, Graduate School of Biomedical Sciences, Program in Biomedical Engineering, Piscataway, NJ 08854-5635. Offers MS, PhD, MD/PhD. MS, PhD offered jointly with Rutgers, The State University of New Jersey, New Brunswick. *Degree requirements:* For master's, thesis, qualifying exam; for doctorate, thesis/dissertation, qualifying exam. *Entrance requirements:* For master's and doctorate, GRE General Test. Additional exam requirements/recommendations for international students: Required—TOEFL. Electronic applications accepted.

St. Cloud State University, School of Graduate Studies, College of Science and Engineering, Program in Regulatory Affairs and Services, St. Cloud, MN 56301-4498. Offers MS. Part-time programs available. *Degree requirements:* For master's, final paper. *Entrance requirements:* For master's, GRE General Test, minimum GPA of 2.75. Additional exam requirements/recommendations for international students: Required—TOEFL (minimum score 550 paper-based; 79 iBT), IELTS (minimum score 6.5). *Expenses:* Contact institution.

Saint Louis University, Graduate Education, Parks College of Engineering, Aviation, and Technology and Graduate Education, Department of Biomedical Engineering, St. Louis, MO 63103-2097. Offers MS, MS-R, PhD. *Degree requirements:* For master's, thesis optional; for doctorate, thesis/dissertation. *Entrance requirements:* For master's, GRE General Test, letters of recommendation, resume, interview; for doctorate, GRE General Test, letters of recommendation, resumé, interview, transcripts, goal statement. Additional exam requirements/recommendations for international students: Required—TOEFL (minimum score 525 paper-based). *Faculty research:* Tissue engineering and biomaterialsneural cardiovascular and orthopedic tissue engineering; tissue engineeringairway remodeling, vasculopathy, and elastic, biodegradable scaffolds; biomechanicsorthopedics, trauma biomechanics and biomechanical modeling; biosignalselectrophysiology, signal processing, and biomechanical instrumentation.

South Dakota School of Mines and Technology, Graduate Division, Program in Biomedical Engineering, Rapid City, SD 57701-3995. Offers MS, PhD. Part-time programs available. *Faculty:* 10 full-time (2 women), 2 part-time/adjunct (1 woman). *Students:* 11 full-time (7 women), 1 part-time (0 women), 8 international. Average age 27. 19 applicants, 42% accepted, 6 enrolled. In 2014, 8 master's, 1 doctorate awarded. *Degree requirements:* For master's, thesis (for some programs); for doctorate, thesis/dissertation. *Entrance requirements:* For doctorate, GRE General Test, 3 letters of recommendation, minimum GPA of 3.0. Additional exam requirements/recommendations for international students: Required—TOEFL (minimum score 520 paper-based; 68 iBT). *Application deadline:* For fall admission, 7/1 for domestic students, 4/1 for international students; for spring admission, 11/1 for domestic students, 9/1 for international students. Applications are processed on a rolling basis. Application fee: $35. Electronic applications accepted. *Expenses:* Tuition, state resident: full-time $5050; part-time $210.40 per credit hour. Tuition, nonresident: full-time $11,290; part-time $470.30 per credit hour. *Required fees:* $4680. *Financial support:* In 2014–15, 14 research assistantships with partial tuition reimbursements (averaging $12,821 per year) were awarded; fellowships also available. Financial award application deadline: 5/15. *Unit head:* Dr. Richard R. Sinden, Professor, 605-394-2256, E-mail: richard.sinden@sdsmt.edu. *Application contact:* Rachel Howard, Office of Graduate Education, 605-355-3468, Fax: 605-394-1767, E-mail: rachel.howard@sdsmt.edu.

Southern Illinois University Carbondale, Graduate School, College of Engineering, Program in Biomedical Engineering, Carbondale, IL 62901-4701. Offers ME, MS. *Students:* 16 full-time (9 women), 1 part-time (0 women), 15 international. Average age 29. 43 applicants, 63% accepted, 7 enrolled. In 2014, 7 master's awarded. *Entrance requirements:* Additional exam requirements/recommendations for international students: Required—TOEFL. Application fee: $50. *Expenses:* Tuition, state resident: full-time $10,176; part-time $1153 per credit. Tuition, nonresident: full-time $20,814; part-time $1744 per credit. *Required fees:* $7092; $394 per credit. $2364 per semester. *Unit head:* Dr. John J. Warwick, Interim Dean, 618-453-4321, E-mail: warwick@siu.edu. *Application contact:* Jennifer Langin, Student Contact, 618-453-4321, Fax: 618-453-4235, E-mail: jlangin@siu.edu.

Stanford University, School of Engineering, Department of Mechanical Engineering, Program in Biomechanical Engineering, Stanford, CA 94305-9991. Offers MS. *Entrance requirements:* For master's, GRE General Test, undergraduate degree in engineering, math or sciences. Additional exam requirements/recommendations for international students: Required—TOEFL. *Expenses: Tuition:* Full-time $44,184; part-time $982 per credit hour. *Required fees:* $191.

State University of New York Downstate Medical Center, School of Graduate Studies, Program in Biomedical Engineering, Brooklyn, NY 11203-2098. Offers bioimaging and neuroengineering (PhD); biomedical engineering (MS); MD/PhD. *Degree requirements:* For doctorate, comprehensive exam, thesis/dissertation.

Stevens Institute of Technology, Graduate School, Charles V. Schaefer Jr. School of Engineering, Department of Chemistry, Chemical Biology and Biomedical Engineering, Program in Biomedical Engineering, Hoboken, NJ 07030. Offers M Eng, Certificate.

Stony Brook University, State University of New York, Graduate School, College of Engineering and Applied Sciences, Department of Biomedical Engineering, Stony Brook, NY 11794. Offers biomedical engineering (MS, PhD, Certificate); medical physics (MS, PhD). *Faculty:* 11 full-time (3 women). *Students:* 83 full-time (35 women), 2 part-time (0 women); includes 22 minority (1 Black or African American, non-Hispanic/Latino; 16 Asian, non-Hispanic/Latino; 4 Hispanic/Latino; 1 Two or more races, non-Hispanic/Latino), 31 international. Average age 26. 195 applicants, 25% accepted, 24 enrolled. In 2014, 9 master's, 4 doctorates awarded. *Degree requirements:* For doctorate, thesis/dissertation, qualifying exams. *Entrance requirements:* For master's and doctorate, GRE General Test. Additional exam requirements/recommendations for international students: Required—TOEFL. *Application deadline:* For fall admission, 1/15 for domestic students; for spring admission, 10/1 for domestic students. Application fee: $100. *Expenses:* Tuition, state resident: full-time $10,370; part-time $432 per credit. Tuition, nonresident: full-time $20,190; part-time $841 per credit. *Required fees:* $1431. *Financial support:* In 2014–15, 6 fellowships, 33 research assistantships, 10 teaching assistantships were awarded. *Total annual research expenditures:* $8.1 million. *Unit head:* Dr. Clinton Rubin, Chair, 631-632-1188, Fax: 631-632-8577, E-mail: clinton.rubin@stonybrook.edu. *Application contact:* Jessica Anne Kuhn, Coordinator, 631-632-8371, Fax: 631- 632-8577, E-mail: Jessica.Kuhn@stonybrook.edu. Website: http://www.bme.sunysb.edu/bme/.

Tennessee State University, The School of Graduate Studies and Research, College of Engineering, Nashville, TN 37209-1561. Offers biomedical engineering (ME); civil engineering (ME); computer and information systems engineering (MS, PhD); electrical engineering (ME); environmental engineering (ME); manufacturing engineering (ME); mathematical sciences (MS); mechanical engineering (ME). Part-time and evening/weekend programs available. *Degree requirements:* For master's, project; for doctorate, comprehensive exam, thesis/dissertation. *Entrance requirements:* For doctorate, minimum GPA of 3.3. *Faculty research:* Robotics, intelligent systems, human-computer interaction software systems, biomedical engineering, signal/image processing, probabilistic design, intelligent manufacturing, cooperative mobile robots, condition based maintenance, sensor fusion.

Texas A&M University, College of Engineering, Department of Biomedical Engineering, College Station, TX 77843-3120. Offers M Eng, MS, D Eng, PhD. Part-time programs available. *Faculty:* 20. *Students:* 106 full-time (33 women), 9 part-time (3 women); includes 32 minority (3 Black or African American, non-Hispanic/Latino; 9 Asian, non-Hispanic/Latino; 19 Hispanic/Latino; 1 Two or more races, non-Hispanic/Latino), 30 international. Average age 26. 250 applicants, 26% accepted, 27 enrolled. In 2014, 11 master's, 16 doctorates awarded. *Degree requirements:* For master's, thesis (for MS); for doctorate, dissertation (for PhD). *Entrance requirements:* For master's and doctorate, GRE General Test, leveling courses if non-engineering undergraduate major. Additional exam requirements/recommendations for international students: Required—TOEFL. *Application deadline:* For fall admission, 5/1 for domestic students, 3/1 for international students; for spring admission, 11/1 for domestic students, 7/1 for international students. Applications are processed on a rolling basis. Application fee: $50 ($90 for international students). Electronic applications accepted. *Expenses:* Tuition, state resident: full-time $4078; part-time $226.55 per credit hour. Tuition, nonresident: full-time $10,594; part-time $577.55 per credit hour. *Required fees:* $2813; $237.70 per credit hour. $278.50 per semester. Tuition and fees vary according to degree level and student level. *Financial support:* In 2014–15, 107 students received support, including 25 fellowships with full and partial tuition reimbursements available (averaging $20,854 per year), 58 research assistantships with full and partial tuition reimbursements available (averaging $6,844 per year), 23 teaching assistantships with full and partial tuition reimbursements available (averaging $5,524 per year); career-related internships or fieldwork, institutionally sponsored loans, scholarships/grants, traineeships, health care benefits, tuition waivers (full and partial), and unspecified assistantships also available. Support available to part-time students. Financial award application deadline: 12/20; financial award applicants required to submit FAFSA. *Faculty research:* Medical devices, cardiovascular biomechanics, biomedical optics and sensing, imaging, tissue engineering, biomaterials. *Unit head:* Dr. Gerard L. Cote, Department Head, 979-845-4196, Fax: 979-845-4450, E-mail: gcote@tamu.edu. *Application contact:* Dr. John C. Criscione, Assistant Dean for Graduate Programs, 979-845-5428, Fax: 979-845-4450, E-mail: jccriscione@tamu.edu. Website: http://engineering.tamu.edu/biomedical.

Thomas Jefferson University, Jefferson Graduate School of Biomedical Sciences, PhD Program in Tissue Engineering and Regenerative Medicine, Philadelphia, PA 19107. Offers PhD. *Degree requirements:* For doctorate, comprehensive exam, thesis/dissertation. *Entrance requirements:* For doctorate, GRE General Test, minimum GPA of 3.2. Additional exam requirements/recommendations for international students:

Required—TOEFL (minimum score 100 iBT) or IELTS. Electronic applications accepted. *Faculty research:* Skeletal development, biomaterials, bone implant interaction, tissue engineering, high resolution imaging.

Tufts University, School of Engineering, Department of Biomedical Engineering, Medford, MA 02155. Offers bioengineering (ME, MS), including biomaterials; biomedical engineering (PhD). Part-time programs available. *Faculty:* 10 full-time (2 women), 5 part-time/adjunct (2 women). *Students:* 51 full-time (25 women), 13 part-time (3 women); includes 12 minority (1 Black or African American, non-Hispanic/Latino; 7 Asian, non-Hispanic/Latino; 2 Hispanic/Latino; 2 Two or more races, non-Hispanic/Latino), 19 international. Average age 26. 226 applicants, 18% accepted, 11 enrolled. In 2014, 12 master's, 9 doctorates awarded. Terminal master's awarded for partial completion of doctoral program. *Degree requirements:* For master's, thesis (for some programs); for doctorate, thesis/dissertation. *Entrance requirements:* For master's and doctorate, GRE General Test. Additional exam requirements/recommendations for international students: Required—TOEFL (minimum score 550 paper-based; 80 iBT), IELTS (minimum score 6.5). *Application deadline:* For fall admission, 1/15 priority date for domestic students, 1/15 for international students; for spring admission, 9/15 for domestic and international students. Applications are processed on a rolling basis. Application fee: $75. Electronic applications accepted. *Expenses: Tuition:* Full-time $45,590; part-time $1161 per credit hour. *Required fees:* $782. Full-time tuition and fees vary according to degree level, program and student level. Part-time tuition and fees vary according to course load. *Financial support:* Fellowships with full tuition reimbursements, research assistantships with full and partial tuition reimbursements, teaching assistantships with full and partial tuition reimbursements, Federal Work-Study, scholarships/grants, tuition waivers (partial), and unspecified assistantships available. Financial award application deadline: 1/15; financial award applicants required to submit FAFSA. *Faculty research:* Regenerative medicine with biomaterials and tissue engineering, diffuse optical imaging and spectroscopy, optics in the development of biomedical devices, ultrafast nonlinear optics and biophotonics, optical diagnostics for diseased and engineered tissues. *Unit head:* Dr. Irene Georgakoudi, Graduate Program Director. *Application contact:* Office of Graduate Admissions, 617-627-3395, E-mail: gradadmissions@tufts.edu. Website: http://engineering.tufts.edu/bme.

Tulane University, School of Science and Engineering, Department of Biomedical Engineering, New Orleans, LA 70118-5669. Offers MS, PhD. MS and PhD offered through the Graduate School. Part-time programs available. Terminal master's awarded for partial completion of doctoral program. *Degree requirements:* For master's, thesis (for some programs); for doctorate, thesis/dissertation. *Entrance requirements:* For master's and doctorate, GRE General Test, minimum B average in undergraduate course work. Additional exam requirements/recommendations for international students: Required—TOEFL. Electronic applications accepted. *Expenses: Tuition:* Full-time $46,326; part-time $2574 per credit hour. *Required fees:* $1980; $44.50 per credit hour. $550 per term. Tuition and fees vary according to course load and program. *Faculty research:* Pulmonary and biofluid mechanics and biomechanics of bone, biomaterials science, finite element analysis, electric fields of the brain.

Université de Montréal, Faculty of Medicine, Institute of Biomedical Engineering, Montréal, QC H3C 3J7, Canada. Offers M Sc A, PhD, DESS. M Sc A and PhD programs offered jointly with École Polytechnique de Montréal. *Degree requirements:* For master's, thesis; for doctorate, thesis/dissertation, general exam. *Entrance requirements:* For master's and doctorate, proficiency in French, knowledge of English. Electronic applications accepted. *Faculty research:* Electrophysiology, biomechanics, instrumentation, imaging, simulation.

University at Buffalo, the State University of New York, Graduate School, School of Engineering and Applied Sciences, Department of Biomedical Engineering, Buffalo, NY 14260. Offers MS, PhD. Part-time programs available. *Faculty:* 8 full-time (2 women), 2 part-time/adjunct (0 women). *Students:* 53 full-time (24 women), 1 (woman) part-time; includes 4 minority (1 Black or African American, non-Hispanic/Latino; 3 Asian, non-Hispanic/Latino), 33 international. Average age 24. 172 applicants, 40% accepted, 23 enrolled. In 2014, 1 master's awarded. *Degree requirements:* For master's, thesis (for some programs); for doctorate, comprehensive exam, thesis/dissertation. *Entrance requirements:* For master's and doctorate, GRE General Test. Additional exam requirements/recommendations for international students: Required—TOEFL (minimum score 550 paper-based; 79 iBT). *Application deadline:* For fall admission, 2/1 priority date for domestic and international students; for spring admission, 10/1 priority date for domestic and international students. Applications are processed on a rolling basis. Application fee: $75. Electronic applications accepted. *Financial support:* In 2014–15, 19 students received support, including 4 fellowships with full and partial tuition reimbursements available (averaging $26,330 per year), 6 research assistantships with full and partial tuition reimbursements available (averaging $20,750 per year), 7 teaching assistantships with full and partial tuition reimbursements available (averaging $23,315 per year); institutionally sponsored loans, scholarships/grants, health care benefits, tuition waivers (partial), and unspecified assistantships also available. Support available to part-time students. Financial award application deadline: 2/28; financial award applicants required to submit FAFSA. *Total annual research expenditures:* $822,000. *Unit head:* Dr. Albert H. Titus, Chair, 716-645-1019, Fax: 716-645-3656, E-mail: ahtitus@buffalo.edu. *Application contact:* Dr. Debanjan Sarkar, Director of Graduate Studies, 716-645-8497, Fax: 716-645-3656, E-mail: debanjan@buffalo.edu. Website: http://www.bme.buffalo.edu/.

The University of Akron, Graduate School, College of Engineering, Department of Biomedical Engineering, Akron, OH 44325. Offers biomedical engineering (MS); engineering (PhD). Part-time and evening/weekend programs available. *Faculty:* 12 full-time (4 women). *Students:* 24 full-time (11 women), 2 part-time (1 woman); includes 1 minority (Asian, non-Hispanic/Latino), 9 international. Average age 28. 31 applicants, 58% accepted, 5 enrolled. In 2014, 8 master's, 2 doctorates awarded. *Degree requirements:* For master's, thesis; for doctorate, one foreign language, thesis/dissertation, candidacy exam, qualifying exam. *Entrance requirements:* For master's, GRE, minimum GPA of 2.75, three letters of recommendation, statement of purpose, resume; for doctorate, GRE, minimum GPA of 3.0 with bachelor's degree, 3.5 with master's degree; three letters of recommendation; personal statement, resume. Additional exam requirements/recommendations for international students: Required—TOEFL (minimum score 590 paper-based; 96 iBT). *Application deadline:* For fall admission, 2/1 priority date for domestic and international students; for spring admission, 9/1 priority date for domestic and international students. Applications are processed on a rolling basis. Application fee: $45 ($70 for international students). Electronic applications accepted. *Expenses:* Tuition, state resident: full-time $7578; part-time $421 per credit hour. Tuition, nonresident: full-time $12,977; part-time $721 per credit hour. *Required fees:* $1388; $35 per credit hour. Tuition and fees vary according to course load. *Financial support:* In 2014–15, 1 fellowship with full tuition reimbursement, 9 research assistantships with full tuition reimbursements, 11 teaching assistantships with full tuition reimbursements were awarded. *Faculty research:* Signal and image processing, physiological controls and instrumentation, biomechanics - orthopedic and hemodynamic, biomaterials for gene and drug delivery systems, telemedicine. *Total annual research expenditures:* $1 million. *Unit head:* Dr. Brian Davis,

Biomedical Engineering

Chair, 330-972-6977, E-mail: bdavis3@uakron.edu. *Application contact:* Dr. Rebecca Willits, Program Contact, 330-972-6587, E-mail: willits@uakron.edu. Website: http://www.uakron.edu/engineering/BME/.

The University of Alabama at Birmingham, School of Engineering, Program in Biomedical Engineering, Birmingham, AL 35294. Offers MSBME, PhD. *Students:* 32 full-time (10 women), 13 part-time (3 women); includes 8 minority (2 Black or African American, non-Hispanic/Latino; 2 Asian, non-Hispanic/Latino; 1 Hispanic/Latino; 3 Two or more races, non-Hispanic/Latino), 12 international. Average age 25. In 2014, 8 master's, 6 doctorates awarded. *Degree requirements:* For master's, thesis or alternative; for doctorate, comprehensive exam, thesis/dissertation. *Entrance requirements:* For master's and doctorate, GRE General Test. Additional exam requirements/recommendations for international students: Required—TOEFL (minimum score 90 iBT), IELTS (minimum score 6.5). *Application deadline:* For fall admission, 1/15 for domestic students. *Expenses:* Tuition, state resident: full-time $7090; part-time $370 per credit hour. Tuition, nonresident: full-time $16,072; part-time $869 per credit hour. Full-time tuition and fees vary according to course load and program. *Financial support:* Fellowships with full tuition reimbursements, research assistantships, career-related internships or fieldwork, Federal Work-Study, and institutionally sponsored loans available. *Faculty research:* Biomedical imaging, biomedical implants and devices, cardiac electrophysiology, multiscale computational modeling, tissue engineering and regenerative medicine. *Unit head:* Dr. Timothy M. Wick, Chair, 205-934-8420, E-mail: uabbmegrad@uab.edu. *Application contact:* Susan Noblitt Banks, Director of Graduate School Operations, 205-934-8227, Fax: 205-934-8413, E-mail: gradschool@uab.edu. Website: http://www.eng.uab.edu/BME/.

University of Alberta, Faculty of Medicine and Dentistry and Faculty of Graduate Studies and Research, Graduate Programs in Medicine, Department of Biomedical Engineering, Edmonton, AB T6G 2E1, Canada. Offers biomedical engineering (M Sc); medical sciences (PhD). *Degree requirements:* For master's, thesis; for doctorate, thesis/dissertation. Electronic applications accepted. *Faculty research:* Medical imaging, rehabilitation engineering, biomaterials and tissue engineering, biomechanics, cryobiology.

The University of Arizona, Graduate Interdisciplinary Programs, Graduate Interdisciplinary Program in Biomedical Engineering, Tucson, AZ 85721. Offers MS, PhD. *Entrance requirements:* For master's, GRE, 3 letters of recommendation; for doctorate, GRE, 3 letters of recommendation, statement of purpose. Additional exam requirements/recommendations for international students: Required—TOEFL (minimum score 600 paper-based). Electronic applications accepted.

University of Arkansas, Graduate School, College of Engineering, Department of Biological and Agricultural Engineering, Program in Biomedical Engineering, Fayetteville, AR 72701-1201. Offers MSBME. Electronic applications accepted.

University of Bridgeport, School of Engineering, Department of Biomedical Engineering, Bridgeport, CT 06604. Offers MS. Part-time and evening/weekend programs available. *Degree requirements:* For master's, thesis optional. *Entrance requirements:* Additional exam requirements/recommendations for international students: Recommended—TOEFL (minimum score 550 paper-based; 80 iBT), IELTS (minimum score 6.5). *Expenses:* Contact institution.

University of Calgary, Faculty of Graduate Studies, Schulich School of Engineering, Biomedical Engineering Graduate Program, Calgary, AB T2N 1N4, Canada. Offers M Sc, PhD. *Degree requirements:* For master's, comprehensive exam, thesis, defense exam; for doctorate, comprehensive exam, thesis/dissertation, defense exam. *Entrance requirements:* For master's, B Sc, minimum GPA of 3.2, confirmed faculty supervisor; for doctorate, M Sc, minimum GPA of 3.5, confirmed faculty supervisor. Additional exam requirements/recommendations for international students: Required—TOEFL, IELTS. *Faculty research:* Bioelectricity, biomechanics, cell and tissue engineering (or biomaterials), imaging, bioinstrumentation, clinical engineering, rehabilitation engineering.

University of California, Davis, College of Engineering, Graduate Group in Biomedical Engineering, Davis, CA 95616. Offers MS, PhD. *Degree requirements:* For master's, thesis; for doctorate, thesis/dissertation. *Entrance requirements:* For master's and doctorate, GRE General Test, minimum GPA of 3.25. Additional exam requirements/recommendations for international students: Required—TOEFL (minimum score 550 paper-based), IELTS (minimum score 7). Electronic applications accepted. *Faculty research:* Orthopedic biomechanics, cell/molecular biomechanics and transport, biosensors and instrumentation, human movement, biomedical image analysis, spectroscopy.

University of California, Irvine, Henry Samueli School of Engineering, Department of Biomedical Engineering, Irvine, CA 92697. Offers MS, PhD. Part-time programs available. *Students:* 122 full-time (45 women), 11 part-time (3 women); includes 57 minority (2 Black or African American, non-Hispanic/Latino; 1 American Indian or Alaska Native, non-Hispanic/Latino; 38 Asian, non-Hispanic/Latino; 12 Hispanic/Latino; 4 Two or more races, non-Hispanic/Latino), 34 international. Average age 26. 316 applicants, 26% accepted, 29 enrolled. In 2014, 21 master's, 13 doctorates awarded. Terminal master's awarded for partial completion of doctoral program. *Degree requirements:* For doctorate, thesis/dissertation. *Entrance requirements:* For master's and doctorate, GRE General Test, minimum GPA of 3.0, 3 letters of recommendation. Additional exam requirements/recommendations for international students: Required—TOEFL (minimum score 550 paper-based). *Application deadline:* For fall admission, 1/15 priority date for domestic students, 1/15 for international students. Applications are processed on a rolling basis. Application fee: $90 ($110 for international students). Electronic applications accepted. *Financial support:* Fellowships, research assistantships with full tuition reimbursements, teaching assistantships, institutionally sponsored loans, traineeships, health care benefits, and unspecified assistantships available. Financial award application deadline: 3/1; financial award applicants required to submit FAFSA. *Faculty research:* Biomedical photonics, biomedical imaging, biomedical nano- and micro-scale systems, biomedical computation/modeling, neuroengineering, tissue engineering. *Unit head:* Prof. Abraham P. Lee, Chair, 949-824-8155, Fax: 949-824-1727, E-mail: aplee@uci.edu. *Application contact:* Nadia Ortiz, Assistant Director of Graduate Student Affairs, 949-824-3562, Fax: 949-824-9096, E-mail: nortiz@uci.edu. Website: http://www.eng.uci.edu/dept/bme.

University of California, Los Angeles, Graduate Division, Henry Samueli School of Engineering and Applied Science, Department of Bioengineering, Los Angeles, CA 90095-1600. Offers MS, PhD. *Faculty:* 10 full-time (2 women), 3 part-time/adjunct (0 women). *Students:* 181 full-time (57 women); includes 66 minority (2 Black or African American, non-Hispanic/Latino; 55 Asian, non-Hispanic/Latino; 6 Hispanic/Latino; 3 Two or more races, non-Hispanic/Latino), 64 international. 364 applicants, 41% accepted, 44 enrolled. In 2014, 36 master's, 29 doctorates awarded. *Degree requirements:* For master's, comprehensive exam or thesis; for doctorate, thesis/dissertation, qualifying exams. *Entrance requirements:* For master's, GRE General Test, minimum GPA of 3.0; for doctorate, GRE General Test, minimum GPA of 3.25. Additional exam requirements/recommendations for international students: Required—TOEFL (minimum score 560 paper-based; 87 iBT), IELTS (minimum score 7). *Application deadline:* For fall admission, 12/15 for domestic and international students. Application fee: $80 ($100 for

international students). Electronic applications accepted. *Financial support:* In 2014–15, 73 fellowships, 104 research assistantships, 49 teaching assistantships were awarded; career-related internships or fieldwork, Federal Work-Study, institutionally sponsored loans, and tuition waivers (full and partial) also available. Financial award application deadline: 1/15; financial award applicants required to submit FAFSA. *Faculty research:* biomedical instrumentation; biomedical signal and image processing; biosystems science and engineering; medical imaging informatics; molecular cellular tissue therapeutics; neuroengineering. *Total annual research expenditures:* $6.1 million. *Unit head:* Dr. Benjamin Wu, Chair, 310-794-7094, E-mail: benwu@seas.ucla.edu. *Application contact:* Anne-Marie Dieters, Student Affairs Officer, 310-794-5945, Fax: 310-794-5956, E-mail: adieters@seas.ucla.edu. Website: http://www.bioeng.ucla.edu/.

University of Central Oklahoma, The Jackson College of Graduate Studies, College of Mathematics and Science, Department of Engineering and Physics, Edmond, OK 73034-5209. Offers biomedical engineering (MS); electrical engineering (MS); mechanical systems (MS); physics (MS). Part-time programs available. *Degree requirements:* For master's, thesis optional. *Entrance requirements:* For master's, GRE, 24 hours of course work in physics or equivalent, mathematics through differential equations, minimum GPA of 2.75 overall and 3.0 in last 60 hours attempted. Additional exam requirements/recommendations for international students: Required—TOEFL (minimum score 550 paper-based). Electronic applications accepted.

University of Cincinnati, Graduate School, College of Engineering and Applied Science, Department of Biomedical Engineering, Cincinnati, OH 45221. Offers bioinformatics (PhD); biomechanics (PhD); medical imaging (PhD); tissue engineering (PhD). Part-time programs available. *Degree requirements:* For doctorate, one foreign language, thesis/dissertation. *Entrance requirements:* For doctorate, GRE General Test. Additional exam requirements/recommendations for international students: Required—TOEFL (minimum score 600 paper-based).

University of Connecticut, Graduate School, School of Engineering, Department of Electrical and Computer Engineering, Field of Biomedical Engineering, Storrs, CT 06269. Offers MS, PhD. Terminal master's awarded for partial completion of doctoral program. *Degree requirements:* For master's, comprehensive exam, thesis or alternative; for doctorate, thesis/dissertation. *Entrance requirements:* For master's and doctorate, GRE General Test. Additional exam requirements/recommendations for international students: Required—TOEFL (minimum score 550 paper-based). Electronic applications accepted.

University of Florida, Graduate School, College of Engineering, Department of Biomedical Engineering, Gainesville, FL 32611. Offers biomedical engineering (ME, MS, PhD, Certificate); clinical and translational science (PhD); medical physics (MS, PhD); MD/PhD. *Faculty:* 26 full-time (5 women), 25 part-time/adjunct (6 women). *Students:* 115 full-time (46 women), 23 part-time (10 women); includes 32 minority (5 Black or African American, non-Hispanic/Latino; 10 Asian, non-Hispanic/Latino; 17 Hispanic/Latino), 40 international. 259 applicants, 40% accepted, 36 enrolled. In 2014, 43 master's, 21 doctorates awarded. Terminal master's awarded for partial completion of doctoral program. *Degree requirements:* For master's, comprehensive exam (for some programs), thesis (for some programs); for doctorate, comprehensive exam (for some programs), thesis/dissertation (for some programs). *Entrance requirements:* For master's and doctorate, http://bme.ufl.edu/academics/admissions/entrancerequirements. Additional exam requirements/recommendations for international students: Required—TOEFL (minimum score 550 paper-based; 80 iBT), IELTS (minimum score 6). *Application deadline:* For fall admission, 12/15 priority date for domestic students, 12/15 for international students; for spring admission, 7/31 for domestic and international students. Applications are processed on a rolling basis. Application fee: $30. Electronic applications accepted. *Financial support:* Application deadline: 12/31; applicants required to submit FAFSA. *Faculty research:* Neural engineering, imaging and medical physics, biomaterials and regenerative medicine, biomedical informatics and modeling. *Total annual research expenditures:* $4.9 million. *Unit head:* Christine E. Schmidt, PhD, Chair, 352-273-9222, Fax: 352-392-9791, E-mail: schmidt@bme.ufl.edu. *Application contact:* Hans Van Oostrom, PhD, Associate Professor/Associate Chair/Graduate Coordinator, 352-273-9315, Fax: 352-392-9221, E-mail: oostrom@ufl.edu. Website: http://www.bme.ufl.edu/.

University of Houston, Cullen College of Engineering, Department of Biomedical Engineering, Houston, TX 77204. Offers PhD. Part-time programs available. *Degree requirements:* For doctorate, seminar. *Entrance requirements:* For doctorate, GRE, BS or MS in biomedical engineering or related field, minimum GPA of 3.3 on last 60 hours. Additional exam requirements/recommendations for international students: Required—TOEFL (minimum score 580 paper-based; 92 iBT), IELTS (minimum score 6). Electronic applications accepted.

The University of Iowa, Graduate College, College of Engineering, Department of Biomedical Engineering, Iowa City, IA 52242-1316. Offers MS, PhD. Part-time programs available. *Faculty:* 10 full-time (2 women), 4 part-time/adjunct (0 women). *Students:* 75 full-time (26 women); includes 10 minority (2 Black or African American, non-Hispanic/Latino; 4 Asian, non-Hispanic/Latino; 2 Hispanic/Latino; 2 Two or more races, non-Hispanic/Latino), 24 international. Average age 26. 58 applicants, 33% accepted, 8 enrolled. In 2014, 15 master's, 7 doctorates awarded. Terminal master's awarded for partial completion of doctoral program. *Degree requirements:* For master's, thesis (for some programs), written and oral exam; for doctorate, comprehensive exam, thesis/dissertation, written and oral exam. *Entrance requirements:* For master's, GRE (minimum score: 310 verbal and quantitative), minimum undergraduate GPA of 3.0; for doctorate, GRE (minimum score: 310 verbal and quantitative), minimum undergraduate GPA of 3.25. Additional exam requirements/recommendations for international students: Required—TOEFL (minimum score 553 paper-based; 85 iBT), IELTS (minimum score 7). *Application deadline:* For fall admission, 3/1 for domestic and international students; for spring admission, 8/1 for domestic and international students; for summer admission, 1/1 for domestic and international students. Applications are processed on a rolling basis. Application fee: $60 ($100 for international students). Electronic applications accepted. *Financial support:* In 2014–15, 57 students received support, including 5 fellowships with partial tuition reimbursements available (averaging $23,927 per year), 51 research assistantships with partial tuition reimbursements available (averaging $23,398 per year), 8 teaching assistantships with partial tuition reimbursements available (averaging $18,080 per year); scholarships/grants, traineeships, health care benefits, and unspecified assistantships also available. Support available to part-time students. Financial award application deadline: 3/1. *Faculty research:* Biomaterials, tissue engineering and cellular mechanics; cell motion analysis and modeling; spinal and joint biomechanics, digital human modeling, and biomedical imaging; bioinformatics and computational biology; fluid and cardiovascular biomechanics; wound healing; mechanobiology. *Total annual research expenditures:* $8.6 million. *Unit head:* Dr. Joseph M. Reinhardt, Departmental Executive Officer, 319-335-5634, Fax: 319-335-5631, E-mail: joe-reinhardt@uiowa.edu. *Application contact:* Courtney Bork, Academic Program Specialist, 319-335-5632, Fax: 319-335-5631, E-mail: bme@engineering.uiowa.edu. Website: http://www.engineering.uiowa.edu/bme.

University of Kentucky, Graduate School, College of Engineering, Program in Biomedical Engineering, Lexington, KY 40506-0032. Offers MSBE, PBME, PhD. *Degree requirements:* For master's, comprehensive exam, thesis optional; for doctorate, comprehensive exam, thesis/dissertation. *Entrance requirements:* For master's, GRE General Test, minimum undergraduate GPA of 2.75; for doctorate, GRE General Test, minimum graduate GPA of 3.0. Additional exam requirements/recommendations for international students: Required—TOEFL (minimum score 550 paper-based). Electronic applications accepted. *Faculty research:* Signal processing and dynamical systems, cardiopulmonary mechanics and systems, bioelectromagnetics, neuromotor control and electrical stimulation, biomaterials and musculoskeletal biomechanics.

University of Maine, Graduate School, Graduate School of Biomedical Science and Engineering, Orono, ME 04469. Offers bioinformatics (PSM); biomedical engineering (PhD); biomedical science (PhD). *Faculty:* 151 full-time (45 women). *Students:* 27 full-time (17 women), 8 part-time (6 women), 11 international. Average age 31. 59 applicants, 8% accepted, 4 enrolled. In 2014, 3 doctorates awarded. *Degree requirements:* For doctorate, comprehensive exam, thesis/dissertation. *Entrance requirements:* For doctorate, GRE General Test, master's degree. Additional exam requirements/recommendations for international students: Required—TOEFL. *Application deadline:* For fall admission, 12/31 for domestic students. Application fee: $65. *Expenses:* Tuition, state resident: part-time $658 per credit hour. Tuition, nonresident: part-time $1550 per credit hour. *Financial support:* In 2014–15, 18 students received support, including 1 fellowship with full tuition reimbursement available (averaging $20,000 per year), 15 research assistantships with full tuition reimbursements available (averaging $23,000 per year), 1 teaching assistantship (averaging $7,500 per year). *Faculty research:* Molecular and cellular biology, neuroscience, biomedical engineering, toxicology, bioinformatics and computational biology. *Total annual research expenditures:* $62 million. *Unit head:* Dr. David Neivandt, Director, 207-581-2803. *Application contact:* Scott G. Delcourt, Assistant Vice President for Graduate Studies and Senior Associate Dean, 207-581-3291, Fax: 207-581-3232, E-mail: graduate@maine.edu.
Website: http://gsbse.umaine.edu/.

University of Massachusetts Boston, College of Science and Mathematics, Program in Biomedical Engineering and Biotechnology, Boston, MA 02125-3393. Offers PhD. *Expenses:* Tuition, state resident: full-time $2590; part-time $108 per credit. Tuition, nonresident: full-time $9758; part-time $406.50 per credit. Tuition and fees vary according to course load and program. *Unit head:* Dr. William Hagar, Interim Dean, 617-287-5777. *Application contact:* Peggy Roldan Patel, Graduate Admissions Coordinator, 617-287-6400, Fax: 617-287-6236, E-mail: bos.gadm@dpc.umassp.edu.

University of Massachusetts Dartmouth, Graduate School, College of Engineering, Program in Biomedical Engineering and Biotechnology, North Dartmouth, MA 02747-2300. Offers bioengineering (PhD); biology (PhD); biomedical engineering/biotechnology (MS, PhD); chemistry (PhD); civil engineering (PhD); computer and information science (PhD); electrical/computer engineering (PhD); mathematics (PhD); mechanical engineering (PhD); medical laboratory science (MS); physics (PhD). Part-time programs available. *Students:* 8 full-time (2 women), 12 part-time (6 women); includes 1 minority (Hispanic/Latino), 10 international. Average age 31. 46 applicants, 22% accepted, 1 enrolled. In 2014, 2 master's, 4 doctorates awarded. *Degree requirements:* For doctorate, comprehensive exam, thesis/dissertation. *Entrance requirements:* For master's and doctorate, GRE, statement of purpose (minimum of 300 words), resume, 3 letters of recommendation, official transcripts. Additional exam requirements/recommendations for international students: Required—TOEFL (minimum score 550 paper-based). *Application deadline:* For fall admission, 2/15 priority date for domestic students, 1/15 priority date for international students; for spring admission, 11/15 priority date for domestic students, 10/15 priority date for international students. Applications are processed on a rolling basis. Application fee: $60. Electronic applications accepted. *Expenses:* Tuition, state resident: full-time $2071; part-time $86.29 per credit. Tuition, nonresident: full-time $8099; part-time $337.46 per credit. *Required fees:* $16,520; $712.33 per credit. Tuition and fees vary according to course load and reciprocity agreements. *Financial support:* In 2014–15, 1 fellowship with full tuition reimbursement (averaging $24,000 per year), 5 research assistantships with full tuition reimbursements (averaging $11,630 per year), 1 teaching assistantship with full tuition reimbursement (averaging $16,000 per year) were awarded; Federal Work-Study and unspecified assistantships also available. Support available to part-time students. Financial award application deadline: 3/1; financial award applicants required to submit FAFSA. *Faculty research:* Comparative immunology, vaccine design, biosensors, biomimetic materials, polymer science, soft electronics, hydrogels, regenerative biological materials. *Total annual research expenditures:* $2 million. *Unit head:* Sankha Bhowmick, Graduate Program Director for Engineering Options, 508-999-8619, Fax: 508-999-8881, E-mail: sbhowmick@umassd.edu. *Application contact:* Steven Briggs, Director of Marketing and Recruitment for Graduate Studies, 508-999-8604, Fax: 508-999-8183, E-mail: graduate@umassd.edu.
Website: http://www.umassd.edu/engineering/graduate/doctoraldegreeprograms/biomedicalengineeringandbiotechnology/.

University of Memphis, Graduate School, Herff College of Engineering, Program in Biomedical Engineering, Memphis, TN 38152. Offers MS, PhD. *Faculty:* 7 full-time (2 women). *Students:* 22 full-time (8 women), 10 part-time (3 women); includes 4 minority (2 Black or African American, non-Hispanic/Latino; 2 Asian, non-Hispanic/Latino), 4 international. Average age 30. 22 applicants, 55% accepted, 1 enrolled. In 2014, 8 master's, 2 doctorates awarded. *Degree requirements:* For master's, thesis or alternative, oral exam; for doctorate, thesis/dissertation, exams. *Entrance requirements:* For master's, GRE General Test or MAT, minimum undergraduate GPA of 3.0; for doctorate, GRE General Test, minimum undergraduate GPA of 3.25 or master's degree in biomedical engineering. *Application deadline:* For fall admission, 8/1 priority date for domestic students; for spring admission, 12/1 for domestic students. Applications are processed on a rolling basis. Application fee: $35 ($60 for international students). Electronic applications accepted. *Financial support:* In 2014–15, 8 students received support. Fellowships with full tuition reimbursements available, research assistantships with full tuition reimbursements available, career-related internships or fieldwork, Federal Work-Study, scholarships/grants, and unspecified assistantships available. Financial award application deadline: 2/15; financial award applicants required to submit FAFSA. *Faculty research:* Biomaterials and cell/tissue engineering, especially for orthopedic applications; biosensors; biomechanics (hemodynamics, soft tissue, lung, gait); electrophysiology; novel medical image-acquisition devices. *Unit head:* Dr. Eugene C. Eckstein, Chairman, 901-678-3733, Fax: 901-678-5281, E-mail: eckstein@memphis.edu. *Application contact:* Dr. Steven M. Slack, Associate Dean, 901-678-4791, Fax: 901-678-5281, E-mail: sslack@memphis.edu.
Website: http://www.memphis.edu/bme/index.php.

University of Miami, Graduate School, College of Engineering, Department of Biomedical Engineering, Coral Gables, FL 33124. Offers MSBE, PhD. Part-time programs available. *Degree requirements:* For master's, thesis (for some programs); for doctorate, comprehensive exam, thesis/dissertation. *Entrance requirements:* For master's and doctorate, GRE General Test, minimum GPA of 3.0. Additional exam requirements/recommendations for international students: Required—TOEFL (minimum score 550 paper-based). Electronic applications accepted. *Faculty research:* Biomedical signal processing and instrumentation, cardiovascular engineering, optics and lasers, rehabilitation engineering, tissue mechanics.

University of Michigan, College of Engineering, Department of Biomedical Engineering, Ann Arbor, MI 48109. Offers MS, MSE, PhD. Part-time programs available. *Students:* 226 full-time (88 women). 725 applicants, 31% accepted, 113 enrolled. In 2014, 61 master's, 25 doctorates awarded. *Degree requirements:* For master's, thesis optional; for doctorate, comprehensive exam, oral defense of dissertation. *Entrance requirements:* For master's, GRE General Test; for doctorate, GRE General Test, master's degree. Additional exam requirements/recommendations for international students: Required—TOEFL. *Application deadline:* Applications are processed on a rolling basis. Electronic applications accepted. *Financial support:* Fellowships, research assistantships, teaching assistantships, Federal Work-Study, scholarships/grants, traineeships, and tuition waivers (partial) available. Financial award applicants required to submit FAFSA. *Faculty research:* Cellular and tissue engineering, biotechnology, biomedical materials, biomechanics, biomedical imaging, rehabilitation engineering. *Total annual research expenditures:* $35.2 million. *Unit head:* Lonnie Shea, Department Chair, 734-764-7149, Fax: 734-936-1905, E-mail: biomede@umich.edu. *Application contact:* Maria E. Steele, Senior Student Administration Assistant, 734-647-1091, Fax: 734-936-1905, E-mail: msteele@umich.edu.
Website: http://www.bme.umich.edu/.

University of Minnesota, Twin Cities Campus, College of Science and Engineering and Medical School, Department of Biomedical Engineering, Minneapolis, MN 55455-0213. Offers MS, PhD, MD/PhD. Part-time programs available. Terminal master's awarded for partial completion of doctoral program. *Degree requirements:* For master's, thesis optional; for doctorate, thesis/dissertation. *Entrance requirements:* For master's and doctorate, GRE General Test. Additional exam requirements/recommendations for international students: Required—TOEFL. Electronic applications accepted. *Faculty research:* Bioinstrumentation and medical devices; biomaterials; biomechanics; biomedical optics and imaging; biomolecular, cellular, and tissue engineering; cardiovascular engineering; neural engineering.

University of Nebraska–Lincoln, Graduate College, College of Engineering, Department of Mechanical and Materials Engineering, Lincoln, NE 68588-0526. Offers biomedical engineering (PhD); engineering mechanics (MS); materials engineering (PhD); mechanical engineering (MS), including materials science engineering, metallurgical engineering; mechanical engineering and applied mechanics (PhD); MS/MS. MS/MS offered with University of Rouen-France. *Degree requirements:* For master's, thesis optional; for doctorate, comprehensive exam, thesis/dissertation. *Entrance requirements:* For master's and doctorate, GRE General Test. Additional exam requirements/recommendations for international students: Required—TOEFL (minimum score 550 paper-based). Electronic applications accepted. *Faculty research:* Medical robotics, rehabilitation dynamics, and design; combustion, fluid mechanics, and heat transfer; nano-materials, manufacturing, and devices; fiber, tissue, bio-polymer, and adaptive composites; blast, impact, fracture, and failure; electro-active and magnetic materials and devices; functional materials, design, and added manufacturing; materials characterization, modeling, and computational simulation.

University of Nevada, Las Vegas, Graduate College, Howard R. Hughes College of Engineering, Department of Mechanical Engineering, Las Vegas, NV 89154-4027. Offers biomedical engineering (MS); materials and nuclear engineering (MS); mechanical engineering (MS); nuclear criticality safety engineering (Certificate). Part-time programs available. *Faculty:* 13 full-time (0 women), 1 (woman) part-time/adjunct. *Students:* 33 full-time (13 women), 13 part-time (3 women); includes 8 minority (1 Asian, non-Hispanic/Latino; 2 Hispanic/Latino; 5 Two or more races, non-Hispanic/Latino), 12 international. Average age 29. 43 applicants, 51% accepted, 11 enrolled. In 2014, 9 master's, 6 doctorates, 3 other advanced degrees awarded. *Degree requirements:* For master's, comprehensive exam, thesis (for some programs), project; for doctorate, comprehensive exam, thesis/dissertation. *Entrance requirements:* For master's, doctorate, and Certificate, GRE General Test. Additional exam requirements/recommendations for international students: Required—TOEFL (minimum score 550 paper-based; 80 iBT), IELTS (minimum score 7). *Application deadline:* For fall admission, 8/1 for domestic students, 5/1 for international students; for spring admission, 12/1 for domestic students, 10/1 for international students. Application fee: $60 ($95 for international students). Electronic applications accepted. *Financial support:* In 2014–15, 33 students received support, including 6 research assistantships with partial tuition reimbursements available (averaging $15,198 per year), 27 teaching assistantships with partial tuition reimbursements available (averaging $14,029 per year); institutionally sponsored loans, scholarships/grants, health care benefits, and unspecified assistantships also available. Financial award application deadline: 3/1. *Faculty research:* Dynamics and control systems; energy systems including renewable and nuclear; computational fluid and solid mechanics; structures, materials and manufacturing; vibrations and acoustics. *Total annual research expenditures:* $1.9 million. *Unit head:* Dr. Brendan O'Toole, Chair/Professor, 702-895-3885, Fax: 702-895-3936, E-mail: brendan.otoole@unlv.edu. *Application contact:* Graduate College Admissions Evaluator, 702-895-3320, Fax: 702-895-4180, E-mail: gradcollege@unlv.edu.
Website: http://me.unlv.edu/.

University of Nevada, Reno, Graduate School, Interdisciplinary Program in Biomedical Engineering, Reno, NV 89557. Offers MS, PhD. Terminal master's awarded for partial completion of doctoral program. *Degree requirements:* For master's, thesis optional; for doctorate, thesis/dissertation. *Entrance requirements:* For master's, GRE General Test (recommended), minimum GPA of 2.75; for doctorate, GRE General Test (recommended), minimum GPA of 3.0. Additional exam requirements/recommendations for international students: Required—TOEFL (minimum score 500 paper-based; 61 iBT), IELTS (minimum score 6). Electronic applications accepted. *Faculty research:* Bioengineering, biophysics, biomedical instrumentation, biosensors.

University of New Mexico, Graduate School, School of Engineering, Program in Biomedical Engineering, Albuquerque, NM 87131-2039. Offers MS, PhD. Part-time programs available. *Faculty:* 1 full-time (0 women). *Students:* 8 full-time (6 women), 14 part-time (6 women); includes 9 minority (1 Asian, non-Hispanic/Latino; 8 Hispanic/Latino), 3 international. Average age 29. 4 applicants, 50% accepted, 1 enrolled. In 2014, 3 master's, 2 doctorates awarded. Terminal master's awarded for partial completion of doctoral program. *Degree requirements:* For master's, thesis (for some programs); for doctorate, comprehensive exam, thesis/dissertation. *Entrance requirements:* For master's and doctorate, GRE General Test, letters of recommendation, letter of intent. *Application deadline:* Applications are processed on a rolling basis. Application fee: $50. *Unit head:* Dr. Steven Graves, Program Director, 505-277-5521, E-mail: graves@unm.edu. *Application contact:* Jocelyn White, Program Coordinator for Advisement, 505-277-5606, Fax: 505-277-5433, E-mail: jowhite@unm.edu.
Website: http://bme.unm.edu/academic-programs.html.

The University of North Carolina at Chapel Hill, School of Medicine and Graduate School, Graduate Programs in Medicine, Joint Department of Biomedical Engineering UNC-Chapel Hill and NC State, Chapel Hill, NC 27599. Offers MS, PhD. Terminal master's awarded for partial completion of doctoral program. *Degree requirements:* For master's, comprehensive exam, thesis, ethics seminar; for doctorate, comprehensive exam, thesis/dissertation, qualifying exam, teaching and ethics seminar. *Entrance requirements:* For master's, GRE General Test, minimum GPA of 3.0; for doctorate, GRE General Test, minimum GPA of 3.3. Additional exam requirements/recommendations for international students: Required—TOEFL. Electronic applications accepted. *Faculty research:* Biomedical imaging, rehabilitation engineering, microsystems engineering.

University of North Texas, Robert B. Toulouse School of Graduate Studies, Denton, TX 76203-5459. Offers accounting (MS); applied anthropology (MA, MS); applied behavior analysis (Certificate); applied geography (MA); applied technology and performance improvement (M Ed, MS); art education (MA); art history (MA); art museum education (Certificate); arts leadership (Certificate); audiology (Au D); behavior analysis (MS); behavioral science (PhD); biochemistry and molecular biology (MS); biology (MA, MS); biomedical engineering (MS); business analysis (MS); chemistry (MS); clinical health psychology (PhD); communication studies (MA, MS); computer engineering (MS); computer science (MS); counseling (M Ed, MS), including clinical mental health counseling (MS), college and university counseling, elementary school counseling, secondary school counseling; creative writing (MA); criminal justice (MS); curriculum and instruction (M Ed); decision sciences (MBA); design (MA, MFA), including fashion design (MFA), innovation studies, interior design (MFA); early childhood studies (MS); economics (MS); educational leadership (M Ed, Ed D); educational psychology (MS, PhD), including family studies (MS), gifted and talented (MS), human development (MS), learning and cognition (MS), research, measurement and evaluation (MS); electrical engineering (MS); emergency management (MPA); engineering technology (MS); English (MA); English as a second language (MA); environmental science (MS); finance (MBA, MS); financial management (MPA); French (MA); health services management (MBA); higher education (M Ed, Ed D); history (MA, MS); hospitality management (MS); human resources management (MPA); information science (MS); information systems (PhD); information technologies (MBA); interdisciplinary studies (MA, MS); international studies (MA); international sustainable tourism (MS); jazz studies (MM); journalism (MA, MJ, Graduate Certificate), including interactive and virtual digital communication (Graduate Certificate), narrative journalism (Graduate Certificate), public relations (Graduate Certificate); kinesiology (MS); linguistics (MA); local government management (MPA); logistics (PhD); logistics and supply chain management (MBA); long-term care, senior housing, and aging services (MA); management (PhD); marketing (MBA); mathematics (MA, MS); mechanical and energy engineering (MS, PhD); music (MA), including ethnomusicology, music theory, musicology, performance; music composition (PhD); music education (MM Ed, PhD); nonprofit management (MPA); operations and supply chain management (MBA); performance (MM, DMA); philosophy (MA); political science (MA); professional and technical communication (MA); radio, television and film (MA, MFA); rehabilitation counseling (Certificate); sociology (MA); Spanish (MA); special education (M Ed); speech-language pathology (MA); strategic management (MBA); studio art (MFA); teaching (M Ed); MBA/MS. Part-time and evening/weekend programs available. Postbaccalaureate distance learning degree programs offered. *Faculty:* 651 full-time (215 women), 233 part-time/adjunct (139 women). *Students:* 3,040 full-time (1,598 women), 3,401 part-time (2,097 women); includes 1,740 minority (533 Black or African American, non-Hispanic/Latino; 15 American Indian or Alaska Native, non-Hispanic/Latino; 286 Asian, non-Hispanic/Latino; 746 Hispanic/Latino; 3 Native Hawaiian or other Pacific Islander, non-Hispanic/Latino; 157 Two or more races, non-Hispanic/Latino), 1,145 international. Terminal master's awarded for partial completion of doctoral program. *Degree requirements:* For master's, variable foreign language requirement, comprehensive exam (for some programs), thesis (for some programs); for doctorate, variable foreign language requirement, comprehensive exam (for some programs), thesis/dissertation; for other advanced degree, variable foreign language requirement, comprehensive exam (for some programs). *Entrance requirements:* For master's and doctorate, GRE, GMAT. Additional exam requirements/recommendations for international students: Required—TOEFL (minimum score 550 paper-based; 79 iBT). *Application deadline:* For fall admission, 7/15 for domestic students, 3/15 for international students; for spring admission, 11/15 for domestic students, 9/15 for international students; for summer admission, 5/1 for domestic students. Applications are processed on a rolling basis. Application fee: $60. Electronic applications accepted. *Expenses:* Tuition, state resident: full-time $5450; part-time $3633 per year. Tuition, nonresident: full-time $11,966; part-time $7977 per year. *Required fees:* $1301; $398 per credit hour. $685 per semester. Tuition and fees vary according to program and reciprocity agreements. *Financial support:* Fellowships with partial tuition reimbursements, research assistantships with partial tuition reimbursements, teaching assistantships, career-related internships or fieldwork, Federal Work-Study, institutionally sponsored loans, scholarships/grants, health care benefits, and library assistantships available. Support available to part-time students. Financial award applicants required to submit FAFSA. *Unit head:* Mark Wardell, Dean, 940-565-2383, E-mail: mark.wardell@unt.edu. *Application contact:* Toulouse School of Graduate Studies, 940-565-2383, Fax: 940-565-2141, E-mail: gradsch@unt.edu.
Website: http://tsgs.unt.edu/.

University of Ottawa, Faculty of Graduate and Postdoctoral Studies, Ottawa—Carlton Joint Program in Biomedical Engineering, Ottawa, ON K1N 6N5, Canada. Offers MA Sc. *Degree requirements:* For master's, thesis or alternative. *Entrance requirements:* For master's, honors degree or equivalent, minimum B average.

University of Portland, School of Engineering, Portland, OR 97203-5798. Offers biomedical engineering (MBME); civil engineering (ME); computer science (ME); electrical engineering (ME); mechanical engineering (ME). Part-time and evening/weekend programs available. *Faculty:* 10 full-time (2 women), 1 part-time/adjunct (0 women). *Students:* 4 full-time (1 woman), 2 part-time (0 women); includes 1 minority (Two or more races, non-Hispanic/Latino), 1 international. Average age 27. In 2014, 2 master's awarded. *Degree requirements:* For master's, thesis optional. *Entrance requirements:* For master's, GRE General Test, minimum GPA of 3.0, 3 letters of recommendation, resume, statement of goals, official transcripts. Additional exam requirements/recommendations for international students: Required—TOEFL (minimum score 550 paper-based; 80 iBT), IELTS (minimum score 7). *Application deadline:* For fall admission, 7/15 priority date for domestic and international students; for spring admission, 12/15 priority date for domestic and international students. Applications are processed on a rolling basis. Application fee: $50. *Expenses:* Expenses: Contact institution. *Financial support:* Career-related internships or fieldwork, Federal Work-Study, and scholarships/grants available. Support available to part-time students. Financial award application deadline: 3/1; financial award applicants required to submit FAFSA. *Unit head:* Dr. Sharon Jones, Dean, 503-943-8169, E-mail: joness@up.edu. *Application contact:* Allison Able, Graduate Program Coordinator, 503-943-7107, Fax: 503-943-7315, E-mail: able@up.edu.
Website: http://engineering.up.edu/default.aspx?cid-6464&pid-2432.

University of Rhode Island, Graduate School, College of Engineering, Department of Electrical, Computer and Biomedical Engineering, Kingston, RI 02881. Offers MS, PhD, Graduate Certificate. Part-time programs available. *Faculty:* 20 full-time (2 women). *Students:* 30 full-time (6 women), 25 part-time (4 women); includes 4 minority (1 Black or African American, non-Hispanic/Latino; 2 Asian, non-Hispanic/Latino; 1 Hispanic/Latino), 23 international. In 2014, 18 master's, 2 doctorates awarded. *Degree requirements:* For master's, comprehensive exam (for some programs), thesis optional; for doctorate, comprehensive exam, thesis/dissertation. *Entrance requirements:* For master's and doctorate, GRE, 2 letters of recommendation (3 for international applicants). Additional exam requirements/recommendations for international students: Required—TOEFL (minimum score 550 paper-based). *Application deadline:* For fall admission, 7/15 for domestic students, 2/1 for international students; for spring admission, 11/15 for domestic students, 7/15 for international students. Application fee: $65. Electronic applications accepted. *Expenses:* Tuition, state resident: full-time $11,532; part-time $641 per credit. Tuition, nonresident: full-time $23,606; part-time $1311 per credit. *Required fees:* $1442; $39 per credit. $35 per semester. One-time fee: $155. *Financial support:* In 2014–15, 6 research assistantships with full and partial tuition reimbursements (averaging $8,108 per year), 4 teaching assistantships with full and partial tuition reimbursements (averaging $8,093 per year) were awarded. Financial award application deadline: 7/15; financial award applicants required to submit FAFSA. *Faculty research:* Biomedical instrumentation, cardiac physiology and computational modeling, analog/digital CMOS circuits, neural-machine interface, digital circuit design and VLSI testing. *Total annual research expenditures:* $2.2 million. *Unit head:* Dr. Godi Fischer, Chair, 401-874-5879, Fax: 401-782-6422, E-mail: fischer@ele.uri.edu. *Application contact:* Dr. Frederick J. Vetter, Graduate Director, 401-874-5141, Fax: 401-874-6422, E-mail: fred@uri.edu.
Website: http://www.ele.uri.edu/.

University of Rochester, Hajim School of Engineering and Applied Sciences, Department of Biomedical Engineering, Rochester, NY 14627. Offers MS, PhD. Part-time programs available. *Faculty:* 9 full-time (5 women). *Students:* 76 full-time (34 women), 3 part-time (0 women); includes 7 minority (1 Black or African American, non-Hispanic/Latino; 4 Asian, non-Hispanic/Latino; 2 Hispanic/Latino), 24 international. 197 applicants, 42% accepted, 19 enrolled. In 2014, 15 master's, 4 doctorates awarded. Terminal master's awarded for partial completion of doctoral program. *Degree requirements:* For master's, comprehensive exam; for doctorate, thesis/dissertation, qualifying exam. *Entrance requirements:* For master's and doctorate, GRE General Test. Additional exam requirements/recommendations for international students: Required—TOEFL. *Application deadline:* For fall admission, 1/1 for domestic students. Application fee: $60. Electronic applications accepted. *Expenses: Tuition:* Full-time $46,150; part-time $1442 per credit hour. *Required fees:* $504. *Financial support:* Fellowships, research assistantships, teaching assistantships, and tuition waivers (full and partial) available. Financial award application deadline: 1/1. *Faculty research:* Biomechanics, biomedical optics, cell and tissue engineering, medical imaging, neuroengineering. *Unit head:* Dr. Richard Waugh, Chair, 585-275-3768. *Application contact:* Donna Porcelli, Graduate Program Coordinator, 585-275-3891.
Website: http://www.urmc.rochester.edu/bme/graduate/.

University of Rochester, Hajim School of Engineering and Applied Sciences, Master of Science in Technical Entrepreneurship and Management Program, Rochester, NY 14642. Offers biomedical engineering (MS); chemical engineering (MS); computer science (MS); electrical and computer engineering (MS); energy and the environment (MS); materials science (MS); mechanical engineering (MS); optics (MS). Program offered in collaboration with the Simon School of Business. Part-time programs available. *Students:* 36 full-time (12 women), 7 part-time (1 woman); includes 3 minority (2 Hispanic/Latino; 1 Two or more races, non-Hispanic/Latino), 33 international. Average age 24. 152 applicants, 68% accepted, 27 enrolled. In 2014, 28 master's awarded. *Degree requirements:* For master's, comprehensive exam. *Entrance requirements:* For master's, GRE or GMAT, 3 letters of recommendation; personal statement; official transcript; bachelor's degree (or equivalent for international students) in engineering, science, or mathematics. Additional exam requirements/recommendations for international students: Required—TOEFL or IELTS. *Application deadline:* For fall admission, 2/1 for domestic and international students. Applications are processed on a rolling basis. Application fee: $60. Electronic applications accepted. *Expenses: Tuition:* Full-time $46,150; part-time $1442 per credit hour. *Required fees:* $504. *Financial support:* Career-related internships or fieldwork and scholarships/grants available. Financial award application deadline: 2/1. *Faculty research:* High efficiency solar cells, macromolecular self-assembly, digital signal processing, memory hierarchy management, molecular and physical mechanisms in cell migration, optical imaging systems. *Unit head:* Duncan T. Moore, Vice Provost for Entrepreneurship, 585-275-5248, Fax: 585-473-6745, E-mail: moore@optics.rochester.edu. *Application contact:* Andrea M. Galati, Executive Director, 585-276-3407, Fax: 585-276-2357, E-mail: andrea.galati@rochester.edu.
Website: http://www.rochester.edu/team.

University of Saskatchewan, College of Graduate Studies and Research, College of Engineering, Biomedical Engineering Program, Saskatoon, SK S7N 5A9, Canada. Offers M Eng, M Sc, PhD. Part-time programs available. *Degree requirements:* For master's, thesis (for some programs), 30 credits (for M Eng); thesis and 12 credits (for MS); for doctorate, comprehensive exam, thesis/dissertation, qualifying exam, 18 credits. *Entrance requirements:* For master's and doctorate, GRE. Additional exam requirements/recommendations for international students: Required—TOEFL, TOEFL (minimum iBT score of 80), IELTS (6.5), CanTEST (4.5), or PTE (59). Electronic applications accepted. *Faculty research:* Bioinformatics, biomechanics, biomedical signal and image processing, biosensor, medical instrumentation, medical imaging, nano-drug delivery system, systems biology, tissue engineering.

University of Southern California, Graduate School, Viterbi School of Engineering, Department of Biomedical Engineering, Los Angeles, CA 90089. Offers biomedical engineering (PhD); medical device and diagnostic engineering (MS); medical imaging and imaging informatics (MS). Postbaccalaureate distance learning degree programs offered (minimal on-campus study). Terminal master's awarded for partial completion of doctoral program. *Degree requirements:* For master's, thesis optional; for doctorate, thesis/dissertation. *Entrance requirements:* For master's and doctorate, GRE General Test. Additional exam requirements/recommendations for international students: Recommended—TOEFL. Electronic applications accepted. *Faculty research:* Medical ultrasound, BioMEMS, neural prosthetics, computational bioengineering, bioengineering of vision, medical devices.

University of South Florida, College of Engineering, Department of Chemical and Biomedical Engineering, Tampa, FL 33620. Offers biomedical engineering (MSBE, PhD); chemical engineering (M Ch E, MSCH, PhD); MSBE/MS; PhD/MD. Part-time programs available. *Faculty:* 15 full-time (2 women). *Students:* 90 full-time (37 women), 17 part-time (6 women); includes 27 minority (9 Black or African American, non-Hispanic/Latino; 2 Asian, non-Hispanic/Latino; 13 Hispanic/Latino; 3 Two or more races, non-Hispanic/Latino), 46 international. Average age 28. 157 applicants, 45% accepted, 33 enrolled. In 2014, 26 master's, 9 doctorates awarded. Terminal master's awarded for partial completion of doctoral program. *Degree requirements:* For master's, comprehensive exam, thesis (for some programs); for doctorate, comprehensive exam, thesis/dissertation. *Entrance requirements:* For master's, GRE General Test (minimum recommended scores of 3.0 in analytical writing and 99th percentile quantitative), undergraduate degree in engineering, science, or chemical engineering with minimum GPA of 3.0; at least two letters of recommendation; current resume; statement of

research interests (for students who wish to pursue thesis option); for doctorate, GRE General Test (minimum recommended scores of 3.0 in analytical writing and 99th percentile quantitative), undergraduate degree in engineering, science, or chemical engineering with minimum GPA of 3.0; three letters of recommendation; current resume; statement of research interests. Additional exam requirements/recommendations for international students: Required—TOEFL (minimum score 550 paper-based; 79 iBT) or IELTS (minimum score 6.5). *Application deadline:* For fall admission, 2/15 for domestic students, 1/2 priority date for international students; for spring admission, 10/15 for domestic students, 6/1 priority date for international students. Application fee: $30. Electronic applications accepted. *Financial support:* In 2014–15, 41 students received support, including 29 research assistantships with tuition reimbursements available (averaging $13,171 per year), 12 teaching assistantships with tuition reimbursements available (averaging $14,017 per year); unspecified assistantships also available. Financial award applicants required to submit FAFSA. *Faculty research:* Neuroengineering, tissue engineering, biomedicine and biotechnology, engineering education, functional materials and nanotechnology, energy, environment/sustainability. *Total annual research expenditures:* $689,262. *Unit head:* Dr. Venkat R. Bhethanabotla, Professor and Department Chair, 813-974-3997, E-mail: bhethana@usf.edu. *Application contact:* Dr. Robert Frisina, Jr., Professor and Graduate Program Director, 813-974-4013, Fax: 813-974-3651, E-mail: rfrisina@usf.edu.
Website: http://che.eng.usf.edu/.

University of South Florida, University College/Distance Education, Tampa, FL 33620-9951. *Unit head:* Kathy Barnes, Interdisciplinary Programs Coordinator, 813-974-8031, Fax: 813-974-7061, E-mail: barnesk@usf.edu. *Application contact:* Karen Tylinski, Metro Initiatives, 813-974-9943, Fax: 813-974-7061, E-mail: ktylinsk@usf.edu.
Website: http://www.usf.edu/innovative-education/.

The University of Tennessee, Graduate School, College of Engineering, Department of Mechanical, Aerospace and Biomedical Engineering, Program in Biomedical Engineering, Knoxville, TN 37996. Offers MS, PhD, MS/PhD. Part-time programs available. Postbaccalaureate distance learning degree programs offered (minimal on-campus study). *Faculty:* 18 full-time (2 women). *Students:* 28 full-time (13 women), 3 part-time (0 women); includes 2 minority (both Asian, non-Hispanic/Latino), 5 international. Average age 28. 45 applicants, 24% accepted, 8 enrolled. In 2014, 7 master's, 10 doctorates awarded. *Degree requirements:* For master's, thesis or alternative; for doctorate, comprehensive exam, thesis/dissertation. *Entrance requirements:* For master's, GRE General Test (for MS students pursuing research thesis), minimum GPA of 2.7 (for U.S. degree holders), 3.0 (for international degree holders); 3 references; statement of purpose; for doctorate, GRE General Test (for all PhD candidates), minimum GPA of 3.0 on previous graduate course work; 3 references; statement of purpose. Additional exam requirements/recommendations for international students: Required—TOEFL (minimum score 550 paper-based). *Application deadline:* For fall admission, 2/1 priority date for domestic and international students; for spring admission, 6/15 for domestic and international students. Applications are processed on a rolling basis. Application fee: $35. Electronic applications accepted. *Financial support:* In 2014–15, 18 students received support, including 4 research assistantships with full tuition reimbursements available (averaging $22,497 per year), 8 teaching assistantships with full tuition reimbursements available (averaging $19,677 per year); fellowships with full tuition reimbursements available, career-related internships or fieldwork, Federal Work-Study, institutionally sponsored loans, health care benefits, and unspecified assistantships also available. Financial award application deadline: 2/1; financial award applicants required to submit FAFSA. *Faculty research:* Bioimaging, biomechanics, biorobotics, biosensors, biomaterials. *Unit head:* Dr. Matthew Mench, Head, 865-974-5115, Fax: 865-974-5274, E-mail: mmench@utk.edu. *Application contact:* Dr. Gary V. Smith, Associate Head, 865-974-5271, Fax: 865-974-5274, E-mail: gvsmith@utk.edu.
Website: http://www.engr.utk.edu/mabe.

The University of Tennessee, The University of Tennessee Space Institute, Tullahoma, TN 37388. Offers aerospace engineering (MS, PhD); biomedical engineering (MS, PhD); engineering science (MS, PhD); industrial and systems engineering/engineering management (MS, PhD); mechanical engineering (MS, PhD); physics (MS, PhD). Part-time programs available. Postbaccalaureate distance learning degree programs offered. *Faculty:* 19 full-time (3 women), 4 part-time/adjunct. *Students:* 31 full-time (6 women), 82 part-time (11 women); includes 10 minority (6 Black or African American, non-Hispanic/Latino; 1 American Indian or Alaska Native, non-Hispanic/Latino; 2 Asian, non-Hispanic/Latino; 1 Hispanic/Latino), 11 international. 60 applicants, 55% accepted, 22 enrolled. In 2014, 25 master's, 5 doctorates awarded. Terminal master's awarded for partial completion of doctoral program. *Degree requirements:* For doctorate, one foreign language, thesis/dissertation. *Entrance requirements:* Additional exam requirements/recommendations for international students: Required—TOEFL (minimum score 550 paper-based; 80 iBT), IELTS (minimum score 6.5). *Application deadline:* For fall admission, 2/1 for international students; for spring admission, 6/15 for international students. Applications are processed on a rolling basis. Application fee: $60. Electronic applications accepted. *Financial support:* In 2014–15, 6 fellowships with full tuition reimbursements (averaging $2,451 per year), 24 research assistantships with full tuition reimbursements (averaging $20,244 per year) were awarded; career-related internships or fieldwork, Federal Work-Study, institutionally sponsored loans, health care benefits, and unspecified assistantships also available. *Faculty research:* Fluid mechanics/aerodynamics, chemical and electric propulsion and laser diagnostics, computational mechanics and simulations, carbon fiber production and composite materials. *Total annual research expenditures:* $1.8 million. *Unit head:* Dr. Charles Johnson, Associate Executive Director, 931-393-7318, Fax: 931-393-7211, E-mail: cjohnson@utsi.edu. *Application contact:* Dee Merriman, Director, 931-393-7213, Fax: 931-393-7211, E-mail: dmerrima@utsi.edu.
Website: http://www.utsi.edu/.

The University of Tennessee Health Science Center, College of Graduate Health Sciences, Memphis, TN 38163-0002. Offers biomedical engineering (MS, PhD); biomedical sciences (PhD); dental sciences (MDS); epidemiology (MS); health outcomes and policy research (PhD); laboratory research and management (MS); nursing science (PhD); pharmaceutical sciences (PhD); pharmacology (MS); speech and hearing science (PhD); DDS/PhD; DNP/PhD; MD/PhD; Pharm D/PhD. Terminal master's awarded for partial completion of doctoral program. *Degree requirements:* For master's, comprehensive exam, thesis; for doctorate, comprehensive exam, thesis/dissertation, oral and written preliminary and comprehensive exams. *Entrance requirements:* For master's and doctorate, GRE General Test, minimum GPA of 3.0. Additional exam requirements/recommendations for international students: Required—TOEFL (minimum score 79 iBT); Recommended—IELTS (minimum score 6.5). Electronic applications accepted.

The University of Texas at Austin, Graduate School, Cockrell School of Engineering, Department of Biomedical Engineering, Austin, TX 78712-1111. Offers MS, PhD, MD/PhD. MD/PhD offered jointly with The University of Texas Medical Branch. Part-time programs available. *Degree requirements:* For master's, thesis optional; for doctorate, comprehensive exam, thesis/dissertation. *Entrance requirements:* For master's and doctorate, GRE General Test. Additional exam requirements/recommendations for

international students: Required—TOEFL (minimum score 550 paper-based). Electronic applications accepted. *Faculty research:* Biomechanics, bioengineering, tissue engineering, tissue optics, biothermal studies.

The University of Texas at Dallas, Erik Jonsson School of Engineering and Computer Science, Department of Bioengineering, Richardson, TX 75080. Offers biomedical engineering (MS, PhD). *Faculty:* 13 full-time (5 women). *Students:* 70 full-time (28 women), 4 part-time (3 women); includes 8 minority (3 Black or African American, non-Hispanic/Latino; 3 Asian, non-Hispanic/Latino; 2 Hispanic/Latino), 43 international. Average age 26. 120 applicants, 43% accepted, 34 enrolled. In 2014, 21 master's awarded. *Degree requirements:* For master's, thesis (for some programs); for doctorate, comprehensive exam, thesis/dissertation. *Entrance requirements:* For master's, GRE (minimum scores of 500 in verbal, 700 in quantitative and 4 in analytical writing), minimum GPA of 3.0 in upper-division quantitative course work; for doctorate, GRE (minimum scores of 500 in verbal, 700 in quantitative and 4 in analytical writing), minimum GPA of 3.5 in upper-division quantitative course work. Additional exam requirements/recommendations for international students: Required—TOEFL (minimum score 550 paper-based). *Application deadline:* For fall admission, 7/15 for domestic students, 5/1 priority date for international students; for spring admission, 11/15 for domestic students, 9/1 priority date for international students. Applications are processed on a rolling basis. Application fee: $50 ($100 for international students). Electronic applications accepted. *Expenses:* Tuition, state resident: full-time $11,940; part-time $663 per credit. Tuition, nonresident: full-time $22,282; part-time $1238 per credit. *Financial support:* In 2014–15, 56 students received support, including 5 fellowships (averaging $9,900 per year), 21 research assistantships with partial tuition reimbursements available (averaging $19,622 per year), 22 teaching assistantships with partial tuition reimbursements available (averaging $16,650 per year); career-related internships or fieldwork, Federal Work-Study, institutionally sponsored loans, scholarships/grants, and unspecified assistantships also available. Support available to part-time students. Financial award application deadline: 4/30; financial award applicants required to submit FAFSA. *Faculty research:* Bio-nanotechnology, organic electronics, system-level design for medical devices, computational geometry and biomedical computing. *Unit head:* Dr. Robert L. Rennaker, Department Head, 972-883-3562, E-mail: renn@utdallas.edu. *Application contact:* Claire Troy, Graduate Program Coordinator, 972-883-4615, E-mail: cct130230@utdallas.edu.
Website: http://be.utdallas.edu.

The University of Texas at El Paso, Graduate School, College of Engineering, El Paso, TX 79968-0001. Offers biomedical engineering (PhD); civil engineering (MEENE, MS, MSENE, PhD, Certificate), including civil engineering (MS), civil engineering (PhD), construction management (MS, Certificate), environmental engineering (MEENE, MSENE); computer science (MS, MSIT, PhD), including computer science (MS, PhD), information technology (MSIT); education engineering (M Eng); electrical and computer engineering (MS, PhD), including computer engineering (MS), electrical and computer engineering (PhD), electrical engineering (MS); industrial engineering (MS, Certificate), including industrial engineering (MS), manufacturing engineering (MS), systems engineering; mechanical engineering (MS, PhD), including environmental science and engineering (PhD), mechanical engineering (MS); metallurgical and materials engineering (MS, PhD), including materials science and engineering (PhD), metallurgical and materials engineering (MS); software engineering (M Eng). Part-time and evening/weekend programs available. *Degree requirements:* For master's, thesis optional; for doctorate, thesis/dissertation. *Entrance requirements:* For master's, GRE, minimum GPA of 3.0, letters of reference; for doctorate, GRE, statement of purpose, letters of reference. Additional exam requirements/recommendations for international students: Required—TOEFL; Recommended—IELTS. Electronic applications accepted. *Expenses:* Contact institution.

The University of Texas at San Antonio, College of Engineering, Department of Biomedical Engineering, San Antonio, TX 78249. Offers MS, PhD. Part-time programs available. *Faculty:* 7 full-time (0 women), 1 (woman) part-time/adjunct. *Students:* 53 full-time (24 women), 27 part-time (9 women); includes 25 minority (3 Black or African American, non-Hispanic/Latino; 9 Asian, non-Hispanic/Latino; 12 Hispanic/Latino; 1 Two or more races, non-Hispanic/Latino), 34 international. Average age 28. 97 applicants, 45% accepted, 31 enrolled. In 2014, 9 master's, 4 doctorates awarded. Terminal master's awarded for partial completion of doctoral program. *Degree requirements:* For master's, comprehensive exam, thesis; for doctorate, comprehensive exam, thesis/dissertation. *Entrance requirements:* For master's, GRE, three letters of recommendation, statement of purpose, BS in any of the science or engineering disciplines; for doctorate, GRE, resume, three letters of recommendation, statement of purpose, BS in any of the science or engineering disciplines. Additional exam requirements/recommendations for international students: Required—TOEFL (minimum score 550 paper-based; 79 iBT), IELTS (minimum score 6.5). *Application deadline:* For fall admission, 2/1 for domestic and international students; for spring admission, 10/1 for domestic and international students. Applications are processed on a rolling basis. Application fee: $45 ($80 for international students). Electronic applications accepted. *Expenses:* Expenses: Contact institution. *Financial support:* In 2014–15, 11 students received support, including 11 fellowships with full tuition reimbursements available (averaging $21,000 per year); unspecified assistantships also available. Financial award application deadline: 2/1. *Faculty research:* Tissue engineering and biomaterials, ocular biomechanics and cardiovascular biomechanics, biophotonics, cellular bioengineering, nanobiomaterials and nanobiotechnology. *Unit head:* Dr. Joo L. Ong, Department Chair/Professor, 210-458-7084, Fax: 210-458-7007, E-mail: anson.ong@utsa.edu. *Application contact:* Monica Rodriguez, Director of the Graduate School, 210-458-4331, E-mail: graduateadmissions@utsa.edu.
Website: http://engineering.utsa.edu/bme/BME_program/index.html.

The University of Texas Health Science Center at San Antonio, Graduate School of Biomedical Sciences, Biomedical Engineering Program, San Antonio, TX 78229-3900. Offers MS, PhD. Program offered jointly with The University of Texas at San Antonio. Part-time programs available. Terminal master's awarded for partial completion of doctoral program. *Degree requirements:* For master's, comprehensive exam, thesis; for doctorate, comprehensive exam, thesis/dissertation. *Application deadline:* For fall admission, 2/1 for domestic and international students; for spring admission, 10/1 for domestic and international students.
Website: http://engineering.utsa.edu/BME/BME_Program.

The University of Texas Southwestern Medical Center, Southwestern Graduate School of Biomedical Sciences, Division of Basic Science, Biomedical Engineering Program, Dallas, TX 75390. Offers MS, PhD. Programs offered jointly with The University of Texas at Arlington. *Degree requirements:* For master's, comprehensive exam or thesis; for doctorate, comprehensive exam, thesis/dissertation. *Entrance requirements:* For master's, GRE General Test, minimum GPA of 3.0; for doctorate, GRE General Test, minimum GPA of 3.4. Additional exam requirements/recommendations for international students: Required—TOEFL. Electronic applications accepted. *Faculty research:* Noninvasive image analysis, biomaterials development, rehabilitation engineering, biomechanics, bioinstrumentation.

The University of Toledo, College of Graduate Studies, College of Engineering and College of Medicine and Life Sciences, PhD Program in Biomedical Engineering,

Toledo, OH 43606-3390. Offers PhD. *Degree requirements:* For doctorate, thesis/dissertation, qualifying exam. *Entrance requirements:* For doctorate, GRE General Test, minimum GPA of 3.3. Additional exam requirements/recommendations for international students: Required—TOEFL (minimum score 550 paper-based; 80 iBT). Electronic applications accepted. *Faculty research:* Biomechanics, biomaterials, tissue engineering, artificial organs, biosensors.

University of Toronto, School of Graduate Studies, Faculty of Applied Science and Engineering, Institute of Biomaterials and Biomedical Engineering, Toronto, ON M5S 2J7, Canada. Offers biomedical engineering (MA Sc, PhD); clinical engineering (MH Sc, PhD). Part-time programs available. *Degree requirements:* For master's, thesis (for some programs), research project (MH Sc), oral presentation (MA Sc); for doctorate, thesis/dissertation, qualifying exam. *Entrance requirements:* For master's, minimum A-average; bachelor's degree or equivalent in engineering, physical or biological science (for MA Sc), applied science or engineering (for MH Sc); for doctorate, master's degree in engineering, engineering science, medicine, dentistry, or a physical or biological science. Additional exam requirements/recommendations for international students: Required—TOEFL (minimum score 600 paper-based), TWE (minimum score 4), IELTS, Michigan English Language Assessment Battery, or COPE. Electronic applications accepted.

University of Vermont, Graduate College, College of Engineering and Mathematics, Program in Bioengineering, Burlington, VT 05405. Offers PhD. *Entrance requirements:* For doctorate, GRE General Test. Additional exam requirements/recommendations for international students: Required—TOEFL (minimum score 550 paper-based; 80 iBT). Electronic applications accepted.

University of Virginia, School of Engineering and Applied Science, Department of Biomedical Engineering, Charlottesville, VA 22903. Offers ME, MS, PhD. *Faculty:* 9 full-time (0 women), 1 part-time/adjunct (0 women). *Students:* 66 full-time (26 women); includes 15 minority (2 Black or African American, non-Hispanic/Latino; 7 Asian, non-Hispanic/Latino; 4 Hispanic/Latino; 2 Two or more races, non-Hispanic/Latino), 11 international. Average age 25. 199 applicants, 20% accepted, 12 enrolled. In 2014, 7 master's, 15 doctorates awarded. *Degree requirements:* For master's, project or thesis; for doctorate, thesis/dissertation. *Entrance requirements:* For master's, GRE General Test, 3 letters of recommendation; for doctorate, GRE General Test, 3 letters of recommendation, essay. Additional exam requirements/recommendations for international students: Required—TOEFL (minimum score 600 paper-based; 90 iBT), IELTS (minimum score 7). *Application deadline:* For fall admission, 8/1 for domestic students, 4/1 for international students; for winter admission, 12/1 for domestic students, 8/1 for international students; for spring admission, 5/1 for domestic students, 1/1 for international students. Applications are processed on a rolling basis. Application fee: $60. Electronic applications accepted. *Expenses:* Tuition, state resident: full-time $14,164; part-time $349 per credit hour. Tuition, nonresident: full-time $23,722; part-time $1300 per credit hour. *Required fees:* $2514. *Financial support:* Fellowships, research assistantships, and teaching assistantships available. Financial award application deadline: 1/15; financial award applicants required to submit FAFSA. *Faculty research:* Cardiopulmonary and neural engineering, cellular engineering, image processing, orthopedics and rehabilitation engineering. *Unit head:* Frederick Epstein, Chair, 434-924-5101, Fax: 434-982-3870, E-mail: bme-dept@virginia.edu. *Application contact:* Jason Papin, Director of Graduate Programs, 434-243-6906, Fax: 434-982-3870, E-mail: bmegrad@virginia.edu.
Website: http://bme.virginia.edu/grad/.

University of Wisconsin–Madison, Graduate School, College of Engineering, Department of Biomedical Engineering, Madison, WI 53706. Offers MS, PhD. Part-time programs available. *Faculty:* 20 full-time (7 women), 57 part-time/adjunct (11 women). *Students:* 104 full-time (34 women), 4 part-time (2 women); includes 18 minority (1 Black or African American, non-Hispanic/Latino; 1 American Indian or Alaska Native, non-Hispanic/Latino; 12 Asian, non-Hispanic/Latino; 4 Hispanic/Latino), 21 international. Average age 25. 413 applicants, 11% accepted, 20 enrolled. In 2014, 23 master's, 13 doctorates awarded. Terminal master's awarded for partial completion of doctoral program. *Degree requirements:* For master's, thesis optional; for doctorate, comprehensive exam, thesis/dissertation, 60 credits of coursework. *Entrance requirements:* For master's and doctorate, GRE, bachelor's degree in engineering or a physical science (chemistry or physics). Additional exam requirements/recommendations for international students: Recommended—TOEFL (minimum score 625 paper-based), IELTS. *Application deadline:* For fall admission, 12/31 for domestic and international students; for spring admission, 10/1 for domestic and international students. Application fee: $56. Electronic applications accepted. *Expenses:* Tuition, state resident: full-time $10,723; part-time $745 per credit. Tuition, nonresident: full-time $24,054; part-time $1578 per credit. *Required fees:* $374 per semester. Tuition and fees vary according to course load, program and reciprocity agreements. *Financial support:* In 2014–15, 53 students received support, including 7 fellowships with full tuition reimbursements available (averaging $23,376 per year), 32 research assistantships with full tuition reimbursements available (averaging $42,448 per year), 14 teaching assistantships with full tuition reimbursements available (averaging $29,492 per year); career-related internships or fieldwork, Federal Work-Study, scholarships/grants, traineeships, and health care benefits also available. *Faculty research:* Biomaterials; bioinstrumentation; cellular scale; biomechanics; biomedical imaging; ergonomics; design, fabrication, and testing of novel micro fabrication techniques; magnetic resonance; tissue engineering; biomedical optics. *Total annual research expenditures:* $5.2 million. *Unit head:* Dr. Elizabeth Meyerand, Professor and Chair, 608-263-1685, Fax: 608-263-1352, E-mail: bme@engr.wisc.edu. *Application contact:* Deidre Vincevineus, Graduate Admissions Coordinator, 608-265-1452, Fax: 608-890-2204, E-mail: vincevineus@wisc.edu.
Website: http://www.engr.wisc.edu/bme.html.

Vanderbilt University, School of Engineering and Graduate School, Department of Biomedical Engineering, Nashville, TN 37240-1001. Offers M Eng, MS, PhD, MD/PhD. *Degree requirements:* For master's, thesis (for some programs); for doctorate, thesis/dissertation. *Entrance requirements:* For master's, GRE General Test (for all except M Eng); for doctorate, GRE General Test. Additional exam requirements/recommendations for international students: Required—TOEFL. Electronic applications accepted. *Expenses: Tuition:* Full-time $42,768; part-time $1782 per credit hour. *Required fees:* $422. One-time fee: $30 full-time. *Faculty research:* Bio-medical imaging, cell bioengineering, biomedical optics, technology-guided therapy, laser-tissue interaction and spectroscopy.

Virginia Commonwealth University, Graduate School, School of Engineering, Department of Biomedical Engineering, Richmond, VA 23284-9005. Offers MS, PhD, MD/PhD. *Degree requirements:* For master's, thesis; for doctorate, thesis/dissertation, comprehensive oral and written exams. *Entrance requirements:* For master's and doctorate, GRE General Test. Additional exam requirements/recommendations for international students: Required—TOEFL (minimum score 600 paper-based; 100 iBT). Electronic applications accepted. *Faculty research:* Clinical instrumentation, mathematical modeling, neurosciences, radiation physics and rehabilitation.

Virginia Polytechnic Institute and State University, Graduate School, College of Engineering, Blacksburg, VA 24061. Offers aerospace engineering (ME, MS, PhD); biological systems engineering (ME, MS, PhD); biomedical engineering (MS, PhD); chemical engineering (ME, MS, PhD); civil engineering (ME, MS, PhD); computer engineering (ME, MS, PhD); computer science (MS, PhD); electrical engineering (ME, PhD); engineering education (PhD); engineering mechanics (ME, MS, PhD); environmental engineering (MS); environmental science and engineering (MS); industrial and systems engineering (ME, MS, PhD); materials science and engineering (ME, MS, PhD); mechanical engineering (ME, MS, PhD); mining and minerals engineering (PhD); mining engineering (ME, MS); nuclear engineering (MS, PhD); ocean engineering (MS); systems engineering (ME, MS). *Accreditation:* ABET (one or more programs are accredited). *Faculty:* 356 full-time (60 women), 3 part-time/adjunct (1 woman). *Students:* 1,700 full-time (398 women), 345 part-time (58 women); includes 213 minority (43 Black or African American, non-Hispanic/Latino; 1 American Indian or Alaska Native, non-Hispanic/Latino; 87 Asian, non-Hispanic/Latino; 58 Hispanic/Latino; 1 Native Hawaiian or other Pacific Islander, non-Hispanic/Latino; 23 Two or more races, non-Hispanic/Latino), 1,079 international. Average age 27. 5,228 applicants, 18% accepted, 471 enrolled. In 2014, 438 master's, 211 doctorates awarded. *Degree requirements:* For master's, comprehensive exam (for some programs), thesis (for some programs); for doctorate, comprehensive exam (for some programs), thesis/dissertation (for some programs). *Entrance requirements:* For master's and doctorate, GRE/GMAT (may vary by department). Additional exam requirements/recommendations for international students: Required—TOEFL (minimum score 550 paper-based). *Application deadline:* For fall admission, 8/1 for domestic students, 4/1 for international students; for spring admission, 1/1 for domestic students, 9/1 for international students. Applications are processed on a rolling basis. Application fee: $75. Electronic applications accepted. *Expenses:* Tuition, state resident: full-time $11,656; part-time $647.50 per credit hour. Tuition, nonresident: full-time $23,351; part-time $1297.25 per credit hour. *Required fees:* $2533; $465.75 per semester. Tuition and fees vary according to course load, campus/location and program. *Financial support:* In 2014–15, 148 fellowships with full tuition reimbursements (averaging $8,031 per year), 855 research assistantships with full tuition reimbursements (averaging $22,855 per year), 288 teaching assistantships with full tuition reimbursements (averaging $20,291 per year) were awarded. Financial award application deadline: 3/1; financial award applicants required to submit FAFSA. *Total annual research expenditures:* $90.5 million. *Unit head:* Dr. Richard C. Benson, Dean, 540-231-9752, Fax: 540-231-3031, E-mail: deaneng@vt.edu. *Application contact:* Linda Perkins, Executive Assistant, 540-231-9752, Fax: 540-231-3031, E-mail: lperkins@vt.edu.
Website: http://www.eng.vt.edu/.

Wake Forest University, Virginia Tech-Wake Forest University School of Biomedical Engineering and Sciences, Winston-Salem, NC 27109. Offers biomedical engineering (MS, PhD); DVM/PhD; MD/PhD. Terminal master's awarded for partial completion of doctoral program. *Degree requirements:* For master's, comprehensive exam, thesis; for doctorate, comprehensive exam, thesis/dissertation. *Entrance requirements:* For master's and doctorate, GRE, 3 letters of recommendation. Additional exam requirements/recommendations for international students: Required—TOEFL (minimum score 603 paper-based). Electronic applications accepted. *Faculty research:* Biomechanics, cell and tissue engineering, medical imaging, medical physics.

Washington University in St. Louis, School of Engineering and Applied Science, Department of Biomedical Engineering, St. Louis, MO 63130-4899. Offers MS, D Sc, PhD. Terminal master's awarded for partial completion of doctoral program. *Degree requirements:* For master's, thesis optional; for doctorate, thesis/dissertation. *Entrance requirements:* For master's, GRE, minimum GPA of 3.0; for doctorate, GRE General Test, minimum GPA of 3.5. Additional exam requirements/recommendations for international students: Required—TOEFL. Electronic applications accepted. *Faculty research:* Cell and tissue engineering, molecular engineering, neural engineering.

Wayne State University, College of Engineering, Department of Biomedical Engineering, Detroit, MI 48202. Offers biomedical engineering (MS, PhD); injury biomechanics (Graduate Certificate). *Students:* 80 full-time (38 women), 29 part-time (10 women); includes 17 minority (3 Black or African American, non-Hispanic/Latino; 11 Asian, non-Hispanic/Latino; 1 Hispanic/Latino; 2 Two or more races, non-Hispanic/Latino), 44 international. Average age 28. 166 applicants, 44% accepted, 24 enrolled. In 2014, 51 master's, 3 doctorates awarded. Terminal master's awarded for partial completion of doctoral program. *Degree requirements:* For master's, thesis optional; for doctorate, thesis/dissertation. *Entrance requirements:* For master's, GRE (recommended), bachelor's degree, minimum undergraduate GPA of 3.0, one-page statement of purpose, completion of prerequisite coursework in calculus and engineering physics; for doctorate, GRE, bachelor's degree with minimum undergraduate GPA of 3.5, undergraduate major or substantial specialized work in proposed doctoral major field, personal statement, three letters of recommendation; for Graduate Certificate, minimum undergraduate GPA of 3.5, bachelor's degree in biomedical engineering or mathematics. Additional exam requirements/recommendations for international students: Required—TOEFL (minimum score 550 paper-based; 79 iBT), TWE (minimum score 5.5), Michigan English Language Assessment Battery (minimum score 85); Recommended—IELTS (minimum score 6.5). *Application deadline:* For fall admission, 6/1 priority date for domestic students, 5/1 priority date for international students; for winter admission, 10/1 priority date for domestic students, 9/1 priority date for international students; for spring admission, 2/1 priority date for domestic students, 1/1 priority date for international students. Applications are processed on a rolling basis. Application fee: $0. Electronic applications accepted. *Expenses:* Expenses: Contact institution. *Financial support:* In 2014–15, 57 students received support, including 5 fellowships with tuition reimbursements available (averaging $15,258 per year), 11 research assistantships with tuition reimbursements available (averaging $18,479 per year), 7 teaching assistantships with tuition reimbursements available (averaging $18,432 per year); Federal Work-Study, scholarships/grants, health care benefits, and unspecified assistantships also available. Support available to part-time students. Financial award application deadline: 3/31; financial award applicants required to submit FAFSA. *Faculty research:* Injury and orthopedic biomechanics, neurophysiology of pain, smart sensors, biomaterials and imaging. *Total annual research expenditures:* $3.7 million. *Unit head:* Dr. Juri Gelovani, Chair, 313-577-1346, E-mail: fg0846@wayne.edu. *Application contact:* 313-577-1345, Fax: 313-577-8333, E-mail: bmeinfo@eng.wayne.edu.
Website: http://engineering.wayne.edu/bme/.

Widener University, Graduate Programs in Engineering, Program in Biomedical Engineering, Chester, PA 19013-5792. Offers M Eng. *Entrance requirements:* For master's, BS in engineering.

Worcester Polytechnic Institute, Graduate Studies and Research, Department of Biomedical Engineering, Worcester, MA 01609-2280. Offers M Eng, MS, PhD, Graduate Certificate. Part-time and evening/weekend programs available. *Faculty:* 9 full-time (3 women), 2 part-time/adjunct (0 women). *Students:* 43 full-time (19 women), 5 part-time (1 woman); includes 9 minority (1 Black or African American, non-Hispanic/Latino; 4 Asian, non-Hispanic/Latino; 2 Hispanic/Latino; 2 Two or more races, non-Hispanic/Latino), 5 international. 155 applicants, 41% accepted, 23 enrolled. In 2014, 13 master's, 3 doctorates awarded. Terminal master's awarded for partial completion of doctoral program. *Degree requirements:* For master's, thesis optional; for doctorate,

comprehensive exam, thesis/dissertation. *Entrance requirements:* For master's and doctorate, GRE General Test, 3 letters of recommendation, statement of purpose. Additional exam requirements/recommendations for international students: Required—TOEFL (minimum score 563 paper-based; 84 iBT), IELTS (minimum score 7). *Application deadline:* For fall admission, 1/1 priority date for domestic and international students. Application fee: $70. Electronic applications accepted. *Financial support:* Research assistantships, teaching assistantships, career-related internships or fieldwork, institutionally sponsored loans, scholarships/grants, and unspecified assistantships available. Financial award application deadline: 1/1; financial award applicants required to submit FAFSA. *Unit head:* Dr. Yitzhak Mendelson, Head, 508-831-5447, Fax: 508-831-5541, E-mail: ym@wpi.edu. *Application contact:* Dr. Marsha Rolle, Graduate Coordinator, 508-831-5447, Fax: 508-831-5447, E-mail: mrolle@wpi.edu.
Website: http://www.wpi.edu/Academics/Depts/BME/.

Wright State University, School of Graduate Studies, College of Engineering and Computer Science, Programs in Engineering, Program in Biomedical and Human Factors Engineering, Dayton, OH 45435. Offers biomedical engineering (MSE); human factors engineering (MSE). Part-time programs available. *Degree requirements:* For master's, thesis or course option alternative. *Entrance requirements:* Additional exam requirements/recommendations for international students: Required—TOEFL. *Faculty research:* Medical imaging, functional electrical stimulation, implantable aids, man-machine interfaces, expert systems.

Yale University, Graduate School of Arts and Sciences, School of Engineering and Applied Science, Department of Biomedical Engineering, New Haven, CT 06520. Offers MS, PhD. *Faculty research:* Biomedical imaging and biosignals; biomechanics; biomolecular engineering and biotechnology.

Biotechnology

Arizona State University at the Tempe campus, Sandra Day O'Connor College of Law, Tempe, AZ 85287-7906. Offers biotechnology and genomics (LL M); global legal studies (LL M); law (MLS, JD); law (customized) (LL M); tribal policy, law and government (LL M); JD/MBA; JD/MD; JD/PhD. JD/MD offered jointly with Mayo Medical School. Accreditation: ABA. *Faculty:* 59 full-time (24 women), 67 part-time/adjunct (16 women). *Students:* 616 full-time (249 women), 45 part-time (18 women); includes 181 minority (28 Black or African American, non-Hispanic/Latino; 21 American Indian or Alaska Native, non-Hispanic/Latino; 23 Asian, non-Hispanic/Latino; 76 Hispanic/Latino; 3 Native Hawaiian or other Pacific Islander, non-Hispanic/Latino; 30 Two or more races, non-Hispanic/Latino), 20 international. Average age 28. 1,410 applicants, 44% accepted, 143 enrolled. In 2014, 9 master's, 198 doctorates awarded. *Degree requirements:* For doctorate, papers. *Entrance requirements:* For master's, bachelor's degree and JD (for LL M); for doctorate, LSAT, bachelor's degree. Additional exam requirements/recommendations for international students: Required—TOEFL (minimum score 550 paper-based; 80 iBT). *Application deadline:* For fall admission, 2/1 priority date for domestic and international students. Applications are processed on a rolling basis. Application fee: $65. Electronic applications accepted. *Expenses:* Expenses: Contact institution. *Financial support:* Research assistantships, teaching assistantships, career-related internships or fieldwork, Federal Work-Study, institutionally sponsored loans, scholarships/grants, tuition waivers (full and partial), and unspecified assistantships available. Financial award application deadline: 3/15; financial award applicants required to submit FAFSA. *Faculty research:* Emerging technologies and the law, Indian law, law and philosophy, international law, intellectual property. *Total annual research expenditures:* $1.3 million. *Unit head:* Douglas Sylvester, Dean/Professor, 480-965-6188, Fax: 480-965-6521, E-mail: douglas.sylvester@asu.edu. *Application contact:* Chitra Damania, Director of Operations, 480-965-1474, Fax: 480-727-7930, E-mail: law.admissions@asu.edu.
Website: http://www.law.asu.edu/.

Arkansas State University, Graduate School, College of Sciences and Mathematics, Department of Biological Sciences, State University, AR 72467. Offers biological sciences (MA); biology (MS); biology education (MSE, SCCT); biotechnology (PSM). Part-time programs available. *Faculty:* 22 full-time (7 women). *Students:* 15 full-time (4 women), 15 part-time (7 women); includes 2 minority (both Black or African American, non-Hispanic/Latino), 1 international. Average age 27. 40 applicants, 38% accepted, 13 enrolled. In 2014, 11 master's awarded. *Degree requirements:* For master's, comprehensive exam, thesis (for some programs); for SCCT, comprehensive exam. *Entrance requirements:* For master's, GRE General Test, appropriate bachelor's degree, letters of reference, interview, official transcripts, immunization records, statement of educational objectives and career goals, teaching certificate (MSE); for SCCT, GRE General Test or MAT, interview, master's degree, letters of reference, official transcript, personal statement, immunization records. Additional exam requirements/recommendations for international students: Required—TOEFL (minimum score 550 paper-based; 79 iBT), IELTS (minimum score 6), PTE (minimum score 56). *Application deadline:* For fall admission, 7/1 for domestic and international students; for spring admission, 11/15 for domestic students, 11/14 for international students. Applications are processed on a rolling basis. Application fee: $30 ($40 for international students). Electronic applications accepted. *Expenses:* Tuition, state resident: full-time $4392; part-time $244 per credit hour. Tuition, nonresident: full-time $8784; part-time $488 per credit hour. International tuition: $9484 full-time. *Required fees:* $1134; $63 per credit hour. $25 per term. Tuition and fees vary according to course load and program. *Financial support:* In 2014–15, 20 students received support. Research assistantships, career-related internships or fieldwork, scholarships/grants, and unspecified assistantships available. Financial award application deadline: 7/1; financial award applicants required to submit FAFSA. *Unit head:* Dr. Thomas Risch, Chair, 870-972-3082, Fax: 870-972-2638, E-mail: trisch@astate.edu. *Application contact:* Vickey Ring, Graduate Admissions Coordinator, 870-972-3029, Fax: 870-972-3857, E-mail: vickeyring@astate.edu.
Website: http://www.astate.edu/college/sciences-and-mathematics/departments/biology/.

Brandeis University, Graduate School of Arts and Sciences, Program in Biotechnology, Waltham, MA 02454-9110. Offers MS. *Degree requirements:* For master's, poster presentation; summer internship. *Entrance requirements:* For master's, GRE, official transcript(s), 3 recommendation letters, curriculum vitae or resume, statement of purpose. Additional exam requirements/recommendations for international students: Required—TOEFL (minimum score 600 paper-based; 100 iBT), PTE (minimum score 68); Recommended—IELTS (minimum score 7). Electronic applications accepted. *Expenses:* Contact institution.

Brigham Young University, Graduate Studies, College of Life Sciences, Department of Plant and Wildlife Sciences, Provo, UT 84602. Offers environmental science (MS); genetics and biotechnology (MS); wildlife and wildlands conservation (MS, PhD). *Faculty:* 25 full-time (1 woman), 1 (woman) part-time/adjunct. *Students:* 48 full-time (16 women); includes 6 minority (3 Asian, non-Hispanic/Latino; 2 Hispanic/Latino; 1 Native Hawaiian or other Pacific Islander, non-Hispanic/Latino). Average age 25. 22 applicants, 36% accepted, 8 enrolled. In 2014, 16 master's, 2 doctorates awarded. *Degree requirements:* For master's, thesis; for doctorate, comprehensive exam, thesis/dissertation, minimum GPA of 3.2, 54 hours (18 dissertation, 36 coursework). *Entrance requirements:* For master's, GRE General Test, minimum GPA of 3.2; for doctorate, GRE, minimum GPA of 3.2. Additional exam requirements/recommendations for international students: Required—TOEFL (minimum score 580 paper-based; 85 iBT). *Application deadline:* 2/1 for domestic and international students. Applications are processed on a rolling basis. Application fee: $50. Electronic applications accepted. *Expenses:* Tuition: Full-time $6310; part-time $371 per credit hour. Tuition and fees vary

according to program and student's religious affiliation. *Financial support:* In 2014–15, 42 students received support, including 64 research assistantships with partial tuition reimbursements available (averaging $19,000 per year), 52 teaching assistantships with partial tuition reimbursements available (averaging $19,000 per year); scholarships/grants and tuition waivers (partial) also available. Financial award application deadline: 2/1. *Faculty research:* Environmental science, plant genetics, plant ecology, plant nutrition and pathology, wildlife and wildlands conservation. *Total annual research expenditures:* $2.6 million. *Unit head:* Dr. Eric N. Jellen, Chair, 801-422-3527, Fax: 801-422-0008, E-mail: rick_jellen@byu.edu. *Application contact:* Dr. Brock R. McMillan, Graduate Coordinator, 801-422-1228, Fax: 801-422-0008, E-mail: brock_mcmillan@byu.edu.
Website: http://pws.byu.edu/home/.

Brock University, Faculty of Graduate Studies, Faculty of Mathematics and Science, Program in Biotechnology, St. Catharines, ON L2S 3A1, Canada. Offers M Sc, PhD. Part-time programs available. *Degree requirements:* For master's, thesis; for doctorate, thesis/dissertation. *Entrance requirements:* For master's, honors B Sc; for doctorate, M Sc. Additional exam requirements/recommendations for international students: Required—TOEFL (minimum score 550 paper-based; 80 iBT), IELTS (minimum score 6.5), TWE (minimum score 4). Electronic applications accepted. *Faculty research:* Bioorganic chemistry, structural chemistry, electrochemistry, cell and molecular biology, plant sciences, oenology, and viticulture.

Brown University, Graduate School, Division of Biology and Medicine, Department of Molecular Pharmacology, Physiology and Biotechnology, Providence, RI 02912. Offers biomedical engineering (Sc M, PhD); biotechnology (PhD); molecular pharmacology and physiology (PhD); MD/PhD. *Degree requirements:* For doctorate, thesis/dissertation, preliminary exam. *Entrance requirements:* For master's and doctorate, GRE General Test, GRE Subject Test. Additional exam requirements/recommendations for international students: Required—TOEFL. Electronic applications accepted. *Faculty research:* Structural biology, antiplatelet drugs, nicotinic receptor structure/function.

California State Polytechnic University, Pomona, Program in Applied Biotechnology, Pomona, CA 91768-2557. Offers MBT. *Students:* 24 full-time (11 women); includes 3 minority (1 Black or African American, non-Hispanic/Latino; 2 Asian, non-Hispanic/Latino), 11 international. Average age 29. 27 applicants, 89% accepted. In 2014, 8 master's awarded. *Application deadline:* Applications are processed on a rolling basis. Application fee: $55. Electronic applications accepted. *Expenses:* Tuition, state resident: full-time $6738. Tuition, nonresident: full-time $12,300. *Required fees:* $1400. *Unit head:* Dr. David L. Dyer, Program Director, 909-869-5508, Fax: 909-869-4078, E-mail: dldyer@cpp.edu.
Website: https://www.cpp.edu/~sci/biological-sciences/pabs/index.shtml.

California State University Channel Islands, Extended University and International Programs, Programs in Biotechnology, Camarillo, CA 93012. Offers biotechnology and bioinformatics (MS); MS/MBA. *Entrance requirements:* Additional exam requirements/recommendations for international students: Required—TOEFL (minimum score 550 paper-based; 80 iBT), IELTS (minimum score 6).

California State University, Fullerton, Graduate Studies, College of Natural Science and Mathematics, Department of Biological Science, Fullerton, CA 92834-9480. Offers biology (MS); biotechnology (MBT). Part-time programs available. *Students:* 9 full-time (7 women), 41 part-time (20 women); includes 26 minority (2 Black or African American, non-Hispanic/Latino; 16 Asian, non-Hispanic/Latino; 6 Hispanic/Latino; 2 Two or more races, non-Hispanic/Latino), 4 international. Average age 26. 70 applicants, 31% accepted, 15 enrolled. In 2014, 21 master's awarded. *Degree requirements:* For master's, thesis. *Entrance requirements:* For master's, GRE General and Subject Tests, MCAT, or DAT, minimum GPA of 3.0 in biology. Application fee: $55. *Financial support:* Research assistantships, teaching assistantships, career-related internships or fieldwork, Federal Work-Study, institutionally sponsored loans, and scholarships/grants available. Support available to part-time students. Financial award application deadline: 3/1; financial award applicants required to submit FAFSA. *Faculty research:* Glycosidase release and the block to polyspermy in ascidian eggs. *Unit head:* Dr. Katherine Dickson, Acting Chair, 657-278-3614. *Application contact:* Admissions/Applications, 657-278-2371.

Carnegie Mellon University, H. John Heinz III College, School of Public Policy and Management, Master of Science Program in Biotechnology and Management, Pittsburgh, PA 15213-3891. Offers MS. Accreditation: AACSB. *Entrance requirements:* For master's, GRE or GMAT, college-level course in advanced algebra/pre-calculus; college-level courses in economics and statistics (recommended). Additional exam requirements/recommendations for international students: Required—TOEFL or IELTS.

Claflin University, Graduate Programs, Orangeburg, SC 29115. Offers biotechnology (MS); business administration (MBA). Part-time programs available. *Degree requirements:* For master's, comprehensive exam, thesis. *Entrance requirements:* For master's, GRE, GMAT, baccalaureate degree, 3 letters of recommendation, resume, statement of purpose. Additional exam requirements/recommendations for international students: Recommended—TOEFL (minimum score 550 paper-based).

Clarkson University, Graduate School, School of Arts and Sciences, Program in Interdisciplinary Bioscience and Biotechnology, Potsdam, NY 13699. Offers PhD. Part-time programs available. *Students:* 6 full-time (2 women), 4 international. Average age 28. 12 applicants, 25% accepted, 2 enrolled. In 2014, 1 doctorate awarded. *Degree requirements:* For doctorate, thesis/dissertation, departmental qualifying exam. *Entrance requirements:* For doctorate, GRE, transcripts of all college coursework, resume, personal statement, three letters of recommendation. Additional exam requirements/recommendations for international students: Required—TOEFL, IELTS.

Biotechnology

Application deadline: For fall admission, 1/30 priority date for domestic and international students; for spring admission, 9/1 priority date for domestic and international students. Applications are processed on a rolling basis. Application fee: $25 ($35 for international students). Electronic applications accepted. *Expenses: Tuition:* Full-time $16,680; part-time $1390 per credit. *Required fees:* $295 per semester. *Financial support:* In 2014–15, 6 students received support, including fellowships with full tuition reimbursements available (averaging $24,029 per year), 1 research assistantship with full tuition reimbursement available (averaging $24,029 per year), 5 teaching assistantships with full tuition reimbursements available (averaging $24,029 per year); scholarships/grants, tuition waivers (partial), and unspecified assistantships also available. *Faculty research:* Regenerative medicine. *Unit head:* Dr. James A. Schulte, II, Director, 315-268-4401, Fax: 315-268-7118, E-mail: jschulte@clarkson.edu. *Application contact:* Jennifer Reed, Graduate Coordinator, School of Arts and Sciences, 315-268-3802, Fax: 315-268-3989, E-mail: sciencegrad@clarkson.edu.
Website: http://www.clarkson.edu/biology/graduate/.

Columbia University, Graduate School of Arts and Sciences, New York, NY 10027. Offers African-American studies (MA); American studies (MA); anthropology (MA, PhD); art history and archaeology (MA, PhD); astronomy (PhD); biological sciences (PhD); biotechnology (MA); chemical physics (PhD); chemistry (PhD); classical studies (MA, PhD); classics (MA, PhD); climate and society (MA); earth and environmental sciences (PhD); East Asia: regional studies (MA); East Asian languages and cultures (MA, PhD); ecology, evolution and environmental biology (MA), including conservation biology; ecology, evolution, and environmental biology (PhD), including ecology and evolutionary biology, evolutionary primatology; economics (PhD); English and comparative literature (MA, PhD); French and Romance philology (MA, PhD); Germanic languages (MA, PhD); global French studies (MA); Hispanic cultural studies (MA); history (PhD); history and literature (MA); human rights studies (MA); Islamic studies (MA); Italian (MA, PhD); Japanese pedagogy (MA); Jewish studies (MA); Latin America and the Caribbean: regional studies (MA); Latin American and Iberian cultures (PhD); mathematics (MA, PhD), including finance (MA); medieval and Renaissance studies (MA); Middle Eastern, South Asian, and African studies (MA, PhD); modern art: critical and curatorial studies (MA); modern European studies (MA); museum anthropology (MA); music (DMA, PhD); oral history (MA); philosophical foundations of physics (MA); philosophy (MA, PhD); physics (PhD); political science (MA, PhD); psychology (PhD); quantitative methods in the social sciences (MA); religion (MA, PhD); Russia, Eurasia and East Europe: regional studies (MA); Russian translation (MA); Slavic cultures (MA); Slavic languages (MA, PhD); sociology (MA, PhD); South Asian studies (MA); statistics (MA, PhD); theatre (PhD); JD/PhD; MA/MS; MD/PhD; MPA/MA. Dual-degree programs require admission to both Graduate School of Arts and Sciences and another Columbia school. Part-time and evening/weekend programs available. Terminal master's awarded for partial completion of doctoral program. *Degree requirements:* For master's, thesis (for some programs); for doctorate, comprehensive exam, thesis/dissertation. *Entrance requirements:* For master's and doctorate, GRE General Test, GRE Subject Test (for some programs). Electronic applications accepted. *Faculty research:* Humanities, natural sciences, social sciences.

Concordia University, School of Graduate Studies, Faculty of Arts and Science, Department of Biology, Montréal, QC H3G 1M8, Canada. Offers biology (M Sc, PhD); biotechnology and genomics (Diploma). *Degree requirements:* For master's, thesis; for doctorate, thesis/dissertation, pedagogical training. *Entrance requirements:* For master's, honors degree in biology; for doctorate, M Sc in life science. *Faculty research:* Cell biology, animal physiology, ecology, microbiology/molecular biology, plant physiology/biochemistry and biotechnology.

Cornell University, Graduate School, Graduate Fields of Agriculture and Life Sciences and Graduate Fields of Engineering, Field of Biological and Environmental Engineering, Ithaca, NY 14853-0001. Offers bioenergy and integrated energy systems (M Eng, MPS, MS, PhD); biological engineering (M Eng, MPS, MS, PhD); bioprocess engineering (M Eng, MPS, MS, PhD); ecohydrology (M Eng, MPS, MS, PhD); environmental engineering (M Eng, MPS, MS, PhD); environmental management (MPS); food engineering (M Eng, MPS, MS, PhD); industrial biotechnology (M Eng, MPS, MS, PhD); nanobiotechnology (M Eng, MPS, MS, PhD); sustainable systems (M Eng, MPS, MS, PhD); synthetic biology (MS); syntheticbiology (M Eng, MPS, PhD). Terminal master's awarded for partial completion of doctoral program. *Degree requirements:* For master's, thesis (MS); for doctorate, comprehensive exam, thesis/dissertation. *Entrance requirements:* For master's, letters of recommendation (3 for MS, 2 for M Eng and MPS); for doctorate, GRE General Test, 3 letters of recommendation. Additional exam requirements/recommendations for international students: Required—TOEFL (minimum score 550 paper-based; 77 iBT). Electronic applications accepted. *Faculty research:* Biological and food engineering, environmental, soil and water engineering, international agricultural engineering, structures and controlled environments, machine systems and energy.

Dartmouth College, Thayer School of Engineering, Program in Biotechnology and Biochemical Engineering, Hanover, NH 03755. Offers MS, PhD. *Degree requirements:* For master's, thesis; for doctorate, thesis/dissertation, candidacy oral exam. *Entrance requirements:* For master's and doctorate, GRE General Test. *Application deadline:* For fall admission, 1/1 priority date for domestic students. Application fee: $45. *Financial support:* Fellowships, research assistantships, teaching assistantships, career-related internships or fieldwork, Federal Work-Study, institutionally sponsored loans, and tuition waivers (full and partial) available. Financial award application deadline: 1/15. *Faculty research:* Biomass processing, metabolic engineering, kinetics and reactor design, applied microbiology, resource and environmental analysis. *Total annual research expenditures:* $2.5 million. *Unit head:* Dr. Joseph J. Helbie, Dean, 603-646-2238, Fax: 603-646-2580, E-mail: joseph.j.helbie@dartmouth.edu. *Application contact:* Candace S. Potter, Graduate Admissions Administrator, 603-646-3844, Fax: 603-646-1620, E-mail: candace.s.potter@dartmouth.edu.
Website: http://engineering.dartmouth.edu/.

Duquesne University, Bayer School of Natural and Environmental Sciences, Program in Biotechnology, Pittsburgh, PA 15282-0001. Offers MS. Part-time programs available. *Faculty:* 1 full-time (0 women), 2 part-time/adjunct (0 women). *Students:* 15 full-time (7 women), 2 part-time (1 woman); includes 1 minority (Two or more races, non-Hispanic/Latino), 9 international. Average age 24. 39 applicants, 59% accepted, 12 enrolled. In 2014, 9 master's awarded. *Entrance requirements:* For master's, GRE General Test, statement of purpose, 3 letters of recommendation, official transcripts. Additional exam requirements/recommendations for international students: Required—TOEFL (minimum score 80 iBT). *Application deadline:* For fall admission, 5/1 priority date for domestic students, 5/1 for international students; for spring admission, 10/1 priority date for domestic students, 10/1 for international students. Applications are processed on a rolling basis. Application fee: $0. Electronic applications accepted. *Expenses:* Expenses: $1,077 per credit; fees: $100 per credit. *Financial support:* In 2014–15, 16 students received support. Career-related internships or fieldwork and tuition waivers (partial) available. *Unit head:* Dr. Alan W. Seadler, Director, 412-396-1568, E-mail: seadlera@

duq.edu. *Application contact:* Heather Costello, Graduate Academic Advisor, 412-396-6339, Fax: 412-396-4881, E-mail: costelloh@duq.edu.
Website: http://www.duq.edu/academics/schools/natural-and-environmental -sciences/academic-programs/biotechnology.

East Carolina University, Graduate School, Thomas Harriot College of Arts and Sciences, Department of Biology, Greenville, NC 27858-4353. Offers biology (MS); molecular biology and biotechnology (MS). Part-time programs available. *Degree requirements:* For master's, one foreign language, comprehensive exam, thesis. *Entrance requirements:* For master's, GRE General Test, GRE Subject Test. Additional exam requirements/recommendations for international students: Required—TOEFL. *Expenses:* Tuition, state resident: full-time $4223. Tuition, nonresident: full-time $16,540. *Required fees:* $2184. *Faculty research:* Biochemistry, microbiology, cell biology.

Eastern Virginia Medical School, Biotechnology Program, Norfolk, VA 23501-1980. Offers MS. *Entrance requirements:* For master's, GRE. Additional exam requirements/recommendations for international students: Required—TOEFL. Electronic applications accepted.

Florida Atlantic University, Charles E. Schmidt College of Science, Department of Biological Sciences, Boca Raton, FL 33431-0991. Offers biology (MS, MST); business biotechnology (MS); environmental science (MS); integrative biology (PhD). Part-time programs available. *Degree requirements:* For master's, thesis (for some programs). *Entrance requirements:* For master's, GRE General Test, minimum GPA of 3.0. Additional exam requirements/recommendations for international students: Required— TOEFL (minimum score 500 paper-based; 61 iBT), IELTS (minimum score 6). *Expenses:* Tuition, state resident: full-time $7396; part-time $369.82 per credit hour. Tuition, nonresident: full-time $19,392; part-time $1024.81 per credit hour. Tuition and fees vary according to course load. *Faculty research:* Ecology of the Everglades, molecular biology and biotechnology, marine biology.

Florida Institute of Technology, Graduate Programs, College of Science, Program in Biological Sciences, Melbourne, FL 32901-6975. Offers biological science (PhD); biotechnology (MS); cell and molecular biology (MS); ecology (MS); marine biology (MS). Part-time programs available. *Students:* 71 full-time (34 women), 11 part-time (6 women); includes 4 minority (2 Asian, non-Hispanic/Latino; 1 Hispanic/Latino; 1 Two or more races, non-Hispanic/Latino), 39 international. Average age 26. 201 applicants, 28% accepted, 15 enrolled. In 2014, 24 master's, 4 doctorates awarded. *Degree requirements:* For master's, comprehensive exam (for some programs), thesis (for some programs), research, seminar, internship, or summer lab; for doctorate, comprehensive exam, thesis/dissertation, dissertations seminar, publications. *Entrance requirements:* For master's, GRE General Test, 3 letters of recommendation, minimum GPA of 3.0, statement of objectives; for doctorate, GRE General Test, resume, 3 letters of recommendation, minimum GPA of 3.2, statement of objectives. Additional exam requirements/recommendations for international students: Required—TOEFL (minimum score 550 paper-based; 79 iBT). *Application deadline:* For fall admission, 3/1 for domestic students, 4/1 for international students; for spring admission, 9/1 for domestic and international students. Applications are processed on a rolling basis. Electronic applications accepted. *Expenses:* Tuition: Part-time $1179 per credit hour. Tuition and fees vary according to campus/location. *Financial support:* Career-related internships or fieldwork, institutionally sponsored loans, tuition waivers (partial), unspecified assistantships, and tuition remissions available. Support available to part-time students. Financial award application deadline: 3/1; financial award applicants required to submit FAFSA. *Faculty research:* Initiation of protein synthesis in eukaryotic cells, fixation of radioactive carbon, changes in DNA molecule, endangered or threatened avian and mammalian species, hydroacoustics and feeding preference of the West Indian manatee. *Unit head:* Dr. Richard B. Aronson, Department Head, 321-674-8034, Fax: 321-674-7238, E-mail: raronson@fit.edu. *Application contact:* Cheryl A. Brown, Associate Director of Graduate Admissions, 321-674-7581, Fax: 321-723-9468, E-mail: cbrown@fit.edu.
Website: http://cos.fit.edu/biology/.

The George Washington University, College of Professional Studies, Program in Molecular Biotechnology, Washington, DC 20052. Offers MPS. *Students:* 1 (woman) full-time, 2 part-time (both women); includes 1 minority (Hispanic/Latino), 1 international. Average age 29. 21 applicants. In 2014, 1 master's awarded. *Application deadline:* For fall admission, 4/1 for domestic and international students. Application fee: $25. Electronic applications accepted. *Financial support:* In 2014–15, 3 students received support. Tuition waivers available. *Unit head:* Dr. Mark Reeves, Director, 202-994-6279, Fax: 202-994-3001, E-mail: reevesme@gwu.edu. *Application contact:* Kristin Williams, Assistant Vice President for Graduate and Special Enrollment Management, 202-994-0467, Fax: 202-994-0371, E-mail: ksw@gwu.edu.
Website: http://cps.gwu.edu/mmb/index.html.

The George Washington University, School of Medicine and Health Sciences, Health Sciences Programs, Washington, DC 20052. Offers clinical practice management (MSHS); clinical research administration (MSHS); emergency services management (MSHS); end-of-life care (MSHS); immunohematology (MSHS); immunohematology and biotechnology (MSHS); physical therapy (DPT); physician assistant (MSHS). Postbaccalaureate distance learning degree programs offered (no on-campus study). *Students:* 265 full-time (200 women), 2 part-time (1 woman); includes 63 minority (9 Black or African American, non-Hispanic/Latino; 2 American Indian or Alaska Native, non-Hispanic/Latino; 30 Asian, non-Hispanic/Latino; 19 Hispanic/Latino; 2 Native Hawaiian or other Pacific Islander, non-Hispanic/Latino; 1 Two or more races, non-Hispanic/Latino), 1 international. Average age 28. 1,868 applicants, 13% accepted, 112 enrolled. *Entrance requirements:* Additional exam requirements/recommendations for international students: Required—TOEFL (minimum score 550 paper-based). *Application deadline:* Applications are processed on a rolling basis. Application fee: $75. *Expenses:* Expenses: Contact institution. *Unit head:* Jean E. Johnson, Senior Associate Dean, 202-994-3725, E-mail: jejohns@gwu.edu. *Application contact:* Joke Ogundiran, Director of Admission, 202-994-1668, Fax: 202-994-0870, E-mail: jokeogun@gwu.edu.

Harvard University, Extension School, Cambridge, MA 02138-3722. Offers applied sciences (CAS); biotechnology (ALM); educational technologies (ALM); educational technology (CET); English for graduate and professional studies (DGP); environmental management (ALM, CEM); information technology (ALM); journalism (ALM); liberal arts (ALM); management (ALM, CM); mathematics for teaching (ALM); museum studies (ALM); premedical studies (Diploma); publication and communication (CPC). Part-time and evening/weekend programs available. *Degree requirements:* For master's, thesis. *Entrance requirements:* For master's, 3 completed graduate courses with grade of B or higher. Additional exam requirements/recommendations for international students: Required—TOEFL (minimum score 600 paper-based), TWE (minimum score 5). *Expenses:* Contact institution.

Hood College, Graduate School, Program in Biomedical Science, Frederick, MD 21701-8575. Offers biomedical science (MS), including biotechnology/molecular biology, microbiology/immunology/virology, regulatory compliance; regulatory compliance (Certificate). Part-time and evening/weekend programs available. *Degree requirements:* For master's, comprehensive exam, thesis or alternative. *Entrance* *requirements:* For master's, bachelor's degree in biology; minimum GPA of 2.75; undergraduate course work in cell biology, chemistry, organic chemistry, and genetics. Additional exam requirements/recommendations for international students: Required—TOEFL (minimum score 575 paper-based; 89 iBT), IELTS (minimum score 6.5). Electronic applications accepted. Application fee is waived when completed online.

Howard University, College of Medicine, Department of Biochemistry and Molecular Biology, Washington, DC 20059-0002. Offers biochemistry and molecular biology (PhD); biotechnology (MS); MD/PhD. Part-time programs available. *Degree requirements:* For master's, externship; for doctorate, comprehensive exam, thesis/dissertation. *Entrance requirements:* For master's and doctorate, GRE General Test, minimum GPA of 3.0. *Faculty research:* Cellular and molecular biology of olfaction, gene regulation and expression, enzymology, NMR spectroscopy of molecular structure, hormone regulation/metabolism.

Illinois State University, Graduate School, College of Arts and Sciences, Department of Biological Sciences, Program in Biotechnology, Normal, IL 61790-2200. Offers MS. *Degree requirements:* For master's, thesis or alternative. *Entrance requirements:* For master's, GRE General Test, minimum GPA of 2.6 in last 60 hours of course work.

Indiana University Bloomington, University Graduate School, College of Arts and Sciences, Department of Biology, Bloomington, IN 47405. Offers biology teaching (MAT); biotechnology (MA); evolution, ecology, and behavior (MA, PhD); genetics (PhD); microbiology (MA, PhD); molecular, cellular, and developmental biology (PhD); plant sciences (MA, PhD); zoology (MA, PhD). *Faculty:* 58 full-time (15 women), 21 part-time/adjunct (6 women). *Students:* 166 full-time (90 women), 2 part-time (1 woman); includes 25 minority (8 Black or African American, non-Hispanic/Latino; 4 Asian, non-Hispanic/Latino; 12 Hispanic/Latino; 1 Two or more races, non-Hispanic/Latino), 45 international. Average age 27. 272 applicants, 24% accepted, 33 enrolled. In 2014, 4 master's, 26 doctorates awarded. Terminal master's awarded for partial completion of doctoral program. *Degree requirements:* For master's, thesis, oral defense; for doctorate, thesis/dissertation, oral defense. *Entrance requirements:* For master's and doctorate, GRE General Test. Additional exam requirements/recommendations for international students: Required—TOEFL (minimum score 100 iBT). *Application deadline:* For fall admission, 1/5 priority date for domestic students, 12/1 priority date for international students. Application fee: $55 ($65 for international students). Electronic applications accepted. *Financial support:* In 2014–15, fellowships with tuition reimbursements (averaging $24,000 per year), research assistantships with tuition reimbursements (averaging $21,000 per year), teaching assistantships with tuition reimbursements (averaging $22,000 per year) were awarded; scholarships/grants, traineeships, health care benefits, and unspecified assistantships also available. Financial award application deadline: 1/5. *Faculty research:* Evolution, ecology and behavior; microbiology; molecular biology and genetics; plant biology. *Unit head:* Dr. Clay Fuqua, Chair, 812-856-6005, Fax: 812-855-6082, E-mail: cfuqua@indiana.edu. *Application contact:* Tracey D. Stohr, Graduate Student Recruitment Coordinator, 812-856-6303, Fax: 812-855-6082, E-mail: gradbio@indiana.edu. Website: http://www.bio.indiana.edu/.

Instituto Tecnológico y de Estudios Superiores de Monterrey, Campus Monterrey, Graduate and Research Division, Program in Natural and Social Sciences, Monterrey, Mexico. Offers biotechnology (MS); chemistry (MS, PhD); communications (MS); education (MA). Part-time programs available. *Degree requirements:* For master's, one foreign language, thesis; for doctorate, one foreign language, thesis/dissertation. *Entrance requirements:* For master's, EXADEP; for doctorate, EXADEP, master's degree in related field. Additional exam requirements/recommendations for international students: Required—TOEFL. *Faculty research:* Cultural industries, mineral substances, bioremediation, food processing, CQ in industrial chemical processing.

Inter American University of Puerto Rico, Bayamón Campus, Graduate School, Bayamón, PR 00957. Offers biology (MS), including environmental sciences and ecology, molecular biotechnology; human resources (MBA). Part-time and evening/weekend programs available. *Degree requirements:* For master's, comprehensive exam, research project. *Entrance requirements:* For master's, EXADEP, GRE General Test, letters of recommendation.

Johns Hopkins University, G. W. C. Whiting School of Engineering, Master of Science in Engineering Management Program, Baltimore, MD 21218-2699. Offers biomaterials (MSEM); civil engineering (MSEM); communications science (MSEM); computer science (MSEM); environmental systems analysis, economics and public policy (MSEM); fluid mechanics (MSEM); materials science and engineering (MSEM); mechanical engineering (MSEM); mechanics and materials (MSEM); nano-biotechnology (MSEM); nanomaterials and nanotechnology (MSEM); operations research (MSEM); probability and statistics (MSEM); smart product and device design (MSEM). *Entrance requirements:* For master's, GRE, 3 letters of recommendation, resume. Additional exam requirements/recommendations for international students: Required—TOEFL (minimum score 600 paper-based; 100 iBT) or IELTS (minimum score 7). Electronic applications accepted.

Johns Hopkins University, Zanvyl Krieger School of Arts and Sciences, Advanced Academic Programs, Program in Biotechnology, Washington, DC 20036. Offers MS, MS/MBA. Part-time and evening/weekend programs available. Postbaccalaureate distance learning degree programs offered (minimal on-campus study). *Degree requirements:* For master's, thesis (for some programs). *Entrance requirements:* For master's, minimum GPA of 3.0; coursework in biology and chemistry. Additional exam requirements/recommendations for international students: Required—TOEFL (minimum score 100 iBT). Electronic applications accepted.

Johns Hopkins University, Zanvyl Krieger School of Arts and Sciences, Advanced Academic Programs, Program in Biotechnology Enterprise and Entrepreneurship, Washington, DC 20036. Offers MBEE. Part-time and evening/weekend programs available. Postbaccalaureate distance learning degree programs offered (no on-campus study). *Degree requirements:* For master's, practicum. *Entrance requirements:* For master's, minimum GPA of 3.0, coursework in biochemistry and cell biology. Additional exam requirements/recommendations for international students: Required—TOEFL (minimum score 100 iBT). Electronic applications accepted.

Kean University, New Jersey Center for Science, Technology and Mathematics, Program in Biotechnology Science, Union, NJ 07083. Offers MS. Part-time programs available. *Faculty:* 7 full-time (1 woman). *Students:* 14 full-time (8 women), 11 part-time (7 women); includes 18 minority (3 Black or African American, non-Hispanic/Latino; 11 Asian, non-Hispanic/Latino; 4 Hispanic/Latino), 3 international. Average age 28. 14 applicants, 64% accepted, 6 enrolled. In 2014, 13 master's awarded. *Degree requirements:* For master's, written research project paper, presentation of research. *Entrance requirements:* For master's, GRE General Test, minimum GPA of 3.0 cumulative and in all science and math courses; official transcripts from all institutions attended; three letters of recommendation; professional resume/curriculum vitae; personal statement. Additional exam requirements/recommendations for international students: Required—TOEFL (minimum score 550 paper-based; 79 iBT). *Application deadline:* For fall admission, 6/1 for domestic and international students; for spring admission, 12/1 for domestic and international students. Applications are processed on a rolling basis. Application fee: $75 ($150 for international students). Electronic

applications accepted. *Expenses:* Tuition, state resident: full-time $12,461; part-time $607 per credit. Tuition, nonresident: full-time $16,889; part-time $744 per credit. *Required fees:* $3141; $143 per credit. Tuition and fees vary according to course load, degree level and program. *Financial support:* In 2014–15, 2 research assistantships with full tuition reimbursements (averaging $3,742 per year) were awarded; scholarships/grants and unspecified assistantships also available. Financial award applicants required to submit FAFSA. *Unit head:* Dr. Salvatore Coniglio, Program Coordinator, 908-737-7216, E-mail: coniglsa@kean.edu. *Application contact:* Reenat Hasan, Pre-Admissions Coordinator, 908-737-7134, Fax: 908-737-7135, E-mail: rhasan@exchange.kean.edu. Website: http://grad.kean.edu/masters-programs/biotechnology.

Marywood University, Academic Affairs, Munley College of Liberal Arts and Sciences, Science Department, Scranton, PA 18509-1598. Offers biotechnology (MS). Part-time programs available. *Students:* 12 full-time (7 women), 1 part-time (0 women); includes 1 minority (Asian, non-Hispanic/Latino), 3 international. Average age 23. In 2014, 12 master's awarded. *Application deadline:* Applications are processed on a rolling basis. Application fee: $35. Electronic applications accepted. *Expenses: Tuition:* Part-time $775 per credit. *Required fees:* $688 per semester. Tuition and fees vary according to degree level and campus/location. *Financial support:* Application deadline: 6/30; applicants required to submit FAFSA. *Unit head:* Dr. Michael C. Kiel, Chair, 570-348-6211 Ext. 2478, E-mail: mkiel@marywood.edu. *Application contact:* Tammy Manka, Assistant Director of Graduate Admissions, 570-348-6211 Ext. 2322, E-mail: tmanka@marywood.edu. Website: http://www.marywood.edu/science/.

McGill University, Faculty of Graduate and Postdoctoral Studies, Faculty of Agricultural and Environmental Sciences, Institute of Parasitology, Montréal, QC H3A 2T5, Canada. Offers biotechnology (M Sc A, Certificate); parasitology (M Sc, PhD).

Middle Tennessee State University, College of Graduate Studies, College of Basic and Applied Sciences, Program in Professional Science, Murfreesboro, TN 37132. Offers actuarial sciences (MS); biostatistics (MS); biotechnology (MS); engineering management (MS); health care informatics (MS). Part-time and evening/weekend programs available. Postbaccalaureate distance learning degree programs offered. *Degree requirements:* For master's, comprehensive exam. *Entrance requirements:* For master's, GRE. Additional exam requirements/recommendations for international students: Required—TOEFL (minimum score 525 paper-based; 71 iBT) or IELTS (minimum score 6). *Faculty research:* Biotechnology, biostatistics, informatics.

Mount St. Mary's University, Program in Biotechnology and Management, Emmitsburg, MD 21727-7799. Offers MS. *Faculty:* 1 part-time/adjunct (0 women). *Students:* 10 part-time (4 women); includes 1 minority (Black or African American, non-Hispanic/Latino). Average age 30. 15 applicants, 67% accepted, 10 enrolled. *Entrance requirements:* For master's, bachelor's degree in biology or related field, undergraduate transcripts from accredited four-year institution with minimum GPA of 2.75, two letters of recommendation. Application fee: $35. Electronic applications accepted. *Expenses: Tuition:* Full-time $10,242; part-time $569 per credit hour. Tuition and fees vary according to program. *Unit head:* Dr. Matthew Rittler, Advisor, 301-447-5716, E-mail: rittler@msmary.edu. *Application contact:* Joseph Lebherz, Director, Center for Professional and Continuing Studies, 301-682-8315, Fax: 301-682-5247, E-mail: lebherz@msmary.edu. Website: http://msmary.edu/School_of_natural_science_and_math /Graduate_Programs/index.html.

New Mexico State University, College of Arts and Sciences, Department of Biology, Las Cruces, NM 88003-8001. Offers biology (MS, PhD); biotechnology (MS). Part-time programs available. *Faculty:* 23 full-time (11 women). *Students:* 49 full-time (26 women), 14 part-time (8 women); includes 18 minority (1 Black or African American, non-Hispanic/Latino; 2 American Indian or Alaska Native, non-Hispanic/Latino; 2 Asian, non-Hispanic/Latino; 13 Hispanic/Latino), 19 international. Average age 31. 50 applicants, 34% accepted, 10 enrolled. In 2014, 20 master's, 3 doctorates awarded. *Degree requirements:* For master's, thesis (for some programs), defense or oral exam; for doctorate, comprehensive exam, thesis/dissertation, qualifying exam. *Entrance requirements:* For master's and doctorate, GRE. Additional exam requirements/recommendations for international students: Required—TOEFL (minimum score 550 paper-based; 79 iBT), IELTS (minimum score 6.5). *Application deadline:* For fall admission, 1/15 priority date for domestic students, 1/15 for international students; for spring admission, 10/4 priority date for domestic students, 10/4 for international students. Applications are processed on a rolling basis. Application fee: $40 ($50 for international students). Electronic applications accepted. *Expenses:* Tuition, state resident: full-time $3969; part-time $220.50 per credit hour. Tuition, nonresident: full-time $13,838; part-time $768.80 per credit hour. *Required fees:* $853; $47.40 per credit hour. *Financial support:* In 2014–15, 48 students received support, including 4 fellowships (averaging $3,970 per year), 11 research assistantships (averaging $19,925 per year), 30 teaching assistantships (averaging $16,972 per year); career-related internships or fieldwork, Federal Work-Study, scholarships/grants, traineeships, health care benefits, and unspecified assistantships also available. Support available to part-time students. Financial award application deadline: 3/1. *Faculty research:* Microbiology, cell and organismal physiology, ecology and ethology, evolution, genetics, developmental biology. *Total annual research expenditures:* $2.6 million. *Unit head:* Dr. Ralph Preszler, Academic Department Head, 575-646-3611, Fax: 575-646-5665, E-mail: rpreszle@nmsu.edu. *Application contact:* Dr. Angus Dawe, Associate Professor, 575-646-3611, Fax: 575-646-5665, E-mail: biologygrads@nmsu.edu. Website: http://bio.nmsu.edu.

New York University, Polytechnic School of Engineering, Department of Chemical and Biomolecular Engineering, Major in Biotechnology, New York, NY 10012-1019. Offers MS. *Students:* 37 full-time (23 women), 10 part-time (4 women); includes 4 minority (1 Black or African American, non-Hispanic/Latino; 2 Asian, non-Hispanic/Latino; 1 Hispanic/Latino), 40 international. Average age 24. 117 applicants, 46% accepted, 20 enrolled. In 2014, 30 master's awarded. *Entrance requirements:* Additional exam requirements/recommendations for international students: Required—TOEFL (minimum score 550 paper-based; 80 iBT); Recommended—IELTS (minimum score 6.5). *Application deadline:* For fall admission, 2/15 priority date for domestic and international students; for spring admission, 11/1 priority date for domestic and international students. Applications are processed on a rolling basis. Application fee: $75. Electronic applications accepted. *Unit head:* Dr. David Pine, Department Head, 718-260-3004, E-mail: pine@nyu.edu. *Application contact:* Raymond Lutzky, Director, Graduate Enrollment Management, 718-637-5984, Fax: 718-260-3624, E-mail: rlutzky@poly.edu.

New York University, Polytechnic School of Engineering, Department of Chemical and Biomolecular Engineering, Major in Biotechnology and Entrepreneurship, New York, NY 10012-1019. Offers MS. *Students:* 14 full-time (7 women), 2 part-time (1 woman); includes 1 minority (Asian, non-Hispanic/Latino), 13 international. Average age 24. 48 applicants, 40% accepted, 7 enrolled. In 2014, 8 master's awarded. *Entrance requirements:* Additional exam requirements/recommendations for international students: Required—TOEFL (minimum score 550 paper-based; 80 iBT); Recommended—IELTS (minimum score 6.5). *Application deadline:* For fall admission, 2/15 priority date for domestic and international students; for spring admission, 11/1 priority date for domestic and international students. Applications are processed on a rolling basis. Application fee: $75. Electronic applications accepted. *Financial support:* Institutionally sponsored loans, scholarships/grants, and unspecified assistantships available. Support available to part-time students. *Unit head:* Dr. Evgency Vulfson, Program Director, 718-260-3096, E-mail: ev494@nyu.edu. *Application contact:* Raymond Lutzky, Director, Graduate Enrollment Management, 718-260-3004, Fax: 718-260-3624, E-mail: rlutzky@poly.edu.

North Carolina State University, Graduate School, College of Agriculture and Life Sciences, Department of Microbiology, Program in Microbial Biotechnology, Raleigh, NC 27695. Offers MMB. *Entrance requirements:* For master's, GRE. Electronic applications accepted.

Northeastern University, Bouvé College of Health Sciences, Boston, MA 02115-5096. Offers audiology (Au D); biotechnology (MS); counseling psychology (MS, PhD, CAGS); counseling/school psychology (PhD); exercise physiology (MS), including exercise physiology, public health; health informatics (MS); nursing (MS, PhD, CAGS), including acute care (MS), administration (MS), anesthesia (MS), primary care (MS), psychiatric mental health (MS); pharmaceutical sciences (PhD); pharmaceutics and drug delivery systems (MS); pharmacology (MS); physical therapy (DPT); physician assistant (MS); school psychology (PhD, CAGS); school/counseling psychology (PhD); speech language pathology (MS); urban public health (MPH); MS/MBA. *Accreditation:* ACPE (one or more programs are accredited). Part-time and evening/weekend programs available. *Degree requirements:* For doctorate, thesis/dissertation (for some programs); for CAGS, comprehensive exam.

Northeastern University, College of Science, Department of Biology, Master of Science in Biotechnology Program, Boston, MA 02115-5096. Offers MS, PSM. Part-time and evening/weekend programs available. *Entrance requirements:* For master's, GRE. Additional exam requirements/recommendations for international students: Required—TOEFL (minimum score 600 paper-based; 100 iBT). Electronic applications accepted. *Expenses:* Contact institution. *Faculty research:* Genomics, proteomics, gene expression analysis (molecular biotechnology), drug discovery, development, delivery (pharmaceutical biotechnology), bioprocess development and optimization (process development).

Northwestern University, The Graduate School, Interdisciplinary Biological Sciences Program (IBiS), Evanston, IL 60208. Offers biochemistry (PhD); bioengineering and biotechnology (PhD); biotechnology (PhD); cell and molecular biology (PhD); developmental and systems biology (PhD); nanotechnology (PhD); neurobiology (PhD); structural biology and biophysics (PhD). *Degree requirements:* For doctorate, thesis/dissertation, qualifying exam. *Entrance requirements:* For doctorate, GRE General Test. Additional exam requirements/recommendations for international students: Required—TOEFL (minimum score 600 paper-based). Electronic applications accepted. *Faculty research:* Biophysics/structural biology, cell/molecular biology, synthetic biology, developmental systems biology, chemical biology/nanotechnology.

Northwestern University, McCormick School of Engineering and Applied Science, MS in Biotechnology Program, Evanston, IL 60208. Offers MS. *Students:* 73 full-time (34 women); includes 4 minority (all Asian, non-Hispanic/Latino), 8 international. Average age 24. 138 applicants, 53% accepted, 34 enrolled. In 2014, 27 master's awarded. *Entrance requirements:* For master's, GRE General Test. Additional exam requirements/recommendations for international students: Required—TOEFL, IELTS. *Application deadline:* For fall admission, 5/31 for domestic and international students. Application fee: $50. Electronic applications accepted. *Financial support:* Career-related internships or fieldwork, institutionally sponsored loans, scholarships/grants, and health care benefits available. Financial award application deadline: 1/15; financial award applicants required to submit FAFSA. *Unit head:* Dr. William M. Miller, Director, 847-491-7399. *Application contact:* Kristen Stevens, Communications Specialist, 847-467-1586, E-mail: kristen.stevens@northwestern.edu.
Website: http://www.mbp.northwestern.edu/.

Oregon State University, Interdisciplinary/Institutional Programs, Program in Applied Biotechnology, Corvallis, OR 97331. Offers PSM. Part-time programs available. In 2014, 6 master's awarded. *Entrance requirements:* For master's, GRE. Additional exam requirements/recommendations for international students: Required—TOEFL (minimum score 80 iBT), IELTS (minimum score 6.5). *Application deadline:* For fall admission, 2/15 for domestic students. Application fee: $60. *Expenses:* Expenses: $14,135 full-time resident tuition and fees; $22,181 non-resident. *Financial support:* Application deadline: 2/15. *Unit head:* Dr. Dee Denver, Program Director, E-mail: denver@cgrb.oregonstate.edu.
Website: http://psm.science.oregonstate.edu/applied-biotechnology.

Penn State University Park, Graduate School, Eberly College of Science, Department of Biochemistry and Molecular Biology, University Park, PA 16802. Offers biochemistry, microbiology, and molecular biology (MS, PhD); biotechnology (MBIOT). *Unit head:* Dr. Douglas R. Cavener, Interim Dean, 814-865-9591, Fax: 814-865-3634, E-mail: drc9@psu.edu. *Application contact:* Lori A. Stania, Director, Graduate Student Services, 814-867-5278, Fax: 814-863-4627, E-mail: gswww@psu.edu.
Website: http://bmb.psu.edu/.

Purdue University, Graduate School, PULSe - Purdue University Life Sciences Program, West Lafayette, IN 47907. Offers biomolecular structure and biophysics (PhD); biotechnology (PhD); chemical biology (PhD); chromatin and regulation of gene expression (PhD); integrative neuroscience (PhD); integrative plant sciences (PhD); membrane biology (PhD); microbiology (PhD); molecular evolutionary and cancer biology (PhD); molecular evolutionary genetics (PhD); molecular virology (PhD). *Entrance requirements:* For doctorate, GRE, minimum undergraduate GPA of 3.0. Additional exam requirements/recommendations for international students: Required—TOEFL (minimum score 550 paper-based; 77 iBT). Electronic applications accepted.

Purdue University Calumet, Graduate Studies Office, School of Engineering, Mathematics, and Science, Department of Biological Sciences, Program in Biotechnology, Hammond, IN 46323-2094. Offers MS. *Degree requirements:* For master's, thesis (for some programs). *Entrance requirements:* For master's, GRE General Test, 3 letters of recommendation.

Regis College, Program in Regulatory and Clinical Research Management, Weston, MA 02493. Offers MS. Part-time and evening/weekend programs available. *Degree requirements:* For master's, thesis optional, internship. *Entrance requirements:* For master's, GRE or MAT. Additional exam requirements/recommendations for international students: Required—TOEFL (minimum score 550 paper-based). *Expenses:* Contact institution. *Faculty research:* FDA regulatory affairs medical device.

Roosevelt University, Graduate Division, College of Arts and Sciences, Department of Biological, Chemical, and Physical Sciences, Chicago, IL 60605. Offers biotechnology and chemical science (MS). Part-time and evening/weekend programs available. *Degree requirements:* For master's, thesis optional. *Entrance requirements:* For master's, minimum GPA of 2.7, undergraduate course work in science and mathematics. *Faculty research:* Phase-transfer catalysts, bioinorganic chemistry, long chain dicarboxylic acids, organosilicon compounds, spectroscopic studies.

St. John's University, Institute for Biotechnology, Queens, NY 11439. Offers biological/pharmaceutical biotechnology (MS). *Students:* 12 full-time (7 women), 9 part-time (3 women); includes 4 minority (1 Black or African American, non-Hispanic/Latino; 3 Asian, non-Hispanic/Latino), 13 international. Average age 26. 34 applicants, 47% accepted, 5 enrolled. In 2014, 5 master's awarded. *Degree requirements:* For master's, comprehensive exam, thesis optional. *Entrance requirements:* For master's, GRE General Test, minimum GPA of 3.0, 2 letters of recommendation, bachelor's degree in major life or physical sciences. Additional exam requirements/recommendations for international students: Required—TOEFL (minimum score 600 paper-based; 100 iBT), IELTS (minimum score 7). *Application deadline:* For fall admission, 5/1 priority date for domestic and international students; for spring admission, 11/1 priority date for domestic and international students. Applications are processed on a rolling basis. Application fee: $70. Electronic applications accepted. *Expenses:* Expenses: Contact institution. *Financial support:* In 2014–15, 1 teaching assistantship with full tuition reimbursement (averaging $15,975 per year) was awarded. Financial award application deadline: 3/1; financial award applicants required to submit FAFSA. *Unit head:* Dr. Vijaya L. Korlipara, Director, 718-990-5369, E-mail: korlipav@stjohns.edu. *Application contact:* Robert Medrano, Director of Graduate Admission, 718-990-1601, Fax: 718-990-5686, E-mail: gradhelp@stjohns.edu.
Website: http://www.stjohns.edu/about/administrative-offices/provost/institute-biotechnology.

San Francisco State University, Division of Graduate Studies, College of Science and Engineering, Department of Biology, Professional Science Master's Program, San Francisco, CA 94132-1722. Offers biotechnology (PSM); stem cell science (PSM). *Expenses:* Tuition, state resident: full-time $6738. Tuition, nonresident: full-time $17,898; part-time $372 per credit hour. *Required fees:* $498 per semester. *Unit head:* Dr. Lily Chen, Director, 415-338-6763, Fax: 415-338-2295, E-mail: lilychen@sfsu.edu. *Application contact:* Dr. Linda H. Chen, Associate Director and Program Coordinator, 415-338-1696, Fax: 415-338-2295, E-mail: psm@sfsu.edu.
Website: http://www.sfsu.edu/~psm/.

Simon Fraser University, Office of Graduate Studies, Faculty of Business Administration, Vancouver, BC V6C 1W6, Canada. Offers business administration (EMBA, PhD, Graduate Diploma); finance (M Sc); management of technology (MBA); management of technology/biotechnology (MBA). *Accreditation:* AACSB. Postbaccalaureate distance learning degree programs offered. *Degree requirements:* For master's, thesis (for some programs); for doctorate, comprehensive exam, thesis/dissertation. *Entrance requirements:* For master's, GMAT, minimum GPA of 3.0 (on scale of 4.33), or 3.33 based on last 60 credits of undergraduate courses; for doctorate, minimum GPA of 3.5 (on scale of 4.33); for Graduate Diploma, minimum GPA of 2.5 (on scale of 4.33), or 2.67 based on the last 60 credits of undergraduate courses. Additional exam requirements/recommendations for international students: Recommended—TOEFL (minimum score 580 paper-based; 93 iBT), IELTS (minimum score 7), TWE (minimum score 5). *Expenses:* Contact institution. *Faculty research:* Accounting, management and organizational studies, technology and operations management, finance, international business.

Southeastern Oklahoma State University, School of Arts and Sciences, Durant, OK 74701-0609. Offers biology (MT); computer information systems (MT); occupational safety and health (MT). Part-time and evening/weekend programs available. *Degree requirements:* For master's, thesis optional. *Entrance requirements:* For master's, minimum GPA of 3.0 in last 60 hours or 2.75 overall. Additional exam requirements/recommendations for international students: Required—TOEFL (minimum score 550 paper-based; 79 iBT). Electronic applications accepted.

Stephen F. Austin State University, Graduate School, College of Sciences and Mathematics, Division of Biotechnology, Nacogdoches, TX 75962. Offers MS. *Degree requirements:* For master's, comprehensive exam, thesis. *Entrance requirements:* For master's, GRE General Test, minimum GPA of 2.8 in last 60 hours, 2.5 overall. Additional exam requirements/recommendations for international students: Required—TOEFL.

Temple University, College of Science and Technology, Department of Biology, Philadelphia, PA 19122. Offers biology (MS, PhD); biotechnology (MS). *Faculty:* 31 full-time (11 women), 2 part-time/adjunct (1 woman). *Students:* 42 full-time (26 women), 5 part-time (3 women); includes 13 minority (3 Black or African American, non-Hispanic/Latino; 8 Asian, non-Hispanic/Latino; 2 Hispanic/Latino), 8 international. 86 applicants, 30% accepted, 17 enrolled. In 2014, 5 master's, 8 doctorates awarded. Terminal master's awarded for partial completion of doctoral program. *Degree requirements:* For master's, comprehensive exam (for some programs), thesis (for some programs); for doctorate, comprehensive exam (for some programs), thesis/dissertation. *Entrance requirements:* For master's and doctorate, GRE General Test, minimum GPA of 3.0. Additional exam requirements/recommendations for international students: Required—TOEFL (minimum score 550 paper-based; 79 iBT). *Application deadline:* For fall admission, 1/15 for domestic students, 12/15 for international students; for spring admission, 10/15 for domestic students, 8/1 for international students. Applications are processed on a rolling basis. Application fee: $60. *Expenses:* Tuition, state resident: full-time $14,490; part-time $805 per credit hour. Tuition, nonresident: full-time $19,850; part-time $1103 per credit hour. *Required fees:* $690. Full-time tuition and fees vary according to class time, course load, degree level, campus/location and program. *Financial support:* Fellowships, research assistantships, teaching assistantships, Federal Work-Study, and tuition waivers (full) available. Financial award application deadline: 1/15; financial award applicants required to submit FAFSA. *Faculty research:* Membrane proteins, genetics, molecular biology, neuroscience, aquatic biology. *Unit head:* Dr. Allen Nicholson, Chair, 215-204-8854, Fax: 215-204-6646, E-mail: biology@temple.edu. *Application contact:* Regee Neely, Administrative Assistant, 215-204-8854, E-mail: rneely@temple.edu.
Website: https://bio.cst.temple.edu/.

Tennessee State University, The School of Graduate Studies and Research, College of Agriculture, Human and Natural Sciences, Nashville, TN 37209-1561. Offers agricultural sciences (MS), including agribusiness, agricultural and extension education, animal science, plant and soil science; biological sciences (MS, PhD); biotechnology (PhD); chemistry (MS). Part-time and evening/weekend programs available. *Degree requirements:* For master's, thesis. *Entrance requirements:* For master's, GRE General Test, GRE Subject Test, MAT. *Faculty research:* Small farm economics, ornamental horticulture, beef cattle production, rural elderly.

Texas Tech University, Graduate School, Interdisciplinary Programs, Lubbock, TX 79409-1030. Offers arid land studies (MS); biotechnology (MS); heritage management (MS); interdisciplinary studies (MA, MS); museum science (MA); wind science and engineering (PhD); JD/MS. Part-time programs available. *Faculty:* 4 full-time (3 women). *Students:* 112 full-time (70 women), 122 part-time (70 women); includes 71 minority (20 Black or African American, non-Hispanic/Latino; 1 American Indian or Alaska Native, non-Hispanic/Latino; 4 Asian, non-Hispanic/Latino; 40 Hispanic/Latino; 6 Two or more races, non-Hispanic/Latino), 43 international. Average age 30. 172 applicants, 65% accepted, 70 enrolled. In 2014, 56 master's, 4 doctorates awarded. Terminal master's awarded for partial completion of doctoral program. *Degree requirements:* For master's, comprehensive exam (for some programs), thesis (for some programs); for doctorate,

comprehensive exam, thesis/dissertation (for some programs). *Entrance requirements:* Additional exam requirements/recommendations for international students: Required—TOEFL (minimum score 550 paper-based; 79 iBT). *Application deadline:* For fall admission, 6/1 priority date for domestic students, 1/15 priority date for international students; for spring admission, 9/1 priority date for domestic students, 6/15 priority date for international students. Applications are processed on a rolling basis. Application fee: $60. Electronic applications accepted. *Expenses:* Tuition, state resident: full-time $6310; part-time $262.92 per credit hour. Tuition, nonresident: full-time $14,998; part-time $624.92 per credit hour. *Required fees:* $2701; $36.50 per credit. $912.50 per semester. Tuition and fees vary according to course load. *Financial support:* In 2014–15, 201 students received support, including 196 fellowships (averaging $2,655 per year), 5 research assistantships (averaging $12,144 per year), 2 teaching assistantships (averaging $7,785 per year); scholarships/grants and unspecified assistantships also available. Financial award application deadline: 4/15; financial award applicants required to submit FAFSA. *Total annual research expenditures:* $241,842. *Unit head:* Dr. Mark Sheridan, Vice Provost for Graduate and Postdoctoral Affairs/Dean of the Graduate School, 806-742-2787, Fax: 806-742-1746, E-mail: mark.sheridan@ttu.edu. *Application contact:* Shannon Samson, Coordinator of Graduate School Recruitment, 806-834-5201, Fax: 806-742-1746, E-mail: gradschool@ttu.edu.
Website: http://www.depts.ttu.edu/gradschool/about/INDS/index.php.

Texas Tech University Health Sciences Center, Graduate School of Biomedical Sciences, Program in Biotechnology, Lubbock, TX 79430. Offers MS. *Entrance requirements:* For master's, GRE General Test, minimum GPA of 3.0. Additional exam requirements/recommendations for international students: Required—TOEFL (minimum score 550 paper-based). *Faculty research:* Reproductive endocrinology, immunology, molecular biology and developmental biochemistry, biology of developing systems.

Thomas Jefferson University, Jefferson Graduate School of Biomedical Sciences, PhD Program in Tissue Engineering and Regenerative Medicine, Philadelphia, PA 19107. Offers PhD. *Degree requirements:* For doctorate, comprehensive exam, thesis/dissertation. *Entrance requirements:* For doctorate, GRE General Test, minimum GPA of 3.2. Additional exam requirements/recommendations for international students: Required—TOEFL (minimum score 100 iBT) or IELTS. Electronic applications accepted. *Faculty research:* Skeletal development, biomaterials, bone implant interaction, tissue engineering, high resolution imaging.

Tufts University, Graduate School of Arts and Sciences, Graduate Certificate Programs, Biotechnology Engineering Program, Medford, MA 02155. Offers Certificate. Part-time and evening/weekend programs available. Electronic applications accepted. *Expenses: Tuition:* Full-time $45,590; part-time $1161 per credit hour. *Required fees:* $782. Full-time tuition and fees vary according to degree level, program and student level. Part-time tuition and fees vary according to course load.

Tufts University, Graduate School of Arts and Sciences, Graduate Certificate Programs, Biotechnology Program, Medford, MA 02155. Offers Certificate. Part-time and evening/weekend programs available. Electronic applications accepted. *Expenses: Tuition:* Full-time $45,590; part-time $1161 per credit hour. *Required fees:* $782. Full-time tuition and fees vary according to degree level, program and student level. Part-time tuition and fees vary according to course load.

Tufts University, School of Engineering, Department of Chemical and Biological Engineering, Medford, MA 02155. Offers bioengineering (ME, MS), including cell and bioprocess engineering; biotechnology engineering (PhD); chemical and biological engineering (ME, MS, PhD). Part-time programs available. *Faculty:* 10 full-time (2 women), 1 part-time/adjunct (0 women). *Students:* 35 full-time (11 women), 12 part-time (7 women); includes 6 minority (5 Asian, non-Hispanic/Latino; 1 Hispanic/Latino), 23 international. Average age 27. 152 applicants, 22% accepted, 18 enrolled. In 2014, 5 master's, 1 doctorate awarded. Terminal master's awarded for partial completion of doctoral program. *Degree requirements:* For master's, thesis (for some programs); for doctorate, thesis/dissertation. *Entrance requirements:* For master's and doctorate, GRE General Test. Additional exam requirements/recommendations for international students: Required—TOEFL (minimum score 550 paper-based; 80 iBT), IELTS (minimum score 6.5). *Application deadline:* For fall admission, 1/15 priority date for domestic students, 1/15 for international students; for spring admission, 9/15 for domestic and international students. Applications are processed on a rolling basis. Application fee: $75. Electronic applications accepted. *Expenses: Tuition:* Full-time $45,590; part-time $1161 per credit hour. *Required fees:* $782. Full-time tuition and fees vary according to degree level, program and student level. Part-time tuition and fees vary according to course load. *Financial support:* Fellowships with full tuition reimbursements, research assistantships with full and partial tuition reimbursements, teaching assistantships with full and partial tuition reimbursements, Federal Work-Study, scholarships/grants, tuition waivers (partial), and unspecified assistantships available. Financial award application deadline: 1/15; financial award applicants required to submit FAFSA. *Faculty research:* Clean energy with materials, biomaterials, colloids; metabolic engineering, biotechnology; process control; reaction kinetics, catalysis; transport phenomena. *Unit head:* Dr. Matt Panzer, Graduate Program Director. *Application contact:* Office of Graduate Admissions, 617-627-3395, E-mail: gradadmissions@tufts.edu.
Website: http://engineering.tufts.edu/chbe/.

Universidad de las Américas Puebla, Division of Graduate Studies, School of Sciences, Program in Biotechnology, Puebla, Mexico. Offers MS. *Degree requirements:* For master's, one foreign language, thesis.

University at Buffalo, the State University of New York, Graduate School, School of Medicine and Biomedical Sciences, Graduate Programs in Medicine and Biomedical Sciences, Department of Biotechnical and Clinical Laboratory Sciences, Buffalo, NY 14214. Offers biotechnology (MS). *Accreditation:* NAACLS. Part-time programs available. *Faculty:* 7 full-time (3 women). *Students:* 10 full-time (8 women), 1 (woman) part-time; includes 1 minority (Asian, non-Hispanic/Latino), 6 international. 86 applicants, 20% accepted, 7 enrolled. In 2014, 8 degrees awarded. *Degree requirements:* For master's, thesis. *Entrance requirements:* For master's, GRE General Test (minimum 50th percentile for all three sections), minimum GPA of 3.0. Additional exam requirements/recommendations for international students: Required—TOEFL (minimum score 79 iBT), IELTS. *Application deadline:* For fall admission, 3/1 priority date for domestic students, 2/1 priority date for international students. Applications are processed on a rolling basis. Application fee: $75. Electronic applications accepted. *Financial support:* In 2014–15, 5 students received support, including 5 teaching assistantships with full tuition reimbursements available (averaging $10,000 per year); unspecified assistantships also available. Financial award application deadline: 3/1. *Faculty research:* Immunology, cancer biology, toxicology, clinical chemistry, hematology, chemistry. *Total annual research expenditures:* $741,728. *Unit head:* Dr. Paul J. Kostyniak, Chair, 716-829-5188, Fax: 716-829-3601, E-mail: pjkost@buffalo.edu. *Application contact:* Dr. Stephen T. Koury, Director of Graduate Studies, 716-829-5188, Fax: 716-829-3601, E-mail: stvkoury@buffalo.edu.
Website: http://www.smbs.buffalo.edu/cls/biotech-ms.html.

The University of Alabama at Birmingham, School of Health Professions, Program in Biotechnology, Birmingham, AL 35294. Offers MS. *Students:* 12 full-time (8 women), 3 part-time (2 women); includes 7 minority (5 Black or African American, non-Hispanic/Latino; 1 Asian, non-Hispanic/Latino; 1 Two or more races, non-Hispanic/Latino), 4 international. Average age 26. In 2014, 17 master's awarded. *Entrance requirements:* For master's, GRE (minimum score of 500 in each area), minimum GPA of 3.0 overall or on last 60 hours attempted, interview. Additional exam requirements/recommendations for international students: Required—TOEFL, TWE. *Application deadline:* For fall admission, 5/31 for domestic students. *Expenses:* Tuition, state resident: full-time $7090; part-time $370 per credit hour. Tuition, nonresident: full-time $16,072; part-time $869 per credit hour. Full-time tuition and fees vary according to course load and program. *Unit head:* Dr. Tino Unlap, Interim Program Director, 205-934-7382, E-mail: unlap@uab.edu. *Application contact:* Susan Noblitt Banks, Director of Graduate School Operations, 205-934-8227, Fax: 205-934-8413, E-mail: gradschool@uab.edu.
Website: http://www.uab.edu/shp/cds/biotechnology-m-s-c-l-s-or-certificate.

The University of Alabama in Huntsville, School of Graduate Studies, College of Engineering, Department of Chemical and Materials Engineering, Huntsville, AL 35899. Offers biotechnology science and engineering (PhD); chemical engineering (MSE); materials science (MS, PhD); mechanical engineering (PhD), including chemical engineering. Part-time and evening/weekend programs available. *Degree requirements:* For master's, comprehensive exam, thesis or alternative, oral and written exams; for doctorate, comprehensive exam, thesis/dissertation. *Entrance requirements:* For master's, GRE General Test, appropriate bachelor's degree, minimum GPA of 3.0; for doctorate, GRE General Test, minimum GPA of 3.0. Additional exam requirements/recommendations for international students: Required—TOEFL (minimum score 500 paper-based; 80 iBT), IELTS (minimum score 6.5). Electronic applications accepted. *Faculty research:* Ultrathin films for optical, sensor and biological applications; materials processing including low gravity; hypergolic reactants; computational fluid dynamics; biofuels and renewable resources.

The University of Alabama in Huntsville, School of Graduate Studies, College of Science, Department of Biological Sciences, Huntsville, AL 35899. Offers biology (MS); biotechnology science and engineering (PhD); education (MS). Part-time and evening/weekend programs available. *Degree requirements:* For master's, comprehensive exam, thesis or alternative, oral and written exams. *Entrance requirements:* For master's, GRE General Test, previous course work in biochemistry and organic chemistry, minimum GPA of 3.0. Additional exam requirements/recommendations for international students: Required—TOEFL (minimum score 550 paper-based; 80 iBT), IELTS (minimum score 6.5). Electronic applications accepted. *Faculty research:* Physiology, microbiology, genomics and protemics, ecology and evolution, drug discovery.

The University of Alabama in Huntsville, School of Graduate Studies, College of Science, Department of Chemistry, Huntsville, AL 35899. Offers biotechnology science and engineering (PhD); chemistry (MS); education (MS); materials science (PhD). Part-time and evening/weekend programs available. *Degree requirements:* For master's, comprehensive exam, thesis or alternative, oral and written exams. *Entrance requirements:* For master's, GRE General Test, minimum GPA of 3.0. Additional exam requirements/recommendations for international students: Required—TOEFL (minimum score 550 paper-based; 80 iBT), IELTS (minimum score 6.5). Electronic applications accepted. *Faculty research:* Natural products drug discovery, protein biochemistry, macromolecular biophysics, polymer synthesis, surface modification and analysis of materials.

The University of Alabama in Huntsville, School of Graduate Studies, Interdisciplinary Studies, Interdisciplinary Program in Biotechnology Science and Engineering, Huntsville, AL 35899. Offers PhD. Part-time and evening/weekend programs available. *Degree requirements:* For doctorate, comprehensive exam, thesis/dissertation, oral and written exams. *Entrance requirements:* For doctorate, GRE General Test, bachelor's degree in science or engineering, minimum GPA of 3.0. Additional exam requirements/recommendations for international students: Required—TOEFL (minimum score 550 paper-based; 80 iBT), IELTS (minimum score 6.5). Electronic applications accepted. *Faculty research:* Protein structure and function, natural products drug discovery, NMR spectroscopy, macromolecular crystallization, bioprocessing.

University of Alberta, Faculty of Graduate Studies and Research, Department of Biological Sciences, Edmonton, AB T6G 2E1, Canada. Offers environmental biology and ecology (M Sc, PhD); microbiology and biotechnology (M Sc, PhD); molecular biology and genetics (M Sc, PhD); physiology and cell biology (M Sc, PhD); plant biology (M Sc, PhD); systematics and evolution (M Sc, PhD). Terminal master's awarded for partial completion of doctoral program. *Degree requirements:* For master's, thesis; for doctorate, thesis/dissertation. *Entrance requirements:* Additional exam requirements/recommendations for international students: Required—TOEFL.

University of Calgary, Cumming School of Medicine and Faculty of Graduate Studies, Program in Biomedical Technology, Calgary, AB T2N 1N4, Canada. Offers MBT. Part-time programs available. *Degree requirements:* For master's, comprehensive exam, practicum. *Entrance requirements:* For master's, minimum GPA of 3.2 in last 2 years, B Sc in biological science. Additional exam requirements/recommendations for international students: Required—TOEFL (minimum score 600 paper-based). Electronic applications accepted. *Expenses:* Contact institution. *Faculty research:* Patent law, intellectual propriétorship.

University of California, Irvine, Francisco J. Ayala School of Biological Sciences, Department of Molecular Biology and Biochemistry, Program in Biotechnology, Irvine, CA 92697. Offers MS. *Students:* 28 full-time (12 women), 1 part-time (0 women); includes 7 minority (5 Asian, non-Hispanic/Latino; 2 Hispanic/Latino), 10 international. Average age 25. 164 applicants, 13% accepted, 17 enrolled. In 2014, 11 master's awarded. *Entrance requirements:* For master's, GRE General Test, GRE Subject Test, minimum GPA of 3.0. *Application deadline:* For fall admission, 3/1 priority date for domestic and international students. Applications are processed on a rolling basis. Application fee: $90 ($110 for international students). Electronic applications accepted. *Financial support:* Application deadline: 3/1; applicants required to submit FAFSA. *Unit head:* Michael G. Cumsky, Director, 949-824-7766, Fax: 949-824-8551, E-mail: mgcumsky@uci.edu. *Application contact:* Morgan Oldham, Administrative Contact, 949-824-6034, Fax: 949-824-8551, E-mail: morgano@uci.edu.

University of California, Irvine, Francisco J. Ayala School of Biological Sciences, Department of Molecular Biology and Biochemistry, Program in Biotechnology Management, Irvine, CA 92697. Offers MS. Program offred jointly with the Paul Merage School of Business and the Department of Biomedical Engineering. *Students:* 13 full-time (7 women), 1 (woman) part-time; includes 3 minority (2 Asian, non-Hispanic/Latino; 1 Hispanic/Latino), 9 international. Average age 24. 60 applicants, 25% accepted, 11 enrolled. *Application deadline:* For fall admission, 3/15 for domestic students. Application fee: $90 ($110 for international students). *Unit head:* Michael G. Cumsky, Program Director, 949-824-7766, Fax: 949-824-8551, E-mail: mgcumsky@uci.edu. *Application contact:* Morgan Oldham, Student Affairs Assistant, 949-826-6034, Fax: 949-824-8551, E-mail: morgano@uci.edu.
Website: http://mbb.bio.uci.edu/graduates/masters-science-degree-biotechnology-management/.

Biotechnology

University of California, Santa Barbara, Graduate Division, College of Letters and Sciences, Division of Mathematics, Life, and Physical Sciences, Department of Molecular, Cellular, and Developmental Biology, Santa Barbara, CA 93106-9625. Offers molecular, cellular, and developmental biology (MA, PhD); pharmacology/biotechnology (MA); MA/PhD. Terminal master's awarded for partial completion of doctoral program. *Degree requirements:* For master's, comprehensive exam (for some programs), thesis (for some programs); for doctorate, comprehensive exam, thesis/dissertation. *Entrance requirements:* For master's and doctorate, GRE General Test, 3 letters of recommendation, statement of purpose, personal achievements/contributions statement, resume/curriculum vitae, transcripts for post-secondary institutions attended. Additional exam requirements/recommendations for international students: Required— TOEFL (minimum score 550 paper-based; 80 iBT), IELTS (minimum score 7). Electronic applications accepted. *Faculty research:* Microbiology, neurobiology (including stem cell research), developmental, virology, cell biology.

University of Central Florida, College of Medicine, Burnett School of Biomedical Sciences, Orlando, FL 32816. Offers biomedical sciences (MS, PhD); biotechnology (MS). *Students:* 94 full-time (53 women), 8 part-time (6 women); includes 22 minority (5 Black or African American, non-Hispanic/Latino; 1 American Indian or Alaska Native, non-Hispanic/Latino; 7 Asian, non-Hispanic/Latino; 8 Hispanic/Latino; 1 Two or more races, non-Hispanic/Latino), 25 international. Average age 27. 158 applicants, 36% accepted, 35 enrolled. In 2014, 25 master's, 8 doctorates awarded. *Expenses:* Tuition, state resident: part-time $288.16 per credit hour. Tuition, nonresident: part-time $1073.31 per credit hour. *Financial support:* In 2014–15, 74 students received support, including 26 fellowships with partial tuition reimbursements available (averaging $4,900 per year), 56 research assistantships with partial tuition reimbursements available (averaging $11,000 per year), 35 teaching assistantships with partial tuition reimbursements available (averaging $10,800 per year). *Unit head:* Dr. Richard Peppler, Interim Director, 407-226-1000, E-mail: pep@ucf.edu. *Application contact:* Barbara Rodriguez Lamas, Director, Admissions and Student Services, 407-823-2766, Fax: 407-823-6442, E-mail: gradadmissions@ucf.edu.
Website: http://www.biomed.ucf.edu/.

University of Delaware, College of Arts and Sciences, Department of Biological Sciences, Newark, DE 19716. Offers biotechnology (MS); cancer biology (MS, PhD); cell and extracellular matrix biology (MS, PhD); cell and systems physiology (MS, PhD); developmental biology (MS, PhD); ecology and evolution (MS, PhD); microbiology (MS, PhD); molecular biology and genetics (MS, PhD). Terminal master's awarded for partial completion of doctoral program. *Degree requirements:* For master's, thesis, preliminary exam; for doctorate, comprehensive exam, thesis/dissertation, preliminary exam. *Entrance requirements:* For master's and doctorate, GRE General Test. Additional exam requirements/recommendations for international students: Required—TOEFL (minimum score 600 paper-based); Recommended—TWE. Electronic applications accepted. *Faculty research:* Microorganisms, bone, cancer metastasis, developmental biology, cell biology, DNA.

University of Guelph, Graduate Studies, Ontario Agricultural College, Department of Environmental Biology, Guelph, ON N1G 2W1, Canada. Offers entomology (M Sc, PhD); environmental microbiology and biotechnology (M Sc, PhD); environmental toxicology (M Sc, PhD); plant and forest systems (M Sc, PhD); plant pathology (M Sc, PhD). Part-time programs available. *Degree requirements:* For master's, thesis; for doctorate, comprehensive exam, thesis/dissertation. *Entrance requirements:* For master's, minimum 75% average during previous 2 years of course work; for doctorate, minimum 75% average. Additional exam requirements/recommendations for international students: Required—TOEFL or IELTS. Electronic applications accepted. *Faculty research:* Entomology, environmental microbiology and biotechnology, environmental toxicology, forest ecology, plant pathology.

University of Houston–Clear Lake, School of Science and Computer Engineering, Program in Biotechnology, Houston, TX 77058-1002. Offers MS.

University of Illinois at Chicago, College of Pharmacy, Department of Biopharmaceutical Sciences, Chicago, IL 60607-7173. Offers MS, PhD. *Faculty:* 15 full-time (4 women), 10 part-time/adjunct (2 women). *Students:* 17 full-time (13 women), 12 part-time (6 women); includes 3 minority (all Asian, non-Hispanic/Latino), 19 international. Average age 28. 81 applicants, 9% accepted, 4 enrolled. In 2014, 19 master's, 5 doctorates awarded. *Expenses:* Tuition, state resident: full-time $11,254; part-time $468 per credit hour. Tuition, nonresident: full-time $23,252; part-time $968 per credit hour. *Required fees:* $1217 per term. Part-time tuition and fees vary according to course load, degree level and program. *Faculty research:* Lipid and polymer-based drug delivery systems, targeted drug delivery, pharmacokinetic membrane transport and absorption, behavioral and cardiovascular pharmacology; neuropharmacology, environmental toxicology, cancer chemotherapy. *Total annual research expenditures:* $1.2 million. *Unit head:* Prof. William T. Beck, Head, 312-996-0888, Fax: 312-996-0098, E-mail: wtbeck@uic.edu.
Website: http://www.uic.edu/pharmacy/depts/Biopharmaceutical_Sciences/index.php.

The University of Kansas, University of Kansas Medical Center, School of Health Professions, Program in Molecular Biotechnology, Lawrence, KS 66045. Offers MS. *Students:* 3 full-time (2 women), 4 part-time (3 women), 4 international. Average age 27. 26 applicants, 23% accepted, 3 enrolled. In 2014, 2 master's awarded. *Degree requirements:* For master's, comprehensive exam. *Entrance requirements:* For master's, GRE General Test. Additional exam requirements/recommendations for international students: Required—TOEFL. *Application deadline:* For fall admission, 2/1 priority date for domestic and international students. Application fee: $60. Electronic applications accepted. *Financial support:* Career-related internships or fieldwork available. Financial award application deadline: 3/1; financial award applicants required to submit FAFSA. *Faculty research:* Diabetes, obesity, polycystic kidney disease, protein structure and function, cell signaling pathways. *Total annual research expenditures:* $41,884. *Unit head:* Dr. Eric Elsinghorst, Director of Graduate Studies, 913-588-1089, E-mail: eelsinghorst@kumc.edu. *Application contact:* Alisha Wittstruck, Coordinator of Admissions, 913-588-6594, Fax: 913-588-4697, E-mail: awittstruck@kumc.edu.
Website: http://www.kumc.edu/school-of-health-professions/molecular-biotechnology.html.

The University of Manchester, Faculty of Life Sciences, Manchester, United Kingdom. Offers adaptive organismal biology (M Phil, PhD); animal biology (M Phil, PhD); biochemistry (M Phil, PhD); bioinformatics (M Phil, PhD); biomolecular sciences (M Phil, PhD); biotechnology (M Phil, PhD); cell biology (M Phil, PhD); cell matrix research (M Phil, PhD); channels and transporters (M Phil, PhD); developmental biology (M Phil, PhD); Egyptology (M Phil, PhD); environmental biology (M Phil, PhD); evolutionary biology (M Phil, PhD); gene expression (M Phil, PhD); genetics (M Phil, PhD); history of science, technology and medicine (M Phil, PhD); immunology (M Phil, PhD); integrative neurobiology and behavior (M Phil, PhD); membrane trafficking (M Phil, PhD); microbiology (M Phil, PhD); molecular and cellular neuroscience (M Phil, PhD); molecular biology (M Phil, PhD); molecular cancer studies (M Phil, PhD); neuroscience (M Phil, PhD); ophthalmology (M Phil, PhD); optometry (M Phil, PhD); organelle function (M Phil, PhD); pharmacology (M Phil, PhD); physiology (M Phil, PhD); plant sciences (M Phil, PhD); stem cell research (M Phil, PhD); structural biology (M Phil, PhD); systems neuroscience (M Phil, PhD); toxicology (M Phil, PhD).

University of Maryland, Baltimore County, The Graduate School, College of Natural and Mathematical Sciences, Department of Biological Sciences, Programs in Biotechnology, Baltimore, MD 21250. Offers biotechnology (MPS); biotechnology management (Graduate Certificate). Part-time and evening/weekend programs available. *Faculty:* 17 part-time/adjunct (6 women). *Students:* 8 full-time (5 women), 29 part-time (22 women); includes 15 minority (3 Black or African American, non-Hispanic/Latino; 10 Asian, non-Hispanic/Latino; 2 Hispanic/Latino), 10 international. Average age 29. 37 applicants, 68% accepted, 16 enrolled. In 2014, 9 master's, 2 other advanced degrees awarded. *Entrance requirements:* Additional exam requirements/recommendations for international students: Required—TOEFL (minimum score 99 iBT). *Application deadline:* For fall admission, 8/1 for domestic students, 1/1 for international students; for spring admission, 1/1 for domestic students. Electronic applications accepted. *Expenses:* Tuition, state resident: part-time $557. Tuition, nonresident: part-time $922. *Required fees:* $122 per semester. One-time fee: $200 part-time. *Financial support:* Career-related internships or fieldwork available. Financial award applicants required to submit FAFSA. *Unit head:* Sonya Crosby, Director, Professional Studies, 410-455-3899, E-mail: scrosby@umbc.edu. *Application contact:* Nancy Clements, Program Specialist, 410-455-5536, E-mail: nancyc@umbc.edu.
Website: http://www.umbc.edu/biotech/.

University of Maryland University College, The Graduate School, Program in Biotechnology, Adelphi, MD 20783. Offers MS, Certificate. Part-time and evening/weekend programs available. Postbaccalaureate distance learning degree programs offered (no on-campus study). *Students:* 9 full-time (6 women), 366 part-time (225 women); includes 178 minority (105 Black or African American, non-Hispanic/Latino; 37 Asian, non-Hispanic/Latino; 28 Hispanic/Latino; 8 Two or more races, non-Hispanic/Latino), 15 international. Average age 32. 123 applicants, 100% accepted, 73 enrolled. In 2014, 121 master's, 16 other advanced degrees awarded. *Degree requirements:* For master's, thesis or alternative, capstone course. *Application deadline:* Applications are processed on a rolling basis. Application fee: $50. Electronic applications accepted. *Financial support:* Federal Work-Study and scholarships/grants available. Support available to part-time students. Financial award application deadline: 6/1; financial award applicants required to submit FAFSA. *Unit head:* Rana Khan, Director, 240-684-2400, Fax: 240-684-2401, E-mail: rana.khan@umuc.edu. *Application contact:* Coordinator, Graduate Admissions, 800-888-8682, Fax: 240-684-2151, E-mail: newgrad@umuc.edu.
Website: http://www.umuc.edu/academic-programs/masters-degrees/biotechnology.cfm.

University of Massachusetts Amherst, Graduate School, College of Natural Sciences, Department of Animal Biotechnology and Biomedical Sciences, Amherst, MA 01003. Offers MS, PhD. Part-time programs available. *Faculty:* 24 full-time (12 women). *Students:* 21 full-time (12 women); includes 2 minority (both Hispanic/Latino), 10 international. Average age 31. 30 applicants, 30% accepted, 8 enrolled. In 2014, 2 master's, 3 doctorates awarded. Terminal master's awarded for partial completion of doctoral program. *Degree requirements:* For master's, thesis or alternative; for doctorate, comprehensive exam, thesis/dissertation. *Entrance requirements:* For doctorate, GRE General Test. Additional exam requirements/recommendations for international students: Required—TOEFL (minimum score 550 paper-based; 80 iBT), IELTS (minimum score 6.5). *Application deadline:* For fall admission, 1/15 for domestic and international students; for spring admission, 10/1 for domestic and international students. Applications are processed on a rolling basis. Application fee: $75. Electronic applications accepted. *Expenses:* Tuition, state resident: full-time $1980; part-time $110 per credit. Tuition, nonresident: full-time $14,644; part-time $414 per credit. *Required fees:* $11,417. One-time fee: $357. *Financial support:* Fellowships with full and partial tuition reimbursements, research assistantships with full and partial tuition reimbursements, teaching assistantships with full and partial tuition reimbursements, career-related internships or fieldwork, Federal Work-Study, scholarships/grants, traineeships, health care benefits, tuition waivers (full and partial), and unspecified assistantships available. Support available to part-time students. Financial award application deadline: 1/15. *Unit head:* Dr. Cynthia Baldwin, Graduate Program Director, 413-577-1193, Fax: 413-577-1150. *Application contact:* Lindsay DeSantis, Supervisor of Admissions, 413-545-0722, Fax: 413-577-0010, E-mail: gradadm@grad.umass.edu.
Website: http://www.vasci.umass.edu/graduate-program-overview.

University of Massachusetts Boston, College of Science and Mathematics, Program in Biomedical Engineering and Biotechnology, Boston, MA 02125-3393. Offers PhD. *Expenses:* Tuition, state resident: full-time $2590; part-time $108 per credit. Tuition, nonresident: full-time $9758; part-time $406.50 per credit. Tuition and fees vary according to course load and program. *Unit head:* Dr. William Hagar, Interim Dean, 617-287-5777. *Application contact:* Peggy Roldan Patel, Graduate Admissions Coordinator, 617-287-6400, Fax: 617-287-6236, E-mail: bos.gadm@dpc.umassp.edu.

University of Massachusetts Boston, College of Science and Mathematics, Program in Biotechnology and Biomedical Sciences, Boston, MA 02125-3393. Offers MS. Part-time and evening/weekend programs available. *Degree requirements:* For master's, comprehensive exam, thesis optional, oral exams. *Entrance requirements:* For master's, GRE General Test, GRE Subject Test, minimum GPA of 2.75, 3.0 in science and math. *Application deadline:* For fall admission, 3/1 for domestic students; for spring admission, 11/1 for domestic students. *Expenses:* Tuition, state resident: full-time $2590; part-time $108 per credit. Tuition, nonresident: full-time $9758; part-time $406.50 per credit. Tuition and fees vary according to course load and program. *Financial support:* Research assistantships with full tuition reimbursements, teaching assistantships with full tuition reimbursements, career-related internships or fieldwork, Federal Work-Study, and unspecified assistantships available. Support available to part-time students. Financial award application deadline: 3/1; financial award applicants required to submit FAFSA. *Faculty research:* Evolutionary and molecular immunology, molecular genetics, tissue culture, computerized laboratory technology. *Unit head:* Dr. Greg Beck, Director, 617-287-6600. *Application contact:* Peggy Roldan Patel, Graduate Admissions Coordinator, 617-287-6400, Fax: 617-287-6236, E-mail: bos.gadm@dpc.umassp.edu.

University of Massachusetts Dartmouth, Graduate School, College of Engineering, Program in Biomedical Engineering and Biotechnology, North Dartmouth, MA 02747-2300. Offers bioengineering (PhD); biology (PhD); biomedical engineering/biotechnology (MS, PhD); chemistry (PhD); civil engineering (PhD); computer and information science (PhD); electrical/computer engineering (PhD); mathematics (PhD); mechanical engineering (PhD); medical laboratory science (MS); physics (PhD). Part-time programs available. *Students:* 8 full-time (2 women), 12 part-time (6 women); includes 1 minority (Hispanic/Latino), 10 international. Average age 31. 46 applicants, 22% accepted, 1 enrolled. In 2014, 2 master's, 4 doctorates awarded. *Degree requirements:* For doctorate, comprehensive exam, thesis/dissertation. *Entrance requirements:* For master's and doctorate, GRE, statement of purpose (minimum of 300 words), resume, 3 letters of recommendation, official transcripts. Additional exam requirements/recommendations for international students: Required—TOEFL (minimum score 550 paper-based). *Application deadline:* For fall admission, 2/15 priority date for domestic students, 1/15 priority date for international students; for spring admission, 11/

15 priority date for domestic students, 10/15 priority date for international students. Applications are processed on a rolling basis. Application fee: $60. Electronic applications accepted. *Expenses:* Tuition, state resident: full-time $2071; part-time $86.29 per credit. Tuition, nonresident: full-time $8099; part-time $337.46 per credit. *Required fees:* $16,520; $712.33 per credit. Tuition and fees vary according to course load and reciprocity agreements. *Financial support:* In 2014–15, 1 fellowship with full tuition reimbursement (averaging $24,000 per year), 5 research assistantships with full tuition reimbursements (averaging $11,630 per year), 1 teaching assistantship with full tuition reimbursement (averaging $16,000 per year) were awarded; Federal Work-Study and unspecified assistantships also available. Support available to part-time students. Financial award application deadline: 3/1; financial award applicants required to submit FAFSA. *Faculty research:* Comparative immunology, vaccine design, biosensors, biomimetic materials, polymer science, soft electronics, hydrogels, regenerative biological materials. *Total annual research expenditures:* $2 million. *Unit head:* Sankha Bhowmick, Graduate Program Director for Engineering Options, 508-999-8619, Fax: 508-999-8881, E-mail: sbhowmick@umassd.edu. *Application contact:* Steven Briggs, Director of Marketing and Recruitment for Graduate Studies, 508-999-8604, Fax: 508-999-8183, E-mail: graduate@umassd.edu.
Website: http://www.umassd.edu/engineering/graduate/doctoraldegreeprograms/biomedicalengineeringandbiotechnology/.

University of Massachusetts Lowell, College of Sciences, Department of Biological Sciences, Lowell, MA 01854. Offers biochemistry (PhD); biological sciences (MS); biotechnology (MS). Part-time programs available. *Degree requirements:* For master's, thesis; for doctorate, thesis/dissertation. *Entrance requirements:* For master's and doctorate, GRE General Test. Electronic applications accepted.

University of Minnesota, Twin Cities Campus, Graduate School, Program in Microbial Engineering, Minneapolis, MN 55455-0213. Offers MS. Part-time programs available. *Degree requirements:* For master's, thesis. *Entrance requirements:* For master's, GRE General Test. Additional exam requirements/recommendations for international students: Required—TOEFL. *Faculty research:* Microbial genetics, oncogenesis, gene transfer, fermentation, bioreactors, genetics of antibiotic biosynthesis.

University of Nevada, Reno, Graduate School, College of Agriculture, Biotechnology and Natural Resources, Program in Biotechnology, Reno, NV 89557. Offers MS. 5 year degree; students are admitted to as undergraduates. *Degree requirements:* For master's, thesis. *Entrance requirements:* For master's, GRE, minimum GPA of 2.75. Additional exam requirements/recommendations for international students: Required—TOEFL (minimum score 500 paper-based; 61 iBT), IELTS (minimum score 6). Electronic applications accepted. *Faculty research:* Cancer biology, plant virology.

University of North Texas Health Science Center at Fort Worth, Graduate School of Biomedical Sciences, Fort Worth, TX 76107-2699. Offers anatomy and cell biology (MS, PhD); biochemistry and molecular biology (MS, PhD); biomedical sciences (MS, PhD); biotechnology (MS); forensic genetics (MS); integrative physiology (MS, PhD); medical science (MS); microbiology and immunology (MS, PhD); pharmacology (MS, PhD); science education (MS); DO/MS; DO/PhD. Terminal master's awarded for partial completion of doctoral program. *Degree requirements:* For master's, thesis; for doctorate, thesis/dissertation. *Entrance requirements:* For master's and doctorate, GRE General Test. Additional exam requirements/recommendations for international students: Required—TOEFL. *Expenses:* Contact institution. *Faculty research:* Alzheimer's disease, aging, eye diseases, cancer, cardiovascular disease.

University of Pennsylvania, School of Engineering and Applied Science, Program in Biotechnology, Philadelphia, PA 19104. Offers MS. Part-time programs available. *Students:* 65 full-time (37 women), 23 part-time (17 women); includes 11 minority (1 Black or African American, non-Hispanic/Latino; 9 Asian, non-Hispanic/Latino; 1 Hispanic/Latino), 57 international. 171 applicants, 43% accepted, 48 enrolled. In 2014, 71 master's awarded. *Entrance requirements:* For master's, GRE General Test, bachelor's degree in science or undergraduate course work in molecular biology. Additional exam requirements/recommendations for international students: Required—TOEFL. *Application deadline:* For fall admission, 6/1 priority date for domestic students, 5/1 priority date for international students. Applications are processed on a rolling basis. Application fee: $70. Electronic applications accepted. *Unit head:* Eduardo D. Glandt, Dean, 215-898-7244, E-mail: seasdean@seas.upenn.edu. *Application contact:* School of Engineering and Applied Science Graduate Admissions, 215-898-4542, E-mail: gradstudies@seas.upenn.edu.
Website: http://www.seas.upenn.edu.

University of Rhode Island, Graduate School, College of the Environment and Life Sciences, Department of Cell and Molecular Biology, Kingston, RI 02881. Offers biochemistry (MS, PhD); clinical laboratory sciences (MS), including biotechnology, clinical laboratory science, cytopathology; microbiology (MS, PhD); molecular genetics (MS, PhD). Part-time programs available. *Faculty:* 17 full-time (8 women), 3 part-time/adjunct (2 women). *Students:* 14 full-time (8 women), 35 part-time (24 women); includes 10 minority (4 Black or African American, non-Hispanic/Latino; 5 Asian, non-Hispanic/Latino; 1 Hispanic/Latino), 8 international. In 2014, 24 master's, 3 doctorates awarded. *Degree requirements:* For master's, comprehensive exam (for some programs), thesis optional; for doctorate, comprehensive exam, thesis/dissertation. *Entrance requirements:* For master's and doctorate, GRE, 2 letters of recommendation. Additional exam requirements/recommendations for international students: Required—TOEFL (minimum score 550 paper-based). *Application deadline:* For fall admission, 7/15 for domestic students, 2/1 for international students; for spring admission, 11/15 for domestic students, 7/15 for international students. Application fee: $65. Electronic applications accepted. *Expenses:* Tuition, state resident: full-time $11,532; part-time $641 per credit. Tuition, nonresident: full-time $23,606; part-time $1311 per credit. *Required fees:* $1442; $39 per credit. $35 per semester. One-time fee: $155. *Financial support:* In 2014–15, 3 research assistantships with full and partial tuition reimbursements (averaging $10,159 per year), 3 teaching assistantships with full and partial tuition reimbursements (averaging $15,844 per year) were awarded. Financial award application deadline: 2/1; financial award applicants required to submit FAFSA. *Faculty research:* Genomics. *Total annual research expenditures:* $6.7 million. *Unit head:* Dr. Gongqing Sun, Chairperson, 401-874-5937, Fax: 401-874-2202, E-mail: gsun@mail.uri.edu. *Application contact:* Graduate Admissions, 401-874-2872, E-mail: gradadm@etal.uri.edu.
Website: http://cels.uri.edu/cmb/.

University of San Francisco, College of Arts and Sciences, Biotechnology Program, San Francisco, CA 94117-1080. Offers PSM. *Faculty:* 3 full-time (2 women). *Students:* 33 full-time (14 women), 5 part-time (3 women); includes 12 minority (2 Black or African American, non-Hispanic/Latino; 5 Asian, non-Hispanic/Latino; 4 Hispanic/Latino; 1 Two or more races, non-Hispanic/Latino), 7 international. Average age 25. 88 applicants, 61% accepted, 19 enrolled. In 2014, 4 master's awarded. *Application deadline:* For fall admission, 3/15 for domestic students; for spring admission, 10/15 for domestic students. *Expenses:* Tuition: Full-time $21,762; part-time $1209 per credit hour. Tuition and fees vary according to degree level, campus/location and program. *Financial support:* In 2014–15, 4 students received support. *Unit head:* Dr. Jennifer Dever, Director, 415-422-6755, E-mail: dever@usfca.edu. *Application contact:* Mark Landerghini, Information Contact, 415-422-5101, Fax: 415-422-2217, E-mail: asgraduate@usfca.edu.
Website: http://www.usfca.edu/biotech/.

University of Saskatchewan, College of Graduate Studies and Research, Edwards School of Business, Program in Business Administration, Saskatoon, SK S7N 5A2, Canada. Offers agribusiness management (MBA); biotechnology management (MBA); health services management (MBA); indigenous management (MBA); international business management (MBA).

University of South Florida, Morsani College of Medicine and Graduate School, Graduate Programs in Medical Sciences, Tampa, FL 33620-9951. Offers aging and neuroscience (MSMS); allergy, immunology and infectious disease (PhD); anatomy (MSMS, PhD); athletic training (MSMS); bioinformatics and computational biology (MSBCB); biotechnology (MSB); clinical and translational research (MSMS, PhD); health informatics (MSHI, MSMS); health science (MSMS); interdisciplinary medical sciences (MSMS); medical microbiology and immunology (MSMS); metabolic and nutritional medicine (MSMS); molecular medicine (MSMS, PhD); molecular pharmacology and physiology (PhD); neurology (PhD); pathology and laboratory medicine (PhD); pharmacology and therapeutics (PhD); physiology and biophysics (PhD); women's health (MSMS). *Students:* 338 full-time (162 women), 36 part-time (25 women); includes 173 minority (43 Black or African American, non-Hispanic/Latino; 65 Asian, non-Hispanic/Latino; 58 Hispanic/Latino; 7 Two or more races, non-Hispanic/Latino), 24 international. Average age 26. 1,188 applicants, 41% accepted, 271 enrolled. In 2014, 216 master's awarded. Terminal master's awarded for partial completion of doctoral program. *Degree requirements:* For master's, comprehensive exam, thesis; for doctorate, comprehensive exam, thesis/dissertation. *Entrance requirements:* For master's, GRE General Test or GMAT, bachelor's degree or equivalent from regionally-accredited university with minimum GPA of 3.0 in upper-division sciences coursework; prerequisites in general biology, general chemistry, general physics, organic chemistry, quantitative analysis, and integral and differential calculus; for doctorate, GRE General Test (minimum score of 32nd percentile quantitative), bachelor's degree from regionally-accredited university with minimum GPA of 3.0 in upper-division sciences coursework; 3 letters of recommendation; personal interview; 1-2 page personal statement; prerequisites in biology, chemistry, physics, organic chemistry, quantitative analysis, and integral/differential calculus. Additional exam requirements/recommendations for international students: Required—TOEFL (minimum score 550 paper-based; 79 iBT) or IELTS (minimum score 6.5). *Application deadline:* For fall admission, 2/15 for domestic students, 1/2 for international students. Application fee: $30. *Expenses:* Expenses: Contact institution. *Faculty research:* Anatomy, biochemistry, cancer biology, cardiovascular disease, cell biology, immunology, microbiology, molecular biology, neuroscience, pharmacology, physiology. *Unit head:* Dr. Michael Barber, Professor and Associate Dean for Graduate and Postdoctoral Affairs, 813-974-9908, Fax: 813-974-4317, E-mail: mbarber@health.usf.edu. *Application contact:* Dr. Eric Bennett, Graduate Director, PhD Program in Medical Sciences, 813-974-1545, Fax: 813-974-4317, E-mail: esbennet@health.usf.edu.
Website: http://health.usf.edu/nocms/medicine/graduatestudies/.

University of South Florida, University College/Distance Education, Tampa, FL 33620-9951. *Unit head:* Kathy Barnes, Interdisciplinary Programs Coordinator, 813-974-8031, Fax: 813-974-7061, E-mail: barnesk@usf.edu. *Application contact:* Karen Tylinski, Metro Initiatives, 813-974-9943, Fax: 813-974-7061, E-mail: ktylinsk@usf.edu.
Website: http://www.usf.edu/innovative-education/.

The University of Texas at Dallas, School of Natural Sciences and Mathematics, Department of Biology, Richardson, TX 75080. Offers bioinformatics and computational biology (MS); biotechnology (MS); molecular and cell biology (MS, PhD). Part-time and evening/weekend programs available. *Faculty:* 20 full-time (4 women). *Students:* 107 full-time (66 women), 15 part-time (9 women); includes 13 minority (3 Black or African American, non-Hispanic/Latino; 7 Asian, non-Hispanic/Latino; 3 Hispanic/Latino), 85 international. Average age 27. 398 applicants, 27% accepted, 42 enrolled. In 2014, 41 master's, 5 doctorates awarded. *Degree requirements:* For master's, thesis optional; for doctorate, thesis/dissertation, publishable paper. *Entrance requirements:* For master's and doctorate, GRE (minimum combined score of 1000 on verbal and quantitative). Additional exam requirements/recommendations for international students: Required—TOEFL (minimum score 550 paper-based; 80 iBT). *Application deadline:* For fall admission, 7/15 for domestic students, 5/1 priority date for international students; for spring admission, 11/15 for domestic students, 9/1 priority date for international students. Applications are processed on a rolling basis. Application fee: $50 ($100 for international students). Electronic applications accepted. *Expenses:* Tuition, state resident: full-time $11,940; part-time $663 per credit. Tuition, nonresident: full-time $22,282; part-time $1238 per credit. *Financial support:* In 2014–15, 61 students received support, including 15 research assistantships with partial tuition reimbursements available (averaging $16,650 per year), 50 teaching assistantships with partial tuition reimbursements available (averaging $16,200 per year); career-related internships or fieldwork, Federal Work-Study, institutionally sponsored loans, scholarships/grants, and unspecified assistantships also available. Support available to part-time students. Financial award application deadline: 4/30; financial award applicants required to submit FAFSA. *Faculty research:* Role of mitochondria in neurodegenerative diseases, protein-DNA interactions in site-specific recombination, eukaryotic gene expression, bio-nanotechnology, sickle cell research. *Unit head:* Dr. Stephen Spiro, Department Head, 972-883-6032, Fax: 972-883-2409, E-mail: stephen.spiro@utdallas.edu. *Application contact:* Dr. Lawrence Reitzer, Graduate Advisor, 972-883-2502, Fax: 972-883-2409, E-mail: reitzer@utdallas.edu.
Website: http://www.utdallas.edu/biology/.

The University of Texas at San Antonio, College of Sciences, Department of Biology, San Antonio, TX 78249-0617. Offers biology (MS); biotechnology (MS); cell and molecular biology (PhD); neurobiology (PhD). *Faculty:* 36 full-time (8 women), 2 part-time/adjunct (0 women). *Students:* 102 full-time (54 women), 64 part-time (32 women); includes 71 minority (5 Black or African American, non-Hispanic/Latino; 8 Asian, non-Hispanic/Latino; 56 Hispanic/Latino; 2 Two or more races, non-Hispanic/Latino), 31 international. Average age 28. 196 applicants, 45% accepted, 49 enrolled. In 2014, 37 master's, 4 doctorates awarded. Terminal master's awarded for partial completion of doctoral program. *Degree requirements:* For master's, comprehensive exam, thesis or alternative; for doctorate, comprehensive exam, thesis/dissertation. *Entrance requirements:* For master's, GRE General Test, bachelor's degree with 18 credit hours in field of study or in another appropriate field of study; for doctorate, GRE General Test, 3 letters of recommendation, statement of purpose, resume. Additional exam requirements/recommendations for international students: Required—TOEFL (minimum score 500 paper-based; 100 iBT), IELTS (minimum score 5). *Application deadline:* For fall admission, 7/1 for domestic students, 4/1 for international students; for spring admission, 11/1 for domestic students, 9/1 for international students. Application fee: $45 ($80 for international students). Electronic applications accepted. *Expenses:* Tuition, state resident: full-time $4671; part-time $260 per credit hour. Tuition, nonresident: full-time $18,022; part-time $1001 per credit hour. *Faculty research:* Development of human and veterinary vaccines against a fungal disease, mammalian germ cells and stem cells, dopamine neuron physiology and addiction, plant

biochemistry, dendritic computation and synaptic plasticity. *Unit head:* Dr. Edwin J. Barea-Rodriguez, Chair, 210-458-4511, Fax: 210-458-5658, E-mail: edwin.barea@utsa.edu. *Application contact:* Rene Munguia, Jr., Senior Program Coordinator, 210-458-4642, Fax: 210-458-5658, E-mail: rene.munguia@utsa.edu.
Website: http://bio.utsa.edu/.

University of the Sciences, College of Graduate Studies, Program in Cell Biology and Biotechnology, Philadelphia, PA 19104-4495. Offers cell and molecular biology (PhD); cell biology (MS). Part-time and evening/weekend programs available. *Degree requirements:* For master's, thesis (for some programs). *Entrance requirements:* For master's, GRE General Test. Additional exam requirements/recommendations for international students: Required—TOEFL, TWE. *Expenses:* Contact institution. *Faculty research:* Invertebrate cell adhesion, plant-microbe interactions, natural product mechanisms, cell signal transduction, gene regulation and organization.

University of Toronto, School of Graduate Studies, Program in Biotechnology, Toronto, ON M5S 2J7, Canada. Offers MBiotech. *Entrance requirements:* For master's, minimum B+ average in the last two years of study and/or GRE. Additional exam requirements/recommendations for international students: Required—TOEFL (minimum score 580 paper-based; 93 iBT), TWE (minimum score 5). Electronic applications accepted.

University of Utah, Graduate School, Professional Master of Science and Technology Program, Salt Lake City, UT 84112-9016. Offers biotechnology (PSM); computational science (PSM); environmental science (PSM); science instrumentation (PSM). Part-time programs available. *Students:* 17 full-time (9 women), 43 part-time (13 women); includes 6 minority (4 Asian, non-Hispanic/Latino; 1 Hispanic/Latino; 1 Two or more races, non-Hispanic/Latino), 2 international. Average age 33. 48 applicants, 77% accepted, 20 enrolled. In 2014, 13 master's awarded. *Degree requirements:* For master's, internship. *Entrance requirements:* For master's, GRE (recommended), minimum undergraduate GPA of 3.0, bachelor's degree from accredited university or college. Additional exam requirements/recommendations for international students: Required—TOEFL (minimum score 550 paper-based; 80 iBT), IELTS (minimum score 6.5). *Application deadline:* For fall admission, 2/1 for domestic and international students. Application fee: $55 ($65 for international students). Electronic applications accepted. *Expenses:* Expenses: Contact institution. *Financial support:* Fellowships, research assistantships, teaching assistantships, and unspecified assistantships available. *Unit head:* Jennifer Schmidt, Program Director, 801-585-5630, E-mail: jennifer.schmidt@gradschool.utah.edu. *Application contact:* Jay Derek Payne, Project Coordinator, 801-585-3650, E-mail: derek.payne@gradschool.utah.edu.
Website: http://pmst.utah.edu/.

University of Washington, Graduate School, School of Medicine, Graduate Programs in Medicine, Department of Genome Sciences, Seattle, WA 98195. Offers PhD. *Degree requirements:* For doctorate, thesis/dissertation, general exam. *Entrance requirements:* For doctorate, GRE General Test, minimum GPA of 3.0. Additional exam requirements/recommendations for international students: Required—TOEFL. Electronic applications accepted. *Faculty research:* Model organism genetics, human and medical genetics, genomics and proteomics, computational biology.

University of West Florida, College of Arts and Sciences: Sciences, School of Allied Health and Life Sciences, Department of Biology, Pensacola, FL 32514-5750. Offers biological chemistry (MS); biology (MS); biology education (MST); biotechnology (MS); coastal zone studies (MS); environmental biology (MS). *Degree requirements:* For master's, thesis. *Entrance requirements:* For master's, GRE (minimum score: verbal 450, quantitative 550), official transcripts; BS in biology or related field; letter of interest; relevant past experience; three letters of recommendation from individuals who can evaluate applicant's academic ability. Additional exam requirements/recommendations for international students: Required—TOEFL (minimum score 550 paper-based).

University of Wyoming, Graduate Program in Molecular and Cellular Life Sciences, Laramie, WY 82071. Offers PhD. *Degree requirements:* For doctorate, thesis/dissertation, four eight-week laboratory rotations, comprehensive basic practical exam, two-part qualifying exam, seminars, symposium.

Virginia Polytechnic Institute and State University, Graduate School, College of Science, Blacksburg, VA 24061. Offers biological sciences (MS, PhD); biomedical technology development and management (MS); chemistry (MS, PhD); economics (MA, PhD); geosciences (MS, PhD); mathematics (MS, PhD); physics (MS, PhD); psychology (MS, PhD); statistics (MS, PhD). *Faculty:* 274 full-time (75 women), 3 part-time/adjunct (all women). *Students:* 544 full-time (212 women), 29 part-time (12 women); includes 54 minority (14 Black or African American, non-Hispanic/Latino; 9 Asian, non-Hispanic/Latino; 16 Hispanic/Latino; 15 Two or more races, non-Hispanic/Latino), 243 international. Average age 27. 1,105 applicants, 22% accepted, 104 enrolled. In 2014, 83 master's, 67 doctorates awarded. *Median time to degree:* Of those who began their doctoral program in fall 2006, 54% received their degree in 8 years or less. *Degree requirements:* For master's, comprehensive exam (for some programs), thesis (for some programs); for doctorate, comprehensive exam (for some programs), thesis/dissertation (for some programs). *Entrance requirements:* For master's and doctorate, GRE/GMAT (may vary by department). Additional exam requirements/recommendations for international students: Required—TOEFL (minimum score 550 paper-based). *Application deadline:* For fall admission, 8/1 for domestic students, 4/1 for international students; for spring admission, 1/1 for domestic students, 9/1 for international students. Applications are processed on a rolling basis. Application fee: $75. Electronic applications accepted. *Expenses:* Tuition, state resident: full-time $11,656; part-time $647.50 per credit hour. Tuition, nonresident: full-time $23,351; part-time $1297.25 per credit hour. *Required fees:* $2533; $465.75 per semester. Tuition and fees vary according to course load, campus/location and program. *Financial support:* In 2014–15, 1 fellowship with full tuition reimbursement (averaging $5,938 per year), 143 research assistantships with full tuition reimbursements (averaging $22,569 per year), 355 teaching assistantships with full tuition reimbursements (averaging $21,476 per year) were awarded. Financial award application deadline: 3/1; financial award applicants required to submit FAFSA. *Total annual research expenditures:* $24.3 million. *Unit head:* Dr. Lay Nam Chang, Dean, 540-231-5422, Fax: 540-231-3380, E-mail: laynam@vt.edu. *Application contact:* Diane Stearns, Assistant to the Dean, 540-231-7515, Fax: 540-231-3380, E-mail: dstearns@vt.edu.
Website: http://www.science.vt.edu/.

Wayne State University, College of Liberal Arts and Sciences, Department of Biological Sciences, Detroit, MI 48202. Offers biological sciences (MA, MS); cell development and neurobiology (PhD); evolution and organismal biology (PhD); molecular biology and biotechnology (PhD); molecular biotechnology (MS). PhD and MS programs admit for fall only. *Faculty:* 26 full-time (9 women). *Students:* 61 full-time (32 women), 17 part-time (8 women); includes 10 minority (4 Black or African American, non-Hispanic/Latino; 5 Asian, non-Hispanic/Latino; 1 Two or more races, non-Hispanic/Latino), 38 international. Average age 28. 247 applicants, 19% accepted, 25 enrolled. In 2014, 13 master's, 2 doctorates awarded. *Degree requirements:* For master's, thesis (for some programs); for doctorate, thesis/dissertation. *Entrance requirements:* For master's, GRE (for MS applicants), minimum GPA of 3.0; adequate preparation in biological sciences and supporting courses in chemistry, physics and mathematics; curriculum vitae; personal statement; three letters of recommendation (two for MA); for doctorate, GRE, curriculum vitae, statement of goals and career objectives, three letters of reference, bachelor's or master's degree in biological or other science. Additional exam requirements/recommendations for international students: Required—TOEFL (minimum score 550 paper-based; 79 iBT), TWE (minimum score 5.5), Michigan English Language Assessment Battery (minimum score 85); Recommended—IELTS (minimum score 6.5). *Application deadline:* For fall admission, 6/1 priority date for domestic students, 5/1 priority date for international students; for winter admission, 10/1 priority date for domestic students, 9/1 priority date for international students. Application fee: $0. Electronic applications accepted. *Expenses:* Tuition, state resident: full-time $10,294; part-time $571.90 per credit hour. Tuition, nonresident: full-time $29,730; part-time $1238.75 per credit hour. *Required fees:* $1365; $43.50 per credit hour. $291.10 per semester. Tuition and fees vary according to course load and program. *Financial support:* In 2014–15, 55 students received support, including 3 fellowships with tuition reimbursements available (averaging $16,842 per year), 9 research assistantships with tuition reimbursements available (averaging $18,582 per year), 49 teaching assistantships with tuition reimbursements available (averaging $18,488 per year); institutionally sponsored loans, scholarships/grants, health care benefits, and unspecified assistantships also available. Financial award application deadline: 3/31; financial award applicants required to submit FAFSA. *Faculty research:* Transcription and chromatin remodeling, genomic and developmental evolution, community and landscape ecology and environmental degradation, microbiology and virology, cell and neurobiology. *Total annual research expenditures:* $1.9 million. *Unit head:* Dr. David Njus, Professor and Chair, 313-577-2783, Fax: 313-577-6891, E-mail: dnjus@wayne.edu. *Application contact:* Rose Mary Priest, Office Services Clerk, 313-577-6818, Fax: 313-577-6891, E-mail: rpriest@wayne.edu.
Website: http://clasweb.clas.wayne.edu/biology.

West Virginia State University, Biotechnology Graduate Program, Institute, WV 25112-1000. Offers MA, MS. *Degree requirements:* For master's, comprehensive exam. *Entrance requirements:* For master's, GRE (Verbal 140, Quantitative 150), International Students: Affidavit of Support, Proof of Immunization, TOEFL (80), evaluation of academic transcripts. Additional exam requirements/recommendations for international students: Required—TOEFL. Electronic applications accepted. *Faculty research:* Plant physiology, microbiology, molecular biology, social insect biology, insect population biology, ecology, fish biology, aquaculture, nutrigenomics, nutritional immunology, tumor biology, gene therapy, muscle physiology, environmental microbiology, microbial genomics, biofilms, anaeromic digestion, plant genomics, parasitic platyhelminths, environmental parasitology, horticulture, plant breeding and genetics, plant reproductive barriers, sustainable agriculture, DNA-assisted plant breeding.

William Paterson University of New Jersey, College of Science and Health, Wayne, NJ 07470-8420. Offers biology (MS); biotechnology (MS); communication disorders (MS); exercise and sports studies (MS); nursing (MSN); nursing practice (DNP). Part-time and evening/weekend programs available. *Faculty:* 31 full-time (16 women), 17 part-time/adjunct (5 women). *Students:* 72 full-time (58 women), 199 part-time (173 women); includes 89 minority (19 Black or African American, non-Hispanic/Latino; 33 Asian, non-Hispanic/Latino; 36 Hispanic/Latino; 1 Two or more races, non-Hispanic/Latino), 2 international. Average age 34. 578 applicants, 36% accepted, 122 enrolled. In 2014, 68 master's, 10 doctorates awarded. *Degree requirements:* For master's, comprehensive exam (for some programs), thesis (for some programs), non-thesis internship/practicum (for some programs). *Entrance requirements:* For master's, GRE/MAT, minimum GPA of 3.0; 2 letters of recommendation; personal statement; work experience (for some programs); for doctorate, GRE/MAT, minimum GPA of 3.3; work experience; 3 letters of recommendation, interview; master's degree in nursing. Additional exam requirements/recommendations for international students: Required—TOEFL (minimum score 550 paper-based; 79 iBT), IELTS (minimum score 6). *Application deadline:* For fall admission, 6/1 for domestic students, 3/1 for international students; for spring admission, 11/1 for domestic students, 10/1 for international students. Applications are processed on a rolling basis. Application fee: $50. Electronic applications accepted. *Expenses:* Tuition, state resident: full-time $12,413; part-time $564.21 per credit. Tuition, nonresident: full-time $20,487; part-time $931.21 per credit. *Required fees:* $2107; $95.79 per credit. $478.95 per semester. Tuition and fees vary according to course load and degree level. *Financial support:* Research assistantships with full tuition reimbursements, career-related internships or fieldwork, Federal Work-Study, scholarships/grants, and unspecified assistantships available. Support available to part-time students. Financial award application deadline: 4/1; financial award applicants required to submit FAFSA. *Faculty research:* Human biomechanics, autism, nanomaterials, health and environment, neurophysiology and neurobiology. *Unit head:* Dr. Kenneth Wolf, Dean, 973-720-2194, Fax: 973-720-3414, E-mail: wolfk@wpunj.edu. *Application contact:* Christina Aiello, Assistant Director, Graduate Admissions, 973-720-2506, Fax: 973-720-2035, E-mail: aielloc@wpunj.edu.
Website: http://www.wpunj.edu/cosh.

Worcester Polytechnic Institute, Graduate Studies and Research, Department of Biology and Biotechnology, Worcester, MA 01609-2280. Offers biology and biotechnology (MS); biotechnology (PhD). *Faculty:* 9 full-time (5 women). *Students:* 21 full-time (10 women); includes 1 minority (Asian, non-Hispanic/Latino), 7 international. 80 applicants, 16% accepted, 9 enrolled. In 2014, 2 master's, 3 doctorates awarded. Terminal master's awarded for partial completion of doctoral program. *Degree requirements:* For master's, thesis; for doctorate, comprehensive exam, thesis/dissertation, qualifying exam. *Entrance requirements:* For master's and doctorate, GRE General Test, 3 letters of recommendation, statement of purpose. Additional exam requirements/recommendations for international students: Required—TOEFL (minimum score 563 paper-based; 84 iBT), IELTS (minimum score 7). *Application deadline:* For fall admission, 1/1 priority date for domestic and international students. Application fee: $70. Electronic applications accepted. *Financial support:* Research assistantships, teaching assistantships, career-related internships or fieldwork, institutionally sponsored loans, scholarships/grants, and unspecified assistantships available. Financial award application deadline: 1/1; financial award applicants required to submit FAFSA. *Unit head:* Dr. Joseph Duffy, Head, 508-831-4111, Fax: 508-831-5936, E-mail: jduffy@wpi.edu. *Application contact:* Dr. Reeta Rao, Graduate Coordinator, 508-831-5538, Fax: 508-831-5936, E-mail: rpr@wpi.edu.
Website: http://www.wpi.edu/Academics/Depts/BBT/.

Worcester State University, Graduate Studies, Program in Biotechnology, Worcester, MA 01602-2597. Offers MS. Part-time and evening/weekend programs available. *Faculty:* 5 full-time (3 women), 1 part-time/adjunct (0 women). *Students:* 3 full-time (1 woman), 18 part-time (12 women); includes 6 minority (1 Black or African American, non-Hispanic/Latino; 3 Asian, non-Hispanic/Latino; 1 Hispanic/Latino; 1 Two or more races, non-Hispanic/Latino), 3 international. Average age 30. 14 applicants, 64% accepted, 3 enrolled. In 2014, 8 master's awarded. *Degree requirements:* For master's, comprehensive exam, thesis. *Entrance requirements:* For master's, GRE General Test or MAT, baccalaureate degree in biology, biotechnology, chemistry or similar majors; minimum GPA of 2.75 in all undergraduate work, 3.0 in all course work within major at the junior and senior level. Additional exam requirements/recommendations for international students: Required—TOEFL (minimum score 550 paper-based; 79 iBT). *Application deadline:* For fall admission, 6/15 for domestic and international students; for spring admission, 11/1 for domestic and international students; for summer admission, 4/1 for domestic and international students. Applications are processed on a rolling basis. Application fee: $50. Electronic applications accepted. *Expenses: Tuition, area resident:* Part-time $150 per credit. Tuition, state resident: part-time $150 per credit. Tuition, nonresident: part-time $150 per credit. *Financial support:* In 2014–15, 1 research assistantship (averaging $4,800 per year) was awarded. Financial award application deadline: 3/1; financial award applicants required to submit FAFSA. *Unit head:* Dr. Peter Bradley, Program Coordinator, 508-929-8571, Fax: 508-929-8171, E-mail: pbradley@worcester.edu. *Application contact:* Sara Grady, Acting Associate Dean of Graduate and Continuing Education, 508-929-8787, Fax: 508-929-8100, E-mail: sara.grady@worcester.edu.

Nanotechnology

Arizona State University at the Tempe campus, College of Liberal Arts and Sciences, Department of Chemistry and Biochemistry, Tempe, AZ 85287-1604. Offers biochemistry (MS, PhD); chemistry (MS, PhD); nanoscience (PSM). Terminal master's awarded for partial completion of doctoral program. *Degree requirements:* For master's, thesis, interactive Program of Study (iPOS) submitted before completing 50 percent of required credit hours; for doctorate, comprehensive exam, thesis/dissertation, interactive Program of Study (iPOS) submitted before completing 50 percent of required credit hours. *Entrance requirements:* For master's and doctorate, GRE, minimum GPA of 3.0 or equivalent in last 2 years of work leading to bachelor's degree. Additional exam requirements/recommendations for international students: Required—TOEFL, IELTS, or PTE. Electronic applications accepted.

Arizona State University at the Tempe campus, College of Liberal Arts and Sciences, Department of Physics, Tempe, AZ 85287-1504. Offers nanoscience (PSM); physics (MNS, PhD). Part-time programs available. Terminal master's awarded for partial completion of doctoral program. *Degree requirements:* For master's, comprehensive exam, thesis or alternative, interactive Program of Study (iPOS) submitted before completing 50 percent of required credit hours; for doctorate, comprehensive exam, thesis/dissertation, interactive Program of Study (iPOS) submitted before completing 50 percent of required credit hours. *Entrance requirements:* For master's and doctorate, GRE, minimum GPA of 3.0 or equivalent in last 2 years of work leading to bachelor's degree. Additional exam requirements/recommendations for international students: Required—TOEFL, IELTS, or PTE. Electronic applications accepted. *Expenses:* Contact institution.

Carnegie Mellon University, Mellon College of Science, Department of Chemistry, Pittsburgh, PA 15213-3891. Offers atmospheric chemistry (PhD); bioinorganic chemistry (PhD); bioorganic chemistry and chemical biology (PhD); biophysical chemistry (PhD); catalysis (PhD); green and environmental chemistry (PhD); materials and nanoscience (PhD); renewable energy (PhD); sensors, probes, and imaging (PhD); spectroscopy and single molecule analysis (PhD); theoretical and computational chemistry (PhD). Part-time programs available. Terminal master's awarded for partial completion of doctoral program. *Degree requirements:* For doctorate, thesis/dissertation, departmental qualifying and oral exams, teaching experience. *Entrance requirements:* For doctorate, GRE General Test, GRE Subject Test. Additional exam requirements/recommendations for international students: Required—TOEFL. Electronic applications accepted. *Faculty research:* Physical and theoretical chemistry, chemical synthesis, biophysical/ bioinorganic chemistry.

The College of William and Mary, Faculty of Arts and Sciences, Department of Applied Science, Williamsburg, VA 23187-8795. Offers accelerator science (PhD); applied mathematics (PhD); applied mechanics (PhD); applied robotics (PhD); applied science (MS); interface, thin film and surface science (PhD); lasers and optics (PhD); magnetic resonance (PhD); nanotechnology (PhD); non-destructive evaluation (PhD); polymer chemistry (PhD); remote sensing (PhD). Part-time programs available. *Faculty:* 8 full-time (2 women), 2 part-time/adjunct (0 women). *Students:* 28 full-time (11 women), 5 part-time (2 women); includes 5 minority (2 Black or African American, non-Hispanic/ Latino; 2 Asian, non-Hispanic/Latino; 1 Hispanic/Latino), 13 international. Average age 28. 32 applicants, 38% accepted, 7 enrolled. In 2014, 6 master's, 4 doctorates awarded. Terminal master's awarded for partial completion of doctoral program. *Degree requirements:* For master's, comprehensive exam, thesis; for doctorate, comprehensive exam, thesis/dissertation, 4 core courses. *Entrance requirements:* For master's and doctorate, GRE General Test, GRE Subject Test. Additional exam requirements/ recommendations for international students: Required—TOEFL, TWE. *Application deadline:* For fall admission, 2/3 priority date for domestic students, 2/3 for international students; for spring admission, 10/15 priority date for domestic students, 10/14 for international students. Applications are processed on a rolling basis. Application fee: $45. Electronic applications accepted. *Financial support:* Fellowships, research assistantships, teaching assistantships, Federal Work-Study, health care benefits, tuition waivers (full), and unspecified assistantships available. Financial award application deadline: 4/15; financial award applicants required to submit FAFSA. *Faculty research:* Computational biology, non-destructive evaluation, neurophysiology, lasers and optics. *Total annual research expenditures:* $1.7 million. *Unit head:* Dr. Christopher Del Negro, Chair, 757-221-7808, Fax: 757-221-2050, E-mail: cadeln@wm.edu. *Application contact:* Lianne Rios Ashburne, Graduate Program Coordinator, 757-221-2563, Fax: 757-221-2050, E-mail: lrashburne@wm.edu.
Website: http://www.wm.edu/as/appliedscience.

Cornell University, Graduate School, Graduate Fields of Agriculture and Life Sciences and Graduate Fields of Engineering, Field of Biological and Environmental Engineering, Ithaca, NY 14853-0001. Offers bioenergy and integrated energy systems (M Eng, MPS, MS, PhD); biological engineering (M Eng, MPS, MS, PhD); bioprocess engineering (M Eng, MPS, MS, PhD); ecohydrology (M Eng, MPS, MS, PhD); environmental engineering (M Eng, MPS, MS, PhD); environmental management (MPS); food engineering (M Eng, MPS, MS, PhD); industrial biotechnology (M Eng, MPS, MS, PhD); nanobiotechnology (M Eng, MPS, MS, PhD); sustainable systems (M Eng, MPS, MS, PhD); synthetic biology (MS); syntheticbiology (M Eng, MPS, PhD). Terminal master's awarded for partial completion of doctoral program. *Degree requirements:* For master's, thesis (MS); for doctorate, comprehensive exam, thesis/dissertation. *Entrance requirements:* For master's, letters of recommendation (3 for MS, 2 for M Eng and MPS); for doctorate, GRE General Test, 3 letters of recommendation. Additional exam requirements/recommendations for international students: Required—TOEFL (minimum score 550 paper-based; 77 iBT). Electronic applications accepted. *Faculty research:* Biological and food engineering, environmental, soil and water engineering, international agricultural engineering, structures and controlled environments, machine systems and energy.

Indiana University of Pennsylvania, School of Graduate Studies and Research, College of Natural Sciences and Mathematics, Department of Physics, Program in Nanoscience/Industrial Materials, Indiana, PA 15705-1087. Offers PSM. Part-time programs available. *Faculty:* 3 full-time (0 women). *Students:* 1 full-time (0 women), 4 part-time (1 woman), 1 international. Average age 24. 12 applicants, 50% accepted, 2 enrolled. In 2014, 3 master's awarded. *Degree requirements:* For master's, comprehensive exam (for some programs), thesis (for some programs). *Entrance*

requirements: Additional exam requirements/recommendations for international students: Required—TOEFL (minimum score 540 paper-based). *Application deadline:* Applications are processed on a rolling basis. Application fee: $50. Electronic applications accepted. *Financial support:* In 2014–15, 1 fellowship with full tuition reimbursement (averaging $1,000 per year), 1 research assistantship with full and partial tuition reimbursement (averaging $1,000 per year) were awarded; career-related internships or fieldwork, Federal Work-Study, and scholarships/grants also available. Support available to part-time students. Financial award application deadline: 4/15; financial award applicants required to submit FAFSA. *Unit head:* Dr. John Bradshaw, Graduate Coordinator, 724-357-7731, E-mail: bradshaw@iup.edu.

Johns Hopkins University, G. W. C. Whiting School of Engineering, Master of Science in Engineering Management Program, Baltimore, MD 21218-2699. Offers biomaterials (MSEM); civil engineering (MSEM); communications science (MSEM); computer science (MSEM); environmental systems analysis, economics and public policy (MSEM); fluid mechanics (MSEM); materials science and engineering (MSEM); mechanical engineering (MSEM); mechanics and materials (MSEM); nano-biotechnology (MSEM); nanomaterials and nanotechnology (MSEM); operations research (MSEM); probability and statistics (MSEM); smart product and device design (MSEM). *Entrance requirements:* For master's, GRE, 3 letters of recommendation, resume. Additional exam requirements/recommendations for international students: Required—TOEFL (minimum score 600 paper-based; 100 iBT) or IELTS (minimum score 7). Electronic applications accepted.

North Dakota State University, College of Graduate and Interdisciplinary Studies, Interdisciplinary Program in Materials and Nanotechnology, Fargo, ND 58108. Offers MS, PhD. *Entrance requirements:* For doctorate, GRE General Test. Additional exam requirements/recommendations for international students: Required—TOEFL (minimum score 525 paper-based; 71 iBT).

South Dakota School of Mines and Technology, Graduate Division, Program in Nanoscience and Nanoengineering, Rapid City, SD 57701-3995. Offers PhD. Part-time programs available. *Faculty:* 4 full-time (0 women). *Students:* 10 full-time (5 women), 6 international. Average age 27. 8 applicants, 63% accepted. In 2014, 2 doctorates awarded. *Degree requirements:* For doctorate, thesis/dissertation. *Entrance requirements:* Additional exam requirements/recommendations for international students: Required—TOEFL (minimum score 520 paper-based; 68 iBT). *Application deadline:* For fall admission, 7/1 for domestic students, 4/1 for international students; for spring admission, 11/1 for domestic students, 9/1 for international students. Applications are processed on a rolling basis. Application fee: $35. Electronic applications accepted. *Expenses:* Tuition, state resident: full-time $5050; part-time $210.40 per credit hour. Tuition, nonresident: full-time $11,290; part-time $470.30 per credit hour. *Required fees:* $4680. *Financial support:* In 2014–15, 1 fellowship (averaging $8,700 per year), 19 research assistantships with partial tuition reimbursements (averaging $9,157 per year) were awarded; teaching assistantships also available. Financial award application deadline: 5/15. *Total annual research expenditures:* $25,572. *Unit head:* Dr. Steve Smith, Director, 605-394-5268, E-mail: steve.smith@sdsmt.edu. *Application contact:* Rachel Howard, Office of Graduate Education, 605-355-3468, Fax: 605-394-1767, E-mail: rachel.howard@sdsmt.edu.
Website: http://www.sdsmt.edu/Academics/Departments/Nanoscience-and -Nanoengineering/Graduate-Education/.

University at Albany, State University of New York, College of Nanoscale Science and Engineering, Albany, NY 12222-0001. Offers MS, PhD. *Entrance requirements:* Additional exam requirements/recommendations for international students: Required— TOEFL (minimum score 550 paper-based). *Faculty research:* Thin film material structures, optoelectronic materials, design and fabrication of nano-mechanical systems, materials characterization.

University of Alberta, Faculty of Graduate Studies and Research, Department of Electrical and Computer Engineering, Edmonton, AB T6G 2E1, Canada. Offers communications (M Eng, M Sc, PhD); computer engineering (M Eng, M Sc, PhD); electromagnetics (M Eng, M Sc, PhD); nanotechnology and microdevices (M Eng, M Sc, PhD); power/power electronics (M Eng, M Sc, PhD); systems (M Eng, M Sc, PhD). Terminal master's awarded for partial completion of doctoral program. *Degree requirements:* For master's, thesis; for doctorate, thesis/dissertation. *Entrance requirements:* Additional exam requirements/recommendations for international students: Required—TOEFL. Electronic applications accepted. *Faculty research:* Controls, communications, microelectronics, electromagnetics.

University of California, Riverside, Graduate Division, Materials Science and Engineering Program, Riverside, CA 92521. Offers MS, PhD. *Entrance requirements:* For master's and doctorate, GRE. Additional exam requirements/recommendations for international students: Required—TOEFL (minimum score 550 paper-based; 80 iBT). Electronic applications accepted. *Expenses:* Tuition, state resident: full-time $5399. Tuition, nonresident: full-time $10,433.

University of California, San Diego, Graduate Division, Department of Electrical and Computer Engineering, La Jolla, CA 92093. Offers applied ocean science (MS, PhD); applied physics (MS, PhD); communication theory and systems (MS, PhD); computer engineering (MS, PhD); electronic circuits and systems (MS, PhD); intelligent systems, robotics and control (MS, PhD); medical devices and systems (MS, PhD); nanoscale devices and systems (MS, PhD); photonics (MS, PhD); signal and image processing (MS, PhD). *Students:* 435 full-time (81 women), 43 part-time (8 women); includes 78 minority (2 Black or African American, non-Hispanic/Latino; 1 American Indian or Alaska Native, non-Hispanic/Latino; 69 Asian, non-Hispanic/Latino; 6 Hispanic/Latino), 306 international. 2,710 applicants, 18% accepted, 177 enrolled. In 2014, 109 master's, 50 doctorates awarded. *Degree requirements:* For master's, thesis or written exam; for doctorate, comprehensive exam, thesis/dissertation. *Entrance requirements:* For master's and doctorate, GRE General Test, minimum GPA of 3.0. Additional exam requirements/recommendations for international students: Required—TOEFL (minimum score 550 paper-based; 80 iBT), IELTS. *Application deadline:* For fall admission, 12/15 for domestic students. Application fee: $90 ($110 for international students). Electronic applications accepted. *Expenses:* Tuition, state resident: full-time $11,220; part-time $5610 per quarter. Tuition, nonresident: full-time $26,322; part-time $13,161 per

quarter. *Required fees:* $570 per quarter. Tuition and fees vary according to program. *Financial support:* Fellowships, research assistantships, teaching assistantships, scholarships/grants, and unspecified assistantships available. Financial award applicants required to submit FAFSA. *Faculty research:* Applied ocean science; applied physics; communication theory and systems; computer,engineering; electronic circuits and systems; intelligent systems, robotics and control; medical devices and systems; nanoscale devices and systems; photonics; signal and image processing. *Unit head:* Truong Nguyen, Chair, 858-822-5554, E-mail: nguyent@ece.ucsd.edu. *Application contact:* Shana Slebioda, Graduate Coordinator, 858-822-2513, E-mail: ecegradapps@ece.ucsd.edu.
Website: http://ece.ucsd.edu/.

University of California, San Diego, Graduate Division, Department of Nanoengineering, La Jolla, CA 92093. Offers MS, PhD. *Students:* 78 full-time (26 women), 6 part-time (2 women); includes 18 minority (1 American Indian or Alaska Native, non-Hispanic/Latino; 15 Asian, non-Hispanic/Latino; 2 Hispanic/Latino), 45 international. 244 applicants, 43% accepted, 39 enrolled. In 2014, 20 master's awarded. *Degree requirements:* For master's, thesis or comprehensive exam; for doctorate, comprehensive exam, thesis/dissertation, 1-quarter teaching assistantship. *Entrance requirements:* For master's and doctorate, GRE General Test, 3 letters of recommendation, statement of purpose, resume. Additional exam requirements/recommendations for international students: Required—TOEFL (minimum score 550 paper-based; 80 iBT), IELTS (minimum score 7). *Application deadline:* For fall admission, 12/15 for domestic students. Application fee: $90 ($110 for international students). *Expenses:* Tuition, state resident: full-time $11,220; part-time $5610 per quarter. Tuition, nonresident: full-time $26,322; part-time $13,161 per quarter. *Required fees:* $570 per quarter. Tuition and fees vary according to program. *Financial support:* Fellowships, research assistantships, teaching assistantships, and scholarships/grants available. Financial award applicants required to submit FAFSA. *Faculty research:* Nanostructured materials, assembly of nanoscale materials, nanomanufacturing, cancer nanotechnology, nanophotonic sensors and devices. *Unit head:* Joseph Wang, Chair, 858-246-0128, E-mail: josephwang@ucsd.edu. *Application contact:* Dana Jimenez, Graduate Coordinator, 858-822-7981, E-mail: dljimenez@ucsd.edu.
Website: http://nanoengineering.ucsd.edu.

University of New Mexico, Graduate School, School of Engineering, Program in Nanoscience and Microsystems Engineering, Albuquerque, NM 87131. Offers MS, PhD. Part-time programs available. *Students:* 30 full-time (10 women), 24 part-time (4 women); includes 19 minority (2 Black or African American, non-Hispanic/Latino; 3 Asian, non-Hispanic/Latino; 11 Hispanic/Latino; 3 Two or more races, non-Hispanic/Latino), 2 international. Average age 33. 18 applicants, 39% accepted, 1 enrolled. In 2014, 6 master's, 5 doctorates awarded. *Degree requirements:* For master's, comprehensive exam, thesis; for doctorate, comprehensive exam, thesis/dissertation. *Entrance requirements:* For master's and doctorate, GRE. Additional exam requirements/recommendations for international students: Required—TOEFL. *Application deadline:* For fall admission, 7/30 for domestic students, 2/1 for international students; for spring admission, 11/30 for domestic students, 6/1 for international students. Applications are processed on a rolling basis. Application fee: $50. Electronic applications accepted. *Financial support:* In 2014–15, 48 students received support, including 39 research assistantships with full tuition reimbursements available (averaging $17,556 per year), 9 teaching assistantships with full tuition reimbursements available (averaging $7,505 per year). *Unit head:* Dr. Abhaya Datye, Professor, 505-277-0477, Fax: 505-277-1024, E-mail: datye@unm.edu. *Application contact:* Heather Elizabeth Armstrong, Program Specialist, 505-277-6824, Fax: 505-277-1024, E-mail: heathera@unm.edu.
Website: http://nsms.unm.edu.

University of Washington, Graduate School, College of Engineering and School of Medicine, Department of Bioengineering, Seattle, WA 98195-5061. Offers bioengineering (MS, PhD); bioengineering and nanotechnology (PhD); pharmaceutical bioengineering (MS). Evening/weekend programs available. *Faculty:* 23 full-time (7 women). *Students:* 130 full-time (46 women), 23 part-time (14 women). Average age 26. 536 applicants, 12% accepted, 28 enrolled. In 2014, 29 master's, 16 doctorates awarded. *Degree requirements:* For master's, comprehensive exam, thesis; for doctorate, comprehensive exam, thesis/dissertation, qualifying exam, general exam, thesis defense. *Entrance requirements:* For master's and doctorate, GRE General Test, minimum GPA of 3.0, transcripts, statement of purpose, letters of recommendation. Additional exam requirements/recommendations for international students: Required—TOEFL (minimum score 580 paper-based; 92 iBT); Recommended—IELTS (minimum score 7). *Application deadline:* For fall admission, 12/1 for domestic and international students. Application fee: $85. Electronic applications accepted. *Expenses:* Expenses: Contact institution. *Financial support:* In 2014–15, 136 students received support, including 22 fellowships with full tuition reimbursements available, 97 research assistantships with full tuition reimbursements available, 7 teaching assistantships with full tuition reimbursements available; Federal Work-Study, institutionally sponsored loans, traineeships, health care benefits, and tuition waivers (full) also available. Support available to part-time students. Financial award application deadline: 12/1; financial award applicants required to submit FAFSA. *Faculty research:* Imaging and image guided therapy, molecular and cellular engineering, biomaterials and regenerative medicine, technology for expanding access to healthcare, synthetic and quantitative biology. *Total annual research expenditures:* $24 million. *Unit head:* Dr. Cecilia Giachelli, Professor/Chair, 206-685-2000, Fax: 206-685-3300, E-mail: ceci@uw.edu. *Application contact:* Senior Academic Counselor, 206-685-3494, Fax: 206-685-3300, E-mail: bioeng@uw.edu.
Website: http://depts.washington.edu/bioe/.

University of Washington, Graduate School, College of Engineering, Department of Chemical Engineering, Seattle, WA 98195-1750. Offers chemical engineering (MS, MSE, PhD); chemical engineering and nanotechnology (PhD). *Faculty:* 21 full-time (3 women). *Students:* 97 full-time (25 women). Average age 25. 258 applicants, 31% accepted, 35 enrolled. In 2014, 15 master's, 19 doctorates awarded. Terminal master's awarded for partial completion of doctoral program. *Degree requirements:* For master's, thesis, final exam, research project, degree requirements must be completed in 6 years; for doctorate, thesis/dissertation, general and final exams, research project, completion of all work within 10 years. *Entrance requirements:* For master's and doctorate, GRE General Test (minimum Quantitative score of 159), minimum GPA of 3.0, official transcripts, personal statement, confidential evaluations by 3 professors or other technical professional, high rank (top 5%) in respected chemical engineering program. Additional exam requirements/recommendations for international students: Required—TOEFL (minimum score 580 paper-based; 92 iBT); Recommended—IELTS (minimum score 7). *Application deadline:* For fall admission, 1/1 priority date for domestic students, 12/15 priority date for international students. Applications are processed on a rolling basis. Application fee: $85. Electronic applications accepted. *Expenses:* Expenses: Contact institution. *Financial support:* In 2014–15, 84 students received support, including 15 fellowships with full tuition reimbursements available, 55 research assistantships with full tuition reimbursements available, 14 teaching assistantships with full tuition reimbursements available; career-related internships or fieldwork, Federal Work-Study, health care benefits, and unspecified assistantships also available. Financial award application deadline: 1/15; financial award applicants required to submit FAFSA. *Faculty research:* Materials processing and characterization, optical and electronic polymers, surface science, biochemical engineering and bioengineering, computational chemistry, environmental studies. *Total annual research expenditures:* $12.2 million. *Unit head:* Dr. Francois Baneyx, Professor/Chair, 206-543-2250, Fax: 206-543-3778, E-mail: baneyx@uw.edu. *Application contact:* Allison Sherrill, Graduate Program Advisor, 206-685-9785, E-mail: sherra@uw.edu.
Website: http://www.cheme.washington.edu/.

University of Washington, Graduate School, College of Engineering, Department of Electrical Engineering, Seattle, WA 98195-2500. Offers electrical engineering (MS, PhD); electrical engineering and nanotechnology (PhD). Part-time programs available. Postbaccalaureate distance learning degree programs offered (no on-campus study). *Faculty:* 37 full-time (5 women). *Students:* 233 full-time (50 women), 115 part-time (14 women). Average age 28. 1,318 applicants, 17% accepted, 118 enrolled. In 2014, 72 master's, 30 doctorates awarded. Terminal master's awarded for partial completion of doctoral program. *Degree requirements:* For master's, thesis optional; for doctorate, thesis/dissertation, qualifying, general, and final exams. *Entrance requirements:* For master's, GRE General Test (recommended minimum Quantitative score of 160), GPA of 3.5 recommended; resume or curriculum vitae, statement of purpose, 3 letters of recommendation, undergraduate and graduate transcripts; for doctorate, GRE General Test (recommended minimum Quantitative score of 160), GPA of 3.5 recommended, resume or curriculum vitae, statement of purpose, 3 letters of recommendation, undergraduate and graduate transcripts. Additional exam requirements/recommendations for international students: Required—TOEFL (minimum score 600 paper-based; 92 iBT); Recommended—IELTS (minimum score 7). *Application deadline:* For fall admission, 12/15 for domestic and international students. Applications are processed on a rolling basis. Application fee: $85. Electronic applications accepted. *Expenses:* Expenses: Contact institution. *Financial support:* In 2014–15, 199 students received support, including 15 fellowships with full tuition reimbursements available, 122 research assistantships with full tuition reimbursements available, 62 teaching assistantships with full tuition reimbursements available; career-related internships or fieldwork, Federal Work-Study, and institutionally sponsored loans also available. Financial award application deadline: 1/1; financial award applicants required to submit FAFSA. *Faculty research:* Smart grid, advanced wireless networks and communications, nanotechnology, biorobotics, signal processing and compression. *Total annual research expenditures:* $18.5 million. *Unit head:* Dr. Radha Poovendran, Professor/Chair, 206-543-6515, Fax: 206-543-3842, E-mail: chair@ee.washington.edu. *Application contact:* Brenda Larson, Lead Graduate Program Academic Counselor, 206-616-1351, Fax: 206-543-3842, E-mail: brenda@ee.washington.edu.
Website: http://www.ee.washington.edu/.

Virginia Commonwealth University, Graduate School, College of Humanities and Sciences, Department of Physics, Richmond, VA 23284-9005. Offers medical physics (MS, PhD); nanoscience and nanotechnology (PhD); physics and applied physics (MS). Part-time programs available. *Degree requirements:* For master's, comprehensive exam, thesis optional. *Entrance requirements:* For master's, GRE. Additional exam requirements/recommendations for international students: Required—TOEFL (minimum score 600 paper-based; 100 iBT); Recommended—IELTS (minimum score 6.5). Electronic applications accepted. *Faculty research:* Condensed-matter theory and experimentation, electronic instrumentation, relativity.

Virginia Commonwealth University, Graduate School, College of Humanities and Sciences, Program in Nanosciences, Richmond, VA 23284-9005. Offers PhD. *Entrance requirements:* For doctorate, GRE General Test. Additional exam requirements/recommendations for international students: Required—TOEFL (minimum score 600 paper-based; 100 iBT); Recommended—IELTS (minimum score 6.5). Electronic applications accepted. *Faculty research:* Nanotechnology, nanoscience.

CASE WESTERN RESERVE UNIVERSITY
Department of Biomedical Engineering

Programs of Study

The Department offers many exceptional and innovative educational programs leading to career opportunities in biomedical engineering (BME) research, development, and design in industry, medical centers, and academic institutions. Graduate degrees offered include the M.S. and Ph.D. in BME, a combined M.D./M.S. degree offered to students admitted to the School of Medicine, and combined M.D./Ph.D. degrees in BME offered through the Physician Engineer Training Program or the Medical Scientist Training Program. Individualized BME programs of study allow students to develop strength in an engineering specialty and apply this expertise to an important biomedical problem under the supervision of a Faculty Guidance Committee. Students can choose from more than forty-three courses regularly taught in BME, as well as many courses in other departments. Typically, an M.S. program consists of seven to nine courses, and a Ph.D. program consists of about thirteen courses beyond the B.S. Students can select research projects from among the many strengths of the Department, including neural engineering and neural prostheses, biomaterials, tissue engineering, drug and gene delivery, biomedical imaging, sensors, optical imaging and diagnostics, the cardiovascular system, biomechanics, mass and heat transport, and metabolic systems. Collaborative research and training in basic biomedical sciences, as well as clinical and translational research, are available through primary faculty members, associated faculty members, and researchers in the nearby major medical centers.

Research Facilities

The primary faculty members have laboratories focusing on cardiovascular and skeletal biomaterials; cardiovascular, orthopaedic, and neural tissue engineering; materials and nanoparticles for drug and gene delivery, biomedical image processing, biomedical imaging in several modalities, cellular and tissue cardiac bioelectricity, ion channel function, electrochemical and fiber-optic sensors, neural engineering and brain electrophysiology, and neural prostheses. BME faculty members and students also make extensive use of campus research centers for special purposes such as microelectronic fabrication, biomedical imaging, and material analyses. Associated faculty members have labs devoted to eye movement control, gait analysis, implantable sensors/actuators, biomedical imaging, metabolism, and tissue pathology. These are located at four major medical centers and teaching hospitals that (with one exception) are within walking distance.

Financial Aid

Graduate students pursuing the Ph.D. may receive financial support from faculty members as research assistants, from training grants (NIH, NSF, DoE GAANN), or from the School of Medicine (M.D./Ph.D. only). These positions are awarded on a competitive basis. There are also opportunities for research assistantships in order to pursue the M.S.

Cost of Study

Tuition at Case in 2015–16 for graduate students is $1,714 per credit hour. A full load for graduate students is a minimum of 9 credits per semester. Fees for health insurance and activities are estimated at $880 per semester.

Living and Housing Costs

Within a 2-mile radius of the campus, numerous apartments are available for married and single graduate students, with rent ranging from $450 to $900 per month.

Student Group

The Department of Biomedical Engineering has 154 graduate students, of whom about 75 percent are advancing toward the Ph.D. At Case Western Reserve University, approximately 4,677 students are enrolled as undergraduates, 2,967 in graduate studies, and 2,825 in the professional schools.

Location

Case is located on the eastern boundary of Cleveland in University Circle, which is the city's cultural center. The area includes Severance Hall (home of the Cleveland Orchestra), the Museum of Art, the Museum of Natural History, the Garden Center, the Institute of Art, the Institute of Music, the Western Reserve Historical Society, and the Crawford Auto-Aviation Museum. Metropolitan Cleveland has a population of almost 2 million. The Cleveland Hopkins International Airport is 30 minutes away by rail transit. A network of parks encircles the greater Cleveland area. Opportunities are available for sailing on Lake Erie and for hiking and skiing nearby in Ohio, Pennsylvania, and New York. Major-league sports, theater, and all types of music provide a full range of entertainment.

The University and The Department

The Department of Biomedical Engineering at Case Western Reserve University is part of both the Case School of Engineering and the School of Medicine, which are located on the same campus. Established in 1967, the Department is one of the pioneers in biomedical engineering education and is currently among the nation's largest and highest rated (according to *U.S. News & World Report*). Case Western Reserve University was formed in 1967 by a federation of Western Reserve College and Case Institute of Technology. Numerous interdisciplinary programs exist with the professional Schools of Medicine, Dentistry, Nursing, Law, Social Work, and Management.

Applying

Applications that request financial aid should be submitted before February 1. The completed application requires official transcripts, scores on the GRE General Test, and three letters of reference. Application forms can be downloaded from the Case website (https://app.applyyourself.com/AYApplicantLogin/ApplicantConnectLogin.asp?id=casegrad). Applicants for the M.D./M.S. and M.D./Ph.D. programs can apply through the School of Medicine.

Correspondence and Information

Admissions Coordinator
Department of Biomedical Engineering
Wickenden Building 310
Case Western Reserve University
10900 Euclid Avenue
Cleveland, Ohio 44106-7207
Phone: 216-368-4094
Fax: 216-368-4969
Website: http://bme.case.edu

THE FACULTY AND THEIR RESEARCH

Primary Faculty

A. Bolu Ajiboye, Ph.D., Assistant Professor. Development and control of brain-computer-interface (BCI) technologies for restoring function to individuals with nervous system injuries.

Eben Alsberg, Ph.D., Associate Professor. Biomimetic tissue engineering, innovative biomaterials and drug delivery vehicles for functional tissue regeneration and cancer therapy, control of stem cell differentiation, mechanotransduction and the influence of mechanics on cell and tissue function, cell-cell interactions.

James P. Basilion, Ph.D., Associate Professor of BME and Radiology. Molecular imaging, biomarkers, diagnosis and treatment of cancer.

Patrick E. Crago, Ph.D., Professor. Control of neuroprostheses for motor function, neuromuscular control systems.

Jeffrey L. Duerk, Ph.D., Dean and Professor. Radiology, MRI, fast MRI pulse sequence design, interventional MRI, MRI reconstruction.

Dominique M. Durand, Ph.D., Professor. Neural engineering, neuro-prostheses, neural dynamics, magnetic and electric stimulation of the nervous system, neural interfaces with electronic devices, analysis and control of epilepsy.

Steven J. Eppell, Ph.D., Associate Professor. Nanoscale instrumentation for biomaterials, bone and cartilage structure and function.

Miklos Gratzl, Ph.D., Associate Professor. Fine chemical manipulation of microdroplets and single cells, cancer research and neurochemistry at the single-cell level, cost-effective biochemical diagnostics in microliter body fluids.

Kenneth Gustafson, Ph.D., Associate Professor. Neural engineering, neural prostheses, neurophysiology and neural control of genitourinary function, devices to restore genitourinary function, functional neuromuscular stimulation.

Efstathios Karathanasis, Ph.D., Assistant Professor. Fabricating multifunctional agents that facilitate diagnosing, treating, and monitoring of therapies in a patient-specific manner.

Robert Kirsch, Ph.D., Professor and Chair, Executive Director, FES Center. Functional neuromuscular stimulation, biomechanics and neural control of human movement, modeling and simulation of musculoskeletal systems, identification of physiological systems.

Erin Lavik, Sc.D., Associate Professor. Biomaterials and synthesis of new degradable polymers, tissue engineering, spinal cord repair, retinal regeneration, drug delivery for optic nerve preservation and repair.

SECTION 5: BIOMEDICAL ENGINEERING AND BIOTECHNOLOGY

Case Western Reserve University

Zheng-Rong Lu, Ph.D., Professor. Molecular imaging and drug delivery using novel nanotechnology.

Anant Madabhushi, Ph.D., Professor. Quantitative image analysis; multi-modal, multi-scale correlation of massive data sets for disease diagnostics, prognostics, theragnostics; cancer applications.

Cameron McIntyre, Ph.D., Associate Professor. Theoretical modeling of the interaction between electric fields and the nervous system, deep brain stimulation.

J. Thomas Mortimer, Ph.D., Professor Emeritus. Neural prostheses, electrical activation of the nervous system, bowel and bladder assist device, respiratory assist device, selective stimulation and electrode development, electrochemical aspects of electrical stimulation.

P. Hunter Peckham, Ph.D., Professor. Neural prostheses, implantable stimulation and control of movement, rehabilitation engineering.

Andrew M. Rollins, Ph.D., Associate Professor. Biomedical diagnosis; novel optical methods for high-resolution, minimally invasive imaging; tissue characterization and analyte sensing; real-time microstructural and functional imaging using coherence tomography; endoscopy.

Gerald M. Saidel, Ph.D., Professor and Director of the Center for Modeling Integrated Metabolic Systems. Mass and heat transport and metabolic analysis in cells, tissues, and organs; mathematical modeling, simulation, and parameter estimation; optimal experimental design; metabolic dynamics; minimally invasive thermal tumor ablation; slow-release drug delivery.

Nicole Seiberlich, Ph.D., Assistant Professor. Advanced signal processing and data acquisition techniques for rapid Magnetic Resonance Imaging (MRI).

Anirban Sen Gupta, Ph.D., Associate Professor. Targeted drug delivery, targeted molecular imaging, image-guided therapy, platelet substitutes, novel polymeric biomaterials for tissue engineering scaffolds.

Nicole F. Steinmetz, Ph.D., Assistant Professor. Engineering of viral nanoparticles as smart devices for applications in medicine: tissue-specific imaging, drug-delivery, and tissue engineering.

Dustin Tyler, Ph.D., Associate Professor. Neuromimetic neuroprostheses, laryngeal neuroprostheses, clinical implementation of nerve electrodes, cortical neuroprostheses, minimally invasive implantation techniques, modeling of neural stimulation and neuroprostheses.

Horst von Recum, Ph.D., Associate Professor. Tissue-engineered epithelia, prevascularized polymer scaffolds, directed stem cell differentiation, novel stimuli-responsive biomaterials for gene and drug delivery, systems biology approaches to the identification of angiogenic factors.

David L. Wilson, Ph.D., Professor. In vivo microscopic and molecular imaging; medical image processing; image segmentation, registration, and analysis; quantitative image quality of X-ray fluoroscopy and fast MRI; interventional MRI treatment of cancer.

Xin Yu, Sc.D., Associate Professor. Cardiovascular physiology, magnetic resonance imaging and spectroscopy, characterization of the structure-function and energy-function relationships in normal and diseased hearts, small-animal imaging and spectroscopy.

Associated Faculty (partial list)

Jay Alberts, Ph.D., Assistant Professor (BME, Cleveland Clinic Foundation). Neural basis of upper-extremity motor function and deep-brain stimulation in Parkinson's disease.

James M. Anderson, M.D./Ph.D., Professor (Pathology, University Hospitals). Biocompatibility of implants, human vascular grafts.

Harihara Baskaran, Ph.D., Associate Professor of BME and Chemical Engineering. Tissue engineering; cell/cellular transport processes in inflammation, wound healing, and cancer metastasis.

Richard C. Burgess, M.D./Ph.D., Adjunct Professor (Staff Physician, Neurology, Cleveland Clinic Foundation). Electrophysiological monitoring, EEG processing.

Arnold Caplan, Ph.D., Professor of Biology. Tissue engineering.

John Chae, M.D., Professor (MED–Physical Medicine and Rehabilitation). Application of neuroprostheses in hemiplegia.

Hillel J. Chiel, Ph.D., Professor. Biomechanical and neural basis of feeding behavior in *Aplysia californica*, neuromechanical system modeling.

Guy Chisolm, Ph.D., Professor (Vice Chairman, Lerner Research Institute, and Staff, Cell Biology, Cleveland Clinic Foundation). Cell and molecular mechanisms in vascular disease and vascular biology; role of lipoprotein oxidation in atherosclerosis; lipoprotein transport into, accumulation in, and injury to arterial tissue.

Margot Damaser, Ph.D., Associate Professor of Molecular Medicine (BME, Cleveland Clinic Foundation). Biomechanics as it relates to function and dysfunction of the lower urinary tract.

Kathleen Derwin, Ph.D., Assistant Professor (BME, Cleveland Clinic Foundation). Tendon mechanobiology and tissue engineering.

Isabelle Deschenes, Ph.D., Associate Professor (Cardiology, MED–Medicine). Molecular imaging, ion channel structure and function, genetic regulation of ion channels, cellular and molecular mechanisms of cardiac arrhythmias.

Agata Exner, Ph.D., Associate Professor (Radiology, University Hospitals). Image-guided drug delivery, polymers for interventional radiology, models of cancer.

Elizabeth Fisher, Ph.D., Associate Professor (BME, Cleveland Clinic Foundation). Quantitative image analysis for monitoring multiple sclerosis.

Mark Griswold, Ph.D., Professor (Radiology, University Hospitals). Rapid magnetic resonance imaging, image reconstruction and processing, MRI hardware/instrumentation.

Elizabeth C. Hardin, Ph.D., Adjunct Assistant Professor (Rehabilitation Research and Development, VA Medical Center). Neural prostheses and gait mechanics, improving gait performance with neural prostheses using strategies developed in conjunction with forward dynamics musculoskeletal models.

Michael W. Keith, M.D., Professor (Orthopaedics, MED–Medicine). Restoration of motor function in hands.

Kevin Kilgore, Ph.D., Adjunct Assistant Professor (MED–Medicine). Functional electrical stimulation, restoration of hand function.

Kandice Kottke-Marchant, M.D./Ph.D., Professor (Staff, Clinical Pathology, Cleveland Clinic Foundation). Interaction of blood and materials, endothelial cell function on biomaterials.

Kenneth R. Laurita, Ph.D., Associate Professor (Heart and Vascular Research Center, MED–Medicine). Cardiac electrophysiology, arrhythmia mechanisms, intracellular calcium homeostasis, fluorescence imaging, instrumentation and software for potential mapping.

Zhenghong Lee, Ph.D., Associate Professor (Radiology, University Hospitals). Quantitative PET and SPECT imaging, multimodal image registration, 3-D visualization, molecular imaging, small-animal imaging systems.

George Muschler, M.D., Professor (Staff, BME, Cleveland Clinic Foundation). Musculoskeletal oncology, adult reconstructive orthopaedic surgery, fracture nonunion, research in bone healing and bone-grafting materials.

Raymond Muzic, Ph.D., Associate Professor (Radiology, University Hospitals). Modeling and experiment design for PET, image reconstruction.

Clare Rimnac, Ph.D., Professor and Director of the Musculoskeletal Mechanics and Materials Laboratories, Mechanical and Aerospace Engineering. Orthopaedic implant performance and design, mechanical behavior of hand tissues.

Mark S. Rzeszotarski, Ph.D., Professor (Radiology, MED–Medicine). Computers in radiology: MRI/CT/nuclear medicine, ultrasound.

Dawn Taylor, Ph.D., Assistant Professor (BME, Cleveland Clinic Foundation). Brain-computer interfaces for control of computers, neural prostheses, and robotic devices; invasive and noninvasive brain signal acquisition; adaptive decoding algorithms for retraining the brain to control alternative devices after paralysis.

Ronald Triolo, Ph.D., Professor (Orthopaedics, VA Medical Center). Rehabilitation engineering, neuroprostheses, orthopaedic biomechanics.

Antonie J. van den Bogert, Ph.D., Adjunct Associate Professor (Assistant Staff, BME, Cleveland Clinic Foundation). Biomechanics of human movement.

Albert L. Waldo, M.D., Professor (Medicine, University Hospitals). Cardiac electrophysiology, cardiac excitation mapping, mechanisms of cardiac arrhythmias and conduction.

Barry W. Wessels, Ph.D., Professor (Radiation Oncology, University Hospitals). Radio-labeled antibody therapy (dosimeter and clinical trials); image-guided radiotherapy; intensity-modulated radiation therapy; image fusion of CT, MR, SPECT, and PET for adaptive radiation therapy treatment planning.

Guang H. Yue, Ph.D., Adjunct Associate Professor (Assistant Staff, BME, Cleveland Clinic Foundation). Neural control of movement, electrophysiology, MRI.

Marcie Zborowski, Ph.D., Adjunct Associate Professor (Assistant Staff, BME, Cleveland Clinic Foundation). High-speed magnetic cell sorting.

Nicholas P. Ziats, Ph.D., Associate Professor (Pathology, University Hospitals). Vascular grafts, cell-material interactions, extracellular matrix, tissue engineering, blood compatibility.

Section 6
Chemical Engineering

This section contains a directory of institutions offering graduate work in chemical engineering, followed by an in-depth entry submitted by an institution that chose to prepare a detailed program description. Additional information about programs listed in the directory but not augmented by an in-depth entry may be obtained by writing directly to the dean of a graduate school or chair of a department at the address given in the directory.

For programs offering related work, see also in this book *Engineering and Applied Sciences; Geological, Mineral/Mining, and Petroleum Engineering; Management of Engineering and Technology;* and *Materials Sciences and Engineering*. In the other guides in this series:

Graduate Programs in the Humanities, Arts & Social Sciences
See *Family and Consumer Sciences (Clothing and Textiles)*

Graduate Programs in the Biological/Biomedical Sciences & Health-Related Medical Professions
See *Biochemistry*

Graduate Programs in the Physical Sciences, Mathematics, Agricultural Sciences, the Environment & Natural Resources
See *Chemistry* and *Geosciences (Geochemistry* and *Geology)*

CONTENTS

Biochemical Engineering

Brown University, Graduate School, School of Engineering, Providence, RI 02912. Offers biomedical engineering (Sc M, PhD); chemical and biochemical engineering (Sc M, PhD); electrical sciences and computer engineering (Sc M, PhD); fluid and thermal sciences (Sc M, PhD); materials science and engineering (Sc M, PhD); mechanics of solids and structures (Sc M, PhD). *Degree requirements:* For doctorate, thesis/dissertation, preliminary exam.

Cornell University, Graduate School, Graduate Fields of Engineering, Field of Chemical Engineering, Ithaca, NY 14853-0001. Offers advanced materials processing (M Eng, MS, PhD); applied mathematics and computational methods (M Eng, MS, PhD); biochemical engineering (M Eng, MS, PhD); chemical reaction engineering (M Eng, MS, PhD); classical and statistical thermodynamics (M Eng, MS, PhD); fluid dynamics, rheology and biorheology (M Eng, MS, PhD); heat and mass transfer (M Eng, MS, PhD); kinetics and catalysis (M Eng, MS, PhD); polymers (M Eng, MS, PhD); surface science (M Eng, MS, PhD). *Degree requirements:* For master's, thesis (MS); for doctorate, comprehensive exam, thesis/dissertation. *Entrance requirements:* For master's and doctorate, GRE General Test, 2 letters of recommendation. Additional exam requirements/recommendations for international students: Required—TOEFL (minimum score 600 paper-based; 77 iBT). Electronic applications accepted. *Faculty research:* Biochemical, biomedical and metabolic engineering; fluid and polymer dynamics; surface science and chemical kinetics; electronics materials; microchemical systems and nanotechnology.

Dartmouth College, Thayer School of Engineering, Program in Biotechnology and Biochemical Engineering, Hanover, NH 03755. Offers MS, PhD. *Degree requirements:* For master's, thesis; for doctorate, thesis/dissertation, candidacy oral exam. *Entrance requirements:* For master's and doctorate, GRE General Test. *Application deadline:* For fall admission, 1/1 priority date for domestic students. Application fee: $45. *Financial support:* Fellowships, research assistantships, teaching assistantships, career-related internships or fieldwork, Federal Work-Study, institutionally sponsored loans, and tuition waivers (full and partial) available. Financial award application deadline: 1/15. *Faculty research:* Biomass processing, metabolic engineering, kinetics and reactor design, applied microbiology, resource and environmental analysis. *Total annual research expenditures:* $2.5 million. *Unit head:* Dr. Joseph J. Helbie, Dean, 603-646-2238, Fax: 603-646-2580, E-mail: joseph.j.helbie@dartmouth.edu. *Application contact:* Candace S. Potter, Graduate Admissions Administrator, 603-646-3844, Fax: 603-646-1620, E-mail: candace.s.potter@dartmouth.edu.
Website: http://engineering.dartmouth.edu/.

Drexel University, College of Engineering, Department of Chemical and Biological Engineering, Program in Biochemical Engineering, Philadelphia, PA 19104-2875. Offers MS. Part-time and evening/weekend programs available. *Degree requirements:* For master's, thesis. *Entrance requirements:* For master's, minimum GPA of 3.0 in chemical engineering or biological sciences. Additional exam requirements/recommendations for international students: Required—TOEFL. Electronic applications accepted. *Faculty research:* Monitoring and control of bioreactors, sensors for bioreactors, large-scale production of monoclonal antibodies.

Rutgers, The State University of New Jersey, New Brunswick, Graduate School-New Brunswick, Program in Chemical and Biochemical Engineering, Piscataway, NJ 08854-8097. Offers MS, PhD. Part-time and evening/weekend programs available. Terminal master's awarded for partial completion of doctoral program. *Degree requirements:* For master's, thesis or alternative; for doctorate, thesis/dissertation. *Entrance requirements:* For master's and doctorate, GRE General Test. Additional exam requirements/recommendations for international students: Required—TOEFL. *Faculty research:* Biotechnology, pharmaceutical engineering, nanotechnology, process system engineering, materials and polymer science, chemical engineering sciences.

University of California, Irvine, Henry Samueli School of Engineering, Department of Chemical Engineering and Materials Science, Irvine, CA 92697. Offers chemical and biochemical engineering (MS, PhD); materials science and engineering (MS, PhD). Part-time programs available. *Students:* 132 full-time (48 women), 8 part-time (1 woman); includes 45 minority (2 Black or African American, non-Hispanic/Latino; 31 Asian, non-Hispanic/Latino; 7 Hispanic/Latino; 1 Native Hawaiian or other Pacific Islander, non-Hispanic/Latino; 4 Two or more races, non-Hispanic/Latino), 48 international. Average age 26. 549 applicants, 32% accepted, 55 enrolled. In 2014, 29 master's, 11 doctorates awarded. Terminal master's awarded for partial completion of doctoral program. *Degree requirements:* For doctorate, thesis/dissertation. *Entrance requirements:* For master's and doctorate, GRE General Test, minimum GPA of 3.0, 3 letters of recommendation. Additional exam requirements/recommendations for international students: Required—TOEFL (minimum score 550 paper-based). *Application deadline:* For fall admission, 1/15 priority date for domestic students, 1/15 for international students. Applications are processed on a rolling basis. Application fee: $90 ($110 for international students). Electronic applications accepted. *Financial support:* Fellowships with tuition reimbursements, research assistantships with full tuition reimbursements, teaching assistantships with tuition reimbursements, institutionally sponsored loans, traineeships, health care benefits, and unspecified assistantships available. Financial award application deadline: 3/1; financial award applicants required to submit FAFSA. *Faculty research:* Molecular biotechnology, nano-bio-materials, biophotonics, synthesis, superplasticity and mechanical behavior, characterization of advanced and nanostructural materials. *Unit head:* Prof. Vasan Venugopalan, Chair, 949-824-5802, Fax: 949-824-2541, E-mail: vvenugop@uci.edu. *Application contact:* Grace Hai-Chin Chau, Academic Program and Graduate Admission Coordinator, 949-824-3887, Fax: 949-824-2541, E-mail: chaug@uci.edu.
Website: http://www.eng.uci.edu/dept/chems.

University of Georgia, Faculty of Engineering, Athens, GA 30602. Offers MS.

The University of Iowa, Graduate College, College of Engineering, Department of Chemical and Biochemical Engineering, Iowa City, IA 52242-1316. Offers MS, PhD. Part-time programs available. *Faculty:* 10 full-time (2 women), 2 part-time/adjunct (1 woman). *Students:* 33 full-time (10 women); includes 7 minority (3 Black or African American, non-Hispanic/Latino; 2 Asian, non-Hispanic/Latino; 2 Hispanic/Latino), 10 international. Average age 26. 36 applicants, 14% accepted, 3 enrolled. In 2014, 4 master's, 2 doctorates awarded. *Degree requirements:* For master's, comprehensive exam (for some programs), thesis (for some programs); for doctorate, comprehensive exam, thesis/dissertation. *Entrance requirements:* For master's and doctorate, GRE (minimum combined verbal and quantitative score of 1300), minimum undergraduate GPA of 3.0. Additional exam requirements/recommendations for international students: Required—TOEFL (minimum score 600 paper-based; 100 iBT). *Application deadline:* For fall admission, 2/1 priority date for domestic and international students; for spring admission, 10/1 for domestic and international students. Applications are processed on a rolling basis. Application fee: $60 ($100 for international students). Electronic applications accepted. *Financial support:* In 2014–15, 28 students received support, including 6 fellowships with full tuition reimbursements available, 22 research assistantships with full tuition reimbursements available (averaging $22,150 per year), 4 teaching assistantships with full tuition reimbursements available (averaging $21,970 per year); health care benefits and unspecified assistantships also available. Financial award application deadline: 2/1; financial award applicants required to submit FAFSA. *Faculty research:* Polymeric materials, photopolymerization, atmospheric chemistry and air pollution, biochemical engineering, bioprocessing and biomedical engineering. *Total annual research expenditures:* $4.4 million. *Unit head:* Dr. C. Allan Guymon, Department Executive Officer, 319-335-5015, Fax: 319-335-1415, E-mail: allan-guymon@uiowa.edu. *Application contact:* Katie Schnedler, Academic Program Specialist, 319-335-1215, Fax: 319-335-1415, E-mail: chemical-engineering@uiowa.edu.
Website: http://www.engineering.uiowa.edu/cbe.

The University of Manchester, School of Chemical Engineering and Analytical Science, Manchester, United Kingdom. Offers biocatalysis (M Phil, PhD); chemical engineering (M Phil, PhD); chemical engineering and analytical science (M Phil, D Eng, PhD); colloids, crystals, interfaces and materials (M Phil, PhD); environment and sustainable technology (M Phil, PhD); instrumentation (M Phil, PhD); multi-scale modeling (M Phil, PhD); process integration (M Phil, PhD); systems biology (M Phil, PhD).

University of Maryland, Baltimore County, The Graduate School, College of Engineering and Information Technology, Department of Chemical, Biochemical, and Environmental Engineering, Post Baccalaureate Certificate Program in Biochemical Regulatory Engineering, Baltimore, MD 21250. Offers Postbaccalaureate Certificate. Part-time programs available. *Students:* 1 applicant. In 2014, 9 Postbaccalaureate Certificates awarded. *Application deadline:* For fall admission, 7/1 for domestic and international students; for spring admission, 2/1 for domestic students, 12/1 for international students. Applications are processed on a rolling basis. Application fee: $70. Electronic applications accepted. *Expenses:* Tuition, state resident: part-time $557. Tuition, nonresident: part-time $922. *Required fees:* $122 per semester. One-time fee: $200 part-time. *Unit head:* Dr. Antonio Moreira, Vice Provost for Academic Affairs, 410-455-6576, E-mail: moreira@umbc.edu. *Application contact:* 410-455-3400, Fax: 410-455-1049.
Website: http://umbc.edu/cbe/grad/certificate.php.

University of Maryland, Baltimore County, The Graduate School, College of Engineering and Information Technology, Department of Chemical, Biochemical, and Environmental Engineering, Program in Chemical and Biochemical Engineering, Baltimore, MD 21250. Offers MS, PhD. Part-time programs available. *Students:* 17 full-time (10 women), 5 part-time (2 women); includes 6 minority (3 Black or African American, non-Hispanic/Latino; 2 Asian, non-Hispanic/Latino; 1 Native Hawaiian or other Pacific Islander, non-Hispanic/Latino), 7 international. Average age 27. 41 applicants, 15% accepted, 3 enrolled. In 2014, 4 master's, 3 doctorates awarded. *Degree requirements:* For master's, comprehensive exam (for some programs), thesis (for some programs); for doctorate, comprehensive exam, thesis/dissertation. *Entrance requirements:* For master's, GRE General Test, minimum GPA of 3.0, strong mathematical background; for doctorate, GRE General Test (within last 5 years), minimum GPA of 3.0. Additional exam requirements/recommendations for international students: Required—TOEFL (minimum score 550 paper-based; 80 iBT). *Application deadline:* For fall admission, 6/1 for domestic students, 1/1 for international students; for spring admission, 11/1 for domestic students, 6/1 for international students. Applications are processed on a rolling basis. Application fee: $70. Electronic applications accepted. Application fee is waived when completed online. *Expenses:* Tuition, state resident: part-time $557. Tuition, nonresident: part-time $922. *Required fees:* $122 per semester. One-time fee: $200 part-time. *Financial support:* In 2014–15, 3 students received support, including 1 fellowship with full tuition reimbursement available (averaging $25,000 per year), 9 research assistantships with full tuition reimbursements available (averaging $23,000 per year), 6 teaching assistantships with full tuition reimbursements available (averaging $17,000 per year); career-related internships or fieldwork, Federal Work-Study, scholarships/grants, health care benefits, tuition waivers (partial), and unspecified assistantships also available. Support available to part-time students. Financial award application deadline: 6/30; financial award applicants required to submit FAFSA. *Faculty research:* Biomaterials engineering, bioprocess engineering, cellular engineering, education, education and outreach, sensors and monitoring, systems biology and functional genomics. *Unit head:* Dr. Brian E. Reed, Professor and Chair, 410-455-3400, Fax: 410-455-1049, E-mail: reedb@umbc.edu. *Application contact:* Dr. Mariajose Castellanos, Lecturer/Graduate Program Director, 410-455-8151, Fax: 410-455-1049, E-mail: mariajose@umbc.edu.
Website: http://www.umbc.edu/engineering/cbe/.

The University of Western Ontario, Faculty of Graduate Studies, Physical Sciences Division, Faculty of Engineering, London, ON N6A 5B8, Canada. Offers chemical and biochemical engineering (ME Sc, PhD); civil and environmental engineering (M Eng, ME Sc, PhD); electrical and computer engineering (M Eng, ME Sc, PhD); mechanical and materials engineering (M Eng, ME Sc, PhD). Part-time programs available. Terminal master's awarded for partial completion of doctoral program. *Degree requirements:* For master's, thesis; for doctorate, thesis/dissertation. *Entrance requirements:* For master's, minimum B average; for doctorate, minimum B+ average. *Faculty research:* Wind, geotechnical, chemical reactor engineering, applied electrostatics, biochemical engineering.

Villanova University, College of Engineering, Department of Chemical Engineering, Villanova, PA 19085-1699. Offers biochemical engineering (Certificate); chemical engineering (MSChE); environmental protection in the chemical process industries (Certificate). Part-time and evening/weekend programs available. *Degree requirements:* For master's, comprehensive exam, thesis optional. *Entrance requirements:* For master's, GRE General Test (for applicants with degrees from foreign universities), B Ch E, minimum GPA of 3.0. Additional exam requirements/recommendations for international students: Required—TOEFL (minimum score 600 paper-based; 100 iBT). *Faculty research:* Heat transfer, advanced materials, chemical vapor deposition, pyrolysis and combustion chemistry, industrial waste treatment.

Chemical Engineering

American University of Sharjah, Graduate Programs, Sharjah, United Arab Emirates. Offers accounting (MS); business (EMBA, MBA); chemical engineering (MS Ch E); civil engineering (MSCE); computer engineering (MS); electrical engineering (MSEE); engineering systems management (MS); mathematics (MS); mechanical engineering (MSME); mechatronics engineering (MS); teaching English to speakers of other languages (MA); translation and interpreting (MA); urban planning (MUP). Part-time and evening/weekend programs available. *Degree requirements:* For master's, thesis (for some programs). *Entrance requirements:* For master's, GMAT (for MBA). Additional exam requirements/recommendations for international students: Required—TOEFL (minimum score 550 paper-based; 80 iBT), TWE (minimum score 5); Recommended—IELTS (minimum score 6.5). Electronic applications accepted. *Faculty research:* Water pollution, management and waste water treatment, energy and sustainability, air pollution, Islamic finance, family business and small and medium enterprises.

Arizona State University at the Tempe campus, Ira A. Fulton Schools of Engineering, School for Engineering of Matter, Transport and Energy, Tempe, AZ 85281. Offers aerospace engineering (MS, PhD); chemical engineering (MS, PhD); materials science and engineering (MS, PhD); mechanical engineering (MS, PhD); solar energy engineering and commercialization (PSM). Part-time and evening/weekend programs available. Postbaccalaureate distance learning degree programs offered (minimal on-campus study). Terminal master's awarded for partial completion of doctoral program. *Degree requirements:* For master's, thesis and oral defense (MS); applied project or comprehensive exam (MSE); interactive Program of Study (iPOS) submitted before completing 50 percent of required credit hours; for doctorate, comprehensive exam, thesis/dissertation, interactive Program of Study (iPOS) submitted before completing 50 percent of required credit hours. *Entrance requirements:* For master's, GRE, minimum GPA of 3.0 or equivalent in last 2 years of work leading to bachelor's degree; for doctorate, GRE, minimum GPA of 3.0 in last 2 years of work leading to bachelor's degree. Additional exam requirements/recommendations for international students: Required—TOEFL, IELTS, or PTE. Electronic applications accepted. *Expenses:* Contact institution. *Faculty research:* Electronic materials and packaging, materials for energy (batteries), adaptive/intelligent materials and structures, multiscale fluid mechanics, membranes, therapeutics and bioseparations, flexible structures, nanostructured materials, and micro/nano transport.

Auburn University, Graduate School, Ginn College of Engineering, Department of Chemical Engineering, Auburn University, AL 36849. Offers M Ch E, MS, PhD. Part-time programs available. *Faculty:* 15 full-time (3 women), 3 part-time/adjunct (0 women). *Students:* 66 full-time (19 women), 22 part-time (4 women); includes 3 minority (1 American Indian or Alaska Native, non-Hispanic/Latino; 2 Asian, non-Hispanic/Latino), 51 international. Average age 27. 142 applicants, 19% accepted, 20 enrolled. In 2014, 6 master's, 6 doctorates awarded. *Degree requirements:* For master's, thesis (for some programs); for doctorate, comprehensive exam, thesis/dissertation. *Entrance requirements:* For master's and doctorate, GRE General Test. *Application deadline:* For fall admission, 7/7 for domestic students; for spring admission, 11/24 for domestic students. Applications are processed on a rolling basis. Application fee: $50 ($60 for international students). Electronic applications accepted. *Expenses:* Tuition, state resident: full-time $8586; part-time $477 per credit hour. Tuition, nonresident: full-time $25,758; part-time $1431 per credit hour. *Required fees:* $804 per semester. Tuition and fees vary according to degree level and program. *Financial support:* Fellowships, research assistantships, teaching assistantships, and Federal Work-Study available. Support available to part-time students. Financial award application deadline: 3/15; financial award applicants required to submit FAFSA. *Faculty research:* Coal liquefaction, asphalt research, pulp and paper engineering, surface science, biochemical engineering. *Unit head:* Dr. Mario Richard Eden, Chair, 334-844-2064. *Application contact:* Dr. George Flowers, Dean of the Graduate School, 334-844-2125. Website: http://www.eng.auburn.edu/department/che/.

Brigham Young University, Graduate Studies, Ira A. Fulton College of Engineering and Technology, Department of Chemical Engineering, Provo, UT 84602. Offers MS, PhD. *Faculty:* 15 full-time (0 women). *Students:* 47 full-time (7 women), 26 international. Average age 27. 33 applicants, 58% accepted, 13 enrolled. In 2014, 4 master's, 5 doctorates awarded. *Degree requirements:* For master's, comprehensive exam, thesis; for doctorate, comprehensive exam, thesis/dissertation. *Entrance requirements:* For master's and doctorate, GRE, BS in chemical engineering or related engineering field, minimum GPA of 3.3. Additional exam requirements/recommendations for international students: Required—TOEFL (minimum score 580 paper-based; 85 iBT), IELTS (minimum score 7). *Application deadline:* For fall admission, 1/31 for domestic and international students; for winter admission, 6/15 for domestic and international students; for spring admission, 10/15 for domestic and international students; for summer admission, 10/15 for domestic and international students. Application fee: $50. Electronic applications accepted. *Expenses: Tuition:* Full-time $6310; part-time $371 per credit hour. Tuition and fees vary according to program and student's religious affiliation. *Financial support:* In 2014–15, 23 students received support, including 3 fellowships (averaging $10,000 per year), 100 research assistantships with full and partial tuition reimbursements available (averaging $23,614 per year), 41 teaching assistantships with full and partial tuition reimbursements available (averaging $22,500 per year); scholarships/grants also available. Financial award application deadline: 6/30; financial award applicants required to submit FAFSA. *Faculty research:* Energy and combustion, thermodynamics and thermophysical properties, biochemical and biomedical engineering, nano and micro technology, molecular modeling. *Total annual research expenditures:* $1.9 million. *Unit head:* Dr. Randy S. Lewis, Chair, 801-422-2586, Fax: 801-422-0151, E-mail: cheme@byu.edu. *Application contact:* Dr. William G. Pitt, Graduate Coordinator, 801-422-2588, Fax: 801-422-0151, E-mail: pitt@byu.edu. Website: http://www.chemicalengineering.byu.edu.

Brown University, Graduate School, School of Engineering, Providence, RI 02912. Offers biomedical engineering (Sc M, PhD); chemical and biochemical engineering (Sc M, PhD); electrical sciences and computer engineering (Sc M, PhD); fluid and thermal sciences (Sc M, PhD); materials science and engineering (Sc M, PhD); mechanics of solids and structures (Sc M, PhD). *Degree requirements:* For doctorate, thesis/dissertation, preliminary exam.

Bucknell University, Graduate Studies, College of Engineering, Department of Chemical Engineering, Lewisburg, PA 17837. Offers MS Ch E. *Degree requirements:* For master's, thesis. *Entrance requirements:* For master's, GRE General Test, minimum GPA of 3.0. Additional exam requirements/recommendations for international students: Required—TOEFL (minimum score 600 paper-based). *Faculty research:* Computer-aided design, software engineering, applied mathematics and modeling, polymer science, digital process control.

California Institute of Technology, Division of Chemistry and Chemical Engineering, Program in Chemical Engineering, Pasadena, CA 91125-0001. Offers MS, PhD.

Faculty: 12 full-time (3 women). *Students:* 59 full-time (14 women); includes 1 minority (Black or African American, non-Hispanic/Latino). Average age 25. 208 applicants, 5% accepted, 10 enrolled. In 2014, 12 master's, 8 doctorates awarded. Terminal master's awarded for partial completion of doctoral program. *Degree requirements:* For master's, thesis; for doctorate, thesis/dissertation. *Entrance requirements:* For doctorate, GRE, BS. Additional exam requirements/recommendations for international students: Required—TOEFL; Recommended—IELTS, TWE. *Application deadline:* For fall admission, 12/15 for domestic and international students. Application fee: $100. Electronic applications accepted. *Financial support:* Fellowships, research assistantships, teaching assistantships, institutionally sponsored loans, scholarships/grants, traineeships, health care benefits, and unspecified assistantships available. Financial award application deadline: 12/15. *Faculty research:* Fluids, biomolecular engineering, atmospheric chemistry, polymers/materials, catalysis. *Unit head:* Prof. Jacqueline K. Barton, Chair, Chemistry and Chemical Engineering, 626-395-3646, Fax: 626-568-8824, E-mail: jkbarton@caltech.edu. *Application contact:* Kathy J. Bubash, Graduate Option Assistant, 626-395-4193, Fax: 626-568-8743, E-mail: kathy@cheme.caltech.edu. Website: https://www.cce.caltech.edu/content/cheme.

California State University, Long Beach, Graduate Studies, College of Engineering, Department of Chemical Engineering, Long Beach, CA 90840. Offers MS.

Carnegie Mellon University, Carnegie Institute of Technology, Department of Chemical Engineering, Pittsburgh, PA 15213-3891. Offers chemical engineering (M Ch E, MS, PhD); colloids, polymers and surfaces (MS). Part-time and evening/weekend programs available. Terminal master's awarded for partial completion of doctoral program. *Degree requirements:* For doctorate, thesis/dissertation, qualifying exam. *Entrance requirements:* For master's and doctorate, GRE General Test, GRE Subject Test. Additional exam requirements/recommendations for international students: Required—TOEFL. *Faculty research:* Computer-aided design in process engineering, biomedical engineering, biotechnology, complex fluids.

Case Western Reserve University, School of Graduate Studies, Case School of Engineering, Department of Chemical and Biomolecular Engineering, Cleveland, OH 44106. Offers MS, PhD. Part-time and evening/weekend programs available. Postbaccalaureate distance learning degree programs offered. *Faculty:* 10 full-time (1 woman). *Students:* 24 full-time (8 women), 2 part-time (1 woman); includes 2 minority (both Asian, non-Hispanic/Latino), 13 international. In 2014, 3 master's, 9 doctorates awarded. Terminal master's awarded for partial completion of doctoral program. *Degree requirements:* For master's, thesis (for some programs); for doctorate, thesis/dissertation, qualifying exam, research proposal, teaching experience. *Entrance requirements:* For master's and doctorate, GRE General Test. Additional exam requirements/recommendations for international students: Required—TOEFL. *Application deadline:* For fall admission, 2/15 priority date for domestic students; for spring admission, 11/1 for domestic students. Applications are processed on a rolling basis. Application fee: $50. *Financial support:* In 2014–15, 17 research assistantships with full and partial tuition reimbursements were awarded; Federal Work-Study and institutionally sponsored loans also available. Financial award application deadline: 3/1; financial award applicants required to submit FAFSA. *Faculty research:* Advanced separation methods; design, synthesis, processing and characterization of advanced materials; biotransport and bioprocessing; electrochemical engineering, materials engineering; energy storage and fuel cells. *Total annual research expenditures:* $3.1 million. *Unit head:* Uziel Landau, Department Chair, 216-368-4132, Fax: 216-368-3016, E-mail: uziel.landau@case.edu. *Application contact:* Theresa Claytor, Student Affairs Coordinator, 216-368-8555, Fax: 216-368-8555, E-mail: theresa.claytor@case.edu. Website: http://www.case.edu/cse/eche.

City College of the City University of New York, Graduate School, Grove School of Engineering, Department of Chemical Engineering, New York, NY 10031-9198. Offers ME, MS, PhD. PhD program offered jointly with Graduate School and University Center of the City University of New York. Part-time programs available. *Degree requirements:* For master's, thesis optional; for doctorate, one foreign language, comprehensive exam, thesis/dissertation. *Entrance requirements:* For master's and doctorate, GRE General Test. Additional exam requirements/recommendations for international students: Required—TOEFL (minimum score 500 paper-based; 61 iBT). *Faculty research:* Theoretical turbulences, bio-fluid dynamics, polymers, fluidization, transport phenomena.

Clarkson University, Graduate School, Wallace H. Coulter School of Engineering, Department of Chemical and Biomolecular Engineering, Potsdam, NY 13699. Offers chemical engineering (ME, MS, PhD). Part-time programs available. *Faculty:* 17 full-time (4 women), 3 part-time/adjunct (2 women). *Students:* 24 full-time (6 women); includes 1 minority (Asian, non-Hispanic/Latino), 19 international. Average age 26. 28 applicants, 79% accepted, 6 enrolled. In 2014, 4 master's, 5 doctorates awarded. Terminal master's awarded for partial completion of doctoral program. *Degree requirements:* For master's, thesis (for MS); project (for ME); for doctorate, comprehensive exam, thesis/dissertation, departmental qualifying exam. *Entrance requirements:* For master's and doctorate, GRE, transcripts of all college coursework, resume, personal statement, three letters of recommendation. Additional exam requirements/recommendations for international students: Required—TOEFL (minimum score 550 paper-based; 80 iBT), IELTS (minimum score 6.5). *Application deadline:* For fall admission, 1/30 priority date for domestic and international students; for spring admission, 9/1 priority date for domestic and international students. Applications are processed on a rolling basis. Application fee: $25 ($35 for international students). Electronic applications accepted. *Expenses: Tuition:* Full-time $16,680; part-time $1390 per credit. *Required fees:* $295 per semester. *Financial support:* In 2014–15, 22 students received support, including 2 fellowships with full tuition reimbursements available (averaging $24,029 per year), 8 research assistantships with full tuition reimbursements available (averaging $24,029 per year), 8 teaching assistantships with full tuition reimbursements available (averaging $24,029 per year); scholarships/grants, tuition waivers (partial), and unspecified assistantships also available. *Faculty research:* Biodiesel production, consumable evaluation, liquid plasma reactors, Great Lakes fish monitoring, scrubbing technology. *Total annual research expenditures:* $1.2 million. *Unit head:* Dr. John McLaughlin, Chair, 315-268-6650, Fax: 315-268-6654, E-mail: jmclau@clarkson.edu. *Application contact:* Kelly Sharlow, Assistant to the Dean, 315-268-7929, Fax: 315-268-4494, E-mail: ksharlow@clarkson.edu. Website: http://www.clarkson.edu/chemeng/.

Clemson University, Graduate School, College of Engineering and Science, Department of Chemical and Biomolecular Engineering, Clemson, SC 29634. Offers MS, PhD. *Faculty:* 12 full-time (2 women), 6 part-time/adjunct (0 women). *Students:* 33 full-time (13 women), 1 part-time (0 women); includes 1 minority (Asian, non-Hispanic/Latino), 21 international. Average age 26. 157 applicants, 11% accepted, 9 enrolled. In

Chemical Engineering

2014, 1 master's, 7 doctorates awarded. *Degree requirements:* For master's, thesis; for doctorate, comprehensive exam, thesis/dissertation. *Entrance requirements:* For master's and doctorate, GRE General Test. Additional exam requirements/recommendations for international students: Required—TOEFL. *Application deadline:* For fall admission, 6/1 for domestic students, 4/15 for international students; for spring admission, 10/1 for domestic students, 9/15 for international students. Applications are processed on a rolling basis. Application fee: $70 ($80 for international students). Electronic applications accepted. *Financial support:* In 2014–15, 30 students received support, including 4 fellowships with full and partial tuition reimbursements available (averaging $14,200 per year), 19 research assistantships with partial tuition reimbursements available (averaging $24,849 per year), 9 teaching assistantships with partial tuition reimbursements available (averaging $22,849 per year); career-related internships or fieldwork, institutionally sponsored loans, scholarships/grants, health care benefits, and unspecified assistantships also available. Support available to part-time students. Financial award applicants required to submit FAFSA. *Faculty research:* Advanced materials, biotechnology, energy, molecular simulation, chemical and biochemical processing. *Total annual research expenditures:* $1.2 million. *Unit head:* Dr. Douglas E. Hirt, Professor and Chair, 864-656-0822, Fax: 864-656-0784, E-mail: hirtd@clemson.edu. *Application contact:* Dr. Scott M. Husson, Professor and Graduate Coordinator, 864-656-4502, Fax: 864-656-0784, E-mail: shusson@clemson.edu. Website: http://www.clemson.edu/ces/chbe/.

Cleveland State University, College of Graduate Studies, Fenn College of Engineering, Department of Chemical and Biomedical Engineering, Cleveland, OH 44115. Offers applied biomedical engineering (D Eng); chemical engineering (MS, D Eng). Part-time and evening/weekend programs available. *Faculty:* 12 full-time (1 woman), 26 part-time/adjunct (3 women). *Students:* 13 full-time (5 women), 51 part-time (21 women); includes 9 minority (3 Black or African American, non-Hispanic/Latino; 4 Asian, non-Hispanic/Latino; 2 Hispanic/Latino), 21 international. Average age 26. 92 applicants, 52% accepted, 17 enrolled. In 2014, 22 master's awarded. *Degree requirements:* For master's, project or thesis; for doctorate, thesis/dissertation, candidacy and qualifying exams. *Entrance requirements:* For master's, GRE General Test, minimum GPA of 2.75; for doctorate, GRE General Test, minimum GPA of 3.25. Additional exam requirements/recommendations for international students: Required—TOEFL (minimum score 550 paper-based; 78 iBT). *Application deadline:* For fall admission, 4/15 for domestic and international students; for spring admission, 10/15 for domestic and international students. Applications are processed on a rolling basis. Application fee: $30. *Expenses:* Tuition, state resident: full-time $9566; part-time $531 per credit hour. Tuition, nonresident: full-time $17,980; part-time $999 per credit hour. *Required fees:* $25 per semester. Tuition and fees vary according to degree level and program. *Financial support:* In 2014–15, 34 students received support, including 1 fellowship, 24 research assistantships with full and partial tuition reimbursements available (averaging $21,000 per year), 9 teaching assistantships with full and partial tuition reimbursements available (averaging $15,000 per year); career-related internships or fieldwork, Federal Work-Study, institutionally sponsored loans, scholarships/grants, tuition waivers (full and partial), and unspecified assistantships also available. Financial award application deadline: 3/30. *Faculty research:* Absorption equilibrium and dynamics, advanced materials processing, biomaterials surface characterization, bioprocessing, cardiovascular mechanics, magnetic resonance imaging, mechanics of biomolecules, metabolic modeling, molecular simulation, process systems engineering, statistical mechanics. *Unit head:* Dr. Joanne M. Belovich, Chairperson, 216-687-3502, Fax: 216-687-9220, E-mail: j.belovich@csuohio.edu. *Application contact:* Becky Laird, Administrative Coordinator, 216-687-2571, Fax: 216-687-9220, E-mail: b.laird@csuohio.edu. Website: http://www.csuohio.edu/engineering/chemical/.

Colorado School of Mines, Graduate School, Department of Chemical and Biological Engineering, Golden, CO 80401. Offers MS, PhD. Part-time programs available. *Faculty:* 34 full-time (12 women), 10 part-time/adjunct (1 woman). *Students:* 77 full-time (17 women), 4 part-time (1 woman); includes 5 minority (1 Asian, non-Hispanic/Latino; 1 Hispanic/Latino; 3 Two or more races, non-Hispanic/Latino), 33 international. Average age 29. 162 applicants, 36% accepted, 27 enrolled. In 2014, 7 master's, 3 doctorates awarded. Terminal master's awarded for partial completion of doctoral program. *Degree requirements:* For master's, thesis (for some programs); for doctorate, comprehensive exam, thesis/dissertation. *Entrance requirements:* For master's and doctorate, GRE General Test. Additional exam requirements/recommendations for international students: Required—TOEFL (minimum score 550 paper-based; 80 iBT). *Application deadline:* For fall admission, 12/15 priority date for domestic and international students; for spring admission, 10/15 for domestic and international students. Application fee: $50 ($70 for international students). Electronic applications accepted. *Financial support:* In 2014–15, 69 students received support, including fellowships with full tuition reimbursements available (averaging $21,120 per year), 45 research assistantships with full tuition reimbursements available (averaging $21,120 per year), 20 teaching assistantships with full tuition reimbursements available (averaging $21,120 per year); scholarships/grants, health care benefits, and unspecified assistantships also available. Financial award application deadline: 12/15; financial award applicants required to submit FAFSA. *Faculty research:* Liquid fuels for the future, responsible management of hazardous substances, surface and interfacial engineering, advanced computational methods and process control, gas hydrates. *Total annual research expenditures:* $6.3 million. *Unit head:* Dr. David Marr, Head, 303-273-3008, E-mail: dmarr@mines.edu. *Application contact:* Dr. Deanna Jacobs, Program Assistant, 303-273-3720, E-mail: Djacobs@mines.edu. Website: http://chemeng.mines.edu/.

Colorado State University, Graduate School, College of Engineering, Department of Chemical and Biological Engineering, Fort Collins, CO 80523-1370. Offers chemical engineering (MS, PhD); engineering (ME). Part-time programs available. *Faculty:* 12 full-time (1 woman). *Students:* 6 full-time (3 women), 15 part-time (6 women), 9 international. Average age 29. 51 applicants, 8% accepted, 4 enrolled. In 2014, 3 master's, 1 doctorate awarded. Terminal master's awarded for partial completion of doctoral program. *Degree requirements:* For master's, comprehensive exam, thesis (for some programs), preliminary exam (first-year); for doctorate, comprehensive exam, thesis/dissertation, exams. *Entrance requirements:* For master's and doctorate, GRE General Test, minimum GPA of 3.0. Additional exam requirements/recommendations for international students: Required—TOEFL (minimum score 550 paper-based; 80 iBT), IELTS (minimum score 5.5). *Application deadline:* For fall admission, 1/15 priority date for domestic and international students; for spring admission, 9/15 priority date for domestic and international students. Application fee: $50. Electronic applications accepted. *Expenses:* Tuition, state resident: full-time $9348; part-time $519 per credit. Tuition, nonresident: full-time $22,916; part-time $1273 per credit. *Required fees:* $1584. *Financial support:* In 2014–15, 5 students received support, including 2 fellowships (averaging $22,201 per year), 3 research assistantships with tuition reimbursements available (averaging $21,250 per year); teaching assistantships and unspecified assistantships also available. Financial award application deadline: 2/1. *Faculty research:* Advanced materials, biofuels and biorenewables, biosensors, systems and synthetic biology, tissue engineering and biomaterials. *Total annual research

expenditures:* $2.2 million. *Unit head:* Dr. David S. Dandy, Department Head, 970-491-7437, Fax: 970-491-7369, E-mail: david.dandy@colostate.edu. *Application contact:* Denise Morgan, Graduate Contact, 970-491-5252, Fax: 970-491-7369, E-mail: denise.morgan@colostate.edu. Website: http://www.engr.colostate.edu/cheme/.

Columbia University, Fu Foundation School of Engineering and Applied Science, Department of Chemical Engineering, New York, NY 10027. Offers MS, Eng Sc D, PhD. PhD offered through the Graduate School of Arts and Sciences. Part-time programs available. Postbaccalaureate distance learning degree programs offered (no on-campus study). *Faculty:* 15 full-time (3 women), 7 part-time/adjunct (1 woman). *Students:* 117 full-time (39 women), 46 part-time (22 women); includes 17 minority (5 Black or African American, non-Hispanic/Latino; 7 Asian, non-Hispanic/Latino; 4 Hispanic/Latino; 1 Two or more races, non-Hispanic/Latino), 128 international. 336 applicants, 40% accepted, 74 enrolled. In 2014, 53 master's, 7 doctorates awarded. *Degree requirements:* For doctorate, thesis/dissertation, qualifying exam. *Entrance requirements:* For master's and doctorate, GRE General Test. Additional exam requirements/recommendations for international students: Required—TOEFL, IELTS, PTE. *Application deadline:* For fall admission, 12/15 priority date for domestic and international students; for spring admission, 10/1 priority date for domestic and international students. Application fee: $85. Electronic applications accepted. *Financial support:* In 2014–15, 35 students received support, including 23 research assistantships with full tuition reimbursements available (averaging $30,000 per year), 12 teaching assistantships with full tuition reimbursements available (averaging $23,350 per year); health care benefits and tuition waivers also available. Financial award application deadline: 12/15; financial award applicants required to submit FAFSA. *Faculty research:* Molecular design and modification of material surfaces, biophysics and soft matter physics, genomics engineering, interfacial engineering and electrochemistry, protein and metabolic engineering. *Unit head:* Dr. Sanat K. Kumar, Professor and Chair, Chemical Engineering, 212-854-2193, Fax: 212-854-3054, E-mail: sk2794@columbia.edu. *Application contact:* Dr. Robert Bozic, Director, MS Programs, 212-854-9637, Fax: 212-854-3054, E-mail: rb2335@columbia.edu. Website: http://www.cheme.columbia.edu/.

Cooper Union for the Advancement of Science and Art, Albert Nerken School of Engineering, New York, NY 10003-7120. Offers chemical engineering (ME); civil engineering (ME); electrical engineering (ME); mechanical engineering (ME). Part-time programs available. *Faculty:* 27 full-time (1 woman), 15 part-time/adjunct (2 women). *Students:* 45 full-time (10 women), 20 part-time (4 women); includes 24 minority (3 Black or African American, non-Hispanic/Latino; 15 Asian, non-Hispanic/Latino; 4 Hispanic/Latino; 2 Two or more races, non-Hispanic/Latino), 4 international. Average age 23. 86 applicants, 71% accepted, 44 enrolled. In 2014, 22 master's awarded. *Degree requirements:* For master's, thesis (for some programs). *Entrance requirements:* For master's, BE or BS in engineering discipline, high school and college transcripts, two letters of recommendation, resume. Additional exam requirements/recommendations for international students: Required—TOEFL (minimum score 600 paper-based; 100 iBT). *Application deadline:* For fall admission, 4/1 for domestic and international students. Application fee: $70. Electronic applications accepted. *Expenses: Tuition:* Full-time $39,600; part-time $1173 per credit. *Required fees:* $925 per semester. One-time fee: $250. *Financial support:* In 2014–15, 65 students received support, including 4 fellowships with full and partial tuition reimbursements available (averaging $11,000 per year); career-related internships or fieldwork, Federal Work-Study, tuition waivers (full and partial), and tuition scholarships offered to exceptional students also available. Support available to part-time students. Financial award application deadline: 5/1; financial award applicants required to submit FAFSA. *Faculty research:* Civil infrastructure, imaging and sensing technology, biomedical engineering, encryption technology, process engineering. *Unit head:* Dr. Teresa Dahlberg, Dean of Engineering, 212-353-4285, E-mail: dahlberg@cooper.edu. *Application contact:* Student Contact, 212-353-4120, E-mail: admissions@cooper.edu. Website: http://cooper.edu/engineering.

Cornell University, Graduate School, Graduate Fields of Engineering, Field of Chemical Engineering, Ithaca, NY 14853-0001. Offers advanced materials processing (M Eng, MS, PhD); applied mathematics and computational methods (M Eng, MS, PhD); biochemical engineering (M Eng, MS, PhD); chemical reaction engineering (M Eng, MS, PhD); classical and statistical thermodynamics (M Eng, MS, PhD); fluid dynamics, rheology and biorheology (M Eng, MS, PhD); heat and mass transfer (M Eng, MS, PhD); kinetics and catalysis (M Eng, MS, PhD); polymers (M Eng, MS, PhD); surface science (M Eng, MS, PhD). *Degree requirements:* For master's, thesis (MS); for doctorate, comprehensive exam, thesis/dissertation. *Entrance requirements:* For master's and doctorate, GRE General Test, 2 letters of recommendation. Additional exam requirements/recommendations for international students: Required—TOEFL (minimum score 600 paper-based; 77 iBT). Electronic applications accepted. *Faculty research:* Biochemical, biomedical and metabolic engineering; fluid and polymer dynamics; surface science and chemical kinetics; electronics materials; microchemical systems and nanotechnology.

Dalhousie University, Faculty of Engineering, Department of Chemical Engineering, Halifax, NS B3J 1Z1, Canada. Offers M Eng, MA Sc, PhD. *Degree requirements:* For master's, thesis; for doctorate, thesis/dissertation. *Entrance requirements:* Additional exam requirements/recommendations for international students: Required—TOEFL, IELTS, CANTEST, CAEL, or Michigan English Language Assessment Battery. Electronic applications accepted. *Faculty research:* Explosions, process optimization, combustion synthesis of materials, waste minimization, treatment of industrial wastewater.

Drexel University, College of Engineering, Department of Chemical and Biological Engineering, Program in Chemical Engineering, Philadelphia, PA 19104-2875. Offers MS, PhD. *Degree requirements:* For doctorate, thesis/dissertation. *Entrance requirements:* For master's, minimum GPA of 3.0; for doctorate, minimum GPA of 3.5, MS in chemical engineering. Additional exam requirements/recommendations for international students: Required—TOEFL. Electronic applications accepted.

École Polytechnique de Montréal, Graduate Programs, Department of Chemical Engineering, Montréal, QC H3C 3A7, Canada. Offers M Eng, M Sc A, PhD, DESS. Part-time and evening/weekend programs available. Terminal master's awarded for partial completion of doctoral program. *Degree requirements:* For master's, one foreign language, thesis; for doctorate, one foreign language, thesis/dissertation. *Entrance requirements:* For master's, minimum GPA of 2.75; for doctorate, minimum GPA of 3.0. Electronic applications accepted. *Faculty research:* Polymer engineering, biochemical and food engineering, reactor engineering and industrial processes pollution control engineering, gas technology.

Fairleigh Dickinson University, College at Florham, Silberman College of Business, Program in Pharmaceutical Studies, Madison, NJ 07940-1099. Offers MBA, Certificate.

Florida Agricultural and Mechanical University, Division of Graduate Studies, Research, and Continuing Education, FAMU-FSU College of Engineering, Department of Chemical and Biomedical Engineering, Tallahassee, FL 32307-3200. Offers biomedical engineering (MS, PhD); chemical engineering (MS, PhD). *Degree *requirements:* For master's, thesis optional; for doctorate, thesis/dissertation, paper presentation at professional meeting. *Entrance requirements:* For master's, GRE General Test, minimum GPA of 3.3, letters of recommendation (3); for doctorate, minimum GPA of 3.3. Additional exam requirements/recommendations for international students: Required—TOEFL (minimum score 550 paper-based). *Faculty research:* Cellular signaling, cancer therapy, drug delivery, cellular and tissue engineering, brain physiology.

Florida Institute of Technology, Graduate Programs, College of Engineering, Program in Chemical Engineering, Melbourne, FL 32901-6975. Offers MS, PhD. Part-time programs available. *Students:* 8 full-time (0 women), 5 part-time (1 woman); includes 3 minority (1 American Indian or Alaska Native, non-Hispanic/Latino; 1 Asian, non-Hispanic/Latino; 1 Hispanic/Latino), 8 international. Average age 30. 65 applicants, 17% accepted, 4 enrolled. In 2014, 9 master's awarded. Terminal master's awarded for partial completion of doctoral program. *Degree requirements:* For master's, comprehensive exam (for some programs), seminar, independent research project, thesis or final exam, written report, oral presentation; for doctorate, comprehensive exam, thesis/dissertation, oral exam, original research project, written exam. *Entrance requirements:* For master's, GRE, minimum GPA of 3.0, resume, 3 letters of recommendation, statement of objectives, undergraduate transcript; for doctorate, GRE General Test, GRE Subject Test, minimum GPA of 3.5, resume, 3 letters of recommendation, statement of objectives. Additional exam requirements/recommendations for international students: Required—TOEFL (minimum score 550 paper-based; 79 iBT). *Application deadline:* For fall admission, 4/1 for international students; for spring admission, 9/30 for international students. Applications are processed on a rolling basis. Electronic applications accepted. *Expenses: Tuition:* Part-time $1179 per credit hour. Tuition and fees vary according to campus/location. *Financial support:* In 2014–15, 1 research assistantship with full and partial tuition reimbursement, 5 teaching assistantships with full and partial tuition reimbursements were awarded; career-related internships or fieldwork, institutionally sponsored loans, tuition waivers (partial), unspecified assistantships, and tuition remissions also available. Support available to part-time students. Financial award application deadline: 3/1; financial award applicants required to submit FAFSA. *Faculty research:* Space technology, biotechnology, materials synthesis and processing, supercritical fluids, water treatment, process control. *Unit head:* Dr. Manolis M. Tomadakis, Department Head, 321-674-7243, Fax: 321-674-7565, E-mail: tomadaki@fit.edu. *Application contact:* Cheryl A. Brown, Associate Director of Graduate Admissions, 321-674-7581, Fax: 321-723-9468, E-mail: cbrown@fit.edu.
Website: http://coe.fit.edu/chemical/.

Florida State University, The Graduate School, FAMU-FSU College of Engineering, Department of Chemical and Biomedical Engineering, Tallahassee, FL 32310-6046. Offers biomedical engineering (MS, PhD); chemical engineering (MS, PhD). Part-time programs available. Terminal master's awarded for partial completion of doctoral program. *Degree requirements:* For master's, thesis (for some programs); for doctorate, comprehensive exam, thesis/dissertation, qualifying exam. *Entrance requirements:* For master's, GRE General Test (recommended minimum scores: verbal 151/8th percentile; quantitative: 158/75th percentile), BS in chemical engineering or other physical science/engineering, minimum GPA of 3.0; for doctorate, GRE General Test (recommended minimum scores: verbal 151/8th percentile; quantitative: 158/75th percentile), BS in chemical engineering or other physical science/engineering, minimum GPA of 3.0, or MS in chemical or biomedical engineering. Additional exam requirements/recommendations for international students: Required—TOEFL (minimum score 550 paper-based; 80 iBT), Michigan English Language Assessment Battery (minimum score 77); Recommended—IELTS (minimum score 6.5). Electronic applications accepted. *Expenses:* Contact institution. *Faculty research:* Macromolecular transport and reaction; polymer characterization and processing; solid NMR-MRI for solid state spectroscopy and cell microscopy; protein, cell, and tissue engineering; electrochemical and fuel cell engineering.

Georgia Institute of Technology, Graduate Studies, College of Engineering, School of Chemical and Biomolecular Engineering, Atlanta, GA 30332-0001. Offers chemical engineering (MS, PhD). *Students:* 182 full-time (50 women), 7 part-time (2 women); includes 38 minority (5 Black or African American, non-Hispanic/Latino; 1 American Indian or Alaska Native, non-Hispanic/Latino; 21 Asian, non-Hispanic/Latino; 10 Hispanic/Latino; 1 Two or more races, non-Hispanic/Latino), 93 international. Average age 25. 543 applicants, 23% accepted, 36 enrolled. In 2014, 27 master's, 36 doctorates awarded. Terminal master's awarded for partial completion of doctoral program. *Degree requirements:* For master's, thesis; for doctorate, comprehensive exam, thesis/dissertation. *Entrance requirements:* For master's, GRE, http://www.grad.gatech.edu/che; for doctorate, GRE, http://www.chbe.gatech.edu/graduate/apply. Additional exam requirements/recommendations for international students: Required—TOEFL (minimum score 550 paper-based; 85 iBT). *Application deadline:* For fall admission, 2/1 for domestic and international students. Applications are processed on a rolling basis. Application fee: $75. Electronic applications accepted. *Expenses:* Tuition, state resident: full-time $12,344; part-time $515 per credit hour. Tuition, nonresident: full-time $27,600; part-time $1150 per credit hour. *Required fees:* $1196 per term. Part-time tuition and fees vary according to course load. *Financial support:* Fellowships with tuition reimbursements, research assistantships with tuition reimbursements, teaching assistantships with tuition reimbursements, career-related internships or fieldwork, Federal Work-Study, institutionally sponsored loans, tuition waivers (partial), and unspecified assistantships available. Support available to part-time students. Financial award application deadline: 5/1. *Faculty research:* Biochemical engineering; process modeling, synthesis, and control; polymer science and engineering; thermodynamics and separations; surface and particle science. *Total annual research expenditures:* $16.2 million. *Unit head:* J. Carson Meredith, Director, 404-385-2151, E-mail: carson.meredith@chbe.gatech.edu. *Application contact:* Janice Whatley-Nwanze, Graduate Coordinator, 404-894-2877, E-mail: janice.whatley@chbe.gatech.edu.
Website: http://www.chbe.gatech.edu.

The Graduate Center, City University of New York, Graduate Studies, Program in Engineering, New York, NY 10016-4039. Offers biomedical engineering (PhD); chemical engineering (PhD); civil engineering (PhD); electrical engineering (PhD); mechanical engineering (PhD). *Degree requirements:* For doctorate, thesis/dissertation. *Entrance requirements:* For doctorate, GRE General Test. Additional exam requirements/recommendations for international students: Required—TOEFL. Electronic applications accepted.

Howard University, College of Engineering, Architecture, and Computer Sciences, School of Engineering and Computer Science, Department of Chemical Engineering, Washington, DC 20059-0002. Offers MS. Offered through the Graduate School of Arts and Sciences. Part-time programs available. *Degree requirements:* For master's, thesis. *Entrance requirements:* For master's, GRE General Test, minimum GPA of 2.75. Additional exam requirements/recommendations for international students: Required—TOEFL. *Faculty research:* Bioengineering, reactor modeling, environmental engineering, nanotechnology, fuel cells.

Illinois Institute of Technology, Graduate College, Armour College of Engineering, Department of Chemical and Biological Engineering, Chicago, IL 60616. Offers biological engineering (MAS); chemical engineering (MAS, MS, PhD); MS/MAS. Part-time and evening/weekend programs available. Postbaccalaureate distance learning degree programs offered (minimal on-campus study). *Faculty:* 18 full-time (2 women), 1 part-time/adjunct (0 women). *Students:* 128 full-time (42 women), 20 part-time (8 women); includes 5 minority (1 Black or African American, non-Hispanic/Latino; 4 Asian, non-Hispanic/Latino), 127 international. Average age 26. 618 applicants, 40% accepted, 42 enrolled. In 2014, 42 master's, 11 doctorates awarded. Terminal master's awarded for partial completion of doctoral program. *Degree requirements:* For master's, comprehensive exam (for some programs), thesis (for some programs); for doctorate, comprehensive exam, thesis/dissertation. *Entrance requirements:* For master's, GRE General Test with minimum score of 950 Quantitative and Verbal, 2.5 Analytical Writing (for MAS); GRE General Test with minimum score of 1100 Quantitative and Verbal, 3.0 Analytical Writing (for MS), minimum undergraduate GPA of 3.0; for doctorate, GRE General Test (minimum score 1100 Quantitative and Verbal, 3.0 Analytical Writing), minimum undergraduate GPA of 3.0. Additional exam requirements/recommendations for international students: Required—TOEFL (minimum score 550 paper-based; 80 iBT). *Application deadline:* For fall admission, 5/1 for domestic and international students; for spring admission, 10/15 for domestic and international students. Applications are processed on a rolling basis. Application fee: $50. Electronic applications accepted. *Expenses: Tuition:* Full-time $22,500; part-time $1250 per credit hour. *Required fees:* $30 per course. $260 per semester. One-time fee: $235. Tuition and fees vary according to course load and program. *Financial support:* Fellowships with partial tuition reimbursements, research assistantships with full and partial tuition reimbursements, teaching assistantships with full tuition reimbursements, Federal Work-Study, institutionally sponsored loans, scholarships/grants, health care benefits, and unspecified assistantships available. Support available to part-time students. Financial award applicants required to submit FAFSA. *Faculty research:* Energy and sustainability, biological engineering, advanced materials, systems engineering. *Unit head:* Dr. Sohail Murad, Chair and Professor of Chemical Engineering, 312-567-3867, Fax: 312-567-8874, E-mail: smurad1@iit.edu. *Application contact:* Rishab Malhotra, Director, Graduate Admission, 866-472-3448, Fax: 312-567-3138, E-mail: inquiry.grad@iit.edu.
Website: http://engineering.iit.edu/chbe.

Instituto Tecnológico y de Estudios Superiores de Monterrey, Campus Monterrey, Graduate and Research Division, Programs in Engineering, Monterrey, Mexico. Offers applied statistics (M Eng); artificial intelligence (PhD); automation engineering (M Eng); chemical engineering (M Eng); civil engineering (M Eng); electrical engineering (M Eng); electronic engineering (M Eng); environmental engineering (M Eng); industrial engineering (M Eng, PhD); manufacturing engineering (M Eng); mechanical engineering (M Eng); systems and quality engineering (M Eng). M Eng program offered jointly with University of Waterloo; PhD in industrial engineering with Texas A&M University. Part-time and evening/weekend programs available. Terminal master's awarded for partial completion of doctoral program. *Degree requirements:* For master's, one foreign language, thesis; for doctorate, one foreign language, thesis/dissertation. *Entrance requirements:* For master's, EXADEP; for doctorate, GRE, master's degree in related field. Additional exam requirements/recommendations for international students: Required—TOEFL. *Faculty research:* Flexible manufacturing cells, materials, statistical methods, environmental prevention, control and evaluation.

Iowa State University of Science and Technology, Department of Chemical and Biological Engineering, Ames, IA 50011. Offers M Eng, MS, PhD. *Degree requirements:* For master's, thesis (for some programs); for doctorate, thesis/dissertation. *Entrance requirements:* For master's and doctorate, GRE General Test. Additional exam requirements/recommendations for international students: Recommended—TOEFL (minimum score 587 paper-based; 94 iBT), IELTS (minimum score 7). Electronic applications accepted.

Johns Hopkins University, Engineering Program for Professionals, Part-time Program in Chemical and Biomolecular Engineering, Baltimore, MD 21218-2699. Offers M Ch E. Part-time and evening/weekend programs available. Electronic applications accepted.

Johns Hopkins University, G. W. C. Whiting School of Engineering, Department of Chemical and Biomolecular Engineering, Baltimore, MD 21218. Offers MSE, PhD. Part-time programs available. Terminal master's awarded for partial completion of doctoral program. *Degree requirements:* For master's, essay presentation; for doctorate, thesis/dissertation, oral exam; thesis presentation. *Entrance requirements:* For master's and doctorate, GRE General Test. Additional exam requirements/recommendations for international students: Required—TOEFL (minimum score 600 paper-based; 100 iBT). Electronic applications accepted. *Faculty research:* Nanotechnology, materials by design, alternative energy, smart molecules and devices, biomolecular design and engineering, physics of cancer.

Kansas State University, Graduate School, College of Engineering, Department of Chemical Engineering, Manhattan, KS 66506. Offers MS, PhD, Graduate Certificate. Postbaccalaureate distance learning degree programs offered (minimal on-campus study). *Faculty:* 8 full-time (2 women), 4 part-time/adjunct (0 women). *Students:* 24 full-time (5 women), 14 part-time (4 women); includes 7 minority (1 Black or African American, non-Hispanic/Latino; 2 Asian, non-Hispanic/Latino; 1 Hispanic/Latino; 3 Two or more races, non-Hispanic/Latino), 13 international. Average age 28. 43 applicants, 33% accepted, 6 enrolled. In 2014, 1 master's, 4 doctorates, 1 other advanced degree awarded. Terminal master's awarded for partial completion of doctoral program. *Degree requirements:* For master's, 24 hours of coursework; 6 hours of thesis; for doctorate, thesis/dissertation, 90 hours of credit. *Entrance requirements:* For doctorate, GRE. Additional exam requirements/recommendations for international students: Required—TOEFL. *Application deadline:* For fall admission, 2/1 priority date for domestic students, 1/1 priority date for international students; for spring admission, 8/1 priority date for domestic and international students. Applications are processed on a rolling basis. Application fee: $50 ($75 for international students). Electronic applications accepted. *Financial support:* In 2014–15, 12 research assistantships with full tuition reimbursements (averaging $22,205 per year), 3 teaching assistantships with partial tuition reimbursements (averaging $22,300 per year) were awarded; fellowships with partial tuition reimbursements, scholarships/grants, and tuition waivers (full) also available. Financial award application deadline: 3/1; financial award applicants required to submit FAFSA. *Faculty research:* Renewable sustainable energy, molecular engineering, advanced materials. *Unit head:* Dr. James Edgar, Head, 785-532-5584, Fax: 785-532-7372, E-mail: che@ksu.edu.
Website: http://www.che.ksu.edu/.

Lamar University, College of Graduate Studies, College of Engineering, Dan F. Smith Department of Chemical Engineering, Beaumont, TX 77710. Offers PhD. *Faculty:* 11 full-time (1 woman). *Students:* 52 full-time (10 women), 24 part-time (8 women); includes 5 minority (2 Black or African American, non-Hispanic/Latino; 2 Asian, non-Hispanic/Latino; 1 Hispanic/Latino), 66 international. Average age 26. 93 applicants, 84% accepted, 45 enrolled. In 2014, 6 doctorates awarded. *Degree requirements:* For doctorate, comprehensive exam, thesis/dissertation. *Entrance requirements:* For doctorate, GRE General Test. Additional exam requirements/recommendations for international students: Required—TOEFL (minimum score 550 paper-based; 79 iBT), IELTS (minimum score 6.5). *Application deadline:* For fall admission, 8/10 for domestic

students, 7/1 for international students; for spring admission, 1/5 for domestic students, 12/1 for international students. Applications are processed on a rolling basis. Application fee: $25 ($50 for international students). *Expenses:* Tuition, state resident: full-time $5724; part-time $1908 per semester. Tuition, nonresident: full-time $12,240; part-time $4080 per semester. *Required fees:* $1940; $318 per credit hour. *Financial support:* In 2014–15, 49 fellowships with partial tuition reimbursements (averaging $1,000 per year), 15 research assistantships with partial tuition reimbursements (averaging $6,000 per year), 8 teaching assistantships with partial tuition reimbursements (averaging $12,600 per year) were awarded; tuition waivers (full and partial) also available. Financial award application deadline: 4/1. *Faculty research:* Flare minimization, process optimization, process integration. *Unit head:* Dr. Thomas C. Ho, Chair, 409-880-8784, Fax: 409-880-2197, E-mail: che_dept@lamar.edu. *Application contact:* Melissa Gallien, Director, Admissions and Academic Services, 409-880-8888, Fax: 409-880-7419, E-mail: gradmissions@lamar.edu.
Website: http://engineering.lamar.edu/chemical.

Lehigh University, P.C. Rossin College of Engineering and Applied Science, Department of Chemical and Biomolecular Engineering, Bethlehem, PA 18015. Offers M Eng, MS, PhD, MBA/E. Part-time programs available. Postbaccalaureate distance learning degree programs offered (no on-campus study). *Faculty:* 20 full-time (3 women), 2 part-time/adjunct (0 women). *Students:* 41 full-time (14 women), 32 part-time (14 women); includes 13 minority (2 Black or African American, non-Hispanic/Latino; 6 Asian, non-Hispanic/Latino; 5 Hispanic/Latino), 30 international. Average age 28. 186 applicants, 28% accepted, 16 enrolled. In 2014, 11 master's, 6 doctorates awarded. Terminal master's awarded for partial completion of doctoral program. *Degree requirements:* For master's, thesis (for some programs); for doctorate, comprehensive exam, thesis/dissertation. *Entrance requirements:* For master's and doctorate, GRE General Test. Additional exam requirements/recommendations for international students: Required—TOEFL (minimum score 570 paper-based; 79 iBT). *Application deadline:* For fall admission, 7/15 for domestic students, 1/15 priority date for international students; for spring admission, 12/1 for domestic and international students. Applications are processed on a rolling basis. Application fee: $75. Electronic applications accepted. *Expenses:* Expenses: $1,340 per credit. *Financial support:* In 2014–15, 38 students received support, including 4 fellowships with full tuition reimbursements available (averaging $26,560 per year), 31 research assistantships with full tuition reimbursements available (averaging $26,560 per year), 5 teaching assistantships with full tuition reimbursements available (averaging $27,316 per year); career-related internships or fieldwork, institutionally sponsored loans, scholarships/grants, health care benefits, and unspecified assistantships also available. Financial award application deadline: 1/15. *Faculty research:* Process control, energy, biotechnology, catalysis, emulsion polymers. *Total annual research expenditures:* $2.6 million. *Unit head:* Dr. Mayuresh V. Kothare, Chairman, 610-758-6654, Fax: 610-758-5057, E-mail: mvk2@lehigh.edu. *Application contact:* Barbara A. Kessler, Graduate Coordinator, 610-758-4261, Fax: 610-758-5057, E-mail: inchegs@mail.lehigh.edu.
Website: http://www.che.lehigh.edu/.

Louisiana State University and Agricultural & Mechanical College, Graduate School, College of Engineering, Cain Department of Chemical Engineering, Baton Rouge, LA 70803. Offers MS Ch E, PhD. Part-time and evening/weekend programs available. *Faculty:* 17 full-time (1 woman). *Students:* 50 full-time (14 women), 3 part-time (1 woman); includes 3 minority (all Asian, non-Hispanic/Latino), 34 international. Average age 26. 189 applicants, 11% accepted, 12 enrolled. In 2014, 9 master's, 8 doctorates awarded. Terminal master's awarded for partial completion of doctoral program. *Degree requirements:* For master's, comprehensive exam or thesis; for doctorate, thesis/dissertation, general exam, qualifying exam. *Entrance requirements:* For master's and doctorate, GRE General Test, minimum GPA of 3.0. Additional exam requirements/recommendations for international students: Required—TOEFL (minimum score 550 paper-based; 79 IBT), IELTS (minimum score 6.5), or PTE (minimum score 59). *Application deadline:* For fall admission, 1/1 priority date for domestic students, 5/15 priority date for international students; for spring admission, 10/15 for domestic and international students; for summer admission, 5/15 for domestic and international students. Applications are processed on a rolling basis. Application fee: $50 ($70 for international students). Electronic applications accepted. *Financial support:* In 2014–15, 51 students received support, including 1 fellowship (averaging $27,454 per year), 45 research assistantships with full and partial tuition reimbursements available (averaging $23,422 per year); teaching assistantships, Federal Work-Study, health care benefits, and tuition waivers (full and partial) also available. Financial award application deadline: 4/15; financial award applicants required to submit FAFSA. *Faculty research:* Reaction engineering, control, thermodynamic and transport phenomena, polymer processing and properties, biochemical engineering. *Total annual research expenditures:* $5 million. *Unit head:* Dr. Mary Julia Wornat, Chair, 225-578-1426, Fax: 225-578-1476, E-mail: mjwornat@lsu.edu. *Application contact:* Dr. John Flake, Director of Graduate Instruction, 225-578-1426, Fax: 225-578-1476, E-mail: johnflake@lsu.edu.
Website: http://www.che.lsu.edu/.

Louisiana Tech University, Graduate School, College of Engineering and Science, Department of Chemical Engineering, Ruston, LA 71272. Offers MS, PhD. Part-time programs available. Terminal master's awarded for partial completion of doctoral program. *Degree requirements:* For master's, thesis; for doctorate, thesis/dissertation. *Entrance requirements:* For master's, GRE General Test, minimum GPA of 3.0 in last 60 hours; for doctorate, minimum graduate GPA of 3.25 (with MS) or GRE General Test. Additional exam requirements/recommendations for international students: Required—TOEFL. *Faculty research:* Artificial intelligence, biotechnology, hazardous waste process safety.

Manhattan College, Graduate Programs, School of Engineering, Program in Chemical Engineering, Riverdale, NY 10471. Offers chemical engineering (MS); cosmetic engineering (MS). Part-time programs available. *Faculty:* 3 full-time (1 woman), 1 part-time/adjunct (0 women). *Students:* 11 full-time (5 women), 7 part-time (5 women); includes 3 minority (2 Asian, non-Hispanic/Latino; 1 Two or more races, non-Hispanic/Latino). Average age 22. 19 applicants, 100% accepted, 12 enrolled. In 2014, 9 master's awarded. *Degree requirements:* For master's, thesis or alternative. *Entrance requirements:* For master's, GRE (recommended), minimum GPA of 3.0. Additional exam requirements/recommendations for international students: Required—TOEFL (minimum score 550 paper-based; 80 iBT), IELTS (minimum score 6). *Application deadline:* For fall admission, 8/10 priority date for domestic students, 8/10 for international students; for spring admission, 1/7 for domestic and international students. Applications are processed on a rolling basis. Application fee: $60. *Financial support:* In 2014–15, 6 students received support, including 6 teaching assistantships with partial tuition reimbursements available (averaging $8,000 per year); career-related internships or fieldwork, Federal Work-Study, scholarships/grants, and unspecified assistantships also available. Support available to part-time students. Financial award application deadline: 2/1. *Faculty research:* Advanced separation processes, environmental management, combustion, pollution prevention. *Unit head:* Dr. Gennaro Maffia, Chairperson, 718-862-7192, Fax: 718-862-7819, E-mail: chmldept@manhattan.edu. *Application contact:* Kathy Ciarletta, Information Contact, 718-862-7185, Fax: 718-862-7819, E-mail: chmldept@manhattan.edu.

Massachusetts Institute of Technology, School of Engineering, Department of Chemical Engineering, Cambridge, MA 02139. Offers chemical engineering (SM, PhD, Sc D); chemical engineering practice (SM, PhD); SM/MBA. *Faculty:* 34 full-time (5 women). *Students:* 236 full-time (76 women); includes 49 minority (2 Black or African American, non-Hispanic/Latino; 32 Asian, non-Hispanic/Latino; 11 Hispanic/Latino; 4 Two or more races, non-Hispanic/Latino), 92 international. Average age 25. 546 applicants, 14% accepted, 50 enrolled. In 2014, 42 master's, 35 doctorates awarded. Terminal master's awarded for partial completion of doctoral program. *Degree requirements:* For master's, thesis (for some programs), one semester of the Practice School (for SM in chemical engineering practice); for doctorate, comprehensive exam, thesis/dissertation, Ph.D./Sc.D.: Minor program in a related field outside of chemical engineering; Ph.D.CEP: Practice School requirements. *Entrance requirements:* For master's and doctorate, GRE General Test. Additional exam requirements/recommendations for international students: Required—TOEFL (minimum score 600 paper-based; 100 iBT), IELTS (minimum score 7). *Application deadline:* For fall admission, 12/15 for domestic and international students. Application fee: $75. Electronic applications accepted. *Expenses: Tuition:* Full-time $44,720; part-time $699 per unit. *Required fees:* $296. *Financial support:* In 2014–15, 222 students received support, including 97 fellowships (averaging $40,300 per year), 117 research assistantships (averaging $37,100 per year), 20 teaching assistantships (averaging $39,500 per year); Federal Work-Study, institutionally sponsored loans, scholarships/grants, traineeships, health care benefits, and unspecified assistantships also available. Financial award application deadline: 4/15; financial award applicants required to submit FAFSA. *Faculty research:* Catalysis and reaction engineering, biological engineering, materials and polymers, surfaces and nanostructures, thermodynamics and molecular computation. *Total annual research expenditures:* $47.3 million. *Unit head:* Prof. Klavs F. Jensen, Department Head, 617-253-4561, Fax: 617-258-8992. *Application contact:* Graduate Admissions, 617-253-4577, Fax: 617-253-9695, E-mail: chemegrad@mit.edu.
Website: http://web.mit.edu/cheme/.

McGill University, Faculty of Graduate and Postdoctoral Studies, Faculty of Engineering, Department of Chemical Engineering, Montréal, QC H3A 2T5, Canada. Offers chemical engineering (M Eng, PhD); environmental engineering (M Eng).

McMaster University, School of Graduate Studies, Faculty of Engineering, Department of Chemical Engineering, Hamilton, ON L8S 4M2, Canada. Offers M Eng, MA Sc, PhD. *Degree requirements:* For master's, thesis; for doctorate, comprehensive exam, thesis/dissertation. *Entrance requirements:* For master's, minimum B average in the last two years. Additional exam requirements/recommendations for international students: Required—TOEFL (minimum score 550 paper-based). *Faculty research:* Biomaterials, computer process control, polymer processing, environmental biotechnology, reverse osmosis.

McNeese State University, Doré School of Graduate Studies, College of Engineering and Engineering Technology, Department of Engineering, Master of Engineering Program, Lake Charles, LA 70609. Offers chemical engineering (M Eng); civil engineering (M Eng); electrical engineering (M Eng); engineering management (M Eng); mechanical engineering (M Eng). Part-time and evening/weekend programs available. *Degree requirements:* For master's, thesis or alternative. *Entrance requirements:* For master's, GRE, baccalaureate degree, minimum overall GPA of 3.0. Additional exam requirements/recommendations for international students: Required—TOEFL (minimum score 560 paper-based; 83 iBT).

Miami University, College of Engineering and Computing, Department of Chemical, Paper and Biomedical Engineering, Oxford, OH 45056. Offers MS. *Students:* 15 full-time (6 women), 12 international. Average age 24. In 2014, 7 master's awarded. *Entrance requirements:* Additional exam requirements/recommendations for international students: Recommended—TOEFL (minimum score 80 iBT), IELTS (minimum score 6.5), TSE (minimum score 54). *Application deadline:* For fall admission, 3/1 for domestic and international students. Application fee: $50. Electronic applications accepted. *Expenses:* Tuition, state resident: full-time $12,887; part-time $537 per credit hour. Tuition, nonresident: full-time $28,449; part-time $1186 per credit hour. *Required fees:* $530; $24 per credit hour. $30 per quarter. Part-time tuition and fees vary according to course load and program. *Financial support:* Fellowships with full and partial tuition reimbursements, research assistantships with full and partial tuition reimbursements, and teaching assistantships with full and partial tuition reimbursements available. Financial award application deadline: 2/15; financial award applicants required to submit FAFSA. *Unit head:* Dr. Shashi Lalvani, Chair, 513-529-0763, E-mail: lalvansb@miamioh.edu. *Application contact:* Department of Chemical, Paper and Biomedical Engineering, 513-529-0760, E-mail: paper@miamioh.edu.
Website: http://miamioh.edu/cec/academics/departments/cpb/.

Michigan State University, The Graduate School, College of Engineering, Department of Chemical Engineering and Materials Science, East Lansing, MI 48824. Offers chemical engineering (MS, PhD); materials science and engineering (MS, PhD). *Entrance requirements:* Additional exam requirements/recommendations for international students: Required—TOEFL. Electronic applications accepted.

Michigan Technological University, Graduate School, College of Engineering, Department of Chemical Engineering, Houghton, MI 49931. Offers MS, PhD. Part-time programs available. *Faculty:* 18 full-time (4 women). *Students:* 42 full-time (15 women), 6 part-time (2 women); includes 3 minority (1 Black or African American, non-Hispanic/Latino; 2 Two or more races, non-Hispanic/Latino), 32 international. Average age 28. 145 applicants, 46% accepted, 12 enrolled. In 2014, 17 master's, 6 doctorates awarded. Terminal master's awarded for partial completion of doctoral program. *Degree requirements:* For master's, comprehensive exam (for some programs), thesis (for some programs); for doctorate, comprehensive exam, thesis/dissertation. *Entrance requirements:* For master's and doctorate, GRE, statement of purpose, official transcripts, 2 letters of recommendation. Additional exam requirements/recommendations for international students: Required—TOEFL (minimum score 94 iBT) or IELTS. *Application deadline:* For fall admission, 1/15 priority date for domestic and international students. Applications are processed on a rolling basis. Electronic applications accepted. *Expenses:* Expenses: Contact institution. *Financial support:* In 2014–15, 31 students received support, including 1 fellowship with full and partial tuition reimbursement available (averaging $13,824 per year), 8 research assistantships with full and partial tuition reimbursements available (averaging $13,824 per year), 10 teaching assistantships with full and partial tuition reimbursements available (averaging $13,824 per year); career-related internships or fieldwork, Federal Work-Study, scholarships/grants, health care benefits, unspecified assistantships, and cooperative program also available. Financial award applicants required to submit FAFSA. *Faculty research:* Polymer engineering, thermodynamics, chemical process safety, surface science/catalysis, environmental chemical engineering. *Total annual research expenditures:* $1.3 million. *Unit head:* Dr. Komar Kawatra, Chair, 906-487-3132, Fax: 906-487-3213, E-mail: skkawatr@mtu.edu. *Application contact:* Alexis E. Snell, Secretary 3, 906-487-3132, Fax: 906-487-3213, E-mail: aesnell@mtu.edu.
Website: http://www.chem.mtu.edu/chem_eng/.

Mississippi State University, Bagley College of Engineering, Dave C. Swalm School of Chemical Engineering, Mississippi State, MS 39762. Offers chemical engineering (MS);

engineering (PhD), including chemical engineering. *Faculty:* 9 full-time (2 women), 1 part-time/adjunct (0 women). *Students:* 18 full-time (5 women), 5 part-time (2 women); includes 3 minority (1 Black or African American, non-Hispanic/Latino; 2 Asian, non-Hispanic/Latino), 16 international. Average age 28. 32 applicants, 25% accepted, 4 enrolled. In 2014, 4 master's, 1 doctorate awarded. *Degree requirements:* For master's, comprehensive exam or thesis; for doctorate, comprehensive exam, thesis/dissertation. *Entrance requirements:* For master's, GRE, minimum GPA of 3.0 on last 64 undergraduate hours; for doctorate, GRE, minimum GPA of 3.2 on last 64 undergraduate hours. Additional exam requirements/recommendations for international students: Required—TOEFL (minimum score 550 paper-based; 79 iBT); Recommended—IELTS (minimum score 6.5). *Application deadline:* For fall admission, 4/1 priority date for domestic students, 5/1 for international students; for spring admission, 8/1 priority date for domestic students, 9/1 for international students. Applications are processed on a rolling basis. Application fee: $60. Electronic applications accepted. *Expenses:* Tuition, state resident: full-time $7140; part-time $783 per credit hour. Tuition, nonresident: full-time $18,478; part-time $2043 per credit hour. *Financial support:* In 2014–15, 14 research assistantships with full tuition reimbursements (averaging $14,751 per year), 1 teaching assistantship with full tuition reimbursement (averaging $14,724 per year) were awarded; Federal Work-Study, institutionally sponsored loans, and unspecified assistantships also available. Financial award application deadline: 4/1; financial award applicants required to submit FAFSA. *Faculty research:* Thermodynamics, composite materials, catalysis, surface science, environmental engineering. *Total annual research expenditures:* $2.9 million. *Unit head:* Dr. Bill Elmore, Interim Director, 662-325-2480, Fax: 662-325-2482, E-mail: gradstudies@che.msstate.edu. *Application contact:* Dr. Todd French, Graduate Coordinator, 662-325-2480, Fax: 662-325-2482, E-mail: gradstudies@che.msstate.edu.
Website: http://www.che.msstate.edu/.

Missouri University of Science and Technology, Graduate School, Department of Chemical and Biological Engineering, Rolla, MO 65409. Offers chemical engineering (MS, DE, PhD). *Degree requirements:* For master's, thesis optional; for doctorate, comprehensive exam. *Entrance requirements:* For master's, GRE (minimum score 1100 verbal and quantitative, 4 writing); for doctorate, GRE (minimum score: verbal and quantitative 1200, writing 4). Additional exam requirements/recommendations for international students: Required—TOEFL (minimum score 550 paper-based). *Faculty research:* Mixing, fluid mechanics, bioengineering, freeze-drying, extraction.

Montana State University, The Graduate School, College of Engineering, Department of Chemical and Biological Engineering, Bozeman, MT 59717. Offers chemical engineering (MS); engineering (PhD), including chemical engineering option, environmental engineering option; environmental engineering (MS). Part-time programs available. *Degree requirements:* For master's, comprehensive exam, thesis (for some programs); for doctorate, comprehensive exam, thesis/dissertation. *Entrance requirements:* For master's and doctorate, GRE General Test. Additional exam requirements/recommendations for international students: Required—TOEFL (minimum score 550 paper-based). Electronic applications accepted. *Faculty research:* Biofuels, extremophilic bioprocessing, and situ biocatalyzed heavy metal transformations; metabolic network analysis and engineering; magnetic resonance microscopy; modeling of biological systems; the development of protective coatings on planar solid oxide fuel cell (SOFC) metallic interconnects; characterizing corrosion mechanisms of materials in precisely-controlled exposures; testing materials in poly-crystalline silicon production environments; environmental biotechnology and bioremediation.

New Jersey Institute of Technology, Newark College of Engineering, Newark, NJ 07102. Offers biomedical engineering (MS, PhD); chemical engineering (MS, PhD); computer engineering (MS, PhD); electrical engineering (MS, PhD); engineering management (MS); healthcare systems management (MS); industrial engineering (MS, PhD); Internet engineering (MS); manufacturing engineering (MS); mechanical engineering (MS, PhD); occupational safety and health engineering (MS); pharmaceutical bioprocessing (MS); pharmaceutical engineering (MS); pharmaceutical systems management (MS); power and energy systems (MS); telecommunications (MS); transportation (MS, PhD). Part-time and evening/weekend programs available. Terminal master's awarded for partial completion of doctoral program. *Degree requirements:* For master's, thesis optional; for doctorate, thesis/dissertation. *Entrance requirements:* For master's, GRE General Test; for doctorate, GRE General Test, minimum graduate GPA of 3.5. Additional exam requirements/recommendations for international students: Required—TOEFL (minimum score 550 paper-based; 79 iBT). Electronic applications accepted.

New Mexico State University, College of Engineering, Department of Chemical and Materials Engineering, Las Cruces, NM 88003-8001. Offers MS Ch E, PhD. Part-time programs available. *Faculty:* 9 full-time (3 women). *Students:* 46 full-time (15 women), 7 part-time (1 woman); includes 5 minority (1 Asian, non-Hispanic/Latino; 3 Hispanic/Latino; 1 Two or more races, non-Hispanic/Latino), 40 international. Average age 28. 43 applicants, 44% accepted, 11 enrolled. In 2014, 8 master's, 3 doctorates awarded. Terminal master's awarded for partial completion of doctoral program. *Degree requirements:* For master's, thesis (for some programs); for doctorate, comprehensive exam, thesis/dissertation. *Entrance requirements:* For master's and doctorate, GRE General Test. Additional exam requirements/recommendations for international students: Required—TOEFL (minimum score 550 paper-based; 79 iBT), IELTS (minimum score 6.5). *Application deadline:* For fall admission, 3/1 priority date for domestic and international students; for spring admission, 11/1 priority date for domestic and international students. Applications are processed on a rolling basis. Application fee: $40 ($50 for international students). Electronic applications accepted. *Expenses:* Tuition, state resident: full-time $3969; part-time $220.50 per credit hour. Tuition, nonresident: full-time $13,838; part-time $768.80 per credit hour. *Required fees:* $853; $47.40 per credit hour. *Financial support:* In 2014–15, 50 students received support, including 2 fellowships (averaging $3,970 per year), 22 research assistantships (averaging $15,713 per year), 9 teaching assistantships (averaging $12,461 per year); career-related internships or fieldwork, Federal Work-Study, scholarships/grants, traineeships, health care benefits, and unspecified assistantships also available. Support available to part-time students. Financial award application deadline: 3/1. *Faculty research:* Separations, advanced materials, computer modeling and simulation, energy, biomaterials, polymers/rheology. *Total annual research expenditures:* $829,360. *Unit head:* Dr. David A. Rockstraw, Academic Department Head, 575-646-1213, Fax: 575-646-7706, E-mail: drockstr@nmsu.edu. *Application contact:* Dr. Hongmei A. Luo, Graduate Student Admissions Coordinator, 575-646-4204, Fax: 575-646-7706, E-mail: hluo@nmsu.edu.
Website: http://chme.nmsu.edu/.

New York University, Polytechnic School of Engineering, Department of Chemical and Biomolecular Engineering, Major in Chemical Engineering, New York, NY 10012-1019. Offers MS, PhD. Part-time and evening/weekend programs available. *Students:* 13 full-time (7 women), 2 part-time (1 woman); includes 2 minority (1 Black or African American, non-Hispanic/Latino; 1 Asian, non-Hispanic/Latino), 9 international. Average age 25. 142 applicants, 17% accepted, 5 enrolled. In 2014, 6 master's, 2 doctorates awarded. *Degree requirements:* For master's, comprehensive exam (for some programs), thesis (for some programs); for doctorate, comprehensive exam, thesis/dissertation. *Entrance requirements:* For master's, GRE General Test, BS in chemical engineering; for doctorate, GRE General Test. Additional exam requirements/recommendations for international students: Required—TOEFL (minimum score 550 paper-based; 80 iBT); Recommended—IELTS (minimum score 6.5). *Application deadline:* For fall admission, 2/15 priority date for domestic and international students; for spring admission, 11/1 priority date for domestic and international students. Applications are processed on a rolling basis. Application fee: $75. Electronic applications accepted. *Financial support:* Fellowships, research assistantships, teaching assistantships, institutionally sponsored loans, scholarships/grants, and unspecified assistantships available. Support available to part-time students. Financial award applicants required to submit FAFSA. *Faculty research:* Plasma polymerization, crystallization of organic compounds, dipolar relaxations in reactive polymers. *Unit head:* Dr. Jovan Mijovic, Academic Director, 718-260-3097, E-mail: jovan.mijovic@nyu.edu. *Application contact:* Raymond Lutzky, Director, Graduate Enrollment Management, 718-637-5984, Fax: 718-260-3624, E-mail: rlutzky@poly.edu.

North Carolina Agricultural and Technical State University, School of Graduate Studies, College of Engineering, Department of Chemical and Bioengineering, Greensboro, NC 27411. Offers bioengineering (MS); biological engineering (MS); chemical engineering (MS).

North Carolina State University, Graduate School, College of Engineering, Department of Chemical and Biomolecular Engineering, Raleigh, NC 27695. Offers chemical engineering (M Ch E, MS, PhD). Part-time programs available. Terminal master's awarded for partial completion of doctoral program. *Degree requirements:* For master's, thesis optional; for doctorate, thesis/dissertation. *Entrance requirements:* For master's and doctorate, GRE General Test. Additional exam requirements/recommendations for international students: Required—TOEFL. Electronic applications accepted. *Faculty research:* Molecular themodynamics and computer simulation, catalysis, kinetics, electrochemical reaction engineering, biochemical engineering.

Northeastern University, College of Engineering, Boston, MA 02115-5096. Offers bioengineering (PhD); chemical engineering (MS, PhD); civil engineering (MS, PhD); computer engineering (PhD); computer systems engineering (MS); electrical and computer engineering (MS); electrical and engineering leadership (MS); electrical engineering (PhD); energy systems (MS); engineering leadership (Certificate); engineering management (MRTP); industrial engineering (MS, PhD); information assurance (PhD); information systems (MS); interdisciplinary (PhD); mechanical engineering (MS, PhD); operations research (MS); telecommunication systems management (MS). Part-time programs available. *Expenses:* Contact institution.

Northwestern University, McCormick School of Engineering and Applied Science, Department of Chemical and Biological Engineering, Evanston, IL 60208. Offers chemical engineering (MS, PhD). Admissions and degrees offered through The Graduate School. Part-time programs available. *Faculty:* 16 full-time (2 women). *Students:* 126 full-time (49 women), 2 part-time (0 women); includes 33 minority (4 Black or African American, non-Hispanic/Latino; 1 American Indian or Alaska Native, non-Hispanic/Latino; 12 Asian, non-Hispanic/Latino; 15 Hispanic/Latino; 1 Two or more races, non-Hispanic/Latino), 41 international. Average age 26. 427 applicants, 21% accepted, 30 enrolled. In 2014, 18 master's, 9 doctorates awarded. Terminal master's awarded for partial completion of doctoral program. *Degree requirements:* For master's, comprehensive exam (for some programs), thesis optional; for doctorate, comprehensive exam, thesis/dissertation. *Entrance requirements:* For master's and doctorate, GRE General Test. Additional exam requirements/recommendations for international students: Required—TOEFL (minimum score 577 paper-based; 90 iBT), IELTS (minimum score 7). *Application deadline:* For fall admission, 12/31 for domestic and international students. Application fee: $95. Electronic applications accepted. *Financial support:* Fellowships with full tuition reimbursements, research assistantships with full tuition reimbursements, teaching assistantships with full tuition reimbursements, career-related internships or fieldwork, institutionally sponsored loans, traineeships, health care benefits, and unspecified assistantships available. Financial award application deadline: 1/15; financial award applicants required to submit FAFSA. *Faculty research:* Biotechnology and bioengineering; complex systems; environmental catalysis, kinetics and reaction engineering; modeling, theory, and simulation; polymer science and engineering; transport processes. *Unit head:* Dr. Linda Broadbelt, Chair, 847-491-2890, Fax: 847-491-3728, E-mail: broadbelt@northwestern.edu. *Application contact:* Dr. Luis Amaral, Admissions Officer, 847-491-7850, Fax: 847-491-3728, E-mail: amaral@northwestern.edu.
Website: http://www.chbe.northwestern.edu/.

The Ohio State University, Graduate School, College of Engineering, Department of Chemical and Biomolecular Engineering, Columbus, OH 43210. Offers chemical engineering (MS, PhD). *Faculty:* 24. *Students:* 92 full-time (28 women), 3 part-time (1 woman); includes 11 minority (2 Black or African American, non-Hispanic/Latino; 1 American Indian or Alaska Native, non-Hispanic/Latino; 4 Asian, non-Hispanic/Latino; 3 Hispanic/Latino; 1 Two or more races, non-Hispanic/Latino), 56 international. Average age 25. In 2014, 6 master's, 16 doctorates awarded. *Degree requirements:* For master's, thesis; for doctorate, thesis/dissertation. *Entrance requirements:* For master's, GRE; for doctorate, GRE (highly recommend minimum score of 75% in Verbal and Quantitative and 4.0 in Analytical Writing). Additional exam requirements/recommendations for international students: Required—TOEFL (minimum score 600 paper-based; 100 iBT), Michigan English Language Assessment Battery (minimum score 86); Recommended—IELTS (minimum score 8). *Application deadline:* For fall admission, 12/13 priority date for domestic students, 11/30 priority date for international students; for spring admission, 11/1 for domestic students, 10/1 for international students. Applications are processed on a rolling basis. Application fee: $60 ($70 for international students). Electronic applications accepted. *Financial support:* Fellowships with tuition reimbursements, research assistantships with tuition reimbursements, teaching assistantships with tuition reimbursements, career-related internships or fieldwork, Federal Work-Study, institutionally sponsored loans, and unspecified assistantships available. Support available to part-time students. *Unit head:* Dr. Andre Palmer, Interim Chair, 614-292-6033, E-mail: palmer.351@osu.edu. *Application contact:* Graduate and Professional Admissions, 614-292-9444, Fax: 614-292-3895, E-mail: gpadmissions@osu.edu.
Website: http://www.cbe.osu.edu.

Ohio University, Graduate College, Russ College of Engineering and Technology, Department of Chemical and Biomolecular Engineering, Athens, OH 45701-2979. Offers biomedical engineering (MS); chemical engineering (MS, PhD). Part-time programs available. *Degree requirements:* For master's, comprehensive exam (for some programs), thesis; for doctorate, comprehensive exam, thesis/dissertation, qualifying exams. *Entrance requirements:* For master's and doctorate, GRE General Test. Additional exam requirements/recommendations for international students: Required—TOEFL (minimum score 590 paper-based; 96 iBT) or IELTS (minimum score 7). Electronic applications accepted. *Faculty research:* Corrosion and multiphase flow, biochemical engineering, thin film materials, air pollution modeling and control, biomedical engineering.

Chemical Engineering

Oklahoma State University, College of Engineering, Architecture and Technology, School of Chemical Engineering, Stillwater, OK 74078. Offers MS, PhD. *Faculty:* 15 full-time (2 women), 1 part-time/adjunct (0 women). *Students:* 28 full-time (7 women), 22 part-time (10 women); includes 4 minority (1 Black or African American, non-Hispanic/Latino; 2 American Indian or Alaska Native, non-Hispanic/Latino; 1 Hispanic/Latino), 35 international. Average age 28. 116 applicants, 12% accepted, 12 enrolled. In 2014, 12 master's, 9 doctorates awarded. *Degree requirements:* For master's, thesis or alternative; for doctorate, comprehensive exam, thesis/dissertation. *Entrance requirements:* For master's and doctorate, GRE or GMAT. Additional exam requirements/recommendations for international students: Required—TOEFL (minimum score 550 paper-based; 79 iBT). *Application deadline:* For fall admission, 3/1 priority date for international students; for spring admission, 8/1 priority date for international students. Applications are processed on a rolling basis. Application fee: $40 ($75 for international students). Electronic applications accepted. *Expenses:* Tuition, state resident: full-time $4488; part-time $187 per credit hour. Tuition, nonresident: full-time $18,360; part-time $765 per credit hour. *Required fees:* $2413; $100.55 per credit hour. Tuition and fees vary according to campus/location. *Financial support:* In 2014–15, 30 research assistantships (averaging $21,594 per year), 19 teaching assistantships (averaging $18,853 per year) were awarded; fellowships, career-related internships or fieldwork, Federal Work-Study, scholarships/grants, health care benefits, tuition waivers (partial), and unspecified assistantships also available. Support available to part-time students. Financial award application deadline: 3/1; financial award applicants required to submit FAFSA. *Unit head:* Dr. Rob Whiteley, Head, 405-744-5280, Fax: 405-744-6338, E-mail: rob.whiteley@okstate.edu.
Website: http://che.okstate.edu/.

Oregon State University, College of Engineering, Program in Chemical Engineering, Corvallis, OR 97331. Offers M Eng, MS, PhD. *Faculty:* 24 full-time (2 women), 1 (woman) part-time/adjunct. *Students:* 59 full-time (19 women), 16 part-time (2 women); includes 5 minority (2 Black or African American, non-Hispanic/Latino; 3 Two or more races, non-Hispanic/Latino), 40 international. Average age 28. 118 applicants, 44% accepted, 22 enrolled. In 2014, 18 master's, 8 doctorates awarded. *Entrance requirements:* For master's, GRE. Additional exam requirements/recommendations for international students: Required—TOEFL (minimum score 92 iBT). *Application deadline:* For fall admission, 1/1 for domestic students. Application fee: $60. *Expenses:* Expenses: $15,359 full-time resident tuition and fees; $23,405 non-resident. *Financial support:* Application deadline: 1/1. *Unit head:* Dr. James Sweeney, School Head/Professor, 541-737-3769. *Application contact:* Elisha Brackett, Chemical Engineering Advisor, 541-737-6149, E-mail: cbee-gradinfo@engr.orst.edu.
Website: http://cbee.oregonstate.edu/che-graduate-program.

Penn State University Park, Graduate School, College of Engineering, Department of Chemical Engineering, University Park, PA 16802. Offers MS, PhD. *Unit head:* Dr. Amr S. Elnashai, Dean, 814-865-7537, Fax: 814-863-4749, E-mail: ase2@psu.edu. *Application contact:* Lori A. Stania, Director, Graduate Student Services, 814-867-5278, Fax: 814-863-4627, E-mail: gswww@psu.edu.
Website: http://www.che.psu.edu/.

Princeton University, Graduate School, School of Engineering and Applied Science, Department of Chemical Engineering, Princeton, NJ 08544-1019. Offers M Eng, MSE, PhD. Terminal master's awarded for partial completion of doctoral program. *Degree requirements:* For master's, thesis (MSE); for doctorate, thesis/dissertation, general exam. *Entrance requirements:* For master's, GRE General Test, 3 letters of recommendation; for doctorate, GRE General Test, official transcript(s), 3 letters of recommendation, personal statement. Additional exam requirements/recommendations for international students: Required—TOEFL. Electronic applications accepted. *Faculty research:* Applied and computational mathematics, bioengineering, environmental and energy science and technology, fluid mechanics and transport phenomena, materials science.

Purdue University, College of Engineering, School of Chemical Engineering, West Lafayette, IN 47907-2050. Offers MSChE, PhD. Terminal master's awarded for partial completion of doctoral program. *Entrance requirements:* For master's and doctorate, GRE, minimum GPA of 3.0. Additional exam requirements/recommendations for international students: Required—TOEFL (minimum score 550 paper-based); Recommended—TWE. Electronic applications accepted. *Faculty research:* Biochemical and biomedical processes, polymer materials, interfacial and surface phenomena, applied thermodynamics, process systems engineering.

Queen's University at Kingston, School of Graduate Studies, Faculty of Applied Science, Department of Chemical Engineering, Kingston, ON K7L 3N6, Canada. Offers M Sc, PhD. Part-time programs available. *Degree requirements:* For master's, thesis or alternative; for doctorate, comprehensive exam, thesis/dissertation. *Entrance requirements:* Additional exam requirements/recommendations for international students: Required—TOEFL (minimum score 580 paper-based). Electronic applications accepted. *Faculty research:* Polymers and reaction engineering, process control and applied statistics, combustion, fermentation and bioremediation, biomaterials.

Rensselaer Polytechnic Institute, Graduate School, School of Engineering, Program in Chemical Engineering, Troy, NY 12180-3590. Offers M Eng, MS, D Eng, PhD. *Faculty:* 34 full-time (4 women), 2 part-time/adjunct (1 woman). *Students:* 69 full-time (20 women), 4 part-time (0 women); includes 9 minority (8 Asian, non-Hispanic/Latino; 1 Two or more races, non-Hispanic/Latino), 36 international. Average age 26. 182 applicants, 19% accepted, 10 enrolled. In 2014, 3 master's, 13 doctorates awarded. Terminal master's awarded for partial completion of doctoral program. *Entrance requirements:* For master's, GRE; for doctorate, GRE. Additional exam requirements/recommendations for international students: Required—TOEFL (minimum score 570 paper-based; 88 iBT), IELTS (minimum score 6.5), PTE (minimum score 60). *Application deadline:* For fall admission, 1/1 priority date for domestic and international students; for spring admission, 8/15 priority date for domestic and international students. Applications are processed on a rolling basis. Electronic applications accepted. *Expenses:* Tuition: Full-time $46,700; part-time $1945 per credit. Tuition and fees vary according to course load. *Financial support:* In 2014–15, 33 students received support, including research assistantships with full tuition reimbursements available (averaging $18,500 per year), teaching assistantships with full tuition reimbursements available (averaging $18,500 per year); fellowships also available. Financial award application deadline: 1/1. *Faculty research:* Advanced materials, biochemical engineering; biomedical engineering; biotechnology; drug delivery; energy; fluid mechanics; interfacial phenomena; mass transport; molecular simulations; molecular thermodynamics; nanotechnology; polymers; process control, design, and optimization; separation and bioseparation processes; systems biology; systems engineering; transport phenomena. *Total annual research expenditures:* $5.5 million. *Unit head:* Dr. Ravi Kane, Graduate Program Director, 518-276-2536, E-mail: kaner@rpi.edu. *Application contact:* Office of Graduate Admissions, 518-276-6216, E-mail: gradadmissions@rpi.edu.
Website: http://cbe.rpi.edu/graduate.

Rice University, Graduate Programs, George R. Brown School of Engineering, Department of Chemical and Biomolecular Engineering, Houston, TX 77251-1892.

Offers chemical and biomolecular engineering (MS, PhD); chemical engineering (M Ch E). Part-time programs available. *Degree requirements:* For master's, thesis (for some programs); for doctorate, thesis/dissertation. *Entrance requirements:* For master's and doctorate, GRE General Test, minimum GPA of 3.0. Additional exam requirements/recommendations for international students: Required—TOEFL (minimum score 600 paper-based; 90 iBT). Electronic applications accepted. *Faculty research:* Thermodynamics, phase equilibria, rheology, fluid mechanics, polymers, biomedical engineering, interfacial phenomena, process control, petroleum engineering, reaction engineering and catalysis, biomaterials, metabolic engineering.

Rose-Hulman Institute of Technology, Faculty of Engineering and Applied Sciences, Department of Chemical Engineering, Terre Haute, IN 47803-3999. Offers M Eng, MS. Part-time programs available. *Faculty:* 10 full-time (3 women), 3 part-time/adjunct (1 woman). *Students:* 3 full-time (1 woman); includes 1 minority (Two or more races, non-Hispanic/Latino), 2 international. Average age 23. 13 applicants, 69% accepted, 2 enrolled. In 2014, 3 master's awarded. *Degree requirements:* For master's, thesis. *Entrance requirements:* For master's, GRE, minimum GPA of 3.0. Additional exam requirements/recommendations for international students: Required—TOEFL (minimum score 580 paper-based; 92 iBT). *Application deadline:* For fall admission, 2/1 priority date for domestic students. Applications are processed on a rolling basis. Application fee: $0. *Expenses:* Tuition: Full-time $40,449. *Financial support:* In 2014–15, 3 students received support. Fellowships with full and partial tuition reimbursements available, research assistantships with full and partial tuition reimbursements available, institutionally sponsored loans, scholarships/grants, and tuition waivers (full and partial) available. *Faculty research:* Thermodynamics and interfacial phenomena, reaction kinetics and separations, particle technology and materials, process systems and control, petrochemical processes. *Total annual research expenditures:* $28,726. *Unit head:* Dr. Adam Nolte, Chairman, 812-877-8096, Fax: 812-877-8992, E-mail: nolte@rose-hulman.edu. *Application contact:* Dr. Azad Siahmakoun, Associate Dean of the Faculty, 812-877-8400, Fax: 812-877-8061, E-mail: siahmako@rose-hulman.edu.
Website: http://www.rose-hulman.edu/academics/academic-departments/chemical-engineering.aspx.

Rowan University, Graduate School, College of Engineering, Department of Chemical Engineering, Glassboro, NJ 08028-1701. Offers MS. *Faculty:* 4 full-time (0 women). *Students:* 7 full-time (3 women), 10 part-time (2 women); includes 4 minority (all Asian, non-Hispanic/Latino), 1 international. Average age 27. 8 applicants, 75% accepted, 5 enrolled. *Application deadline:* For fall admission, 8/1 for domestic and international students; for spring admission, 11/1 for domestic and international students; for summer admission, 4/1 for domestic and international students. Applications are processed on a rolling basis. Application fee: $65. Electronic applications accepted. *Expenses:* Tuition, area resident: Part-time $648 per credit. Tuition, state resident: part-time $648 per credit. Tuition, nonresident: part-time $648 per credit. *Required fees:* $145 per credit. Tuition and fees vary according to degree level, campus/location, program and student level. *Unit head:* Dr. Steve Chin, Dean, 856-256-5301. *Application contact:* Dr. Ralph Dusseau, Program Adviser, 856-256-5332.

Royal Military College of Canada, Division of Graduate Studies and Research, Science Division, Department of Chemistry and Chemical and Materials Engineering, Kingston, ON K7K 7B4, Canada. Offers chemical engineering (M Eng, MA Sc, PhD); chemistry (M Sc, PhD). *Degree requirements:* For master's, thesis; for doctorate, comprehensive exam, thesis/dissertation. *Entrance requirements:* For master's, honour's degree with second-class standing; for doctorate, master's degree. Electronic applications accepted.

Rutgers, The State University of New Jersey, New Brunswick, Graduate School-New Brunswick, Program in Chemical and Biochemical Engineering, Piscataway, NJ 08854-8097. Offers MS, PhD. Part-time and evening/weekend programs available. Terminal master's awarded for partial completion of doctoral program. *Degree requirements:* For master's, thesis or alternative; for doctorate, thesis/dissertation. *Entrance requirements:* For master's and doctorate, GRE General Test. Additional exam requirements/recommendations for international students: Required—TOEFL. *Faculty research:* Biotechnology, pharmaceutical engineering, nanotechnology, process system engineering, materials and polymer science, chemical engineering sciences.

San Jose State University, Graduate Studies and Research, Charles W. Davidson College of Engineering, Department of Chemical and Materials Engineering, Program in Chemical Engineering, San Jose, CA 95192-0001. Offers MS. *Degree requirements:* For master's, thesis or alternative. Electronic applications accepted.

South Dakota School of Mines and Technology, Graduate Division, Program in Chemical and Biological Engineering, Rapid City, SD 57701-3995. Offers PhD. Part-time programs available. *Faculty:* 13 full-time (6 women). *Students:* 16 full-time (3 women), 2 part-time (0 women); includes 2 minority (both Black or African American, non-Hispanic/Latino), 9 international. Average age 31. 8 applicants, 13% accepted, 1 enrolled. In 2014, 7 doctorates awarded. *Degree requirements:* For doctorate, thesis/dissertation. *Entrance requirements:* Additional exam requirements/recommendations for international students: Required—TOEFL (minimum score 520 paper-based; 68 iBT). *Application deadline:* For fall admission, 7/1 priority date for domestic students, 4/1 for international students; for spring admission, 11/1 for domestic students, 9/1 for international students. Applications are processed on a rolling basis. Application fee: $35. Electronic applications accepted. *Expenses:* Tuition, state resident: full-time $5050; part-time $210.40 per credit hour. Tuition, nonresident: full-time $11,290; part-time $470.30 per credit hour. *Required fees:* $4680. *Financial support:* In 2014–15, 3 fellowships (averaging $5,138 per year), 30 research assistantships with partial tuition reimbursements (averaging $9,284 per year) were awarded; teaching assistantships with partial tuition reimbursements also available. Financial award application deadline: 5/15. *Faculty research:* Polymer synthesis, processing, and characterization; composite material processing; characterization and prototyping. *Total annual research expenditures:* $408,983. *Unit head:* Dr. Robb Winter, Department Head, 605-394-1237, E-mail: robb.winter@sdsmt.edu. *Application contact:* Rachel Howard, Office of Graduate Education, 605-355-3468, Fax: 605-394-1767, E-mail: rachel.howard@sdsmt.edu.
Website: http://www.sdsmt.edu/Academics/Departments/Chemical-and-Biological-Engineering/Graduate-Education/Chemical-and-Biological-Engineering—PhD/.

South Dakota School of Mines and Technology, Graduate Division, Program in Chemical Engineering, Rapid City, SD 57701-3995. Offers MS. Part-time programs available. *Faculty:* 8 full-time (1 woman), 2 part-time/adjunct (1 woman). *Students:* 12 full-time (4 women); includes 1 minority (Hispanic/Latino), 1 international. Average age 25. 2 applicants. In 2014, 2 master's awarded. *Degree requirements:* For master's, thesis. *Entrance requirements:* For master's, GRE General Test. Additional exam requirements/recommendations for international students: Required—TOEFL (minimum score 520 paper-based; 68 iBT), TWE. *Application deadline:* For fall admission, 7/1 priority date for domestic students, 4/1 for international students; for spring admission, 11/1 for domestic students, 9/1 for international students. Applications are processed on a rolling basis. Application fee: $35. Electronic applications accepted. *Expenses:* Tuition, state resident: full-time $5050; part-time $210.40 per credit hour. Tuition, nonresident: full-time $11,290; part-time $470.30 per credit hour. *Required fees:* $4680. *Financial support:* In 2014–15, 90 research assistantships with partial tuition

reimbursements were awarded; fellowships, teaching assistantships with partial tuition reimbursements, Federal Work-Study, and institutionally sponsored loans also available. Support available to part-time students. Financial award application deadline: 5/15. *Faculty research:* Incineration chemistry, environmental chemistry, polymer surface chemistry. *Total annual research expenditures:* $301,749. *Unit head:* Dr. Robb Winter, Department Head, 605-394-1237, E-mail: robb.winter@sdsmt.edu. *Application contact:* Rachel Howard, Office of Graduate Education, 605-355-3468, Fax: 605-394-1767, E-mail: rachel.howard@sdsmt.edu.
Website: http://www.sdsmt.edu/Academics/Departments/Chemical-and-Biological -Engineering/Graduate-Education/Chemical-Engineering-MS/.

Stanford University, School of Engineering, Department of Chemical Engineering, Stanford, CA 94305-9991. Offers MS, PhD. Terminal master's awarded for partial completion of doctoral program. *Degree requirements:* For doctorate, thesis/ dissertation. *Entrance requirements:* For master's and doctorate, GRE General Test. Additional exam requirements/recommendations for international students: Required— TOEFL. Electronic applications accepted. *Expenses: Tuition:* Full-time $44,184; part-time $982 per credit hour. *Required fees:* $191.

Stevens Institute of Technology, Graduate School, Charles V. Schaefer Jr. School of Engineering, Department of Chemical Engineering and Materials Science, Program in Chemical Engineering, Hoboken, NJ 07030. Offers M Eng, PhD, Engr.

Syracuse University, L. C. Smith College of Engineering and Computer Science, Program in Chemical Engineering, Syracuse, NY 13244. Offers MS, PhD. Part-time programs available. *Students:* 46 full-time (15 women), 1 part-time (0 women); includes 3 minority (1 Black or African American, non-Hispanic/Latino; 1 Asian, non-Hispanic/ Latino; 1 Two or more races, non-Hispanic/Latino), 38 international. Average age 25. 111 applicants, 54% accepted, 19 enrolled. In 2014, 11 master's, 4 doctorates awarded. *Degree requirements:* For master's, comprehensive exam (for some programs), thesis (for some programs); for doctorate, comprehensive exam, thesis/dissertation. *Entrance requirements:* For master's, GRE General Test. Additional exam requirements/ recommendations for international students: Required—TOEFL (minimum score 100 iBT). *Application deadline:* For fall admission, 7/1 priority date for domestic students, 6/1 priority date for international students. Applications are processed on a rolling basis. Application fee: $75. Electronic applications accepted. *Expenses: Tuition:* Part-time $1341 per credit. *Required fees:* $1341 per credit. *Financial support:* Fellowships with full tuition reimbursements, research assistantships with full and partial tuition reimbursements, teaching assistantships with full and partial tuition reimbursements, and tuition waivers (partial) available. Financial award application deadline: 1/1; financial award applicants required to submit FAFSA. *Unit head:* Dr. Radhakrishna Sureshkumar, Department Chair, 315-443-1931, E-mail: topgrads@syr.edu. *Application contact:* Kathleen Joyce, Assistant Dean, 314-443-2219, E-mail: topgrads@syr.edu.
Website: http://lcs.syr.edu/.

Tennessee Technological University, College of Graduate Studies, College of Engineering, Department of Chemical Engineering, Cookeville, TN 38505. Offers MS. Part-time programs available. *Faculty:* 8 full-time (0 women). *Students:* 8 full-time (3 women), 8 part-time (5 women), 6 international. Average age 26. 33 applicants, 76% accepted, 5 enrolled. In 2014, 4 master's awarded. *Degree requirements:* For master's, thesis. *Entrance requirements:* For master's, GRE General Test. Additional exam requirements/recommendations for international students: Required—TOEFL (minimum score 550 paper-based; 79 iBT), IELTS (minimum score 5.5), PTE (minimum score 53), or TOEIC (Test of English as an International Communication). *Application deadline:* For fall admission, 8/1 for domestic students, 5/1 for international students; for spring admission, 12/1 for domestic students, 10/1 for international students. Applications are processed on a rolling basis. Application fee: $35 ($40 for international students). Electronic applications accepted. *Expenses: Tuition,* state resident: full-time $9783; part-time $492 per credit hour. Tuition, nonresident: full-time $24,071; part-time $1179 per credit hour. *Financial support:* In 2014–15, fellowships (averaging $8,000 per year), 7 research assistantships (averaging $7,000 per year), 5 teaching assistantships (averaging $5,433 per year) were awarded; career-related internships or fieldwork also available. Financial award application deadline: 4/1. *Faculty research:* Biochemical conversion, insulation, fuel reprocessing. *Unit head:* Dr. Pedro Arce, Chairperson, 931-372-3297, Fax: 931-372-6372, E-mail: parce@tntech.edu. *Application contact:* Shelia K. Kendrick, Coordinator of Graduate Studies, 931-372-3808, Fax: 931-372-3497, E-mail: skendrick@tntech.edu.

Texas A&M University, College of Engineering, Artie McFerrin Department of Chemical Engineering, College Station, TX 77843. Offers M Eng, MS, PhD. *Faculty:* 30. *Students:* 159 full-time (58 women), 22 part-time (8 women); includes 22 minority (5 Black or African American, non-Hispanic/Latino; 11 Asian, non-Hispanic/Latino; 3 Hispanic/ Latino; 3 Two or more races, non-Hispanic/Latino), 123 international. Average age 27. 517 applicants, 27% accepted, 59 enrolled. In 2014, 26 master's, 14 doctorates awarded. Terminal master's awarded for partial completion of doctoral program. *Degree requirements:* For master's, thesis (MS); for doctorate, thesis/dissertation. *Entrance requirements:* For master's and doctorate, GRE General Test. Additional exam requirements/recommendations for international students: Required—TOEFL. *Application deadline:* For fall admission, 12/15 for domestic students, 3/1 priority date for international students; for spring admission, 8/1 for domestic students, 10/1 for international students. Applications are processed on a rolling basis. Application fee: $50 ($90 for international students). Electronic applications accepted. *Expenses: Tuition,* state resident: full-time $4078; part-time $226.55 per credit hour. Tuition, nonresident: full-time $10,594; part-time $577.55 per credit hour. *Required fees:* $2813; $237.70 per credit hour. $278.50 per semester. Tuition and fees vary according to degree level and student level. *Financial support:* In 2014–15, 161 students received support, including 23 fellowships with full and partial tuition reimbursements available (averaging $3,884 per year), 109 research assistantships with full and partial tuition reimbursements available (averaging $8,708 per year), 3 teaching assistantships with full and partial tuition reimbursements available (averaging $4,050 per year); career-related internships or fieldwork, institutionally sponsored loans, scholarships/grants, traineeships, health care benefits, tuition waivers (full and partial), and unspecified assistantships also available. Support available to part-time students. Financial award application deadline: 3/31; financial award applicants required to submit FAFSA. *Faculty research:* Reaction engineering, interface phenomena, environmental applications, biochemical engineering, polymers. *Unit head:* Dr. M. Nazmul Karim, Head, 979-845-9806, E-mail: nazkarim@che.tamu.edu. *Application contact:* Dr. Hae-Kwon Jeong, Graduate Recruitment and Admissions Coordinator, 979-862-4850, E-mail: jeong@ chemail.tamu.edu.
Website: http://engineering.tamu.edu/chemical.

Texas A&M University–Kingsville, College of Graduate Studies, College of Engineering, Wayne H. King Department of Chemical and Natural Gas Engineering, Program in Chemical Engineering, Kingsville, TX 78363. Offers ME, MS. *Students:* 40 full-time (8 women), 7 part-time (0 women); includes 6 minority (2 Black or African American, non-Hispanic/Latino; 3 Hispanic/Latino; 1 Two or more races, non-Hispanic/ Latino), 39 international. Average age 26. 69 applicants, 75% accepted, 23 enrolled. In 2014, 2 master's awarded. *Degree requirements:* For master's, variable foreign

language requirement, comprehensive exam, thesis (for some programs). *Entrance requirements:* For master's, GRE, MAT, GMAT, minimum GPA of 2.75, minimum GRE quantitative score of 150, minimum GRE verbal score of 145. Additional exam requirements/recommendations for international students: Required—TOEFL (minimum score 550 paper-based; 79 iBT). *Application deadline:* For fall admission, 8/15 for domestic students, 6/1 for international students; for spring admission, 12/15 for domestic students, 10/1 for international students; for summer admission, 5/15 for domestic students, 4/1 for international students. Applications are processed on a rolling basis. Application fee: $35 ($50 for international students). Electronic applications accepted. *Financial support:* In 2014–15, 21 students received support, including 1 teaching assistantship (averaging $5,153 per year); career-related internships or fieldwork, Federal Work-Study, institutionally sponsored loans, scholarships/grants, health care benefits, tuition waivers (full and partial), and unspecified assistantships also available. Support available to part-time students. Financial award application deadline: 5/15; financial award applicants required to submit FAFSA. *Unit head:* Dr. Ali A. Pilehvari, Professor and Chair, 361-593-2089, Fax: 361-593-4026, E-mail: a-pilehvari@ tamuk.edu. *Application contact:* Dr. Mohamed Abdelrahman, Dean, College of Graduate Studies, 361-593-2809, E-mail: mohamed.abdelrahman@tamuk.edu.

Texas Tech University, Graduate School, Edward E. Whitacre Jr. College of Engineering, Department of Chemical Engineering, Lubbock, TX 79409-3121. Offers MS Ch E, PhD. *Faculty:* 14 full-time (3 women). *Students:* 72 full-time (29 women), 3 part-time (1 woman); includes 6 minority (3 Asian, non-Hispanic/Latino; 3 Hispanic/ Latino), 62 international. Average age 26. 221 applicants, 16% accepted, 23 enrolled. In 2014, 3 master's, 10 doctorates awarded. Terminal master's awarded for partial completion of doctoral program. *Degree requirements:* For master's, comprehensive exam, thesis (for some programs); for doctorate, comprehensive exam, thesis/ dissertation. *Entrance requirements:* For master's and doctorate, GRE (Verbal and Quantitative). Additional exam requirements/recommendations for international students: Required—TOEFL (minimum score 550 paper-based; 79 iBT). *Application deadline:* For fall admission, 6/1 priority date for domestic students, 1/15 priority date for international students; for spring admission, 9/1 priority date for domestic students, 6/15 priority date for international students. Applications are processed on a rolling basis. Application fee: $60. Electronic applications accepted. *Expenses: Tuition,* state resident: full-time $6310; part-time $262.92 per credit hour. Tuition, nonresident: full-time $14,998; part-time $624.92 per credit hour. *Required fees:* $2701; $36.50 per credit. $912.50 per semester. Tuition and fees vary according to course load. *Financial support:* In 2014–15, 75 students received support, including 74 fellowships (averaging $780 per year), 42 research assistantships (averaging $27,500 per year), 14 teaching assistantships (averaging $20,625 per year); scholarships/grants, tuition waivers (partial), and unspecified assistantships also available. Financial award application deadline: 4/15; financial award applicants required to submit FAFSA. *Faculty research:* Bioengineering; energy and sustainability; polymers and materials; simulation and modeling in chemical engineering. *Total annual research expenditures:* $3.5 million. *Unit head:* Dr. Sindee Simon, Department Chair, 806-742-3553, Fax: 806-742-3552, E-mail: sindee.simon@ttu.edu. *Application contact:* Dr. Siva Vanapalli, Associate Professor, 806-742-3553, Fax: 806-742-3552, E-mail: siva.vanapalli@ttu.edu.
Website: http://www.depts.ttu.edu/che/.

Tufts University, School of Engineering, Department of Chemical and Biological Engineering, Medford, MA 02155. Offers bioengineering (ME, MS), including cell and bioprocess engineering; biotechnology engineering (PhD); chemical and biological engineering (ME, MS, PhD). Part-time programs available. *Faculty:* 10 full-time (2 women), 1 part-time/adjunct (0 women). *Students:* 35 full-time (11 women), 12 part-time (7 women); includes 6 minority (5 Asian, non-Hispanic/Latino; 1 Hispanic/Latino), 23 international. Average age 27. 152 applicants, 22% accepted, 18 enrolled. In 2014, 5 master's, 1 doctorate awarded. Terminal master's awarded for partial completion of doctoral program. *Degree requirements:* For master's, thesis (for some programs); for doctorate, thesis/dissertation. *Entrance requirements:* For master's and doctorate, GRE General Test. Additional exam requirements/recommendations for international students: Required—TOEFL (minimum score 550 paper-based; 80 iBT), IELTS (minimum score 6.5). *Application deadline:* For fall admission, 1/15 priority date for domestic students, 1/15 for international students; for spring admission, 9/15 for domestic and international students. Applications are processed on a rolling basis. Application fee: $75. Electronic applications accepted. *Expenses: Tuition:* Full-time $45,590; part-time $1161 per credit hour. *Required fees:* $782. Full-time tuition and fees vary according to degree level, program and student level. Part-time tuition and fees vary according to course load. *Financial support:* Fellowships with full tuition reimbursements, research assistantships with full and partial tuition reimbursements, teaching assistantships with full and partial tuition reimbursements, Federal Work-Study, scholarships/grants, tuition waivers (partial), and unspecified assistantships available. Financial award application deadline: 1/15; financial award applicants required to submit FAFSA. *Faculty research:* Clean energy with materials, biomaterials, colloids; metabolic engineering, biotechnology; process control; reaction kinetics, catalysis; transport phenomena. *Unit head:* Dr. Matt Panzer, Graduate Program Director. *Application contact:* Office of Graduate Admissions, 617-627-3395, E-mail: gradadmissions@ tufts.edu.
Website: http://engineering.tufts.edu/chbe/.

Tulane University, School of Science and Engineering, Department of Chemical and Biomolecular Engineering, New Orleans, LA 70118-5669. Offers PhD. Part-time programs available. Terminal master's awarded for partial completion of doctoral program. *Degree requirements:* For doctorate, thesis/dissertation. *Entrance requirements:* For doctorate, GRE General Test, minimum B average in undergraduate course work. Additional exam requirements/recommendations for international students: Required—TOEFL. Electronic applications accepted. *Expenses: Tuition:* Full-time $46,326; part-time $2574 per credit hour. *Required fees:* $1980; $44.50 per credit hour. $550 per term. Tuition and fees vary according to course load and program. *Faculty research:* Interfacial phenomena catalysis, electrochemical engineering, environmental science.

Universidad de las Américas Puebla, Division of Graduate Studies, School of Engineering, Program in Chemical Engineering, Puebla, Mexico. Offers chemical engineering (MS); food technology (MS). Part-time and evening/weekend programs available. *Degree requirements:* For master's, one foreign language, thesis. *Faculty research:* Food science, reactors, oil industry, biotechnology.

Université de Sherbrooke, Faculty of Engineering, Department of Chemical Engineering, Sherbrooke, QC J1K 2R1, Canada. Offers M Sc A, PhD. *Degree requirements:* For master's, one foreign language, thesis; for doctorate, comprehensive exam, thesis/dissertation. *Entrance requirements:* For doctorate, master's degree in engineering or equivalent. Electronic applications accepted. *Faculty research:* Conversion processes, high-temperature plasma technologies, system engineering, environmental engineering, textile technologies.

Université Laval, Faculty of Sciences and Engineering, Department of Chemical Engineering, Programs in Chemical Engineering, Québec, QC G1K 7P4, Canada. Offers M Sc, PhD. Terminal master's awarded for partial completion of doctoral program. *Degree requirements:* For master's, thesis (for some programs); for doctorate, comprehensive exam, thesis/dissertation. *Entrance requirements:* Additional exam requirements/recommendations for international students: Required—TOEFL (minimum score 500 paper-based). Electronic applications accepted.

University at Buffalo, the State University of New York, Graduate School, School of Engineering and Applied Sciences, Department of Chemical and Biological Engineering, Buffalo, NY 14260. Offers ME, MS, PhD. Part-time programs available. *Faculty:* 17 full-time (1 woman), 5 part-time/adjunct (1 woman). *Students:* 109 full-time (32 women), 4 part-time (2 women); includes 4 minority (1 Black or African American, non-Hispanic/Latino; 2 Asian, non-Hispanic/Latino; 1 Two or more races, non-Hispanic/Latino), 89 international. Average age 26. 411 applicants, 29% accepted, 20 enrolled. In 2014, 27 master's, 15 doctorates awarded. *Degree requirements:* For master's, thesis (for some programs); for doctorate, comprehensive exam, thesis/dissertation. *Entrance requirements:* For master's and doctorate, GRE General Test. Additional exam requirements/recommendations for international students: Required—TOEFL (minimum score 550 paper-based; 79 iBT). *Application deadline:* For fall admission, 2/1 priority date for domestic and international students; for spring admission, 10/1 priority date for domestic and international students. Applications are processed on a rolling basis. Application fee: $75. Electronic applications accepted. *Financial support:* In 2014–15, 55 students received support, including 3 fellowships with full and partial tuition reimbursements available (averaging $25,000 per year), 40 research assistantships with full and partial tuition reimbursements available (averaging $21,120 per year); teaching assistantships with full and partial tuition reimbursements available, institutionally sponsored loans, scholarships/grants, health care benefits, tuition waivers (full and partial), and unspecified assistantships also available. Support available to part-time students. Financial award application deadline: 2/28; financial award applicants required to submit FAFSA. *Faculty research:* Transport, polymers, nanomaterials, biochemical engineering, catalysis. *Total annual research expenditures:* $7.8 million. *Unit head:* Dr. Stylianos Andreadis, Chairman, 716-645-2911, Fax: 716-645-3822, E-mail: sandread@buffalo.edu. *Application contact:* Dr. Paschalis Alexandridis, Director of Graduate Studies, 716-645-1183, Fax: 716-645-3822, E-mail: cegrad@buffalo.edu.
Website: http://www.cbe.buffalo.edu/.

The University of Akron, Graduate School, College of Engineering, Department of Chemical and Biomolecular Engineering, Akron, OH 44325. Offers chemical engineering (MS); engineering (PhD). Part-time and evening/weekend programs available. *Faculty:* 17 full-time (4 women), 2 part-time/adjunct (0 women). *Students:* 90 full-time (31 women), 8 part-time (2 women); includes 4 minority (2 Asian, non-Hispanic/Latino; 2 Hispanic/Latino), 78 international. Average age 28. 89 applicants, 57% accepted, 17 enrolled. In 2014, 5 master's, 14 doctorates awarded. *Degree requirements:* For master's, thesis optional; for doctorate, one foreign language, thesis/dissertation, candidacy exam, qualifying exam. *Entrance requirements:* For master's, GRE, minimum GPA of 2.75, letters of recommendation, statement of purpose, resume; for doctorate, GRE, minimum GPA of 3.0 with bachelor's degree, 3.5 with master's degree; letters of recommendation; personal statement. Additional exam requirements/recommendations for international students: Required—TOEFL (minimum score 550 paper-based; 79 iBT), IELTS (minimum score 6.5). *Application deadline:* For fall admission, 5/1 priority date for domestic and international students; for spring admission, 10/31 priority date for domestic and international students; for summer admission, 2/15 for domestic and international students. Application fee: $45 ($70 for international students). Electronic applications accepted. *Expenses:* Tuition, state resident: full-time $7578; part-time $421 per credit hour. Tuition, nonresident: full-time $12,977; part-time $721 per credit hour. *Required fees:* $1388; $35 per credit hour. Tuition and fees vary according to course load. *Financial support:* In 2014–15, 56 research assistantships with full tuition reimbursements, 24 teaching assistantships with full tuition reimbursements were awarded; scholarships/grants also available. *Faculty research:* Renewable energy, fuel cell and CO2 sequestration, nanofiber synthesis and applications, materials for biomedical applications, engineering, surface characterization and modification. *Total annual research expenditures:* $2.7 million. *Unit head:* Dr. H. Michael Cheung, Chair, 330-972-7282, E-mail: cheung@uakron.edu.
Website: http://www.uakron.edu/engineering/CBE/.

The University of Alabama, Graduate School, College of Engineering, Department of Chemical and Biological Engineering, Tuscaloosa, AL 35487. Offers MS Ch E, PhD. *Faculty:* 14 full-time (3 women), 1 part-time/adjunct (0 women). *Students:* 22 full-time (7 women), 1 part-time (0 women); includes 1 minority (Asian, non-Hispanic/Latino), 11 international. Average age 27. 31 applicants, 26% accepted, 5 enrolled. In 2014, 7 master's, 3 doctorates awarded. Terminal master's awarded for partial completion of doctoral program. *Degree requirements:* For master's, comprehensive exam, thesis; for doctorate, comprehensive exam, thesis/dissertation. *Entrance requirements:* For master's, GRE, minimum GPA of 3.0 overall; for doctorate, GRE, minimum GPA of 3.0. Additional exam requirements/recommendations for international students: Required—TOEFL (minimum score 550 paper-based); Recommended—IELTS (minimum score 6.5). *Application deadline:* For fall admission, 1/31 priority date for domestic and international students; for winter admission, 9/15 priority date for domestic and international students. Applications are processed on a rolling basis. Application fee: $50 ($60 for international students). Electronic applications accepted. *Expenses:* Tuition, state resident: full-time $9826. Tuition, nonresident: full-time $24,950. *Financial support:* In 2014–15, 2 fellowships with full tuition reimbursements (averaging $25,000 per year), 14 research assistantships with full tuition reimbursements (averaging $25,000 per year), 4 teaching assistantships with full tuition reimbursements (averaging $25,000 per year) were awarded; Federal Work-Study also available. *Faculty research:* Nanotechnology, materials, electrochemistry, alternative energy, biological. *Total annual research expenditures:* $1.2 million. *Unit head:* Dr. Christopher S. Brazel, Associate Professor, 205-348-6450, Fax: 205-348-6579, E-mail: cbrazel@eng.ua.edu. *Application contact:* Dr. Christoffer H. Turner, Professor, 205-348-1733, Fax: 205-348-6579, E-mail: hturner@eng.ua.edu.
Website: http://www.eng.ua.edu/~chedept/.

The University of Alabama in Huntsville, School of Graduate Studies, College of Engineering, Department of Chemical and Materials Engineering, Huntsville, AL 35899. Offers biotechnology science and engineering (PhD); chemical engineering (MSE); materials science (MS, PhD); mechanical engineering (PhD), including chemical engineering. Part-time and evening/weekend programs available. *Degree requirements:* For master's, comprehensive exam, thesis or alternative, oral and written exams; for doctorate, comprehensive exam, thesis/dissertation. *Entrance requirements:* For master's, GRE General Test, appropriate bachelor's degree, minimum GPA of 3.0; for doctorate, GRE General Test, minimum GPA of 3.0. Additional exam requirements/recommendations for international students: Required—TOEFL (minimum score 500 paper-based; 80 iBT), IELTS (minimum score 6.5). Electronic applications accepted. *Faculty research:* Ultrathin films for optical, sensor and biological applications; materials processing including low gravity; hypergolic reactants; computational fluid dynamics; biofuels and renewable resources.

University of Alberta, Faculty of Graduate Studies and Research, Department of Chemical and Materials Engineering, Edmonton, AB T6G 2E1, Canada. Offers chemical engineering (M Eng, M Sc, PhD); materials engineering (M Eng, M Sc, PhD); process control (M Eng, M Sc, PhD); welding (M Eng). Part-time programs available. Postbaccalaureate distance learning degree programs offered (minimal on-campus study). Terminal master's awarded for partial completion of doctoral program. *Degree requirements:* For master's, thesis; for doctorate, thesis/dissertation. *Faculty research:* Advanced materials and polymers, catalytic and reaction engineering, mineral processing, physical metallurgy, fluid mechanics.

The University of Arizona, College of Engineering, Department of Chemical and Environmental Engineering, Program in Chemical Engineering, Tucson, AZ 85721. Offers MS, PhD. *Entrance requirements:* For master's and doctorate, GRE, 3 letters of recommendation, resume, statement of purpose. Additional exam requirements/recommendations for international students: Required—TOEFL (minimum score 550 paper-based; 79 iBT). Electronic applications accepted.

University of Arkansas, Graduate School, College of Engineering, Department of Chemical Engineering, Fayetteville, AR 72701-1201. Offers MS Ch E, MSE, PhD. Part-time programs available. *Degree requirements:* For master's, thesis optional; for doctorate, one foreign language, thesis/dissertation. *Entrance requirements:* For master's and doctorate, GRE General Test. Electronic applications accepted.

The University of British Columbia, Faculty of Applied Science, Program in Chemical and Biological Engineering, Vancouver, BC V6T 1Z1, Canada. Offers chemical engineering (M Eng, M Sc, MA Sc, PhD). Part-time and evening/weekend programs available. *Degree requirements:* For master's, thesis (for some programs); for doctorate, thesis/dissertation. *Entrance requirements:* Additional exam requirements/recommendations for international students: Required—TOEFL, IELTS. Electronic applications accepted. *Faculty research:* Biotechnology, catalysis, polymers, fluidization, pulp and paper.

University of Calgary, Faculty of Graduate Studies, Schulich School of Engineering, Department of Chemical and Petroleum Engineering, Calgary, AB T2N 1N4, Canada. Offers chemical engineering (M Eng, M Sc, PhD); energy and environment engineering (M Eng, M Sc, PhD); energy and environmental systems (M Eng, M Sc, PhD); environmental engineering (M Eng, M Sc, PhD); petroleum engineering (M Eng, M Sc, PhD); reservoir characterization (M Eng, M Sc). Part-time programs available. *Degree requirements:* For master's, thesis (for some programs); for doctorate, comprehensive exam, thesis/dissertation, candidacy exam. *Entrance requirements:* For master's, minimum GPA of 3.0 or equivalent; for doctorate, minimum GPA of 3.5 or equivalent. Additional exam requirements/recommendations for international students: Required—TOEFL (minimum score 550 paper-based; 80 iBT), IELTS (minimum score 7). Electronic applications accepted. *Faculty research:* Environmental engineering, biomedical engineering modeling, simulation and control, petroleum recovery and reservoir engineering, phase equilibria and transport properties.

University of California, Berkeley, Graduate Division, College of Chemistry, Department of Chemical Engineering, Berkeley, CA 94720-1500. Offers MS, PhD. *Degree requirements:* For master's, thesis; for doctorate, thesis/dissertation, qualifying exam. *Entrance requirements:* For master's and doctorate, GRE General Test, minimum GPA of 3.0, 3 letters of recommendation. Additional exam requirements/recommendations for international students: Required—TOEFL. *Faculty research:* Biochemical engineering, electrochemical engineering, electronic materials, heterogeneous catalysis and reaction engineering, complex fluids.

University of California, Davis, College of Engineering, Program in Chemical Engineering, Davis, CA 95616. Offers MS, PhD. Terminal master's awarded for partial completion of doctoral program. *Degree requirements:* For master's, comprehensive exam (for some programs), thesis (for some programs); for doctorate, thesis/dissertation. *Entrance requirements:* For master's and doctorate, GRE General Test, minimum GPA of 3.0. Additional exam requirements/recommendations for international students: Required—TOEFL (minimum score 550 paper-based). Electronic applications accepted. *Faculty research:* Transport phenomena, colloid science, catalysis, biotechnology, materials.

University of California, Irvine, Henry Samueli School of Engineering, Department of Chemical Engineering and Materials Science, Irvine, CA 92697. Offers chemical and biochemical engineering (MS, PhD); materials science and engineering (MS, PhD). Part-time programs available. *Students:* 132 full-time (48 women), 8 part-time (1 woman); includes 45 minority (2 Black or African American, non-Hispanic/Latino; 31 Asian, non-Hispanic/Latino; 7 Hispanic/Latino; 1 Native Hawaiian or other Pacific Islander, non-Hispanic/Latino; 4 Two or more races, non-Hispanic/Latino), 48 international. Average age 26. 549 applicants, 32% accepted, 55 enrolled. In 2014, 29 master's, 11 doctorates awarded. Terminal master's awarded for partial completion of doctoral program. *Degree requirements:* For doctorate, thesis/dissertation. *Entrance requirements:* For master's and doctorate, GRE General Test, minimum GPA of 3.0, 3 letters of recommendation. Additional exam requirements/recommendations for international students: Required—TOEFL (minimum score 550 paper-based). *Application deadline:* For fall admission, 1/15 priority date for domestic students, 1/15 for international students. Applications are processed on a rolling basis. Application fee: $90 ($110 for international students). Electronic applications accepted. *Financial support:* Fellowships with tuition reimbursements, research assistantships with full tuition reimbursements, teaching assistantships with tuition reimbursements, institutionally sponsored loans, traineeships, health care benefits, and unspecified assistantships available. Financial award application deadline: 3/1; financial award applicants required to submit FAFSA. *Faculty research:* Molecular biotechnology, nano-bio-materials, biophotonics, synthesis, superplasticity and mechanical behavior, characterization of advanced and nanostructural materials. *Unit head:* Prof. Vasan Venugopalan, Chair, 949-824-5802, Fax: 949-824-2541, E-mail: vvenugop@uci.edu. *Application contact:* Grace Hai-Chin Chau, Academic Program and Graduate Admission Coordinator, 949-824-3887, Fax: 949-824-2541, E-mail: chaug@uci.edu.
Website: http://www.eng.uci.edu/dept/chems.

University of California, Los Angeles, Graduate Division, Henry Samueli School of Engineering and Applied Science, Department of Chemical and Biomolecular Engineering, Los Angeles, CA 90095-1592. Offers MS, PhD. *Faculty:* 13 full-time (2 women), 5 part-time/adjunct (0 women). *Students:* 100 full-time (29 women); includes 31 minority (1 Black or African American, non-Hispanic/Latino; 1 American Indian or Alaska Native, non-Hispanic/Latino; 23 Asian, non-Hispanic/Latino; 5 Hispanic/Latino; 1 Two or more races, non-Hispanic/Latino), 46 international. 410 applicants, 11% accepted, 23 enrolled. In 2014, 6 master's, 6 doctorates awarded. *Degree requirements:* For master's, comprehensive exam (for some programs), thesis (for some programs); for doctorate, thesis/dissertation, qualifying exams. *Entrance requirements:* For master's, GRE General Test, minimum GPA of 3.0; for doctorate, GRE General Test, minimum GPA of 3.25. Additional exam requirements/recommendations for international students: Required—TOEFL (minimum score 560 paper-based; 87 iBT), IELTS (minimum score 7). *Application deadline:* For fall admission, 1/15 for domestic and international students; for winter admission, 10/1 for domestic and international students; for spring admission, 12/31 for domestic and international students. Application fee: $80 ($100 for international students). Electronic applications accepted. *Financial support:* In 2014–15, 73 fellowships, 177 research assistantships, 62 teaching assistantships were awarded; Federal Work-Study, institutionally sponsored loans, and tuition waivers (full and partial) also available. Financial award application deadline: 1/15; financial award applicants

required to submit FAFSA. *Faculty research:* Biomolecular engineering, renewable energy, water technology, advanced materials processing, process systems engineering. *Total annual research expenditures:* $11.2 million. *Unit head:* Dr. James C. Liao, Chair, 310-825-1656, E-mail: liaoj@ucla.edu. *Application contact:* John Berger, Student Affairs Officer, 310-825-9063, Fax: 310-206-4107, E-mail: jpberger@ea.ucla.edu.
Website: http://www.chemeng.ucla.edu/.

University of California, Riverside, Graduate Division, Department of Chemical and Environmental Engineering, Riverside, CA 92521-0102. Offers MS, PhD. Part-time programs available. Terminal master's awarded for partial completion of doctoral program. *Degree requirements:* For master's, thesis (for some programs); for doctorate, comprehensive exam, thesis/dissertation. *Entrance requirements:* For master's and doctorate, GRE General Test, minimum GPA of 3.0. Additional exam requirements/recommendations for international students: Required—TOEFL (minimum score 550 paper-based; 80 iBT). Electronic applications accepted. *Expenses:* Tuition, state resident: full-time $5399. Tuition, nonresident: full-time $10,433. *Faculty research:* Air quality systems, water quality systems, advanced materials and nanotechnology, energy systems/alternative fuels, theory and molecular modeling.

University of California, San Diego, Graduate Division, Program in Chemical Engineering, La Jolla, CA 92093. Offers MS, PhD. *Students:* 33 full-time (6 women), 1 part-time (0 women); includes 8 minority (6 Asian, non-Hispanic/Latino; 2 Hispanic/Latino), 17 international. 176 applicants, 40% accepted, 15 enrolled. In 2014, 10 master's, 1 doctorate awarded. *Degree requirements:* For master's, comprehensive exam (for some programs), thesis (for some programs), thesis or comprehensive exam; for doctorate, comprehensive exam, thesis/dissertation, 1-quarter teaching assistantship. *Entrance requirements:* For master's and doctorate, GRE General Test. Additional exam requirements/recommendations for international students: Required—TOEFL (minimum score 550 paper-based; 80 iBT), IELTS (minimum score 7). *Application deadline:* For fall admission, 12/14 for domestic students. Application fee: $90 ($110 for international students). Electronic applications accepted. *Expenses:* Tuition, state resident: full-time $11,220; part-time $5610 per quarter. Tuition, nonresident: full-time $26,322; part-time $13,161 per quarter. *Required fees:* $570 per quarter. Tuition and fees vary according to program. *Financial support:* Fellowships, research assistantships, teaching assistantships, and scholarships/grants available. Financial award application deadline: 1/31; financial award applicants required to submit FAFSA. *Faculty research:* Regenerative medicine, development of new microfluidic devices, biomedical modeling, solar thermochemical hydrogen production. *Unit head:* Joseph Wang, Chair, 858-246-0128, E-mail: josephwang@ucsd.edu. *Application contact:* Dana Jimenez, Graduate Coordinator, 858-822-7981, E-mail: dljimenez@ucsd.edu.
Website: http://nanoengineering.ucsd.edu/graduate-programs/degree/chemical-engineering.

University of California, Santa Barbara, Graduate Division, College of Engineering, Department of Chemical Engineering, Santa Barbara, CA 93106-5080. Offers MS, PhD. *Degree requirements:* For master's, thesis or comprehensive exam; for doctorate, thesis/dissertation, research progress reports (prior to candidacy), candidacy exam, thesis defense, seminar. *Entrance requirements:* For master's and doctorate, GRE. Additional exam requirements/recommendations for international students: Required—TOEFL (minimum score 560 paper-based; 83 iBT), IELTS (minimum score 7). Electronic applications accepted. *Faculty research:* Biomaterials and bioengineering; energy, catalysis and reaction engineering; complex fluids and polymers; electronic and optical materials; fluids and transport phenomena; molecular thermodynamics and simulation; process systems engineering; surfaces and interfacial phenomena.

University of Cincinnati, Graduate School, College of Engineering and Applied Science, Department of Chemical and Materials Engineering, Program in Chemical Engineering, Cincinnati, OH 45221. Offers MS, PhD. Part-time and evening/weekend programs available. Terminal master's awarded for partial completion of doctoral program. *Degree requirements:* For master's, thesis; for doctorate, thesis/dissertation. *Entrance requirements:* For master's and doctorate, GRE General Test. Additional exam requirements/recommendations for international students: Required—TOEFL (minimum score 600 paper-based).

University of Colorado Boulder, Graduate School, College of Engineering and Applied Science, Department of Chemical and Biological Engineering, Boulder, CO 80309. Offers ME, MS, PhD. *Faculty:* 19 full-time (4 women). *Students:* 86 full-time (31 women), 37 part-time (14 women); includes 15 minority (2 American Indian or Alaska Native, non-Hispanic/Latino; 9 Asian, non-Hispanic/Latino; 4 Hispanic/Latino), 30 international. Average age 26. 511 applicants, 22% accepted, 39 enrolled. In 2014, 13 master's, 15 doctorates awarded. Terminal master's awarded for partial completion of doctoral program. *Degree requirements:* For master's, comprehensive exam, thesis; for doctorate, thesis/dissertation. *Entrance requirements:* For master's, minimum undergraduate GPA of 3.0. *Application deadline:* For fall admission, 1/5 for domestic and international students. Applications are processed on a rolling basis. Application fee: $50 ($70 for international students). Electronic applications accepted. *Financial support:* In 2014–15, 289 students received support, including 42 fellowships (averaging $15,036 per year), 85 research assistantships with full and partial tuition reimbursements available (averaging $31,793 per year), 29 teaching assistantships with full and partial tuition reimbursements available (averaging $30,922 per year); institutionally sponsored loans, scholarships/grants, health care benefits, and unspecified assistantships also available. Financial award applicants required to submit FAFSA. *Faculty research:* Chemical engineering, materials engineering, interfacial phenomena, reaction engineering, biomedical engineering. *Total annual research expenditures:* $12.7 million.
Website: http://www.colorado.edu/chbe.

University of Connecticut, Graduate School, School of Engineering, Department of Chemical, Materials and Biomolecular Engineering, Field of Chemical Engineering, Storrs, CT 06269. Offers MS, PhD. Terminal master's awarded for partial completion of doctoral program. *Degree requirements:* For master's, comprehensive exam, thesis or alternative; for doctorate, thesis/dissertation. *Entrance requirements:* For master's and doctorate, GRE General Test. Additional exam requirements/recommendations for international students: Required—TOEFL (minimum score 550 paper-based). Electronic applications accepted.

University of Dayton, Department of Chemical Engineering, Dayton, OH 45469. Offers bioengineering (MS); chemical engineering (MS Ch E). Part-time and evening/weekend programs available. *Faculty:* 9 full-time (2 women), 5 part-time/adjunct (1 woman). *Students:* 42 full-time (13 women), 6 part-time (2 women); includes 1 minority (Black or African American, non-Hispanic/Latino), 36 international. Average age 26. 91 applicants, 54% accepted, 16 enrolled. In 2014, 42 master's awarded. *Degree requirements:* For master's, comprehensive exam (for some programs), thesis optional. *Entrance requirements:* For master's, GRE (for bioengineering). Additional exam requirements/recommendations for international students: Required—TOEFL (minimum score 550 paper-based; 80 iBT). *Application deadline:* For fall admission, 8/1 for domestic students, 5/1 for international students; for spring admission, 11/1 for international students. Applications are processed on a rolling basis. Application fee: $0 ($50 for international students). Electronic applications accepted. *Expenses: Tuition:* Full-time $10,176; part-time $848 per credit. *Required fees:* $25; $25 per course. Part-time tuition and fees vary according to course level, course load, degree level and program. *Financial support:* In 2014–15, 4 research assistantships with full tuition reimbursements (averaging $12,329 per year) were awarded; institutionally sponsored loans, health care benefits, and unspecified assistantships also available. Financial award application deadline: 3/1; financial award applicants required to submit FAFSA. *Faculty research:* Vertically-aligned carbon nanotubes infiltrated with temperature-responsive polymers: smart nanocomposite films for self-cleaning and controlled release, bilayer and bulk heterojunction solar cells using liquid crystalline porphyrins as donors by solution processing, DNA damage induced by multiwalled carbon nanotubes in mouse embryonic stem cells. *Unit head:* Dr. Charles Browning, Chair, 937-229-2627, E-mail: cbrowning1@udayton.edu. *Application contact:* Dr. Kevin Myers, Graduate Program Director, 937-229-2627, E-mail: kmyers1@udayton.edu.
Website: https://www.udayton.edu/engineering/departments/chemical_and_materials/index.php.

University of Delaware, College of Engineering, Department of Chemical Engineering, Newark, DE 19716. Offers M Ch E, PhD. Part-time and evening/weekend programs available. Postbaccalaureate distance learning degree programs offered (minimal on-campus study). Terminal master's awarded for partial completion of doctoral program. *Degree requirements:* For master's, thesis (for some programs); for doctorate, thesis/dissertation. *Entrance requirements:* For master's and doctorate, GRE General Test. Additional exam requirements/recommendations for international students: Required—TOEFL. Electronic applications accepted. *Faculty research:* Biochemical/biomedical engineer, thermodynamics, polymers/composites, materials, catalysis/reactions, colloid/interfaces, expert systems/process control.

University of Florida, Graduate School, College of Engineering, Department of Chemical Engineering, Gainesville, FL 32611. Offers ME, MS, PhD, Engr. Part-time programs available. *Faculty:* 19 full-time (1 woman), 13 part-time/adjunct (0 women). *Students:* 175 full-time (43 women), 20 part-time (5 women); includes 22 minority (2 Black or African American, non-Hispanic/Latino; 12 Asian, non-Hispanic/Latino; 8 Hispanic/Latino), 143 international. 453 applicants, 42% accepted, 56 enrolled. In 2014, 85 master's, 10 doctorates awarded. Terminal master's awarded for partial completion of doctoral program. *Degree requirements:* For master's, thesis optional; for doctorate, comprehensive exam, thesis/dissertation. *Entrance requirements:* For master's and doctorate, minimum GPA of 3.0. Additional exam requirements/recommendations for international students: Required—TOEFL (minimum score 550 paper-based; 80 iBT), IELTS (minimum score 6). *Application deadline:* For fall admission, 1/15 priority date for domestic students, 1/14 priority date for international students; for spring admission, 11/1 for domestic and international students. Applications are processed on a rolling basis. Application fee: $30. Electronic applications accepted. *Financial support:* Federal Work-Study, institutionally sponsored loans, scholarships/grants, and unspecified assistantships available. Financial award application deadline: 1/28; financial award applicants required to submit FAFSA. *Faculty research:* Complex fluids and interfacial and colloidal phenomena; materials for biological, energy and microelectronic applications; catalysis and reaction kinetics; transport and electrochemistry; biomolecular research including biomechanics, signal transduction, and tissue engineering. *Total annual research expenditures:* $4.8 million. *Unit head:* Richard B. Dickinson, PhD, Chair, 352-392-0898, Fax: 352-392-9513, E-mail: dickinson@che.ufl.edu. *Application contact:* Anuj Chauhan, Graduate Coordinator, 352-392-2592, Fax: 352-392-9513, E-mail: chauhan@che.ufl.edu.
Website: http://www.che.ufl.edu/.

University of Houston, Cullen College of Engineering, Department of Chemical and Biomolecular Engineering, Houston, TX 77204. Offers chemical engineering (MCHE, PhD); petroleum engineering (M Pet E). Part-time programs available. Terminal master's awarded for partial completion of doctoral program. *Entrance requirements:* For master's and doctorate, GRE General Test. Additional exam requirements/recommendations for international students: Required—TOEFL (minimum score 550 paper-based; 79 iBT), IELTS (minimum score 6.5). *Faculty research:* Chemical engineering.

University of Idaho, College of Graduate Studies, College of Engineering, Department of Chemical and Materials Engineering, Moscow, ID 83844-1021. Offers chemical engineering (M Engr, MS, PhD); materials science and engineering (MS, PhD). *Faculty:* 8 full-time. *Students:* 13 full-time, 6 part-time. Average age 32. In 2014, 7 master's, 4 doctorates awarded. *Degree requirements:* For master's, thesis; for doctorate, one foreign language, thesis/dissertation. *Entrance requirements:* For master's, GRE, minimum GPA of 2.8; for doctorate, GRE, minimum undergraduate GPA of 2.8, 3.0 graduate. *Application deadline:* For fall admission, 8/1 for domestic students; for spring admission, 12/15 for domestic students. Applications are processed on a rolling basis. Application fee: $60. Electronic applications accepted. *Expenses:* Tuition, state resident: full-time $4784; part-time $280.50 per credit hour. Tuition, nonresident: full-time $18,314; part-time $957.50 per credit hour. *Required fees:* $2000; $58.50 per credit hour. Tuition and fees vary according to program. *Financial support:* Fellowships, research assistantships, and teaching assistantships available. Financial award applicants required to submit FAFSA. *Faculty research:* Geothermal energy utilization, alcohol production from agriculture waste material, energy conservation in pulp and paper mills. *Unit head:* Dr. Eric Aston, Interim Chair, 208-885-7572, E-mail: che@uidaho.edu. *Application contact:* Sean Scoggin, Graduate Recruitment Coordinator, 208-885-4001, Fax: 208-885-4406, E-mail: graduateadmissions@uidaho.edu.
Website: http://www.uidaho.edu/engr/cme/about/materials.

University of Illinois at Chicago, Graduate College, College of Engineering, Department of Chemical Engineering, Chicago, IL 60607-7128. Offers MS, PhD. Part-time programs available. *Faculty:* 7 full-time (2 women), 3 part-time/adjunct (1 woman). *Students:* 47 full-time (23 women), 6 part-time (4 women); includes 8 minority (4 Asian, non-Hispanic/Latino; 4 Hispanic/Latino), 35 international. Average age 27. 159 applicants, 53% accepted, 18 enrolled. In 2014, 8 master's, 5 doctorates awarded. *Degree requirements:* For master's, thesis or project; for doctorate, thesis/dissertation, departmental qualifying exam. *Entrance requirements:* For master's and doctorate, GRE General Test, minimum GPA of 2.75. Additional exam requirements/recommendations for international students: Required—TOEFL. *Application deadline:* For fall admission, 1/15 for domestic students, 1/15 priority date for international students; for spring admission, 11/1 for domestic students, 7/15 for international students. Application fee: $40 ($50 for international students). *Expenses:* Expenses: $17,602 in-state, $29,600 out-of-state. *Financial support:* In 2014–15, 1 fellowship with full tuition reimbursement was awarded; research assistantships with full tuition reimbursements, teaching assistantships with full tuition reimbursements, Federal Work-Study, scholarships/grants, traineeships, tuition waivers (full), and unspecified assistantships also available. Financial award application deadline: 1/15; financial award applicants required to submit FAFSA. *Faculty research:* Multiphase flows, interfacial transport, heterogeneous catalysis, coal technology, molecular and static thermodynamics. *Total annual research expenditures:* $305,000. *Unit head:* Prof. Sohail Murad, Head, 312-996-5593, E-mail:

Chemical Engineering

murad@uic.edu. *Application contact:* Prof. Lewis R. Wedgewood, Director of Graduate Studies, 312-996-5228, Fax: 312-996-0808, E-mail: wedge@uic.edu.
Website: http://www.uic.edu/depts/chme/.

University of Illinois at Urbana–Champaign, Graduate College, College of Liberal Arts and Sciences, School of Chemical Sciences, Department of Chemical and Biomolecular Engineering, Champaign, IL 61820. Offers bioinformatics: chemical and biomolecular engineering (MS); chemical engineering (MS, PhD). *Students:* 84 (29 women). *Entrance requirements:* For master's, minimum GPA of 3.0. Application fee: $70 ($90 for international students). *Unit head:* Paul Kenis, Head, 217-244-9214, Fax: 217-333-5052, E-mail: kenis@illinois.edu. *Application contact:* Christine M. Bowser, Office Manager, 217-244-9214, Fax: 217-333-5052, E-mail: cbowser@illinois.edu.
Website: http://chbe.illinois.edu/.

The University of Iowa, Graduate College, College of Engineering, Department of Chemical and Biochemical Engineering, Iowa City, IA 52242-1316. Offers MS, PhD. Part-time programs available. *Faculty:* 10 full-time (2 women), 2 part-time/adjunct (1 woman). *Students:* 33 full-time (10 women); includes 7 minority (3 Black or African American, non-Hispanic/Latino; 2 Asian, non-Hispanic/Latino; 2 Hispanic/Latino), 10 international. Average age 26. 36 applicants, 14% accepted, 3 enrolled. In 2014, 4 master's, 2 doctorates awarded. *Degree requirements:* For master's, comprehensive exam (for some programs), thesis (for some programs); for doctorate, comprehensive exam, thesis/dissertation. *Entrance requirements:* For master's and doctorate, GRE (minimum combined verbal and quantitative score of 1300), minimum undergraduate GPA of 3.0. Additional exam requirements/recommendations for international students: Required—TOEFL (minimum score 600 paper-based; 100 iBT). *Application deadline:* For fall admission, 2/1 priority date for domestic and international students; for spring admission, 10/1 for domestic and international students. Applications are processed on a rolling basis. Application fee: $60 ($100 for international students). Electronic applications accepted. *Financial support:* In 2014–15, 28 students received support, including 6 fellowships with full tuition reimbursements available, 22 research assistantships with full tuition reimbursements available (averaging $22,150 per year), 4 teaching assistantships with full tuition reimbursements available (averaging $21,970 per year); health care benefits and unspecified assistantships also available. Financial award application deadline: 2/1; financial award applicants required to submit FAFSA. *Faculty research:* Polymeric materials, photopolymerization, atmospheric chemistry and air pollution, biochemical engineering, bioprocessing and biomedical engineering. *Total annual research expenditures:* $4.4 million. *Unit head:* Dr. C. Allan Guymon, Department Executive Officer, 319-335-5015, Fax: 319-335-1415, E-mail: allan-guymon@uiowa.edu. *Application contact:* Katie Schnedler, Academic Program Specialist, 319-335-1215, Fax: 319-335-1415, E-mail: chemical-engineering@uiowa.edu.
Website: http://www.engineering.uiowa.edu/cbe.

The University of Kansas, Graduate Studies, School of Engineering, Program in Chemical and Petroleum Engineering, Lawrence, KS 66045. Offers MS, PhD. *Faculty:* 19 full-time, 4 part-time/adjunct. *Students:* 29 full-time (8 women), 1 part-time (0 women); includes 1 minority (American Indian or Alaska Native, non-Hispanic/Latino), 19 international. Average age 28. 58 applicants, 26% accepted, 5 enrolled. In 2014, 3 doctorates awarded. *Degree requirements:* For master's, thesis (for some programs), exam; for doctorate, comprehensive exam, thesis/dissertation, qualifying exams. *Entrance requirements:* For master's, GRE General Test, minimum GPA of 3.0; for doctorate, GRE General Test, minimum GPA of 3.5. Additional exam requirements/recommendations for international students: Required—TOEFL. *Application deadline:* For fall admission, 1/10 priority date for domestic students, 1/10 for international students; for spring admission, 6/10 priority date for domestic students, 6/10 for international students. Applications are processed on a rolling basis. Application fee: $55 ($65 for international students). Electronic applications accepted. *Financial support:* Fellowships, research assistantships with full and partial tuition reimbursements, teaching assistantships with full and partial tuition reimbursements, career-related internships or fieldwork, Federal Work-Study, scholarships/grants, traineeships, and unspecified assistantships available. Financial award application deadline: 4/1; financial award applicants required to submit FAFSA. *Faculty research:* Enhanced oil recovery, catalysis and kinetics, electrochemical engineering, biomedical engineering, semiconductor materials processing. *Unit head:* Laurence Weatherley, Chair, 785-864-3553, E-mail: lweather@ku.edu. *Application contact:* Carol Miner, Graduate Program Assistant, 785-864-2900, E-mail: cminer@ku.edu.
Website: http://www.cpe.engr.ku.edu.

The University of Kansas, Graduate Studies, School of Engineering, Program in Chemical Engineering, Lawrence, KS 66045. Offers MS. *Faculty:* 19 full-time, 4 part-time/adjunct. *Students:* 5 full-time (0 women), 1 part-time (0 women); includes 1 minority (Two or more races, non-Hispanic/Latino), 2 international. Average age 24. 27 applicants, 26% accepted, 1 enrolled. In 2014, 1 master's awarded. *Unit head:* Laurence Weatherley, Chair, 785-864-3553, E-mail: lweather@ku.edu. *Application contact:* Carol Miner, Graduate Admissions Contact, 785-864-4965, E-mail: cminer@ku.edu.
Website: http://www.cpe.engr.ku.edu/.

University of Kentucky, Graduate School, College of Engineering, Program in Chemical Engineering, Lexington, KY 40506-0032. Offers MS, PhD. *Degree requirements:* For master's, comprehensive exam, thesis optional; for doctorate, comprehensive exam, thesis/dissertation. *Entrance requirements:* For master's, GRE General Test, minimum undergraduate GPA of 2.75; for doctorate, GRE General Test, minimum undergraduate GPA of 3.0. Additional exam requirements/recommendations for international students: Required—TOEFL (minimum score 550 paper-based). Electronic applications accepted. *Faculty research:* Aerosol physics and chemistry, biocellular engineering fuel science, poly and membrane science.

University of Louisiana at Lafayette, College of Engineering, Department of Chemical Engineering, Lafayette, LA 70504. Offers MSE. Evening/weekend programs available. *Degree requirements:* For master's, comprehensive exam, thesis or alternative. *Entrance requirements:* For master's, GRE General Test, BS in chemical engineering, minimum GPA of 2.85. Additional exam requirements/recommendations for international students: Required—TOEFL (minimum score 550 paper-based). Electronic applications accepted. *Faculty research:* Corrosion, transport phenomena and thermodynamics in the oil and gas industry.

University of Louisville, J. B. Speed School of Engineering, Department of Chemical Engineering, Louisville, KY 40292-0001. Offers M Eng, MS, PhD. *Accreditation:* ABET (one or more programs are accredited). Part-time programs available. Postbaccalaureate distance learning degree programs offered (no on-campus study). *Students:* 36 full-time (8 women), 7 part-time (0 women); includes 6 minority (1 Black or African American, non-Hispanic/Latino; 2 Hispanic/Latino; 3 Two or more races, non-Hispanic/Latino), 13 international. Average age 26. 16 applicants, 69% accepted, 3 enrolled. In 2014, 13 master's, 1 doctorate awarded. Terminal master's awarded for partial completion of doctoral program. *Degree requirements:* For master's, comprehensive exam (for some programs), thesis optional, minimum GPA of 3.0; for doctorate, comprehensive exam, thesis/dissertation, minimum GPA of 3.0. *Entrance requirements:* For master's and doctorate, GRE, letters of recommendation, final official transcripts. Additional exam requirements/recommendations for international students: Required—PTE (minimum score 550), TOEFL (minimum score 80 iBT) or IELTS. *Application deadline:* For fall admission, 6/15 for domestic students, 5/1 priority date for international students; for spring admission, 11/22 for domestic students, 11/1 priority date for international students; for summer admission, 3/31 for domestic students, 4/1 priority date for international students. Application fee: $60. Electronic applications accepted. *Expenses:* Tuition, state resident: full-time $11,326; part-time $630 per credit hour. Tuition, nonresident: full-time $23,568; part-time $1311 per credit hour. *Required fees:* $196. Tuition and fees vary according to program and reciprocity agreements. *Financial support:* Fellowships with full tuition reimbursements, research assistantships with full tuition reimbursements, and teaching assistantships with full tuition reimbursements available. Financial award application deadline: 2/3. *Faculty research:* Mixing in chemical and biochemical systems; nanomaterials processing; nanoparticles; surface science; materials including polymers, thin films, and rapid prototyping. *Total annual research expenditures:* $1.4 million. *Unit head:* Dr. James C. Waters, Chair, 502-852-0802, Fax: 502-852-6355, E-mail: jcwatt01@louisville.edu. *Application contact:* Dr. Michael Harris, Director of Academic Programs, J. B. Speed School of Engineering, 502-852-6278, Fax: 502-852-7294, E-mail: mharris@louisville.edu.
Website: http://louisville.edu/speed/chemical/.

University of Maine, Graduate School, College of Engineering, Department of Chemical and Biological Engineering, Orono, ME 04469. Offers chemical engineering (MS, PhD). Part-time programs available. *Faculty:* 10 full-time (0 women). *Students:* 26 full-time (12 women), 7 part-time (3 women); includes 4 minority (1 Black or African American, non-Hispanic/Latino; 2 Asian, non-Hispanic/Latino; 1 Native Hawaiian or other Pacific Islander, non-Hispanic/Latino), 10 international. Average age 33. 30 applicants, 50% accepted, 4 enrolled. In 2014, 1 master's awarded. Terminal master's awarded for partial completion of doctoral program. *Degree requirements:* For master's, thesis; for doctorate, comprehensive exam, thesis/dissertation. *Entrance requirements:* For master's and doctorate, GRE General Test. Additional exam requirements/recommendations for international students: Required—TOEFL. *Application deadline:* For fall admission, 6/1 priority date for domestic students. Applications are processed on a rolling basis. Application fee: $65. Electronic applications accepted. *Expenses:* Tuition, state resident: part-time $658 per credit hour. Tuition, nonresident: part-time $1550 per credit hour. *Financial support:* In 2014–15, 16 students received support, including 9 research assistantships with full tuition reimbursements available (averaging $14,600 per year), 1 teaching assistantship (averaging $14,600 per year); Federal Work-Study and tuition waivers (full and partial) also available. Financial award application deadline: 3/1. *Faculty research:* Biomass conservation, nanoparticles, microscopy and spectroscopy, paper coating, transport phenomena, process modeling, polymer science and engineering, material characterization, unit operations in pulp and paper. *Total annual research expenditures:* $608,977. *Unit head:* Dr. Hemant Pendse, Chair, 207-581-2290, Fax: 207-581-2323, E-mail: pendse@maine.edu. *Application contact:* Scott G. Delcourt, Assistant Vice President for Graduate Studies and Senior Associate Dean, 207-581-3291, Fax: 207-581-3232, E-mail: graduate@maine.edu.
Website: http://www.umche.maine.edu/chb/.

The University of Manchester, School of Chemical Engineering and Analytical Science, Manchester, United Kingdom. Offers biocatalysis (M Phil, PhD); chemical engineering (M Phil, PhD); chemical engineering and analytical science (M Phil, D Eng, PhD); colloids, crystals, interfaces and materials (M Phil, PhD); environment and sustainable technology (M Phil, PhD); instrumentation (M Phil, PhD); multi-scale modeling (M Phil, PhD); process integration (M Phil, PhD); systems biology (M Phil, PhD).

University of Maryland, Baltimore County, The Graduate School, College of Engineering and Information Technology, Department of Chemical, Biochemical, and Environmental Engineering, Program in Chemical and Biochemical Engineering, Baltimore, MD 21250. Offers MS, PhD. Part-time programs available. *Students:* 17 full-time (10 women), 5 part-time (2 women); includes 6 minority (3 Black or African American, non-Hispanic/Latino; 2 Asian, non-Hispanic/Latino; 1 Native Hawaiian or other Pacific Islander, non-Hispanic/Latino), 7 international. Average age 27. 41 applicants, 15% accepted, 3 enrolled. In 2014, 4 master's, 3 doctorates awarded. *Degree requirements:* For master's, comprehensive exam (for some programs), thesis (for some programs); for doctorate, comprehensive exam, thesis/dissertation. *Entrance requirements:* For master's, GRE General Test, minimum GPA of 3.0, strong mathematical background; for doctorate, GRE General Test (within last 5 years), minimum GPA of 3.0. Additional exam requirements/recommendations for international students: Required—TOEFL (minimum score 550 paper-based; 80 iBT). *Application deadline:* For fall admission, 6/1 for domestic students, 1/1 for international students; for spring admission, 11/1 for domestic students, 6/1 for international students. Applications are processed on a rolling basis. Application fee: $70. Electronic applications accepted. Application fee is waived when completed online. *Expenses:* Tuition, state resident: part-time $557. Tuition, nonresident: part-time $922. *Required fees:* $122 per semester. One-time fee: $200 part-time. *Financial support:* In 2014–15, 3 students received support, including 1 fellowship with full tuition reimbursement available (averaging $25,000 per year), 9 research assistantships with full tuition reimbursements available (averaging $23,000 per year), 6 teaching assistantships with full tuition reimbursements available (averaging $17,000 per year); career-related internships or fieldwork, Federal Work-Study, scholarships/grants, health care benefits, tuition waivers (partial), and unspecified assistantships also available. Support available to part-time students. Financial award application deadline: 6/30; financial award applicants required to submit FAFSA. *Faculty research:* Biomaterials engineering, bioprocess engineering, cellular engineering, education, education and outreach, sensors and monitoring, systems biology and functional genomics. *Unit head:* Dr. Brian E. Reed, Professor and Chair, 410-455-3400, Fax: 410-455-1049, E-mail: reedb@umbc.edu. *Application contact:* Dr. Mariajose Castellanos, Lecturer/Graduate Program Director, 410-455-8151, Fax: 410-455-1049, E-mail: mariajose@umbc.edu.
Website: http://www.umbc.edu/engineering/cbe/.

University of Maryland, College Park, Academic Affairs, A. James Clark School of Engineering, Department of Chemical and Biomolecular Engineering, College Park, MD 20742. Offers bioengineering (MS, PhD); chemical engineering (M Eng, MS, PhD). Part-time and evening/weekend programs available. *Degree requirements:* For master's, thesis optional; for doctorate, variable foreign language requirement, thesis/dissertation, exam, oral presentation. *Entrance requirements:* For master's and doctorate, GRE General Test, 3 letters of recommendation. Additional exam requirements/recommendations for international students: Required—TOEFL. Electronic applications accepted. *Faculty research:* Applied polymer science, biochemical engineering, thermal properties, bioprocess monitoring.

University of Massachusetts Amherst, Graduate School, College of Engineering, Department of Chemical Engineering, Amherst, MA 01003. Offers MSChE, PhD. Part-time programs available. *Faculty:* 25 full-time (6 women). *Students:* 60 full-time (20 women), 3 part-time (2 women); includes 6 minority (3 Asian, non-Hispanic/Latino; 1 Hispanic/Latino; 2 Two or more races, non-Hispanic/Latino), 38 international. Average age 26. 288 applicants, 15% accepted, 19 enrolled. In 2014, 1 master's, 8 doctorates awarded. Terminal master's awarded for partial completion of doctoral program. *Degree requirements:* For master's, thesis; for doctorate, comprehensive exam, thesis/

dissertation. *Entrance requirements:* For master's and doctorate, GRE General Test. Additional exam requirements/recommendations for international students: Required— TOEFL (minimum score 550 paper-based; 80 iBT), IELTS (minimum score 6.5). *Application deadline:* For fall admission, 1/15 for domestic and international students. Applications are processed on a rolling basis. Application fee: $75. Electronic applications accepted. *Expenses:* Tuition, state resident: full-time $1980; part-time $110 per credit. Tuition, nonresident: full-time $14,644; part-time $414 per credit. *Required fees:* $11,417. One-time fee: $357. *Financial support:* Fellowships with full and partial tuition reimbursements, research assistantships with full and partial tuition reimbursements, teaching assistantships with full and partial tuition reimbursements, career-related internships or fieldwork, Federal Work-Study, scholarships/grants, traineeships, health care benefits, tuition waivers (full and partial), and unspecified assistantships available. Support available to part-time students. Financial award application deadline: 1/15. *Unit head:* Dr. Neil Forbes, Graduate Program Director, 413-577-6164, Fax: 413-545-1647. *Application contact:* Lindsay DeSantis, Supervisor of Admissions, 413-545-0722, Fax: 413-577-0010, E-mail: gradadm@grad.umass.edu. Website: http://che.umass.edu/.

University of Massachusetts Lowell, Francis College of Engineering, Department of Chemical Engineering, Lowell, MA 01854. Offers MS Eng, D Eng, PhD. Part-time programs available. *Degree requirements:* For master's, thesis; for doctorate, thesis/dissertation, seminar, qualifying examination. *Entrance requirements:* For master's, GRE General Test. Electronic applications accepted. *Faculty research:* Biotechnology/bioprocessing, nanomaterials, ceramic materials, materials characterization.

University of Michigan, College of Engineering, Department of Chemical Engineering, Ann Arbor, MI 48109. Offers MSE, PhD, Ch E. Part-time programs available. Postbaccalaureate distance learning degree programs offered (no on-campus study). *Students:* 145 full-time (49 women), 3 part-time (2 women). 466 applicants, 30% accepted, 48 enrolled. In 2014, 31 master's, 17 doctorates awarded. Terminal master's awarded for partial completion of doctoral program. *Degree requirements:* For doctorate, thesis/dissertation, oral defense of dissertation, preliminary exams. *Entrance requirements:* For master's and doctorate, GRE General Test. Additional exam requirements/recommendations for international students: Required—TOEFL (minimum score 600 paper-based). *Application deadline:* Applications are processed on a rolling basis. Electronic applications accepted. *Financial support:* Fellowships, research assistantships, teaching assistantships, scholarships/grants, traineeships, health care benefits, tuition waivers (partial), and unspecified assistantships available. Financial award applicants required to submit FAFSA. *Faculty research:* Life sciences and biotechnology, energy and environment, complex fluids and nanostructured materials. *Total annual research expenditures:* $11.9 million. *Unit head:* Mark Burns, Department Chair, 734-764-1516, E-mail: maburns@umich.edu. *Application contact:* Sue Hamlin, Graduate Program Coordinator, 734-763-1148, Fax: 734-764-7453, E-mail: hamlins@umich.edu.
Website: http://www.engin.umich.edu/che.

University of Minnesota, Twin Cities Campus, College of Science and Engineering, Department of Chemical Engineering and Materials Science, Program in Chemical Engineering, Minneapolis, MN 55455-0132. Offers M Ch E, MS Ch E, PhD. Part-time programs available. Terminal master's awarded for partial completion of doctoral program. *Degree requirements:* For master's, thesis; for doctorate, thesis/dissertation. *Entrance requirements:* For master's and doctorate, GRE General Test. Additional exam requirements/recommendations for international students: Required—TOEFL. Electronic applications accepted. *Faculty research:* Biotechnology and bioengineering, chemical kinetics, reaction engineering and chemical process synthesis.

University of Missouri, Office of Research and Graduate Studies, College of Engineering, Department of Chemical Engineering, Columbia, MO 65211. Offers MS, PhD. *Faculty:* 9 full-time (1 woman), 1 part-time/adjunct (0 women). *Students:* 21 full-time (8 women), 10 part-time (3 women), 27 international. Average age 26. 122 applicants, 21% accepted, 20 enrolled. In 2014, 9 master's, 1 doctorate awarded. *Degree requirements:* For master's, thesis; for doctorate, thesis/dissertation. *Entrance requirements:* For master's and doctorate, GRE General Test, minimum GPA of 3.0. Additional exam requirements/recommendations for international students: Required— TOEFL (minimum score 550 paper-based; 80 iBT). *Application deadline:* For fall admission, 3/15 for domestic and international students; for winter admission, 10/15 for domestic and international students. Applications are processed on a rolling basis. Application fee: $55 ($75 for international students). Electronic applications accepted. *Financial support:* Fellowships, research assistantships, teaching assistantships, institutionally sponsored loans, scholarships/grants, traineeships, health care benefits, and unspecified assistantships available. Support available to part-time students. *Faculty research:* Batteries, biochemical engineering, biomaterials, carbon, ceramics, catalysis, corrosion, electrochemistry, environmental sciences, ionic liquids, materials science, computational modeling and simulation, nanomaterials, nuclear materials, polymers, separations, solar energy, surface science. *Unit head:* Dr. Baolin Deng, Department Chair, 573-884-7414, E-mail: dengb@missouri.edu. *Application contact:* Ryan Johnson, Administrative Assistant, 573-882-3563, E-mail: johnsonryan@missouri.edu.
Website: http://engineering.missouri.edu/chemical/.

University of Nebraska–Lincoln, Graduate College, College of Engineering, Department of Chemical and Biomolecular Engineering, Lincoln, NE 68588. Offers MS, PhD. *Degree requirements:* For master's, thesis; for doctorate, comprehensive exam, thesis/dissertation. *Entrance requirements:* For master's and doctorate, GRE. Additional exam requirements/recommendations for international students: Required—TOEFL (minimum score 550 paper-based). Electronic applications accepted. *Faculty research:* Fermentation, radioactive waste remediation, chemical fuels from renewable feedstocks.

University of Nevada, Reno, Graduate School, College of Engineering, Department of Chemical and Materials Engineering, Program in Chemical Engineering, Reno, NV 89557. Offers MS, PhD. Terminal master's awarded for partial completion of doctoral program. *Degree requirements:* For master's, comprehensive exam, thesis optional; for doctorate, thesis/dissertation. *Entrance requirements:* For master's, GRE General Test, minimum GPA of 2.75; for doctorate, GRE General Test, minimum GPA of 3.0. Additional exam requirements/recommendations for international students: Required— TOEFL (minimum score 500 paper-based; 61 iBT), IELTS (minimum score 6). Electronic applications accepted. *Faculty research:* Energy conservation, fuel efficiency, development and fabrication of new materials.

University of New Brunswick Fredericton, School of Graduate Studies, Faculty of Engineering, Department of Chemical Engineering, Fredericton, NB E3B 5A3, Canada. Offers chemical engineering (M Eng, M Sc E, PhD); environmental studies (M Eng). Part-time programs available. *Faculty:* 14 full-time (3 women). *Students:* 50 full-time (15 women), 9 part-time (3 women). In 2014, 14 master's, 5 doctorates awarded. *Degree requirements:* For master's, thesis; for doctorate, comprehensive exam, thesis/dissertation, qualifying exam. *Entrance requirements:* For master's and doctorate, minimum GPA of 3.0. Additional exam requirements/recommendations for international students: Required—TOEFL (minimum score 580 paper-based), TWE (minimum score

5), Michigan English Language Assessment Battery (minimum score 85) or CanTest (minimum score 4.5). *Application deadline:* For fall admission, 3/1 for domestic students. Applications are processed on a rolling basis. Application fee: $50 Canadian dollars. Electronic applications accepted. *Financial support:* In 2014–15, 65 fellowships, 65 research assistantships with tuition reimbursements, 47 teaching assistantships were awarded. *Faculty research:* Processing and characterizing nanoengineered composite materials based on carbon nanotubes, enhanced oil recovery processes and oil sweep strategies for conventional and heavy oils, pulp and paper, waste-water treatment, chemistry and corrosion of high and lower temperature water systems, adsorption, aquaculture systems, bioprocessing and biomass refining, nanotechnologies, nuclear, oil and gas, polymer and recirculation. *Unit head:* Dr. Ying Zheng, Director of Graduate Studies, 506-447-3329, Fax: 506-453-3591, E-mail: yzheng@unb.ca. *Application contact:* Sylvia Demerson, Graduate Secretary, 506-453-4520, Fax: 506-453-3591, E-mail: sdemerso@unb.ca.
Website: http://go.unb.ca/gradprograms.

University of New Hampshire, Graduate School, College of Engineering and Physical Sciences, Department of Chemical Engineering, Durham, NH 03824. Offers M Engr, MS, PhD. *Faculty:* 7 full-time (1 woman). *Students:* 8 full-time (3 women), 12 part-time (5 women); includes 1 minority (Asian, non-Hispanic/Latino), 11 international. Average age 25. 33 applicants, 36% accepted, 7 enrolled. In 2014, 5 master's, 1 doctorate awarded. *Degree requirements:* For master's, thesis; for doctorate, thesis/dissertation. *Entrance requirements:* For master's and doctorate, GRE. Additional exam requirements/recommendations for international students: Required—TOEFL (minimum score 550 paper-based). *Application deadline:* For fall admission, 6/1 priority date for domestic students, 4/1 for international students; for spring admission, 12/1 for domestic students. Applications are processed on a rolling basis. Application fee: $65. Electronic applications accepted. *Expenses:* Tuition, state resident: full-time $13,500; part-time $750 per credit hour. Tuition, nonresident: full-time $26,460; part-time $1110 per credit hour. *Required fees:* $1788; $447 per semester. *Financial support:* In 2014–15, 12 students received support, including 3 research assistantships, 8 teaching assistantships; fellowships, Federal Work-Study, scholarships/grants, and tuition waivers (full and partial) also available. Support available to part-time students. Financial award application deadline: 2/15. *Unit head:* Dr. Russell Carr, Chairperson, 603-862-1429. *Application contact:* Jennie Allen, Administrative Assistant, 603-862-3654, E-mail: chemeng.grad@unh.edu.
Website: http://www.unh.edu/chemical-engineering/.

University of New Mexico, Graduate School, School of Engineering, Program in Chemical Engineering, Albuquerque, NM 87131-2039. Offers MS, PhD. Part-time programs available. *Faculty:* 5 full-time (0 women), 1 part-time/adjunct (0 women). *Students:* 4 full-time (2 women), 3 part-time (1 woman); includes 4 minority (all Hispanic/Latino). Average age 26. 10 applicants. In 2014, 6 master's, 7 doctorates awarded. Terminal master's awarded for partial completion of doctoral program. *Degree requirements:* For master's, thesis (for some programs); for doctorate, comprehensive exam, thesis/dissertation, qualifying exam. *Entrance requirements:* For master's, GRE General Test, minimum GPA of 3.0, 3 letters of reference, letter of intent; for doctorate, GRE General Test, 3 letters of reference, minimum GPA of 3.0, letter of intent. Additional exam requirements/recommendations for international students: Required— TOEFL. *Application deadline:* For fall admission, 1/15 priority date for domestic and international students; for spring admission, 7/15 priority date for domestic and international students. Application fee: $50. Electronic applications accepted. *Financial support:* In 2014–15, 1 fellowship (averaging $19,909 per year), 30 research assistantships with full tuition reimbursements (averaging $21,900 per year) were awarded; scholarships/grants, traineeships, and health care benefits also available. Financial award application deadline: 1/15; financial award applicants required to submit FAFSA. *Faculty research:* Bioanalytical systems, ceramics, catalysis, colloidal science, bioengineering, biomaterials, fuel cells, protein engineering, semiconductors, tissue engineering. *Total annual research expenditures:* $7.8 million. *Unit head:* Dr. Timothy Ward, Chair, 505-277-5431, Fax: 505-277-5433, E-mail: tward@unm.edu. *Application contact:* Jocelyn White, Coordinator/Program Advisor, 505-277-5606, Fax: 505-277-5433, E-mail: jowhite@unm.edu.
Website: http://www.chne.unm.edu/chemicalgraduate.html.

University of North Dakota, Graduate School, School of Engineering and Mines, Department of Chemical Engineering, Grand Forks, ND 58202. Offers M Engr, MS. Part-time programs available. *Degree requirements:* For master's, comprehensive exam, thesis or alternative. *Entrance requirements:* For master's, GRE General Test, minimum GPA of 3.0 (MS), 2.5 (M Engr). Additional exam requirements/recommendations for international students: Required—TOEFL (minimum score 550 paper-based; 79 iBT), IELTS (minimum score 6.5). Electronic applications accepted. *Faculty research:* Catalysis, fluid flow and heat transfer, application of fractals, modeling and simulation, reaction engineering.

University of Notre Dame, Graduate School, College of Engineering, Department of Chemical and Biomolecular Engineering, Notre Dame, IN 46556. Offers MS Ch E, PhD. *Degree requirements:* For master's, comprehensive exam, thesis; for doctorate, comprehensive exam, thesis/dissertation, candidacy exam. *Entrance requirements:* For master's, GRE General Test; for doctorate, GRE General Test, GRE Subject Test (strongly recommended). Additional exam requirements/recommendations for international students: Required—TOEFL (minimum score 600 paper-based; 80 iBT). Electronic applications accepted. *Faculty research:* Biomolecular engineering, green chemistry and engineering for the environment, advanced materials, nanoengineering, catalysis and reaction engineering.

University of Oklahoma, Gallogly College of Engineering, School of Chemical, Biological and Materials Engineering, Norman, OK 73019. Offers chemical engineering (MS, PhD). *Faculty:* 16 full-time (1 woman), 1 part-time/adjunct (0 women). *Students:* 44 full-time (12 women), 10 part-time (4 women); includes 3 minority (1 Black or African American, non-Hispanic/Latino; 1 American Indian or Alaska Native, non-Hispanic/Latino; 1 Two or more races, non-Hispanic/Latino), 30 international. Average age 26. 64 applicants, 17% accepted, 11 enrolled. In 2014, 5 master's, 5 doctorates awarded. Terminal master's awarded for partial completion of doctoral program. *Degree requirements:* For master's, comprehensive exam, thesis, oral defense of thesis; for doctorate, comprehensive exam, thesis/dissertation, oral defense of dissertation. *Entrance requirements:* Additional exam requirements/recommendations for international students: Required—TOEFL (minimum score 79 iBT), IELTS. *Application deadline:* For fall admission, 4/1 for domestic and international students; for winter admission, 10/1 for international students; for spring admission, 11/1 for domestic students, 10/1 for international students. Applications are processed on a rolling basis. Application fee: $50 ($100 for international students). Electronic applications accepted. *Expenses:* Tuition, state resident: full-time $4394; part-time $183.10 per credit hour. Tuition, nonresident: full-time $16,970; part-time $707.10 per credit hour. *Required fees:* $2892; $109.95 per credit hour. $126.50 per semester. *Financial support:* In 2014–15, 50 students received support, including 1 fellowship with full tuition reimbursement available (averaging $2,500 per year), 48 research assistantships with partial tuition reimbursements available (averaging $17,419 per year), 3 teaching assistantships with partial tuition reimbursements available (averaging $25,457 per year); career-related

internships or fieldwork and assistantships (with tuition waivers and health insurance) also available. Financial award application deadline: 6/1; financial award applicants required to submit FAFSA. *Faculty research:* Applied surfactant technologies, biofuels and bio-refining, biomedical and biochemical engineering, catalysis and surface characterization, nanomaterials, polymer processing and characterization. *Total annual research expenditures:* $4.4 million. *Unit head:* Dr. Brian Grady, Director, 405-325-5814, Fax: 405-325-5813, E-mail: cbme@ou.edu. *Application contact:* Dr. M. Ulli Nollert, Graduate Program Coordinator and Associate Professor, 405-325-4366, Fax: 405-325-5813, E-mail: nollert@ou.edu.
Website: http://www.ou.edu/content/coe/cbme.html.

University of Ottawa, Faculty of Graduate and Postdoctoral Studies, Faculty of Engineering, Department of Chemical and Biological Engineering, Ottawa, ON K1N 6N5, Canada. Offers M Eng, MA Sc, PhD. *Degree requirements:* For master's, thesis or alternative; for doctorate, comprehensive exam, thesis/dissertation. *Entrance requirements:* For master's, honors degree or equivalent, minimum B average; for doctorate, master's degree, minimum B+ average. Electronic applications accepted. *Faculty research:* Material development, process engineering, clean technologies.

University of Pennsylvania, School of Engineering and Applied Science, Department of Chemical Engineering, Philadelphia, PA 19104. Offers MSE, PhD, MSE/MBA. Part-time programs available. *Faculty:* 21 full-time (4 women), 5 part-time/adjunct (0 women). *Students:* 98 full-time (30 women), 9 part-time (3 women); includes 11 minority (all Asian, non-Hispanic/Latino), 66 international. 471 applicants, 24% accepted, 41 enrolled. In 2014, 38 master's, 10 doctorates awarded. Terminal master's awarded for partial completion of doctoral program. *Degree requirements:* For doctorate, thesis/dissertation. *Entrance requirements:* Additional exam requirements/recommendations for international students: Required—TOEFL. *Application deadline:* For fall admission, 6/1 priority date for domestic students. Applications are processed on a rolling basis. Application fee: $70. Electronic applications accepted. *Financial support:* Fellowships, research assistantships, teaching assistantships, institutionally sponsored loans, scholarships/grants, traineeships, health care benefits, and unspecified assistantships available. *Faculty research:* Biochemical engineering, surface and interfacial phenomena, process and design control, zeolites, molecular dynamics. *Unit head:* Eduardo D. Glandt, Dean, 215-898-7244, E-mail: seasdean@seas.upenn.edu. *Application contact:* School of Engineering and Applied Science Graduate Admissions, 215-898-4542, E-mail: gradstudies@seas.upenn.edu.
Website: http://www.cbe.seas.upenn.edu/.

University of Pittsburgh, Swanson School of Engineering, Department of Chemical and Petroleum Engineering, Pittsburgh, PA 15260. Offers petroleum engineering (MSPE); MS Ch E/MSPE. Part-time programs available. Postbaccalaureate distance learning degree programs offered. *Faculty:* 21 full-time (4 women), 28 part-time/adjunct (2 women). *Students:* 84 full-time (25 women), 7 part-time (0 women); includes 11 minority (3 Black or African American, non-Hispanic/Latino; 4 Asian, non-Hispanic/Latino; 1 Hispanic/Latino; 3 Two or more races, non-Hispanic/Latino), 51 international. 337 applicants, 38% accepted, 41 enrolled. In 2014, 9 master's, 5 doctorates awarded. *Degree requirements:* For master's, thesis; for doctorate, comprehensive exam, thesis/dissertation, final oral exams. *Entrance requirements:* For master's and doctorate, GRE General Test, minimum GPA of 3.0. Additional exam requirements/recommendations for international students: Required—TOEFL (minimum score 550 paper-based; 80 iBT). *Application deadline:* For fall admission, 3/1 priority date for domestic and international students; for spring admission, 7/1 priority date for domestic and international students. Applications are processed on a rolling basis. Application fee: $50. Electronic applications accepted. *Expenses:* Tuition, state resident: full-time $20,742; part-time $838 per credit. Tuition, nonresident: full-time $33,960; part-time $1389 per credit. *Required fees:* $800; $205 per term. Tuition and fees vary according to program. *Financial support:* In 2014–15, 52 students received support, including 6 fellowships with full tuition reimbursements available (averaging $29,376 per year), 21 research assistantships with full tuition reimbursements available (averaging $27,000 per year), 25 teaching assistantships with full tuition reimbursements available (averaging $26,004 per year); scholarships/grants, traineeships, and tuition waivers (full and partial) also available. Financial award application deadline: 4/15. *Faculty research:* Biotechnology, polymers, catalysis, energy and environment, computational modeling. *Total annual research expenditures:* $8.6 million. *Unit head:* Dr. Steven R. Little, Chairman, 412-624-9614, Fax: 412-624-9639, E-mail: srlittle@pitt.edu. *Application contact:* Dr. Joseph John McCarthy, Professor/Graduate Coordinator, 412-624-7362, Fax: 412-624-9639, E-mail: jjmcc@pitt.edu.
Website: http://www.engineering.pitt.edu/Chemical/.

University of Puerto Rico, Mayagüez Campus, Graduate Studies, College of Engineering, Department of Chemical Engineering, Mayagüez, PR 00681-9000. Offers ME, MS, PhD. Part-time programs available. *Faculty:* 21 full-time (6 women), 1 (woman) part-time/adjunct. *Students:* 42 full-time (20 women). 12 applicants, 50% accepted, 3 enrolled. In 2014, 3 master's, 6 doctorates awarded. *Degree requirements:* For master's, comprehensive exam, thesis; for doctorate, comprehensive exam, thesis/dissertation. *Entrance requirements:* For master's, BS in chemical engineering or its equivalent. Additional exam requirements/recommendations for international students: Required—TOEFL. *Application deadline:* For fall admission, 2/15 for domestic and international students; for spring admission, 9/15 for domestic and international students. Applications are processed on a rolling basis. Application fee: $25. *Expenses: Tuition, area resident:* Full-time $2466; part-time $822 per credit. *International tuition:* $6371 full-time. *Required fees:* $1095; $1095 per year. Tuition and fees vary according to course level, course load and reciprocity agreements. *Financial support:* In 2014–15, 37 students received support, including 31 research assistantships (averaging $12,514 per year), 16 teaching assistantships (averaging $4,318 per year); fellowships with full tuition reimbursements available, Federal Work-Study, institutionally sponsored loans, and unspecified assistantships also available. *Faculty research:* Process simulation and optimization, air and water pollution control, mass transport, biochemical engineering. *Unit head:* Dr. Aldo Acevedo, Chairperson, 787-832-4040 Ext. 2587, Fax: 787-834-3655, E-mail: aldo.acevedo@upr.edu. *Application contact:* Dr. Arturo Hernandez, Graduate Coordinator, 787-832-4040 Ext. 3748, Fax: 787-834-3655, E-mail: arturoj.hernandez@upr.edu.
Website: http://atomo.uprm.edu.

University of Rhode Island, Graduate School, College of Engineering, Department of Chemical Engineering, Kingston, RI 02881. Offers MS, PhD. Part-time programs available. *Faculty:* 8 full-time (2 women). *Students:* 19 full-time (7 women), 6 part-time (1 woman), 15 international. In 2014, 4 master's, 1 doctorate awarded. *Degree requirements:* For master's, comprehensive exam (for some programs), thesis optional; for doctorate, comprehensive exam, thesis/dissertation. *Entrance requirements:* For master's and doctorate, 3 letters of recommendation. Additional exam requirements/recommendations for international students: Required—TOEFL (minimum score 550 paper-based). *Application deadline:* For fall admission, 1/15 for domestic and international students; for spring admission, 7/15 for domestic and international students. Application fee: $65. Electronic applications accepted. *Expenses:* Tuition, state resident: full-time $11,532; part-time $641 per credit. Tuition, nonresident: full-time $23,606; part-time $1311 per credit. *Required fees:* $1442; $39 per credit. $35 per semester. One-time fee: $155. *Financial support:* In 2014–15, 5 research assistantships with full and partial tuition reimbursements (averaging $8,173 per year), 2 teaching assistantships with full and partial tuition reimbursements (averaging $8,150 per year) were awarded. Financial award application deadline: 1/15; financial award applicants required to submit FAFSA. *Faculty research:* Photobioreactors, colloidal and interfacial engineering, biomembrane thermodynamics and transport, degradation of materials, closed loop recycling systems. *Total annual research expenditures:* $1.4 million. *Unit head:* Dr. Richard Brown, Chair, 401-874-2707, Fax: 401-874-4689, E-mail: david_h_brown@mail.uri.edu. *Application contact:* Graduate Admission, 401-874-2872, E-mail: gradadm@etal.uri.edu.
Website: http://egr.uri.edu/che/.

University of Rochester, Hajim School of Engineering and Applied Sciences, Master of Science in Technical Entrepreneurship and Management Program, Rochester, NY 14642. Offers biomedical engineering (MS); chemical engineering (MS); computer science (MS); electrical and computer engineering (MS); energy and the environment (MS); materials science (MS); mechanical engineering (MS); optics (MS). Program offered in collaboration with the Simon School of Business. Part-time programs available. *Students:* 36 full-time (12 women), 7 part-time (1 woman); includes 3 minority (2 Hispanic/Latino; 1 Two or more races, non-Hispanic/Latino), 33 international. Average age 24. 152 applicants, 68% accepted, 27 enrolled. In 2014, 28 master's awarded. *Degree requirements:* For master's, comprehensive exam. *Entrance requirements:* For master's, GRE or GMAT, 3 letters of recommendation; personal statement; official transcript; bachelor's degree (or equivalent for international students) in engineering, science, or mathematics. Additional exam requirements/recommendations for international students: Required—TOEFL or IELTS. *Application deadline:* For fall admission, 2/1 for domestic and international students. Applications are processed on a rolling basis. Application fee: $60. Electronic applications accepted. *Expenses: Tuition:* Full-time $46,150; part-time $1442 per credit hour. *Required fees:* $504. *Financial support:* Career-related internships or fieldwork and scholarships/grants available. Financial award application deadline: 2/1. *Faculty research:* High efficiency solar cells, macromolecular self-assembly, digital signal processing, memory hierarchy management, molecular and physical mechanisms in cell migration, optical imaging systems. *Unit head:* Duncan T. Moore, Vice Provost for Entrepreneurship, 585-275-5248, Fax: 585-473-6745, E-mail: moore@optics.rochester.edu. *Application contact:* Andrea M. Galati, Executive Director, 585-276-3407, Fax: 585-276-2357, E-mail: andrea.galati@rochester.edu.
Website: http://www.rochester.edu/team.

★ **University of Rochester,** Hajim School of Engineering and Applied Sciences, Program in Chemical Engineering, Rochester, NY 14627. Offers MS, PhD. Part-time programs available. *Faculty:* 11 full-time (1 woman). *Students:* 49 full-time (16 women), 1 part-time (0 women); includes 6 minority (4 Asian, non-Hispanic/Latino; 2 Hispanic/Latino), 33 international. 111 applicants, 58% accepted, 17 enrolled. In 2014, 16 master's, 4 doctorates awarded. Terminal master's awarded for partial completion of doctoral program. *Degree requirements:* For master's, comprehensive exam; for doctorate, thesis/dissertation, preliminary and oral exams. *Entrance requirements:* For master's and doctorate, GRE. Additional exam requirements/recommendations for international students: Required—TOEFL. *Application deadline:* For fall admission, 1/15 for domestic students. Application fee: $60. *Expenses: Tuition:* Full-time $46,150; part-time $1442 per credit hour. *Required fees:* $504. *Financial support:* Fellowships, research assistantships, teaching assistantships, and tuition waivers (full and partial) available. Financial award application deadline: 2/1. *Faculty research:* Advanced materials, nanotechnology, alternative energy, biotechnology, photovoltaics. *Unit head:* Matthew Yates, Chairman, 585-273-2335. *Application contact:* Gina Eagan, Graduate Program Coordinator, 585-275-4913.
Website: http://www.che.rochester.edu/graduate/index.html.

See Display on next page and Close-Up on page 167.

University of Saskatchewan, College of Graduate Studies and Research, College of Engineering, Chemical Engineering Program, Saskatoon, SK S7N 5A9, Canada. Offers M Eng, M Sc, PhD. Part-time programs available. *Degree requirements:* For master's, thesis (for some programs), 30 credits (for M Eng); thesis and 12 credits (for MS); for doctorate, comprehensive exam, thesis/dissertation, qualifying exam, 18 credits. *Entrance requirements:* For master's and doctorate, GRE. Additional exam requirements/recommendations for international students: Required—TOEFL, TOEFL (minimum iBT score of 80), IELTS (6.5), CanTEST (4.5), or PTE (59). Electronic applications accepted. *Faculty research:* Applied thermodynamics, biochemical engineering, biosorption, chemical reaction engineering and catalysis, corrosion, environmental remediation, fluidization, fuel cell and microbial fuel cell technology, mineral processing, petroleum processing, process engineering, renewable energy.

University of South Africa, College of Science, Engineering and Technology, Pretoria, South Africa. Offers chemical engineering (M Tech); information technology (M Tech).

University of South Alabama, College of Engineering, Department of Chemical Engineering, Mobile, AL 36688. Offers MS Ch E. *Faculty:* 5 full-time (1 woman). *Students:* 14 full-time (4 women), 3 part-time (all women); includes 5 minority (1 Black or African American, non-Hispanic/Latino; 1 Asian, non-Hispanic/Latino; 2 Hispanic/Latino; 1 Two or more races, non-Hispanic/Latino), 7 international. Average age 25. 35 applicants, 49% accepted, 6 enrolled. In 2014, 1 master's awarded. *Degree requirements:* For master's, comprehensive exam, project or thesis. *Entrance requirements:* For master's, GRE General Test, BS in engineering, minimum GPA of 3.0. Additional exam requirements/recommendations for international students: Required—TOEFL (minimum score 525 paper-based; 71 iBT). *Application deadline:* For fall admission, 7/15 priority date for domestic students, 6/15 priority date for international students; for spring admission, 12/1 priority date for domestic students, 11/1 priority date for international students. Applications are processed on a rolling basis. Application fee: $35. Electronic applications accepted. *Expenses:* Expenses: Contact institution. *Financial support:* Fellowships, research assistantships, teaching assistantships, career-related internships or fieldwork, Federal Work-Study, institutionally sponsored loans, scholarships/grants, and unspecified assistantships available. Support available to part-time students. Financial award application deadline: 5/31; financial award applicants required to submit FAFSA. *Faculty research:* Molecular imaging, novel catalyst synthesis, gas separation and storage, lipidic ionic liquids. *Unit head:* Dr. Srinivas Palanki, Department Chair, 251-460-6160, Fax: 251-461-1485, E-mail: spalanki@southalabama.edu. *Application contact:* Dr. Thomas G. Thomas, Jr., Graduate Studies, College of Engineering, 251-460-6140, Fax: 251-460-6343, E-mail: engineering@southalabama.edu.
Website: http://www.southalabama.edu/colleges/engineering/chbe/index.html.

University of South Carolina, The Graduate School, College of Engineering and Computing, Department of Chemical Engineering, Columbia, SC 29208. Offers ME, MS, PhD. Part-time and evening/weekend programs available. Postbaccalaureate distance learning degree programs offered (minimal on-campus study). *Degree requirements:* For master's, comprehensive exam, thesis (for some programs); for doctorate, comprehensive exam, thesis/dissertation. *Entrance requirements:* For master's and doctorate, GRE General Test. Additional exam requirements/recommendations for international students: Required—TOEFL. Electronic applications accepted. *Faculty* *research:* Rheology, liquid and supercritical extractions, electrochemistry, corrosion, heterogeneous and homogeneous catalysis.

University of Southern California, Graduate School, Viterbi School of Engineering, Mork Family Department of Chemical Engineering and Materials Science, Los Angeles, CA 90089. Offers chemical engineering (MS, PhD, Engr); geoscience technologies (MS); materials engineering (MS); materials science (MS, PhD, Engr); petroleum engineering (MS, PhD, Engr); smart oilfield technologies (MS, Graduate Certificate). Terminal master's awarded for partial completion of doctoral program. *Degree requirements:* For master's, thesis optional; for doctorate, thesis/dissertation. *Entrance requirements:* For master's and doctorate, GRE General Test. Additional exam requirements/recommendations for international students: Recommended—TOEFL. Electronic applications accepted. *Expenses:* Contact institution. *Faculty research:* Heterogeneous materials and porous media, statistical mechanics, molecular simulation, polymer science and engineering, advanced materials, reaction engineering and catalysis, membrane processes and separation, biochemical engineering, cell culture, bioreactor modeling, petroleum engineering.

University of South Florida, College of Engineering, Department of Chemical and Biomedical Engineering, Tampa, FL 33620. Offers biomedical engineering (MSBE, PhD); chemical engineering (M Ch E, MSCH, PhD); MSBE/MS; PhD/MD. Part-time programs available. *Faculty:* 15 full-time (2 women). *Students:* 90 full-time (37 women), 17 part-time (6 women); includes 27 minority (9 Black or African American, non-Hispanic/Latino; 2 Asian, non-Hispanic/Latino; 13 Hispanic/Latino; 3 Two or more races, non-Hispanic/Latino), 46 international. Average age 28. 157 applicants, 45% accepted, 33 enrolled. In 2014, 26 master's, 9 doctorates awarded. Terminal master's awarded for partial completion of doctoral program. *Degree requirements:* For master's, comprehensive exam, thesis (for some programs); for doctorate, comprehensive exam, thesis/dissertation. *Entrance requirements:* For master's, GRE General Test (minimum recommended scores of 3.0 in analytical writing and 99th percentile quantitative), undergraduate degree in engineering, science, or chemical engineering with minimum GPA of 3.0; at least two letters of recommendation; current resume; statement of research interests (for students who wish to pursue thesis option); for doctorate, GRE General Test (minimum recommended scores of 3.0 in analytical writing and 99th percentile quantitative), undergraduate degree in engineering, science, or chemical engineering with minimum GPA of 3.0; three letters of recommendation; current resume; statement of research interests. Additional exam requirements/recommendations for international students: Required—TOEFL (minimum score 550 paper-based; 79 iBT) or IELTS (minimum score 6.5). *Application deadline:* For fall admission, 2/15 for domestic students, 1/2 priority date for international students; for spring admission, 10/15 for domestic students, 6/1 priority date for international students. Application fee: $30. Electronic applications accepted. *Financial support:* In 2014–15, 41 students received support, including 29 research assistantships with tuition reimbursements available (averaging $13,171 per year), 12 teaching assistantships with tuition reimbursements available (averaging $14,017 per year); unspecified assistantships also available. Financial award applicants required to submit FAFSA. *Faculty research:* Neuroengineering, tissue engineering, biomedicine and biotechnology, engineering education, functional materials and nanotechnology, energy, environment/sustainability. *Total annual research expenditures:* $689,262. *Unit head:* Dr. Venkat R. Bhethanabotla, Professor and Department Chair, 813-974-3997, E-mail: bhethana@usf.edu. *Application contact:* Dr. Robert Frisina, Jr., Professor and Graduate Program Director, 813-974-4013, Fax: 813-974-3651, E-mail: rfrisina@usf.edu. Website: http://che.eng.usf.edu/.

University of South Florida, University College/Distance Education, Tampa, FL 33620-9951. *Unit head:* Kathy Barnes, Interdisciplinary Programs Coordinator, 813-974-8031, Fax: 813-974-7061, E-mail: barnesk@usf.edu. *Application contact:* Karen Tylinski, Metro Initiatives, 813-974-9943, Fax: 813-974-7061, E-mail: ktylinsk@usf.edu. Website: http://www.usf.edu/innovative-education/.

The University of Tennessee, Graduate School, College of Engineering, Department of Chemical and Biomolecular Engineering, Knoxville, TN 37996. Offers chemical engineering (MS, PhD); reliability and maintainability engineering (MS); MS/MBA. Part-time programs available. *Faculty:* 30 full-time (0 women). *Students:* 54 full-time (16 women), 2 part-time (0 women); includes 7 minority (1 Black or African American, non-Hispanic/Latino; 1 Asian, non-Hispanic/Latino; 2 Hispanic/Latino; 3 Two or more races, non-Hispanic/Latino), 24 international. Average age 26. 104 applicants, 29% accepted, 14 enrolled. In 2014, 11 master's, 10 doctorates awarded. *Degree requirements:* For master's, thesis or alternative; for doctorate, comprehensive exam, thesis/dissertation. *Entrance requirements:* For master's, GRE General Test (for MS students pursuing research thesis), minimum GPA of 2.7 (for U.S. degree holders), 3.0 (for international degree holders); for doctorate, GRE General Test (for all PhD candidates), minimum GPA of 3.0 on previous graduate course work. Additional exam requirements/recommendations for international students: Required—TOEFL (minimum score 550 paper-based). *Application deadline:* For fall admission, 2/1 priority date for domestic and international students; for spring admission, 6/15 for domestic and international students. Applications are processed on a rolling basis. Application fee: $35. Electronic applications accepted. *Financial support:* In 2014–15, 50 students received support, including 3 fellowships (averaging $25,333 per year), 29 research assistantships with full tuition reimbursements available (averaging $24,097 per year), 18 teaching assistantships with full tuition reimbursements available (averaging $24,033 per year); career-related internships or fieldwork, Federal Work-Study, institutionally sponsored loans, health care benefits, and unspecified assistantships also available. Financial award application deadline: 2/1; financial award applicants required to submit FAFSA. *Faculty research:* Bio-fuels; engineering of soft, functional and structural materials; fuel cells and energy storage devices; molecular and cellular bioengineering; molecular modeling and simulations. *Total annual research expenditures:* $4 million. *Unit head:* Dr. Bamin Khomami, Head, 865-974-2421, Fax: 865-974-7076, E-mail: bkhomami@utk.edu. *Application contact:* Dr. Paul Frymier, Graduate Program Coordinator, 865-974-4961, Fax: 865-974-7076, E-mail: pdf@utk.edu. Website: http://www.engr.utk.edu/cbe/.

The University of Tennessee at Chattanooga, Program in Engineering, Chattanooga, TN 37403. Offers chemical engineering (MS Engr); civil engineering (MS Engr); computational engineering (MS Engr); electrical engineering (MS Engr); industrial engineering (MS Engr); mechanical engineering (MS Engr). Part-time and evening/weekend programs available. *Faculty:* 20 full-time (3 women), 3 part-time/adjunct (0 women). *Students:* 42 full-time (7 women), 41 part-time (5 women); includes 6 minority (2 Black or African American, non-Hispanic/Latino; 1 Asian, non-Hispanic/Latino; 2 Hispanic/Latino; 1 Two or more races, non-Hispanic/Latino), 30 international. Average age 29. 96 applicants, 32% accepted, 17 enrolled. In 2014, 29 master's awarded. *Degree requirements:* For master's, comprehensive exam, thesis or alternative, engineering project. *Entrance requirements:* For master's, GRE General Test, minimum undergraduate GPA of 2.5 or 3.0 in last 30 hours of coursework. Additional exam requirements/recommendations for international students: Required—TOEFL (minimum score 550 paper-based; 79 iBT), IELTS (minimum score 6). *Application deadline:* For fall admission, 6/13 priority date for domestic students, 6/1 for international students; for spring admission, 10/15 priority date for domestic students, 10/1 for international students. Applications are processed on a rolling basis. Application fee: $30 ($35 for international students). Electronic applications accepted. *Expenses:* Tuition, state resident: full-time $7708; part-time $428 per credit hour. Tuition, nonresident: full-time $23,826; part-time $1323 per credit hour. *Required fees:* $1708; $252 per credit hour. *Financial support:* In

Chemical Engineering

2014–15, 24 research assistantships with tuition reimbursements (averaging $7,669 per year), 7 teaching assistantships with tuition reimbursements (averaging $5,735 per year) were awarded; career-related internships or fieldwork, scholarships/grants, and unspecified assistantships also available. Support available to part-time students. *Faculty research:* Quality control and reliability engineering, financial management, thermal science, energy conservation, structural analysis. *Total annual research expenditures:* $1.6 million. *Unit head:* Dr. William Sutton, Dean, 423-425-2256, Fax: 423-425-5229, E-mail: will-sutton@utc.edu. *Application contact:* Dr. J. Randy Walker, Interim Dean of Graduate Studies, 423-425-4478, Fax: 423-425-5223, E-mail: randy-walker@utc.edu.
Website: http://www.utc.edu/Departments/engrcs/ms_engr.php.

The University of Texas at Austin, Graduate School, Cockrell School of Engineering, Department of Chemical Engineering, Austin, TX 78712-1111. Offers MSE, PhD. Terminal master's awarded for partial completion of doctoral program. *Degree requirements:* For master's, thesis (for some programs); for doctorate, comprehensive exam, thesis/dissertation. *Entrance requirements:* For master's and doctorate, GRE General Test. Electronic applications accepted.

The University of Toledo, College of Graduate Studies, College of Engineering, Department of Chemical and Environmental Engineering, Toledo, OH 43606-3390. Offers chemical engineering (MS, PhD). Part-time and evening/weekend programs available. *Degree requirements:* For master's, thesis optional; for doctorate, thesis/dissertation, qualifying exam. *Entrance requirements:* For master's, GRE General Test, minimum GPA of 3.0; for doctorate, GRE General Test, minimum GPA of 3.3. Additional exam requirements/recommendations for international students: Required—TOEFL (minimum score 550 paper-based; 80 iBT). Electronic applications accepted. *Faculty research:* Polymers, applied computing, membranes, alternative energy (fuel cells).

University of Toronto, School of Graduate Studies, Faculty of Applied Science and Engineering, Department of Chemical Engineering and Applied Chemistry, Toronto, ON M5S 2J7, Canada. Offers M Eng, MA Sc, PhD. Part-time programs available. *Degree requirements:* For master's, thesis (for some programs); for doctorate, thesis/dissertation. *Entrance requirements:* For master's, minimum B+ average in final 2 years, four-year degree in engineering (M Eng, MA Sc) or physical sciences (MA Sc), 2 letters of reference; for doctorate, research master's degree, minimum B+ average, 2 letters of reference. Additional exam requirements/recommendations for international students: Required—TOEFL (minimum score 580 paper-based; 93 iBT), TWE (minimum score 4). Electronic applications accepted.

The University of Tulsa, Graduate School, College of Engineering and Natural Sciences, Department of Chemical Engineering, Tulsa, OK 74104-3189. Offers ME, MSE, PhD. Part-time programs available. *Faculty:* 9 full-time (3 women). *Students:* 13 full-time (4 women), 6 part-time (4 women), 13 international. Average age 26. 45 applicants, 51% accepted, 3 enrolled. In 2014, 8 master's, 1 doctorate awarded. Terminal master's awarded for partial completion of doctoral program. *Degree requirements:* For master's, thesis (for some programs); for doctorate, comprehensive exam, thesis/dissertation. *Entrance requirements:* For master's and doctorate, GRE General Test. Additional exam requirements/recommendations for international students: Required—TOEFL (minimum score 550 paper-based; 80 iBT), IELTS (minimum score 6). *Application deadline:* Applications are processed on a rolling basis. Application fee: $55. Electronic applications accepted. *Expenses: Tuition:* Full-time $20,160; part-time $1120 per credit hour. *Required fees:* $6 per credit hour. Tuition and fees vary according to course level and course load. *Financial support:* In 2014–15, 21 students received support, including 6 fellowships (averaging $8,863 per year), 13 research assistantships with full and partial tuition reimbursements available (averaging $10,275 per year), 9 teaching assistantships with full and partial tuition reimbursements available (averaging $9,135 per year); career-related internships or fieldwork, Federal Work-Study, scholarships/grants, health care benefits, tuition waivers (full and partial), and unspecified assistantships also available. Support available to part-time students. Financial award application deadline: 2/1; financial award applicants required to submit FAFSA. *Faculty research:* Environment, surface science, catalysis, transport phenomena, process systems engineering, bioengineering, alternative energy, petrochemical processes. *Total annual research expenditures:* $759,358. *Unit head:* Dr. Geoffrey Price, Chairperson, 918-631-2575, Fax: 918-631-3268, E-mail: chegradadvisor@utulsa.edu. *Application contact:* Dr. Selen Cremaschi, Advisor, 918-631-3422, Fax: 918-631-3268, E-mail: chegradadvisor@utulsa.edu.
Website: http://engineering.utulsa.edu/academics/chemical-engineering/.

University of Utah, Graduate School, College of Engineering, Department of Chemical Engineering, Salt Lake City, UT 84112-5820. Offers chemical engineering (MS, PhD); petroleum engineering (MS); MS/MBA. Part-time and evening/weekend programs available. Postbaccalaureate distance learning degree programs offered (minimal on-campus study). *Faculty:* 13 full-time (1 woman), 10 part-time/adjunct (1 woman). *Students:* 76 full-time (15 women), 23 part-time (2 women); includes 12 minority (4 Black or African American, non-Hispanic/Latino; 2 Asian, non-Hispanic/Latino; 5 Hispanic/Latino; 1 Native Hawaiian or other Pacific Islander, non-Hispanic/Latino), 41 international. Average age 30. 201 applicants, 30% accepted, 28 enrolled. In 2014, 6 master's, 7 doctorates awarded. *Degree requirements:* For master's, comprehensive exam, thesis (for some programs); for doctorate, comprehensive exam, thesis/dissertation. *Entrance requirements:* For master's, GRE General Test, minimum GPA of 3.0; for doctorate, GRE General Test, minimum GPA of 3.0, degree or course work in chemical engineering. Additional exam requirements/recommendations for international students: Required—TOEFL (minimum score 550 paper-based; 80 iBT), IELTS (minimum score 6.5). *Application deadline:* For fall admission, 1/15 priority date for domestic and international students; for spring admission, 10/1 priority date for domestic and international students; for summer admission, 2/1 priority date for domestic and international students. Applications are processed on a rolling basis. Application fee: $0 ($15 for international students). Electronic applications accepted. Application fee is waived when completed online. *Expenses:* Expenses: Contact institution. *Financial support:* In 2014–15, 5 fellowships with full tuition reimbursements (averaging $25,450 per year), 41 research assistantships with full tuition reimbursements (averaging $24,444 per year), 6 teaching assistantships (averaging $6,848 per year) were awarded; Federal Work-Study, institutionally sponsored loans, scholarships/grants, and unspecified assistantships also available. Financial award application deadline: 4/1; financial award applicants required to submit FAFSA. *Faculty research:* Drug delivery, fossil fuel and biomass combustion and gasification, oil and gas reservoir characteristics and management, multi-scale simulation, micro-scale synthesis. *Unit head:* Dr. Milind D. Deo, Chair, 801-581-6915, Fax: 801-585-9291, E-mail: milind.deo@utah.edu. *Application contact:* Rachelle L. Reed, Graduate Coordinator, 801-587-3610, Fax: 801-585-9291, E-mail: rachelle@chemeng.utah.edu.
Website: http://www.che.utah.edu/.

University of Virginia, School of Engineering and Applied Science, Department of Chemical Engineering, Charlottesville, VA 22903. Offers ME, MS, PhD. Postbaccalaureate distance learning degree programs offered (no on-campus study). *Faculty:* 10 full-time (1 woman). *Students:* 47 full-time (13 women); includes 4 minority (all Asian, non-Hispanic/Latino), 19 international. Average age 25. 141 applicants, 18% accepted, 14 enrolled. In 2014, 1 master's, 9 doctorates awarded. *Degree requirements:* For master's, thesis (for some programs); for doctorate, thesis/dissertation. *Entrance requirements:* For master's, GRE General Test, 3 recommendations; for doctorate, GRE General Test, 3 recommendations, essay. Additional exam requirements/recommendations for international students: Required—TOEFL (minimum score 600 paper-based; 90 iBT), IELTS (minimum score 7). *Application deadline:* For fall admission, 8/1 for domestic students, 4/1 for international students; for winter admission, 12/1 for domestic students, 8/1 for international students; for spring admission, 5/1 for domestic students, 1/1 for international students. Applications are processed on a rolling basis. Application fee: $60. Electronic applications accepted. *Expenses:* Tuition, state resident: full-time $14,164; part-time $349 per credit hour. Tuition, nonresident: full-time $23,722; part-time $1300 per credit hour. *Required fees:* $2514. *Financial support:* Fellowships, research assistantships, and teaching assistantships available. Financial award application deadline: 1/15; financial award applicants required to submit FAFSA. *Faculty research:* Fluid mechanics, heat and mass transfer, chemical reactor analysis and engineering, biochemical engineering and biotechnology. *Unit head:* Roseanne Ford, Chair, 434-924-7778, Fax: 434-982-2658, E-mail: rmf3f@virginia.edu. *Application contact:* David Green, Graduate Admissions Coordinator, 434-924-7778, Fax: 434-982-2658, E-mail: dlg9s@virginia.edu.
Website: http://www.che.virginia.edu/.

University of Washington, Graduate School, College of Engineering, Department of Chemical Engineering, Seattle, WA 98195-1750. Offers chemical engineering (MS, MSE, PhD); chemical engineering and nanotechnology (PhD). *Faculty:* 21 full-time (3 women). *Students:* 97 full-time (25 women). Average age 25. 258 applicants, 31% accepted, 35 enrolled. In 2014, 15 master's, 19 doctorates awarded. Terminal master's awarded for partial completion of doctoral program. *Degree requirements:* For master's, thesis, final exam, research project, degree requirements must be completed in 6 years; for doctorate, thesis/dissertation, general and final exams, research project, completion of all work within 10 years. *Entrance requirements:* For master's and doctorate, GRE General Test (minimum Quantitative score of 159), minimum GPA of 3.0, official transcripts, personal statement, confidential evaluations by 3 professors or other technical professional, high rank (top 5%) in respected chemical engineering program. Additional exam requirements/recommendations for international students: Required—TOEFL (minimum score 580 paper-based; 92 iBT); Recommended—IELTS (minimum score 7). *Application deadline:* For fall admission, 1/1 priority date for domestic students, 12/15 priority date for international students. Applications are processed on a rolling basis. Application fee: $85. Electronic applications accepted. *Expenses:* Expenses: Contact institution. *Financial support:* In 2014–15, 84 students received support, including 15 fellowships with full tuition reimbursements available, 55 research assistantships with full tuition reimbursements available, 14 teaching assistantships with full tuition reimbursements available; career-related internships or fieldwork, Federal Work-Study, health care benefits, and unspecified assistantships also available. Financial award application deadline: 1/15; financial award applicants required to submit FAFSA. *Faculty research:* Materials processing and characterization, optical and electronic polymers, surface science, biochemical engineering and bioengineering, computational chemistry, environmental studies. *Total annual research expenditures:* $12.2 million. *Unit head:* Dr. Francois Baneyx, Professor/Chair, 206-543-2250, Fax: 206-543-3778, E-mail: baneyx@uw.edu. *Application contact:* Allison Sherrill, Graduate Program Advisor, 206-685-9785, E-mail: sherra@uw.edu.
Website: http://www.cheme.washington.edu/.

University of Waterloo, Graduate Studies, Faculty of Engineering, Department of Chemical Engineering, Waterloo, ON N2L 3G1, Canada. Offers M Eng, MA Sc, PhD. Part-time programs available. *Degree requirements:* For master's, research project or thesis, seminar; for doctorate, comprehensive exam, thesis/dissertation. *Entrance requirements:* For master's, honors degree, minimum B average; for doctorate, master's degree, minimum A- average. Additional exam requirements/recommendations for international students: Required—TOEFL, TWE. Electronic applications accepted. *Faculty research:* Biotechnical and environmental engineering, mathematical analysis, statistics and control, polymer science and engineering.

The University of Western Ontario, Faculty of Graduate Studies, Physical Sciences Division, Faculty of Engineering, London, ON N6A 5B8, Canada. Offers chemical and biochemical engineering (ME Sc, PhD); civil and environmental engineering (M Eng, ME Sc, PhD); electrical and computer engineering (M Eng, ME Sc, PhD); mechanical and materials engineering (M Eng, ME Sc, PhD). Part-time programs available. Terminal master's awarded for partial completion of doctoral program. *Degree requirements:* For master's, thesis; for doctorate, thesis/dissertation. *Entrance requirements:* For master's, minimum B average; for doctorate, minimum B+ average. *Faculty research:* Wind, geotechnical, chemical reactor engineering, applied electrostatics, biochemical engineering.

University of Wisconsin–Madison, Graduate School, College of Engineering, Department of Chemical and Biological Engineering, Madison, WI 53706-0607. Offers chemical engineering (PhD). *Faculty:* 19 full-time (2 women). *Students:* 101 full-time (23 women); includes 13 minority (1 American Indian or Alaska Native, non-Hispanic/Latino; 6 Asian, non-Hispanic/Latino; 6 Hispanic/Latino), 43 international. Average age 27. 415 applicants, 17% accepted, 19 enrolled. In 2014, 26 doctorates awarded. *Median time to degree:* Of those who began their doctoral program in fall 2006, 97% received their degree in 8 years or less. *Degree requirements:* For doctorate, thesis/dissertation, 2 semesters of teaching assistantship. *Entrance requirements:* For doctorate, GRE General Test, electronic application, official transcripts, personal statement, 3 letters of recommendation, resume. Additional exam requirements/recommendations for international students: Required—TOEFL (minimum score 580 paper-based; 92 iBT). *Application deadline:* For fall admission, 12/30 for domestic and international students; for spring admission, 10/15 for domestic and international students. Application fee: $56. Electronic applications accepted. *Expenses:* Tuition, state resident: full-time $10,723; part-time $745 per credit. Tuition, nonresident: full-time $24,054; part-time $1578 per credit. *Required fees:* $374 per semester. Tuition and fees vary according to course load, program and reciprocity agreements. *Financial support:* In 2014–15, 98 students received support, including 4 fellowships with full tuition reimbursements available (averaging $19,365 per year), 116 research assistantships with full tuition reimbursements available (averaging $29,000 per year), 39 teaching assistantships with full tuition reimbursements available (averaging $7,521 per year); traineeships and health care benefits also available. Financial award application deadline: 12/30. *Faculty research:* Biotechnology, nanotechnology, complex fluids, molecular and systems modeling, renewable energy and chemicals: materials and processes. *Total annual research expenditures:* $6.9 million. *Unit head:* Prof. Manos Mavrikakis, Chair, 608-263-2922, Fax: 608-262-5434, E-mail: emavrikakis@wisc.edu. *Application contact:* Kathy M. Heinzen, Senior Student Services Coordinator, 608-263-3138, Fax: 608-262-5434, E-mail: gradoffice@che.wisc.edu.
Website: http://www.engr.wisc.edu/che/.

University of Wyoming, College of Engineering and Applied Sciences, Department of Chemical and Petroleum Engineering, Program in Chemical Engineering, Laramie, WY 82071. Offers MS, PhD. Part-time programs available. Terminal master's awarded for partial completion of doctoral program. *Degree requirements:* For master's, thesis; for doctorate, thesis/dissertation. *Entrance requirements:* For master's and doctorate, GRE

General Test, minimum GPA of 3.0. Additional exam requirements/recommendations for international students: Required—TOEFL (minimum score 600 paper-based; 76 iBT). Electronic applications accepted. *Faculty research:* Microwave reactor systems, synthetic fuels, fluidization, coal combustion/gasification, flue-gas cleanup.

Vanderbilt University, School of Engineering, Department of Chemical and Biomolecular Engineering, Nashville, TN 37240-1001. Offers M Eng, MS, PhD. MS and PhD offered through the Graduate School. Part-time programs available. *Degree requirements:* For master's, thesis; for doctorate, thesis/dissertation. *Entrance requirements:* For master's and doctorate, GRE General Test. Additional exam requirements/recommendations for international students: Required—TOEFL. Electronic applications accepted. *Expenses: Tuition:* Full-time $42,768; part-time $1782 per credit hour. *Required fees:* $422. One-time fee: $30 full-time. *Faculty research:* Adsorption and surface chemistry; biochemical engineering and biotechnology; chemical reaction engineering, environment, materials, process modeling and control; molecular modeling and thermodynamics.

Villanova University, College of Engineering, Department of Chemical Engineering, Villanova, PA 19085-1699. Offers biochemical engineering (Certificate); chemical engineering (MSChE); environmental protection in the chemical process industries (Certificate). Part-time and evening/weekend programs available. *Degree requirements:* For master's, comprehensive exam, thesis optional. *Entrance requirements:* For master's, GRE General Test (for applicants with degrees from foreign universities), B Ch E, minimum GPA of 3.0. Additional exam requirements/recommendations for international students: Required—TOEFL (minimum score 600 paper-based; 100 iBT). *Faculty research:* Heat transfer, advanced materials, chemical vapor deposition, pyrolysis and combustion chemistry, industrial waste treatment.

Virginia Commonwealth University, Graduate School, School of Engineering, Department of Chemical and Life Science Engineering, Richmond, VA 23284-9005. Offers MS, PhD. *Entrance requirements:* For master's and doctorate, GRE. Additional exam requirements/recommendations for international students: Required—TOEFL (minimum score 600 paper-based; 100 iBT). Electronic applications accepted. *Faculty research:* Advanced polymers, including biopolymers and polymers in medicine; chemical and biochemical reactor analysis; the study of supercritical fluids for environmentally favorable processes; systems biological engineering; stem cell engineering; biosensors and biochips; computational bioinformatics and rational drug design.

Virginia Polytechnic Institute and State University, Graduate School, College of Engineering, Blacksburg, VA 24061. Offers aerospace engineering (ME, MS, PhD); biological systems engineering (ME, MS, PhD); biomedical engineering (MS, PhD); chemical engineering (ME, MS, PhD); civil engineering (ME, MS, PhD); computer engineering (ME, MS, PhD); computer science (MS, PhD); electrical engineering (ME, PhD); engineering education (PhD); engineering mechanics (ME, MS, PhD); environmental engineering (MS); environmental science and engineering (MS); industrial and systems engineering (ME, MS, PhD); materials science and engineering (ME, MS, PhD); mechanical engineering (ME, MS, PhD); mining and minerals engineering (PhD); mining engineering (ME, MS); nuclear engineering (MS, PhD); ocean engineering (MS); systems engineering (ME, MS). *Accreditation:* ABET (one or more programs are accredited). *Faculty:* 356 full-time (60 women), 3 part-time/adjunct (1 woman). *Students:* 1,700 full-time (398 women), 345 part-time (58 women); includes 213 minority (43 Black or African American, non-Hispanic/Latino; 1 American Indian or Alaska Native, non-Hispanic/Latino; 87 Asian, non-Hispanic/Latino; 58 Hispanic/Latino; 1 Native Hawaiian or other Pacific Islander, non-Hispanic/Latino; 23 Two or more races, non-Hispanic/Latino), 1,079 international. Average age 27. 5,228 applicants, 18% accepted, 471 enrolled. In 2014, 438 master's, 211 doctorates awarded. *Degree requirements:* For master's, comprehensive exam (for some programs), thesis (for some programs); for doctorate, comprehensive exam (for some programs), thesis/dissertation (for some programs). *Entrance requirements:* For master's and doctorate, GRE/GMAT (may vary by department). Additional exam requirements/recommendations for international students: Required—TOEFL (minimum score 550 paper-based). *Application deadline:* For fall admission, 8/1 for domestic students, 4/1 for international students; for spring admission, 1/1 for domestic students, 9/1 for international students. Applications are processed on a rolling basis. Application fee: $75. Electronic applications accepted. *Expenses:* Tuition, state resident: full-time $11,656; part-time $647.50 per credit hour. Tuition, nonresident: full-time $23,351; part-time $1297.25 per credit hour. *Required fees:* $2533; $465.75 per semester. Tuition and fees vary according to course load, campus/location and program. *Financial support:* In 2014–15, 148 fellowships with full tuition reimbursements (averaging $8,031 per year), 855 research assistantships with full tuition reimbursements (averaging $22,855 per year), 288 teaching assistantships with full tuition reimbursements (averaging $20,291 per year) were awarded. Financial award application deadline: 3/1; financial award applicants required to submit FAFSA. *Total annual research expenditures:* $90.5 million. *Unit head:* Dr. Richard C. Benson, Dean, 540-231-9752, Fax: 540-231-3031, E-mail: deaneng@vt.edu. *Application contact:* Linda Perkins, Executive Assistant, 540-231-9752, Fax: 540-231-3031, E-mail: lperkins@vt.edu.
Website: http://www.eng.vt.edu/.

Washington State University, Voiland College of Engineering and Architecture, The Gene and Linda Voiland School of Chemical Engineering and Bioengineering, Pullman, WA 99164-6515. Offers MS, PhD. *Faculty:* 22 full-time (4 women), 18 part-time/adjunct (0 women). *Students:* 58 full-time (26 women), 4 part-time (0 women); includes 8 minority (2 Black or African American, non-Hispanic/Latino; 5 Asian, non-Hispanic/Latino; 1 Hispanic/Latino), 34 international. Average age 28. 102 applicants, 25% accepted, 19 enrolled. In 2014, 3 master's, 2 doctorates awarded. Terminal master's awarded for partial completion of doctoral program. *Degree requirements:* For master's, comprehensive exam, thesis (for some programs), oral exam; for doctorate, one foreign language, comprehensive exam, thesis/dissertation, oral exam. *Entrance requirements:* For master's and doctorate, minimum GPA of 3.0, 3 letters of recommendation by faculty. Additional exam requirements/recommendations for international students: Required—TOEFL (minimum score 580 paper-based). *Application deadline:* For fall admission, 3/1 priority date for domestic students, 3/1 for international students; for spring admission, 7/1 priority date for domestic students, 7/1 for international students. Applications are processed on a rolling basis. Application fee: $75. *Expenses:* Tuition, state resident: full-time $11,768. Tuition, nonresident: full-time $25,200. *Required fees:* $960. Tuition and fees vary according to program. *Financial support:* In 2014–15, 10 students received support, including 5 fellowships (averaging $4,991 per year), 32 research assistantships with full and partial tuition reimbursements available (averaging $16,467 per year), 15 teaching assistantships with full and partial tuition reimbursements available (averaging $17,090 per year); career-related internships or fieldwork, Federal Work-Study, institutionally sponsored loans, tuition waivers (partial), and teaching associateships also available. Financial award application deadline: 4/1; financial award applicants required to submit FAFSA. *Faculty research:* Kinetics and catalysis, biofilm engineering, muscle systems, engineering education. *Total annual research expenditures:* $4.1 million. *Unit head:* Dr. James Peterson, Director, 509-335-4332, Fax: 509-335-4806, E-mail: jnp@wsu.edu. *Application contact:* Graduate School Admissions, 800-GRADWSU, Fax: 509-335-1949, E-mail: gradsch@wsu.edu.
Website: http://voiland.wsu.edu/.

Washington University in St. Louis, School of Engineering and Applied Science, Department of Energy, Environmental and Chemical Engineering, St. Louis, MO 63130-4899. Offers chemical engineering (MS, D Sc); environmental engineering (MS, D Sc). Part-time programs available. Terminal master's awarded for partial completion of doctoral program. *Degree requirements:* For master's, thesis optional; for doctorate, thesis/dissertation, preliminary exam, qualifying exam. *Entrance requirements:* For master's and doctorate, GRE, minimum B average during final 2 years of course work. Additional exam requirements/recommendations for international students: Required—TOEFL, TWE. Electronic applications accepted. *Faculty research:* Reaction engineering, materials processing, catalysis, process control, air pollution control.

Wayne State University, College of Engineering, Department of Chemical Engineering and Materials Science, Program in Chemical Engineering, Detroit, MI 48202. Offers MS, PhD. *Students:* 28 full-time (10 women), 10 part-time (2 women); includes 7 minority (2 Black or African American, non-Hispanic/Latino; 5 Asian, non-Hispanic/Latino), 19 international. Average age 26. 92 applicants, 21% accepted, 11 enrolled. In 2014, 2 master's, 5 doctorates awarded. *Degree requirements:* For master's, thesis optional; for doctorate, thesis/dissertation. *Entrance requirements:* For master's, GRE (if applying for financial support), three letters of recommendation, resume, personal statement, bachelor's degree in engineering or other mathematics-based science; for doctorate, GRE, three letters of recommendation; resume; personal statement. Additional exam requirements/recommendations for international students: Required—TOEFL (minimum score 550 paper-based; 79 iBT), TWE (minimum score 5.5), Michigan English Language Assessment Battery (minimum score 85); Recommended—IELTS (minimum score 6.5). *Application deadline:* For fall admission, 6/1 priority date for domestic students, 5/1 priority date for international students; for winter admission, 10/1 priority date for domestic students, 9/1 priority date for international students; for spring admission, 2/1 priority date for domestic students, 1/1 priority date for international students. Applications are processed on a rolling basis. Application fee: $0. Electronic applications accepted. *Expenses:* Expenses: Contact institution. *Financial support:* In 2014–15, 21 students received support. Fellowships with tuition reimbursements available, research assistantships with tuition reimbursements available, teaching assistantships with tuition reimbursements available, scholarships/grants, health care benefits, and unspecified assistantships available. Support available to part-time students. Financial award application deadline: 3/31; financial award applicants required to submit FAFSA. *Faculty research:* Environmental management, biochemical engineering, supercritical technology, polymer process catalysis. *Unit head:* Dr. Charles Manke, Chair, 313-577-3800, E-mail: cmanke@eng.wayne.edu. *Application contact:* Dr. Yinlun Huang, Director of Materials Science Graduate Program, 313-577-3771, E-mail: yhuang@eng.wayne.edu.
Website: http://engineering.wayne.edu/che/.

Western Michigan University, Graduate College, College of Engineering and Applied Sciences, Department of Chemical and Paper Engineering, Kalamazoo, MI 49008. Offers MS, MSE, PhD. *Degree requirements:* For master's, thesis optional; for doctorate, one foreign language, comprehensive exam, thesis/dissertation. *Application deadline:* For fall admission, 2/15 for domestic students. *Financial support:* Application deadline: 2/15. *Application contact:* Admissions and Orientation, 269-387-2000, Fax: 269-387-2096.

West Virginia University, College of Engineering and Mineral Resources, Department of Chemical Engineering, Morgantown, WV 26506. Offers MS Ch E, PhD. Part-time programs available. Terminal master's awarded for partial completion of doctoral program. *Degree requirements:* For master's, thesis; for doctorate, comprehensive exam, thesis/dissertation, original research proposal, dissertation research proposal. *Entrance requirements:* For master's and doctorate, minimum GPA of 3.0. Additional exam requirements/recommendations for international students: Required—TOEFL (minimum score 550 paper-based; 80 iBT). Electronic applications accepted. *Faculty research:* Biocatalysis and catalysis, fluid-particle systems, high-value non-fuel uses of coal, opto-electronic materials processing, polymer and polymer-composite nanotechnology.

Widener University, Graduate Programs in Engineering, Program in Chemical Engineering, Chester, PA 19013-5792. Offers M Eng. Part-time and evening/weekend programs available. *Degree requirements:* For master's, thesis optional. *Faculty research:* Biotechnology, environmental engineering, computational fluid mechanics, reaction kinetics, process design.

Worcester Polytechnic Institute, Graduate Studies and Research, Department of Chemical Engineering, Worcester, MA 01609-2280. Offers MS, PhD. Part-time and evening/weekend programs available. *Faculty:* 9 full-time (2 women), 1 (woman) part-time/adjunct. *Students:* 31 full-time (11 women), 2 part-time (1 woman); includes 2 minority (1 Asian, non-Hispanic/Latino; 1 Hispanic/Latino), 20 international. 100 applicants, 40% accepted, 7 enrolled. In 2014, 5 master's awarded. Terminal master's awarded for partial completion of doctoral program. *Degree requirements:* For master's, thesis; for doctorate, comprehensive exam, thesis/dissertation. *Entrance requirements:* For master's and doctorate, GRE (recommended), 3 letters of recommendation. Additional exam requirements/recommendations for international students: Required—TOEFL (minimum score 563 paper-based; 84 iBT), IELTS (minimum score 7). *Application deadline:* For fall admission, 1/1 priority date for domestic and international students; for spring admission, 10/1 priority date for domestic and international students. Applications are processed on a rolling basis. Application fee: $70. Electronic applications accepted. *Financial support:* Fellowships, research assistantships, career-related internships or fieldwork, institutionally sponsored loans, scholarships/grants, and unspecified assistantships available. Financial award application deadline: 1/1; financial award applicants required to submit FAFSA. *Unit head:* Dr. David DiBiasio, Head, 508-831-5250, Fax: 508-831-5853, E-mail: dibiasio@wpi.edu. *Application contact:* Dr. Aaron Deskins, Graduate Coordinator, 508-831-5250, Fax: 508-831-5853, E-mail: nadeskinswp.edu.
Website: http://www.wpi.edu/academics/che.

Yale University, Graduate School of Arts and Sciences, School of Engineering and Applied Science, Department of Chemical Engineering, New Haven, CT 06520. Offers MS, PhD. Terminal master's awarded for partial completion of doctoral program. *Degree requirements:* For doctorate, thesis/dissertation, exam. *Entrance requirements:* For master's and doctorate, GRE General Test. Additional exam requirements/recommendations for international students: Required—TOEFL. *Faculty research:* Biochemical engineering, heterogeneous catalysis, high-temperature chemical reaction engineering, separation science and technology, colloids and complex fluids.

UNIVERSITY OF ROCHESTER

Edmund A. Hajim School of Engineering and Applied Sciences
Department of Chemical Engineering

★ For more information, visit http://petersons.to/rochesterchemengineering

Programs of Study

The interdisciplinary nature of the University of Rochester's chemical engineering program manifests itself in active collaborations with other departments at the school. The faculty enjoys generous research support from government agencies and private industries. The University's graduate programs are among the highest ranked in the nation according to the 2010 National Research Council survey report (www.nap.edu/rdp).

To earn a Ph.D., students must complete 90 credit hours. It typically takes five years to complete the program, which includes successful defense of a dissertation. The first two semesters are devoted to graduate courses in chemical engineering and other sciences. Students are expected to provide undergraduate teaching assistance. At the end of this period, students take a first-year examination as a transition from classroom to full-time research.

Students without prior backgrounds in chemical engineering are encouraged to apply. The Department has a graduate curriculum devised for students with a background in science, such as chemistry, physics, and biology. The curriculum combines courses at the undergraduate and graduate levels and is designed to foster interdisciplinary research in advanced materials, nanotechnology, alternative energy, and biotechnology.

The Master of Science degree may be obtained through either a full-time or a part-time program. Graduate students may complete a thesis (Plan A) or choose a nonthesis (Plan B) option. All students who pursue Plan A are expected to earn 30 hours of credit, of which a minimum of 18 and a maximum of 24 hours should be formal course work. The balance of credit hours required for the degree is earned through M.S. research and/or reading courses. Satisfactory completion of the master thesis is also required. All students who pursue Plan B must earn a minimum of 32 credits of course work. At least 18 credits should be taken from courses within the Department. Overall, no more than 6 credits toward a degree may be earned by research and/or reading courses. Plan B students are required to pass a comprehensive oral exam toward the end of their program.

The Department of Chemical Engineering also awards the Master of Science degree in Alternative Energy. Courses and research projects focus on the fundamentals and applications of the generation, storage, and utilization of various forms of alternative energy as well as their impact on sustainability and energy conservation. This program is designed for graduate students with a bachelor's degree in engineering or science who are interested in pursuing a technical career in alternative energy. As with the other M.S. programs, the M.S. degree in Alternative Energy is available as a full- or part-time program, with a thesis (Plan A) or nonthesis (Plan B) option. All students who pursue Plan A are expected to earn 30 hours of credit; at least 18 should be attributed to 400-level courses. The balance of the credit-hour requirement can be satisfied through independent reading (no more than 4 credit hours) and thesis research (at least 6 credit hours), culminating in a master thesis. All students who pursue Plan B must earn a minimum of 32 credits of course work, with at least 18 credits from 400-level courses and no more than 4 through independent reading. Students may opt for industrial internship (1 credit hour), for which a final essay must be submitted as a part of their degree requirements. In addition to course work and the essay, all Plan B students must pass a comprehensive oral exam toward the end of their program.

Research Facilities

The River Campus Libraries hold approximately 2.5 million volumes and provide access to an extensive collection of electronic, multimedia, and interlibrary loan resources. Miner Library includes more than 230,000 volumes of journals, books, theses, and government documents for health-care and medical research. Located at the Medical Center, the library also maintains access to online databases and electronic resources.

The Laboratory for Laser Energetics and the Center for Optoelectronics and Imaging are two state-of-the-art facilities in which specialized material science research is conducted. The Laboratory for Laser Energetics was established in 1970 for the investigation of the interaction of intense radiation with matter, to conduct experiments in support of the National Inertial Confinement Fusion (ICF) program; develop new laser and materials technologies; provide education in electro-optics, high-power lasers, high-energy-density physics, plasma physics, and nuclear fusion technology; operate the National Laser User's Facility; and conduct research in advanced technology related to high-energy-density phenomena.

The renowned Medical Center, which is a few minutes' walk from the River Campus, houses the Peptide Sequencing/Mass Spectrometry Facilities, Cell Sorting Facility, Nucleic Acid Laboratory, Real-Time and Static Confocal Imaging Facility, Functional Genomics Center, and a network of nearly 1,000 investigators providing research, clinical trial, and education services. In addition, a recently founded research institute, the Aab Institute of Biomedical Sciences, is the centerpiece of a ten-year, $400-million strategic plan to expand the Medical Center's research programs in the basic sciences. It is headquartered in a 240,000-square-foot research building on the Medical Center campus.

Financial Aid

The University offers fellowships, scholarships, and assistantships for full-time graduate students, and individual departments provide support through research assistantships. Applicants are encouraged to apply for outside funding such as NSF or New York State fellowships. Full-time Ph.D. students receive an annual stipend of $26,000 plus full graduate tuition.

Cost of Study

In the 2015–16 academic year, tuition is $1,462 per credit hour. Students must also pay additional yearly fees of $528 for health services and $2,400 for optional health insurance. All amounts are subject to change.

Living and Housing Costs

Students are eligible to lease a University apartment if enrolled as a full-time graduate student or postgraduate trainee. In the 2015–16 academic year, rent, utilities, food, and supplies are estimated at $15,382 per year; books at $1,380; and personal expenses at $2,400. All amounts are subject to change.

Student Group

The chemical engineering discipline appeals to students who are proficient at both analytical and descriptive sciences, and are intrigued by the prospect of investigating new phenomena, and devising new materials and devices for the technologies of the future. Students in the master's degree program should have acquired technical background in chemistry, mathematics, and physics. For students interested in biotechnology, a technical background in biology is desirable.

Student Outcomes

In addition to the traditional jobs in the chemical process and petrochemical industries, chemical engineers work in pharmaceuticals, health care, pulp and paper, food processing, polymers, biotechnology, and environmental health and safety industries. Their expertise is also applied in law, education, publishing, finance, and medicine. Chemical engineers also are well equipped to analyze environmental issues and develop solutions to environmental problems, such as pollution control and remediation.

Location

Located at a bend of the Genesee River, the 85-acre River Campus is about 2 miles south of downtown Rochester, New York. Rochester has been ranked as one of the Northeast's ten "Best Places to Live in America" by *Money* magazine, Rochester has also been listed as one of the "Most Livable Cities" in America by the Partners for Livable Communities. Rochester claims more sites on the National Register of Historic Places than any other city its size. With Lake Ontario on its northern border and the scenic Finger Lakes to the south, the Rochester area of about 1 million people offers a wide variety of cultural and recreational opportunities through its museums, parks, orchestras, planetarium, theater companies, and professional sports teams.

The University

Founded in 1850, the University of Rochester ranks among the most highly regarded universities in the country, offering degree programs at the bachelor's, master's, and doctoral levels, as well as in several professional disciplines. In the last eighteen years, 27 faculty members have been named Guggenheim Fellows. Present faculty members include a MacArthur Foundation fellowship recipient and 6 National Endowment for the Humanities Senior Fellows. Past alumni have included 7 Nobel Prize winners and 11 Pulitzer Prize winners. The University's Eastman School of Music is consistently ranked as one of the top music schools in the nation.

University of Rochester

Applying

The official graduate application can be found online at **https://apply.grad. rochester.edu**. The entire application must be received by January 15 for fall admission. Late applications are considered for exceptional applicants only if scholarship slots are available. Applicants are required to send college transcripts, letters of recommendation, personal/research statement, curriculum vitae, and standardized test results along with a $60 application fee to the Department of Chemical Engineering.

Correspondence and Information

Graduate Program Coordinator
Department of Chemical Engineering
206 Gavett Hall, Box 270166
University of Rochester
Rochester, New York 14627-0166
United States
Phone: 585-275-4913
Fax: 585-273-1348
E-mail: chegradinfo@che.rochester.edu
Website: http://www.che.rochester.edu

THE FACULTY AND THEIR RESEARCH

Mitchell Anthamatten, Associate Professor and Scientist, LLE; Ph.D., MIT, 2001. Macromolecular self-assembly, associative and functional polymers, nanostructured materials, liquid crystals, interfacial phenomena, optoelectronic materials, vapor deposition polymerization, fuel cell membranes.

Danielle S. W. Benoit, Assistant Professor Biomedical Engineering and Chemical Engineering; Ph.D., Colorado, 2006. The rational design, synthesis, characterization, and employment of materials to treat diseases or control cell behavior for applications in drug therapy, regenerative medicine, and tissue engineering.

Shaw H. Chen, Professor and Senior Scientist, LLE; Ph.D., Minnesota, 1981. Organic semiconductors, green chemical engineering, glassy liquid crystals, photoalignment of conjugated molecules, bipolar hosts for phosphorescent OLEDs, geometric surfactancy for bulk heterojunction solar cells.

Eldred H. Chimowitz, Professor; Ph.D., Connecticut, 1982. Critical phenomena, statistical mechanics of fluids, computer-aided design, supercritical fluids.

David G. Foster, Associate Professor; Ph.D., Rochester, 1999. Principles of transport phenomena, classic chemical engineering as well as biomedical engineering research, creation of nanoparticle coatings for enhanced capture of flowing cells in microtubes, capture cancer cells in blood flow, creating state-of-the-art videos for curricular purposes of fundamental fluid mechanics principles.

David R. Harding, Professor of Chemical Engineering and Senior Scientist, LLE; Ph.D., Cambridge, 1986. Thin-film deposition, properties of films and composite structures, and developing cryogenic fuel capsules for nuclear fusion experiments.

Jacob Jornè, Professor; Ph.D., Berkeley, 1972. Electrochemical engineering, microelectronics processing, fuel cells, polymer electrolyte membrane fuel cell, lithium batteries, green energy, copper electrodeposition, and reaction-diffusion interactions.

F. Douglas Kelley, Associate Professor; Ph.D., Rochester, 1990. Ways to exploit the divergent transport properties of fluids near the critical point, energy storage technologies that can be useful in balancing energy demand with sustainable energy generation, polymer mixtures and composites.

Hitomi Mukaibo, Assistant Professor, Ph.D., Waseda (Japan), 2006. Template synthesis, microstructured/nanostructured materials, electrochemistry, nanoporous thin film, cell/nanostructure interface, gene delivery, energy storage and production, biosensors and bioanalytical chemistry.

Lewis Rothberg, Professor of Chemistry and Chemical Engineering; Ph.D., Harvard, 1984. Polymer electronics, optoelectronic devices, light-emitting diodes, thin-film transistors, organic photovoltaics and solar cells, biomolecular sensors, plasmon-enhanced devices.

Yonathon Shapir, Professor of Physics and Chemical Engineering; Ph.D., Tel-Aviv, 1981. Critical phenomena in ordered and disordered systems, classical and quantum transport in dirty metals and the metal-insulator transition, statistical properties of different polymer configurations, fractal properties of percolation and other clusters, kinetic models of growth and aggregation.

Alexander A. Shestopalov, Assistant Professor; Ph.D., Duke, 2009. Development of new unconventional fabrication and patterning techniques and their use in preparation of functional micro- and nanostructured devices, organic chemistry and colloidal self-assembly.

Ching W. Tang, Professor of Chemical Engineering, Chemistry, and Physics; Ph.D., Cornell, 1975. Applications of organic electronic devices—organic light-emitting diodes, solar cells, photoconductors, image sensors, photoreceptors; basic studies of organic thin-film devices: charge injection, transport, recombination and luminescence properties; metal-organic and organic-organic junction phenomena; development of flat-panel display technology based on organic light-emitting diodes.

Wyatt Tenhaeff, Assistant Professor; Ph.D., MIT, 2009. Electrochemical energy storage, solid-state lithium batteries, solid electrolytes, polymer thin films and interfaces, thin film synthesis and characterization, vacuum deposition techniques.

Andrew D. White, Assistant Professor; Ph.D., Washington (Seattle), 2013. Computer simulation and data informatics design of material design for self-assembly, machine learning.

J. H. David Wu, Professor of Chemical Engineering and Biomedical Engineering and Associate Professor of Microbiology and Immunology; Ph.D., MIT, 1987. Biofuels development, molecular enzymology, transcriptional network, genomics and systems biology of biomass degradation for bioenergy conversion, artificial bone marrow and lymphoid tissue engineering, molecular control of hematopoiesis and immune response, stem cell and lymphocyte culture, biochemical engineering, fermentation, molecular biology.

Matthew Z. Yates, Professor, Chair, and Scientist, LLE; Ph.D., Texas, 1999. Particle synthesis and assembly, crystallization, fuel cell membranes, microemulsions and microencapsulation, supercritical fluids, microencapsulation, colloids and interfaces.

Fun in the snow

Rochester fall colors.

Section 7
Civil and Environmental Engineering

This section contains a directory of institutions offering graduate work in civil and environmental engineering. Additional information about programs listed in the directory may be obtained by writing directly to the dean of a graduate school or chair of a department at the address given in the directory.

For programs offering related work, see also in this book *Agricultural Engineering and Bioengineering, Biomedical Engineering and Biotechnology, Engineering and Applied Sciences, Management of Engineering and Technology,* and *Ocean Engineering.* In the other guides in this series:

Graduate Programs in the Humanities, Arts & Social Sciences
See *Public, Regional, and Industrial Affairs (Urban and Regional Planning and Urban Studies)*

Graduate Programs in the Biological/Biomedical Sciences & Health-Related Medical Professions
See *Ecology, Environmental Biology,* and *Evolutionary Biology*

Graduate Programs in the Physical Sciences, Mathematics, Agricultural Sciences, the Environment & Natural Resources
See *Agricultural and Food Sciences, Environmental Sciences and Management, Geosciences,* and *Marine Sciences and Oceanography*

CONTENTS

Program Directories

Civil Engineering

American University of Beirut, Graduate Programs, Faculty of Engineering and Architecture, Beirut, Lebanon. Offers applied energy (ME); civil engineering (PhD); electrical and computer engineering (PhD); engineering management (MEM); environmental and water resources (ME); environmental technology (MSES); mechanical engineering (ME, PhD); urban design (MUD); urban planning and policy (MUPP). Part-time programs available. *Faculty:* 93 full-time (18 women), 3 part-time/adjunct (1 woman). *Students:* 268 full-time (111 women), 58 part-time (27 women). Average age 26. 225 applicants, 68% accepted, 79 enrolled. In 2014, 114 master's, 9 doctorates awarded. Terminal master's awarded for partial completion of doctoral program. *Degree requirements:* For master's, one foreign language, comprehensive exam, thesis (for some programs); for doctorate, one foreign language, comprehensive exam, thesis/dissertation, publications. *Entrance requirements:* For master's, letters of recommendation; for doctorate, GRE, letters of recommendation, master's degree, transcripts, curriculum vitae, interview. Additional exam requirements/recommendations for international students: Required—TOEFL (minimum score 600 paper-based; 100 iBT), IELTS (minimum score 7.5). *Application deadline:* For fall admission, 2/5 priority date for domestic and international students; for spring admission, 11/1 priority date for domestic students, 11/1 for international students. Application fee: $50. Electronic applications accepted. *Expenses: Tuition:* Full-time $15,462; part-time $859 per credit. *Required fees:* $692. Tuition and fees vary according to course load and program. *Financial support:* In 2014–15, 190 students received support, including 2 fellowships with full tuition reimbursements available (averaging $24,800 per year), 64 research assistantships with full tuition reimbursements available (averaging $24,800 per year), 124 teaching assistantships with full tuition reimbursements available (averaging $9,800 per year); career-related internships or fieldwork, institutionally sponsored loans, scholarships/grants, health care benefits, and unspecified assistantships also available. *Total annual research expenditures:* $1.5 million. *Unit head:* Prof. Makram T. Suidan, Dean, 961-1350000 Ext. 3400, Fax: 961-1744462, E-mail: msuidan@aub.edu.lb. *Application contact:* Dr. Salim Kanaan, Director, Admissions Office, 961-1350000 Ext. 2594, Fax: 961-1750775, E-mail: sk00@aub.edu.lb.
Website: http://staff.aub.edu.lb/~webfea.

American University of Sharjah, Graduate Programs, Sharjah, United Arab Emirates. Offers accounting (MS); business (EMBA, MBA); chemical engineering (MS Ch E); civil engineering (MSCE); computer engineering (MS); electrical engineering (MSEE); engineering systems management (MS); mathematics (MS); mechanical engineering (MSME); mechatronics engineering (MS); teaching English to speakers of other languages (MA); translation and interpreting (MA); urban planning (MUP). Part-time and evening/weekend programs available. *Degree requirements:* For master's, thesis (for some programs). *Entrance requirements:* For master's, GMAT (for MBA). Additional exam requirements/recommendations for international students: Required—TOEFL (minimum score 550 paper-based; 80 iBT), TWE (minimum score 5); Recommended—IELTS (minimum score 6.5). Electronic applications accepted. *Faculty research:* Water pollution, management and waste water treatment, energy and sustainability, air pollution, Islamic finance, family business and small and medium enterprises.

Arizona State University at the Tempe campus, Ira A. Fulton Schools of Engineering, School of Sustainable Engineering and the Built Environment, Tempe, AZ 85287-5306. Offers civil, environmental and sustainable engineering (MS, MSE, PhD); construction engineering (MSE); construction management (MS, PhD). Part-time and evening/weekend programs available. Postbaccalaureate distance learning degree programs offered (minimal on-campus study). Terminal master's awarded for partial completion of doctoral program. *Degree requirements:* For master's, thesis optional, comprehensive exams (MSE); interactive Program of Study (iPOS) submitted before completing 50 percent of required credit hours; for doctorate, comprehensive exam, thesis/dissertation, interactive Program of Study (iPOS) submitted before completing 50 percent of required credit hours. *Entrance requirements:* For master's, GRE, minimum GPA of 3.0 or equivalent in last 2 years of work leading to bachelor's degree; for doctorate, GRE, minimum GPA of 3.0 in last 2 years of work leading to bachelor's degree, 3.2 in all graduate-level coursework with master's degree; 3 letters of recommendation; resume/curriculum vitae; letter of intent; thesis (if applicable); statement of research interests. Additional exam requirements/recommendations for international students: Required—TOEFL, IELTS, or PTE. Electronic applications accepted. *Expenses:* Contact institution. *Faculty research:* Water purification, transportation (safety and materials), construction management, environmental biotechnology, environmental nanotechnology, earth systems engineering and management, SMART innovations, project performance metrics, and underground infrastructure.

Auburn University, Graduate School, Ginn College of Engineering, Department of Civil Engineering, Auburn University, AL 36849. Offers construction engineering and management (MCE, MS, PhD); environmental engineering (MCE, MS, PhD); geotechnical/materials engineering (MCE, MS, PhD); hydraulics/hydrology (MCE, MS, PhD); structural engineering (MCE, MS, PhD); transportation engineering (MCE, MS, PhD). Part-time programs available. *Faculty:* 27 full-time (3 women), 1 part-time/adjunct (0 women). *Students:* 59 full-time (15 women), 46 part-time (6 women); includes 10 minority (4 Black or African American, non-Hispanic/Latino; 4 Asian, non-Hispanic/Latino; 2 Hispanic/Latino), 40 international. Average age 26. 134 applicants, 46% accepted, 20 enrolled. In 2014, 40 master's, 7 doctorates awarded. *Degree requirements:* For master's, project (MCE), thesis (MS); for doctorate, comprehensive exam, thesis/dissertation. *Entrance requirements:* For master's and doctorate, GRE General Test. *Application deadline:* For fall admission, 7/7 for domestic students; for spring admission, 11/24 for domestic students. Applications are processed on a rolling basis. Application fee: $50 ($60 for international students). Electronic applications accepted. *Expenses: Tuition,* state resident: full-time $8586; part-time $477 per credit hour. Tuition, nonresident: full-time $25,758; part-time $1431 per credit hour. *Required fees:* $804 per semester. Tuition and fees vary according to degree level and program. *Financial support:* Fellowships, research assistantships, teaching assistantships, and Federal Work-Study available. Support available to part-time students. Financial award application deadline: 3/15; financial award applicants required to submit FAFSA. *Unit head:* Dr. Andy Nowak, Head, 334-844-4320. *Application contact:* Dr. George Flowers, Dean of the Graduate School, 334-844-2125.

Boise State University, College of Engineering, Department of Civil Engineering, Boise, ID 83725-0399. Offers M Engr, MS. Part-time and evening/weekend programs available. *Faculty:* 9 full-time, 4 part-time/adjunct. *Students:* 19 full-time (7 women), 13 part-time (3 women), 3 international. 36 applicants, 72% accepted, 8 enrolled. In 2014, 17 master's awarded. *Degree requirements:* For master's, thesis. *Entrance requirements:* For master's, GRE General Test, minimum GPA of 3.0. Additional exam requirements/recommendations for international students: Required—TOEFL. *Application deadline:* For fall admission, 3/1 priority date for domestic students; for spring admission, 10/1 priority date for domestic students. Applications are processed on a rolling basis. Application fee: $55. Electronic applications accepted. *Expenses:*

Tuition, state resident: part-time $331 per credit hour. Tuition, nonresident: part-time $531 per credit hour. *Financial support:* In 2014–15, 4 students received support, including 2 research assistantships; career-related internships or fieldwork, Federal Work-Study, institutionally sponsored loans, scholarships/grants, and unspecified assistantships also available. Support available to part-time students. Financial award application deadline: 3/1; financial award applicants required to submit FAFSA. *Unit head:* Mandar Khanal, Department Chair, 208-426-1430, E-mail: mkhanal@boisestate.edu. *Application contact:* Linda Platt, Supervisor, Graduate Admission and Degree Services, 208-426-1074, E-mail: lplatt@boisestate.edu.
Website: http://coen.boisestate.edu/ce/graduate-students/.

Bradley University, Graduate School, College of Engineering and Technology, Department of Civil Engineering and Construction, Peoria, IL 61625-0002. Offers MSCE. Part-time and evening/weekend programs available. *Faculty:* 6 full-time (1 woman). *Students:* 24 full-time (4 women), 10 part-time (0 women), 28 international. 86 applicants, 45% accepted, 18 enrolled. In 2014, 8 master's awarded. *Degree requirements:* For master's, comprehensive exam. *Entrance requirements:* Additional exam requirements/recommendations for international students: Required—TOEFL (minimum score 550 paper-based; 79 iBT), IELTS (minimum score 6.5). *Application deadline:* For fall admission, 5/15 priority date for domestic and international students; for spring admission, 10/15 priority date for domestic and international students. Applications are processed on a rolling basis. Application fee: $40 ($50 for international students). Electronic applications accepted. *Expenses: Tuition:* Full-time $14,580; part-time $810 per credit. *Required fees:* $224. Full-time tuition and fees vary according to course load. *Financial support:* In 2014–15, 11 research assistantships with full and partial tuition reimbursements (averaging $10,130 per year) were awarded; teaching assistantships, scholarships/grants, tuition waivers (partial), and unspecified assistantships also available. Support available to part-time students. Financial award application deadline: 4/1. *Application contact:* Kayla Carroll, Director of International Admissions and Student Services, 309-677-2375, E-mail: klcarroll@fsmail.bradley.edu.

Brigham Young University, Graduate Studies, Ira A. Fulton College of Engineering and Technology, Department of Civil and Environmental Engineering, Provo, UT 84602. Offers civil engineering (MS, PhD). *Faculty:* 17 full-time (0 women). *Students:* 74 full-time (14 women); includes 8 minority (1 Black or African American, non-Hispanic/Latino; 1 Asian, non-Hispanic/Latino; 2 Hispanic/Latino; 4 Two or more races, non-Hispanic/Latino), 12 international. Average age 28. 33 applicants, 91% accepted, 25 enrolled. In 2014, 42 master's, 2 doctorates awarded. *Degree requirements:* For master's, thesis (for some programs), Fundamentals of Engineering (FE) Exam; for doctorate, comprehensive exam, thesis/dissertation. *Entrance requirements:* For master's and doctorate, GRE General Test, minimum cumulative GPA of 3.0 in last 60 hours of upper-division course work. Additional exam requirements/recommendations for international students: Required—TOEFL (minimum score 580 paper-based; 85 iBT), IELTS (minimum score 7). *Application deadline:* For fall admission, 2/15 for domestic and international students; for winter admission, 9/5 for domestic students, 9/15 for international students; for spring admission, 2/15 for domestic and international students; for summer admission, 2/15 for domestic and international students. Application fee: $50. Electronic applications accepted. *Expenses: Tuition:* Full-time $6310; part-time $371 per credit hour. Tuition and fees vary according to program and student's religious affiliation. *Financial support:* In 2014–15, 40 students received support, including 1 fellowship (averaging $10,000 per year), 71 research assistantships (averaging $6,784 per year), 50 teaching assistantships (averaging $3,498 per year); scholarships/grants also available. Financial award application deadline: 3/1; financial award applicants required to submit FAFSA. *Faculty research:* Structural optimization; finite element modeling and earthquake resistant analysis; groundwater, surface water, watershed and hydrologic modeling and visualization; subsurface environmental issues including transport, remediation, monitoring and characterization; capacity of deep foundations under static and dynamic loading and the behavior and mitigation of liquefiable soils. *Total annual research expenditures:* $3 million. *Unit head:* Dr. Rollin H. Hotchkiss, Department Chair, 801-422-2811, Fax: 801-422-0159, E-mail: rhh@byu.edu. *Application contact:* Dr. Fernando S. Fonseca, Graduate Coordinator, 801-422-2811, Fax: 801-422-0159, E-mail: ffonseca@byu.edu.
Website: http://ceen.et.byu.edu/.

Bucknell University, Graduate Studies, College of Engineering, Department of Civil and Environmental Engineering, Lewisburg, PA 17837. Offers MSCE, MSEV. *Degree requirements:* For master's, thesis. *Entrance requirements:* For master's, GRE General Test, minimum GPA of 3.0. Additional exam requirements/recommendations for international students: Required—TOEFL (minimum score 600 paper-based). *Faculty research:* Pile foundations, rehabilitation of bridges, deep-shaft biological-waste treatment, pre-cast concrete structures.

California Institute of Technology, Division of Engineering and Applied Science, Option in Civil Engineering, Pasadena, CA 91125-0001. Offers MS, PhD, Engr. *Degree requirements:* For doctorate, thesis/dissertation. *Faculty research:* Earthquake engineering, soil mechanics, finite-element analysis, hydraulics, coastal engineering.

California Polytechnic State University, San Luis Obispo, College of Engineering, Department of Civil and Environmental Engineering, San Luis Obispo, CA 93407. Offers MS. Part-time programs available. *Faculty:* 12 full-time (2 women), 1 part-time/adjunct (0 women). *Students:* 45 full-time (8 women), 8 part-time (0 women); includes 19 minority (1 Black or African American, non-Hispanic/Latino; 9 Asian, non-Hispanic/Latino; 8 Hispanic/Latino; 1 Two or more races, non-Hispanic/Latino), 1 international. Average age 24. 76 applicants, 70% accepted, 33 enrolled. In 2014, 28 master's awarded. *Degree requirements:* For master's, comprehensive exam (for some programs), thesis (for some programs). *Application deadline:* For fall admission, 3/1 for domestic and international students; for winter admission, 10/1 for domestic students, 6/30 for international students; for spring admission, 1/1 for domestic students. Applications are processed on a rolling basis. Application fee: $55. Electronic applications accepted. *Expenses:* Tuition, state resident: full-time $6738; part-time $3906 per year. Tuition, nonresident: full-time $15,666; part-time $8370 per year. *Required fees:* $3447; $1001 per quarter. One-time fee: $3447 full-time; $3003 part-time. *Financial support:* Fellowships, research assistantships, teaching assistantships, career-related internships or fieldwork, Federal Work-Study, and scholarships/grants available. Support available to part-time students. Financial award application deadline: 3/2; financial award applicants required to submit FAFSA. *Faculty research:* Transportation and traffic, environmental protection, geotechnology, water engineering. *Unit head:* Dr. Robb Moss, Graduate Coordinator, 805-756-6427, Fax: 805-756-6330, E-mail: rmoss@calpoly.edu. *Application contact:* Dr. James Maraviglia, Associate Vice Provost for Marketing and Enrollment Development, 805-756-2311, Fax: 805-756-5400, E-mail: admissions@calpoly.edu.
Website: http://ceenve.calpoly.edu.

California State Polytechnic University, Pomona, Program in Civil Engineering, Pomona, CA 91768-2557. Offers MS. *Students:* 22 full-time (3 women), 83 part-time (18 women); includes 54 minority (1 Black or African American, non-Hispanic/Latino; 30 Asian, non-Hispanic/Latino; 19 Hispanic/Latino; 2 Native Hawaiian or other Pacific Islander, non-Hispanic/Latino; 2 Two or more races, non-Hispanic/Latino), 9 international. Average age 27. 105 applicants, 67% accepted, 35 enrolled. In 2014, 38 master's awarded. *Degree requirements:* For master's, project or thesis. *Application deadline:* Applications are processed on a rolling basis. Application fee: $55. Electronic applications accepted. *Expenses:* Tuition, state resident: full-time $6738. Tuition, nonresident: full-time $12,300. *Required fees:* $1400. *Unit head:* Dr. Ronald Yeung, Graduate Coordinator, 909-869-2640, Fax: 909-869-4342, E-mail: mryeung@cpp.edu.
Website: http://www.cpp.edu/~ce/.

California State University, Fresno, Division of Graduate Studies, College of Engineering and Computer Science, Department of Civil Engineering, Fresno, CA 93740-8027. Offers MS. Part-time and evening/weekend programs available. *Degree requirements:* For master's, thesis or alternative. *Entrance requirements:* For master's, GRE General Test, minimum GPA of 2.75. Additional exam requirements/recommendations for international students: Required—TOEFL. Electronic applications accepted. *Faculty research:* Surveying, water damage, instrumentation equipment, agricultural drainage, aerial triangulation, dairy manure particles.

California State University, Fullerton, Graduate Studies, College of Engineering and Computer Science, Department of Civil and Environmental Engineering, Fullerton, CA 92834-9480. Offers civil engineering (MS); environmental engineering (MS). Part-time programs available. *Students:* 72 full-time (20 women), 195 part-time (42 women); includes 114 minority (14 Black or African American, non-Hispanic/Latino; 47 Asian, non-Hispanic/Latino; 44 Hispanic/Latino; 2 Native Hawaiian or other Pacific Islander, non-Hispanic/Latino; 7 Two or more races, non-Hispanic/Latino), 68 international. Average age 29. 264 applicants, 73% accepted, 113 enrolled. In 2014, 75 master's awarded. *Degree requirements:* For master's, comprehensive exam, project or thesis. *Entrance requirements:* For master's, minimum undergraduate GPA of 2.5. Application fee: $55. *Financial support:* Career-related internships or fieldwork, Federal Work-Study, institutionally sponsored loans, and scholarships/grants available. Support available to part-time students. Financial award application deadline: 3/1; financial award applicants required to submit FAFSA. *Faculty research:* Soil-structure interaction, finite-element analysis, computer-aided analysis and design. *Unit head:* Dr. Prasada Rao, Chair, 657-278-3012. *Application contact:* Admissions/Applications, 657-278-2371.
Website: http://www.fullerton.edu/ecs/cee/.

California State University, Long Beach, Graduate Studies, College of Engineering, Department of Civil Engineering and Construction Engineering Management, Long Beach, CA 90840. Offers civil engineering (MSCE). Part-time programs available. *Degree requirements:* For master's, comprehensive exam or thesis. *Entrance requirements:* Additional exam requirements/recommendations for international students: Required—TOEFL. Electronic applications accepted. *Faculty research:* Soils, hydraulics, seismic structures, composite metals, computer-aided manufacturing.

California State University, Los Angeles, Graduate Studies, College of Engineering, Computer Science, and Technology, Department of Civil Engineering, Los Angeles, CA 90032-8530. Offers MS. Part-time and evening/weekend programs available. *Degree requirements:* For master's, comprehensive exam or thesis. *Entrance requirements:* For master's, GRE or minimum GPA of 2.4. Additional exam requirements/recommendations for international students: Required—TOEFL (minimum score 550 paper-based). *Expenses:* Tuition, state resident: full-time $6738; part-time $3609 per year. Tuition, nonresident: full-time $15,666; part-time $8073 per year. Tuition and fees vary according to course load, degree level and program. *Faculty research:* Structure, hydraulics, hydrology, soil mechanics.

California State University, Northridge, Graduate Studies, College of Engineering and Computer Science, Department of Civil Engineering and Applied Mechanics, Northridge, CA 91330. Offers engineering (MS), including structural engineering. Part-time and evening/weekend programs available. *Students:* 21 full-time (3 women), 39 part-time (8 women); includes 18 minority (5 Asian, non-Hispanic/Latino; 9 Hispanic/Latino; 4 Two or more races, non-Hispanic/Latino), 15 international. Average age 26. *Degree requirements:* For master's, thesis. *Entrance requirements:* Additional exam requirements/recommendations for international students: Required—TOEFL. *Application deadline:* For fall admission, 11/30 for domestic students. Application fee: $55. *Expenses: Required fees:* $12,402. *Financial support:* Teaching assistantships available. Financial award application deadline: 3/1. *Faculty research:* Composite study. *Unit head:* Dr. Nazaret Dermendjian, Chair, 818-677-2166.
Website: http://www.csun.edu/~ceam/.

California State University, Sacramento, Office of Graduate Studies, College of Engineering and Computer Science, Department of Civil Engineering, Sacramento, CA 95819. Offers MS. Part-time and evening/weekend programs available. *Degree requirements:* For master's, thesis, project, direct study, or comprehensive exam; writing proficiency exam. *Entrance requirements:* Additional exam requirements/recommendations for international students: Required—TOEFL. Electronic applications accepted.

Carleton University, Faculty of Graduate Studies, Faculty of Engineering and Design, Department of Civil and Environmental Engineering, Ottawa, ON K1S 5B6, Canada. Offers M Eng, MA Sc, PhD. *Degree requirements:* For master's, thesis optional; for doctorate, thesis/dissertation. *Entrance requirements:* For master's, honors degree; for doctorate, MA Sc or M Eng. Additional exam requirements/recommendations for international students: Required—TOEFL. *Faculty research:* Pollution and wastewater management, fire safety engineering, earthquake engineering, structural design, bridge engineering.

Carnegie Mellon University, Carnegie Institute of Technology, Department of Civil and Environmental Engineering, Pittsburgh, PA 15213. Offers advanced infrastructure systems (MS, PhD); advanced infrastructure systems technology development and application (MS); air quality engineering and science (MS); civil and environmental engineering (MS, PhD); civil and environmental engineering/engineering and public policy (PhD); civil engineering (MS, PhD); computational mechanics (MS, PhD); computational modeling and monitoring for resilient structural and material systems (MS); energy infrastructure systems (MS); environmental engineering (MS, PhD); environmental management and science (MS, PhD); IT-based sustainable global infrastructure and construction management (MS); sustainability and green design (MS); water quality engineering and science (MS). Part-time programs available. *Faculty:* 21 full-time (5 women), 12 part-time/adjunct (3 women). *Students:* 229 full-time (99 women), 31 part-time (11 women); includes 18 minority (4 Black or African American, non-Hispanic/Latino; 13 Asian, non-Hispanic/Latino; 1 Hispanic/Latino), 193 international. Average age 26. 590 applicants, 68% accepted, 124 enrolled. In 2014, 85 master's, 11 doctorates awarded. Terminal master's awarded for partial completion of doctoral program. *Degree requirements:* For master's, thesis optional; for doctorate, comprehensive exam, thesis/dissertation, two-part qualifying exam, public defense of dissertation. *Entrance requirements:* For master's, GRE General Test, BS in engineering, science or mathematics; for doctorate, GRE General Test, BS or MS in engineering, science or mathematics. Additional exam requirements/recommendations for international students: Required—TOEFL (minimum score 84 iBT) or IELTS. *Application deadline:* For fall admission, 1/5 priority date for domestic and international students; for spring admission, 9/15 priority date for domestic and international students. Application fee: $65. Electronic applications accepted. *Financial support:* In 2014–15, 169 students received support. Fellowships with full and partial tuition reimbursements available, research assistantships with full and partial tuition reimbursements available, scholarships/grants, tuition waivers (full and partial), unspecified assistantships, and service assistantships available. Financial award application deadline: 1/5. *Faculty research:* Advanced infrastructure systems; environmental engineering, sustainability, and science; mechanics, materials, and computing. *Total annual research expenditures:* $4.9 million. *Unit head:* Dr. David A. Dzombak, Head, 412-268-2941, Fax: 412-268-7813, E-mail: dzombak@cmu.edu. *Application contact:* Melissa L. Brown, Director of Graduate Admissions & Recruiting, 412-268-8762, Fax: 412-268-7813, E-mail: mlb2@andrew.cmu.edu.
Website: http://www.cmu.edu/cee/.

Case Western Reserve University, School of Graduate Studies, Case School of Engineering, Department of Civil Engineering, Cleveland, OH 44106. Offers civil engineering (MS, PhD). Part-time programs available. Postbaccalaureate distance learning degree programs offered (minimal on-campus study). *Faculty:* 8 full-time (1 woman). *Students:* 19 full-time (7 women), 1 part-time (0 women), 13 international. In 2014, 8 master's, 1 doctorate awarded. *Degree requirements:* For master's, thesis (for some programs); for doctorate, thesis/dissertation, qualifying exam, teaching experience. *Entrance requirements:* For master's and doctorate, GRE General Test. Additional exam requirements/recommendations for international students: Required—TOEFL. *Application deadline:* For fall admission, 8/1 priority date for domestic students; for spring admission, 1/1 for domestic students. Application fee: $50. *Financial support:* In 2014–15, 8 research assistantships with full and partial tuition reimbursements, 5 teaching assistantships were awarded; institutionally sponsored loans also available. Financial award application deadline: 8/1; financial award applicants required to submit FAFSA. *Faculty research:* Infrastructure performance and reliability, environmental, geotechnical, infrastructure reliability, mechanics, structures. *Total annual research expenditures:* $940,000. *Unit head:* Dr. David Zeng, Chairman/Professor, 216-368-2923, Fax: 216-368-5229, E-mail: xxz16@case.edu. *Application contact:* Carla Wilson, Student Affairs Coordinator, 216-368-4580, Fax: 216-368-3007, E-mail: cxw75@case.edu.
Website: http://civil.case.edu.

The Catholic University of America, School of Engineering, Department of Civil Engineering, Washington, DC 20064. Offers environmental engineering (PhD). Part-time programs available. *Faculty:* 7 full-time (0 women), 9 part-time/adjunct (1 woman). *Students:* 11 full-time (2 women), 29 part-time (9 women); includes 13 minority (9 Black or African American, non-Hispanic/Latino; 2 Asian, non-Hispanic/Latino; 2 Two or more races, non-Hispanic/Latino), 18 international. Average age 39. 42 applicants, 69% accepted, 11 enrolled. In 2014, 7 master's, 2 doctorates awarded. *Degree requirements:* For master's, thesis optional; for doctorate, comprehensive exam, thesis/dissertation. *Entrance requirements:* For master's and doctorate, statement of purpose, official copies of academic transcripts, three letters of recommendation. Additional exam requirements/recommendations for international students: Required—TOEFL (minimum score 580 paper-based). *Application deadline:* For fall admission, 7/15 priority date for domestic students, 7/1 for international students; for spring admission, 11/15 priority date for domestic students, 11/1 for international students. Applications are processed on a rolling basis. Application fee: $55. Electronic applications accepted. *Expenses:* Expenses: Contact institution. *Financial support:* Fellowships, research assistantships, teaching assistantships, Federal Work-Study, scholarships/grants, tuition waivers (full and partial), and unspecified assistantships available. Financial award application deadline: 2/1; financial award applicants required to submit FAFSA. *Faculty research:* Geotechnical engineering, solid mechanics, construction engineering and management, environmental engineering, structural engineering. *Total annual research expenditures:* $363,826. *Unit head:* Dr. Lu Sun, Chair, 202-319-6671, Fax: 202-319-6677, E-mail: sunl@cua.edu. *Application contact:* Director of Graduate Admissions, 202-319-5057, Fax: 202-319-6533, E-mail: cua-admissions@cua.edu.
Website: http://civil.cua.edu/.

The Citadel, The Military College of South Carolina, Citadel Graduate College, Engineering Leadership and Program Management Department, Charleston, SC 29409. Offers technical project management (MS). Part-time and evening/weekend programs available. *Entrance requirements:* For master's, GRE or GMAT, evidence of a minimum of one year of professional experience, or permission from department head; two letters of reference; resume detailing previous work. Additional exam requirements/recommendations for international students: Required—TOEFL (minimum score 550 paper-based; 79 iBT). Electronic applications accepted.

City College of the City University of New York, Graduate School, Grove School of Engineering, Department of Civil Engineering, New York, NY 10031-9198. Offers ME, MS, PhD. PhD program offered jointly with Graduate School and University Center of the City University of New York. Part-time programs available. *Degree requirements:* For master's, thesis optional; for doctorate, one foreign language, comprehensive exam, thesis/dissertation. *Entrance requirements:* For master's and doctorate, GRE General Test. Additional exam requirements/recommendations for international students: Required—TOEFL (minimum score 500 paper-based; 61 iBT). *Faculty research:* Earthquake engineering, transportation systems, groundwater, environmental systems, highway systems.

Clarkson University, Graduate School, Wallace H. Coulter School of Engineering, Department of Civil and Environmental Engineering, Potsdam, NY 13699. Offers ME, MS, PhD. Part-time programs available. *Faculty:* 34 full-time (6 women), 9 part-time/adjunct (1 woman). *Students:* 31 full-time (9 women); includes 1 minority (Black or African American, non-Hispanic/Latino), 23 international. Average age 27. 64 applicants, 66% accepted, 10 enrolled. In 2014, 9 master's, 2 doctorates awarded. Terminal master's awarded for partial completion of doctoral program. *Degree requirements:* For master's, thesis (for MS); project (for ME); for doctorate, comprehensive exam, thesis/dissertation, departmental qualifying exam. *Entrance requirements:* For master's and doctorate, GRE, transcripts of all college coursework, resume, personal statement, three letters of recommendation. Additional exam requirements/recommendations for international students: Required—TOEFL (minimum score 550 paper-based; 80 iBT), IELTS (minimum score 6.5). *Application deadline:* For fall admission, 1/30 priority date for domestic and international students; for spring admission, 9/1 priority date for domestic and international students. Applications are processed on a rolling basis. Application fee: $25 ($35 for international students). Electronic applications accepted. *Expenses: Tuition:* Full-time $16,680; part-time $1390 per credit. *Required fees:* $295 per semester. *Financial support:* In 2014–15, 29 students received support, including 2 fellowships with full tuition reimbursements available (averaging $24,029 per year), 15 research assistantships with full tuition reimbursements available (averaging $24,029 per year), 7 teaching assistantships with full tuition reimbursements available (averaging $24,029 per year); scholarships/grants, tuition waivers (partial), and unspecified assistantships also available. *Faculty research:* Structural fatigue, deep water oil spill prediction, hydration kinetics and property evolution, ice-flow modeling. *Total annual research expenditures:* $3.5 million. *Unit head:* Dr. Stefan Grimberg, Chair, 315-268-6529, Fax: 315-268-7985, E-mail: grimberg@clarkson.edu. *Application contact:* Kelly Sharlow, Assistant to the Dean, 315-268-7929, Fax: 315-268-4494, E-mail: ksharlow@clarkson.edu.

Website: http://www.clarkson.edu/cee/.

Clemson University, Graduate School, College of Engineering and Science, Department of Civil Engineering, Clemson, SC 29634. Offers MS, PhD. Part-time programs available. *Faculty:* 26 full-time (3 women), 1 part-time/adjunct (0 women). *Students:* 130 full-time (29 women), 13 part-time (2 women); includes 7 minority (5 Black or African American, non-Hispanic/Latino; 1 Asian, non-Hispanic/Latino; 1 Two or more races, non-Hispanic/Latino), 83 international. Average age 27. 275 applicants, 59% accepted, 72 enrolled. In 2014, 41 master's, 13 doctorates awarded. *Degree requirements:* For master's, thesis or alternative, oral exam, seminar; for doctorate, comprehensive exam, thesis/dissertation, oral exam, seminar. *Entrance requirements:* For master's and doctorate, GRE General Test, minimum GPA of 3.0. Additional exam requirements/recommendations for international students: Required—TOEFL. *Application deadline:* For fall admission, 6/1 for domestic students, 4/15 for international students; for spring admission, 9/15 for international students. Applications are processed on a rolling basis. Application fee: $70 ($80 for international students). Electronic applications accepted. *Financial support:* In 2014–15, 73 students received support, including 29 fellowships with full and partial tuition reimbursements available (averaging $6,074 per year), 31 research assistantships with partial tuition reimbursements available (averaging $16,807 per year), 2 teaching assistantships with partial tuition reimbursements available (averaging $16,983 per year); career-related internships or fieldwork, institutionally sponsored loans, scholarships/grants, health care benefits, and unspecified assistantships also available. Support available to part-time students. Financial award application deadline: 2/15; financial award applicants required to submit FAFSA. *Faculty research:* Applied fluid mechanics, construction materials, project management, structural and geotechnical engineering, transportation. *Total annual research expenditures:* $3.2 million. *Unit head:* Dr. Nadim Aziz, Chair, 864-656-3300, Fax: 864-656-2670, E-mail: aziz@clemson.edu. *Application contact:* Dr. Ronald D. Andrus, Graduate Program Coordinator, 864-656-0488, Fax: 864-656-2670, E-mail: randrus@clemson.edu.

Website: http://www.clemson.edu/ce/.

Cleveland State University, College of Graduate Studies, Fenn College of Engineering, Department of Civil and Environmental Engineering, Cleveland, OH 44115. Offers accelerated civil engineering (MS); accelerated environmental engineering (MS); civil engineering (MS, D Eng); engineering mechanics (MS); environmental engineering (MS). Part-time and evening/weekend programs available. *Faculty:* 8 full-time (2 women). *Students:* 20 full-time (0 women), 46 part-time (6 women); includes 2 minority (both Asian, non-Hispanic/Latino), 41 international. Average age 26. 113 applicants, 53% accepted, 22 enrolled. In 2014, 18 master's, 2 doctorates awarded. *Degree requirements:* For master's, project or thesis; for doctorate, comprehensive exam, thesis/dissertation, candidacy and qualifying exams. *Entrance requirements:* For master's, GRE General Test, GRE Subject Test, minimum GPA of 2.75; for doctorate, GRE General Test, GRE Subject Test, minimum GPA of 3.25. Additional exam requirements/recommendations for international students: Required—TOEFL (minimum score 525 paper-based). *Application deadline:* For fall admission, 7/15 priority date for domestic students. Applications are processed on a rolling basis. Application fee: $30. *Expenses:* Tuition, state resident: full-time $9566; part-time $531 per credit hour. Tuition, nonresident: full-time $17,980; part-time $999 per credit hour. *Required fees:* $25 per semester. Tuition and fees vary according to degree level and program. *Financial support:* In 2014–15, 9 research assistantships with full and partial tuition reimbursements (averaging $3,920 per year) were awarded; teaching assistantships with tuition reimbursements, career-related internships or fieldwork, scholarships/grants, and unspecified assistantships also available. Financial award application deadline: 9/1. *Faculty research:* Solid-waste disposal, constitutive modeling, transportation, safety engineering, concrete materials. *Total annual research expenditures:* $800,000. *Unit head:* Dr. Norbert Joseph Delatte, Chairperson, 216-687-9259, Fax: 216-687-5395, E-mail: n.delatte@csuohio.edu. *Application contact:* Deborah L. Brown, Interim Assistant Director, Graduate Admissions, 216-523-7572, Fax: 216-687-9214, E-mail: d.l.brown@csuohio.edu.

Website: http://www.csuohio.edu/engineering/civil.

Colorado School of Mines, Graduate School, Department of Civil and Environmental Engineering, Golden, CO 80401. Offers civil and environmental engineering (MS, PhD); environmental engineering science (MS, PhD); underground construction and tunneling (MS, PhD). Part-time programs available. *Faculty:* 40 full-time (14 women), 17 part-time/adjunct (8 women). *Students:* 120 full-time (40 women), 32 part-time (13 women); includes 23 minority (1 Black or African American, non-Hispanic/Latino; 8 Asian, non-Hispanic/Latino; 12 Hispanic/Latino; 2 Two or more races, non-Hispanic/Latino), 19 international. Average age 29. 158 applicants, 55% accepted, 44 enrolled. In 2014, 69 master's, 6 doctorates awarded. *Degree requirements:* For master's, thesis (for some programs); for doctorate, comprehensive exam, thesis/dissertation. *Entrance requirements:* For master's and doctorate, GRE General Test. Additional exam requirements/recommendations for international students: Required—TOEFL (minimum score 550 paper-based; 80 iBT). *Application deadline:* For fall admission, 12/15 priority date for domestic students, 1/15 priority date for international students; for spring admission, 9/1 priority date for domestic and international students. Application fee: $50 ($70 for international students). Electronic applications accepted. *Financial support:* In 2014–15, 82 students received support, including 11 fellowships with full tuition reimbursements available (averaging $21,120 per year), 54 research assistantships with full tuition reimbursements available (averaging $21,120 per year), 6 teaching assistantships with full tuition reimbursements available (averaging $21,120 per year); scholarships/grants, health care benefits, and unspecified assistantships also available. Financial award application deadline: 12/15; financial award applicants required to submit FAFSA. *Faculty research:* Treatment of water and wastes, environmental law: policy and practice, natural environment systems, hazardous waste management, environmental data analysis. *Total annual research expenditures:* $6.7 million. *Unit head:* Dr. John McCray, Deptartment Head, 303-384-3490, Fax: 303-273-3413, E-mail: jmccray@mines.edu. *Application contact:* Tim VanHaverbeke, Research Faculty, 303-273-3467, Fax: 303-273-3413, E-mail: tvanhave@mines.edu.

Colorado State University, Graduate School, College of Engineering, Department of Civil and Environmental Engineering, Fort Collins, CO 80523-1372. Offers civil engineering (ME, MS, PhD). Part-time programs available. Postbaccalaureate distance learning degree programs offered (no on-campus study). *Faculty:* 27 full-time (4 women). *Students:* 100 full-time (23 women), 140 part-time (48 women); includes 11 minority (1 Black or African American, non-Hispanic/Latino; 3 Asian, non-Hispanic/Latino; 5 Hispanic/Latino; 2 Two or more races, non-Hispanic/Latino), 104 international. Average age 30. 290 applicants, 68% accepted, 56 enrolled. In 2014, 42 master's, 9 doctorates awarded. Terminal master's awarded for partial completion of doctoral program. *Degree requirements:* For master's, comprehensive exam (for some programs), thesis or alternative, Publication; for doctorate, comprehensive exam, thesis/dissertation, Publication. *Entrance requirements:* For master's and doctorate, GRE, TOEFL or IELTS (international), 3.0 GPA. Additional exam requirements/recommendations for international students: Required—TOEFL (minimum score 550 paper-based; 80 iBT), IELTS (minimum score 6.5). *Application deadline:* For fall admission, 2/15 priority date for domestic and international students; for spring admission, 9/1 priority date for domestic and international students. Applications are processed on a rolling basis. Application fee: $50. Electronic applications accepted. *Expenses:* Expenses: Contact institution. *Financial support:* In 2014–15, 66 students received support, including 4 fellowships (averaging $26,238 per year), 52 research assistantships with full tuition reimbursements available (averaging $15,868 per year), 10 teaching assistantships with full tuition reimbursements available (averaging $8,648 per year); unspecified assistantships also available. Financial award application deadline: 1/1; financial award applicants required to submit FAFSA. *Faculty research:* Urban water sustainability, community resiliency, shale oil and gas development, fatigue and fracture of steel structures, natural and anthropogenic hazard mitigation of infrastructure. *Total annual research expenditures:* $15.2 million. *Unit head:* Dr. Charles Shackelford, Head, 970-491-5051, Fax: 970-491-7727, E-mail: charles.shackelford@colostate.edu. *Application contact:* Laurie Alburn, Academic Advisor, 970-491-5844, Fax: 970-491-7727, E-mail: laurie.alburn@colostate.edu.

Website: http://www.engr.colostate.edu/ce/.

Columbia University, Fu Foundation School of Engineering and Applied Science, Department of Civil Engineering and Engineering Mechanics, New York, NY 10027. Offers civil engineering (MS, Eng Sc D, PhD); construction engineering and management (MS); engineering mechanics (MS, Eng Sc D, PhD). Part-time programs available. Postbaccalaureate distance learning degree programs offered (no on-campus study). *Faculty:* 19 full-time (4 women), 27 part-time/adjunct (2 women). *Students:* 153 full-time (40 women), 100 part-time (27 women); includes 19 minority (1 Black or African American, non-Hispanic/Latino; 11 Asian, non-Hispanic/Latino; 6 Hispanic/Latino; 1 Two or more races, non-Hispanic/Latino), 194 international. 504 applicants, 38% accepted, 110 enrolled. In 2014, 131 master's, 7 doctorates awarded. Terminal master's awarded for partial completion of doctoral program. *Degree requirements:* For doctorate, thesis/dissertation, qualifying exam. *Entrance requirements:* For master's and doctorate, GRE General Test. Additional exam requirements/recommendations for international students: Required—TOEFL, IELTS, PTE. *Application deadline:* For fall admission, 12/15 priority date for domestic and international students; for spring admission, 10/1 priority date for domestic and international students. Application fee: $85. Electronic applications accepted. *Financial support:* In 2014–15, 44 students received support, including 13 fellowships with full tuition reimbursements available (averaging $27,500 per year), 18 research assistantships with full tuition reimbursements available (averaging $32,448 per year), 13 teaching assistantships with full tuition reimbursements available (averaging $32,448 per year); health care benefits also available. Financial award application deadline: 12/15; financial award applicants required to submit FAFSA. *Faculty research:* Structural dynamics, structural health and monitoring, fatigue and fracture mechanics, geo-environmental engineering, multiscale science and engineering. *Unit head:* Dr. George Deodatis, Professor and Chair, Civil Engineering and Engineering Mechanics, 212-854-6267, E-mail: deodatis@civil.columbia.edu. *Application contact:* Scott Kelly, Graduate Admissions and Student Affairs, 212-854-3219, E-mail: kelly@civil.columbia.edu.

Website: http://www.civil.columbia.edu/.

Concordia University, School of Graduate Studies, Faculty of Engineering and Computer Science, Department of Building, Civil and Environmental Engineering, Montréal, QC H3G 1M8, Canada. Offers building engineering (M Eng, MA Sc, PhD, Certificate); civil engineering (M Eng, MA Sc, PhD); environmental engineering (Certificate). *Degree requirements:* For master's, thesis or alternative; for doctorate, comprehensive exam, thesis/dissertation. *Faculty research:* Structural engineering, geotechnical engineering, water resources and fluid engineering, transportation engineering, systems engineering.

Cooper Union for the Advancement of Science and Art, Albert Nerken School of Engineering, New York, NY 10003-7120. Offers chemical engineering (ME); civil engineering (ME); electrical engineering (ME); mechanical engineering (ME). Part-time programs available. *Faculty:* 27 full-time (1 woman), 15 part-time/adjunct (2 women). *Students:* 45 full-time (10 women), 20 part-time (4 women); includes 24 minority (3 Black or African American, non-Hispanic/Latino; 15 Asian, non-Hispanic/Latino; 4 Hispanic/Latino; 2 Two or more races, non-Hispanic/Latino), 4 international. Average age 23. 86 applicants, 71% accepted, 44 enrolled. In 2014, 22 master's awarded. *Degree requirements:* For master's, thesis (for some programs). *Entrance requirements:* For master's, BE or BS in engineering discipline, high school and college transcripts, two letters of recommendation, resume. Additional exam requirements/recommendations for international students: Required—TOEFL (minimum score 600 paper-based; 100 iBT). *Application deadline:* For fall admission, 4/1 for domestic and international students. Application fee: $70. Electronic applications accepted. *Expenses: Tuition:* Full-time $39,600; part-time $1173 per credit. *Required fees:* $925 per semester. One-time fee: $250. *Financial support:* In 2014–15, 65 students received support, including 4 fellowships with full and partial tuition reimbursements available (averaging $11,000 per year); career-related internships or fieldwork, Federal Work-Study, tuition waivers (full and partial), and tuition scholarships offered to exceptional students also available. Support available to part-time students. Financial award application deadline: 5/1; financial award applicants required to submit FAFSA. *Faculty research:* Civil infrastructure, imaging and sensing technology, biomedical engineering, encryption technology, process engineering. *Unit head:* Dr. Teresa Dahlberg, Dean of Engineering, 212-353-4285, E-mail: dahlberg@cooper.edu. *Application contact:* Student Contact, 212-353-4120, E-mail: admissions@cooper.edu.

Website: http://cooper.edu/engineering.

Cornell University, Graduate School, Graduate Fields of Engineering, Field of Civil and Environmental Engineering, Ithaca, NY 14853-0001. Offers engineering management (M Eng, MS, PhD); environmental engineering (M Eng, MS, PhD); environmental fluid mechanics and hydrology (M Eng, MS, PhD); environmental systems engineering (M Eng, MS, PhD); geotechnical engineering (M Eng, MS, PhD); remote sensing (M Eng, MS, PhD); structural engineering (M Eng, MS, PhD); structural mechanics (M Eng, MS); transportation engineering (MS, PhD); transportation systems engineering (M Eng); water resource systems (M Eng, MS, PhD). Terminal master's awarded for partial completion of doctoral program. *Degree requirements:* For master's, thesis (MS); for doctorate, comprehensive exam, thesis/dissertation. *Entrance requirements:* For master's and doctorate, GRE General Test (recommended), 2 letters of recommendation. Additional exam requirements/recommendations for international students: Required—TOEFL (minimum score 600 paper-based; 77 iBT). Electronic applications accepted. *Faculty research:* Environmental engineering, geotechnical engineering, remote sensing, environmental fluid mechanics and hydrology, structural engineering.

Dalhousie University, Faculty of Engineering, Department of Civil and Resource Engineering, Halifax, NS B3J 2X4, Canada. Offers M Eng, MA Sc, PhD. *Degree requirements:* For master's, thesis; for doctorate, thesis/dissertation. *Entrance requirements:* Additional exam requirements/recommendations for international students: Required—TOEFL, IELTS, CANTEST, CAEL, or Michigan English Language

Assessment Battery. Electronic applications accepted. *Faculty research:* Environmental/water resources, bridge engineering, geotechnical engineering, pavement design and management/highway materials, composite materials.

Drexel University, College of Engineering, Department of Civil, Architectural, and Environmental Engineering, Program in Civil Engineering, Philadelphia, PA 19104-2875. Offers MS, PhD. Part-time and evening/weekend programs available. *Degree requirements:* For master's, thesis optional; for doctorate, thesis/dissertation. *Entrance requirements:* For master's, minimum GPA of 3.0; for doctorate, minimum GPA of 3.5, MS in civil engineering. Additional exam requirements/recommendations for international students: Required—TOEFL. Electronic applications accepted.

Duke University, Graduate School, Pratt School of Engineering, Department of Civil and Environmental Engineering, Durham, NC 27708. Offers civil and environmental engineering (MS, PhD); environmental engineering (MS, PhD). *Faculty:* 18 full-time (3 women). *Students:* 50 full-time (26 women); includes 10 minority (4 Black or African American, non-Hispanic/Latino; 3 Asian, non-Hispanic/Latino; 3 Hispanic/Latino), 22 international. 176 applicants, 17% accepted, 12 enrolled. In 2014, 9 master's, 11 doctorates awarded. Terminal master's awarded for partial completion of doctoral program. *Degree requirements:* For doctorate, thesis/dissertation. *Entrance requirements:* For master's and doctorate, GRE General Test. Additional exam requirements/recommendations for international students: Required—TOEFL (minimum score 550 paper-based; 90 iBT), IELTS (minimum score 7). *Application deadline:* For fall admission, 12/8 priority date for domestic and international students; for spring admission, 10/15 for domestic students. Application fee: $80. Electronic applications accepted. *Expenses: Tuition:* Full-time $45,760; part-time $2765 per credit. *Required fees:* $978. Full-time tuition and fees vary according to program. *Financial support:* Fellowships, research assistantships, and Federal Work-Study available. Financial award application deadline: 12/8. *Faculty research:* Environmental process engineering, hydrology and fluid dynamics, materials, structures and geo-systems. *Unit head:* Prof. John Dolbow, Director of Graduate Studies, 919-660-5200, Fax: 919-660-5219, E-mail: john.dolbow@duke.edu. *Application contact:* Ruby Nell Carpenter, DGSA, DUSA, DMSA, Staff assistant, 919-660-5200, Fax: 919-660-5219, E-mail: rubync@duke.edu.
Website: http://www.cee.duke.edu/graduate-studies/.

Duke University, Graduate School, Pratt School of Engineering, Master of Engineering Program, Durham, NC 27708-0271. Offers biomedical engineering (M Eng); civil engineering (M Eng); electrical and computer engineering (M Eng); environmental engineering (M Eng); materials science and engineering (M Eng); mechanical engineering (M Eng); photonics and optical sciences (M Eng). Part-time programs available. *Students:* 45 full-time (17 women); includes 5 minority (1 Black or African American, non-Hispanic/Latino; 2 Asian, non-Hispanic/Latino; 2 Hispanic/Latino), 23 international. Average age 24. 285 applicants, 43% accepted, 45 enrolled. In 2014, 45 master's awarded. *Entrance requirements:* For master's, GRE General Test, resume, 3 letters of recommendation, statement of purpose, transcripts. Additional exam requirements/recommendations for international students: Required—TOEFL. *Application deadline:* For fall admission, 6/15 for domestic students, 2/15 for international students; for spring admission, 11/1 for domestic students, 9/1 for international students. Application fee: $75. *Expenses: Tuition:* Full-time $45,760; part-time $2765 per credit. *Required fees:* $978. Full-time tuition and fees vary according to program. *Financial support:* Merit scholarships/grants available. *Unit head:* Dr. Bradley A. Fox, Executive Director, 919-660-5455, Fax: 919-660-5456. *Application contact:* Susan Brown, Assistant Director of Admissions, 919-660-8451, Fax: 919-660-5456, E-mail: susan.brown@duke.edu.
Website: http://meng.pratt.duke.edu/.

École Polytechnique de Montréal, Graduate Programs, Department of Civil, Geological and Mining Engineering, Montréal, QC H3C 3A7, Canada. Offers civil, geological and mining engineering (DESS); environmental engineering (M Eng, M Sc A, PhD); geotechnical engineering (M Eng, M Sc A, PhD); hydraulics engineering (M Eng, M Sc A, PhD); structural engineering (M Eng, M Sc A, PhD); transportation engineering (M Eng, M Sc A, PhD). Part-time programs available. *Degree requirements:* For master's, one foreign language, thesis; for doctorate, one foreign language, thesis/dissertation. *Entrance requirements:* For master's, minimum GPA of 2.75; for doctorate, minimum GPA of 3.0. *Faculty research:* Water resources management, characteristics of building materials, aging of dams, pollution control.

Florida Agricultural and Mechanical University, Division of Graduate Studies, Research, and Continuing Education, FAMU-FSU College of Engineering, Department of Civil and Environmental Engineering, Tallahassee, FL 32307-3200. Offers civil engineering (M Eng, MS, PhD). *Degree requirements:* For master's, comprehensive exam, thesis optional; for doctorate, comprehensive exam, thesis/dissertation. *Entrance requirements:* For master's, GRE General Test, minimum GPA of 3.0; for doctorate, GRE General Test, minimum GPA of 3.0, letters of recommendation (3). Additional exam requirements/recommendations for international students: Required—TOEFL (minimum score 550 paper-based). *Faculty research:* Geotechnical, environmental, hydraulic, construction materials, and structures.

Florida Atlantic University, College of Engineering and Computer Science, Department of Civil, Environmental and Geomatics Engineering, Boca Raton, FL 33431-0991. Offers civil engineering (MS); environmental engineering (MS). Part-time and evening/weekend programs available. *Degree requirements:* For master's, thesis optional. *Entrance requirements:* For master's, GRE General Test, minimum GPA of 3.0 in last 60 hours of undergraduate course work. Additional exam requirements/recommendations for international students: Required—TOEFL (minimum score 550 paper-based; 61 iBT), IELTS (minimum score 6). *Expenses:* Tuition, state resident: full-time $7396; part-time $369.82 per credit hour. Tuition, nonresident: full-time $19,392; part-time $1024.81 per credit hour. Tuition and fees vary according to course load. *Faculty research:* Structures, geotechnical engineering, environmental and water resources engineering, transportation engineering, materials.

Florida Institute of Technology, Graduate Programs, College of Engineering, Program in Civil Engineering, Melbourne, FL 32901-6975. Offers MS, PhD. Part-time programs available. *Students:* 30 full-time (9 women), 8 part-time (3 women); includes 1 minority (Hispanic/Latino), 30 international. Average age 29. 179 applicants, 27% accepted, 10 enrolled. In 2014, 14 master's awarded. *Degree requirements:* For master's, comprehensive exam (for some programs), thesis (for some programs), teaching/internship (for thesis) or final examinations (for non-thesis); for doctorate, comprehensive exam, thesis/dissertation, research project, preliminary examination. *Entrance requirements:* For master's, GRE, 2 letters of recommendation, minimum GPA of 3.0, statement of objectives; for doctorate, GRE, 3 letters of recommendation, minimum GPA of 3.2, resume, statement of objectives. Additional exam requirements/recommendations for international students: Required—TOEFL (minimum score 550 paper-based; 79 iBT). *Application deadline:* For fall admission, 4/1 for international students; for spring admission, 9/30 for international students. Applications are processed on a rolling basis. Electronic applications accepted. *Expenses: Tuition:* Part-time $1179 per credit hour. Tuition and fees vary according to campus/location. *Financial support:* In 2014–15, 7 research assistantships, 5 teaching assistantships were awarded; career-related internships or fieldwork, institutionally sponsored loans, tuition waivers (partial), unspecified assistantships, and tuition remissions also available. Support available to part-time students. Financial award application deadline: 3/1; financial award applicants required to submit FAFSA. *Faculty research:* Groundwater and surface water modeling, pavements, waste materials, in situ soil testing, fiber optic sensors. *Total annual research expenditures:* $286,567. *Unit head:* Dr. Ashok Pandit, Department Head, 321-674-7151, Fax: 321-768-7565, E-mail: apandit@fit.edu. *Application contact:* Cheryl A. Brown, Associate Director of Graduate Admissions, 321-674-7581, Fax: 321-723-9468, E-mail: cbrown@fit.edu.
Website: http://coe.fit.edu/civil/.

Florida International University, College of Engineering and Computing, Department of Civil and Environmental Engineering, Program in Civil Engineering, Miami, FL 33175. Offers MS, PhD. Part-time and evening/weekend programs available. Postbaccalaureate distance learning degree programs offered (no on-campus study). *Degree requirements:* For master's, thesis optional; for doctorate, comprehensive exam, thesis/dissertation. *Entrance requirements:* For master's, bachelor's degree in related field, minimum GPA of 3.0; for doctorate, GRE General Test, minimum graduate GPA of 3.3, master's degree, resume, letters of recommendation, statement of objectives. Additional exam requirements/recommendations for international students: Required—TOEFL (minimum score 550 paper-based; 80 iBT). Electronic applications accepted. *Faculty research:* Structural engineering, wind engineering, sustainable infrastructure engineering, water resources engineering, transportation engineering.

Florida State University, The Graduate School, FAMU-FSU College of Engineering, Department of Civil and Environmental Engineering, Tallahassee, FL 32310. Offers M Eng, MS, PhD. Part-time programs available. *Degree requirements:* For master's, comprehensive exam, thesis optional; for doctorate, thesis/dissertation. *Entrance requirements:* For master's, GRE General Test (minimum score 1000 in old version), BS in engineering or related field, minimum GPA of 3.0; for doctorate, GRE General Test, master's degree in engineering or related field, minimum GPA of 3.0. Additional exam requirements/recommendations for international students: Required—TOEFL (minimum score 550 paper-based; 80 iBT); Recommended—IELTS (minimum score 6.5). *Expenses:* Tuition, state resident: part-time $403.51 per credit hour. Tuition, nonresident: part-time $1004.85 per credit hour. *Required fees:* $75.81 per credit hour. One-time fee: $20 part-time. Tuition and fees vary according to campus/location. *Faculty research:* Tidal hydraulics, temperature effects on bridge girders, codes for coastal construction, field performance of pine bridges, river basin management, transportation pavement design, soil dynamics, structural analysis.

George Mason University, Volgenau School of Engineering, Sid and Reva Dewberry Department of Civil, Environmental, and Infrastructure Engineering, Fairfax, VA 22030. Offers construction project management (MS); environmental and water resources engineering (MS); geotechnical, construction, and structural engineering (M Eng); transportation engineering (MS, PhD). *Faculty:* 12 full-time (4 women), 16 part-time/adjunct (3 women). *Students:* 28 full-time (7 women), 51 part-time (13 women); includes 25 minority (12 Black or African American, non-Hispanic/Latino; 8 Asian, non-Hispanic/Latino; 5 Hispanic/Latino), 14 international. Average age 30. 90 applicants, 58% accepted, 25 enrolled. In 2014, 28 master's, 3 doctorates awarded. *Degree requirements:* For master's, thesis (for some programs), 30 credits, departmental seminars; for doctorate, thesis/dissertation, qualifying exams. *Entrance requirements:* For master's, GRE, photocopy of passport; 2 official college transcripts; resume; official bank statement; proof of financial support; expanded goals statement; self-evaluation form; BS in engineering or other related science; 3 letters of recommendation; for doctorate, GRE (for those who received degree outside of the U.S.), photocopy of passport; 2 official college transcripts; resume; official bank statement; proof of financial support; expanded goals statement; self-evaluation form; baccalaureate degree in engineering or related science; master's degree (preferred); 3 letters of recommendation. Additional exam requirements/recommendations for international students: Required—TOEFL (minimum score 575 paper-based; 80 iBT), IELTS (minimum score 6.5), PTE. *Application deadline:* For fall admission, 1/15 priority date for domestic students; for spring admission, 8/1 priority date for domestic students. Application fee: $65 ($80 for international students). Electronic applications accepted. *Expenses:* Expenses: Contact institution. *Financial support:* In 2014–15, 19 students received support, including 1 fellowship (averaging $5,000 per year), 9 research assistantships with full and partial tuition reimbursements available (averaging $23,846 per year), 10 teaching assistantships with full and partial tuition reimbursements available (averaging $21,200 per year); career-related internships or fieldwork, Federal Work-Study, scholarships/grants, unspecified assistantships, and health care benefits (for full-time research or teaching assistantship recipients) also available. Support available to part-time students. Financial award application deadline: 3/1; financial award applicants required to submit FAFSA. *Faculty research:* Evolutionary design, infrastructure security, intelligent transportation systems, national transportation networks, water quality modeling. *Total annual research expenditures:* $159,347. *Unit head:* Dr. Deborah J. Goodings, Chair, 703-993-1675, Fax: 703-993-9790, E-mail: goodings@gmu.edu. *Application contact:* Kristin Amaya, Administrative Assistant, 703-993-1675, Fax: 703-993-9790, E-mail: kfairch1@gmu.edu.
Website: http://civil.gmu.edu/.

The George Washington University, School of Engineering and Applied Science, Department of Civil and Environmental Engineering, Washington, DC 20052. Offers MS, PhD, App Sc, Engr, Graduate Certificate. Part-time and evening/weekend programs available. *Faculty:* 12 full-time (3 women), 15 part-time/adjunct (0 women). *Students:* 17 full-time (4 women), 27 part-time (6 women); includes 3 minority (1 Black or African American, non-Hispanic/Latino; 1 Asian, non-Hispanic/Latino; 1 Hispanic/Latino), 30 international. Average age 30. 134 applicants, 51% accepted, 7 enrolled. In 2014, 14 master's, 4 doctorates awarded. *Degree requirements:* For master's, thesis optional; for doctorate, thesis/dissertation, final and qualifying exams. *Entrance requirements:* For master's, appropriate bachelor's degree, minimum GPA of 3.0; for doctorate, GRE (if highest earned degree is BS), appropriate bachelor's or master's degree, minimum GPA of 3.4; for other advanced degree, appropriate master's degree, minimum GPA of 3.0. Additional exam requirements/recommendations for international students: Required—TOEFL or The George Washington University English as a Foreign Language Test. *Application deadline:* For fall admission, 3/1 priority date for domestic students; for spring admission, 10/1 for domestic students. Applications are processed on a rolling basis. Application fee: $75. *Financial support:* In 2014–15, 42 students received support. Fellowships with tuition reimbursements available, research assistantships, teaching assistantships with tuition reimbursements available, career-related internships or fieldwork, Federal Work-Study, institutionally sponsored loans, and tuition waivers available. Financial award application deadline: 3/1; financial award applicants required to submit FAFSA. *Faculty research:* Computer-integrated manufacturing, materials engineering, electronic materials, fatigue and fracture, reliability. *Unit head:* Dr. Majid Manzari, Chair, 202-994-8515, Fax: 202-994-0127, E-mail: manzari@gwu.edu. *Application contact:* Adina Lav, Marketing, Recruiting and Admissions, 202-994-5827, Fax: 202-994-0909, E-mail: engineering@gwu.edu.
Website: http://www.cee.seas.gwu.edu/.

Georgia Institute of Technology, Graduate Studies, College of Engineering, School of Civil and Environmental Engineering, Program in Civil Engineering, Atlanta, GA 30332-0001. Offers MS, PhD. Part-time programs available. *Students:* 226 full-time (57

women), 37 part-time (8 women); includes 34 minority (8 Black or African American, non-Hispanic/Latino; 10 Asian, non-Hispanic/Latino; 14 Hispanic/Latino; 2 Two or more races, non-Hispanic/Latino), 161 international. Average age 25. 658 applicants, 34% accepted, 67 enrolled. In 2014, 89 master's, 22 doctorates awarded. Terminal master's awarded for partial completion of doctoral program. *Degree requirements:* For master's, thesis optional; for doctorate, comprehensive exam, thesis/dissertation. *Entrance requirements:* For master's and doctorate, GRE, http://www.grad.gatech.edu/ce. Additional exam requirements/recommendations for international students: Required—TOEFL (minimum score 550 paper-based; 79 iBT). *Application deadline:* For fall admission, 12/15 for domestic and international students; for spring admission, 8/31 for domestic and international students; for summer admission, 12/15 for domestic and international students. Applications are processed on a rolling basis. Application fee: $75. Electronic applications accepted. *Expenses:* Tuition, state resident: full-time $12,344; part-time $515 per credit hour. Tuition, nonresident: full-time $27,600; part-time $1150 per credit hour. *Required fees:* $1196 per term. Part-time tuition and fees vary according to course load. *Financial support:* Fellowships, research assistantships, teaching assistantships, career-related internships or fieldwork, Federal Work-Study, institutionally sponsored loans, tuition waivers (partial), and unspecified assistantships available. Support available to part-time students. Financial award application deadline: 5/1. *Faculty research:* Structural analysis, fluid mechanics, geotechnical engineering, construction management, transportation engineering. *Unit head:* Jim Mulholland, Director, 404-894-1695, E-mail: james.mulholland@ce.gatech.edu. *Application contact:* Robert Simon, Graduate Coordinator, 404-894-1660, E-mail: robert.simon@gatech.edu.
Website: http://www.ce.gatech.edu.

The Graduate Center, City University of New York, Graduate Studies, Program in Engineering, New York, NY 10016-4039. Offers biomedical engineering (PhD); chemical engineering (PhD); civil engineering (PhD); electrical engineering (PhD); mechanical engineering (PhD). *Degree requirements:* For doctorate, thesis/dissertation. *Entrance requirements:* For doctorate, GRE General Test. Additional exam requirements/recommendations for international students: Required—TOEFL. Electronic applications accepted.

Howard University, College of Engineering, Architecture, and Computer Sciences, School of Engineering and Computer Science, Department of Civil Engineering, Washington, DC 20059-0002. Offers M Eng. Offered through the Graduate School of Arts and Sciences. *Degree requirements:* For master's, comprehensive exam, thesis. *Entrance requirements:* For master's, GRE General Test, minimum GPA of 3.0, bachelor's degree in engineering or related field. Additional exam requirements/recommendations for international students: Required—TOEFL. Electronic applications accepted. *Faculty research:* Modeling of concrete, structures, transportation planning, structural analysis, environmental and water resources.

Idaho State University, Office of Graduate Studies, College of Science and Engineering, Civil and Environmental Engineering Department, Pocatello, ID 83209-8060. Offers civil engineering (MS); environmental engineering (MS); environmental science and management (MS). Part-time programs available. *Degree requirements:* For master's, comprehensive exam (for some programs), thesis optional, thesis project, 2 semesters of seminar. *Entrance requirements:* For master's, GRE. Additional exam requirements/recommendations for international students: Required—TOEFL (minimum score 550 paper-based; 80 iBT). Electronic applications accepted. *Faculty research:* Floor vibration investigations, earthquake engineering, base isolation systems and seismic risk assessment, infrastructure revitalization (building foundations and damage, bridge structures, highways, and dams), slope stability and soil erosion, pavement rehabilitation, computational fluid dynamics and flood control structures, microbial fuel cells, water treatment and water quality modeling, environmental risk assessment, biotechnology, nanotechnology.

Illinois Institute of Technology, Graduate College, Armour College of Engineering, Department of Civil, Architectural and Environmental Engineering, Chicago, IL 60616. Offers architectural engineering (M Arch E); civil engineering (MS, PhD), including architectural engineering (MS), construction engineering and management (MS), geoenvironmental engineering (MS), geotechnical engineering (MS), structural engineering (MS), transportation engineering (MS); construction engineering and management (MCEM); environmental engineering (M Env E, MS, PhD); geoenvironmental engineering (M Geoenv E); geotechnical engineering (MGE); infrastructure engineering and management (MPW); structural engineering (MSE); transportation engineering (M Trans E). Part-time and evening/weekend programs available. Postbaccalaureate distance learning degree programs offered (minimal on-campus study). *Faculty:* 12 full-time (1 woman), 15 part-time/adjunct (1 woman). *Students:* 165 full-time (48 women), 54 part-time (11 women); includes 31 minority (2 Black or African American, non-Hispanic/Latino; 21 Asian, non-Hispanic/Latino; 7 Hispanic/Latino; 1 Native Hawaiian or other Pacific Islander, non-Hispanic/Latino), 157 international. Average age 29. 1,039 applicants, 42% accepted, 82 enrolled. In 2014, 94 master's, 7 doctorates awarded. Terminal master's awarded for partial completion of doctoral program. *Degree requirements:* For master's, thesis (for some programs); for doctorate, comprehensive exam, thesis/dissertation. *Entrance requirements:* For master's, GRE General Test (minimum score 900 Quantitative and Verbal, 2.5 Analytical Writing), minimum undergraduate GPA of 3.0; for doctorate, GRE General Test (minimum score 1000 Quantitative and Verbal, 3.0 Analytical Writing), minimum undergraduate GPA of 3.0. Additional exam requirements/recommendations for international students: Required—TOEFL (minimum score 550 paper-based; 80 iBT). *Application deadline:* For fall admission, 5/1 for domestic and international students; for spring admission, 10/15 for domestic and international students. Applications are processed on a rolling basis. Application fee: $50. Electronic applications accepted. *Expenses: Tuition:* Full-time $22,500; part-time $1250 per credit hour. *Required fees:* $30 per course. $260 per semester. One-time fee: $235. Tuition and fees vary according to course load and program. *Financial support:* Fellowships with full and partial tuition reimbursements, research assistantships with full and partial tuition reimbursements, teaching assistantships with full and partial tuition reimbursements, Federal Work-Study, institutionally sponsored loans, scholarships/grants, health care benefits, tuition waivers (partial), and unspecified assistantships available. Support available to part-time students. Financial award applicants required to submit FAFSA. *Faculty research:* Structural, architectural, geotechnical and geoenvironmental engineering; construction engineering and management; transportation engineering; environmental engineering and public works. *Unit head:* Dr. Gongkang Fu, Professor and Chairman, 312-567-3540, Fax: 312-567-3519, E-mail: gfu2@iit.edu. *Application contact:* Rishab Malhotra, Director, Graduate Admission, 866-472-3448, Fax: 312-567-3138, E-mail: inquiry.grad@iit.edu.
Website: http://engineering.iit.edu/caee.

Indiana University–Purdue University Fort Wayne, College of Engineering, Technology, and Computer Science, Department of Engineering, Fort Wayne, IN 46805-1499. Offers civil engineering (MSE); computer engineering (MSE); electrical engineering (MSE); mechanical engineering (MSE); systems engineering (MSE). Part-time programs available. *Faculty:* 21 full-time (2 women). *Students:* 4 full-time (1 woman), 15 part-time (1 woman); includes 3 minority (2 Black or African American, non-Hispanic/Latino; 1 Asian, non-Hispanic/Latino), 2 international. Average age 30. 13 applicants, 100% accepted, 10 enrolled. In 2014, 17 master's awarded. *Entrance requirements:* For master's, minimum GPA of 3.0, bachelor's degree in engineering discipline. Additional exam requirements/recommendations for international students: Required—TOEFL (minimum score 550 paper-based; 79 iBT); Recommended—TWE. *Application deadline:* For fall admission, 7/15 priority date for domestic students, 5/15 priority date for international students; for spring admission, 12/1 priority date for domestic students, 10/15 priority date for international students. Applications are processed on a rolling basis. Application fee: $55 ($60 for international students). Electronic applications accepted. *Financial support:* In 2014–15, 3 research assistantships with partial tuition reimbursements (averaging $13,522 per year), 1 teaching assistantship with partial tuition reimbursement (averaging $13,522 per year) were awarded. Financial award application deadline: 3/1; financial award applicants required to submit FAFSA. *Faculty research:* Continuous space language model, sensor networks, wireless cloud architecture. *Total annual research expenditures:* $841,333. *Unit head:* Dr. Nashwan Younis, Chair, 260-481-6887, Fax: 260-481-6281, E-mail: younis@engr.ipfw.edu. *Application contact:* Dr. Abdullah Eroglu, Program Director/Professor, 260-481-0273, Fax: 260-481-5734, E-mail: eroglua@ipfw.edu.
Website: http://www.ipfw.edu/engr.

Instituto Tecnológico y de Estudios Superiores de Monterrey, Campus Monterrey, Graduate and Research Division, Programs in Engineering, Monterrey, Mexico. Offers applied statistics (M Eng); artificial intelligence (PhD); automation engineering (M Eng); chemical engineering (M Eng); civil engineering (M Eng); electrical engineering (M Eng); electronic engineering (M Eng); environmental engineering (M Eng); industrial engineering (M Eng, PhD); manufacturing engineering (M Eng); mechanical engineering (M Eng); systems and quality engineering (M Eng). M Eng program offered jointly with University of Waterloo; PhD in industrial engineering with Texas A&M University. Part-time and evening/weekend programs available. Terminal master's awarded for partial completion of doctoral program. *Degree requirements:* For master's, one foreign language, thesis; for doctorate, one foreign language, thesis/dissertation. *Entrance requirements:* For master's, EXADEP; for doctorate, GRE, master's degree in related field. Additional exam requirements/recommendations for international students: Required—TOEFL. *Faculty research:* Flexible manufacturing cells, materials, statistical methods, environmental prevention, control and evaluation.

Iowa State University of Science and Technology, Department of Civil and Construction Engineering, Ames, IA 50011. Offers civil engineering (MS, PhD), including civil engineering materials, construction engineering and management, environmental engineering, geometronics, geotechnical engineering, structural engineering, transportation engineering. *Degree requirements:* For master's, thesis or alternative; for doctorate, thesis/dissertation. *Entrance requirements:* For master's and doctorate, GRE General Test. Additional exam requirements/recommendations for international students: Required—TOEFL (minimum score 550 paper-based; 82 iBT), IELTS (minimum score 6.5). Electronic applications accepted.

Johns Hopkins University, Engineering Program for Professionals, Part-time Program in Civil Engineering, Baltimore, MD 21218-2699. Offers MCE. Part-time and evening/weekend programs available. Electronic applications accepted.

Johns Hopkins University, G. W. C. Whiting School of Engineering, Department of Civil Engineering, Baltimore, MD 21218. Offers MSE, PhD. Terminal master's awarded for partial completion of doctoral program. *Degree requirements:* For master's, thesis (for some programs); for doctorate, comprehensive exam, thesis/dissertation, qualifying and oral exams. *Entrance requirements:* For master's and doctorate, GRE General Test. Additional exam requirements/recommendations for international students: Required—TOEFL. Electronic applications accepted. *Faculty research:* Structural engineering, structural mechanics, probabilistic modeling, coastal engineering, computational mechanics and computational materials science, topology optimization, systems dynamic modeling, earthquake engineering, stochastic simulation, Equilibrium Problems with Equilibrium Constraints (EPECs).

Johns Hopkins University, G. W. C. Whiting School of Engineering, Master of Science in Engineering Management Program, Baltimore, MD 21218-2699. Offers biomaterials (MSEM); civil engineering (MSEM); communications science (MSEM); computer science (MSEM); environmental systems analysis, economics and public policy (MSEM); fluid mechanics (MSEM); materials science and engineering (MSEM); mechanical engineering (MSEM); mechanics and materials (MSEM); nano-biotechnology (MSEM); nanomaterials and nanotechnology (MSEM); operations research (MSEM); probability and statistics (MSEM); smart product and device design (MSEM). *Entrance requirements:* For master's, GRE, 3 letters of recommendation, resume. Additional exam requirements/recommendations for international students: Required—TOEFL (minimum score 600 paper-based; 100 iBT) or IELTS (minimum score 7). Electronic applications accepted.

Kansas State University, Graduate School, College of Engineering, Department of Civil Engineering, Manhattan, KS 66506. Offers civil engineering (MS, PhD); environmental engineering (MS, PhD); geotechnical engineering (MS, PhD); structural engineering (MS, PhD); transportation engineering (MS, PhD); water resources engineering (MS, PhD). Part-time and evening/weekend programs available. Postbaccalaureate distance learning degree programs offered (no on-campus study). *Faculty:* 14 full-time (4 women), 3 part-time/adjunct (1 woman). *Students:* 37 full-time (12 women), 37 part-time (9 women); includes 6 minority (3 Black or African American, non-Hispanic/Latino; 3 Hispanic/Latino), 23 international. Average age 30. 62 applicants, 39% accepted, 10 enrolled. In 2014, 14 master's, 4 doctorates awarded. *Degree requirements:* For master's, thesis or alternative; for doctorate, thesis/dissertation. *Entrance requirements:* For master's, GRE General Test, bachelor's degree or course work in related engineering fields; for doctorate, GRE General Test. Additional exam requirements/recommendations for international students: Required—TOEFL (minimum score 550 paper-based; 79 iBT). *Application deadline:* For fall admission, 2/1 priority date for domestic students, 1/1 priority date for international students; for spring admission, 8/1 priority date for domestic and international students. Applications are processed on a rolling basis. Application fee: $50 ($75 for international students). Electronic applications accepted. *Financial support:* In 2014–15, 19 research assistantships with partial tuition reimbursements (averaging $13,431 per year), 12 teaching assistantships with partial tuition reimbursements (averaging $15,058 per year) were awarded; institutionally sponsored loans and scholarships/grants also available. Support available to part-time students. Financial award application deadline: 3/1; financial award applicants required to submit FAFSA. *Faculty research:* Transportation and materials engineering, water resources engineering, environmental engineering, geotechnical engineering, structural engineering. *Total annual research expenditures:* $2.4 million. *Unit head:* Dr. Robert Stokes, Head, 785-532-1595, Fax: 785-532-7717, E-mail: drbobb@k-state.edu. *Application contact:* Dr. Dunja Peric, Graduate Coordinator, 785-532-2468, Fax: 785-532-7717, E-mail: peric@k-state.edu.
Website: http://www.ce.ksu.edu/.

Lawrence Technological University, College of Engineering, Southfield, MI 48075-1058. Offers architectural engineering (MS); automotive engineering (MS); civil engineering (MA, MS, PhD); construction engineering management (MA); electrical and computer engineering (MS); engineering management (MEM); industrial engineering (MS); manufacturing systems (ME, DE); mechanical engineering (MS, DE); mechatronic

systems engineering (MS). Part-time and evening/weekend programs available. *Faculty:* 24 full-time (5 women), 15 part-time/adjunct (0 women). *Students:* 16 full-time (6 women), 478 part-time (71 women); includes 295 minority (15 Black or African American, non-Hispanic/Latino; 271 Asian, non-Hispanic/Latino; 7 Hispanic/Latino; 2 Two or more races, non-Hispanic/Latino), 38 international. Average age 27. 1,786 applicants, 40% accepted, 218 enrolled. In 2014, 106 master's awarded. *Degree requirements:* For master's, thesis (for some programs). *Entrance requirements:* Additional exam requirements/recommendations for international students: Required—TOEFL (minimum score 550 paper-based; 79 iBT). *Application deadline:* For fall admission, 8/1 priority date for domestic students, 5/29 for international students; for spring admission, 12/1 priority date for domestic students, 10/15 for international students. Applications are processed on a rolling basis. Application fee: $50. Electronic applications accepted. *Expenses: Tuition:* Full-time $14,700; part-time $1050 per credit hour. *Required fees:* $150. One-time fee: $150 part-time. *Financial support:* In 2014–15, 31 students received support, including 8 research assistantships (averaging $9,338 per year); Federal Work-Study and institutionally sponsored loans also available. Support available to part-time students. Financial award application deadline: 4/1; financial award applicants required to submit FAFSA. *Faculty research:* Advanced composite materials in bridges, strengthening existing bridges with carbon and glass fiber sheets, development of drive shafts using composite materials. *Unit head:* Dr. Nabil Grace, Dean, 248-204-2500, Fax: 248-204-2509, E-mail: engrdean@ltu.edu. *Application contact:* Jane Rohrback, Director of Admissions, 248-204-3160, Fax: 248-204-2228, E-mail: admissions@ltu.edu.
Website: http://www.ltu.edu/engineering/index.asp.

Lehigh University, P.C. Rossin College of Engineering and Applied Science, Department of Civil and Environmental Engineering, Bethlehem, PA 18015. Offers M Eng, MS, PhD. Part-time programs available. *Faculty:* 21 full-time (4 women), 1 part-time/adjunct (0 women). *Students:* 75 full-time (20 women), 15 part-time (2 women); includes 3 minority (1 Black or African American, non-Hispanic/Latino; 1 Asian, non-Hispanic/Latino; 1 Hispanic/Latino), 52 international. Average age 27. 225 applicants, 41% accepted, 11 enrolled. In 2014, 44 master's, 3 doctorates awarded. Terminal master's awarded for partial completion of doctoral program. *Degree requirements:* For master's, thesis (for some programs); for doctorate, comprehensive exam, thesis/dissertation. *Entrance requirements:* For master's and doctorate, GRE. Additional exam requirements/recommendations for international students: Required—TOEFL (minimum score 550 paper-based; 79 iBT). *Application deadline:* For fall admission, 7/15 priority date for domestic and international students; for spring admission, 12/1 priority date for domestic and international students; for summer admission, 5/30 for domestic and international students. Applications are processed on a rolling basis. Application fee: $75. Electronic applications accepted. *Expenses:* Expenses: $24,120. *Financial support:* In 2014–15, 47 students received support, including 7 fellowships with full tuition reimbursements available (averaging $19,920 per year), 31 research assistantships with full tuition reimbursements available (averaging $23,100 per year), 7 teaching assistantships with full tuition reimbursements available (averaging $20,490 per year); institutionally sponsored loans, scholarships/grants, tuition waivers, and unspecified assistantships also available. Financial award application deadline: 1/15; financial award applicants required to submit FAFSA. *Faculty research:* Structural engineering, geotechnical engineering, water resources engineering, environmental engineering. *Total annual research expenditures:* $5.8 million. *Unit head:* Dr. Panayiotis Diplas, Chair, 610-758-3554, E-mail: pad313@lehigh.edu. *Application contact:* Prisca Vidanage, Graduate Coordinator, 610-758-3530, E-mail: pmv1@lehigh.edu.
Website: http://www.lehigh.edu/~incee/.

Louisiana State University and Agricultural & Mechanical College, Graduate School, College of Engineering, Department of Civil and Environmental Engineering, Baton Rouge, LA 70803. Offers environmental engineering (MSCE, PhD); geotechnical engineering (MSCE, PhD); structural engineering and mechanics (MSCE, PhD); transportation engineering (MSCE, PhD); water resources (MSCE, PhD). Part-time programs available. *Faculty:* 26 full-time (1 woman). *Students:* 90 full-time (24 women), 28 part-time (6 women); includes 12 minority (5 Black or African American, non-Hispanic/Latino; 1 American Indian or Alaska Native, non-Hispanic/Latino; 5 Asian, non-Hispanic/Latino; 1 Two or more races, non-Hispanic/Latino), 67 international. Average age 30. 147 applicants, 50% accepted, 23 enrolled. In 2014, 26 master's, 8 doctorates awarded. *Degree requirements:* For master's, thesis optional; for doctorate, one foreign language, thesis/dissertation. *Entrance requirements:* For master's and doctorate, GRE General Test, minimum GPA of 3.0. Additional exam requirements/recommendations for international students: Required—TOEFL (minimum score 550 paper-based; 79 IBT), IELTS (minimum score 6.5), or PTE (minimum score 59). *Application deadline:* For fall admission, 1/1 priority date for domestic students, 5/15 for international students; for spring admission, 10/15 for domestic and international students; for summer admission, 5/15 for domestic and international students. Applications are processed on a rolling basis. Application fee: $50 ($70 for international students). Electronic applications accepted. *Financial support:* In 2014–15, 88 students received support, including 7 fellowships with full and partial tuition reimbursements available (averaging $26,784 per year), 59 research assistantships with full and partial tuition reimbursements available (averaging $16,992 per year), 13 teaching assistantships with full and partial tuition reimbursements available (averaging $16,290 per year); career-related internships or fieldwork, institutionally sponsored loans, scholarships/grants, and health care benefits also available. Financial award application deadline: 3/1; financial award applicants required to submit FAFSA. *Faculty research:* Mechanics and structures, environmental, geotechnical transportation, water resources. *Total annual research expenditures:* $3.2 million. *Unit head:* Dr. George Z. Voyiadjis, Chair/Professor, 225-578-8442, Fax: 225-578-8652, E-mail: voyaidjis@lsu.edu. *Application contact:* Dr. Ayman Ikeli, Professor, 225-578-7048, E-mail: aokeli@lsu.edu.
Website: http://www.cee.lsu.edu/.

Louisiana Tech University, Graduate School, College of Engineering and Science, Department of Civil Engineering, Ruston, LA 71272. Offers MS, PhD. Part-time programs available. Terminal master's awarded for partial completion of doctoral program. *Degree requirements:* For master's, thesis or alternative; for doctorate, thesis/dissertation. *Entrance requirements:* For master's, GRE General Test, minimum GPA of 3.0 in last 60 hours; for doctorate, minimum graduate GPA of 3.25 (with MS) or GRE General Test. Additional exam requirements/recommendations for international students: Required—TOEFL. *Faculty research:* Environmental engineering, trenchless excavation construction, structural mechanics, transportation materials and planning, water quality modeling.

Loyola Marymount University, College of Science and Engineering, Department of Civil Engineering and Environmental Science, Program in Civil Engineering, Los Angeles, CA 90045. Offers MSE. Part-time programs available. *Degree requirements:* For master's, comprehensive exam. *Entrance requirements:* For master's, 2 letters of recommendation, personal statement. Additional exam requirements/recommendations for international students: Required—TOEFL (minimum score 550 paper-based; 80 iBT). Electronic applications accepted.

Manhattan College, Graduate Programs, School of Engineering, Program in Civil Engineering, Riverdale, NY 10471. Offers MS. Part-time and evening/weekend programs available. *Faculty:* 3 full-time (1 woman), 15 part-time/adjunct (3 women). *Students:* 9 full-time (3 women), 86 part-time (20 women); includes 6 minority (4 Asian, non-Hispanic/Latino; 1 Hispanic/Latino; 1 Two or more races, non-Hispanic/Latino). Average age 24. 41 applicants, 76% accepted, 22 enrolled. In 2014, 15 master's awarded. *Degree requirements:* For master's, thesis or alternative. *Entrance requirements:* For master's, GRE (recommended), minimum GPA of 3.0. Additional exam requirements/recommendations for international students: Required—TOEFL (minimum score 550 paper-based; 80 iBT), IELTS (minimum score 6). *Application deadline:* For fall admission, 8/10 priority date for domestic students, 8/10 for international students; for spring admission, 1/7 for domestic and international students. Applications are processed on a rolling basis. Application fee: $60. *Financial support:* In 2014–15, 2 students received support, including 5 teaching assistantships (averaging $7,600 per year); fellowships, research assistantships, career-related internships or fieldwork, Federal Work-Study, scholarships/grants, unspecified assistantships, and laboratory assistantships also available. Support available to part-time students. Financial award application deadline: 2/1. *Faculty research:* Compressible-inclusion function for geofoams used with rigid walls under static loading, validation of sediment criteria. *Unit head:* Dr. Moujalli Hourani, Chair, 718-862-7172, Fax: 718-862-8035, E-mail: moujalli.hourani@manhattan.edu. *Application contact:* Janet Horgan, Information Contact, 718-862-7171, Fax: 718-862-8035, E-mail: civildept@manhattan.edu.
Website: http://www.engineering.manhattan.edu.

Marquette University, Graduate School, Opus College of Engineering, Department of Civil, Construction and Environmental Engineering, Milwaukee, WI 53201-1881. Offers construction engineering and management (MS, PhD, Certificate); environmental engineering (MS, PhD); structural design (Certificate); structural engineering and structural mechanics (MS, PhD); transportation (Certificate); transportation engineering and materials (MS, PhD); waste and wastewater treatment processes (Certificate); water resources engineering (Certificate). Part-time and evening/weekend programs available. Terminal master's awarded for partial completion of doctoral program. *Degree requirements:* For master's, comprehensive exam (for some programs), thesis or alternative; for doctorate, thesis/dissertation. *Entrance requirements:* For master's, GRE General Test (recommended), minimum GPA of 3.0, official transcripts from all current and previous colleges/universities except Marquette, three letters of recommendation; for doctorate, GRE General Test, minimum GPA of 3.0, official transcripts from all current and previous colleges/universities except Marquette, three letters of recommendation, brief statement of purpose, submission of any English language publications authored by applicant (strongly recommended). Additional exam requirements/recommendations for international students: Required—TOEFL (minimum score 530 paper-based). Electronic applications accepted. *Faculty research:* Highway safety, highway performance, and intelligent transportation systems; surface mount technology; watershed management.

Massachusetts Institute of Technology, School of Engineering, Department of Civil and Environmental Engineering, Cambridge, MA 02139. Offers biological oceanography (PhD, Sc D); chemical oceanography (PhD, Sc D); civil and environmental engineering (M Eng, SM, PhD, Sc D); civil and environmental systems (PhD, Sc D); civil engineering (PhD, Sc D, CE); coastal engineering (PhD, Sc D); construction engineering and management (PhD, Sc D); environmental biology (PhD, Sc D); environmental chemistry (PhD, Sc D); environmental engineering (PhD, Sc D); environmental fluid mechanics (PhD, Sc D); geotechnical and geoenvironmental engineering (PhD, Sc D); hydrology (PhD, Sc D); information technology (PhD, Sc D); oceanographic engineering (PhD, Sc D); structures and materials (PhD, Sc D); transportation (PhD, Sc D); SM/MBA. *Faculty:* 34 full-time (8 women), 1 part-time/adjunct (0 women). *Students:* 216 full-time (82 women); includes 25 minority (1 Black or African American, non-Hispanic/Latino; 10 Asian, non-Hispanic/Latino; 8 Hispanic/Latino; 6 Two or more races, non-Hispanic/Latino), 117 international. Average age 26. 565 applicants, 22% accepted, 85 enrolled. In 2014, 76 master's, 18 doctorates awarded. *Degree requirements:* For master's and CE, thesis; for doctorate, comprehensive exam, thesis/dissertation. *Entrance requirements:* For master's and doctorate, GRE General Test. Additional exam requirements/recommendations for international students: Required—TOEFL (minimum score 577 paper-based; 100 iBT), IELTS (minimum score 7). *Application deadline:* For fall admission, 12/15 for domestic and international students. Application fee: $75. Electronic applications accepted. *Expenses: Tuition:* Full-time $44,720; part-time $699 per unit. *Required fees:* $296. *Financial support:* In 2014–15, 170 students received support, including 32 fellowships (averaging $32,800 per year), 132 research assistantships (averaging $33,800 per year), 13 teaching assistantships (averaging $32,900 per year); Federal Work-Study, institutionally sponsored loans, scholarships/grants, traineeships, health care benefits, and unspecified assistantships also available. Financial award application deadline: 4/15; financial award applicants required to submit FAFSA. *Faculty research:* Environmental chemistry, environmental fluid mechanics and coastal engineering, environmental microbiology, geotechnical engineering and geomechanics, hydrology and hydroclimatology, infrastructure systems, mechanics of materials and structures, transportation systems. *Total annual research expenditures:* $22.9 million. *Unit head:* Prof. Markus Buehler, Department Head, 617-324-6488. *Application contact:* Graduate Admissions Coordinator, 617-253-7119, E-mail: cee-admissions@mit.edu.
Website: http://cee.mit.edu/.

McGill University, Faculty of Graduate and Postdoctoral Studies, Faculty of Engineering, Department of Civil Engineering and Applied Mechanics, Montréal, QC H3A 2T5, Canada. Offers environmental engineering (M Eng, M Sc, PhD); fluid mechanics (M Sc); fluid mechanics and hydraulic engineering (M Eng, PhD); materials engineering (M Eng, PhD); rehabilitation of urban infrastructure (M Eng, PhD); soil behavior (M Eng, PhD); soil mechanics and foundations (M Eng, PhD); structures and structural mechanics (M Eng, PhD); water resources (M Sc); water resources engineering (M Eng, PhD).

McMaster University, School of Graduate Studies, Faculty of Engineering, Department of Civil Engineering, Hamilton, ON L8S 4M2, Canada. Offers M Eng, MA Sc, PhD. *Degree requirements:* For master's, thesis; for doctorate, comprehensive exam, thesis/dissertation. *Entrance requirements:* Additional exam requirements/recommendations for international students: Required—TOEFL (minimum score 550 paper-based). *Faculty research:* Building science, environmental hydrology, bolted steel connections, research on highway materials, earthquake engineering.

McNeese State University, Doré School of Graduate Studies, College of Engineering and Engineering Technology, Department of Engineering, Master of Engineering Program, Lake Charles, LA 70609. Offers chemical engineering (M Eng); civil engineering (M Eng); electrical engineering (M Eng); engineering management (M Eng); mechanical engineering (M Eng). Part-time and evening/weekend programs available. *Degree requirements:* For master's, thesis or alternative. *Entrance requirements:* For master's, GRE, baccalaureate degree, minimum overall GPA of 3.0. Additional exam requirements/recommendations for international students: Required—TOEFL (minimum score 560 paper-based; 83 iBT).

Memorial University of Newfoundland, School of Graduate Studies, Faculty of Engineering and Applied Science, St. John's, NL A1C 5S7, Canada. Offers civil engineering (M Eng, PhD); electrical and computer engineering (M Eng, PhD); mechanical engineering (M Eng, PhD); ocean and naval architecture engineering (M Eng, PhD). Part-time programs available. *Degree requirements:* For master's, thesis; for doctorate, comprehensive exam, thesis/dissertation, oral thesis defense. *Entrance requirements:* For master's, 2nd class degree; for doctorate, master's degree in engineering. Electronic applications accepted. *Faculty research:* Engineering analysis, environmental and hydrotechnical studies, manufacturing and robotics, mechanics, structures and materials.

Michigan State University, The Graduate School, College of Engineering, Department of Civil and Environmental Engineering, East Lansing, MI 48824. Offers civil engineering (MS, PhD); environmental engineering (MS, PhD); environmental engineering-environmental toxicology (PhD). Part-time programs available. *Entrance requirements:* Additional exam requirements/recommendations for international students: Required—TOEFL. Electronic applications accepted.

Michigan Technological University, Graduate School, College of Engineering, Department of Civil and Environmental Engineering, Houghton, MI 49931. Offers civil engineering (M Eng, MS, PhD); environmental engineering (M Eng, MS); environmental engineering science (MS). Part-time programs available. *Faculty:* 41 full-time, 10 part-time/adjunct. *Students:* 101 full-time (38 women), 17 part-time (8 women); includes 10 minority (2 Black or African American, non-Hispanic/Latino; 2 Asian, non-Hispanic/Latino; 4 Hispanic/Latino; 1 Native Hawaiian or other Pacific Islander, non-Hispanic/Latino; 1 Two or more races, non-Hispanic/Latino), 48 international. Average age 26. 389 applicants, 51% accepted, 46 enrolled. In 2014, 31 master's, 4 doctorates awarded. *Degree requirements:* For master's, comprehensive exam (for some programs), thesis (for some programs); for doctorate, comprehensive exam, thesis/dissertation. *Entrance requirements:* For master's and doctorate, GRE (Michigan Tech students exempt), statement of purpose, official transcripts, 2 letters of recommendation. Additional exam requirements/recommendations for international students: Required—TOEFL (recommended score 100 iBT) or IELTS. *Application deadline:* For fall admission, 1/15 priority date for domestic and international students; for spring admission, 9/15 priority date for domestic and international students; for summer admission, 2/15 priority date for domestic and international students. Applications are processed on a rolling basis. Electronic applications accepted. *Expenses:* Expenses: Contact institution. *Financial support:* In 2014–15, 90 students received support, including 8 fellowships with full and partial tuition reimbursements available (averaging $13,824 per year), 19 research assistantships with full and partial tuition reimbursements available (averaging $13,824 per year), 9 teaching assistantships with full and partial tuition reimbursements available (averaging $13,824 per year); career-related internships or fieldwork, Federal Work-Study, scholarships/grants, health care benefits, unspecified assistantships, and cooperative program also available. Financial award applicants required to submit FAFSA. *Faculty research:* Water resources, construction engineering, transportation engineering, structural engineering, geotechnical engineering. *Total annual research expenditures:* $2.4 million. *Unit head:* Dr. David Hand, Chair, 906-487-2777, Fax: 906-487-2943, E-mail: dwhand@mtu.edu. *Application contact:* Angela Keranen, Administrative Aide, 906-487-2474, Fax: 906-487-2943, E-mail: amkerane@mtu.edu.
Website: http://www.mtu.edu/cee/.

Milwaukee School of Engineering, Civil and Architectural Engineering and Construction Management Department, Program in Civil Engineering, Milwaukee, WI 53202-3109. Offers MS. Five-year freshman-to-master's degree program. Part-time and evening/weekend programs available. *Faculty:* 1 full-time (0 women). *Students:* 1 full-time (0 women), all international. Average age 23. 4 applicants. *Degree requirements:* For master's, thesis. *Entrance requirements:* For master's, GRE General Test or GMAT if undergraduate GPA less than 3.0, 2 letters of recommendation; BS in architectural, structural, or civil engineering. Additional exam requirements/recommendations for international students: Required—TOEFL (minimum score 90 iBT), IELTS (minimum score 6.5). *Application deadline:* Applications are processed on a rolling basis. Electronic applications accepted. Application fee is waived when completed online. *Expenses: Tuition:* Part-time $732 per credit. *Financial support:* Application deadline: 3/15; applicants required to submit FAFSA. *Unit head:* Dr. Francis Mahuta, Director, 414-277-7599, E-mail: mahuta@msoe.edu. *Application contact:* Ian Dahlinghaus, Graduate Program Associate, 414-277-7208, E-mail: dahlinghaus@msoe.edu.
Website: http://www.msoe.edu/community/academics/engineering/page/2495/mscve-overview.

See Display on page 58 and Close-Up on page 83.

Mississippi State University, Bagley College of Engineering, Department of Civil and Environmental Engineering, Mississippi State, MS 39762. Offers civil engineering (MS); engineering (PhD), including civil engineering. Part-time programs available. Postbaccalaureate distance learning degree programs offered (no on-campus study). *Faculty:* 12 full-time (0 women), 3 part-time/adjunct (1 woman). *Students:* 30 full-time (8 women), 72 part-time (21 women); includes 25 minority (9 Black or African American, non-Hispanic/Latino; 16 Hispanic/Latino), 16 international. Average age 30. 61 applicants, 36% accepted, 15 enrolled. In 2014, 16 master's, 2 doctorates awarded. Terminal master's awarded for partial completion of doctoral program. *Degree requirements:* For master's, thesis optional; for doctorate, thesis/dissertation, research on an approved topic, minimum 20 hours of dissertation research. *Entrance requirements:* For master's and doctorate, GRE (for graduates from program not accredited by EAC/ABET), minimum GPA of 3.0. Additional exam requirements/recommendations for international students: Required—TOEFL (minimum score 550 paper-based; 79 iBT); Recommended—IELTS (minimum score 6.5). *Application deadline:* For fall admission, 7/1 for domestic students, 5/1 for international students; for spring admission, 11/1 for domestic students, 9/1 for international students. Applications are processed on a rolling basis. Application fee: $60. Electronic applications accepted. *Expenses:* Tuition, state resident: full-time $7140; part-time $783 per credit hour. Tuition, nonresident: full-time $18,478; part-time $2043 per credit hour. *Financial support:* In 2014–15, 12 research assistantships with full tuition reimbursements (averaging $13,966 per year), 3 teaching assistantships with full tuition reimbursements (averaging $13,579 per year) were awarded; Federal Work-Study, institutionally sponsored loans, and unspecified assistantships also available. Financial award application deadline: 4/1; financial award applicants required to submit FAFSA. *Faculty research:* Transportation, water modeling, construction materials, structures. *Total annual research expenditures:* $4.2 million. *Unit head:* Dr. Dennis D. Truax, Department Head, 662-325-7187, Fax: 662-325-7189, E-mail: truax@cee.msstate.edu. *Application contact:* Dr. James L. Martin, Professor and Graduate Coordinator, 662-325-7194, Fax: 662-325-7189, E-mail: jmartin@cee.msstate.edu.
Website: http://www.cee.msstate.edu/.

Missouri University of Science and Technology, Graduate School, Department of Civil, Architectural, and Environmental Engineering, Rolla, MO 65409. Offers civil engineering (MS, DE, PhD); construction engineering (MS, DE, PhD); environmental engineering (MS); fluid mechanics (MS, DE, PhD); geotechnical engineering (MS, DE, PhD); hydrology and hydraulic engineering (MS, DE, PhD). Part-time and evening/weekend programs available. Terminal master's awarded for partial completion of doctoral program. *Degree requirements:* For master's, thesis optional; for doctorate, comprehensive exam, thesis/dissertation. *Entrance requirements:* For master's, GRE General Test (minimum combined score 1100), minimum GPA of 3.0; for doctorate, GRE General Test (minimum score: verbal and quantitative 400, writing 3.5), minimum GPA of 3.0. Additional exam requirements/recommendations for international students: Required—TOEFL. Electronic applications accepted. *Faculty research:* Earthquake engineering, structural optimization and control systems, structural health monitoring/damage detection, soil-structure interaction, soil mechanics and foundation engineering.

Montana State University, The Graduate School, College of Engineering, Department of Civil Engineering, Bozeman, MT 59717. Offers civil engineering (MS); construction engineering management (MCEM); engineering (PhD), including applied mechanics option, civil engineering option. Part-time programs available. *Degree requirements:* For master's, comprehensive exam, thesis (for some programs); for doctorate, comprehensive exam, thesis/dissertation. *Entrance requirements:* For master's and doctorate, GRE General Test. Additional exam requirements/recommendations for international students: Required—TOEFL (minimum score 550 paper-based). Electronic applications accepted. *Faculty research:* Snow and ice mechanics, biofilm engineering, transportation, structural and geo materials, water resources.

Morgan State University, School of Graduate Studies, Clarence M. Mitchell, Jr. School of Engineering, Baltimore, MD 21251. Offers civil engineering (M Eng, D Eng); electrical and computer engineering (M Eng, MS, D Eng); industrial and systems engineering (M Eng, D Eng); transportation (MS). Part-time and evening/weekend programs available. *Degree requirements:* For master's, thesis, comprehensive exam or equivalent; for doctorate, thesis/dissertation, comprehensive exam or equivalent. *Entrance requirements:* For master's, GRE, minimum undergraduate GPA of 2.5; for doctorate, GRE, minimum GPA of 3.0. Additional exam requirements/recommendations for international students: Required—TOEFL (minimum score 550 paper-based).

New Mexico State University, College of Engineering, Department of Civil and Geological Engineering, Las Cruces, NM 88003-8001. Offers MS Env E, MSCE, PhD. Part-time programs available. Postbaccalaureate distance learning degree programs offered (minimal on-campus study). *Faculty:* 14 full-time (3 women). *Students:* 58 full-time (17 women), 19 part-time (3 women); includes 22 minority (2 Black or African American, non-Hispanic/Latino; 3 American Indian or Alaska Native, non-Hispanic/Latino; 1 Asian, non-Hispanic/Latino; 15 Hispanic/Latino; 1 Two or more races, non-Hispanic/Latino), 36 international. Average age 30. 74 applicants, 41% accepted, 16 enrolled. In 2014, 14 master's awarded. *Degree requirements:* For master's, thesis (for some programs); for doctorate, comprehensive exam (for some programs), thesis/dissertation, qualifying exam. *Entrance requirements:* For master's and doctorate, BS in engineering, minimum GPA of 3.0. Additional exam requirements/recommendations for international students: Required—TOEFL (minimum score 550 paper-based; 79 iBT), IELTS (minimum score 6.5). *Application deadline:* For fall admission, 4/1 priority date for domestic and international students; for spring admission, 9/1 priority date for domestic and international students. Applications are processed on a rolling basis. Application fee: $40 ($50 for international students). Electronic applications accepted. *Expenses:* Tuition, state resident: full-time $3969; part-time $220.50 per credit hour. Tuition, nonresident: full-time $13,838; part-time $768.80 per credit hour. *Required fees:* $853; $47.40 per credit hour. *Financial support:* In 2014–15, 59 students received support, including 8 fellowships (averaging $2,510 per year), 24 research assistantships (averaging $12,168 per year), 27 teaching assistantships (averaging $9,444 per year); career-related internships or fieldwork, Federal Work-Study, scholarships/grants, traineeships, health care benefits, and unspecified assistantships also available. Support available to part-time students. Financial award application deadline: 3/1. *Faculty research:* Structural engineering, water resources engineering, environmental engineering, geotechnical engineering, transportation. *Total annual research expenditures:* $2.1 million. *Unit head:* Dr. Peter T. Martin, Head, 575-646-3801, E-mail: wales@nmsu.edu. *Application contact:* 575-646-3801, E-mail: civil@nmsu.edu.
Website: http://ce.nmsu.edu.

New York University, Polytechnic School of Engineering, Department of Civil and Urban Engineering, Major in Civil Engineering, New York, NY 10012-1019. Offers MS, PhD. Part-time and evening/weekend programs available. *Students:* 49 full-time (11 women), 26 part-time (9 women); includes 18 minority (2 Black or African American, non-Hispanic/Latino; 11 Asian, non-Hispanic/Latino; 4 Hispanic/Latino; 1 Two or more races, non-Hispanic/Latino), 30 international. Average age 28. 209 applicants, 45% accepted, 34 enrolled. In 2014, 27 master's, 6 doctorates awarded. *Degree requirements:* For master's, comprehensive exam (for some programs), thesis (for some programs); for doctorate, comprehensive exam, thesis/dissertation, qualifying exam. *Entrance requirements:* For doctorate, MS in civil engineering. Additional exam requirements/recommendations for international students: Required—TOEFL (minimum score 550 paper-based; 80 iBT); Recommended—IELTS (minimum score 6.5). *Application deadline:* For fall admission, 2/15 priority date for domestic and international students; for spring admission, 11/1 priority date for domestic and international students. Applications are processed on a rolling basis. Application fee: $75. Electronic applications accepted. *Financial support:* Fellowships, research assistantships, teaching assistantships, institutionally sponsored loans, scholarships/grants, and unspecified assistantships available. Support available to part-time students. Financial award applicants required to submit FAFSA. *Unit head:* Dr. Mohsen Hossein, Department Head, 718-260-3766, Fax: 718-260-3433, E-mail: mhossein@nyu.edu. *Application contact:* Raymond Lutzky, Director of Graduate Enrollment Management, 718-637-5984, Fax: 718-260-3624, E-mail: rlutzky@poly.edu.

North Carolina Agricultural and Technical State University, School of Graduate Studies, College of Engineering, Department of Civil, Architectural, Agricultural and Environmental Engineering, Greensboro, NC 27411. Offers civil engineering (MSCE). Part-time programs available. *Degree requirements:* For master's, thesis optional. *Entrance requirements:* For master's, GRE General Test, GRE Subject Test (recommended). Additional exam requirements/recommendations for international students: Required—TOEFL. *Faculty research:* Lightning, indoor air quality, material behavior HVAC controls, structural masonry systems.

North Carolina State University, Graduate School, College of Engineering, Department of Civil, Construction, and Environmental Engineering, Raleigh, NC 27695. Offers civil engineering (MCE, MS, PhD). Part-time programs available. Postbaccalaureate distance learning degree programs offered. *Degree requirements:* For master's, thesis optional, oral exams; for doctorate, thesis/dissertation, oral exams. *Entrance requirements:* For master's, GRE General Test, minimum B average in major; for doctorate, GRE General Test. Additional exam requirements/recommendations for international students: Required—TOEFL. Electronic applications accepted. *Faculty research:* Materials; systems, environmental, geotechnical, structural, transportation and water rescue engineering.

North Dakota State University, College of Graduate and Interdisciplinary Studies, College of Engineering and Architecture, Department of Civil Engineering, Fargo, ND 58108. Offers civil engineering (MS, PhD); environmental engineering (MS, PhD); transportation and logistics (PhD). PhD in transportation and logistics offered jointly with Upper Great Plains Transportation Institute. Part-time programs available. Postbaccalaureate distance learning degree programs offered (minimal on-campus study). *Degree requirements:* For master's, thesis; for doctorate, comprehensive exam, thesis/dissertation. *Entrance requirements:* Additional exam requirements/

recommendations for international students: Required—TOEFL (minimum score 525 paper-based; 71 iBT). Electronic applications accepted. *Faculty research:* Wastewater, solid waste, composites, nanotechnology.

Northeastern University, College of Engineering, Boston, MA 02115-5096. Offers bioengineering (PhD); chemical engineering (MS, PhD); civil engineering (MS, PhD); computer engineering (PhD); computer systems engineering (MS); electrical and computer engineering (MS); electrical and engineering leadership (MS); electrical engineering (PhD); energy systems (MS); engineering leadership (Certificate); engineering management (MRTP); industrial engineering (MS, PhD); information assurance (PhD); information systems (MS); interdisciplinary (PhD); mechanical engineering (MS, PhD); operations research (MS); telecommunication systems management (MS). Part-time programs available. *Expenses:* Contact institution.

Northern Arizona University, Graduate College, College of Engineering, Forestry and Natural Sciences, Programs in Engineering, Flagstaff, AZ 86011. Offers civil and environmental engineering (M Eng); civil engineering (MSE); computer science (MSE); electrical engineering (M Eng, MSE); engineering (M Eng, MSE); environmental engineering (M Eng, MSE); mechanical engineering (M Eng, MSE). Part-time programs available. Postbaccalaureate distance learning degree programs offered (no on-campus study). *Degree requirements:* For master's, thesis. *Entrance requirements:* For master's, GRE General Test. Additional exam requirements/recommendations for international students: Required—TOEFL (minimum score 550 paper-based; 80 iBT), IELTS (minimum score 7). Electronic applications accepted.

Northwestern University, McCormick School of Engineering and Applied Science, Department of Civil and Environmental Engineering, Evanston, IL 60208-3109. Offers environmental engineering and science (MS, PhD); geotechnical engineering (MS, PhD); mechanics of materials and solids (MS, PhD); project management (MS, PhD); structural engineering and materials (MS, PhD); transportation systems analysis and planning (MS, PhD). MS and PhD admissions and degrees offered through The Graduate School. Part-time programs available. *Faculty:* 19 full-time (2 women). *Students:* 118 full-time (36 women), 5 part-time (2 women); includes 7 minority (3 Black or African American, non-Hispanic/Latino; 2 Asian, non-Hispanic/Latino; 1 Hispanic/Latino; 1 Two or more races, non-Hispanic/Latino), 95 international. Average age 24. 412 applicants, 36% accepted, 49 enrolled. In 2014, 42 master's, 10 doctorates awarded. Terminal master's awarded for partial completion of doctoral program. *Degree requirements:* For master's, thesis (for some programs); for doctorate, comprehensive exam, thesis/dissertation. *Entrance requirements:* For master's and doctorate, GRE General Test, minimum 2 letters of recommendation, transcripts from all academic institutions attended. Additional exam requirements/recommendations for international students: Required—TOEFL (minimum score 577 paper-based; 90 iBT), IELTS (minimum score 7). *Application deadline:* For fall admission, 12/31 for domestic and international students; for winter admission, 11/15 for domestic and international students; for spring admission, 1/15 for domestic and international students. Application fee: $95. Electronic applications accepted. *Financial support:* Fellowships with full tuition reimbursements, research assistantships with full tuition reimbursements, teaching assistantships with full tuition reimbursements, career-related internships or fieldwork, institutionally sponsored loans, health care benefits, and unspecified assistantships available. Financial award application deadline: 12/31; financial award applicants required to submit FAFSA. *Faculty research:* Environmental engineering and science, geotechnics, mechanics of materials and solids, structural engineering and materials, transportation systems analysis and planning. *Total annual research expenditures:* $5.8 million. *Unit head:* Dr. Jianmin Qu, Chair, 847-467-4528, Fax: 847-491-4011, E-mail: j-qu@northwestern.edu. *Application contact:* Dr. David Corr, Academic Coordinator, 847-467-0890, Fax: 847-491-4011, E-mail: d-corr@u.northwestern.edu.
Website: http://www.civil.northwestern.edu/.

Norwich University, College of Graduate and Continuing Studies, Master of Civil Engineering Program, Northfield, VT 05663. Offers construction management engineering (MCE); environmental/water resources engineering (MCE); geotechnical engineering (MCE); structural engineering (MCE). Evening/weekend programs available. Postbaccalaureate distance learning degree programs offered (minimal on-campus study). *Faculty:* 14 part-time/adjunct (2 women). *Students:* 111 full-time (17 women); includes 28 minority (16 Black or African American, non-Hispanic/Latino; 2 American Indian or Alaska Native, non-Hispanic/Latino; 7 Asian, non-Hispanic/Latino; 3 Hispanic/Latino). Average age 36. 61 applicants, 100% accepted, 42 enrolled. In 2014, 57 master's awarded. *Entrance requirements:* For master's, minimum undergraduate GPA of 2.75. Additional exam requirements/recommendations for international students: Required—TOEFL (minimum score 550 paper-based; 80 iBT), IELTS (minimum score 6.5). *Application deadline:* For fall admission, 8/8 for domestic and international students; for spring admission, 2/16 for domestic and international students. Applications are processed on a rolling basis. Electronic applications accepted. *Expenses:* Expenses: Contact institution. *Financial support:* In 2014–15, 27 students received support. Scholarships/grants available. Financial award applicants required to submit FAFSA. *Unit head:* Dr. Thomas Descoteaux, Program Director, 802-485-2730, Fax: 802-485-2533, E-mail: tdescote@norwich.edu. *Application contact:* Rija Ramahatra, Associate Program Director, 802-485-2892, Fax: 802-485-2533, E-mail: ramahatr@norwich.edu.
Website: http://online.norwich.edu/degree-programs/masters/master-civil-engineering/overview.

The Ohio State University, Graduate School, College of Engineering, Department of Civil, Environmental and Geodetic Engineering, Columbus, OH 43210. Offers civil engineering (MS, PhD). *Faculty:* 22. *Students:* 84 full-time (23 women), 16 part-time (5 women); includes 9 minority (3 Black or African American, non-Hispanic/Latino; 4 Asian, non-Hispanic/Latino; 1 Hispanic/Latino; 1 Two or more races, non-Hispanic/Latino), 47 international. Average age 27. In 2014, 22 master's, 3 doctorates awarded. *Degree requirements:* For doctorate, thesis/dissertation. *Entrance requirements:* For master's and doctorate, GRE General Test (for all applicants whose undergraduate GPA is below 3.0 or whose undergraduate degree is not from an accredited U.S.-ABET or Canadian-CEAB institution). Additional exam requirements/recommendations for international students: Required—TOEFL (minimum score 550 paper-based; 79 iBT), Michigan English Language Assessment Battery (minimum score 82); Recommended—IELTS (minimum score 7). *Application deadline:* For fall admission, 12/13 priority date for domestic students, 11/30 priority date for international students. Applications are processed on a rolling basis. Application fee: $60 ($70 for international students). Electronic applications accepted. *Financial support:* Fellowships with tuition reimbursements, research assistantships with tuition reimbursements, teaching assistantships with tuition reimbursements, institutionally sponsored loans, and unspecified assistantships available. *Unit head:* Dr. Dorota Grejner-Brzezinska, Chair, 614-3455, E-mail: grejner-brzezinska.1@osu.edu. *Application contact:* Graduate and Professional Admissions, 614-292-9444, Fax: 614-292-3895, E-mail: gpadmissions@osu.edu.
Website: http://ceg.osu.edu/.

Ohio University, Graduate College, Russ College of Engineering and Technology, Department of Civil Engineering, Athens, OH 45701-2979. Offers civil engineering

(PhD); construction engineering and management (MS); environmental (MS); geotechnical and geoenvironmental (MS); mechanics (MS); structures (MS); transportation (MS); water resources (MS). Part-time programs available. *Degree requirements:* For master's, comprehensive exam (for some programs), thesis or alternative; for doctorate, comprehensive exam, thesis/dissertation. *Entrance requirements:* For master's, GRE General Test, minimum GPA of 3.0, 3 letters of recommendation; for doctorate, GRE General Test. Additional exam requirements/recommendations for international students: Required—TOEFL (minimum score 550 paper-based; 80 iBT) or IELTS (minimum score 6.5). Electronic applications accepted. *Faculty research:* Noise abatement, materials and environment, highway infrastructure, subsurface investigation (pavements, pipes, bridges).

Oklahoma State University, College of Engineering, Architecture and Technology, School of Civil and Environmental Engineering, Stillwater, OK 74078. Offers civil engineering (MS, PhD); environmental engineering (MS). *Faculty:* 17 full-time (1 woman), 3 part-time/adjunct (1 woman). *Students:* 49 full-time (10 women), 32 part-time (8 women); includes 7 minority (1 Black or African American, non-Hispanic/Latino; 2 American Indian or Alaska Native, non-Hispanic/Latino; 2 Hispanic/Latino; 2 Two or more races, non-Hispanic/Latino), 61 international. Average age 27. 146 applicants, 28% accepted, 18 enrolled. In 2014, 22 master's, 3 doctorates awarded. *Degree requirements:* For master's, thesis or alternative; for doctorate, comprehensive exam, thesis/dissertation. *Entrance requirements:* For master's and doctorate, GRE or GMAT. Additional exam requirements/recommendations for international students: Required—TOEFL (minimum score 550 paper-based; 79 iBT). *Application deadline:* For fall admission, 3/1 priority date for international students; for spring admission, 8/1 priority date for international students. Applications are processed on a rolling basis. Application fee: $40 ($75 for international students). Electronic applications accepted. *Expenses:* Tuition, state resident: full-time $4488; part-time $187 per credit hour. Tuition, nonresident: full-time $18,360; part-time $765 per credit hour. *Required fees:* $2413; $100.55 per credit hour. Tuition and fees vary according to campus/location. *Financial support:* In 2014–15, 30 research assistantships (averaging $17,682 per year), 15 teaching assistantships (averaging $16,496 per year) were awarded; career-related internships or fieldwork, Federal Work-Study, scholarships/grants, health care benefits, tuition waivers (partial), and unspecified assistantships also available. Support available to part-time students. Financial award application deadline: 3/1; financial award applicants required to submit FAFSA. *Unit head:* Dr. John Veenstra, Department Head, 405-744-5190, Fax: 405-744-7554, E-mail: jveenst@okstate.edu.
Website: http://cive.okstate.edu.

Old Dominion University, Frank Batten College of Engineering and Technology, Program in Civil and Environmental Engineering, Norfolk, VA 23529. Offers D Eng, PhD. Part-time and evening/weekend programs available. Postbaccalaureate distance learning degree programs offered (minimal on-campus study). *Faculty:* 13 full-time (1 woman), 7 part-time/adjunct (0 women). *Students:* 10 full-time (3 women), 16 part-time (0 women); includes 2 minority (both Asian, non-Hispanic/Latino), 15 international. Average age 37. 12 applicants, 100% accepted, 2 enrolled. In 2014, 5 doctorates awarded. *Degree requirements:* For doctorate, thesis/dissertation, candidacy exam. *Entrance requirements:* For doctorate, GRE, minimum GPA of 3.5. Additional exam requirements/recommendations for international students: Required—TOEFL (minimum score 550 paper-based; 80 iBT). *Application deadline:* For fall admission, 6/1 priority date for domestic students, 4/15 priority date for international students; for spring admission, 11/1 priority date for domestic students, 10/1 priority date for international students. Applications are processed on a rolling basis. Application fee: $50. Electronic applications accepted. *Expenses:* Tuition, state resident: full-time $10,488; part-time $437 per credit. Tuition, nonresident: full-time $26,136; part-time $1089 per credit. *Required fees:* $64 per semester. One-time fee: $50. *Financial support:* In 2014–15, 10 research assistantships with full and partial tuition reimbursements (averaging $15,439 per year), 8 teaching assistantships with full and partial tuition reimbursements (averaging $14,244 per year) were awarded; scholarships/grants and unspecified assistantships also available. Support available to part-time students. Financial award application deadline: 4/1. *Faculty research:* Structural engineering, coastal engineering, environmental engineering, geotechnical engineering, water resources, transportation engineering. *Total annual research expenditures:* $941,621. *Unit head:* Dr. Isao Ishibashi, Graduate Program Director, 757-683-4641, Fax: 757-683-5354, E-mail: cegpd@odu.edu. *Application contact:* Dr. Linda Vahala, Associate Dean, 757-683-3789, Fax: 757-683-4898, E-mail: lvahala@odu.edu.
Website: http://eng.odu.edu/cee/.

Old Dominion University, Frank Batten College of Engineering and Technology, Program in Civil Engineering, Norfolk, VA 23529. Offers ME, MS. Part-time and evening/weekend programs available. Postbaccalaureate distance learning degree programs offered (minimal on-campus study). *Faculty:* 13 full-time (1 woman), 7 part-time/adjunct (0 women). *Students:* 10 full-time (3 women), 41 part-time (12 women); includes 5 minority (1 Black or African American, non-Hispanic/Latino; 1 Asian, non-Hispanic/Latino; 1 Hispanic/Latino; 2 Two or more races, non-Hispanic/Latino), 13 international. Average age 29. 23 applicants, 96% accepted, 8 enrolled. In 2014, 21 master's awarded. *Degree requirements:* For master's, comprehensive exam, thesis optional. *Entrance requirements:* For master's, GRE, minimum GPA of 3.0. Additional exam requirements/recommendations for international students: Required—TOEFL (minimum score 550 paper-based; 80 iBT). *Application deadline:* For fall admission, 6/1 priority date for domestic students, 4/15 priority date for international students; for spring admission, 11/1 priority date for domestic students, 10/1 priority date for international students. Applications are processed on a rolling basis. Application fee: $50. Electronic applications accepted. *Expenses:* Tuition, state resident: full-time $10,488; part-time $437 per credit. Tuition, nonresident: full-time $26,136; part-time $1089 per credit. *Required fees:* $64 per semester. One-time fee: $50. *Financial support:* In 2014–15, 4 research assistantships with full and partial tuition reimbursements (averaging $12,177 per year), 1 teaching assistantship (averaging $12,800 per year) were awarded; scholarships/grants and unspecified assistantships also available. Support available to part-time students. Financial award application deadline: 4/1; financial award applicants required to submit FAFSA. *Faculty research:* Structural engineering, coastal engineering, environmental engineering, geotechnical engineering, water resources, transportation engineering. *Total annual research expenditures:* $941,621. *Unit head:* Dr. Isao Ishibashi, Graduate Program Director, 757-683-4641, Fax: 757-683-5354, E-mail: cegpd@odu.edu. *Application contact:* Dr. Linda Vahala, Associate Dean, 757-683-3789, Fax: 757-683-4898, E-mail: lvahala@odu.edu.
Website: http://eng.odu.edu/cee/.

Oregon State University, College of Engineering, Program in Civil Engineering, Corvallis, OR 97331. Offers M Eng, MS, PhD. *Faculty:* 34 full-time (3 women), 1 part-time/adjunct (0 women). *Students:* 144 full-time (38 women), 25 part-time (5 women); includes 15 minority (7 Asian, non-Hispanic/Latino; 4 Hispanic/Latino; 4 Two or more races, non-Hispanic/Latino), 89 international. Average age 28. 405 applicants, 36% accepted, 57 enrolled. In 2014, 49 master's, 7 doctorates awarded. *Entrance requirements:* For master's and doctorate, GRE. Additional exam requirements/recommendations for international students: Required—TOEFL (minimum score 80 iBT), IELTS (minimum score 6.5). *Application deadline:* For fall admission, 8/1 for domestic students, 4/1 for international students; for winter admission, 12/1 for domestic

students, 7/1 for international students; for spring admission, 2/1 for domestic students, 10/1 for international students; for summer admission, 5/1 for domestic students, 1/1 for international students. Application fee: $60. *Expenses:* Expenses: $15,359 full-time resident tuition and fees; $23,405 non-resident. *Financial support:* Application deadline: 1/15. *Unit head:* Dr. Michael Scott, Interim Head/Associate Professor, 541-737-6996. *Application contact:* Chris Bell, Civil Engineering Advisor, 541-737-3794, E-mail: chris.a.bell@oregonstate.edu.
Website: http://cce.oregonstate.edu/graduate-academics.

Penn State University Park, Graduate School, College of Engineering, Department of Civil and Environmental Engineering, University Park, PA 16802. Offers civil engineering (M Eng, MS, PhD); environmental engineering (M Eng, MS, PhD). *Unit head:* Dr. Amr S. Elnashai, Dean, 814-865-7537, Fax: 814-863-4749, E-mail: ase2@psu.edu. *Application contact:* Lori A. Stania, Director, Graduate Student Services, 814-867-5278, Fax: 814-863-4627, E-mail: gswww@psu.edu.
Website: http://www.engr.psu.edu/CE/.

Polytechnic University of Puerto Rico, Graduate School, Hato Rey, PR 00919. Offers business administration (MBA), including computer information systems, general management, management of information systems, management of international enterprises; civil engineering (ME, MS); computer engineering (ME, MS); computer science (MCS, MS); electrical engineering (ME, MS); engineering management (MEM); environmental management (MEM); landscape architecture (M Land Arch); manufacturing competitiveness (MMC, MS); manufacturing engineering (ME, MS); mechanical engineering (M Mech E). Part-time and evening/weekend programs available. *Entrance requirements:* For master's, 3 letters of recommendation.

Portland State University, Graduate Studies, College of Liberal Arts and Sciences, Systems Science Program, Portland, OR 97207-0751. Offers computational intelligence (Certificate); computer modeling and simulation (Certificate); systems science (MS); systems science/anthropology (PhD); systems science/business administration (PhD); systems science/civil engineering (PhD); systems science/economics (PhD); systems science/engineering management (PhD); systems science/general (PhD); systems science/mathematical sciences (PhD); systems science/mechanical engineering (PhD); systems science/psychology (PhD); systems science/sociology (PhD). *Faculty:* 2 full-time (0 women), 1 part-time/adjunct (0 women). *Students:* 6 full-time (2 women), 29 part-time (8 women); includes 6 minority (1 Black or African American, non-Hispanic/Latino; 1 American Indian or Alaska Native, non-Hispanic/Latino; 1 Asian, non-Hispanic/Latino; 3 Hispanic/Latino). Average age 41. 32 applicants, 19% accepted, 6 enrolled. In 2014, 10 master's, 3 doctorates awarded. *Degree requirements:* For master's, comprehensive exam (for some programs), thesis optional; for doctorate, variable foreign language requirement, comprehensive exam (for some programs), thesis/dissertation. *Entrance requirements:* For master's, GRE/GMAT scores are recommended but not required., GPA 3.0 for undergraduate or 3.0 for graduate work, 2 letters of recommendation, and statement of interest; for doctorate, GMAT, GRE General Test, GPA requirement is 3.0 for undergraduate and 3.25 for graduate, 2 letters of recommendation and statement of interest. Additional exam requirements/recommendations for international students: Required—TOEFL (minimum score 550 paper-based; 80 iBT). *Application deadline:* For fall admission, 1/15 for domestic and international students; for spring admission, 11/1 for domestic students. Application fee: $50. Electronic applications accepted. *Expenses:* Tuition, state resident: part-time $222 per credit. Tuition, nonresident: part-time $527 per credit. *Required fees:* $22 per contact hour. $100 per quarter. Tuition and fees vary according to program. *Financial support:* In 2014–15, 1 research assistantship with full and partial tuition reimbursement (averaging $2,358 per year) was awarded; teaching assistantships with full and partial tuition reimbursements, career-related internships or fieldwork, Federal Work-Study, scholarships/grants, and unspecified assistantships also available. Support available to part-time students. Financial award application deadline: 3/1; financial award applicants required to submit FAFSA. *Faculty research:* Systems theory and methodology, artificial intelligence neural networks, information theory, nonlinear dynamics/chaos, modeling and simulation. *Total annual research expenditures:* $137,833. *Unit head:* Prof. Wayne Wakeland, PhD, Chair, 503-725-4975, E-mail: wakeland@pdx.edu.
Website: http://www.pdx.edu/sysc/.

Portland State University, Graduate Studies, Maseeh College of Engineering and Computer Science, Department of Civil and Environmental Engineering, Portland, OR 97207-0751. Offers civil and environmental engineering (M Eng, MS, PhD); civil and environmental engineering management (M Eng); environmental sciences and resources (PhD); systems science (PhD). Part-time and evening/weekend programs available. *Faculty:* 16 full-time (3 women), 1 part-time/adjunct (0 women). *Students:* 71 full-time (18 women), 42 part-time (6 women); includes 9 minority (4 Black or African American, non-Hispanic/Latino; 1 Asian, non-Hispanic/Latino; 2 Hispanic/Latino; 2 Two or more races, non-Hispanic/Latino), 45 international. Average age 31. 119 applicants, 54% accepted, 29 enrolled. In 2014, 29 master's, 3 doctorates awarded. *Degree requirements:* For master's, comprehensive exam (for some programs), thesis (for some programs); for doctorate, one foreign language, comprehensive exam, thesis/dissertation, oral and written exams. *Entrance requirements:* For master's, B.S degree in an engineering field, science, or closely related area with a minimum GPA of 3.00; for doctorate, M.S. degree in an engineering field, science, or closely related area. Additional exam requirements/recommendations for international students: Required—TOEFL (minimum score 550 paper-based). *Application deadline:* For fall admission, 1/4 priority date for domestic and international students; for winter admission, 9/1 for domestic and international students; for spring admission, 11/1 for domestic and international students. Applications are processed on a rolling basis. Application fee: $50. *Expenses:* Tuition, state resident: part-time $222 per credit. Tuition, nonresident: part-time $527 per credit. *Required fees:* $22 per contact hour. $100 per quarter. Tuition and fees vary according to program. *Financial support:* In 2014–15, 15 research assistantships with full and partial tuition reimbursements (averaging $6,105 per year), 12 teaching assistantships with full and partial tuition reimbursements (averaging $2,471 per year) were awarded; career-related internships or fieldwork, Federal Work-Study, scholarships/grants, and unspecified assistantships also available. Support available to part-time students. Financial award application deadline: 3/1; financial award applicants required to submit FAFSA. *Faculty research:* Structures, water resources, geotechnical engineering, environmental engineering, transportation. *Total annual research expenditures:* $3.1 million. *Unit head:* Dr. Chris Monsere, Acting Chair, 503-725-9746, Fax: 503-725-4298, E-mail: monserec@cecs.pdx.edu. *Application contact:* Ariel Lewis, Department Manager, 503-725-4244, Fax: 503-725-4298, E-mail: ariel.lewis@pdx.edu.
Website: http://www.pdx.edu/cee/.

Princeton University, Graduate School, School of Engineering and Applied Science, Department of Civil and Environmental Engineering, Princeton, NJ 08544-1019. Offers M Eng, MSE, PhD. Terminal master's awarded for partial completion of doctoral program. *Degree requirements:* For master's, thesis (MSE); for doctorate, thesis/dissertation, general exam. *Entrance requirements:* For master's, GRE General Test, 3 letters of recommendation; for doctorate, GRE General Test, official transcript(s), 3 letters of recommendation, personal statement. Additional exam requirements/recommendations for international students: Required—TOEFL. Electronic applications accepted. *Faculty research:* Carbon mitigation; civil engineering materials and structures; climate and atmospheric dynamics; computational mechanics and risk assessment; hydrology, remote sensing, and sustainability.

Purdue University, College of Engineering, School of Civil Engineering, West Lafayette, IN 47907-2051. Offers MS, MSCE, MSE, PhD. Part-time programs available. Terminal master's awarded for partial completion of doctoral program. *Degree requirements:* For master's, thesis (for some programs); for doctorate, thesis/dissertation. *Entrance requirements:* For master's and doctorate, GRE General Test, minimum GPA of 3.0. Additional exam requirements/recommendations for international students: Required—TOEFL (minimum score 575 paper-based; 90 iBT); Recommended—TWE. Electronic applications accepted. *Faculty research:* Environmental and hydraulic engineering, geotechnical and materials engineering, structural engineering, construction engineering, infrastructure and transportation systems engineering.

Queen's University at Kingston, School of Graduate Studies, Faculty of Applied Science, Department of Civil Engineering, Kingston, ON K7L 3N6, Canada. Offers M Eng, M Sc Eng, PhD. Part-time programs available. *Degree requirements:* For master's, thesis (for some programs); for doctorate, comprehensive exam, thesis/dissertation. *Entrance requirements:* Additional exam requirements/recommendations for international students: Required—TOEFL. *Faculty research:* Structural, geotechnical, transportation, hydrotechnical, and environmental engineering.

Rensselaer Polytechnic Institute, Graduate School, School of Engineering, Program in Civil Engineering, Troy, NY 12180-3590. Offers M Eng, MS, D Eng, PhD. Part-time programs available. *Faculty:* 23 full-time (3 women), 5 part-time/adjunct (1 woman). *Students:* 21 full-time (8 women), 1 (woman) part-time; includes 1 minority (Asian, non-Hispanic/Latino), 20 international. Average age 27. 85 applicants, 26% accepted, 13 enrolled. In 2014, 15 master's, 4 doctorates awarded. Terminal master's awarded for partial completion of doctoral program. *Degree requirements:* For master's, thesis (for some programs); for doctorate, thesis/dissertation. *Entrance requirements:* For master's and doctorate, GRE. Additional exam requirements/recommendations for international students: Required—TOEFL (minimum score 570 paper-based; 88 iBT), IELTS (minimum score 6.5), PTE (minimum score 60). *Application deadline:* For fall admission, 1/1 priority date for domestic and international students; for spring admission, 8/15 priority date for domestic and international students. Applications are processed on a rolling basis. Electronic applications accepted. *Expenses: Tuition:* Full-time $46,700; part-time $1945 per credit. Tuition and fees vary according to course load. *Financial support:* In 2014–15, 16 students received support, including research assistantships (averaging $18,500 per year), teaching assistantships (averaging $18,500 per year); fellowships also available. Financial award application deadline: 1/1. *Faculty research:* Geotechnical, structural, transportation. *Total annual research expenditures:* $2.7 million. *Unit head:* Dr. Michael O'Rourke, Graduate Program Director, 518-276-6933, E-mail: orourm@rpi.edu. *Application contact:* Office of Graduate Admissions, 518-276-6216, E-mail: gradadmissions@rpi.edu.
Website: http://cee.rpi.edu/graduate.

Rice University, Graduate Programs, George R. Brown School of Engineering, Department of Civil and Environmental Engineering, Houston, TX 77251-1892. Offers civil engineering (MCE, MS, PhD); environmental engineering (MEE, MES, MS, PhD); environmental science (MEE, MES, MS, PhD). Part-time programs available. *Degree requirements:* For master's, thesis (for some programs); for doctorate, thesis/dissertation. *Entrance requirements:* For master's and doctorate, GRE General Test, GRE Subject Test, minimum GPA of 3.25. Additional exam requirements/recommendations for international students: Required—TOEFL (minimum score 600 paper-based; 90 iBT). Electronic applications accepted. *Faculty research:* Biology and chemistry of groundwater, pollutant fate in groundwater systems, water quality monitoring, urban storm water runoff, urban air quality.

Rose-Hulman Institute of Technology, Faculty of Engineering and Applied Sciences, Department of Civil Engineering, Terre Haute, IN 47803-3999. Offers civil engineering (MS); environmental engineering (MS). Part-time programs available. *Faculty:* 9 full-time (2 women), 1 part-time/adjunct (0 women). *Students:* 4 full-time (1 woman). Average age 23. 9 applicants, 100% accepted, 2 enrolled. In 2014, 2 master's awarded. *Degree requirements:* For master's, thesis (for some programs). *Entrance requirements:* For master's, GRE, minimum GPA of 3.0. Additional exam requirements/recommendations for international students: Required—TOEFL (minimum score 580 paper-based; 92 iBT). *Application deadline:* For fall admission, 2/1 priority date for domestic students. Applications are processed on a rolling basis. Application fee: $0. *Expenses: Tuition:* Full-time $40,449. *Financial support:* In 2014–15, 3 students received support. Fellowships with full and partial tuition reimbursements available, research assistantships with full and partial tuition reimbursements available, institutionally sponsored loans, scholarships/grants, and tuition waivers (full and partial) available. Financial award application deadline: 2/1. *Faculty research:* Transportation, hydraulics/hydrology, environmental, construction, geotechnical, structural. *Total annual research expenditures:* $25,939. *Unit head:* Dr. Kevin Sutterer, Chairman, 812-877-8959, Fax: 812-877-8440, E-mail: sutterer@rose-hulman.edu. *Application contact:* Dr. Azad Siahmakoun, Associate Dean of the Faculty, 812-877-8400, Fax: 812-877-8061, E-mail: siahmako@rose-hulman.edu.
Website: http://www.rose-hulman.edu/ce/.

Rowan University, Graduate School, College of Engineering, Department of Civil Engineering, Glassboro, NJ 08028-1701. Offers MEM, MS. *Faculty:* 9 full-time (2 women). *Students:* 9 full-time (2 women), 33 part-time (6 women); includes 9 minority (2 Black or African American, non-Hispanic/Latino; 4 Asian, non-Hispanic/Latino; 3 Hispanic/Latino). Average age 30. 18 applicants, 94% accepted, 11 enrolled. In 2014, 12 master's awarded. *Application deadline:* For fall admission, 8/1 for domestic students, 5/1 for international students; for spring admission, 11/1 for domestic and international students; for summer admission, 4/1 for domestic students, 2/15 for international students. Applications are processed on a rolling basis. Application fee: $65. Electronic applications accepted. *Expenses: Tuition, area resident:* Part-time $648 per credit. Tuition, state resident: part-time $648 per credit. Tuition, nonresident: part-time $648 per credit. *Required fees:* $145 per credit. Tuition and fees vary according to degree level, campus/location, program and student level. *Unit head:* Dr. Steve Chin, Dean, 856-256-5301. *Application contact:* Dr. Ralph Dusseau, Program Adviser, 856-256-5332.

Royal Military College of Canada, Division of Graduate Studies and Research, Engineering Division, Department of Civil Engineering, Kingston, ON K7K 7B4, Canada. Offers M Eng, MA Sc, PhD. *Degree requirements:* For master's, thesis; for doctorate, comprehensive exam, thesis/dissertation. *Entrance requirements:* For master's, honours degree with second-class standing; for doctorate, master's degree. Electronic applications accepted.

Rutgers, The State University of New Jersey, New Brunswick, Graduate School-New Brunswick, Department of Civil and Environmental Engineering, Piscataway, NJ 08854-8097. Offers MS, PhD. Part-time and evening/weekend programs available. Terminal master's awarded for partial completion of doctoral program. *Degree requirements:* For master's, comprehensive exam, thesis or alternative; for doctorate, comprehensive exam, thesis/dissertation. *Entrance requirements:* For master's and doctorate, GRE General Test. Additional exam requirements/recommendations for international students: Required—TOEFL (minimum score 580 paper-based). Electronic applications accepted. *Faculty research:* Civil engineering materials research, non-destructive evaluation of transportation infrastructure, transportation planning, intelligent transportation systems.

Saint Martin's University, Office of Graduate Studies, Program in Civil Engineering, Lacey, WA 98503. Offers MCE. Part-time and evening/weekend programs available. *Faculty:* 2 full-time (0 women), 2 part-time/adjunct (0 women). *Students:* 8 full-time (0 women), 2 part-time (0 women); includes 3 minority (2 Asian, non-Hispanic/Latino; 1 Two or more races, non-Hispanic/Latino), 5 international. Average age 27. 21 applicants, 76% accepted, 7 enrolled. In 2014, 3 master's awarded. *Degree requirements:* For master's, thesis optional. *Entrance requirements:* For master's, minimum GPA of 2.8 in undergraduate work; BS in civil engineering or other engineering/science with completion of calculus, differential equations, physics, chemistry, statistics, mechanics of materials and dynamics. Additional exam requirements/recommendations for international students: Required—TOEFL (minimum score 550 paper-based; 79 iBT); Recommended—IELTS (minimum score 6.5). *Application deadline:* For fall admission, 4/1 priority date for domestic students, 4/1 for international students; for spring admission, 11/1 priority date for domestic students, 11/1 for international students. Applications are processed on a rolling basis. Application fee: $50. Electronic applications accepted. *Expenses: Tuition:* Part-time $1045 per credit. *Financial support:* Scholarships/grants and tuition waivers (partial) available. Support available to part-time students. Financial award application deadline: 3/1; financial award applicants required to submit FAFSA. *Faculty research:* Transportation engineering, metal fatigue and fracture, environmental engineering. *Unit head:* Dr. Pius O. Igharo, Program Chair, 360-438-4322, Fax: 360-438-4548, E-mail: pigharo@stmartin.edu. *Application contact:* Bailey Craft, Assistant Director for Graduate Recruitment, 360-412-6142, E-mail: gradstudies@stmartin.edu.
Website: http://www.stmartin.edu/gradstudies/MCE.

San Diego State University, Graduate and Research Affairs, College of Engineering, Department of Civil and Environmental Engineering, San Diego, CA 92182. Offers civil engineering (MS). Part-time and evening/weekend programs available. *Degree requirements:* For master's, thesis optional. *Entrance requirements:* For master's, GRE General Test. Additional exam requirements/recommendations for international students: Required—TOEFL. Electronic applications accepted. *Faculty research:* Hydraulics, hydrology, transportation, smart material, concrete material.

San Jose State University, Graduate Studies and Research, Charles W. Davidson College of Engineering, Department of Civil and Environmental Engineering, San Jose, CA 95192-0001. Offers civil engineering (MS). *Degree requirements:* For master's, thesis or alternative. *Entrance requirements:* For master's, minimum GPA of 2.7. Electronic applications accepted.

Santa Clara University, School of Engineering, Santa Clara, CA 95053. Offers analog circuit design (Certificate); applied mathematics (MS); ASIC design and test (Certificate); bioengineering (MS); civil engineering (MS); computer science and engineering (MS, PhD); controls (Certificate); digital signal processing (Certificate); dynamics (Certificate); electrical engineering (MS, PhD); engineering (Engineer); engineering management (MS); fundamentals of electrical engineering (Certificate); information assurance (Certificate); materials engineering (Certificate); mechanical design analysis (Certificate); mechanical engineering (MS, PhD); mechatronics systems engineering (Certificate); microwave and antennas (Certificate); networking (Certificate); renewable energy (Certificate); software engineering (Certificate); sustainable energy (MS); technology jump-start (Certificate); thermofluids (Certificate). Part-time and evening/weekend programs available. *Faculty:* 59 full-time (23 women), 80 part-time/adjunct (14 women). *Students:* 584 full-time (239 women), 353 part-time (102 women); includes 224 minority (7 Black or African American, non-Hispanic/Latino; 144 Asian, non-Hispanic/Latino; 50 Hispanic/Latino; 2 Native Hawaiian or other Pacific Islander, non-Hispanic/Latino; 21 Two or more races, non-Hispanic/Latino), 548 international. Average age 27. 1,248 applicants, 51% accepted, 375 enrolled. In 2014, 283 master's, 5 doctorates, 1 other advanced degree awarded. *Degree requirements:* For master's, thesis (for some programs); for doctorate, thesis/dissertation; for other advanced degree, thesis. *Entrance requirements:* For master's, GRE, transcript; for doctorate, GRE, master's degree or equivalent; for other advanced degree, master's degree, published paper. Additional exam requirements/recommendations for international students: Required—TOEFL (minimum score 550 paper-based; 79 iBT). *Application deadline:* For fall admission, 8/1 for domestic students, 7/15 for international students; for winter admission, 10/28 for domestic students, 9/23 for international students; for spring admission, 2/25 for domestic students, 1/21 for international students. Applications are processed on a rolling basis. Application fee: $60. Electronic applications accepted. *Expenses:* Expenses: Contact institution. *Financial support:* In 2014–15, 94 students received support. Fellowships with full and partial tuition reimbursements available, research assistantships with full and partial tuition reimbursements available, teaching assistantships with full tuition reimbursements available, career-related internships or fieldwork, Federal Work-Study, institutionally sponsored loans, and scholarships/grants available. Support available to part-time students. Financial award application deadline: 3/2; financial award applicants required to submit FAFSA. *Faculty research:* Video encoding, nanostructures, robotics, microfluidics, water resources. *Total annual research expenditures:* $1.6 million. *Unit head:* Dr. Alex Zecevic, Associate Dean for Graduate Studies, 408-554-2394, E-mail: azecevic@scu.edu. *Application contact:* Stacey Tinker, Director of Enrollment Management, 408-554-4748, Fax: 408-554-4323, E-mail: stinker@scu.edu.
Website: http://www.scu.edu/engineering/graduate/.

South Carolina State University, College of Graduate and Professional Studies, Department of Civil and Mechanical Engineering Technology, Orangeburg, SC 29117-0001. Offers MS. Part-time and evening/weekend programs available. *Faculty:* 3 full-time (1 woman), 1 part-time/adjunct (0 women). *Students:* 14 full-time (6 women); includes 13 minority (all Black or African American, non-Hispanic/Latino), 1 international. Average age 29. 7 applicants, 100% accepted, 6 enrolled. In 2014, 3 master's awarded. *Degree requirements:* For master's, comprehensive exam, thesis, departmental qualifying exam. *Entrance requirements:* For master's, GRE. Additional exam requirements/recommendations for international students: Recommended—TOEFL. *Application deadline:* For fall admission, 6/15 for domestic and international students; for spring admission, 11/1 for domestic and international students. Application fee: $25. Electronic applications accepted. *Expenses:* Tuition, state resident: full-time $7290; part-time $405 per credit. Tuition, nonresident: full-time $17,058; part-time $948 per credit. *Required fees:* $2798; $155 per credit hour. *Financial support:* Fellowships, research assistantships, career-related internships or fieldwork, Federal Work-Study, institutionally sponsored loans, and unspecified assistantships available. Financial award application deadline: 6/1. *Unit head:* Dr. Ali Akbar Eliadorani, Chair, 803-536-7117, Fax: 803-516-4607, E-mail: aeliadorani@scsu.edu. *Application contact:* Curtis Foskey, Coordinator of Graduate Admission, 803-536-8419, Fax: 803-536-8812, E-mail: cfoskey@scsu.edu.
Website: http://www.scsu.edu/schoolofgraduatestudies.aspx.

South Dakota School of Mines and Technology, Graduate Division, Program in Civil and Environmental Engineering, Rapid City, SD 57701-3995. Offers MS. Part-time programs available. Postbaccalaureate distance learning degree programs offered. *Faculty:* 12 full-time (3 women), 3 part-time/adjunct (1 woman). *Students:* 17 full-time (5 women), 6 part-time (2 women), 3 international. Average age 24. 31 applicants, 55% accepted, 11 enrolled. In 2014, 14 master's awarded. *Degree requirements:* For master's, thesis (for some programs). *Entrance requirements:* Additional exam requirements/recommendations for international students: Required—TOEFL (minimum score 520 paper-based; 68 iBT), TWE. *Application deadline:* For fall admission, 7/1 priority date for domestic students, 4/1 for international students; for spring admission, 11/1 for domestic students, 9/1 for international students. Applications are processed on a rolling basis. Application fee: $35. Electronic applications accepted. *Expenses:* Tuition, state resident: full-time $5050; part-time $210.40 per credit hour. Tuition, nonresident: full-time $11,290; part-time $470.30 per credit hour. *Required fees:* $4680. *Financial support:* In 2014–15, 1 fellowship (averaging $3,475 per year), 6 research assistantships with partial tuition reimbursements (averaging $9,363 per year), 16 teaching assistantships with full and partial tuition reimbursements (averaging $4,772 per year) were awarded; Federal Work-Study and institutionally sponsored loans also available. Support available to part-time students. Financial award application deadline: 5/15. *Faculty research:* Concrete technology, environmental and sanitation engineering, water resources engineering, composite materials, geotechnical engineering. *Total annual research expenditures:* $360,606. *Unit head:* Dr. Molly M. Gribb, Graduate Coordinator, 605-394-1697, E-mail: molly.gribb@sdsmt.edu. *Application contact:* Rachel Howard, Office of Graduate Education, 605-355-3468, Fax: 605-394-1767, E-mail: rachel.howard@sdsmt.edu.
Website: http://graded.sdsmt.edu/academics/programs/ce/.

South Dakota State University, Graduate School, College of Engineering, Department of Civil and Environmental Engineering, Brookings, SD 57007. Offers engineering (MS). Part-time programs available. Postbaccalaureate distance learning degree programs offered (minimal on-campus study). *Degree requirements:* For master's, thesis (for some programs), oral exam. *Entrance requirements:* Additional exam requirements/recommendations for international students: Required—TOEFL (minimum score 525 paper-based). *Faculty research:* Structural, environmental, geotechnical, transportation engineering and water resources.

Southern Illinois University Carbondale, Graduate School, College of Engineering, Department of Civil and Environmental Engineering, Carbondale, IL 62901-4701. Offers civil engineering (MS). *Faculty:* 10 full-time (1 woman). *Students:* 34 full-time (2 women), 10 part-time (1 woman); includes 3 minority (all Hispanic/Latino), 27 international. Average age 26. 74 applicants, 24% accepted, 8 enrolled. In 2014, 10 master's awarded. *Degree requirements:* For master's, comprehensive exam, thesis. *Entrance requirements:* For master's, minimum GPA of 2.7. Additional exam requirements/recommendations for international students: Required—TOEFL. *Application deadline:* Applications are processed on a rolling basis. Application fee: $50. *Expenses:* Tuition, state resident: full-time $10,176; part-time $1153 per credit. Tuition, nonresident: full-time $20,814; part-time $1744 per credit. *Required fees:* $7092; $394 per credit. $2364 per semester. *Financial support:* In 2014–15, 21 students received support, including 5 research assistantships with full tuition reimbursements available, 9 teaching assistantships with full tuition reimbursements available; fellowships with full tuition reimbursements available, Federal Work-Study, institutionally sponsored loans, and tuition waivers (full) also available. Support available to part-time students. Financial award application deadline: 7/1. *Faculty research:* Composite materials, wastewater treatment, solid waste disposal, slurry transport, geotechnical engineering. *Total annual research expenditures:* $230,856. *Unit head:* Dr. Sanjeev Kumar, Chair, 618-453-7815, E-mail: kumars@ce.siu.edu. *Application contact:* Christine O'Dell, Office Support Specialist, 618-536-2369, E-mail: codell@siu.edu.
Website: http://engineering.siu.edu/civil/.

Southern Illinois University Edwardsville, Graduate School, School of Engineering, Department of Civil Engineering, Edwardsville, IL 62026. Offers environmental engineering (MS); geotechnical engineering (MS); structural engineering (MS); transportation engineering (MS). Part-time and evening/weekend programs available. *Faculty:* 10 full-time (3 women). *Students:* 15 full-time (2 women), 42 part-time (6 women); includes 3 minority (1 Black or African American, non-Hispanic/Latino; 1 Asian, non-Hispanic/Latino; 1 Hispanic/Latino), 25 international. 82 applicants, 61% accepted. In 2014, 13 master's awarded. *Degree requirements:* For master's, thesis (for some programs), research paper. *Entrance requirements:* For master's, minimum undergraduate GPA of 2.75 in science, math, and engineering courses. Additional exam requirements/recommendations for international students: Required—TOEFL (minimum score 550 paper-based; 79 iBT), IELTS (minimum score 6.5). *Application deadline:* For fall admission, 7/24 for domestic students, 7/15 for international students; for spring admission, 12/11 for domestic students, 11/15 for international students; for summer admission, 4/29 for domestic students, 4/15 for international students. Applications are processed on a rolling basis. Application fee: $30. Electronic applications accepted. *Expenses:* Tuition, state resident: full-time $5026. Tuition, nonresident: full-time $12,566. *International tuition:* $25,136 full-time. *Required fees:* $1682. Tuition and fees vary according to course load, campus/location and program. *Financial support:* In 2014–15, 28 students received support, including 1 fellowship with full tuition reimbursement available (averaging $8,370 per year), 16 research assistantships with full tuition reimbursements available, 11 teaching assistantships with full tuition reimbursements available; institutionally sponsored loans, scholarships/grants, and unspecified assistantships also available. Financial award application deadline: 3/1; financial award applicants required to submit FAFSA. *Unit head:* Dr. Jim Zhou, Chair, 618-650-2533, E-mail: jzhou@siue.edu. *Application contact:* Melissa K Mace, Assistant Director of Admissions for Graduate and International Recruitment, 618-650-2756, Fax: 618-650-3618, E-mail: mmace@siue.edu.
Website: http://www.siue.edu/engineering/civilengineering.

Southern Methodist University, Bobby B. Lyle School of Engineering, Department of Environmental and Civil Engineering, Dallas, TX 75275-0340. Offers air pollution control and atmospheric sciences (PhD); civil engineering (MS); environmental engineering (MS); environmental science (MS); structural engineering (PhD); sustainability and development (MA); water and wastewater engineering (PhD). Part-time and evening/weekend programs available. Postbaccalaureate distance learning degree programs offered (no on-campus study). Terminal master's awarded for partial completion of doctoral program. *Degree requirements:* For master's, thesis optional; for doctorate, thesis/dissertation, oral and written qualifying exams. *Entrance requirements:* For master's, GRE General Test, minimum GPA of 3.0 in last 2 years; bachelor's degree in engineering, mathematics, or sciences; for doctorate, GRE, BS and MS in related field, minimum GPA of 3.3. Additional exam requirements/recommendations for international students: Required—TOEFL. Electronic applications accepted. *Faculty research:* Human and environmental health effects of endocrine disrupters, development of air pollution control systems for diesel engines, structural analysis and design, modeling and design of waste treatment systems.

Stanford University, School of Engineering, Department of Civil and Environmental Engineering, Stanford, CA 94305-9991. Offers atmosphere and energy (MS, PhD);

construction (MS), including construction engineering and management, design-construction integration, sustainable design and construction; environmental engineering and science (MS, PhD, Eng); environmental fluid mechanics and hydrology (PhD); geomechanics (MS); structural engineering (MS). Terminal master's awarded for partial completion of doctoral program. *Degree requirements:* For doctorate, thesis/dissertation, qualifying exam; for Eng, thesis. *Entrance requirements:* For master's, doctorate, and Eng, GRE General Test. Additional exam requirements/recommendations for international students: Required—TOEFL. Electronic applications accepted. *Expenses: Tuition:* Full-time $44,184; part-time $982 per credit hour. *Required fees:* $191.

Stevens Institute of Technology, Graduate School, Charles V. Schaefer Jr. School of Engineering, Department of Civil, Environmental, and Ocean Engineering, Program in Civil Engineering, Hoboken, NJ 07030. Offers civil engineering (PhD); geotechnical engineering (Certificate); geotechnical/geoenvironmental engineering (M Eng, Engr); hydrologic modeling (M Eng); stormwater management (M Eng); structural engineering (M Eng, Engr); water resources engineering (M Eng). *Degree requirements:* For master's, thesis optional; for doctorate, variable foreign language requirement, thesis/dissertation; for other advanced degree, project or thesis. *Entrance requirements:* For doctorate, GRE. Additional exam requirements/recommendations for international students: Required—TOEFL. Electronic applications accepted.

Syracuse University, L. C. Smith College of Engineering and Computer Science, Program in Civil Engineering, Syracuse, NY 13244. Offers MS, PhD. Part-time programs available. *Students:* 92 full-time (27 women), 10 part-time (2 women); includes 3 minority (1 Black or African American, non-Hispanic/Latino; 2 Asian, non-Hispanic/Latino), 87 international. Average age 26. 151 applicants, 64% accepted, 42 enrolled. In 2014, 16 master's, 5 doctorates awarded. *Degree requirements:* For master's, comprehensive exam (for some programs), thesis (for some programs); for doctorate, comprehensive exam, thesis/dissertation. *Entrance requirements:* For master's and doctorate, GRE General Test. Additional exam requirements/recommendations for international students: Required—TOEFL (minimum score 100 iBT). *Application deadline:* For fall admission, 7/1 priority date for domestic students, 6/1 priority date for international students; for spring admission, 11/15 priority date for domestic students, 10/15 priority date for international students. Applications are processed on a rolling basis. Application fee: $75. Electronic applications accepted. *Expenses: Tuition:* Part-time $1341 per credit. *Required fees:* $1341 per credit. *Financial support:* Fellowships with full tuition reimbursements, research assistantships with full and partial tuition reimbursements, teaching assistantships with full and partial tuition reimbursements, and tuition waivers (partial) available. Financial award application deadline: 1/1. *Faculty research:* Fate and transport of pollutants, methods for characterization and remediation of hazardous wastes, response of eco-systems to disturbances, water quality and engineering. *Unit head:* Dr. Ossama Sam Salem, Chair, 315-443-2311, E-mail: omsalem@syr.edu,. *Application contact:* Elizabeth Buchanan, Information Contact, 315-443-2558, E-mail: ebuchana@syr.edu.
Website: http://lcs.syr.edu/.

Temple University, College of Engineering, Department of Civil and Environmental Engineering, Philadelphia, PA 19122-6096. Offers civil engineering (MSCE); engineering (PhD); environmental engineering (MS Env E); storm water management (Graduate Certificate). Part-time and evening/weekend programs available. *Faculty:* 20 full-time (4 women). *Students:* 12 full-time (4 women), 12 part-time (3 women); includes 7 minority (4 Black or African American, non-Hispanic/Latino; 3 Asian, non-Hispanic/Latino), 10 international. 43 applicants, 67% accepted, 7 enrolled. In 2014, 1 master's, 1 other advanced degree awarded. Terminal master's awarded for partial completion of doctoral program. *Degree requirements:* For master's, thesis optional; for doctorate, thesis/dissertation, preliminary exam, dissertation proposal and defense. *Entrance requirements:* For master's, GRE General Test, minimum GPA of 3.0; BS in engineering from ABET-accredited or equivalent institution; resume; goals statement; three letters of reference; official transcripts; for doctorate, GRE General Test, minimum GPA of 3.0; MS in engineering from ABET-accredited or equivalent institution (preferred); resume; goals statement; three letters of reference; official transcripts. Additional exam requirements/recommendations for international students: Required—TOEFL (minimum score 550 paper-based; 79 iBT), IELTS (minimum score 6.5). *Application deadline:* For fall admission, 3/1 priority date for domestic and international students; for spring admission, 11/1 priority date for domestic students, 8/1 priority date for international students. Applications are processed on a rolling basis. Application fee: $60. Electronic applications accepted. *Expenses:* Expenses: $913 per credit hour in-state; $1,210 per credit hour out-of-state. *Financial support:* Fellowships with full and partial tuition reimbursements, research assistantships with full and partial tuition reimbursements, teaching assistantships with full and partial tuition reimbursements, Federal Work-Study, scholarships/grants, health care benefits, and unspecified assistantships available. Financial award application deadline: 3/1; financial award applicants required to submit FAFSA. *Faculty research:* Analysis of the effect of scour on bridge stability, design of sustainable buildings, development of new highway pavement material using plastic waste, characterization of by-products and waste materials for pavement and geotechnical engineering applications, development of effective traffic signals in urban and rural settings, development of techniques for effective construction management. *Unit head:* Dr. Rominder Suri, Acting Chair, 215-204-2378, Fax: 215-204-6936, E-mail: rominder.suri@temple.edu. *Application contact:* Mojan Arshad, Assistant Coordinator, Graduate Studies, 215-204-7800, Fax: 215-204-6936, E-mail: gradengr@temple.edu.
Website: http://engineering.temple.edu/department/civil-environmental-engineering.

Tennessee State University, The School of Graduate Studies and Research, College of Engineering, Nashville, TN 37209-1561. Offers biomedical engineering (ME); civil engineering (ME); computer and information systems engineering (MS, PhD); electrical engineering (ME); environmental engineering (ME); manufacturing engineering (ME); mathematical sciences (MS); mechanical engineering (ME). Part-time and evening/weekend programs available. *Degree requirements:* For master's, project; for doctorate, comprehensive exam, thesis/dissertation. *Entrance requirements:* For doctorate, minimum GPA of 3.3. *Faculty research:* Robotics, intelligent systems, human-computer interaction software systems, biomedical engineering, signal/image processing, probabilistic design, intelligent manufacturing, cooperative mobile robots, condition based maintenance, sensor fusion.

Tennessee Technological University, College of Graduate Studies, College of Engineering, Department of Civil and Environmental Engineering, Cookeville, TN 38505. Offers MS. Part-time programs available. *Faculty:* 17 full-time (0 women). *Students:* 12 full-time (5 women), 7 part-time (1 woman); includes 1 minority (Black or African American, non-Hispanic/Latino), 7 international. Average age 27. 46 applicants, 41% accepted, 6 enrolled. In 2014, 11 master's awarded. *Degree requirements:* For master's, thesis. *Entrance requirements:* For master's, GRE. Additional exam requirements/recommendations for international students: Required—TOEFL (minimum score 550 paper-based; 79 iBT), IELTS (minimum score 5.5), PTE (minimum score 53), or TOEIC (Test of English as an International Communication). *Application deadline:* For fall admission, 8/1 for domestic students, 5/1 for international students; for spring admission, 12/1 for domestic students, 10/1 for international students. Applications are processed on a rolling basis. Application fee: $35 ($40 for international students). Electronic applications accepted. *Expenses:* Tuition, state resident: full-time $9783; part-time $492 per credit hour. Tuition, nonresident: full-time $24,071; part-time $1179 per credit hour. *Financial support:* In 2014–15, 6 research assistantships (averaging $8,227 per year), 5 teaching assistantships (averaging $7,200 per year) were awarded; career-related internships or fieldwork also available. Financial award application deadline: 4/1. *Faculty research:* Environmental engineering, transportation, structural engineering, water resources. *Unit head:* Dr. Ben Mohr, Interim Chairperson, 931-372-3454, Fax: 931-372-6352, E-mail: bmohr@tntech.edu. *Application contact:* Shelia K. Kendrick, Coordinator of Graduate Studies, 931-372-3808, Fax: 931-372-3497, E-mail: skendrick@tntech.edu.

Texas A&M University, College of Engineering, Zachry Department of Civil Engineering, College Station, TX 77843. Offers civil engineering (M Eng, MS, PhD); ocean engineering (M Eng, MS, PhD). Part-time programs available. *Faculty:* 52. *Students:* 431 full-time (123 women), 58 part-time (15 women); includes 42 minority (5 Black or African American, non-Hispanic/Latino; 2 American Indian or Alaska Native, non-Hispanic/Latino; 15 Asian, non-Hispanic/Latino; 17 Hispanic/Latino; 3 Two or more races, non-Hispanic/Latino), 337 international. Average age 27. 904 applicants, 53% accepted, 176 enrolled. In 2014, 101 master's, 37 doctorates awarded. *Degree requirements:* For master's, thesis (MS); for doctorate, dissertation (PhD), internship (D Eng). *Entrance requirements:* For master's and doctorate, GRE General Test. Additional exam requirements/recommendations for international students: Required—TOEFL. *Application deadline:* Applications are processed on a rolling basis. Application fee: $50 ($90 for international students). Electronic applications accepted. *Expenses:* Tuition, state resident: full-time $4078; part-time $226.55 per credit hour. Tuition, nonresident: full-time $10,594; part-time $577.55 per credit hour. *Required fees:* $2813; $237.70 per credit hour. $278.50 per semester. Tuition and fees vary according to degree level and student level. *Financial support:* In 2014–15, 362 students received support, including 59 fellowships with full and partial tuition reimbursements available (averaging $3,445 per year), 156 research assistantships with full and partial tuition reimbursements available (averaging $6,404 per year), 55 teaching assistantships with full and partial tuition reimbursements available (averaging $4,665 per year); career-related internships or fieldwork, institutionally sponsored loans, scholarships/grants, traineeships, health care benefits, tuition waivers (full and partial), and unspecified assistantships also available. Support available to part-time students. Financial award application deadline: 4/15; financial award applicants required to submit FAFSA. *Unit head:* Dr. Robin Autenrieth, Interim Head, 979-845-2438, E-mail: rautenrieth@civil.tamu.edu. *Application contact:* Laura Byrd, Program Assistant, Graduate Student Services, 979-845-2498, E-mail: lbyrd@civil.tamu.edu.
Website: http://engineering.tamu.edu/civil/.

Texas A&M University–Kingsville, College of Graduate Studies, College of Engineering, Department of Civil Engineering, Kingsville, TX 78363. Offers ME, MS. *Faculty:* 4 full-time (0 women), 1 part-time/adjunct (0 women). *Students:* 53 full-time (10 women), 28 part-time (11 women); includes 15 minority (all Hispanic/Latino), 63 international. Average age 25. 142 applicants, 43% accepted, 20 enrolled. In 2014, 23 master's awarded. *Degree requirements:* For master's, variable foreign language requirement, comprehensive exam, thesis (for some programs). *Entrance requirements:* For master's, GRE (minimum Quantitative and Verbal score of 950 on old scale), MAT, GMAT, minimum GPA of 2.6. Additional exam requirements/recommendations for international students: Required—TOEFL (minimum score 550 paper-based; 79 iBT). *Application deadline:* For fall admission, 8/15 for domestic students, 6/1 for international students; for spring admission, 12/15 for domestic students, 11/1 for international students; for summer admission, 5/15 for domestic students, 4/1 for international students. Applications are processed on a rolling basis. Application fee: $35 ($50 for international students). Electronic applications accepted. *Financial support:* In 2014–15, 21 students received support, including 3 research assistantships (averaging $1,668 per year), 9 teaching assistantships (averaging $3,282 per year); career-related internships or fieldwork, Federal Work-Study, institutionally sponsored loans, scholarships/grants, health care benefits, tuition waivers (full and partial), and unspecified assistantships also available. Support available to part-time students. Financial award application deadline: 5/15; financial award applicants required to submit FAFSA. *Faculty research:* Dam restoration. *Unit head:* Dr. Joseph O. Sai, Department Chair, 361-593-2266, Fax: 361-593-2069, E-mail: j-sai@tamuk.edu. *Application contact:* Dr. Dazhi Sun, Graduate Coordinator, 361-593-2270, Fax: 361-593-2069, E-mail: dazhi.sun@tamuk.edu.

Texas Tech University, Graduate School, Edward E. Whitacre Jr. College of Engineering, Department of Civil and Environmental Engineering, Lubbock, TX 79409-1023. Offers civil engineering (MSCE, PhD); environmental engineering (MENVEGR). *Accreditation:* ABET. Part-time programs available. *Faculty:* 23 full-time (3 women), 1 part-time/adjunct (0 women). *Students:* 76 full-time (25 women), 8 part-time (0 women); includes 19 minority (1 Black or African American, non-Hispanic/Latino; 4 Asian, non-Hispanic/Latino; 13 Hispanic/Latino; 1 Two or more races, non-Hispanic/Latino), 42 international. Average age 26. 129 applicants, 67% accepted, 29 enrolled. In 2014, 36 master's, 4 doctorates awarded. Terminal master's awarded for partial completion of doctoral program. *Degree requirements:* For master's, comprehensive exam, thesis or alternative; for doctorate, comprehensive exam, thesis/dissertation, preliminary examination. *Entrance requirements:* For master's and doctorate, GRE (Verbal and Quantitative). Additional exam requirements/recommendations for international students: Required—TOEFL (minimum score 550 paper-based; 79 iBT), IELTS (minimum score 6.5). *Application deadline:* For fall admission, 6/1 priority date for domestic students, 1/15 priority date for international students; for spring admission, 9/1 priority date for domestic students, 6/15 priority date for international students. Applications are processed on a rolling basis. Application fee: $60. Electronic applications accepted. *Expenses:* Tuition, state resident: full-time $6310; part-time $262.92 per credit hour. Tuition, nonresident: full-time $14,998; part-time $624.92 per credit hour. *Required fees:* $2701; $36.50 per credit. $912.50 per semester. Tuition and fees vary according to course load. *Financial support:* In 2014–15, 61 students received support, including 59 fellowships (averaging $3,102 per year), 3 research assistantships (averaging $17,500 per year), 21 teaching assistantships (averaging $18,170 per year); scholarships/grants, tuition waivers (partial), and unspecified assistantships also available. Financial award application deadline: 3/1; financial award applicants required to submit FAFSA. *Faculty research:* Geotechnical engineering, transportation engineering, water resources engineering, environmental engineering, wind engineering. *Total annual research expenditures:* $830,395. *Unit head:* Dr. David Ernst, Interim Chair, 806-834-8657, E-mail: david.ernst@ttu.edu. *Application contact:* Dr. Priyantha Jayawickrama, Associate Professor, 806-742-3523 Ext. 245, Fax: 806-742-3488, E-mail: priyantha.jayawickrama@ttu.edu.
Website: http://www.depts.ttu.edu/ceweb/.

Trine University, Allen School of Engineering and Technology, Angola, IN 46703-1764. Offers civil engineering (ME); engineering management (MS). Part-time and evening/weekend programs available. *Students:* 2 full-time (0 women). In 2014, 4 master's awarded. *Degree requirements:* For master's, comprehensive exam, thesis. *Entrance requirements:* Additional exam requirements/recommendations for international students: Required—TOEFL. *Application deadline:* For fall admission, 6/30 for domestic students. Application fee: $100. *Expenses: Tuition:* Full-time $12,000; part-time $670 per credit hour. Tuition and fees vary according to degree level, campus/location, program and student level. *Financial support:* Career-related internships or fieldwork and traineeships available. Financial award application deadline: 3/1; financial award applicants required to submit FAFSA. *Faculty research:* CAD, computer numerical control, parametric modeling, megatronics. *Unit head:* Dr. VK Sharma, Dean, Allen School of Engineering and Technology, 260-665-4432, E-mail: sharmavk@trine.edu. *Application contact:* Dr. Earl D. Brooks, II, President, 260-665-4101, E-mail: brookse@trine.edu.

Tufts University, School of Engineering, Department of Civil and Environmental Engineering, Medford, MA 02155. Offers bioengineering (ME, MS), including environmental technology; civil engineering (ME, MS, PhD), including geotechnical engineering, structural engineering, water diplomacy (PhD); environmental engineering (ME, MS, PhD), including environmental engineering and environmental sciences, environmental geotechnology, environmental health, environmental science and management, hazardous materials management, water diplomacy (PhD), water resources engineering. Part-time programs available. *Faculty:* 24 full-time (5 women), 6 part-time/adjunct (1 woman). *Students:* 66 full-time (29 women), 19 part-time (6 women); includes 5 minority (1 Black or African American, non-Hispanic/Latino; 2 Asian, non-Hispanic/Latino; 1 Hispanic/Latino; 1 Two or more races, non-Hispanic/Latino), 25 international. Average age 29. 166 applicants, 42% accepted, 27 enrolled. In 2014, 21 master's, 6 doctorates awarded. Terminal master's awarded for partial completion of doctoral program. *Degree requirements:* For master's, thesis or alternative; for doctorate, thesis/dissertation. *Entrance requirements:* For master's and doctorate, GRE General Test. Additional exam requirements/recommendations for international students: Required—TOEFL (minimum score 550 paper-based; 80 iBT), IELTS (minimum score 6.5). *Application deadline:* For fall admission, 1/15 priority date for domestic students, 1/15 for international students; for spring admission, 9/15 for domestic and international students. Applications are processed on a rolling basis. Application fee: $75. Electronic applications accepted. *Expenses: Tuition:* Full-time $45,590; part-time $1161 per credit hour. *Required fees:* $782. Full-time tuition and fees vary according to degree level, program and student level. Part-time tuition and fees vary according to course load. *Financial support:* Fellowships with full tuition reimbursements, research assistantships with full and partial tuition reimbursements, teaching assistantships with full and partial tuition reimbursements, Federal Work-Study, scholarships/grants, tuition waivers (partial), and unspecified assistantships available. Financial award application deadline: 5/15; financial award applicants required to submit FAFSA. *Faculty research:* Environmental and water resources engineering, environmental health, geotechnical and geoenvironmental engineering, structural engineering and mechanics, water diplomacy. *Unit head:* Dr. Kurt Pennell, Graduate Program Director. *Application contact:* Office of Graduate Admissions, 617-627-3395, E-mail: gradadmissions@tufts.edu. Website: http://www.ase.tufts.edu/cee/.

United States Merchant Marine Academy, Graduate Program, Kings Point, NY 11024-1699. Offers MS.

Université de Moncton, Faculty of Engineering, Program in Civil Engineering, Moncton, NB E1A 3E9, Canada. Offers M Sc A. *Degree requirements:* For master's, thesis, proficiency in French. *Faculty research:* Structures and materials, hydrology and water resources, soil mechanics and statistical analysis, environment, transportation.

Université de Sherbrooke, Faculty of Engineering, Department of Civil Engineering, Sherbrooke, QC J1K 2R1, Canada. Offers M Sc A, PhD. *Degree requirements:* For master's, one foreign language, thesis; for doctorate, comprehensive exam, thesis/dissertation. *Entrance requirements:* For master's, bachelor's degree in engineering or equivalent; for doctorate, master's degree in engineering or equivalent. Electronic applications accepted. *Faculty research:* High-strength concrete, dynamics of structures, solid mechanics, geotechnical engineering, wastewater treatment.

Université Laval, Faculty of Sciences and Engineering, Department of Civil Engineering, Program in Urban Infrastructure Engineering, Québec, QC G1K 7P4, Canada. Offers Diploma. Part-time and evening/weekend programs available. *Entrance requirements:* For degree, knowledge of French. Electronic applications accepted.

Université Laval, Faculty of Sciences and Engineering, Department of Civil Engineering, Programs in Civil Engineering, Québec, QC G1K 7P4, Canada. Offers civil engineering (M Sc, PhD); environmental technology (M Sc). Terminal master's awarded for partial completion of doctoral program. *Degree requirements:* For master's, thesis (for some programs); for doctorate, comprehensive exam, thesis/dissertation. *Entrance requirements:* For master's and doctorate, knowledge of French and English. Electronic applications accepted.

University at Buffalo, the State University of New York, Graduate School, School of Engineering and Applied Sciences, Department of Civil, Structural, and Environmental Engineering, Buffalo, NY 14260. Offers civil engineering (ME, MS, PhD); engineering science (MS). Part-time programs available. Postbaccalaureate distance learning degree programs offered (minimal on-campus study). *Faculty:* 31 full-time (5 women), 1 part-time/adjunct (0 women). *Students:* 166 full-time (43 women), 16 part-time (3 women); includes 15 minority (2 Black or African American, non-Hispanic/Latino; 1 American Indian or Alaska Native, non-Hispanic/Latino; 5 Asian, non-Hispanic/Latino; 4 Hispanic/Latino; 3 Two or more races, non-Hispanic/Latino), 111 international. Average age 27. 714 applicants, 33% accepted, 55 enrolled. In 2014, 59 master's, 17 doctorates awarded. Terminal master's awarded for partial completion of doctoral program. *Degree requirements:* For master's, project, thesis, or comprehensive exam; for doctorate, thesis/dissertation. *Entrance requirements:* For master's and doctorate, GRE General Test, letters of reference. Additional exam requirements/recommendations for international students: Required—TOEFL (minimum score 550 paper-based; 79 iBT). *Application deadline:* For fall admission, 1/15 priority date for domestic and international students; for spring admission, 9/15 for domestic and international students. Applications are processed on a rolling basis. Application fee: $75. Electronic applications accepted. *Financial support:* In 2014–15, 87 students received support, including 3 fellowships with full and partial tuition reimbursements available (averaging $30,000 per year), 28 research assistantships with full and partial tuition reimbursements available (averaging $20,090 per year), 28 teaching assistantships with full and partial tuition reimbursements available (averaging $21,420 per year); career-related internships or fieldwork, Federal Work-Study, institutionally sponsored loans, scholarships/grants, traineeships, health care benefits, tuition waivers (full and partial), and unspecified assistantships also available. Support available to part-time students. Financial award application deadline: 1/15; financial award applicants required to submit FAFSA. *Faculty research:* Environmental engineering and fluid mechanics, structural dynamics, geomechanics, earthquake engineering computational mechanics. *Total annual research expenditures:* $4.4 million. *Unit head:* Dr. Andrew S. Whittaker, Chairman, 716-645-2114, Fax: 716-645-3733, E-mail: awhittak@buffalo.edu. *Application contact:* Dr. Joseph Atkinson, Director of Graduate Studies, 716-645-2220, Fax: 716-645-3733, E-mail: atkinson@buffalo.edu. Website: http://www.csee.buffalo.edu/.

The University of Akron, Graduate School, College of Engineering, Department of Civil Engineering, Akron, OH 44325. Offers civil engineering (MS); engineering (PhD). Evening/weekend programs available. *Faculty:* 19 full-time (1 woman), 5 part-time/adjunct (0 women). *Students:* 84 full-time (20 women), 21 part-time (1 woman); includes 5 minority (1 Black or African American, non-Hispanic/Latino; 2 Asian, non-Hispanic/Latino; 1 Hispanic/Latino; 1 Two or more races, non-Hispanic/Latino), 66 international. Average age 30. 75 applicants, 65% accepted, 16 enrolled. In 2014, 22 master's, 7 doctorates awarded. *Degree requirements:* For master's, thesis optional; for doctorate, thesis/dissertation, candidacy exam, qualifying exam. *Entrance requirements:* For master's, GRE, minimum GPA of 2.75, statement of purpose, three letters of recommendation, resume; for doctorate, GRE, minimum GPA of 3.0 with bachelor's degree, 3.5 with master's degree; three letters of recommendation; statement of purpose, resume. Additional exam requirements/recommendations for international students: Required—TOEFL (minimum score 550 paper-based; 79 iBT), IELTS (minimum score 6.5). *Application deadline:* Applications are processed on a rolling basis. Application fee: $45 ($70 for international students). Electronic applications accepted. *Expenses:* Tuition, state resident: full-time $7578; part-time $421 per credit hour. Tuition, nonresident: full-time $12,977; part-time $721 per credit hour. *Required fees:* $1388; $35 per credit hour. Tuition and fees vary according to course load. *Financial support:* In 2014–15, 16 research assistantships with full tuition reimbursements, 47 teaching assistantships with full tuition reimbursements were awarded; fellowships also available. *Faculty research:* Development of constitutive laws for numerical analysis of nonlinear problems in structural mechanics, multiscale modeling and simulation of novel materials, water quality and distribution system analysis, safety-related traffic control, dynamic pile testing and analysis. *Total annual research expenditures:* $3.4 million. *Unit head:* Dr. Wieslaw K. Binienda, Chair, 330-972-6693, E-mail: wbinienda@uakron.edu. *Application contact:* Dr. Ernian Pan, Graduate Director, 330-972-6739, E-mail: pan2@uakron.edu. Website: http://www.uakron.edu/engineering/CE/.

The University of Alabama, Graduate School, College of Engineering, Department of Civil, Construction and Environmental Engineering, Tuscaloosa, AL 35487-0205. Offers civil engineering (MSCE, PhD); environmental engineering (MS). Part-time programs available. *Faculty:* 22 full-time (2 women). *Students:* 58 full-time (20 women), 4 part-time (0 women); includes 4 minority (2 Black or African American, non-Hispanic/Latino; 1 Asian, non-Hispanic/Latino; 1 Hispanic/Latino), 22 international. Average age 28. 76 applicants, 43% accepted, 16 enrolled. In 2014, 23 master's, 4 doctorates awarded. Terminal master's awarded for partial completion of doctoral program. *Degree requirements:* For master's, thesis or alternative; for doctorate, one foreign language, comprehensive exam, thesis/dissertation. *Entrance requirements:* For master's and doctorate, GRE General Test (minimum combined score of 300), minimum GPA of 3.0 in last 60 hours of course work. Additional exam requirements/recommendations for international students: Required—TOEFL (minimum score 550 paper-based; 79 iBT), IELTS (minimum score 6.5), PTE (minimum score 59). *Application deadline:* For fall admission, 7/10 for domestic students, 1/15 for international students; for spring admission, 11/1 for domestic students, 6/1 for international students. Applications are processed on a rolling basis. Application fee: $50 ($60 for international students). Electronic applications accepted. *Expenses:* Tuition, state resident: full-time $9826. Tuition, nonresident: full-time $24,950. *Financial support:* In 2014–15, 40 students received support, including 2 fellowships with full tuition reimbursements available (averaging $30,000 per year), 17 research assistantships with full tuition reimbursements available (averaging $13,275 per year), 20 teaching assistantships with full tuition reimbursements available (averaging $13,275 per year); scholarships/grants, tuition waivers (partial), and unspecified assistantships also available. Financial award application deadline: 2/15. *Faculty research:* Experimental structures, modeling of structures, bridge management systems, geotechnological engineering, environmental remediation. *Total annual research expenditures:* $2.7 million. *Unit head:* Dr. W. Edward Back, Head and Professor, 205-348-6550, Fax: 205-348-0783, E-mail: eback@eng.ua.edu. *Application contact:* Dr. Andrew Graettinger, Associate Professor and Graduate Program Director, 205-348-1707, Fax: 205-348-0783, E-mail: andrewg@eng.ua.edu. Website: http://cce.eng.ua.edu/.

The University of Alabama at Birmingham, School of Engineering, Program in Civil Engineering, Birmingham, AL 35294. Offers MSCE, PhD. Program offered jointly with The University of Alabama in Huntsville. *Students:* 22 full-time (3 women), 24 part-time (6 women); includes 6 minority (5 Black or African American, non-Hispanic/Latino; 1 Two or more races, non-Hispanic/Latino), 29 international. Average age 30. In 2014, 8 master's, 1 doctorate awarded. *Degree requirements:* For master's, comprehensive exam, thesis optional; for doctorate, comprehensive exam, thesis/dissertation. *Entrance requirements:* For master's, GRE General Test preferred (minimum score of 500 on each component), minimum GPA of 3.0 in all undergraduate degree major courses attempted, letters of evaluation. Additional exam requirements/recommendations for international students: Required—TOEFL (minimum score 550 paper-based), TWE (minimum score 3.5). *Expenses:* Tuition, state resident: full-time $7090; part-time $370 per credit hour. Tuition, nonresident: full-time $16,072; part-time $869 per credit hour. Full-time tuition and fees vary according to course load and program. *Unit head:* Dr. Fouad H. Fouad, Chair, 205-934-8430, Fax: 205-934-9855, E-mail: ffouad@uab.edu. *Application contact:* Susan Noblitt Banks, Director of Graduate School Operations, 205-834-8227, Fax: 205-934-8413, E-mail: gradschool@uab.edu. Website: https://www.uab.edu/engineering/home/graduate-civil.

The University of Alabama in Huntsville, School of Graduate Studies, College of Engineering, Department of Civil and Environmental Engineering, Huntsville, AL 35899. Offers civil and environmental engineering (PhD); civil engineering (MSE), including civil engineering, environmental and water resource engineering, geotechnical engineering, structural engineering and structural mechanics, transportation engineering. PhD offered jointly with The University of Alabama at Birmingham. Part-time and evening/weekend programs available. *Degree requirements:* For master's, comprehensive exam, thesis or alternative, oral and written exams; for doctorate, comprehensive exam, thesis/dissertation, oral and written exams. *Entrance requirements:* For master's, GRE General Test, BSE, minimum GPA of 3.0; for doctorate, GRE General Test, minimum GPA of 3.0. Additional exam requirements/recommendations for international students: Required—TOEFL (minimum score 500 paper-based; 80 iBT), IELTS (minimum score 6.5). Electronic applications accepted. *Faculty research:* Smart materials and smart structures, fiber-reinforced cementitious composites, processing and mechanics of composites, geographic information systems, environmental engineering.

University of Alaska Anchorage, School of Engineering, Program in Civil Engineering, Anchorage, AK 99508. Offers civil engineering (MCE, MS); coastal, ocean, and port engineering (Certificate). Part-time and evening/weekend programs available. *Degree requirements:* For master's, thesis (for some programs). *Entrance requirements:* For master's, bachelor's degree in engineering. Additional exam requirements/recommendations for international students: Required—TOEFL (minimum score 550 paper-based). *Faculty research:* Structural engineering, engineering education, astronomical observations related to engineering.

University of Alaska Fairbanks, College of Engineering and Mines, Department of Civil and Environmental Engineering, Fairbanks, AK 99775-5900. Offers arctic engineering (MS); civil engineering (MCE, MS); design and construction management

(Graduate Certificate); engineering and science management (MS), including engineering management, science management; environmental engineering (MS, PhD); environmental quality science (MS), including environmental contaminants, environmental science and management, water supply and waste treatment. Part-time programs available. *Faculty:* 10 full-time (2 women). *Students:* 14 full-time (7 women), 8 part-time (2 women); includes 4 minority (1 Black or African American, non-Hispanic/Latino; 1 American Indian or Alaska Native, non-Hispanic/Latino; 1 Hispanic/Latino; 1 Two or more races, non-Hispanic/Latino), 5 international. Average age 30. 19 applicants, 37% accepted, 5 enrolled. In 2014, 3 master's, 1 other advanced degree awarded. *Degree requirements:* For master's, comprehensive exam, thesis (for some programs), oral defense of project or thesis; for doctorate, comprehensive exam, thesis/dissertation. *Entrance requirements:* For master's, bachelor's degree from accredited institution with minimum cumulative undergraduate and major GPA of 3.0. Additional exam requirements/recommendations for international students: Required—TOEFL, IELTS. *Application deadline:* For fall admission, 6/1 for domestic students, 3/1 for international students; for spring admission, 10/15 for domestic students, 9/1 for international students. Applications are processed on a rolling basis. Application fee: $60. Electronic applications accepted. *Expenses:* Tuition, state resident: full-time $7614; part-time $423 per credit. Tuition, nonresident: full-time $15,552; part-time $864 per credit. Tuition and fees vary according to course level, course load and reciprocity agreements. *Financial support:* In 2014–15, 7 research assistantships with full tuition reimbursements (averaging $8,189 per year), 6 teaching assistantships with full tuition reimbursements (averaging $5,809 per year) were awarded; fellowships with full tuition reimbursements, career-related internships or fieldwork, Federal Work-Study, scholarships/grants, health care benefits, and unspecified assistantships also available. Support available to part-time students. Financial award application deadline: 7/1; financial award applicants required to submit FAFSA. *Faculty research:* Soils, structures, culvert thawing with solar power, pavement drainage, contaminant hydrogeology. *Unit head:* Dr. Robert Perkins, Department Chair, 907-474-7241, Fax: 907-474-6087, E-mail: fycee@uaf.edu. *Application contact:* Mary Kreta, Director of Admissions, 907-474-7500, Fax: 907-474-7097, E-mail: admissions@uaf.edu.
Website: http://cem.uaf.edu/cee.

University of Alberta, Faculty of Graduate Studies and Research, Department of Civil and Environmental Engineering, Edmonton, AB T6G 2E1, Canada. Offers construction engineering and management (M Eng, M Sc, PhD); environmental engineering (M Eng, M Sc, PhD); environmental science (M Sc, PhD); geoenvironmental engineering (M Eng, M Sc, PhD); geotechnical engineering (M Eng, M Sc, PhD); mining engineering (M Eng, M Sc, PhD); petroleum engineering (M Eng, M Sc, PhD); structural engineering (M Eng, M Sc, PhD); water resources (M Eng, M Sc, PhD). Part-time programs available. Postbaccalaureate distance learning degree programs offered (minimal on-campus study). *Degree requirements:* For master's, thesis (for some programs); for doctorate, thesis/dissertation. *Entrance requirements:* For master's, minimum GPA of 3.0 in last 2 years of undergraduate studies; for doctorate, minimum GPA of 3.0. Additional exam requirements/recommendations for international students: Required—TOEFL (minimum score 550 paper-based). Electronic applications accepted. *Faculty research:* Mining.

University of Arkansas, Graduate School, College of Engineering, Department of Civil Engineering, Program in Civil Engineering, Fayetteville, AR 72701-1201. Offers MSCE, MSE, PhD. *Degree requirements:* For master's, thesis optional; for doctorate, one foreign language, thesis/dissertation. Electronic applications accepted.

The University of British Columbia, Faculty of Applied Science, Department of Civil Engineering, Vancouver, BC V6T 1Z1, Canada. Offers M Eng, MA Sc, PhD. Part-time programs available. *Degree requirements:* For master's, thesis; for doctorate, thesis/dissertation. *Entrance requirements:* Additional exam requirements/recommendations for international students: Required—TOEFL (minimum score 600 paper-based), IELTS (minimum score 7), TWE (minimum score 5). Electronic applications accepted. *Faculty research:* Geotechnology; structural, water, and environmental engineering; transportation; materials and construction engineering.

University of Calgary, Faculty of Graduate Studies, Schulich School of Engineering, Department of Civil Engineering, Calgary, AB T2N 1N4, Canada. Offers avalanche mechanics (M Sc, PhD); civil engineering (M Eng, M Sc, PhD); energy and environment engineering (M Eng, M Sc, PhD); environmental engineering (M Eng, M Sc, PhD); geotechnical engineering (M Eng, M Sc, PhD); materials science (M Eng, M Sc, PhD); project management (M Eng, M Sc, PhD); structures and solid mechanics (M Eng, M Sc, PhD); transportation engineering (M Eng, M Sc, PhD); water resources (M Eng, M Sc, PhD). Part-time programs available. *Degree requirements:* For master's, thesis; for doctorate, thesis/dissertation, written and oral candidacy exam. *Entrance requirements:* For master's, minimum GPA of 3.0; for doctorate, minimum GPA of 3.5. Additional exam requirements/recommendations for international students: Required—TOEFL (minimum score 580 paper-based; 93 iBT), IELTS (minimum score 7). Electronic applications accepted. *Faculty research:* Geotechnical engineering, energy and environment, transportation, project management, structures and solid mechanics.

University of California, Berkeley, Graduate Division, College of Engineering, Department of Civil and Environmental Engineering, Berkeley, CA 94720-1500. Offers engineering and project management (M Eng, MS, D Eng, PhD); environmental engineering (M Eng, MS, D Eng, PhD); geoengineering (M Eng, MS, D Eng, PhD); structural engineering, mechanics and materials (M Eng, MS, D Eng, PhD); transportation engineering (M Eng, MS, D Eng, PhD); M Arch/MS; MCP/MS; MPP/MS. *Degree requirements:* For master's, comprehensive exam or thesis (MS); for doctorate, thesis/dissertation, qualifying exam. *Entrance requirements:* For master's, GRE General Test, minimum GPA of 3.0, 3 letters of recommendation; for doctorate, GRE General Test, minimum GPA of 3.5, 3 letters of recommendation. Additional exam requirements/recommendations for international students: Required—TOEFL (minimum score 570 paper-based). Electronic applications accepted.

University of California, Davis, College of Engineering, Program in Civil and Environmental Engineering, Davis, CA 95616. Offers M Engr, MS, D Engr, PhD, Certificate, M Engr/MBA. *Degree requirements:* For master's, comprehensive exam (for some programs), thesis (for some programs); for doctorate, thesis/dissertation. *Entrance requirements:* For master's, GRE General Test, minimum GPA of 3.0; for doctorate, GRE, minimum graduate GPA of 3.5. Additional exam requirements/recommendations for international students: Required—TOEFL (minimum score 550 paper-based). Electronic applications accepted. *Faculty research:* Environmental water resources, transportation, structural mechanics, structural engineering, geotechnical engineering.

University of California, Irvine, Henry Samueli School of Engineering, Department of Civil and Environmental Engineering, Irvine, CA 92697. Offers MS, PhD. Part-time programs available. *Students:* 180 full-time (65 women), 26 part-time (9 women); includes 38 minority (2 Black or African American, non-Hispanic/Latino; 21 Asian, non-Hispanic/Latino; 13 Hispanic/Latino; 2 Two or more races, non-Hispanic/Latino), 115 international. Average age 26. 543 applicants, 58% accepted, 93 enrolled. In 2014, 36 master's, 14 doctorates awarded. Terminal master's awarded for partial completion of doctoral program. *Degree requirements:* For doctorate, thesis/dissertation. *Entrance requirements:* For master's and doctorate, GRE General Test, minimum GPA of 3.0, 3 letters of recommendation. Additional exam requirements/recommendations for international students: Required—TOEFL (minimum score 550 paper-based). *Application deadline:* For fall admission, 1/15 priority date for domestic students, 1/15 for international students. Applications are processed on a rolling basis. Application fee: $90 ($110 for international students). Electronic applications accepted. *Financial support:* Fellowships, research assistantships with full tuition reimbursements, teaching assistantships, institutionally sponsored loans, traineeships, health care benefits, and unspecified assistantships available. Financial award application deadline: 3/1; financial award applicants required to submit FAFSA. *Faculty research:* Intelligent transportation systems and transportation economics, risk and reliability, fluid mechanics, environmental hydrodynamics, hydrological and climate systems, water resources. *Unit head:* Prof. Brett F. Sanders, Chair and Professor, 949-824-4327, Fax: 949-824-3672, E-mail: bsanders@uci.edu. *Application contact:* Nadia Ortiz, Assistant Director, 949-824-3562, Fax: 949-824-9096, E-mail: nortiz@uci.edu.
Website: http://www.eng.uci.edu/dept/cee.

University of California, Los Angeles, Graduate Division, Henry Samueli School of Engineering and Applied Science, Department of Civil and Environmental Engineering, Los Angeles, CA 90095-1593. Offers MS, PhD. *Faculty:* 16 full-time (3 women), 27 part-time/adjunct (0 women). *Students:* 139 full-time (60 women); includes 33 minority (1 Black or African American, non-Hispanic/Latino; 19 Asian, non-Hispanic/Latino; 11 Hispanic/Latino; 2 Two or more races, non-Hispanic/Latino), 73 international. 433 applicants, 57% accepted, 85 enrolled. In 2014, 86 master's, 22 doctorates awarded. *Degree requirements:* For master's, comprehensive exam or thesis; for doctorate, thesis/dissertation, qualifying exams. *Entrance requirements:* For master's, GRE General Test, minimum GPA of 3.0; for doctorate, GRE General Test, minimum GPA of 3.25. Additional exam requirements/recommendations for international students: Required—TOEFL (minimum score 560 paper-based; 87 iBT), IELTS (minimum score 7). *Application deadline:* For fall admission, 12/15 priority date for domestic and international students. Application fee: $80 ($100 for international students). Electronic applications accepted. *Financial support:* In 2014–15, 109 fellowships, 45 research assistantships, 66 teaching assistantships were awarded; Federal Work-Study, institutionally sponsored loans, and tuition waivers (full and partial) also available. Financial award application deadline: 12/15; financial award applicants required to submit FAFSA. *Faculty research:* Civil engineering materials, environmental engineering, geotechnical engineering, hydrology and water resources, structures. *Total annual research expenditures:* $3.5 million. *Unit head:* Dr. Jonathan P. Stewart, Chair, 310-206-2990, E-mail: jstewart@seas.ucla.edu. *Application contact:* Jesse Miller Murphy, Graduate Affairs Officer, 310-825-1851, Fax: 310-206-2222, E-mail: jmurphy@seas.ucla.edu.
Website: http://cee.ucla.edu/.

University of Central Florida, College of Engineering and Computer Science, Department of Civil, Environmental, and Construction Engineering, Program in Civil Engineering, Orlando, FL 32816. Offers MS, MSCE, PhD, Certificate. Part-time and evening/weekend programs available. *Students:* 83 full-time (17 women), 78 part-time (22 women); includes 44 minority (8 Black or African American, non-Hispanic/Latino; 6 Asian, non-Hispanic/Latino; 26 Hispanic/Latino; 4 Two or more races, non-Hispanic/Latino), 67 international. Average age 30. 136 applicants, 57% accepted, 44 enrolled. In 2014, 34 master's, 8 doctorates, 1 other advanced degree awarded. *Degree requirements:* For master's, thesis or alternative; for doctorate, thesis/dissertation, departmental qualifying exam, candidacy exam. *Entrance requirements:* For master's, GRE General Test, minimum GPA of 3.0 in last 60 hours; for doctorate, GRE General Test, minimum GPA of 3.5 in last 60 hours. Additional exam requirements/recommendations for international students: Required—TOEFL. *Application deadline:* For fall admission, 7/15 priority date for domestic students; for spring admission, 12/15 priority date for domestic students. Application fee: $30. Electronic applications accepted. *Expenses:* Tuition, state resident: part-time $288.16 per credit hour. Tuition, nonresident: part-time $1073.31 per credit hour. *Financial support:* In 2014–15, 37 students received support, including 16 fellowships with partial tuition reimbursements available (averaging $3,400 per year), 31 research assistantships with partial tuition reimbursements available (averaging $9,200 per year), 9 teaching assistantships with partial tuition reimbursements available (averaging $8,900 per year); career-related internships or fieldwork, Federal Work-Study, institutionally sponsored loans, tuition waivers (partial), and unspecified assistantships also available. Financial award application deadline: 3/1; financial award applicants required to submit FAFSA. *Unit head:* Dr. Mohamed Abdel-Aty, Chair, 407-823-5657, E-mail: m.aty@ucf.edu. *Application contact:* Barbara Rodriguez Lamas, Director, Admissions and Student Services, 407-823-2766, Fax: 407-823-6442, E-mail: gradadmissions@ucf.edu.
Website: http://cece.ucf.edu/.

University of Cincinnati, Graduate School, College of Engineering and Applied Science, Department of Civil and Environmental Engineering, Program in Civil Engineering, Cincinnati, OH 45221. Offers MS, PhD. Part-time programs available. Terminal master's awarded for partial completion of doctoral program. *Degree requirements:* For master's, project or thesis; for doctorate, one foreign language, thesis/dissertation. *Entrance requirements:* For master's and doctorate, GRE General Test. Additional exam requirements/recommendations for international students: Required—TOEFL (minimum score 580 paper-based; 92 iBT). Electronic applications accepted. *Faculty research:* Soil mechanics and foundations, structures, transportation, water resources systems and hydraulics.

University of Colorado Boulder, Graduate School, College of Engineering and Applied Science, Department of Civil, Environmental, and Architectural Engineering, Boulder, CO 80309. Offers building systems engineering (MS, PhD); construction engineering management (MS, PhD); environmental engineering (MS, PhD); geotechnical engineering and geomechanics (MS, PhD); hydrology, water resources and environmental fluid mechanics (MS, PhD); structural engineering and structural mechanics (MS, PhD). *Faculty:* 37 full-time (8 women). *Students:* 235 full-time (81 women), 36 part-time (9 women); includes 24 minority (9 Asian, non-Hispanic/Latino; 6 Hispanic/Latino; 9 Two or more races, non-Hispanic/Latino), 83 international. Average age 28. 391 applicants, 63% accepted, 68 enrolled. In 2014, 76 master's, 30 doctorates awarded. Terminal master's awarded for partial completion of doctoral program. *Degree requirements:* For master's, comprehensive exam, thesis or alternative; for doctorate, thesis/dissertation. *Entrance requirements:* For master's, GRE General Test, minimum undergraduate GPA of 3.0. *Application deadline:* For fall admission, 1/31 for domestic and international students; for spring admission, 10/1 for domestic and international students. Application fee: $50 ($70 for international students). Electronic applications accepted. *Financial support:* In 2014–15, 387 students received support, including 75 fellowships (averaging $11,889 per year), 92 research assistantships with full and partial tuition reimbursements available (averaging $34,669 per year), 17 teaching assistantships with full and partial tuition reimbursements available (averaging $28,513 per year); institutionally sponsored loans, scholarships/grants, health care benefits, and unspecified assistantships also available. Financial award application deadline: 1/15; financial award applicants required to submit FAFSA. *Faculty research:* Civil engineering, environmental engineering, architectural engineering, geotechnical engineering, hydrology. *Total annual research expenditures:* $13 million.
Website: http://civil.colorado.edu/.

University of Colorado Denver, College of Engineering and Applied Science, Department of Civil Engineering, Denver, CO 80217. Offers civil engineering (EASPh D); civil engineering systems (PhD); environmental and sustainability engineering (MS, PhD); geographic information systems (MS); geotechnical engineering (MS, PhD); hydrology and hydraulics (MS, PhD); structural engineering (MS, PhD); transportation engineering (MS, PhD). Part-time and evening/weekend programs available. *Faculty:* 15 full-time (4 women), 11 part-time/adjunct (2 women). *Students:* 64 full-time (15 women), 43 part-time (8 women); includes 15 minority (3 Black or African American, non-Hispanic/Latino; 3 Asian, non-Hispanic/Latino; 6 Hispanic/Latino; 3 Two or more races, non-Hispanic/Latino), 34 international. Average age 32. 136 applicants, 54% accepted, 28 enrolled. In 2014, 35 master's, 9 doctorates awarded. *Degree requirements:* For master's, comprehensive exam, 30 credit hours, project or thesis; for doctorate, comprehensive exam, thesis/dissertation, 60 credit hours (30 of which are dissertation research). *Entrance requirements:* For master's, GRE, statement of purpose, transcripts, three references; for doctorate, GRE, statement of purpose, transcripts, references, letter of support from faculty stating willingness to serve as dissertation advisor and outlining plan for financial support. Additional exam requirements/recommendations for international students: Required—TOEFL (minimum score 537 paper-based; 75 iBT); Recommended—IELTS (minimum score 6.5). *Application deadline:* For fall admission, 5/1 for domestic students, 4/1 for international students; for spring admission, 10/1 for domestic students, 9/1 for international students; for summer admission, 2/15 for domestic students, 1/15 for international students. Application fee: $50 ($75 for international students). Electronic applications accepted. *Expenses:* Expenses: Contact institution. *Financial support:* In 2014–15, 26 students received support. Fellowships, research assistantships, teaching assistantships, career-related internships or fieldwork, Federal Work-Study, institutionally sponsored loans, scholarships/grants, traineeships, and unspecified assistantships available. Financial award application deadline: 4/1; financial award applicants required to submit FAFSA. *Faculty research:* Earthquake source physics, environmental biotechnology, hydrologic and hydraulic engineering, sustainability assessments, transportation energy use and greenhouse gas emissions. *Unit head:* Dr. Kevin Rens, Chair, 303-556-8017, E-mail: kevin.rens@ucdenver.edu. *Application contact:* Tammy Southern, Program Assistant, 303-556-6712, E-mail: tamara.southern@ucdenver.edu.
Website: http://www.ucdenver.edu/academics/colleges/Engineering/Programs /Civil-Engineering/Pages/CivilEngineering.aspx.

University of Colorado Denver, College of Engineering and Applied Science, Master of Engineering Program, Denver, CO 80217-3364. Offers civil engineering (M Eng), including civil engineering, geographic information systems, transportation systems; electrical engineering (M Eng); mechanical engineering (M Eng). Part-time programs available. *Students:* 30 full-time (9 women), 20 part-time (7 women); includes 3 minority (1 Black or African American, non-Hispanic/Latino; 2 Hispanic/Latino), 8 international. Average age 34. 35 applicants, 83% accepted, 15 enrolled. In 2014, 14 master's awarded. *Degree requirements:* For master's, comprehensive exam, 27 credit hours of course work, 3 credit hours of report or thesis work. *Entrance requirements:* For master's, GRE (for those with GPA below 2.75), transcripts, references, statement of purpose. Additional exam requirements/recommendations for international students: Required—TOEFL (minimum score 537 paper-based; 75 iBT); Recommended—IELTS (minimum score 6.5). *Application deadline:* For fall admission, 4/1 for domestic students, 3/1 for international students; for spring admission, 10/1 for domestic students, 9/15 for international students. Applications are processed on a rolling basis. Application fee: $50 ($75 for international students). Electronic applications accepted. *Expenses:* Expenses: Contact institution. *Financial support:* In 2014–15, 4 students received support. Fellowships, research assistantships, teaching assistantships, Federal Work-Study, institutionally sponsored loans, scholarships/grants, traineeships, and unspecified assistantships available. Financial award application deadline: 4/1; financial award applicants required to submit FAFSA. *Faculty research:* Civil, electrical and mechanical engineering. *Unit head:* 303-556-2870, Fax: 303-556-2511, E-mail: engineering@ucdenver.edu. *Application contact:* Graduate School Admissions, 303-556-2704, E-mail: admissions@ucdenver.edu.
Website: http://www.ucdenver.edu/academics/colleges/Engineering/admissions/ Masters/Pages/MastersAdmissions.aspx.

University of Connecticut, Graduate School, School of Engineering, Department of Civil and Environmental Engineering, Field of Civil Engineering, Storrs, CT 06269. Offers MS, PhD. Terminal master's awarded for partial completion of doctoral program. *Degree requirements:* For master's, comprehensive exam, thesis or alternative; for doctorate, thesis/dissertation. *Entrance requirements:* Additional exam requirements/recommendations for international students: Required—TOEFL (minimum score 550 paper-based). Electronic applications accepted.

University of Dayton, Department of Civil and Environmental Engineering and Engineering Mechanics, Dayton, OH 45469. Offers engineering mechanics (MSEM); environmental engineering (MSCE); geotechnical engineering (MSCE); structural engineering (MSCE); transportation engineering (MSCE); water resources engineering (MSCE). Part-time and evening/weekend programs available. *Faculty:* 9 full-time (2 women), 3 part-time/adjunct (1 woman). *Students:* 23 full-time (4 women), 6 part-time (2 women), 22 international. Average age 26. 70 applicants, 39% accepted, 4 enrolled. In 2014, 11 master's awarded. *Degree requirements:* For master's, thesis optional. *Entrance requirements:* For master's, minimum GPA of 3.0 in undergraduate work. Additional exam requirements/recommendations for international students: Required—TOEFL (minimum score 550 paper-based; 80 iBT). *Application deadline:* For fall admission, 8/1 priority date for domestic students, 5/1 priority date for international students; for winter admission, 7/1 priority date for international students; for spring admission, 11/1 priority date for international students. Applications are processed on a rolling basis. Application fee: $0 ($50 for international students). Electronic applications accepted. *Expenses:* Tuition: Full-time $10,176; part-time $848 per credit. *Required fees:* $25; $25 per course. Part-time tuition and fees vary according to course level, course load, degree level and program. *Financial support:* In 2014–15, 3 students received support. Institutionally sponsored loans, scholarships/grants, and department-funded awards (averaging $2448 per year) available. Financial award application deadline: 3/1; financial award applicants required to submit FAFSA. *Faculty research:* Physical modeling of water resource systems, finite element methods, mechanics of composite materials, transportation systems safety, biological treatment processes, fiber reinforced concrete. *Total annual research expenditures:* $250,000. *Unit head:* Dr. Donald V. Chase, Chair, 937-229-3847, Fax: 937-229-3491, E-mail: dchase1@ udayton.edu. *Application contact:* 937-229-4462, E-mail: graduateadmission@ udayton.edu.
Website: https://www.udayton.edu/engineering/departments/civil/index.php.

University of Delaware, College of Engineering, Department of Civil and Environmental Engineering, Newark, DE 19716. Offers environmental engineering (MAS, MCE, PhD); geotechnical engineering (MAS, MCE, PhD); ocean engineering (MAS, MCE, PhD); structural engineering (MAS, MCE, PhD); transportation engineering (MAS, MCE, PhD); water resource engineering (MAS, MCE, PhD). Part-time programs available. Terminal master's awarded for partial completion of doctoral program. *Degree requirements:* For master's, thesis; for doctorate, thesis/dissertation. *Entrance requirements:* For master's and doctorate, GRE General Test. Additional exam requirements/recommendations for

international students: Required—TOEFL. Electronic applications accepted. *Faculty research:* Structural engineering and mechanics; transportation engineering; ocean engineering; soil mechanics and foundation; water resources and environmental engineering.

University of Detroit Mercy, College of Engineering and Science, Department of Civil and Environmental Engineering, Detroit, MI 48221. Offers ME, DE. Evening/weekend programs available. *Faculty research:* Geotechnical engineering.

University of Florida, Graduate School, College of Engineering, Department of Civil and Coastal Engineering, Gainesville, FL 32611. Offers civil engineering (ME, MS, PhD), including civil engineering; coastal and oceanographic engineering (ME, MS, PhD). Part-time programs available. Postbaccalaureate distance learning degree programs offered (no on-campus study). *Faculty:* 44 full-time (5 women), 22 part-time/adjunct (3 women). *Students:* 140 full-time (27 women), 43 part-time (11 women); includes 26 minority (7 Black or African American, non-Hispanic/Latino; 1 American Indian or Alaska Native, non-Hispanic/Latino; 5 Asian, non-Hispanic/Latino; 13 Hispanic/Latino), 87 international. 418 applicants, 41% accepted, 54 enrolled. In 2014, 145 master's, 17 doctorates awarded. Terminal master's awarded for partial completion of doctoral program. *Degree requirements:* For master's, thesis (for some programs); for doctorate, comprehensive exam, thesis/dissertation. *Entrance requirements:* For master's and doctorate, minimum GPA of 3.0. Additional exam requirements/recommendations for international students: Required—TOEFL (minimum score 550 paper-based; 80 iBT), IELTS (minimum score 6). *Application deadline:* For fall admission, 8/1 priority date for domestic students, 1/31 for international students; for winter admission, 9/30 for international students; for spring admission, 12/1 for domestic students, 1/31 for international students. Applications are processed on a rolling basis. Application fee: $30. Electronic applications accepted. *Financial support:* Unspecified assistantships available. Financial award application deadline: 1/31; financial award applicants required to submit FAFSA. *Faculty research:* Traffic congestion mitigation, wind mitigation, sustainable infrastructure materials, improved sensors for in situ measurements, storm surge modeling. *Unit head:* Kirk Hatfield, PhD, Director, Engineering School of Sustainable Infrastructure and Environment, 352-392-9537 Ext. 1400, Fax: 352-392-3394, E-mail: director@essie.ufl.edu. *Application contact:* Ariel Drescher, Coordinator, Graduate Programs, 352-392-9537 Ext. 1435, Fax: 352-392-3394, E-mail: ariel.drescher@essie.ufl.edu.
Website: http://www.essie.ufl.edu/departments/civil_and_coastal_engineering/ cce_grad_student_info/.

University of Hawaii at Manoa, Graduate Division, College of Engineering, Department of Civil and Environmental Engineering, Honolulu, HI 96822. Offers MS, PhD. Part-time programs available. *Degree requirements:* For master's, comprehensive exam, thesis; for doctorate, comprehensive exam, thesis/dissertation. *Entrance requirements:* For master's and doctorate, GRE General Test or EIT Exam. Additional exam requirements/recommendations for international students: Required—TOEFL (minimum score 540 paper-based; 76 iBT), IELTS (minimum score 5). *Faculty research:* Structures, transportation, environmental engineering, geotechnical engineering, construction.

University of Houston, Cullen College of Engineering, Department of Civil and Environmental Engineering, Houston, TX 77204. Offers civil engineering (MCE, PhD). Part-time programs available. Terminal master's awarded for partial completion of doctoral program. *Entrance requirements:* For master's and doctorate, GRE General Test. Additional exam requirements/recommendations for international students: Required—TOEFL (minimum score 550 paper-based; 79 iBT), IELTS (minimum score 6.5). Electronic applications accepted. *Faculty research:* Civil engineering.

University of Idaho, College of Graduate Studies, College of Engineering, Department of Civil Engineering, Moscow, ID 83844-1022. Offers civil engineering (M Engr, MS, PhD); engineering management (M Engr); geological engineering (MS). *Faculty:* 13 full-time, 3 part-time/adjunct. *Students:* 24 full-time, 86 part-time. Average age 37. In 2014, 25 master's, 3 doctorates awarded. *Degree requirements:* For master's, thesis; for doctorate, thesis/dissertation. *Entrance requirements:* For master's, minimum GPA of 2.8; for doctorate, minimum undergraduate GPA of 2.8, 3.0 graduate. *Application deadline:* For fall admission, 8/1 for domestic students; for spring admission, 12/15 for domestic students. Applications are processed on a rolling basis. Application fee: $60. Electronic applications accepted. *Expenses:* Tuition: state resident: full-time $4784; part-time $280.50 per credit hour. Tuition, nonresident: full-time $18,314; part-time $957.50 per credit hour. *Required fees:* $2000; $58.50 per credit hour. Tuition and fees vary according to program. *Financial support:* Fellowships, research assistantships, teaching assistantships, and career-related internships or fieldwork available. Financial award applicants required to submit FAFSA. *Faculty research:* Water resources systems, structural analysis and design, soil mechanics, transportation technology. *Unit head:* Richard J. Nielsen, Chair, 208-885-6782, E-mail: civilengr@uidaho.edu. *Application contact:* Sean Scoggin, Graduate Recruitment Coordinator, 208-885-4001, Fax: 208-885-4406, E-mail: graduateadmissions@uidaho.edu.
Website: http://www.uidaho.edu/engr/ce/.

University of Illinois at Chicago, Graduate College, College of Engineering, Department of Civil and Materials Engineering, Chicago, IL 60607-7128. Offers MS, PhD. Evening/weekend programs available. *Faculty:* 17 full-time (2 women), 5 part-time/adjunct (0 women). *Students:* 74 full-time (15 women), 30 part-time (6 women); includes 12 minority (7 Asian, non-Hispanic/Latino; 5 Hispanic/Latino), 61 international. Average age 30. 285 applicants, 54% accepted, 26 enrolled. In 2014, 20 master's, 4 doctorates awarded. *Degree requirements:* For master's, thesis (for some programs); for doctorate, thesis/dissertation, preliminary and qualifying exams. *Entrance requirements:* For master's and doctorate, GRE General Test, minimum GPA of 3.0. Additional exam requirements/recommendations for international students: Required—TOEFL. *Application deadline:* For fall admission, 5/15 for domestic students, 3/15 for international students; for spring admission, 11/1 for domestic students, 7/15 for international students. Applications are processed on a rolling basis. Application fee: $60. Electronic applications accepted. *Expenses:* Expenses: $17,602 in-state; $29,600 out-of-state. *Financial support:* Fellowships with full tuition reimbursements, research assistantships with full tuition reimbursements, teaching assistantships with full tuition reimbursements, Federal Work-Study, and tuition waivers (full) available. Financial award application deadline: 3/1; financial award applicants required to submit FAFSA. *Faculty research:* Integrated fiber optic, acoustic emission and MEMS-based sensors development; monitoring the state of repaired and strengthened structures; development of weigh-in-motion (WIM) systems; image processing techniques for characterization of concrete entrained air bubble systems. *Total annual research expenditures:* $1.8 million. *Unit head:* Prof. Farhad Ansaru, Head, 312-996-3428, Fax: 312-996-2426. *Application contact:* J. Ernesto Indacochea, Director of Graduate Studies, 312-996-5283, E-mail: jeindaco@uic.edu.
Website: http://www.uic.edu/depts/cme/.

University of Illinois at Urbana–Champaign, Graduate College, College of Engineering, Department of Civil and Environmental Engineering, Champaign, IL 61820. Offers civil engineering (MS); environmental engineering in civil engineering (MS, PhD); M Arch/MS; MBA/MS. Part-time and evening/weekend programs available. Postbaccalaureate distance learning degree programs offered (no on-campus study). *Students:* 608 (153 women). Application fee: $70 ($90 for international students). *Unit*

head: Benito Marinas, Head, 217-333-6961, Fax: 217-265-8040, E-mail: marinas@illinois.edu. *Application contact:* Maxine M. Peyton, Office Manager, 217-333-6636, Fax: 217-333-9464, E-mail: mpeyton@illinois.edu.
Website: http://cee.illinois.edu/.

The University of Iowa, Graduate College, College of Engineering, Department of Civil and Environmental Engineering, Iowa City, IA 52242-1316. Offers MS, PhD. Part-time programs available. *Faculty:* 21 full-time (2 women), 3 part-time/adjunct (0 women). *Students:* 72 full-time (21 women); includes 3 minority (1 Black or African American, non-Hispanic/Latino; 2 Asian, non-Hispanic/Latino), 28 international. Average age 28. 142 applicants, 22% accepted, 9 enrolled. In 2014, 18 master's, 11 doctorates awarded. Terminal master's awarded for partial completion of doctoral program. *Degree requirements:* For master's, thesis optional, exam; for doctorate, comprehensive exam, thesis/dissertation, exam. *Entrance requirements:* For master's, GRE, minimum undergraduate GPA of 3.0; for doctorate, GRE, master's degree or equivalent with minimum GPA of 3.0. Additional exam requirements/recommendations for international students: Required—TOEFL (minimum score 550 paper-based; 81 iBT). *Application deadline:* For fall admission, 1/15 priority date for domestic and international students; for spring admission, 12/1 for domestic students, 10/1 for international students; for summer admission, 4/15 for domestic students, 3/1 for international students. Applications are processed on a rolling basis. Application fee: $60 ($100 for international students). Electronic applications accepted. *Financial support:* In 2014–15, 6 fellowships with partial tuition reimbursements, 40 research assistantships with partial tuition reimbursements (averaging $20,000 per year), 10 teaching assistantships with partial tuition reimbursements (averaging $18,080 per year) were awarded; career-related internships or fieldwork, Federal Work-Study, scholarships/grants, traineeships, and unspecified assistantships also available. Support available to part-time students. Financial award application deadline: 1/15; financial award applicants required to submit FAFSA. *Faculty research:* Water resources; environmental engineering and science; hydraulics and hydrology; structures, mechanics, and materials; transportation engineering. *Total annual research expenditures:* $19.3 million. *Unit head:* Dr. Michelle Scherer, Department Executive Officer, 319-335-5654, Fax: 319-335-5660, E-mail: michelle-scherer@uiowa.edu. *Application contact:* Kim Lebeck, Academic Program Specialist, 319-335-5647, Fax: 319-335-5660, E-mail: cee@engineering.uiowa.edu.
Website: http://www.engineering.uiowa.edu/cee.

The University of Kansas, Graduate Studies, School of Engineering, Program in Civil Engineering, Lawrence, KS 66045. Offers MCE, MS, DE, PhD. Part-time and evening/weekend programs available. *Faculty:* 25 full-time, 8 part-time/adjunct. *Students:* 78 full-time (20 women), 25 part-time (8 women); includes 1 minority (Asian, non-Hispanic/Latino), 54 international. Average age 28. 122 applicants, 60% accepted, 24 enrolled. In 2014, 23 master's, 6 doctorates awarded. *Degree requirements:* For master's, thesis or alternative, exam; for doctorate, comprehensive exam, thesis/dissertation. *Entrance requirements:* For master's and doctorate, GRE, BS in engineering. Additional exam requirements/recommendations for international students: Required—TOEFL. *Application deadline:* For fall admission, 7/1 priority date for domestic students, 3/1 priority date for international students; for spring admission, 12/1 priority date for domestic students, 8/15 priority date for international students. Applications are processed on a rolling basis. Application fee: $55 ($65 for international students). Electronic applications accepted. *Financial support:* Fellowships with full tuition reimbursements, research assistantships with full tuition reimbursements, teaching assistantships with full and partial tuition reimbursements, and career-related internships or fieldwork available. Financial award application deadline: 2/7. *Faculty research:* Structural engineering, geotechnical engineering, transportation engineering, water resources engineering, construction engineering. *Unit head:* David Darwin, Chair, 785-864-3827, E-mail: daved@ku.edu. *Application contact:* Susan Scott, Graduate Admissions Contact, 785-864-3826, E-mail: sbscott@ku.edu.
Website: http://www.ceae.ku.edu/.

University of Kentucky, Graduate School, College of Engineering, Program in Civil Engineering, Lexington, KY 40506-0032. Offers MSCE, PhD. *Degree requirements:* For master's, comprehensive exam, thesis optional; for doctorate, comprehensive exam, thesis/dissertation. *Entrance requirements:* For master's, GRE General Test, minimum undergraduate GPA of 2.75; for doctorate, GRE General Test, minimum undergraduate GPA of 3.0. Additional exam requirements/recommendations for international students: Required—TOEFL (minimum score 550 paper-based). Electronic applications accepted. *Faculty research:* Geotechnical engineering, structures, construction engineering and management, environmental engineering and water resources, transportation and materials.

University of Louisiana at Lafayette, College of Engineering, Department of Civil Engineering, Lafayette, LA 70504. Offers MSE. Evening/weekend programs available. *Degree requirements:* For master's, comprehensive exam, thesis or alternative. *Entrance requirements:* For master's, GRE General Test, BS in civil engineering, minimum GPA of 2.85. *Faculty research:* Structural mechanics, computer-aided design, environmental engineering.

University of Louisville, J. B. Speed School of Engineering, Department of Civil and Environmental Engineering, Louisville, KY 40292-0001. Offers civil engineering (M Eng, MS, PhD); environmental engineering (Graduate Certificate). *Accreditation:* ABET (one or more programs are accredited). Part-time programs available. Postbaccalaureate distance learning degree programs offered (no on-campus study). *Students:* 34 full-time (10 women), 17 part-time (4 women); includes 5 minority (2 Black or African American, non-Hispanic/Latino; 1 Asian, non-Hispanic/Latino; 2 Two or more races, non-Hispanic/Latino), 15 international. Average age 27. 26 applicants, 65% accepted, 7 enrolled. In 2014, 15 master's, 1 doctorate, 5 other advanced degrees awarded. Terminal master's awarded for partial completion of doctoral program. *Degree requirements:* For master's, comprehensive exam (for some programs), thesis optional, minimum GPA of 3.0; for doctorate, comprehensive exam, thesis/dissertation, minimum GPA of 3.0. *Entrance requirements:* For master's and doctorate, GRE, letters of recommendation, final official transcripts; for Graduate Certificate, pursuit of graduate degree (M Eng, MS, PhD) at J.B. Speed School of Engineering; undergraduate degree. Additional exam requirements/recommendations for international students: Required—TOEFL (minimum score 80 iBT) or IELTS. *Application deadline:* For fall admission, 6/15 for domestic students, 5/1 priority date for international students; for spring admission, 11/3 for domestic students, 11/1 priority date for international students; for summer admission, 3/31 for domestic students, 4/1 priority date for international students. Application fee: $60. Electronic applications accepted. *Expenses:* Tuition, state resident: full-time $11,326; part-time $630 per credit hour. Tuition, nonresident: full-time $23,568; part-time $1311 per credit hour. *Required fees:* $196. Tuition and fees vary according to program and reciprocity agreements. *Financial support:* Fellowships with full tuition reimbursements, research assistantships with full tuition reimbursements, and teaching assistantships with full tuition reimbursements available. Financial award application deadline: 2/3. *Faculty research:* Structures, hydraulics, transportation, environmental engineering, geomechanics. *Total annual research expenditures:* $1.8 million. *Unit head:* Dr. J. P. Mohsen, Chair, 502-852-4596, Fax: 502-852-8851, E-mail: jpm@louisville.edu. *Application contact:* Dr. Michael Harris, Director of Academic Programs, J. B. Speed School of Engineering, 502-852-6278, Fax: 502-852-7294, E-mail: mharris@louisville.edu.
Website: http://louisville.edu/speed/civil/.

University of Maine, Graduate School, College of Engineering, Department of Civil and Environmental Engineering, Orono, ME 04469. Offers civil engineering (MS, PhD). *Faculty:* 12 full-time (3 women). *Students:* 33 full-time (8 women), 7 part-time (2 women); includes 2 minority (both American Indian or Alaska Native, non-Hispanic/Latino), 7 international. Average age 31. 68 applicants, 84% accepted, 19 enrolled. In 2014, 6 master's, 2 doctorates awarded. Terminal master's awarded for partial completion of doctoral program. *Degree requirements:* For master's, thesis (for some programs); for doctorate, comprehensive exam, thesis/dissertation. *Entrance requirements:* For master's and doctorate, GRE General Test. Additional exam requirements/recommendations for international students: Required—TOEFL. *Application deadline:* For fall admission, 1/5 priority date for domestic students. Applications are processed on a rolling basis. Application fee: $65. Electronic applications accepted. *Expenses:* Tuition, state resident: part-time $658 per credit hour. Tuition, nonresident: part-time $1550 per credit hour. *Financial support:* In 2014–15, 26 students received support, including 3 fellowships (averaging $25,200 per year), 12 research assistantships with full tuition reimbursements available (averaging $14,600 per year), 6 teaching assistantships with full tuition reimbursements available (averaging $14,600 per year); Federal Work-Study, institutionally sponsored loans, scholarships/grants, and tuition waivers (full and partial) also available. Financial award application deadline: 3/1. *Faculty research:* Structural engineering, environmental engineering, water resources, transportation engineering, geotechnical engineering. *Total annual research expenditures:* $3 million. *Unit head:* Dr. Bill Davids, Chair, 207-581-2170, E-mail: william.davids@umit.maine.edu. *Application contact:* Scott G. Delcourt, Assistant Vice President for Graduate Studies and Senior Associate Dean, 207-581-3291, Fax: 207-581-3232, E-mail: graduate@maine.edu.
Website: http://www.civil.umaine.edu/.

The University of Manchester, School of Mechanical, Aerospace and Civil Engineering, Manchester, United Kingdom. Offers advanced manufacturing technology (M Ent); aerospace engineering (M Phil, M Sc, PhD); civil engineering (M Phil, M Sc, PhD); environmental engineering (M Phil, PhD); management of projects (M Phil, M Sc, PhD); mechanical engineering (M Phil, M Sc, PhD); mechanical engineering design (M Ent); nuclear engineering (M Phil, D Eng, PhD).

University of Manitoba, Faculty of Graduate Studies, Faculty of Engineering, Department of Civil Engineering, Winnipeg, MB R3T 2N2, Canada. Offers M Eng, M Sc, PhD. *Degree requirements:* For master's, thesis.

University of Maryland, College Park, Academic Affairs, A. James Clark School of Engineering, Department of Civil and Environmental Engineering, College Park, MD 20742. Offers M Eng, MS, PhD. Part-time and evening/weekend programs available. Postbaccalaureate distance learning degree programs offered. *Degree requirements:* For master's, thesis optional; for doctorate, thesis/dissertation, qualifying exam. *Entrance requirements:* For master's and doctorate, GRE General Test, 3 letters of recommendation. Electronic applications accepted. *Faculty research:* Transportation and urban systems, environmental engineering, geotechnical engineering, construction engineering and management, hydraulics.

University of Massachusetts Amherst, Graduate School, College of Engineering, Department of Civil and Environmental Engineering, Amherst, MA 01003. Offers civil engineering (MSCE, PhD); environmental and water resources engineering (MSCE); geotechnical engineering (MSCE); structural engineering and mechanics (MSCE); transportation engineering (MSCE). Part-time programs available. *Faculty:* 32 full-time (8 women). *Students:* 104 full-time (43 women), 15 part-time (7 women); includes 16 minority (3 Black or African American, non-Hispanic/Latino; 4 Asian, non-Hispanic/Latino; 7 Hispanic/Latino; 2 Two or more races, non-Hispanic/Latino), 44 international. Average age 26. 219 applicants, 62% accepted, 40 enrolled. In 2014, 36 master's, 4 doctorates awarded. Terminal master's awarded for partial completion of doctoral program. *Degree requirements:* For master's, thesis or alternative; for doctorate, comprehensive exam, thesis/dissertation. *Entrance requirements:* For master's and doctorate, GRE General Test. Additional exam requirements/recommendations for international students: Required—TOEFL (minimum score 550 paper-based; 80 iBT), IELTS (minimum score 6.5). *Application deadline:* For fall admission, 1/2 for domestic and international students; for spring admission, 10/1 for domestic and international students. Applications are processed on a rolling basis. Application fee: $75. Electronic applications accepted. *Expenses:* Tuition, state resident: full-time $1980; part-time $110 per credit. Tuition, nonresident: full-time $14,644; part-time $414 per credit. *Required fees:* $11,417. One-time fee: $357. *Financial support:* Fellowships with full and partial tuition reimbursements, research assistantships with full and partial tuition reimbursements, teaching assistantships with full and partial tuition reimbursements, career-related internships or fieldwork, Federal Work-Study, scholarships/grants, traineeships, health care benefits, tuition waivers (full and partial), and unspecified assistantships available. Support available to part-time students. Financial award application deadline: 1/2. *Unit head:* Dr. Sanjay Arwade, Graduate Program Director, 413-545-0686, Fax: 413-545-2840. *Application contact:* Lindsay DeSantis, Supervisor of Admissions, 413-545-0722, Fax: 413-577-0100, E-mail: gradadm@grad.umass.edu.
Website: http://cee.umass.edu/.

University of Massachusetts Amherst, Graduate School, Interdisciplinary Programs, Dual Degree Programs in Management and Engineering, Amherst, MA 01003. Offers MBA/MIE, MBA/MSEWRE, MSCE/MBA, MSME/MBA. Part-time programs available. *Students:* 1 full-time (0 women). Average age 27. 4 applicants, 25% accepted, 1 enrolled. *Entrance requirements:* Additional exam requirements/recommendations for international students: Required—TOEFL (minimum score 600 paper-based; 100 iBT), IELTS (minimum score 7). *Application deadline:* For fall admission, 1/2 for domestic and international students. Applications are processed on a rolling basis. Application fee: $75. Electronic applications accepted. *Expenses:* Tuition, state resident: full-time $1980; part-time $110 per credit. Tuition, nonresident: full-time $14,644; part-time $414 per credit. *Required fees:* $11,417. One-time fee: $357. *Financial support:* Career-related internships or fieldwork, Federal Work-Study, scholarships/grants, traineeships, health care benefits, tuition waivers (full), and unspecified assistantships available. Support available to part-time students. Financial award application deadline: 1/2. *Unit head:* Dr. Ana Muriel, Associate Professor, MBA/MS Degree Coordinator, 413-545-4242, Fax: 413-545-2840, E-mail: muriel@ecs.umass.edu. *Application contact:* Lindsay DeSantis, Supervisor of Admissions, 413-545-0722, Fax: 413-577-0010, E-mail: gradadm@grad.umass.edu.
Website: http://engineering.umass.edu/mbams-dual-degrees-management-and-engineering.

University of Massachusetts Dartmouth, Graduate School, College of Engineering, Department of Civil and Environmental Engineering, North Dartmouth, MA 02747-2300. Offers MS. Part-time programs available. *Faculty:* 7 full-time (1 woman), 4 part-time/adjunct (0 women). *Students:* 4 full-time (0 women), 5 part-time (0 women), 4 international. Average age 27. 17 applicants, 24% accepted. In 2014, 5 master's awarded. *Degree requirements:* For master's, thesis or project. *Entrance requirements:* For master's, GRE (UMass Dartmouth civil engineering bachelor's degree recipients are exempt), statement of purpose (minimum of 300 words), resume, 3 letters of

recommendation, official transcripts. Additional exam requirements/recommendations for international students: Required—TOEFL (minimum score 550 paper-based). *Application deadline:* For fall admission, 2/15 priority date for domestic students, 1/15 priority date for international students; for spring admission, 11/15 priority date for domestic students, 10/15 priority date for international students. Applications are processed on a rolling basis. Application fee: $60. Electronic applications accepted. *Expenses:* Tuition, state resident: full-time $2071; part-time $86.29 per credit. Tuition, nonresident: full-time $8099; part-time $337.46 per credit. *Required fees:* $16,520; $712.33 per credit. Tuition and fees vary according to course load and reciprocity agreements. *Financial support:* In 2014–15, 2 teaching assistantships with full tuition reimbursements (averaging $11,250 per year) were awarded; Federal Work-Study and unspecified assistantships also available. Support available to part-time students. Financial award application deadline: 3/1; financial award applicants required to submit FAFSA. *Faculty research:* Water/wastewater treatment systems, highway sustainability, structural analysis, cold-region engineering. *Total annual research expenditures:* $1.5 million. *Unit head:* Mazdak Tootkaboni, Graduate Program Director, 508-999-8465, Fax: 508-999-8964, E-mail: mtootkaboni@umassd.edu. *Application contact:* Steven Briggs, Director of Marketing and Recruitment for Graduate Studies, 508-999-8604, Fax: 508-999-8183, E-mail: graduate@umassd.edu.
Website: http://www.umassd.edu/engineering/cen/.

University of Massachusetts Lowell, Francis College of Engineering, Department of Civil and Environmental Engineering, Lowell, MA 01854. Offers civil and environmental engineering (MS Eng, Certificate); environmental engineering (D Eng); environmental studies (MSES, PhD, Certificate), including environmental engineering (MSES), environmental studies (PhD, Certificate); sustainable infrastructure for developing nations (Certificate). Part-time programs available. *Degree requirements:* For master's, thesis optional. *Entrance requirements:* For master's, GRE General Test. *Faculty research:* Bridge design, traffic control, groundwater remediation, pile capacity.

University of Memphis, Graduate School, Herff College of Engineering, Department of Civil Engineering, Memphis, TN 38152. Offers civil engineering (PhD); environmental engineering (MS); foundation engineering (MS); structural engineering (MS); transportation engineering (MS); water resources engineering (MS). *Faculty:* 11 full-time (1 woman), 2 part-time/adjunct (0 women). *Students:* 12 full-time (5 women), 8 part-time (1 woman); includes 2 minority (both Black or African American, non-Hispanic/Latino), 4 international. Average age 27. 18 applicants, 100% accepted, 4 enrolled. In 2014, 8 master's awarded. Terminal master's awarded for partial completion of doctoral program. *Degree requirements:* For master's, comprehensive exam, thesis optional; for doctorate, comprehensive exam, thesis/dissertation. *Entrance requirements:* For master's, GRE General Test or MAT, minimum undergraduate GPA of 2.5; for doctorate, GRE, 3 letters of recommendation. Additional exam requirements/recommendations for international students: Required—TOEFL (minimum score 550 paper-based; 79 iBT). *Application deadline:* For fall admission, 1/7 for domestic students, 1/5 for international students; for spring admission, 12/1 for domestic students, 9/15 for international students. Application fee: $35 ($60 for international students). *Financial support:* In 2014–15, 6 students received support. Fellowships with full tuition reimbursements available, research assistantships with full tuition reimbursements available, career-related internships or fieldwork, Federal Work-Study, scholarships/grants, and unspecified assistantships available. Financial award application deadline: 2/15; financial award applicants required to submit FAFSA. *Faculty research:* Structural response to earthquakes, pavement design, water quality, transportation safety, intermodal transportation. *Unit head:* Dr. Sharam Pezeshk, Interim Chair, 901-678-2746, Fax: 901-678-3026. *Application contact:* Dr. Roger Meier, Coordinator of Graduate Studies, 901-678-3284.
Website: http://www.ce.memphis.edu.

University of Miami, Graduate School, College of Engineering, Department of Civil, Architectural, and Environmental Engineering, Coral Gables, FL 33124. Offers architectural engineering (MSAE); civil engineering (MSCE, PhD). Part-time programs available. Terminal master's awarded for partial completion of doctoral program. *Degree requirements:* For master's, thesis (for some programs); for doctorate, comprehensive exam, thesis/dissertation. *Entrance requirements:* For master's, GRE General Test (minimum score 1000 verbal and quantitative), minimum GPA of 3.0; for doctorate, GRE General Test, minimum GPA of 3.5 in preceding degree. Additional exam requirements/recommendations for international students: Required—TOEFL (minimum score 550 paper-based). Electronic applications accepted. *Faculty research:* Structural assessment and wind engineering, sustainable construction and materials, moisture transport and management, wastewater and waste engineering, water management and risk analysis.

University of Michigan, College of Engineering, Department of Civil and Environmental Engineering, Ann Arbor, MI 48109. Offers civil engineering (MSE, PhD, CE); construction engineering and management (M Eng, MSE); environmental engineering (MSE, PhD); structural engineering (M Eng); MBA/MSE. Part-time programs available. *Students:* 184 full-time (69 women), 5 part-time (0 women). 691 applicants, 36% accepted, 62 enrolled. In 2014, 59 master's, 12 doctorates awarded. *Degree requirements:* For master's, thesis optional; for doctorate, comprehensive exam, thesis/dissertation, oral defense of dissertation, preliminary and written exams. *Entrance requirements:* For master's and doctorate, GRE General Test. Additional exam requirements/recommendations for international students: Required—TOEFL (minimum score 560 paper-based). *Application deadline:* Applications are processed on a rolling basis. Electronic applications accepted. *Financial support:* Fellowships, research assistantships, teaching assistantships, institutionally sponsored loans, and tuition waivers (partial) available. Financial award application deadline: 1/19. *Faculty research:* Construction engineering and management, geotechnical engineering, earthquake-resistant design of structures, environmental chemistry and microbiology, cost engineering, environmental and water resources engineering. *Total annual research expenditures:* $10.4 million. *Unit head:* Kim Hayes, Department Chair, 734-764-8495, Fax: 734-764-4292, E-mail: ford@umich.edu. *Application contact:* Jessica Taylor, Graduate Coordinator, 734-764-8405, Fax: 734-647-2127, E-mail: jrand@umich.edu.
Website: http://cee.engin.umich.edu/.

University of Michigan, College of Engineering, Department of Naval Architecture and Marine Engineering, Ann Arbor, MI 48109. Offers MS, MSE, PhD, Mar Eng, Nav Arch, MBA/MSE. Part-time programs available. *Students:* 79 full-time (12 women), 5 part-time (1 woman). 138 applicants, 43% accepted, 36 enrolled. In 2014, 43 master's, 12 doctorates awarded. Terminal master's awarded for partial completion of doctoral program. *Degree requirements:* For master's, thesis (for some programs); for doctorate, comprehensive exam, thesis/dissertation, oral defense of dissertation, written and oral preliminary exams; for other advanced degree, comprehensive exam, thesis, oral defense of thesis. *Entrance requirements:* For doctorate, GRE General Test, master's degree; for other advanced degree, GRE General Test. Additional exam requirements/recommendations for international students: Required—TOEFL (minimum score 560 paper-based). *Application deadline:* Applications are processed on a rolling basis. Electronic applications accepted. *Financial support:* Fellowships, research assistantships, teaching assistantships, career-related internships or fieldwork, Federal Work-Study, institutionally sponsored loans, scholarships/grants, and unspecified assistantships available. *Faculty research:* System and structural reliability, design and analysis of offshore structures and vehicles, marine systems design, remote sensing of ship wakes and sea surfaces, marine hydrodynamics, nonlinear seakeeping analysis. *Total annual research expenditures:* $12.2 million. *Unit head:* Dr. Steven Ceccio, Department Chair, 734-936-7636, Fax: 734-936-8820, E-mail: ceccio@umich.edu. *Application contact:* Nathalie Fiveland, Graduate Program Coordinator, 734-936-0566, Fax: 734-936-8820, E-mail: fiveland@umich.edu.
Website: http://name.engin.umich.edu/.

University of Minnesota, Twin Cities Campus, College of Science and Engineering, Department of Civil, Environmental, and Geo-Engineering, Minneapolis, MN 55455-0213. Offers civil engineering (MCE, MS, PhD); geological engineering (M Geo E, MS); stream restoration science and engineering (Certificate). Part-time programs available. *Degree requirements:* For master's, thesis optional; for doctorate, thesis/dissertation. *Entrance requirements:* For master's and doctorate, GRE General Test. Additional exam requirements/recommendations for international students: Required—TOEFL. Electronic applications accepted. *Faculty research:* Environmental engineering, geomechanics, structural engineering, transportation, water resources.

University of Missouri, Office of Research and Graduate Studies, College of Engineering, Department of Civil and Environmental Engineering, Columbia, MO 65211. Offers civil engineering (MS, PhD); environmental engineering (MS, PhD); geotechnical engineering (MS, PhD); structural engineering (MS, PhD); transportation and highway engineering (MS); water resources (MS, PhD). *Faculty:* 18 full-time (2 women), 1 part-time/adjunct (0 women). *Students:* 42 full-time (8 women), 27 part-time (6 women); includes 4 minority (1 Black or African American, non-Hispanic/Latino; 1 Asian, non-Hispanic/Latino; 2 Hispanic/Latino), 45 international. Average age 31. 102 applicants, 48% accepted, 22 enrolled. In 2014, 14 master's, 2 doctorates awarded. *Degree requirements:* For master's, report or thesis; for doctorate, thesis/dissertation. *Entrance requirements:* For master's and doctorate, GRE General Test. Additional exam requirements/recommendations for international students: Required—TOEFL (minimum score 550 paper-based; 79 iBT). *Application deadline:* For fall admission, 2/15 priority date for domestic students, 2/15 for international students; for winter admission, 9/15 priority date for domestic students, 9/15 for international students. Application fee: $55 ($75 for international students). *Financial support:* Fellowships, research assistantships, teaching assistantships, and institutionally sponsored loans available. *Unit head:* Dr. Mark Virkler, Department Chair, 573-882-7434, E-mail: virklerm@missouri.edu. *Application contact:* Jennifer Keyzer-Andre, Administrative Associate I, 573-882-4442, E-mail: keyzerandrej@missouri.edu.
Website: http://engineering.missouri.edu/civil/.

University of Missouri–Kansas City, School of Computing and Engineering, Kansas City, MO 64110-2499. Offers civil engineering (MS); computer and electrical engineering (PhD); computer science (MS), including bioinformatics, software engineering, telecommunications networking; computer science and informatics (PhD); computing (PhD); electrical engineering (MS); engineering (PhD); engineering and construction management (Graduate Certificate); mechanical engineering (MS); telecommunications and computer networking (PhD). PhD (interdisciplinary) offered through the School of Graduate Studies. Part-time programs available. *Faculty:* 39 full-time (5 women), 26 part-time/adjunct (3 women). *Students:* 500 full-time (143 women), 136 part-time (28 women); includes 18 minority (5 Black or African American, non-Hispanic/Latino; 8 Asian, non-Hispanic/Latino; 4 Hispanic/Latino; 1 Two or more races, non-Hispanic/Latino), 551 international. Average age 24. 1,924 applicants, 39% accepted, 200 enrolled. In 2014, 124 master's, 1 other advanced degree awarded. *Degree requirements:* For doctorate, thesis/dissertation. *Entrance requirements:* For master's, GRE General Test, minimum GPA of 3.0, 3 letters of recommendation from professors; for doctorate, GRE General Test, minimum GPA of 3.5. Additional exam requirements/recommendations for international students: Required—TOEFL (minimum score 550 paper-based; 80 iBT). *Application deadline:* For fall admission, 1/15 priority date for domestic students, 1/15 for international students. Applications are processed on a rolling basis. Application fee: $45 ($50 for international students). *Financial support:* In 2014–15, 34 research assistantships with partial tuition reimbursements (averaging $15,602 per year), 24 teaching assistantships with partial tuition reimbursements (averaging $15,090 per year) were awarded; career-related internships or fieldwork, Federal Work-Study, scholarships/grants, tuition waivers (partial), and unspecified assistantships also available. Support available to part-time students. Financial award application deadline: 3/1; financial award applicants required to submit FAFSA. *Faculty research:* Algorithms, bioinformatics and medical informatics, biomechanics/biomaterials, civil engineering materials, networking and telecommunications, thermal science. *Unit head:* Dr. Kevin Z. Truman, Dean, 816-235-2399, Fax: 816-235-5159. *Application contact:* 816-235-2399, Fax: 816-235-5159.
Website: http://sce.umkc.edu/.

University of Nebraska–Lincoln, Graduate College, College of Engineering, Department of Civil Engineering, Lincoln, NE 68588. Offers MS, PhD. *Degree requirements:* For master's, thesis optional; for doctorate, comprehensive exam, thesis/dissertation. *Entrance requirements:* For master's and doctorate, GRE General Test. Additional exam requirements/recommendations for international students: Required—TOEFL (minimum score 550 paper-based). Electronic applications accepted. *Faculty research:* Water resources engineering, sediment transport, steel bridge systems, highway safety.

University of Nevada, Las Vegas, Graduate College, Howard R. Hughes College of Engineering, Department of Civil and Environmental Engineering and Construction, Las Vegas, NV 89154-4015. Offers civil and environmental engineering (PhD); transportation (MS). Part-time programs available. *Faculty:* 13 full-time (2 women), 2 part-time/adjunct (0 women). *Students:* 48 full-time (14 women), 30 part-time (14 women); includes 17 minority (3 Black or African American, non-Hispanic/Latino; 4 Asian, non-Hispanic/Latino; 7 Hispanic/Latino; 3 Two or more races, non-Hispanic/Latino), 37 international. Average age 32. 51 applicants, 75% accepted, 18 enrolled. In 2014, 19 master's, 3 doctorates awarded. *Degree requirements:* For master's, comprehensive exam (for some programs); thesis (for some programs); for doctorate, comprehensive exam, thesis/dissertation. *Entrance requirements:* For master's and doctorate, GRE General Test. Additional exam requirements/recommendations for international students: Required—TOEFL (minimum score 550 paper-based; 80 iBT), IELTS (minimum score 7). *Application deadline:* For fall admission, 6/15 for domestic students, 3/15 for international students; for spring admission, 11/15 for domestic students, 8/30 for international students. Application fee: $60 ($95 for international students). Electronic applications accepted. *Financial support:* In 2014–15, 45 students received support, including 15 research assistantships with partial tuition reimbursements available (averaging $15,678 per year), 30 teaching assistantships with partial tuition reimbursements available (averaging $13,553 per year); institutionally sponsored loans, scholarships/grants, health care benefits, and unspecified assistantships also available. Financial award application deadline: 3/1. *Total annual research expenditures:* $747,749. *Unit head:* Donald Hayes, Chair/Professor, 702-895-4723, Fax: 702-895-3936, E-mail: donald.hayes@unlv.edu. *Application contact:*

Civil Engineering

Graduate College Admissions Evaluator, 702-895-3320, Fax: 702-895-4180, E-mail: gradcollege@unlv.edu.
Website: http://www.unlv.edu/ceec.

University of Nevada, Reno, Graduate School, College of Engineering, Department of Civil and Environmental Engineering, Reno, NV 89557. Offers MS, PhD. Terminal master's awarded for partial completion of doctoral program. *Degree requirements:* For master's, thesis optional; for doctorate, thesis/dissertation. *Entrance requirements:* For master's, GRE General Test, minimum GPA of 3.0; for doctorate, GRE General Test, minimum GPA of 3.25. Additional exam requirements/recommendations for international students: Required—TOEFL (minimum score 500 paper-based; 61 iBT), IELTS (minimum score 6). Electronic applications accepted. *Faculty research:* Structural and earthquake engineering, geotechnical engineering, environmental engineering, transportation, pavements/materials.

University of New Brunswick Fredericton, School of Graduate Studies, Faculty of Engineering, Department of Civil Engineering, Fredericton, NB E3B 5A3, Canada. Offers construction engineering and management (M Eng, M Sc E, PhD); environmental engineering (M Eng, M Sc E, PhD); environmental studies (M Eng); geotechnical engineering (M Eng, M Sc E, PhD); groundwater/hydrology (M Eng, M Sc E, PhD); materials (M Eng, M Sc E, PhD); pavements (M Eng, M Sc E, PhD); structures (M Eng, M Sc E, PhD); transportation (M Eng, M Sc E, PhD). Part-time programs available. *Faculty:* 12 full-time (1 woman), 4 part-time/adjunct (0 women). *Students:* 16 full-time (4 women), 15 part-time (5 women). In 2014, 9 master's, 3 doctorates awarded. *Degree requirements:* For master's, thesis, proposal; for doctorate, comprehensive exam, thesis/dissertation, qualifying exam; 27 credit hours of courses. *Entrance requirements:* For master's, minimum GPA of 3.0; B Sc E in civil engineering or related engineering degree; for doctorate, minimum GPA of 3.0; graduate degree in engineering or applied science. Additional exam requirements/recommendations for international students: Required—IELTS (minimum score 7.5), TWE (minimum score 4), Michigan English Language Assessment Battery (minimum score 85) or CanTest (minimum score 4.5); Recommended—TOEFL (minimum score 580 paper-based). *Application deadline:* For fall admission, 5/1 for domestic students; for winter admission, 11/1 for domestic students. Applications are processed on a rolling basis. Application fee: $50 Canadian dollars. Electronic applications accepted. *Financial support:* In 2014–15, 35 fellowships, 48 research assistantships, 35 teaching assistantships were awarded; career-related internships or fieldwork and scholarships/grants also available. *Faculty research:* Construction engineering and management; engineering materials and infrastructure renewal; highway and pavement research; structures and solid mechanics; geotechnical and geoenvironmental engineering; structure interaction; transportation and planning; environment, solid waste management; structural engineering; water and environmental engineering. *Unit head:* Dr. Kerry MacQuarrie, Director of Graduate Studies, 506-453-5121, Fax: 506-453-3568, E-mail: ktm@unb.ca. *Application contact:* Joyce Moore, Graduate Secretary, 506-452-6127, Fax: 506-453-3568, E-mail: joycem@unb.ca.
Website: http://go.unb.ca/gradprograms.

University of New Hampshire, Graduate School, College of Engineering and Physical Sciences, Department of Civil Engineering, Durham, NH 03824. Offers M Engr, MS, PhD. Part-time programs available. *Faculty:* 15 full-time (4 women). *Students:* 30 full-time (8 women), 42 part-time (17 women); includes 6 minority (1 Black or African American, non-Hispanic/Latino; 3 Asian, non-Hispanic/Latino; 2 Two or more races, non-Hispanic/Latino), 14 international. Average age 27. 90 applicants, 73% accepted, 24 enrolled. In 2014, 20 master's, 1 doctorate awarded. *Degree requirements:* For master's, thesis or alternative; for doctorate, thesis/dissertation. *Entrance requirements:* For master's and doctorate, GRE. Additional exam requirements/recommendations for international students: Required—TOEFL (minimum score 550 paper-based; 80 iBT). *Application deadline:* For fall admission, 4/1 priority date for domestic students, 4/1 for international students; for spring admission, 12/1 for domestic students. Applications are processed on a rolling basis. Application fee: $65. Electronic applications accepted. *Expenses:* Tuition, state resident: full-time $13,500; part-time $750 per credit hour. Tuition, nonresident: full-time $26,460; part-time $1110 per credit hour. *Required fees:* $1788; $447 per semester. *Financial support:* In 2014–15, 30 students received support, including 1 fellowship, 7 research assistantships, 19 teaching assistantships; Federal Work-Study, scholarships/grants, and tuition waivers (full and partial) also available. Support available to part-time students. Financial award application deadline: 2/15. *Faculty research:* Environmental, structural materials, geotechnical engineering, water resources, systems analysis. *Unit head:* Dr. Erin Bell, Chairperson, 603-862-3850. *Application contact:* Michelle Mancini, Administrative Assistant, 603-862-1428, E-mail: michelle.mancini@unh.edu.
Website: http://www.unh.edu/civil-engineering/.

University of New Mexico, Graduate School, School of Engineering, Program in Civil Engineering, Albuquerque, NM 87131-0001. Offers civil engineering (M Eng, MSCE); construction management (MCM); engineering (PhD). Part-time programs available. *Faculty:* 11 full-time (2 women), 4 part-time/adjunct (1 woman). *Students:* 26 full-time (9 women), 28 part-time (14 women); includes 15 minority (1 American Indian or Alaska Native, non-Hispanic/Latino; 13 Hispanic/Latino; 1 Two or more races, non-Hispanic/Latino), 11 international. Average age 28. 72 applicants, 39% accepted, 17 enrolled. In 2014, 20 master's, 4 doctorates awarded. Terminal master's awarded for partial completion of doctoral program. *Degree requirements:* For master's, comprehensive exam, thesis (for some programs); for doctorate, comprehensive exam, thesis/dissertation. *Entrance requirements:* For master's, GRE General Test (for MSCE and M Eng); GRE or GMAT (for MCM), minimum GPA of 3.0; for doctorate, GRE General Test, minimum GPA of 3.0. Additional exam requirements/recommendations for international students: Required—TOEFL (minimum score 550 paper-based; 80 iBT), IELTS (minimum score 6.5). *Application deadline:* For fall admission, 7/15 for domestic students, 3/1 for international students; for spring admission, 11/10 for domestic students, 8/1 for international students. Applications are processed on a rolling basis. Application fee: $50. Electronic applications accepted. *Financial support:* In 2014–15, research assistantships with full and partial tuition reimbursements (averaging $19,944 per year), teaching assistantships with full and partial tuition reimbursements (averaging $15,000 per year) were awarded; scholarships/grants, health care benefits, and unspecified assistantships also available. Support available to part-time students. Financial award application deadline: 3/1; financial award applicants required to submit FAFSA. *Faculty research:* Integrating design and construction, project delivery methods, sustainable design and construction, leadership and management in construction, project management and project supervision, production management and improvement. *Total annual research expenditures:* $2.6 million. *Unit head:* Dr. John C. Stormont, Chair, 505-277-2722, Fax: 505-277-1988, E-mail: jcstorm@unm.edu. *Application contact:* Missy Garoza, Professional Academic Advisor, 505-277-2722, Fax: 505-277-1988, E-mail: civil@unm.edu.
Website: http://civil.unm.edu.

The University of North Carolina at Charlotte, The William States Lee College of Engineering, Department of Civil and Environmental Engineering, Charlotte, NC 28223-0001. Offers civil engineering (MSCE); infrastructure and environmental systems (PhD), including infrastructure and environmental systems design. Part-time and evening/weekend programs available. *Faculty:* 24 full-time (4 women). *Students:* 58 full-time (17 women), 44 part-time (13 women); includes 15 minority (8 Black or African American, non-Hispanic/Latino; 2 Asian, non-Hispanic/Latino; 5 Hispanic/Latino), 35 international. Average age 29. 105 applicants, 49% accepted, 22 enrolled. In 2014, 18 master's, 3 doctorates awarded. Terminal master's awarded for partial completion of doctoral program. *Degree requirements:* For master's, thesis or project; for doctorate, comprehensive exam, thesis/dissertation. *Entrance requirements:* For master's, GRE General Test, minimum GPA of 3.0 in undergraduate major, 2.75 overall; for doctorate, GRE General Test, minimum undergraduate GPA of 3.2, graduate 3.5; three letters of recommendation. Additional exam requirements/recommendations for international students: Required—TOEFL (minimum score 557 paper-based; 83 iBT). *Application deadline:* For fall admission, 5/1 priority date for domestic students, 5/1 for international students; for spring admission, 10/1 priority date for domestic students, 10/1 for international students. Applications are processed on a rolling basis. Application fee: $75. Electronic applications accepted. *Expenses:* Tuition, state resident: full-time $4008. Tuition, nonresident: full-time $16,295. *Required fees:* $2755. Tuition and fees vary according to course load and program. *Financial support:* In 2014–15, 37 students received support, including 1 fellowship (averaging $23,545 per year), 24 research assistantships (averaging $7,949 per year), 12 teaching assistantships (averaging $4,663 per year); career-related internships or fieldwork, institutionally sponsored loans, scholarships/grants, and unspecified assistantships also available. Support available to part-time students. Financial award application deadline: 4/1; financial award applicants required to submit FAFSA. *Faculty research:* Structural analysis and design, civil design for sustainability, structural materials, transportation engineering, geotechnical engineering, environmental management, water resources. *Total annual research expenditures:* $973,550. *Unit head:* Dr. John L. Daniels, Chair, 704-687-1219, Fax: 704-687-6953, E-mail: jodaniels@uncc.edu. *Application contact:* Kathy B. Giddings, Director of Graduate Admissions, 704-687-5503, Fax: 704-687-1668, E-mail: gradadm@uncc.edu.
Website: https://cee.uncc.edu/graduate-program.

University of North Dakota, Graduate School, School of Engineering and Mines, Department of Civil Engineering, Grand Forks, ND 58202. Offers civil engineering (M Engr); sanitary engineering (M Engr), including soils and structures engineering, surface mining engineering. Part-time programs available. *Degree requirements:* For master's, comprehensive exam, thesis or alternative. *Entrance requirements:* For master's, GRE General Test, minimum GPA of 2.5. Additional exam requirements/recommendations for international students: Required—TOEFL (minimum score 550 paper-based; 79 iBT), IELTS (minimum score 6.5). Electronic applications accepted. *Faculty research:* Soil-structures, environmental-water resources.

University of North Florida, College of Computing, Engineering, and Construction, School of Engineering, Jacksonville, FL 32224. Offers MSCE, MSEE, MSME. Part-time programs available. *Faculty:* 17 full-time (1 woman), 1 part-time/adjunct (0 women). *Students:* 9 full-time (2 women), 22 part-time (7 women); includes 8 minority (1 Black or African American, non-Hispanic/Latino; 4 Asian, non-Hispanic/Latino; 2 Hispanic/Latino; 1 Two or more races, non-Hispanic/Latino), 4 international. Average age 28. 60 applicants, 28% accepted, 8 enrolled. In 2014, 14 master's awarded. *Application deadline:* For fall admission, 7/1 for domestic students, 5/1 for international students; for spring admission, 11/1 for domestic students, 10/1 for international students. Application fee: $30. *Expenses:* Tuition, state resident: full-time $9794; part-time $408.10 per credit hour. Tuition, nonresident: full-time $22,383; part-time $932.61 per credit hour. *Required fees:* $2047; $85.29 per credit hour. Tuition and fees vary according to course load and program. *Financial support:* In 2014–15, 16 students received support, including 2 research assistantships (averaging $2,775 per year); teaching assistantships, Federal Work-Study, scholarships/grants, tuition waivers, and unspecified assistantships also available. Financial award application deadline: 4/1; financial award applicants required to submit FAFSA. *Total annual research expenditures:* $863,034. *Unit head:* Dr. Murat Tiryakioglo, Associate Dean, 904-620-2504, E-mail: m.tiryakioglo@unf.edu. *Application contact:* Dr. Amanda Pascale, Director, The Graduate School, 904-320-1360, Fax: 904-620-1362, E-mail: graduateschool@unf.edu.
Website: http://www.unf.edu/ccec/engineering/.

University of Notre Dame, Graduate School, College of Engineering, Department of Civil Engineering and Geological Sciences, Notre Dame, IN 46556. Offers bioengineering (MS Bio E); civil engineering (MSCE); civil engineering and geological sciences (PhD); environmental engineering (MS Env E); geological sciences (MS). Terminal master's awarded for partial completion of doctoral program. *Degree requirements:* For master's, comprehensive exam; for doctorate, thesis/dissertation, candidacy exam. *Entrance requirements:* For master's and doctorate, GRE General Test. Additional exam requirements/recommendations for international students: Required—TOEFL (minimum score 600 paper-based; 80 iBT). Electronic applications accepted. *Faculty research:* Environmental modeling, biological-waste treatment, petrology, environmental geology, geochemistry.

University of Oklahoma, Gallogly College of Engineering, School of Civil Engineering and Environmental Science, Program in Civil Engineering, Norman, OK 73019. Offers MS, PhD. Part-time programs available. *Students:* 20 full-time (5 women), 20 part-time (6 women); includes 5 minority (2 Black or African American, non-Hispanic/Latino; 1 Asian, non-Hispanic/Latino; 1 Hispanic/Latino; 1 Two or more races, non-Hispanic/Latino), 21 international. Average age 27. 33 applicants, 33% accepted, 6 enrolled. In 2014, 11 master's, 3 doctorates awarded. Terminal master's awarded for partial completion of doctoral program. *Degree requirements:* For master's, comprehensive exam, thesis; for doctorate, comprehensive exam, thesis/dissertation. *Entrance requirements:* For master's, GRE, minimum GPA of 3.0, statement of goals, 2 letters of recommendation; for doctorate, GRE, minimum graduate GPA of 3.0, statement of goals, 2 letters of recommendation. Additional exam requirements/recommendations for international students: Required—TOEFL (minimum score 79 iBT). *Application deadline:* For fall admission, 1/15 for domestic and international students; for spring admission, 5/15 for domestic and international students. Application fee: $50 ($100 for international students). Electronic applications accepted. *Expenses:* Tuition, state resident: full-time $4394; part-time $183.10 per credit hour. Tuition, nonresident: full-time $16,970; part-time $707.10 per credit hour. *Required fees:* $2892; $109.95 per credit hour. $126.50 per semester. *Financial support:* In 2014–15, 36 students received support. Scholarships/grants available. Financial award application deadline: 6/1; financial award applicants required to submit FAFSA. *Faculty research:* Intelligent structures, composites, earthquake engineering, intelligent compaction, bridge engineering. *Unit head:* Dr. Randall Kolar, Director, 405-325-4267, Fax: 405-325-4217, E-mail: kolar@ou.edu. *Application contact:* Susan Williams, Graduate Programs Assistant, 405-325-2344, Fax: 405-325-4217, E-mail: srwilliams@ou.edu.
Website: http://www.ou.edu/coe/cees.html.

University of Ottawa, Faculty of Graduate and Postdoctoral Studies, Faculty of Engineering, Ottawa-Carleton Institute for Civil Engineering, Ottawa, ON K1N 6N5, Canada. Offers M Eng, MA Sc, PhD. PhD, M Eng, MA Sc offered jointly with Carleton University. *Degree requirements:* For master's, thesis or alternative; for doctorate, comprehensive exam, thesis/dissertation, seminar series. *Entrance requirements:* For master's, honors degree or equivalent, minimum B average; for doctorate, master's degree, minimum B+ average. Electronic applications accepted. *Faculty research:* Environmental engineering, geotechnical engineering, structural engineering, transportation engineering, water resources engineering.

University of Pittsburgh, Dietrich School of Arts and Sciences, Program in Computational Modeling and Simulation, Pittsburgh, PA 15260. Offers bioengineering (PhD); biological science (PhD); civil and environmental engineering (PhD); computer science (PhD); economics (PhD); industrial engineering (PhD); mathematics (PhD); mechanical engineering and materials science (PhD); physics and astronomy (PhD); psychology (PhD); statistics (PhD). Part-time programs available. *Faculty:* 4 full-time (0 women). *Students:* 5 full-time (2 women), 1 part-time (0 women), 5 international. Average age 22. 14 applicants, 14% accepted, 2 enrolled. *Degree requirements:* For doctorate, comprehensive exam, thesis/dissertation, preliminary exam. *Entrance requirements:* For doctorate, GRE, statement of purpose, transcripts for all college-level institutions attended, three letters of reference. Additional exam requirements/recommendations for international students: Required—TOEFL (minimum score 90 iBT), IELTS (minimum score 7). *Application deadline:* For fall admission, 2/21 for domestic and international students. Applications are processed on a rolling basis. Application fee: $0 ($50 for international students). Electronic applications accepted. *Expenses:* Tuition, state resident: full-time $20,742; part-time $838 per credit. Tuition, nonresident: full-time $33,960; part-time $1389 per credit. *Required fees:* $800; $205 per term. Tuition and fees vary according to program. *Financial support:* In 2014–15, 5 students received support, including 3 fellowships with tuition reimbursements available (averaging $25,500 per year), 2 research assistantships with tuition reimbursements available (averaging $26,000 per year). *Unit head:* Kathleen Blee, Associate Dean, Graduate Studies and Research, 412-624-3939, Fax: 412-624-6855. *Application contact:* Dave R. Carmen, Administrative Secretary, 412-624-6094, Fax: 412-624-6855, E-mail: drc41@pitt.edu.
Website: http://cmsp.pitt.edu/.

University of Pittsburgh, Swanson School of Engineering, Department of Civil and Environmental Engineering, Pittsburgh, PA 15260. Offers MSCEE, PhD. Part-time programs available. Postbaccalaureate distance learning degree programs offered. *Faculty:* 17 full-time (3 women), 15 part-time/adjunct (1 woman). *Students:* 104 full-time (25 women), 48 part-time (11 women); includes 2 minority (1 Black or African American, non-Hispanic/Latino; 1 Asian, non-Hispanic/Latino), 93 international. 343 applicants, 57% accepted, 32 enrolled. In 2014, 52 master's, 15 doctorates awarded. Terminal master's awarded for partial completion of doctoral program. *Degree requirements:* For master's, thesis optional; for doctorate, comprehensive exam, thesis/dissertation, final oral exams. *Entrance requirements:* For master's and doctorate, minimum GPA of 3.0. Additional exam requirements/recommendations for international students: Required—TOEFL (minimum score 550 paper-based; 80 iBT). *Application deadline:* For fall admission, 3/1 priority date for domestic and international students; for spring admission, 7/1 priority date for domestic and international students. Applications are processed on a rolling basis. Application fee: $50. Electronic applications accepted. *Expenses:* Tuition, state resident: full-time $20,742; part-time $838 per credit. Tuition, nonresident: full-time $33,960; part-time $1389 per credit. *Required fees:* $800; $205 per term. Tuition and fees vary according to program. *Financial support:* In 2014–15, 47 students received support, including 7 fellowships with full tuition reimbursements available (averaging $29,376 per year), 28 research assistantships with full tuition reimbursements available (averaging $24,000 per year), 12 teaching assistantships with full tuition reimbursements available (averaging $25,692 per year); scholarships/grants, traineeships, and tuition waivers (full and partial) also available. Financial award application deadline: 4/15. *Faculty research:* Environmental and water resources, structures and infrastructures, construction management. *Total annual research expenditures:* $5.5 million. *Unit head:* Dr. Radisav Vidic, Chairman, 412-624-9870, Fax: 412-624-0135. *Application contact:* Dr. Leonard Casson, Academic Coordinator, 412-624-9868, Fax: 412-624-0135, E-mail: casson@pitt.edu.
Website: http://www.engineering.pitt.edu/Civil/.

University of Portland, School of Engineering, Portland, OR 97203-5798. Offers biomedical engineering (MBME); civil engineering (ME); computer science (ME); electrical engineering (ME); mechanical engineering (ME). Part-time and evening/weekend programs available. *Faculty:* 10 full-time (2 women), 1 part-time/adjunct (0 women). *Students:* 4 full-time (1 woman), 2 part-time (0 women); includes 1 minority (Two or more races, non-Hispanic/Latino), 1 international. Average age 27. In 2014, 2 master's awarded. *Degree requirements:* For master's, thesis optional. *Entrance requirements:* For master's, GRE General Test, minimum GPA of 3.0, 3 letters of recommendation, resume, statement of goals, official transcripts. Additional exam requirements/recommendations for international students: Required—TOEFL (minimum score 550 paper-based; 80 iBT), IELTS (minimum score 7). *Application deadline:* For fall admission, 7/15 priority date for domestic and international students; for spring admission, 12/15 priority date for domestic and international students. Applications are processed on a rolling basis. Application fee: $50. *Expenses:* Expenses: Contact institution. *Financial support:* Career-related internships or fieldwork, Federal Work-Study, and scholarships/grants available. Support available to part-time students. Financial award application deadline: 3/1; financial award applicants required to submit FAFSA. *Unit head:* Dr. Sharon Jones, Dean, 503-943-8169, E-mail: joness@up.edu. *Application contact:* Allison Able, Graduate Program Coordinator, 503-943-7107, Fax: 503-943-7315, E-mail: able@up.edu.
Website: http://engineering.up.edu/default.aspx?cid-6464&pid-2432.

University of Puerto Rico, Mayagüez Campus, Graduate Studies, College of Engineering, Department of Civil Engineering and Surveying, Mayagüez, PR 00681-9000. Offers civil engineering (ME, MS, PhD). Part-time programs available. *Faculty:* 30 full-time (5 women), 2 part-time/adjunct (1 woman). *Students:* 133 full-time (40 women), 8 part-time (1 woman). 55 applicants, 82% accepted, 31 enrolled. In 2014, 33 master's, 3 doctorates awarded. *Degree requirements:* For master's, comprehensive exam, thesis (MS); for doctorate, one foreign language, thesis/dissertation. *Entrance requirements:* For master's, proficiency in English and Spanish, BS in civil engineering or its equivalent; for doctorate, proficiency in English and Spanish. *Application deadline:* For fall admission, 2/15 for domestic and international students; for spring admission, 9/15 for domestic and international students. Applications are processed on a rolling basis. Application fee: $25. *Expenses: Tuition, area resident:* Full-time $2466; part-time $822 per credit. *International tuition:* $6371 full-time. *Required fees:* $1095; $1095 per year. Tuition and fees vary according to course level, course load and reciprocity agreements. *Financial support:* In 2014–15, 101 students received support, including 64 research assistantships (averaging $8,648 per year), 40 teaching assistantships (averaging $5,650 per year); fellowships with full tuition reimbursements available, Federal Work-Study, institutionally sponsored loans, and unspecified assistantships also available. *Faculty research:* Structural design, concrete structure, finite elements, dynamic analysis, transportation, soils. *Unit head:* Prof. Ismael Pagan Trinidad, Chairperson, 787-832-4040 Ext. 3434, Fax: 787-833-8260, E-mail: ismael.pagan@upr.edu. *Application contact:* Dr. Ricardo Lopez, Associate Director, 787-832-4040 Ext. 2178, Fax: 787-833-8260, E-mail: rilopez@upr.edu.
Website: http://civil.uprm.edu.

University of Rhode Island, Graduate School, College of Engineering, Department of Civil and Environmental Engineering, Kingston, RI 02881. Offers MS, PhD. Part-time programs available. *Faculty:* 9 full-time (3 women), 2 part-time/adjunct (0 women). *Students:* 19 full-time (5 women), 12 part-time (4 women); includes 4 minority (1 Black or African American, non-Hispanic/Latino; 3 Hispanic/Latino), 11 international. In 2014, 27 master's, 3 doctorates awarded. *Degree requirements:* For master's, comprehensive exam (for some programs), thesis optional; for doctorate, comprehensive exam, thesis/dissertation. *Entrance requirements:* For master's and doctorate, 2 letters of recommendation. Additional exam requirements/recommendations for international students: Required—TOEFL (minimum score 550 paper-based). *Application deadline:* For fall admission, 7/15 for domestic students, 2/1 for international students; for spring admission, 11/15 for domestic students, 7/15 for international students. Application fee: $65. Electronic applications accepted. *Expenses:* Tuition, state resident: full-time $11,532; part-time $641 per credit. Tuition, nonresident: full-time $23,606; part-time $1311 per credit. *Required fees:* $1442; $39 per credit. $35 per semester. One-time fee: $155. *Financial support:* In 2014–15, 5 research assistantships with full and partial tuition reimbursements (averaging $10,381 per year), 3 teaching assistantships with full and partial tuition reimbursements (averaging $10,131 per year) were awarded. Financial award application deadline: 7/15; financial award applicants required to submit FAFSA. *Faculty research:* Industrial waste treatment, structural health monitoring, traffic and transit system operations, computational mechanics, engineering materials design. *Total annual research expenditures:* $300,577. *Unit head:* Dr. George E. Tsiatas, Chair, 401-874-5117, Fax: 401-874-2786, E-mail: gt@uri.edu. *Application contact:* Graduate Admissions, 401-874-2872, E-mail: gradadm@etal.uri.edu.
Website: http://www.uri.edu/cve/.

University of Saskatchewan, College of Graduate Studies and Research, College of Engineering, Civil and Geological Engineering Program, Saskatoon, SK S7N 5A9, Canada. Offers M Eng, M Sc, PhD. Part-time programs available. *Degree requirements:* For master's, thesis (for some programs), 30 credits (for M Eng); thesis and 12 credits (for MS); for doctorate, comprehensive exam, thesis/dissertation, qualifying exam, 18 credits. *Entrance requirements:* For master's, GRE, minimum GPA of 5.0 on an 8.0 scale; for doctorate, GRE. Additional exam requirements/recommendations for international students: Required—TOEFL, TOEFL (minimum iBT score of 80), IELTS (6.5), CanTEST (4.5), or PTE (59). Electronic applications accepted. *Faculty research:* Geotechnical/geo-environmental engineering, structural engineering, water resources engineering, civil engineering materials, environmental/sanitary engineering, hydrogeology, rock mechanics and mining, transportation engineering.

University of South Alabama, College of Engineering, Department of Civil Engineering, Mobile, AL 36688. Offers MSCE. *Faculty:* 6 full-time (0 women). *Students:* 16 full-time (5 women), 6 part-time (0 women); includes 3 minority (1 Black or African American, non-Hispanic/Latino; 2 Hispanic/Latino), 7 international. Average age 29. 40 applicants, 43% accepted, 9 enrolled. In 2014, 9 master's awarded. *Degree requirements:* For master's, comprehensive exam, thesis or project. *Entrance requirements:* For master's, GRE, minimum GPA of 3.0, three references, portfolio. Additional exam requirements/recommendations for international students: Required—TOEFL (minimum score 525 paper-based; 71 iBT). *Application deadline:* For fall admission, 7/15 priority date for domestic students, 6/15 priority date for international students; for spring admission, 12/1 priority date for domestic students, 11/1 priority date for international students. Applications are processed on a rolling basis. Application fee: $35. Electronic applications accepted. *Expenses:* Expenses: Contact institution. *Financial support:* Fellowships, research assistantships, teaching assistantships, career-related internships or fieldwork, Federal Work-Study, institutionally sponsored loans, scholarships/grants, and unspecified assistantships available. Support available to part-time students. Financial award application deadline: 5/31; financial award applicants required to submit FAFSA. *Faculty research:* Roadway runoff treatment, roundabout operational guidelines, multimodal freight networks, velocity and bathymetry mapping, pile driving vibration monitoring. *Unit head:* Dr. Kevin White, Department Chair, 251-460-6174, Fax: 251-461-1400, E-mail: kwhite@southalabama.edu. *Application contact:* Dr. Thomas G. Thomas, Jr., Graduate Studies, College of Engineering, 251-460-6140, Fax: 251-460-6343, E-mail: engineering@alabama.edu.
Website: http://www.southalabama.edu/colleges/engineering/ce/index.html.

University of South Carolina, The Graduate School, College of Engineering and Computing, Department of Civil and Environmental Engineering, Columbia, SC 29208. Offers civil engineering (ME, MS, PhD). Part-time and evening/weekend programs available. Postbaccalaureate distance learning degree programs offered (minimal on-campus study). *Degree requirements:* For master's, comprehensive exam, thesis (for some programs); for doctorate, thesis/dissertation. *Entrance requirements:* For master's and doctorate, GRE General Test, 2 letters of recommendation. Additional exam requirements/recommendations for international students: Required—TOEFL (minimum score 570 paper-based). Electronic applications accepted. *Faculty research:* Structures, water resources.

University of Southern California, Graduate School, Viterbi School of Engineering, Sonny Astani Department of Civil Engineering, Los Angeles, CA 90089. Offers applied mechanics (MS); civil engineering (MS, PhD); computer-aided engineering (ME, Graduate Certificate); construction management (MCM); engineering technology commercialization (Graduate Certificate); environmental engineering (MS, PhD); environmental quality management (ME); structural design (ME); sustainable cities (Graduate Certificate); transportation systems (MS, Graduate Certificate); water and waste management (MS). Part-time and evening/weekend programs available. Terminal master's awarded for partial completion of doctoral program. *Degree requirements:* For master's, thesis optional; for doctorate, thesis/dissertation. *Entrance requirements:* For master's and doctorate, GRE General Test. Additional exam requirements/recommendations for international students: Recommended—TOEFL. Electronic applications accepted. *Faculty research:* Geotechnical engineering, transportation engineering, structural engineering, construction management, environmental engineering, water resources.

University of South Florida, College of Engineering, Department of Civil and Environmental Engineering, Tampa, FL 33620-9951. Offers civil engineering (MCE, MSCE, PhD), including environmental engineering (MSES, PhD), geotechnical engineering (MCE, MSCE, MSES, PhD), interdisciplinary transportation (MSCE), materials engineering and science, structural engineering, transportation engineering, water resources; engineering science (MSES), including environmental engineering (MSES, PhD), geotechnical engineering (MCE, MSCE, MSES, PhD); environmental engineering (MEVE, MSEV, PhD). Part-time programs available. *Faculty:* 19 full-time (5 women). *Students:* 97 full-time (35 women), 83 part-time (25 women); includes 41 minority (6 Black or African American, non-Hispanic/Latino; 1 American Indian or Alaska Native, non-Hispanic/Latino; 3 Asian, non-Hispanic/Latino; 25 Hispanic/Latino; 6 Two or more races, non-Hispanic/Latino), 39 international. Average age 30. 229 applicants, 51% accepted, 43 enrolled. In 2014, 68 master's, 9 doctorates awarded. Terminal master's awarded for partial completion of doctoral program. *Degree requirements:* For master's, comprehensive exam, thesis (for some programs); for doctorate, comprehensive exam, thesis/dissertation. *Entrance requirements:* For master's, GRE General Test (preferred minimum scores of 20th percentile verbal, 50th percentile

quantitative, and 10th percentile in analytical writing), minimum GPA of 3.0 in major, two letters of reference, statement of purpose; for doctorate, GRE General Test (preferred minimum scores of 45th percentile verbal, 65th percentile quantitative, and 50th percentile in analytical writing), three letters of recommendation, statement of purpose, resume. Additional exam requirements/recommendations for international students: Required—TOEFL (minimum score 550 paper-based; 79 iBT) or IELTS (minimum score 6.5). *Application deadline:* For fall admission, 2/15 for domestic students, 1/2 priority date for international students; for spring admission, 10/15 for domestic students, 6/1 priority date for international students. Application fee: $30. Electronic applications accepted. *Financial support:* In 2014–15, 65 students received support, including 44 research assistantships (averaging $14,123 per year), 21 teaching assistantships with tuition reimbursements available (averaging $15,329 per year). *Faculty research:* Environmental and water resources engineering, geotechnics and geoenvironmental systems, structures and materials systems, transportation systems. *Total annual research expenditures:* $3.3 million. *Unit head:* Dr. Manjriker Gunaratne, Professor and Department Chair, 813-974-5818, Fax: 813-974-2957, E-mail: gunaratn@usf.edu. *Application contact:* Dr. Sarina J. Ergas, Professor and Graduate Program Coordinator, 813-974-1119, Fax: 813-974-2957, E-mail: sergas@usf.edu.
Website: http://ce.eng.usf.edu/.

University of South Florida, University College/Distance Education, Tampa, FL 33620-9951. *Unit head:* Kathy Barnes, Interdisciplinary Programs Coordinator, 813-974-8031, Fax: 813-974-7061, E-mail: barnesk@usf.edu. *Application contact:* Karen Tylinski, Metro Initiatives, 813-974-9943, Fax: 813-974-7061, E-mail: ktylinsk@usf.edu.
Website: http://www.usf.edu/innovative-education/.

The University of Tennessee, Graduate School, College of Engineering, Department of Civil and Environmental Engineering, Program in Civil Engineering, Knoxville, TN 37996. Offers MS, PhD, MS/MBA. Part-time programs available. Postbaccalaureate distance learning degree programs offered (minimal on-campus study). *Faculty:* 18 full-time (3 women), 19 part-time/adjunct (3 women). *Students:* 74 full-time (19 women), 48 part-time (9 women); includes 14 minority (6 Black or African American, non-Hispanic/Latino; 2 Asian, non-Hispanic/Latino; 1 Hispanic/Latino; 5 Two or more races, non-Hispanic/Latino), 33 international. Average age 29. 173 applicants, 52% accepted, 61 enrolled. In 2014, 38 master's, 13 doctorates awarded. *Degree requirements:* For master's, thesis or alternative; for doctorate, comprehensive exam, thesis/dissertation. *Entrance requirements:* For master's, GRE General Test (for MS students pursuing research thesis), minimum GPA of 2.7 (for U.S. degree holders), 3.0 (for international degree holders); 3 references; statement of purpose; resume; for doctorate, GRE General Test (for all PhD candidates), minimum GPA of 3.0 on previous graduate course work; 3 references; statement of purpose; resume. Additional exam requirements/recommendations for international students: Required—TOEFL (minimum score 550 paper-based). *Application deadline:* For fall admission, 2/1 priority date for domestic and international students; for spring admission, 6/15 for domestic and international students. Applications are processed on a rolling basis. Application fee: $35. Electronic applications accepted. *Financial support:* In 2014–15, 61 students received support, including 21 research assistantships with full tuition reimbursements available (averaging $21,318 per year), 31 teaching assistantships with full tuition reimbursements available (averaging $19,782 per year); fellowships, career-related internships or fieldwork, Federal Work-Study, institutionally sponsored loans, health care benefits, and unspecified assistantships also available. Financial award application deadline: 2/1; financial award applicants required to submit FAFSA. *Faculty research:* Multi-functional composites and mechanics of materials, geohydrologic investigations and monitoring, structures and vibrations, geotechnical and earthquake engineering, transportation system planning and design. *Unit head:* Dr. Greg Reed, Head, 865-974-2503, Fax: 865-974-2669, E-mail: gdreed@utk.edu. *Application contact:* Dr. Chris Cox, Associate Head, 865-974-7729, Fax: 865-974-2355, E-mail: ccox9@utk.edu.
Website: http://www.engr.utk.edu/civil.

The University of Tennessee at Chattanooga, Program in Engineering, Chattanooga, TN 37403. Offers chemical engineering (MS Engr); civil engineering (MS Engr); computational engineering (MS Engr); electrical engineering (MS Engr); industrial engineering (MS Engr); mechanical engineering (MS Engr). Part-time and evening/weekend programs available. *Faculty:* 20 full-time (3 women), 3 part-time/adjunct (0 women). *Students:* 42 full-time (7 women), 41 part-time (5 women); includes 6 minority (2 Black or African American, non-Hispanic/Latino; 1 Asian, non-Hispanic/Latino; 2 Hispanic/Latino; 1 Two or more races, non-Hispanic/Latino), 30 international. Average age 29. 96 applicants, 32% accepted, 17 enrolled. In 2014, 29 master's awarded. *Degree requirements:* For master's, comprehensive exam, thesis or alternative, engineering project. *Entrance requirements:* For master's, GRE General Test, minimum undergraduate GPA of 2.5 or 3.0 in last 30 hours of coursework. Additional exam requirements/recommendations for international students: Required—TOEFL (minimum score 550 paper-based; 79 iBT), IELTS (minimum score 6). *Application deadline:* For fall admission, 6/13 priority date for domestic students, 6/1 for international students; for spring admission, 10/15 priority date for domestic students, 10/1 for international students. Applications are processed on a rolling basis. Application fee: $30 ($35 for international students). Electronic applications accepted. *Expenses:* Tuition, state resident: full-time $7708; part-time $428 per credit hour. Tuition, nonresident: full-time $23,826; part-time $1323 per credit hour. *Required fees:* $1708; $252 per credit hour. *Financial support:* In 2014–15, 24 research assistantships with tuition reimbursements (averaging $7,669 per year), 7 teaching assistantships with tuition reimbursements (averaging $5,735 per year) were awarded; career-related internships or fieldwork, scholarships/grants, and unspecified assistantships also available. Support available to part-time students. *Faculty research:* Quality control and reliability engineering, financial management, thermal science, energy conservation, structural analysis. *Total annual research expenditures:* $1.6 million. *Unit head:* Dr. William Sutton, Dean, 423-425-2256, Fax: 423-425-5229, E-mail: will-sutton@utc.edu. *Application contact:* Dr. J. Randy Walker, Interim Dean of Graduate Studies, 423-425-4478, Fax: 423-425-5223, E-mail: randy-walker@utc.edu.
Website: http://www.utc.edu/Departments/engrcs/ms_engr.php.

The University of Texas at Arlington, Graduate School, College of Engineering, Department of Civil Engineering, Arlington, TX 76019. Offers civil engineering (M Engr, MS, PhD); construction management (MCM). Part-time and evening/weekend programs available. Postbaccalaureate distance learning degree programs offered (minimal on-campus study). Terminal master's awarded for partial completion of doctoral program. *Degree requirements:* For master's, comprehensive exam, thesis (for some programs), oral and written exams; for doctorate, comprehensive exam, thesis/dissertation, oral and written defense of dissertation. *Entrance requirements:* For master's, GRE General Test, minimum GPA of 3.0 in last 60 hours of undergraduate course work; for doctorate, GRE General Test, minimum GPA of 3.5. Additional exam requirements/recommendations for international students: Required—TOEFL. Electronic applications accepted. *Faculty research:* Environmental and water resources structures, geotechnical, transportation.

The University of Texas at Austin, Graduate School, Cockrell School of Engineering, Department of Civil, Architectural and Environmental Engineering, Austin, TX 78712-1111. Offers architectural engineering (MSE); civil engineering (MS, PhD); environmental and water resources engineering (MS, PhD). Part-time programs available. *Degree requirements:* For master's, thesis or alternative; for doctorate, comprehensive exam, thesis/dissertation. *Entrance requirements:* For master's and doctorate, GRE General Test. Additional exam requirements/recommendations for international students: Required—TOEFL. Electronic applications accepted. *Faculty research:* Geotechnical structural engineering, transportation engineering, construction engineering/project management.

The University of Texas at El Paso, Graduate School, College of Engineering, Department of Civil Engineering, El Paso, TX 79968-0001. Offers civil engineering (MS, PhD); construction management (MS, Certificate); environmental engineering (MEENE, MSENE). Part-time and evening/weekend programs available. *Degree requirements:* For master's, comprehensive exam, thesis optional; for doctorate, comprehensive exam, thesis/dissertation. *Entrance requirements:* For master's, GRE, minimum GPA of 3.0; for doctorate, GRE. Additional exam requirements/recommendations for international students: Required—TOEFL. Electronic applications accepted. *Faculty research:* Non-destructive testing for geotechnical and pavement applications, transportation systems, wastewater treatment systems, air quality, linear and non-linear modeling of structures, structural reliability.

The University of Texas at San Antonio, College of Engineering, Department of Civil and Environmental Engineering, San Antonio, TX 78249. Offers civil engineering (MCE, MSCE); environmental science and engineering (PhD). Part-time programs available. *Faculty:* 12 full-time (2 women), 1 part-time/adjunct (0 women). *Students:* 28 full-time (8 women), 27 part-time (6 women); includes 12 minority (3 Black or African American, non-Hispanic/Latino; 2 Asian, non-Hispanic/Latino; 6 Hispanic/Latino; 1 Two or more races, non-Hispanic/Latino), 24 international. Average age 30. 66 applicants, 74% accepted, 21 enrolled. In 2014, 21 master's, 5 doctorates awarded. *Degree requirements:* For master's, comprehensive exam, thesis (for some programs); for doctorate, comprehensive exam, thesis/dissertation, written qualifying exam, dissertation proposal. *Entrance requirements:* For master's, GRE General Test, BS in civil engineering or related field from accredited institution, statement of research/specialization interest, favorable recommendation by the Civil Engineering Master's Program Admissions Committee; for doctorate, GRE, BS and MS from accredited institution, minimum GPA of 3.0 in upper-division and graduate courses, three letters of recommendation, letter of research interest, resume/curriculum vitae. Additional exam requirements/recommendations for international students: Required—TOEFL (minimum score 550 paper-based; 79 iBT), IELTS (minimum score 6.5). *Application deadline:* For fall admission, 7/1 for domestic students, 4/1 for international students; for spring admission, 11/1 for domestic students, 9/1 for international students. Application fee: $45 ($80 for international students). Electronic applications accepted. *Expenses:* Expenses: Contact institution. *Financial support:* In 2014–15, 42 students received support, including 28 research assistantships with full tuition reimbursements available (averaging $20,000 per year), 14 teaching assistantships (averaging $4,680 per year); scholarships/grants also available. Financial award application deadline: 2/1. *Faculty research:* Structures, application of geographic information systems in water resources, geotechnical engineering, pavement traffic loading, hydrogeology. *Total annual research expenditures:* $774,040. *Unit head:* Dr. Heather Shipley, Department Chair, 210-458-7517, Fax: 210-458-6475, E-mail: heather.shipley@utsa.edu. *Application contact:* Jessica Perez, Administrative Associate I, 210-458-4428, Fax: 210-458-7469, E-mail: jessica.perez@utsa.edu.
Website: http://engineering.utsa.edu/CE/.

The University of Texas at Tyler, College of Engineering and Computer Science, Department of Civil Engineering, Tyler, TX 75799-0001. Offers environmental engineering (MS); industrial safety (MS); structural engineering (MS); transportation engineering (MS); water resources engineering (MS). Part-time and evening/weekend programs available. *Degree requirements:* For master's, thesis optional. *Entrance requirements:* For master's, GRE General Test, bachelor's degree in engineering, associated science degree. Additional exam requirements/recommendations for international students: Required—TOEFL. *Faculty research:* Non-destructive strength testing, indoor air quality, transportation routing and signaling, pavement replacement criteria, flood water routing, construction and long-term behavior of innovative geotechnical foundation and embankment construction used in highway construction, engineering education.

The University of Toledo, College of Graduate Studies, College of Engineering, Department of Civil Engineering, Toledo, OH 43606-3390. Offers MS, PhD. Part-time programs available. Terminal master's awarded for partial completion of doctoral program. *Degree requirements:* For master's, thesis or alternative; for doctorate, thesis/dissertation, qualifying exam. *Entrance requirements:* For master's, GRE General Test, minimum GPA of 3.0; for doctorate, GRE General Test, minimum GPA of 3.3. Additional exam requirements/recommendations for international students: Required—TOEFL (minimum score 550 paper-based; 80 iBT). Electronic applications accepted. *Faculty research:* Environmental modeling, soil/pavement interaction, structural mechanics, earthquakes, transportation engineering.

University of Toronto, School of Graduate Studies, Faculty of Applied Science and Engineering, Department of Civil Engineering, Toronto, ON M5S 2J7, Canada. Offers M Eng, MA Sc, PhD. Part-time programs available. *Degree requirements:* For master's, thesis and oral presentation (MA Sc); for doctorate, thesis/dissertation, oral presentation. *Entrance requirements:* For master's, bachelor's degree in civil engineering, proficiency in computer usage, minimum B average in final 2 years, 3 letters of reference; for doctorate, proficiency in computer usage, minimum B average in final 2 years, 3 letters of reference. Additional exam requirements/recommendations for international students: Required—TOEFL (minimum score 580 paper-based; 93 iBT). Electronic applications accepted.

University of Utah, Graduate School, College of Engineering, Department of Civil and Environmental Engineering, Salt Lake City, UT 84112. Offers civil and environmental engineering (MS, PhD); environmental engineering (PhD); nuclear engineering (MS, PhD). Part-time programs available. *Faculty:* 20 full-time (7 women), 16 part-time/adjunct (1 woman). *Students:* 89 full-time (25 women), 40 part-time (8 women); includes 7 minority (1 Black or African American, non-Hispanic/Latino; 2 Asian, non-Hispanic/Latino; 4 Two or more races, non-Hispanic/Latino), 54 international. Average age 30. 121 applicants, 57% accepted, 21 enrolled. In 2014, 36 master's, 8 doctorates awarded. Terminal master's awarded for partial completion of doctoral program. *Degree requirements:* For master's, comprehensive exam (for some programs), thesis (for some programs); for doctorate, comprehensive exam, thesis/dissertation, departmental qualifying exam, preliminary exam. *Entrance requirements:* For master's and doctorate, GRE General Test, minimum GPA of 3.0. Additional exam requirements/recommendations for international students: Required—TOEFL (minimum score 550 paper-based; 80 iBT). *Application deadline:* For fall admission, 1/15 for domestic students, 12/15 for international students; for spring admission, 10/1 for domestic and international students. Applications are processed on a rolling basis. Application fee: $10 ($25 for international students). Electronic applications accepted. *Expenses:* Expenses: Contact institution. *Financial support:* In 2014–15, 62 students received support, including 2 fellowships with full tuition reimbursements available (averaging $15,000 per year), 45 research assistantships with full tuition reimbursements available (averaging $21,068 per year), 15 teaching assistantships with full tuition reimbursements available (averaging $21,068 per year); career-related internships or fieldwork, Federal Work-Study, institutionally sponsored loans, scholarships/grants, traineeships, health care benefits, tuition waivers (full and partial), and unspecified assistantships also available. Support available to part-time students. Financial award application deadline: 12/15; financial award applicants required to submit FAFSA. *Faculty research:* Structural engineering, geotechnical engineering, transportation engineering, environmental engineering, water resources. *Total annual research expenditures:* $14.1 million. *Unit head:* Dr. Michael Barber, Chair, 801-581-6931, Fax: 801-585-5477, E-mail: barber@civil.utah.edu. *Application contact:* Bonnie Ogden, Academic Advisor, 801-581-6678, Fax: 801-585-5477, E-mail: bonnie.ogden@utah.edu. Website: http://www.civil.utah.edu.

University of Vermont, Graduate College, College of Engineering and Mathematics, Department of Civil and Environmental Engineering, Burlington, VT 05405. Offers MS, PhD. *Degree requirements:* For master's, thesis or alternative; for doctorate, thesis/dissertation. *Entrance requirements:* For master's and doctorate, GRE General Test. Additional exam requirements/recommendations for international students: Required—TOEFL (minimum score 550 paper-based; 80 iBT). Electronic applications accepted.

University of Virginia, School of Engineering and Applied Science, Department of Civil and Environmental Engineering, Charlottesville, VA 22903. Offers ME, MS, PhD. Part-time programs available. Postbaccalaureate distance learning degree programs offered (no on-campus study). *Faculty:* 13 full-time (2 women), 1 part-time/adjunct (0 women). *Students:* 49 full-time (18 women), 3 part-time (1 woman); includes 3 minority (1 Black or African American, non-Hispanic/Latino; 1 Asian, non-Hispanic/Latino; 1 Two or more races, non-Hispanic/Latino), 21 international. Average age 27. 112 applicants, 39% accepted, 18 enrolled. In 2014, 16 master's, 10 doctorates awarded. Terminal master's awarded for partial completion of doctoral program. *Degree requirements:* For master's, thesis (for some programs); for doctorate, comprehensive exam, thesis/dissertation. *Entrance requirements:* For master's and doctorate, GRE General Test, 3 letters of recommendation. Additional exam requirements/recommendations for international students: Required—TOEFL (minimum score 600 paper-based; 90 iBT), IELTS (minimum score 7). *Application deadline:* For fall admission, 8/1 for domestic students, 4/1 for international students; for winter admission, 12/1 for domestic students, 8/1 for international students; for spring admission, 5/1 for domestic students, 1/1 for international students. Applications are processed on a rolling basis. Application fee: $60. Electronic applications accepted. *Expenses:* Tuition, state resident: full-time $14,164; part-time $349 per credit hour. Tuition, nonresident: full-time $23,722; part-time $1300 per credit hour. *Required fees:* $2514. *Financial support:* Fellowships with full tuition reimbursements, research assistantships with full tuition reimbursements, and teaching assistantships with full tuition reimbursements available. Financial award application deadline: 1/15. *Faculty research:* Groundwater, surface water, traffic engineering, composite materials. *Unit head:* Brian L. Smith, Chair, 434-924-7464, Fax: 434-982-2951, E-mail: civil@virginia.edu. *Application contact:* Graduate Program Coordinator, 434-924-7464, Fax: 434-982-2951, E-mail: civil@virginia.edu. Website: http://www.ce.virginia.edu/.

University of Washington, Graduate School, College of Engineering, Department of Civil and Environmental Engineering, Seattle, WA 98195-2700. Offers civil engineering (PhD); construction engineering (MSCE); environmental engineering (MSCE, PhD); hydrology, water resources, and environmental fluid mechanics (MSCE, PhD); structural and geotechnical engineering and mechanics (MSCE, PhD); transportation and construction engineering (PhD); transportation engineering (MSCE). Part-time programs available. Postbaccalaureate distance learning degree programs offered (no on-campus study). *Faculty:* 35 full-time (9 women). *Students:* 220 full-time (81 women), 147 part-time (50 women); includes 61 minority (9 Black or African American, non-Hispanic/Latino; 2 American Indian or Alaska Native, non-Hispanic/Latino; 34 Asian, non-Hispanic/Latino; 14 Hispanic/Latino; 2 Native Hawaiian or other Pacific Islander, non-Hispanic/Latino), 91 international. Average age 28. 901 applicants, 49% accepted, 162 enrolled. In 2014, 110 master's, 12 doctorates awarded. Terminal master's awarded for partial completion of doctoral program. *Degree requirements:* For master's, thesis (for some programs); for doctorate, comprehensive exam, thesis/dissertation, general, qualifying, and final exams; completion of degree within 10 years. *Entrance requirements:* For master's, GRE General Test, minimum GPA of 3.0, statement of purpose, letters of recommendation, transcripts; for doctorate, GRE General Test, minimum GPA of 3.5, statement of purpose, letters of recommendation, transcripts. Additional exam requirements/recommendations for international students: Required—TOEFL (minimum score 580 paper-based; 92 iBT); Recommended—IELTS (minimum score 7). *Application deadline:* For fall admission, 12/15 for domestic and international students. Applications are processed on a rolling basis. Application fee: $85. Electronic applications accepted. *Expenses:* Expenses: Contact institution. *Financial support:* In 2014–15, 179 students received support, including 41 fellowships with full and partial tuition reimbursements available, 77 research assistantships with full tuition reimbursements available, 58 teaching assistantships with full tuition reimbursements available; scholarships/grants also available. Financial award application deadline: 1/10; financial award applicants required to submit FAFSA. *Faculty research:* Structural and geotechnical engineering, transportation and construction engineering, water and environmental engineering. *Total annual research expenditures:* $14.1 million. *Unit head:* Dr. Gregory R. Miller, Professor/Chair, 206-543-0350, Fax: 206-543-1543, E-mail: gmiller@uw.edu. *Application contact:* Lorna Latal, Graduate Adviser, 206-543-2574, Fax: 206-543-1543, E-mail: llatal@u.washington.edu. Website: http://www.ce.washington.edu/.

University of Waterloo, Graduate Studies, Faculty of Engineering, Department of Civil and Environmental Engineering, Waterloo, ON N2L 3G1, Canada. Offers M Eng, MA Sc, PhD. Part-time programs available. *Degree requirements:* For master's, research paper or thesis; for doctorate, comprehensive exam, thesis/dissertation. *Entrance requirements:* For master's, honors degree, minimum B average; for doctorate, master's degree, minimum A- average. Additional exam requirements/recommendations for international students: Required—TOEFL, TWE. Electronic applications accepted. *Faculty research:* Water resources, structures, construction management, transportation, geotechnical engineering.

The University of Western Ontario, Faculty of Graduate Studies, Physical Sciences Division, Faculty of Engineering, London, ON N6A 5B8, Canada. Offers chemical and biochemical engineering (ME Sc, PhD); civil and environmental engineering (M Eng, ME Sc, PhD); electrical and computer engineering (M Eng, ME Sc, PhD); mechanical and materials engineering (M Eng, ME Sc, PhD). Part-time programs available. Terminal master's awarded for partial completion of doctoral program. *Degree requirements:* For master's, thesis; for doctorate, thesis/dissertation. *Entrance requirements:* For master's, minimum B average; for doctorate, minimum B+ average. *Faculty research:* Wind, geotechnical, chemical reactor engineering, applied electrostatics, biochemical engineering.

University of Windsor, Faculty of Graduate Studies, Faculty of Engineering, Department of Civil and Environmental Engineering, Windsor, ON N9B 3P4, Canada. Offers civil engineering (M Eng, MA Sc, PhD); environmental engineering (M Eng, MA Sc, PhD). Part-time programs available. *Degree requirements:* For master's, thesis; for doctorate, comprehensive exam, thesis/dissertation. *Entrance requirements:* For master's, minimum B average; for doctorate, master's degree, minimum A average. Additional exam requirements/recommendations for international students: Required—TOEFL (minimum score 580 paper-based). Electronic applications accepted. *Faculty research:* Odors: sampling, measurement, control; drinking water disinfection, hydrocarbon contaminated soil remediation, structural dynamics, numerical simulation of piezoelectric materials.

University of Wisconsin–Madison, Graduate School, College of Engineering, Department of Civil and Environmental Engineering, Madison, WI 53706. Offers MS, PhD. Part-time programs available. Terminal master's awarded for partial completion of doctoral program. *Degree requirements:* For master's, thesis or alternative; for doctorate, thesis/dissertation, preliminary exam, qualifying exams. *Entrance requirements:* For master's and doctorate, GRE General Test, minimum GPA of 3.0 for last 60 credits of course work. Additional exam requirements/recommendations for international students: Required—TOEFL (minimum score 550 paper-based; 92 iBT). Electronic applications accepted. *Expenses:* Tuition, state resident: full-time $10,723; part-time $745 per credit. Tuition, nonresident: full-time $24,054; part-time $1578 per credit. *Required fees:* $374 per semester. Tuition and fees vary according to course load, program and reciprocity agreements. *Faculty research:* Environmental geotechnics and soil mechanics, design and analysis of structures, traffic engineering and intelligent transport systems, industrial pollution control, hydrological monitoring.

University of Wisconsin–Milwaukee, Graduate School, College of Engineering and Applied Science, Program in Engineering, Milwaukee, WI 53201-0413. Offers civil engineering (MS); electrical and computer engineering (MS); energy engineering (Certificate); engineering (PhD); engineering management (MS); engineering mechanics (MS); ergonomics (Certificate); industrial and management engineering (MS); manufacturing engineering (MS); materials engineering (MS); mechanical engineering (MS); MUP/MS. Part-time programs available. *Degree requirements:* For master's, comprehensive exam (for some programs), thesis or alternative; for doctorate, comprehensive exam, thesis/dissertation, internship. *Entrance requirements:* For master's, GRE, minimum GPA of 2.75; for doctorate, GRE, minimum GPA of 3.5. Additional exam requirements/recommendations for international students: Required—TOEFL (minimum score 550 paper-based; 79 iBT), IELTS (minimum score 6.5).

University of Wyoming, College of Engineering and Applied Sciences, Department of Civil and Architectural Engineering, Program in Civil Engineering, Laramie, WY 82071. Offers MS, PhD. Part-time programs available. Terminal master's awarded for partial completion of doctoral program. *Degree requirements:* For master's, thesis (for some programs); for doctorate, variable foreign language requirement, comprehensive exam, thesis/dissertation. *Entrance requirements:* For master's, GRE General Test (minimum score 900), minimum GPA of 3.0; for doctorate, GRE General Test (minimum score: 1000), minimum GPA of 3.0. Additional exam requirements/recommendations for international students: Required—TOEFL. Electronic applications accepted. *Faculty research:* Structures, water, resources, geotechnical, transportation.

Utah State University, School of Graduate Studies, College of Engineering, Department of Civil and Environmental Engineering, Logan, UT 84322. Offers ME, MS, PhD, CE. *Degree requirements:* For master's, thesis (for some programs); for doctorate, thesis/dissertation. *Entrance requirements:* For master's and doctorate, GRE General Test, minimum GPA of 3.0. Additional exam requirements/recommendations for international students: Required—TOEFL. Electronic applications accepted. *Faculty research:* Hazardous waste treatment, large space structures, river basin management, earthquake engineering, environmental impact.

Vanderbilt University, School of Engineering, Department of Civil and Environmental Engineering, Program in Civil Engineering, Nashville, TN 37240-1001. Offers M Eng, MS, PhD. MS and PhD offered through the Graduate School. Part-time programs available. Terminal master's awarded for partial completion of doctoral program. *Degree requirements:* For master's, thesis; for doctorate, thesis/dissertation. *Entrance requirements:* For master's and doctorate, GRE General Test. Additional exam requirements/recommendations for international students: Required—TOEFL. Electronic applications accepted. *Expenses: Tuition:* Full-time $42,768; part-time $1782 per credit hour. *Required fees:* $422. One-time fee: $30 full-time. *Faculty research:* Structural mechanics, finite element analysis, urban transportation, hazardous material transport.

Villanova University, College of Engineering, Department of Civil and Environmental Engineering, Program in Civil Engineering, Villanova, PA 19085-1699. Offers MSCE. Part-time and evening/weekend programs available. *Degree requirements:* For master's, thesis optional. *Entrance requirements:* For master's, GRE General Test (for applicants with degrees from foreign universities), minimum GPA of 3.0. Additional exam requirements/recommendations for international students: Required—TOEFL (minimum score 600 paper-based; 100 iBT). Electronic applications accepted. *Faculty research:* Bridge inspection, environment maintenance, economy and risk.

Virginia Polytechnic Institute and State University, Graduate School, College of Engineering, Blacksburg, VA 24061. Offers aerospace engineering (ME, MS, PhD); biological systems engineering (ME, MS, PhD); biomedical engineering (MS, PhD); chemical engineering (ME, MS, PhD); civil engineering (ME, MS, PhD); computer engineering (ME, MS, PhD); computer science (MS, PhD); electrical engineering (ME, PhD); engineering education (PhD); engineering mechanics (ME, MS, PhD); environmental engineering (MS); environmental science and engineering (MS); industrial and systems engineering (ME, MS, PhD); materials science and engineering (ME, MS, PhD); mechanical engineering (ME, MS, PhD); mining and minerals engineering (PhD); mining engineering (ME, MS); nuclear engineering (MS, PhD); ocean engineering (MS); systems engineering (ME, MS). *Accreditation:* ABET (one or more programs are accredited). *Faculty:* 356 full-time (60 women), 3 part-time/adjunct (1 woman). *Students:* 1,700 full-time (398 women), 345 part-time (58 women); includes 213 minority (43 Black or African American, non-Hispanic/Latino; 1 American Indian or Alaska Native, non-Hispanic/Latino; 87 Asian, non-Hispanic/Latino; 58 Hispanic/Latino; 1 Native Hawaiian or other Pacific Islander, non-Hispanic/Latino; 23 Two or more races, non-Hispanic/Latino), 1,079 international. Average age 27. 5,228 applicants, 18% accepted, 471 enrolled. In 2014, 438 master's, 211 doctorates awarded. *Degree requirements:* For master's, comprehensive exam (for some programs), thesis (for some programs); for doctorate, comprehensive exam (for some programs), thesis/dissertation (for some programs). *Entrance requirements:* For master's and doctorate, GRE/GMAT (may vary by department). Additional exam requirements/recommendations for international students: Required—TOEFL (minimum score 550 paper-based). *Application deadline:* For fall admission, 8/1 for domestic students, 4/1 for international students; for spring admission, 1/1 for domestic students, 9/1 for international students. Applications are processed on a rolling basis. Application fee: $75. Electronic applications accepted. *Expenses:* Tuition, state resident: full-time $11,656; part-time $647.50 per credit hour. Tuition, nonresident: full-time $23,351; part-time $1297.25 per credit hour. *Required fees:* $2533; $465.75 per semester. Tuition and fees vary according to course load, campus/location and program. *Financial support:* In 2014–15, 148 fellowships with full tuition reimbursements (averaging $8,031 per year), 855 research assistantships with full tuition reimbursements (averaging $22,855 per year), 288 teaching assistantships with full tuition reimbursements (averaging $20,291 per

year) were awarded. Financial award application deadline: 3/1; financial award applicants required to submit FAFSA. *Total annual research expenditures:* $90.5 million. *Unit head:* Dr. Richard C. Benson, Dean, 540-231-9752, Fax: 540-231-3031, E-mail: deaneng@vt.edu. *Application contact:* Linda Perkins, Executive Assistant, 540-231-9752, Fax: 540-231-3031, E-mail: lperkins@vt.edu.
Website: http://www.eng.vt.edu/.

Virginia Polytechnic Institute and State University, VT Online, Blacksburg, VA 24061. Offers advanced transportation systems (Certificate); aerospace engineering (MS); agricultural and life sciences (MSLFS); business information systems (Graduate Certificate); career and technical education (MS); civil engineering (MS); computer engineering (M Eng, MS); decision support systems (Graduate Certificate); eLearning leadership (MA); electrical engineering (M Eng, MS); engineering administration (MEA); environmental engineering (Certificate); environmental politics and policy (Graduate Certificate); environmental sciences and engineering (MS); foundations of political analysis (Graduate Certificate); health product risk management (Graduate Certificate); industrial and systems engineering (MS); information policy and society (Graduate Certificate); information security (Graduate Certificate); information technology (MIT); instructional technology (MA); integrative STEM education (MA Ed); liberal arts (Graduate Certificate); life sciences: health product risk management (MS); natural resources (MNR, Graduate Certificate); networking (Graduate Certificate); nonprofit and nongovernmental organization management (Graduate Certificate); ocean engineering (MS); political science (MA); security studies (Graduate Certificate); software development (Graduate Certificate). *Expenses:* Tuition, state resident: full-time $11,656; part-time $647.50 per credit hour. Tuition, nonresident: full-time $23,351; part-time $1297.25 per credit hour. *Required fees:* $2533; $465.75 per semester. Tuition and fees vary according to course load, campus/location and program.

Washington State University, Voiland College of Engineering and Architecture, Department of Civil and Environmental Engineering, Pullman, WA 99164-2910. Offers civil engineering (MS, PhD); environmental engineering (MS). MS programs also offered at Tri-Cities campus. Part-time programs available. *Faculty:* 38 full-time (7 women), 4 part-time/adjunct (1 woman). *Students:* 66 full-time (18 women), 13 part-time (7 women); includes 13 minority (3 Black or African American, non-Hispanic/Latino; 1 American Indian or Alaska Native, non-Hispanic/Latino; 5 Asian, non-Hispanic/Latino; 3 Hispanic/Latino; 1 Two or more races, non-Hispanic/Latino), 32 international. Average age 29. 135 applicants, 26% accepted, 18 enrolled. In 2014, 28 master's, 8 doctorates awarded. Terminal master's awarded for partial completion of doctoral program. *Degree requirements:* For master's, comprehensive exam (for some programs), thesis (for some programs), oral exam; for doctorate, comprehensive exam, thesis/dissertation, oral exam, written exam. *Entrance requirements:* For master's, minimum GPA of 3.0, 3 letters of recommendation, statement of purpose; for doctorate, minimum GPA of 3.4, 3 letters of recommendation, statement of purpose. Additional exam requirements/recommendations for international students: Required—TOEFL (minimum score 550 paper-based), IELTS. *Application deadline:* For fall admission, 2/1 for domestic students, 3/1 for international students; for spring admission, 9/1 for domestic students. Applications are processed on a rolling basis. Application fee: $75. Electronic applications accepted. *Expenses:* Tuition, state resident: full-time $11,768. Tuition, nonresident: full-time $25,200. *Required fees:* $960. Tuition and fees vary according to program. *Financial support:* In 2014–15, 62 students received support, including 4 fellowships with full tuition reimbursements available (averaging $22,000 per year), 27 research assistantships with full tuition reimbursements available (averaging $13,659 per year), 20 teaching assistantships with full tuition reimbursements available (averaging $14,135 per year); career-related internships or fieldwork, Federal Work-Study, and institutionally sponsored loans also available. Financial award application deadline: 4/1; financial award applicants required to submit FAFSA. *Faculty research:* Environmental engineering, water resources, structural engineering, geotechnical, transportation. *Total annual research expenditures:* $8.3 million. *Unit head:* Dr. Balasingam Muhunthan, Chair, 509-335-9578, Fax: 509-335-7632, E-mail: muhuntha@wsu.edu. *Application contact:* Ryan Lancaster, Graduate School Admissions, 509-335-2576, Fax: 509-335-7632, E-mail: ryan.lancaster@wsu.edu.
Website: http://www.ce.wsu.edu/.

Wayne State University, College of Engineering, Department of Civil and Environmental Engineering, Detroit, MI 48202. Offers civil engineering (MS). *Faculty:* 10 full-time (1 woman), 9 part-time/adjunct (0 women). *Students:* 61 full-time (17 women), 35 part-time (5 women); includes 9 minority (2 Black or African American, non-Hispanic/Latino; 6 Asian, non-Hispanic/Latino; 1 Hispanic/Latino), 40 international. Average age 29. 186 applicants, 48% accepted, 25 enrolled. In 2014, 26 master's, 4 doctorates awarded. *Degree requirements:* For master's, thesis optional; for doctorate, thesis/dissertation. *Entrance requirements:* For master's, BS in civil engineering from ABET-accredited institution with minimum GPA of 3.0; for doctorate, BS in civil engineering from ABET-accredited institution with minimum GPA of 3.2 and 3.4 last two years, or MS in civil engineering with minimum GPA of 3.5; letters of recommendation (for international applicants). Additional exam requirements/recommendations for international students: Required—TOEFL (minimum score 550 paper-based; 79 iBT), TWE (minimum score 5.5), Michigan English Language Assessment Battery (minimum score 85); Recommended—IELTS (minimum score 6.5). *Application deadline:* For fall admission, 6/1 priority date for domestic students, 5/1 priority date for international students; for winter admission, 10/1 priority date for domestic students, 9/1 priority date for international students; for spring admission, 2/1 priority date for domestic students, 1/1 priority date for international students. Applications are processed on a rolling basis. Application fee: $0. Electronic applications accepted. *Expenses:* Expenses: Contact institution. *Financial support:* In 2014–15, 29 students received support, including 1 fellowship with tuition reimbursement available (averaging $16,000 per year), 12 research assistantships with tuition reimbursements available (averaging $19,375 per year), 5 teaching assistantships with tuition reimbursements available (averaging $18,746 per year); scholarships/grants, health care benefits, and unspecified assistantships also available. Support available to part-time students. Financial award application deadline: 3/31; financial award applicants required to submit FAFSA. *Faculty research:* Traffic engineering and safety, infrastructure information systems using GIS, intelligent transportation systems, non-destructive evaluation of structures, infrastructure appraisal and upgrade, geosynthetics, water quality modeling, waste containment systems, liquefaction effects on piles and underground utilities, construction safety and quality management. *Total annual research expenditures:* $3 million. *Unit head:* Dr. Joseph E. Hummer, Professor and Chair, 313-577-3790, E-mail: joseph.hummer@wayne.edu. *Application contact:* Casey Rue, Advisor, 313-577-2163, E-mail: crue@wayne.edu.
Website: http://engineering.wayne.edu/cee/.

Western Michigan University, Graduate College, College of Engineering and Applied Sciences, Department of Civil and Construction Engineering, Kalamazoo, MI 49008. Offers MSE. *Application deadline:* For fall admission, 2/15 for domestic students. *Financial support:* Application deadline: 2/15. *Application contact:* Admissions and Orientation, 269-387-2000, Fax: 269-387-2096.

West Virginia University, College of Engineering and Mineral Resources, Department of Civil and Environmental Engineering, Morgantown, WV 26506. Offers civil engineering (MSCE, MSE, PhD). Part-time programs available. *Degree requirements:* For master's, thesis; for doctorate, comprehensive exam, thesis/dissertation. *Entrance requirements:* For master's and doctorate, minimum GPA of 3.0. Additional exam requirements/recommendations for international students: Required—TOEFL. *Faculty research:* Habitat restoration, advanced materials for civil infrastructure, pavement modeling, infrastructure condition assessment.

Widener University, Graduate Programs in Engineering, Program in Civil Engineering, Chester, PA 19013-5792. Offers M Eng. Part-time and evening/weekend programs available. *Degree requirements:* For master's, thesis optional. *Faculty research:* Environmental engineering, laws and water supply, structural analysis and design.

Worcester Polytechnic Institute, Graduate Studies and Research, Department of Civil and Environmental Engineering, Worcester, MA 01609-2280. Offers civil and environmental engineering (Advanced Certificate, Graduate Certificate); civil engineering (ME, MS, PhD); construction project management (MS); environmental engineering (M Eng, MS); master builder (M Eng). Part-time and evening/weekend programs available. Postbaccalaureate distance learning degree programs offered (no on-campus study). *Faculty:* 27 full-time (1 woman), 24 part-time/adjunct (3 women). *Students:* 36 full-time (14 women), 13 part-time (5 women); includes 4 minority (1 Hispanic/Latino; 3 Two or more races, non-Hispanic/Latino), 20 international. 160 applicants, 65% accepted, 26 enrolled. In 2014, 30 master's, 1 doctorate awarded. *Degree requirements:* For master's, thesis optional; for doctorate, comprehensive exam, thesis/dissertation. *Entrance requirements:* For master's and doctorate, GRE (recommended), 3 letters of recommendation. Additional exam requirements/recommendations for international students: Required—TOEFL (minimum score 563 paper-based; 84 iBT), IELTS (minimum score 7). *Application deadline:* For fall admission, 1/1 priority date for domestic and international students; for spring admission, 10/1 priority date for domestic and international students. Applications are processed on a rolling basis. Application fee: $70. Electronic applications accepted. *Financial support:* Research assistantships, teaching assistantships, career-related internships or fieldwork, institutionally sponsored loans, scholarships/grants, and unspecified assistantships available. Financial award application deadline: 1/1; financial award applicants required to submit FAFSA. *Unit head:* Dr. Tahar El-Korchi, Interim Head, 508-831-5530, Fax: 508-831-5808, E-mail: tek@wpi.edu. *Application contact:* Dr. Rajib Mallick, Graduate Coordinator, 508-831-5530, Fax: 508-831-5808, E-mail: rajib@wpi.edu.
Website: http://www.wpi.edu/academics/cee.

Youngstown State University, Graduate School, College of Science, Technology, Engineering and Mathematics, Department of Civil and Environmental Engineering, Youngstown, OH 44555-0001. Offers MSE. Part-time and evening/weekend programs available. *Degree requirements:* For master's, thesis optional. *Entrance requirements:* For master's, minimum GPA of 2.75 in field. Additional exam requirements/recommendations for international students: Required—TOEFL. *Faculty research:* Structural mechanics, water quality modeling, surface and ground water hydrology, physical and chemical processes in aquatic systems.

Construction Engineering

The American University in Cairo, School of Sciences and Engineering, Department of Construction and Architectural Engineering, Cairo, Egypt. Offers construction engineering (M Eng, MS). *Degree requirements:* For master's, thesis. *Entrance requirements:* Additional exam requirements/recommendations for international students: Required—English entrance exam and/or TOEFL. Tuition and fees vary according to course load and program. *Faculty research:* Composite materials, superelasticity, expert systems, materials selection.

Arizona State University at the Tempe campus, Ira A. Fulton Schools of Engineering, School of Sustainable Engineering and the Built Environment, Tempe, AZ 85287-5306. Offers civil, environmental and sustainable engineering (MS, MSE, PhD); construction engineering (MSE); construction management (MS, PhD). Part-time and evening/weekend programs available. Postbaccalaureate distance learning degree programs offered (minimal on-campus study). Terminal master's awarded for partial completion of doctoral program. *Degree requirements:* For master's, thesis optional, comprehensive exams (MSE); interactive Program of Study (iPOS) submitted before completing 50 percent of required credit hours; for doctorate, comprehensive exam, thesis/dissertation, interactive Program of Study (iPOS) submitted before completing 50 percent of required credit hours. *Entrance requirements:* For master's, GRE, minimum GPA of 3.0 or equivalent in last 2 years of work leading to bachelor's degree; for doctorate, GRE, minimum GPA of 3.0 in last 2 years of work leading to bachelor's degree, 3.2 in all graduate-level coursework with master's degree; 3 letters of recommendation; resume/curriculum vitae; letter of intent; thesis (if applicable); statement of research interests. Additional exam requirements/recommendations for international students: Required—TOEFL, IELTS, or PTE. Electronic applications accepted. *Expenses:* Contact institution. *Faculty research:* Water purification, transportation (safety and materials), construction management, environmental biotechnology, environmental nanotechnology, earth systems engineering and management, SMART innovations, project performance metrics, and underground infrastructure.

Auburn University, Graduate School, College of Architecture, Design, and Construction, Department of Building Science, Auburn University, AL 36849. Offers building construction (MBC); construction management (MBC); integrated design and construction (MIDC). *Faculty:* 17 full-time (1 woman), 2 part-time/adjunct (1 woman). *Students:* 25 full-time (4 women), 47 part-time (13 women); includes 9 minority (3 Black or African American, non-Hispanic/Latino; 2 Asian, non-Hispanic/Latino; 4 Hispanic/Latino), 4 international. Average age 33. 84 applicants, 85% accepted, 52 enrolled. In 2014, 36 master's awarded. *Entrance requirements:* For master's, GRE General Test. *Application deadline:* For fall admission, 7/7 for domestic students; for spring admission, 11/24 for domestic students. Applications are processed on a rolling basis. Application fee: $50 ($60 for international students). Electronic applications accepted. *Expenses:* Tuition, state resident: full-time $8586; part-time $477 per credit hour. Tuition, nonresident: full-time $25,758; part-time $1431 per credit hour. *Required fees:* $804 per semester. Tuition and fees vary according to degree level and program. *Financial*

support: Application deadline: 3/15; applicants required to submit FAFSA. *Unit head:* Dr. Richard Burt, Head, 334-844-5260. *Application contact:* Dr. George Flowers, Dean of the Graduate School, 334-844-2125.
Website: http://cadc.auburn.edu/bsci/Pages/default.aspx.

Auburn University, Graduate School, Ginn College of Engineering, Department of Civil Engineering, Auburn University, AL 36849. Offers construction engineering and management (MCE, MS, PhD); environmental engineering (MCE, MS, PhD); geotechnical/materials engineering (MCE, MS, PhD); hydraulics/hydrology (MCE, MS, PhD); structural engineering (MCE, MS, PhD); transportation engineering (MCE, MS, PhD). Part-time programs available. *Faculty:* 27 full-time (3 women), 1 part-time/adjunct (0 women). *Students:* 59 full-time (15 women), 46 part-time (6 women); includes 10 minority (4 Black or African American, non-Hispanic/Latino; 4 Asian, non-Hispanic/Latino; 2 Hispanic/Latino), 40 international. Average age 26. 134 applicants, 46% accepted, 20 enrolled. In 2014, 40 master's, 7 doctorates awarded. *Degree requirements:* For master's, project (MCE), thesis (MS); for doctorate, comprehensive exam, thesis/dissertation. *Entrance requirements:* For master's and doctorate, GRE General Test. *Application deadline:* For fall admission, 7/7 for domestic students; for spring admission, 11/24 for domestic students. Applications are processed on a rolling basis. Application fee: $50 ($60 for international students). Electronic applications accepted. *Expenses:* Tuition, state resident: full-time $8586; part-time $477 per credit hour. Tuition, nonresident: full-time $25,758; part-time $1431 per credit hour. *Required fees:* $804 per semester. Tuition and fees vary according to degree level and program. *Financial support:* Fellowships, research assistantships, teaching assistantships, and Federal Work-Study available. Support available to part-time students. Financial award application deadline: 3/15; financial award applicants required to submit FAFSA. *Unit head:* Dr. Andy Nowak, Head, 334-844-4320. *Application contact:* Dr. George Flowers, Dean of the Graduate School, 334-844-2125.

Bradley University, Graduate School, College of Engineering and Technology, Department of Civil Engineering and Construction, Peoria, IL 61625-0002. Offers MSCE. Part-time and evening/weekend programs available. *Faculty:* 6 full-time (1 woman). *Students:* 24 full-time (4 women), 10 part-time (0 women), 28 international. 86 applicants, 45% accepted, 18 enrolled. In 2014, 8 master's awarded. *Degree requirements:* For master's, comprehensive exam. *Entrance requirements:* Additional exam requirements/recommendations for international students: Required—TOEFL (minimum score 550 paper-based; 79 iBT), IELTS (minimum score 6.5). *Application deadline:* For fall admission, 5/15 priority date for domestic and international students; for spring admission, 10/15 priority date for domestic and international students. Applications are processed on a rolling basis. Application fee: $40 ($50 for international students). Electronic applications accepted. *Expenses: Tuition:* Full-time $14,580; part-time $810 per credit. *Required fees:* $224. Full-time tuition and fees vary according to course load. *Financial support:* In 2014–15, 11 research assistantships with full and partial tuition reimbursements (averaging $10,130 per year) were awarded; teaching assistantships, scholarships/grants, tuition waivers (partial), and unspecified assistantships also available. Support available to part-time students. Financial award application deadline: 4/1. *Application contact:* Kayla Carroll, Director of International Admissions and Student Services, 309-677-2375, E-mail: klcarroll@fsmail.bradley.edu.

Colorado School of Mines, Graduate School, Department of Civil and Environmental Engineering, Golden, CO 80401. Offers civil and environmental engineering (MS, PhD); environmental engineering science (MS, PhD); underground construction and tunneling (MS, PhD). Part-time programs available. *Faculty:* 40 full-time (14 women), 17 part-time/adjunct (8 women). *Students:* 120 full-time (40 women), 32 part-time (13 women); includes 23 minority (1 Black or African American, non-Hispanic/Latino; 8 Asian, non-Hispanic/Latino; 12 Hispanic/Latino; 2 Two or more races, non-Hispanic/Latino), 19 international. Average age 29. 158 applicants, 55% accepted, 44 enrolled. In 2014, 69 master's, 6 doctorates awarded. *Degree requirements:* For master's, thesis (for some programs); for doctorate, comprehensive exam, thesis/dissertation. *Entrance requirements:* For master's and doctorate, GRE General Test. Additional exam requirements/recommendations for international students: Required—TOEFL (minimum score 550 paper-based; 80 iBT). *Application deadline:* For fall admission, 12/15 priority date for domestic students, 1/15 priority date for international students; for spring admission, 9/1 priority date for domestic and international students. Application fee: $50 ($70 for international students). Electronic applications accepted. *Financial support:* In 2014–15, 82 students received support, including 11 fellowships with full tuition reimbursements available (averaging $21,120 per year), 54 research assistantships with full tuition reimbursements available (averaging $21,120 per year), 6 teaching assistantships with full tuition reimbursements available (averaging $21,120 per year); scholarships/grants, health care benefits, and unspecified assistantships also available. Financial award application deadline: 12/15; financial award applicants required to submit FAFSA. *Faculty research:* Treatment of water and wastes, environmental law: policy and practice, natural environment systems, hazardous waste management, environmental data analysis. *Total annual research expenditures:* $6.7 million. *Unit head:* Dr. John McCray, Deptartment Head, 303-384-3490, Fax: 303-273-3413, E-mail: jmccray@mines.edu. *Application contact:* Tim VanHaverbeke, Research Faculty, 303-273-3467, Fax: 303-273-3413, E-mail: tvanhave@mines.edu.

Colorado School of Mines, Graduate School, Department of Mining Engineering, Golden, CO 80401. Offers engineer of mines (ME); mining and earth systems engineering (MS); mining engineering (PhD); underground construction and tunneling (MS, PhD). Part-time programs available. *Faculty:* 13 full-time (2 women), 10 part-time/adjunct (2 women). *Students:* 33 full-time (3 women), 9 part-time (1 woman); includes 2 minority (1 Black or African American, non-Hispanic/Latino; 1 Hispanic/Latino), 22 international. Average age 33. 44 applicants, 82% accepted, 14 enrolled. In 2014, 12 master's, 4 doctorates awarded. *Degree requirements:* For master's, thesis (for some programs); for doctorate, one foreign language, comprehensive exam, thesis/dissertation. *Entrance requirements:* For master's and doctorate, GRE General Test. Additional exam requirements/recommendations for international students: Required—TOEFL (minimum score 550 paper-based; 80 iBT). *Application deadline:* For fall admission, 12/15 priority date for domestic and international students; for spring admission, 9/1 priority date for domestic and international students. Application fee: $50 ($70 for international students). Electronic applications accepted. *Financial support:* In 2014–15, 17 students received support, including 4 fellowships with full tuition reimbursements available (averaging $21,120 per year), 6 research assistantships with full tuition reimbursements available (averaging $21,120 per year), 7 teaching assistantships with full tuition reimbursements available (averaging $21,120 per year); scholarships/grants, health care benefits, and unspecified assistantships also available. Financial award application deadline: 12/15; financial award applicants required to submit FAFSA. *Faculty research:* Mine evaluation and planning, geostatistics, mining robotics, water jet cutting, rock mechanics. *Total annual research expenditures:* $4.7 million. *Unit head:* Dr. Priscella Nelson, Head, 303-273-2606, E-mail: pnelson@mines.edu. *Application contact:* Melanie Barnhart, Program Assistant, 303-273-3768, E-mail: barnhart@mines.edu.
Website: http://mining.mines.edu.

Columbia University, Fu Foundation School of Engineering and Applied Science, Department of Civil Engineering and Engineering Mechanics, New York, NY 10027.

Offers civil engineering (MS, Eng Sc D, PhD); construction engineering and management (MS); engineering mechanics (MS, Eng Sc D, PhD). Part-time programs available. Postbaccalaureate distance learning degree programs offered (no on-campus study). *Faculty:* 19 full-time (4 women), 27 part-time/adjunct (2 women). *Students:* 153 full-time (40 women), 100 part-time (27 women); includes 19 minority (1 Black or African American, non-Hispanic/Latino; 11 Asian, non-Hispanic/Latino; 6 Hispanic/Latino; 1 Two or more races, non-Hispanic/Latino), 194 international. 504 applicants, 38% accepted, 110 enrolled. In 2014, 131 master's, 7 doctorates awarded. Terminal master's awarded for partial completion of doctoral program. *Degree requirements:* For doctorate, thesis/dissertation, qualifying exam. *Entrance requirements:* For master's and doctorate, GRE General Test. Additional exam requirements/recommendations for international students: Required—TOEFL, IELTS, PTE. *Application deadline:* For fall admission, 12/15 priority date for domestic and international students; for spring admission, 10/1 priority date for domestic and international students. Application fee: $85. Electronic applications accepted. *Financial support:* In 2014–15, 44 students received support, including 13 fellowships with full tuition reimbursements available (averaging $27,500 per year), 18 research assistantships with full tuition reimbursements available (averaging $32,448 per year), 13 teaching assistantships with full tuition reimbursements available (averaging $32,448 per year); health care benefits also available. Financial award application deadline: 12/15; financial award applicants required to submit FAFSA. *Faculty research:* Structural dynamics, structural health and monitoring, fatigue and fracture mechanics, geo-environmental engineering, multiscale science and engineering. *Unit head:* Dr. George Deodatis, Professor and Chair, Civil Engineering and Engineering Mechanics, 212-854-6267, E-mail: deodatis@civil.columbia.edu. *Application contact:* Scott Kelly, Graduate Admissions and Student Affairs, 212-854-3219, E-mail: kelly@civil.columbia.edu.
Website: http://www.civil.columbia.edu/.

Concordia University, School of Graduate Studies, Faculty of Engineering and Computer Science, Department of Building, Civil and Environmental Engineering, Montréal, QC H3G 1M8, Canada. Offers building engineering (M Eng, MA Sc, PhD, Certificate); civil engineering (M Eng, MA Sc, PhD); environmental engineering (Certificate). *Degree requirements:* For master's, thesis or alternative; for doctorate, comprehensive exam, thesis/dissertation. *Faculty research:* Structural engineering, geotechnical engineering, water resources and fluid engineering, transportation engineering, systems engineering.

George Mason University, Volgenau School of Engineering, Sid and Reva Dewberry Department of Civil, Environmental, and Infrastructure Engineering, Fairfax, VA 22030. Offers construction project management (MS); environmental and water resources engineering (MS); geotechnical, construction, and structural engineering (M Eng); transportation engineering (MS, PhD). *Faculty:* 12 full-time (4 women), 16 part-time/adjunct (3 women). *Students:* 28 full-time (7 women), 51 part-time (13 women); includes 25 minority (12 Black or African American, non-Hispanic/Latino; 8 Asian, non-Hispanic/Latino; 5 Hispanic/Latino), 14 international. Average age 30. 90 applicants, 58% accepted, 25 enrolled. In 2014, 28 master's, 3 doctorates awarded. *Degree requirements:* For master's, thesis (for some programs), 30 credits, departmental seminars; for doctorate, thesis/dissertation, qualifying exams. *Entrance requirements:* For master's, GRE, photocopy of passport; 2 official college transcripts; resume; official bank statement; proof of financial support; expanded goals statement; self-evaluation form; BS in engineering or other related science; 3 letters of recommendation; for doctorate, GRE (for those who received degree outside of the U.S.), photocopy of passport; 2 official college transcripts; resume; official bank statement; proof of financial support; expanded goals statement; self-evaluation form; baccalaureate degree in engineering or related science; master's degree (preferred); 3 letters of recommendation. Additional exam requirements/recommendations for international students: Required—TOEFL (minimum score 575 paper-based; 80 iBT), IELTS (minimum score 6.5), PTE. *Application deadline:* For fall admission, 1/15 priority date for domestic students; for spring admission, 8/1 priority date for domestic students. Application fee: $65 ($80 for international students). Electronic applications accepted. *Expenses:* Expenses: Contact institution. *Financial support:* In 2014–15, 19 students received support, including 1 fellowship (averaging $5,000 per year), 9 research assistantships with full and partial tuition reimbursements available (averaging $23,846 per year), 10 teaching assistantships with full and partial tuition reimbursements available (averaging $21,200 per year); career-related internships or fieldwork, Federal Work-Study, scholarships/grants, unspecified assistantships, and health care benefits (for full-time research or teaching assistantship recipients) also available. Support available to part-time students. Financial award application deadline: 3/1; financial award applicants required to submit FAFSA. *Faculty research:* Evolutionary design, infrastructure security, intelligent transportation systems, national transportation networks, water quality modeling. *Total annual research expenditures:* $159,347. *Unit head:* Dr. Deborah J. Goodings, Chair, 703-993-1675, Fax: 703-993-9790, E-mail: goodings@gmu.edu. *Application contact:* Kristin Amaya, Administrative Assistant, 703-993-1675, Fax: 703-993-9790, E-mail: kfairch1@gmu.edu.
Website: http://civil.gmu.edu/.

Illinois Institute of Technology, Graduate College, Armour College of Engineering, Department of Civil, Architectural and Environmental Engineering, Chicago, IL 60616. Offers architectural engineering (M Arch E); civil engineering (MS, PhD), including architectural engineering (MS), construction engineering and management (MS), geoenvironmental engineering (MS), geotechnical engineering (MS), structural engineering (MS), transportation engineering (MS); construction engineering and management (MCEM); environmental engineering (M Env E, MS, PhD); geoenvironmental engineering (M Geoenv E); geotechnical engineering (MGE); infrastructure engineering and management (MPW); structural engineering (MSE); transportation engineering (M Trans E). Part-time and evening/weekend programs available. Postbaccalaureate distance learning degree programs offered (minimal on-campus study). *Faculty:* 12 full-time (1 woman), 15 part-time/adjunct (1 woman). *Students:* 165 full-time (48 women), 54 part-time (11 women); includes 31 minority (2 Black or African American, non-Hispanic/Latino; 21 Asian, non-Hispanic/Latino; 7 Hispanic/Latino; 1 Native Hawaiian or other Pacific Islander, non-Hispanic/Latino), 157 international. Average age 29. 1,039 applicants, 42% accepted, 82 enrolled. In 2014, 94 master's, 7 doctorates awarded. Terminal master's awarded for partial completion of doctoral program. *Degree requirements:* For master's, thesis (for some programs); for doctorate, comprehensive exam, thesis/dissertation. *Entrance requirements:* For master's, GRE General Test (minimum score 900 Quantitative and Verbal, 2.5 Analytical Writing), minimum undergraduate GPA of 3.0; for doctorate, GRE General Test (minimum score 1000 Quantitative and Verbal, 3.0 Analytical Writing), minimum undergraduate GPA of 3.0. Additional exam requirements/recommendations for international students: Required—TOEFL (minimum score 550 paper-based; 80 iBT). *Application deadline:* For fall admission, 5/1 for domestic and international students; for spring admission, 10/15 for domestic and international students. Applications are processed on a rolling basis. Application fee: $50. Electronic applications accepted. *Expenses: Tuition:* Full-time $22,500; part-time $1250 per credit hour. *Required fees:* $30 per course. $260 per semester. One-time fee: $235. Tuition and fees vary according to course load and program. *Financial support:* Fellowships with full and partial tuition reimbursements, research assistantships with full and partial tuition reimbursements,

teaching assistantships with full and partial tuition reimbursements, Federal Work-Study, institutionally sponsored loans, scholarships/grants, health care benefits, tuition waivers (partial), and unspecified assistantships available. Support available to part-time students. Financial award applicants required to submit FAFSA. *Faculty research:* Structural, architectural, geotechnical and geoenvironmental engineering; construction engineering and management; transportation engineering; environmental engineering and public works. *Unit head:* Dr. Gongkang Fu, Professor and Chairman, 312-567-3540, Fax: 312-567-3519, E-mail: gfu2@iit.edu. *Application contact:* Rishab Malhotra, Director, Graduate Admission, 866-472-3448, Fax: 312-567-3138, E-mail: inquiry.grad@iit.edu.
Website: http://engineering.iit.edu/caee.

Iowa State University of Science and Technology, Department of Civil and Construction Engineering, Ames, IA 50011. Offers civil engineering (MS, PhD), including civil engineering materials, construction engineering and management, environmental engineering, geometronics, geotechnical engineering, structural engineering, transportation engineering. *Degree requirements:* For master's, thesis or alternative; for doctorate, thesis/dissertation. *Entrance requirements:* For master's and doctorate, GRE General Test. Additional exam requirements/recommendations for international students: Required—TOEFL (minimum score 550 paper-based; 82 iBT), IELTS (minimum score 6.5). Electronic applications accepted.

Lawrence Technological University, College of Engineering, Southfield, MI 48075-1058. Offers architectural engineering (MS); automotive engineering (MS); civil engineering (MA, MS, PhD); construction engineering management (MA); electrical and computer engineering (MS); engineering management (MEM); industrial engineering (MS); manufacturing systems (ME, DE); mechanical engineering (MS, DE); mechatronic systems engineering (MS). Part-time and evening/weekend programs available. *Faculty:* 24 full-time (5 women), 15 part-time/adjunct (0 women). *Students:* 16 full-time (6 women), 478 part-time (71 women); includes 295 minority (15 Black or African American, non-Hispanic/Latino; 271 Asian, non-Hispanic/Latino; 7 Hispanic/Latino; 2 Two or more races, non-Hispanic/Latino), 38 international. Average age 27. 1,786 applicants, 40% accepted, 218 enrolled. In 2014, 106 master's awarded. *Degree requirements:* For master's, thesis (for some programs). *Entrance requirements:* Additional exam requirements/recommendations for international students: Required—TOEFL (minimum score 550 paper-based; 79 iBT). *Application deadline:* For fall admission, 8/1 priority date for domestic students, 5/29 for international students; for spring admission, 12/1 priority date for domestic students, 10/15 for international students. Applications are processed on a rolling basis. Application fee: $50. Electronic applications accepted. *Expenses: Tuition:* Full-time $14,700; part-time $1050 per credit hour. *Required fees:* $150. One-time fee: $150 part-time. *Financial support:* In 2014–15, 31 students received support, including 8 research assistantships (averaging $9,338 per year); Federal Work-Study and institutionally sponsored loans also available. Support available to part-time students. Financial award application deadline: 4/1; financial award applicants required to submit FAFSA. *Faculty research:* Advanced composite materials in bridges, strengthening existing bridges with carbon and glass fiber sheets, development of drive shafts using composite materials. *Unit head:* Dr. Nabil Grace, Dean, 248-204-2500, Fax: 248-204-2509, E-mail: engrdean@ltu.edu. *Application contact:* Jane Rohrback, Director of Admissions, 248-204-3160, Fax: 248-204-2228, E-mail: admissions@ltu.edu.
Website: http://www.ltu.edu/engineering/index.asp.

Marquette University, Graduate School, Opus College of Engineering, Department of Civil, Construction and Environmental Engineering, Milwaukee, WI 53201-1881. Offers construction engineering and management (MS, PhD, Certificate); environmental engineering (MS, PhD); structural design (Certificate); structural engineering and structural mechanics (MS, PhD); transportation (Certificate); transportation engineering and materials (MS, PhD); waste and wastewater treatment processes (Certificate); water resources engineering (Certificate). Part-time and evening/weekend programs available. Terminal master's awarded for partial completion of doctoral program. *Degree requirements:* For master's, comprehensive exam (for some programs), thesis or alternative; for doctorate, thesis/dissertation. *Entrance requirements:* For master's, GRE General Test (recommended), minimum GPA of 3.0, official transcripts from all current and previous colleges/universities except Marquette, three letters of recommendation; for doctorate, GRE General Test, minimum GPA of 3.0, official transcripts from all current and previous colleges/universities except Marquette, three letters of recommendation, brief statement of purpose, submission of any English language publications authored by applicant (strongly recommended). Additional exam requirements/recommendations for international students: Required—TOEFL (minimum score 530 paper-based). Electronic applications accepted. *Faculty research:* Highway safety, highway performance, and intelligent transportation systems; surface mount technology; watershed management.

Massachusetts Institute of Technology, School of Engineering, Department of Civil and Environmental Engineering, Cambridge, MA 02139. Offers biological oceanography (PhD, Sc D); chemical oceanography (PhD, Sc D); civil and environmental engineering (M Eng, SM, PhD, Sc D); civil and environmental systems (PhD, Sc D); civil engineering (PhD, Sc D, CE); coastal engineering (PhD, Sc D); construction engineering and management (PhD, Sc D); environmental biology (PhD, Sc D); environmental chemistry (PhD, Sc D); environmental engineering (PhD, Sc D); environmental fluid mechanics (PhD, Sc D); geotechnical and geoenvironmental engineering (PhD, Sc D); hydrology (PhD, Sc D); information technology (PhD, Sc D); oceanographic engineering (PhD, Sc D); structures and materials (PhD, Sc D); transportation (PhD, Sc D); SM/MBA. *Faculty:* 34 full-time (8 women), 1 part-time/adjunct (0 women). *Students:* 216 full-time (82 women); includes 25 minority (1 Black or African American, non-Hispanic/Latino; 10 Asian, non-Hispanic/Latino; 8 Hispanic/Latino; 6 Two or more races, non-Hispanic/Latino), 117 international. Average age 26. 565 applicants, 22% accepted, 85 enrolled. In 2014, 76 master's, 18 doctorates awarded. *Degree requirements:* For master's and CE, thesis; for doctorate, comprehensive exam, thesis/dissertation. *Entrance requirements:* For master's and doctorate, GRE General Test. Additional exam requirements/recommendations for international students: Required—TOEFL (minimum score 577 paper-based; 100 iBT), IELTS (minimum score 7). *Application deadline:* For fall admission, 12/15 for domestic and international students. Application fee: $75. Electronic applications accepted. *Expenses: Tuition:* Full-time $44,720; part-time $699 per unit. *Required fees:* $296. *Financial support:* In 2014–15, 170 students received support, including 32 fellowships (averaging $32,800 per year), 132 research assistantships (averaging $33,800 per year), 13 teaching assistantships (averaging $32,900 per year); Federal Work-Study, institutionally sponsored loans, scholarships/grants, traineeships, health care benefits, and unspecified assistantships also available. Financial award application deadline: 4/15; financial award applicants required to submit FAFSA. *Faculty research:* Environmental chemistry, environmental fluid mechanics and coastal engineering, environmental microbiology, geotechnical engineering and geomechanics, hydrology and hydroclimatology, infrastructure systems, mechanics of materials and structures, transportation systems. *Total annual research expenditures:* $22.9 million. *Unit head:* Prof. Markus Buehler, Department Head, 617-324-6488. *Application contact:* Graduate Admissions Coordinator, 617-253-7119, E-mail: cee-admissions@mit.edu.
Website: http://cee.mit.edu/.

Missouri University of Science and Technology, Graduate School, Department of Civil, Architectural, and Environmental Engineering, Rolla, MO 65409. Offers civil engineering (MS, DE, PhD); construction engineering (MS, DE, PhD); environmental engineering (MS); fluid mechanics (MS, DE, PhD); geotechnical engineering (MS, DE, PhD); hydrology and hydraulic engineering (MS, DE, PhD). Part-time and evening/weekend programs available. Terminal master's awarded for partial completion of doctoral program. *Degree requirements:* For master's, thesis optional; for doctorate, comprehensive exam, thesis/dissertation. *Entrance requirements:* For master's, GRE General Test (minimum combined score 1100), minimum GPA of 3.0; for doctorate, GRE General Test (minimum score: verbal and quantitative 400, writing 3.5), minimum GPA of 3.0. Additional exam requirements/recommendations for international students: Required—TOEFL. Electronic applications accepted. *Faculty research:* Earthquake engineering, structural optimization and control systems, structural health monitoring/damage detection, soil-structure interaction, soil mechanics and foundation engineering.

Montana State University, The Graduate School, College of Engineering, Department of Civil Engineering, Bozeman, MT 59717. Offers civil engineering (MS); construction engineering management (MCEM); engineering (PhD), including applied mechanics option, civil engineering option. Part-time programs available. *Degree requirements:* For master's, comprehensive exam, thesis (for some programs); for doctorate, comprehensive exam, thesis/dissertation. *Entrance requirements:* For master's and doctorate, GRE General Test. Additional exam requirements/recommendations for international students: Required—TOEFL (minimum score 550 paper-based). Electronic applications accepted. *Faculty research:* Snow and ice mechanics, biofilm engineering, transportation, structural and geo materials, water resources.

Ohio University, Graduate College, Russ College of Engineering and Technology, Department of Civil Engineering, Athens, OH 45701-2979. Offers civil engineering (PhD); construction engineering and management (MS); environmental (MS); geotechnical and geoenvironmental (MS); mechanics (MS); structures (MS); transportation (MS); water resources (MS). Part-time programs available. *Degree requirements:* For master's, comprehensive exam (for some programs), thesis or alternative; for doctorate, comprehensive exam, thesis/dissertation. *Entrance requirements:* For master's, GRE General Test, minimum GPA of 3.0, 3 letters of recommendation; for doctorate, GRE General Test. Additional exam requirements/recommendations for international students: Required—TOEFL (minimum score 550 paper-based; 80 iBT) or IELTS (minimum score 6.5). Electronic applications accepted. *Faculty research:* Noise abatement, materials and environment, highway infrastructure, subsurface investigation (pavements, pipes, bridges).

Pittsburg State University, Graduate School, College of Technology, Department of Construction Management and Construction Engineering Technologies, Pittsburg, KS 66762. Offers construction (MET).

Stanford University, School of Engineering, Department of Civil and Environmental Engineering, Stanford, CA 94305-9991. Offers atmosphere and energy (MS, PhD); construction (MS), including construction engineering and management, design-construction integration, sustainable design and construction; environmental engineering and science (MS, PhD, Eng); environmental fluid mechanics and hydrology (PhD); geomechanics (MS); structural engineering (MS). Terminal master's awarded for partial completion of doctoral program. *Degree requirements:* For doctorate, thesis/dissertation, qualifying exam; for Eng, thesis. *Entrance requirements:* For master's, doctorate, and Eng, GRE General Test. Additional exam requirements/recommendations for international students: Required—TOEFL. Electronic applications accepted. *Expenses: Tuition:* Full-time $44,184; part-time $982 per credit hour. *Required fees:* $191.

Stevens Institute of Technology, Graduate School, Charles V. Schaefer Jr. School of Engineering, Department of Civil, Environmental, and Ocean Engineering, Program in Construction Management, Hoboken, NJ 07030. Offers construction accounting/estimating (Certificate); construction engineering (Certificate); construction law/disputes (Certificate); construction management (MS); construction/quality management (Certificate). *Degree requirements:* For master's, thesis optional. *Entrance requirements:* For master's, GMAT, GRE General Test. Additional exam requirements/recommendations for international students: Required—TOEFL. Electronic applications accepted.

The University of Alabama, Graduate School, College of Engineering, Department of Civil, Construction and Environmental Engineering, Tuscaloosa, AL 35487-0205. Offers civil engineering (MSCE, PhD); environmental engineering (MS). Part-time programs available. *Faculty:* 22 full-time (2 women). *Students:* 58 full-time (20 women), 4 part-time (0 women); includes 4 minority (2 Black or African American, non-Hispanic/Latino; 1 Asian, non-Hispanic/Latino; 1 Hispanic/Latino), 22 international. Average age 28. 76 applicants, 43% accepted, 16 enrolled. In 2014, 23 master's, 4 doctorates awarded. Terminal master's awarded for partial completion of doctoral program. *Degree requirements:* For master's, thesis or alternative; for doctorate, one foreign language, comprehensive exam, thesis/dissertation. *Entrance requirements:* For master's and doctorate, GRE General Test (minimum combined score of 300), minimum GPA of 3.0 in last 60 hours of course work. Additional exam requirements/recommendations for international students: Required—TOEFL (minimum score 550 paper-based; 79 iBT), IELTS (minimum score 6.5), PTE (minimum score 59). *Application deadline:* For fall admission, 7/10 for domestic students, 1/15 for international students; for spring admission, 11/1 for domestic students, 6/1 for international students. Applications are processed on a rolling basis. Application fee: $50 ($60 for international students). Electronic applications accepted. *Expenses:* Tuition, state resident: full-time $9826. Tuition, nonresident: full-time $24,950. *Financial support:* In 2014–15, 40 students received support, including 2 fellowships with full tuition reimbursements available (averaging $30,000 per year), 17 research assistantships with full tuition reimbursements available (averaging $13,275 per year), 20 teaching assistantships with full tuition reimbursements available (averaging $13,275 per year); scholarships/grants, tuition waivers (partial), and unspecified assistantships also available. Financial award application deadline: 2/15. *Faculty research:* Experimental structures, modeling of structures, bridge management systems, geotechnological engineering, environmental remediation. *Total annual research expenditures:* $2.7 million. *Unit head:* Dr. W. Edward Back, Head and Professor, 205-348-6550, Fax: 205-348-0783, E-mail: eback@eng.ua.edu. *Application contact:* Dr. Andrew Graettinger, Associate Professor and Graduate Program Director, 205-348-1707, Fax: 205-348-0783, E-mail: andrewg@eng.ua.edu.
Website: http://cce.eng.ua.edu/.

The University of Alabama at Birmingham, School of Engineering, Program in Engineering, Birmingham, AL 35294. Offers advanced safety engineering and management (M Eng); construction engineering management (M Eng); information engineering management (M Eng). Part-time programs available. Postbaccalaureate distance learning degree programs offered (no on-campus study). *Students:* 14 full-time (4 women), 237 part-time (44 women); includes 91 minority (71 Black or African

American, non-Hispanic/Latino; 1 American Indian or Alaska Native, non-Hispanic/Latino; 3 Asian, non-Hispanic/Latino; 8 Hispanic/Latino; 8 Two or more races, non-Hispanic/Latino), 6 international. Average age 38. In 2014, 90 master's awarded. *Entrance requirements:* Additional exam requirements/recommendations for international students: Required—TOEFL. *Expenses:* Tuition, state resident: full-time $7090; part-time $370 per credit hour. Tuition, nonresident: full-time $16,072; part-time $869 per credit hour. Full-time tuition and fees vary according to course load and program. *Unit head:* Dr. J. Iwan Alexander, Dean, 205-934-8400, Fax: 205-934-8437, E-mail: ialex@uab.edu. *Application contact:* Susan Noblitt Banks, Director of Graduate School Operations, 205-934-8227, Fax: 205-934-8413, E-mail: gradschool@uab.edu. Website: http://www.uab.edu/engineering/home/professional-programs.

University of Alberta, Faculty of Graduate Studies and Research, Department of Civil and Environmental Engineering, Edmonton, AB T6G 2E1, Canada. Offers construction engineering and management (M Eng, M Sc, PhD); environmental engineering (M Eng, M Sc, PhD); environmental science (M Sc, PhD); geoenvironmental engineering (M Eng, M Sc, PhD); geotechnical engineering (M Eng, M Sc, PhD); mining engineering (M Eng, M Sc, PhD); petroleum engineering (M Eng, M Sc, PhD); structural engineering (M Eng, M Sc, PhD); water resources (M Eng, M Sc, PhD). Part-time programs available. Postbaccalaureate distance learning degree programs offered (minimal on-campus study). *Degree requirements:* For master's, thesis (for some programs); for doctorate, thesis/dissertation. *Entrance requirements:* For master's, minimum GPA of 3.0 in last 2 years of undergraduate studies; for doctorate, minimum GPA of 3.0. Additional exam requirements/recommendations for international students: Required—TOEFL (minimum score 550 paper-based). Electronic applications accepted. *Faculty research:* Mining.

University of Central Florida, College of Engineering and Computer Science, Department of Civil, Environmental, and Construction Engineering, Orlando, FL 32816. Offers civil engineering (MS, MSCE, PhD, Certificate), including civil engineering (MS, MSCE, PhD), construction engineering (Certificate), structural engineering (Certificate), transportation engineering (Certificate); construction engineering (Certificate); environmental engineering (MS, MS Env E, PhD). Part-time and evening/weekend programs available. *Faculty:* 27 full-time (2 women), 13 part-time/adjunct (0 women). *Students:* 107 full-time (28 women), 95 part-time (30 women); includes 53 minority (9 Black or African American, non-Hispanic/Latino; 7 Asian, non-Hispanic/Latino; 30 Hispanic/Latino; 7 Two or more races, non-Hispanic/Latino), 74 international. Average age 30. 172 applicants, 56% accepted, 53 enrolled. In 2014, 48 master's, 9 doctorates, 1 other advanced degree awarded. *Degree requirements:* For master's, thesis or alternative; for doctorate, thesis/dissertation, departmental qualifying exam, candidacy exam. *Entrance requirements:* For master's, GRE General Test, minimum GPA of 3.0 in last 60 hours of course work; for doctorate, GRE General Test, minimum GPA of 3.5 in last 60 hours of course work. Additional exam requirements/recommendations for international students: Required—TOEFL. *Application deadline:* For fall admission, 7/15 priority date for domestic students; for spring admission, 12/1 priority date for domestic students. Application fee: $30. Electronic applications accepted. *Expenses:* Tuition, state resident: part-time $288.16 per credit hour. Tuition, nonresident: part-time $1073.31 per credit hour. *Financial support:* In 2014–15, 51 students received support, including 18 fellowships with partial tuition reimbursements available (averaging $3,900 per year), 44 research assistantships with partial tuition reimbursements available (averaging $9,750 per year), 14 teaching assistantships with partial tuition reimbursements available (averaging $8,900 per year); career-related internships or fieldwork, Federal Work-Study, institutionally sponsored loans, tuition waivers (partial), and unspecified assistantships also available. Financial award application deadline: 3/1; financial award applicants required to submit FAFSA. *Unit head:* Dr. Mohamed Abdel-Aty, Chair, 407-823-2841, E-mail: m.aty@ucf.edu. *Application contact:* Barbara Rodriguez Lamas, Director, Admissions and Student Services, 407-823-2766, Fax: 407-823-6442, E-mail: gradadmissions@ucf.edu.
Website: http://cece.ucf.edu/.

University of Colorado Boulder, Graduate School, College of Engineering and Applied Science, Department of Civil, Environmental, and Architectural Engineering, Boulder, CO 80309. Offers building systems engineering (MS, PhD); construction engineering management (MS, PhD); environmental engineering (MS, PhD); geotechnical engineering and geomechanics (MS, PhD); hydrology, water resources and environmental fluid mechanics (MS, PhD); structural engineering and structural mechanics (MS, PhD). *Faculty:* 37 full-time (8 women). *Students:* 235 full-time (81 women), 36 part-time (9 women); includes 24 minority (9 Asian, non-Hispanic/Latino; 6 Hispanic/Latino; 9 Two or more races, non-Hispanic/Latino), 83 international. Average age 28. 391 applicants, 63% accepted, 68 enrolled. In 2014, 76 master's, 30 doctorates awarded. Terminal master's awarded for partial completion of doctoral program. *Degree requirements:* For master's, comprehensive exam, thesis or alternative; for doctorate, thesis/dissertation. *Entrance requirements:* For master's, GRE General Test, minimum undergraduate GPA of 3.0. *Application deadline:* For fall admission, 1/31 for domestic and international students; for spring admission, 10/1 for domestic and international students. Application fee: $50 ($70 for international students). Electronic applications accepted. *Financial support:* In 2014–15, 387 students received support, including 75 fellowships (averaging $11,889 per year), 92 research assistantships with full and partial tuition reimbursements available (averaging $34,669 per year), 17 teaching assistantships with full and partial tuition reimbursements available (averaging $28,513 per year); institutionally sponsored loans, scholarships/grants, health care benefits, and unspecified assistantships also available. Financial award application deadline: 1/15; financial award applicants required to submit FAFSA. *Faculty research:* Civil engineering, environmental engineering, architectural engineering, geotechnical engineering, hydrology. *Total annual research expenditures:* $13 million.
Website: http://civil.colorado.edu/.

University of Michigan, College of Engineering, Department of Civil and Environmental Engineering, Ann Arbor, MI 48109. Offers civil engineering (MSE, PhD, CE); construction engineering and management (M Eng, MSE); environmental engineering (MSE, PhD); structural engineering (M Eng); MBA/MSE. Part-time programs available. *Students:* 184 full-time (69 women), 5 part-time (0 women). 691 applicants, 36% accepted, 62 enrolled. In 2014, 59 master's, 12 doctorates awarded. *Degree requirements:* For master's, thesis optional; for doctorate, comprehensive exam, thesis/dissertation, oral defense of dissertation, preliminary and written exams. *Entrance requirements:* For master's and doctorate, GRE General Test. Additional exam requirements/recommendations for international students: Required—TOEFL (minimum score 560 paper-based). *Application deadline:* Applications are processed on a rolling basis. Electronic applications accepted. *Financial support:* Fellowships, research assistantships, teaching assistantships, institutionally sponsored loans, and tuition waivers (partial) available. Financial award application deadline: 1/19. *Faculty research:* Construction engineering and management, geotechnical engineering, earthquake-resistant design of structures, environmental chemistry and microbiology, cost engineering, environmental and water resources engineering. *Total annual research expenditures:* $10.4 million. *Unit head:* Kim Hayes, Department Chair, 734-764-8495, Fax: 734-764-4292, E-mail: ford@umich.edu. *Application contact:* Jessica Taylor, Graduate Coordinator, 734-764-8405, Fax: 734-647-2127, E-mail: jrand@umich.edu.
Website: http://cee.engin.umich.edu/.

University of Missouri–Kansas City, School of Computing and Engineering, Kansas City, MO 64110-2499. Offers civil engineering (MS); computer and electrical engineering (PhD); computer science (MS), including bioinformatics, software engineering, telecommunications networking; computer science and informatics (PhD); computing (PhD); electrical engineering (MS); engineering (PhD); engineering and construction management (Graduate Certificate); mechanical engineering (MS); telecommunications and computer networking (PhD). PhD (interdisciplinary) offered through the School of Graduate Studies. Part-time programs available. *Faculty:* 39 full-time (5 women), 26 part-time/adjunct (3 women). *Students:* 500 full-time (143 women), 136 part-time (28 women); includes 18 minority (5 Black or African American, non-Hispanic/Latino; 8 Asian, non-Hispanic/Latino; 4 Hispanic/Latino; 1 Two or more races, non-Hispanic/Latino), 551 international. Average age 24. 1,924 applicants, 39% accepted, 200 enrolled. In 2014, 124 master's, 1 other advanced degree awarded. *Degree requirements:* For doctorate, thesis/dissertation. *Entrance requirements:* For master's, GRE General Test, minimum GPA of 3.0, 3 letters of recommendation from professors; for doctorate, GRE General Test, minimum GPA of 3.5. Additional exam requirements/recommendations for international students: Required—TOEFL (minimum score 550 paper-based; 80 iBT). *Application deadline:* For fall admission, 1/15 priority date for domestic students, 1/15 for international students. Applications are processed on a rolling basis. Application fee: $45 ($50 for international students). *Financial support:* In 2014–15, 34 research assistantships with partial tuition reimbursements (averaging $15,602 per year), 24 teaching assistantships with partial tuition reimbursements (averaging $15,090 per year) were awarded; career-related internships or fieldwork, Federal Work-Study, scholarships/grants, tuition waivers (partial), and unspecified assistantships also available. Support available to part-time students. Financial award application deadline: 3/1; financial award applicants required to submit FAFSA. *Faculty research:* Algorithms, bioinformatics and medical informatics, biomechanics/biomaterials, civil engineering materials, networking and telecommunications, thermal science. *Unit head:* Dr. Kevin Z. Truman, Dean, 816-235-2399, Fax: 816-235-5159. *Application contact:* 816-235-2399, Fax: 816-235-5159.
Website: http://sce.umkc.edu/.

University of New Brunswick Fredericton, School of Graduate Studies, Faculty of Engineering, Department of Civil Engineering, Fredericton, NB E3B 5A3, Canada. Offers construction engineering and management (M Eng, M Sc E, PhD); environmental engineering (M Eng, M Sc E, PhD); environmental studies (M Eng); geotechnical engineering (M Eng, M Sc E, PhD); groundwater/hydrology (M Eng, M Sc E, PhD); materials (M Eng, M Sc E, PhD); pavements (M Eng, M Sc E, PhD); structures (M Eng, M Sc E, PhD); transportation (M Eng, M Sc E, PhD). Part-time programs available. *Faculty:* 12 full-time (1 woman), 4 part-time/adjunct (0 women). *Students:* 16 full-time (4 women), 15 part-time (5 women). In 2014, 9 master's, 3 doctorates awarded. *Degree requirements:* For master's, thesis, proposal; for doctorate, comprehensive exam, thesis/dissertation, qualifying exam; 27 credit hours of courses. *Entrance requirements:* For master's, minimum GPA of 3.0; B Sc E in civil engineering or related engineering degree; for doctorate, minimum GPA of 3.0; graduate degree in engineering or applied science. Additional exam requirements/recommendations for international students: Required—IELTS (minimum score 7.5), TWE (minimum score 4), Michigan English Language Assessment Battery (minimum score 85) or CanTest (minimum score 4.5); Recommended—TOEFL (minimum score 580 paper-based). *Application deadline:* For fall admission, 5/1 for domestic students; for winter admission, 11/1 for domestic students. Applications are processed on a rolling basis. Application fee: $50 Canadian dollars. Electronic applications accepted. *Financial support:* In 2014–15, 35 fellowships, 48 research assistantships, 35 teaching assistantships were awarded; career-related internships or fieldwork and scholarships/grants also available. *Faculty research:* Construction engineering and management; engineering materials and infrastructure renewal; highway and pavement research; structures and solid mechanics; geotechnical and geoenvironmental engineering; structure interaction; transportation and planning; environment, solid waste management; structural engineering; water and environmental engineering. *Unit head:* Dr. Kerry MacQuarrie, Director of Graduate Studies, 506-453-5121, Fax: 506-453-3568, E-mail: ktm@unb.ca. *Application contact:* Joyce Moore, Graduate Secretary, 506-452-6127, Fax: 506-453-3568, E-mail: joycem@unb.ca.
Website: http://go.unb.ca/gradprograms.

University of Southern Mississippi, Graduate School, College of Science and Technology, School of Construction, Hattiesburg, MS 39406-0001. Offers logistics, trade and transportation (MS). Part-time programs available. *Degree requirements:* For master's, comprehensive exam, thesis optional. *Entrance requirements:* For master's, GMAT or GRE General Test, minimum GPA of 2.75 in last 60 hours. Additional exam requirements/recommendations for international students: Required—TOEFL, IELTS. *Faculty research:* Robotics; CAD/CAM; simulation; computer-integrated manufacturing processes; construction scheduling, estimating, and computer systems.

University of Virginia, School of Architecture, Program in the Constructed Environment, Charlottesville, VA 22903. Offers PhD. *Students:* 5 full-time (all women), 1 international. Average age 28. 53 applicants, 15% accepted, 5 enrolled. *Degree requirements:* For doctorate, thesis/dissertation. *Entrance requirements:* For doctorate, GRE, master's degree or equivalent, official transcripts, sample of academic writing, three letters of recommendation, resume or curriculum vitae, graphic portfolio. Additional exam requirements/recommendations for international students: Required—TOEFL. *Expenses:* Tuition, state resident: full-time $14,164; part-time $349 per credit hour. Tuition, nonresident: full-time $23,722; part-time $1300 per credit hour. *Required fees:* $2514. *Unit head:* Nana Last, Director, 434-924-6446, E-mail: ndl5g@virginia.edu. *Application contact:* Kristine Nelson, Director of Graduate Admissions and Financial Aid, 434-924-6442, Fax: 434-982-2678, E-mail: arch-admissions@virginia.edu.
Website: http://www.arch.virginia.edu/academics/phd.

University of Washington, Graduate School, College of Engineering, Department of Civil and Environmental Engineering, Seattle, WA 98195-2700. Offers civil engineering (PhD); construction engineering (MSCE); environmental engineering (MSCE, PhD); hydrology, water resources, and environmental fluid mechanics (MSCE, PhD); structural and geotechnical engineering and mechanics (MSCE, PhD); transportation and construction engineering (PhD); transportation engineering (MSCE). Part-time programs available. Postbaccalaureate distance learning degree programs offered (no on-campus study). *Faculty:* 35 full-time (9 women). *Students:* 220 full-time (81 women), 147 part-time (50 women); includes 61 minority (9 Black or African American, non-Hispanic/Latino; 2 American Indian or Alaska Native, non-Hispanic/Latino; 34 Asian, non-Hispanic/Latino; 14 Hispanic/Latino; 2 Native Hawaiian or other Pacific Islander, non-Hispanic/Latino), 91 international. Average age 28. 901 applicants, 49% accepted, 162 enrolled. In 2014, 110 master's, 12 doctorates awarded. Terminal master's awarded for partial completion of doctoral program. *Degree requirements:* For master's, thesis (for some programs); for doctorate, comprehensive exam, thesis/dissertation, general, qualifying, and final exams; completion of degree within 10 years. *Entrance requirements:* For master's, GRE General Test, minimum GPA of 3.0, statement of purpose, letters of recommendation, transcripts; for doctorate, GRE General Test,

minimum GPA of 3.5, statement of purpose, letters of recommendation, transcripts. Additional exam requirements/recommendations for international students: Required—TOEFL (minimum score 580 paper-based; 92 iBT); Recommended—IELTS (minimum score 7). *Application deadline:* For fall admission, 12/15 for domestic and international students. Applications are processed on a rolling basis. Application fee: $85. Electronic applications accepted. *Expenses:* Expenses: Contact institution. *Financial support:* In 2014–15, 179 students received support, including 41 fellowships with full and partial tuition reimbursements available, 77 research assistantships with full tuition reimbursements available, 58 teaching assistantships with full tuition reimbursements available; scholarships/grants also available. Financial award application deadline: 1/10; financial award applicants required to submit FAFSA. *Faculty research:* Structural and geotechnical engineering, transportation and construction engineering, water and environmental engineering. *Total annual research expenditures:* $14.1 million. *Unit head:* Dr. Gregory R. Miller, Professor/Chair, 206-543-0350, Fax: 206-543-1543, E-mail: gmiller@uw.edu. *Application contact:* Lorna Latal, Graduate Adviser, 206-543-2574, Fax: 206-543-1543, E-mail: llatal@u.washington.edu.
Website: http://www.ce.washington.edu/.

Virginia Polytechnic Institute and State University, Graduate School, College of Architecture and Urban Studies, Blacksburg, VA 24061. Offers architecture (MS Arch); architecture and design research (PhD); building/construction science and management (MS); creative technologies (MFA); environmental design and planning (PhD); landscape architecture (MLA); planning, governance, and globalization (PhD); public administration (MPA); public administration/public affairs (PhD, Certificate); public and international affairs (MPIA); urban and regional planning (MURP); MS/MA. *Accreditation:* ASLA (one or more programs are accredited). *Faculty:* 133 full-time (54 women), 2 part-time/adjunct (1 woman). *Students:* 316 full-time (166 women), 237 part-time (108 women); includes 104 minority (46 Black or African American, non-Hispanic/Latino; 1 American Indian or Alaska Native, non-Hispanic/Latino; 20 Asian, non-Hispanic/Latino; 21 Hispanic/Latino; 16 Two or more races, non-Hispanic/Latino), 108 international. Average age 32. 609 applicants, 50% accepted, 108 enrolled. In 2014, 155 master's, 29 doctorates awarded. *Degree requirements:* For master's, comprehensive exam (for some programs), thesis (for some programs); for doctorate, comprehensive exam (for some programs), thesis/dissertation (for some programs). *Entrance requirements:* For master's and doctorate, GRE/GMAT (may vary by department). Additional exam requirements/recommendations for international students: Required—TOEFL (minimum score 550 paper-based). *Application deadline:* For fall admission, 8/1 for domestic students, 4/1 for international students; for spring admission, 1/1 for domestic students, 9/1 for international students. Applications are processed on a rolling basis. Application fee: $75. Electronic applications accepted. *Expenses:* Tuition, state resident: full-time $11,656; part-time $647.50 per credit hour. Tuition, nonresident: full-time $23,351; part-time $1297.25 per credit hour. *Required fees:* $2533; $465.75 per semester. Tuition and fees vary according to course load, campus/location and program. *Financial support:* In 2014–15, 13 research assistantships with full tuition reimbursements (averaging $20,302 per year), 44 teaching assistantships with full tuition reimbursements (averaging $19,484 per year) were awarded. Financial award application deadline: 3/1; financial award applicants required to submit FAFSA. *Total annual research expenditures:* $3.2 million. *Unit head:* Dr. A. J. Davis, Dean, 540-231-6416, Fax: 540-231-6332, E-mail: davisa@vt.edu. *Application contact:* Christine Mattsson-Coon, Executive Assistant, 540-231-6416, Fax: 540-231-6332, E-mail: cmattsso@vt.edu.
Website: http://www.caus.vt.edu/.

Environmental Engineering

Air Force Institute of Technology, Graduate School of Engineering and Management, Department of Systems and Engineering Management, Dayton, OH 45433-7765. Offers cost analysis (MS); environmental and engineering management (MS); environmental engineering science (MS); information resource/systems management (MS). *Accreditation:* ABET. Part-time programs available. *Degree requirements:* For master's, thesis. *Entrance requirements:* For master's, GRE, GMAT, minimum GPA of 3.0.

Arizona State University at the Tempe campus, Ira A. Fulton Schools of Engineering, School of Sustainable Engineering and the Built Environment, Tempe, AZ 85287-5306. Offers civil, environmental and sustainable engineering (MS, MSE, PhD); construction engineering (MSE); construction management (MS, PhD). Part-time and evening/weekend programs available. Postbaccalaureate distance learning degree programs offered (minimal on-campus study). Terminal master's awarded for partial completion of doctoral program. *Degree requirements:* For master's, thesis optional, comprehensive exams (MSE); interactive Program of Study (iPOS) submitted before completing 50 percent of required credit hours; for doctorate, comprehensive exam, thesis/dissertation, interactive Program of Study (iPOS) submitted before completing 50 percent of required credit hours. *Entrance requirements:* For master's, GRE, minimum GPA of 3.0 or equivalent in last 2 years of work leading to bachelor's degree; for doctorate, GRE, minimum GPA of 3.0 in last 2 years of work leading to bachelor's degree, 3.2 in all graduate-level coursework with master's degree; 3 letters of recommendation; resume/curriculum vitae; letter of intent; thesis (if applicable); statement of research interests. Additional exam requirements/recommendations for international students: Required—TOEFL, IELTS, or PTE. Electronic applications accepted. *Expenses:* Contact institution. *Faculty research:* Water purification, transportation (safety and materials), construction management, environmental biotechnology, environmental nanotechnology, earth systems engineering and management, SMART innovations, project performance metrics, and underground infrastructure.

Auburn University, Graduate School, Ginn College of Engineering, Department of Civil Engineering, Auburn University, AL 36849. Offers construction engineering and management (MCE, MS, PhD); environmental engineering (MCE, MS, PhD); geotechnical/materials engineering (MCE, MS, PhD); hydraulics/hydrology (MCE, MS, PhD); structural engineering (MCE, MS, PhD); transportation engineering (MCE, MS, PhD). Part-time programs available. *Faculty:* 27 full-time (3 women), 1 part-time/adjunct (0 women). *Students:* 59 full-time (15 women), 46 part-time (6 women); includes 10 minority (4 Black or African American, non-Hispanic/Latino; 4 Asian, non-Hispanic/Latino; 2 Hispanic/Latino), 40 international. Average age 26. 134 applicants, 46% accepted, 20 enrolled. In 2014, 40 master's, 7 doctorates awarded. *Degree requirements:* For master's, project (MCE), thesis (MS); for doctorate, comprehensive exam, thesis/dissertation. *Entrance requirements:* For master's and doctorate, GRE General Test. *Application deadline:* For fall admission, 7/7 for domestic students; for spring admission, 11/24 for domestic students. Applications are processed on a rolling basis. Application fee: $50 ($60 for international students). Electronic applications accepted. *Expenses:* Tuition, state resident: full-time $8586; part-time $477 per credit hour. Tuition, nonresident: full-time $25,758; part-time $1431 per credit hour. *Required fees:* $804 per semester. Tuition and fees vary according to degree level and program. *Financial support:* Fellowships, research assistantships, teaching assistantships, and Federal Work-Study available. Support available to part-time students. Financial award application deadline: 3/15; financial award applicants required to submit FAFSA. *Unit head:* Dr. Andy Nowak, Head, 334-844-4320. *Application contact:* Dr. George Flowers, Dean of the Graduate School, 334-844-2125.

California Institute of Technology, Division of Engineering and Applied Science, Option in Environmental Science and Engineering, Pasadena, CA 91125-0001. Offers MS, PhD. *Degree requirements:* For doctorate, thesis/dissertation. Electronic applications accepted. *Faculty research:* Chemistry of natural waters, physics and chemistry of particulates, fluid mechanics of the natural environment, pollutant formation and control, environmental modeling systems.

California Institute of Technology, Division of Geological and Planetary Sciences, Pasadena, CA 91125-0001. Offers environmental science and engineering (MS, PhD); geobiology (MS, PhD); geochemistry (MS, PhD); geology (MS, PhD); geophysics (MS, PhD); planetary science (MS, PhD). *Degree requirements:* For doctorate, thesis/dissertation. *Entrance requirements:* For doctorate, GRE General Test. Additional exam requirements/recommendations for international students: Required—TOEFL; Recommended—IELTS, TWE. Electronic applications accepted. *Faculty research:* Planetary surfaces, evolution of anaerobic respiratory processes, structural geology and tectonics, theoretical and numerical seismology, global biogeochemical cycles.

California Polytechnic State University, San Luis Obispo, College of Engineering, Department of Civil and Environmental Engineering, San Luis Obispo, CA 93407. Offers MS. Part-time programs available. *Faculty:* 12 full-time (2 women), 1 part-time/adjunct (0 women). *Students:* 45 full-time (8 women), 8 part-time (0 women); includes 19 minority (1 Black or African American, non-Hispanic/Latino; 9 Asian, non-Hispanic/Latino; 8 Hispanic/Latino; 1 Two or more races, non-Hispanic/Latino), 1 international. Average age 24. 76 applicants, 70% accepted, 33 enrolled. In 2014, 28 master's awarded. *Degree requirements:* For master's, comprehensive exam (for some programs), thesis (for some programs). *Application deadline:* For fall admission, 3/1 for domestic and international students; for winter admission, 10/1 for domestic students, 6/30 for international students; for spring admission, 1/1 for domestic students. Applications are processed on a rolling basis. Application fee: $55. Electronic applications accepted. *Expenses:* Tuition, state resident: full-time $6738; part-time $3906 per year. Tuition, nonresident: full-time $15,666; part-time $8370 per year. *Required fees:* $3447; $1001 per quarter. One-time fee: $3447 full-time; $3003 part-time. *Financial support:* Fellowships, research assistantships, teaching assistantships, career-related internships or fieldwork, Federal Work-Study, and scholarships/grants available. Support available to part-time students. Financial award application deadline: 3/2; financial award applicants required to submit FAFSA. *Faculty research:* Transportation and traffic, environmental protection, geotechnology, water engineering. *Unit head:* Dr. Robb Moss, Graduate Coordinator, 805-756-6427, Fax: 805-756-6330, E-mail: rmoss@calpoly.edu. *Application contact:* Dr. James Maraviglia, Associate Vice Provost for Marketing and Enrollment Development, 805-756-2311, Fax: 805-756-5400, E-mail: admissions@calpoly.edu.
Website: http://ceenve.calpoly.edu.

California State University, Fullerton, Graduate Studies, College of Engineering and Computer Science, Department of Civil and Environmental Engineering, Fullerton, CA 92834-9480. Offers civil engineering (MS); environmental engineering (MS). Part-time programs available. *Students:* 72 full-time (20 women), 195 part-time (42 women); includes 114 minority (14 Black or African American, non-Hispanic/Latino; 47 Asian, non-Hispanic/Latino; 44 Hispanic/Latino; 2 Native Hawaiian or other Pacific Islander, non-Hispanic/Latino; 7 Two or more races, non-Hispanic/Latino), 68 international. Average age 29. 264 applicants, 73% accepted, 113 enrolled. In 2014, 75 master's awarded. *Degree requirements:* For master's, comprehensive exam, project or thesis. *Entrance requirements:* For master's, minimum undergraduate GPA of 2.5. Application fee: $55. *Financial support:* Career-related internships or fieldwork, Federal Work-Study, institutionally sponsored loans, and scholarships/grants available. Support available to part-time students. Financial award application deadline: 3/1; financial award applicants required to submit FAFSA. *Faculty research:* Soil-structure interaction, finite-element analysis, computer-aided analysis and design. *Unit head:* Dr. Prasada Rao, Chair, 657-278-3012. *Application contact:* Admissions/Applications, 657-278-2371.
Website: http://www.fullerton.edu/ecs/cee/.

Carleton University, Faculty of Graduate Studies, Faculty of Engineering and Design, Department of Civil and Environmental Engineering, Ottawa, ON K1S 5B6, Canada. Offers M Eng, MA Sc, PhD. *Degree requirements:* For master's, thesis optional; for doctorate, thesis/dissertation. *Entrance requirements:* For master's, honors degree; for doctorate, MA Sc or M Eng. Additional exam requirements/recommendations for international students: Required—TOEFL. *Faculty research:* Pollution and wastewater management, fire safety engineering, earthquake engineering, structural design, bridge engineering.

Carnegie Mellon University, Carnegie Institute of Technology, Department of Civil and Environmental Engineering, Pittsburgh, PA 15213. Offers advanced infrastructure systems (MS, PhD); advanced infrastructure systems technology development and application (MS); air quality engineering and science (MS); civil and environmental engineering (MS, PhD); civil and environmental engineering/engineering and public policy (PhD); civil engineering (MS, PhD); computational mechanics (MS, PhD); computational modeling and monitoring for resilient structural and material systems (MS); energy infrastructure systems (MS); environmental engineering (MS, PhD); environmental management and science (MS, PhD); IT-based sustainable global infrastructure and construction management (MS); sustainability and green design (MS); water quality engineering and science (MS). Part-time programs available. *Faculty:* 21 full-time (5 women), 12 part-time/adjunct (3 women). *Students:* 229 full-time (99 women), 31 part-time (11 women); includes 18 minority (4 Black or African American, non-Hispanic/Latino; 13 Asian, non-Hispanic/Latino; 1 Hispanic/Latino), 193 international. Average age 26. 590 applicants, 68% accepted, 124 enrolled. In 2014, 85 master's, 11 doctorates awarded. Terminal master's awarded for partial completion of doctoral program. *Degree requirements:* For master's, thesis optional; for doctorate, comprehensive exam, thesis/dissertation, two-part qualifying exam, public defense of dissertation. *Entrance requirements:* For master's, GRE General Test, BS in engineering, science or mathematics; for doctorate, GRE General Test, BS or MS in engineering, science or mathematics. Additional exam requirements/recommendations for international students: Required—TOEFL (minimum score 84 iBT) or IELTS. *Application deadline:* For fall admission, 1/5 priority date for domestic and international

students; for spring admission, 9/15 priority date for domestic and international students. Application fee: $65. Electronic applications accepted. *Financial support:* In 2014–15, 169 students received support. Fellowships with full and partial tuition reimbursements available, research assistantships with full and partial tuition reimbursements available, scholarships/grants, tuition waivers (full and partial), unspecified assistantships, and service assistantships available. Financial award application deadline: 1/5. *Faculty research:* Advanced infrastructure systems; environmental engineering, sustainability, and science; mechanics, materials, and computing. *Total annual research expenditures:* $4.9 million. *Unit head:* Dr. David A. Dzombak, Head, 412-268-2941, Fax: 412-268-7813, E-mail: dzombak@cmu.edu. *Application contact:* Melissa L. Brown, Director of Graduate Admissions & Recruiting, 412-268-8762, Fax: 412-268-7813, E-mail: mlb2@andrew.cmu.edu.
Website: http://www.cmu.edu/cee/.

Carnegie Mellon University, Tepper School of Business, Pittsburgh, PA 15213-3891. Offers accounting (PhD); business management and software engineering (MBMSE); business technologies (PhD); civil engineering and industrial management (MS); computational finance (MSCF); economics (PhD); environmental engineering and management (MEEM); financial economics (PhD); industrial administration (MBA), including administration and public management; marketing (PhD); mathematical finance (PhD); operations management (PhD); operations research (PhD); organizational behavior and theory (PhD); production and operations management (PhD); public policy and management (MS, MSED); software engineering and business management (MS); JD/MS; JD/MSIA; M Div/MS; MOM/MSIA; MSCF/MSIA. JD/MSIA offered jointly with University of Pittsburgh. Part-time programs available. Terminal master's awarded for partial completion of doctoral program. *Degree requirements:* For doctorate, thesis/dissertation. *Entrance requirements:* For master's, GMAT. Additional exam requirements/recommendations for international students: Required—TOEFL. *Expenses:* Contact institution.

The Catholic University of America, School of Engineering, Department of Civil Engineering, Washington, DC 20064. Offers environmental engineering (PhD). Part-time programs available. *Faculty:* 7 full-time (0 women), 9 part-time/adjunct (1 woman). *Students:* 11 full-time (2 women), 29 part-time (9 women); includes 13 minority (9 Black or African American, non-Hispanic/Latino; 2 Asian, non-Hispanic/Latino; 2 Two or more races, non-Hispanic/Latino), 18 international. Average age 39. 42 applicants, 69% accepted, 11 enrolled. In 2014, 7 master's, 2 doctorates awarded. *Degree requirements:* For master's, thesis optional; for doctorate, comprehensive exam, thesis/dissertation. *Entrance requirements:* For master's and doctorate, statement of purpose, official copies of academic transcripts, three letters of recommendation. Additional exam requirements/recommendations for international students: Required—TOEFL (minimum score 580 paper-based). *Application deadline:* For fall admission, 7/15 priority date for domestic students, 7/1 for international students; for spring admission, 11/15 priority date for domestic students, 11/1 for international students. Applications are processed on a rolling basis. Application fee: $55. Electronic applications accepted. *Expenses:* Expenses: Contact institution. *Financial support:* Fellowships, research assistantships, teaching assistantships, Federal Work-Study, scholarships/grants, tuition waivers (full and partial), and unspecified assistantships available. Financial award application deadline: 2/1; financial award applicants required to submit FAFSA. *Faculty research:* Geotechnical engineering, solid mechanics, construction engineering and management, environmental engineering, structural engineering. *Total annual research expenditures:* $363,826. *Unit head:* Dr. Lu Sun, Chair, 202-319-6671, Fax: 202-319-6677, E-mail: sunl@cua.edu. *Application contact:* Director of Graduate Admissions, 202-319-5057, Fax: 202-319-6533, E-mail: cua-admissions@cua.edu.
Website: http://civil.cua.edu/.

Clarkson University, Graduate School, Institute for a Sustainable Environment, Program in Environmental Science and Engineering, Potsdam, NY 13699. Offers MS, PhD. Part-time programs available. *Students:* 23 full-time (11 women), 4 part-time (1 woman), 13 international. Average age 28. 30 applicants, 60% accepted, 6 enrolled. In 2014, 10 master's, 3 doctorates awarded. Terminal master's awarded for partial completion of doctoral program. *Degree requirements:* For master's, thesis; for doctorate, comprehensive exam, thesis/dissertation, departmental qualifying exam. *Entrance requirements:* For master's and doctorate, GRE, transcripts of all college coursework, resume, personal statement, three letters of recommendation. Additional exam requirements/recommendations for international students: Required—TOEFL (minimum score 550 paper-based; 80 iBT), IELTS (minimum score 6.5). *Application deadline:* For fall admission, 1/30 priority date for domestic and international students; for spring admission, 9/1 priority date for domestic and international students. Applications are processed on a rolling basis. Application fee: $25 ($35 for international students). Electronic applications accepted. *Expenses: Tuition:* Full-time $16,680; part-time $1390 per credit. *Required fees:* $295 per semester. *Financial support:* In 2014–15, 25 students received support, including fellowships with full tuition reimbursements available (averaging $24,029 per year), 12 research assistantships with full tuition reimbursements available (averaging $24,029 per year), 4 teaching assistantships with full tuition reimbursements available (averaging $24,029 per year); scholarships/grants, tuition waivers (partial), and unspecified assistantships also available. *Faculty research:* Biological, chemical, physical and social systems, renewable energy, environmental health. *Unit head:* Dr. Philip Hopke, Director, 315-268-3856, Fax: 315-268-4291, E-mail: hopkepk@clarkson.edu. *Application contact:* Mary Jane Smalling, Administrative Assistant, 315-268-2318, Fax: 315-268-4291, E-mail: isegrad@clarkson.edu.
Website: http://www.clarkson.edu/ese/.

Clarkson University, Graduate School, Wallace H. Coulter School of Engineering, Department of Civil and Environmental Engineering, Potsdam, NY 13699. Offers ME, MS, PhD. Part-time programs available. *Faculty:* 34 full-time (6 women), 9 part-time/adjunct (1 woman). *Students:* 31 full-time (9 women); includes 1 minority (Black or African American, non-Hispanic/Latino), 23 international. Average age 27. 64 applicants, 66% accepted, 10 enrolled. In 2014, 9 master's, 2 doctorates awarded. Terminal master's awarded for partial completion of doctoral program. *Degree requirements:* For master's, thesis (for MS); project (for ME); for doctorate, comprehensive exam, thesis/dissertation, departmental qualifying exam. *Entrance requirements:* For master's and doctorate, GRE, transcripts of all college coursework, resume, personal statement, three letters of recommendation. Additional exam requirements/recommendations for international students: Required—TOEFL (minimum score 550 paper-based; 80 iBT), IELTS (minimum score 6.5). *Application deadline:* For fall admission, 1/30 priority date for domestic and international students; for spring admission, 9/1 priority date for domestic and international students. Applications are processed on a rolling basis. Application fee: $25 ($35 for international students). Electronic applications accepted. *Expenses: Tuition:* Full-time $16,680; part-time $1390 per credit. *Required fees:* $295 per semester. *Financial support:* In 2014–15, 29 students received support, including 2 fellowships with full tuition reimbursements available (averaging $24,029 per year), 15 research assistantships with full tuition reimbursements available (averaging $24,029 per year), 7 teaching assistantships with full tuition reimbursements available (averaging $24,029 per year); scholarships/grants, tuition waivers (partial), and unspecified assistantships also available. *Faculty research:* Structural fatigue, deep water oil spill prediction, hydration kinetics and property evolution, ice-flow modeling. *Total annual research expenditures:* $3.5 million. *Unit head:* Dr. Stefan Grimberg, Chair, 315-268-

6529, Fax: 315-268-7985, E-mail: grimberg@clarkson.edu. *Application contact:* Kelly Sharlow, Assistant to the Dean, 315-268-7929, Fax: 315-268-4494, E-mail: ksharlow@clarkson.edu.
Website: http://www.clarkson.edu/cee/.

Clemson University, Graduate School, College of Engineering and Science, Department of Environmental Engineering and Earth Sciences, Programs in Environmental Engineering and Science, Clemson, SC 29634. Offers MS, PhD. *Accreditation:* ABET. *Students:* 63 full-time (32 women), 15 part-time (2 women); includes 5 minority (2 Black or African American, non-Hispanic/Latino; 1 Asian, non-Hispanic/Latino; 2 Two or more races, non-Hispanic/Latino), 32 international. Average age 28. 134 applicants, 45% accepted, 27 enrolled. In 2014, 18 master's, 5 doctorates awarded. *Degree requirements:* For master's, thesis; for doctorate, comprehensive exam, thesis/dissertation, qualifying exam. *Entrance requirements:* For master's, GRE General Test, minimum GPA of 3.0; 4 semesters of calculus, 2 semesters each of chemistry and calculus-based physics; for doctorate, GRE General Test, minimum GPA of 3.0. Additional exam requirements/recommendations for international students: Required—TOEFL. *Application deadline:* For fall admission, 2/15 priority date for domestic and international students; for spring admission, 9/15 for international students. Applications are processed on a rolling basis. Application fee: $70 ($80 for international students). Electronic applications accepted. *Financial support:* In 2014–15, 41 students received support, including 4 fellowships with full and partial tuition reimbursements available (averaging $8,934 per year), 27 research assistantships with full and partial tuition reimbursements available (averaging $18,780 per year), 12 teaching assistantships with full and partial tuition reimbursements available (averaging $19,891 per year); career-related internships or fieldwork, institutionally sponsored loans, scholarships/grants, health care benefits, and unspecified assistantships also available. Financial award applicants required to submit FAFSA. *Faculty research:* Drinking water treatment, hazardous waste treatment, environmental chemistry and microbiology, containment transport modeling, life cycle assessment and sustainable systems. *Unit head:* Dr. Tanju Karanfil, Chair, 864-656-1005, E-mail: tkaranf@clemson.edu. *Application contact:* Dr. Cindy Lee, Graduate Program Coordinator, 864-656-1006, Fax: 864-656-0672, E-mail: lc@clemson.edu.
Website: http://www.clemson.edu/ces/departments/eees/.

Cleveland State University, College of Graduate Studies, Fenn College of Engineering, Department of Civil and Environmental Engineering, Cleveland, OH 44115. Offers accelerated civil engineering (MS); accelerated environmental engineering (MS); civil engineering (MS, D Eng); engineering mechanics (MS); environmental engineering (MS). Part-time and evening/weekend programs available. *Faculty:* 8 full-time (2 women). *Students:* 20 full-time (0 women), 46 part-time (6 women); includes 2 minority (both Asian, non-Hispanic/Latino), 41 international. Average age 26. 113 applicants, 53% accepted, 22 enrolled. In 2014, 18 master's, 2 doctorates awarded. *Degree requirements:* For master's, project or thesis; for doctorate, comprehensive exam, thesis/dissertation, candidacy and qualifying exams. *Entrance requirements:* For master's, GRE General Test, GRE Subject Test, minimum GPA of 2.75; for doctorate, GRE General Test, GRE Subject Test, minimum GPA of 3.25. Additional exam requirements/recommendations for international students: Required—TOEFL (minimum score 525 paper-based). *Application deadline:* For fall admission, 7/15 priority date for domestic students. Applications are processed on a rolling basis. Application fee: $30. *Expenses:* Tuition, state resident: full-time $9566; part-time $531 per credit hour. Tuition, nonresident: full-time $17,980; part-time $999 per credit hour. *Required fees:* $25 per semester. Tuition and fees vary according to degree level and program. *Financial support:* In 2014–15, 9 research assistantships with full and partial tuition reimbursements (averaging $3,920 per year) were awarded; teaching assistantships with tuition reimbursements, career-related internships or fieldwork, scholarships/grants, and unspecified assistantships also available. Financial award application deadline: 9/1. *Faculty research:* Solid-waste disposal, constitutive modeling, transportation, safety engineering, concrete materials. *Total annual research expenditures:* $800,000. *Unit head:* Dr. Norbert Joseph Delatte, Chairperson, 216-687-9259, Fax: 216-687-5395, E-mail: n.delatte@csuohio.edu. *Application contact:* Deborah L. Brown, Interim Assistant Director, Graduate Admissions, 216-523-7572, Fax: 216-687-9214, E-mail: d.l.brown@csuohio.edu.
Website: http://www.csuohio.edu/engineering/civil.

Colorado School of Mines, Graduate School, Department of Civil and Environmental Engineering, Golden, CO 80401. Offers civil and environmental engineering (MS, PhD); environmental engineering science (MS, PhD); underground construction and tunneling (MS, PhD). Part-time programs available. *Faculty:* 40 full-time (14 women), 17 part-time/adjunct (8 women). *Students:* 120 full-time (40 women), 32 part-time (13 women); includes 23 minority (1 Black or African American, non-Hispanic/Latino; 8 Asian, non-Hispanic/Latino; 12 Hispanic/Latino; 2 Two or more races, non-Hispanic/Latino), 19 international. Average age 29. 158 applicants, 55% accepted, 44 enrolled. In 2014, 69 master's, 6 doctorates awarded. *Degree requirements:* For master's, thesis (for some programs); for doctorate, comprehensive exam, thesis/dissertation. *Entrance requirements:* For master's and doctorate, GRE General Test. Additional exam requirements/recommendations for international students: Required—TOEFL (minimum score 550 paper-based; 80 iBT). *Application deadline:* For fall admission, 12/15 priority date for domestic students, 1/15 priority date for international students; for spring admission, 9/1 priority date for domestic and international students. Application fee: $50 ($70 for international students). Electronic applications accepted. *Financial support:* In 2014–15, 82 students received support, including 11 fellowships with full tuition reimbursements available (averaging $21,120 per year), 54 research assistantships with full tuition reimbursements available (averaging $21,120 per year), 6 teaching assistantships with full tuition reimbursements available (averaging $21,120 per year); scholarships/grants, health care benefits, and unspecified assistantships also available. Financial award application deadline: 12/15; financial award applicants required to submit FAFSA. *Faculty research:* Treatment of water and wastes, environmental law: policy and practice, natural environment systems, hazardous waste management, environmental data analysis. *Total annual research expenditures:* $6.7 million. *Unit head:* Dr. John McCray, Deptartment Head, 303-384-3490, Fax: 303-273-3413, E-mail: jmccray@mines.edu. *Application contact:* Tim VanHaverbeke, Research Faculty, 303-273-3467, Fax: 303-273-3413, E-mail: tvanhave@mines.edu.

Columbia University, Fu Foundation School of Engineering and Applied Science, Department of Earth and Environmental Engineering, New York, NY 10027. Offers earth and environmental engineering (MS, Eng Sc D, PhD); MS/MBA. Part-time programs available. Postbaccalaureate distance learning degree programs offered (minimal on-campus study). *Faculty:* 12 full-time (1 woman), 7 part-time/adjunct (0 women). *Students:* 75 full-time (28 women), 18 part-time (13 women); includes 9 minority (4 Asian, non-Hispanic/Latino; 4 Hispanic/Latino; 1 Two or more races, non-Hispanic/Latino), 69 international. 225 applicants, 39% accepted, 34 enrolled. In 2014, 29 master's, 10 doctorates awarded. Terminal master's awarded for partial completion of doctoral program. *Degree requirements:* For master's, thesis; for doctorate, thesis/dissertation, qualifying exam. *Entrance requirements:* For master's and doctorate, GRE General Test. Additional exam requirements/recommendations for international students: Required—TOEFL, IELTS, PTE. *Application deadline:* For fall admission, 12/15 priority date for domestic and international students; for spring admission, 10/1

priority date for domestic and international students. Application fee: $85. Electronic applications accepted. *Financial support:* In 2014–15, 39 students received support, including 6 fellowships with full and partial tuition reimbursements available (averaging $16,478 per year), 26 research assistantships with full tuition reimbursements available (averaging $27,733 per year), 7 teaching assistantships with full tuition reimbursements available (averaging $22,500 per year); health care benefits and unspecified assistantships also available. Financial award application deadline: 12/15; financial award applicants required to submit FAFSA. *Faculty research:* Sustainable energy and materials, waste to energy, water resources and climate risks, environmental health engineering, life cycle analysis. *Unit head:* Dr. Paul F. Duby, Professor and Chair, Earth and Environmental Engineering, 212-854-2928, Fax: 212-854-7081, E-mail: pfd1@columbia.edu. *Application contact:* Elizabeth Allende, Administrative Assistant, 212-854-2905, Fax: 212-854-7081, E-mail: ea2516@columbia.edu.
Website: http://www.eee.columbia.edu/.

Concordia University, School of Graduate Studies, Faculty of Engineering and Computer Science, Department of Building, Civil and Environmental Engineering, Montréal, QC H3G 1M8, Canada. Offers building engineering (M Eng, MA Sc, PhD, Certificate); civil engineering (M Eng, MA Sc, PhD); environmental engineering (Certificate). *Degree requirements:* For master's, thesis or alternative; for doctorate, comprehensive exam, thesis/dissertation. *Faculty research:* Structural engineering, geotechnical engineering, water resources and fluid engineering, transportation engineering, systems engineering.

Cornell University, Graduate School, Graduate Fields of Engineering, Field of Civil and Environmental Engineering, Ithaca, NY 14853-0001. Offers engineering management (M Eng, MS, PhD); environmental engineering (M Eng, MS, PhD); environmental fluid mechanics and hydrology (M Eng, MS, PhD); environmental systems engineering (M Eng, MS, PhD); geotechnical engineering (M Eng, MS, PhD); remote sensing (M Eng, MS, PhD); structural engineering (M Eng, MS, PhD); structural mechanics (M Eng, MS); transportation engineering (MS, PhD); transportation systems engineering (M Eng); water resource systems (M Eng, MS, PhD). Terminal master's awarded for partial completion of doctoral program. *Degree requirements:* For master's, thesis (MS); for doctorate, comprehensive exam, thesis/dissertation. *Entrance requirements:* For master's and doctorate, GRE General Test (recommended), 2 letters of recommendation. Additional exam requirements/recommendations for international students: Required—TOEFL (minimum score 600 paper-based; 77 iBT). Electronic applications accepted. *Faculty research:* Environmental engineering, geotechnical engineering, remote sensing, environmental fluid mechanics and hydrology, structural engineering.

Dalhousie University, Faculty of Engineering, Department of Environmental Engineering, Halifax, NS B3J 2X4, Canada. Offers M Eng, MA Sc, PhD. *Entrance requirements:* Additional exam requirements/recommendations for international students: Required—TOEFL, IELTS, CANTEST, CAEL, or Michigan English Language Assessment Battery. Electronic applications accepted.

Dartmouth College, Thayer School of Engineering, Program in Environmental Engineering, Hanover, NH 03755. Offers MS, PhD. Application fee: $45. *Faculty research:* Resource and environmental analysis, decision theory, risk assessment and public policy, environmental fluid mechanics. *Unit head:* Dr. Joseph J. Helbie, Dean, 603-646-2238, Fax: 603-646-2580, E-mail: joseph.j.helbie@dartmouth.edu. *Application contact:* Candace S. Potter, Graduate Admissions Administrator, 603-646-3844, Fax: 603-646-1620, E-mail: candace.s.potter@dartmouth.edu.

Drexel University, College of Engineering, Department of Civil, Architectural, and Environmental Engineering, Program in Environmental Engineering, Philadelphia, PA 19104-2875. Offers MS, PhD. Part-time and evening/weekend programs available. Terminal master's awarded for partial completion of doctoral program. *Degree requirements:* For master's, thesis optional; for doctorate, thesis/dissertation. Electronic applications accepted.

Drexel University, College of Engineering, Department of Civil, Architectural, and Environmental Engineering, Program in Geotechnical, Geoenvironmental and Geosynthetics Engineering, Philadelphia, PA 19104-2875. Offers MS, PhD.

Duke University, Graduate School, Pratt School of Engineering, Department of Civil and Environmental Engineering, Durham, NC 27708. Offers civil and environmental engineering (MS, PhD); environmental engineering (MS, PhD). *Faculty:* 18 full-time (3 women). *Students:* 50 full-time (26 women); includes 10 minority (4 Black or African American, non-Hispanic/Latino; 3 Asian, non-Hispanic/Latino; 3 Hispanic/Latino), 22 international. 176 applicants, 17% accepted, 12 enrolled. In 2014, 9 master's, 11 doctorates awarded. Terminal master's awarded for partial completion of doctoral program. *Degree requirements:* For doctorate, thesis/dissertation. *Entrance requirements:* For master's and doctorate, GRE General Test. Additional exam requirements/recommendations for international students: Required—TOEFL (minimum score 550 paper-based; 90 iBT), IELTS (minimum score 7). *Application deadline:* For fall admission, 12/8 priority date for domestic and international students; for spring admission, 10/15 for domestic students. Application fee: $80. Electronic applications accepted. *Expenses: Tuition:* Full-time $45,760; part-time $2765 per credit. *Required fees:* $978. Full-time tuition and fees vary according to program. *Financial support:* Fellowships, research assistantships, and Federal Work-Study available. Financial award application deadline: 12/8. *Faculty research:* Environmental process engineering, hydrology and fluid dynamics, materials, structures and geo-systems. *Unit head:* Prof. John Dolbow, Director of Graduate Studies, 919-660-5200, Fax: 919-660-5219, E-mail: john.dolbow@duke.edu. *Application contact:* Ruby Nell Carpenter, DGSA, DUSA, DMSA, Staff assistant, 919-660-5200, Fax: 919-660-5219, E-mail: rubync@duke.edu.
Website: http://www.cee.duke.edu/graduate-studies/.

Duke University, Graduate School, Pratt School of Engineering, Master of Engineering Program, Durham, NC 27708-0271. Offers biomedical engineering (M Eng); civil engineering (M Eng); electrical and computer engineering (M Eng); environmental engineering (M Eng); materials science and engineering (M Eng); mechanical engineering (M Eng); photonics and optical sciences (M Eng). Part-time programs available. *Students:* 45 full-time (17 women); includes 5 minority (1 Black or African American, non-Hispanic/Latino; 2 Asian, non-Hispanic/Latino; 2 Hispanic/Latino), 23 international. Average age 24. 285 applicants, 43% accepted, 45 enrolled. In 2014, 45 master's awarded. *Entrance requirements:* For master's, GRE General Test, resume, 3 letters of recommendation, statement of purpose, transcripts. Additional exam requirements/recommendations for international students: Required—TOEFL. *Application deadline:* For fall admission, 6/15 for domestic students, 2/15 for international students; for spring admission, 11/1 for domestic students, 9/1 for international students. Application fee: $75. *Expenses: Tuition:* Full-time $45,760; part-time $2765 per credit. *Required fees:* $978. Full-time tuition and fees vary according to program. *Financial support:* Merit scholarships/grants available. *Unit head:* Dr. Bradley A. Fox, Executive Director, 919-660-5455, Fax: 919-660-5456. *Application contact:* Susan Brown, Assistant Director of Admissions, 919-660-8451, Fax: 919-660-5456, E-mail: susan.brown@duke.edu.
Website: http://meng.pratt.duke.edu/.

École Polytechnique de Montréal, Graduate Programs, Department of Civil, Geological and Mining Engineering, Montréal, QC H3C 3A7, Canada. Offers civil, geological and mining engineering (DESS); environmental engineering (M Eng, M Sc A, PhD); geotechnical engineering (M Eng, M Sc A, PhD); hydraulics engineering (M Eng, M Sc A, PhD); structural engineering (M Eng, M Sc A, PhD); transportation engineering (M Eng, M Sc A, PhD). Part-time programs available. *Degree requirements:* For master's, one foreign language, thesis; for doctorate, one foreign language, thesis/dissertation. *Entrance requirements:* For master's, minimum GPA of 2.75; for doctorate, minimum GPA of 3.0. *Faculty research:* Water resources management, characteristics of building materials, aging of dams, pollution control.

Florida Atlantic University, College of Engineering and Computer Science, Department of Civil, Environmental and Geomatics Engineering, Boca Raton, FL 33431-0991. Offers civil engineering (MS); environmental engineering (MS). Part-time and evening/weekend programs available. *Degree requirements:* For master's, thesis optional. *Entrance requirements:* For master's, GRE General Test, minimum GPA of 3.0 in last 60 hours of undergraduate course work. Additional exam requirements/recommendations for international students: Required—TOEFL (minimum score 550 paper-based; 61 iBT), IELTS (minimum score 6). *Expenses:* Tuition, state resident: full-time $7396; part-time $369.82 per credit hour. Tuition, nonresident: full-time $19,392; part-time $1024.81 per credit hour. Tuition and fees vary according to course load. *Faculty research:* Structures, geotechnical engineering, environmental and water resources engineering, transportation engineering, materials.

Florida International University, College of Engineering and Computing, Department of Civil and Environmental Engineering, Program in Environmental Engineering, Miami, FL 33175. Offers MS. Part-time and evening/weekend programs available. Postbaccalaureate distance learning degree programs offered (no on-campus study). *Degree requirements:* For master's, thesis optional. *Entrance requirements:* For master's, minimum GPA of 3.0; resume, 3 letters of recommendation. Additional exam requirements/recommendations for international students: Required—TOEFL (minimum score 550 paper-based; 80 iBT). Electronic applications accepted. *Faculty research:* Water and wastewater treatment, water quality, solid and hazardous waste, sustainability and green engineering, clean up, remediation and restoration.

Florida State University, The Graduate School, FAMU-FSU College of Engineering, Department of Civil and Environmental Engineering, Tallahassee, FL 32310. Offers M Eng, MS, PhD. Part-time programs available. *Degree requirements:* For master's, comprehensive exam, thesis optional; for doctorate, thesis/dissertation. *Entrance requirements:* For master's, GRE General Test (minimum score 1000 in old version), BS in engineering or related field, minimum GPA of 3.0; for doctorate, GRE General Test, master's degree in engineering or related field, minimum GPA of 3.0. Additional exam requirements/recommendations for international students: Required—TOEFL (minimum score 550 paper-based; 80 iBT); Recommended—IELTS (minimum score 6.5). *Expenses:* Tuition, state resident: part-time $403.51 per credit hour. Tuition, nonresident: part-time $1004.85 per credit hour. *Required fees:* $75.81 per credit hour. One-time fee: $20 part-time. Tuition and fees vary according to campus/location. *Faculty research:* Tidal hydraulics, temperature effects on bridge girders, codes for coastal construction, field performance of pine bridges, river basin management, transportation pavement design, soil dynamics, structural analysis.

Gannon University, School of Graduate Studies, College of Engineering and Business, School of Engineering and Computer Science, Program in Environmental Science and Engineering, Erie, PA 16541-0001. Offers environmental health and engineering (MS). Part-time and evening/weekend programs available. *Degree requirements:* For master's, thesis (for some programs), research paper or project (for some programs). *Entrance requirements:* For master's, GRE, bachelor's degree in science or engineering. Additional exam requirements/recommendations for international students: Required—TOEFL (minimum score 79 iBT). Electronic applications accepted.

George Mason University, Volgenau School of Engineering, Sid and Reva Dewberry Department of Civil, Environmental, and Infrastructure Engineering, Fairfax, VA 22030. Offers construction project management (MS); environmental and water resources engineering (MS); geotechnical, construction, and structural engineering (M Eng); transportation engineering (MS, PhD). *Faculty:* 12 full-time (4 women), 16 part-time/adjunct (3 women). *Students:* 28 full-time (7 women), 51 part-time (13 women); includes 25 minority (12 Black or African American, non-Hispanic/Latino; 8 Asian, non-Hispanic/Latino; 5 Hispanic/Latino), 14 international. Average age 30. 90 applicants, 58% accepted, 25 enrolled. In 2014, 28 master's, 3 doctorates awarded. *Degree requirements:* For master's, thesis (for some programs), 30 credits, departmental seminars; for doctorate, thesis/dissertation, qualifying exams. *Entrance requirements:* For master's, GRE, photocopy of passport; 2 official college transcripts; resume; official bank statement; proof of financial support; expanded goals statement; self-evaluation form; BS in engineering or other related science; 3 letters of recommendation; for doctorate, GRE (for those who received degree outside of the U.S.), photocopy of passport; 2 official college transcripts; resume; official bank statement; proof of financial support; expanded goals statement; self-evaluation form; baccalaureate degree in engineering or related science; master's degree (preferred); 3 letters of recommendation. Additional exam requirements/recommendations for international students: Required—TOEFL (minimum score 575 paper-based; 80 iBT), IELTS (minimum score 6.5), PTE. *Application deadline:* For fall admission, 1/15 priority date for domestic students; for spring admission, 8/1 priority date for domestic students. Application fee: $65 ($80 for international students). Electronic applications accepted. *Expenses:* Expenses: Contact institution. *Financial support:* In 2014–15, 19 students received support, including 1 fellowship (averaging $5,000 per year), 9 research assistantships with full and partial tuition reimbursements available (averaging $23,846 per year), 10 teaching assistantships with full and partial tuition reimbursements available (averaging $21,200 per year); career-related internships or fieldwork, Federal Work-Study, scholarships/grants, unspecified assistantships, and health care benefits (for full-time research or teaching assistantship recipients) also available. Support available to part-time students. Financial award application deadline: 3/1; financial award applicants required to submit FAFSA. *Faculty research:* Evolutionary design, infrastructure security, intelligent transportation systems, national transportation networks, water quality modeling. *Total annual research expenditures:* $159,347. *Unit head:* Dr. Deborah J. Goodings, Chair, 703-993-1675, Fax: 703-993-9790, E-mail: goodings@gmu.edu. *Application contact:* Kristin Amaya, Administrative Assistant, 703-993-1675, Fax: 703-993-9790, E-mail: kfairch1@gmu.edu.
Website: http://civil.gmu.edu/.

The George Washington University, School of Engineering and Applied Science, Department of Civil and Environmental Engineering, Washington, DC 20052. Offers MS, PhD, App Sc, Engr, Graduate Certificate. Part-time and evening/weekend programs available. *Faculty:* 12 full-time (3 women), 15 part-time/adjunct (0 women). *Students:* 17 full-time (4 women), 27 part-time (6 women); includes 3 minority (1 Black or African American, non-Hispanic/Latino; 1 Asian, non-Hispanic/Latino; 1 Hispanic/Latino), 30 international. Average age 30. 134 applicants, 51% accepted, 7 enrolled. In 2014, 14 master's, 4 doctorates awarded. *Degree requirements:* For master's, thesis optional; for doctorate, thesis/dissertation, final and qualifying exams. *Entrance requirements:* For master's, appropriate bachelor's degree, minimum GPA of 3.0; for doctorate, GRE (if

highest earned degree is BS), appropriate bachelor's or master's degree, minimum GPA of 3.4; for other advanced degree, appropriate master's degree, minimum GPA of 3.0. Additional exam requirements/recommendations for international students: Required—TOEFL or The George Washington University English as a Foreign Language Test. *Application deadline:* For fall admission, 3/1 priority date for domestic students; for spring admission, 10/1 for domestic students. Applications are processed on a rolling basis. Application fee: $75. *Financial support:* In 2014–15, 42 students received support. Fellowships with tuition reimbursements available, research assistantships, teaching assistantships with tuition reimbursements available, career-related internships or fieldwork, Federal Work-Study, institutionally sponsored loans, and tuition waivers available. Financial award application deadline: 3/1; financial award applicants required to submit FAFSA. *Faculty research:* Computer-integrated manufacturing, materials engineering, electronic materials, fatigue and fracture, reliability. *Unit head:* Dr. Majid Manzari, Chair, 202-994-8515, Fax: 202-994-0127, E-mail: manzari@gwu.edu. *Application contact:* Adina Lav, Marketing, Recruiting and Admissions, 202-994-5827, Fax: 202-994-0909, E-mail: engineering@gwu.edu.
Website: http://www.cee.seas.gwu.edu/.

Georgia Institute of Technology, Graduate Studies, College of Engineering, School of Civil and Environmental Engineering, Program in Environmental Engineering, Atlanta, GA 30332-0001. Offers MS, PhD. Part-time programs available. *Students:* 108 full-time (62 women), 18 part-time (8 women); includes 21 minority (2 Black or African American, non-Hispanic/Latino; 12 Asian, non-Hispanic/Latino; 6 Hispanic/Latino; 1 Two or more races, non-Hispanic/Latino), 77 international. Average age 23. 211 applicants, 76% accepted, 50 enrolled. In 2014, 29 master's, 15 doctorates awarded. Terminal master's awarded for partial completion of doctoral program. *Degree requirements:* For master's, thesis optional; for doctorate, comprehensive exam, thesis/dissertation. *Entrance requirements:* For master's and doctorate, GRE, http://www.grad.gatech.edu/enve. Additional exam requirements/recommendations for international students: Required—TOEFL (minimum score 550 paper-based; 79 iBT). *Application deadline:* For fall admission, 12/15 for domestic and international students; for spring admission, 8/31 for domestic and international students; for summer admission, 12/15 for domestic and international students. Applications are processed on a rolling basis. Application fee: $75. Electronic applications accepted. *Expenses:* Tuition, state resident: full-time $12,344; part-time $515 per credit hour. Tuition, nonresident: full-time $27,600; part-time $1150 per credit hour. *Required fees:* $1196 per term. Part-time tuition and fees vary according to course load. *Financial support:* Fellowships, research assistantships, teaching assistantships, career-related internships or fieldwork, Federal Work-Study, institutionally sponsored loans, tuition waivers (partial), and unspecified assistantships available. Support available to part-time students. Financial award application deadline: 5/1. *Faculty research:* Advanced microbiology of water and wastes, industrial waste treatment and disposal, air pollution measurements and control. *Unit head:* Jim Mulholland, Director, 404-894-1695, E-mail: james.mulholland@ce.gatech.edu. *Application contact:* Robert Simon, Graduate Coordinator, 404-894-1660, E-mail: robert.simon@gatech.edu.
Website: http://www.ce.gatech.edu.

Idaho State University, Office of Graduate Studies, College of Science and Engineering, Civil and Environmental Engineering Department, Pocatello, ID 83209-8060. Offers civil engineering (MS); environmental engineering (MS); environmental science and management (MS). Part-time programs available. *Degree requirements:* For master's, comprehensive exam (for some programs), thesis optional, thesis project, 2 semesters of seminar. *Entrance requirements:* For master's, GRE. Additional exam requirements/recommendations for international students: Required—TOEFL (minimum score 550 paper-based; 80 iBT). Electronic applications accepted. *Faculty research:* Floor vibration investigations, earthquake engineering, base isolation systems and seismic risk assessment, infrastructure revitalization (building foundations and damage, bridge structures, highways, and dams), slope stability and soil erosion, pavement rehabilitation, computational fluid dynamics and flood control structures, microbial fuel cells, water treatment and water quality modeling, environmental risk assessment, biotechnology, nanotechnology.

Illinois Institute of Technology, Graduate College, Armour College of Engineering, Department of Civil, Architectural and Environmental Engineering, Chicago, IL 60616. Offers architectural engineering (M Arch E); civil engineering (MS, PhD), including architectural engineering (MS), construction engineering and management (MS), geoenvironmental engineering (MS), geotechnical engineering (MS), structural engineering (MS), transportation engineering (MS); construction engineering and management (MCEM); environmental engineering (M Env E, MS, PhD); geoenvironmental engineering (M Geoenv E); geotechnical engineering (MGE); infrastructure engineering and management (MPW); structural engineering (MSE); transportation engineering (M Trans E). Part-time and evening/weekend programs available. Postbaccalaureate distance learning degree programs offered (minimal on-campus study). *Faculty:* 12 full-time (1 woman), 15 part-time/adjunct (1 woman). *Students:* 165 full-time (48 women), 54 part-time (11 women); includes 31 minority (2 Black or African American, non-Hispanic/Latino; 21 Asian, non-Hispanic/Latino; 7 Hispanic/Latino; 1 Native Hawaiian or other Pacific Islander, non-Hispanic/Latino), 157 international. Average age 29. 1,039 applicants, 42% accepted, 82 enrolled. In 2014, 94 master's, 7 doctorates awarded. Terminal master's awarded for partial completion of doctoral program. *Degree requirements:* For master's, thesis (for some programs); for doctorate, comprehensive exam, thesis/dissertation. *Entrance requirements:* For master's, GRE General Test (minimum score 900 Quantitative and Verbal, 2.5 Analytical Writing), minimum undergraduate GPA of 3.0; for doctorate, GRE General Test (minimum score 1000 Quantitative and Verbal, 3.0 Analytical Writing), minimum undergraduate GPA of 3.0. Additional exam requirements/recommendations for international students: Required—TOEFL (minimum score 550 paper-based; 80 iBT). *Application deadline:* For fall admission, 5/1 for domestic and international students; for spring admission, 10/15 for domestic and international students. Applications are processed on a rolling basis. Application fee: $50. Electronic applications accepted. *Expenses: Tuition:* Full-time $22,500; part-time $1250 per credit hour. *Required fees:* $30 per course. $260 per semester. One-time fee: $235. Tuition and fees vary according to course load and program. *Financial support:* Fellowships with full and partial tuition reimbursements, research assistantships with full and partial tuition reimbursements, teaching assistantships with full and partial tuition reimbursements, Federal Work-Study, institutionally sponsored loans, scholarships/grants, health care benefits, tuition waivers (partial), and unspecified assistantships available. Support available to part-time students. Financial award applicants required to submit FAFSA. *Faculty research:* Structural, architectural, geotechnical and geoenvironmental engineering; construction engineering and management; transportation engineering; environmental engineering and public works. *Unit head:* Dr. Gongkang Fu, Professor and Chairman, 312-567-3540, Fax: 312-567-3519, E-mail: gfu2@iit.edu. *Application contact:* Rishab Malhotra, Director, Graduate Admission, 866-472-3448, Fax: 312-567-3138, E-mail: inquiry.grad@iit.edu.
Website: http://engineering.iit.edu/caee.

Instituto Tecnologico de Santo Domingo, Graduate School, Area of Engineering, Santo Domingo, Dominican Republic. Offers construction administration (MS, Certificate); data telecommunications (M Eng, MS, Certificate); industrial engineering (M Eng, Certificate); industrial management (M Mgmt); information technology (Certificate); maintenance engineering (M Eng); occupational hazard prevention (M Mgmt); production management (Certificate); quantitative methods (Certificate); sanitary and environmental engineering (M Eng); structural engineering (M Eng); systems engineering and electronic data processing (Certificate); transportation (Certificate).

Instituto Tecnológico y de Estudios Superiores de Monterrey, Campus Ciudad de México, Virtual University Division, Ciudad de Mexico, Mexico. Offers administration of information technologies (MA); computer sciences (MA); education (MA, PhD); educational technology (MA); environmental engineering (MA); environmental systems (MA); humanistic studies (MA); industrial engineering (MA); international business for Latin America (MA); quality systems (MA); quality systems and productivity (MA). Part-time and evening/weekend programs available. Postbaccalaureate distance learning degree programs offered (minimal on-campus study). *Entrance requirements:* For master's and doctorate, Instituto entrance exam. Additional exam requirements/recommendations for international students: Required—TOEFL.

Instituto Tecnológico y de Estudios Superiores de Monterrey, Campus Monterrey, Graduate and Research Division, Programs in Engineering, Monterrey, Mexico. Offers applied statistics (M Eng); artificial intelligence (PhD); automation engineering (M Eng); chemical engineering (M Eng); civil engineering (M Eng); electrical engineering (M Eng); electronic engineering (M Eng); environmental engineering (M Eng); industrial engineering (M Eng, PhD); manufacturing engineering (M Eng); mechanical engineering (M Eng); systems and quality engineering (M Eng). M Eng program offered jointly with University of Waterloo; PhD in industrial engineering with Texas A&M University. Part-time and evening/weekend programs available. Terminal master's awarded for partial completion of doctoral program. *Degree requirements:* For master's, one foreign language, thesis; for doctorate, one foreign language, thesis/dissertation. *Entrance requirements:* For master's, EXADEP; for doctorate, GRE, master's degree in related field. Additional exam requirements/recommendations for international students: Required—TOEFL. *Faculty research:* Flexible manufacturing cells, materials, statistical methods, environmental prevention, control and evaluation.

Iowa State University of Science and Technology, Department of Civil and Construction Engineering, Ames, IA 50011. Offers civil engineering (MS, PhD), including civil engineering materials, construction engineering and management, environmental engineering, geometronics, geotechnical engineering, structural engineering, transportation engineering. *Degree requirements:* For master's, thesis or alternative; for doctorate, thesis/dissertation. *Entrance requirements:* For master's and doctorate, GRE General Test. Additional exam requirements/recommendations for international students: Required—TOEFL (minimum score 550 paper-based; 82 iBT), IELTS (minimum score 6.5). Electronic applications accepted.

Johns Hopkins University, Bloomberg School of Public Health, Department of Environmental Health Sciences, Baltimore, MD 21218-2699. Offers environmental health engineering (PhD); environmental health sciences (MHS, Dr PH); occupational and environmental health (PhD); physiology (PhD); toxicology (PhD). Postbaccalaureate distance learning degree programs offered (minimal on-campus study). *Degree requirements:* For master's, essay, presentation; for doctorate, comprehensive exam, thesis/dissertation, 1-year full-time residency, oral and written exams. *Entrance requirements:* For master's, GRE General Test or MCAT, 3 letters of recommendation, transcripts; for doctorate, GRE General Test or MCAT, 3 letters of recommendation. Additional exam requirements/recommendations for international students: Required—TOEFL (minimum score 600 paper-based). Electronic applications accepted. *Faculty research:* Chemical carcinogenesis/toxicology, lung disease, occupational and environmental health, nuclear imaging, molecular epidemiology.

Johns Hopkins University, Engineering Program for Professionals, Part-time Program in Environmental Engineering, Baltimore, MD 21218-2699. Offers MS, Graduate Certificate, Post-Master's Certificate. Part-time and evening/weekend programs available.

Johns Hopkins University, Engineering Program for Professionals, Part-time Program in Environmental Engineering and Science, Baltimore, MD 21218-2699. Offers MEE, MS, Graduate Certificate, Post-Master's Certificate. Part-time and evening/weekend programs available. Electronic applications accepted.

Johns Hopkins University, G. W. C. Whiting School of Engineering, Department of Geography and Environmental Engineering, Baltimore, MD 21218-2699. Offers MA, MS, MSE, PhD. Terminal master's awarded for partial completion of doctoral program. *Degree requirements:* For master's, thesis (for some programs), 1-year full-time residency; for doctorate, comprehensive exam, thesis/dissertation, oral exam, 2-year full-time residency. *Entrance requirements:* For master's and doctorate, GRE General Test. Additional exam requirements/recommendations for international students: Required—TOEFL (minimum score 670 paper-based; 120 iBT); Recommended—IELTS. Electronic applications accepted. *Faculty research:* Environmental engineering; environmental chemistry; water resources engineering; systems analysis and economics for public decision-making; geomorphology, hydrology and ecology.

Kansas State University, Graduate School, College of Engineering, Department of Civil Engineering, Manhattan, KS 66506. Offers civil engineering (MS, PhD); environmental engineering (MS, PhD); geotechnical engineering (MS, PhD); structural engineering (MS, PhD); transportation engineering (MS, PhD); water resources engineering (MS, PhD). Part-time and evening/weekend programs available. Postbaccalaureate distance learning degree programs offered (no on-campus study). *Faculty:* 14 full-time (4 women), 3 part-time/adjunct (1 woman). *Students:* 37 full-time (12 women), 37 part-time (9 women); includes 6 minority (3 Black or African American, non-Hispanic/Latino; 3 Hispanic/Latino), 23 international. Average age 30. 62 applicants, 39% accepted, 10 enrolled. In 2014, 14 master's, 4 doctorates awarded. *Degree requirements:* For master's, thesis or alternative; for doctorate, thesis/dissertation. *Entrance requirements:* For master's, GRE General Test, bachelor's degree or course work in related engineering fields; for doctorate, GRE General Test. Additional exam requirements/recommendations for international students: Required—TOEFL (minimum score 550 paper-based; 79 iBT). *Application deadline:* For fall admission, 2/1 priority date for domestic students, 1/1 priority date for international students; for spring admission, 8/1 priority date for domestic and international students. Applications are processed on a rolling basis. Application fee: $50 ($75 for international students). Electronic applications accepted. *Financial support:* In 2014–15, 19 research assistantships with partial tuition reimbursements (averaging $13,431 per year), 12 teaching assistantships with partial tuition reimbursements (averaging $15,058 per year) were awarded; institutionally sponsored loans and scholarships/grants also available. Support available to part-time students. Financial award application deadline: 3/1; financial award applicants required to submit FAFSA. *Faculty research:* Transportation and materials engineering, water resources engineering, environmental engineering, geotechnical engineering, structural engineering. *Total annual research expenditures:* $2.4 million. *Unit head:* Dr. Robert Stokes, Head, 785-532-1595, Fax: 785-532-7717, E-mail: drbobb@k-state.edu. *Application contact:* Dr. Dunja Peric, Graduate Coordinator, 785-532-2468, Fax: 785-532-7717, E-mail: peric@k-state.edu.
Website: http://www.ce.ksu.edu/.

Environmental Engineering

Lakehead University, Graduate Studies, Faculty of Engineering, Thunder Bay, ON P7B 5E1, Canada. Offers control engineering (M Sc Engr); electrical/computer engineering (M Sc Engr); environmental engineering (M Sc Engr). Part-time programs available. *Degree requirements:* For master's, thesis. *Entrance requirements:* For master's, bachelor's degree in chemical, electrical or mechanical engineering, minimum B average. Additional exam requirements/recommendations for international students: Required—TOEFL. *Faculty research:* Pulp and paper, adaptive/process control, robust/interactive learning control, vibration control.

Lamar University, College of Graduate Studies, College of Engineering, Department of Civil and Environmental Engineering, Beaumont, TX 77710. Offers environmental engineering (MS); environmental studies (MS). Part-time programs available. *Faculty:* 5 full-time (1 woman), 2 part-time/adjunct (0 women). *Students:* 78 full-time (15 women), 14 part-time (3 women); includes 7 minority (1 Black or African American, non-Hispanic/Latino; 5 Asian, non-Hispanic/Latino; 1 Hispanic/Latino), 78 international. Average age 25. 136 applicants, 75% accepted, 47 enrolled. In 2014, 10 master's awarded. *Degree requirements:* For master's, thesis optional. *Entrance requirements:* For master's, GRE General Test. Additional exam requirements/recommendations for international students: Required—TOEFL (minimum score 550 paper-based; 79 iBT), IELTS (minimum score 6.5). *Application deadline:* For fall admission, 8/1 for domestic students, 7/1 for international students; for spring admission, 1/5 for domestic students, 12/1 for international students. Applications are processed on a rolling basis. Application fee: $25 ($50 for international students). *Expenses:* Tuition, state resident: full-time $5724; part-time $1908 per semester. Tuition, nonresident: full-time $12,240; part-time $4080 per semester. *Required fees:* $1940; $318 per credit hour. *Financial support:* In 2014–15, 45 fellowships with partial tuition reimbursements (averaging $1,000 per year), 10 research assistantships with partial tuition reimbursements (averaging $7,200 per year), 3 teaching assistantships with partial tuition reimbursements (averaging $7,200 per year) were awarded; scholarships/grants and tuition waivers (partial) also available. Financial award application deadline: 4/1. *Faculty research:* Environmental remediations, construction productivity, geotechnical soil stabilization, lake/reservoir hydrodynamics, air pollution. *Unit head:* Dr. Robert Yuan, Chair, 409-880-8759, Fax: 409-880-8121. *Application contact:* Melissa Gallien, Director, Admissions and Academic Services, 409-880-8888, Fax: 409-880-7419, E-mail: gradmissions@lamar.edu. Website: http://engineering.lamar.edu/civil.

Lehigh University, P.C. Rossin College of Engineering and Applied Science, Department of Civil and Environmental Engineering, Bethlehem, PA 18015. Offers M Eng, MS, PhD. Part-time programs available. *Faculty:* 21 full-time (4 women), 1 part-time/adjunct (0 women). *Students:* 75 full-time (20 women), 15 part-time (2 women); includes 3 minority (1 Black or African American, non-Hispanic/Latino; 1 Asian, non-Hispanic/Latino; 1 Hispanic/Latino), 52 international. Average age 27. 225 applicants, 41% accepted, 11 enrolled. In 2014, 44 master's, 3 doctorates awarded. Terminal master's awarded for partial completion of doctoral program. *Degree requirements:* For master's, thesis (for some programs); for doctorate, comprehensive exam, thesis/dissertation. *Entrance requirements:* For master's and doctorate, GRE. Additional exam requirements/recommendations for international students: Required—TOEFL (minimum score 550 paper-based; 79 iBT). *Application deadline:* For fall admission, 7/15 priority date for domestic and international students; for spring admission, 12/1 priority date for domestic and international students; for summer admission, 5/30 for domestic and international students. Applications are processed on a rolling basis. Application fee: $75. Electronic applications accepted. *Expenses:* Expenses: $24,120. *Financial support:* In 2014–15, 47 students received support, including 7 fellowships with full tuition reimbursements available (averaging $19,920 per year), 31 research assistantships with full tuition reimbursements available (averaging $23,100 per year), 7 teaching assistantships with full tuition reimbursements available (averaging $20,490 per year); institutionally sponsored loans, scholarships/grants, tuition waivers, and unspecified assistantships also available. Financial award application deadline: 1/15; financial award applicants required to submit FAFSA. *Faculty research:* Structural engineering, geotechnical engineering, water resources engineering, environmental engineering. *Total annual research expenditures:* $5.8 million. *Unit head:* Dr. Panayiotis Diplas, Chair, 610-758-3554, E-mail: pad313@lehigh.edu. *Application contact:* Prisca Vidanage, Graduate Coordinator, 610-758-3530, E-mail: pmv1@lehigh.edu. Website: http://www.lehigh.edu/~incee/.

Louisiana State University and Agricultural & Mechanical College, Graduate School, College of Engineering, Department of Civil and Environmental Engineering, Baton Rouge, LA 70803. Offers environmental engineering (MSCE, PhD); geotechnical engineering (MSCE, PhD); structural engineering and mechanics (MSCE, PhD); transportation engineering (MSCE, PhD); water resources (MSCE, PhD). Part-time programs available. *Faculty:* 26 full-time (1 woman). *Students:* 90 full-time (24 women), 28 part-time (6 women); includes 12 minority (5 Black or African American, non-Hispanic/Latino; 1 American Indian or Alaska Native, non-Hispanic/Latino; 5 Asian, non-Hispanic/Latino; 1 Two or more races, non-Hispanic/Latino), 67 international. Average age 30. 147 applicants, 50% accepted, 23 enrolled. In 2014, 26 master's, 8 doctorates awarded. *Degree requirements:* For master's, thesis optional; for doctorate, one foreign language, thesis/dissertation. *Entrance requirements:* For master's and doctorate, GRE General Test, minimum GPA of 3.0. Additional exam requirements/recommendations for international students: Required—TOEFL (minimum score 550 paper-based; 79 iBT), IELTS (minimum score 6.5), or PTE (minimum score 59). *Application deadline:* For fall admission, 1/1 priority date for domestic students, 5/15 for international students; for spring admission, 10/15 for domestic and international students; for summer admission, 5/15 for domestic and international students. Applications are processed on a rolling basis. Application fee: $50 ($70 for international students). Electronic applications accepted. *Financial support:* In 2014–15, 88 students received support, including 7 fellowships with full and partial tuition reimbursements available (averaging $26,784 per year), 59 research assistantships with full and partial tuition reimbursements available (averaging $16,992 per year), 13 teaching assistantships with full and partial tuition reimbursements available (averaging $16,290 per year); career-related internships or fieldwork, institutionally sponsored loans, scholarships/grants, and health care benefits also available. Financial award application deadline: 3/1; financial award applicants required to submit FAFSA. *Faculty research:* Mechanics and structures, environmental, geotechnical transportation, water resources. *Total annual research expenditures:* $3.2 million. *Unit head:* Dr. George Z. Voyiadjis, Chair/Professor, 225-578-8442, Fax: 225-578-8652, E-mail: voyaidjis@lsu.edu. *Application contact:* Dr. Ayman Ikeli, Professor, 225-578-7048, E-mail: aokeli@lsu.edu. Website: http://www.cee.lsu.edu/.

Manhattan College, Graduate Programs, School of Engineering, Program in Environmental Engineering, Riverdale, NY 10471. Offers ME, MS. *Accreditation:* ABET. Part-time and evening/weekend programs available. *Faculty:* 5 full-time (1 woman), 2 part-time/adjunct (1 woman). *Students:* 17 full-time (6 women), 12 part-time (4 women); includes 4 minority (3 Asian, non-Hispanic/Latino; 1 Hispanic/Latino). Average age 24. 22 applicants, 100% accepted, 15 enrolled. In 2014, 9 master's awarded. *Degree requirements:* For master's, thesis optional, 30 credits, minimum GPA of 3.0. *Entrance requirements:* For master's, GRE (recommended), minimum GPA of 3.0. Additional exam requirements/recommendations for international students: Required—TOEFL (minimum score 550 paper-based; 80 iBT), IELTS (minimum score 6). *Application deadline:* For fall admission, 8/10 priority date for domestic students, 8/10 for international students; for spring admission, 1/7 for domestic and international students. Applications are processed on a rolling basis. Application fee: $60. *Financial support:* In 2014–15, 15 students received support, including 3 fellowships with full tuition reimbursements available (averaging $15,000 per year), 6 research assistantships with full tuition reimbursements available (averaging $18,000 per year), 2 teaching assistantships with partial tuition reimbursements available (averaging $8,800 per year); career-related internships or fieldwork, Federal Work-Study, scholarships/grants, unspecified assistantships, and laboratory assistantships also available. Support available to part-time students. Financial award application deadline: 3/1. *Faculty research:* Water quality modeling, environmental chemistry, air modeling, biological treatment, environmental chemistry. *Total annual research expenditures:* $400,000. *Unit head:* Dr. Robert Sharp, Graduate Program Director, 718-862-7169, Fax: 718-862-8035, E-mail: robert.sharp@manhattan.edu. *Application contact:* Janet Horgan, Information Contact, 718-862-7171, Fax: 718-862-8035, E-mail: janet.horgan@manhattan.edu. Website: http://www.engineering.manhattan.edu.

Marquette University, Graduate School, Opus College of Engineering, Department of Civil, Construction and Environmental Engineering, Milwaukee, WI 53201-1881. Offers construction engineering and management (MS, PhD, Certificate); environmental engineering (MS, PhD); structural design (Certificate); structural engineering and structural mechanics (MS, PhD); transportation (Certificate); transportation engineering and materials (MS, PhD); waste and wastewater treatment processes (Certificate); water resources engineering (Certificate). Part-time and evening/weekend programs available. Terminal master's awarded for partial completion of doctoral program. *Degree requirements:* For master's, comprehensive exam (for some programs), thesis or alternative; for doctorate, thesis/dissertation. *Entrance requirements:* For master's, GRE General Test (recommended), minimum GPA of 3.0, official transcripts from all current and previous colleges/universities except Marquette, three letters of recommendation; for doctorate, GRE General Test, minimum GPA of 3.0, official transcripts from all current and previous colleges/universities except Marquette, three letters of recommendation, brief statement of purpose, submission of any English language publications authored by applicant (strongly recommended). Additional exam requirements/recommendations for international students: Required—TOEFL (minimum score 530 paper-based). Electronic applications accepted. *Faculty research:* Highway safety, highway performance, and intelligent transportation systems; surface mount technology; watershed management.

Marshall University, Academic Affairs Division, College of Information Technology and Engineering, Weisbert Division of Engineering, Huntington, WV 25755. Offers engineering management (MSE); environmental engineering (MSE); mechanical engineering (MS); transportation and infrastructure engineering (MSE). Part-time and evening/weekend programs available. *Students:* 30 full-time (5 women), 28 part-time (7 women); includes 3 minority (all Black or African American, non-Hispanic/Latino), 22 international. Average age 29. In 2014, 11 master's awarded. *Degree requirements:* For master's, final project, oral exam. *Entrance requirements:* For master's, GMAT or GRE General Test, minimum undergraduate GPA of 2.75. Application fee: $40. *Financial support:* Tuition waivers (full) available. Support available to part-time students. Financial award application deadline: 8/1; financial award applicants required to submit FAFSA. *Unit head:* Dr. William Pierson, Chair, 304-696-2695, E-mail: pierson@marshall.edu. *Application contact:* Information Contact, 304-746-1900, Fax: 304-746-1902, E-mail: services@marshall.edu. Website: http://www.marshall.edu/cite/.

Massachusetts Institute of Technology, School of Engineering, Department of Civil and Environmental Engineering, Cambridge, MA 02139. Offers biological oceanography (PhD, Sc D); chemical oceanography (PhD, Sc D); civil and environmental engineering (M Eng, SM, PhD, Sc D); civil and environmental systems (PhD, Sc D); civil engineering (PhD, Sc D, CE); coastal engineering (PhD, Sc D); construction engineering and management (PhD, Sc D); environmental biology (PhD, Sc D); environmental chemistry (PhD, Sc D); environmental engineering (PhD, Sc D); environmental fluid mechanics (PhD, Sc D); geotechnical and geoenvironmental engineering (PhD, Sc D); hydrology (PhD, Sc D); information technology (PhD, Sc D); oceanographic engineering (PhD, Sc D); structures and materials (PhD, Sc D); transportation (PhD, Sc D); SM/MBA. *Faculty:* 34 full-time (8 women), 1 part-time/adjunct (0 women). *Students:* 216 full-time (82 women); includes 25 minority (1 Black or African American, non-Hispanic/Latino; 10 Asian, non-Hispanic/Latino; 8 Hispanic/Latino; 6 Two or more races, non-Hispanic/Latino), 117 international. Average age 26. 565 applicants, 22% accepted, 85 enrolled. In 2014, 76 master's, 18 doctorates awarded. *Degree requirements:* For master's and CE, thesis; for doctorate, comprehensive exam, thesis/dissertation. *Entrance requirements:* For master's and doctorate, GRE General Test. Additional exam requirements/recommendations for international students: Required—TOEFL (minimum score 577 paper-based; 100 iBT), IELTS (minimum score 7). *Application deadline:* For fall admission, 12/15 for domestic and international students. Application fee: $75. Electronic applications accepted. *Expenses:* Tuition: full-time $44,720; part-time $699 per unit. *Required fees:* $296. *Financial support:* In 2014–15, 170 students received support, including 32 fellowships (averaging $32,800 per year), 132 research assistantships (averaging $33,800 per year), 13 teaching assistantships (averaging $32,900 per year); Federal Work-Study, institutionally sponsored loans, scholarships/grants, traineeships, health care benefits, and unspecified assistantships also available. Financial award application deadline: 4/15; financial award applicants required to submit FAFSA. *Faculty research:* Environmental chemistry, environmental fluid mechanics and coastal engineering, environmental microbiology, geotechnical engineering and geomechanics, hydrology and hydroclimatology, infrastructure systems, mechanics of materials and structures, transportation systems. *Total annual research expenditures:* $22.9 million. *Unit head:* Prof. Markus Buehler, Department Head, 617-324-6488. *Application contact:* Graduate Admissions Coordinator, 617-253-7119, E-mail: cee-admissions@mit.edu. Website: http://cee.mit.edu/.

McGill University, Faculty of Graduate and Postdoctoral Studies, Faculty of Engineering, Department of Chemical Engineering, Montréal, QC H3A 2T5, Canada. Offers chemical engineering (M Eng, PhD); environmental engineering (M Eng).

McGill University, Faculty of Graduate and Postdoctoral Studies, Faculty of Engineering, Department of Civil Engineering and Applied Mechanics, Montréal, QC H3A 2T5, Canada. Offers environmental engineering (M Eng, M Sc, PhD); fluid mechanics (M Sc); fluid mechanics and hydraulic engineering (M Eng, PhD); materials engineering (M Eng, PhD); rehabilitation of urban infrastructure (M Eng, PhD); soil behavior (M Eng, PhD); soil mechanics and foundations (M Eng, PhD); structures and structural mechanics (M Eng, PhD); water resources (M Sc); water resources engineering (M Eng, PhD).

Memorial University of Newfoundland, School of Graduate Studies, Interdisciplinary Program in Environmental Systems Engineering and Management, St. John's, NL A1C 5S7, Canada. Offers MA Sc. *Degree requirements:* For master's, project course. *Entrance requirements:* For master's, 2nd class engineering degree.

Mercer University, Graduate Studies, Macon Campus, School of Engineering, Macon, GA 31207. Offers biomedical engineering (MSE); computer engineering (MSE);

electrical engineering (MSE); engineering management (MSE); environmental engineering (MSE); environmental systems (MS); mechanical engineering (MSE); software engineering (MSE); software systems (MS); technical communications management (MS); technical management (MS). Part-time and evening/weekend programs available. Postbaccalaureate distance learning degree programs offered (no on-campus study). *Faculty:* 20 full-time (6 women), 2 part-time/adjunct (0 women). *Students:* 10 full-time (4 women), 75 part-time (16 women); includes 10 minority (5 Black or African American, non-Hispanic/Latino; 4 Asian, non-Hispanic/Latino; 1 Hispanic/Latino), 4 international. Average age 42. In 2014, 70 master's awarded. *Degree requirements:* For master's, thesis or alternative. *Entrance requirements:* For master's, minimum undergraduate GPA of 3.0. Additional exam requirements/recommendations for international students: Required—TOEFL (minimum score 550 paper-based; 80 iBT). *Application deadline:* For fall admission, 4/1 priority date for domestic and international students; for spring admission, 11/1 priority date for domestic and international students. Applications are processed on a rolling basis. Application fee: $75. *Expenses:* Expenses: Contact institution. *Financial support:* Federal Work-Study available. *Unit head:* Dr. Wade H. Shaw, Dean, 478-301-2459, Fax: 478-301-5593, E-mail: shaw_wh@mercer.edu. *Application contact:* Dr. Richard O. Mines, Program Director, 478-301-2347, Fax: 478-301-5433, E-mail: mines_ro@mercer.edu. Website: http://engineering.mercer.edu/.

Michigan State University, The Graduate School, College of Engineering, Department of Civil and Environmental Engineering, East Lansing, MI 48824. Offers civil engineering (MS, PhD); environmental engineering (MS, PhD); environmental engineering-environmental toxicology (PhD). Part-time programs available. *Entrance requirements:* Additional exam requirements/recommendations for international students: Required—TOEFL. Electronic applications accepted.

Michigan Technological University, Graduate School, College of Engineering, Department of Civil and Environmental Engineering, Houghton, MI 49931. Offers civil engineering (M Eng, MS, PhD); environmental engineering (M Eng, MS); environmental engineering science (MS). Part-time programs available. *Faculty:* 41 full-time, 10 part-time/adjunct. *Students:* 101 full-time (38 women), 17 part-time (8 women); includes 10 minority (2 Black or African American, non-Hispanic/Latino; 2 Asian, non-Hispanic/Latino; 4 Hispanic/Latino; 1 Native Hawaiian or other Pacific Islander, non-Hispanic/Latino; 1 Two or more races, non-Hispanic/Latino), 48 international. Average age 26. 389 applicants, 51% accepted, 46 enrolled. In 2014, 31 master's, 4 doctorates awarded. *Degree requirements:* For master's, comprehensive exam (for some programs), thesis (for some programs); for doctorate, comprehensive exam, thesis/dissertation. *Entrance requirements:* For master's and doctorate, GRE (Michigan Tech students exempt), statement of purpose, official transcripts, 2 letters of recommendation. Additional exam requirements/recommendations for international students: Required—TOEFL (recommended score 100 iBT) or IELTS. *Application deadline:* For fall admission, 1/15 priority date for domestic and international students; for spring admission, 9/15 priority date for domestic and international students; for summer admission, 2/15 priority date for domestic and international students. Applications are processed on a rolling basis. Electronic applications accepted. *Expenses:* Expenses: Contact institution. *Financial support:* In 2014–15, 90 students received support, including 8 fellowships with full and partial tuition reimbursements available (averaging $13,824 per year), 19 research assistantships with full and partial tuition reimbursements available (averaging $13,824 per year), 9 teaching assistantships with full and partial tuition reimbursements available (averaging $13,824 per year); career-related internships or fieldwork, Federal Work-Study, scholarships/grants, health care benefits, unspecified assistantships, and cooperative program also available. Financial award applicants required to submit FAFSA. *Faculty research:* Water resources, construction engineering, transportation engineering, structural engineering, geotechnical engineering. *Total annual research expenditures:* $2.4 million. *Unit head:* Dr. David Hand, Chair, 906-487-2777, Fax: 906-487-2943, E-mail: dwhand@mtu.edu. *Application contact:* Angela Keranen, Administrative Aide, 906-487-2474, Fax: 906-487-2943, E-mail: amkerane@mtu.edu. Website: http://www.mtu.edu/cee/.

Michigan Technological University, Graduate School, Interdisciplinary Programs, Houghton, MI 49931. Offers atmospheric sciences (PhD); biochemistry and molecular biology (PhD); computational science and engineering (PhD); environmental engineering (PhD); interdisciplinary studies (M Ed, MS, Graduate Certificate). Part-time programs available. *Faculty:* 6 full-time, 3 part-time/adjunct. *Students:* 46 full-time (20 women), 6 part-time (3 women); includes 2 minority (1 Asian, non-Hispanic/Latino; 1 Two or more races, non-Hispanic/Latino), 35 international. Average age 30. 239 applicants, 16% accepted, 9 enrolled. In 2014, 4 doctorates awarded. Terminal master's awarded for partial completion of doctoral program. *Degree requirements:* For master's, comprehensive exam (for some programs), thesis (for some programs); for doctorate, comprehensive exam, thesis/dissertation. *Entrance requirements:* For master's, doctorate, and Graduate Certificate, GRE, statement of purpose, official transcripts, 2-3 letters of recommendation. Additional exam requirements/recommendations for international students: Required—TOEFL or IELTS. *Application deadline:* Applications are processed on a rolling basis. Electronic applications accepted. *Expenses:* Tuition, state resident: full-time $14,769; part-time $820.50 per credit. Tuition, nonresident: full-time $14,769; part-time $820.50 per credit. *Required fees:* $248; $248 per year. Tuition and fees vary according to course load and program. *Financial support:* In 2014–15, 42 students received support, including 6 fellowships with full and partial tuition reimbursements available (averaging $13,824 per year), 25 research assistantships with full and partial tuition reimbursements available (averaging $13,824 per year), 4 teaching assistantships with full and partial tuition reimbursements available (averaging $13,824 per year); career-related internships or fieldwork, Federal Work-Study, scholarships/grants, health care benefits, unspecified assistantships, and cooperative program also available. Financial award applicants required to submit FAFSA. *Faculty research:* Big data, atmospheric sciences, bioinformatics and systems biology, molecular dynamics. *Unit head:* Dr. Jacqueline E. Huntoon, Dean, 906-487-2327, Fax: 906-487-2284, E-mail: jeh@mtu.edu. *Application contact:* Carol T. Wingerson, Administrative Aide, 906-487-2328, Fax: 906-487-2284, E-mail: gradadms@mtu.edu.

Missouri University of Science and Technology, Graduate School, Department of Civil, Architectural, and Environmental Engineering, Rolla, MO 65409. Offers civil engineering (MS, DE, PhD); construction engineering (MS, DE, PhD); environmental engineering (MS); fluid mechanics (MS, DE, PhD); geotechnical engineering (MS, DE, PhD); hydrology and hydraulic engineering (MS, DE, PhD). Part-time and evening/weekend programs available. Terminal master's awarded for partial completion of doctoral program. *Degree requirements:* For master's, thesis optional; for doctorate, comprehensive exam, thesis/dissertation. *Entrance requirements:* For master's, GRE General Test (minimum combined score 1100), minimum GPA of 3.0; for doctorate, GRE General Test (minimum score: verbal and quantitative 400, writing 3.5), minimum GPA of 3.0. Additional exam requirements/recommendations for international students: Required—TOEFL. Electronic applications accepted. *Faculty research:* Earthquake engineering, structural optimization and control systems, structural health monitoring/damage detection, soil-structure interaction, soil mechanics and foundation engineering.

Montana State University, The Graduate School, College of Engineering, Department of Chemical and Biological Engineering, Bozeman, MT 59717. Offers chemical

engineering (MS); engineering (PhD), including chemical engineering option, environmental engineering option; environmental engineering (MS). Part-time programs available. *Degree requirements:* For master's, comprehensive exam, thesis (for some programs); for doctorate, comprehensive exam, thesis/dissertation. *Entrance requirements:* For master's and doctorate, GRE General Test. Additional exam requirements/recommendations for international students: Required—TOEFL (minimum score 550 paper-based). Electronic applications accepted. *Faculty research:* Biofuels, extremophilic bioprocessing, and situ biocatalyzed heavy metal transformations; metabolic network analysis and engineering; magnetic resonance microscopy; modeling of biological systems; the development of protective coatings on planar solid oxide fuel cell (SOFC) metallic interconnects; characterizing corrosion mechanisms of materials in precisely-controlled exposures; testing materials in poly-crystalline silicon production environments; environmental biotechnology and bioremediation.

Montana Tech of The University of Montana, Graduate School, Department of Environmental Engineering, Butte, MT 59701-8997. Offers MS. Part-time programs available. *Degree requirements:* For master's, thesis. *Entrance requirements:* For master's, GRE General Test, minimum GPA of 3.0. Additional exam requirements/recommendations for international students: Required—TOEFL (minimum score 525 paper-based; 71 iBT). Electronic applications accepted. *Expenses:* Tuition, state resident: full-time $5802; part-time $241 per credit. Tuition, nonresident: full-time $15,895; part-time $662 per credit. *Required fees:* $1516; $414 per credit. $207 per semester. One-time fee: $30. *Faculty research:* Mine waste reclamation, modeling, air pollution control, wetlands, water pollution control.

National University, Academic Affairs, School of Engineering and Computing, La Jolla, CA 92037-1011. Offers computer science (MS), including advanced computing, database engineering, software engineering; cyber security and information assurance (MS), including computer forensics, ethical hacking and penetration testing, health information assurance, information assurance and security; data analytics (MS); engineering management (MS), including enterprise architecture, project management, systems engineering, technology management; environmental engineering (MS); homeland security and emergency management (MS); management information systems (MS); project management (Certificate); sustainability management (MS); wireless communications (MS). Part-time and evening/weekend programs available. Postbaccalaureate distance learning degree programs offered (no on-campus study). *Faculty:* 24 full-time (5 women), 21 part-time/adjunct (5 women). *Students:* 275 full-time (72 women), 86 part-time (24 women); includes 147 minority (41 Black or African American, non-Hispanic/Latino; 48 Asian, non-Hispanic/Latino; 37 Hispanic/Latino; 7 Native Hawaiian or other Pacific Islander, non-Hispanic/Latino; 14 Two or more races, non-Hispanic/Latino), 95 international. Average age 33. In 2014, 281 master's awarded. *Degree requirements:* For master's, thesis (for some programs). *Entrance requirements:* For master's, interview, minimum GPA of 2.5. Additional exam requirements/recommendations for international students: Required—TOEFL (minimum score 550 paper-based; 79 iBT), IELTS (minimum score 6). *Application deadline:* Applications are processed on a rolling basis. Application fee: $60 ($65 for international students). Electronic applications accepted. *Expenses: Tuition:* Full-time $14,184; part-time $1773 per course. *Financial support:* Career-related internships or fieldwork, institutionally sponsored loans, scholarships/grants, and tuition waivers (partial) available. Support available to part-time students. Financial award application deadline: 6/30; financial award applicants required to submit FAFSA. *Faculty research:* Educational technology, scholarships in science. *Unit head:* School of Engineering and Computing, 800-628-8648, E-mail: soec@nu.edu. *Application contact:* Frank Rojas, Vice President for Enrollment Services, 800-628-8648, E-mail: advisor@nu.edu. Website: http://www.nu.edu/OurPrograms/SchoolOfEngineeringAndTechnology.html.

New Mexico Institute of Mining and Technology, Graduate Studies, Department of Civil and Environmental Engineering, Socorro, NM 87801. Offers environmental engineering (MS), including air quality engineering and science, hazardous waste engineering, water quality engineering and science. *Degree requirements:* For master's, thesis. *Entrance requirements:* For master's, GRE General Test. Additional exam requirements/recommendations for international students: Required—TOEFL (minimum score 540 paper-based). *Faculty research:* Air quality, hazardous waste management, wastewater management and treatment, site remediation.

New York Institute of Technology, School of Engineering and Computing Sciences, Department of Environmental Technology, Old Westbury, NY 11568-8000. Offers MS. Part-time and evening/weekend programs available. *Degree requirements:* For master's, thesis or alternative. *Entrance requirements:* For master's, minimum QPA of 2.85. Additional exam requirements/recommendations for international students: Required—TOEFL (minimum score 550 paper-based; 79 iBT), IELTS (minimum score 6). Electronic applications accepted. *Faculty research:* Clean water, pathways to cleaner production, development and testing of methodology to assess health risks and environmental impacts from separate sanitary sewage, introduction of technology innovation (including geographical information systems).

New York University, Polytechnic School of Engineering, Department of Civil and Urban Engineering, Major in Environmental Engineering, New York, NY 10012-1019. Offers MS. Part-time and evening/weekend programs available. *Students:* 15 full-time (8 women), 6 part-time (2 women); includes 4 minority (3 Asian, non-Hispanic/Latino; 1 Hispanic/Latino), 15 international. Average age 26. 54 applicants, 41% accepted, 21 enrolled. In 2014, 10 master's awarded. *Degree requirements:* For master's, comprehensive exam (for some programs), thesis (for some programs). *Entrance requirements:* Additional exam requirements/recommendations for international students: Required—TOEFL (minimum score 550 paper-based; 80 iBT); Recommended—IELTS (minimum score 6.5). *Application deadline:* For fall admission, 2/15 priority date for domestic and international students; for spring admission, 11/1 priority date for domestic and international students. Applications are processed on a rolling basis. Application fee: $75. Electronic applications accepted. *Financial support:* Fellowships, research assistantships, teaching assistantships, institutionally sponsored loans, scholarships/grants, and unspecified assistantships available. Support available to part-time students. Financial award applicants required to submit FAFSA. *Unit head:* Dr. Magued Iskander, Head, 718-260-3016, E-mail: iskander@nyu.edu. *Application contact:* Raymond Lutzky, Director, Graduate Enrollment Management, 718-637-5984, Fax: 718-260-3624, E-mail: rlutzky@poly.edu.

North Dakota State University, College of Graduate and Interdisciplinary Studies, College of Engineering and Architecture, Department of Civil Engineering, Fargo, ND 58108. Offers civil engineering (MS, PhD); environmental engineering (MS, PhD); transportation and logistics (PhD). PhD in transportation and logistics offered jointly with Upper Great Plains Transportation Institute. Part-time programs available. Postbaccalaureate distance learning degree programs offered (minimal on-campus study). *Degree requirements:* For master's, thesis; for doctorate, comprehensive exam, thesis/dissertation. *Entrance requirements:* Additional exam requirements/recommendations for international students: Required—TOEFL (minimum score 525 paper-based; 71 iBT). Electronic applications accepted. *Faculty research:* Wastewater, solid waste, composites, nanotechnology.

Northern Arizona University, Graduate College, College of Engineering, Forestry and Natural Sciences, Programs in Engineering, Flagstaff, AZ 86011. Offers civil and environmental engineering (M Eng); civil engineering (MSE); computer science (MSE); electrical engineering (M Eng, MSE); engineering (M Eng, MSE); environmental engineering (M Eng, MSE); mechanical engineering (M Eng, MSE). Part-time programs available. Postbaccalaureate distance learning degree programs offered (no on-campus study). *Degree requirements:* For master's, thesis. *Entrance requirements:* For master's, GRE General Test. Additional exam requirements/recommendations for international students: Required—TOEFL (minimum score 550 paper-based; 80 iBT), IELTS (minimum score 7). Electronic applications accepted.

Northwestern University, McCormick School of Engineering and Applied Science, Department of Civil and Environmental Engineering, Evanston, IL 60208-3109. Offers environmental engineering and science (MS, PhD); geotechnical engineering (MS, PhD); mechanics of materials and solids (MS, PhD); project management (MS, PhD); structural engineering and materials (MS, PhD); transportation systems analysis and planning (MS, PhD). MS and PhD admissions and degrees offered through The Graduate School. Part-time programs available. *Faculty:* 19 full-time (2 women). *Students:* 118 full-time (36 women), 5 part-time (2 women); includes 7 minority (3 Black or African American, non-Hispanic/Latino; 2 Asian, non-Hispanic/Latino; 1 Hispanic/Latino; 1 Two or more races, non-Hispanic/Latino), 95 international. Average age 24. 412 applicants, 36% accepted, 49 enrolled. In 2014, 42 master's, 10 doctorates awarded. Terminal master's awarded for partial completion of doctoral program. *Degree requirements:* For master's, thesis (for some programs); for doctorate, comprehensive exam, thesis/dissertation. *Entrance requirements:* For master's and doctorate, GRE General Test, minimum 2 letters of recommendation, transcripts from all academic institutions attended. Additional exam requirements/recommendations for international students: Required—TOEFL (minimum score 577 paper-based; 90 iBT), IELTS (minimum score 7). *Application deadline:* For fall admission, 12/31 for domestic and international students; for winter admission, 11/15 for domestic and international students; for spring admission, 1/15 for domestic and international students. Application fee: $95. Electronic applications accepted. *Financial support:* Fellowships with full tuition reimbursements, research assistantships with full tuition reimbursements, teaching assistantships with full tuition reimbursements, career-related internships or fieldwork, institutionally sponsored loans, health care benefits, and unspecified assistantships available. Financial award application deadline: 12/31; financial award applicants required to submit FAFSA. *Faculty research:* Environmental engineering and science, geotechnics, mechanics of materials and solids, structural engineering and materials, transportation systems analysis and planning. *Total annual research expenditures:* $5.8 million. *Unit head:* Dr. Jianmin Qu, Chair, 847-467-4528, Fax: 847-491-4011, E-mail: j-qu@northwestern.edu. *Application contact:* Dr. David Corr, Academic Coordinator, 847-467-0890, Fax: 847-491-4011, E-mail: d-corr@u.northwestern.edu.
Website: http://www.civil.northwestern.edu/.

Norwich University, College of Graduate and Continuing Studies, Master of Civil Engineering Program, Northfield, VT 05663. Offers construction management engineering (MCE); environmental/water resources engineering (MCE); geotechnical engineering (MCE); structural engineering (MCE). Evening/weekend programs available. Postbaccalaureate distance learning degree programs offered (minimal on-campus study). *Faculty:* 14 part-time/adjunct (2 women). *Students:* 111 full-time (17 women); includes 28 minority (16 Black or African American, non-Hispanic/Latino; 2 American Indian or Alaska Native, non-Hispanic/Latino; 7 Asian, non-Hispanic/Latino; 3 Hispanic/Latino). Average age 36. 61 applicants, 100% accepted, 42 enrolled. In 2014, 57 master's awarded. *Entrance requirements:* For master's, minimum undergraduate GPA of 2.75. Additional exam requirements/recommendations for international students: Required—TOEFL (minimum score 550 paper-based; 80 iBT), IELTS (minimum score 6.5). *Application deadline:* For fall admission, 8/8 for domestic and international students; for spring admission, 2/16 for domestic and international students. Applications are processed on a rolling basis. Electronic applications accepted. *Expenses:* Expenses: Contact institution. *Financial support:* In 2014–15, 27 students received support. Scholarships/grants available. Financial award applicants required to submit FAFSA. *Unit head:* Dr. Thomas Descoteaux, Program Director, 802-485-2730, Fax: 802-485-2533, E-mail: tdescote@norwich.edu. *Application contact:* Rija Ramahatra, Associate Program Director, 802-485-2892, Fax: 802-485-2533, E-mail: ramahatr@norwich.edu.
Website: http://online.norwich.edu/degree-programs/masters/master-civil-engineering/overview.

Ohio University, Graduate College, Russ College of Engineering and Technology, Department of Civil Engineering, Athens, OH 45701-2979. Offers civil engineering (PhD); construction engineering and management (MS); environmental (MS); geotechnical and geoenvironmental (MS); mechanics (MS); structures (MS); transportation (MS); water resources (MS). Part-time programs available. *Degree requirements:* For master's, comprehensive exam (for some programs), thesis or alternative; for doctorate, comprehensive exam, thesis/dissertation. *Entrance requirements:* For master's, GRE General Test, minimum GPA of 3.0, 3 letters of recommendation; for doctorate, GRE General Test. Additional exam requirements/recommendations for international students: Required—TOEFL (minimum score 550 paper-based; 80 iBT) or IELTS (minimum score 6.5). Electronic applications accepted. *Faculty research:* Noise abatement, materials and environment, highway infrastructure, subsurface investigation (pavements, pipes, bridges).

Oklahoma State University, College of Agricultural Science and Natural Resources, Department of Biosystems and Agricultural Engineering, Stillwater, OK 74078. Offers biosystems engineering (MS, PhD); environmental and natural resources (MS, PhD). *Faculty:* 26 full-time (3 women). *Students:* 19 full-time (13 women), 23 part-time (5 women); includes 5 minority (2 American Indian or Alaska Native, non-Hispanic/Latino; 2 Hispanic/Latino; 1 Two or more races, non-Hispanic/Latino), 19 international. Average age 29. 43 applicants, 30% accepted, 8 enrolled. In 2014, 4 master's, 6 doctorates awarded. *Degree requirements:* For master's, thesis; for doctorate, comprehensive exam, thesis/dissertation. *Entrance requirements:* For master's and doctorate, GRE or GMAT. Additional exam requirements/recommendations for international students: Required—TOEFL (minimum score 550 paper-based; 79 iBT). *Application deadline:* For fall admission, 3/1 priority date for international students; for spring admission, 8/1 priority date for international students. Applications are processed on a rolling basis. Application fee: $40 ($75 for international students). Electronic applications accepted. *Expenses:* Tuition, state resident: full-time $4488; part-time $187 per credit hour. Tuition, nonresident: full-time $18,360; part-time $765 per credit hour. *Required fees:* $2413; $100.55 per credit hour. Tuition and fees vary according to campus/location. *Financial support:* In 2014–15, 33 research assistantships (averaging $17,683 per year), 2 teaching assistantships (averaging $14,100 per year) were awarded; career-related internships or fieldwork, Federal Work-Study, scholarships/grants, health care benefits, tuition waivers (partial), and unspecified assistantships also available. Support available to part-time students. Financial award application deadline: 3/1; financial award applicants required to submit FAFSA. *Unit head:* Dr. Daniel Thomas, Department Head, 405-744-5431, Fax: 405-744-6059, E-mail: daniel.thomas@okstate.edu. *Application contact:* Glenn Brown, Professor/Graduate Coordinator, 405-744-8425, E-mail: gbrown@okstate.edu.
Website: http://bae.okstate.edu/.

Oklahoma State University, College of Engineering, Architecture and Technology, School of Civil and Environmental Engineering, Stillwater, OK 74078. Offers civil engineering (MS, PhD); environmental engineering (MS). *Faculty:* 17 full-time (1 woman), 3 part-time/adjunct (1 woman). *Students:* 49 full-time (10 women), 32 part-time (8 women); includes 7 minority (1 Black or African American, non-Hispanic/Latino; 2 American Indian or Alaska Native, non-Hispanic/Latino; 2 Hispanic/Latino; 2 Two or more races, non-Hispanic/Latino), 61 international. Average age 27. 146 applicants, 28% accepted, 18 enrolled. In 2014, 22 master's, 3 doctorates awarded. *Degree requirements:* For master's, thesis or alternative; for doctorate, comprehensive exam, thesis/dissertation. *Entrance requirements:* For master's and doctorate, GRE or GMAT. Additional exam requirements/recommendations for international students: Required—TOEFL (minimum score 550 paper-based; 79 iBT). *Application deadline:* For fall admission, 3/1 priority date for international students; for spring admission, 8/1 priority date for international students. Applications are processed on a rolling basis. Application fee: $40 ($75 for international students). Electronic applications accepted. *Expenses:* Tuition, state resident: full-time $4488; part-time $187 per credit hour. Tuition, nonresident: full-time $18,360; part-time $765 per credit hour. *Required fees:* $2413; $100.55 per credit hour. Tuition and fees vary according to campus/location. *Financial support:* In 2014–15, 30 research assistantships (averaging $17,682 per year), 15 teaching assistantships (averaging $16,496 per year) were awarded; career-related internships or fieldwork, Federal Work-Study, scholarships/grants, health care benefits, tuition waivers (partial), and unspecified assistantships also available. Support available to part-time students. Financial award application deadline: 3/1; financial award applicants required to submit FAFSA. *Unit head:* Dr. John Veenstra, Department Head, 405-744-5190, Fax: 405-744-7554, E-mail: jveenst@okstate.edu.
Website: http://cive.okstate.edu.

Old Dominion University, Frank Batten College of Engineering and Technology, Program in Civil and Environmental Engineering, Norfolk, VA 23529. Offers D Eng, PhD. Part-time and evening/weekend programs available. Postbaccalaureate distance learning degree programs offered (minimal on-campus study). *Faculty:* 13 full-time (1 woman), 7 part-time/adjunct (0 women). *Students:* 10 full-time (3 women), 16 part-time (0 women); includes 2 minority (both Asian, non-Hispanic/Latino), 15 international. Average age 37. 12 applicants, 100% accepted, 2 enrolled. In 2014, 5 doctorates awarded. *Degree requirements:* For doctorate, thesis/dissertation, candidacy exam. *Entrance requirements:* For doctorate, GRE, minimum GPA of 3.5. Additional exam requirements/recommendations for international students: Required—TOEFL (minimum score 550 paper-based; 80 iBT). *Application deadline:* For fall admission, 6/1 priority date for domestic students, 4/15 priority date for international students; for spring admission, 11/1 priority date for domestic students, 10/1 priority date for international students. Applications are processed on a rolling basis. Application fee: $50. Electronic applications accepted. *Expenses:* Tuition, state resident: full-time $10,488; part-time $437 per credit. Tuition, nonresident: full-time $26,136; part-time $1089 per credit. *Required fees:* $64 per semester. One-time fee: $50. *Financial support:* In 2014–15, 10 research assistantships with full and partial tuition reimbursements (averaging $15,439 per year), 8 teaching assistantships with full and partial tuition reimbursements (averaging $14,244 per year) were awarded; scholarships/grants and unspecified assistantships also available. Support available to part-time students. Financial award application deadline: 4/1. *Faculty research:* Structural engineering, coastal engineering, environmental engineering, geotechnical engineering, water resources, transportation engineering. *Total annual research expenditures:* $941,621. *Unit head:* Dr. Isao Ishibashi, Graduate Program Director, 757-683-4641, Fax: 757-683-5354, E-mail: cegpd@odu.edu. *Application contact:* Dr. Linda Vahala, Associate Dean, 757-683-3789, Fax: 757-683-4898, E-mail: lvahala@odu.edu.
Website: http://eng.odu.edu/cee/.

Old Dominion University, Frank Batten College of Engineering and Technology, Program in Environmental Engineering, Norfolk, VA 23529. Offers ME, MS. Part-time and evening/weekend programs available. Postbaccalaureate distance learning degree programs offered (minimal on-campus study). *Faculty:* 13 full-time (1 woman), 7 part-time/adjunct (0 women). *Students:* 12 full-time (1 woman), 21 part-time (8 women); includes 6 minority (2 Black or African American, non-Hispanic/Latino; 2 Asian, non-Hispanic/Latino; 2 Hispanic/Latino), 6 international. Average age 32. 18 applicants, 83% accepted, 7 enrolled. In 2014, 11 master's awarded. *Degree requirements:* For master's, comprehensive exam, thesis optional. *Entrance requirements:* For master's, GRE, minimum GPA of 3.0. Additional exam requirements/recommendations for international students: Required—TOEFL (minimum score 550 paper-based; 80 iBT). *Application deadline:* For fall admission, 6/1 priority date for domestic students, 4/15 priority date for international students; for spring admission, 11/1 priority date for domestic students, 10/1 priority date for international students. Applications are processed on a rolling basis. Application fee: $50. Electronic applications accepted. *Expenses:* Tuition, state resident: full-time $10,488; part-time $437 per credit. Tuition, nonresident: full-time $26,136; part-time $1089 per credit. *Required fees:* $64 per semester. One-time fee: $50. *Financial support:* In 2014–15, 3 research assistantships with partial tuition reimbursements (averaging $12,050 per year), 1 teaching assistantship with partial tuition reimbursement (averaging $12,800 per year) were awarded; scholarships/grants and unspecified assistantships also available. Support available to part-time students. Financial award application deadline: 4/1; financial award applicants required to submit FAFSA. *Faculty research:* Aquatic chemistry, physiochemical treatment, waste water treatment, hazardous waste treatment, environmental microbiology. *Total annual research expenditures:* $941,621. *Unit head:* Dr. Isao Ishibashi, Graduate Program Director, 757-683-4641, Fax: 757-683-5354, E-mail: cegpd@odu.edu. *Application contact:* Dr. Linda Vahala, Associate Dean, 757-683-3789, Fax: 757-683-4898, E-mail: lvahala@odu.edu.
Website: http://eng.odu.edu/cee/.

Oregon Health & Science University, School of Medicine, Graduate Programs in Medicine, Department of Environmental and Biomolecular Systems, Portland, OR 97239-3098. Offers biochemistry and molecular biology (MS, PhD); environmental science and engineering (MS, PhD). Part-time programs available. *Faculty:* 13 full-time (4 women). *Students:* 33 full-time (23 women), 1 part-time (0 women); includes 8 minority (1 Black or African American, non-Hispanic/Latino; 2 American Indian or Alaska Native, non-Hispanic/Latino; 2 Asian, non-Hispanic/Latino; 3 Hispanic/Latino), 5 international. Average age 30. 46 applicants, 28% accepted, 13 enrolled. In 2014, 10 master's, 5 doctorates awarded. Terminal master's awarded for partial completion of doctoral program. *Degree requirements:* For master's, thesis (for some programs); for doctorate, comprehensive exam, thesis/dissertation, qualifying exam. *Entrance requirements:* For master's and doctorate, GRE General Test (minimum scores: 500 Verbal/600 Quantitative/4.5 Analytical) or MCAT (for some programs). Additional exam requirements/recommendations for international students: Required—TOEFL. *Application deadline:* For fall admission, 7/15 for domestic students, 5/15 for international students; for winter admission, 10/15 for domestic students, 9/15 for international students; for spring admission, 1/15 for domestic students, 12/15 for international students. Applications are processed on a rolling basis. Application fee:

$70. Electronic applications accepted. *Financial support:* Health care benefits and full tuition and stipends (for PhD students) available. *Faculty research:* Metalloprotein biochemistry, molecular microbiology, environmental microbiology, environmental chemistry, biogeochemistry. *Unit head:* Dr. Paul Tratnyek, Program Director, 503-748-1070, E-mail: info@ebs.ogi.edu. *Application contact:* Vanessa Green, Program Coordinator, 503-346-3411, E-mail: info@ebs.ogi.edu.

Oregon State University, College of Engineering, Program in Environmental Engineering, Corvallis, OR 97331. Offers M Eng, MS, PhD. *Faculty:* 24 full-time (2 women), 1 (woman) part-time/adjunct. *Students:* 36 full-time (19 women), 1 part-time (0 women); includes 1 minority (Hispanic/Latino), 15 international. Average age 27. 81 applicants, 43% accepted, 18 enrolled. In 2014, 9 master's, 1 doctorate awarded. *Entrance requirements:* For master's, GRE; for doctorate, GRE. Additional exam requirements/recommendations for international students: Required—TOEFL (minimum score 92 iBT). *Application deadline:* For fall admission, 1/1 for domestic students. Application fee: $60. Electronic applications accepted. *Expenses:* Expenses: $15,359 full-time resident tuition and fees; $23,405 non-resident. *Financial support:* Unspecified assistantships available. Financial award application deadline: 1/1. *Unit head:* Dr. James Sweeney, School Head/Professor, 541-737-3769. *Application contact:* Elisha Brackett, Graduate Student Coordinator for Environmental Engineering, 541-737-6149, E-mail: elisha.brackett@oregonstate.edu.
Website: http://cbee.oregonstate.edu/enve-graduate-program.

Penn State Harrisburg, Graduate School, School of Science, Engineering and Technology, Middletown, PA 17057-4898. Offers computer science (MS); electrical engineering (M Eng, MS); engineering management (MPS); engineering science (M Eng); environmental engineering (M Eng); structural engineering (Certificate). Part-time and evening/weekend programs available. *Unit head:* Dr. Mukund S. Kulkarni, Chancellor, 717-948-6105, Fax: 717-948-6452, E-mail: msk5@psu.edu. *Application contact:* Robert W. Coffman, Jr., Director of Enrollment Management, Admissions, 717-948-6250, Fax: 717-948-6325, E-mail: ric1@psu.edu.
Website: http://harrisburg.psu.edu/science-engineering-technology.

Penn State University Park, Graduate School, College of Engineering, Department of Civil and Environmental Engineering, University Park, PA 16802. Offers civil engineering (M Eng, MS, PhD); environmental engineering (M Eng, MS, PhD). *Unit head:* Dr. Amr S. Elnashai, Dean, 814-865-7537, Fax: 814-863-4749, E-mail: ase2@psu.edu. *Application contact:* Lori A. Stania, Director, Graduate Student Services, 814-867-5278, Fax: 814-863-4627, E-mail: gswww@psu.edu.
Website: http://www.engr.psu.edu/CE/.

Polytechnic University of Puerto Rico, Miami Campus, Graduate School, Miami, FL 33166. Offers accounting (MBA); business administration (MBA); construction management (MEM); environmental management (MEM); finance (MBA); human resources management (MBA); logistics and supply chain management (MBA); management of international enterprises (MBA); manufacturing management (MEM); marketing management (MBA); project management (MBA). Part-time and evening/weekend programs available. Postbaccalaureate distance learning degree programs offered (no on-campus study). *Entrance requirements:* For master's, minimum GPA of 3.0. Electronic applications accepted.

Polytechnic University of Puerto Rico, Orlando Campus, Graduate School, Winter Park, FL 32792. Offers accounting (MBA); business administration (MBA); construction management (MEM); engineering management (MEM); environmental management (MEM); finance (MBA); human resources management (MBA); management of international enterprises (MBA); management of technology (MBA); manufacturing management (MEM). Part-time and evening/weekend programs available. Postbaccalaureate distance learning degree programs offered (no on-campus study). *Entrance requirements:* For master's, minimum GPA of 3.0. Additional exam requirements/recommendations for international students: Recommended—TOEFL. Electronic applications accepted.

Portland State University, Graduate Studies, Maseeh College of Engineering and Computer Science, Department of Civil and Environmental Engineering, Portland, OR 97207-0751. Offers civil and environmental engineering (M Eng, MS, PhD); civil and environmental engineering management (M Eng); environmental sciences and resources (PhD); systems science (PhD). Part-time and evening/weekend programs available. *Faculty:* 16 full-time (3 women), 1 part-time/adjunct (0 women). *Students:* 71 full-time (18 women), 42 part-time (6 women); includes 9 minority (4 Black or African American, non-Hispanic/Latino; 1 Asian, non-Hispanic/Latino; 2 Hispanic/Latino; 2 Two or more races, non-Hispanic/Latino), 45 international. Average age 31. 119 applicants, 54% accepted, 29 enrolled. In 2014, 29 master's, 3 doctorates awarded. *Degree requirements:* For master's, comprehensive exam (for some programs), thesis (for some programs); for doctorate, one foreign language, comprehensive exam, thesis/dissertation, oral and written exams. *Entrance requirements:* For master's, B.S degree in an engineering field, science, or closely related area with a minimum GPA of 3.00; for doctorate, M.S. degree in an engineering field, science, or closely related area. Additional exam requirements/recommendations for international students: Required—TOEFL (minimum score 550 paper-based). *Application deadline:* For fall admission, 1/4 priority date for domestic and international students; for winter admission, 9/1 for domestic and international students; for spring admission, 11/1 for domestic and international students. Applications are processed on a rolling basis. Application fee: $50. *Expenses:* Tuition, state resident: part-time $222 per credit. Tuition, nonresident: part-time $527 per credit. *Required fees:* $22 per contact hour. $100 per quarter. Tuition and fees vary according to program. *Financial support:* In 2014–15, 15 research assistantships with full and partial tuition reimbursements (averaging $6,105 per year), 12 teaching assistantships with full and partial tuition reimbursements (averaging $2,471 per year) were awarded; career-related internships or fieldwork, Federal Work-Study, scholarships/grants, and unspecified assistantships also available. Support available to part-time students. Financial award application deadline: 3/1; financial award applicants required to submit FAFSA. *Faculty research:* Structures, water resources, geotechnical engineering, environmental engineering, transportation. *Total annual research expenditures:* $3.1 million. *Unit head:* Dr. Chris Monsere, Acting Chair, 503-725-9746, Fax: 503-725-4298, E-mail: monserec@cecs.pdx.edu. *Application contact:* Ariel Lewis, Department Manager, 503-725-4244, Fax: 503-725-4298, E-mail: ariel.lewis@pdx.edu.
Website: http://www.pdx.edu/cee/.

Princeton University, Graduate School, School of Engineering and Applied Science, Department of Civil and Environmental Engineering, Princeton, NJ 08544-1019. Offers M Eng, MSE, PhD. Terminal master's awarded for partial completion of doctoral program. *Degree requirements:* For master's, thesis (MSE); for doctorate, thesis/dissertation, general exam. *Entrance requirements:* For master's, GRE General Test, 3 letters of recommendation; for doctorate, GRE General Test, official transcript(s), 3 letters of recommendation, personal statement. Additional exam requirements/recommendations for international students: Required—TOEFL. Electronic applications accepted. *Faculty research:* Carbon mitigation; civil engineering materials and structures; climate and atmospheric dynamics; computational mechanics and risk assessment; hydrology, remote sensing, and sustainability.

Rensselaer Polytechnic Institute, Graduate School, School of Engineering, Program in Environmental Engineering, Troy, NY 12180-3590. Offers M Eng, MS, D Eng, PhD. *Faculty:* 8 full-time (4 women), 1 part-time/adjunct (0 women). *Students:* 5 full-time (4 women), 1 part-time (0 women); includes 1 minority (Hispanic/Latino), 1 international. Average age 25. 36 applicants, 31% accepted, 3 enrolled. In 2014, 6 master's awarded. Terminal master's awarded for partial completion of doctoral program. *Degree requirements:* For master's, thesis (for some programs); for doctorate, thesis/dissertation. *Entrance requirements:* For master's and doctorate, GRE. Additional exam requirements/recommendations for international students: Required—TOEFL (minimum score 570 paper-based; 88 iBT), IELTS (minimum score 6.5), PTE (minimum score 60). *Application deadline:* For fall admission, 1/1 priority date for domestic students, 1/1 for international students; for spring admission, 8/15 for domestic and international students. Applications are processed on a rolling basis. Application fee: $75. Electronic applications accepted. *Expenses: Tuition:* Full-time $46,700; part-time $1945 per credit. Tuition and fees vary according to course load. *Financial support:* In 2014–15, 5 students received support, including research assistantships (averaging $18,500 per year), teaching assistantships with full tuition reimbursements available (averaging $18,500 per year); fellowships also available. Financial award application deadline: 1/1. *Faculty research:* Environmental systems, pollutant fate and transport, site remediation and bioremediation, waste treatment, water treatment. *Total annual research expenditures:* $21,880. *Unit head:* Dr. Marianne Nyman, Graduate Program Director, 518-276-2268, E-mail: nymanm@rpi.edu. *Application contact:* Office of Graduate Admissions, 518-276-6216, E-mail: gradadmissions@rpi.edu.
Website: http://eng.rpi.edu/.

Rice University, Graduate Programs, George R. Brown School of Engineering, Department of Civil and Environmental Engineering, Houston, TX 77251-1892. Offers civil engineering (MCE, MS, PhD); environmental engineering (MEE, MES, MS, PhD); environmental science (MEE, MES, MS, PhD). Part-time programs available. *Degree requirements:* For master's, thesis (for some programs); for doctorate, thesis/dissertation. *Entrance requirements:* For master's and doctorate, GRE General Test, GRE Subject Test, minimum GPA of 3.25. Additional exam requirements/recommendations for international students: Required—TOEFL (minimum score 600 paper-based; 90 iBT). Electronic applications accepted. *Faculty research:* Biology and chemistry of groundwater, pollutant fate in groundwater systems, water quality monitoring, urban storm water runoff, urban air quality.

Rose-Hulman Institute of Technology, Faculty of Engineering and Applied Sciences, Department of Civil Engineering, Terre Haute, IN 47803-3999. Offers civil engineering (MS); environmental engineering (MS). Part-time programs available. *Faculty:* 9 full-time (2 women), 1 part-time/adjunct (0 women). *Students:* 4 full-time (1 woman). Average age 23. 9 applicants, 100% accepted, 2 enrolled. In 2014, 2 master's awarded. *Degree requirements:* For master's, thesis (for some programs). *Entrance requirements:* For master's, GRE, minimum GPA of 3.0. Additional exam requirements/recommendations for international students: Required—TOEFL (minimum score 580 paper-based; 92 iBT). *Application deadline:* For fall admission, 2/1 priority date for domestic students. Applications are processed on a rolling basis. Application fee: $0. *Expenses: Tuition:* Full-time $40,449. *Financial support:* In 2014–15, 3 students received support. Fellowships with full and partial tuition reimbursements available, research assistantships with full and partial tuition reimbursements available, institutionally sponsored loans, scholarships/grants, and tuition waivers (full and partial) available. Financial award application deadline: 2/1. *Faculty research:* Transportation, hydraulics/hydrology, environmental, construction, geotechnical, structural. *Total annual research expenditures:* $25,939. *Unit head:* Dr. Kevin Sutterer, Chairman, 812-877-8959, Fax: 812-877-8440, E-mail: sutterer@rose-hulman.edu. *Application contact:* Dr. Azad Siahmakoun, Associate Dean of the Faculty, 812-877-8400, Fax: 812-877-8061, E-mail: siahmako@rose-hulman.edu.
Website: http://www.rose-hulman.edu/ce/.

Royal Military College of Canada, Division of Graduate Studies and Research, Engineering Division, Department of Chemistry and Chemical Engineering, Program in Environmental Engineering, Kingston, ON K7K 7B4, Canada. Offers chemical and materials (M Eng); chemistry (M Eng); environmental (PhD); nuclear (PhD). *Degree requirements:* For master's, thesis; for doctorate, comprehensive exam, thesis/dissertation. *Entrance requirements:* For master's, honours degree with second-class standing; for doctorate, master's degree. Electronic applications accepted.

Rutgers, The State University of New Jersey, New Brunswick, Graduate School-New Brunswick, Department of Civil and Environmental Engineering, Piscataway, NJ 08854-8097. Offers MS, PhD. Part-time and evening/weekend programs available. Terminal master's awarded for partial completion of doctoral program. *Degree requirements:* For master's, comprehensive exam, thesis or alternative; for doctorate, comprehensive exam, thesis/dissertation. *Entrance requirements:* For master's and doctorate, GRE General Test. Additional exam requirements/recommendations for international students: Required—TOEFL (minimum score 580 paper-based). Electronic applications accepted. *Faculty research:* Civil engineering materials research, non-destructive evaluation of transportation infrastructure, transportation planning, intelligent transportation systems.

Southern Illinois University Edwardsville, Graduate School, School of Engineering, Department of Civil Engineering, Program in Environmental Engineering, Edwardsville, IL 62026. Offers MS. Part-time and evening/weekend programs available. *Degree requirements:* For master's, thesis (for some programs), research paper. *Entrance requirements:* For master's, minimum undergraduate GPA of 2.75 in science, math, and engineering courses. Additional exam requirements/recommendations for international students: Required—TOEFL (minimum score 550 paper-based, 79 iBT), IELTS (minimum score 6.5), Michigan Test of English Language Proficiency or PTE. *Application deadline:* For fall admission, 7/18 for domestic students, 6/1 for international students; for spring admission, 12/12 for domestic students, 10/1 for international students; for summer admission, 4/24 for domestic students, 3/1 for international students. Applications are processed on a rolling basis. Application fee: $30. Electronic applications accepted. *Expenses:* Tuition, state resident: full-time $5026. Tuition, nonresident: full-time $12,566. *International tuition:* $25,136 full-time. *Required fees:* $1682. Tuition and fees vary according to course load, campus/location and program. *Financial support:* Institutionally sponsored loans, scholarships/grants, and unspecified assistantships available. *Unit head:* Dr. Jim Zhou, Chair, 618-650-2533, E-mail: jzhou@siue.edu. *Application contact:* Dr. Ryan Fries, Director, 618-650-5026, E-mail: rfries@siue.edu.
Website: http://www.siue.edu/engineering/civilengineering/.

Southern Methodist University, Bobby B. Lyle School of Engineering, Department of Environmental and Civil Engineering, Dallas, TX 75275-0340. Offers air pollution control and atmospheric sciences (PhD); civil engineering (MS); environmental engineering (MS); environmental science (MS); structural engineering (PhD); sustainability and development (MA); water and wastewater engineering (PhD). Part-time and evening/weekend programs available. Postbaccalaureate distance learning degree programs offered (no on-campus study). Terminal master's awarded for partial completion of doctoral program. *Degree requirements:* For master's, thesis optional; for doctorate, thesis/dissertation, oral and written qualifying exams. *Entrance requirements:* For master's, GRE General Test, minimum GPA of 3.0 in last 2 years; bachelor's degree in engineering, mathematics, or sciences; for doctorate, GRE, BS and MS in related field, minimum GPA of 3.3. Additional exam requirements/recommendations for international students: Required—TOEFL. Electronic applications accepted. *Faculty research:* Human and environmental health effects of endocrine disrupters, development of air pollution control systems for diesel engines, structural analysis and design, modeling and design of waste treatment systems.

Stanford University, School of Engineering, Department of Civil and Environmental Engineering, Stanford, CA 94305-9991. Offers atmosphere and energy (MS, PhD); construction (MS), including construction engineering and management, design-construction integration, sustainable design and construction; environmental engineering and science (MS, PhD, Eng); environmental fluid mechanics and hydrology (PhD); geomechanics (MS); structural engineering (MS). Terminal master's awarded for partial completion of doctoral program. *Degree requirements:* For doctorate, thesis/dissertation, qualifying exam; for Eng, thesis. *Entrance requirements:* For master's, doctorate, and Eng, GRE General Test. Additional exam requirements/recommendations for international students: Required—TOEFL. Electronic applications accepted. *Expenses: Tuition:* Full-time $44,184; part-time $982 per credit hour. *Required fees:* $191.

State University of New York College of Environmental Science and Forestry, Department of Environmental Resources Engineering, Syracuse, NY 13210-2779. Offers ecological engineering (MPS, MS, PhD); environmental management (MPS); environmental resources engineering (MPS, MS, PhD); geospatial information science and engineering (MPS, MS, PhD); water resources engineering (MPS, MS, PhD). Part-time programs available. *Degree requirements:* For master's, thesis (for some programs); for doctorate, comprehensive exam, thesis/dissertation. *Entrance requirements:* For master's and doctorate, GRE General Test, minimum GPA of 3.0. Additional exam requirements/recommendations for international students: Required—TOEFL (minimum score 550 paper-based; 80 iBT), IELTS (minimum score 6). *Faculty research:* Ecological engineering, environmental resources engineering, geospatial information science and engineering, water resources engineering, environmental science.

Stevens Institute of Technology, Graduate School, Charles V. Schaefer Jr. School of Engineering, Department of Civil, Environmental, and Ocean Engineering, Program in Environmental Engineering, Hoboken, NJ 07030. Offers environmental compatibility in engineering (Certificate); environmental engineering (PhD); environmental processes (M Eng, Certificate); groundwater and soil pollution control (M Eng, Certificate); inland and coastal environmental hydrodynamics (M Eng, Certificate); water quality control (Certificate). *Degree requirements:* For master's, thesis optional; for doctorate, variable foreign language requirement, thesis/dissertation; for Certificate, project or thesis. *Entrance requirements:* For doctorate, GRE. Additional exam requirements/recommendations for international students: Required—TOEFL. Electronic applications accepted.

Syracuse University, L. C. Smith College of Engineering and Computer Science, Program in Environmental Engineering, Syracuse, NY 13244. Offers MS. Part-time programs available. *Students:* 17 full-time (9 women), 2 part-time (0 women); includes 1 minority (Hispanic/Latino), 15 international. Average age 24. 35 applicants, 49% accepted, 7 enrolled. In 2014, 6 master's awarded. *Degree requirements:* For master's, thesis optional. *Entrance requirements:* For master's, GRE General Test. Additional exam requirements/recommendations for international students: Required—TOEFL (minimum score 100 iBT). *Application deadline:* For fall admission, 7/1 priority date for domestic students, 6/1 priority date for international students. Applications are processed on a rolling basis. Application fee: $75. Electronic applications accepted. *Expenses: Tuition:* Part-time $1341 per credit. *Required fees:* $1341 per credit. *Financial support:* Fellowships with full tuition reimbursements, research assistantships with full and partial tuition reimbursements, teaching assistantships with full and partial tuition reimbursements, and tuition waivers available. Financial award application deadline: 1/1. *Unit head:* Dr. Cliff Davidson, Program Director, 315-443-2311, E-mail: davidson@syr.edu. *Application contact:* Elizabeth Buchanan, Information Contact, 314-443-2558, E-mail: topgrads@syr.edu.
Website: http://lcs.syr.edu.

Syracuse University, L. C. Smith College of Engineering and Computer Science, Program in Environmental Engineering Science, Syracuse, NY 13244. Offers MS. Part-time programs available. *Students:* 8 full-time (4 women), 5 international. Average age 24. 10 applicants, 50% accepted, 2 enrolled. In 2014, 2 master's awarded. *Degree requirements:* For master's, thesis optional. *Entrance requirements:* For master's, GRE General Test. Additional exam requirements/recommendations for international students: Required—TOEFL (minimum score 100 iBT). *Application deadline:* For fall admission, 7/1 for domestic students, 6/1 priority date for international students. Applications are processed on a rolling basis. Application fee: $75. Electronic applications accepted. *Expenses: Tuition:* Part-time $1341 per credit. *Required fees:* $1341 per credit. *Financial support:* Fellowships with full tuition reimbursements, research assistantships with full and partial tuition reimbursements, teaching assistantships with full and partial tuition reimbursements, and tuition waivers available. *Unit head:* Dr. Cliff Davidson, Program Director, 315-443-2311, E-mail: davidson@syr.edu. *Application contact:* Elizabeth Buchanan, Information Contact, 315-443-2558, E-mail: ebuchana@syr.edu.
Website: http://lcs.syr.edu/.

Temple University, College of Engineering, Department of Civil and Environmental Engineering, Philadelphia, PA 19122-6096. Offers civil engineering (MSCE); engineering (PhD); environmental engineering (MS Env E); storm water management (Graduate Certificate). Part-time and evening/weekend programs available. *Faculty:* 20 full-time (4 women). *Students:* 12 full-time (4 women), 12 part-time (3 women); includes 7 minority (4 Black or African American, non-Hispanic/Latino; 3 Asian, non-Hispanic/Latino), 10 international. 43 applicants, 67% accepted, 7 enrolled. In 2014, 1 master's, 1 other advanced degree awarded. Terminal master's awarded for partial completion of doctoral program. *Degree requirements:* For master's, thesis optional; for doctorate, thesis/dissertation, preliminary exam, dissertation proposal and defense. *Entrance requirements:* For master's, GRE General Test, minimum GPA of 3.0; BS in engineering from ABET-accredited or equivalent institution; resume, goals statement; three letters of reference; official transcripts; for doctorate, GRE General Test, minimum GPA of 3.0; MS in engineering from ABET-accredited or equivalent institution (preferred); resume; goals statement; three letters of reference; official transcripts. Additional exam requirements/recommendations for international students: Required—TOEFL (minimum score 550 paper-based; 79 iBT), IELTS (minimum score 6.5). *Application deadline:* For fall admission, 3/1 priority date for domestic and international students; for spring admission, 11/1 priority date for domestic students, 8/1 priority date for international students. Applications are processed on a rolling basis. Application fee: $60. Electronic applications accepted. *Expenses:* Expenses: $913 per credit hour in-state; $1,210 per credit hour out-of-state. *Financial support:* Fellowships with full and partial tuition reimbursements, research assistantships with full and partial tuition reimbursements, teaching assistantships with full and partial tuition reimbursements, Federal Work-Study, scholarships/grants, health care benefits, and unspecified assistantships available. Financial award application deadline: 3/1; financial award applicants required to submit FAFSA. *Faculty research:* Analysis of the effect of scour on bridge stability, design of sustainable buildings, development of new highway pavement material using plastic waste, characterization of by-products and waste materials for pavement and geotechnical engineering applications, development of effective traffic signals in urban and rural settings, development of techniques for effective construction management. *Unit head:* Dr. Rominder Suri, Acting Chair, 215-204-2378, Fax: 215-204-6936, E-mail: rominder.suri@temple.edu. *Application contact:* Mojan Arshad, Assistant Coordinator, Graduate Studies, 215-204-7800, Fax: 215-204-6936, E-mail: gradengr@temple.edu.
Website: http://engineering.temple.edu/department/civil-environmental-engineering.

Tennessee State University, The School of Graduate Studies and Research, College of Engineering, Nashville, TN 37209-1561. Offers biomedical engineering (ME); civil engineering (ME); computer and information systems engineering (MS, PhD); electrical engineering (ME); environmental engineering (ME); manufacturing engineering (ME); mathematical sciences (MS); mechanical engineering (ME). Part-time and evening/weekend programs available. *Degree requirements:* For master's, project; for doctorate, comprehensive exam, thesis/dissertation. *Entrance requirements:* For doctorate, minimum GPA of 3.3. *Faculty research:* Robotics, intelligent systems, human-computer interaction software systems, biomedical engineering, signal/image processing, probabilistic design, intelligent manufacturing, cooperative mobile robots, condition based maintenance, sensor fusion.

Texas A&M University–Kingsville, College of Graduate Studies, College of Engineering, Department of Environmental Engineering, Kingsville, TX 78363. Offers ME, MS, PhD. *Faculty:* 7 full-time (1 woman), 1 (woman) part-time/adjunct. *Students:* 55 full-time (14 women), 12 part-time (7 women); includes 11 minority (4 Black or African American, non-Hispanic/Latino; 6 Hispanic/Latino; 1 Two or more races, non-Hispanic/Latino), 51 international. Average age 29. 77 applicants, 74% accepted, 23 enrolled. In 2014, 9 master's, 4 doctorates awarded. *Degree requirements:* For master's, variable foreign language requirement, comprehensive exam, thesis (for some programs); for doctorate, variable foreign language requirement, comprehensive exam, thesis/dissertation (for some programs). *Entrance requirements:* For master's, GRE, MAT, GMAT, minimum undergraduate GPA of 2.8, GRE (Q+V) score of 294; for doctorate, GRE, MAT, GMAT. Additional exam requirements/recommendations for international students: Required—TOEFL (minimum score 550 paper-based; 79 iBT). *Application deadline:* For fall admission, 8/15 for domestic students, 6/1 for international students; for spring admission, 12/15 for domestic students, 10/1 for international students; for summer admission, 5/15 for domestic students, 4/1 for international students. Applications are processed on a rolling basis. Application fee: $35 ($50 for international students). Electronic applications accepted. *Financial support:* In 2014–15, 37 students received support, including 23 research assistantships (averaging $8,163 per year), 8 teaching assistantships (averaging $5,339 per year); career-related internships or fieldwork, Federal Work-Study, institutionally sponsored loans, scholarships/grants, health care benefits, tuition waivers (full and partial), and unspecified assistantships also available. Support available to part-time students. Financial award application deadline: 5/15; financial award applicants required to submit FAFSA. *Faculty research:* Water sampling in the Lower Rio Grande, urban stormwater management. *Unit head:* Dr. Kim D. Jones, Department Chair, 361-593-2187, Fax: 361-593-2069, E-mail: kjones@tamuk.edu. *Application contact:* Dr. Mohamed Abdelrahman, Dean, College of Graduate Studies, 361-593-2809, E-mail: mohamed.abdelrahman@tamuk.edu.

Texas Tech University, Graduate School, Edward E. Whitacre Jr. College of Engineering, Department of Civil and Environmental Engineering, Lubbock, TX 79409-1023. Offers civil engineering (MSCE, PhD); environmental engineering (MENVEGR). *Accreditation:* ABET. Part-time programs available. *Faculty:* 23 full-time (3 women), 1 part-time/adjunct (0 women). *Students:* 76 full-time (25 women), 8 part-time (0 women); includes 19 minority (1 Black or African American, non-Hispanic/Latino; 4 Asian, non-Hispanic/Latino; 13 Hispanic/Latino; 1 Two or more races, non-Hispanic/Latino), 42 international. Average age 26. 129 applicants, 67% accepted, 29 enrolled. In 2014, 36 master's, 4 doctorates awarded. Terminal master's awarded for partial completion of doctoral program. *Degree requirements:* For master's, comprehensive exam, thesis or alternative; for doctorate, comprehensive exam, thesis/dissertation, preliminary examination. *Entrance requirements:* For master's and doctorate, GRE (Verbal and Quantitative). Additional exam requirements/recommendations for international students: Required—TOEFL (minimum score 550 paper-based; 79 iBT), IELTS (minimum score 6.5). *Application deadline:* For fall admission, 6/1 priority date for domestic students, 1/15 priority date for international students; for spring admission, 9/1 priority date for domestic students, 6/15 priority date for international students. Applications are processed on a rolling basis. Application fee: $60. Electronic applications accepted. *Expenses:* Tuition, state resident: full-time $6310; part-time $262.92 per credit hour. Tuition, nonresident: full-time $14,998; part-time $624.92 per credit hour. *Required fees:* $2701; $36.50 per credit. $912.50 per semester. Tuition and fees vary according to course load. *Financial support:* In 2014–15, 61 students received support, including 59 fellowships (averaging $3,102 per year), 3 research assistantships (averaging $17,500 per year), 21 teaching assistantships (averaging $18,170 per year); scholarships/grants, tuition waivers (partial), and unspecified assistantships also available. Financial award application deadline: 3/1; financial award applicants required to submit FAFSA. *Faculty research:* Geotechnical engineering, transportation engineering, water resources engineering, environmental engineering, wind engineering. *Total annual research expenditures:* $830,395. *Unit head:* Dr. David Ernst, Interim Chair, 806-834-8657, E-mail: david.ernst@ttu.edu. *Application contact:* Dr. Priyantha Jayawickrama, Associate Professor, 806-742-3523 Ext. 245, Fax: 806-742-3488, E-mail: priyantha.jayawickrama@ttu.edu.
Website: http://www.depts.ttu.edu/ceweb/.

Tufts University, School of Engineering, Department of Civil and Environmental Engineering, Medford, MA 02155. Offers bioengineering (ME, MS), including environmental technology; civil engineering (ME, MS, PhD), including geotechnical engineering, structural engineering, water diplomacy (PhD); environmental engineering (ME, MS, PhD), including environmental engineering and environmental sciences, environmental geotechnology, environmental health, environmental science and management, hazardous materials management, water diplomacy (PhD), water resources engineering. Part-time programs available. *Faculty:* 24 full-time (5 women), 6 part-time/adjunct (1 woman). *Students:* 66 full-time (29 women), 19 part-time (6 women); includes 5 minority (1 Black or African American, non-Hispanic/Latino; 2 Asian, non-Hispanic/Latino; 1 Hispanic/Latino; 1 Two or more races, non-Hispanic/Latino), 25 international. Average age 29. 166 applicants, 42% accepted, 27 enrolled. In 2014, 21 master's, 6 doctorates awarded. Terminal master's awarded for partial completion of doctoral program. *Degree requirements:* For master's, thesis or alternative; for doctorate, thesis/dissertation. *Entrance requirements:* For master's and doctorate, GRE General Test. Additional exam requirements/recommendations for international students: Required—TOEFL (minimum score 550 paper-based; 80 iBT), IELTS (minimum score 6.5). *Application deadline:* For fall admission, 1/15 priority date for domestic students, 1/15 for international students; for spring admission, 9/15 for domestic and international students. Applications are processed on a rolling basis. Application fee: $75. Electronic applications accepted. *Expenses: Tuition:* Full-time $45,590; part-time $1161 per credit hour. *Required fees:* $782. Full-time tuition and fees

vary according to degree level, program and student level. Part-time tuition and fees vary according to course load. *Financial support:* Fellowships with full tuition reimbursements, research assistantships with full and partial tuition reimbursements, teaching assistantships with full and partial tuition reimbursements, Federal Work-Study, scholarships/grants, tuition waivers (partial), and unspecified assistantships available. Financial award application deadline: 5/15; financial award applicants required to submit FAFSA. *Faculty research:* Environmental and water resources engineering, environmental health, geotechnical and geoenvironmental engineering, structural engineering and mechanics, water diplomacy. *Unit head:* Dr. Kurt Pennell, Graduate Program Director. *Application contact:* Office of Graduate Admissions, 617-627-3395, E-mail: gradadmissions@tufts.edu.
Website: http://www.ase.tufts.edu/cee/.

Universidad Central del Este, Graduate School, San Pedro de Macoris, Dominican Republic. Offers environmental engineering (ME); financial management (M Ad); higher education (M Ed), including higher education management, higher education pedagogy; human resources (M Ad). *Entrance requirements:* For master's, letters of recommendation.

Universidad Nacional Pedro Henriquez Urena, Graduate School, Santo Domingo, Dominican Republic. Offers agricultural diversity (MS), including horticultural/fruit production, tropical animal production; conservation of monuments and cultural assets (M Arch); ecology and environment (MS); environmental engineering (MEE); international relations (MA); natural resource management (MS); political science (MA); project optimization (MPM); project feasibility (MPM); project management (MPM); sanitation engineering (ME); science for teachers (MS); tropical Caribbean architecture (M Arch).

Université de Sherbrooke, Faculty of Engineering, Program in the Environment, Sherbrooke, QC J1K 2R1, Canada. Offers M Env. *Degree requirements:* For master's, thesis.

Université Laval, Faculty of Sciences and Engineering, Department of Civil Engineering, Programs in Civil Engineering, Québec, QC G1K 7P4, Canada. Offers civil engineering (M Sc, PhD); environmental technology (M Sc). Terminal master's awarded for partial completion of doctoral program. *Degree requirements:* For master's, thesis (for some programs); for doctorate, comprehensive exam, thesis/dissertation. *Entrance requirements:* For master's and doctorate, knowledge of French and English. Electronic applications accepted.

University at Buffalo, the State University of New York, Graduate School, School of Engineering and Applied Sciences, Department of Civil, Structural, and Environmental Engineering, Buffalo, NY 14260. Offers civil engineering (ME, MS, PhD); engineering science (MS). Part-time programs available. Postbaccalaureate distance learning degree programs offered (minimal on-campus study). *Faculty:* 31 full-time (5 women), 1 part-time/adjunct (0 women). *Students:* 166 full-time (43 women), 16 part-time (3 women); includes 15 minority (2 Black or African American, non-Hispanic/Latino; 1 American Indian or Alaska Native, non-Hispanic/Latino; 5 Asian, non-Hispanic/Latino; 4 Hispanic/Latino; 3 Two or more races, non-Hispanic/Latino), 111 international. Average age 27. 714 applicants, 33% accepted, 55 enrolled. In 2014, 59 master's, 17 doctorates awarded. Terminal master's awarded for partial completion of doctoral program. *Degree requirements:* For master's, project, thesis, or comprehensive exam; for doctorate, thesis/dissertation. *Entrance requirements:* For master's and doctorate, GRE General Test, letters of reference. Additional exam requirements/recommendations for international students: Required—TOEFL (minimum score 550 paper-based; 79 iBT). *Application deadline:* For fall admission, 1/15 priority date for domestic and international students; for spring admission, 9/15 for domestic and international students. Applications are processed on a rolling basis. Application fee: $75. Electronic applications accepted. *Financial support:* In 2014–15, 87 students received support, including 3 fellowships with full and partial tuition reimbursements available (averaging $30,000 per year), 28 research assistantships with full and partial tuition reimbursements available (averaging $20,090 per year), 28 teaching assistantships with full and partial tuition reimbursements available (averaging $21,420 per year); career-related internships or fieldwork, Federal Work-Study, institutionally sponsored loans, scholarships/grants, traineeships, health care benefits, tuition waivers (full and partial), and unspecified assistantships also available. Support available to part-time students. Financial award application deadline: 1/15; financial award applicants required to submit FAFSA. *Faculty research:* Environmental engineering and fluid mechanics, structural dynamics, geomechanics, earthquake engineering computational mechanics. *Total annual research expenditures:* $4.4 million. *Unit head:* Dr. Andrew S. Whittaker, Chairman, 716-645-2114, Fax: 716-645-3733, E-mail: awhittak@buffalo.edu. *Application contact:* Dr. Joseph Atkinson, Director of Graduate Studies, 716-645-2220, Fax: 716-645-3733, E-mail: atkinson@buffalo.edu.
Website: http://www.csee.buffalo.edu/.

The University of Alabama, Graduate School, College of Engineering, Department of Civil, Construction and Environmental Engineering, Tuscaloosa, AL 35487-0205. Offers civil engineering (MSCE, PhD); environmental engineering (MS). Part-time programs available. *Faculty:* 22 full-time (2 women). *Students:* 58 full-time (20 women), 4 part-time (0 women); includes 4 minority (2 Black or African American, non-Hispanic/Latino; 1 Asian, non-Hispanic/Latino; 1 Hispanic/Latino), 22 international. Average age 28. 76 applicants, 43% accepted, 16 enrolled. In 2014, 23 master's, 4 doctorates awarded. Terminal master's awarded for partial completion of doctoral program. *Degree requirements:* For master's, thesis or alternative; for doctorate, one foreign language, comprehensive exam, thesis/dissertation. *Entrance requirements:* For master's and doctorate, GRE General Test (minimum combined score of 300), minimum GPA of 3.0 in last 60 hours of course work. Additional exam requirements/recommendations for international students: Required—TOEFL (minimum score 550 paper-based; 79 iBT), IELTS (minimum score 6.5), PTE (minimum score 59). *Application deadline:* For fall admission, 7/10 for domestic students, 1/15 for international students; for spring admission, 11/1 for domestic students, 6/1 for international students. Applications are processed on a rolling basis. Application fee: $50 ($60 for international students). Electronic applications accepted. *Expenses:* Tuition, state resident: full-time $9826. Tuition, nonresident: full-time $24,950. *Financial support:* In 2014–15, 40 students received support, including 2 fellowships with full tuition reimbursements available (averaging $30,000 per year), 17 research assistantships with full tuition reimbursements available (averaging $13,275 per year), 20 teaching assistantships with full tuition reimbursements available (averaging $13,275 per year); scholarships/grants, tuition waivers (partial), and unspecified assistantships also available. Financial award application deadline: 2/15. *Faculty research:* Experimental structures, modeling of structures, bridge management systems, geotechnological engineering, environmental remediation. *Total annual research expenditures:* $2.7 million. *Unit head:* Dr. W. Edward Back, Head and Professor, 205-348-6550, Fax: 205-348-0783, E-mail: eback@eng.ua.edu. *Application contact:* Dr. Andrew Graettinger, Associate Professor and Graduate Program Director, 205-348-1707, Fax: 205-348-0783, E-mail: andrewg@eng.ua.edu.
Website: http://cce.eng.ua.edu/.

The University of Alabama at Birmingham, School of Engineering, Program in Interdisciplinary Engineering, Birmingham, AL 35294. Offers computational engineering (PhD); environmental health and safety engineering (PhD). *Students:* 12 full-time (1 woman), 26 part-time (7 women); includes 9 minority (6 Black or African American, non-Hispanic/Latino; 2 Asian, non-Hispanic/Latino; 1 Hispanic/Latino), 7 international. Average age 38. In 2014, 4 doctorates awarded. *Degree requirements:* For doctorate, comprehensive exam, thesis/dissertation. *Entrance requirements:* For doctorate, GRE (minimum rank 50% in both Quantitative Reasoning and Verbal Reasoning sections), undergraduate degree in a supporting field, official transcripts, minimum undergraduate GPA of 3.0. Additional exam requirements/recommendations for international students: Required—TOEFL (minimum score 100 iBT). *Application deadline:* For fall admission, 7/1 for domestic students; for spring admission, 11/1 for domestic students; for summer admission, 4/1 for domestic students. *Expenses:* Tuition, state resident: full-time $7090; part-time $370 per credit hour. Tuition, nonresident: full-time $16,072; part-time $869 per credit hour. Full-time tuition and fees vary according to course load and program. *Unit head:* Dr. David Littlefield, Graduate Program Director, 205-934-8460, E-mail: littlefield@uab.edu. *Application contact:* Susan Noblitt Banks, Director of Graduate School Operations, 205-934-8227, Fax: 205-934-8413, E-mail: gradschool@uab.edu.
Website: http://www.uab.edu/engineering/home/degrees-cert/phd?id=189:phd-in-interdisciplinary-engineering&catid=3.

The University of Alabama in Huntsville, School of Graduate Studies, College of Engineering, Department of Civil and Environmental Engineering, Huntsville, AL 35899. Offers civil and environmental engineering (PhD); civil engineering (MSE), including civil engineering, environmental and water resource engineering, geotechnical engineering, structural engineering and structural mechanics, transportation engineering. PhD offered jointly with The University of Alabama at Birmingham. Part-time and evening/weekend programs available. *Degree requirements:* For master's, comprehensive exam, thesis or alternative, oral and written exams; for doctorate, comprehensive exam, thesis/dissertation, oral and written exams. *Entrance requirements:* For master's, GRE General Test, BSE, minimum GPA of 3.0; for doctorate, GRE General Test, minimum GPA of 3.0. Additional exam requirements/recommendations for international students: Required—TOEFL (minimum score 500 paper-based; 80 iBT), IELTS (minimum score 6.5). Electronic applications accepted. *Faculty research:* Smart materials and smart structures, fiber-reinforced cementitious composites, processing and mechanics of composites, geographic information systems, environmental engineering.

University of Alaska Anchorage, School of Engineering, Program in Applied Environmental Science and Technology, Anchorage, AK 99508. Offers M AEST, MS. Part-time and evening/weekend programs available. *Degree requirements:* For master's, comprehensive exam, thesis (for some programs). *Entrance requirements:* For master's, GRE General Test. Additional exam requirements/recommendations for international students: Required—TOEFL (minimum score 550 paper-based). *Faculty research:* Wastewater treatment, environmental regulations, water resources management, justification of public facilities, rural sanitation, biological treatment process.

University of Alaska Fairbanks, College of Engineering and Mines, Department of Civil and Environmental Engineering, Program in Environmental Engineering, Fairbanks, AK 99775-5900. Offers MS, PhD. Part-time programs available. *Students:* 4 full-time (2 women), 2 international. Average age 27. 4 applicants, 75% accepted, 2 enrolled. *Degree requirements:* For master's, comprehensive exam, oral defense of project or thesis; for doctorate, comprehensive exam, thesis/dissertation. *Entrance requirements:* For master's, BS in engineering from ABET-accredited institution with minimum GPA of 3.0, basic computer techniques course. Additional exam requirements/recommendations for international students: Required—TOEFL (minimum score 575 paper-based). *Application deadline:* For fall admission, 6/1 for domestic students, 3/1 for international students; for spring admission, 10/15 for domestic students, 9/1 for international students. Applications are processed on a rolling basis. Application fee: $60. Electronic applications accepted. *Expenses:* Tuition, state resident: full-time $7614; part-time $423 per credit. Tuition, nonresident: full-time $15,552; part-time $864 per credit. Tuition and fees vary according to course level, course load and reciprocity agreements. *Financial support:* In 2014–15, 2 research assistantships with full tuition reimbursements (averaging $9,746 per year), 2 teaching assistantships with full tuition reimbursements (averaging $5,477 per year) were awarded; fellowships with full tuition reimbursements, career-related internships or fieldwork, Federal Work-Study, scholarships/grants, health care benefits, and unspecified assistantships also available. Support available to part-time students. Financial award application deadline: 7/1; financial award applicants required to submit FAFSA. *Unit head:* Dr. Robert Perkins, Department Chair, 907-474-7241, Fax: 907-474-6087, E-mail: fycee@uaf.edu. *Application contact:* Mary Kreta, Director of Admissions, 907-474-7500, Fax: 907-474-7097, E-mail: admissions@uaf.edu.
Website: http://cem.uaf.edu/cee/environmental-engineering.aspx.

University of Alberta, Faculty of Graduate Studies and Research, Department of Civil and Environmental Engineering, Edmonton, AB T6G 2E1, Canada. Offers construction engineering and management (M Eng, M Sc, PhD); environmental engineering (M Eng, M Sc, PhD); environmental science (M Sc, PhD); geoenvironmental engineering (M Eng, M Sc, PhD); geotechnical engineering (M Eng, M Sc, PhD); mining engineering (M Eng, M Sc, PhD); petroleum engineering (M Eng, M Sc, PhD); structural engineering (M Eng, M Sc, PhD); water resources (M Eng, M Sc, PhD). Part-time programs available. Postbaccalaureate distance learning degree programs offered (minimal on-campus study). *Degree requirements:* For master's, thesis (for some programs); for doctorate, thesis/dissertation. *Entrance requirements:* For master's, minimum GPA of 3.0 in last 2 years of undergraduate studies; for doctorate, minimum GPA of 3.0. Additional exam requirements/recommendations for international students: Required—TOEFL (minimum score 550 paper-based). Electronic applications accepted. *Faculty research:* Mining.

The University of Arizona, College of Engineering, Department of Chemical and Environmental Engineering, Program in Environmental Engineering, Tucson, AZ 85721. Offers MS, PhD. *Entrance requirements:* For master's and doctorate, GRE, 3 letters of recommendation, resume, statement of purpose. Additional exam requirements/recommendations for international students: Required—TOEFL (minimum score 550 paper-based; 79 iBT). Electronic applications accepted.

University of Arkansas, Graduate School, College of Engineering, Department of Civil Engineering, Program in Environmental Engineering, Fayetteville, AR 72701-1201. Offers MS En E, MSE. *Accreditation:* ABET. *Degree requirements:* For master's, thesis optional. Electronic applications accepted.

University of Calgary, Faculty of Graduate Studies, Schulich School of Engineering, Department of Chemical and Petroleum Engineering, Calgary, AB T2N 1N4, Canada. Offers chemical engineering (M Eng, M Sc, PhD); energy and environment engineering (M Eng, M Sc, PhD); energy and environmental systems (M Eng, M Sc, PhD); environmental engineering (M Eng, M Sc, PhD); petroleum engineering (M Eng, M Sc, PhD); reservoir characterization (M Eng, M Sc). Part-time programs available. *Degree requirements:* For master's, thesis (for some programs); for doctorate, comprehensive exam, thesis/dissertation, candidacy exam. *Entrance requirements:* For master's, minimum GPA of 3.0 or equivalent; for doctorate, minimum GPA of 3.5 or equivalent. Additional exam requirements/recommendations for international students: Required—TOEFL (minimum score 550 paper-based; 80 iBT), IELTS (minimum score 7). Electronic applications accepted. *Faculty research:* Environmental engineering, biomedical engineering modeling, simulation and control, petroleum recovery and reservoir engineering, phase equilibria and transport properties.

University of Calgary, Faculty of Graduate Studies, Schulich School of Engineering, Department of Civil Engineering, Calgary, AB T2N 1N4, Canada. Offers avalanche mechanics (M Sc, PhD); civil engineering (M Eng, M Sc, PhD); energy and environment engineering (M Eng, M Sc, PhD); environmental engineering (M Eng, M Sc, PhD); geotechnical engineering (M Eng, M Sc, PhD); materials science (M Eng, M Sc, PhD); project management (M Eng, M Sc, PhD); structures and solid mechanics (M Eng, M Sc, PhD); transportation engineering (M Eng, M Sc, PhD); water resources (M Eng, M Sc, PhD). Part-time programs available. *Degree requirements:* For master's, thesis; for doctorate, thesis/dissertation, written and oral candidacy exam. *Entrance requirements:* For master's, minimum GPA of 3.0; for doctorate, minimum GPA of 3.5. Additional exam requirements/recommendations for international students: Required—TOEFL (minimum score 580 paper-based; 93 iBT), IELTS (minimum score 7). Electronic applications accepted. *Faculty research:* Geotechnical engineering, energy and environment, transportation, project management, structures and solid mechanics.

University of California, Berkeley, Graduate Division, College of Engineering, Department of Civil and Environmental Engineering, Berkeley, CA 94720-1500. Offers engineering and project management (M Eng, MS, D Eng, PhD); environmental engineering (M Eng, MS, D Eng, PhD); geoengineering (M Eng, MS, D Eng, PhD); structural engineering, mechanics and materials (M Eng, MS, D Eng, PhD); transportation engineering (M Eng, MS, D Eng, PhD); M Arch/MS; MCP/MS; MPP/MS. *Degree requirements:* For master's, comprehensive exam or thesis (MS); for doctorate, thesis/dissertation, qualifying exam. *Entrance requirements:* For master's, GRE General Test, minimum GPA of 3.0, 3 letters of recommendation; for doctorate, GRE General Test, minimum GPA of 3.5, 3 letters of recommendation. Additional exam requirements/recommendations for international students: Required—TOEFL (minimum score 570 paper-based). Electronic applications accepted.

University of California, Davis, College of Engineering, Program in Civil and Environmental Engineering, Davis, CA 95616. Offers M Engr, MS, D Engr, PhD, Certificate, M Engr/MBA. *Degree requirements:* For master's, comprehensive exam (for some programs), thesis (for some programs); for doctorate, thesis/dissertation. *Entrance requirements:* For master's, GRE General Test, minimum GPA of 3.0; for doctorate, GRE, minimum graduate GPA of 3.5. Additional exam requirements/recommendations for international students: Required—TOEFL (minimum score 550 paper-based). Electronic applications accepted. *Faculty research:* Environmental water resources, transportation, structural mechanics, structural engineering, geotechnical engineering.

University of California, Irvine, Henry Samueli School of Engineering, Department of Civil and Environmental Engineering, Irvine, CA 92697. Offers MS, PhD. Part-time programs available. *Students:* 180 full-time (65 women), 26 part-time (9 women); includes 38 minority (2 Black or African American, non-Hispanic/Latino; 21 Asian, non-Hispanic/Latino; 13 Hispanic/Latino; 2 Two or more races, non-Hispanic/Latino), 115 international. Average age 26. 543 applicants, 58% accepted, 93 enrolled. In 2014, 36 master's, 14 doctorates awarded. Terminal master's awarded for partial completion of doctoral program. *Degree requirements:* For doctorate, thesis/dissertation. *Entrance requirements:* For master's and doctorate, GRE General Test, minimum GPA of 3.0, 3 letters of recommendation. Additional exam requirements/recommendations for international students: Required—TOEFL (minimum score 550 paper-based). *Application deadline:* For fall admission, 1/15 priority date for domestic students, 1/15 for international students. Applications are processed on a rolling basis. Application fee: $90 ($110 for international students). Electronic applications accepted. *Financial support:* Fellowships, research assistantships with full tuition reimbursements, teaching assistantships, institutionally sponsored loans, traineeships, health care benefits, and unspecified assistantships available. Financial award application deadline: 3/1; financial award applicants required to submit FAFSA. *Faculty research:* Intelligent transportation systems and transportation economics, risk and reliability, fluid mechanics, environmental hydrodynamics, hydrological and climate systems, water resources. *Unit head:* Prof. Brett F. Sanders, Chair and Professor, 949-824-4327, Fax: 949-824-3672, E-mail: bsanders@uci.edu. *Application contact:* Nadia Ortiz, Assistant Director, 949-824-3562, Fax: 949-824-9096, E-mail: nortiz@uci.edu.
Website: http://www.eng.uci.edu/dept/cee.

University of California, Los Angeles, Graduate Division, Henry Samueli School of Engineering and Applied Science, Department of Civil and Environmental Engineering, Los Angeles, CA 90095-1593. Offers MS, PhD. *Faculty:* 16 full-time (3 women), 27 part-time/adjunct (0 women). *Students:* 139 full-time (60 women); includes 33 minority (1 Black or African American, non-Hispanic/Latino; 19 Asian, non-Hispanic/Latino; 11 Hispanic/Latino; 2 Two or more races, non-Hispanic/Latino), 73 international. 433 applicants, 57% accepted, 85 enrolled. In 2014, 86 master's, 22 doctorates awarded. *Degree requirements:* For master's, comprehensive exam or thesis; for doctorate, thesis/dissertation, qualifying exams. *Entrance requirements:* For master's, GRE General Test, minimum GPA of 3.0; for doctorate, GRE General Test, minimum GPA of 3.25. Additional exam requirements/recommendations for international students: Required—TOEFL (minimum score 560 paper-based; 87 iBT), IELTS (minimum score 7). *Application deadline:* For fall admission, 12/15 priority date for domestic and international students. Application fee: $80 ($100 for international students). Electronic applications accepted. *Financial support:* In 2014–15, 109 fellowships, 45 research assistantships, 66 teaching assistantships were awarded; Federal Work-Study, institutionally sponsored loans, and tuition waivers (full and partial) also available. Financial award application deadline: 12/15; financial award applicants required to submit FAFSA. *Faculty research:* Civil engineering materials, environmental engineering, geotechnical engineering, hydrology and water resources, structures. *Total annual research expenditures:* $3.5 million. *Unit head:* Dr. Jonathan P. Stewart, Chair, 310-206-2990, E-mail: jstewart@seas.ucla.edu. *Application contact:* Jesse Miller Murphy, Graduate Affairs Officer, 310-825-1851, Fax: 310-206-2222, E-mail: jmurphy@seas.ucla.edu.
Website: http://cee.ucla.edu/.

University of California, Los Angeles, Graduate Division, Institute of the Environment and Sustainability, Los Angeles, CA 90095-1496. Offers environmental science and engineering (D Env). *Degree requirements:* For doctorate, thesis/dissertation, oral and written qualifying exams. *Entrance requirements:* For doctorate, GRE General Test, minimum undergraduate GPA of 3.0, master's degree or equivalent in a natural science, engineering, or public health. *Faculty research:* Toxic and hazardous substances, air and water pollution, risk assessment/management, water resources, marine science.

University of California, Los Angeles, Graduate Division, School of Public Health, Department of Environmental Health Sciences, Los Angeles, CA 90095. Offers environmental health sciences (MS, PhD); environmental science and engineering (D Env); molecular toxicology (PhD); JD/MPH. *Accreditation:* ABET (one or more programs are accredited). *Degree requirements:* For master's, comprehensive exam or thesis; for doctorate, thesis/dissertation, oral and written qualifying exams. *Entrance requirements:* For master's, GRE General Test, minimum GPA of 3.0; for doctorate, GRE General Test, minimum undergraduate GPA of 3.0. Electronic applications accepted.

University of California, Merced, Graduate Division, School of Engineering, Merced, CA 95343. Offers biological engineering and small scale technologies (MS, PhD); electrical engineering and computer science (MS, PhD); environmental systems (MS, PhD); mechanical engineering (MS); mechanical engineering and applied mechanics (PhD). *Faculty:* 38 full-time (6 women), 1 part-time/adjunct (0 women). *Students:* 128 full-time (36 women), 2 part-time (0 women); includes 21 minority (1 Black or African American, non-Hispanic/Latino; 11 Asian, non-Hispanic/Latino; 6 Hispanic/Latino; 3 Two or more races, non-Hispanic/Latino), 72 international. Average age 28. 230 applicants, 39% accepted, 38 enrolled. In 2014, 5 master's, 18 doctorates awarded. *Degree requirements:* For master's, variable foreign language requirement, comprehensive exam, thesis (for some programs); for doctorate, variable foreign language requirement, comprehensive exam, thesis/dissertation. *Entrance requirements:* For master's and doctorate, GRE. Additional exam requirements/recommendations for international students: Required—TOEFL (minimum score 550 paper-based; 68 iBT); Recommended—IELTS. Application fee: $80 ($100 for international students). *Expenses:* Tuition, state resident: full-time $11,220; part-time $2805 per semester. *Required fees:* $1940; $970 per semester hour. *Financial support:* In 2014–15, 19 fellowships with full and partial tuition reimbursements (averaging $6,683 per year) were awarded; scholarships/grants also available. *Faculty research:* Artificial intelligence, biomedical imaging, thermal science, ecology, nanotechnology. *Unit head:* Dr. Erik Rolland, Interim Dean, 209-228-4296, Fax: 209-228-4047, E-mail: erolland@ucmerced.edu. *Application contact:* Tsu Ya, Graduate Admissions and Academic Services Manager, 209-228-4521, Fax: 209-228-6906, E-mail: tya@ucmerced.edu.

University of California, Riverside, Graduate Division, Department of Chemical and Environmental Engineering, Riverside, CA 92521-0102. Offers MS, PhD. Part-time programs available. Terminal master's awarded for partial completion of doctoral program. *Degree requirements:* For master's, thesis (for some programs); for doctorate, comprehensive exam, thesis/dissertation. *Entrance requirements:* For master's and doctorate, GRE General Test, minimum GPA of 3.0. Additional exam requirements/recommendations for international students: Required—TOEFL (minimum score 550 paper-based; 80 iBT). Electronic applications accepted. *Expenses:* Tuition, state resident: full-time $5399. Tuition, nonresident: full-time $10,433. *Faculty research:* Air quality systems, water quality systems, advanced materials and nanotechnology, energy systems/alternative fuels, theory and molecular modeling.

University of Central Florida, College of Engineering and Computer Science, Department of Civil, Environmental, and Construction Engineering, Program in Environmental Engineering, Orlando, FL 32816. Offers MS, MS Env E, PhD. Part-time and evening/weekend programs available. *Students:* 24 full-time (11 women), 17 part-time (8 women); includes 10 minority (1 Black or African American, non-Hispanic/Latino; 2 Asian, non-Hispanic/Latino; 4 Hispanic/Latino; 3 Two or more races, non-Hispanic/Latino), 7 international. Average age 30. 36 applicants, 53% accepted, 9 enrolled. In 2014, 14 master's, 1 doctorate awarded. *Degree requirements:* For master's, thesis or alternative; for doctorate, thesis/dissertation, departmental qualifying exam, candidacy exam. *Entrance requirements:* For master's, GRE General Test, minimum GPA of 3.0 in last 60 hours of course work; for doctorate, GRE General Test, minimum GPA of 3.5 in last 60 hours of course work, interview. Additional exam requirements/recommendations for international students: Required—TOEFL. *Application deadline:* For fall admission, 7/15 priority date for domestic students; for spring admission, 12/15 priority date for domestic students. Application fee: $30. Electronic applications accepted. *Expenses:* Tuition, state resident: part-time $288.16 per credit hour. Tuition, nonresident: part-time $1073.31 per credit hour. *Financial support:* In 2014–15, 14 students received support, including 2 fellowships with partial tuition reimbursements available (averaging $7,800 per year), 13 research assistantships with partial tuition reimbursements available (averaging $11,000 per year), 5 teaching assistantships with partial tuition reimbursements available (averaging $8,900 per year); career-related internships or fieldwork, Federal Work-Study, institutionally sponsored loans, tuition waivers (partial), and unspecified assistantships also available. Financial award application deadline: 3/1; financial award applicants required to submit FAFSA. *Unit head:* Dr. Mohamed Abdel-Aty, Chair, 407-823-5657, E-mail: m.aty@ucf.edu. *Application contact:* Barbara Rodriguez Lamas, Director, Admissions and Student Services, 407-823-2766, Fax: 407-823-6442, E-mail: gradadmissions@ucf.edu.
Website: http://cece.ucf.edu/.

University of Cincinnati, Graduate School, College of Engineering and Applied Science, Department of Civil and Environmental Engineering, Program in Environmental Engineering, Cincinnati, OH 45221. Offers MS, PhD. *Accreditation:* ABET (one or more programs are accredited). Part-time programs available. *Degree requirements:* For master's, project or thesis; for doctorate, one foreign language, thesis/dissertation. *Entrance requirements:* For master's and doctorate, GRE General Test. Additional exam requirements/recommendations for international students: Required—TOEFL (minimum score 580 paper-based; 92 iBT). Electronic applications accepted. *Faculty research:* Environmental microbiology, solid-waste management, air pollution control, water pollution control, aerosols.

University of Colorado Boulder, Graduate School, College of Engineering and Applied Science, Department of Civil, Environmental, and Architectural Engineering, Boulder, CO 80309. Offers building systems engineering (MS, PhD); construction engineering management (MS, PhD); environmental engineering (MS, PhD); geotechnical engineering and geomechanics (MS, PhD); hydrology, water resources and environmental fluid mechanics (MS, PhD); structural engineering and structural mechanics (MS, PhD). *Faculty:* 37 full-time (8 women). *Students:* 235 full-time (81 women), 36 part-time (9 women); includes 24 minority (9 Asian, non-Hispanic/Latino; 6 Hispanic/Latino; 9 Two or more races, non-Hispanic/Latino), 83 international. Average age 28. 391 applicants, 63% accepted, 68 enrolled. In 2014, 76 master's, 30 doctorates awarded. Terminal master's awarded for partial completion of doctoral program. *Degree requirements:* For master's, comprehensive exam, thesis or alternative; for doctorate, thesis/dissertation. *Entrance requirements:* For master's, GRE General Test, minimum undergraduate GPA of 3.0. *Application deadline:* For fall admission, 1/31 for domestic and international students; for spring admission, 10/1 for domestic and international students. Application fee: $50 ($70 for international students). Electronic applications accepted. *Financial support:* In 2014–15, 387 students received support, including 75 fellowships (averaging $11,889 per year), 92 research assistantships with full and partial tuition reimbursements available (averaging $34,669 per year), 17 teaching assistantships with full and partial tuition reimbursements available (averaging $28,513 per year); institutionally sponsored loans, scholarships/grants, health care benefits, and unspecified assistantships also available. Financial award application deadline: 1/15; financial award applicants required to submit FAFSA. *Faculty research:* Civil engineering, environmental engineering, architectural engineering, geotechnical engineering, hydrology. *Total annual research expenditures:* $13 million.
Website: http://civil.colorado.edu/.

University of Colorado Denver, College of Engineering and Applied Science, Department of Civil Engineering, Denver, CO 80217. Offers civil engineering (EASPh D); civil engineering systems (PhD); environmental and sustainability engineering (MS, PhD); geographic information systems (MS); geotechnical engineering (MS, PhD); hydrology and hydraulics (MS, PhD); structural engineering (MS, PhD);

transportation engineering (MS, PhD). Part-time and evening/weekend programs available. *Faculty:* 15 full-time (4 women), 11 part-time/adjunct (2 women). *Students:* 64 full-time (15 women), 43 part-time (8 women); includes 15 minority (3 Black or African American, non-Hispanic/Latino; 3 Asian, non-Hispanic/Latino; 6 Hispanic/Latino; 3 Two or more races, non-Hispanic/Latino), 34 international. Average age 32. 136 applicants, 54% accepted, 28 enrolled. In 2014, 35 master's, 9 doctorates awarded. *Degree requirements:* For master's, comprehensive exam, 30 credit hours, project or thesis; for doctorate, comprehensive exam, thesis/dissertation, 60 credit hours (30 of which are dissertation research). *Entrance requirements:* For master's, GRE, statement of purpose, transcripts, three references; for doctorate, GRE, statement of purpose, transcripts, references, letter of support from faculty stating willingness to serve as dissertation advisor and outlining plan for financial support. Additional exam requirements/recommendations for international students: Required—TOEFL (minimum score 537 paper-based; 75 iBT); Recommended—IELTS (minimum score 6.5). *Application deadline:* For fall admission, 5/1 for domestic students, 4/1 for international students; for spring admission, 10/1 for domestic students, 9/1 for international students; for summer admission, 2/15 for domestic students, 1/15 for international students. Application fee: $50 ($75 for international students). Electronic applications accepted. *Expenses:* Expenses: Contact institution. *Financial support:* In 2014–15, 26 students received support. Fellowships, research assistantships, teaching assistantships, career-related internships or fieldwork, Federal Work-Study, institutionally sponsored loans, scholarships/grants, traineeships, and unspecified assistantships available. Financial award application deadline: 4/1; financial award applicants required to submit FAFSA. *Faculty research:* Earthquake source physics, environmental biotechnology, hydrologic and hydraulic engineering, sustainability assessments, transportation energy use and greenhouse gas emissions. *Unit head:* Dr. Kevin Rens, Chair, 303-556-8017, E-mail: kevin.rens@ucdenver.edu. *Application contact:* Tammy Southern, Program Assistant, 303-556-6712, E-mail: tamara.southern@ucdenver.edu.
Website: http://www.ucdenver.edu/academics/colleges/Engineering/Programs/Civil-Engineering/Pages/CivilEngineering.aspx.

University of Connecticut, Graduate School, School of Engineering, Department of Civil and Environmental Engineering, Field of Environmental Engineering, Storrs, CT 06269. Offers MS, PhD. *Degree requirements:* For master's, comprehensive exam; for doctorate, thesis/dissertation. *Entrance requirements:* For master's and doctorate, GRE General Test. Additional exam requirements/recommendations for international students: Required—TOEFL (minimum score 550 paper-based). Electronic applications accepted.

University of Dayton, Department of Civil and Environmental Engineering and Engineering Mechanics, Dayton, OH 45469. Offers engineering mechanics (MSEM); environmental engineering (MSCE); geotechnical engineering (MSCE); structural engineering (MSCE); transportation engineering (MSCE); water resources engineering (MSCE). Part-time and evening/weekend programs available. *Faculty:* 9 full-time (2 women), 3 part-time/adjunct (1 woman). *Students:* 23 full-time (4 women), 6 part-time (2 women), 22 international. Average age 26. 70 applicants, 39% accepted, 4 enrolled. In 2014, 11 master's awarded. *Degree requirements:* For master's, thesis optional. *Entrance requirements:* For master's, minimum GPA of 3.0 in undergraduate work. Additional exam requirements/recommendations for international students: Required—TOEFL (minimum score 550 paper-based; 80 iBT). *Application deadline:* For fall admission, 8/1 priority date for domestic students, 5/1 priority date for international students; for winter admission, 7/1 priority date for international students; for spring admission, 11/1 priority date for international students. Applications are processed on a rolling basis. Application fee: $0 ($50 for international students). Electronic applications accepted. *Expenses: Tuition:* Full-time $10,176; part-time $848 per credit. *Required fees:* $25; $25 per course. Part-time tuition and fees vary according to course level, course load, degree level and program. *Financial support:* In 2014–15, 3 students received support. Institutionally sponsored loans, scholarships/grants, and department-funded awards (averaging $2448 per year) available. Financial award application deadline: 3/1; financial award applicants required to submit FAFSA. *Faculty research:* Physical modeling of water resource systems, finite element methods, mechanics of composite materials, transportation systems safety, biological treatment processes, fiber reinforced concrete. *Total annual research expenditures:* $250,000. *Unit head:* Dr. Donald V. Chase, Chair, 937-229-3847, Fax: 937-229-3491, E-mail: dchase1@udayton.edu. *Application contact:* 937-229-4462, E-mail: graduateadmission@udayton.edu.
Website: https://www.udayton.edu/engineering/departments/civil/index.php.

University of Delaware, College of Engineering, Department of Civil and Environmental Engineering, Newark, DE 19716. Offers environmental engineering (MAS, MCE, PhD); geotechnical engineering (MAS, MCE, PhD); ocean engineering (MAS, MCE, PhD); structural engineering (MAS, MCE, PhD); transportation engineering (MAS, MCE, PhD); water resource engineering (MAS, MCE, PhD). Part-time programs available. Terminal master's awarded for partial completion of doctoral program. *Degree requirements:* For master's, thesis; for doctorate, thesis/dissertation. *Entrance requirements:* For master's and doctorate, GRE General Test. Additional exam requirements/recommendations for international students: Required—TOEFL. Electronic applications accepted. *Faculty research:* Structural engineering and mechanics; transportation engineering; ocean engineering; soil mechanics and foundation; water resources and environmental engineering.

University of Detroit Mercy, College of Engineering and Science, Department of Civil and Environmental Engineering, Detroit, MI 48221. Offers ME, DE. Evening/weekend programs available. *Faculty research:* Geotechnical engineering.

University of Florida, Graduate School, College of Engineering, Department of Environmental Engineering Sciences, Gainesville, FL 32611. Offers ME, MS, PhD, Engr, JD/MS. Part-time and evening/weekend programs available. Postbaccalaureate distance learning degree programs offered (no on-campus study). *Faculty:* 44 full-time (5 women), 22 part-time/adjunct (3 women). *Students:* 91 full-time (42 women), 66 part-time (25 women); includes 28 minority (5 Black or African American, non-Hispanic/Latino; 1 American Indian or Alaska Native, non-Hispanic/Latino; 8 Asian, non-Hispanic/Latino; 14 Hispanic/Latino), 47 international. 182 applicants, 50% accepted, 54 enrolled. In 2014, 43 master's, 20 doctorates awarded. Terminal master's awarded for partial completion of doctoral program. *Degree requirements:* For master's, comprehensive exam (for some programs), thesis (for some programs), project, thesis or coursework; for doctorate, comprehensive exam, thesis/dissertation; for Engr, project or thesis. *Entrance requirements:* For master's and doctorate, minimum GPA of 3.0; for Engr, GRE General Test. Additional exam requirements/recommendations for international students: Required—TOEFL (minimum score 550 paper-based; 80 iBT), IELTS (minimum score 6). *Application deadline:* For fall admission, 7/1 priority date for domestic students, 5/1 for international students; for spring admission, 11/15 for domestic students, 9/1 for international students. Applications are processed on a rolling basis. Application fee: $30. Electronic applications accepted. *Financial support:* Career-related internships or fieldwork and unspecified assistantships available. Financial award application deadline: 2/1; financial award applicants required to submit FAFSA. *Faculty research:* Air resources; system ecology and ecological engineering; water systems; geosystems engineering; environmental nanotechnology. *Total annual research expenditures:* $1.9 million. *Unit head:* Paul A. Chadik, PhD, Chair, 352-392-0841, Fax: 352-392-3076, E-mail: pchadik@ufl.edu. *Application contact:* Chang-Yu Wu, PhD, Graduate Program Contact, 352-392-0845, Fax: 352-392-3076, E-mail: cywu@ufl.edu.
Website: http://www.ees.ufl.edu/.

University of Georgia, Faculty of Engineering, Athens, GA 30602. Offers MS.

University of Guelph, Graduate Studies, College of Physical and Engineering Science, School of Engineering, Guelph, ON N1G 2W1, Canada. Offers biological engineering (M Eng, M Sc, MA Sc, PhD); engineering systems and computing (M Eng, M Sc, MA Sc, PhD); environmental engineering (M Eng, M Sc, MA Sc, PhD); water resources engineering (M Eng, M Sc, MA Sc, PhD). Part-time programs available. *Degree requirements:* For master's, thesis (for some programs); for doctorate, comprehensive exam, thesis/dissertation. *Entrance requirements:* For master's, minimum B- average during previous 2 years of course work; for doctorate, minimum B average. Additional exam requirements/recommendations for international students: Required—TOEFL (minimum score 550 paper-based; 89 iBT), IELTS (minimum score 6.5). Electronic applications accepted. *Faculty research:* Water and food safety, environmental contaminant fates and mechanisms, computer systems, robotics and mechatronics, waste treatment.

University of Hawaii at Manoa, Graduate Division, College of Engineering, Department of Civil and Environmental Engineering, Honolulu, HI 96822. Offers MS, PhD. Part-time programs available. *Degree requirements:* For master's, comprehensive exam, thesis; for doctorate, comprehensive exam, thesis/dissertation. *Entrance requirements:* For master's and doctorate, GRE General Test or EIT Exam. Additional exam requirements/recommendations for international students: Required—TOEFL (minimum score 540 paper-based; 76 iBT), IELTS (minimum score 5). *Faculty research:* Structures, transportation, environmental engineering, geotechnical engineering, construction.

University of Idaho, College of Graduate Studies, College of Engineering, Department of Engineering, Moscow, ID 83844-1011. Offers environmental engineering (M Engr, MS); nuclear engineering (M Engr, MS, PhD); technology management (MS). *Faculty:* 4 full-time, 2 part-time/adjunct. *Students:* 1 full-time, 12 part-time. Average age 44. In 2014, 5 master's awarded. *Application deadline:* Applications are processed on a rolling basis. Application fee: $60. Electronic applications accepted. *Expenses:* Tuition, state resident: full-time $4784; part-time $280.50 per credit hour. Tuition, nonresident: full-time $18,314; part-time $957.50 per credit hour. *Required fees:* $2000; $58.50 per credit hour. Tuition and fees vary according to program. *Financial support:* Applicants required to submit FAFSA. *Unit head:* Dr. Larry Stauffer, Interim Dean, 208-885-6479. *Application contact:* Stephanie Thomas, Graduate Recruitment Coordinator, 208-885-4001, Fax: 208-885-4406, E-mail: gadms@uidaho.edu.
Website: http://www.uidaho.edu/engr/.

University of Illinois at Urbana–Champaign, Graduate College, College of Engineering, Department of Civil and Environmental Engineering, Champaign, IL 61820. Offers civil engineering (MS); environmental engineering in civil engineering (MS, PhD); M Arch/MS; MBA/MS. Part-time and evening/weekend programs available. Postbaccalaureate distance learning degree programs offered (no on-campus study). *Students:* 608 (153 women). Application fee: $70 ($90 for international students). *Unit head:* Benito Marinas, Head, 217-333-6961, Fax: 217-265-8040, E-mail: marinas@illinois.edu. *Application contact:* Maxine M. Peyton, Office Manager, 217-333-6636, Fax: 217-333-9464, E-mail: mpeyton@illinois.edu.
Website: http://cee.illinois.edu/.

The University of Iowa, Graduate College, College of Engineering, Department of Civil and Environmental Engineering, Iowa City, IA 52242-1316. Offers MS, PhD. Part-time programs available. *Faculty:* 21 full-time (2 women), 3 part-time/adjunct (0 women). *Students:* 72 full-time (21 women); includes 3 minority (1 Black or African American, non-Hispanic/Latino; 2 Asian, non-Hispanic/Latino), 28 international. Average age 28. 142 applicants, 22% accepted, 9 enrolled. In 2014, 18 master's, 11 doctorates awarded. Terminal master's awarded for partial completion of doctoral program. *Degree requirements:* For master's, thesis optional, exam; for doctorate, comprehensive exam, thesis/dissertation, exam. *Entrance requirements:* For master's, GRE, minimum undergraduate GPA of 3.0; for doctorate, GRE, master's degree or equivalent with minimum GPA of 3.0. Additional exam requirements/recommendations for international students: Required—TOEFL (minimum score 550 paper-based; 81 iBT). *Application deadline:* For fall admission, 1/15 priority date for domestic and international students; for spring admission, 12/1 for domestic students, 10/1 for international students; for summer admission, 4/15 for domestic students, 3/1 for international students. Applications are processed on a rolling basis. Application fee: $60 ($100 for international students). Electronic applications accepted. *Financial support:* In 2014–15, 6 fellowships with partial tuition reimbursements, 40 research assistantships with partial tuition reimbursements (averaging $20,000 per year), 10 teaching assistantships with partial tuition reimbursements (averaging $18,080 per year) were awarded; career-related internships or fieldwork, Federal Work-Study, scholarships/grants, traineeships, and unspecified assistantships also available. Support available to part-time students. Financial award application deadline: 1/15; financial award applicants required to submit FAFSA. *Faculty research:* Water resources; environmental engineering and science; hydraulics and hydrology; structures, mechanics, and materials; transportation engineering. *Total annual research expenditures:* $19.3 million. *Unit head:* Dr. Michelle Scherer, Department Executive Officer, 319-335-5654, Fax: 319-335-5660, E-mail: michelle-scherer@uiowa.edu. *Application contact:* Kim Lebeck, Academic Program Specialist, 319-335-5647, Fax: 319-335-5660, E-mail: cee@engineering.uiowa.edu.
Website: http://www.engineering.uiowa.edu/cee.

The University of Kansas, Graduate Studies, School of Engineering, Program in Environmental Engineering, Lawrence, KS 66045. Offers MS, PhD. Part-time programs available. *Faculty:* 25 full-time, 8 part-time/adjunct. *Students:* 8 full-time (6 women), 9 part-time (2 women), 8 international. Average age 31. 12 applicants, 75% accepted, 3 enrolled. In 2014, 3 master's awarded. *Degree requirements:* For master's, thesis or alternative, exam; for doctorate, comprehensive exam, thesis/dissertation. *Entrance requirements:* For master's and doctorate, GRE, BS in engineering. Additional exam requirements/recommendations for international students: Required—TOEFL. *Application deadline:* For fall admission, 3/1 priority date for domestic and international students; for spring admission, 12/1 priority date for domestic students, 8/15 priority date for international students. Applications are processed on a rolling basis. Application fee: $55 ($65 for international students). Electronic applications accepted. *Financial support:* Fellowships with full tuition reimbursements, research assistantships with full tuition reimbursements, teaching assistantships with full and partial tuition reimbursements, and career-related internships or fieldwork available. Financial award application deadline: 2/7. *Faculty research:* Water quality, water treatment, wastewater treatment, air quality, air pollution control, solid waste, hazardous waste, water resources engineering. *Unit head:* David Darwin, Chair, 785-864-3827, E-mail: daved@ku.edu. *Application contact:* Susan Scott, Administrative Assistant, 785-864-3826, E-mail: sbscott@ku.edu.
Website: http://ceae.ku.edu/overview-3.

Environmental Engineering

University of Louisville, J. B. Speed School of Engineering, Department of Civil and Environmental Engineering, Louisville, KY 40292-0001. Offers civil engineering (M Eng, MS, PhD); environmental engineering (Graduate Certificate). *Accreditation:* ABET (one or more programs are accredited). Part-time programs available. Postbaccalaureate distance learning degree programs offered (no on-campus study). *Students:* 34 full-time (10 women), 17 part-time (4 women); includes 5 minority (2 Black or African American, non-Hispanic/Latino; 1 Asian, non-Hispanic/Latino; 2 Two or more races, non-Hispanic/Latino), 15 international. Average age 27. 26 applicants, 65% accepted, 7 enrolled. In 2014, 15 master's, 1 doctorate, 5 other advanced degrees awarded. Terminal master's awarded for partial completion of doctoral program. *Degree requirements:* For master's, comprehensive exam (for some programs), thesis optional, minimum GPA of 3.0; for doctorate, comprehensive exam, thesis/dissertation, minimum GPA of 3.0. *Entrance requirements:* For master's and doctorate, GRE, letters of recommendation, final official transcripts; for Graduate Certificate, pursuit of graduate degree (M Eng, MS, PhD) at J.B. Speed School of Engineering; undergraduate degree. Additional exam requirements/recommendations for international students: Required—TOEFL (minimum score 80 iBT) or IELTS. *Application deadline:* For fall admission, 6/15 for domestic students, 5/1 priority date for international students; for spring admission, 11/3 for domestic students, 11/1 priority date for international students; for summer admission, 3/31 for domestic students, 4/1 priority date for international students. Application fee: $60. Electronic applications accepted. *Expenses:* Tuition, state resident: full-time $11,326; part-time $630 per credit hour. Tuition, nonresident: full-time $23,568; part-time $1311 per credit hour. *Required fees:* $196. Tuition and fees vary according to program and reciprocity agreements. *Financial support:* Fellowships with full tuition reimbursements, research assistantships with full tuition reimbursements, and teaching assistantships with full tuition reimbursements available. Financial award application deadline: 2/3. *Faculty research:* Structures, hydraulics, transportation, environmental engineering, geomechanics. *Total annual research expenditures:* $1.8 million. *Unit head:* Dr. J. P. Mohsen, Chair, 502-852-4596, Fax: 502-852-8851, E-mail: jpm@louisville.edu. *Application contact:* Dr. Michael Harris, Director of Academic Programs, J. B. Speed School of Engineering, 502-852-6278, Fax: 502-852-7294, E-mail: mharris@louisville.edu.
Website: http://louisville.edu/speed/civil/.

The University of Manchester, School of Mechanical, Aerospace and Civil Engineering, Manchester, United Kingdom. Offers advanced manufacturing technology (M Ent); aerospace engineering (M Phil, M Sc, PhD); civil engineering (M Phil, M Sc, PhD); environmental engineering (M Phil, PhD); management of projects (M Phil, M Sc, PhD); mechanical engineering (M Phil, M Sc, PhD); mechanical engineering design (M Ent); nuclear engineering (M Phil, D Eng, PhD).

University of Maryland, Baltimore County, The Graduate School, College of Engineering and Information Technology, Department of Chemical, Biochemical, and Environmental Engineering, Program in Environmental Engineering, Baltimore, MD 21250. Offers MS, PhD. Part-time programs available. *Students:* 13 full-time (6 women), 5 part-time (3 women); includes 4 minority (1 Asian, non-Hispanic/Latino; 2 Hispanic/Latino; 1 Two or more races, non-Hispanic/Latino), 9 international. Average age 28. 32 applicants, 22% accepted, 3 enrolled. In 2014, 2 master's, 1 doctorate awarded. *Degree requirements:* For master's, comprehensive exam (for some programs), thesis (for some programs); for doctorate, comprehensive exam, thesis/dissertation. *Entrance requirements:* For master's and doctorate, GRE General Test, BS in civil and environmental engineering or related field of engineering. Additional exam requirements/recommendations for international students: Required—TOEFL (minimum score 550 paper-based; 80 iBT). *Application deadline:* For fall admission, 6/1 for domestic students, 1/1 for international students; for spring admission, 11/1 for domestic students, 6/1 for international students. Applications are processed on a rolling basis. Application fee: $70. Electronic applications accepted. *Expenses:* Tuition, state resident: part-time $557. Tuition, nonresident: part-time $922. *Required fees:* $122 per semester. One-time fee: $200 part-time. *Financial support:* In 2014–15, 5 research assistantships with full tuition reimbursements (averaging $23,000 per year), teaching assistantships with full tuition reimbursements (averaging $17,000 per year) were awarded; career-related internships or fieldwork, Federal Work-Study, scholarships/grants, health care benefits, tuition waivers (partial), and unspecified assistantships also available. Support available to part-time students. Financial award application deadline: 6/30; financial award applicants required to submit FAFSA. *Faculty research:* Environmental fate and transport, water resources treatment/remediation. *Unit head:* Dr. Brian E. Reed, Professor and Chair, 410-455-3400, Fax: 410-455-1049, E-mail: reedb@umbc.edu. *Application contact:* Dr. Mariajose Castellanos, Lecturer/Graduate Program Director, 410-455-8151, Fax: 410-455-6500, E-mail: mariajose@umbc.edu.
Website: http://www.umbc.edu/cbe.

University of Maryland, College Park, Academic Affairs, A. James Clark School of Engineering, Department of Civil and Environmental Engineering, College Park, MD 20742. Offers M Eng, MS, PhD. Part-time and evening/weekend programs available. Postbaccalaureate distance learning degree programs offered. *Degree requirements:* For master's, thesis optional; for doctorate, thesis/dissertation, qualifying exam. *Entrance requirements:* For master's and doctorate, GRE General Test, 3 letters of recommendation. Electronic applications accepted. *Faculty research:* Transportation and urban systems, environmental engineering, geotechnical engineering, construction engineering and management, hydraulics.

University of Massachusetts Amherst, Graduate School, College of Engineering, Department of Civil and Environmental Engineering, Amherst, MA 01003. Offers civil engineering (MSCE, PhD); environmental and water resources engineering (MSCE); geotechnical engineering (MSCE); structural engineering and mechanics (MSCE); transportation engineering (MSCE). Part-time programs available. *Faculty:* 32 full-time (8 women). *Students:* 104 full-time (43 women), 15 part-time (7 women); includes 16 minority (3 Black or African American, non-Hispanic/Latino; 4 Asian, non-Hispanic/Latino; 7 Hispanic/Latino; 2 Two or more races, non-Hispanic/Latino), 44 international. Average age 26. 219 applicants, 62% accepted, 40 enrolled. In 2014, 36 master's, 4 doctorates awarded. Terminal master's awarded for partial completion of doctoral program. *Degree requirements:* For master's, thesis or alternative; for doctorate, comprehensive exam, thesis/dissertation. *Entrance requirements:* For master's and doctorate, GRE General Test. Additional exam requirements/recommendations for international students: Required—TOEFL (minimum score 550 paper-based; 80 iBT), IELTS (minimum score 6.5). *Application deadline:* For fall admission, 1/2 for domestic and international students; for spring admission, 10/1 for domestic and international students. Applications are processed on a rolling basis. Application fee: $75. Electronic applications accepted. *Expenses:* Tuition, state resident: full-time $1980; part-time $110 per credit. Tuition, nonresident: full-time $14,644; part-time $414 per credit. *Required fees:* $11,417. One-time fee: $357. *Financial support:* Fellowships with full and partial tuition reimbursements, research assistantships with full and partial tuition reimbursements, teaching assistantships with full and partial tuition reimbursements, career-related internships or fieldwork, Federal Work-Study, scholarships/grants, traineeships, health care benefits, tuition waivers (full and partial), and unspecified assistantships available. Support available to part-time students. Financial award application deadline: 1/2. *Unit head:* Dr. Sanjay Arwade, Graduate Program Director, 413-545-0686, Fax: 413-545-2840. *Application contact:* Lindsay DeSantis, Supervisor of Admissions, 413-545-0722, Fax: 413-577-0100, E-mail: gradadm@grad.umass.edu.
Website: http://cee.umass.edu/.

University of Massachusetts Lowell, Francis College of Engineering, Department of Civil and Environmental Engineering and College of Sciences, Program in Environmental Studies, Lowell, MA 01854. Offers environmental engineering (MSES); environmental studies (PhD, Certificate). Part-time programs available. *Degree requirements:* For master's, thesis optional. *Entrance requirements:* For master's, GRE General Test. *Faculty research:* Remote sensing of air pollutants, atmospheric deposition of toxic metals, contaminant transport in groundwater, soil remediation.

University of Memphis, Graduate School, Herff College of Engineering, Department of Civil Engineering, Memphis, TN 38152. Offers civil engineering (PhD); environmental engineering (MS); foundation engineering (MS); structural engineering (MS); transportation engineering (MS); water resources engineering (MS). *Faculty:* 11 full-time (1 woman), 2 part-time/adjunct (0 women). *Students:* 12 full-time (5 women), 8 part-time (1 woman); includes 2 minority (both Black or African American, non-Hispanic/Latino), 4 international. Average age 27. 18 applicants, 100% accepted, 4 enrolled. In 2014, 8 master's awarded. Terminal master's awarded for partial completion of doctoral program. *Degree requirements:* For master's, comprehensive exam, thesis optional; for doctorate, comprehensive exam, thesis/dissertation. *Entrance requirements:* For master's, GRE General Test or MAT, minimum undergraduate GPA of 2.5; for doctorate, GRE, 3 letters of recommendation. Additional exam requirements/recommendations for international students: Required—TOEFL (minimum score 550 paper-based; 79 iBT). *Application deadline:* For fall admission, 1/7 for domestic students, 1/5 for international students; for spring admission, 12/1 for domestic students, 9/15 for international students. Application fee: $35 ($60 for international students). *Financial support:* In 2014–15, 6 students received support. Fellowships with full tuition reimbursements available, research assistantships with full tuition reimbursements available, career-related internships or fieldwork, Federal Work-Study, scholarships/grants, and unspecified assistantships available. Financial award application deadline: 2/15; financial award applicants required to submit FAFSA. *Faculty research:* Structural response to earthquakes, pavement design, water quality, transportation safety, intermodal transportation. *Unit head:* Dr. Sharam Pezeshk, Interim Chair, 901-678-2746, Fax: 901-678-3026. *Application contact:* Dr. Roger Meier, Coordinator of Graduate Studies, 901-678-3284.
Website: http://www.ce.memphis.edu.

University of Michigan, College of Engineering, Department of Civil and Environmental Engineering, Ann Arbor, MI 48109. Offers civil engineering (MSE, PhD, CE); construction engineering and management (M Eng, MSE); environmental engineering (MSE, PhD); structural engineering (M Eng); MBA/MSE. Part-time programs available. *Students:* 184 full-time (69 women), 5 part-time (0 women). 691 applicants, 36% accepted, 62 enrolled. In 2014, 59 master's, 12 doctorates awarded. *Degree requirements:* For master's, thesis optional; for doctorate, comprehensive exam, thesis/dissertation, oral defense of dissertation, preliminary and written exams. *Entrance requirements:* For master's and doctorate, GRE General Test. Additional exam requirements/recommendations for international students: Required—TOEFL (minimum score 560 paper-based). *Application deadline:* Applications are processed on a rolling basis. Electronic applications accepted. *Financial support:* Fellowships, research assistantships, teaching assistantships, institutionally sponsored loans, and tuition waivers (partial) available. Financial award application deadline: 1/19. *Faculty research:* Construction engineering and management, geotechnical engineering, earthquake-resistant design of structures, environmental chemistry and microbiology, cost engineering, environmental and water resources engineering. *Total annual research expenditures:* $10.4 million. *Unit head:* Kim Hayes, Department Chair, 734-764-8495, Fax: 734-764-4292, E-mail: ford@umich.edu. *Application contact:* Jessica Taylor, Graduate Coordinator, 734-764-8405, Fax: 734-647-2127, E-mail: jrand@umich.edu.
Website: http://cee.engin.umich.edu/.

University of Missouri, Office of Research and Graduate Studies, College of Engineering, Department of Civil and Environmental Engineering, Columbia, MO 65211. Offers civil engineering (MS, PhD); environmental engineering (MS, PhD); geotechnical engineering (MS, PhD); structural engineering (MS, PhD); transportation and highway engineering (MS); water resources (MS, PhD). *Faculty:* 18 full-time (2 women), 1 part-time/adjunct (0 women). *Students:* 42 full-time (8 women), 27 part-time (6 women); includes 4 minority (1 Black or African American, non-Hispanic/Latino; 1 Asian, non-Hispanic/Latino; 2 Hispanic/Latino), 45 international. Average age 31. 102 applicants, 48% accepted, 22 enrolled. In 2014, 14 master's, 2 doctorates awarded. *Degree requirements:* For master's, report or thesis; for doctorate, thesis/dissertation. *Entrance requirements:* For master's and doctorate, GRE General Test. Additional exam requirements/recommendations for international students: Required—TOEFL (minimum score 550 paper-based; 79 iBT). *Application deadline:* For fall admission, 2/15 priority date for domestic students, 2/15 for international students; for winter admission, 9/15 priority date for domestic students, 9/15 for international students. Application fee: $55 ($75 for international students). *Financial support:* Fellowships, research assistantships, teaching assistantships, and institutionally sponsored loans available. *Unit head:* Dr. Mark Virkler, Department Chair, 573-882-7434, E-mail: virklerm@missouri.edu. *Application contact:* Jennifer Keyzer-Andre, Administrative Associate I, 573-882-4442, E-mail: keyzerandrej@missouri.edu.
Website: http://engineering.missouri.edu/civil/.

University of Nebraska–Lincoln, Graduate College, College of Engineering, Interdepartmental Area of Environmental Engineering, Lincoln, NE 68588. Offers MS, PhD. *Degree requirements:* For master's, thesis optional; for doctorate, comprehensive exam, thesis/dissertation. *Entrance requirements:* For master's and doctorate, GRE General Test. Additional exam requirements/recommendations for international students: Required—TOEFL (minimum score 550 paper-based). Electronic applications accepted. *Faculty research:* Wastewater engineering, hazardous waste management, solid waste management, groundwater engineering.

University of Nevada, Las Vegas, Graduate College, Howard R. Hughes College of Engineering, Department of Civil and Environmental Engineering and Construction, Las Vegas, NV 89154-4015. Offers civil and environmental engineering (PhD); transportation (MS). Part-time programs available. *Faculty:* 13 full-time (2 women), 2 part-time/adjunct (0 women). *Students:* 48 full-time (14 women), 30 part-time (14 women); includes 17 minority (3 Black or African American, non-Hispanic/Latino; 4 Asian, non-Hispanic/Latino; 7 Hispanic/Latino; 3 Two or more races, non-Hispanic/Latino), 37 international. Average age 32. 51 applicants, 75% accepted, 18 enrolled. In 2014, 19 master's, 3 doctorates awarded. *Degree requirements:* For master's, comprehensive exam (for some programs), thesis (for some programs); for doctorate, comprehensive exam, thesis/dissertation. *Entrance requirements:* For master's and doctorate, GRE General Test. Additional exam requirements/recommendations for international students: Required—TOEFL (minimum score 550 paper-based; 80 iBT), IELTS (minimum score 7). *Application deadline:* For fall admission, 6/15 for domestic students, 3/15 for international students; for spring admission, 11/15 for domestic students, 8/30 for international students. Application fee: $60 ($95 for international students). Electronic applications accepted. *Financial support:* In 2014–15, 45 students

received support, including 15 research assistantships with partial tuition reimbursements available (averaging $15,678 per year), 30 teaching assistantships with partial tuition reimbursements available (averaging $13,553 per year); institutionally sponsored loans, scholarships/grants, health care benefits, and unspecified assistantships also available. Financial award application deadline: 3/1. *Total annual research expenditures:* $747,749. *Unit head:* Donald Hayes, Chair/Professor, 702-895-4723, Fax: 702-895-3936, E-mail: donald.hayes@unlv.edu. *Application contact:* Graduate College Admissions Evaluator, 702-895-3320, Fax: 702-895-4180, E-mail: gradcollege@unlv.edu.
Website: http://www.unlv.edu/ceec.

University of New Brunswick Fredericton, School of Graduate Studies, Faculty of Engineering, Department of Civil Engineering, Fredericton, NB E3B 5A3, Canada. Offers construction engineering and management (M Eng, M Sc E, PhD); environmental engineering (M Eng, M Sc E, PhD); environmental studies (M Eng); geotechnical engineering (M Eng, M Sc E, PhD); groundwater/hydrology (M Eng, M Sc E, PhD); materials (M Eng, M Sc E, PhD); pavements (M Eng, M Sc E, PhD); structures (M Eng, M Sc E, PhD); transportation (M Eng, M Sc E, PhD). Part-time programs available. *Faculty:* 12 full-time (1 woman), 4 part-time/adjunct (0 women). *Students:* 16 full-time (4 women), 15 part-time (5 women). In 2014, 9 master's, 3 doctorates awarded. *Degree requirements:* For master's, thesis, proposal; for doctorate, comprehensive exam, thesis/dissertation, qualifying exam; 27 credit hours of courses. *Entrance requirements:* For master's, minimum GPA of 3.0; B Sc E in civil engineering or related engineering degree; for doctorate, minimum GPA of 3.0; graduate degree in engineering or applied science. Additional exam requirements/recommendations for international students: Required—IELTS (minimum score 7.5), TWE (minimum score 4), Michigan English Language Assessment Battery (minimum score 85) or CanTest (minimum score 4.5); Recommended—TOEFL (minimum score 580 paper-based). *Application deadline:* For fall admission, 5/1 for domestic students; for winter admission, 11/1 for domestic students. Applications are processed on a rolling basis. Application fee: $50 Canadian dollars. Electronic applications accepted. *Financial support:* In 2014–15, 35 fellowships, 48 research assistantships, 35 teaching assistantships were awarded; career-related internships or fieldwork and scholarships/grants also available. *Faculty research:* Construction engineering and management; engineering materials and infrastructure renewal; highway and pavement research; structures and solid mechanics; geotechnical and geoenvironmental engineering; structure interaction; transportation and planning; environment, solid waste management; structural engineering; water and environmental engineering. *Unit head:* Dr. Kerry MacQuarrie, Director of Graduate Studies, 506-453-5121, Fax: 506-453-3568, E-mail: ktm@unb.ca. *Application contact:* Joyce Moore, Graduate Secretary, 506-452-6127, Fax: 506-453-3568, E-mail: joycem@unb.ca.
Website: http://go.unb.ca/gradprograms.

University of New Haven, Graduate School, Tagliatela College of Engineering, Program in Environmental Engineering, West Haven, CT 06516-1916. Offers environmental engineering (MS); industrial and hazardous wastes (MS); water and wastewater treatment (MS); water resources (MS). Part-time and evening/weekend programs available. *Degree requirements:* For master's, thesis or alternative, research project. *Entrance requirements:* For master's, bachelor's degree in engineering. Additional exam requirements/recommendations for international students: Required—TOEFL (minimum score 75 iBT), IELTS, PTE (minimum score 50). Electronic applications accepted. Application fee is waived when completed online.

The University of North Carolina at Chapel Hill, Graduate School, Gillings School of Global Public Health, Department of Environmental Sciences and Engineering, Chapel Hill, NC 27599. Offers air, radiation and industrial hygiene (MPH, MS, MSEE, MSPH, PhD); aquatic and atmospheric sciences (MPH, MS, MSPH, PhD); environmental engineering (MPH, MS, MSEE, MSPH, PhD); environmental health sciences (MPH, MS, MSPH, PhD); environmental management and policy (MPH, MS, MSPH, PhD). Terminal master's awarded for partial completion of doctoral program. *Degree requirements:* For master's, comprehensive exam, thesis (for some programs), research paper; for doctorate, comprehensive exam, thesis/dissertation. *Entrance requirements:* For master's and doctorate, GRE General Test, minimum GPA of 3.0 (recommended). Additional exam requirements/recommendations for international students: Required—TOEFL. Electronic applications accepted. *Faculty research:* Air, radiation and industrial hygiene, aquatic and atmospheric sciences, environmental health sciences, environmental management and policy, water resources engineering.

The University of North Carolina at Charlotte, The William States Lee College of Engineering, Department of Civil and Environmental Engineering, Charlotte, NC 28223-0001. Offers civil engineering (MSCE); infrastructure and environmental systems (PhD), including infrastructure and environmental systems design. Part-time and evening/weekend programs available. *Faculty:* 24 full-time (4 women). *Students:* 58 full-time (17 women), 44 part-time (13 women); includes 15 minority (8 Black or African American, non-Hispanic/Latino; 2 Asian, non-Hispanic/Latino; 5 Hispanic/Latino), 35 international. Average age 29. 105 applicants, 49% accepted, 22 enrolled. In 2014, 18 master's, 3 doctorates awarded. Terminal master's awarded for partial completion of doctoral program. *Degree requirements:* For master's, thesis or project; for doctorate, comprehensive exam, thesis/dissertation. *Entrance requirements:* For master's, GRE General Test, minimum GPA of 3.0 in undergraduate major, 2.75 overall; for doctorate, GRE General Test, minimum undergraduate GPA of 3.2, graduate 3.5; three letters of recommendation. Additional exam requirements/recommendations for international students: Required—TOEFL (minimum score 557 paper-based; 83 iBT). *Application deadline:* For fall admission, 5/1 priority date for domestic students, 5/1 for international students; for spring admission, 10/1 priority date for domestic students, 10/1 for international students. Applications are processed on a rolling basis. Application fee: $75. Electronic applications accepted. *Expenses:* Tuition, state resident: full-time $4008. Tuition, nonresident: full-time $16,295. *Required fees:* $2755. Tuition and fees vary according to course load and program. *Financial support:* In 2014–15, 37 students received support, including 1 fellowship (averaging $23,545 per year), 24 research assistantships (averaging $7,949 per year), 12 teaching assistantships (averaging $4,663 per year); career-related internships or fieldwork, institutionally sponsored loans, scholarships/grants, and unspecified assistantships also available. Support available to part-time students. Financial award application deadline: 4/1; financial award applicants required to submit FAFSA. *Faculty research:* Structural analysis and design, civil design for sustainability, structural materials, transportation engineering, geotechnical engineering, environmental management, water resources. *Total annual research expenditures:* $973,550. *Unit head:* Dr. John L. Daniels, Chair, 704-687-1219, Fax: 704-687-6953, E-mail: jodaniels@uncc.edu. *Application contact:* Kathy B. Giddings, Director of Graduate Admissions, 704-687-5503, Fax: 704-687-1668, E-mail: gradadm@uncc.edu.
Website: https://cee.uncc.edu/graduate-program.

The University of North Carolina at Charlotte, The William States Lee College of Engineering, Department of Systems Engineering and Engineering Management, Charlotte, NC 28223-0001. Offers energy analytics (Graduate Certificate); engineering management (MSEM); engineering science (MS); infrastructure and environmental systems (PhD); Lean Six Sigma (Graduate Certificate); logistics and supply chains (Graduate Certificate); systems analytics (Graduate Certificate). Part-time and evening/

weekend programs available. Postbaccalaureate distance learning degree programs offered. *Faculty:* 7 full-time (2 women), 1 part-time/adjunct (0 women). *Students:* 33 full-time (8 women), 47 part-time (14 women); includes 15 minority (9 Black or African American, non-Hispanic/Latino; 3 Asian, non-Hispanic/Latino; 3 Hispanic/Latino), 33 international. Average age 29. 146 applicants, 51% accepted, 42 enrolled. In 2014, 19 master's awarded. *Degree requirements:* For master's, thesis or alternative, project. *Entrance requirements:* For master's, GRE or GMAT, letters of recommendation. Additional exam requirements/recommendations for international students: Required—TOEFL (minimum score 557 paper-based; 83 iBT). *Application deadline:* For fall admission, 5/1 priority date for domestic students, 5/1 for international students; for spring admission, 10/1 priority date for domestic students, 10/1 for international students. Application fee: $75. Electronic applications accepted. *Expenses:* Tuition, state resident: full-time $4008. Tuition, nonresident: full-time $16,295. *Required fees:* $2755. Tuition and fees vary according to course load and program. *Financial support:* In 2014–15, 5 students received support, including 3 research assistantships (averaging $5,317 per year), 2 teaching assistantships (averaging $3,125 per year); career-related internships or fieldwork, institutionally sponsored loans, scholarships/grants, and unspecified assistantships also available. Support available to part-time students. Financial award application deadline: 4/1; financial award applicants required to submit FAFSA. *Faculty research:* Sustainable material and renewable technology; thermal analysis; large scale optimization; project risk management; supply chains; leans systems; global product innovation; quality and reliability analysis and management; productivity and project management; business forecasting, market analyses and feasibility studies. *Total annual research expenditures:* $106,777. *Unit head:* Dr. Robert E. Johnson, Dean, 704-687-8242, Fax: 704-687-2352, E-mail: robejohn@uncc.edu. *Application contact:* Kathy B. Giddings, Director of Graduate Admissions, 704-687-5503, Fax: 704-687-1668, E-mail: gradadm@uncc.edu.
Website: http://seem.uncc.edu/.

University of North Dakota, Graduate School, School of Engineering and Mines, Department of Environmental Engineering, Grand Forks, ND 58202. Offers M Engr, MS. *Degree requirements:* For master's, thesis. *Entrance requirements:* For master's, GRE General Test, minimum GPA of 3.0. Additional exam requirements/recommendations for international students: Required—TOEFL (minimum score 550 paper-based; 79 iBT), IELTS (minimum score 6.5). Electronic applications accepted.

University of Notre Dame, Graduate School, College of Engineering, Department of Civil Engineering and Geological Sciences, Notre Dame, IN 46556. Offers bioengineering (MS Bio E); civil engineering (MSCE); civil engineering and geological sciences (PhD); environmental engineering (MS Env E); geological sciences (MS). Terminal master's awarded for partial completion of doctoral program. *Degree requirements:* For master's, comprehensive exam; for doctorate, thesis/dissertation, candidacy exam. *Entrance requirements:* For master's and doctorate, GRE General Test. Additional exam requirements/recommendations for international students: Required—TOEFL (minimum score 600 paper-based; 80 iBT). Electronic applications accepted. *Faculty research:* Environmental modeling, biological-waste treatment, petrology, environmental geology, geochemistry.

University of Oklahoma, Gallogly College of Engineering, School of Civil Engineering and Environmental Science, Program in Environmental Engineering, Norman, OK 73019. Offers MS, PhD. Part-time programs available. *Students:* 5 full-time (3 women), 6 part-time (2 women); includes 2 minority (1 Black or African American, non-Hispanic/Latino; 1 American Indian or Alaska Native, non-Hispanic/Latino), 4 international. Average age 28. 11 applicants, 36% accepted, 4 enrolled. In 2014, 2 master's, 1 doctorate awarded. Terminal master's awarded for partial completion of doctoral program. *Degree requirements:* For master's, comprehensive exam, thesis; for doctorate, comprehensive exam, thesis/dissertation. *Entrance requirements:* For master's and doctorate, GRE, statement of goals, 2 letters of recommendation, minimum GPA of 3.0. Additional exam requirements/recommendations for international students: Required—TOEFL (minimum score 79 iBT). *Application deadline:* For fall admission, 1/15 for domestic and international students; for spring admission, 5/15 for domestic and international students. Application fee: $50 ($100 for international students). Electronic applications accepted. *Expenses:* Tuition, state resident: full-time $4394; part-time $183.10 per credit hour. Tuition, nonresident: full-time $16,970; part-time $707.10 per credit hour. *Required fees:* $2892; $109.95 per credit hour. $126.50 per semester. *Financial support:* In 2014–15, 11 students received support. Scholarships/grants available. Financial award application deadline: 6/1. *Faculty research:* Coastal zone flood prediction, inland runoff modeling, flooding and drought due to climate change, water treatment. *Unit head:* Dr. Randall Kolar, Director, 405-325-4267, Fax: 405-325-4217, E-mail: kolar@ou.edu. *Application contact:* Susan Williams, Graduate Programs Specialist, 405-325-2344, Fax: 405-325-4217, E-mail: srwilliams@ou.edu.
Website: http://www.ou.edu/content/coe/cees.html.

University of Pittsburgh, Dietrich School of Arts and Sciences, Program in Computational Modeling and Simulation, Pittsburgh, PA 15260. Offers bioengineering (PhD); biological science (PhD); civil and environmental engineering (PhD); computer science (PhD); economics (PhD); industrial engineering (PhD); mathematics (PhD); mechanical engineering and materials science (PhD); physics and astronomy (PhD); psychology (PhD); statistics (PhD). Part-time programs available. *Faculty:* 4 full-time (0 women). *Students:* 5 full-time (2 women), 1 part-time (0 women), 5 international. Average age 22. 14 applicants, 14% accepted, 2 enrolled. *Degree requirements:* For doctorate, comprehensive exam, thesis/dissertation, preliminary exam. *Entrance requirements:* For doctorate, GRE, statement of purpose, transcripts for all college-level institutions attended, three letters of reference. Additional exam requirements/recommendations for international students: Required—TOEFL (minimum score 90 iBT), IELTS (minimum score 7). *Application deadline:* For fall admission, 2/21 for domestic and international students. Applications are processed on a rolling basis. Application fee: $0 ($50 for international students). Electronic applications accepted. *Expenses:* Tuition, state resident: full-time $20,742; part-time $838 per credit. Tuition, nonresident: full-time $33,960; part-time $1389 per credit. *Required fees:* $800; $205 per term. Tuition and fees vary according to program. *Financial support:* In 2014–15, 5 students received support, including 3 fellowships with tuition reimbursements available (averaging $25,500 per year), 2 research assistantships with tuition reimbursements available (averaging $26,000 per year). *Unit head:* Kathleen Blee, Associate Dean, Graduate Studies and Research, 412-624-3939, Fax: 412-624-6855. *Application contact:* Dave R. Carmen, Administrative Secretary, 412-624-6094, Fax: 412-624-6855, E-mail: drc41@pitt.edu.
Website: http://cmsp.pitt.edu/.

University of Pittsburgh, Swanson School of Engineering, Department of Civil and Environmental Engineering, Pittsburgh, PA 15260. Offers MSCEE, PhD. Part-time programs available. Postbaccalaureate distance learning degree programs offered. *Faculty:* 17 full-time (3 women), 15 part-time/adjunct (1 woman). *Students:* 104 full-time (25 women), 48 part-time (11 women); includes 2 minority (1 Black or African American, non-Hispanic/Latino; 1 Asian, non-Hispanic/Latino), 93 international. 343 applicants, 57% accepted, 32 enrolled. In 2014, 52 master's, 15 doctorates awarded. Terminal master's awarded for partial completion of doctoral program. *Degree requirements:* For

master's, thesis optional; for doctorate, comprehensive exam, thesis/dissertation, final oral exams. *Entrance requirements:* For master's and doctorate, minimum GPA of 3.0. Additional exam requirements/recommendations for international students: Required—TOEFL (minimum score 550 paper-based; 80 iBT). *Application deadline:* For fall admission, 3/1 priority date for domestic and international students; for spring admission, 7/1 priority date for domestic and international students. Applications are processed on a rolling basis. Application fee: $50. Electronic applications accepted. *Expenses:* Tuition, state resident: full-time $20,742; part-time $838 per credit. Tuition, nonresident: full-time $33,960; part-time $1389 per credit. *Required fees:* $800; $205 per term. Tuition and fees vary according to program. *Financial support:* In 2014–15, 47 students received support, including 7 fellowships with full tuition reimbursements available (averaging $29,376 per year), 28 research assistantships with full tuition reimbursements available (averaging $24,000 per year), 12 teaching assistantships with full tuition reimbursements available (averaging $25,692 per year); scholarships/grants, traineeships, and tuition waivers (full and partial) also available. Financial award application deadline: 4/15. *Faculty research:* Environmental and water resources, structures and infrastructures, construction management. *Total annual research expenditures:* $5.5 million. *Unit head:* Dr. Radisav Vidic, Chairman, 412-624-9870, Fax: 412-624-0135. *Application contact:* Dr. Leonard Casson, Academic Coordinator, 412-624-9868, Fax: 412-624-0135, E-mail: casson@pitt.edu.
Website: http://www.engineering.pitt.edu/Civil/.

University of Regina, Faculty of Graduate Studies and Research, Faculty of Engineering and Applied Science, Program in Environmental Systems Engineering, Regina, SK S4S 0A2, Canada. Offers M Eng, MA Sc, PhD. Part-time programs available. *Faculty:* 39 full-time (7 women), 24 part-time/adjunct (0 women). *Students:* 54 full-time (25 women), 6 part-time (4 women). 75 applicants, 27% accepted. In 2014, 18 master's, 4 doctorates awarded. *Degree requirements:* For master's, thesis, project, report; for doctorate, thesis/dissertation. *Entrance requirements:* For doctorate, master's degree. Additional exam requirements/recommendations for international students: Required—TOEFL (minimum score 550 paper-based; 80 iBT), IELTS (minimum score 6.5), PTE (minimum score 59). *Application deadline:* For fall admission, 3/31 for domestic and international students; for winter admission, 7/31 for domestic and international students; for spring admission, 11/30 for domestic and international students. Application fee: $100. Electronic applications accepted. *Expenses:* Expenses: $2,588.85 per semester of full time study (M Eng); $1,633.35 (for MA Sc); $1,755.60 (for PhD). *Financial support:* In 2014–15, 13 fellowships (averaging $6,462 per year), 12 teaching assistantships (averaging $2,496 per year) were awarded; research assistantships, career-related internships or fieldwork, and scholarships/grants also available. Financial award application deadline: 6/15. *Faculty research:* Design of water and wastewater treatment systems, urban and regional transportation planning, environmental fluid mechanics, air quality management, environmental modeling and decision-making. *Unit head:* Dr. Raphael Idem, Associate Dean, Research and Graduate Studies, 306-585-4770, Fax: 306-585-4855, E-mail: raphael.idem@uregina.ca. *Application contact:* Dr. Amornvadee (Amy) Veawab, Graduate Coordinator, 306-585-5665, Fax: 306-585-4855, E-mail: veawab@uregina.ca.
Website: http://www.uregina.ca/engineering/.

University of Rhode Island, Graduate School, College of Engineering, Department of Civil and Environmental Engineering, Kingston, RI 02881. Offers MS, PhD. Part-time programs available. *Faculty:* 9 full-time (3 women), 2 part-time/adjunct (0 women). *Students:* 19 full-time (5 women), 12 part-time (4 women); includes 4 minority (1 Black or African American, non-Hispanic/Latino; 3 Hispanic/Latino), 11 international. In 2014, 27 master's, 3 doctorates awarded. *Degree requirements:* For master's, comprehensive exam (for some programs), thesis optional; for doctorate, comprehensive exam, thesis/dissertation. *Entrance requirements:* For master's and doctorate, 2 letters of recommendation. Additional exam requirements/recommendations for international students: Required—TOEFL (minimum score 550 paper-based). *Application deadline:* For fall admission, 7/15 for domestic students, 2/1 for international students; for spring admission, 11/15 for domestic students, 7/15 for international students. Application fee: $65. Electronic applications accepted. *Expenses:* Tuition, state resident: full-time $11,532; part-time $641 per credit. Tuition, nonresident: full-time $23,606; part-time $1311 per credit. *Required fees:* $1442; $39 per credit. $35 per semester. One-time fee: $155. *Financial support:* In 2014–15, 5 research assistantships with full and partial tuition reimbursements (averaging $10,381 per year), 3 teaching assistantships with full and partial tuition reimbursements (averaging $10,131 per year) were awarded. Financial award application deadline: 7/15; financial award applicants required to submit FAFSA. *Faculty research:* Industrial waste treatment, structural health monitoring, traffic and transit system operations, computational mechanics, engineering materials design. *Total annual research expenditures:* $300,577. *Unit head:* Dr. George E. Tsiatas, Chair, 401-874-5117, Fax: 401-874-2786, E-mail: gt@uri.edu. *Application contact:* Graduate Admissions, 401-874-2872, E-mail: gradadm@etal.uri.edu.
Website: http://www.uri.edu/cve/.

University of Southern California, Graduate School, Viterbi School of Engineering, Sonny Astani Department of Civil Engineering, Los Angeles, CA 90089. Offers applied mechanics (MS); civil engineering (MS, PhD); computer-aided engineering (ME, Graduate Certificate); construction management (MCM); engineering technology commercialization (Graduate Certificate); environmental engineering (MS, PhD); environmental quality management (ME); structural design (ME); sustainable cities (Graduate Certificate); transportation systems (MS, Graduate Certificate); water and waste management (MS). Part-time and evening/weekend programs available. Terminal master's awarded for partial completion of doctoral program. *Degree requirements:* For master's, thesis optional; for doctorate, thesis/dissertation. *Entrance requirements:* For master's and doctorate, GRE General Test. Additional exam requirements/recommendations for international students: Recommended—TOEFL. Electronic applications accepted. *Faculty research:* Geotechnical engineering, transportation engineering, structural engineering, construction management, environmental engineering, water resources.

University of South Florida, College of Engineering, Department of Civil and Environmental Engineering, Tampa, FL 33620-9951. Offers civil engineering (MCE, MSCE, PhD), including environmental engineering (MSES, PhD), geotechnical engineering (MCE, MSCE, MSES, PhD), interdisciplinary transportation (MSCE), materials engineering and science, structural engineering, transportation engineering, water resources; engineering science (MSES), including environmental engineering (MSES, PhD), geotechnical engineering (MCE, MSCE, MSES, PhD); environmental engineering (MEVE, MSEV, PhD). Part-time programs available. *Faculty:* 19 full-time (5 women). *Students:* 97 full-time (35 women), 83 part-time (25 women); includes 41 minority (6 Black or African American, non-Hispanic/Latino; 1 American Indian or Alaska Native, non-Hispanic/Latino; 3 Asian, non-Hispanic/Latino; 25 Hispanic/Latino; 6 Two or more races, non-Hispanic/Latino), 39 international. Average age 30. 229 applicants, 51% accepted, 43 enrolled. In 2014, 68 master's, 9 doctorates awarded. Terminal master's awarded for partial completion of doctoral program. *Degree requirements:* For master's, comprehensive exam, thesis (for some programs); for doctorate, comprehensive exam, thesis/dissertation. *Entrance requirements:* For master's, GRE General Test (preferred minimum scores of 20th percentile verbal, 50th percentile quantitative, and 10th percentile in analytical writing), minimum GPA of 3.0 in major, two letters of reference, statement of purpose; for doctorate, GRE General Test (preferred minimum scores of 45th percentile verbal, 65th percentile quantitative, and 50th percentile in analytical writing), three letters of recommendation, statement of purpose, resume. Additional exam requirements/recommendations for international students: Required—TOEFL (minimum score 550 paper-based; 79 iBT) or IELTS (minimum score 6.5). *Application deadline:* For fall admission, 2/15 for domestic students, 1/2 priority date for international students; for spring admission, 10/15 for domestic students, 6/1 priority date for international students. Application fee: $30. Electronic applications accepted. *Financial support:* In 2014–15, 65 students received support, including 44 research assistantships (averaging $14,123 per year), 21 teaching assistantships with tuition reimbursements available (averaging $15,329 per year). *Faculty research:* Environmental and water resources engineering, geotechnics and geoenvironmental systems, structures and materials systems, transportation systems. *Total annual research expenditures:* $3.3 million. *Unit head:* Dr. Manjriker Gunaratne, Professor and Department Chair, 813-974-5818, Fax: 813-974-2957, E-mail: gunaratn@usf.edu. *Application contact:* Dr. Sarina J. Ergas, Professor and Graduate Program Coordinator, 813-974-1119, Fax: 813-974-2957, E-mail: sergas@usf.edu.
Website: http://ce.eng.usf.edu/.

The University of Tennessee, Graduate School, College of Engineering, Department of Civil and Environmental Engineering, Program in Environmental Engineering, Knoxville, TN 37996. Offers MS, MS/MBA. Part-time programs available. Postbaccalaureate distance learning degree programs offered (minimal on-campus study). *Faculty:* 17 full-time (2 women), 5 part-time/adjunct (0 women). *Students:* 7 full-time (2 women), 4 part-time (0 women). Average age 25. 19 applicants, 26% accepted, 4 enrolled. In 2014, 12 master's awarded. *Degree requirements:* For master's, thesis or alternative. *Entrance requirements:* For master's, GRE General Test (for MS students pursuing research thesis), minimum GPA of 2.7 (for U.S. degree holders), 3.0 (for international degree holders); 3 references; statement of purpose; resume. Additional exam requirements/recommendations for international students: Required—TOEFL (minimum score 550 paper-based). *Application deadline:* For fall admission, 2/1 priority date for domestic and international students; for spring admission, 6/15 for domestic and international students. Applications are processed on a rolling basis. Application fee: $35. Electronic applications accepted. *Financial support:* In 2014–15, 6 students received support, including 5 research assistantships with full tuition reimbursements available (averaging $18,588 per year), 1 teaching assistantship with full tuition reimbursement available (averaging $18,000 per year); career-related internships or fieldwork, Federal Work-Study, institutionally sponsored loans, health care benefits, and unspecified assistantships also available. Financial award application deadline: 2/1; financial award applicants required to submit FAFSA. *Faculty research:* Air pollution control technologies; climate change and engineering impact on environment; environmental sampling, monitoring, and restoration; soil erosion prediction and control; waste management and utilization. *Unit head:* Dr. Greg Reed, Head, 865-974-2503, Fax: 865-974-2669, E-mail: gdreed@utk.edu. *Application contact:* Dr. Chris Cox, Associate Head, 865-974-7729, Fax: 865-974-2355, E-mail: ccox9@utk.edu.
Website: http://www.engr.utk.edu/civil/.

The University of Texas at Austin, Graduate School, Cockrell School of Engineering, Department of Civil, Architectural and Environmental Engineering, Program in Environmental and Water Resources Engineering, Austin, TX 78712-1111. Offers MS, PhD. Part-time programs available. *Degree requirements:* For master's, thesis or alternative. *Entrance requirements:* For master's, GRE General Test. Additional exam requirements/recommendations for international students: Required—TOEFL. Electronic applications accepted.

The University of Texas at El Paso, Graduate School, College of Engineering, Department of Civil Engineering, El Paso, TX 79968-0001. Offers civil engineering (MS, PhD); construction management (MS, Certificate); environmental engineering (MEENE, MSENE). Part-time and evening/weekend programs available. *Degree requirements:* For master's, comprehensive exam, thesis optional; for doctorate, comprehensive exam, thesis/dissertation. *Entrance requirements:* For master's, GRE, minimum GPA of 3.0; for doctorate, GRE. Additional exam requirements/recommendations for international students: Required—TOEFL. Electronic applications accepted. *Faculty research:* Non-destructive testing for geotechnical and pavement applications, transportation systems, wastewater treatment systems, air quality, linear and non-linear modeling of structures, structural reliability.

The University of Texas at El Paso, Graduate School, College of Engineering, Department of Mechanical Engineering, El Paso, TX 79968-0001. Offers environmental science and engineering (PhD); mechanical engineering (MS). Part-time programs available. *Degree requirements:* For master's, thesis optional; for doctorate, thesis/dissertation. *Entrance requirements:* For master's, GRE, minimum GPA of 3.0, letter of reference; for doctorate, GRE, minimum GPA of 3.5, letters of reference, BS or equivalent. Additional exam requirements/recommendations for international students: Required—TOEFL; Recommended—IELTS. Electronic applications accepted. *Faculty research:* Aerospace, energy, combustion and propulsion, design engineering, high temperature materials.

The University of Texas at El Paso, Graduate School, Interdisciplinary Program in Environmental Science and Engineering, El Paso, TX 79968-0001. Offers PhD. Part-time and evening/weekend programs available. *Degree requirements:* For doctorate, thesis/dissertation. *Entrance requirements:* For doctorate, GRE, letters of recommendation. Additional exam requirements/recommendations for international students: Required—TOEFL; Recommended—IELTS. Electronic applications accepted.

The University of Texas at San Antonio, College of Engineering, Department of Civil and Environmental Engineering, San Antonio, TX 78249. Offers civil engineering (MCE, MSCE); environmental science and engineering (PhD). Part-time programs available. *Faculty:* 12 full-time (2 women), 1 part-time/adjunct (0 women). *Students:* 28 full-time (8 women), 27 part-time (6 women); includes 12 minority (3 Black or African American, non-Hispanic/Latino; 2 Asian, non-Hispanic/Latino; 6 Hispanic/Latino; 1 Two or more races, non-Hispanic/Latino), 24 international. Average age 30. 66 applicants, 74% accepted, 21 enrolled. In 2014, 21 master's, 5 doctorates awarded. *Degree requirements:* For master's, comprehensive exam, thesis (for some programs); for doctorate, comprehensive exam, thesis/dissertation, written qualifying exam, dissertation proposal. *Entrance requirements:* For master's, GRE General Test, BS in civil engineering or related field from accredited institution, statement of research/specialization interest, favorable recommendation by the Civil Engineering Master's Program Admissions Committee; for doctorate, GRE, BS and MS from accredited institution, minimum GPA of 3.0 in upper-division and graduate courses, three letters of recommendation, letter of research interest, resume/curriculum vitae. Additional exam requirements/recommendations for international students: Required—TOEFL (minimum score 550 paper-based; 79 iBT), IELTS (minimum score 6.5). *Application deadline:* For fall admission, 7/1 for domestic students, 4/1 for international students; for spring admission, 11/1 for domestic students, 9/1 for international students. Application fee: $45 ($80 for international students). Electronic applications accepted. *Expenses:* Expenses: Contact institution. *Financial support:* In 2014–15, 42 students received support, including 28 research assistantships with full tuition reimbursements available (averaging $20,000 per year), 14 teaching assistantships (averaging $4,680 per year);

scholarships/grants also available. Financial award application deadline: 2/1. *Faculty research:* Structures, application of geographic information systems in water resources, geotechnical engineering, pavement traffic loading, hydrogeology. *Total annual research expenditures:* $774,040. *Unit head:* Dr. Heather Shipley, Department Chair, 210-458-7517, Fax: 210-458-6475, E-mail: heather.shipley@utsa.edu. *Application contact:* Jessica Perez, Administrative Associate I, 210-458-4428, Fax: 210-458-7469, E-mail: jessica.perez@utsa.edu.
Website: http://engineering.utsa.edu/CE/.

The University of Texas at Tyler, College of Engineering and Computer Science, Department of Civil Engineering, Tyler, TX 75799-0001. Offers environmental engineering (MS); industrial safety (MS); structural engineering (MS); transportation engineering (MS); water resources engineering (MS). Part-time and evening/weekend programs available. *Degree requirements:* For master's, thesis optional. *Entrance requirements:* For master's, GRE General Test, bachelor's degree in engineering, associated science degree. Additional exam requirements/recommendations for international students: Required—TOEFL. *Faculty research:* Non-destructive strength testing, indoor air quality, transportation routing and signaling, pavement replacement criteria, flood water routing, construction and long-term behavior of innovative geotechnical foundation and embankment construction used in highway construction, engineering education.

University of Utah, Graduate School, College of Engineering, Department of Civil and Environmental Engineering, Interdepartmental Program in Environmental Engineering, Salt Lake City, UT 84112. Offers PhD. Part-time programs available. *Students:* 1 (woman) part-time. *Degree requirements:* For doctorate, comprehensive exam, thesis/dissertation, qualifying exam. *Entrance requirements:* For doctorate, GRE, minimum undergraduate GPA of 3.0. Additional exam requirements/recommendations for international students: Required—TOEFL (minimum score 500 paper-based; 80 iBT). *Application deadline:* For fall admission, 4/1 for domestic and international students; for spring admission, 10/1 for domestic and international students. Applications are processed on a rolling basis. Application fee: $55 ($65 for international students). Electronic applications accepted. *Expenses:* Expenses: Contact institution. *Financial support:* Application deadline: 12/15; applicants required to submit FAFSA. *Unit head:* Dr. Michael Barber, Chair, 801-581-6931, Fax: 801-585-5477, E-mail: barber@civil.utah.edu. *Application contact:* Bonnie Ogden, Academic Advisor, 801-581-6678, Fax: 850-585-5477, E-mail: bonnie.ogden@utah.edu.
Website: http://www.civil.utah.edu.

University of Utah, Graduate School, College of Mines and Earth Sciences, Department of Geology and Geophysics, Salt Lake City, UT 84112. Offers environmental engineering (ME, MS, PhD); geological engineering (ME, MS, PhD); geology (MS, PhD); geophysics (MS, PhD). *Faculty:* 23 full-time (5 women), 9 part-time/adjunct (3 women). *Students:* 50 full-time (20 women), 36 part-time (18 women); includes 6 minority (1 Black or African American, non-Hispanic/Latino; 1 American Indian or Alaska Native, non-Hispanic/Latino; 4 Hispanic/Latino), 17 international. Average age 29. 228 applicants, 14% accepted, 22 enrolled. In 2014, 26 master's, 5 doctorates awarded. Terminal master's awarded for partial completion of doctoral program. *Degree requirements:* For master's, comprehensive exam, thesis; for doctorate, thesis/dissertation, qualifying exam (written and oral). *Entrance requirements:* For master's and doctorate, GRE General Test, minimum GPA of 3.25. Additional exam requirements/recommendations for international students: Required—TOEFL (minimum score 500 paper-based; 61 iBT). *Application deadline:* For fall admission, 1/15 priority date for domestic and international students. Application fee: $55 ($65 for international students). Electronic applications accepted. *Financial support:* In 2014–15, 62 students received support, including 14 fellowships with full tuition reimbursements available (averaging $17,500 per year), 32 research assistantships with full tuition reimbursements available (averaging $23,000 per year), 16 teaching assistantships with full tuition reimbursements available (averaging $17,500 per year); career-related internships or fieldwork, institutionally sponsored loans, scholarships/grants, unspecified assistantships, and stipends also available. Financial award application deadline: 1/15; financial award applicants required to submit FAFSA. *Faculty research:* Igneous, metamorphic, and sedimentary petrology; stratigraphy; paleoclimatology; hydrology; seismology. *Total annual research expenditures:* $4.1 million. *Unit head:* Dr. John Bartley, Chair, 801-585-1670, Fax: 801-581-7065, E-mail: john.bartley@utah.edu. *Application contact:* Dr. Gabriel J. Bowen, Director of Graduate Studies, 801-585-7925, Fax: 801-581-7065, E-mail: gabe.bowen@utah.edu.
Website: http://www.earth.utah.edu/.

University of Vermont, Graduate College, College of Engineering and Mathematics, Department of Civil and Environmental Engineering, Burlington, VT 05405. Offers MS, PhD. *Degree requirements:* For master's, thesis or alternative; for doctorate, thesis/dissertation. *Entrance requirements:* For master's and doctorate, GRE General Test. Additional exam requirements/recommendations for international students: Required—TOEFL (minimum score 550 paper-based; 80 iBT). Electronic applications accepted.

University of Washington, Graduate School, College of Engineering, Department of Civil and Environmental Engineering, Seattle, WA 98195-2700. Offers civil engineering (PhD); construction engineering (MSCE); environmental engineering (MSCE, PhD); hydrology, water resources, and environmental fluid mechanics (MSCE, PhD); structural and geotechnical engineering and mechanics (MSCE, PhD); transportation and construction engineering (PhD); transportation engineering (MSCE). Part-time programs available. Postbaccalaureate distance learning degree programs offered (no on-campus study). *Faculty:* 35 full-time (9 women). *Students:* 220 full-time (81 women), 147 part-time (50 women); includes 61 minority (9 Black or African American, non-Hispanic/Latino; 2 American Indian or Alaska Native, non-Hispanic/Latino; 34 Asian, non-Hispanic/Latino; 14 Hispanic/Latino; 2 Native Hawaiian or other Pacific Islander, non-Hispanic/Latino), 91 international. Average age 28. 901 applicants, 49% accepted, 162 enrolled. In 2014, 110 master's, 12 doctorates awarded. Terminal master's awarded for partial completion of doctoral program. *Degree requirements:* For master's, thesis (for some programs); for doctorate, comprehensive exam, thesis/dissertation, general, qualifying, and final exams; completion of degree within 10 years. *Entrance requirements:* For master's, GRE General Test, minimum GPA of 3.0, statement of purpose, letters of recommendation, transcripts; for doctorate, GRE General Test, minimum GPA of 3.5, statement of purpose, letters of recommendation, transcripts. Additional exam requirements/recommendations for international students: Required—TOEFL (minimum score 580 paper-based; 92 iBT); Recommended—IELTS (minimum score 7). *Application deadline:* For fall admission, 12/15 for domestic and international students. Applications are processed on a rolling basis. Application fee: $85. Electronic applications accepted. *Expenses:* Expenses: Contact institution. *Financial support:* In 2014–15, 179 students received support, including 41 fellowships with full and partial tuition reimbursements available, 77 research assistantships with full tuition reimbursements available, 58 teaching assistantships with full tuition reimbursements available; scholarships/grants also available. Financial award application deadline: 1/10; financial award applicants required to submit FAFSA. *Faculty research:* Structural and geotechnical engineering, transportation and construction engineering, water and environmental engineering. *Total annual research expenditures:* $14.1 million. *Unit head:* Dr. Gregory R. Miller, Professor/Chair, 206-543-0350, Fax: 206-543-1543, E-mail: gmiller@uw.edu. *Application contact:* Lorna Latal, Graduate Adviser, 206-543-2574, Fax: 206-543-1543, E-mail: llatal@u.washington.edu.
Website: http://www.ce.washington.edu/.

University of Waterloo, Graduate Studies, Faculty of Engineering, Department of Civil and Environmental Engineering, Waterloo, ON N2L 3G1, Canada. Offers M Eng, MA Sc, PhD. Part-time programs available. *Degree requirements:* For master's, research paper or thesis; for doctorate, comprehensive exam, thesis/dissertation. *Entrance requirements:* For master's, honors degree, minimum B average; for doctorate, master's degree, minimum A- average. Additional exam requirements/recommendations for international students: Required—TOEFL, TWE. Electronic applications accepted. *Faculty research:* Water resources, structures, construction management, transportation, geotechnical engineering.

The University of Western Ontario, Faculty of Graduate Studies, Physical Sciences Division, Faculty of Engineering, London, ON N6A 5B8, Canada. Offers chemical and biochemical engineering (ME Sc, PhD); civil and environmental engineering (M Eng, ME Sc, PhD); electrical and computer engineering (M Eng, ME Sc, PhD); mechanical and materials engineering (M Eng, ME Sc, PhD). Part-time programs available. Terminal master's awarded for partial completion of doctoral program. *Degree requirements:* For master's, thesis; for doctorate, thesis/dissertation. *Entrance requirements:* For master's, minimum B average; for doctorate, minimum B+ average. *Faculty research:* Wind, geotechnical, chemical reactor engineering, applied electrostatics, biochemical engineering.

University of Windsor, Faculty of Graduate Studies, Faculty of Engineering, Department of Civil and Environmental Engineering, Windsor, ON N9B 3P4, Canada. Offers civil engineering (M Eng, MA Sc, PhD); environmental engineering (M Eng, MA Sc, PhD). Part-time programs available. *Degree requirements:* For master's, thesis; for doctorate, comprehensive exam, thesis/dissertation. *Entrance requirements:* For master's, minimum B average; for doctorate, master's degree, minimum A average. Additional exam requirements/recommendations for international students: Required—TOEFL (minimum score 580 paper-based). Electronic applications accepted. *Faculty research:* Odors: sampling, measurement, control; drinking water disinfection, hydrocarbon contaminated soil remediation, structural dynamics, numerical simulation of piezoelectric materials.

University of Wisconsin–Madison, Graduate School, College of Engineering, Department of Civil and Environmental Engineering, Madison, WI 53706. Offers MS, PhD. Part-time programs available. Terminal master's awarded for partial completion of doctoral program. *Degree requirements:* For master's, thesis or alternative; for doctorate, thesis/dissertation, preliminary exam, qualifying exams. *Entrance requirements:* For master's and doctorate, GRE General Test, minimum GPA of 3.0 for last 60 credits of course work. Additional exam requirements/recommendations for international students: Required—TOEFL (minimum score 550 paper-based; 92 iBT). Electronic applications accepted. *Expenses:* Tuition, state resident: full-time $10,723; part-time $745 per credit. Tuition, nonresident: full-time $24,054; part-time $1578 per credit. *Required fees:* $374 per semester. Tuition and fees vary according to course load, program and reciprocity agreements. *Faculty research:* Environmental geotechnics and soil mechanics, design and analysis of structures, traffic engineering and intelligent transport systems, industrial pollution control, hydrological monitoring.

University of Wyoming, College of Engineering and Applied Sciences, Department of Civil and Architectural Engineering and Department of Chemical and Petroleum Engineering, Program in Environmental Engineering, Laramie, WY 82071. Offers MS. Part-time programs available. *Degree requirements:* For master's, thesis optional. *Entrance requirements:* For master's, GRE General Test, minimum GPA of 3.0. Additional exam requirements/recommendations for international students: Required—TOEFL (minimum score 550 paper-based). Electronic applications accepted. *Faculty research:* Water and waste water, solid and hazardous waste management, air pollution control, flue-gas cleanup.

Utah State University, School of Graduate Studies, College of Engineering, Department of Civil and Environmental Engineering, Logan, UT 84322. Offers ME, MS, PhD, CE. *Degree requirements:* For master's, thesis (for some programs); for doctorate, thesis/dissertation. *Entrance requirements:* For master's and doctorate, GRE General Test, minimum GPA of 3.0. Additional exam requirements/recommendations for international students: Required—TOEFL. Electronic applications accepted. *Faculty research:* Hazardous waste treatment, large space structures, river basin management, earthquake engineering, environmental impact.

Vanderbilt University, School of Engineering, Department of Civil and Environmental Engineering, Program in Environmental Engineering, Nashville, TN 37240-1001. Offers environmental engineering (M Eng); environmental management (MS, PhD). MS and PhD offered through the Graduate School. Part-time programs available. Terminal master's awarded for partial completion of doctoral program. *Degree requirements:* For master's, thesis or alternative; for doctorate, thesis/dissertation. *Entrance requirements:* For master's and doctorate, GRE General Test. Additional exam requirements/recommendations for international students: Required—TOEFL. Electronic applications accepted. *Expenses: Tuition:* Full-time $42,768; part-time $1782 per credit hour. *Required fees:* $422. One-time fee: $30 full-time. *Faculty research:* Waste treatment, hazardous waste management, chemical waste treatment, water quality.

Villanova University, College of Engineering, Department of Civil and Environmental Engineering, Program in Water Resources and Environmental Engineering, Villanova, PA 19085-1699. Offers urban water resources design (Certificate); water resources and environmental engineering (MSWREE). Part-time and evening/weekend programs available. Postbaccalaureate distance learning degree programs offered (no on-campus study). *Degree requirements:* For master's, thesis optional. *Entrance requirements:* For master's, GRE General Test (for applicants with degrees from foreign universities), BCE or bachelor's degree in science or related engineering field, minimum GPA of 3.0. Additional exam requirements/recommendations for international students: Required—TOEFL (minimum score 600 paper-based; 100 iBT). Electronic applications accepted. *Faculty research:* Photocatalytic decontamination and disinfection of water, urban storm water wetlands, economy and risk, removal and destruction of organic acids in water, sludge treatment.

Virginia Polytechnic Institute and State University, Graduate School, College of Engineering, Blacksburg, VA 24061. Offers aerospace engineering (ME, MS, PhD); biological systems engineering (ME, MS, PhD); biomedical engineering (MS, PhD); chemical engineering (ME, MS, PhD); civil engineering (ME, MS, PhD); computer engineering (ME, MS, PhD); computer science (MS, PhD); electrical engineering (ME, PhD); engineering education (PhD); engineering mechanics (ME, MS, PhD); environmental engineering (MS); environmental science and engineering (MS); industrial and systems engineering (ME, MS, PhD); materials science and engineering (ME, MS, PhD); mechanical engineering (ME, MS, PhD); mining and minerals engineering (PhD); mining engineering (ME, MS); nuclear engineering (MS, PhD); ocean engineering (MS); systems engineering (ME, MS). *Accreditation:* ABET (one or more programs are accredited). *Faculty:* 356 full-time (60 women), 3 part-time/adjunct (1 woman). *Students:* 1,700 full-time (398 women), 345 part-time (58 women); includes 213 minority (43 Black or African American, non-Hispanic/Latino; 1 American Indian or

Alaska Native, non-Hispanic/Latino; 87 Asian, non-Hispanic/Latino; 58 Hispanic/Latino; 1 Native Hawaiian or other Pacific Islander, non-Hispanic/Latino; 23 Two or more races, non-Hispanic/Latino), 1,079 international. Average age 27. 5,228 applicants, 18% accepted, 471 enrolled. In 2014, 438 master's, 211 doctorates awarded. *Degree requirements:* For master's, comprehensive exam (for some programs), thesis (for some programs); for doctorate, comprehensive exam (for some programs), thesis/dissertation (for some programs). *Entrance requirements:* For master's and doctorate, GRE/GMAT (may vary by department). Additional exam requirements/recommendations for international students: Required—TOEFL (minimum score 550 paper-based). *Application deadline:* For fall admission, 8/1 for domestic students, 4/1 for international students; for spring admission, 1/1 for domestic students, 9/1 for international students. Applications are processed on a rolling basis. Application fee: $75. Electronic applications accepted. *Expenses:* Tuition, state resident: full-time $11,656; part-time $647.50 per credit hour. Tuition, nonresident: full-time $23,351; part-time $1297.25 per credit hour. *Required fees:* $2533; $465.75 per semester. Tuition and fees vary according to course load, campus/location and program. *Financial support:* In 2014–15, 148 fellowships with full tuition reimbursements (averaging $8,031 per year), 855 research assistantships with full tuition reimbursements (averaging $22,855 per year), 288 teaching assistantships with full tuition reimbursements (averaging $20,291 per year) were awarded. Financial award application deadline: 3/1; financial award applicants required to submit FAFSA. *Total annual research expenditures:* $90.5 million. *Unit head:* Dr. Richard C. Benson, Dean, 540-231-9752, Fax: 540-231-3031, E-mail: deaneng@vt.edu. *Application contact:* Linda Perkins, Executive Assistant, 540-231-9752, Fax: 540-231-3031, E-mail: lperkins@vt.edu.
Website: http://www.eng.vt.edu/.

Virginia Polytechnic Institute and State University, VT Online, Blacksburg, VA 24061. Offers advanced transportation systems (Certificate); aerospace engineering (MS); agricultural and life sciences (MSLFS); business information systems (Graduate Certificate); career and technical education (MS); civil engineering (MS); computer engineering (M Eng, MS); decision support systems (Graduate Certificate); eLearning leadership (MA); electrical engineering (M Eng, MS); engineering administration (MEA); environmental engineering (Certificate); environmental politics and policy (Graduate Certificate); environmental sciences and engineering (MS); foundations of political analysis (Graduate Certificate); health product risk management (Graduate Certificate); industrial and systems engineering (MS); information policy and society (Graduate Certificate); information security (Graduate Certificate); information technology (MIT); instructional technology (MA); integrative STEM education (MA Ed); liberal arts (Graduate Certificate); life sciences: health product risk management (MS); natural resources (MNR, Graduate Certificate); networking (Graduate Certificate); nonprofit and nongovernmental organization management (Graduate Certificate); ocean engineering (MS); political science (MA); security studies (Graduate Certificate); software development (Graduate Certificate). *Expenses:* Tuition, state resident: full-time $11,656; part-time $647.50 per credit hour. Tuition, nonresident: full-time $23,351; part-time $1297.25 per credit hour. *Required fees:* $2533; $465.75 per semester. Tuition and fees vary according to course load, campus/location and program.

Washington State University, Voiland College of Engineering and Architecture, Department of Civil and Environmental Engineering, Pullman, WA 99164-2910. Offers civil engineering (MS, PhD); environmental engineering (MS). MS programs also offered at Tri-Cities campus. Part-time programs available. *Faculty:* 38 full-time (7 women), 4 part-time/adjunct (1 woman). *Students:* 66 full-time (18 women), 13 part-time (7 women); includes 13 minority (3 Black or African American, non-Hispanic/Latino; 1 American Indian or Alaska Native, non-Hispanic/Latino; 5 Asian, non-Hispanic/Latino; 3 Hispanic/Latino; 1 Two or more races, non-Hispanic/Latino), 32 international. Average age 29. 135 applicants, 26% accepted, 18 enrolled. In 2014, 28 master's, 8 doctorates awarded. Terminal master's awarded for partial completion of doctoral program. *Degree requirements:* For master's, comprehensive exam (for some programs), thesis (for some programs), oral exam; for doctorate, comprehensive exam, thesis/dissertation, oral exam, written exam. *Entrance requirements:* For master's, minimum GPA of 3.0, 3 letters of recommendation, statement of purpose; for doctorate, minimum GPA of 3.4, 3 letters of recommendation, statement of purpose. Additional exam requirements/recommendations for international students: Required—TOEFL (minimum score 550 paper-based), IELTS. *Application deadline:* For fall admission, 2/1 for domestic students, 3/1 for international students; for spring admission, 9/1 for domestic students. Applications are processed on a rolling basis. Application fee: $75. Electronic applications accepted. *Expenses:* Tuition, state resident: full-time $11,768. Tuition, nonresident: full-time $25,200. *Required fees:* $960. Tuition and fees vary according to program. *Financial support:* In 2014–15, 62 students received support, including 4 fellowships with full tuition reimbursements available (averaging $22,000 per year), 27 research assistantships with full tuition reimbursements available (averaging $13,659 per year), 20 teaching assistantships with full tuition reimbursements available (averaging $14,135 per year); career-related internships or fieldwork, Federal Work-Study, and institutionally sponsored loans also available. Financial award application deadline: 4/1; financial award applicants required to submit FAFSA. *Faculty research:* Environmental engineering, water resources, structural engineering, geotechnical, transportation. *Total annual research expenditures:* $8.3 million. *Unit head:* Dr. Balasingam Muhunthan, Chair, 509-335-9578, Fax: 509-335-7632, E-mail: muhuntha@wsu.edu. *Application contact:* Ryan Lancaster, Graduate School Admissions, 509-335-2576, Fax: 509-335-7632, E-mail: ryan.lancaster@wsu.edu.
Website: http://www.ce.wsu.edu/.

Washington University in St. Louis, School of Engineering and Applied Science, Department of Energy, Environmental and Chemical Engineering, St. Louis, MO 63130-4899. Offers chemical engineering (MS, D Sc); environmental engineering (MS, D Sc). Part-time programs available. Terminal master's awarded for partial completion of doctoral program. *Degree requirements:* For master's, thesis optional; for doctorate, thesis/dissertation, preliminary exam, qualifying exam. *Entrance requirements:* For master's and doctorate, GRE, minimum B average during final 2 years of course work. Additional exam requirements/recommendations for international students: Required—TOEFL, TWE. Electronic applications accepted. *Faculty research:* Reaction engineering, materials processing, catalysis, process control, air pollution control.

West Virginia University, College of Engineering and Mineral Resources, Department of Civil and Environmental Engineering, Morgantown, WV 26506. Offers civil engineering (MSCE, MSE, PhD). Part-time programs available. *Degree requirements:* For master's, thesis; for doctorate, comprehensive exam, thesis/dissertation. *Entrance requirements:* For master's and doctorate, minimum GPA of 3.0. Additional exam requirements/recommendations for international students: Required—TOEFL. *Faculty research:* Habitat restoration, advanced materials for civil infrastructure, pavement modeling, infrastructure condition assessment.

Worcester Polytechnic Institute, Graduate Studies and Research, Department of Civil and Environmental Engineering, Worcester, MA 01609-2280. Offers civil and environmental engineering (Advanced Certificate, Graduate Certificate); civil engineering (ME, MS, PhD); construction project management (MS); environmental engineering (M Eng, MS); master builder (M Eng). Part-time and evening/weekend programs available. Postbaccalaureate distance learning degree programs offered (no on-campus study). *Faculty:* 27 full-time (1 woman), 24 part-time/adjunct (3 women). *Students:* 36 full-time (14 women), 13 part-time (5 women); includes 4 minority (1 Hispanic/Latino; 3 Two or more races, non-Hispanic/Latino), 20 international. 160 applicants, 65% accepted, 26 enrolled. In 2014, 30 master's, 1 doctorate awarded. *Degree requirements:* For master's, thesis optional; for doctorate, comprehensive exam, thesis/dissertation. *Entrance requirements:* For master's and doctorate, GRE (recommended), 3 letters of recommendation. Additional exam requirements/recommendations for international students: Required—TOEFL (minimum score 563 paper-based; 84 iBT), IELTS (minimum score 7). *Application deadline:* For fall admission, 1/1 priority date for domestic and international students; for spring admission, 10/1 priority date for domestic and international students. Applications are processed on a rolling basis. Application fee: $70. Electronic applications accepted. *Financial support:* Research assistantships, teaching assistantships, career-related internships or fieldwork, institutionally sponsored loans, scholarships/grants, and unspecified assistantships available. Financial award application deadline: 1/1; financial award applicants required to submit FAFSA. *Unit head:* Dr. Tahar El-Korchi, Interim Head, 508-831-5530, Fax: 508-831-5808, E-mail: tek@wpi.edu. *Application contact:* Dr. Rajib Mallick, Graduate Coordinator, 508-831-5530, Fax: 508-831-5808, E-mail: rajib@wpi.edu.
Website: http://www.wpi.edu/academics/cee.

Worcester Polytechnic Institute, Graduate Studies and Research, Programs in Interdisciplinary Studies, Worcester, MA 01609-2280. Offers bioscience administration (MS); impact engineering (MS); manufacturing engineering management (MS); power systems management (MS); social science (PhD); systems modeling (MS). Part-time and evening/weekend programs available. *Faculty:* 1 part-time/adjunct (0 women). *Students:* 2 full-time (0 women), 74 part-time (15 women); includes 18 minority (3 Black or African American, non-Hispanic/Latino; 7 Asian, non-Hispanic/Latino; 3 Hispanic/Latino; 5 Two or more races, non-Hispanic/Latino), 5 international. 37 applicants, 97% accepted, 29 enrolled. In 2014, 10 master's, 1 doctorate awarded. *Degree requirements:* For master's, thesis; for doctorate, comprehensive exam, thesis/dissertation. *Entrance requirements:* For master's and doctorate, 3 letters of recommendation. Additional exam requirements/recommendations for international students: Required—TOEFL (minimum score 563 paper-based; 84 iBT), IELTS (minimum score 7). *Application deadline:* For fall admission, 1/1 priority date for domestic students, 1/1 for international students; for spring admission, 10/1 priority date for domestic students, 10/1 for international students. Application fee: $70. *Financial support:* Institutionally sponsored loans, scholarships/grants, and unspecified assistantships available. Financial award application deadline: 1/1; financial award applicants required to submit FAFSA. *Unit head:* Dr. Fred J. Looft, Head, 508-831-5231, Fax: 508-831-5491, E-mail: fjlooft@wpi.edu. *Application contact:* Lynne Dougherty, Administrative Assistant, 508-831-5301, Fax: 508-831-5717, E-mail: grad@wpi.edu.

Yale University, Graduate School of Arts and Sciences, School of Engineering and Applied Science, Program in Environmental Engineering, New Haven, CT 06520. Offers MS, PhD.

Youngstown State University, Graduate School, College of Science, Technology, Engineering and Mathematics, Department of Civil and Environmental Engineering, Youngstown, OH 44555-0001. Offers MSE. Part-time and evening/weekend programs available. *Degree requirements:* For master's, thesis optional. *Entrance requirements:* For master's, minimum GPA of 2.75 in field. Additional exam requirements/recommendations for international students: Required—TOEFL. *Faculty research:* Structural mechanics, water quality modeling, surface and ground water hydrology, physical and chemical processes in aquatic systems.

Fire Protection Engineering

Anna Maria College, Graduate Division, Program in Fire Science, Paxton, MA 01612. Offers MA. Part-time and evening/weekend programs available. *Degree requirements:* For master's, thesis, internship, research project. *Entrance requirements:* For master's, minimum GPA of 2.7, resume, bachelor's degree in fire science or employment in a fire science organization. Additional exam requirements/recommendations for international students: Required—TOEFL (minimum score 500 paper-based). Electronic applications accepted.

Oklahoma State University, College of Arts and Sciences, Department of Political Science, Stillwater, OK 74078. Offers fire and emergency management administration (MS, PhD); political science (MA). *Faculty:* 21 full-time (7 women), 2 part-time/adjunct (0 women). *Students:* 11 full-time (5 women), 62 part-time (12 women); includes 14 minority (4 Black or African American, non-Hispanic/Latino; 7 Hispanic/Latino; 3 Two or more races, non-Hispanic/Latino), 4 international. Average age 39. 42 applicants, 40% accepted, 14 enrolled. In 2014, 20 master's awarded. *Degree requirements:* For master's, comprehensive exam, thesis or creative component; for doctorate, comprehensive exam, thesis/dissertation. *Entrance requirements:* For master's, GRE; for doctorate, GRE. Additional exam requirements/recommendations for international students: Required—TOEFL (minimum score 550 paper-based; 79 iBT). *Application deadline:* For fall admission, 3/1 priority date for international students, for spring admission, 8/1 priority date for international students. Applications are processed on a rolling basis. Application fee: $40 ($75 for international students). Electronic applications accepted. *Expenses:* Tuition, state resident: full-time $4488; part-time $187 per credit hour. Tuition, nonresident: full-time $18,360; part-time $765 per credit hour. *Required fees:* $2413; $100.55 per credit hour. Tuition and fees vary according to campus/location. *Financial support:* In 2014–15, 1 research assistantship (averaging $19,644 per year), 10 teaching assistantships (averaging $16,961 per year) were awarded; career-related internships or fieldwork, Federal Work-Study, scholarships/grants, health care benefits, tuition waivers (partial), and unspecified assistantships also available. Support available to part-time students. Financial award application deadline: 3/1; financial award applicants required to submit FAFSA. *Faculty research:* Fire and emergency management, environmental dispute resolution, voting and elections, women and politics, urban politics. *Unit head:* Dr. Anthony Brown, Interim Department Head, 405-744-0420, Fax: 405-744-6534, E-mail: anthony.brown@okstate.edu.

Application contact: Dr. Rebekah Herrick, Interim Director of Graduate Studies, 405-744-8437, Fax: 405-744-6534, E-mail: rebekah.herrick@okstate.edu.
Website: http://polsci.okstate.edu.

University of Maryland, College Park, Academic Affairs, A. James Clark School of Engineering, Department of Fire Protection Engineering, College Park, MD 20742. Offers M Eng, MS. Part-time and evening/weekend programs available. *Degree requirements:* For master's, thesis optional. *Entrance requirements:* For master's, GRE General Test, minimum GPA of 3.0, BS in any engineering or physical science area, 3 letters of recommendation. Electronic applications accepted. *Faculty research:* Fire and thermal degradation of materials, fire modeling, fire dynamics, smoke detection and management, fire resistance.

University of New Haven, Graduate School, Henry C. Lee College of Criminal Justice and Forensic Sciences, Program in Fire Science, West Haven, CT 06516-1916. Offers emergency management (MS, Certificate); fire administration (MS); fire science (MS); fire science technology (Certificate); fire/arson investigation (MS, Certificate); forensic science/fire science (Certificate); public safety management (MS, Certificate). Part-time and evening/weekend programs available. *Degree requirements:* For master's, thesis or alternative, research project or internship. *Entrance requirements:* Additional exam requirements/recommendations for international students: Required—TOEFL (minimum score 80 iBT), IELTS, PTE (minimum score 53). Electronic applications accepted. Application fee is waived when completed online.

The University of North Carolina at Charlotte, The William States Lee College of Engineering, Department of Engineering Technology and Construction Management, Charlotte, NC 28223-0001. Offers applied energy and electromechanical systems (MS); construction and facilities management (MS); fire protection and administration (MS). *Faculty:* 26 full-time (5 women). *Students:* 30 full-time (6 women), 15 part-time (1 woman); includes 7 minority (3 Black or African American, non-Hispanic/Latino; 1 American Indian or Alaska Native, non-Hispanic/Latino; 1 Asian, non-Hispanic/Latino; 1 Hispanic/Latino; 1 Two or more races, non-Hispanic/Latino), 13 international. Average age 27. 69 applicants, 78% accepted, 27 enrolled. In 2014, 8 master's awarded. *Degree requirements:* For master's, comprehensive exam, thesis optional. *Entrance requirements:* Additional exam requirements/recommendations for international students: Required—TOEFL (minimum score 557 paper-based; 83 iBT). *Application deadline:* For fall admission, 5/1 for domestic and international students; for spring admission, 10/1 for domestic and international students. Application fee: $75. Electronic applications accepted. *Expenses:* Tuition, state resident: full-time $4008. Tuition, nonresident: full-time $16,295. *Required fees:* $2755. Tuition and fees vary according to course load and program. *Financial support:* In 2014–15, 24 students received support, including 22 research assistantships (averaging $6,665 per year), 2 teaching assistantships (averaging $14,250 per year); career-related internships or fieldwork, institutionally sponsored loans, scholarships/grants, and unspecified assistantships also available. Support available to part-time students. Financial award application deadline: 4/1; financial award applicants required to submit FAFSA. *Total annual research expenditures:* $1.1 million. *Unit head:* Dr. Cheng Liu, Chair Emeritus, 704-687-2474, E-mail: liu@uncc.edu. *Application contact:* Kathy B. Giddings, Director of Graduate Admissions, 704-687-5503, Fax: 704-687-1668, E-mail: gradadm@uncc.edu.
Website: http://et.uncc.edu/.

Worcester Polytechnic Institute, Graduate Studies and Research, Department of Fire Protection Engineering, Worcester, MA 01609-2280. Offers MS, PhD, Advanced Certificate, Graduate Certificate. Part-time and evening/weekend programs available. Postbaccalaureate distance learning degree programs offered (no on-campus study). *Faculty:* 3 full-time (0 women), 2 part-time/adjunct (0 women). *Students:* 45 full-time (14 women), 34 part-time (6 women); includes 8 minority (1 Black or African American, non-Hispanic/Latino; 1 Asian, non-Hispanic/Latino; 6 Hispanic/Latino), 15 international. 42 applicants, 88% accepted, 25 enrolled. In 2014, 49 master's, 2 doctorates awarded. *Degree requirements:* For master's, thesis optional; for doctorate, comprehensive exam, thesis/dissertation. *Entrance requirements:* For master's, GRE General Test (recommended), BS in engineering or physical sciences, 3 letters of recommendation, work experience or statement of purpose; for doctorate, GRE General Test, 3 letters of recommendation, statement of purpose. Additional exam requirements/recommendations for international students: Required—TOEFL (minimum score 563 paper-based; 84 iBT), IELTS (minimum score 7). *Application deadline:* For fall admission, 1/1 priority date for domestic students, 1/1 for international students; for spring admission, 10/1 priority date for domestic students, 10/1 for international students. Applications are processed on a rolling basis. Electronic applications accepted. *Financial support:* Research assistantships, teaching assistantships, career-related internships or fieldwork, institutionally sponsored loans, scholarships/grants, and unspecified assistantships available. Financial award application deadline: 1/1; financial award applicants required to submit FAFSA. *Unit head:* Dr. Tahar El-Korchi, Head, 508-831-5593, Fax: 508-831-5862, E-mail: tek@wpi.edu. *Application contact:* Dr. Ali Rangwala, Graduate Coordinator, 508-831-5593, Fax: 508-831-5862, E-mail: rangwala@wpi.edu.
Website: http://www.wpi.edu/academics/fpe.

Geotechnical Engineering

Auburn University, Graduate School, Ginn College of Engineering, Department of Civil Engineering, Auburn University, AL 36849. Offers construction engineering and management (MCE, MS, PhD); environmental engineering (MCE, MS, PhD); geotechnical/materials engineering (MCE, MS, PhD); hydraulics/hydrology (MCE, MS, PhD); structural engineering (MCE, MS, PhD); transportation engineering (MCE, MS, PhD). Part-time programs available. *Faculty:* 27 full-time (3 women), 1 part-time/adjunct (0 women). *Students:* 59 full-time (15 women), 46 part-time (6 women); includes 10 minority (4 Black or African American, non-Hispanic/Latino; 4 Asian, non-Hispanic/Latino; 2 Hispanic/Latino), 40 international. Average age 26. 134 applicants, 46% accepted, 20 enrolled. In 2014, 40 master's, 7 doctorates awarded. *Degree requirements:* For master's, project (MCE), thesis (MS); for doctorate, comprehensive exam, thesis/dissertation. *Entrance requirements:* For master's and doctorate, GRE General Test. *Application deadline:* For fall admission, 7/7 for domestic students; for spring admission, 11/24 for domestic students. Applications are processed on a rolling basis. Application fee: $50 ($60 for international students). Electronic applications accepted. *Expenses:* Tuition, state resident: full-time $8586; part-time $477 per credit hour. Tuition, nonresident: full-time $25,758; part-time $1431 per credit hour. *Required fees:* $804 per semester. Tuition and fees vary according to degree level and program. *Financial support:* Fellowships, research assistantships, teaching assistantships, and Federal Work-Study available. Support available to part-time students. Financial award application deadline: 3/15; financial award applicants required to submit FAFSA. *Unit head:* Dr. Andy Nowak, Head, 334-844-4320. *Application contact:* Dr. George Flowers, Dean of the Graduate School, 334-844-2125.

Cornell University, Graduate School, Graduate Fields of Engineering, Field of Civil and Environmental Engineering, Ithaca, NY 14853-0001. Offers engineering management (M Eng, MS, PhD); environmental engineering (M Eng, MS, PhD); environmental fluid mechanics and hydrology (M Eng, MS, PhD); environmental systems engineering (M Eng, MS, PhD); geotechnical engineering (M Eng, MS, PhD); remote sensing (M Eng, MS, PhD); structural engineering (M Eng, MS, PhD); structural mechanics (M Eng, MS); transportation engineering (MS, PhD); transportation systems engineering (M Eng); water resource systems (M Eng, MS, PhD). Terminal master's awarded for partial completion of doctoral program. *Degree requirements:* For master's, thesis (MS); for doctorate, comprehensive exam, thesis/dissertation. *Entrance requirements:* For master's and doctorate, GRE General Test (recommended), 2 letters of recommendation. Additional exam requirements/recommendations for international students: Required—TOEFL (minimum score 600 paper-based; 77 iBT). Electronic applications accepted. *Faculty research:* Environmental engineering, geotechnical engineering, remote sensing, environmental fluid mechanics and hydrology, structural engineering.

Drexel University, College of Engineering, Department of Civil, Architectural, and Environmental Engineering, Program in Geotechnical, Geoenvironmental and Geosynthetics Engineering, Philadelphia, PA 19104-2875. Offers MS, PhD.

École Polytechnique de Montréal, Graduate Programs, Department of Civil, Geological and Mining Engineering, Montréal, QC H3C 3A7, Canada. Offers civil, geological and mining engineering (DESS); environmental engineering (M Eng, M Sc A, PhD); geotechnical engineering (M Eng, M Sc A, PhD); hydraulics engineering (M Eng, M Sc A, PhD); structural engineering (M Eng, M Sc A, PhD); transportation engineering (M Eng, M Sc A, PhD). Part-time programs available. *Degree requirements:* For master's, one foreign language, thesis; for doctorate, one foreign language, thesis/dissertation. *Entrance requirements:* For master's, minimum GPA of 2.75; for doctorate, minimum GPA of 3.0. *Faculty research:* Water resources management, characteristics of building materials, aging of dams, pollution control.

Illinois Institute of Technology, Graduate College, Armour College of Engineering, Department of Civil, Architectural and Environmental Engineering, Chicago, IL 60616. Offers architectural engineering (M Arch E); civil engineering (MS, PhD), including architectural engineering (MS), construction engineering and management (MS), geoenvironmental engineering (MS), geotechnical engineering (MS), structural engineering (MS), transportation engineering (MS); construction engineering and management (MCEM); environmental engineering (M Env E, MS, PhD); geoenvironmental engineering (M Geoenv E); geotechnical engineering (MGE); infrastructure engineering and management (MPW); structural engineering (MSE); transportation engineering (M Trans E). Part-time and evening/weekend programs available. Postbaccalaureate distance learning degree programs offered (minimal on-campus study). *Faculty:* 12 full-time (1 woman), 15 part-time/adjunct (1 woman). *Students:* 165 full-time (48 women), 54 part-time (11 women); includes 31 minority (2 Black or African American, non-Hispanic/Latino; 21 Asian, non-Hispanic/Latino; 7 Hispanic/Latino; 1 Native Hawaiian or other Pacific Islander, non-Hispanic/Latino), 157 international. Average age 29. 1,039 applicants, 42% accepted, 82 enrolled. In 2014, 94 master's, 7 doctorates awarded. Terminal master's awarded for partial completion of doctoral program. *Degree requirements:* For master's, thesis (for some programs); for doctorate, comprehensive exam, thesis/dissertation. *Entrance requirements:* For master's, GRE General Test (minimum score 900 Quantitative and Verbal, 2.5 Analytical Writing), minimum undergraduate GPA of 3.0; for doctorate, GRE General Test (minimum score 1000 Quantitative and Verbal, 3.0 Analytical Writing), minimum undergraduate GPA of 3.0. Additional exam requirements/recommendations for international students: Required—TOEFL (minimum score 550 paper-based; 80 iBT). *Application deadline:* For fall admission, 5/1 for domestic and international students; for spring admission, 10/15 for domestic and international students. Applications are processed on a rolling basis. Application fee: $50. Electronic applications accepted. *Expenses: Tuition:* Full-time $22,500; part-time $1250 per credit hour. *Required fees:* $30 per course. $260 per semester. One-time fee: $235. Tuition and fees vary according to course load and program. *Financial support:* Fellowships with full and partial tuition reimbursements, research assistantships with full and partial tuition reimbursements, teaching assistantships with full and partial tuition reimbursements, Federal Work-Study, institutionally sponsored loans, scholarships/grants, health care benefits, tuition waivers (partial), and unspecified assistantships available. Support available to part-time students. Financial award applicants required to submit FAFSA. *Faculty research:* Structural, architectural, geotechnical and geoenvironmental engineering; construction engineering and management; transportation engineering; environmental engineering and public works. *Unit head:* Dr. Gongkang Fu, Professor and Chairman, 312-567-3540, Fax: 312-567-3519, E-mail: gfu2@iit.edu. *Application contact:* Rishab Malhotra, Director, Graduate Admission, 866-472-3448, Fax: 312-567-3138, E-mail: inquiry.grad@iit.edu.
Website: http://engineering.iit.edu/caee.

Iowa State University of Science and Technology, Department of Civil and Construction Engineering, Ames, IA 50011. Offers civil engineering (MS, PhD), including civil engineering materials, construction engineering and management, environmental engineering, geometronics, geotechnical engineering, structural engineering, transportation engineering. *Degree requirements:* For master's, thesis or alternative; for doctorate, thesis/dissertation. *Entrance requirements:* For master's and doctorate, GRE General Test. Additional exam requirements/recommendations for international students: Required—TOEFL (minimum score 550 paper-based; 82 iBT), IELTS (minimum score 6.5). Electronic applications accepted.

Kansas State University, Graduate School, College of Engineering, Department of Civil Engineering, Manhattan, KS 66506. Offers civil engineering (MS, PhD); environmental engineering (MS, PhD); geotechnical engineering (MS, PhD); structural engineering (MS, PhD); transportation engineering (MS, PhD); water resources engineering (MS, PhD). Part-time and evening/weekend programs available. Postbaccalaureate distance learning degree programs offered (no on-campus study). *Faculty:* 14 full-time (4 women), 3 part-time/adjunct (1 woman). *Students:* 37 full-time (12 women), 37 part-time (9 women); includes 6 minority (3 Black or African American, non-Hispanic/Latino; 3 Hispanic/Latino), 23 international. Average age 30. 62 applicants, 39% accepted, 10 enrolled. In 2014, 14 master's, 4 doctorates awarded. *Degree requirements:* For master's, thesis or alternative; for doctorate, thesis/dissertation. *Entrance requirements:* For master's, GRE General Test, bachelor's

degree or course work in related engineering fields; for doctorate, GRE General Test. Additional exam requirements/recommendations for international students: Required—TOEFL (minimum score 550 paper-based; 79 iBT). *Application deadline:* For fall admission, 2/1 priority date for domestic students, 1/1 priority date for international students; for spring admission, 8/1 priority date for domestic and international students. Applications are processed on a rolling basis. Application fee: $50 ($75 for international students). Electronic applications accepted. *Financial support:* In 2014–15, 19 research assistantships with partial tuition reimbursements (averaging $13,431 per year), 12 teaching assistantships with partial tuition reimbursements (averaging $15,058 per year) were awarded; institutionally sponsored loans and scholarships/grants also available. Support available to part-time students. Financial award application deadline: 3/1; financial award applicants required to submit FAFSA. *Faculty research:* Transportation and materials engineering, water resources engineering, environmental engineering, geotechnical engineering, structural engineering. *Total annual research expenditures:* $2.4 million. *Unit head:* Dr. Robert Stokes, Head, 785-532-1595, Fax: 785-532-7717, E-mail: drbobb@k-state.edu. *Application contact:* Dr. Dunja Peric, Graduate Coordinator, 785-532-2468, Fax: 785-532-7717, E-mail: peric@k-state.edu.
Website: http://www.ce.ksu.edu/.

Louisiana State University and Agricultural & Mechanical College, Graduate School, College of Engineering, Department of Civil and Environmental Engineering, Baton Rouge, LA 70803. Offers environmental engineering (MSCE, PhD); geotechnical engineering (MSCE, PhD); structural engineering and mechanics (MSCE, PhD); transportation engineering (MSCE, PhD); water resources (MSCE, PhD). Part-time programs available. *Faculty:* 26 full-time (1 woman). *Students:* 90 full-time (24 women), 28 part-time (6 women); includes 12 minority (5 Black or African American, non-Hispanic/Latino; 1 American Indian or Alaska Native, non-Hispanic/Latino; 5 Asian, non-Hispanic/Latino; 1 Two or more races, non-Hispanic/Latino), 67 international. Average age 30. 147 applicants, 50% accepted, 23 enrolled. In 2014, 26 master's, 8 doctorates awarded. *Degree requirements:* For master's, thesis optional; for doctorate, one foreign language, thesis/dissertation. *Entrance requirements:* For master's and doctorate, GRE General Test, minimum GPA of 3.0. Additional exam requirements/recommendations for international students: Required—TOEFL (minimum score 550 paper-based; 79 IBT), IELTS (minimum score 6.5), or PTE (minimum score 59). *Application deadline:* For fall admission, 1/1 priority date for domestic students, 5/15 for international students; for spring admission, 10/15 for domestic and international students; for summer admission, 5/15 for domestic and international students. Applications are processed on a rolling basis. Application fee: $50 ($70 for international students). Electronic applications accepted. *Financial support:* In 2014–15, 88 students received support, including 7 fellowships with full and partial tuition reimbursements available (averaging $26,784 per year), 59 research assistantships with full and partial tuition reimbursements available (averaging $16,992 per year), 13 teaching assistantships with full and partial tuition reimbursements available (averaging $16,290 per year); career-related internships or fieldwork, institutionally sponsored loans, scholarships/grants, and health care benefits also available. Financial award application deadline: 3/1; financial award applicants required to submit FAFSA. *Faculty research:* Mechanics and structures, environmental, geotechnical transportation, water resources. *Total annual research expenditures:* $3.2 million. *Unit head:* Dr. George Z. Voyiadjis, Chair/Professor, 225-578-8442, Fax: 225-578-8652, E-mail: voyaidjis@lsu.edu. *Application contact:* Dr. Ayman Ikeli, Professor, 225-578-7048, E-mail: aokeli@lsu.edu.
Website: http://www.cee.lsu.edu/.

Massachusetts Institute of Technology, School of Engineering, Department of Civil and Environmental Engineering, Cambridge, MA 02139. Offers biological oceanography (PhD, Sc D); chemical oceanography (PhD, Sc D); civil and environmental engineering (M Eng, SM, PhD, Sc D); civil and environmental systems (PhD, Sc D); civil engineering (PhD, Sc D, CE); coastal engineering (PhD, Sc D); construction engineering and management (PhD, Sc D); environmental biology (PhD, Sc D); environmental chemistry (PhD, Sc D); environmental engineering (PhD, Sc D); environmental fluid mechanics (PhD, Sc D); geotechnical and geoenvironmental engineering (PhD, Sc D); hydrology (PhD, Sc D); information technology (PhD, Sc D); oceanographic engineering (PhD, Sc D); structures and materials (PhD, Sc D); transportation (PhD, Sc D); SM/MBA. *Faculty:* 34 full-time (8 women), 1 part-time/adjunct (0 women). *Students:* 216 full-time (82 women); includes 25 minority (1 Black or African American, non-Hispanic/Latino; 10 Asian, non-Hispanic/Latino; 8 Hispanic/Latino; 6 Two or more races, non-Hispanic/Latino), 117 international. Average age 26. 565 applicants, 22% accepted, 85 enrolled. In 2014, 76 master's, 18 doctorates awarded. *Degree requirements:* For master's and CE, thesis; for doctorate, comprehensive exam, thesis/dissertation. *Entrance requirements:* For master's and doctorate, GRE General Test. Additional exam requirements/recommendations for international students: Required—TOEFL (minimum score 577 paper-based; 100 iBT), IELTS (minimum score 7). *Application deadline:* For fall admission, 12/15 for domestic and international students. Application fee: $75. Electronic applications accepted. *Expenses: Tuition:* Full-time $44,720; part-time $699 per unit. *Required fees:* $296. *Financial support:* In 2014–15, 170 students received support, including 32 fellowships (averaging $32,800 per year), 132 research assistantships (averaging $33,800 per year), 13 teaching assistantships (averaging $32,900 per year); Federal Work-Study, institutionally sponsored loans, scholarships/grants, traineeships, health care benefits, and unspecified assistantships also available. Financial award application deadline: 4/15; financial award applicants required to submit FAFSA. *Faculty research:* Environmental chemistry, environmental fluid mechanics and coastal engineering, environmental microbiology, geotechnical engineering and geomechanics, hydrology and hydroclimatology, infrastructure systems, mechanics of materials and structures, transportation systems. *Total annual research expenditures:* $22.9 million. *Unit head:* Prof. Markus Buehler, Department Head, 617-324-6488. *Application contact:* Graduate Admissions Coordinator, 617-253-7119, E-mail: cee-admissions@mit.edu.
Website: http://cee.mit.edu/.

McGill University, Faculty of Graduate and Postdoctoral Studies, Faculty of Engineering, Department of Civil Engineering and Applied Mechanics, Montréal, QC H3A 2T5, Canada. Offers environmental engineering (M Eng, M Sc, PhD); fluid mechanics (M Sc); fluid mechanics and hydraulic engineering (M Eng, PhD); materials engineering (M Eng, PhD); rehabilitation of urban infrastructure (M Eng, PhD); soil behavior (M Eng, PhD); soil mechanics and foundations (M Eng, PhD); structures and structural mechanics (M Eng, PhD); water resources (M Sc); water resources engineering (M Eng, PhD).

Missouri University of Science and Technology, Graduate School, Department of Civil, Architectural, and Environmental Engineering, Rolla, MO 65409. Offers civil engineering (MS, DE, PhD); construction engineering (MS, DE, PhD); environmental engineering (MS); fluid mechanics (MS, DE, PhD); geotechnical engineering (MS, DE, PhD); hydrology and hydraulic engineering (MS, DE, PhD). Part-time and evening/weekend programs available. Terminal master's awarded for partial completion of doctoral program. *Degree requirements:* For master's, thesis optional; for doctorate, comprehensive exam, thesis/dissertation. *Entrance requirements:* For master's, GRE General Test (minimum combined score 1100), minimum GPA of 3.0; for doctorate, GRE General Test (minimum score: verbal and quantitative 400, writing 3.5), minimum GPA of 3.0. Additional exam requirements/recommendations for international students: Required—TOEFL. Electronic applications accepted. *Faculty research:* Earthquake engineering, structural optimization and control systems, structural health monitoring/damage detection, soil-structure interaction, soil mechanics and foundation engineering.

Northwestern University, McCormick School of Engineering and Applied Science, Department of Civil and Environmental Engineering, Evanston, IL 60208-3109. Offers environmental engineering and science (MS, PhD); geotechnical engineering (MS, PhD); mechanics of materials and solids (MS, PhD); project management (MS, PhD); structural engineering and materials (MS, PhD); transportation systems analysis and planning (MS, PhD). MS and PhD admissions and degrees offered through The Graduate School. Part-time programs available. *Faculty:* 19 full-time (2 women). *Students:* 118 full-time (36 women), 5 part-time (2 women); includes 7 minority (3 Black or African American, non-Hispanic/Latino; 2 Asian, non-Hispanic/Latino; 1 Hispanic/Latino; 1 Two or more races, non-Hispanic/Latino), 95 international. Average age 24. 412 applicants, 36% accepted, 49 enrolled. In 2014, 42 master's, 10 doctorates awarded. Terminal master's awarded for partial completion of doctoral program. *Degree requirements:* For master's, thesis (for some programs); for doctorate, comprehensive exam, thesis/dissertation. *Entrance requirements:* For master's and doctorate, GRE General Test, minimum 2 letters of recommendation, transcripts from all academic institutions attended. Additional exam requirements/recommendations for international students: Required—TOEFL (minimum score 577 paper-based; 90 iBT), IELTS (minimum score 7). *Application deadline:* For fall admission, 12/31 for domestic and international students; for winter admission, 11/15 for domestic and international students; for spring admission, 1/15 for domestic and international students. Application fee: $95. Electronic applications accepted. *Financial support:* Fellowships with full tuition reimbursements, research assistantships with full tuition reimbursements, teaching assistantships with full tuition reimbursements, career-related internships or fieldwork, institutionally sponsored loans, health care benefits, and unspecified assistantships available. Financial award application deadline: 12/31; financial award applicants required to submit FAFSA. *Faculty research:* Environmental engineering and science, geotechnics, mechanics of materials and solids, structural engineering and materials, transportation systems analysis and planning. *Total annual research expenditures:* $5.8 million. *Unit head:* Dr. Jianmin Qu, Chair, 847-467-4528, Fax: 847-491-4011, E-mail: j-qu@northwestern.edu. *Application contact:* Dr. David Corr, Academic Coordinator, 847-467-0890, Fax: 847-491-4011, E-mail: d-corr@u.northwestern.edu.
Website: http://www.civil.northwestern.edu/.

Norwich University, College of Graduate and Continuing Studies, Master of Civil Engineering Program, Northfield, VT 05663. Offers construction management engineering (MCE); environmental/water resources engineering (MCE); geotechnical engineering (MCE); structural engineering (MCE). Evening/weekend programs available. Postbaccalaureate distance learning degree programs offered (minimal on-campus study). *Faculty:* 14 part-time/adjunct (2 women). *Students:* 111 full-time (17 women); includes 28 minority (16 Black or African American, non-Hispanic/Latino; 2 American Indian or Alaska Native, non-Hispanic/Latino; 7 Asian, non-Hispanic/Latino; 3 Hispanic/Latino). Average age 36. 61 applicants, 100% accepted, 42 enrolled. In 2014, 57 master's awarded. *Entrance requirements:* For master's, minimum undergraduate GPA of 2.75. Additional exam requirements/recommendations for international students: Required—TOEFL (minimum score 550 paper-based; 80 iBT), IELTS (minimum score 6.5). *Application deadline:* For fall admission, 8/8 for domestic and international students; for spring admission, 2/16 for domestic and international students. Applications are processed on a rolling basis. Electronic applications accepted. *Expenses:* Expenses: Contact institution. *Financial support:* In 2014–15, 27 students received support. Scholarships/grants available. Financial award applicants required to submit FAFSA. *Unit head:* Dr. Thomas Descoteaux, Program Director, 802-485-2730, Fax: 802-485-2533, E-mail: tdescote@norwich.edu. *Application contact:* Rija Ramahatra, Associate Program Director, 802-485-2892, Fax: 802-485-2533, E-mail: ramahatr@norwich.edu.
Website: http://online.norwich.edu/degree-programs/masters/master-civil-engineering/overview.

Ohio University, Graduate College, Russ College of Engineering and Technology, Department of Civil Engineering, Athens, OH 45701-2979. Offers civil engineering (PhD); construction engineering and management (MS); environmental (MS); geotechnical and geoenvironmental (MS); mechanics (MS); structures (MS); transportation (MS); water resources (MS). Part-time programs available. *Degree requirements:* For master's, comprehensive exam (for some programs), thesis or alternative; for doctorate, comprehensive exam, thesis/dissertation. *Entrance requirements:* For master's, GRE General Test, minimum GPA of 3.0, 3 letters of recommendation; for doctorate, GRE General Test. Additional exam requirements/recommendations for international students: Required—TOEFL (minimum score 550 paper-based; 80 iBT) or IELTS (minimum score 6.5). Electronic applications accepted. *Faculty research:* Noise abatement, materials and environment, highway infrastructure, subsurface investigation (pavements, pipes, bridges).

Penn State University Park, Graduate School, College of Earth and Mineral Sciences, Department of Energy and Mineral Engineering, University Park, PA 16802. Offers MS, PhD. *Unit head:* Dr. William E. Easterling, III, Dean, 814-865-7482, Fax: 814-863-7708, E-mail: wee2@psu.edu. *Application contact:* Lori A. Stania, Director, Graduate Student Services, 814-867-5278, Fax: 814-863-4627, E-mail: gswww@psu.edu.
Website: http://www.eme.psu.edu/.

Southern Illinois University Edwardsville, Graduate School, School of Engineering, Department of Civil Engineering, Program in Geotechnical Engineering, Edwardsville, IL 62026. Offers MS. Part-time and evening/weekend programs available. *Degree requirements:* For master's, thesis (for some programs), research paper. *Entrance requirements:* For master's, minimum undergraduate GPA of 2.75 in science, math, and engineering courses. Additional exam requirements/recommendations for international students: Required—TOEFL (minimum score 550 paper-based, 79 iBT), IELTS (minimum score 6.5), Michigan Test of English Language Proficiency or PTE. *Application deadline:* For fall admission, 7/18 for domestic students, 6/1 for international students; for spring admission, 12/12 for domestic students, 10/1 for international students; for summer admission, 4/24 for domestic students, 3/1 for international students. Applications are processed on a rolling basis. Application fee: $30. Electronic applications accepted. *Expenses:* Tuition, state resident: full-time $5026. Tuition, nonresident: full-time $12,566. *International tuition:* $25,136 full-time. *Required fees:* $1682. Tuition and fees vary according to course load, campus/location and program. *Financial support:* Institutionally sponsored loans, scholarships/grants, and unspecified assistantships available. Financial award application deadline: 3/1; financial award applicants required to submit FAFSA. *Unit head:* Dr. Jim Zhou, Chair, 618-650-2533, E-mail: jzhou@siue.edu. *Application contact:* Dr. Ryan Fries, Director, 618-650-5026, E-mail: rfries@siue.edu.
Website: http://www.siue.edu/engineering/civilengineering/.

Stanford University, School of Engineering, Department of Civil and Environmental Engineering, Stanford, CA 94305-9991. Offers atmosphere and energy (MS, PhD); construction (MS), including construction engineering and management, design-construction integration, sustainable design and construction; environmental engineering and science (MS, PhD, Eng); environmental fluid mechanics and hydrology (PhD); geomechanics (MS); structural engineering (MS). Terminal master's awarded for partial completion of doctoral program. *Degree requirements:* For doctorate, thesis/dissertation, qualifying exam; for Eng, thesis. *Entrance requirements:* For master's, doctorate, and Eng, GRE General Test. Additional exam requirements/recommendations for international students: Required—TOEFL. Electronic applications accepted. *Expenses: Tuition:* Full-time $44,184; part-time $982 per credit hour. *Required fees:* $191.

Tufts University, School of Engineering, Department of Civil and Environmental Engineering, Medford, MA 02155. Offers bioengineering (ME, MS), including environmental technology; civil engineering (ME, MS, PhD), including geotechnical engineering, structural engineering, water diplomacy (PhD); environmental engineering (ME, MS, PhD), including environmental engineering and environmental sciences, environmental geotechnology, environmental health, environmental science and management, hazardous materials management, water diplomacy (PhD), water resources engineering. Part-time programs available. *Faculty:* 24 full-time (5 women), 6 part-time/adjunct (1 woman). *Students:* 66 full-time (29 women), 19 part-time (6 women); includes 5 minority (1 Black or African American, non-Hispanic/Latino; 2 Asian, non-Hispanic/Latino; 1 Hispanic/Latino; 1 Two or more races, non-Hispanic/Latino), 25 international. Average age 29. 166 applicants, 42% accepted, 27 enrolled. In 2014, 21 master's, 6 doctorates awarded. Terminal master's awarded for partial completion of doctoral program. *Degree requirements:* For master's, thesis or alternative; for doctorate, thesis/dissertation. *Entrance requirements:* For master's and doctorate, GRE General Test. Additional exam requirements/recommendations for international students: Required—TOEFL (minimum score 550 paper-based; 80 iBT), IELTS (minimum score 6.5). *Application deadline:* For fall admission, 1/15 priority date for domestic students, 1/15 for international students; for spring admission, 9/15 for domestic and international students. Applications are processed on a rolling basis. Application fee: $75. Electronic applications accepted. *Expenses: Tuition:* Full-time $45,590; part-time $1161 per credit hour. *Required fees:* $782. Full-time tuition and fees vary according to degree level, program and student level. Part-time tuition and fees vary according to course load. *Financial support:* Fellowships with full tuition reimbursements, research assistantships with full and partial tuition reimbursements, teaching assistantships with full and partial tuition reimbursements, Federal Work-Study, scholarships/grants, tuition waivers (partial), and unspecified assistantships available. Financial award application deadline: 5/15; financial award applicants required to submit FAFSA. *Faculty research:* Environmental and water resources engineering, environmental health, geotechnical and geoenvironmental engineering, structural engineering and mechanics, water diplomacy. *Unit head:* Dr. Kurt Pennell, Graduate Program Director. *Application contact:* Office of Graduate Admissions, 617-627-3395, E-mail: gradadmissions@tufts.edu.
Website: http://www.ase.tufts.edu/cee/.

The University of Alabama in Huntsville, School of Graduate Studies, College of Engineering, Department of Civil and Environmental Engineering, Huntsville, AL 35899. Offers civil and environmental engineering (PhD); civil engineering (MSE), including civil engineering, environmental and water resource engineering, geotechnical engineering, structural engineering and structural mechanics, transportation engineering. PhD offered jointly with The University of Alabama at Birmingham. Part-time and evening/weekend programs available. *Degree requirements:* For master's, comprehensive exam, thesis or alternative, oral and written exams; for doctorate, comprehensive exam, thesis/dissertation, oral and written exams. *Entrance requirements:* For master's, GRE General Test, BSE, minimum GPA of 3.0; for doctorate, GRE General Test, minimum GPA of 3.0. Additional exam requirements/recommendations for international students: Required—TOEFL (minimum score 500 paper-based; 80 iBT), IELTS (minimum score 6.5). Electronic applications accepted. *Faculty research:* Smart materials and smart structures, fiber-reinforced cementitious composites, processing and mechanics of composites, geographic information systems, environmental engineering.

University of Alberta, Faculty of Graduate Studies and Research, Department of Civil and Environmental Engineering, Edmonton, AB T6G 2E1, Canada. Offers construction engineering and management (M Eng, M Sc, PhD); environmental engineering (M Eng, M Sc, PhD); environmental science (M Sc, PhD); geoenvironmental engineering (M Eng, M Sc, PhD); geotechnical engineering (M Eng, M Sc, PhD); mining engineering (M Eng, M Sc, PhD); petroleum engineering (M Eng, M Sc, PhD); structural engineering (M Eng, M Sc, PhD); water resources (M Eng, M Sc, PhD). Part-time programs available. Postbaccalaureate distance learning degree programs offered (minimal on-campus study). *Degree requirements:* For master's, thesis (for some programs); for doctorate, thesis/dissertation. *Entrance requirements:* For master's, minimum GPA of 3.0 in last 2 years of undergraduate studies; for doctorate, minimum GPA of 3.0. Additional exam requirements/recommendations for international students: Required—TOEFL (minimum score 550 paper-based). Electronic applications accepted. *Faculty research:* Mining.

University of Calgary, Faculty of Graduate Studies, Schulich School of Engineering, Department of Civil Engineering, Calgary, AB T2N 1N4, Canada. Offers avalanche mechanics (M Sc, PhD); civil engineering (M Eng, M Sc, PhD); energy and environment engineering (M Eng, M Sc, PhD); environmental engineering (M Eng, M Sc, PhD); geotechnical engineering (M Eng, M Sc, PhD); materials science (M Eng, M Sc, PhD); project management (M Eng, M Sc, PhD); structures and solid mechanics (M Eng, M Sc, PhD); transportation engineering (M Eng, M Sc, PhD); water resources (M Eng, M Sc, PhD). Part-time programs available. *Degree requirements:* For master's, thesis; for doctorate, thesis/dissertation, written and oral candidacy exam. *Entrance requirements:* For master's, minimum GPA of 3.0; for doctorate, minimum GPA of 3.5. Additional exam requirements/recommendations for international students: Required—TOEFL (minimum score 580 paper-based; 93 iBT), IELTS (minimum score 7). Electronic applications accepted. *Faculty research:* Geotechnical engineering, energy and environment, transportation, project management, structures and solid mechanics.

University of Calgary, Faculty of Graduate Studies, Schulich School of Engineering, Department of Geomatics Engineering, Calgary, AB T2N 1N4, Canada. Offers M Eng, M Sc, PhD. Part-time programs available. *Degree requirements:* For master's, thesis (for some programs), minimum of 4 half-courses, completion of seminar course; for doctorate, comprehensive exam, thesis/dissertation, minimum of 3 half-courses, completion of two seminar courses, candidacy exam. *Entrance requirements:* For master's, B Sc or equivalent with minimum GPA of 3.0; for doctorate, M Sc or transfer from M Sc program with minimum GPA of 3.5. Additional exam requirements/recommendations for international students: Required—TOEFL (minimum score 550 paper-based; 80 iBT) or IELTS (minimum score 7). Electronic applications accepted. *Faculty research:* Digital imaging systems, earth observation, geospatial information systems, and land tenure positioning, navigation and wireless location.

University of California, Berkeley, Graduate Division, College of Engineering, Department of Civil and Environmental Engineering, Berkeley, CA 94720-1500. Offers engineering and project management (M Eng, MS, D Eng, PhD); environmental engineering (M Eng, MS, D Eng, PhD); geoengineering (M Eng, MS, D Eng, PhD); structural engineering, mechanics and materials (M Eng, MS, D Eng, PhD); transportation engineering (M Eng, MS, D Eng, PhD); M Arch/MS; MCP/MS; MPP/MS.

Degree requirements: For master's, comprehensive exam or thesis (MS); for doctorate, thesis/dissertation, qualifying exam. *Entrance requirements:* For master's, GRE General Test, minimum GPA of 3.0, 3 letters of recommendation; for doctorate, GRE General Test, minimum GPA of 3.5, 3 letters of recommendation. Additional exam requirements/recommendations for international students: Required—TOEFL (minimum score 570 paper-based). Electronic applications accepted.

University of Colorado Boulder, Graduate School, College of Engineering and Applied Science, Department of Civil, Environmental, and Architectural Engineering, Boulder, CO 80309. Offers building systems engineering (MS, PhD); construction engineering management (MS, PhD); environmental engineering (MS, PhD); geotechnical engineering and geomechanics (MS, PhD); hydrology, water resources and environmental fluid mechanics (MS, PhD); structural engineering and structural mechanics (MS, PhD). *Faculty:* 37 full-time (8 women). *Students:* 235 full-time (81 women), 36 part-time (9 women); includes 24 minority (9 Asian, non-Hispanic/Latino; 6 Hispanic/Latino; 9 Two or more races, non-Hispanic/Latino), 83 international. Average age 28. 391 applicants, 63% accepted, 68 enrolled. In 2014, 76 master's, 30 doctorates awarded. Terminal master's awarded for partial completion of doctoral program. *Degree requirements:* For master's, comprehensive exam, thesis or alternative; for doctorate, thesis/dissertation. *Entrance requirements:* For master's, GRE General Test, minimum undergraduate GPA of 3.0. *Application deadline:* For fall admission, 1/31 for domestic and international students; for spring admission, 10/1 for domestic and international students. Application fee: $50 ($70 for international students). Electronic applications accepted. *Financial support:* In 2014–15, 387 students received support, including 75 fellowships (averaging $11,889 per year), 92 research assistantships with full and partial tuition reimbursements available (averaging $34,669 per year), 17 teaching assistantships with full and partial tuition reimbursements available (averaging $28,513 per year); institutionally sponsored loans, scholarships/grants, health care benefits, and unspecified assistantships also available. Financial award application deadline: 1/15; financial award applicants required to submit FAFSA. *Faculty research:* Civil engineering, environmental engineering, architectural engineering, geotechnical engineering, hydrology. *Total annual research expenditures:* $13 million.
Website: http://civil.colorado.edu/.

University of Colorado Denver, College of Engineering and Applied Science, Department of Civil Engineering, Denver, CO 80217. Offers civil engineering (EASPh D); civil engineering systems (PhD); environmental and sustainability engineering (MS, PhD); geographic information systems (MS); geotechnical engineering (MS, PhD); hydrology and hydraulics (MS, PhD); structural engineering (MS, PhD); transportation engineering (MS, PhD). Part-time and evening/weekend programs available. *Faculty:* 15 full-time (4 women), 11 part-time/adjunct (2 women). *Students:* 64 full-time (15 women), 43 part-time (8 women); includes 15 minority (3 Black or African American, non-Hispanic/Latino; 3 Asian, non-Hispanic/Latino; 6 Hispanic/Latino; 3 Two or more races, non-Hispanic/Latino), 34 international. Average age 32. 136 applicants, 54% accepted, 28 enrolled. In 2014, 35 master's, 9 doctorates awarded. *Degree requirements:* For master's, comprehensive exam, 30 credit hours, project or thesis; for doctorate, comprehensive exam, thesis/dissertation, 60 credit hours (30 of which are dissertation research). *Entrance requirements:* For master's, GRE, statement of purpose, transcripts, three references; for doctorate, GRE, statement of purpose, transcripts, references, letter of support from faculty stating willingness to serve as dissertation advisor and outlining plan for financial support. Additional exam requirements/recommendations for international students: Required—TOEFL (minimum score 537 paper-based; 75 iBT); Recommended—IELTS (minimum score 6.5). *Application deadline:* For fall admission, 5/1 for domestic students, 4/1 for international students; for spring admission, 10/1 for domestic students, 9/1 for international students; for summer admission, 2/15 for domestic students, 1/15 for international students. Application fee: $50 ($75 for international students). Electronic applications accepted. *Expenses:* Expenses: Contact institution. *Financial support:* In 2014–15, 26 students received support. Fellowships, research assistantships, teaching assistantships, career-related internships or fieldwork, Federal Work-Study, institutionally sponsored loans, scholarships/grants, traineeships, and unspecified assistantships available. Financial award application deadline: 4/1; financial award applicants required to submit FAFSA. *Faculty research:* Earthquake source physics, environmental biotechnology, hydrologic and hydraulic engineering, sustainability assessments, transportation energy use and greenhouse gas emissions. *Unit head:* Dr. Kevin Rens, Chair, 303-556-8017, E-mail: kevin.rens@ucdenver.edu. *Application contact:* Tammy Southern, Program Assistant, 303-556-6712, E-mail: tamara.southern@ucdenver.edu.
Website: http://www.ucdenver.edu/academics/colleges/Engineering/Programs/Civil-Engineering/Pages/CivilEngineering.aspx.

University of Dayton, Department of Civil and Environmental Engineering and Engineering Mechanics, Dayton, OH 45469. Offers engineering mechanics (MSEM); environmental engineering (MSCE); geotechnical engineering (MSCE); structural engineering (MSCE); transportation engineering (MSCE); water resources engineering (MSCE). Part-time and evening/weekend programs available. *Faculty:* 9 full-time (2 women), 3 part-time/adjunct (1 woman). *Students:* 23 full-time (4 women), 6 part-time (2 women), 22 international. Average age 26. 70 applicants, 39% accepted, 4 enrolled. In 2014, 11 master's awarded. *Degree requirements:* For master's, thesis optional. *Entrance requirements:* For master's, minimum GPA of 3.0 in undergraduate work. Additional exam requirements/recommendations for international students: Required—TOEFL (minimum score 550 paper-based; 80 iBT). *Application deadline:* For fall admission, 8/1 priority date for domestic students, 5/1 priority date for international students; for winter admission, 7/1 priority date for international students; for spring admission, 11/1 priority date for international students. Applications are processed on a rolling basis. Application fee: $0 ($50 for international students). Electronic applications accepted. *Expenses: Tuition:* Full-time $10,176; part-time $848 per credit. *Required fees:* $25; $25 per course. Part-time tuition and fees vary according to course level, course load, degree level and program. *Financial support:* In 2014–15, 3 students received support. Institutionally sponsored loans, scholarships/grants, and department-funded awards (averaging $2448 per year) available. Financial award application deadline: 3/1; financial award applicants required to submit FAFSA. *Faculty research:* Physical modeling of water resource systems, finite element methods, mechanics of composite materials, transportation systems safety, biological treatment processes, fiber reinforced concrete. *Total annual research expenditures:* $250,000. *Unit head:* Dr. Donald V. Chase, Chair, 937-229-3847, Fax: 937-229-3491, E-mail: dchase1@udayton.edu. *Application contact:* 937-229-4462, E-mail: graduateadmission@udayton.edu.
Website: https://www.udayton.edu/engineering/departments/civil/index.php.

University of Delaware, College of Engineering, Department of Civil and Environmental Engineering, Newark, DE 19716. Offers environmental engineering (MAS, MCE, PhD); geotechnical engineering (MAS, MCE, PhD); ocean engineering (MAS, MCE, PhD); structural engineering (MAS, MCE, PhD); transportation engineering (MAS, MCE, PhD); water resource engineering (MAS, MCE, PhD). Part-time programs available. Terminal master's awarded for partial completion of doctoral program. *Degree requirements:* For master's, thesis; for doctorate, thesis/dissertation. *Entrance requirements:* For master's and doctorate, GRE General Test. Additional exam requirements/recommendations for international students: Required—TOEFL. Electronic applications accepted. *Faculty* *research:* Structural engineering and mechanics; transportation engineering; ocean engineering; soil mechanics and foundation; water resources and environmental engineering.

University of Massachusetts Amherst, Graduate School, College of Engineering, Department of Civil and Environmental Engineering, Amherst, MA 01003. Offers civil engineering (MSCE, PhD); environmental and water resources engineering (MSCE); geotechnical engineering (MSCE); structural engineering and mechanics (MSCE); transportation engineering (MSCE). Part-time programs available. *Faculty:* 32 full-time (8 women). *Students:* 104 full-time (43 women), 15 part-time (7 women); includes 16 minority (3 Black or African American, non-Hispanic/Latino; 4 Asian, non-Hispanic/Latino; 7 Hispanic/Latino; 2 Two or more races, non-Hispanic/Latino), 44 international. Average age 26. 219 applicants, 62% accepted, 40 enrolled. In 2014, 36 master's, 4 doctorates awarded. Terminal master's awarded for partial completion of doctoral program. *Degree requirements:* For master's, thesis or alternative; for doctorate, comprehensive exam, thesis/dissertation. *Entrance requirements:* For master's and doctorate, GRE General Test. Additional exam requirements/recommendations for international students: Required—TOEFL (minimum score 550 paper-based; 80 iBT), IELTS (minimum score 6.5). *Application deadline:* For fall admission, 1/2 for domestic and international students; for spring admission, 10/1 for domestic and international students. Applications are processed on a rolling basis. Application fee: $75. Electronic applications accepted. *Expenses:* Tuition, state resident: full-time $1980; part-time $110 per credit. Tuition, nonresident: full-time $14,644; part-time $414 per credit. *Required fees:* $11,417. One-time fee: $357. *Financial support:* Fellowships with full and partial tuition reimbursements, research assistantships with full and partial tuition reimbursements, teaching assistantships with full and partial tuition reimbursements, career-related internships or fieldwork, Federal Work-Study, scholarships/grants, traineeships, health care benefits, tuition waivers (full and partial), and unspecified assistantships available. Support available to part-time students. Financial award application deadline: 1/2. *Unit head:* Dr. Sanjay Arwade, Graduate Program Director, 413-545-0686, Fax: 413-545-2840. *Application contact:* Lindsay DeSantis, Supervisor of Admissions, 413-545-0722, Fax: 413-577-0100, E-mail: gradadm@grad.umass.edu.
Website: http://cee.umass.edu/.

University of Missouri, Office of Research and Graduate Studies, College of Engineering, Department of Civil and Environmental Engineering, Columbia, MO 65211. Offers civil engineering (MS, PhD); environmental engineering (MS, PhD); geotechnical engineering (MS, PhD); structural engineering (MS, PhD); transportation and highway engineering (MS); water resources (MS, PhD). *Faculty:* 18 full-time (2 women), 1 part-time/adjunct (0 women). *Students:* 42 full-time (8 women), 27 part-time (6 women); includes 4 minority (1 Black or African American, non-Hispanic/Latino; 1 Asian, non-Hispanic/Latino; 2 Hispanic/Latino), 45 international. Average age 31. 102 applicants, 48% accepted, 22 enrolled. In 2014, 14 master's, 2 doctorates awarded. *Degree requirements:* For master's, report or thesis; for doctorate, thesis/dissertation. *Entrance requirements:* For master's and doctorate, GRE General Test. Additional exam requirements/recommendations for international students: Required—TOEFL (minimum score 550 paper-based; 79 iBT). *Application deadline:* For fall admission, 2/15 priority date for domestic students, 2/15 for international students; for winter admission, 9/15 priority date for domestic students, 9/15 for international students. Application fee: $55 ($75 for international students). *Financial support:* Fellowships, research assistantships, teaching assistantships, and institutionally sponsored loans available. *Unit head:* Dr. Mark Virkler, Department Chair, 573-882-7434, E-mail: virklerm@missouri.edu. *Application contact:* Jennifer Keyzer-Andre, Administrative Associate I, 573-882-4442, E-mail: keyzerandrej@missouri.edu.
Website: http://engineering.missouri.edu/civil/.

University of New Brunswick Fredericton, School of Graduate Studies, Faculty of Engineering, Department of Civil Engineering, Fredericton, NB E3B 5A3, Canada. Offers construction engineering and management (M Eng, M Sc E, PhD); environmental engineering (M Eng, M Sc E, PhD); environmental studies (M Eng); geotechnical engineering (M Eng, M Sc E, PhD); groundwater/hydrology (M Eng, M Sc E, PhD); materials (M Eng, M Sc E, PhD); pavements (M Eng, M Sc E, PhD); structures (M Eng, M Sc E, PhD); transportation (M Eng, M Sc E, PhD). Part-time programs available. *Faculty:* 12 full-time (1 woman), 4 part-time/adjunct (0 women). *Students:* 16 full-time (4 women), 15 part-time (5 women). In 2014, 9 master's, 3 doctorates awarded. *Degree requirements:* For master's, thesis, proposal; for doctorate, comprehensive exam, thesis/dissertation, qualifying exam; 27 credit hours of courses. *Entrance requirements:* For master's, minimum GPA of 3.0; B Sc E in civil engineering or related engineering degree; for doctorate, minimum GPA of 3.0; graduate degree in engineering or applied science. Additional exam requirements/recommendations for international students: Required—IELTS (minimum score 7.5), TWE (minimum score 4), Michigan English Language Assessment Battery (minimum score 85) or CanTest (minimum score 4.5); Recommended—TOEFL (minimum score 580 paper-based). *Application deadline:* For fall admission, 5/1 for domestic students; for winter admission, 11/1 for domestic students. Applications are processed on a rolling basis. Application fee: $50 Canadian dollars. Electronic applications accepted. *Financial support:* In 2014–15, 35 fellowships, 48 research assistantships, 35 teaching assistantships were awarded; career-related internships or fieldwork and scholarships/grants also available. *Faculty research:* Construction engineering and management; engineering materials and infrastructure renewal; highway and pavement research; structures and solid mechanics; geotechnical and geoenvironmental engineering; structure interaction; transportation and planning; environment, solid waste management; structural engineering; water and environmental engineering. *Unit head:* Dr. Kerry MacQuarrie, Director of Graduate Studies, 506-453-5121, Fax: 506-453-3568, E-mail: ktm@unb.ca. *Application contact:* Joyce Moore, Graduate Secretary, 506-452-6127, Fax: 506-453-3568, E-mail: joycem@unb.ca.
Website: http://go.unb.ca/gradprograms.

University of Southern California, Graduate School, Viterbi School of Engineering, Mork Family Department of Chemical Engineering and Materials Science, Los Angeles, CA 90089. Offers chemical engineering (MS, PhD, Engr); geoscience technologies (MS); materials engineering (MS); materials science (MS, PhD, Engr); petroleum engineering (MS, PhD, Engr); smart oilfield technologies (MS, Graduate Certificate). Terminal master's awarded for partial completion of doctoral program. *Degree requirements:* For master's, thesis optional; for doctorate, thesis/dissertation. *Entrance requirements:* For master's and doctorate, GRE General Test. Additional exam requirements/recommendations for international students: Recommended—TOEFL. Electronic applications accepted. *Expenses:* Contact institution. *Faculty research:* Heterogeneous materials and porous media, statistical mechanics, molecular simulation, polymer science and engineering, advanced materials, reaction engineering and catalysis, membrane processes and separation, biochemical engineering, cell culture, bioreactor modeling, petroleum engineering.

University of South Florida, College of Engineering, Department of Civil and Environmental Engineering, Tampa, FL 33620-9951. Offers civil engineering (MCE, MSCE, PhD), including environmental engineering (MSES, PhD), geotechnical engineering (MCE, MSCE, MSES, PhD), interdisciplinary transportation (MSCE), materials engineering and science, structural engineering, transportation engineering, water resources; engineering science (MSES), including environmental engineering (MSES, PhD), geotechnical engineering (MCE, MSCE, MSES, PhD); environmental engineering (MEVE, MSEV, PhD). Part-time programs available. *Faculty:* 19 full-time (5 women). *Students:* 97 full-time (35 women), 83 part-time (25 women); includes 41 minority (6 Black or African American, non-Hispanic/Latino; 1 American Indian or Alaska Native, non-Hispanic/Latino; 3 Asian, non-Hispanic/Latino; 25 Hispanic/Latino; 6 Two or more races, non-Hispanic/Latino), 39 international. Average age 30. 229 applicants, 51% accepted, 43 enrolled. In 2014, 68 master's, 9 doctorates awarded. Terminal master's awarded for partial completion of doctoral program. *Degree requirements:* For master's, comprehensive exam, thesis (for some programs); for doctorate, comprehensive exam, thesis/dissertation. *Entrance requirements:* For master's, GRE General Test (preferred minimum scores of 20th percentile verbal, 50th percentile quantitative, and 10th percentile in analytical writing), minimum GPA of 3.0 in major, two letters of reference, statement of purpose; for doctorate, GRE General Test (preferred minimum scores of 45th percentile verbal, 65th percentile quantitative, and 50th percentile in analytical writing), three letters of recommendation, statement of purpose, resume. Additional exam requirements/recommendations for international students: Required—TOEFL (minimum score 550 paper-based; 79 iBT) or IELTS (minimum score 6.5). *Application deadline:* For fall admission, 2/15 for domestic students, 1/2 priority date for international students; for spring admission, 10/15 for domestic students, 6/1 priority date for international students. Application fee: $30. Electronic applications accepted. *Financial support:* In 2014–15, 65 students received support, including 44 research assistantships (averaging $14,123 per year), 21 teaching assistantships with tuition reimbursements available (averaging $15,329 per year). *Faculty research:* Environmental and water resources engineering, geotechnics and geoenvironmental systems, structures and materials systems, transportation systems. *Total annual research expenditures:* $3.3 million. *Unit head:* Dr. Manjriker Gunaratne, Professor and Department Chair, 813-974-5818, Fax: 813-974-2957, E-mail: gunaratn@usf.edu. *Application contact:* Dr. Sarina J. Ergas, Professor and Graduate Program Coordinator, 813-974-1119, Fax: 813-974-2957, E-mail: sergas@usf.edu.
Website: http://ce.eng.usf.edu/.

The University of Texas at Austin, Graduate School, Cockrell School of Engineering, Department of Petroleum and Geosystems Engineering, Austin, TX 78712-1111. Offers energy and earth resources (MA); petroleum engineering (MS, PhD). Evening/weekend programs available. Postbaccalaureate distance learning degree programs offered (no on-campus study). *Entrance requirements:* For master's and doctorate, GRE General Test. Electronic applications accepted.

University of Washington, Graduate School, College of Engineering, Department of Civil and Environmental Engineering, Seattle, WA 98195-2700. Offers civil engineering (PhD); construction engineering (MSCE); environmental engineering (MSCE, PhD); hydrology, water resources, and environmental fluid mechanics (MSCE, PhD); structural and geotechnical engineering and mechanics (MSCE, PhD); transportation and construction engineering (PhD); transportation engineering (MSCE). Part-time programs available. Postbaccalaureate distance learning degree programs offered (no on-campus study). *Faculty:* 35 full-time (9 women). *Students:* 220 full-time (81 women), 147 part-time (50 women); includes 61 minority (9 Black or African American, non-Hispanic/Latino; 2 American Indian or Alaska Native, non-Hispanic/Latino; 34 Asian, non-Hispanic/Latino; 14 Hispanic/Latino; 2 Native Hawaiian or other Pacific Islander, non-Hispanic/Latino), 91 international. Average age 28. 901 applicants, 49% accepted, 162 enrolled. In 2014, 110 master's, 12 doctorates awarded. Terminal master's awarded for partial completion of doctoral program. *Degree requirements:* For master's, thesis (for some programs); for doctorate, comprehensive exam, thesis/dissertation, general, qualifying, and final exams; completion of degree within 10 years. *Entrance requirements:* For master's, GRE General Test, minimum GPA of 3.0, statement of purpose, letters of recommendation, transcripts; for doctorate, GRE General Test, minimum GPA of 3.5, statement of purpose, letters of recommendation, transcripts. Additional exam requirements/recommendations for international students: Required—TOEFL (minimum score 580 paper-based; 92 iBT); Recommended—IELTS (minimum score 7). *Application deadline:* For fall admission, 12/15 for domestic and international students. Applications are processed on a rolling basis. Application fee: $85. Electronic applications accepted. *Expenses:* Expenses: Contact institution. *Financial support:* In 2014–15, 179 students received support, including 41 fellowships with full and partial tuition reimbursements available, 77 research assistantships with full tuition reimbursements available, 58 teaching assistantships with full tuition reimbursements available; scholarships/grants also available. Financial award application deadline: 1/10; financial award applicants required to submit FAFSA. *Faculty research:* Structural and geotechnical engineering, transportation and construction engineering, water and environmental engineering. *Total annual research expenditures:* $14.1 million. *Unit head:* Dr. Gregory R. Miller, Professor/Chair, 206-543-0350, Fax: 206-543-1543, E-mail: gmiller@uw.edu. *Application contact:* Lorna Latal, Graduate Adviser, 206-543-2574, Fax: 206-543-1543, E-mail: llatal@u.washington.edu.
Website: http://www.ce.washington.edu/.

Hazardous Materials Management

Humboldt State University, Academic Programs, College of Natural Resources and Sciences, Programs in Natural Resources, Arcata, CA 95521-8299. Offers natural resources (MS), including fisheries, forestry, natural resources planning and interpretation, rangeland resources and wildland soils, wastewater utilization, watershed management, wildlife. *Students:* 60 full-time (34 women), 17 part-time (7 women); includes 8 minority (1 Asian, non-Hispanic/Latino; 6 Hispanic/Latino; 1 Two or more races, non-Hispanic/Latino), 2 international. Average age 29. 125 applicants, 21% accepted, 20 enrolled. In 2014, 21 master's awarded. *Degree requirements:* For master's, thesis or alternative. *Entrance requirements:* For master's, GRE, appropriate bachelor's degree, minimum GPA of 2.5, 3 letters of recommendation, resume. Additional exam requirements/recommendations for international students: Required—TOEFL (minimum score 500 paper-based). *Application deadline:* For fall admission, 2/1 for domestic and international students; for spring admission, 9/30 for domestic and international students. Applications are processed on a rolling basis. Application fee: $55. *Expenses:* Tuition, state resident: full-time $6738; part-time $3906 per year. Tuition, nonresident: full-time $13,434; part-time $6138 per year. *Required fees:* $1690;

$1266 per year. Tuition and fees vary according to program. *Financial support:* Fellowships, career-related internships or fieldwork, and Federal Work-Study available. Support available to part-time students. Financial award application deadline: 3/1; financial award applicants required to submit FAFSA. *Faculty research:* Spotted owl habitat, pre-settlement vegetation, hardwood utilization, tree physiology, fisheries. *Unit head:* Dr. Yvonne Everett, Coordinator, 707-826-4188, E-mail: yvonne.everett@humboldt.edu. *Application contact:* Loraine Taggart, Administrative Support Coordinator, 707-826-3256, E-mail: cnrsmast@humboldt.edu.
Website: http://www.humboldt.edu/cnrs/graduate_programs.

Idaho State University, Office of Graduate Studies, Department of Interdisciplinary Studies, Pocatello, ID 83209. Offers general interdisciplinary (M Ed, MA, MNS); waste management and environmental science (MS). Part-time programs available. *Degree requirements:* For master's, comprehensive exam, thesis optional. *Entrance requirements:* For master's, GRE General Test or MAT, minimum GPA of 3.0. Additional exam requirements/recommendations for international students: Required—TOEFL (minimum score 550 paper-based; 80 iBT).

Marquette University, Graduate School, Opus College of Engineering, Department of Civil, Construction and Environmental Engineering, Milwaukee, WI 53201-1881. Offers construction engineering and management (MS, PhD, Certificate); environmental engineering (MS, PhD); structural design (Certificate); structural engineering and structural mechanics (MS, PhD); transportation (Certificate); transportation engineering and materials (MS, PhD); waste and wastewater treatment processes (Certificate); water resources engineering (Certificate). Part-time and evening/weekend programs available. Terminal master's awarded for partial completion of doctoral program. *Degree requirements:* For master's, comprehensive exam (for some programs), thesis or alternative; for doctorate, thesis/dissertation. *Entrance requirements:* For master's, GRE General Test (recommended), minimum GPA of 3.0, official transcripts from all current and previous colleges/universities except Marquette, three letters of recommendation; for doctorate, GRE General Test, minimum GPA of 3.0, official transcripts from all current and previous colleges/universities except Marquette, three letters of recommendation, brief statement of purpose, submission of any English language publications authored by applicant (strongly recommended). Additional exam requirements/recommendations for international students: Required—TOEFL (minimum score 530 paper-based). Electronic applications accepted. *Faculty research:* Highway safety, highway performance, and intelligent transportation systems; surface mount technology; watershed management.

New Mexico Institute of Mining and Technology, Graduate Studies, Department of Civil and Environmental Engineering, Socorro, NM 87801. Offers environmental engineering (MS), including air quality engineering and science, hazardous waste engineering, water quality engineering and science. *Degree requirements:* For master's, thesis. *Entrance requirements:* For master's, GRE General Test. Additional exam requirements/recommendations for international students: Required—TOEFL (minimum score 540 paper-based). *Faculty research:* Air quality, hazardous waste management, wastewater management and treatment, site remediation.

Rutgers, The State University of New Jersey, New Brunswick, Graduate School-New Brunswick, Department of Environmental Sciences, Piscataway, NJ 08854-8097. Offers air pollution and resources (MS, PhD); aquatic biology (MS, PhD); aquatic chemistry (MS, PhD); atmospheric science (MS, PhD); chemistry and physics of aerosol and hydrosol systems (MS, PhD); environmental chemistry (MS, PhD); environmental microbiology (MS, PhD); environmental toxicology (PhD); exposure assessment (PhD); fate and effects of pollutants (MS, PhD); pollution prevention and control (MS, PhD); water and wastewater treatment (MS, PhD); water resources (MS, PhD). Terminal master's awarded for partial completion of doctoral program. *Degree requirements:* For master's, comprehensive exam, thesis or alternative, oral final exam; for doctorate, comprehensive exam, thesis/dissertation, thesis defense, qualifying exam. *Entrance requirements:* For master's and doctorate, GRE General Test. Additional exam requirements/recommendations for international students: Required—TOEFL. Electronic applications accepted. *Faculty research:* Biological waste treatment; contaminant fate and transport; air, soil and water quality.

Tufts University, School of Engineering, Department of Civil and Environmental Engineering, Medford, MA 02155. Offers bioengineering (ME, MS), including environmental technology; civil engineering (ME, MS, PhD), including geotechnical engineering, structural engineering, water diplomacy (PhD); environmental engineering (ME, MS, PhD), including environmental engineering and environmental sciences, environmental geotechnology, environmental health, environmental science and management, hazardous materials management, water diplomacy (PhD), water resources engineering. Part-time programs available. *Faculty:* 24 full-time (5 women), 6 part-time/adjunct (1 woman). *Students:* 66 full-time (29 women), 19 part-time (6 women); includes 5 minority (1 Black or African American, non-Hispanic/Latino; 2 Asian, non-Hispanic/Latino; 1 Hispanic/Latino; 1 Two or more races, non-Hispanic/Latino), 25 international. Average age 29. 166 applicants, 42% accepted, 27 enrolled. In 2014, 21 master's, 6 doctorates awarded. Terminal master's awarded for partial completion of doctoral program. *Degree requirements:* For master's, thesis or alternative; for doctorate, thesis/dissertation. *Entrance requirements:* For master's and doctorate, GRE General Test. Additional exam requirements/recommendations for international students: Required—TOEFL (minimum score 550 paper-based; 80 iBT), IELTS (minimum score 6.5). *Application deadline:* For fall admission, 1/15 priority date for domestic students, 1/15 for international students; for spring admission, 9/15 for domestic and international students. Applications are processed on a rolling basis. Application fee: $75. Electronic applications accepted. *Expenses: Tuition:* Full-time $45,590; part-time $1161 per credit hour. *Required fees:* $782. Full-time tuition and fees vary according to degree level, program and student level. Part-time tuition and fees vary according to course load. *Financial support:* Fellowships with full tuition reimbursements, research assistantships with full and partial tuition reimbursements, teaching assistantships with full and partial tuition reimbursements, Federal Work-Study, scholarships/grants, tuition waivers (partial), and unspecified assistantships available. Financial award application deadline: 5/15; financial award applicants required to submit FAFSA. *Faculty research:* Environmental and water resources engineering, environmental health, geotechnical and geoenvironmental engineering, structural engineering and mechanics, water diplomacy. *Unit head:* Dr. Kurt Pennell, Graduate Program Director. *Application contact:* Office of Graduate Admissions, 617-627-3395, E-mail: gradadmissions@tufts.edu.
Website: http://www.ase.tufts.edu/cee/.

University of Alaska Fairbanks, College of Engineering and Mines, Department of Civil and Environmental Engineering, Fairbanks, AK 99775-5900. Offers arctic engineering (MS); civil engineering (MCE, MS); design and construction management (Graduate Certificate); engineering and science management (MS), including engineering management, science management; environmental engineering (MS, PhD); environmental quality science (MS), including environmental contaminants, environmental science and management, water supply and waste treatment. Part-time programs available. *Faculty:* 10 full-time (2 women). *Students:* 14 full-time (7 women), 8 part-time (2 women); includes 4 minority (1 Black or African American, non-Hispanic/Latino; 1 American Indian or Alaska Native, non-Hispanic/Latino; 1 Hispanic/Latino; 1 Two or more races, non-Hispanic/Latino), 5 international. Average age 30. 19 applicants, 37% accepted, 5 enrolled. In 2014, 3 master's, 1 other advanced degree awarded. *Degree requirements:* For master's, comprehensive exam, thesis (for some programs), oral defense of project or thesis; for doctorate, comprehensive exam, thesis/dissertation. *Entrance requirements:* For master's, bachelor's degree from accredited institution with minimum cumulative undergraduate and major GPA of 3.0. Additional exam requirements/recommendations for international students: Required—TOEFL, IELTS. *Application deadline:* For fall admission, 6/1 for domestic students, 3/1 for international students; for spring admission, 10/15 for domestic students, 9/1 for international students. Applications are processed on a rolling basis. Application fee: $60. Electronic applications accepted. *Expenses:* Tuition, state resident: full-time $7614; part-time $423 per credit. Tuition, nonresident: full-time $15,552; part-time $864 per credit. Tuition and fees vary according to course level, course load and reciprocity agreements. *Financial support:* In 2014–15, 7 research assistantships with full tuition reimbursements (averaging $8,189 per year), 6 teaching assistantships with full tuition reimbursements (averaging $5,809 per year) were awarded; fellowships with full tuition reimbursements, career-related internships or fieldwork, Federal Work-Study, scholarships/grants, health care benefits, and unspecified assistantships also available. Support available to part-time students. Financial award application deadline: 7/1; financial award applicants required to submit FAFSA. *Faculty research:* Soils, structures, culvert thawing with solar power, pavement drainage, contaminant hydrogeology. *Unit head:* Dr. Robert Perkins, Department Chair, 907-474-7241, Fax: 907-474-6087, E-mail: fycee@uaf.edu. *Application contact:* Mary Kreta, Director of Admissions, 907-474-7500, Fax: 907-474-7097, E-mail: admissions@uaf.edu.
Website: http://cem.uaf.edu/cee.

University of Colorado Denver, College of Liberal Arts and Sciences, Department of Geography and Environmental Sciences, Denver, CO 80217. Offers environmental sciences (MS), including air quality, ecosystems, environmental health, environmental science education, geo-spatial analysis, hazardous waste, water quality. Part-time and evening/weekend programs available. *Faculty:* 11 full-time (4 women), 3 part-time/adjunct. *Students:* 39 full-time (29 women), 9 part-time (6 women); includes 6 minority (1 Black or African American, non-Hispanic/Latino; 1 Asian, non-Hispanic/Latino; 3 Hispanic/Latino; 1 Two or more races, non-Hispanic/Latino), 8 international. Average age 29. 40 applicants, 65% accepted, 14 enrolled. In 2014, 10 master's awarded. *Degree requirements:* For master's, thesis or alternative, 30 credits including 21 of core requirements and 9 of environmental science electives. *Entrance requirements:* For master's, GRE General Test, BA in one of the natural/physical sciences or engineering (or equivalent background); prerequisite coursework in calculus and physics (one semester each), general chemistry with lab and general biology with lab (two semesters each), three letters of recommendation. Additional exam requirements/recommendations for international students: Required—TOEFL (minimum score 537 paper-based; 75 iBT); Recommended—IELTS (minimum score 6.5). *Application deadline:* For fall admission, 1/20 for domestic and international students; for spring admission, 10/1 for domestic and international students. Application fee: $50 ($75 for international students). Electronic applications accepted. *Financial support:* In 2014–15, 4 students received support. Fellowships, research assistantships, teaching assistantships, Federal Work-Study, institutionally sponsored loans, scholarships/grants, and traineeships available. Financial award application deadline: 4/1; financial award applicants required to submit FAFSA. *Faculty research:* Air quality, environmental health, ecosystems, hazardous waste, water quality, geo-spatial analysis and environmental science education. *Unit head:* Dr. Frederick Chambers, Director of MS in Environmental Sciences Program, 303-556-2619, E-mail: frederick.chambers@ucdenver.edu. *Application contact:* Sue Eddleman, Program Assistant, 303-352-3698, E-mail: sue.eddleman@ucdenver.edu.
Website: http://www.ucdenver.edu/academics/colleges/CLAS/Departments/ges/Programs/MasterofScience/Pages/MasterofScience.aspx.

The University of Manchester, School of Materials, Manchester, United Kingdom. Offers advanced aerospace materials engineering (M Sc); advanced metallic systems (PhD); biomedical materials (M Phil, M Sc, PhD); ceramics and glass (M Phil, M Sc, PhD); composite materials (M Sc, PhD); corrosion and protection (M Phil, M Sc, PhD); materials (M Phil, PhD); metallic materials (M Phil, M Sc, PhD); nanostructural materials (M Phil, M Sc, PhD); paper science (M Phil, M Sc, PhD); polymer science and engineering (M Phil, M Sc, PhD); technical textiles (M Sc); textile design, fashion and management (M Phil, M Sc, PhD); textile science and technology (M Phil, M Sc, PhD); textiles (M Phil, PhD); textiles and fashion (M Ent).

University of New Haven, Graduate School, Tagliatela College of Engineering, Program in Environmental Engineering, West Haven, CT 06516-1916. Offers environmental engineering (MS); industrial and hazardous wastes (MS); water and wastewater treatment (MS); water resources (MS). Part-time and evening/weekend programs available. *Degree requirements:* For master's, thesis or alternative, research project. *Entrance requirements:* For master's, bachelor's degree in engineering. Additional exam requirements/recommendations for international students: Required—TOEFL (minimum score 75 iBT), IELTS, PTE (minimum score 50). Electronic applications accepted. Application fee is waived when completed online.

University of South Carolina, The Graduate School, Arnold School of Public Health, Department of Environmental Health Sciences, Program in Hazardous Materials Management, Columbia, SC 29208. Offers MPH, MSPH, PhD. *Degree requirements:* For master's, comprehensive exam, thesis (for some programs), practicum (MPH); for doctorate, one foreign language, comprehensive exam, thesis/dissertation. *Entrance requirements:* Additional exam requirements/recommendations for international students: Required—TOEFL (minimum score 570 paper-based). Electronic applications accepted. *Faculty research:* Environmental/human health protection; use and disposal of hazardous materials; site safety; exposure assessment; migration, fate and transformation of materials.

University of Southern California, Graduate School, Viterbi School of Engineering, Sonny Astani Department of Civil Engineering, Los Angeles, CA 90089. Offers applied mechanics (MS); civil engineering (MS, PhD); computer-aided engineering (ME, Graduate Certificate); construction management (MCM); engineering technology commercialization (Graduate Certificate); environmental engineering (MS, PhD); environmental quality management (ME); structural design (ME); sustainable cities (Graduate Certificate); transportation systems (MS, Graduate Certificate); water and waste management (MS). Part-time and evening/weekend programs available. Terminal master's awarded for partial completion of doctoral program. *Degree requirements:* For master's, thesis optional; for doctorate, thesis/dissertation. *Entrance requirements:* For master's and doctorate, GRE General Test. Additional exam requirements/recommendations for international students: Recommended—TOEFL. Electronic applications accepted. *Faculty research:* Geotechnical engineering, transportation engineering, structural engineering, construction management, environmental engineering, water resources.

Hydraulics

Auburn University, Graduate School, Ginn College of Engineering, Department of Civil Engineering, Auburn University, AL 36849. Offers construction engineering and management (MCE, MS, PhD); environmental engineering (MCE, MS, PhD); geotechnical/materials engineering (MCE, MS, PhD); hydraulics/hydrology (MCE, MS, PhD); structural engineering (MCE, MS, PhD); transportation engineering (MCE, MS, PhD). Part-time programs available. *Faculty:* 27 full-time (3 women), 1 part-time/adjunct (0 women). *Students:* 59 full-time (15 women), 46 part-time (6 women); includes 10 minority (4 Black or African American, non-Hispanic/Latino; 4 Asian, non-Hispanic/Latino; 2 Hispanic/Latino), 40 international. Average age 26. 134 applicants, 46% accepted, 20 enrolled. In 2014, 40 master's, 7 doctorates awarded. *Degree requirements:* For master's, project (MCE), thesis (MS); for doctorate, comprehensive exam, thesis/dissertation. *Entrance requirements:* For master's and doctorate, GRE General Test. *Application deadline:* For fall admission, 7/7 for domestic students; for spring admission, 11/24 for domestic students. Applications are processed on a rolling basis. Application fee: $50 ($60 for international students). Electronic applications accepted. *Expenses:* Tuition, state resident: full-time $8586; part-time $477 per credit hour. Tuition, nonresident: full-time $25,758; part-time $1431 per credit hour. *Required fees:* $804 per semester. Tuition and fees vary according to degree level and program. *Financial support:* Fellowships, research assistantships, teaching assistantships, and Federal Work-Study available. Support available to part-time students. Financial award application deadline: 3/15; financial award applicants required to submit FAFSA. *Unit head:* Dr. Andy Nowak, Head, 334-844-4320. *Application contact:* Dr. George Flowers, Dean of the Graduate School, 334-844-2125.

Drexel University, College of Engineering, Department of Civil, Architectural, and Environmental Engineering, Philadelphia, PA 19104-2875. Offers architectural / building systems engineering (PhD); architectural/building systems engineering (MS); civil engineering (MS, PhD); environmental engineering (MS, PhD); geotechnical, geoenvironmental and geosynthetics engineering (MS, PhD); hydraulics, hydrology and water resources engineering (MS, PhD); structures (MS). Part-time and evening/weekend programs available. *Degree requirements:* For master's, thesis optional; for doctorate, thesis/dissertation. *Entrance requirements:* For master's, minimum GPA of 3.0; for doctorate, minimum GPA of 3.5, MS in civil engineering. Additional exam requirements/recommendations for international students: Required—TOEFL. Electronic applications accepted. *Faculty research:* Structural dynamics, hazardous wastes, water resources, pavement materials, groundwater.

École Polytechnique de Montréal, Graduate Programs, Department of Civil, Geological and Mining Engineering, Montréal, QC H3C 3A7, Canada. Offers civil, geological and mining engineering (DESS); environmental engineering (M Eng, M Sc A, PhD); geotechnical engineering (M Eng, M Sc A, PhD); hydraulics engineering (M Eng, M Sc A, PhD); structural engineering (M Eng, M Sc A, PhD); transportation engineering (M Eng, M Sc A, PhD). Part-time programs available. *Degree requirements:* For master's, one foreign language, thesis; for doctorate, one foreign language, thesis/dissertation. *Entrance requirements:* For master's, minimum GPA of 2.75; for doctorate, minimum GPA of 3.0. *Faculty research:* Water resources management, characteristics of building materials, aging of dams, pollution control.

McGill University, Faculty of Graduate and Postdoctoral Studies, Faculty of Engineering, Department of Civil Engineering and Applied Mechanics, Montréal, QC H3A 2T5, Canada. Offers environmental engineering (M Eng, M Sc, PhD); fluid mechanics (M Sc); fluid mechanics and hydraulic engineering (M Eng, PhD); materials engineering (M Eng, PhD); rehabilitation of urban infrastructure (M Eng, PhD); soil behavior (M Eng, PhD); soil mechanics and foundations (M Eng, PhD); structures and structural mechanics (M Eng, PhD); water resources (M Sc); water resources engineering (M Eng, PhD).

Missouri University of Science and Technology, Graduate School, Department of Civil, Architectural, and Environmental Engineering, Rolla, MO 65409. Offers civil engineering (MS, DE, PhD); construction engineering (MS, DE, PhD); environmental engineering (MS); fluid mechanics (MS, DE, PhD); geotechnical engineering (MS, DE, PhD); hydrology and hydraulic engineering (MS, DE, PhD). Part-time and evening/weekend programs available. Terminal master's awarded for partial completion of doctoral program. *Degree requirements:* For master's, thesis optional; for doctorate, comprehensive exam, thesis/dissertation. *Entrance requirements:* For master's, GRE General Test (minimum combined score 1100), minimum GPA of 3.0; for doctorate, GRE General Test (minimum score: verbal and quantitative 400, writing 3.5), minimum GPA of 3.0. Additional exam requirements/recommendations for international students: Required—TOEFL. Electronic applications accepted. *Faculty research:* Earthquake engineering, structural optimization and control systems, structural health monitoring/damage detection, soil-structure interaction, soil mechanics and foundation engineering.

University of Colorado Denver, College of Engineering and Applied Science, Department of Civil Engineering, Denver, CO 80217. Offers civil engineering (EASPh D); civil engineering systems (PhD); environmental and sustainability engineering (MS, PhD); geographic information systems (MS); geotechnical engineering (MS, PhD); hydrology and hydraulics (MS, PhD); structural engineering (MS, PhD); transportation engineering (MS, PhD). Part-time and evening/weekend programs available. *Faculty:* 15 full-time (4 women), 11 part-time/adjunct (2 women). *Students:* 64 full-time (15 women), 43 part-time (8 women); includes 15 minority (3 Black or African American, non-Hispanic/Latino; 3 Asian, non-Hispanic/Latino; 6 Hispanic/Latino; 3 Two or more races, non-Hispanic/Latino), 34 international. Average age 32. 136 applicants, 54% accepted, 28 enrolled. In 2014, 35 master's, 9 doctorates awarded. *Degree requirements:* For master's, comprehensive exam, 30 credit hours, project or thesis; for doctorate, comprehensive exam, thesis/dissertation, 60 credit hours (30 of which are dissertation research). *Entrance requirements:* For master's, GRE, statement of purpose, transcripts, three references; for doctorate, GRE, statement of purpose, transcripts, references, letter of support from faculty stating willingness to serve as dissertation advisor and outlining plan for financial support. Additional exam requirements/recommendations for international students: Required—TOEFL (minimum score 537 paper-based; 75 iBT); Recommended—IELTS (minimum score 6.5). *Application deadline:* For fall admission, 5/1 for domestic students, 4/1 for international students; for spring admission, 10/1 for domestic students, 9/1 for international students; for summer admission, 2/15 for domestic students, 1/15 for international students. Application fee: $50 ($75 for international students). Electronic applications accepted. *Expenses:* Expenses: Contact institution. *Financial support:* In 2014–15, 26 students received support. Fellowships, research assistantships, teaching assistantships, career-related internships or fieldwork, Federal Work-Study, institutionally sponsored loans, scholarships/grants, traineeships, and unspecified assistantships available. Financial award application deadline: 4/1; financial award applicants required to submit FAFSA. *Faculty research:* Earthquake source physics, environmental biotechnology, hydrologic and hydraulic engineering, sustainability assessments, transportation energy use and greenhouse gas emissions. *Unit head:* Dr. Kevin Rens, Chair, 303-556-8017, E-mail: kevin.rens@ucdenver.edu. *Application contact:* Tammy Southern, Program Assistant, 303-556-6712, E-mail: tamara.southern@ucdenver.edu.
Website: http://www.ucdenver.edu/academics/colleges/Engineering/Programs/Civil-Engineering/Pages/CivilEngineering.aspx.

Structural Engineering

Auburn University, Graduate School, Ginn College of Engineering, Department of Civil Engineering, Auburn University, AL 36849. Offers construction engineering and management (MCE, MS, PhD); environmental engineering (MCE, MS, PhD); geotechnical/materials engineering (MCE, MS, PhD); hydraulics/hydrology (MCE, MS, PhD); structural engineering (MCE, MS, PhD); transportation engineering (MCE, MS, PhD). Part-time programs available. *Faculty:* 27 full-time (3 women), 1 part-time/adjunct (0 women). *Students:* 59 full-time (15 women), 46 part-time (6 women); includes 10 minority (4 Black or African American, non-Hispanic/Latino; 4 Asian, non-Hispanic/Latino; 2 Hispanic/Latino), 40 international. Average age 26. 134 applicants, 46% accepted, 20 enrolled. In 2014, 40 master's, 7 doctorates awarded. *Degree requirements:* For master's, project (MCE), thesis (MS); for doctorate, comprehensive exam, thesis/dissertation. *Entrance requirements:* For master's and doctorate, GRE General Test. *Application deadline:* For fall admission, 7/7 for domestic students; for spring admission, 11/24 for domestic students. Applications are processed on a rolling basis. Application fee: $50 ($60 for international students). Electronic applications accepted. *Expenses:* Tuition, state resident: full-time $8586; part-time $477 per credit hour. Tuition, nonresident: full-time $25,758; part-time $1431 per credit hour. *Required fees:* $804 per semester. Tuition and fees vary according to degree level and program. *Financial support:* Fellowships, research assistantships, teaching assistantships, and Federal Work-Study available. Support available to part-time students. Financial award application deadline: 3/15; financial award applicants required to submit FAFSA. *Unit head:* Dr. Andy Nowak, Head, 334-844-4320. *Application contact:* Dr. George Flowers, Dean of the Graduate School, 334-844-2125.

California State University, Northridge, Graduate Studies, College of Engineering and Computer Science, Department of Civil Engineering and Applied Mechanics, Northridge, CA 91330. Offers engineering (MS), including structural engineering. Part-time and evening/weekend programs available. *Students:* 21 full-time (3 women), 39 part-time (8 women); includes 18 minority (5 Asian, non-Hispanic/Latino; 9 Hispanic/Latino; 4 Two or more races, non-Hispanic/Latino), 15 international. Average age 26. *Degree requirements:* For master's, thesis. *Entrance requirements:* Additional exam requirements/recommendations for international students: Required—TOEFL. *Application deadline:* For fall admission, 11/30 for domestic students. Application fee: $55. *Expenses: Required fees:* $12,402. *Financial support:* Teaching assistantships available. Financial award application deadline: 3/1. *Faculty research:* Composite study. *Unit head:* Dr. Nazaret Dermendjian, Chair, 818-677-2166.
Website: http://www.csun.edu/~ceam/.

Cornell University, Graduate School, Graduate Fields of Engineering, Field of Civil and Environmental Engineering, Ithaca, NY 14853-0001. Offers engineering management (M Eng, MS, PhD); environmental engineering (M Eng, MS, PhD); environmental fluid mechanics and hydrology (M Eng, MS, PhD); environmental systems engineering (M Eng, MS, PhD); geotechnical engineering (M Eng, MS, PhD); remote sensing (M Eng, MS, PhD); structural engineering (M Eng, MS, PhD); structural mechanics (M Eng, MS); transportation engineering (MS, PhD); transportation systems engineering (M Eng); water resource systems (M Eng, MS, PhD). Terminal master's awarded for partial completion of doctoral program. *Degree requirements:* For master's, thesis (MS); for doctorate, comprehensive exam, thesis/dissertation. *Entrance requirements:* For master's and doctorate, GRE General Test (recommended), 2 letters of recommendation. Additional exam requirements/recommendations for international students: Required—TOEFL (minimum score 600 paper-based; 77 iBT). Electronic applications accepted. *Faculty research:* Environmental engineering, geotechnical engineering, remote sensing, environmental fluid mechanics and hydrology, structural engineering.

Drexel University, College of Engineering, Department of Civil, Architectural, and Environmental Engineering, Philadelphia, PA 19104-2875. Offers architectural / building systems engineering (PhD); architectural/building systems engineering (MS); civil engineering (MS, PhD); environmental engineering (MS, PhD); geotechnical, geoenvironmental and geosynthetics engineering (MS, PhD); hydraulics, hydrology and water resources engineering (MS, PhD); structures (MS). Part-time and evening/weekend programs available. *Degree requirements:* For master's, thesis optional; for doctorate, thesis/dissertation. *Entrance requirements:* For master's, minimum GPA of 3.0; for doctorate, minimum GPA of 3.5, MS in civil engineering. Additional exam requirements/recommendations for international students: Required—TOEFL. Electronic applications accepted. *Faculty research:* Structural dynamics, hazardous wastes, water resources, pavement materials, groundwater.

École Polytechnique de Montréal, Graduate Programs, Department of Civil, Geological and Mining Engineering, Montréal, QC H3C 3A7, Canada. Offers civil, geological and mining engineering (DESS); environmental engineering (M Eng, M Sc A, PhD); geotechnical engineering (M Eng, M Sc A, PhD); hydraulics engineering (M Eng, M Sc A, PhD); structural engineering (M Eng, M Sc A, PhD); transportation engineering (M Eng, M Sc A, PhD). Part-time programs available. *Degree requirements:* For master's, one foreign language, thesis; for doctorate, one foreign language, thesis/dissertation. *Entrance requirements:* For master's, minimum GPA of 2.75; for doctorate, minimum GPA of 3.0. *Faculty research:* Water resources management, characteristics of building materials, aging of dams, pollution control.

George Mason University, Volgenau School of Engineering, Sid and Reva Dewberry Department of Civil, Environmental, and Infrastructure Engineering, Fairfax, VA 22030. Offers construction project management (MS); environmental and water resources engineering (MS); geotechnical, construction, and structural engineering (M Eng); transportation engineering (MS, PhD). *Faculty:* 12 full-time (4 women), 16 part-time/

adjunct (3 women). *Students:* 28 full-time (7 women), 51 part-time (13 women); includes 25 minority (12 Black or African American, non-Hispanic/Latino; 8 Asian, non-Hispanic/Latino; 5 Hispanic/Latino), 14 international. Average age 30. 90 applicants, 58% accepted, 25 enrolled. In 2014, 28 master's, 3 doctorates awarded. *Degree requirements:* For master's, thesis (for some programs), 30 credits, departmental seminars; for doctorate, thesis/dissertation, qualifying exams. *Entrance requirements:* For master's, GRE, photocopy of passport; 2 official college transcripts; resume; official bank statement; proof of financial support; expanded goals statement; self-evaluation form; BS in engineering or other related science; 3 letters of recommendation; for doctorate, GRE (for those who received degree outside of the U.S.), photocopy of passport; 2 official college transcripts; resume; official bank statement; proof of financial support; expanded goals statement; self-evaluation form; baccalaureate degree in engineering or related science; master's degree (preferred); 3 letters of recommendation. Additional exam requirements/recommendations for international students: Required—TOEFL (minimum score 575 paper-based; 80 iBT), IELTS (minimum score 6.5), PTE. *Application deadline:* For fall admission, 1/15 priority date for domestic students; for spring admission, 8/1 priority date for domestic students. Application fee: $65 ($80 for international students). Electronic applications accepted. *Expenses:* Expenses: Contact institution. *Financial support:* In 2014–15, 19 students received support, including 1 fellowship (averaging $5,000 per year), 9 research assistantships with full and partial tuition reimbursements available (averaging $23,846 per year), 10 teaching assistantships with full and partial tuition reimbursements available (averaging $21,200 per year); career-related internships or fieldwork, Federal Work-Study, scholarships/grants, unspecified assistantships, and health care benefits (for full-time research or teaching assistantship recipients) also available. Support available to part-time students. Financial award application deadline: 3/1; financial award applicants required to submit FAFSA. *Faculty research:* Evolutionary design, infrastructure security, intelligent transportation systems, national transportation networks, water quality modeling. *Total annual research expenditures:* $159,347. *Unit head:* Dr. Deborah J. Goodings, Chair, 703-993-1675, Fax: 703-993-9790, E-mail: goodings@gmu.edu. *Application contact:* Kristin Amaya, Administrative Assistant, 703-993-1675, Fax: 703-993-9790, E-mail: kfairch1@gmu.edu.
Website: http://civil.gmu.edu/.

Illinois Institute of Technology, Graduate College, Armour College of Engineering, Department of Civil, Architectural and Environmental Engineering, Chicago, IL 60616. Offers architectural engineering (M Arch E); civil engineering (MS, PhD), including architectural engineering (MS), construction engineering and management (MS), geoenvironmental engineering (MS), geotechnical engineering (MS), structural engineering (MS), transportation engineering (MS); construction engineering and management (MCEM); environmental engineering (M Env E, MS, PhD); geoenvironmental engineering (M Geoenv E); geotechnical engineering (MGE); infrastructure engineering and management (MPW); structural engineering (MSE); transportation engineering (M Trans E). Part-time and evening/weekend programs available. Postbaccalaureate distance learning degree programs offered (minimal on-campus study). *Faculty:* 12 full-time (1 woman), 15 part-time/adjunct (1 woman). *Students:* 165 full-time (48 women), 54 part-time (11 women); includes 31 minority (2 Black or African American, non-Hispanic/Latino; 21 Asian, non-Hispanic/Latino; 7 Hispanic/Latino; 1 Native Hawaiian or other Pacific Islander, non-Hispanic/Latino), 157 international. Average age 29. 1,039 applicants, 42% accepted, 82 enrolled. In 2014, 94 master's, 7 doctorates awarded. Terminal master's awarded for partial completion of doctoral program. *Degree requirements:* For master's, thesis (for some programs); for doctorate, comprehensive exam, thesis/dissertation. *Entrance requirements:* For master's, GRE General Test (minimum score 900 Quantitative and Verbal, 2.5 Analytical Writing), minimum undergraduate GPA of 3.0; for doctorate, GRE General Test (minimum score 1000 Quantitative and Verbal, 3.0 Analytical Writing), minimum undergraduate GPA of 3.0. Additional exam requirements/recommendations for international students: Required—TOEFL (minimum score 550 paper-based; 80 iBT). *Application deadline:* For fall admission, 5/1 for domestic and international students; for spring admission, 10/15 for domestic and international students. Applications are processed on a rolling basis. Application fee: $50. Electronic applications accepted. *Expenses: Tuition:* Full-time $22,500; part-time $1250 per credit hour. *Required fees:* $30 per course. $260 per semester. One-time fee: $235. Tuition and fees vary according to course load and program. *Financial support:* Fellowships with full and partial tuition reimbursements, research assistantships with full and partial tuition reimbursements, teaching assistantships with full and partial tuition reimbursements, Federal Work-Study, institutionally sponsored loans, scholarships/grants, health care benefits, tuition waivers (partial), and unspecified assistantships available. Support available to part-time students. Financial award applicants required to submit FAFSA. *Faculty research:* Structural, architectural, geotechnical and geoenvironmental engineering; construction engineering and management; transportation engineering; environmental engineering and public works. *Unit head:* Dr. Gongkang Fu, Professor and Chairman, 312-567-3540, Fax: 312-567-3519, E-mail: gfu2@iit.edu. *Application contact:* Rishab Malhotra, Director, Graduate Admission, 866-472-3448, Fax: 312-567-3138, E-mail: inquiry.grad@iit.edu.
Website: http://engineering.iit.edu/caee.

Instituto Tecnologico de Santo Domingo, Graduate School, Area of Engineering, Santo Domingo, Dominican Republic. Offers construction administration (MS, Certificate); data telecommunications (M Eng, MS, Certificate); industrial engineering (M Eng, Certificate); industrial management (M Mgmt); information technology (Certificate); maintenance engineering (M Eng); occupational hazard prevention (M Mgmt); production management (Certificate); quantitative methods (Certificate); sanitary and environmental engineering (M Eng); structural engineering (M Eng); systems engineering and electronic data processing (Certificate); transportation (Certificate).

Iowa State University of Science and Technology, Department of Civil and Construction Engineering, Ames, IA 50011. Offers civil engineering (MS, PhD), including civil engineering materials, construction engineering and management, environmental engineering, geometronics, geotechnical engineering, structural engineering, transportation engineering. *Degree requirements:* For master's, thesis or alternative; for doctorate, thesis/dissertation. *Entrance requirements:* For master's and doctorate, GRE General Test. Additional exam requirements/recommendations for international students: Required—TOEFL (minimum score 550 paper-based; 82 iBT), IELTS (minimum score 6.5). Electronic applications accepted.

Kansas State University, Graduate School, College of Engineering, Department of Civil Engineering, Manhattan, KS 66506. Offers civil engineering (MS, PhD); environmental engineering (MS, PhD); geotechnical engineering (MS, PhD); structural engineering (MS, PhD); transportation engineering (MS, PhD); water resources engineering (MS, PhD). Part-time and evening/weekend programs available. Postbaccalaureate distance learning degree programs offered (no on-campus study). *Faculty:* 14 full-time (4 women), 3 part-time/adjunct (1 woman). *Students:* 37 full-time (12 women), 37 part-time (9 women); includes 6 minority (3 Black or African American, non-Hispanic/Latino; 3 Hispanic/Latino), 23 international. Average age 30. 62 applicants, 39% accepted, 10 enrolled. In 2014, 14 master's, 4 doctorates awarded. *Degree requirements:* For master's, thesis or alternative; for doctorate, thesis/dissertation. *Entrance requirements:* For master's, GRE General Test, bachelor's degree or course work in related engineering fields; for doctorate, GRE General Test. Additional exam requirements/recommendations for international students: Required—TOEFL (minimum score 550 paper-based; 79 iBT). *Application deadline:* For fall admission, 2/1 priority date for domestic students, 1/1 priority date for international students; for spring admission, 8/1 priority date for domestic and international students. Applications are processed on a rolling basis. Application fee: $50 ($75 for international students). Electronic applications accepted. *Financial support:* In 2014–15, 19 research assistantships with partial tuition reimbursements (averaging $13,431 per year), 12 teaching assistantships with partial tuition reimbursements (averaging $15,058 per year) were awarded; institutionally sponsored loans and scholarships/grants also available. Support available to part-time students. Financial award application deadline: 3/1; financial award applicants required to submit FAFSA. *Faculty research:* Transportation and materials engineering, water resources engineering, environmental engineering, geotechnical engineering, structural engineering. *Total annual research expenditures:* $2.4 million. *Unit head:* Dr. Robert Stokes, Head, 785-532-1595, Fax: 785-532-7717, E-mail: drbobb@k-state.edu. *Application contact:* Dr. Dunja Peric, Graduate Coordinator, 785-532-2468, Fax: 785-532-7717, E-mail: peric@k-state.edu.
Website: http://www.ce.ksu.edu/.

Louisiana State University and Agricultural & Mechanical College, Graduate School, College of Engineering, Department of Civil and Environmental Engineering, Baton Rouge, LA 70803. Offers environmental engineering (MSCE, PhD); geotechnical engineering (MSCE, PhD); structural engineering and mechanics (MSCE, PhD); transportation engineering (MSCE, PhD); water resources (MSCE, PhD). Part-time programs available. *Faculty:* 26 full-time (1 woman). *Students:* 90 full-time (24 women), 28 part-time (6 women); includes 12 minority (5 Black or African American, non-Hispanic/Latino; 1 American Indian or Alaska Native, non-Hispanic/Latino; 5 Asian, non-Hispanic/Latino; 1 Two or more races, non-Hispanic/Latino), 67 international. Average age 30. 147 applicants, 50% accepted, 23 enrolled. In 2014, 26 master's, 8 doctorates awarded. *Degree requirements:* For master's, thesis optional; for doctorate, one foreign language, thesis/dissertation. *Entrance requirements:* For master's and doctorate, GRE General Test, minimum GPA of 3.0. Additional exam requirements/recommendations for international students: Required—TOEFL (minimum score 550 paper-based; 79 IBT), IELTS (minimum score 6.5), or PTE (minimum score 59). *Application deadline:* For fall admission, 1/1 priority date for domestic students, 5/15 for international students; for spring admission, 10/15 for domestic and international students; for summer admission, 5/15 for domestic and international students. Applications are processed on a rolling basis. Application fee: $50 ($70 for international students). Electronic applications accepted. *Financial support:* In 2014–15, 88 students received support, including 7 fellowships with full and partial tuition reimbursements available (averaging $26,784 per year), 59 research assistantships with full and partial tuition reimbursements available (averaging $16,992 per year), 13 teaching assistantships with full and partial tuition reimbursements available (averaging $16,290 per year); career-related internships or fieldwork, institutionally sponsored loans, scholarships/grants, and health care benefits also available. Financial award application deadline: 3/1; financial award applicants required to submit FAFSA. *Faculty research:* Mechanics and structures, environmental, geotechnical transportation, water resources. *Total annual research expenditures:* $3.2 million. *Unit head:* Dr. George Z. Voyiadjis, Chair/Professor, 225-578-8442, Fax: 225-578-8652, E-mail: voyaidjis@lsu.edu. *Application contact:* Dr. Ayman Ikeli, Professor, 225-578-7048, E-mail: aokeli@lsu.edu.
Website: http://www.cee.lsu.edu/.

Marquette University, Graduate School, Opus College of Engineering, Department of Civil, Construction and Environmental Engineering, Milwaukee, WI 53201-1881. Offers construction engineering and management (MS, PhD, Certificate); environmental engineering (MS, PhD); structural design (Certificate); structural engineering and structural mechanics (MS, PhD); transportation (Certificate); transportation engineering and materials (MS, PhD); waste and wastewater treatment processes (Certificate); water resources engineering (Certificate). Part-time and evening/weekend programs available. Terminal master's awarded for partial completion of doctoral program. *Degree requirements:* For master's, comprehensive exam (for some programs), thesis or alternative; for doctorate, thesis/dissertation. *Entrance requirements:* For master's, GRE General Test (recommended), minimum GPA of 3.0, official transcripts from all current and previous colleges/universities except Marquette, three letters of recommendation; for doctorate, GRE General Test, minimum GPA of 3.0, official transcripts from all current and previous colleges/universities except Marquette, three letters of recommendation, brief statement of purpose, submission of any English language publications authored by applicant (strongly recommended). Additional exam requirements/recommendations for international students: Required—TOEFL (minimum score 530 paper-based). Electronic applications accepted. *Faculty research:* Highway safety, highway performance, and intelligent transportation systems; surface mount technology; watershed management.

Massachusetts Institute of Technology, School of Engineering, Department of Civil and Environmental Engineering, Cambridge, MA 02139. Offers biological oceanography (PhD, Sc D); chemical oceanography (PhD, Sc D); civil and environmental engineering (M Eng, SM, PhD, Sc D); civil and environmental systems (PhD, Sc D); civil engineering (PhD, Sc D, CE); coastal engineering (PhD, Sc D); construction engineering and management (PhD, Sc D); environmental biology (PhD, Sc D); environmental chemistry (PhD, Sc D); environmental engineering (PhD, Sc D); environmental fluid mechanics (PhD, Sc D); geotechnical and geoenvironmental engineering (PhD, Sc D); hydrology (PhD, Sc D); information technology (PhD, Sc D); oceanographic engineering (PhD, Sc D); structures and materials (PhD, Sc D); transportation (PhD, Sc D); SM/MBA. *Faculty:* 34 full-time (8 women), 1 part-time/adjunct (0 women). *Students:* 216 full-time (82 women); includes 25 minority (1 Black or African American, non-Hispanic/Latino; 10 Asian, non-Hispanic/Latino; 8 Hispanic/Latino; 6 Two or more races, non-Hispanic/Latino), 117 international. Average age 26. 565 applicants, 22% accepted, 85 enrolled. In 2014, 76 master's, 18 doctorates awarded. *Degree requirements:* For master's and CE, thesis; for doctorate, comprehensive exam, thesis/dissertation. *Entrance requirements:* For master's and doctorate, GRE General Test. Additional exam requirements/recommendations for international students: Required—TOEFL (minimum score 577 paper-based; 100 iBT), IELTS (minimum score 7). *Application deadline:* For fall admission, 12/15 for domestic and international students. Application fee: $75. Electronic applications accepted. *Expenses: Tuition:* Full-time $44,720; part-time $699 per unit. *Required fees:* $296. *Financial support:* In 2014–15, 170 students received support, including 32 fellowships (averaging $32,800 per year), 132 research assistantships (averaging $33,800 per year), 13 teaching assistantships (averaging $32,900 per year); Federal Work-Study, institutionally sponsored loans, scholarships/grants, traineeships, health care benefits, and unspecified assistantships also available. Financial award application deadline: 4/15; financial award applicants required to submit FAFSA. *Faculty research:* Environmental chemistry, environmental fluid mechanics and coastal engineering, environmental microbiology, geotechnical engineering and geomechanics, hydrology and hydroclimatology, infrastructure systems, mechanics of materials and structures, transportation systems. *Total annual research expenditures:* $22.9 million. *Unit head:* Prof. Markus Buehler, Department Head, 617-324-6488.

Structural Engineering

Application contact: Graduate Admissions Coordinator, 617-253-7119, E-mail: cee-admissions@mit.edu.
Website: http://cee.mit.edu/.

McGill University, Faculty of Graduate and Postdoctoral Studies, Faculty of Engineering, Department of Civil Engineering and Applied Mechanics, Montréal, QC H3A 2T5, Canada. Offers environmental engineering (M Eng, M Sc, PhD); fluid mechanics (M Sc); fluid mechanics and hydraulic engineering (M Eng, PhD); materials engineering (M Eng, PhD); rehabilitation of urban infrastructure (M Eng, PhD); soil behavior (M Eng, PhD); soil mechanics and foundations (M Eng, PhD); structures and structural mechanics (M Eng, PhD); water resources (M Sc); water resources engineering (M Eng, PhD).

Northwestern University, McCormick School of Engineering and Applied Science, Department of Civil and Environmental Engineering, Evanston, IL 60208-3109. Offers environmental engineering and science (MS, PhD); geotechnical engineering (MS, PhD); mechanics of materials and solids (MS, PhD); project management (MS, PhD); structural engineering and materials (MS, PhD); transportation systems analysis and planning (MS, PhD). MS and PhD admissions and degrees offered through The Graduate School. Part-time programs available. *Faculty:* 19 full-time (2 women). *Students:* 118 full-time (36 women), 5 part-time (2 women); includes 7 minority (3 Black or African American, non-Hispanic/Latino; 2 Asian, non-Hispanic/Latino; 1 Hispanic/Latino; 1 Two or more races, non-Hispanic/Latino), 95 international. Average age 24. 412 applicants, 36% accepted, 49 enrolled. In 2014, 42 master's, 10 doctorates awarded. Terminal master's awarded for partial completion of doctoral program. *Degree requirements:* For master's, thesis (for some programs); for doctorate, comprehensive exam, thesis/dissertation. *Entrance requirements:* For master's and doctorate, GRE General Test, minimum 2 letters of recommendation, transcripts from all academic institutions attended. Additional exam requirements/recommendations for international students: Required—TOEFL (minimum score 577 paper-based; 90 iBT), IELTS (minimum score 7). *Application deadline:* For fall admission, 12/31 for domestic and international students; for winter admission, 11/15 for domestic and international students; for spring admission, 1/15 for domestic and international students. Application fee: $95. Electronic applications accepted. *Financial support:* Fellowships with full tuition reimbursements, research assistantships with full tuition reimbursements, teaching assistantships with full tuition reimbursements, career-related internships or fieldwork, institutionally sponsored loans, health care benefits, and unspecified assistantships available. Financial award application deadline: 12/31; financial award applicants required to submit FAFSA. *Faculty research:* Environmental engineering and science, geotechnics, mechanics of materials and solids, structural engineering and materials, transportation systems analysis and planning. *Total annual research expenditures:* $5.8 million. *Unit head:* Dr. Jianmin Qu, Chair, 847-467-4528, Fax: 847-491-4011, E-mail: j-qu@northwestern.edu. *Application contact:* Dr. David Corr, Academic Coordinator, 847-467-0890, Fax: 847-491-4011, E-mail: d-corr@u.northwestern.edu.
Website: http://www.civil.northwestern.edu/.

Norwich University, College of Graduate and Continuing Studies, Master of Civil Engineering Program, Northfield, VT 05663. Offers construction management engineering (MCE); environmental/water resources engineering (MCE); geotechnical engineering (MCE); structural engineering (MCE). Evening/weekend programs available. Postbaccalaureate distance learning degree programs offered (minimal on-campus study). *Faculty:* 14 part-time/adjunct (2 women). *Students:* 111 full-time (17 women); includes 28 minority (16 Black or African American, non-Hispanic/Latino; 2 American Indian or Alaska Native, non-Hispanic/Latino; 7 Asian, non-Hispanic/Latino; 3 Hispanic/Latino). Average age 36. 61 applicants, 100% accepted, 42 enrolled. In 2014, 57 master's awarded. *Entrance requirements:* For master's, minimum undergraduate GPA of 2.75. Additional exam requirements/recommendations for international students: Required—TOEFL (minimum score 550 paper-based; 80 iBT), IELTS (minimum score 6.5). *Application deadline:* For fall admission, 8/8 for domestic and international students; for spring admission, 2/16 for domestic and international students. Applications are processed on a rolling basis. Electronic applications accepted. *Expenses:* Expenses: Contact institution. *Financial support:* In 2014–15, 27 students received support. Scholarships/grants available. Financial award applicants required to submit FAFSA. *Unit head:* Dr. Thomas Descoteaux, Program Director, 802-485-2730, Fax: 802-485-2533, E-mail: tdescote@norwich.edu. *Application contact:* Rija Ramahatra, Associate Program Director, 802-485-2892, Fax: 802-485-2533, E-mail: ramahatr@norwich.edu.
Website: http://online.norwich.edu/degree-programs/masters/master-civil-engineering/overview.

Ohio University, Graduate College, Russ College of Engineering and Technology, Department of Civil Engineering, Athens, OH 45701-2979. Offers civil engineering (PhD); construction engineering and management (MS); environmental (MS); geotechnical and geoenvironmental (MS); mechanics (MS); structures (MS); transportation (MS); water resources (MS). Part-time programs available. *Degree requirements:* For master's, comprehensive exam (for some programs), thesis or alternative; for doctorate, comprehensive exam, thesis/dissertation. *Entrance requirements:* For master's, GRE General Test, minimum GPA of 3.0, 3 letters of recommendation; for doctorate, GRE General Test. Additional exam requirements/recommendations for international students: Required—TOEFL (minimum score 550 paper-based; 80 iBT) or IELTS (minimum score 6.5). Electronic applications accepted. *Faculty research:* Noise abatement, materials and environment, highway infrastructure, subsurface investigation (pavements, pipes, bridges).

Penn State Harrisburg, Graduate School, School of Science, Engineering and Technology, Middletown, PA 17057-4898. Offers computer science (MS); electrical engineering (M Eng, MS); engineering management (MPS); engineering science (M Eng); environmental engineering (M Eng); structural engineering (Certificate). Part-time and evening/weekend programs available. *Unit head:* Dr. Mukund S. Kulkarni, Chancellor, 717-948-6105, Fax: 717-948-6452, E-mail: msk5@psu.edu. *Application contact:* Robert W. Coffman, Jr., Director of Enrollment Management, Admissions, 717-948-6250, Fax: 717-948-6325, E-mail: ric1@psu.edu.
Website: http://harrisburg.psu.edu/science-engineering-technology.

Pontificia Universidad Catolica Madre y Maestra, Graduate School, Faculty of Engineering Sciences, Santiago, Dominican Republic. Offers earthquake engineering (ME); logistics management (ME).

Southern Illinois University Edwardsville, Graduate School, School of Engineering, Department of Civil Engineering, Program in Structural Engineering, Edwardsville, IL 62026. Offers MS. Part-time and evening/weekend programs available. *Degree requirements:* For master's, thesis (for some programs), research paper. *Entrance requirements:* For master's, minimum undergraduate GPA of 2.75 in science, math, and engineering courses. Additional exam requirements/recommendations for international students: Required—TOEFL (minimum score 550 paper-based, 79 iBT), IELTS (minimum score 6.5), Michigan Test of English Language Proficiency or PTE. *Application deadline:* For fall admission, 7/18 for domestic students, 6/1 for international students; for spring admission, 12/12 for domestic students, 10/1 for international students; for summer admission, 4/24 for domestic students, 3/1 for international students. Applications are processed on a rolling basis. Application fee: $30. Electronic applications accepted. *Expenses:* Tuition, state resident: full-time $5026. Tuition, nonresident: full-time $12,566. *International tuition:* $25,136 full-time. *Required fees:* $1682. Tuition and fees vary according to course load, campus/location and program. *Financial support:* Institutionally sponsored loans, scholarships/grants, and unspecified assistantships available. Financial award application deadline: 3/1; financial award applicants required to submit FAFSA. *Unit head:* Dr. Jim Zhou, Chair, 618-650-2533, E-mail: jzhou@siue.edu. *Application contact:* Dr. Ryan Fries, Director, 618-650-5026, E-mail: rfries@siue.edu.
Website: http://www.siue.edu/engineering/civilengineering.

Southern Methodist University, Bobby B. Lyle School of Engineering, Department of Environmental and Civil Engineering, Dallas, TX 75275-0340. Offers air pollution control and atmospheric sciences (PhD); civil engineering (MS); environmental engineering (MS); environmental science (MS); structural engineering (PhD); sustainability and development (MA); water and wastewater engineering (PhD). Part-time and evening/weekend programs available. Postbaccalaureate distance learning degree programs offered (no on-campus study). Terminal master's awarded for partial completion of doctoral program. *Degree requirements:* For master's, thesis optional; for doctorate, thesis/dissertation, oral and written qualifying exams. *Entrance requirements:* For master's, GRE General Test, minimum GPA of 3.0 in last 2 years; bachelor's degree in engineering, mathematics, or sciences; for doctorate, GRE, BS and MS in related field, minimum GPA of 3.3. Additional exam requirements/recommendations for international students: Required—TOEFL. Electronic applications accepted. *Faculty research:* Human and environmental health effects of endocrine disrupters, development of air pollution control systems for diesel engines, structural analysis and design, modeling and design of waste treatment systems.

Stanford University, School of Engineering, Department of Civil and Environmental Engineering, Stanford, CA 94305-9991. Offers atmosphere and energy (MS, PhD); construction (MS), including construction engineering and management, design-construction integration, sustainable design and construction; environmental engineering and science (MS, PhD, Eng); environmental fluid mechanics and hydrology (PhD); geomechanics (MS); structural engineering (MS). Terminal master's awarded for partial completion of doctoral program. *Degree requirements:* For doctorate, thesis/dissertation, qualifying exam; for Eng, thesis. *Entrance requirements:* For master's, doctorate, and Eng, GRE General Test. Additional exam requirements/recommendations for international students: Required—TOEFL. Electronic applications accepted. *Expenses: Tuition:* Full-time $44,184; part-time $982 per credit hour. *Required fees:* $191.

Stevens Institute of Technology, Graduate School, Charles V. Schaefer Jr. School of Engineering, Department of Civil, Environmental, and Ocean Engineering, Program in Civil Engineering, Hoboken, NJ 07030. Offers civil engineering (PhD); geotechnical engineering (Certificate); geotechnical/geoenvironmental engineering (M Eng, Engr); hydrologic modeling (M Eng); stormwater management (M Eng); structural engineering (M Eng, Engr); water resources engineering (M Eng). *Degree requirements:* For master's, thesis optional; for doctorate, variable foreign language requirement, thesis/dissertation; for other advanced degree, project or thesis. *Entrance requirements:* For doctorate, GRE. Additional exam requirements/recommendations for international students: Required—TOEFL. Electronic applications accepted.

Tufts University, School of Engineering, Department of Civil and Environmental Engineering, Medford, MA 02155. Offers bioengineering (ME, MS), including environmental technology; civil engineering (ME, MS, PhD), including geotechnical engineering, structural engineering, water diplomacy (PhD); environmental engineering (ME, MS, PhD), including environmental engineering and environmental sciences, environmental geotechnology, environmental health, environmental science and management, hazardous materials management, water diplomacy (PhD), water resources engineering. Part-time programs available. *Faculty:* 24 full-time (5 women), 6 part-time/adjunct (1 woman). *Students:* 66 full-time (29 women), 19 part-time (6 women); includes 5 minority (1 Black or African American, non-Hispanic/Latino; 2 Asian, non-Hispanic/Latino; 1 Hispanic/Latino; 1 Two or more races, non-Hispanic/Latino), 25 international. Average age 29. 166 applicants, 42% accepted, 27 enrolled. In 2014, 21 master's, 6 doctorates awarded. Terminal master's awarded for partial completion of doctoral program. *Degree requirements:* For master's, thesis or alternative; for doctorate, thesis/dissertation. *Entrance requirements:* For master's and doctorate, GRE General Test. Additional exam requirements/recommendations for international students: Required—TOEFL (minimum score 550 paper-based; 80 iBT), IELTS (minimum score 6.5). *Application deadline:* For fall admission, 1/15 priority date for domestic students, 1/15 for international students; for spring admission, 9/15 for domestic and international students. Applications are processed on a rolling basis. Application fee: $75. Electronic applications accepted. *Expenses: Tuition:* Full-time $45,590; part-time $1161 per credit hour. *Required fees:* $782. Full-time tuition and fees vary according to degree level, program and student level. Part-time tuition and fees vary according to course load. *Financial support:* Fellowships with full tuition reimbursements, research assistantships with full and partial tuition reimbursements, teaching assistantships with full and partial tuition reimbursements, Federal Work-Study, scholarships/grants, tuition waivers (partial), and unspecified assistantships available. Financial award application deadline: 5/15; financial award applicants required to submit FAFSA. *Faculty research:* Environmental and water resources engineering, environmental health, geotechnical and geoenvironmental engineering, structural engineering and mechanics, water diplomacy. *Unit head:* Dr. Kurt Pennell, Graduate Program Director. *Application contact:* Office of Graduate Admissions, 617-627-3395, E-mail: gradadmissions@tufts.edu.
Website: http://www.ase.tufts.edu/cee/.

University at Buffalo, the State University of New York, Graduate School, School of Engineering and Applied Sciences, Department of Civil, Structural, and Environmental Engineering, Buffalo, NY 14260. Offers civil engineering (ME, MS, PhD); engineering science (MS). Part-time programs available. Postbaccalaureate distance learning degree programs offered (minimal on-campus study). *Faculty:* 31 full-time (5 women), 1 part-time/adjunct (0 women). *Students:* 166 full-time (43 women), 16 part-time (3 women); includes 15 minority (2 Black or African American, non-Hispanic/Latino; 1 American Indian or Alaska Native, non-Hispanic/Latino; 5 Asian, non-Hispanic/Latino; 4 Hispanic/Latino; 3 Two or more races, non-Hispanic/Latino), 111 international. Average age 27. 714 applicants, 33% accepted, 55 enrolled. In 2014, 59 master's, 17 doctorates awarded. Terminal master's awarded for partial completion of doctoral program. *Degree requirements:* For master's, project, thesis, or comprehensive exam; for doctorate, thesis/dissertation. *Entrance requirements:* For master's and doctorate, GRE General Test, letters of reference. Additional exam requirements/recommendations for international students: Required—TOEFL (minimum score 550 paper-based; 79 iBT). *Application deadline:* For fall admission, 1/15 priority date for domestic and international students; for spring admission, 9/15 for domestic and international students. Applications are processed on a rolling basis. Application fee: $75. Electronic applications accepted. *Financial support:* In 2014–15, 87 students received support, including 3 fellowships with full and partial tuition reimbursements available (averaging $30,000 per year), 28 research assistantships with full and partial tuition

reimbursements available (averaging $20,090 per year), 28 teaching assistantships with full and partial tuition reimbursements available (averaging $21,420 per year); career-related internships or fieldwork, Federal Work-Study, institutionally sponsored loans, scholarships/grants, traineeships, health care benefits, tuition waivers (full and partial), and unspecified assistantships also available. Support available to part-time students. Financial award application deadline: 1/15; financial award applicants required to submit FAFSA. *Faculty research:* Environmental engineering and fluid mechanics, structural dynamics, geomechanics, earthquake engineering computational mechanics. *Total annual research expenditures:* $4.4 million. *Unit head:* Dr. Andrew S. Whittaker, Chairman, 716-645-2114, Fax: 716-645-3733, E-mail: awhittak@buffalo.edu. *Application contact:* Dr. Joseph Atkinson, Director of Graduate Studies, 716-645-2220, Fax: 716-645-3733, E-mail: atkinson@buffalo.edu.
Website: http://www.csee.buffalo.edu/.

The University of Alabama in Huntsville, School of Graduate Studies, College of Engineering, Department of Civil and Environmental Engineering, Huntsville, AL 35899. Offers civil and environmental engineering (PhD); civil engineering (MSE), including civil engineering, environmental and water resource engineering, geotechnical engineering, structural engineering and structural mechanics, transportation engineering. PhD offered jointly with The University of Alabama at Birmingham. Part-time and evening/weekend programs available. *Degree requirements:* For master's, comprehensive exam, thesis or alternative, oral and written exams; for doctorate, comprehensive exam, thesis/dissertation, oral and written exams. *Entrance requirements:* For master's, GRE General Test, BSE, minimum GPA of 3.0; for doctorate, GRE General Test, minimum GPA of 3.0. Additional exam requirements/recommendations for international students: Required—TOEFL (minimum score 500 paper-based; 80 iBT), IELTS (minimum score 6.5). Electronic applications accepted. *Faculty research:* Smart materials and smart structures, fiber-reinforced cementitious composites, processing and mechanics of composites, geographic information systems, environmental engineering.

University of Alberta, Faculty of Graduate Studies and Research, Department of Civil and Environmental Engineering, Edmonton, AB T6G 2E1, Canada. Offers construction engineering and management (M Eng, M Sc, PhD); environmental engineering (M Eng, M Sc, PhD); environmental science (M Sc, PhD); geoenvironmental engineering (M Eng, M Sc, PhD); geotechnical engineering (M Eng, M Sc, PhD); mining engineering (M Eng, M Sc, PhD); petroleum engineering (M Eng, M Sc, PhD); structural engineering (M Eng, M Sc, PhD); water resources (M Eng, M Sc, PhD). Part-time programs available. Postbaccalaureate distance learning degree programs offered (minimal on-campus study). *Degree requirements:* For master's, thesis (for some programs); for doctorate, thesis/dissertation. *Entrance requirements:* For master's, minimum GPA of 3.0 in last 2 years of undergraduate studies; for doctorate, minimum GPA of 3.0. Additional exam requirements/recommendations for international students: Required—TOEFL (minimum score 550 paper-based). Electronic applications accepted. *Faculty research:* Mining.

University of Calgary, Faculty of Graduate Studies, Schulich School of Engineering, Department of Civil Engineering, Calgary, AB T2N 1N4, Canada. Offers avalanche mechanics (M Sc, PhD); civil engineering (M Eng, M Sc, PhD); energy and environment engineering (M Eng, M Sc, PhD); environmental engineering (M Eng, M Sc, PhD); geotechnical engineering (M Eng, M Sc, PhD); materials science (M Eng, M Sc, PhD); project management (M Eng, M Sc, PhD); structures and solid mechanics (M Eng, M Sc, PhD); transportation engineering (M Eng, M Sc, PhD); water resources (M Eng, M Sc, PhD). Part-time programs available. *Degree requirements:* For master's, thesis; for doctorate, thesis/dissertation, written and oral candidacy exam. *Entrance requirements:* For master's, minimum GPA of 3.0; for doctorate, minimum GPA of 3.5. Additional exam requirements/recommendations for international students: Required—TOEFL (minimum score 580 paper-based; 93 iBT), IELTS (minimum score 7). Electronic applications accepted. *Faculty research:* Geotechnical engineering, energy and environment, transportation, project management, structures and solid mechanics.

University of California, Berkeley, Graduate Division, College of Engineering, Department of Civil and Environmental Engineering, Berkeley, CA 94720-1500. Offers engineering and project management (M Eng, MS, D Eng, PhD); environmental engineering (M Eng, MS, D Eng, PhD); geoengineering (M Eng, MS, D Eng, PhD); structural engineering, mechanics and materials (M Eng, MS, D Eng, PhD); transportation engineering (M Eng, MS, D Eng, PhD); M Arch/MS; MCP/MS; MPP/MS. *Degree requirements:* For master's, comprehensive exam or thesis (MS); for doctorate, thesis/dissertation, qualifying exam. *Entrance requirements:* For master's, GRE General Test, minimum GPA of 3.0, 3 letters of recommendation; for doctorate, GRE General Test, minimum GPA of 3.5, 3 letters of recommendation. Additional exam requirements/recommendations for international students: Required—TOEFL (minimum score 570 paper-based). Electronic applications accepted.

University of California, San Diego, Graduate Division, Department of Structural Engineering, La Jolla, CA 92093. Offers computational neuroscience (PhD); structural engineering (MS, PhD); structural health monitoring, prognosis, and validated simulations (MS). PhD in engineering sciences offered jointly with San Diego State University. *Students:* 166 full-time (33 women), 3 part-time (0 women); includes 48 minority (1 Black or African American, non-Hispanic/Latino; 1 American Indian or Alaska Native, non-Hispanic/Latino; 32 Asian, non-Hispanic/Latino; 14 Hispanic/Latino), 74 international. 381 applicants, 52% accepted, 84 enrolled. In 2014, 66 master's, 6 doctorates awarded. *Degree requirements:* For master's, comprehensive exam or thesis; for doctorate, comprehensive exam, thesis/dissertation, 1-quarter teaching assistantship. *Entrance requirements:* For master's and doctorate, GRE General Test. Additional exam requirements/recommendations for international students: Required—TOEFL (minimum score 550 paper-based; 80 iBT), IELTS (minimum score 7). *Application deadline:* For fall admission, 12/15 for domestic students. Application fee: $90 ($110 for international students). Electronic applications accepted. *Expenses:* Tuition, state resident: full-time $11,220; part-time $5610 per quarter. Tuition, nonresident: full-time $26,322; part-time $13,161 per quarter. *Required fees:* $570 per quarter. Tuition and fees vary according to program. *Financial support:* Fellowships, research assistantships, teaching assistantships, scholarships/grants, and readerships available. Financial award application deadline: 3/2; financial award applicants required to submit FAFSA. *Faculty research:* Geotechnical, marine/offshore engineering; structural design and analysis; structural materials; computational mechanics; solid mechanics. *Unit head:* J. Enrique Luco, Chair, 858-534-4338, E-mail: jeluco@ucsd.edu. *Application contact:* Yvonne C. Wilson, Graduate Coordinator, 858-822-1421, E-mail: ywilson@ucsd.edu.
Website: http://www.structures.ucsd.edu/.

University of Central Florida, College of Engineering and Computer Science, Department of Civil, Environmental, and Construction Engineering, Orlando, FL 32816. Offers civil engineering (MS, MSCE, PhD, Certificate), including civil engineering (MS, MSCE, PhD), construction engineering (Certificate), structural engineering (Certificate), transportation engineering (Certificate); construction engineering (Certificate); environmental engineering (MS, MS Env E, PhD). Part-time and evening/weekend programs available. *Faculty:* 27 full-time (2 women), 13 part-time/adjunct (0 women). *Students:* 107 full-time (28 women), 95 part-time (30 women); includes 53 minority (9 Black or African American, non-Hispanic/Latino; 7 Asian, non-Hispanic/Latino; 30 Hispanic/Latino; 7 Two or more races, non-Hispanic/Latino), 74 international. Average age 30. 172 applicants, 56% accepted, 53 enrolled. In 2014, 48 master's, 9 doctorates, 1 other advanced degree awarded. *Degree requirements:* For master's, thesis or alternative; for doctorate, thesis/dissertation, departmental qualifying exam, candidacy exam. *Entrance requirements:* For master's, GRE General Test, minimum GPA of 3.0 in last 60 hours of course work; for doctorate, GRE General Test, minimum GPA of 3.5 in last 60 hours of course work. Additional exam requirements/recommendations for international students: Required—TOEFL. *Application deadline:* For fall admission, 7/15 priority date for domestic students; for spring admission, 12/1 priority date for domestic students. Application fee: $30. Electronic applications accepted. *Expenses:* Tuition, state resident: part-time $288.16 per credit hour. Tuition, nonresident: part-time $1073.31 per credit hour. *Financial support:* In 2014–15, 51 students received support, including 18 fellowships with partial tuition reimbursements available (averaging $3,900 per year), 44 research assistantships with partial tuition reimbursements available (averaging $9,750 per year), 14 teaching assistantships with partial tuition reimbursements available (averaging $8,900 per year); career-related internships or fieldwork, Federal Work-Study, institutionally sponsored loans, tuition waivers (partial), and unspecified assistantships also available. Financial award application deadline: 3/1; financial award applicants required to submit FAFSA. *Unit head:* Dr. Mohamed Abdel-Aty, Chair, 407-823-2841, E-mail: m.aty@ucf.edu. *Application contact:* Barbara Rodriguez Lamas, Director, Admissions and Student Services, 407-823-2766, Fax: 407-823-6442, E-mail: gradadmissions@ucf.edu.
Website: http://cece.ucf.edu/.

University of Colorado Boulder, Graduate School, College of Engineering and Applied Science, Department of Civil, Environmental, and Architectural Engineering, Boulder, CO 80309. Offers building systems engineering (MS, PhD); construction engineering management (MS, PhD); environmental engineering (MS, PhD); geotechnical engineering and geomechanics (MS, PhD); hydrology, water resources and environmental fluid mechanics (MS, PhD); structural engineering and structural mechanics (MS, PhD). *Faculty:* 37 full-time (8 women). *Students:* 235 full-time (81 women), 36 part-time (9 women); includes 24 minority (9 Asian, non-Hispanic/Latino; 6 Hispanic/Latino; 9 Two or more races, non-Hispanic/Latino), 83 international. Average age 28. 391 applicants, 63% accepted, 68 enrolled. In 2014, 76 master's, 30 doctorates awarded. Terminal master's awarded for partial completion of doctoral program. *Degree requirements:* For master's, comprehensive exam, thesis or alternative; for doctorate, thesis/dissertation. *Entrance requirements:* For master's, GRE General Test, minimum undergraduate GPA of 3.0. *Application deadline:* For fall admission, 1/31 for domestic and international students; for spring admission, 10/1 for domestic and international students. Application fee: $50 ($70 for international students). Electronic applications accepted. *Financial support:* In 2014–15, 387 students received support, including 75 fellowships (averaging $11,889 per year), 92 research assistantships with full and partial tuition reimbursements available (averaging $34,669 per year), 17 teaching assistantships with full and partial tuition reimbursements available (averaging $28,513 per year); institutionally sponsored loans, scholarships/grants, health care benefits, and unspecified assistantships also available. Financial award application deadline: 1/15; financial award applicants required to submit FAFSA. *Faculty research:* Civil engineering, environmental engineering, architectural engineering, geotechnical engineering, hydrology. *Total annual research expenditures:* $13 million.
Website: http://civil.colorado.edu/.

University of Colorado Denver, College of Engineering and Applied Science, Department of Civil Engineering, Denver, CO 80217. Offers civil engineering (EASPh D); civil engineering systems (PhD); environmental and sustainability engineering (MS, PhD); geographic information systems (MS); geotechnical engineering (MS, PhD); hydrology and hydraulics (MS, PhD); structural engineering (MS, PhD); transportation engineering (MS, PhD). Part-time and evening/weekend programs available. *Faculty:* 15 full-time (4 women), 11 part-time/adjunct (2 women). *Students:* 64 full-time (15 women), 43 part-time (8 women); includes 15 minority (3 Black or African American, non-Hispanic/Latino; 3 Asian, non-Hispanic/Latino; 6 Hispanic/Latino; 3 Two or more races, non-Hispanic/Latino), 34 international. Average age 32. 136 applicants, 54% accepted, 28 enrolled. In 2014, 35 master's, 9 doctorates awarded. *Degree requirements:* For master's, comprehensive exam, 30 credit hours, project or thesis; for doctorate, comprehensive exam, thesis/dissertation, 60 credit hours (30 of which are dissertation research). *Entrance requirements:* For master's, GRE, statement of purpose, transcripts, three references; for doctorate, GRE, statement of purpose, transcripts, references, letter of support from faculty stating willingness to serve as dissertation advisor and outlining plan for financial support. Additional exam requirements/recommendations for international students: Required—TOEFL (minimum score 537 paper-based; 75 iBT); Recommended—IELTS (minimum score 6.5). *Application deadline:* For fall admission, 5/1 for domestic students, 4/1 for international students; for spring admission, 10/1 for domestic students, 9/1 for international students; for summer admission, 2/15 for domestic students, 1/15 for international students. Application fee: $50 ($75 for international students). Electronic applications accepted. *Expenses:* Expenses: Contact institution. *Financial support:* In 2014–15, 26 students received support. Fellowships, research assistantships, teaching assistantships, career-related internships or fieldwork, Federal Work-Study, institutionally sponsored loans, scholarships/grants, traineeships, and unspecified assistantships available. Financial award application deadline: 4/1; financial award applicants required to submit FAFSA. *Faculty research:* Earthquake source physics, environmental biotechnology, hydrologic and hydraulic engineering, sustainability assessments, transportation energy use and greenhouse gas emissions. *Unit head:* Dr. Kevin Rens, Chair, 303-556-8017, E-mail: kevin.rens@ucdenver.edu. *Application contact:* Tammy Southern, Program Assistant, 303-556-6712, E-mail: tamara.southern@ucdenver.edu.
Website: http://www.ucdenver.edu/academics/colleges/Engineering/Programs/Civil-Engineering/Pages/CivilEngineering.aspx.

University of Dayton, Department of Civil and Environmental Engineering and Engineering Mechanics, Dayton, OH 45469. Offers engineering mechanics (MSEM); environmental engineering (MSCE); geotechnical engineering (MSCE); structural engineering (MSCE); transportation engineering (MSCE); water resources engineering (MSCE). Part-time and evening/weekend programs available. *Faculty:* 9 full-time (2 women), 3 part-time/adjunct (1 woman). *Students:* 23 full-time (4 women), 6 part-time (2 women), 22 international. Average age 26. 70 applicants, 39% accepted, 4 enrolled. In 2014, 11 master's awarded. *Degree requirements:* For master's, thesis optional. *Entrance requirements:* For master's, minimum GPA of 3.0 in undergraduate work. Additional exam requirements/recommendations for international students: Required—TOEFL (minimum score 550 paper-based; 80 iBT). *Application deadline:* For fall admission, 8/1 priority date for domestic students, 5/1 priority date for international students; for winter admission, 7/1 priority date for international students; for spring admission, 11/1 priority date for international students. Applications are processed on a rolling basis. Application fee: $0 ($50 for international students). Electronic applications accepted. *Expenses: Tuition:* Full-time $10,176; part-time $848 per credit. *Required fees:* $25; $25 per course. Part-time tuition and fees vary according to course level, course load, degree level and program. *Financial support:* In 2014–15, 3 students received support. Institutionally sponsored loans, scholarships/grants, and department-funded awards (averaging $2448 per year) available. Financial award application

Structural Engineering

deadline: 3/1; financial award applicants required to submit FAFSA. *Faculty research:* Physical modeling of water resource systems, finite element methods, mechanics of composite materials, transportation systems safety, biological treatment processes, fiber reinforced concrete. *Total annual research expenditures:* $250,000. *Unit head:* Dr. Donald V. Chase, Chair, 937-229-3847, Fax: 937-229-3491, E-mail: dchase1@udayton.edu. *Application contact:* 937-229-4462, E-mail: graduateadmission@udayton.edu.
Website: https://www.udayton.edu/engineering/departments/civil/index.php.

University of Delaware, College of Engineering, Department of Civil and Environmental Engineering, Newark, DE 19716. Offers environmental engineering (MAS, MCE, PhD); geotechnical engineering (MAS, MCE, PhD); ocean engineering (MAS, MCE, PhD); structural engineering (MAS, MCE, PhD); transportation engineering (MAS, MCE, PhD); water resource engineering (MAS, MCE, PhD). Part-time programs available. Terminal master's awarded for partial completion of doctoral program. *Degree requirements:* For master's, thesis; for doctorate, thesis/dissertation. *Entrance requirements:* For master's and doctorate, GRE General Test. Additional exam requirements/recommendations for international students: Required—TOEFL. Electronic applications accepted. *Faculty research:* Structural engineering and mechanics; transportation engineering; ocean engineering; soil mechanics and foundation; water resources and environmental engineering.

The University of Manchester, School of Materials, Manchester, United Kingdom. Offers advanced aerospace materials engineering (M Sc); advanced metallic systems (PhD); biomedical materials (M Phil, M Sc, PhD); ceramics and glass (M Phil, M Sc, PhD); composite materials (M Sc, PhD); corrosion and protection (M Phil, M Sc, PhD); materials (M Phil, PhD); metallic materials (M Phil, M Sc, PhD); nanostructural materials (M Phil, M Sc, PhD); paper science (M Phil, M Sc, PhD); polymer science and engineering (M Phil, M Sc, PhD); technical textiles (M Sc); textile design, fashion and management (M Phil, M Sc, PhD); textile science and technology (M Phil, M Sc, PhD); textiles (M Phil, PhD); textiles and fashion (M Ent).

University of Massachusetts Amherst, Graduate School, College of Engineering, Department of Civil and Environmental Engineering, Amherst, MA 01003. Offers civil engineering (MSCE, PhD); environmental and water resources engineering (MSCE); geotechnical engineering (MSCE); structural engineering and mechanics (MSCE); transportation engineering (MSCE). Part-time programs available. *Faculty:* 32 full-time (8 women). *Students:* 104 full-time (43 women), 15 part-time (7 women); includes 16 minority (3 Black or African American, non-Hispanic/Latino; 4 Asian, non-Hispanic/Latino; 7 Hispanic/Latino; 2 Two or more races, non-Hispanic/Latino), 44 international. Average age 26. 219 applicants, 62% accepted, 40 enrolled. In 2014, 36 master's, 4 doctorates awarded. Terminal master's awarded for partial completion of doctoral program. *Degree requirements:* For master's, thesis or alternative; for doctorate, comprehensive exam, thesis/dissertation. *Entrance requirements:* For master's and doctorate, GRE General Test. Additional exam requirements/recommendations for international students: Required—TOEFL (minimum score 550 paper-based; 80 iBT), IELTS (minimum score 6.5). *Application deadline:* For fall admission, 1/2 for domestic and international students; for spring admission, 10/1 for domestic and international students. Applications are processed on a rolling basis. Application fee: $75. Electronic applications accepted. *Expenses:* Tuition, state resident: full-time $1980; part-time $110 per credit. Tuition, nonresident: full-time $14,644; part-time $414 per credit. *Required fees:* $11,417. One-time fee: $357. *Financial support:* Fellowships with full and partial tuition reimbursements, research assistantships with full and partial tuition reimbursements, teaching assistantships with full and partial tuition reimbursements, career-related internships or fieldwork, Federal Work-Study, scholarships/grants, traineeships, health care benefits, tuition waivers (full and partial), and unspecified assistantships available. Support available to part-time students. Financial award application deadline: 1/2. *Unit head:* Dr. Sanjay Arwade, Graduate Program Director, 413-545-0686, Fax: 413-545-2840. *Application contact:* Lindsay DeSantis, Supervisor of Admissions, 413-545-0722, Fax: 413-577-0100, E-mail: gradadm@grad.umass.edu. Website: http://cee.umass.edu/.

University of Memphis, Graduate School, Herff College of Engineering, Department of Civil Engineering, Memphis, TN 38152. Offers civil engineering (PhD); environmental engineering (MS); foundation engineering (MS); structural engineering (MS); transportation engineering (MS); water resources engineering (MS). *Faculty:* 11 full-time (1 woman), 2 part-time/adjunct (0 women). *Students:* 12 full-time (5 women), 8 part-time (1 woman); includes 2 minority (both Black or African American, non-Hispanic/Latino), 4 international. Average age 27. 18 applicants, 100% accepted, 4 enrolled. In 2014, 8 master's awarded. Terminal master's awarded for partial completion of doctoral program. *Degree requirements:* For master's, comprehensive exam, thesis optional; for doctorate, comprehensive exam, thesis/dissertation. *Entrance requirements:* For master's, GRE General Test or MAT, minimum undergraduate GPA of 2.5; for doctorate, GRE, 3 letters of recommendation. Additional exam requirements/recommendations for international students: Required—TOEFL (minimum score 550 paper-based; 79 iBT). *Application deadline:* For fall admission, 1/7 for domestic students, 1/5 for international students; for spring admission, 12/1 for domestic students, 9/15 for international students. Application fee: $35 ($60 for international students). *Financial support:* In 2014–15, 6 students received support. Fellowships with full tuition reimbursements available, research assistantships with full tuition reimbursements available, career-related internships or fieldwork, Federal Work-Study, scholarships/grants, and unspecified assistantships available. Financial award application deadline: 2/15; financial award applicants required to submit FAFSA. *Faculty research:* Structural response to earthquakes, pavement design, water quality, transportation safety, intermodal transportation. *Unit head:* Dr. Sharam Pezeshk, Interim Chair, 901-678-2746, Fax: 901-678-3026. *Application contact:* Dr. Roger Meier, Coordinator of Graduate Studies, 901-678-3284.
Website: http://www.ce.memphis.edu.

University of Michigan, College of Engineering, Department of Civil and Environmental Engineering, Ann Arbor, MI 48109. Offers civil engineering (MSE, PhD, CE); construction engineering and management (M Eng, MSE); environmental engineering (MSE, PhD); structural engineering (M Eng); MBA/MSE. Part-time programs available. *Students:* 184 full-time (69 women), 5 part-time (0 women). 691 applicants, 36% accepted, 62 enrolled. In 2014, 59 master's, 12 doctorates awarded. *Degree requirements:* For master's, thesis optional; for doctorate, comprehensive exam, thesis/dissertation, oral defense of dissertation, preliminary and written exams. *Entrance requirements:* For master's and doctorate, GRE General Test. Additional exam requirements/recommendations for international students: Required—TOEFL (minimum score 560 paper-based). *Application deadline:* Applications are processed on a rolling basis. Electronic applications accepted. *Financial support:* Fellowships, research assistantships, teaching assistantships, institutionally sponsored loans, and tuition waivers (partial) available. Financial award application deadline: 1/19. *Faculty research:* Construction engineering and management, geotechnical engineering, earthquake-resistant design of structures, environmental chemistry and microbiology, cost engineering, environmental and water resources engineering. *Total annual research expenditures:* $10.4 million. *Unit head:* Kim Hayes, Department Chair, 734-764-8495,

Fax: 734-764-4292, E-mail: ford@umich.edu. *Application contact:* Jessica Taylor, Graduate Coordinator, 734-764-8405, Fax: 734-647-2127, E-mail: jrand@umich.edu.
Website: http://cee.engin.umich.edu/.

University of Missouri, Office of Research and Graduate Studies, College of Engineering, Department of Civil and Environmental Engineering, Columbia, MO 65211. Offers civil engineering (MS, PhD); environmental engineering (MS, PhD); geotechnical engineering (MS, PhD); structural engineering (MS, PhD); transportation and highway engineering (MS); water resources (MS, PhD). *Faculty:* 18 full-time (2 women), 1 part-time/adjunct (0 women). *Students:* 42 full-time (8 women), 27 part-time (6 women); includes 4 minority (1 Black or African American, non-Hispanic/Latino; 1 Asian, non-Hispanic/Latino; 2 Hispanic/Latino), 45 international. Average age 31. 102 applicants, 48% accepted, 22 enrolled. In 2014, 14 master's, 2 doctorates awarded. *Degree requirements:* For master's, report or thesis; for doctorate, thesis/dissertation. *Entrance requirements:* For master's and doctorate, GRE General Test. Additional exam requirements/recommendations for international students: Required—TOEFL (minimum score 550 paper-based; 79 iBT). *Application deadline:* For fall admission, 2/15 priority date for domestic students, 2/15 for international students; for winter admission, 9/15 priority date for domestic students, 9/15 for international students. Application fee: $55 ($75 for international students). *Financial support:* Fellowships, research assistantships, teaching assistantships, and institutionally sponsored loans available. *Unit head:* Dr. Mark Virkler, Department Chair, 573-882-7434, E-mail: virklerm@missouri.edu. *Application contact:* Jennifer Keyzer-Andre, Administrative Associate I, 573-882-4442, E-mail: keyzerandrej@missouri.edu.
Website: http://engineering.missouri.edu/civil/.

University of New Brunswick Fredericton, School of Graduate Studies, Faculty of Engineering, Department of Civil Engineering, Fredericton, NB E3B 5A3, Canada. Offers construction engineering and management (M Eng, M Sc E, PhD); environmental engineering (M Eng, M Sc E, PhD); environmental studies (M Eng); geotechnical engineering (M Eng, M Sc E, PhD); groundwater/hydrology (M Eng, M Sc E, PhD); materials (M Eng, M Sc E, PhD); pavements (M Eng, M Sc E, PhD); structures (M Eng, M Sc E, PhD); transportation (M Eng, M Sc E, PhD). Part-time programs available. *Faculty:* 12 full-time (1 woman), 4 part-time/adjunct (0 women). *Students:* 16 full-time (4 women), 15 part-time (5 women). In 2014, 9 master's, 3 doctorates awarded. *Degree requirements:* For master's, thesis, proposal; for doctorate, comprehensive exam, thesis/dissertation, qualifying exam; 27 credit hours of courses. *Entrance requirements:* For master's, minimum GPA of 3.0; B Sc E in civil engineering or related engineering degree; for doctorate, minimum GPA of 3.0; graduate degree in engineering or applied science. Additional exam requirements/recommendations for international students: Required—IELTS (minimum score 7.5), TWE (minimum score 4), Michigan English Language Assessment Battery (minimum score 85) or CanTest (minimum score 4.5); Recommended—TOEFL (minimum score 580 paper-based). *Application deadline:* For fall admission, 5/1 for domestic students; for winter admission, 11/1 for domestic students. Applications are processed on a rolling basis. Application fee: $50 Canadian dollars. Electronic applications accepted. *Financial support:* In 2014–15, 35 fellowships, 48 research assistantships, 35 teaching assistantships were awarded; career-related internships or fieldwork and scholarships/grants also available. *Faculty research:* Construction engineering and management; engineering materials and infrastructure renewal; highway and pavement research; structures and solid mechanics; geotechnical and geoenvironmental engineering; structure interaction; transportation and planning; environment, solid waste management; structural engineering; water and environmental engineering. *Unit head:* Dr. Kerry MacQuarrie, Director of Graduate Studies, 506-453-5121, Fax: 506-453-3568, E-mail: ktm@unb.ca. *Application contact:* Joyce Moore, Graduate Secretary, 506-452-6127, Fax: 506-453-3568, E-mail: joycem@unb.ca.
Website: http://go.unb.ca/gradprograms.

University of North Dakota, Graduate School, School of Engineering and Mines, Department of Civil Engineering, Grand Forks, ND 58202. Offers civil engineering (M Engr); sanitary engineering (M Engr), including soils and structures engineering, surface mining engineering. Part-time programs available. *Degree requirements:* For master's, comprehensive exam, thesis or alternative. *Entrance requirements:* For master's, GRE General Test, minimum GPA of 2.5. Additional exam requirements/recommendations for international students: Required—TOEFL (minimum score 550 paper-based; 79 iBT), IELTS (minimum score 6.5). Electronic applications accepted. *Faculty research:* Soil-structures, environmental-water resources.

University of South Florida, College of Engineering, Department of Civil and Environmental Engineering, Tampa, FL 33620-9951. Offers civil engineering (MCE, MSCE, PhD), including environmental engineering (MSES, PhD), geotechnical engineering (MCE, MSCE, MSES, PhD), interdisciplinary transportation (MSCE), materials engineering and science, structural engineering, transportation engineering, water resources; engineering science (MSES), including environmental engineering (MSES, PhD), geotechnical engineering (MCE, MSCE, MSES, PhD); environmental engineering (MEVE, MSEV, PhD). Part-time programs available. *Faculty:* 19 full-time (5 women). *Students:* 97 full-time (35 women), 83 part-time (25 women); includes 41 minority (6 Black or African American, non-Hispanic/Latino; 1 American Indian or Alaska Native, non-Hispanic/Latino; 3 Asian, non-Hispanic/Latino; 25 Hispanic/Latino; 6 Two or more races, non-Hispanic/Latino), 39 international. Average age 30. 229 applicants, 51% accepted, 43 enrolled. In 2014, 68 master's, 9 doctorates awarded. Terminal master's awarded for partial completion of doctoral program. *Degree requirements:* For master's, comprehensive exam, thesis (for some programs); for doctorate, comprehensive exam, thesis/dissertation. *Entrance requirements:* For master's, GRE General Test (preferred minimum scores of 20th percentile verbal, 50th percentile quantitative, and 10th percentile in analytical writing), minimum GPA of 3.0 in major, two letters of reference, statement of purpose; for doctorate, GRE General Test (preferred minimum scores of 45th percentile verbal, 65th percentile quantitative, and 50th percentile in analytical writing), three letters of recommendation, statement of purpose, resume. Additional exam requirements/recommendations for international students: Required—TOEFL (minimum score 550 paper-based; 79 iBT) or IELTS (minimum score 6.5). *Application deadline:* For fall admission, 2/15 for domestic students, 1/2 priority date for international students; for spring admission, 10/15 for domestic students, 6/1 priority date for international students. Application fee: $30. Electronic applications accepted. *Financial support:* In 2014–15, 65 students received support, including 44 research assistantships (averaging $14,123 per year), 21 teaching assistantships with tuition reimbursements available (averaging $15,329 per year). *Faculty research:* Environmental and water resources engineering, geotechnics and geoenvironmental systems, structures and materials systems, transportation systems. *Total annual research expenditures:* $3.3 million. *Unit head:* Dr. Manjriker Gunaratne, Professor and Department Chair, 813-974-5818, Fax: 813-974-2957, E-mail: gunaratn@usf.edu. *Application contact:* Dr. Sarina J. Ergas, Professor and Graduate Program Coordinator, 813-974-1119, Fax: 813-974-2957, E-mail: sergas@usf.edu.
Website: http://ce.eng.usf.edu/.

The University of Texas at Tyler, College of Engineering and Computer Science, Department of Civil Engineering, Tyler, TX 75799-0001. Offers environmental engineering (MS); industrial safety (MS); structural engineering (MS); transportation engineering (MS); water resources engineering (MS). Part-time and evening/weekend programs available. *Degree requirements:* For master's, thesis optional. *Entrance requirements:* For master's, GRE General Test, bachelor's degree in engineering, associated science degree. Additional exam requirements/recommendations for international students: Required—TOEFL. *Faculty research:* Non-destructive strength testing, indoor air quality, transportation routing and signaling, pavement replacement criteria, flood water routing, construction and long-term behavior of innovative geotechnical foundation and embankment construction used in highway construction, engineering education.

University of Washington, Graduate School, College of Engineering, Department of Civil and Environmental Engineering, Seattle, WA 98195-2700. Offers civil engineering (PhD); construction engineering (MSCE); environmental engineering (MSCE, PhD); hydrology, water resources, and environmental fluid mechanics (MSCE, PhD); structural and geotechnical engineering and mechanics (MSCE, PhD); transportation and construction engineering (PhD); transportation engineering (MSCE). Part-time programs available. Postbaccalaureate distance learning degree programs offered (no on-campus study). *Faculty:* 35 full-time (9 women). *Students:* 220 full-time (81 women), 147 part-time (50 women); includes 61 minority (9 Black or African American, non-Hispanic/Latino; 2 American Indian or Alaska Native, non-Hispanic/Latino; 34 Asian, non-Hispanic/Latino; 14 Hispanic/Latino; 2 Native Hawaiian or other Pacific Islander, non-Hispanic/Latino), 91 international. Average age 28. 901 applicants, 49% accepted, 162 enrolled. In 2014, 110 master's, 12 doctorates awarded. Terminal master's awarded for partial completion of doctoral program. *Degree requirements:* For master's, thesis (for some programs); for doctorate, comprehensive exam, thesis/dissertation, general, qualifying, and final exams; completion of degree within 10 years. *Entrance requirements:* For master's, GRE General Test, minimum GPA of 3.0, statement of purpose, letters of recommendation, transcripts; for doctorate, GRE General Test, minimum GPA of 3.5, statement of purpose, letters of recommendation, transcripts. Additional exam requirements/recommendations for international students: Required—TOEFL (minimum score 580 paper-based; 92 iBT); Recommended—IELTS (minimum score 7). *Application deadline:* For fall admission, 12/15 for domestic and international students. Applications are processed on a rolling basis. Application fee: $85. Electronic applications accepted. *Expenses:* Expenses: Contact institution. *Financial support:* In 2014–15, 179 students received support, including 41 fellowships with full and partial tuition reimbursements available, 77 research assistantships with full tuition reimbursements available, 58 teaching assistantships with full tuition reimbursements available; scholarships/grants also available. Financial award application deadline: 1/10; financial award applicants required to submit FAFSA. *Faculty research:* Structural and geotechnical engineering, transportation and construction engineering, water and environmental engineering. *Total annual research expenditures:* $14.1 million. *Unit head:* Dr. Gregory R. Miller, Professor/Chair, 206-543-0350, Fax: 206-543-1543, E-mail: gmiller@uw.edu. *Application contact:* Lorna Latal, Graduate Adviser, 206-543-2574, Fax: 206-543-1543, E-mail: llatal@u.washington.edu.
Website: http://www.ce.washington.edu/.

Surveying Science and Engineering

University of New Brunswick Fredericton, School of Graduate Studies, Faculty of Engineering, Department of Geodesy and Geomatics Engineering, Fredericton, NB E3B 5A3, Canada. Offers M Eng, M Sc E, PhD. *Faculty:* 9 full-time (1 woman), 11 part-time/adjunct (3 women). *Students:* 37 full-time (8 women), 11 part-time (2 women). In 2014, 16 master's, 3 doctorates awarded. *Degree requirements:* For master's, thesis; for doctorate, comprehensive exam, thesis/dissertation, qualifying exam. *Entrance requirements:* For master's and doctorate, minimum GPA of 3.0. Additional exam requirements/recommendations for international students: Required—TOEFL (minimum score 550 paper-based; 80 iBT), IELTS (minimum score 7), TWE (minimum score 4), Michigan English Language Assessment Battery (minimum score 85) or CanTest (minimum score 4.5). *Application deadline:* For fall admission, 3/1 for domestic students. Applications are processed on a rolling basis. Application fee: $50 Canadian dollars. Electronic applications accepted. *Financial support:* In 2014–15, 28 fellowships, 28 research assistantships, 27 teaching assistantships were awarded. *Faculty research:* GIS, GPS, remote sensing, ocean mapping, land administration, hydrography, engineering surveys. *Unit head:* Dr. Emmanuel Stefanakis, Director of Graduate Studies, 506-453-5137, Fax: 506-453-4943, E-mail: estef@unb.ca. *Application contact:* Sylvia Whitaker, Graduate Secretary, 506-458-7085, Fax: 506-453-4943, E-mail: swhitake@unb.ca.
Website: http://go.unb.ca/gradprograms.

Transportation and Highway Engineering

Arizona State University at the Tempe campus, College of Liberal Arts and Sciences, School of Geographical Sciences and Urban Planning, Tempe, AZ 85287-5302. Offers geographic information systems (MAS); geographical information science (Graduate Certificate); geography (MA, PhD); transportation systems (Graduate Certificate); urban and environmental planning (MUEP); urban planning (PhD). Terminal master's awarded for partial completion of doctoral program. *Degree requirements:* For master's, thesis, interactive Program of Study (iPOS) submitted before completing 50 percent of required credit hours; for doctorate, comprehensive exam, thesis/dissertation, interactive Program of Study (iPOS) submitted before completing 50 percent of required credit hours. *Entrance requirements:* For master's and doctorate, GRE, minimum GPA of 3.0 or equivalent in last 2 years of work leading to bachelor's degree. Additional exam requirements/recommendations for international students: Required—TOEFL, IELTS, or PTE. Electronic applications accepted. *Expenses:* Contact institution.

Art Center College of Design, Graduate Transportation Design Program, Pasadena, CA 91103. Offers transportation systems (MS); vehicle design (MS). *Students:* 15 full-time (0 women), 5 part-time (1 woman); includes 4 minority (3 Asian, non-Hispanic/Latino; 1 Hispanic/Latino), 11 international. Average age 28. 26 applicants, 54% accepted, 7 enrolled. *Degree requirements:* For master's, thesis. *Entrance requirements:* For master's, portfolio. Additional exam requirements/recommendations for international students: Required—TOEFL (minimum score 100 iBT), IELTS (minimum score 7). *Application deadline:* For fall admission, 2/1 priority date for domestic and international students. Application fee: $50 ($70 for international students). Electronic applications accepted. *Financial support:* Application deadline: 2/1; applicants required to submit FAFSA. *Unit head:* Geoff Wardle, Executive Director, 626-396-2421, E-mail: gwardle@artcenter.edu. *Application contact:* Tom Stern, Managing Director, Admissions, 626-396-2369, E-mail: tom.stern@artcenter.edu.

Auburn University, Graduate School, Ginn College of Engineering, Department of Civil Engineering, Auburn University, AL 36849. Offers construction engineering and management (MCE, MS, PhD); environmental engineering (MCE, MS, PhD); geotechnical/materials engineering (MCE, MS, PhD); hydraulics/hydrology (MCE, MS, PhD); structural engineering (MCE, MS, PhD); transportation engineering (MCE, MS, PhD). Part-time programs available. *Faculty:* 27 full-time (3 women), 1 part-time/adjunct (0 women). *Students:* 59 full-time (15 women), 46 part-time (6 women); includes 10 minority (4 Black or African American, non-Hispanic/Latino; 4 Asian, non-Hispanic/Latino; 2 Hispanic/Latino), 40 international. Average age 26. 134 applicants, 46% accepted, 20 enrolled. In 2014, 40 master's, 7 doctorates awarded. *Degree requirements:* For master's, project (MCE), thesis (MS); for doctorate, comprehensive exam, thesis/dissertation. *Entrance requirements:* For master's and doctorate, GRE General Test. *Application deadline:* For fall admission, 7/7 for domestic students; for spring admission, 11/24 for domestic students. Applications are processed on a rolling basis. Application fee: $50 ($60 for international students). Electronic applications accepted. *Expenses:* Tuition, state resident: full-time $8586; part-time $477 per credit hour. Tuition, nonresident: full-time $25,758; part-time $1431 per credit hour. *Required fees:* $804 per semester. Tuition and fees vary according to degree level and program. *Financial support:* Fellowships, research assistantships, teaching assistantships, and Federal Work-Study available. Support available to part-time students. Financial award application deadline: 3/15; financial award applicants required to submit FAFSA. *Unit head:* Dr. Andy Nowak, Head, 334-844-4320. *Application contact:* Dr. George Flowers, Dean of the Graduate School, 334-844-2125.

College for Creative Studies, Graduate Programs, Detroit, MI 48202-4034. Offers interdisciplinary design (MFA); transportation design (MFA).

Cornell University, Graduate School, Graduate Fields of Engineering, Field of Civil and Environmental Engineering, Ithaca, NY 14853-0001. Offers engineering management (M Eng, MS, PhD); environmental engineering (M Eng, MS, PhD); environmental fluid mechanics and hydrology (M Eng, MS, PhD); environmental systems engineering (M Eng, MS, PhD); geotechnical engineering (M Eng, MS, PhD); remote sensing (M Eng, MS, PhD); structural engineering (M Eng, MS, PhD); structural mechanics (M Eng, MS); transportation engineering (MS, PhD); transportation systems engineering (M Eng); water resource systems (M Eng, MS, PhD). Terminal master's awarded for partial completion of doctoral program. *Degree requirements:* For master's, thesis (MS); for doctorate, comprehensive exam, thesis/dissertation. *Entrance requirements:* For master's and doctorate, GRE General Test (recommended), 2 letters of recommendation. Additional exam requirements/recommendations for international students: Required—TOEFL (minimum score 600 paper-based; 77 iBT). Electronic applications accepted. *Faculty research:* Environmental engineering, geotechnical engineering, remote sensing, environmental fluid mechanics and hydrology, structural engineering.

École Polytechnique de Montréal, Graduate Programs, Department of Civil, Geological and Mining Engineering, Montréal, QC H3C 3A7, Canada. Offers civil, geological and mining engineering (DESS); environmental engineering (M Eng, M Sc A, PhD); geotechnical engineering (M Eng, M Sc A, PhD); hydraulics engineering (M Eng, M Sc A, PhD); structural engineering (M Eng, M Sc A, PhD); transportation engineering (M Eng, M Sc A, PhD). Part-time programs available. *Degree requirements:* For master's, one foreign language, thesis; for doctorate, one foreign language, thesis/dissertation. *Entrance requirements:* For master's, minimum GPA of 2.75; for doctorate, minimum GPA of 3.0. *Faculty research:* Water resources management, characteristics of building materials, aging of dams, pollution control.

George Mason University, Volgenau School of Engineering, Sid and Reva Dewberry Department of Civil, Environmental, and Infrastructure Engineering, Fairfax, VA 22030. Offers construction project management (MS); environmental and water resources engineering (MS); geotechnical, construction, and structural engineering (M Eng); transportation engineering (MS, PhD). *Faculty:* 12 full-time (4 women), 16 part-time/adjunct (3 women). *Students:* 28 full-time (7 women), 51 part-time (13 women); includes 25 minority (12 Black or African American, non-Hispanic/Latino; 8 Asian, non-Hispanic/Latino; 5 Hispanic/Latino), 14 international. Average age 30. 90 applicants, 58% accepted, 25 enrolled. In 2014, 28 master's, 3 doctorates awarded. *Degree requirements:* For master's, thesis (for some programs), 30 credits, departmental seminars; for doctorate, thesis/dissertation, qualifying exams. *Entrance requirements:* For master's, GRE, photocopy of passport; 2 official college transcripts; resume; official bank statement; proof of financial support; expanded goals statement; self-evaluation form; BS in engineering or other related science; 3 letters of recommendation; for doctorate, GRE (for those who received degree outside of the U.S.), photocopy of passport; 2 official college transcripts; resume; official bank statement; proof of financial support; expanded goals statement; self-evaluation form; baccalaureate degree in engineering or related science; master's degree (preferred); 3 letters of recommendation. Additional exam requirements/recommendations for international students: Required—TOEFL (minimum score 575 paper-based; 80 iBT), IELTS (minimum score 6.5), PTE. *Application deadline:* For fall admission, 1/15 priority date for domestic students; for spring admission, 8/1 priority date for domestic students. Application fee: $65 ($80 for international students). Electronic applications accepted. *Expenses:* Expenses: Contact institution. *Financial support:* In 2014–15, 19 students received support, including 1 fellowship (averaging $5,000 per year), 9 research assistantships with full and partial tuition reimbursements available (averaging $23,846 per year), 10 teaching assistantships with full and partial tuition reimbursements available (averaging $21,200 per year); career-related internships or fieldwork, Federal Work-Study, scholarships/grants, unspecified assistantships, and health care benefits (for full-time research or teaching assistantship recipients) also available. Support available to part-time students. Financial award application deadline: 3/1; financial

Transportation and Highway Engineering

award applicants required to submit FAFSA. *Faculty research:* Evolutionary design, infrastructure security, intelligent transportation systems, national transportation networks, water quality modeling. *Total annual research expenditures:* $159,347. *Unit head:* Dr. Deborah J. Goodings, Chair, 703-993-1675, Fax: 703-993-9790, E-mail: goodings@gmu.edu. *Application contact:* Kristin Amaya, Administrative Assistant, 703-993-1675, Fax: 703-993-9790, E-mail: kfairch1@gmu.edu.
Website: http://civil.gmu.edu/.

Illinois Institute of Technology, Graduate College, Armour College of Engineering, Department of Civil, Architectural and Environmental Engineering, Chicago, IL 60616. Offers architectural engineering (M Arch E); civil engineering (MS, PhD), including architectural engineering (MS), construction engineering and management (MS), geoenvironmental engineering (MS), geotechnical engineering (MS), structural engineering (MS), transportation engineering (MS); construction engineering and management (MCEM); environmental engineering (M Env E, MS, PhD); geoenvironmental engineering (M Geoenv E); geotechnical engineering (MGE); infrastructure engineering and management (MPW); structural engineering (MSE); transportation engineering (M Trans E). Part-time and evening/weekend programs available. Postbaccalaureate distance learning degree programs offered (minimal on-campus study). *Faculty:* 12 full-time (1 woman), 15 part-time/adjunct (1 woman). *Students:* 165 full-time (48 women), 54 part-time (11 women); includes 31 minority (2 Black or African American, non-Hispanic/Latino; 21 Asian, non-Hispanic/Latino; 7 Hispanic/Latino; 1 Native Hawaiian or other Pacific Islander, non-Hispanic/Latino), 157 international. Average age 29. 1,039 applicants, 42% accepted, 82 enrolled. In 2014, 94 master's, 7 doctorates awarded. Terminal master's awarded for partial completion of doctoral program. *Degree requirements:* For master's, thesis (for some programs); for doctorate, comprehensive exam, thesis/dissertation. *Entrance requirements:* For master's, GRE General Test (minimum score 900 Quantitative and Verbal, 2.5 Analytical Writing), minimum undergraduate GPA of 3.0; for doctorate, GRE General Test (minimum score 1000 Quantitative and Verbal, 3.0 Analytical Writing), minimum undergraduate GPA of 3.0. Additional exam requirements/recommendations for international students: Required—TOEFL (minimum score 550 paper-based; 80 iBT). *Application deadline:* For fall admission, 5/1 for domestic and international students; for spring admission, 10/15 for domestic and international students. Applications are processed on a rolling basis. Application fee: $50. Electronic applications accepted. *Expenses: Tuition:* Full-time $22,500; part-time $1250 per credit hour. *Required fees:* $30 per course. $260 per semester. One-time fee: $235. Tuition and fees vary according to course load and program. *Financial support:* Fellowships with full and partial tuition reimbursements, research assistantships with full and partial tuition reimbursements, teaching assistantships with full and partial tuition reimbursements, Federal Work-Study, institutionally sponsored loans, scholarships/grants, health care benefits, tuition waivers (partial), and unspecified assistantships available. Support available to part-time students. Financial award applicants required to submit FAFSA. *Faculty research:* Structural, architectural, geotechnical and geoenvironmental engineering; construction engineering and management; transportation engineering; environmental engineering and public works. *Unit head:* Dr. Gongkang Fu, Professor and Chairman, 312-567-3540, Fax: 312-567-3519, E-mail: gfu2@iit.edu. *Application contact:* Rishab Malhotra, Director, Graduate Admission, 866-472-3448, Fax: 312-567-3138, E-mail: inquiry.grad@iit.edu.
Website: http://engineering.iit.edu/caee.

Iowa State University of Science and Technology, Department of Civil and Construction Engineering, Ames, IA 50011. Offers civil engineering (MS, PhD), including civil engineering materials, construction engineering and management, environmental engineering, geometronics, geotechnical engineering, structural engineering, transportation engineering. *Degree requirements:* For master's, thesis or alternative; for doctorate, thesis/dissertation. *Entrance requirements:* For master's and doctorate, GRE General Test. Additional exam requirements/recommendations for international students: Required—TOEFL (minimum score 550 paper-based; 82 iBT), IELTS (minimum score 6.5). Electronic applications accepted.

Kansas State University, Graduate School, College of Engineering, Department of Civil Engineering, Manhattan, KS 66506. Offers civil engineering (MS, PhD); environmental engineering (MS, PhD); geotechnical engineering (MS, PhD); structural engineering (MS, PhD); transportation engineering (MS, PhD); water resources engineering (MS, PhD). Part-time and evening/weekend programs available. Postbaccalaureate distance learning degree programs offered (no on-campus study). *Faculty:* 14 full-time (4 women), 3 part-time/adjunct (1 woman). *Students:* 37 full-time (12 women), 37 part-time (9 women); includes 6 minority (3 Black or African American, non-Hispanic/Latino; 3 Hispanic/Latino), 23 international. Average age 30. 62 applicants, 39% accepted, 10 enrolled. In 2014, 14 master's, 4 doctorates awarded. *Degree requirements:* For master's, thesis or alternative; for doctorate, thesis/dissertation. *Entrance requirements:* For master's, GRE General Test, bachelor's degree or course work in related engineering fields; for doctorate, GRE General Test. Additional exam requirements/recommendations for international students: Required—TOEFL (minimum score 550 paper-based; 79 iBT). *Application deadline:* For fall admission, 2/1 priority date for domestic students, 1/1 priority date for international students; for spring admission, 8/1 priority date for domestic and international students. Applications are processed on a rolling basis. Application fee: $50 ($75 for international students). Electronic applications accepted. *Financial support:* In 2014–15, 19 research assistantships with partial tuition reimbursements (averaging $13,431 per year), 12 teaching assistantships with partial tuition reimbursements (averaging $15,058 per year) were awarded; institutionally sponsored loans and scholarships/grants also available. Support available to part-time students. Financial award application deadline: 3/1; financial award applicants required to submit FAFSA. *Faculty research:* Transportation and materials engineering, water resources engineering, environmental engineering, geotechnical engineering, structural engineering. *Total annual research expenditures:* $2.4 million. *Unit head:* Dr. Robert Stokes, Head, 785-532-1595, Fax: 785-532-7717, E-mail: drbobb@k-state.edu. *Application contact:* Dr. Dunja Peric, Graduate Coordinator, 785-532-2468, Fax: 785-532-7717, E-mail: peric@k-state.edu.
Website: http://www.ce.ksu.edu/.

Louisiana State University and Agricultural & Mechanical College, Graduate School, College of Engineering, Department of Civil and Environmental Engineering, Baton Rouge, LA 70803. Offers environmental engineering (MSCE, PhD); geotechnical engineering (MSCE, PhD); structural engineering and mechanics (MSCE, PhD); transportation engineering (MSCE, PhD); water resources (MSCE, PhD). Part-time programs available. *Faculty:* 26 full-time (1 woman). *Students:* 90 full-time (24 women), 28 part-time (6 women); includes 12 minority (5 Black or African American, non-Hispanic/Latino; 1 American Indian or Alaska Native, non-Hispanic/Latino; 5 Asian, non-Hispanic/Latino; 1 Two or more races, non-Hispanic/Latino), 67 international. Average age 30. 147 applicants, 50% accepted, 23 enrolled. In 2014, 26 master's, 8 doctorates awarded. *Degree requirements:* For master's, thesis optional; for doctorate, one foreign language, thesis/dissertation. *Entrance requirements:* For master's and doctorate, GRE General Test, minimum GPA of 3.0. Additional exam requirements/recommendations for international students: Required—TOEFL (minimum score 550 paper-based; 79 iBT), IELTS (minimum score 6.5), or PTE (minimum score 59). *Application deadline:* For fall admission, 1/1 priority date for domestic students, 5/15 for international students; for spring admission, 10/15 for domestic and international students; for summer admission, 5/15 for domestic and international students. Applications are processed on a rolling basis. Application fee: $50 ($70 for international students). Electronic applications accepted. *Financial support:* In 2014–15, 88 students received support, including 7 fellowships with full and partial tuition reimbursements available (averaging $26,784 per year), 59 research assistantships with full and partial tuition reimbursements available (averaging $16,992 per year), 13 teaching assistantships with full and partial tuition reimbursements available (averaging $16,290 per year); career-related internships or fieldwork, institutionally sponsored loans, scholarships/grants, and health care benefits also available. Financial award application deadline: 3/1; financial award applicants required to submit FAFSA. *Faculty research:* Mechanics and structures, environmental, geotechnical transportation, water resources. *Total annual research expenditures:* $3.2 million. *Unit head:* Dr. George Z. Voyiadjis, Chair/Professor, 225-578-8442, Fax: 225-578-8652, E-mail: voyaidjis@lsu.edu. *Application contact:* Dr. Ayman Ikeli, Professor, 225-578-7048, E-mail: aokeli@lsu.edu.
Website: http://www.cee.lsu.edu/.

Marquette University, Graduate School, Opus College of Engineering, Department of Civil, Construction and Environmental Engineering, Milwaukee, WI 53201-1881. Offers construction engineering and management (MS, PhD, Certificate); environmental engineering (MS, PhD); structural design (Certificate); structural engineering and structural mechanics (MS, PhD); transportation (Certificate); transportation engineering and materials (MS, PhD); waste and wastewater treatment processes (Certificate); water resources engineering (Certificate). Part-time and evening/weekend programs available. Terminal master's awarded for partial completion of doctoral program. *Degree requirements:* For master's, comprehensive exam (for some programs), thesis or alternative; for doctorate, thesis/dissertation. *Entrance requirements:* For master's, GRE General Test (recommended), minimum GPA of 3.0, official transcripts from all current and previous colleges/universities except Marquette, three letters of recommendation; for doctorate, GRE General Test, minimum GPA of 3.0, official transcripts from all current and previous colleges/universities except Marquette, three letters of recommendation, brief statement of purpose, submission of any English language publications authored by applicant (strongly recommended). Additional exam requirements/recommendations for international students: Required—TOEFL (minimum score 530 paper-based). Electronic applications accepted. *Faculty research:* Highway safety, highway performance, and intelligent transportation systems; surface mount technology; watershed management.

Marshall University, Academic Affairs Division, College of Information Technology and Engineering, Weisbert Division of Engineering, Huntington, WV 25755. Offers engineering management (MSE); environmental engineering (MSE); mechanical engineering (MS); transportation and infrastructure engineering (MSE). Part-time and evening/weekend programs available. *Students:* 30 full-time (5 women), 28 part-time (7 women); includes 3 minority (all Black or African American, non-Hispanic/Latino), 22 international. Average age 29. In 2014, 11 master's awarded. *Degree requirements:* For master's, final project, oral exam. *Entrance requirements:* For master's, GMAT or GRE General Test, minimum undergraduate GPA of 2.75. Application fee: $40. *Financial support:* Tuition waivers (full) available. Support available to part-time students. Financial award application deadline: 8/1; financial award applicants required to submit FAFSA. *Unit head:* Dr. William Pierson, Chair, 304-696-2695, E-mail: pierson@marshall.edu. *Application contact:* Information Contact, 304-746-1900, Fax: 304-746-1902, E-mail: services@marshall.edu.
Website: http://www.marshall.edu/cite/.

Massachusetts Institute of Technology, School of Engineering, Department of Civil and Environmental Engineering, Cambridge, MA 02139. Offers biological oceanography (PhD, Sc D); chemical oceanography (PhD, Sc D); civil and environmental engineering (M Eng, SM, PhD, Sc D); civil and environmental systems (PhD, Sc D); civil engineering (PhD, Sc D, CE); coastal engineering (PhD, Sc D); construction engineering and management (PhD, Sc D); environmental biology (PhD, Sc D); environmental chemistry (PhD, Sc D); environmental engineering (PhD, Sc D); environmental fluid mechanics (PhD, Sc D); geotechnical and geoenvironmental engineering (PhD, Sc D); hydrology (PhD, Sc D); information technology (PhD, Sc D); oceanographic engineering (PhD, Sc D); structures and materials (PhD, Sc D); transportation (PhD, Sc D); SM/MBA. *Faculty:* 34 full-time (8 women), 1 part-time/adjunct (0 women). *Students:* 216 full-time (82 women); includes 25 minority (1 Black or African American, non-Hispanic/Latino; 10 Asian, non-Hispanic/Latino; 8 Hispanic/Latino; 6 Two or more races, non-Hispanic/Latino), 117 international. Average age 26. 565 applicants, 22% accepted, 85 enrolled. In 2014, 76 master's, 18 doctorates awarded. *Degree requirements:* For master's and CE, thesis; for doctorate, comprehensive exam, thesis/dissertation. *Entrance requirements:* For master's and doctorate, GRE General Test. Additional exam requirements/recommendations for international students: Required—TOEFL (minimum score 577 paper-based; 100 iBT), IELTS (minimum score 7). *Application deadline:* For fall admission, 12/15 for domestic and international students. Application fee: $75. Electronic applications accepted. *Expenses: Tuition:* Full-time $44,720; part-time $699 per unit. *Required fees:* $296. *Financial support:* In 2014–15, 170 students received support, including 32 fellowships (averaging $32,800 per year), 132 research assistantships (averaging $33,800 per year), 13 teaching assistantships (averaging $32,900 per year); Federal Work-Study, institutionally sponsored loans, scholarships/grants, traineeships, health care benefits, and unspecified assistantships also available. Financial award application deadline: 4/15; financial award applicants required to submit FAFSA. *Faculty research:* Environmental chemistry, environmental fluid mechanics and coastal engineering, environmental microbiology, geotechnical engineering and geomechanics, hydrology and hydroclimatology, infrastructure systems, mechanics of materials and structures, transportation systems. *Total annual research expenditures:* $22.9 million. *Unit head:* Prof. Markus Buehler, Department Head, 617-324-6488. *Application contact:* Graduate Admissions Coordinator, 617-253-7119, E-mail: cee-admissions@mit.edu.
Website: http://cee.mit.edu/.

Morgan State University, School of Graduate Studies, Clarence M. Mitchell, Jr. School of Engineering, Department of Transportation, Baltimore, MD 21251. Offers MS. Part-time and evening/weekend programs available. *Degree requirements:* For master's, thesis optional, comprehensive exam or equivalent. *Entrance requirements:* For master's, minimum undergraduate GPA of 2.5. Additional exam requirements/recommendations for international students: Required—TOEFL (minimum score 550 paper-based). *Faculty research:* Distributional impacts of congestion, pricing education and training for intelligent vehicle highway systems.

New Jersey Institute of Technology, Newark College of Engineering, Newark, NJ 07102. Offers biomedical engineering (MS, PhD); chemical engineering (MS, PhD); computer engineering (MS, PhD); electrical engineering (MS, PhD); engineering management (MS); healthcare systems management (MS); industrial engineering (MS, PhD); Internet engineering (MS); manufacturing engineering (MS); mechanical engineering (MS, PhD); occupational safety and health engineering (MS); pharmaceutical bioprocessing (MS); pharmaceutical engineering (MS); pharmaceutical systems management (MS); power and energy systems (MS); telecommunications (MS); transportation (MS, PhD). Part-time and evening/weekend programs available.

Terminal master's awarded for partial completion of doctoral program. *Degree requirements:* For master's, thesis optional; for doctorate, thesis/dissertation. *Entrance requirements:* For master's, GRE General Test; for doctorate, GRE General Test, minimum graduate GPA of 3.5. Additional exam requirements/recommendations for international students: Required—TOEFL (minimum score 550 paper-based; 79 iBT). Electronic applications accepted.

New York University, Polytechnic School of Engineering, Department of Civil and Urban Engineering, Major in Transportation Planning and Engineering, New York, NY 10012-1019. Offers MS, PhD. Part-time and evening/weekend programs available. *Students:* 28 full-time (7 women), 10 part-time (5 women); includes 6 minority (2 Black or African American, non-Hispanic/Latino; 2 Asian, non-Hispanic/Latino; 2 Hispanic/Latino), 21 international. Average age 29. 45 applicants, 47% accepted, 8 enrolled. In 2014, 13 master's awarded. *Degree requirements:* For master's, comprehensive exam (for some programs), thesis (for some programs); for doctorate, comprehensive exam, thesis/dissertation. *Entrance requirements:* Additional exam requirements/recommendations for international students: Required—TOEFL (minimum score 550 paper-based; 80 iBT); Recommended—IELTS (minimum score 6.5). *Application deadline:* For fall admission, 2/15 priority date for domestic and international students; for spring admission, 11/1 priority date for domestic and international students. Applications are processed on a rolling basis. Application fee: $75. Electronic applications accepted. *Financial support:* Fellowships, research assistantships, teaching assistantships, institutionally sponsored loans, scholarships/grants, and unspecified assistantships available. Support available to part-time students. Financial award applicants required to submit FAFSA. *Unit head:* Dr. Magued Iskander, Head, 718-260-3016, E-mail: iskander@nyu.edu. *Application contact:* Raymond Lutzky, Director of Graduate Enrollment Management, 718-637-5984, Fax: 718-260-3624, E-mail: rlutzky@poly.edu.

Northwestern University, McCormick School of Engineering and Applied Science, Department of Civil and Environmental Engineering, Evanston, IL 60208-3109. Offers environmental engineering and science (MS, PhD); geotechnical engineering (MS, PhD); mechanics of materials and solids (MS, PhD); project management (MS, PhD); structural engineering and materials (MS, PhD); transportation systems analysis and planning (MS, PhD). MS and PhD admissions and degrees offered through The Graduate School. Part-time programs available. *Faculty:* 19 full-time (2 women). *Students:* 118 full-time (36 women), 5 part-time (2 women); includes 7 minority (3 Black or African American, non-Hispanic/Latino; 2 Asian, non-Hispanic/Latino; 1 Hispanic/Latino; 1 Two or more races, non-Hispanic/Latino), 95 international. Average age 24. 412 applicants, 36% accepted, 49 enrolled. In 2014, 42 master's, 10 doctorates awarded. Terminal master's awarded for partial completion of doctoral program. *Degree requirements:* For master's, thesis (for some programs); for doctorate, comprehensive exam, thesis/dissertation. *Entrance requirements:* For master's and doctorate, GRE General Test, minimum 2 letters of recommendation, transcripts from all academic institutions attended. Additional exam requirements/recommendations for international students: Required—TOEFL (minimum score 577 paper-based; 90 iBT), IELTS (minimum score 7). *Application deadline:* For fall admission, 12/31 for domestic and international students; for winter admission, 11/15 for domestic and international students; for spring admission, 1/15 for domestic and international students. Application fee: $95. Electronic applications accepted. *Financial support:* Fellowships with full tuition reimbursements, research assistantships with full tuition reimbursements, teaching assistantships with full tuition reimbursements, career-related internships or fieldwork, institutionally sponsored loans, health care benefits, and unspecified assistantships available. Financial award application deadline: 12/31; financial award applicants required to submit FAFSA. *Faculty research:* Environmental engineering and science, geotechnics, mechanics of materials and solids, structural engineering and materials, transportation systems analysis and planning. *Total annual research expenditures:* $5.8 million. *Unit head:* Dr. Jianmin Qu, Chair, 847-467-4528, Fax: 847-491-4011, E-mail: j-qu@northwestern.edu. *Application contact:* Dr. David Corr, Academic Coordinator, 847-467-0890, Fax: 847-491-4011, E-mail: d-corr@u.northwestern.edu. Website: http://www.civil.northwestern.edu/.

Ohio University, Graduate College, Russ College of Engineering and Technology, Department of Civil Engineering, Athens, OH 45701-2979. Offers civil engineering (PhD); construction engineering and management (MS); environmental (MS); geotechnical and geoenvironmental (MS); mechanics (MS); structures (MS); transportation (MS); water resources (MS). Part-time programs available. *Degree requirements:* For master's, comprehensive exam (for some programs), thesis or alternative; for doctorate, comprehensive exam, thesis/dissertation. *Entrance requirements:* For master's, GRE General Test, minimum GPA of 3.0, 3 letters of recommendation; for doctorate, GRE General Test. Additional exam requirements/recommendations for international students: Required—TOEFL (minimum score 550 paper-based; 80 iBT) or IELTS (minimum score 6.5). Electronic applications accepted. *Faculty research:* Noise abatement, materials and environment, highway infrastructure, subsurface investigation (pavements, pipes, bridges).

Rensselaer Polytechnic Institute, Graduate School, School of Engineering, Program in Transportation Engineering, Troy, NY 12180-3590. Offers M Eng, MS, D Eng, PhD. *Faculty:* 14 full-time (3 women), 2 part-time/adjunct (0 women). *Students:* 5 full-time (3 women), 1 (woman) part-time; includes 1 minority (Hispanic/Latino), 4 international. Average age 30. 11 applicants, 9% accepted. In 2014, 2 master's, 3 doctorates awarded. Terminal master's awarded for partial completion of doctoral program. *Degree requirements:* For master's, thesis (for some programs); for doctorate, thesis/dissertation. *Entrance requirements:* For master's and doctorate, GRE. Additional exam requirements/recommendations for international students: Required—TOEFL (minimum score 570 paper-based; 88 iBT), IELTS (minimum score 6.5), PTE (minimum score 60). *Application deadline:* For fall admission, 1/1 priority date for domestic and international students; for spring admission, 8/15 priority date for domestic and international students. Applications are processed on a rolling basis. Application fee: $75. Electronic applications accepted. *Expenses: Tuition:* Full-time $46,700; part-time $1945 per credit. Tuition and fees vary according to course load. *Financial support:* In 2014–15, 3 students received support, including research assistantships (averaging $18,500 per year), teaching assistantships (averaging $18,500 per year); fellowships also available. Financial award application deadline: 1/1. *Faculty research:* Advanced econometrics, freight transportation systems: operations and modeling, intelligent transportation systems, traffic simulation and network modeling, transportation economics, transportation planning. *Total annual research expenditures:* $965,565. *Unit head:* Dr. Michael O'Rourke, Graduate Program Director, 518-276-6933, E-mail: orourm@rpi.edu. *Application contact:* Office of Graduate Admissions, 518-276-6216, E-mail: gradadmissions@rpi.edu. Website: http://eng.rpi.edu/.

Southern Illinois University Edwardsville, Graduate School, School of Engineering, Department of Civil Engineering, Program in Transportation Engineering, Edwardsville, IL 62026. Offers MS. Part-time and evening/weekend programs available. *Degree requirements:* For master's, thesis (for some programs), research paper. *Entrance requirements:* For master's, minimum undergraduate GPA of 2.75 in science, math, and engineering courses. Additional exam requirements/recommendations for international students: Required—TOEFL (minimum score 550 paper-based, 79 iBT), IELTS (minimum score 6.5), Michigan Test of English Language Proficiency or PTE. *Application deadline:* For fall admission, 7/18 for domestic students, 6/1 for international students; for spring admission, 12/12 for domestic students, 10/1 for international students; for summer admission, 4/24 for domestic students, 3/1 for international students. Applications are processed on a rolling basis. Application fee: $30. Electronic applications accepted. *Expenses:* Tuition, state resident: full-time $5026. Tuition, nonresident: full-time $12,566. *International tuition:* $25,136 full-time. *Required fees:* $1682. Tuition and fees vary according to course load, campus/location and program. *Financial support:* Institutionally sponsored loans, scholarships/grants, and unspecified assistantships available. Financial award application deadline: 3/1; financial award applicants required to submit FAFSA. *Unit head:* Dr. Jim Zhou, Chair, 618-650-2533, E-mail: jzhou@siue.edu. *Application contact:* Dr. Ryan Fries, Director, 618-650-5026, E-mail: rfries@siue.edu. Website: http://www.siue.edu/engineering/civilengineering.

Texas Southern University, School of Science and Technology, Program in Transportation, Planning and Management, Houston, TX 77004-4584. Offers MS. Part-time and evening/weekend programs available. *Degree requirements:* For master's, comprehensive exam, thesis optional. *Entrance requirements:* For master's, GRE General Test, minimum GPA of 2.5. Additional exam requirements/recommendations for international students: Required—TOEFL. Electronic applications accepted. *Faculty research:* Highway traffic operations, transportation and policy planning, air quality in transportation, transportation modeling.

The University of Alabama in Huntsville, School of Graduate Studies, College of Engineering, Department of Civil and Environmental Engineering, Huntsville, AL 35899. Offers civil and environmental engineering (PhD); civil engineering (MSE), including civil engineering, environmental and water resource engineering, geotechnical engineering, structural engineering and structural mechanics, transportation engineering. PhD offered jointly with The University of Alabama at Birmingham. Part-time and evening/weekend programs available. *Degree requirements:* For master's, comprehensive exam, thesis or alternative, oral and written exams; for doctorate, comprehensive exam, thesis/dissertation, oral and written exams. *Entrance requirements:* For master's, GRE General Test, BSE, minimum GPA of 3.0; for doctorate, GRE General Test, minimum GPA of 3.0. Additional exam requirements/recommendations for international students: Required—TOEFL (minimum score 500 paper-based; 80 iBT), IELTS (minimum score 6.5). Electronic applications accepted. *Faculty research:* Smart materials and smart structures, fiber-reinforced cementitious composites, processing and mechanics of composites, geographic information systems, environmental engineering.

University of Arkansas, Graduate School, College of Engineering, Department of Civil Engineering, Fayetteville, AR 72701-1201. Offers civil engineering (MSCE, MSE, PhD); environmental engineering (MS En E, MSE); transportation engineering (MSE, MSTE). *Degree requirements:* For master's, thesis optional; for doctorate, one foreign language, thesis/dissertation. Electronic applications accepted.

University of Calgary, Faculty of Graduate Studies, Schulich School of Engineering, Department of Civil Engineering, Calgary, AB T2N 1N4, Canada. Offers avalanche mechanics (M Sc, PhD); civil engineering (M Eng, M Sc, PhD); energy and environment engineering (M Eng, M Sc, PhD); environmental engineering (M Eng, M Sc, PhD); geotechnical engineering (M Eng, M Sc, PhD); materials science (M Eng, M Sc, PhD); project management (M Eng, M Sc, PhD); structures and solid mechanics (M Eng, M Sc, PhD); transportation engineering (M Eng, M Sc, PhD); water resources (M Eng, M Sc, PhD). Part-time programs available. *Degree requirements:* For master's, thesis; for doctorate, thesis/dissertation, written and oral candidacy exam. *Entrance requirements:* For master's, minimum GPA of 3.0; for doctorate, minimum GPA of 3.5. Additional exam requirements/recommendations for international students: Required—TOEFL (minimum score 580 paper-based; 93 iBT), IELTS (minimum score 7). Electronic applications accepted. *Faculty research:* Geotechnical engineering, energy and environment, transportation, project management, structures and solid mechanics.

University of California, Berkeley, Graduate Division, College of Engineering, Department of Civil and Environmental Engineering, Berkeley, CA 94720-1500. Offers engineering and project management (M Eng, MS, D Eng, PhD); environmental engineering (M Eng, MS, D Eng, PhD); geoengineering (M Eng, MS, D Eng, PhD); structural engineering, mechanics and materials (M Eng, MS, D Eng, PhD); transportation engineering (M Eng, MS, D Eng, PhD); M Arch/MS; MCP/MS; MPP/MS. *Degree requirements:* For master's, comprehensive exam or thesis (MS); for doctorate, thesis/dissertation, qualifying exam. *Entrance requirements:* For master's, GRE General Test, minimum GPA of 3.0, 3 letters of recommendation; for doctorate, GRE General Test, minimum GPA of 3.5, 3 letters of recommendation. Additional exam requirements/recommendations for international students: Required—TOEFL (minimum score 570 paper-based). Electronic applications accepted.

University of California, Davis, College of Engineering, Graduate Group in Transportation Technology and Policy, Davis, CA 95616. Offers MS, PhD. Terminal master's awarded for partial completion of doctoral program. *Degree requirements:* For master's, comprehensive exam (for some programs), thesis (for some programs); for doctorate, thesis/dissertation. *Entrance requirements:* For master's, GRE General Test, minimum GPA of 3.0; for doctorate, GRE General Test, minimum GPA of 3.5. Additional exam requirements/recommendations for international students: Required—TOEFL (minimum score 550 paper-based). Electronic applications accepted.

University of California, Irvine, Institute of Transportation Studies, Irvine, CA 92697. Offers MA, PhD. *Students:* 11 full-time (7 women); includes 4 minority (all Asian, non-Hispanic/Latino), 6 international. Average age 31. 20 applicants, 60% accepted, 2 enrolled. In 2014, 3 doctorates awarded. *Entrance requirements:* For master's and doctorate, GRE General Test, minimum GPA of 3.0. *Application deadline:* For fall admission, 1/15 for domestic and international students. Application fee: $90 ($110 for international students). *Financial support:* Fellowships, research assistantships with full tuition reimbursements, teaching assistantships, institutionally sponsored loans, traineeships, health care benefits, and unspecified assistantships available. Financial award application deadline: 3/1. *Unit head:* Jean-Daniel Saphores, Director, 949-824-7334, E-mail: saphores@uci.edu. *Application contact:* Anne Marie DeFeo, Administrative Manager, 949-824-6564, E-mail: amdefeo@uci.edu. Website: http://www.its.uci.edu/.

University of Central Florida, College of Engineering and Computer Science, Department of Civil, Environmental, and Construction Engineering, Orlando, FL 32816. Offers civil engineering (MS, MSCE, PhD, Certificate), including civil engineering (MS, MSCE, PhD), construction engineering (Certificate), structural engineering (Certificate); transportation engineering (Certificate); construction engineering (Certificate); environmental engineering (MS, MS Env E, PhD). Part-time and evening/weekend programs available. *Faculty:* 27 full-time (2 women), 13 part-time/adjunct (0 women). *Students:* 107 full-time (28 women), 95 part-time (30 women); includes 53 minority (9 Black or African American, non-Hispanic/Latino; 7 Asian, non-Hispanic/Latino; 30 Hispanic/Latino; 7 Two or more races, non-Hispanic/Latino), 74 international. Average age 30. 172 applicants, 56% accepted, 53 enrolled. In 2014, 48 master's, 9 doctorates, 1 other advanced degree awarded. *Degree requirements:* For master's, thesis or alternative; for doctorate, thesis/dissertation, departmental qualifying exam, candidacy

exam. *Entrance requirements:* For master's, GRE General Test, minimum GPA of 3.0 in last 60 hours of course work; for doctorate, GRE General Test, minimum GPA of 3.5 in last 60 hours of course work. Additional exam requirements/recommendations for international students: Required—TOEFL. *Application deadline:* For fall admission, 7/15 priority date for domestic students; for spring admission, 12/1 priority date for domestic students. Application fee: $30. Electronic applications accepted. *Expenses:* Tuition, state resident: part-time $288.16 per credit hour. Tuition, nonresident: part-time $1073.31 per credit hour. *Financial support:* In 2014–15, 51 students received support, including 18 fellowships with partial tuition reimbursements available (averaging $3,900 per year), 44 research assistantships with partial tuition reimbursements available (averaging $9,750 per year), 14 teaching assistantships with partial tuition reimbursements available (averaging $8,900 per year); career-related internships or fieldwork, Federal Work-Study, institutionally sponsored loans, tuition waivers (partial), and unspecified assistantships also available. Financial award application deadline: 3/1; financial award applicants required to submit FAFSA. *Unit head:* Dr. Mohamed Abdel-Aty, Chair, 407-823-2841, E-mail: m.aty@ucf.edu. *Application contact:* Barbara Rodriguez Lamas, Director, Admissions and Student Services, 407-823-2766, Fax: 407-823-6442, E-mail: gradadmissions@ucf.edu.
Website: http://cece.ucf.edu/.

University of Colorado Denver, College of Engineering and Applied Science, Department of Civil Engineering, Denver, CO 80217. Offers civil engineering (EASPh D); civil engineering systems (PhD); environmental and sustainability engineering (MS, PhD); geographic information systems (MS); geotechnical engineering (MS, PhD); hydrology and hydraulics (MS, PhD); structural engineering (MS, PhD); transportation engineering (MS, PhD). Part-time and evening/weekend programs available. *Faculty:* 15 full-time (4 women), 11 part-time/adjunct (2 women). *Students:* 64 full-time (15 women), 43 part-time (8 women); includes 15 minority (3 Black or African American, non-Hispanic/Latino; 3 Asian, non-Hispanic/Latino; 6 Hispanic/Latino; 3 Two or more races, non-Hispanic/Latino), 34 international. Average age 32. 136 applicants, 54% accepted, 28 enrolled. In 2014, 35 master's, 9 doctorates awarded. *Degree requirements:* For master's, comprehensive exam, 30 credit hours, project or thesis; for doctorate, comprehensive exam, thesis/dissertation, 60 credit hours (30 of which are dissertation research). *Entrance requirements:* For master's, GRE, statement of purpose, transcripts, three references; for doctorate, GRE, statement of purpose, transcripts, references, letter of support from faculty stating willingness to serve as dissertation advisor and outlining plan for financial support. Additional exam requirements/recommendations for international students: Required—TOEFL (minimum score 537 paper-based; 75 iBT); Recommended—IELTS (minimum score 6.5). *Application deadline:* For fall admission, 5/1 for domestic students, 4/1 for international students; for spring admission, 10/1 for domestic students, 9/1 for international students; for summer admission, 2/15 for domestic students, 1/15 for international students. Application fee: $50 ($75 for international students). Electronic applications accepted. *Expenses:* Expenses: Contact institution. *Financial support:* In 2014–15, 26 students received support. Fellowships, research assistantships, teaching assistantships, career-related internships or fieldwork, Federal Work-Study, institutionally sponsored loans, scholarships/grants, traineeships, and unspecified assistantships available. Financial award application deadline: 4/1; financial award applicants required to submit FAFSA. *Faculty research:* Earthquake source physics, environmental biotechnology, hydrologic and hydraulic engineering, sustainability assessments, transportation energy use and greenhouse gas emissions. *Unit head:* Dr. Kevin Rens, Chair, 303-556-8017, E-mail: kevin.rens@ucdenver.edu. *Application contact:* Tammy Southern, Program Assistant, 303-556-6712, E-mail: tamara.southern@ucdenver.edu.
Website: http://www.ucdenver.edu/academics/colleges/Engineering/Programs/Civil-Engineering/Pages/CivilEngineering.aspx.

University of Colorado Denver, College of Engineering and Applied Science, Master of Engineering Program, Denver, CO 80217-3364. Offers civil engineering (M Eng), including civil engineering, geographic information systems, transportation systems; electrical engineering (M Eng); mechanical engineering (M Eng). Part-time programs available. *Students:* 30 full-time (9 women), 20 part-time (7 women); includes 3 minority (1 Black or African American, non-Hispanic/Latino; 2 Hispanic/Latino), 8 international. Average age 34. 35 applicants, 83% accepted, 15 enrolled. In 2014, 14 master's awarded. *Degree requirements:* For master's, comprehensive exam, 27 credit hours of course work, 3 credit hours of report or thesis work. *Entrance requirements:* For master's, GRE (for those with GPA below 2.75), transcripts, references, statement of purpose. Additional exam requirements/recommendations for international students: Required—TOEFL (minimum score 537 paper-based; 75 iBT); Recommended—IELTS (minimum score 6.5). *Application deadline:* For fall admission, 4/1 for domestic students, 3/1 for international students; for spring admission, 10/1 for domestic students, 9/15 for international students. Applications are processed on a rolling basis. Application fee: $50 ($75 for international students). Electronic applications accepted. *Expenses:* Expenses: Contact institution. *Financial support:* In 2014–15, 4 students received support. Fellowships, research assistantships, teaching assistantships, Federal Work-Study, institutionally sponsored loans, scholarships/grants, traineeships, and unspecified assistantships available. Financial award application deadline: 4/1; financial award applicants required to submit FAFSA. *Faculty research:* Civil, electrical and mechanical engineering. *Unit head:* 303-556-2870, Fax: 303-556-2511, E-mail: engineering@ucdenver.edu. *Application contact:* Graduate School Admissions, 303-556-2704, E-mail: admissions@ucdenver.edu.
Website: http://www.ucdenver.edu/academics/colleges/Engineering/admissions/Masters/Pages/MastersAdmissions.aspx.

University of Dayton, Department of Civil and Environmental Engineering and Engineering Mechanics, Dayton, OH 45469. Offers engineering mechanics (MSEM); environmental engineering (MSCE); geotechnical engineering (MSCE); structural engineering (MSCE); transportation engineering (MSCE); water resources engineering (MSCE). Part-time and evening/weekend programs available. *Faculty:* 9 full-time (2 women), 3 part-time/adjunct (1 woman). *Students:* 23 full-time (4 women), 6 part-time (2 women), 22 international. Average age 26. 70 applicants, 39% accepted, 4 enrolled. In 2014, 11 master's awarded. *Degree requirements:* For master's, thesis optional. *Entrance requirements:* For master's, minimum GPA of 3.0 in undergraduate work. Additional exam requirements/recommendations for international students: Required—TOEFL (minimum score 550 paper-based; 80 iBT). *Application deadline:* For fall admission, 8/1 priority date for domestic students, 5/1 priority date for international students; for winter admission, 7/1 priority date for international students; for spring admission, 11/1 priority date for international students. Applications are processed on a rolling basis. Application fee: $0 ($50 for international students). Electronic applications accepted. *Expenses: Tuition:* Full-time $10,176; part-time $848 per credit. *Required fees:* $25; $25 per course. Part-time tuition and fees vary according to course level, course load, degree level and program. *Financial support:* In 2014–15, 3 students received support. Institutionally sponsored loans, scholarships/grants, and department-funded awards (averaging $2448 per year) available. Financial award application deadline: 3/1; financial award applicants required to submit FAFSA. *Faculty research:* Physical modeling of water resource systems, finite element methods, mechanics of composite materials, transportation systems safety, biological treatment processes, fiber reinforced concrete. *Total annual research expenditures:* $250,000. *Unit head:* Dr. Donald V. Chase, Chair, 937-229-3847, Fax: 937-229-3491, E-mail: dchase1@udayton.edu. *Application contact:* 937-229-4462, E-mail: graduateadmission@udayton.edu.
Website: https://www.udayton.edu/engineering/departments/civil/index.php.

University of Delaware, College of Engineering, Department of Civil and Environmental Engineering, Newark, DE 19716. Offers environmental engineering (MAS, MCE, PhD); geotechnical engineering (MAS, MCE, PhD); ocean engineering (MAS, MCE, PhD); structural engineering (MAS, MCE, PhD); transportation engineering (MAS, MCE, PhD); water resource engineering (MAS, MCE, PhD). Part-time programs available. Terminal master's awarded for partial completion of doctoral program. *Degree requirements:* For master's, thesis; for doctorate, thesis/dissertation. *Entrance requirements:* For master's and doctorate, GRE General Test. Additional exam requirements/recommendations for international students: Required—TOEFL. Electronic applications accepted. *Faculty research:* Structural engineering and mechanics; transportation engineering; ocean engineering; soil mechanics and foundation; water resources and environmental engineering.

University of Massachusetts Amherst, Graduate School, College of Engineering, Department of Civil and Environmental Engineering, Amherst, MA 01003. Offers civil engineering (MSCE, PhD); environmental and water resources engineering (MSCE); geotechnical engineering (MSCE); structural engineering and mechanics (MSCE); transportation engineering (MSCE). Part-time programs available. *Faculty:* 32 full-time (8 women). *Students:* 104 full-time (43 women), 15 part-time (7 women); includes 16 minority (3 Black or African American, non-Hispanic/Latino; 4 Asian, non-Hispanic/Latino; 7 Hispanic/Latino; 2 Two or more races, non-Hispanic/Latino), 44 international. Average age 26. 219 applicants, 62% accepted, 40 enrolled. In 2014, 36 master's, 4 doctorates awarded. Terminal master's awarded for partial completion of doctoral program. *Degree requirements:* For master's, thesis or alternative; for doctorate, comprehensive exam, thesis/dissertation. *Entrance requirements:* For master's and doctorate, GRE General Test. Additional exam requirements/recommendations for international students: Required—TOEFL (minimum score 550 paper-based; 80 iBT), IELTS (minimum score 6.5). *Application deadline:* For fall admission, 1/2 for domestic and international students; for spring admission, 10/1 for domestic and international students. Applications are processed on a rolling basis. Application fee: $75. Electronic applications accepted. *Expenses:* Tuition, state resident: full-time $1980; part-time $110 per credit. Tuition, nonresident: full-time $14,644; part-time $414 per credit. *Required fees:* $11,417. One-time fee: $357. *Financial support:* Fellowships with full and partial tuition reimbursements, research assistantships with full and partial tuition reimbursements, teaching assistantships with full and partial tuition reimbursements, career-related internships or fieldwork, Federal Work-Study, scholarships/grants, traineeships, health care benefits, tuition waivers (full and partial), and unspecified assistantships available. Support available to part-time students. Financial award application deadline: 1/2. *Unit head:* Dr. Sanjay Arwade, Graduate Program Director, 413-545-0686, Fax: 413-545-2840. *Application contact:* Lindsay DeSantis, Supervisor of Admissions, 413-545-0722, Fax: 413-577-0100, E-mail: gradadm@grad.umass.edu.
Website: http://cee.umass.edu/.

University of Memphis, Graduate School, Herff College of Engineering, Department of Civil Engineering, Memphis, TN 38152. Offers civil engineering (PhD); environmental engineering (MS); foundation engineering (MS); structural engineering (MS); transportation engineering (MS); water resources engineering (MS). *Faculty:* 11 full-time (1 woman), 2 part-time/adjunct (0 women). *Students:* 12 full-time (5 women), 8 part-time (1 woman); includes 2 minority (both Black or African American, non-Hispanic/Latino), 4 international. Average age 27. 18 applicants, 100% accepted, 4 enrolled. In 2014, 8 master's awarded. Terminal master's awarded for partial completion of doctoral program. *Degree requirements:* For master's, comprehensive exam, thesis optional; for doctorate, comprehensive exam, thesis/dissertation. *Entrance requirements:* For master's, GRE General Test or MAT, minimum undergraduate GPA of 2.5; for doctorate, GRE, 3 letters of recommendation. Additional exam requirements/recommendations for international students: Required—TOEFL (minimum score 550 paper-based; 79 iBT). *Application deadline:* For fall admission, 1/7 for domestic students, 1/5 for international students; for spring admission, 12/1 for domestic students, 9/15 for international students. Application fee: $35 ($60 for international students). *Financial support:* In 2014–15, 6 students received support. Fellowships with full tuition reimbursements available, research assistantships with full tuition reimbursements available, career-related internships or fieldwork, Federal Work-Study, scholarships/grants, and unspecified assistantships available. Financial award application deadline: 2/15; financial award applicants required to submit FAFSA. *Faculty research:* Structural response to earthquakes, pavement design, water quality, transportation safety, intermodal transportation. *Unit head:* Dr. Sharam Pezeshk, Interim Chair, 901-678-2746, Fax: 901-678-3026. *Application contact:* Dr. Roger Meier, Coordinator of Graduate Studies, 901-678-3284.
Website: http://www.ce.memphis.edu.

University of Missouri, Office of Research and Graduate Studies, College of Engineering, Department of Civil and Environmental Engineering, Columbia, MO 65211. Offers civil engineering (MS, PhD); environmental engineering (MS, PhD); geotechnical engineering (MS, PhD); structural engineering (MS, PhD); transportation and highway engineering (MS); water resources (MS, PhD). *Faculty:* 18 full-time (2 women), 1 part-time/adjunct (0 women). *Students:* 42 full-time (8 women), 27 part-time (6 women); includes 4 minority (1 Black or African American, non-Hispanic/Latino; 1 Asian, non-Hispanic/Latino; 2 Hispanic/Latino), 45 international. Average age 31. 102 applicants, 48% accepted, 22 enrolled. In 2014, 14 master's, 2 doctorates awarded. *Degree requirements:* For master's, report or thesis; for doctorate, thesis/dissertation. *Entrance requirements:* For master's and doctorate, GRE General Test. Additional exam requirements/recommendations for international students: Required—TOEFL (minimum score 550 paper-based; 79 iBT). *Application deadline:* For fall admission, 2/15 priority date for domestic students, 2/15 for international students; for winter admission, 9/15 priority date for domestic students, 9/15 for international students. Application fee: $55 ($75 for international students). *Financial support:* Fellowships, research assistantships, teaching assistantships, and institutionally sponsored loans available. *Unit head:* Dr. Mark Virkler, Department Chair, 573-882-7434, E-mail: virklerm@missouri.edu. *Application contact:* Jennifer Keyzer-Andre, Administrative Associate I, 573-882-4442, E-mail: keyzerandrej@missouri.edu.
Website: http://engineering.missouri.edu/civil/.

University of Nevada, Las Vegas, Graduate College, Howard R. Hughes College of Engineering, Department of Civil and Environmental Engineering and Construction, Las Vegas, NV 89154-4015. Offers civil and environmental engineering (PhD); transportation (MS). Part-time programs available. *Faculty:* 13 full-time (2 women), 2 part-time/adjunct (0 women). *Students:* 48 full-time (14 women), 30 part-time (14 women); includes 17 minority (3 Black or African American, non-Hispanic/Latino; 4 Asian, non-Hispanic/Latino; 7 Hispanic/Latino; 3 Two or more races, non-Hispanic/Latino), 37 international. Average age 32. 51 applicants, 75% accepted, 18 enrolled. In 2014, 19 master's, 3 doctorates awarded. *Degree requirements:* For master's, comprehensive exam (for some programs), thesis (for some programs); for doctorate, comprehensive exam, thesis/dissertation. *Entrance requirements:* For master's and

doctorate, GRE General Test. Additional exam requirements/recommendations for international students: Required—TOEFL (minimum score 550 paper-based; 80 iBT), IELTS (minimum score 7). *Application deadline:* For fall admission, 6/15 for domestic students, 3/15 for international students; for spring admission, 11/15 for domestic students, 8/30 for international students. Application fee: $60 ($95 for international students). Electronic applications accepted. *Financial support:* In 2014–15, 45 students received support, including 15 research assistantships with partial tuition reimbursements available (averaging $15,678 per year), 30 teaching assistantships with partial tuition reimbursements available (averaging $13,553 per year); institutionally sponsored loans, scholarships/grants, health care benefits, and unspecified assistantships also available. Financial award application deadline: 3/1. *Total annual research expenditures:* $747,749. *Unit head:* Donald Hayes, Chair/Professor, 702-895-4723, Fax: 702-895-3936, E-mail: donald.hayes@unlv.edu. *Application contact:* Graduate College Admissions Evaluator, 702-895-3320, Fax: 702-895-4180, E-mail: gradcollege@unlv.edu.
Website: http://www.unlv.edu/ceec.

University of New Brunswick Fredericton, School of Graduate Studies, Faculty of Engineering, Department of Civil Engineering, Fredericton, NB E3B 5A3, Canada. Offers construction engineering and management (M Eng, M Sc E, PhD); environmental engineering (M Eng, M Sc E, PhD); environmental studies (M Eng); geotechnical engineering (M Eng, M Sc E, PhD); groundwater/hydrology (M Eng, M Sc E, PhD); materials (M Eng, M Sc E, PhD); pavements (M Eng, M Sc E, PhD); structures (M Eng, M Sc E, PhD); transportation (M Eng, M Sc E, PhD). Part-time programs available. *Faculty:* 12 full-time (1 woman), 4 part-time/adjunct (0 women). *Students:* 16 full-time (4 women), 15 part-time (5 women). In 2014, 9 master's, 3 doctorates awarded. *Degree requirements:* For master's, thesis, proposal; for doctorate, comprehensive exam, thesis/dissertation, qualifying exam; 27 credit hours of courses. *Entrance requirements:* For master's, minimum GPA of 3.0; B Sc E in civil engineering or related engineering degree; for doctorate, minimum GPA of 3.0; graduate degree in engineering or applied science. Additional exam requirements/recommendations for international students: Required—IELTS (minimum score 7.5), TWE (minimum score 4), Michigan English Language Assessment Battery (minimum score 85) or CanTest (minimum score 4.5); Recommended—TOEFL (minimum score 580 paper-based). *Application deadline:* For fall admission, 5/1 for domestic students; for winter admission, 11/1 for domestic students. Applications are processed on a rolling basis. Application fee: $50 Canadian dollars. Electronic applications accepted. *Financial support:* In 2014–15, 35 fellowships, 48 research assistantships, 35 teaching assistantships were awarded; career-related internships or fieldwork and scholarships/grants also available. *Faculty research:* Construction engineering and management; engineering materials and infrastructure renewal; highway and pavement research; structures and solid mechanics; geotechnical and geoenvironmental engineering; structure interaction; transportation and planning; environment, solid waste management; structural engineering; water and environmental engineering. *Unit head:* Dr. Kerry MacQuarrie, Director of Graduate Studies, 506-453-5121, Fax: 506-453-3568, E-mail: ktm@unb.ca. *Application contact:* Joyce Moore, Graduate Secretary, 506-452-6127, Fax: 506-453-3568, E-mail: joycem@unb.ca.
Website: http://go.unb.ca/gradprograms.

University of Southern California, Graduate School, School of Policy, Planning, and Development, Master of Planning Program, Los Angeles, CA 90089. Offers sustainable cities (Graduate Certificate); transportation systems (Graduate Certificate); urban planning (M Pl); M Arch/M Pl; M Pl/MA; M Pl/MPP; M Pl/MRED; M Pl/MS; M Pl/MSW; MBA/M Pl; ML Arch/M Pl; MPA/M Pl. *Accreditation:* ACSP. Part-time programs available. *Degree requirements:* For master's, comprehensive exam, internship. *Entrance requirements:* For master's, GRE, GMAT. Additional exam requirements/recommendations for international students: Required—TOEFL (minimum score 600 paper-based; 100 iBT). Electronic applications accepted. *Faculty research:* Transportation and infrastructure, comparative international development, healthy communities, social economic development, sustainable community planning.

University of Southern California, Graduate School, Viterbi School of Engineering, Daniel J. Epstein Department of Industrial and Systems Engineering, Los Angeles, CA 90089. Offers digital supply chain management (MS); engineering management (MS); engineering technology communication (Graduate Certificate); health systems operations (Graduate Certificate); industrial and systems engineering (MS, PhD, Engr); manufacturing engineering (MS); operations research engineering (MS); optimization and supply chain management (Graduate Certificate); product development engineering (MS); safety systems and security (MS); systems architecting and engineering (MS, Graduate Certificate); systems safety and security (Graduate Certificate); transportation systems (Graduate Certificate); MS/MBA. Part-time and evening/weekend programs available. Postbaccalaureate distance learning degree programs offered (no on-campus study). Terminal master's awarded for partial completion of doctoral program. *Degree requirements:* For master's, thesis optional; for doctorate, thesis/dissertation. *Entrance requirements:* For master's and doctorate, GRE General Test. Additional exam requirements/recommendations for international students: Recommended—TOEFL. Electronic applications accepted. *Faculty research:* Health systems, music cognition and retrieval, transportation and logistics, manufacturing and automation, engineering systems design, risk and economic analysis.

University of Southern California, Graduate School, Viterbi School of Engineering, Sonny Astani Department of Civil Engineering, Los Angeles, CA 90089. Offers applied mechanics (MS); civil engineering (MS, PhD); computer-aided engineering (ME, Graduate Certificate); construction management (MCM); engineering technology commercialization (Graduate Certificate); environmental engineering (MS, PhD); environmental quality management (ME); structural design (ME); sustainable cities (Graduate Certificate); transportation systems (MS, Graduate Certificate); water and waste management (MS). Part-time and evening/weekend programs available. Terminal master's awarded for partial completion of doctoral program. *Degree requirements:* For master's, thesis optional; for doctorate, thesis/dissertation. *Entrance requirements:* For master's and doctorate, GRE General Test. Additional exam requirements/recommendations for international students: Recommended—TOEFL. Electronic applications accepted. *Faculty research:* Geotechnical engineering, transportation engineering, structural engineering, construction management, environmental engineering, water resources.

University of Southern Mississippi, Graduate School, College of Science and Technology, School of Construction, Hattiesburg, MS 39406-0001. Offers logistics, trade and transportation (MS). Part-time programs available. *Degree requirements:* For master's, comprehensive exam, thesis optional. *Entrance requirements:* For master's, GMAT or GRE General Test, minimum GPA of 2.75 in last 60 hours. Additional exam requirements/recommendations for international students: Required—TOEFL, IELTS. *Faculty research:* Robotics; CAD/CAM; simulation; computer-integrated manufacturing processes; construction scheduling, estimating, and computer systems.

University of South Florida, College of Engineering, Department of Civil and Environmental Engineering, Tampa, FL 33620-9951. Offers civil engineering (MCE, MSCE, PhD), including environmental engineering (MSES, PhD), geotechnical engineering (MCE, MSCE, MSES, PhD), interdisciplinary transportation (MSCE); materials engineering and science, structural engineering, transportation engineering, water resources; engineering science (MSES), including environmental engineering (MSES, PhD), geotechnical engineering (MCE, MSCE, MSES, PhD); environmental engineering (MEVE, MSEV, PhD). Part-time programs available. *Faculty:* 19 full-time (5 women). *Students:* 97 full-time (35 women), 83 part-time (25 women); includes 41 minority (6 Black or African American, non-Hispanic/Latino; 1 American Indian or Alaska Native, non-Hispanic/Latino; 3 Asian, non-Hispanic/Latino; 25 Hispanic/Latino; 6 Two or more races, non-Hispanic/Latino), 39 international. Average age 30. 229 applicants, 51% accepted, 43 enrolled. In 2014, 68 master's, 9 doctorates awarded. Terminal master's awarded for partial completion of doctoral program. *Degree requirements:* For master's, comprehensive exam, thesis (for some programs); for doctorate, comprehensive exam, thesis/dissertation. *Entrance requirements:* For master's, GRE General Test (preferred minimum scores of 20th percentile verbal, 50th percentile quantitative, and 10th percentile in analytical writing), minimum GPA of 3.0 in major, two letters of reference, statement of purpose; for doctorate, GRE General Test (preferred minimum scores of 45th percentile verbal, 65th percentile quantitative, and 50th percentile in analytical writing), three letters of recommendation, statement of purpose, resume. Additional exam requirements/recommendations for international students: Required—TOEFL (minimum score 550 paper-based; 79 iBT) or IELTS (minimum score 6.5). *Application deadline:* For fall admission, 2/15 for domestic students, 1/2 priority date for international students; for spring admission, 10/15 for domestic students, 6/1 priority date for international students. Application fee: $30. Electronic applications accepted. *Financial support:* In 2014–15, 65 students received support, including 44 research assistantships (averaging $14,123 per year), 21 teaching assistantships with tuition reimbursements available (averaging $15,329 per year). *Faculty research:* Environmental and water resources engineering, geotechnics and geoenvironmental systems, structures and materials systems, transportation systems. *Total annual research expenditures:* $3.3 million. *Unit head:* Dr. Manjriker Gunaratne, Professor and Department Chair, 813-974-5818, Fax: 813-974-2957, E-mail: gunaratn@usf.edu. *Application contact:* Dr. Sarina J. Ergas, Professor and Graduate Program Coordinator, 813-974-1119, Fax: 813-974-2957, E-mail: sergas@usf.edu.
Website: http://ce.eng.usf.edu/.

University of South Florida, University College/Distance Education, Tampa, FL 33620-9951. *Unit head:* Kathy Barnes, Interdisciplinary Programs Coordinator, 813-974-8031, Fax: 813-974-7061, E-mail: barnesk@usf.edu. *Application contact:* Karen Tylinski, Metro Initiatives, 813-974-9943, Fax: 813-974-7061, E-mail: ktylinsk@usf.edu.
Website: http://www.usf.edu/innovative-education/.

The University of Texas at Tyler, College of Engineering and Computer Science, Department of Civil Engineering, Tyler, TX 75799-0001. Offers environmental engineering (MS); industrial safety (MS); structural engineering (MS); transportation engineering (MS); water resources engineering (MS). Part-time and evening/weekend programs available. *Degree requirements:* For master's, thesis optional. *Entrance requirements:* For master's, GRE General Test, bachelor's degree in engineering, associated science degree. Additional exam requirements/recommendations for international students: Required—TOEFL. *Faculty research:* Non-destructive strength testing, indoor air quality, transportation routing and signaling, pavement replacement criteria, flood water routing, construction and long-term behavior of innovative geotechnical foundation and embankment construction used in highway construction, engineering education.

University of Washington, Graduate School, College of Engineering, Department of Civil and Environmental Engineering, Seattle, WA 98195-2700. Offers civil engineering (PhD); construction engineering (MSCE); environmental engineering (MSCE, PhD); hydrology, water resources, and environmental fluid mechanics (MSCE, PhD); structural and geotechnical engineering and mechanics (MSCE, PhD); transportation and construction engineering (PhD); transportation engineering (MSCE). Part-time programs available. Postbaccalaureate distance learning degree programs offered (no on-campus study). *Faculty:* 35 full-time (9 women). *Students:* 220 full-time (81 women), 147 part-time (50 women); includes 61 minority (9 Black or African American, non-Hispanic/Latino; 2 American Indian or Alaska Native, non-Hispanic/Latino; 34 Asian, non-Hispanic/Latino; 14 Hispanic/Latino; 2 Native Hawaiian or other Pacific Islander, non-Hispanic/Latino), 91 international. Average age 28. 901 applicants, 49% accepted, 162 enrolled. In 2014, 110 master's, 12 doctorates awarded. Terminal master's awarded for partial completion of doctoral program. *Degree requirements:* For master's, thesis (for some programs); for doctorate, comprehensive exam, thesis/dissertation, general, qualifying, and final exams; completion of degree within 10 years. *Entrance requirements:* For master's, GRE General Test, minimum GPA of 3.0, statement of purpose, letters of recommendation, transcripts; for doctorate, GRE General Test, minimum GPA of 3.5, statement of purpose, letters of recommendation, transcripts. Additional exam requirements/recommendations for international students: Required—TOEFL (minimum score 580 paper-based; 92 iBT); Recommended—IELTS (minimum score 7). *Application deadline:* For fall admission, 12/15 for domestic and international students. Applications are processed on a rolling basis. Application fee: $85. Electronic applications accepted. *Expenses:* Expenses: Contact institution. *Financial support:* In 2014–15, 179 students received support, including 41 fellowships with full and partial tuition reimbursements available, 77 research assistantships with full tuition reimbursements available, 58 teaching assistantships with full tuition reimbursements available; scholarships/grants also available. Financial award application deadline: 1/10; financial award applicants required to submit FAFSA. *Faculty research:* Structural and geotechnical engineering, transportation and construction engineering, water and environmental engineering. *Total annual research expenditures:* $14.1 million. *Unit head:* Dr. Gregory R. Miller, Professor/Chair, 206-543-0350, Fax: 206-543-1543, E-mail: gmiller@uw.edu. *Application contact:* Lorna Latal, Graduate Adviser, 206-543-2574, Fax: 206-543-1543, E-mail: llatal@u.washington.edu.
Website: http://www.ce.washington.edu/.

Virginia Polytechnic Institute and State University, VT Online, Blacksburg, VA 24061. Offers advanced transportation systems (Certificate); aerospace engineering (MS); agricultural and life sciences (MSLFS); business information systems (Graduate Certificate); career and technical education (MS); civil engineering (MS); computer engineering (M Eng, MS); decision support systems (Graduate Certificate); eLearning leadership (MA); electrical engineering (M Eng, MS); engineering administration (MEA); environmental engineering (Certificate); environmental politics and policy (Graduate Certificate); environmental sciences and engineering (MS); foundations of political analysis (Graduate Certificate); health product risk management (Graduate Certificate); industrial and systems engineering (MS); information policy and society (Graduate Certificate); information security (Graduate Certificate); information technology (MIT); instructional technology (MA); integrative STEM education (MA Ed); liberal arts (Graduate Certificate); life sciences: health product risk management (MS); natural resources (MNR, Graduate Certificate); networking (Graduate Certificate); nonprofit and nongovernmental organization management (Graduate Certificate); ocean engineering (MS); political science (MA); security studies (Graduate Certificate); software development (Graduate Certificate). *Expenses:* Tuition, state resident: full-time $11,656; part-time $647.50 per credit hour. Tuition, nonresident: full-time $23,351; part-time $1297.25 per credit hour. *Required fees:* $2533; $465.75 per semester. Tuition and fees vary according to course load, campus/location and program.

Water Resources Engineering

American University of Beirut, Graduate Programs, Faculty of Engineering and Architecture, Beirut, Lebanon. Offers applied energy (ME); civil engineering (PhD); electrical and computer engineering (PhD); engineering management (MEM); environmental and water resources (ME); environmental technology (MSES); mechanical engineering (ME, PhD); urban design (MUD); urban planning and policy (MUPP). Part-time programs available. *Faculty:* 93 full-time (18 women), 3 part-time/adjunct (1 woman). *Students:* 268 full-time (111 women), 58 part-time (27 women). Average age 26. 225 applicants, 68% accepted, 79 enrolled. In 2014, 114 master's, 9 doctorates awarded. Terminal master's awarded for partial completion of doctoral program. *Degree requirements:* For master's, one foreign language, comprehensive exam, thesis (for some programs); for doctorate, one foreign language, comprehensive exam, thesis/dissertation, publications. *Entrance requirements:* For master's, letters of recommendation; for doctorate, GRE, letters of recommendation, master's degree, transcripts, curriculum vitae, interview. Additional exam requirements/recommendations for international students: Required—TOEFL (minimum score 600 paper-based; 100 iBT), IELTS (minimum score 7.5). *Application deadline:* For fall admission, 2/5 priority date for domestic and international students; for spring admission, 11/1 priority date for domestic students, 11/1 for international students. Application fee: $50. Electronic applications accepted. *Expenses: Tuition:* Full-time $15,462; part-time $859 per credit. *Required fees:* $692. Tuition and fees vary according to course load and program. *Financial support:* In 2014–15, 190 students received support, including 2 fellowships with full tuition reimbursements available (averaging $24,800 per year), 64 research assistantships with full tuition reimbursements available (averaging $24,800 per year), 124 teaching assistantships with full tuition reimbursements available (averaging $9,800 per year); career-related internships or fieldwork, institutionally sponsored loans, scholarships/grants, health care benefits, and unspecified assistantships also available. *Total annual research expenditures:* $1.5 million. *Unit head:* Prof. Makram T. Suidan, Dean, 961-1350000 Ext. 3400, Fax: 961-1744462, E-mail: msuidan@aub.edu.lb. *Application contact:* Dr. Salim Kanaan, Director, Admissions Office, 961-1350000 Ext. 2594, Fax: 961-1750775, E-mail: sk00@aub.edu.lb.
Website: http://staff.aub.edu.lb/~webfea.

Carnegie Mellon University, Carnegie Institute of Technology, Department of Civil and Environmental Engineering, Pittsburgh, PA 15213. Offers advanced infrastructure systems (MS, PhD); advanced infrastructure systems technology development and application (MS); air quality engineering and science (MS); civil and environmental engineering (MS, PhD); civil and environmental engineering/engineering and public policy (PhD); civil engineering (MS, PhD); computational mechanics (MS, PhD); computational modeling and monitoring for resilient structural and material systems (MS); energy infrastructure systems (MS); environmental engineering (MS, PhD); environmental management and science (MS, PhD); IT-based sustainable global infrastructure and construction management (MS); sustainability and green design (MS); water quality engineering and science (MS). Part-time programs available. *Faculty:* 21 full-time (5 women), 12 part-time/adjunct (3 women). *Students:* 229 full-time (99 women), 31 part-time (11 women); includes 18 minority (4 Black or African American, non-Hispanic/Latino; 13 Asian, non-Hispanic/Latino; 1 Hispanic/Latino), 193 international. Average age 26. 590 applicants, 68% accepted, 124 enrolled. In 2014, 85 master's, 11 doctorates awarded. Terminal master's awarded for partial completion of doctoral program. *Degree requirements:* For master's, thesis optional; for doctorate, comprehensive exam, thesis/dissertation, two-part qualifying exam, public defense of dissertation. *Entrance requirements:* For master's, GRE General Test, BS in engineering, science or mathematics; for doctorate, GRE General Test, BS or MS in engineering, science or mathematics. Additional exam requirements/recommendations for international students: Required—TOEFL (minimum score 84 iBT) or IELTS. *Application deadline:* For fall admission, 1/5 priority date for domestic and international students; for spring admission, 9/15 priority date for domestic and international students. Application fee: $65. Electronic applications accepted. *Financial support:* In 2014–15, 169 students received support. Fellowships with full and partial tuition reimbursements available, research assistantships with full and partial tuition reimbursements available, scholarships/grants, tuition waivers (full and partial), unspecified assistantships, and service assistantships available. Financial award application deadline: 1/5. *Faculty research:* Advanced infrastructure systems; environmental engineering, sustainability, and science; mechanics, materials, and computing. *Total annual research expenditures:* $4.9 million. *Unit head:* Dr. David A. Dzombak, Head, 412-268-2941, Fax: 412-268-7813, E-mail: dzombak@cmu.edu. *Application contact:* Melissa L. Brown, Director of Graduate Admissions & Recruiting, 412-268-8762, Fax: 412-268-7813, E-mail: mlb2@andrew.cmu.edu.
Website: http://www.cmu.edu/cee/.

Cornell University, Graduate School, Graduate Fields of Engineering, Field of Civil and Environmental Engineering, Ithaca, NY 14853-0001. Offers engineering management (M Eng, MS, PhD); environmental engineering (M Eng, MS, PhD); environmental fluid mechanics and hydrology (M Eng, MS, PhD); environmental systems engineering (M Eng, MS, PhD); geotechnical engineering (M Eng, MS, PhD); remote sensing (M Eng, MS, PhD); structural engineering (M Eng, MS, PhD); structural mechanics (M Eng, MS); transportation engineering (MS, PhD); transportation systems engineering (M Eng); water resource systems (M Eng, MS, PhD). Terminal master's awarded for partial completion of doctoral program. *Degree requirements:* For master's, thesis (MS); for doctorate, comprehensive exam, thesis/dissertation. *Entrance requirements:* For master's and doctorate, GRE General Test (recommended), 2 letters of recommendation. Additional exam requirements/recommendations for international students: Required—TOEFL (minimum score 600 paper-based; 77 iBT). Electronic applications accepted. *Faculty research:* Environmental engineering, geotechnical engineering, remote sensing, environmental fluid mechanics and hydrology, structural engineering.

George Mason University, Volgenau School of Engineering, Sid and Reva Dewberry Department of Civil, Environmental, and Infrastructure Engineering, Fairfax, VA 22030. Offers construction project management (MS); environmental and water resources engineering (MS); geotechnical, construction, and structural engineering (M Eng); transportation engineering (MS, PhD). *Faculty:* 12 full-time (4 women), 16 part-time/adjunct (3 women). *Students:* 28 full-time (7 women), 51 part-time (13 women); includes 25 minority (12 Black or African American, non-Hispanic/Latino; 8 Asian, non-Hispanic/Latino; 5 Hispanic/Latino), 14 international. Average age 30. 90 applicants, 58% accepted, 25 enrolled. In 2014, 28 master's, 3 doctorates awarded. *Degree requirements:* For master's, thesis (for some programs), 30 credits, departmental seminars; for doctorate, thesis/dissertation, qualifying exams. *Entrance requirements:* For master's, GRE, photocopy of passport; 2 official college transcripts; resume; official bank statement; proof of financial support; expanded goals statement; self-evaluation form; BS in engineering or other related science; 3 letters of recommendation; for doctorate, GRE (for those who received degree outside of the U.S.), photocopy of passport; 2 official college transcripts; resume; official bank statement; proof of financial support; expanded goals statement; self-evaluation form; baccalaureate degree in engineering or related science; master's degree (preferred); 3 letters of recommendation. Additional exam requirements/recommendations for international students: Required—TOEFL (minimum score 575 paper-based; 80 iBT), IELTS (minimum score 6.5), PTE. *Application deadline:* For fall admission, 1/15 priority date for domestic students; for spring admission, 8/1 priority date for domestic students. Application fee: $65 ($80 for international students). Electronic applications accepted. *Expenses:* Expenses: Contact institution. *Financial support:* In 2014–15, 19 students received support, including 1 fellowship (averaging $5,000 per year), 9 research assistantships with full and partial tuition reimbursements available (averaging $23,846 per year), 10 teaching assistantships with full and partial tuition reimbursements available (averaging $21,200 per year); career-related internships or fieldwork, Federal Work-Study, scholarships/grants, unspecified assistantships, and health care benefits (for full-time research or teaching assistantship recipients) also available. Support available to part-time students. Financial award application deadline: 3/1; financial award applicants required to submit FAFSA. *Faculty research:* Evolutionary design, infrastructure security, intelligent transportation systems, national transportation networks, water quality modeling. *Total annual research expenditures:* $159,347. *Unit head:* Dr. Deborah J. Goodings, Chair, 703-993-1675, Fax: 703-993-9790, E-mail: goodings@gmu.edu. *Application contact:* Kristin Amaya, Administrative Assistant, 703-993-1675, Fax: 703-993-9790, E-mail: kfairch1@gmu.edu.
Website: http://civil.gmu.edu/.

Indiana University Bloomington, School of Public and Environmental Affairs, Environmental Science Programs, Bloomington, IN 47405. Offers applied ecology (MSES); energy (MSES); environmental chemistry, toxicology, and risk assessment (MSES); environmental science (PhD); hazardous materials management (Certificate); specialized environmental science (MSES); water resources (MSES); JD/MSES; MSES/MA; MSES/MPA; MSES/MS. Part-time programs available. Terminal master's awarded for partial completion of doctoral program. *Degree requirements:* For master's, capstone or thesis; internship; for doctorate, comprehensive exam, thesis/dissertation. *Entrance requirements:* For master's, GRE General Test or GMAT, official transcripts, 3 letters of recommendation, resume, personal statement; for doctorate, GRE General Test or LSAT, official transcripts, 3 letters of recommendation, resume or curriculum vitae, statement of purpose. Additional exam requirements/recommendations for international students: Required—TOEFL (minimum score 600 paper-based; 96 iBT); Recommended—IELTS (minimum score 7). Electronic applications accepted. *Faculty research:* Applied ecology, bio-geochemistry, toxicology, wetlands ecology, environmental microbiology, forest ecology, environmental chemistry.

Kansas State University, Graduate School, College of Engineering, Department of Civil Engineering, Manhattan, KS 66506. Offers civil engineering (MS, PhD); environmental engineering (MS, PhD); geotechnical engineering (MS, PhD); structural engineering (MS, PhD); transportation engineering (MS, PhD); water resources engineering (MS, PhD). Part-time and evening/weekend programs available. Postbaccalaureate distance learning degree programs offered (no on-campus study). *Faculty:* 14 full-time (4 women), 3 part-time/adjunct (1 woman). *Students:* 37 full-time (12 women), 37 part-time (9 women); includes 6 minority (3 Black or African American, non-Hispanic/Latino; 3 Hispanic/Latino), 23 international. Average age 30. 62 applicants, 39% accepted, 10 enrolled. In 2014, 14 master's, 4 doctorates awarded. *Degree requirements:* For master's, thesis or alternative; for doctorate, thesis/dissertation. *Entrance requirements:* For master's, GRE General Test, bachelor's degree or course work in related engineering fields; for doctorate, GRE General Test. Additional exam requirements/recommendations for international students: Required—TOEFL (minimum score 550 paper-based; 79 iBT). *Application deadline:* For fall admission, 2/1 priority date for domestic students, 1/1 priority date for international students; for spring admission, 8/1 priority date for domestic and international students. Applications are processed on a rolling basis. Application fee: $50 ($75 for international students). Electronic applications accepted. *Financial support:* In 2014–15, 19 research assistantships with partial tuition reimbursements (averaging $13,431 per year), 12 teaching assistantships with partial tuition reimbursements (averaging $15,058 per year) were awarded; institutionally sponsored loans and scholarships/grants also available. Support available to part-time students. Financial award application deadline: 3/1; financial award applicants required to submit FAFSA. *Faculty research:* Transportation and materials engineering, water resources engineering, environmental engineering, geotechnical engineering, structural engineering. *Total annual research expenditures:* $2.4 million. *Unit head:* Dr. Robert Stokes, Head, 785-532-1595, Fax: 785-532-7717, E-mail: drbobb@k-state.edu. *Application contact:* Dr. Dunja Peric, Graduate Coordinator, 785-532-2468, Fax: 785-532-7717, E-mail: peric@k-state.edu.
Website: http://www.ce.ksu.edu/.

Louisiana State University and Agricultural & Mechanical College, Graduate School, College of Engineering, Department of Civil and Environmental Engineering, Baton Rouge, LA 70803. Offers environmental engineering (MSCE, PhD); geotechnical engineering (MSCE, PhD); structural engineering and mechanics (MSCE, PhD); transportation engineering (MSCE, PhD); water resources (MSCE, PhD). Part-time programs available. *Faculty:* 26 full-time (1 woman). *Students:* 90 full-time (24 women), 28 part-time (6 women); includes 12 minority (5 Black or African American, non-Hispanic/Latino; 1 American Indian or Alaska Native, non-Hispanic/Latino; 5 Asian, non-Hispanic/Latino; 1 Two or more races, non-Hispanic/Latino), 67 international. Average age 30. 147 applicants, 50% accepted, 23 enrolled. In 2014, 26 master's, 8 doctorates awarded. *Degree requirements:* For master's, thesis optional; for doctorate, one foreign language, thesis/dissertation. *Entrance requirements:* For master's and doctorate, GRE General Test, minimum GPA of 3.0. Additional exam requirements/recommendations for international students: Required—TOEFL (minimum score 550 paper-based; 79 IBT), IELTS (minimum score 6.5), or PTE (minimum score 59). *Application deadline:* For fall admission, 1/1 priority date for domestic students, 5/15 for international students; for spring admission, 10/15 for domestic and international students; for summer admission, 5/15 for domestic and international students. Applications are processed on a rolling basis. Application fee: $50 ($70 for international students). Electronic applications accepted. *Financial support:* In 2014–15, 88 students received support, including 7 fellowships with full and partial tuition reimbursements available (averaging $26,784 per year), 59 research assistantships with full and partial tuition reimbursements available (averaging $16,992 per year), 13 teaching assistantships with full and partial tuition reimbursements available (averaging $16,290 per year); career-related internships or fieldwork, institutionally sponsored loans, scholarships/grants, and health care benefits also available. Financial award application deadline: 3/1; financial award applicants required to submit FAFSA. *Faculty research:* Mechanics and structures, environmental, geotechnical transportation, water resources. *Total annual research expenditures:* $3.2 million. *Unit head:* Dr. George Z. Voyiadjis, Chair/Professor, 225-578-8442, Fax: 225-578-8652, E-mail: voyaidjis@lsu.edu. *Application contact:* Dr. Ayman Ikeli, Professor, 225-578-7048, E-mail: aokeli@lsu.edu.
Website: http://www.cee.lsu.edu/.

Marquette University, Graduate School, Opus College of Engineering, Department of Civil, Construction and Environmental Engineering, Milwaukee, WI 53201-1881. Offers construction engineering and management (MS, PhD, Certificate); environmental engineering (MS, PhD); structural design (Certificate); structural engineering and structural mechanics (MS, PhD); transportation (Certificate); transportation engineering and materials (MS, PhD); waste and wastewater treatment processes (Certificate); water resources engineering (Certificate). Part-time and evening/weekend programs available. Terminal master's awarded for partial completion of doctoral program. *Degree requirements:* For master's, comprehensive exam (for some programs), thesis or alternative; for doctorate, thesis/dissertation. *Entrance requirements:* For master's, GRE General Test (recommended), minimum GPA of 3.0, official transcripts from all current and previous colleges/universities except Marquette, three letters of recommendation; for doctorate, GRE General Test, minimum GPA of 3.0, official transcripts from all current and previous colleges/universities except Marquette, three letters of recommendation, brief statement of purpose, submission of any English language publications authored by applicant (strongly recommended). Additional exam requirements/recommendations for international students: Required—TOEFL (minimum score 530 paper-based). Electronic applications accepted. *Faculty research:* Highway safety, highway performance, and intelligent transportation systems; surface mount technology; watershed management.

McGill University, Faculty of Graduate and Postdoctoral Studies, Faculty of Engineering, Department of Civil Engineering and Applied Mechanics, Montréal, QC H3A 2T5, Canada. Offers environmental engineering (M Eng, M Sc, PhD); fluid mechanics (M Sc); fluid mechanics and hydraulic engineering (M Eng, PhD); materials engineering (M Eng, PhD); rehabilitation of urban infrastructure (M Eng, PhD); soil behavior (M Eng, PhD); soil mechanics and foundations (M Eng, PhD); structures and structural mechanics (M Eng, PhD); water resources (M Sc); water resources engineering (M Eng, PhD).

New Mexico Institute of Mining and Technology, Graduate Studies, Department of Civil and Environmental Engineering, Socorro, NM 87801. Offers environmental engineering (MS), including air quality engineering and science, hazardous waste engineering, water quality engineering and science. *Degree requirements:* For master's, thesis. *Entrance requirements:* For master's, GRE General Test. Additional exam requirements/recommendations for international students: Required—TOEFL (minimum score 540 paper-based). *Faculty research:* Air quality, hazardous waste management, wastewater management and treatment, site remediation.

Norwich University, College of Graduate and Continuing Studies, Master of Civil Engineering Program, Northfield, VT 05663. Offers construction management engineering (MCE); environmental/water resources engineering (MCE); geotechnical engineering (MCE); structural engineering (MCE). Evening/weekend programs available. Postbaccalaureate distance learning degree programs offered (minimal on-campus study). *Faculty:* 14 part-time/adjunct (2 women). *Students:* 111 full-time (17 women); includes 28 minority (16 Black or African American, non-Hispanic/Latino; 2 American Indian or Alaska Native, non-Hispanic/Latino; 7 Asian, non-Hispanic/Latino; 3 Hispanic/Latino). Average age 36. 61 applicants, 100% accepted, 42 enrolled. In 2014, 57 master's awarded. *Entrance requirements:* For master's, minimum undergraduate GPA of 2.75. Additional exam requirements/recommendations for international students: Required—TOEFL (minimum score 550 paper-based; 80 iBT), IELTS (minimum score 6.5). *Application deadline:* For fall admission, 8/8 for domestic and international students; for spring admission, 2/16 for domestic and international students. Applications are processed on a rolling basis. Electronic applications accepted. *Expenses:* Expenses: Contact institution. *Financial support:* In 2014–15, 27 students received support. Scholarships/grants available. Financial award applicants required to submit FAFSA. *Unit head:* Dr. Thomas Descoteaux, Program Director, 802-485-2730, Fax: 802-485-2533, E-mail: tdescote@norwich.edu. *Application contact:* Rija Ramahatra, Associate Program Director, 802-485-2892, Fax: 802-485-2533, E-mail: ramahatr@norwich.edu.
Website: http://online.norwich.edu/degree-programs/masters/master-civil-engineering/overview.

Ohio University, Graduate College, Russ College of Engineering and Technology, Department of Civil Engineering, Athens, OH 45701-2979. Offers civil engineering (PhD); construction engineering and management (MS); environmental (MS); geotechnical and geoenvironmental (MS); mechanics (MS); structures (MS); transportation (MS); water resources (MS). Part-time programs available. *Degree requirements:* For master's, comprehensive exam (for some programs), thesis or alternative; for doctorate, comprehensive exam, thesis/dissertation. *Entrance requirements:* For master's, GRE General Test, minimum GPA of 3.0, 3 letters of recommendation; for doctorate, GRE General Test. Additional exam requirements/recommendations for international students: Required—TOEFL (minimum score 550 paper-based; 80 iBT) or IELTS (minimum score 6.5). Electronic applications accepted. *Faculty research:* Noise abatement, materials and environment, highway infrastructure, subsurface investigation (pavements, pipes, bridges).

Oregon State University, College of Engineering, Program in Biological and Ecological Engineering, Corvallis, OR 97331. Offers M Eng, MS, PhD. Part-time programs available. *Faculty:* 8 full-time (2 women), 4 part-time/adjunct (0 women). *Students:* 12 full-time (2 women), 1 part-time (0 women), 8 international. Average age 30. 21 applicants, 14% accepted, 1 enrolled. In 2014, 1 master's, 3 doctorates awarded. Terminal master's awarded for partial completion of doctoral program. *Degree requirements:* For master's, thesis or alternative; for doctorate, thesis/dissertation. *Entrance requirements:* For master's and doctorate, GRE, minimum GPA of 3.0 in last 90 hours. Additional exam requirements/recommendations for international students: Required—TOEFL (minimum score 80 iBT), IELTS (minimum score 6.5). *Application deadline:* For fall admission, 8/1 for domestic students, 4/1 for international students; for winter admission, 12/1 for domestic students, 7/1 for international students; for spring admission, 2/1 for domestic students, 10/1 for international students; for summer admission, 5/1 for domestic students, 1/1 for international students. Application fee: $60. *Expenses:* Expenses: $15,359 full-time resident tuition and fees; $23,405 non-resident. *Financial support:* Fellowships with full tuition reimbursements, research assistantships with full tuition reimbursements, teaching assistantships, Federal Work-Study, and institutionally sponsored loans available. Support available to part-time students. Financial award application deadline: 2/1. *Faculty research:* Bioengineering, water resources engineering, food engineering, cell culture and fermentation, vadose zone transport. *Unit head:* Dr. John P. Bolte, Head, 541-737-6303, Fax: 541-737-2082, E-mail: info-bee@engr.orst.edu. *Application contact:* Ganti Murthy, Biological and Ecological Engineering Advisor, 541-737-6291, E-mail: info-bee@engr.orst.edu.
Website: http://bee.oregonstate.edu/programs/graduate.

Oregon State University, Interdisciplinary/Institutional Programs, Program in Water Resources Engineering, Corvallis, OR 97331. Offers MS, PhD. Part-time programs available. *Students:* 23 full-time (10 women), 2 part-time (1 woman); includes 5 minority (1 Asian, non-Hispanic/Latino; 2 Hispanic/Latino; 2 Two or more races, non-Hispanic/Latino), 2 international. Average age 30. 39 applicants, 38% accepted, 8 enrolled. In 2014, 3 master's, 4 doctorates awarded. *Entrance requirements:* For master's and doctorate, GRE. Additional exam requirements/recommendations for international students: Required—TOEFL (minimum score 80 iBT), IELTS (minimum score 6.5). *Application deadline:* For fall admission, 1/5 for domestic students. Application fee: $60. *Expenses:* Tuition, state resident: full-time $11,907; part-time $189 per credit hour. Tuition, nonresident: full-time $19,953; part-time $441 per credit hour. *Required fees:* $1472; $449 per term. One-time fee: $350. Tuition and fees vary according to course load and program. *Unit head:* Dr. Mary Santelmann, Director, Water Resources Graduate Program, 541-737-1215, E-mail: santelmm@oregonstate.edu.
Website: http://oregonstate.edu/gradwater/.

Southern Methodist University, Bobby B. Lyle School of Engineering, Department of Environmental and Civil Engineering, Dallas, TX 75275-0340. Offers air pollution control and atmospheric sciences (PhD); civil engineering (MS); environmental engineering (MS); environmental science (MS); structural engineering (PhD); sustainability and development (MA); water and wastewater engineering (PhD). Part-time and evening/weekend programs available. Postbaccalaureate distance learning degree programs offered (no on-campus study). Terminal master's awarded for partial completion of doctoral program. *Degree requirements:* For master's, thesis optional; for doctorate, thesis/dissertation, oral and written qualifying exams. *Entrance requirements:* For master's, GRE General Test, minimum GPA of 3.0 in last 2 years; bachelor's degree in engineering, mathematics, or sciences; for doctorate, GRE, BS and MS in related field, minimum GPA of 3.3. Additional exam requirements/recommendations for international students: Required—TOEFL. Electronic applications accepted. *Faculty research:* Human and environmental health effects of endocrine disrupters, development of air pollution control systems for diesel engines, structural analysis and design, modeling and design of waste treatment systems.

State University of New York College of Environmental Science and Forestry, Department of Environmental Resources Engineering, Syracuse, NY 13210-2779. Offers ecological engineering (MPS, MS, PhD); environmental management (MPS); environmental resources engineering (MPS, MS, PhD); geospatial information science and engineering (MPS, MS, PhD); water resources engineering (MPS, MS, PhD). Part-time programs available. *Degree requirements:* For master's, thesis (for some programs); for doctorate, comprehensive exam, thesis/dissertation. *Entrance requirements:* For master's and doctorate, GRE General Test, minimum GPA of 3.0. Additional exam requirements/recommendations for international students: Required—TOEFL (minimum score 550 paper-based; 80 iBT), IELTS (minimum score 6). *Faculty research:* Ecological engineering, environmental resources engineering, geospatial information science and engineering, water resources engineering, environmental science.

Stevens Institute of Technology, Graduate School, Charles V. Schaefer Jr. School of Engineering, Department of Civil, Environmental, and Ocean Engineering, Program in Civil Engineering, Hoboken, NJ 07030. Offers civil engineering (PhD); geotechnical engineering (Certificate); geotechnical/geoenvironmental engineering (M Eng, Engr); hydrologic modeling (M Eng); stormwater management (M Eng); structural engineering (M Eng, Engr); water resources engineering (M Eng). *Degree requirements:* For master's, thesis optional; for doctorate, variable foreign language requirement, thesis/dissertation; for other advanced degree, project or thesis. *Entrance requirements:* For doctorate, GRE. Additional exam requirements/recommendations for international students: Required—TOEFL. Electronic applications accepted.

Tufts University, School of Engineering, Department of Civil and Environmental Engineering, Medford, MA 02155. Offers bioengineering (ME, MS), including environmental technology; civil engineering (ME, MS, PhD), including geotechnical engineering, structural engineering, water diplomacy (PhD); environmental engineering (ME, MS, PhD), including environmental engineering and environmental sciences, environmental geotechnology, environmental health, environmental science and management, hazardous materials management, water diplomacy (PhD), water resources engineering. Part-time programs available. *Faculty:* 24 full-time (5 women), 6 part-time/adjunct (1 woman). *Students:* 66 full-time (29 women), 19 part-time (6 women); includes 5 minority (1 Black or African American, non-Hispanic/Latino; 2 Asian, non-Hispanic/Latino; 1 Hispanic/Latino; 1 Two or more races, non-Hispanic/Latino), 25 international. Average age 29. 166 applicants, 42% accepted, 27 enrolled. In 2014, 21 master's, 6 doctorates awarded. Terminal master's awarded for partial completion of doctoral program. *Degree requirements:* For master's, thesis or alternative; for doctorate, thesis/dissertation. *Entrance requirements:* For master's and doctorate, GRE General Test. Additional exam requirements/recommendations for international students: Required—TOEFL (minimum score 550 paper-based; 80 iBT), IELTS (minimum score 6.5). *Application deadline:* For fall admission, 1/15 priority date for domestic students, 1/15 for international students; for spring admission, 9/15 for domestic and international students. Applications are processed on a rolling basis. Application fee: $75. Electronic applications accepted. *Expenses: Tuition:* Full-time $45,590; part-time $1161 per credit hour. *Required fees:* $782. Full-time tuition and fees vary according to degree level, program and student level. Part-time tuition and fees vary according to course load. *Financial support:* Fellowships with full tuition reimbursements, research assistantships with full and partial tuition reimbursements, teaching assistantships with full and partial tuition reimbursements, Federal Work-Study, scholarships/grants, tuition waivers (partial), and unspecified assistantships available. Financial award application deadline: 5/15; financial award applicants required to submit FAFSA. *Faculty research:* Environmental and water resources engineering, environmental health, geotechnical and geoenvironmental engineering, structural engineering and mechanics, water diplomacy. *Unit head:* Dr. Kurt Pennell, Graduate Program Director. *Application contact:* Office of Graduate Admissions, 617-627-3395, E-mail: gradadmissions@tufts.edu.
Website: http://www.ase.tufts.edu/cee/.

The University of Alabama in Huntsville, School of Graduate Studies, College of Engineering, Department of Civil and Environmental Engineering, Huntsville, AL 35899. Offers civil and environmental engineering (PhD); civil engineering (MSE), including civil engineering, environmental and water resource engineering, geotechnical engineering, structural engineering and structural mechanics, transportation engineering. PhD offered jointly with The University of Alabama at Birmingham. Part-time and evening/weekend programs available. *Degree requirements:* For master's, comprehensive exam, thesis or alternative, oral and written exams; for doctorate, comprehensive exam, thesis/dissertation, oral and written exams. *Entrance requirements:* For master's, GRE General Test, BSE, minimum GPA of 3.0; for doctorate, GRE General Test, minimum GPA of 3.0. Additional exam requirements/recommendations for international students: Required—TOEFL (minimum score 500 paper-based; 80 iBT), IELTS (minimum score 6.5). Electronic applications accepted. *Faculty research:* Smart materials and smart structures, fiber-reinforced cementitious composites, processing and mechanics of composites, geographic information systems, environmental engineering.

University of Alberta, Faculty of Graduate Studies and Research, Department of Civil and Environmental Engineering, Edmonton, AB T6G 2E1, Canada. Offers construction engineering and management (M Eng, M Sc, PhD); environmental engineering (M Eng, M Sc, PhD); environmental science (M Sc, PhD); geoenvironmental engineering (M Eng, M Sc, PhD); geotechnical engineering (M Eng, M Sc, PhD); mining engineering (M Eng, M Sc, PhD); petroleum engineering (M Eng, M Sc, PhD); structural engineering (M Eng, M Sc, PhD); water resources (M Eng, M Sc, PhD). Part-time programs available. Postbaccalaureate distance learning degree programs offered (minimal on-campus study). *Degree requirements:* For master's, thesis (for some programs); for doctorate, thesis/dissertation. *Entrance requirements:* For master's, minimum GPA of 3.0 in last 2 years of undergraduate studies; for doctorate, minimum GPA of 3.0. Additional exam requirements/recommendations for international students: Required—TOEFL (minimum score 550 paper-based). Electronic applications accepted. *Faculty research:* Mining.

University of California, Berkeley, Graduate Division, College of Engineering, Department of Civil and Environmental Engineering, Berkeley, CA 94720-1500. Offers engineering and project management (M Eng, MS, D Eng, PhD); environmental engineering (M Eng, MS, D Eng, PhD); geoengineering (M Eng, MS, D Eng, PhD); structural engineering, mechanics and materials (M Eng, MS, D Eng, PhD); transportation engineering (M Eng, MS, D Eng, PhD); M Arch/MS; MCP/MS; MPP/MS. *Degree requirements:* For master's, comprehensive exam or thesis (MS); for doctorate, thesis/dissertation, qualifying exam. *Entrance requirements:* For master's, GRE General Test, minimum GPA of 3.0, 3 letters of recommendation; for doctorate, GRE General Test, minimum GPA of 3.5, 3 letters of recommendation. Additional exam requirements/recommendations for international students: Required—TOEFL (minimum score 570 paper-based). Electronic applications accepted.

University of Colorado Boulder, Graduate School, College of Engineering and Applied Science, Department of Civil, Environmental, and Architectural Engineering, Boulder, CO 80309. Offers building systems engineering (MS, PhD); construction engineering management (MS, PhD); environmental engineering (MS, PhD); geotechnical engineering and geomechanics (MS, PhD); hydrology, water resources and environmental fluid mechanics (MS, PhD); structural engineering and structural mechanics (MS, PhD). *Faculty:* 37 full-time (8 women). *Students:* 235 full-time (81 women), 36 part-time (9 women); includes 24 minority (9 Asian, non-Hispanic/Latino; 6 Hispanic/Latino; 9 Two or more races, non-Hispanic/Latino), 83 international. Average age 28. 391 applicants, 63% accepted, 68 enrolled. In 2014, 76 master's, 30 doctorates awarded. Terminal master's awarded for partial completion of doctoral program. *Degree requirements:* For master's, comprehensive exam, thesis or alternative; for doctorate, thesis/dissertation. *Entrance requirements:* For master's, GRE General Test, minimum undergraduate GPA of 3.0. *Application deadline:* For fall admission, 1/31 for domestic and international students; for spring admission, 10/1 for domestic and international students. Application fee: $50 ($70 for international students). Electronic applications accepted. *Financial support:* In 2014–15, 387 students received support, including 75 fellowships (averaging $11,889 per year), 92 research assistantships with full and partial tuition reimbursements available (averaging $34,669 per year), 17 teaching assistantships with full and partial tuition reimbursements available (averaging $28,513 per year); institutionally sponsored loans, scholarships/grants, health care benefits, and unspecified assistantships also available. Financial award application deadline: 1/15; financial award applicants required to submit FAFSA. *Faculty research:* Civil engineering, environmental engineering, architectural engineering, geotechnical engineering, hydrology. *Total annual research expenditures:* $13 million.
Website: http://civil.colorado.edu/.

University of Dayton, Department of Civil and Environmental Engineering and Engineering Mechanics, Dayton, OH 45469. Offers engineering mechanics (MSEM); environmental engineering (MSCE); geotechnical engineering (MSCE); structural engineering (MSCE); transportation engineering (MSCE); water resources engineering (MSCE). Part-time and evening/weekend programs available. *Faculty:* 9 full-time (2 women), 3 part-time/adjunct (1 woman). *Students:* 23 full-time (4 women), 6 part-time (2 women), 22 international. Average age 26. 70 applicants, 39% accepted, 4 enrolled. In 2014, 11 master's awarded. *Degree requirements:* For master's, thesis optional. *Entrance requirements:* For master's, minimum GPA of 3.0 in undergraduate work. Additional exam requirements/recommendations for international students: Required—TOEFL (minimum score 550 paper-based; 80 iBT). *Application deadline:* For fall admission, 8/1 priority date for domestic students, 5/1 priority date for international students; for winter admission, 7/1 priority date for international students; for spring admission, 11/1 priority date for international students. Applications are processed on a rolling basis. Application fee: $0 ($50 for international students). Electronic applications accepted. *Expenses: Tuition:* Full-time $10,176; part-time $848 per credit. *Required fees:* $25; $25 per course. Part-time tuition and fees vary according to course level, course load, degree level and program. *Financial support:* In 2014–15, 3 students received support. Institutionally sponsored loans, scholarships/grants, and department-funded awards (averaging $2448 per year) available. Financial award application deadline: 3/1; financial award applicants required to submit FAFSA. *Faculty research:* Physical modeling of water resource systems, finite element methods, mechanics of composite materials, transportation systems safety, biological treatment processes, fiber reinforced concrete. *Total annual research expenditures:* $250,000. *Unit head:* Dr. Donald V. Chase, Chair, 937-229-3847, Fax: 937-229-3491, E-mail: dchase1@udayton.edu. *Application contact:* 937-229-4462, E-mail: graduateadmission@udayton.edu.
Website: https://www.udayton.edu/engineering/departments/civil/index.php.

University of Delaware, College of Engineering, Department of Civil and Environmental Engineering, Newark, DE 19716. Offers environmental engineering (MAS, MCE, PhD); geotechnical engineering (MAS, MCE, PhD); ocean engineering (MAS, MCE, PhD); structural engineering (MAS, MCE, PhD); transportation engineering (MAS, MCE, PhD); water resource engineering (MAS, MCE, PhD). Part-time programs available. Terminal master's awarded for partial completion of doctoral program. *Degree requirements:* For master's, thesis; for doctorate, thesis/dissertation. *Entrance requirements:* For master's and doctorate, GRE General Test. Additional exam requirements/recommendations for international students: Required—TOEFL. Electronic applications accepted. *Faculty research:* Structural engineering and mechanics; transportation engineering; ocean engineering; soil mechanics and foundation; water resources and environmental engineering.

University of Guelph, Graduate Studies, College of Physical and Engineering Science, School of Engineering, Guelph, ON N1G 2W1, Canada. Offers biological engineering (M Eng, M Sc, MA Sc, PhD); engineering systems and computing (M Eng, M Sc, MA Sc, PhD); environmental engineering (M Eng, M Sc, MA Sc, PhD); water resources engineering (M Eng, M Sc, MA Sc, PhD). Part-time programs available. *Degree requirements:* For master's, thesis (for some programs); for doctorate, comprehensive exam, thesis/dissertation. *Entrance requirements:* For master's, minimum B- average during previous 2 years of course work; for doctorate, minimum B average. Additional exam requirements/recommendations for international students: Required—TOEFL (minimum score 550 paper-based; 89 iBT), IELTS (minimum score 6.5). Electronic applications accepted. *Faculty research:* Water and food safety, environmental contaminant fates and mechanisms, computer systems, robotics and mechatronics, waste treatment.

University of Idaho, College of Graduate Studies, Water Resources Program, Moscow, ID 83844-1130. Offers engineering and science (PhD); engineering and science (MS); MS/JD. *Faculty:* 10 full-time, 1 part-time/adjunct. *Students:* 18 full-time, 11 part-time. Average age 34. In 2014, 12 master's, 2 doctorates awarded. *Entrance requirements:* Additional exam requirements/recommendations for international students: Required—TOEFL. *Application deadline:* Applications are processed on a rolling basis. Application fee: $60. Electronic applications accepted. *Expenses:* Tuition, state resident: full-time $4784; part-time $280.50 per credit hour. Tuition, nonresident: full-time $18,314; part-time $957.50 per credit hour. *Required fees:* $2000; $58.50 per credit hour. Tuition and fees vary according to program. *Financial support:* Applicants required to submit FAFSA. *Faculty research:* Water resource systems, biological wastewater treatment and water reclamation, invasive species, aquatics ecosystem restoration, watershed science and management. *Unit head:* Dr. Jan Boll, Director, 208-885-9694, E-mail: water@uidaho.edu. *Application contact:* Sean Scoggin, Graduate Recruitment Coordinator, 208-885-4001, Fax: 208-885-4406, E-mail: graduateadmissions@uidaho.edu.
Website: http://www.uidaho.edu/cogs/envs/water-resources.

University of Massachusetts Amherst, Graduate School, College of Engineering, Department of Civil and Environmental Engineering, Amherst, MA 01003. Offers civil engineering (MSCE, PhD); environmental and water resources engineering (MSCE); geotechnical engineering (MSCE); structural engineering and mechanics (MSCE); transportation engineering (MSCE). Part-time programs available. *Faculty:* 32 full-time (8 women). *Students:* 104 full-time (43 women), 15 part-time (7 women); includes 16 minority (3 Black or African American, non-Hispanic/Latino; 4 Asian, non-Hispanic/Latino; 7 Hispanic/Latino; 2 Two or more races, non-Hispanic/Latino), 44 international. Average age 26. 219 applicants, 62% accepted, 40 enrolled. In 2014, 36 master's, 4 doctorates awarded. Terminal master's awarded for partial completion of doctoral program. *Degree requirements:* For master's, thesis or alternative; for doctorate, comprehensive exam, thesis/dissertation. *Entrance requirements:* For master's and doctorate, GRE General Test. Additional exam requirements/recommendations for international students: Required—TOEFL (minimum score 550 paper-based; 80 iBT), IELTS (minimum score 6.5). *Application deadline:* For fall admission, 1/2 for domestic and international students; for spring admission, 10/1 for domestic and international students. Applications are processed on a rolling basis. Application fee: $75. Electronic applications accepted. *Expenses:* Tuition, state resident: full-time $1980; part-time $110 per credit. Tuition, nonresident: full-time $14,644; part-time $414 per credit. *Required fees:* $11,417. One-time fee: $357. *Financial support:* Fellowships with full and partial tuition reimbursements, research assistantships with full and partial tuition reimbursements, teaching assistantships with full and partial tuition reimbursements, career-related internships or fieldwork, Federal Work-Study, scholarships/grants, traineeships, health care benefits, tuition waivers (full and partial), and unspecified assistantships available. Support available to part-time students. Financial award application deadline: 1/2. *Unit head:* Dr. Sanjay Arwade, Graduate Program Director, 413-545-0686, Fax: 413-545-2840. *Application contact:* Lindsay DeSantis, Supervisor of Admissions, 413-545-0722, Fax: 413-577-0100, E-mail: gradadm@grad.umass.edu.
Website: http://cee.umass.edu/.

University of Memphis, Graduate School, Herff College of Engineering, Department of Civil Engineering, Memphis, TN 38152. Offers civil engineering (PhD); environmental engineering (MS); foundation engineering (MS); structural engineering (MS); transportation engineering (MS); water resources engineering (MS). *Faculty:* 11 full-time (1 woman), 2 part-time/adjunct (0 women). *Students:* 12 full-time (5 women), 8 part-time (1 woman); includes 2 minority (both Black or African American, non-Hispanic/Latino), 4 international. Average age 27. 18 applicants, 100% accepted, 4 enrolled. In 2014, 8 master's awarded. Terminal master's awarded for partial completion of doctoral program. *Degree requirements:* For master's, comprehensive exam, thesis optional; for doctorate, comprehensive exam, thesis/dissertation. *Entrance requirements:* For master's, GRE General Test or MAT, minimum undergraduate GPA of 2.5; for doctorate, GRE, 3 letters of recommendation. Additional exam requirements/recommendations for international students: Required—TOEFL (minimum score 550 paper-based; 79 iBT). *Application deadline:* For fall admission, 1/7 for domestic students, 1/5 for international students; for spring admission, 12/1 for domestic students, 9/15 for international students. Application fee: $35 ($60 for international students). *Financial support:* In 2014–15, 6 students received support. Fellowships with full tuition reimbursements available, research assistantships with full tuition reimbursements available, career-related internships or fieldwork, Federal Work-Study, scholarships/grants, and unspecified assistantships available. Financial award application deadline: 2/15; financial award applicants required to submit FAFSA. *Faculty research:* Structural response to earthquakes, pavement design, water quality, transportation safety, intermodal transportation. *Unit head:* Dr. Sharam Pezeshk, Interim Chair, 901-678-2746, Fax: 901-678-3026. *Application contact:* Dr. Roger Meier, Coordinator of Graduate Studies, 901-678-3284.
Website: http://www.ce.memphis.edu.

University of Missouri, Office of Research and Graduate Studies, College of Engineering, Department of Civil and Environmental Engineering, Columbia, MO 65211. Offers civil engineering (MS, PhD); environmental engineering (MS, PhD); geotechnical engineering (MS, PhD); structural engineering (MS, PhD); transportation and highway engineering (MS); water resources (MS, PhD). *Faculty:* 18 full-time (2 women), 1 part-time/adjunct (0 women). *Students:* 42 full-time (8 women), 27 part-time (6 women); includes 4 minority (1 Black or African American, non-Hispanic/Latino; 1 Asian, non-Hispanic/Latino; 2 Hispanic/Latino), 45 international. Average age 31. 102 applicants, 48% accepted, 22 enrolled. In 2014, 14 master's, 2 doctorates awarded. *Degree requirements:* For master's, report or thesis; for doctorate, thesis/dissertation. *Entrance requirements:* For master's and doctorate, GRE General Test. Additional exam requirements/recommendations for international students: Required—TOEFL (minimum score 550 paper-based; 79 iBT). *Application deadline:* For fall admission, 2/15 priority date for domestic students, 2/15 for international students; for winter admission, 9/15 priority date for domestic students, 9/15 for international students. Application fee: $55 ($75 for international students). *Financial support:* Fellowships, research assistantships, teaching assistantships, and institutionally sponsored loans available. *Unit head:* Dr. Mark Virkler, Department Chair, 573-882-7434, E-mail: virklerm@missouri.edu. *Application contact:* Jennifer Keyzer-Andre, Administrative Associate I, 573-882-4442, E-mail: keyzerandrej@missouri.edu.
Website: http://engineering.missouri.edu/civil/.

University of New Haven, Graduate School, Tagliatela College of Engineering, Program in Environmental Engineering, West Haven, CT 06516-1916. Offers environmental engineering (MS); industrial and hazardous wastes (MS); water and wastewater treatment (MS); water resources (MS). Part-time and evening/weekend programs available. *Degree requirements:* For master's, thesis or alternative, research project. *Entrance requirements:* For master's, bachelor's degree in engineering. Additional exam requirements/recommendations for international students: Required—TOEFL (minimum score 75 iBT), IELTS, PTE (minimum score 50). Electronic applications accepted. Application fee is waived when completed online.

University of South Florida, College of Engineering, Department of Civil and Environmental Engineering, Tampa, FL 33620-9951. Offers civil engineering (MCE, MSCE, PhD), including environmental engineering (MSES, PhD), geotechnical engineering (MCE, MSCE, MSES, PhD), interdisciplinary transportation (MSCE), materials engineering and science, structural engineering, transportation engineering, water resources; engineering science (MSES), including environmental engineering (MSES, PhD), geotechnical engineering (MCE, MSCE, MSES, PhD); environmental engineering (MEVE, MSEV, PhD). Part-time programs available. *Faculty:* 19 full-time (5 women). *Students:* 97 full-time (35 women), 83 part-time (25 women); includes 41 minority (6 Black or African American, non-Hispanic/Latino; 1 American Indian or Alaska

Native, non-Hispanic/Latino; 3 Asian, non-Hispanic/Latino; 25 Hispanic/Latino; 6 Two or more races, non-Hispanic/Latino), 39 international. Average age 30. 229 applicants, 51% accepted, 43 enrolled. In 2014, 68 master's, 9 doctorates awarded. Terminal master's awarded for partial completion of doctoral program. *Degree requirements:* For master's, comprehensive exam, thesis (for some programs); for doctorate, comprehensive exam, thesis/dissertation. *Entrance requirements:* For master's, GRE General Test (preferred minimum scores of 20th percentile verbal, 50th percentile quantitative, and 10th percentile in analytical writing), minimum GPA of 3.0 in major, two letters of reference, statement of purpose; for doctorate, GRE General Test (preferred minimum scores of 45th percentile verbal, 65th percentile quantitative, and 50th percentile in analytical writing), three letters of recommendation, statement of purpose, resume. Additional exam requirements/recommendations for international students: Required—TOEFL (minimum score 550 paper-based; 79 iBT) or IELTS (minimum score 6.5). *Application deadline:* For fall admission, 2/15 for domestic students, 1/2 priority date for international students; for spring admission, 10/15 for domestic students, 6/1 priority date for international students. Application fee: $30. Electronic applications accepted. *Financial support:* In 2014–15, 65 students received support, including 44 research assistantships (averaging $14,123 per year), 21 teaching assistantships with tuition reimbursements available (averaging $15,329 per year). *Faculty research:* Environmental and water resources engineering, geotechnics and geoenvironmental systems, structures and materials systems, transportation systems. *Total annual research expenditures:* $3.3 million. *Unit head:* Dr. Manjriker Gunaratne, Professor and Department Chair, 813-974-5818, Fax: 813-974-2957, E-mail: gunaratn@usf.edu. *Application contact:* Dr. Sarina J. Ergas, Professor and Graduate Program Coordinator, 813-974-1119, Fax: 813-974-2957, E-mail: sergas@usf.edu.
Website: http://ce.eng.usf.edu/.

University of South Florida, College of Global Sustainability, Tampa, FL 33620-9951. Offers entrepreneurship (MA); sustainable energy (MA); sustainable tourism (MA); water (MA); MA/MS. *Faculty:* 5 full-time (0 women). *Students:* 30 full-time (16 women), 43 part-time (28 women); includes 23 minority (4 Black or African American, non-Hispanic/Latino; 3 Asian, non-Hispanic/Latino; 14 Hispanic/Latino; 2 Two or more races, non-Hispanic/Latino), 15 international. Average age 30. 88 applicants, 68% accepted, 44 enrolled. In 2014, 3 master's awarded. *Degree requirements:* For master's, comprehensive exam (for some programs), thesis or alternative, internship. *Entrance requirements:* For master's, minimum GPA of 3.0 in undergraduate coursework; at least two letters of recommendation (one must be academic); 200-250-word essay on student's background, professional goals, and reasons for seeking degree. Additional exam requirements/recommendations for international students: Required—TOEFL (minimum score 550 paper-based; 79 iBT). *Faculty research:* Global sustainability, integrated resource management, systems thinking, green communities, entrepreneurship, ecotourism. *Total annual research expenditures:* $125,823. *Unit head:* Dr. Rafael Perez, Interim Dean, 813-974-9694, E-mail: perez@usf.edu.
Website: http://psgs.usf.edu/.

University of South Florida, University College/Distance Education, Tampa, FL 33620-9951. *Unit head:* Kathy Barnes, Interdisciplinary Programs Coordinator, 813-974-8031, Fax: 813-974-7061, E-mail: barnesk@usf.edu. *Application contact:* Karen Tylinski, Metro Initiatives, 813-974-9943, Fax: 813-974-7061, E-mail: ktylinsk@usf.edu.
Website: http://www.usf.edu/innovative-education/.

The University of Texas at Austin, Graduate School, Cockrell School of Engineering, Department of Civil, Architectural and Environmental Engineering, Program in Environmental and Water Resources Engineering, Austin, TX 78712-1111. Offers MS, PhD. Part-time programs available. *Degree requirements:* For master's, thesis or alternative. *Entrance requirements:* For master's, GRE General Test. Additional exam requirements/recommendations for international students: Required—TOEFL. Electronic applications accepted.

The University of Texas at Tyler, College of Engineering and Computer Science, Department of Civil Engineering, Tyler, TX 75799-0001. Offers environmental engineering (MS); industrial safety (MS); structural engineering (MS); transportation engineering (MS); water resources engineering (MS). Part-time and evening/weekend programs available. *Degree requirements:* For master's, thesis optional. *Entrance requirements:* For master's, GRE General Test, bachelor's degree in engineering, associated science degree. Additional exam requirements/recommendations for

international students: Required—TOEFL. *Faculty research:* Non-destructive strength testing, indoor air quality, transportation routing and signaling, pavement replacement criteria, flood water routing, construction and long-term behavior of innovative geotechnical foundation and embankment construction used in highway construction, engineering education.

University of Washington, Graduate School, College of Engineering, Department of Civil and Environmental Engineering, Seattle, WA 98195-2700. Offers civil engineering (PhD); construction engineering (MSCE); environmental engineering (MSCE, PhD); hydrology, water resources, and environmental fluid mechanics (MSCE, PhD); structural and geotechnical engineering and mechanics (MSCE, PhD); transportation and construction engineering (PhD); transportation engineering (MSCE). Part-time programs available. Postbaccalaureate distance learning degree programs available (minimal on-campus study). *Faculty:* 35 full-time (9 women). *Students:* 220 full-time (81 women), 147 part-time (50 women); includes 61 minority (9 Black or African American, non-Hispanic/Latino; 2 American Indian or Alaska Native, non-Hispanic/Latino; 34 Asian, non-Hispanic/Latino; 14 Hispanic/Latino; 2 Native Hawaiian or other Pacific Islander, non-Hispanic/Latino), 91 international. Average age 28. 901 applicants, 49% accepted, 162 enrolled. In 2014, 110 master's, 12 doctorates awarded. Terminal master's awarded for partial completion of doctoral program. *Degree requirements:* For master's, thesis (for some programs); for doctorate, comprehensive exam, thesis/dissertation, general, qualifying, and final exams; completion of degree within 10 years. *Entrance requirements:* For master's, GRE General Test, minimum GPA of 3.0, statement of purpose, letters of recommendation, transcripts; for doctorate, GRE General Test, minimum GPA of 3.5, statement of purpose, letters of recommendation, transcripts. Additional exam requirements/recommendations for international students: Required—TOEFL (minimum score 580 paper-based; 92 iBT); Recommended—IELTS (minimum score 7). *Application deadline:* For fall admission, 12/15 for domestic and international students. Applications are processed on a rolling basis. Application fee: $85. Electronic applications accepted. *Expenses:* Expenses: Contact institution. *Financial support:* In 2014–15, 179 students received support, including 41 fellowships with full and partial tuition reimbursements available, 77 research assistantships with full tuition reimbursements available, 58 teaching assistantships with full tuition reimbursements available; scholarships/grants also available. Financial award application deadline: 1/10; financial award applicants required to submit FAFSA. *Faculty research:* Structural and geotechnical engineering, transportation and construction engineering, water and environmental engineering. *Total annual research expenditures:* $14.1 million. *Unit head:* Dr. Gregory R. Miller, Professor/Chair, 206-543-0350, Fax: 206-543-1543, E-mail: gmiller@uw.edu. *Application contact:* Lorna Latal, Graduate Adviser, 206-543-2574, Fax: 206-543-1543, E-mail: llatal@u.washington.edu.
Website: http://www.ce.washington.edu/.

Utah State University, School of Graduate Studies, College of Engineering, Department of Biological and Irrigation Engineering, Logan, UT 84322. Offers biological and agricultural engineering (MS, PhD); irrigation engineering (MS, PhD). Part-time programs available. Terminal master's awarded for partial completion of doctoral program. *Degree requirements:* For master's, thesis (for some programs); for doctorate, thesis/dissertation. *Entrance requirements:* For master's and doctorate, GRE General Test, minimum GPA of 3.0. Additional exam requirements/recommendations for international students: Required—TOEFL. *Faculty research:* On-farm water management, crop-water yield modeling, irrigation, biosensors, biological engineering.

Villanova University, College of Engineering, Department of Civil and Environmental Engineering, Program in Water Resources and Environmental Engineering, Villanova, PA 19085-1699. Offers urban water resources design (Certificate); water resources and environmental engineering (MSWREE). Part-time and evening/weekend programs available. Postbaccalaureate distance learning degree programs offered (no on-campus study). *Degree requirements:* For master's, thesis optional. *Entrance requirements:* For master's, GRE General Test (for applicants with degrees from foreign universities), BCE or bachelor's degree in science or related engineering field, minimum GPA of 3.0. Additional exam requirements/recommendations for international students: Required—TOEFL (minimum score 600 paper-based; 100 iBT). Electronic applications accepted. *Faculty research:* Photocatalytic decontamination and disinfection of water, urban storm water wetlands, economy and risk, removal and destruction of organic acids in water, sludge treatment.

Section 8
Computer Science and Information Technology

This section contains a directory of institutions offering graduate work in computer science and information technology, followed by in-depth entries submitted by institutions that chose to prepare detailed program descriptions. Additional information about programs listed in the directory but not augmented by an in-depth entry may be obtained by writing directly to the dean of a graduate school or chair of a department at the address given in the directory.

For programs offering related work, see also in this book *Electrical and Computer Engineering, Engineering and Applied Sciences,* and *Industrial Engineering.* In the other guides in this series:

Graduate Programs in the Humanities, Arts & Social Sciences
See *Communication and Media*

Graduate Programs in the Biological/Biomedical Sciences & Health-Related Medical Professions
See *Allied Health*

Graduate Programs in the Physical Sciences, Mathematics, Agricultural Sciences, the Environment & Natural Resources
See *Mathematical Sciences*

Graduate Programs in Business, Education, Information Studies, Law & Social Work
See *Business Administration and Management* and *Library and Information Studies*

CONTENTS

Artificial Intelligence/Robotics

California State University, Northridge, Graduate Studies, College of Engineering and Computer Science, Department of Manufacturing Systems Engineering and Management, Northridge, CA 91330. Offers engineering automation (MS); engineering management (MS); manufacturing systems engineering (MS); materials engineering (MS). Postbaccalaureate distance learning degree programs offered. *Students:* 180 full-time (38 women), 56 part-time (15 women); includes 24 minority (11 Asian, non-Hispanic/Latino; 8 Hispanic/Latino; 5 Two or more races, non-Hispanic/Latino), 172 international. Average age 26. *Entrance requirements:* For master's, GRE (if cumulative undergraduate GPA less than 3.0). *Application deadline:* For fall admission, 3/30 for domestic students; for spring admission, 9/30 for domestic students. Application fee: $55. *Expenses: Required fees:* $12,402. *Unit head:* Kang Chang, Acting Chair, 818-677-2167.
Website: http://www.csun.edu/~msem/.

Carnegie Mellon University, Dietrich College of Humanities and Social Sciences, Department of Statistics, Pittsburgh, PA 15213-3891. Offers machine learning and statistics (PhD); mathematical finance (PhD); statistics (MS, PhD), including applied statistics (PhD), computational statistics (PhD), theoretical statistics (PhD); statistics and public policy (PhD). Terminal master's awarded for partial completion of doctoral program. *Degree requirements:* For doctorate, comprehensive exam, thesis/dissertation. *Entrance requirements:* For master's and doctorate, GRE General Test. Additional exam requirements/recommendations for international students: Required—TOEFL. *Faculty research:* Stochastic processes, Bayesian statistics, statistical computing, decision theory, psychiatric statistics.

Carnegie Mellon University, School of Computer Science, Department of Machine Learning, Pittsburgh, PA 15213-3891. Offers MS, PhD.

Carnegie Mellon University, School of Computer Science and Carnegie Institute of Technology, Robotics Institute, Pittsburgh, PA 15213-3891. Offers computer vision (MS); robotic systems development (MS); robotics (MS, PhD); robotics technology (MS). *Degree requirements:* For doctorate, thesis/dissertation. *Entrance requirements:* For doctorate, GRE General Test, GRE Subject Test. Additional exam requirements/recommendations for international students: Required—TOEFL. *Faculty research:* Perception, cognition, manipulation, robot systems, manufacturing.

The College of William and Mary, Faculty of Arts and Sciences, Department of Applied Science, Williamsburg, VA 23187-8795. Offers accelerator science (PhD); applied mathematics (PhD); applied mechanics (PhD); applied robotics (PhD); applied science (MS); interface, thin film and surface science (PhD); lasers and optics (PhD); magnetic resonance (PhD); nanotechnology (PhD); non-destructive evaluation (PhD); polymer chemistry (PhD); remote sensing (PhD). Part-time programs available. *Faculty:* 8 full-time (2 women), 2 part-time/adjunct (0 women). *Students:* 28 full-time (11 women), 5 part-time (2 women); includes 5 minority (2 Black or African American, non-Hispanic/Latino; 2 Asian, non-Hispanic/Latino; 1 Hispanic/Latino), 13 international. Average age 28. 32 applicants, 38% accepted, 7 enrolled. In 2014, 6 master's, 4 doctorates awarded. Terminal master's awarded for partial completion of doctoral program. *Degree requirements:* For master's, comprehensive exam, thesis; for doctorate, comprehensive exam, thesis/dissertation, 4 core courses. *Entrance requirements:* For master's and doctorate, GRE General Test, GRE Subject Test. Additional exam requirements/recommendations for international students: Required—TOEFL, TWE. *Application deadline:* For fall admission, 2/3 priority date for domestic students, 2/3 for international students; for spring admission, 10/15 priority date for domestic students, 10/14 for international students. Applications are processed on a rolling basis. Application fee: $45. Electronic applications accepted. *Financial support:* Fellowships, research assistantships, teaching assistantships, Federal Work-Study, health care benefits, tuition waivers (full), and unspecified assistantships available. Financial award application deadline: 4/15; financial award applicants required to submit FAFSA. *Faculty research:* Computational biology, non-destructive evaluation, neurophysiology, lasers and optics. *Total annual research expenditures:* $1.7 million. *Unit head:* Dr. Christopher Del Negro, Chair, 757-221-7808, Fax: 757-221-2050, E-mail: cadeln@wm.edu. *Application contact:* Lianne Rios Ashburne, Graduate Program Coordinator, 757-221-2563, Fax: 757-221-2050, E-mail: lrashburne@wm.edu.
Website: http://www.wm.edu/as/appliedscience.

Cornell University, Graduate School, Graduate Fields of Engineering, Field of Computer Science, Ithaca, NY 14853-0001. Offers algorithms (M Eng, PhD); applied logic and automated reasoning (M Eng, PhD); artificial intelligence (M Eng, PhD); computer graphics (M Eng, PhD); computer science (M Eng, PhD); computer vision (M Eng, PhD); concurrency and distributed computing (M Eng, PhD); information organization and retrieval (M Eng, PhD); operating systems (M Eng, PhD); parallel computing (M Eng, PhD); programming environments (M Eng, PhD); programming languages and methodology (M Eng, PhD); robotics (M Eng, PhD); scientific computing (M Eng, PhD); theory of computation (M Eng, PhD). *Degree requirements:* For doctorate, comprehensive exam, thesis/dissertation. *Entrance requirements:* For master's, GRE General Test, 2 letters of recommendation; for doctorate, GRE General Test, GRE Subject Test (computer science or mathematics), 3 letters of recommendation. Additional exam requirements/recommendations for international students: Required—TOEFL (minimum score 505 paper-based; 77 iBT). Electronic applications accepted. *Faculty research:* Artificial intelligence, operating systems and databases, programming languages and security, scientific computing, theory of computing, computational biology and graphics.

Eastern Michigan University, Graduate School, College of Arts and Sciences, Department of English Language and Literature, Ypsilanti, MI 48197. Offers children's literature (MA); creative writing (MA); English linguistics (MA); English studies for teachers (MA); language technology (Graduate Certificate); literature (MA); teaching of writing (Graduate Certificate); written communication (MA, Graduate Certificate), including technical communications, written communications (MA). Part-time and evening/weekend programs available. Postbaccalaureate distance learning degree programs offered (minimal on-campus study). *Faculty:* 47 full-time (26 women). *Students:* 20 full-time (14 women), 72 part-time (47 women); includes 13 minority (8 Black or African American, non-Hispanic/Latino; 1 Asian, non-Hispanic/Latino; 1 Hispanic/Latino; 3 Two or more races, non-Hispanic/Latino), 8 international. Average age 31. 93 applicants, 48% accepted, 27 enrolled. In 2014, 31 master's, 1 other advanced degree awarded. *Entrance requirements:* Additional exam requirements/recommendations for international students: Required—TOEFL. *Application deadline:* Applications are processed on a rolling basis. Application fee: $45. *Financial support:* Fellowships, research assistantships with full tuition reimbursements, teaching assistantships with full tuition reimbursements, career-related internships or fieldwork, Federal Work-Study, institutionally sponsored loans, scholarships/grants, tuition waivers (partial), and unspecified assistantships available. Support available to part-time students. Financial award applicants required to submit FAFSA. *Unit head:* Dr. Mary Ramsey, Department Head, 734-487-4220, Fax: 734-483-9744, E-mail: mary.ramsey@

emich.edu. *Application contact:* Dr. Christine Neufeld, Graduate Coordinator, 734-487-2670, Fax: 734-487-9744, E-mail: cneufeld@emich.edu.
Website: http://www.emich.edu/english.

Georgia Institute of Technology, Graduate Studies, College of Computing, Multidisciplinary Program in Robotics, Atlanta, GA 30332-0001. Offers PhD. Program offered jointly with College of Computing, School of Aerospace Engineering, Wallace H. Coulter Department of Biomedical Engineering, George W. Woodruff School of Mechanical Engineering, and School of Electrical and Computer Engineering. Part-time programs available. *Students:* 54 full-time (8 women), 2 part-time; includes 8 minority (7 Asian, non-Hispanic/Latino; 1 Hispanic/Latino), 22 international. Average age 27. 171 applicants, 25% accepted, 8 enrolled. In 2014, 8 doctorates awarded. *Degree requirements:* For doctorate, comprehensive exam, thesis/dissertation. *Entrance requirements:* For doctorate, GRE General Test, requirements. Additional exam requirements/recommendations for international students: Required—TOEFL (minimum score 600 paper-based; 100 iBT). *Application deadline:* For fall admission, 12/1 priority date for domestic and international students. Applications are processed on a rolling basis. Application fee: $75. Electronic applications accepted. *Expenses:* Tuition, state resident: full-time $12,344; part-time $515 per credit hour. Tuition, nonresident: full-time $27,600; part-time $1150 per credit hour. *Required fees:* $1196 per term. Part-time tuition and fees vary according to course load. *Financial support:* Fellowships, research assistantships, teaching assistantships, career-related internships or fieldwork, Federal Work-Study, institutionally sponsored loans, tuition waivers (partial), and unspecified assistantships available. Support available to part-time students. Financial award application deadline: 5/1. *Unit head:* Frank Dellaert, Director, E-mail: frank.dellaert@cc.gatech.edu. *Application contact:* Graduate Coordinator, 404-894-1610, E-mail: gradinfo@mail.gatech.edu.
Website: http://robotics.gatech.edu.

Illinois Institute of Technology, Graduate College, College of Science, Department of Computer Science, Chicago, IL 60616. Offers business (MCS); computational intelligence (MCS); computer networking and communications (MCS); computer science (MCS, MS, PhD); cyber-physical systems (MCS); data analytics (MCS); data science (MAS); database systems (MCS); distributed and cloud computing (MCS); education (MCS); finance (MCS); information security and assurance (MCS); software engineering (MCS); telecommunications and software engineering (MAS); MS/MAS. Part-time and evening/weekend programs available. Postbaccalaureate distance learning degree programs offered (no on-campus study). *Faculty:* 29 full-time (5 women), 8 part-time/adjunct (1 woman). *Students:* 432 full-time (108 women), 117 part-time (27 women); includes 11 minority (3 Black or African American, non-Hispanic/Latino; 7 Asian, non-Hispanic/Latino; 1 Two or more races, non-Hispanic/Latino), 495 international. Average age 26. 2,573 applicants, 42% accepted, 244 enrolled. In 2014, 164 master's, 2 doctorates awarded. Terminal master's awarded for partial completion of doctoral program. *Degree requirements:* For master's, thesis optional; for doctorate, comprehensive exam, thesis/dissertation. *Entrance requirements:* For master's, MS GRE General Test (minimum scores: 298 Quantitative and Verbal, 3.0 Analytical Writing); MAS GRE General Test (minimum scores: 292 Quantitative and Verbal, 2.5 Analytical Writing), minimum undergraduate GPA of 3.0; for doctorate, GRE General Test (minimum scores: 304 Quantitative and Verbal, 3.5 Analytical Writing), minimum undergraduate GPA of 3.0. Additional exam requirements/recommendations for international students: Required—TOEFL (minimum score 523 paper-based; 70 iBT). *Application deadline:* For fall admission, 5/1 for domestic and international students; for spring admission, 10/15 for domestic and international students. Applications are processed on a rolling basis. Application fee: $50. Electronic applications accepted. *Expenses:* Tuition: Full-time $22,500; part-time $1250 per credit hour. *Required fees:* $30 per course. $260 per semester. One-time fee: $235. Tuition and fees vary according to course load and program. *Financial support:* Fellowships with partial tuition reimbursements, research assistantships with full and partial tuition reimbursements, teaching assistantships with full and partial tuition reimbursements, career-related internships or fieldwork, Federal Work-Study, institutionally sponsored loans, scholarships/grants, traineeships, health care benefits, tuition waivers (partial), and unspecified assistantships available. Support available to part-time students. Financial award applicants required to submit FAFSA. *Faculty research:* Parallel and distributed processing, high-performance computing, computational linguistics, information retrieval, data mining, grid computing. *Unit head:* Dr. Eunice Santos, Chair/Professor, 312-567-5150, E-mail: eunice.santos@iit.edu. *Application contact:* Rishab Malhotra, Director, Graduate Admission, 866-472-3448, Fax: 312-567-3138, E-mail: inquiry.grad@iit.edu.
Website: http://www.iit.edu/csl/cs/.

Indiana University Bloomington, School of Informatics and Computing, Program in Informatics, Bloomington, IN 47408. Offers informatics (MS, PhD), including bioinformatics, cheminformatics (PhD), complex systems (PhD), health informatics (PhD), human-computer interaction (MS), human-computer interaction design (PhD), logic and mathematical foundations of informatics (PhD), music informatics (PhD), robotics (PhD), security informatics, social informatics (PhD). Part-time programs available. *Students:* 206 full-time (78 women), 7 part-time (1 woman); includes 25 minority (9 Black or African American, non-Hispanic/Latino; 12 Asian, non-Hispanic/Latino; 2 Hispanic/Latino; 2 Two or more races, non-Hispanic/Latino), 101 international. 287 applicants, 52% accepted, 65 enrolled. In 2014, 65 master's, 13 doctorates awarded. Terminal master's awarded for partial completion of doctoral program. *Degree requirements:* For master's, thesis; for doctorate, thesis/dissertation. *Entrance requirements:* For master's and doctorate, GRE, TOEFL if international and no US degree. Additional exam requirements/recommendations for international students: Required—TOEFL (minimum score 600 paper-based; 100 iBT). *Application deadline:* For fall admission, 12/1 priority date for domestic and international students. Application fee: $55 ($65 for international students). Electronic applications accepted. *Financial support:* Application deadline: 12/1. *Unit head:* Dr. Howard Rosenbaum, Associate Dean for Graduate Studies, 812-855-3250, E-mail: hrosenba@indiana.edu. *Application contact:* Patty Reyes-Cooksey, Director of Graduate Administration, 812-856-3622, E-mail: patreyes@indiana.edu.
Website: http://www.soic.indiana.edu/informatics/index.shtml.

Instituto Tecnológico y de Estudios Superiores de Monterrey, Campus Monterrey, Graduate and Research Division, Program in Computer Science, Monterrey, Mexico. Offers artificial intelligence (PhD); computer science (MS); information systems (MS); information technology (MS). Part-time programs available. *Degree requirements:* For master's, one foreign language, thesis; for doctorate, one foreign language, thesis/dissertation. *Entrance requirements:* For master's, EXADEP; for doctorate, master's degree in related field. Additional exam requirements/recommendations for international students: Required—TOEFL. *Faculty research:* Distributed systems, software engineering, decision support systems.

Instituto Tecnológico y de Estudios Superiores de Monterrey, Campus Monterrey, Graduate and Research Division, Programs in Engineering, Monterrey, Mexico. Offers applied statistics (M Eng); artificial intelligence (PhD); automation engineering (M Eng); chemical engineering (M Eng); civil engineering (M Eng); electrical engineering (M Eng); electronic engineering (M Eng); environmental engineering (M Eng); industrial engineering (M Eng, PhD); manufacturing engineering (M Eng); mechanical engineering (M Eng); systems and quality engineering (M Eng). M Eng program offered jointly with University of Waterloo; PhD in industrial engineering with Texas A&M University. Part-time and evening/weekend programs available. Terminal master's awarded for partial completion of doctoral program. *Degree requirements:* For master's, one foreign language, thesis; for doctorate, one foreign language, thesis/dissertation. *Entrance requirements:* For master's, EXADEP; for doctorate, GRE, master's degree in related field. Additional exam requirements/recommendations for international students: Required—TOEFL. *Faculty research:* Flexible manufacturing cells, materials, statistical methods, environmental prevention, control and evaluation.

Johns Hopkins University, G. W. C. Whiting School of Engineering, Laboratory for Computational Sensing and Robotics, Baltimore, MD 21218-2699. Offers robotics (MSE). *Degree requirements:* For master's, thesis optional, 10 courses or 8 courses and an essay. *Entrance requirements:* For master's, GRE, proficiencies in: multivariable integral and differential calculus, linear algebra, ordinary differential equations, physics, probability and statistics, basic numerical methods using existing programming environments, standard programming languages (C++, Java, or MATLAB). Additional exam requirements/recommendations for international students: Required—TOEFL (minimum score 600 paper-based; 100 iBT), IELTS (minimum score 7). Electronic applications accepted. *Faculty research:* Medical robotics, human machine intervention, extreme environments robotics, robotics and biological systems.

Oregon State University, College of Engineering, Program in Robotics, Corvallis, OR 97331. Offers M Eng, MS, PhD. *Faculty:* 8 full-time (1 woman). *Students:* 17 full-time (1 woman), 3 international. Average age 27. 4 applicants, 100% accepted, 4 enrolled. *Entrance requirements:* For master's and doctorate, GRE. *Application deadline:* For fall admission, 8/1 for domestic students. *Expenses:* Expenses: $15,359 full-time resident tuition and fees; $23,405 non-resident. *Financial support:* Application deadline: 1/15. *Unit head:* Dr. Robert Stone, Professor and School Head, 541-737-3638. *Application contact:* Jean Robinson, Mechanical Engineering Advisor, 541-737-9191, E-mail: jean.robinson@oregonstate.edu.
Website: http://robotics.oregonstate.edu/graduate-program-robotics.

Portland State University, Graduate Studies, College of Liberal Arts and Sciences, Systems Science Program, Portland, OR 97207-0751. Offers computational intelligence (Certificate); computer modeling and simulation (Certificate); systems science (MS); systems science/anthropology (PhD); systems science/business administration (PhD); systems science/civil engineering (PhD); systems science/economics (PhD); systems science/engineering management (PhD); systems science/general (PhD); systems science/mathematical sciences (PhD); systems science/mechanical engineering (PhD); systems science/psychology (PhD); systems science/sociology (PhD). *Faculty:* 2 full-time (0 women), 1 part-time/adjunct (0 women). *Students:* 6 full-time (2 women), 29 part-time (8 women); includes 6 minority (1 Black or African American, non-Hispanic/Latino; 1 American Indian or Alaska Native, non-Hispanic/Latino; 1 Asian, non-Hispanic/Latino; 3 Hispanic/Latino). Average age 41. 32 applicants, 19% accepted, 6 enrolled. In 2014, 10 master's, 3 doctorates awarded. *Degree requirements:* For master's, comprehensive exam (for some programs), thesis optional; for doctorate, variable foreign language requirement, comprehensive exam (for some programs), thesis/dissertation. *Entrance requirements:* For master's, GRE/GMAT scores are recommended but not required., GPA 3.0 for undergraduate or 3.0 for graduate work, 2 letters of recommendation, and statement of interest; for doctorate, GMAT, GRE General Test, GPA requirement is 3.0 for undergraduate and 3.25 for graduate, 2 letters of recommendation and statement of interest. Additional exam requirements/recommendations for international students: Required—TOEFL (minimum score 550 paper-based; 80 iBT). *Application deadline:* For fall admission, 1/15 for domestic and international students; for spring admission, 11/1 for domestic students. Application fee: $50. Electronic applications accepted. *Expenses:* Tuition, state resident: part-time $222 per credit. Tuition, nonresident: part-time $527 per credit. *Required fees:* $22 per contact hour. $100 per quarter. Tuition and fees vary according to program. *Financial support:* In 2014–15, 1 research assistantship with full and partial tuition reimbursement (averaging $2,358 per year) was awarded; teaching assistantships with full and partial tuition reimbursements, career-related internships or fieldwork, Federal Work-Study, scholarships/grants, and unspecified assistantships also available. Support available to part-time students. Financial award application deadline: 3/1; financial award applicants required to submit FAFSA. *Faculty research:* Systems theory and methodology, artificial intelligence neural networks, information theory, nonlinear dynamics/chaos, modeling and simulation. *Total annual research expenditures:* $137,833. *Unit head:* Prof. Wayne Wakeland, PhD, Chair, 503-725-4975, E-mail: wakeland@pdx.edu.
Website: http://www.pdx.edu/sysc/.

South Dakota School of Mines and Technology, Graduate Division, Program in Computational Sciences and Robotics, Rapid City, SD 57701-3995. Offers MS. Part-time programs available. *Faculty:* 14 full-time (5 women). *Students:* 10 full-time (4 women), 1 part-time (0 women), 8 international. Average age 24. 17 applicants, 59% accepted, 7 enrolled. In 2014, 5 master's awarded. *Entrance requirements:* Additional exam requirements/recommendations for international students: Required—TOEFL (minimum score 520 paper-based; 68 iBT), TWE. *Application deadline:* For fall admission, 7/1 priority date for domestic students, 4/1 for international students; for spring admission, 11/1 for domestic students, 9/1 for international students. Applications are processed on a rolling basis. Application fee: $35. Electronic applications accepted. *Expenses:* Tuition, state resident: full-time $5050; part-time $210.40 per credit hour. Tuition, nonresident: full-time $11,290; part-time $470.30 per credit hour. *Required fees:* $4680. *Financial support:* In 2014–15, 1 fellowship (averaging $3,374 per year), 6 research assistantships with partial tuition reimbursements (averaging $3,504 per year), 11 teaching assistantships with partial tuition reimbursements (averaging $3,709 per year) were awarded; Federal Work-Study and institutionally sponsored loans also available. Support available to part-time students. Financial award application deadline: 5/15. *Faculty research:* Database systems, remote sensing, numerical modeling, artificial intelligence, neural networks. *Total annual research expenditures:* $49,014. *Unit head:* Dr. Kyle Riley, Chair, 605-394-6147, E-mail: kyle.riley@sdsmt.edu. *Application contact:* Rachel Howard, Office of Graduate Education, 605-355-3468, Fax: 605-394-1767, E-mail: rachel.howard@sdsmt.edu.

University of California, Riverside, Graduate Division, Department of Electrical Engineering, Riverside, CA 92521-0102. Offers electrical engineering (MS, PhD), including computer engineering (MS), control and robotics, intelligent systems, nano-materials, devices and circuits, signal processing and communications. Terminal master's awarded for partial completion of doctoral program. *Degree requirements:* For master's, thesis optional; for doctorate, thesis/dissertation, qualifying exams. *Entrance requirements:* For master's and doctorate, GRE General Test, minimum GPA of 3.25. Additional exam requirements/recommendations for international students: Required—TOEFL (minimum score 550 paper-based; 80 iBT). Electronic applications accepted. *Expenses:* Tuition, state resident: full-time $5399. Tuition, nonresident: full-time $10,433. *Faculty research:* Solid state devices, integrated circuits, signal processing.

University of California, San Diego, Graduate Division, Department of Electrical and Computer Engineering, La Jolla, CA 92093. Offers applied ocean science (MS, PhD); applied physics (MS, PhD); communication theory and systems (MS, PhD); computer engineering (MS, PhD); electronic circuits and systems (MS, PhD); intelligent systems, robotics and control (MS, PhD); medical devices and systems (MS, PhD); nanoscale devices and systems (MS, PhD); photonics (MS, PhD); signal and image processing (MS, PhD). *Students:* 435 full-time (81 women), 43 part-time (8 women); includes 78 minority (2 Black or African American, non-Hispanic/Latino; 1 American Indian or Alaska Native, non-Hispanic/Latino; 69 Asian, non-Hispanic/Latino; 6 Hispanic/Latino), 306 international. 2,710 applicants, 18% accepted, 177 enrolled. In 2014, 109 master's, 50 doctorates awarded. *Degree requirements:* For master's, thesis or written exam; for doctorate, comprehensive exam, thesis/dissertation. *Entrance requirements:* For master's and doctorate, GRE General Test, minimum GPA of 3.0. Additional exam requirements/recommendations for international students: Required—TOEFL (minimum score 550 paper-based; 80 iBT), IELTS. *Application deadline:* For fall admission, 12/15 for domestic students. Application fee: $90 ($110 for international students). Electronic applications accepted. *Expenses:* Tuition, state resident: full-time $11,220; part-time $5610 per quarter. Tuition, nonresident: full-time $26,322; part-time $13,161 per quarter. *Required fees:* $570 per quarter. Tuition and fees vary according to program. *Financial support:* Fellowships, research assistantships, teaching assistantships, scholarships/grants, and unspecified assistantships available. Financial award applicants required to submit FAFSA. *Faculty research:* Applied ocean science; applied physics; communication theory and systems; computer engineering; electronic circuits and systems; intelligent systems, robotics and control; medical devices and systems; nanoscale devices and systems; photonics; signal and image processing. *Unit head:* Truong Nguyen, Chair, 858-822-5554, E-mail: nguyent@ece.ucsd.edu. *Application contact:* Shana Slebioda, Graduate Coordinator, 858-822-2513, E-mail: ecegradapps@ece.ucsd.edu.
Website: http://ece.ucsd.edu/.

University of Georgia, Franklin College of Arts and Sciences, Artificial Intelligence Center, Athens, GA 30602. Offers MS. *Degree requirements:* For master's, thesis. *Entrance requirements:* For master's, GRE General Test. Electronic applications accepted.

University of Michigan, College of Engineering, Interpro Programs in Engineering, Ann Arbor, MI 48109. Offers automotive engineering (M Eng); design science (PhD); energy systems engineering (MS); financial engineering (MS); global automotive and manufacturing engineering (M Eng); manufacturing engineering (M Eng, D Eng); pharmaceutical engineering (M Eng); robotics and autonomous vehicles (M Eng); MBA/M Eng; MSE/MS. Part-time programs available. Postbaccalaureate distance learning degree programs offered (no on-campus study). *Students:* 187 full-time (46 women), 250 part-time (40 women). 364 applicants, 2% accepted, 3 enrolled. In 2014, 171 master's, 1 doctorate awarded. Terminal master's awarded for partial completion of doctoral program. *Degree requirements:* For master's, capstone project; for doctorate, thesis/dissertation. *Entrance requirements:* For master's, GRE; for doctorate, GRE, 2 years of work experience. Additional exam requirements/recommendations for international students: Required—TOEFL (minimum score 560 paper-based). *Application deadline:* Applications are processed on a rolling basis. Electronic applications accepted. *Financial support:* Fellowships, research assistantships with full tuition reimbursements, teaching assistantships with full tuition reimbursements, career-related internships or fieldwork, scholarships/grants, and unspecified assistantships available. Financial award application deadline: 2/15; financial award applicants required to submit FAFSA. *Faculty research:* Automotive engineering, design science, energy systems engineering, engineering sustainable systems, financial engineering, global automotive and manufacturing engineering, integrated microsystems, manufacturing engineering, pharmaceutical engineering, robotics and autonomous vehicles. *Total annual research expenditures:* $263,643. *Unit head:* Prof. Panos Papalambros, Director, 734-647-8401, Fax: 734-647-0079, E-mail: pyp@umich.edu. *Application contact:* Patti Mackmiller, Program Manager, 734-764-3071, Fax: 734-647-2243, E-mail: pmackmil@umich.edu.
Website: http://www.isd.engin.umich.edu.

University of Michigan, College of Engineering, Program in Robotics, Ann Arbor, MI 48109. Offers MS, PhD. *Students:* 8 full-time (4 women). *Entrance requirements:* For master's and doctorate, GRE General Test. Additional exam requirements/recommendations for international students: Required—TOEFL. *Unit head:* Prof. David C. Munson, Chair, 734-647-7008, Fax: 734-647-7009, E-mail: munson@umich.edu. *Application contact:* Andria Rose, Recruiting Contact, 734-647-7030, Fax: 734-647-7045, E-mail: ajrose@umich.edu.
Website: http://www.robotics.umich.edu/academic-program/.

University of Nebraska at Omaha, Graduate Studies, College of Information Science and Technology, Department of Computer Science, Omaha, NE 68182. Offers artificial intelligence (Certificate); communication networks (Certificate); computer science (MA, MS); software engineering (Certificate); systems and architecture (Certificate). Part-time and evening/weekend programs available. *Faculty:* 17 full-time (3 women). *Students:* 58 full-time (18 women), 51 part-time (16 women); includes 6 minority (1 Black or African American, non-Hispanic/Latino; 3 Asian, non-Hispanic/Latino; 1 Hispanic/Latino; 1 Two or more races, non-Hispanic/Latino), 80 international. Average age 26. 196 applicants, 54% accepted, 50 enrolled. In 2014, 24 master's awarded. *Degree requirements:* For master's, comprehensive exam, thesis (for some programs). *Entrance requirements:* For master's, GRE General Test, minimum GPA of 3.0, prior course work in computer science, official transcripts, resume, 2 letters of recommendation; for Certificate, minimum GPA of 3.0, resume. Additional exam requirements/recommendations for international students: Required—TOEFL, IELTS, PTE. *Application deadline:* For fall admission, 7/1 priority date for domestic students; for spring admission, 11/1 priority date for domestic and international students; for summer admission, 3/1 for domestic and international students. Applications are processed on a rolling basis. Application fee: $45. Electronic applications accepted. *Financial support:* In 2014–15, 6 students received support, including 6 research assistantships with tuition reimbursements available; teaching assistantships with tuition reimbursements available, Federal Work-Study, institutionally sponsored loans, scholarships/grants, tuition waivers (full), and unspecified assistantships also available. Support available to part-time students. Financial award application deadline: 3/1; financial award applicants required to submit FAFSA. *Unit head:* Dr. Qiuming Zhu, Chairperson, 402-554-2341, E-mail: graduate@unomaha.edu. *Application contact:* Dr. Jong-Hoon Youn, Graduate Program Chair, 402-554-2341, E-mail: graduate@unomaha.edu.

University of Pittsburgh, Dietrich School of Arts and Sciences, Intelligent Systems Program, Pittsburgh, PA 15260. Offers MS, PhD. *Faculty:* 28 full-time (9 women). *Students:* 25 full-time (9 women); includes 1 minority (Native Hawaiian or other Pacific Islander, non-Hispanic/Latino), 18 international. Average age 28. 33 applicants, 15% accepted, 4 enrolled. In 2014, 1 master's awarded. Terminal master's awarded for partial completion of doctoral program. *Degree requirements:* For master's, thesis; for doctorate, comprehensive exam, thesis/dissertation. *Entrance requirements:* For

master's and doctorate, GRE General Test. Additional exam requirements/recommendations for international students: Required—TOEFL. *Application deadline:* For fall admission, 2/1 priority date for domestic and international students. Application fee: $50. Electronic applications accepted. *Expenses:* Expenses: Contact institution. *Financial support:* In 2014–15, 4 fellowships with full tuition reimbursements, 10 research assistantships with full tuition reimbursements were awarded; Federal Work-Study, institutionally sponsored loans, scholarships/grants, traineeships, health care benefits, and unspecified assistantships also available. Financial award application deadline: 2/1. *Faculty research:* Natural language processing and information retrieval, intelligent tutoring systems and educational technology, machine learning and decision-making, biomedical informatics, artificial intelligence and law. *Unit head:* Janyce M. Wiebe, Director, 412-624-9590, Fax: 412-624-8561, E-mail: wiebe@cs.pitt.edu. *Application contact:* Michele Lee Thomas, Administrator, 412-624-5755, Fax: 412-624-8561, E-mail: paum4b@pitt.edu.
Website: http://www.isp.pitt.edu/.

University of Southern California, Graduate School, Viterbi School of Engineering, Department of Computer Science, Los Angeles, CA 90089. Offers computer networks (MS); computer science (MS, PhD); computer security (MS); game development (MS); high performance computing and simulations (MS); human language technology (MS); intelligent robotics (MS); multimedia and creative technologies (MS); software engineering (MS). Part-time and evening/weekend programs available. Postbaccalaureate distance learning degree programs offered (no on-campus study). *Entrance requirements:* For master's and doctorate, GRE General Test. Additional exam requirements/recommendations for international students: Required—TOEFL. Electronic applications accepted. *Faculty research:* Databases, computer graphics and computer vision, software engineering, networks and security, robotics, multimedia and virtual reality.

Villanova University, College of Engineering, Department of Electrical and Computer Engineering, Program in Computer Engineering, Villanova, PA 19085-1699. Offers computer architectures (Certificate); computer engineering (MSCPE); intelligent control systems (Certificate). Part-time and evening/weekend programs available. *Degree requirements:* For master's, thesis optional. *Entrance requirements:* For master's, GRE General Test (for applicants with degrees from foreign universities), BEE, minimum GPA of 3.0. Additional exam requirements/recommendations for international students: Required—TOEFL (minimum score 600 paper-based; 100 iBT). Electronic applications accepted. *Faculty research:* Expert systems, computer vision, neural networks, image processing, computer architectures.

Villanova University, College of Engineering, Department of Electrical and Computer Engineering, Program in Electrical Engineering, Villanova, PA 19085-1699. Offers electric power systems (Certificate); electrical engineering (MSEE); electro mechanical systems (Certificate); high frequency systems (Certificate); intelligent control systems (Certificate); wireless and digital communications (Certificate). Part-time and evening/weekend programs available. *Degree requirements:* For master's, thesis optional. *Entrance requirements:* For master's, GRE General Test (for applicants with degrees from foreign universities), BEE, minimum GPA of 3.0. Additional exam requirements/recommendations for international students: Required—TOEFL (minimum score 600 paper-based; 100 iBT). *Faculty research:* Signal processing, communications, antennas, devices.

Worcester Polytechnic Institute, Graduate Studies and Research, Program in Robotics Engineering, Worcester, MA 01609-2280. Offers MS, PhD. Part-time and evening/weekend programs available. Postbaccalaureate distance learning degree programs offered (no on-campus study). *Students:* 56 full-time (3 women), 14 part-time (0 women); includes 7 minority (4 Asian, non-Hispanic/Latino; 3 Hispanic/Latino), 31 international. 227 applicants, 60% accepted, 35 enrolled. In 2014, 22 master's awarded. *Degree requirements:* For master's, thesis or capstone design project; for doctorate, thesis/dissertation. *Entrance requirements:* For master's and doctorate, GRE, 3 letters of recommendation, statement of purpose. Additional exam requirements/recommendations for international students: Required—TOEFL (minimum score 563 paper-based; 84 iBT), IELTS (minimum score 7). *Application deadline:* For fall admission, 1/1 priority date for domestic and international students; for spring admission, 10/1 priority date for domestic and international students. Applications are processed on a rolling basis. Electronic applications accepted. *Financial support:* Research assistantships, teaching assistantships, career-related internships or fieldwork, institutionally sponsored loans, scholarships/grants, and unspecified assistantships available. Financial award application deadline: 1/1; financial award applicants required to submit FAFSA. *Unit head:* Dr. Michael Gennert, Director, 508-831-5357, Fax: 508-831-5776, E-mail: michaelg@wpi.edu. *Application contact:* Tracy Coetzee, Graduate Coordinator, 508-831-5357, Fax: 508-831-5776, E-mail: tcoetzee@wpi.edu.
Website: http://www.wpi.edu/academics/robotics/gradprograms.html.

Bioinformatics

Arizona State University at the Tempe campus, College of Health Solutions, Department of Biomedical Informatics, Phoenix, AZ 85004. Offers MS, PhD. Terminal master's awarded for partial completion of doctoral program. *Degree requirements:* For master's, interactive Program of Study (iPOS) submitted before completing 50 percent of required credit hours; for doctorate, comprehensive exam, thesis/dissertation, interactive Program of Study (iPOS) submitted before completing 50 percent of required credit hours. *Entrance requirements:* For master's, GRE or MCAT, bachelor's degree with minimum GPA of 3.25 in computer science, biology, physiology, nursing, statistics, engineering, related fields, or unrelated fields with appropriate academic backgrounds; resume/curriculum vitae; statement of purpose; 3 letters of recommendation; all official transcripts; for doctorate, GRE or MCAT, bachelor's degree with minimum GPA of 3.5 in computer science, biology, physiology, nursing, statistics, engineering, related fields, or unrelated fields with appropriate academic backgrounds; resume/curriculum vitae; statement of purpose; 3 letters of recommendation; all official transcripts. Additional exam requirements/recommendations for international students: Required—TOEFL (minimum score 550 paper-based; 83 iBT), IELTS (minimum score 6.5). Electronic applications accepted.

Boston University, Graduate School of Arts and Sciences and College of Engineering, Intercollegiate Program in Bioinformatics, Boston, MA 02215. Offers MS, PhD. *Students:* 67 full-time (19 women), 13 part-time (5 women); includes 26 minority (4 Black or African American, non-Hispanic/Latino; 16 Asian, non-Hispanic/Latino; 6 Hispanic/Latino), 21 international. Average age 28. 179 applicants, 29% accepted, 18 enrolled. In 2014, 10 master's, 19 doctorates awarded. *Degree requirements:* For doctorate, thesis/dissertation. *Entrance requirements:* For master's, 3 letters of recommendation, resume; for doctorate, GRE General Test, 3 letters of recommendation, resume. Additional exam requirements/recommendations for international students: Required—TOEFL (minimum score 550 paper-based; 84 iBT). *Application deadline:* For fall admission, 12/1 for domestic and international students; for spring admission, 12/15 for domestic and international students. Application fee: $80. Electronic applications accepted. *Expenses: Tuition:* Full-time $45,686; part-time $1428 per credit hour. *Required fees:* $660; $60 per semester. Tuition and fees vary according to program. *Financial support:* In 2014–15, 46 students received support, including 17 fellowships with full tuition reimbursements available (averaging $20,500 per year), 29 research assistantships with full tuition reimbursements available (averaging $20,500 per year); career-related internships or fieldwork, Federal Work-Study, scholarships/grants, traineeships, health care benefits, and unspecified assistantships also available. Financial award application deadline: 12/1. *Unit head:* Tom Tullius, Director, 617-353-2482, E-mail: tullius@bu.edu. *Application contact:* David King, Administrator, 617-358-0751, Fax: 617-353-5929, E-mail: dking@bu.edu.
Website: http://www.bu.edu/bioinformatics.

Brandeis University, Rabb School of Continuing Studies, Division of Graduate Professional Studies, Master of Science in Bioinformatics Program, Waltham, MA 02454-9110. Offers MS. Part-time programs available. Postbaccalaureate distance learning degree programs offered (no on-campus study). *Faculty:* 2 full-time (1 woman), 36 part-time/adjunct (13 women). *Students:* 21 part-time (9 women); includes 9 minority (1 Black or African American, non-Hispanic/Latino; 8 Asian, non-Hispanic/Latino). Average age 35. 11 applicants, 91% accepted, 6 enrolled. In 2014, 2 master's awarded. *Entrance requirements:* For master's, four-year bachelor's degree from regionally-accredited U.S. institution or equivalent; official transcript(s) from every college or university attended; resume or curriculum vitae; statement of goals; letter of recommendation. Additional exam requirements/recommendations for international students: Required—TOEFL (minimum scores: 600 paper-based, 100 iBT), IELTS (7), or PTE. *Application deadline:* For fall admission, 8/11 priority date for domestic and international students; for winter admission, 11/15 for domestic students; for spring admission, 12/15 priority date for domestic and international students; for summer admission, 4/14 priority date for domestic students, 4/14 for international students. Applications are processed on a rolling basis. Application fee: $50. Electronic applications accepted. *Unit head:* Dr. Alan Cheng, Program Chair, 781-736-8787, Fax: 781-736-3420, E-mail: acheng@brandeis.edu. *Application contact:* Frances Stearns, Director of Admissions and Recruitment, 781-736-8785, Fax: 781-736-3420, E-mail: fstearns@brandeis.edu.
Website: http://www.brandeis.edu/gps.

California State University Channel Islands, Extended University and International Programs, Programs in Biotechnology, Camarillo, CA 93012. Offers biotechnology and bioinformatics (MS); MS/MBA. *Entrance requirements:* Additional exam requirements/recommendations for international students: Required—TOEFL (minimum score 550 paper-based; 80 iBT), IELTS (minimum score 6).

California State University, Dominguez Hills, College of Natural and Behavioral Sciences, Department of Biology, Carson, CA 90747-0001. Offers MS. Part-time and evening/weekend programs available. *Faculty:* 3 full-time (1 woman). *Students:* 3 full-time (2 women), 17 part-time (8 women); includes 13 minority (3 Black or African American, non-Hispanic/Latino; 2 Asian, non-Hispanic/Latino; 6 Hispanic/Latino; 2 Two or more races, non-Hispanic/Latino), 3 international. Average age 32. 14 applicants, 64% accepted, 5 enrolled. In 2014, 10 master's awarded. *Degree requirements:* For master's, thesis. *Entrance requirements:* For master's, minimum GPA of 2.75. Additional exam requirements/recommendations for international students: Required—TOEFL (minimum score 550 paper-based). *Application deadline:* For fall admission, 6/1 for domestic students, 5/1 for international students; for spring admission, 12/15 for domestic students, 10/1 for international students. Application fee: $55. Electronic applications accepted. *Expenses:* Tuition, state resident: full-time $6738; part-time $3960 per year. Tuition, nonresident: full-time $13,434; part-time $8370 per year. *Required fees:* $623; $623 per year. *Faculty research:* Cancer biology, infectious diseases, ecology of native plants, remediation, community ecology. *Unit head:* Dr. Helen Chun, Chair, 310-243-3381, Fax: 310-243-2350, E-mail: hchun@csudh.edu. *Application contact:* Dr. Getachew Kidane, Graduate Program Coordinator, 310-243-3564, Fax: 310-243-2350, E-mail: gkidane@csudh.edu.
Website: http://www4.csudh.edu/biology/.

Dalhousie University, Faculty of Computer Science, Halifax, NS B3H 1W5, Canada. Offers computational biology and bioinformatics (M Sc); computer science (MA Sc, MC Sc, PhD); electronic commerce (MEC); health informatics (MHI). *Degree requirements:* For master's, thesis (for some programs); for doctorate, thesis/dissertation. *Entrance requirements:* Additional exam requirements/recommendations for international students: Required—1 of 5 approved tests: TOEFL, IELTS, CANTEST, CAEL, Michigan English Language Assessment Battery. Electronic applications accepted.

Duke University, Graduate School, Department of Computational Biology and Bioinformatics, Durham, NC 27708. Offers PhD, Certificate. *Degree requirements:* For doctorate, thesis/dissertation. *Entrance requirements:* For doctorate, GRE General Test. Additional exam requirements/recommendations for international students: Required—TOEFL (minimum score 577 paper-based; 90 iBT) or IELTS (minimum score 7). Electronic applications accepted. *Expenses: Tuition:* Full-time $45,760; part-time $2765 per credit. *Required fees:* $978. Full-time tuition and fees vary according to program.

Emory University, Rollins School of Public Health, Department of Biostatistics and Bioinformatics, Atlanta, GA 30322-1100. Offers bioinformatics (PhD); biostatistics (MPH, MSPH); public health informatics (MSPH). PhD offered through the Graduate School of Arts and Sciences. Part-time programs available. *Degree requirements:* For master's, thesis, practicum. *Entrance requirements:* For master's, GRE General Test. Additional exam requirements/recommendations for international students: Required—TOEFL (minimum score 550 paper-based; 80 iBT). Electronic applications accepted.

Florida State University, The Graduate School, College of Arts and Sciences, Department of Scientific Computing, Tallahassee, FL 32306-4120. Offers computational science (MS, PSM, PhD), including atmospheric science (PhD), biochemistry (PhD), biological science (PhD), computational molecular biology/bioinformatics (PSM), computational science (PhD), geological science (PhD), materials science (PhD), physics (PhD). Part-time programs available. *Faculty:* 14 full-time (2 women). *Students:* 30 full-time (5 women); includes 13 minority (1 Black or African American, non-Hispanic/Latino; 7 Asian, non-Hispanic/Latino; 4 Hispanic/Latino; 1 Two or more races, non-Hispanic/Latino). Average age 27. 28 applicants, 43% accepted, 7 enrolled. In 2014, 9

master's, 7 doctorates awarded. Terminal master's awarded for partial completion of doctoral program. *Degree requirements:* For master's, thesis (for some programs); for doctorate, comprehensive exam, thesis/dissertation. *Entrance requirements:* For master's and doctorate, GRE General Test, knowledge of at least one object-oriented computing language, 3 letters of recommendation. Additional exam requirements/ recommendations for international students: Required—TOEFL (minimum score 550 paper-based; 80 iBT). *Application deadline:* For fall admission, 1/15 for domestic and international students. Application fee: $30. Electronic applications accepted. *Expenses:* Tuition, state resident: part-time $403.51 per credit hour. Tuition, nonresident: part-time $1004.85 per credit hour. *Required fees:* $75.81 per credit hour. One-time fee: $20 part-time. Tuition and fees vary according to campus/location. *Financial support:* In 2014–15, 32 students received support, including 10 research assistantships with full tuition reimbursements available (averaging $20,000 per year), 23 teaching assistantships with full tuition reimbursements available (averaging $20,000 per year); scholarships/grants and unspecified assistantships also available. Financial award application deadline: 4/15. *Faculty research:* Morphometrics, mathematical and systems biology, mining proteomic and metabolic data, computational materials research, advanced 4-D Var data-assimilation methods in dynamic meteorology and oceanography, computational fluid dynamics, astrophysics. *Unit head:* Dr. Max Gunzburger, Chair, 850-644-1010, E-mail: mgunzburger@fsu.edu. *Application contact:* Mark Howard, Academic Program Specialist, 850-644-0143, Fax: 850-644-0098, E-mail: mlhoward@fsu.edu.
Website: http://www.sc.fsu.edu.

George Mason University, College of Science, School of Systems Biology, Manassas, VA 20109. Offers bioinformatics and computational biology (MS); biology (MS), including microbiology and infectious diseases, molecular biology. *Faculty:* 8 full-time (1 woman), 1 part-time/adjunct (0 women). *Students:* 76 full-time (42 women), 69 part-time (35 women); includes 41 minority (4 Black or African American, non-Hispanic/Latino; 2 American Indian or Alaska Native, non-Hispanic/Latino; 26 Asian, non-Hispanic/Latino; 7 Hispanic/Latino; 1 Native Hawaiian or other Pacific Islander, non-Hispanic/Latino; 1 Two or more races, non-Hispanic/Latino), 27 international. Average age 31. 173 applicants, 42% accepted, 31 enrolled. In 2014, 20 master's, 9 doctorates, 1 other advanced degree awarded. *Degree requirements:* For master's, research project or thesis; for doctorate, comprehensive exam, thesis/dissertation. *Entrance requirements:* For master's, GRE, resume; 3 letters of recommendation; expanded goals statement; 2 copies of official transcripts; bachelor's degree in related field with minimum GPA of 3.0 in last 60 hours; for doctorate, GRE, self-assessment form; resume; 3 letters of recommendation; expanded goals statement; 2 copies of official transcripts; bachelor's degree in related field with minimum GPA of 3.0 in last 60 hours; for Advanced Certificate, resume; 2 copies of official transcripts. Additional exam requirements/ recommendations for international students: Required—TOEFL (minimum score 570 paper-based; 80 iBT), IELTS (minimum score 6.5), PTE. Application fee: $65 ($80 for international students). Electronic applications accepted. *Expenses:* Tuition, state resident: full-time $9794; part-time $408 per credit hour. Tuition, nonresident: full-time $26,978; part-time $1124 per credit hour. *Required fees:* $2820; $118 per credit hour. Tuition and fees vary according to course load and program. *Financial support:* In 2014–15, 56 students received support, including 11 fellowships (averaging $6,670 per year), 25 research assistantships with full and partial tuition reimbursements available (averaging $15,025 per year), 34 teaching assistantships with full and partial tuition reimbursements available (averaging $14,320 per year); career-related internships or fieldwork, Federal Work-Study, scholarships/grants, unspecified assistantships, and health care benefits (for full-time research or teaching assistantship recipients) also available. Support available to part-time students. Financial award application deadline: 3/1; financial award applicants required to submit FAFSA. *Faculty research:* Functional genomics of chronic human diseases, ecology of vector-borne infectious diseases, neurogenetics, molecular biology, computational modeling, proteomics, chronic metabolic diseases, nanotechnology. *Total annual research expenditures:* $696,868. *Unit head:* Dr. James D. Willett, Director, 703-993-8311, Fax: 703-993-8976, E-mail: jwillett@gmu.edu. *Application contact:* Diane St. Germain, Graduate Student Services Coordinator, 703-993-4263, Fax: 703-993-8976, E-mail: dstgerma@gmu.edu.
Website: http://ssb.gmu.edu/.

Georgetown University, Graduate School of Arts and Sciences, Department of Biostatistics, Bioinformatics and Biomathematics, Washington, DC 20057-1484. Offers biostatistics (MS, Certificate), including bioinformatics (MS), epidemiology (MS); epidemiology (Certificate). *Entrance requirements:* For master's, GRE General Test. Additional exam requirements/recommendations for international students: Required—TOEFL. *Faculty research:* Occupation epidemiology, cancer.

The George Washington University, School of Medicine and Health Sciences, Program in Molecular Biochemistry and Bioinformatics, Washington, DC 20052. Offers bioinformatics (MS). Part-time programs available. *Entrance requirements:* For master's, GRE General Test, minimum GPA of 3.0. Additional exam requirements/ recommendations for international students: Required—TOEFL (minimum score 550 paper-based). *Application deadline:* For fall admission, 4/1 priority date for domestic and international students; for spring admission, 10/1 priority date for domestic and international students. Applications are processed on a rolling basis. Electronic applications accepted. *Unit head:* Dr. Jack Vanderhoek, Director, 202-994-2929, E-mail: jyvdh@gwu.edu. *Application contact:* Dr. Fatah Kashanchi, Director, 202-994-1781, Fax: 202-994-6213, E-mail: bcmfxk@gwumc.edu.
Website: http://www.gwumc.edu/bioinformatics/.

Georgia Institute of Technology, Graduate Studies, Multidisciplinary Program in Bioinformatics, Atlanta, GA 30332-0001. Offers MS, PhD. Program offered jointly with School of Biology, Wallace H. Coulter Department of Biomedical Engineering, School of Chemistry and Biochemistry, School of Computational Science and Engineering, School of Mathematics, and School of Industrial and Systems Engineering. Part-time programs available. *Students:* 54 full-time (22 women), 3 part-time (1 woman); includes 9 minority (1 Black or African American, non-Hispanic/Latino; 6 Asian, non-Hispanic/Latino; 2 Two or more races, non-Hispanic/Latino), 36 international. Average age 25. 92 applicants, 47% accepted, 20 enrolled. In 2014, 20 master's, 5 doctorates awarded. Terminal master's awarded for partial completion of doctoral program. *Degree requirements:* For master's, research with faculty, professional internships, co-op work experience; for doctorate, comprehensive exam, thesis/dissertation. *Entrance requirements:* For master's, GRE General Test, http://bioinformatics.gatech.edu/professional-masters-admission; for doctorate, GRE General Test, http://bioinformatics.gatech.edu/phd-admission. Additional exam requirements/recommendations for international students: Required—TOEFL (minimum score 600 paper-based; 100 iBT). *Application deadline:* For fall admission, 1/1 priority date for domestic and international students; for spring admission, 10/1 for domestic and international students. Applications are processed on a rolling basis. Application fee: $75. Electronic applications accepted. *Expenses:* Expenses: $13,743 per term in-state, $19,176 out-of-state plus fees of $1,196 per term (for MS). *Financial support:* Fellowships, research assistantships, teaching assistantships, career-related internships or fieldwork, Federal Work-Study, institutionally sponsored loans, tuition waivers (partial), and unspecified assistantships available. Support available to part-time students. Financial award application deadline: 5/1. *Unit head:* King Jordan, Director, E-mail: king.jordan@biology.gatech.edu. *Application contact:* Lisa Redding, Graduate Coordinator, 404-385-1720, E-mail: lisa.redding@biology.gatech.edu.
Website: http://bioinformatics.gatech.edu.

Georgia State University, College of Arts and Sciences, Department of Biology, Program in Applied and Environmental Microbiology, Atlanta, GA 30302-3083. Offers applied and environmental microbiology (MS, PhD); bioinformatics (MS). Part-time programs available. Terminal master's awarded for partial completion of doctoral program. *Degree requirements:* For master's, comprehensive exam (for some programs), thesis optional; for doctorate, comprehensive exam, thesis/dissertation. *Entrance requirements:* For master's and doctorate, GRE. Additional exam requirements/recommendations for international students: Required—TOEFL (minimum score 550 paper-based; 82 iBT) or IELTS (minimum score 7). *Application deadline:* For fall admission, 7/1 priority date for domestic students, 6/1 priority date for international students; for spring admission, 11/15 priority date for domestic students, 10/15 priority date for international students. Applications are processed on a rolling basis. Application fee: $50. Electronic applications accepted. *Expenses:* Tuition, state resident: full-time $6516; part-time $362 per credit hour. Tuition, nonresident: full-time $22,014; part-time $1223 per credit hour. *Required fees:* $2128 per semester. Tuition and fees vary according to course load and program. *Financial support:* In 2014–15, fellowships with full tuition reimbursements (averaging $22,000 per year), research assistantships with full tuition reimbursements (averaging $20,000 per year) were awarded. Financial award application deadline: 12/3. *Faculty research:* Bioremediation, biofilms, indoor air quality control, environmental toxicology, product biosynthesis. *Unit head:* Dr. George Pierce, Professor, 404-413-5315, Fax: 404-413-5301, E-mail: gpierce@gsu.edu. *Application contact:* LaTesha Warren, Graduate Coordinator, 404-413-5314, Fax: 404-413-5301, E-mail: lwarren@gsu.edu.
Website: http://biology.gsu.edu/.

Georgia State University, College of Arts and Sciences, Department of Biology, Program in Cellular and Molecular Biology and Physiology, Atlanta, GA 30302-3083. Offers bioinformatics (MS); cellular and molecular biology and physiology (MS, PhD). Part-time programs available. Terminal master's awarded for partial completion of doctoral program. *Degree requirements:* For master's, comprehensive exam (for some programs), thesis optional; for doctorate, comprehensive exam, thesis/dissertation. *Entrance requirements:* For master's and doctorate, GRE. Additional exam requirements/recommendations for international students: Required—TOEFL (minimum score 550 paper-based; 82 iBT) or IELTS (minimum score 7). *Application deadline:* For fall admission, 7/1 priority date for domestic students, 6/1 priority date for international students; for spring admission, 11/15 priority date for domestic students, 10/15 priority date for international students. Applications are processed on a rolling basis. Application fee: $50. Electronic applications accepted. *Expenses:* Tuition, state resident: full-time $6516; part-time $362 per credit hour. Tuition, nonresident: full-time $22,014; part-time $1223 per credit hour. *Required fees:* $2128 per semester. Tuition and fees vary according to course load and program. *Financial support:* In 2014–15, fellowships with full tuition reimbursements (averaging $22,000 per year), research assistantships with full tuition reimbursements (averaging $20,000 per year) were awarded. Financial award application deadline: 12/3. *Faculty research:* Membrane transport, viral infection, molecular immunology, protein modeling, gene regulation. *Unit head:* Dr. Julia Hilliard, Professor, 404-413-6560, Fax: 404-413-5301, E-mail: jhilliard@gsu.edu. *Application contact:* LaTesha Warren, Graduate Coordinator, 404-413-5314, Fax: 404-413-5301, E-mail: lwarren@gsu.edu.
Website: http://biology.gsu.edu/.

Georgia State University, College of Arts and Sciences, Department of Biology, Program in Molecular Genetics and Biochemistry, Atlanta, GA 30302-3083. Offers bioinformatics (MS); molecular genetics and biochemistry (MS, PhD). Part-time programs available. Terminal master's awarded for partial completion of doctoral program. *Degree requirements:* For master's, comprehensive exam (for some programs), thesis optional; for doctorate, comprehensive exam, thesis/dissertation. *Entrance requirements:* For master's and doctorate, GRE. Additional exam requirements/recommendations for international students: Required—TOEFL (minimum score 550 paper-based; 82 iBT) or IELTS (minimum score 7). *Application deadline:* For fall admission, 7/1 priority date for domestic students, 6/1 priority date for international students; for spring admission, 11/15 priority date for domestic students, 10/15 priority date for international students. Applications are processed on a rolling basis. Application fee: $50. Electronic applications accepted. *Expenses:* Tuition, state resident: full-time $6516; part-time $362 per credit hour. Tuition, nonresident: full-time $22,014; part-time $1223 per credit hour. *Required fees:* $2128 per semester. Tuition and fees vary according to course load and program. *Financial support:* In 2014–15, fellowships with full tuition reimbursements (averaging $22,000 per year), research assistantships with full tuition reimbursements (averaging $20,000 per year) were awarded. Financial award application deadline: 12/3. *Faculty research:* Gene regulation, microbial pathogenesis, molecular transport, protein modeling, viral pathogenesis. *Unit head:* Dr. Parjit Kaur, Professor, 404-413-5432, Fax: 404-413-5301. *Application contact:* LaTesha Warren, Graduate Coordinator, 404-413-5314, Fax: 404-413-5301, E-mail: lwarren@gsu.edu.
Website: http://biology.gsu.edu/.

Georgia State University, College of Arts and Sciences, Department of Biology, Program in Neurobiology and Behavior, Atlanta, GA 30302-3083. Offers bioinformatics (MS); neurobiology and behavior (MS, PhD). Part-time programs available. Terminal master's awarded for partial completion of doctoral program. *Degree requirements:* For master's, comprehensive exam (for some programs), thesis optional; for doctorate, comprehensive exam, thesis/dissertation. *Entrance requirements:* For master's and doctorate, GRE. Additional exam requirements/recommendations for international students: Required—TOEFL (minimum score 550 paper-based; 82 iBT) or IELTS (minimum score 7). *Application deadline:* For fall admission, 7/1 priority date for domestic students, 6/1 priority date for international students; for spring admission, 11/15 priority date for domestic students, 10/15 priority date for international students. Applications are processed on a rolling basis. Application fee: $50. Electronic applications accepted. *Expenses:* Tuition, state resident: full-time $6516; part-time $362 per credit hour. Tuition, nonresident: full-time $22,014; part-time $1223 per credit hour. *Required fees:* $2128 per semester. Tuition and fees vary according to course load and program. *Financial support:* In 2014–15, fellowships with full tuition reimbursements (averaging $22,000 per year), research assistantships with full tuition reimbursements (averaging $20,000 per year) were awarded. Financial award application deadline: 12/3. *Faculty research:* Behavior, Circadian and Circa-annual rhythms, developmental genetics, neuroendocrinology, cytoskeletal dynamics. *Unit head:* Dr. Vincent Rehder, Professor, 404-413-5307, Fax: 404-413-5301, E-mail: vrehder@gsu.edu. *Application contact:* LaTesha Warren, Graduate Coordinator, 404-413-5314, Fax: 404-413-5301, E-mail: lwarren@gsu.edu.
Website: http://biology.gsu.edu/.

Georgia State University, College of Arts and Sciences, Department of Chemistry, Atlanta, GA 30302-3083. Offers analytical chemistry (MS, PhD); biochemistry (MS, PhD); bioinformatics (MS, PhD); biophysical chemistry (PhD); computational chemistry (MS, PhD); geochemistry (PhD); organic/medicinal chemistry (MS, PhD); physical chemistry (MS). PhD in geochemistry offered jointly with Department of Geosciences.

Part-time programs available. *Faculty:* 26 full-time (4 women). *Students:* 158 full-time (68 women), 5 part-time (2 women); includes 42 minority (20 Black or African American, non-Hispanic/Latino; 1 American Indian or Alaska Native, non-Hispanic/Latino; 8 Asian, non-Hispanic/Latino; 8 Hispanic/Latino; 5 Two or more races, non-Hispanic/Latino), 81 international. Average age 27. 112 applicants, 55% accepted, 43 enrolled. In 2014, 19 master's, 18 doctorates awarded. Terminal master's awarded for partial completion of doctoral program. *Degree requirements:* For master's, one foreign language, comprehensive exam (for some programs), thesis (for some programs); for doctorate, one foreign language, comprehensive exam, thesis/dissertation. *Entrance requirements:* For master's and doctorate, GRE. Additional exam requirements/recommendations for international students: Required—TOEFL (minimum score 550 paper-based; 80 iBT) or IELTS (minimum score 6.5). *Application deadline:* For fall admission, 7/1 priority date for domestic and international students; for winter admission, 11/15 priority date for domestic and international students; for spring admission, 4/15 priority date for domestic and international students. Applications are processed on a rolling basis. Application fee: $50. Electronic applications accepted. *Expenses:* Tuition, state resident: full-time $6516; part-time $362 per credit hour. Tuition, nonresident: full-time $22,014; part-time $1223 per credit hour. *Required fees:* $2128 per semester. Tuition and fees vary according to course load and program. *Financial support:* Fellowships with full tuition reimbursements, research assistantships with full tuition reimbursements, and teaching assistantships with full tuition reimbursements available. *Faculty research:* Analytical chemistry, biological/biochemistry, biophysical/computational chemistry, chemical education, organic/medicinal chemistry. *Unit head:* Dr. Binghe Wang, Department Chair, 404-413-5500, Fax: 404-413-5506, E-mail: chemchair@gsu.edu. *Application contact:* Rita S. Bennett, Academic Specialist, 404-413-5497, Fax: 404-413-5505, E-mail: rsb423@gsu.edu.
Website: http://chemistry.gsu.edu/.

Georgia State University, College of Arts and Sciences, Department of Computer Science, Atlanta, GA 30302-3083. Offers bioinformatics (MS, PhD); computer science (MS, PhD). Part-time programs available. *Faculty:* 16 full-time (2 women). *Students:* 136 full-time (54 women), 26 part-time (8 women); includes 15 minority (8 Black or African American, non-Hispanic/Latino; 4 Asian, non-Hispanic/Latino; 1 Hispanic/Latino; 2 Two or more races, non-Hispanic/Latino), 126 international. Average age 29. 303 applicants, 27% accepted, 36 enrolled. In 2014, 42 master's, 8 doctorates awarded. Terminal master's awarded for partial completion of doctoral program. *Degree requirements:* For master's, comprehensive exam, thesis (for some programs); for doctorate, comprehensive exam, thesis/dissertation, proposal defense. *Entrance requirements:* For master's and doctorate, GRE General Test. Additional exam requirements/ recommendations for international students: Required—TOEFL (minimum score 550 paper-based; 80 iBT). *Application deadline:* For fall admission, 3/15 for domestic and international students; for spring admission, 10/15 for domestic and international students. Application fee: $50. Electronic applications accepted. *Expenses:* Tuition, state resident: full-time $6516; part-time $362 per credit hour. Tuition, nonresident: full-time $22,014; part-time $1223 per credit hour. *Required fees:* $2128 per semester. Tuition and fees vary according to course load and program. *Financial support:* In 2014–15, fellowships with full tuition reimbursements (averaging $22,000 per year), research assistantships with full tuition reimbursements (averaging $16,000 per year), teaching assistantships with full tuition reimbursements (averaging $16,000 per year) were awarded; institutionally sponsored loans, health care benefits, and unspecified assistantships also available. Financial award application deadline: 2/15. *Faculty research:* Artificial intelligence and computational intelligence, bioinformatics, computer software systems, databases, graphics and human computer interaction, networks and parallel and distributed computing. *Unit head:* Dr. Yi Pan, Professor/Chair, 404-413-5700, Fax: 404-413-5717, E-mail: pan@cs.gsu.edu. *Application contact:* Dr. Rajshekhar Sunderraman, Director of Graduate Studies, 404-413-5726, Fax: 404-413-5717, E-mail: grad@cs.gsu.edu.
Website: http://www.cs.gsu.edu/.

Georgia State University, College of Arts and Sciences, Department of Mathematics and Statistics, Atlanta, GA 30302-3083. Offers bioinformatics (MS, PhD); biostatistics (MS, PhD); discrete mathematics (MS); mathematics (MS, PhD); scientific computing (MS); statistics (MS). Part-time programs available. *Faculty:* 22 full-time (7 women). *Students:* 75 full-time (38 women), 30 part-time (9 women); includes 31 minority (13 Black or African American, non-Hispanic/Latino; 15 Asian, non-Hispanic/Latino; 3 Hispanic/Latino), 46 international. Average age 33. 95 applicants, 51% accepted, 19 enrolled. In 2014, 21 master's, 4 doctorates awarded. Terminal master's awarded for partial completion of doctoral program. *Degree requirements:* For master's, comprehensive exam (for some programs), thesis optional; for doctorate, comprehensive exam, thesis/dissertation. *Entrance requirements:* For master's and doctorate, GRE. Additional exam requirements/recommendations for international students: Required—TOEFL (minimum score 550 paper-based; 80 iBT). *Application deadline:* For fall admission, 7/1 priority date for domestic and international students; for spring admission, 11/15 priority date for domestic and international students. Application fee: $50. Electronic applications accepted. *Expenses:* Tuition, state resident: full-time $6516; part-time $362 per credit hour. Tuition, nonresident: full-time $22,014; part-time $1223 per credit hour. *Required fees:* $2128 per semester. Tuition and fees vary according to course load and program. *Financial support:* In 2014–15, fellowships with full tuition reimbursements (averaging $22,000 per year), research assistantships with full tuition reimbursements (averaging $9,000 per year), teaching assistantships with full tuition reimbursements (averaging $9,000 per year) were awarded; institutionally sponsored loans, scholarships/grants, health care benefits, and unspecified assistantships also available. Financial award application deadline: 2/1. *Faculty research:* Algebra, matrix theory, graph theory and combinatorics; applied mathematics and analysis; collegiate mathematics education; statistics, biostatistics and applications; bioinformatics, dynamical systems. *Unit head:* Dr. Guantao Chen, Chair, 404-413-6436, Fax: 404-413-6403, E-mail: gchen@gsu.edu. *Application contact:* Dr. Zhongshan Li, Graduate Director, 404-413-6437, Fax: 404-413-6403, E-mail: zli@gsu.edu.
Website: http://www2.gsu.edu/~wwwmat/.

Grand Valley State University, Padnos College of Engineering and Computing, Medical and Bioinformatics Program, Allendale, MI 49401-9403. Offers MS. Part-time and evening/weekend programs available. *Students:* 15 full-time (7 women), 8 part-time (5 women); includes 5 minority (2 Asian, non-Hispanic/Latino; 3 Hispanic/Latino), 12 international. Average age 29. 17 applicants, 100% accepted, 10 enrolled. In 2014, 3 master's awarded. *Degree requirements:* For master's, thesis or alternative. Application fee: $30. *Expenses:* Tuition, state resident: full-time $10,602; part-time $589 per credit hour. Tuition, nonresident: full-time $14,022; part-time $779 per credit hour. Tuition and fees vary according to degree level and program. *Financial support:* In 2014–15, 8 students received support, including 2 fellowships (averaging $1,610 per year), 7 research assistantships with full and partial tuition reimbursements available (averaging $7,390 per year); career-related internships or fieldwork, tuition waivers (full), and unspecified assistantships also available. *Faculty research:* Biomedical informatics, information visualization, data mining, high-performance computing, computational biology. *Unit head:* Paul Leidig, Director, 616-331-2308, Fax: 616-331-2106, E-mail: leidigp@gvsu.edu. *Application contact:* Dr. David Elrod, Coordinator, 616-331-8643, E-mail: elrod@gvsu.edu.

Indiana University Bloomington, School of Informatics and Computing, Program in Informatics, Bloomington, IN 47408. Offers informatics (MS, PhD), including bioinformatics, cheminformatics (PhD), complex systems (PhD), health informatics (PhD), human-computer interaction (MS), human-computer interaction design (PhD), logic and mathematical foundations of informatics (PhD), music informatics (PhD), robotics (PhD), security informatics, social informatics (PhD). Part-time programs available. *Students:* 206 full-time (78 women), 7 part-time (1 woman); includes 25 minority (9 Black or African American, non-Hispanic/Latino; 12 Asian, non-Hispanic/ Latino; 2 Hispanic/Latino; 2 Two or more races, non-Hispanic/Latino), 101 international. 287 applicants, 52% accepted, 65 enrolled. In 2014, 65 master's, 13 doctorates awarded. Terminal master's awarded for partial completion of doctoral program. *Degree requirements:* For master's, thesis; for doctorate, thesis/dissertation. *Entrance requirements:* For master's and doctorate, GRE, TOEFL if international and no US degree. Additional exam requirements/recommendations for international students: Required—TOEFL (minimum score 600 paper-based; 100 iBT). *Application deadline:* For fall admission, 12/1 priority date for domestic and international students. Application fee: $55 ($65 for international students). Electronic applications accepted. *Financial support:* Application deadline: 12/1. *Unit head:* Dr. Howard Rosenbaum, Associate Dean for Graduate Studies, 812-855-3250, E-mail: hrosenba@indiana.edu. *Application contact:* Patty Reyes-Cooksey, Director of Graduate Administration, 812-856-3622, E-mail: patreyes@indiana.edu.
Website: http://www.soic.indiana.edu/informatics/index.shtml.

Indiana University–Purdue University Indianapolis, School of Informatics and Computing, Indianapolis, IN 46202. Offers bioinformatics (MS, PhD); health informatics (MS, PhD); human-computer interaction (MS, PhD); information and library science (MLS); media arts and science (MS). Part-time and evening/weekend programs available. *Faculty:* 3 full-time (0 women). *Students:* 199 full-time (101 women), 229 part-time (159 women); includes 49 minority (18 Black or African American, non-Hispanic/ Latino; 15 Asian, non-Hispanic/Latino; 10 Hispanic/Latino; 6 Two or more races, non-Hispanic/Latino), 102 international. Average age 34. 268 applicants, 63% accepted, 133 enrolled. In 2014, 144 master's awarded. *Degree requirements:* For master's, thesis optional; for doctorate, thesis/dissertation. *Entrance requirements:* For master's, minimum undergraduate GPA of 3.0, graduate 3.2. Additional exam requirements/ recommendations for international students: Required—TOEFL. *Application deadline:* For fall admission, 3/15 for domestic students; for spring admission, 10/15 for domestic students. Application fee: $60 ($65 for international students). Electronic applications accepted. *Financial support:* Fellowships, research assistantships, teaching assistantships, career-related internships or fieldwork, Federal Work-Study, institutionally sponsored loans, and scholarships/grants available. Support available to part-time students. *Unit head:* Dr. Robert B. Schnabel, Dean. *Application contact:* Elizabeth Bunge, Graduate Admissions Coordinator, 317-278-9200, E-mail: ebunge@iupui.edu.
Website: http://soic.iupui.edu/.

Iowa State University of Science and Technology, Bioinformatics and Computational Biology Program, Ames, IA 50011. Offers MS, PhD. *Degree requirements:* For doctorate, thesis/dissertation. *Entrance requirements:* For master's and doctorate, GRE General Test. Additional exam requirements/recommendations for international students: Recommended—TOEFL, IELTS. Electronic applications accepted. *Faculty research:* Functional and structural genomics, genome evolution, macromolecular structure and function, mathematical biology and biological statistics, metabolic and developmental networks.

Johns Hopkins University, Bloomberg School of Public Health, Department of Biostatistics, Baltimore, MD 21205-2179. Offers bioinformatics (MHS); biostatistics (MHS, Sc M, PhD). Part-time programs available. *Degree requirements:* For master's, comprehensive exam (for some programs), thesis (for some programs), written exam, final project; for doctorate, comprehensive exam, thesis/dissertation, 1-year full-time residency, oral and written exams. *Entrance requirements:* For master's and doctorate, GRE General Test, course work in calculus and matrix algebra, 3 letters of recommendation, curriculum vitae. Additional exam requirements/recommendations for international students: Required—TOEFL (minimum score 600 paper-based). Electronic applications accepted. *Faculty research:* Statistical genetics, bioinformatics, statistical computing, statistical methods, environmental statistics.

Johns Hopkins University, Engineering Program for Professionals and Advanced Academic Programs, Part-time Program in Bioinformatics, Baltimore, MD 21218-2699. Offers MS, Post-Master's Certificate. Part-time and evening/weekend programs available.

Johns Hopkins University, Engineering Program for Professionals, Part-time Program in Computer Science, Baltimore, MD 21218-2699. Offers bioinformatics (MS); computer science (MS, Post-Master's Certificate); telecommunications and networking (MS). Part-time and evening/weekend programs available. Postbaccalaureate distance learning degree programs offered (no on-campus study). Electronic applications accepted.

Johns Hopkins University, Zanvyl Krieger School of Arts and Sciences, Advanced Academic Programs, Program in Bioinformatics, Washington, DC 20036. Offers MS. Part-time and evening/weekend programs available. Postbaccalaureate distance learning degree programs offered (no on-campus study). *Degree requirements:* For master's, thesis (for some programs). *Entrance requirements:* For master's, minimum GPA of 3.0; coursework in programming and data structures, biology, and chemistry. Additional exam requirements/recommendations for international students: Required—TOEFL (minimum score 100 iBT). Electronic applications accepted.

Marquette University, Graduate School, College of Arts and Sciences, Department of Mathematics, Statistics, and Computer Science, Milwaukee, WI 53201-1881. Offers bioinformatics (MS); computational sciences (MS, PhD); computing (MS); mathematics education (MS). Part-time and evening/weekend programs available. Postbaccalaureate distance learning degree programs offered (minimal on-campus study). Terminal master's awarded for partial completion of doctoral program. *Degree requirements:* For master's, thesis (for some programs), essay with oral presentation; for doctorate, comprehensive exam, thesis/dissertation, qualifying examination. *Entrance requirements:* For master's, official transcripts from all current and previous colleges/ universities except Marquette, three letters of recommendation; for doctorate, GRE General Test, official transcripts from all current and previous colleges/universities except Marquette, three letters of recommendation. Additional exam requirements/ recommendations for international students: Required—TOEFL (minimum score 530 paper-based). Electronic applications accepted. *Faculty research:* Models of physiological systems, mathematical immunology, computational group theory, mathematical logic, computational science.

Marquette University, Graduate School, College of Arts and Sciences, Program in Bioinformatics, Milwaukee, WI 53201-1881. Offers MS. Program offered jointly with Medical College of Wisconsin. Part-time and evening/weekend programs available. Postbaccalaureate distance learning degree programs offered (minimal on-campus study). *Degree requirements:* For master's, research practicum or thesis. *Entrance requirements:* For master's, GRE (strongly recommended), official transcripts from all current and previous colleges/universities except Marquette; essay outlining relevant work experience or education, career goals, possible areas of interest, and reasons for seeking admission; three letters of reference. Additional exam requirements/recommendations for international students: Required—TOEFL (minimum score 530 paper-based). Electronic applications accepted.

Massachusetts Institute of Technology, School of Engineering, Harvard-MIT Health Sciences and Technology Program, Cambridge, MA 02139. Offers health sciences and technology (SM, PhD, Sc D), including bioastronautics (PhD, Sc D), bioinformatics and integrative genomics (PhD, Sc D), medical engineering and medical physics (PhD, Sc D), speech and hearing bioscience and technology (PhD, Sc D). *Faculty:* 131 full-time (23 women). *Students:* 231 full-time (87 women), 51 part-time (16 women); includes 80 minority (2 Black or African American, non-Hispanic/Latino; 1 American Indian or Alaska Native, non-Hispanic/Latino; 64 Asian, non-Hispanic/Latino; 9 Hispanic/Latino; 4 Two or more races, non-Hispanic/Latino), 52 international. Average age 26. 213 applicants, 16% accepted, 23 enrolled. In 2014, 2 master's, 19 doctorates awarded. Terminal master's awarded for partial completion of doctoral program. *Degree requirements:* For master's, thesis; for doctorate, comprehensive exam, thesis/dissertation. *Entrance requirements:* For doctorate, GRE General Test (for medical engineering and medical physics). Additional exam requirements/recommendations for international students: Required—TOEFL (minimum score 600 paper-based; 100 iBT), IELTS (minimum score 7). *Application deadline:* For fall admission, 12/15 for domestic and international students. Application fee: $75. Electronic applications accepted. *Expenses: Tuition:* Full-time $44,720; part-time $699 per unit. *Required fees:* $296. *Financial support:* In 2014–15, 127 students received support, including 41 fellowships (averaging $34,000 per year), 65 research assistantships (averaging $34,100 per year), 3 teaching assistantships (averaging $29,400 per year); Federal Work-Study, institutionally sponsored loans, scholarships/grants, traineeships, health care benefits, and unspecified assistantships also available. Financial award application deadline: 4/15; financial award applicants required to submit FAFSA. *Faculty research:* Signal processing, biomedical imaging, drug delivery, medical devices, medical diagnostics, regenerative biomedical technologies. *Unit head:* Emery N. Brown, Director, 617-452-4091. *Application contact:* Emery N. Brown, Director, 617-452-4091.
Website: http://hst.mit.edu/.

McGill University, Faculty of Graduate and Postdoctoral Studies, Faculty of Science, Department of Biology, Montréal, QC H3A 2T5, Canada. Offers bioinformatics (M Sc, PhD); environment (M Sc, PhD); neo-tropical environment (M Sc, PhD).

Medical College of Wisconsin, Graduate School of Biomedical Sciences, Program in Bioinformatics, Milwaukee, WI 53226-0509. Offers MS. *Entrance requirements:* For master's, GRE, official transcripts, three letters of recommendation. Additional exam requirements/recommendations for international students: Required—TOEFL.

Mississippi Valley State University, Department of Natural Science and Environmental Health, Itta Bena, MS 38941-1400. Offers bioinformatics (MS); environmental health (MS). Part-time and evening/weekend programs available. *Entrance requirements:* For master's, GRE, minimum GPA of 3.0. *Faculty research:* Toxicology, water equality, microbiology, ecology.

Morgan State University, School of Graduate Studies, School of Computer, Mathematical, and Natural Sciences, Department of Computer Science, Baltimore, MD 21251. Offers bioinformatics (MS). *Entrance requirements:* Additional exam requirements/recommendations for international students: Required—TOEFL (minimum score 550 paper-based).

New Jersey Institute of Technology, College of Computing Science, Newark, NJ 07102. Offers computer science (MS, PhD), including bioinformatics (MS), computer science, computing and business (MS), cyber security and privacy (MS), software engineering (MS); information systems (MS, PhD), including business and information systems (MS), emergency management and business continuity (MS), information systems; information technology administration and security (MS). Part-time and evening/weekend programs available. Terminal master's awarded for partial completion of doctoral program. *Degree requirements:* For master's, thesis optional; for doctorate, thesis/dissertation. *Entrance requirements:* For master's, GRE General Test; for doctorate, GRE General Test, minimum graduate GPA of 3.5. Additional exam requirements/recommendations for international students: Required—TOEFL (minimum score 550 paper-based; 79 iBT). Electronic applications accepted. *Faculty research:* Computer systems, communications and networking, artificial intelligence, database engineering, systems analysis.

New Mexico State University, College of Arts and Sciences, Department of Computer Science, Las Cruces, NM 88003-8001. Offers bioinformatics (MS); computer science (MS, PhD). Part-time programs available. *Faculty:* 10 full-time (2 women), 1 part-time/adjunct (0 women). *Students:* 86 full-time (30 women), 15 part-time (2 women); includes 12 minority (2 Black or African American, non-Hispanic/Latino; 3 Asian, non-Hispanic/Latino; 7 Hispanic/Latino), 76 international. Average age 29. 273 applicants, 55% accepted, 36 enrolled. In 2014, 13 master's, 5 doctorates awarded. Terminal master's awarded for partial completion of doctoral program. *Degree requirements:* For master's, comprehensive exam, thesis or alternative; for doctorate, comprehensive exam, thesis/dissertation, qualifying examination, thesis proposal. *Entrance requirements:* For master's and doctorate, BS in computer science. Additional exam requirements/recommendations for international students: Required—TOEFL (minimum score 550 paper-based; 79 iBT), IELTS (minimum score 6.5). *Application deadline:* For fall admission, 3/1 priority date for domestic and international students; for spring admission, 11/1 priority date for domestic and international students. Applications are processed on a rolling basis. Application fee: $40 ($50 for international students). Electronic applications accepted. *Expenses:* Tuition, state resident: full-time $3969; part-time $220.50 per credit hour. Tuition, nonresident: full-time $13,838; part-time $768.80 per credit hour. *Required fees:* $853; $47.40 per credit hour. *Financial support:* In 2014–15, 67 students received support, including 1 fellowship (averaging $3,970 per year), 13 research assistantships (averaging $10,537 per year), 18 teaching assistantships (averaging $9,106 per year); career-related internships or fieldwork, Federal Work-Study, scholarships/grants, traineeships, health care benefits, and unspecified assistantships also available. Support available to part-time students. Financial award application deadline: 3/1. *Faculty research:* Bioinformatics, database and data mining, networks and systems optimization, artificial intelligence, human factors and user interfaces. *Total annual research expenditures:* $1.1 million. *Unit head:* Dr. Son Tran, Academic Department Head, 575-646-3723, Fax: 575-646-1002, E-mail: stran@cs.nmsu.edu. *Application contact:* Dr. Joe Song, Associate Professor, 575-646-3723, Fax: 575-646-1002, E-mail: gradcs@cs.nmsu.edu.
Website: http://www.cs.nmsu.edu/.

New York University, Polytechnic School of Engineering, Major in Bioinformatics, New York, NY 10012-1019. Offers MS. Part-time programs available. Postbaccalaureate distance learning degree programs offered (no on-campus study). *Students:* 5 full-time (2 women), 7 part-time (4 women); includes 7 minority (1 Black or African American, non-Hispanic/Latino; 6 Asian, non-Hispanic/Latino), 2 international. Average age 27. 24 applicants, 46% accepted, 3 enrolled. In 2014, 6 master's awarded. *Entrance requirements:* Additional exam requirements/recommendations for international students: Required—TOEFL (minimum score 550 paper-based; 80 iBT). *Application deadline:* For fall admission, 2/15 for domestic and international students; for spring admission, 11/1 for domestic and international students. Applications are processed on a rolling basis. Application fee: $75. Electronic applications accepted. *Unit head:* Prof. Mgavi Elombe Brathwaite, Program Manager, 718-260-3950, E-mail: m.brathwaite@nyu.edu. *Application contact:* Raymond Lutzky, Director, Graduate Enrollment Management, 718-637-5984, Fax: 718-260-3624, E-mail: rlutzky@poly.edu.
Website: http://engineering.nyu.edu/academics/programs/bioinformatics-ms.

New York University, School of Medicine and Graduate School of Arts and Science, Sackler Institute of Graduate Biomedical Sciences, Program in Biomedical Informatics, New York, NY 10012-1019. Offers PhD. *Faculty:* 13 full-time (0 women). *Students:* 4 full-time (2 women), 4 international. Average age 28. *Degree requirements:* For doctorate, comprehensive exam, thesis/dissertation, qualifying exam. *Faculty research:* Microbiomics, molecular signatures, sequencing informatics, evidence based medicine and scientometrics, computational proteomics. *Unit head:* Dr. Naoko Tanese, Associate Dean for Biomedical Sciences; Director, Sackler Institute, 212-263-8945, Fax: 212-263-7600, E-mail: naoko.tanese@nyumc.org. *Application contact:* Michael Escosia, Project Manager, 212-263-5648, Fax: 212-263-7600, E-mail: sackler-info@nyumc.org.
Website: http://www.med.nyu.edu/sackler/phd-program/training-programs/biomedical-informatics.

North Carolina State University, Graduate School, College of Agriculture and Life Sciences and College of Engineering, Program in Bioinformatics, Raleigh, NC 27695. Offers MB, PhD. *Degree requirements:* For master's, thesis optional; for doctorate, thesis/dissertation. *Entrance requirements:* For master's and doctorate, GRE, minimum B average. Additional exam requirements/recommendations for international students: Required—TOEFL. Electronic applications accepted. *Faculty research:* Statistical genetics, molecular evolution, pedigree analysis, quantitative genetics, protein structure.

North Dakota State University, College of Graduate and Interdisciplinary Studies, Interdisciplinary Program in Genomics and Bioinformatics, Fargo, ND 58108. Offers MS, PhD. Part-time programs available. *Degree requirements:* For master's, thesis; for doctorate, comprehensive exam, thesis/dissertation. *Entrance requirements:* For master's and doctorate, minimum GPA of 3.0. Additional exam requirements/recommendations for international students: Required—TOEFL (minimum score 525 paper-based; 71 iBT). Electronic applications accepted. *Faculty research:* Genome evolution, genome mapping, genome expression, bioinformatics, data mining.

Northeastern University, College of Science, Department of Biology, Master of Science in Bioinformatics Program, Boston, MA 02115-5096. Offers MS, PSM. Part-time programs available. Postbaccalaureate distance learning degree programs offered (minimal on-campus study). *Degree requirements:* For master's, internship. *Entrance requirements:* For master's, GRE General Test. Additional exam requirements/recommendations for international students: Required—TOEFL (minimum score 100 iBT). Electronic applications accepted. *Expenses:* Contact institution.

Nova Southeastern University, College of Osteopathic Medicine, Fort Lauderdale, FL 33328. Offers biomedical informatics (MS, Graduate Certificate), including biomedical informatics (MS), clinical informatics (Graduate Certificate), public health informatics (Graduate Certificate); disaster and emergency preparedness (MS); osteopathic medicine (DO); public health (MPH). *Accreditation:* AOsA. *Faculty:* 107 full-time (55 women), 1,235 part-time/adjunct (297 women). *Students:* 1,027 full-time (436 women), 189 part-time (124 women); includes 560 minority (92 Black or African American, non-Hispanic/Latino; 260 Asian, non-Hispanic/Latino; 174 Hispanic/Latino; 1 Native Hawaiian or other Pacific Islander, non-Hispanic/Latino; 33 Two or more races, non-Hispanic/Latino), 45 international. Average age 28. 4,012 applicants, 12% accepted, 246 enrolled. In 2014, 75 master's, 237 doctorates, 4 other advanced degrees awarded. *Entrance requirements:* For master's, GRE, licensed healthcare professional or GRE; for doctorate, MCAT, biology, chemistry, organic chemistry, physics (all with labs), and English. *Application deadline:* For fall admission, 1/15 for domestic students. Applications are processed on a rolling basis. Application fee: $50. Electronic applications accepted. *Expenses:* Expenses: Contact institution. *Financial support:* In 2014–15, 39 students received support, including 24 fellowships (averaging $45,593 per year); research assistantships, teaching assistantships, Federal Work-Study, and scholarships/grants also available. Financial award application deadline: 6/1; financial award applicants required to submit FAFSA. *Faculty research:* Teaching strategies, simulated patient use, HIV/AIDS education, minority health issues, managed care education. *Unit head:* Elaine M. Wallace, DO, Dean, 954-262-1407, E-mail: ewallace@nova.edu. *Application contact:* Monica Sanchez, Admissions Counselor, College of Osteopathic Medicine, 954-262-1110, Fax: 954-262-2282, E-mail: mh1156@nova.edu.
Website: http://www.medicine.nova.edu/.

Rice University, Graduate Programs, George R. Brown School of Engineering, Department of Statistics, Houston, TX 77251-1892. Offers bioinformatics (PhD); biostatistics (PhD); computational finance (PhD); general statistics (PhD); statistics (M Stat, MA); MBA/M Stat. Part-time programs available. *Degree requirements:* For master's, comprehensive exam; for doctorate, comprehensive exam, thesis/dissertation. *Entrance requirements:* For master's and doctorate, GRE General Test, minimum GPA of 3.0. Additional exam requirements/recommendations for international students: Required—TOEFL (minimum score 630 paper-based; 90 iBT). Electronic applications accepted. *Faculty research:* Statistical genetics, non parametric function estimation, computational statistics and visualization, stochastic processes.

Rochester Institute of Technology, Graduate Enrollment Services, College of Science, School of Life Sciences, MS Program in Bioinformatics, Rochester, NY 14623-5603. Offers MS. Part-time programs available. *Students:* 15 full-time (10 women), 4 part-time (2 women), 12 international. Average age 28. 47 applicants, 45% accepted, 6 enrolled. In 2014, 6 master's awarded. *Degree requirements:* For master's, thesis. *Entrance requirements:* For master's, TOEFL, IELTS, or PTE for non-native English speakers, GRE, recommended minimum GPA of 3.2. Additional exam requirements/recommendations for international students: Required—PTE (minimum score 58), TOEFL (minimum score 550 paper-based; 79 iBT) or IELTS (minimum score 6.5). *Application deadline:* For fall admission, 2/15 priority date for domestic and international students; for spring admission, 12/15 priority date for domestic and international students. Applications are processed on a rolling basis. Application fee: $60. Electronic applications accepted. *Expenses:* Expenses: $1,673 per credit hour. *Financial support:* In 2014–15, 19 students received support. Research assistantships with partial tuition reimbursements available, teaching assistantships with partial tuition reimbursements available, career-related internships or fieldwork, Federal Work-Study, institutionally sponsored loans, scholarships/grants, and unspecified assistantships available. Support available to part-time students. Financial award applicants required to submit FAFSA. *Faculty research:* Metabolomics analysis, data mining of NHANES III, categorizing mitochondrial genome variation, evolution of viral genomes. *Unit head:* Dr. Michael Osier, Graduate Program Director, 585-475-4392, Fax: 585-475-6970, E-mail: mvosd@rit.edu. *Application contact:* Diane Ellison, Associate Vice President, Graduate Enrollment Services, 585-475-2229, Fax: 585-475-7164, E-mail: gradinfo@rit.edu.
Website: https://www.rit.edu/science/programs/ms/bioinformatics.

Rowan University, Graduate School, College of Science and Mathematics, Program in Bioinformatics, Glassboro, NJ 08028-1701. Offers MS. *Faculty:* 3 full-time (0 women), 3 part-time/adjunct (0 women). *Students:* 5 part-time (2 women). Average age 28. 6 applicants, 83% accepted, 5 enrolled. *Entrance requirements:* For master's, GRE, BS in biology, biochemistry, chemistry, computer science, or related field with minimum GPA of 2.5. Additional exam requirements/recommendations for international students: Required—TOEFL. *Application deadline:* For fall admission, 6/1 for domestic and international students. Applications are processed on a rolling basis. Application fee: $65. Electronic applications accepted. *Expenses: Tuition, area resident:* Part-time $648 per credit. Tuition, state resident: part-time $648 per credit. Tuition, nonresident: part-time $648 per credit. *Required fees:* $145 per credit. Tuition and fees vary according to degree level, campus/location, program and student level. *Unit head:* Dr. Horacio Sosa, Dean, College of Graduate and Continuing Education, 856-256-4747, Fax: 856-256-5638, E-mail: sosa@rowan.edu. *Application contact:* Admissions and Enrollment Services, 856-256-4747, Fax: 856-256-5637, E-mail: globaladmissions@rowan.edu.

Rutgers, The State University of New Jersey, Newark, School of Health Related Professions, Department of Health Informatics, Program in Biomedical Informatics, Newark, NJ 07102. Offers MS, PhD, DMD/MS, MD/MS. Part-time and evening/weekend programs available. Postbaccalaureate distance learning degree programs offered (minimal on-campus study). *Degree requirements:* For master's, thesis; for doctorate, comprehensive exam, thesis/dissertation. *Entrance requirements:* For master's, BS, transcript of highest degree, statement of research interests, curriculum vitae, basic understanding of database concepts and calculus, 3 reference letters; for doctorate, master's degree, transcripts of highest degree, statement of research interests, curriculum vitae, basic understanding of database concepts and calculus, 3 reference letters. Additional exam requirements/recommendations for international students: Required—TOEFL. Electronic applications accepted.

Simon Fraser University, Office of Graduate Studies, Faculty of Science, Department of Biological Sciences, Burnaby, BC V5A 1S6, Canada. Offers bioinformatics (Graduate Diploma); biological sciences (M Sc, PhD); environmental toxicology (MET); pest management (MPM). *Degree requirements:* For master's, thesis; for doctorate, thesis/dissertation, candidacy exam; for Graduate Diploma, practicum. *Entrance requirements:* For master's, minimum GPA of 3.0 (on scale of 4.33), or 3.33 based on last 60 credits of undergraduate courses; for doctorate, minimum GPA of 3.5 (on scale of 4.33); for Graduate Diploma, minimum GPA of 2.5 (on scale of 4.33), or 2.67 based on the last 60 credits of undergraduate courses. Additional exam requirements/recommendations for international students: Recommended—TOEFL (minimum score 580 paper-based; 93 iBT), IELTS (minimum score 7), TWE (minimum score 5). Electronic applications accepted. *Faculty research:* Cell biology, wildlife ecology, environmental and evolutionary physiology, environmental toxicology, pest management.

Simon Fraser University, Office of Graduate Studies, Faculty of Science, Department of Molecular Biology and Biochemistry, Burnaby, BC V5A 1S6, Canada. Offers bioinformatics (Graduate Diploma); molecular biology and biochemistry (M Sc, PhD). *Degree requirements:* For master's, thesis; for doctorate, thesis/dissertation; for Graduate Diploma, practicum. *Entrance requirements:* For master's, minimum GPA of 3.0 (on scale of 4.33), or 3.33 based on last 60 credits of undergraduate courses; for doctorate, minimum GPA of 3.5; for Graduate Diploma, minimum GPA of 2.5 (on scale of 4.33), or 2.67 based on the last 60 credits of undergraduate courses. Additional exam requirements/recommendations for international students: Recommended—TOEFL (minimum score 580 paper-based; 100 iBT), IELTS (minimum score 7.5), TWE (minimum score 5). Electronic applications accepted. *Faculty research:* Genomics and bioinformatics, cell and developmental biology, structural biology/biochemistry, immunology, nucleic acid function.

Stevens Institute of Technology, Graduate School, Charles V. Schaefer Jr. School of Engineering, Department of Chemistry, Chemical Biology and Biomedical Engineering, Hoboken, NJ 07030. Offers analytical chemistry (PhD, Certificate); bioinformatics (PhD, Certificate); biomedical chemistry (Certificate); biomedical engineering (M Eng, Certificate); chemical biology (MS, PhD, Certificate); chemical physiology (Certificate); chemistry (MS, PhD); organic chemistry (PhD); physical chemistry (PhD); polymer chemistry (PhD, Certificate). Part-time and evening/weekend programs available. Postbaccalaureate distance learning degree programs offered (no on-campus study). Terminal master's awarded for partial completion of doctoral program. *Degree requirements:* For master's, thesis or alternative; for doctorate, one foreign language, thesis/dissertation; for Certificate, project or thesis. *Entrance requirements:* Additional exam requirements/recommendations for international students: Required—TOEFL. Electronic applications accepted. *Faculty research:* Biochemical reaction engineering, polymerization engineering, reactor design, biochemical process control and synthesis.

Stony Brook University, State University of New York, Stony Brook University Medical Center, Health Sciences Center, School of Medicine and Graduate School, Graduate Programs in Medicine and College of Engineering and Applied Sciences, Department of Biomedical Informatics, Stony Brook, NY 11794. Offers MS, PhD. *Entrance requirements:* For doctorate, GRE, https://www.grad.stonybrook.edu/ProspectiveStudents/faq.shtml#scores. Additional exam requirements/recommendations for international students: Required—TOEFL. *Application deadline:* For fall admission, 1/15 for domestic students; for spring admission, 10/1 for domestic students. *Expenses:* Tuition, state resident: full-time $10,370; part-time $432 per credit. Tuition, nonresident: full-time $20,190; part-time $841 per credit. *Required fees:* $1431. *Financial support:* In 2014–15, 1 research assistantship was awarded. *Total annual research expenditures:* $197,283. *Unit head:* Dr. Joel H. Saltz, Chair, 631-638-1420, E-mail: joel.saltz@stonybrook.edu. *Application contact:* Melissa Jordan, Assistant Dean, 631-632-9712, Fax: 631-632-7243, E-mail: melissa.jordan@stonybrook.edu.
Website: http://bmi.stonybrookmedicine.edu/.

Tufts University, School of Engineering, Department of Computer Science, Medford, MA 02155. Offers bioengineering (ME, MS), including bioinformatics; cognitive science (PhD); computer science (MS, PhD). Part-time programs available. *Students:* 57 full-time (17 women), 19 part-time (4 women); includes 13 minority (1 Black or African American, non-Hispanic/Latino; 4 Asian, non-Hispanic/Latino; 2 Hispanic/Latino; 6 Two or more races, non-Hispanic/Latino), 25 international. Average age 29. 218 applicants, 24% accepted, 23 enrolled. In 2014, 18 master's, 4 doctorates awarded. Terminal master's awarded for partial completion of doctoral program. *Degree requirements:* For master's, thesis (for some programs); for doctorate, thesis/dissertation. *Entrance requirements:* For master's and doctorate, GRE General Test. Additional exam requirements/recommendations for international students: Required—TOEFL (minimum score 550 paper-based; 80 iBT), IELTS (minimum score 6.5). *Application deadline:* For fall admission, 1/15 for domestic and international students; for spring admission, 9/15 for domestic and international students. Applications are processed on a rolling basis. Application fee: $75. Electronic applications accepted. *Expenses: Tuition:* Full-time $45,590; part-time $1161 per credit hour. *Required fees:* $782. Full-time tuition and fees vary according to degree level, program and student level. Part-time tuition and fees vary according to course load. *Financial support:* Fellowships with full tuition reimbursements, research assistantships with full and partial tuition reimbursements, teaching assistantships with full and partial tuition reimbursements, Federal Work-Study, scholarships/grants, tuition waivers (partial), and unspecified assistantships available. Financial award application deadline: 4/15; financial award applicants required to submit FAFSA. *Faculty research:* Computational biology, computational geometry, and computational systems biology; cognitive sciences, human-computer interaction, and human-robotic interaction; visualization and graphics, educational technologies; machine learning and data mining; programming languages and systems. *Unit head:* Dr. Samuel Guyer, Graduate Program Director. *Application contact:* Office of Graduate Admissions, 617-623-3395, E-mail: gradadmissions@cs.tufts.edu.
Website: http://www.cs.tufts.edu/.

Tufts University, School of Engineering, Department of Mechanical Engineering, Medford, MA 02155. Offers bioengineering (ME, MS), including bioinformatics, biomechanical systems and devices, signals and systems; bioinformatics (MS); human factors (MS); mechanical engineering (ME, MS, PhD). Part-time programs available. *Faculty:* 15 full-time (1 woman), 7 part-time/adjunct (1 woman). *Students:* 35 full-time (12 women), 23 part-time (11 women); includes 11 minority (3 Black or African American, non-Hispanic/Latino; 1 American Indian or Alaska Native, non-Hispanic/Latino; 3 Asian, non-Hispanic/Latino; 2 Hispanic/Latino; 2 Two or more races, non-Hispanic/Latino), 14 international. Average age 27. 112 applicants, 47% accepted, 16 enrolled. In 2014, 18 master's, 6 doctorates awarded. Terminal master's awarded for partial completion of doctoral program. *Degree requirements:* For master's, thesis; for doctorate, thesis/dissertation. *Entrance requirements:* For master's and doctorate, GRE General Test. Additional exam requirements/recommendations for international students: Required—TOEFL (minimum score 550 paper-based; 80 iBT), IELTS (minimum score 6.5). *Application deadline:* For fall admission, 1/15 priority date for domestic students, 1/15 for international students; for spring admission, 9/15 for domestic and international students. Applications are processed on a rolling basis. Application fee: $75. Electronic applications accepted. *Expenses: Tuition:* Full-time $45,590; part-time $1161 per credit hour. *Required fees:* $782. Full-time tuition and fees vary according to degree level, program and student level. Part-time tuition and fees vary according to course load. *Financial support:* Fellowships with full tuition reimbursements, research assistantships with full and partial tuition reimbursements, teaching assistantships with full and partial tuition reimbursements, Federal Work-Study, scholarships/grants, tuition waivers (partial), and unspecified assistantships available. Financial award application deadline: 5/15; financial award applicants required to submit FAFSA. *Faculty research:* Applied mechanics, biomaterials, controls/robotics, design/systems, human factors. *Unit head:* Dr. Robert C. White, Graduate Program Director. *Application contact:* Office of Graduate Admissions, 617-627-3395, E-mail: gradadmissions@tufts.edu.
Website: http://engineering.tufts.edu/me.

Université de Montréal, Faculty of Medicine, Biochemistry Department, Montréal, QC H3C 3J7, Canada. Offers M Sc, PhD. Electronic applications accepted.

Université de Montréal, Faculty of Medicine, Program in Bioinformatics, Montréal, QC H3C 3J7, Canada. Offers M Sc, PhD.

University at Buffalo, the State University of New York, Graduate School, School of Medicine and Biomedical Sciences, Graduate Programs in Medicine and Biomedical Sciences, Program in Genetics, Genomics and Bioinformatics, Buffalo, NY 14260. Offers MS, PhD.

The University of Alabama at Birmingham, Graduate Programs in Joint Health Sciences, Genetics, Genomics and Bioinformatics Theme, Birmingham, AL 35294. Offers PhD. *Students:* 29 full-time (14 women); includes 3 minority (1 Black or African American, non-Hispanic/Latino; 1 Hispanic/Latino; 1 Two or more races, non-Hispanic/Latino), 3 international. Average age 26. *Degree requirements:* For doctorate, comprehensive exam, thesis/dissertation. *Entrance requirements:* For doctorate, GRE General Test, interview, previous research experience. Additional exam requirements/recommendations for international students: Required—TOEFL. *Application deadline:* For fall admission, 12/1 priority date for domestic and international students. Application fee: $0 ($60 for international students). Electronic applications accepted. *Expenses:* Tuition, state resident: full-time $7090; part-time $370 per credit hour. Tuition, nonresident: full-time $16,072; part-time $869 per credit hour. Full-time tuition and fees vary according to course load and program. *Financial support:* Fellowships, scholarships/grants, health care benefits, and competitive annual stipends, health insurance, and fully-paid tuition and fees available. *Unit head:* Dr. Daniel C. Bullard, Program Director, 205-934-7768, E-mail: dcbullard@uab.edu. *Application contact:* Nan Travis, Graduate Program Manager, 205-934-1003, Fax: 205-996-6749, E-mail: ntravis@uab.edu.
Website: http://www.uab.edu/gbs/genomic/.

University of Arkansas at Little Rock, Graduate School, George W. Donaghey College of Engineering and Information Technology, Program in Bioinformatics, Little Rock, AR 72204-1099. Offers MS, PhD. *Entrance requirements:* For doctorate, MS in bioinformatics. Additional exam requirements/recommendations for international students: Required—TOEFL. Application fee: $40. *Expenses:* Tuition, state resident: full-time $6000; part-time $300 per credit hour. Tuition, nonresident: full-time $13,800; part-time $690 per credit hour. *Required fees:* $1126; $603 per term. One-time fee: $40 full-time. *Unit head:* Dr. Mary Yang, Coordinator, 501-683-2035, E-mail: mqyang@ualr.edu.
Website: http://ualr.edu/bioinformatics/.

University of Arkansas for Medical Sciences, Graduate School, Little Rock, AR 72205. Offers biochemistry and molecular biology (MS, PhD); bioinformatics (MS, PhD); cellular physiology and molecular biophysics (MS, PhD); clinical nutrition (MS); interdisciplinary biomedical sciences (MS, PhD, Certificate); interdisciplinary toxicology (MS); microbiology and immunology (PhD); neurobiology and developmental sciences (PhD); pharmacology (PhD); MD/PhD. Bioinformatics programs hosted jointly with the University of Arkansas at Little Rock. Part-time programs available. Terminal master's awarded for partial completion of doctoral program. *Degree requirements:* For master's, comprehensive exam (for some programs), thesis (for some programs); for doctorate, thesis/dissertation. *Entrance requirements:* For master's and doctorate, GRE. Additional exam requirements/recommendations for international students: Required—TOEFL. Electronic applications accepted. *Expenses:* Contact institution.

University of California, Los Angeles, Graduate Division, College of Letters and Science, Interdepartmental Program in Bioinformatics, Los Angeles, CA 90095. Offers MS, PhD. Terminal master's awarded for partial completion of doctoral program. *Degree requirements:* For master's, comprehensive exam, thesis, one quarter of teaching experience; for doctorate, thesis/dissertation, oral and written qualifying exams; one quarter of teaching experience. *Entrance requirements:* For doctorate, GRE General Test, bachelor's degree; minimum undergraduate GPA of 3.0 (or its equivalent if letter grade system not used). Additional exam requirements/recommendations for international students: Required—TOEFL. Electronic applications accepted.

University of California, Riverside, Graduate Division, Graduate Program in Genetics, Genomics, and Bioinformatics, Riverside, CA 92521-0102. Offers genomics and bioinformatics (PhD). *Faculty:* 72 full-time (20 women). *Students:* 32 full-time (18 women); includes 2 minority (1 Black or African American, non-Hispanic/Latino; 1 Hispanic/Latino), 15 international. Average age 30. In 2014, 2 doctorates awarded. *Degree requirements:* For doctorate, thesis/dissertation, qualifying exams, teaching experience. *Entrance requirements:* For doctorate, GRE General Test, minimum GPA of 3.2. Additional exam requirements/recommendations for international students: Required—TOEFL (minimum score 550 paper-based; 80 iBT). *Application deadline:* For fall admission, 12/1 priority date for domestic students, 1/1 priority date for international students; for winter admission, 9/1

for domestic students, 7/1 for international students; for spring admission, 12/1 for domestic students, 10/1 for international students. Applications are processed on a rolling basis. Application fee: $85 ($100 for international students). Electronic applications accepted. *Expenses:* Tuition, state resident: full-time $5399. Tuition, nonresident: full-time $10,433. *Financial support:* In 2014–15, fellowships with tuition reimbursements (averaging $18,000 per year), research assistantships with tuition reimbursements (averaging $18,000 per year), teaching assistantships with tuition reimbursements (averaging $16,500 per year) were awarded; career-related internships or fieldwork, Federal Work-Study, institutionally sponsored loans, and tuition waivers (full and partial) also available. *Faculty research:* Molecular genetics, evolution and population genetics, genomics and bioinformatics. *Unit head:* Dr. Hailing Jin, Director, 951-827-7378. *Application contact:* Deidra Kornfeld, Graduate Program Assistant, 800-735-0717, Fax: 951-827-5517, E-mail: deidra.kornfeld@ucr.edu.
Website: http://ggb.ucr.edu/.

University of California, San Diego, Graduate Division, Department of Mathematics, La Jolla, CA 92093. Offers applied mathematics (MA); bioinformatics (PhD); computational science (PhD); mathematics (MA, PhD); statistics (MS, PhD). *Students:* 127 full-time (26 women), 4 part-time (1 woman); includes 16 minority (11 Asian, non-Hispanic/Latino; 5 Hispanic/Latino), 66 international. 676 applicants, 20% accepted, 39 enrolled. In 2014, 31 master's, 16 doctorates awarded. *Degree requirements:* For master's, comprehensive exam; for doctorate, one foreign language, comprehensive exam, thesis/dissertation. *Entrance requirements:* For master's, GRE General Test, GRE Subject Test, minimum GPA of 3.0; GRE Subject Test not required for MS in Statistics; for doctorate, GRE General Test, GRE Subject Test, minimum GPA of 3.0. Additional exam requirements/recommendations for international students: Required—TOEFL (minimum score 550 paper-based; 80 iBT), IELTS. Application fee: $90 ($110 for international students). Electronic applications accepted. *Expenses:* Tuition, state resident: full-time $11,220; part-time $5610 per quarter. Tuition, nonresident: full-time $26,322; part-time $13,161 per quarter. *Required fees:* $570 per quarter. Tuition and fees vary according to program. *Financial support:* Fellowships, research assistantships, teaching assistantships, and scholarships/grants available. Financial award applicants required to submit FAFSA. *Faculty research:* Combinatorics, graph theory, differential geometry, image processing, operator theory. *Unit head:* Peter Ebenfelt, Chair, 858-822-4961, E-mail: pebenfelt@ucsd.edu. *Application contact:* Terry Le, Admissions Contact, 858-534-6887, E-mail: mathgradadmissions@math.ucsd.edu.
Website: http://math.ucsd.edu/.

University of California, San Diego, Graduate Division, Division of Biological Sciences, La Jolla, CA 92093. Offers anthropogeny (PhD); bioinformatics (PhD); biology (PhD). PhD in biology offered jointly with San Diego State University. *Students:* 267 full-time (147 women), 13 part-time (9 women); includes 104 minority (2 Black or African American, non-Hispanic/Latino; 1 American Indian or Alaska Native, non-Hispanic/Latino; 75 Asian, non-Hispanic/Latino; 25 Hispanic/Latino; 1 Native Hawaiian or other Pacific Islander, non-Hispanic/Latino), 65 international. 638 applicants, 26% accepted, 84 enrolled. In 2014, 30 doctorates awarded. *Degree requirements:* For doctorate, thesis/dissertation, 3 quarters of teaching assistantship. *Entrance requirements:* For doctorate, GRE General Test; GRE Subject Test (recommended: biology, biochemistry, cell and molecular biology, chemistry). Additional exam requirements/recommendations for international students: Required—TOEFL (minimum score 550 paper-based; 80 iBT), IELTS (minimum score 7). *Application deadline:* For fall admission, 12/3 for domestic students. Application fee: $90 ($110 for international students). Electronic applications accepted. *Expenses:* Tuition, state resident: full-time $11,220; part-time $5610 per quarter. Tuition, nonresident: full-time $26,322; part-time $13,161 per quarter. *Required fees:* $570 per quarter. Tuition and fees vary according to program. *Financial support:* Fellowships, research assistantships, teaching assistantships, scholarships/grants, and unspecified assistantships available. Financial award applicants required to submit FAFSA. *Faculty research:* Ecology, behavior and evolution; microbiology; bioinformatics; multi-scale biology; signal transduction. *Unit head:* Jens Lykke-Andersen, Vice Chair, 858-822-3659, E-mail: jlykkeandersen@ucsd.edu. *Application contact:* Cathy Pugh, Graduate Coordinator, 858-534-0181, E-mail: gradprog@biology.ucsd.edu.
Website: http://biology.ucsd.edu/.

University of California, San Diego, Graduate Division, Program in Bioinformatics and Systems Biology, La Jolla, CA 92093. Offers biomedical informatics (PhD). *Students:* 62 full-time (15 women), 1 part-time (0 women); includes 17 minority (1 Black or African American, non-Hispanic/Latino; 16 Asian, non-Hispanic/Latino), 12 international. 204 applicants, 12% accepted, 7 enrolled. In 2014, 10 doctorates awarded. *Degree requirements:* For doctorate, comprehensive exam, thesis/dissertation. *Entrance requirements:* For doctorate, GRE General Test. Additional exam requirements/recommendations for international students: Required—TOEFL (minimum score 550 paper-based; 80 iBT), IELTS (minimum score 7). *Application deadline:* For fall admission, 12/15 for domestic students. Application fee: $90 ($110 for international students). Electronic applications accepted. *Expenses:* Tuition, state resident: full-time $11,220; part-time $5610 per quarter. Tuition, nonresident: full-time $26,322; part-time $13,161 per quarter. *Required fees:* $570 per quarter. Tuition and fees vary according to program. *Financial support:* Fellowships, research assistantships, and scholarships/grants available. Financial award applicants required to submit FAFSA. *Faculty research:* Quantitative foundations of computational biology, structural bioinformatics and systems pharmacology, proteomics and metabolomics, epigenomics and gene expression control, genetic and molecular networks. *Unit head:* Bing Ren, Chair, 858-822-5766, E-mail: biren@ucsd.edu. *Application contact:* Risa Shibata, Graduate Coordinator, 858-822-4948, E-mail: bioinfo@ucsd.edu.
Website: http://bioinformatics.ucsd.edu/.

University of California, San Diego, School of Medicine and Graduate Division, Graduate Studies in Biomedical Sciences, La Jolla, CA 92093. Offers anthropogeny (PhD); bioinformatics (PhD); multi-scale biology (PhD). *Students:* 183 full-time (99 women); includes 77 minority (8 Black or African American, non-Hispanic/Latino; 2 American Indian or Alaska Native, non-Hispanic/Latino; 49 Asian, non-Hispanic/Latino; 18 Hispanic/Latino), 3 international. 412 applicants, 22% accepted, 33 enrolled. In 2014, 23 doctorates awarded. *Degree requirements:* For doctorate, comprehensive exam, thesis/dissertation, 1-quarter teaching assistantship. *Entrance requirements:* For doctorate, GRE General Test; GRE Subject Test in either biology, biochemistry, cell and molecular biology or chemistry (recommended). Additional exam requirements/recommendations for international students: Required—TOEFL (minimum score 550 paper-based; 80 iBT), IELTS (minimum score 7). *Application deadline:* For fall admission, 12/2 for domestic students. Application fee: $90 ($110 for international students). Electronic applications accepted. *Expenses:* Tuition, state resident: full-time $11,220; part-time $5610 per quarter. Tuition, nonresident: full-time $26,322; part-time $13,161 per quarter. *Required fees:* $570 per quarter. Tuition and fees vary according to program. *Financial support:* Fellowships, research assistantships, teaching assistantships, scholarships/grants, unspecified assistantships, and stipends available. Financial award applicants required to submit FAFSA. *Faculty research:* Genetics, microbiology and immunology, molecular cell biology, molecular pharmacology, molecular pathology. *Unit head:* Deborah Spector, Chair, 858-822-4003, E-mail:

dspector@ucsd.edu. *Application contact:* Leanne Nordeman, Graduate Coordinator, 858-534-3982, E-mail: biomedsci@ucsd.edu.
Website: http://biomedsci.ucsd.edu.

University of California, San Francisco, School of Pharmacy and Graduate Division, Program in Bioinformatics, San Francisco, CA 94158-2517. Offers PhD. Terminal master's awarded for partial completion of doctoral program. *Degree requirements:* For doctorate, thesis/dissertation, cumulative qualifying exams, proposal defense. *Entrance requirements:* For doctorate, GRE General Test, minimum GPA of 3.0, bachelor's degree. Additional exam requirements/recommendations for international students: Required—TOEFL (minimum score 550 paper-based; 80 iBT). *Faculty research:* Bioinformatics and computational biology, genetics and genomics, systems biology.

University of California, Santa Cruz, Division of Graduate Studies, Jack Baskin School of Engineering, Program in Bioinformatics, Santa Cruz, CA 95064. Offers MS, PhD. *Degree requirements:* For master's, research project with written report; for doctorate, thesis/dissertation. *Entrance requirements:* For master's and doctorate, GRE General Test. Additional exam requirements/recommendations for international students: Required—TOEFL (minimum score 570 paper-based; 89 iBT); Recommended—IELTS (minimum score 8). Electronic applications accepted. *Faculty research:* Bioinformatics, genomics, nanopore, stem cell.

University of Cincinnati, Graduate School, College of Engineering and Applied Science, Department of Biomedical Engineering, Cincinnati, OH 45221. Offers bioinformatics (PhD); biomechanics (PhD); medical imaging (PhD); tissue engineering (PhD). Part-time programs available. *Degree requirements:* For doctorate, one foreign language, thesis/dissertation. *Entrance requirements:* For doctorate, GRE General Test. Additional exam requirements/recommendations for international students: Required—TOEFL (minimum score 600 paper-based).

University of Colorado Denver, School of Medicine, Program in Pharmacology, Aurora, CO 80045. Offers bioinformatics (PhD); biomolecular structure (PhD); pharmacology (PhD). *Students:* 19 full-time (13 women); includes 5 minority (3 Asian, non-Hispanic/Latino; 1 Hispanic/Latino; 1 Two or more races, non-Hispanic/Latino). Average age 26. 34 applicants, 12% accepted, 4 enrolled. In 2014, 2 doctorates awarded. *Degree requirements:* For doctorate, comprehensive exam, thesis/dissertation, major seminar, 3 research rotations in the first year, 30 hours each of course work and thesis. *Entrance requirements:* For doctorate, GRE General Test, three letters of recommendation, personal statement. Additional exam requirements/recommendations for international students: Required—TOEFL (minimum score 550 paper-based; 80 iBT). *Application deadline:* For fall admission, 12/15 for domestic students, 11/15 for international students. Application fee: $50 ($75 for international students). Electronic applications accepted. *Expenses:* Expenses: Contact institution. *Financial support:* In 2014–15, 19 students received support. Fellowships, research assistantships, teaching assistantships, institutionally sponsored loans, scholarships/grants, traineeships, health care benefits, tuition waivers (full), and unspecified assistantships available. Financial award application deadline: 3/15; financial award applicants required to submit FAFSA. *Faculty research:* Cancer biology, drugs of abuse, neuroscience, signal transduction, structural biology. *Total annual research expenditures:* $16.7 million. *Unit head:* Dr. Andrew Thorburn, Interim Chair, 303-724-3290, Fax: 303-724-3663, E-mail: andrew.thorburn@ucdenver.edu. *Application contact:* Elizabeth Bowen, Graduate Program Coordinator, 303-724-3565, E-mail: elizabeth.bowen@ucdenver.edu.
Website: http://www.ucdenver.edu/academics/colleges/medicalschool/departments/Pharmacology/Pages/Pharmacology.aspx.

University of Georgia, Institute of Bioinformatics, Athens, GA 30602. Offers MS, PhD, Graduate Certificate.

University of Idaho, College of Graduate Studies, Program in Bioinformatics and Computational Biology, Moscow, ID 83844-3051. Offers MS, PhD. *Faculty:* 14 full-time. *Students:* 16 full-time, 2 part-time. Average age 30. In 2014, 5 master's awarded. *Entrance requirements:* For master's, GRE, minimum GPA of 2.8. Additional exam requirements/recommendations for international students: Required—TOEFL. *Application deadline:* For fall admission, 8/1 for domestic students; for spring admission, 12/15 for domestic students. Applications are processed on a rolling basis. Application fee: $60. Electronic applications accepted. *Expenses:* Tuition, state resident: full-time $4784; part-time $280.50 per credit hour. Tuition, nonresident: full-time $18,314; part-time $957.50 per credit hour. *Required fees:* $2000; $58.50 per credit hour. Tuition and fees vary according to program. *Financial support:* Applicants required to submit FAFSA. *Unit head:* Dr. Eva Top, Director, 208-885-6010, E-mail: bcb@uidaho.edu. *Application contact:* Sean Scoggin, Graduate Recruitment Coordinator, 208-885-4001, Fax: 208-885-4406, E-mail: graduateadmissions@uidaho.edu.
Website: http://www.uidaho.edu/cogs/bcb.

University of Illinois at Chicago, Graduate College, College of Engineering, Department of Bioengineering, Chicago, IL 60607-7128. Offers MS, PhD. *Faculty:* 21 full-time (5 women), 10 part-time/adjunct (4 women). *Students:* 125 full-time (52 women), 16 part-time (6 women); includes 42 minority (2 Black or African American, non-Hispanic/Latino; 1 American Indian or Alaska Native, non-Hispanic/Latino; 28 Asian, non-Hispanic/Latino; 9 Hispanic/Latino; 2 Two or more races, non-Hispanic/Latino), 67 international. Average age 27. 225 applicants, 36% accepted, 28 enrolled. In 2014, 14 master's, 10 doctorates awarded. Terminal master's awarded for partial completion of doctoral program. *Degree requirements:* For master's, thesis; for doctorate, thesis/dissertation. *Entrance requirements:* For master's and doctorate, GRE Subject Test, minimum GPA of 3.0. Additional exam requirements/recommendations for international students: Required—TOEFL. *Application deadline:* For fall admission, 3/15 for domestic students, 1/1 for international students; for spring admission, 10/1 for domestic students. Applications are processed on a rolling basis. Application fee: $60. Electronic applications accepted. *Expenses:* Expenses: $17,602 in-state; $29,600 out-of-state. *Financial support:* In 2014–15, 3 fellowships with full tuition reimbursements were awarded; research assistantships with full tuition reimbursements, teaching assistantships with full tuition reimbursements, career-related internships or fieldwork, Federal Work-Study, scholarships/grants, traineeships, tuition waivers (full), and unspecified assistantships also available. Financial award application deadline: 3/1; financial award applicants required to submit FAFSA. *Faculty research:* Imaging systems, bioinstrumentation, electrophysiology, biological control, laser scattering. *Total annual research expenditures:* $3.6 million. *Unit head:* Dr. Thomas J. Royston, Head, 312-996-2335, E-mail: troyston@uic.edu. *Application contact:* Receptionist, 312-413-2550, E-mail: gradcoll@uic.edu.
Website: http://www.bioe.uic.edu/BIOE/WebHome.

University of Illinois at Urbana–Champaign, Graduate College, College of Agricultural, Consumer and Environmental Sciences, Department of Crop Sciences, Champaign, IL 61820. Offers bioinformatics: crop sciences (MS); crop sciences (MS, PhD). Postbaccalaureate distance learning degree programs offered (no on-campus study). *Students:* 112 full-time (48 women). Application fee: $70 ($90 for international students). *Unit head:* German A. Bollero, Head, 217-333-9475, Fax: 217-333-9817,

E-mail: gbollero@illinois.edu. *Application contact:* S. Dianne Carson, Office Support Specialist, 217-244-0396, Fax: 217-333-9817, E-mail: sdcarson@illinois.edu.
Website: http://cropsci.illinois.edu/.

University of Illinois at Urbana–Champaign, Graduate College, College of Engineering, Department of Computer Science, Champaign, IL 61820. Offers bioinformatics (MS); computer science (MCS, MS, PhD); MCS/JD; MCS/M Arch; MCS/MBA. Part-time and evening/weekend programs available. Postbaccalaureate distance learning degree programs offered (no on-campus study). *Students:* 530 (118 women). Application fee: $70 ($90 for international students). *Unit head:* Robin A. Rutenbar, Head, 217-333-3373, Fax: 217-333-3501, E-mail: rutenbar@illinois.edu. *Application contact:* Kara L. MacGregor, Graduate Academic Advisor, 217-333-9706, Fax: 217-244-6073, E-mail: kmacgreg@illinois.edu.
Website: http://cs.illinois.edu/.

University of Illinois at Urbana–Champaign, Graduate College, Graduate School of Library and Information Science, Champaign, IL 61820. Offers bioinformatics (MS); digital libraries (CAS); library and information science (MS, PhD, CAS). *Accreditation:* ALA (one or more programs are accredited). Part-time programs available. Postbaccalaureate distance learning degree programs offered (minimal on-campus study). *Students:* 283 (208 women). *Entrance requirements:* For degree, master's degree in library and information science or related field with minimum GPA of 3.0. Application fee: $70 ($90 for international students). *Unit head:* Allen Renear, Interim Dean, 217-265-5216, Fax: 217-244-3302, E-mail: renear@illinois.edu. *Application contact:* Penny Ames, Graduate Contact, 217-333-7197, E-mail: pames@illinois.edu.
Website: http://www.lis.illinois.edu.

The University of Iowa, Graduate College, Program in Informatics, Iowa City, IA 52242-1316. Offers bioinformatics (MS, PhD); bioinformatics and computational biology (Certificate); geoinformatics (MS, PhD, Certificate); health informatics (MS, PhD, Certificate); information science (MS, PhD, Certificate). *Degree requirements:* For master's, thesis optional; for doctorate, comprehensive exam, thesis/dissertation. *Entrance requirements:* For master's and doctorate, GRE General Test, minimum GPA of 3.0. Additional exam requirements/recommendations for international students: Required—TOEFL (minimum score 550 paper-based; 81 iBT). Electronic applications accepted.

The University of Kansas, Graduate Studies, College of Liberal Arts and Sciences, Bioinformatics Program, Lawrence, KS 66047. Offers PhD. *Faculty:* 6 full-time. *Students:* 20 full-time (10 women); includes 2 minority (both Asian, non-Hispanic/Latino), 13 international. Average age 29. 25 applicants, 28% accepted, 6 enrolled. In 2014, 1 doctorate awarded. *Entrance requirements:* For doctorate, bachelor's or master's degree in natural sciences, mathematics, engineering, or another relevant field. Additional exam requirements/recommendations for international students: Required—TOEFL. *Application deadline:* For fall admission, 12/15 for domestic and international students. Application fee: $55 ($65 for international students). *Faculty research:* Life sciences, computational modeling tools, community-wide activities in bioinformatics, education for the new generation of researchers. *Unit head:* Illya Vakser, Director, 785-864-1057, E-mail: vakser@ku.edu. *Application contact:* Debbie Douglass-Metsker, Office Manager, 785-864-1057, E-mail: douglass@ku.edu.
Website: http://www.bioinformatics.ku.edu/.

University of Maine, Graduate School, Graduate School of Biomedical Science and Engineering, Orono, ME 04469. Offers bioinformatics (PSM); biomedical engineering (PhD); biomedical science (PhD). *Faculty:* 151 full-time (45 women). *Students:* 27 full-time (17 women), 8 part-time (6 women), 11 international. Average age 31. 59 applicants, 8% accepted, 4 enrolled. In 2014, 3 doctorates awarded. *Degree requirements:* For doctorate, comprehensive exam, thesis/dissertation. *Entrance requirements:* For doctorate, GRE General Test, master's degree. Additional exam requirements/recommendations for international students: Required—TOEFL. *Application deadline:* For fall admission, 12/31 for domestic students. Application fee: $65. *Expenses:* Tuition, state resident: part-time $658 per credit hour. Tuition, nonresident: part-time $1550 per credit hour. *Financial support:* In 2014–15, 18 students received support, including 1 fellowship with full tuition reimbursement available (averaging $20,000 per year), 15 research assistantships with full tuition reimbursements available (averaging $23,000 per year), 1 teaching assistantship (averaging $7,500 per year). *Faculty research:* Molecular and cellular biology, neuroscience, biomedical engineering, toxicology, bioinformatics and computational biology. *Total annual research expenditures:* $62 million. *Unit head:* Dr. David Neivandt, Director, 207-581-2803. *Application contact:* Scott G. Delcourt, Assistant Vice President for Graduate Studies and Senior Associate Dean, 207-581-3291, Fax: 207-581-3232, E-mail: graduate@maine.edu.
Website: http://gsbse.umaine.edu/.

The University of Manchester, Faculty of Life Sciences, Manchester, United Kingdom. Offers adaptive organismal biology (M Phil, PhD); animal biology (M Phil, PhD); biochemistry (M Phil, PhD); bioinformatics (M Phil, PhD); biomolecular sciences (M Phil, PhD); biotechnology (M Phil, PhD); cell biology (M Phil, PhD); cell matrix research (M Phil, PhD); channels and transporters (M Phil, PhD); developmental biology (M Phil, PhD); Egyptology (M Phil, PhD); environmental biology (M Phil, PhD); evolutionary biology (M Phil, PhD); gene expression (M Phil, PhD); genetics (M Phil, PhD); history of science, technology and medicine (M Phil, PhD); immunology (M Phil, PhD); integrative neurobiology and behavior (M Phil, PhD); membrane trafficking (M Phil, PhD); microbiology (M Phil, PhD); molecular and cellular neuroscience (M Phil, PhD); molecular biology (M Phil, PhD); molecular cancer studies (M Phil, PhD); neuroscience (M Phil, PhD); ophthalmology (M Phil, PhD); optometry (M Phil, PhD); organelle function (M Phil, PhD); pharmacology (M Phil, PhD); physiology (M Phil, PhD); plant sciences (M Phil, PhD); stem cell research (M Phil, PhD); structural biology (M Phil, PhD); systems neuroscience (M Phil, PhD); toxicology (M Phil, PhD).

University of Maryland, College Park, Academic Affairs, College of Computer, Mathematical and Natural Sciences, Department of Biology, PhD Program in Biological Sciences, College Park, MD 20742. Offers behavior, ecology, evolution, and systematics (PhD); computational biology, bioinformatics, and genomics (PhD); molecular and cellular biology (PhD); physiological systems (PhD). *Degree requirements:* For doctorate, comprehensive exam, thesis/dissertation, thesis work presentation in seminar. *Entrance requirements:* For doctorate, GRE General Test; GRE Subject Test in biology (recommended), academic transcripts, statement of purpose/research interests, 3 letters of recommendation. Additional exam requirements/recommendations for international students: Required—TOEFL. Electronic applications accepted.

University of Massachusetts Worcester, Graduate School of Biomedical Sciences, Worcester, MA 01655-0115. Offers biochemistry and molecular pharmacology (PhD); bioinformatics and computational biology (PhD); biomedical sciences (millennium program) (PhD); cancer biology (PhD); cell biology (PhD); clinical and population health research (PhD); clinical investigation (MS); immunology and microbiology (PhD); interdisciplinary graduate research (PhD); neuroscience (PhD); translational science (PhD). *Faculty:* 1,367 full-time (516 women), 294 part-time/adjunct (186 women). *Students:* 372 full-time (191 women), 11 part-time (7 women); includes 60 minority (12 Black or African American, non-Hispanic/Latino; 33 Asian, non-Hispanic/Latino; 15 Hispanic/Latino), 139 international. Average age 29. 481 applicants, 22% accepted, 41 enrolled. In 2014, 4 master's, 54 doctorates awarded. Terminal master's awarded for partial completion of doctoral program. *Degree requirements:* For master's, comprehensive exam, thesis; for doctorate, comprehensive exam, thesis/dissertation. *Entrance requirements:* For master's, MD, PhD, DVM, or PharmD; for doctorate, GRE General Test, bachelor's degree. Additional exam requirements/recommendations for international students: Required—TOEFL (minimum score 100 iBT) or IELTS (minimum score 7.5). *Application deadline:* For fall admission, 12/15 for domestic and international students; for spring admission, 5/15 for domestic students. Application fee: $80. Electronic applications accepted. *Expenses:* Expenses: $6,942 state resident; $14,158 nonresident. *Financial support:* In 2014–15, 383 students received support, including research assistantships with full tuition reimbursements available (averaging $30,000 per year); scholarships/grants, health care benefits, tuition waivers (full), and unspecified assistantships also available. Financial award application deadline: 5/16. *Faculty research:* RNA interference, cell/molecular/developmental biology, bioinformatics, clinical/translational research, infectious disease. *Total annual research expenditures:* $241.9 million. *Unit head:* Dr. Anthony Carruthers, Dean, 508-856-4135, E-mail: anthony.carruthers@umassmed.edu. *Application contact:* Dr. Kendall Knight, Assistant Vice Provost for Admissions, 508-856-5628, Fax: 508-856-3659, E-mail: kendall.knight@umassmed.edu.
Website: http://www.umassmed.edu/gsbs/.

University of Michigan, Horace H. Rackham School of Graduate Studies, Program in Biomedical Sciences (PIBS) and Horace H. Rackham School of Graduate Studies, Program in Bioinformatics, Ann Arbor, MI 48109-2218. Offers MS, PhD. Part-time programs available. *Faculty:* 132 full-time (34 women). *Students:* 51 full-time (20 women), 3 part-time (0 women); includes 7 minority (2 Black or African American, non-Hispanic/Latino; 3 Asian, non-Hispanic/Latino; 2 Hispanic/Latino), 31 international. Average age 29. 108 applicants, 37% accepted, 14 enrolled. In 2014, 1 master's, 2 doctorates awarded. Terminal master's awarded for partial completion of doctoral program. *Degree requirements:* For master's, thesis optional, summer internship or rotation; for doctorate, thesis/dissertation, oral defense of dissertation, preliminary exam, two rotations. *Entrance requirements:* For master's and doctorate, GRE or MCAT. Additional exam requirements/recommendations for international students: Required—TOEFL (minimum score 100 iBT). *Application deadline:* For fall admission, 12/1 for domestic and international students. Application fee: $75 ($90 for international students). Electronic applications accepted. *Financial support:* In 2014–15, 47 students received support, including 16 fellowships with full tuition reimbursements available (averaging $28,500 per year), 25 research assistantships with full tuition reimbursements available (averaging $28,500 per year), 6 teaching assistantships with full tuition reimbursements available (averaging $28,500 per year); scholarships/grants, traineeships, health care benefits, and unspecified assistantships also available. Financial award application deadline: 12/1. *Faculty research:* Biophysics, structural and chemical informatics, clinical and biomedical informatics, databases and computing, evolutionary and population genetics, genomics, human and statistical genetics, medical and translational research, modeling immunological and infectious disease systems, molecular biology, neuroscience and psychiatry, proteomics and metabolomics, statistical and bioinformatics applications and software, systemic modeling and systems biology. *Unit head:* Dr. Dan Burns, Co-Director, 734-615-5510, Fax: 734-615-6553, E-mail: dburns@umich.edu. *Application contact:* Michelle S. Melis, Director of Student Life, 734-615-6538, Fax: 734-647-7022, E-mail: msmtegan@umich.edu.
Website: http://medicine.umich.edu/medschool/education/phd-programs/about-pibs/programs/bioinformatics.

University of Missouri, Office of Research and Graduate Studies, Informatics Institute, Columbia, MO 65211. Offers PhD. *Students:* 16 full-time (8 women), 19 part-time (5 women); includes 2 minority (1 Black or African American, non-Hispanic/Latino; 1 Asian, non-Hispanic/Latino), 20 international. Average age 34. 24 applicants, 38% accepted, 8 enrolled. In 2014, 5 doctorates awarded. *Entrance requirements:* Additional exam requirements/recommendations for international students: Required—TOEFL (minimum score 577 paper-based; 90 iBT). *Application deadline:* For fall admission, 1/15 priority date for domestic and international students. Applications are processed on a rolling basis. Application fee: $55 ($75 for international students). Electronic applications accepted. *Financial support:* Scholarships/grants, health care benefits, and unspecified assistantships available. Support available to part-time students. *Faculty research:* Human-computer interaction, human factors, information technology standards, IT sophistication in nursing homes, data mining and knowledge discovery in genomics and epigenomics, pathology decision support systems, digital image analysis, pathology text mining, computational biophysics, RNA folding and gene regulation, computer graphics and scientific visualization, biomedical imaging and computer vision, 3D shape modeling. *Unit head:* Dr. Chi-Ren Shyu, Director, 573-882-3884, E-mail: shyuc@missouri.edu. *Application contact:* Robert Sanders, Academic Advisor, 573-882-9007, E-mail: sandersrl@missouri.edu.
Website: http://muii.missouri.edu/.

University of Missouri–Kansas City, School of Computing and Engineering, Kansas City, MO 64110-2499. Offers civil engineering (MS); computer and electrical engineering (PhD); computer science (MS), including bioinformatics, software engineering, telecommunications networking; computer science and informatics (PhD); computing (PhD); electrical engineering (MS); engineering (PhD); engineering and construction management (Graduate Certificate); mechanical engineering (MS); telecommunications and computer networking (PhD). PhD (interdisciplinary) offered through the School of Graduate Studies. Part-time programs available. *Faculty:* 39 full-time (5 women), 26 part-time/adjunct (3 women). *Students:* 500 full-time (143 women), 136 part-time (28 women); includes 18 minority (5 Black or African American, non-Hispanic/Latino; 8 Asian, non-Hispanic/Latino; 4 Hispanic/Latino; 1 Two or more races, non-Hispanic/Latino), 551 international. Average age 24. 1,924 applicants, 39% accepted, 200 enrolled. In 2014, 124 master's, 1 other advanced degree awarded. *Degree requirements:* For doctorate, thesis/dissertation. *Entrance requirements:* For master's, GRE General Test, minimum GPA of 3.0, 3 letters of recommendation from professors; for doctorate, GRE General Test, minimum GPA of 3.5. Additional exam requirements/recommendations for international students: Required—TOEFL (minimum score 550 paper-based; 80 iBT). *Application deadline:* For fall admission, 1/15 priority date for domestic students, 1/15 for international students. Applications are processed on a rolling basis. Application fee: $45 ($50 for international students). *Financial support:* In 2014–15, 34 research assistantships with partial tuition reimbursements (averaging $15,602 per year), 24 teaching assistantships with partial tuition reimbursements (averaging $15,090 per year) were awarded; career-related internships or fieldwork, Federal Work-Study, scholarships/grants, tuition waivers (partial), and unspecified assistantships also available. Support available to part-time students. Financial award application deadline: 3/1; financial award applicants required to submit FAFSA. *Faculty research:* Algorithms, bioinformatics and medical informatics, biomechanics/biomaterials, civil engineering materials, networking and telecommunications, thermal science. *Unit head:* Dr. Kevin Z. Truman, Dean, 816-235-2399, Fax: 816-235-5159. *Application contact:* 816-235-2399, Fax: 816-235-5159.
Website: http://sce.umkc.edu/.

University of Missouri–Kansas City, School of Medicine, Kansas City, MO 64110-2499. Offers anesthesia (MS); bioinformatics (MS); health professions education (MS); medicine (MD); physician assistant (MMS); MD/PhD. *Accreditation:* LCME/AMA. *Faculty:* 48 full-time (20 women), 13 part-time/adjunct (6 women). *Students:* 497 full-time (260 women), 15 part-time (8 women); includes 263 minority (32 Black or African American, non-Hispanic/Latino; 2 American Indian or Alaska Native, non-Hispanic/Latino; 193 Asian, non-Hispanic/Latino; 15 Hispanic/Latino; 1 Native Hawaiian or other Pacific Islander, non-Hispanic/Latino; 20 Two or more races, non-Hispanic/Latino), 7 international. Average age 24. 973 applicants, 12% accepted, 113 enrolled. In 2014, 21 master's, 90 doctorates awarded. *Degree requirements:* For doctorate, one foreign language, United States Medical Licensing Exam Step 1 and 2. *Entrance requirements:* For doctorate, interview. *Application deadline:* For fall admission, 11/15 for domestic and international students. Application fee: $50. *Expenses:* Expenses: Contact institution. *Financial support:* In 2014–15, 2 fellowships (averaging $40,255 per year), 2 research assistantships (averaging $14,339 per year) were awarded; career-related internships or fieldwork, Federal Work-Study, institutionally sponsored loans, scholarships/grants, and tuition waivers (partial) also available. Financial award application deadline: 3/1; financial award applicants required to submit FAFSA. *Faculty research:* Cardiovascular disease, women's and children's health, trauma and infectious diseases, neurological, metabolic disease. *Unit head:* Dr. Steven L. Kanter, MD, Dean, 816-235-1803, E-mail: kantersl@umkc.edu. *Application contact:* Janine Kluckhohn, Admissions Coordinator, 816-235-1870, Fax: 816-235-6579, E-mail: kluckhohnj@umkc.edu. Website: http://www.med.umkc.edu/.

University of Nebraska at Omaha, Graduate Studies, College of Information Science and Technology, Department of Information Systems and Quantitative Analysis, Omaha, NE 68182. Offers biomedical informatics (MS, PhD); information assurance (MS, Certificate); information technology (PhD); management information systems (MS); project management (Certificate); systems analysis and design (Certificate). Part-time and evening/weekend programs available. *Faculty:* 25 full-time (8 women). *Students:* 137 full-time (50 women), 125 part-time (31 women); includes 36 minority (14 Black or African American, non-Hispanic/Latino; 1 American Indian or Alaska Native, non-Hispanic/Latino; 15 Asian, non-Hispanic/Latino; 2 Hispanic/Latino; 4 Two or more races, non-Hispanic/Latino), 143 international. Average age 29. 404 applicants, 50% accepted, 101 enrolled. In 2014, 46 master's, 3 doctorates, 21 other advanced degrees awarded. *Degree requirements:* For master's, comprehensive exam, thesis (for some programs); for doctorate, comprehensive exam, thesis/dissertation. *Entrance requirements:* For master's, GRE General Test, minimum GPA of 3.0, 3 letters of recommendation, writing sample, resume, official transcripts; for doctorate, GMAT or GRE General Test, minimum GPA of 3.0, 3 letters of recommendation, writing sample, resume, official transcripts; for Certificate, minimum GPA of 3.0, official transcripts. Additional exam requirements/recommendations for international students: Required—TOEFL, IELTS, PTE. *Application deadline:* For fall admission, 2/15 for domestic and international students; for spring admission, 9/15 for domestic and international students; for summer admission, 4/1 for domestic and international students. Applications are processed on a rolling basis. Application fee: $45. Electronic applications accepted. *Financial support:* In 2014–15, 35 students received support, including 28 research assistantships with tuition reimbursements available, 7 teaching assistantships with tuition reimbursements available; fellowships, career-related internships or fieldwork, Federal Work-Study, scholarships/grants, tuition waivers (partial), and unspecified assistantships also available. Financial award application deadline: 3/1; financial award applicants required to submit FAFSA. *Unit head:* Dr. Peter Wolcott, Chairperson, 402-554-2341, E-mail: graduate@unomaha.edu. *Application contact:* Dr. Leah Pietron, Graduate Program Chair, 402-554-2341, E-mail: graduate@unomaha.edu.

University of Nebraska–Lincoln, Graduate College, College of Arts and Sciences and College of Engineering, Department of Computer Science and Engineering, Lincoln, NE 68588. Offers bioinformatics (MS, PhD); computer engineering (MS, PhD); computer science (MS, PhD); information technology (PhD). *Degree requirements:* For master's, thesis optional; for doctorate, comprehensive exam, thesis/dissertation. *Entrance requirements:* For master's and doctorate, GRE General Test. Additional exam requirements/recommendations for international students: Required—TOEFL (minimum score 600 paper-based). Electronic applications accepted. *Faculty research:* Software engineering, geo- and bio-informatics, scientific computation, secure communication.

University of Nebraska Medical Center, Program in Biomedical Informatics, Omaha, NE 68198-1150. Offers MS, PhD. *Students:* 5 full-time (2 women), 6 part-time (3 women); includes 1 minority (Asian, non-Hispanic/Latino), 3 international. Average age 38. 8 applicants, 38% accepted, 3 enrolled. *Degree requirements:* For master's, comprehensive exam, thesis; for doctorate, comprehensive exam, thesis/dissertation. *Entrance requirements:* For master's and doctorate, GRE, Clinical training and experience (medicine, nursing, dentistry, or allied health degree). Additional exam requirements/recommendations for international students: Required—TOEFL (minimum score 550 paper-based). *Application deadline:* For fall admission, 6/1 for domestic students, 5/1 for international students; for spring admission, 10/15 for domestic students, 9/15 for international students; for summer admission, 3/1 for domestic students, 2/1 for international students. Application fee: $45. Electronic applications accepted. *Expenses:* Tuition, state resident: full-time $7695; part-time $285 per credit hour. Tuition, nonresident: full-time $22,005; part-time $815 per credit hour. Tuition and fees vary according to course load and program. *Financial support:* In 2014–15, 2 fellowships with full tuition reimbursements (averaging $23,100 per year) were awarded; scholarships/grants also available. Support available to part-time students. Financial award applicants required to submit FAFSA. *Unit head:* Dr. Jim McClay, Director, 402-559-3587, E-mail: jmcclay@unmc.edu. Website: http://www.unmc.edu/bmi/.

The University of North Carolina at Chapel Hill, School of Medicine and Graduate School, Graduate Programs in Medicine, Curriculum in Bioinformatics and Computational Biology, Chapel Hill, NC 27599. Offers PhD. *Degree requirements:* For doctorate, comprehensive exam, thesis/dissertation. *Entrance requirements:* For doctorate, GRE, minimum GPA of 3.0. Additional exam requirements/recommendations for international students: Required—TOEFL. Electronic applications accepted. *Faculty research:* Protein folding, design and evolution and molecular biophysics of disease; mathematical modeling of signaling pathways and regulatory networks; bioinformatics, medical informatics, user interface design; statistical genetics and genetic epidemiology datamining, classification and clustering analysis of gene-expression data.

The University of North Carolina at Charlotte, College of Computing and Informatics, Department of Bioinformatics and Genomics, Charlotte, NC 28223-0001. Offers bioinformatics (PSM); bioinformatics and computational biology (PhD); bioinformatics applications (Graduate Certificate); bioinformatics technology (Graduate Certificate). Part-time programs available. *Faculty:* 15 full-time (7 women). *Students:* 40 full-time (17 women), 22 part-time (14 women); includes 18 minority (4 Black or African American, non-Hispanic/Latino; 4 Asian, non-Hispanic/Latino; 6 Hispanic/Latino; 1 Native Hawaiian or other Pacific Islander, non-Hispanic/Latino; 3 Two or more races, non-Hispanic/Latino), 10 international. Average age 29. 55 applicants, 71% accepted, 21 enrolled. In 2014, 12 master's, 3 doctorates, 2 other advanced degrees awarded. Terminal master's awarded for partial completion of doctoral program. *Degree requirements:* For master's,

internship, research project, or thesis; for doctorate, comprehensive exam, thesis/dissertation. *Entrance requirements:* For master's, GRE, minimum undergraduate GPA of 3.0 overall and in major; for doctorate, GRE, letters of recommendation. Additional exam requirements/recommendations for international students: Required—TOEFL (minimum score 557 paper-based; 83 iBT). *Application deadline:* For fall admission, 5/1 priority date for domestic and international students; for spring admission, 10/1 priority date for domestic and international students. Applications are processed on a rolling basis. Application fee: $75. Electronic applications accepted. *Expenses:* Tuition, state resident: full-time $4008. Tuition, nonresident: full-time $16,295. *Required fees:* $2755. Tuition and fees vary according to course load and program. *Financial support:* In 2014–15, 28 students received support, including 5 fellowships (averaging $43,315 per year), 15 research assistantships (averaging $9,756 per year), 8 teaching assistantships (averaging $17,531 per year); career-related internships or fieldwork, institutionally sponsored loans, scholarships/grants, and unspecified assistantships also available. Support available to part-time students. *Faculty research:* Big data in bioinformatics, computational biophysics, computational mass spectrometry, genome-wide association analysis, high-throughput studies, metagenomics, plant genomics, structural bioinformatics, systems biology. *Total annual research expenditures:* $1.8 million. *Unit head:* Dr. Yi Deng, Chairman, 704-687-8450, Fax: 704-687-6979, E-mail: yi.deng@uncc.edu. *Application contact:* Kathy B. Giddings, Director of Graduate Admissions, 704-687-5503, Fax: 704-687-1668, E-mail: gradadm@uncc.edu. Website: http://bioinformatics.uncc.edu/.

University of Oklahoma, College of Arts and Sciences, Department of Biology, Program in Biology, Norman, OK 73019. Offers bioinformatics (MS, PhD); biology (MS, PhD); natural science (M Nat Sci). *Students:* 16 full-time (6 women), 12 part-time (3 women); includes 1 minority (Asian, non-Hispanic/Latino), 7 international. Average age 27. 23 applicants, 65% accepted, 7 enrolled. In 2014, 5 master's, 1 doctorate awarded. *Degree requirements:* For master's, thesis, course in biostatistics; for doctorate, comprehensive exam, thesis/dissertation, course in biostatistics; 2 semesters as teaching assistant. *Entrance requirements:* For master's and doctorate, GRE, transcripts, 3 letters of recommendation, personal statement, curriculum vitae. Additional exam requirements/recommendations for international students: Required—TOEFL (minimum score 79 iBT). *Application deadline:* For fall admission, 12/15 for domestic and international students. Application fee: $50 ($100 for international students). Electronic applications accepted. *Expenses:* Tuition, state resident: full-time $4394; part-time $183.10 per credit hour. Tuition, nonresident: full-time $16,970; part-time $707.10 per credit hour. *Required fees:* $2892; $109.95 per credit hour. $126.50 per semester. *Financial support:* In 2014–15, 24 students received support. Scholarships/grants, health care benefits, and unspecified assistantships available. Financial award application deadline: 6/1; financial award applicants required to submit FAFSA. *Faculty research:* Geographical ecology; evolution, cellular and behavioral neurobiology; evolutionary and molecular genetics; evolution of development. *Unit head:* Dr. Randall Hewes, Chair, 405-325-6200, Fax: 405-325-6202, E-mail: biology@ou.edu. *Application contact:* Dr. Rosemary Knapp, Director of Graduate Studies, 405-325-4389, Fax: 405-325-6202, E-mail: biologygrad@ou.edu. Website: http://www.ou.edu/cas/biology.

University of Oklahoma, College of Arts and Sciences, Department of Chemistry and Biochemistry, Norman, OK 73019. Offers bioinformatics (MS); chemistry (PhD). Part-time programs available. *Faculty:* 29 full-time (8 women). *Students:* 67 full-time (30 women), 23 part-time (7 women); includes 14 minority (5 Black or African American, non-Hispanic/Latino; 1 American Indian or Alaska Native, non-Hispanic/Latino; 2 Asian, non-Hispanic/Latino; 5 Hispanic/Latino; 1 Two or more races, non-Hispanic/Latino), 27 international. Average age 26. 96 applicants, 34% accepted, 19 enrolled. In 2014, 12 master's, 8 doctorates awarded. Terminal master's awarded for partial completion of doctoral program. *Degree requirements:* For master's, comprehensive exam (for some programs), thesis (for some programs); for doctorate, comprehensive exam, thesis/dissertation. *Entrance requirements:* For master's and doctorate, GRE, minimum GPA of 3.0. Additional exam requirements/recommendations for international students: Required—TOEFL (minimum score 79 iBT). *Application deadline:* For fall admission, 1/15 for domestic and international students; for spring admission, 9/1 for domestic and international students. Application fee: $50 ($100 for international students). Electronic applications accepted. *Expenses:* Tuition, state resident: full-time $4394; part-time $183.10 per credit hour. Tuition, nonresident: full-time $16,970; part-time $707.10 per credit hour. *Required fees:* $2892; $109.95 per credit hour. $126.50 per semester. *Financial support:* In 2014–15, 90 students received support, including 5 fellowships with full tuition reimbursements available (averaging $4,500 per year), 18 research assistantships with partial tuition reimbursements available (averaging $17,026 per year), 69 teaching assistantships with partial tuition reimbursements available (averaging $16,650 per year); scholarships/grants, health care benefits, and unspecified assistantships also available. Support available to part-time students. Financial award application deadline: 6/1; financial award applicants required to submit FAFSA. *Faculty research:* Structural biology, synthesis and catalysis, natural products, membrane biochemistry, genomics. *Total annual research expenditures:* $6.6 million. *Unit head:* Dr. Ronald L. Halterman, Department Chairperson, 405-325-4812, Fax: 405-325-6111, E-mail: rhalterman@ou.edu. *Application contact:* Angelika Tietz, Graduate Program Assistant, 405-325-4811 Ext. 62946, Fax: 405-325-6111, E-mail: atietz@ou.edu. Website: http://chem.ou.edu.

University of Oklahoma, College of Arts and Sciences, Department of Microbiology and Plant Biology, Program in Botany, Norman, OK 73019. Offers bioinformatics (MS, PhD); botany (MS, PhD). *Students:* 18 full-time (8 women), 8 part-time (5 women); includes 7 minority (2 American Indian or Alaska Native, non-Hispanic/Latino; 1 Asian, non-Hispanic/Latino; 3 Hispanic/Latino; 1 Two or more races, non-Hispanic/Latino), 7 international. Average age 28. 15 applicants, 27% accepted, 3 enrolled. In 2014, 3 master's, 2 doctorates awarded. Terminal master's awarded for partial completion of doctoral program. *Degree requirements:* For master's, thesis; for doctorate, one foreign language, comprehensive exam, thesis/dissertation. *Entrance requirements:* For master's and doctorate, GRE, 3 recommendation letters, letter of intent, bachelor's degree. Additional exam requirements/recommendations for international students: Required—TOEFL (minimum score 80 iBT). *Application deadline:* For fall admission, 3/1 for domestic and international students; for spring admission, 9/1 for domestic and international students. Application fee: $50 ($100 for international students). Electronic applications accepted. *Expenses:* Tuition, state resident: full-time $4394; part-time $183.10 per credit hour. Tuition, nonresident: full-time $16,970; part-time $707.10 per credit hour. *Required fees:* $2892; $109.95 per credit hour. $126.50 per semester. *Financial support:* In 2014–15, 20 students received support. Federal Work-Study, institutionally sponsored loans, scholarships/grants, health care benefits, and unspecified assistantships available. Support available to part-time students. Financial award application deadline: 6/1; financial award applicants required to submit FAFSA. *Faculty research:* Ecology, evolution, and systematics of plants; molecular biology of plant stress and reproduction; global change biology and ecosystem modeling; plant structure and development; science education. *Unit head:* Dr. Michael McInerney, Professor/Department Chair, 405-325-4321, Fax: 405-325-7619, E-mail: mcinerney@

ou.edu. *Application contact:* Adell Hopper, Staff Assistant, 405-325-4322, Fax: 405-325-7619, E-mail: ahopper@ou.edu.
Website: http://mpbio.ou.edu/.

University of Pittsburgh, School of Medicine, Biomedical Informatics Training Program, Pittsburgh, PA 15260. Offers MS, PhD, Certificate. Part-time programs available. *Faculty:* 16 full-time (6 women), 14 part-time/adjunct (5 women). *Students:* 26 full-time (7 women), 1 part-time (0 women); includes 7 minority (1 Black or African American, non-Hispanic/Latino; 5 Asian, non-Hispanic/Latino; 1 Hispanic/Latino), 7 international. Average age 27. 69 applicants, 22% accepted, 10 enrolled. In 2014, 4 master's awarded. Terminal master's awarded for partial completion of doctoral program. *Degree requirements:* For master's, comprehensive exam, thesis, written research report; for doctorate, comprehensive exam, thesis/dissertation. *Entrance requirements:* For master's, doctorate, and Certificate, GRE. Additional exam requirements/recommendations for international students: Required—TOEFL. *Application deadline:* For fall admission, 2/1 priority date for domestic and international students. Application fee: $50. Electronic applications accepted. *Expenses:* Tuition, state resident: full-time $20,742; part-time $838 per credit. Tuition, nonresident: full-time $33,960; part-time $1389 per credit. *Required fees:* $800; $205 per term. Tuition and fees vary according to program. *Financial support:* In 2014–15, 19 students received support, including 12 fellowships with full tuition reimbursements available (averaging $27,000 per year), 7 research assistantships with full tuition reimbursements available (averaging $27,000 per year); health care benefits also available. Financial award application deadline: 2/1. *Faculty research:* Biomedical informatics; bioinformatics; global health informatics; artificial intelligence; probability theory; data mining; machine learning; evaluation methods; dental, radiology, and pathology imaging. *Unit head:* Dr. Rebecca Jacobson, Director, 412-624-5100, Fax: 412-648-9118, E-mail: crowleyrs@upmc.edu. *Application contact:* Toni L. Porterfield, Coordinator, 412-648-9203, Fax: 412-648-9118, E-mail: tls18@pitt.edu.
Website: http://www.dbmi.pitt.edu.

University of Southern California, Graduate School, Dana and David Dornsife College of Letters, Arts and Sciences, Department of Biological Sciences, Program in Molecular and Computational Biology, Los Angeles, CA 90089. Offers computational biology and bioinformatics (PhD); molecular biology (PhD). *Degree requirements:* For doctorate, comprehensive exam, thesis/dissertation, qualifying examination, dissertation defense. *Entrance requirements:* For doctorate, GRE, 3 letters of recommendation, personal statement, resume, minimum GPA of 3.0. Additional exam requirements/recommendations for international students: Required—TOEFL (minimum score 600 paper-based; 100 iBT). Electronic applications accepted. *Faculty research:* Biochemistry and molecular biology; genomics; computational biology and bioinformatics; cell and developmental biology, and genetics; DNA replication and repair, and cancer biology.

University of South Florida, Morsani College of Medicine and Graduate School, Graduate Programs in Medical Sciences, Tampa, FL 33620-9951. Offers aging and neuroscience (MSMS); allergy, immunology and infectious disease (PhD); anatomy (MSMS, PhD); athletic training (MSMS); bioinformatics and computational biology (MSBCB); biotechnology (MSB); clinical and translational research (MSMS, PhD); health informatics (MSHI, MSMS); health science (MSMS); interdisciplinary medical sciences (MSMS); medical microbiology and immunology (MSMS); metabolic and nutritional medicine (MSMS); molecular medicine (MSMS, PhD); molecular pharmacology and physiology (PhD); neurology (PhD); pathology and laboratory medicine (PhD); pharmacology and therapeutics (PhD); physiology and biophysics (PhD); women's health (MSMS). *Students:* 338 full-time (162 women), 36 part-time (25 women); includes 173 minority (43 Black or African American, non-Hispanic/Latino; 65 Asian, non-Hispanic/Latino; 58 Hispanic/Latino; 7 Two or more races, non-Hispanic/Latino), 24 international. Average age 26. 1,188 applicants, 41% accepted, 271 enrolled. In 2014, 216 master's awarded. Terminal master's awarded for partial completion of doctoral program. *Degree requirements:* For master's, comprehensive exam, thesis; for doctorate, comprehensive exam, thesis/dissertation. *Entrance requirements:* For master's, GRE General Test or GMAT, bachelor's degree or equivalent from regionally-accredited university with minimum GPA of 3.0 in upper-division sciences coursework; prerequisites in general biology, general chemistry, general physics, organic chemistry, quantitative analysis, and integral and differential calculus; for doctorate, GRE General Test (minimum score of 32nd percentile quantitative), bachelor's degree from regionally-accredited university with minimum GPA of 3.0 in upper-division sciences coursework; 3 letters of recommendation; personal interview; 1-2 page personal statement; prerequisites in biology, chemistry, physics, organic chemistry, quantitative analysis, and integral/differential calculus. Additional exam requirements/recommendations for international students: Required—TOEFL (minimum score 550 paper-based; 79 iBT) or IELTS (minimum score 6.5). *Application deadline:* For fall admission, 2/15 for domestic students, 1/2 for international students. Application fee: $30. *Expenses:* Expenses: Contact institution. *Faculty research:* Anatomy, biochemistry, cancer biology, cardiovascular disease, cell biology, immunology, microbiology, molecular biology, neuroscience, pharmacology, physiology. *Unit head:* Dr. Michael Barber, Professor and Associate Dean for Graduate and Postdoctoral Affairs, 813-974-9908, Fax: 813-974-4317, E-mail: mbarber@health.usf.edu. *Application contact:* Dr. Eric Bennett, Graduate Director, PhD Program in Medical Sciences, 813-974-1545, Fax: 813-974-4317, E-mail: esbennet@health.usf.edu.
Website: http://health.usf.edu/nocms/medicine/graduatestudies/.

University of South Florida, University College/Distance Education, Tampa, FL 33620-9951. *Unit head:* Kathy Barnes, Interdisciplinary Programs Coordinator, 813-974-8031, Fax: 813-974-7061, E-mail: barnesk@usf.edu. *Application contact:* Karen Tylinski, Metro Initiatives, 813-974-9943, Fax: 813-974-7061, E-mail: ktylinsk@usf.edu.
Website: http://www.usf.edu/innovative-education/.

The University of Texas at El Paso, Graduate School, College of Science, Department of Biological Sciences, El Paso, TX 79968-0001. Offers bioinformatics (MS); biological sciences (MS, PhD). Part-time and evening/weekend programs available. *Degree requirements:* For master's, thesis; for doctorate, thesis/dissertation. *Entrance requirements:* For master's, GRE, minimum GPA of 3.0, letters of recommendation; for doctorate, GRE, statement of purpose, letters of recommendation. Additional exam requirements/recommendations for international students: Required—TOEFL; Recommended—IELTS. Electronic applications accepted.

The University of Texas at El Paso, Graduate School, College of Science, Program in Bioinformatics, El Paso, TX 79968-0001. Offers MS. Part-time programs available. *Entrance requirements:* For master's, GRE, minimum GPA of 3.0. Additional exam requirements/recommendations for international students: Required—TOEFL. Electronic applications accepted.

The University of Texas Medical Branch, Graduate School of Biomedical Sciences, Program in Biochemistry and Molecular Biology, Galveston, TX 77555. Offers biochemistry (PhD); bioinformatics (PhD); biophysics (PhD); cell biology (PhD); computational biology (PhD); structural biology (PhD). *Degree requirements:* For doctorate, thesis/dissertation. *Entrance requirements:* Additional exam requirements/recommendations for international students: Required—TOEFL (minimum score 550 paper-based). Electronic applications accepted.

University of the Sciences, College of Graduate Studies, Program in Bioinformatics, Philadelphia, PA 19104-4495. Offers MS. Part-time and evening/weekend programs available. *Entrance requirements:* Additional exam requirements/recommendations for international students: Required—TOEFL, TWE. *Expenses:* Contact institution. *Faculty research:* Genomics, microarray analysis, computer-aided drug design, molecular biophysics, cell structure, molecular dynamics, computational chemistry.

The University of Toledo, College of Graduate Studies, College of Medicine and Life Sciences, Interdepartmental Programs, Toledo, OH 43606-3390. Offers bioinformatics and proteomics/genomics (MSBS); biomarkers and bioinformatics (Certificate); biomarkers and diagnostics (PSM); human donation sciences (MSBS); medical sciences (MSBS); MD/MSBS. *Degree requirements:* For master's, thesis or alternative. *Entrance requirements:* For master's, GRE, minimum undergraduate GPA of 3.0, three letters of recommendation, statement of purpose, transcripts from all prior institutions attended, resume; for Certificate, minimum undergraduate GPA of 3.0, three letters of recommendation, statement of purpose, transcripts from all prior institutions attended, resume. Additional exam requirements/recommendations for international students: Required—TOEFL (minimum score 550 paper-based; 80 iBT). Electronic applications accepted.

University of Utah, School of Medicine and Graduate School, Graduate Programs in Medicine, Department of Biomedical Informatics, Salt Lake City, UT 84112-1107. Offers MS, PhD, Certificate. Part-time programs available. Postbaccalaureate distance learning degree programs offered (minimal on-campus study). *Degree requirements:* For master's, comprehensive exam, thesis; for doctorate, comprehensive exam, thesis/dissertation, qualifying exam. *Entrance requirements:* For master's and doctorate, GRE General Test (minimum 60th percentile), minimum GPA of 3.3. Additional exam requirements/recommendations for international students: Required—TOEFL (minimum score 600 paper-based). Electronic applications accepted. *Faculty research:* Health information systems and expert systems, genetic epidemiology, medical imaging, bioinformatics, public health informatics.

University of Washington, Graduate School, School of Medicine, Graduate Programs in Medicine, Department of Medical Education and Biomedical Informatics, Division of Biomedical and Health Informatics, Seattle, WA 98195. Offers MS, PhD. *Entrance requirements:* For master's and doctorate, GRE General Test, minimum GPA of 3.0; previous undergraduate course work in biology, computer programming, and mathematics. Additional exam requirements/recommendations for international students: Required—TOEFL (minimum score 580 paper-based; 70 iBT). Electronic applications accepted. *Faculty research:* Bio-clinical informatics, information retrieval, human-computer interaction, knowledge-based systems, telehealth.

Vanderbilt University, Graduate School, Department of Biomedical Informatics, Nashville, TN 37240-1001. Offers MS, PhD, MD/MS, MD/PhD. Part-time programs available. *Faculty:* 19 full-time (4 women). *Students:* 29 full-time (9 women), 2 part-time (1 woman); includes 8 minority (1 Black or African American, non-Hispanic/Latino; 6 Asian, non-Hispanic/Latino; 1 Hispanic/Latino), 2 international. Average age 33. 64 applicants, 20% accepted, 11 enrolled. In 2014, 2 master's awarded. Terminal master's awarded for partial completion of doctoral program. *Degree requirements:* For master's, thesis; for doctorate, thesis/dissertation, final and qualifying exams. *Entrance requirements:* For master's and doctorate, GRE General Test. Additional exam requirements/recommendations for international students: Required—TOEFL (minimum score 570 paper-based; 88 iBT). *Application deadline:* For fall admission, 1/15 for domestic and international students. Electronic applications accepted. *Expenses: Tuition:* Full-time $42,768; part-time $1782 per credit hour. *Required fees:* $422. One-time fee: $30 full-time. *Financial support:* Fellowships with full and partial tuition reimbursements, research assistantships with full and partial tuition reimbursements, teaching assistantships with full and partial tuition reimbursements, Federal Work-Study, institutionally sponsored loans, scholarships/grants, traineeships, and health care benefits available. Financial award application deadline: 1/15; financial award applicants required to submit CSS PROFILE or FAFSA. *Faculty research:* Organizational informatics, the application of informatics to the role of information technology in organizational change, clinical research and translational informatics, applications of informatics to facilitating "bench to bedside" translational research. *Unit head:* Dr. Cindy Gadd, Director of Graduate Studies, 615-936-5951, Fax: 615-936-1427, E-mail: cindy.gadd@vanderbilt.edu. *Application contact:* Rischelle Jenkins, Administrative Assistant, 615-936-1068, Fax: 615-936-1427, E-mail: rischelle.jenkins@vanderbilt.edu.
Website: https://medschool.vanderbilt.edu/dbmi/.

Virginia Commonwealth University, Graduate School, School of Life Sciences, Center for the Study of Biological Complexity, Richmond, VA 23284-9005. Offers bioinformatics (MS); integrative life sciences (PhD). *Degree requirements:* For master's, thesis optional. *Entrance requirements:* For master's and doctorate, GRE. Additional exam requirements/recommendations for international students: Required—TOEFL (minimum score 600 paper-based; 100 iBT). Electronic applications accepted.

Virginia Polytechnic Institute and State University, Graduate School, Intercollege, Blacksburg, VA 24061. Offers genetics, bioinformatics and computational biology (PhD); information technology (MIT); macromolecular science and engineering (MS, PhD). *Students:* 173 full-time (89 women), 657 part-time (229 women); includes 186 minority (65 Black or African American, non-Hispanic/Latino; 64 Asian, non-Hispanic/Latino; 33 Hispanic/Latino; 2 Native Hawaiian or other Pacific Islander, non-Hispanic/Latino; 22 Two or more races, non-Hispanic/Latino), 89 international. Average age 32. 599 applicants, 75% accepted, 343 enrolled. In 2014, 102 master's, 19 doctorates awarded. *Degree requirements:* For master's, comprehensive exam (for some programs), thesis (for some programs); for doctorate, comprehensive exam (for some programs), thesis/dissertation (for some programs). *Entrance requirements:* For master's and doctorate, GRE/GMAT (may vary by department). Additional exam requirements/recommendations for international students: Required—TOEFL (minimum score 550 paper-based). *Application deadline:* For fall admission, 8/1 for domestic students, 4/1 for international students; for spring admission, 1/1 for domestic students, 9/1 for international students. Applications are processed on a rolling basis. Application fee: $75. Electronic applications accepted. *Expenses:* Tuition, state resident: full-time $11,656; part-time $647.50 per credit hour. Tuition, nonresident: full-time $23,351; part-time $1297.25 per credit hour. *Required fees:* $2533; $465.75 per semester. Tuition and fees vary according to course load, campus/location and program. *Financial support:* In 2014–15, 102 research assistantships with full tuition reimbursements (averaging $25,419 per year), 13 teaching assistantships with full tuition reimbursements (averaging $21,101 per year) were awarded. Financial award application deadline: 3/1; financial award applicants required to submit FAFSA. *Unit head:* Dr. Karen P. DePauw, Vice President and Dean for Graduate Education, 540-231-7581, Fax: 540-231-1670, E-mail: kpdepauw@vt.edu. *Application contact:* Graduate Admissions and Academic Progress, 540-231-8636, Fax: 540-231-2039, E-mail: grads@vt.edu.
Website: http://www.graduateschool.vt.edu/graduate_catalog/colleges.htm.

Wayne State University, College of Engineering, Department of Computer Science, Detroit, MI 48202. Offers computer science (MS, PhD), including bioinformatics (PhD), computational biology (PhD), computer science (PhD); scientific computing (Graduate

Certificate). *Students:* 139 full-time (41 women), 60 part-time (21 women); includes 23 minority (1 Black or African American, non-Hispanic/Latino; 20 Asian, non-Hispanic/Latino; 1 Hispanic/Latino; 1 Two or more races, non-Hispanic/Latino), 154 international. Average age 28. 566 applicants, 38% accepted, 54 enrolled. In 2014, 37 master's, 8 doctorates awarded. *Degree requirements:* For master's, thesis (for some programs); for doctorate, thesis/dissertation. *Entrance requirements:* For master's, GRE, minimum GPA of 3.0, three letters of recommendation, adequate preparation in computer science and mathematics courses, personal statement; for doctorate, GRE, minimum GPA of 3.3 in most recent degree; three letters of recommendation; personal statement; adequate preparation in computer science and mathematics courses. Additional exam requirements/recommendations for international students: Required—TOEFL (minimum score 550 paper-based; 79 iBT), TWE (minimum score 5.5), Michigan English Language Assessment Battery (minimum score 85); Recommended—IELTS (minimum score 6.5). *Application deadline:* For fall admission, 6/1 priority date for domestic students, 5/1 priority date for international students; for winter admission, 10/1 priority date for domestic students, 9/1 priority date for international students; for spring admission, 2/1 priority date for domestic students, 1/2 priority date for international students. Applications are processed on a rolling basis. Application fee: $0. Electronic applications accepted. *Expenses:* Expenses: Contact institution. *Financial support:* In 2014–15, 99 students received support, including 5 fellowships with tuition reimbursements available (averaging $16,000 per year), 26 research assistantships with tuition reimbursements available (averaging $19,371 per year), 26 teaching assistantships with tuition reimbursements available (averaging $18,645 per year); scholarships/grants, health care benefits, and unspecified assistantships also available. Financial award application deadline: 3/31; financial award applicants required to submit FAFSA. *Faculty research:* Software engineering, databases, bioinformatics, artificial intelligence, networking, distributed and parallel computing, security, graphics, visualizations. *Total annual research expenditures:* $2.7 million. *Unit head:* Dr. Xuewen Chen, Chair, 313-577-2478, E-mail: xwchen@wayne.edu.
Website: http://engineering.wayne.edu/cs/.

Wayne State University, School of Medicine, Office of Biomedical Graduate Programs, Program in Molecular Biology and Genetics, Detroit, MI 48201. Offers bioinformatics and computational biology (PhD); cellular neuroscience (PhD); MD/PhD. *Students:* 45 applicants, 13% accepted, 4 enrolled. In 2014, 5 doctorates awarded. Terminal master's awarded for partial completion of doctoral program. *Degree requirements:* For doctorate, thesis/dissertation. *Entrance requirements:* For doctorate, GRE General Test, GRE Subject Test (chemistry or biology), minimum GPA of 3.0, strong background in one of the chemical or biological sciences, three letters of recommendation, personal statement, interview. Additional exam requirements/recommendations for international students: Required—TOEFL (minimum score 550 paper-based; 79 iBT), Michigan English Language Assessment Battery (minimum score 85); Recommended—IELTS (minimum score 6.5), TWE (minimum score 5.5). *Application deadline:* For fall admission, 3/1 for domestic students, 5/1 for international students; for winter admission, 10/1 for domestic students, 9/1 for international students; for spring admission, 2/1 for domestic students, 1/1 for international students. Applications are processed on a rolling basis. Application fee: $0. Electronic applications accepted. *Expenses:* Tuition, state resident: full-time $10,294; part-time $571.90 per credit hour. Tuition, nonresident: full-time $29,730; part-time $1238.75 per credit hour. *Required fees:* $1365; $43.50 per credit hour. $291.10 per semester. Tuition and fees vary according to course load and program. *Financial support:* In 2014–15, 18 students received support. Fellowships with tuition reimbursements available, research assistantships with tuition reimbursements available, teaching assistantships with tuition reimbursements available, scholarships/grants, and unspecified assistantships available. Financial award application deadline: 3/31; financial award applicants required to submit FAFSA. *Faculty research:* Human gene mapping, genome organization and sequencing, gene regulation, molecular evolution. *Total annual research expenditures:* $2.6 million. *Unit head:* Dr. Lawrence Grossman, Director, 313-577-5323, E-mail: l.grossman@wayne.edu. *Application contact:* Dr. Gregory Kapatos, Professor, Director for Education, and Graduate Officer, 313-577-5965, Fax: 313-993-4269, E-mail: gkapato@med.wayne.edu.
Website: http://genetics.wayne.edu/students/mdphd.php.

Worcester Polytechnic Institute, Graduate Studies and Research, Program in Bioinformatics and Computational Biology, Worcester, MA 01609-2280. Offers MS, PhD. *Students:* 5 full-time (3 women), 1 international. 7 applicants, 71% accepted, 2 enrolled. In 2014, 1 master's awarded. *Entrance requirements:* For master's and doctorate, GRE, 3 letters of recommendation, statement of purpose. Additional exam requirements/recommendations for international students: Required—TOEFL (minimum score 563 paper-based; 84 iBT), IELTS (minimum score 7). *Application deadline:* For fall admission, 1/1 priority date for domestic and international students; for spring admission, 10/1 priority date for domestic and international students. Applications are processed on a rolling basis. Electronic applications accepted. *Financial support:* Research assistantships, teaching assistantships, and career-related internships or fieldwork available. Financial award application deadline: 1/1; financial award applicants required to submit FAFSA. *Unit head:* Elizabeth Ryder, Professor, 508-831-5543, Fax: 508-831-5936, E-mail: ryder@wpi.edu. *Application contact:* Jenny McGarty, Administrative Assistant, 508-831-5543, Fax: 508-831-5936, E-mail: jrmcgourty@wpi.edu.
Website: http://www.wpi.edu/academics/bcb.

Yale University, School of Medicine and Graduate School of Arts and Sciences, Combined Program in Biological and Biomedical Sciences (BBS), Computational Biology and Bioinformatics Track, New Haven, CT 06520. Offers PhD, MD/PhD. *Entrance requirements:* Additional exam requirements/recommendations for international students: Required—TOEFL.

Computer and Information Systems Security

American InterContinental University Online, Program in Information Technology, Schaumburg, IL 60173. Offers Internet security (MIT); IT project management (MIT). Evening/weekend programs available. Postbaccalaureate distance learning degree programs offered (no on-campus study). *Entrance requirements:* Additional exam requirements/recommendations for international students: Required—TOEFL (minimum score 550 paper-based). Electronic applications accepted.

American Public University System, AMU/APU Graduate Programs, Charles Town, WV 25414. Offers accounting (MBA, MS); criminal justice (MA), including business administration, emergency and disaster management, general (MA, MS); educational leadership (M Ed); emergency and disaster management (MA); entrepreneurship (MBA); environmental policy and management (MS), including environmental planning, environmental sustainability, fish and wildlife management, general (MA, MS), global environmental management; finance (MBA); general (MBA); global business management (MBA); history (MA), including American history, ancient and classical history, European history, global history, public history; homeland security (MA), including business administration, counter-terrorism studies, criminal justice, cyber, emergency management and public health, intelligence studies, transportation security; homeland security resource allocation (MBA); humanities (MA); information technology (MS), including digital forensics, enterprise software development, information assurance and security, IT project management; information technology management (MBA); intelligence studies (MA), including criminal intelligence, cyber, general (MA, MS), homeland security, intelligence analysis, intelligence collection, intelligence management, intelligence operations, terrorism studies; international relations and conflict resolution (MA), including comparative and security issues, conflict resolution, international and transnational security issues, peacekeeping; legal studies (MA); management (MA), including defense management, general (MA, MS), human resource management, organizational leadership, public administration; marketing (MBA); military history (MA), including American military history, American Revolution, civil war, war since 1945, World War II; military studies (MA), including joint warfare, strategic leadership; national security studies (MA), including general (MA, MS), homeland security, regional security studies, security and intelligence analysis, terrorism studies; nonprofit management (MBA); political science (MA), including American politics and government, comparative government and development, general (MA, MS), international relations, public policy; psychology (MA); public administration (MPA), including disaster management, environmental policy, health policy, human resources, national security, organizational management, security management; public health (MPH); reverse logistics management (MA); school counseling (M Ed); security management (MA); space studies (MS), including aerospace science, general (MA, MS), planetary science; sports and health sciences (MS); teaching (M Ed), including curriculum and instruction for elementary teachers, elementary reading, English language learners, instructional leadership, online learning, special education; transportation and logistics management (MA), including general (MA, MS), maritime engineering management, reverse logistics management. Programs offered via distance learning only. Part-time and evening/weekend programs available. Postbaccalaureate distance learning degree programs offered (no on-campus study). *Faculty:* 426 full-time (236 women), 1,864 part-time/adjunct (880 women). *Students:* 475 full-time (215 women), 10,067 part-time (4,085 women); includes 3,462 minority (1,863 Black or African American, non-Hispanic/Latino; 74 American Indian or Alaska Native, non-Hispanic/Latino; 273 Asian, non-Hispanic/Latino; 831 Hispanic/Latino; 78 Native Hawaiian or other Pacific Islander, non-Hispanic/Latino; 343 Two or more races, non-Hispanic/Latino), 131 international. Average age 36. In 2014, 3,740 master's awarded. *Degree requirements:* For master's, comprehensive exam or practicum. *Entrance requirements:* For master's, official transcript showing earned bachelor's degree from institution accredited by recognized accrediting body. Additional exam requirements/recommendations for international students: Required—TOEFL (minimum score 550 paper-based), IELTS (minimum score 6.5). *Application deadline:* Applications are processed on a rolling basis. Application fee: $0. Electronic applications accepted. *Financial support:* Applicants required to submit FAFSA. *Faculty research:* Military history, criminal justice, management performance, national security. *Unit head:* Dr. Karan Powell, Executive Vice President and Provost, 877-468-6268, Fax: 304-724-3780. *Application contact:* Terry Grant, Vice President of Enrollment Management, 877-468-6268, Fax: 304-724-3780, E-mail: info@apus.edu.
Website: http://www.apus.edu.

Armstrong State University, School of Graduate Studies, Program in Criminal Justice, Savannah, GA 31419-1997. Offers criminal justice (MS); cyber crime (Certificate). Part-time and evening/weekend programs available. *Faculty:* 8 full-time (4 women), 2 part-time/adjunct (1 woman). *Students:* 10 full-time (2 women), 12 part-time (7 women); includes 5 minority (2 Black or African American, non-Hispanic/Latino; 3 Hispanic/Latino). Average age 31. 15 applicants, 53% accepted, 6 enrolled. In 2014, 3 master's, 5 other advanced degrees awarded. *Degree requirements:* For master's, comprehensive exam, field practicum or thesis. *Entrance requirements:* For master's, GRE General Test (minimum score 150 on verbal, 141 on quantitative, or 4 on analytical section) or MAT, minimum GPA of 2.5, 2 letters of recommendation, letter of intent (500-1000 words). Additional exam requirements/recommendations for international students: Required—TOEFL (minimum score 523 paper-based). *Application deadline:* For fall admission, 6/1 priority date for domestic students, 5/1 priority date for international students; for spring admission, 11/15 priority date for domestic students, 9/15 priority date for international students; for summer admission, 4/15 priority date for domestic students, 9/15 for international students. Applications are processed on a rolling basis. Application fee: $30. Electronic applications accepted. *Expenses:* Tuition, state resident: part-time $206 per credit hour. Tuition, nonresident: part-time $763 per credit hour. *Required fees:* $612 per semester. Tuition and fees vary according to course load, campus/location and program. *Financial support:* In 2014–15, research assistantships with full tuition reimbursements (averaging $5,000 per year) were awarded; career-related internships or fieldwork, Federal Work-Study, scholarships/grants, and unspecified assistantships also available. Support available to part-time students. Financial award application deadline: 3/15; financial award applicants required to submit FAFSA. *Faculty research:* International crime/globalization, cyber-crime, influence of social science research on judicial decision-making. *Unit head:* Dr. Daniel Skidmore-Hess, Department Head, 912-344-2532, Fax: 912-344-3438, E-mail: daniel.skidmore-hess@armstrong.edu. *Application contact:* Kathy Ingram, Associate Director of Graduate/Adult and Nontraditional Students, 912-344-2503, Fax: 912-344-3417, E-mail: graduate@armstrong.edu.
Website: http://www.armstrong.edu/Liberal_Arts/criminal_justice_soc_and_pol_science/cjsocpols_graduate_program.

Auburn University at Montgomery, College of Arts and Sciences, Informatics Institute, Montgomery, AL 36124-4023. Offers cybersystems and information security (MS). *Faculty:* 1 full-time (0 women), 1 part-time/adjunct (0 women). *Students:* 4 part-time (2 women), all international. Average age 27. 8 applicants, 38% accepted, 1 enrolled. In 2014, 4 master's awarded. *Expenses:* Tuition, state resident: full-time $6264; part-time $348 per credit hour. Tuition, nonresident: full-time $14,094; part-time $783 per credit hour. *Financial support:* In 2014–15, 4 teaching assistantships were awarded. *Unit head:* Dr. Karen Stine, Dean, 334-244-3689, Fax: 334-244-3826, E-mail: kstine@aum.edu. *Application contact:* Dr. Pamela Tidwell, Associate Dean, 334-244-3362, Fax: 334-244-3826, E-mail: ptidwell@aum.edu.

Bay Path University, Program in Cybersecurity Management, Longmeadow, MA 01106-2292. Offers MS. Part-time and evening/weekend programs available.

Postbaccalaureate distance learning degree programs offered (no on-campus study). *Students:* 8 full-time (4 women), 19 part-time (10 women); includes 7 minority (5 Black or African American, non-Hispanic/Latino; 2 Hispanic/Latino). Average age 37. 32 applicants, 81% accepted, 20 enrolled. *Degree requirements:* For master's, 12 core courses. *Application deadline:* Applications are processed on a rolling basis. Application fee: $45. Electronic applications accepted. Application fee is waived when completed online. *Financial support:* In 2014–15, 8 students received support. Applicants required to submit FAFSA. *Unit head:* Dr. Larry Snyder, Director, 413-565-1294, E-mail: lsnyder@baypath.edu. *Application contact:* Diane Ranaldi, Dean of Graduate Admissions, 413-565-1332, Fax: 413-565-1250, E-mail: dranaldi@baypath.edu.
Website: http://graduate.baypath.edu/graduate-programs/programs-online/ms-programs/cybersecurity-management.

Benedictine University, Graduate Programs, Program in Business Administration, Lisle, IL 60532-0900. Offers accounting (MBA); entrepreneurship and managing innovation (MBA); financial management (MBA); health administration (MBA); human resource management (MBA); information systems security (MBA); international business (MBA); management consulting (MBA); management information systems (MBA); marketing management (MBA); operations management and logistics (MBA); organizational leadership (MBA). Part-time and evening/weekend programs available. Postbaccalaureate distance learning degree programs offered (minimal on-campus study). *Entrance requirements:* For master's, GMAT. Additional exam requirements/recommendations for international students: Required—TOEFL (minimum score 550 paper-based). Electronic applications accepted. *Faculty research:* Strategic leadership in professional organizations, sociology of professions, organizational change, social identity theory, applications to change management.

Boston University, Graduate School of Arts and Sciences, Department of Computer Science, Boston, MA 02215. Offers computer science (MS); cyber security (MS); MS/PhD. *Students:* 92 full-time (31 women), 6 part-time (0 women); includes 5 minority (4 Asian, non-Hispanic/Latino; 1 Hispanic/Latino), 68 international. Average age 26. 650 applicants, 8% accepted, 29 enrolled. In 2014, 55 master's awarded. *Degree requirements:* For master's, one foreign language, thesis optional, project. *Entrance requirements:* For master's, GRE General Test, 3 letters of recommendation. Additional exam requirements/recommendations for international students: Required—TOEFL (minimum score 550 paper-based; 84 iBT). *Application deadline:* For fall admission, 12/15 for domestic and international students; for spring admission, 11/1 for domestic and international students. Application fee: $80. *Expenses: Tuition:* Full-time $45,686; part-time $1428 per credit hour. *Required fees:* $660; $60 per semester. Tuition and fees vary according to program. *Financial support:* In 2014–15, 54 students received support, including 3 fellowships with full tuition reimbursements available (averaging $20,500 per year), 27 research assistantships with full tuition reimbursements available (averaging $20,500 per year), 21 teaching assistantships with full tuition reimbursements available (averaging $20,500 per year); Federal Work-Study, scholarships/grants, and health care benefits also available. Support available to part-time students. Financial award application deadline: 12/15. *Unit head:* Mark Crovella, Chairman, 617-353-8919, Fax: 617-353-6457, E-mail: crovella@bu.edu. *Application contact:* Jennifer Streubel, Program Coordinator, 617-353-8919, Fax: 617-353-6457, E-mail: jenn4@bu.edu.
Website: http://cs-www.bu.edu/.

Boston University, Metropolitan College, Department of Computer Science, Boston, MA 02215. Offers computer information systems (MS), including computer networks, database management and business intelligence, health informatics, IT project management, security, Web application development; computer networks (Certificate); digital forensics (Certificate); health informatics (Certificate); information technology project management (Certificate); software engineering in health care systems (Certificate); telecommunications (MS), including security. Part-time and evening/weekend programs available. Postbaccalaureate distance learning degree programs offered (no on-campus study). *Faculty:* 13 full-time (3 women), 43 part-time/adjunct (3 women). *Students:* 76 full-time (22 women), 768 part-time (188 women); includes 251 minority (68 Black or African American, non-Hispanic/Latino; 1 American Indian or Alaska Native, non-Hispanic/Latino; 117 Asian, non-Hispanic/Latino; 57 Hispanic/Latino; 2 Native Hawaiian or other Pacific Islander, non-Hispanic/Latino; 6 Two or more races, non-Hispanic/Latino), 130 international. Average age 34. 463 applicants, 79% accepted, 248 enrolled. In 2014, 222 master's, 25 other advanced degrees awarded. *Degree requirements:* For master's, thesis optional. *Entrance requirements:* For master's and Certificate, official transcripts from regionally-accredited bachelor's degree program, 3 letters of recommendation, professional resume, personal statement. Additional exam requirements/recommendations for international students: Required—TOEFL (minimum score 84 iBT), IELTS. *Application deadline:* For fall admission, 6/1 priority date for international students; for spring admission, 10/1 priority date for international students. Applications are processed on a rolling basis. Application fee: $80. Electronic applications accepted. *Expenses:* Expenses: $800 per credit part-time; student services fees: $60 per semester; technology fee of $60 per credit (for online courses). *Financial support:* In 2014–15, 11 research assistantships (averaging $8,400 per year) were awarded; unspecified assistantships also available. Support available to part-time students. Financial award applicants required to submit FAFSA. *Faculty research:* Medical informatics, Web technologies, telecom and networks, security and forensics, software engineering, programming languages, multimedia and artificial intelligence (AI), information systems and IT project management. *Unit head:* Dr. Anatoly Temkin, Chairman, 617-353-2566, Fax: 617-353-2367, E-mail: csinfo@bu.edu. *Application contact:* Lesley Moreau, Academic Program Coordinator, 617-353-2566, Fax: 617-353-2367, E-mail: metcs@bu.edu.
Website: http://www.bu.edu/csmet/.

Brandeis University, Rabb School of Continuing Studies, Division of Graduate Professional Studies, Master of Science in Information Security Program, Waltham, MA 02454-9110. Offers MS. Part-time programs available. Postbaccalaureate distance learning degree programs offered (no on-campus study). *Faculty:* 2 full-time (1 woman), 36 part-time/adjunct (13 women). *Students:* 35 part-time (7 women); includes 8 minority (3 Black or African American, non-Hispanic/Latino; 1 Asian, non-Hispanic/Latino; 3 Hispanic/Latino; 1 Two or more races, non-Hispanic/Latino). Average age 35. 9 applicants, 100% accepted, 7 enrolled. In 2014, 7 master's awarded. *Entrance requirements:* For master's, four-year bachelor's degree from regionally-accredited U.S. institution or equivalent; official transcript(s) from every college or university attended; resume or curriculum vitae; statement of goals; letter of recommendation. Additional exam requirements/recommendations for international students: Required—TOEFL (minimum scores: 600 paper-based, 100 iBT), IELTS (7), or PTE. *Application deadline:* For fall admission, 8/11 priority date for domestic and international students; for winter admission, 11/15 for domestic students; for spring admission, 12/15 priority date for domestic and international students; for summer admission, 4/14 priority date for domestic and international students. Applications are processed on a rolling basis. Application fee: $50. Electronic applications accepted. *Unit head:* Michael Corn, Program Chair, 781-736-8787, Fax: 781-736-3420, E-mail: mcorn@brandeis.edu. *Application contact:* Frances Stearns, Director of Admissions and Recruitment, 781-736-8785, Fax: 781-736-3420, E-mail: fstearns@brandeis.edu.
Website: http://www.brandeis.edu/gps.

California State University, San Bernardino, Graduate Studies, College of Business and Public Administration, MBA Program, San Bernardino, CA 92407-2318. Offers accounting (MBA); entrepreneurship (MBA); finance (MBA); global business (MBA); information management (MBA); information security (MBA); management (MBA); supply chain management (MBA). *Accreditation:* AACSB. Part-time and evening/weekend programs available. Postbaccalaureate distance learning degree programs offered (no on-campus study). *Students:* 85 full-time (37 women), 170 part-time (68 women); includes 86 minority (10 Black or African American, non-Hispanic/Latino; 2 American Indian or Alaska Native, non-Hispanic/Latino; 17 Asian, non-Hispanic/Latino; 54 Hispanic/Latino; 3 Two or more races, non-Hispanic/Latino), 91 international. Average age 27. 507 applicants, 31% accepted, 91 enrolled. In 2014, 111 degrees awarded. *Degree requirements:* For master's, comprehensive exam, thesis. *Entrance requirements:* Additional exam requirements/recommendations for international students: Required—TOEFL. *Application deadline:* For fall admission, 7/17 for domestic students, 7/20 for international students; for winter admission, 10/20 for domestic and international students; for spring admission, 1/20 for domestic and international students. Application fee: $55. *Expenses:* Expenses: Contact institution. *Financial support:* Application deadline: 3/1. *Unit head:* Dr. Lawrence C. Rose, Dean, 909-537-3703, Fax: 909-537-7026, E-mail: lrose@csusb.edu. *Application contact:* Dr. Vipin Gupta, Associate Dean/MBA Director, 909-537-7380, Fax: 909-537-7026, E-mail: vgupta@csusb.edu.
Website: http://mba.csusb.edu/.

Capella University, School of Business and Technology, Doctoral Programs in Technology, Minneapolis, MN 55402. Offers general information technology (PhD); global operations and supply chain management (DBA); information assurance and security (PhD); information technology education (PhD); information technology management (DBA, PhD).

Capella University, School of Business and Technology, Master's Programs in Technology, Minneapolis, MN 55402. Offers enterprise software architecture (MS); general information systems and technology management (MS); global operations and supply chain management (MBA); information assurance and security (MS); information technology management (MBA); network management (MS).

Capitol Technology University, Graduate Programs, Laurel, MD 20708-9759. Offers business administration (MBA); computer science (MS); electrical engineering (MS); information and telecommunications systems management (MS); information architecture (MS); network security (MS). Part-time and evening/weekend programs available. Postbaccalaureate distance learning degree programs offered (no on-campus study). *Entrance requirements:* For master's, minimum GPA of 3.0. Electronic applications accepted.

Carlow University, College of Leadership and Social Change, Program in Fraud and Forensics, Pittsburgh, PA 15213-3165. Offers MS. Postbaccalaureate distance learning degree programs offered (no on-campus study). *Students:* 40 full-time (31 women), 1 part-time (0 women); includes 10 minority (8 Black or African American, non-Hispanic/Latino; 2 Two or more races, non-Hispanic/Latino). Average age 33. 61 applicants, 92% accepted, 41 enrolled. In 2014, 40 master's awarded. *Entrance requirements:* For master's, minimum undergraduate GPA of 3.0; essay; resume; transcripts; two recommendations. Additional exam requirements/recommendations for international students: Required—TOEFL (minimum score 550 paper-based). *Application deadline:* For fall admission, 7/1 for domestic students. Electronic applications accepted. Application fee is waived when completed online. *Expenses: Tuition:* Full-time $9750; part-time $785 per credit. Part-time tuition and fees vary according to degree level and program. *Unit head:* Dr. Diane Matthews, Director, Fraud and Forensics Program, 412-578-6384, Fax: 412-587-6367, E-mail: damatthews@carlow.edu. *Application contact:* Kimberly Lipniskis, Associate Director Graduate Enrollment Management, 412-578-6671, Fax: 412-578-6321, E-mail: klipniskis@carlow.edu.
Website: http://www.carlow.edu/Fraud_and_Forensics_(MS).aspx.

Carnegie Mellon University, Carnegie Institute of Technology, Information Networking Institute, Pittsburgh, PA 15213. Offers information networking (MS); information security (MS); information technology - information security (MS); information technology - mobility (MS); information technology - software management (MS). *Degree requirements:* For master's, thesis optional. *Entrance requirements:* For master's, GRE General Test, bachelor's degree in computer science, computer engineering, or electrical engineering, or related technology degree; programming skills (C/C++ fluency for some programs). Additional exam requirements/recommendations for international students: Required—TOEFL. *Faculty research:* Computer forensics and incident response; dependable systems, embedded systems, mobile systems, and sensor networks; computer and information networks, network and information security, human and socio-economic factors in secure system design; wireless sensor networks, survivable embedded systems, signal processing/compression; strategic management, international strategic management, group dynamics and decision-making structures, simulated competitive environments.

Carnegie Mellon University, H. John Heinz III College, School of Information Systems and Management, Master of Science in Information Security Policy and Management Program, Pittsburgh, PA 15213-3891. Offers MSISPM. *Entrance requirements:* For master's, GRE or GMAT, college-level course in advanced algebra/pre-calculus; college-level courses in economics and statistics (recommended). Additional exam requirements/recommendations for international students: Required—TOEFL or IELTS.

Central Michigan University, Central Michigan University Global Campus, Program in Cybersecurity, Mount Pleasant, MI 48859. Offers Certificate. Part-time and evening/weekend programs available. Electronic applications accepted. *Financial support:* Scholarships/grants available. Support available to part-time students. *Unit head:* Karl Smart, Chairperson, Business Information Systems, 989-774-6447, E-mail: smart1kl@cmich.edu. *Application contact:* Global Campus Call Center, 877-268-4636, Fax: 989-774-2461, E-mail: cmuglobal@cmich.edu.

City University of Seattle, Graduate Division, School of Management, Seattle, WA 98121. Offers accounting (Certificate); change leadership (MBA, Certificate); computer systems (MS); finance (Certificate); financial management (MBA); general management (MBA); general management-Europe (MBA); global marketing (MBA); human resources management (Certificate); individualized study (MBA); information security (MS); information systems (MBA); leadership (MA); marketing (MBA, Certificate); project management (MBA, MS, Certificate); sustainable business (Certificate); technology management (MBA, Certificate). Part-time and evening/weekend programs available. Postbaccalaureate distance learning degree programs offered (no on-campus study). *Faculty:* 4 full-time (1 woman), 168 part-time/adjunct (63 women). *Students:* 445 full-time (227 women), 249 part-time (130 women); includes 115 minority (42 Black or African American, non-Hispanic/Latino; 3 American Indian or Alaska Native, non-Hispanic/Latino; 41 Asian, non-Hispanic/Latino; 22 Hispanic/Latino; 4 Native Hawaiian or other Pacific Islander, non-Hispanic/Latino; 3 Two or more races, non-Hispanic/Latino), 227 international. Average age 33. 127 applicants, 100% accepted, 127 enrolled. In 2014,

200 master's, 15 other advanced degrees awarded. *Degree requirements:* For master's, comprehensive exam (for some programs), thesis (for some programs). *Entrance requirements:* For master's, baccalaureate degree or equivalent from an accredited or otherwise recognized institution. Additional exam requirements/recommendations for international students: Required—TOEFL (minimum score 567 paper-based; 87 iBT); Recommended—IELTS. *Application deadline:* For fall admission, 9/1 for international students; for winter admission, 12/1 for international students; for spring admission, 3/1 for international students. Applications are processed on a rolling basis. Application fee: $50. Electronic applications accepted. *Expenses: Tuition:* Full-time $30,000; part-time $600 per credit. One-time fee: $50. Tuition and fees vary according to degree level and program. *Financial support:* In 2014–15, 47 students received support. Federal Work-Study and scholarships/grants available. Support available to part-time students. Financial award applicants required to submit FAFSA. *Unit head:* Dr. Kurt Kirstein, Dean, 206-239-4860 Ext. 5456, E-mail: kdkirstein@cityu.edu. *Application contact:* 888-422-4898, Fax: 425-709-5363, E-mail: info@cityu.edu.

Colorado Christian University, Program in Business Administration, Lakewood, CO 80226. Offers corporate training (MBA); information security (MA); leadership (MBA); project management (MBA). Part-time and evening/weekend programs available. Postbaccalaureate distance learning degree programs offered (minimal on-campus study). *Degree requirements:* For master's, thesis optional. *Entrance requirements:* For master's, GMAT, 2 letters of recommendation, resume. Additional exam requirements/recommendations for international students: Required—TOEFL. Electronic applications accepted. *Expenses:* Contact institution.

Colorado Technical University Colorado Springs, Graduate Studies, Program in Computer Science, Colorado Springs, CO 80907-3896. Offers computer science (DCS); computer systems security (MSCS); database systems (MSCS); software engineering (MSCS). Part-time and evening/weekend programs available. Postbaccalaureate distance learning degree programs offered. *Degree requirements:* For master's, thesis or alternative; for doctorate, thesis/dissertation. *Entrance requirements:* For doctorate, minimum graduate GPA of 3.0, 5 years of related work experience. *Faculty research:* Software engineering, systems engineering.

Colorado Technical University Colorado Springs, Graduate Studies, Program in Information Science, Colorado Springs, CO 80907-3896. Offers information systems security (MSM). Postbaccalaureate distance learning degree programs offered.

Colorado Technical University Denver South, Program in Computer Science, Aurora, CO 80014. Offers computer systems security (MSCS); database systems (MSCS); software engineering (MSCS). Part-time and evening/weekend programs available. *Degree requirements:* For master's, thesis or alternative. *Entrance requirements:* For master's, minimum undergraduate GPA of 3.0, resume.

Colorado Technical University Denver South, Program in Information Science, Aurora, CO 80014. Offers information systems security (MSM).

Columbus State University, Graduate Studies, D. Abbott Turner College of Business and Computer Science, Columbus, GA 31907-5645. Offers applied computer science (MS); business administration (MBA); information systems security (Certificate); modeling and simulation (Certificate); organizational leadership (MS). *Accreditation:* AACSB. *Faculty:* 9 full-time (3 women), 2 part-time/adjunct (1 woman). *Students:* 86 full-time (21 women), 134 part-time (47 women); includes 68 minority (37 Black or African American, non-Hispanic/Latino; 2 American Indian or Alaska Native, non-Hispanic/Latino; 15 Asian, non-Hispanic/Latino; 10 Hispanic/Latino; 4 Two or more races, non-Hispanic/Latino), 12 international. Average age 32. 149 applicants, 51% accepted, 49 enrolled. In 2014, 141 master's awarded. *Entrance requirements:* For master's, GMAT, GRE, minimum undergraduate GPA of 2.75, letters of recommendation. Additional exam requirements/recommendations for international students: Required—TOEFL (minimum score 550 paper-based; 79 iBT). *Application deadline:* For fall admission, 6/30 for domestic students, 5/1 for international students; for spring admission, 11/1 for domestic and international students; for summer admission, 3/1 for domestic and international students. Applications are processed on a rolling basis. Application fee: $50. Electronic applications accepted. *Financial support:* In 2014–15, 66 students received support, including 16 research assistantships (averaging $3,000 per year). Financial award application deadline: 5/1; financial award applicants required to submit FAFSA. *Unit head:* Dr. Linda U. Hadley, Dean, 706-507-8153, Fax: 706-568-2184, E-mail: hadley_linda@columbusstate.edu. *Application contact:* Kristin Williams, Director of International and Graduate Recruitment, 706-507-8848, Fax: 706-568-5091, E-mail: thornton_katie@colstate.edu.
Website: http://turner.columbusstate.edu/.

Concordia University, School of Graduate Studies, Faculty of Engineering and Computer Science, Concordia Institute for Information Systems Engineering (CIISE), Montréal, QC H3G 1M8, Canada. Offers 3D graphics and game development (Certificate); information systems security (M Eng, MA Sc); quality systems engineering (M Eng, MA Sc); service engineering and network management (Certificate).

Concordia University College of Alberta, Program in Information Systems Security Management, Edmonton, AB T5B 4E4, Canada. Offers MA.

Davenport University, Sneden Graduate School, Grand Rapids, MI 49512. Offers accounting (MBA); business administration (EMBA); finance (MBA); health care management (MBA); human resources (MBA); information assurance (MS); public health (MPH); strategic management (MBA). Evening/weekend programs available. *Entrance requirements:* For master's, GMAT, minimum undergraduate GPA of 2.75. Additional exam requirements/recommendations for international students: Required—TOEFL. Electronic applications accepted. *Faculty research:* Leadership, management, marketing, organizational culture.

DePaul University, College of Computing and Digital Media, Chicago, IL 60604. Offers animation (MA, MFA); business information technology (MS); cinema (MFA); cinema production (MS); computational finance (MS); computer and information sciences (PhD); computer game development (MS); computer information and network security (MS); computer science (MS); e-commerce technology (MS); health informatics (MS); human-computer interaction (MS); information systems (MS); information technology project management (MS); network engineering and management (MS); predictive analytics (MS); screenwriting (MFA); software engineering (MS); JD/MS. Part-time and evening/weekend programs available. Postbaccalaureate distance learning degree programs offered (no on-campus study). *Degree requirements:* For master's, thesis (for some programs); for doctorate, comprehensive exam, thesis/dissertation. *Entrance requirements:* For master's, GRE or GMAT (for MS in computational finance only), bachelor's degree, resume (MS in predictive analytics only), IT experience (MS in information technology project management only), portfolio review (all MFA programs and MA in animation); for doctorate, GRE, master's degree in computer science. Additional exam requirements/recommendations for international students: Required—TOEFL (minimum score 590 paper-based; 80 iBT), IELTS (minimum score 6.5), PTE (minimum score 53). Electronic applications accepted. *Expenses:* Contact institution. *Faculty research:* Data mining, computer science, human-computer interaction, security, animation and film.

East Carolina University, Graduate School, College of Engineering and Technology, Department of Technology Systems, Greenville, NC 27858-4353. Offers computer network professional (Certificate); information assurance (Certificate); Lean Six Sigma Black Belt (Certificate); network technology (MS), including computer networking management, digital communications technology, information security, Web technologies; occupational safety (MS); technology management (PhD); technology systems (MS), including industrial distribution and logistics, manufacturing systems, performance improvement, quality systems; Website developer (Certificate). *Entrance requirements:* For master's and Certificate, GRE General Test or MAT, minimum GPA of 2.5; for doctorate, GRE General Test, related work experience. *Expenses:* Tuition, state resident: full-time $4223. Tuition, nonresident: full-time $16,540. *Required fees:* $2184.

Eastern Illinois University, Graduate School, Lumpkin College of Business and Applied Sciences, School of Technology, Charleston, IL 61920. Offers computer technology (Certificate); quality systems (Certificate); technology (MS); technology security (Certificate); work performance improvement (Certificate); MS/MBA; MS/MS. Part-time and evening/weekend programs available. *Faculty:* 28. *Students:* 133 full-time (43 women), 68 part-time (39 women); includes 17 minority (11 Black or African American, non-Hispanic/Latino; 2 Asian, non-Hispanic/Latino; 2 Hispanic/Latino; 2 Two or more races, non-Hispanic/Latino), 124 international. Average age 28. 449 applicants, 31% accepted, 58 enrolled. In 2014, 61 master's awarded. *Application deadline:* For fall admission, 3/31 priority date for domestic students. Applications are processed on a rolling basis. Application fee: $30. *Expenses:* Tuition, state resident: full-time $3113; part-time $283 per credit hour. Tuition, nonresident: full-time $7469; part-time $679 per credit hour. *Required fees:* $2287; $96 per credit hour. Tuition and fees vary according to course load. *Financial support:* In 2014–15, 107 students received support, including 7 research assistantships with tuition reimbursements available, 6 teaching assistantships with tuition reimbursements available. *Unit head:* Austin Cheney, Chair, 217-581-3226, Fax: 217-581-6607, E-mail: acheney@eiu.edu. *Application contact:* Peter Ping Liu, Coordinator, 217-581-6267, Fax: 217-581-6607, E-mail: pliu@eiu.edu. Website: http://www.eiu.edu/tech/.

Eastern Michigan University, Graduate School, College of Technology, School of Information Security and Applied Computing, Programs in Information Assurance, Ypsilanti, MI 48197. Offers Graduate Certificate. *Students:* 1 part-time (0 women). Average age 45. 2 applicants, 50% accepted. Application fee: $45. *Application contact:* James Banfield, Program Coordinator, 734-487-1161, Fax: 734-483-8755, E-mail: jbanfield@emich.edu.

Embry-Riddle Aeronautical University–Daytona, Department of Electrical, Computer, Software and Systems Engineering, Daytona Beach, FL 32114-3900. Offers cybersecurity engineering (MS); electrical and computer engineering (MSECE); software engineering (MSE); unmanned and autonomous systems engineering (MSUASE). MS in unmanned and autonomous systems engineering held jointly with Department of Electrical, Computer, Software and Systems Engineering. Part-time and evening/weekend programs available. *Faculty:* 13 full-time (0 women), 1 (woman) part-time/adjunct. *Students:* 56 full-time (15 women), 8 part-time (0 women); includes 6 minority (4 Black or African American, non-Hispanic/Latino; 1 Asian, non-Hispanic/Latino; 1 Hispanic/Latino), 41 international. Average age 25. 46 applicants, 61% accepted, 23 enrolled. In 2014, 16 master's awarded. *Degree requirements:* For master's, thesis or alternative, MS UASE students are required to complete a two-semester capstone project. *Entrance requirements:* For master's, Applicants to the MSE program are strongly encouraged to complete the GRE for this degree program; Applicants to the MSUASE program must complete the GRE; For consideration of fellowship and assistantship award programs offered by the Department of Computing, GRE scores are required., minimum CGPA of 3.0; course work in computer science. Additional exam requirements/recommendations for international students: Required—TOEFL (minimum score 550 paper-based; 79 iBT). *Application deadline:* For fall admission, 6/1 priority date for domestic and international students; for spring admission, 11/1 priority date for domestic students, 10/1 priority date for international students. Applications are processed on a rolling basis. Application fee: $50. Electronic applications accepted. *Expenses: Tuition:* Full-time $15,360; part-time $1280 per credit hour. *Required fees:* $1334. *Financial support:* In 2014–15, 24 students received support. Research assistantships with full and partial tuition reimbursements available, teaching assistantships with full and partial tuition reimbursements available, career-related internships or fieldwork, and unspecified assistantships available. Financial award application deadline: 4/15. *Faculty research:* Cybersecurity and assured systems engineering, radar, unmanned and autonomous systems, modeling and simulation, cyber-physical systems. *Unit head:* Dr. Timothy Wilson, Professor of Electrical and Computer Engineering and Chair, ECSSE Dept., 386-226-6994, E-mail: timothy.wilson@erau.edu. *Application contact:* International and Graduate Admissions, 800-388-3728, Fax: 386-226-7070, E-mail: graduate.admissions@erau.edu. Website: http://daytonabeach.erau.edu/college-engineering/electrical-computer-software-systems/index.html.

Embry-Riddle Aeronautical University–Daytona, Department of Security Studies and International Affairs, Daytona Beach, FL 32114-3900. Offers cybersecurity management and policy (MS); human security and resilience (MS). *Degree requirements:* For master's, Capstone projects are required. *Entrance requirements:* Additional exam requirements/recommendations for international students: Required—TOEFL (minimum score 550 paper-based; 79 iBT). *Application deadline:* Applications are processed on a rolling basis. Application fee: $50. Electronic applications accepted. *Expenses: Tuition:* Full-time $15,360; part-time $1280 per credit hour. *Required fees:* $1334. *Financial support:* Research assistantships, teaching assistantships, career-related internships or fieldwork, and unspecified assistantships available. *Faculty research:* Cybersecurity education and curriculum, and the practice of digital forensics and information security; intelligence and homeland security, military intervention and nation building, and international relations theory; environmental and human security, resilience and their relationship to domestic and national security; African political culture and governance; military rule; regional cooperation; mass media and democratization. *Unit head:* James Ramsay, PhD, Professor of Homeland Security and Chair, Department of Security Studies and International Affairs, 386-226-7153, E-mail: james.ramsay@erau.edu. *Application contact:* International and Graduate Admissions, 386-226-6176, Fax: 386-226-7070, E-mail: graduate.admissions@erau.edu. Website: http://daytonabeach.erau.edu/college-arts-sciences/security-studies/index.html.

Fairfield University, School of Engineering, Fairfield, CT 06824. Offers automated manufacturing (CAS); database management (CAS); electrical and computer engineering (MS); information security (CAS); management of technology (MS); mechanical engineering (MS); network technology (CAS); software engineering (MS); Web application development (CAS). Part-time and evening/weekend programs available. *Faculty:* 4 full-time (1 woman), 18 part-time/adjunct (5 women). *Students:* 193 full-time (50 women), 69 part-time (11 women); includes 20 minority (4 Black or African American, non-Hispanic/Latino; 6 Asian, non-Hispanic/Latino; 10 Hispanic/Latino), 199 international. Average age 27. 516 applicants, 64% accepted, 124 enrolled. In 2014, 38 master's awarded. *Degree requirements:* For master's, thesis, capstone course. *Entrance requirements:* For master's, interview, minimum GPA of 2.8, resume, 2

recommendations. Additional exam requirements/recommendations for international students: Required—TOEFL (minimum score 550 paper-based; 80 iBT) or IELTS (minimum score 6.5). *Application deadline:* For fall admission, 5/15 for international students; for spring admission, 10/15 for international students. Applications are processed on a rolling basis. Application fee: $60. Electronic applications accepted. *Expenses:* Expenses: $750 per credit hour. *Financial support:* In 2014–15, 30 students received support. Scholarships/grants and unspecified assistantships available. Financial award applicants required to submit FAFSA. *Faculty research:* Ocean dynamics modeling, thermo fluids, Web/mobile software applications, microwaves/electromagnetics, micro/nano manufacturing. *Unit head:* Dr. Bruce Berdanier, Dean, 203-254-4147, Fax: 203-254-4013, E-mail: bberdanier@fairfield.edu. *Application contact:* Marianne Gumpper, Director of Graduate and Continuing Studies Admission, 203-254-4184, Fax: 203-254-4073, E-mail: gradadmis@fairfield.edu.
Website: http://www.fairfield.edu/academics/schoolscollegescenters/schoolofengineering/graduateprograms/.

Ferris State University, College of Business, Big Rapids, MI 49307. Offers business intelligence (MBA); design and innovation management (MBA); incident response (MBA); information security and intelligence (MS), including business intelligence, incident response, project management; management tools and concepts (MBA); project management (MBA). *Accreditation:* ACBSP. Part-time and evening/weekend programs available. Postbaccalaureate distance learning degree programs offered (minimal on-campus study). *Faculty:* 9 full-time (3 women), 6 part-time/adjunct (2 women). *Students:* 44 full-time (9 women), 90 part-time (44 women); includes 17 minority (6 Black or African American, non-Hispanic/Latino; 1 American Indian or Alaska Native, non-Hispanic/Latino; 1 Asian, non-Hispanic/Latino; 3 Hispanic/Latino; 6 Two or more races, non-Hispanic/Latino), 30 international. Average age 33. 121 applicants, 81% accepted, 52 enrolled. In 2014, 47 master's awarded. *Degree requirements:* For master's, comprehensive exam, thesis (for MS). *Entrance requirements:* For master's, GRE or GMAT (waived if GPA is 3.5 or better), minimum GPA of 3.0 in junior/senior level classes, 2.75 overall; statement of purpose; 3 letters of reference; resume. Additional exam requirements/recommendations for international students: Required—TOEFL (minimum score 500 paper-based; 67 iBT). *Application deadline:* For fall admission, 7/1 priority date for domestic students, 6/15 for international students; for winter admission, 11/1 priority date for domestic students, 10/15 for international students; for spring admission, 3/1 priority date for domestic students, 2/15 for international students. Applications are processed on a rolling basis. Application fee: $0 ($30 for international students). Electronic applications accepted. Application fee is waived when completed online. Tuition and fees vary according to degree level and program. *Financial support:* Career-related internships or fieldwork, Federal Work-Study, scholarships/grants, and unspecified assistantships available. Support available to part-time students. Financial award application deadline: 3/15; financial award applicants required to submit FAFSA. *Faculty research:* Quality improvement, client/server end-user computing, security and digital forensics, performance metrics and sustainability. *Unit head:* Dr. David Nicol, College of Business Dean, 231-591-2168, Fax: 231-591-3521, E-mail: davidnicol@ferris.edu. *Application contact:* Shannon Yost, Department Secretary, 231-591-2168, Fax: 231-591-3521, E-mail: yosts@ferris.edu.
Website: http://cbgp.ferris.edu/.

Florida Institute of Technology, Graduate Programs, College of Engineering, Program in Information Assurance and Cybersecurity, Melbourne, FL 32901-6975. Offers MS. *Students:* 7 full-time (3 women), 5 part-time (1 woman); includes 1 minority (Hispanic/Latino), 8 international. Average age 27. 37 applicants, 46% accepted, 5 enrolled. *Degree requirements:* For master's, comprehensive exam (for some programs), thesis or final exam. *Entrance requirements:* For master's, GRE General Test, transcripts, 3 credit hours of differential and integral calculus, and discrete mathematics. *Application deadline:* Applications are processed on a rolling basis. Electronic applications accepted. *Expenses: Tuition:* Part-time $1179 per credit hour. Tuition and fees vary according to campus/location. *Financial support:* Applicants required to submit FAFSA. *Unit head:* Dr. Richard Newman, Department Head, 321-674-7478, E-mail: jrnewman@fit.edu. *Application contact:* Cheryl A. Brown, Associate Director of Graduate Admissions, 321-674-7581, Fax: 321-723-9468, E-mail: cbrown@fit.edu.
Website: http://www.fit.edu/programs/8098/ms-information-assurance-cybersecurity/classes#.VT_oKE10ypo.

Florida State University, The Graduate School, College of Arts and Sciences, Department of Computer Science, Tallahassee, FL 32306-4530. Offers computer criminology (MS); computer network and system administration (MS); computer science (MS, PhD); information security (MS). Part-time programs available. *Faculty:* 23 full-time (3 women), 1 part-time/adjunct (0 women). *Students:* 161 full-time (33 women), 11 part-time (4 women); includes 19 minority (7 Black or African American, non-Hispanic/Latino; 3 American Indian or Alaska Native, non-Hispanic/Latino; 4 Asian, non-Hispanic/Latino; 4 Hispanic/Latino; 1 Two or more races, non-Hispanic/Latino), 112 international. Average age 28. 455 applicants, 51% accepted, 32 enrolled. In 2014, 30 master's, 7 doctorates awarded. Terminal master's awarded for partial completion of doctoral program. *Degree requirements:* For master's, comprehensive exam (for some programs), thesis (for some programs); for doctorate, comprehensive exam, thesis/dissertation, qualifying exam, preliminary exam, prospectus defense. *Entrance requirements:* For master's, GRE General Test, minimum undergraduate GPA of 3.0; for doctorate, GRE General Test, minimum GPA of 3.0. Additional exam requirements/recommendations for international students: Required—TOEFL (minimum score 550 paper-based; 80 iBT), IELTS (minimum score 6.5). *Application deadline:* For fall admission, 7/1 for domestic students, 3/1 priority date for international students; for spring admission, 11/1 for domestic students, 9/1 priority date for international students. Application fee: $30. Electronic applications accepted. *Expenses:* Tuition, state resident: part-time $403.51 per credit hour. Tuition, nonresident: part-time $1004.85 per credit hour. *Required fees:* $75.81 per credit hour. One-time fee: $20 part-time. Tuition and fees vary according to campus/location. *Financial support:* In 2014–15, 106 students received support, including 11 fellowships with full tuition reimbursements available (averaging $21,000 per year), 15 research assistantships with full tuition reimbursements available (averaging $23,670 per year), 53 teaching assistantships with full tuition reimbursements available (averaging $17,220 per year); scholarships/grants, health care benefits, tuition waivers (full and partial), and unspecified assistantships also available. Financial award application deadline: 3/1; financial award applicants required to submit FAFSA. *Faculty research:* Embedded systems, high performance computing, networking, operating systems, security, databases, algorithms, big data, visualization. *Unit head:* Dr. Xin Yuan, Chairman, 850-644-9133, Fax: 850-644-0058, E-mail: xyuan@cs.fsu.edu. *Application contact:* Daniel B. Clawson, Graduate Coordinator, 850-645-4975, Fax: 850-644-0058, E-mail: clawson@cs.fsu.edu.
Website: http://www.cs.fsu.edu/.

George Mason University, School of Business, Fairfax, VA 22030. Offers accounting (MS, Certificate); business administration (EMBA, MBA); management of secure information systems (MS); real estate development (MS); technology management (MS). MS in management of secure information systems offered jointly with Volgenau School of Engineering. Part-time and evening/weekend programs available. Postbaccalaureate distance learning degree programs offered. *Faculty:* 83 full-time (26 women), 54 part-time/adjunct (17 women). *Students:* 375 full-time (153 women), 132 part-time (53 women); includes 151 minority (53 Black or African American, non-Hispanic/Latino; 2 American Indian or Alaska Native, non-Hispanic/Latino; 43 Asian, non-Hispanic/Latino; 37 Hispanic/Latino; 4 Native Hawaiian or other Pacific Islander, non-Hispanic/Latino; 12 Two or more races, non-Hispanic/Latino), 33 international. Average age 32. 545 applicants, 55% accepted, 173 enrolled. In 2014, 245 master's, 3 other advanced degrees awarded. *Entrance requirements:* For master's, GMAT. Additional exam requirements/recommendations for international students: Required—TOEFL (minimum score 570 paper-based; 80 iBT), IELTS (minimum score 6.5), PTE. *Application deadline:* Applications are processed on a rolling basis. Application fee: $65 ($80 for international students). Electronic applications accepted. *Expenses:* Expenses: Contact institution. *Financial support:* In 2014–15, 19 students received support, including 13 research assistantships with full and partial tuition reimbursements available (averaging $8,231 per year), 10 teaching assistantships with full and partial tuition reimbursements available (averaging $7,849 per year); career-related internships or fieldwork, Federal Work-Study, scholarships/grants, unspecified assistantships, and health care benefits (for full-time research or teaching assistantship recipients) also available. Support available to part-time students. Financial award application deadline: 3/1; financial award applicants required to submit FAFSA. *Faculty research:* Current leading global issues: offshore outsourcing, international financial risk, comparative systems of innovation. *Total annual research expenditures:* $369,778. *Unit head:* Sarah E. Nutter, Dean, 703-993-1807, Fax: 703-993-1867, E-mail: snutter@gmu.edu. *Application contact:* Nancy Doernhoefer, Admissions Specialist, 703-993-4128, Fax: 703-993-1778, E-mail: ndoernho@gmu.edu.
Website: http://business.gmu.edu/.

George Mason University, Volgenau School of Engineering, Department of Computer Science, Fairfax, VA 22030. Offers computer science (MS, PhD, Certificate); information security and assurance (MS); information systems (MS); software engineering (MS). MS programs offered jointly with Old Dominion University, University of Virginia, Virginia Commonwealth University, and Virginia Polytechnic Institute and State University. *Faculty:* 46 full-time (10 women), 17 part-time/adjunct (1 woman). *Students:* 236 full-time (68 women), 246 part-time (50 women); includes 77 minority (13 Black or African American, non-Hispanic/Latino; 48 Asian, non-Hispanic/Latino; 11 Hispanic/Latino; 5 Two or more races, non-Hispanic/Latino), 231 international. Average age 29. 874 applicants, 42% accepted, 119 enrolled. In 2014, 171 master's, 8 doctorates, 22 other advanced degrees awarded. *Degree requirements:* For master's, thesis optional; for doctorate, comprehensive exam, thesis/dissertation. *Entrance requirements:* For master's, GRE, proof of financial support; 2 official college transcripts; resume; self-evaluation form; official bank statement; photocopy of passport; 3 letters of recommendation; baccalaureate degree related to computer science; minimum GPA of 3.0 in last 2 years of undergraduate work; 1 year beyond 1st-year calculus; personal goals statement; for doctorate, GRE, personal goals statement; 2 official copies of transcripts; self-evaluation form; 3 letters of recommendation; photocopy of passport; proof of financial support; official bank statement; resume; 4-year baccalaureate degree with strong background in computer science. Additional exam requirements/recommendations for international students: Required—TOEFL (minimum score 575 paper-based; 80 iBT), IELTS (minimum score 6.5), PTE. *Application deadline:* For fall admission, 1/15 priority date for domestic students; for spring admission, 8/15 priority date for domestic students. Application fee: $65 ($80 for international students). Electronic applications accepted. *Expenses:* Expenses: Contact institution. *Financial support:* In 2014–15, 113 students received support, including 1 fellowship (averaging $9,302 per year), 46 research assistantships (averaging $19,727 per year), 67 teaching assistantships (averaging $14,678 per year); career-related internships or fieldwork, Federal Work-Study, scholarships/grants, unspecified assistantships, and health care benefits (for full-time research or teaching assistantship recipients) also available. Support available to part-time students. Financial award application deadline: 3/1; financial award applicants required to submit FAFSA. *Faculty research:* Artificial intelligence, image processing/graphics, parallel/distributed systems, software engineering systems. *Total annual research expenditures:* $3.4 million. *Unit head:* Sanjeev Setia, Chair, 703-993-4098, Fax: 703-993-1710, E-mail: setia@gmu.edu. *Application contact:* Michele Pieper, Office Manager, 703-993-9483, Fax: 703-993-1710, E-mail: mpieper@gmu.edu.
Website: http://cs.gmu.edu/.

George Mason University, Volgenau School of Engineering, Program in Management of Secure Information Systems, Fairfax, VA 22030. Offers MS. Program offered jointly with School of Business. *Expenses:* Tuition, state resident: full-time $9794; part-time $408 per credit hour. Tuition, nonresident: full-time $26,978; part-time $1124 per credit hour. *Required fees:* $2820; $118 per credit hour. Tuition and fees vary according to course load and program. *Unit head:* Kenneth S. Ball, Dean, 703-993-1498, Fax: 703-993-1734, E-mail: vsdean@gmu.edu. *Application contact:* Jade T. Perez, Director, Graduate Services, 703-993-2426, E-mail: jperezc@gmu.edu.

The George Washington University, School of Engineering and Applied Science, Department of Computer Science, Washington, DC 20052. Offers computer science (MS, D Sc); cybersecurity (MS). Part-time and evening/weekend programs available. *Faculty:* 19 full-time (6 women), 48 part-time/adjunct (6 women). *Students:* 276 full-time (82 women), 157 part-time (44 women); includes 40 minority (10 Black or African American, non-Hispanic/Latino; 18 Asian, non-Hispanic/Latino; 9 Hispanic/Latino; 1 Native Hawaiian or other Pacific Islander, non-Hispanic/Latino; 2 Two or more races, non-Hispanic/Latino), 312 international. Average age 28. 662 applicants, 62% accepted, 141 enrolled. In 2014, 199 master's, 5 doctorates, 41 other advanced degrees awarded. *Degree requirements:* For master's, thesis optional; for doctorate, thesis/dissertation, dissertation defense, qualifying exam. *Entrance requirements:* For master's, appropriate bachelor's degree, minimum GPA of 3.0; for doctorate, GRE (if highest earned degree is BS), appropriate bachelor's or master's degree, minimum GPA of 3.3; for other advanced degree, appropriate master's degree, minimum GPA of 3.4. Additional exam requirements/recommendations for international students: Required—TOEFL or The George Washington University English as a Foreign Language Test. *Application deadline:* For fall admission, 3/1 priority date for domestic students; for spring admission, 10/1 for domestic students. Applications are processed on a rolling basis. Application fee: $75. *Financial support:* In 2014–15, 49 students received support. Fellowships with tuition reimbursements available, research assistantships, teaching assistantships with tuition reimbursements available, career-related internships or fieldwork, institutionally sponsored loans, and tuition waivers available. Financial award application deadline: 3/1; financial award applicants required to submit FAFSA. *Faculty research:* Computer graphics, multimedia, VLSI, parallel processing. *Unit head:* Abdou Youssef, Chair, 202-994-7181, E-mail: ayoussef@gwu.edu. *Application contact:* Adina Lav, Marketing, Recruiting and Admissions, 202-994-5827, Fax: 202-994-0909, E-mail: engineering@gwu.edu.
Website: http://www.cs.gwu.edu/.

Georgia Institute of Technology, Graduate Studies, College of Computing, Program in Information Security, Atlanta, GA 30332-0001. Offers MS. Part-time programs available. *Students:* 24 full-time (9 women), 56 part-time (4 women); includes 6 minority (2 Black or African American, non-Hispanic/Latino; 2 Asian, non-Hispanic/Latino; 2 Two or more races, non-Hispanic/Latino), 60 international. Average age 27. 97 applicants, 31% accepted, 13 enrolled. In 2014, 20 master's awarded. *Degree requirements:* For master's, http://www.scs.gatech.edu/future/msinfosec/program. *Entrance requirements:* For master's, GRE General Test, http://www.scs.gatech.edu/future/msinfosec/ admissions. Additional exam requirements/recommendations for international students: Required—TOEFL (minimum score 600 paper-based; 100 iBT). *Application deadline:* For fall admission, 2/1 for domestic and international students. Applications are processed on a rolling basis. Application fee: $75. Electronic applications accepted. *Expenses:* Tuition, state resident: full-time $12,344; part-time $515 per credit hour. Tuition, nonresident: full-time $27,600; part-time $1150 per credit hour. *Required fees:* $1196 per term. Part-time tuition and fees vary according to course load. *Financial support:* Fellowships, research assistantships, teaching assistantships, career-related internships or fieldwork, Federal Work-Study, institutionally sponsored loans, tuition waivers (partial), and unspecified assistantships available. Support available to part-time students. Financial award application deadline: 5/1. *Unit head:* H Venkatewaran, Director, 404-894-3658, E-mail: venkat@cc.gatech.edu. *Application contact:* Tiffany Jordan, Graduate Coordinator, 404-385-7481, E-mail: tjordan3@cc.gatech.edu. Website: http://www.scs.gatech.edu/future/msinfosec.

Hampton University, School of Science, Program in Information Assurance, Hampton, VA 23668. Offers MS. *Expenses: Tuition:* Full-time $20,526; part-time $522 per credit. *Required fees:* $100. *Unit head:* Dr. Calvin Lowe, Vice President for Research and Dean, 757-727-5310, Fax: 757-727-5084. *Application contact:* Erika Henderson, Director, Graduate Programs, 757-727-5454, Fax: 757-727-5084.

Hofstra University, School of Engineering and Applied Science, Hempstead, NY 11549. Offers computer science (MS), including cybersecurity, Web engineering. Part-time and evening/weekend programs available. Postbaccalaureate distance learning degree programs offered (no on-campus study). *Faculty:* 7 full-time (2 women), 3 part-time/adjunct. *Students:* 13 full-time (3 women), 17 part-time (3 women); includes 4 minority (all Asian, non-Hispanic/Latino), 8 international. Average age 30. 27 applicants, 59% accepted, 12 enrolled. In 2014, 6 master's awarded. *Degree requirements:* For master's, thesis optional, 30 credits, 3.0 GPA. *Entrance requirements:* For master's, GRE, Minimum GPA of 3.0. Additional exam requirements/recommendations for international students: Required—TOEFL (minimum score 550 paper-based; 80 iBT). *Application deadline:* Applications are processed on a rolling basis. Application fee: $70 ($75 for international students). Electronic applications accepted. *Expenses: Tuition:* Full-time $20,610; part-time $1145 per credit hour. *Required fees:* $970; $165 per term. Tuition and fees vary according to program. *Financial support:* In 2014–15, 10 students received support, including 4 fellowships with full and partial tuition reimbursements available (averaging $4,300 per year), 1 research assistantship with full and partial tuition reimbursement available (averaging $8,147 per year); Federal Work-Study, institutionally sponsored loans, scholarships/grants, tuition waivers (full and partial), and unspecified assistantships also available. Support available to part-time students. Financial award applicants required to submit FAFSA. *Faculty research:* Semantic web, software engineering, data mining and machine learning, programming languages, cybersecurity. *Unit head:* Dr. Sina Rabbany, Acting Dean, 516-463-6672, E-mail: eggsyr@hofstra.edu. *Application contact:* Sunil Samuel, Assistant Vice President of Admissions, 516-463-4723, Fax: 516-463-4664, E-mail: graduateadmission@hofstra.edu.
Website: http://www.hofstra.edu/academics/colleges/seas/.

Hood College, Graduate School, Programs in Computer and Information Sciences, Frederick, MD 21701-8575. Offers computer and information sciences (MS); computer science (MS); information security (Certificate). Part-time and evening/weekend programs available. *Degree requirements:* For master's, thesis. *Entrance requirements:* For master's, minimum GPA of 2.75. Additional exam requirements/recommendations for international students: Required—TOEFL (minimum score 575 paper-based; 89 iBT), IELTS (minimum score 6.5). Electronic applications accepted. Application fee is waived when completed online. *Faculty research:* Systems engineering, natural language, processing, database design, artificial intelligence and parallel distributed computing.

Illinois Institute of Technology, Graduate College, College of Science, Department of Computer Science, Chicago, IL 60616. Offers business (MCS); computational intelligence (MCS); computer networking and communications (MCS); computer science (MCS, MS, PhD); cyber-physical systems (MCS); data analytics (MCS); data science (MAS); database systems (MCS); distributed and cloud computing (MCS); education (MCS); finance (MCS); information security and assurance (MCS); software engineering (MCS); telecommunications and software engineering (MAS); MS/MAS. Part-time and evening/weekend programs available. Postbaccalaureate distance learning degree programs offered (no on-campus study). *Faculty:* 29 full-time (5 women), 8 part-time/adjunct (1 woman). *Students:* 432 full-time (108 women), 117 part-time (27 women); includes 11 minority (3 Black or African American, non-Hispanic/Latino; 7 Asian, non-Hispanic/Latino; 1 Two or more races, non-Hispanic/Latino), 495 international. Average age 26. 2,573 applicants, 42% accepted, 244 enrolled. In 2014, 164 master's, 2 doctorates awarded. Terminal master's awarded for partial completion of doctoral program. *Degree requirements:* For master's, thesis optional; for doctorate, comprehensive exam, thesis/dissertation. *Entrance requirements:* For master's, MS GRE General Test (minimum scores: 298 Quantitative and Verbal, 3.0 Analytical Writing); MAS GRE General Test (minimum scores: 292 Quantitative and Verbal, 2.5 Analytical Writing), minimum undergraduate GPA of 3.0; for doctorate, GRE General Test (minimum scores: 304 Quantitative and Verbal, 3.5 Analytical Writing), minimum undergraduate GPA of 3.0. Additional exam requirements/recommendations for international students: Required—TOEFL (minimum score 523 paper-based; 70 iBT). *Application deadline:* For fall admission, 5/1 for domestic and international students; for spring admission, 10/15 for domestic and international students. Applications are processed on a rolling basis. Application fee: $50. Electronic applications accepted. *Expenses: Tuition:* Full-time $22,500; part-time $1250 per credit hour. *Required fees:* $30 per course. $260 per semester. One-time fee: $235. Tuition and fees vary according to course load and program. *Financial support:* Fellowships with partial tuition reimbursements, research assistantships with full and partial tuition reimbursements, teaching assistantships with full and partial tuition reimbursements, career-related internships or fieldwork, Federal Work-Study, institutionally sponsored loans, scholarships/grants, traineeships, health care benefits, tuition waivers (partial), and unspecified assistantships available. Support available to part-time students. Financial award applicants required to submit FAFSA. *Faculty research:* Parallel and distributed processing, high-performance computing, computational linguistics, information retrieval, data mining, grid computing. *Unit head:* Dr. Eunice Santos, Chair/Professor, 312-567-5150, E-mail: eunice.santos@iit.edu. *Application contact:* Rishab Malhotra, Director, Graduate Admission, 866-472-3448, Fax: 312-567-3138, E-mail: inquiry.grad@iit.edu.
Website: http://www.iit.edu/csl/cs/.

Illinois Institute of Technology, Graduate College, School of Applied Technology, Department of Information Technology and Management, Wheaton, IL 60189. Offers cyber forensics and security (MAS); information technology and management (MAS). Part-time and evening/weekend programs available. Postbaccalaureate distance learning degree programs offered (no on-campus study). *Faculty:* 8 full-time (1 woman),

13 part-time/adjunct (1 woman). *Students:* 222 full-time (89 women), 62 part-time (21 women); includes 24 minority (5 Black or African American, non-Hispanic/Latino; 9 Asian, non-Hispanic/Latino; 7 Hispanic/Latino; 3 Two or more races, non-Hispanic/Latino), 229 international. Average age 27. 771 applicants, 57% accepted, 132 enrolled. In 2014, 96 master's awarded. *Entrance requirements:* For master's, GRE (minimum score 300 Quantitative and Verbal, 2.5 Analytical Writing), bachelor's degree with minimum cumulative undergraduate GPA of 3.0 (or its equivalent) from accredited institution. Additional exam requirements/recommendations for international students: Required—TOEFL (minimum score 523 paper-based; 70 iBT); Recommended—IELTS (minimum score 5.5). *Application deadline:* For fall admission, 8/1 for domestic students, 5/1 for international students; for spring admission, 12/15 for domestic students, 10/15 for international students. Applications are processed on a rolling basis. Application fee: $50. Electronic applications accepted. *Expenses: Tuition:* Full-time $22,500; part-time $1250 per credit hour. *Required fees:* $30 per course. $260 per semester. One-time fee: $235. Tuition and fees vary according to course load and program. *Financial support:* Fellowships with partial tuition reimbursements, teaching assistantships with partial tuition reimbursements, career-related internships or fieldwork, Federal Work-Study, institutionally sponsored loans, scholarships/grants, traineeships, health care benefits, tuition waivers (partial), and unspecified assistantships available. Support available to part-time students. Financial award applicants required to submit FAFSA. *Faculty research:* Database design, voice over IP, process engineering, object-oriented programming, computer networking, online design, system administration. *Unit head:* C. Robert Carlson, Director, 630-682-6002, Fax: 630-682-6010, E-mail: carlson@iit.edu. *Application contact:* Rishab Malhotra, Director, Graduate Admission, 866-472-3448, Fax: 312-567-3138, E-mail: inquiry.grad@iit.edu.
Website: http://appliedtech.iit.edu/information-technology-and-management.

Indiana University Bloomington, School of Informatics and Computing, Program in Informatics, Bloomington, IN 47408. Offers informatics (MS, PhD), including bioinformatics, cheminformatics (PhD), complex systems (PhD), health informatics (PhD), human-computer interaction (MS), human-computer interaction design (PhD), logic and mathematical foundations of informatics (PhD), music informatics (PhD), robotics (PhD), security informatics, social informatics (PhD). Part-time programs available. *Students:* 206 full-time (78 women), 7 part-time (1 woman); includes 25 minority (9 Black or African American, non-Hispanic/Latino; 12 Asian, non-Hispanic/Latino; 2 Hispanic/Latino; 2 Two or more races, non-Hispanic/Latino), 101 international. 287 applicants, 52% accepted, 65 enrolled. In 2014, 65 master's, 13 doctorates awarded. Terminal master's awarded for partial completion of doctoral program. *Degree requirements:* For master's, thesis; for doctorate, thesis/dissertation. *Entrance requirements:* For master's and doctorate, GRE, TOEFL if international and no US degree. Additional exam requirements/recommendations for international students: Required—TOEFL (minimum score 600 paper-based; 100 iBT). *Application deadline:* For fall admission, 12/1 priority date for domestic and international students. Application fee: $55 ($65 for international students). Electronic applications accepted. *Financial support:* Application deadline: 12/1. *Unit head:* Dr. Howard Rosenbaum, Associate Dean for Graduate Studies, 812-855-3250, E-mail: hrosenba@indiana.edu. *Application contact:* Patty Reyes-Cooksey, Director of Graduate Administration, 812-856-3622, E-mail: patreyes@indiana.edu.
Website: http://www.soic.indiana.edu/informatics/index.shtml.

Inter American University of Puerto Rico, Guayama Campus, Department of Natural and Applied Sciences, Guayama, PR 00785. Offers computer security and networks (MS); networking and security (MCS).

Iona College, School of Arts and Science, Department of Computer Science, New Rochelle, NY 10801-1890. Offers computer science (MS); cyber security (MS). Part-time and evening/weekend programs available. *Faculty:* 4 full-time (2 women). *Students:* 4 full-time (1 woman), 9 part-time (1 woman); includes 6 minority (3 Black or African American, non-Hispanic/Latino; 3 Hispanic/Latino), 1 international. Average age 26. 15 applicants, 93% accepted, 7 enrolled. In 2014, 1 master's awarded. *Degree requirements:* For master's, thesis optional. *Entrance requirements:* For master's, minimum GPA of 3.0. Additional exam requirements/recommendations for international students: Required—TOEFL (minimum score 550 paper-based; 80 iBT), IELTS (minimum score 6.5). *Application deadline:* For fall admission, 8/1 priority date for domestic students, 5/1 priority date for international students; for spring admission, 1/1 priority date for domestic students, 9/1 priority date for international students. Applications are processed on a rolling basis. Application fee: $50. Electronic applications accepted. *Expenses:* Expenses: Contact institution. *Financial support:* In 2014–15, 2 research assistantships with full tuition reimbursements were awarded; tuition waivers (partial) and unspecified assistantships also available. Support available to part-time students. Financial award application deadline: 4/15; financial award applicants required to submit FAFSA. *Faculty research:* Parallel procession, data mining, machine learning, cyber security, medical imaging. *Unit head:* Robert Schiaffino, PhD, Chair, 914-633-2338, E-mail: rschiaffino@iona.edu. *Application contact:* Amanda St. Bernard, Assistant Director, Graduate Admissions, 914-633-2440, Fax: 914-633-2277, E-mail: astbernard@iona.edu.
Website: http://www.iona.edu/Academics/School-of-Arts-Science/Departments/Computer-Science/Graduate-Programs.aspx.

John Marshall Law School, Graduate and Professional Programs, Chicago, IL 60604-3968. Offers employee benefits (LL M, MS); estate planning (LL M); information technology (MS); information technology and privacy law (LL M); intellectual property (LL M, MS); international business and trade (LL M); law (JD); real estate (LL M, MS); taxation (LL M, MS); trial advocacy (LL M); U.S. legal studies (LL M); JD/LL M; JD/MA; JD/MBA; JD/MPA. *Accreditation:* ABA. Part-time and evening/weekend programs available. Postbaccalaureate distance learning degree programs offered (no on-campus study). *Faculty:* 70 full-time (26 women), 165 part-time/adjunct (54 women). *Students:* 912 full-time (453 women), 407 part-time (203 women); includes 393 minority (162 Black or African American, non-Hispanic/Latino; 5 American Indian or Alaska Native, non-Hispanic/Latino; 85 Asian, non-Hispanic/Latino; 121 Hispanic/Latino; 3 Native Hawaiian or other Pacific Islander, non-Hispanic/Latino; 17 Two or more races, non-Hispanic/Latino), 44 international. Average age 27. 2,095 applicants, 73% accepted, 380 enrolled. In 2014, 77 master's, 420 doctorates awarded. *Degree requirements:* For master's, 24 credits; for doctorate, 90 credits. *Entrance requirements:* For master's, JD; for doctorate, LSAT. Additional exam requirements/recommendations for international students: Required—TOEFL (minimum score 90 iBT), IELTS (minimum score 7). *Application deadline:* For fall admission, 3/1 priority date for domestic and international students; for spring admission, 10/15 priority date for domestic and international students. Applications are processed on a rolling basis. Application fee: $0. Electronic applications accepted. *Expenses: Tuition:* Full-time $44,850. *Required fees:* $270. *Financial support:* In 2014–15, 785 students received support. Federal Work-Study, scholarships/grants, and tuition waivers (full and partial) available. Support available to part-time students. Financial award application deadline: 4/1; financial award applicants required to submit FAFSA. *Unit head:* John Corkery, Dean, 312-427-2737. *Application contact:* William B. Powers, Associate Dean of Admission and Student Affairs, 800-537-4280, Fax: 312-427-5136, E-mail: admission@jmls.edu.

Computer and Information Systems Security

Johns Hopkins University, Engineering Program for Professionals, Part-time Program in Cybersecurity, Baltimore, MD 21218-2699. Offers MS, Post-Master's Certificate. Electronic applications accepted.

Johns Hopkins University, Engineering Program for Professionals, Part-time Program in Information Assurance, Baltimore, MD 21218-2699. Offers MS. Part-time and evening/weekend programs available.

Johns Hopkins University, G. W. C. Whiting School of Engineering, Information Security Institute, Baltimore, MD 21218-2699. Offers MSSI. Part-time programs available. *Degree requirements:* For master's, 10 courses, capstone project. *Entrance requirements:* For master's, GRE, minimum GPA of 3.0. Additional exam requirements/recommendations for international students: Required—TOEFL. Electronic applications accepted. *Faculty research:* Critical infrastructure protection, cryptography, information security policy, computing privacy, system and software security, medical information security, computer forensics, application security, risk management.

Kaplan University, Davenport Campus, School of Information Technology, Davenport, IA 52807-2095. Offers decision support systems (MS); information security and assurance (MS). Part-time and evening/weekend programs available. Postbaccalaureate distance learning degree programs offered (no on-campus study). *Entrance requirements:* Additional exam requirements/recommendations for international students: Required—TOEFL (minimum score 550 paper-based; 80 iBT).

Keiser University, Master of Business Administration Program, Ft. Lauderdale, FL 33309. Offers accounting (MBA); health services management (MBA); information security management (MBA); international business (MBA); leadership for managers (MBA); marketing (MBA). All concentrations except information security management also offered in Mandarin; leadership for managers and international business also offered in Spanish. Part-time programs available. Postbaccalaureate distance learning degree programs offered (minimal on-campus study).

Keiser University, MS in Information Security Program, Ft. Lauderdale, FL 33309. Offers MS.

Kent State University, School of Digital Sciences, Kent, OH 44242-0001. Offers digital sciences (MDS); enterprise architecture (Certificate). Part-time programs available. Postbaccalaureate distance learning degree programs offered. *Students:* 134 full-time (31 women), 29 part-time (11 women); includes 3 minority (1 Black or African American, non-Hispanic/Latino; 1 Asian, non-Hispanic/Latino; 1 Hispanic/Latino), 139 international. Average age 25. 465 applicants, 69% accepted, 182 enrolled. In 2014, 9 master's awarded. *Degree requirements:* For master's, thesis optional. *Entrance requirements:* For master's, minimum GPA of 3.0, transcripts, goal statement, resume, 3 letters of recommendation; for Certificate, minimum GPA of 3.0, transcripts. Additional exam requirements/recommendations for international students: Required—TOEFL (minimum score: paper-based 525, iBT 71), Michigan English Language Assessment Battery (minimum score of 75), IELTS (minimum score of 6.0), PTE Academic (minimum score of 48), or completion of ELS level 112 Intensive Program. *Application deadline:* For fall admission, 7/1 for domestic students; for spring admission, 11/15 for domestic students; for summer admission, 4/15 priority date for domestic students. Applications are processed on a rolling basis. Application fee: $45 ($70 for international students). Electronic applications accepted. *Expenses:* Tuition, state resident: full-time $8730; part-time $485 per credit hour. Tuition, nonresident: full-time $14,886; part-time $827 per credit hour. Tuition and fees vary according to campus/location and program. *Financial support:* Research assistantships with full tuition reimbursements, teaching assistantships with full tuition reimbursements, career-related internships or fieldwork, Federal Work-Study, and unspecified assistantships available. *Unit head:* Robert A. Walker, Director, 330-672-9105, E-mail: rawalke1@kent.edu. *Application contact:* 330-672-9069, E-mail: digital-sciences@kent.edu.
Website: http://www.kent.edu/dsci.

Lewis University, College of Arts and Sciences, Program in Information Security, Romeoville, IL 60446. Offers management (MS); technical (MS). Program offered jointly with College of Business. Part-time and evening/weekend programs available. Postbaccalaureate distance learning degree programs offered (no on-campus study). *Students:* 34 full-time (8 women), 87 part-time (19 women); includes 33 minority (14 Black or African American, non-Hispanic/Latino; 5 Asian, non-Hispanic/Latino; 6 Hispanic/Latino; 3 Native Hawaiian or other Pacific Islander, non-Hispanic/Latino; 5 Two or more races, non-Hispanic/Latino), 23 international. Average age 32. *Entrance requirements:* For master's, bachelor's degree, minimum GPA of 3.0, resume, 2-page statement of purpose, 3 letters of recommendation. Additional exam requirements/recommendations for international students: Required—TOEFL (minimum score 550 paper-based; 80 iBT). *Application deadline:* For fall admission, 5/1 priority date for international students; for spring admission, 11/15 priority date for international students. Applications are processed on a rolling basis. Application fee: $40. Electronic applications accepted. *Financial support:* Application deadline: 5/1; applicants required to submit FAFSA. *Unit head:* Dr. Raymond Klump, Program Director, 815-836-5528, E-mail: klumpra@lewisu.edu. *Application contact:* Office of Graduate Admission, 800-897-9000 Ext. 5610, E-mail: grad@lewisu.edu.
Website: http://www.lewisu.edu/academics/msinfosec/index.htm.

Liberty University, School of Business, Lynchburg, VA 24515. Offers accounting (MBA, MS, DBA); business administration (MBA); criminal justice (MBA); cyber security (MS); executive leadership (MA); healthcare (MBA); human resources (DBA); information systems (MS), including information assurance, technology management; international business (MBA, DBA); leadership (MBA, DBA); marketing (MBA, MS, DBA), including digital marketing and advertising (MS), project management (MS), public relations (MS), sports marketing and media (MS); project management (MBA, DBA); public administration (MBA); public relations (MBA). Part-time programs available. Postbaccalaureate distance learning degree programs offered (minimal on-campus study). *Students:* 1,520 full-time (813 women), 4,179 part-time (1,982 women); includes 1,402 minority (1,110 Black or African American, non-Hispanic/Latino; 30 American Indian or Alaska Native, non-Hispanic/Latino; 82 Asian, non-Hispanic/Latino; 59 Hispanic/Latino; 7 Native Hawaiian or other Pacific Islander, non-Hispanic/Latino; 114 Two or more races, non-Hispanic/Latino), 119 international. Average age 35. 5,645 applicants, 49% accepted, 1445 enrolled. In 2014, 1,474 master's, 63 other advanced degrees awarded. *Entrance requirements:* For master's, minimum undergraduate GPA of 3.0, 15 hours of upper-level business courses. Additional exam requirements/recommendations for international students: Required—TOEFL (minimum score 600 paper-based; 100 iBT). *Application deadline:* Applications are processed on a rolling basis. Application fee: $50. Electronic applications accepted. *Expenses:* Expenses: Contact institution. *Unit head:* Dr. Scott Hicks, Dean, 434-592-4808, Fax: 434-582-2366, E-mail: smhicks@liberty.edu. *Application contact:* Jay Bridge, Director of Graduate Admissions, 800-424-9595, Fax: 800-628-7977, E-mail: gradadmissions@liberty.edu.
Website: http://www.liberty.edu/academics/business/index.cfm?PID-149.

Liberty University, School of Engineering and Computational Sciences, Lynchburg, VA 24515. Offers cyber security (MS). Part-time programs available. Postbaccalaureate distance learning degree programs offered (no on-campus study). *Students:* 26 full-time (4 women), 44 part-time (10 women); includes 18 minority (14 Black or African American, non-Hispanic/Latino; 1 American Indian or Alaska Native, non-Hispanic/Latino; 1 Asian, non-Hispanic/Latino; 2 Two or more races, non-Hispanic/Latino). Average age 37. 258 applicants, 41% accepted, 58 enrolled. *Entrance requirements:* For master's, baccalaureate degree or its equivalent in computer science, information technology, or other technical degree, or baccalaureate degree in any field along with significant technical work experience. *Application deadline:* Applications are processed on a rolling basis. Application fee: $50. Electronic applications accepted. *Unit head:* David Donahoo, Dean, 434-592-7150. *Application contact:* Jay Bridge, Director of Admissions, 800-424-9595, Fax: 800-628-7977, E-mail: gradadmissions@liberty.edu.

Lipscomb University, Graduate School of Business, Nashville, TN 37204-3951. Offers accountancy (M Acc); accounting (MBA); conflict management (MBA); financial services (MBA); health care informatics (MBA); healthcare management (MBA); human resources (MHR); information security (MBA); leadership (MBA); nonprofit management (MBA); professional accountancy (Certificate); sports management (MBA); strategic human resources (MBA); sustainability (MBA); MBA/MS. *Accreditation:* ACBSP. Part-time and evening/weekend programs available. *Faculty:* 14 full-time (1 woman), 15 part-time/adjunct (4 women). *Students:* 121 full-time (71 women), 113 part-time (47 women); includes 36 minority (23 Black or African American, non-Hispanic/Latino; 11 Hispanic/Latino; 2 Two or more races, non-Hispanic/Latino), 7 international. Average age 32. 145 applicants, 79% accepted, 69 enrolled. In 2014, 106 master's awarded. *Entrance requirements:* For master's, GMAT, transcripts, interview, 2 references, resume. Additional exam requirements/recommendations for international students: Required—TOEFL (minimum score 570 paper-based). *Application deadline:* For fall admission, 6/15 for domestic students, 2/1 for international students; for winter admission, 6/1 for international students; for spring admission, 11/15 for domestic students. Applications are processed on a rolling basis. Application fee: $50 ($75 for international students). Electronic applications accepted. *Expenses:* Expenses: $1,230 per credit hour (for MBA and PMBA); $1,150 (for M Acc); $1,125 (for MHR); $1,100 (for MM). *Financial support:* Career-related internships or fieldwork, scholarships/grants, tuition waivers (partial), and unspecified assistantships available. Support available to part-time students. Financial award application deadline: 7/1; financial award applicants required to submit FAFSA. *Faculty research:* Impact of spirituality on organization commitment, women in corporate leadership, psychological empowerment, training. *Unit head:* Joe Ivey, Associate Dean of Graduate Business Programs, 615-966-6229, Fax: 615-966-1818, E-mail: joe.ivey@lipscomb.edu. *Application contact:* Lisa Shacklett, Assistant Dean of Enrollment and Marketing, 615-966-5968, E-mail: lisa.shacklett@lipscomb.edu.
Website: http://www.lipscomb.edu/business/Graduate-Programs.

Loyola University Maryland, Graduate Programs, Sellinger School of Business and Management, Program in Cyber Security, Baltimore, MD 21210-2699. Offers Certificate. Part-time programs available.

Marymount University, School of Business Administration, Program in Cybersecurity, Arlington, VA 22207-4299. Offers MS. Part-time and evening/weekend programs available. *Faculty:* 3 full-time (2 women), 4 part-time/adjunct (0 women). *Students:* 13 full-time (2 women), 18 part-time (9 women); includes 23 minority (12 Black or African American, non-Hispanic/Latino; 4 Asian, non-Hispanic/Latino; 6 Hispanic/Latino; 1 Two or more races, non-Hispanic/Latino). Average age 32. 17 applicants, 88% accepted, 8 enrolled. *Entrance requirements:* For master's, resume, certification or demonstrated work experience in computer networking. Additional exam requirements/recommendations for international students: Required—TOEFL (minimum score 600 paper-based; 96 iBT), IELTS (minimum score 6.5). *Application deadline:* For fall admission, 7/15 priority date for domestic students, 7/1 priority date for international students; for spring admission, 11/15 priority date for domestic and international students. Applications are processed on a rolling basis. Application fee: $40. Electronic applications accepted. *Expenses:* Expenses: Contact institution. *Financial support:* In 2014–15, 5 students received support, including 2 research assistantships with full and partial tuition reimbursements available; career-related internships or fieldwork, Federal Work-Study, scholarships/grants, and unspecified assistantships also available. Support available to part-time students. Financial award applicants required to submit FAFSA. *Unit head:* Dr. Diane Murphy, Chair, 703-284-5958, Fax: 703-527-3830, E-mail: diane.murphy@marymount.edu. *Application contact:* Francesca Reed, Director, Graduate Admissions, 703-284-5901, Fax: 703-527-3815, E-mail: grad.admissions@marymount.edu.
Website: http://www.marymount.edu/Academics/School-of-Business-Administration/Graduate-Programs/Cybersecurity-(M-S-).

Marymount University, School of Business Administration, Program in Information Technology, Arlington, VA 22207-4299. Offers computer security and information assurance (Certificate); health care informatics (Certificate); information technology (MS, Certificate); information technology project management and technology leadership (Certificate). Part-time and evening/weekend programs available. *Faculty:* 6 full-time (3 women), 7 part-time/adjunct (1 woman). *Students:* 34 full-time (15 women), 30 part-time (11 women); includes 21 minority (14 Black or African American, non-Hispanic/Latino; 4 Asian, non-Hispanic/Latino; 3 Hispanic/Latino), 28 international. Average age 30. 53 applicants, 96% accepted, 31 enrolled. In 2014, 36 master's, 13 other advanced degrees awarded. *Degree requirements:* For master's, thesis or alternative. *Entrance requirements:* For master's, interview, resume, bachelor's degree in computer-related field or degree in another subject with a post-baccalaureate certificate in a computer-related field; for Certificate, resume. Additional exam requirements/recommendations for international students: Required—TOEFL (minimum score 600 paper-based; 96 iBT), IELTS (minimum score 6.5). *Application deadline:* For fall admission, 7/15 priority date for domestic students, 7/1 for international students; for spring admission, 11/15 priority date for domestic students, 11/15 for international students. Applications are processed on a rolling basis. Application fee: $40. Electronic applications accepted. *Expenses:* Expenses: Contact institution. *Financial support:* In 2014–15, 5 students received support, including 1 research assistantship with full and partial tuition reimbursement available, 1 teaching assistantship with full and partial tuition reimbursement available; career-related internships or fieldwork, Federal Work-Study, scholarships/grants, and unspecified assistantships also available. Support available to part-time students. Financial award applicants required to submit FAFSA. *Unit head:* Dr. Diane Murphy, Chair, 703-284-5958, Fax: 703-527-3830, E-mail: diane.murphy@marymount.edu. *Application contact:* Francesca Reed, Director, Graduate Admissions, 703-284-5901, Fax: 703-527-3815, E-mail: grad.admissions@marymount.edu.
Website: http://www.marymount.edu/Academics/School-of-Business-Administration/Graduate-Programs/Information-Technology-(M-S-).

Marywood University, Academic Affairs, Munley College of Liberal Arts and Sciences, Department of Mathematics and Computer Science, Scranton, PA 18509-1598. Offers information security (MS). *Expenses: Tuition:* Part-time $775 per credit. *Required fees:* $688 per semester. Tuition and fees vary according to degree level and campus/location. *Unit head:* Dr. Chaogui Zhang, Chair, 570-961-4598, E-mail: czhang@marywood.edu. *Application contact:* Marcia Gaughan, Secretary, 570-348-6265, E-mail: mgaughan@marywood.edu.
Website: http://www.marywood.edu/math/.

Mercy College, School of Liberal Arts, Program in Cybersecurity, Dobbs Ferry, NY 10522-1189. Offers MS. Part-time and evening/weekend programs available. Postbaccalaureate distance learning degree programs offered (no on-campus study). *Students:* 24 full-time (4 women), 17 part-time (1 woman); includes 25 minority (15 Black or African American, non-Hispanic/Latino; 4 Asian, non-Hispanic/Latino; 5 Hispanic/Latino; 1 Two or more races, non-Hispanic/Latino), 4 international. Average age 35. 30 applicants, 77% accepted, 17 enrolled. In 2014, 13 master's awarded. *Entrance requirements:* For master's, essay, letter of recommendation, undergraduate transcripts. Additional exam requirements/recommendations for international students: Required—TOEFL (minimum score 600 paper-based; 100 iBT), IELTS (minimum score 8). *Application deadline:* For fall admission, 8/1 for international students. Applications are processed on a rolling basis. Application fee: $40. Electronic applications accepted. *Expenses:* Expenses: Contact institution. *Financial support:* Career-related internships or fieldwork, Federal Work-Study, scholarships/grants, and unspecified assistantships available. Support available to part-time students. Financial award applicants required to submit FAFSA. *Unit head:* Dr. Nagaraj Rao, Dean, School of Liberal Arts, 914-674-7593, E-mail: nrao@mercy.edu. *Application contact:* Allison Gurdineer, Senior Director of Admissions, 877-637-2946, Fax: 914-674-7382, E-mail: admissions@mercy.edu. Website: https://www.mercy.edu/degrees-programs/ms-cybersecurity.

Metropolitan State University, College of Management, St. Paul, MN 55106-5000. Offers business administration (MBA, DBA); database administration (Graduate Certificate); healthcare information technology management (Graduate Certificate); information assurance security (Graduate Certificate); management information systems (MMIS); MIS generalist (Graduate Certificate); MIS systems analysis and design (Graduate Certificate); project management (Graduate Certificate); public and nonprofit administration (MPNA). Part-time and evening/weekend programs available. *Degree requirements:* For master's, thesis optional, computer language (MMIS). *Entrance requirements:* For master's, GMAT (for MBA), resume. Additional exam requirements/recommendations for international students: Required—TOEFL (minimum score 550 paper-based). Electronic applications accepted. *Faculty research:* Yugoslav economic system, workers' cooperatives, participative management and job enrichment, global business systems.

Missouri Western State University, Program in Information Technology Assurance Administration, St. Joseph, MO 64507-2294. Offers MS. Part-time programs available. *Entrance requirements:* For master's, minimum GPA of 3.0. Additional exam requirements/recommendations for international students: Recommended—TOEFL (minimum score 70 iBT), IELTS (minimum score 6). *Application deadline:* For fall admission, 7/15 for domestic and international students; for spring admission, 11/1 for domestic students, 10/15 for international students; for summer admission, 4/29 for domestic students. Applications are processed on a rolling basis. Application fee: $45 ($50 for international students). Electronic applications accepted. *Expenses:* Tuition, state resident: full-time $5506; part-time $305.91 per credit hour. Tuition, nonresident: full-time $10,075; part-time $559.71 per credit hour. *Required fees:* $504; $99 per credit hour. $176 per semester. Tuition and fees vary according to course load and program. *Financial support:* Scholarships/grants and unspecified assistantships available. Support available to part-time students. *Application contact:* Dr. Benjamin D. Caldwell, Dean of the Graduate School, 816-271-4394, Fax: 816-271-4525, E-mail: graduate@missouriwestern.edu. Website: https://www.missouriwestern.edu/itaa/.

National University, Academic Affairs, School of Engineering and Computing, La Jolla, CA 92037-1011. Offers computer science (MS), including advanced computing, database engineering, software engineering; cyber security and information assurance (MS), including computer forensics, ethical hacking and penetration testing, health information assurance, information assurance and security; data analytics (MS); engineering management (MS), including enterprise architecture, project management, systems engineering, technology management; environmental engineering (MS); homeland security and emergency management (MS); management information systems (MS); project management (Certificate); sustainability management (MS); wireless communications (MS). Part-time and evening/weekend programs available. Postbaccalaureate distance learning degree programs offered (no on-campus study). *Faculty:* 24 full-time (5 women), 21 part-time/adjunct (5 women). *Students:* 275 full-time (72 women), 86 part-time (24 women); includes 147 minority (41 Black or African American, non-Hispanic/Latino; 48 Asian, non-Hispanic/Latino; 37 Hispanic/Latino; 7 Native Hawaiian or other Pacific Islander, non-Hispanic/Latino; 14 Two or more races, non-Hispanic/Latino), 95 international. Average age 33. In 2014, 281 master's awarded. *Degree requirements:* For master's, thesis (for some programs). *Entrance requirements:* For master's, interview, minimum GPA of 2.5. Additional exam requirements/recommendations for international students: Required—TOEFL (minimum score 550 paper-based; 79 iBT), IELTS (minimum score 6). *Application deadline:* Applications are processed on a rolling basis. Application fee: $60 ($65 for international students). Electronic applications accepted. *Expenses:* Tuition: Full-time $14,184; part-time $1773 per course. *Financial support:* Career-related internships or fieldwork, institutionally sponsored loans, scholarships/grants, and tuition waivers (partial) available. Support available to part-time students. Financial award application deadline: 6/30; financial award applicants required to submit FAFSA. *Faculty research:* Educational technology, scholarships in science. *Unit head:* School of Engineering and Computing, 800-628-8648, E-mail: soec@nu.edu. *Application contact:* Frank Rojas, Vice President for Enrollment Services, 800-628-8648, E-mail: advisor@nu.edu. Website: http://www.nu.edu/OurPrograms/SchoolOfEngineeringAndTechnology.html.

Naval Postgraduate School, Departments and Academic Groups, Department of Computer Science, Monterey, CA 93943. Offers computer science (MS, PhD); identity management and cyber security (MA); modeling of virtual environments and simulations (MS, PhD); software engineering (MS, PhD). Program only open to commissioned officers of the United States and friendly nations and selected United States federal civilian employees. Part-time programs available. Postbaccalaureate distance learning degree programs offered (minimal on-campus study). *Degree requirements:* For master's, thesis; for doctorate, thesis/dissertation.

New Jersey City University, Graduate Studies and Continuing Education, College of Professional Studies, Program in National Security Studies, Jersey City, NJ 07305-1597. Offers civil security leadership (D Sc); national security studies (MS). Part-time programs available. *Faculty:* 2 full-time (0 women), 5 part-time/adjunct (0 women). *Students:* 17 full-time (5 women), 79 part-time (15 women); includes 40 minority (22 Black or African American, non-Hispanic/Latino; 6 Asian, non-Hispanic/Latino; 11 Hispanic/Latino; 1 Two or more races, non-Hispanic/Latino), 2 international. Average age 38. 39 applicants, 100% accepted, 34 enrolled. In 2014, 12 master's awarded. *Entrance requirements:* Additional exam requirements/recommendations for international students: Required—TOEFL (minimum score 79 iBT). Application fee: $50. *Expenses:* Tuition, area resident: Part-time $538 per credit. Tuition, state resident: part-time $538 per credit. Tuition, nonresident: part-time $948 per credit. *Unit head:* Dr. Tsung (Bill) Soo Hoo, Chair, 201-200-3492, E-mail: bsoohoo@njcu.edu. *Application contact:* Jose Balda, Director of Admission, E-mail: jbalda@njcu.edu. Website: http://www.njcu.edu/grad/national-security-studies/.

New Jersey Institute of Technology, College of Computing Science, Newark, NJ 07102. Offers computer science (MS, PhD), including bioinformatics (MS), computer science, computing and business (MS), cyber security and privacy (MS), software engineering (MS); information systems (MS, PhD), including business and information systems (MS), emergency management and business continuity (MS), information systems; information technology administration and security (MS). Part-time and evening/weekend programs available. Terminal master's awarded for partial completion of doctoral program. *Degree requirements:* For master's, thesis optional; for doctorate, thesis/dissertation. *Entrance requirements:* For master's, GRE General Test; for doctorate, GRE General Test, minimum graduate GPA of 3.5. Additional exam requirements/recommendations for international students: Required—TOEFL (minimum score 550 paper-based; 79 iBT). Electronic applications accepted. *Faculty research:* Computer systems, communications and networking, artificial intelligence, database engineering, systems analysis.

New York Institute of Technology, School of Engineering and Computing Sciences, Department of Computer Science, Old Westbury, NY 11568-8000. Offers computer science (MS); information, network, and computer security (MS). Part-time and evening/weekend programs available. *Degree requirements:* For master's, project. *Entrance requirements:* For master's, GRE General Test (if QPA less than 2.85), minimum QPA of 2.85, BS in computer science or related field. Additional exam requirements/recommendations for international students: Required—TOEFL (minimum score 550 paper-based; 79 iBT), IELTS (minimum score 6). Electronic applications accepted. *Faculty research:* Detection of physical node capture in wireless sensor networks, sensing cloud system for cybersecurity, energy efficiency and high performance networks, cognitive rhythms as a new modality for continuous authentication, cloud-enabled and cloud source disaster detection.

New York University, Polytechnic School of Engineering, Department of Computer Science and Engineering, Major in Cyber Security, New York, NY 10012-1019. Offers Graduate Certificate. Postbaccalaureate distance learning degree programs offered (no on-campus study). *Students:* 24 full-time (4 women), 77 part-time (15 women); includes 31 minority (10 Black or African American, non-Hispanic/Latino; 10 Asian, non-Hispanic/Latino; 8 Hispanic/Latino; 3 Two or more races, non-Hispanic/Latino), 21 international. Average age 33. 142 applicants, 37% accepted, 27 enrolled. *Application deadline:* For fall admission, 2/15 priority date for domestic and international students; for spring admission, 11/1 priority date for domestic and international students. Applications are processed on a rolling basis. Application fee: $75. Electronic applications accepted. *Unit head:* Dr. Nasir Memon, Program Director, 718-260-3970, E-mail: memon@nyu.edu. *Application contact:* Raymond Lutzky, Director, Graduate Enrollment Management, 718-637-5984, Fax: 718-260-3624, E-mail: rlutzky@poly.edu.

Northeastern University, College of Computer and Information Science, Boston, MA 02115-5096. Offers computer science (MS, PhD); health informatics (MS); information assurance (MS, PhD). Part-time and evening/weekend programs available. Terminal master's awarded for partial completion of doctoral program. *Degree requirements:* For master's, thesis optional; for doctorate, comprehensive exam, thesis/dissertation.

Northeastern University, College of Engineering, Boston, MA 02115-5096. Offers bioengineering (PhD); chemical engineering (MS, PhD); civil engineering (MS, PhD); computer engineering (PhD); computer systems engineering (MS); electrical and computer engineering (MS); electrical and engineering leadership (MS); electrical engineering (PhD); energy systems (MS); engineering leadership (Certificate); engineering management (MRTP); industrial engineering (MS, PhD); information assurance (PhD); information systems (MS); interdisciplinary (PhD); mechanical engineering (MS, PhD); operations research (MS); telecommunication systems management (MS). Part-time programs available. *Expenses:* Contact institution.

Northern Kentucky University, Office of Graduate Programs, College of Informatics, Department of Business Informatics, Highland Heights, KY 41099. Offers business informatics (MS, Certificate); corporate information security (Certificate); enterprise resource planning (Certificate). Part-time and evening/weekend programs available. *Faculty:* 7 full-time (2 women), 2 part-time/adjunct (0 women). *Students:* 10 full-time (3 women), 41 part-time (15 women); includes 5 minority (3 Black or African American, non-Hispanic/Latino; 1 Asian, non-Hispanic/Latino; 1 Hispanic/Latino), 6 international. Average age 34. In 2014, 20 master's awarded. *Entrance requirements:* For master's, GRE or GMAT. Additional exam requirements/recommendations for international students: Required—TOEFL (minimum score 79 iBT); Recommended—IELTS (minimum score 6.5). *Application deadline:* For fall admission, 8/1 for domestic students, 6/1 for international students; for spring admission, 12/1 for domestic students, 10/1 for international students; for summer admission, 5/1 for domestic students, 3/1 for international students. Applications are processed on a rolling basis. Application fee: $40. Electronic applications accepted. *Expenses:* Tuition, area resident: Part-time $518 per credit hour. Tuition, state resident: part-time $630 per credit hour. Tuition, nonresident: part-time $797 per credit hour. *Required fees:* $192 per semester. Tuition and fees vary according to course load, degree level, campus/location, program and reciprocity agreements. *Financial support:* In 2014–15, 15 students received support. Unspecified assistantships available. Financial award applicants required to submit FAFSA. *Faculty research:* Data analytics, cloud computing, healthcare informatics, information systems security. *Unit head:* Dr. Teuta Cata, Department Chair, 859-572-5626, E-mail: catat@nku.edu. *Application contact:* Alison Swanson, Graduate Admissions Coordinator, 859-572-6971, E-mail: swansona1@nku.edu. Website: http://informatics.nku.edu/departments/business-informatics.html.

Northwestern University, School of Professional Studies, Program in Information Systems, Evanston, IL 60208. Offers analytics and business intelligence (MS); database and Internet technologies (MS); information systems (MS); information systems management (MS); information systems security (MS); medical informatics (MS); software project management and development (MS).

Norwich University, College of Graduate and Continuing Studies, Master of Science in Information Security and Assurance Program, Northfield, VT 05663. Offers investigation/incident response team management (MS). Evening/weekend programs available. Postbaccalaureate distance learning degree programs offered (minimal on-campus study). *Faculty:* 11 part-time/adjunct (1 woman). *Students:* 65 full-time (10 women); includes 15 minority (8 Black or African American, non-Hispanic/Latino; 5 Asian, non-Hispanic/Latino; 1 Hispanic/Latino; 1 Two or more races, non-Hispanic/Latino). Average age 40. 51 applicants, 100% accepted, 36 enrolled. In 2014, 44 master's awarded. *Entrance requirements:* For master's, minimum undergraduate GPA of 2.75. Additional exam requirements/recommendations for international students: Required—TOEFL (minimum score 550 paper-based; 80 iBT), IELTS (minimum score 6.5). *Application deadline:* For fall admission, 8/8 for domestic and international students; for winter admission, 11/7 for domestic and international students; for spring admission, 2/16 for domestic and international students; for summer admission, 5/18 for domestic and international students. Applications are processed on a rolling basis. Electronic applications accepted. *Expenses:* Expenses: Contact institution. *Financial support:* In 2014–15, 37 students received support. Scholarships/grants available. Financial award applicants required to submit FAFSA. *Unit head:* Dr. Rosemarie Pelletier, Program Director, 802-485-2767, Fax: 802-485-2533, E-mail: rpellet2@norwich.edu. *Application*

contact: Lars Nielsen, Associate Program Director, 802-485-2853, Fax: 802-485-2533, E-mail: lnielsen@norwich.edu.
Website: http://online.norwich.edu/degree-programs/masters/master-science-information-security-assurance/overview.

Nova Southeastern University, College of Engineering and Computing, Fort Lauderdale, FL 33314-7796. Offers computer science (MS, PhD); information assurance (PhD); information security (MS); information systems (PhD); information technology (MS); management information systems (MS); software engineering (MS). Part-time and evening/weekend programs available. Postbaccalaureate distance learning degree programs offered (minimal on-campus study). *Faculty:* 20 full-time (6 women), 24 part-time/adjunct (3 women). *Students:* 106 full-time (35 women), 758 part-time (227 women); includes 417 minority (183 Black or African American, non-Hispanic/Latino; 2 American Indian or Alaska Native, non-Hispanic/Latino; 59 Asian, non-Hispanic/Latino; 159 Hispanic/Latino; 14 Two or more races, non-Hispanic/Latino), 90 international. Average age 40. 390 applicants, 74% accepted. In 2014, 146 master's, 67 doctorates awarded. Terminal master's awarded for partial completion of doctoral program. *Degree requirements:* For master's, thesis optional; for doctorate, thesis/dissertation. *Entrance requirements:* For master's, minimum undergraduate GPA of 2.5; 3.0 in major; for doctorate, master's degree, minimum graduate GPA of 3.25. Additional exam requirements/recommendations for international students: Required—TOEFL (minimum score 80 iBT), IELTS (minimum score 6). *Application deadline:* Applications are processed on a rolling basis. Application fee: $50. Electronic applications accepted. *Expenses:* Expenses: $675/credit hour (for MS), $975 (for PhD). *Financial support:* Application deadline: 5/1; applicants required to submit FAFSA. *Faculty research:* Artificial intelligence, database management, human-computer interaction, distance education, information security. *Unit head:* Dr. Eric S. Ackerman, Dean, 954-262-2000, Fax: 954-262-2752, E-mail: esa@nova.edu. *Application contact:* Nancy Ruidiaz, Director, Admissions, 954-262-2026, Fax: 954-262-2752, E-mail: azoulayn@nova.edu.
Website: http://scis.nova.edu.

Our Lady of the Lake University of San Antonio, School of Business and Leadership, Program in Information Systems and Security, San Antonio, TX 78207-4689. Offers MS. Part-time programs available. Postbaccalaureate distance learning degree programs offered (no on-campus study). *Entrance requirements:* For master's, GMAT, GRE General Test, or MAT. Additional exam requirements/recommendations for international students: Required—TOEFL. Electronic applications accepted. *Faculty research:* Innovative programming, data management, systems analysis, computer network security, information assurance.

Pace University, Seidenberg School of Computer Science and Information Systems, New York, NY 10038. Offers computer science (MS); computing science (DPS); information systems (MS); Internet technology (MS); large computing systems (Certificate); network administration (Certificate); security and information assurance (Certificate); software development and engineering (MS, Certificate); telecommunications (Certificate); telecommunications systems and networks (MS). Part-time and evening/weekend programs available. *Faculty:* 26 full-time (7 women), 7 part-time/adjunct (2 women). *Students:* 167 full-time (57 women), 324 part-time (90 women); includes 182 minority (83 Black or African American, non-Hispanic/Latino; 1 American Indian or Alaska Native, non-Hispanic/Latino; 46 Asian, non-Hispanic/Latino; 47 Hispanic/Latino; 5 Two or more races, non-Hispanic/Latino), 132 international. Average age 35. 441 applicants, 84% accepted, 157 enrolled. In 2014, 115 master's, 7 doctorates, 9 other advanced degrees awarded. *Degree requirements:* For master's, thesis or alternative, capstone course; for doctorate, comprehensive exam (for some programs), thesis/dissertation. *Entrance requirements:* For master's, GRE General Test. Additional exam requirements/recommendations for international students: Required—TOEFL. *Application deadline:* For fall admission, 8/1 priority date for domestic students, 6/1 for international students; for spring admission, 12/1 for domestic students, 10/1 for international students. Applications are processed on a rolling basis. Application fee: $70. Electronic applications accepted. *Expenses:* Expenses: Contact institution. *Financial support:* Research assistantships and career-related internships or fieldwork available. Support available to part-time students. Financial award applicants required to submit FAFSA. *Faculty research:* Computer security and forensics, cybersecurity, telehealth, mobile computing, distributed teams, robotics. *Total annual research expenditures:* $685,824. *Unit head:* Dr. Amar Gupta, Dean, Seidenberg School of Computer Science and Information Systems, 914-773-3750, Fax: 914-773-3533, E-mail: agupta@pace.edu. *Application contact:* Susan Ford-Goldschein, Director of Graduate Admissions, 914-422-4283, Fax: 914-422-4287, E-mail: gradwp@pace.edu.
Website: http://www.pace.edu/seidenberg.

Purdue University, Graduate School, Interdisciplinary Program in Information Security, West Lafayette, IN 47907. Offers MS. *Entrance requirements:* For master's, GRE, minimum undergraduate GPA of 3.0 or equivalent. Additional exam requirements/recommendations for international students: Required—TOEFL (minimum score 550 paper-based; 100 iBT); Recommended—TWE. Electronic applications accepted.

Regis University, College for Professional Studies, School of Computer and Information Sciences, Denver, CO 80221-1099. Offers database development (Certificate); enterprise Java software development (Certificate); enterprise resource planning (Certificate); executive information technology (Certificate); information assurance (M Sc); information technology management (M Sc); software engineering (Certificate); software engineering and database technologies (M Sc); storage area networks (Certificate); systems engineering (M Sc, Certificate). Part-time and evening/weekend programs available. Postbaccalaureate distance learning degree programs offered (no on-campus study). *Faculty:* 8 full-time (3 women), 46 part-time/adjunct (9 women). *Students:* 254 full-time (69 women), 221 part-time (59 women); includes 159 minority (57 Black or African American, non-Hispanic/Latino; 4 American Indian or Alaska Native, non-Hispanic/Latino; 39 Asian, non-Hispanic/Latino; 49 Hispanic/Latino; 1 Native Hawaiian or other Pacific Islander, non-Hispanic/Latino; 9 Two or more races, non-Hispanic/Latino), 22 international. Average age 38. 204 applicants, 87% accepted, 128 enrolled. In 2014, 176 master's awarded. *Degree requirements:* For master's, thesis (for some programs), final research project. *Entrance requirements:* For master's, official transcript reflecting baccalaureate degree awarded from regionally-accredited college or university, 2 years of related experience, resume, interview. Additional exam requirements/recommendations for international students: Required—TOEFL (minimum score 550 paper-based; 82 iBT). *Application deadline:* For fall admission, 8/13 for domestic students, 7/13 for international students; for winter admission, 10/8 for domestic students, 9/8 for international students; for spring admission, 12/17 for domestic students, 11/17 for international students. Applications are processed on a rolling basis. Application fee: $75. Electronic applications accepted. *Expenses:* Expenses: $710 per credit hour (for M Sc). *Financial support:* In 2014–15, 16 students received support. Federal Work-Study and scholarships/grants available. Financial award application deadline: 4/15; financial award applicants required to submit FAFSA. *Faculty research:* Information policy, knowledge management, software architectures. *Unit head:* Donald Archer, Interim Dean, 303-458-4335, E-mail: archer@regis.edu. *Application contact:* Sarah Engel, Director of Admissions, 303-458-4900, Fax: 303-964-5534, E-mail: regisadm@regis.edu.
Website: http://regis.edu/CCIS.aspx.

Robert Morris University, Graduate Studies, School of Communications and Information Systems, Moon Township, PA 15108-1189. Offers communication and information systems (MS); competitive intelligence systems (MS); information security and assurance (MS); information systems and communications (D Sc); information systems management (MS); information technology project management (MS); Internet information systems (MS); organizational leadership (MS). Part-time and evening/weekend programs available. Postbaccalaureate distance learning degree programs offered (no on-campus study). *Faculty:* 25 full-time (10 women), 4 part-time/adjunct (0 women). *Students:* 320 part-time (117 women); includes 71 minority (38 Black or African American, non-Hispanic/Latino; 1 American Indian or Alaska Native, non-Hispanic/Latino; 6 Asian, non-Hispanic/Latino; 4 Hispanic/Latino; 22 Two or more races, non-Hispanic/Latino), 46 international. Average age 34. 267 applicants, 42% accepted, 85 enrolled. In 2014, 84 master's, 14 doctorates awarded. *Degree requirements:* For doctorate, thesis/dissertation. *Entrance requirements:* For doctorate, employer letter of endorsement, interview. Additional exam requirements/recommendations for international students: Required—TOEFL (minimum score 550 paper-based; 79 iBT). *Application deadline:* For fall admission, 7/1 priority date for domestic and international students; for spring admission, 11/1 priority date for domestic and international students. Applications are processed on a rolling basis. Application fee: $35. Electronic applications accepted. *Expenses:* Expenses: Contact institution. *Financial support:* Research assistantships with partial tuition reimbursements, institutionally sponsored loans, and unspecified assistantships available. Support available to part-time students. Financial award application deadline: 5/1. *Unit head:* Dr. Barbara J. Levine, Dean, 412-397-6460, Fax: 412-397-6469, E-mail: levine@rmu.edu. *Application contact:* 412-397-5200, Fax: 412-397-5915, E-mail: graduateadmissions@rmu.edu.
Website: http://www.rmu.edu/web/cms/schools/scis/Pages/default.aspx.

Robert Morris University Illinois, Morris Graduate School of Management, Chicago, IL 60605. Offers accounting (MBA); accounting/finance (MBA); business analytics (MIS); design and media (MM); educational technology (MM); health care administration (MM); higher education administration (MM); human resource management (MBA); information security (MIS); information systems (MIS); law enforcement administration (MM); management (MBA); management/finance (MBA); management/human resource management (MBA); mobile computing (MIS); sports administration (MM). Part-time and evening/weekend programs available. *Faculty:* 5 full-time (2 women), 27 part-time/adjunct (8 women). *Students:* 237 full-time (122 women), 180 part-time (109 women); includes 222 minority (128 Black or African American, non-Hispanic/Latino; 2 American Indian or Alaska Native, non-Hispanic/Latino; 18 Asian, non-Hispanic/Latino; 68 Hispanic/Latino; 1 Native Hawaiian or other Pacific Islander, non-Hispanic/Latino; 5 Two or more races, non-Hispanic/Latino), 26 international. Average age 33. 191 applicants, 63% accepted, 104 enrolled. In 2014, 234 master's awarded. *Entrance requirements:* For master's, official transcripts, two letters of recommendation. Additional exam requirements/recommendations for international students: Required—TOEFL (minimum score 550 paper-based). *Application deadline:* Applications are processed on a rolling basis. Application fee: $20 ($100 for international students). Electronic applications accepted. *Expenses: Tuition:* Full-time $14,400; part-time $2400 per course. *Financial support:* In 2014–15, 339 students received support. Federal Work-Study and scholarships/grants available. Support available to part-time students. Financial award applicants required to submit FAFSA. *Unit head:* Kayed Akkawi, Dean, 312-935-6050, Fax: 312-935-6020, E-mail: kakkawi@robertmorris.edu. *Application contact:* Catherine Lockwood, Vice President of Adult Undergraduate and Graduate Education, 312-935-6050, Fax: 312-935-6020, E-mail: clockwood@robertmorris.edu.

Rochester Institute of Technology, Graduate Enrollment Services, Golisano College of Computing and Information Sciences, Computing Security Department, Advanced Certificate Program in Information Assurance, Rochester, NY 14623-5608. Offers Advanced Certificate. Part-time programs available. In 2014, 12 Advanced Certificates awarded. *Entrance requirements:* For degree, TOEFL, IELTS, or PTE for non-native English speakers, Recommended minimum GPA of 3.0. Additional exam requirements/recommendations for international students: Required—PTE (minimum score 58), TOEFL (minimum score 550 paper-based; 79 iBT) or IELTS (minimum score 6.5). *Application deadline:* Applications are processed on a rolling basis. Electronic applications accepted. *Expenses:* Expenses: $1,673 per credit hour. *Financial support:* Federal Work-Study, institutionally sponsored loans, and scholarships/grants available. Support available to part-time students. Financial award applicants required to submit FAFSA. *Faculty research:* Enterprise level network security and computer system security, forensics. *Unit head:* Sumita Mishra, Graduate Program Director, 585-475-4475, Fax: 585-475-6584, E-mail: sumita.mishra@rit.edu. *Application contact:* Diane Ellison, Associate Vice President, Graduate Enrollment Services, 585-475-2229, Fax: 585-475-7164, E-mail: gradinfo@rit.edu.
Website: https://www.rit.edu/gccis/computingsecurity/academics/ms/certificates.

Rochester Institute of Technology, Graduate Enrollment Services, Golisano College of Computing and Information Sciences, Computing Security Department, MS Program in Computing Security, Rochester, NY 14623-5608. Offers MS. Part-time programs available. *Students:* 21 full-time (3 women), 11 part-time (2 women); includes 2 minority (both Asian, non-Hispanic/Latino), 26 international. Average age 25. 131 applicants, 49% accepted, 14 enrolled. In 2014, 15 master's awarded. *Degree requirements:* For master's, thesis or alternative. *Entrance requirements:* For master's, GRE and TOEFL, IELTS, or PTE for non-native English speakers, Recommended minimum GPA of 3.0. Additional exam requirements/recommendations for international students: Required—PTE (minimum score 58), TOEFL (minimum score 550 paper-based; 79 iBT) or IELTS (minimum score 6.5). *Application deadline:* For fall admission, 2/15 priority date for domestic and international students; for spring admission, 12/15 priority date for domestic and international students. Applications are processed on a rolling basis. Electronic applications accepted. *Expenses:* Expenses: $1,673 per credit hour. *Financial support:* In 2014–15, 23 students received support. Research assistantships with partial tuition reimbursements available, teaching assistantships with partial tuition reimbursements available, career-related internships or fieldwork, Federal Work-Study, institutionally sponsored loans, scholarships/grants, and unspecified assistantships available. Support available to part-time students. Financial award applicants required to submit FAFSA. *Faculty research:* Forensics; cryptography; critical infrastructure protection; building virtual research, interactive, service, and experiential learning modules for cyber security education; gamified digital forensics. *Unit head:* Sumita Mishra, Graduate Program Director, 585-475-4475, Fax: 585-475-6584, E-mail: sumita.mishra@rit.edu. *Application contact:* Diane Ellison, Associate Vice President, Graduate Enrollment Services, 585-475-2229, Fax: 585-475-7164, E-mail: gradinfo@rit.edu.
Website: http://www.rit.edu/gccis/computingsecurity/academics/ms/overview.

Roger Williams University, School of Justice Studies, Bristol, RI 02809. Offers criminal justice (MS); cybersecurity (MS); leadership (MS), including health care administration (MPA, MS), public management (MPA, MS); public administration (MPA), including health care administration (MPA, MS), public management (MPA, MS); MS/JD. Part-time and evening/weekend programs available. Postbaccalaureate distance learning degree programs offered. *Faculty:* 4 full-time (2 women), 5 part-time/adjunct (0 women). *Students:* 13 full-time (7 women), 88 part-time (41 women); includes 10 minority (4 Black or African American, non-Hispanic/Latino; 2 Asian, non-Hispanic/Latino; 4 Hispanic/Latino), 5 international. Average age 36. 69 applicants, 61% accepted, 24 enrolled. In 2014, 30 master's awarded. *Degree requirements:* For master's, comprehensive exam,

thesis optional. *Entrance requirements:* For master's, 2 letters of recommendation. Additional exam requirements/recommendations for international students: Recommended—TOEFL (minimum score 85 iBT), IELTS. *Application deadline:* Applications are processed on a rolling basis. Application fee: $50. Electronic applications accepted. *Expenses:* Expenses: $14,724. *Financial support:* Application deadline: 6/15; applicants required to submit FAFSA. *Unit head:* Dr. Stephanie Manzi, Dean, 401-254-3021, Fax: 401-254-3431, E-mail: smanzi@rwu.edu. *Application contact:* Lori Vales, Graduate Admissions Coordinator, 401-254-6200, Fax: 401-254-3557, E-mail: gradadmit@rwu.edu.
Website: http://www.rwu.edu/academics/departments/criminaljustice.htm#graduate.

Sacred Heart University, Graduate Programs, College of Arts and Sciences, Department of Computer Science, Fairfield, CT 06825-1000. Offers computer game design and development (Graduate Certificate); computer science and information technology (MS); computer science gaming (MS); cybersecurity (MS); database design (Graduate Certificate); information technology (Graduate Certificate); information technology and network security (Graduate Certificate); interactive multimedia (Graduate Certificate); Web development (Graduate Certificate). Part-time and evening/weekend programs available. *Faculty:* 6 full-time (2 women), 18 part-time/adjunct (5 women). *Students:* 266 full-time (100 women), 69 part-time (15 women); includes 30 minority (11 Black or African American, non-Hispanic/Latino; 7 Asian, non-Hispanic/Latino; 12 Hispanic/Latino), 265 international. Average age 26. 1,010 applicants, 56% accepted, 166 enrolled. In 2014, 50 master's awarded. *Degree requirements:* For master's, thesis or alternative. *Entrance requirements:* For master's, bachelor's degree, minimum GPA of 3.0. Additional exam requirements/recommendations for international students: Required—PTE; Recommended—TOEFL (minimum score 570 paper-based; 80 iBT), IELTS (minimum score 6.5). *Application deadline:* For fall admission, 5/15 for international students; for spring admission, 10/30 for international students. Applications are processed on a rolling basis. Application fee: $60. Electronic applications accepted. *Expenses: Tuition:* Full-time $24,559; part-time $649 per credit. *Financial support:* Unspecified assistantships available. Financial award applicants required to submit FAFSA. *Unit head:* Domenick Pinto, Academic Director and Chairperson, 203-371-7789, Fax: 203-371-0506, E-mail: pintod@sacredheart.edu. *Application contact:* Kathy Dilks, Executive Director of Graduate Admissions, 203-365-7619, Fax: 203-365-4732, E-mail: gradstudies@sacredheart.edu.
Website: http://www.sacredheart.edu/academics/collegeofartssciences/academicdepartments/computerscienceinformationtechnology/graduatedegreesandcertificates/.

St. Cloud State University, School of Graduate Studies, College of Science and Engineering, Program in Information Assurance, St. Cloud, MN 56301-4498. Offers MS. Part-time programs available. *Degree requirements:* For master's, 30 to 33 credits of coursework. *Entrance requirements:* For master's, minimum overall GPA of 2.75 in previous undergraduate and graduate records or in last half of undergraduate work. Electronic applications accepted.

St. Cloud State University, School of Graduate Studies, Herberger Business School, Program in Business Administration, St. Cloud, MN 56301-4498. Offers business administration (MBA); information assurance (MS). Part-time and evening/weekend programs available. *Degree requirements:* For master's, thesis or alternative. *Entrance requirements:* For master's, GMAT, minimum GPA of 2.75. Additional exam requirements/recommendations for international students: Required—Michigan English Language Assessment Battery; Recommended—TOEFL (minimum score 550 paper-based), IELTS (minimum score 6.5).

Saint Leo University, Graduate Business Studies, Saint Leo, FL 33574-6665. Offers accounting (M Acc, MBA); health care management (MBA); human resource management (MBA); information security management (MBA); marketing (MBA); marketing research and social media analytics (MBA); project management (MBA); sport business (MBA). Part-time and evening/weekend programs available. Postbaccalaureate distance learning degree programs offered (no on-campus study). *Faculty:* 49 full-time (12 women), 63 part-time/adjunct (24 women). *Students:* 1,887 full-time (1,024 women), 7 part-time (3 women); includes 821 minority (603 Black or African American, non-Hispanic/Latino; 5 American Indian or Alaska Native, non-Hispanic/Latino; 35 Asian, non-Hispanic/Latino; 156 Hispanic/Latino; 2 Native Hawaiian or other Pacific Islander, non-Hispanic/Latino; 20 Two or more races, non-Hispanic/Latino), 35 international. Average age 38. In 2014, 782 master's awarded. *Entrance requirements:* For master's, GMAT (minimum score 500 if applicant has less than 3.0 in the last two years of undergraduate study), bachelor's degree with minimum GPA of 3.0 in the last 60 hours of coursework from regionally-accredited college or university; 2 years of professional work experience; resume; 2 letters of recommendation. Additional exam requirements/recommendations for international students: Required—TOEFL (minimum score 550 paper-based; 80 iBT). *Application deadline:* For fall admission, 7/1 priority date for domestic and international students; for spring admission, 11/12 priority date for domestic students, 11/1 for international students. Applications are processed on a rolling basis. Application fee: $80. Electronic applications accepted. *Expenses: Tuition:* Full-time $12,114; part-time $673 per semester hour. Tuition and fees vary according to course level, campus/location and program. *Financial support:* In 2014–15, 137 students received support. Career-related internships or fieldwork, scholarships/grants, and health care benefits available. Financial award application deadline: 3/1; financial award applicants required to submit FAFSA. *Unit head:* Dr. Lorrie McGovern, Assistant Dean, Graduate Studies in Business, 352-588-7390, Fax: 352-588-8912, E-mail: mbaslu@saintleo.edu. *Application contact:* Joshua Stagner, Director of Graduate Admission, 800-707-8846, Fax: 352-588-7873, E-mail: grad.admissions@saintleo.edu.
Website: http://www.saintleo.edu/academics/graduate.aspx.

Salem International University, School of Business, Salem, WV 26426-0500. Offers information security (MBA); international business (MBA). Part-time programs available. Postbaccalaureate distance learning degree programs offered (no on-campus study). *Entrance requirements:* For master's, minimum undergraduate GPA of 2.5, course work in business, resume. Additional exam requirements/recommendations for international students: Recommended—TOEFL (minimum score 550 paper-based), IELTS (minimum score 6.5). Electronic applications accepted. *Expenses:* Contact institution. *Faculty research:* Organizational behavior strategy, marketing services.

Salve Regina University, Program in Administration of Justice and Homeland Security, Newport, RI 02840-4192. Offers administration of justice and homeland security (MS); cybersecurity and intelligence (CGS); leadership in justice (CGS). Part-time and evening/weekend programs available. Postbaccalaureate distance learning degree programs offered (no on-campus study). *Faculty:* 2 full-time (0 women), 6 part-time/adjunct (1 woman). *Students:* 18 full-time (10 women), 58 part-time (15 women); includes 6 minority (1 Black or African American, non-Hispanic/Latino; 4 Hispanic/Latino; 1 Two or more races, non-Hispanic/Latino). Average age 31. 15 applicants, 100% accepted, 15 enrolled. In 2014, 23 master's awarded. *Entrance requirements:* For master's, GMAT, GRE General Test, or MAT. Additional exam requirements/recommendations for international students: Required—TOEFL (minimum score 600 paper-based; 100 iBT). *Application deadline:* For fall admission, 3/5 priority date for domestic students, 3/15 priority date for international students; for spring admission, 9/15 priority date for domestic students, 9/5 priority date for international students. Applications are processed on a rolling basis. Application fee: $60. Electronic applications accepted. *Expenses: Tuition:* Full-time $8550; part-time $475 per credit. *Required fees:* $50 per term. Tuition and fees vary according to course level, course load and degree level. *Financial support:* Career-related internships or fieldwork and Federal Work-Study available. Support available to part-time students. Financial award application deadline: 3/1; financial award applicants required to submit FAFSA. *Unit head:* David Smith, Director, 401-341-3210, E-mail: david.smith@salve.edu. *Application contact:* Nicole Ferreira, Associate Director of Graduate Admissions, 401-341-2462, Fax: 401-341-2973, E-mail: nicole.ferreira@salve.edu.
Website: http://www.salve.edu/graduate-studies/administration-of-justice-and-homeland-security.

Salve Regina University, Program in Business Administration, Newport, RI 02840-4192. Offers cybersecurity issues in business (MBA); entrepreneurial enterprise (MBA); health care administration and management (MBA); social ventures (MBA). Part-time and evening/weekend programs available. Postbaccalaureate distance learning degree programs offered (no on-campus study). *Faculty:* 3 full-time (2 women), 12 part-time/adjunct (7 women). *Students:* 47 full-time (20 women), 61 part-time (30 women); includes 13 minority (7 Black or African American, non-Hispanic/Latino; 1 American Indian or Alaska Native, non-Hispanic/Latino; 1 Asian, non-Hispanic/Latino; 2 Hispanic/Latino; 1 Native Hawaiian or other Pacific Islander, non-Hispanic/Latino; 1 Two or more races, non-Hispanic/Latino), 3 international. Average age 29. 25 applicants, 96% accepted, 24 enrolled. In 2014, 56 master's awarded. *Entrance requirements:* For master's, GMAT, GRE General Test, or MAT, 6 undergraduate credits each in accounting, economics, quantitative analysis and calculus or statistics. Additional exam requirements/recommendations for international students: Required—TOEFL (minimum score 600 paper-based; 100 iBT) or IELTS. *Application deadline:* For fall admission, 3/15 priority date for domestic and international students; for spring admission, 9/15 priority date for domestic and international students. Applications are processed on a rolling basis. Application fee: $60. Electronic applications accepted. *Expenses: Tuition:* Full-time $8550; part-time $475 per credit. *Required fees:* $50 per term. Tuition and fees vary according to course level, course load and degree level. *Financial support:* Career-related internships or fieldwork and Federal Work-Study available. Support available to part-time students. Financial award application deadline: 3/1; financial award applicants required to submit FAFSA. *Unit head:* Dr. Arlene Nicholas, Director, 401-341-3280, E-mail: arlene.nicholas@salve.edu. *Application contact:* Nicole Ferreira, Associate Director of Graduate Admissions, 401-341-2462, Fax: 401-341-2973, E-mail: nicole.ferreira@salve.edu.
Website: http://salve.edu/graduate-studies/business-administration-and-management.

Sam Houston State University, College of Sciences, Department of Computer Science, Huntsville, TX 77341. Offers computing and information science (MS); digital forensics (MS); information assurance and security (MS). Part-time programs available. *Faculty:* 12 full-time (3 women), 1 (woman) part-time/adjunct. *Students:* 37 full-time (8 women), 49 part-time (10 women); includes 25 minority (12 Black or African American, non-Hispanic/Latino; 3 Asian, non-Hispanic/Latino; 9 Hispanic/Latino; 1 Two or more races, non-Hispanic/Latino), 32 international. Average age 32. 73 applicants, 40% accepted, 21 enrolled. In 2014, 7 master's awarded. *Degree requirements:* For master's, comprehensive exam, thesis optional, internship; for doctorate, comprehensive exam, thesis/dissertation. *Entrance requirements:* For master's, GRE General Test, letters of recommendation. Additional exam requirements/recommendations for international students: Required—TOEFL (minimum score 550 paper-based; 79 iBT), IELTS (minimum score 6.5). *Application deadline:* For fall admission, 8/1 for domestic students, 6/25 for international students; for spring admission, 12/1 for domestic students, 11/12 for international students; for summer admission, 5/15 for domestic students, 4/9 for international students. Applications are processed on a rolling basis. Application fee: $45 ($75 for international students). Electronic applications accepted. *Expenses:* Tuition, state resident: full-time $2286; part-time $254 per credit hour. Tuition, nonresident: full-time $5544; part-time $616 per credit hour. *Required fees:* $440 per semester. Tuition and fees vary according to course load and campus/location. *Financial support:* In 2014–15, 19 research assistantships (averaging $6,013 per year) were awarded; career-related internships or fieldwork, Federal Work-Study, scholarships/grants, tuition waivers (partial), and unspecified assistantships also available. Support available to part-time students. Financial award application deadline: 3/15; financial award applicants required to submit FAFSA. *Unit head:* Dr. Peter Cooper, Chair/Professor, 936-294-1569, Fax: 936-294-4312, E-mail: css_pac@shsu.edu. *Application contact:* Dr. Jihuang Ji, Associate Professor/Graduate Advisor, 936-294-1579, Fax: 936-294-4312, E-mail: csc_jxj@shsu.edu.
Website: http://cs.shsu.edu/.

Santa Clara University, School of Engineering, Santa Clara, CA 95053. Offers analog circuit design (Certificate); applied mathematics (MS); ASIC design and test (Certificate); bioengineering (MS); civil engineering (MS); computer science and engineering (MS, PhD); controls (Certificate); digital signal processing (Certificate); dynamics (Certificate); electrical engineering (MS, PhD); engineering (Engineer); engineering management (MS); fundamentals of electrical engineering (Certificate); information assurance (Certificate); materials engineering (Certificate); mechanical design analysis (Certificate); mechanical engineering (MS, PhD); mechatronics systems engineering (Certificate); microwave and antennas (Certificate); networking (Certificate); renewable energy (Certificate); software engineering (Certificate); sustainable energy (MS); technology jump-start (Certificate); thermofluids (Certificate). Part-time and evening/weekend programs available. *Faculty:* 59 full-time (23 women), 80 part-time/adjunct (14 women). *Students:* 584 full-time (239 women), 353 part-time (102 women); includes 224 minority (7 Black or African American, non-Hispanic/Latino; 144 Asian, non-Hispanic/Latino; 50 Hispanic/Latino; 2 Native Hawaiian or other Pacific Islander, non-Hispanic/Latino; 21 Two or more races, non-Hispanic/Latino), 548 international. Average age 27. 1,248 applicants, 51% accepted, 375 enrolled. In 2014, 283 master's, 5 doctorates, 1 other advanced degree awarded. *Degree requirements:* For master's, thesis (for some programs); for doctorate, thesis/dissertation; for other advanced degree, thesis. *Entrance requirements:* For master's, GRE, transcript; for doctorate, GRE, master's degree or equivalent; for other advanced degree, master's degree, published paper. Additional exam requirements/recommendations for international students: Required—TOEFL (minimum score 550 paper-based; 79 iBT). *Application deadline:* For fall admission, 8/1 for domestic students, 7/15 for international students; for winter admission, 10/28 for domestic students, 9/23 for international students; for spring admission, 2/25 for domestic students, 1/21 for international students. Applications are processed on a rolling basis. Application fee: $60. Electronic applications accepted. *Expenses:* Expenses: Contact institution. *Financial support:* In 2014–15, 94 students received support. Fellowships with full and partial tuition reimbursements available, research assistantships with full and partial tuition reimbursements available, teaching assistantships with full tuition reimbursements available, career-related internships or fieldwork, Federal Work-Study, institutionally sponsored loans, and scholarships/grants available. Support available to part-time students. Financial award application deadline: 3/2; financial award applicants required to submit FAFSA. *Faculty research:* Video encoding, nanostructures, robotics, microfluidics, water resources. *Total annual research expenditures:* $1.6 million. *Unit head:* Dr. Alex Zecevic, Associate Dean for Graduate Studies, 408-554-2394, E-mail:

azecevic@scu.edu. *Application contact:* Stacey Tinker, Director of Enrollment Management, 408-554-4748, Fax: 408-554-4323, E-mail: stinker@scu.edu.
Website: http://www.scu.edu/engineering/graduate/.

Southern Polytechnic State University, School of Computing and Software Engineering, Department of Information Technology, Marietta, GA 30060-2896. Offers health information technology (Postbaccalaureate Certificate); information security and assurance (Graduate Certificate); information technology (MSIT, Graduate Certificate); information technology fundamentals (Postbaccalaureate Certificate). Part-time and evening/weekend programs available. Postbaccalaureate distance learning degree programs offered (no on-campus study). *Degree requirements:* For master's, thesis optional. *Entrance requirements:* For master's, minimum GPA of 2.75; for other advanced degree, bachelor's degree. Additional exam requirements/recommendations for international students: Required—TOEFL (minimum score 550 paper-based; 79 iBT), IELTS (minimum score 6.5). Electronic applications accepted. *Faculty research:* IT ethics, user interface design, IT security, IT integration, IT management, health information technology, business intelligence, networks, business continuity.

State University of New York Polytechnic Institute, Program in Network and Computer Security, Utica, NY 13504-3050. Offers MS. Part-time programs available. *Degree requirements:* For master's, thesis or project. *Entrance requirements:* For master's, GRE General Test, minimum GPA of 3.0, letter of reference, resume, BS in network and computer security or related field. Additional exam requirements/recommendations for international students: Required—TOEFL (minimum score 550 paper-based; 79 iBT), IELTS (minimum score 6.5). Electronic applications accepted. *Faculty research:* Cloud security, virtualization, wireless networks, cyber physical system.

Stevens Institute of Technology, Graduate School, Charles V. Schaefer Jr. School of Engineering, Department of Computer Science, Hoboken, NJ 07030. Offers computer graphics (Certificate); computer science (MS, PhD); computer systems (Certificate); database management systems (Certificate); distributed systems (Certificate); elements of computer science (Certificate); enterprise computing (Certificate); enterprise security and information assurance (Certificate); health informatics (Certificate); multimedia experience and management (Certificate); networks and systems administration (Certificate); security and privacy (Certificate); service oriented computing (Certificate); software design (Certificate); theoretical computer science (Certificate). Part-time and evening/weekend programs available. Terminal master's awarded for partial completion of doctoral program. *Degree requirements:* For master's, thesis optional; for doctorate, variable foreign language requirement, comprehensive exam, thesis/dissertation. *Entrance requirements:* For master's and doctorate, GRE, minimum GPA of 3.0. Additional exam requirements/recommendations for international students: Required—TOEFL. Electronic applications accepted. *Faculty research:* Semantics, reliability theory, programming language, cyber security.

Stevens Institute of Technology, Graduate School, Wesley J. Howe School of Technology Management, Program in Information Systems, Hoboken, NJ 07030. Offers computer science (MS); e-commerce (MS); enterprise systems (MS); entrepreneurial information technology (MS); information architecture (MS); information management (MS, Certificate); information security (MS); information technology in financial services industry (MS); information technology in the pharmaceutical industry (MS); information technology outsourcing management (MS); project management (MS, Certificate); software engineering (MS); telecommunications (MS). *Degree requirements:* For master's, thesis optional. *Entrance requirements:* For master's, GMAT, GRE General Test. Additional exam requirements/recommendations for international students: Required—TOEFL. Electronic applications accepted.

Stevenson University, Program in Cyber Forensics, Owings Mills, MD 21117. Offers MS. *Faculty:* 5 part-time/adjunct (0 women). *Students:* 3 full-time (0 women), 27 part-time (11 women); includes 10 minority (all Black or African American, non-Hispanic/Latino). Average age 36. 16 applicants, 63% accepted, 7 enrolled. *Degree requirements:* For master's, capstone. *Entrance requirements:* For master's, official transcripts, minimum cumulative GPA of 3.0, two letters of recommendation. Additional exam requirements/recommendations for international students: Required—TOEFL (minimum score 550 paper-based), IELTS (minimum score 6.5). *Application deadline:* Applications are processed on a rolling basis. Electronic applications accepted. *Expenses:* Expenses: $645 per credit, $125 fee. *Unit head:* Michael Robinson, Coordinator, Fax: 443-394-0538, E-mail: mrobinson4614@stevenson.edu. *Application contact:* William Wellein, Enrollment Counselor, 443-352-5843, Fax: 443-394-0538, E-mail: wwellein@stevenson.edu.
Website: http://www.stevenson.edu.

Stratford University, School of Graduate Studies, Falls Church, VA 22043. Offers accounting (MS); business administration (IMBA, MBA); enterprise business management (MS); entrepreneurial management (MS); information assurance (MS); information systems (MS); software engineering (MS); telecommunications (MS). Part-time and evening/weekend programs available. Postbaccalaureate distance learning degree programs offered (no on-campus study). *Degree requirements:* For master's, comprehensive exam, capstone project. *Entrance requirements:* For master's, GRE or GMAT, baccalaureate degree. Additional exam requirements/recommendations for international students: Required—TOEFL (minimum score 79 iBT) or IELTS (6.5). Electronic applications accepted.

Strayer University, Graduate Studies, Washington, DC 20005-2603. Offers accounting (MS); acquisition (MBA); business administration (MBA); communications technology (MS); educational management (M Ed); finance (MBA); health services administration (MHSA); hospitality and tourism management (MBA); human resource management (MBA); information systems (MS), including computer security management, decision support system management, enterprise resource management, network management, software engineering management, systems development management; management (MBA); management information systems (MS); marketing (MBA); professional accounting (MS), including accounting information systems, controllership, taxation; public administration (MPA); supply chain management (MBA); technology in education (M Ed). Programs also offered at campus locations in Birmingham, AL; Chamblee, GA; Cobb County, GA; Morrow, GA; White Marsh, MD; Charleston, SC; Columbia, SC; Greensboro, NC; Greenville, SC; Lexington, KY; Louisville, KY; Nashville, TN; North Raleigh, NC; Washington, DC. Part-time and evening/weekend programs available. Postbaccalaureate distance learning degree programs offered (minimal on-campus study). *Degree requirements:* For master's, thesis. *Entrance requirements:* For master's, GMAT, GRE General Test, bachelor's degree from an accredited college or university, minimum undergraduate GPA of 2.75. Electronic applications accepted.

Syracuse University, L. C. Smith College of Engineering and Computer Science, Program in Cybersecurity, Syracuse, NY 13244. Offers MS, CAS. Part-time and evening/weekend programs available. *Students:* 7 applicants. *Entrance requirements:* Additional exam requirements/recommendations for international students: Required—TOEFL (minimum score 100 iBT). *Application deadline:* For fall admission, 7/1 priority date for domestic students, 6/1 priority date for international students; for spring admission, 11/15 for domestic students, 10/15 priority date for international students. Applications are processed on a rolling basis. Application fee: $75. Electronic applications accepted. *Expenses: Tuition:* Part-time $1341 per credit. *Required fees:* $1341 per credit. *Financial support:* Application deadline: 1/1. *Unit head:* Dr. Kishan Mehrotra, Professor and Chair, 315-443-2811, E-mail: mehrotra@syr.edu. *Application contact:* Kathleen Joyce, Assistant Dean, 315-443-2219, E-mail: topgrads@syr.edu.
Website: http://eng-cs.syr.edu/.

Syracuse University, School of Information Studies, Program in Information Security Management, Syracuse, NY 13244. Offers CAS. Part-time and evening/weekend programs available. Postbaccalaureate distance learning degree programs offered. *Students:* 1 full-time (0 women), 3 part-time (1 woman). Average age 26. 28 applicants, 71% accepted, 3 enrolled. In 2014, 42 CASs awarded. *Entrance requirements:* Additional exam requirements/recommendations for international students: Required—TOEFL (minimum score 100 iBT). *Application deadline:* For fall admission, 1/1 priority date for domestic and international students; for spring admission, 10/15 priority date for domestic and international students. Applications are processed on a rolling basis. Application fee: $75. Electronic applications accepted. *Expenses: Tuition:* Part-time $1341 per credit. *Required fees:* $1341 per credit. *Financial support:* Application deadline: 1/1. *Unit head:* Carsten Oesterlund, Program Director, 315-443-2911, E-mail: igrad@syr.edu. *Application contact:* Susan Corieri, Director of Enrollment Management, 315-443-2575, E-mail: ischool@syr.edu.
Website: http://ischool.syr.edu/.

Texas A&M University–San Antonio, School of Business, San Antonio, TX 78224. Offers business administration (MBA); enterprise resource planning systems (MBA); finance (MBA); healthcare management (MBA); human resources management (MBA); information assurance and security (MBA); international business (MBA); professional accounting (MPA); project management (MBA); supply chain management (MBA). Part-time and evening/weekend programs available. *Entrance requirements:* For master's, GMAT. Additional exam requirements/recommendations for international students: Required—TOEFL (minimum score 550 paper-based; 80 iBT), IELTS (minimum score 6). Electronic applications accepted.

Towson University, Program in Applied Information Technology, Towson, MD 21252-0001. Offers applied information technology (MS, D Sc); database management systems (Postbaccalaureate Certificate); information security and assurance (Postbaccalaureate Certificate); information systems management (Postbaccalaureate Certificate); Internet applications development (Postbaccalaureate Certificate); networking technologies (Postbaccalaureate Certificate); software engineering (Postbaccalaureate Certificate). *Students:* 132 full-time (44 women), 219 part-time (73 women); includes 118 minority (71 Black or African American, non-Hispanic/Latino; 1 American Indian or Alaska Native, non-Hispanic/Latino; 23 Asian, non-Hispanic/Latino; 12 Hispanic/Latino; 2 Native Hawaiian or other Pacific Islander, non-Hispanic/Latino; 9 Two or more races, non-Hispanic/Latino), 85 international. *Entrance requirements:* For master's and Postbaccalaureate Certificate, bachelor's degree, minimum GPA of 3.0; for doctorate, master's degree in computer science, information systems, information technology, or closely-related areas; minimum GPA of 3.0; 2 letters of recommendation; resume. Additional exam requirements/recommendations for international students: Required—TOEFL. *Application deadline:* Applications are processed on a rolling basis. Application fee: $45. Electronic applications accepted. *Unit head:* Dr. Suranjan Chakraborty, Graduate Program Director, 410-704-4769, E-mail: schakraborty@towson.edu. *Application contact:* Alicia Arkell-Kleis, Information Contact, 410-704-6004, E-mail: grads@towson.edu.
Website: http://grad.towson.edu/program/master/ait-ms/.

Trident University International, College of Business Administration, Program in Business Administration, Cypress, CA 90630. Offers business administration (PhD); conflict and negotiation management (MBA); criminal justice administration (MBA); entrepreneurship (MBA); finance (MBA); general management (MBA); government accounting (MBA); human resource management (MBA); information security and digital assurance management (MBA); information technology management (MBA); international business (MBA); logistics management (MBA); marketing (MBA); project management (MBA); public management (MBA); quality management (MBA); strategic leadership (MBA). Part-time and evening/weekend programs available. Postbaccalaureate distance learning degree programs offered (no on-campus study). *Degree requirements:* For doctorate, comprehensive exam, thesis/dissertation, defense of dissertation. *Entrance requirements:* For master's, minimum GPA of 2.5 (students with GPA 3.0 or greater may transfer up to 30% of graduate level credits); for doctorate, minimum GPA of 3.4, curriculum vitae, course work in research methods or statistics. Additional exam requirements/recommendations for international students: Required—TOEFL. Electronic applications accepted.

Tuskegee University, Graduate Programs, Andrew F. Brimmer College of Business and Information Science, Tuskegee, AL 36088. Offers information systems and security management (MS). *Degree requirements:* For master's, thesis. *Entrance requirements:* For master's, GRE or GMAT, baccalaureate degree in computer science, management information systems, accounting, finance, management, information technology, or a closely-related field. *Expenses: Tuition:* Full-time $18,560; part-time $1542 per credit hour. *Required fees:* $2910; $1455 per semester.

Universidad del Este, Graduate School, Carolina, PR 00984. Offers accounting (MBA); adult education (M Ed); agribusiness (MBA); criminal justice and criminology (MA); curriculum and instruction - early education (M Ed); curriculum and instruction - elementary (M Ed); curriculum and instruction - English (M Ed); curriculum and instruction - Spanish (M Ed); human resources (MBA); information security management (MBA); information technology and Web business development (MBA); management (MBA); public policy (MPA); social work (MA), including clinical social work; special education (M Ed); strategic leadership (MBA).

Université de Sherbrooke, Faculty of Administration, Program in Governance, Audit and Security of Information Technology, Longueuil, QC J4K0A8, Canada. Offers M Adm. Part-time and evening/weekend programs available. Postbaccalaureate distance learning degree programs offered. *Degree requirements:* For master's, thesis. *Entrance requirements:* For master's, bachelor's degree, related work experience. Electronic applications accepted.

University of Advancing Technology, Master of Science Program in Technology, Tempe, AZ 85283-1042. Offers advancing computer science (MS); emerging technologies (MS); game production and management (MS); information assurance (MS); technology leadership (MS). *Degree requirements:* For master's, project or thesis. *Entrance requirements:* Additional exam requirements/recommendations for international students: Required—TOEFL (minimum score 550 paper-based). Electronic applications accepted. *Faculty research:* Artificial intelligence, fractals, organizational management.

The University of Alabama at Birmingham, College of Arts and Sciences, Program in Computer Forensics and Security Management, Birmingham, AL 35294. Offers MS. Interdisciplinary program offered jointly with College of Arts and Sciences and School of Business. *Students:* 4 full-time (1 woman), 6 part-time (2 women); includes 2 minority (1 Black or African American, non-Hispanic/Latino; 1 Hispanic/Latino), 3 international. Average age 34. In 2014, 3 master's awarded. *Degree requirements:* For master's, field practicum (internship). *Entrance requirements:* For master's, GRE General Test (minimum combined score of 320) or GMAT (minimum total score of 550), minimum GPA of 3.0. *Application deadline:* For fall admission, 3/1 for domestic students. Application fee: $45 ($60 for international students). Electronic applications accepted. *Expenses:* Tuition, state resident: full-time $7090; part-time $370 per credit hour. Tuition, nonresident: full-time $16,072; part-time $869 per credit hour. Full-time tuition and fees vary according to course load and program. *Unit head:* Dr. Anthony Skjellum, Program Co-Director, Computer and Information Sciences, 205-934-2213, Fax: 205-934-5473, E-mail: tony@cis.uab.edu. *Application contact:* Dr. John J. Sloan, III, Program Co-Director, Justice Sciences, 205-934-2069, E-mail: prof@uab.edu. Website: http://www.uab.edu/cas/justice-sciences/graduate-programs/master-of-science-in-computer-forensics-and-security-management-mscfsm.

The University of Alabama at Birmingham, School of Business, Program in Management Information Systems, Birmingham, AL 35294. Offers management information systems (MS), including information security, information technology management, Web and mobile development. Part-time programs available. Postbaccalaureate distance learning degree programs offered (no on-campus study). *Students:* 44 part-time (17 women); includes 27 minority (19 Black or African American, non-Hispanic/Latino; 1 American Indian or Alaska Native, non-Hispanic/Latino; 3 Asian, non-Hispanic/Latino; 1 Hispanic/Latino; 3 Two or more races, non-Hispanic/Latino). Average age 37. *Entrance requirements:* For master's, GMAT. Additional exam requirements/recommendations for international students: Required—TOEFL. *Application deadline:* For fall admission, 7/15 for domestic and international students; for spring admission, 11/15 for domestic students, 12/15 for international students; for summer admission, 4/15 for domestic and international students. Application fee: $45 ($60 for international students). *Expenses:* Tuition, state resident: full-time $7090; part-time $370 per credit hour. Tuition, nonresident: full-time $16,072; part-time $869 per credit hour. Full-time tuition and fees vary according to course load and program. *Unit head:* Dr. Eric Jack, Dean, 205-934-8800, Fax: 205-934-8886, E-mail: ejack@uab.edu. *Application contact:* Wendy England, Online Program Coordinator, 205-934-8813, Fax: 205-975-4429.
Website: http://businessdegrees.uab.edu/mis-degree/.

The University of Alabama in Huntsville, School of Graduate Studies, College of Business Administration, Programs in Information Systems, Huntsville, AL 35899. Offers enterprise resource planning (Certificate); information assurance (MS, Certificate); information systems (MSIS); supply chain management (Certificate). Part-time and evening/weekend programs available. *Degree requirements:* For master's, comprehensive exam, thesis or alternative. *Entrance requirements:* For master's, GMAT (minimum score 500), minimum AACSB index of 1080. Additional exam requirements/recommendations for international students: Required—TOEFL (minimum score 550 paper-based; 80 iBT), IELTS (minimum score 6.5). Electronic applications accepted. *Faculty research:* Supply chain information systems, information assurance and security, databases and conceptual schema, workflow management, inter-organizational information sharing.

The University of Alabama in Huntsville, School of Graduate Studies, College of Engineering, Department of Electrical and Computer Engineering, Huntsville, AL 35899. Offers computer engineering (MSE, PhD); electrical engineering (MSE, PhD), including optics and photonics technology (MSE), opto-electronics (MSE); information assurance (MS); optical science and engineering (PhD); optics and photonics (MSE); software engineering (MSSE). Part-time and evening/weekend programs available. *Degree requirements:* For master's, comprehensive exam, thesis or alternative, oral and written exams; for doctorate, comprehensive exam, thesis/dissertation, oral and written exams. *Entrance requirements:* For master's, GRE General Test, appropriate bachelor's degree, minimum GPA of 3.0; for doctorate, GRE General Test, minimum GPA of 3.0. Additional exam requirements/recommendations for international students: Required—TOEFL (minimum score 500 paper-based; 80 iBT), IELTS (minimum score 6.5). Electronic applications accepted. *Faculty research:* Advanced computer architecture and systems, fault tolerant computing and verification, computational electro-magnetics, nano-photonics and plasmonics, micro electro-mechanical (MEMS) systems.

The University of Alabama in Huntsville, School of Graduate Studies, College of Science, Department of Computer Science, Huntsville, AL 35899. Offers computer science (MS, PhD); information assurance (MS); modeling and simulation (MS, PhD); software engineering (MSSE, Certificate). Part-time and evening/weekend programs available. Postbaccalaureate distance learning degree programs offered (minimal on-campus study). *Degree requirements:* For master's, comprehensive exam, thesis or alternative, oral and written exams; for doctorate, comprehensive exam, thesis/dissertation, oral and written exams. *Entrance requirements:* For master's, doctorate, and Certificate, GRE General Test, minimum GPA of 3.0. Additional exam requirements/recommendations for international students: Required—TOEFL (minimum score 550 paper-based; 80 iBT), IELTS (minimum score 6.5). Electronic applications accepted. *Faculty research:* Information assurance and cyber security, modeling and simulation, data science, computer graphics and visualization, multimedia systems.

University of Colorado Colorado Springs, College of Engineering and Applied Science, Program in General Engineering, Colorado Springs, CO 80933-7150. Offers energy engineering (ME); engineering management (ME); information assurance (ME); software engineering (ME); space operations (ME); systems engineering (ME). Part-time and evening/weekend programs available. Postbaccalaureate distance learning degree programs offered (minimal on-campus study). *Faculty:* 2 full-time (0 women), 8 part-time/adjunct (2 women). *Students:* 15 full-time (2 women), 159 part-time (30 women); includes 29 minority (3 Black or African American, non-Hispanic/Latino; 1 American Indian or Alaska Native, non-Hispanic/Latino; 10 Asian, non-Hispanic/Latino; 12 Hispanic/Latino; 3 Two or more races, non-Hispanic/Latino), 63 international. Average age 36. 113 applicants, 65% accepted, 39 enrolled. In 2014, 29 master's, 6 doctorates awarded. *Degree requirements:* For master's, thesis, portfolio, or project; for doctorate, comprehensive exam, thesis/dissertation. *Entrance requirements:* For master's, GRE (minimum score of 148 new grading scale on quantitative portion if GPA is less than 3.0); for doctorate, GRE (minimum score of 148 new grading scale on the quantitative portion if the applicant has not graduated from a program of recognized standing), minimum GPA of 3.3 in the bachelor or master degree program attempted. Additional exam requirements/recommendations for international students: Required—TOEFL (minimum score 80 iBT), IELTS (minimum score 6). *Application deadline:* For fall admission, 6/1 for domestic and international students; for spring admission, 11/1 for domestic and international students; for summer admission, 4/15 for domestic and international students. Application fee: $60 ($100 for international students). Electronic applications accepted. *Expenses:* Expenses: Contact institution. *Financial support:* In 2014–15, 10 students received support, including 2 fellowships (averaging $6,000 per year), 16 research assistantships (averaging $11,600 per year); teaching assistantships, Federal Work-Study, and scholarships/grants also available. Support available to part-time students. Financial award application deadline: 3/1; financial award applicants required to submit FAFSA. *Total annual research expenditures:* $91,458. *Unit head:* Dr. Ramaswami Dandapani, Dean, 719-255-3543, Fax: 719-255-3542, E-mail: rdan@cas.uccs.edu. *Application contact:* Dawn House, Coordinator, 719-255-3246, E-mail: dhouse@uccs.edu.

University of Dayton, School of Business Administration, Dayton, OH 45469. Offers accounting (MBA); cyber security (MBA); finance (MBA); marketing (MBA); JD/MBA. *Accreditation:* AACSB. Part-time and evening/weekend programs available. *Faculty:* 22 full-time (6 women), 10 part-time/adjunct (2 women). *Students:* 108 full-time (46 women), 70 part-time (28 women); includes 15 minority (3 Black or African American, non-Hispanic/Latino; 5 Asian, non-Hispanic/Latino; 7 Hispanic/Latino), 50 international. Average age 29. 437 applicants, 44% accepted, 53 enrolled. In 2014, 142 master's awarded. *Entrance requirements:* For master's, GMAT or GRE. Additional exam requirements/recommendations for international students: Required—TOEFL (minimum score 550 paper-based; 80 iBT); Recommended—IELTS (minimum score 6.5). *Application deadline:* For fall admission, 5/1 priority date for international students; for winter admission, 7/1 for international students; for spring admission, 11/1 priority date for international students. Applications are processed on a rolling basis. Application fee: $0 ($50 for international students). Electronic applications accepted. *Expenses:* Expenses: Contact institution. *Financial support:* In 2014–15, 10 research assistantships with partial tuition reimbursements (averaging $8,053 per year) were awarded; institutionally sponsored loans, health care benefits, and unspecified assistantships also available. Financial award application deadline: 3/1; financial award applicants required to submit FAFSA. *Faculty research:* Management information systems, economics, finance, entrepreneurship, marketing, accounting and cyber security. *Unit head:* John M. Gentner, Director, MBA Program, 937-229-3733, Fax: 937-229-3882, E-mail: jgentner1@udayton.edu. *Application contact:* Mandy Schrank, Program Manager, MBA Program, 937-229-3733, Fax: 937-229-3882, E-mail: mschrank2@udayton.edu.
Website: https://www.udayton.edu/business/academics/master_of_business_administration/index.php.

University of Denver, University College, Denver, CO 80208. Offers geographic information systems (Certificate); global affairs (Certificate), including translation studies, world history and culture; information and communications technology (MCIS), including geographic information systems, information systems security, project management (MCIS, Certificate), software design and programming, technology management, telecommunications technology, Web design and development; leadership and organizations (Certificate), including human capital in organizations, philanthropic leadership, project management (MCIS, Certificate), strategic innovation and change; organizational and professional communication (MPS), including alternative dispute resolution, organizational communication, organizational development and training, public relations and marketing; security management (MAS, Certificate), including emergency planning and response, information security (MAS), organizational security. Part-time and evening/weekend programs available. Postbaccalaureate distance learning degree programs offered (no on-campus study). *Faculty:* 8 full-time (4 women), 133 part-time/adjunct (46 women). *Students:* 54 full-time (21 women), 1,327 part-time (775 women); includes 272 minority (106 Black or African American, non-Hispanic/Latino; 6 American Indian or Alaska Native, non-Hispanic/Latino; 26 Asian, non-Hispanic/Latino; 108 Hispanic/Latino; 1 Native Hawaiian or other Pacific Islander, non-Hispanic/Latino; 25 Two or more races, non-Hispanic/Latino), 116 international. Average age 35. 768 applicants, 95% accepted, 620 enrolled. In 2014, 391 master's, 196 other advanced degrees awarded. *Degree requirements:* For master's, capstone project. *Entrance requirements:* For master's, transcripts, two letters of recommendation, personal statement, resume. Additional exam requirements/recommendations for international students: Required—TOEFL (minimum score 550 paper-based; 80 iBT). *Application deadline:* For fall admission, 6/21 priority date for domestic students, 5/1 priority date for international students; for winter admission, 9/14 priority date for domestic students, 9/19 priority date for international students; for spring admission, 1/11 for domestic students, 12/12 for international students; for summer admission, 3/29 priority date for domestic students, 3/6 priority date for international students. Applications are processed on a rolling basis. Application fee: $75. Electronic applications accepted. *Expenses:* Expenses: $959 per credit hour. *Financial support:* In 2014–15, 19 students received support. Applicants required to submit FAFSA. *Unit head:* Dr. Michael McGuire, Interim Dean, 303-871-3518, E-mail: mmcguire@du.edu. *Application contact:* Information Contact, 303-871-2291, E-mail: ucoladm@du.edu. Website: http://www.universitycollege.du.edu/.

University of Houston, College of Technology, Department of Information and Logistics Technology, Houston, TX 77204. Offers information security (MS); supply chain and logistics technology (MS); technology project management (MS). Part-time programs available. *Degree requirements:* For master's, project or thesis (most programs). *Entrance requirements:* For master's, GMAT. Additional exam requirements/recommendations for international students: Required—TOEFL (minimum score 550 paper-based; 79 iBT). Electronic applications accepted.

University of Louisville, J. B. Speed School of Engineering, Department of Computer Engineering and Computer Science, Louisville, KY 40292-0001. Offers computer engineering and computer science (M Eng, MS); computer science and engineering (PhD); data mining (Certificate); network and information security (Certificate). *Accreditation:* ABET (one or more programs are accredited). Part-time programs available. Postbaccalaureate distance learning degree programs offered (no on-campus study). *Students:* 77 full-time (22 women), 68 part-time (14 women); includes 17 minority (8 Black or African American, non-Hispanic/Latino; 6 Asian, non-Hispanic/Latino; 2 Hispanic/Latino; 1 Two or more races, non-Hispanic/Latino), 51 international. Average age 29. 92 applicants, 54% accepted, 29 enrolled. In 2014, 8 master's, 3 doctorates, 6 other advanced degrees awarded. Terminal master's awarded for partial completion of doctoral program. *Degree requirements:* For master's, comprehensive exam (for some programs), thesis optional, minimum GPA of 3.0; for doctorate, comprehensive exam, thesis/dissertation, minimum GPA of 3.0. *Entrance requirements:* For master's and doctorate, GRE, letters of recommendation, final official transcripts; for Certificate, undergraduate degree. Additional exam requirements/recommendations for international students: Required—TOEFL (minimum score 80 iBT) or IELTS. *Application deadline:* For fall admission, 6/15 for domestic students, 5/1 priority date for international students; for spring admission, 11/22 for domestic students, 11/1 priority date for international students; for summer admission, 3/31 for domestic students, 4/1 priority date for international students. Application fee: $60. Electronic applications accepted. *Expenses:* Tuition, state resident: full-time $11,326; part-time $630 per credit hour. Tuition, nonresident: full-time $23,568; part-time $1311 per credit hour. *Required fees:* $196. Tuition and fees vary according to program and reciprocity agreements. *Financial support:* Fellowships with full tuition reimbursements, research assistantships with full tuition reimbursements, and teaching assistantships with full tuition reimbursements available. Financial award application deadline: 2/3. *Faculty research:* Software systems engineering, information security and forensics, multimedia and vision, mobile and distributed computing, intelligent systems. *Total annual research expenditures:* $1.3 million. *Unit head:* Dr. Adel S. Elmaghraby, Chair, 502-852-6304, Fax: 502-852-4713, E-mail: adel@louisville.edu. *Application contact:* Dr. Michael Harris, Director of Academic Programs, J. B. Speed School of Engineering, 502-852-6278, Fax: 502-852-6294, E-mail: mharris@louisville.edu.
Website: http://louisville.edu/speed/computer.

Computer and Information Systems Security

University of Maryland, Baltimore County, The Graduate School, College of Engineering and Information Technology, Department of Computer Science and Electrical Engineering, Program in Cybersecurity, Baltimore, MD 21250. Offers cybersecurity (MPS); cybersecurity strategy and policy (Postbaccalaureate Certificate). Part-time programs available. *Students:* 25 full-time (6 women), 134 part-time (33 women); includes 56 minority (27 Black or African American, non-Hispanic/Latino; 17 Asian, non-Hispanic/Latino; 8 Hispanic/Latino; 4 Two or more races, non-Hispanic/Latino), 5 international. Average age 38. 104 applicants, 73% accepted, 48 enrolled. In 2014, 36 master's, 31 other advanced degrees awarded. *Degree requirements:* For master's, comprehensive exam (for some programs). *Entrance requirements:* For master's, bachelor's degree in computer science, computer engineering, engineering, math, or information systems, or in other field with relevant work experience; curriculum vitae and two letters of recommendation (for international students). *Application deadline:* For fall admission, 8/1 for domestic and international students; for spring admission, 11/1 for international students. Applications are processed on a rolling basis. Application fee: $70. Electronic applications accepted. *Expenses:* Tuition, state resident: part-time $557. Tuition, nonresident: part-time $922. *Required fees:* $122 per semester. One-time fee: $200 part-time. *Financial support:* In 2014–15, 1 teaching assistantship was awarded; career-related internships or fieldwork, Federal Work-Study, scholarships/grants, health care benefits, and unspecified assistantships also available. Support available to part-time students. Financial award application deadline: 6/30; financial award applicants required to submit FAFSA. *Faculty research:* Cyber-security strategy and policy. *Unit head:* Dr. Gary Carter, Professor and Chair, 410-455-3500, E-mail: carter@cs.umbc.edu. *Application contact:* Dr. Richard Forno, Graduate Program Director, 410-455-5536, Fax: 410-455-3969, E-mail: richard.forno@umbc.edu. Website: http://www.umbc.edu/cyber/.

University of Maryland University College, The Graduate School, Program in Cybersecurity, Adelphi, MD 20783. Offers MS, Certificate. Part-time and evening/weekend programs available. Postbaccalaureate distance learning degree programs offered (no on-campus study). *Students:* 5 full-time (1 woman), 1,445 part-time (403 women); includes 743 minority (470 Black or African American, non-Hispanic/Latino; 6 American Indian or Alaska Native, non-Hispanic/Latino; 101 Asian, non-Hispanic/Latino; 118 Hispanic/Latino; 7 Native Hawaiian or other Pacific Islander, non-Hispanic/Latino; 41 Two or more races, non-Hispanic/Latino), 9 international. Average age 35. 573 applicants, 100% accepted, 382 enrolled. In 2014, 431 master's, 255 other advanced degrees awarded. *Degree requirements:* For master's, thesis or alternative, capstone course. *Application deadline:* Applications are processed on a rolling basis. Application fee: $50. Electronic applications accepted. *Financial support:* Federal Work-Study and scholarships/grants available. Support available to part-time students. Financial award application deadline: 6/1; financial award applicants required to submit FAFSA. *Unit head:* Dr. Emma Garrison-Alexander, Chair, 240-684-2400, Fax: 240-684-2401, E-mail: emma.garrison-alexander@umuc.edu. *Application contact:* Coordinator, Graduate Admissions, 800-888-8682, Fax: 240-684-2151, E-mail: newgrad@umuc.edu. Website: http://www.umuc.edu/academic-programs/masters-degrees/cybersecurity.cfm.

University of Maryland University College, The Graduate School, Program in Cybersecurity Policy, Adelphi, MD 20783. Offers MS, Certificate. Part-time and evening/weekend programs available. Postbaccalaureate distance learning degree programs offered (no on-campus study). *Students:* 1 full-time (0 women), 212 part-time (94 women); includes 111 minority (78 Black or African American, non-Hispanic/Latino; 1 American Indian or Alaska Native, non-Hispanic/Latino; 9 Asian, non-Hispanic/Latino; 12 Hispanic/Latino; 1 Native Hawaiian or other Pacific Islander, non-Hispanic/Latino; 10 Two or more races, non-Hispanic/Latino). Average age 37. 64 applicants, 100% accepted, 28 enrolled. In 2014, 81 master's awarded. *Degree requirements:* For master's, thesis or alternative, capstone course. *Application deadline:* Applications are processed on a rolling basis. Application fee: $50. Electronic applications accepted. *Financial support:* Federal Work-Study and scholarships/grants available. Support available to part-time students. Financial award application deadline: 6/1; financial award applicants required to submit FAFSA. *Unit head:* Dr. Bruce deGrazia, Program Chair, 240-684-2400, Fax: 240-684-2401, E-mail: bruce.degrazia@umuc.edu. *Application contact:* Coordinator, Graduate Admissions, 800-888-UMUC, Fax: 240-684-2151, E-mail: newgrad@umuc.edu. Website: http://www.umuc.edu/academic-programs/masters-degrees/cybersecurity-policy.cfm.

University of Maryland University College, The Graduate School, Program in Digital Forensics and Cyber Investigation, Adelphi, MD 20783. Offers MS, Postbaccalaureate Certificate. Part-time and evening/weekend programs available. Postbaccalaureate distance learning degree programs offered (no on-campus study). *Students:* 266 part-time (133 women); includes 128 minority (86 Black or African American, non-Hispanic/Latino; 2 American Indian or Alaska Native, non-Hispanic/Latino; 9 Asian, non-Hispanic/Latino; 14 Hispanic/Latino; 17 Two or more races, non-Hispanic/Latino), 2 international. Average age 34. 111 applicants, 100% accepted, 74 enrolled. In 2014, 15 master's, 7 other advanced degrees awarded. *Degree requirements:* For master's, thesis or alternative, capstone course. *Application deadline:* Applications are processed on a rolling basis. Application fee: $50. Electronic applications accepted. *Financial support:* Federal Work-Study and scholarships/grants available. Support available to part-time students. Financial award application deadline: 6/1; financial award applicants required to submit FAFSA. *Unit head:* Dr. Rosemary Shumba, Director, 240-684-2400, Fax: 240-684-2401, E-mail: rosemary.shumba@umuc.edu. *Application contact:* Coordinator, Graduate Admissions, 800-888-8682, Fax: 240-684-2151, E-mail: newgrad@umuc.edu. Website: http://www.umuc.edu/academic-programs/masters-degrees/digital-forensics-and-cyber-investigations.cfm.

University of Minnesota, Twin Cities Campus, College of Science and Engineering, Technological Leadership Institute, Program in Security Technologies, Minneapolis, MN 55455-0213. Offers MSST. Part-time programs available. *Degree requirements:* For master's, capstone project. *Entrance requirements:* Additional exam requirements/recommendations for international students: Required—TOEFL (minimum score 580 paper-based; 90 iBT). Electronic applications accepted.

University of Nebraska at Omaha, Graduate Studies, College of Information Science and Technology, Department of Information Systems and Quantitative Analysis, Omaha, NE 68182. Offers biomedical informatics (MS, PhD); information assurance (MS, Certificate); information technology (PhD); management information systems (MS); project management (Certificate); systems analysis and design (Certificate). Part-time and evening/weekend programs available. *Faculty:* 25 full-time (8 women). *Students:* 137 full-time (50 women), 125 part-time (31 women); includes 36 minority (14 Black or African American, non-Hispanic/Latino; 1 American Indian or Alaska Native, non-Hispanic/Latino; 15 Asian, non-Hispanic/Latino; 2 Hispanic/Latino; 4 Two or more races, non-Hispanic/Latino), 143 international. Average age 29. 404 applicants, 50% accepted, 101 enrolled. In 2014, 46 master's, 3 doctorates, 21 other advanced degrees awarded. *Degree requirements:* For master's, comprehensive exam, thesis (for some programs); for doctorate, comprehensive exam, thesis/dissertation. *Entrance requirements:* For master's, GRE General Test, minimum GPA of 3.0, 3 letters of recommendation, writing sample, resume, official transcripts; for doctorate, GMAT or GRE General Test,

minimum GPA of 3.0, 3 letters of recommendation, writing sample, resume, official transcripts; for Certificate, minimum GPA of 3.0, official transcripts. Additional exam requirements/recommendations for international students: Required—TOEFL, IELTS, PTE. *Application deadline:* For fall admission, 2/15 for domestic and international students; for spring admission, 9/15 for domestic and international students; for summer admission, 4/1 for domestic and international students. Applications are processed on a rolling basis. Application fee: $45. Electronic applications accepted. *Financial support:* In 2014–15, 35 students received support, including 28 research assistantships with tuition reimbursements available, 7 teaching assistantships with tuition reimbursements available; fellowships, career-related internships or fieldwork, Federal Work-Study, scholarships/grants, tuition waivers (partial), and unspecified assistantships also available. Financial award application deadline: 3/1; financial award applicants required to submit FAFSA. *Unit head:* Dr. Peter Wolcott, Chairperson, 402-554-2341, E-mail: graduate@unomaha.edu. *Application contact:* Dr. Leah Pietron, Graduate Program Chair, 402-554-2341, E-mail: graduate@unomaha.edu.

University of New Haven, Graduate School, Henry C. Lee College of Criminal Justice and Forensic Sciences, National Security Program, West Haven, CT 06516-1916. Offers information protection and security (MS, Certificate); national security (MS, Certificate); national security administration (Certificate). Part-time and evening/weekend programs available. *Degree requirements:* For master's, thesis or alternative, research project or internship. *Entrance requirements:* Additional exam requirements/recommendations for international students: Required—TOEFL (minimum score 70 iBT), IELTS, or PTE (minimum score of 53). Electronic applications accepted. Application fee is waived when completed online.

University of New Haven, Graduate School, Henry C. Lee College of Criminal Justice and Forensic Sciences, Program in Criminal Justice, West Haven, CT 06516-1916. Offers crime analysis (MS); criminal justice (MS, PhD); criminal justice management (MS, Certificate); forensic computer investigation (MS, Certificate); forensic psychology (MS); information protection and security (Certificate); victim advocacy and services management (Certificate); victimology (MS). Part-time and evening/weekend programs available. Postbaccalaureate distance learning degree programs offered (no on-campus study). *Degree requirements:* For master's, thesis or alternative. *Entrance requirements:* Additional exam requirements/recommendations for international students: Required—TOEFL (minimum score 80 iBT), IELTS, PTE (minimum score 53). Electronic applications accepted. Application fee is waived when completed online.

University of New Haven, Graduate School, Tagliatela College of Engineering, Program in Cyber Systems, West Haven, CT 06516-1916. Offers MS.

University of New Mexico, Robert O. Anderson Graduate School of Management, Department of Accounting, Albuquerque, NM 87131. Offers accounting (MBA); advanced accounting (M Acct); information assurance (M Acct); professional accounting (M Acct); tax accounting (M Acct); JD/M Acct. *Accreditation:* AACSB. Part-time and evening/weekend programs available. *Faculty:* 12 full-time (5 women), 1 (woman) part-time/adjunct. In 2014, 63 master's awarded. *Entrance requirements:* For master's, GMAT or GRE, minimum GPA of 3.0 on last 60 hours of coursework. Additional exam requirements/recommendations for international students: Required—TOEFL (minimum score 550 paper-based; 79 iBT). *Application deadline:* For fall admission, 4/1 priority date for domestic and international students; for spring admission, 10/1 priority date for domestic and international students. Applications are processed on a rolling basis. Application fee: $50. Electronic applications accepted. *Expenses:* Expenses: Contact institution. *Financial support:* Fellowships, research assistantships, career-related internships or fieldwork, Federal Work-Study, scholarships/grants, and unspecified assistantships available. Support available to part-time students. Financial award application deadline: 6/1; financial award applicants required to submit FAFSA. *Faculty research:* Critical accounting, accounting pedagogy, theory, taxation, information fraud. *Unit head:* Dr. Leslie Oakes, Chair, 505-277-6471, Fax: 505-277-7108, E-mail: loakes@unm.edu. *Application contact:* Tina Armijo, Office Administrator, 505-277-6471, Fax: 505-277-7108, E-mail: tmarmijo@unm.edu. Website: http://mba.mgt.unm.edu/default.asp.

University of New Mexico, Robert O. Anderson Graduate School of Management, Department of Marketing, Information and Decision Sciences, Albuquerque, NM 87131. Offers information assurance (MBA); information systems and assurance (MS); management information systems (MBA); marketing management (MBA); operations management (MBA). Part-time and evening/weekend programs available. *Faculty:* 14 full-time (2 women), 6 part-time/adjunct (2 women). In 2014, 106 master's awarded. *Entrance requirements:* For master's, GMAT or GRE, minimum GPA of 3.0 on last 60 hours of coursework. Additional exam requirements/recommendations for international students: Required—TOEFL (minimum score 550 paper-based; 79 iBT). *Application deadline:* For fall admission, 4/1 priority date for domestic and international students; for spring admission, 10/1 priority date for domestic and international students. Applications are processed on a rolling basis. Application fee: $50. Electronic applications accepted. *Expenses:* Expenses: Contact institution. *Financial support:* Fellowships, research assistantships, career-related internships or fieldwork, Federal Work-Study, scholarships/grants, and unspecified assistantships available. Support available to part-time students. Financial award application deadline: 6/1; financial award applicants required to submit FAFSA. *Faculty research:* Marketing, operations management, information systems, information assurance. *Unit head:* Dr. Steve Yourstone, Chair, 505-277-6471, Fax: 505-277-7108, E-mail: yourstone@unm.edu. *Application contact:* Tracy Wilkey, Manager, Academic Advisement, 505-277-3290, Fax: 505-277-8436, E-mail: andersonadvising@unm.edu. Website: http://mba.mgt.unm.edu/default.asp.

The University of North Carolina at Charlotte, College of Computing and Informatics, Department of Software and Information Systems, Charlotte, NC 28223-0001. Offers computing and information systems (PhD); information security/privacy (Graduate Certificate); information technology (MS, Graduate Certificate); management of information technology (Graduate Certificate). Part-time and evening/weekend programs available. *Faculty:* 17 full-time (5 women), 4 part-time/adjunct (0 women). *Students:* 223 full-time (80 women), 60 part-time (18 women); includes 17 minority (8 Black or African American, non-Hispanic/Latino; 5 Asian, non-Hispanic/Latino; 2 Hispanic/Latino; 2 Two or more races, non-Hispanic/Latino), 215 international. Average age 27. 457 applicants, 63% accepted, 135 enrolled. In 2014, 30 master's, 17 doctorates, 24 other advanced degrees awarded. Terminal master's awarded for partial completion of doctoral program. *Degree requirements:* For master's, thesis or alternative, practica; for doctorate, comprehensive exam, thesis/dissertation. *Entrance requirements:* For master's, GRE or GMAT, minimum undergraduate GPA of 2.8 overall, 2.0 in last 2 years; for doctorate, GRE or GMAT, working knowledge of 2 high-level programming languages, letters of recommendation. Additional exam requirements/recommendations for international students: Required—TOEFL (minimum score 557 paper-based; 83 iBT). *Application deadline:* For fall admission, 5/1 for domestic and international students; for spring admission, 10/1 for domestic and international students. Applications are processed on a rolling basis. Application fee: $75. Electronic applications accepted. *Expenses:* Tuition, state resident: full-time $4008. Tuition, nonresident: full-time $16,295. *Required fees:* $2755. Tuition and fees vary according to course load and program. *Financial support:* In 2014–15, 34 students received support,

including 1 fellowship (averaging $50,000 per year), 20 research assistantships (averaging $12,139 per year), 13 teaching assistantships (averaging $11,089 per year); career-related internships or fieldwork, institutionally sponsored loans, scholarships/grants, and unspecified assistantships also available. Support available to part-time students. Financial award application deadline: 4/1; financial award applicants required to submit FAFSA. *Faculty research:* Information security, information privacy, information assurance, cryptography, software engineering, enterprise integration, intelligent information systems, human-computer interaction. *Total annual research expenditures:* $2.5 million. *Unit head:* Dr. Mary Lou Maher, Chair, 704-687-1940, E-mail: mmaher9@uncc.edu. *Application contact:* Kathy B. Giddings, Director of Graduate Admissions, 704-687-5503, Fax: 704-687-1668, E-mail: gradadm@uncc.edu.
Website: http://sis.uncc.edu/.

University of Pittsburgh, School of Information Sciences, Information Science and Technology Program, Pittsburgh, PA 15260. Offers big data (Postbaccalaureate Certificate); information science (MSIS, PhD), including information science (PhD), telecommunications (PhD); information science and technology (Certificate); security assured information systems (Post-Master's Certificate). Part-time programs available. *Faculty:* 15 full-time (2 women), 11 part-time/adjunct (3 women). *Students:* 202 full-time (92 women), 62 part-time (19 women); includes 13 minority (2 Black or African American, non-Hispanic/Latino; 7 Asian, non-Hispanic/Latino; 3 Hispanic/Latino; 1 Two or more races, non-Hispanic/Latino), 200 international. 491 applicants, 77% accepted, 113 enrolled. In 2014, 87 master's, 9 doctorates awarded. *Degree requirements:* For master's, thesis optional; for doctorate, comprehensive exam, thesis/dissertation. *Entrance requirements:* For master's, GRE General Test, GMAT, bachelor's degree with minimum GPA of 3.0; course work in structured programming language, statistics, mathematics; for doctorate, GRE General Test, GMAT, master's degree; minimum QPA of 3.3; course work in statistics or mathematics, programming, cognitive psychology, systems analysis and design, data structures database management; for other advanced degree, master's degree in information science, telecommunications, or related field. Additional exam requirements/recommendations for international students: Required—TOEFL (minimum score 550 paper-based; 80 iBT). *Application deadline:* For fall admission, 7/15 priority date for domestic students, 1/15 priority date for international students; for winter admission, 11/1 priority date for domestic students, 6/15 priority date for international students; for spring admission, 11/1 priority date for domestic students, 6/15 priority date for international students; for summer admission, 3/15 priority date for domestic students, 12/15 priority date for international students. Applications are processed on a rolling basis. Application fee: $50. Electronic applications accepted. *Expenses:* Expenses: $21,810 in-state, $35,710 out-of-state; $889 per credit in-state, $1,470 out-of-state (for summer); mandatory fees: $900. *Financial support:* Fellowships with full and partial tuition reimbursements, research assistantships with full and partial tuition reimbursements, teaching assistantships with full and partial tuition reimbursements, career-related internships or fieldwork, scholarships/grants, traineeships, health care benefits, tuition waivers (full and partial), and unspecified assistantships available. Financial award application deadline: 1/15; financial award applicants required to submit FAFSA. *Faculty research:* Big data, systems analysis and design, geoinformatics, database and Web systems, information assurance and security. *Unit head:* Dr. Peter Brusilovsky, Program Chair, 412-624-9404, Fax: 421-624-5231, E-mail: peterb@sis.pitt.edu. *Application contact:* Shabana Reza, Enrollment Manager, 412-624-3988, Fax: 412-624-5231, E-mail: isinq@sis.pitt.edu.
Website: http://www.ischool.pitt.edu/ist/.

University of St. Thomas, Graduate Studies, Graduate Programs in Software, Saint Paul, MN 55105. Offers advanced studies in software engineering (Certificate); big data (Certificate); business analysis (Certificate); computer security (Certificate); information systems (Certificate); information technology (MS); software design and development (Certificate); software engineering (MS); software management (MS); software systems (MSS); MS/MBA. Part-time and evening/weekend programs available. *Degree requirements:* For master's, thesis optional. *Entrance requirements:* For master's, bachelor's degree earned in U.S. or equivalent international degree. Additional exam requirements/recommendations for international students: Required—TOEFL (minimum score 80 iBT). Electronic applications accepted. *Expenses:* Contact institution. *Faculty research:* Data mining, distributed databases, computer security, big data.

University of Southern California, Graduate School, Viterbi School of Engineering, Department of Computer Science, Los Angeles, CA 90089. Offers computer networks (MS); computer science (MS, PhD); computer security (MS); game development (MS); high performance computing and simulations (MS); human language technology (MS); intelligent robotics (MS); multimedia and creative technologies (MS); software engineering (MS). Part-time and evening/weekend programs available. Postbaccalaureate distance learning degree programs offered (no on-campus study). *Entrance requirements:* For master's and doctorate, GRE General Test. Additional exam requirements/recommendations for international students: Required—TOEFL. Electronic applications accepted. *Faculty research:* Databases, computer graphics and computer vision, software engineering, networks and security, robotics, multimedia and virtual reality.

The University of Texas at San Antonio, College of Business, Department of Information Systems and Cyber Security, San Antonio, TX 78249-0617. Offers cyber security (MSIT); information technology (MS, PhD), including cyber security (MS); management of technology (MBA). Part-time and evening/weekend programs available. *Faculty:* 9 full-time (2 women), 3 part-time/adjunct (0 women). *Students:* 33 full-time (8 women), 75 part-time (21 women); includes 26 minority (1 Black or African American, non-Hispanic/Latino; 1 American Indian or Alaska Native, non-Hispanic/Latino; 3 Asian, non-Hispanic/Latino; 18 Hispanic/Latino; 1 Native Hawaiian or other Pacific Islander, non-Hispanic/Latino; 2 Two or more races, non-Hispanic/Latino), 22 international. Average age 31. 107 applicants, 56% accepted, 33 enrolled. In 2014, 33 master's, 3 doctorates awarded. *Degree requirements:* For master's, comprehensive exam (for some programs), thesis optional; for doctorate, comprehensive exam, thesis/dissertation. *Entrance requirements:* For master's and doctorate, GMAT/GRE, TOEFL/IELTS, official transcripts, statement of purpose, letters of recommendation. Additional exam requirements/recommendations for international students: Required—TOEFL (minimum score 550 paper-based; 79 iBT), IELTS (minimum score 6.5). *Application deadline:* For fall admission, 7/1 for domestic students, 4/1 for international students; for spring admission, 11/1 for domestic students, 9/1 for international students. Applications are processed on a rolling basis. Application fee: $45 ($80 for international students). Electronic applications accepted. *Expenses:* Expenses: Contact institution. *Financial support:* In 2014–15, 15 students received support, including 1 fellowship with full tuition reimbursement available (averaging $25,000 per year), 10 research assistantships with full and partial tuition reimbursements available (averaging $9,000 per year), 12 teaching assistantships with full and partial tuition reimbursements available (averaging $9,000 per year); scholarships/grants, health care benefits, and unspecified assistantships also available. Support available to part-time students. Financial award application deadline: 2/15. *Faculty research:* Cyber security, digital forensics, economics of information systems, information systems privacy, information technology adoption. *Total annual research expenditures:* $1.5 million. *Unit head:* Dr. Yoris A. Au, Chair/Associate Professor, 210-458-6337, Fax: 210-458-6305, E-mail: yoris.au@utsa.edu. *Application contact:* Graduate Advisor of Record.
Website: http://business.utsa.edu/directory/index.aspx?DepID=16.

University of Utah, Graduate School, David Eccles School of Business, Department of Operations and Information Systems, Salt Lake City, UT 84112. Offers information systems (MS, Graduate Certificate), including business intelligence and analytics, IT security, product and process management, software and systems architecture. Part-time and evening/weekend programs available. *Faculty:* 11 full-time (4 women), 6 part-time/adjunct (0 women). *Students:* 77 full-time (18 women), 63 part-time (7 women); includes 19 minority (2 Black or African American, non-Hispanic/Latino; 5 Asian, non-Hispanic/Latino; 10 Hispanic/Latino; 2 Two or more races, non-Hispanic/Latino), 27 international. Average age 31. 148 applicants, 72% accepted, 71 enrolled. In 2014, 63 master's awarded. *Degree requirements:* For master's, capstone project. *Entrance requirements:* For master's, GMAT/GRE, minimum undergraduate GPA of 3.0. Additional exam requirements/recommendations for international students: Required—TOEFL (minimum score 550 paper-based; 80 iBT), IELTS (minimum score 6.5). *Application deadline:* For fall admission, 7/28 for domestic students, 3/1 for international students; for spring admission, 12/7 for domestic students, 8/16 for international students. Applications are processed on a rolling basis. Application fee: $55 ($65 for international students). Electronic applications accepted. *Expenses:* Expenses: Contact institution. *Financial support:* In 2014–15, 5 students received support, including 3 fellowships with partial tuition reimbursements available (averaging $5,160 per year), 2 teaching assistantships with partial tuition reimbursements available (averaging $5,160 per year); tuition waivers (partial) and unspecified assistantships also available. Financial award application deadline: 4/14; financial award applicants required to submit FAFSA. *Faculty research:* Business intelligence and analytics, software and system architecture, product and process management, IT security, Web and data mining, applications and management of IT in healthcare. *Unit head:* Bradden Blair, Director of the MSIS Program, 801-587-9489, Fax: 801-581-3666, E-mail: b.blair@business.utah.edu. *Application contact:* Andrea Miller, Director of Admissions, 801-585-7366, Fax: 801-581-3666, E-mail: andrea.miller@business.utah.edu.
Website: http://msis.business.utah.edu.

University of Wisconsin–Madison, Graduate School, Wisconsin School of Business, Wisconsin Full-Time MBA Program, Madison, WI 53706. Offers applied security analysis (MBA); arts administration (MBA); brand and product management (MBA); corporate finance and investment banking (MBA); marketing research (MBA); operations and technology management (MBA); real estate (MBA); risk management and insurance (MBA); strategic human resource management (MBA); supply chain management (MBA). *Faculty:* 55 full-time (9 women), 13 part-time/adjunct (4 women). *Students:* 199 full-time (72 women); includes 30 minority (11 Black or African American, non-Hispanic/Latino; 1 American Indian or Alaska Native, non-Hispanic/Latino; 3 Asian, non-Hispanic/Latino; 12 Hispanic/Latino; 3 Two or more races, non-Hispanic/Latino), 39 international. Average age 28. 473 applicants, 29% accepted, 100 enrolled. In 2014, 92 master's awarded. *Entrance requirements:* For master's, GMAT or GRE, bachelor's or equivalent degree, 2 years of work experience, essay, one letter of recommendation, resume. Additional exam requirements/recommendations for international students: Required—TOEFL (minimum score 100 iBT), IELTS (minimum score 7.5). *Application deadline:* For fall admission, 11/4 for domestic and international students; for winter admission, 2/3 for domestic and international students; for spring admission, 4/28 for domestic students, 4/2 for international students. Applications are processed on a rolling basis. Application fee: $56. Electronic applications accepted. *Expenses:* Expenses: Contact institution. *Financial support:* In 2014–15, 157 students received support, including 10 fellowships with full tuition reimbursements available (averaging $37,956 per year), 82 research assistantships with full tuition reimbursements available (averaging $28,175 per year), 50 teaching assistantships with full tuition reimbursements available (averaging $28,175 per year); scholarships/grants, health care benefits, and unspecified assistantships also available. Financial award application deadline: 4/28; financial award applicants required to submit FAFSA. *Faculty research:* Market consequences of International Financial Reporting Standards (IFRS), inter-firm relationships and strategic partnerships, application of Bayesian statistical methods and applied probability models to understanding individuals' behaviors in the context of customer relationship management (CRM) applications, liquidity provision and the structure of financial markets, strategic management of global startups. *Unit head:* Prof. Ella Mae Matsumura, Associate Dean Full-time MBA Program, 608-262-9731, E-mail: ematsumura@bus.wisc.edu. *Application contact:* Betsy Kacizak, Director of Admissions and Recruiting, Full-time MBA Program, 608-262-4000, E-mail: mlewitzke@bus.wisc.edu.
Website: http://www.bus.wisc.edu/mba.

Utica College, Program in Cybersecurity, Utica, NY 13502-4892. Offers MS. Part-time and evening/weekend programs available. Postbaccalaureate distance learning degree programs offered. *Faculty:* 5 full-time (0 women), 8 part-time/adjunct (0 women). *Students:* 2 full-time (0 women), 285 part-time (85 women); includes 74 minority (29 Black or African American, non-Hispanic/Latino; 6 American Indian or Alaska Native, non-Hispanic/Latino; 14 Asian, non-Hispanic/Latino; 21 Hispanic/Latino; 4 Two or more races, non-Hispanic/Latino). Average age 35. 194 applicants, 97% accepted, 153 enrolled. In 2014, 70 master's awarded. *Entrance requirements:* For master's, BS, minimum GPA of 3.0. Additional exam requirements/recommendations for international students: Recommended—TOEFL (minimum score 525 paper-based). *Application deadline:* Applications are processed on a rolling basis. Electronic applications accepted. *Expenses: Tuition:* Full-time $33,216; part-time $706 per credit hour. *Required fees:* $520; $50 per course. Tuition and fees vary according to course load, degree level, campus/location and program. *Financial support:* Application deadline: 3/15; applicants required to submit FAFSA. *Faculty research:* Steganography and data hiding, cryptography. *Unit head:* Joseph Giordano, Chair, 315-792-2521. *Application contact:* John D. Rowe, Director of Graduate Admissions, 315-792-3824, Fax: 315-792-3003, E-mail: jrowe@utica.edu.
Website: http://www.onlineuticacollege.com/programs/masters-cybersecurity.asp.

Valparaiso University, Graduate School, Program in Cyber Security, Valparaiso, IN 46383. Offers MS. Part-time and evening/weekend programs available. *Students:* 1 full-time (0 women), 3 part-time (0 women), all international. Average age 25. *Degree requirements:* For master's, internship or research project. *Entrance requirements:* Additional exam requirements/recommendations for international students: Required—TOEFL (minimum score 550 paper-based; 80 iBT), IELTS (minimum score 6). *Application deadline:* Applications are processed on a rolling basis. Application fee: $30 ($50 for international students). Electronic applications accepted. *Expenses: Tuition:* Full-time $10,710; part-time $595 per credit hour. *Required fees:* $378; $101 per term. Tuition and fees vary according to course load and program. *Financial support:* Available to part-time students. Applicants required to submit FAFSA. *Unit head:* Dr. Jennifer A. Ziegler, Dean, Graduate School and Continuing Education, 219-464-5313, Fax: 219-464-5381, E-mail: jennifer.ziegler@valpo.edu. *Application contact:* Jessica Choquette, Graduate Admissions Specialist, 219-464-5313, Fax: 219-464-5381, E-mail: jessica.choquette@valpo.edu.
Website: http://www.valpo.edu/grad/it/cybersecurity1.php.

Virginia Polytechnic Institute and State University, VT Online, Blacksburg, VA 24061. Offers advanced transportation systems (Certificate); aerospace engineering (MS); agricultural and life sciences (MSLFS); business information systems (Graduate Certificate); career and technical education (MS); civil engineering (MS); computer engineering (M Eng, MS); decision support systems (Graduate Certificate); eLearning leadership (MA); electrical engineering (M Eng, MS); engineering administration (MEA); environmental engineering (Certificate); environmental politics and policy (Graduate Certificate); environmental sciences and engineering (MS); foundations of political analysis (Graduate Certificate); health product risk management (Graduate Certificate); industrial and systems engineering (MS); information policy and society (Graduate Certificate); information security (Graduate Certificate); information technology (MIT); instructional technology (MA); integrative STEM education (MA Ed); liberal arts (Graduate Certificate); life sciences: health product risk management (MS); natural resources (MNR, Graduate Certificate); networking (Graduate Certificate); nonprofit and nongovernmental organization management (Graduate Certificate); ocean engineering (MS); political science (MA); security studies (Graduate Certificate); software development (Graduate Certificate). *Expenses:* Tuition, state resident: full-time $11,656; part-time $647.50 per credit hour. Tuition, nonresident: full-time $23,351; part-time $1297.25 per credit hour. *Required fees:* $2533; $465.75 per semester. Tuition and fees vary according to course load, campus/location and program.

Walden University, Graduate Programs, School of Information Systems and Technology, Minneapolis, MN 55401. Offers information systems (Graduate Certificate); information systems management (MISM); information technology (MS, DIT), including health informatics (MS), information assurance and cyber security (MS), information systems (MS), software engineering (MS). Part-time and evening/weekend programs available. Postbaccalaureate distance learning degree programs offered (no on-campus study). *Faculty:* 4 full-time (1 woman), 31 part-time/adjunct (9 women). *Students:* 329 full-time (107 women), 199 part-time (70 women); includes 262 minority (202 Black or African American, non-Hispanic/Latino; 16 Asian, non-Hispanic/Latino; 27 Hispanic/Latino; 17 Two or more races, non-Hispanic/Latino), 13 international. Average age 38. 314 applicants, 99% accepted, 290 enrolled. In 2014, 62 master's, 18 other advanced degrees awarded. *Degree requirements:* For doctorate, thesis/dissertation (for some programs), residency. *Entrance requirements:* For master's, bachelor's degree or higher; minimum GPA of 2.5; official transcripts; goal statement (for some programs); access to computer and Internet; for doctorate, master's degree or higher; three years of related professional or academic experience (preferred); minimum GPA of 3.0; goal statement and current resume (for select programs); official transcripts; access to computer and Internet; for Graduate Certificate, relevant work experience; access to computer and Internet. Additional exam requirements/recommendations for international students: Required—TOEFL (minimum score 550 paper-based, 79 iBT), IELTS (minimum score 6.5), Michigan English Language Assessment Battery (minimum score 82), or PTE (minimum score 53). *Application deadline:* Applications are processed on a rolling basis. Application fee: $0. Electronic applications accepted. *Expenses: Tuition:* Full-time $11,925; part-time $500 per credit hour. *Required fees:* $647. *Financial support:* Fellowships, Federal Work-Study, scholarships/grants, unspecified assistantships, and family tuition reduction, active duty/veteran tuition reduction, group tuition reduction, interest-free payment plans, employee tuition reduction available. Support available to part-time students. Financial award applicants required to submit FAFSA. *Unit head:* Dr. Karlyn A. Barilovits, Associate Dean, 866-492-5336. *Application contact:* Meghan Thomas, Vice President of Enrollment Management, 866-492-5336, E-mail: info@waldenu.edu.
Website: http://www.waldenu.edu/programs/colleges-schools/information-systems-and-technology.

West Chester University of Pennsylvania, College of Arts and Sciences, Department of Computer Science, West Chester, PA 19383. Offers computer science (MS); computer security (Certificate); information systems (Certificate); Web technology (Certificate). Part-time and evening/weekend programs available. *Faculty:* 8 full-time (2 women). *Students:* 13 full-time (5 women), 34 part-time (5 women); includes 6 minority (3 Black or African American, non-Hispanic/Latino; 3 Asian, non-Hispanic/Latino), 13 international. Average age 30. 19 applicants, 89% accepted, 12 enrolled. In 2014, 6 master's awarded. *Degree requirements:* For master's, thesis optional, 33 credits; for Certificate, 18 credits. *Entrance requirements:* For master's, GRE, two letters of recommendation; for Certificate, BS. Additional exam requirements/recommendations for international students: Required—TOEFL (minimum score 550 paper-based; 80 iBT). *Application deadline:* For fall admission, 4/15 priority date for domestic students, 3/15 for international students; for spring admission, 10/15 priority date for domestic students, 9/1 for international students. Applications are processed on a rolling basis. Application fee: $45. Electronic applications accepted. *Expenses:* Tuition, state resident: full-time $8172; part-time $454 per credit. Tuition, nonresident: full-time $12,258; part-time $681 per credit. *Required fees:* $2231; $110.78 per credit. Tuition and fees vary according to campus/location and program. *Financial support:* Unspecified assistantships available. Support available to part-time students. Financial award application deadline: 2/15; financial award applicants required to submit FAFSA. *Faculty research:* Security in sensor and mobile ad-hoc networks, intrusion detection, security and trust in pervasive computing, cloud, computing, wireless sensor networks. *Unit head:* Dr. James Fabrey, Chair, 610-436-2204, E-mail: jfabrey@wcupa.edu. *Application contact:* Dr. Afrand Agah, Graduate Coordinator, 610-430-4419, E-mail: aagah@wcupa.edu.
Website: http://www.cs.wcupa.edu/.

Western Governors University, College of Information Technology, Salt Lake City, UT 84107. Offers information security and assurance (MS); information technology (MS). Postbaccalaureate distance learning degree programs offered. *Degree requirements:* For master's, capstone project.

Wilmington University, College of Technology, New Castle, DE 19720-6491. Offers geographic information systems (MS); information assurance (MS); information systems technologies (MS); Internet/Web design (MS); management and management information systems (MS). Part-time and evening/weekend programs available. *Faculty:* 5 full-time (2 women), 53 part-time/adjunct (14 women). *Students:* 674 full-time (197 women), 131 part-time (55 women); includes 48 minority (35 Black or African American, non-Hispanic/Latino; 3 American Indian or Alaska Native, non-Hispanic/Latino; 6 Asian, non-Hispanic/Latino; 4 Hispanic/Latino), 708 international. Average age 27. 679 applicants, 100% accepted, 423 enrolled. In 2014, 102 master's awarded. *Entrance requirements:* Additional exam requirements/recommendations for international students: Required—TOEFL (minimum score 500 paper-based). *Application deadline:* Applications are processed on a rolling basis. Application fee: $35. Electronic applications accepted. *Unit head:* Dr. Edward L. Guthrie, Dean, 302-356-6870. *Application contact:* Laura Morris, Director of Admissions, 877-967-5464, E-mail: infocenter@wilmu.edu.
Website: http://www.wilmu.edu/technology/.

Computer Science

Acadia University, Faculty of Pure and Applied Science, Jodrey School of Computer Science, Wolfville, NS B4P 2R6, Canada. Offers M Sc. *Degree requirements:* For master's, thesis. *Entrance requirements:* For master's, honors degree in computer science. Additional exam requirements/recommendations for international students: Required—TOEFL (minimum score 580 paper-based; 93 iBT), IELTS (minimum score 6.5). *Faculty research:* Visual and object-oriented programming, concurrency, artificial intelligence, hypertext and multimedia, algorithm analysis, xml.

Air Force Institute of Technology, Graduate School of Engineering and Management, Department of Electrical and Computer Engineering, Dayton, OH 45433-7765. Offers computer engineering (MS, PhD); computer systems/science (MS); electrical engineering (MS, PhD); electro-optics (MS, PhD). *Accreditation:* ABET (one or more programs are accredited). Part-time programs available. *Degree requirements:* For master's, thesis; for doctorate, thesis/dissertation. *Entrance requirements:* For master's and doctorate, GRE General Test, minimum GPA of 3.0, U.S. citizenship. *Faculty research:* Remote sensing, information survivability, microelectronics, computer networks, artificial intelligence.

Alabama Agricultural and Mechanical University, School of Graduate Studies, School of Engineering and Technology, Department of Computer Science, Huntsville, AL 35811. Offers MS. Evening/weekend programs available. *Degree requirements:* For master's, comprehensive exam, thesis optional. *Entrance requirements:* For master's, GRE General Test. Additional exam requirements/recommendations for international students: Required—TOEFL (minimum score 500 paper-based; 61 iBT). Electronic applications accepted. *Faculty research:* Computer-assisted instruction, database management, software engineering, operating systems, neural networks.

Alcorn State University, School of Graduate Studies, School of Arts and Sciences, Department of Mathematical Sciences, Lorman, MS 39096-7500. Offers computer and information sciences (MS).

American Sentinel University, Graduate Programs, Aurora, CO 80014. Offers business administration (MBA); business intelligence (MS); computer science (MSCS); health information management (MS); healthcare (MBA); information systems (MSIS); nursing (MSN). Part-time and evening/weekend programs available. Postbaccalaureate distance learning degree programs offered (no on-campus study). *Entrance requirements:* Additional exam requirements/recommendations for international students: Required—TOEFL (minimum score 600 paper-based). Electronic applications accepted.

The American University in Cairo, School of Sciences and Engineering, Department of Computer Science and Engineering, Cairo, Egypt. Offers computer science (Graduate Diploma); computing (M Comp). *Degree requirements:* For master's, thesis. *Entrance requirements:* Additional exam requirements/recommendations for international students: Required—English entrance exam and/or TOEFL. Tuition and fees vary according to course load and program. *Faculty research:* Software engineering, artificial intelligence, robotics, data and knowledge bases.

American University of Armenia, Graduate Programs, Yerevan, Armenia. Offers business administration (MBA); computer and information science (MS), including business management, design and manufacturing, energy (ME, MS), industrial engineering and systems management; economics (MS); industrial engineering and systems management (ME), including business, computer aided design/manufacturing, energy (ME, MS), information technology; law (LL M); political science and international affairs (MPSIA); public health (MPH); teaching English as a foreign language (MA). Part-time and evening/weekend programs available. *Degree requirements:* For master's, thesis (for some programs), capstone/project. *Entrance requirements:* For master's, GRE, GMAT, or LSAT. Additional exam requirements/recommendations for international students: Recommended—TOEFL (minimum score 79 iBT), IELTS (minimum score 6.5). *Faculty research:* Microfinance, finance (rural/development, international, corporate), firm life cycle theory, TESOL, language proficiency testing, public policy, administrative law, economic development, cryptography, artificial intelligence, energy efficiency/renewable energy, computer-aided design/manufacturing, health financing, tuberculosis control, mother/child health, preventive ophthalmology, post-earthquake psychopathological investigations, tobacco control, environmental health risk assessments.

American University of Beirut, Graduate Programs, Faculty of Arts and Sciences, Beirut, Lebanon. Offers anthropology (MA); Arab and Middle Eastern history (PhD); Arabic language and literature (MA, PhD); archaeology (MA); biology (MS); cell and molecular biology (PhD); chemistry (MS); clinical psychology (MA); computational sciences (MS); computer science (MS); economics (MA); English language (MA); English literature (MA); environmental policy planning (MS); financial economics (MAFE); geology (MS); history (MA); mathematics (MA, MS); media studies (MA); Middle Eastern studies (MA); physics (MS); political studies (MA); psychology (MA); public administration (MA); sociology (MA); statistics (MA, MS); theoretical physics (PhD); transnational American studies (MA). Part-time programs available. *Faculty:* 107 full-time (32 women), 6 part-time/adjunct (2 women). *Students:* 230 full-time (161 women), 209 part-time (146 women). Average age 26. 261 applicants, 70% accepted, 83 enrolled. In 2014, 68 master's, 2 doctorates awarded. *Degree requirements:* For master's, one foreign language, comprehensive exam, thesis (for some programs); for doctorate, one foreign language, comprehensive exam, thesis/dissertation. *Entrance requirements:* For master's, GRE (for some MA/MS programs), letter of recommendation; for doctorate, GRE, letters of recommendation. Additional exam requirements/recommendations for international students: Required—TOEFL (minimum score 600 paper-based; 97 iBT), IELTS (minimum score 7). *Application deadline:* For fall admission, 4/1 for domestic and international students; for spring admission, 11/1 for domestic and international students. Application fee: $50. Electronic applications accepted. *Expenses: Tuition:* Full-time $15,462; part-time $859 per credit. *Required fees:* $692. Tuition and fees vary according to course load and program. *Financial support:* Research assistantships, career-related internships or fieldwork, institutionally sponsored loans, scholarships/grants, health care benefits, and unspecified assistantships available. Financial award application deadline: 2/4; financial award applicants required to submit FAFSA. *Faculty research:* Determinants of language proficiency among Arab learners of English as a foreign language; opinion mining, information retrieval, runtime verification, high performance computing; solar and fuel cells, self-organizing systems, heterocyclic chemistry, air and water chemistry; complex analysis, harmonic analysis, number theory; social and political psychology, clinical psychology; thin films physics and technology; theory of soft matter; religious and ethnic conflict; sports and politics. *Total annual research expenditures:* $966,000. *Unit head:* Dr. Patrick McGreevy, Dean, 961-1374374 Ext. 3800, Fax: 961-1744461, E-mail: pm07@aub.edu.lb. *Application contact:* Dr. Salim Kanaan, Director, Admissions Office, 961-1350000 Ext. 2590, Fax: 961-1750775, E-mail: sk00@aub.edu.lb. Website: http://www.aub.edu.lb/fas/.

Appalachian State University, Cratis D. Williams Graduate School, Department of Computer Science, Boone, NC 28608. Offers MS. Part-time programs available. *Degree requirements:* For master's, comprehensive exam, thesis. *Entrance requirements:* For master's, GRE General Test, 3 letters of recommendation. Additional exam requirements/recommendations for international students: Required—TOEFL (minimum score 570 paper-based; 79 iBT), IELTS (minimum score 6.5). Electronic applications accepted. *Faculty research:* Graph theory, compilers, parallel architecture, image processing.

Arizona State University at the Tempe campus, Ira A. Fulton Schools of Engineering, The Polytechnic School, Department of Engineering, Mesa, AZ 85212. Offers simulation, modeling, and applied cognitive science (PhD). Part-time programs available. *Degree requirements:* For doctorate, comprehensive exam, thesis/dissertation, interactive Program of Study (iPOS) submitted before completing 50 percent of required credit hours. *Entrance requirements:* For doctorate, GRE, master's degree in psychology, engineering, cognitive science, or computer science; 3 letters of recommendation; statement of research interests. Additional exam requirements/recommendations for international students: Required—TOEFL, IELTS, or PTE. Electronic applications accepted. *Faculty research:* Software process and automated workflow, software architecture, dotal technologies, relational database systems, embedded systems.

Arizona State University at the Tempe campus, Ira A. Fulton Schools of Engineering, School of Computing, Informatics, and Decision Systems Engineering, Tempe, AZ 85287-8809. Offers computer engineering (MS, PhD); computer science (MCS, MS, PhD); industrial engineering (MS, PhD); software engineering (MS). Part-time and evening/weekend programs available. Postbaccalaureate distance learning degree programs offered (minimal on-campus study). Terminal master's awarded for partial completion of doctoral program. *Degree requirements:* For master's, comprehensive exam (for some programs), portfolio (MCS); interactive Program of Study (iPOS) submitted before completing 50 percent of required credit hours; for doctorate, comprehensive exam, thesis/dissertation, interactive Program of Study (iPOS) submitted before completing 50 percent of required credit hours. *Entrance requirements:* For master's, GRE, minimum GPA of 3.0 or equivalent in last 2 years of work leading to bachelor's degree; for doctorate, GRE, minimum GPA of 3.0 in last 2 years of work leading to bachelor's degree. Additional exam requirements/recommendations for international students: Required—TOEFL, IELTS, or PTE. Electronic applications accepted. *Expenses:* Contact institution. *Faculty research:* Artificial intelligence, cyberphysical and embedded systems, health informatics, information assurance and security, information management/multimedia/visualization, network science, personalized learning/educational games, production logistics, software and systems engineering, statistical modeling and data mining.

Arkansas State University, Graduate School, College of Sciences and Mathematics, Department of Computer Science, State University, AR 72467. Offers MS. Part-time programs available. *Faculty:* 5 full-time (1 woman). *Students:* 45 full-time (13 women), 6 part-time (2 women), 46 international. Average age 24. 312 applicants, 49% accepted, 35 enrolled. In 2014, 14 master's awarded. *Degree requirements:* For master's, comprehensive exam, thesis or alternative. *Entrance requirements:* For master's, GRE General Test or MAT, appropriate bachelor's degree, official transcripts, immunization records. Additional exam requirements/recommendations for international students: Required—TOEFL (minimum score 550 paper-based; 79 iBT), IELTS (minimum score 6), PTE (minimum score 56). *Application deadline:* For fall admission, 7/1 for domestic and international students; for spring admission, 11/15 for domestic students, 11/14 for international students. Applications are processed on a rolling basis. Application fee: $30 ($40 for international students). Electronic applications accepted. *Expenses:* Tuition, state resident: full-time $4392; part-time $244 per credit hour. Tuition, nonresident: full-time $8784; part-time $488 per credit hour. *International tuition:* $9484 full-time. *Required fees:* $1134; $63 per credit hour. $25 per term. Tuition and fees vary according to course load and program. *Financial support:* In 2014–15, 14 students received support. Career-related internships or fieldwork, scholarships/grants, and unspecified assistantships available. Financial award application deadline: 7/1; financial award applicants required to submit FAFSA. *Unit head:* Dr. Debra Ingram, Chair, 870-972-3978, Fax: 870-972-3950, E-mail: dingram@astate.edu. *Application contact:* Vickey Ring, Graduate Admissions Coordinator, 870-972-3029, Fax: 870-972-3857, E-mail: vickeyring@astate.edu.
Website: http://www.astate.edu/college/sciences-and-mathematics/departments/computer-science/.

Armstrong State University, School of Graduate Studies, Program in Computer Science, Savannah, GA 31419-1997. Offers MSCIS. Part-time programs available. *Faculty:* 3 full-time (0 women). *Students:* 1 (woman) full-time, 1 (woman) part-time; includes 1 minority (Black or African American, non-Hispanic/Latino), 1 international. Average age 28. 4 applicants, 25% accepted. *Degree requirements:* For master's, project. *Entrance requirements:* For master's, GRE (minimum scores: verbal 156, quantitative 144, and writing 4), minimum GPA of 2.7, letters of recommendation, BS in computer science or related field. Additional exam requirements/recommendations for international students: Required—TOEFL (minimum score 523 paper-based). *Application deadline:* For fall admission, 6/30 priority date for domestic students, 5/1 priority date for international students; for spring admission, 11/15 priority date for domestic students, 9/15 priority date for international students; for summer admission, 4/15 priority date for domestic students, 9/15 for international students. Applications are processed on a rolling basis. Application fee: $30. Electronic applications accepted. *Expenses:* Tuition, state resident: part-time $206 per credit hour. Tuition, nonresident: part-time $763 per credit hour. *Required fees:* $612 per semester. Tuition and fees vary according to course load, campus/location and program. *Financial support:* In 2014–15, research assistantships with full tuition reimbursements (averaging $5,000 per year) were awarded; career-related internships or fieldwork, Federal Work-Study, scholarships/grants, and unspecified assistantships also available. Support available to part-time students. Financial award application deadline: 3/15; financial award applicants required to submit FAFSA. *Faculty research:* Bioinformatics, data mining, graph theory, image processing, machine learning. *Unit head:* Dr. Hong Zhang, Department Head, 912-344-3151, E-mail: hong.zhang@armstrong.edu. *Application contact:* Kathy Ingram, Associate Director of Graduate/Adult and Nontraditional Students, 912-344-2503, Fax: 912-344-3417, E-mail: graduate@armstrong.edu.
Website: http://www.armstrong.edu/Science_and_Technology/deans_office/computer_science1.

Auburn University, Graduate School, Ginn College of Engineering, Department of Computer Science and Software Engineering, Auburn University, AL 36849. Offers MS, MSWE, PhD. Part-time programs available. *Faculty:* 18 full-time (3 women). *Students:* 70 full-time (17 women), 54 part-time (13 women); includes 15 minority (10 Black or African American, non-Hispanic/Latino; 5 Asian, non-Hispanic/Latino), 50 international. Average age 30. 198 applicants, 34% accepted, 21 enrolled. In 2014, 26 master's, 9 doctorates awarded. *Degree requirements:* For master's, thesis (for some programs); for doctorate, thesis/dissertation. *Entrance requirements:* For master's and doctorate, GRE General Test, GRE Subject Test. *Application deadline:* For fall admission, 7/7 for domestic students; for spring admission, 11/24 for domestic students. Applications are processed on a rolling basis. Application fee: $50 ($60 for international students). Electronic applications accepted. *Expenses:* Tuition, state resident: full-time $8586; part-time $477 per credit hour. Tuition, nonresident: full-time $25,758; part-time $1431 per credit hour. *Required fees:* $804 per semester. Tuition and fees vary according to degree level and program. *Financial support:* Research assistantships, teaching assistantships, and Federal Work-Study available. Support available to part-time students. Financial award application deadline: 3/15; financial award applicants required to submit FAFSA. *Faculty research:* Parallelizable, scalable software translations; graphical representations of algorithms, structures, and processes; graph drawing. *Total annual research expenditures:* $400,000. *Unit head:* Dr. Kai Chang, Chair, 334-844-6310. *Application contact:* Dr. George Flowers, Dean of the Graduate School, 334-844-2125.
Website: http://www.eng.auburn.edu/department/cse/.

Ball State University, Graduate School, College of Sciences and Humanities, Department of Computer Science, Muncie, IN 47306-1099. Offers MA, MS. *Faculty:* 3 full-time (0 women). *Students:* 31 full-time (5 women), 6 part-time (0 women); includes 3 minority (2 Black or African American, non-Hispanic/Latino; 1 Hispanic/Latino), 29 international. Average age 26. 4,928 applicants, 1% accepted, 16 enrolled. In 2014, 18 master's awarded. *Entrance requirements:* For master's, GRE General Test. Application fee: $50. *Financial support:* In 2014–15, 12 students received support, including 2 research assistantships with partial tuition reimbursements available (averaging $10,268 per year), 7 teaching assistantships with partial tuition reimbursements available (averaging $12,929 per year); unspecified assistantships also available. Financial award application deadline: 3/1. *Faculty research:* Numerical methods, programmer productivity, graphics. *Unit head:* Dr. Paul Buis, Chairperson, 765-285-8641, Fax: 765-285-2614, E-mail: 00pebuis@bsu.edu. *Application contact:* Dr. J. Michael McGrew, Graduate Program Director, 765-285-3469, Fax: 765-285-2614, E-mail: mmcgrew@bsu.edu.
Website: http://www.cs.bsu.edu/.

Baylor University, Graduate School, School of Engineering and Computer Science, Department of Computer Science, Waco, TX 76798. Offers MS. Part-time programs available. *Degree requirements:* For master's, thesis (for some programs). *Entrance requirements:* For master's, GRE, course training in computer science equivalent to BS in computer science from Baylor University. Additional exam requirements/recommendations for international students: Required—TOEFL (minimum score 550 paper-based; 90 iBT). Electronic applications accepted. *Faculty research:* Bioinformatics, databases, machine learning, software engineering, networking.

Binghamton University, State University of New York, Graduate School, Thomas J. Watson School of Engineering and Applied Science, Department of Computer Science, Vestal, NY 13850. Offers MS, PhD. Part-time programs available. *Faculty:* 23 full-time (3 women), 11 part-time/adjunct (4 women). *Students:* 273 full-time (66 women), 84 part-time (10 women); includes 10 minority (3 Asian, non-Hispanic/Latino; 4 Hispanic/Latino; 3 Native Hawaiian or other Pacific Islander, non-Hispanic/Latino), 304 international. Average age 26. 861 applicants, 54% accepted, 133 enrolled. In 2014, 79 master's, 9 doctorates awarded. *Degree requirements:* For master's, comprehensive exam (for some programs), thesis or alternative; for doctorate, comprehensive exam, thesis/dissertation. *Entrance requirements:* For master's and doctorate, GRE General Test. Additional exam requirements/recommendations for international students: Required—TOEFL (minimum score 550 paper-based; 80 iBT). *Application deadline:* For fall admission, 4/15 priority date for domestic students, 1/15 priority date for international students; for spring admission, 11/1 for domestic students, 10/1 priority date for international students. Applications are processed on a rolling basis. Application fee: $75. Electronic applications accepted. *Expenses:* Expenses: $5,435 resident; $11,105 non-resident. *Financial support:* In 2014–15, 59 students received support, including 1 fellowship (averaging $10,000 per year), 16 research assistantships with full tuition reimbursements available (averaging $16,500 per year), 27 teaching assistantships with full tuition reimbursements available (averaging $16,500 per year); career-related internships or fieldwork, Federal Work-Study, institutionally sponsored loans, scholarships/grants, health care benefits, and unspecified assistantships also available. Financial award application deadline: 2/15; financial award applicants required to submit FAFSA. *Unit head:* Ellen Tilden, Coordinator of Graduate Studies, 607-777-2873, E-mail: etilden@binghamton.edu. *Application contact:* Kishan Zuber, Recruiting and Admissions Coordinator, 607-777-2151, Fax: 607-777-2501, E-mail: kzuber@binghamton.edu.

Boise State University, College of Engineering, Program in Computer Science, Boise, ID 83725-0399. Offers MS. Part-time programs available. *Faculty:* 8 full-time (0 women), 2 part-time/adjunct (0 women). *Students:* 11 full-time (2 women), 16 part-time (4 women); includes 4 minority (1 Asian, non-Hispanic/Latino; 3 Hispanic/Latino), 7 international. 33 applicants, 55% accepted, 11 enrolled. In 2014, 4 master's awarded. *Degree requirements:* For master's, comprehensive exam, thesis. *Entrance requirements:* For master's, GRE General Test, minimum GPA of 3.0. *Application deadline:* For fall admission, 7/17 priority date for domestic students; for spring admission, 12/5 priority date for domestic students. Applications are processed on a rolling basis. Application fee: $55. Electronic applications accepted. *Expenses:* Tuition, state resident: part-time $331 per credit hour. Tuition, nonresident: part-time $531 per credit hour. *Financial support:* In 2014–15, 8 students received support, including 2 research assistantships (averaging $13,200 per year), 5 teaching assistantships (averaging $12,810 per year); career-related internships or fieldwork, Federal Work-Study, and institutionally sponsored loans also available. Support available to part-time students. Financial award application deadline: 3/1. *Unit head:* Dr. Tim Andersen, Department Chair, 208-426-5768, E-mail: tim@cs.boisestate.edu. *Application contact:* Linda Platt, Office Services Supervisor, Graduate Admission and Degree Services, 208-426-1074, Fax: 208-426-2789, E-mail: lplatt@boisestate.edu.
Website: http://coen.boisestate.edu/cs/.

Boston University, Graduate School of Arts and Sciences, Department of Computer Science, Boston, MA 02215. Offers computer science (MS); cyber security (MS); MS/PhD. *Students:* 92 full-time (31 women), 6 part-time (0 women); includes 5 minority (4 Asian, non-Hispanic/Latino; 1 Hispanic/Latino), 68 international. Average age 26. 650 applicants, 8% accepted, 29 enrolled. In 2014, 55 master's awarded. *Degree requirements:* For master's, one foreign language, thesis optional, project. *Entrance requirements:* For master's, GRE General Test, 3 letters of recommendation. Additional exam requirements/recommendations for international students: Required—TOEFL (minimum score 550 paper-based; 84 iBT). *Application deadline:* For fall admission, 12/15 for domestic and international students; for spring admission, 11/1 for domestic and international students. Application fee: $80. *Expenses:* Tuition: Full-time $45,686; part-time $1428 per credit hour. *Required fees:* $660; $60 per semester. Tuition and fees

vary according to program. *Financial support:* In 2014–15, 54 students received support, including 3 fellowships with full tuition reimbursements available (averaging $20,500 per year), 27 research assistantships with full tuition reimbursements available (averaging $20,500 per year), 21 teaching assistantships with full tuition reimbursements available (averaging $20,500 per year); Federal Work-Study, scholarships/grants, and health care benefits also available. Support available to part-time students. Financial award application deadline: 12/15. *Unit head:* Mark Crovella, Chairman, 617-353-8919, Fax: 617-353-6457, E-mail: crovella@bu.edu. *Application contact:* Jennifer Streubel, Program Coordinator, 617-353-8919, Fax: 617-353-6457, E-mail: jenn4@bu.edu.
Website: http://cs-www.bu.edu/.

Boston University, Metropolitan College, Department of Computer Science, Boston, MA 02215. Offers computer information systems (MS), including computer networks, database management and business intelligence, health informatics, IT project management, security, Web application development; computer networks (Certificate); digital forensics (Certificate); health informatics (Certificate); information technology project management (Certificate); software engineering in health care systems (Certificate); telecommunications (MS), including security. Part-time and evening/weekend programs available. Postbaccalaureate distance learning degree programs offered (no on-campus study). *Faculty:* 13 full-time (3 women), 43 part-time/adjunct (3 women). *Students:* 76 full-time (22 women), 768 part-time (188 women); includes 251 minority (68 Black or African American, non-Hispanic/Latino; 1 American Indian or Alaska Native, non-Hispanic/Latino; 117 Asian, non-Hispanic/Latino; 57 Hispanic/Latino; 2 Native Hawaiian or other Pacific Islander, non-Hispanic/Latino; 6 Two or more races, non-Hispanic/Latino), 130 international. Average age 34. 463 applicants, 79% accepted, 248 enrolled. In 2014, 222 master's, 25 other advanced degrees awarded. *Degree requirements:* For master's, thesis optional. *Entrance requirements:* For master's and Certificate, official transcripts from regionally-accredited bachelor's degree program, 3 letters of recommendation, professional resume, personal statement. Additional exam requirements/recommendations for international students: Required—TOEFL (minimum score 84 iBT), IELTS. *Application deadline:* For fall admission, 6/1 priority date for international students; for spring admission, 10/1 priority date for international students. Applications are processed on a rolling basis. Application fee: $80. Electronic applications accepted. *Expenses:* Expenses: $800 per credit part-time; student services fees: $60 per semester; technology fee of $60 per credit (for online courses). *Financial support:* In 2014–15, 11 research assistantships (averaging $8,400 per year) were awarded; unspecified assistantships also available. Support available to part-time students. Financial award applicants required to submit FAFSA. *Faculty research:* Medical informatics, Web technologies, telecom and networks, security and forensics, software engineering, programming languages, multimedia and artificial intelligence (AI), information systems and IT project management. *Unit head:* Dr. Anatoly Temkin, Chairman, 617-353-2566, Fax: 617-353-2367, E-mail: csinfo@bu.edu. *Application contact:* Lesley Moreau, Academic Program Coordinator, 617-353-2566, Fax: 617-353-2367, E-mail: metcs@bu.edu.
Website: http://www.bu.edu/csmet/.

Bowie State University, Graduate Programs, Department of Computer Science, Bowie, MD 20715-9465. Offers MS. Part-time and evening/weekend programs available. *Students:* 9 full-time (4 women), 18 part-time (7 women); includes 22 minority (16 Black or African American, non-Hispanic/Latino; 6 Hispanic/Latino), 4 international. Average age 29. 13 applicants, 100% accepted, 9 enrolled. In 2014, 10 master's awarded. *Degree requirements:* For master's, comprehensive exam, thesis optional, research paper. *Entrance requirements:* For master's, minimum undergraduate GPA of 2.5. *Application deadline:* For fall admission, 4/1 priority date for domestic and international students; for spring admission, 11/1 priority date for domestic and international students. Applications are processed on a rolling basis. Application fee: $40. Electronic applications accepted. *Expenses:* Tuition, state resident: full-time $8928; part-time $372 per credit. Tuition, nonresident: full-time $16,176; part-time $674 per credit. *Required fees:* $2141. *Financial support:* Career-related internships or fieldwork and institutionally sponsored loans available. Financial award application deadline: 4/1. *Faculty research:* Holographics, launch vehicle ground truth ephemera. *Unit head:* Dr. Sadanand Srivatava, Chairperson, 301-860-3962, E-mail: ssrivatava@bowiestate.edu. *Application contact:* Angela Issac, Information Contact, 301-860-4000.

Bowie State University, Graduate Programs, Program in Computer Science, Bowie, MD 20715-9465. Offers App Sc D. Part-time and evening/weekend programs available. *Students:* 13 full-time (8 women), 40 part-time (20 women); includes 46 minority (40 Black or African American, non-Hispanic/Latino; 2 American Indian or Alaska Native, non-Hispanic/Latino; 4 Hispanic/Latino), 5 international. Average age 33. *Application deadline:* For fall admission, 4/1 priority date for domestic and international students; for spring admission, 11/1 priority date for domestic and international students. Applications are processed on a rolling basis. Application fee: $50. Electronic applications accepted. *Expenses:* Tuition, state resident: full-time $8928; part-time $372 per credit. Tuition, nonresident: full-time $16,176; part-time $674 per credit. *Required fees:* $2141. *Unit head:* Dr. Manohar Mareboyana, Director of Doctoral Programs, 301-860-3971, E-mail: manohar@bowiestate.edu. *Application contact:* Angela Issac, Information Contact, 301-860-4000.

Bowling Green State University, Graduate College, College of Arts and Sciences, Department of Computer Science, Bowling Green, OH 43403. Offers computer science (MS), including operations research, parallel and distributed computing, software engineering. Part-time programs available. *Degree requirements:* For master's, thesis or alternative. *Entrance requirements:* For master's, GRE General Test. Additional exam requirements/recommendations for international students: Required—TOEFL. Electronic applications accepted. *Faculty research:* Artificial intelligence, real time and concurrent programming languages, behavioral aspects of computing, network protocols.

Bradley University, Graduate School, College of Liberal Arts and Sciences, Department of Computer Science and Information Systems, Peoria, IL 61625-0002. Offers computer information systems (MS); computer science (MS). Part-time and evening/weekend programs available. *Faculty:* 9 full-time (1 woman), 3 part-time/adjunct (1 woman). *Students:* 82 full-time (31 women), 66 part-time (27 women), 143 international. 425 applicants, 42% accepted, 63 enrolled. In 2014, 25 master's awarded. *Degree requirements:* For master's, comprehensive exam, thesis or alternative, programming test. *Entrance requirements:* For master's, GRE. Additional exam requirements/recommendations for international students: Required—TOEFL (minimum score 550 paper-based; 79 iBT), IELTS (minimum score 6.5). *Application deadline:* For fall admission, 5/15 priority date for domestic and international students; for spring admission, 10/15 priority date for domestic and international students. Applications are processed on a rolling basis. Application fee: $40 ($50 for international students). Electronic applications accepted. *Expenses: Tuition:* Full-time $14,580; part-time $810 per credit. *Required fees:* $224. Full-time tuition and fees vary according to course load. *Financial support:* In 2014–15, 18 research assistantships with full and partial tuition reimbursements (averaging $9,820 per year) were awarded; teaching assistantships, scholarships/grants, tuition waivers (partial), and unspecified assistantships also available. Support available to part-time students. Financial award application deadline: 4/1. *Unit head:* Dr. Steven Dolins, Chair, 309-677-3284, E-mail: sdolins@bradley.edu. *Application contact:* Kayla Carroll, Director of International Admissions and Student Services, 309-677-2375, E-mail: klcarroll@fsmail.bradley.edu.

Brandeis University, Graduate School of Arts and Sciences, Program in Computational Linguistics, Waltham, MA 02454-9110. Offers MA. *Degree requirements:* For master's, internship in computational linguistics or thesis. *Entrance requirements:* For master's, GRE (recommended), statement of purpose, 2 letters of recommendation, official transcript(s), resume or curriculum vitae. Additional exam requirements/recommendations for international students: Required—TOEFL (minimum score 650 paper-based; 100 iBT), PTE (minimum score 68); Recommended—IELTS (minimum score 7). Electronic applications accepted.

Bridgewater State University, College of Graduate Studies, School of Arts and Sciences, Department of Mathematics and Computer Science, Bridgewater, MA 02325-0001. Offers computer science (MS); mathematics (MAT). Part-time and evening/weekend programs available. *Entrance requirements:* For master's, GRE General Test.

Brigham Young University, Graduate Studies, College of Physical and Mathematical Sciences, Department of Computer Science, Provo, UT 84602-1001. Offers MS, PhD. *Faculty:* 28 full-time (0 women), 3 part-time/adjunct (0 women). *Students:* 81 full-time (5 women); includes 14 minority (all Asian, non-Hispanic/Latino). Average age 30. 31 applicants, 55% accepted, 12 enrolled. In 2014, 18 master's, 8 doctorates awarded. Terminal master's awarded for partial completion of doctoral program. *Degree requirements:* For master's, thesis; for doctorate, comprehensive exam, thesis/dissertation, residency. *Entrance requirements:* For master's, GRE General Test, minimum GPA of 3.25 in last 60 hours; for doctorate, GRE General Test, minimum GPA of 3.5 in last 60 hours, undergraduate degree in computer science. Additional exam requirements/recommendations for international students: Required—TOEFL (minimum score 600 paper-based; 85 iBT). *Application deadline:* For fall admission, 12/15 for domestic and international students; for winter admission, 7/15 for domestic and international students. Application fee: $50. Electronic applications accepted. *Expenses: Tuition:* Full-time $6310; part-time $371 per credit hour. Tuition and fees vary according to program and student's religious affiliation. *Financial support:* In 2014–15, 102 students received support, including fellowships with full tuition reimbursements available (averaging $32,000 per year), 78 research assistantships with full and partial tuition reimbursements available (averaging $15,000 per year), 24 teaching assistantships with partial tuition reimbursements available (averaging $13,000 per year); scholarships/grants and health care benefits also available. Financial award application deadline: 3/1. *Faculty research:* Graphics, image processing, neural networks and machine learning, formal methods. *Total annual research expenditures:* $1 million. *Unit head:* Dr. Michael A. Goodrich, Chair, 801-422-6468, Fax: 801-422-0169, E-mail: mike@cs.byu.edu. *Application contact:* Dr. Quinn Snell, Graduate Coordinator, 801-422-5098, Fax: 801-422-0169, E-mail: snell@cs.byu.edu.
Website: http://www.cs.byu.edu/.

Brock University, Faculty of Graduate Studies, Faculty of Mathematics and Science, Program in Computer Science, St. Catharines, ON L2S 3A1, Canada. Offers M Sc. Part-time programs available. *Degree requirements:* For master's, thesis. *Entrance requirements:* For master's, honors degree. Additional exam requirements/recommendations for international students: Required—TOEFL (minimum score 550 paper-based; 80 iBT), IELTS (minimum score 6.5), TWE (minimum score 4).

Brooklyn College of the City University of New York, School of Natural and Behavioral Sciences, Department of Computer and Information Science, Brooklyn, NY 11210-2889. Offers computer science (MA); health informatics (MS); information systems (MS); parallel and distributed computing (Advanced Certificate). Part-time and evening/weekend programs available. *Degree requirements:* For master's, comprehensive exam, thesis or alternative. *Entrance requirements:* For master's, previous course work in computer science, 2 letters of recommendation. Additional exam requirements/recommendations for international students: Required—TOEFL (minimum score 525 paper-based; 70 iBT). Electronic applications accepted. *Faculty research:* Networks and distributed systems, programming languages, modeling and computer applications, algorithms, artificial intelligence, theoretical computer science.

Brown University, Graduate School, Department of Computer Science, Providence, RI 02912. Offers Sc M, PhD. *Degree requirements:* For master's, thesis or alternative; for doctorate, one foreign language, comprehensive exam, thesis/dissertation. *Entrance requirements:* For master's and doctorate, GRE General Test, GRE Subject Test.

California Institute of Technology, Division of Engineering and Applied Science, Option in Computer Science, Pasadena, CA 91125-0001. Offers MS, PhD. *Degree requirements:* For master's, thesis; for doctorate, thesis/dissertation. Electronic applications accepted. *Faculty research:* VLSI systems, concurrent computation, high-level programming languages, signal and image processing, graphics.

California Polytechnic State University, San Luis Obispo, College of Engineering, Department of Computer Science, San Luis Obispo, CA 93407. Offers MS. Part-time programs available. *Faculty:* 10 full-time (1 woman), 1 part-time/adjunct (0 women). *Students:* 29 full-time (5 women), 13 part-time (2 women); includes 10 minority (5 Asian, non-Hispanic/Latino; 3 Hispanic/Latino; 2 Two or more races, non-Hispanic/Latino), 1 international. Average age 25. 72 applicants, 21% accepted, 11 enrolled. In 2014, 15 master's awarded. *Degree requirements:* For master's, thesis. *Application deadline:* For fall admission, 4/1 for domestic and international students; for winter admission, 9/1 for domestic students, 6/30 for international students. Applications are processed on a rolling basis. Application fee: $55. Electronic applications accepted. *Expenses:* Tuition, state resident: full-time $6738; part-time $3906 per year. Tuition, nonresident: full-time $15,666; part-time $8370 per year. *Required fees:* $3447; $1001 per quarter. One-time fee: $3447 full-time; $3003 part-time. *Financial support:* Fellowships, research assistantships, teaching assistantships, career-related internships or fieldwork, Federal Work-Study, institutionally sponsored loans, scholarships/grants, and unspecified assistantships available. Support available to part-time students. Financial award application deadline: 3/2; financial award applicants required to submit FAFSA. *Faculty research:* Human-computer interaction, artificial intelligence, programming languages, computer graphics, database systems. *Unit head:* Dr. Alex Dekhtyar, Graduate Coordinator, 805-756-2387, Fax: 805-756-2956, E-mail: dekhtyar@calpoly.edu. *Application contact:* Dr. James Maraviglia, Associate Vice Provost for Marketing and Enrollment Development, 805-756-2311, Fax: 805-756-5400, E-mail: admissions@calpoly.edu.
Website: http://www.csc.calpoly.edu/programs/ms-csc/.

California State Polytechnic University, Pomona, Program in Computer Science, Pomona, CA 91768-2557. Offers MS. Part-time programs available. *Students:* 17 full-time (3 women), 46 part-time (11 women); includes 26 minority (2 Black or African American, non-Hispanic/Latino; 19 Asian, non-Hispanic/Latino; 4 Hispanic/Latino; 1 Two or more races, non-Hispanic/Latino), 24 international. Average age 27. 122 applicants, 39% accepted, 20 enrolled. In 2014, 15 master's awarded. *Degree requirements:* For master's, thesis. *Entrance requirements:* For master's, GRE General Test. *Application deadline:* For fall admission, 5/1 priority date for domestic students; for winter admission, 10/15 priority date for domestic students; for spring admission, 1/20 priority date for domestic students. Applications are processed on a rolling basis. Application fee: $55.

Electronic applications accepted. *Expenses:* Tuition, state resident: full-time $6738. Tuition, nonresident: full-time $12,300. *Required fees:* $1400. *Financial support:* Career-related internships or fieldwork, Federal Work-Study, and institutionally sponsored loans available. Support available to part-time students. Financial award application deadline: 3/2; financial award applicants required to submit FAFSA. *Unit head:* Dr. Daisy Tang, Graduate Coordinator, 909-869-2157, Fax: 909-869-4733, E-mail: ftang@cpp.edu. Website: http://www.cpp.edu/~cs/ms/.

California State University Channel Islands, Extended University and International Programs, Program in Computer Science, Camarillo, CA 93012. Offers MS. Part-time and evening/weekend programs available. *Entrance requirements:* Additional exam requirements/recommendations for international students: Required—TOEFL (minimum score 550 paper-based; 80 iBT), IELTS (minimum score 6).

California State University, Chico, Office of Graduate Studies, College of Engineering, Computer Science, and Technology, Department of Computer Science, Chico, CA 95929-0722. Offers MS. Postbaccalaureate distance learning degree programs offered. *Faculty:* 66 full-time (32 women), 18 part-time/adjunct (10 women). *Students:* 60 full-time (12 women), 7 part-time (1 woman), 63 international. Average age 26. 184 applicants, 67% accepted, 49 enrolled. In 2014, 11 master's awarded. *Degree requirements:* For master's, thesis or project and oral defense. *Entrance requirements:* For master's, GRE General Test (waived if graduated from ABET-accredited institution), 2 letters of recommendation, statement of purpose. Additional exam requirements/recommendations for international students: Required—TOEFL (minimum score 550 paper-based; 80 iBT), IELTS (minimum score 6.5). *Application deadline:* For fall admission, 3/1 priority date for domestic students, 3/1 for international students; for spring admission, 9/15 priority date for domestic students, 9/15 for international students. Application fee: $55. Electronic applications accepted. *Expenses:* Tuition, state resident: full-time $7002. Tuition, nonresident: full-time $18,162. *Required fees:* $1530. Tuition and fees vary according to program. *Financial support:* Fellowships, research assistantships, teaching assistantships, career-related internships or fieldwork, scholarships/grants, and traineeships available. Financial award application deadline: 3/1; financial award applicants required to submit FAFSA. *Unit head:* Dr. Melody J. Stapleton, Chair, 530-898-6442, Fax: 530-898-5995, E-mail: csci@csuchico.edu. *Application contact:* Judy L. Rice, Graduate Admissions Coordinator, 530-898-5416, Fax: 530-898-3342, E-mail: jlrice@csuchico.edu. Website: http://csci.ecst.csuchico.edu.

California State University, Dominguez Hills, College of Natural and Behavioral Sciences, Department of Computer Science, Carson, CA 90747-0001. Offers MSCS. *Faculty:* 3 full-time (0 women), 1 part-time/adjunct (0 women). *Students:* 22 full-time (5 women), 18 part-time (5 women); includes 14 minority (2 Black or African American, non-Hispanic/Latino; 7 Asian, non-Hispanic/Latino; 5 Hispanic/Latino), 13 international. Average age 32. 27 applicants, 85% accepted, 13 enrolled. In 2014, 4 master's awarded. *Degree requirements:* For master's, comprehensive exam (for some programs), thesis (for some programs). *Entrance requirements:* For master's, GRE (minimum score 900), minimum GPA of 2.75. Additional exam requirements/recommendations for international students: Required—TOEFL (minimum score 550 paper-based). Application fee: $55. Electronic applications accepted. *Expenses:* Tuition, state resident: full-time $6738; part-time $3960 per year. Tuition, nonresident: full-time $13,434; part-time $8370 per year. *Required fees:* $623; $623 per year. *Unit head:* Dr. Mohsen Beheshti, Department Chair, 310-243-3398, E-mail: mbeheshti@csudh.edu. *Application contact:* Brandy McLelland, Director of Student Information Services/Registrar, 310-243-3654, E-mail: bmclelland@csudh.edu. Website: http://csc.csudh.edu/.

California State University, East Bay, Office of Academic Programs and Graduate Studies, College of Science, Department of Mathematics and Computer Science, Computer Science Program, Hayward, CA 94542-3000. Offers computer networks (MS); computer science (MS). Part-time programs available. *Degree requirements:* For master's, thesis or capstone experience. *Entrance requirements:* For master's, GRE, minimum GPA of 3.0 in field, 2.75 overall; baccalaureate degree in computer science or related field. Additional exam requirements/recommendations for international students: Required—TOEFL (minimum score 550 paper-based). *Application deadline:* For fall admission, 6/30 for domestic and international students. Application fee: $55. Electronic applications accepted. *Expenses:* Tuition, state resident: full-time $7830; part-time $1302 per credit hour. Tuition, nonresident: full-time $16,368. *Required fees:* $327 per quarter. Tuition and fees vary according to course load and program. *Financial support:* Fellowships, career-related internships or fieldwork, Federal Work-Study, institutionally sponsored loans, and scholarships/grants available. Support available to part-time students. Financial award application deadline: 3/2; financial award applicants required to submit FAFSA. *Unit head:* Matthew Johnson, Chair, 510-885-3414, E-mail: matt.johnson@csueastbay.edu. *Application contact:* Dr. Donna Wiley, Interim Associate Vice President for Academic Programs and Graduate Studies, 510-885-3716, Fax: 510-885-4777, E-mail: donna.wiley@csueastbay.edu. Website: http://www20.csueastbay.edu/csci/departments/math-cs/.

California State University, Fresno, Division of Graduate Studies, College of Science and Mathematics, Department of Computer Science, Fresno, CA 93740-8027. Offers MS. Part-time and evening/weekend programs available. *Degree requirements:* For master's, thesis or alternative. *Entrance requirements:* For master's, GRE General Test, minimum GPA of 2.75. Additional exam requirements/recommendations for international students: Required—TOEFL. Electronic applications accepted. *Faculty research:* Software design, parallel processing, computer engineering, autoline research.

California State University, Fullerton, Graduate Studies, College of Engineering and Computer Science, Department of Computer Science, Fullerton, CA 92834-9480. Offers computer science (MS); software engineering (MS). Part-time programs available. Postbaccalaureate distance learning degree programs offered. *Students:* 164 full-time (49 women), 376 part-time (96 women); includes 130 minority (11 Black or African American, non-Hispanic/Latino; 84 Asian, non-Hispanic/Latino; 28 Hispanic/Latino; 7 Two or more races, non-Hispanic/Latino), 354 international. Average age 27. 1,060 applicants, 39% accepted, 216 enrolled. In 2014, 138 master's awarded. *Degree requirements:* For master's, comprehensive exam, project or thesis. *Entrance requirements:* For master's, GRE General Test, minimum undergraduate GPA of 2.5. Application fee: $55. *Financial support:* Career-related internships or fieldwork, Federal Work-Study, institutionally sponsored loans, and scholarships/grants available. Support available to part-time students. Financial award application deadline: 3/1; financial award applicants required to submit FAFSA. *Faculty research:* Software engineering, development of computer networks. *Unit head:* Dr. Shawn Wang, Chair, 657-278-7258. *Application contact:* Admissions/Applications, 657-278-2371.

California State University, Long Beach, Graduate Studies, College of Engineering, Department of Computer Engineering and Computer Science, Long Beach, CA 90840. Offers computer engineering (MSCS); computer science (MSCS). Part-time programs available. *Degree requirements:* For master's, thesis or alternative. *Entrance requirements:* Additional exam requirements/recommendations for international students: Required—TOEFL. Electronic applications accepted. *Faculty research:*

Artificial intelligence, software engineering, computer simulation and modeling, user-interface design, networking.

California State University, Los Angeles, Graduate Studies, College of Engineering, Computer Science, and Technology, Department of Computer Science, Los Angeles, CA 90032-8530. Offers MS. *Entrance requirements:* Additional exam requirements/recommendations for international students: Required—TOEFL (minimum score 550 paper-based). Electronic applications accepted. *Expenses:* Tuition, state resident: full-time $6738; part-time $3609 per year. Tuition, nonresident: full-time $15,666; part-time $8073 per year. Tuition and fees vary according to course load, degree level and program.

California State University, Northridge, Graduate Studies, College of Engineering and Computer Science, Department of Computer Science, Northridge, CA 91330. Offers computer science (MS); software engineering (MS). Part-time and evening/weekend programs available. *Students:* 46 full-time (10 women), 36 part-time (8 women); includes 20 minority (1 Black or African American, non-Hispanic/Latino; 7 Asian, non-Hispanic/Latino; 9 Hispanic/Latino; 3 Two or more races, non-Hispanic/Latino), 14 international. Average age 30. *Degree requirements:* For master's, thesis. *Entrance requirements:* For master's, GRE General Test, minimum GPA of 2.5. Additional exam requirements/recommendations for international students: Required—TOEFL. *Application deadline:* For fall admission, 11/30 for domestic students. Application fee: $55. *Expenses: Required fees:* $12,402. *Financial support:* Application deadline: 3/1. *Faculty research:* Radar data processing. *Unit head:* Rick Covington, Chair, 818-677-3398. Website: http://www.csun.edu/computerscience/.

California State University, Sacramento, Office of Graduate Studies, College of Engineering and Computer Science, Department of Computer Science, Sacramento, CA 95819. Offers computer science (MS); software engineering (MS). Part-time and evening/weekend programs available. *Degree requirements:* For master's, thesis or comprehensive exam; writing proficiency exam. *Entrance requirements:* For master's, GRE. Additional exam requirements/recommendations for international students: Required—TOEFL. Electronic applications accepted.

California State University, San Bernardino, Graduate Studies, College of Natural Sciences, Department of Computer Science, San Bernardino, CA 92407-2397. Offers MS. *Students:* 23 full-time (6 women), 29 part-time (7 women); includes 4 minority (2 Asian, non-Hispanic/Latino; 1 Hispanic/Latino; 1 Two or more races, non-Hispanic/Latino), 46 international. Average age 23. 190 applicants, 34% accepted, 17 enrolled. In 2014, 13 master's awarded. *Entrance requirements:* Additional exam requirements/recommendations for international students: Required—TOEFL. *Application deadline:* For fall admission, 7/17 for domestic students. Application fee: $55. *Expenses:* Tuition, state resident: full-time $6738; part-time $1302 per term. Tuition, nonresident: full-time $17,898; part-time $248 per unit. *Required fees:* $365 per quarter. Tuition and fees vary according to degree level and program. *Unit head:* Dr. Haiyan Qiao, Director, 909-537-5415, Fax: 909-537-7004, E-mail: hqiao@csusb.edu. *Application contact:* Dr. Jeffrey Thompson, Dean of Graduate Studies, 909-537-5058, E-mail: jthompso@csusb.edu.

California State University, San Marcos, College of Science and Mathematics, Program in Computer Science, San Marcos, CA 92096-0001. Offers MS. Part-time programs available. *Entrance requirements:* For master's, GRE General Test, statement of purpose, letters of recommendation. Additional exam requirements/recommendations for international students: Required—TOEFL (minimum score 550 paper-based; 80 iBT). *Application deadline:* For fall admission, 5/30 for domestic students; for spring admission, 8/30 for domestic students, 11/1 for international students. Application fee: $55. *Expenses:* Tuition, state resident: full-time $6738. *Required fees:* $1692. Tuition and fees vary according to program. *Financial support:* Research assistantships and teaching assistantships available. *Faculty research:* Networks, multimedia, parallel algorithms, software engineering, artificial intelligence. *Unit head:* Xiaoyu Zhang, Graduate Coordinator, 760-750-4187, E-mail: xiaoyu@csusm.edu. Website: http://www.csusm.edu/cs/master/.

Capitol Technology University, Graduate Programs, Laurel, MD 20708-9759. Offers business administration (MBA); computer science (MS); electrical engineering (MS); information and telecommunications systems management (MS); information architecture (MS); network security (MS). Part-time and evening/weekend programs available. Postbaccalaureate distance learning degree programs offered (no on-campus study). *Entrance requirements:* For master's, minimum GPA of 3.0. Electronic applications accepted.

Carleton University, Faculty of Graduate Studies, Faculty of Science, School of Computer Science, Ottawa, ON K1S 5B6, Canada. Offers computer science (MCS, PhD); information and system science (M Sc). MCS and PhD programs offered jointly with University of Ottawa. Part-time programs available. *Degree requirements:* For master's, thesis optional, project; for doctorate, comprehensive exam, thesis/dissertation. *Entrance requirements:* For master's, honors degree. Additional exam requirements/recommendations for international students: Required—TOEFL. *Faculty research:* Programming systems, theory of computing, computer applications, computer systems.

Carnegie Mellon University, School of Computer Science, Department of Computer Science, Pittsburgh, PA 15213-3891. Offers algorithms, combinatorics, and optimization (PhD); computer science (MS, PhD); pure and applied logic (PhD). *Degree requirements:* For doctorate, thesis/dissertation. *Entrance requirements:* For doctorate, GRE General Test, GRE Subject Test, BS in computer science or equivalent. Additional exam requirements/recommendations for international students: Required—TOEFL. *Faculty research:* Software systems, theory of computations, artificial intelligence, computer systems, programming languages.

Carnegie Mellon University, School of Computer Science, Language Technologies Institute, Pittsburgh, PA 15213-3891. Offers MLT, MS, PhD. Terminal master's awarded for partial completion of doctoral program. *Degree requirements:* For doctorate, thesis/dissertation. *Entrance requirements:* For master's and doctorate, GRE General Test, GRE Subject Test. Additional exam requirements/recommendations for international students: Required—TOEFL. *Faculty research:* Machine translation, natural language processing, speech and information retrieval, literacy.

Case Western Reserve University, School of Graduate Studies, Case School of Engineering, Department of Electrical Engineering and Computer Science, Cleveland, OH 44106. Offers computer engineering (MS, PhD); computing and information sciences (MS, PhD); electrical engineering (MS, PhD); systems and control engineering (MS, PhD). Part-time and evening/weekend programs available. Postbaccalaureate distance learning degree programs offered (minimal on-campus study). *Faculty:* 33 full-time (3 women). *Students:* 158 full-time (35 women), 18 part-time (5 women); includes 5 minority (1 Black or African American, non-Hispanic/Latino; 3 Asian, non-Hispanic/Latino; 1 Hispanic/Latino), 122 international. In 2014, 37 master's, 11 doctorates awarded. Terminal master's awarded for partial completion of doctoral program. *Degree requirements:* For master's, thesis; for doctorate, thesis/dissertation, qualifying exam, teaching experience. *Entrance requirements:* For master's and doctorate, GRE General Test. Additional exam requirements/recommendations for international students: Required—TOEFL. *Application deadline:* For fall admission, 2/1 for domestic students; for spring admission, 11/1 for domestic students. Applications are processed on a rolling

basis. Application fee: $50. *Financial support:* In 2014–15, 51 research assistantships with full and partial tuition reimbursements, 10 teaching assistantships were awarded; fellowships with full and partial tuition reimbursements, career-related internships or fieldwork, Federal Work-Study, and institutionally sponsored loans also available. Support available to part-time students. Financial award application deadline: 3/1; financial award applicants required to submit FAFSA. *Faculty research:* Micro/nano systems; robotics and haptics, applied artificial intelligence; automation, computer-aided design and testing of digital systems. *Total annual research expenditures:* $6 million. *Unit head:* Dr. Kenneth Loparo, Department Chair, 216-368-4115, E-mail: kal4@case.edu. *Application contact:* Kimberly Yurchick, Student Affairs Specialist, 216-368-2920, Fax: 216-368-2801, E-mail: ksy4@case.edu.
Website: http://eecs.cwru.edu/.

The Catholic University of America, School of Engineering, Department of Electrical Engineering and Computer Science, Washington, DC 20064. Offers MEE, MSCS, PhD. Part-time programs available. *Faculty:* 12 full-time (2 women), 9 part-time/adjunct (3 women). *Students:* 13 full-time (5 women), 44 part-time (8 women); includes 9 minority (3 Black or African American, non-Hispanic/Latino; 3 Asian, non-Hispanic/Latino; 2 Hispanic/Latino; 1 Two or more races, non-Hispanic/Latino), 30 international. Average age 33. 56 applicants, 52% accepted, 13 enrolled. In 2014, 16 master's, 5 doctorates awarded. *Degree requirements:* For master's, thesis or alternative; for doctorate, comprehensive exam, thesis/dissertation, oral exams. *Entrance requirements:* For master's and doctorate, statement of purpose, official copies of academic transcripts, three letters of recommendation. Additional exam requirements/recommendations for international students: Required—TOEFL (minimum score 580 paper-based). *Application deadline:* For fall admission, 7/15 priority date for domestic students, 7/1 for international students; for spring admission, 11/15 priority date for domestic students, 11/1 for international students. Applications are processed on a rolling basis. Application fee: $55. Electronic applications accepted. *Expenses:* Expenses: Contact institution. *Financial support:* Fellowships, research assistantships, teaching assistantships, Federal Work-Study, scholarships/grants, tuition waivers (full and partial), and unspecified assistantships available. Financial award application deadline: 2/1; financial award applicants required to submit FAFSA. *Faculty research:* Signal and image processing, computer communications, robotics, intelligent controls, bioelectromagnetics. *Total annual research expenditures:* $216,563. *Unit head:* Dr. Ozlem Kilic, Chair, 202-319-5879, Fax: 202-319-5195, E-mail: regalia@cua.edu. *Application contact:* Director of Graduate Admissions, 202-319-5057, Fax: 202-319-6533, E-mail: cua-admissions@cua.edu.
Website: http://eecs.cua.edu/.

Central Connecticut State University, School of Graduate Studies, School of Engineering, Science and Technology, Department of Computer Science, New Britain, CT 06050-4010. Offers computer information technology (MS). Part-time and evening/weekend programs available. *Faculty:* 6 full-time (4 women). *Students:* 25 full-time (13 women), 46 part-time (13 women); includes 24 minority (3 Black or African American, non-Hispanic/Latino; 1 American Indian or Alaska Native, non-Hispanic/Latino; 12 Asian, non-Hispanic/Latino; 5 Hispanic/Latino; 3 Two or more races, non-Hispanic/Latino), 19 international. Average age 31. 73 applicants, 56% accepted, 25 enrolled. In 2014, 15 master's awarded. *Degree requirements:* For master's, comprehensive exam, thesis or alternative. *Entrance requirements:* For master's, minimum undergraduate GPA of 2.7, letters of recommendation, resume. Additional exam requirements/recommendations for international students: Required—TOEFL (minimum score 550 paper-based; 79 iBT). *Application deadline:* For fall admission, 6/1 for domestic students, 5/1 for international students; for spring admission, 11/1 for domestic and international students. Applications are processed on a rolling basis. Application fee: $50. Electronic applications accepted. *Expenses: Tuition, area resident:* Full-time $5730; part-time $534 per credit. Tuition, state resident: full-time $8596; part-time $534 per credit. Tuition, nonresident: full-time $15,964; part-time $548 per credit. *Required fees:* $4211; $215 per credit. *Financial support:* In 2014–15, 5 research assistantships were awarded; career-related internships or fieldwork, Federal Work-Study, scholarships/grants, and unspecified assistantships also available. Support available to part-time students. Financial award application deadline: 3/1; financial award applicants required to submit FAFSA. *Unit head:* Dr. Stanislav Kurkovsky, Chair, 860-832-2710, E-mail: kurkovsky@ccsu.edu. *Application contact:* Patricia Gardner, Associate Director of Graduate Studies, 860-832-2350, Fax: 860-832-2362, E-mail: graduateadmissions@ccsu.edu.
Website: http://www.cs.ccsu.edu/.

Central Connecticut State University, School of Graduate Studies, School of Engineering, Science and Technology, Department of Mathematical Sciences, New Britain, CT 06050-4010. Offers data mining (MS, Certificate); mathematics (MA, MS, Certificate, Sixth Year Certificate), including actuarial science (MA), computer science (MA), statistics (MA). Part-time and evening/weekend programs available. *Faculty:* 13 full-time (4 women). *Students:* 11 full-time (3 women), 68 part-time (31 women); includes 18 minority (4 Black or African American, non-Hispanic/Latino; 1 American Indian or Alaska Native, non-Hispanic/Latino; 6 Asian, non-Hispanic/Latino; 5 Hispanic/Latino; 2 Two or more races, non-Hispanic/Latino), 4 international. Average age 37. 55 applicants, 64% accepted, 19 enrolled. In 2014, 33 master's, 5 other advanced degrees awarded. *Degree requirements:* For master's, comprehensive exam, thesis or alternative; for other advanced degree, qualifying exam. *Entrance requirements:* For master's, minimum undergraduate GPA of 2.7; for other advanced degree, minimum undergraduate GPA of 3.0, essay, letters of recommendation. Additional exam requirements/recommendations for international students: Required—TOEFL (minimum score 550 paper-based; 79 iBT). *Application deadline:* For fall admission, 5/1 for domestic and international students; for spring admission, 11/1 for domestic and international students. Applications are processed on a rolling basis. Application fee: $50. Electronic applications accepted. *Expenses: Tuition, area resident:* Full-time $5730; part-time $534 per credit. Tuition, state resident: full-time $8596; part-time $534 per credit. Tuition, nonresident: full-time $15,964; part-time $548 per credit. *Required fees:* $4211; $215 per credit. *Financial support:* In 2014–15, 4 students received support, including 1 research assistantship; career-related internships or fieldwork, Federal Work-Study, scholarships/grants, and unspecified assistantships also available. Support available to part-time students. Financial award application deadline: 3/1; financial award applicants required to submit FAFSA. *Faculty research:* Statistics, actuarial mathematics, computer systems and engineering, computer programming techniques, operations research. *Unit head:* Dr. Jeffrey McGowan, Chair, 860-832-2835, E-mail: mcgowan@ccsu.edu. *Application contact:* Patricia Gardner, Associate Director of Graduate Studies, 860-832-2350, Fax: 860-832-2362, E-mail: graduateadmissions@ccsu.edu.
Website: http://www.math.ccsu.edu/.

Central Michigan University, College of Graduate Studies, College of Science and Technology, Department of Computer Science, Mount Pleasant, MI 48859. Offers MS. Part-time programs available. *Degree requirements:* For master's, thesis or alternative. *Entrance requirements:* For master's, bachelor's degree from accredited institution with minimum GPA of 3.0 in last two years of study. Electronic applications accepted. *Faculty research:* Artificial intelligence, biocomputing, data mining, software engineering, operating systems, mobile applications.

Chicago State University, School of Graduate and Professional Studies, College of Arts and Sciences, Department of Mathematics and Computer Science, Chicago, IL 60628. Offers computer science (MS); mathematics (MS). *Degree requirements:* For master's, thesis optional, oral exam. *Entrance requirements:* For master's, minimum GPA of 2.75.

Christopher Newport University, Graduate Studies, Department of Physics, Computer Science, and Engineering, Newport News, VA 23606-3072. Offers applied physics and computer science (MS). Part-time and evening/weekend programs available. *Faculty:* 15 full-time (2 women), 1 part-time/adjunct (0 women). *Students:* 10 full-time (1 woman), 13 part-time (3 women); includes 5 minority (1 Black or African American, non-Hispanic/Latino; 4 Hispanic/Latino). Average age 27. 9 applicants, 89% accepted, 5 enrolled. In 2014, 4 master's awarded. *Degree requirements:* For master's, comprehensive exam (for some programs), thesis optional. *Entrance requirements:* For master's, GRE General Test, minimum GPA of 3.0. Additional exam requirements/recommendations for international students: Required—TOEFL (minimum score 580 paper-based; 92 iBT). *Application deadline:* For fall admission, 7/15 priority date for domestic students, 4/1 for international students; for spring admission, 11/1 for domestic students, 10/1 for international students; for summer admission, 2/15 for domestic students, 3/1 for international students. Applications are processed on a rolling basis. Application fee: $50. Electronic applications accepted. *Expenses:* Tuition, state resident: full-time $5886; part-time $327 per credit hour. Tuition, nonresident: full-time $13,410; part-time $745 per credit hour. *Required fees:* $3528; $196 per credit hour. Full-time tuition and fees vary according to course load. *Financial support:* In 2014–15, 8 students received support, including 2 fellowships with full tuition reimbursements available (averaging $30,000 per year), 3 research assistantships with full tuition reimbursements available (averaging $2,000 per year), 5 teaching assistantships (averaging $1,000 per year); career-related internships or fieldwork, Federal Work-Study, and unspecified assistantships also available. Financial award application deadline: 3/1; financial award applicants required to submit FAFSA. *Faculty research:* Advanced programming methodologies, experimental nuclear physics, computer architecture, semiconductor nanophysics, laser and optical fiber sensors. *Total annual research expenditures:* $425,256. *Unit head:* Dr. Antonio Siochi, Coordinator, 757-594-7569, Fax: 757-594-7919, E-mail: siochi@cnu.edu. *Application contact:* Lyn Sawyer, Associate Director, Graduate Admissions and Records, 757-594-7544, Fax: 757-594-7649, E-mail: gradstdy@cnu.edu.

The Citadel, The Military College of South Carolina, Citadel Graduate College, Department of Mathematics and Computer Science, Charleston, SC 29409. Offers computer and information science (MS); mathematics education (MAE). *Accreditation:* NCATE (one or more programs are accredited). Part-time and evening/weekend programs available. *Degree requirements:* For master's, comprehensive exam (for some programs), thesis (for some programs). *Entrance requirements:* For master's, GRE General Test with minimum combined score of 300 on the verbal and quantitative sections [1000 under the old grading system], 4.0 on the writing assessment (for MS); MAT with minimum raw score of 396 (for MA Ed), minimum undergraduate GPA of 3.0 (MS) or 2.5 (MAT); competency, demonstrated through coursework, approved work experience, or a program-administrated competency exam, in the areas of basic computer architecture, object-oriented programming, discrete mathematics, and data structures (MS); successful completion of 7 courses (MAT). Additional exam requirements/recommendations for international students: Required—TOEFL (minimum score 550 paper-based; 79 iBT). Electronic applications accepted. *Faculty research:* Mathematics: numerical linear algebra, inverse problems, operator algebras, geometric group theory, integral equations; computer science: computer networks, database systems, software engineering, computational systems biology, mobile systems.

City College of the City University of New York, Graduate School, Grove School of Engineering, Department of Computer Sciences, New York, NY 10031-9198. Offers MS, PhD. PhD program offered jointly with Graduate School and University Center of the City University of New York. *Degree requirements:* For master's, thesis optional; for doctorate, one foreign language, comprehensive exam, thesis/dissertation. *Entrance requirements:* For master's and doctorate, GRE General Test. Additional exam requirements/recommendations for international students: Required—TOEFL (minimum score 500 paper-based; 61 iBT). *Faculty research:* Complexities of algebraic research, human issues in computer science, scientific computing, supercompilers, parallel algorithms.

City University of Seattle, Graduate Division, School of Management, Seattle, WA 98121. Offers accounting (Certificate); change leadership (MBA, Certificate); computer systems (MS); finance (Certificate); financial management (MBA); general management (MBA); general management-Europe (MBA); global marketing (MBA); human resources management (Certificate); individualized study (MBA); information security (MS); information systems (MBA); leadership (MA); marketing (MBA, Certificate); project management (MBA, MS, Certificate); sustainable business (Certificate); technology management (MBA, Certificate). Part-time and evening/weekend programs available. Postbaccalaureate distance learning degree programs offered (no on-campus study). *Faculty:* 4 full-time (1 woman), 168 part-time/adjunct (63 women). *Students:* 445 full-time (227 women), 249 part-time (130 women); includes 115 minority (42 Black or African American, non-Hispanic/Latino; 3 American Indian or Alaska Native, non-Hispanic/Latino; 41 Asian, non-Hispanic/Latino; 22 Hispanic/Latino; 4 Native Hawaiian or other Pacific Islander, non-Hispanic/Latino; 3 Two or more races, non-Hispanic/Latino), 227 international. Average age 33. 127 applicants, 100% accepted, 127 enrolled. In 2014, 200 master's, 15 other advanced degrees awarded. *Degree requirements:* For master's, comprehensive exam (for some programs), thesis (for some programs). *Entrance requirements:* For master's, baccalaureate degree or equivalent from an accredited or otherwise recognized institution. Additional exam requirements/recommendations for international students: Required—TOEFL (minimum score 567 paper-based; 87 iBT); Recommended—IELTS. *Application deadline:* For fall admission, 9/1 for international students; for winter admission, 12/1 for international students; for spring admission, 3/1 for international students. Applications are processed on a rolling basis. Application fee: $50. Electronic applications accepted. *Expenses: Tuition:* Full-time $30,000; part-time $600 per credit. One-time fee: $50. Tuition and fees vary according to degree level and program. *Financial support:* In 2014–15, 47 students received support. Federal Work-Study and scholarships/grants available. Support available to part-time students. Financial award applicants required to submit FAFSA. *Unit head:* Dr. Kurt Kirstein, Dean, 206-239-4860 Ext. 5456, E-mail: kdkirstein@cityu.edu. *Application contact:* 888-422-4898, Fax: 425-709-5363, E-mail: info@cityu.edu.

Clark Atlanta University, School of Arts and Sciences, Department of Computer and Information Science, Atlanta, GA 30314. Offers MS. Part-time programs available. *Faculty:* 3 full-time (0 women). *Students:* 23 full-time (9 women), 5 part-time (2 women); includes 13 minority (7 Black or African American, non-Hispanic/Latino; 2 American Indian or Alaska Native, non-Hispanic/Latino; 4 Asian, non-Hispanic/Latino), 10 international. Average age 29. 27 applicants, 96% accepted, 14 enrolled. In 2014, 9 master's awarded. *Degree requirements:* For master's, one foreign language, thesis. *Entrance requirements:* For master's, GRE General Test, minimum GPA of 2.5.

Additional exam requirements/recommendations for international students: Required—TOEFL (minimum score 500 paper-based; 61 iBT). *Application deadline:* For fall admission, 4/1 for domestic and international students; for spring admission, 11/1 for domestic and international students. Applications are processed on a rolling basis. Application fee: $40 ($55 for international students). *Expenses: Tuition:* Full-time $14,904; part-time $828 per credit hour. *Required fees:* $746; $373 per semester. *Financial support:* In 2014–15, 4 fellowships were awarded; career-related internships or fieldwork, Federal Work-Study, scholarships/grants, and unspecified assistantships also available. Support available to part-time students. Financial award application deadline: 4/30; financial award applicants required to submit FAFSA. *Unit head:* Dr. Olugbemiga Olatidoye, Chairperson, 404-880-6940, E-mail: oolatidoye@cau.edu. *Application contact:* Michelle Clark-Davis, Graduate Program Admissions, 404-880-6605, E-mail: cauadmissions@cau.edu.

Clarkson University, Graduate School, School of Arts and Sciences, Department of Computer Science, Potsdam, NY 13699. Offers MS, PhD. Part-time programs available. *Faculty:* 7 full-time (2 women). *Students:* 12 full-time (3 women), 6 part-time (0 women), 7 international. Average age 29. 19 applicants, 79% accepted, 4 enrolled. In 2014, 3 master's, 2 doctorates awarded. *Degree requirements:* For doctorate, thesis/dissertation, departmental qualifying exam. *Entrance requirements:* For master's and doctorate, GRE, transcripts of all college coursework, resume, personal statement, three letters of recommendation. Additional exam requirements/recommendations for international students: Required—TOEFL, IELTS. *Application deadline:* For fall admission, 1/30 priority date for domestic and international students; for spring admission, 9/1 priority date for domestic and international students. Applications are processed on a rolling basis. Application fee: $25 ($35 for international students). Electronic applications accepted. *Expenses: Tuition:* Full-time $16,680; part-time $1390 per credit. *Required fees:* $295 per semester. *Financial support:* In 2014–15, 10 students received support, including 1 fellowship with full tuition reimbursement available (averaging $24,029 per year), research assistantships with full tuition reimbursements available (averaging $24,029 per year), 4 teaching assistantships with full tuition reimbursements available (averaging $24,029 per year); scholarships/grants, tuition waivers (partial), and unspecified assistantships also available. *Faculty research:* Image enhancement, cryptographic protocol, green data. *Total annual research expenditures:* $77,227. *Unit head:* Dr. Christopher Lynch, Chair, 315-268-2395, Fax: 315-268-2371, E-mail: clynch@clarkson.edu. *Application contact:* Jennifer Reed, Graduate Coordinator, School of Arts and Sciences, 315-268-3802, Fax: 315-268-3989, E-mail: sciencegrad@clarkson.edu.
Website: http://www.clarkson.edu/cs/.

Clemson University, Graduate School, College of Engineering and Science, School of Computing, Program in Computer Science, Clemson, SC 29634. Offers MS, PhD. *Students:* 133 full-time (40 women), 31 part-time (4 women); includes 15 minority (5 Black or African American, non-Hispanic/Latino; 1 Asian, non-Hispanic/Latino; 2 Hispanic/Latino; 1 Native Hawaiian or other Pacific Islander, non-Hispanic/Latino; 6 Two or more races, non-Hispanic/Latino), 104 international. Average age 27. 468 applicants, 29% accepted, 76 enrolled. In 2014, 54 master's, 2 doctorates awarded. Terminal master's awarded for partial completion of doctoral program. *Degree requirements:* For master's, thesis optional; for doctorate, thesis/dissertation. *Entrance requirements:* For master's and doctorate, GRE General Test. Additional exam requirements/recommendations for international students: Required—TOEFL. *Application deadline:* Applications are processed on a rolling basis. Application fee: $70 ($80 for international students). Electronic applications accepted. *Financial support:* In 2014–15, 45 students received support, including 7 fellowships with full and partial tuition reimbursements available (averaging $5,048 per year), 34 research assistantships with partial tuition reimbursements available (averaging $23,565 per year), 11 teaching assistantships with partial tuition reimbursements available (averaging $26,640 per year); career-related internships or fieldwork, institutionally sponsored loans, scholarships/grants, health care benefits, and unspecified assistantships also available. Support available to part-time students. Financial award application deadline: 3/1; financial award applicants required to submit FAFSA. *Unit head:* Dr. Larry F. Hodges, Director, School of Computing, 864-656-7552, Fax: 864-656-0145, E-mail: lfh@clemson.edu. *Application contact:* Dr. Mark Smootherman, Director of Graduate Programs, 864-656-5878, Fax: 864-656-0145, E-mail: mark@clemson.edu.
Website: http://www.clemson.edu/ces/departments/computing/index.html.

Cleveland State University, College of Graduate Studies, Monte Ahuja College of Business, Department of Computer and Information Science, Cleveland, OH 44115. Offers computer and information science (MCIS); information systems (DBA). Part-time and evening/weekend programs available. *Faculty:* 12 full-time (2 women), 3 part-time/adjunct (2 women). *Students:* 29 full-time (12 women), 81 part-time (29 women); includes 5 minority (2 Black or African American, non-Hispanic/Latino; 3 Asian, non-Hispanic/Latino), 77 international. Average age 27. 447 applicants, 56% accepted, 54 enrolled. In 2014, 22 master's awarded. Terminal master's awarded for partial completion of doctoral program. *Degree requirements:* For master's, thesis optional; for doctorate, comprehensive exam, thesis/dissertation. *Entrance requirements:* For master's, GRE or GMAT, minimum GPA of 2.75; for doctorate, GRE or GMAT, MBA, MCIS or equivalent. Additional exam requirements/recommendations for international students: Required—TOEFL (minimum score 525 paper-based; 78 iBT). *Application deadline:* For fall admission, 7/15 priority date for domestic students, 5/15 priority date for international students; for spring admission, 12/15 priority date for domestic students. Applications are processed on a rolling basis. Application fee: $30. Electronic applications accepted. *Expenses:* Tuition, state resident: full-time $9566; part-time $531 per credit hour. Tuition, nonresident: full-time $17,980; part-time $999 per credit hour. *Required fees:* $25 per semester. Tuition and fees vary according to degree level and program. *Financial support:* In 2014–15, 21 students received support, including 7 research assistantships with full and partial tuition reimbursements available (averaging $7,800 per year), 2 teaching assistantships with full and partial tuition reimbursements available (averaging $16,000 per year); career-related internships or fieldwork, tuition waivers (full), and unspecified assistantships also available. *Faculty research:* Artificial intelligence, object-oriented analysis, database design, software efficiency, distributed system, geographical information systems. *Total annual research expenditures:* $7,500. *Unit head:* Dr. Santosh K. Misra, Chairman, 216-687-4760, Fax: 216-687-5448, E-mail: s.misra@csuohio.edu. *Application contact:* 216-687-4760, Fax: 216-687-9354, E-mail: s.misra@csuohio.edu.
Website: http://cis.csuohio.edu/.

Coastal Carolina University, College of Science, Conway, SC 29528-6054. Offers applied computing and information systems (Certificate); coastal marine and wetland studies (MS). Part-time and evening/weekend programs available. *Faculty:* 19 full-time (4 women), 1 part-time/adjunct (0 women). *Students:* 14 full-time (8 women), 17 part-time (8 women); includes 1 minority (Hispanic/Latino), 1 international. Average age 26. 22 applicants, 68% accepted, 10 enrolled. In 2014, 12 master's, 1 other advanced degree awarded. *Degree requirements:* For master's, thesis or internship; for doctorate, comprehensive exam, thesis/dissertation. *Entrance requirements:* For master's, GRE, 2 letters of recommendation, resume, official transcripts, written statement of educational and career goals, baccalaureate degree; for doctorate, GRE, official transcripts;

baccalaureate or master's degree; minimum GPA of 3.0 for all collegiate coursework; successful completion of at least two semesters of college-level calculus, physics, and chemistry; 3 letters of recommendation; written statement of educational and career goals; resume; for Certificate, 2 letters of reference, official transcripts, minimum GPA of 3.0 in all computing and information systems courses, documentation of graduation from accredited four-year college or university. Additional exam requirements/recommendations for international students: Required—TOEFL (minimum score 575 paper-based; 89 iBT). *Application deadline:* For fall admission, 1/15 priority date for domestic and international students; for spring admission, 11/1 priority date for domestic and international students. Applications are processed on a rolling basis. Application fee: $45. Electronic applications accepted. *Expenses:* Tuition, state resident: full-time $12,384; part-time $516 per credit hour. Tuition, nonresident: full-time $22,560; part-time $940 per credit hour. *Required fees:* $5 per credit hour. *Financial support:* Fellowships, research assistantships, and unspecified assistantships available. Support available to part-time students. Financial award application deadline: 3/1; financial award applicants required to submit FAFSA. *Unit head:* Dr. Michael H. Roberts, Dean, 843-349-2282, Fax: 843-349-2545, E-mail: mroberts@coastal.edu. *Application contact:* Dr. James O. Luken, Associate Provost/Director of Graduate Studies, 843-349-2235, Fax: 843-349-6444, E-mail: joluken@coastal.edu.
Website: http://www.coastal.edu/science/.

College of Charleston, Graduate School, School of Sciences and Mathematics, Program in Computer and Information Sciences, Charleston, SC 29424-0001. Offers MS. Program offered jointly with The Citadel, The Military College of South Carolina. Part-time and evening/weekend programs available. *Degree requirements:* For master's, thesis optional. *Entrance requirements:* For master's, GRE. Additional exam requirements/recommendations for international students: Required—TOEFL (minimum score 81 iBT). Electronic applications accepted.

The College of Saint Rose, Graduate Studies, School of Mathematics and Sciences, Program in Computer Information Systems, Albany, NY 12203-1419. Offers MS. Part-time and evening/weekend programs available. *Degree requirements:* For master's, comprehensive exam, research component. *Entrance requirements:* For master's, minimum GPA of 3.0, 9 undergraduate credits in math. Additional exam requirements/recommendations for international students: Required—TOEFL (minimum score 550 paper-based). Electronic applications accepted.

College of Staten Island of the City University of New York, Graduate Programs, Division of Science and Technology, Program in Computer Science, Staten Island, NY 10314-6600. Offers MS. Part-time and evening/weekend programs available. *Faculty:* 6 full-time (3 women). *Students:* 7 full-time, 32 part-time. Average age 27. 91 applicants, 34% accepted, 18 enrolled. In 2014, 24 master's awarded. *Degree requirements:* For master's, 10 courses (30 credits) with minimum GPA of 3.0 or thesis. *Entrance requirements:* For master's, GRE General Test, BS in computer science or related area with minimum B average overall and in major. Additional exam requirements/recommendations for international students: Required—TOEFL (minimum score 550 paper-based; 79 iBT), IELTS (minimum score 6.5). *Application deadline:* For fall admission, 4/22 priority date for domestic and international students; for spring admission, 11/19 priority date for domestic and international students. Applications are processed on a rolling basis. Application fee: $125. Electronic applications accepted. *Expenses:* Tuition, state resident: full-time $9650; part-time $405 per credit. Tuition, nonresident: full-time $17,880; part-time $745 per credit. *Required fees:* $141.10 per semester. Tuition and fees vary according to program. *Financial support:* In 2014–15, 3 students received support. Career-related internships or fieldwork, Federal Work-Study, and scholarships/grants available. Support available to part-time students. Financial award applicants required to submit FAFSA. *Faculty research:* Spatial temporal information fusion and real-time sensor data assimilation using Sequential Monte Carlo methods. *Total annual research expenditures:* $160,448. *Unit head:* Dr. Anatoliy Gordonov, Graduate Program Coordinator, 718-982-2852, Fax: 718-982-2856, E-mail: anatoliy.gordonov@csi.cuny.edu. *Application contact:* Sasha Spence, Assistant Director for Graduate Admissions, 718-982-2019, Fax: 718-982-2500, E-mail: sasha.spence@csi.cuny.edu.
Website: http://www.cs.csi.cuny.edu/content/grad.cs.csi.cuny.new.htm.

The College of William and Mary, Faculty of Arts and Sciences, Department of Computer Science, Williamsburg, VA 23187-8795. Offers computational operations research (MS), including computer science; computer science (MS, PhD), including computational science (PhD). Part-time programs available. *Faculty:* 14 full-time (3 women). *Students:* 78 full-time (17 women), 5 part-time (2 women); includes 3 minority (1 Asian, non-Hispanic/Latino; 1 Hispanic/Latino; 1 Two or more races, non-Hispanic/Latino), 60 international. Average age 28. 95 applicants, 56% accepted, 23 enrolled. In 2014, 9 master's, 6 doctorates awarded. *Degree requirements:* For master's, comprehensive exam, thesis optional, research project; for doctorate, comprehensive exam, thesis/dissertation. *Entrance requirements:* For master's, GRE General Test, minimum GPA of 2.5; for doctorate, GRE General Test, minimum GPA of 3.0. Additional exam requirements/recommendations for international students: Required—TOEFL, TWE. *Application deadline:* For fall admission, 3/1 priority date for domestic students, 3/1 for international students; for spring admission, 11/1 for domestic and international students. Applications are processed on a rolling basis. Application fee: $45. Electronic applications accepted. *Financial support:* In 2014–15, 6 fellowships with full tuition reimbursements (averaging $9,000 per year), 35 research assistantships with full tuition reimbursements (averaging $24,000 per year), 24 teaching assistantships with full tuition reimbursements (averaging $24,000 per year) were awarded; scholarships/grants and unspecified assistantships also available. Financial award application deadline: 3/1; financial award applicants required to submit FAFSA. *Faculty research:* High-performance computing, wireless computing, algorithms, computer systems and network computing, modeling, simulation, and graphics. *Total annual research expenditures:* $2.1 million. *Unit head:* Dr. Robert Lewis, Chair, 757-221-3460, Fax: 757-221-1717, E-mail: rmlewi@wm.edu. *Application contact:* Vanessa Godwin, Administrative Director, 757-221-3455, Fax: 757-221-1717, E-mail: gradinfo@cs.wm.edu.
Website: http://www.wm.edu/computerscience.

Colorado School of Mines, Graduate School, Department of Electrical Engineering and Computer Science, Golden, CO 80401. Offers computer science (MS, PhD); electrical engineering (MS, PhD). Part-time programs available. *Faculty:* 22 full-time (5 women), 8 part-time/adjunct (2 women). *Students:* 60 full-time (9 women), 22 part-time (3 women); includes 7 minority (1 Black or African American, non-Hispanic/Latino; 2 Asian, non-Hispanic/Latino; 3 Hispanic/Latino; 1 Two or more races, non-Hispanic/Latino), 31 international. Average age 30. 122 applicants, 58% accepted, 26 enrolled. In 2014, 43 master's, 9 doctorates awarded. *Degree requirements:* For master's, thesis (for some programs); for doctorate, comprehensive exam, thesis/dissertation. *Entrance requirements:* For master's and doctorate, GRE General Test. Additional exam requirements/recommendations for international students: Required—TOEFL (minimum score 550 paper-based; 80 iBT). *Application deadline:* For fall admission, 12/15 priority date for domestic and international students; for spring admission, 9/1 priority date for domestic and international students. Application fee: $50 ($70 for international students). Electronic applications accepted. *Financial support:* In 2014–15, 36 students

Computer Science

received support, including 4 fellowships (averaging $21,120 per year), 19 research assistantships (averaging $21,120 per year), 7 teaching assistantships (averaging $21,120 per year); career-related internships or fieldwork, Federal Work-Study, institutionally sponsored loans, scholarships/grants, health care benefits, and unspecified assistantships also available. Financial award application deadline: 12/15; financial award applicants required to submit FAFSA. *Total annual research expenditures:* $1.4 million. *Unit head:* Dr. Randy Haupt, Head, 303-273-3721, E-mail: rhaupt@mines.edu. *Application contact:* Lori Sisneros, Graduate Program Administrator, 303-384-3658, E-mail: sisneros@mines.edu.
Website: http://eecs.mines.edu/.

Colorado State University, Graduate School, College of Natural Sciences, Department of Computer Science, Fort Collins, CO 80523-1873. Offers MCS, MS, PhD. Part-time programs available. Postbaccalaureate distance learning degree programs offered (no on-campus study). *Faculty:* 23 full-time (5 women). *Students:* 69 full-time (17 women), 130 part-time (22 women); includes 20 minority (13 Asian, non-Hispanic/Latino; 7 Hispanic/Latino), 107 international. Average age 32. 160 applicants, 66% accepted, 54 enrolled. In 2014, 39 master's, 11 doctorates awarded. Terminal master's awarded for partial completion of doctoral program. *Degree requirements:* For master's, comprehensive exam (for some programs), thesis (for MS), coursework (for MCS); for doctorate, comprehensive exam, thesis/dissertation, qualifying, preliminary, and final exams. *Entrance requirements:* For master's, GRE, minimum GPA of 3.0, undergraduate experience in computer science, transcripts; for doctorate, GRE General Test, BSC or master's degree in computer science, minimum GPA of 3.0, transcripts. Additional exam requirements/recommendations for international students: Required—TOEFL (minimum score 580 paper-based; 92 iBT), IELTS (minimum score 6.5). *Application deadline:* For fall admission, 1/15 priority date for domestic and international students; for spring admission, 10/1 priority date for domestic and international students. Applications are processed on a rolling basis. Application fee: $50. Electronic applications accepted. *Expenses:* Tuition, state resident: full-time $9348; part-time $519 per credit. Tuition, nonresident: full-time $22,916; part-time $1273 per credit. *Required fees:* $1584. *Financial support:* In 2014–15, 60 students received support, including 33 research assistantships with full tuition reimbursements available (averaging $13,555 per year), 27 teaching assistantships with full tuition reimbursements available (averaging $12,077 per year); fellowships and unspecified assistantships also available. Financial award application deadline: 1/15; financial award applicants required to submit FAFSA. *Faculty research:* Artificial intelligence, software engineering/human-computer interaction networking and security, high performance computing, bioinformatics. *Total annual research expenditures:* $5 million. *Unit head:* Dr. L. Darrell Whitley, Department Chair, 970-491-5373, Fax: 970-491-2466, E-mail: whitley@cs.colostate.edu. *Application contact:* Dr. Bruce Draper, Director of Graduate Studies, 970-491-7873, E-mail: draper@cs.colostate.edu.
Website: http://www.cs.colostate.edu/cstop/index.

Colorado Technical University Colorado Springs, Graduate Studies, Program in Computer Science, Colorado Springs, CO 80907-3896. Offers computer science (DCS); computer systems security (MSCS); database systems (MSCS); software engineering (MSCS). Part-time and evening/weekend programs available. Postbaccalaureate distance learning degree programs offered. *Degree requirements:* For master's, thesis or alternative; for doctorate, thesis/dissertation. *Entrance requirements:* For doctorate, minimum graduate GPA of 3.0, 5 years of related work experience. *Faculty research:* Software engineering, systems engineering.

Colorado Technical University Denver South, Program in Computer Science, Aurora, CO 80014. Offers computer systems security (MSCS); database systems (MSCS); software engineering (MSCS). Part-time and evening/weekend programs available. *Degree requirements:* For master's, thesis or alternative. *Entrance requirements:* For master's, minimum undergraduate GPA of 3.0, resume.

★ **Columbia University,** Fu Foundation School of Engineering and Applied Science, Department of Computer Science, New York, NY 10027. Offers computer science (MS, Eng Sc D, PhD); computer science and journalism (MS). PhD offered through the Graduate School of Arts and Sciences. Part-time programs available. Postbaccalaureate distance learning degree programs offered (no on-campus study). *Faculty:* 46 full-time (8 women), 32 part-time/adjunct (4 women). *Students:* 333 full-time (95 women), 229 part-time (58 women); includes 61 minority (2 Black or African American, non-Hispanic/Latino; 45 Asian, non-Hispanic/Latino; 6 Hispanic/Latino; 8 Two or more races, non-Hispanic/Latino), 418 international. 1,818 applicants, 25% accepted, 227 enrolled. In 2014, 182 master's, 12 doctorates awarded. Terminal master's awarded for partial completion of doctoral program. *Degree requirements:* For master's, thesis optional; for doctorate, comprehensive exam, thesis/dissertation, candidacy exam. *Entrance requirements:* For master's and doctorate, GRE General Test. Additional exam requirements/recommendations for international students: Required—TOEFL, IELTS, PTE. *Application deadline:* For fall admission, 12/15 priority date for domestic and international students; for spring admission, 10/1 priority date for domestic and international students. Application fee: $85. Electronic applications accepted. *Financial support:* In 2014–15, 135 students received support, including 9 fellowships with full tuition reimbursements available (averaging $32,059 per year), 108 research assistantships with full tuition reimbursements available (averaging $28,809 per year), 18 teaching assistantships with full tuition reimbursements available (averaging $6,000 per year); health care benefits also available. Financial award application deadline: 12/15; financial award applicants required to submit FAFSA. *Faculty research:* Natural language processing, machine learning, software systems, network systems, computer security, computational biology, foundations of computer science, vision and graphics. *Unit head:* Dr. Julia B. Hirschberg, Professor and Chair, Computer Science, 212-939-7114, E-mail: julia@cs.columbia.edu. *Application contact:* Remiko O. Moss, Assistant Director, 212-939-7002, Fax: 212-666-0140, E-mail: remimoss@cs.columbia.edu.
Website: http://www.cs.columbia.edu/.

See Display on next page and Close-Up on page 347.

Columbus State University, Graduate Studies, D. Abbott Turner College of Business and Computer Science, Columbus, GA 31907-5645. Offers applied computer science (MS); business administration (MBA); information systems security (Certificate); modeling and simulation (Certificate); organizational leadership (MS). *Accreditation:* AACSB. *Faculty:* 9 full-time (3 women), 2 part-time/adjunct (1 woman). *Students:* 86 full-time (21 women), 134 part-time (47 women); includes 68 minority (37 Black or African American, non-Hispanic/Latino; 2 American Indian or Alaska Native, non-Hispanic/Latino; 15 Asian, non-Hispanic/Latino; 10 Hispanic/Latino; 4 Two or more races, non-Hispanic/Latino), 12 international. Average age 32. 149 applicants, 51% accepted, 49 enrolled. In 2014, 141 master's awarded. *Entrance requirements:* For master's, GMAT, GRE, minimum undergraduate GPA of 2.75, letters of recommendation. Additional exam requirements/recommendations for international students: Required—TOEFL (minimum score 550 paper-based; 79 iBT). *Application deadline:* For fall admission, 6/30 for domestic students, 5/1 for international students; for spring admission, 11/1 for domestic

and international students; for summer admission, 3/1 for domestic and international students. Applications are processed on a rolling basis. Application fee: $50. Electronic applications accepted. *Financial support:* In 2014–15, 66 students received support, including 16 research assistantships (averaging $3,000 per year). Financial award application deadline: 5/1; financial award applicants required to submit FAFSA. *Unit head:* Dr. Linda U. Hadley, Dean, 706-507-8153, Fax: 706-568-2184, E-mail: hadley_linda@columbusstate.edu. *Application contact:* Kristin Williams, Director of International and Graduate Recruitment, 706-507-8848, Fax: 706-568-5091, E-mail: thornton_katie@colstate.edu.
Website: http://turner.columbusstate.edu/.

Concordia University, School of Graduate Studies, Faculty of Engineering and Computer Science, Department of Computer Science and Software Engineering, Montréal, QC H3G 1M8, Canada. Offers computer science (M App Comp Sc, M Comp Sc, PhD, Diploma); software engineering (MA Sc). *Degree requirements:* For master's, one foreign language, thesis optional; for doctorate, one foreign language, comprehensive exam, thesis/dissertation. *Faculty research:* Computer systems and applications, mathematics of computation, pattern recognition, artificial intelligence and robotics.

Cornell University, Graduate School, Graduate Fields of Engineering, Field of Computer Science, Ithaca, NY 14853-0001. Offers algorithms (M Eng, PhD); applied logic and automated reasoning (M Eng, PhD); artificial intelligence (M Eng, PhD); computer graphics (M Eng, PhD); computer science (M Eng, PhD); computer vision (M Eng, PhD); concurrency and distributed computing (M Eng, PhD); information organization and retrieval (M Eng, PhD); operating systems (M Eng, PhD); parallel computing (M Eng, PhD); programming environments (M Eng, PhD); programming languages and methodology (M Eng, PhD); robotics (M Eng, PhD); scientific computing (M Eng, PhD); theory of computation (M Eng, PhD). *Degree requirements:* For doctorate, comprehensive exam, thesis/dissertation. *Entrance requirements:* For master's, GRE General Test, 2 letters of recommendation; for doctorate, GRE General Test, GRE Subject Test (computer science or mathematics), 3 letters of recommendation. Additional exam requirements/recommendations for international students: Required—TOEFL (minimum score 505 paper-based; 77 iBT). Electronic applications accepted. *Faculty research:* Artificial intelligence, operating systems and databases, programming languages and security, scientific computing, theory of computing, computational biology and graphics.

Dakota State University, College of Business and Information Systems, Madison, SD 57042-1799. Offers applied computer science (MSACS); general management (MBA); health informatics (MSHI); information assurance (MSIA); information systems (MSIS, D Sc IS). *Accreditation:* ACBSP. Part-time and evening/weekend programs available. Postbaccalaureate distance learning degree programs offered (minimal on-campus study). *Faculty:* 25 full-time (6 women), 1 part-time/adjunct (0 women). *Students:* 84 full-time (16 women), 165 part-time (45 women); includes 48 minority (17 Black or African American, non-Hispanic/Latino; 3 American Indian or Alaska Native, non-Hispanic/Latino; 17 Asian, non-Hispanic/Latino; 3 Hispanic/Latino; 1 Native Hawaiian or other Pacific Islander, non-Hispanic/Latino; 7 Two or more races, non-Hispanic/Latino), 76 international. Average age 35. 236 applicants, 65% accepted, 100 enrolled. In 2014, 58 master's, 7 doctorates, 4 other advanced degrees awarded. *Degree requirements:* For master's, comprehensive exam, thesis optional, examination, integrative project; for doctorate, comprehensive exam, thesis/dissertation, portfolio. *Entrance requirements:* For master's, GRE General Test, demonstration of information systems skills, minimum GPA of 2.7; for doctorate, GRE General Test, demonstration of information systems skills; for Graduate Certificate, GMAT, MBA. Additional exam requirements/recommendations for international students: Required—TOEFL (minimum score 550 paper-based; 79 iBT), IELTS (minimum score 6.5). *Application deadline:* For fall admission, 6/15 for domestic and international students; for spring admission, 11/15 for domestic and international students; for summer admission, 4/15 for domestic and international students. Applications are processed on a rolling basis. Application fee: $35. *Expenses:* Tuition, state resident: full-time $3633; part-time $201.85 per credit hour. Tuition, nonresident: full-time $7691; part-time $427.30 per credit hour. *Required fees:* $2108; $117.10 per credit hour. Tuition and fees vary according to course load, campus/location, program and reciprocity agreements. *Financial support:* In 2014–15, 32 students received support, including 18 fellowships with partial tuition reimbursements available (averaging $13,344 per year), 13 research assistantships with partial tuition reimbursements available (averaging $32,782 per year), 1 teaching assistantship with partial tuition reimbursement available (averaging $10,927 per year); Federal Work-Study, scholarships/grants, and unspecified assistantships also available. Support available to part-time students. Financial award applicants required to submit FAFSA. *Faculty research:* Data mining and data warehousing, effectiveness of hybrid learning environments, biometrics and information assurance, decision support systems, analytics, health informatics. *Unit head:* Dr. Omar El-Gayar, Dean of Graduate Studies and Research, 605-256-5799, Fax: 605-256-5093, E-mail: omar.el-gayar@dsu.edu. *Application contact:* Erin Blankespoor, Secretary, Office of Graduate Studies and Research, 605-256-5799, Fax: 605-256-5093, E-mail: erin.blankespoor@dsu.edu. Website: http://dsu.edu/graduate-students.

Dalhousie University, Faculty of Computer Science, Halifax, NS B3H 1W5, Canada. Offers computational biology and bioinformatics (M Sc); computer science (MA Sc, MC Sc, PhD); electronic commerce (MEC); health informatics (MHI). *Degree requirements:* For master's, thesis (for some programs); for doctorate, thesis/dissertation. *Entrance requirements:* Additional exam requirements/recommendations for international students: Required—1 of 5 approved tests: TOEFL, IELTS, CANTEST, CAEL, Michigan English Language Assessment Battery. Electronic applications accepted.

Dartmouth College, Arts and Sciences Graduate Programs, Department of Computer Science, Hanover, NH 03755. Offers MS, PhD. *Faculty:* 17 full-time (4 women), 3 part-time/adjunct (1 woman). *Students:* 96 full-time (23 women); includes 8 minority (3 Asian, non-Hispanic/Latino; 1 Hispanic/Latino; 4 Two or more races, non-Hispanic/Latino), 76 international. Average age 26. 442 applicants, 24% accepted, 33 enrolled. In 2014, 22 master's, 3 doctorates awarded. Terminal master's awarded for partial completion of doctoral program. *Degree requirements:* For master's, thesis; for doctorate, thesis/dissertation. *Entrance requirements:* For master's and doctorate, GRE General Test, GRE Subject Test. *Application deadline:* For fall admission, 1/15 priority date for domestic students. Application fee: $40. *Financial support:* Fellowships with full tuition reimbursements, research assistantships with full tuition reimbursements, teaching assistantships with full tuition reimbursements, career-related internships or fieldwork, institutionally sponsored loans, scholarships/grants, and tuition waivers (full and partial) available. Support available to part-time students. Financial award application deadline: 2/1. *Faculty research:* Algorithms, computational geometry and learning, computer vision, information retrieval, robotics. *Unit head:* Dr. Thomas H. Cormen, Chair, 603-646-2206. *Application contact:* Joseph Elsener, Department Administrator, 603-646-2206.
Website: http://www.cs.dartmouth.edu/.

DePaul University, College of Computing and Digital Media, Chicago, IL 60604. Offers animation (MA, MFA); business information technology (MS); cinema (MFA); cinema production (MS); computational finance (MS); computer and information sciences (PhD); computer game development (MS); computer information and network security (MS); computer science (MS); e-commerce technology (MS); health informatics (MS); human-computer interaction (MS); information systems (MS); information technology project management (MS); network engineering and management (MS); predictive analytics (MS); screenwriting (MFA); software engineering (MS); JD/MS. Part-time and evening/weekend programs available. Postbaccalaureate distance learning degree programs offered (no on-campus study). *Degree requirements:* For master's, thesis (for some programs); for doctorate, comprehensive exam, thesis/dissertation. *Entrance requirements:* For master's, GRE or GMAT (for MS in computational finance only), bachelor's degree, resume (MS in predictive analytics only), IT experience (MS in information technology project management only), portfolio review (all MFA programs and MA in animation); for doctorate, GRE, master's degree in computer science. Additional exam requirements/recommendations for international students: Required—TOEFL (minimum score 590 paper-based; 80 iBT), IELTS (minimum score 6.5), PTE (minimum score 53). Electronic applications accepted. *Expenses:* Contact institution. *Faculty research:* Data mining, computer science, human-computer interaction, security, animation and film.

DigiPen Institute of Technology, Graduate Programs, Redmond, WA 98052. Offers computer science (MS); digital arts (MFA). Part-time and evening/weekend programs available. *Faculty:* 25 full-time (5 women), 7 part-time/adjunct (0 women). *Students:* 63 full-time (13 women), 22 part-time (3 women); includes 35 minority (2 Black or African American, non-Hispanic/Latino; 1 American Indian or Alaska Native, non-Hispanic/Latino; 20 Asian, non-Hispanic/Latino; 12 Hispanic/Latino), 27 international. Average age 26. 204 applicants, 23% accepted, 30 enrolled. In 2014, 7 master's awarded. *Degree requirements:* For master's, comprehensive exam (for some programs), thesis (for some programs). *Entrance requirements:* For master's, GRE General Test or DigiPen computer science exam for applicants with non-computer science degrees (for MS), art portfolio (for MFA). Additional exam requirements/recommendations for international students: Required—TOEFL (minimum score 550 paper-based; 80 iBT). *Application deadline:* For fall admission, 2/1 priority date for domestic and international students; for spring admission, 7/1 for domestic and international students. Applications are processed on a rolling basis. Application fee: $35. Electronic applications accepted. *Expenses:* Expenses: $17,100, $18,920 international (for MS in computer science); $23,200, $25,200 international (for MFA in digital arts). *Financial support:* In 2014–15, 1 student received support, including 1 fellowship (averaging $15,450 per year); career-related internships or fieldwork and scholarships/grants also available. Financial award application deadline: 5/1; financial award applicants required to submit FAFSA. *Faculty research:* Procedural modeling, computer graphics and visualization, human-computer interaction, fuzzy numbers and fuzzy analysis, modeling under spistemic uncertainty, nonlinear image processing, mathematical representation of surfaces, advanced computer graphic rendering techniques, mathematical physics, computer music and sound synthesis. *Unit head:* Angela Kugler, Vice President of External Affairs, 425-895-4438, Fax: 425-558-0378, E-mail: akugler@digipen.edu. *Application contact:* Danial Powers, Director of Admissions, 425-629-5071, Fax: 425-558-0378, E-mail: dpowers@digipen.edu.

Drexel University, College of Computing and Informatics, Department of Computer Science, Philadelphia, PA 19104-2875. Offers MS, PhD. Part-time programs available. Postbaccalaureate distance learning degree programs offered (no on-campus study). *Faculty:* 17 full-time (3 women), 4 part-time/adjunct (0 women). *Students:* 43 full-time (7 women), 47 part-time (3 women); includes 12 minority (1 Black or African American, non-Hispanic/Latino; 8 Asian, non-Hispanic/Latino; 3 Hispanic/Latino), 21 international. Average age 28. 195 applicants, 33% accepted, 17 enrolled. In 2014, 20 master's, 4 doctorates awarded. Terminal master's awarded for partial completion of doctoral program. *Degree requirements:* For doctorate, thesis/dissertation. *Entrance requirements:* For master's, GRE General Test. Additional exam requirements/recommendations for international students: Required—TOEFL (minimum score 600 paper-based; 100 iBT). *Application deadline:* For fall admission, 8/22 for domestic students, 8/1 for international students. Applications are processed on a rolling basis. Electronic applications accepted. Application fee is waived when completed online. *Financial support:* In 2014–15, 36 students received support, including 13 research assistantships with full tuition reimbursements available (averaging $23,500 per year), 8 teaching assistantships with full tuition reimbursements available (averaging $23,500 per year); tuition waivers (partial) also available. Financial award application deadline: 2/1; financial award applicants required to submit FAFSA. *Unit head:* Dr. Spiros Mancoridis, Interim Dean/Professor of Computer Science, 215-895-6824, E-mail: spiros@drexel.edu. *Application contact:* Matthew Lechtenberg, Graduate Admissions Manager, 215-895-1951, Fax: 215-895-2303, E-mail: ml333@drexel.edu.

Duke University, Graduate School, Department of Computer Science, Durham, NC 27708. Offers MS, PhD. Spring admission applies to MS program only. *Degree requirements:* For doctorate, thesis/dissertation. *Entrance requirements:* For master's, GRE General Test; for doctorate, GRE General Test, GRE Subject Test (recommended). Additional exam requirements/recommendations for international students: Required—TOEFL (minimum score 577 paper-based; 90 iBT) or IELTS (minimum score 7). Electronic applications accepted. *Expenses: Tuition:* Full-time $45,760; part-time $2765 per credit. *Required fees:* $978. Full-time tuition and fees vary according to program.

East Carolina University, Graduate School, College of Engineering and Technology, Department of Computer Science, Greenville, NC 27858-4353. Offers computer science (MS); software engineering (MS). Part-time and evening/weekend programs available. *Degree requirements:* For master's, comprehensive exam, thesis or alternative. *Entrance requirements:* For master's, GRE General Test. Additional exam requirements/recommendations for international students: Required—TOEFL. Electronic applications accepted. *Expenses:* Tuition, state resident: full-time $4223. Tuition, nonresident: full-time $16,540. *Required fees:* $2184. *Faculty research:* Software development, software engineering, artificial intelligence, bioinformatics, cryptography.

East Carolina University, Graduate School, College of Engineering and Technology, Department of Technology Systems, Greenville, NC 27858-4353. Offers computer network professional (Certificate); information assurance (Certificate); Lean Six Sigma Black Belt (Certificate); network technology (MS), including computer networking management, digital communications technology, information security, Web technologies; occupational safety (MS); technology management (PhD); technology systems (MS), including industrial distribution and logistics, manufacturing systems, performance improvement, quality systems; Website developer (Certificate). *Entrance requirements:* For master's and Certificate, GRE General Test or MAT, minimum GPA of 2.5; for doctorate, GRE General Test, related work experience. *Expenses:* Tuition, state resident: full-time $4223. Tuition, nonresident: full-time $16,540. *Required fees:* $2184.

Eastern Illinois University, Graduate School, Lumpkin College of Business and Applied Sciences, School of Technology, Program in Technology, Charleston, IL 61920. Offers MS. Part-time and evening/weekend programs available. *Faculty:* 28. *Students:* 119 full-time (39 women), 66 part-time (37 women); includes 17 minority (11 Black or African American, non-Hispanic/Latino; 2 Asian, non-Hispanic/Latino; 2 Hispanic/Latino; 2 Two or more races, non-Hispanic/Latino), 111 international. Average age 29. 418

applicants, 28% accepted, 47 enrolled. In 2014, 57 master's awarded. *Degree requirements:* For master's, comprehensive exam (for some programs), thesis (for some programs). *Entrance requirements:* For master's, GMAT or GRE. Additional exam requirements/recommendations for international students: Required—TOEFL (minimum score 500 paper-based; 61 iBT), IELTS (minimum score 6). *Application deadline:* For fall admission, 5/15 for domestic and international students; for spring admission, 10/15 for domestic and international students. Applications are processed on a rolling basis. Application fee: $30. Electronic applications accepted. *Expenses:* Tuition, state resident: full-time $3113; part-time $283 per credit hour. Tuition, nonresident: full-time $7469; part-time $679 per credit hour. *Required fees:* $2287; $96 per credit hour. Tuition and fees vary according to course load. *Financial support:* In 2014–15, 89 students received support, including 2 research assistantships with full tuition reimbursements available (averaging $7,830 per year), 6 teaching assistantships with full tuition reimbursements available (averaging $7,830 per year); career-related internships or fieldwork, Federal Work-Study, and unspecified assistantships also available. Support available to part-time students. Financial award application deadline: 3/1; financial award applicants required to submit FAFSA. *Unit head:* Austin Cheney, Chair School of Technology, 217-581-3226, Fax: 217-581-6607, E-mail: acheney@eiu.edu. *Application contact:* Peter Ping Liu, Graduate Coordinator, 217-581-6267, Fax: 217-581-6607, E-mail: pliu@eiu.edu.
Website: http://www.eiu.edu/techgrad/.

Eastern Michigan University, Graduate School, College of Arts and Sciences, Department of Computer Science, Ypsilanti, MI 48197. Offers computer science (MS). Part-time and evening/weekend programs available. Postbaccalaureate distance learning degree programs offered (no on-campus study). *Faculty:* 12 full-time (5 women). *Students:* 45 full-time (28 women), 16 part-time (3 women); includes 2 minority (both Asian, non-Hispanic/Latino), 42 international. Average age 26. 89 applicants, 51% accepted, 24 enrolled. In 2014, 10 master's, 1 other advanced degree awarded. *Degree requirements:* For master's, thesis or alternative. *Entrance requirements:* For master's, at least 18 credit hours of computer science courses including data structures, programming languages like java, C or C++, computer organization; courses in discrete mathematics, probability and statistics, linear algebra and calculus; minimum GPA of 2.75 in computer science. Additional exam requirements/recommendations for international students: Required—TOEFL. *Application deadline:* For fall admission, 8/1 for domestic students, 5/1 for international students; for winter admission, 12/1 for domestic students, 10/1 for international students; for spring admission, 4/1 for domestic students, 2/1 for international students. Application fee: $45. *Financial support:* Fellowships, research assistantships with full tuition reimbursements, teaching assistantships with full tuition reimbursements, career-related internships or fieldwork, Federal Work-Study, institutionally sponsored loans, scholarships/grants, tuition waivers (partial), and unspecified assistantships available. Support available to part-time students. Financial award applicants required to submit FAFSA. *Unit head:* Dr. Augustine C. Ikeji, Department Head, 734-487-1063, Fax: 734-487-6824, E-mail: aikeji@emich.edu. *Application contact:* Pamela Moore, Graduate Coordinator, 734-487-3205, Fax: 734-487-6824, E-mail: pmoore@emich.edu.
Website: http://www.emich.edu/compsci.

Eastern Washington University, Graduate Studies, College of Science, Health and Engineering, Department of Computer Science, Cheney, WA 99004-2431. Offers computer and technology-supported education (M Ed); computer science (MS). Part-time programs available. *Degree requirements:* For master's, comprehensive exam, thesis or alternative. *Entrance requirements:* For master's, minimum GPA of 3.0.

East Stroudsburg University of Pennsylvania, Graduate College, College of Arts and Sciences, Department of Computer Science, East Stroudsburg, PA 18301-2999. Offers MS. Part-time and evening/weekend programs available. *Degree requirements:* For master's, comprehensive exam, thesis or alternative. *Entrance requirements:* For master's, bachelor's degree in computer science or related field. Additional exam requirements/recommendations for international students: Required—TOEFL (minimum score 560 paper-based; 83 iBT) or IELTS. Electronic applications accepted.

East Tennessee State University, School of Graduate Studies, College of Business and Technology, Department of Computing, Johnson City, TN 37614. Offers MS, Postbaccalaureate Certificate. Part-time and evening/weekend programs available. *Faculty:* 15 full-time (3 women). *Students:* 33 full-time (4 women), 8 part-time (1 woman); includes 6 minority (2 Black or African American, non-Hispanic/Latino; 1 Asian, non-Hispanic/Latino; 2 Hispanic/Latino; 1 Two or more races, non-Hispanic/Latino), 9 international. Average age 30. 69 applicants, 39% accepted, 15 enrolled. In 2014, 13 master's awarded. *Degree requirements:* For master's, comprehensive exam, thesis optional, capstone. *Entrance requirements:* For master's, GRE General Test, minimum GPA of 2.5, three letters of recommendation. Additional exam requirements/recommendations for international students: Required—TOEFL (minimum score 550 paper-based; 79 iBT). *Application deadline:* For fall admission, 6/1 for domestic students, 4/30 for international students; for spring admission, 11/1 for domestic students, 9/30 for international students. Application fee: $35 ($45 for international students). Electronic applications accepted. *Financial support:* In 2014–15, 27 students received support, including 14 research assistantships with full tuition reimbursements available (averaging $9,000 per year), 16 teaching assistantships with full and partial tuition reimbursements available (averaging $9,300 per year); career-related internships or fieldwork, institutionally sponsored loans, scholarships/grants, and unspecified assistantships also available. Financial award application deadline: 7/1; financial award applicants required to submit FAFSA. *Faculty research:* Data mining, security and forensics, numerical optimization, computer gaming, enterprise resource planning. *Unit head:* Dr. Terry Countermine, Chair, 423-439-5328, Fax: 423-439-7119, E-mail: counter@etsu.edu. *Application contact:* Kimberly Brockman, Graduate Specialist, 423-439-6165, Fax: 423-439-5624, E-mail: brockmank@etsu.edu.
Website: http://www-cs.etsu.edu/.

École Polytechnique de Montréal, Graduate Programs, Department of Electrical and Computer Engineering, Montréal, QC H3C 3A7, Canada. Offers automation (M Eng, M Sc A, PhD); computer science (M Eng, M Sc A, PhD); electrical engineering (DESS); electrotechnology (M Eng, M Sc A, PhD); microelectronics (M Eng, M Sc A, PhD); microwave technology (M Eng, M Sc A, PhD). Part-time and evening/weekend programs available. *Degree requirements:* For master's, one foreign language, thesis; for doctorate, one foreign language, thesis/dissertation. *Entrance requirements:* For master's, minimum GPA of 2.75; for doctorate, minimum GPA of 3.0. *Faculty research:* Microwaves, telecommunications, software engineering.

Emory University, Laney Graduate School, Department of Mathematics and Computer Science, Atlanta, GA 30322-1100. Offers computer science (MS); computer science and informatics (PhD); mathematics (MS, PhD). Terminal master's awarded for partial completion of doctoral program. *Degree requirements:* For master's, thesis; for doctorate, one foreign language, comprehensive exam, thesis/dissertation. *Entrance requirements:* For master's and doctorate, GRE General Test. Additional exam requirements/recommendations for international students: Recommended—TOEFL. Electronic applications accepted.

Fairleigh Dickinson University, College at Florham, Maxwell Becton College of Arts and Sciences, Department of Computer Science, Madison, NJ 07940-1099. Offers MS.

Fairleigh Dickinson University, Metropolitan Campus, University College: Arts, Sciences, and Professional Studies, School of Computer Sciences and Engineering, Program in Computer Science, Teaneck, NJ 07666-1914. Offers MS.

Fitchburg State University, Division of Graduate and Continuing Education, Program in Computer Science, Fitchburg, MA 01420-2697. Offers MS. Part-time and evening/weekend programs available. *Entrance requirements:* Additional exam requirements/recommendations for international students: Required—TOEFL (minimum score 550 paper-based; 79 iBT). Electronic applications accepted.

Florida Atlantic University, College of Engineering and Computer Science, Department of Computer and Electrical Engineering and Computer Science, Boca Raton, FL 33431-0991. Offers bioengineering (MS); computer engineering (MS, PhD); computer science (MS, PhD); electrical engineering (MS, PhD); information technology and management (MS). Part-time and evening/weekend programs available. Terminal master's awarded for partial completion of doctoral program. *Degree requirements:* For master's, thesis optional; for doctorate, thesis/dissertation, qualifying exam. *Entrance requirements:* For master's, GRE General Test, minimum GPA of 3.0; for doctorate, GRE General Test, master's degree, minimum GPA of 3.5. Additional exam requirements/recommendations for international students: Required—TOEFL (minimum score 500 paper-based; 61 iBT), IELTS (minimum score 6). *Expenses:* Tuition, state resident: full-time $7396; part-time $369.82 per credit hour. Tuition, nonresident: full-time $19,392; part-time $1024.81 per credit hour. Tuition and fees vary according to course load. *Faculty research:* VLSI and neural networks, communication networks, software engineering, computer architecture, multimedia and video processing.

Florida Gulf Coast University, Lutgert College of Business, Program in Computer and Information Systems, Fort Myers, FL 33965-6565. Offers MS. *Faculty:* 55 full-time (17 women), 24 part-time/adjunct (7 women). *Students:* 2 part-time (0 women). Average age 32. *Entrance requirements:* For master's, GMAT, minimum GPA of 3.0. Additional exam requirements/recommendations for international students: Required—TOEFL (minimum score 550 paper-based). *Application deadline:* For fall admission, 6/1 priority date for domestic students; for spring admission, 11/1 for domestic students. Applications are processed on a rolling basis. Application fee: $30. Electronic applications accepted. *Expenses:* Tuition, state resident: full-time $6974. Tuition, nonresident: full-time $28,170. *Required fees:* $1987. Tuition and fees vary according to course load. *Financial support:* Application deadline: 6/30; applicants required to submit FAFSA. *Faculty research:* Advanced distributed learning technologies, object-oriented systems analysis, database management systems, workgroup support systems, software engineering project management. *Unit head:* Dr. Rajesh Srivastava, Chair, 239-590-7372, Fax: 239-590-7330, E-mail: rsrivast@fgcu.edu. *Application contact:* Marisa Ouverson, Director of Enrollment Management, 239-590-7403, Fax: 239-590-7330, E-mail: mouverso@fgcu.edu.

Florida Institute of Technology, Graduate Programs, College of Engineering, Program in Computer Science, Melbourne, FL 32901-6975. Offers MS, PhD. Part-time and evening/weekend programs available. *Students:* 102 full-time (24 women), 34 part-time (7 women); includes 3 minority (1 Black or African American, non-Hispanic/Latino; 2 Asian, non-Hispanic/Latino), 120 international. Average age 29. 587 applicants, 43% accepted, 41 enrolled. In 2014, 14 master's awarded. *Degree requirements:* For master's, comprehensive exam (for some programs), thesis, final exam, seminar, or internship; for doctorate, comprehensive exam, thesis/dissertation, publication in journal, teaching experience (strongly encouraged), specialized research program. *Entrance requirements:* For master's, GRE General Test, minimum GPA of 3.0, 3 letters of recommendation, transcript, differential and integral calculus courses, 12 credits of advanced coursework; for doctorate, GRE General Test, GRE Subject Test in computer science (recommended), 3 letters of recommendation, minimum GPA of 3.5, resume, statement of objectives. Additional exam requirements/recommendations for international students: Required—TOEFL (minimum score 550 paper-based; 79 iBT). *Application deadline:* For fall admission, 4/1 for international students; for spring admission, 9/30 for international students. Applications are processed on a rolling basis. Electronic applications accepted. *Expenses: Tuition:* Part-time $1179 per credit hour. Tuition and fees vary according to campus/location. *Financial support:* Career-related internships or fieldwork, institutionally sponsored loans, tuition waivers (partial), unspecified assistantships, and tuition remissions available. Support available to part-time students. Financial award application deadline: 3/1; financial award applicants required to submit FAFSA. *Faculty research:* Artificial intelligence, software engineering, management and processes, programming languages, database systems. *Unit head:* Dr. Richard Ford, Department Head, 321-674-7473, Fax: 321-674-7046, E-mail: rford@fit.edu. *Application contact:* Cheryl A. Brown, Associate Director of Graduate Admissions, 321-674-7581, Fax: 321-723-9468, E-mail: cbrown@fit.edu.
Website: http://coe.fit.edu/cs.

Florida Institute of Technology, Graduate Programs, Extended Studies Division, Melbourne, FL 32901-6975. Offers acquisition and contract management (MS); aerospace engineering (MS); business administration (MBA, DBA); computer information systems (MS); computer science (MS); electrical engineering (MS); engineering management (MS); human resources management (MS); logistics management (MS), including humanitarian and disaster relief logistics; management (MS), including acquisition and contract management, e-business, human resources management, information systems, logistics management, management, transportation management; material acquisition management (MS); mechanical engineering (MS); operations research (MS); project management (MS), including information systems, operations research; public administration (MPA); quality management (MS); software engineering (MS); space systems (MS); space systems management (MS); supply chain management (MS); systems management (MS), including information systems, operations research; technology management (MS). Part-time and evening/weekend programs available. Postbaccalaureate distance learning degree programs offered (no on-campus study). *Faculty:* 7 full-time (1 woman), 112 part-time/adjunct (29 women). *Students:* 98 full-time (45 women), 975 part-time (396 women); includes 440 minority (292 Black or African American, non-Hispanic/Latino; 13 American Indian or Alaska Native, non-Hispanic/Latino; 32 Asian, non-Hispanic/Latino; 79 Hispanic/Latino; 1 Native Hawaiian or other Pacific Islander, non-Hispanic/Latino; 23 Two or more races, non-Hispanic/Latino), 4 international. Average age 37. 807 applicants, 56% accepted, 258 enrolled. In 2014, 457 master's awarded. *Degree requirements:* For master's, comprehensive exam (for some programs), capstone course. *Entrance requirements:* For master's, GMAT or resume showing 8 years of supervised experience, minimum GPA of 3.0, 2 letters of recommendation, resume. Additional exam requirements/recommendations for international students: Required—TOEFL (minimum score 550 paper-based; 79 iBT). *Application deadline:* For fall admission, 4/1 for international students; for spring admission, 9/30 for international students. Applications are processed on a rolling basis. Electronic applications accepted. *Expenses:* Expenses: Contact institution. *Financial support:* Application deadline: 3/1; applicants required to submit FAFSA. *Unit head:* Dr. Theodore R. Richardson, III, Senior Associate Dean, 321-674-8123, Fax: 321-674-7597, E-mail: trichardson@fit.edu. *Application contact:* Carolyn

Farrior, Director of Graduate Admissions, Online Learning and Off-Campus Programs, 321-674-7118, Fax: 321-674-8216, E-mail: cfarrior@fit.edu.
Website: http://es.fit.edu.

Florida International University, College of Engineering and Computing, School of Computing and Information Sciences, Miami, FL 33199. Offers computer science (MS, PhD); information technology (MS); telecommunications and networking (MS). Part-time and evening/weekend programs available. *Degree requirements:* For master's, thesis or alternative; for doctorate, comprehensive exam, thesis/dissertation. *Entrance requirements:* For master's and doctorate, GRE General Test, 3 letters of recommendation, minimum GPA of 3.0. Additional exam requirements/ recommendations for international students: Required—TOEFL (minimum score 550 paper-based; 80 iBT). Electronic applications accepted. *Faculty research:* Database systems, software engineering, operating systems, networks, bioinformatics and computational biology.

Florida State University, The Graduate School, College of Arts and Sciences, Department of Computer Science, Tallahassee, FL 32306-4530. Offers computer criminology (MS); computer network and system administration (MS); computer science (MS, PhD); information security (MS). Part-time programs available. *Faculty:* 23 full-time (3 women), 1 part-time/adjunct (0 women). *Students:* 161 full-time (33 women), 11 part-time (4 women); includes 19 minority (7 Black or African American, non-Hispanic/Latino; 3 American Indian or Alaska Native, non-Hispanic/Latino; 4 Asian, non-Hispanic/Latino; 4 Hispanic/Latino; 1 Two or more races, non-Hispanic/Latino), 112 international. Average age 28. 455 applicants, 51% accepted, 32 enrolled. In 2014, 30 master's, 7 doctorates awarded. Terminal master's awarded for partial completion of doctoral program. *Degree requirements:* For master's, comprehensive exam (for some programs), thesis (for some programs); for doctorate, comprehensive exam, thesis/ dissertation, qualifying exam, preliminary exam, prospectus defense. *Entrance requirements:* For master's, GRE General Test, minimum undergraduate GPA of 3.0; for doctorate, GRE General Test, minimum GPA of 3.0. Additional exam requirements/ recommendations for international students: Required—TOEFL (minimum score 550 paper-based; 80 iBT), IELTS (minimum score 6.5). *Application deadline:* For fall admission, 7/1 for domestic students, 3/1 priority date for international students; for spring admission, 11/1 for domestic students, 9/1 priority date for international students. Application fee: $30. Electronic applications accepted. *Expenses:* Tuition, state resident: part-time $403.51 per credit hour. Tuition, nonresident: part-time $1004.85 per credit hour. *Required fees:* $75.81 per credit hour. One-time fee: $20 part-time. Tuition and fees vary according to campus/location. *Financial support:* In 2014–15, 106 students received support, including 11 fellowships with full tuition reimbursements available (averaging $21,000 per year), 15 research assistantships with full tuition reimbursements available (averaging $23,670 per year), 53 teaching assistantships with full tuition reimbursements available (averaging $17,220 per year); scholarships/grants, health care benefits, tuition waivers (full and partial), and unspecified assistantships also available. Financial award application deadline: 3/1; financial award applicants required to submit FAFSA. *Faculty research:* Embedded systems, high performance computing, networking, operating systems, security, databases, algorithms, big data, visualization. *Unit head:* Dr. Xin Yuan, Chairman, 850-644-9133, Fax: 850-644-0058, E-mail: xyuan@ cs.fsu.edu. *Application contact:* Daniel B. Clawson, Graduate Coordinator, 850-645-4975, Fax: 850-644-0058, E-mail: clawson@cs.fsu.edu.
Website: http://www.cs.fsu.edu/.

Fordham University, Graduate School of Arts and Sciences, Department of Computer and Information Sciences, New York, NY 10458. Offers biomedical informatics (Advanced Certificate); computer science (MS). Part-time and evening/weekend programs available. *Faculty:* 11 full-time (1 woman). *Students:* 12 full-time (3 women), 9 part-time (4 women); includes 1 minority (Hispanic/Latino), 7 international. Average age 31. 43 applicants, 67% accepted, 12 enrolled. In 2014, 10 master's awarded. *Degree requirements:* For master's, thesis optional. *Entrance requirements:* For master's, GRE General Test. Additional exam requirements/recommendations for international students: Required—TOEFL (minimum score 550 paper-based). *Application deadline:* For fall admission, 1/4 priority date for domestic students; for spring admission, 11/1 for domestic students. Application fee: $70. Electronic applications accepted. *Financial support:* In 2014–15, 5 students received support, including 5 research assistantships with full and partial tuition reimbursements available (averaging $18,960 per year); career-related internships or fieldwork, institutionally sponsored loans, tuition waivers (full and partial), and unspecified assistantships also available. Financial award application deadline: 1/4; financial award applicants required to submit CSS PROFILE or FAFSA. *Faculty research:* Robotics and computer vision, data mining and informatics, information and networking, computation and algorithms, biomedical informatics. *Total annual research expenditures:* $213,000. *Unit head:* Dr. Yangjun Li, Chair, 718-817-5196, Fax: 718-817-4488, E-mail: yli@fordham.edu. *Application contact:* Bernadette Valentino-Morrison, Director of Graduate Admissions, 718-817-4420, Fax: 718-817-3566, E-mail: valentinomor@fordham.edu.

Franklin University, Computer Science Program, Columbus, OH 43215-5399. Offers MS. Part-time and evening/weekend programs available. *Entrance requirements:* For master's, minimum undergraduate GPA of 2.75. Additional exam requirements/ recommendations for international students: Required—TOEFL (minimum score 550 paper-based). Electronic applications accepted. *Expenses:* Contact institution.

Frostburg State University, Graduate School, College of Liberal Arts and Sciences, Department of Computer Science, Program in Applied Computer Science, Frostburg, MD 21532-1099. Offers MS. *Entrance requirements:* Additional exam requirements/ recommendations for international students: Required—TOEFL. Electronic applications accepted.

Gannon University, School of Graduate Studies, College of Engineering and Business, School of Engineering and Computer Science, Program in Computer and Information Science, Erie, PA 16541-0001. Offers applied computer science (MSCIS); information systems (MSCIS); Web development (MSCIS). Part-time and evening/weekend programs available. *Degree requirements:* For master's, thesis (for some programs), directed research. *Entrance requirements:* For master's, GRE or GMAT, letters of recommendation, resume, transcripts, baccalaureate degree in computer and information science or related field, minimum GPA of 2.5. Additional exam requirements/ recommendations for international students: Required—TOEFL (minimum score 79 iBT). Electronic applications accepted.

George Mason University, Volgenau School of Engineering, Department of Computer Science, Fairfax, VA 22030. Offers computer science (MS, PhD, Certificate); information security and assurance (MS); information systems (MS); software engineering (MS). MS programs offered jointly with Old Dominion University, University of Virginia, Virginia Commonwealth University, and Virginia Polytechnic Institute and State University. *Faculty:* 46 full-time (10 women), 17 part-time/adjunct (1 woman). *Students:* 236 full-time (68 women), 246 part-time (50 women); includes 77 minority (13 Black or African American, non-Hispanic/Latino; 48 Asian, non-Hispanic/Latino; 11 Hispanic/Latino; 5 Two or more races, non-Hispanic/Latino), 231 international. Average age 29. 874 applicants, 42% accepted, 119 enrolled. In 2014, 171 master's, 8 doctorates, 22 other advanced degrees awarded. *Degree requirements:* For master's, thesis optional; for doctorate, comprehensive exam, thesis/dissertation. *Entrance requirements:* For master's, GRE, proof of financial support; 2 official college transcripts; resume; self-evaluation form; official bank statement; photocopy of passport; 3 letters of recommendation; baccalaureate degree related to computer science; minimum GPA of 3.0 in last 2 years of undergraduate work; 1 year beyond 1st-year calculus; personal goals statement; for doctorate, GRE, personal goals statement; 2 official copies of transcripts; self-evaluation form; 3 letters of recommendation; photocopy of passport; proof of financial support; official bank statement; resume; 4-year baccalaureate degree with strong background in computer science. Additional exam requirements/ recommendations for international students: Required—TOEFL (minimum score 575 paper-based; 80 iBT), IELTS (minimum score 6.5), PTE. *Application deadline:* For fall admission, 1/15 priority date for domestic students; for spring admission, 8/15 priority date for domestic students. Application fee: $65 ($80 for international students). Electronic applications accepted. *Expenses:* Expenses: Contact institution. *Financial support:* In 2014–15, 113 students received support, including 1 fellowship (averaging $9,302 per year), 46 research assistantships (averaging $19,727 per year), 67 teaching assistantships (averaging $14,678 per year); career-related internships or fieldwork, Federal Work-Study, scholarships/grants, unspecified assistantships, and health care benefits (for full-time research or teaching assistantship recipients) also available. Support available to part-time students. Financial award application deadline: 3/1; financial award applicants required to submit FAFSA. *Faculty research:* Artificial intelligence, image processing/graphics, parallel/distributed systems, software engineering systems. *Total annual research expenditures:* $3.4 million. *Unit head:* Sanjeev Setia, Chair, 703-993-4098, Fax: 703-993-1710, E-mail: setia@gmu.edu. *Application contact:* Michele Pieper, Office Manager, 703-993-9483, Fax: 703-993-1710, E-mail: mpieper@gmu.edu.
Website: http://cs.gmu.edu/.

Georgetown University, Graduate School of Arts and Sciences, Department of Computer Science, Washington, DC 20057. Offers MS, PhD. Part-time and evening/ weekend programs available. *Degree requirements:* For master's, thesis optional. *Entrance requirements:* For master's, GRE, basic course work in data structures, advanced math, and programming; 3 letters of recommendation. Additional exam requirements/recommendations for international students: Required—TOEFL. Electronic applications accepted. *Faculty research:* Data mining, artificial intelligence, software engineering, security.

The George Washington University, School of Engineering and Applied Science, Department of Computer Science, Washington, DC 20052. Offers computer science (MS, D Sc); cybersecurity (MS). Part-time and evening/weekend programs available. *Faculty:* 19 full-time (6 women), 48 part-time/adjunct (6 women). *Students:* 276 full-time (82 women), 157 part-time (44 women); includes 40 minority (10 Black or African American, non-Hispanic/Latino; 18 Asian, non-Hispanic/Latino; 9 Hispanic/Latino; 1 Native Hawaiian or other Pacific Islander, non-Hispanic/Latino; 2 Two or more races, non-Hispanic/Latino), 312 international. Average age 28. 662 applicants, 62% accepted, 141 enrolled. In 2014, 199 master's, 5 doctorates, 41 other advanced degrees awarded. *Degree requirements:* For master's, thesis optional; for doctorate, thesis/dissertation, dissertation defense, qualifying exam. *Entrance requirements:* For master's, appropriate bachelor's degree, minimum GPA of 3.0; for doctorate, GRE (if highest earned degree is BS), appropriate bachelor's or master's degree, minimum GPA of 3.3; for other advanced degree, appropriate master's degree, minimum GPA of 3.4. Additional exam requirements/recommendations for international students: Required—TOEFL or The George Washington University English as a Foreign Language Test. *Application deadline:* For fall admission, 3/1 priority date for domestic students; for spring admission, 10/1 for domestic students. Applications are processed on a rolling basis. Application fee: $75. *Financial support:* In 2014–15, 49 students received support. Fellowships with tuition reimbursements available, research assistantships, teaching assistantships with tuition reimbursements available, career-related internships or fieldwork, institutionally sponsored loans, and tuition waivers available. Financial award application deadline: 3/1; financial award applicants required to submit FAFSA. *Faculty research:* Computer graphics, multimedia, VLSI, parallel processing. *Unit head:* Abdou Youssef, Chair, 202-994-7181, E-mail: ayoussef@gwu.edu. *Application contact:* Adina Lav, Marketing, Recruiting and Admissions, 202-994-5827, Fax: 202-994-0909, E-mail: engineering@gwu.edu.
Website: http://www.cs.gwu.edu/.

Georgia Institute of Technology, Graduate Studies, College of Computing, Program in Computer Science, Atlanta, GA 30332-0001. Offers MS, PhD. Part-time programs available. Postbaccalaureate distance learning degree programs offered (no on-campus study). *Students:* 445 full-time (98 women), 1,289 part-time (141 women); includes 414 minority (70 Black or African American, non-Hispanic/Latino; 1 American Indian or Alaska Native, non-Hispanic/Latino; 208 Asian, non-Hispanic/Latino; 86 Hispanic/Latino; 2 Native Hawaiian or other Pacific Islander, non-Hispanic/Latino; 47 Two or more races, non-Hispanic/Latino), 486 international. Average age 29. 3,861 applicants, 31% accepted, 736 enrolled. In 2014, 153 master's, 39 doctorates awarded. Terminal master's awarded for partial completion of doctoral program. *Degree requirements:* For master's, thesis optional; for doctorate, comprehensive exam, thesis/dissertation. *Entrance requirements:* For master's, GRE General Test and Subject Test in Computer Science, http://www.grad.gatech.edu/cs; for doctorate, GRE General Test and Subject Tests in Computer Science, Mathematics, or Physics, http://www.grad.gatech.edu/cs. Additional exam requirements/recommendations for international students: Required—TOEFL (minimum score 600 paper-based; 100 iBT). *Application deadline:* For fall admission, 2/1 priority date for domestic and international students. Applications are processed on a rolling basis. Application fee: $75. Electronic applications accepted. *Expenses:* Expenses: $134 per semester credit hour plus fees of $301 per semester (for online MS). *Financial support:* Fellowships, research assistantships, teaching assistantships, career-related internships or fieldwork, Federal Work-Study, institutionally sponsored loans, tuition waivers (partial), and unspecified assistantships available. Support available to part-time students. Financial award application deadline: 5/1. *Unit head:* David White, Faculty Director/Coordinator, 404-385-4301, E-mail: david.white@cc.gatech.edu. *Application contact:* Rebecca Wilson, Graduate Coordinator, 404-385-1728, E-mail: rebecca.wilson@cc.gatech.edu.
Website: http://www.scs.gatech.edu/.

Georgia Southern University, Jack N. Averitt College of Graduate Studies, Allen E. Paulson College of Engineering and Information Technology, Program in Computer Science, Statesboro, GA 30460. Offers MS. Part-time programs available. Postbaccalaureate distance learning degree programs offered (no on-campus study). *Students:* 1 full-time (0 women), 41 part-time (6 women); includes 18 minority (10 Black or African American, non-Hispanic/Latino; 7 Hispanic/Latino; 1 Two or more races, non-Hispanic/Latino), 3 international. Average age 33. 36 applicants, 42% accepted, 6 enrolled. In 2014, 9 master's awarded. *Degree requirements:* For master's, thesis (for some programs). *Entrance requirements:* For master's, GRE. Additional exam requirements/recommendations for international students: Required—TOEFL (minimum score 80 iBT). *Application deadline:* For fall admission, 7/31 for domestic and international students. Application fee: $50. *Expenses:* Tuition, state resident: full-time $7236; part-time $277 per semester hour. Tuition, nonresident: full-time $27,118; part-

time $1105 per semester hour. *Required fees:* $2092. *Financial support:* In 2014–15, 1 student received support. Unspecified assistantships available. *Faculty research:* Cyber physical systems, big data, data mining and analytics, cloud computing. *Total annual research expenditures:* $663. *Unit head:* Lixin Li, Program Coordinator, 912-478-7646, E-mail: lli@georgiasouthern.edu.
Website: http://ceit.georgiasouthern.edu/cs/.

Georgia Southwestern State University, Graduate Studies, School of Computing and Mathematics, Americus, GA 31709-4693. Offers computer science (MS). Part-time programs available. Postbaccalaureate distance learning degree programs offered (no on-campus study). *Faculty:* 2 full-time (0 women), 1 part-time/adjunct (0 women). *Students:* 6 full-time (1 woman), 19 part-time (7 women); includes 9 minority (5 Black or African American, non-Hispanic/Latino; 3 Asian, non-Hispanic/Latino; 1 Two or more races, non-Hispanic/Latino), 11 international. Average age 37. 11 applicants, 100% accepted, 4 enrolled. In 2014, 12 master's awarded. *Degree requirements:* For master's, thesis (for some programs). *Entrance requirements:* For master's, GRE, undergraduate degree from accredited college; minimum undergraduate GPA of 2.5 as reported on official final transcripts from all institutions attended; letters of recommendation; for Graduate Certificate, GRE, undergraduate degree from accredited college; minimum undergraduate GPA of 2.5 as reported on official final transcripts from all institutions attended; letters of recommendation. Additional exam requirements/recommendations for international students: Required—TOEFL (minimum score 523 paper-based; 69 iBT), IELTS (minimum score 6.5). *Application deadline:* For fall admission, 5/31 for domestic students; for spring admission, 10/15 for domestic students; for summer admission, 3/15 for domestic students. Applications are processed on a rolling basis. Application fee: $25. Electronic applications accepted. *Expenses:* Expenses: $250 per credit hour. *Financial support:* Application deadline: 6/1; applicants required to submit FAFSA. *Unit head:* Dr. Boris V. Peltsverger, Dean, 229-931-2100. *Application contact:* Office of Graduate Admission, 229-931-4206, Fax: 229-931-2983.
Website: https://gsw.edu/Academics/Schools-and-Departments/School-of-Computing-and-Mathematics/index.

Georgia State University, College of Arts and Sciences, Department of Computer Science, Atlanta, GA 30302-3083. Offers bioinformatics (MS, PhD); computer science (MS, PhD). Part-time programs available. *Faculty:* 16 full-time (2 women). *Students:* 136 full-time (54 women), 26 part-time (8 women); includes 15 minority (8 Black or African American, non-Hispanic/Latino; 4 Asian, non-Hispanic/Latino; 1 Hispanic/Latino; 2 Two or more races, non-Hispanic/Latino), 126 international. Average age 29. 303 applicants, 27% accepted, 36 enrolled. In 2014, 42 master's, 8 doctorates awarded. Terminal master's awarded for partial completion of doctoral program. *Degree requirements:* For master's, comprehensive exam, thesis (for some programs); for doctorate, comprehensive exam, thesis/dissertation, proposal defense. *Entrance requirements:* For master's and doctorate, GRE General Test. Additional exam requirements/recommendations for international students: Required—TOEFL (minimum score 550 paper-based; 80 iBT). *Application deadline:* For fall admission, 3/15 for domestic and international students; for spring admission, 10/15 for domestic and international students. Application fee: $50. Electronic applications accepted. *Expenses:* Tuition, state resident: full-time $6516; part-time $362 per credit hour. Tuition, nonresident: full-time $22,014; part-time $1223 per credit hour. *Required fees:* $2128 per semester. Tuition and fees vary according to course load and program. *Financial support:* In 2014–15, fellowships with full tuition reimbursements (averaging $22,000 per year), research assistantships with full tuition reimbursements (averaging $16,000 per year), teaching assistantships with full tuition reimbursements (averaging $16,000 per year) were awarded; institutionally sponsored loans, health care benefits, and unspecified assistantships also available. Financial award application deadline: 2/15. *Faculty research:* Artificial intelligence and computational intelligence, bioinformatics, computer software systems, databases, graphics and human computer interaction, networks and parallel and distributed computing. *Unit head:* Dr. Yi Pan, Professor/Chair, 404-413-5700, Fax: 404-413-5717, E-mail: pan@cs.gsu.edu. *Application contact:* Dr. Rajshekhar Sunderraman, Director of Graduate Studies, 404-413-5726, Fax: 404-413-5717, E-mail: grad@cs.gsu.edu.
Website: http://www.cs.gsu.edu/.

Georgia State University, College of Arts and Sciences, Department of Mathematics and Statistics, Atlanta, GA 30302-3083. Offers bioinformatics (MS, PhD); biostatistics (MS, PhD); discrete mathematics (MS); mathematics (MS, PhD); scientific computing (MS); statistics (MS). Part-time programs available. *Faculty:* 22 full-time (7 women). *Students:* 75 full-time (38 women), 30 part-time (9 women); includes 31 minority (13 Black or African American, non-Hispanic/Latino; 15 Asian, non-Hispanic/Latino; 3 Hispanic/Latino), 46 international. Average age 33. 95 applicants, 51% accepted, 19 enrolled. In 2014, 21 master's, 4 doctorates awarded. Terminal master's awarded for partial completion of doctoral program. *Degree requirements:* For master's, comprehensive exam (for some programs), thesis optional; for doctorate, comprehensive exam, thesis/dissertation. *Entrance requirements:* For master's and doctorate, GRE. Additional exam requirements/recommendations for international students: Required—TOEFL (minimum score 550 paper-based; 80 iBT). *Application deadline:* For fall admission, 7/1 priority date for domestic and international students; for spring admission, 11/15 priority date for domestic and international students. Application fee: $50. Electronic applications accepted. *Expenses:* Tuition, state resident: full-time $6516; part-time $362 per credit hour. Tuition, nonresident: full-time $22,014; part-time $1223 per credit hour. *Required fees:* $2128 per semester. Tuition and fees vary according to course load and program. *Financial support:* In 2014–15, fellowships with full tuition reimbursements (averaging $22,000 per year), research assistantships with full tuition reimbursements (averaging $9,000 per year), teaching assistantships with full tuition reimbursements (averaging $9,000 per year) were awarded; institutionally sponsored loans, scholarships/grants, health care benefits, and unspecified assistantships also available. Financial award application deadline: 2/1. *Faculty research:* Algebra, matrix theory, graph theory and combinatorics; applied mathematics and analysis; collegiate mathematics education; statistics, biostatistics and applications; bioinformatics, dynamical systems. *Unit head:* Dr. Guantao Chen, Chair, 404-413-6436, Fax: 404-413-6403, E-mail: gchen@gsu.edu. *Application contact:* Dr. Zhongshan Li, Graduate Director, 404-413-6437, Fax: 404-413-6403, E-mail: zli@gsu.edu.
Website: http://www2.gsu.edu/~wwwmat/.

Governors State University, College of Arts and Sciences, Program in Computer Science, University Park, IL 60484. Offers MS. Part-time and evening/weekend programs available. *Degree requirements:* For master's, thesis or alternative. *Entrance requirements:* For master's, minimum GPA of 2.75.

The Graduate Center, City University of New York, Graduate Studies, Program in Computer Science, New York, NY 10016-4039. Offers PhD. Program offered jointly with College of Staten Island of the City University of New York. *Degree requirements:* For doctorate, one foreign language, thesis/dissertation. *Entrance requirements:* For doctorate, GRE General Test. Additional exam requirements/recommendations for international students: Required—TOEFL. Electronic applications accepted.

Grand Valley State University, Padnos College of Engineering and Computing, School of Computing and Information Systems, Allendale, MI 49401-9403. Offers computer information systems (MS), including databases, distributed systems, management of information systems, object-oriented systems, software engineering. Part-time and evening/weekend programs available. *Faculty:* 8 full-time (0 women). *Students:* 26 full-time (10 women), 57 part-time (12 women); includes 10 minority (7 Asian, non-Hispanic/Latino; 3 Hispanic/Latino), 21 international. Average age 32. 44 applicants, 82% accepted, 18 enrolled. In 2014, 29 master's awarded. *Degree requirements:* For master's, thesis or alternative. *Entrance requirements:* For master's, GMAT or GRE General Test. Additional exam requirements/recommendations for international students: Required—TOEFL. *Application deadline:* For fall admission, 6/1 for international students; for winter admission, 9/1 for international students. Applications are processed on a rolling basis. Application fee: $30. Electronic applications accepted. *Expenses:* Tuition, state resident: full-time $10,602; part-time $589 per credit hour. Tuition, nonresident: full-time $14,022; part-time $779 per credit hour. Tuition and fees vary according to degree level and program. *Financial support:* In 2014–15, 17 students received support, including 10 fellowships (averaging $1,856 per year), 7 research assistantships with full and partial tuition reimbursements available (averaging $10,134 per year). *Faculty research:* Object technology, distributed computing, information systems management database, software engineering. *Unit head:* Paul Leidig, Director, 616-331-2038, Fax: 616-331-2106, E-mail: leidigp@gvsu.edu. *Application contact:* D. Robert Adams, Graduate Program Chair, 616-331-3885, Fax: 616-331-2106, E-mail: adams@cis.gvsu.edu.
Website: http://www.cis.gvsu.edu/.

Hampton University, School of Science, Department of Computer Science, Hampton, VA 23668. Offers MS. Part-time and evening/weekend programs available. *Faculty:* 8 full-time (3 women). *Students:* 9 full-time (3 women), 2 part-time (both women); includes 9 minority (6 Black or African American, non-Hispanic/Latino; 3 Asian, non-Hispanic/Latino), 5 international. Average age 22. 8 applicants, 63% accepted, 5 enrolled. *Degree requirements:* For master's, thesis or alternative. *Entrance requirements:* For master's, GRE General Test, TOEFL or IELTS. Additional exam requirements/recommendations for international students: Required—TOEFL (minimum score 525 paper-based), IELTS (minimum score 6.5). *Application deadline:* For fall admission, 6/1 priority date for domestic students, 4/1 priority date for international students; for spring admission, 11/1 priority date for domestic students, 9/1 priority date for international students; for summer admission, 4/1 priority date for domestic students, 2/1 priority date for international students. Applications are processed on a rolling basis. Application fee: $35. Electronic applications accepted. *Expenses: Tuition:* Full-time $20,526; part-time $522 per credit. *Required fees:* $100. *Financial support:* In 2014–15, 5 fellowships (averaging $38,900 per year), 1 research assistantship were awarded; career-related internships or fieldwork, Federal Work-Study, and scholarships/grants also available. Support available to part-time students. Financial award application deadline: 6/30; financial award applicants required to submit FAFSA. *Faculty research:* Software testing, neural networks, parallel processing, computer graphics, natural language processing. *Unit head:* Dr. Jean Muhammad, Chair, 757-727-5552.

Harvard University, Graduate School of Arts and Sciences, School of Engineering and Applied Sciences, Cambridge, MA 02138. Offers applied mathematics (ME, SM, PhD); applied physics (ME, SM, PhD); computer science (ME, SM, PhD); engineering science (ME); engineering sciences (SM, PhD). Part-time programs available. Terminal master's awarded for partial completion of doctoral program. *Degree requirements:* For master's, thesis optional; for doctorate, comprehensive exam, thesis/dissertation. *Entrance requirements:* For master's and doctorate, GRE General Test, GRE Subject Test (recommended), 3 letters of recommendation. Additional exam requirements/recommendations for international students: Required—TOEFL (minimum score 80 iBT). Electronic applications accepted. *Faculty research:* Applied mathematics, applied physics, computer science and electrical engineering, environmental engineering, mechanical and biomedical engineering.

Hood College, Graduate School, Programs in Computer and Information Sciences, Frederick, MD 21701-8575. Offers computer and information sciences (MS); computer science (MS); information security (Certificate). Part-time and evening/weekend programs available. *Degree requirements:* For master's, thesis. *Entrance requirements:* For master's, minimum GPA of 2.75. Additional exam requirements/recommendations for international students: Required—TOEFL (minimum score 575 paper-based; 89 iBT), IELTS (minimum score 6.5). Electronic applications accepted. Application fee is waived when completed online. *Faculty research:* Systems engineering, natural language, processing, database design, artificial intelligence and parallel distributed computing.

Howard University, College of Engineering, Architecture, and Computer Sciences, School of Engineering and Computer Science, Department of Systems and Computer Science, Washington, DC 20059-0002. Offers MCS. Offered through the Graduate School of Arts and Sciences. Part-time programs available. *Degree requirements:* For master's, thesis. *Entrance requirements:* For master's, GRE General Test, minimum GPA of 3.0. Additional exam requirements/recommendations for international students: Required—TOEFL. Electronic applications accepted. *Faculty research:* Software engineering, software fault-tolerance, software reliability, artificial intelligence.

Illinois Institute of Technology, Graduate College, College of Science, Department of Computer Science, Chicago, IL 60616. Offers business (MCS); computational intelligence (MCS); computer networking and communications (MCS); computer science (MCS, MS, PhD); cyber-physical systems (MCS); data analytics (MCS); data science (MAS); database systems (MCS); distributed and cloud computing (MCS); education (MCS); finance (MCS); information security and assurance (MCS); software engineering (MCS); telecommunications and software engineering (MAS); MS/MAS. Part-time and evening/weekend programs available. Postbaccalaureate distance learning degree programs offered (no on-campus study). *Faculty:* 29 full-time (5 women), 8 part-time/adjunct (1 woman). *Students:* 432 full-time (108 women), 117 part-time (27 women); includes 11 minority (3 Black or African American, non-Hispanic/Latino; 7 Asian, non-Hispanic/Latino; 1 Two or more races, non-Hispanic/Latino), 495 international. Average age 26. 2,573 applicants, 42% accepted, 244 enrolled. In 2014, 164 master's, 2 doctorates awarded. Terminal master's awarded for partial completion of doctoral program. *Degree requirements:* For master's, thesis optional; for doctorate, comprehensive exam, thesis/dissertation. *Entrance requirements:* For master's, MS GRE General Test (minimum scores: 298 Quantitative and Verbal, 3.0 Analytical Writing); MAS GRE General Test (minimum scores: 292 Quantitative and Verbal, 2.5 Analytical Writing), minimum undergraduate GPA of 3.0; for doctorate, GRE General Test (minimum scores: 304 Quantitative and Verbal, 3.5 Analytical Writing), minimum undergraduate GPA of 3.0. Additional exam requirements/recommendations for international students: Required—TOEFL (minimum score 523 paper-based; 70 iBT). *Application deadline:* For fall admission, 5/1 for domestic and international students; for spring admission, 10/15 for domestic and international students. Applications are processed on a rolling basis. Application fee: $50. Electronic applications accepted. *Expenses: Tuition:* Full-time $22,500; part-time $1250 per credit hour. *Required fees:* $30 per course. $260 per semester. One-time fee: $235. Tuition and fees vary according to course load and program. *Financial support:* Fellowships with partial tuition reimbursements, research assistantships with full and partial tuition reimbursements, teaching assistantships with full and partial tuition reimbursements, career-related internships or fieldwork, Federal Work-Study, institutionally sponsored loans, scholarships/grants, traineeships, health care benefits, tuition waivers (partial), and

unspecified assistantships available. Support available to part-time students. Financial award applicants required to submit FAFSA. *Faculty research:* Parallel and distributed processing, high-performance computing, computational linguistics, information retrieval, data mining, grid computing. *Unit head:* Dr. Eunice Santos, Chair/Professor, 312-567-5150, E-mail: eunice.santos@iit.edu. *Application contact:* Rishab Malhotra, Director, Graduate Admission, 866-472-3448, Fax: 312-567-3138, E-mail: inquiry.grad@iit.edu.
Website: http://www.iit.edu/csl/cs/.

Indiana State University, College of Graduate and Professional Studies, College of Arts and Sciences, Department of Mathematics and Computer Science, Terre Haute, IN 47809. Offers math teaching (MA, MS); mathematics and computer science (MA); mathematics and computer sciences (MS). Part-time programs available. *Degree requirements:* For master's, thesis or alternative. *Entrance requirements:* For master's, 24 semester hours of course work in undergraduate mathematics. Electronic applications accepted.

Indiana University Bloomington, School of Informatics and Computing, Program in Computer Science, Bloomington, IN 47405. Offers MS, PhD. *Faculty:* 40 full-time (5 women), 12 part-time/adjunct (1 woman). *Students:* 358 full-time (77 women); includes 11 minority (3 Black or African American, non-Hispanic/Latino; 3 Asian, non-Hispanic/Latino; 5 Hispanic/Latino), 318 international. Average age 27. 1,179 applicants, 37% accepted, 143 enrolled. In 2014, 175 master's, 12 doctorates awarded. Terminal master's awarded for partial completion of doctoral program. *Degree requirements:* For master's, thesis optional; for doctorate, comprehensive exam, thesis/dissertation, oral and written exams. *Entrance requirements:* For master's and doctorate, GRE General Test. Additional exam requirements/recommendations for international students: Required—TOEFL. *Application deadline:* For fall admission, 1/15 priority date for domestic students, 12/1 priority date for international students. Application fee: $55 ($65 for international students). Electronic applications accepted. *Financial support:* In 2014–15, 1 fellowship with full tuition reimbursement (averaging $25,000 per year), 66 research assistantships with full tuition reimbursements (averaging $19,150 per year), 38 teaching assistantships with full tuition reimbursements (averaging $19,150 per year) were awarded; health care benefits and unspecified assistantships also available. *Faculty research:* Bioinformatics, high-performance computing, applied logic and computational theory, programming languages, security, compilers, networking, databases. *Unit head:* Dr. Funda Ergun, CS Director of Graduate Studies, E-mail: fergun@indiana.edu. *Application contact:* Rachel Harris, Admissions and Records Coordinator, 812-855-6487, E-mail: graduate-cs@soic.indiana.edu.
Website: http://www.cs.indiana.edu.

Indiana University–Purdue University Fort Wayne, College of Engineering, Technology, and Computer Science, Department of Computer Science, Fort Wayne, IN 46805-1499. Offers applied computer science (MS). Part-time programs available. *Faculty:* 7 full-time (0 women). *Students:* 6 full-time (2 women), 17 part-time (3 women); includes 4 minority (1 Black or African American, non-Hispanic/Latino; 2 Asian, non-Hispanic/Latino; 1 Hispanic/Latino), 4 international. Average age 32. 10 applicants, 100% accepted, 8 enrolled. In 2014, 15 master's awarded. *Entrance requirements:* For master's, GRE General Test, minimum GPA of 3.0. Additional exam requirements/recommendations for international students: Required—TOEFL (minimum score 550 paper-based; 79 iBT); Recommended—TWE. *Application deadline:* For fall admission, 7/15 for domestic students, 5/15 for international students; for spring admission, 12/1 for domestic students, 10/15 for international students. Applications are processed on a rolling basis. Application fee: $55 ($60 for international students). Electronic applications accepted. *Financial support:* In 2014–15, 1 research assistantship with partial tuition reimbursement (averaging $13,522 per year), 3 teaching assistantships with partial tuition reimbursements (averaging $13,522 per year) were awarded; career-related internships or fieldwork, scholarships/grants, and unspecified assistantships also available. Support available to part-time students. Financial award application deadline: 3/1; financial award applicants required to submit FAFSA. *Faculty research:* Architecture, cloud computing and security. *Total annual research expenditures:* $9,979. *Unit head:* Dr. Peter Ng, Chair, 260-481-6237, Fax: 260-481-5734, E-mail: ngp@ipfw.edu. *Application contact:* Dr. Jin Soung Yoo, Graduate Program Director, 260-481-6946, Fax: 260-481-5734, E-mail: yooj@ipfw.edu.
Website: http://www.ipfw.edu/cs.

Indiana University–Purdue University Indianapolis, School of Science, Department of Computer and Information Science, Indianapolis, IN 46202-5132. Offers computer science (MS, PhD). Part-time programs available. *Faculty:* 15 full-time (2 women), 2 part-time/adjunct (1 woman). *Students:* 106 full-time (42 women), 54 part-time (12 women); includes 9 minority (3 Black or African American, non-Hispanic/Latino; 4 Asian, non-Hispanic/Latino; 1 Hispanic/Latino; 1 Two or more races, non-Hispanic/Latino), 132 international. Average age 28. 292 applicants, 37% accepted, 55 enrolled. In 2014, 63 master's awarded. Terminal master's awarded for partial completion of doctoral program. *Degree requirements:* For master's and Graduate Certificate, thesis optional; for doctorate, thesis/dissertation. *Entrance requirements:* For master's, doctorate, and Graduate Certificate, BS in computer science or the equivalent with a minimum GPA of 3.0 (or equivalent). Additional exam requirements/recommendations for international students: Required—TOEFL (minimum score 550 paper-based; 79 iBT), IELTS (minimum score 6.5), PTE (minimum score 58). *Application deadline:* For fall admission, 1/15 priority date for domestic and international students; for spring admission, 9/15 for domestic students. Application fee: $60 ($65 for international students). Electronic applications accepted. *Expenses:* Expenses: $1325 per course (3 credits) resident, $3268 per course (3 credits) non-resident. *Financial support:* In 2014–15, 40 students received support, including 2 fellowships with full tuition reimbursements available (averaging $20,000 per year), 10 research assistantships with full and partial tuition reimbursements available (averaging $14,000 per year), 20 teaching assistantships with full and partial tuition reimbursements available (averaging $14,000 per year); institutionally sponsored loans, scholarships/grants, health care benefits, tuition waivers (full and partial), and unspecified assistantships also available. Financial award application deadline: 1/15. *Faculty research:* Imaging and visualization; networking and security; software engineering; distributed and parallel computing; database, data mining and machine learning. *Unit head:* Dr. Shiaofen Fang, Chair, 317-274-9727, Fax: 317-274-9742, E-mail: sfang@cs.iupui.edu. *Application contact:* Nicole Wittlief, Graduate Admissions & Program Coordinator, 317-274-3883, Fax: 317-274-9742, E-mail: wittlief@cs.iupui.edu.
Website: http://www.cs.iupui.edu/.

Indiana University South Bend, College of Liberal Arts and Sciences, South Bend, IN 46634-7111. Offers applied mathematics and computer science (MS); English (MA); liberal studies (MLS); public affairs (MPA). Part-time and evening/weekend programs available. *Faculty:* 79 full-time (33 women). *Students:* 41 full-time (26 women), 89 part-time (59 women); includes 24 minority (12 Black or African American, non-Hispanic/Latino; 1 Asian, non-Hispanic/Latino; 3 Hispanic/Latino; 1 Native Hawaiian or other Pacific Islander, non-Hispanic/Latino; 7 Two or more races, non-Hispanic/Latino), 15 international. Average age 37. 58 applicants, 72% accepted, 33 enrolled. In 2014, 33 master's awarded. *Degree requirements:* For master's, thesis (for some programs). *Entrance requirements:* For master's, minimum GPA of 3.0. Additional exam requirements/recommendations for international students: Required—TOEFL. *Application deadline:* For fall admission, 7/31 priority date for domestic students, 7/1 priority date for international students; for spring admission, 3/31 priority date for domestic students, 11/1 priority date for international students. Applications are processed on a rolling basis. *Financial support:* In 2014–15, 5 teaching assistantships were awarded; Federal Work-Study also available. Support available to part-time students. *Faculty research:* Artificial intelligence, bioinformatics, English language and literature, creative writing, computer networks. *Total annual research expenditures:* $127,000. *Unit head:* Dr. Elizabeth E. Dunn, Dean, 574-520-4290, E-mail: elizdunn@iusb.edu. *Application contact:* Admissions Counselor, 574-520-4839, Fax: 574-520-4834, E-mail: graduate@iusb.edu.
Website: https://www.iusb.edu/clas/academics/index.php.

Instituto Tecnológico y de Estudios Superiores de Monterrey, Campus Central de Veracruz, Graduate Programs, Córdoba, Mexico. Offers administration (MA); administration of information technologies (MTI); computer sciences (MCC); education (MEE); educational institution administration (MAD); educational technology (MTE); electronic commerce (MCE); finance (MAF); humanistic studies (MEH); international business for Latin America (MNL); marketing (MMT); science (MCP). Part-time and evening/weekend programs available. Postbaccalaureate distance learning degree programs offered (minimal on-campus study). *Degree requirements:* For master's, thesis (for some programs). *Entrance requirements:* For master's, PAEP College Board. Electronic applications accepted.

Instituto Tecnológico y de Estudios Superiores de Monterrey, Campus Ciudad de México, Virtual University Division, Ciudad de Mexico, Mexico. Offers administration of information technologies (MA); computer sciences (MA); education (MA, PhD); educational technology (MA); environmental engineering (MA); environmental systems (MA); humanistic studies (MA); industrial engineering (MA); international business for Latin America (MA); quality systems (MA); quality systems and productivity (MA). Part-time and evening/weekend programs available. Postbaccalaureate distance learning degree programs offered (minimal on-campus study). *Entrance requirements:* For master's and doctorate, Instituto entrance exam. Additional exam requirements/recommendations for international students: Required—TOEFL.

Instituto Tecnológico y de Estudios Superiores de Monterrey, Campus Cuernavaca, Programs in Information Science, Temixco, Mexico. Offers administration of information technology (MATI); computer science (MCC, DCC); information technology (MTI).

Instituto Tecnológico y de Estudios Superiores de Monterrey, Campus Estado de México, Professional and Graduate Division, Estado de Mexico, Mexico. Offers administration of information technologies (MITA); architecture (M Arch); business administration (GMBA, MBA); computer sciences (MCS, PhD); education (M Ed); educational institution administration (MAD); educational technology and innovation (PhD); electronic commerce (MEC); environmental systems (MS); finance (MAF); humanistic studies (MHS); information sciences and knowledge management (MISKM); information systems (MS); manufacturing systems (MS); marketing (MEM); quality systems and productivity (MS); science and materials engineering (PhD); telecommunications management (MTM). Part-time programs available. Postbaccalaureate distance learning degree programs offered (minimal on-campus study). *Degree requirements:* For master's, one foreign language, thesis (for some programs); for doctorate, one foreign language, thesis/dissertation. *Entrance requirements:* For master's, E-PAEP 500, interview; for doctorate, E-PAEP 500, research proposal. Additional exam requirements/recommendations for international students: Required—TOEFL (minimum score 550 paper-based). *Faculty research:* Surface treatments by plasmas, mechanical properties, robotics, graphical computing, mechatronics security protocols.

Instituto Tecnológico y de Estudios Superiores de Monterrey, Campus Irapuato, Graduate Programs, Irapuato, Mexico. Offers administration (MBA); administration of information technology (MAIT); administration of telecommunications (MAT); architecture (M Arch); computer science (MCS); education (M Ed); educational administration (MEA); educational innovation and technology (DEIT); educational technology (MET); electronic commerce (MBA); environmental administration and planning (MEAP); environmental systems (MES); finances (MBA); humanistic studies (MHS); international management for Latin American executives (MIMLAE); library and information science (MLIS); manufacturing quality management (MMQM); marketing research (MBA).

Instituto Tecnológico y de Estudios Superiores de Monterrey, Campus Monterrey, Graduate and Research Division, Program in Computer Science, Monterrey, Mexico. Offers artificial intelligence (PhD); computer science (MS); information systems (MS); information technology (MS). Part-time programs available. *Degree requirements:* For master's, one foreign language, thesis; for doctorate, one foreign language, thesis/dissertation. *Entrance requirements:* For master's, EXADEP; for doctorate, master's degree in related field. Additional exam requirements/recommendations for international students: Required—TOEFL. *Faculty research:* Distributed systems, software engineering, decision support systems.

Inter American University of Puerto Rico, Fajardo Campus, Graduate Programs, Fajardo, PR 00738-7003. Offers computer science (MS); educational management and leadership (MA Ed); elementary education (MA Ed); general business (MBA); management information systems (MBA); marketing (MBA); special education (MA Ed).

Inter American University of Puerto Rico, Guayama Campus, Department of Natural and Applied Sciences, Guayama, PR 00785. Offers computer security and networks (MS); networking and security (MCS).

Inter American University of Puerto Rico, Metropolitan Campus, Graduate Programs, Program in Open Information Systems, San Juan, PR 00919-1293. Offers MS. *Degree requirements:* For master's, 2 foreign languages.

Iona College, School of Arts and Science, Department of Computer Science, New Rochelle, NY 10801-1890. Offers computer science (MS); cyber security (MS). Part-time and evening/weekend programs available. *Faculty:* 4 full-time (2 women). *Students:* 4 full-time (1 woman), 9 part-time (1 woman); includes 6 minority (3 Black or African American, non-Hispanic/Latino; 3 Hispanic/Latino), 1 international. Average age 26. 15 applicants, 93% accepted, 7 enrolled. In 2014, 1 master's awarded. *Degree requirements:* For master's, thesis optional. *Entrance requirements:* For master's, minimum GPA of 3.0. Additional exam requirements/recommendations for international students: Required—TOEFL (minimum score 550 paper-based; 80 iBT), IELTS (minimum score 6.5). *Application deadline:* For fall admission, 8/1 priority date for domestic students, 5/1 priority date for international students; for spring admission, 1/1 priority date for domestic students, 9/1 priority date for international students. Applications are processed on a rolling basis. Application fee: $50. Electronic applications accepted. *Expenses:* Expenses: Contact institution. *Financial support:* In 2014–15, 2 research assistantships with full tuition reimbursements were awarded; tuition waivers (partial) and unspecified assistantships also available. Support available to part-time students. Financial award application deadline: 4/15; financial award applicants required to submit FAFSA. *Faculty research:* Parallel procession, data mining, machine learning, cyber security, medical imaging. *Unit head:* Robert Schiaffino,

Computer Science

PhD, Chair, 914-633-2338, E-mail: rschiaffino@iona.edu. *Application contact:* Amanda St. Bernard, Assistant Director, Graduate Admissions, 914-633-2440, Fax: 914-633-2277, E-mail: astbernard@iona.edu.
Website: http://www.iona.edu/Academics/School-of-Arts-Science/Departments/Computer-Science/Graduate-Programs.aspx.

Iowa State University of Science and Technology, Department of Computer Science, Ames, IA 50011. Offers MS, PhD. *Degree requirements:* For master's, thesis; for doctorate, thesis/dissertation. *Entrance requirements:* For master's and doctorate, GRE General Test. Additional exam requirements/recommendations for international students: Recommended—TOEFL (minimum score 550 paper-based; 79 iBT), IELTS (minimum score 6.5). Electronic applications accepted.

Jackson State University, Graduate School, College of Science, Engineering and Technology, Department of Computer Science, Jackson, MS 39217. Offers MS. Part-time and evening/weekend programs available. *Degree requirements:* For master's, comprehensive exam, thesis. *Entrance requirements:* For master's, GRE General Test. Additional exam requirements/recommendations for international students: Required—TOEFL (minimum score 520 paper-based; 67 iBT).

Jacksonville State University, College of Graduate Studies and Continuing Education, College of Arts and Sciences, Program in Computer Systems and Software Design, Jacksonville, AL 36265-1602. Offers MS. Part-time and evening/weekend programs available. *Faculty:* 11 full-time (5 women). *Students:* 1 (woman) full-time, 13 part-time (3 women); includes 1 minority (Hispanic/Latino), 3 international. Average age 30. 11 applicants, 45% accepted, 3 enrolled. In 2014, 13 master's awarded. *Degree requirements:* For master's, comprehensive exam, thesis (for some programs). *Entrance requirements:* Additional exam requirements/recommendations for international students: Required—TOEFL (minimum score 500 paper-based; 61 iBT). *Application deadline:* Applications are processed on a rolling basis. Application fee: $35. Electronic applications accepted. *Financial support:* In 2014–15, 5 students received support, including 3 teaching assistantships. Support available to part-time students. Financial award application deadline: 4/1; financial award applicants required to submit FAFSA. *Unit head:* Dr. Donnie Ford, Head, 256-782-5242, E-mail: dford@jsu.edu. *Application contact:* Dr. Jean Pugliese, Associate Dean, 256-782-8278, Fax: 256-782-5321, E-mail: pugliese@jsu.edu.

James Madison University, The Graduate School, College of Integrated Science and Technology, Department of Computer Science, Harrisonburg, VA 22807. Offers MS. Postbaccalaureate distance learning degree programs offered. *Degree requirements:* For master's, thesis or alternative. *Entrance requirements:* For master's, GRE General Test. Additional exam requirements/recommendations for international students: Required—TOEFL. Electronic applications accepted.

Johns Hopkins University, Engineering Program for Professionals, Part-time Program in Computer Science, Baltimore, MD 21218-2699. Offers bioinformatics (MS); computer science (MS, Post-Master's Certificate); telecommunications and networking (MS). Part-time and evening/weekend programs available. Postbaccalaureate distance learning degree programs offered (no on-campus study). Electronic applications accepted.

Johns Hopkins University, G. W. C. Whiting School of Engineering, Department of Computer Science, Baltimore, MD 21218-2699. Offers MSE, MSSI, PhD. Terminal master's awarded for partial completion of doctoral program. *Degree requirements:* For master's, thesis optional; for doctorate, comprehensive exam, thesis/dissertation, oral exam. *Entrance requirements:* For master's and doctorate, GRE General Test. Additional exam requirements/recommendations for international students: Required—TOEFL (minimum score 600 paper-based). Electronic applications accepted. *Faculty research:* Computer medical systems, networks/distributed systems, algorithms, security, natural language processing.

Johns Hopkins University, G. W. C. Whiting School of Engineering, Master of Science in Engineering Management Program, Baltimore, MD 21218-2699. Offers biomaterials (MSEM); civil engineering (MSEM); communications science (MSEM); computer science (MSEM); environmental systems analysis, economics and public policy (MSEM); fluid mechanics (MSEM); materials science and engineering (MSEM); mechanical engineering (MSEM); mechanics and materials (MSEM); nano-biotechnology (MSEM); nanomaterials and nanotechnology (MSEM); operations research (MSEM); probability and statistics (MSEM); smart product and device design (MSEM). *Entrance requirements:* For master's, GRE, 3 letters of recommendation, resume. Additional exam requirements/recommendations for international students: Required—TOEFL (minimum score 600 paper-based; 100 iBT) or IELTS (minimum score 7). Electronic applications accepted.

Kansas State University, Graduate School, College of Engineering, Department of Computing and Information Sciences, Manhattan, KS 66506. Offers MS, MSE, PhD. Part-time programs available. Postbaccalaureate distance learning degree programs offered (no on-campus study). *Faculty:* 17 full-time (1 woman), 5 part-time/adjunct (2 women). *Students:* 63 full-time (20 women), 21 part-time (2 women); includes 6 minority (2 Black or African American, non-Hispanic/Latino; 1 American Indian or Alaska Native, non-Hispanic/Latino; 3 Asian, non-Hispanic/Latino), 53 international. Average age 28. 200 applicants, 28% accepted, 26 enrolled. In 2014, 28 master's, 7 doctorates awarded. Terminal master's awarded for partial completion of doctoral program. *Degree requirements:* For master's, thesis or alternative; for doctorate, thesis/dissertation. *Entrance requirements:* For master's, GRE General Test, bachelor's degree in computer science, minimum GPA of 3.0; for doctorate, GRE General Test, master's degree in computer science or bachelor's degree and strong advanced computer knowledge. Additional exam requirements/recommendations for international students: Required—TOEFL (minimum score 575 paper-based; 90 iBT), IELTS, or PTE. *Application deadline:* For fall admission, 2/1 priority date for domestic students, 1/1 priority date for international students; for spring admission, 9/1 priority date for domestic students, 8/1 priority date for international students. Applications are processed on a rolling basis. Application fee: $50 ($75 for international students). Electronic applications accepted. *Financial support:* In 2014–15, 23 research assistantships with tuition reimbursements (averaging $21,900 per year), 25 teaching assistantships with full tuition reimbursements (averaging $14,208 per year) were awarded; fellowships, career-related internships or fieldwork, institutionally sponsored loans, scholarships/grants, health care benefits, and unspecified assistantships also available. Support available to part-time students. Financial award application deadline: 3/15; financial award applicants required to submit FAFSA. *Faculty research:* High-assurance software and programming languages, data mining, parallel and distributed computing, computer security, embedded systems. *Total annual research expenditures:* $3.2 million. *Unit head:* Dr. Scott DeLoach, Interim Head, 785-532-6350, Fax: 785-532-7353, E-mail: sdeloach@ksu.edu. *Application contact:* Ami Ratzlaff, Program Coordinator, 785-532-6350, Fax: 785-532-7353, E-mail: cis-gradapps@ksu.edu.
Website: http://www.cis.k-state.edu/.

Kennesaw State University, College of Science and Mathematics, Program in Computer Science, Kennesaw, GA 30144. Offers MS. Part-time programs available. Postbaccalaureate distance learning degree programs offered (minimal on-campus study). *Students:* 28 full-time (19 women), 10 part-time (2 women); includes 22 minority (15 Black or African American, non-Hispanic/Latino; 3 Asian, non-Hispanic/Latino; 2

Hispanic/Latino; 2 Two or more races, non-Hispanic/Latino), 8 international. Average age 27. 52 applicants, 54% accepted, 19 enrolled. In 2014, 3 master's awarded. *Degree requirements:* For master's, thesis optional. *Entrance requirements:* For master's, GMAT or GRE, minimum GPA of 2.75. Additional exam requirements/recommendations for international students: Required—TOEFL (minimum score 550 paper-based; 80 iBT), IELTS (minimum score 6.5). *Application deadline:* For fall admission, 6/1 priority date for domestic students, 6/1 for international students; for spring admission, 11/1 priority date for domestic students, 11/1 for international students. Applications are processed on a rolling basis. Application fee: $60. Electronic applications accepted. *Expenses:* Contact institution. *Financial support:* In 2014–15, 5 research assistantships with full tuition reimbursements (averaging $12,000 per year) were awarded; Federal Work-Study and unspecified assistantships also available. Support available to part-time students. Financial award application deadline: 4/1; financial award applicants required to submit FAFSA. *Unit head:* Dr. Ying Xie, Director, 470-578-2143, E-mail: yxie2@kennesaw.edu. *Application contact:* Admissions Counselor, 470-578-4377, Fax: 470-578-9172, E-mail: ksugrad@kennesaw.edu.

Kent State University, College of Arts and Sciences, Department of Computer Science, Kent, OH 44242-0001. Offers MA, MS, PhD. Part-time programs available. *Faculty:* 13 full-time (1 woman). *Students:* 194 full-time (60 women), 19 part-time (2 women); includes 5 minority (1 Black or African American, non-Hispanic/Latino; 2 Asian, non-Hispanic/Latino; 1 Hispanic/Latino; 1 Two or more races, non-Hispanic/Latino), 190 international. Average age 26. 12,922 applicants, 3% accepted, 146 enrolled. In 2014, 53 master's, 5 doctorates awarded. *Degree requirements:* For master's, thesis (for some programs); for doctorate, comprehensive exam, thesis/dissertation, preliminary examination. *Entrance requirements:* For master's and doctorate, GRE General Test, minimum GPA of 3.0, transcript, statement of purpose, 3 letters of recommendation. Additional exam requirements/recommendations for international students: Required—TOEFL (minimum score: paper-based 525, iBT 71), Michigan English Language Assessment Battery (minimum score of 75), IELTS (minimum score of 6.0), PTE Academic (minimum score of 48), or completion of ELS level 112 Intensive Program. *Application deadline:* Applications are processed on a rolling basis. Application fee: $45 ($70 for international students). Electronic applications accepted. *Expenses:* Tuition, state resident: full-time $8730; part-time $485 per credit hour. Tuition, nonresident: full-time $14,886; part-time $827 per credit hour. Tuition and fees vary according to campus/location and program. *Financial support:* Fellowships with full tuition reimbursements, research assistantships with full tuition reimbursements, teaching assistantships with full tuition reimbursements, Federal Work-Study, and unspecified assistantships available. Financial award application deadline: 9/15. *Unit head:* Dr. Javed Khan, Professor and Chair, 330-672-9038, E-mail: javed@kent.edu. *Application contact:* Graduate Coordinator, 330-672-9980, E-mail: cs-gradcoord@kent.edu.
Website: http://www.kent.edu/cas/cs/.

Kentucky State University, College of Agriculture, Food Science and Sustainable Systems, Frankfort, KY 40601. Offers aquaculture (MS); environmental studies (MS). Part-time and evening/weekend programs available. *Faculty:* 9 full-time (1 woman). *Students:* 14 full-time (3 women), 10 part-time (3 women); includes 5 minority (all Black or African American, non-Hispanic/Latino), 1 international. Average age 31. 12 applicants, 58% accepted, 5 enrolled. In 2014, 12 master's awarded. *Degree requirements:* For master's, comprehensive exam, thesis optional. *Entrance requirements:* For master's, GRE, GMAT. Additional exam requirements/recommendations for international students: Required—TOEFL (minimum score 525 paper-based). *Application deadline:* Applications are processed on a rolling basis. Application fee: $30 ($100 for international students). Electronic applications accepted. *Expenses:* Tuition, state resident: full-time $7164; part-time $398 per credit hour. Tuition, nonresident: full-time $10,782; part-time $599 per credit hour. Tuition and fees vary according to course load. *Financial support:* In 2014–15, 3 students received support, including 3 research assistantships (averaging $5,391 per year); scholarships/grants, tuition waivers (partial), and unspecified assistantships also available. Financial award application deadline: 4/15; financial award applicants required to submit FAFSA. *Unit head:* Dr. Teferi Tsegaye, Associate VP for Agriculture Administration and Land Grant Programs, Dean of CAFSS, 502-597-6310, E-mail: teferi.tsegaye@kysu.edu. *Application contact:* Dr. James Obielodan, Director of Graduate Studies, 502-597-4723, E-mail: james.obielodan@kysu.edu.
Website: http://www.kysu.edu/academics/CAFSSS/.

Kentucky State University, College of Business and Computer Science, Frankfort, KY 40601. Offers business administration (MBA); computer science technology (MS). *Accreditation:* ACBSP. Part-time and evening/weekend programs available. Postbaccalaureate distance learning degree programs offered. *Faculty:* 9 full-time (2 women). *Students:* 20 full-time (8 women), 18 part-time (6 women); includes 12 minority (11 Black or African American, non-Hispanic/Latino; 1 Native Hawaiian or other Pacific Islander, non-Hispanic/Latino), 12 international. Average age 33. 19 applicants, 68% accepted, 10 enrolled. In 2014, 13 master's awarded. *Degree requirements:* For master's, comprehensive exam, thesis optional. *Entrance requirements:* For master's, GMAT, GRE. Additional exam requirements/recommendations for international students: Required—TOEFL (minimum score 525 paper-based). *Application deadline:* Applications are processed on a rolling basis. Application fee: $30 ($100 for international students). Electronic applications accepted. *Expenses:* Tuition, state resident: full-time $7164; part-time $398 per credit hour. Tuition, nonresident: full-time $10,782; part-time $599 per credit hour. Tuition and fees vary according to course load. *Financial support:* In 2014–15, 10 students received support, including 9 research assistantships (averaging $3,589 per year); scholarships/grants, tuition waivers (partial), and unspecified assistantships also available. Financial award application deadline: 4/15; financial award applicants required to submit FAFSA. *Unit head:* Dr. Lorna Shaw-Berbick, Dean, 502-597-6443. *Application contact:* Dr. James Obielodan, Director of Graduate Studies, 502-597-4723, E-mail: james.obielodan@kysu.edu.
Website: http://kysu.edu/academics/college-of-business-and-computer-science/.

Knowledge Systems Institute, Program in Computer and Information Sciences, Skokie, IL 60076. Offers MS. Part-time and evening/weekend programs available. Postbaccalaureate distance learning degree programs offered (minimal on-campus study). *Degree requirements:* For master's, comprehensive exam, thesis. *Entrance requirements:* Additional exam requirements/recommendations for international students: Required—TOEFL (minimum score 550 paper-based; 79 iBT). Electronic applications accepted. *Faculty research:* Data mining, web development, database programming and administration.

Kutztown University of Pennsylvania, College of Liberal Arts and Sciences, Program in Computer Science, Kutztown, PA 19530-0730. Offers MS. Part-time and evening/weekend programs available. *Faculty:* 7 full-time (0 women). *Students:* 6 full-time (3 women), 15 part-time (4 women); includes 3 minority (2 Asian, non-Hispanic/Latino; 1 Hispanic/Latino), 4 international. Average age 28. 10 applicants, 70% accepted, 7 enrolled. In 2014, 3 master's awarded. *Degree requirements:* For master's, comprehensive exam or thesis. *Entrance requirements:* For master's, GRE General Test. Additional exam requirements/recommendations for international students: Required—TOEFL (minimum score 550 paper-based; 79 iBT). *Application deadline:* For fall admission, 8/1 priority date for domestic and international students; for spring admission, 12/1 priority date for domestic and international students. Applications are processed on a rolling basis. Application fee: $35. Electronic applications accepted. *Expenses: Tuition, area resident:* Part-time $454 per credit. Tuition, state resident: part-time $454 per credit. Tuition, nonresident: part-time $681 per credit. *Required fees:* $85 per credit. *Financial support:* Career-related internships or fieldwork, Federal Work-Study, scholarships/grants, and unspecified assistantships available. Financial award application deadline: 3/1; financial award applicants required to submit FAFSA. *Faculty research:* Artificial intelligence, expert systems, neural networks. *Unit head:* Dr. Lisa Frye, Chairperson, 610-683-4422, Fax: 610-683-4129, E-mail: frye@kutztown.edu. *Application contact:* Kelly Hish, Admissions Clerk, 610-683-4200, Fax: 610-683-1393, E-mail: graduate@kutztown.edu.

Lakehead University, Graduate Studies, School of Mathematical Sciences, Thunder Bay, ON P7B 5E1, Canada. Offers computer science (M Sc); mathematical science (MA). Part-time and evening/weekend programs available. *Degree requirements:* For master's, thesis optional. *Entrance requirements:* For master's, minimum B average, honours degree in mathematics or computer science. Additional exam requirements/recommendations for international students: Required—TOEFL. *Faculty research:* Numerical analysis, classical analysis, theoretical computer science, abstract harmonic analysis, functional analysis.

Lamar University, College of Graduate Studies, College of Arts and Sciences, Department of Computer Science, Beaumont, TX 77710. Offers MS. Part-time programs available. *Faculty:* 9 full-time (2 women). *Students:* 88 full-time (22 women), 12 part-time (4 women); includes 5 minority (1 Black or African American, non-Hispanic/Latino; 3 Asian, non-Hispanic/Latino; 1 Two or more races, non-Hispanic/Latino), 93 international. Average age 25. 303 applicants, 51% accepted, 51 enrolled. In 2014, 8 master's awarded. *Degree requirements:* For master's, comprehensive exams and project or thesis. *Entrance requirements:* For master's, GRE General Test, minimum GPA of 3.3 in last 60 hours of undergraduate course work or 3.0 overall. Additional exam requirements/recommendations for international students: Required—TOEFL (minimum score 550 paper-based; 79 iBT), IELTS (minimum score 6.5). *Application deadline:* For fall admission, 8/10 for domestic students, 7/1 for international students; for spring admission, 1/5 for domestic students, 12/1 for international students. Applications are processed on a rolling basis. Application fee: $25 ($50 for international students). *Expenses:* Tuition, state resident: full-time $5724; part-time $1908 per semester. Tuition, nonresident: full-time $12,240; part-time $4080 per semester. *Required fees:* $1940; $318 per credit hour. *Financial support:* In 2014–15, 2 research assistantships with partial tuition reimbursements (averaging $6,000 per year), 4 teaching assistantships with partial tuition reimbursements (averaging $6,000 per year) were awarded; institutionally sponsored loans, scholarships/grants, and tuition waivers (partial) also available. Financial award application deadline: 4/1. *Faculty research:* Computer architecture, network security. *Unit head:* Dr. Stefan Andrei, Chair, 409-880-8775, Fax: 409-880-2364. *Application contact:* Melissa Gallien, Director, Admissions and Academic Services, 409-880-8888, Fax: 409-880-7419, E-mail: gradmissions@lamar.edu.
Website: http://artssciences.lamar.edu/computer-science.

La Salle University, School of Arts and Sciences, Program in Computer Information Science, Philadelphia, PA 19141-1199. Offers application development (Certificate); computer information science (MS). Part-time and evening/weekend programs available. Postbaccalaureate distance learning degree programs offered (minimal on-campus study). *Degree requirements:* For master's, capstone project. *Entrance requirements:* For master's, GRE, MAT, or GMAT, minimum undergraduate GPA of 3.0; two letters of recommendation; resume; telephone or in-person interview. Additional exam requirements/recommendations for international students: Required—TOEFL. Electronic applications accepted. Application fee is waived when completed online. *Expenses:* Contact institution. *Faculty research:* Human-computer interaction, networks, technology trends, databases, groupware.

Lawrence Technological University, College of Arts and Sciences, Southfield, MI 48075-1058. Offers computer science (MS); educational technology (MA); science education (MA); technical communication (MS); training and performance (MA). Part-time and evening/weekend programs available. *Faculty:* 8 full-time (4 women), 16 part-time/adjunct (7 women). *Students:* 108 part-time (49 women); includes 46 minority (12 Black or African American, non-Hispanic/Latino; 31 Asian, non-Hispanic/Latino; 1 Hispanic/Latino; 2 Two or more races, non-Hispanic/Latino), 5 international. Average age 31. 765 applicants, 22% accepted, 43 enrolled. In 2014, 28 master's awarded. *Degree requirements:* For master's, thesis (for some programs). *Entrance requirements:* Additional exam requirements/recommendations for international students: Required—TOEFL (minimum score 550 paper-based; 79 iBT). *Application deadline:* For fall admission, 8/1 priority date for domestic students, 5/29 for international students; for spring admission, 12/1 priority date for domestic students, 10/15 for international students. Applications are processed on a rolling basis. Application fee: $50. Electronic applications accepted. *Expenses: Tuition:* Full-time $14,700; part-time $1050 per credit hour. *Required fees:* $150. One-time fee: $150 part-time. *Financial support:* In 2014–15, 8 students received support, including 2 research assistantships (averaging $6,338 per year); Federal Work-Study also available. Financial award application deadline: 4/1; financial award applicants required to submit FAFSA. *Unit head:* Dr. Hsiao-Ping Moore, Dean, 248-204-3500, Fax: 248-204-3518, E-mail: scidean@ltu.edu. *Application contact:* Jane Rohrback, Director of Admissions, 248-204-3160, Fax: 248-204-2228, E-mail: admissions@ltu.edu.
Website: http://www.ltu.edu/arts_sciences/graduate.asp.

Lebanese American University, School of Arts and Sciences, Beirut, Lebanon. Offers computer science (MS); international affairs (MA).

Lehigh University, P.C. Rossin College of Engineering and Applied Science, Department of Computer Science and Engineering, Bethlehem, PA 18015. Offers computer engineering (M Eng, MS, PhD); computer science (M Eng, MS, PhD); MBA/E. Part-time programs available. *Faculty:* 12 full-time (2 women), 1 (woman) part-time/adjunct. *Students:* 57 full-time (8 women), 6 part-time (0 women); includes 6 minority (4 Asian, non-Hispanic/Latino; 2 Two or more races, non-Hispanic/Latino), 40 international. Average age 25. 252 applicants, 22% accepted, 21 enrolled. In 2014, 18 master's, 6 doctorates awarded. *Degree requirements:* For master's, oral presentation of thesis; for doctorate, thesis/dissertation, qualifying, general, and oral exams. *Entrance requirements:* For master's, GRE General Test, minimum GPA of 3.0; for doctorate, GRE General Test, minimum GPA of 3.5. Additional exam requirements/recommendations for international students: Required—TOEFL (minimum score 550 paper-based; 79 iBT). *Application deadline:* For fall admission, 4/1 for domestic and international students; for spring admission, 11/1 for domestic and international students. Applications are processed on a rolling basis. Application fee: $75. Electronic applications accepted. *Expenses:* Expenses: $1,340 per credit. *Financial support:* In 2014–15, 19 students received support, including 2 fellowships with full tuition reimbursements available (averaging $19,920 per year), 6 research assistantships with full tuition reimbursements available (averaging $18,920 per year), 5 teaching assistantships with full tuition reimbursements available (averaging $20,490 per year). Financial award application deadline: 1/15. *Faculty research:* Artificial intelligence, networking-pattern recognition, multimedia e-learning/data mining/Web search, mobile robotics, bioinformatics, computer vision. *Total annual research expenditures:* $1.3 million. *Unit head:* Dr. Hank Korth, Interim Chair, 610-758-5782, Fax: 610-758-4096, E-mail: hfk2@lehigh.edu. *Application contact:* Heidi Wegrzyn, Graduate Coordinator, 610-758-3065, Fax: 610-758-4096, E-mail: hew207@lehigh.edu.
Website: http://www.cse.lehigh.edu/.

Lehman College of the City University of New York, School of Natural and Social Sciences, Department of Mathematics and Computer Science, Program in Computer Science, Bronx, NY 10468-1589. Offers MS. *Degree requirements:* For master's, one foreign language, thesis or alternative.

Long Island University–LIU Brooklyn, School of Business, Public Administration and Information Sciences, Brooklyn, NY 11201-8423. Offers accounting (MBA); accounting (MS); computer science (MS); entrepreneurship (MBA); finance (MBA); health administration (MPA); human resources management (MS); international business (MBA); management (MBA); management information systems (MBA); marketing (MBA); public administration (MPA); taxation (MS). Part-time and evening/weekend programs available. *Faculty:* 16 full-time (7 women), 29 part-time/adjunct (6 women). *Students:* 230 full-time (155 women), 239 part-time (166 women); includes 321 minority (210 Black or African American, non-Hispanic/Latino; 2 American Indian or Alaska Native, non-Hispanic/Latino; 46 Asian, non-Hispanic/Latino; 56 Hispanic/Latino; 2 Native Hawaiian or other Pacific Islander, non-Hispanic/Latino; 5 Two or more races, non-Hispanic/Latino), 69 international. Average age 37. 481 applicants, 79% accepted, 153 enrolled. In 2014, 158 master's awarded. *Degree requirements:* For master's, thesis optional. *Entrance requirements:* For master's, GMAT or GRE General Test (Excluding MPA), 2 letters of recommendation, personal statement & resume. Additional exam requirements/recommendations for international students: Required—TOEFL (minimum score 550 paper-based; 79 iBT). *Application deadline:* For fall admission, 5/1 for international students; for spring admission, 11/1 for international students. Applications are processed on a rolling basis. Application fee: $30. Electronic applications accepted. *Expenses: Tuition:* Part-time $1132 per credit. *Required fees:* $434 per semester. *Financial support:* Scholarships/grants and unspecified assistantships available. Support available to part-time students. Financial award application deadline: 2/15; financial award applicants required to submit FAFSA. *Unit head:* Dr. Edward Rogoff, Dean, 718-488-1130. *Application contact:* Richard Sunday, Dean of Admissions, 718-488-1011, Fax: 718-780-6110, E-mail: bkln-admissions@liu.edu.
Website: http://www.liu.edu/.

Louisiana State University and Agricultural & Mechanical College, Graduate School, College of Engineering, Division of Computer Science, Baton Rouge, LA 70803. Offers computer science (MSSS, PhD); systems science (MSSS). Part-time programs available. *Faculty:* 18 full-time (2 women). *Students:* 68 full-time (10 women), 16 part-time (2 women); includes 6 minority (2 Black or African American, non-Hispanic/Latino; 1 American Indian or Alaska Native, non-Hispanic/Latino; 3 Asian, non-Hispanic/Latino), 56 international. Average age 30. 154 applicants, 45% accepted, 17 enrolled. In 2014, 29 master's, 9 doctorates awarded. Terminal master's awarded for partial completion of doctoral program. *Degree requirements:* For master's, thesis; for doctorate, thesis/dissertation. *Entrance requirements:* For master's and doctorate, GRE General Test, minimum GPA of 3.0. Additional exam requirements/recommendations for international students: Required—TOEFL (minimum score 550 paper-based; 79 IBT), IELTS (minimum score 6.5), or PTE (minimum score 59). *Application deadline:* For fall admission, 1/1 priority date for domestic students, 5/15 for international students; for spring admission, 10/15 for domestic and international students; for summer admission, 5/15 for domestic students. Applications are processed on a rolling basis. Application fee: $50 ($70 for international students). Electronic applications accepted. *Financial support:* In 2014–15, 71 students received support, including 1 fellowship with full tuition reimbursement available (averaging $9,575 per year), 22 research assistantships with full and partial tuition reimbursements available (averaging $17,323 per year), 34 teaching assistantships with full and partial tuition reimbursements available (averaging $15,335 per year); Federal Work-Study, institutionally sponsored loans, health care benefits, and unspecified assistantships also available. Financial award application deadline: 2/1; financial award applicants required to submit FAFSA. *Faculty research:* Robotics, artificial intelligence, algorithms, database software engineering, high-performance computing. *Total annual research expenditures:* $2.3 million. *Unit head:* Dr. Bijaya S. Karki, Interim Chair, 225-578-1495, Fax: 225-578-1465, E-mail: bbkarki@lsu.edu. *Application contact:* Dr. Seung-John Park, Graduate Coordinator, 225-578-3179, Fax: 225-578-1465, E-mail: sjpark@lsu.edu.
Website: http://www.cse.lsu.edu/.

Louisiana State University in Shreveport, College of Arts and Sciences, Program in Computer Systems Technology, Shreveport, LA 71115-2399. Offers MS. Part-time and evening/weekend programs available. *Students:* 6 full-time (2 women), 4 part-time (0 women); includes 3 minority (1 Asian, non-Hispanic/Latino; 2 Hispanic/Latino), 2 international. Average age 31. 13 applicants, 100% accepted, 4 enrolled. In 2014, 12 master's awarded. *Degree requirements:* For master's, comprehensive exam (for some programs), thesis or alternative. *Entrance requirements:* For master's, GRE, programming course in high-level language, interview. Additional exam requirements/recommendations for international students: Required—TOEFL (minimum score 550 paper-based; 80 iBT). *Application deadline:* For fall admission, 6/30 for domestic and international students; for spring admission, 11/30 for domestic and international students; for summer admission, 4/30 for domestic and international students. Applications are processed on a rolling basis. Application fee: $20 ($30 for international students). Electronic applications accepted. *Expenses:* Tuition, state resident: full-time $5234; part-time $290.80 per credit hour. Tuition, nonresident: full-time $16,774; part-time $879.61 per credit hour. *Required fees:* $52.28 per credit hour. *Financial support:* In 2014–15, 2 research assistantships (averaging $5,000 per year) were awarded. *Unit head:* Dr. Krishna Agarwal, Program Director, 318-795-4283, Fax: 318-795-2419, E-mail: krishna.agarwal@lsus.edu. *Application contact:* Kimberly Thornton, Director of Admissions, 318-795-2405, Fax: 318-797-5286, E-mail: kimberly.thornton@lsus.edu.

Louisiana Tech University, Graduate School, College of Engineering and Science, Department of Computer Science, Ruston, LA 71272. Offers MS. Part-time programs available. *Degree requirements:* For master's, thesis or alternative. *Entrance requirements:* For master's, GRE General Test, minimum GPA of 3.0 in last 60 hours. Additional exam requirements/recommendations for international students: Required—TOEFL. *Faculty research:* Computer systems organization, artificial intelligence, expert systems, graphics, program language.

Loyola University Chicago, Graduate School, Department of Computer Science, Chicago, IL 60660. Offers computer science (MS); information technology (MS); software engineering (MS); software technology (MS). Part-time and evening/weekend programs available. *Faculty:* 10 full-time (1 woman), 10 part-time/adjunct (2 women). *Students:* 86 full-time (30 women), 40 part-time (16 women); includes 24 minority (8 Black or African American, non-Hispanic/Latino; 10 Asian, non-Hispanic/Latino; 6 Hispanic/Latino), 45 international. Average age 29. 218 applicants, 45% accepted, 60 enrolled. In 2014, 46 master's awarded. *Degree requirements:* For master's, thesis optional, ten courses; thesis (for computer science). *Entrance requirements:* For master's, 3 letters of recommendation, transcripts, statement of purpose. Additional exam requirements/recommendations for international students: Required—TOEFL

(minimum score 550 paper-based; 79 iBT) or IELTS (minimum score 6.5). *Application deadline:* For fall admission, 8/10 for domestic students, 5/15 for international students; for spring admission, 12/20 for domestic students, 9/15 for international students. Applications are processed on a rolling basis. Electronic applications accepted. Application fee is waived when completed online. *Expenses: Tuition:* Full-time $17,370; part-time $965 per credit. *Required fees:* $138 per semester. *Financial support:* In 2014–15, 20 students received support, including 1 fellowship (averaging $3,000 per year), 16 teaching assistantships with partial tuition reimbursements available (averaging $4,000 per year); career-related internships or fieldwork, Federal Work-Study, scholarships/grants, tuition waivers (partial), and unspecified assistantships also available. Financial award application deadline: 3/15. *Faculty research:* Software engineering, high performance computing, algorithms and complexity, parallel and distributed computing, databases and computer networks. *Total annual research expenditures:* $22,000. *Unit head:* Dr. Chandra Sekharan, Chair, 312-915-7985, Fax: 312-915-7998, E-mail: csekhar@luc.edu. *Application contact:* Cecilia Murphy, Graduate Program Secretary, 312-915-7990, Fax: 312-915-7998, E-mail: gradinfo-cs@luc.edu.
Website: http://cs.luc.edu.

Loyola University Maryland, Graduate Programs, Loyola College of Arts and Sciences, Department of Computer Science and Software Engineering, Baltimore, MD 21210-2699. Offers computer science (MS); software engineering (MS). Part-time programs available. *Entrance requirements:* For master's, essay, letter of recommendation, transcripts, resume. Additional exam requirements/recommendations for international students: Required—TOEFL. Electronic applications accepted.

Maharishi University of Management, Graduate Studies, Program in Computer Science, Fairfield, IA 52557. Offers MS. *Degree requirements:* For master's, thesis or alternative. *Entrance requirements:* For master's, GRE General Test, minimum GPA of 3.0. Additional exam requirements/recommendations for international students: Required—TOEFL. *Faculty research:* Parallel processing, computer systems in architecture.

Marist College, Graduate Programs, School of Computer Science and Mathematics, Poughkeepsie, NY 12601-1387. Offers computer science/software development (MS); information systems (MS, Adv C); technology management (MS). Part-time and evening/weekend programs available. Postbaccalaureate distance learning degree programs offered (minimal on-campus study). *Entrance requirements:* For master's, resume. Additional exam requirements/recommendations for international students: Required—TOEFL (minimum score 550 paper-based; 80 iBT); Recommended—IELTS (minimum score 6.5). Electronic applications accepted. *Faculty research:* Data quality, artificial intelligence, imaging, analysis of algorithms, distributed systems and applications.

Marquette University, Graduate School, College of Arts and Sciences, Department of Mathematics, Statistics, and Computer Science, Milwaukee, WI 53201-1881. Offers bioinformatics (MS); computational sciences (MS, PhD); computing (MS); mathematics education (MS). Part-time and evening/weekend programs available. Postbaccalaureate distance learning degree programs offered (minimal on-campus study). Terminal master's awarded for partial completion of doctoral program. *Degree requirements:* For master's, thesis (for some programs), essay with oral presentation; for doctorate, comprehensive exam, thesis/dissertation, qualifying examination. *Entrance requirements:* For master's, official transcripts from all current and previous colleges/universities except Marquette, three letters of recommendation; for doctorate, GRE General Test, official transcripts from all current and previous colleges/universities except Marquette, three letters of recommendation. Additional exam requirements/recommendations for international students: Required—TOEFL (minimum score 530 paper-based). Electronic applications accepted. *Faculty research:* Models of physiological systems, mathematical immunology, computational group theory, mathematical logic, computational science.

Marquette University, Graduate School, College of Arts and Sciences, Program in Computing, Milwaukee, WI 53201-1881. Offers MS. Part-time and evening/weekend programs available. Postbaccalaureate distance learning degree programs offered (minimal on-campus study). *Degree requirements:* For master's, thesis optional, enrollment in the Professional Seminar in Computing each term. *Entrance requirements:* For master's, official transcripts from all current and previous colleges/universities except Marquette, essay, three letters of reference. Additional exam requirements/recommendations for international students: Required—TOEFL (minimum score 530 paper-based). Electronic applications accepted.

Marshall University, Academic Affairs Division, College of Information Technology and Engineering, Weisberg Division of Computer Science, Huntington, WV 25755. Offers computer science (MS); information systems (MS). *Students:* 1 full-time (0 women), 2 part-time (0 women). Average age 31. *Degree requirements:* For master's, thesis or project. *Entrance requirements:* Additional exam requirements/recommendations for international students: Required—IELTS (minimum score 5.5). *Unit head:* Dr. Venkat Gudivada, Interim Chair, E-mail: gudivada@marshall.edu. *Application contact:* Information Contact, 304-746-1900, Fax: 304-746-1902, E-mail: services@marshall.edu.
Website: http://www.marshall.edu/cite/home/academic/divisions/wdcs/.

Massachusetts Institute of Technology, School of Engineering, Department of Electrical Engineering and Computer Science, Cambridge, MA 02139. Offers computer science (PhD, Sc D, ECS); computer science and engineering (PhD, Sc D); electrical engineering (PhD, Sc D, EE); electrical engineering and computer science (M Eng, SM, PhD, Sc D); SM/MBA. *Faculty:* 120 full-time (19 women). *Students:* 795 full-time (185 women), 4 part-time (0 women); includes 193 minority (13 Black or African American, non-Hispanic/Latino; 2 American Indian or Alaska Native, non-Hispanic/Latino; 119 Asian, non-Hispanic/Latino; 40 Hispanic/Latino; 19 Two or more races, non-Hispanic/Latino), 390 international. Average age 26. 2,971 applicants, 13% accepted, 277 enrolled. In 2014, 219 master's, 101 doctorates, 4 other advanced degrees awarded. Terminal master's awarded for partial completion of doctoral program. *Degree requirements:* For master's and other advanced degree, thesis; for doctorate, comprehensive exam, thesis/dissertation. *Entrance requirements:* Additional exam requirements/recommendations for international students: Required—TOEFL (minimum score 100 iBT), IELTS (minimum score 7). *Application deadline:* For fall admission, 12/15 for domestic and international students. Application fee: $75. Electronic applications accepted. *Expenses: Tuition:* Full-time $44,720; part-time $699 per unit. *Required fees:* $296. *Financial support:* In 2014–15, 743 students received support, including 124 fellowships (averaging $36,900 per year), 493 research assistantships (averaging $34,100 per year), 142 teaching assistantships (averaging $34,800 per year); Federal Work-Study, institutionally sponsored loans, scholarships/grants, traineeships, health care benefits, and unspecified assistantships also available. Financial award application deadline: 4/15; financial award applicants required to submit FAFSA. *Faculty research:* Information systems, circuits, biomedical sciences and engineering, computer science: artificial intelligence, systems, theory. *Total annual research expenditures:* $112 million. *Unit head:* Prof. Anantha P. Chandrakasan, Department Head, 617-253-4600. *Application contact:* Graduate Admissions, 617-253-4603, Fax: 617-258-7354, E-mail: grad-ap@eecs.mit.edu.
Website: http://www.eecs.mit.edu/.

McGill University, Faculty of Graduate and Postdoctoral Studies, Faculty of Science, School of Computer Science, Montréal, QC H3A 2T5, Canada. Offers M Sc, PhD.

McMaster University, School of Graduate Studies, Faculty of Engineering, Department of Computing and Software, Hamilton, ON L8S 4M2, Canada. Offers computer science (M Sc, PhD); software engineering (M Eng, MA Sc, PhD). Part-time programs available. *Degree requirements:* For master's, thesis. *Entrance requirements:* Additional exam requirements/recommendations for international students: Required—TOEFL (minimum score 550 paper-based). *Faculty research:* Software engineering; theory of non-sequential systems; parallel and distributed computing; artificial intelligence; complexity, design, and analysis of algorithms; combinatorial computing, especially applications to molecular biology.

McNeese State University, Doré School of Graduate Studies, College of Science, Department of Mathematics, Computer Science, and Statistics, Lake Charles, LA 70609. Offers computer science (MS); mathematics (MS); statistics (MS). Evening/weekend programs available. *Degree requirements:* For master's, comprehensive exam, thesis or alternative, written exam. *Entrance requirements:* For master's, GRE.

Memorial University of Newfoundland, School of Graduate Studies, Department of Computer Science, St. John's, NL A1C 5S7, Canada. Offers M Sc, PhD. Part-time programs available. *Degree requirements:* For master's, thesis; for doctorate, comprehensive exam, thesis/dissertation, oral thesis defense. *Entrance requirements:* For master's, GRE (strongly recommended), honors degree in computer science or related field; for doctorate, GRE (strongly recommended), master's degree in computer science. Electronic applications accepted. *Faculty research:* Theoretical computer science, parallel and distributed computing, scientific computing, software systems and artificial intelligence.

Metropolitan State University, College of Arts and Sciences, St. Paul, MN 55106-5000. Offers computer science (MS); liberal studies (MA); technical communication (MS). Part-time and evening/weekend programs available. *Entrance requirements:* For master's, minimum GPA of 2.75, resume. Additional exam requirements/recommendations for international students: Required—TOEFL (minimum score 550 paper-based). Electronic applications accepted.

Michigan State University, The Graduate School, College of Engineering, Department of Computer Science and Engineering, East Lansing, MI 48824. Offers computer science (MS, PhD). *Entrance requirements:* Additional exam requirements/recommendations for international students: Required—TOEFL. Electronic applications accepted.

Michigan Technological University, Graduate School, College of Sciences and Arts, Department of Computer Science, Houghton, MI 49931. Offers MS, PhD. Part-time programs available. *Faculty:* 15 full-time, 8 part-time/adjunct. *Students:* 29 full-time, 6 part-time, 22 international. Average age 29. 626 applicants, 16% accepted, 7 enrolled. In 2014, 6 master's, 1 doctorate awarded. *Degree requirements:* For master's, comprehensive exam (for some programs), thesis (for some programs); for doctorate, comprehensive exam, thesis/dissertation. *Entrance requirements:* For master's and doctorate, GRE, statement of purpose, official transcripts, 3 letters of recommendation. Additional exam requirements/recommendations for international students: Required—TOEFL (recommended score 90 iBT) or IELTS. *Application deadline:* For fall admission, 5/1 priority date for domestic and international students; for spring admission, 10/1 priority date for domestic and international students. Applications are processed on a rolling basis. Electronic applications accepted. *Expenses:* Expenses: Contact institution. *Financial support:* In 2014–15, 27 students received support, including 5 research assistantships with full and partial tuition reimbursements available (averaging $13,824 per year), 20 teaching assistantships with full and partial tuition reimbursements available (averaging $13,824 per year); career-related internships or fieldwork, Federal Work-Study, scholarships/grants, health care benefits, unspecified assistantships, and cooperative program also available. Financial award applicants required to submit FAFSA. *Faculty research:* Artificial intelligence, graphics/visualization, software engineering, architecture and compiler optimization, human computing interaction. *Total annual research expenditures:* $646,907. *Unit head:* Dr. Min Song, Chair, 906-487-2602, Fax: 906-487-2283, E-mail: mins@mtu.edu. *Application contact:* Jennifer Franke, Office Assistant, 906-487-2209, Fax: 906-487-2283, E-mail: jbfranke@mtu.edu.
Website: http://www.mtu.edu/cs/.

Middle Tennessee State University, College of Graduate Studies, College of Basic and Applied Sciences, Department of Computer Science, Murfreesboro, TN 37132. Offers MS. Part-time and evening/weekend programs available. Postbaccalaureate distance learning degree programs offered. *Degree requirements:* For master's, comprehensive exam, thesis. *Entrance requirements:* For master's, GRE. Additional exam requirements/recommendations for international students: Required—TOEFL (minimum score 525 paper-based; 71 iBT) or IELTS (minimum score 6). Electronic applications accepted. *Faculty research:* Computational science, parallel processing, artificial intelligence.

Midwestern State University, Billie Doris McAda Graduate School, College of Science and Mathematics, Department of Computer Science, Wichita Falls, TX 76308. Offers MS. Part-time and evening/weekend programs available. *Degree requirements:* For master's, comprehensive exam, thesis. *Entrance requirements:* For master's, GRE General Test. Additional exam requirements/recommendations for international students: Required—TOEFL (minimum score 573 paper-based). *Application deadline:* For fall admission, 7/1 priority date for domestic students, 4/1 for international students; for spring admission, 11/1 priority date for domestic students, 8/1 for international students. Applications are processed on a rolling basis. Application fee: $35 ($50 for international students). Electronic applications accepted. *Financial support:* Teaching assistantships with partial tuition reimbursements, career-related internships or fieldwork, Federal Work-Study, institutionally sponsored loans, scholarships/grants, tuition waivers (partial), and unspecified assistantships available. Support available to part-time students. Financial award application deadline: 3/1; financial award applicants required to submit FAFSA. *Faculty research:* Software engineering, genetic algorithms and graphics, computational epidemiology, new ways of using GPS. *Unit head:* Antoinette Brown, Secretary, 940-397-4702, E-mail: antoinette.brown@mwsu.edu.
Website: http://www.mwsu.edu/academics/scienceandmath/computerscience/index.

Mills College, Graduate Studies, Program in Computer Science, Oakland, CA 94613-1000. Offers computer science (Certificate); interdisciplinary computer science (MA). Part-time programs available. *Faculty:* 4 full-time (3 women), 2 part-time/adjunct (1 woman). *Students:* 16 full-time (all women); includes 9 minority (4 Asian, non-Hispanic/Latino; 4 Hispanic/Latino; 1 Two or more races, non-Hispanic/Latino). Average age 28. 26 applicants, 85% accepted, 9 enrolled. In 2014, 2 master's awarded. *Degree requirements:* For master's, thesis. *Entrance requirements:* For master's, three letters of recommendation. Additional exam requirements/recommendations for international students: Required—TOEFL (minimum score 600 paper-based; 100 iBT) or IELTS

(minimum score 7). *Application deadline:* For fall admission, 2/1 priority date for domestic students, 12/15 for international students; for spring admission, 11/1 priority date for domestic students, 10/1 for international students. Applications are processed on a rolling basis. Application fee: $50. Electronic applications accepted. *Expenses: Tuition:* Full-time $31,620; part-time $7905 per course. *Required fees:* $1118. *Financial support:* In 2014–15, 4 students received support, including 13 fellowships with full and partial tuition reimbursements available (averaging $4,173 per year), 4 teaching assistantships with full and partial tuition reimbursements available (averaging $1,866 per year); career-related internships or fieldwork, institutionally sponsored loans, and scholarships/grants also available. Support available to part-time students. Financial award application deadline: 2/1; financial award applicants required to submit FAFSA. *Faculty research:* Dynamical systems, linear programming, theory of computer viruses, interface design, intelligent tutoring systems. *Total annual research expenditures:* $7,483. *Unit head:* Susan S. Wang, Department Head, 510-430-2138, E-mail: wang@mills.edu. *Application contact:* Shrim Bathey, Director of Graduate Admission, 510-430-3309, Fax: 510-430-2159, E-mail: grad-admission@mills.edu.
Website: http://www.mills.edu/ics.

Mississippi College, Graduate School, College of Arts and Sciences, School of Science and Mathematics, Department of Computer Science, Clinton, MS 39058. Offers M Ed, MS. Part-time programs available. *Degree requirements:* For master's, comprehensive exam, thesis or alternative. *Entrance requirements:* For master's, GRE. Additional exam requirements/recommendations for international students: Recommended—TOEFL, IELTS.

Mississippi State University, Bagley College of Engineering, Department of Computer Science and Engineering, Mississippi State, MS 39762. Offers computer science (MS, PhD). Part-time programs available. Postbaccalaureate distance learning degree programs offered (minimal on-campus study). *Faculty:* 17 full-time (4 women), 1 part-time/adjunct (0 women). *Students:* 51 full-time (14 women), 14 part-time (1 woman); includes 9 minority (5 Black or African American, non-Hispanic/Latino; 2 Asian, non-Hispanic/Latino; 2 Two or more races, non-Hispanic/Latino), 24 international. Average age 29. 127 applicants, 31% accepted, 16 enrolled. In 2014, 23 master's, 4 doctorates awarded. *Degree requirements:* For master's, thesis optional, comprehensive oral exam; for doctorate, thesis/dissertation, comprehensive oral or written exam. *Entrance requirements:* For master's, GRE, minimum GPA of 2.75; for doctorate, GRE. Additional exam requirements/recommendations for international students: Required—TOEFL (minimum score 550 paper-based; 79 iBT); Recommended—IELTS (minimum score 6.5). *Application deadline:* For fall admission, 7/1 for domestic students, 5/1 for international students; for spring admission, 11/1 for domestic students, 9/1 for international students. Applications are processed on a rolling basis. Application fee: $60. Electronic applications accepted. *Expenses:* Tuition, state resident: full-time $7140; part-time $783 per credit hour. Tuition, nonresident: full-time $18,478; part-time $2043 per credit hour. *Financial support:* In 2014–15, 12 research assistantships with full tuition reimbursements (averaging $15,010 per year), 16 teaching assistantships with full tuition reimbursements (averaging $13,245 per year) were awarded; Federal Work-Study, institutionally sponsored loans, and unspecified assistantships also available. Financial award application deadline: 4/1; financial award applicants required to submit FAFSA. *Faculty research:* Artificial intelligence, software engineering, visualization, high performance computing. *Total annual research expenditures:* $5.7 million. *Unit head:* Dr. Donna Reese, Professor and Department Head, 662-325-2756, Fax: 662-325-8997, E-mail: office@cse.msstate.edu. *Application contact:* Dr. T.J. Jankun-Kelly, Graduate Coordinator, 662-325-7504, Fax: 662-325-8997, E-mail: office@cse.msstate.edu.
Website: http://www.cse.msstate.edu/.

Missouri State University, Graduate College, College of Natural and Applied Sciences, Department of Computer Science, Springfield, MO 65897. Offers MNAS. Part-time programs available. *Faculty:* 6 full-time (1 woman). *Students:* 2 full-time (0 women), both international. Average age 26. 10 applicants, 30% accepted, 1 enrolled. *Degree requirements:* For master's, comprehensive exam, thesis or alternative. *Entrance requirements:* For master's, GRE, minimum GPA of 3.0. Additional exam requirements/recommendations for international students: Required—TOEFL (minimum score 550 paper-based; 79 iBT). *Application deadline:* For fall admission, 7/20 priority date for domestic students, 5/1 for international students; for spring admission, 12/20 priority date for domestic students, 9/1 for international students. Applications are processed on a rolling basis. Application fee: $35 ($50 for international students). Electronic applications accepted. *Expenses:* Tuition, state resident: full-time $2250; part-time $250 per credit hour. Tuition, nonresident: full-time $4509; part-time $501 per credit hour. Tuition and fees vary according to course level, course load and program. *Financial support:* Federal Work-Study, institutionally sponsored loans, scholarships/grants, and unspecified assistantships available. Financial award application deadline: 3/31; financial award applicants required to submit FAFSA. *Faculty research:* Floating point numbers, data compression, graph theory. *Unit head:* Dr. Kenneth Vollmar, Head, 417-836-4157, Fax: 417-836-6659, E-mail: computerscience@missouristate.edu. *Application contact:* Misty Stewart, Coordinator of Graduate Recruitment, 417-836-6079, Fax: 417-836-6200, E-mail: mistystewart@missouristate.edu.
Website: http://computerscience.missouristate.edu/.

Missouri University of Science and Technology, Graduate School, Department of Computer Science, Rolla, MO 65409. Offers MS, PhD. Part-time programs available. Terminal master's awarded for partial completion of doctoral program. *Degree requirements:* For doctorate, thesis/dissertation, departmental qualifying exam. *Entrance requirements:* For master's, GRE General Test (minimum score 700 quantitative, 4 writing); for doctorate, GRE Subject Test (minimum score: quantitative 600, writing 3.5). Electronic applications accepted. *Faculty research:* Intelligent systems, artificial intelligence software engineering, distributed systems, database systems, computer systems.

Monmouth University, The Graduate School, Department of Computer Science, West Long Branch, NJ 07764-1898. Offers computer science (MS); computer science software design and development (Certificate); information systems (MS). Part-time and evening/weekend programs available. *Faculty:* 4 full-time (2 women), 6 part-time/adjunct (0 women). *Students:* 56 full-time (21 women), 21 part-time (9 women); includes 4 minority (1 Black or African American, non-Hispanic/Latino; 2 Hispanic/Latino; 1 Two or more races, non-Hispanic/Latino), 63 international. Average age 25. 238 applicants, 55% accepted, 39 enrolled. In 2014, 14 master's awarded. *Degree requirements:* For master's, thesis (for some programs), practicum. *Entrance requirements:* For master's, minimum GPA of 3.0 in major, 2.75 overall; two letters of recommendation; calculus I and II with minimum C grade; two semesters of computer programming courses within the past five years with minimum B grade; IS-minimum 2.75 overall GPA, 3.0 in major, UG degree in major that requires substantial component of software development and/or business adm; for Certificate, minimum GPA of 3.0 in major, 2.75 overall; two letters of recommendation; calculus I and II with minimum C grade; two semesters of computer programming courses within the past five years with minimum B grade. Additional exam requirements/recommendations for international students: Required—TOEFL (minimum score 550 paper-based, 79 iBT), IELTS (minimum score 6), Michigan English Language Assessment Battery (minimum score 77) or Certificate of Advanced English (minimum score B2). *Application deadline:* For fall admission, 7/15 priority date for domestic students, 6/1 for international students; for spring admission, 11/15 priority date for domestic students, 11/1 for international students. Applications are processed on a rolling basis. Application fee: $50. Electronic applications accepted. *Expenses: Tuition:* Full-time $18,072; part-time $1004 per credit. *Required fees:* $157 per semester. *Financial support:* In 2014–15, 64 students received support, including 64 fellowships (averaging $3,184 per year), 23 research assistantships (averaging $5,888 per year); career-related internships or fieldwork, scholarships/grants, and unspecified assistantships also available. Support available to part-time students. Financial award application deadline: 3/1; financial award applicants required to submit FAFSA. *Faculty research:* Databases, natural language processing, protocols, performance analysis, communications networks (systems), cybersecurity. *Unit head:* Dr. Cui Yu, Program Director, 732-571-4460, Fax: 732-263-5202, E-mail: cyu@monmouth.edu. *Application contact:* Andrea Thompson, Graduate Admission Counselor, 732-571-3452, Fax: 732-263-5123, E-mail: gradadm@monmouth.edu.
Website: http://www.monmouth.edu/academics/CSSE/mscs.asp.

Montana State University, The Graduate School, College of Engineering, Department of Computer Science, Bozeman, MT 59717. Offers computer science (MS, PhD). Part-time programs available. *Degree requirements:* For master's, comprehensive exam; for doctorate, comprehensive exam, thesis/dissertation. *Entrance requirements:* For master's and doctorate, GRE. Additional exam requirements/recommendations for international students: Required—TOEFL (minimum score 550 paper-based). Electronic applications accepted. *Faculty research:* Applied algorithms, artificial intelligence, data mining, software engineering, Web-based learning, wireless networking and robotics.

Montclair State University, The Graduate School, College of Science and Mathematics, CISCO Certificate Program, Montclair, NJ 07043-1624. Offers Certificate. *Students:* 1 (woman) part-time; minority (Hispanic/Latino). Average age 31. 1 applicant, 100% accepted, 1 enrolled. *Expenses:* Tuition, state resident: full-time $9960; part-time $553.35 per credit. Tuition, nonresident: full-time $15,074; part-time $837.43 per credit. *Required fees:* $1595; $88.63 per credit. Tuition and fees vary according to degree level and program. *Unit head:* Dr. Robert Prezant, Dean, 973-655-5108. *Application contact:* Amy Aiello, Director of Graduate Admissions and Operations, 973-655-5147, Fax: 973-655-7869, E-mail: graduate.school@montclair.edu.

Montclair State University, The Graduate School, College of Science and Mathematics, MS Program in Computer Science, Montclair, NJ 07043-1624. Offers computer science (MS); information technology (MS). Part-time and evening/weekend programs available. *Students:* 11 full-time (6 women), 19 part-time (4 women); includes 7 minority (3 Black or African American, non-Hispanic/Latino; 3 Asian, non-Hispanic/Latino; 1 Hispanic/Latino), 7 international. Average age 30. 40 applicants, 45% accepted, 9 enrolled. In 2014, 4 degrees awarded. *Degree requirements:* For master's, comprehensive exam, thesis or alternative. *Entrance requirements:* For master's, GRE General Test, 2 letters of recommendation, essay. Additional exam requirements/recommendations for international students: Required—TOEFL (minimum score 83 iBT) or IELTS (minimum score 6.5). *Application deadline:* For fall admission, 6/1 for international students; for spring admission, 10/1 for international students. Applications are processed on a rolling basis. Application fee: $60. Electronic applications accepted. *Expenses:* Tuition, state resident: full-time $9960; part-time $553.35 per credit. Tuition, nonresident: full-time $15,074; part-time $837.43 per credit. *Required fees:* $1595; $88.63 per credit. Tuition and fees vary according to degree level and program. *Financial support:* In 2014–15, 3 research assistantships with full tuition reimbursements (averaging $7,000 per year) were awarded; Federal Work-Study, scholarships/grants, and unspecified assistantships also available. Support available to part-time students. Financial award application deadline: 3/1; financial award applicants required to submit FAFSA. *Faculty research:* Software engineering, parallel and distributed systems, artificial intelligence, databases, human-computer interaction. *Unit head:* Dr. Michael Oudshoorn, Chairperson, 973-655-4166. *Application contact:* Amy Aiello, Director of Graduate Admissions and Operations, 973-655-5147, Fax: 973-655-7869, E-mail: graduate.school@montclair.edu.
Website: http://cs.montclair.edu/.

National University, Academic Affairs, School of Engineering and Computing, La Jolla, CA 92037-1011. Offers computer science (MS), including advanced computing, database engineering, software engineering; cyber security and information assurance (MS), including computer forensics, ethical hacking and penetration testing, health information assurance, information assurance and security; data analytics (MS); engineering management (MS), including enterprise architecture, project management, systems engineering, technology management; environmental engineering (MS); homeland security and emergency management (MS); management information systems (MS); project management (Certificate); sustainability management (MS); wireless communications (MS). Part-time and evening/weekend programs available. Postbaccalaureate distance learning degree programs offered (no on-campus study). *Faculty:* 24 full-time (5 women), 21 part-time/adjunct (5 women). *Students:* 275 full-time (72 women), 86 part-time (24 women); includes 147 minority (41 Black or African American, non-Hispanic/Latino; 48 Asian, non-Hispanic/Latino; 37 Hispanic/Latino; 7 Native Hawaiian or other Pacific Islander, non-Hispanic/Latino; 14 Two or more races, non-Hispanic/Latino), 95 international. Average age 33. In 2014, 281 master's awarded. *Degree requirements:* For master's, thesis (for some programs). *Entrance requirements:* For master's, interview, minimum GPA of 2.5. Additional exam requirements/recommendations for international students: Required—TOEFL (minimum score 550 paper-based; 79 iBT), IELTS (minimum score 6). *Application deadline:* Applications are processed on a rolling basis. Application fee: $60 ($65 for international students). Electronic applications accepted. *Expenses: Tuition:* Full-time $14,184; part-time $1773 per course. *Financial support:* Career-related internships or fieldwork, institutionally sponsored loans, scholarships/grants, and tuition waivers (partial) available. Support available to part-time students. Financial award application deadline: 6/30; financial award applicants required to submit FAFSA. *Faculty research:* Educational technology, scholarships in science. *Unit head:* School of Engineering and Computing, 800-628-8648, E-mail: soec@nu.edu. *Application contact:* Frank Rojas, Vice President for Enrollment Services, 800-628-8648, E-mail: advisor@nu.edu.
Website: http://www.nu.edu/OurPrograms/SchoolOfEngineeringAndTechnology.html.

Naval Postgraduate School, Departments and Academic Groups, Department of Computer Science, Monterey, CA 93943. Offers computer science (MS, PhD); identity management and cyber security (MA); modeling of virtual environments and simulations (MS, PhD); software engineering (MS, PhD). Program only open to commissioned officers of the United States and friendly nations and selected United States federal civilian employees. Part-time programs available. Postbaccalaureate distance learning degree programs offered (minimal on-campus study). *Degree requirements:* For master's, thesis; for doctorate, thesis/dissertation.

Naval Postgraduate School, Departments and Academic Groups, Space Systems Academic Group, Monterey, CA 93943. Offers applied physics (MS); astronautical engineering (MS); computer science (MS); electrical engineering (MS); mechanical engineering (MS); space systems (Engr); space systems operations (MS). Program only open to commissioned officers of the United States and friendly nations and selected United States federal civilian employees. Part-time programs available. *Degree* *requirements:* For master's and Engr, thesis; for doctorate, thesis/dissertation. *Faculty research:* Military applications for space; space reconnaissance and remote sensing; radiation-hardened electronics for space; design, construction and operations of small satellites; satellite communications systems.

New Jersey Institute of Technology, College of Computing Science, Newark, NJ 07102. Offers computer science (MS, PhD), including bioinformatics (MS), computer science, computing and business (MS), cyber security and privacy (MS), software engineering (MS); information systems (MS, PhD), including business and information systems (MS), emergency management and business continuity (MS), information systems; information technology administration and security (MS). Part-time and evening/weekend programs available. Terminal master's awarded for partial completion of doctoral program. *Degree requirements:* For master's, thesis optional; for doctorate, thesis/dissertation. *Entrance requirements:* For master's, GRE General Test; for doctorate, GRE General Test, minimum graduate GPA of 3.5. Additional exam requirements/recommendations for international students: Required—TOEFL (minimum score 550 paper-based; 79 iBT). Electronic applications accepted. *Faculty research:* Computer systems, communications and networking, artificial intelligence, database engineering, systems analysis.

New Mexico Highlands University, Graduate Studies, College of Arts and Sciences, Department of Computer Sciences, Las Vegas, NM 87701. Offers media arts and computer science (MS), including computer science. *Faculty:* 4 full-time (0 women). *Students:* 6 full-time (2 women), 9 part-time (3 women); includes 3 minority (all Hispanic/Latino), 12 international. Average age 28. 3 applicants, 100% accepted, 3 enrolled. In 2014, 9 master's awarded. *Degree requirements:* For master's, comprehensive exam, thesis. *Entrance requirements:* For master's, minimum undergraduate GPA of 3.0. Additional exam requirements/recommendations for international students: Required—TOEFL (minimum score 540 paper-based). Application fee: $15. *Financial support:* In 2014–15, 7 students received support, including 8 research assistantships, 12 teaching assistantships; career-related internships or fieldwork, Federal Work-Study, institutionally sponsored loans, scholarships/grants, tuition waivers (full and partial), and unspecified assistantships also available. Support available to part-time students. Financial award application deadline: 3/1; financial award applicants required to submit FAFSA. *Faculty research:* Advanced digital compositing, photographic installations and exhibition design, pattern recognition, parallel and distributed computing, computer security education. *Unit head:* Dr. John Jeffries, Department Chair, 505-454-3480, E-mail: jjeffries@nmhu.edu. *Application contact:* Diane Trujillo, Administrative Assistant for Graduate Studies, 505-454-3266, Fax: 505-426-2117, E-mail: dtrujillo@nmhu.edu.
Website: http://www.nmhu.edu/current-students/graduate/arts-and-sciences/masters-in-computer-and-mathematical-sciences/.

New Mexico Institute of Mining and Technology, Graduate Studies, Department of Computer Science and Engineering, Socorro, NM 87801. Offers computer science (MS, PhD). Part-time programs available. *Degree requirements:* For master's, thesis optional; for doctorate, thesis/dissertation. *Entrance requirements:* For master's, GRE General Test; for doctorate, GRE General Test, GRE Subject Test. Additional exam requirements/recommendations for international students: Required—TOEFL. Electronic applications accepted.

New Mexico State University, College of Arts and Sciences, Department of Computer Science, Las Cruces, NM 88003-8001. Offers bioinformatics (MS); computer science (MS, PhD). Part-time programs available. *Faculty:* 10 full-time (2 women), 1 part-time/adjunct (0 women). *Students:* 86 full-time (30 women), 15 part-time (2 women); includes 12 minority (2 Black or African American, non-Hispanic/Latino; 3 Asian, non-Hispanic/Latino; 7 Hispanic/Latino), 76 international. Average age 29. 273 applicants, 55% accepted, 36 enrolled. In 2014, 13 master's, 5 doctorates awarded. Terminal master's awarded for partial completion of doctoral program. *Degree requirements:* For master's, comprehensive exam, thesis or alternative; for doctorate, comprehensive exam, thesis/dissertation, qualifying examination, thesis proposal. *Entrance requirements:* For master's and doctorate, BS in computer science. Additional exam requirements/recommendations for international students: Required—TOEFL (minimum score 550 paper-based; 79 iBT), IELTS (minimum score 6.5). *Application deadline:* For fall admission, 3/1 priority date for domestic and international students; for spring admission, 11/1 priority date for domestic and international students. Applications are processed on a rolling basis. Application fee: $40 ($50 for international students). Electronic applications accepted. *Expenses:* Tuition, state resident: full-time $3969; part-time $220.50 per credit hour. Tuition, nonresident: full-time $13,838; part-time $768.80 per credit hour. *Required fees:* $853; $47.40 per credit hour. *Financial support:* In 2014–15, 67 students received support, including 1 fellowship (averaging $3,970 per year), 13 research assistantships (averaging $10,537 per year), 18 teaching assistantships (averaging $9,106 per year); career-related internships or fieldwork, Federal Work-Study, scholarships/grants, traineeships, health care benefits, and unspecified assistantships also available. Support available to part-time students. Financial award application deadline: 3/1. *Faculty research:* Bioinformatics, database and data mining, networks and systems optimization, artificial intelligence, human factors and user interfaces. *Total annual research expenditures:* $1.1 million. *Unit head:* Dr. Son Tran, Academic Department Head, 575-646-3723, Fax: 575-646-1002, E-mail: stran@cs.nmsu.edu. *Application contact:* Dr. Joe Song, Associate Professor, 575-646-3723, Fax: 575-646-1002, E-mail: gradcs@cs.nmsu.edu.
Website: http://www.cs.nmsu.edu/.

New York Institute of Technology, School of Engineering and Computing Sciences, Department of Computer Science, Old Westbury, NY 11568-8000. Offers computer science (MS); information, network, and computer security (MS). Part-time and evening/weekend programs available. *Degree requirements:* For master's, project. *Entrance requirements:* For master's, GRE General Test (if QPA less than 2.85), minimum QPA of 2.85, BS in computer science or related field. Additional exam requirements/recommendations for international students: Required—TOEFL (minimum score 550 paper-based; 79 iBT), IELTS (minimum score 6). Electronic applications accepted. *Faculty research:* Detection of physical node capture in wireless sensor networks, sensing cloud system for cybersecurity, energy efficiency and high performance networks, cognitive rhythms as a new modality for continuous authentication, cloud-enabled and cloud source disaster detection.

New York University, Graduate School of Arts and Science, Courant Institute of Mathematical Sciences, Department of Computer Science, New York, NY 10012-1019. Offers computer science (MS, PhD); information systems (MS); scientific computing (MS). Part-time and evening/weekend programs available. *Faculty:* 30 full-time (1 woman). *Students:* 237 full-time (54 women), 113 part-time (27 women); includes 43 minority (3 Black or African American, non-Hispanic/Latino; 29 Asian, non-Hispanic/Latino; 10 Hispanic/Latino; 1 Two or more races, non-Hispanic/Latino), 245 international. Average age 27. 1,373 applicants, 27% accepted, 124 enrolled. In 2014, 144 master's, 12 doctorates awarded. *Degree requirements:* For doctorate, thesis/dissertation, oral and written exams. *Entrance requirements:* For master's and doctorate, GRE General Test. Additional exam requirements/recommendations for international students: Required—TOEFL. *Application deadline:* For fall admission, 12/12 for domestic and international students; for spring admission, 10/1 for domestic and international students. Application fee: $100. *Financial support:* Fellowships with tuition reimbursements, research assistantships with tuition reimbursements, teaching assistantships with tuition reimbursements, Federal Work-Study, institutionally sponsored loans, scholarships/grants, health care benefits, and unspecified assistantships available. Financial award application deadline: 12/12; financial award applicants required to submit FAFSA. *Faculty research:* Distributed parallel and secure computing, computer graphics and vision, algorithmic and theory of computation, natural language processing, computational biology. *Unit head:* Oded Regev, Director of Graduate Studies, PhD Program, 212-998-3011, Fax: 212-995-4124, E-mail: admissions@cs.nyu.edu. *Application contact:* Benjamin Goldberg, Director of Graduate Studies, Master's Program, 212-998-3011, Fax: 212-995-4124, E-mail: admissions@cs.nyu.edu.
Website: http://cs.nyu.edu/.

New York University, Polytechnic School of Engineering, Department of Computer Science and Engineering, Major in Computer Science, New York, NY 10012-1019. Offers MS, PhD. Part-time and evening/weekend programs available. *Students:* 585 full-time (136 women), 91 part-time (21 women); includes 42 minority (2 Black or African American, non-Hispanic/Latino; 29 Asian, non-Hispanic/Latino; 8 Hispanic/Latino; 3 Two or more races, non-Hispanic/Latino), 595 international. Average age 25. 2,034 applicants, 32% accepted, 251 enrolled. In 2014, 189 master's, 3 doctorates awarded. *Degree requirements:* For master's, comprehensive exam (for some programs), thesis (for some programs); for doctorate, comprehensive exam, thesis/dissertation, qualifying exam. *Entrance requirements:* For master's, BA or BS in computer science, mathematics, science, or engineering; working knowledge of a high-level program; for doctorate, GRE General Test, GRE Subject Test, BA or BS in science, engineering, or management; MS or 1 year of graduate course work. Additional exam requirements/recommendations for international students: Required—TOEFL (minimum score 550 paper-based; 80 iBT); Recommended—IELTS (minimum score 6.5). *Application deadline:* For fall admission, 2/15 priority date for domestic and international students; for spring admission, 11/1 priority date for domestic and international students. Applications are processed on a rolling basis. Application fee: $75. Electronic applications accepted. *Financial support:* Research assistantships, teaching assistantships, institutionally sponsored loans, scholarships/grants, and unspecified assistantships available. Support available to part-time students. Financial award applicants required to submit FAFSA. *Unit head:* Dr. Edward Wong, Program Director, 718-260-3523, E-mail: ewong@nyu.edu. *Application contact:* Raymond Lutzky, Director of Graduate Enrollment Management, 718-637-5984, Fax: 718-260-3624, E-mail: rlutzky@poly.edu.

Nicholls State University, Graduate Studies, College of Arts and Sciences, Department of Mathematics and Computer Science, Thibodaux, LA 70310. Offers community/technical college mathematics (MS). Part-time and evening/weekend programs available. *Degree requirements:* For master's, comprehensive exam. *Entrance requirements:* For master's, GRE General Test. Electronic applications accepted. *Faculty research:* Operations research, statistics, numerical analysis, algebra, topology.

Norfolk State University, School of Graduate Studies, School of Science and Technology, Department of Computer Science, Norfolk, VA 23504. Offers MS.

North Carolina Agricultural and Technical State University, School of Graduate Studies, College of Engineering, Department of Computer Science, Greensboro, NC 27411. Offers MSCS. Part-time programs available. *Degree requirements:* For master's, thesis optional. *Faculty research:* Object-oriented analysis, artificial intelligence, distributed computing, societal implications of computing, testing.

North Carolina Agricultural and Technical State University, School of Graduate Studies, School of Technology, Department of Electronics, Computer, and Information Technology, Greensboro, NC 27411. Offers electronics and computer technology (MSIT, MSTM); information technology (MSIT, MSTM).

North Carolina State University, Graduate School, College of Engineering, Department of Computer Science, Raleigh, NC 27695. Offers MC Sc, MS, PhD. Part-time programs available. Postbaccalaureate distance learning degree programs offered. *Degree requirements:* For master's, thesis optional; for doctorate, thesis/dissertation. *Entrance requirements:* For master's, GRE General Test, GRE Subject Test, minimum GPA of 3.0; for doctorate, GRE General Test, GRE Subject Test (recommended), minimum GPA of 3.5. Additional exam requirements/recommendations for international students: Required—TOEFL. Electronic applications accepted. *Faculty research:* Networking and performance analysis, theory and algorithms of computation, data mining, graphics and human computer interaction, software engineering and information security.

North Carolina State University, Graduate School, College of Engineering, Department of Electrical and Computer Engineering and Department of Computer Science, Program in Computer Networking, Raleigh, NC 27695. Offers MS. *Degree requirements:* For master's, thesis optional. *Entrance requirements:* For master's, GRE General Test, GRE Subject Test (recommended). Electronic applications accepted. *Faculty research:* High-speed networks, performance modelling, security, wireless and mobile.

North Central College, Graduate and Continuing Studies Programs, Department of Computer Science, Naperville, IL 60566-7063. Offers Web and Internet applications (MS). Part-time and evening/weekend programs available. *Faculty:* 4 full-time (2 women). *Students:* 3 full-time (0 women), 6 part-time (1 woman); includes 1 minority (Asian, non-Hispanic/Latino), 1 international. Average age 27. 15 applicants, 47% accepted, 2 enrolled. In 2014, 5 master's awarded. *Degree requirements:* For master's, thesis optional, project. *Entrance requirements:* For master's, interview. Additional exam requirements/recommendations for international students: Required—TOEFL (minimum score 550 paper-based; 80 iBT). *Application deadline:* For fall admission, 8/15 for domestic students, 7/15 for international students; for winter admission, 12/1 for domestic students, 11/1 for international students; for spring admission, 2/1 for domestic students, 12/1 for international students. Applications are processed on a rolling basis. Application fee: $25. Electronic applications accepted. Application fee is waived when completed online. *Expenses:* Expenses: Contact institution. *Financial support:* Scholarships/grants available. Support available to part-time students. Financial award applicants required to submit FAFSA. *Unit head:* Dr. Caroline St. Clair, Program Coordinator, Web and Internet Applications, 630-637-5171, Fax: 630-637-5172, E-mail: cstclair@noctrl.edu. *Application contact:* Wendy Kulpinski, Director of Graduate and Continuing Education Admission, 630-637-5808, Fax: 630-637-5819, E-mail: wekulpinski@noctrl.edu.

North Dakota State University, College of Graduate and Interdisciplinary Studies, College of Science and Mathematics, Department of Computer Science, Fargo, ND 58108. Offers computer science (MS, PhD); digital enterprise (Certificate); operations research (MS); software engineering (MS, PhD, Certificate). Part-time programs available. *Degree requirements:* For master's, comprehensive exam, thesis optional; for doctorate, thesis/dissertation, qualifying exam. *Entrance requirements:* For master's, minimum GPA of 3.0, BS in computer science or related field; for doctorate, minimum GPA of 3.25, MS in computer science or related field. Additional exam requirements/recommendations for international students: Required—TOEFL (minimum score 550 paper-based; 79 iBT). Electronic applications accepted. *Faculty research:* Networking, software engineering, artificial intelligence, database, programming languages.

Northeastern Illinois University, College of Graduate Studies and Research, College of Arts and Sciences, Program in Computer Science, Chicago, IL 60625-4699. Offers MS. Part-time and evening/weekend programs available. *Degree requirements:* For master's, comprehensive exam, research project or thesis. *Entrance requirements:* For master's, minimum GPA of 2.75, proficiency in 2 higher-level computer languages, 1 course in discrete mathematics. Additional exam requirements/recommendations for international students: Required—TOEFL (minimum score 550 paper-based; 79 iBT). Electronic applications accepted. *Faculty research:* Telecommunications, database inference problems, decision-making under uncertainty, belief networks, analysis of algorithms.

Northeastern University, College of Computer and Information Science, Boston, MA 02115-5096. Offers computer science (MS, PhD); health informatics (MS); information assurance (MS, PhD). Part-time and evening/weekend programs available. Terminal master's awarded for partial completion of doctoral program. *Degree requirements:* For master's, thesis optional; for doctorate, comprehensive exam, thesis/dissertation.

Northern Arizona University, Graduate College, College of Engineering, Forestry and Natural Sciences, Programs in Engineering, Flagstaff, AZ 86011. Offers civil and environmental engineering (M Eng); civil engineering (MSE); computer science (MSE); electrical engineering (M Eng, MSE); engineering (M Eng, MSE); environmental engineering (M Eng, MSE); mechanical engineering (M Eng, MSE). Part-time programs available. Postbaccalaureate distance learning degree programs offered (no on-campus study). *Degree requirements:* For master's, thesis. *Entrance requirements:* For master's, GRE General Test. Additional exam requirements/recommendations for international students: Required—TOEFL (minimum score 550 paper-based; 80 iBT), IELTS (minimum score 7). Electronic applications accepted.

Northern Illinois University, Graduate School, College of Liberal Arts and Sciences, Department of Computer Science, De Kalb, IL 60115-2854. Offers MS. Part-time and evening/weekend programs available. *Faculty:* 14 full-time (3 women). *Students:* 148 full-time (47 women), 45 part-time (10 women); includes 8 minority (2 Black or African American, non-Hispanic/Latino; 6 Asian, non-Hispanic/Latino), 155 international. Average age 24. 580 applicants, 54% accepted, 101 enrolled. In 2014, 64 master's awarded. *Degree requirements:* For master's, comprehensive exam. *Entrance requirements:* For master's, GRE General Test, minimum GPA of 2.75. Additional exam requirements/recommendations for international students: Required—TOEFL (minimum score 550 paper-based). *Application deadline:* For fall admission, 6/1 for domestic students, 5/1 for international students; for spring admission, 11/1 for domestic students, 10/1 for international students. Applications are processed on a rolling basis. Application fee: $40. Electronic applications accepted. *Financial support:* In 2014–15, 5 research assistantships with full tuition reimbursements, 30 teaching assistantships with full tuition reimbursements were awarded; fellowships with full tuition reimbursements, career-related internships or fieldwork, Federal Work-Study, scholarships/grants, tuition waivers (full), and unspecified assistantships also available. Support available to part-time students. Financial award applicants required to submit FAFSA. *Faculty research:* Databases, theorem proving, artificial intelligence, neural networks, computer ethics. *Unit head:* Dr. Nicholas Karonis, Chair, 815-753-0349, Fax: 815-753-0342, E-mail: karonis@niu.edu. *Application contact:* Graduate School Office, 815-753-0395, E-mail: gradsch@niu.edu.
Website: http://www.cs.niu.edu/.

Northern Kentucky University, Office of Graduate Programs, College of Informatics, Department of Computer Science, Highland Heights, KY 41099. Offers computer science (MSCS); geographic information systems (Certificate); secure software engineering (Certificate). Part-time and evening/weekend programs available. *Faculty:* 6 full-time (0 women), 2 part-time/adjunct (0 women). *Students:* 5 full-time (1 woman), 21 part-time (4 women); includes 4 minority (1 Black or African American, non-Hispanic/Latino; 2 Asian, non-Hispanic/Latino; 1 Two or more races, non-Hispanic/Latino), 2 international. Average age 29. 33 applicants, 42% accepted, 8 enrolled. In 2014, 11 master's awarded. *Degree requirements:* For master's, thesis optional. *Entrance requirements:* For master's, GRE, minimum GPA of 3.0, at least 4 semesters of undergraduate study in computer science including intermediate computer programming and data structures, one year of calculus, one course in discrete mathematics. Additional exam requirements/recommendations for international students: Required—TOEFL (minimum score 550 paper-based; 79 iBT); Recommended—IELTS (minimum score 6.5). *Application deadline:* For fall admission, 8/1 for domestic students, 6/1 for international students; for spring admission, 12/1 for domestic students, 10/1 for international students; for summer admission, 5/1 for domestic students, 3/1 for international students. Applications are processed on a rolling basis. Application fee: $40. Electronic applications accepted. *Expenses:* Tuition, area resident: Part-time $518 per credit hour. Tuition, state resident: part-time $630 per credit hour. Tuition, nonresident: part-time $797 per credit hour. *Required fees:* $192 per semester. Tuition and fees vary according to course load, degree level, campus/location, program and reciprocity agreements. *Financial support:* In 2014–15, 4 students received support. Scholarships/grants and unspecified assistantships available. Financial award applicants required to submit FAFSA. *Faculty research:* Data privacy, data mining, wireless security, secure software engineering, secure networking. *Unit head:* Dr. Jeff Ward, Interim Director, 859-572-1453, E-mail: wardj1@nku.edu. *Application contact:* Alison Swanson, Graduate Admissions Coordinator, 859-572-6971, E-mail: swansona1@nku.edu.
Website: http://informatics.nku.edu/departments/computer-science.html.

Northwestern Polytechnic University, School of Engineering, Fremont, CA 94539-7482. Offers computer science (MS); computer systems engineering (MS); electrical engineering (MS). Part-time and evening/weekend programs available. *Degree requirements:* For master's, thesis optional. *Entrance requirements:* For master's, minimum GPA of 3.0. Additional exam requirements/recommendations for international students: Required—TOEFL (minimum score 550 paper-based; 79 iBT). *Faculty research:* Computer networking, database design, Internet technology, software engineering, digital signal processing.

Northwestern University, McCormick School of Engineering and Applied Science, Department of Electrical Engineering and Computer Science, Evanston, IL 60208. Offers electrical engineering, computer engineering, and computer science (MS, PhD); information technology (MS). MS and PhD admissions and degrees offered through The Graduate School. Part-time programs available. *Faculty:* 47 full-time (3 women). *Students:* 301 full-time (61 women), 57 part-time (11 women); includes 27 minority (3 Black or African American, non-Hispanic/Latino; 13 Asian, non-Hispanic/Latino; 9 Hispanic/Latino; 2 Two or more races, non-Hispanic/Latino), 299 international. Average age 26. 1,544 applicants, 24% accepted, 123 enrolled. In 2014, 42 master's, 27 doctorates awarded. Terminal master's awarded for partial completion of doctoral program. *Degree requirements:* For master's, comprehensive exam (for some programs), thesis optional; for doctorate, comprehensive exam, thesis/dissertation. *Entrance requirements:* For master's and doctorate, GRE General Test. Additional exam requirements/recommendations for international students: Required—TOEFL (minimum

score 577 paper-based; 90 iBT) or IELTS (minimum score of 7.0). *Application deadline:* For fall admission, 12/31 for domestic and international students; for winter admission, 11/15 for domestic students, 11/1 for international students; for spring admission, 2/15 for domestic students, 2/1 for international students. Application fee: $95. Electronic applications accepted. *Financial support:* Fellowships with full tuition reimbursements, research assistantships with full tuition reimbursements, teaching assistantships with full tuition reimbursements, career-related internships or fieldwork, institutionally sponsored loans, health care benefits, and unspecified assistantships available. Financial award application deadline: 1/15; financial award applicants required to submit FAFSA. *Faculty research:* Solid state and photonics; computing, algorithms, and applications; computer engineering and systems; cognitive systems; graphics and interactive media; signals and systems. *Total annual research expenditures:* $14.7 million. *Unit head:* Dr. Alan Sahakian, Chair, 847-491-7007, Fax: 847-491-4455, E-mail: sahakian@ece.northwestern.edu. *Application contact:* Dr. Allen Taflove, Director of Graduate Admissions, 847-491-4127, Fax: 847-491-4455, E-mail: taflove@ece.northwestern.edu. Website: http://www.eecs.northwestern.edu/.

Northwest Missouri State University, Graduate School, College of Arts and Sciences, Department of Mathematics and Statistics, Maryville, MO 64468-6001. Offers applied computer science (MS); instructional technology (MS); mathematics (MS); teaching mathematics (MS Ed). Part-time programs available. *Degree requirements:* For master's, comprehensive exam. *Entrance requirements:* For master's, GRE General Test, minimum undergraduate GPA of 2.5, writing sample. Additional exam requirements/recommendations for international students: Required—TOEFL (minimum score 550 paper-based). *Application deadline:* For fall admission, 7/1 for domestic and international students; for spring admission, 11/15 for domestic and international students. Applications are processed on a rolling basis. Application fee: $0 ($50 for international students). *Expenses:* Tuition, state resident: full-time $4464; part-time $346 per credit hour. Tuition, nonresident: full-time $8920; part-time $593 per credit hour. *Required fees:* $1763; $98 per credit hour. *Financial support:* Teaching assistantships with full tuition reimbursements available. Financial award application deadline: 4/1; financial award applicants required to submit FAFSA. *Application contact:* Jeanne Crawford, Office Manager, 660-562-1600, Fax: 660-562-1963, E-mail: jcrawfo@nwmissouri.edu.
Website: http://www.nwmissouri.edu/mathcsis/.

Notre Dame College, Graduate Programs, South Euclid, OH 44121-4293. Offers mild/moderate needs (M Ed); reading (M Ed); security policy studies (MA, Graduate Certificate); technology (M Ed). Part-time and evening/weekend programs available. *Degree requirements:* For master's, thesis. *Entrance requirements:* For master's, GRE General Test, MAT, minimum undergraduate GPA of 2.75, valid teaching certificate, bachelor's degree in an education-related field from accredited college or university, official transcripts of most recent college work. *Faculty research:* Cognitive psychology, teaching critical thinking in the classroom.

Notre Dame de Namur University, Division of Academic Affairs, College of Arts and Sciences, Program in Computer and Information Science, Belmont, CA 94002-1908. Offers MS. Part-time and evening/weekend programs available. Postbaccalaureate distance learning degree programs offered (no on-campus study). *Entrance requirements:* For master's, minimum GPA of 2.5, interview (for some programs). Additional exam requirements/recommendations for international students: Required—TOEFL (minimum score 550 paper-based; 79 iBT). Electronic applications accepted.

Nova Southeastern University, College of Engineering and Computing, Fort Lauderdale, FL 33314-7796. Offers computer science (MS, PhD); information assurance (PhD); information security (MS); information systems (PhD); information technology (MS); management information systems (MS); software engineering (MS). Part-time and evening/weekend programs available. Postbaccalaureate distance learning degree programs offered (minimal on-campus study). *Faculty:* 20 full-time (6 women), 24 part-time/adjunct (3 women). *Students:* 106 full-time (35 women), 758 part-time (227 women); includes 417 minority (183 Black or African American, non-Hispanic/Latino; 2 American Indian or Alaska Native, non-Hispanic/Latino; 59 Asian, non-Hispanic/Latino; 159 Hispanic/Latino; 14 Two or more races, non-Hispanic/Latino), 90 international. Average age 40. 390 applicants, 74% accepted. In 2014, 146 master's, 67 doctorates awarded. Terminal master's awarded for partial completion of doctoral program. *Degree requirements:* For master's, thesis optional; for doctorate, thesis/dissertation. *Entrance requirements:* For master's, minimum undergraduate GPA of 2.5; 3.0 in major; for doctorate, master's degree, minimum graduate GPA of 3.25. Additional exam requirements/recommendations for international students: Required—TOEFL (minimum score 80 iBT), IELTS (minimum score 6). *Application deadline:* Applications are processed on a rolling basis. Application fee: $50. Electronic applications accepted. *Expenses:* Expenses: $675/credit hour (for MS), $975 (for PhD). *Financial support:* Application deadline: 5/1; applicants required to submit FAFSA. *Faculty research:* Artificial intelligence, database management, human-computer interaction, distance education; information security. *Unit head:* Dr. Eric S. Ackerman, Dean, 954-262-2000, Fax: 954-262-2752, E-mail: esa@nova.edu. *Application contact:* Nancy Ruidiaz, Director, Admissions, 954-262-2026, Fax: 954-262-2752, E-mail: azoulayn@nova.edu.
Website: http://scis.nova.edu.

Oakland University, Graduate Study and Lifelong Learning, School of Engineering and Computer Science, Department of Computer Science and Engineering, Rochester, MI 48309-4401. Offers computer science (MS); embedded systems (MS); information systems engineering (MS); software engineering (MS). Part-time and evening/weekend programs available. *Entrance requirements:* For master's, minimum GPA of 3.0. Electronic applications accepted. *Expenses:* Contact institution. *Faculty research:* Urinary continence index for prediction of urinary incontinence in older women.

The Ohio State University, Graduate School, College of Engineering, Department of Computer Science and Engineering, Columbus, OH 43210. Offers computer science and engineering (MS, PhD). *Faculty:* 43. *Students:* 321 full-time (55 women), 17 part-time (3 women); includes 8 minority (2 Black or African American, non-Hispanic/Latino; 4 Asian, non-Hispanic/Latino; 1 Hispanic/Latino; 1 Two or more races, non-Hispanic/Latino), 293 international. Average age 26. In 2014, 93 master's, 26 doctorates awarded. *Degree requirements:* For master's, thesis optional; for doctorate, thesis/dissertation. *Entrance requirements:* For master's and doctorate, GRE (minimum score Quantitative 750 old, 159 new, Verbal 500 old, 155 new, Analytical Writing 3.0); GRE CS subject test is strongly recommended for those whose undergraduate degree is not in computer science. Additional exam requirements/recommendations for international students: Required—TOEFL (minimum score 550 paper-based; 79 iBT), Michigan English Language Assessment Battery (minimum score 82); Recommended—IELTS (minimum score 7). *Application deadline:* For fall admission, 12/13 priority date for domestic students, 11/30 priority date for international students; for winter admission, 12/1 for domestic students, 11/1 for international students; for spring admission, 10/15 priority date for domestic and international students. Applications are processed on a rolling basis. Application fee: $60 ($70 for international students). Electronic applications accepted. *Financial support:* Fellowships with tuition reimbursements, research assistantships with tuition reimbursements, teaching assistantships with tuition reimbursements, career-related internships or fieldwork, Federal Work-Study, institutionally sponsored loans, unspecified assistantships, and administrative

assistantships available. Support available to part-time students. Financial award application deadline: 1/15. *Unit head:* Dr. Xiadong Zhang, Chair, 614-292-2770, E-mail: zhang.574@osu.edu. *Application contact:* Graduate and Professional Admissions, 614-292-9444, Fax: 614-292-3895, E-mail: gpadmissions@osu.edu.
Website: http://www.cse.osu.edu.

Ohio University, Graduate College, Russ College of Engineering and Technology, School of Electrical Engineering and Computer Science, Athens, OH 45701-2979. Offers computer science (MS); electrical engineering (MS); electrical engineering and computer science (PhD). *Degree requirements:* For master's, comprehensive exam (for some programs), thesis; for doctorate, comprehensive exam, thesis/dissertation, qualifying exams. *Entrance requirements:* For master's, GRE, BSEE or BSCS, minimum GPA of 3.0; for doctorate, GRE, MSEE or MSCS, minimum GPA of 3.0. Additional exam requirements/recommendations for international students: Required—TOEFL (minimum score 550 paper-based; 80 iBT) or IELTS (minimum score 6.5). Electronic applications accepted. *Faculty research:* Avionics, networking/communications, intelligent distribution, real-time computing, control systems, optical properties of semiconductors.

Oklahoma City University, Meinders School of Business, Program in Computer Science, Oklahoma City, OK 73106-1402. Offers MSCS. Part-time and evening/weekend programs available. *Faculty:* 3 full-time (0 women), 1 part-time/adjunct (0 women). *Students:* 78 full-time (19 women), 9 part-time (4 women); includes 2 minority (both Asian, non-Hispanic/Latino), 82 international. Average age 24. 465 applicants, 56% accepted, 55 enrolled. In 2014, 7 master's awarded. *Degree requirements:* For master's, comprehensive exam, thesis optional. *Entrance requirements:* Additional exam requirements/recommendations for international students: Required—TOEFL (minimum score 550 paper-based; 80 iBT). *Application deadline:* Applications are processed on a rolling basis. Application fee: $50. Electronic applications accepted. *Expenses:* Expenses: Contact institution. *Financial support:* In 2014–15, 2 students received support. Career-related internships or fieldwork and Federal Work-Study available. Support available to part-time students. Financial award application deadline: 6/1; financial award applicants required to submit FAFSA. *Faculty research:* Parallel processing, pedagogical techniques, databases, numerical analysis, gesture recognition. *Unit head:* Dr. Steve Agee, Dean, 405-208-5130, Fax: 405-208-5098, E-mail: sagee@okcu.edu. *Application contact:* Michael Harrington, Director, Graduate Admissions, 800-633-7242, Fax: 405-208-5916, E-mail: gadmissions@okcu.edu.
Website: http://msb.okcu.edu/graduate.

Oklahoma State University, College of Arts and Sciences, Department of Computer Science, Stillwater, OK 74078. Offers MS, PhD. *Faculty:* 14 full-time (3 women). *Students:* 48 full-time (15 women), 41 part-time (12 women); includes 3 minority (all Two or more races, non-Hispanic/Latino), 76 international. Average age 28. 438 applicants, 13% accepted, 16 enrolled. In 2014, 15 master's, 3 doctorates awarded. *Degree requirements:* For master's, thesis optional; for doctorate, comprehensive exam, thesis/dissertation. *Entrance requirements:* For master's, GRE; for doctorate, GRE General Test, GRE Subject Test in computer science (recommended), 3 letters of recommendation. Additional exam requirements/recommendations for international students: Required—TOEFL (minimum score 550 paper-based; 79 iBT). *Application deadline:* For fall admission, 3/1 priority date for international students; for spring admission, 8/1 priority date for international students. Applications are processed on a rolling basis. Application fee: $40 ($75 for international students). Electronic applications accepted. *Expenses:* Tuition, state resident: full-time $4488; part-time $187 per credit hour. Tuition, nonresident: full-time $18,360; part-time $765 per credit hour. *Required fees:* $2413; $100.55 per credit hour. Tuition and fees vary according to campus/location. *Financial support:* In 2014–15, 6 research assistantships (averaging $15,993 per year), 25 teaching assistantships (averaging $18,297 per year) were awarded; career-related internships or fieldwork, Federal Work-Study, scholarships/grants, health care benefits, tuition waivers (partial), and unspecified assistantships also available. Support available to part-time students. Financial award application deadline: 3/1; financial award applicants required to submit FAFSA. *Unit head:* Dr. K. M. George, Department Head, 405-744-5668, Fax: 405-774-9097, E-mail: kmg@cs.okstate.edu. *Application contact:* Dr. Nohphill Park, Graduate Coordinator, 405-744-7937, Fax: 405-744-0355, E-mail: npark@cs.okstate.edu.
Website: http://cs.okstate.edu/.

Old Dominion University, College of Sciences, Program in Computer Science, Norfolk, VA 23529. Offers MS, PhD. Part-time programs available. *Faculty:* 16 full-time (2 women). *Students:* 71 full-time (19 women), 68 part-time (18 women); includes 17 minority (6 Black or African American, non-Hispanic/Latino; 6 Asian, non-Hispanic/Latino; 3 Hispanic/Latino; 2 Two or more races, non-Hispanic/Latino), 93 international. Average age 30. 180 applicants, 71% accepted, 32 enrolled. In 2014, 38 master's, 3 doctorates awarded. Terminal master's awarded for partial completion of doctoral program. *Degree requirements:* For master's, comprehensive exam, thesis optional; for doctorate, comprehensive exam, thesis/dissertation. *Entrance requirements:* For master's, GRE General Test, minimum GPA of 3.0; for doctorate, GRE General Test, MS in computer science. Additional exam requirements/recommendations for international students: Required—TOEFL. *Application deadline:* For fall admission, 7/1 for domestic students. Applications are processed on a rolling basis. Application fee: $50. *Expenses:* Tuition, state resident: full-time $10,488; part-time $437 per credit. Tuition, nonresident: full-time $26,136; part-time $1089 per credit. *Required fees:* $64 per semester. One-time fee: $50. *Financial support:* In 2014–15, 98 students received support, including 1 fellowship (averaging $2,021 per year), 27 research assistantships with tuition reimbursements available (averaging $8,736 per year), 28 teaching assistantships with tuition reimbursements available (averaging $7,926 per year); career-related internships or fieldwork, scholarships/grants, and tuition waivers (partial) also available. Support available to part-time students. Financial award application deadline: 2/15; financial award applicants required to submit FAFSA. *Faculty research:* Software engineering, foundations, high-performance computing, networking and mobile computing, bioinformatics, medical image computing, Web science. *Total annual research expenditures:* $1.4 million. *Unit head:* Dr. Mohammed Zubair, PhD Director, 757-683-3917, Fax: 757-683-4900, E-mail: csgpd@odu.edu. *Application contact:* Dr. Michele Weigle, MS Director, 757-683-6001, E-mail: mweigle@odu.edu.
Website: http://www.cs.odu.edu/.

Oregon Health & Science University, School of Medicine, Graduate Programs in Medicine, Department of Computer Science and Engineering, Portland, OR 97239-3098. Offers computer science and engineering (MS, PhD); electrical engineering (MS, PhD). Part-time programs available. *Faculty:* 7 full-time (2 women), 1 part-time/adjunct (0 women). *Students:* 18 full-time (8 women), 10 international. Average age 32. 10 applicants, 60% accepted, 5 enrolled. In 2014, 1 master's, 3 doctorates awarded. Terminal master's awarded for partial completion of doctoral program. *Degree requirements:* For master's, thesis (for some programs); for doctorate, comprehensive exam, thesis/dissertation, qualifying exam. *Entrance requirements:* For master's and doctorate, GRE General Test (minimum scores: 153 Verbal/148 Quantitative/4.5 Analytical). Additional exam requirements/recommendations for international students: Required—IELTS or TOEFL. *Application deadline:* For fall admission, 7/15 for domestic students, 5/15 for international students; for winter admission, 10/15 for domestic students, 9/15 for international students; for spring admission, 1/15 for domestic students, 12/15 for international students. Applications are processed on a rolling basis. Application fee: $70. Electronic applications accepted. *Financial support:* Health care benefits, tuition waivers (full), and full tuition and stipends (for PhD students) available. *Faculty research:* Natural language processing, speech signal processing, computational biology, autism spectrum disorders, hearing and speaking disorders. *Unit head:* Dr. Peter Heeman, Program Director, 503-748-1635, E-mail: cseedept@csee.ogi.edu. *Application contact:* Pat Dickerson, Administrative Coordinator, 503-748-1635, E-mail: cseedept@csee.ogi.edu.

Oregon State University, College of Engineering, Program in Computer Science, Corvallis, OR 97331. Offers M Eng, MS, PhD. *Faculty:* 49 full-time (7 women), 2 part-time/adjunct (both women). *Students:* 157 full-time (35 women), 9 part-time (2 women); includes 8 minority (4 Asian, non-Hispanic/Latino; 2 Hispanic/Latino; 2 Two or more races, non-Hispanic/Latino), 120 international. Average age 28. 479 applicants, 16% accepted, 53 enrolled. In 2014, 31 master's, 12 doctorates awarded. *Entrance requirements:* For master's and doctorate, GRE. Additional exam requirements/recommendations for international students: Required—TOEFL (minimum score 600 paper-based; 80 iBT), IELTS (minimum score 6.5). *Application deadline:* For fall admission, 1/15 for domestic students. Application fee: $60. *Expenses:* Expenses: $15,359 full-time resident tuition and fees; $23,405 non-resident. *Financial support:* Application deadline: 1/15. *Unit head:* Bella Bose, Professor/Interim School Head, 541-737-5573. *Application contact:* Graduate Coordinator, 541-737-7234, E-mail: eecs.gradinfo@oregonstate.edu.
Website: http://eecs.oregonstate.edu/current-students/graduate/cs-program.

Pace University, Seidenberg School of Computer Science and Information Systems, New York, NY 10038. Offers computer science (MS); computing science (DPS); information systems (MS); Internet technology (MS); large computing systems (Certificate); network administration (Certificate); security and information assurance (Certificate); software development and engineering (MS, Certificate); telecommunications (Certificate); telecommunications systems and networks (MS). Part-time and evening/weekend programs available. *Faculty:* 26 full-time (7 women), 7 part-time/adjunct (2 women). *Students:* 167 full-time (57 women), 324 part-time (90 women); includes 182 minority (83 Black or African American, non-Hispanic/Latino; 1 American Indian or Alaska Native, non-Hispanic/Latino; 46 Asian, non-Hispanic/Latino; 47 Hispanic/Latino; 5 Two or more races, non-Hispanic/Latino), 132 international. Average age 35. 441 applicants, 84% accepted, 157 enrolled. In 2014, 115 master's, 7 doctorates, 9 other advanced degrees awarded. *Degree requirements:* For master's, thesis or alternative, capstone course; for doctorate, comprehensive exam (for some programs), thesis/dissertation. *Entrance requirements:* For master's, GRE General Test. Additional exam requirements/recommendations for international students: Required—TOEFL. *Application deadline:* For fall admission, 8/1 priority date for domestic students, 6/1 for international students; for spring admission, 12/1 for domestic students, 10/1 for international students. Applications are processed on a rolling basis. Application fee: $70. Electronic applications accepted. *Expenses:* Expenses: Contact institution. *Financial support:* Research assistantships and career-related internships or fieldwork available. Support available to part-time students. Financial award applicants required to submit FAFSA. *Faculty research:* Computer security and forensics, cybersecurity, telehealth, mobile computing, distributed teams, robotics. *Total annual research expenditures:* $685,824. *Unit head:* Dr. Amar Gupta, Dean, Seidenberg School of Computer Science and Information Systems, 914-773-3750, Fax: 914-773-3533, E-mail: agupta@pace.edu. *Application contact:* Susan Ford-Goldschein, Director of Graduate Admissions, 914-422-4283, Fax: 914-422-4287, E-mail: gradwp@pace.edu.
Website: http://www.pace.edu/seidenberg.

Pacific States University, College of Computer Science and Information Systems, Los Angeles, CA 90006. Offers computer science (MS); information systems (MS). Part-time and evening/weekend programs available. *Entrance requirements:* For master's, bachelor's degree in physics, engineering, computer science, or applied mathematics; minimum undergraduate GPA of 2.5 during last 90 hours of course work. Additional exam requirements/recommendations for international students: Required—TOEFL (minimum score 500 paper-based; 61 iBT), IELTS (minimum score 5.5).

Penn State Harrisburg, Graduate School, School of Science, Engineering and Technology, Middletown, PA 17057-4898. Offers computer science (MS); electrical engineering (M Eng, MS); engineering management (MPS); engineering science (M Eng); environmental engineering (M Eng); structural engineering (Certificate). Part-time and evening/weekend programs available. *Unit head:* Dr. Mukund S. Kulkarni, Chancellor, 717-948-6105, Fax: 717-948-6452, E-mail: msk5@psu.edu. *Application contact:* Robert W. Coffman, Jr., Director of Enrollment Management, Admissions, 717-948-6250, Fax: 717-948-6325, E-mail: ric1@psu.edu.
Website: http://harrisburg.psu.edu/science-engineering-technology.

Penn State University Park, Graduate School, College of Engineering, Department of Computer Science and Engineering, University Park, PA 16802. Offers M Eng, MS, PhD. *Unit head:* Dr. Amr S. Elnashai, Dean, 814-865-7537, Fax: 814-863-4749, E-mail: ase2@psu.edu. *Application contact:* Lori A. Stania, Director, Graduate Student Services, 814-867-5278, Fax: 814-863-4627, E-mail: gswww@psu.edu.
Website: http://www.cse.psu.edu/.

Polytechnic University of Puerto Rico, Graduate School, Hato Rey, PR 00919. Offers business administration (MBA), including computer information systems, general management, management of information systems, management of international enterprises; civil engineering (ME, MS); computer engineering (ME, MS); computer science (MCS, MS); electrical engineering (ME, MS); engineering management (MEM); environmental management (MEM); landscape architecture (M Land Arch); manufacturing competitiveness (MMC, MS); manufacturing engineering (ME, MS); mechanical engineering (M Mech E). Part-time and evening/weekend programs available. *Entrance requirements:* For master's, 3 letters of recommendation.

Portland State University, Graduate Studies, Maseeh College of Engineering and Computer Science, Department of Computer Science, Portland, OR 97207-0751. Offers computer science (MS, PhD); software engineering (MSE). Part-time programs available. *Faculty:* 25 full-time (5 women), 5 part-time/adjunct (0 women). *Students:* 84 full-time (31 women), 50 part-time (18 women); includes 15 minority (1 Black or African American, non-Hispanic/Latino; 10 Asian, non-Hispanic/Latino; 1 Hispanic/Latino; 3 Two or more races, non-Hispanic/Latino), 73 international. Average age 30. 231 applicants, 27% accepted, 36 enrolled. In 2014, 35 master's, 5 doctorates awarded. *Degree requirements:* For master's, thesis or alternative; for doctorate, comprehensive exam, thesis/dissertation. *Entrance requirements:* For master's, GRE scores are required. The minimum for acceptance as an MS student is 60th percentile in Quantitative and 25th percentile in Verbal., 3.0 or equivalent GPA, 2 letters of recommendation and a personal statement; for doctorate, GRE scores are required. The minimum for acceptance is above 60th percentile in Quantitative and 25th percentile in Verbal., MS in computer science or allied field. Additional exam requirements/recommendations for international students: Required—TOEFL (minimum score 550 paper-based). *Application deadline:* For fall admission, 3/1 for domestic and international students; for winter admission, 5/15 for domestic and international students; for spring admission, 11/1 for domestic students, 10/1 for international students. Applications are processed on a rolling basis.

Application fee: $50. *Expenses:* Tuition, state resident: part-time $222 per credit. Tuition, nonresident: part-time $527 per credit. *Required fees:* $22 per contact hour. $100 per quarter. Tuition and fees vary according to program. *Financial support:* In 2014–15, 18 research assistantships with full and partial tuition reimbursements (averaging $8,688 per year), 18 teaching assistantships with full and partial tuition reimbursements (averaging $6,231 per year) were awarded; career-related internships or fieldwork, Federal Work-Study, scholarships/grants, tuition waivers (partial), and unspecified assistantships also available. Support available to part-time students. Financial award application deadline: 3/1; financial award applicants required to submit FAFSA. *Faculty research:* Formal methods, database systems, parallel programming environments, computer security, software tools. *Total annual research expenditures:* $2 million. *Unit head:* Dr. Warren Harrison, Chair, 503-725-3108, Fax: 503-725-3211, E-mail: warren@cs.pdx.edu. *Application contact:* Sara Smith, Graduate Coordinator, 503-725-4036, Fax: 503-725-3211, E-mail: gc@cs.pdx.edu.
Website: http://www.pdx.edu/computer-science/.

Prairie View A&M University, College of Engineering, Prairie View, TX 77446-0519. Offers computer information systems (MSCIS); computer science (MSCS); electrical engineering (MSEE, PhDEE); engineering (MS Engr). Part-time and evening/weekend programs available. *Faculty:* 29 full-time (5 women), 1 (woman) part-time/adjunct. *Students:* 113 full-time (46 women), 55 part-time (23 women); includes 72 minority (49 Black or African American, non-Hispanic/Latino; 1 American Indian or Alaska Native, non-Hispanic/Latino; 18 Asian, non-Hispanic/Latino; 3 Hispanic/Latino; 1 Two or more races, non-Hispanic/Latino), 73 international. Average age 32. 106 applicants, 98% accepted, 64 enrolled. In 2014, 37 master's, 5 doctorates awarded. *Degree requirements:* For master's, thesis (for some programs); for doctorate, comprehensive exam, thesis/dissertation. *Entrance requirements:* For master's, GRE General Test (minimum score of 900), bachelor's degree in engineering from ABET-accredited institution; for doctorate, minimum GPA of 3.0. Additional exam requirements/recommendations for international students: Required—TOEFL (minimum score 550 paper-based; 79 iBT). *Application deadline:* For fall admission, 7/1 priority date for domestic students, 6/1 priority date for international students; for spring admission, 11/1 priority date for domestic students, 10/1 priority date for international students; for summer admission, 3/1 priority date for domestic students, 2/1 priority date for international students. Application fee: $50. Electronic applications accepted. *Expenses:* Expenses: $6,686 tuition and fees. *Financial support:* In 2014–15, 14 research assistantships with partial tuition reimbursements (averaging $8,000 per year), 14 teaching assistantships with partial tuition reimbursements (averaging $7,500 per year) were awarded; career-related internships or fieldwork, institutionally sponsored loans, scholarships/grants, health care benefits, tuition waivers (partial), and unspecified assistantships also available. Financial award application deadline: 3/1; financial award applicants required to submit FAFSA. *Faculty research:* Applied radiation research, thermal science, computational fluid dynamics, analog mixed signal, aerial space battlefield. *Unit head:* Dr. Kendall T. Harris, Dean, 936-261-9956, Fax: 936-261-9869, E-mail: tharris@pvamu.edu. *Application contact:* Pauline Walker, Administrative Assistant II, Research and Graduate Studies, 936-261-3521, Fax: 936-261-3529, E-mail: pmwalker@pvamu.edu.

Princeton University, Graduate School, School of Engineering and Applied Science, Department of Computer Science, Princeton, NJ 08544-1019. Offers MSE, PhD. Terminal master's awarded for partial completion of doctoral program. *Degree requirements:* For master's, thesis; for doctorate, thesis/dissertation, general exam. *Entrance requirements:* For master's, GRE General Test, GRE Subject Test (recommended), 3 letters of recommendation; for doctorate, GRE General Test, GRE Subject Test (recommended), official transcript(s), 3 letters of recommendation, personal statement. Additional exam requirements/recommendations for international students: Required—TOEFL. Electronic applications accepted. *Faculty research:* Computational biology and bioinformatics; computer and network systems; graphics, vision, and sound; machine learning, programming languages and security; theory.

Purdue University, Graduate School, College of Science, Department of Computer Sciences, West Lafayette, IN 47907. Offers MS, PhD. Part-time programs available. Terminal master's awarded for partial completion of doctoral program. *Degree requirements:* For master's, thesis optional; for doctorate, comprehensive exam, thesis/dissertation. *Entrance requirements:* For master's and doctorate, minimum GPA of 3.5. Additional exam requirements/recommendations for international students: Required—TOEFL (minimum score 600 paper-based; 95 iBT), TWE (minimum score 5). Electronic applications accepted. *Faculty research:* Bioinformatics and computational biology, computational science and engineering, databases, data mining, distributed systems, graphics and visualization, information retrieval, information security and assurance, machine learning, networking and operation systems, programming languages and compilers, software engineering, theory of computing and algorithms.

Purdue University Calumet, Graduate Studies Office, School of Engineering, Mathematics, and Science, Department of Mathematics, Computer Science, and Statistics, Hammond, IN 46323-2094. Offers computer science (MS); mathematics (MAT, MS). Part-time programs available. *Entrance requirements:* Additional exam requirements/recommendations for international students: Required—TOEFL. *Faculty research:* Topology, analysis, algebra, mathematics education.

Queens College of the City University of New York, Division of Graduate Studies, Mathematics and Natural Sciences Division, Department of Computer Science, Flushing, NY 11367-1597. Offers MA. Part-time and evening/weekend programs available. *Degree requirements:* For master's, comprehensive exam, thesis optional. *Entrance requirements:* For master's, GRE, minimum GPA of 3.0. Additional exam requirements/recommendations for international students: Required—TOEFL.

Queen's University at Kingston, School of Graduate Studies, Faculty of Arts and Sciences, School of Computing, Kingston, ON K7L 3N6, Canada. Offers M Sc, PhD. *Degree requirements:* For master's, thesis; for doctorate, comprehensive exam, thesis/dissertation. *Entrance requirements:* For master's, honours B Sc in computer science; for doctorate, M Sc in computer science. Additional exam requirements/recommendations for international students: Required—TOEFL, TWE. *Faculty research:* Software engineering, human computer interaction, data base, networks, computational geometry.

Regis University, College for Professional Studies, School of Computer and Information Sciences, Denver, CO 80221-1099. Offers database development (Certificate); enterprise Java software development (Certificate); enterprise resource planning (Certificate); executive information technology (Certificate); information assurance (M Sc); information technology management (M Sc); software engineering (Certificate); software engineering and database technologies (M Sc); storage area networks (Certificate); systems engineering (M Sc, Certificate). Part-time and evening/weekend programs available. Postbaccalaureate distance learning degree programs offered (no on-campus study). *Faculty:* 8 full-time (3 women), 46 part-time/adjunct (9 women). *Students:* 254 full-time (69 women), 221 part-time (59 women); includes 159 minority (57 Black or African American, non-Hispanic/Latino; 4 American Indian or Alaska Native, non-Hispanic/Latino; 39 Asian, non-Hispanic/Latino; 49 Hispanic/Latino; 1 Native Hawaiian or other Pacific Islander, non-Hispanic/Latino; 9 Two or more races, non-Hispanic/Latino), 22 international. Average age 38. 204 applicants, 87% accepted, 128 enrolled. In 2014, 176 master's awarded. *Degree requirements:* For master's, thesis (for some programs), final research project. *Entrance requirements:* For master's, official transcript reflecting baccalaureate degree awarded from regionally-accredited college or university, 2 years of related experience, resume, interview. Additional exam requirements/recommendations for international students: Required—TOEFL (minimum score 550 paper-based; 82 iBT). *Application deadline:* For fall admission, 8/13 for domestic students, 7/13 for international students; for winter admission, 10/8 for domestic students, 9/8 for international students; for spring admission, 12/17 for domestic students, 11/17 for international students. Applications are processed on a rolling basis. Application fee: $75. Electronic applications accepted. *Expenses:* Expenses: $710 per credit hour (for M Sc). *Financial support:* In 2014–15, 16 students received support. Federal Work-Study and scholarships/grants available. Financial award application deadline: 4/15; financial award applicants required to submit FAFSA. *Faculty research:* Information policy, knowledge management, software architectures. *Unit head:* Donald Archer, Interim Dean, 303-458-4335, E-mail: archer@regis.edu. *Application contact:* Sarah Engel, Director of Admissions, 303-458-4900, Fax: 303-964-5534, E-mail: regisadm@regis.edu.
Website: http://regis.edu/CCIS.aspx.

Rensselaer at Hartford, Department of Computer and Information Science, Hartford, CT 06120-2991. Offers computer science (MS); information technology (MS). Part-time and evening/weekend programs available. *Degree requirements:* For master's, thesis optional. *Entrance requirements:* For master's, GRE. Additional exam requirements/recommendations for international students: Required—TOEFL (minimum score 600 paper-based; 100 iBT). Electronic applications accepted.

Rensselaer Polytechnic Institute, Graduate School, School of Science, Program in Computer Science, Troy, NY 12180-3590. Offers MS, PhD. Part-time programs available. *Faculty:* 24 full-time (5 women), 4 part-time/adjunct (1 woman). *Students:* 91 full-time (14 women), 10 part-time (1 woman); includes 12 minority (2 Black or African American, non-Hispanic/Latino; 5 Asian, non-Hispanic/Latino; 3 Hispanic/Latino; 2 Two or more races, non-Hispanic/Latino), 50 international. Average age 29. 276 applicants, 20% accepted, 20 enrolled. In 2014, 15 master's, 6 doctorates awarded. Terminal master's awarded for partial completion of doctoral program. *Degree requirements:* For master's, thesis; for doctorate, comprehensive exam, thesis/dissertation. *Entrance requirements:* For master's and doctorate, GRE. Additional exam requirements/recommendations for international students: Required—TOEFL (minimum score 570 paper-based; 88 iBT), IELTS (minimum score 6.5), PTE (minimum score 60). *Application deadline:* For fall admission, 1/1 priority date for domestic and international students; for spring admission, 8/15 priority date for domestic and international students. Applications are processed on a rolling basis. Application fee: $75. Electronic applications accepted. *Expenses: Tuition:* Full-time $46,700; part-time $1945 per credit. Tuition and fees vary according to course load. *Financial support:* In 2014–15, 63 students received support, including research assistantships (averaging $18,500 per year), teaching assistantships (averaging $18,500 per year); fellowships also available. Financial award application deadline: 1/1. *Faculty research:* Algorithms and theory; artificial intelligence; bioinformatics; computational science and engineering; computer vision, graphics, and robotics; data mining and machine and computational learning; database systems; pervasive computing and networking; programming languages and software engineering; security; semantic web; social networking. *Total annual research expenditures:* $4.3 million. *Unit head:* Dr. Mark Goldberg, Graduate Program Director, 518-276-2609, E-mail: goldberg@cs.rpi.edu. *Application contact:* Office of Graduate Admissions, 518-276-6216, E-mail: gradadmissions@rpi.edu.
Website: http://www.cs.rpi.edu/.

Rice University, Graduate Programs, George R. Brown School of Engineering, Department of Computer Science, Houston, TX 77251-1892. Offers MCS, MS, PhD. Terminal master's awarded for partial completion of doctoral program. *Degree requirements:* For master's, comprehensive exam; for doctorate, comprehensive exam, thesis/dissertation. *Entrance requirements:* For master's and doctorate, bachelor's degree. Additional exam requirements/recommendations for international students: Required—TOEFL. Electronic applications accepted. *Faculty research:* Programming languages and compiler construction; robotics, bioinformatics, algorithms - motion planning with emphasis on high-dimensional systems; network protocols, distributed systems, and operating systems - adaptive protocols for wireless; computer architecture, aperating systems - virtual machine monitors; computer graphics - application of computers to geometric problems and centered around general problem of representing geometric shapes.

Rivier University, School of Graduate Studies, Department of Computer Science and Mathematics, Nashua, NH 03060. Offers computer science (MS); mathematics (MAT). Part-time and evening/weekend programs available. *Entrance requirements:* For master's, GRE Subject Test. Electronic applications accepted.

Rochester Institute of Technology, Graduate Enrollment Services, Golisano College of Computing and Information Sciences, Computing and Information Sciences Department, PhD Program in Computing and Information Sciences, Rochester, NY 14623-5608. Offers PhD. *Students:* 23 full-time (4 women), 16 part-time (4 women); includes 3 minority (1 Asian, non-Hispanic/Latino; 1 Hispanic/Latino; 1 Two or more races, non-Hispanic/Latino), 31 international. Average age 30. 74 applicants, 27% accepted, 12 enrolled. In 2014, 3 doctorates awarded. *Degree requirements:* For doctorate, thesis/dissertation. *Entrance requirements:* For doctorate, GRE and TOEFL, IELTS, or PTE for non-native English speakers, minimum GPA of 3.0. Additional exam requirements/recommendations for international students: Required—PTE (minimum score 58), TOEFL (minimum score 550 paper-based; 79 iBT) or IELTS (minimum score 6.5). *Application deadline:* For fall admission, 1/15 priority date for domestic and international students. Applications are processed on a rolling basis. Application fee: $60. Electronic applications accepted. *Expenses:* Expenses: $1,673 per credit hour. *Financial support:* In 2014–15, 26 students received support. Research assistantships with full tuition reimbursements available, teaching assistantships with full tuition reimbursements available, career-related internships or fieldwork, Federal Work-Study, institutionally sponsored loans, scholarships/grants, health care benefits, and unspecified assistantships available. Support available to part-time students. Financial award applicants required to submit FAFSA. *Faculty research:* Cyber infrastructure as applied to multiple domains, astro-informatics, biomedical informatics, environmental informatics, computational biology, computational science, services sciences, electronic commerce. *Unit head:* Dr. Pengcheng Shi, Director, 585-475-6193, E-mail: ljtdps@rit.edu. *Application contact:* Diane Ellison, Associate Vice President, Graduate Enrollment Services, 585-475-2229, Fax: 585-475-7164, E-mail: gradinfo@rit.edu.
Website: http://www.rit.edu/gccis/phd.

Rochester Institute of Technology, Graduate Enrollment Services, Golisano College of Computing and Information Sciences, Information Science and Technologies Department, MS Program in Networking and Systems Administration, Rochester, NY 14623-5608. Offers MS. Part-time programs available. Postbaccalaureate distance learning degree programs offered (no on-campus study). *Students:* 37 full-time (6 women), 47 part-time (7 women); includes 4 minority (1 Black or African American, non-Hispanic/Latino; 2 Asian, non-Hispanic/Latino; 1 Hispanic/Latino), 45 international. Average age 26. 133 applicants, 32% accepted, 16 enrolled. In 2014, 12 master's

awarded. *Degree requirements:* For master's, thesis or alternative. *Entrance requirements:* For master's, GRE and TOEFL, IELTS, or PTE for non-native English speakers, minimum GPA of 3.0. Additional exam requirements/recommendations for international students: Required—PTE (minimum score 58), TOEFL (minimum score 550 paper-based; 79 iBT) or IELTS (minimum score 6.5). *Application deadline:* For fall admission, 2/15 priority date for domestic and international students; for spring admission, 12/15 priority date for domestic and international students. Applications are processed on a rolling basis. Application fee: $60. Electronic applications accepted. *Expenses:* Expenses: $1,673 per credit hour. *Financial support:* In 2014–15, 4 students received support. Research assistantships with partial tuition reimbursements available, teaching assistantships with partial tuition reimbursements available, career-related internships or fieldwork, Federal Work-Study, institutionally sponsored loans, scholarships/grants, and unspecified assistantships available. Support available to part-time students. Financial award applicants required to submit FAFSA. *Faculty research:* Network communications, unifying wired and wireless infrastructures, Cloud computing, scalability, collaboration tools, enterprise scale networking, emerging network technologies, network processing, high performance computing, network programming, security. *Unit head:* Dr. Peter Lutz, Graduate Program Director, 585-475-2700, Fax: 585-475-6584, E-mail: informaticsgrad@rit.edu. *Application contact:* Diane Ellison, Associate Vice President, Graduate Enrollment Services, 585-475-2229, Fax: 585-475-7164, E-mail: gradinfo@rit.edu.
Website: http://nsa.rit.edu/.

Roosevelt University, Graduate Division, College of Arts and Sciences, Department of Computer Science and Telecommunications, Program in Computer Science, Chicago, IL 60605. Offers MSC. Part-time and evening/weekend programs available. *Faculty research:* Artificial intelligence, software engineering, distributed databases, parallel processing.

Rowan University, Graduate School, College of Science and Mathematics, Program in Computer Science, Glassboro, NJ 08028-1701. Offers MS. *Faculty:* 5 full-time (1 woman), 3 part-time/adjunct (1 woman). *Students:* 5 full-time (1 woman), 30 part-time (3 women); includes 3 minority (all Asian, non-Hispanic/Latino), 2 international. Average age 36. 13 applicants, 77% accepted, 6 enrolled. In 2014, 21 master's awarded. *Degree requirements:* For master's, thesis optional. *Entrance requirements:* For master's, bachelor's degree (or its equivalent) in related field from accredited institution; official transcripts from all colleges attended; current professional resume; two letters of recommendation; statement of professional objectives; minimum undergraduate cumulative GPA of 3.0. *Application deadline:* For fall admission, 8/1 for domestic students; for spring admission, 11/1 for domestic students; for summer admission, 4/1 for domestic students. Applications are processed on a rolling basis. Application fee: $65. Electronic applications accepted. *Expenses: Tuition, area resident:* Part-time $648 per credit. Tuition, state resident: part-time $648 per credit. Tuition, nonresident: part-time $648 per credit. *Required fees:* $145 per credit. Tuition and fees vary according to degree level, campus/location, program and student level. *Unit head:* Dr. Horacio Sosa, Vice President, Global Learning and Partnerships, 856-256-4747, Fax: 856-256-5638, E-mail: sosa@rowan.edu. *Application contact:* Admissions and Enrollment Services, 856-256-4747, Fax: 856-256-5637, E-mail: globaladmissions@rowan.edu.
Website: http://www.rowan.edu/colleges/csm/departments/computerscience/.

Royal Military College of Canada, Division of Graduate Studies and Research, Science Division, Department of Mathematics and Computer Science, Kingston, ON K7K 7B4, Canada. Offers computer science (M Sc); mathematics (M Sc). *Degree requirements:* For master's, thesis. *Entrance requirements:* For master's, honours degree with second-class standing. Electronic applications accepted.

Rutgers, The State University of New Jersey, Camden, Graduate School of Arts and Sciences, Program in Computer Science, Camden, NJ 08102. Offers MS. Part-time and evening/weekend programs available. *Degree requirements:* For master's, comprehensive exam, thesis (for some programs), 30 credits. *Entrance requirements:* For master's, GRE, 3 letters of recommendation; statement of personal, professional, and academic goals; computer science undergraduate degree (preferred). Additional exam requirements/recommendations for international students: Required—TOEFL, IELTS. Electronic applications accepted. *Faculty research:* Cryptography and computer security, approximation algorithms, optical networks and wireless communications, computational geometry, data compression and encoding.

Rutgers, The State University of New Jersey, New Brunswick, Graduate School-New Brunswick, Program in Computer Science, Piscataway, NJ 08854-8097. Offers MS, PhD. Part-time programs available. Terminal master's awarded for partial completion of doctoral program. *Degree requirements:* For master's, comprehensive exam, thesis; for doctorate, comprehensive exam, thesis/dissertation. *Entrance requirements:* For master's and doctorate, GRE General Test, GRE Subject Test. Additional exam requirements/recommendations for international students: Required—TOEFL. *Faculty research:* Artificial intelligence and machine learning, bioinformatics, algorithms and complexity, networking and operating systems, computational graphics and vision.

Sacred Heart University, Graduate Programs, College of Arts and Sciences, Department of Computer Science, Fairfield, CT 06825-1000. Offers computer game design and development (Graduate Certificate); computer science and information technology (MS); computer science gaming (MS); cybersecurity (MS); database design (Graduate Certificate); information technology (Graduate Certificate); information technology and network security (Graduate Certificate); interactive multimedia (Graduate Certificate); Web development (Graduate Certificate). Part-time and evening/weekend programs available. *Faculty:* 6 full-time (2 women), 18 part-time/adjunct (5 women). *Students:* 266 full-time (100 women), 69 part-time (15 women); includes 30 minority (11 Black or African American, non-Hispanic/Latino; 7 Asian, non-Hispanic/Latino; 12 Hispanic/Latino), 265 international. Average age 26. 1,010 applicants, 56% accepted, 166 enrolled. In 2014, 50 master's awarded. *Degree requirements:* For master's, thesis or alternative. *Entrance requirements:* For master's, bachelor's degree, minimum GPA of 3.0. Additional exam requirements/recommendations for international students: Required—PTE; Recommended—TOEFL (minimum score 570 paper-based; 80 iBT), IELTS (minimum score 6.5). *Application deadline:* For fall admission, 5/15 for international students; for spring admission, 10/30 for international students. Applications are processed on a rolling basis. Application fee: $60. Electronic applications accepted. *Expenses: Tuition:* Full-time $24,559; part-time $649 per credit. *Financial support:* Unspecified assistantships available. Financial award applicants required to submit FAFSA. *Unit head:* Domenick Pinto, Academic Director and Chairperson, 203-371-7789, Fax: 203-371-0506, E-mail: pintod@sacredheart.edu. *Application contact:* Kathy Dilks, Executive Director of Graduate Admissions, 203-365-7619, Fax: 203-365-4732, E-mail: gradstudies@sacredheart.edu.
Website: http://www.sacredheart.edu/academics/collegeofartssciences/academicdepartments/computerscienceinformationtechnology/graduatedegreesandcertificates/.

St. Cloud State University, School of Graduate Studies, College of Science and Engineering, Department of Computer Science and Information Technology, St. Cloud, MN 56301-4498. Offers computer science (MS). *Degree requirements:* For master's, thesis or alternative. *Entrance requirements:* For master's, GRE General Test, minimum GPA of 2.75. Additional exam requirements/recommendations for international students: Required—Michigan English Language Assessment Battery; Recommended—TOEFL (minimum score 550 paper-based), IELTS (minimum score 6.5). Electronic applications accepted.

St. Francis Xavier University, Graduate Studies, Department of Mathematics, Statistics and Computer Science, Antigonish, NS B2G 2W5, Canada. Offers computer science (M Sc). *Degree requirements:* For master's, thesis. *Entrance requirements:* For master's, bachelor's degree or equivalent in computer science with minimum B average, 2 letters of recommendation. Additional exam requirements/recommendations for international students: Required—TOEFL (minimum score 580 paper-based).

Saint Joseph's University, College of Arts and Sciences, Department of Mathematics and Computer Science, Philadelphia, PA 19131-1395. Offers computer science (MS); mathematics and computer science (Post-Master's Certificate). Part-time and evening/weekend programs available. *Faculty:* 4 full-time (2 women), 2 part-time/adjunct (1 woman). *Students:* 26 full-time (16 women), 19 part-time (6 women); includes 2 minority (1 Black or African American, non-Hispanic/Latino; 1 Two or more races, non-Hispanic/Latino), 31 international. Average age 27. 91 applicants, 54% accepted, 16 enrolled. In 2014, 17 master's awarded. *Entrance requirements:* For master's, 2 letters of recommendation, resume, personal statement, official transcripts. Additional exam requirements/recommendations for international students: Required—TOEFL (minimum score 550 paper-based; 80 iBT), IELTS (minimum score 6.2). *Application deadline:* For fall admission, 7/15 priority date for domestic students, 4/15 for international students; for winter admission, 4/15 for domestic students, 1/15 for international students; for spring admission, 11/15 priority date for domestic students, 10/15 for international students. Applications are processed on a rolling basis. Application fee: $35. Electronic applications accepted. *Financial support:* In 2014–15, 16 students received support. Teaching assistantships with partial tuition reimbursements available and unspecified assistantships available. Financial award applicants required to submit FAFSA. *Faculty research:* Enhancing the 5-year Math and Science Education program, nonnegative curvature on lie groups and bundles, Regional Noyce Partnership, PACMACS Bridge Expansion Program, STEM teacher preparation. *Total annual research expenditures:* $270,393. *Unit head:* Dr. Babak Forouraghi. *Application contact:* Elisabeth Woodward, Director of Marketing and Admissions, Graduate Arts and Sciences, 610-660-3131, Fax: 610-660-3230, E-mail: gradstudies@sju.edu.
Website: http://sju.edu/majors-programs/graduate-arts-sciences/masters/computer-science-ms.

St. Mary's University, Graduate School, Department of Computer Science, Program in Computer Information Systems, San Antonio, TX 78228-8507. Offers MS. Part-time programs available. *Faculty:* 4 full-time (2 women). *Students:* 11 full-time (3 women), 6 part-time (2 women); includes 4 minority (2 Asian, non-Hispanic/Latino; 2 Hispanic/Latino), 11 international. Average age 30. 26 applicants, 23% accepted, 5 enrolled. In 2014, 6 master's awarded. *Degree requirements:* For master's, comprehensive exam. *Entrance requirements:* For master's, GMAT or GRE General Test, Minimum GPA of 2.7 in a bachelor's degree, minimum GRE quantitative score of 143 or better, or minimum GMAT score of 334, completed application form to include the following: written statement of purpose indicating interest and objective, two letters of recommendation, official transcripts of all college-level work. Additional exam requirements/recommendations for international students: Required—TOEFL (minimum score 530 paper-based; 80 iBT). *Application deadline:* Applications are processed on a rolling basis. Electronic applications accepted. *Expenses: Tuition:* Full-time $15,070; part-time $800 per credit hour. *Required fees:* $156 per semester. *Financial support:* Career-related internships or fieldwork, Federal Work-Study, institutionally sponsored loans, scholarships/grants, health care benefits, and unspecified assistantships available. Financial award application deadline: 3/31; financial award applicants required to submit FAFSA. *Faculty research:* Data integrity in cloud computing systems, artificial intelligence, computer science education, replicating data over cloud servers, intelligent systems, critical thinking and learning, expert systems/knowledge engineering. *Unit head:* Dr. Carol Redfield, Graduate Program Director, 210-436-3298, E-mail: credfield@stmarytx.edu.
Website: https://www.stmarytx.edu/academics/set/graduate/cis/.

St. Mary's University, Graduate School, Department of Computer Science, Program in Computer Science, San Antonio, TX 78228-8507. Offers MS, JD/MS. Part-time programs available. *Faculty:* 4 full-time (2 women). *Students:* 45 full-time (9 women), 19 part-time (6 women); includes 4 minority (all Hispanic/Latino), 58 international. Average age 25. 92 applicants, 22% accepted, 17 enrolled. In 2014, 22 master's awarded. *Degree requirements:* For master's, comprehensive exam. *Entrance requirements:* For master's, GRE or GMAT, Minimum GPA of 2.7 in a bachelor's degree, minimum GRE quantitative score of 143 or better, written statement of purpose indicating interest and objective, two letters of recommendation, and official transcripts of all college-level work. Additional exam requirements/recommendations for international students: Required—TOEFL (minimum score 550 paper-based; 80 iBT); Recommended—IELTS (minimum score 6). *Application deadline:* Applications are processed on a rolling basis. Electronic applications accepted. *Expenses: Tuition:* Full-time $15,070; part-time $800 per credit hour. *Required fees:* $156 per semester. *Financial support:* In 2014–15, 2 students received support. Fellowships, research assistantships, career-related internships or fieldwork, Federal Work-Study, institutionally sponsored loans, scholarships/grants, and health care benefits available. Financial award application deadline: 3/31; financial award applicants required to submit FAFSA. *Faculty research:* Data integrity in cloud computing systems, artificial intelligence, computer science education, replicating data over cloud servers, intelligent systems, critical thinking and learning, expert systems/knowledge engineering. *Unit head:* Dr. Carol Redfield, Graduate Program Director, 210-436-3298, E-mail: credfield@stmarytx.edu. *Application contact:* Dean of the Graduate School.
Website: https://www.stmarytx.edu/academics/set/graduate/computer-science/.

St. Mary's University, Graduate School, Department of Education, Program in Education, San Antonio, TX 78228-8507. Offers computer science (MA); education (MA); English literature and language (MA); international relations (MA); political science (MA). *Students:* 1 (woman) part-time; minority (Black or African American, non-Hispanic/Latino). Average age 28. 12 applicants, 17% accepted. In 2014, 3 master's awarded. *Entrance requirements:* For master's, GRE or MAT, 200 X GPA + Average GRE [(Verbal + Quantitative)/2]= 1050; or 10 X GPA + MAT = 68. *Expenses: Tuition:* Full-time $15,070; part-time $800 per credit hour. *Required fees:* $156 per semester. *Faculty research:* Bronfenbrenner's ecological systems theory: implications for education today. *Unit head:* Dr. Dan Higgins, Department Chair, 210-436-3121, E-mail: dhiggins@stmarytx.edu.
Website: https://www.stmarytx.edu/academics/graduate/masters/education/.

Saint Xavier University, Graduate Studies, College of Arts and Sciences, Department of Computer Science, Chicago, IL 60655-3105. Offers MACS. *Degree requirements:* For master's, thesis optional.

Sam Houston State University, College of Sciences, Department of Computer Science, Huntsville, TX 77341. Offers computing and information science (MS); digital

forensics (MS); information assurance and security (MS). Part-time programs available. *Faculty:* 12 full-time (3 women), 1 (woman) part-time/adjunct. *Students:* 37 full-time (8 women), 49 part-time (10 women); includes 25 minority (12 Black or African American, non-Hispanic/Latino; 3 Asian, non-Hispanic/Latino; 9 Hispanic/Latino; 1 Two or more races, non-Hispanic/Latino), 32 international. Average age 32. 73 applicants, 40% accepted, 21 enrolled. In 2014, 7 master's awarded. *Degree requirements:* For master's, comprehensive exam, thesis optional, internship; for doctorate, comprehensive exam, thesis/dissertation. *Entrance requirements:* For master's, GRE General Test, letters of recommendation. Additional exam requirements/recommendations for international students: Required—TOEFL (minimum score 550 paper-based; 79 iBT), IELTS (minimum score 6.5). *Application deadline:* For fall admission, 8/1 for domestic students, 6/25 for international students; for spring admission, 12/1 for domestic students, 11/12 for international students; for summer admission, 5/15 for domestic students, 4/9 for international students. Applications are processed on a rolling basis. Application fee: $45 ($75 for international students). Electronic applications accepted. *Expenses:* Tuition, state resident: full-time $2286; part-time $254 per credit hour. Tuition, nonresident: full-time $5544; part-time $616 per credit hour. *Required fees:* $440 per semester. Tuition and fees vary according to course load and campus/location. *Financial support:* In 2014–15, 19 research assistantships (averaging $6,013 per year) were awarded; career-related internships or fieldwork, Federal Work-Study, scholarships/grants, tuition waivers (partial), and unspecified assistantships also available. Support available to part-time students. Financial award application deadline: 3/15; financial award applicants required to submit FAFSA. *Unit head:* Dr. Peter Cooper, Chair/Professor, 936-294-1569, Fax: 936-294-4312, E-mail: css_pac@shsu.edu. *Application contact:* Dr. Jihuang Ji, Associate Professor/Graduate Advisor, 936-294-1579, Fax: 936-294-4312, E-mail: csc_jxj@shsu.edu.
Website: http://cs.shsu.edu/.

San Diego State University, Graduate and Research Affairs, College of Sciences, Program in Computer Science, San Diego, CA 92182. Offers MS. Part-time programs available. *Degree requirements:* For master's, comprehensive exam or thesis. *Entrance requirements:* For master's, GRE General Test. Additional exam requirements/recommendations for international students: Required—TOEFL. Electronic applications accepted.

San Francisco State University, Division of Graduate Studies, College of Science and Engineering, Department of Computer Science, San Francisco, CA 94132-1722. Offers computing and business (MS); computing for life sciences (MS). Part-time programs available. *Application deadline:* Applications are processed on a rolling basis. *Expenses:* Tuition, state resident: full-time $6738. Tuition, nonresident: full-time $17,898; part-time $372 per credit hour. *Required fees:* $498 per semester. *Unit head:* Dr. Dragutin Petkovic, Chair, 415-338-2156, Fax: 415-338-6826, E-mail: petkovic@sfsu.edu. *Application contact:* Prof. Kaz Okada, Acting Graduate Coordinator, 415-338-7687, Fax: 415-338-6826, E-mail: kazokada@sfsu.edu.
Website: http://cs.sfsu.edu/grad/graduate.html.

San Jose State University, Graduate Studies and Research, College of Science, Department of Computer Science, San Jose, CA 95192-0001. Offers MS. Electronic applications accepted.

Santa Clara University, School of Engineering, Santa Clara, CA 95053. Offers analog circuit design (Certificate); applied mathematics (MS); ASIC design and test (Certificate); bioengineering (MS); civil engineering (MS); computer science and engineering (MS, PhD); controls (Certificate); digital signal processing (Certificate); dynamics (Certificate); electrical engineering (MS, PhD); engineering (Engineer); engineering management (MS); fundamentals of electrical engineering (Certificate); information assurance (Certificate); materials engineering (Certificate); mechanical design analysis (Certificate); mechanical engineering (MS, PhD); mechatronics systems engineering (Certificate); microwave and antennas (Certificate); networking (Certificate); renewable energy (Certificate); software engineering (Certificate); sustainable energy (MS); technology jump-start (Certificate); thermofluids (Certificate). Part-time and evening/weekend programs available. *Faculty:* 59 full-time (23 women), 80 part-time/adjunct (14 women). *Students:* 584 full-time (239 women), 353 part-time (102 women); includes 224 minority (7 Black or African American, non-Hispanic/Latino; 144 Asian, non-Hispanic/Latino; 50 Hispanic/Latino; 2 Native Hawaiian or other Pacific Islander, non-Hispanic/Latino; 21 Two or more races, non-Hispanic/Latino), 548 international. Average age 27. 1,248 applicants, 51% accepted, 375 enrolled. In 2014, 283 master's, 5 doctorates, 1 other advanced degree awarded. *Degree requirements:* For master's, thesis (for some programs); for doctorate, thesis/dissertation; for other advanced degree, thesis. *Entrance requirements:* For master's, GRE, transcript; for doctorate, GRE, master's degree or equivalent; for other advanced degree, master's degree, published paper. Additional exam requirements/recommendations for international students: Required—TOEFL (minimum score 550 paper-based; 79 iBT). *Application deadline:* For fall admission, 8/1 for domestic students, 7/15 for international students; for winter admission, 10/28 for domestic students, 9/23 for international students; for spring admission, 2/25 for domestic students, 1/21 for international students. Applications are processed on a rolling basis. Application fee: $60. Electronic applications accepted. *Expenses:* Expenses: Contact institution. *Financial support:* In 2014–15, 94 students received support. Fellowships with full and partial tuition reimbursements available, research assistantships with full and partial tuition reimbursements available, teaching assistantships with full tuition reimbursements available, career-related internships or fieldwork, Federal Work-Study, institutionally sponsored loans, and scholarships/grants available. Support available to part-time students. Financial award application deadline: 3/2; financial award applicants required to submit FAFSA. *Faculty research:* Video encoding, nanostructures, robotics, microfluidics, water resources. *Total annual research expenditures:* $1.6 million. *Unit head:* Dr. Alex Zecevic, Associate Dean for Graduate Studies, 408-554-2394, E-mail: azecevic@scu.edu. *Application contact:* Stacey Tinker, Director of Enrollment Management, 408-554-4748, Fax: 408-554-4323, E-mail: stinker@scu.edu.
Website: http://www.scu.edu/engineering/graduate/.

Seattle University, College of Science and Engineering, Program in Computer Science, Seattle, WA 98122-1090. Offers MSCS. *Faculty:* 8 full-time (3 women), 2 part-time/adjunct (0 women). *Students:* 17 full-time (11 women), 29 part-time (11 women); includes 13 minority (1 Black or African American, non-Hispanic/Latino; 8 Asian, non-Hispanic/Latino; 2 Hispanic/Latino; 2 Two or more races, non-Hispanic/Latino), 15 international. Average age 28. 67 applicants, 36% accepted, 14 enrolled. In 2014, 13 master's awarded. *Entrance requirements:* For master's, GRE, bachelor's degree in computer science or related discipline from regionally-accredited institution; minimum GPA of 3.0; letter of intent; 2 academic or professional recommendations; official transcripts. Additional exam requirements/recommendations for international students: Required—TOEFL (minimum score 580 paper-based; 92 iBT). *Application deadline:* For fall admission, 7/20 for domestic students, 4/1 for international students; for winter admission, 11/20 for domestic students, 9/1 for international students; for spring admission, 2/20 for domestic students, 12/1 for international students. *Financial support:* In 2014–15, 6 students received support. *Unit head:* Dr. Richard LeBlanc, Chair, 206-296-5510, Fax: 206-296-2071, E-mail: leblanc@seattleu.edu. *Application contact:* Janet Shandley, Director of Graduate Admissions, 206-296-5900, Fax: 206-298-5656, E-mail: grad_admissions@seattleu.edu.
Website: https://www.seattleu.edu/scieng/comsci/.

Shippensburg University of Pennsylvania, School of Graduate Studies, College of Arts and Sciences, Department of Computer Science, Shippensburg, PA 17257-2299. Offers MS. Part-time and evening/weekend programs available. *Faculty:* 5 full-time (3 women). *Students:* 13 full-time (6 women), 11 part-time (6 women); includes 1 minority (Hispanic/Latino), 16 international. Average age 27. 66 applicants, 61% accepted, 20 enrolled. In 2014, 5 master's awarded. *Entrance requirements:* For master's, GRE (if GPA less than 2.75), professional resume. Additional exam requirements/recommendations for international students: Required—TOEFL (minimum score 580 paper-based; 70 iBT); Recommended—IELTS (minimum score 6). *Application deadline:* For fall admission, 4/30 for international students; for spring admission, 9/30 for international students. Applications are processed on a rolling basis. Application fee: $45. Electronic applications accepted. *Expenses: Tuition, area resident:* Part-time $454 per credit. Tuition, state resident: part-time $454 per credit. Tuition, nonresident: part-time $681 per credit. *Required fees:* $133 per credit. *Financial support:* In 2014–15, 4 research assistantships with full tuition reimbursements (averaging $5,000 per year) were awarded; career-related internships or fieldwork, scholarships/grants, unspecified assistantships, and resident hall director and student payroll positions also available. Support available to part-time students. Financial award application deadline: 3/1; financial award applicants required to submit FAFSA. *Unit head:* Dr. Jeonghwa Lee, Program Coordinator, 717-477-1178, Fax: 717-477-4002, E-mail: jlee@ship.edu. *Application contact:* Jeremy R. Goshorn, Assistant Dean of Graduate Admissions, 717-477-1231, Fax: 717-477-4016, E-mail: jrgoshorn@ship.edu.
Website: http://www.cs.ship.edu/.

Silicon Valley University, Graduate Programs, San Jose, CA 95131. Offers business administration (MBA); computer engineering (MSCE); computer science (MSCS). *Degree requirements:* For master's, project (MSCS).

Simon Fraser University, Office of Graduate Studies, Faculty of Applied Sciences, School of Computing Science, Burnaby, BC V5A 1S6, Canada. Offers M Sc, PhD, M Sc/MSE. M Sc/MSE offered jointly with Zhejiang University. *Degree requirements:* For master's, comprehensive exam, thesis or alternative; for doctorate, comprehensive exam, thesis/dissertation, qualifying exams. *Entrance requirements:* For master's, minimum GPA of 3.0 (on scale of 4.33), or 3.33 based on last 60 credits of undergraduate courses; for doctorate, minimum GPA of 3.5 (on scale of 4.33). Additional exam requirements/recommendations for international students: Recommended—TOEFL (minimum score 580 paper-based; 93 iBT), IELTS (minimum score 7), TWE (minimum score 5). Electronic applications accepted. *Faculty research:* Artificial intelligence, computer hardware, computer systems, database systems, theory.

Simon Fraser University, Office of Graduate Studies, School of Interactive Arts and Technology, Surrey, BC V3T 2W1, Canada. Offers M Sc, MA, PhD. *Degree requirements:* For master's, thesis, seminar presentation; for doctorate, comprehensive exam, thesis/dissertation, seminar presentations. *Entrance requirements:* For master's, minimum GPA of 3.0 (on scale of 4.33), or 3.33 based on last 60 credits of undergraduate courses; for doctorate, minimum GPA of 3.5 (on scale of 4.33). Additional exam requirements/recommendations for international students: Required—TOEFL (minimum score 580 paper-based; 93 iBT), IELTS (minimum score 7), TWE (minimum score 5). Electronic applications accepted. *Faculty research:* Media and culture, scientific methods, social and human experience, knowledge computation, media art.

Southern Arkansas University–Magnolia, School of Graduate Studies, Magnolia, AR 71753. Offers agriculture (MS); business administration (MBA); computer and information sciences (MS); education (M Ed), including counseling and development, curriculum and instruction, educational administration and supervision, elementary education, reading, secondary education, TESOL; kinesiology (M Ed); library media and information specialist (M Ed); mental health and clinical counseling (MS); public administration (MPA); school counseling (M Ed); teaching (MAT). *Accreditation:* NCATE. Part-time and evening/weekend programs available. Postbaccalaureate distance learning degree programs offered. *Faculty:* 32 full-time (16 women), 18 part-time/adjunct (12 women). *Students:* 121 full-time (65 women), 356 part-time (234 women); includes 101 minority (76 Black or African American, non-Hispanic/Latino; 14 American Indian or Alaska Native, non-Hispanic/Latino; 5 Asian, non-Hispanic/Latino; 2 Hispanic/Latino; 4 Two or more races, non-Hispanic/Latino), 65 international. Average age 33. 204 applicants, 78% accepted, 160 enrolled. In 2014, 149 master's awarded. *Degree requirements:* For master's, comprehensive exam (for some programs), thesis optional. *Entrance requirements:* For master's, GRE, MAT or GMAT, minimum GPA of 2.5. Additional exam requirements/recommendations for international students: Required—TOEFL, IELTS. *Application deadline:* For fall admission, 7/20 for domestic students, 7/10 for international students; for winter admission, 12/1 for domestic and international students; for spring admission, 12/1 for domestic and international students; for summer admission, 4/1 for domestic and international students. Applications are processed on a rolling basis. Application fee: $25 ($50 for international students). Electronic applications accepted. *Expenses:* Tuition, state resident: full-time $4716; part-time $262 per credit. Tuition, nonresident: full-time $7020; part-time $390 per credit. *Required fees:* $831; $277 per course. Tuition and fees vary according to class time, course level, course load, degree level, campus/location, program, student level and student's religious affiliation. *Financial support:* Career-related internships or fieldwork, Federal Work-Study, scholarships/grants, tuition waivers (full), and unspecified assistantships available. Financial award applicants required to submit FAFSA. *Faculty research:* Alternative certification for teachers, supervision of instruction, instructional leadership, counseling. *Unit head:* Dr. Kim Bloss, Dean, School of Graduate Studies, 870-235-4150, Fax: 870-235-5227, E-mail: kkbloss@saumag.edu. *Application contact:* Shrijana Malakar, Admissions Specialist, 870-235-4150, Fax: 870-235-5227, E-mail: smalakar@saumag.edu.
Website: http://www.saumag.edu/graduate.

Southern Connecticut State University, School of Graduate Studies, School of Arts and Sciences, Department of Computer Science, New Haven, CT 06515-1355. Offers MS. *Entrance requirements:* For master's, GRE. Electronic applications accepted.

Southern Illinois University Carbondale, Graduate School, College of Science, Department of Computer Science, Carbondale, IL 62901-4701. Offers MS, PhD. *Faculty:* 12 full-time (0 women). *Students:* 123 full-time (41 women), 29 part-time (6 women); includes 4 minority (3 Asian, non-Hispanic/Latino; 1 Hispanic/Latino), 134 international. 483 applicants, 24% accepted, 41 enrolled. In 2014, 25 master's, 5 doctorates awarded. *Degree requirements:* For master's, thesis. *Entrance requirements:* For master's, previous undergraduate course work in computer science, minimum GPA of 2.7. Additional exam requirements/recommendations for international students: Required—TOEFL. *Application deadline:* Applications are processed on a rolling basis. Application fee: $50. *Expenses:* Tuition, state resident: full-time $10,176; part-time $1153 per credit. Tuition, nonresident: full-time $20,814; part-time $1744 per credit. *Required fees:* $7092; $394 per credit. $2364 per semester. *Financial support:* In 2014–15, 32 students received support, including 3 research assistantships with full tuition

reimbursements available, 22 teaching assistantships with full tuition reimbursements available; fellowships with full tuition reimbursements available, Federal Work-Study, institutionally sponsored loans, and tuition waivers (full) also available. Support available to part-time students. Financial award application deadline: 3/1. *Faculty research:* Analysis of algorithms, VLSI testing, database systems, artificial intelligence, computer architecture. *Unit head:* Dr. Norman Carver, Director of Graduate Studies, 618-453-6048, E-mail: carver@cs.siu.edu. *Application contact:* Terri Elliot, Office Manager, 618-453-6041, E-mail: terri@cs.siu.edu.
Website: http://www.cs.siu.edu/.

Southern Illinois University Edwardsville, Graduate School, School of Engineering, Department of Computer Science, Edwardsville, IL 62026. Offers MS. Part-time and evening/weekend programs available. *Faculty:* 11 full-time (0 women). *Students:* 17 full-time (7 women), 21 part-time (5 women); includes 6 minority (1 Black or African American, non-Hispanic/Latino; 3 Asian, non-Hispanic/Latino; 1 Hispanic/Latino; 1 Two or more races, non-Hispanic/Latino), 20 international. 210 applicants, 23% accepted. In 2014, 12 master's awarded. *Degree requirements:* For master's, thesis (for some programs), final exam, final project. *Entrance requirements:* Additional exam requirements/recommendations for international students: Required—TOEFL (minimum score 550 paper-based; 79 iBT), IELTS (minimum score 6.5). *Application deadline:* For fall admission, 7/24 for domestic students, 7/15 for international students; for spring admission, 12/11 for domestic students, 11/15 for international students; for summer admission, 4/29 for domestic students, 4/15 for international students. Applications are processed on a rolling basis. Application fee: $30. Electronic applications accepted. *Expenses:* Tuition, state resident: full-time $5026. Tuition, nonresident: full-time $12,566. *International tuition:* $25,136 full-time. *Required fees:* $1682. Tuition and fees vary according to course load, campus/location and program. *Financial support:* In 2014–15, 16 students received support, including 1 fellowship with full tuition reimbursement available (averaging $8,370 per year), 9 research assistantships with full tuition reimbursements available, 6 teaching assistantships with full tuition reimbursements available; institutionally sponsored loans, scholarships/grants, and unspecified assistantships also available. Financial award application deadline: 3/1; financial award applicants required to submit FAFSA. *Unit head:* Dr. Dennis Bouvier, Chair, 618-650-2369, E-mail: dbouvie@siue.edu. *Application contact:* Melissa K Mace, Assistant Director of Admissions for Graduate and International Recruitment, 618-650-2756, Fax: 618-650-3618, E-mail: mmace@siue.edu.
Website: http://www.cs.siue.edu/.

Southern Methodist University, Bobby B. Lyle School of Engineering, Department of Computer Science and Engineering, Dallas, TX 75275-0122. Offers computer engineering (MS, PhD); computer science (MS, PhD); security engineering (MS); software engineering (MS, DE). Part-time and evening/weekend programs available. Postbaccalaureate distance learning degree programs offered (no on-campus study). Terminal master's awarded for partial completion of doctoral program. *Degree requirements:* For master's, thesis optional; for doctorate, thesis/dissertation, oral and written qualifying exams, oral final exam (PhD). *Entrance requirements:* For master's, GRE General Test, minimum GPA of 3.0 in last 2 years; bachelor's degree in engineering, mathematics, or sciences; for doctorate, preliminary counseling exam (PhD), minimum GPA of 3.0, bachelor's degree in related field, MA (for DE). Additional exam requirements/recommendations for international students: Required—TOEFL (minimum score 550 paper-based). *Faculty research:* Trusted and high performance network computing, software engineering and management, knowledge engineering and management, computer arithmetic, computer architecture and CAD.

Southern Oregon University, Graduate Studies, Department of Computer Science, Ashland, OR 97520. Offers applied computer science (PSM). Part-time programs available. Postbaccalaureate distance learning degree programs offered (minimal on-campus study). *Faculty:* 3 full-time (1 woman), 3 part-time/adjunct (1 woman). *Students:* 1 full-time (0 women). Average age 36. 4 applicants, 25% accepted. In 2014, 1 master's awarded. *Degree requirements:* For master's, thesis (for some programs). *Entrance requirements:* For master's, GRE General Test, minimum cumulative GPA of 3.0 in the last 90 quarter credits (60 semester credits) of undergraduate coursework. Additional exam requirements/recommendations for international students: Required—TOEFL (minimum score 540 paper-based; 76 iBT), IELTS (minimum score 6), ELPT (minimum score 964) or ELS (minimum score 112). *Application deadline:* For fall admission, 7/31 priority date for domestic students, 7/30 priority date for international students; for winter admission, 11/15 priority date for domestic and international students; for spring admission, 1/7 priority date for domestic and international students. Applications are processed on a rolling basis. Application fee: $50. Electronic applications accepted. *Expenses:* Tuition, state resident: full-time $10,225; part-time $1515 per quarter. Tuition, nonresident: full-time $12,782; part-time $1894 per quarter. *Required fees:* $1395; $261 per quarter. *Financial support:* In 2014–15, 1 student received support, including 1 research assistantship with partial tuition reimbursement available; career-related internships or fieldwork, institutionally sponsored loans, scholarships/grants, and unspecified assistantships also available. *Unit head:* Dr. Kevin Sahr, Graduate Program Coordinator, 541-552-6978. *Application contact:* Kelly Moutsatson, Director of Admissions, 541-552-6411, Fax: 541-552-8403, E-mail: admissions@sou.edu.
Website: http://www.sou.edu/cs/.

Southern Polytechnic State University, School of Computing and Software Engineering, Department of Computer Science and Software Engineering, Marietta, GA 30060-2896. Offers computer science (MS, Graduate Transition Certificate); software engineering (MSSWE, Graduate Certificate); software engineering fundamentals (Postbaccalaureate Certificate). Part-time and evening/weekend programs available. Postbaccalaureate distance learning degree programs offered (no on-campus study). *Degree requirements:* For master's, thesis optional, capstone (software engineering). *Entrance requirements:* For master's, GRE (recommended). Additional exam requirements/recommendations for international students: Required—TOEFL (minimum score 550 paper-based; 79 iBT), IELTS (minimum score 6.5). Electronic applications accepted. *Faculty research:* Image processing and artificial intelligence, distributed computing, telemedicine applications, enterprise architectures, databases, software requirements engineering, software quality and metrics, usability, parallel and distributed computing, information security.

Southern University and Agricultural and Mechanical College, Graduate School, College of Sciences, Department of Computer Science, Baton Rouge, LA 70813. Offers information systems (MS); micro/minicomputer architecture (MS); operating systems (MS). Part-time programs available. Postbaccalaureate distance learning degree programs offered (minimal on-campus study). *Degree requirements:* For master's, thesis. *Entrance requirements:* For master's, GRE General Test, minimum GPA of 3.0, bachelor's degree in computer science or related field. Additional exam requirements/recommendations for international students: Required—TOEFL (minimum score 525 paper-based). *Faculty research:* Network theory, computational complexity, high speed computing, neural networking, data warehousing/mining.

Stanford University, School of Engineering, Department of Computer Science, Stanford, CA 94305-9991. Offers MS, PhD. Terminal master's awarded for partial completion of doctoral program. *Degree requirements:* For doctorate, thesis/dissertation. *Entrance requirements:* For master's, GRE General Test; for doctorate, GRE General Test, GRE Computer Science Subject Test. Additional exam requirements/recommendations for international students: Required—TOEFL. Electronic applications accepted. *Expenses: Tuition:* Full-time $44,184; part-time $982 per credit hour. *Required fees:* $191.

Stanford University, School of Engineering, Institute for Computational and Mathematical Engineering, Stanford, CA 94305-9991. Offers MS, PhD. Terminal master's awarded for partial completion of doctoral program. *Degree requirements:* For doctorate, thesis/dissertation, qualifying exam. *Entrance requirements:* For master's, GRE General Test; for doctorate, GRE General Test, GRE Subject Test. Additional exam requirements/recommendations for international students: Required—TOEFL. Electronic applications accepted. *Expenses: Tuition:* Full-time $44,184; part-time $982 per credit hour. *Required fees:* $191.

State University of New York at New Paltz, Graduate School, School of Science and Engineering, Department of Computer Science, New Paltz, NY 12561. Offers MS. Part-time and evening/weekend programs available. *Faculty:* 4 full-time (1 woman), 2 part-time/adjunct (0 women). *Students:* 39 full-time (7 women), 11 part-time (1 woman); includes 4 minority (1 Black or African American, non-Hispanic/Latino; 1 Asian, non-Hispanic/Latino; 1 Hispanic/Latino; 1 Native Hawaiian or other Pacific Islander, non-Hispanic/Latino), 37 international. Average age 26. 203 applicants, 45% accepted, 25 enrolled. In 2014, 13 master's awarded. *Degree requirements:* For master's, comprehensive exam, thesis. *Entrance requirements:* For master's, minimum GPA of 3.0, proficiency in program assembly. Additional exam requirements/recommendations for international students: Required—TOEFL (minimum score 550 paper-based; 80 iBT), IELTS (minimum score 6.5). *Application deadline:* For fall admission, 5/15 for domestic and international students; for spring admission, 11/15 for domestic and international students. Applications are processed on a rolling basis. Application fee: $50. Electronic applications accepted. *Financial support:* In 2014–15, 3 teaching assistantships with partial tuition reimbursements (averaging $5,000 per year) were awarded. Financial award application deadline: 8/1. *Unit head:* Dr. Andrew Pletch, Chair, 845-257-3990, Fax: 845-257-3996, E-mail: pletcha@newpaltz.edu. *Application contact:* Dr. Paul Zuckerman, Graduate Coordinator, 845-257-3516, E-mail: zuckerpr@newpaltz.edu.
Website: http://www.newpaltz.edu/compsci/.

State University of New York Polytechnic Institute, Program in Computer and Information Science, Utica, NY 13504-3050. Offers MS. Part-time and evening/weekend programs available. *Degree requirements:* For master's, thesis or project. *Entrance requirements:* For master's, GRE General Test, minimum GPA of 3.0, one letter of reference, resume, BS in computer science or a related field. Additional exam requirements/recommendations for international students: Required—TOEFL (minimum score 550 paper-based; 79 iBT), IELTS (minimum score 6.5). Electronic applications accepted. *Faculty research:* Cryptography, distributed systems, computer-aided system theory, reasoning with uncertainty, grid computing.

Stephen F. Austin State University, Graduate School, College of Business, Department of Computer Science, Nacogdoches, TX 75962. Offers MS. Part-time programs available. *Degree requirements:* For master's, comprehensive exam, thesis optional. *Entrance requirements:* For master's, GRE General Test. Additional exam requirements/recommendations for international students: Required—TOEFL.

Stevens Institute of Technology, Graduate School, Charles V. Schaefer Jr. School of Engineering, Department of Computer Science, Program in Computer Science, Hoboken, NJ 07030. Offers MS, PhD.

Stevens Institute of Technology, Graduate School, Wesley J. Howe School of Technology Management, Program in Information Systems, Hoboken, NJ 07030. Offers computer science (MS); e-commerce (MS); enterprise systems (MS); entrepreneurial information technology (MS); information architecture (MS); information management (MS, Certificate); information security (MS); information technology in financial services industry (MS); information technology in the pharmaceutical industry (MS); information technology outsourcing management (MS); project management (MS, Certificate); software engineering (MS); telecommunications (MS). *Degree requirements:* For master's, thesis optional. *Entrance requirements:* For master's, GMAT, GRE General Test. Additional exam requirements/recommendations for international students: Required—TOEFL. Electronic applications accepted.

Stony Brook University, State University of New York, Graduate School, College of Engineering and Applied Sciences, Department of Computer Science, Stony Brook, NY 11794. Offers computer science (MS, PhD); information systems (Certificate); information systems engineering (MS); software engineering (Certificate). *Faculty:* 46 full-time (8 women), 1 part-time/adjunct (0 women). *Students:* 417 full-time (79 women), 76 part-time (13 women); includes 22 minority (1 Black or African American, non-Hispanic/Latino; 18 Asian, non-Hispanic/Latino; 3 Hispanic/Latino), 450 international. Average age 25. 2,476 applicants, 23% accepted, 214 enrolled. In 2014, 131 master's, 15 doctorates awarded. *Degree requirements:* For master's, thesis or alternative; for doctorate, comprehensive exam, thesis/dissertation. *Entrance requirements:* For master's and doctorate, GRE General Test. Additional exam requirements/recommendations for international students: Required—TOEFL. *Application deadline:* For fall admission, 1/15 for domestic students; for spring admission, 10/1 for domestic students. Application fee: $100. *Expenses:* Tuition, state resident: full-time $10,370; part-time $432 per credit. Tuition, nonresident: full-time $20,190; part-time $841 per credit. *Required fees:* $1431. *Financial support:* In 2014–15, 12 fellowships, 92 research assistantships, 46 teaching assistantships were awarded. *Faculty research:* Artificial intelligence, computer architecture, database management systems, VLSI, operating systems. *Total annual research expenditures:* $6.6 million. *Unit head:* Prof. Arie Kauffman, Chairman, 631-632-8428, Fax: 631-632-8334, E-mail: arie.kaufman@stonybrook.edu. *Application contact:* Cynthia Scalzo, Coordinator, 631-632-1521, Fax: 631-632-8334, E-mail: graduate@cs.stonybrook.edu.
Website: http://www.cs.sunysb.edu/.

Syracuse University, L. C. Smith College of Engineering and Computer Science, Program in Computer Science, Syracuse, NY 13244. Offers MS. Part-time programs available. *Students:* 170 full-time (45 women), 8 part-time (3 women); includes 4 minority (1 Black or African American, non-Hispanic/Latino; 3 Asian, non-Hispanic/Latino), 163 international. Average age 25. 1,001 applicants, 34% accepted, 82 enrolled. In 2014, 53 master's awarded. *Degree requirements:* For master's, comprehensive exam (for some programs), thesis (for some programs). *Entrance requirements:* For master's, GRE General Test. Additional exam requirements/recommendations for international students: Required—TOEFL (minimum score 100 iBT). *Application deadline:* For fall admission, 7/1 priority date for domestic students, 6/1 priority date for international students; for spring admission, 11/15 priority date for domestic students, 10/15 priority date for international students. Applications are processed on a rolling basis. Application fee: $75. Electronic applications accepted. *Expenses: Tuition:* Part-time $1341 per credit. *Required fees:* $1341 per credit. *Financial support:* Fellowships with full tuition reimbursements, research assistantships with full and partial tuition reimbursements, teaching assistantships with full and partial tuition reimbursements, and tuition waivers (partial) available. Financial award application deadline: 1/1; financial award applicants required to submit FAFSA. *Unit head:* Dr. Susan Older,, Program director, 315-443-4679, Fax: 315-443-2583, E-mail: sueo@ecs.syr.edu. *Application*

contact: Brenda Flowers, Information Contact, 315-443-4408, E-mail: topgrads@syr.edu.
Website: http://lcs.syr.edu/.

Télé-université, Graduate Programs, Québec, QC G1K 9H5, Canada. Offers computer science (PhD); corporate finance (MS); distance learning (MS). Part-time programs available.

Temple University, College of Science and Technology, Department of Computer and Information Sciences, Philadelphia, PA 19140. Offers computer and information science (PhD); computer science (MS); information science and technology (MS). Part-time and evening/weekend programs available. *Faculty:* 28 full-time (4 women), 5 part-time/adjunct (1 woman). *Students:* 92 full-time (24 women), 24 part-time (8 women); includes 7 minority (2 Black or African American, non-Hispanic/Latino; 5 Asian, non-Hispanic/Latino), 81 international. 102 applicants, 71% accepted, 31 enrolled. In 2014, 29 master's, 8 doctorates awarded. Terminal master's awarded for partial completion of doctoral program. *Degree requirements:* For doctorate, thesis/dissertation. *Entrance requirements:* For master's and doctorate, GRE General Test, minimum GPA of 3.0. Additional exam requirements/recommendations for international students: Required—TOEFL (minimum score 550 paper-based; 79 iBT). *Application deadline:* For fall admission, 2/1 for domestic students, 12/15 for international students; for spring admission, 8/1 for domestic and international students. Applications are processed on a rolling basis. Application fee: $60. Electronic applications accepted. *Expenses:* Tuition, state resident: full-time $14,490; part-time $805 per credit hour. Tuition, nonresident: full-time $19,850; part-time $1103 per credit hour. *Required fees:* $690. Full-time tuition and fees vary according to class time, course load, degree level, campus/location and program. *Financial support:* Fellowships, research assistantships with tuition reimbursements, teaching assistantships with tuition reimbursements, career-related internships or fieldwork, institutionally sponsored loans, and unspecified assistantships available. Financial award application deadline: 1/15; financial award applicants required to submit FAFSA. *Faculty research:* Artificial intelligence, information systems, software engineering, network-distributed systems. *Unit head:* Dr. Jie Wu, Chair, 215-204-8450, Fax: 215-204-5082, E-mail: cis@temple.edu. *Application contact:* Marilyn Grandshaw, Administrative Coordinator, 215-204-8450, E-mail: marilyng@temple.edu.
Website: http://www.temple.edu/cis.

Tennessee Technological University, College of Graduate Studies, College of Engineering, Department of Computer Science, Cookeville, TN 38505. Offers computer software and scientific applications (MS); Internet-based computing (MS). Part-time programs available. *Students:* 8 full-time (0 women), 6 part-time (1 woman), 6 international. 125 applicants, 10% accepted, 7 enrolled. In 2014, 8 master's awarded. *Degree requirements:* For master's, thesis or alternative. *Entrance requirements:* For master's, GRE. Additional exam requirements/recommendations for international students: Required—TOEFL (minimum score 550 paper-based; 79 iBT), IELTS (minimum score 5.5), PTE (minimum score 53), or TOEIC (Test of English as an International Communication). *Application deadline:* For fall admission, 8/1 for domestic students, 5/1 for international students; for spring admission, 12/1 for domestic students, 10/1 for international students. Applications are processed on a rolling basis. Application fee: $35 ($40 for international students). Electronic applications accepted. *Expenses:* Tuition, state resident: full-time $9783; part-time $492 per credit hour. Tuition, nonresident: full-time $24,071; part-time $1179 per credit hour. *Financial support:* In 2014–15, 4 research assistantships (averaging $7,500 per year), 3 teaching assistantships (averaging $7,500 per year) were awarded. Financial award application deadline: 4/1. *Unit head:* Dr. Doug Talbert, Interim Chairperson, 931-372-3691, Fax: 931-372-3686, E-mail: dtalbert@tntech.edu. *Application contact:* Shelia K. Kendrick, Coordinator of Graduate Studies, 931-372-3808, Fax: 931-372-3497, E-mail: skendrick@tntech.edu.

Texas A&M University, College of Engineering, Department of Computer Science and Engineering, College Station, TX 77843. Offers computer engineering (M Eng, MS, PhD); computer science (MCS, MS, PhD). Part-time programs available. *Faculty:* 36. *Students:* 267 full-time (54 women), 53 part-time (10 women); includes 32 minority (4 Black or African American, non-Hispanic/Latino; 12 Asian, non-Hispanic/Latino; 14 Hispanic/Latino; 1 Native Hawaiian or other Pacific Islander, non-Hispanic/Latino; 1 Two or more races, non-Hispanic/Latino), 234 international. Average age 27. 1,740 applicants, 11% accepted, 79 enrolled. In 2014, 51 master's, 24 doctorates awarded. *Degree requirements:* For master's, thesis (for some programs); for doctorate, thesis/dissertation. *Entrance requirements:* For master's and doctorate, GRE General Test. Additional exam requirements/recommendations for international students: Required—TOEFL. *Application deadline:* For fall admission, 3/1 priority date for domestic and international students; for spring admission, 8/1 priority date for domestic and international students. Applications are processed on a rolling basis. Application fee: $50 ($90 for international students). Electronic applications accepted. *Expenses:* Tuition, state resident: full-time $4078; part-time $226.55 per credit hour. Tuition, nonresident: full-time $10,594; part-time $577.55 per credit hour. *Required fees:* $2813; $237.70 per credit hour. $278.50 per semester. Tuition and fees vary according to degree level and student level. *Financial support:* In 2014–15, 226 students received support, including 5 fellowships with full and partial tuition reimbursements available (averaging $20,100 per year), 107 research assistantships with full and partial tuition reimbursements available (averaging $6,861 per year), 72 teaching assistantships with full and partial tuition reimbursements available (averaging $6,784 per year); career-related internships or fieldwork, institutionally sponsored loans, scholarships/grants, traineeships, health care benefits, tuition waivers (full and partial), and unspecified assistantships also available. Support available to part-time students. Financial award application deadline: 3/1; financial award applicants required to submit FAFSA. *Faculty research:* Software, systems, informatics, human-centered systems, theory. *Unit head:* Dr. Dilma Da Silva, Department Head, E-mail: dilma@cse.tamu.edu. *Application contact:* Dr. Andreas Klappenecker, Graduate Advisor, 979-458-0608, E-mail: klappi@cse.tamu.edu.
Website: http://engineering.tamu.edu/cse/.

Texas A&M University–Corpus Christi, College of Graduate Studies, College of Science and Engineering, Program in Computer Science, Corpus Christi, TX 78412-5503. Offers MS. Part-time and evening/weekend programs available. *Students:* 95 full-time (31 women), 8 part-time (2 women); includes 6 minority (1 American Indian or Alaska Native, non-Hispanic/Latino; 5 Hispanic/Latino), 94 international. Average age 24. 415 applicants, 26% accepted, 25 enrolled. In 2014, 16 master's awarded. *Degree requirements:* For master's, comprehensive exam, thesis optional. *Entrance requirements:* For master's, GRE General Test, Essay (500-1000 words). Additional exam requirements/recommendations for international students: Required—TOEFL (minimum score 550 paper-based; 79 iBT), IELTS (minimum score 6.5). *Application deadline:* For fall admission, 2/1 priority date for domestic and international students; for spring admission, 11/15 priority date for domestic students, 10/1 priority date for international students; for summer admission, 4/15 priority date for domestic students, 2/1 priority date for international students. Applications are processed on a rolling basis. Application fee: $50 ($70 for international students). Electronic applications accepted. *Financial support:* In 2014–15, 7 students received support, including 29 research assistantships (averaging $8,721 per year); career-related internships or fieldwork,

Federal Work-Study, institutionally sponsored loans, scholarships/grants, health care benefits, and unspecified assistantships also available. Support available to part-time students. Financial award application deadline: 3/15; financial award applicants required to submit FAFSA. *Unit head:* Dr. Scott King, Associate Professor, 361-825-5877, E-mail: Scott.King@tamucc.edu. *Application contact:* Graduate Admissions Coordinator, 361-825-2177, Fax: 361-825-2755, E-mail: gradweb@tamucc.edu.
Website: http://cs.tamucc.edu/masters.html.

Texas A&M University–Kingsville, College of Graduate Studies, College of Engineering, Department of Electrical Engineering and Computer Science, Program in Computer Science, Kingsville, TX 78363. Offers MS. *Students:* 492 full-time (112 women), 98 part-time (23 women); includes 2 minority (1 Asian, non-Hispanic/Latino; 1 Hispanic/Latino), 588 international. Average age 23. 1,128 applicants, 73% accepted, 253 enrolled. In 2014, 109 master's awarded. *Degree requirements:* For master's, variable foreign language requirement, comprehensive exam, thesis (for some programs). *Entrance requirements:* For master's, GRE (minimum Quantitative and Verbal score of 288), MAT, GMAT, minimum undergraduate GPA of 3.0. Additional exam requirements/recommendations for international students: Required—TOEFL (minimum score 550 paper-based; 79 iBT). *Application deadline:* For fall admission, 8/15 for domestic students, 7/1 for international students; for spring admission, 12/15 for domestic students, 11/1 for international students; for summer admission, 5/15 for domestic students, 4/1 for international students. Applications are processed on a rolling basis. Application fee: $35 ($50 for international students). Electronic applications accepted. *Financial support:* In 2014–15, 129 students received support, including 6 research assistantships (averaging $402 per year), 23 teaching assistantships (averaging $1,539 per year); career-related internships or fieldwork, Federal Work-Study, institutionally sponsored loans, scholarships/grants, health care benefits, tuition waivers (full and partial), and unspecified assistantships also available. Support available to part-time students. Financial award application deadline: 5/15; financial award applicants required to submit FAFSA. *Unit head:* Dr. Rajab Challoo, Coordinator, 361-593-2001, E-mail: r-challoo@tamuk.edu. *Application contact:* Dr. Mohamed Abdelrahman, Dean of Graduate Studies, 361-593-2809, E-mail: mohamed.abdelrahman@tamuk.edu.

Texas Southern University, School of Science and Technology, Department of Computer Science, Houston, TX 77004-4584. Offers MS. Electronic applications accepted.

Texas State University, The Graduate College, College of Science and Engineering, Department of Computer Science, San Marcos, TX 78666. Offers computer science (MA, MS); software engineering (MS). Part-time programs available. *Faculty:* 16 full-time (4 women). *Students:* 85 full-time (35 women), 47 part-time (12 women); includes 32 minority (5 Black or African American, non-Hispanic/Latino; 12 Asian, non-Hispanic/Latino; 13 Hispanic/Latino; 2 Two or more races, non-Hispanic/Latino), 74 international. Average age 28. 183 applicants, 69% accepted, 56 enrolled. In 2014, 55 master's awarded. *Degree requirements:* For master's, comprehensive exam, thesis (for some programs). *Entrance requirements:* For master's, GRE General Test, minimum GPA of 2.75 in last 60 hours of course work. Additional exam requirements/recommendations for international students: Required—TOEFL (minimum score 550 paper-based; 78 iBT). *Application deadline:* For fall admission, 6/15 priority date for domestic students, 6/1 priority date for international students; for spring admission, 10/15 priority date for domestic students, 10/1 priority date for international students. Applications are processed on a rolling basis. Application fee: $40 ($90 for international students). Electronic applications accepted. *Financial support:* In 2014–15, 54 students received support, including 9 research assistantships (averaging $10,384 per year), 18 teaching assistantships (averaging $11,311 per year); career-related internships or fieldwork, Federal Work-Study, institutionally sponsored loans, scholarships/grants, health care benefits, and unspecified assistantships also available. Support available to part-time students. Financial award application deadline: 4/1; financial award applicants required to submit FAFSA. *Faculty research:* Usability assessment, power consumption, hidden Web databases, REU sites, wireless networks. *Total annual research expenditures:* $531,298. *Unit head:* Dr. Hongchi Shi, Chair, 512-245-3409, Fax: 512-245-8750, E-mail: hs15@txstate.edu. *Application contact:* Dr. Andrea Golato, Dean of the Graduate College, 512-245-2581, Fax: 512-245-8365, E-mail: gradcollege@txstate.edu.
Website: http://www.cs.txstate.edu/.

Texas Tech University, Graduate School, Edward E. Whitacre Jr. College of Engineering, Department of Computer Science, Lubbock, TX 79409-3104. Offers computer science (MS, PhD); software engineering (MS). Part-time programs available. Postbaccalaureate distance learning degree programs offered (minimal on-campus study). *Faculty:* 16 full-time (3 women). *Students:* 97 full-time (26 women), 33 part-time (6 women); includes 6 minority (1 Asian, non-Hispanic/Latino; 4 Hispanic/Latino; 1 Two or more races, non-Hispanic/Latino), 95 international. Average age 27. 451 applicants, 47% accepted, 53 enrolled. In 2014, 23 master's, 6 doctorates awarded. Terminal master's awarded for partial completion of doctoral program. *Degree requirements:* For master's, comprehensive exam, thesis (for some programs); for doctorate, comprehensive exam, thesis/dissertation. *Entrance requirements:* For master's and doctorate, GRE (Verbal and Quantitative). Additional exam requirements/recommendations for international students: Required—TOEFL (minimum score 550 paper-based; 79 iBT). *Application deadline:* For fall admission, 6/1 priority date for domestic students, 1/15 priority date for international students; for spring admission, 9/1 priority date for domestic students, 6/15 priority date for international students. Applications are processed on a rolling basis. Application fee: $60. Electronic applications accepted. *Expenses:* Tuition, state resident: full-time $6310; part-time $262.92 per credit hour. Tuition, nonresident: full-time $14,998; part-time $624.92 per credit hour. *Required fees:* $2701; $36.50 per credit. $912.50 per semester. Tuition and fees vary according to course load. *Financial support:* In 2014–15, 58 students received support, including 58 fellowships (averaging $1,818 per year), 1 research assistantship (averaging $26,004 per year), 11 teaching assistantships (averaging $20,625 per year); scholarships/grants, tuition waivers (partial), and unspecified assistantships also available. Financial award application deadline: 4/15; financial award applicants required to submit FAFSA. *Faculty research:* High performance and parallel computing; cyber security and data science; software engineering (quality assurance, testing, design specification); artificial intelligence (intelligent systems, knowledge representation); mobile and computer networks. *Total annual research expenditures:* $748,066. *Unit head:* Dr. Rattikorn Hewett, Professor and Chair, 806-742-3527, Fax: 806-742-3519, E-mail: rattikorn.hewett@ttu.edu. *Application contact:* Jessica Lunsford, Staff Graduate Advisor, 806-742-3527, Fax: 806-742-3519, E-mail: jessica.lunsford@ttu.edu.
Website: http://www.cs.ttu.edu/.

Towson University, Program in Computer Science, Towson, MD 21252-0001. Offers MS. Part-time and evening/weekend programs available. *Students:* 75 full-time (23 women), 109 part-time (28 women); includes 39 minority (21 Black or African American, non-Hispanic/Latino; 12 Asian, non-Hispanic/Latino; 4 Hispanic/Latino; 2 Two or more races, non-Hispanic/Latino), 56 international. *Degree requirements:* For master's, thesis optional. *Entrance requirements:* For master's, minimum GPA of 3.0, bachelor's degree in computer science or bachelor's degree in any other field and completion of 1-3 preparatory courses. *Application deadline:* Applications are processed on a rolling basis.

Application fee: $45. Electronic applications accepted. *Financial support:* Application deadline: 4/1. *Unit head:* Dr. Yanggon Kim, Graduate Program Director, 410-704-3782, E-mail: ykim@towson.edu. *Application contact:* Alicia Arkell-Kleis, Information Contact, 410-704-6004, E-mail: grads@towson.edu.
Website: http://grad.towson.edu/program/master/cosc-ms/.

Toyota Technological Institute of Chicago, Program in Computer Science, Chicago, IL 60637. Offers PhD. *Degree requirements:* For doctorate, thesis/dissertation.

Trent University, Graduate Studies, Program in Applications of Modeling in the Natural and Social Sciences, Department of Computer Studies, Peterborough, ON K9J 7B8, Canada. Offers M Sc. *Degree requirements:* For master's, thesis. *Entrance requirements:* For master's, honours degree.

Troy University, Graduate School, College of Arts and Sciences, Program in Computer Science, Troy, AL 36082. Offers MS. Part-time and evening/weekend programs available. *Faculty:* 10 full-time (0 women), 1 part-time/adjunct (0 women). *Students:* 69 full-time (15 women), 33 part-time (9 women); includes 13 minority (5 Black or African American, non-Hispanic/Latino; 7 Asian, non-Hispanic/Latino; 1 Hispanic/Latino). Average age 26. 362 applicants, 52% accepted, 4 enrolled. In 2014, 14 master's awarded. *Degree requirements:* For master's, thesis or research paper and comprehensive exam; minimum GPA of 3.0; admission to candidacy. *Entrance requirements:* For master's, GRE (minimum score of 850 on old exam or 286 on new exam), MAT (minimum score of 385) or GMAT (minimum score of 380), bachelor's degree; minimum undergraduate GPA of 2.5 or 3.0 on last 30 semester hours. Additional exam requirements/recommendations for international students: Required—TOEFL (minimum score 523 paper-based; 70 iBT), IELTS (minimum score 6). *Application deadline:* For fall admission, 6/1 for international students; for spring admission, 10/15 for international students. Applications are processed on a rolling basis. Application fee: $50. Electronic applications accepted. *Expenses:* Tuition, state resident: full-time $6570; part-time $365 per credit hour. Tuition, nonresident: full-time $13,140; part-time $730 per credit hour. *Required fees:* $365 per credit hour. *Unit head:* Dr. Bill Zhong, Department Chairman/Professor, 334-670-3388, Fax: 334-670-3796, E-mail: jzhong@troy.edu. *Application contact:* Jessica A. Kimbro, Director of Graduate Admissions, 334-670-3178, E-mail: jacord@troy.edu.

Tufts University, Graduate School of Arts and Sciences, Graduate Certificate Programs, Computer Science Program, Medford, MA 02155. Offers Certificate. Part-time and evening/weekend programs available. Electronic applications accepted. *Expenses: Tuition:* Full-time $45,590; part-time $1161 per credit hour. *Required fees:* $782. Full-time tuition and fees vary according to degree level, program and student level. Part-time tuition and fees vary according to course load.

Tufts University, Graduate School of Arts and Sciences, Graduate Certificate Programs, Post-Baccalaureate Minor Program in Computer Science, Medford, MA 02155. Offers Certificate. Part-time and evening/weekend programs available. Electronic applications accepted. *Expenses: Tuition:* Full-time $45,590; part-time $1161 per credit hour. *Required fees:* $782. Full-time tuition and fees vary according to degree level, program and student level. Part-time tuition and fees vary according to course load.

Tufts University, School of Engineering, Department of Computer Science, Medford, MA 02155. Offers bioengineering (ME, MS), including bioinformatics; cognitive science (PhD); computer science (MS, PhD). Part-time programs available. *Students:* 57 full-time (17 women), 19 part-time (4 women); includes 13 minority (1 Black or African American, non-Hispanic/Latino; 4 Asian, non-Hispanic/Latino; 2 Hispanic/Latino; 6 Two or more races, non-Hispanic/Latino), 25 international. Average age 29. 218 applicants, 24% accepted, 23 enrolled. In 2014, 18 master's, 4 doctorates awarded. Terminal master's awarded for partial completion of doctoral program. *Degree requirements:* For master's, thesis (for some programs); for doctorate, thesis/dissertation. *Entrance requirements:* For master's and doctorate, GRE General Test. Additional exam requirements/recommendations for international students: Required—TOEFL (minimum score 550 paper-based; 80 iBT), IELTS (minimum score 6.5). *Application deadline:* For fall admission, 1/15 for domestic and international students; for spring admission, 9/15 for domestic and international students. Applications are processed on a rolling basis. Application fee: $75. Electronic applications accepted. *Expenses: Tuition:* Full-time $45,590; part-time $1161 per credit hour. *Required fees:* $782. Full-time tuition and fees vary according to degree level, program and student level. Part-time tuition and fees vary according to course load. *Financial support:* Fellowships with full tuition reimbursements, research assistantships with full and partial tuition reimbursements, teaching assistantships with full and partial tuition reimbursements, Federal Work-Study, scholarships/grants, tuition waivers (partial), and unspecified assistantships available. Financial award application deadline: 4/15; financial award applicants required to submit FAFSA. *Faculty research:* Computational biology, computational geometry, and computational systems biology; cognitive sciences, human-computer interaction, and human-robotic interaction; visualization and graphics, educational technologies; machine learning and data mining; programming languages and systems. *Unit head:* Dr. Samuel Guyer, Graduate Program Director. *Application contact:* Office of Graduate Admissions, 617-623-3395, E-mail: gradadmissions@cs.tufts.edu.
Website: http://www.cs.tufts.edu/.

Union Graduate College, School of Engineering and Computer Science, Schenectady, NY 12308-3107. Offers computer science (MS); electrical engineering (MS); engineering and management systems (MS); mechanical engineering (MS). Part-time and evening/weekend programs available. *Degree requirements:* For master's, capstone course. *Entrance requirements:* For master's, minimum GPA of 3.0, letters of recommendation. Additional exam requirements/recommendations for international students: Required—TOEFL (minimum score 550 paper-based). Electronic applications accepted. *Expenses:* Contact institution.

Universidad Autonoma de Guadalajara, Graduate Programs, Guadalajara, Mexico. Offers administrative law and justice (LL M); advertising and corporate communications (MA); architecture (M Arch); business (MBA); computational science (MCC); education (Ed M, Ed D); English-Spanish translation (MA); entrepreneurship and management (MBA); integrated management of digital animation (MA); international business (MIB); international corporate law (LL M); internet technologies (MS); manufacturing systems (MMS); occupational health (MS); philosophy (MA, PhD); power electronics (MS); quality systems (MQS); renewable energy (MS); social evaluation of projects (MBA); strategic market research (MBA); tax law (MA); teaching mathematics (MA).

Universidad de las Américas Puebla, Division of Graduate Studies, School of Engineering, Program in Computer Engineering, Puebla, Mexico. Offers computer science (MS). Part-time and evening/weekend programs available. *Degree requirements:* For master's, one foreign language, thesis. *Faculty research:* Computers in education, robotics, artificial intelligence.

Universidad de las Américas Puebla, Division of Graduate Studies, School of Engineering, Program in Computer Science, Puebla, Mexico. Offers PhD.

Université de Moncton, Faculty of Sciences, Information Technology Programs, Moncton, NB E1A 3E9, Canada. Offers M Sc, Certificate, Diploma. Part-time programs available. *Degree requirements:* For master's, thesis. Electronic applications accepted. *Faculty research:* Programming, databases, networks.

Université de Montréal, Faculty of Arts and Sciences, Department of Computer Science and Operational Research, Montréal, QC H3C 3J7, Canada. Offers computer systems (M Sc, PhD); electronic commerce (M Sc). Part-time programs available. Terminal master's awarded for partial completion of doctoral program. *Degree requirements:* For master's, one foreign language, thesis; for doctorate, one foreign language, thesis/dissertation, general exam. *Entrance requirements:* For master's, B Sc in related field; for doctorate, MA or M Sc in related field. Electronic applications accepted. *Faculty research:* Optimization statistics, programming languages, telecommunications, theoretical computer science, artificial intelligence.

Université du Québec à Trois-Rivières, Graduate Programs, Program in Mathematics and Computer Science, Trois-Rivières, QC G9A 5H7, Canada. Offers M Sc. *Faculty research:* Probability, statistics.

Université du Québec en Outaouais, Graduate Programs, Program in Computer Network, Gatineau, QC J8X 3X7, Canada. Offers computer science (M Sc, PhD, DESS). Part-time and evening/weekend programs available. *Students:* 28 full-time, 48 part-time, 5 international. *Degree requirements:* For master's, thesis; for doctorate, thesis/dissertation. *Application deadline:* For fall admission, 6/1 for domestic students, 4/15 for international students; for winter admission, 11/1 for domestic students, 9/15 for international students. Application fee: $30 Canadian dollars. *Unit head:* Benyahia Ilham, Director, 819-595-3900 Ext. 1600, Fax: 819-773-1875, E-mail: ilham.benyahia@uqo.ca. *Application contact:* Registrar's Office, 819-773-1850, Fax: 819-773-1835, E-mail: registraire@uqo.ca.

Université Laval, Faculty of Sciences and Engineering, Department of Computer Science, Programs in Computer Science, Québec, QC G1K 7P4, Canada. Offers M Sc, PhD. Terminal master's awarded for partial completion of doctoral program. *Degree requirements:* For master's, thesis; for doctorate, thesis/dissertation. *Entrance requirements:* For master's and doctorate, knowledge of French and English. Electronic applications accepted.

University at Albany, State University of New York, College of Computing and Information, Department of Computer Science, Albany, NY 12222-0001. Offers MS, PhD. *Degree requirements:* For master's, comprehensive exam, project or thesis; for doctorate, comprehensive exam, thesis/dissertation, area exams. *Entrance requirements:* For master's and doctorate, GRE General Test. Additional exam requirements/recommendations for international students: Required—TOEFL (minimum score 550 paper-based). Electronic applications accepted. *Faculty research:* Algorithm design and analysis, artificial intelligence, computational logic, databases, numerical analysis.

University at Buffalo, the State University of New York, Graduate School, School of Engineering and Applied Sciences, Department of Computer Science and Engineering, Buffalo, NY 14260. Offers computer science and engineering (MS, PhD); information assurance (Certificate). Part-time programs available. *Faculty:* 35 full-time (3 women), 4 part-time/adjunct (1 woman). *Students:* 693 full-time (116 women), 9 part-time (1 woman); includes 15 minority (3 Black or African American, non-Hispanic/Latino; 10 Asian, non-Hispanic/Latino; 2 Hispanic/Latino), 653 international. Average age 25. 3,316 applicants, 21% accepted, 262 enrolled. In 2014, 152 master's, 25 doctorates awarded. Terminal master's awarded for partial completion of doctoral program. *Degree requirements:* For master's, thesis or alternative; for doctorate, thesis/dissertation, comprehensive qualifying exam. *Entrance requirements/recommendations:* For master's and doctorate, GRE General Test. Additional exam requirements/recommendations for international students: Required—TOEFL (minimum score 550 paper-based; 79 iBT). *Application deadline:* For fall admission, 2/1 priority date for domestic and international students; for spring admission, 10/1 priority date for domestic and international students. Applications are processed on a rolling basis. Application fee: $75. Electronic applications accepted. *Financial support:* In 2014–15, 138 students received support, including 3 fellowships with full and partial tuition reimbursements available (averaging $24,000 per year), 55 research assistantships with full and partial tuition reimbursements available (averaging $20,784 per year), 60 teaching assistantships with full and partial tuition reimbursements available (averaging $21,320 per year); career-related internships or fieldwork, Federal Work-Study, institutionally sponsored loans, health care benefits, tuition waivers (partial), and unspecified assistantships also available. Financial award application deadline: 12/15; financial award applicants required to submit FAFSA. *Faculty research:* Bioinformatics, pattern recognition, computer networks and security, theory and algorithms, databases and data mining. *Total annual research expenditures:* $6.4 million. *Unit head:* Dr. Aidong Zhang, Chairman, 716-645-3180, Fax: 716-645-3464, E-mail: azhang@buffalo.edu. *Application contact:* Dr. Hung Ngo, Director of Graduate Studies, 716-645-4750, Fax: 716-645-3464, E-mail: hungngo@buffalo.edu.
Website: http://www.cse.buffalo.edu/.

University of Advancing Technology, Master of Science Program in Technology, Tempe, AZ 85283-1042. Offers advancing computer science (MS); emerging technologies (MS); game production and management (MS); information assurance (MS); technology leadership (MS). *Degree requirements:* For master's, project or thesis. *Entrance requirements:* Additional exam requirements/recommendations for international students: Required—TOEFL (minimum score 550 paper-based). Electronic applications accepted. *Faculty research:* Artificial intelligence, fractals, organizational management.

The University of Akron, Graduate School, Buchtel College of Arts and Sciences, Department of Computer Science, Akron, OH 44325. Offers MS. *Faculty:* 8 full-time (3 women). *Students:* 60 full-time (18 women), 12 part-time (4 women); includes 1 minority (Asian, non-Hispanic/Latino), 57 international. Average age 25. 183 applicants, 21% accepted, 13 enrolled. In 2014, 21 master's awarded. *Degree requirements:* For master's, seminar and comprehensive exam or thesis. *Entrance requirements:* For master's, baccalaureate degree in computer science or a related field, minimum GPA of 3.0, three letters of recommendation, statement of purpose, resume, knowledge of one high-level programming language, mathematical maturity, proficiency in data structures, computer organization, and operating systems. Additional exam requirements/recommendations for international students: Required—TOEFL (minimum score 550 paper-based; 79 iBT), IELTS (minimum score 6.5). *Application deadline:* For fall admission, 3/15 for domestic and international students; for spring admission, 10/15 for domestic and international students. Application fee: $45 ($70 for international students). Electronic applications accepted. *Expenses:* Tuition, state resident: full-time $7578; part-time $421 per credit hour. Tuition, nonresident: full-time $12,977; part-time $721 per credit hour. *Required fees:* $1388; $35 per credit hour. Tuition and fees vary according to course load. *Financial support:* In 2014–15, 8 research assistantships with full tuition reimbursements, 23 teaching assistantships with full tuition reimbursements were awarded; unspecified assistantships also available. *Faculty research:* Bioinformatics, database/data mining, networking, parallel computing, visualization. *Total annual research expenditures:* $100,590. *Unit head:* Dr. Timothy Norfolk, Interim Chair, 330-972-6121, E-mail: norfolk@uakron.edu. *Application contact:* Dr. Kathy Liszka, Graduate Program Coordinator, 330-972-8017, E-mail: liszka@uakron.edu.
Website: http://www.uakron.edu/computer-science/.

The University of Alabama, Graduate School, College of Engineering, Department of Computer Science, Tuscaloosa, AL 35487-0290. Offers MS, PhD. Part-time programs available. *Faculty:* 15 full-time (2 women). *Students:* 31 full-time (6 women), 13 part-time (0 women); includes 4 minority (2 Black or African American, non-Hispanic/Latino; 1 Asian, non-Hispanic/Latino; 1 Two or more races, non-Hispanic/Latino), 21 international. Average age 29. 43 applicants, 19% accepted, 5 enrolled. In 2014, 12 master's, 6 doctorates awarded. Terminal master's awarded for partial completion of doctoral program. *Degree requirements:* For master's, comprehensive exam, thesis (for some programs); for doctorate, comprehensive exam, thesis/dissertation. *Entrance requirements:* For master's and doctorate, GRE. Additional exam requirements/recommendations for international students: Required—TOEFL. *Application deadline:* For fall admission, 7/1 priority date for domestic students, 3/1 for international students; for winter admission, 8/1 for international students; for spring admission, 11/1 priority date for domestic students, 7/1 for international students; for summer admission, 1/1 for international students. Applications are processed on a rolling basis. Application fee: $50 ($60 for international students). Electronic applications accepted. *Expenses:* Tuition, state resident: full-time $9826. Tuition, nonresident: full-time $24,950. *Financial support:* In 2014–15, 28 students received support, including 2 fellowships with full tuition reimbursements available (averaging $15,000 per year), 10 research assistantships with full tuition reimbursements available (averaging $15,750 per year), 15 teaching assistantships with full tuition reimbursements available (averaging $15,750 per year); health care benefits and unspecified assistantships also available. Financial award application deadline: 3/15. *Faculty research:* Software engineering, networking, database management, robotics, security, algorithms. *Total annual research expenditures:* $13.3 million. *Unit head:* Dr. David Cordes, Professor and Department Head, 205-348-6363, Fax: 205-348-0219, E-mail: david.cordes@ua.edu. *Application contact:* Dr. Susan Vrbsky, Associate Professor and Graduate Program Director, 205-348-6363, Fax: 205-348-0219, E-mail: vrbsky@cs.ua.edu.
Website: http://cs.ua.edu/.

The University of Alabama at Birmingham, College of Arts and Sciences, Program in Computer and Information Sciences, Birmingham, AL 35294. Offers MS, PhD. *Students:* 47 full-time (8 women), 11 part-time (2 women); includes 2 minority (1 Asian, non-Hispanic/Latino; 1 Hispanic/Latino), 34 international. Average age 29. In 2014, 15 master's, 1 doctorate awarded. Terminal master's awarded for partial completion of doctoral program. *Degree requirements:* For master's, thesis optional; for doctorate, thesis/dissertation. *Entrance requirements:* For master's, GRE General Test, minimum GPA of 3.0, letters of recommendation; for doctorate, GRE General Test, minimum GPA of 3.5 overall or on last 60 hours; letters of recommendation. Additional exam requirements/recommendations for international students: Required—TOEFL, IELTS. *Application deadline:* For fall admission, 2/1 for domestic students; for spring admission, 9/1 for domestic students. Applications are processed on a rolling basis. Application fee: $45 ($60 for international students). Electronic applications accepted. *Expenses:* Tuition, state resident: full-time $7090; part-time $370 per credit hour. Tuition, nonresident: full-time $16,072; part-time $869 per credit hour. Full-time tuition and fees vary according to course load and program. *Financial support:* Fellowships with full tuition reimbursements, research assistantships with full tuition reimbursements, teaching assistantships with full tuition reimbursements, career-related internships or fieldwork, Federal Work-Study, institutionally sponsored loans, scholarships/grants, traineeships, health care benefits, and unspecified assistantships available. Support available to part-time students. Financial award application deadline: 3/10. *Faculty research:* Theory and software systems, intelligent systems, systems architecture, high performance computing, computer architecture, computer graphics, data mining, software engineering. *Unit head:* Dr. Chengcui Zhang, Graduate Program Director, 205-934-8606, Fax: 205-934-5473, E-mail: czhang02@uab.edu. *Application contact:* Susan Noblitt Banks, Director of Graduate School Operations, 205-934-8227, Fax: 205-934-8413, E-mail: gradschool@uab.edu.
Website: https://cis.uab.edu/academics/graduates/.

The University of Alabama in Huntsville, School of Graduate Studies, College of Science, Department of Computer Science, Huntsville, AL 35899. Offers computer science (MS, PhD); information assurance (MS); modeling and simulation (MS, PhD); software engineering (MSSE, Certificate). Part-time and evening/weekend programs available. Postbaccalaureate distance learning degree programs offered (minimal on-campus study). *Degree requirements:* For master's, comprehensive exam, thesis or alternative, oral and written exams; for doctorate, comprehensive exam, thesis/dissertation, oral and written exams. *Entrance requirements:* For master's, doctorate, and Certificate, GRE General Test, minimum GPA of 3.0. Additional exam requirements/recommendations for international students: Required—TOEFL (minimum score 550 paper-based; 80 iBT), IELTS (minimum score 6.5). Electronic applications accepted. *Faculty research:* Information assurance and cyber security, modeling and simulation, data science, computer graphics and visualization, multimedia systems.

University of Alaska Fairbanks, College of Engineering and Mines, Department of Computer Science, Fairbanks, AK 99775-6670. Offers computer science (MS). Part-time programs available. *Faculty:* 6 full-time (1 woman), 1 part-time/adjunct (0 women). *Students:* 2 full-time (0 women), 4 part-time (1 woman); includes 2 minority (1 American Indian or Alaska Native, non-Hispanic/Latino; 1 Hispanic/Latino). Average age 29. 10 applicants, 40% accepted, 1 enrolled. In 2014, 3 master's awarded. *Degree requirements:* For master's, comprehensive exam, oral defense of project or thesis. *Entrance requirements:* For master's, GRE General Test, GRE Subject Test (computer science), bachelor's degree from accredited institution with minimum cumulative undergraduate and major GPA of 3.0. Additional exam requirements/recommendations for international students: Required—TOEFL (minimum score 600 paper-based). *Application deadline:* For fall admission, 6/1 for domestic students, 3/1 for international students; for spring admission, 10/15 for domestic students, 9/1 for international students. Applications are processed on a rolling basis. Application fee: $60. Electronic applications accepted. *Expenses:* Tuition, state resident: full-time $7614; part-time $423 per credit. Tuition, nonresident: full-time $15,552; part-time $864 per credit. Tuition and fees vary according to course level, course load and reciprocity agreements. *Financial support:* In 2014–15, 2 teaching assistantships with full tuition reimbursements (averaging $4,564 per year) were awarded; fellowships with full tuition reimbursements, research assistantships with full tuition reimbursements, career-related internships or fieldwork, Federal Work-Study, scholarships/grants, health care benefits, and unspecified assistantships also available. Support available to part-time students. Financial award application deadline: 7/1; financial award applicants required to submit FAFSA. *Faculty research:* Interaction with a virtual reality environment, synthetic aperture radar interferometry software. *Unit head:* Dr. Jon Genetti, Department Chair, 907-474-2777, Fax: 907-474-5030, E-mail: uaf-cs-dept@alaska.edu. *Application contact:* Mary Kreta, Director of Admissions, 907-474-7500, Fax: 907-474-7097, E-mail: admissions@uaf.edu.
Website: http://www.cs.uaf.edu.

University of Alberta, Faculty of Graduate Studies and Research, Department of Computing Science, Edmonton, AB T6G 2E1, Canada. Offers M Sc, PhD. Part-time programs available. Terminal master's awarded for partial completion of doctoral program. *Degree requirements:* For master's, thesis (for some programs), oral exam, seminar; for doctorate, thesis/dissertation, oral exam, seminar. *Entrance requirements:* For master's and doctorate, GRE General Test. Additional exam requirements/recommendations for international students: Required—TOEFL. *Faculty research:* Artificial intelligence, multimedia, distributed computing, theory, software engineering.

The University of Arizona, College of Science, Department of Computer Science, Tucson, AZ 85721. Offers MS, PhD. Part-time programs available. *Faculty:* 13 full-time (0 women). *Students:* 58 full-time (13 women), 7 part-time (2 women); includes 7 minority (1 Asian, non-Hispanic/Latino; 4 Hispanic/Latino; 2 Two or more races, non-Hispanic/Latino), 41 international. Average age 29. 184 applicants, 33% accepted, 30 enrolled. In 2014, 28 master's, 4 doctorates awarded. Terminal master's awarded for partial completion of doctoral program. *Degree requirements:* For master's, thesis optional; for doctorate, comprehensive exam, thesis/dissertation. *Entrance requirements:* For master's, GRE General Test, minimum GPA of 3.2; for doctorate, GRE General Test, minimum undergraduate GPA of 3.5. Additional exam requirements/recommendations for international students: Required—TOEFL (minimum score 600 paper-based; 100 iBT). *Application deadline:* For fall admission, 1/15 for domestic and international students; for spring admission, 9/15 for domestic students. Application fee: $75. Electronic applications accepted. *Financial support:* In 2014–15, 46 students received support, including 4 fellowships with full tuition reimbursements available (averaging $25,000 per year), 30 research assistantships with full tuition reimbursements available (averaging $16,597 per year), 12 teaching assistantships with full tuition reimbursements available (averaging $14,858 per year); scholarships/grants, health care benefits, tuition waivers (full and partial), and unspecified assistantships also available. Financial award application deadline: 1/15. *Faculty research:* Operating systems, theory of computation, programming languages, databases, algorithms, networks, cloud computing, green computing, computational biology, parallel and distributed computing, data visualization. *Total annual research expenditures:* $2.9 million. *Unit head:* Dr. Todd Proebsting, Department Head, 520-621-4324, Fax: 520-626-5997. *Application contact:* Bridget Radcliff, Manager, Academic Services and Student Support, 520-621-4049, Fax: 520-626-5997, E-mail: gradadmissions@cs.arizona.edu.
Website: http://www.cs.arizona.edu/.

University of Arkansas, Graduate School, College of Engineering, Department of Computer Science and Computer Engineering, Program in Computer Science, Fayetteville, AR 72701-1201. Offers MS, PhD. *Degree requirements:* For doctorate, thesis/dissertation. Electronic applications accepted.

University of Arkansas at Little Rock, Graduate School, George W. Donughey College of Engineering and Information Technology, Department of Computer Science, Little Rock, AR 72204-1099. Offers MS, PhD. Part-time and evening/weekend programs available. *Degree requirements:* For master's, thesis optional. *Entrance requirements:* For master's, GRE General Test, minimum GPA of 3.0; bachelor's degree in computer science, mathematics, or appropriate alternative. *Expenses:* Tuition, state resident: full-time $6000; part-time $300 per credit hour. Tuition, nonresident: full-time $13,800; part-time $690 per credit hour. *Required fees:* $1126; $603 per term. One-time fee: $40 full-time. *Financial support:* Research assistantships with tuition reimbursements, teaching assistantships, Federal Work-Study, institutionally sponsored loans, and unspecified assistantships available. Support available to part-time students. *Unit head:* Dr. Kenji Yoshigoe, Chair, 501-569-8150, E-mail: kxyoshigoe@ualr.edu.
Website: http:/ualr.edu/computerscience/.

University of Bridgeport, School of Engineering, Departments of Computer Science and Computer Engineering, Bridgeport, CT 06604. Offers computer engineering (MS); computer science (MS); computer science and engineering (PhD). *Degree requirements:* For master's, thesis optional; for doctorate, comprehensive exam, thesis/dissertation. *Entrance requirements:* Additional exam requirements/recommendations for international students: Recommended—TOEFL (minimum score 550 paper-based; 80 iBT), IELTS (minimum score 6.5). Electronic applications accepted. *Expenses:* Contact institution.

The University of British Columbia, Faculty of Science, Department of Computer Science, Vancouver, BC V6T 1Z4, Canada. Offers M Sc, PhD. Part-time programs available. *Degree requirements:* For doctorate, comprehensive exam, thesis/dissertation. *Entrance requirements:* Additional exam requirements/recommendations for international students: Required—TOEFL (minimum score 600 paper-based; 100 iBT). Electronic applications accepted. *Faculty research:* Computational intelligence, data management and mining, theory, graphics, network security and systems.

University of Calgary, Faculty of Graduate Studies, Faculty of Science, Department of Computer Science, Calgary, AB T2N 1N4, Canada. Offers computer science (M Sc, PhD); software engineering (M Sc). Part-time programs available. *Degree requirements:* For master's, comprehensive exam (for some programs), thesis (for some programs); for doctorate, thesis/dissertation, oral and written departmental exam. *Entrance requirements:* For master's, bachelor's degree in computer science; for doctorate, M Sc in computer science. Additional exam requirements/recommendations for international students: Required—TOEFL (minimum score 600 paper-based); Recommended—TWE. Electronic applications accepted. *Faculty research:* Visual and interactive computing, quantum computing and cryptography, evolutionary software engineering, distributed systems and algorithms.

University of California, Berkeley, Graduate Division, College of Engineering, Department of Electrical Engineering and Computer Sciences, Berkeley, CA 94720-1500. Offers computer science (MS, PhD); electrical engineering (MS, PhD). *Degree requirements:* For master's, comprehensive exam or thesis; for doctorate, thesis/dissertation, qualifying exam. *Entrance requirements:* For master's and doctorate, GRE General Test, minimum GPA of 3.0, 3 letters of recommendation. Additional exam requirements/recommendations for international students: Required—TOEFL. Electronic applications accepted.

University of California, Davis, College of Engineering, Graduate Group in Computer Science, Davis, CA 95616. Offers MS, PhD. Terminal master's awarded for partial completion of doctoral program. *Degree requirements:* For master's, comprehensive exam (for some programs), thesis optional; for doctorate, comprehensive exam, thesis/dissertation. *Entrance requirements:* For master's and doctorate, GRE General Test, GRE Subject Test, minimum GPA of 3.0. Additional exam requirements/recommendations for international students: Required—TOEFL (minimum score 550 paper-based). Electronic applications accepted. *Faculty research:* Intrusion detection, malicious code detection, next generation light wave computer networks, biological algorithms, parallel processing.

University of California, Irvine, Donald Bren School of Information and Computer Sciences, Department of Computer Science, Irvine, CA 92697. Offers MS, PhD. *Students:* 221 full-time (31 women), 24 part-time (3 women); includes 29 minority (24 Asian, non-Hispanic/Latino; 3 Hispanic/Latino; 2 Two or more races, non-Hispanic/Latino), 175 international. Average age 27. 2,123 applicants, 11% accepted, 90 enrolled. In 2014, 69 master's, 23 doctorates awarded. Application fee: $90 ($110 for international students). *Unit head:* Alexandru Nicolau, Chair, 949-824-4079, E-mail: nicolau@

ics.uci.edu. *Application contact:* Holly Byrnes, Department Manager, 949-824-6753, E-mail: hbyrnes@uci.edu.
Website: http://www.cs.uci.edu/.

University of California, Irvine, Donald Bren School of Information and Computer Sciences, Program in Networked Systems, Irvine, CA 92697. Offers MS, PhD. *Students:* 33 full-time (6 women), 3 part-time (1 woman); includes 1 minority (Asian, non-Hispanic/Latino), 34 international. Average age 26. 257 applicants, 16% accepted, 18 enrolled. In 2014, 7 master's, 2 doctorates awarded. *Application deadline:* For fall admission, 1/15 for domestic students. Application fee: $90 ($110 for international students). *Financial support:* Fellowships, research assistantships, and teaching assistantships available. *Unit head:* Athina Markopoulou, Director, 949-824-0357 Ext. 1637, Fax: 949-824-3203, E-mail: athina@uci.edu. *Application contact:* Gene Tsudik, Faculty Graduate Advisor, 949-824-3410, Fax: 949-824-4056, E-mail: gene.tsudik@uci.edu.
Website: http://www.networkedsystems.uci.edu/.

University of California, Irvine, Henry Samueli School of Engineering, Department of Electrical Engineering and Computer Science, Irvine, CA 92697. Offers electrical engineering and computer science (MS, PhD); networked systems (MS, PhD). Part-time programs available. *Students:* 322 full-time (84 women), 29 part-time (4 women); includes 25 minority (23 Asian, non-Hispanic/Latino; 1 Hispanic/Latino; 1 Two or more races, non-Hispanic/Latino), 292 international. Average age 27. 2,452 applicants, 14% accepted, 139 enrolled. In 2014, 74 master's, 25 doctorates awarded. Terminal master's awarded for partial completion of doctoral program. *Degree requirements:* For doctorate, thesis/dissertation. *Entrance requirements:* For master's and doctorate, GRE General Test, minimum GPA of 3.0, 3 letters of recommendation. Additional exam requirements/recommendations for international students: Required—TOEFL (minimum score 550 paper-based). *Application deadline:* For fall admission, 1/15 priority date for domestic students, 1/15 for international students. Applications are processed on a rolling basis. Application fee: $90 ($110 for international students). Electronic applications accepted. *Financial support:* Fellowships, research assistantships with full tuition reimbursements, teaching assistantships, institutionally sponsored loans, traineeships, health care benefits, and unspecified assistantships available. Financial award application deadline: 3/1; financial award applicants required to submit FAFSA. *Faculty research:* Optics and electronic devices and circuits, signal processing, communications, machine vision, power electronics. *Unit head:* Prof. K. Kumar Wickramasinghe, Chair, 949-824-2213, E-mail: hkwick@uci.edu. *Application contact:* Jean Bennett, Director of Graduate Student Affairs, 949-824-6475, Fax: 949-824-8200, E-mail: jean.bennett@uci.edu.
Website: http://www.eng.uci.edu/dept/eecs.

University of California, Los Angeles, Graduate Division, Henry Samueli School of Engineering and Applied Science, Department of Computer Science, Los Angeles, CA 90095-1596. Offers MS, PhD, MBA/MS. *Faculty:* 28 full-time (3 women), 2 part-time/adjunct (0 women). *Students:* 360 full-time (77 women); includes 77 minority (1 Black or African American, non-Hispanic/Latino; 58 Asian, non-Hispanic/Latino; 13 Hispanic/Latino; 1 Native Hawaiian or other Pacific Islander, non-Hispanic/Latino; 4 Two or more races, non-Hispanic/Latino), 239 international. 1,534 applicants, 21% accepted, 180 enrolled. In 2014, 75 master's, 37 doctorates awarded. *Degree requirements:* For master's, comprehensive exam or thesis; for doctorate, thesis/dissertation, qualifying exams. *Entrance requirements:* For master's, GRE General Test, GRE Subject Test, minimum GPA of 3.0; for doctorate, GRE General Test, GRE Subject Test, minimum GPA of 3.25. Additional exam requirements/recommendations for international students: Required—TOEFL (minimum score 560 paper-based; 87 iBT), IELTS (minimum score 7). *Application deadline:* For fall admission, 12/1 for domestic and international students. Application fee: $80 ($100 for international students). Electronic applications accepted. *Financial support:* In 2014–15, 36 fellowships, 208 research assistantships, 186 teaching assistantships were awarded; Federal Work-Study, institutionally sponsored loans, and tuition waivers (full and partial) also available. Financial award application deadline: 1/15; financial award applicants required to submit FAFSA. *Faculty research:* Artificial intelligence, computational systems biology, computer network systems, computer systems architecture, information and data management. *Total annual research expenditures:* $12.9 million. *Unit head:* Dr. Jens Palsberg, Chair, 310-825-3886. *Application contact:* Steve Arbuckle, Student Affairs Officer, 310-825-6830, Fax: 310-206-8133, E-mail: arbuckle@cs.ucla.edu.
Website: http://www.cs.ucla.edu/.

University of California, Merced, Graduate Division, School of Engineering, Merced, CA 95343. Offers biological engineering and small scale technologies (MS, PhD); electrical engineering and computer science (MS, PhD); environmental systems (MS, PhD); mechanical engineering (MS); mechanical engineering and applied mechanics (PhD). *Faculty:* 38 full-time (6 women), 1 part-time/adjunct (0 women). *Students:* 128 full-time (36 women), 2 part-time (0 women); includes 21 minority (1 Black or African American, non-Hispanic/Latino; 11 Asian, non-Hispanic/Latino; 6 Hispanic/Latino; 3 Two or more races, non-Hispanic/Latino), 72 international. Average age 28. 230 applicants, 39% accepted, 38 enrolled. In 2014, 5 master's, 18 doctorates awarded. *Degree requirements:* For master's, variable foreign language requirement, comprehensive exam, thesis (for some programs); for doctorate, variable foreign language requirement, comprehensive exam, thesis/dissertation. *Entrance requirements:* For master's and doctorate, GRE. Additional exam requirements/recommendations for international students: Required—TOEFL (minimum score 550 paper-based; 68 iBT); Recommended—IELTS. Application fee: $80 ($100 for international students). *Expenses:* Tuition, state resident: full-time $11,220; part-time $2805 per semester. *Required fees:* $1940; $970 per semester hour. *Financial support:* In 2014–15, 19 fellowships with full and partial tuition reimbursements (averaging $6,683 per year) were awarded; scholarships/grants also available. *Faculty research:* Artificial intelligence, biomedical imaging, thermal science, ecology, nanotechnology. *Unit head:* Dr. Erik Rolland, Interim Dean, 209-228-4296, Fax: 209-228-4047, E-mail: erolland@ucmerced.edu. *Application contact:* Tsu Ya, Graduate Admissions and Academic Services Manager, 209-228-4521, Fax: 209-228-6906, E-mail: tya@ucmerced.edu.

University of California, Riverside, Graduate Division, Department of Computer Science and Engineering, Riverside, CA 92521. Offers computer engineering (MS); computer science (MS, PhD). Part-time programs available. Terminal master's awarded for partial completion of doctoral program. *Degree requirements:* For master's, thesis or project; for doctorate, thesis/dissertation, qualifying exams. *Entrance requirements:* For master's and doctorate, GRE General Test (minimum score of 1100 or 300 for new format), minimum GPA of 3.2 in junior/senior years of undergraduate study (last two years). Additional exam requirements/recommendations for international students: Required—TOEFL (minimum score 550 paper-based; 80 iBT). Electronic applications accepted. *Expenses:* Tuition, state resident: full-time $5399. Tuition, nonresident: full-time $10,433. *Faculty research:* Algorithms, bioinformatics, logic; architecture, compilers, embedded systems, verification; databases, data mining, artificial intelligence, graphics; systems, networks.

University of California, San Diego, Graduate Division, Department of Computer Science and Engineering, La Jolla, CA 92093. Offers computer engineering (MS, PhD); computer science (MS, PhD). *Students:* 338 full-time (58 women), 22 part-time (4 women); includes 60 minority (4 Black or African American, non-Hispanic/Latino; 50 Asian, non-Hispanic/Latino; 6 Hispanic/Latino), 219 international. 2,663 applicants, 13% accepted, 121 enrolled. In 2014, 75 master's, 24 doctorates awarded. *Degree requirements:* For master's, comprehensive exam (for some programs), thesis (for some programs), comprehensive exam or thesis; for doctorate, comprehensive exam, thesis/dissertation, 1-quarter teaching assistantship. *Entrance requirements:* For master's and doctorate, GRE General Test, GRE Subject Test (recommended). Additional exam requirements/recommendations for international students: Required—TOEFL (minimum score 550 paper-based; 80 iBT), IELTS. *Application deadline:* For fall admission, 12/14 for domestic students. Application fee: $90 ($110 for international students). Electronic applications accepted. *Expenses:* Tuition, state resident: full-time $11,220; part-time $5610 per quarter. Tuition, nonresident: full-time $26,322; part-time $13,161 per quarter. *Required fees:* $570 per quarter. Tuition and fees vary according to program. *Financial support:* Fellowships, research assistantships, teaching assistantships, career-related internships or fieldwork, and scholarships/grants available. Financial award applicants required to submit FAFSA. *Faculty research:* Algorithms and complexity; artificial intelligence and machine learning, bioinformatics, computer architecture, computer graphics, computer vision, databases, embedded systems and software, high-performance computing, programming languages and compilers, security and cryptography, software engineering, systems and networking, ubiquitous computing, VLSI/CAD. *Unit head:* Rajesh Gupta, Chair, 858-822-4391, E-mail: gupta@cs.ucsd.edu. *Application contact:* Julie Connor, Graduate Coordinator, 858-534-3622, E-mail: gradinfo@cs.ucsd.edu.
Website: http://cse.ucsd.edu.

University of California, Santa Barbara, Graduate Division, College of Engineering, Department of Computer Science, Santa Barbara, CA 93106-5110. Offers cognitive science (PhD); computational science and engineering (PhD); computer science (MS, PhD); technology and society (PhD). Terminal master's awarded for partial completion of doctoral program. *Degree requirements:* For master's, comprehensive exam (for some programs), thesis (for some programs), project (for some programs); for doctorate, thesis/dissertation. *Entrance requirements:* For master's and doctorate, GRE. Additional exam requirements/recommendations for international students: Required—TOEFL (minimum score 600 paper-based; 100 iBT), IELTS (minimum score 7). Electronic applications accepted. *Faculty research:* Bioinformatics, cloud computing, computer architecture, computational science and engineering, database and information systems, foundations and algorithms, intelligent and interactive systems, programming languages, quantum computing, software engineering and security.

University of California, Santa Cruz, Division of Graduate Studies, Jack Baskin School of Engineering, Department of Computer Science, Santa Cruz, CA 95064. Offers MS, PhD. Terminal master's awarded for partial completion of doctoral program. *Degree requirements:* For master's, thesis, project; for doctorate, one foreign language, thesis/dissertation, qualifying exam. *Entrance requirements:* For master's and doctorate, GRE General Test, GRE Subject Test. Additional exam requirements/recommendations for international students: Required—TOEFL (minimum score 570 paper-based; 89 iBT); Recommended—IELTS (minimum score 8). Electronic applications accepted. *Faculty research:* Algorithm analysis, artificial intelligence, scientific visualization, computer graphics and gaming, multimodal human-computer interaction.

University of Central Arkansas, Graduate School, College of Natural Sciences and Math, Department of Applied Computing, Conway, AR 72035-0001. Offers MS. *Entrance requirements:* For master's, GRE, minimum GPA of 2.7. Additional exam requirements/recommendations for international students: Required—TOEFL (minimum score 550 paper-based; 80 iBT). Electronic applications accepted.

University of Central Florida, College of Engineering and Computer Science, Department of Electrical Engineering and Computer Science, Program in Computer Science, Orlando, FL 32816. Offers computer science (MS, PhD); digital forensics (MS). Part-time and evening/weekend programs available. *Students:* 192 full-time (53 women), 122 part-time (22 women); includes 49 minority (11 Black or African American, non-Hispanic/Latino; 12 Asian, non-Hispanic/Latino; 23 Hispanic/Latino; 3 Two or more races, non-Hispanic/Latino), 137 international. Average age 30. 371 applicants, 71% accepted, 99 enrolled. In 2014, 75 master's, 6 doctorates awarded. *Degree requirements:* For master's, thesis or alternative; for doctorate, thesis/dissertation, candidacy exam, departmental qualifying exam. *Entrance requirements:* For master's, GRE General Test, GRE Subject Test, minimum GPA of 3.0 in last 60 hours; for doctorate, GRE Subject Test, minimum GPA of 3.0 in last 60 hours. Additional exam requirements/recommendations for international students: Required—TOEFL. *Application deadline:* For fall admission, 7/15 priority date for domestic students; for spring admission, 12/1 priority date for domestic students. Application fee: $30. Electronic applications accepted. *Expenses:* Tuition, state resident: part-time $288.16 per credit hour. Tuition, nonresident: part-time $1073.31 per credit hour. *Financial support:* In 2014–15, 88 students received support, including 23 fellowships with partial tuition reimbursements available (averaging $6,300 per year), 46 research assistantships with partial tuition reimbursements available (averaging $10,600 per year), 46 teaching assistantships with partial tuition reimbursements available (averaging $11,100 per year); career-related internships or fieldwork, Federal Work-Study, institutionally sponsored loans, tuition waivers (partial), and unspecified assistantships also available. Financial award application deadline: 3/1; financial award applicants required to submit FAFSA. *Faculty research:* Parallel processing, databases, algorithms, virtual reality. *Unit head:* Dr. Gary Leavens, Chair, 407-882-0185, E-mail: leavens@ucf.edu. *Application contact:* Barbara Rodriguez Lamas, Director, Admissions and Student Services, 407-823-2766, Fax: 407-823-6442, E-mail: gradadmissions@ucf.edu.
Website: http://web.eecs.ucf.edu/.

University of Central Missouri, The Graduate School, Warrensburg, MO 64093. Offers accountancy (MA); accounting (MBA); applied mathematics (MS); aviation safety (MA); biology (MS); business administration (MBA); career and technical education leadership (MS); college student personnel administration (MS); communication (MA); computer science (MS); counseling (MS); criminal justice (MS); educational leadership (Ed D); educational technology (MS); elementary and early childhood education (MSE); English (MA); environmental studies (MA); finance (MBA); history (MA); human services/educational technology (Ed S); human services/learning resources (Ed S); human services/professional counseling (Ed S); industrial hygiene (MS); industrial management (MS); information systems (MBA); information technology (MS); kinesiology (MS); library science and information services (MS); literacy education (MSE); marketing (MBA); mathematics (MS); music (MA); occupational safety management (MS); psychology (MS); rural family nursing (MS); school administration (MSE); social gerontology (MS); sociology (MA); special education (MSE); speech language pathology (MS); superintendency (Ed S); teaching (MAT); teaching English as a second language (MA); technology (MS); technology management (PhD); theatre (MA). Part-time programs available. *Faculty:* 314 full-time (137 women), 24 part-time/adjunct (14 women). *Students:* 1,624 full-time (542 women), 1,773 part-time (1,055 women); includes 194 minority (104 Black or African American, non-Hispanic/Latino; 6 American Indian or Alaska Native, non-Hispanic/Latino; 23 Asian, non-Hispanic/Latino; 41 Hispanic/Latino; 3 Native Hawaiian or other Pacific Islander, non-Hispanic/Latino; 17 Two or more races, non-Hispanic/Latino), 1,592 international. Average age 31. 2,800 applicants, 63% accepted, 1223 enrolled. In 2014, 796 master's, 81 other advanced degrees awarded.

Degree requirements: For master's and Ed S, comprehensive exam (for some programs), thesis (for some programs). *Entrance requirements:* Additional exam requirements/recommendations for international students: Required—TOEFL (minimum score 550 paper-based; 79 iBT). *Application deadline:* For fall admission, 6/1 for domestic students; for spring admission, 10/1 for domestic and international students. Applications are processed on a rolling basis. Application fee: $30 ($75 for international students). Electronic applications accepted. *Expenses:* Tuition, state resident: full-time $6630; part-time $276.25 per credit hour. Tuition, nonresident: full-time $13,260; part-time $552.50 per credit hour. *Required fees:* $29 per credit hour. Tuition and fees vary according to campus/location. *Financial support:* In 2014–15, 118 students received support, including 271 research assistantships with full and partial tuition reimbursements available (averaging $7,500 per year), 109 teaching assistantships with full and partial tuition reimbursements available (averaging $7,500 per year); career-related internships or fieldwork, Federal Work-Study, scholarships/grants, and administrative and laboratory assistantships also available. Support available to part-time students. Financial award application deadline: 3/1; financial award applicants required to submit FAFSA. *Unit head:* Tina Church-Hockett, Director of Graduate School and International Admissions, 660-543-4621, Fax: 660-543-4778, E-mail: church@ucmo.edu. *Application contact:* Brittany Lawrence, Graduate Student Services Coordinator, 660-543-4621, Fax: 660-543-4778, E-mail: gradinfo@ucmo.edu. Website: http://www.ucmo.edu/graduate/.

University of Central Oklahoma, The Jackson College of Graduate Studies, College of Mathematics and Science, Department of Mathematics and Statistics, Edmond, OK 73034-5209. Offers applied mathematical sciences (MS), including computer science, mathematics, statistics, teaching. Part-time programs available. *Degree requirements:* For master's, comprehensive exam (for some programs), thesis (for some programs). *Entrance requirements:* For master's, GRE. Additional exam requirements/recommendations for international students: Required—TOEFL (minimum score 550 paper-based; 79 iBT), IELTS (minimum score 6.5). Electronic applications accepted.

University of Chicago, Division of the Physical Sciences, Master's Program in Computer Science, Chicago, IL 60637-1513. Offers MS. Part-time and evening/weekend programs available. *Students:* 53 full-time (11 women), 80 part-time (12 women); includes 23 minority (2 Black or African American, non-Hispanic/Latino; 17 Asian, non-Hispanic/Latino; 3 Hispanic/Latino; 1 Two or more races, non-Hispanic/Latino), 45 international. 588 applicants, 30% accepted, 66 enrolled. *Entrance requirements:* For master's, GRE General Test. Additional exam requirements/recommendations for international students: Required—TOEFL (minimum score 600 paper-based; 90 iBT), IELTS (minimum score 7). *Application deadline:* For fall admission, 8/1 priority date for domestic students; 2/1 for international students; for winter admission, 12/1 priority date for domestic students; 10/1 for international students; for spring admission, 3/1 for domestic students, 12/31 for international students; for summer admission, 5/1 priority date for domestic students, 2/1 for international students. Applications are processed on a rolling basis. Application fee: $90. Electronic applications accepted. *Expenses: Tuition:* Full-time $46,899. *Required fees:* $347. *Financial support:* Institutionally sponsored loans available. Financial award applicants required to submit FAFSA. *Unit head:* Dr. Anne Rogers, Associate Professor/Director, 773-702-8487, Fax: 773-702-8487, E-mail: masters-admin@cs.uchicago.edu. *Application contact:* Karin M. Czaplewski, Student Support Representative, 773-834-8587, Fax: 773-702-8487, E-mail: masters-admin@cs.uchicago.edu.

University of Chicago, Division of the Physical Sciences, PhD Program in Computer Science, Chicago, IL 60637. Offers PhD. *Students:* 58 full-time (13 women); includes 7 minority (2 Black or African American, non-Hispanic/Latino; 2 Asian, non-Hispanic/Latino; 3 Hispanic/Latino), 37 international. 247 applicants, 21% accepted, 16 enrolled. *Entrance requirements:* For doctorate, GRE General Test. Additional exam requirements/recommendations for international students: Required—TOEFL (minimum score 90 iBT), IELTS (minimum score 7). *Application deadline:* For fall admission, 1/7 for domestic and international students. Application fee: $55. Electronic applications accepted. *Expenses: Tuition:* Full-time $46,899. *Required fees:* $347. *Financial support:* In 2014–15, fellowships with full tuition reimbursements (averaging $22,950 per year), research assistantships with full tuition reimbursements (averaging $22,950 per year), teaching assistantships with full tuition reimbursements (averaging $22,950 per year) were awarded; institutionally sponsored loans, scholarships/grants, traineeships, health care benefits, and unspecified assistantships also available. Financial award applicants required to submit FAFSA. *Faculty research:* Systems, theoretical computer science, machine learning, programming languages, scientific computing and visualization. *Unit head:* Todd DuPont, Chair, 773-702-7950. *Application contact:* Margaret Jaffey, Student Support Representative, 773-702-6011, E-mail: admissions@cs.uchicago.edu. Website: http://csphd.sites.uchicago.edu/.

University of Cincinnati, Graduate School, College of Engineering and Applied Science, Department of Electrical and Computer Engineering and Computer Science, Program in Computer Science, Cincinnati, OH 45221. Offers MS. *Degree requirements:* For master's, thesis. *Entrance requirements:* For master's, GRE General Test, GRE Subject Test or BS in computer science. Additional exam requirements/recommendations for international students: Required—TOEFL (minimum score 550 paper-based).

University of Cincinnati, Graduate School, College of Engineering and Applied Science, Department of Electrical and Computer Engineering and Computer Science, Program in Computer Science and Engineering, Cincinnati, OH 45221. Offers PhD. *Degree requirements:* For doctorate, thesis/dissertation. *Entrance requirements:* For doctorate, GRE General Test. Additional exam requirements/recommendations for international students: Required—TOEFL.

University of Colorado Boulder, Graduate School, College of Engineering and Applied Science, Department of Computer Science, Boulder, CO 80309. Offers ME, MS, PhD. *Faculty:* 28 full-time (6 women). *Students:* 157 full-time (42 women), 70 part-time (7 women); includes 32 minority (2 Black or African American, non-Hispanic/Latino; 2 American Indian or Alaska Native, non-Hispanic/Latino; 10 Asian, non-Hispanic/Latino; 14 Hispanic/Latino; 4 Two or more races, non-Hispanic/Latino), 88 international. Average age 29. 710 applicants, 34% accepted, 71 enrolled. In 2014, 53 master's, 15 doctorates awarded. Terminal master's awarded for partial completion of doctoral program. *Degree requirements:* For master's, comprehensive exam, thesis or alternative; for doctorate, one foreign language, thesis/dissertation. *Entrance requirements:* For master's, minimum undergraduate GPA of 3.0. *Application deadline:* For fall admission, 12/15 for domestic and international students; for spring admission, 10/15 for domestic students, 9/1 for international students. Applications are processed on a rolling basis. Application fee: $50 ($70 for international students). Electronic applications accepted. *Financial support:* In 2014–15, 343 students received support, including 48 fellowships (averaging $6,933 per year), 67 research assistantships with full and partial tuition reimbursements available (averaging $38,393 per year), 28 teaching assistantships with full and partial tuition reimbursements available (averaging $38,743 per year); institutionally sponsored loans, scholarships/grants, health care benefits, and unspecified assistantships also available. Financial award applicants required to submit

FAFSA. *Faculty research:* Computer science, distributed systems, computer interface, computer software, networking. *Total annual research expenditures:* $5.7 million. Website: http://www.cs.colorado.edu/.

University of Colorado Colorado Springs, College of Engineering and Applied Science, Department of Computer Science, Colorado Springs, CO 80933-7150. Offers MS. Part-time programs available. *Faculty:* 16 full-time (3 women), 10 part-time/adjunct (2 women). *Students:* 11 full-time (5 women), 59 part-time (10 women); includes 5 minority (2 American Indian or Alaska Native, non-Hispanic/Latino; 3 Hispanic/Latino), 31 international. Average age 31. 53 applicants, 62% accepted, 11 enrolled. In 2014, 18 master's awarded. *Degree requirements:* For master's, thesis optional, oral final exam. *Entrance requirements:* For master's, GRE General Test, minimum undergraduate GPA of 3.0, 2 semesters of course work in calculus, 1 other math course, course work in computer science. Additional exam requirements/recommendations for international students: Required—TOEFL (minimum score 550 paper-based; 80 iBT). *Application deadline:* For fall admission, 6/1 priority date for domestic students, 4/1 for international students; for spring admission, 11/1 priority date for domestic students, 10/1 for international students; for summer admission, 4/15 priority date for domestic students. Applications are processed on a rolling basis. Application fee: $60 ($100 for international students). *Expenses:* Tuition, state resident: full-time $9900; part-time $1892 per course. Tuition, nonresident: full-time $18,792; part-time $3375 per course. One-time fee: $100. Tuition and fees vary according to course load, program and reciprocity agreements. *Financial support:* In 2014–15, 4 students received support, including 11 research assistantships (averaging $12,000 per year); fellowships, teaching assistantships, career-related internships or fieldwork, Federal Work-Study, and scholarships/grants also available. Financial award application deadline: 3/1; financial award applicants required to submit FAFSA. *Faculty research:* Neural networks, computer vision, pattern recognition, networking, medical imaging, computer game design and development, human motion tracking and reasoning, natural language processing, medical imaging, distributed systems, dynamic process, migration. *Total annual research expenditures:* $788,579. *Unit head:* Dr. Xiaobo Zhou, Chair, 719-255-3493, Fax: 719-255-3369, E-mail: xzhou@uccs.edu. *Application contact:* Ali Langfels, Program Assistant, 719-255-3243, E-mail: alangfel@uccs.edu. Website: http://eas.uccs.edu/cs/.

University of Colorado Denver, Business School, Program in Computer Science and Information Systems, Denver, CO 80217. Offers PhD. *Students:* 11 full-time (2 women), 3 part-time (1 woman); includes 2 minority (1 Black or African American, non-Hispanic/Latino; 1 Asian, non-Hispanic/Latino), 6 international. Average age 39. 22 applicants, 14% accepted, 1 enrolled. In 2014, 2 doctorates awarded. *Degree requirements:* For doctorate, comprehensive exam, thesis/dissertation. *Entrance requirements:* For doctorate, GMAT or GRE General Test, letters of recommendation, portfolio, essay describing applicant's motivation and initial plan for doctoral study, resume. Additional exam requirements/recommendations for international students: Required—TOEFL (minimum score 525 paper-based; 71 iBT); Recommended—IELTS (minimum score 6.5). *Application deadline:* For fall admission, 3/1 priority date for domestic and international students; for spring admission, 10/15 for domestic students, 10/1 for international students. Applications are processed on a rolling basis. Application fee: $50 ($75 for international students). Electronic applications accepted. *Expenses:* Expenses: Contact institution. *Financial support:* In 2014–15, 11 students received support. Fellowships, research assistantships, teaching assistantships, Federal Work-Study, institutionally sponsored loans, scholarships/grants, and traineeships available. Financial award application deadline: 4/1; financial award applicants required to submit FAFSA. *Faculty research:* Design science of information systems, information system economics, organizational impacts of information technology, high performance parallel and distributed systems, performance measurement and prediction. *Unit head:* Dr. Michael Mannino, Associate Professor/Co-Director, 303-315-8427, E-mail: michael.mannino@ucdenver.edu. *Application contact:* Shelly Townley, Director of Graduate Admissions, Business School, 303-315-8202, Fax: 303-556-5904, E-mail: shelly.townley@ucdenver.edu. Website: http://www.ucdenver.edu/academics/colleges/business/degrees/phd/Pages/default.aspx.

University of Colorado Denver, College of Engineering and Applied Science, Department of Computer Science and Engineering, Denver, CO 80217. Offers computer science (MS); computer science and engineering (EASPh D); computer science and information systems (PhD). Part-time and evening/weekend programs available. *Faculty:* 9 full-time (2 women), 3 part-time/adjunct (1 woman). *Students:* 113 full-time (44 women), 28 part-time (6 women); includes 9 minority (3 Black or African American, non-Hispanic/Latino; 3 Asian, non-Hispanic/Latino; 2 Hispanic/Latino; 1 Two or more races, non-Hispanic/Latino), 104 international. Average age 29. 394 applicants, 46% accepted, 64 enrolled. In 2014, 28 master's awarded. *Degree requirements:* For master's, thesis or alternative, at least 30 semester hours of computer science courses while maintaining minimum GPA of 3.0; for doctorate, comprehensive exam, thesis/dissertation, at least 60 hours beyond the master's degree level, 30 of which are dissertation research. *Entrance requirements:* For master's, GRE, minimum GPA of 3.0, 10 semester hours of university-level calculus, at least one math course beyond calculus, statement of purpose, letters of recommendation; for doctorate, GRE or GMAT. Additional exam requirements/recommendations for international students: Required—TOEFL (minimum score 537 paper-based; 75 iBT). *Application deadline:* For fall admission, 5/1 for domestic students, 4/1 for international students; for spring admission, 10/1 for domestic students, 9/1 for international students. Application fee: $50 ($75 for international students). Electronic applications accepted. *Financial support:* In 2014–15, 8 students received support. Research assistantships, teaching assistantships, Federal Work-Study, institutionally sponsored loans, scholarships/grants, traineeships, and unspecified assistantships available. Financial award application deadline: 4/1; financial award applicants required to submit FAFSA. *Faculty research:* Algorithms, automata theory, artificial intelligence, communication networks, combinatorial geometry, computational geometry, computer architectures, computer graphics, distributed computing, high performance computing, graph theory, Internet, operating systems, parallel processing, simulation and software engineering. *Unit head:* Dr. Gita Alaghband, Chair, 303-315-1400, E-mail: gita.alaghband@ucdenver.edu. *Application contact:* Sarah Mandos, Program Assistant, 303-315-1411, E-mail: sarah.mandos@ucdenver.edu. Website: http://www.ucdenver.edu/academics/colleges/Engineering/Programs/Computer-Science-and-Engineering/Pages/ComputerScienceEngineering.aspx.

University of Colorado Denver, College of Liberal Arts and Sciences, Program in Integrated Sciences, Denver, CO 80217. Offers applied science (MIS); computer science (MIS); mathematics (MIS). Part-time and evening/weekend programs available. *Faculty:* 1 (woman) full-time. *Students:* 6 full-time (2 women), 4 part-time (2 women); includes 2 minority (both Asian, non-Hispanic/Latino). Average age 33. 7 applicants, 57% accepted, 3 enrolled. In 2014, 2 master's awarded. *Degree requirements:* For master's, 30 credit hours; thesis or project. *Entrance requirements:* For master's, GRE if undergraduate GPA is 3.0 or less, minimum of 40 semester hours in mathematics, computer science, physics, biology, chemistry and/or geology; essay; three letters of recommendation. Additional exam requirements/recommendations for international

students: Required—TOEFL (minimum score 537 paper-based; 75 iBT); Recommended—IELTS (minimum score 6.5). *Application deadline:* For fall admission, 4/15 for domestic students, 4/15 priority date for international students; for spring admission, 10/15 for domestic students, 10/15 priority date for international students. Application fee: $50 ($75 for international students). Electronic applications accepted. *Financial support:* In 2014–15, 4 students received support. Fellowships, research assistantships, teaching assistantships, Federal Work-Study, institutionally sponsored loans, scholarships/grants, and traineeships available. Financial award application deadline: 4/1; financial award applicants required to submit FAFSA. *Faculty research:* Computer science, applied science, mathematics. *Unit head:* Dr. Martin Huber, Director of Integrated Sciences, 303-556-3561, E-mail: martin.huber@ucdenver.edu. *Application contact:* Marissa Tornatore, Graduate School Application Specialist, 303-315-0049, E-mail: marissa.tornatore@ucdenver.edu.
Website: http://www.ucdenver.edu/academics/colleges/CLAS/Programs/MastersofIntegratedSciences/Pages/ProgramOverview.aspx.

University of Connecticut, Graduate School, School of Engineering, Department of Computer Science and Engineering, Storrs, CT 06269. Offers computer science (MS, PhD), including artificial intelligence, computer architecture, computer science, operating systems, robotics, software engineering. Terminal master's awarded for partial completion of doctoral program. *Degree requirements:* For master's, comprehensive exam, thesis or alternative; for doctorate, thesis/dissertation. *Entrance requirements:* For master's and doctorate, GRE General Test. Additional exam requirements/recommendations for international students: Required—TOEFL (minimum score 550 paper-based). Electronic applications accepted.

University of Dayton, Department of Computer Science, Dayton, OH 45469. Offers MCS. Part-time and evening/weekend programs available. *Faculty:* 9 full-time (2 women), 3 part-time/adjunct (1 woman). *Students:* 52 full-time (16 women), 1 part-time (0 women); includes 2 minority (1 Hispanic/Latino; 1 Two or more races, non-Hispanic/Latino), 46 international. Average age 25. 203 applicants, 42% accepted, 13 enrolled. In 2014, 17 master's awarded. *Degree requirements:* For master's, thesis optional, software project, additional coursework, or thesis. *Entrance requirements:* For master's, GRE General Test. Additional exam requirements/recommendations for international students: Required—TOEFL (minimum score 550 paper-based; 80 iBT), IELTS (minimum score 6.5). *Application deadline:* For fall admission, 8/1 for domestic students, 5/1 priority date for international students; for winter admission, 7/1 for international students; for spring admission, 11/1 priority date for international students. Applications are processed on a rolling basis. Application fee: $0. Electronic applications accepted. *Expenses: Tuition:* Full-time $10,176; part-time $848 per credit. *Required fees:* $25; $25 per course. Part-time tuition and fees vary according to course level, course load, degree level and program. *Financial support:* In 2014–15, 5 teaching assistantships with full tuition reimbursements (averaging $10,548 per year) were awarded; institutionally sponsored loans, health care benefits, and unspecified assistantships also available. Financial award application deadline: 3/1; financial award applicants required to submit FAFSA. *Faculty research:* Graph theory, peer-to-peer (P2P) networking, database systems, human-computer interaction, machine learning, virtual reality. *Total annual research expenditures:* $3,000. *Unit head:* Dr. Mehdi Zargham, Chair, 937-229-3831, E-mail: mzargham1@udayton.edu. *Application contact:* 937-229-4462, E-mail: graduateadmission@udayton.edu.
Website: https://www.udayton.edu/artssciences/academics/computerscience/welcome/index.php.

University of Delaware, College of Engineering, Department of Computer and Information Sciences, Newark, DE 19716. Offers MS, PhD. Part-time programs available. Terminal master's awarded for partial completion of doctoral program. *Degree requirements:* For master's, thesis optional; for doctorate, comprehensive exam, thesis/dissertation. *Entrance requirements:* For master's and doctorate, GRE General Test. Additional exam requirements/recommendations for international students: Required—TOEFL (minimum score 550 paper-based). Electronic applications accepted. *Faculty research:* Artificial intelligence, computational theory, graphics and computer vision, networks, systems.

University of Denver, Daniel Felix Ritchie School of Engineering and Computer Science, Department of Computer Science, Denver, CO 80208. Offers MS, PhD. Part-time programs available. *Faculty:* 12 full-time (2 women), 2 part-time/adjunct (1 woman). *Students:* 2 full-time (1 woman), 34 part-time (4 women); includes 3 minority (1 Black or African American, non-Hispanic/Latino; 2 Asian, non-Hispanic/Latino), 20 international. Average age 29. 65 applicants, 74% accepted, 12 enrolled. In 2014, 7 master's, 1 doctorate awarded. *Degree requirements:* For doctorate, variable foreign language requirement, comprehensive exam, thesis/dissertation, reading competency in two languages, modern typesetting system, or additional coursework. *Entrance requirements:* For master's, GRE General Test, bachelor's degree, transcripts, personal statement, resume or curriculum vitae, three letters of recommendation; for doctorate, GRE General Test, bachelor's degree in computer science or a related discipline, transcripts, personal statement, resume or curriculum vitae, three letters of recommendation. Additional exam requirements/recommendations for international students: Required—TOEFL (minimum score 550 paper-based; 80 iBT). *Application deadline:* For fall admission, 2/15 priority date for domestic and international students. Applications are processed on a rolling basis. Application fee: $65. Electronic applications accepted. *Expenses:* Expenses: $1,199 per credit hour. *Financial support:* In 2014–15, 8 students received support, including 8 teaching assistantships with full and partial tuition reimbursements available (averaging $11,320 per year); career-related internships or fieldwork, Federal Work-Study, institutionally sponsored loans, scholarships/grants, and unspecified assistantships also available. Financial award application deadline: 2/15; financial award applicants required to submit FAFSA. *Faculty research:* Gaming, unified modeling language (UML) designs, humane games, information security and privacy, software engineering. *Unit head:* Dr. Ramakrishna Thurimella, Chair, 303-871-3329, E-mail: ramki@cs.du.edu. *Application contact:* Information Contact, 303-871-2458, E-mail: info@cs.du.edu.
Website: http://www.du.edu/rsecs/departments/cs/index.html.

University of Detroit Mercy, College of Engineering and Science, Department of Mathematics and Computer Science, Program in Computer Science, Detroit, MI 48221. Offers computer systems applications (MSCS); software engineering (MSCS). Evening/weekend programs available. *Entrance requirements:* For master's, minimum GPA of 3.0.

University of Florida, Graduate School, College of Engineering and College of Liberal Arts and Sciences, Department of Computer and Information Science and Engineering, Gainesville, FL 32611. Offers computer engineering (ME, MS, PhD); computer science (MS); digital arts and sciences (MS). Part-time programs available. Postbaccalaureate distance learning degree programs offered (minimal on-campus study). *Faculty:* 42 full-time (6 women), 32 part-time/adjunct (4 women). *Students:* 364 full-time (91 women), 90 part-time (9 women); includes 30 minority (8 Black or African American, non-Hispanic/Latino; 1 American Indian or Alaska Native, non-Hispanic/Latino; 12 Asian, non-Hispanic/Latino; 9 Hispanic/Latino), 370 international. 2,043 applicants, 22% accepted, 156 enrolled. In 2014, 218 master's, 18 doctorates awarded. Terminal master's awarded for partial completion of doctoral program. *Degree requirements:* For master's, comprehensive exam, thesis optional; for doctorate, comprehensive exam, thesis/dissertation. *Entrance requirements:* For master's and doctorate, minimum GPA of 3.0. Additional exam requirements/recommendations for international students: Required—TOEFL (minimum score 550 paper-based; 80 iBT), IELTS (minimum score 6). *Application deadline:* For fall admission, 12/15 priority date for domestic students, 2/1 for international students; for spring admission, 9/1 for domestic and international students. Applications are processed on a rolling basis. Application fee: $30. Electronic applications accepted. *Financial support:* Unspecified assistantships available. Financial award application deadline: 2/1; financial award applicants required to submit FAFSA. *Faculty research:* Computer systems and computer networking; high-performance computing and algorithm; database and machine learning; computer graphics, vision, and intelligent systems; human center computing and digital art. *Unit head:* Paul Gader, PhD, Chair, 352-392-1527, Fax: 352-392-1220, E-mail: pgader@cise.ufl.edu. *Application contact:* Jih-Kwon Peir, PhD, Graduate Coordinator, 352-505-1573, Fax: 352-392-1220, E-mail: peir@cise.ufl.edu.
Website: http://www.cise.ufl.edu/.

University of Georgia, Franklin College of Arts and Sciences, Department of Computer Science, Athens, GA 30602. Offers applied mathematical science (MAMS); computer science (MS, PhD). *Degree requirements:* For doctorate, thesis/dissertation. *Entrance requirements:* For master's and doctorate, GRE General Test. Electronic applications accepted.

University of Guelph, Graduate Studies, College of Physical and Engineering Science, Department of Computing and Information Science, Guelph, ON N1G 2W1, Canada. Offers applied computer science (M Sc); computer science (PhD). *Degree requirements:* For master's, thesis; for doctorate, comprehensive exam, thesis/dissertation. *Entrance requirements:* For master's, major or minor in computer science, honors degree; for doctorate, M Sc in computer science or related discipline. Additional exam requirements/recommendations for international students: Required—TOEFL (minimum score 600 paper-based; 89 iBT), IELTS (minimum score 6.5). Electronic applications accepted. *Faculty research:* Modeling and theory, distributed computing, soft computing, software and information systems, data and knowledge management.

University of Hawaii at Manoa, Graduate Division, College of Natural Sciences, Department of Information and Computer Sciences, Honolulu, HI 96822. Offers computer science (MS, PhD); library and information science (MLI Sc, Graduate Certificate), including advanced library and information science (Graduate Certificate), library and information science (MLI Sc). Part-time programs available. *Degree requirements:* For master's, thesis optional; for doctorate, comprehensive exam, thesis/dissertation. *Entrance requirements:* For master's and doctorate, GRE. Additional exam requirements/recommendations for international students: Required—TOEFL (minimum score 580 paper-based; 92 iBT), IELTS (minimum score 5). *Faculty research:* Software engineering, telecommunications, artificial intelligence, multimedia.

University of Houston, College of Natural Sciences and Mathematics, Department of Computer Science, Houston, TX 77204. Offers MA, PhD. Part-time programs available. Terminal master's awarded for partial completion of doctoral program. *Degree requirements:* For master's, thesis or alternative; for doctorate, comprehensive exam, thesis/dissertation. *Entrance requirements:* For master's and doctorate, GRE. Additional exam requirements/recommendations for international students: Required—TOEFL (minimum score 550 paper-based; 79 iBT), IELTS (minimum score 6.5). Electronic applications accepted. *Faculty research:* Databases, networks, image analysis, security, animation.

University of Houston–Clear Lake, School of Science and Computer Engineering, Program in Computer Science, Houston, TX 77058-1002. Offers MS. Part-time and evening/weekend programs available. *Entrance requirements:* For master's, GRE General Test. Additional exam requirements/recommendations for international students: Required—TOEFL (minimum score 550 paper-based).

University of Houston–Victoria, School of Arts and Sciences, Department of Computer Science, Victoria, TX 77901-4450. Offers computer information systems (MS); computer science (MS). Part-time and evening/weekend programs available. Postbaccalaureate distance learning degree programs offered (no on-campus study). *Degree requirements:* For master's, comprehensive exam (for some programs), thesis (for some programs). *Entrance requirements:* For master's, GRE. Additional exam requirements/recommendations for international students: Required—TOEFL (minimum score 550 paper-based).

University of Idaho, College of Graduate Studies, College of Engineering, Department of Computer Science, Moscow, ID 83844-1010. Offers MS, PhD. *Faculty:* 9 full-time. *Students:* 16 full-time, 16 part-time. Average age 35. In 2014, 14 master's, 3 doctorates awarded. *Degree requirements:* For master's, thesis; for doctorate, thesis/dissertation. *Entrance requirements:* For master's, GRE General Test, minimum GPA of 3.0; for doctorate, minimum undergraduate GPA of 2.8, 3.0 graduate. Additional exam requirements/recommendations for international students: Required—TOEFL. *Application deadline:* For fall admission, 8/1 for domestic students; for spring admission, 12/15 for domestic students. Applications are processed on a rolling basis. Application fee: $60. Electronic applications accepted. *Expenses:* Tuition, state resident: full-time $4784; part-time $280.50 per credit hour. Tuition, nonresident: full-time $18,314; part-time $957.50 per credit hour. *Required fees:* $2000; $58.50 per credit hour. Tuition and fees vary according to program. *Financial support:* Research assistantships, teaching assistantships, and career-related internships or fieldwork available. Financial award applicants required to submit FAFSA. *Faculty research:* Artificial intelligence, computer and network security, software engineering. *Unit head:* Dr. Greg Donahoe, Chair, 208-885-6589, E-mail: csinfo@uidaho.edu. *Application contact:* Sean Scoggin, Graduate Recruitment Coordinator, 208-885-4001, Fax: 208-885-4406, E-mail: graduateadmissions@uidaho.edu.
Website: http://www.uidaho.edu/engr/cs/.

University of Illinois at Chicago, Graduate College, College of Engineering, Department of Computer Science, Chicago, IL 60607-7128. Offers MS, PhD. Part-time programs available. *Faculty:* 30 full-time (5 women), 8 part-time/adjunct (1 woman). *Students:* 195 full-time (58 women), 34 part-time (9 women); includes 42 minority (2 Black or African American, non-Hispanic/Latino; 1 American Indian or Alaska Native, non-Hispanic/Latino; 28 Asian, non-Hispanic/Latino; 9 Hispanic/Latino; 2 Two or more races, non-Hispanic/Latino), 190 international. Average age 26. 1,512 applicants, 23% accepted, 73 enrolled. In 2014, 110 master's, 11 doctorates awarded. *Degree requirements:* For master's, thesis or alternative; for doctorate, thesis/dissertation, departmental qualifying exam. *Entrance requirements:* For master's, BS in related field, minimum GPA of 2.75; for doctorate, GRE General Test, minimum GPA of 2.75, MS in related field. Additional exam requirements/recommendations for international students: Required—TOEFL. *Application deadline:* For fall admission, 1/1 priority date for domestic students, 2/15 for international students; for spring admission, 11/1 for domestic students, 7/15 for international students. Application fee: $60. *Expenses:* Expenses: $17,602 in-state; $29,600 out-of-state. *Financial support:* In 2014–15, 3 fellowships were awarded; research assistantships, teaching assistantships, and tuition waivers (full) also available. Financial award application deadline: 3/1. *Faculty research:* Artificial intelligence; deployment of Natural Language discourse/dialogue coordinated

with graphics tools; data management and mining, information retrieval; computational techniques for population biology; systems security research; scientific visualization. *Total annual research expenditures:* $8.3 million. *Unit head:* Prof. Robert Sloan, Professor and Head, 312-996-2369, E-mail: sloan@uic.edu. *Application contact:* Receptionist, 312-413-2550, E-mail: gradcoll@uic.edu.
Website: http://www.cs.uic.edu/.

University of Illinois at Chicago, Graduate College, College of Liberal Arts and Sciences, Department of Mathematics, Statistics, and Computer Science, Chicago, IL 60607-7128. Offers probability and statistics (PhD); statistics (MS). Part-time programs available. *Faculty:* 73 full-time (20 women), 3 part-time/adjunct (0 women). *Students:* 118 full-time (30 women), 19 part-time (9 women); includes 19 minority (7 Asian, non-Hispanic/Latino; 9 Hispanic/Latino; 3 Two or more races, non-Hispanic/Latino), 51 international. Average age 28. 202 applicants, 32% accepted, 25 enrolled. In 2014, 42 master's, 22 doctorates awarded. *Degree requirements:* For master's, comprehensive exam; for doctorate, one foreign language, thesis/dissertation. *Entrance requirements:* For master's and doctorate, GRE General Test, minimum GPA of 3.0. Additional exam requirements/recommendations for international students: Required—TOEFL (minimum score 100 iBT). *Application deadline:* For fall admission, 1/1 for domestic and international students; for spring admission, 10/1 for domestic students, 7/15 for international students. Applications are processed on a rolling basis. Application fee: $60. Electronic applications accepted. *Expenses:* Tuition, state resident: full-time $11,254; part-time $468 per credit hour. Tuition, nonresident: full-time $23,252; part-time $968 per credit hour. *Required fees:* $1217 per term. Part-time tuition and fees vary according to course load, degree level and program. *Financial support:* In 2014–15, 109 students received support, including 2 fellowships with full tuition reimbursements available (averaging $20,000 per year), 8 research assistantships with full tuition reimbursements available (averaging $17,000 per year), 87 teaching assistantships with full tuition reimbursements available (averaging $17,000 per year); Federal Work-Study, scholarships/grants, and tuition waivers (full) also available. Financial award application deadline: 1/1. *Total annual research expenditures:* $2.4 million. *Unit head:* Prof. Brooke Shipley, Head, 312-996-3044, E-mail: shipley@math.uic.edu. *Application contact:* Ramin Takloo-Bighash, Director of Graduate Studies, 312-996-5119, E-mail: dgs@math.uic.edu.
Website: http://www.math.uic.edu/.

University of Illinois at Springfield, Graduate Programs, College of Liberal Arts and Sciences, Program in Computer Science, Springfield, IL 62703-5407. Offers MS. Part-time and evening/weekend programs available. Postbaccalaureate distance learning degree programs offered (no on-campus study). *Faculty:* 13 full-time (4 women), 5 part-time/adjunct (0 women). *Students:* 387 full-time (107 women), 313 part-time (69 women); includes 70 minority (15 Black or African American, non-Hispanic/Latino; 1 American Indian or Alaska Native, non-Hispanic/Latino; 37 Asian, non-Hispanic/Latino; 11 Hispanic/Latino; 1 Native Hawaiian or other Pacific Islander, non-Hispanic/Latino; 5 Two or more races, non-Hispanic/Latino), 427 international. Average age 28. 1,054 applicants, 57% accepted, 323 enrolled. In 2014, 120 master's awarded. *Degree requirements:* For master's, research seminar. *Entrance requirements:* For master's, GRE General Test, minimum undergraduate GPA of 2.7. Additional exam requirements/recommendations for international students: Required—TOEFL (minimum score 550 paper-based; 79 iBT). *Application deadline:* Applications are processed on a rolling basis. Application fee: $60 ($75 for international students). Electronic applications accepted. *Expenses:* Tuition, state resident: full-time $7662; part-time $319.25 per credit hour. Tuition, nonresident: full-time $15,966; part-time $665.25 per credit hour. *Financial support:* In 2014–15, fellowships with full tuition reimbursements (averaging $9,900 per year), research assistantships with full tuition reimbursements (averaging $9,600 per year), teaching assistantships with full tuition reimbursements (averaging $9,600 per year) were awarded; career-related internships or fieldwork, Federal Work-Study, scholarships/grants, health care benefits, and unspecified assistantships also available. Support available to part-time students. Financial award application deadline: 11/15; financial award applicants required to submit FAFSA. *Unit head:* Dr. Ted Mims, Program Administrator, 217-206-7326, Fax: 217-206-6217, E-mail: mims.ted@uis.edu. *Application contact:* Dr. Lynn Pardie, Office of Graduate Studies, 800-252-8533, Fax: 217-206-7623, E-mail: lpard1@uis.edu.

University of Illinois at Urbana–Champaign, Graduate College, College of Engineering, Department of Computer Science, Champaign, IL 61820. Offers bioinformatics (MS); computer science (MCS, MS, PhD); MCS/JD; MCS/M Arch; MCS/MBA. Part-time and evening/weekend programs available. Postbaccalaureate distance learning degree programs offered (no on-campus study). *Students:* 530 (118 women). Application fee: $70 ($90 for international students). *Unit head:* Robin A. Rutenbar, Head, 217-333-3373, Fax: 217-333-3501, E-mail: rutenbar@illinois.edu. *Application contact:* Kara L. MacGregor, Graduate Academic Advisor, 217-333-9706, Fax: 217-244-6073, E-mail: kmacgreg@illinois.edu.
Website: http://cs.illinois.edu/.

The University of Iowa, Graduate College, College of Liberal Arts and Sciences, Department of Computer Science, Iowa City, IA 52242-1316. Offers MCS, PhD. *Degree requirements:* For master's, thesis optional, exam; for doctorate, comprehensive exam, thesis/dissertation. *Entrance requirements:* For master's, minimum GPA of 3.0; for doctorate, GRE General Test, minimum GPA of 3.0. Additional exam requirements/recommendations for international students: Required—TOEFL (minimum score 550 paper-based; 81 iBT). Electronic applications accepted.

The University of Kansas, Graduate Studies, School of Engineering, Program in Computer Science, Lawrence, KS 66045. Offers MS, PhD. Part-time and evening/weekend programs available. *Faculty:* 33 full-time, 1 part-time/adjunct. *Students:* 62 full-time (14 women), 20 part-time (2 women); includes 3 minority (1 Black or African American, non-Hispanic/Latino; 1 Asian, non-Hispanic/Latino; 1 Two or more races, non-Hispanic/Latino), 57 international. Average age 27. 150 applicants, 52% accepted, 25 enrolled. In 2014, 7 master's, 4 doctorates awarded. Terminal master's awarded for partial completion of doctoral program. *Degree requirements:* For master's, thesis optional, exam; for doctorate, one foreign language, comprehensive exam, thesis/dissertation, qualifying exams. *Entrance requirements:* For master's, GRE (minimum scores: 146 verbal and 155 quantitative), minimum GPA of 3.0; for doctorate, GRE (minimum scores: 146 verbal and 155 quantitative), minimum GPA of 3.5. Additional exam requirements/recommendations for international students: Required—TOEFL (minimum score 600 paper-based; 100 iBT). *Application deadline:* For fall admission, 3/1 priority date for domestic students, 3/1 for international students; for spring admission, 10/1 priority date for domestic students, 10/1 for international students. Applications are processed on a rolling basis. Application fee: $55 ($65 for international students). Electronic applications accepted. *Financial support:* Fellowships with full and partial tuition reimbursements, research assistantships with full and partial tuition reimbursements, teaching assistantships with full and partial tuition reimbursements, career-related internships or fieldwork, scholarships/grants, and unspecified assistantships available. Financial award application deadline: 1/1. *Faculty research:* Communication systems and networking, computer systems design, interactive intelligent systems, bioinformatics. *Unit head:* James Stiles, Associate Chair for

Graduate Studies, 785-864-8803, E-mail: jstiles@eecs.ku.edu. *Application contact:* Pam Shadoin, Graduate Admissions Contact, 785-864-4487, E-mail: pshadoin@ku.edu. Website: http://www.eecs.ku.edu/prospective_students/graduate.

University of Kentucky, Graduate School, College of Engineering, Program in Computer Science, Lexington, KY 40506-0032. Offers MS, PhD. *Degree requirements:* For master's, comprehensive exam, thesis optional; for doctorate, one foreign language, comprehensive exam, thesis/dissertation. *Entrance requirements:* For master's, GRE General Test, minimum undergraduate GPA of 2.75; for doctorate, GRE General Test, minimum undergraduate GPA of 3.0. Additional exam requirements/recommendations for international students: Required—TOEFL (minimum score 550 paper-based). Electronic applications accepted. *Faculty research:* Artificial intelligence and databases, communication networks and operating systems, graphics and vision, numerical analysis, theory.

University of Lethbridge, School of Graduate Studies, Lethbridge, AB T1K 3M4, Canada. Offers addictions counseling (M Sc); agricultural biotechnology (M Sc); agricultural studies (M Sc, MA); anthropology (MA); archaeology (M Sc, MA); art (MA, MFA); biochemistry (M Sc); biological sciences (M Sc); biomolecular science (PhD); biosystems and biodiversity (PhD); Canadian studies (MA); chemistry (M Sc); computer science (M Sc); computer science and geographical information science (M Sc); counseling (MC); counseling psychology (M Ed); dramatic arts (MA); earth, space, and physical science (PhD); economics (MA); education (MA); educational leadership (M Ed); English (MA); environmental science (M Sc); evolution and behavior (PhD); exercise science (M Sc); French (MA); French/German (MA); French/Spanish (MA); general education (M Ed); geography (M Sc, MA); German (MA); health sciences (M Sc); individualized multidisciplinary (M Sc, MA); kinesiology (M Sc, MA); management (M Sc), including accounting, finance, general management, human resource management and labor relations, information systems, international management, marketing, policy and strategy; mathematics (M Sc); modern languages (MA); music (M Mus, MA); Native American studies (MA); neuroscience (M Sc, PhD); new media (MA, MFA); nursing (M Sc, MN); philosophy (MA); physics (M Sc); political science (MA); psychology (M Sc, MA); religious studies (MA); sociology (MA); theatre and dramatic arts (MFA); theoretical and computational science (PhD); urban and regional studies (MA); women and gender studies (MA). Part-time and evening/weekend programs available. *Faculty:* 358. *Students:* 445 full-time (243 women), 116 part-time (72 women). Average age 31. 351 applicants, 26% accepted, 87 enrolled. In 2014, 129 master's, 13 doctorates awarded. *Degree requirements:* For master's, thesis (for some programs); for doctorate, comprehensive exam, thesis/dissertation. *Entrance requirements:* For master's, GMAT (for M Sc in management), bachelor's degree in related field, minimum GPA of 3.0 during previous 20 graded semester courses, 2 years' teaching or related experience (M Ed); for doctorate, master's degree, minimum graduate GPA of 3.5. Additional exam requirements/recommendations for international students: Required—TOEFL. Application fee: $100 Canadian dollars. *Financial support:* Fellowships, research assistantships, teaching assistantships, scholarships/grants, health care benefits, and unspecified assistantships available. *Faculty research:* Movement and brain plasticity, gibberellin physiology, photosynthesis, carbon cycling, molecular properties of main-group ring components. *Application contact:* School of Graduate Studies, 403-329-5194, E-mail: sgsinquiries@uleth.ca.
Website: http://www.uleth.ca/graduatestudies/.

University of Louisiana at Lafayette, College of Engineering, Center for Advanced Computer Studies, Lafayette, LA 70504. Offers computer engineering (MS, PhD); computer science (MS, PhD). Part-time programs available. Terminal master's awarded for partial completion of doctoral program. *Degree requirements:* For master's, thesis or alternative; for doctorate, comprehensive exam, thesis/dissertation, final oral exam. *Entrance requirements:* For master's, GRE General Test, minimum GPA of 2.75; for doctorate, GRE General Test, minimum GPA of 3.0. Additional exam requirements/recommendations for international students: Required—TOEFL. Electronic applications accepted.

University of Louisville, J. B. Speed School of Engineering, Department of Computer Engineering and Computer Science, Louisville, KY 40292-0001. Offers computer engineering and computer science (M Eng, MS); computer science and engineering (PhD); data mining (Certificate); network and information security (Certificate). *Accreditation:* ABET (one or more programs are accredited). Part-time programs available. Postbaccalaureate distance learning degree programs offered (no on-campus study). *Students:* 77 full-time (22 women), 68 part-time (14 women); includes 17 minority (8 Black or African American, non-Hispanic/Latino; 6 Asian, non-Hispanic/Latino; 2 Hispanic/Latino; 1 Two or more races, non-Hispanic/Latino), 51 international. Average age 29. 92 applicants, 54% accepted, 29 enrolled. In 2014, 8 master's, 3 doctorates, 6 other advanced degrees awarded. Terminal master's awarded for partial completion of doctoral program. *Degree requirements:* For master's, comprehensive exam (for some programs), thesis optional, minimum GPA of 3.0; for doctorate, comprehensive exam, thesis/dissertation, minimum GPA of 3.0. *Entrance requirements:* For master's and doctorate, GRE, letters of recommendation, final official transcripts; for Certificate, undergraduate degree. Additional exam requirements/recommendations for international students: Required—TOEFL (minimum score 80 iBT) or IELTS. *Application deadline:* For fall admission, 6/15 for domestic students, 5/1 priority date for international students; for spring admission, 11/22 for domestic students, 11/1 priority date for international students; for summer admission, 3/31 for domestic students, 4/1 priority date for international students. Application fee: $60. Electronic applications accepted. *Expenses:* Tuition, state resident: full-time $11,326; part-time $630 per credit hour. Tuition, nonresident: full-time $23,568; part-time $1311 per credit hour. *Required fees:* $196. Tuition and fees vary according to program and reciprocity agreements. *Financial support:* Fellowships with full tuition reimbursements, research assistantships with full tuition reimbursements, and teaching assistantships with full tuition reimbursements available. Financial award application deadline: 2/3. *Faculty research:* Software systems engineering, information security and forensics, multimedia and vision, mobile and distributed computing, intelligent systems. *Total annual research expenditures:* $1.3 million. *Unit head:* Dr. Adel S. Elmaghraby, Chair, 502-852-6304, Fax: 502-852-4713, E-mail: adel@louisville.edu. *Application contact:* Dr. Michael Harris, Director of Academic Programs, J. B. Speed School of Engineering, 502-852-6278, Fax: 502-852-6294, E-mail: mharris@louisville.edu.
Website: http://louisville.edu/speed/computer.

University of Maine, Graduate School, College of Liberal Arts and Sciences, School of Computing and Information Science, Orono, ME 04469. Offers computer science (MS, PhD); geographic information systems (CGS); information systems (MS); spatial information science and engineering (MS, PhD). Part-time programs available. *Faculty:* 13 full-time (2 women). *Students:* 30 full-time (6 women), 9 part-time (2 women); includes 1 minority (Asian, non-Hispanic/Latino), 10 international. Average age 34. 46 applicants, 37% accepted, 3 enrolled. In 2014, 9 master's, 3 doctorates awarded. Terminal master's awarded for partial completion of doctoral program. *Degree requirements:* For master's, thesis (for some programs); for doctorate, comprehensive exam, thesis/dissertation. *Entrance requirements:* For master's and doctorate, GRE General Test, GRE Subject Test. Additional exam requirements/recommendations for international students: Required—TOEFL. *Application deadline:* For fall admission, 2/1

priority date for domestic students. Applications are processed on a rolling basis. Application fee: $65. Electronic applications accepted. *Expenses:* Tuition, state resident: part-time $658 per credit hour. Tuition, nonresident: part-time $1550 per credit hour. *Financial support:* In 2014–15, 18 students received support, including 3 fellowships (averaging $21,600 per year), 7 research assistantships with full tuition reimbursements available (averaging $14,600 per year), 8 teaching assistantships with full tuition reimbursements available (averaging $14,600 per year); career-related internships or fieldwork, Federal Work-Study, institutionally sponsored loans, and tuition waivers (full) also available. Financial award application deadline: 3/1. *Faculty research:* Geographic information science, virtual reality, robotics, sensor networks, ice sheet modeling. *Total annual research expenditures:* $436,973. *Unit head:* Dr. Max Egenhofer, Acting Director, 207-581-2114, Fax: 207-581-2206. *Application contact:* Scott G. Delcourt, Assistant Vice President for Graduate Studies and Senior Associate Dean, 207-581-3291, Fax: 207-581-3232, E-mail: graduate@maine.edu.
Website: http://umaine.edu/cis/.

University of Management and Technology, Program in Computer Science, Arlington, VA 22209. Offers computer science (MS); information technology (AC); project management (AC); software engineering (MS). Part-time and evening/weekend programs available. Postbaccalaureate distance learning degree programs offered (no on-campus study). *Entrance requirements:* For master's, 3 recommendations, resume. Additional exam requirements/recommendations for international students: Required—TOEFL (minimum score 530 paper-based; 71 iBT). Electronic applications accepted.

The University of Manchester, School of Computer Science, Manchester, United Kingdom. Offers M Phil, PhD.

University of Manitoba, Faculty of Graduate Studies, Faculty of Science, Department of Computer Science, Winnipeg, MB R3T 2N2, Canada. Offers M Sc, PhD. *Degree requirements:* For master's, thesis or alternative; for doctorate, thesis/dissertation.

University of Maryland, Baltimore County, The Graduate School, College of Engineering and Information Technology, Department of Computer Science and Electrical Engineering, Program in Computer Science, Baltimore, MD 21250. Offers MS, PhD. Part-time programs available. *Students:* 107 full-time (28 women), 59 part-time (13 women); includes 25 minority (4 Black or African American, non-Hispanic/Latino; 1 American Indian or Alaska Native, non-Hispanic/Latino; 13 Asian, non-Hispanic/Latino; 5 Hispanic/Latino; 2 Two or more races, non-Hispanic/Latino), 88 international. Average age 28. 404 applicants, 23% accepted, 36 enrolled. In 2014, 28 master's, 9 doctorates awarded. *Degree requirements:* For master's, comprehensive exam (for some programs), thesis (for some programs); for doctorate, comprehensive exam, thesis/dissertation. *Entrance requirements:* For master's, GRE General Test, strong background in computer science and math courses; for doctorate, GRE General Test, MS in computer science (strongly recommended). Additional exam requirements/recommendations for international students: Required—TOEFL (minimum score 550 paper-based; 80 iBT). *Application deadline:* For fall admission, 6/1 for domestic students, 1/1 for international students; for spring admission, 11/1 for domestic students, 6/1 for international students. Applications are processed on a rolling basis. Application fee: $70. Electronic applications accepted. *Expenses:* Tuition, state resident: part-time $557. Tuition, nonresident: part-time $922. *Required fees:* $122 per semester. One-time fee: $200 part-time. *Financial support:* In 2014–15, 1 fellowship with full tuition reimbursement (averaging $18,000 per year), 26 research assistantships with full tuition reimbursements (averaging $18,000 per year), 44 teaching assistantships with full tuition reimbursements (averaging $16,000 per year) were awarded; career-related internships or fieldwork, Federal Work-Study, scholarships/grants, health care benefits, tuition waivers (partial), and unspecified assistantships also available. Support available to part-time students. Financial award application deadline: 6/30; financial award applicants required to submit FAFSA. *Faculty research:* Artificial intelligence, graphics and visualization, high performance computing, information and knowledge management, networking and systems, security, theory and algorithms. *Unit head:* Dr. Gary Carter, Professor and Chair, 410-455-3500, Fax: 410-455-3969, E-mail: carter@cs.umbc.edu. *Application contact:* Dr. Kostas Kalpakis, Professor and Graduate Program Director, 410-455-3000, Fax: 410-455-3969, E-mail: kalpakis@cs.umbc.edu.
Website: http://www.csee.umbc.edu/.

University of Maryland, Baltimore County, The Graduate School, College of Engineering and Information Technology, Department of Information Systems, Program in Human-Centered Computing, Baltimore, MD 21250. Offers MS, PhD. Part-time and evening/weekend programs available. *Students:* 29 full-time (16 women), 28 part-time (12 women); includes 9 minority (7 Black or African American, non-Hispanic/Latino; 1 Asian, non-Hispanic/Latino; 1 Hispanic/Latino), 17 international. Average age 32. 56 applicants, 54% accepted, 12 enrolled. In 2014, 20 master's, 2 doctorates awarded. Terminal master's awarded for partial completion of doctoral program. *Degree requirements:* For master's, comprehensive exam (for some programs), thesis optional; for doctorate, comprehensive exam, thesis/dissertation. *Entrance requirements:* For master's, minimum GPA of 3.0; for doctorate, GRE General Test or GMAT, competence in statistical analysis and experimental design. Additional exam requirements/recommendations for international students: Required—TOEFL (minimum score 550 paper-based; 80 iBT). *Application deadline:* For fall admission, 6/1 for domestic students, 1/1 for international students; for spring admission, 11/1 for domestic students, 6/1 for international students. Applications are processed on a rolling basis. Application fee: $70. Electronic applications accepted. *Expenses:* Tuition, state resident: part-time $557. Tuition, nonresident: part-time $922. *Required fees:* $122 per semester. One-time fee: $200 part-time. *Financial support:* In 2014–15, 2 fellowships with full tuition reimbursements (averaging $20,000 per year), 12 research assistantships with full tuition reimbursements (averaging $20,000 per year), 4 teaching assistantships with full tuition reimbursements (averaging $20,000 per year) were awarded; career-related internships or fieldwork, Federal Work-Study, scholarships/grants, health care benefits, tuition waivers (partial), and unspecified assistantships also available. Support available to part-time students. Financial award application deadline: 6/30; financial award applicants required to submit FAFSA. *Faculty research:* Human-centered computing. *Unit head:* Dr. Arrya Gangopadhyay, Professor and Chair, 410-455-2620, Fax: 410-455-1217, E-mail: gangopad@umbc.edu. *Application contact:* Dr. Anita Komlodi, Associate Professor and Graduate Program Director, 410-455-3212, Fax: 410-455-1217, E-mail: komlodi@umbc.edu.
Website: http://www.is.umbc.edu/.

University of Maryland, College Park, Academic Affairs, College of Computer, Mathematical and Natural Sciences, Department of Computer Science, College Park, MD 20742. Offers MS, PhD. Part-time and evening/weekend programs available. Terminal master's awarded for partial completion of doctoral program. *Degree requirements:* For master's, thesis or scholarly paper and exam; for doctorate, thesis/dissertation. *Entrance requirements:* For master's and doctorate, GRE General Test, GRE Subject Test (recommended), minimum GPA of 3.0, 3 letters of recommendation. Additional exam requirements/recommendations for international students: Required—TOEFL; Recommended—TWE. Electronic applications accepted. *Faculty research:* Artificial intelligence, computer applications, information processing, bioinformatics and computational biology, human-computer interaction.

University of Maryland Eastern Shore, Graduate Programs, Department of Mathematics and Computer Sciences, Princess Anne, MD 21853-1299. Offers applied computer science (MS). Part-time and evening/weekend programs available. *Degree requirements:* For master's, thesis or alternative, research project. *Entrance requirements:* For master's, GRE General Test, minimum GPA of 3.0. Additional exam requirements/recommendations for international students: Required—TOEFL (minimum score 80 iBT). Electronic applications accepted.

University of Massachusetts Amherst, Graduate School, College of Natural Sciences, School of Computer Science, Amherst, MA 01003. Offers MS, PhD. Part-time programs available. *Faculty:* 60 full-time (9 women). *Students:* 168 full-time (51 women), 56 part-time (13 women); includes 15 minority (3 Black or African American, non-Hispanic/Latino; 8 Asian, non-Hispanic/Latino; 1 Hispanic/Latino; 3 Two or more races, non-Hispanic/Latino), 126 international. Average age 27. 1,082 applicants, 15% accepted, 55 enrolled. In 2014, 42 master's, 19 doctorates awarded. Terminal master's awarded for partial completion of doctoral program. *Degree requirements:* For master's, thesis or alternative; for doctorate, comprehensive exam, thesis/dissertation. *Entrance requirements:* For master's and doctorate, GRE General Test. Additional exam requirements/recommendations for international students: Required—TOEFL (minimum score 550 paper-based; 80 iBT), IELTS (minimum score 6.5), TWE. *Application deadline:* For fall admission, 12/15 for domestic and international students. Applications are processed on a rolling basis. Application fee: $75. Electronic applications accepted. *Expenses:* Tuition, state resident: full-time $1980; part-time $110 per credit. Tuition, nonresident: full-time $14,644; part-time $414 per credit. *Required fees:* $11,417. One-time fee: $357. *Financial support:* Fellowships with full and partial tuition reimbursements, research assistantships with full and partial tuition reimbursements, teaching assistantships with full and partial tuition reimbursements, career-related internships or fieldwork, Federal Work-Study, scholarships/grants, traineeships, health care benefits, tuition waivers (full and partial), and unspecified assistantships available. Support available to part-time students. Financial award application deadline: 12/15. *Faculty research:* Artificial intelligence, robotics, computer vision, and wearable computing; autonomous and multiagent systems; information retrieval, data mining and machine learning; networking, distributed systems and security. *Unit head:* Dr. J. Eliot Moss, Graduate Program Director, 413-545-3640, Fax: 413-545-1249, E-mail: csinfo@cs.umass.edu. *Application contact:* Lindsay DeSantis, Supervisor of Admissions, 413-545-0721, Fax: 413-577-0010, E-mail: gradadm@grad.umass.edu.
Website: http://www.cs.umass.edu/.

University of Massachusetts Boston, College of Science and Mathematics, Program in Computer Science, Boston, MA 02125-3393. Offers MS, PhD. Part-time and evening/weekend programs available. *Degree requirements:* For master's, comprehensive exam, thesis optional, capstone final project; for doctorate, comprehensive exam, thesis/dissertation, oral exams. *Entrance requirements:* For master's and doctorate, GRE General Test, minimum GPA of 2.75. Additional exam requirements/recommendations for international students: Required—TOEFL (minimum score 80 iBT). *Application deadline:* For fall admission, 3/1 for domestic students; for spring admission, 11/1 for domestic students. *Expenses:* Tuition, state resident: full-time $2590; part-time $108 per credit. Tuition, nonresident: full-time $9758; part-time $406.50 per credit. Tuition and fees vary according to course load and program. *Financial support:* Research assistantships with full tuition reimbursements, teaching assistantships with full tuition reimbursements, career-related internships or fieldwork, Federal Work-Study, and unspecified assistantships available. Support available to part-time students. Financial award application deadline: 3/1; financial award applicants required to submit FAFSA. *Faculty research:* Queuing theory, database design theory, computer networks, theory of database query languages, real-time systems. *Unit head:* Dr. Dan Simovici, Director, 617-287-6440. *Application contact:* Peggy Roldan Patel, Graduate Admissions Coordinator, 617-287-6400, Fax: 617-287-6236, E-mail: bos.gadm@dpc.umassp.edu.

University of Massachusetts Dartmouth, Graduate School, College of Engineering, Department of Computer Science, North Dartmouth, MA 02747-2300. Offers MS, Postbaccalaureate Certificate. Part-time programs available. Postbaccalaureate distance learning degree programs offered (no on-campus study). *Faculty:* 7 full-time (1 woman), 2 part-time/adjunct (0 women). *Students:* 62 full-time (20 women), 20 part-time (5 women); includes 3 minority (1 Asian, non-Hispanic/Latino; 1 Hispanic/Latino; 1 Two or more races, non-Hispanic/Latino), 67 international. Average age 25. 149 applicants, 77% accepted, 38 enrolled. In 2014, 15 master's awarded. *Degree requirements:* For master's, thesis or project. *Entrance requirements:* For master's, GRE (UMass Dartmouth computer information science bachelor's degree recipients are exempt), statement of purpose (minimum of 300 words), resume, 3 letters of recommendation, official transcripts; for Postbaccalaureate Certificate, statement of purpose (minimum of 300 words), resume, official transcripts. Additional exam requirements/recommendations for international students: Required—TOEFL (minimum score 533 paper-based; 72 iBT), IELTS (minimum score 6). *Application deadline:* For fall admission, 2/15 priority date for domestic students, 1/15 priority date for international students; for spring admission, 11/15 priority date for domestic students, 10/15 priority date for international students. Applications are processed on a rolling basis. Application fee: $60. Electronic applications accepted. *Expenses:* Tuition, state resident: full-time $2071; part-time $86.29 per credit. Tuition, nonresident: full-time $8099; part-time $337.46 per credit. *Required fees:* $16,520; $712.33 per credit. Tuition and fees vary according to course load and reciprocity agreements. *Financial support:* In 2014–15, 2 research assistantships with full tuition reimbursements (averaging $18,000 per year), 4 teaching assistantships with full tuition reimbursements (averaging $7,500 per year) were awarded; Federal Work-Study and unspecified assistantships also available. Support available to part-time students. Financial award application deadline: 3/1; financial award applicants required to submit FAFSA. *Faculty research:* Human-computer interaction, visualization and imaging, software engineering, multi-agent systems, informatics and data processing, computer networks. *Total annual research expenditures:* $140,000. *Unit head:* Dr. Xiaoqin (Shelley) Zhang, Graduate Program Director, 508-999-8294, Fax: 508-999-9144, E-mail: x2zhang@umassd.edu. *Application contact:* Steven Briggs, Director of Marketing and Recruitment for Graduate Studies, 508-999-8604, Fax: 508-999-8183, E-mail: graduate@umassd.edu.
Website: http://www.umassd.edu/engineering/cis/.

University of Massachusetts Dartmouth, Graduate School, College of Engineering, Program in Engineering and Applied Science, North Dartmouth, MA 02747-2300. Offers applied mechanics and materials (PhD); computational science and engineering (PhD); computer science and information systems (PhD); industrial and systems engineering (PhD). Part-time programs available. *Students:* 21 full-time (6 women), 1 (woman) part-time; includes 2 minority (1 Black or African American, non-Hispanic/Latino; 1 Two or more races, non-Hispanic/Latino), 12 international. Average age 30. 23 applicants, 65% accepted, 5 enrolled. In 2014, 1 doctorate awarded. *Degree requirements:* For doctorate, comprehensive exam, thesis/dissertation. *Entrance requirements:* For doctorate, GRE, statement of purpose (minimum of 300 words), resume, 3 letters of recommendation, official transcripts. Additional exam requirements/recommendations for international students: Required—TOEFL (minimum score 550 paper-based; 79 iBT). *Application deadline:* For fall admission, 2/15 priority date for domestic students, 1/15 priority date for international students; for spring admission, 11/15 priority date for

domestic students, 10/15 priority date for international students. Applications are processed on a rolling basis. Application fee: $60. Electronic applications accepted. *Expenses:* Tuition, state resident: full-time $2071; part-time $86.29 per credit. Tuition, nonresident: full-time $8099; part-time $337.46 per credit. *Required fees:* $16,520; $712.33 per credit. Tuition and fees vary according to course load and reciprocity agreements. *Financial support:* In 2014–15, 8 fellowships with full tuition reimbursements (averaging $16,577 per year), 8 research assistantships with full tuition reimbursements (averaging $13,627 per year), 5 teaching assistantships with full tuition reimbursements (averaging $12,400 per year) were awarded; Federal Work-Study and unspecified assistantships also available. Support available to part-time students. Financial award application deadline: 3/1; financial award applicants required to submit FAFSA. *Faculty research:* Tissue/cell engineering, biotransport sensors/networks, marine systems biomimetic materials, composite/polymeric materials, resilient infrastructure robotics, renewable energy. *Total annual research expenditures:* $1.7 million. *Unit head:* Gaurav Khanna, Graduate Program Director, 508-910-6605, Fax: 508-999-9115, E-mail: gkhanna@umassd.edu. *Application contact:* Steven Briggs, Director of Marketing and Recruitment for Graduate Studies, 508-999-8604, Fax: 508-999-8183, E-mail: graduate@umassd.edu.
Website: http://www.umassd.edu/engineering/graduate/doctoraldegreeprograms/egrandappliedsciencephd/.

University of Massachusetts Lowell, College of Sciences, Department of Computer Science, Lowell, MA 01854. Offers MS, PhD, Sc D. Part-time programs available. *Degree requirements:* For master's, thesis optional; for doctorate, thesis/dissertation. *Entrance requirements:* For master's and doctorate, GRE General Test. *Faculty research:* Networks, multimedia systems, human-computer interaction, graphics and visualization databases.

University of Memphis, Graduate School, College of Arts and Sciences, Department of Computer Science, Memphis, TN 38152. Offers computer science (MS). *Faculty:* 11 full-time (1 woman), 3 part-time/adjunct (0 women). *Students:* 54 full-time (11 women), 16 part-time (4 women); includes 5 minority (4 Black or African American, non-Hispanic/Latino; 1 Asian, non-Hispanic/Latino), 58 international. Average age 28. 64 applicants, 77% accepted, 13 enrolled. In 2014, 14 master's, 4 doctorates awarded. *Degree requirements:* For master's, comprehensive exam, thesis; for doctorate, comprehensive exam, thesis/dissertation. *Entrance requirements:* For master's and doctorate, GRE, letters of recommendation. Additional exam requirements/recommendations for international students: Required—TOEFL (minimum score 550 paper-based; 80 iBT). Application fee: $35 ($60 for international students). *Financial support:* In 2014–15, 9 students received support. Research assistantships with full tuition reimbursements available, teaching assistantships with full tuition reimbursements available, Federal Work-Study, scholarships/grants, and unspecified assistantships available. Financial award application deadline: 2/15; financial award applicants required to submit FAFSA. *Faculty research:* Network security, biomolecular and distributed computing, wireless sensor networks, artificial intelligence. *Unit head:* Dr. Sajjan Shiva, Chair, 901-678-5667, Fax: 901-678-2480, E-mail: info@cs.memphis.edu. *Application contact:* Dr. David Lin, Graduate Studies Coordinator, 901-678-3135, E-mail: davidlin@memphis.edu.
Website: http://www.cs.memphis.edu.

University of Memphis, Graduate School, College of Arts and Sciences, Department of Mathematical Sciences, Memphis, TN 38152. Offers applied mathematics (MS); applied statistics (PhD); bioinformatics (MS); computer sciences (MS); statistics (MS). Part-time programs available. *Faculty:* 20 full-time (5 women), 2 part-time/adjunct (0 women). *Students:* 42 full-time (12 women), 21 part-time (10 women); includes 20 minority (9 Black or African American, non-Hispanic/Latino; 10 Asian, non-Hispanic/Latino; 1 Hispanic/Latino), 19 international. Average age 32. 36 applicants, 89% accepted, 14 enrolled. In 2014, 12 master's, 6 doctorates awarded. Terminal master's awarded for partial completion of doctoral program. *Degree requirements:* For master's, comprehensive exam; for doctorate, one foreign language, thesis/dissertation, oral exams. *Entrance requirements:* For master's and doctorate, GRE General Test, minimum GPA of 2.5. Additional exam requirements/recommendations for international students: Required—TOEFL (minimum score 550 paper-based). *Application deadline:* For fall admission, 8/1 for domestic students, 5/1 priority date for international students; for spring admission, 12/1 for domestic students, 9/1 priority date for international students. Applications are processed on a rolling basis. Application fee: $35 ($60 for international students). Electronic applications accepted. *Financial support:* In 2014–15, 22 students received support. Fellowships with full tuition reimbursements available, research assistantships with full tuition reimbursements available, teaching assistantships with full tuition reimbursements available, career-related internships or fieldwork, Federal Work-Study, scholarships/grants, and unspecified assistantships available. Financial award application deadline: 2/15; financial award applicants required to submit FAFSA. *Faculty research:* Combinatorics, ergodic theory, graph theory, Ramsey theory, applied statistics. *Unit head:* Dr. Irena Lasiecka, Chairman, 901-678-2482, Fax: 901-678-2480, E-mail: lasiecka@memphis.edu. *Application contact:* Dr. Fernanda Botelho, Coordinator of Graduate Studies, 901-678-3131, Fax: 901-678-2480, E-mail: mbotelho@memphis.edu.
Website: http://www.MSCI.memphis.edu/.

University of Miami, Graduate School, College of Arts and Sciences, Department of Computer Science, Coral Gables, FL 33124. Offers MS, PhD. Part-time programs available. Postbaccalaureate distance learning degree programs offered (no on-campus study). *Degree requirements:* For master's, comprehensive exam (for some programs), thesis. *Entrance requirements:* For master's, GRE. Additional exam requirements/recommendations for international students: Required—TOEFL. Electronic applications accepted. *Faculty research:* Algorithm engineering, automated reasoning, computer graphics, cryptography, security network.

University of Michigan, College of Engineering, Department of Computer Science and Engineering, Ann Arbor, MI 48109. Offers MS, MSE, PhD. *Students:* 284 full-time (44 women), 4 part-time (2 women). 1,451 applicants, 17% accepted, 90 enrolled. In 2014, 70 master's, 19 doctorates awarded. *Faculty research:* Solid state electronics and optics; communications, control, signal process; sensors and integrated circuitry; software systems; artificial intelligence; hardware systems. *Total annual research expenditures:* $22.5 million. *Unit head:* Prof. Marios Papaefthymiou, Interim Chair, 734-764-8504, Fax: 734-763-1503, E-mail: marios@umich.edu. *Application contact:* Dawn Freysinger, Graduate Programs Coordinator, 734-647-1807, Fax: 734-763-1503, E-mail: dawnf@umich.edu.
Website: http://eecs.umich.edu/cse/.

University of Michigan, College of Engineering, Department of Electrical Engineering and Computer Science, Ann Arbor, MI 48109. Offers MS, MSE, PhD. *Students:* 598 full-time (96 women), 9 part-time (2 women). 1,997 applicants, 26% accepted, 241 enrolled. In 2014, 199 master's, 49 doctorates awarded. *Faculty research:* Solid state electronics and optics; communications, control, signal process; sensors and integrated circuitry; software systems; artificial intelligence; hardware systems. *Total annual research expenditures:* $39.3 million. *Unit head:* Prof. Khalil Najafi, Department Chair, 734-647-7010, Fax: 734-647-7009, E-mail: najafi@umich.edu. *Application contact:* Steven

Pejuan, Graduate Coordinator, 734-647-1758, Fax: 734-763-1503, E-mail: spejuan@umich.edu.
Website: http://www.eecs.umich.edu.

University of Michigan–Flint, College of Arts and Sciences, Program in Computer Science and Information Systems, Flint, MI 48502-1950. Offers computer science (MS); information systems (MS). Part-time programs available. *Faculty:* 25 full-time (6 women), 12 part-time/adjunct (8 women). *Students:* 62 full-time (23 women), 160 part-time (27 women); includes 4 minority (1 Black or African American, non-Hispanic/Latino; 1 Asian, non-Hispanic/Latino; 1 Hispanic/Latino; 1 Two or more races, non-Hispanic/Latino), 174 international. Average age 25. 380 applicants, 69% accepted, 134 enrolled. In 2014, 30 master's awarded. *Degree requirements:* For master's, thesis optional. *Entrance requirements:* For master's, minimum undergraduate GPA of 3.0; BS from accredited institution in computer science, computer information systems, or computer engineering (preferred). Additional exam requirements/recommendations for international students: Required—TOEFL (minimum score 84 iBT), IELTS (minimum score 6.5). *Application deadline:* For fall admission, 8/1 for domestic students, 5/1 for international students; for winter admission, 11/15 for domestic students, 9/1 for international students; for spring admission, 3/15 for domestic students, 1/1 for international students. Applications are processed on a rolling basis. Application fee: $55. Electronic applications accepted. *Expenses:* Expenses: Contact institution. *Financial support:* Federal Work-Study, scholarships/grants, and unspecified assistantships available. Support available to part-time students. Financial award application deadline: 3/1; financial award applicants required to submit FAFSA. *Unit head:* Dr. Michael Farmer, Director, 810-762-3131, Fax: 810-766-6780. *Application contact:* Bradley T. Maki, Director of Graduate Admissions, 810-762-3171, Fax: 810-766-6789, E-mail: bmaki@umflint.edu.
Website: http://www.umflint.edu/graduateprograms/computer-science-information-systems-ms.

University of Minnesota, Duluth, Graduate School, Swenson College of Science and Engineering, Department of Computer Science, Duluth, MN 55812-2496. Offers MS. Part-time programs available. *Entrance requirements:* For master's, GRE General Test, minimum GPA of 3.0. Additional exam requirements/recommendations for international students: Required—TOEFL (minimum score 550 paper-based). Electronic applications accepted. *Faculty research:* Information retrieval, artificial intelligence, machine learning, parallel/distributed computing, graphics.

University of Minnesota, Twin Cities Campus, College of Science and Engineering, Department of Computer Science and Engineering, Minneapolis, MN 55455-0213. Offers computer science (MCS, MS, PhD); data science (MS); software engineering (MSSE). Part-time programs available. Terminal master's awarded for partial completion of doctoral program. *Degree requirements:* For doctorate, thesis/dissertation. *Entrance requirements:* For master's and doctorate, GRE General Test. Additional exam requirements/recommendations for international students: Required—TOEFL. Electronic applications accepted. *Faculty research:* Computer architecture, bioinformatics and computational biology, data mining, graphics and visualization, high performance computing, human-computer interaction, networks, software systems, theory, artificial intelligence.

University of Minnesota, Twin Cities Campus, College of Science and Engineering, Scientific Computation Program, Minneapolis, MN 55455-0213. Offers MS, PhD. Part-time programs available. *Degree requirements:* For master's, thesis; for doctorate, thesis/dissertation. *Entrance requirements:* For master's and doctorate, GRE General Test. Additional exam requirements/recommendations for international students: Required—TOEFL (minimum score 550 paper-based; 79 iBT), IELTS (minimum score 6.5). Electronic applications accepted. *Faculty research:* Parallel computations, quantum mechanical dynamics, computational materials science, computational fluid dynamics, computational neuroscience.

University of Missouri, Office of Research and Graduate Studies, College of Engineering, Department of Computer Science, Columbia, MO 65211. Offers MS, PhD. Part-time programs available. *Faculty:* 19 full-time (4 women). *Students:* 64 full-time (14 women), 60 part-time (9 women); includes 1 minority (Asian, non-Hispanic/Latino), 96 international. Average age 27. 143 applicants, 39% accepted, 33 enrolled. In 2014, 17 master's, 4 doctorates awarded. *Degree requirements:* For doctorate, thesis/dissertation. *Entrance requirements:* For master's, GRE General Test, minimum GPA of 3.0; for doctorate, GRE General Test. Additional exam requirements/recommendations for international students: Required—TOEFL (minimum score 577 paper-based; 90 iBT). *Application deadline:* For fall admission, 1/15 priority date for domestic students, 1/15 for international students; for winter admission, 10/1 priority date for domestic students, 10/1 for international students. Applications are processed on a rolling basis. Application fee: $55 ($75 for international students). Electronic applications accepted. *Financial support:* Fellowships, research assistantships, teaching assistantships, institutionally sponsored loans, scholarships/grants, traineeships, health care benefits, and unspecified assistantships available. Support available to part-time students. *Faculty research:* Computational biology and bioinformatics, cybersecurity, distributed computing, geospatial information mining and retrieval, intelligent systems, multimedia communications, large dataset scientific visualization, networking, spoken language processing and human-machine interfaces, wireless sensor networks. *Unit head:* Dr. Dong Xu, Department Chair, 573-882-2299, E-mail: xudong@missouri.edu. *Application contact:* Jodie Lenser, Graduate Academic Advisor, 573-882-7037, E-mail: lenserj@missouri.edu.
Website: http://engineering.missouri.edu/cs/degree-programs/.

University of Missouri–Kansas City, School of Computing and Engineering, Kansas City, MO 64110-2499. Offers civil engineering (MS); computer and electrical engineering (PhD); computer science (MS), including bioinformatics, software engineering, telecommunications networking; computer science and informatics (PhD); computing (PhD); electrical engineering (MS); engineering (PhD); engineering and construction management (Graduate Certificate); mechanical engineering (MS); telecommunications and computer networking (PhD). PhD (interdisciplinary) offered through the School of Graduate Studies. Part-time programs available. *Faculty:* 39 full-time (5 women), 26 part-time/adjunct (3 women). *Students:* 500 full-time (143 women), 136 part-time (28 women); includes 18 minority (5 Black or African American, non-Hispanic/Latino; 8 Asian, non-Hispanic/Latino; 4 Hispanic/Latino; 1 Two or more races, non-Hispanic/Latino), 551 international. Average age 24. 1,924 applicants, 39% accepted, 200 enrolled. In 2014, 124 master's, 1 other advanced degree awarded. *Degree requirements:* For doctorate, thesis/dissertation. *Entrance requirements:* For master's, GRE General Test, minimum GPA of 3.0, 3 letters of recommendation from professors; for doctorate, GRE General Test, minimum GPA of 3.5. Additional exam requirements/recommendations for international students: Required—TOEFL (minimum score 550 paper-based; 80 iBT). *Application deadline:* For fall admission, 1/15 priority date for domestic students, 1/15 for international students. Applications are processed on a rolling basis. Application fee: $45 ($50 for international students). *Financial support:* In 2014–15, 34 research assistantships with partial tuition reimbursements (averaging $15,602 per year), 24 teaching assistantships with partial tuition reimbursements (averaging $15,090 per year) were awarded; career-related internships or fieldwork, Federal Work-Study, scholarships/grants, tuition waivers (partial), and unspecified

assistantships also available. Support available to part-time students. Financial award application deadline: 3/1; financial award applicants required to submit FAFSA. *Faculty research:* Algorithms, bioinformatics and medical informatics, biomechanics/ biomaterials, civil engineering materials, networking and telecommunications, thermal science. *Unit head:* Dr. Kevin Z. Truman, Dean, 816-235-2399, Fax: 816-235-5159. *Application contact:* 816-235-2399, Fax: 816-235-5159.
Website: http://sce.umkc.edu/.

University of Missouri–St. Louis, College of Arts and Sciences, Department of Mathematics and Computer Science, St. Louis, MO 63121. Offers computer science (MS). Part-time and evening/weekend programs available. *Faculty:* 14 full-time (1 woman), 2 part-time/adjunct (0 women). *Students:* 28 full-time (17 women), 42 part-time (13 women); includes 5 minority (1 Black or African American, non-Hispanic/Latino; 3 Asian, non-Hispanic/Latino; 1 Hispanic/Latino), 23 international. Average age 31. 64 applicants, 70% accepted, 15 enrolled. In 2014, 7 master's, 2 doctorates awarded. *Degree requirements:* For master's, thesis optional; for doctorate, thesis/dissertation. *Entrance requirements:* For master's, GRE (for teaching assistantships), 2 letters of recommendation; C programming, C++ or Java (for computer science); for doctorate, GRE General Test, 3 letters of recommendation. Additional exam requirements/ recommendations for international students: Required—TOEFL (minimum score 550 paper-based; 79 iBT), IELTS (minimum score 6.5). *Application deadline:* For fall admission, 7/1 priority date for domestic and international students; for spring admission, 12/1 priority date for domestic and international students. Applications are processed on a rolling basis. Application fee: $50 ($40 for international students). Electronic applications accepted. *Expenses:* Tuition, state resident: full-time $7364; part-time $409.10 per hour. Tuition, nonresident: full-time $18,153; part-time $1008.50 per hour. *Financial support:* In 2014–15, 3 research assistantships with full and partial tuition reimbursements (averaging $13,500 per year), 11 teaching assistantships with full and partial tuition reimbursements (averaging $13,500 per year) were awarded. Financial award applicants required to submit FAFSA. *Faculty research:* Statistics, algebra, analysis. *Unit head:* Dr. Qingtang Jiang, Director of Graduate Studies, 314-516-5741, Fax: 314-516-5400, E-mail: jiangq@umsl.edu. *Application contact:* 314-516-5458, Fax: 314-516-6996, E-mail: gradadm@umsl.edu.

The University of Montana, Graduate School, College of Humanities and Sciences, Department of Computer Science, Missoula, MT 59812-0002. Offers MS. Part-time programs available. *Degree requirements:* For master's, project or thesis. *Entrance requirements:* For master's, GRE General Test. Additional exam requirements/ recommendations for international students: Required—TOEFL (minimum score 525 paper-based). *Faculty research:* Parallel and distributed systems, neural networks, genetic algorithms, machine learning, data visualization, artificial intelligence.

University of Nebraska at Omaha, Graduate Studies, College of Information Science and Technology, Department of Computer Science, Omaha, NE 68182. Offers artificial intelligence (Certificate); communication networks (Certificate); computer science (MA, MS); software engineering (Certificate); systems and architecture (Certificate). Part-time and evening/weekend programs available. *Faculty:* 17 full-time (3 women). *Students:* 58 full-time (18 women), 51 part-time (16 women); includes 6 minority (1 Black or African American, non-Hispanic/Latino; 3 Asian, non-Hispanic/Latino; 1 Hispanic/Latino; 1 Two or more races, non-Hispanic/Latino), 80 international. Average age 26. 196 applicants, 54% accepted, 50 enrolled. In 2014, 24 master's awarded. *Degree requirements:* For master's, comprehensive exam, thesis (for some programs). *Entrance requirements:* For master's, GRE General Test, minimum GPA of 3.0, prior course work in computer science, official transcripts, resume, 2 letters of recommendation; for Certificate, minimum GPA of 3.0, resume. Additional exam requirements/recommendations for international students: Required—TOEFL, IELTS, PTE. *Application deadline:* For fall admission, 7/1 priority date for domestic students; for spring admission, 11/1 priority date for domestic and international students; for summer admission, 3/1 for domestic and international students. Applications are processed on a rolling basis. Application fee: $45. Electronic applications accepted. *Financial support:* In 2014–15, 6 students received support, including 6 research assistantships with tuition reimbursements available; teaching assistantships with tuition reimbursements available, Federal Work-Study, institutionally sponsored loans, scholarships/grants, tuition waivers (full), and unspecified assistantships also available. Support available to part-time students. Financial award application deadline: 3/1; financial award applicants required to submit FAFSA. *Unit head:* Dr. Qiuming Zhu, Chairperson, 402-554-2341, E-mail: graduate@unomaha.edu. *Application contact:* Dr. Jong-Hoon Youn, Graduate Program Chair, 402-554-2341, E-mail: graduate@unomaha.edu.

University of Nebraska–Lincoln, Graduate College, College of Arts and Sciences and College of Engineering, Department of Computer Science and Engineering, Lincoln, NE 68588. Offers bioinformatics (MS, PhD); computer engineering (MS, PhD); computer science (MS, PhD); information technology (PhD). *Degree requirements:* For master's, thesis optional; for doctorate, comprehensive exam, thesis/dissertation. *Entrance requirements:* For master's and doctorate, GRE General Test. Additional exam requirements/recommendations for international students: Required—TOEFL (minimum score 600 paper-based). Electronic applications accepted. *Faculty research:* Software engineering, geo- and bio-informatics, scientific computation, secure communication.

University of Nevada, Las Vegas, Graduate College, Howard R. Hughes College of Engineering, School of Computer Science, Las Vegas, NV 89154-4019. Offers MSCS, PhD. Part-time programs available. *Faculty:* 11 full-time (1 woman). *Students:* 34 full-time (7 women), 18 part-time (4 women); includes 8 minority (2 Black or African American, non-Hispanic/Latino; 1 Asian, non-Hispanic/Latino; 1 Hispanic/Latino; 4 Two or more races, non-Hispanic/Latino), 31 international. Average age 30. 49 applicants, 65% accepted, 22 enrolled. In 2014, 14 master's awarded. *Degree requirements:* For master's, comprehensive exam, thesis optional, project; for doctorate, comprehensive exam, thesis/dissertation. *Entrance requirements:* For master's, GRE General Test; for doctorate, GRE General Test, GRE Subject Test (computer science). Additional exam requirements/recommendations for international students: Required—TOEFL (minimum score 550 paper-based; 80 iBT), IELTS (minimum score 7). *Application deadline:* For fall admission, 6/1 for domestic students, 2/1 for international students; for spring admission, 11/1 for domestic students, 10/1 for international students. Application fee: $60 ($95 for international students). Electronic applications accepted. *Financial support:* In 2014–15, 32 students received support, including 15 research assistantships with partial tuition reimbursements available (averaging $13,270 per year), 17 teaching assistantships with partial tuition reimbursements available (averaging $10,559 per year); institutionally sponsored loans, scholarships/grants, health care benefits, and unspecified assistantships also available. Financial award application deadline: 3/1. *Faculty research:* Algorithms, computer graphics, databases and data mining, distributed systems and networks, parallel algorithms. *Total annual research expenditures:* $206,446. *Unit head:* Dr. Laxmi Gewali, Director/Associate Professor, 702-895-4028, Fax: 702-895-2639, E-mail: laxmi.gewali@unlv.edu. *Application contact:* Graduate College Admissions Evaluator, 702-895-3320, Fax: 702-895-4180, E-mail: gradcollege@unlv.edu.
Website: http://cs.unlv.edu/.

University of Nevada, Reno, Graduate School, College of Engineering, Department of Computer Science and Engineering, Reno, NV 89557. Offers MS, PhD. Terminal master's awarded for partial completion of doctoral program. *Degree requirements:* For master's, thesis optional; for doctorate, thesis/dissertation. *Entrance requirements:* For master's, GRE General Test, minimum GPA of 2.75; for doctorate, GRE General Test, minimum GPA of 3.0. Additional exam requirements/recommendations for international students: Required—TOEFL (minimum score 500 paper-based; 61 iBT), IELTS (minimum score 6). Electronic applications accepted. *Faculty research:* Evolutionary computing systems, computer vision/virtual reality, software engineering.

University of New Brunswick Fredericton, School of Graduate Studies, Faculty of Computer Science, Fredericton, NB E3B 5A3, Canada. Offers M Sc CS, PhD. Part-time programs available. *Faculty:* 27 full-time (8 women), 18 part-time/adjunct (1 woman). *Students:* 120 full-time (27 women), 18 part-time (5 women). In 2014, 27 master's, 2 doctorates awarded. *Degree requirements:* For master's, thesis; for doctorate, comprehensive exam, thesis/dissertation, qualifying exam. *Entrance requirements:* For master's, minimum GPA of 3.0; undergraduate degree with sufficient computer science background; for doctorate, research-based master's degree in computer science or related area. Additional exam requirements/recommendations for international students: Required—TOEFL (minimum score 550 paper-based; 80 iBT), IELTS (minimum score 7), TWE (minimum score 4.5), Michigan English Language Assessment Battery (minimum score 85) or CanTest (minimum score 4.5). *Application deadline:* For fall admission, 8/31 priority date for domestic students; for winter admission, 2/28 priority date for domestic students. Applications are processed on a rolling basis. Application fee: $50 Canadian dollars. Electronic applications accepted. *Financial support:* In 2014–15, 1 fellowship, 94 research assistantships, 40 teaching assistantships were awarded. *Faculty research:* Computer hardware, software engineering, embedded systems, e-business, e-learning, security, artificial intelligence, bioinformatics, computer-assisted drug design, high performance computing, Web services. *Unit head:* Dr. Patricia Evans, Director of Graduate Studies, 506-458-7276, Fax: 506-453-3566, E-mail: pevans@unb.ca. *Application contact:* Jody McDonald, Graduate Secretary, 506-458-7285, Fax: 506-453-3566, E-mail: jody.m@unb.ca.
Website: http://go.unb.ca/gradprograms.

University of New Hampshire, Graduate School, College of Engineering and Physical Sciences, Department of Computer Science, Durham, NH 03824. Offers MS, PhD, Postbaccalaureate Certificate. Part-time and evening/weekend programs available. *Faculty:* 9 full-time (1 woman). *Students:* 36 full-time (13 women), 37 part-time (5 women), 34 international. Average age 28. 88 applicants, 78% accepted, 28 enrolled. In 2014, 6 master's, 2 doctorates, 5 other advanced degrees awarded. *Degree requirements:* For master's, thesis or alternative; for doctorate, thesis/dissertation. *Entrance requirements:* For master's and doctorate, GRE General Test. Additional exam requirements/recommendations for international students: Required—TOEFL (minimum score 550 paper-based; 80 iBT). *Application deadline:* For fall admission, 4/1 priority date for domestic students, 4/1 for international students; for spring admission, 12/1 for domestic students. Applications are processed on a rolling basis. Application fee: $65. Electronic applications accepted. *Expenses:* Tuition, state resident: full-time $13,500; part-time $750 per credit hour. Tuition, nonresident: full-time $26,460; part-time $1110 per credit hour. *Required fees:* $1788; $447 per semester. *Financial support:* In 2014–15, 43 students received support, including 2 fellowships, 12 research assistantships, 12 teaching assistantships; career-related internships or fieldwork, Federal Work-Study, scholarships/grants, and tuition waivers (full and partial) also available. Support available to part-time students. *Faculty research:* Programming languages, compiler design, parallel algorithms, computer graphics, artificial intelligence. *Unit head:* Radim Bartos, Department Chair, 603-862-3792. *Application contact:* Carolyn Kirkpatrick, Administrative Assistant, 603-862-3778, E-mail: office@cs.unh.edu.
Website: http://www.cs.unh.edu/.

University of New Haven, Graduate School, Henry C. Lee College of Criminal Justice and Forensic Sciences, Program in Criminal Justice, West Haven, CT 06516-1916. Offers crime analysis (MS); criminal justice (MS, PhD); criminal justice management (MS, Certificate); forensic computer investigation (MS, Certificate); forensic psychology (MS); information protection and security (Certificate); victim advocacy and services management (Certificate); victimology (MS). Part-time and evening/weekend programs available. Postbaccalaureate distance learning degree programs offered (no on-campus study). *Degree requirements:* For master's, thesis or alternative. *Entrance requirements:* Additional exam requirements/recommendations for international students: Required—TOEFL (minimum score 80 iBT), IELTS, PTE (minimum score 53). Electronic applications accepted. Application fee is waived when completed online.

University of New Haven, Graduate School, Tagliatela College of Engineering, Program in Computer and Information Science, West Haven, CT 06516-1916. Offers computer and information science (MS); computer programming (Certificate); computer systems (MS); database and information systems (MS); network systems (MS); software engineering and development (MS). Part-time and evening/weekend programs available. *Degree requirements:* For master's, thesis or alternative. *Entrance requirements:* Additional exam requirements/recommendations for international students: Required—TOEFL (minimum score 75 iBT), IELTS, PTE (minimum score 50). Electronic applications accepted. Application fee is waived when completed online.

University of New Mexico, Graduate School, School of Engineering, Program in Computer Science, Albuquerque, NM 87131-2039. Offers MS, PhD. Part-time programs available. *Faculty:* 16 full-time (3 women), 3 part-time/adjunct (1 woman). *Students:* 161 full-time (32 women), 35 part-time (6 women); includes 23 minority (2 Black or African American, non-Hispanic/Latino; 2 Asian, non-Hispanic/Latino; 14 Hispanic/Latino; 5 Two or more races, non-Hispanic/Latino), 113 international. Average age 30. 298 applicants, 40% accepted, 85 enrolled. In 2014, 33 master's, 11 doctorates awarded. Terminal master's awarded for partial completion of doctoral program. *Degree requirements:* For master's, thesis or alternative; for doctorate, thesis/dissertation. *Entrance requirements:* For master's and doctorate, GRE General Test, minimum GPA of 3.0. Additional exam requirements/recommendations for international students: Required—TOEFL (minimum score 550 paper-based; 79 iBT), IELTS (minimum score 6.5). *Application deadline:* For fall admission, 1/15 for domestic students, 3/1 for international students; for spring admission, 8/1 for domestic and international students. Applications are processed on a rolling basis. Application fee: $50. Electronic applications accepted. *Financial support:* In 2014–15, 60 students received support, including 3 fellowships with full tuition reimbursements available (averaging $16,020 per year), 45 research assistantships with full tuition reimbursements available (averaging $16,020 per year), 12 teaching assistantships with full tuition reimbursements available (averaging $13,450 per year); career-related internships or fieldwork, scholarships/grants, and health care benefits also available. Financial award application deadline: 1/15; financial award applicants required to submit FAFSA. *Faculty research:* Artificial life, genetic algorithms, computer security, complexity theory, interactive computer graphics, operating systems and networking, biology and computation, machine learning, automated reasoning, quantum computation. *Total annual research expenditures:* $3.7 million. *Unit head:* Dr. Michalis Faloutsos, Chairperson, 505-277-3112, Fax: 505-277-6927, E-mail: michalis@cs.unm.edu. *Application contact:* Lynne Jacobsen, Coordinator, Program Advisement, 505-277-3112, Fax: 505-277-6927, E-mail: ljake@cs.unm.edu.
Website: http://www.cs.unm.edu/.

University of New Orleans, Graduate School, College of Sciences, Department of Computer Science, New Orleans, LA 70148. Offers MS. *Entrance requirements:* For master's, GRE General Test. Additional exam requirements/recommendations for international students: Required—TOEFL (minimum score 550 paper-based; 79 iBT), IELTS (minimum score 6.5). Electronic applications accepted.

The University of North Carolina at Chapel Hill, Graduate School, College of Arts and Sciences, Department of Computer Science, Chapel Hill, NC 27599. Offers MS, PhD. Part-time programs available. Postbaccalaureate distance learning degree programs offered. Terminal master's awarded for partial completion of doctoral program. *Degree requirements:* For master's, comprehensive exam, thesis or alternative, programming product; for doctorate, comprehensive exam, thesis/dissertation, programming product, teaching requirement. *Entrance requirements:* For master's and doctorate, GRE General Test, minimum GPA of 3.0. Additional exam requirements/recommendations for international students: Required—TOEFL (minimum score 575 paper-based). Electronic applications accepted. *Faculty research:* Bioinformatics, graphics, hardware, systems, theory.

The University of North Carolina at Charlotte, College of Computing and Informatics, Department of Computer Science, Charlotte, NC 28223-0001. Offers advanced databases and knowledge discovery (Graduate Certificate); computer science (MS); game design and development (Graduate Certificate). Part-time and evening/weekend programs available. *Faculty:* 27 full-time (5 women), 5 part-time/adjunct (3 women). *Students:* 197 full-time (50 women), 48 part-time (14 women); includes 6 minority (2 Asian, non-Hispanic/Latino; 3 Hispanic/Latino; 1 Two or more races, non-Hispanic/Latino), 220 international. Average age 24. 1,113 applicants, 33% accepted, 104 enrolled. In 2014, 118 master's awarded. *Degree requirements:* For master's, thesis optional. *Entrance requirements:* For master's, GRE General Test, minimum GPA of 3.0 during previous 2 years, 2.8 overall. Additional exam requirements/recommendations for international students: Required—TOEFL (minimum score 557 paper-based; 83 iBT). *Application deadline:* For fall admission, 5/1 for domestic and international students; for spring admission, 10/1 for domestic and international students. Applications are processed on a rolling basis. Application fee: $75. Electronic applications accepted. *Expenses:* Tuition, state resident: full-time $4008. Tuition, nonresident: full-time $16,295. *Required fees:* $2755. Tuition and fees vary according to course load and program. *Financial support:* In 2014–15, 45 students received support, including 2 fellowships (averaging $30,438 per year), 22 research assistantships (averaging $9,562 per year), 21 teaching assistantships (averaging $6,300 per year); career-related internships or fieldwork, Federal Work-Study, institutionally sponsored loans, scholarships/grants, and unspecified assistantships also available. Support available to part-time students. Financial award application deadline: 4/1; financial award applicants required to submit FAFSA. *Faculty research:* Visualization; visual analytics and computer graphics; intelligent and interactive systems; data mining theory, systems, and application; networked systems; computer game design. *Total annual research expenditures:* $2.4 million. *Unit head:* William Ribarsky, Chair, 704-687-8559, Fax: 704-687-3516, E-mail: ribarsky@uncc.edu. *Application contact:* Kathy B. Giddings, Director of Graduate Admissions, 704-687-3366, Fax: 704-687-3279, E-mail: gradadm@uncc.edu.
Website: http://cs.uncc.edu/.

The University of North Carolina at Greensboro, Graduate School, College of Arts and Sciences, Department of Computer Science, Greensboro, NC 27412-5001. Offers MS.

The University of North Carolina Wilmington, Interdisciplinary Program in Computer Science and Information Systems, Wilmington, NC 28403-3297. Offers MS. *Faculty:* 12 full-time (2 women). *Students:* 15 full-time (4 women), 13 part-time (2 women); includes 6 minority (3 Black or African American, non-Hispanic/Latino; 1 Asian, non-Hispanic/Latino; 2 Two or more races, non-Hispanic/Latino), 2 international. 15 applicants, 53% accepted, 7 enrolled. In 2014, 18 master's awarded. *Entrance requirements:* For master's, GMAT or GRE, 3 letters of recommendation, resume. *Application deadline:* For fall admission, 6/1 for domestic students; for spring admission, 11/1 for domestic students. Application fee: $60. *Expenses:* Tuition, state resident: full-time $3240. Tuition, nonresident: full-time $9208. *Required fees:* $1967. *Financial support:* Applicants required to submit FAFSA. *Unit head:* Dr. Laurie Patterson, Director, 910-962-3906, E-mail: pattersonl@uncw.edu. *Application contact:* Karen Barnhill, Graduate Coordinator, 910-962-3903, Fax: 910-962-7457, E-mail: barnhillk@uncw.edu.
Website: http://csb.uncw.edu/mscsis/.

University of North Dakota, Graduate School, John D. Odegard School of Aerospace Sciences, Department of Computer Science, Grand Forks, ND 58202. Offers MS, PhD. Part-time programs available. *Degree requirements:* For master's, comprehensive exam, thesis or alternative. *Entrance requirements:* For master's, GRE General Test, minimum GPA of 3.0. Additional exam requirements/recommendations for international students: Required—TOEFL (minimum score 550 paper-based; 79 iBT), IELTS (minimum score 6.5). Electronic applications accepted. *Faculty research:* Operating systems, simulation, parallel computation, hypermedia, graph theory.

University of Northern British Columbia, Office of Graduate Studies, Prince George, BC V2N 4Z9, Canada. Offers business administration (Diploma); community health science (M Sc); disability management (MA); education (M Ed); first nations studies (MA); gender studies (MA); history (MA); interdisciplinary studies (MA); international studies (MA); mathematical, computer and physical sciences (M Sc); natural resources and environmental studies (M Sc, MA, MNRES, PhD); political science (MA); psychology (M Sc, PhD); social work (MSW). Part-time and evening/weekend programs available. Postbaccalaureate distance learning degree programs offered (no on-campus study). *Degree requirements:* For master's, thesis; for doctorate, thesis/dissertation. *Entrance requirements:* For master's, GRE, minimum B average in undergraduate course work; for doctorate, candidacy exam, minimum A average in graduate course work.

University of North Florida, College of Computing, Engineering, and Construction, School of Computing, Jacksonville, FL 32224. Offers computer science (MS); information systems (MS); software engineering (MS). Part-time programs available. *Faculty:* 13 full-time (2 women). *Students:* 27 full-time (12 women), 48 part-time (13 women); includes 17 minority (5 Black or African American, non-Hispanic/Latino; 8 Asian, non-Hispanic/Latino; 2 Hispanic/Latino; 2 Two or more races, non-Hispanic/Latino), 18 international. Average age 30. 73 applicants, 37% accepted, 17 enrolled. In 2014, 6 master's awarded. *Degree requirements:* For master's, thesis. *Entrance requirements:* For master's, GRE General Test, minimum GPA of 3.0 in last 60 hours of course work. Additional exam requirements/recommendations for international students: Required—TOEFL (minimum score 500 paper-based; 61 iBT). *Application deadline:* For fall admission, 7/1 for domestic students, 5/1 for international students; for spring admission, 11/1 for domestic students, 10/1 for international students. Application fee: $30. Electronic applications accepted. *Expenses:* Tuition, state resident: full-time $9794; part-time $408.10 per credit hour. Tuition, nonresident: full-time $22,383; part-time $932.61 per credit hour. *Required fees:* $2047; $85.29 per credit hour. Tuition and fees vary according to course load and program. *Financial support:* In 2014–15, 11 students received support, including 4 research assistantships (averaging $1,238 per

year); teaching assistantships, Federal Work-Study, scholarships/grants, and unspecified assistantships also available. Financial award application deadline: 4/1; financial award applicants required to submit FAFSA. *Total annual research expenditures:* $94,179. *Unit head:* Dr. Asai Asaithambi, Dean, 904-620-2985, E-mail: asai.asaithambi@unf.edu. *Application contact:* Dr. Amanda Pascale, Director, The Graduate School, 904-620-1360, Fax: 904-620-1362, E-mail: graduateschool@unf.edu. Website: http://www.unf.edu/ccec/computing/.

University of North Texas, Robert B. Toulouse School of Graduate Studies, Denton, TX 76203-5459. Offers accounting (MS); applied anthropology (MA, MS); applied behavior analysis (Certificate); applied geography (MA); applied technology and performance improvement (M Ed, MS); art education (MA); art history (MA); art museum education (Certificate); arts leadership (Certificate); audiology (Au D); behavior analysis (MS); behavioral science (PhD); biochemistry and molecular biology (MS); biology (MA, MS); biomedical engineering (MS); business analysis (MS); chemistry (MS); clinical health psychology (PhD); communication studies (MA, MS); computer engineering (MS); computer science (MS); counseling (M Ed, MS), including clinical mental health counseling (MS), college and university counseling, elementary school counseling, secondary school counseling; creative writing (MA); criminal justice (MS); curriculum and instruction (M Ed); decision sciences (MBA); design (MA, MFA), including fashion design (MFA), innovation studies, interior design (MFA); early childhood studies (MS); economics (MS); educational leadership (M Ed, Ed D); educational psychology (MS, PhD), including family studies (MS), gifted and talented (MS), human development (MS), learning and cognition (MS), research, measurement and evaluation (MS); electrical engineering (MS); emergency management (MPA); engineering technology (MS); English (MA); English as a second language (MA); environmental science (MS); finance (MBA, MS); financial management (MPA); French (MA); health services management (MBA); higher education (M Ed, Ed D); history (MA, MS); hospitality management (MS); human resources management (MPA); information science (MS); information systems (PhD); information technologies (MBA); interdisciplinary studies (MA, MS); international studies (MA); international sustainable tourism (MS); jazz studies (MM); journalism (MA, MJ, Graduate Certificate), including interactive and virtual digital communication (Graduate Certificate), narrative journalism (Graduate Certificate), public relations (Graduate Certificate); kinesiology (MS); linguistics (MA); local government management (MPA); logistics (PhD); logistics and supply chain management (MBA); long-term care, senior housing, and aging services (MA); management (PhD); marketing (MBA); mathematics (MA, MS); mechanical and energy engineering (MS, PhD); music (MA), including ethnomusicology, music theory, musicology, performance; music composition (PhD); music education (MM Ed, PhD); nonprofit management (MPA); operations and supply chain management (MBA); performance (MM, DMA); philosophy (MA); political science (MA); professional and technical communication (MA); radio, television and film (MA, MFA); rehabilitation counseling (Certificate); sociology (MA); Spanish (MA); special education (M Ed); speech-language pathology (MA); strategic management (MBA); studio art (MFA); teaching (M Ed); MBA/MS. Part-time and evening/weekend programs available. Postbaccalaureate distance learning degree programs offered. *Faculty:* 651 full-time (215 women), 233 part-time/adjunct (139 women). *Students:* 3,040 full-time (1,598 women), 3,401 part-time (2,097 women); includes 1,740 minority (533 Black or African American, non-Hispanic/Latino; 15 American Indian or Alaska Native, non-Hispanic/Latino; 286 Asian, non-Hispanic/Latino; 746 Hispanic/Latino; 3 Native Hawaiian or other Pacific Islander, non-Hispanic/Latino; 157 Two or more races, non-Hispanic/Latino), 1,145 international. Terminal master's awarded for partial completion of doctoral program. *Degree requirements:* For master's, variable foreign language requirement, comprehensive exam (for some programs), thesis (for some programs); for doctorate, variable foreign language requirement, comprehensive exam (for some programs), thesis/dissertation; for other advanced degree, variable foreign language requirement, comprehensive exam (for some programs). *Entrance requirements:* For master's and doctorate, GRE, GMAT. Additional exam requirements/recommendations for international students: Required—TOEFL (minimum score 550 paper-based; 79 iBT). *Application deadline:* For fall admission, 7/15 for domestic students, 3/15 for international students; for spring admission, 11/15 for domestic students, 9/15 for international students; for summer admission, 5/1 for domestic students. Applications are processed on a rolling basis. Application fee: $60. Electronic applications accepted. *Expenses:* Tuition, state resident: full-time $5450; part-time $3633 per year. Tuition, nonresident: full-time $11,966; part-time $7977 per year. *Required fees:* $1301; $398 per credit hour. $685 per semester. Tuition and fees vary according to program and reciprocity agreements. *Financial support:* Fellowships with partial tuition reimbursements, research assistantships with partial tuition reimbursements, teaching assistantships, career-related internships or fieldwork, Federal Work-Study, institutionally sponsored loans, scholarships/grants, health care benefits, and library assistantships available. Support available to part-time students. Financial award applicants required to submit FAFSA. *Unit head:* Mark Wardell, Dean, 940-565-2383, E-mail: mark.wardell@unt.edu. *Application contact:* Toulouse School of Graduate Studies, 940-565-2383, Fax: 940-565-2141, E-mail: gradsch@unt.edu. Website: http://tsgs.unt.edu/.

University of Notre Dame, Graduate School, College of Engineering, Department of Computer Science and Engineering, Notre Dame, IN 46556. Offers MSCSE, PhD. Terminal master's awarded for partial completion of doctoral program. *Degree requirements:* For master's, comprehensive exam; for doctorate, thesis/dissertation, candidacy exam. *Entrance requirements:* For master's and doctorate, GRE General Test. Additional exam requirements/recommendations for international students: Required—TOEFL (minimum score 600 paper-based; 80 iBT). Electronic applications accepted. *Faculty research:* Algorithms and theory of computer science, artificial intelligence, behavior-based robotics, biometrics, computer vision.

University of Oklahoma, Gallogly College of Engineering, School of Computer Science, Norman, OK 73019. Offers MS, PhD. Part-time programs available. *Faculty:* 17 full-time (3 women). *Students:* 68 full-time (11 women), 25 part-time (8 women); includes 5 minority (2 American Indian or Alaska Native, non-Hispanic/Latino; 1 Asian, non-Hispanic/Latino; 1 Hispanic/Latino; 1 Two or more races, non-Hispanic/Latino), 64 international. Average age 26. 131 applicants, 40% accepted, 26 enrolled. In 2014, 23 master's, 5 doctorates awarded. Terminal master's awarded for partial completion of doctoral program. *Degree requirements:* For master's, comprehensive exam (for some programs), thesis optional, 5 seminars; exit exam (for some programs); for doctorate, comprehensive exam, thesis/dissertation, 5 seminars. *Entrance requirements:* For master's and doctorate, GRE, bachelor's degree, resume, statement of purpose, 3 letters of recommendation, transcripts. Additional exam requirements/recommendations for international students: Required—TOEFL (minimum score 79 iBT). *Application deadline:* For fall admission, 4/1 for domestic students, 3/1 for international students; for spring admission, 10/1 for domestic students, 9/1 for international students. Application fee: $50 ($100 for international students). Electronic applications accepted. *Expenses:* Tuition, state resident: full-time $4394; part-time $183.10 per credit hour. Tuition, nonresident: full-time $16,970; part-time $707.10 per credit hour. *Required fees:* $2892; $109.95 per credit hour. $126.50 per semester. *Financial support:* In 2014–15, 62 students received support, including 13 research assistantships with partial tuition reimbursements available (averaging $13,251 per year), 16 teaching assistantships with partial tuition reimbursements available (averaging $14,550 per year); Federal Work-

Study, scholarships/grants, health care benefits, tuition waivers, and unspecified assistantships also available. Support available to part-time students. Financial award application deadline: 6/1; financial award applicants required to submit FAFSA. *Faculty research:* Algorithms and theory, computational science, data mining, robotics, wireless and mobile networks, computer security. *Total annual research expenditures:* $1.7 million. *Unit head:* Dr. Sridhar Radhakrishnan, Professor and Director, 405-325-3078, Fax: 405-325-4044, E-mail: sridhar@ou.edu. *Application contact:* Virginie Perez Woods, Academic Programs Coordinator, 405-325-0145, Fax: 405-325-4044, E-mail: vpw@ou.edu.
Website: http://cs.ou.edu/.

University of Oregon, Graduate School, College of Arts and Sciences, Department of Computer and Information Science, Eugene, OR 97403. Offers MA, MS, PhD. Part-time programs available. Terminal master's awarded for partial completion of doctoral program. *Degree requirements:* For doctorate, thesis/dissertation. *Entrance requirements:* For master's and doctorate, GRE General Test, minimum GPA of 3.0. Additional exam requirements/recommendations for international students: Required—TOEFL. *Faculty research:* Artificial intelligence, graphics, natural-language processing, expert systems, operating systems.

University of Ottawa, Faculty of Graduate and Postdoctoral Studies, Faculty of Engineering, Ottawa-Carleton Institute for Computer Science, Ottawa, ON K1N 6N5, Canada. Offers MCS, PhD. MCS, PhD offered jointly with Carleton University. *Degree requirements:* For master's, thesis or alternative; for doctorate, comprehensive exam, thesis/dissertation, two seminars. *Entrance requirements:* For master's, honors degree or equivalent, minimum B average; for doctorate, minimum B+ average. Electronic applications accepted. *Faculty research:* Knowledge-based and intelligent systems, algorithms, parallel and distributed systems.

University of Pennsylvania, School of Engineering and Applied Science, Department of Computer and Information Science, Philadelphia, PA 19104. Offers MCIT, MSE, PhD. Part-time programs available. *Faculty:* 54 full-time (6 women), 6 part-time/adjunct (1 woman). *Students:* 287 full-time (74 women), 77 part-time (27 women); includes 42 minority (5 Black or African American, non-Hispanic/Latino; 28 Asian, non-Hispanic/Latino; 6 Hispanic/Latino; 3 Two or more races, non-Hispanic/Latino), 223 international. 1,831 applicants, 16% accepted, 156 enrolled. In 2014, 178 master's, 15 doctorates awarded. Terminal master's awarded for partial completion of doctoral program. *Degree requirements:* For master's, thesis optional; for doctorate, thesis/dissertation. *Entrance requirements:* For master's and doctorate, GRE General Test. Additional exam requirements/recommendations for international students: Required—TOEFL. *Application deadline:* For fall admission, 6/1 priority date for domestic students, 5/1 priority date for international students. Applications are processed on a rolling basis. Application fee: $70. Electronic applications accepted. *Financial support:* Fellowships with full tuition reimbursements, research assistantships with full tuition reimbursements, teaching assistantships, institutionally sponsored loans, scholarships/grants, traineeships, health care benefits, and unspecified assistantships available. *Faculty research:* Artificial intelligence, computer systems graphics, information management, robotics, software systems theory. *Unit head:* Eduardo D. Glandt, Dean, 215-898-7244, E-mail: seasdean@seas.upenn.edu. *Application contact:* School of Engineering and Applied Science Graduate Admissions, 215-898-4542, E-mail: gradstudies@seas.upenn.edu.
Website: http://www.seas.upenn.edu.

University of Pittsburgh, Dietrich School of Arts and Sciences, Department of Computer Science, Pittsburgh, PA 15260. Offers MS, PhD. Part-time programs available. *Faculty:* 21 full-time (4 women). *Students:* 98 full-time (19 women), 5 part-time (1 woman); includes 23 minority (1 Black or African American, non-Hispanic/Latino; 21 Asian, non-Hispanic/Latino; 1 Hispanic/Latino), 50 international. Average age 27. 385 applicants, 16% accepted, 31 enrolled. In 2014, 12 master's, 7 doctorates awarded. Terminal master's awarded for partial completion of doctoral program. *Degree requirements:* For master's, thesis or alternative; for doctorate, comprehensive exam, thesis/dissertation, preliminary exams. *Entrance requirements:* For master's and doctorate, GRE General Test. Additional exam requirements/recommendations for international students: Required—TOEFL or IELTS. *Application deadline:* For fall admission, 1/15 for domestic and international students; for winter admission, 9/15 for domestic and international students. Applications are processed on a rolling basis. Application fee: $50. Electronic applications accepted. *Expenses:* Tuition, state resident: full-time $20,742; part-time $838 per credit. Tuition, nonresident: full-time $33,960; part-time $1389 per credit. *Required fees:* $800; $205 per term. Tuition and fees vary according to program. *Financial support:* In 2014–15, 57 students received support, including 5 fellowships with full tuition reimbursements available (averaging $21,262 per year), 23 research assistantships with full tuition reimbursements available (averaging $18,400 per year), 29 teaching assistantships with full tuition reimbursements available (averaging $17,130 per year); career-related internships or fieldwork, Federal Work-Study, scholarships/grants, health care benefits, and tuition waivers (partial) also available. Financial award application deadline: 1/15. *Faculty research:* Algorithms and theory, artificial intelligence, parallel and distributed systems, software systems and interfaces. *Unit head:* Dr. Daniel Mosse, Chairman, 412-624-8493, Fax: 412-624-8854, E-mail: mosse@cs.pitt.edu. *Application contact:* Keena M. Walker, Graduate Administrator, 412-624-8495, Fax: 412-624-8854, E-mail: keena@cs.pitt.edu.
Website: http://www.cs.pitt.edu/.

University of Pittsburgh, Dietrich School of Arts and Sciences, Program in Computational Modeling and Simulation, Pittsburgh, PA 15260. Offers bioengineering (PhD); biological science (PhD); civil and environmental engineering (PhD); computer science (PhD); economics (PhD); industrial engineering (PhD); mathematics (PhD); mechanical engineering and materials science (PhD); physics and astronomy (PhD); psychology (PhD); statistics (PhD). Part-time programs available. *Faculty:* 4 full-time (0 women). *Students:* 5 full-time (2 women), 1 part-time (0 women), 5 international. Average age 22. 14 applicants, 14% accepted, 2 enrolled. *Degree requirements:* For doctorate, comprehensive exam, thesis/dissertation, preliminary exam. *Entrance requirements:* For doctorate, GRE, statement of purpose, transcripts for all college-level institutions attended, three letters of reference. Additional exam requirements/recommendations for international students: Required—TOEFL (minimum score 90 iBT), IELTS (minimum score 7). *Application deadline:* For fall admission, 2/21 for domestic and international students. Applications are processed on a rolling basis. Application fee: $0 ($50 for international students). Electronic applications accepted. *Expenses:* Tuition, state resident: full-time $20,742; part-time $838 per credit. Tuition, nonresident: full-time $33,960; part-time $1389 per credit. *Required fees:* $800; $205 per term. Tuition and fees vary according to program. *Financial support:* In 2014–15, 5 students received support, including 3 fellowships with tuition reimbursements available (averaging $25,500 per year), 2 research assistantships with tuition reimbursements available (averaging $26,000 per year). *Unit head:* Kathleen Blee, Associate Dean, Graduate Studies and Research, 412-624-3939, Fax: 412-624-6855. *Application contact:* Dave R. Carmen, Administrative Secretary, 412-624-6094, Fax: 412-624-6855, E-mail: drc41@pitt.edu.
Website: http://cmsp.pitt.edu/.

University of Portland, School of Engineering, Portland, OR 97203-5798. Offers biomedical engineering (MBME); civil engineering (ME); computer science (ME); electrical engineering (ME); mechanical engineering (ME). Part-time and evening/weekend programs available. *Faculty:* 10 full-time (2 women), 1 part-time/adjunct (0 women). *Students:* 4 full-time (1 woman), 2 part-time (0 women); includes 1 minority (Two or more races, non-Hispanic/Latino), 1 international. Average age 27. In 2014, 2 master's awarded. *Degree requirements:* For master's, thesis optional. *Entrance requirements:* For master's, GRE General Test, minimum GPA of 3.0, 3 letters of recommendation, resume, statement of goals, official transcripts. Additional exam requirements/recommendations for international students: Required—TOEFL (minimum score 550 paper-based; 80 iBT), IELTS (minimum score 7). *Application deadline:* For fall admission, 7/15 priority date for domestic and international students; for spring admission, 12/15 priority date for domestic and international students. Applications are processed on a rolling basis. Application fee: $50. *Expenses:* Expenses: Contact institution. *Financial support:* Career-related internships or fieldwork, Federal Work-Study, and scholarships/grants available. Support available to part-time students. Financial award application deadline: 3/1; financial award applicants required to submit FAFSA. *Unit head:* Dr. Sharon Jones, Dean, 503-943-8169, E-mail: joness@up.edu. *Application contact:* Allison Able, Graduate Program Coordinator, 503-943-7107, Fax: 503-943-7315, E-mail: able@up.edu.
Website: http://engineering.up.edu/default.aspx?cid-6464&pid-2432.

University of Puerto Rico, Mayagüez Campus, Graduate Studies, College of Engineering, Department of Electrical and Computer Engineering, Mayagüez, PR 00681-9000. Offers computer engineering (ME, MS); computing and information sciences and engineering (PhD); electrical engineering (ME, MS). Part-time programs available. *Faculty:* 43 full-time (5 women). *Students:* 70 full-time (8 women), 7 part-time (0 women). 36 applicants, 83% accepted, 18 enrolled. In 2014, 13 master's awarded. *Degree requirements:* For master's, comprehensive exam, thesis; for doctorate, comprehensive exam, thesis/dissertation. *Entrance requirements:* For master's, proficiency in English and Spanish, BS in electrical or computer engineering or equivalent, minimum GPA of 3.0; for doctorate, GRE. *Application deadline:* For fall admission, 2/15 for domestic and international students; for spring admission, 9/15 for domestic and international students. Applications are processed on a rolling basis. Application fee: $25. *Expenses: Tuition, area resident:* Full-time $2466; part-time $822 per credit. *International tuition:* $6371 full-time. *Required fees:* $1095; $1095 per year. Tuition and fees vary according to course level, course load and reciprocity agreements. *Financial support:* In 2014–15, 54 students received support, including 32 research assistantships (averaging $7,499 per year), 32 teaching assistantships (averaging $7,614 per year); fellowships with full tuition reimbursements available, Federal Work-Study, institutionally sponsored loans, and unspecified assistantships also available. *Faculty research:* Microcomputer interfacing, control systems, power systems, electronics. *Unit head:* Dr. Pedro Rivera, Chairperson, 787-832-4040 Ext. 3821, E-mail: p.rivera@upr.edu. *Application contact:* Sandra Montalvo, Administrative Staff, 787-832-4040 Ext. 3094, Fax: 787-831-7564, E-mail: sandra@ece.uprm.edu.
Website: http://www.ece.uprm.edu.

University of Regina, Faculty of Graduate Studies and Research, Faculty of Science, Department of Computer Science, Regina, SK S4S 0A2, Canada. Offers M Sc, PhD. Part-time programs available. *Faculty:* 15 full-time (3 women), 10 part-time/adjunct (0 women). *Students:* 71 full-time (16 women), 5 part-time (3 women). 163 applicants, 23% accepted. In 2014, 10 master's, 4 doctorates awarded. *Degree requirements:* For master's, thesis (for some programs), project, report; for doctorate, thesis/dissertation. *Entrance requirements:* Additional exam requirements/recommendations for international students: Required—TOEFL (minimum score 580 paper-based; 80 iBT), IELTS (minimum score 6.5), PTE (minimum score 59). *Application deadline:* For fall admission, 3/31 for domestic and international students; for winter admission, 7/31 for domestic and international students; for spring admission, 11/30 for domestic and international students. Application fee: $100. Electronic applications accepted. *Expenses: Tuition, area resident:* Full-time $4900 Canadian dollars; part-time $837.65 Canadian dollars per semester. *International tuition:* $7900 Canadian dollars full-time. *Required fees:* $396 Canadian dollars; $86.90 Canadian dollars per semester. *Financial support:* In 2014–15, 7 fellowships (averaging $6,429 per year), 8 teaching assistantships (averaging $2,501 per year) were awarded; research assistantships, career-related internships or fieldwork, and scholarships/grants also available. Financial award application deadline: 6/15. *Faculty research:* Information retrieval, machine learning, computer visualization, theory and application of rough sets, human-computer interaction. *Unit head:* Dr. Howard Hamilton, Head, 306-585-4079, Fax: 306-585-4745, E-mail: hamilton@cs.uregina.ca. *Application contact:* Dr. Orland Hoeber, Graduate Program Coordinator, 306-585-4598, Fax: 306-585-4745, E-mail: orland.hoeber@uregina.ca.
Website: http://www.cs.uregina.ca.

University of Rhode Island, Graduate School, College of Arts and Sciences, Department of Computer Science and Statistics, Kingston, RI 02881. Offers applied mathematics (PhD), including computer science, statistics; computer science (MS, PhD); digital forensics (Graduate Certificate); statistics (MS). Part-time programs available. *Faculty:* 12 full-time (6 women). *Students:* 30 full-time (10 women), 49 part-time (8 women); includes 15 minority (5 Black or African American, non-Hispanic/Latino; 1 American Indian or Alaska Native, non-Hispanic/Latino; 7 Asian, non-Hispanic/Latino; 2 Hispanic/Latino), 16 international. In 2014, 5 master's, 3 doctorates awarded. *Degree requirements:* For master's, comprehensive exam (for some programs), thesis optional; for doctorate, comprehensive exam, thesis/dissertation. *Entrance requirements:* For master's and doctorate, GRE, 2 letters of recommendation. Additional exam requirements/recommendations for international students: Required—TOEFL (minimum score 550 paper-based). *Application deadline:* For fall admission, 7/15 for domestic students, 2/1 for international students; for spring admission, 11/15 for domestic students, 7/15 for international students. Application fee: $65. Electronic applications accepted. *Expenses:* Tuition, state resident: full-time $11,532; part-time $641 per credit. Tuition, nonresident: full-time $23,606; part-time $1311 per credit. *Required fees:* $1442; $39 per credit. $35 per semester. One-time fee: $155. *Financial support:* In 2014–15, 4 research assistantships with full and partial tuition reimbursements (averaging $14,430 per year), 12 teaching assistantships with full and partial tuition reimbursements (averaging $15,298 per year) were awarded. Financial award application deadline: 2/1; financial award applicants required to submit FAFSA. *Faculty research:* Bioinformatics, computer and digital forensics, behavioral model of pedestrian dynamics, real-time distributed object computing, cryptography. *Total annual research expenditures:* $371,046. *Unit head:* Dr. Joan Peckham, Chair, 401-874-2701, Fax: 401-874-4617, E-mail: joan@cs.uri.edu. *Application contact:* E-mail: grad-inquiries@cs.uri.edu.
Website: http://www.cs.uri.edu/.

University of Rochester, Hajim School of Engineering and Applied Sciences, Department of Computer Science, Rochester, NY 14627. Offers MS, PhD. *Faculty:* 19 full-time (1 woman). *Students:* 64 full-time (12 women), 4 part-time (0 women); includes 3 minority (2 Asian, non-Hispanic/Latino; 1 Hispanic/Latino), 44 international. 400 applicants, 10% accepted, 20 enrolled. In 2014, 13 master's, 13 doctorates awarded.

Entrance requirements: Additional exam requirements/recommendations for international students: Required—TOEFL. *Application deadline:* For fall admission, 1/15 for domestic students. Application fee: $60. Electronic applications accepted. *Expenses: Tuition:* Full-time $46,150; part-time $1442 per credit hour. *Required fees:* $504. *Faculty research:* Artificial intelligence, human-computer interaction, systems research, theory research. *Unit head:* Henry Kautz, Chair, 585-275-3772. *Application contact:* JoMarie Carpenter, Graduate Coordinator, 585-275-7737.
Website: http://www.cs.rochester.edu/.

University of Rochester, Hajim School of Engineering and Applied Sciences, Master of Science in Technical Entrepreneurship and Management Program, Rochester, NY 14642. Offers biomedical engineering (MS); chemical engineering (MS); computer science (MS); electrical and computer engineering (MS); energy and the environment (MS); materials science (MS); mechanical engineering (MS); optics (MS). Program offered in collaboration with the Simon School of Business. Part-time programs available. *Students:* 36 full-time (12 women), 7 part-time (1 woman); includes 3 minority (2 Hispanic/Latino; 1 Two or more races, non-Hispanic/Latino), 33 international. Average age 24. 152 applicants, 68% accepted, 27 enrolled. In 2014, 28 master's awarded. *Degree requirements:* For master's, comprehensive exam. *Entrance requirements:* For master's, GRE or GMAT, 3 letters of recommendation; personal statement; official transcript; bachelor's degree (or equivalent for international students) in engineering, science, or mathematics. Additional exam requirements/ recommendations for international students: Required—TOEFL or IELTS. *Application deadline:* For fall admission, 2/1 for domestic and international students. Applications are processed on a rolling basis. Application fee: $60. Electronic applications accepted. *Expenses: Tuition:* Full-time $46,150; part-time $1442 per credit hour. *Required fees:* $504. *Financial support:* Career-related internships or fieldwork and scholarships/grants available. Financial award application deadline: 2/1. *Faculty research:* High efficiency solar cells, macromolecular self-assembly, digital signal processing, memory hierarchy management, molecular and physical mechanisms in cell migration, optical imaging systems. *Unit head:* Duncan T. Moore, Vice Provost for Entrepreneurship, 585-275-5248, Fax: 585-473-6745, E-mail: moore@optics.rochester.edu. *Application contact:* Andrea M. Galati, Executive Director, 585-276-3407, Fax: 585-276-2357, E-mail: andrea.galati@rochester.edu.
Website: http://www.rochester.edu/team.

University of San Francisco, College of Arts and Sciences, Computer Science Program, San Francisco, CA 94117-1080. Offers MS. Part-time programs available. *Faculty:* 8 full-time (4 women). *Students:* 55 full-time (13 women), 10 part-time (4 women); includes 2 minority (1 Asian, non-Hispanic/Latino; 1 Hispanic/Latino), 54 international. Average age 26. 196 applicants, 28% accepted, 25 enrolled. In 2014, 19 master's awarded. *Degree requirements:* For master's, thesis optional. *Entrance requirements:* For master's, GRE General Test, GRE Subject Test, BS in computer science or related field. Additional exam requirements/recommendations for international students: Required—TOEFL. *Application deadline:* For fall admission, 3/1 for domestic students; for spring admission, 10/15 for domestic students. Applications are processed on a rolling basis. Application fee: $55 ($65 for international students). *Expenses: Tuition:* Full-time $21,762; part-time $1209 per credit hour. Tuition and fees vary according to degree level, campus/location and program. *Financial support:* In 2014–15, 17 students received support. Fellowships, teaching assistantships, career-related internships or fieldwork, and Federal Work-Study available. Financial award application deadline: 3/2; financial award applicants required to submit FAFSA. *Faculty research:* Software engineering, computer graphics, computer networks. *Unit head:* Dr. Sophie Engle, Chairman, 415-422-6530. *Application contact:* Mark Landerghini, Graduate Adviser, 415-422-5101, E-mail: asgraduate@usfca.edu.
Website: http://www.usfca.edu/artsci/csg/.

University of Saskatchewan, College of Graduate Studies and Research, College of Arts and Science, Department of Computer Science, Saskatoon, SK S7N 5A2, Canada. Offers M Sc, PhD. *Degree requirements:* For master's, thesis; for doctorate, comprehensive exam (for some programs), thesis/dissertation. *Entrance requirements:* For master's and doctorate, GRE. Additional exam requirements/recommendations for international students: Required—TOEFL (minimum score 80 iBT); Recommended—IELTS (minimum score 6.5). Electronic applications accepted.

University of South Alabama, School of Computing, Mobile, AL 36688. Offers computer science (MS); information systems (MS). Part-time and evening/weekend programs available. *Faculty:* 15 full-time (2 women), 3 part-time/adjunct (0 women). *Students:* 120 full-time (33 women), 13 part-time (1 woman); includes 12 minority (4 Black or African American, non-Hispanic/Latino; 4 Asian, non-Hispanic/Latino; 3 Hispanic/Latino; 1 Native Hawaiian or other Pacific Islander, non-Hispanic/Latino), 89 international. Average age 27. 321 applicants, 47% accepted, 48 enrolled. In 2014, 25 master's awarded. *Degree requirements:* For master's, comprehensive exam, project, thesis, or coursework only with additional credit hours earned; for doctorate, comprehensive exam, thesis/dissertation, minimum GPA of 3.0. *Entrance requirements:* For master's, GRE General Test, undergraduate degree, official transcripts, three letters of recommendation, statement of purpose; for doctorate, GRE, master's degree in related discipline, minimum graduate GPA of 3.5, statement of purpose, three letters of recommendation, curriculum vitae, official transcripts. Additional exam requirements/ recommendations for international students: Required—TOEFL (minimum score 525 paper-based; 71 iBT). *Application deadline:* For fall admission, 7/15 priority date for domestic students, 6/15 priority date for international students; for spring admission, 12/1 priority date for domestic students, 11/1 priority date for international students; for summer admission, 5/1 priority date for domestic students, 4/1 priority date for international students. Applications are processed on a rolling basis. Application fee: $35. Electronic applications accepted. *Expenses:* Tuition, state resident: full-time $9288; part-time $387 per credit hour. Tuition, nonresident: full-time $18,576; part-time $774 per credit hour. Part-time tuition and fees vary according to course load and program. *Financial support:* Fellowships, research assistantships, teaching assistantships, career-related internships or fieldwork, Federal Work-Study, institutionally sponsored loans, scholarships/grants, and unspecified assistantships available. Support available to part-time students. Financial award application deadline: 5/31; financial award applicants required to submit FAFSA. *Faculty research:* Numerical analysis, artificial intelligence, simulation, medical applications, software engineering. *Unit head:* Dr. Alec Yasinsac, Dean, School of Computing, 251-460-6390, Fax: 251-460-7274, E-mail: yasinsac@southalabama.edu. *Application contact:* Dr. Harold Pardue, Director of School of Computing Graduate Studies, 251-460-7634, Fax: 251-460-7274, E-mail: hpardue@southalabama.edu.
Website: http://www.cis.usouthal.edu.

University of South Carolina, The Graduate School, College of Engineering and Computing, Department of Computer Science and Engineering, Columbia, SC 29208. Offers computer science and engineering (ME, MS, PhD); software engineering (MS). Part-time and evening/weekend programs available. Postbaccalaureate distance learning degree programs offered (minimal on-campus study). *Degree requirements:* For master's, comprehensive exam, thesis (for some programs); for doctorate, comprehensive exam, thesis/dissertation. *Entrance requirements:* For master's and doctorate, GRE General Test. Additional exam requirements/recommendations for international students: Required—TOEFL (minimum score 570 paper-based). Electronic applications accepted. *Faculty research:* Computer security, computer vision, artificial intelligence, multiagent systems, bioinformatics.

The University of South Dakota, Graduate School, College of Arts and Sciences, Department of Computer Science, Vermillion, SD 57069-2390. Offers MS. Part-time programs available. *Degree requirements:* For master's, thesis optional. *Entrance requirements:* For master's, GRE General Test, GRE Subject Test (recommended), minimum GPA of 2.7. Additional exam requirements/recommendations for international students: Required—TOEFL (minimum score 550 paper-based; 79 iBT). Electronic applications accepted.

University of Southern California, Graduate School, Viterbi School of Engineering, Department of Computer Science, Los Angeles, CA 90089. Offers computer networks (MS); computer science (MS, PhD); computer security (MS); game development (MS); high performance computing and simulations (MS); human language technology (MS); intelligent robotics (MS); multimedia and creative technologies (MS); software engineering (MS). Part-time and evening/weekend programs available. Postbaccalaureate distance learning degree programs offered (no on-campus study). *Entrance requirements:* For master's and doctorate, GRE General Test. Additional exam requirements/recommendations for international students: Required—TOEFL. Electronic applications accepted. *Faculty research:* Databases, computer graphics and computer vision, software engineering, networks and security, robotics, multimedia and virtual reality.

University of Southern Maine, School of Applied Science, Engineering, and Technology, Department of Computer Science, Portland, ME 04104-9300. Offers computer science (MS); software systems (CGS). Part-time programs available. *Faculty:* 1 full-time, 1 part-time/adjunct (0 women). *Students:* 6 full-time (2 women), 5 part-time; includes 1 minority (Asian, non-Hispanic/Latino). Average age 37. 14 applicants, 71% accepted, 7 enrolled. In 2014, 5 master's, 1 other advanced degree awarded. *Degree requirements:* For master's, thesis. *Entrance requirements:* For master's, GRE General Test, minimum GPA of 3.0. Additional exam requirements/recommendations for international students: Required—TOEFL. *Application deadline:* For fall admission, 3/1 priority date for domestic students; for spring admission, 10/1 for domestic students. Application fee: $65. Electronic applications accepted. *Expenses: Tuition, area resident:* Full-time $6840; part-time $380 per credit hour. Tuition, state resident: full-time $10,260; part-time $570 per credit hour. Tuition, nonresident: full-time $18,468; part-time $1026 per credit hour. *Required fees:* $830; $83 per credit hour. Tuition and fees vary according to course load and program. *Financial support:* Research assistantships, teaching assistantships, and Federal Work-Study available. Support available to part-time students. Financial award application deadline: 4/1; financial award applicants required to submit FAFSA. *Faculty research:* Software engineering, database systems, formal methods, object-oriented technology, artificial intelligence, bioinformatics, data analysis and data mining, health information systems. *Unit head:* Dr. Saud Alagic, Director, 207-780-4841, Fax: 207-780-4933, E-mail: alagic@usm.maine.edu. *Application contact:* Mary Sloan, Assistant Dean of Graduate Studies and Director of Graduate Admissions, 207-780-4812, Fax: 207-780-4969, E-mail: gradstudies@usm.maine.edu.
Website: http://www.usm.maine.edu/cos.

University of Southern Mississippi, Graduate School, College of Science and Technology, School of Computing, Hattiesburg, MS 39406-0001. Offers computational science (MS, PhD); computer science (MS). *Degree requirements:* For master's, comprehensive exam, thesis; for doctorate, comprehensive exam, thesis/dissertation. *Entrance requirements:* For master's, GRE General Test, minimum GPA of 2.75 in last 60 hours; for doctorate, GRE General Test, minimum GPA of 3.5. Additional exam requirements/recommendations for international students: Required—TOEFL, IELTS. Electronic applications accepted. *Faculty research:* Satellite telecommunications, advanced life-support systems, artificial intelligence.

University of South Florida, College of Engineering, Department of Computer Science and Engineering, Tampa, FL 33620-9951. Offers computer engineering (MSCP); computer science (MSCS); computer science and engineering (PhD). Part-time programs available. *Faculty:* 18 full-time (3 women). *Students:* 116 full-time (29 women), 30 part-time (7 women); includes 15 minority (2 Black or African American, non-Hispanic/Latino; 5 Asian, non-Hispanic/Latino; 8 Hispanic/Latino), 91 international. Average age 27. 504 applicants, 27% accepted, 45 enrolled. In 2014, 30 master's, 7 doctorates awarded. Terminal master's awarded for partial completion of doctoral program. *Degree requirements:* For master's, comprehensive exam, thesis or alternative; for doctorate, comprehensive exam, thesis/dissertation, teaching of at least one undergraduate computer science and engineering course. *Entrance requirements:* For master's, GRE General Test, minimum GPA of 3.0 in last 60 hours of coursework, three letters of recommendation, statement of purpose; for doctorate, GRE General Test, minimum GPA of 3.0 in last 60 hours of coursework, three letters of recommendation, statement of purpose that includes three areas of research interest. Additional exam requirements/recommendations for international students: Required—TOEFL (minimum score 550 paper-based; 79 iBT) or IELTS (minimum score 6.5). *Application deadline:* For fall admission, 2/15 for domestic students, 1/2 for international students; for spring admission, 10/15 for domestic students, 6/1 for international students. Application fee: $30. Electronic applications accepted. *Financial support:* In 2014–15, 65 students received support, including 30 research assistantships with tuition reimbursements available (averaging $14,942 per year), 35 teaching assistantships with tuition reimbursements available (averaging $14,003 per year); unspecified assistantships also available. Financial award application deadline: 1/1; financial award applicants required to submit FAFSA. *Faculty research:* Artificial intelligence/intelligence systems; computational biology and bioinformatics; computer vision and pattern recognition; databases; distributed systems; graphics; information systems (networks) and location-aware information systems; robotics (biomorphic robotics and robot perception and action); software security; VLSI, computer architecture, and parallel processing. *Total annual research expenditures:* $1.4 million. *Unit head:* Dr. Lawrence Hall, Professor and Department Chair, 813-974-4195, Fax: 813-974-5094, E-mail: hall@cse.usf.edu. *Application contact:* Dr. Srivinas Katkoori, Associate Professor and Graduate Program Director, 813-974-5737, Fax: 813-974-5094, E-mail: katkoori@cse.usf.edu.
Website: http://www.cse.usf.edu/.

The University of Tennessee, Graduate School, College of Arts and Sciences, Department of Computer Science, Knoxville, TN 37996. Offers MS, PhD. Part-time programs available. *Degree requirements:* For master's, thesis or alternative; for doctorate, thesis/dissertation. *Entrance requirements:* For master's and doctorate, GRE General Test, minimum GPA of 2.7. Additional exam requirements/recommendations for international students: Required—TOEFL. Electronic applications accepted.

The University of Tennessee, Graduate School, College of Engineering, Department of Electrical Engineering and Computer Science, Program in Computer Science, Knoxville, TN 37966. Offers MS, PhD. Part-time programs available. *Faculty:* 32 full-time (5 women), 5 part-time/adjunct (4 women). *Students:* 43 full-time (11 women), 18 part-time (2 women); includes 8 minority (1 Black or African American, non-Hispanic/Latino;

4 Asian, non-Hispanic/Latino; 2 Hispanic/Latino; 1 Two or more races, non-Hispanic/ Latino), 23 international. Average age 29. 165 applicants, 14% accepted, 13 enrolled. In 2014, 11 master's, 3 doctorates awarded. *Degree requirements:* For master's, thesis or alternative; for doctorate, comprehensive exam, thesis/dissertation. *Entrance requirements:* For master's, GRE General Test (for MS students pursuing research thesis), minimum GPA of 2.7 (for U.S. degree holders), 3.0 (for international degree holders); 3 references; personal statement; for doctorate, GRE General Test (for all PhD candidates), minimum GPA of 3.0 on previous graduate coursework; 3 references; personal statement. Additional exam requirements/recommendations for international students: Required—TOEFL (minimum score 550 paper-based). *Application deadline:* For fall admission, 2/1 priority date for domestic and international students; for spring admission, 6/15 for domestic and international students. Applications are processed on a rolling basis. Application fee: $35. Electronic applications accepted. *Financial support:* In 2014–15, 40 students received support, including 15 research assistantships with full tuition reimbursements available (averaging $23,369 per year), 20 teaching assistantships with full tuition reimbursements available (averaging $17,806 per year); fellowships with full tuition reimbursements available, career-related internships or fieldwork, Federal Work-Study, institutionally sponsored loans, health care benefits, and unspecified assistantships also available. Financial award application deadline: 2/1; financial award applicants required to submit FAFSA. *Unit head:* Dr. Leon Tolbert, Head, 865-974-3461, Fax: 865-974-5483, E-mail: tolbert@utk.edu. *Application contact:* Dr. Lynne E. Parker, Associate Head, 865-974-4394, Fax: 865-974-5483, E-mail: parker@eecs.utk.edu.
Website: http://www.eecs.utk.edu.

The University of Tennessee at Chattanooga, Program in Computer Science, Chattanooga, TN 37403-2598. Offers MS, Graduate Certificate. Part-time and evening/weekend programs available. *Faculty:* 5 full-time (2 women). *Students:* 17 full-time (1 woman), 17 part-time (4 women); includes 11 minority (5 Black or African American, non-Hispanic/Latino; 3 Asian, non-Hispanic/Latino; 2 Hispanic/Latino; 1 Two or more races, non-Hispanic/Latino), 9 international. Average age 29. 59 applicants, 54% accepted, 12 enrolled. In 2014, 6 master's awarded. *Degree requirements:* For master's, comprehensive exam, thesis. *Entrance requirements:* For master's, GRE General Test. Additional exam requirements/recommendations for international students: Required—TOEFL (minimum score 550 paper-based; 79 iBT), IELTS (minimum score 6). *Application deadline:* For fall admission, 6/13 priority date for domestic students, 6/1 for international students; for spring admission, 10/15 priority date for domestic students, 10/1 for international students. Applications are processed on a rolling basis. Application fee: $30 ($35 for international students). Electronic applications accepted. *Expenses:* Tuition, state resident: full-time $7708; part-time $428 per credit hour. Tuition, nonresident: full-time $23,826; part-time $1323 per credit hour. *Required fees:* $1708; $252 per credit hour. *Financial support:* In 2014–15, 6 research assistantships with tuition reimbursements (averaging $6,468 per year), 1 teaching assistantship with tuition reimbursement (averaging $4,579 per year) were awarded; career-related internships or fieldwork, scholarships/grants, and unspecified assistantships also available. Support available to part-time students. *Faculty research:* Power systems, computer architecture, pattern recognition, artificial intelligence, statistical data analysis. *Total annual research expenditures:* $1.1 million. *Unit head:* Dr. Joseph Kizza, Department Head, 423-425-4349, Fax: 423-425-5442, E-mail: joseph-kizza@utc.edu. *Application contact:* Dr. J. Randy Walker, Interim Dean of Graduate Studies, 423-425-4478, Fax: 423-425-5223, E-mail: randy-walker@utc.edu.
Website: http://www.utc.edu/college-engineering-computer-science/departments/computer-science-engineering/graduateprogram.php.

The University of Texas at Arlington, Graduate School, College of Engineering, Department of Computer Science and Engineering, Arlington, TX 76019. Offers computer engineering (MS, PhD); computer science (MS, PhD); mathematical sciences, computer science (PhD); software engineering (MS). Part-time programs available. Postbaccalaureate distance learning degree programs offered (minimal on-campus study). Terminal master's awarded for partial completion of doctoral program. *Degree requirements:* For master's, comprehensive exam (for some programs), thesis; for doctorate, comprehensive exam, thesis/dissertation. *Entrance requirements:* For master's, GRE General Test, minimum GPA of 3.0 (3.2 in computer science-related classes); for doctorate, GRE General Test, minimum GPA of 3.5. Additional exam requirements/recommendations for international students: Required—TOEFL (minimum score 550 paper-based; 92 iBT), IELTS (minimum score 6.5). *Faculty research:* Algorithms, homeland security, mobile pervasive computing, high performance computing bioinformation.

The University of Texas at Austin, Graduate School, College of Natural Sciences, Department of Computer Sciences, Austin, TX 78712-1111. Offers MSCS, PhD. *Degree requirements:* For master's, thesis optional; for doctorate, thesis/dissertation, oral proposal, final defense. *Entrance requirements:* For master's and doctorate, GRE General Test, GRE Subject Test, bachelor's degree in computer sciences (preferred). Additional exam requirements/recommendations for international students: Required—TOEFL. Electronic applications accepted. *Faculty research:* Artificial intelligence, distributed computing, networks, algorithms, experimental systems.

The University of Texas at Brownsville, Graduate Studies, College of Science, Mathematics and Technology, Brownsville, TX 78520-4991. Offers biological sciences (MS); biology (MSIS); computer science (MSIS); computer sciences (MS); mathematics (MS); physics (MS). Part-time and evening/weekend programs available. Postbaccalaureate distance learning degree programs offered (no on-campus study). *Degree requirements:* For master's, comprehensive exam (for some programs), thesis optional, project (for some programs). *Entrance requirements:* For master's, GRE General Test, letters of recommendation. Additional exam requirements/recommendations for international students: Required—TOEFL (minimum score 550 paper-based; 77 iBT). Electronic applications accepted. *Faculty research:* Fish, insects, barrier islands, algae.

The University of Texas at Dallas, Erik Jonsson School of Engineering and Computer Science, Department of Computer Science, Richardson, TX 75080. Offers computer science (MS, PhD); software engineering (MS, PhD). Part-time and evening/weekend programs available. *Faculty:* 47 full-time (7 women), 11 part-time/adjunct (2 women). *Students:* 990 full-time (269 women), 273 part-time (75 women); includes 59 minority (6 Black or African American, non-Hispanic/Latino; 39 Asian, non-Hispanic/Latino; 10 Hispanic/Latino; 4 Two or more races, non-Hispanic/Latino), 1,111 international. Average age 26. 2,985 applicants, 39% accepted, 505 enrolled. In 2014, 315 master's, 28 doctorates awarded. *Degree requirements:* For master's, thesis optional; for doctorate, comprehensive exam, thesis/dissertation. *Entrance requirements:* For master's, GRE General Test, minimum GPA of 3.0 in undergraduate course work, 3.3 in quantitative course work; for doctorate, GRE General Test, minimum GPA of 3.5. Additional exam requirements/recommendations for international students: Required—TOEFL (minimum score 550 paper-based). *Application deadline:* For fall admission, 7/15 for domestic students, 5/1 priority date for international students; for spring admission, 11/15 for domestic students, 9/1 priority date for international students. Applications are processed on a rolling basis. Application fee: $50 ($100 for international students). Electronic applications accepted. *Expenses:* Tuition, state resident: full-time $11,940; part-time $663 per credit. Tuition, nonresident: full-time $22,282; part-time $1238 per credit. *Financial support:* In 2014–15, 240 students received support, including 13 fellowships with partial tuition reimbursements available (averaging $8,300 per year), 71 research assistantships with partial tuition reimbursements available (averaging $17,442 per year), 66 teaching assistantships with partial tuition reimbursements available (averaging $16,650 per year); career-related internships or fieldwork, Federal Work-Study, institutionally sponsored loans, and scholarships/grants also available. Support available to part-time students. Financial award application deadline: 4/30; financial award applicants required to submit FAFSA. *Faculty research:* AI-based automated software synthesis and testing, quality of service in computer networks, wireless networks, cloud computing and IT security, speech recognition. *Unit head:* Dr. Gopal Gupta, Department Head, 972-883-4107, Fax: 972-883-2399, E-mail: gupta@utdallas.edu. *Application contact:* Dr. Balaji Raghavachari, Associate Department Head/Director of Graduate Studies, 972-883-2136, Fax: 972-883-2399, E-mail: gradecs@utdallas.edu.
Website: http://cs.utdallas.edu/.

The University of Texas at El Paso, Graduate School, College of Engineering, Department of Computer Science, El Paso, TX 79968-0001. Offers computer science (MS, PhD); information technology (MSIT). Part-time and evening/weekend programs available. *Degree requirements:* For master's, thesis optional; for doctorate, thesis/dissertation. *Entrance requirements:* For master's, GRE, minimum GPA of 3.0; for doctorate, GRE, statement of purpose, letters of reference. Additional exam requirements/recommendations for international students: Required—TOEFL; Recommended—IELTS. Electronic applications accepted.

The University of Texas at San Antonio, College of Sciences, Department of Computer Science, San Antonio, TX 78249-0617. Offers MS, PhD. Part-time programs available. *Faculty:* 21 full-time (2 women). *Students:* 101 full-time (31 women), 40 part-time (8 women); includes 24 minority (5 Black or African American, non-Hispanic/Latino; 7 Asian, non-Hispanic/Latino; 11 Hispanic/Latino; 1 Two or more races, non-Hispanic/Latino), 86 international. Average age 29. 222 applicants, 54% accepted, 37 enrolled. In 2014, 22 master's, 15 doctorates awarded. Terminal master's awarded for partial completion of doctoral program. *Degree requirements:* For master's, 36 credits of coursework; thesis or comprehensive exam within 6 years; minimum GPA of 3.0; for doctorate, comprehensive exam, thesis/dissertation, continuous enrollment until time of graduation; admission to candidacy; oral examination; 90 credits of coursework and research; minimum GPA of 3.0 on all coursework. *Entrance requirements:* For master's and doctorate, GRE General Test, bachelor's degree in computer science offered by UTSA or an equivalent academic preparation from an accredited college or university in the United States or a comparable foreign institution; minimum GPA of 3.0; at least 24 semester credit hours (12 of which must be at the upper-division level) in the area. Additional exam requirements/recommendations for international students: Required—TOEFL (minimum score 550 paper-based; 79 iBT), IELTS (minimum score 6.5). *Application deadline:* For fall admission, 7/1 for domestic students, 4/1 for international students; for spring admission, 11/1 for domestic students, 9/1 for international students. Application fee: $45 ($80 for international students). Electronic applications accepted. *Expenses:* Expenses: $3700 per semester in-state, $10,400 per semester out-of-state and international. *Financial support:* In 2014–15, 82 students received support, including 19 fellowships (averaging $1,000 per year), 3 research assistantships with full tuition reimbursements available (averaging $28,465 per year), 37 teaching assistantships with full tuition reimbursements available (averaging $28,465 per year); career-related internships or fieldwork, scholarships/grants, and unspecified assistantships also available. Financial award application deadline: 10/1; financial award applicants required to submit FAFSA. *Faculty research:* Cyber security, cloud computing, software engineering, data science, bioinformatics and computational biology, high performance computing and storage systems, programming languages, operating systems, real-time systems, embedded computing, human-computer interaction, augmented reality, computer vision and multimedia, wireless networks, AI and machine learning. *Total annual research expenditures:* $2 million. *Unit head:* Dr. Rajendra V. Boppana, Department Chair, 210-458-4436, Fax: 210-458-4437, E-mail: rajendra.boppana@utsa.edu. *Application contact:* Dr. Weining Zhang, Graduate Advisor of Record, 210-458-5557, E-mail: wzhang@cs.utsa.edu.
Website: http://www.cs.utsa.edu/.

The University of Texas at Tyler, College of Engineering and Computer Science, Department of Computer Science, Tyler, TX 75799-0001. Offers computer science (MS); interdisciplinary studies (MSIS). *Degree requirements:* For master's, comprehensive exam, thesis optional. *Entrance requirements:* For master's, GRE General Test, previous course work in data structures and computer organization, 6 hours of course work in calculus and statistics. Additional exam requirements/recommendations for international students: Required—TOEFL. Electronic applications accepted. *Faculty research:* Database design, software engineering, client-server architecture, visual programming, data mining, computer security, digital image processing, simulation and modeling, computer science education.

The University of Texas of the Permian Basin, Office of Graduate Studies, College of Arts and Sciences, Department of Math and Computer Science, Odessa, TX 79762-0001. Offers computer science (MS). Part-time and evening/weekend programs available. *Degree requirements:* For master's, comprehensive exam, thesis or alternative. *Entrance requirements:* For master's, GRE General Test. Additional exam requirements/recommendations for international students: Required—TOEFL (minimum score 550 paper-based).

The University of Texas–Pan American, College of Engineering and Computer Science, Department of Computer Science, Edinburg, TX 78539. Offers computer science (MS); information technology (MS). Part-time and evening/weekend programs available. Postbaccalaureate distance learning degree programs offered (minimal on-campus study). *Degree requirements:* For master's, final written exam, project. *Entrance requirements:* For master's, GRE General Test, minimum GPA of 3.0 in last 60 hours. Additional exam requirements/recommendations for international students: Required—TOEFL. *Expenses:* Tuition, state resident: full-time $4187; part-time $232.60 per credit hour. Tuition, nonresident: full-time $10,857; part-time $603.16 per credit hour. *Required fees:* $782; $27.50 per credit hour. $143.35 per semester. *Faculty research:* Artificial intelligence, distributed systems, Internet computing, theoretical computer sciences, information visualization.

University of the District of Columbia, School of Engineering and Applied Science, Department of Computer Science and Information Technology, Program in Computer Science, Washington, DC 20008-1175. Offers MS. *Degree requirements:* For master's, thesis optional.

The University of Toledo, College of Graduate Studies, College of Engineering, Department of Electrical Engineering and Computer Science, Toledo, OH 43606-3390. Offers computer science (MS, PhD); electrical engineering (MS, PhD). Part-time and evening/weekend programs available. *Degree requirements:* For master's, thesis or alternative; for doctorate, thesis/dissertation, qualifying exam. *Entrance requirements:* For master's, GRE General Test, minimum GPA of 3.0; for doctorate, GRE General Test, minimum GPA of 3.3. Additional exam requirements/recommendations for international students: Required—TOEFL (minimum score 550 paper-based; 80 iBT). Electronic applications accepted. *Faculty research:* Communication and signal processing, high performance computing systems, intelligent systems, power electronics and energy systems, RF and microwave systems, sensors and medical devices, solid state devices.

University of Toronto, School of Graduate Studies, Faculty of Arts and Science, Department of Computer Science, Toronto, ON M5S 2J7, Canada. Offers applied computing (M Sc AC); computer science (M Sc, PhD). Part-time programs available. *Degree requirements:* For master's, thesis; for doctorate, thesis/dissertation, thesis defense/oral exam. *Entrance requirements:* For master's, GRE (recommended), minimum B+ average overall and in final year; resume; 3 letters of reference; background in computer science and mathematics (preferred); for doctorate, minimum B+ average overall and in final year; resume; 3 letters of reference; background in computer science and mathematics (preferred). Additional exam requirements/recommendations for international students: Required—TOEFL (minimum score 580 paper-based), TWE (minimum score 5). Electronic applications accepted.

The University of Tulsa, Graduate School, College of Engineering and Natural Sciences, Tandy School of Computer Science, Tulsa, OK 74104-3189. Offers MS, PhD, JD/MS, MBA/MS. Part-time programs available. *Faculty:* 12 full-time (1 woman). *Students:* 38 full-time (8 women), 13 part-time (4 women); includes 5 minority (2 Black or African American, non-Hispanic/Latino; 2 American Indian or Alaska Native, non-Hispanic/Latino; 1 Two or more races, non-Hispanic/Latino), 12 international. Average age 28. 45 applicants, 73% accepted, 16 enrolled. In 2014, 18 master's, 7 doctorates awarded. Terminal master's awarded for partial completion of doctoral program. *Degree requirements:* For master's, thesis (for some programs); for doctorate, comprehensive exam, thesis/dissertation. *Entrance requirements:* For master's and doctorate, GRE General Test. Additional exam requirements/recommendations for international students: Required—TOEFL (minimum score 550 paper-based; 80 iBT), IELTS (minimum score 6). *Application deadline:* Applications are processed on a rolling basis. Application fee: $55. Electronic applications accepted. *Expenses: Tuition:* Full-time $20,160; part-time $1120 per credit hour. *Required fees:* $6 per credit hour. Tuition and fees vary according to course level and course load. *Financial support:* In 2014–15, 32 students received support, including 3 fellowships with full and partial tuition reimbursements available (averaging $5,625 per year), 17 research assistantships with full and partial tuition reimbursements available (averaging $11,090 per year), 12 teaching assistantships with full and partial tuition reimbursements available (averaging $9,832 per year); career-related internships or fieldwork, Federal Work-Study, scholarships/grants, health care benefits, tuition waivers (full and partial), and unspecified assistantships also available. Support available to part-time students. Financial award application deadline: 2/1; financial award applicants required to submit FAFSA. *Faculty research:* Robotics, human-computer interaction, systems security, information assurance, machine learning, intelligent systems, software engineering, distributed systems, evolutionary computation, computational biology, bioinformatics. *Total annual research expenditures:* $2.9 million. *Unit head:* Dr. Roger Wainwright, Chairperson, 918-631-3143, E-mail: rogerw@utulsa.edu. *Application contact:* Dr. Sandip Sen, Advisor, 918-631-2985, Fax: 918-631-3077, E-mail: sandip-sen@utulsa.edu.
Website: http://engineering.utulsa.edu/academics/computer-science/.

The University of Tulsa, Graduate School, Collins College of Business, Business Administration/Computer Science Program, Tulsa, OK 74104-3189. Offers MBA/MS. Part-time programs available. *Students:* 1 full-time (0 women), all international. Average age 24. 2 applicants, 50% accepted. *Entrance requirements:* Additional exam requirements/recommendations for international students: Required—TOEFL (minimum score 577 paper-based; 91 iBT), IELTS (minimum score 6.5). *Application deadline:* Applications are processed on a rolling basis. Application fee: $55. Electronic applications accepted. *Expenses: Tuition:* Full-time $20,160; part-time $1120 per credit hour. *Required fees:* $6 per credit hour. Tuition and fees vary according to course level and course load. *Financial support:* Career-related internships or fieldwork, Federal Work-Study, institutionally sponsored loans, scholarships/grants, health care benefits, tuition waivers, and unspecified assistantships available. Support available to part-time students. Financial award application deadline: 2/1; financial award applicants required to submit FAFSA. *Unit head:* Dr. Linda Nichols, Associate Dean, 918-631-2242, Fax: 918-631-2142, E-mail: linda-nichols@utulsa.edu. *Application contact:* Information Contact, 918-631-2242, E-mail: graduate-business@utulsa.edu.

University of Utah, Graduate School, College of Engineering, School of Computing, Salt Lake City, UT 84112-9205. Offers computational engineering and science (MS); computer science (MS, PhD); computing (MS, PhD); MS/MBA. *Faculty:* 33 full-time (5 women), 11 part-time/adjunct (0 women). *Students:* 231 full-time (51 women), 56 part-time (10 women); includes 15 minority (2 Black or African American, non-Hispanic/Latino; 10 Asian, non-Hispanic/Latino; 2 Hispanic/Latino; 1 Two or more races, non-Hispanic/Latino), 192 international. Average age 28. 616 applicants, 36% accepted, 95 enrolled. In 2014, 56 master's, 19 doctorates awarded. Terminal master's awarded for partial completion of doctoral program. *Degree requirements:* For master's, comprehensive exam (for some programs), thesis (for some programs); for doctorate, comprehensive exam, thesis/dissertation. *Entrance requirements:* For master's and doctorate, GRE General Test, minimum GPA of 3.0. Additional exam requirements/recommendations for international students: Required—TOEFL (minimum score 500 paper-based; 61 iBT), IELTS (minimum score 6.5). *Application deadline:* For fall admission, 12/15 for domestic and international students. Application fee: $55 ($65 for international students). Electronic applications accepted. *Expenses:* Expenses: Contact institution. *Financial support:* In 2014–15, 3 students received support, including 3 fellowships with full tuition reimbursements available (averaging $25,000 per year), 125 research assistantships with full tuition reimbursements available (averaging $33,375 per year), 55 teaching assistantships with full tuition reimbursements available (averaging $16,800 per year); Federal Work-Study, scholarships/grants, health care benefits, and unspecified assistantships also available. Financial award application deadline: 12/15; financial award applicants required to submit FAFSA. *Faculty research:* Operating systems, programming languages, formal methods, natural language processing, architecture, networks, image analysis, data analysis, visualization, graphics, scientific computing, robotics. *Total annual research expenditures:* $7.9 million. *Unit head:* Dr. Ross Whitaker, Director, 801-581-8224, Fax: 801-581-5843, E-mail: whitaker@cs.utah.edu. *Application contact:* Ann Carlstrom, Graduate Advisor, 801-581-7631, Fax: 801-581-5843, E-mail: annc@cs.utah.edu.
Website: http://www.cs.utah.edu.

University of Vermont, Graduate College, College of Engineering and Mathematics, Program in Computer Science, Burlington, VT 05405. Offers MS, PhD. *Degree requirements:* For master's, thesis or alternative. *Entrance requirements:* For master's and doctorate, GRE General Test. Additional exam requirements/recommendations for international students: Required—TOEFL (minimum score 550 paper-based; 80 iBT). Electronic applications accepted.

University of Victoria, Faculty of Graduate Studies, Faculty of Engineering, Department of Computer Science, Victoria, BC V8W 2Y2, Canada. Offers M Sc, PhD. Part-time programs available. Terminal master's awarded for partial completion of doctoral program. *Degree requirements:* For master's, thesis or alternative; for doctorate, thesis/dissertation, candidacy exam. *Entrance requirements:* For master's, GRE (recommended), B Sc in computer science/software engineering or the equivalent or bachelor's degree in mathematics with emphasis on computer science (recommended); for doctorate, GRE (recommended), MS in computer science or equivalent (recommended). Additional exam requirements/recommendations for international students: Required—TOEFL (minimum score 575 paper-based), IELTS (minimum score 7). Electronic applications accepted. *Faculty research:* Functional and logic programming, numerical analysis, parallel and distributed computing, software systems, theoretical computer science, VLSI design and testing.

University of Virginia, School of Engineering and Applied Science, Department of Computer Science, Charlottesville, VA 22903. Offers MCS, MS, PhD. *Faculty:* 26 full-time (3 women). *Students:* 61 full-time (14 women), 1 part-time (0 women); includes 4 minority (all Asian, non-Hispanic/Latino), 42 international. Average age 26. 367 applicants, 14% accepted, 10 enrolled. In 2014, 14 master's, 8 doctorates awarded. *Degree requirements:* For master's, thesis (for some programs); for doctorate, comprehensive exam, thesis/dissertation. *Entrance requirements:* For master's, GRE General Test, 3 letters of recommendation; for doctorate, GRE General Test, 3 letters of recommendation; essay. Additional exam requirements/recommendations for international students: Required—TOEFL (minimum score 650 paper-based; 90 iBT), IELTS (minimum score 7). *Application deadline:* For fall admission, 8/1 for domestic students, 4/1 for international students; for winter admission, 12/1 for domestic students, 8/1 for international students; for spring admission, 5/1 for domestic students, 1/1 for international students. Applications are processed on a rolling basis. Application fee: $60. Electronic applications accepted. *Expenses:* Tuition, state resident: full-time $14,164; part-time $349 per credit hour. Tuition, nonresident: full-time $23,722; part-time $1300 per credit hour. *Required fees:* $2514. *Financial support:* Fellowships available. Financial award application deadline: 10/15; financial award applicants required to submit FAFSA. *Faculty research:* Systems programming, operating systems, analysis of programs and computation theory, programming languages, software engineering. *Unit head:* Kevin Skadron, Chair, 434-982-2200, Fax: 434-982-2214, E-mail: inquiry@cs.virginia.edu. *Application contact:* Pamela M. Morris, Associate Dean for Research and Graduate Programs, 434-243-7683, Fax: 434-982-3044, E-mail: pamela@virginia.edu.
Website: http://www.cs.virginia.edu/.

University of Washington, Graduate School, College of Engineering, Department of Computer Science and Engineering, Seattle, WA 98195-2350. Offers MS, PhD. Part-time and evening/weekend programs available. *Faculty:* 51 full-time (9 women). *Students:* 231 full-time (56 women), 141 part-time (18 women). Average age 28. 1,287 applicants, 13% accepted, 83 enrolled. In 2014, 86 master's, 18 doctorates awarded. *Degree requirements:* For doctorate, thesis/dissertation, independent project. *Entrance requirements:* For master's, GRE General Test; for doctorate, GRE General Test, minimum GPA of 3.0, statement of purpose, curriculum vitae, letters of recommendation, transcript. Additional exam requirements/recommendations for international students: Required—TOEFL (minimum score 580 paper-based; 92 iBT); Recommended—IELTS (minimum score 7). *Application deadline:* For fall admission, 12/15 for domestic and international students. Applications are processed on a rolling basis. Application fee: $85. Electronic applications accepted. *Expenses:* Expenses: Contact institution. *Financial support:* In 2014–15, 200 students received support, including 40 fellowships with full tuition reimbursements available, 127 research assistantships with full tuition reimbursements available, 33 teaching assistantships with full tuition reimbursements available; career-related internships or fieldwork, traineeships, and health care benefits also available. Financial award application deadline: 12/15. *Faculty research:* Theory, systems, artificial intelligence, graphics, databases. *Total annual research expenditures:* $32.7 million. *Unit head:* Henry M. Levy, Professor/Chair, 206-543-9204, Fax: 206-543-2969, E-mail: levy@cs.washington.edu. *Application contact:* Elise deGoede Dorough, Graduate Admissions Information Contact, 206-543-1695, Fax: 206-543-2969, E-mail: elised@cs.washington.edu.
Website: http://www.cs.washington.edu/.

University of Waterloo, Graduate Studies, Faculty of Mathematics, David R. Cheriton School of Computer Science, Waterloo, ON N2L 3G1, Canada. Offers computer science (M Math, PhD); software engineering (M Math); statistics and computing (M Math). Part-time programs available. *Degree requirements:* For master's, research paper or thesis; for doctorate, comprehensive exam, thesis/dissertation. *Entrance requirements:* For master's, honors degree in field, minimum B+ average; for doctorate, master's degree, minimum B+ average. *Faculty research:* Computer graphics, artificial intelligence, algorithms and complexity, distributed computing and networks, software engineering.

The University of Western Ontario, Faculty of Graduate Studies, Physical Sciences Division, Department of Computer Science, London, ON N6A 5B8, Canada. Offers M Sc, PhD. Part-time programs available. *Degree requirements:* For master's, thesis, project, or course work; for doctorate, thesis/dissertation. *Entrance requirements:* For master's, B Sc in computer science or comparable academic qualifications; for doctorate, M Sc in computer science or comparable academic qualifications. Additional exam requirements/recommendations for international students: Required—TOEFL. *Faculty research:* Artificial intelligence and logic programming, graphics and image processing, software and systems, theory of computing, symbolic mathematical computation.

University of West Florida, College of Arts and Sciences: Sciences, Department of Computer Science, Pensacola, FL 32514-5750. Offers computer science (MS); database systems (MS); software engineering (MS). Part-time and evening/weekend programs available. *Degree requirements:* For master's, thesis optional. *Entrance requirements:* For master's, GRE, MAT, or GMAT, official transcripts; minimum undergraduate GPA of 3.0; letter of intent; three letters of recommendation. Additional exam requirements/recommendations for international students: Required—TOEFL (minimum score 550 paper-based).

University of West Georgia, College of Science and Mathematics, Department of Computer Science, Carrollton, GA 30118. Offers applied computer science (MS). Part-time and evening/weekend programs available. Postbaccalaureate distance learning degree programs offered (no on-campus study). *Faculty:* 7 full-time (2 women). *Students:* 1 full-time (0 women), 82 part-time (26 women); includes 20 minority (8 Black or African American, non-Hispanic/Latino; 6 Asian, non-Hispanic/Latino; 4 Hispanic/Latino; 1 Native Hawaiian or other Pacific Islander, non-Hispanic/Latino; 1 Two or more races, non-Hispanic/Latino), 7 international. Average age 34. 87 applicants, 59% accepted, 37 enrolled. In 2014, 7 master's awarded. *Degree requirements:* For master's, comprehensive exam. *Entrance requirements:* For master's, bachelor's degree, minimum overall undergraduate GPA of 2.5, 3 letters of reference, resume or curriculum vitae, personal narrative. Additional exam requirements/recommendations for international students: Recommended—TOEFL (minimum score 523 paper-based; 69 iBT), IELTS (minimum score 6). *Application deadline:* For fall admission, 7/15 for domestic and international students. Applications are processed on a rolling basis. Application fee: $40. Electronic applications accepted. *Expenses:* Expenses: Contact institution. *Financial support:* In 2014–15, 1 research assistantship with full tuition reimbursement (averaging $9,000 per year) was awarded; unspecified assistantships

also available. Financial award application deadline: 4/1; financial award applicants required to submit FAFSA. *Faculty research:* Artificial intelligence, software engineering, Web technologies, database, networks, computer science education. *Unit head:* Dr. Adel M. Abunawass, Chair, 678-839-6485, Fax: 678-839-6486, E-mail: adel@westga.edu. *Application contact:* Jane Wood, Departmental Assistant, 678-839-6485, Fax: 678-839-6486, E-mail: jwood@westga.edu.
Website: http://www.cs.westga.edu/.

University of Windsor, Faculty of Graduate Studies, Faculty of Science, School of Computer Science, Windsor, ON N9B 3P4, Canada. Offers M Sc, PhD. Part-time programs available. *Degree requirements:* For master's, thesis; for doctorate, comprehensive exam, thesis/dissertation. *Entrance requirements:* For master's, GRE, minimum B average; for doctorate, master's degree in computer science, minimum B+ average. Additional exam requirements/recommendations for international students: Required—TOEFL (minimum score 580 paper-based). Electronic applications accepted. *Faculty research:* Data mining, distributed query optimization, distributed object based systems, grid computing, querying multimedia database systems.

University of Wisconsin–Madison, Graduate School, College of Letters and Science, Department of Computer Sciences, Madison, WI 53706-1380. Offers MS, PhD. Part-time programs available. Terminal master's awarded for partial completion of doctoral program. *Degree requirements:* For doctorate, thesis/dissertation. *Entrance requirements:* For master's and doctorate, GRE General Test, GRE Subject Test. Electronic applications accepted. *Expenses:* Tuition, state resident: full-time $10,723; part-time $745 per credit. Tuition, nonresident: full-time $24,054; part-time $1578 per credit. *Required fees:* $374 per semester. Tuition and fees vary according to course load, program and reciprocity agreements.

University of Wisconsin–Milwaukee, Graduate School, College of Engineering and Applied Science, Program in Computer Science, Milwaukee, WI 53201-0413. Offers MS. Part-time programs available. *Degree requirements:* For master's, comprehensive exam (for some programs), thesis or alternative. *Entrance requirements:* For master's, GRE, minimum GPA of 2.75. Additional exam requirements/recommendations for international students: Required—TOEFL (minimum score 550 paper-based; 79 iBT), IELTS (minimum score 6.5). Electronic applications accepted.

University of Wisconsin–Parkside, School of Business and Technology, Program in Computer and Information Systems, Kenosha, WI 53141-2000. Offers MSCIS. *Entrance requirements:* For master's, GRE General Test or GMAT, 3 letters of recommendation, minimum GPA of 3.0. *Faculty research:* Distributed systems, data bases, natural language processing, event-driven systems.

University of Wisconsin–Platteville, School of Graduate Studies, College of Engineering, Mathematics and Science, Program in Computer Science, Platteville, WI 53818-3099. Offers MS. Part-time programs available. *Degree requirements:* For master's, comprehensive exam, thesis or alternative. *Entrance requirements:* Additional exam requirements/recommendations for international students: Required—TOEFL (minimum score 500 paper-based; 61 iBT), IELTS (minimum score 6). Electronic applications accepted.

University of Wyoming, College of Engineering and Applied Sciences, Department of Computer Science, Laramie, WY 82071. Offers MS, PhD. Part-time programs available. Terminal master's awarded for partial completion of doctoral program. *Degree requirements:* For master's, thesis; for doctorate, thesis/dissertation. *Entrance requirements:* For master's and doctorate, GRE General Test, minimum GPA of 3.0. Additional exam requirements/recommendations for international students: Required—TOEFL (minimum score 550 paper-based), IELTS (minimum score 6). Electronic applications accepted. *Faculty research:* Fault-tolerant computing, distributed systems, knowledge representation, automated reasoning, parallel database access, formal methods.

Utah State University, School of Graduate Studies, College of Science, Department of Computer Science, Logan, UT 84322. Offers MCS, MS, PhD. Part-time and evening/weekend programs available. Postbaccalaureate distance learning degree programs offered. *Degree requirements:* For master's, thesis (for some programs), research project; for doctorate, thesis/dissertation. *Entrance requirements:* For master's, GRE General Test, GRE Subject Test, minimum GPA of 3.25, prerequisite coursework in math, 3 recommendation letters; for doctorate, GRE General Test, minimum GPA of 3.25, BS or MS. Additional exam requirements/recommendations for international students: Required—TOEFL. Electronic applications accepted. *Faculty research:* Artificial intelligence, software engineering, parallelism.

Vanderbilt University, School of Engineering, Department of Electrical Engineering and Computer Science, Program in Computer Science, Nashville, TN 37240-1001. Offers M Eng, MS, PhD. MS and PhD offered through the Graduate School. Part-time programs available. Terminal master's awarded for partial completion of doctoral program. *Degree requirements:* For master's, thesis (for some programs); for doctorate, comprehensive exam, thesis/dissertation. *Entrance requirements:* For master's and doctorate, GRE General Test, 3 letters of recommendation. Additional exam requirements/recommendations for international students: Required—TOEFL. Electronic applications accepted. *Expenses: Tuition:* Full-time $42,768; part-time $1782 per credit hour. *Required fees:* $422. One-time fee: $30 full-time. *Faculty research:* Artificial intelligence, performance evaluation, databases, software engineering, computational science.

Villanova University, College of Engineering, Department of Electrical and Computer Engineering, Program in Computer Engineering, Villanova, PA 19085-1699. Offers computer architectures (Certificate); computer engineering (MSCPE); intelligent control systems (Certificate). Part-time and evening/weekend programs available. *Degree requirements:* For master's, thesis optional. *Entrance requirements:* For master's, GRE General Test (for applicants with degrees from foreign universities), BEE, minimum GPA of 3.0. Additional exam requirements/recommendations for international students: Required—TOEFL (minimum score 600 paper-based; 100 iBT). Electronic applications accepted. *Faculty research:* Expert systems, computer vision, neural networks, image processing, computer architectures.

Villanova University, Graduate School of Liberal Arts and Sciences, Department of Computing Sciences, Villanova, PA 19085-1699. Offers computer science (MS); software engineering (MS). Part-time and evening/weekend programs available. *Students:* 116 full-time (56 women), 21 part-time (3 women); includes 5 minority (2 Asian, non-Hispanic/Latino; 1 Hispanic/Latino; 1 Native Hawaiian or other Pacific Islander, non-Hispanic/Latino; 1 Two or more races, non-Hispanic/Latino), 102 international. Average age 27. 75 applicants, 64% accepted, 35 enrolled. In 2014, 32 master's awarded. *Degree requirements:* For master's, thesis optional, independent study project. *Entrance requirements:* For master's, GRE, minimum GPA of 3.0, 3 recommendation letters. Additional exam requirements/recommendations for international students: Required—TOEFL. *Application deadline:* For fall admission, 5/1 priority date for international students; for spring admission, 11/15 priority date for international students. Applications are processed on a rolling basis. Application fee: $50. Electronic applications accepted. *Financial support:* Research assistantships, scholarships/grants, and unspecified assistantships available. Financial award applicants required to submit FAFSA. *Unit head:* Dr. Vijay Geholt, Chair, 610-519-5843.
Website: http://www1.villanova.edu/villanova/artsci/computerscience/graduate.html.

Virginia Commonwealth University, Graduate School, School of Engineering, Department of Computer Science, Richmond, VA 23284-9005. Offers computer science (MS, PhD); engineering (PhD). *Degree requirements:* For master's, thesis optional. *Entrance requirements:* For master's, GRE General Test; for doctorate, GRE. Additional exam requirements/recommendations for international students: Required—TOEFL (minimum score 600 paper-based; 100 iBT). Electronic applications accepted.

Virginia International University, School of Computer Information Systems, Fairfax, VA 22030. Offers computer science (MS); information systems (MS). Part-time programs available. *Entrance requirements:* For master's, bachelor's degree. Additional exam requirements/recommendations for international students: Required—TOEFL (minimum score 550 paper-based; 80 iBT), IELTS. Electronic applications accepted.

Virginia Polytechnic Institute and State University, Graduate School, College of Engineering, Blacksburg, VA 24061. Offers aerospace engineering (ME, MS, PhD); biological systems engineering (ME, MS, PhD); biomedical engineering (MS, PhD); chemical engineering (ME, MS, PhD); civil engineering (ME, MS, PhD); computer engineering (ME, MS, PhD); computer science (MS, PhD); electrical engineering (ME, PhD); engineering education (PhD); engineering mechanics (ME, MS, PhD); environmental engineering (MS); environmental science and engineering (MS); industrial and systems engineering (ME, MS, PhD); materials science and engineering (ME, MS, PhD); mechanical engineering (ME, MS, PhD); mining and minerals engineering (PhD); mining engineering (ME, MS); nuclear engineering (MS, PhD); ocean engineering (MS); systems engineering (ME, MS). *Accreditation:* ABET (one or more programs are accredited). *Faculty:* 356 full-time (60 women), 3 part-time/adjunct (1 woman). *Students:* 1,700 full-time (398 women), 345 part-time (58 women); includes 213 minority (43 Black or African American, non-Hispanic/Latino; 1 American Indian or Alaska Native, non-Hispanic/Latino; 87 Asian, non-Hispanic/Latino; 58 Hispanic/Latino; 1 Native Hawaiian or other Pacific Islander, non-Hispanic/Latino; 23 Two or more races, non-Hispanic/Latino), 1,079 international. Average age 27. 5,228 applicants, 18% accepted, 471 enrolled. In 2014, 438 master's, 211 doctorates awarded. *Degree requirements:* For master's, comprehensive exam (for some programs), thesis (for some programs); for doctorate, comprehensive exam (for some programs), thesis/dissertation (for some programs). *Entrance requirements:* For master's and doctorate, GRE/GMAT (may vary by department). Additional exam requirements/recommendations for international students: Required—TOEFL (minimum score 550 paper-based). *Application deadline:* For fall admission, 8/1 for domestic students, 4/1 for international students; for spring admission, 1/1 for domestic students, 9/1 for international students. Applications are processed on a rolling basis. Application fee: $75. Electronic applications accepted. *Expenses:* Tuition, state resident: full-time $11,656; part-time $647.50 per credit hour. Tuition, nonresident: full-time $23,351; part-time $1297.25 per credit hour. *Required fees:* $2533; $465.75 per semester. Tuition and fees vary according to course load, campus/location and program. *Financial support:* In 2014–15, 148 fellowships with full tuition reimbursements (averaging $8,031 per year), 855 research assistantships with full tuition reimbursements (averaging $22,855 per year), 288 teaching assistantships with full tuition reimbursements (averaging $20,291 per year) were awarded. Financial award application deadline: 3/1; financial award applicants required to submit FAFSA. *Total annual research expenditures:* $90.5 million. *Unit head:* Dr. Richard C. Benson, Dean, 540-231-9752, Fax: 540-231-3031, E-mail: deaneng@vt.edu. *Application contact:* Linda Perkins, Executive Assistant, 540-231-9752, Fax: 540-231-3031, E-mail: lperkins@vt.edu.
Website: http://www.eng.vt.edu/.

Virginia Polytechnic Institute and State University, VT Online, Blacksburg, VA 24061. Offers advanced transportation systems (Certificate); aerospace engineering (MS); agricultural and life sciences (MSLFS); business information systems (Graduate Certificate); career and technical education (MS); civil engineering (MS); computer engineering (M Eng, MS); decision support systems (Graduate Certificate); eLearning leadership (MA); electrical engineering (M Eng, MS); engineering administration (MEA); environmental engineering (Certificate); environmental politics and policy (Graduate Certificate); environmental sciences and engineering (MS); foundations of political analysis (Graduate Certificate); health product risk management (Graduate Certificate); industrial and systems engineering (MS); information policy and society (Graduate Certificate); information security (Graduate Certificate); information technology (MIT); instructional technology (MA); integrative STEM education (MA Ed); liberal arts (Graduate Certificate); life sciences: health product risk management (MS); natural resources (MNR, Graduate Certificate); networking (Graduate Certificate); nonprofit and nongovernmental organization management (Graduate Certificate); ocean engineering (MS); political science (MA); security studies (Graduate Certificate); software development (Graduate Certificate). *Expenses:* Tuition, state resident: full-time $11,656; part-time $647.50 per credit hour. Tuition, nonresident: full-time $23,351; part-time $1297.25 per credit hour. *Required fees:* $2533; $465.75 per semester. Tuition and fees vary according to course load, campus/location and program.

Virginia State University, College of Graduate Studies, College of Engineering and Technology, Department of Mathematics and Computer Science, Petersburg, VA 23806-0001. Offers computer science (MS); mathematics (MS); mathematics education (MS). *Degree requirements:* For master's, thesis (for some programs).

Wake Forest University, Graduate School of Arts and Sciences, Department of Computer Science, Winston-Salem, NC 27109. Offers MS. Part-time programs available. *Degree requirements:* For master's, one foreign language, thesis optional. *Entrance requirements:* For master's, GRE General Test. Additional exam requirements/recommendations for international students: Required—TOEFL (minimum score 79 iBT). Electronic applications accepted.

Washington State University, Voiland College of Engineering and Architecture, Engineering and Computer Science Programs, Vancouver Campus, Pullman, WA 99164. Offers MS. *Students:* 32 full-time (4 women), 9 part-time (1 woman); includes 12 minority (1 Black or African American, non-Hispanic/Latino; 10 Asian, non-Hispanic/Latino; 1 Hispanic/Latino), 11 international. Average age 30. 39 applicants, 36% accepted, 13 enrolled. In 2014, 16 master's awarded. *Degree requirements:* For master's, comprehensive exam, thesis optional. *Entrance requirements:* For master's, official transcripts from all colleges and universities attended; one-page statement of purpose; three letters of recommendation. Additional exam requirements/recommendations for international students: Required—TOEFL; Recommended—IELTS. *Application deadline:* For fall admission, 1/10 priority date for domestic and international students; for spring admission, 7/1 priority date for domestic and international students. Application fee: $75. Electronic applications accepted. *Expenses:* Tuition, state resident: full-time $11,768. Tuition, nonresident: full-time $25,200. *Required fees:* $960. Tuition and fees vary according to program. *Financial support:* In 2014–15, 24 students received support, including 2 fellowships, 4 research assistantships (averaging $13,379 per year), 24 teaching assistantships (averaging $13,379 per year); health care benefits, tuition waivers, and unspecified assistantships also available. Financial award application deadline: 3/1; financial award applicants international students: Required—TOEFL (minimum score 550 paper-based; 80 iBT). Electronic applications accepted. *Faculty research:* Communication and signal processing, high performance computing systems, intelligent systems, power electronics and energy systems, RF and microwave systems, sensors and medical devices, solid state devices.

University of Toronto, School of Graduate Studies, Faculty of Arts and Science, Department of Computer Science, Toronto, ON M5S 2J7, Canada. Offers applied computing (M Sc AC); computer science (M Sc, PhD). Part-time programs available. *Degree requirements:* For master's, thesis; for doctorate, thesis/dissertation, thesis defense/oral exam. *Entrance requirements:* For master's, GRE (recommended), minimum B+ average overall and in final year; resume; 3 letters of reference; background in computer science and mathematics (preferred); for doctorate, minimum B+ average overall and in final year; resume; 3 letters of reference; background in computer science and mathematics (preferred). Additional exam requirements/recommendations for international students: Required—TOEFL (minimum score 580 paper-based), TWE (minimum score 5). Electronic applications accepted.

The University of Tulsa, Graduate School, College of Engineering and Natural Sciences, Tandy School of Computer Science, Tulsa, OK 74104-3189. Offers MS, PhD, JD/MS, MBA/MS. Part-time programs available. *Faculty:* 12 full-time (1 woman). *Students:* 38 full-time (8 women), 13 part-time (4 women); includes 5 minority (2 Black or African American, non-Hispanic/Latino; 2 American Indian or Alaska Native, non-Hispanic/Latino; 1 Two or more races, non-Hispanic/Latino), 12 international. Average age 28. 45 applicants, 73% accepted, 16 enrolled. In 2014, 18 master's, 7 doctorates awarded. Terminal master's awarded for partial completion of doctoral program. *Degree requirements:* For master's, thesis (for some programs); for doctorate, comprehensive exam, thesis/dissertation. *Entrance requirements:* For master's and doctorate, GRE General Test. Additional exam requirements/recommendations for international students: Required—TOEFL (minimum score 550 paper-based; 80 iBT), IELTS (minimum score 6). *Application deadline:* Applications are processed on a rolling basis. Application fee: $55. Electronic applications accepted. *Expenses: Tuition:* Full-time $20,160; part-time $1120 per credit hour. *Required fees:* $6 per credit hour. Tuition and fees vary according to course level and course load. *Financial support:* In 2014–15, 32 students received support, including 3 fellowships with full and partial tuition reimbursements available (averaging $5,625 per year), 17 research assistantships with full and partial tuition reimbursements available (averaging $11,090 per year), 12 teaching assistantships with full and partial tuition reimbursements available (averaging $9,832 per year); career-related internships or fieldwork, Federal Work-Study, scholarships/grants, health care benefits, tuition waivers (full and partial), and unspecified assistantships also available. Support available to part-time students. Financial award application deadline: 2/1; financial award applicants required to submit FAFSA. *Faculty research:* Robotics, human-computer interaction, systems security, information assurance, machine learning, intelligent systems, software engineering, distributed systems, evolutionary computation, computational biology, bioinformatics. *Total annual research expenditures:* $2.9 million. *Unit head:* Dr. Roger Wainwright, Chairperson, 918-631-3143, E-mail: rogerw@utulsa.edu. *Application contact:* Dr. Sandip Sen, Advisor, 918-631-2985, Fax: 918-631-3077, E-mail: sandip-sen@utulsa.edu.
Website: http://engineering.utulsa.edu/academics/computer-science/.

The University of Tulsa, Graduate School, Collins College of Business, Business Administration/Computer Science Program, Tulsa, OK 74104-3189. Offers MBA/MS. Part-time programs available. *Students:* 1 full-time (0 women), all international. Average age 24. 2 applicants, 50% accepted. *Entrance requirements:* Additional exam requirements/recommendations for international students: Required—TOEFL (minimum score 577 paper-based; 91 iBT), IELTS (minimum score 6.5). *Application deadline:* Applications are processed on a rolling basis. Application fee: $55. Electronic applications accepted. *Expenses: Tuition:* Full-time $20,160; part-time $1120 per credit hour. *Required fees:* $6 per credit hour. Tuition and fees vary according to course level and course load. *Financial support:* Career-related internships or fieldwork, Federal Work-Study, institutionally sponsored loans, scholarships/grants, health care benefits, tuition waivers, and unspecified assistantships available. Support available to part-time students. Financial award application deadline: 2/1; financial award applicants required to submit FAFSA. *Unit head:* Dr. Linda Nichols, Associate Dean, 918-631-2242, Fax: 918-631-2142, E-mail: linda-nichols@utulsa.edu. *Application contact:* Information Contact, 918-631-2242, E-mail: graduate-business@utulsa.edu.

University of Utah, Graduate School, College of Engineering, School of Computing, Salt Lake City, UT 84112-9205. Offers computational engineering and science (MS); computer science (MS, PhD); computing (MS, PhD); MS/MBA. *Faculty:* 33 full-time (5 women), 11 part-time/adjunct (0 women). *Students:* 231 full-time (51 women), 56 part-time (10 women); includes 15 minority (2 Black or African American, non-Hispanic/Latino; 10 Asian, non-Hispanic/Latino; 2 Hispanic/Latino; 1 Two or more races, non-Hispanic/Latino), 192 international. Average age 28. 616 applicants, 36% accepted, 95 enrolled. In 2014, 56 master's, 19 doctorates awarded. Terminal master's awarded for partial completion of doctoral program. *Degree requirements:* For master's, comprehensive exam (for some programs), thesis (for some programs); for doctorate, comprehensive exam, thesis/dissertation. *Entrance requirements:* For master's and doctorate, GRE General Test, minimum GPA of 3.0. Additional exam requirements/recommendations for international students: Required—TOEFL (minimum score 500 paper-based; 61 iBT), IELTS (minimum score 6.5). *Application deadline:* For fall admission, 12/15 for domestic and international students. Application fee: $55 ($65 for international students). Electronic applications accepted. *Expenses:* Expenses: Contact institution. *Financial support:* In 2014–15, 3 students received support, including 3 fellowships with full tuition reimbursements available (averaging $25,000 per year), 125 research assistantships with full tuition reimbursements available (averaging $33,375 per year), 55 teaching assistantships with full tuition reimbursements available (averaging $16,800 per year); Federal Work-Study, scholarships/grants, health care benefits, and unspecified assistantships also available. Financial award application deadline: 12/15; financial award applicants required to submit FAFSA. *Faculty research:* Operating systems, programming languages, formal methods, natural language processing, architecture, networks, image analysis, data analysis, visualization, graphics, scientific computing, robotics. *Total annual research expenditures:* $7.9 million. *Unit head:* Dr. Ross Whitaker, Director, 801-581-8224, Fax: 801-581-5843, E-mail: whitaker@cs.utah.edu. *Application contact:* Ann Carlstrom, Graduate Advisor, 801-581-7631, Fax: 801-581-5843, E-mail: annc@cs.utah.edu.
Website: http://www.cs.utah.edu.

University of Vermont, Graduate College, College of Engineering and Mathematics, Program in Computer Science, Burlington, VT 05405. Offers MS, PhD. *Degree requirements:* For master's, thesis or alternative. *Entrance requirements:* For master's and doctorate, GRE General Test. Additional exam requirements/recommendations for international students: Required—TOEFL (minimum score 550 paper-based; 80 iBT). Electronic applications accepted.

University of Victoria, Faculty of Graduate Studies, Faculty of Engineering, Department of Computer Science, Victoria, BC V8W 2Y2, Canada. Offers M Sc, PhD. Part-time programs available. Terminal master's awarded for partial completion of

doctoral program. *Degree requirements:* For master's, thesis or alternative; for doctorate, thesis/dissertation, candidacy exam. *Entrance requirements:* For master's, GRE (recommended), B Sc in computer science/software engineering or the equivalent or bachelor's degree in mathematics with emphasis on computer science (recommended); for doctorate, GRE (recommended), MS in computer science or equivalent (recommended). Additional exam requirements/recommendations for international students: Required—TOEFL (minimum score 575 paper-based), IELTS (minimum score 7). Electronic applications accepted. *Faculty research:* Functional and logic programming, numerical analysis, parallel and distributed computing, software systems, theoretical computer science, VLSI design and testing.

University of Virginia, School of Engineering and Applied Science, Department of Computer Science, Charlottesville, VA 22903. Offers MCS, MS, PhD. *Faculty:* 26 full-time (3 women). *Students:* 61 full-time (14 women), 1 part-time (0 women); includes 4 minority (all Asian, non-Hispanic/Latino), 42 international. Average age 26. 367 applicants, 14% accepted, 10 enrolled. In 2014, 14 master's, 8 doctorates awarded. *Degree requirements:* For master's, thesis (for some programs); for doctorate, comprehensive exam, thesis/dissertation. *Entrance requirements:* For master's, GRE General Test, 3 letters of recommendation; for doctorate, GRE General Test, 3 letters of recommendation; essay. Additional exam requirements/recommendations for international students: Required—TOEFL (minimum score 650 paper-based; 90 iBT), IELTS (minimum score 7). *Application deadline:* For fall admission, 8/1 for domestic students, 4/1 for international students; for winter admission, 12/1 for domestic students, 8/1 for international students; for spring admission, 5/1 for domestic students, 1/1 for international students. Applications are processed on a rolling basis. Application fee: $60. Electronic applications accepted. *Expenses:* Tuition, state resident: full-time $14,164; part-time $349 per credit hour. Tuition, nonresident: full-time $23,722; part-time $1300 per credit hour. *Required fees:* $2514. *Financial support:* Fellowships available. Financial award application deadline: 10/15; financial award applicants required to submit FAFSA. *Faculty research:* Systems programming, operating systems, analysis of programs and computation theory, programming languages, software engineering. *Unit head:* Kevin Skadron, Chair, 434-982-2200, Fax: 434-982-2214, E-mail: inquiry@cs.virginia.edu. *Application contact:* Pamela M. Morris, Associate Dean for Research and Graduate Programs, 434-243-7683, Fax: 434-982-3044, E-mail: pamela@virginia.edu.
Website: http://www.cs.virginia.edu/.

University of Washington, Graduate School, College of Engineering, Department of Computer Science and Engineering, Seattle, WA 98195-2350. Offers MS, PhD. Part-time and evening/weekend programs available. *Faculty:* 51 full-time (9 women). *Students:* 231 full-time (56 women), 141 part-time (18 women). Average age 28. 1,287 applicants, 13% accepted, 83 enrolled. In 2014, 86 master's, 18 doctorates awarded. *Degree requirements:* For doctorate, thesis/dissertation, independent project. *Entrance requirements:* For master's, GRE General Test; for doctorate, GRE General Test, minimum GPA of 3.0, statement of purpose, curriculum vitae, letters of recommendation, transcript. Additional exam requirements/recommendations for international students: Required—TOEFL (minimum score 580 paper-based; 92 iBT); Recommended—IELTS (minimum score 7). *Application deadline:* For fall admission, 12/15 for domestic and international students. Applications are processed on a rolling basis. Application fee: $85. Electronic applications accepted. *Expenses:* Expenses: Contact institution. *Financial support:* In 2014–15, 200 students received support, including 40 fellowships with full tuition reimbursements available, 127 research assistantships with full tuition reimbursements available, 33 teaching assistantships with full tuition reimbursements available; career-related internships or fieldwork, traineeships, and health care benefits also available. Financial award application deadline: 12/15. *Faculty research:* Theory, systems, artificial intelligence, graphics, databases. *Total annual research expenditures:* $32.7 million. *Unit head:* Henry M. Levy, Professor/Chair, 206-543-9204, Fax: 206-543-2969, E-mail: levy@cs.washington.edu. *Application contact:* Elise deGoede Dorough, Graduate Admissions Information Contact, 206-543-1695, Fax: 206-543-2969, E-mail: elised@cs.washington.edu.
Website: http://www.cs.washington.edu/.

University of Waterloo, Graduate Studies, Faculty of Mathematics, David R. Cheriton School of Computer Science, Waterloo, ON N2L 3G1, Canada. Offers computer science (M Math, PhD); software engineering (M Math); statistics and computing (M Math). Part-time programs available. *Degree requirements:* For master's, research paper or thesis; for doctorate, comprehensive exam, thesis/dissertation. *Entrance requirements:* For master's, honors degree in field, minimum B+ average; for doctorate, master's degree, minimum B+ average. *Faculty research:* Computer graphics, artificial intelligence, algorithms and complexity, distributed computing and networks, software engineering.

The University of Western Ontario, Faculty of Graduate Studies, Physical Sciences Division, Department of Computer Science, London, ON N6A 5B8, Canada. Offers M Sc, PhD. Part-time programs available. *Degree requirements:* For master's, thesis, project, or course work; for doctorate, thesis/dissertation. *Entrance requirements:* For master's, B Sc in computer science or comparable academic qualifications; for doctorate, M Sc in computer science or comparable academic qualifications. Additional exam requirements/recommendations for international students: Required—TOEFL. *Faculty research:* Artificial intelligence and logic programming, graphics and image processing, software and systems, theory of computing, symbolic mathematical computation.

University of West Florida, College of Arts and Sciences: Sciences, Department of Computer Science, Pensacola, FL 32514-5750. Offers computer science (MS); database systems (MS); software engineering (MS). Part-time and evening/weekend programs available. *Degree requirements:* For master's, thesis optional. *Entrance requirements:* For master's, GRE, MAT, or GMAT, official transcripts; minimum undergraduate GPA of 3.0; letter of intent; three letters of recommendation. Additional exam requirements/recommendations for international students: Required—TOEFL (minimum score 550 paper-based).

University of West Georgia, College of Science and Mathematics, Department of Computer Science, Carrollton, GA 30118. Offers applied computer science (MS). Part-time and evening/weekend programs available. Postbaccalaureate distance learning degree programs offered (no on-campus study). *Faculty:* 7 full-time (2 women). *Students:* 1 full-time (0 women), 82 part-time (26 women); includes 20 minority (8 Black or African American, non-Hispanic/Latino; 6 Asian, non-Hispanic/Latino; 4 Hispanic/Latino; 1 Native Hawaiian or other Pacific Islander, non-Hispanic/Latino; 1 Two or more races, non-Hispanic/Latino), 7 international. Average age 34. 87 applicants, 59% accepted, 37 enrolled. In 2014, 7 master's awarded. *Degree requirements:* For master's, comprehensive exam. *Entrance requirements:* For master's, bachelor's degree, minimum overall undergraduate GPA of 2.5, 3 letters of reference, resume or curriculum vitae, personal narrative. Additional exam requirements/recommendations for international students: Recommended—TOEFL (minimum score 523 paper-based; 69 iBT), IELTS (minimum score 6). *Application deadline:* For fall admission, 7/15 for domestic and international students. Applications are processed on a rolling basis. Application fee: $40. Electronic applications accepted. *Expenses:* Expenses: Contact institution. *Financial support:* In 2014–15, 1 research assistantship with full tuition reimbursement (averaging $9,000 per year) was awarded; unspecified assistantships

also available. Financial award application deadline: 4/1; financial award applicants required to submit FAFSA. *Faculty research:* Artificial intelligence, software engineering, Web technologies, database, networks, computer science education. *Unit head:* Dr. Adel M. Abunawass, Chair, 678-839-6485, Fax: 678-839-6486, E-mail: adel@westga.edu. *Application contact:* Jane Wood, Departmental Assistant, 678-839-6485, Fax: 678-839-6486, E-mail: jwood@westga.edu.
Website: http://www.cs.westga.edu/.

University of Windsor, Faculty of Graduate Studies, Faculty of Science, School of Computer Science, Windsor, ON N9B 3P4, Canada. Offers M Sc, PhD. Part-time programs available. *Degree requirements:* For master's, thesis; for doctorate, comprehensive exam, thesis/dissertation. *Entrance requirements:* For master's, GRE, minimum B average; for doctorate, master's degree in computer science, minimum B+ average. Additional exam requirements/recommendations for international students: Required—TOEFL (minimum score 580 paper-based). Electronic applications accepted. *Faculty research:* Data mining, distributed query optimization, distributed object based systems, grid computing, querying multimedia database systems.

University of Wisconsin–Madison, Graduate School, College of Letters and Science, Department of Computer Sciences, Madison, WI 53706-1380. Offers MS, PhD. Part-time programs available. Terminal master's awarded for partial completion of doctoral program. *Degree requirements:* For doctorate, thesis/dissertation. *Entrance requirements:* For master's and doctorate, GRE General Test, GRE Subject Test. Electronic applications accepted. *Expenses:* Tuition, state resident: full-time $10,723; part-time $745 per credit. Tuition, nonresident: full-time $24,054; part-time $1578 per credit. *Required fees:* $374 per semester. Tuition and fees vary according to course load, program and reciprocity agreements.

University of Wisconsin–Milwaukee, Graduate School, College of Engineering and Applied Science, Program in Computer Science, Milwaukee, WI 53201-0413. Offers MS. Part-time programs available. *Degree requirements:* For master's, comprehensive exam (for some programs), thesis or alternative. *Entrance requirements:* For master's, GRE, minimum GPA of 2.75. Additional exam requirements/recommendations for international students: Required—TOEFL (minimum score 550 paper-based; 79 iBT), IELTS (minimum score 6.5). Electronic applications accepted.

University of Wisconsin–Parkside, School of Business and Technology, Program in Computer and Information Systems, Kenosha, WI 53141-2000. Offers MSCIS. *Entrance requirements:* For master's, GRE General Test or GMAT, 3 letters of recommendation, minimum GPA of 3.0. *Faculty research:* Distributed systems, data bases, natural language processing, event-driven systems.

University of Wisconsin–Platteville, School of Graduate Studies, College of Engineering, Mathematics and Science, Program in Computer Science, Platteville, WI 53818-3099. Offers MS. Part-time programs available. *Degree requirements:* For master's, comprehensive exam, thesis or alternative. *Entrance requirements:* Additional exam requirements/recommendations for international students: Required—TOEFL (minimum score 500 paper-based; 61 iBT), IELTS (minimum score 6). Electronic applications accepted.

University of Wyoming, College of Engineering and Applied Sciences, Department of Computer Science, Laramie, WY 82071. Offers MS, PhD. Part-time programs available. Terminal master's awarded for partial completion of doctoral program. *Degree requirements:* For master's, thesis; for doctorate, thesis/dissertation. *Entrance requirements:* For master's and doctorate, GRE General Test, minimum GPA of 3.0. Additional exam requirements/recommendations for international students: Required—TOEFL (minimum score 550 paper-based), IELTS (minimum score 6). Electronic applications accepted. *Faculty research:* Fault-tolerant computing, distributed systems, knowledge representation, automated reasoning, parallel database access, formal methods.

Utah State University, School of Graduate Studies, College of Science, Department of Computer Science, Logan, UT 84322. Offers MCS, MS, PhD. Part-time and evening/weekend programs available. Postbaccalaureate distance learning degree programs offered. *Degree requirements:* For master's, thesis (for some programs), research project; for doctorate, thesis/dissertation. *Entrance requirements:* For master's, GRE General Test, GRE Subject Test, minimum GPA of 3.25, prerequisite coursework in math, 3 recommendation letters; for doctorate, GRE General Test, minimum GPA of 3.25, BS or MS. Additional exam requirements/recommendations for international students: Required—TOEFL. Electronic applications accepted. *Faculty research:* Artificial intelligence, software engineering, parallelism.

Vanderbilt University, School of Engineering, Department of Electrical Engineering and Computer Science, Program in Computer Science, Nashville, TN 37240-1001. Offers M Eng, MS, PhD. MS and PhD offered through the Graduate School. Part-time programs available. Terminal master's awarded for partial completion of doctoral program. *Degree requirements:* For master's, thesis (for some programs); for doctorate, comprehensive exam, thesis/dissertation. *Entrance requirements:* For master's and doctorate, GRE General Test, 3 letters of recommendation. Additional exam requirements/recommendations for international students: Required—TOEFL. Electronic applications accepted. *Expenses: Tuition:* Full-time $42,768; part-time $1782 per credit hour. *Required fees:* $422. One-time fee: $30 full-time. *Faculty research:* Artificial intelligence, performance evaluation, databases, software engineering, computational science.

Villanova University, College of Engineering, Department of Electrical and Computer Engineering, Program in Computer Engineering, Villanova, PA 19085-1699. Offers computer architectures (Certificate); computer engineering (MSCPE); intelligent control systems (Certificate). Part-time and evening/weekend programs available. *Degree requirements:* For master's, thesis optional. *Entrance requirements:* For master's, GRE General Test (for applicants with degrees from foreign universities), BEE, minimum GPA of 3.0. Additional exam requirements/recommendations for international students: Required—TOEFL (minimum score 600 paper-based; 100 iBT). Electronic applications accepted. *Faculty research:* Expert systems, computer vision, neural networks, image processing, computer architectures.

Villanova University, Graduate School of Liberal Arts and Sciences, Department of Computing Sciences, Villanova, PA 19085-1699. Offers computer science (MS); software engineering (MS). Part-time and evening/weekend programs available. *Students:* 116 full-time (56 women), 21 part-time (3 women); includes 5 minority (2 Asian, non-Hispanic/Latino; 1 Hispanic/Latino; 1 Native Hawaiian or other Pacific Islander, non-Hispanic/Latino; 1 Two or more races, non-Hispanic/Latino), 102 international. Average age 27. 75 applicants, 64% accepted, 35 enrolled. In 2014, 32 master's awarded. *Degree requirements:* For master's, thesis optional, independent study project. *Entrance requirements:* For master's, GRE, minimum GPA of 3.0, 3 recommendation letters. Additional exam requirements/recommendations for international students: Required—TOEFL. *Application deadline:* For fall admission, 5/1 priority date for international students; for spring admission, 11/15 priority date for international students. Applications are processed on a rolling basis. Application fee: $50. Electronic applications accepted. *Financial support:* Research assistantships, scholarships/grants, and unspecified assistantships available. Financial award applicants required to submit FAFSA. *Unit head:* Dr. Vijay Geholt, Chair, 610-519-5843.
Website: http://www1.villanova.edu/villanova/artsci/computerscience/graduate.html.

Virginia Commonwealth University, Graduate School, School of Engineering, Department of Computer Science, Richmond, VA 23284-9005. Offers computer science (MS, PhD); engineering (PhD). *Degree requirements:* For master's, thesis optional. *Entrance requirements:* For master's, GRE General Test; for doctorate, GRE. Additional exam requirements/recommendations for international students: Required—TOEFL (minimum score 600 paper-based; 100 iBT). Electronic applications accepted.

Virginia International University, School of Computer Information Systems, Fairfax, VA 22030. Offers computer science (MS); information systems (MS). Part-time programs available. *Entrance requirements:* For master's, bachelor's degree. Additional exam requirements/recommendations for international students: Required—TOEFL (minimum score 550 paper-based; 80 iBT), IELTS. Electronic applications accepted.

Virginia Polytechnic Institute and State University, Graduate School, College of Engineering, Blacksburg, VA 24061. Offers aerospace engineering (ME, MS, PhD); biological systems engineering (ME, MS, PhD); biomedical engineering (MS, PhD); chemical engineering (ME, MS, PhD); civil engineering (ME, MS, PhD); computer engineering (ME, MS, PhD); computer science (MS, PhD); electrical engineering (ME, PhD); engineering education (PhD); engineering mechanics (ME, MS, PhD); environmental engineering (MS); environmental science and engineering (MS); industrial and systems engineering (ME, MS, PhD); materials science and engineering (ME, MS, PhD); mechanical engineering (ME, MS, PhD); mining and minerals engineering (PhD); mining engineering (ME, MS); nuclear engineering (MS, PhD); ocean engineering (MS); systems engineering (ME, MS). *Accreditation:* ABET (one or more programs are accredited). *Faculty:* 356 full-time (60 women), 3 part-time/adjunct (1 woman). *Students:* 1,700 full-time (398 women), 345 part-time (58 women); includes 213 minority (43 Black or African American, non-Hispanic/Latino; 1 American Indian or Alaska Native, non-Hispanic/Latino; 87 Asian, non-Hispanic/Latino; 58 Hispanic/Latino; 1 Native Hawaiian or other Pacific Islander, non-Hispanic/Latino; 23 Two or more races, non-Hispanic/Latino), 1,079 international. Average age 27. 5,228 applicants, 18% accepted, 471 enrolled. In 2014, 438 master's, 211 doctorates awarded. *Degree requirements:* For master's, comprehensive exam (for some programs), thesis (for some programs); for doctorate, comprehensive exam (for some programs), thesis/dissertation (for some programs). *Entrance requirements:* For master's and doctorate, GRE/GMAT (may vary by department). Additional exam requirements/recommendations for international students: Required—TOEFL (minimum score 550 paper-based). *Application deadline:* For fall admission, 8/1 for domestic students, 4/1 for international students; for spring admission, 1/1 for domestic students, 9/1 for international students. Applications are processed on a rolling basis. Application fee: $75. Electronic applications accepted. *Expenses:* Tuition, state resident: full-time $11,656; part-time $647.50 per credit hour. Tuition, nonresident: full-time $23,351; part-time $1297.25 per credit hour. *Required fees:* $2533; $465.75 per semester. Tuition and fees vary according to course load, campus/location and program. *Financial support:* In 2014–15, 148 fellowships with full tuition reimbursements (averaging $8,031 per year), 855 research assistantships with full tuition reimbursements (averaging $22,855 per year), 288 teaching assistantships with full tuition reimbursements (averaging $20,291 per year) were awarded. Financial award application deadline: 3/1; financial award applicants required to submit FAFSA. *Total annual research expenditures:* $90.5 million. *Unit head:* Dr. Richard C. Benson, Dean, 540-231-9752, Fax: 540-231-3031, E-mail: deaneng@vt.edu. *Application contact:* Linda Perkins, Executive Assistant, 540-231-9752, Fax: 540-231-3031, E-mail: lperkins@vt.edu.
Website: http://www.eng.vt.edu/.

Virginia Polytechnic Institute and State University, VT Online, Blacksburg, VA 24061. Offers advanced transportation systems (Certificate); aerospace engineering (MS); agricultural and life sciences (MSLFS); business information systems (Graduate Certificate); career and technical education (MS); civil engineering (MS); computer engineering (M Eng, MS); decision support systems (Graduate Certificate); eLearning leadership (MA); electrical engineering (M Eng, MS); engineering administration (MEA); environmental engineering (Certificate); environmental politics and policy (Graduate Certificate); environmental sciences and engineering (MS); foundations of political analysis (Graduate Certificate); health product risk management (Graduate Certificate); industrial and systems engineering (MS); information policy and society (Graduate Certificate); information security (Graduate Certificate); information technology (MIT); instructional technology (MA); integrative STEM education (MA Ed); liberal arts (Graduate Certificate); life sciences: health product risk management (MS); natural resources (MNR, Graduate Certificate); networking (Graduate Certificate); nonprofit and nongovernmental organization management (Graduate Certificate); ocean engineering (MS); political science (MA); security studies (Graduate Certificate); software development (Graduate Certificate). *Expenses:* Tuition, state resident: full-time $11,656; part-time $647.50 per credit hour. Tuition, nonresident: full-time $23,351; part-time $1297.25 per credit hour. *Required fees:* $2533; $465.75 per semester. Tuition and fees vary according to course load, campus/location and program.

Virginia State University, College of Graduate Studies, College of Engineering and Technology, Department of Mathematics and Computer Science, Petersburg, VA 23806-0001. Offers computer science (MS); mathematics (MS); mathematics education (MS). *Degree requirements:* For master's, thesis (for some programs).

Wake Forest University, Graduate School of Arts and Sciences, Department of Computer Science, Winston-Salem, NC 27109. Offers MS. Part-time programs available. *Degree requirements:* For master's, one foreign language, thesis optional. *Entrance requirements:* For master's, GRE General Test. Additional exam requirements/recommendations for international students: Required—TOEFL (minimum score 79 iBT). Electronic applications accepted.

Washington State University, Voiland College of Engineering and Architecture, Engineering and Computer Science Programs, Vancouver Campus, Pullman, WA 99164. Offers MS. *Students:* 32 full-time (4 women), 9 part-time (1 woman); includes 12 minority (1 Black or African American, non-Hispanic/Latino; 10 Asian, non-Hispanic/Latino; 1 Hispanic/Latino), 11 international. Average age 30. 39 applicants, 36% accepted, 13 enrolled. In 2014, 16 master's awarded. *Degree requirements:* For master's, comprehensive exam, thesis optional. *Entrance requirements:* For master's, official transcripts from all colleges and universities attended; one-page statement of purpose; three letters of recommendation. Additional exam requirements/recommendations for international students: Required—TOEFL; Recommended—IELTS. *Application deadline:* For fall admission, 1/10 priority date for domestic and international students; for spring admission, 7/1 priority date for domestic and international students. Application fee: $75. Electronic applications accepted. *Expenses:* Tuition, state resident: full-time $11,768. Tuition, nonresident: full-time $25,200. *Required fees:* $960. Tuition and fees vary according to program. *Financial support:* In 2014–15, 24 students received support, including 2 fellowships, 4 research assistantships (averaging $13,379 per year), 24 teaching assistantships (averaging $13,379 per year); health care benefits, tuition waivers, and unspecified assistantships also available. Financial award application deadline: 3/1; financial award applicants

contact: Marianne Gumpper, Director of Graduate and Continuing Studies Admission, 203-254-4184, Fax: 203-254-4073, E-mail: gradadmis@fairfield.edu.
Website: http://www.fairfield.edu/academics/schoolscollegescenters/schoolofengineering/graduateprograms/.

Ferris State University, College of Business, Big Rapids, MI 49307. Offers business intelligence (MBA); design and innovation management (MBA); incident response (MBA); information security and intelligence (MS), including business intelligence, incident response, project management; management tools and concepts (MBA); project management (MBA). *Accreditation:* ACBSP. Part-time and evening/weekend programs available. Postbaccalaureate distance learning degree programs offered (minimal on-campus study). *Faculty:* 9 full-time (3 women), 6 part-time/adjunct (2 women). *Students:* 44 full-time (9 women), 90 part-time (44 women); includes 17 minority (6 Black or African American, non-Hispanic/Latino; 1 American Indian or Alaska Native, non-Hispanic/Latino; 1 Asian, non-Hispanic/Latino; 3 Hispanic/Latino; 6 Two or more races, non-Hispanic/Latino), 30 international. Average age 33. 121 applicants, 81% accepted, 52 enrolled. In 2014, 47 master's awarded. *Degree requirements:* For master's, comprehensive exam, thesis (for MS). *Entrance requirements:* For master's, GRE or GMAT (waived if GPA is 3.5 or better), minimum GPA of 3.0 in junior/senior level classes, 2.75 overall; statement of purpose; 3 letters of reference; resume. Additional exam requirements/recommendations for international students: Required—TOEFL (minimum score 500 paper-based; 67 iBT). *Application deadline:* For fall admission, 7/1 priority date for domestic students, 6/15 for international students; for winter admission, 11/1 priority date for domestic students, 10/15 for international students; for spring admission, 3/1 priority date for domestic students, 2/15 for international students. Applications are processed on a rolling basis. Application fee: $0 ($30 for international students). Electronic applications accepted. Application fee is waived when completed online. Tuition and fees vary according to degree level and program. *Financial support:* Career-related internships or fieldwork, Federal Work-Study, scholarships/grants, and unspecified assistantships available. Support available to part-time students. Financial award application deadline: 3/15; financial award applicants required to submit FAFSA. *Faculty research:* Quality improvement, client/server end-user computing, security and digital forensics, performance metrics and sustainability. *Unit head:* Dr. David Nicol, College of Business Dean, 231-591-2168, Fax: 231-591-3521, E-mail: davidnicol@ferris.edu. *Application contact:* Shannon Yost, Department Secretary, 231-591-2168, Fax: 231-591-3521, E-mail: yosts@ferris.edu.
Website: http://cbgp.ferris.edu/.

Illinois Institute of Technology, Graduate College, College of Science, Department of Applied Mathematics, Chicago, IL 60616. Offers applied mathematics (MS, PhD); data science (MAS); mathematical finance (MAS). MAS in mathematical finance program held jointly with Stuart School of Business. *Faculty:* 20 full-time (3 women), 7 part-time/adjunct (0 women). *Students:* 52 full-time (17 women), 5 part-time (1 woman); includes 1 minority (Two or more races, non-Hispanic/Latino), 43 international. Average age 27. 218 applicants, 38% accepted, 14 enrolled. In 2014, 9 master's, 1 doctorate awarded. Terminal master's awarded for partial completion of doctoral program. *Degree requirements:* For master's, comprehensive exam, thesis; for doctorate, comprehensive exam, thesis/dissertation. *Entrance requirements:* For master's, GRE General Test (minimum scores: 304 Quantitative and Verbal, 2.5 Analytical Writing), minimum undergraduate GPA of 3.0; three letters of recommendation; interview may be required; for doctorate, GRE General Test (minimum scores: 304 Quantitative and Verbal, 3.0 Analytical Writing), minimum undergraduate GPA of 3.5; three letters of recommendation; interview may be required. Additional exam requirements/recommendations for international students: Required—TOEFL (minimum score 550 paper-based; 80 iBT). *Application deadline:* For fall admission, 5/1 for domestic and international students; for spring admission, 10/15 for domestic and international students. Applications are processed on a rolling basis. Application fee: $50. Electronic applications accepted. *Expenses: Tuition:* Full-time $22,500; part-time $1250 per credit hour. *Required fees:* $30 per course. $260 per semester. One-time fee: $235. Tuition and fees vary according to course load and program. *Financial support:* Fellowships with full and partial tuition reimbursements, research assistantships with full and partial tuition reimbursements, teaching assistantships with full and partial tuition reimbursements, career-related internships or fieldwork, Federal Work-Study, institutionally sponsored loans, scholarships/grants, health care benefits, tuition waivers (partial), and unspecified assistantships available. Support available to part-time students. Financial award applicants required to submit FAFSA. *Faculty research:* Applied analysis, computational mathematics, discrete applied mathematics, stochastics (including financial mathematics). *Unit head:* Dr. Fred J. Hickernell, Chairman/Professor, 312-567-8983, Fax: 312-567-3135, E-mail: hickernell@iit.edu. *Application contact:* Rishab Malhotra, Director, Graduate Admission, 866-472-3448, Fax: 312-567-3138, E-mail: inquiry.grad@iit.edu.
Website: http://www.math.iit.edu.

Illinois Institute of Technology, Graduate College, College of Science, Department of Computer Science, Chicago, IL 60616. Offers business (MCS); computational intelligence (MCS); computer networking and communications (MCS); computer science (MCS, MS, PhD); cyber-physical systems (MCS); data analytics (MCS); data science (MAS); database systems (MCS); distributed and cloud computing (MCS); education (MCS); finance (MCS); information security and assurance (MCS); software engineering (MCS); telecommunications and software engineering (MAS); MS/MAS. Part-time and evening/weekend programs available. Postbaccalaureate distance learning degree programs offered (no on-campus study). *Faculty:* 29 full-time (5 women), 8 part-time/adjunct (1 woman). *Students:* 432 full-time (108 women), 117 part-time (27 women); includes 11 minority (3 Black or African American, non-Hispanic/Latino; 7 Asian, non-Hispanic/Latino; 1 Two or more races, non-Hispanic/Latino), 495 international. Average age 26. 2,573 applicants, 42% accepted, 244 enrolled. In 2014, 164 master's, 2 doctorates awarded. Terminal master's awarded for partial completion of doctoral program. *Degree requirements:* For master's, thesis optional; for doctorate, comprehensive exam, thesis/dissertation. *Entrance requirements:* For master's, MS GRE General Test (minimum scores: 298 Quantitative and Verbal, 3.0 Analytical Writing); MAS GRE General Test (minimum scores: 292 Quantitative and Verbal, 2.5 Analytical Writing), minimum undergraduate GPA of 3.0; for doctorate, GRE General Test (minimum scores: 304 Quantitative and Verbal, 3.5 Analytical Writing), minimum undergraduate GPA of 3.0. Additional exam requirements/recommendations for international students: Required—TOEFL (minimum score 523 paper-based; 70 iBT). *Application deadline:* For fall admission, 5/1 for domestic and international students; for spring admission, 10/15 for domestic and international students. Applications are processed on a rolling basis. Application fee: $50. Electronic applications accepted. *Expenses: Tuition:* Full-time $22,500; part-time $1250 per credit hour. *Required fees:* $30 per course. $260 per semester. One-time fee: $235. Tuition and fees vary according to course load and program. *Financial support:* Fellowships with partial tuition reimbursements, research assistantships with full and partial tuition reimbursements, teaching assistantships with full and partial tuition reimbursements, career-related internships or fieldwork, Federal Work-Study, institutionally sponsored loans, scholarships/grants, traineeships, health care benefits, tuition waivers (partial), and unspecified assistantships available. Support available to part-time students. Financial award applicants required to submit FAFSA. *Faculty research:* Parallel and distributed processing, high-performance computing, computational linguistics, information retrieval, data mining, grid computing. *Unit head:* Dr. Eunice Santos, Chair/Professor, 312-567-5150, E-mail: eunice.santos@iit.edu. *Application contact:* Rishab Malhotra, Director, Graduate Admission, 866-472-3448, Fax: 312-567-3138, E-mail: inquiry.grad@iit.edu.
Website: http://www.iit.edu/csl/cs/.

Lewis University, College of Business, Graduate School of Management, Program in Business Analytics, Romeoville, IL 60446. Offers financial analytics (MS); healthcare analytics (MS); marketing analytics (MS); operations analytics (MS). Postbaccalaureate distance learning degree programs offered (no on-campus study). *Students:* 2 full-time (1 woman), 7 part-time (2 women); includes 4 minority (2 Black or African American, non-Hispanic/Latino; 1 Asian, non-Hispanic/Latino; 1 Hispanic/Latino). Average age 28. *Unit head:* Dr. Rami Khasawneh, Dean, 800-838-0500 Ext. 5360, E-mail: khasawra@lewisu.edu. *Application contact:* Michele Ryan, Director of Admission, 815-836-5384, E-mail: gsm@lewisu.edu.
Website: http://www.lewisu.edu/academics/business-analytics/.

Lipscomb University, College of Computing and Technology, Nashville, TN 37204-3951. Offers information technology (MS), including data science. Part-time and evening/weekend programs available. *Faculty:* 5 full-time (2 women), 8 part-time/adjunct (5 women). *Students:* 11 full-time (4 women), 11 part-time (2 women); includes 3 minority (2 Black or African American, non-Hispanic/Latino; 1 Asian, non-Hispanic/Latino), 1 international. Average age 39. In 2014, 33 master's awarded. *Degree requirements:* For master's, capstone project. *Entrance requirements:* For master's, GRE, 2 references, transcripts, resume, personal statement. Additional exam requirements/recommendations for international students: Required—TOEFL (minimum score 570 paper-based; 80 iBT). *Application deadline:* Applications are processed on a rolling basis. Application fee: $50 ($75 for international students). Electronic applications accepted. *Expenses:* Expenses: $1,225 per credit hour. *Financial support:* Scholarships/grants and employer agreements available. Financial award applicants required to submit FAFSA. *Unit head:* Dr. Fortune S. Mhlanga, Director, 615-966-5073, E-mail: fortune.mhlanga@lipscomb.edu. *Application contact:* Finn Breland, Enrollment Management Specialist, 615-966-1193, E-mail: finn.breland@lipscomb.edu.
Website: http://www.lipscomb.edu/technology/.

Metropolitan State University, College of Management, St. Paul, MN 55106-5000. Offers business administration (MBA, DBA); database administration (Graduate Certificate); healthcare information technology management (Graduate Certificate); information assurance security (Graduate Certificate); management information systems (MMIS); MIS generalist (Graduate Certificate); MIS systems analysis and design (Graduate Certificate); project management (Graduate Certificate); public and nonprofit administration (MPNA). Part-time and evening/weekend programs available. *Degree requirements:* For master's, thesis optional, computer language (MMIS). *Entrance requirements:* For master's, GMAT (for MBA), resume. Additional exam requirements/recommendations for international students: Required—TOEFL (minimum score 550 paper-based). Electronic applications accepted. *Faculty research:* Yugoslav economic system, workers' cooperatives, participative management and job enrichment, global business systems.

Minnesota State University Mankato, College of Graduate Studies, College of Science, Engineering and Technology, Department of Information Systems and Technology, Mankato, MN 56001. Offers database technologies (Certificate); information technology (MS). *Students:* 35 full-time (8 women), 24 part-time (7 women). *Degree requirements:* For master's, comprehensive exam, thesis or alternative. *Entrance requirements:* For master's, GRE General Test, minimum GPA of 3.0 during previous 2 years. Additional exam requirements/recommendations for international students: Required—TOEFL (minimum score 550 paper-based; 80 iBT). *Application deadline:* For fall admission, 7/1 priority date for domestic students; for spring admission, 11/1 for domestic students. Applications are processed on a rolling basis. Electronic applications accepted. *Financial support:* Research assistantships with full tuition reimbursements, teaching assistantships with full tuition reimbursements, and unspecified assistantships available. Financial award application deadline: 3/15; financial award applicants required to submit FAFSA. *Unit head:* Dr. Mahbubur Syed, Graduate Coordinator, 507-389-3226. *Application contact:* 507-389-2321, E-mail: grad@mnsu.edu.
Website: http://cset.mnsu.edu/ist/.

Montclair State University, The Graduate School, College of Humanities and Social Sciences, Data Collection and Management Certificate Program, Montclair, NJ 07043-1624. Offers Certificate. *Students:* 1 (woman) full-time, 7 part-time (5 women); includes 2 minority (both Hispanic/Latino). Average age 27. 12 applicants, 83% accepted, 7 enrolled. *Expenses:* Tuition, state resident: full-time $9960; part-time $553.35 per credit. Tuition, nonresident: full-time $15,074; part-time $837.43 per credit. *Required fees:* $1595; $88.63 per credit. Tuition and fees vary according to degree level and program. *Unit head:* Dr. Jay Livingston, Chairperson. *Application contact:* Amy Aiello, Executive Director of The Graduate School, 973-655-5147, Fax: 973-655-7869, E-mail: graduate.school@montclair.edu.

National University, Academic Affairs, School of Engineering and Computing, La Jolla, CA 92037-1011. Offers computer science (MS), including advanced computing, database engineering, software engineering; cyber security and information assurance (MS), including computer forensics, ethical hacking and penetration testing, health information assurance, information assurance and security; data analytics (MS); engineering management (MS), including enterprise architecture, project management, systems engineering, technology management; environmental engineering (MS); homeland security and emergency management (MS); management information systems (MS); project management (Certificate); sustainability management (MS); wireless communications (MS). Part-time and evening/weekend programs available. Postbaccalaureate distance learning degree programs offered (no on-campus study). *Faculty:* 24 full-time (5 women), 21 part-time/adjunct (5 women). *Students:* 275 full-time (72 women), 86 part-time (24 women); includes 147 minority (41 Black or African American, non-Hispanic/Latino; 48 Asian, non-Hispanic/Latino; 37 Hispanic/Latino; 7 Native Hawaiian or other Pacific Islander, non-Hispanic/Latino; 14 Two or more races, non-Hispanic/Latino), 95 international. Average age 33. In 2014, 281 master's awarded. *Degree requirements:* For master's, thesis (for some programs). *Entrance requirements:* For master's, interview, minimum GPA of 2.5. Additional exam requirements/recommendations for international students: Required—TOEFL (minimum score 550 paper-based; 79 iBT), IELTS (minimum score 6). *Application deadline:* Applications are processed on a rolling basis. Application fee: $60 ($65 for international students). Electronic applications accepted. *Expenses: Tuition:* Full-time $14,184; part-time $1773 per course. *Financial support:* Career-related internships or fieldwork, institutionally sponsored loans, scholarships/grants, and tuition waivers (partial) available. Support available to part-time students. Financial award application deadline: 6/30; financial award applicants required to submit FAFSA. *Faculty research:* Educational technology, scholarships in science. *Unit head:* School of Engineering and Computing, 800-628-8648, E-mail: soec@nu.edu. *Application contact:* Frank Rojas, Vice President for Enrollment Services, 800-628-8648, E-mail: advisor@nu.edu.
Website: http://www.nu.edu/OurPrograms/SchoolOfEngineeringAndTechnology.html.

Database Systems

New York University, Graduate School of Arts and Science, Department of Data Science, New York, NY 10012-1019. Offers MS. *Students:* 49 full-time (20 women), 17 part-time (6 women); includes 5 minority (4 Asian, non-Hispanic/Latino; 1 Two or more races, non-Hispanic/Latino), 51 international. Average age 25. 604 applicants, 15% accepted, 39 enrolled. *Entrance requirements:* For master's, GRE or GMAT. Additional exam requirements/recommendations for international students: Required—TOEFL. *Application deadline:* For fall admission, 2/4 for domestic and international students. Application fee: $100. Electronic applications accepted. *Financial support:* Application deadline: 2/4; applicants required to submit FAFSA. *Unit head:* Roy Lawrence, Director, 212-998-3401, E-mail: datascience-group@nyu.edu. *Application contact:* Varsha Tiger, Administrator, 212-998-3401, E-mail: datascience-group@nyu.edu.

New York University, School of Continuing and Professional Studies, Division of Programs in Business, Graduate Programs in Management and Systems, New York, NY 10012-1019. Offers core business competencies (Advanced Certificate); database technologies (MS); enterprise risk management (MS, Advanced Certificate); information technologies (Advanced Certificate); strategy and leadership (MS, Advanced Certificate); systems management (MS). Part-time and evening/weekend programs available. Postbaccalaureate distance learning degree programs offered (no on-campus study). *Faculty:* 1 full-time (0 women), 36 part-time/adjunct (8 women). *Students:* 69 full-time (32 women), 196 part-time (88 women); includes 75 minority (21 Black or African American, non-Hispanic/Latino; 31 Asian, non-Hispanic/Latino; 20 Hispanic/Latino; 3 Two or more races, non-Hispanic/Latino), 86 international. Average age 31. 198 applicants, 58% accepted, 49 enrolled. In 2014, 66 master's, 8 other advanced degrees awarded. *Degree requirements:* For master's, thesis, capstone project. *Entrance requirements:* For master's, GRE or GMAT only upon request, bachelor's degree, resume with relevant professional work, internship or volunteer experience, two letters of recommendation, statement of purpose. Additional exam requirements/recommendations for international students: Required—TOEFL (minimum score 600 paper-based; 100 iBT); IELTS (minimum score 7). *Application deadline:* For fall admission, 2/1 priority date for domestic and international students; for spring admission, 10/15 priority date for domestic students, 8/15 priority date for international students. Applications are processed on a rolling basis. Application fee: $150. Electronic applications accepted. *Financial support:* In 2014–15, 50 students received support, including 50 fellowships (averaging $1,517 per year); Federal Work-Study and scholarships/grants also available. Support available to part-time students. Financial award application deadline: 4/1; financial award applicants required to submit FAFSA. *Unit head:* Vish Ganpati, Academic Director, 212-992-3664, E-mail: vg36@nyu.edu. *Application contact:* Admissions Office, 212-998-7100, E-mail: sps.gradadmissions@nyu.edu.
Website: http://www.sps.nyu.edu/areas-of-study/information-technology/.

Northwestern University, School of Professional Studies, Program in Information Systems, Evanston, IL 60208. Offers analytics and business intelligence (MS); database and Internet technologies (MS); information systems (MS); information systems management (MS); information systems security (MS); medical informatics (MS); software project management and development (MS).

Regis University, College for Professional Studies, School of Computer and Information Sciences, Denver, CO 80221-1099. Offers database development (Certificate); enterprise Java software development (Certificate); enterprise resource planning (Certificate); executive information technology (Certificate); information assurance (M Sc); information technology management (M Sc); software engineering (Certificate); software engineering and database technologies (M Sc); storage area networks (Certificate); systems engineering (M Sc, Certificate). Part-time and evening/weekend programs available. Postbaccalaureate distance learning degree programs offered (no on-campus study). *Faculty:* 8 full-time (3 women), 46 part-time/adjunct (9 women). *Students:* 254 full-time (69 women), 221 part-time (59 women); includes 159 minority (57 Black or African American, non-Hispanic/Latino; 4 American Indian or Alaska Native, non-Hispanic/Latino; 39 Asian, non-Hispanic/Latino; 49 Hispanic/Latino; 1 Native Hawaiian or other Pacific Islander, non-Hispanic/Latino; 9 Two or more races, non-Hispanic/Latino), 22 international. Average age 38. 204 applicants, 87% accepted, 128 enrolled. In 2014, 176 master's awarded. *Degree requirements:* For master's, thesis (for some programs), final research project. *Entrance requirements:* For master's, official transcript reflecting baccalaureate degree awarded from regionally-accredited college or university, 2 years of related experience, resume, interview. Additional exam requirements/recommendations for international students: Required—TOEFL (minimum score 550 paper-based; 82 iBT). *Application deadline:* For fall admission, 8/13 for domestic students, 7/13 for international students; for winter admission, 10/8 for domestic students, 9/8 for international students; for spring admission, 12/17 for domestic students, 11/17 for international students. Applications are processed on a rolling basis. Application fee: $75. Electronic applications accepted. *Expenses:* Expenses: $710 per credit hour (for M Sc). *Financial support:* In 2014–15, 16 students received support. Federal Work-Study and scholarships/grants available. Financial award application deadline: 4/15; financial award applicants required to submit FAFSA. *Faculty research:* Information policy, knowledge management, software architectures. *Unit head:* Donald Archer, Interim Dean, 303-458-4335, E-mail: archer@regis.edu. *Application contact:* Sarah Engel, Director of Admissions, 303-458-4900, Fax: 303-964-5534, E-mail: regisadm@regis.edu.
Website: http://regis.edu/CCIS.aspx.

Rochester Institute of Technology, Graduate Enrollment Services, Golisano College of Computing and Information Sciences, Computer Science Department, Advanced Certificate Program in Big Data Analytics, Rochester, NY 14623-5608. Offers Advanced Certificate. Part-time programs available. *Students:* 3 applicants. *Entrance requirements:* For degree, TOEFL, IELTS, or PTE for non-native English speakers, Recommended minimum GPA of 3.0. Additional exam requirements/recommendations for international students: Required—PTE (minimum score 58), TOEFL (minimum score 550 paper-based; 79 iBT) or IELTS (minimum score 6.5). *Application deadline:* Applications are processed on a rolling basis. Electronic applications accepted. *Expenses:* Expenses: $1,673 per credit hour. *Financial support:* Federal Work-Study, institutionally sponsored loans, and scholarships/grants available. Support available to part-time students. Financial award applicants required to submit FAFSA. *Faculty research:* Data management, data analytics, data security, data warehousing. *Unit head:* Dr. Hans-Peter Bischof, Graduate Program Director, 585-475-5568, Fax: 585-475-4935, E-mail: hpb@cs.rit.edu. *Application contact:* Diane Ellison, Associate Vice President, Graduate Enrollment Services, 585-475-2229, Fax: 585-475-7164, E-mail: gradinfo@rit.edu.
Website: http://www.cs.rit.edu/programs/BigData.

Sacred Heart University, Graduate Programs, College of Arts and Sciences, Department of Computer Science, Fairfield, CT 06825-1000. Offers computer game design and development (Graduate Certificate); computer science and information technology (MS); computer science gaming (MS); cybersecurity (MS); database design (Graduate Certificate); information technology (Graduate Certificate); information technology and network security (Graduate Certificate); interactive multimedia (Graduate Certificate); Web development (Graduate Certificate). Part-time and evening/weekend programs available. *Faculty:* 6 full-time (2 women), 18 part-time/adjunct (5

women). *Students:* 266 full-time (100 women), 69 part-time (15 women); includes 30 minority (11 Black or African American, non-Hispanic/Latino; 7 Asian, non-Hispanic/Latino; 12 Hispanic/Latino), 265 international. Average age 26. 1,010 applicants, 56% accepted, 166 enrolled. In 2014, 50 master's awarded. *Degree requirements:* For master's, thesis or alternative. *Entrance requirements:* For master's, bachelor's degree, minimum GPA of 3.0. Additional exam requirements/recommendations for international students: Required—PTE; Recommended—TOEFL (minimum score 570 paper-based; 80 iBT), IELTS (minimum score 6.5). *Application deadline:* For fall admission, 5/15 for international students; for spring admission, 10/30 for international students. Applications are processed on a rolling basis. Application fee: $60. Electronic applications accepted. *Expenses: Tuition:* Full-time $24,559; part-time $649 per credit. *Financial support:* Unspecified assistantships available. Financial award applicants required to submit FAFSA. *Unit head:* Domenick Pinto, Academic Director and Chairperson, 203-371-7789, Fax: 203-371-0506, E-mail: pintod@sacredheart.edu. *Application contact:* Kathy Dilks, Executive Director of Graduate Admissions, 203-365-7619, Fax: 203-365-4732, E-mail: gradstudies@sacredheart.edu.
Website: http://www.sacredheart.edu/academics/collegeofartssciences/academicdepartments/computerscienceinformationtechnology/graduatedegreesandcertificates/.

St. John's University, College of Professional Studies, Department of Computer Science, Mathematics and Science (CPS), Queens, NY 11439. Offers MS. Part-time and evening/weekend programs available. *Students:* 9 full-time (4 women), 5 part-time (1 woman); includes 4 minority (2 Black or African American, non-Hispanic/Latino; 2 Hispanic/Latino), 5 international. 47 applicants, 74% accepted, 14 enrolled. *Entrance requirements:* For master's, baccalaureate degree, two letters of recommendation. Additional exam requirements/recommendations for international students: Required—TOEFL (minimum score 600 paper-based; 100 iBT), IELTS (minimum score 7). *Application deadline:* For fall admission, 6/1 priority date for domestic students; for spring admission, 11/1 priority date for domestic students. Applications are processed on a rolling basis. Electronic applications accepted. *Expenses: Tuition:* Full-time $20,610; part-time $1145 per credit. *Required fees:* $170 per semester. *Unit head:* Dr. Ronald Fechter, Associate Professor, 718-990-6473, E-mail: fechterr@stjohns.edu. *Application contact:* Robert Medrano, Director of Graduate Admission, 718-990-1601, E-mail: medranor@stjohns.edu.
Website: http://www.stjohns.edu/academics/schools-and-colleges/college-professional-studies/programs-and-majors/data-mining-and-predictive-analytics-master-sci.

Saint Peter's University, Graduate Business Programs, Program in Data Science, Jersey City, NJ 07306-5997. Offers business analytics (MS). Part-time programs available. *Entrance requirements:* Additional exam requirements/recommendations for international students: Required—TOEFL (minimum score 550 paper-based; 79 iBT), IELTS (minimum score 6.5).

Southern Methodist University, Bobby B. Lyle School of Engineering, Program in Datacenter Systems Engineering, Dallas, TX 75275. Offers MS. Part-time programs available. Postbaccalaureate distance learning degree programs offered (no on-campus study). *Entrance requirements:* For master's, BS in one of the engineering disciplines, computer science, one of the quantitative sciences or mathematics; minimum of two years of college-level mathematics including one year of college-level calculus.

Stevens Institute of Technology, Graduate School, Charles V. Schaefer Jr. School of Engineering, Department of Computer Science, Hoboken, NJ 07030. Offers computer graphics (Certificate); computer science (MS, PhD); computer systems (Certificate); database management systems (Certificate); distributed systems (Certificate); elements of computer science (Certificate); enterprise computing (Certificate); enterprise security and information assurance (Certificate); health informatics (Certificate); multimedia experience and management (Certificate); networks and systems administration (Certificate); security and privacy (Certificate); service oriented computing (Certificate); software design (Certificate); theoretical computer science (Certificate). Part-time and evening/weekend programs available. Terminal master's awarded for partial completion of doctoral program. *Degree requirements:* For master's, thesis optional; for doctorate, variable foreign language requirement, comprehensive exam, thesis/dissertation. *Entrance requirements:* For master's and doctorate, GRE, minimum GPA of 3.0. Additional exam requirements/recommendations for international students: Required—TOEFL. Electronic applications accepted. *Faculty research:* Semantics, reliability theory, programming language, cyber security.

Towson University, Program in Applied Information Technology, Towson, MD 21252-0001. Offers applied information technology (MS, D Sc); database management systems (Postbaccalaureate Certificate); information security and assurance (Postbaccalaureate Certificate); information systems management (Postbaccalaureate Certificate); Internet applications development (Postbaccalaureate Certificate); networking technologies (Postbaccalaureate Certificate); software engineering (Postbaccalaureate Certificate). *Students:* 132 full-time (44 women), 219 part-time (73 women); includes 118 minority (71 Black or African American, non-Hispanic/Latino; 1 American Indian or Alaska Native, non-Hispanic/Latino; 23 Asian, non-Hispanic/Latino; 12 Hispanic/Latino; 2 Native Hawaiian or other Pacific Islander, non-Hispanic/Latino; 9 Two or more races, non-Hispanic/Latino), 85 international. *Entrance requirements:* For master's and Postbaccalaureate Certificate, bachelor's degree, minimum GPA of 3.0; for doctorate, master's degree in computer science, information systems, information technology, or closely-related areas; minimum GPA of 3.0; 2 letters of recommendation; resume. Additional exam requirements/recommendations for international students: Required—TOEFL. *Application deadline:* Applications are processed on a rolling basis. Application fee: $45. Electronic applications accepted. *Unit head:* Dr. Suranjan Chakraborty, Graduate Program Director, 410-704-4769, E-mail: schakraborty@towson.edu. *Application contact:* Alicia Arkell-Kleis, Information Contact, 410-704-6004, E-mail: grads@towson.edu.
Website: http://grad.towson.edu/program/master/ait-ms/.

University of Maryland University College, The Graduate School, Program in Data Analytics, Adelphi, MD 20783. Offers MS, Certificate. Part-time and evening/weekend programs available. Postbaccalaureate distance learning degree programs offered (no on-campus study). *Students:* 216 part-time (84 women); includes 82 minority (39 Black or African American, non-Hispanic/Latino; 18 Asian, non-Hispanic/Latino; 17 Hispanic/Latino; 2 Native Hawaiian or other Pacific Islander, non-Hispanic/Latino; 6 Two or more races, non-Hispanic/Latino), 9 international. Average age 38. 186 applicants, 100% accepted, 96 enrolled. *Degree requirements:* For master's, practicum. *Application deadline:* Applications are processed on a rolling basis. Application fee: $50. Electronic applications accepted. *Financial support:* Federal Work-Study available. Support available to part-time students. Financial award application deadline: 6/1; financial award applicants required to submit FAFSA. *Unit head:* Dr. William Ford, Program Chair, 240-684-2400, Fax: 240-684-2401, E-mail: william.ford@umuc.edu. *Application contact:* Coordinator, Graduate Admissions, 800-888-8682, Fax: 240-684-2151, E-mail: newgrad@umuc.edu.
Website: http://www.umuc.edu/academic-programs/masters-degrees/data-analytics.cfm.

University of Michigan–Dearborn, College of Business, MS Program in Business Analytics, Dearborn, MI 48126. Offers MS. Part-time and evening/weekend programs available. *Faculty:* 47 full-time (21 women), 31 part-time/adjunct (9 women). *Students:* 27 full-time (7 women), 34 part-time (12 women); includes 9 minority (1 American Indian or Alaska Native, non-Hispanic/Latino; 7 Asian, non-Hispanic/Latino; 1 Hispanic/Latino), 34 international. 90 applicants, 57% accepted, 22 enrolled. In 2014, 1 master's awarded. *Entrance requirements:* For master's, GMAT or GRE, equivalent of four-year U.S. bachelor's degree from regionally-accredited institution, undergraduate course in finite math, pre-calculus, or calculus. Additional exam requirements/recommendations for international students: Required—TOEFL (minimum score 560 paper-based; 84 iBT), IELTS (minimum score 6.5). *Application deadline:* For fall admission, 8/1 for domestic students, 5/1 for international students; for winter admission, 12/1 for domestic students, 9/1 for international students; for spring admission, 4/1 for domestic students, 1/1 for international students. Applications are processed on a rolling basis. Application fee: $60. Electronic applications accepted. *Expenses:* Expenses: $822 per credit hour in-state, $560 for ninth credit hour and beyond; $1,324 per credit hour out-state, $933 for ninth credit hour and beyond; $267 in fees per term part-time, $329 full-time. *Financial support:* Career-related internships or fieldwork and scholarships/grants available. Support available to part-time students. Financial award applicants required to submit FAFSA. *Faculty research:* Decision sciences and business intelligence, management information systems, marketing, organization behavior, supply chain management. *Unit head:* Dr. Michael Kamen, Dean, 313-593-5460, E-mail: mkamen@umich.edu. *Application contact:* Joan Doherty, Academic Advisor/Counselor, 313-593-5460, Fax: 313-271-9838, E-mail: umd-gradbusiness@umich.edu.
Website: http://umdearborn.edu/cob/ms-business-analytics/.

University of Minnesota, Twin Cities Campus, College of Science and Engineering, Department of Computer Science and Engineering, Program in Data Science, Minneapolis, MN 55455-0213. Offers MS. *Entrance requirements:* For master's, GRE. Additional exam requirements/recommendations for international students: Required—TOEFL. Electronic applications accepted. *Faculty research:* Data collection and management, data analytics, scalable data-driven pattern discovery, and the fundamental algorithmic and statistical concepts behind these methods.

University of New Haven, Graduate School, Tagliatela College of Engineering, Program in Computer and Information Science, West Haven, CT 06516-1916. Offers computer and information science (MS); computer programming (Certificate); computer systems (MS); database and information systems (MS); network systems (MS); software engineering and development (MS). Part-time and evening/weekend programs available. *Degree requirements:* For master's, thesis or alternative. *Entrance requirements:* Additional exam requirements/recommendations for international students: Required—TOEFL (minimum score 75 iBT), IELTS, PTE (minimum score 50). Electronic applications accepted. Application fee is waived when completed online.

The University of North Carolina at Charlotte, College of Computing and Informatics, Department of Computer Science, Charlotte, NC 28223-0001. Offers advanced databases and knowledge discovery (Graduate Certificate); computer science (MS); game design and development (Graduate Certificate). Part-time and evening/weekend programs available. *Faculty:* 27 full-time (5 women), 5 part-time/adjunct (3 women). *Students:* 197 full-time (50 women), 48 part-time (14 women); includes 6 minority (2 Asian, non-Hispanic/Latino; 3 Hispanic/Latino; 1 Two or more races, non-Hispanic/Latino), 220 international. Average age 24. 1,113 applicants, 33% accepted, 104 enrolled. In 2014, 118 master's awarded. *Degree requirements:* For master's, thesis optional. *Entrance requirements:* For master's, GRE General Test, minimum GPA of 3.0 during previous 2 years, 2.8 overall. Additional exam requirements/recommendations for international students: Required—TOEFL (minimum score 557 paper-based; 83 iBT). *Application deadline:* For fall admission, 5/1 for domestic and international students; for spring admission, 10/1 for domestic and international students. Applications are processed on a rolling basis. Application fee: $75. Electronic applications accepted. *Expenses:* Tuition, state resident: full-time $4008. Tuition, nonresident: full-time $16,295. *Required fees:* $2755. Tuition and fees vary according to course load and program. *Financial support:* In 2014–15, 45 students received support, including 2 fellowships (averaging $30,438 per year), 22 research assistantships (averaging $9,562 per year), 21 teaching assistantships (averaging $6,300 per year); career-related internships or fieldwork, Federal Work-Study, institutionally sponsored loans, scholarships/grants, and unspecified assistantships also available. Support available to part-time students. Financial award application deadline: 4/1; financial award applicants required to submit FAFSA. *Faculty research:* Visualization; visual analytics and computer graphics; intelligent and interactive systems; data mining theory, systems, and application; networked systems; computer game design. *Total annual research expenditures:* $2.4 million. *Unit head:* William Ribarsky, Chair, 704-687-8559, Fax: 704-687-3516, E-mail: ribarsky@uncc.edu. *Application contact:* Kathy B. Giddings, Director of Graduate Admissions, 704-687-3366, Fax: 704-687-3279, E-mail: gradadm@uncc.edu.
Website: http://cs.uncc.edu/.

University of Notre Dame, Mendoza College of Business, Master of Science in Business Analytics Program, Notre Dame, IN 46556. Offers MSBA. *Students:* 33 full-time (6 women); includes 8 minority (2 Black or African American, non-Hispanic/Latino; 3 Asian, non-Hispanic/Latino; 1 Hispanic/Latino; 2 Two or more races, non-Hispanic/Latino). Average age 33. *Degree requirements:* For master's, practicum. *Entrance requirements:* For master's, At least two years work experience is required. *Application deadline:* For fall admission, 10/31 for domestic and international students. Applications are processed on a rolling basis. Application fee: $50. Electronic applications accepted. *Unit head:* Suzanne T. Waller, Director of Degree Programs, 574-631-2717, E-mail: suzanne.waller@nd.edu. *Application contact:* Stacey Dickson, Admissions Coordinator, 574-631-1593, Fax: 574-631-6783, E-mail: sdickso1@nd.edu.
Website: http://mendoza.nd.edu/programs/specialized-masters/ms-in-business-analytics/.

University of San Francisco, College of Arts and Sciences, Analytics Program, San Francisco, CA 94117-1080. Offers MS. Program offered jointly with School of Management. *Faculty:* 4 full-time (1 woman), 2 part-time/adjunct (0 women). *Students:* 34 full-time (11 women); includes 11 minority (2 Asian, non-Hispanic/Latino; 3 Hispanic/Latino; 6 Two or more races, non-Hispanic/Latino), 11 international. Average age 27. 229 applicants, 19% accepted, 34 enrolled. In 2014, 11 master's awarded. *Expenses:* Tuition: Full-time $21,762; part-time $1209 per credit hour. Tuition and fees vary according to degree level, campus/location and program. *Financial support:* In 2014–15, 19 students received support. *Unit head:* Kirsten Keihl, Program Manager, 415-422-2966. *Application contact:* Mark Landerghini, Information Contact, 415-422-5101, Fax: 415-422-2217, E-mail: asgraduate@usfca.edu.
Website: https://www.usfca.edu/artsci/analytics/.

University of Virginia, Data Science Institute, Charlottesville, VA 22903. Offers MS. *Students:* 47 full-time (17 women); includes 4 minority (2 Asian, non-Hispanic/Latino; 1 Hispanic/Latino; 1 Two or more races, non-Hispanic/Latino), 29 international. Average age 24. 170 applicants, 56% accepted, 48 enrolled. *Entrance requirements:* For master's, GRE or GMAT, undergraduate degree, personal statement, official transcripts, two letters of recommendation. Additional exam requirements/recommendations for international students: Required—TOEFL or IELTS. *Application deadline:* Applications are processed on a rolling basis. Application fee: $85. *Expenses:* Tuition, state resident: full-time $14,164; part-time $349 per credit hour. Tuition, nonresident: full-time $23,722; part-time $1300 per credit hour. *Required fees:* $2514. *Unit head:* Donald E. Brown, Director, 434-982-2074, E-mail: deb@virginia.edu. *Application contact:* Jeffrey Holt, Program Director, 434-924-4927, E-mail: jeff@virginia.edu.
Website: http://dsi.virginia.edu/.

University of West Florida, College of Arts and Sciences: Sciences, Department of Computer Science, Pensacola, FL 32514-5750. Offers computer science (MS); database systems (MS); software engineering (MS). Part-time and evening/weekend programs available. *Degree requirements:* For master's, thesis optional. *Entrance requirements:* For master's, GRE, MAT, or GMAT, official transcripts; minimum undergraduate GPA of 3.0; letter of intent; three letters of recommendation. Additional exam requirements/recommendations for international students: Required—TOEFL (minimum score 550 paper-based).

University of West Florida, College of Professional Studies, Department of Research and Advanced Studies, Pensacola, FL 32514-5750. Offers administration (MSA), including acquisition and contract administration, biomedical/pharmaceutical, criminal justice administration, database administration, education leadership, healthcare administration, human performance technology, leadership, nursing administration, public administration, software engineering and administration; college student personnel administration (M Ed), including college personnel administration, guidance and counseling; curriculum and instruction (M Ed, Ed S); educational leadership (M Ed); middle and secondary level education and ESOL (M Ed). Part-time and evening/weekend programs available. *Entrance requirements:* For master's, GRE or MAT, official transcripts; minimum undergraduate GPA of 3.0; letter of intent; three letters of recommendation; resume. Additional exam requirements/recommendations for international students: Required—TOEFL (minimum score 550 paper-based).

University of West Florida, College of Professional Studies, Program in Administration, Pensacola, FL 32514-5750. Offers acquisition and contract administration (MSA); database administration (MSA); health care administration (MSA); human performance technology (MSA); leadership (MSA); public administration (MSA); software engineering administration (MSA). Part-time and evening/weekend programs available. Postbaccalaureate distance learning degree programs offered (no on-campus study). *Entrance requirements:* For master's, GRE General Test, letter of intent, names of references. Additional exam requirements/recommendations for international students: Required—TOEFL (minimum score 550 paper-based).

Villanova University, Villanova School of Business, Master of Science in Analytics Program, Villanova, PA 19085-1699. Offers MSA. Part-time programs available. Postbaccalaureate distance learning degree programs offered (no on-campus study). *Entrance requirements:* For master's, two essays, professional resume, two letters of recommendation, official transcripts, statistics. Additional exam requirements/recommendations for international students: Required—TOEFL.

Washington University in St. Louis, Olin Business School, Program in Customer Analytics, St. Louis, MO 63130-4899. Offers MS. Part-time programs available. *Faculty:* 87 full-time (20 women), 42 part-time/adjunct (7 women). *Students:* 10 full-time (7 women), 3 part-time; includes 3 minority (all Asian, non-Hispanic/Latino), 6 international. Average age 25. 36 applicants, 44% accepted, 12 enrolled. *Entrance requirements:* For master's, GMAT or GRE. Additional exam requirements/recommendations for international students: Required—TOEFL, IELTS. *Application deadline:* For fall admission, 10/1 for domestic and international students; for winter admission, 11/15 for domestic and international students; for spring admission, 1/4 for domestic and international students. Application fee: $100. Electronic applications accepted. *Financial support:* Applicants required to submit FAFSA. *Unit head:* Greg J. Hutchings, Associate Dean/Director of Specialized Master's Programs, 314-935-4464. *Application contact:* Nikki Lemley, Associate Director, Specialized Master's Programs Admissions, 314-935-8469, Fax: 314-935-8469, E-mail: nlemley@wustl.edu.

Worcester Polytechnic Institute, Graduate Studies and Research, Program in Data Science, Worcester, MA 01609-2280. Offers MS, Graduate Certificate. *Students:* 30 full-time (10 women), 1 (woman) part-time; includes 2 minority (1 Asian, non-Hispanic/Latino; 1 Two or more races, non-Hispanic/Latino), 26 international. 121 applicants, 67% accepted, 30 enrolled. *Entrance requirements:* For master's, GRE Required for international students; Highly recommended for all applicants, Statement of purpose required; 3 letters of recommendation. Additional exam requirements/recommendations for international students: Required—TOEFL (minimum score 563 paper-based; 84 iBT), IELTS. *Application deadline:* For fall admission, 1/1 for domestic and international students; for spring admission, 10/1 for domestic and international students. Application fee: $70. Electronic applications accepted. *Unit head:* Dr. Elke Rundensteiner, Director, 508-831-5815, Fax: 508-831-5776, E-mail: rundenst@wpi.edu. *Application contact:* Lynne Dougherty, Administrative Assistant, 508-831-5301, Fax: 508-831-5717, E-mail: grad@wpi.edu.
Website: http://www.wpi.edu/academics/datascience/graduate-program.html.

Financial Engineering

Baruch College of the City University of New York, Weissman School of Arts and Sciences, Program in Financial Engineering, New York, NY 10010-5585. Offers MS. Part-time and evening/weekend programs available. *Faculty:* 13 full-time (3 women), 6 part-time/adjunct (0 women). *Students:* 34 full-time (7 women), 19 part-time (2 women); includes 9 minority (8 Asian, non-Hispanic/Latino; 1 Two or more races, non-Hispanic/Latino), 36 international. Average age 30. 510 applicants, 9% accepted, 34 enrolled. In 2014, 32 master's awarded. *Entrance requirements:* For master's, GRE General Test or GMAT, 3 recommendations. *Application deadline:* For fall admission, 4/1 for domestic and international students. Application fee: $135. Electronic applications accepted. *Financial support:* Applicants required to submit FAFSA. *Faculty research:* Two-dimensional random walks; Brownian motion; financial applications of probability; volatility modeling; modeling equity market micro-structure for algorithmic trading; mathematical physics; properties of spatially disordered systems; stochastic processes; interacting particle systems; algebra and number theory; discrete and computational

geometry; Ramsey theory; additive number theory; numerical methods for financial applications; option pricing; dynamical systems. *Unit head:* Prof. Dan Stefanica, Director, 646-312-1000. *Application contact:* Michael J. Lovaglio, Director of Graduate Programs, 646-312-4490, Fax: 646-312-4491, E-mail: michael.lovaglio@baruch.cuny.edu.
Website: http://mfe.baruch.cuny.edu/.

Claremont Graduate University, Graduate Programs, Financial Engineering Program, Claremont, CA 91711-6160. Offers MSFE, MS/EMBA, MS/MBA, MS/PhD. *Students:* 33 full-time (9 women), 12 part-time (4 women); includes 5 minority (1 Black or African American, non-Hispanic/Latino; 3 Asian, non-Hispanic/Latino; 1 Hispanic/Latino), 33 international. Average age 27. In 2014, 30 master's awarded. *Entrance requirements:* For master's, GRE General Test or GMAT. Additional exam requirements/recommendations for international students: Required—TOEFL (minimum score 550 paper-based; 80 iBT). *Application deadline:* For fall admission, 11/1 for domestic students, 11/1 priority date for international students. Applications are processed on a rolling basis. Application fee: $80. Electronic applications accepted. *Expenses: Tuition:* Full-time $41,784; part-time $1741 per credit. *Required fees:* $600; $300 per semester. *Financial support:* Fellowships, Federal Work-Study, institutionally sponsored loans, and scholarships/grants available. Support available to part-time students. Financial award application deadline: 2/15; financial award applicants required to submit FAFSA. *Unit head:* Jim Mills, Co-Director, 909-607-3310, E-mail: jim.mills@cgu.edu. *Application contact:* Patrick Latimer, Admissions Coordinator, 909-607-5117, E-mail: patrick.latimer@cgu.edu.
Website: http://www.cgu.edu/fineng.

Columbia University, Fu Foundation School of Engineering and Applied Science, Department of Industrial Engineering and Operations Research, New York, NY 10027. Offers financial engineering (MS); industrial engineering and operations research (MS, Eng Sc D, PhD); management science and engineering (MS); MS/MBA. Part-time and evening/weekend programs available. Postbaccalaureate distance learning degree programs offered (no on-campus study). *Faculty:* 22 full-time (3 women), 50 part-time/adjunct (2 women). *Students:* 417 full-time (152 women), 258 part-time (95 women); includes 37 minority (27 Asian, non-Hispanic/Latino; 7 Hispanic/Latino; 3 Two or more races, non-Hispanic/Latino), 598 international. 2,369 applicants, 27% accepted, 364 enrolled. In 2014, 331 master's, 13 doctorates awarded. *Degree requirements:* For doctorate, thesis/dissertation, oral and written qualifying exams. *Entrance requirements:* For master's and doctorate, GRE General Test. Additional exam requirements/recommendations for international students: Required—TOEFL, IELTS, PTE. *Application deadline:* For fall admission, 12/15 priority date for domestic and international students; for spring admission, 10/1 priority date for domestic and international students. Application fee: $85. Electronic applications accepted. *Financial support:* In 2014–15, 49 students received support, including 1 fellowship with full tuition reimbursement available (averaging $25,000 per year), 24 research assistantships with full tuition reimbursements available (averaging $21,485 per year), 23 teaching assistantships with full tuition reimbursements available (averaging $21,485 per year); health care benefits and funding for travel to conferences also available. Financial award application deadline: 12/15; financial award applicants required to submit FAFSA. *Faculty research:* Applied probability and optimization; financial engineering, modeling risk including credit risk and systemic risk, asset allocation, portfolio execution, behavioral finance, agent-based model in finance; revenue management; management and optimization of service systems, call centers, capacity allocation in healthcare systems, inventory control for vaccines; energy, smart grids, demand shaping, managing renewable energy sources, energy-aware scheduling. *Unit head:* Dr. Garud N. Iyengar, Professor and Department Chair, Industrial Engineering and Operations Research, 212-854-4594, Fax: 212-854-8103, E-mail: garud@ieor.columbia.edu. *Application contact:* Adina Berrios Brooks, Associate Director, Graduate Admissions and Student Affairs, 212-854-1934, Fax: 212-854-8103, E-mail: admit@ieor.columbia.edu.
Website: http://www.ieor.columbia.edu/.

HEC Montreal, School of Business Administration, Master of Science Programs in Administration, Program in Financial Engineering, Montréal, QC H3T 2A7, Canada. Offers M Sc. All courses are given in French. *Students:* 61 full-time (15 women), 14 part-time (4 women). 48 applicants, 75% accepted, 24 enrolled. In 2014, 23 master's awarded. *Degree requirements:* For master's, one foreign language, thesis. *Entrance requirements:* For master's, Test de francais international (TFI) with minimum score of 850 (for those who have never studied in French), BBA, undergraduate degree in another field, degree deemed equivalent by program director and minimum GPA of 3.0 on 4.3 scale. *Application deadline:* For fall admission, 3/15 for domestic and international students; for winter admission, 9/15 for domestic and international students. Application fee: $83 Canadian dollars. Electronic applications accepted. *Financial support:* Research assistantships, teaching assistantships, and scholarships/grants available. Financial award application deadline: 9/2. *Unit head:* Dr. Anne Bourhis, Director, 514-340-6873, Fax: 514-340-6880, E-mail: anne.bourhis@hec.ca. *Application contact:* Marianne de Moura, Administrative Director, 514-340-7106, Fax: 514-340-6411, E-mail: marianne.de-moura@hec.ca.
Website: http://www.hec.ca/programmes_formations/msc/options/finance/ingenierie_financiere/index.html.

The International University of Monaco, Graduate Programs, Monte Carlo, Monaco. Offers entrepreneurship (EMBA, MBA); financial engineering (M Sc); hedge fund and private equity (M Sc); international marketing (EMBA, MBA); international wealth management (M Sc); luxury goods and services (EMBA, M Sc, MBA); wealth and asset management (EMBA, MBA). Part-time programs available. *Degree requirements:* For master's, comprehensive exam (for some programs), applied research project. *Entrance requirements:* Additional exam requirements/recommendations for international students: Required—TOEFL (minimum score 550 paper-based), IELTS. Electronic applications accepted. *Faculty research:* Gaming, leadership, disintermediation.

New York University, Polytechnic School of Engineering, Department of Finance and Risk Engineering, New York, NY 10012-1019. Offers financial engineering (MS, Advanced Certificate), including capital markets (MS), computational finance (MS), financial technology (MS); financial technology management (Advanced Certificate); organizational behavior (Advanced Certificate); risk management (Advanced Certificate); technology management (Advanced Certificate). MS program also offered in Manhattan. Part-time and evening/weekend programs available. *Faculty:* 9 full-time (4 women), 13 part-time/adjunct (4 women). *Students:* 270 full-time (80 women), 39 part-time (9 women); includes 19 minority (5 Black or African American, non-Hispanic/Latino; 11 Asian, non-Hispanic/Latino; 2 Hispanic/Latino; 1 Two or more races, non-Hispanic/Latino), 279 international. Average age 25. 782 applicants, 23% accepted, 163 enrolled. In 2014, 125 master's awarded. *Degree requirements:* For master's, comprehensive exam (for some programs), thesis (for some programs). *Entrance requirements:* For master's, GMAT, minimum B average in undergraduate course work. Additional exam requirements/recommendations for international students: Required—TOEFL (minimum score 550 paper-based; 80 iBT); Recommended—IELTS (minimum score 6.5). *Application deadline:* For fall admission, 2/15 priority date for domestic and international students; for spring admission, 11/1 priority date for domestic and international students. Applications are processed on a rolling basis. Application fee: $75. Electronic applications accepted. *Financial support:* Institutionally sponsored loans, scholarships/grants, and unspecified assistantships available. Support available to part-time students. Financial award applicants required to submit FAFSA. *Faculty research:* Optimal control theory, general modeling and analysis, risk parity optimality, a new algorithmic approach to entangled political economy. *Total annual research expenditures:* $387,325. *Unit head:* Dr. Charles S. Tapiero, Department Chair, 718-260-3653, Fax: 718-260-3874, E-mail: cst262@nyu.edu. *Application contact:* Raymond Lutzky, Director, Graduate Enrollment Management, 718-637-5984, Fax: 718-260-3624, E-mail: rlutzky@poly.edu.

North Carolina State University, Graduate School, College of Agriculture and Life Sciences and College of Engineering and College of Physical and Mathematical Sciences, Program in Financial Mathematics, Raleigh, NC 27695. Offers MFM. Part-time programs available. *Degree requirements:* For master's, thesis optional, project/internship. *Entrance requirements:* For master's, GRE General Test. Additional exam requirements/recommendations for international students: Required—TOEFL (minimum score 550 paper-based). Electronic applications accepted. *Faculty research:* Financial mathematics modeling and computation, futures, options and commodities markets, real options, credit risk, portfolio optimization.

Princeton University, Graduate School, School of Engineering and Applied Science, Department of Operations Research and Financial Engineering, Princeton, NJ 08544-1019. Offers M Eng, MSE, PhD. Terminal master's awarded for partial completion of doctoral program. *Degree requirements:* For master's, thesis (MSE); for doctorate, thesis/dissertation, general exam. *Entrance requirements:* For master's and doctorate, GRE General Test, official transcript(s), 3 letters of recommendation, personal statement. Additional exam requirements/recommendations for international students: Required—TOEFL. Electronic applications accepted. *Faculty research:* Applied and computational mathematics; financial mathematics; optimization, queuing theory, and machine learning; statistics and stochastic analysis; transportation and logistics.

Rensselaer Polytechnic Institute, Graduate School, Lally School of Management, Program in Quantitative Finance and Risk Analytics, Troy, NY 12180-3590. Offers MS, MS/MBA. Part-time programs available. *Students:* 361 applicants, 26% accepted, 41 enrolled. In 2014, 61 master's awarded. *Entrance requirements:* For master's, GMAT or GRE. Additional exam requirements/recommendations for international students: Required—TOEFL (minimum score 570 paper-based; 88 iBT), IELTS (minimum score 6.5), PTE (minimum score 60). *Application deadline:* For fall admission, 1/1 for domestic and international students. Applications are processed on a rolling basis. Application fee: $75. Electronic applications accepted. *Expenses: Tuition:* Full-time $46,700; part-time $1945 per credit. Tuition and fees vary according to course load. *Financial support:* Scholarships/grants available. Financial award application deadline: 1/1. *Unit head:* Dr. Gina O'Connor, Graduate Program Director, 518-276-6842, E-mail: oconng@rpi.edu. *Application contact:* Office of Graduate Admissions, 518-276-6216, E-mail: gradadmissions@rpi.edu.
Website: http://lallyschool.rpi.edu/academics/ms_fera.html.

Stevens Institute of Technology, Graduate School, School of Systems and Enterprises, Program in Financial Engineering, Hoboken, NJ 07030. Offers MS.

Temple University, Fox School of Business, Specialized Master's Programs, Philadelphia, PA 19122-6096. Offers accountancy (MS); actuarial science (MS); finance (MS); financial engineering (MS); human resource management (MS); innovation management and entrepreneurship (MS); marketing (MS); statistics (MS). MS in innovation management and entrepreneurship delivered jointly with College of Engineering. *Accreditation:* AACSB. Part-time programs available. *Entrance requirements:* For master's, GRE General Test or GMAT, minimum undergraduate GPA of 3.0. Additional exam requirements/recommendations for international students: Required—TOEFL (minimum score 600 paper-based; 100 iBT), IELTS (minimum score 7.5). *Expenses:* Tuition, state resident: full-time $14,490; part-time $805 per credit hour. Tuition, nonresident: full-time $19,850; part-time $1103 per credit hour. *Required fees:* $690. Full-time tuition and fees vary according to class time, course load, degree level, campus/location and program.

University of California, Berkeley, Graduate Division, Haas School of Business, Master of Financial Engineering Program, Berkeley, CA 94720-1500. Offers MFE. *Students:* 67 full-time (13 women); includes 2 minority (both Asian, non-Hispanic/Latino), 53 international. Average age 27. 383 applicants, 22% accepted, 67 enrolled. In 2014, 67 master's awarded. *Degree requirements:* For master's, comprehensive exam, internship/applied finance project. *Entrance requirements:* For master's, GMAT or GRE (waived if candidate holds PhD), bachelor's degree with minimum GPA of 3.0 or equivalent; two recommendation letters; proficiency in math, statistics, computer science, economics/finance. Additional exam requirements/recommendations for international students: Required—TOEFL (minimum score 570 paper-based; 90 iBT). *Application deadline:* For spring admission, 10/15 for domestic and international students. Applications are processed on a rolling basis. Application fee: $275. Electronic applications accepted. *Expenses:* Expenses: Contact institution. *Financial support:* In 2014–15, 1 student received support, including 1 fellowship (averaging $1,000 per year); research assistantships with partial tuition reimbursements available, teaching assistantships with partial tuition reimbursements available, institutionally sponsored loans, scholarships/grants, and non-resident tuition waivers for some students, such as veterans also available. Financial award application deadline: 4/2. *Faculty research:* Financial economics, modern portfolio theory, valuation of exotic options, mortgage markets. *Unit head:* Linda Kreitzman, Executive Director, 510-643-4329, Fax: 510-643-4345, E-mail: lindak@haas.berkeley.edu. *Application contact:* Christina Henri, Associate Director, 510-642-4417, Fax: 510-643-4345, E-mail: mfe@haas.berkeley.edu.
Website: http://mfe.berkeley.edu.

University of California, Los Angeles, Graduate Division, UCLA Anderson School of Management, Los Angeles, CA 90095-1481. Offers accounting (PhD); Asia Pacific (EMBA); business administration (EMBA, MBA); decisions, operations and technology management (PhD); finance (PhD); financial engineering (MFE); global economics and management (PhD); management and organizations (PhD); marketing (PhD); strategy and policy (PhD); DDS/MBA; MBA/JD; MBA/MD; MBA/MLAS; MBA/MLIS; MBA/MN; MBA/MPH; MBA/MPP; MBA/MSCS. *Accreditation:* AACSB. Part-time and evening/weekend programs available. *Faculty:* 98 full-time (18 women), 61 part-time/adjunct (6 women). *Students:* 820 full-time (272 women), 1,145 part-time (322 women); includes 673 minority (42 Black or African American, non-Hispanic/Latino; 470 Asian, non-Hispanic/Latino; 67 Hispanic/Latino; 6 Native Hawaiian or other Pacific Islander, non-Hispanic/Latino; 88 Two or more races, non-Hispanic/Latino), 465 international. Average age 31. 6,471 applicants, 24% accepted, 895 enrolled. In 2014, 777 master's, 9 doctorates awarded. *Degree requirements:* For master's, comprehensive exam, Field study consulting project (for MBA, FEMA, EMBA, and the two GEMBA programs); Thesis/dissertation (R for MFE); for doctorate, comprehensive exam, thesis/dissertation, Oral and written qualifying exams. *Entrance requirements:* For master's, GMAT or GRE General Test (for MBA, FEMBA, EMBA, MFE programs), 4-year bachelor's degree or equivalent; recommendation letters (1 for MBA, 2 for MFE); essays (1 for MBA, 2 for MFE); interview (by invitation only for MBA); At least eight years of work experience with at least three years at a management level (EMBA); for doctorate, GMAT or GRE General Test, Bachelor's degree from college or university of fully-recognized standing;

minimum B average during junior and senior years of undergraduate years; statement of purpose; three recommendation letters. Additional exam requirements/recommendations for international students: Required—TOEFL (minimum score 560 paper-based, 87 iBT) or IELTS. *Application deadline:* For fall admission, 10/6 priority date for domestic and international students; for winter admission, 1/5 for domestic and international students; for spring admission, 4/12 for domestic and international students. Applications are processed on a rolling basis. Application fee: $200. Electronic applications accepted. *Expenses:* Expenses: $51,159 in-state, $56,159 out-of-state (for MBA); $39,540 (for FEMBA); $69,379 (for EMBA); $52,500 (for GEMBA); $57,268 (for MFE); $30,746 (for PhD). *Financial support:* In 2014–15, 564 students received support, including 470 fellowships (averaging $25,596 per year), 8 research assistantships with partial tuition reimbursements available (averaging $2,418 per year), 83 teaching assistantships with partial tuition reimbursements available (averaging $3,464 per year); career-related internships or fieldwork, institutionally sponsored loans, and scholarships/grants also available. Support available to part-time students. Financial award application deadline: 4/15; financial award applicants required to submit FAFSA. *Faculty research:* Asset pricing, decision-making, behavioral finance, international finance and economics, global macroeconomics. *Total annual research expenditures:* $325,000. *Unit head:* Dr. Judy D. Olian, Dean and John E. Anderson Chair in Management, 310-825-7982, Fax: 310-206-2073, E-mail: judy.olian@anderson.ucla.edu. *Application contact:* Alex Lawrence, Assistant Dean, MBA Admissions and Financial Aid, 310-825-6944, Fax: 310-825-8582, E-mail: mba.admissions@anderson.ucla.edu.
Website: http://www.anderson.ucla.edu/.

University of Hawaii at Manoa, Graduate Division, Shidler College of Business, Program in Financial Engineering, Honolulu, HI 96822. Offers MS. Part-time programs available. *Degree requirements:* For master's, thesis optional. *Entrance requirements:* For master's, GRE General Test. Additional exam requirements/recommendations for international students: Required—TOEFL (minimum score 600 paper-based; 100 iBT), IELTS (minimum score 7).

University of Illinois at Urbana–Champaign, Graduate College, College of Engineering, Joint Program in Financial Engineering, Champaign, IL 61820. Offers MS. Program offered jointly with College of Business. *Students:* 109 (33 women). *Degree requirements:* For master's, thesis or alternative. Application fee: $70 ($90 for international students). *Unit head:* Morton Lane, Director, 217-333-3284, Fax: 217-333-1486, E-mail: msfe@illinois.edu. *Application contact:* Emily Ziegler, Assistant Director, 217-300-5603, E-mail: ekrickl@illinois.edu.
Website: http://msfe.illinois.edu/.

University of Michigan, College of Engineering, Interpro Programs in Engineering, Ann Arbor, MI 48109. Offers automotive engineering (M Eng); design science (PhD); energy systems engineering (MS); financial engineering (MS); global automotive and manufacturing engineering (M Eng); manufacturing engineering (M Eng, D Eng); pharmaceutical engineering (M Eng); robotics and autonomous vehicles (M Eng); MBA/M Eng; MSE/MS. Part-time programs available. Postbaccalaureate distance learning degree programs offered (no on-campus study). *Students:* 187 full-time (46 women), 250 part-time (40 women). 364 applicants, 2% accepted, 3 enrolled. In 2014, 171 master's, 1 doctorate awarded. Terminal master's awarded for partial completion of doctoral program. *Degree requirements:* For master's, capstone project; for doctorate, thesis/dissertation. *Entrance requirements:* For master's, GRE; for doctorate, GRE, 2 years of work experience. Additional exam requirements/recommendations for international students: Required—TOEFL (minimum score 560 paper-based). *Application deadline:* Applications are processed on a rolling basis. Electronic applications accepted. *Financial support:* Fellowships, research assistantships with full tuition reimbursements, teaching assistantships with full tuition reimbursements, career-related internships or fieldwork, scholarships/grants, and unspecified assistantships available. Financial award application deadline: 2/15; financial award applicants required to submit FAFSA. *Faculty research:* Automotive engineering, design science, energy systems engineering, engineering sustainable systems, financial engineering, global automotive and manufacturing engineering, integrated microsystems, manufacturing engineering, pharmaceutical engineering, robotics and autonomous vehicles. *Total annual research expenditures:* $263,643. *Unit head:* Prof. Panos Papalambros, Director, 734-647-8401, Fax: 734-647-0079, E-mail: pyp@umich.edu. *Application contact:* Patti Mackmiller, Program Manager, 734-764-3071, Fax: 734-647-2243, E-mail: pmackmil@umich.edu.
Website: http://www.isd.engin.umich.edu.

The University of Tulsa, Graduate School, Collins College of Business, Program in Finance, Tulsa, OK 74104-3189. Offers corporate finance (MS); investments and portfolio management (MS); risk management (MS); JD/MSF; MBA/MSF; MSF/MSAM. Part-time and evening/weekend programs available. *Faculty:* 9 full-time (1 woman). *Students:* 7 full-time (1 woman), 4 part-time (1 woman); includes 3 minority (2 Hispanic/Latino; 1 Two or more races, non-Hispanic/Latino), 6 international. Average age 24. 83 applicants, 53% accepted, 5 enrolled. In 2014, 25 master's awarded. *Degree requirements:* For master's, thesis optional. *Entrance requirements:* For master's, GMAT. Additional exam requirements/recommendations for international students: Required—TOEFL (minimum score 577 paper-based; 91 iBT), IELTS (minimum score 6.5). *Application deadline:* Applications are processed on a rolling basis. Application fee: $55. Electronic applications accepted. *Expenses:* Tuition: Full-time $20,160; part-time $1120 per credit hour. *Required fees:* $6 per credit hour. Tuition and fees vary according to course level and course load. *Financial support:* In 2014–15, 5 students received support, including 5 teaching assistantships with full and partial tuition reimbursements available (averaging $9,349 per year); fellowships with full and partial tuition reimbursements available, research assistantships with full and partial tuition reimbursements available, career-related internships or fieldwork, Federal Work-Study, institutionally sponsored loans, scholarships/grants, health care benefits, tuition waivers (full and partial), and unspecified assistantships also available. Support available to part-time students. Financial award application deadline: 2/1; financial award applicants required to submit FAFSA. *Unit head:* Dr. Linda Nichols, Associate Dean, 918-631-2242, Fax: 918-631-2142, E-mail: linda-nichols@utulsa.edu. *Application contact:* Information Contact, 918-631-2242, E-mail: graduate-business@utulsa.edu.

Game Design and Development

Academy of Art University, Graduate Program, School of Game Development, San Francisco, CA 94105-3410. Offers MFA. Part-time programs available. Postbaccalaureate distance learning degree programs offered (no on-campus study). *Faculty:* 9 full-time (0 women), 23 part-time/adjunct (2 women). *Students:* 107 full-time (28 women), 46 part-time (6 women); includes 30 minority (6 Black or African American, non-Hispanic/Latino; 12 Asian, non-Hispanic/Latino; 9 Hispanic/Latino; 1 Native Hawaiian or other Pacific Islander, non-Hispanic/Latino; 2 Two or more races, non-Hispanic/Latino), 74 international. Average age 29. 49 applicants, 100% accepted, 24 enrolled. In 2014, 38 master's awarded. *Degree requirements:* For master's, final review. *Entrance requirements:* For master's, statement of intent; resume; portfolio/reel; official college transcripts. *Application deadline:* Applications are processed on a rolling basis. Application fee: $100. Electronic applications accepted. *Expenses:* Tuition: Part-time $910 per unit. *Financial support:* Career-related internships or fieldwork and Federal Work-Study available. Support available to part-time students. Financial award application deadline: 8/10; financial award applicants required to submit FAFSA. *Unit head:* 800-544-ARTS, E-mail: info@academyart.edu. *Application contact:* 800-544-ARTS, E-mail: info@academyart.edu.
Website: http://www.academyart.edu/academics/game-development.

Concordia University, School of Graduate Studies, Faculty of Engineering and Computer Science, Concordia Institute for Information Systems Engineering (CIISE), Montréal, QC H3G 1M8, Canada. Offers 3D graphics and game development (Certificate); information systems security (M Eng, MA Sc); quality systems engineering (M Eng, MA Sc); service engineering and network management (Certificate).

DePaul University, College of Computing and Digital Media, Chicago, IL 60604. Offers animation (MA, MFA); business information technology (MS); cinema (MFA); cinema production (MS); computational finance (MS); computer and information sciences (PhD); computer game development (MS); computer information and network security (MS); computer science (MS); e-commerce technology (MS); health informatics (MS); human-computer interaction (MS); information systems (MS); information technology project management (MS); network engineering and management (MS); predictive analytics (MS); screenwriting (MFA); software engineering (MS); JD/MS. Part-time and evening/weekend programs available. Postbaccalaureate distance learning degree programs offered (no on-campus study). *Degree requirements:* For master's, thesis (for some programs); for doctorate, comprehensive exam, thesis/dissertation. *Entrance requirements:* For master's, GRE or GMAT (for MS in computational finance only), bachelor's degree, resume (MS in predictive analytics only), IT experience (MS in information technology project management only), portfolio review (all MFA programs and MA in animation); for doctorate, GRE, master's degree in computer science. Additional exam requirements/recommendations for international students: Required—TOEFL (minimum score 590 paper-based; 80 iBT), IELTS (minimum score 6.5), PTE (minimum score 53). Electronic applications accepted. *Expenses:* Contact institution. *Faculty research:* Data mining, computer science, human-computer interaction, security, animation and film.

Full Sail University, Game Design Master of Science Program - Campus, Winter Park, FL 32792-7437. Offers MS.

Michigan State University, The Graduate School, College of Communication Arts and Sciences, Department of Telecommunication, Information Studies, and Media, East Lansing, MI 48824. Offers digital media arts and technology (MA); information and telecommunication management (MA); information, policy and society (MA); serious game design (MA). *Entrance requirements:* Additional exam requirements/recommendations for international students: Required—TOEFL. Electronic applications accepted.

New York University, Tisch School of the Arts, Game Center, Brooklyn, NY 11201. Offers MFA. *Students:* 55 full-time (11 women); includes 20 minority (1 Black or African American, non-Hispanic/Latino; 4 Asian, non-Hispanic/Latino; 1 Hispanic/Latino; 14 Two or more races, non-Hispanic/Latino), 23 international. 137 applicants, 39% accepted, 34 enrolled. *Application deadline:* For fall admission, 12/1 for domestic students. *Unit head:* Frank Lantz, Director, 646-997-0746, E-mail: frank.lantz@nyu.edu. *Application contact:* Dan Sandford, Director of Graduate Admissions, 212-998-1918, Fax: 212-995-4060, E-mail: tisch.gradadmissions@nyu.edu.
Website: http://gamecenter.nyu.edu/.

Rochester Institute of Technology, Graduate Enrollment Services, Golisano College of Computing and Information Sciences, Interactive Games and Media School, MS Program in Game Design and Development, Rochester, NY 14623-5608. Offers MS. *Students:* 31 full-time; includes 3 minority (1 Black or African American, non-Hispanic/Latino; 1 Hispanic/Latino; 1 Two or more races, non-Hispanic/Latino), 18 international. Average age 24. 144 applicants, 36% accepted, 15 enrolled. In 2014, 7 master's awarded. *Degree requirements:* For master's, thesis or alternative, capstone experience. *Entrance requirements:* For master's, GRE and TOEFL, IELTS, or PTE for non-native English speakers, portfolio and recommended minimum GPA of 3.0. Additional exam requirements/recommendations for international students: Required—TOEFL, PTE (minimum score 58), TOEFL (minimum score 550 paper-based; 79 iBT) or IELTS (minimum score 6.5). *Application deadline:* For fall admission, 2/15 priority date for domestic and international students. Applications are processed on a rolling basis. Electronic applications accepted. *Expenses:* Expenses: $1,673 per credit hour. *Financial support:* In 2014–15, 29 students received support. Research assistantships with partial tuition reimbursements available, teaching assistantships with partial tuition reimbursements available, career-related internships or fieldwork, Federal Work-Study, institutionally sponsored loans, scholarships/grants, and unspecified assistantships available. Support available to part-time students. Financial award application deadline: 3/31; financial award applicants required to submit FAFSA. *Faculty research:* Experimental game design and development; exploratory research in visualization environments and integrated media frameworks; outreach efforts that surround games and underlying technologies; support of STEM learning through games and interactive entertainment; the application of games and game technology to non-entertainment domains (Serious Games); small, discrete play experiences (Casual Games). *Unit head:* Dr. Jessica Bayliss, Graduate Program Director, 585-475-2507, E-mail: jdbics@rit.edu. *Application contact:* Diane Ellison, Associate Vice President, Graduate Enrollment Services, 585-475-2229, Fax: 585-475-7164, E-mail: gradinfo@rit.edu.
Website: https://www.rit.edu/gccis/igm/ms-game-design-development-overview.

Sacred Heart University, Graduate Programs, College of Arts and Sciences, Department of Computer Science, Fairfield, CT 06825-1000. Offers computer game design and development (Graduate Certificate); computer science and information technology (MS); computer science gaming (MS); cybersecurity (MS); database design (Graduate Certificate); information technology (Graduate Certificate); information technology and network security (Graduate Certificate); interactive multimedia (Graduate Certificate); Web development (Graduate Certificate). Part-time and evening/weekend programs available. *Faculty:* 6 full-time (2 women), 18 part-time/adjunct (5

women). *Students:* 266 full-time (100 women), 69 part-time (15 women); includes 30 minority (11 Black or African American, non-Hispanic/Latino; 7 Asian, non-Hispanic/Latino; 12 Hispanic/Latino), 265 international. Average age 26. 1,010 applicants, 56% accepted, 166 enrolled. In 2014, 50 master's awarded. *Degree requirements:* For master's, thesis or alternative. *Entrance requirements:* For master's, bachelor's degree, minimum GPA of 3.0. Additional exam requirements/recommendations for international students: Required—PTE; Recommended—TOEFL (minimum score 570 paper-based; 80 iBT), IELTS (minimum score 6.5). *Application deadline:* For fall admission, 5/15 for international students; for spring admission, 10/30 for international students. Applications are processed on a rolling basis. Application fee: $60. Electronic applications accepted. *Expenses: Tuition:* Full-time $24,559; part-time $649 per credit. *Financial support:* Unspecified assistantships available. Financial award applicants required to submit FAFSA. *Unit head:* Domenick Pinto, Academic Director and Chairperson, 203-371-7789, Fax: 203-371-0506, E-mail: pintod@sacredheart.edu. *Application contact:* Kathy Dilks, Executive Director of Graduate Admissions, 203-365-7619, Fax: 203-365-4732, E-mail: gradstudies@sacredheart.edu.
Website: http://www.sacredheart.edu/academics/collegeofartssciences/academicdepartments/computerscienceinformationtechnology/graduatedegreesandcertificates/.

Savannah College of Art and Design, Graduate School, Program in Interactive Design and Game Development, Savannah, GA 31402-3146. Offers MA, MFA, Graduate Certificate. Part-time programs available. Postbaccalaureate distance learning degree programs offered (no on-campus study). *Faculty:* 16 full-time (4 women), 5 part-time/adjunct (1 woman). *Students:* 53 full-time (17 women), 44 part-time (14 women); includes 14 minority (6 Black or African American, non-Hispanic/Latino; 6 Asian, non-Hispanic/Latino; 2 Hispanic/Latino), 37 international. Average age 28. 113 applicants, 42% accepted, 24 enrolled. In 2014, 22 master's awarded. *Degree requirements:* For master's, thesis (for some programs), final project (for MA); internship (for MFA). *Entrance requirements:* For master's, portfolio (in digital or multimedia format). Additional exam requirements/recommendations for international students: Required—TOEFL (minimum score 550 paper-based, 85 iBT), IELTS (minimum score 6.5), or ACTFL. *Application deadline:* For fall admission, 4/1 for domestic and international students. Applications are processed on a rolling basis. Application fee: $40. Electronic applications accepted. *Expenses: Tuition:* Full-time $34,605; part-time $3845 per course. One-time fee: $500. Tuition and fees vary according to course load. *Financial support:* Fellowships, career-related internships or fieldwork, Federal Work-Study, and scholarships/grants available. Financial award application deadline: 4/1; financial award applicants required to submit FAFSA. *Unit head:* SuAnne Fu, Interim Chair. *Application contact:* Jenny Jaquillard, Executive Director of Admissions, Recruitment and Events, 912-525-5100, Fax: 912-525-5985, E-mail: admission@scad.edu.
Website: http://www.scad.edu/academics/programs/interactive-design-and-game-development.

Shepherd University, Hollywood CG School of Digital Arts, Los Angeles, CA 90065. Offers game art and design (MSIT); visual effects and animation (MSIT). *Degree requirements:* For master's, exam, thesis, or portfolio.

University of Advancing Technology, Master of Science Program in Technology, Tempe, AZ 85283-1042. Offers advancing computer science (MS); emerging technologies (MS); game production and management (MS); information assurance (MS); technology leadership (MS). *Degree requirements:* For master's, project or thesis. *Entrance requirements:* Additional exam requirements/recommendations for international students: Required—TOEFL (minimum score 550 paper-based). Electronic applications accepted. *Faculty research:* Artificial intelligence, fractals, organizational management.

University of Central Florida, College of Arts and Humanities, Florida Interactive Entertainment Academy, Orlando, FL 32816. Offers MS. *Faculty:* 10 full-time (0 women). *Students:* 65 full-time (16 women), 54 part-time (12 women); includes 36 minority (9 Black or African American, non-Hispanic/Latino; 6 Asian, non-Hispanic/Latino; 13 Hispanic/Latino; 8 Two or more races, non-Hispanic/Latino), 9 international. Average age 25. 135 applicants, 61% accepted, 66 enrolled. In 2014, 57 master's awarded. *Expenses:* Tuition, state resident: part-time $288.16 per credit hour. Tuition, nonresident: part-time $1073.31 per credit hour. *Financial support:* Fellowships with partial tuition reimbursements and research assistantships with partial tuition reimbursements available. *Unit head:* Ben Noel, Executive Director, 407-235-3612, Fax: 407-317-7094, E-mail: bnoel@fiea.ucf.edu. *Application contact:* Barbara Rodriguez Lamas, Director, Admissions and Student Services, 407-823-2766, Fax: 407-823-6442, E-mail: gradadmissions@ucf.edu.
Website: http://www.fiea.ucf.edu/.

The University of North Carolina at Charlotte, College of Computing and Informatics, Department of Computer Science, Charlotte, NC 28223-0001. Offers advanced databases and knowledge discovery (Graduate Certificate); computer science (MS); game design and development (Graduate Certificate). Part-time and evening/weekend programs available. *Faculty:* 27 full-time (5 women), 5 part-time/adjunct (3 women). *Students:* 197 full-time (50 women), 48 part-time (14 women); includes 6 minority (2 Asian, non-Hispanic/Latino; 3 Hispanic/Latino; 1 Two or more races, non-Hispanic/Latino), 220 international. Average age 24. 1,113 applicants, 33% accepted, 104 enrolled. In 2014, 118 master's awarded. *Degree requirements:* For master's, thesis optional. *Entrance requirements:* For master's, GRE General Test, minimum GPA of 3.0 during previous 2 years, 2.8 overall. Additional exam requirements/recommendations for international students: Required—TOEFL (minimum score 557 paper-based; 83 iBT). *Application deadline:* For fall admission, 5/1 for domestic and international students; for spring admission, 10/1 for domestic and international students. Applications are processed on a rolling basis. Application fee: $75. Electronic applications accepted. *Expenses:* Tuition, state resident: full-time $4008. Tuition, nonresident: full-time $16,295. *Required fees:* $2755. Tuition and fees vary according to course load and program. *Financial support:* In 2014–15, 45 students received support, including 2 fellowships (averaging $30,438 per year), 22 research assistantships (averaging $9,562 per year), 21 teaching assistantships (averaging $6,300 per year); career-related internships or fieldwork, Federal Work-Study, institutionally sponsored loans, scholarships/grants, and unspecified assistantships also available. Support available to part-time students. Financial award application deadline: 4/1; financial award applicants required to submit FAFSA. *Faculty research:* Visualization; visual analytics and computer graphics; intelligent and interactive systems; data mining theory, systems, and application; networked systems; computer game design. *Total annual research expenditures:* $2.4 million. *Unit head:* William Ribarsky, Chair, 704-687-8559, Fax: 704-687-3516, E-mail: ribarsky@uncc.edu. *Application contact:* Kathy B. Giddings, Director of Graduate Admissions, 704-687-3366, Fax: 704-687-3279, E-mail: gradadm@uncc.edu.
Website: http://cs.uncc.edu/.

University of Southern California, Graduate School, Viterbi School of Engineering, Department of Computer Science, Los Angeles, CA 90089. Offers computer networks (MS); computer science (MS, PhD); computer security (MS); game development (MS); high performance computing and simulations (MS); human language technology (MS); intelligent robotics (MS); multimedia and creative technologies (MS); software engineering (MS). Part-time and evening/weekend programs available. Postbaccalaureate distance learning degree programs offered (no on-campus study). *Entrance requirements:* For master's and doctorate, GRE General Test. Additional exam requirements/recommendations for international students: Required—TOEFL. Electronic applications accepted. *Faculty research:* Databases, computer graphics and computer vision, software engineering, networks and security, robotics, multimedia and virtual reality.

University of Utah, Graduate School, College of Engineering, Program in Entertainment Arts and Engineering, Salt Lake City, UT 84112. Offers game art (MEAE); game engineering (MEAE); game production (MEAE); technical art (MEAE). Part-time programs available. *Faculty:* 6 full-time, 8 part-time/adjunct (2 women). *Students:* 94 full-time (12 women), 1 (woman) part-time; includes 7 minority (2 Asian, non-Hispanic/Latino; 2 Hispanic/Latino; 1 Native Hawaiian or other Pacific Islander, non-Hispanic/Latino; 2 Two or more races, non-Hispanic/Latino), 38 international. Average age 27. 160 applicants, 50% accepted, 60 enrolled. In 2014, 23 master's awarded. *Entrance requirements:* For master's, GRE (recommended for game engineering and game production track applicants). Additional exam requirements/recommendations for international students: Required—TOEFL (minimum score 550 paper-based; 80 iBT), IELTS (minimum score 6.5). *Application deadline:* For fall admission, 2/28 for domestic and international students. Application fee: $65. Electronic applications accepted. *Expenses:* Expenses: Contact institution. *Financial support:* In 2014–15, 50 research assistantships with partial tuition reimbursements (averaging $6,750 per year), 53 teaching assistantships with partial tuition reimbursements (averaging $6,750 per year) were awarded; career-related internships or fieldwork, health care benefits, tuition waivers (partial), and unspecified assistantships also available. *Faculty research:* Games for health, simulation. *Unit head:* Corrinne Lewis, Academic Program Manager, 801-585-6491, E-mail: corrinne.lewis@utah.edu. *Application contact:* Hallie Huber, Program Coordinator/Academic Advisor, 801-581-5460, E-mail: hallie.huber@utah.edu.
Website: http://eae.utah.edu/.

West Virginia University, College of Engineering and Mineral Resources, Lane Department of Computer Science and Electrical Engineering, Program in Interactive Technologies and Serious Gaming, Morgantown, WV 26506. Offers Graduate Certificate. *Entrance requirements:* Additional exam requirements/recommendations for international students: Required—TOEFL or IELTS. Electronic applications accepted.

Worcester Polytechnic Institute, Graduate Studies and Research, Program in Interactive Media and Game Development, Worcester, MA 01609-2280. Offers MS. Part-time and evening/weekend programs available. *Students:* 21 full-time (6 women), 1 part-time (0 women); includes 2 minority (1 Black or African American, non-Hispanic/Latino; 1 Asian, non-Hispanic/Latino), 14 international. 55 applicants, 73% accepted, 10 enrolled. In 2014, 2 master's awarded. *Entrance requirements:* For master's, GRE (recommended), 3 letters of recommendation, statement of purpose, portfolio (recommended). Additional exam requirements/recommendations for international students: Required—TOEFL (minimum score 563 paper-based; 84 iBT), IELTS (minimum score 7). *Application deadline:* For fall admission, 1/1 for domestic and international students; for spring admission, 10/1 for domestic and international students. Applications are processed on a rolling basis. Electronic applications accepted. *Financial support:* Research assistantships and teaching assistantships available. *Unit head:* Charles Rich, Graduate Coordinator, 508-831-4977, Fax: 508-831-5776, E-mail: rich@wpi.edu. *Application contact:* Tricia Desmarais, Administrative Assistant, 508-831-6470, Fax: 508-831-5776, E-mail: td@wpi.edu.
Website: http://www.wpi.edu/academics/imgd.

Health Informatics

Adelphi University, College of Nursing and Public Health, Program in Health Information Technology, Garden City, NY 11530-0701. Offers MS, Advanced Certificate. *Students:* 3 full-time (2 women), 46 part-time (34 women); includes 37 minority (18 Black or African American, non-Hispanic/Latino; 1 American Indian or Alaska Native, non-Hispanic/Latino; 10 Asian, non-Hispanic/Latino; 3 Hispanic/Latino; 5 Two or more races, non-Hispanic/Latino). Average age 37. *Financial support:* Research assistantships, career-related internships or fieldwork, Federal Work-Study, tuition waivers, and unspecified assistantships available. *Unit head:* Dr. Thomas Virgona, Director, 516-877-4516, E-mail: tvirgona@adelphi.edu. *Application contact:* Christine Murphy, Director of Admissions, 516-877-3050, Fax: 516-877-3039, E-mail: graduateadmissions@adelphi.edu.

American Sentinel University, Graduate Programs, Aurora, CO 80014. Offers business administration (MBA); business intelligence (MS); computer science (MSCS); health information management (MS); healthcare (MBA); information systems (MSIS); nursing (MSN). Part-time and evening/weekend programs available. Postbaccalaureate distance learning degree programs offered (no on-campus study). *Entrance requirements:* Additional exam requirements/recommendations for international students: Required—TOEFL (minimum score 600 paper-based). Electronic applications accepted.

Arkansas Tech University, College of Natural and Health Sciences, Russellville, AR 72801. Offers fisheries and wildlife biology (MS); health informatics (MS); nursing (MSN). Part-time programs available. *Students:* 13 full-time (6 women), 43 part-time (35 women); includes 12 minority (7 Black or African American, non-Hispanic/Latino; 2 Asian, non-Hispanic/Latino; 1 Hispanic/Latino; 2 Two or more races, non-Hispanic/Latino), 1 international. Average age 36. In 2014, 21 master's awarded. *Degree requirements:* For master's, thesis (for some programs), project. *Entrance requirements:* For master's, GRE General Test. Additional exam requirements/recommendations for international students: Required—TOEFL (minimum score 550 paper-based; 79 iBT), IELTS (minimum score 6). *Application deadline:* For fall admission, 3/1 priority date for domestic students, 5/1 priority date for international students; for spring admission, 10/1 priority date for domestic and international students. Applications are processed on a rolling basis. Application fee: $25 ($75 for international students). Electronic applications accepted. *Expenses:* Tuition, state resident: full-time $6264; part-time $261 per credit hour. Tuition, nonresident: full-time $12,528; part-time $522 per credit hour. *Required*

fees: $423 per semester. Tuition and fees vary according to course load. *Financial support:* In 2014–15, research assistantships with full tuition reimbursements (averaging $4,800 per year), teaching assistantships with full tuition reimbursements (averaging $4,800 per year) were awarded; career-related internships or fieldwork, Federal Work-Study, scholarships/grants, health care benefits, and unspecified assistantships also available. Support available to part-time students. Financial award application deadline: 4/15; financial award applicants required to submit FAFSA. *Unit head:* Dr. Jeff Robertson, Dean, 479-968-0498, E-mail: jrobertson@atu.edu. *Application contact:* Dr. Mary B. Gunter, Dean of Graduate College, 479-968-0398, Fax: 479-964-0542, E-mail: gradcollege@atu.edu.
Website: http://www.atu.edu/nhs/.

Barry University, College of Health Sciences, Graduate Certificate Programs, Miami Shores, FL 33161-6695. Offers health care leadership (Certificate); health care planning and informatics (Certificate); histotechnology (Certificate); long term care management (Certificate); medical group practice management (Certificate); quality improvement and outcomes management (Certificate).

Benedictine University, Graduate Programs, Program in Public Health, Lisle, IL 60532-0900. Offers administration of health care institutions (MPH); dietetics (MPH); disaster management (MPH); health education (MPH); health information systems (MPH); MBA/MPH; MPH/MS. Part-time and evening/weekend programs available. Postbaccalaureate distance learning degree programs offered. *Entrance requirements:* For master's, MAT, GRE, or GMAT. Additional exam requirements/recommendations for international students: Required—TOEFL (minimum score 550 paper-based).

Boston University, Metropolitan College, Department of Computer Science, Boston, MA 02215. Offers computer information systems (MS), including computer networks, database management and business intelligence, health informatics, IT project management, security, Web application development; computer networks (Certificate); digital forensics (Certificate); health informatics (Certificate); information technology project management (Certificate); software engineering in health care systems (Certificate); telecommunications (MS), including security. Part-time and evening/weekend programs available. Postbaccalaureate distance learning degree programs offered (no on-campus study). *Faculty:* 13 full-time (3 women), 43 part-time/adjunct (3 women). *Students:* 76 full-time (22 women), 768 part-time (188 women); includes 251 minority (68 Black or African American, non-Hispanic/Latino; 1 American Indian or Alaska Native, non-Hispanic/Latino; 117 Asian, non-Hispanic/Latino; 57 Hispanic/Latino; 2 Native Hawaiian or other Pacific Islander, non-Hispanic/Latino; 6 Two or more races, non-Hispanic/Latino), 130 international. Average age 34. 463 applicants, 79% accepted, 248 enrolled. In 2014, 222 master's, 25 other advanced degrees awarded. *Degree requirements:* For master's, thesis optional. *Entrance requirements:* For master's and Certificate, official transcripts from regionally-accredited bachelor's degree program, 3 letters of recommendation, professional resume, personal statement. Additional exam requirements/recommendations for international students: Required—TOEFL (minimum score 84 iBT), IELTS. *Application deadline:* For fall admission, 6/1 priority date for international students; for spring admission, 10/1 priority date for international students. Applications are processed on a rolling basis. Application fee: $80. Electronic applications accepted. *Expenses:* Expenses: $800 per credit part-time; student services fees: $60 per semester; technology fee of $60 per credit (for online courses). *Financial support:* In 2014–15, 11 research assistantships (averaging $8,400 per year) were awarded; unspecified assistantships also available. Support available to part-time students. Financial award applicants required to submit FAFSA. *Faculty research:* Medical informatics, Web technologies, telecom and networks, security and forensics, software engineering, programming languages, multimedia and artificial intelligence (AI), information systems and IT project management. *Unit head:* Dr. Anatoly Temkin, Chairman, 617-353-2566, Fax: 617-353-2367, E-mail: csinfo@bu.edu. *Application contact:* Lesley Moreau, Academic Program Coordinator, 617-353-2566, Fax: 617-353-2367, E-mail: metcs@bu.edu.
Website: http://www.bu.edu/csmet/.

Brandeis University, Rabb School of Continuing Studies, Division of Graduate Professional Studies, Master of Science in Health and Medical Informatics Program, Waltham, MA 02454-9110. Offers MS. Part-time programs available. Postbaccalaureate distance learning degree programs offered (no on-campus study). *Faculty:* 2 full-time (1 woman), 36 part-time/adjunct (13 women). *Students:* 2 full-time (both women), 29 part-time (15 women); includes 13 minority (6 Black or African American, non-Hispanic/Latino; 5 Asian, non-Hispanic/Latino; 2 Hispanic/Latino). Average age 35. 16 applicants, 100% accepted, 12 enrolled. In 2014, 9 master's awarded. *Entrance requirements:* For master's, four-year bachelor's degree from regionally-accredited U.S. institution or equivalent; official transcript(s) from every college or university attended; resume or curriculum vitae; statement of goals; letter of recommendation. Additional exam requirements/recommendations for international students: Required—TOEFL (minimum scores: 600 paper-based, 100 iBT), IELTS (7), or PTE (68). *Application deadline:* For fall admission, 8/11 priority date for domestic and international students; for winter admission, 11/15 for domestic students; for spring admission, 12/15 priority date for domestic and international students; for summer admission, 4/14 priority date for domestic and international students. Applications are processed on a rolling basis. Application fee: $50. Electronic applications accepted. *Unit head:* Arthur Harvey, Chair, 781-736-8787, Fax: 781-736-3420, E-mail: aharv0001@brandeis.edu. *Application contact:* Frances Stearns, Director of Admissions and Recruitment, 781-736-8785, Fax: 781-736-3420, E-mail: fstearns@brandeis.edu.
Website: http://www.brandeis.edu/gps.

Brooklyn College of the City University of New York, School of Natural and Behavioral Sciences, Department of Computer and Information Science, Brooklyn, NY 11210-2889. Offers computer science (MA); health informatics (MS); information systems (MS); parallel and distributed computing (Advanced Certificate). Part-time and evening/weekend programs available. *Degree requirements:* For master's, comprehensive exam, thesis or alternative. *Entrance requirements:* For master's, previous course work in computer science, 2 letters of recommendation. Additional exam requirements/recommendations for international students: Required—TOEFL (minimum score 525 paper-based; 70 iBT). Electronic applications accepted. *Faculty research:* Networks and distributed systems, programming languages, modeling and computer applications, algorithms, artificial intelligence, theoretical computer science.

Canisius College, Graduate Division, School of Education and Human Services, Office of Professional Studies, Buffalo, NY 14208-1098. Offers applied nutrition (MS, Certificate); community and school health (MS); health and human performance (MS); health information technology (MS); respiratory care (MS). Postbaccalaureate distance learning degree programs offered (no on-campus study). *Faculty:* 17 part-time/adjunct (10 women). *Students:* 37 full-time (26 women), 68 part-time (50 women); includes 19 minority (12 Black or African American, non-Hispanic/Latino; 1 American Indian or Alaska Native, non-Hispanic/Latino; 6 Hispanic/Latino), 4 international. Average age 33. 85 applicants, 65% accepted, 32 enrolled. In 2014, 47 master's awarded. *Entrance requirements:* Additional exam requirements/recommendations for international students: Required—TOEFL (minimum score 550 paper-based, 80 iBT), IELTS (minimum score 6.5), or CAEL (minimum score 70). *Application deadline:* Applications are processed on a rolling basis. Application fee: $25. Electronic applications accepted.

Application fee is waived when completed online. *Financial support:* Career-related internships or fieldwork, Federal Work-Study, scholarships/grants, and unspecified assistantships available. Support available to part-time students. Financial award application deadline: 4/30; financial award applicants required to submit FAFSA. *Faculty research:* Nutrition, community and school health; community and health; health and human performance applied; nutrition and respiratory care. *Unit head:* Dr. Khalid Bibi, Executive Director, 716-888-8296. *Application contact:* Kathleen B. Davis, Vice President of Enrollment Management, 716-888-2500, Fax: 716-888-3195, E-mail: daviskb@canisius.edu.
Website: http://www.canisius.edu/graduate/.

Capella University, School of Public Service Leadership, Master's Programs in Nursing, Minneapolis, MN 55402. Offers diabetes nursing (MSN); general nursing (MSN); gerontology nursing (MSN); health information management (MS); nurse educator (MSN); nursing leadership and administration (MSN).

Claremont Graduate University, Graduate Programs, Center for Information Systems and Technology, Claremont, CA 91711-6160. Offers electronic commerce (MS, PhD); health information management (MS); information systems (Certificate); knowledge management (MS, PhD); systems development (MS, PhD); telecommunications and networking (MS, PhD); MBA/MS. Part-time programs available. *Faculty:* 5 full-time (0 women), 2 part-time/adjunct (0 women). *Students:* 60 full-time (21 women), 65 part-time (22 women); includes 26 minority (5 Black or African American, non-Hispanic/Latino; 1 American Indian or Alaska Native, non-Hispanic/Latino; 15 Asian, non-Hispanic/Latino; 4 Hispanic/Latino; 1 Two or more races, non-Hispanic/Latino), 65 international. Average age 36. In 2014, 17 master's, 1 doctorate awarded. *Degree requirements:* For doctorate, comprehensive exam, thesis/dissertation, portfolio. *Entrance requirements:* For master's and doctorate, GMAT, GRE General Test. Additional exam requirements/recommendations for international students: Required—TOEFL (minimum score 550 paper-based; 80 iBT). *Application deadline:* For fall admission, 2/1 priority date for domestic and international students. Applications are processed on a rolling basis. Application fee: $80. Electronic applications accepted. *Expenses: Tuition:* Full-time $41,784; part-time $1741 per credit. *Required fees:* $600; $300 per semester. *Financial support:* Fellowships, research assistantships, teaching assistantships, Federal Work-Study, institutionally sponsored loans, and scholarships/grants available. Support available to part-time students. Financial award application deadline: 2/15; financial award applicants required to submit FAFSA. *Faculty research:* Man-machine interaction, organizational aspects of computing, implementation of information systems, information systems practice. *Unit head:* Tom Horan, Dean, 909-607-9302, Fax: 909-621-8564, E-mail: tom.horan@cgu.edu. *Application contact:* Leah Litwack, Administrative Assistant, 909-621-8209, E-mail: leah.litwack@cgu.edu.
Website: http://www.cgu.edu/pages/153.asp.

The College of St. Scholastica, Graduate Studies, Department of Health Information Management, Duluth, MN 55811-4199. Offers MA, Certificate. Part-time programs available. *Faculty:* 4 full-time (all women), 12 part-time/adjunct (10 women). *Students:* 209 full-time (175 women), 49 part-time (42 women); includes 105 minority (68 Black or African American, non-Hispanic/Latino; 1 American Indian or Alaska Native, non-Hispanic/Latino; 16 Asian, non-Hispanic/Latino; 12 Hispanic/Latino; 1 Native Hawaiian or other Pacific Islander, non-Hispanic/Latino; 7 Two or more races, non-Hispanic/Latino), 5 international. Average age 40. 95 applicants, 77% accepted, 43 enrolled. In 2014, 37 master's, 56 other advanced degrees awarded. *Degree requirements:* For master's, thesis. *Entrance requirements:* Additional exam requirements/recommendations for international students: Required—TOEFL (minimum score 550 paper-based; 79 iBT). *Application deadline:* For fall admission, 8/1 for domestic and international students; for spring admission, 11/1 for domestic and international students. Applications are processed on a rolling basis. Application fee: $0. Electronic applications accepted. *Expenses:* Expenses: Contact institution. *Financial support:* In 2014–15, 55 students received support. Scholarships/grants available. Support available to part-time students. Financial award applicants required to submit FAFSA. *Faculty research:* Electronic health record implementation, personal health records, Athens Project. *Unit head:* Amy Watters, Director, 218-723-7094, Fax: 218-733-2239, E-mail: awatters@css.edu. *Application contact:* Lindsay Lahti, Director of Graduate and Extended Studies Recruitment, 218-733-2240, Fax: 218-733-2275, E-mail: gradstudies@css.edu.
Website: http://www.css.edu/Graduate/Masters-Doctoral-and-Professional-Programs/Areas-of-Study/MS-Health-Information-Management.html.

Dakota State University, College of Business and Information Systems, Madison, SD 57042-1799. Offers applied computer science (MSACS); general management (MBA); health informatics (MSHI); information assurance (MSIA); information systems (MSIS, D Sc IS). *Accreditation:* ACBSP. Part-time and evening/weekend programs available. Postbaccalaureate distance learning degree programs offered (minimal on-campus study). *Faculty:* 25 full-time (6 women), 1 part-time/adjunct (0 women). *Students:* 84 full-time (16 women), 165 part-time (45 women); includes 48 minority (17 Black or African American, non-Hispanic/Latino; 3 American Indian or Alaska Native, non-Hispanic/Latino; 17 Asian, non-Hispanic/Latino; 3 Hispanic/Latino; 1 Native Hawaiian or other Pacific Islander, non-Hispanic/Latino; 7 Two or more races, non-Hispanic/Latino), 76 international. Average age 35. 236 applicants, 65% accepted, 100 enrolled. In 2014, 58 master's, 7 doctorates, 4 other advanced degrees awarded. *Degree requirements:* For master's, comprehensive exam, thesis optional, examination, integrative project; for doctorate, comprehensive exam, thesis/dissertation, portfolio. *Entrance requirements:* For master's, GRE General Test, demonstration of information systems skills, minimum GPA of 2.7; for doctorate, GRE General Test, demonstration of information systems skills; for Graduate Certificate, GMAT, MBA. Additional exam requirements/recommendations for international students: Required—TOEFL (minimum score 550 paper-based; 79 iBT), IELTS (minimum score 6.5). *Application deadline:* For fall admission, 6/15 for domestic and international students; for spring admission, 11/15 for domestic and international students; for summer admission, 4/15 for domestic and international students. Applications are processed on a rolling basis. Application fee: $35. *Expenses:* Tuition, state resident: full-time $3633; part-time $201.85 per credit hour. Tuition, nonresident: full-time $7691; part-time $427.30 per credit hour. *Required fees:* $2108; $117.10 per credit hour. Tuition and fees vary according to course load, campus/location, program and reciprocity agreements. *Financial support:* In 2014–15, 32 students received support, including 18 fellowships with partial tuition reimbursements available (averaging $13,344 per year), 13 research assistantships with partial tuition reimbursements available (averaging $32,782 per year), 1 teaching assistantship with partial tuition reimbursement available (averaging $10,927 per year); Federal Work-Study, scholarships/grants, and unspecified assistantships also available. Support available to part-time students. Financial award applicants required to submit FAFSA. *Faculty research:* Data mining and data warehousing, effectiveness of hybrid learning environments, biometrics and information assurance, decision support systems, analytics, health informatics. *Unit head:* Dr. Omar El-Gayar, Dean of Graduate Studies and Research, 605-256-5799, Fax: 605-256-5093, E-mail: omar.el-gayar@dsu.edu. *Application contact:* Erin Blankespoor, Secretary, Office of Graduate Studies and Research, 605-256-5799, Fax: 605-256-5093, E-mail: erin.blankespoor@dsu.edu.
Website: http://dsu.edu/graduate-students.

Health Informatics

DePaul University, College of Computing and Digital Media, Chicago, IL 60604. Offers animation (MA, MFA); business information technology (MS); cinema (MFA); cinema production (MS); computational finance (MS); computer and information sciences (PhD); computer game development (MS); computer information and network security (MS); computer science (MS); e-commerce technology (MS); health informatics (MS); human-computer interaction (MS); information systems (MS); information technology project management (MS); network engineering and management (MS); predictive analytics (MS); screenwriting (MFA); software engineering (MS); JD/MS. Part-time and evening/weekend programs available. Postbaccalaureate distance learning degree programs offered (no on-campus study). *Degree requirements:* For master's, thesis (for some programs); for doctorate, comprehensive exam, thesis/dissertation. *Entrance requirements:* For master's, GRE or GMAT (for MS in computational finance only), bachelor's degree, resume (MS in predictive analytics only), IT experience (MS in information technology project management only), portfolio review (all MFA programs and MA in animation); for doctorate, GRE, master's degree in computer science. Additional exam requirements/recommendations for international students: Required—TOEFL (minimum score 590 paper-based; 80 iBT), IELTS (minimum score 6.5), PTE (minimum score 53). Electronic applications accepted. *Expenses:* Contact institution. *Faculty research:* Data mining, computer science, human-computer interaction, security, animation and film.

Drexel University, College of Computing and Informatics, Master of Science in Health Informatics Program, Philadelphia, PA 19104-2875. Offers MSHI. Part-time and evening/weekend programs available. Postbaccalaureate distance learning degree programs offered (no on-campus study). *Faculty:* 8 full-time (6 women), 6 part-time/adjunct (3 women). *Students:* 5 full-time (4 women), 44 part-time (31 women); includes 14 minority (4 Black or African American, non-Hispanic/Latino; 5 Asian, non-Hispanic/Latino; 3 Hispanic/Latino; 2 Two or more races, non-Hispanic/Latino), 1 international. Average age 37. 24 applicants, 83% accepted, 15 enrolled. In 2014, 7 master's awarded. *Entrance requirements:* For master's, GRE General Test. Additional exam requirements/recommendations for international students: Required—TOEFL (minimum score 600 paper-based; 100 iBT). *Application deadline:* For fall admission, 8/22 for domestic students, 8/1 for international students; for spring admission, 3/4 for domestic students, 2/1 for international students. Applications are processed on a rolling basis. Application fee: $0. Electronic applications accepted. *Financial support:* In 2014–15, 14 students received support. Institutionally sponsored loans, scholarships/grants, and tuition waivers (partial) available. Support available to part-time students. Financial award application deadline: 3/1; financial award applicants required to submit FAFSA. *Unit head:* Dr. Spiros Mancoridis, Interim Dean/Professor of Computer Science, 215-895-2475, Fax: 215-895-6378, E-mail: fenske@drexel.edu. *Application contact:* Matthew Lechtenberg, Graduate Admissions Manager, 215-895-1951, Fax: 215-895-2303, E-mail: ml333@drexel.edu.
Website: http://cci.drexel.edu/academics/graduate-programs/ms-in-health-informatics.

East Carolina University, Graduate School, College of Allied Health Sciences, Department of Health Services and Information Management, Greenville, NC 27858-4353. Offers health informatics and information management (MS). *Expenses:* Tuition, state resident: full-time $4223. Tuition, nonresident: full-time $16,540. *Required fees:* $2184.

Emory University, Rollins School of Public Health, Department of Biostatistics and Bioinformatics, Atlanta, GA 30322-1100. Offers bioinformatics (PhD); biostatistics (MPH, MSPH); public health informatics (MSPH). PhD offered through the Graduate School of Arts and Sciences. Part-time programs available. *Degree requirements:* For master's, thesis, practicum. *Entrance requirements:* For master's, GRE General Test. Additional exam requirements/recommendations for international students: Required—TOEFL (minimum score 550 paper-based; 80 iBT). Electronic applications accepted.

Emory University, Rollins School of Public Health, Online Program in Public Health, Atlanta, GA 30322-1100. Offers applied epidemiology (MPH); applied public health informatics (MPH); prevention science (MPH). Part-time and evening/weekend programs available. Postbaccalaureate distance learning degree programs offered (minimal on-campus study). *Degree requirements:* For master's, thesis, practicum. *Entrance requirements:* For master's, GRE. Additional exam requirements/recommendations for international students: Required—TOEFL (minimum score 550 paper-based; 80 iBT). Electronic applications accepted.

George Mason University, College of Health and Human Services, Department of Health Administration and Policy, Fairfax, VA 22030. Offers health and medical policy (MS); health informatics (MS); health systems management (MHA). *Accreditation:* CAHME. *Faculty:* 17 full-time (6 women), 17 part-time/adjunct (8 women). *Students:* 59 full-time (41 women), 117 part-time (85 women); includes 88 minority (34 Black or African American, non-Hispanic/Latino; 38 Asian, non-Hispanic/Latino; 13 Hispanic/Latino; 1 Native Hawaiian or other Pacific Islander, non-Hispanic/Latino; 2 Two or more races, non-Hispanic/Latino), 20 international. Average age 33. 123 applicants, 60% accepted, 45 enrolled. In 2014, 67 master's awarded. *Degree requirements:* For master's, comprehensive exam, internship. *Entrance requirements:* For master's, GRE recommended if undergraduate GPA is below 3.0 (for senior housing administration MS only), 2 official transcripts; expanded goals statement; 3 letters of recommendation; resume; 1 year of work experience (for MHA in health systems management). Additional exam requirements/recommendations for international students: Required—TOEFL (minimum score 570 paper-based; 80 iBT), IELTS (minimum score 6.5), PTE. *Application deadline:* For fall admission, 4/1 priority date for domestic students; for spring admission, 11/1 priority date for domestic students. Applications are processed on a rolling basis. Application fee: $65 ($80 for international students). Electronic applications accepted. *Expenses:* Expenses: Contact institution. *Financial support:* In 2014–15, 6 students received support, including 6 research assistantships with full and partial tuition reimbursements available (averaging $20,833 per year), 1 teaching assistantship (averaging $14,500 per year); career-related internships or fieldwork, Federal Work-Study, scholarships/grants, unspecified assistantships, and health care benefits (for full-time research or teaching assistantship recipients) also available. Support available to part-time students. Financial award application deadline: 3/1; financial award applicants required to submit FAFSA. *Faculty research:* Universal health care, publications, relationships between malpractice pressure and rates of Cesarean section and VBAC, seniors and Wii gaming, relationships between changes in physician's incomes and practice settings and their care to Medicaid and charity patients. *Total annual research expenditures:* $590,779. *Unit head:* Dr. P. J. Maddox, Chair, 703-993-1982, Fax: 703-993-1953, E-mail: pmaddox@gmu.edu. *Application contact:* Tracy Shevlin, Department Manager, 703-993-1929, Fax: 703-993-1953, E-mail: tshevlin@gmu.edu.
Website: http://chhs.gmu.edu/hap/index.

Georgia Regents University, The Graduate School, Program in Public Health–Informatics, Augusta, GA 30912. Offers health informatics (MPH); health management (MPH). Part-time programs available. *Degree requirements:* For master's, thesis (for some programs). *Entrance requirements:* For master's, GRE General Test. Additional exam requirements/recommendations for international students: Required—TOEFL. Electronic applications accepted.

Georgia State University, J. Mack Robinson College of Business, Department of Computer Information Systems, Atlanta, GA 30302-3083. Offers computer information systems (PhD); health informatics (MBA, MS); information systems (MSIS, Certificate); information systems development and project management (MBA); information systems management (MBA); managing information technology (Exec MS); the wireless organization (MBA). Part-time and evening/weekend programs available. *Faculty:* 15 full-time (2 women). *Students:* 123 full-time (48 women), 4 part-time (2 women); includes 44 minority (24 Black or African American, non-Hispanic/Latino; 18 Asian, non-Hispanic/Latino; 2 Two or more races, non-Hispanic/Latino), 59 international. Average age 30. 354 applicants, 55% accepted, 91 enrolled. In 2014, 61 master's, 1 doctorate awarded. *Degree requirements:* For master's, thesis optional; for doctorate, comprehensive exam, thesis/dissertation. *Entrance requirements:* For master's, GRE or GMAT, transcripts from all institutions attended, resume, essays; for doctorate, GRE or GMAT, three letters of recommendation, personal statement, transcripts from all institutions attended, resume. Additional exam requirements/recommendations for international students: Required—TOEFL (minimum score 610 paper-based; 101 iBT), IELTS (minimum score 7). *Application deadline:* For fall admission, 5/1 priority date for domestic students, 2/1 priority date for international students; for spring admission, 9/15 priority date for domestic students, 4/1 priority date for international students. Applications are processed on a rolling basis. Application fee: $50. Electronic applications accepted. *Expenses:* Tuition, state resident: full-time $6516; part-time $362 per credit hour. Tuition, nonresident: full-time $22,014; part-time $1223 per credit hour. *Required fees:* $2128 per semester. Tuition and fees vary according to course load and program. *Financial support:* Research assistantships, teaching assistantships, scholarships/grants, tuition waivers, and unspecified assistantships available. *Faculty research:* Process and technological innovation, strategic IT management, intelligent systems, information systems security, software project risk. *Unit head:* Dr. Ephraim R. McLean, Professor/Chair, 404-413-7360, Fax: 404-413-7394. *Application contact:* Toby McChesney, Assistant Dean for Graduate Recruiting and Student Services, 404-413-7167, Fax: 404-413-7167, E-mail: rcbgradadmissions@gsu.edu.
Website: http://cis.robinson.gsu.edu/.

Georgia State University, J. Mack Robinson College of Business, Institute of Health Administration, Atlanta, GA 30302-3083. Offers health administration (MBA, MSHA); health informatics (MBA, MSCIS); MBA/MHA; PMBA/MHA. *Accreditation:* CAHME. Part-time and evening/weekend programs available. *Faculty:* 5 full-time (1 woman). *Students:* 54 full-time (23 women), 15 part-time (7 women); includes 20 minority (10 Black or African American, non-Hispanic/Latino; 7 Asian, non-Hispanic/Latino; 3 Two or more races, non-Hispanic/Latino), 7 international. Average age 29. 108 applicants, 37% accepted, 16 enrolled. In 2014, 67 master's awarded. *Entrance requirements:* For master's, GRE or GMAT, transcripts from all institutions attended, resume, essays. Additional exam requirements/recommendations for international students: Required—TOEFL (minimum score 610 paper-based; 101 iBT), IELTS (minimum score 7). *Application deadline:* For fall admission, 5/1 priority date for domestic students, 2/1 priority date for international students; for spring admission, 9/15 priority date for domestic students, 4/1 priority date for international students. Applications are processed on a rolling basis. Application fee: $50. Electronic applications accepted. *Expenses:* Tuition, state resident: full-time $6516; part-time $362 per credit hour. Tuition, nonresident: full-time $22,014; part-time $1223 per credit hour. *Required fees:* $2128 per semester. Tuition and fees vary according to course load and program. *Financial support:* Research assistantships, teaching assistantships, scholarships/grants, tuition waivers, and unspecified assistantships available. *Faculty research:* Health information technology, health insurance exchanges, health policy and economic impact, healthcare quality, healthcare transformation. *Unit head:* Dr. Andrew T. Sumner, Chair in Health Administration/Director of the Institute of Health, 404-413-7630, Fax: 404-413-7631. *Application contact:* Toby McChesney, Assistant Dean for Graduate Recruiting and Student Services, 404-413-7167, Fax: 404-413-7162, E-mail: rcbgradadmissions@gsu.edu.
Website: http://www.hagsu.org/.

Golden Gate University, Ageno School of Business, San Francisco, CA 94105-2968. Offers accounting (MBA); business administration (EMBA, MBA, PMBA, DBA); finance (MBA, MS, Certificate); financial planning (MS, Certificate); healthcare information systems (Certificate); human resource management (MBA, MS); human resources management (Certificate); information systems (MS); information technology (MBA); information technology management (Certificate); integrated marketing and communications (MS, Certificate); international business (MBA); management (MBA); marketing (MBA, MS, Certificate); operations supply chain management (Certificate); psychology (MA, Certificate); public administration (EMPA); public relations (MS, Certificate); technical market analysis (Certificate); JD/MBA. Part-time and evening/weekend programs available. *Degree requirements:* For doctorate, thesis/dissertation, qualifying examination. *Entrance requirements:* For master's, GMAT (MBA), minimum GPA of 2.5 (MS). Additional exam requirements/recommendations for international students: Required—TOEFL (minimum score 550 paper-based; 79 iBT). Electronic applications accepted. *Expenses:* Contact institution.

Grand Canyon University, College of Nursing and Health Sciences, Phoenix, AZ 85017-1097. Offers addiction counseling (MS); health care administration (MS); health care informatics (MS); marriage and family therapy (MS); professional counseling (MS); public health (MS). Part-time and evening/weekend programs available. Postbaccalaureate distance learning degree programs offered (no on-campus study). *Entrance requirements:* For master's, undergraduate degree with minimum GPA of 2.8. Additional exam requirements/recommendations for international students: Required—TOEFL (minimum score 575 paper-based; 90 iBT), IELTS (minimum score 7).

Indiana University Bloomington, School of Informatics and Computing, Program in Informatics, Bloomington, IN 47408. Offers informatics (MS, PhD), including bioinformatics, cheminformatics (PhD), complex systems (PhD), health informatics (PhD), human-computer interaction (MS), human-computer interaction design (PhD), logic and mathematical foundations of informatics (PhD), music informatics (PhD), robotics (PhD), security informatics, social informatics (PhD). Part-time programs available. *Students:* 206 full-time (78 women), 7 part-time (1 woman); includes 25 minority (9 Black or African American, non-Hispanic/Latino; 12 Asian, non-Hispanic/Latino; 2 Hispanic/Latino; 2 Two or more races, non-Hispanic/Latino), 101 international. 287 applicants, 52% accepted, 65 enrolled. In 2014, 65 master's, 13 doctorates awarded. Terminal master's awarded for partial completion of doctoral program. *Degree requirements:* For master's, thesis; for doctorate, thesis/dissertation. *Entrance requirements:* For master's and doctorate, GRE, TOEFL if international and no US degree. Additional exam requirements/recommendations for international students: Required—TOEFL (minimum score 600 paper-based; 100 iBT). *Application deadline:* For fall admission, 12/1 priority date for domestic and international students. Application fee: $55 ($65 for international students). Electronic applications accepted. *Financial support:* Application deadline: 12/1. *Unit head:* Dr. Howard Rosenbaum, Associate Dean for Graduate Studies, 812-855-3250, E-mail: hrosenba@indiana.edu. *Application contact:* Patty Reyes-Cooksey, Director of Graduate Administration, 812-856-3622, E-mail: patreyes@indiana.edu.
Website: http://www.soic.indiana.edu/informatics/index.shtml.

Indiana University–Purdue University Indianapolis, School of Informatics and Computing, Indianapolis, IN 46202. Offers bioinformatics (MS, PhD); health informatics (MS, PhD); human-computer interaction (MS, PhD); information and library science (MLS); media arts and science (MS). Part-time and evening/weekend programs available. *Faculty:* 3 full-time (0 women). *Students:* 199 full-time (101 women), 229 part-time (159 women); includes 49 minority (18 Black or African American, non-Hispanic/Latino; 15 Asian, non-Hispanic/Latino; 10 Hispanic/Latino; 6 Two or more races, non-Hispanic/Latino), 102 international. Average age 34. 268 applicants, 63% accepted, 133 enrolled. In 2014, 144 master's awarded. *Degree requirements:* For master's, thesis optional; for doctorate, thesis/dissertation. *Entrance requirements:* For master's, minimum undergraduate GPA of 3.0, graduate 3.2. Additional exam requirements/recommendations for international students: Required—TOEFL. *Application deadline:* For fall admission, 3/15 for domestic students; for spring admission, 10/15 for domestic students. Application fee: $60 ($65 for international students). Electronic applications accepted. *Financial support:* Fellowships, research assistantships, teaching assistantships, career-related internships or fieldwork, Federal Work-Study, institutionally sponsored loans, and scholarships/grants available. Support available to part-time students. *Unit head:* Dr. Robert B. Schnabel, Dean. *Application contact:* Elizabeth Bunge, Graduate Admissions Coordinator, 317-278-9200, E-mail: ebunge@iupui.edu.
Website: http://soic.iupui.edu/.

Johns Hopkins University, School of Medicine, Division of Health Sciences Informatics, Baltimore, MD 21218-2699. Offers applied health sciences informatics (MS); clinical informatics (Certificate); health sciences informatics (PhD); health sciences informatics research (MS). *Degree requirements:* For master's, thesis, publications, practica. *Entrance requirements:* Additional exam requirements/recommendations for international students: Recommended—TOEFL. Electronic applications accepted. *Faculty research:* Decision modeling, consumer health informatics, digital libraries, data standards, patient safety.

Lipscomb University, Graduate School of Business, Nashville, TN 37204-3951. Offers accountancy (M Acc); accounting (MBA); conflict management (MBA); financial services (MBA); health care informatics (MBA); healthcare management (MBA); human resources (MHR); information security (MBA); leadership (MBA); nonprofit management (MBA); professional accountancy (Certificate); sports management (MBA); strategic human resources (MBA); sustainability (MBA); MBA/MS. *Accreditation:* ACBSP. Part-time and evening/weekend programs available. *Faculty:* 14 full-time (1 woman), 15 part-time/adjunct (4 women). *Students:* 121 full-time (71 women), 113 part-time (47 women); includes 36 minority (23 Black or African American, non-Hispanic/Latino; 11 Hispanic/Latino; 2 Two or more races, non-Hispanic/Latino), 7 international. Average age 32. 145 applicants, 79% accepted, 69 enrolled. In 2014, 106 master's awarded. *Entrance requirements:* For master's, GMAT, transcripts, interview, 2 references, resume. Additional exam requirements/recommendations for international students: Required—TOEFL (minimum score 570 paper-based). *Application deadline:* For fall admission, 6/15 for domestic students, 2/1 for international students; for winter admission, 6/1 for international students; for spring admission, 11/15 for domestic students. Applications are processed on a rolling basis. Application fee: $50 ($75 for international students). Electronic applications accepted. *Expenses:* Expenses: $1,230 per credit hour (for MBA and PMBA); $1,150 (for M Acc); $1,125 (for MHR); $1,100 (for MM). *Financial support:* Career-related internships or fieldwork, scholarships/grants, tuition waivers (partial), and unspecified assistantships available. Support available to part-time students. Financial award application deadline: 7/1; financial award applicants required to submit FAFSA. *Faculty research:* Impact of spirituality on organization commitment, women in corporate leadership, psychological empowerment, training. *Unit head:* Joe Ivey, Associate Dean of Graduate Business Programs, 615-966-6229, Fax: 615-966-1818, E-mail: joe.ivey@lipscomb.edu. *Application contact:* Lisa Shacklett, Assistant Dean of Enrollment and Marketing, 615-966-5968, E-mail: lisa.shacklett@lipscomb.edu.
Website: http://www.lipscomb.edu/business/Graduate-Programs.

Logan University, College of Health Sciences, Chesterfield, MO 63017. Offers health informatics (MS); health professionals education (DHPE); nutrition and human performance (MS); sports science and rehabilitation (MS). Part-time programs available. Postbaccalaureate distance learning degree programs offered (no on-campus study). *Faculty:* 7 full-time (2 women), 13 part-time/adjunct (5 women). *Students:* 11 full-time (7 women), 70 part-time (34 women); includes 12 minority (3 Black or African American, non-Hispanic/Latino; 4 Asian, non-Hispanic/Latino; 3 Hispanic/Latino; 2 Two or more races, non-Hispanic/Latino), 3 international. Average age 32. 43 applicants, 65% accepted, 28 enrolled. In 2014, 85 master's awarded. *Degree requirements:* For master's, comprehensive exam. *Entrance requirements:* For master's, GRE (if GPA lower than 3.0), specific undergraduate coursework based on program of interest. Additional exam requirements/recommendations for international students: Required—TOEFL (minimum score 79 iBT). *Application deadline:* For fall admission, 7/15 priority date for domestic and international students; for winter admission, 11/15 priority date for domestic and international students; for spring admission, 3/15 priority date for domestic students, 3/15 for international students. Applications are processed on a rolling basis. Application fee: $50. Electronic applications accepted. *Expenses:* Expenses: Contact institution. *Financial support:* In 2014–15, 1 student received support. Federal Work-Study and scholarships/grants available. Support available to part-time students. Financial award applicants required to submit FAFSA. *Faculty research:* Ankle injury prevention in high school athletes, low back pain in college football players, short arc banding and low back pain, the effects of enzymes on inflammatory blood markers, gait analysis in high school and college athletes. *Unit head:* Dr. Sherri Cole, Dean, College of Health Sciences, 636-227-2100 Ext. 2702, Fax: 636-207-2418, E-mail: sherri.cole@logan.edu. *Application contact:* Stacey Till, Assistant Vice President, Admissions and Development, 636-227-2100 Ext. 1749, Fax: 636-207-2425, E-mail: admissions@logan.edu.
Website: http://www.logan.edu.

Louisiana Tech University, Graduate School, College of Applied and Natural Sciences, Department of Health Informatics and Information Management, Ruston, LA 71272. Offers health informatics (MHI). Postbaccalaureate distance learning degree programs offered (no on-campus study). *Entrance requirements:* For master's, essay or GRE; three reference letters; official transcripts; bachelor's degree from regionally-accredited institution; two years of work experience; resume; personal statement; interview.

Marshall University, Academic Affairs Division, College of Health Professions, Department of Health Informatics, Huntington, WV 25755. Offers MS. Offered jointly with College of Business and College of Information Technology and Engineering. *Students:* 18 full-time (12 women), 4 part-time (1 woman); includes 6 minority (4 Black or African American, non-Hispanic/Latino; 1 Asian, non-Hispanic/Latino; 1 Two or more races, non-Hispanic/Latino), 5 international. Average age 31. In 2014, 8 master's awarded. *Unit head:* Dr. Girmay Berhie, Program Director, 304-696-2718, E-mail: berhie@marshall.edu. *Application contact:* Information Contact, 304-746-1900, Fax: 304-746-1902, E-mail: services@marshall.edu.

Metropolitan State University, College of Management, St. Paul, MN 55106-5000. Offers business administration (MBA, DBA); database administration (Graduate

Certificate); healthcare information technology management (Graduate Certificate); information assurance security (Graduate Certificate); management information systems (MMIS); MIS generalist (Graduate Certificate); MIS systems analysis and design (Graduate Certificate); project management (Graduate Certificate); public and nonprofit administration (MPNA). Part-time and evening/weekend programs available. *Degree requirements:* For master's, thesis optional, computer language (MMIS). *Entrance requirements:* For master's, GMAT (for MBA), resume. Additional exam requirements/recommendations for international students: Required—TOEFL (minimum score 550 paper-based). Electronic applications accepted. *Faculty research:* Yugoslav economic system, workers' cooperatives, participative management and job enrichment, global business systems.

Midwestern State University, Billie Doris McAda Graduate School, Robert D. and Carol Gunn College of Health Sciences and Human Services, Department of Criminal Justice and Health Services Administration, Wichita Falls, TX 76308. Offers criminal justice (MA); health information management (MHA); health services administration (Graduate Certificate); medical practice management (MHA); public and community sector health care management (MHA); rural and urban hospital management (MHA). Part-time and evening/weekend programs available. *Degree requirements:* For master's, comprehensive exam, thesis. *Entrance requirements:* For master's, GRE. Additional exam requirements/recommendations for international students: Required—TOEFL (minimum score 550 paper-based). *Application deadline:* For fall admission, 7/1 priority date for domestic students, 4/1 for international students; for spring admission, 11/1 priority date for domestic students, 8/1 for international students. Applications are processed on a rolling basis. Application fee: $35 ($50 for international students). Electronic applications accepted. *Financial support:* Teaching assistantships with partial tuition reimbursements, career-related internships or fieldwork, Federal Work-Study, institutionally sponsored loans, scholarships/grants, tuition waivers (partial), and unspecified assistantships available. Support available to part-time students. Financial award application deadline: 3/1; financial award applicants required to submit FAFSA. *Faculty research:* Universal service policy, telehealth, bullying, healthcare financial management, public health ethics. *Unit head:* Dr. Nathan Moran, Chair, 940-397-4752, Fax: 940-397-6291, E-mail: nathan.moran@mwsu.edu.
Website: http://www.mwsu.edu/academics/hs2/health-admin/.

Millennia Atlantic University, Graduate Programs, Doral, FL 33178. Offers accounting (MBA); business administration (MBA); health information management (MS); human resource management (MA). Postbaccalaureate distance learning degree programs offered (no on-campus study).

Molloy College, Division of Nursing, Rockville Centre, NY 11571-5002. Offers adult-gerontology primary care nurse practitioner (MS); clinical nurse specialist (MS), including adult-gerontology health; clinical nurse specialist: adult-gerontology (Advanced Certificate), including adult-gerontology; family nurse practitioner (MS, Advanced Certificate), including primary care; family psychiatric mental health nurse practitioner (MS); nursing (DNP, PhD); nursing administration (MS), including informatics; nursing education (MS); pediatric nurse practitioner (MS), including primary care (MS, Advanced Certificate). *Accreditation:* AACN. Part-time and evening/weekend programs available. *Faculty:* 24 full-time (all women), 11 part-time/adjunct (8 women). *Students:* 17 full-time (15 women), 578 part-time (537 women); includes 325 minority (174 Black or African American, non-Hispanic/Latino; 89 Asian, non-Hispanic/Latino; 55 Hispanic/Latino; 3 Native Hawaiian or other Pacific Islander, non-Hispanic/Latino; 4 Two or more races, non-Hispanic/Latino), 2 international. Average age 37. 249 applicants, 68% accepted, 121 enrolled. In 2014, 116 master's, 1 doctorate, 6 other advanced degrees awarded. *Degree requirements:* For master's, thesis optional. *Entrance requirements:* For master's, 3 letters of reference, BS in nursing, minimum undergraduate GPA of 3.0; for Advanced Certificate, 3 letters of reference, master's degree in nursing. *Application deadline:* For fall admission, 9/2 priority date for domestic students; for spring admission, 1/20 priority date for domestic students. Applications are processed on a rolling basis. Application fee: $60. *Expenses: Tuition:* Full-time $17,640; part-time $980 per credit. *Required fees:* $900. *Financial support:* Research assistantships with partial tuition reimbursements, teaching assistantships with partial tuition reimbursements, institutionally sponsored loans, scholarships/grants, and unspecified assistantships available. Support available to part-time students. Financial award application deadline: 4/1; financial award applicants required to submit FAFSA. *Faculty research:* Psychiatric workplace violence, parents of children with special needs, moral distress/ethical dilemmas, obesity and teasing in school-age children, families of children with rare diseases. *Unit head:* Dr. Jeannine Muldoon, Dean of Nursing, 516-323-3651, E-mail: jmuldoon@molloy.edu. *Application contact:* Alina Haitz, Assistant Director of Graduate Admissions, 516-323-4008, E-mail: ahaitz@molloy.edu.

Montana Tech of The University of Montana, Graduate School, Health Care Informatics Program, Butte, MT 59701-8997. Offers Certificate. Part-time and evening/weekend programs available. Postbaccalaureate distance learning degree programs offered (no on-campus study). *Entrance requirements:* Additional exam requirements/recommendations for international students: Required—TOEFL (minimum score 525 paper-based; 71 iBT). Electronic applications accepted. *Expenses:* Tuition, state resident: full-time $5802; part-time $241 per credit. Tuition, nonresident: full-time $15,895; part-time $662 per credit. *Required fees:* $1516; $414 per credit. $207 per semester. One-time fee: $30. *Faculty research:* Informatics, healthcare, computer science.

National University, Academic Affairs, School of Engineering and Computing, La Jolla, CA 92037-1011. Offers computer science (MS), including advanced computing, database engineering, software engineering; cyber security and information assurance (MS), including computer forensics, ethical hacking and penetration testing, health information assurance, information assurance and security; data analytics (MS); engineering management (MS), including enterprise architecture, project management, systems engineering, technology management; environmental engineering (MS); homeland security and emergency management (MS); management information systems (MS); project management (Certificate); sustainability management (MS); wireless communications (MS). Part-time and evening/weekend programs available. Postbaccalaureate distance learning degree programs offered (no on-campus study). *Faculty:* 24 full-time (5 women), 21 part-time/adjunct (5 women). *Students:* 275 full-time (72 women), 86 part-time (24 women); includes 147 minority (41 Black or African American, non-Hispanic/Latino; 48 Asian, non-Hispanic/Latino; 37 Hispanic/Latino; 7 Native Hawaiian or other Pacific Islander, non-Hispanic/Latino; 14 Two or more races, non-Hispanic/Latino), 95 international. Average age 33. In 2014, 281 master's awarded. *Degree requirements:* For master's, thesis (for some programs). *Entrance requirements:* For master's, interview, minimum GPA of 2.5. Additional exam requirements/recommendations for international students: Required—TOEFL (minimum score 550 paper-based; 79 iBT), IELTS (minimum score 6). *Application deadline:* Applications are processed on a rolling basis. Application fee: $60 ($65 for international students). Electronic applications accepted. *Expenses: Tuition:* Full-time $14,184; part-time $1773 per course. *Financial support:* Career-related internships or fieldwork, institutionally sponsored loans, scholarships/grants, and tuition waivers (partial) available. Support available to part-time students. Financial award application deadline: 6/30; financial award applicants required to submit FAFSA. *Faculty research:* Educational technology,

scholarships in science. *Unit head:* School of Engineering and Computing, 800-628-8648, E-mail: soec@nu.edu. *Application contact:* Frank Rojas, Vice President for Enrollment Services, 800-628-8648, E-mail: advisor@nu.edu.
Website: http://www.nu.edu/OurPrograms SchoolOfEngineeringAndTechnology.html.

National University, Academic Affairs, School of Health and Human Services, La Jolla, CA 92037-1011. Offers clinical affairs (MS); clinical informatics (Certificate); clinical regulatory affairs (MS); health and life science analytics (MS); health coaching (Certificate); health informatics (MS); healthcare administration (MHA); nurse anesthesia (MS); nursing (MS), including forensic nursing, nursing administration, nursing informatics; nursing administration (Certificate); nursing informatics (Certificate); nursing practice (DNP); public health (MPH), including health promotion, healthcare administration, mental health. Part-time and evening/weekend programs available. Postbaccalaureate distance learning degree programs offered (no on-campus study). *Faculty:* 26 full-time (14 women), 29 part-time/adjunct (21 women). *Students:* 302 full-time (232 women), 95 part-time (66 women); includes 282 minority (89 Black or African American, non-Hispanic/Latino; 1 American Indian or Alaska Native, non-Hispanic/Latino; 87 Asian, non-Hispanic/Latino; 76 Hispanic/Latino; 7 Native Hawaiian or other Pacific Islander, non-Hispanic/Latino; 22 Two or more races, non-Hispanic/Latino), 21 international. Average age 32. In 2014, 53 master's awarded. *Degree requirements:* For master's, thesis (for some programs). *Entrance requirements:* For master's, interview, minimum GPA of 2.5. Additional exam requirements/recommendations for international students: Required—TOEFL (minimum score 550 paper-based; 79 iBT), IELTS (minimum score 6). *Application deadline:* Applications are processed on a rolling basis. Application fee: $60 ($65 for international students). Electronic applications accepted. *Expenses:* Tuition: Full-time $14,184; part-time $1773 per course. *Financial support:* Career-related internships or fieldwork, institutionally sponsored loans, scholarships/grants, and tuition waivers (partial) available. Support available to part-time students. Financial award application deadline: 6/30; financial award applicants required to submit FAFSA. *Faculty research:* Nursing education, obesity prevention, workforce diversity. *Unit head:* School of Health and Human Services, 800-628-8648, E-mail: shhs@nu.edu. *Application contact:* Frank Rojas, Vice President for Enrollment Services, 800-628-8648, E-mail: advisor@nu.edu.
Website: http://www.nu.edu/OurPrograms/SchoolOfHealthAndHumanServices.html.

Northeastern University, Bouvé College of Health Sciences, Boston, MA 02115-5096. Offers audiology (Au D); biotechnology (MS); counseling psychology (MS, PhD, CAGS); counseling/school psychology (PhD); exercise physiology (MS), including exercise physiology, public health; health informatics (MS); nursing (MS, PhD, CAGS), including acute care (MS), administration (MS), anesthesia (MS), primary care (MS), psychiatric mental health (MS); pharmaceutical sciences (PhD); pharmaceutics and drug delivery systems (MS); pharmacology (MS); physical therapy (DPT); physician assistant (MS); school psychology (PhD, CAGS); school/counseling psychology (PhD); speech language pathology (MS); urban public health (MPH); MS/MBA. *Accreditation:* ACPE (one or more programs are accredited). Part-time and evening/weekend programs available. *Degree requirements:* For doctorate, thesis/dissertation (for some programs); for CAGS, comprehensive exam.

Northeastern University, College of Computer and Information Science, Boston, MA 02115-5096. Offers computer science (MS, PhD); health informatics (MS); information assurance (MS, PhD). Part-time and evening/weekend programs available. Terminal master's awarded for partial completion of doctoral program. *Degree requirements:* For master's, thesis optional; for doctorate, comprehensive exam, thesis/dissertation.

Northern Kentucky University, Office of Graduate Programs, College of Informatics, Program in Health Informatics, Highland Heights, KY 41099. Offers MS, Certificate. Part-time and evening/weekend programs available. Postbaccalaureate distance learning degree programs offered (no on-campus study). *Faculty:* 4 full-time (3 women), 2 part-time/adjunct (0 women). *Students:* 9 full-time (7 women), 44 part-time (24 women); includes 8 minority (2 Black or African American, non-Hispanic/Latino; 3 Asian, non-Hispanic/Latino; 2 Hispanic/Latino; 1 Two or more races, non-Hispanic/Latino), 7 international. Average age 37. In 2014, 29 master's awarded. *Degree requirements:* For master's, capstone, electronic portfolio. *Entrance requirements:* For master's, MAT, GRE, or GMAT, official transcripts from accredited college or university, minimum GPA of 3.0, letter of career goals and background, statement addressing computer proficiencies; references (recommended). Additional exam requirements/recommendations for international students: Required—TOEFL (minimum score 79 iBT); Recommended—IELTS (minimum score 6.5). *Application deadline:* For fall admission, 8/1 for domestic students, 6/1 for international students; for spring admission, 12/1 for domestic students, 10/1 for international students; for summer admission, 5/1 for domestic students, 3/1 for international students. Applications are processed on a rolling basis. Application fee: $40. Electronic applications accepted. *Expenses:* Tuition, area resident: Part-time $518 per credit hour. Tuition, state resident: part-time $630 per credit hour. Tuition, nonresident: part-time $797 per credit hour. *Required fees:* $192 per semester. Tuition and fees vary according to course load, degree level, campus/location, program and reciprocity agreements. *Financial support:* In 2014–15, 20 students received support. Unspecified assistantships available. Financial award applicants required to submit FAFSA. *Faculty research:* Health informatics course development, healthcare analytics, technology acceptance in healthcare, consumer engagement, population health outcome, systems implementation, healthcare operations. *Unit head:* Kevin Gallagher, Department Chair, 859-572-7716, E-mail: gallagherk2@nku.edu. *Application contact:* Alison Swanson, Graduate Admissions Coordinator, 859-572-6971, E-mail: swansona1@nku.edu.
Website: http://informatics.nku.edu/departments/business-informatics/programs/mhi.html.

Northwestern University, Feinberg School of Medicine and Interdepartmental Programs, Integrated Graduate Programs in the Life Sciences, Chicago, IL 60611. Offers biostatistics (PhD); epidemiology (PhD); health and biomedical informatics (PhD); health services and outcomes research (PhD); healthcare quality and patient safety (PhD); translational outcomes in science (PhD). *Degree requirements:* For doctorate, comprehensive exam, thesis/dissertation, written and oral qualifying exams. *Entrance requirements:* For doctorate, GRE General Test. Additional exam requirements/recommendations for international students: Required—TOEFL (minimum score 600 paper-based). Electronic applications accepted.

Nova Southeastern University, College of Osteopathic Medicine, Fort Lauderdale, FL 33328. Offers biomedical informatics (MS, Graduate Certificate), including biomedical informatics (MS), clinical informatics (Graduate Certificate), public health informatics (Graduate Certificate); disaster and emergency preparedness (MS); osteopathic medicine (DO); public health (MPH). *Accreditation:* AOsA. *Faculty:* 107 full-time (55 women), 1,235 part-time/adjunct (297 women). *Students:* 1,027 full-time (436 women), 189 part-time (124 women); includes 560 minority (92 Black or African American, non-Hispanic/Latino; 260 Asian, non-Hispanic/Latino; 174 Hispanic/Latino; 1 Native Hawaiian or other Pacific Islander, non-Hispanic/Latino; 33 Two or more races, non-Hispanic/Latino), 45 international. Average age 28. 4,012 applicants, 12% accepted, 246 enrolled. In 2014, 75 master's, 237 doctorates, 4 other advanced degrees awarded. *Entrance requirements:* For master's, GRE, licensed healthcare professional or GRE; for doctorate, MCAT, biology, chemistry, organic chemistry, physics (all with labs), and

English. *Application deadline:* For fall admission, 1/15 for domestic students. Applications are processed on a rolling basis. Application fee: $50. Electronic applications accepted. *Expenses:* Expenses: Contact institution. *Financial support:* In 2014–15, 39 students received support, including 24 fellowships (averaging $45,593 per year); research assistantships, teaching assistantships, Federal Work-Study, and scholarships/grants also available. Financial award application deadline: 6/1; financial award applicants required to submit FAFSA. *Faculty research:* Teaching strategies, simulated patient use, HIV/AIDS education, minority health issues, managed care education. *Unit head:* Elaine M. Wallace, DO, Dean, 954-262-1407, E-mail: ewallace@nova.edu. *Application contact:* Monica Sanchez, Admissions Counselor, College of Osteopathic Medicine, 954-262-1110, Fax: 954-262-2282, E-mail: mh1156@nova.edu.
Website: http://www.medicine.nova.edu/.

Oregon Health & Science University, School of Medicine, Graduate Programs in Medicine, Department of Medical Informatics and Clinical Epidemiology, Portland, OR 97239-3098. Offers clinical informatics (MS, PhD, Certificate); computational biology (MS, PhD); health information management (Certificate). Part-time programs available. Postbaccalaureate distance learning degree programs offered (minimal on-campus study). *Faculty:* 12 full-time (6 women), 15 part-time/adjunct (7 women). *Students:* 32 full-time (12 women), 92 part-time (41 women); includes 43 minority (7 Black or African American, non-Hispanic/Latino; 26 Asian, non-Hispanic/Latino; 5 Hispanic/Latino; 5 Two or more races, non-Hispanic/Latino), 3 international. Average age 39. 111 applicants, 64% accepted, 52 enrolled. In 2014, 28 master's, 2 doctorates, 25 other advanced degrees awarded. Terminal master's awarded for partial completion of doctoral program. *Degree requirements:* For master's, thesis optional, thesis or capstone project; for doctorate, comprehensive exam, thesis/dissertation, qualifying exam. *Entrance requirements:* For master's and doctorate, GRE General Test (minimum scores: 153 Verbal/148 Quantitative/4.5 Analytical), coursework in computer programming, human anatomy and physiology. Additional exam requirements/recommendations for international students: Required—IELTS or TOEFL. *Application deadline:* For fall admission, 12/1 for domestic students; for winter admission, 11/1 for domestic students; for spring admission, 2/1 for domestic students. Applications are processed on a rolling basis. Application fee: $70. Electronic applications accepted. *Expenses:* Expenses: Contact institution. *Financial support:* Fellowships with full tuition reimbursements, research assistantships, Federal Work-Study, institutionally sponsored loans, scholarships/grants, health care benefits, and full tuition and stipends (for PhD students) available. Financial award application deadline: 3/1; financial award applicants required to submit FAFSA. *Faculty research:* Clinical informatics, computational biology, health information management, genomics, data analytics. *Unit head:* Dr. Allison Fryer, Associate Dean for Graduate Studies, 503-494-6222, Fax: 503-494-3400, E-mail: somgrad@ohsu.edu. *Application contact:* Lauren Ludwig, Administrative Coordinator, 503-494-2252, E-mail: informat@ohsu.edu.
Website: http://www.ohsu.edu/dmice/.

Regis University, Rueckert-Hartman College for Health Professions, Division of Health Services Administration, Denver, CO 80221-1099. Offers health care informatics and information management (MS); health information management (Postbaccalaureate Certificate); health services administration (MS). Part-time and evening/weekend programs available. Postbaccalaureate distance learning degree programs offered (no on-campus study). *Faculty:* 5 full-time (4 women), 16 part-time/adjunct (10 women). *Students:* 41 full-time (30 women), 30 part-time (23 women); includes 17 minority (4 Black or African American, non-Hispanic/Latino; 6 Asian, non-Hispanic/Latino; 4 Hispanic/Latino; 3 Two or more races, non-Hispanic/Latino), 1 international. Average age 38. 28 applicants, 75% accepted, 20 enrolled. In 2014, 15 master's awarded. *Degree requirements:* For master's, thesis, final research project. *Entrance requirements:* For master's, official transcript reflecting baccalaureate degree awarded from regionally-accredited college or university, with minimum cumulative GPA of 3.0 or GRE/GMAT; letters of recommendation; essay; resume; interview. Additional exam requirements/recommendations for international students: Required—TOEFL (minimum score 550 paper-based; 82 iBT). *Application deadline:* Applications are processed on a rolling basis. Application fee: $75. Electronic applications accepted. *Expenses:* Expenses: Contact institution. *Financial support:* In 2014–15, 1 student received support. Federal Work-Study and scholarships/grants available. Financial award application deadline: 4/15; financial award applicants required to submit FAFSA. *Unit head:* Dr. Tristen Amador, Director, 303-458-4146, Fax: 303-964-5430, E-mail: tamador@regis.edu. *Application contact:* Sarah Engel, Director of Admissions, 303-458-4900, Fax: 303-964-5534, E-mail: regisadm@regis.edu.
Website: http://www.regis.edu/RHCHP/Schools/Division-of-Health-Services-Administration.aspx.

Roberts Wesleyan College, Health Administration Programs, Rochester, NY 14624-1997. Offers health administration (MS); healthcare informatics administration (MS). Evening/weekend programs available. Postbaccalaureate distance learning degree programs offered (no on-campus study). *Degree requirements:* For master's, thesis or alternative. *Entrance requirements:* For master's, minimum GPA of 3.0, verifiable work experience or recommendation.

Sacred Heart University, Graduate Programs, College of Health Professions, Program in Healthcare Information Systems, Fairfield, CT 06825-1000. Offers MS. Part-time and evening/weekend programs available. *Faculty:* 1 full-time (0 women), 2 part-time/adjunct (both women). *Students:* 1 full-time (0 women), 22 part-time (15 women); includes 8 minority (5 Black or African American, non-Hispanic/Latino; 2 Asian, non-Hispanic/Latino; 1 Native Hawaiian or other Pacific Islander, non-Hispanic/Latino). Average age 37. 13 applicants, 85% accepted, 10 enrolled. *Degree requirements:* For master's, comprehensive exam (for some programs). *Entrance requirements:* For master's, bachelor's degree, minimum cumulative undergraduate GPA of 3.0, personal essay, two letters of recommendation, resume. Additional exam requirements/recommendations for international students: Required—PTE; Recommended—TOEFL (minimum score 570 paper-based; 80 iBT), IELTS (minimum score 6.5). *Application deadline:* Applications are processed on a rolling basis. Application fee: $60. Electronic applications accepted. *Expenses:* Tuition: Full-time $24,559; part-time $649 per credit. *Financial support:* Unspecified assistantships available. Financial award applicants required to submit FAFSA. *Unit head:* Dr. Stephen C. Burrows, Chair, Health Science and Leadership/Program Director, Healthcare Informatics, 203-416-3948, Fax: 203-416-3951, E-mail: burrowss@sacredheart.edu. *Application contact:* Kathy Dilks, Executive Director of Graduate Admissions, 203-365-7619, Fax: 203-365-4732, E-mail: gradstudies@sacredheart.edu.
Website: http://www.sacredheart.edu/academics/collegeofhealthprofessions/academicprograms/healthcareinformatics/.

Shenandoah University, Eleanor Wade Custer School of Nursing, Winchester, VA 22601-5195. Offers family nurse practitioner (Post-Graduate Certificate); health informatics (Certificate); nursing (MSN, DNP); nursing education (Post-Graduate Certificate). *Accreditation:* AACN; ACNM/ACME. Part-time programs available. *Faculty:* 11 full-time (all women), 13 part-time/adjunct (12 women). *Students:* 30 full-time (27 women), 65 part-time (62 women); includes 21 minority (14 Black or African American, non-Hispanic/Latino; 4 Asian, non-Hispanic/Latino; 3 Hispanic/Latino), 1 international. Average age 37. 54 applicants, 74% accepted, 30 enrolled. In 2014, 27 master's, 3

doctorates, 7 other advanced degrees awarded. *Degree requirements:* For master's, research project, clinical hours; for doctorate, scholarly project, clinical hours; for other advanced degree, clinical hours. *Entrance requirements:* For master's, United States RN license; minimum GPA of 3.0; appropriate clinical experience; curriculum vitae; 3 letters of recommendation, two-to-three page essay; for doctorate, MSN, minimum GPA of 3.0, 3 letters of recommendation, 500-word statement, interview, BSN; for other advanced degree, MSN, minimum GPA of 3.0, 2 letters of recommendation, minimum of one year (2,080 hours) of clinical nursing experience, interview. Additional exam requirements/recommendations for international students: Required—TOEFL (minimum score 558 paper-based; 83 iBT). *Application deadline:* For fall admission, 5/1 priority date for domestic and international students; for spring admission, 11/1 priority date for domestic and international students. Applications are processed on a rolling basis. Application fee: $30. Electronic applications accepted. *Expenses: Tuition:* Full-time $19,512; part-time $813 per credit hour. *Required fees:* $365 per term. Tuition and fees vary according to course level, course load and program. *Financial support:* In 2014–15, 13 students received support, including 3 teaching assistantships with partial tuition reimbursements available (averaging $1,084 per year); career-related internships or fieldwork, scholarships/grants, and unspecified assistantships also available. Support available to part-time students. Financial award application deadline: 3/15; financial award applicants required to submit FAFSA. *Faculty research:* Moral reasoning in nurses, improving health care access to underserved rural women, screening for depression and anxiety in the obese in a rural free clinic, health care outcomes among patients in a free clinic setting cared for by nurse practitioners, effects of depression on diabetes as evidenced by the relationship between the patient healthcare questionnaire (PHQ-9) scores and the patient's glycohemoglobin (HbA1c), policy development, research on a Virginia Nurses Hall of Fame inductee. *Unit head:* Kathryn Ganske, PhD, RN, Director, 540-678-4374, Fax: 540-665-5519, E-mail: kganske@su.edu. *Application contact:* Andrew Woodall, Executive Director of Recruitment and Admissions, 540-665-4581, Fax: 540-665-4627, E-mail: admit@su.edu.
Website: http://www.nursing.su.edu.

Southern Illinois University Edwardsville, Graduate School, Program in Healthcare Informatics, Edwardsville, IL 62026-0001. Offers MS. Part-time and evening/weekend programs available. *Students:* 25 part-time (20 women); includes 7 minority (4 Black or African American, non-Hispanic/Latino; 3 Asian, non-Hispanic/Latino). In 2014, 29 master's awarded. *Degree requirements:* For master's, comprehensive exam. *Entrance requirements:* For master's, completion of healthcare-related baccalaureate degree with minimum GPA of 2.75, completion of statistics course with minimum C grade. Additional exam requirements/recommendations for international students: Required—TOEFL (minimum score 550 paper-based; 79 iBT), IELTS (minimum score 6.5). *Application deadline:* For fall admission, 7/24 for domestic students, 7/15 for international students; for spring admission, 12/11 for domestic students, 11/15 for international students; for summer admission, 4/29 for domestic students, 4/15 for international students. Applications are processed on a rolling basis. Application fee: $30. Electronic applications accepted. *Expenses:* Tuition, state resident: full-time $5026. Tuition, nonresident: full-time $12,566. *International tuition:* $25,136 full-time. *Required fees:* $1682. Tuition and fees vary according to course load, campus/location and program. *Financial support:* Application deadline: 3/1; applicants required to submit FAFSA. *Unit head:* Mary Sumner, Director, 618-650-3093, E-mail: msumner@siue.edu. *Application contact:* Melissa K. Mace, Assistant Director of Admissions for Graduate and International Recruitment, 618-650-2756, Fax: 618-650-3618, E-mail: mmace@siue.edu.
Website: http://www.siue.edu/healthcareinformatics/.

Southern New Hampshire University, School of Business, Manchester, NH 03106-1045. Offers accounting (MBA, MS, Graduate Certificate); accounting finance (MS); accounting/auditing (MS); accounting/forensic accounting (MS); accounting/taxation (MS); athletic administration (MBA, Graduate Certificate); business administration (IMBA, MBA, Certificate, Graduate Certificate), including accounting (Certificate), business administration (MBA), business information systems (Graduate Certificate); human resource management (Certificate); corporate social responsibility (MBA); entrepreneurship (MBA); finance (MBA, MS, Graduate Certificate); finance/corporate finance (MS); finance/investments and securities (MS); forensic accounting (MBA); healthcare informatics (MBA); healthcare management (MBA); human resource management (Graduate Certificate); information technology (MS, Graduate Certificate); information technology management (MBA); international business (Graduate Certificate); international business and information technology (Graduate Certificate); international finance (Graduate Certificate); international sport management (Graduate Certificate); justice studies (MBA); leadership of nonprofit organizations (Graduate Certificate); marketing (MBA, MS, Graduate Certificate); operations and project management (MS); operations and supply chain management (MBA, Graduate Certificate); organizational leadership (MS); project management (MBA, Graduate Certificate); Six Sigma (MBA); Six Sigma quality (Graduate Certificate); social media marketing (MBA); sport management (MBA, MS, Graduate Certificate); sustainability and environmental compliance (MBA); workplace conflict management (MBA); MBA/Certificate. *Accreditation:* ACBSP. Part-time and evening/weekend programs available. Postbaccalaureate distance learning degree programs offered (no on-campus study). Terminal master's awarded for partial completion of doctoral program. *Degree requirements:* For master's, one foreign language, comprehensive exam (for some programs), thesis or alternative. *Entrance requirements:* For master's, minimum GPA of 2.5. Additional exam requirements/recommendations for international students: Required—TOEFL (minimum score 500 paper-based). Electronic applications accepted.

Southern Polytechnic State University, School of Computing and Software Engineering, Department of Information Technology, Marietta, GA 30060-2896. Offers health information technology (Postbaccalaureate Certificate); information security and assurance (Graduate Certificate); information technology (MSIT, Graduate Certificate); information technology fundamentals (Postbaccalaureate Certificate). Part-time and evening/weekend programs available. Postbaccalaureate distance learning degree programs offered (no on-campus study). *Degree requirements:* For master's, thesis optional. *Entrance requirements:* For master's, minimum GPA of 2.75; for other advanced degree, bachelor's degree. Additional exam requirements/recommendations for international students: Required—TOEFL (minimum score 550 paper-based; 79 iBT), IELTS (minimum score 6.5). Electronic applications accepted. *Faculty research:* IT ethics, user interface design, IT security, IT integration, IT management, health information technology, business intelligence, networks, business continuity.

Stephens College, Division of Graduate and Continuing Studies, Columbia, MO 65215-0002. Offers business (MSL); counseling (M Ed, PGC), including counseling; curriculum and instruction (M Ed); health information administration (Postbaccalaureate Certificate). Part-time and evening/weekend programs available. Postbaccalaureate distance learning degree programs offered (minimal on-campus study). *Faculty:* 5 full-time (all women), 21 part-time/adjunct (14 women). *Students:* 156 full-time (135 women), 37 part-time (34 women); includes 26 minority (13 Black or African American, non-Hispanic/Latino; 2 Asian, non-Hispanic/Latino; 1 Hispanic/Latino; 1 Native Hawaiian or other Pacific Islander, non-Hispanic/Latino; 9 Two or more races, non-Hispanic/Latino). Average age 35. 54 applicants, 67% accepted, 33 enrolled. In 2014, 59 master's

awarded. *Entrance requirements:* For master's, minimum GPA of 3.0 in last 60 hours. Additional exam requirements/recommendations for international students: Required—TOEFL. *Application deadline:* For fall admission, 7/25 priority date for domestic and international students; for winter admission, 12/1 priority date for domestic and international students; for spring admission, 4/25 priority date for domestic and international students. Applications are processed on a rolling basis. Application fee: $50. Electronic applications accepted. *Expenses: Tuition:* Full-time $4656; part-time $388 per credit hour. *Required fees:* $540; $45 per credit hour. *Financial support:* In 2014–15, 9 fellowships with full tuition reimbursements (averaging $7,808 per year) were awarded; scholarships/grants and unspecified assistantships also available. Financial award applicants required to submit FAFSA. *Faculty research:* Educational psychology, outcomes assessment. *Unit head:* Lindsey Boudinot, Vice President of Strategic Enrollment Management, 800-388-7579, Fax: 573-876-7237, E-mail: online@stephens.edu.
Website: http://www.stephens.edu/gcs/.

Stevens Institute of Technology, Graduate School, Charles V. Schaefer Jr. School of Engineering, Department of Computer Science, Hoboken, NJ 07030. Offers computer graphics (Certificate); computer science (MS, PhD); computer systems (Certificate); database management systems (Certificate); distributed systems (Certificate); elements of computer science (Certificate); enterprise computing (Certificate); enterprise security and information assurance (Certificate); health informatics (Certificate); multimedia experience and management (Certificate); networks and systems administration (Certificate); security and privacy (Certificate); service oriented computing (Certificate); software design (Certificate); theoretical computer science (Certificate). Part-time and evening/weekend programs available. Terminal master's awarded for partial completion of doctoral program. *Degree requirements:* For master's, thesis optional; for doctorate, variable foreign language requirement, comprehensive exam, thesis/dissertation. *Entrance requirements:* For master's and doctorate, GRE, minimum GPA of 3.0. Additional exam requirements/recommendations for international students: Required—TOEFL. Electronic applications accepted. *Faculty research:* Semantics, reliability theory, programming language, cyber security.

Temple University, College of Health Professions and Social Work, Department of Health Information Management, Philadelphia, PA 19140. Offers health informatics (MS). Part-time and evening/weekend programs available. Postbaccalaureate distance learning degree programs offered. *Faculty:* 7 full-time (all women), 3 part-time/adjunct (1 woman). *Students:* 5 full-time (4 women), 55 part-time (37 women); includes 33 minority (15 Black or African American, non-Hispanic/Latino; 11 Asian, non-Hispanic/Latino; 5 Hispanic/Latino; 1 Native Hawaiian or other Pacific Islander, non-Hispanic/Latino; 1 Two or more races, non-Hispanic/Latino), 1 international. 13 applicants, 92% accepted, 10 enrolled. In 2014, 30 master's awarded. *Entrance requirements:* For master's, two letters of reference, statement of goals. Additional exam requirements/recommendations for international students: Required—TOEFL (minimum score 550 paper-based; 79 iBT). *Application deadline:* For fall admission, 5/1 for domestic students, 4/1 for international students; for spring admission, 11/1 for domestic students, 10/1 for international students. Applications are processed on a rolling basis. Application fee: $60. Electronic applications accepted. *Expenses:* Tuition, state resident: full-time $14,490; part-time $805 per credit hour. Tuition, nonresident: full-time $19,850; part-time $1103 per credit hour. *Required fees:* $690. Full-time tuition and fees vary according to class time, course load, degree level, campus/location and program. *Financial support:* Federal Work-Study, scholarships/grants, and tuition waivers available. Financial award application deadline: 1/15; financial award applicants required to submit FAFSA. *Unit head:* Cathy A. Flite, Department Chair, 215-707-7654, E-mail: cathy.flite@temple.edu. *Application contact:* Joseph Hines, Student Services Coordinator, 215-707-4811, Fax: 215-204-5852, E-mail: hlthinfo@temple.edu.
Website: http://chpsw.temple.edu/him/home.

Trident University International, College of Health Sciences, Program in Health Sciences, Cypress, CA 90630. Offers clinical research administration (MS, Certificate); emergency and disaster management (MS, Certificate); environmental health science (Certificate); health care administration (PhD); health care management (MS), including health informatics; health education (MS, Certificate); health informatics (Certificate); health sciences (PhD); international health (MS); international health: educator or researcher option (PhD); international health: practitioner option (PhD); law and expert witness studies (MS, Certificate); public health (MS); quality assurance (Certificate). Part-time and evening/weekend programs available. Postbaccalaureate distance learning degree programs offered (no on-campus study). *Degree requirements:* For doctorate, comprehensive exam, thesis/dissertation, defense of dissertation. *Entrance requirements:* For master's, minimum GPA of 2.5 (students with GPA 3.0 or greater may transfer up to 30% of graduate level credits); for doctorate, minimum GPA of 3.4, curriculum vitae, course work in research methods or statistics. Additional exam requirements/recommendations for international students: Required—TOEFL. Electronic applications accepted.

University at Buffalo, the State University of New York, Graduate School, School of Medicine and Biomedical Sciences, Program in Medical and Health Informatics, Buffalo, NY 14260. Offers Certificate. Part-time programs available. *Faculty:* 4 part-time/adjunct (0 women). *Students:* 4 part-time (2 women). Average age 35. 1 applicant. In 2014, 1 Certificate awarded. *Degree requirements:* For Certificate, 24 credit hours of coursework (18 required courses, 6 electives). *Entrance requirements:* For degree, all previous college/university transcripts; 2 letters of recommendation; personal letter with career objectives. Additional exam requirements/recommendations for international students: Required—TOEFL (minimum score 600 paper-based). *Application deadline:* For fall admission, 8/15 priority date for domestic students, 7/15 for international students. Application fee: $50. *Faculty research:* Integrated information systems planning and evaluation, management of knowledge-based information resources, scholarly communication in the health sciences, the economic value of health information, electronic health records, natural language understanding, ontologies, telemedicine/telehealth systems of healthcare, quality management information systems, implementation and evaluation of electronic health record systems, ethical and social issues in informatics. *Unit head:* Dr. Michael E. Cain, Dean, 716-829-3955, Fax: 716-829-3395, E-mail: mcain@buffalo.edu. *Application contact:* Elizabeth A. White, Staff Associate, 716-829-3399, Fax: 716-829-2437, E-mail: bethw@buffalo.edu.
Website: http://www.smbs.buffalo.edu/medinformatics/.

The University of Alabama at Birmingham, School of Health Professions, Program in Health Informatics, Birmingham, AL 35294. Offers MSHI. Postbaccalaureate distance learning degree programs offered (minimal on-campus study). *Students:* 41 part-time (28 women); includes 18 minority (13 Black or African American, non-Hispanic/Latino; 3 Asian, non-Hispanic/Latino; 1 Hispanic/Latino; 1 Two or more races, non-Hispanic/Latino), 2 international. Average age 40. In 2014, 15 master's awarded. *Degree requirements:* For master's, thesis, administrative internship, or project. *Entrance requirements:* For master's, GRE General Test, MAT, minimum undergraduate GPA of 3.0, course work in computing fundamentals and programming, letters of recommendation, interview. Additional exam requirements/recommendations for international students: Recommended—TOEFL, IELTS. *Application deadline:* For fall admission, 4/30 priority date for domestic students. Application fee: $45 ($60 for

international students). Electronic applications accepted. *Expenses:* Tuition, state resident: full-time $7090; part-time $370 per credit hour. Tuition, nonresident: full-time $16,072; part-time $869 per credit hour. Full-time tuition and fees vary according to course load and program. *Financial support:* Career-related internships or fieldwork and Federal Work-Study available. *Faculty research:* Healthcare/medical informatics, natural language processing, application of expert systems, graphical user interface design. *Unit head:* Dr. Gerald L. Glandon, Program Director, 205-934-3509, Fax: 205-975-6608. *Application contact:* Susan Noblitt Banks, Director of Graduate School Operations, 205-934-8227, Fax: 205-934-8413, E-mail: gradschool@uab.edu.
Website: http://www.uab.edu/shp/hsa/academic-program/master-of-science-in-health-informatics.

University of Central Florida, College of Health and Public Affairs, Department of Health Management and Informatics, Orlando, FL 32816. Offers health care informatics (MS). *Accreditation:* CAHME. Part-time and evening/weekend programs available. *Faculty:* 19 full-time (10 women), 22 part-time/adjunct (14 women). *Students:* 152 full-time (101 women), 201 part-time (147 women); includes 174 minority (82 Black or African American, non-Hispanic/Latino; 34 Asian, non-Hispanic/Latino; 48 Hispanic/Latino; 1 Native Hawaiian or other Pacific Islander, non-Hispanic/Latino; 9 Two or more races, non-Hispanic/Latino), 6 international. Average age 29. 274 applicants, 67% accepted, 125 enrolled. In 2014, 133 master's awarded. *Degree requirements:* For master's, comprehensive exam, thesis or alternative, research report. *Entrance requirements:* For master's, GRE General Test. Additional exam requirements/recommendations for international students: Required—TOEFL. *Application deadline:* For fall admission, 7/15 for domestic students; for spring admission, 10/1 for domestic students. Application fee: $30. Electronic applications accepted. *Expenses:* Tuition, state resident: part-time $288.16 per credit hour. Tuition, nonresident: part-time $1073.31 per credit hour. *Financial support:* In 2014–15, 1 student received support, including 1 research assistantship with partial tuition reimbursement available (averaging $7,700 per year); career-related internships or fieldwork, Federal Work-Study, institutionally sponsored loans, and unspecified assistantships also available. Financial award application deadline: 3/1; financial award applicants required to submit FAFSA. *Unit head:* Dr. Reid Oetjen, Interim Chair, 407-823-5668, E-mail: reid.oetjen@ucf.edu. *Application contact:* Barbara Rodriguez Lamas, Director, Admissions and Student Services, 407-823-2766, Fax: 407-823-6442, E-mail: gradadmissions@ucf.edu.
Website: http://www.cohpa.ucf.edu/hmi/.

The University of Findlay, Office of Graduate Admissions, Findlay, OH 45840-3653. Offers athletic training (MAT); business (MBA), including health care management, hospitality management, organizational leadership, public management; education (MA Ed), including administration, children's literature, early childhood, human resource development, reading, science, special education, technology; environmental, safety and health management (MSEM); health informatics (MS); occupational therapy (MOT); pharmacy (Pharm D); physical therapy (DPT); physician assistant (MPA); rhetoric and writing (MA); teaching English to speakers of other languages (TESOL) and bilingual education (MA). Part-time and evening/weekend programs available. Postbaccalaureate distance learning degree programs offered (no on-campus study). *Faculty:* 213 full-time (102 women), 62 part-time/adjunct (37 women). *Students:* 690 full-time (385 women), 515 part-time (316 women); includes 101 minority (43 Black or African American, non-Hispanic/Latino; 1 American Indian or Alaska Native, non-Hispanic/Latino; 19 Asian, non-Hispanic/Latino; 27 Hispanic/Latino; 11 Two or more races, non-Hispanic/Latino), 214 international. Average age 28. 765 applicants, 66% accepted, 289 enrolled. In 2014, 225 master's, 104 doctorates awarded. *Degree requirements:* For master's, thesis, cumulative project, capstone project. *Entrance requirements:* For master's, GRE/GMAT, bachelor's degree from accredited institution, minimum undergraduate GPA of 2.5 in last 64 hours of course work; for doctorate, GRE, minimum cumulative GPA of 3.0. Additional exam requirements/recommendations for international students: Required—TOEFL (minimum score 80 iBT). *Application deadline:* Applications are processed on a rolling basis. Application fee: $25. Electronic applications accepted. Tuition and fees vary according to degree level and program. *Financial support:* In 2014–15, 11 research assistantships with full and partial tuition reimbursements (averaging $4,000 per year), 10 teaching assistantships with full and partial tuition reimbursements (averaging $3,600 per year) were awarded; career-related internships or fieldwork, Federal Work-Study, health care benefits, and unspecified assistantships also available. Financial award application deadline: 4/1; financial award applicants required to submit FAFSA. *Unit head:* Christopher M. Harris, Director of Admissions, 419-434-4347, E-mail: harrisc1@findlay.edu. *Application contact:* Austyn Erickson, Graduate Admissions Counselor, 419-434-4693, Fax: 419-434-4898, E-mail: ericksona@findlay.edu.
Website: http://www.findlay.edu/admissions/graduate/Pages/default.aspx.

University of Illinois at Chicago, Graduate College, College of Applied Health Sciences, Program in Health Informatics, Chicago, IL 60607-7128. Offers health informatics (MS, CAS); health information management (Certificate). Part-time programs available. Postbaccalaureate distance learning degree programs offered (no on-campus study). *Students:* 26 full-time (20 women), 470 part-time (342 women); includes 209 minority (93 Black or African American, non-Hispanic/Latino; 1 American Indian or Alaska Native, non-Hispanic/Latino; 85 Asian, non-Hispanic/Latino; 23 Hispanic/Latino; 2 Native Hawaiian or other Pacific Islander, non-Hispanic/Latino; 5 Two or more races, non-Hispanic/Latino), 5 international. Average age 40. 222 applicants, 68% accepted, 100 enrolled. In 2014, 121 master's, 45 other advanced degrees awarded. *Expenses:* Expenses: $21,942 in-state, $33,940 out-of-state. *Faculty research:* Information science, computer science, health informatics, health information management. *Unit head:* Dr. Larry Pawola, Department Head and Professor, 312-996-1446, Fax: 312-996-8342, E-mail: lpawola@uic.edu.
Website: http://healthinformatics.uic.edu/.

University of Illinois at Urbana–Champaign, Graduate College, Graduate School of Library and Information Science, Champaign, IL 61820. Offers bioinformatics (MS); digital libraries (CAS); library and information science (MS, PhD, CAS). *Accreditation:* ALA (one or more programs are accredited). Part-time programs available. Postbaccalaureate distance learning degree programs offered (minimal on-campus study). *Students:* 283 (208 women). *Entrance requirements:* For degree, master's degree in library and information science or related field with minimum GPA of 3.0. Application fee: $70 ($90 for international students). *Unit head:* Allen Renear, Interim Dean, 217-265-5216, Fax: 217-244-3302, E-mail: renear@illinois.edu. *Application contact:* Penny Ames, Graduate Contact, 217-333-7197, E-mail: pames@illinois.edu.
Website: http://www.lis.illinois.edu.

The University of Iowa, Graduate College, Program in Informatics, Iowa City, IA 52242-1316. Offers bioinformatics (MS, PhD); bioinformatics and computational biology (Certificate); geoinformatics (MS, PhD, Certificate); health informatics (MS, PhD, Certificate); information science (MS, PhD, Certificate). *Degree requirements:* For master's, thesis optional; for doctorate, comprehensive exam, thesis/dissertation. *Entrance requirements:* For master's and doctorate, GRE General Test, minimum GPA of 3.0. Additional exam requirements/recommendations for international students: Required—TOEFL (minimum score 550 paper-based; 81 iBT). Electronic applications accepted.

The University of Kansas, University of Kansas Medical Center, Program in Health Informatics, Lawrence, KS 66045. Offers MS. Part-time programs available. Postbaccalaureate distance learning degree programs offered (minimal on-campus study). *Students:* 16 part-time (10 women); includes 4 minority (2 Black or African American, non-Hispanic/Latino; 2 Two or more races, non-Hispanic/Latino), 2 international. Average age 35. 8 applicants, 63% accepted, 4 enrolled. In 2014, 6 master's awarded. *Degree requirements:* For master's, comprehensive exam, thesis or alternative. *Entrance requirements:* For master's, GRE, minimum GPA of 3.0, 3 references, personal statement of career goals. Additional exam requirements/recommendations for international students: Required—TOEFL. *Application deadline:* For fall admission, 3/1 for domestic and international students; for spring admission, 9/1 for domestic and international students. Application fee: $60. Electronic applications accepted. *Financial support:* Application deadline: 3/1; applicants required to submit FAFSA. *Faculty research:* GIS in public health, symbolic representation of health data, smoking cessation, inter-professional education and practice, usability of health systems, electronic health record systems quality and safety. *Unit head:* Dr. Robert Klein, Vice Chancellor for Academic Affairs/Dean of Graduate Studies, 913-588-5071, E-mail: rklein@kumc.edu. *Application contact:* Dr. Eva LaVerne Manos, Director, 913-588-1671, Fax: 913-588-1660, E-mail: lmanos@kumc.edu.
Website: http://www.kumc.edu/health-informatics/master-in-health-informatics.html.

University of Maryland, Baltimore County, The Graduate School, College of Engineering and Information Technology, Department of Information Systems, Program in Health Information Technology, Baltimore, MD 21250. Offers MPS. *Students:* 12 part-time (6 women); includes 8 minority (4 Black or African American, non-Hispanic/Latino; 4 Asian, non-Hispanic/Latino), 1 international. Average age 33. 18 applicants, 89% accepted, 12 enrolled. *Entrance requirements:* For master's, minimum undergraduate GPA of 3.0. Additional exam requirements/recommendations for international students: Required—GRE. *Expenses:* Tuition, state resident: part-time $557. Tuition, nonresident: part-time $922. *Required fees:* $122 per semester. One-time fee: $200 part-time. *Faculty research:* Health information technology. *Unit head:* Dr. Aryya Gangopadhyay, Professor and Chair, 410-455-2620, Fax: 410-455-1217, E-mail: gangopad@umbc.edu. *Application contact:* Dr. George Karabatis, Associate Professor/Associate Chair for Academic Affairs, 410-455-2650, Fax: 410-455-1217, E-mail: georgek@umbc.edu.
Website: http://informationsystems.umbc.edu/home/graduate-programs/master-of-science-programs/master-of-professional-studies-in-health-information-technology/.

University of Maryland University College, The Graduate School, Program in Health Administration Informatics, Adelphi, MD 20783. Offers MS, Certificate. Part-time and evening/weekend programs available. Postbaccalaureate distance learning degree programs offered (no on-campus study). *Students:* 1 (woman) full-time, 211 part-time (141 women); includes 127 minority (93 Black or African American, non-Hispanic/Latino; 16 Asian, non-Hispanic/Latino; 11 Hispanic/Latino; 7 Two or more races, non-Hispanic/Latino), 2 international. Average age 36. 103 applicants, 100% accepted, 62 enrolled. In 2014, 33 master's awarded. *Degree requirements:* For master's, thesis or alternative, capstone course. *Application deadline:* Applications are processed on a rolling basis. Application fee: $50. Electronic applications accepted. *Financial support:* Federal Work-Study and scholarships/grants available. Support available to part-time students. Financial award application deadline: 6/1; financial award applicants required to submit FAFSA. *Unit head:* Dr. Katherine Marconi, Program Chair, 240-684-2400, Fax: 240-684-2401, E-mail: katherine.marconi@umuc.edu. *Application contact:* Coordinator, Graduate Admissions, 800-888-8682, Fax: 240-684-2151, E-mail: newgrad@umuc.edu.
Website: http://www.umuc.edu/academic-programs/masters-degrees/health-informatics-administration.cfm.

University of Massachusetts Lowell, College of Health Sciences, Department of Community Health and Sustainability, Lowell, MA 01854. Offers health informatics and management (MS, Graduate Certificate). Part-time programs available. *Degree requirements:* For master's, thesis optional. *Entrance requirements:* For master's, GRE General Test. *Faculty research:* Alzheimer's disease, total quality management systems, information systems, market analysis.

University of Michigan, Horace H. Rackham School of Graduate Studies, School of Information, Ann Arbor, MI 48109-1285. Offers archives and records management (MSI); health informatics (MS); information (PhD). *Accreditation:* ALA (one or more programs are accredited). Part-time programs available. *Students:* 424 full-time (256 women), 32 part-time (15 women); includes 85 minority (14 Black or African American, non-Hispanic/Latino; 39 Asian, non-Hispanic/Latino; 21 Hispanic/Latino; 11 Two or more races, non-Hispanic/Latino), 178 international. Average age 28. 765 applicants, 55% accepted, 199 enrolled. In 2014, 188 master's, 6 doctorates awarded. Terminal master's awarded for partial completion of doctoral program. *Degree requirements:* For master's, thesis optional, internship requirement; for doctorate, thesis/dissertation. *Entrance requirements:* For master's and doctorate, GRE General Test. Additional exam requirements/recommendations for international students: Required—TOEFL (minimum score 600 paper-based; 100 iBT). *Application deadline:* Applications are processed on a rolling basis. Application fee: $75 ($90 for international students). Electronic applications accepted. *Expenses:* Expenses: MS full time: $12,496/term in-state, $20,657/term out-of-state; MSI full time: $10,039/term in-state, $20,282/term out-of-state; PhD: fully funded. *Financial support:* In 2014–15, 122 students received support, including 2 fellowships (averaging $28,200 per year), 33 research assistantships (averaging $28,200 per year), 41 teaching assistantships (averaging $28,200 per year); scholarships/grants, tuition waivers (full and partial), and all PhD's are funded, merit-based scholarships available for Master's students also available. *Unit head:* Dr. Jeffrey K. Mackie-Mason, Dean, School of Information, 734-647-3576. *Application contact:* School of Information Admissions, 734-763-2285, Fax: 734-615-3587, E-mail: umsi.admissions@umich.edu.
Website: http://www.si.umich.edu/.

See Display on page 324 and Close-Up on page 349.

University of Michigan–Dearborn, College of Education, Health, and Human Services, Master of Science Program in Health Information Technology, Dearborn, MI 48126. Offers MS. *Faculty:* 5 full-time (3 women). *Students:* 1 (woman) full-time, 6 part-time (5 women); includes 2 minority (1 Black or African American, non-Hispanic/Latino; 1 Two or more races, non-Hispanic/Latino). 8 applicants, 88% accepted, 6 enrolled. *Entrance requirements:* Additional exam requirements/recommendations for international students: Required—TOEFL (minimum score 560 paper-based; 84 iBT), IELTS (minimum score 6.5). *Application deadline:* For fall admission, 8/1 for domestic students, 5/1 for international students; for winter admission, 12/1 for domestic students, 9/1 for international students; for spring admission, 4/1 for domestic students, 1/1 for international students. Applications are processed on a rolling basis. Application fee: $60. Electronic applications accepted. *Expenses:* Expenses: $541 per credit hour in-state, $351 for ninth credit hour and beyond; $1,115 per credit hour out-of-state, $724 for ninth credit hour and beyond; $267 in fees per term part-time, $329 full-time. *Financial support:* Career-related internships or fieldwork and scholarships/grants

available. Support available to part-time students. Financial award applicants required to submit FAFSA. *Faculty research:* Behavior and new technology, information quality, technology acceptance, healthcare systems, economics of recovery. *Unit head:* Dr. Stein Brunvand, Director, 313-583-6415, E-mail: sbrunvan@umich.edu. *Application contact:* Kimberly Lewandowski, Graduate Programs Coordinator, 313-593-1494, Fax: 313-436-9156, E-mail: umdgrad@umd.umich.edu.
Website: http://umdearborn.edu/cehhs/cehhs_m_hit/.

University of Minnesota, Twin Cities Campus, Graduate School, Program in Health Informatics, Minneapolis, MN 55455-0213. Offers MHI, MS, PhD, MD/MHI. Part-time programs available. *Degree requirements:* For master's, thesis or alternative; for doctorate, thesis/dissertation. *Entrance requirements:* For master's and doctorate, GRE General Test, previous course work in life sciences, programming, calculus. Additional exam requirements/recommendations for international students: Required—TOEFL (minimum score 550 paper-based). Electronic applications accepted. *Faculty research:* Medical decision making, physiological control systems, population studies, clinical information systems, telemedicine.

University of Missouri, Office of Research and Graduate Studies, Department of Health Management and Informatics, Columbia, MO 65211. Offers health administration (MHA); health ethics (Graduate Certificate); health informatics (MS, Graduate Certificate). *Accreditation:* CAHME. Part-time programs available. *Faculty:* 18 full-time (5 women), 2 part-time/adjunct (0 women). *Students:* 98 full-time (54 women), 27 part-time (14 women); includes 22 minority (8 Black or African American, non-Hispanic/Latino; 8 Asian, non-Hispanic/Latino; 3 Hispanic/Latino; 3 Two or more races, non-Hispanic/Latino), 20 international. Average age 30. 61 applicants, 56% accepted, 31 enrolled. In 2014, 53 master's, 10 other advanced degrees awarded. *Entrance requirements:* For master's, GRE General Test or GMAT, minimum GPA of 3.0. Additional exam requirements/recommendations for international students: Required—TOEFL (minimum score 500 paper-based; 61 iBT). *Application deadline:* Applications are processed on a rolling basis. Application fee: $55 ($75 for international students). Electronic applications accepted. *Financial support:* Fellowships, research assistantships, teaching assistantships, institutionally sponsored loans, scholarships/grants, traineeships, health care benefits, and unspecified assistantships available. Support available to part-time students. *Faculty research:* Application of informatics tools to day-to-day clinical operations, consumer health informatics, decision support, health literacy and numeracy, information interventions for persons with chronic illnesses, use of simulation in the education of health care professionals, statistical bioinformatics, classification, dimension reduction, ethics and end of life care, telehealth and tele-ethics, research ethics, health literacy, clinical informatics, human factors. *Unit head:* Dr. Suzanne Boren, Director of Graduate Studies, 573-882-1492, E-mail: borens@missouri.edu. *Application contact:* Veronica Kramer, Coordinator of Student Recruitment and Admissions, 573-884-0698, E-mail: kramerv@missouri.edu.
Website: http://www.hmi.missouri.edu/.

The University of North Carolina at Charlotte, The Graduate School, Program in Health Informatics, Charlotte, NC 28223-0001. Offers MS, Graduate Certificate. Program offered jointly between College of Computing and Informatics and College of Health and Human Services. *Students:* 18 full-time (11 women), 44 part-time (29 women); includes 28 minority (19 Black or African American, non-Hispanic/Latino; 4 Asian, non-Hispanic/Latino; 1 Hispanic/Latino; 4 Two or more races, non-Hispanic/Latino), 5 international. Average age 36. 38 applicants, 100% accepted, 29 enrolled. In 2014, 3 master's, 19 other advanced degrees awarded. *Expenses:* Tuition, state resident: full-time $4008. Tuition, nonresident: full-time $16,295. *Required fees:* $2755. Tuition and fees vary according to course load and program. *Unit head:* Dr. Thomas L. Reynolds, Dean and Associate Provost, 704-687-7248, Fax: 687-687-3279, E-mail: gradadm@uncc.edu. *Application contact:* Kathy B. Giddings, Director of Graduate Admissions, 704-687-5503, Fax: 704-687-1668, E-mail: gradadm@uncc.edu.
Website: http://www.hi.uncc.edu/.

University of Phoenix–Birmingham Campus, College of Health and Human Services, Birmingham, AL 35242. Offers education (MHA); gerontology (MHA); health administration (MHA); health care management (MBA); informatics (MHA); nursing (MSN); nursing/health care education (MSN); MSN/MBA; MSN/MHA.

University of Phoenix–Charlotte Campus, College of Nursing, Charlotte, NC 28273-3409. Offers education (MHA); gerontology (MHA); health administration (MHA); informatics (MHA, MSN); nursing (MSN); nursing/health care education (MSN). Evening/weekend programs available. *Degree requirements:* For master's, thesis (for some programs). *Entrance requirements:* For master's, minimum undergraduate GPA of 2.5, 3 years work experience. Additional exam requirements/recommendations for international students: Required—TOEFL (minimum score 550 paper-based; 79 iBT). Electronic applications accepted.

University of Phoenix–Des Moines Campus, College of Nursing, Des Moines, IA 50309. Offers education (MHA); gerontology (MHA); health administration (MHA, DHA); informatics (MHA, MSN); nursing (MSN, PhD); nursing/health care education (MSN).

University of Phoenix–Online Campus, College of Health Sciences and Nursing, Phoenix, AZ 85034-7209. Offers family nurse practitioner (Certificate); health care (Certificate); health care education (Certificate); health care informatics (Certificate); informatics (MSN); nursing (MSN); nursing and health care education (MSN); MSN/MBA; MSN/MHA. *Accreditation:* AACN. Evening/weekend programs available. Postbaccalaureate distance learning degree programs offered. *Entrance requirements:* Additional exam requirements/recommendations for international students: Required—TOEFL, TOEIC (Test of English as an International Communication), Berlitz Online English Proficiency Exam, PTE, or IELTS. Electronic applications accepted. *Expenses:* Contact institution.

University of Phoenix–Washington D.C. Campus, College of Nursing, Washington, DC 20001. Offers education (MHA); gerontology (MHA); health administration (MHA, DHA); informatics (MHA, MSN); nursing (MSN, PhD); nursing/health care education (MSN); MSN/MBA; MSN/MHA.

University of Puerto Rico, Medical Sciences Campus, School of Health Professions, Program in Health Information Administration, San Juan, PR 00936-5067. Offers MS. Part-time programs available. *Degree requirements:* For master's, one foreign language, thesis or alternative, internship. *Entrance requirements:* For master's, EXADEP or GRE General Test, minimum GPA of 2.5, interview, fluency in Spanish. *Faculty research:* Quality of medical records, health information data.

University of San Diego, Hahn School of Nursing and Health Science, San Diego, CA 92110-2492. Offers adult-gerontology clinical nurse specialist (MSN); adult-gerontology nurse practitioner/family nurse practitioner (MSN); executive nurse leader (MSN); family nurse practitioner (MSN); family/lifespan psychiatric-mental health nurse practitioner (MSN); healthcare informatics (MS, MSN); nursing (PhD); nursing practice (DNP). *Accreditation:* AACN. Part-time and evening/weekend programs available. *Faculty:* 24 full-time (20 women), 53 part-time/adjunct (49 women). *Students:* 196 full-time (168 women), 163 part-time (143 women); includes 132 minority (23 Black or African American, non-Hispanic/Latino; 3 American Indian or Alaska Native, non-Hispanic/Latino; 51 Asian, non-Hispanic/Latino; 46 Hispanic/Latino; 2 Native Hawaiian or other

Pacific Islander, non-Hispanic/Latino; 7 Two or more races, non-Hispanic/Latino), 4 international. Average age 36. 73,483 applicants, 131 enrolled. In 2014, 95 master's, 41 doctorates awarded. *Degree requirements:* For doctorate, thesis/dissertation (for some programs), residency (DNP). *Entrance requirements:* For master's, GRE General Test (for entry-level nursing), BSN, current California RN licensure (except for entry-level nursing); minimum GPA of 3.0; for doctorate, minimum GPA of 3.5, MSN, current California RN licensure. Additional exam requirements/recommendations for international students: Required—TOEFL (minimum score 580 paper-based; 83 iBT), TWE. *Application deadline:* For fall admission, 3/1 priority date for domestic students, 3/1 for international students; for spring admission, 11/1 priority date for domestic students, 11/1 for international students. Applications are processed on a rolling basis. Application fee: $45. Electronic applications accepted. *Financial support:* In 2014–15, 235 students received support. Scholarships/grants and traineeships available. Support available to part-time students. Financial award application deadline: 4/1; financial award applicants required to submit FAFSA. *Faculty research:* Maternal/neonatal health, palliative and end of life care, adolescent obesity, health disparities, cognitive dysfunction. *Unit head:* Dr. Sally Hardin, Dean, 619-260-4550, Fax: 619-260-6814. *Application contact:* Monica Mahon, Associate Director of Graduate Admissions, 619-260-4524, Fax: 619-260-4158, E-mail: grads@sandiego.edu.
Website: http://www.sandiego.edu/nursing/.

University of South Carolina Upstate, Graduate Programs, Spartanburg, SC 29303-4999. Offers early childhood education (M Ed); elementary education (M Ed); informatics (MS); special education: visual impairment (M Ed). *Accreditation:* NCATE. Part-time and evening/weekend programs available. *Faculty:* 15 full-time (11 women), 6 part-time/adjunct (4 women). *Students:* 11 full-time (8 women), 164 part-time (137 women); includes 39 minority (33 Black or African American, non-Hispanic/Latino; 2 American Indian or Alaska Native, non-Hispanic/Latino; 4 Asian, non-Hispanic/Latino). Average age 38. In 2014, 11 master's awarded. *Degree requirements:* For master's, professional portfolio. *Entrance requirements:* For master's, GRE General Test or MAT, interview, minimum undergraduate GPA of 2.5, teaching certificate, 2 letters of recommendation. *Application deadline:* Applications are processed on a rolling basis. Application fee: $40. *Expenses:* Tuition, state resident: full-time $12,024; part-time $501 per semester hour. Tuition, nonresident: full-time $25,770; part-time $1073.75 per semester hour. *Financial support:* Institutionally sponsored loans and institutional work-study available. Financial award application deadline: 7/15; financial award applicants required to submit FAFSA. *Faculty research:* Promoting university diversity awareness, rough and tumble play, social justice education, American Indian literatures and cultures, diversity and multicultural education, science teaching strategy. *Unit head:* Dr. Tina Herzberg, Director of Graduate Programs, 864-503-5572, Fax: 864-503-5573, E-mail: therzberg@uscupstate.edu. *Application contact:* Donette Stewart, Associate Vice Chancellor for Enrollment Services, 864-503-5280, E-mail: dstewart@uscupstate.edu.
Website: http://www.uscupstate.edu/graduate/.

University of South Florida, Morsani College of Medicine and Graduate School, Graduate Programs in Medical Sciences, Tampa, FL 33620-9951. Offers aging and neuroscience (MSMS); allergy, immunology and infectious disease (PhD); anatomy (MSMS, PhD); athletic training (MSMS); bioinformatics and computational biology (MSBCB); biotechnology (MSB); clinical and translational research (MSMS, PhD); health informatics (MSHI, MSMS); health science (MSMS); interdisciplinary medical sciences (MSMS); medical microbiology and immunology (MSMS); metabolic and nutritional medicine (MSMS); molecular medicine (MSMS, PhD); molecular pharmacology and physiology (PhD); neurology (PhD); pathology and laboratory medicine (PhD); pharmacology and therapeutics (PhD); physiology and biophysics (PhD); women's health (MSMS). *Students:* 338 full-time (162 women), 36 part-time (25 women); includes 173 minority (43 Black or African American, non-Hispanic/Latino; 65 Asian, non-Hispanic/Latino; 58 Hispanic/Latino; 7 Two or more races, non-Hispanic/Latino), 24 international. Average age 26. 1,188 applicants, 41% accepted, 271 enrolled. In 2014, 216 master's awarded. Terminal master's awarded for partial completion of doctoral program. *Degree requirements:* For master's, comprehensive exam, thesis; for doctorate, comprehensive exam, thesis/dissertation. *Entrance requirements:* For master's, GRE General Test or GMAT, bachelor's degree or equivalent from regionally-accredited university with minimum GPA of 3.0 in upper-division sciences coursework; prerequisites in general biology, general chemistry, general physics, organic chemistry, quantitative analysis, and integral and differential calculus; for doctorate, GRE General Test (minimum score of 32nd percentile quantitative), bachelor's degree from regionally-accredited university with minimum GPA of 3.0 in upper-division sciences coursework; 3 letters of recommendation; personal interview; 1-2 page personal statement; prerequisites in biology, chemistry, physics, organic chemistry, quantitative analysis, and integral/differential calculus. Additional exam requirements/recommendations for international students: Required—TOEFL (minimum score 550 paper-based; 79 iBT) or IELTS (minimum score 6.5). *Application deadline:* For fall admission, 2/15 for domestic students, 1/2 for international students. Application fee: $30. *Expenses:* Expenses: Contact institution. *Faculty research:* Anatomy, biochemistry, cancer biology, cardiovascular disease, cell biology, immunology, microbiology, molecular biology, neuroscience, pharmacology, physiology. *Unit head:* Dr. Michael Barber, Professor and Associate Dean for Graduate and Postdoctoral Affairs, 813-974-9908, Fax: 813-974-4317, E-mail: mbarber@health.usf.edu. *Application contact:* Dr. Eric Bennett, Graduate Director, PhD Program in Medical Sciences, 813-974-1545, Fax: 813-974-4317, E-mail: esbennet@health.usf.edu.
Website: http://health.usf.edu/nocms/medicine/graduatestudies/.

University of South Florida, University College/Distance Education, Tampa, FL 33620-9951. *Unit head:* Kathy Barnes, Interdisciplinary Programs Coordinator, 813-974-8031, Fax: 813-974-7061, E-mail: barnesk@usf.edu. *Application contact:* Karen Tylinski, Metro Initiatives, 813-974-9943, Fax: 813-974-7061, E-mail: ktylinsk@usf.edu.
Website: http://www.usf.edu/innovative-education/.

The University of Tennessee Health Science Center, College of Health Professions, Memphis, TN 38163-0002. Offers audiology (MS, Au D); clinical laboratory science (MSCLS); cytopathology practice (MCP); health informatics and information management (MHIIM); occupational therapy (MOT); physical therapy (DPT, ScDPT); physician assistant (MMS); speech-language pathology (MS). *Accreditation:* AOTA; APTA. Part-time and evening/weekend programs available. Postbaccalaureate distance learning degree programs offered (minimal on-campus study). Terminal master's awarded for partial completion of doctoral program. *Degree requirements:* For master's, comprehensive exam, thesis; for doctorate, comprehensive exam, residency. *Entrance requirements:* For master's, GRE (MOT, MSCLS), minimum GPA of 3.0, 3 letters of reference, national accreditation (MSCLS), GRE if GPA is less than 3.0 (MCP); for doctorate, GRE. Additional exam requirements/recommendations for international students: Required—TOEFL (minimum score 550 paper-based; 80 iBT). Electronic applications accepted. *Expenses:* Contact institution. *Faculty research:* Gait deviation, muscular dystrophy and strength, hemophilia and exercise, pediatric neurology, self-efficacy.

The University of Texas Health Science Center at Houston, School of Health Information Sciences, Houston, TX 77225-0036. Offers health informatics (MS, PhD,

Certificate); MPH/MS; MPH/PhD. Part-time programs available. Postbaccalaureate distance learning degree programs offered (no on-campus study). *Degree requirements:* For master's, thesis; for doctorate, thesis/dissertation. *Entrance requirements:* For master's and doctorate, GRE or MAT. Additional exam requirements/recommendations for international students: Required—TOEFL (minimum score 550 paper-based; 87 iBT). Electronic applications accepted. *Expenses:* Tuition, state resident: full-time $4158; part-time $231 per hour. Tuition, nonresident: full-time $12,744; part-time $708 per hour. *Required fees:* $771 per semester. *Faculty research:* Patient safety, human computer interface, artificial intelligence, decision support tools, 3-D visualization, biomedical engineering.

University of Toronto, Faculty of Medicine, Institute of Health Policy, Management and Evaluation, Program in Health Informatics, Toronto, ON M5S 2J7, Canada. Offers MHI. *Entrance requirements:* For master's, minimum B average in last academic year. Additional exam requirements/recommendations for international students: Required—TOEFL (minimum score 580 paper-based; 93 iBT), TWE (minimum score 5). Electronic applications accepted.

University of Victoria, Faculty of Graduate Studies, Faculty of Human and Social Development, School of Health Information Science, Victoria, BC V8W 2Y2, Canada. Offers M Sc. *Degree requirements:* For master's, thesis or research project. *Entrance requirements:* Additional exam requirements/recommendations for international students: Required—TOEFL (minimum score 575 paper-based).

University of Virginia, School of Medicine, Department of Public Health Sciences, Program in Clinical Research, Charlottesville, VA 22903. Offers clinical investigation and patient-oriented research (MS); informatics in medicine (MS). Part-time programs available. *Students:* 5 full-time (4 women), 7 part-time (3 women); includes 2 minority (1 Asian, non-Hispanic/Latino; 1 Two or more races, non-Hispanic/Latino), 2 international. Average age 34. 24 applicants, 50% accepted, 10 enrolled. In 2014, 5 master's awarded. *Degree requirements:* For master's, thesis (for some programs). *Entrance requirements:* For master's, 2 letters of recommendation. Additional exam requirements/ recommendations for international students: Required—TOEFL (minimum score 600 paper-based; 90 iBT). *Application deadline:* For fall admission, 3/1 priority date for domestic and international students. Application fee: $60. Electronic applications accepted. *Expenses:* Tuition, state resident: full-time $14,164; part-time $349 per credit hour. Tuition, nonresident: full-time $23,722; part-time $1300 per credit hour. *Required fees:* $2514. *Financial support:* Career-related internships or fieldwork available. Financial award applicants required to submit FAFSA. *Unit head:* Dr. Jean Eby, Program Director, 434-924-8430, Fax: 434-924-8437, E-mail: jmg5b@virginia.edu. *Application contact:* Tracey L. Brookman, Academic Programs Administrator, 434-924-8430, Fax: 434-924-8437, E-mail: phsdegrees@virginia.edu.
Website: http://www.healthsystem.virginia.edu/internet/phs/ms/mshome.cfm.

University of Washington, Graduate School, School of Medicine, Graduate Programs in Medicine, Department of Medical Education and Biomedical Informatics, Division of Biomedical and Health Informatics, Seattle, WA 98195. Offers MS, PhD. *Entrance requirements:* For master's and doctorate, GRE General Test, minimum GPA of 3.0; previous undergraduate course work in biology, computer programming, and mathematics. Additional exam requirements/recommendations for international students: Required—TOEFL (minimum score 580 paper-based; 70 iBT). Electronic applications accepted. *Faculty research:* Bio-clinical informatics, information retrieval, human-computer interaction, knowledge-based systems, telehealth.

University of Washington, Graduate School, School of Public Health, Department of Health Services, Program in Health Informatics and Health Information Management, Seattle, WA 98195. Offers MHIHIM. Evening/weekend programs available. Postbaccalaureate distance learning degree programs offered (minimal on-campus study). *Students:* 16 full-time (12 women), 23 part-time (12 women); includes 28 minority (6 Black or African American, non-Hispanic/Latino; 3 American Indian or Alaska Native, non-Hispanic/Latino; 16 Asian, non-Hispanic/Latino; 3 Hispanic/Latino), 1 international. Average age 34. 37 applicants, 62% accepted, 16 enrolled. *Degree requirements:* For master's, capstone project. *Entrance requirements:* For master's, resume or curriculum vitae, three recommendations, minimum GPA of 3.0. Additional exam requirements/ recommendations for international students: Required—TOEFL (minimum score 580 paper-based; 92 iBT), IELTS. *Application deadline:* For fall admission, 12/1 for domestic students, 11/1 for international students. Application fee: $85. Electronic applications accepted. *Expenses:* Expenses: Contact institution. *Financial support:* Applicants required to submit FAFSA. *Unit head:* Gretchen Murphy, Program Director, 206-543-8810, E-mail: mhihim@uw.edu. *Application contact:* Emily Karrmarshall, Program Coordinator, 206-543-5380, E-mail: mhihim@uw.edu.
Website: http://www.health-informatics.uw.edu/.

University of Wisconsin–Milwaukee, Graduate School, College of Health Sciences, Interdepartmental Program in Healthcare Informatics, Milwaukee, WI 53201-0413. Offers MS, Certificate. *Degree requirements:* For master's, comprehensive exam, thesis optional. *Entrance requirements:* For master's, GRE General Test. Additional exam requirements/recommendations for international students: Required—TOEFL (minimum score 550 paper-based; 79 iBT), IELTS (minimum score 6.5).

Walden University, Graduate Programs, School of Health Sciences, Minneapolis, MN 55401. Offers clinical research administration (MS, Graduate Certificate); health education and promotion (MS, PhD), including general (MHA, MS), population health (PhD); health informatics (MS); health services (PhD), including community health, healthcare administration, leadership, public health policy, self-designed; healthcare administration (MHA), including general (MHA, MS); public health (MPH, Dr PH, PhD), including community health education (PhD), epidemiology (PhD). Part-time and evening/weekend programs available. Postbaccalaureate distance learning degree programs offered (no on-campus study). *Faculty:* 24 full-time (15 women), 278 part-time/ adjunct (153 women). *Students:* 2,439 full-time (1,738 women), 2,004 part-time (1,378 women); includes 2,642 minority (2,001 Black or African American, non-Hispanic/Latino; 30 American Indian or Alaska Native, non-Hispanic/Latino; 224 Asian, non-Hispanic/ Latino; 295 Hispanic/Latino; 14 Native Hawaiian or other Pacific Islander, non-Hispanic/ Latino; 78 Two or more races, non-Hispanic/Latino), 78 international. Average age 39. 1,178 applicants, 97% accepted, 1067 enrolled. In 2014, 668 master's, 141 doctorates, 13 other advanced degrees awarded. *Degree requirements:* For doctorate, thesis/ dissertation, residency. *Entrance requirements:* For master's, bachelor's degree or higher; minimum GPA of 2.5; official transcripts; goal statement (for some programs); access to computer and Internet; for doctorate, master's degree or higher; three years of related professional or academic experience (preferred); minimum GPA of 3.0; goal statement and current resume (for select programs); official transcripts; access to computer and Internet; for Graduate Certificate, relevant work experience; access to computer and Internet. Additional exam requirements/recommendations for international students: Required—TOEFL (minimum score 550 paper-based, 79 iBT), IELTS (minimum score 6.5), Michigan English Language Assessment Battery (minimum score 82), or PTE (minimum score 53). *Application deadline:* Applications are processed on a rolling basis. Application fee: $0. Electronic applications accepted. *Expenses: Tuition:* Full-time $11,925; part-time $500 per credit hour. *Required fees:* $647. *Financial support:* Fellowships, Federal Work-Study, scholarships/grants, unspecified assistantships, and family tuition reduction, active duty/veteran tuition reduction, group tuition reduction, interest-free payment plans, employee tuition reduction available. Support available to part-time students. Financial award applicants required to submit FAFSA. *Unit head:* Dr. Jorg Westermann, Associate Dean, 866-492-5336. *Application contact:* Meghan M. Thomas, Vice President of Enrollment Management, 866-492-5336, E-mail: info@waldenu.edu.
Website: http://www.waldenu.edu/colleges-schools/school-of-health-sciences.

Walden University, Graduate Programs, School of Information Systems and Technology, Minneapolis, MN 55401. Offers information systems (Graduate Certificate); information systems management (MISM); information technology (MS, DIT), including health informatics (MS), information assurance and cyber security (MS), information systems (MS), software engineering (MS). Part-time and evening/weekend programs available. Postbaccalaureate distance learning degree programs offered (no on-campus study). *Faculty:* 4 full-time (1 woman), 31 part-time/adjunct (9 women). *Students:* 329 full-time (107 women), 199 part-time (70 women); includes 262 minority (202 Black or African American, non-Hispanic/Latino; 16 Asian, non-Hispanic/Latino; 27 Hispanic/ Latino; 17 Two or more races, non-Hispanic/Latino), 13 international. Average age 38. 314 applicants, 99% accepted, 290 enrolled. In 2014, 62 master's, 18 other advanced degrees awarded. *Degree requirements:* For doctorate, thesis/dissertation (for some programs), residency. *Entrance requirements:* For master's, bachelor's degree or higher; minimum GPA of 2.5; official transcripts; goal statement (for some programs); access to computer and Internet; for doctorate, master's degree or higher; three years of related professional or academic experience (preferred); minimum GPA of 3.0; goal statement and current resume (for select programs); official transcripts; access to computer and Internet; for Graduate Certificate, relevant work experience; access to computer and Internet. Additional exam requirements/recommendations for international students: Required—TOEFL (minimum score 550 paper-based, 79 iBT), IELTS (minimum score 6.5), Michigan English Language Assessment Battery (minimum score 82), or PTE (minimum score 53). *Application deadline:* Applications are processed on a rolling basis. Application fee: $0. Electronic applications accepted. *Expenses: Tuition:* Full-time $11,925; part-time $500 per credit hour. *Required fees:* $647. *Financial support:* Fellowships, Federal Work-Study, scholarships/grants, unspecified assistantships, and family tuition reduction, active duty/veteran tuition reduction, group tuition reduction, interest-free payment plans, employee tuition reduction available. Support available to part-time students. Financial award applicants required to submit FAFSA. *Unit head:* Dr. Karlyn A. Barilovits, Associate Dean, 866-492-5336. *Application contact:* Meghan Thomas, Vice President of Enrollment Management, 866-492-5336, E-mail: info@waldenu.edu.
Website: http://www.waldenu.edu/programs/colleges-schools/information -systems-and-technology.

Weill Cornell Medical College, Weill Cornell Graduate School of Medical Sciences, Program in Health Informatics, New York, NY 10065. Offers MS. Part-time programs available. *Students:* 4 full-time (1 woman), 2 part-time (1 woman); includes 3 minority (2 Asian, non-Hispanic/Latino; 1 Hispanic/Latino). In 2014, 4 master's awarded. *Degree requirements:* For master's, thesis. *Entrance requirements:* For master's, GRE, or MCAT, or GMAT, official transcripts, resume, personal statement, 3 letters of reference. Additional exam requirements/recommendations for international students: Required—TOEFL. Application fee: $60. *Expenses:* Expenses: Contact institution. *Unit head:* Dr. David P. Hajjar, Dean, 212-746-6900, E-mail: dphajjar@med.cornell.edu. *Application contact:* Dr. Randi Silver, Associate Dean, 212-746-6565, Fax: 212-746-8906, E-mail: gsms@med.cornell.edu.
Website: http://hpr.weill.cornell.edu/education/.

Human-Computer Interaction

Carnegie Mellon University, School of Computer Science, Department of Human-Computer Interaction, Pittsburgh, PA 15213-3891. Offers MHCI, PhD. *Entrance requirements:* For master's, GRE General Test, GRE Subject Test.

Clemson University, Graduate School, College of Engineering and Science, School of Computing, Program in Human-Centered Computing, Clemson, SC 29634. Offers PhD. *Students:* 27 full-time (12 women), 2 part-time (both women); includes 16 minority (15 Black or African American, non-Hispanic/Latino; 1 Asian, non-Hispanic/Latino), 8 international. Average age 29. 25 applicants, 64% accepted, 12 enrolled. In 2014, 1 doctorate awarded. *Degree requirements:* For doctorate, comprehensive exam, thesis/ dissertation. *Entrance requirements:* For doctorate, GRE General Test. Additional exam requirements/recommendations for international students: Required—TOEFL. *Application deadline:* For fall admission, 1/1 priority date for domestic and international students; for spring admission, 9/15 priority date for domestic students, 9/15 for international students. Applications are processed on a rolling basis. Electronic applications accepted. *Financial support:* In 2014–15, 21 students received support, including 6 fellowships with full and partial tuition reimbursements available (averaging $4,167 per year), 10 research assistantships with partial tuition reimbursements available (averaging $26,946 per year), 11 teaching assistantships with partial tuition reimbursements available (averaging $26,687 per year). Financial award applicants required to submit FAFSA. *Faculty research:* Virtual worlds and virtual humans, user interfaces and user experience, identity science and biometrics, affective computing, advanced learning technologies. *Unit head:* Dr. Larry F. Hodges, Director, 864-656-7552, Fax: 864-656-0145, E-mail: lfh@clemson.edu. *Application contact:* Dr. Juan Gilbert, Professor and Chair, 864-656-4846, E-mail: mark@clemson.edu.
Website: http://www.clemson.edu/ces/computing/current/curr_grad/phd_hcc/.

Cornell University, Graduate School, Graduate Fields of Agriculture and Life Sciences, Field of Communication, Ithaca, NY 14853-0001. Offers communication (MS, PhD); human-computer interaction (MS, PhD); language and communication (MS, PhD); media communication and society (MS, PhD); organizational communication (MS, PhD); science, environment and health communication (MS, PhD); social psychology of communication (MS, PhD). *Degree requirements:* For master's, thesis (MS); for doctorate, comprehensive exam, thesis/dissertation. *Entrance requirements:* For master's and doctorate, GRE General Test, 3 letters of recommendation. Additional exam requirements/recommendations for international students: Required—TOEFL (minimum score 600 paper-based; 100 iBT). Electronic applications accepted. *Faculty research:* Mass communication, communication technologies, science and environmental communication.

Cornell University, Graduate School, Graduate Fields of Arts and Sciences, Field of Information Science, Ithaca, NY 14853-0001. Offers cognition (PhD); human computer interaction (PhD); information science (PhD); information systems (PhD); social aspects of information (PhD). *Degree requirements:* For doctorate, comprehensive exam, thesis/dissertation. *Entrance requirements:* For doctorate, GRE General Test, 3 letters of recommendation. Additional exam requirements/recommendations for international students: Required—TOEFL (minimum score 550 paper-based; 77 iBT). Electronic applications accepted. *Faculty research:* Digital libraries, game theory, data mining, human-computer interaction, computational linguistics.

Dalhousie University, Faculty of Engineering, Department of Internetworking, Halifax, NS B3J 1Z1, Canada. Offers M Eng. *Entrance requirements:* Additional exam requirements/recommendations for international students: Required—TOEFL, IELTS, CANTEST, CAEL, or Michigan English Language Assessment Battery. Electronic applications accepted.

DePaul University, College of Computing and Digital Media, Chicago, IL 60604. Offers animation (MA, MFA); business information technology (MS); cinema (MFA); cinema production (MS); computational finance (MS); computer and information sciences (PhD); computer game development (MS); computer information and network security (MS); computer science (MS); e-commerce technology (MS); health informatics (MS); human-computer interaction (MS); information systems (MS); information technology project management (MS); network engineering and management (MS); predictive analytics (MS); screenwriting (MFA); software engineering (MS); JD/MS. Part-time and evening/weekend programs available. Postbaccalaureate distance learning degree programs offered (no on-campus study). *Degree requirements:* For master's, thesis (for some programs); for doctorate, comprehensive exam, thesis/dissertation. *Entrance requirements:* For master's, GRE or GMAT (for MS in computational finance only), bachelor's degree, resume (MS in predictive analytics only), IT experience (MS in information technology project management only), portfolio review (all MFA programs and MA in animation); for doctorate, GRE, master's degree in computer science. Additional exam requirements/recommendations for international students: Required—TOEFL (minimum score 590 paper-based; 80 iBT), IELTS (minimum score 6.5), PTE (minimum score 53). Electronic applications accepted. *Expenses:* Contact institution. *Faculty research:* Data mining, computer science, human-computer interaction, security, animation and film.

Florida Institute of Technology, Graduate Programs, College of Aeronautics, Program in Aviation Human Factors, Melbourne, FL 32901-6975. Offers MS. *Students:* 8 full-time (2 women), 1 international. Average age 24. 12 applicants, 50% accepted, 3 enrolled. In 2014, 4 master's awarded. *Degree requirements:* For master's, comprehensive exam, thesis, 36 credit hours. *Entrance requirements:* For master's, GRE General Test, 3 letters of recommendation, statement of objectives, resume. *Application deadline:* Applications are processed on a rolling basis. Electronic applications accepted. *Expenses: Tuition:* Part-time $1179 per credit hour. Tuition and fees vary according to campus/location. *Unit head:* Dr. Korhan Oyman, Dean, 321-674-8971, Fax: 321-674-8059, E-mail: koyman@fit.edu. *Application contact:* Cheryl A. Brown, Associate Director of Graduate Admissions, 321-674-7581, Fax: 321-723-9468, E-mail: cbrown@fit.edu.
Website: http://www.fit.edu/programs/8229/ms-aviation-human-factors#.VT_URE10ypo.

Florida Institute of Technology, Graduate Programs, College of Aeronautics, Program in Human Factors in Aeronautics, Melbourne, FL 32901-6975. Offers MS. Postbaccalaureate distance learning degree programs offered (no on-campus study). In 2014, 11 master's awarded. *Degree requirements:* For master's, thesis or capstone project. *Entrance requirements:* For master's, letter of recommednation, resume, statement of objectives. *Application deadline:* Applications are processed on a rolling basis. Electronic applications accepted. *Expenses: Tuition:* Part-time $1179 per credit hour. Tuition and fees vary according to campus/location. *Unit head:* Dr. Korhan Oyman, Dean, 321-674-8971, E-mail: koyman@fit.edu. *Application contact:* Cheryl A. Brown, Associate Director of Graduate Admissions, 321-674-7581, Fax: 321-723-9468, E-mail: cbrown@fit.edu.
Website: http://coa.fit.edu/programs/human-factors.php.

Georgia Institute of Technology, Graduate Studies, Multidisciplinary Program in Human Computer Interaction, Atlanta, GA 30332-0001. Offers MSHCI. Program offered jointly with School of Industrial Design, School of Interactive Computing, School of Psychology, and School of Literature, Media, and Communication. Part-time programs available. *Students:* 85 full-time (43 women), 6 part-time (2 women); includes 13 minority (3 Black or African American, non-Hispanic/Latino; 5 Asian, non-Hispanic/Latino; 3 Hispanic/Latino; 2 Two or more races, non-Hispanic/Latino), 45 international. Average age 24. 344 applicants, 27% accepted, 42 enrolled. In 2014, 29 master's awarded. *Degree requirements:* For master's, seminar and project. *Entrance requirements:* For master's, GRE General Test, http://www.grad.gatech.edu/hci. Additional exam requirements/recommendations for international students: Required—TOEFL (minimum score 600 paper-based; 100 iBT). *Application deadline:* For fall admission, 2/1 for domestic and international students. Applications are processed on a rolling basis. Application fee: $75. Electronic applications accepted. *Expenses:* Expenses: $7,172 per term in-state, $16,934 out-of-state plus fees of $1,196 per term (for MSHCI). *Financial support:* Fellowships, research assistantships, teaching assistantships, career-related internships or fieldwork, Federal Work-Study, institutionally sponsored loans, tuition waivers (partial), and unspecified assistantships available. Support available to part-time students. Financial award application deadline: 5/1. *Unit head:* Jim Foley, Director, 404-385-1467, E-mail: james.foley@cc.gatech.edu. *Application contact:* Jessica Celestine, Graduate Coordinator, 404-385-7205, E-mail: jcelesti@cc.gatech.edu.
Website: http://mshci.gatech.edu.

Indiana University Bloomington, School of Informatics and Computing, Program in Informatics, Bloomington, IN 47408. Offers informatics (MS, PhD), including bioinformatics, cheminformatics (PhD), complex systems (PhD), health informatics (PhD), human-computer interaction (MS), human-computer interaction design (PhD), logic and mathematical foundations of informatics (PhD), music informatics (PhD), robotics (PhD), security informatics, social informatics (PhD). Part-time programs available. *Students:* 206 full-time (78 women), 7 part-time (1 woman); includes 25 minority (9 Black or African American, non-Hispanic/Latino; 12 Asian, non-Hispanic/Latino; 2 Hispanic/Latino; 2 Two or more races, non-Hispanic/Latino), 101 international. 287 applicants, 52% accepted, 65 enrolled. In 2014, 65 master's, 13 doctorates awarded. Terminal master's awarded for partial completion of doctoral program. *Degree requirements:* For master's, thesis; for doctorate, thesis/dissertation. *Entrance requirements:* For master's and doctorate, GRE, TOEFL if international and no US degree. Additional exam requirements/recommendations for international students: Required—TOEFL (minimum score 600 paper-based; 100 iBT). *Application deadline:* For fall admission, 12/1 priority date for domestic and international students. Application fee: $55 ($65 for international students). Electronic applications accepted. *Financial support:* Application deadline: 12/1. *Unit head:* Dr. Howard Rosenbaum, Associate Dean for Graduate Studies, 812-855-3250, E-mail: hrosenba@indiana.edu. *Application contact:* Patty Reyes-Cooksey, Director of Graduate Administration, 812-856-3622, E-mail: patreyes@indiana.edu.
Website: http://www.soic.indiana.edu/informatics/index.shtml.

Indiana University–Purdue University Indianapolis, School of Informatics and Computing, Indianapolis, IN 46202. Offers bioinformatics (MS, PhD); health informatics (MS, PhD); human-computer interaction (MS, PhD); information and library science (MLS); media arts and science (MS). Part-time and evening/weekend programs available. *Faculty:* 3 full-time (0 women). *Students:* 199 full-time (101 women), 229 part-time (159 women); includes 49 minority (18 Black or African American, non-Hispanic/Latino; 15 Asian, non-Hispanic/Latino; 10 Hispanic/Latino; 6 Two or more races, non-Hispanic/Latino), 102 international. Average age 34. 268 applicants, 63% accepted, 133 enrolled. In 2014, 144 master's awarded. *Degree requirements:* For master's, thesis optional; for doctorate, thesis/dissertation. *Entrance requirements:* For master's, minimum undergraduate GPA of 3.0, graduate 3.2. Additional exam requirements/recommendations for international students: Required—TOEFL. *Application deadline:* For fall admission, 3/15 for domestic students; for spring admission, 10/15 for domestic students. Application fee: $60 ($65 for international students). Electronic applications accepted. *Financial support:* Fellowships, research assistantships, teaching assistantships, career-related internships or fieldwork, Federal Work-Study, institutionally sponsored loans, and scholarships/grants available. Support available to part-time students. *Unit head:* Dr. Robert B. Schnabel, Dean. *Application contact:* Elizabeth Bunge, Graduate Admissions Coordinator, 317-278-9200, E-mail: ebunge@iupui.edu.
Website: http://soic.iupui.edu/.

Iowa State University of Science and Technology, Program in Human-Computer Interaction, Ames, IA 50011. Offers MS, PhD. *Degree requirements:* For master's, thesis; for doctorate, thesis/dissertation. *Entrance requirements:* For master's, GRE General Test; for doctorate, GRE General Test, e-portfolio of research. Additional exam requirements/recommendations for international students: Required—TOEFL (minimum score 580 paper-based; 95 iBT), IELTS (minimum score 7). Electronic applications accepted.

Rensselaer Polytechnic Institute, Graduate School, School of Humanities, Arts, and Social Sciences, Program in Human-Computer Interaction, Troy, NY 12180-3590. Offers MS. Part-time programs available. *Faculty:* 4 full-time (3 women), 1 part-time/adjunct (0 women). *Students:* 62 applicants, 13% accepted. In 2014, 2 master's awarded. *Degree requirements:* For master's, thesis optional. *Entrance requirements:* For master's, GRE. Additional exam requirements/recommendations for international students: Required—TOEFL (minimum score 570 paper-based; 88 iBT), IELTS (minimum score 6.5), PTE (minimum score 60). *Application deadline:* For fall admission, 1/1 priority date for domestic and international students; for spring admission, 8/15 priority date for domestic and international students. Applications are processed on a rolling basis. Application fee: $75. Electronic applications accepted. *Expenses: Tuition:* Full-time $46,700; part-time $1945 per credit. Tuition and fees vary according to course load. *Financial support:* Career-related internships or fieldwork and institutionally sponsored loans available. *Faculty research:* Communication, game studies, literary theory, media studies, rhetoric, visual design, writing studies. *Unit head:* Dr. Katya Haskins, Graduate Program Director, 518-276-8120, E-mail: haskie@rpi.edu. *Application contact:* Office of Graduate Admissions, 518-276-6216, E-mail: gradadmissions@rpi.edu.
Website: http://www.cm.rpi.edu/.

Rochester Institute of Technology, Graduate Enrollment Services, Golisano College of Computing and Information Sciences, Information Science and Technologies Department, MS Program in Human Computer Interaction, Rochester, NY 14623-5608. Offers MS. Part-time programs available. Postbaccalaureate distance learning degree programs offered (no on-campus study). *Students:* 26 full-time (11 women), 19 part-time (8 women); includes 8 minority (1 Black or African American, non-Hispanic/Latino; 5 Asian, non-Hispanic/Latino; 1 Hispanic/Latino; 1 Two or more races, non-Hispanic/Latino), 21 international. Average age 29. 137 applicants, 47% accepted, 23 enrolled. In 2014, 5 master's awarded. *Degree requirements:* For master's, thesis or alternative. *Entrance requirements:* For master's, GRE and TOEFL, IELTS, or PTE for non-native English speakers, minimum GPA of 3.0. Additional exam requirements/recommendations for international students: Required—PTE (minimum score 58), TOEFL (minimum score 550 paper-based; 79 iBT) or IELTS (minimum score 6.5). *Application deadline:* For fall admission, 2/15 priority date for domestic and international students; for spring admission, 12/15 priority date for domestic and international students. Applications are processed on a rolling basis. Application fee: $60. Electronic applications accepted. *Expenses:* Expenses: $1,673 per credit hour. *Financial support:* In 2014–15, 28 students received support. Research assistantships with partial tuition reimbursements available, teaching assistantships with partial tuition reimbursements available, career-related internships or fieldwork, Federal Work-Study, institutionally sponsored loans, scholarships/grants, and unspecified assistantships available. Support available to part-time students. Financial award applicants required to submit FAFSA. *Faculty research:* Human computer interaction and accessibility including accessibility and inclusion, wearable and mobile computing, personal fabrication technologies, technology for aging, educational technology for students with disabilities, touch and haptic interaction for users with disabilities, sign language technologies. *Unit head:* Dr. Peter Lutz, Graduate Program Director, 585-475-2700, Fax: 585-475-6584, E-mail: informaticsGrad@rit.edu. *Application contact:* Diane Ellison, Associate Vice President, Graduate Enrollment Services, 585-475-2229, Fax: 585-475-7164, E-mail: gradinfo@rit.edu.
Website: http://hci.rit.edu/index.php.

State University of New York at Oswego, Graduate Studies, College of Liberal Arts and Sciences, Interdisciplinary Program in Human Computer Interaction, Oswego, NY 13126. Offers MA. Part-time programs available. *Entrance requirements:* For master's, GRE, minimum GPA of 3.0. Additional exam requirements/recommendations for international students: Required—TOEFL (minimum score 560 paper-based).

Tufts University, Graduate School of Arts and Sciences, Graduate Certificate Programs, Human-Computer Interaction Program, Medford, MA 02155. Offers Certificate. Part-time and evening/weekend programs available. Electronic applications accepted. *Expenses: Tuition:* Full-time $45,590; part-time $1161 per credit hour. *Required fees:* $782. Full-time tuition and fees vary according to degree level, program and student level. Part-time tuition and fees vary according to course load.

University of Baltimore, Graduate School, Yale Gordon College of Arts and Sciences, Program in Interaction Design and Information Architecture, Baltimore, MD 21201-5779. Offers MS. Part-time and evening/weekend programs available. *Degree requirements:* For master's, project or thesis. *Entrance requirements:* For master's, GRE General Test or Miller Analogy Test, undergraduate GPA of 3.0.

University of Illinois at Urbana–Champaign, Graduate College, Graduate School of Library and Information Science, Champaign, IL 61820. Offers bioinformatics (MS); digital libraries (CAS); library and information science (MS, PhD, CAS). *Accreditation:* ALA (one or more programs are accredited). Part-time programs available.

Postbaccalaureate distance learning degree programs offered (minimal on-campus study). *Students:* 283 (208 women). *Entrance requirements:* For degree, master's degree in library and information science or related field with minimum GPA of 3.0. Application fee: $70 ($90 for international students). *Unit head:* Allen Renear, Interim Dean, 217-265-5216, Fax: 217-244-3302, E-mail: renear@illinois.edu. *Application contact:* Penny Ames, Graduate Contact, 217-333-7197, E-mail: pames@illinois.edu. Website: http://www.lis.illinois.edu.

Information Science

Alcorn State University, School of Graduate Studies, School of Arts and Sciences, Department of Mathematical Sciences, Lorman, MS 39096-7500. Offers computer and information sciences (MS).

American InterContinental University Atlanta, Program in Information Technology, Atlanta, GA 30328. Offers MIT. Part-time and evening/weekend programs available. *Degree requirements:* For master's, technical proficiency demonstration. *Entrance requirements:* For master's, Computer Programmer Aptitude Battery Exam, interview. Electronic applications accepted. *Faculty research:* Operating systems, security issues, networks and routing, computer hardware.

American InterContinental University Online, Program in Information Technology, Schaumburg, IL 60173. Offers Internet security (MIT); IT project management (MIT). Evening/weekend programs available. Postbaccalaureate distance learning degree programs offered (no on-campus study). *Entrance requirements:* Additional exam requirements/recommendations for international students: Required—TOEFL (minimum score 550 paper-based). Electronic applications accepted.

American University of Armenia, Graduate Programs, Yerevan, Armenia. Offers business administration (MBA); computer and information science (MS), including business management, design and manufacturing, energy (ME, MS), industrial engineering and systems management; economics (MS); industrial engineering and systems management (ME), including business, computer aided design/manufacturing, energy (ME, MS), information technology; law (LL M); political science and international affairs (MPSIA); public health (MPH); teaching English as a foreign language (MA). Part-time and evening/weekend programs available. *Degree requirements:* For master's, thesis (for some programs), capstone/project. *Entrance requirements:* For master's, GRE, GMAT, or LSAT. Additional exam requirements/recommendations for international students: Recommended—TOEFL (minimum score 79 iBT), IELTS (minimum score 6.5). *Faculty research:* Microfinance, finance (rural/development, international, corporate), firm life cycle theory, TESOL, language proficiency testing, public policy, administrative law, economic development, cryptography, artificial intelligence, energy efficiency/renewable energy, computer-aided design/manufacturing, health financing, tuberculosis control, mother/child health, preventive ophthalmology, post-earthquake psychopathological investigations, tobacco control, environmental health risk assessments.

Arizona State University at the Tempe campus, Ira A. Fulton Schools of Engineering, The Polytechnic School, Programs in Technology Management, Mesa, AZ 85212. Offers aviation management and human factors (MS); environmental technology management (MS); global technology and development (MS); graphic information technology (MS); management of technology (MS). Part-time and evening/weekend programs available. Postbaccalaureate distance learning degree programs offered (minimal on-campus study). *Degree requirements:* For master's, thesis or applied project and oral defense; interactive Program of Study (iPOS) submitted before completing 50 percent of required credit hours. *Entrance requirements:* For master's, GRE, minimum GPA of 3.0 or equivalent in last 2 years of work leading to bachelor's degree. Additional exam requirements/recommendations for international students: Required—TOEFL, IELTS, or PTE. Electronic applications accepted. *Faculty research:* Digital imaging, digital publishing, Internet development/e-commerce, information aviation human factors, pilot selection, databases, multimedia, commercial digital photography, digital workflow, computer graphics modeling and animation, information design, sociotechnology, visual and technical literacy, environmental management, quality management, project management, industrial ethics, hazardous materials, environmental chemistry.

Arkansas Tech University, College of Engineering and Applied Sciences, Russellville, AR 72801. Offers emergency management (MS); engineering (M Engr); information technology (MS). Part-time programs available. Postbaccalaureate distance learning degree programs offered (no on-campus study). *Students:* 83 full-time (31 women), 48 part-time (16 women); includes 14 minority (5 Black or African American, non-Hispanic/Latino; 1 American Indian or Alaska Native, non-Hispanic/Latino; 1 Asian, non-Hispanic/Latino; 3 Hispanic/Latino; 4 Two or more races, non-Hispanic/Latino), 60 international. Average age 28. In 2014, 39 master's awarded. *Degree requirements:* For master's, comprehensive exam (for some programs), thesis (for some programs), internship. *Entrance requirements:* For master's, GRE General Test. Additional exam requirements/recommendations for international students: Required—TOEFL (minimum score 550 paper-based; 79 iBT), IELTS (minimum score 6). *Application deadline:* For fall admission, 3/1 priority date for domestic students, 5/1 priority date for international students; for spring admission, 10/1 priority date for domestic and international students. Applications are processed on a rolling basis. Application fee: $25 ($75 for international students). Electronic applications accepted. *Expenses:* Tuition, state resident: full-time $6264; part-time $261 per credit hour. Tuition, nonresident: full-time $12,528; part-time $522 per credit hour. *Required fees:* $423 per semester. Tuition and fees vary according to course load. *Financial support:* In 2014-15, research assistantships with full tuition reimbursements (averaging $4,800 per year), teaching assistantships with full tuition reimbursements (averaging $4,800 per year) were awarded; career-related internships or fieldwork, Federal Work-Study, scholarships/grants, health care benefits, and unspecified assistantships also available. Support available to part-time students. Financial award application deadline: 4/15; financial award applicants required to submit FAFSA. *Unit head:* Dr. William Hoefler, Dean, 479-968-0353, E-mail: whoeflerjr@atu.edu. *Application contact:* Dr. Mary B. Gunter, Dean of Graduate College, 479-968-0398, Fax: 479-964-0542, E-mail: gradcollege@atu.edu. Website: http://www.atu.edu/appliedsci/.

Armstrong State University, School of Graduate Studies, Program in Computer Science, Savannah, GA 31419-1997. Offers MSCIS. Part-time programs available. *Faculty:* 3 full-time (0 women). *Students:* 1 (woman) full-time, 1 (woman) part-time; includes 1 minority (Black or African American, non-Hispanic/Latino), 1 international. Average age 28. 4 applicants, 25% accepted. *Degree requirements:* For master's, project. *Entrance requirements:* For master's, GRE (minimum scores: verbal 156, quantitative 144, and writing 4), minimum GPA of 2.7, letters of recommendation, BS in computer science or related field. Additional exam requirements/recommendations for international students: Required—TOEFL (minimum score 523 paper-based). *Application deadline:* For fall admission, 6/30 priority date for domestic students, 5/1 priority date for international students; for spring admission, 11/15 priority date for domestic students, 9/15 priority date for international students; for summer admission, 4/ 15 priority date for domestic students, 9/15 for international students. Applications are processed on a rolling basis. Application fee: $30. Electronic applications accepted. *Expenses:* Tuition, state resident: part-time $206 per credit hour. Tuition, nonresident: part-time $763 per credit hour. *Required fees:* $612 per semester. Tuition and fees vary according to course load, campus/location and program. *Financial support:* In 2014-15, research assistantships with full tuition reimbursements (averaging $5,000 per year) were awarded; career-related internships or fieldwork, Federal Work-Study, scholarships/grants, and unspecified assistantships also available. Support available to part-time students. Financial award application deadline: 3/15; financial award applicants required to submit FAFSA. *Faculty research:* Bioinformatics, data mining, graph theory, image processing, machine learning. *Unit head:* Dr. Hong Zhang, Department Head, 912-344-3151, E-mail: hong.zhang@armstrong.edu. *Application contact:* Kathy Ingram, Associate Director of Graduate/Adult and Nontraditional Students, 912-344-2503, Fax: 912-344-3417, E-mail: graduate@armstrong.edu. Website: http://www.armstrong.edu/Science_and_Technology/deans_office /computer_science1.

Aspen University, Program in Information Technology, Denver, CO 80246-1930. Offers MS, Certificate. Part-time and evening/weekend programs available. Postbaccalaureate distance learning degree programs offered (no on-campus study). Electronic applications accepted.

Athabasca University, School of Computing and Information Systems, Athabasca, AB T9S 3A3, Canada. Offers information systems (M Sc). Part-time programs available. Postbaccalaureate distance learning degree programs offered (no on-campus study). *Degree requirements:* For master's, thesis optional. *Entrance requirements:* For master's, B Sc in computing or other bachelor's degree and IT experience. Electronic applications accepted. *Expenses:* Contact institution. *Faculty research:* Distributed systems multimedia, computer science education, e-services.

Auburn University at Montgomery, College of Arts and Sciences, Informatics Institute, Montgomery, AL 36124-4023. Offers cybersystems and information security (MS). *Faculty:* 1 full-time (0 women), 1 part-time/adjunct (0 women). *Students:* 4 part-time (2 women), all international. Average age 27. 8 applicants, 38% accepted, 1 enrolled. In 2014, 4 master's awarded. *Expenses:* Tuition, state resident: full-time $6264; part-time $348 per credit hour. Tuition, nonresident: full-time $14,094; part-time $783 per credit hour. *Financial support:* In 2014-15, 4 teaching assistantships were awarded. *Unit head:* Dr. Karen Stine, Dean, 334-244-3689, Fax: 334-244-3826, E-mail: kstine@aum.edu. *Application contact:* Dr. Pamela Tidwell, Associate Dean, 334-244-3362, Fax: 334-244-3826, E-mail: ptidwell@aum.edu.

Ball State University, Graduate School, College of Communication, Information, and Media, Center for Information and Communication Sciences, Muncie, IN 47306-1099. Offers MS. *Faculty:* 6 full-time (0 women). *Students:* 59 full-time (12 women), 14 part-time (3 women); includes 4 minority (3 Black or African American, non-Hispanic/Latino; 1 Hispanic/Latino), 4 international. Average age 26. 90 applicants, 87% accepted, 52 enrolled. In 2014, 47 master's awarded. Application fee: $50. *Financial support:* In 2014-15, 40 students received support, including 22 research assistantships with partial tuition reimbursements available (averaging $7,722 per year), 3 teaching assistantships with partial tuition reimbursements available (averaging $10,417 per year); unspecified assistantships also available. Financial award application deadline: 3/1. *Unit head:* Dr. Stephan Jones, Director, 765-285-5930, Fax: 765-285-1516, E-mail: sjones@bsu.edu. *Application contact:* Dr. Robert Morris, Associate Provost for Research and Dean of the Graduate School, 765-285-4723, Fax: 765-285-1328, E-mail: rmorris@bsu.edu. Website: http://cms.bsu.edu/academics/collegesanddepartments/cics.

Barry University, School of Adult and Continuing Education, Program in Information Technology, Miami Shores, FL 33161-6695. Offers MS. Part-time and evening/weekend programs available. *Entrance requirements:* For master's, GMAT, GRE or MAT, bachelor's degree in information technology, related area or professional experience. Electronic applications accepted.

Bellevue University, Graduate School, College of Information Technology, Bellevue, NE 68005-3098. Offers computer information systems (MS); cybersecurity (MS); management of information systems (MS); project management (MPM).

Bentley University, Graduate School of Business, Program in Information Technology, Waltham, MA 02452-4705. Offers MSIT. Part-time and evening/weekend programs available. *Faculty:* 85 full-time (28 women), 26 part-time/adjunct (9 women). *Students:* 45 full-time (17 women), 21 part-time (8 women); includes 5 minority (1 Black or African American, non-Hispanic/Latino; 4 Asian, non-Hispanic/Latino), 47 international. Average age 27. 128 applicants, 72% accepted, 32 enrolled. In 2014, 39 master's awarded. *Entrance requirements:* For master's, GMAT or GRE General Test. Additional exam requirements/recommendations for international students: Required—TOEFL (minimum score 600 paper-based; 100 iBT) or IELTS (minimum score 7). *Application deadline:* For fall admission, 12/1 priority date for domestic and international students; for spring admission, 10/1 for domestic and international students. Applications are processed on a rolling basis. Application fee: $50. Electronic applications accepted. *Expenses: Tuition:* Full-time $31,320. *Required fees:* $437. *Financial support:* In 2014-15, 11 students received support. Scholarships/grants and unspecified assistantships available. Financial award application deadline: 6/1; financial award applicants required to submit CSS PROFILE or FAFSA. *Faculty research:* Business intelligence, enterprise networks and services, telemedicine, enterprise resource planning usability, information visualization, system design quality. *Unit head:* Dr. Wendy Lucas, Director, 781-891-2554, E-mail: wlucas@bentley.edu. *Application contact:* Sharon Hill, Director of Graduate Admissions, 781-891-2108, Fax: 781-891-2464, E-mail: bentleygraduateadmissions@bentley.edu. Website: http://www.bentley.edu/graduate/ms-programs/information-technology.

Bradley University, Graduate School, College of Liberal Arts and Sciences, Department of Computer Science and Information Systems, Peoria, IL 61625-0002. Offers computer information systems (MS); computer science (MS). Part-time and evening/weekend programs available. *Faculty:* 9 full-time (1 woman), 3 part-time/adjunct (1 woman). *Students:* 82 full-time (31 women), 66 part-time (27 women), 143 international. 425 applicants, 42% accepted, 63 enrolled. In 2014, 25 master's awarded. *Degree requirements:* For master's, comprehensive exam, thesis or alternative, programming test. *Entrance requirements:* For master's, GRE. Additional exam requirements/recommendations for international students: Required—TOEFL (minimum score 550 paper-based; 79 iBT), IELTS (minimum score 6.5). *Application deadline:* For fall admission, 5/15 priority date for domestic and international students; for spring admission, 10/15 priority date for domestic and international students. Applications are processed on a rolling basis. Application fee: $40 ($50 for international students). Electronic applications accepted. *Expenses: Tuition:* Full-time $14,580; part-time $810 per credit. *Required fees:* $224. Full-time tuition and fees vary according to course load. *Financial support:* In 2014–15, 18 research assistantships with full and partial tuition reimbursements (averaging $9,820 per year) were awarded; teaching assistantships, scholarships/grants, tuition waivers (partial), and unspecified assistantships also available. Support available to part-time students. Financial award application deadline: 4/1. *Unit head:* Dr. Steven Dolins, Chair, 309-677-3284, E-mail: sdolins@bradley.edu. *Application contact:* Kayla Carroll, Director of International Admissions and Student Services, 309-677-2375, E-mail: klcarroll@fsmail.bradley.edu.

Brigham Young University, Graduate Studies, Ira A. Fulton College of Engineering and Technology, School of Technology, Provo, UT 84602-1001. Offers construction management (MS); information technology (MS); manufacturing systems (MS); technology and engineering education (MS). *Faculty:* 27 full-time (0 women). *Students:* 40 full-time (4 women); includes 6 minority (3 Asian, non-Hispanic/Latino; 2 Hispanic/Latino; 1 Native Hawaiian or other Pacific Islander, non-Hispanic/Latino), 1 international. Average age 30. 19 applicants, 63% accepted, 12 enrolled. In 2014, 12 master's awarded. *Degree requirements:* For master's, thesis. *Entrance requirements:* For master's, GRE General Test; GMAT or GRE (for construction management emphasis), minimum GPA of 3.0 in last 60 hours of course work. Additional exam requirements/recommendations for international students: Required—TOEFL (minimum score 580 paper-based; 85 iBT). *Application deadline:* For fall admission, 2/15 for domestic and international students; for winter admission, 9/10 for domestic students, 9/15 for international students; for spring admission, 2/15 for domestic and international students; for summer admission, 2/15 for domestic students. Application fee: $50. Electronic applications accepted. *Expenses: Tuition:* Full-time $6310; part-time $371 per credit hour. Tuition and fees vary according to program and student's religious affiliation. *Financial support:* In 2014–15, 40 students received support, including 17 research assistantships (averaging $4,305 per year), 18 teaching assistantships (averaging $4,257 per year); scholarships/grants also available. *Faculty research:* Information assurance and security, HEI and databases, manufacturing materials, processes and systems, innovation in construction management scheduling and delivery methods. *Total annual research expenditures:* $534,164. *Unit head:* Richard E. Fry, Director, 801-422-4445, Fax: 801-422-0490, E-mail: rfry@byu.edu. *Application contact:* Barry M. Lunt, Graduate Coordinator, 801-422-2264, Fax: 801-422-0490, E-mail: sotadminasst@byu.edu.
Website: http://www.et.byu.edu/sot/.

Brooklyn College of the City University of New York, School of Natural and Behavioral Sciences, Department of Computer and Information Science, Brooklyn, NY 11210-2889. Offers computer science (MA); health informatics (MS); information systems (MS); parallel and distributed computing (Advanced Certificate). Part-time and evening/weekend programs available. *Degree requirements:* For master's, comprehensive exam, thesis or alternative. *Entrance requirements:* For master's, previous course work in computer science, 2 letters of recommendation. Additional exam requirements/recommendations for international students: Required—TOEFL (minimum score 525 paper-based; 70 iBT). Electronic applications accepted. *Faculty research:* Networks and distributed systems, programming languages, modeling and computer applications, algorithms, artificial intelligence, theoretical computer science.

California State University, Fullerton, Graduate Studies, College of Business and Economics, Department of Information Systems and Decision Sciences, Fullerton, CA 92834-9480. Offers decision science (MBA); information systems (MBA, MS); information systems and decision sciences (MS); information systems and e-commerce (MS); information technology (MS). Part-time programs available. *Students:* 52 full-time (15 women), 68 part-time (20 women); includes 45 minority (2 Black or African American, non-Hispanic/Latino; 29 Asian, non-Hispanic/Latino; 11 Hispanic/Latino; 3 Two or more races, non-Hispanic/Latino), 48 international. Average age 29. 248 applicants, 45% accepted, 42 enrolled. In 2014, 31 master's awarded. *Degree requirements:* For master's, project or thesis. *Entrance requirements:* For master's, GMAT, minimum AACSB index of 950. Application fee: $55. *Financial support:* Career-related internships or fieldwork, Federal Work-Study, institutionally sponsored loans, and scholarships/grants available. Support available to part-time students. Financial award application deadline: 3/1; financial award applicants required to submit FAFSA. *Unit head:* Dr. Bhushan Kapoor, Chair, 657-278-2221. *Application contact:* Admissions/Applications, 657-278-2371.
Website: http://business.fullerton.edu/isds/.

Capitol Technology University, Graduate Programs, Laurel, MD 20708-9759. Offers business administration (MBA); computer science (MS); electrical engineering (MS); information and telecommunications systems management (MS); information architecture (MS); network security (MS). Part-time and evening/weekend programs available. Postbaccalaureate distance learning degree programs offered (no on-campus study). *Entrance requirements:* For master's, minimum GPA of 3.0. Electronic applications accepted.

Carleton University, Faculty of Graduate Studies, Faculty of Engineering and Design, Ottawa-Carleton Institute for Electrical Engineering, Department of Systems and Computer Engineering, Program in Information and Systems Science, Ottawa, ON K1S 5B6, Canada. Offers M Sc.

Carleton University, Faculty of Graduate Studies, Faculty of Science, Information and Systems Science Program, Ottawa, ON K1S 5B6, Canada. Offers M Sc. *Degree requirements:* For master's, thesis optional. *Entrance requirements:* For master's, honors degree. Additional exam requirements/recommendations for international students: Required—TOEFL. *Faculty research:* Software engineering, real-time and microprocessor programming, computer communications.

Carleton University, Faculty of Graduate Studies, Faculty of Science, School of Computer Science, Ottawa, ON K1S 5B6, Canada. Offers computer science (MCS, PhD); information and system science (M Sc). MCS and PhD programs offered jointly with University of Ottawa. Part-time programs available. *Degree requirements:* For master's, thesis optional, project; for doctorate, comprehensive exam, thesis/dissertation. *Entrance requirements:* For master's, honors degree. Additional exam requirements/recommendations for international students: Required—TOEFL. *Faculty research:* Programming systems, theory of computing, computer applications, computer systems.

Carnegie Mellon University, Heinz College Australia, Master of Science in Information Technology Program (Adelaide, South Australia), Adelaide, PA 5000, Australia. Offers MSIT. *Entrance requirements:* For master's, GRE or GMAT, college-level course in advanced algebra/pre-calculus; college-level courses in economics and statistics (recommended). Additional exam requirements/recommendations for international students: Required—TOEFL or IELTS.

Carnegie Mellon University, H. John Heinz III College, School of Information Systems and Management, Master of Information Systems Management Program, Pittsburgh, PA

15213-3891. Offers MISM. *Entrance requirements:* For master's, GRE or GMAT, college-level course in advanced algebra/pre-calculus; college-level courses in economics and statistics (recommended). Additional exam requirements/recommendations for international students: Required—TOEFL or IELTS.

Carnegie Mellon University, School of Computer Science, Language Technologies Institute, Pittsburgh, PA 15213-3891. Offers MLT, MS, PhD. Terminal master's awarded for partial completion of doctoral program. *Degree requirements:* For doctorate, thesis/dissertation. *Entrance requirements:* For master's and doctorate, GRE General Test, GRE Subject Test. Additional exam requirements/recommendations for international students: Required—TOEFL. *Faculty research:* Machine translation, natural language processing, speech and information retrieval, literacy.

Case Western Reserve University, School of Graduate Studies, Case School of Engineering, Department of Electrical Engineering and Computer Science, Cleveland, OH 44106. Offers computer engineering (MS, PhD); computing and information sciences (MS, PhD); electrical engineering (MS, PhD); systems and control engineering (MS, PhD). Part-time and evening/weekend programs available. Postbaccalaureate distance learning degree programs offered (minimal on-campus study). *Faculty:* 33 full-time (3 women). *Students:* 158 full-time (35 women), 18 part-time (5 women); includes 5 minority (1 Black or African American, non-Hispanic/Latino; 3 Asian, non-Hispanic/Latino; 1 Hispanic/Latino), 122 international. In 2014, 37 master's, 11 doctorates awarded. Terminal master's awarded for partial completion of doctoral program. *Degree requirements:* For master's, thesis; for doctorate, thesis/dissertation, qualifying exam, teaching experience. *Entrance requirements:* For master's and doctorate, GRE General Test. Additional exam requirements/recommendations for international students: Required—TOEFL. *Application deadline:* For fall admission, 2/1 for domestic students; for spring admission, 11/1 for domestic students. Applications are processed on a rolling basis. Application fee: $50. *Financial support:* In 2014–15, 51 research assistantships with full and partial tuition reimbursements, 10 teaching assistantships were awarded; fellowships with full and partial tuition reimbursements, career-related internships or fieldwork, Federal Work-Study, and institutionally sponsored loans also available. Support available to part-time students. Financial award application deadline: 3/1; financial award applicants required to submit FAFSA. *Faculty research:* Micro/nano systems; robotics and haptics, applied artificial intelligence; automation, computer-aided design and testing of digital systems. *Total annual research expenditures:* $6 million. *Unit head:* Dr. Kenneth Loparo, Department Chair, 216-368-4115, E-mail: kal4@case.edu. *Application contact:* Kimberly Yurchick, Student Affairs Specialist, 216-368-2920, Fax: 216-368-2801, E-mail: ksy4@case.edu.
Website: http://eecs.cwru.edu/.

The Citadel, The Military College of South Carolina, Citadel Graduate College, Department of Mathematics and Computer Science, Charleston, SC 29409. Offers computer and information science (MS); mathematics education (MAE). *Accreditation:* NCATE (one or more programs are accredited). Part-time and evening/weekend programs available. *Degree requirements:* For master's, comprehensive exam (for some programs), thesis (for some programs). *Entrance requirements:* For master's, GRE General Test with minimum combined score of 300 on the verbal and quantitative sections [1000 under the old grading system], 4.0 on the writing assessment (for MS); MAT with minimum raw score of 396 (for MA Ed), minimum undergraduate GPA of 3.0 (MS) or 2.5 (MAT); competency, demonstrated through coursework, approved work experience, or a program-administrated competency exam, in the areas of basic computer architecture, object-oriented programming, discrete mathematics, and data structures (MS); successful completion of 7 courses (MAT). Additional exam requirements/recommendations for international students: Required—TOEFL (minimum score 550 paper-based; 79 iBT). Electronic applications accepted. *Faculty research:* Mathematics: numerical linear algebra, inverse problems, operator algebras, geometric group theory, integral equations; computer science: computer networks, database systems, software engineering, computational systems biology, mobile systems.

Claremont Graduate University, Graduate Programs, Center for Information Systems and Technology, Claremont, CA 91711-6160. Offers electronic commerce (MS, PhD); health information management (MS); information systems (Certificate); knowledge management (MS, PhD); systems development (MS, PhD); telecommunications and networking (MS, PhD); MBA/MS. Part-time programs available. *Faculty:* 5 full-time (0 women), 2 part-time/adjunct (0 women). *Students:* 60 full-time (21 women), 65 part-time (22 women); includes 26 minority (5 Black or African American, non-Hispanic/Latino; 1 American Indian or Alaska Native, non-Hispanic/Latino; 15 Asian, non-Hispanic/Latino; 4 Hispanic/Latino; 1 Two or more races, non-Hispanic/Latino), 65 international. Average age 36. In 2014, 17 master's, 1 doctorate awarded. *Degree requirements:* For doctorate, comprehensive exam, thesis/dissertation, portfolio. *Entrance requirements:* For master's and doctorate, GMAT, GRE General Test. Additional exam requirements/recommendations for international students: Required—TOEFL (minimum score 550 paper-based; 80 iBT). *Application deadline:* For fall admission, 2/1 priority date for domestic and international students. Applications are processed on a rolling basis. Application fee: $80. Electronic applications accepted. *Expenses: Tuition:* Full-time $41,784; part-time $1741 per credit. *Required fees:* $600; $300 per semester. *Financial support:* Fellowships, research assistantships, teaching assistantships, Federal Work-Study, institutionally sponsored loans, and scholarships/grants available. Support available to part-time students. Financial award application deadline: 2/15; financial award applicants required to submit FAFSA. *Faculty research:* Man-machine interaction, organizational aspects of computing, implementation of information systems, information systems practice. *Unit head:* Tom Horan, Dean, 909-607-9302, Fax: 909-621-8564, E-mail: tom.horan@cgu.edu. *Application contact:* Leah Litwack, Administrative Assistant, 909-621-8209, E-mail: leah.litwack@cgu.edu.
Website: http://www.cgu.edu/pages/153.asp.

Clark Atlanta University, School of Arts and Sciences, Department of Computer and Information Science, Atlanta, GA 30314. Offers MS. Part-time programs available. *Faculty:* 3 full-time (0 women). *Students:* 23 full-time (9 women), 5 part-time (2 women); includes 13 minority (7 Black or African American, non-Hispanic/Latino; 2 American Indian or Alaska Native, non-Hispanic/Latino; 4 Asian, non-Hispanic/Latino), 10 international. Average age 29. 27 applicants, 96% accepted, 14 enrolled. In 2014, 9 master's awarded. *Degree requirements:* For master's, one foreign language, thesis. *Entrance requirements:* For master's, GRE General Test, minimum GPA of 2.5. Additional exam requirements/recommendations for international students: Required—TOEFL (minimum score 500 paper-based; 61 iBT). *Application deadline:* For fall admission, 4/1 for domestic and international students; for spring admission, 11/1 for domestic and international students. Applications are processed on a rolling basis. Application fee: $40 ($55 for international students). *Expenses: Tuition:* Full-time $14,904; part-time $828 per credit hour. *Required fees:* $746; $373 per semester. *Financial support:* In 2014–15, 4 fellowships were awarded; career-related internships or fieldwork, Federal Work-Study, scholarships/grants, and unspecified assistantships also available. Support available to part-time students. Financial award application deadline: 4/30; financial award applicants required to submit FAFSA. *Unit head:* Dr. Olugbemiga Olatidoye, Chairperson, 404-880-6940, E-mail: oolatidoye@cau.edu. *Application contact:* Michelle Clark-Davis, Graduate Program Admissions, 404-880-6605, E-mail: cauadmissions@cau.edu.

Information Science

Clarkson University, Graduate School, School of Arts and Sciences, Program in Information Technology, Potsdam, NY 13699. Offers MS. Part-time programs available. *Students:* 1 (woman) full-time, 1 (woman) part-time, 1 international. Average age 24. 13 applicants, 54% accepted, 2 enrolled. In 2014, 2 master's awarded. *Entrance requirements:* For master's, GRE, transcripts of all college coursework, resume, personal statement, three letters of recommendation. Additional exam requirements/recommendations for international students: Required—TOEFL, IELTS. *Application deadline:* For fall admission, 1/30 priority date for domestic and international students; for spring admission, 9/1 priority date for domestic and international students. Applications are processed on a rolling basis. Application fee: $25 ($35 for international students). Electronic applications accepted. *Expenses: Tuition:* Full-time $16,680; part-time $1390 per credit. *Required fees:* $295 per semester. *Financial support:* In 2014–15, 2 students received support, including research assistantships with full tuition reimbursements available (averaging $24,029 per year); scholarships/grants, tuition waivers (partial), and unspecified assistantships also available. *Unit head:* Dr. William Dennis Horn, Director, 315-268-6420, Fax: 315-268-2335, E-mail: horn@clarkson.edu. *Application contact:* Jennifer Reed, Graduate Coordinator, School of Arts and Sciences, 315-268-3802, Fax: 315-268-3989, E-mail: sciencegrad@clarkson.edu.
Website: http://www.clarkson.edu/it/.

See Close-Up on page 345.

Clark University, Graduate School, College of Professional and Continuing Education, Program in Information Technology, Worcester, MA 01610-1477. Offers MSIT. *Students:* 24 full-time (15 women), 17 part-time (5 women); includes 4 minority (2 Black or African American, non-Hispanic/Latino; 1 Hispanic/Latino; 1 Two or more races, non-Hispanic/Latino), 29 international. Average age 31. 39 applicants, 77% accepted, 17 enrolled. In 2014, 22 master's awarded. *Degree requirements:* For master's, thesis or alternative. *Entrance requirements:* Additional exam requirements/recommendations for international students: Required—TOEFL. *Application deadline:* Applications are processed on a rolling basis. Application fee: $75. Electronic applications accepted. *Expenses: Tuition:* Full-time $40,380; part-time $1262 per credit hour. *Required fees:* $30. *Financial support:* Tuition waivers (partial) available. *Unit head:* Dr. William Fisher, Dean, 508-793-7676. *Application contact:* Ethan Bernstein, Director of Graduate Admissions, 508-793-7373, E-mail: gradadmissions@clarku.edu.
Website: http://copace.clarku.edu/graduate-programs/masters-information-technology/index.cfm.

Cleveland State University, College of Graduate Studies, Monte Ahuja College of Business, Department of Computer and Information Science, Cleveland, OH 44115. Offers computer and information science (MCIS); information systems (DBA). Part-time and evening/weekend programs available. *Faculty:* 12 full-time (2 women), 3 part-time/adjunct (2 women). *Students:* 29 full-time (12 women), 81 part-time (29 women); includes 5 minority (2 Black or African American, non-Hispanic/Latino; 3 Asian, non-Hispanic/Latino), 77 international. Average age 27. 447 applicants, 56% accepted, 54 enrolled. In 2014, 22 master's awarded. Terminal master's awarded for partial completion of doctoral program. *Degree requirements:* For master's, thesis optional; for doctorate, comprehensive exam, thesis/dissertation. *Entrance requirements:* For master's, GRE or GMAT, minimum GPA of 2.75; for doctorate, GRE or GMAT, MBA, MCIS or equivalent. Additional exam requirements/recommendations for international students: Required—TOEFL (minimum score 525 paper-based; 78 iBT). *Application deadline:* For fall admission, 7/15 priority date for domestic students, 5/15 priority date for international students; for spring admission, 12/15 priority date for domestic students. Applications are processed on a rolling basis. Application fee: $30. Electronic applications accepted. *Expenses: Tuition,* state resident: full-time $9566; part-time $531 per credit hour. Tuition, nonresident: full-time $17,980; part-time $999 per credit hour. *Required fees:* $25 per semester. Tuition and fees vary according to degree level and program. *Financial support:* In 2014–15, 21 students received support, including 7 research assistantships with full and partial tuition reimbursements available (averaging $7,800 per year), 2 teaching assistantships with full and partial tuition reimbursements available (averaging $16,000 per year); career-related internships or fieldwork, tuition waivers (full), and unspecified assistantships also available. *Faculty research:* Artificial intelligence, object-oriented analysis, database design, software efficiency, distributed system, geographical information systems. *Total annual research expenditures:* $7,500. *Unit head:* Dr. Santosh K. Misra, Chairman, 216-687-4760, Fax: 216-687-5448, E-mail: s.misra@csuohio.edu. *Application contact:* 216-687-4760, Fax: 216-687-9354, E-mail: s.misra@csuohio.edu.
Website: http://cis.csuohio.edu/.

Coleman University, Program in Information Technology, San Diego, CA 92123. Offers MSIT. Evening/weekend programs available. *Entrance requirements:* For master's, bachelor's degree in computer field, minimum GPA of 3.0. Additional exam requirements/recommendations for international students: Required—TOEFL (minimum score 500 paper-based).

The College of Saint Rose, Graduate Studies, School of Mathematics and Sciences, Program in Computer Information Systems, Albany, NY 12203-1419. Offers MS. Part-time and evening/weekend programs available. *Degree requirements:* For master's, comprehensive exam, research component. *Entrance requirements:* For master's, minimum GPA of 3.0, 9 undergraduate credits in math. Additional exam requirements/recommendations for international students: Required—TOEFL (minimum score 550 paper-based). Electronic applications accepted.

Cornell University, Graduate School, Graduate Fields of Arts and Sciences, Field of Information Science, Ithaca, NY 14853-0001. Offers cognition (PhD); human computer interaction (PhD); information science (PhD); information systems (PhD); social aspects of information (PhD). *Degree requirements:* For doctorate, comprehensive exam, thesis/dissertation. *Entrance requirements:* For doctorate, GRE General Test, 3 letters of recommendation. Additional exam requirements/recommendations for international students: Required—TOEFL (minimum score 550 paper-based; 77 iBT). Electronic applications accepted. *Faculty research:* Digital libraries, game theory, data mining, human-computer interaction, computational linguistics.

Dakota State University, College of Business and Information Systems, Madison, SD 57042-1799. Offers applied computer science (MSACS); general management (MBA); health informatics (MSHI); information assurance (MSIA); information systems (MSIS, D Sc IS). *Accreditation:* ACBSP. Part-time and evening/weekend programs available. Postbaccalaureate distance learning degree programs offered (minimal on-campus study). *Faculty:* 25 full-time (6 women), 1 part-time/adjunct (0 women). *Students:* 84 full-time (16 women), 165 part-time (45 women); includes 48 minority (17 Black or African American, non-Hispanic/Latino; 3 American Indian or Alaska Native, non-Hispanic/Latino; 17 Asian, non-Hispanic/Latino; 3 Hispanic/Latino; 1 Native Hawaiian or other Pacific Islander, non-Hispanic/Latino; 7 Two or more races, non-Hispanic/Latino), 76 international. Average age 35. 236 applicants, 65% accepted, 100 enrolled. In 2014, 58 master's, 7 doctorates, 4 other advanced degrees awarded. *Degree requirements:* For master's, comprehensive exam, thesis optional, examination, integrative project; for doctorate, comprehensive exam, thesis/dissertation, portfolio. *Entrance requirements:* For master's, GRE General Test, demonstration of information systems skills, minimum

GPA of 2.7; for doctorate, GRE General Test, demonstration of information systems skills; for Graduate Certificate, GMAT, MBA. Additional exam requirements/recommendations for international students: Required—TOEFL (minimum score 550 paper-based; 79 iBT), IELTS (minimum score 6.5). *Application deadline:* For fall admission, 6/15 for domestic and international students; for spring admission, 11/15 for domestic and international students; for summer admission, 4/15 for domestic and international students. Applications are processed on a rolling basis. Application fee: $35. *Expenses: Tuition,* state resident: full-time $3633; part-time $201.85 per credit hour. Tuition, nonresident: full-time $7691; part-time $427.30 per credit hour. *Required fees:* $2108; $117.10 per credit hour. Tuition and fees vary according to course load, campus/location, program and reciprocity agreements. *Financial support:* In 2014–15, 32 students received support, including 18 fellowships with partial tuition reimbursements available (averaging $13,344 per year), 13 research assistantships with partial tuition reimbursements available (averaging $32,782 per year), 1 teaching assistantship with partial tuition reimbursement available (averaging $10,927 per year); Federal Work-Study, scholarships/grants, and unspecified assistantships also available. Support available to part-time students. Financial award applicants required to submit FAFSA. *Faculty research:* Data mining and data warehousing, effectiveness of hybrid learning environments, biometrics and information assurance, decision support systems, analytics, health informatics. *Unit head:* Dr. Omar El-Gayar, Dean of Graduate Studies and Research, 605-256-5799, Fax: 605-256-5093, E-mail: omar.el-gayar@dsu.edu. *Application contact:* Erin Blankespoor, Secretary, Office of Graduate Studies and Research, 605-256-5799, Fax: 605-256-5093, E-mail: erin.blankespoor@dsu.edu.
Website: http://dsu.edu/graduate-students.

DePaul University, College of Computing and Digital Media, Chicago, IL 60604. Offers animation (MA, MFA); business information technology (MS); cinema (MFA); cinema production (MS); computational finance (MS); computer and information sciences (PhD); computer game development (MS); computer information and network security (MS); computer science (MS); e-commerce technology (MS); health informatics (MS); human-computer interaction (MS); information systems (MS); information technology project management (MS); network engineering and management (MS); predictive analytics (MS); screenwriting (MFA); software engineering (MS); JD/MS. Part-time and evening/weekend programs available. Postbaccalaureate distance learning degree programs offered (no on-campus study). *Degree requirements:* For master's, thesis (for some programs); for doctorate, comprehensive exam, thesis/dissertation. *Entrance requirements:* For master's, GRE or GMAT (for MS in computational finance only), bachelor's degree, resume (MS in predictive analytics only), IT experience (MS in information technology project management only), portfolio review (all MFA programs and MA in animation); for doctorate, GRE, master's degree in computer science. Additional exam requirements/recommendations for international students: Required—TOEFL (minimum score 590 paper-based; 80 iBT), IELTS (minimum score 6.5), PTE (minimum score 53). Electronic applications accepted. *Expenses:* Contact institution. *Faculty research:* Data mining, computer science, human-computer interaction, security, animation and film.

DeSales University, Graduate Division, Division of Healthcare and Natural Sciences, Program in Information Systems, Center Valley, PA 18034-9568. Offers MSIS. Part-time programs available. *Students:* 32 part-time. *Degree requirements:* For master's, comprehensive exam, thesis optional. *Entrance requirements:* Additional exam requirements/recommendations for international students: Required—TOEFL. *Application deadline:* Applications are processed on a rolling basis. Application fee: $35. Electronic applications accepted. *Financial support:* Applicants required to submit FAFSA. *Faculty research:* Digital communication, numerical analysis, database design. *Unit head:* Dr. Daniel Wisniewski, Department Chair of Mathematics and Computer Science, 610-282-1100 Ext. 1269, E-mail: daniel.wisniewski@desales.edu. *Application contact:* Abigail Wernicki, Director of Graduate Admissions, 610-282-1100 Ext. 1768, Fax: 610-282-2869, E-mail: gradadmissions@desales.edu.

Drexel University, College of Computing and Informatics, Master of Science in Library and Information Science Program, Philadelphia, PA 19104-2875. Offers competitive intelligence and knowledge management (MS); school library media (MS). Part-time and evening/weekend programs available. Postbaccalaureate distance learning degree programs offered (no on-campus study). *Faculty:* 15 full-time (14 women), 2 part-time/adjunct (both women). *Students:* 68 full-time (55 women), 264 part-time (215 women); includes 50 minority (14 Black or African American, non-Hispanic/Latino; 7 Asian, non-Hispanic/Latino; 15 Hispanic/Latino; 14 Two or more races, non-Hispanic/Latino), 9 international. Average age 34. 223 applicants, 88% accepted, 101 enrolled. In 2014, 207 master's awarded. *Entrance requirements:* For master's, GRE General Test. Additional exam requirements/recommendations for international students: Required—TOEFL (minimum score 600 paper-based; 100 iBT). *Application deadline:* For fall admission, 8/22 for domestic students, 8/1 for international students; for spring admission, 3/4 for domestic students, 2/1 for international students. Applications are processed on a rolling basis. Application fee: $0. Electronic applications accepted. *Financial support:* In 2014–15, 87 students received support. Institutionally sponsored loans, scholarships/grants, and tuition waivers (partial) available. Support available to part-time students. Financial award application deadline: 3/1; financial award applicants required to submit FAFSA. *Faculty research:* Library and information resources and services, knowledge organization and representation, information retrieval/information visualization/bibliometrics, information needs and behaviors, digital libraries. *Unit head:* Dr. Spiros Mancoridis, Dean/Professor of Information Science, 215-895-6824, Fax: 215-895-0545, E-mail: spiros@drexel.edu. *Application contact:* Matthew Lechtenberg, Graduate Admissions Manager, 215-895-1951, Fax: 215-895-2303, E-mail: ml333@drexel.edu.
Website: http://drexel.edu/cci/programs/graduate-programs/ms-in-library-and-information-science/.

Drexel University, College of Computing and Informatics, PhD in Information Studies, Philadelphia, PA 19104-2875. Offers PhD. Part-time and evening/weekend programs available. *Faculty:* 18 full-time (10 women). *Students:* 37 full-time (19 women), 8 part-time (5 women); includes 5 minority (2 Black or African American, non-Hispanic/Latino; 3 Asian, non-Hispanic/Latino), 23 international. Average age 32. 41 applicants, 46% accepted, 12 enrolled. In 2014, 11 doctorates awarded. *Degree requirements:* For doctorate, thesis/dissertation. *Entrance requirements:* For doctorate, GRE General Test. Additional exam requirements/recommendations for international students: Required—TOEFL (minimum score 600 paper-based; 100 iBT). *Application deadline:* For fall admission, 2/1 for domestic and international students. Applications are processed on a rolling basis. Application fee: $0. Electronic applications accepted. *Financial support:* In 2014–15, 35 students received support, including 20 research assistantships with full tuition reimbursements available (averaging $22,500 per year), 12 teaching assistantships with full tuition reimbursements available (averaging $22,500 per year); career-related internships or fieldwork, institutionally sponsored loans, scholarships/grants, traineeships, health care benefits, tuition waivers (partial), and unspecified assistantships also available. Financial award application deadline: 2/1; financial award applicants required to submit FAFSA. *Faculty research:* Information retrieval/information visualization/bibliometrics, human-computer interaction, digital libraries, databases, text/data mining, healthcare informatics, school library media, social media, information behavior, information ethics, information policy and archives. *Unit head:* Dr. Sprios

Mancoridis, Interim Dean/Professor of Computer Science, 215-895-6824, Fax: 215-895-0545, E-mail: sprios@drexel.edu. *Application contact:* Matthew Lechtenberg, Graduate Admissions Manager, 215-895-1951, Fax: 215-895-2303, E-mail: ml333@drexel.edu.

East Tennessee State University, School of Graduate Studies, College of Business and Technology, Department of Computing, Johnson City, TN 37614. Offers MS, Postbaccalaureate Certificate. Part-time and evening/weekend programs available. *Faculty:* 15 full-time (3 women). *Students:* 33 full-time (4 women), 8 part-time (1 woman); includes 6 minority (2 Black or African American, non-Hispanic/Latino; 1 Asian, non-Hispanic/Latino; 2 Hispanic/Latino; 1 Two or more races, non-Hispanic/Latino), 9 international. Average age 30. 69 applicants, 39% accepted, 15 enrolled. In 2014, 13 master's awarded. *Degree requirements:* For master's, comprehensive exam, thesis optional, capstone. *Entrance requirements:* For master's, GRE General Test, minimum GPA of 2.5, three letters of recommendation. Additional exam requirements/recommendations for international students: Required—TOEFL (minimum score 550 paper-based; 79 iBT). *Application deadline:* For fall admission, 6/1 for domestic students, 4/30 for international students; for spring admission, 11/1 for domestic students, 9/30 for international students. Application fee: $35 ($45 for international students). Electronic applications accepted. *Financial support:* In 2014–15, 27 students received support, including 14 research assistantships with full tuition reimbursements available (averaging $9,000 per year), 16 teaching assistantships with full and partial tuition reimbursements available (averaging $9,300 per year); career-related internships or fieldwork, institutionally sponsored loans, scholarships/grants, and unspecified assistantships also available. Financial award application deadline: 7/1; financial award applicants required to submit FAFSA. *Faculty research:* Data mining, security and forensics, numerical optimization, computer gaming, enterprise resource planning. *Unit head:* Dr. Terry Countermine, Chair, 423-439-5328, Fax: 423-439-7119, E-mail: counter@etsu.edu. *Application contact:* Kimberly Brockman, Graduate Specialist, 423-439-6165, Fax: 423-439-5624, E-mail: brockmank@etsu.edu.
Website: http://www-cs.etsu.edu/.

Everglades University, Graduate Programs, Program in Information Technology, Boca Raton, FL 33431. Offers MIT. *Entrance requirements:* Additional exam requirements/recommendations for international students: Recommended—TOEFL (minimum score 500 paper-based). Electronic applications accepted.

Florida Gulf Coast University, Lutgert College of Business, Program in Computer and Information Systems, Fort Myers, FL 33965-6565. Offers MS. *Faculty:* 55 full-time (17 women), 24 part-time/adjunct (7 women). *Students:* 2 part-time (0 women). Average age 32. *Entrance requirements:* For master's, GMAT, minimum GPA of 3.0. Additional exam requirements/recommendations for international students: Required—TOEFL (minimum score 550 paper-based). *Application deadline:* For fall admission, 6/1 priority date for domestic students; for spring admission, 11/1 for domestic students. Applications are processed on a rolling basis. Application fee: $30. Electronic applications accepted. *Expenses:* Tuition, state resident: full-time $6974. Tuition, nonresident: full-time $28,170. *Required fees:* $1987. Tuition and fees vary according to course load. *Financial support:* Application deadline: 6/30; applicants required to submit FAFSA. *Faculty research:* Advanced distributed learning technologies, object-oriented systems analysis, database management systems, workgroup support systems, software engineering project management. *Unit head:* Dr. Rajesh Srivastava, Chair, 239-590-7372, Fax: 239-590-7330, E-mail: rsrivast@fgcu.edu. *Application contact:* Marisa Ouverson, Director of Enrollment Management, 239-590-7403, Fax: 239-590-7330, E-mail: mouverso@fgcu.edu.

Florida International University, College of Engineering and Computing, School of Computing and Information Sciences, Miami, FL 33199. Offers computer science (MS, PhD); information technology (MS); telecommunications and networking (MS). Part-time and evening/weekend programs available. *Degree requirements:* For master's, thesis or alternative; for doctorate, comprehensive exam, thesis/dissertation. *Entrance requirements:* For master's and doctorate, GRE General Test, 3 letters of recommendation, minimum GPA of 3.0. Additional exam requirements/recommendations for international students: Required—TOEFL (minimum score 550 paper-based; 80 iBT). Electronic applications accepted. *Faculty research:* Database systems, software engineering, operating systems, networks, bioinformatics and computational biology.

Gannon University, School of Graduate Studies, College of Engineering and Business, School of Engineering and Computer Science, Program in Computer and Information Science, Erie, PA 16541-0001. Offers applied computer science (MSCIS); information systems (MSCIS); Web development (MSCIS). Part-time and evening/weekend programs available. *Degree requirements:* For master's, thesis (for some programs), directed research. *Entrance requirements:* For master's, GRE or GMAT, letters of recommendation, resume, transcripts, baccalaureate degree in computer and information science or related field, minimum GPA of 2.5. Additional exam requirements/recommendations for international students: Required—TOEFL (minimum score 79 iBT). Electronic applications accepted.

Gannon University, School of Graduate Studies, College of Engineering and Business, School of Engineering and Computer Science, Program in Information Analytics, Erie, PA 16541-0001. Offers MSCIS. Part-time and evening/weekend programs available. Electronic applications accepted.

George Mason University, College of Humanities and Social Sciences, Department of History and Art History, Program in History, Fairfax, VA 22030. Offers history (MA); new media and information technology (PhD); public and applied history (PhD). *Faculty:* 45 full-time (18 women), 8 part-time/adjunct (4 women). *Students:* 66 full-time (32 women), 136 part-time (58 women); includes 19 minority (4 Black or African American, non-Hispanic/Latino; 3 Asian, non-Hispanic/Latino; 9 Hispanic/Latino; 3 Two or more races, non-Hispanic/Latino), 4 international. Average age 36. 145 applicants, 54% accepted, 42 enrolled. In 2014, 42 master's, 4 doctorates awarded. *Degree requirements:* For master's, comprehensive exam, translation language exam; for doctorate, comprehensive exam, thesis/dissertation. *Entrance requirements:* For master's, GRE (waived for students who received their undergraduate degree 10 or more years ago or hold another graduate degree), expanded goals statement; 2 letters of recommendation; resume; official transcript; for doctorate, GRE, expanded goals statement; 3 letters of recommendation; writing sample; official transcripts. Additional exam requirements/recommendations for international students: Required—TOEFL (minimum score 570 paper-based; 80 iBT), IELTS (minimum score 6.5), PTE. *Application deadline:* For fall admission, 3/15 priority date for domestic students; for spring admission, 11/1 priority date for domestic students. Application fee: $65 ($80 for international students). Electronic applications accepted. *Expenses:* Tuition, state resident: full-time $9794; part-time $408 per credit hour. Tuition, nonresident: full-time $26,978; part-time $1124 per credit hour. *Required fees:* $2820; $118 per credit hour. Tuition and fees vary according to course load and program. *Financial support:* In 2014–15, 31 students received support, including 2 fellowships with full tuition reimbursements available (averaging $7,151 per year), 16 research assistantships with full and partial tuition reimbursements available (averaging $17,210 per year), 14 teaching assistantships with full and partial tuition reimbursements available (averaging $14,330 per year); career-related internships or fieldwork, Federal Work-Study, scholarships/grants, unspecified assistantships, and health care benefits (for full-time research or teaching assistantship

recipients) also available. Support available to part-time students. Financial award application deadline: 3/1; financial award applicants required to submit FAFSA. *Faculty research:* History and new media, American history (digital), building digital archives in the 1930's. *Unit head:* Randolph Scully, History Program Director, 703-993-1259, Fax: 703-993-1251, E-mail: rscully@gmu.edu. *Application contact:* Nicole Anne Roth, Graduate Program Coordinator, 703-993-1248, Fax: 703-993-1251, E-mail: nroth@gmu.edu.
Website: http://historyarthistory.gmu.edu/programs/la-ma-hist.

George Mason University, Volgenau School of Engineering, Department of Information Sciences and Technology, Fairfax, VA 22030. Offers applied information technology (MS); information sciences and technology (Certificate). *Faculty:* 20 full-time (5 women), 63 part-time/adjunct (12 women). *Students:* 54 full-time (19 women), 99 part-time (27 women); includes 68 minority (7 Black or African American, non-Hispanic/Latino; 47 Asian, non-Hispanic/Latino; 11 Hispanic/Latino; 1 Native Hawaiian or other Pacific Islander, non-Hispanic/Latino; 2 Two or more races, non-Hispanic/Latino), 18 international. Average age 30. 101 applicants, 68% accepted, 47 enrolled. In 2014, 65 master's, 2 other advanced degrees awarded. *Degree requirements:* For master's, capstone course. *Entrance requirements:* For master's, GRE/GMAT, personal goals statement; 2 copies of official transcripts; 3 letters of recommendation; resume; official bank statement; proof of financial support; photocopy of passport; baccalaureate degree from an accredited program with minimum B average in last 60 credit hours. Additional exam requirements/recommendations for international students: Required—TOEFL (minimum score 575 paper-based; 80 iBT), IELTS (minimum score 6.5), PTE. *Application deadline:* For fall admission, 1/15 priority date for domestic students; for spring admission, 8/15 priority date for domestic students. Application fee: $65 ($80 for international students). Electronic applications accepted. *Expenses:* Expenses: Contact institution. *Financial support:* In 2014–15, 7 students received support, including 1 research assistantship (averaging $13,500 per year), 6 teaching assistantships with full and partial tuition reimbursements available (averaging $10,711 per year); career-related internships or fieldwork, Federal Work-Study, scholarships/grants, unspecified assistantships, and health care benefits (for full-time research or teaching assistantship recipients) also available. Support available to part-time students. Financial award application deadline: 3/1; financial award applicants required to submit FAFSA. *Faculty research:* Secure information systems, document forensics, IT entrepreneurship, learning agents. *Total annual research expenditures:* $66,808. *Unit head:* Aditya Johri, Chair, 703-993-5397, Fax: 703-993-2972, E-mail: ajohri3@gmu.edu. *Application contact:* Krystal Dains, Academic Advisor, 703-993-2799, Fax: 703-993-8450, E-mail: kdains@gmu.edu.
Website: http://ist.gmu.edu.

George Mason University, Volgenau School of Engineering, Program in Data Analytics Engineering, Fairfax, VA 22030. Offers MS. *Expenses:* Tuition, state resident: full-time $9794; part-time $408 per credit hour. Tuition, nonresident: full-time $26,978; part-time $1124 per credit hour. *Required fees:* $2820; $118 per credit hour. Tuition and fees vary according to course load and program. *Unit head:* Kenneth S. Ball, Dean, 703-993-1498, Fax: 703-993-1734, E-mail: vsdean@gmu.edu. *Application contact:* Jade T. Perez, Director, Graduate Services, 703-993-2426, E-mail: jperezc@gmu.edu.

George Mason University, Volgenau School of Engineering, Program in Information Technology, Fairfax, VA 22030. Offers PhD. *Faculty:* 40 full-time (9 women), 17 part-time/adjunct (0 women). *Students:* 42 full-time (12 women), 53 part-time (8 women); includes 16 minority (4 Black or African American, non-Hispanic/Latino; 10 Asian, non-Hispanic/Latino; 2 Hispanic/Latino), 32 international. Average age 38. 64 applicants, 28% accepted, 7 enrolled. In 2014, 18 doctorates awarded. *Degree requirements:* For doctorate, comprehensive exam, thesis/dissertation, internship. *Entrance requirements:* For doctorate, GRE, MS and BS in a related field; 2 official copies of transcripts; 3 letters of recommendation; resume; expanded goals statement; self assessment. Additional exam requirements/recommendations for international students: Required—TOEFL (minimum score 575 paper-based; 80 iBT), IELTS (minimum score 6.5), PTE. *Application deadline:* For fall admission, 1/1 priority date for domestic students; for spring admission, 8/1 priority date for domestic students. Application fee: $65 ($80 for international students). Electronic applications accepted. *Expenses:* Expenses: Contact institution. *Financial support:* In 2014–15, 23 students received support, including 1 fellowship (averaging $9,302 per year), 4 research assistantships with full and partial tuition reimbursements available (averaging $16,250 per year), 15 teaching assistantships with full and partial tuition reimbursements available (averaging $16,772 per year); career-related internships or fieldwork, Federal Work-Study, scholarships/grants, unspecified assistantships, and health care benefits (for full-time research or teaching assistantship recipients) also available. Support available to part-time students. Financial award application deadline: 3/1; financial award applicants required to submit FAFSA. *Faculty research:* Rapid pace of technological innovation, need for efficient and effective technology development, unwavering interoperability challenges, the scope and complexity of major system design requirements. *Unit head:* Stephen Nash, Senior Associate Dean, 703-993-1505, Fax: 703-993-1633, E-mail: snash@gmu.edu. *Application contact:* Lisa Nolder, Director of Graduate Student Services, 703-993-1499, Fax: 703-993-1633, E-mail: snolder@gmu.edu.
Website: http://volgenau.gmu.edu/students/graduates/phd-in-information-technology.

Georgia State University, J. Mack Robinson College of Business, Department of Computer Information Systems, Atlanta, GA 30302-3083. Offers computer information systems (PhD); health informatics (MBA, MS); information systems (MSIS, Certificate); information systems development and project management (MBA); information systems management (MBA); managing information technology (Exec MS); the wireless organization (MBA). Part-time and evening/weekend programs available. *Faculty:* 15 full-time (2 women). *Students:* 123 full-time (48 women), 4 part-time (2 women); includes 44 minority (24 Black or African American, non-Hispanic/Latino; 18 Asian, non-Hispanic/Latino; 2 Two or more races, non-Hispanic/Latino), 59 international. Average age 30. 354 applicants, 55% accepted, 91 enrolled. In 2014, 61 master's, 1 doctorate awarded. *Degree requirements:* For master's, thesis optional; for doctorate, comprehensive exam, thesis/dissertation. *Entrance requirements:* For master's, GRE or GMAT, transcripts from all institutions attended, resume, essays; for doctorate, GRE or GMAT, three letters of recommendation, personal statement, transcripts from all institutions attended, resume. Additional exam requirements/recommendations for international students: Required—TOEFL (minimum score 610 paper-based; 101 iBT), IELTS (minimum score 7). *Application deadline:* For fall admission, 5/1 priority date for domestic students, 2/1 priority date for international students; for spring admission, 9/15 priority date for domestic students, 4/1 priority date for international students. Applications are processed on a rolling basis. Application fee: $50. Electronic applications accepted. *Expenses:* Tuition, state resident: full-time $6516; part-time $362 per credit hour. Tuition, nonresident: full-time $22,014; part-time $1223 per credit hour. *Required fees:* $2128 per semester. Tuition and fees vary according to course load and program. *Financial support:* Research assistantships, teaching assistantships, scholarships/grants, tuition waivers, and unspecified assistantships available. *Faculty research:* Process and technological innovation, strategic IT management, intelligent systems, information systems security, software project risk. *Unit head:* Dr. Ephraim R. McLean, Professor/Chair, 404-413-7360, Fax: 404-413-7394. *Application contact:* Toby

McChesney, Assistant Dean for Graduate Recruiting and Student Services, 404-413-7167, Fax: 404-413-7167, E-mail: rcbgradadmissions@gsu.edu. Website: http://cis.robinson.gsu.edu/.

Grand Valley State University, Padnos College of Engineering and Computing, School of Computing and Information Systems, Allendale, MI 49401-9403. Offers computer information systems (MS), including databases, distributed systems, management of information systems, object-oriented systems, software engineering. Part-time and evening/weekend programs available. *Faculty:* 8 full-time (0 women). *Students:* 26 full-time (10 women), 57 part-time (12 women); includes 10 minority (7 Asian, non-Hispanic/Latino; 3 Hispanic/Latino), 21 international. Average age 32. 44 applicants, 82% accepted, 18 enrolled. In 2014, 29 master's awarded. *Degree requirements:* For master's, thesis or alternative. *Entrance requirements:* For master's, GMAT or GRE General Test. Additional exam requirements/recommendations for international students: Required—TOEFL. *Application deadline:* For fall admission, 6/1 for international students; for winter admission, 9/1 for international students. Applications are processed on a rolling basis. Application fee: $30. Electronic applications accepted. *Expenses:* Tuition, state resident: full-time $10,602; part-time $589 per credit hour. Tuition, nonresident: full-time $14,022; part-time $779 per credit hour. Tuition and fees vary according to degree level and program. *Financial support:* In 2014–15, 17 students received support, including 10 fellowships (averaging $1,856 per year), 7 research assistantships with full and partial tuition reimbursements available (averaging $10,134 per year). *Faculty research:* Object technology, distributed computing, information systems management database, software engineering. *Unit head:* Paul Leidig, Director, 616-331-2038, Fax: 616-331-2106, E-mail: leidigp@gvsu.edu. *Application contact:* D. Robert Adams, Graduate Program Chair, 616-331-3885, Fax: 616-331-2106, E-mail: adams@cis.gvsu.edu.
Website: http://www.cis.gvsu.edu/.

Harvard University, Extension School, Cambridge, MA 02138-3722. Offers applied sciences (CAS); biotechnology (ALM); educational technologies (ALM); educational technology (CET); English for graduate and professional studies (DGP); environmental management (ALM, CEM); information technology (ALM); journalism (ALM); liberal arts (ALM); management (ALM, CM); mathematics for teaching (ALM); museum studies (ALM); premedical studies (Diploma); publication and communication (CPC). Part-time and evening/weekend programs available. *Degree requirements:* For master's, thesis. *Entrance requirements:* For master's, 3 completed graduate courses with grade of B or higher. Additional exam requirements/recommendations for international students: Required—TOEFL (minimum score 600 paper-based), TWE (minimum score 5). *Expenses:* Contact institution.

Harvard University, Graduate School of Arts and Sciences, Program in Information, Technology and Management, Cambridge, MA 02138. Offers PhD.

Hood College, Graduate School, Program in Management of Information Technology, Frederick, MD 21701-8575. Offers MS. Part-time and evening/weekend programs available. *Degree requirements:* For master's, thesis. *Entrance requirements:* For master's, minimum GPA of 2.75. Additional exam requirements/recommendations for international students: Required—TOEFL (minimum score 575 paper-based; 89 iBT), IELTS (minimum score 6.5). Electronic applications accepted. Application fee is waived when completed online. *Faculty research:* Systems engineering, parallel distributed computing, strategy, business ethics, entrepreneurship.

Hood College, Graduate School, Programs in Computer and Information Sciences, Frederick, MD 21701-8575. Offers computer and information sciences (MS); computer science (MS); information security (Certificate). Part-time and evening/weekend programs available. *Degree requirements:* For master's, thesis. *Entrance requirements:* For master's, minimum GPA of 2.75. Additional exam requirements/recommendations for international students: Required—TOEFL (minimum score 575 paper-based; 89 iBT), IELTS (minimum score 6.5). Electronic applications accepted. Application fee is waived when completed online. *Faculty research:* Systems engineering, natural language, processing, database design, artificial intelligence and parallel distributed computing.

Indiana University Bloomington, School of Informatics and Computing, Department of Information and Library Science, Bloomington, IN 47405-3907. Offers information science (MIS, PhD); library and information science (Sp LIS); library science (MLS); JD/MLS; MIS/MA; MLS/MA; MPA/MIS; MPA/MLS. *Accreditation:* ALA (one or more programs are accredited). Part-time programs available. *Faculty:* 16 full-time (7 women). *Students:* 136 full-time (83 women), 49 part-time (36 women); includes 21 minority (6 Black or African American, non-Hispanic/Latino; 8 Asian, non-Hispanic/Latino; 2 Hispanic/Latino; 5 Two or more races, non-Hispanic/Latino), 31 international. Average age 29. 192 applicants, 84% accepted, 53 enrolled. In 2014, 107 master's, 3 doctorates, 2 other advanced degrees awarded. *Degree requirements:* For doctorate, thesis/dissertation. *Entrance requirements:* For master's and doctorate, GRE General Test, 3 letters of reference. Additional exam requirements/recommendations for international students: Required—TOEFL (minimum score 600 paper-based; 100 iBT). *Application deadline:* For fall admission, 5/15 priority date for domestic students, 12/1 priority date for international students; for spring admission, 10/15 priority date for domestic students, 9/1 priority date for international students. Applications are processed on a rolling basis. Application fee: $55 ($65 for international students). Electronic applications accepted. *Expenses:* Expenses: Contact institution. *Financial support:* Fellowships with full and partial tuition reimbursements, research assistantships with full and partial tuition reimbursements, career-related internships or fieldwork, Federal Work-Study, institutionally sponsored loans, scholarships/grants, tuition waivers (partial), and unspecified assistantships available. Support available to part-time students. Financial award application deadline: 1/15. *Faculty research:* Scholarly communication, interface design, library and management policy, computer-mediated communication, information retrieval. *Unit head:* Dr. Howard Rosenbaum, Associate Dean for Graduate Studies, 812-855-3250, E-mail: hrosenba@indiana.edu. *Application contact:* Rhonda Spencer, Director of Admissions, 812-855-2018, Fax: 812-855-6166, E-mail: slis@indiana.edu.
Website: http://ils.indiana.edu/.

Indiana University Bloomington, School of Informatics and Computing, Program in Informatics, Bloomington, IN 47408. Offers informatics (MS, PhD), including bioinformatics, cheminformatics (PhD), complex systems (PhD), health informatics (PhD), human-computer interaction (MS), human-computer interaction design (PhD), logic and mathematical foundations of informatics (PhD), music informatics (PhD), robotics (PhD), security informatics, social informatics (PhD). Part-time programs available. *Students:* 206 full-time (78 women), 7 part-time (1 woman); includes 25 minority (9 Black or African American, non-Hispanic/Latino; 12 Asian, non-Hispanic/Latino; 2 Hispanic/Latino; 2 Two or more races, non-Hispanic/Latino), 101 international. 287 applicants, 52% accepted, 65 enrolled. In 2014, 65 master's, 13 doctorates awarded. Terminal master's awarded for partial completion of doctoral program. *Degree requirements:* For master's, thesis; for doctorate, thesis/dissertation. *Entrance requirements:* For master's and doctorate, GRE, TOEFL if international and no US degree. Additional exam requirements/recommendations for international students: Required—TOEFL (minimum score 600 paper-based; 100 iBT). *Application deadline:* For fall admission, 12/1 priority date for domestic and international students. Application fee: $55 ($65 for international students). Electronic applications accepted. *Financial*

support: Application deadline: 12/1. *Unit head:* Dr. Howard Rosenbaum, Associate Dean for Graduate Studies, 812-855-3250, E-mail: hrosenba@indiana.edu. *Application contact:* Patty Reyes-Cooksey, Director of Graduate Administration, 812-856-3622, E-mail: patreyes@indiana.edu.
Website: http://www.soic.indiana.edu/informatics/index.shtml.

Indiana University–Purdue University Fort Wayne, College of Engineering, Technology, and Computer Science, Program in Technology, Fort Wayne, IN 46805-1499. Offers industrial technology/manufacturing (MS); information technology/advanced computer applications (MS). Part-time programs available. *Faculty:* 14 full-time (5 women). *Students:* 4 full-time (2 women), 8 part-time (2 women); includes 3 minority (2 Black or African American, non-Hispanic/Latino; 1 American Indian or Alaska Native, non-Hispanic/Latino), 4 international. Average age 34. 7 applicants, 100% accepted, 5 enrolled. In 2014, 11 master's awarded. *Entrance requirements:* For master's, minimum GPA of 3.0. Additional exam requirements/recommendations for international students: Required—TOEFL (minimum score 550 paper-based; 79 iBT), TWE. *Application deadline:* For fall admission, 7/15 for domestic students, 5/15 for international students; for spring admission, 12/1 for domestic students, 10/15 for international students. Applications are processed on a rolling basis. Application fee: $55 ($60 for international students). Electronic applications accepted. *Financial support:* In 2014–15, 2 teaching assistantships with partial tuition reimbursements (averaging $13,522 per year) were awarded; career-related internships or fieldwork, scholarships/grants, and unspecified assistantships also available. Support available to part-time students. Financial award application deadline: 3/1; financial award applicants required to submit FAFSA. *Unit head:* Dr. Max Yen, Dean, 260-481-6839, Fax: 260-481-5734, E-mail: yens@ipfw.edu. *Application contact:* Dr. Ali Alavizadeh, Director, 260-481-0234, Fax: 260-481-5734, E-mail: alavizaa@ipfw.edu.
Website: http://www.ipfw.edu/etcs.

Indiana University–Purdue University Indianapolis, School of Informatics and Computing, Department of Information and Library Science, Indianapolis, IN 46202. Offers MLS. Part-time and evening/weekend programs available. *Faculty:* 3 full-time (2 women). *Students:* 53 full-time (42 women), 131 part-time (108 women); includes 9 minority (3 Black or African American, non-Hispanic/Latino; 3 Hispanic/Latino; 3 Two or more races, non-Hispanic/Latino). Average age 34. 78 applicants, 90% accepted, 59 enrolled. In 2014, 55 master's awarded. *Entrance requirements:* For master's, GRE General Test. Additional exam requirements/recommendations for international students: Required—TOEFL (minimum score 600 paper-based). *Application deadline:* For fall admission, 7/15 priority date for domestic students; for spring admission, 11/15 priority date for domestic students. Applications are processed on a rolling basis. Application fee: $55 ($65 for international students). *Financial support:* Teaching assistantships, career-related internships or fieldwork, Federal Work-Study, institutionally sponsored loans, and scholarships/grants available. Support available to part-time students. *Unit head:* Dr. Rachel Applegate, Chair, 317-278-2395, E-mail: rapplega@iupui.edu. *Application contact:* Elizabeth Bunge, Graduate Admissions Coordinator, 317-278-9200, E-mail: ebunge@iupui.edu.
Website: http://soic.iupui.edu/departments/lis/.

Instituto Tecnologico de Santo Domingo, Graduate School, Area of Engineering, Santo Domingo, Dominican Republic. Offers construction administration (MS, Certificate); data telecommunications (M Eng, MS, Certificate); industrial engineering (M Eng, Certificate); industrial management (M Mgmt); information technology (Certificate); maintenance engineering (M Eng); occupational hazard prevention (M Mgmt); production management (Certificate); quantitative methods (Certificate); sanitary and environmental engineering (M Eng); structural engineering (M Eng); systems engineering and electronic data processing (Certificate); transportation (Certificate).

Instituto Tecnológico y de Estudios Superiores de Monterrey, Campus Cuernavaca, Programs in Information Science, Temixco, Mexico. Offers administration of information technology (MATI); computer science (MCC, DCC); information technology (MTI).

Instituto Tecnológico y de Estudios Superiores de Monterrey, Campus Estado de México, Professional and Graduate Division, Estado de Mexico, Mexico. Offers administration of information technologies (MITA); architecture (M Arch); business administration (GMBA, MBA); computer sciences (MCS, PhD); education (M Ed); educational institution administration (MAD); educational technology and innovation (PhD); electronic commerce (MEC); environmental systems (MS); finance (MAF); humanistic studies (MHS); information sciences and knowledge management (MISKM); information systems (MS); manufacturing systems (MS); marketing (MEM); quality systems and productivity (MS); science and materials engineering (PhD); telecommunications management (MTM). Part-time programs available. Postbaccalaureate distance learning degree programs offered (minimal on-campus study). *Degree requirements:* For master's, one foreign language, thesis (for some programs); for doctorate, one foreign language, thesis/dissertation. *Entrance requirements:* For master's, E-PAEP 500, interview; for doctorate, E-PAEP 500, research proposal. Additional exam requirements/recommendations for international students: Required—TOEFL (minimum score 550 paper-based). *Faculty research:* Surface treatments by plasmas, mechanical properties, robotics, graphical computing, mechatronics security protocols.

Instituto Tecnológico y de Estudios Superiores de Monterrey, Campus Irapuato, Graduate Programs, Irapuato, Mexico. Offers administration (MBA); administration of information technology (MAIT); administration of telecommunications (MAT); architecture (M Arch); computer science (MCS); education (M Ed); educational administration (MEA); educational innovation and technology (DEIT); educational technology (MET); electronic commerce (MBA); environmental administration and planning (MEAP); environmental systems (MES); finances (MBA); humanistic studies (MHS); international management for Latin American executives (MIMLAE); library and information science (MLIS); manufacturing quality management (MMQM); marketing research (MBA).

Instituto Tecnológico y de Estudios Superiores de Monterrey, Campus Monterrey, Graduate and Research Division, Program in Computer Science, Monterrey, Mexico. Offers artificial intelligence (PhD); computer science (MS); information systems (MS); information technology (MS). Part-time programs available. *Degree requirements:* For master's, one foreign language, thesis; for doctorate, one foreign language, thesis/dissertation. *Entrance requirements:* For master's, EXADEP; for doctorate, master's degree in related field. Additional exam requirements/recommendations for international students: Required—TOEFL. *Faculty research:* Distributed systems, software engineering, decision support systems.

Instituto Tecnológico y de Estudios Superiores de Monterrey, Campus Monterrey, Graduate and Research Division, Program in Informatics, Monterrey, Mexico. Offers PhD. Part-time programs available. *Degree requirements:* For doctorate, one foreign language, thesis/dissertation, technological project, arbitrated publication of articles. *Entrance requirements:* For doctorate, GRE General Test, GRE Subject Test, master's degree in related field. Additional exam requirements/recommendations for international students: Required—TOEFL. *Faculty research:* Artificial intelligence, distributed systems, software engineering, decision support systems.

Instituto Tecnológico y de Estudios Superiores de Monterrey, Campus Sonora Norte, Program in Technological Information Management, Hermosillo, Mexico. Offers MA.

Iowa State University of Science and Technology, Program in Information Assurance, Ames, IA 50011. Offers MS. *Degree requirements:* For master's, thesis or alternative. *Entrance requirements:* For master's, GRE General Test. Additional exam requirements/recommendations for international students: Required—TOEFL (minimum score 570 paper-based; 79 iBT), IELTS (minimum score 6.5). Electronic applications accepted.

Johns Hopkins University, G. W. C. Whiting School of Engineering, Information Security Institute, Baltimore, MD 21218-2699. Offers MSSI. Part-time programs available. *Degree requirements:* For master's, 10 courses, capstone project. *Entrance requirements:* For master's, GRE, minimum GPA of 3.0. Additional exam requirements/recommendations for international students: Required—TOEFL. Electronic applications accepted. *Faculty research:* Critical infrastructure protection, cryptography, information security policy, computing privacy, system and software security, medical information security, computer forensics, application security, risk management.

Kansas State University, Graduate School, College of Engineering, Department of Computing and Information Sciences, Manhattan, KS 66506. Offers MS, MSE, PhD. Part-time programs available. Postbaccalaureate distance learning degree programs offered (no on-campus study). *Faculty:* 17 full-time (1 woman), 5 part-time/adjunct (2 women). *Students:* 63 full-time (20 women), 21 part-time (2 women); includes 6 minority (2 Black or African American, non-Hispanic/Latino; 1 American Indian or Alaska Native, non-Hispanic/Latino; 3 Asian, non-Hispanic/Latino), 53 international. Average age 28. 200 applicants, 28% accepted, 26 enrolled. In 2014, 28 master's, 7 doctorates awarded. Terminal master's awarded for partial completion of doctoral program. *Degree requirements:* For master's, thesis or alternative; for doctorate, thesis/dissertation. *Entrance requirements:* For master's, GRE General Test, bachelor's degree in computer science, minimum GPA of 3.0; for doctorate, GRE General Test, master's degree in computer science or bachelor's degree and strong advanced computer knowledge. Additional exam requirements/recommendations for international students: Required—TOEFL (minimum score 575 paper-based; 90 iBT), IELTS, or PTE. *Application deadline:* For fall admission, 2/1 priority date for domestic students, 1/1 priority date for international students; for spring admission, 9/1 priority date for domestic students, 8/1 priority date for international students. Applications are processed on a rolling basis. Application fee: $50 ($75 for international students). Electronic applications accepted. *Financial support:* In 2014–15, 23 research assistantships with tuition reimbursements (averaging $21,900 per year), 25 teaching assistantships with full tuition reimbursements (averaging $14,208 per year) were awarded; fellowships, career-related internships or fieldwork, institutionally sponsored loans, scholarships/grants, health care benefits, and unspecified assistantships also available. Support available to part-time students. Financial award application deadline: 3/15; financial award applicants required to submit FAFSA. *Faculty research:* High-assurance software and programming languages, data mining, parallel and distributed computing, computer security, embedded systems. *Total annual research expenditures:* $3.2 million. *Unit head:* Dr. Scott DeLoach, Interim Head, 785-532-6350, Fax: 785-532-7353, E-mail: sdeloach@ksu.edu. *Application contact:* Ami Ratzlaff, Program Coordinator, 785-532-6350, Fax: 785-532-7353, E-mail: cis-gradapps@ksu.edu.
Website: http://www.cis.k-state.edu/.

Kennesaw State University, Michael J. Coles College of Business, Program in Information Systems, Kennesaw, GA 30144. Offers MSIS. Part-time programs available. *Students:* 16 full-time (7 women), 34 part-time (14 women); includes 14 minority (9 Black or African American, non-Hispanic/Latino; 3 Asian, non-Hispanic/Latino; 2 Hispanic/Latino), 9 international. Average age 33. 34 applicants, 56% accepted, 15 enrolled. In 2014, 25 master's awarded. *Entrance requirements:* For master's, GMAT or GRE General Test, minimum GPA of 2.75. Additional exam requirements/recommendations for international students: Required—TOEFL (minimum score 550 paper-based; 80 iBT), IELTS (minimum score 6.5). *Application deadline:* For fall admission, 6/1 for domestic and international students; for spring admission, 11/1 for domestic and international students; for summer admission, 5/1 for domestic and international students. Applications are processed on a rolling basis. Application fee: $60. Electronic applications accepted. *Expenses:* Tuition, state resident: part-time $275 per semester hour. Tuition, nonresident: part-time $990 per semester hour. *Financial support:* In 2014–15, 2 research assistantships with full tuition reimbursements (averaging $8,000 per year) were awarded; Federal Work-Study and unspecified assistantships also available. Support available to part-time students. Financial award application deadline: 4/1; financial award applicants required to submit FAFSA. *Unit head:* Dr. Tridib Bandyopadhyay, Director, 470-578-2144, E-mail: tbandyop@kennesaw.edu. *Application contact:* Timothy Isles, Admissions Counselor, 470-578-4470, Fax: 770-578-9172, E-mail: ksugrad@kennesaw.edu.
Website: http://www.kennesaw.edu/.

Kent State University, College of Communication and Information, School of Library and Information Science, Kent, OH 44242-0001. Offers MLIS, MS, Certificate. *Accreditation:* ALA (one or more programs are accredited). Part-time and evening/weekend programs available. Postbaccalaureate distance learning degree programs offered. *Faculty:* 22 full-time (16 women). *Students:* 230 full-time (183 women), 583 part-time (439 women); includes 103 minority (42 Black or African American, non-Hispanic/Latino; 2 American Indian or Alaska Native, non-Hispanic/Latino; 9 Asian, non-Hispanic/Latino; 27 Hispanic/Latino; 23 Two or more races, non-Hispanic/Latino), 9 international. Average age 34. 652 applicants, 90% accepted, 445 enrolled. In 2014, 257 master's, 5 other advanced degrees awarded. *Degree requirements:* For master's, thesis, project, or internship; for Certificate, individual investigation. *Entrance requirements:* For master's, minimum GPA of 3.0, transcripts, goal statement, resume, 3 letters of recommendation; biographical sketch and interview (for MLIS). Additional exam requirements/recommendations for international students: Required—TOEFL (minimum score: paper-based 525, iBT 71), Michigan English Language Assessment Battery (minimum score of 75), IELTS (minimum score of 6.0), PTE Academic (minimum score of 48), or completion of ELS level 112 Intensive Program. *Application deadline:* For fall admission, 3/15 for domestic students; for spring admission, 9/15 for domestic students; for summer admission, 1/15 for domestic students. Application fee: $45 ($70 for international students). Electronic applications accepted. *Expenses:* Tuition, state resident: full-time $8730; part-time $485 per credit hour. Tuition, nonresident: full-time $14,886; part-time $827 per credit hour. Tuition and fees vary according to campus/location and program. *Financial support:* Research assistantships with full tuition reimbursements, teaching assistantships with full tuition reimbursements, career-related internships or fieldwork, Federal Work-Study, scholarships/grants, and unspecified assistantships available. Financial award application deadline: 2/1. *Unit head:* Jeff Fruit, Professor and Interim Director, 330-672-0890, E-mail: jfruit@kent.edu. *Application contact:* 330-672-2782, E-mail: slisinform@kent.edu.
Website: http://www.kent.edu/slis/.

Knowledge Systems Institute, Program in Computer and Information Sciences, Skokie, IL 60076. Offers MS. Part-time and evening/weekend programs available. Postbaccalaureate distance learning degree programs offered (minimal on-campus study). *Degree requirements:* For master's, comprehensive exam, thesis. *Entrance requirements:* Additional exam requirements/recommendations for international students: Required—TOEFL (minimum score 550 paper-based; 79 iBT). Electronic applications accepted. *Faculty research:* Data mining, web development, database programming and administration.

Lehigh University, College of Business and Economics, Department of Accounting, Bethlehem, PA 18015. Offers accounting and information analysis (MS). *Accreditation:* AACSB. *Faculty:* 9 full-time (3 women), 1 part-time/adjunct (0 women). *Students:* 84 full-time (65 women), 2 part-time (both women), 77 international. Average age 23. 150 applicants, 35% accepted, 19 enrolled. In 2014, 35 master's awarded. *Entrance requirements:* For master's, GMAT. Additional exam requirements/recommendations for international students: Required—TOEFL (minimum score 105 iBT). *Application deadline:* For fall admission, 2/28 for domestic and international students. Applications are processed on a rolling basis. Application fee: $100. Electronic applications accepted. *Expenses:* Expenses: $1,200 per credit. *Financial support:* In 2014–15, 10 research assistantships with partial tuition reimbursements (averaging $2,500 per year) were awarded; scholarships/grants and tuition waivers (partial) also available. Financial award application deadline: 1/15. *Faculty research:* Behavioral accounting, internal control, information systems, supply chain management, financial accounting. *Unit head:* Dr. Parveen Gupta, Chairman, 610-758-3443, Fax: 610-758-6429, E-mail: ppg0@lehigh.edu. *Application contact:* Michael Tarantino, Director of Recruitment and Admissions, 610-758-3418, Fax: 610-758-5283, E-mail: mgt215@lehigh.edu.
Website: http://www4.lehigh.edu/business/academics/depts/accounting.

Long Island University–LIU Post, College of Education, Information and Technology, Brookville, NY 11548-1300. Offers adolescence education (MS); art education (MS); childhood education (MS); childhood education literacy B-6 (MS); childhood/special education (MS); clinical mental health counseling (AC); early childhood education (MS); early childhood education/childhood education (MS); education (MS Ed); educational leadership (AC); educational technology (MS); information systems (MS); information technology education (MS); informational studies (PhD); public library administration (AC); student with disabilities, 7-12 generalist (AC); teaching students with speech language disabilities (MA). *Accreditation:* Teacher Education Accreditation Council. Part-time and evening/weekend programs available. *Faculty:* 62 full-time (35 women), 131 part-time/adjunct (49 women). *Students:* 422 full-time (359 women), 732 part-time (564 women); includes 257 minority (109 Black or African American, non-Hispanic/Latino; 31 Asian, non-Hispanic/Latino; 104 Hispanic/Latino; 1 Native Hawaiian or other Pacific Islander, non-Hispanic/Latino; 12 Two or more races, non-Hispanic/Latino), 44 international. Average age 31. 1,130 applicants, 65% accepted, 368 enrolled. In 2014, 366 master's, 17 doctorates, 140 other advanced degrees awarded. Terminal master's awarded for partial completion of doctoral program. *Degree requirements:* For master's, comprehensive exam (for some programs), thesis (for some programs); for doctorate, comprehensive exam, thesis/dissertation; for AC, internship. *Entrance requirements:* For master's, GRE (for some programs if GPA less than 3.0). Additional exam requirements/recommendations for international students: Required—TOEFL (minimum score 550 paper-based; 79 iBT), IELTS (minimum score 6.5). *Application deadline:* Applications are processed on a rolling basis. Application fee: $50. Electronic applications accepted. *Expenses:* Expenses: $1,132 per credit, $1,153 for speech language pathology (for master's programs); $1,505 per credit (for doctoral programs); $867 in fees for 12+ credits per term, $434 for less than 12 credits. *Financial support:* Career-related internships or fieldwork and Federal Work-Study available. Support available to part-time students. Financial award application deadline: 5/15; financial award applicants required to submit CSS PROFILE or FAFSA. *Total annual research expenditures:* $97,964. *Unit head:* Dr. Barbara Garii, Dean, 516-299-2210, Fax: 516-299-4167, E-mail: barbara.garii@liu.edu. *Application contact:* Carol Zerah, Director of Graduate and International Admissions, 516-299-2900 Ext. 3952, Fax: 516-299-3952, E-mail: enroll@cwpost.liu.edu.

Loyola University Chicago, Graduate School, Department of Computer Science, Chicago, IL 60660. Offers computer science (MS); information technology (MS); software engineering (MS); software technology (MS). Part-time and evening/weekend programs available. *Faculty:* 10 full-time (1 woman), 10 part-time/adjunct (2 women). *Students:* 86 full-time (30 women), 40 part-time (16 women); includes 24 minority (8 Black or African American, non-Hispanic/Latino; 10 Asian, non-Hispanic/Latino; 6 Hispanic/Latino), 45 international. Average age 29. 218 applicants, 45% accepted, 60 enrolled. In 2014, 46 master's awarded. *Degree requirements:* For master's, thesis optional, ten courses; thesis (for computer science). *Entrance requirements:* For master's, 3 letters of recommendation, transcripts, statement of purpose. Additional exam requirements/recommendations for international students: Required—TOEFL (minimum score 550 paper-based; 79 iBT) or IELTS (minimum score 6.5). *Application deadline:* For fall admission, 8/10 for domestic students, 5/15 for international students; for spring admission, 12/20 for domestic students, 9/15 for international students. Applications are processed on a rolling basis. Electronic applications accepted. Application fee is waived when completed online. *Expenses: Tuition:* Full-time $17,370; part-time $965 per credit. *Required fees:* $138 per semester. *Financial support:* In 2014–15, 20 students received support, including 1 fellowship (averaging $3,000 per year), 16 teaching assistantships with partial tuition reimbursements available (averaging $4,000 per year); career-related internships or fieldwork, Federal Work-Study, scholarships/grants, tuition waivers (partial), and unspecified assistantships also available. Financial award application deadline: 3/15. *Faculty research:* Software engineering, high performance computing, algorithms and complexity, parallel and distributed computing, databases and computer networks. *Total annual research expenditures:* $22,000. *Unit head:* Dr. Chandra Sekharan, Chair, 312-915-7985, Fax: 312-915-7998, E-mail: csekhar@luc.edu. *Application contact:* Cecilia Murphy, Graduate Program Secretary, 312-915-7990, Fax: 312-915-7998, E-mail: gradinfo-cs@luc.edu.
Website: http://cs.luc.edu.

Marlboro College, Graduate and Professional Studies, Program in Information Technologies, Marlboro, VT 05344. Offers information technologies (MS); open source Web development (Certificate); project management (MS, Certificate). Part-time and evening/weekend programs available. Postbaccalaureate distance learning degree programs offered (minimal on-campus study). *Degree requirements:* For master's, 30 credits including capstone project. *Entrance requirements:* For master's, letter of intent, 2 letters of recommendation, transcripts. Electronic applications accepted. *Expenses: Tuition:* Full-time $45,900; part-time $765 per credit.

Marshall University, Academic Affairs Division, College of Information Technology and Engineering, Weisberg Division of Computer Science, Program in Information Systems, Huntington, WV 25755. Offers MS. Part-time and evening/weekend programs available. *Students:* 18 full-time (4 women), 5 part-time (4 women); includes 1 minority (Black or African American, non-Hispanic/Latino), 15 international. Average age 27. In 2014, 6 master's awarded. *Degree requirements:* For master's, final project, oral exam. *Entrance requirements:* For master's, GRE General Test or MAT, minimum undergraduate GPA of 2.5. Application fee: $40. *Financial support:* Tuition waivers (full)

available. Support available to part-time students. Financial award application deadline: 8/1; financial award applicants required to submit FAFSA. *Unit head:* Dr. William Pierson, Professor, 304-696-2695, E-mail: pierson@marshall.edu. *Application contact:* Information Contact, 304-746-1900, Fax: 304-746-1902, E-mail: services@marshall.edu.
Website: http://www.marshall.edu/cite/.

Massachusetts Institute of Technology, School of Engineering, Department of Civil and Environmental Engineering, Cambridge, MA 02139. Offers biological oceanography (PhD, Sc D); chemical oceanography (PhD, Sc D); civil and environmental engineering (M Eng, SM, PhD, Sc D); civil and environmental systems (PhD, Sc D); civil engineering (PhD, Sc D, CE); coastal engineering (PhD, Sc D); construction engineering and management (PhD, Sc D); environmental biology (PhD, Sc D); environmental chemistry (PhD, Sc D); environmental engineering (PhD, Sc D); environmental fluid mechanics (PhD, Sc D); geotechnical and geoenvironmental engineering (PhD, Sc D); hydrology (PhD, Sc D); information technology (PhD, Sc D); oceanographic engineering (PhD, Sc D); structures and materials (PhD, Sc D); transportation (PhD, Sc D); SM/MBA. *Faculty:* 34 full-time (8 women), 1 part-time/adjunct (0 women). *Students:* 216 full-time (82 women); includes 25 minority (1 Black or African American, non-Hispanic/Latino; 10 Asian, non-Hispanic/Latino; 8 Hispanic/Latino; 6 Two or more races, non-Hispanic/Latino), 117 international. Average age 26. 565 applicants, 22% accepted, 85 enrolled. In 2014, 76 master's, 18 doctorates awarded. *Degree requirements:* For master's and CE, thesis; for doctorate, comprehensive exam, thesis/dissertation. *Entrance requirements:* For master's and doctorate, GRE General Test. Additional exam requirements/recommendations for international students: Required—TOEFL (minimum score 577 paper-based; 100 iBT), IELTS (minimum score 7). *Application deadline:* For fall admission, 12/15 for domestic and international students. Application fee: $75. Electronic applications accepted. *Expenses: Tuition:* Full-time $44,720; part-time $699 per unit. *Required fees:* $296. *Financial support:* In 2014–15, 170 students received support, including 32 fellowships (averaging $32,800 per year), 132 research assistantships (averaging $33,800 per year), 13 teaching assistantships (averaging $32,900 per year); Federal Work-Study, institutionally sponsored loans, scholarships/grants, traineeships, health care benefits, and unspecified assistantships also available. Financial award application deadline: 4/15; financial award applicants required to submit FAFSA. *Faculty research:* Environmental chemistry, environmental fluid mechanics and coastal engineering, environmental microbiology, geotechnical engineering and geomechanics, hydrology and hydroclimatology, infrastructure systems, mechanics of materials and structures, transportation systems. *Total annual research expenditures:* $22.9 million. *Unit head:* Prof. Markus Buehler, Department Head, 617-324-6488. *Application contact:* Graduate Admissions Coordinator, 617-253-7119, E-mail: cee-admissions@mit.edu.
Website: http://cee.mit.edu/.

Missouri University of Science and Technology, Graduate School, Department of Business and Information Technology, Rolla, MO 65409. Offers business and information technology (MBA); information science and technology (MS). *Degree requirements:* For master's, thesis or alternative. *Entrance requirements:* Additional exam requirements/recommendations for international students: Required—TOEFL (minimum score 600 paper-based).

Naval Postgraduate School, Departments and Academic Groups, Department of Information Sciences, Monterey, CA 93943. Offers electronic warfare systems engineering (MS); information sciences (PhD); information systems and operations (MS); information technology management (MS); information warfare systems engineering (MS); knowledge superiority (Certificate); remote sensing intelligence (MS); system technology (command, control and communications) (MS). Program open only to commissioned officers of the United States and friendly nations and selected United States federal civilian employees. Part-time programs available. *Degree requirements:* For master's, thesis (for some programs); for doctorate, thesis/dissertation. *Faculty research:* Designing inter-organisational collectivities for dynamic fit: stability, manoeuvrability and application in disaster relief endeavours; system self-awareness and related methods for Improving the use and understanding of data within DoD; evaluating a macrocognition model of team collaboration using real-world data from the Haiti relief effort; cyber distortion in command and control; performance and QoS in service-based systems.

New Jersey Institute of Technology, College of Computing Science, Newark, NJ 07102. Offers computer science (MS, PhD), including bioinformatics (MS), computer science, computing and business (MS), cyber security and privacy (MS), software engineering (MS); information systems (MS, PhD), including business and information systems (MS), emergency management and business continuity (MS), information systems; information technology administration and security (MS). Part-time and evening/weekend programs available. Terminal master's awarded for partial completion of doctoral program. *Degree requirements:* For master's, thesis optional; for doctorate, thesis/dissertation. *Entrance requirements:* For master's, GRE General Test; for doctorate, GRE General Test, minimum graduate GPA of 3.5. Additional exam requirements/recommendations for international students: Required—TOEFL (minimum score 550 paper-based; 79 iBT). Electronic applications accepted. *Faculty research:* Computer systems, communications and networking, artificial intelligence, database engineering, systems analysis.

Northeastern University, College of Engineering, Boston, MA 02115-5096. Offers bioengineering (PhD); chemical engineering (MS, PhD); civil engineering (MS, PhD); computer engineering (PhD); computer systems engineering (MS); electrical and computer engineering (MS); electrical and engineering leadership (MS); electrical engineering (PhD); energy systems (MS); engineering leadership (Certificate); engineering management (MRTP); industrial engineering (MS, PhD); information assurance (PhD); information systems (MS); interdisciplinary (PhD); mechanical engineering (MS, PhD); operations research (MS); telecommunication systems management (MS). Part-time programs available. *Expenses:* Contact institution.

Northern Kentucky University, Office of Graduate Programs, College of Informatics, Department of Business Informatics, Highland Heights, KY 41099. Offers business informatics (MS, Certificate); corporate information security (Certificate); enterprise resource planning (Certificate). Part-time and evening/weekend programs available. *Faculty:* 7 full-time (2 women), 2 part-time/adjunct (0 women). *Students:* 10 full-time (3 women), 41 part-time (15 women); includes 5 minority (3 Black or African American, non-Hispanic/Latino; 1 Asian, non-Hispanic/Latino; 1 Hispanic/Latino), 6 international. Average age 34. In 2014, 20 master's awarded. *Entrance requirements:* For master's, GRE or GMAT. Additional exam requirements/recommendations for international students: Required—TOEFL (minimum score 79 iBT); Recommended—IELTS (minimum score 6.5). *Application deadline:* For fall admission, 8/1 for domestic students, 6/1 for international students; for spring admission, 12/1 for domestic students, 10/1 for international students; for summer admission, 5/1 for domestic students, 3/1 for international students. Applications are processed on a rolling basis. Application fee: $40. Electronic applications accepted. *Expenses: Tuition, area resident:* Part-time $518 per credit hour. Tuition, state resident: part-time $630 per credit hour. Tuition, nonresident: part-time $797 per credit hour. *Required fees:* $192 per semester. Tuition and fees vary according to course load, degree level, campus/location, program and reciprocity agreements. *Financial support:* In 2014–15, 15 students received support. Unspecified assistantships available. Financial award applicants required to submit FAFSA. *Faculty research:* Data analytics, cloud computing, healthcare informatics, information systems security. *Unit head:* Dr. Teuta Cata, Department Chair, 859-572-5626, E-mail: catat@nku.edu. *Application contact:* Alison Swanson, Graduate Admissions Coordinator, 859-572-6971, E-mail: swansona1@nku.edu.
Website: http://informatics.nku.edu/departments/business-informatics.html.

Northwestern University, McCormick School of Engineering and Applied Science, Department of Electrical Engineering and Computer Science, MS in Information Technology Program, Evanston, IL 60208. Offers MS. Part-time and evening/weekend programs available. *Faculty:* 15 part-time/adjunct (0 women). *Students:* 13 full-time (5 women), 32 part-time (7 women); includes 19 minority (8 Black or African American, non-Hispanic/Latino; 9 Asian, non-Hispanic/Latino; 1 Hispanic/Latino; 1 Two or more races, non-Hispanic/Latino), 19 international. Average age 32. 134 applicants, 27% accepted, 21 enrolled. In 2014, 26 master's awarded. *Entrance requirements:* For master's, GRE (recommended), work experience in an IT-related position. Additional exam requirements/recommendations for international students: Required—TOEFL (minimum score 80 iBT), IELTS (minimum score 7). *Application deadline:* For fall admission, 8/1 for domestic students, 6/1 for international students. Applications are processed on a rolling basis. Application fee: $50. Electronic applications accepted. *Financial support:* Institutionally sponsored loans available. Financial award application deadline: 1/15; financial award applicants required to submit FAFSA. *Unit head:* Dr. Randy Berry, Co-Director, 847-491-7074, Fax: 847-467-3550, E-mail: rberry@eecs.northwestern.edu. *Application contact:* Abi Shay, Associate Director, 847-467-6557, Fax: 847-467-3550, E-mail: abigayle.shay@northwestern.edu.
Website: http://msit.northwestern.edu/.

Notre Dame de Namur University, Division of Academic Affairs, College of Arts and Sciences, Program in Computer and Information Science, Belmont, CA 94002-1908. Offers MS. Part-time and evening/weekend programs available. Postbaccalaureate distance learning degree programs offered (no on-campus study). *Entrance requirements:* For master's, minimum GPA of 2.5, interview (for some programs). Additional exam requirements/recommendations for international students: Required—TOEFL (minimum score 550 paper-based; 79 iBT). Electronic applications accepted.

Nova Southeastern University, College of Engineering and Computing, Fort Lauderdale, FL 33314-7796. Offers computer science (MS, PhD); information assurance (PhD); information security (MS); information systems (PhD); information technology (MS); management information systems (MS); software engineering (MS). Part-time and evening/weekend programs available. Postbaccalaureate distance learning degree programs offered (minimal on-campus study). *Faculty:* 20 full-time (6 women), 24 part-time/adjunct (3 women). *Students:* 106 full-time (35 women), 758 part-time (227 women); includes 417 minority (183 Black or African American, non-Hispanic/Latino; 2 American Indian or Alaska Native, non-Hispanic/Latino; 59 Asian, non-Hispanic/Latino; 159 Hispanic/Latino; 14 Two or more races, non-Hispanic/Latino), 90 international. Average age 40. 390 applicants, 74% accepted. In 2014, 146 master's, 67 doctorates awarded. Terminal master's awarded for partial completion of doctoral program. *Degree requirements:* For master's, thesis optional; for doctorate, thesis/dissertation. *Entrance requirements:* For master's, minimum undergraduate GPA of 2.5; 3.0 in major; for doctorate, master's degree, minimum graduate GPA of 3.25. Additional exam requirements/recommendations for international students: Required—TOEFL (minimum score 80 iBT), IELTS (minimum score 6). *Application deadline:* Applications are processed on a rolling basis. Application fee: $50. Electronic applications accepted. *Expenses:* Expenses: $675/credit hour (for MS), $975 (for PhD). *Financial support:* Application deadline: 5/1; applicants required to submit FAFSA. *Faculty research:* Artificial intelligence, database management, human-computer interaction, distance education, information security. *Unit head:* Dr. Eric S. Ackerman, Dean, 954-262-2000, Fax: 954-262-2752, E-mail: esa@nova.edu. *Application contact:* Nancy Ruidiaz, Director, Admissions, 954-262-2026, Fax: 954-262-2752, E-mail: azoulayn@nova.edu.
Website: http://scis.nova.edu.

Oklahoma State University, Spears School of Business, Department of Management Science and Information Systems, Stillwater, OK 74078. Offers management information systems (MS); management science and information systems (PhD); telecommunications management (MS). Part-time programs available. Postbaccalaureate distance learning degree programs offered. *Faculty:* 18 full-time (2 women), 5 part-time/adjunct (1 woman). *Students:* 121 full-time (25 women), 101 part-time (17 women); includes 13 minority (5 Black or African American, non-Hispanic/Latino; 1 Asian, non-Hispanic/Latino; 3 Hispanic/Latino; 4 Two or more races, non-Hispanic/Latino), 160 international. Average age 28. 883 applicants, 14% accepted, 81 enrolled. In 2014, 131 master's, 2 doctorates awarded. *Degree requirements:* For master's, thesis or alternative; for doctorate, comprehensive exam, thesis/dissertation. *Entrance requirements:* For master's and doctorate, GRE or GMAT. Additional exam requirements/recommendations for international students: Required—TOEFL (minimum score 550 paper-based; 79 iBT). *Application deadline:* For fall admission, 3/1 priority date for international students; for spring admission, 8/1 priority date for international students. Applications are processed on a rolling basis. Application fee: $40 ($75 for international students). Electronic applications accepted. *Expenses:* Tuition, state resident: full-time $4488; part-time $187 per credit hour. Tuition, nonresident: full-time $18,360; part-time $765 per credit hour. *Required fees:* $2413; $100.55 per credit hour. Tuition and fees vary according to campus/location. *Financial support:* In 2014–15, 2 research assistantships (averaging $6,000 per year), 22 teaching assistantships (averaging $11,906 per year) were awarded; career-related internships or fieldwork, Federal Work-Study, scholarships/grants, health care benefits, tuition waivers (partial), and unspecified assistantships also available. Support available to part-time students. Financial award application deadline: 3/1; financial award applicants required to submit FAFSA. *Unit head:* Dr. Rick Wilson, Department Head, 405-744-3551, Fax: 405-744-5180, E-mail: rick.wilson@okstate.edu. *Application contact:* Dr. Rathin Sarathy, Graduate Coordinator, 405-744-8646, Fax: 405-744-5180, E-mail: rathin.sarathy@okstate.edu.
Website: http://spears.okstate.edu/msis.

Old Dominion University, Strome College of Business, Doctoral Program in Business Administration, Norfolk, VA 23529. Offers finance (PhD); information technology (PhD); marketing (PhD); strategic management (PhD). *Accreditation:* AACSB. *Faculty:* 29 full-time (6 women). *Students:* 29 full-time (9 women), 28 part-time (10 women); includes 3 minority (2 Asian, non-Hispanic/Latino; 1 Native Hawaiian or other Pacific Islander, non-Hispanic/Latino), 40 international. Average age 33. 71 applicants, 17% accepted, 12 enrolled. In 2014, 5 doctorates awarded. *Degree requirements:* For doctorate, comprehensive exam, thesis/dissertation. *Entrance requirements:* For doctorate, GMAT. Additional exam requirements/recommendations for international students: Required—TOEFL (minimum score 550 paper-based; 79 iBT). *Application deadline:* For fall admission, 1/1 priority date for domestic and international students. Application fee: $50. Electronic applications accepted. *Expenses:* Tuition, state resident: full-time $10,488; part-time $437 per credit. Tuition, nonresident: full-time $26,136; part-time $1089 per credit. *Required fees:* $64 per semester. One-time fee: $50. *Financial support:* In 2014–15, 27 students received support, including 14 fellowships with full tuition

reimbursements available (averaging $7,500 per year), 24 research assistantships with full tuition reimbursements available (averaging $7,500 per year), 16 teaching assistantships with full tuition reimbursements available (averaging $7,500 per year); scholarships/grants and unspecified assistantships also available. Financial award application deadline: 1/1; financial award applicants required to submit FAFSA. *Faculty research:* International business, buyer behavior, financial markets, strategy, operations research. *Unit head:* Dr. John B. Ford, Graduate Program Director, 757-683-3587, Fax: 757-683-4076, E-mail: jbford@odu.edu. *Application contact:* Katrina Davenport, Program Coordinator, 757-683-5138, Fax: 757-683-4076, E-mail: kdavenpo@odu.edu.
Website: http://www.odu.edu/business/academics/graduate/scb-phd.

Pace University, Seidenberg School of Computer Science and Information Systems, New York, NY 10038. Offers computer science (MS); computing science (DPS); information systems (MS); Internet technology (MS); large computing systems (Certificate); network administration (Certificate); security and information assurance (Certificate); software development and engineering (MS, Certificate); telecommunications (Certificate); telecommunications systems and networks (MS). Part-time and evening/weekend programs available. *Faculty:* 26 full-time (7 women), 7 part-time/adjunct (2 women). *Students:* 167 full-time (57 women), 324 part-time (90 women); includes 182 minority (83 Black or African American, non-Hispanic/Latino; 1 American Indian or Alaska Native, non-Hispanic/Latino; 46 Asian, non-Hispanic/Latino; 47 Hispanic/Latino; 5 Two or more races, non-Hispanic/Latino), 132 international. Average age 35. 441 applicants, 84% accepted, 157 enrolled. In 2014, 115 master's, 7 doctorates, 9 other advanced degrees awarded. *Degree requirements:* For master's, thesis or alternative, capstone course; for doctorate, comprehensive exam (for some programs), thesis/dissertation. *Entrance requirements:* For master's, GRE General Test. Additional exam requirements/recommendations for international students: Required—TOEFL. *Application deadline:* For fall admission, 8/1 priority date for domestic students, 6/1 for international students; for spring admission, 12/1 for domestic students, 10/1 for international students. Applications are processed on a rolling basis. Application fee: $70. Electronic applications accepted. *Expenses:* Expenses: Contact institution. *Financial support:* Research assistantships and career-related internships or fieldwork available. Support available to part-time students. Financial award applicants required to submit FAFSA. *Faculty research:* Computer security and forensics, cybersecurity, telehealth, mobile computing, distributed teams, robotics. *Total annual research expenditures:* $685,824. *Unit head:* Dr. Amar Gupta, Dean, Seidenberg School of Computer Science and Information Systems, 914-773-3750, Fax: 914-773-3533, E-mail: agupta@pace.edu. *Application contact:* Susan Ford-Goldschein, Director of Graduate Admissions, 914-422-4283, Fax: 914-422-4287, E-mail: gradwp@pace.edu.
Website: http://www.pace.edu/seidenberg.

Penn State University Park, Graduate School, College of Information Sciences and Technology, University Park, PA 16802. Offers MS, PhD. Part-time and evening/weekend programs available. Postbaccalaureate distance learning degree programs offered. *Students:* 140 (46 women). Average age 29. 161 applicants, 45% accepted, 35 enrolled. In 2014, 13 master's, 13 doctorates awarded. *Entrance requirements:* Additional exam requirements/recommendations for international students: Required—TOEFL (minimum score 550 paper-based; 80 iBT), IELTS. *Application deadline:* For fall admission, 12/15 for domestic and international students. Applications are processed on a rolling basis. Application fee: $65. Electronic applications accepted. *Financial support:* Fellowships, research assistantships, teaching assistantships, Federal Work-Study, institutionally sponsored loans, scholarships/grants, traineeships, health care benefits, and unspecified assistantships available. Support available to part-time students. Financial award application deadline: 3/1; financial award applicants required to submit FAFSA. *Application contact:* 814-865-8711, E-mail: graduateprograms@ist.psu.edu.
Website: http://ist.psu.edu/.

Regis University, College for Professional Studies, School of Computer and Information Sciences, Denver, CO 80221-1099. Offers database development (Certificate); enterprise Java software development (Certificate); enterprise resource planning (Certificate); executive information technology (Certificate); information assurance (M Sc); information technology management (M Sc); software engineering (Certificate); software engineering and database technologies (M Sc); storage area networks (Certificate); systems engineering (M Sc, Certificate). Part-time and evening/weekend programs available. Postbaccalaureate distance learning degree programs offered (no on-campus study). *Faculty:* 8 full-time (3 women), 46 part-time/adjunct (9 women). *Students:* 254 full-time (69 women), 221 part-time (59 women); includes 159 minority (57 Black or African American, non-Hispanic/Latino; 4 American Indian or Alaska Native, non-Hispanic/Latino; 39 Asian, non-Hispanic/Latino; 49 Hispanic/Latino; 1 Native Hawaiian or other Pacific Islander, non-Hispanic/Latino; 9 Two or more races, non-Hispanic/Latino), 22 international. Average age 38. 204 applicants, 87% accepted, 128 enrolled. In 2014, 176 master's awarded. *Degree requirements:* For master's, thesis (for some programs), final research project. *Entrance requirements:* For master's, official transcript reflecting baccalaureate degree awarded from regionally-accredited college or university, 2 years of related experience, resume, interview. Additional exam requirements/recommendations for international students: Required—TOEFL (minimum score 550 paper-based; 82 iBT). *Application deadline:* For fall admission, 8/13 for domestic students, 7/13 for international students; for winter admission, 10/8 for domestic students, 9/8 for international students; for spring admission, 12/17 for domestic students, 11/17 for international students. Applications are processed on a rolling basis. Application fee: $75. Electronic applications accepted. *Expenses:* Expenses: $710 per credit hour (for M Sc). *Financial support:* In 2014–15, 16 students received support. Federal Work-Study and scholarships/grants available. Financial award application deadline: 4/15; financial award applicants required to submit FAFSA. *Faculty research:* Information policy, knowledge management, software architectures. *Unit head:* Donald Archer, Interim Dean, 303-458-4335, E-mail: archer@regis.edu. *Application contact:* Sarah Engel, Director of Admissions, 303-458-4900, Fax: 303-964-5534, E-mail: regisadm@regis.edu.
Website: http://regis.edu/CCIS.aspx.

Rensselaer at Hartford, Department of Computer and Information Science, Program in Information Technology, Hartford, CT 06120-2991. Offers MS. Part-time and evening/weekend programs available. *Entrance requirements:* For master's, GRE. Additional exam requirements/recommendations for international students: Required—TOEFL (minimum score 600 paper-based; 100 iBT). Electronic applications accepted.

Rensselaer Polytechnic Institute, Graduate School, School of Science, Program in Information Technology and Web Science, Troy, NY 12180-3590. Offers MS. Part-time programs available. *Faculty:* 52 full-time (14 women), 12 part-time/adjunct (2 women). *Students:* 46 full-time (16 women), 4 part-time (2 women); includes 3 minority (1 Black or African American, non-Hispanic/Latino; 1 Asian, non-Hispanic/Latino; 1 Hispanic/Latino), 39 international. Average age 28. 156 applicants, 37% accepted, 30 enrolled. In 2014, 29 master's awarded. *Entrance requirements:* For master's, GRE, IT Background Evaluation Form. Additional exam requirements/recommendations for international students: Required—TOEFL (minimum score 570 paper-based; 88 iBT), IELTS (minimum score 6.5), PTE (minimum score 60). *Application deadline:* For fall admission, 1/1 priority date for domestic and international students; for spring admission, 8/15 priority date for domestic and international students. Applications are processed on a rolling basis. Application fee: $75. Electronic applications accepted. *Expenses: Tuition:* Full-time $46,700; part-time $1945 per credit. Tuition and fees vary according to course load. *Financial support:* In 2014–15, 49 students received support, including teaching assistantships with full tuition reimbursements available (averaging $18,500 per year). Financial award application deadline: 1/1. *Faculty research:* Database and intelligent systems, data science and analytics, financial engineering, human computer interaction, information dominance, information security, information systems engineering, management information systems, networking, software design and engineering, Web science. *Unit head:* Dr. Peter Fox, Graduate Program Director, 518-276-4862, E-mail: pfox@cs.rpi.edu. *Application contact:* Office of Graduate Admissions, 518-276-6216, E-mail: gradadmissions@rpi.edu.
Website: http://www.it.rpi.edu/graduate/index.html.

Robert Morris University, Graduate Studies, School of Communications and Information Systems, Moon Township, PA 15108-1189. Offers communication and information systems (MS); competitive intelligence systems (MS); information security and assurance (MS); information systems and communications (D Sc); information systems management (MS); information technology project management (MS); Internet information systems (MS); organizational leadership (MS). Part-time and evening/weekend programs available. Postbaccalaureate distance learning degree programs offered (no on-campus study). *Faculty:* 25 full-time (10 women), 4 part-time/adjunct (0 women). *Students:* 320 part-time (117 women); includes 71 minority (38 Black or African American, non-Hispanic/Latino; 1 American Indian or Alaska Native, non-Hispanic/Latino; 6 Asian, non-Hispanic/Latino; 4 Hispanic/Latino; 22 Two or more races, non-Hispanic/Latino), 46 international. Average age 34. 267 applicants, 42% accepted, 85 enrolled. In 2014, 84 master's, 14 doctorates awarded. *Degree requirements:* For doctorate, thesis/dissertation. *Entrance requirements:* For doctorate, employer letter of endorsement, interview. Additional exam requirements/recommendations for international students: Required—TOEFL (minimum score 550 paper-based; 79 iBT). *Application deadline:* For fall admission, 7/1 priority date for domestic and international students; for spring admission, 11/1 priority date for domestic and international students. Applications are processed on a rolling basis. Application fee: $35. Electronic applications accepted. *Expenses:* Expenses: Contact institution. *Financial support:* Research assistantships with partial tuition reimbursements, institutionally sponsored loans, and unspecified assistantships available. Support available to part-time students. Financial award application deadline: 5/1. *Unit head:* Dr. Barbara J. Levine, Dean, 412-397-6460, Fax: 412-397-6469, E-mail: levine@rmu.edu. *Application contact:* 412-397-5200, Fax: 412-397-5915, E-mail: graduateadmissions@rmu.edu.
Website: http://www.rmu.edu/web/cms/schools/scis/Pages/default.aspx.

Rochester Institute of Technology, Graduate Enrollment Services, Golisano College of Computing and Information Sciences, Computing and Information Sciences Department, PhD Program in Computing and Information Sciences, Rochester, NY 14623-5608. Offers PhD. *Students:* 23 full-time (4 women), 16 part-time (4 women); includes 3 minority (1 Asian, non-Hispanic/Latino; 1 Hispanic/Latino; 1 Two or more races, non-Hispanic/Latino), 31 international. Average age 30. 74 applicants, 27% accepted, 12 enrolled. In 2014, 3 doctorates awarded. *Degree requirements:* For doctorate, thesis/dissertation. *Entrance requirements:* For doctorate, GRE and TOEFL, IELTS, or PTE for non-native English speakers, minimum GPA of 3.0. Additional exam requirements/recommendations for international students: Required—PTE (minimum score 58), TOEFL (minimum score 550 paper-based; 79 iBT) or IELTS (minimum score 6.5). *Application deadline:* For fall admission, 1/15 priority date for domestic and international students. Applications are processed on a rolling basis. Application fee: $60. Electronic applications accepted. *Expenses:* Expenses: $1,673 per credit hour. *Financial support:* In 2014–15, 26 students received support. Research assistantships with full tuition reimbursements available, teaching assistantships with full tuition reimbursements available, career-related internships or fieldwork, Federal Work-Study, institutionally sponsored loans, scholarships/grants, health care benefits, and unspecified assistantships available. Support available to part-time students. Financial award applicants required to submit FAFSA. *Faculty research:* Cyber infrastructure as applied to multiple domains, astro-informatics, biomedical informatics, environmental informatics, computational biology, computational science, services sciences, electronic commerce. *Unit head:* Dr. Pengcheng Shi, Director, 585-475-6193, E-mail: ljtdps@rit.edu. *Application contact:* Diane Ellison, Associate Vice President, Graduate Enrollment Services, 585-475-2229, Fax: 585-475-7164, E-mail: gradinfo@rit.edu.
Website: http://www.rit.edu/gccis/phd.

Rochester Institute of Technology, Graduate Enrollment Services, Golisano College of Computing and Information Sciences, Information Science and Technologies Department, MS Program in Information Sciences and Technologies, Rochester, NY 14623-5608. Offers MS. Part-time programs available. *Students:* 67 full-time (18 women), 28 part-time (3 women); includes 5 minority (1 American Indian or Alaska Native, non-Hispanic/Latino; 2 Asian, non-Hispanic/Latino; 1 Hispanic/Latino; 1 Two or more races, non-Hispanic/Latino), 78 international. Average age 27. 248 applicants, 39% accepted, 28 enrolled. In 2014, 26 master's awarded. *Degree requirements:* For master's, thesis or alternative. *Entrance requirements:* For master's, GRE and TOEFL, IELTS, or PTE for non-native English speakers, minimum GPA of 3.0. Additional exam requirements/recommendations for international students: Required—PTE (minimum score 58), TOEFL (minimum score 550 paper-based; 79 iBT) or IELTS (minimum score 6.5). *Application deadline:* For fall admission, 2/15 priority date for domestic and international students; for spring admission, 12/15 priority date for domestic and international students. Applications are processed on a rolling basis. Application fee: $60. Electronic applications accepted. *Expenses:* Expenses: $1,673 per credit hour. *Financial support:* In 2014–15, 73 students received support. Research assistantships with partial tuition reimbursements available, teaching assistantships with partial tuition reimbursements available, career-related internships or fieldwork, Federal Work-Study, institutionally sponsored loans, scholarships/grants, and unspecified assistantships available. Support available to part-time students. Financial award applicants required to submit FAFSA. *Faculty research:* Cloud computing, virtualization, big data, NoSQL, geospatial technologies. *Unit head:* Dr. Peter Lutz, Graduate Program Director, 585-475-2700, E-mail: informaticsGrad@rit.edu. *Application contact:* Diane Ellison, Associate Vice President, Graduate Enrollment Services, 585-475-2229, Fax: 585-475-7164, E-mail: gradinfo@rit.edu.
Website: http://www.ist.rit.edu/degrees/graduate/ms-in-it/overview.php.

Sacred Heart University, Graduate Programs, College of Arts and Sciences, Department of Computer Science, Fairfield, CT 06825-1000. Offers computer game design and development (Graduate Certificate); computer science and information technology (MS); computer science gaming (MS); cybersecurity (MS); database design (Graduate Certificate); information technology (Graduate Certificate); information technology and network security (Graduate Certificate); interactive multimedia (Graduate Certificate); Web development (Graduate Certificate). Part-time and evening/weekend programs available. *Faculty:* 6 full-time (2 women), 18 part-time/adjunct (5 women). *Students:* 266 full-time (100 women), 69 part-time (15 women); includes 30 minority (11 Black or African American, non-Hispanic/Latino; 7 Asian, non-Hispanic/Latino; 12 Hispanic/Latino), 265 international. Average age 26. 1,010 applicants, 56% accepted, 166 enrolled. In 2014, 50 master's awarded. *Degree requirements:* For

master's, thesis or alternative. *Entrance requirements:* For master's, bachelor's degree, minimum GPA of 3.0. Additional exam requirements/recommendations for international students: Required—PTE; Recommended—TOEFL (minimum score 570 paper-based; 80 iBT), IELTS (minimum score 6.5). *Application deadline:* For fall admission, 5/15 for international students; for spring admission, 10/30 for international students. Applications are processed on a rolling basis. Application fee: $60. Electronic applications accepted. *Expenses: Tuition:* Full-time $24,559; part-time $649 per credit. *Financial support:* Unspecified assistantships available. Financial award applicants required to submit FAFSA. *Unit head:* Domenick Pinto, Academic Director and Chairperson, 203-371-7789, Fax: 203-371-0506, E-mail: pintod@sacredheart.edu. *Application contact:* Kathy Dilks, Executive Director of Graduate Admissions, 203-365-7619, Fax: 203-365-4732, E-mail: gradstudies@sacredheart.edu.
Website: http://www.sacredheart.edu/academics/collegeofartssciences/academicdepartments/computerscienceinformationtechnology/graduatedegreesandcertificates/.

St. John's University, St. John's College of Liberal Arts and Sciences, Department of Government and Politics and Division of Library and Information Science, Program in Government and Library and Information Science, Queens, NY 11439. Offers MA/MS. Part-time and evening/weekend programs available. *Students:* 2 full-time (1 woman). Average age 24. 3 applicants, 33% accepted, 1 enrolled. *Entrance requirements:* Additional exam requirements/recommendations for international students: Required—TOEFL (minimum score 600 paper-based; 100 iBT), IELTS (minimum score 7). *Application deadline:* For fall admission, 5/1 priority date for domestic and international students; for spring admission, 11/1 priority date for domestic and international students. Applications are processed on a rolling basis. Application fee: $70. Electronic applications accepted. *Expenses: Tuition:* Full-time $20,610; part-time $1145 per credit. *Required fees:* $170 per semester. *Financial support:* Research assistantships, career-related internships or fieldwork, and scholarships/grants available. Support available to part-time students. Financial award application deadline: 3/1; financial award applicants required to submit FAFSA. *Unit head:* Dr. Diane Heith, Chair, 718-990-6329, E-mail: heithd@stjohns.edu. *Application contact:* Robert Medrano, Director of Graduate Admission, 718-990-1601, Fax: 718-990-5686, E-mail: gradhelp@stjohns.edu.

St. Mary's University, Graduate School, Department of Computer Science, Program in Computer Information Systems, San Antonio, TX 78228-8507. Offers MS. Part-time programs available. *Faculty:* 4 full-time (2 women). *Students:* 11 full-time (3 women), 6 part-time (2 women); includes 4 minority (2 Asian, non-Hispanic/Latino; 2 Hispanic/Latino), 11 international. Average age 30. 26 applicants, 23% accepted, 5 enrolled. In 2014, 6 master's awarded. *Degree requirements:* For master's, comprehensive exam. *Entrance requirements:* For master's, GMAT or GRE General Test, Minimum GPA of 2.7 in a bachelor's degree, minimum GRE quantitative score of 143 or better, or minimum GMAT score of 334, completed application form to include the following: written statement of purpose indicating interest and objective, two letters of recommendation, official transcripts of all college-level work. Additional exam requirements/recommendations for international students: Required—TOEFL (minimum score 530 paper-based; 80 iBT). *Application deadline:* Applications are processed on a rolling basis. Electronic applications accepted. *Expenses: Tuition:* Full-time $15,070; part-time $800 per credit hour. *Required fees:* $156 per semester. *Financial support:* Career-related internships or fieldwork, Federal Work-Study, institutionally sponsored loans, scholarships/grants, health care benefits, and unspecified assistantships available. Financial award application deadline: 3/31; financial award applicants required to submit FAFSA. *Faculty research:* Data integrity in cloud computing systems, artificial intelligence, computer science education, replicating data over cloud servers, intelligent systems, critical thinking and learning, expert systems/knowledge engineering. *Unit head:* Dr. Carol Redfield, Graduate Program Director, 210-436-3298, E-mail: credfield@stmarytx.edu.
Website: https://www.stmarytx.edu/academics/set/graduate/cis/.

Sam Houston State University, College of Sciences, Department of Computer Science, Huntsville, TX 77341. Offers computing and information science (MS); digital forensics (MS); information assurance and security (MS). Part-time programs available. *Faculty:* 12 full-time (3 women), 1 (woman) part-time/adjunct. *Students:* 37 full-time (8 women), 49 part-time (10 women); includes 25 minority (12 Black or African American, non-Hispanic/Latino; 3 Asian, non-Hispanic/Latino; 9 Hispanic/Latino; 1 Two or more races, non-Hispanic/Latino), 32 international. Average age 32. 73 applicants, 40% accepted, 21 enrolled. In 2014, 7 master's awarded. *Degree requirements:* For master's, comprehensive exam, thesis optional, internship; for doctorate, comprehensive exam, thesis/dissertation. *Entrance requirements:* For master's, GRE General Test, letters of recommendation. Additional exam requirements/recommendations for international students: Required—TOEFL (minimum score 550 paper-based; 79 iBT), IELTS (minimum score 6.5). *Application deadline:* For fall admission, 8/1 for domestic students, 6/25 for international students; for spring admission, 12/1 for domestic students, 11/12 for international students; for summer admission, 5/15 for domestic students, 4/9 for international students. Applications are processed on a rolling basis. Application fee: $45 ($75 for international students). Electronic applications accepted. *Expenses:* Tuition, state resident: full-time $2286; part-time $254 per credit hour. Tuition, nonresident: full-time $5544; part-time $616 per credit hour. *Required fees:* $440 per semester. Tuition and fees vary according to course load and campus/location. *Financial support:* In 2014–15, 19 research assistantships (averaging $6,013 per year) were awarded; career-related internships or fieldwork, Federal Work-Study, scholarships/grants, tuition waivers (partial), and unspecified assistantships also available. Support available to part-time students. Financial award application deadline: 3/15; financial award applicants required to submit FAFSA. *Unit head:* Dr. Peter Cooper, Chair/Professor, 936-294-1569, Fax: 936-294-4312, E-mail: css_pac@shsu.edu. *Application contact:* Dr. Jihuang Ji, Associate Professor/Graduate Advisor, 936-294-1579, Fax: 936-294-4312, E-mail: csc_jxj@shsu.edu.
Website: http://cs.shsu.edu/.

Simmons College, Graduate School of Library and Information Science, Boston, MA 02115. Offers information science and technology (MS); MA/MA; MA/MAT; MA/MFA; MS/MA. *Accreditation:* ALA (one or more programs are accredited). Part-time and evening/weekend programs available. Postbaccalaureate distance learning degree programs offered (no on-campus study). *Faculty:* 62 full-time (46 women), 30 part-time/adjunct (19 women). *Students:* 65 full-time (55 women), 677 part-time (551 women); includes 87 minority (16 Black or African American, non-Hispanic/Latino; 15 Asian, non-Hispanic/Latino; 39 Hispanic/Latino; 17 Two or more races, non-Hispanic/Latino), 15 international. 540 applicants, 98% accepted, 288 enrolled. In 2014, 281 master's, 4 doctorates awarded. *Degree requirements:* For master's, thesis optional, capstone project experience; for doctorate, comprehensive exam, 36 credit hours (includes 3-credit dissertation). *Entrance requirements:* For doctorate, GRE, transcripts, personal statement, resume, recommendations, master's degree. Additional exam requirements/recommendations for international students: Required—TOEFL (minimum score 550 paper-based; 79 iBT), IELTS (minimum score 7). *Application deadline:* For fall admission, 3/1 for domestic and international students; for spring admission, 9/1 for domestic and international students; for summer admission, 2/1 for domestic and international students. Applications are processed on a rolling basis. Application fee: $65. Electronic applications accepted. *Expenses: Tuition:* Full-time $19,500; part-time $975 per credit. *Financial support:* Fellowships with partial tuition reimbursements, research assistantships, teaching assistantships with full and partial tuition reimbursements, scholarships/grants, tuition waivers, and unspecified assistantships available. Financial award application deadline: 2/1; financial award applicants required to submit FAFSA. *Faculty research:* Archives and social justice, information-seeking behavior, information retrieval, organization of information, cultural heritage informatics. *Unit head:* Dr. Eileen G. Abels, Dean, 617-521-2869. *Application contact:* Sarah Petrakos, Assistant Dean for Admission and Recruitment, 617-521-2868, Fax: 617-521-3192, E-mail: gslisadm@simmons.edu.
Website: http://www.simmons.edu/slis/.

Southern Methodist University, Bobby B. Lyle School of Engineering, Department of Engineering Management, Information, and Systems, Dallas, TX 75275. Offers engineering management (MSEM, DE); information engineering and management (MSIEM); operations research (MS, PhD); systems engineering (MS, PhD). Part-time and evening/weekend programs available. Postbaccalaureate distance learning degree programs offered. Terminal master's awarded for partial completion of doctoral program. *Degree requirements:* For master's, thesis optional; for doctorate, thesis/dissertation, oral and written qualifying exams. *Entrance requirements:* For master's, minimum GPA of 3.0 in last 2 years; bachelor's degree in engineering, mathematics, sciences, or technical area; for doctorate, GRE General Test (operations research, engineering management), bachelor's degree in related field. Additional exam requirements/recommendations for international students: Required—TOEFL. *Faculty research:* Telecommunications, decision systems, information engineering, operations research, software.

Southern Polytechnic State University, School of Arts and Sciences, Department of English, Technical Communication, and Media Arts, Marietta, GA 30060-2896. Offers communications management (Postbaccalaureate Certificate); content development (Postbaccalaureate Certificate); information and instructional design (MSIID); information design and communication (MS); instructional design (Postbaccalaureate Certificate); technical communication (Graduate Certificate); visual communication and graphics (Postbaccalaureate Certificate). Part-time and evening/weekend programs available. Postbaccalaureate distance learning degree programs offered (no on-campus study). *Degree requirements:* For master's, thesis optional; for other advanced degree, thesis optional, 18 hours completed through thesis option (6 hours), internship option (6 hours) or advanced coursework option (6 hours). *Entrance requirements:* For master's, GRE, statement of purpose, writing sample, timed essay; for other advanced degree, writing sample, professional recommendations. Additional exam requirements/recommendations for international students: Required—TOEFL (minimum score 550 paper-based; 79 iBT), IELTS (minimum score 6.5). Electronic applications accepted. *Faculty research:* Usability, user-centered design, instructional design, information architecture, information design, content strategy.

Southern Polytechnic State University, School of Computing and Software Engineering, Department of Information Technology, Marietta, GA 30060-2896. Offers health information technology (Postbaccalaureate Certificate); information security and assurance (Graduate Certificate); information technology (MSIT, Graduate Certificate); information technology fundamentals (Postbaccalaureate Certificate). Part-time and evening/weekend programs available. Postbaccalaureate distance learning degree programs offered (no on-campus study). *Degree requirements:* For master's, thesis optional. *Entrance requirements:* For master's, minimum GPA of 2.75; for other advanced degree, bachelor's degree. Additional exam requirements/recommendations for international students: Required—TOEFL (minimum score 550 paper-based; 79 iBT), IELTS (minimum score 6.5). Electronic applications accepted. *Faculty research:* IT ethics, user interface design, IT security, IT integration, IT management, health information technology, business intelligence, networks, business continuity.

State University of New York Polytechnic Institute, Program in Computer and Information Science, Utica, NY 13504-3050. Offers MS. Part-time and evening/weekend programs available. *Degree requirements:* For master's, thesis or project. *Entrance requirements:* For master's, GRE General Test, minimum GPA of 3.0, one letter of reference, resume, BS in computer science or a related field. Additional exam requirements/recommendations for international students: Required—TOEFL (minimum score 550 paper-based; 79 iBT), IELTS (minimum score 6.5). Electronic applications accepted. *Faculty research:* Cryptography, distributed systems, computer-aided system theory, reasoning with uncertainty, grid computing.

State University of New York Polytechnic Institute, Program in Information Design and Technology, Utica, NY 13504-3050. Offers MS. Part-time programs available. Postbaccalaureate distance learning degree programs offered (no on-campus study). *Degree requirements:* For master's, thesis or project. *Entrance requirements:* For master's, minimum GPA of 3.0; 2 letters of reference; writing samples or portfolio; resume, educational objective. Additional exam requirements/recommendations for international students: Required—TOEFL (minimum score 550 paper-based; 79 iBT), IELTS (minimum score 6.5). Electronic applications accepted. *Faculty research:* Textual-visualization, ethics and technology, behavioral information security.

Stevens Institute of Technology, Graduate School, Wesley J. Howe School of Technology Management, Program in Information Systems, Hoboken, NJ 07030. Offers computer science (MS); e-commerce (MS); enterprise systems (MS); entrepreneurial information technology (MS); information architecture (MS); information management (MS, Certificate); information security (MS); information technology in financial services industry (MS); information technology in the pharmaceutical industry (MS); information technology outsourcing management (MS); project management (MS, Certificate); software engineering (MS); telecommunications (MS). *Degree requirements:* For master's, thesis optional. *Entrance requirements:* For master's, GMAT, GRE General Test. Additional exam requirements/recommendations for international students: Required—TOEFL. Electronic applications accepted.

Strayer University, Graduate Studies, Washington, DC 20005-2603. Offers accounting (MS); acquisition (MBA); business administration (MBA); communications technology (MS); educational management (M Ed); finance (MBA); health services administration (MHSA); hospitality and tourism management (MBA); human resource management (MBA); information systems (MS), including computer security management, decision support system management, enterprise resource management, network management, software engineering management, systems development management; management (MBA); management information systems (MS); marketing (MBA); professional accounting (MS), including accounting information systems, controllership, taxation; public administration (MPA); supply chain management (MBA); technology in education (M Ed). Programs also offered at campus locations in Birmingham, AL; Chamblee, GA; Cobb County, GA; Morrow, GA; White Marsh, MD; Charleston, SC; Columbia, SC; Greensboro, NC; Greenville, SC; Lexington, KY; Louisville, KY; Nashville, TN; North Raleigh, NC; Washington, DC. Part-time and evening/weekend programs available. Postbaccalaureate distance learning degree programs offered (minimal on-campus study). *Degree requirements:* For master's, thesis. *Entrance requirements:* For master's, GMAT, GRE General Test, bachelor's degree from an accredited college or university, minimum undergraduate GPA of 2.75. Electronic applications accepted.

Syracuse University, L. C. Smith College of Engineering and Computer Science, Program in Computer and Information Science and Engineering, Syracuse, NY 13244. Offers PhD. Part-time programs available. *Students:* 26 full-time (5 women), 8 part-time (3 women); includes 2 minority (both Asian, non-Hispanic/Latino), 25 international. Average age 29. 69 applicants, 17% accepted, 8 enrolled. In 2014, 3 doctorates awarded. *Degree requirements:* For doctorate, comprehensive exam, thesis/dissertation. *Entrance requirements:* For doctorate, GRE General Test, GRE Subject Test (computer science). Additional exam requirements/recommendations for international students: Required—TOEFL (minimum score 100 iBT). *Application deadline:* For fall admission, 7/1 priority date for domestic students, 6/1 priority date for international students; for spring admission, 11/15 priority date for domestic students, 10/15 priority date for international students. Applications are processed on a rolling basis. Application fee: $75. Electronic applications accepted. *Expenses: Tuition:* Part-time $1341 per credit. *Required fees:* $1341 per credit. *Financial support:* Fellowships with full tuition reimbursements, research assistantships with full and partial tuition reimbursements, teaching assistantships with full and partial tuition reimbursements, and tuition waivers (partial) available. Financial award application deadline: 1/1; financial award applicants required to submit FAFSA. *Unit head:* Dr. Chilukuri Mohan, Department Chair, 315-443-2322, Fax: 315-443-2583, E-mail: ckmohan@syr.edu. *Application contact:* Brenda Flowers, Information Contact, 315-443-4408, E-mail: topgrads@syr.edu.
Website: http://lcs.syr.edu/.

Syracuse University, School of Information Studies, Program in Information Science and Technology, Syracuse, NY 13244. Offers PhD. *Students:* 26 full-time (13 women), 9 part-time (7 women); includes 9 minority (5 Black or African American, non-Hispanic/Latino; 2 Asian, non-Hispanic/Latino; 1 Hispanic/Latino; 1 Two or more races, non-Hispanic/Latino), 16 international. Average age 35. 44 applicants, 11% accepted, 3 enrolled. In 2014, 4 doctorates awarded. *Degree requirements:* For doctorate, comprehensive exam, thesis/dissertation. *Entrance requirements:* For doctorate, GRE General Test, interview, writing sample of scholarly work. Additional exam requirements/recommendations for international students: Required—TOEFL (minimum score 100 iBT). *Application deadline:* For fall admission, 1/10 priority date for domestic and international students. Application fee: $75. Electronic applications accepted. *Expenses: Tuition:* Part-time $1341 per credit. *Required fees:* $1341 per credit. *Financial support:* Fellowships with full tuition reimbursements, research assistantships with partial tuition reimbursements, and teaching assistantships with partial tuition reimbursements available. Financial award application deadline: 1/1. *Unit head:* Dr. Steve Sawyer, Director, 315-443-6147, Fax: 315-443-6886, E-mail: ssawyer@syr.edu. *Application contact:* Susan Corieri, Director of Enrollment Management, 315-443-2575, E-mail: ischool@syr.edu.
Website: http://ischool.syr.edu/.

Temple University, College of Science and Technology, Department of Computer and Information Sciences, Philadelphia, PA 19140. Offers computer and information science (PhD); computer science (MS); information science and technology (MS). Part-time and evening/weekend programs available. *Faculty:* 28 full-time (4 women), 5 part-time/adjunct (1 woman). *Students:* 92 full-time (24 women), 24 part-time (8 women); includes 7 minority (2 Black or African American, non-Hispanic/Latino; 5 Asian, non-Hispanic/Latino), 81 international. 102 applicants, 71% accepted, 31 enrolled. In 2014, 29 master's, 8 doctorates awarded. Terminal master's awarded for partial completion of doctoral program. *Degree requirements:* For doctorate, thesis/dissertation. *Entrance requirements:* For master's and doctorate, GRE General Test, minimum GPA of 3.0. Additional exam requirements/recommendations for international students: Required—TOEFL (minimum score 550 paper-based; 79 iBT). *Application deadline:* For fall admission, 2/1 for domestic students, 12/15 for international students; for spring admission, 8/1 for domestic and international students. Applications are processed on a rolling basis. Application fee: $60. Electronic applications accepted. *Expenses:* Tuition, state resident: full-time $14,490; part-time $805 per credit hour. Tuition, nonresident: full-time $19,850; part-time $1103 per credit hour. *Required fees:* $690. Full-time tuition and fees vary according to class time, course load, degree level, campus/location and program. *Financial support:* Fellowships, research assistantships with tuition reimbursements, teaching assistantships with tuition reimbursements, career-related internships or fieldwork, institutionally sponsored loans, and unspecified assistantships available. Financial award application deadline: 1/15; financial award applicants required to submit FAFSA. *Faculty research:* Artificial intelligence, information systems, software engineering, network-distributed systems. *Unit head:* Dr. Jie Wu, Chair, 215-204-8450, Fax: 215-204-5082, E-mail: cis@temple.edu. *Application contact:* Marilyn Grandshaw, Administrative Coordinator, 215-204-8450, E-mail: marilyng@temple.edu.
Website: http://www.temple.edu/cis.

Towson University, Program in Applied Information Technology, Towson, MD 21252-0001. Offers applied information technology (MS, D Sc); database management systems (Postbaccalaureate Certificate); information security and assurance (Postbaccalaureate Certificate); information systems management (Postbaccalaureate Certificate); Internet applications development (Postbaccalaureate Certificate); networking technologies (Postbaccalaureate Certificate); software engineering (Postbaccalaureate Certificate). *Students:* 132 full-time (44 women), 219 part-time (73 women); includes 118 minority (71 Black or African American, non-Hispanic/Latino; 1 American Indian or Alaska Native, non-Hispanic/Latino; 23 Asian, non-Hispanic/Latino; 12 Hispanic/Latino; 2 Native Hawaiian or other Pacific Islander, non-Hispanic/Latino; 9 Two or more races, non-Hispanic/Latino), 85 international. *Entrance requirements:* For master's and Postbaccalaureate Certificate, bachelor's degree, minimum GPA of 3.0; for doctorate, master's degree in computer science, information systems, information technology, or closely-related areas; minimum GPA of 3.0; 2 letters of recommendation; resume. Additional exam requirements/recommendations for international students: Required—TOEFL. *Application deadline:* Applications are processed on a rolling basis. Application fee: $45. Electronic applications accepted. *Unit head:* Dr. Suranjan Chakraborty, Graduate Program Director, 410-704-4769, E-mail: schakraborty@towson.edu. *Application contact:* Alicia Arkell-Kleis, Information Contact, 410-704-6004, E-mail: grads@towson.edu.
Website: http://grad.towson.edu/program/master/ait-ms/.

Trevecca Nazarene University, Graduate Education Program, Nashville, TN 37210-2877. Offers curriculum, assessment, and instruction K-12 (M Ed); educational leadership (M Ed); leadership and professional practice (Ed D); library and information science (MLI Sc); teaching (MAE, MAT), including teaching 7-12 (MAT), teaching K-6 (MAT); turnaround school leadership (M Ed); visual impairments special education (M Ed). *Accreditation:* NCATE. Part-time and evening/weekend programs available. Postbaccalaureate distance learning degree programs offered. *Faculty:* 9 full-time (all women), 18 part-time/adjunct (10 women). *Students:* 249 full-time (191 women), 72 part-time (55 women); includes 114 minority (104 Black or African American, non-Hispanic/Latino; 2 Asian, non-Hispanic/Latino; 2 Hispanic/Latino; 1 Native Hawaiian or other Pacific Islander, non-Hispanic/Latino; 5 Two or more races, non-Hispanic/Latino), 1 international. Average age 37. In 2014, 112 master's, 21 doctorates awarded. *Degree requirements:* For master's, comprehensive exam, exit assessment/e-portfolio; for doctorate, thesis/dissertation, proposal study, symposium presentation. *Entrance requirements:* For master's, GRE with minimum score of 378 or MAT with minimum score of 290, ACT with minimum score of 22 or SAT with minimum score of 1020 (for MAT programs only); PRAXIS (for MAT and MAE programs), minimum GPA of 2.7, official transcript from regionally-accredited institution, 3+ years' successful teaching experience (for M Ed in teacher leader and educational leadership majors); for doctorate, GRE or MAT, minimum GPA of 3.4, official transcript from regionally-accredited institution, resume, writing sample, interview, reference forms. Additional exam requirements/recommendations for international students: Required—TOEFL (minimum score 550 paper-based). *Application deadline:* Applications are processed on a rolling basis. *Expenses:* Expenses: Contact institution. *Financial support:* Applicants required to submit FAFSA. *Unit head:* Dr. Suzie Harris, Dean, School of Education/Director of Graduate Education Programs, 615-248-1201, Fax: 615-248-1597, E-mail: admissions_ged@trevecca.edu. *Application contact:* 615-248-1529, E-mail: cll@trevecca.edu.
Website: http://trevecca.edu/academics/program/educational-leadership (address varies by major).

Université de Sherbrooke, Faculty of Sciences, Department of Informatics, Sherbrooke, QC J1K 2R1, Canada. Offers M Sc, PhD. *Degree requirements:* For master's, thesis. Electronic applications accepted.

University at Albany, State University of New York, College of Computing and Information, Albany, NY 12222-0001. Offers computer science (MS, PhD); information science (PhD); information studies (MS, CAS), including information science. *Accreditation:* ALA (one or more programs are accredited). Part-time programs available. *Degree requirements:* For doctorate, thesis/dissertation. *Entrance requirements:* For doctorate, GRE General Test. Additional exam requirements/recommendations for international students: Required—TOEFL (minimum score 550 paper-based). Electronic applications accepted. *Faculty research:* Human-computer interaction, government information management, library information science, Web development, social implications of technology.

The University of Alabama at Birmingham, College of Arts and Sciences, Program in Computer and Information Sciences, Birmingham, AL 35294. Offers MS, PhD. *Students:* 47 full-time (8 women), 11 part-time (2 women); includes 2 minority (1 Asian, non-Hispanic/Latino; 1 Hispanic/Latino), 34 international. Average age 29. In 2014, 15 master's, 1 doctorate awarded. Terminal master's awarded for partial completion of doctoral program. *Degree requirements:* For master's, thesis optional; for doctorate, thesis/dissertation. *Entrance requirements:* For master's, GRE General Test, minimum GPA of 3.0, letters of recommendation; for doctorate, GRE General Test, minimum GPA of 3.5 overall or on last 60 hours; letters of recommendation. Additional exam requirements/recommendations for international students: Required—TOEFL, IELTS. *Application deadline:* For fall admission, 2/1 for domestic students; for spring admission, 9/1 for domestic students. Applications are processed on a rolling basis. Application fee: $45 ($60 for international students). Electronic applications accepted. *Expenses:* Tuition, state resident: full-time $7090; part-time $370 per credit hour. Tuition, nonresident: full-time $16,072; part-time $869 per credit hour. Full-time tuition and fees vary according to course load and program. *Financial support:* Fellowships with full tuition reimbursements, research assistantships with full tuition reimbursements, teaching assistantships with full tuition reimbursements, career-related internships or fieldwork, Federal Work-Study, institutionally sponsored loans, scholarships/grants, traineeships, health care benefits, and unspecified assistantships available. Support available to part-time students. Financial award application deadline: 3/10. *Faculty research:* Theory and software systems, intelligent systems, systems architecture, high performance computing, computer architecture, computer graphics, data mining, software engineering. *Unit head:* Dr. Chengcui Zhang, Graduate Program Director, 205-934-8606, Fax: 205-934-5473, E-mail: czhang02@uab.edu. *Application contact:* Susan Noblitt Banks, Director of Graduate School Operations, 205-934-8227, Fax: 205-934-8413, E-mail: gradschool@uab.edu.
Website: https://cis.uab.edu/academics/graduates/.

University of Arkansas at Little Rock, Graduate School, George W. Donaghey College of Engineering and Information Technology, Program in Information Quality, Little Rock, AR 72204-1099. Offers MS, PhD, Graduate Certificate. *Expenses:* Tuition, state resident: full-time $6000; part-time $300 per credit hour. Tuition, nonresident: full-time $13,800; part-time $690 per credit hour. *Required fees:* $1126; $603 per term. One-time fee: $40 full-time. *Unit head:* Dr. John R. Talburt, Chair, 501-371-7616, Fax: 501-683-7049, E-mail: jrtalburt@ualr.edu.
Website: http:/ualr.edu/informationquality/.

University of California, Irvine, Donald Bren School of Information and Computer Sciences, Department of Informatics, Irvine, CA 92697. Offers information and computer science (MS, PhD). *Students:* 105 full-time (41 women), 7 part-time (2 women); includes 16 minority (1 Black or African American, non-Hispanic/Latino; 6 Asian, non-Hispanic/Latino; 5 Hispanic/Latino; 4 Two or more races, non-Hispanic/Latino), 67 international. Average age 28. 469 applicants, 19% accepted, 43 enrolled. In 2014, 20 master's, 7 doctorates awarded. Application fee: $90 ($110 for international students). *Unit head:* Andre van der Hoek, Chair, 949-824-6326, Fax: 949-824-4056, E-mail: andre@uci.edu. *Application contact:* Gillian Hayes, Vice Chair of Graduate Affairs, 949-824-1483, E-mail: gillianrh@ics.uci.edu.
Website: http://www.informatics.uci.edu/.

University of California, Merced, Graduate Division, School of Social Sciences, Humanities and Arts, Merced, CA 95343. Offers cognitive and information sciences (MA, PhD); psychology (MA, PhD); social sciences (MA, PhD); world cultures (MA, PhD). *Faculty:* 89 full-time (40 women). *Students:* 114 full-time (79 women), 2 part-time (1 woman); includes 43 minority (3 Black or African American, non-Hispanic/Latino; 1 American Indian or Alaska Native, non-Hispanic/Latino; 10 Asian, non-Hispanic/Latino; 24 Hispanic/Latino; 1 Native Hawaiian or other Pacific Islander, non-Hispanic/Latino; 4 Two or more races, non-Hispanic/Latino), 13 international. Average age 32. 127 applicants, 34% accepted, 22 enrolled. In 2014, 3 master's, 11 doctorates awarded. *Degree requirements:* For master's, variable foreign language requirement, comprehensive exam, thesis; for doctorate, variable foreign language requirement, comprehensive exam, thesis/dissertation. *Entrance requirements:* For master's and doctorate, GRE. Additional exam requirements/recommendations for international students: Required—TOEFL (minimum score 550 paper-based; 68 iBT); Recommended—IELTS. *Application deadline:* For fall admission, 1/15 for domestic and international students. Application fee: $80 ($100 for international students). Electronic applications accepted. *Expenses:* Tuition, state resident: full-time $11,220; part-time $2805 per semester. *Required fees:* $1940; $970 per semester hour. *Financial support:* In 2014–15, 29 fellowships with full and partial tuition reimbursements (averaging $7,056 per year) were awarded; scholarships/grants also available. *Faculty research:* Psychology, political science, social inequality, interdisciplinary, humanities, cognitive sciences. *Unit head:* Dr. Mark Aldenderfer, Dean, 209-228-7843, Fax: 209-228-4007, E-mail: maldenderfer@ucmerced.edu. *Application contact:* Tsu Ya, Graduate Admissions and Academic Services Manager, 209-228-4521, Fax: 209-228-6906, E-mail: tya@ucmerced.edu.

Information Science

University of Central Missouri, The Graduate School, Warrensburg, MO 64093. Offers accountancy (MA); accounting (MBA); applied mathematics (MS); aviation safety (MA); biology (MS); business administration (MBA); career and technical education leadership (MS); college student personnel administration (MS); communication (MA); computer science (MS); counseling (MS); criminal justice (MS); educational leadership (Ed D); educational technology (MS); elementary and early childhood education (MSE); English (MA); environmental studies (MA); finance (MBA); history (MA); human services/educational technology (Ed S); human services/learning resources (Ed S); human services/professional counseling (Ed S); industrial hygiene (MS); industrial management (MS); information systems (MBA); information technology (MS); kinesiology (MS); library science and information services (MS); literacy education (MSE); marketing (MBA); mathematics (MS); music (MA); occupational safety management (MS); psychology (MS); rural family nursing (MS); school administration (MSE); social gerontology (MS); sociology (MA); special education (MSE); speech language pathology (MS); superintendency (Ed S); teaching (MAT); teaching English as a second language (MA); technology (MS); technology management (PhD); theatre (MA). Part-time programs available. *Faculty:* 314 full-time (137 women), 24 part-time/adjunct (14 women). *Students:* 1,624 full-time (542 women), 1,773 part-time (1,055 women); includes 194 minority (104 Black or African American, non-Hispanic/Latino; 6 American Indian or Alaska Native, non-Hispanic/Latino; 23 Asian, non-Hispanic/Latino; 41 Hispanic/Latino; 3 Native Hawaiian or other Pacific Islander, non-Hispanic/Latino; 17 Two or more races, non-Hispanic/Latino), 1,592 international. Average age 31. 2,800 applicants, 63% accepted, 1223 enrolled. In 2014, 796 master's, 81 other advanced degrees awarded. *Degree requirements:* For master's and Ed S, comprehensive exam (for some programs), thesis (for some programs). *Entrance requirements:* Additional exam requirements/recommendations for international students: Required—TOEFL (minimum score 550 paper-based; 79 iBT). *Application deadline:* For fall admission, 6/1 for domestic students; for spring admission, 10/1 for domestic and international students. Applications are processed on a rolling basis. Application fee: $30 ($75 for international students). Electronic applications accepted. *Expenses:* Tuition, state resident: full-time $6630; part-time $276.25 per credit hour. Tuition, nonresident: full-time $13,260; part-time $552.50 per credit hour. *Required fees:* $29 per credit hour. Tuition and fees vary according to campus/location. *Financial support:* In 2014–15, 118 students received support, including 271 research assistantships with full and partial tuition reimbursements available (averaging $7,500 per year), 109 teaching assistantships with full and partial tuition reimbursements available (averaging $7,500 per year); career-related internships or fieldwork, Federal Work-Study, scholarships/grants, and administrative and laboratory assistantships also available. Support available to part-time students. Financial award application deadline: 3/1; financial award applicants required to submit FAFSA. *Unit head:* Tina Church-Hockett, Director of Graduate School and International Admissions, 660-543-4621, Fax: 660-543-4778, E-mail: church@ucmo.edu. *Application contact:* Brittany Lawrence, Graduate Student Services Coordinator, 660-543-4621, Fax: 660-543-4778, E-mail: gradinfo@ucmo.edu. Website: http://www.ucmo.edu/graduate/.

University of Colorado Denver, College of Engineering and Applied Science, Department of Computer Science and Engineering, Denver, CO 80217. Offers computer science (MS); computer science and engineering (EASPh D); computer science and information systems (PhD). Part-time and evening/weekend programs available. *Faculty:* 9 full-time (2 women), 3 part-time/adjunct (1 woman). *Students:* 113 full-time (44 women), 28 part-time (6 women); includes 9 minority (3 Black or African American, non-Hispanic/Latino; 3 Asian, non-Hispanic/Latino; 2 Hispanic/Latino; 1 Two or more races, non-Hispanic/Latino), 104 international. Average age 29. 394 applicants, 46% accepted, 64 enrolled. In 2014, 28 master's awarded. *Degree requirements:* For master's, thesis or alternative, at least 30 semester hours of computer science courses while maintaining minimum GPA of 3.0; for doctorate, comprehensive exam, thesis/dissertation, at least 60 hours beyond the master's degree level, 30 of which are dissertation research. *Entrance requirements:* For master's, GRE, minimum GPA of 3.0, 10 semester hours of university-level calculus, at least one math course beyond calculus, statement of purpose, letters of recommendation; for doctorate, GRE or GMAT. Additional exam requirements/recommendations for international students: Required—TOEFL (minimum score 537 paper-based; 75 iBT). *Application deadline:* For fall admission, 5/1 for domestic students, 4/1 for international students; for spring admission, 10/1 for domestic students, 9/1 for international students. Application fee: $50 ($75 for international students). Electronic applications accepted. *Financial support:* In 2014–15, 8 students received support. Research assistantships, teaching assistantships, Federal Work-Study, institutionally sponsored loans, scholarships/grants, traineeships, and unspecified assistantships available. Financial award application deadline: 4/1; financial award applicants required to submit FAFSA. *Faculty research:* Algorithms, automata theory, artificial intelligence, communication networks, combinatorial geometry, computational geometry, computer architectures, computer graphics, distributed computing, high performance computing, graph theory, Internet, operating systems, parallel processing, simulation and software engineering. *Unit head:* Dr. Gita Alaghband, Chair, 303-315-1400, E-mail: gita.alaghband@ucdenver.edu. *Application contact:* Sarah Mandos, Program Assistant, 303-315-1411, E-mail: sarah.mandos@ucdenver.edu. Website: http://www.ucdenver.edu/academics/colleges/Engineering/Programs/Computer-Science-and-Engineering/Pages/ComputerScienceEngineering.aspx.

University of Delaware, College of Engineering, Department of Computer and Information Sciences, Newark, DE 19716. Offers MS, PhD. Part-time programs available. Terminal master's awarded for partial completion of doctoral program. *Degree requirements:* For master's, thesis optional; for doctorate, comprehensive exam, thesis/dissertation. *Entrance requirements:* For master's and doctorate, GRE General Test. Additional exam requirements/recommendations for international students: Required—TOEFL (minimum score 550 paper-based). Electronic applications accepted. *Faculty research:* Artificial intelligence, computational theory, graphics and computer vision, networks, systems.

University of Detroit Mercy, College of Business Administration, Program in Information Assurance, Detroit, MI 48221. Offers MS.

University of Florida, Graduate School, College of Engineering and College of Liberal Arts and Sciences, Department of Computer and Information Science and Engineering, Gainesville, FL 32611. Offers computer engineering (ME, MS, PhD); computer science (MS); digital arts and sciences (MS). Part-time programs available. Postbaccalaureate distance learning degree programs offered (minimal on-campus study). *Faculty:* 42 full-time (6 women), 32 part-time/adjunct (4 women). *Students:* 364 full-time (91 women), 90 part-time (9 women); includes 30 minority (8 Black or African American, non-Hispanic/Latino; 1 American Indian or Alaska Native, non-Hispanic/Latino; 12 Asian, non-Hispanic/Latino; 9 Hispanic/Latino), 370 international. 2,043 applicants, 22% accepted, 156 enrolled. In 2014, 218 master's, 18 doctorates awarded. Terminal master's awarded for partial completion of doctoral program. *Degree requirements:* For master's, comprehensive exam, thesis optional; for doctorate, comprehensive exam, thesis/dissertation. *Entrance requirements:* For master's and doctorate, minimum GPA of 3.0. Additional exam requirements/recommendations for international students: Required—TOEFL (minimum score 550 paper-based; 80 iBT), IELTS (minimum score 6).

Application deadline: For fall admission, 12/15 priority date for domestic students, 2/1 for international students; for spring admission, 9/1 for domestic and international students. Applications are processed on a rolling basis. Application fee: $30. Electronic applications accepted. *Financial support:* Unspecified assistantships available. Financial award application deadline: 2/1; financial award applicants required to submit FAFSA. *Faculty research:* Computer systems and computer networking; high-performance computing and algorithm; database and machine learning; computer graphics, vision, and intelligent systems; human center computing and digital art. *Unit head:* Paul Gader, PhD, Chair, 352-392-1527, Fax: 352-392-1220, E-mail: pgader@cise.ufl.edu. *Application contact:* Jih-Kwon Peir, PhD, Graduate Coordinator, 352-505-1573, Fax: 352-392-1220, E-mail: peir@cise.ufl.edu. Website: http://www.cise.ufl.edu/.

University of Hawaii at Manoa, Graduate Division, Interdisciplinary Program in Communication and Information Sciences, Honolulu, HI 96822. Offers PhD. Part-time programs available. *Degree requirements:* For doctorate, comprehensive exam, thesis/dissertation. *Entrance requirements:* For doctorate, GRE or GMAT. Additional exam requirements/recommendations for international students: Required—TOEFL (minimum score 600 paper-based; 100 iBT), IELTS (minimum score 7).

University of Hawaii at Manoa, Graduate Division, Shidler College of Business, Program in Business Administration, Honolulu, HI 96822. Offers Asian business studies (MBA); Chinese business studies (MBA); decision sciences (MBA); entrepreneurship (MBA); finance (MBA); finance and banking (MBA); human resources management (MBA); information management (MBA); information technology (MBA); international business (MBA); Japanese business studies (MBA); marketing (MBA); organizational behavior (MBA); organizational management (MBA); real estate (MBA); student-designed track (MBA). *Accreditation:* AACSB. Part-time and evening/weekend programs available. *Degree requirements:* For master's, thesis optional. *Entrance requirements:* For master's, GMAT, minimum GPA of 3.0. Additional exam requirements/recommendations for international students: Required—TOEFL (minimum score 600 paper-based; 100 iBT), IELTS (minimum score 7). *Expenses:* Contact institution.

University of Houston, Bauer College of Business, Decision and Information Sciences Program, Houston, TX 77204. Offers PhD. Evening/weekend programs available.

University of Houston, College of Technology, Department of Information and Logistics Technology, Houston, TX 77204. Offers information security (MS); supply chain and logistics technology (MS); technology project management (MS). Part-time programs available. *Degree requirements:* For master's, project or thesis (most programs). *Entrance requirements:* For master's, GMAT. Additional exam requirements/recommendations for international students: Required—TOEFL (minimum score 550 paper-based; 79 iBT). Electronic applications accepted.

University of Houston–Clear Lake, School of Science and Computer Engineering, Program in Computer Information Systems, Houston, TX 77058-1002. Offers MS. Part-time and evening/weekend programs available. *Entrance requirements:* For master's, GRE General Test. Additional exam requirements/recommendations for international students: Required—TOEFL (minimum score 550 paper-based).

University of Illinois at Urbana–Champaign, Graduate College, Graduate School of Library and Information Science, Champaign, IL 61820. Offers bioinformatics (MS); digital libraries (CAS); library and information science (MS, PhD, CAS). *Accreditation:* ALA (one or more programs are accredited). Part-time programs available. Postbaccalaureate distance learning degree programs offered (minimal on-campus study). *Students:* 283 (208 women). *Entrance requirements:* For degree, master's degree in library and information science or related field with minimum GPA of 3.0. Application fee: $70 ($90 for international students). *Unit head:* Allen Renear, Interim Dean, 217-265-5216, Fax: 217-244-3302, E-mail: renear@illinois.edu. *Application contact:* Penny Ames, Graduate Contact, 217-333-7197, E-mail: pames@illinois.edu. Website: http://www.lis.illinois.edu.

University of Illinois at Urbana–Champaign, Informatics Institute, Champaign, IL 61820. Offers PhD. *Students:* 27 (6 women). *Degree requirements:* For doctorate, thesis/dissertation. Application fee: $70 ($90 for international students). *Unit head:* Guy Garnett, Director, 217-333-3281, E-mail: garnett@illinois.edu. *Application contact:* Karin Readel, Coordinator for Informatics Education Programs, 217-244-1220, E-mail: kereadel@illinois.edu. Website: http://www.informatics.illinois.edu/.

The University of Iowa, Graduate College, Program in Informatics, Iowa City, IA 52242-1316. Offers bioinformatics (MS, PhD); bioinformatics and computational biology (Certificate); geoinformatics (MS, PhD, Certificate); health informatics (MS, PhD, Certificate); information science (MS, PhD, Certificate). *Degree requirements:* For master's, thesis optional; for doctorate, comprehensive exam, thesis/dissertation. *Entrance requirements:* For master's and doctorate, GRE General Test, minimum GPA of 3.0. Additional exam requirements/recommendations for international students: Required—TOEFL (minimum score 550 paper-based; 81 iBT). Electronic applications accepted.

University of Kentucky, Graduate School, College of Communication and Information, Program in Library and Information Science, Lexington, KY 40506-0032. Offers MA, MSLS. *Accreditation:* ALA (one or more programs are accredited). Part-time programs available. *Degree requirements:* For master's, variable foreign language requirement, comprehensive exam. *Entrance requirements:* For master's, GRE General Test, minimum undergraduate GPA of 2.75. Additional exam requirements/recommendations for international students: Required—TOEFL (minimum score 550 paper-based). *Faculty research:* Information retrieval systems, information-seeking behavior, organizational behavior, computer cataloging, library resource sharing.

University of Maine, Graduate School, College of Liberal Arts and Sciences, School of Computing and Information Science, Orono, ME 04469. Offers computer science (MS, PhD); geographic information systems (CGS); information systems (MS); spatial information science and engineering (MS, PhD). Part-time programs available. *Faculty:* 13 full-time (2 women). *Students:* 30 full-time (6 women), 9 part-time (2 women); includes 1 minority (Asian, non-Hispanic/Latino), 10 international. Average age 34. 46 applicants, 37% accepted, 3 enrolled. In 2014, 9 master's, 3 doctorates awarded. Terminal master's awarded for partial completion of doctoral program. *Degree requirements:* For master's, thesis (for some programs); for doctorate, comprehensive exam, thesis/dissertation. *Entrance requirements:* For master's and doctorate, GRE General Test, GRE Subject Test. Additional exam requirements/recommendations for international students: Required—TOEFL. *Application deadline:* For fall admission, 2/1 priority date for domestic students. Applications are processed on a rolling basis. Application fee: $65. Electronic applications accepted. *Expenses:* Tuition, state resident: part-time $658 per credit hour. Tuition, nonresident: part-time $1550 per credit hour. *Financial support:* In 2014–15, 18 students received support, including 3 fellowships (averaging $21,600 per year), 7 research assistantships with full tuition reimbursements available (averaging $14,600 per year), 8 teaching assistantships with full tuition reimbursements available (averaging $14,600 per year); career-related internships or fieldwork, Federal Work-Study, institutionally sponsored loans, and tuition waivers (full) also available. Financial award application deadline: 3/1. *Faculty research:*

Geographic information science, virtual reality, robotics, sensor networks, ice sheet modeling. *Total annual research expenditures:* $436,973. *Unit head:* Dr. Max Egenhofer, Acting Director, 207-581-2114, Fax: 207-581-2206. *Application contact:* Scott G. Delcourt, Assistant Vice President for Graduate Studies and Senior Associate Dean, 207-581-3291, Fax: 207-581-3232, E-mail: graduate@maine.edu.
Website: http://umaine.edu/cis/.

University of Maryland, Baltimore County, The Graduate School, College of Engineering and Information Technology, Department of Information Systems, Program in Information Systems, Baltimore, MD 21250. Offers MS, PhD. Part-time programs available. Postbaccalaureate distance learning degree programs offered (no on-campus study). *Students:* 171 full-time (68 women), 230 part-time (79 women); includes 93 minority (45 Black or African American, non-Hispanic/Latino; 1 American Indian or Alaska Native, non-Hispanic/Latino; 38 Asian, non-Hispanic/Latino; 5 Hispanic/Latino; 4 Two or more races, non-Hispanic/Latino), 168 international. Average age 32. 464 applicants, 54% accepted, 101 enrolled. In 2014, 93 master's, 6 doctorates awarded. *Degree requirements:* For master's, comprehensive exam (for some programs), thesis optional; for doctorate, comprehensive exam, thesis/dissertation. *Entrance requirements:* For master's, minimum GPA of 3.0; for doctorate, GRE General Test or GMAT, competence in statistical analysis, experimental design, programming, databases, and computer networks. Additional exam requirements/recommendations for international students: Required—TOEFL (minimum score 550 paper-based; 80 iBT). *Application deadline:* For fall admission, 6/1 for domestic students, 1/1 for international students; for spring admission, 11/1 for domestic students, 6/1 for international students. Applications are processed on a rolling basis. Application fee: $70. Electronic applications accepted. *Expenses:* Tuition, state resident: part-time $557. Tuition, nonresident: part-time $922. *Required fees:* $122 per semester. One-time fee: $200 part-time. *Financial support:* In 2014–15, 4 fellowships with full tuition reimbursements (averaging $20,000 per year), 17 research assistantships with full tuition reimbursements (averaging $20,000 per year), 11 teaching assistantships with full tuition reimbursements (averaging $17,000 per year) were awarded; career-related internships or fieldwork, Federal Work-Study, scholarships/grants, health care benefits, tuition waivers (partial), and unspecified assistantships also available. Support available to part-time students. Financial award application deadline: 6/30; financial award applicants required to submit FAFSA. *Faculty research:* Artificial intelligence/knowledge management, database/data mining, software engineering. *Unit head:* Dr. Arrya Gangopadhyay, Professor and Chair, 410-455-2620, Fax: 410-455-1217, E-mail: gangopad@umbc.edu. *Application contact:* Dr. Zhiyuan Chen, Associate Professor and Graduate Program Director, 410-455-8833, Fax: 410-455-1217, E-mail: zhchen@umbc.edu.
Website: http://www.is.umbc.edu/.

University of Maryland University College, The Graduate School, Program in Information Technology, Adelphi, MD 20783. Offers MS, Certificate. Part-time and evening/weekend programs available. Postbaccalaureate distance learning degree programs offered (no on-campus study). *Students:* 34 full-time (11 women), 1,569 part-time (540 women); includes 804 minority (545 Black or African American, non-Hispanic/Latino; 8 American Indian or Alaska Native, non-Hispanic/Latino; 111 Asian, non-Hispanic/Latino; 97 Hispanic/Latino; 5 Native Hawaiian or other Pacific Islander, non-Hispanic/Latino; 38 Two or more races, non-Hispanic/Latino), 40 international. Average age 36. 557 applicants, 100% accepted, 332 enrolled. In 2014, 404 master's, 92 other advanced degrees awarded. *Degree requirements:* For master's, thesis or alternative, capstone course. *Application deadline:* Applications are processed on a rolling basis. Application fee: $50. Electronic applications accepted. *Financial support:* Federal Work-Study and scholarships/grants available. Support available to part-time students. Financial award application deadline: 6/1; financial award applicants required to submit FAFSA. *Unit head:* Dr. Garth MacKenzie, Program Chair, 240-684-2400, Fax: 240-684-2401, E-mail: garth.mackenzie@umuc.edu. *Application contact:* Coordinator, Graduate Admissions, 800-888-8682, Fax: 240-684-2151, E-mail: newgrad@umuc.edu.
Website: http://www.umuc.edu/academic-programs/masters-degrees/information-technology.cfm.

University of Massachusetts Dartmouth, Graduate School, College of Engineering, Program in Engineering and Applied Science, North Dartmouth, MA 02747-2300. Offers applied mechanics and materials (PhD); computational science and engineering (PhD); computer science and information systems (PhD); industrial and systems engineering (PhD). Part-time programs available. *Students:* 21 full-time (6 women), 1 (woman) part-time; includes 2 minority (1 Black or African American, non-Hispanic/Latino; 1 Two or more races, non-Hispanic/Latino), 12 international. Average age 30. 23 applicants, 65% accepted, 5 enrolled. In 2014, 1 doctorate awarded. *Degree requirements:* For doctorate, comprehensive exam, thesis/dissertation. *Entrance requirements:* For doctorate, GRE, statement of purpose (minimum of 300 words), resume, 3 letters of recommendation, official transcripts. Additional exam requirements/recommendations for international students: Required—TOEFL (minimum score 550 paper-based; 79 iBT). *Application deadline:* For fall admission, 2/15 priority date for domestic students, 1/15 priority date for international students; for spring admission, 11/15 priority date for domestic students, 10/15 priority date for international students. Applications are processed on a rolling basis. Application fee: $60. Electronic applications accepted. *Expenses:* Tuition, state resident: full-time $2071; part-time $86.29 per credit. Tuition, nonresident: full-time $8099; part-time $337.46 per credit. *Required fees:* $16,520; $712.33 per credit. Tuition and fees vary according to course load and reciprocity agreements. *Financial support:* In 2014–15, 8 fellowships with full tuition reimbursements (averaging $16,577 per year), 8 research assistantships with full tuition reimbursements (averaging $13,627 per year), 5 teaching assistantships with full tuition reimbursements (averaging $12,400 per year) were awarded; Federal Work-Study and unspecified assistantships also available. Support available to part-time students. Financial award application deadline: 3/1; financial award applicants required to submit FAFSA. *Faculty research:* Tissue/cell engineering, biotransport sensors/networks, marine systems biomimetic materials, composite/polymeric materials, resilient infrastructure robotics, renewable energy. *Total annual research expenditures:* $1.7 million. *Unit head:* Gaurav Khanna, Graduate Program Director, 508-910-6605, Fax: 508-999-9115, E-mail: gkhanna@umassd.edu. *Application contact:* Steven Briggs, Director of Marketing and Recruitment for Graduate Studies, 508-999-8604, Fax: 508-999-8183, E-mail: graduate@umassd.edu.
Website: http://www.umassd.edu/engineering/graduate/doctoraldegreeprograms/egrandappliedsciencephd/

⭐ **University of Michigan,** Horace H. Rackham School of Graduate Studies, School of Information, Ann Arbor, MI 48109-1285. Offers archives and records management (MSI); health informatics (MS); information (PhD). *Accreditation:* ALA (one or more programs are accredited). Part-time programs available. *Students:* 424 full-time (256 women), 32 part-time (15 women); includes 85 minority (14 Black or African American, non-Hispanic/Latino; 39 Asian, non-Hispanic/Latino; 21 Hispanic/Latino; 11 Two or more races, non-Hispanic/Latino), 178 international. Average age 28. 765 applicants, 55% accepted, 199 enrolled. In 2014, 188 master's, 6 doctorates awarded. Terminal master's awarded for partial completion of doctoral program. *Degree requirements:* For master's, thesis optional, internship requirement; for

doctorate, thesis/dissertation. *Entrance requirements:* For master's and doctorate, GRE General Test. Additional exam requirements/recommendations for international students: Required—TOEFL (minimum score 600 paper-based; 100 iBT). *Application deadline:* Applications are processed on a rolling basis. Application fee: $75 ($90 for international students). Electronic applications accepted. *Expenses:* Expenses: MS full time: $12,496/term in state, $20,657/term out-of-state; MSI full time: $10,039/term in-state, $20,282/term out-of-state; PhD: fully funded. *Financial support:* In 2014–15, 122 students received support, including 2 fellowships (averaging $28,200 per year), 33 research assistantships (averaging $28,200 per year), 41 teaching assistantships (averaging $28,200 per year); scholarships/grants, tuition waivers (full and partial), and all PhD's are funded, merit-based scholarships available for Master's students also available. *Unit head:* Dr. Jeffrey K. Mackie-Mason, Dean, School of Information, 734-647-3576. *Application contact:* School of Information Admissions, 734-763-2285, Fax: 734-615-3587, E-mail: umsi.admissions@umich.edu.
Website: http://www.si.umich.edu/.

See Display on next page and Close-Up on page 349.

University of Michigan–Dearborn, College of Engineering and Computer Science, Master of Science Program in Computer and Information Science, Dearborn, MI 48128. Offers MS. Part-time and evening/weekend programs available. Postbaccalaureate distance learning degree programs offered (minimal on-campus study). *Faculty:* 15 full-time (1 woman), 3 part-time/adjunct (0 women). *Students:* 21 full-time (13 women), 25 part-time (10 women); includes 8 minority (1 Black or African American, non-Hispanic/Latino; 5 Asian, non-Hispanic/Latino; 2 Hispanic/Latino), 29 international. 63 applicants, 49% accepted, 16 enrolled. In 2014, 17 master's awarded. *Degree requirements:* For master's, thesis optional. *Entrance requirements:* For master's, bachelor's degree with a minimum GPA of 3.0. Additional exam requirements/recommendations for international students: Required—TOEFL (minimum score 560 paper-based; 84 iBT), IELTS (minimum score 6.5). *Application deadline:* For fall admission, 8/1 priority date for domestic students, 5/1 for international students; for winter admission, 12/1 priority date for domestic students, 9/1 for international students; for spring admission, 4/1 priority date for domestic students, 1/1 for international students. Application fee: $60. *Expenses:* Tuition, state resident: full-time $12,202; part-time $707 per credit hour. Tuition, nonresident: full-time $20,980; part-time $1209 per credit hour. *Required fees:* $798; $302 per term. Tuition and fees vary according to course level, course load, degree level and program. *Financial support:* In 2014–15, 2 research assistantships with full tuition reimbursements (averaging $14,228 per year), 1 teaching assistantship with full tuition reimbursement (averaging $14,228 per year) were awarded; career-related internships or fieldwork, scholarships/grants, and unspecified assistantships also available. Support available to part-time students. Financial award application deadline: 4/1; financial award applicants required to submit FAFSA. *Faculty research:* Data science, analytics, connected vehicles, software engineering, security. *Unit head:* Dr. William I. Grosky, Chair, 313-583-6424, Fax: 313-593-4256, E-mail: wgrosky@umich.edu. *Application contact:* Leyla O. Field, Intermediate Academic Records Assistant, 313-436-9145, Fax: 313-593-4256, E-mail: leylaf@umich.edu.
Website: http://umdearborn.edu/cecs/CIS/grad_prog/index.php.

University of Michigan–Flint, College of Arts and Sciences, Program in Computer Science and Information Systems, Flint, MI 48502-1950. Offers computer science (MS); information systems (MS). Part-time programs available. *Faculty:* 25 full-time (6 women), 12 part-time/adjunct (8 women). *Students:* 62 full-time (23 women), 160 part-time (27 women); includes 4 minority (1 Black or African American, non-Hispanic/Latino; 1 Asian, non-Hispanic/Latino; 1 Hispanic/Latino; 1 Two or more races, non-Hispanic/Latino), 174 international. Average age 25. 380 applicants, 69% accepted, 134 enrolled. In 2014, 30 master's awarded. *Degree requirements:* For master's, thesis optional. *Entrance requirements:* For master's, minimum undergraduate GPA of 3.0; BS from accredited institution in computer science, computer information systems, or computer engineering (preferred). Additional exam requirements/recommendations for international students: Required—TOEFL (minimum score 84 iBT), IELTS (minimum score 6.5). *Application deadline:* For fall admission, 8/1 for domestic students, 5/1 for international students; for winter admission, 11/15 for domestic students, 9/1 for international students; for spring admission, 3/15 for domestic students, 1/1 for international students. Applications are processed on a rolling basis. Application fee: $55. Electronic applications accepted. *Expenses:* Expenses: Contact institution. *Financial support:* Federal Work-Study, scholarships/grants, and unspecified assistantships available. Support available to part-time students. Financial award application deadline: 3/1; financial award applicants required to submit FAFSA. *Unit head:* Dr. Michael Farmer, Director, 810-762-3131, Fax: 810-766-6780. *Application contact:* Bradley T. Maki, Director of Graduate Admissions, 810-762-3171, Fax: 810-766-6789, E-mail: bmaki@umflint.edu.
Website: http://www.umflint.edu/graduateprograms/computer-science-information-systems-ms.

University of Nebraska at Omaha, Graduate Studies, College of Information Science and Technology, Department of Information Systems and Quantitative Analysis, Omaha, NE 68182. Offers biomedical informatics (MS, PhD); information assurance (MS, Certificate); information technology (PhD); management information systems (MS); project management (Certificate); systems analysis and design (Certificate). Part-time and evening/weekend programs available. *Faculty:* 25 full-time (8 women). *Students:* 137 full-time (50 women), 125 part-time (31 women); includes 36 minority (14 Black or African American, non-Hispanic/Latino; 1 American Indian or Alaska Native, non-Hispanic/Latino; 15 Asian, non-Hispanic/Latino; 2 Hispanic/Latino; 4 Two or more races, non-Hispanic/Latino), 143 international. Average age 29. 404 applicants, 50% accepted, 101 enrolled. In 2014, 46 master's, 3 doctorates, 21 other advanced degrees awarded. *Degree requirements:* For master's, comprehensive exam, thesis (for some programs); for doctorate, comprehensive exam, thesis/dissertation. *Entrance requirements:* For master's, GRE General Test, minimum GPA of 3.0, 3 letters of recommendation, writing sample, resume, official transcripts; for doctorate, GMAT or GRE General Test, minimum GPA of 3.0, 3 letters of recommendation, writing sample, resume, official transcripts; for Certificate, minimum GPA of 3.0, official transcripts. Additional exam requirements/recommendations for international students: Required—TOEFL, IELTS, PTE. *Application deadline:* For fall admission, 2/15 for domestic and international students; for spring admission, 9/15 for domestic and international students; for summer admission, 4/1 for domestic and international students. Applications are processed on a rolling basis. Application fee: $45. Electronic applications accepted. *Financial support:* In 2014–15, 35 students received support, including 28 research assistantships with tuition reimbursements available, 7 teaching assistantships with tuition reimbursements available; fellowships, career-related internships or fieldwork, Federal Work-Study, scholarships/grants, tuition waivers (partial), and unspecified assistantships also available. Financial award application deadline: 3/1; financial award applicants required to submit FAFSA. *Unit head:* Dr. Peter Wolcott, Chairperson, 402-554-2341, E-mail: graduate@unomaha.edu. *Application contact:* Dr. Leah Pietron, Graduate Program Chair, 402-554-2341, E-mail: graduate@unomaha.edu.

University of Nebraska–Lincoln, Graduate College, College of Arts and Sciences and College of Engineering, Department of Computer Science and Engineering, Lincoln, NE 68588. Offers bioinformatics (MS, PhD); computer engineering (MS, PhD); computer

Information Science

science (MS, PhD); information technology (PhD). *Degree requirements:* For master's, thesis optional; for doctorate, comprehensive exam, thesis/dissertation. *Entrance requirements:* For master's and doctorate, GRE General Test. Additional exam requirements/recommendations for international students: Required—TOEFL (minimum score 600 paper-based). Electronic applications accepted. *Faculty research:* Software engineering, geo- and bio-informatics, scientific computation, secure communication.

University of New Haven, Graduate School, Tagliatela College of Engineering, Program in Computer and Information Science, West Haven, CT 06516-1916. Offers computer and information science (MS); computer programming (Certificate); computer systems (MS); database and information systems (MS); network systems (MS); software engineering and development (MS). Part-time and evening/weekend programs available. *Degree requirements:* For master's, thesis or alternative. *Entrance requirements:* Additional exam requirements/recommendations for international students: Required—TOEFL (minimum score 75 iBT), IELTS, PTE (minimum score 50). Electronic applications accepted. Application fee is waived when completed online.

The University of North Carolina at Charlotte, College of Computing and Informatics, Department of Software and Information Systems, Charlotte, NC 28223-0001. Offers computing and information systems (PhD); information security/privacy (Graduate Certificate); information technology (MS, Graduate Certificate); management of information technology (Graduate Certificate). Part-time and evening/weekend programs available. *Faculty:* 17 full-time (5 women), 4 part-time/adjunct (0 women). *Students:* 223 full-time (80 women), 60 part-time (18 women); includes 17 minority (8 Black or African American, non-Hispanic/Latino; 5 Asian, non-Hispanic/Latino; 2 Hispanic/Latino; 2 Two or more races, non-Hispanic/Latino), 215 international. Average age 27. 457 applicants, 63% accepted, 135 enrolled. In 2014, 30 master's, 17 doctorates, 24 other advanced degrees awarded. Terminal master's awarded for partial completion of doctoral program. *Degree requirements:* For master's, thesis or alternative, practica; for doctorate, comprehensive exam, thesis/dissertation. *Entrance requirements:* For master's, GRE or GMAT, minimum undergraduate GPA of 2.8 overall, 2.0 in last 2 years; for doctorate, GRE or GMAT, working knowledge of 2 high-level programming languages, letters of recommendation. Additional exam requirements/recommendations for international students: Required—TOEFL (minimum score 557 paper-based; 83 iBT). *Application deadline:* For fall admission, 5/1 for domestic and international students; for spring admission, 10/1 for domestic and international students. Applications are processed on a rolling basis. Application fee: $75. Electronic applications accepted. *Expenses:* Tuition, state resident: full-time $4008. Tuition, nonresident: full-time $16,295. *Required fees:* $2755. Tuition and fees vary according to course load and program. *Financial support:* In 2014–15, 34 students received support, including 1 fellowship (averaging $50,000 per year), 20 research assistantships (averaging $12,139 per year), 13 teaching assistantships (averaging $11,089 per year); career-related internships or fieldwork, institutionally sponsored loans, scholarships/grants, and unspecified assistantships also available. Support available to part-time students. Financial award application deadline: 4/1; financial award applicants required to submit FAFSA. *Faculty research:* Information security, information privacy, information assurance, cryptography, software engineering, enterprise integration, intelligent information systems, human-computer interaction. *Total annual research expenditures:* $2.5 million. *Unit head:* Dr. Mary Lou Maher, Chair, 704-687-1940, E-mail: mmaher9@uncc.edu. *Application contact:* Kathy B. Giddings, Director of Graduate Admissions, 704-687-5503, Fax: 704-687-1668, E-mail: gradadm@uncc.edu. Website: http://sis.uncc.edu/.

University of North Texas, Robert B. Toulouse School of Graduate Studies, Denton, TX 76203-5459. Offers accounting (MS); applied anthropology (MA, MS); applied behavior analysis (Certificate); applied geography (MA); applied technology and performance improvement (M Ed, MS); art education (MA); art history (MA); art museum education (Certificate); arts leadership (Certificate); audiology (Au D); behavior analysis (MS); behavioral science (PhD); biochemistry and molecular biology (MS); biology (MA, MS); biomedical engineering (MS); business analysis (MS); chemistry (MS); clinical health psychology (PhD); communication studies (MA, MS); computer engineering (MS); computer science (MS); counseling (M Ed, MS), including clinical mental health counseling (MS), college and university counseling, elementary school counseling, secondary school counseling; creative writing (MA); criminal justice (MS); curriculum and instruction (M Ed); decision sciences (MBA); design (MA, MFA), including fashion design (MFA), innovation studies, interior design (MFA); early childhood studies (MS); economics (MS); educational leadership (M Ed, Ed D); educational psychology (MS, PhD), including family studies (MS), gifted and talented (MS), human development (MS), learning and cognition (MS), research, measurement and evaluation (MS); electrical engineering (MS); emergency management (MPA); engineering technology (MS); English (MA); English as a second language (MA); environmental science (MS); finance (MBA, MS); financial management (MPA); French (MA); health services management (MBA); higher education (M Ed, Ed D); history (MA, MS); hospitality management (MS); human resources management (MPA); information science (MS); information systems (PhD); information technologies (MBA); interdisciplinary studies (MA, MS); international studies (MA); international sustainable tourism (MS); jazz studies (MM); journalism (MA, MJ, Graduate Certificate), including interactive and virtual digital communication (Graduate Certificate), narrative journalism (Graduate Certificate), public relations (Graduate Certificate); kinesiology (MS); linguistics (MA); local government management (MPA); logistics (PhD); logistics and supply chain management (MBA); long-term care, senior housing, and aging services (MA); management (PhD); marketing (MBA); mathematics (MA, MS); mechanical and energy engineering (MS, PhD); music (MA), including ethnomusicology, music theory, musicology, performance; music composition (PhD); music education (MM Ed, PhD); nonprofit management (MPA); operations and supply chain management (MBA); performance (MM, DMA); philosophy (MA); political science (MA); professional and technical communication (MA); radio, television and film (MA, MFA); rehabilitation counseling (Certificate); sociology (MA); Spanish (MA); special education (M Ed); speech-language pathology (MA); strategic management (MBA); studio art (MFA); teaching (M Ed); MBA/MS. Part-time and evening/weekend programs available. Postbaccalaureate distance learning degree programs offered. *Faculty:* 651 full-time (215 women), 233 part-time/adjunct (139 women). *Students:* 3,040 full-time (1,598 women), 3,401 part-time (2,097 women); includes 1,740 minority (533 Black or African American, non-Hispanic/Latino; 15 American Indian or Alaska Native, non-Hispanic/Latino; 286 Asian, non-Hispanic/Latino; 746 Hispanic/Latino; 3 Native Hawaiian or other Pacific Islander, non-Hispanic/Latino; 157 Two or more races, non-Hispanic/Latino), 1,145 international. Terminal master's awarded for partial completion of doctoral program. *Degree requirements:* For master's, variable foreign language requirement, comprehensive exam (for some programs), thesis (for some programs); for doctorate, variable foreign language requirement, comprehensive exam (for some programs), thesis/dissertation; for other advanced degree, variable foreign language requirement, comprehensive exam (for some programs). *Entrance requirements:* For master's and doctorate, GRE, GMAT. Additional exam requirements/recommendations for international students: Required—TOEFL (minimum score 550 paper-based; 79 iBT). *Application deadline:* For fall admission, 7/15 for domestic students, 3/15 for international students; for spring admission, 11/15 for domestic students, 9/15 for international students; for summer admission, 5/1 for domestic students. Applications are processed on a rolling basis. Application fee: $60. Electronic applications accepted. *Expenses:* Tuition, state resident: full-time $5450; part-time $3633 per year. Tuition, nonresident: full-time $11,966; part-time $7977 per year. *Required fees:* $1301; $398 per credit hour. $685 per semester. Tuition and fees vary according to program and reciprocity agreements. *Financial support:* Fellowships with partial tuition reimbursements, research assistantships with partial tuition

reimbursements, teaching assistantships, career-related internships or fieldwork, Federal Work-Study, institutionally sponsored loans, scholarships/grants, health care benefits, and library assistantships available. Support available to part-time students. Financial award applicants required to submit FAFSA. *Unit head:* Mark Wardell, Dean, 940-565-2383, E-mail: mark.wardell@unt.edu. *Application contact:* Toulouse School of Graduate Studies, 940-565-2383, Fax: 940-565-2141, E-mail: gradsch@unt.edu.
Website: http://tsgs.unt.edu/.

University of Oregon, Graduate School, College of Arts and Sciences, Department of Computer and Information Science, Eugene, OR 97403. Offers MA, MS, PhD. Part-time programs available. Terminal master's awarded for partial completion of doctoral program. *Degree requirements:* For doctorate, thesis/dissertation. *Entrance requirements:* For master's and doctorate, GRE General Test, minimum GPA of 3.0. Additional exam requirements/recommendations for international students: Required—TOEFL. *Faculty research:* Artificial intelligence, graphics, natural-language processing, expert systems, operating systems.

University of Ottawa, Faculty of Graduate and Postdoctoral Studies, Faculty of Engineering, Engineering Management Program, Ottawa, ON K1N 6N5, Canada. Offers engineering management (M Eng); information technology (Certificate); project management (Certificate). *Degree requirements:* For master's, thesis or alternative. *Entrance requirements:* For master's and Certificate, honors degree or equivalent, minimum B average. Electronic applications accepted.

University of Pennsylvania, School of Engineering and Applied Science, Department of Computer and Information Science, Philadelphia, PA 19104. Offers MCIT, MSE, PhD. Part-time programs available. *Faculty:* 54 full-time (6 women), 6 part-time/adjunct (1 woman). *Students:* 287 full-time (74 women), 77 part-time (27 women); includes 42 minority (5 Black or African American, non-Hispanic/Latino; 28 Asian, non-Hispanic/Latino; 6 Hispanic/Latino; 3 Two or more races, non-Hispanic/Latino), 223 international. 1,831 applicants, 16% accepted, 156 enrolled. In 2014, 178 master's, 15 doctorates awarded. Terminal master's awarded for partial completion of doctoral program. *Degree requirements:* For master's, thesis optional; for doctorate, thesis/dissertation. *Entrance requirements:* For master's and doctorate, GRE General Test. Additional exam requirements/recommendations for international students: Required—TOEFL. *Application deadline:* For fall admission, 6/1 priority date for domestic students, 5/1 priority date for international students. Applications are processed on a rolling basis. Application fee: $70. Electronic applications accepted. *Financial support:* Fellowships with full tuition reimbursements, research assistantships with full tuition reimbursements, teaching assistantships, institutionally sponsored loans, scholarships/grants, traineeships, health care benefits, and unspecified assistantships available. *Faculty research:* Artificial intelligence, computer systems graphics, information management, robotics, software systems theory. *Unit head:* Eduardo D. Glandt, Dean, 215-898-7244, E-mail: seasdean@seas.upenn.edu. *Application contact:* School of Engineering and Applied Science Graduate Admissions, 215-898-4542, E-mail: gradstudies@seas.upenn.edu.
Website: http://www.seas.upenn.edu.

University of Pittsburgh, School of Information Sciences, Information Science and Technology Program, Pittsburgh, PA 15260. Offers big data (Postbaccalaureate Certificate); information science (MSIS, PhD), including information science (PhD), telecommunications (PhD); information science and technology (Certificate); security assured information systems (Post-Master's Certificate). Part-time programs available. *Faculty:* 15 full-time (2 women), 11 part-time/adjunct (3 women). *Students:* 202 full-time (92 women), 62 part-time (19 women); includes 13 minority (2 Black or African American, non-Hispanic/Latino; 7 Asian, non-Hispanic/Latino; 3 Hispanic/Latino; 1 Two or more races, non-Hispanic/Latino), 200 international. 491 applicants, 77% accepted, 113 enrolled. In 2014, 87 master's, 9 doctorates awarded. *Degree requirements:* For master's, thesis optional; for doctorate, comprehensive exam, thesis/dissertation. *Entrance requirements:* For master's, GRE General Test, GMAT, bachelor's degree with minimum GPA of 3.0; course work in structured programming language, statistics, mathematics; for doctorate, GRE General Test, GMAT, master's degree; minimum QPA of 3.3; course work in statistics or mathematics, programming, cognitive psychology, systems analysis and design, data structures database management; for other advanced degree, master's degree in information science, telecommunications, or related field. Additional exam requirements/recommendations for international students: Required—TOEFL (minimum score 550 paper-based; 80 iBT). *Application deadline:* For fall admission, 7/15 priority date for domestic students, 1/15 priority date for international students; for winter admission, 11/1 priority date for domestic students, 6/15 priority date for international students; for spring admission, 11/1 priority date for domestic students, 6/15 priority date for international students; for summer admission, 3/15 priority date for domestic students, 12/15 priority date for international students. Applications are processed on a rolling basis. Application fee: $50. Electronic applications accepted. *Expenses:* Expenses: $21,810 in-state, $35,710 out-of-state; $889 per credit in-state, $1,470 out-of-state (for summer); mandatory fees: $900. *Financial support:* Fellowships with full and partial tuition reimbursements, research assistantships with full and partial tuition reimbursements, teaching assistantships with full and partial tuition reimbursements, career-related internships or fieldwork, scholarships/grants, traineeships, health care benefits, tuition waivers (full and partial), and unspecified assistantships available. Financial award application deadline: 1/15; financial award applicants required to submit FAFSA. *Faculty research:* Big data, systems analysis and design, geoinformatics, database and Web systems, information assurance and security. *Unit head:* Dr. Peter Brusilovsky, Program Chair, 412-624-9404, Fax: 421-624-5231, E-mail: peterb@sis.pitt.edu. *Application contact:* Shabana Reza, Enrollment Manager, 412-624-3988, Fax: 412-624-5231, E-mail: isinq@sis.pitt.edu.
Website: http://www.ischool.pitt.edu/ist/.

University of Pittsburgh, School of Information Sciences, Telecommunications and Networking Program, Pittsburgh, PA 15260. Offers information science (PhD), including telecommunications; telecommunications and networking (MST, Certificate). Part-time programs available. *Faculty:* 4 full-time (0 women), 2 part-time/adjunct (0 women). *Students:* 67 full-time (17 women), 7 part-time (1 woman); includes 2 minority (both Asian, non-Hispanic/Latino), 65 international. 132 applicants, 71% accepted, 24 enrolled. In 2014, 31 master's, 4 doctorates, 1 other advanced degree awarded. *Degree requirements:* For master's, thesis optional; for doctorate, comprehensive exam, thesis/dissertation. *Entrance requirements:* For master's, GRE General Test, GMAT, undergraduate degree with minimum GPA of 3.0; previous course work in computer programming, calculus, and probability; for doctorate, GRE, GMAT, master's degree; minimum GPA of 3.3; course work in computer programming (2 languages), differential and integral calculus, and probability and statistics; for Certificate, MSIS, MST from accredited university. Additional exam requirements/recommendations for international students: Required—TOEFL (minimum score 550 paper-based; 80 iBT). *Application deadline:* For fall admission, 1/15 priority date for domestic and international students; for winter admission, 9/15 priority date for domestic students, 6/15 priority date for international students; for spring admission, 9/15 priority date for domestic students, 6/15 priority date for international students; for summer admission, 1/15 priority date for domestic students, 12/15 priority date for international students. Applications are processed on a rolling basis. Application fee: $50. Electronic applications accepted. *Expenses:* Expenses: $21,810 in-state, $35,710 out-of-state; $889 per credit in-state, $1,470 out-of-state (for summer); mandatory fees: $900. *Financial support:* Fellowships with full and partial tuition reimbursements, research assistantships with full and partial tuition reimbursements, teaching assistantships with full and partial tuition reimbursements, career-related internships or fieldwork, scholarships/grants, health care benefits, tuition waivers (full and partial), and unspecified assistantships available. Financial award application deadline: 1/15; financial award applicants required to submit FAFSA. *Faculty research:* Telecommunication systems, telecommunications policy, network design and management, wireless information systems, network security. *Unit head:* Dr. David Tipper, Program Chair, 412-624-9421, Fax: 412-624-2788, E-mail: tipper@tele.pitt.edu. *Application contact:* Shabana Reza, Enrollment Manager, 412-624-3988, Fax: 412-624-5231, E-mail: teleinq@sis.pitt.edu.
Website: http://www.ischool.pitt.edu/tele/.

University of Puerto Rico, Mayagüez Campus, Graduate Studies, College of Engineering, Department of Electrical and Computer Engineering, Mayagüez, PR 00681-9000. Offers computer engineering (ME, MS); computing and information sciences and engineering (PhD); electrical engineering (ME, MS). Part-time programs available. *Faculty:* 43 full-time (5 women). *Students:* 70 full-time (8 women), 7 part-time (0 women). 36 applicants, 83% accepted, 18 enrolled. In 2014, 13 master's awarded. *Degree requirements:* For master's, comprehensive exam, thesis; for doctorate, comprehensive exam, thesis/dissertation. *Entrance requirements:* For master's, proficiency in English and Spanish, BS in electrical or computer engineering or equivalent, minimum GPA of 3.0; for doctorate, GRE. *Application deadline:* For fall admission, 2/15 for domestic and international students; for spring admission, 9/15 for domestic and international students. Applications are processed on a rolling basis. Application fee: $25. *Expenses: Tuition, area resident:* Full-time $2466; part-time $822 per credit. *International tuition:* $6371 full-time. *Required fees:* $1095; $1095 per year. Tuition and fees vary according to course level, course load and reciprocity agreements. *Financial support:* In 2014–15, 54 students received support, including 32 research assistantships (averaging $7,499 per year), 32 teaching assistantships (averaging $7,614 per year); fellowships with full tuition reimbursements available, Federal Work-Study, institutionally sponsored loans, and unspecified assistantships also available. *Faculty research:* Microcomputer interfacing, control systems, power systems, electronics. *Unit head:* Dr. Pedro Rivera, Chairperson, 787-832-4040 Ext. 3821, E-mail: p.rivera@upr.edu. *Application contact:* Sandra Montalvo, Administrative Staff, 787-832-4040 Ext. 3094, Fax: 787-831-7564, E-mail: sandra@ece.uprm.edu.
Website: http://www.ece.uprm.edu.

University of Puerto Rico, Mayagüez Campus, Graduate Studies, College of Engineering, Program in Computing and Information Sciences and Engineering, Mayagüez, PR 00681-9000. Offers PhD. Part-time programs available. *Faculty:* 20 full-time (3 women). *Students:* 13 full-time (1 woman), 1 part-time (0 women). 3 applicants, 67% accepted, 1 enrolled. In 2014, 1 doctorate awarded. *Degree requirements:* For doctorate, comprehensive exam, thesis/dissertation. *Entrance requirements:* For doctorate, GRE, BS in engineering or science; the equivalent of undergraduate courses in data structures, programming language, calculus III and linear algebra. *Application deadline:* For fall admission, 2/15 for domestic and international students; for spring admission, 9/15 for domestic and international students. Application fee: $25. *Expenses: Tuition, area resident:* Full-time $2466; part-time $822 per credit. *International tuition:* $6371 full-time. *Required fees:* $1095; $1095 per year. Tuition and fees vary according to course level, course load and reciprocity agreements. *Financial support:* In 2014–15, 10 students received support, including 5 research assistantships (averaging $4,414 per year), 10 teaching assistantships (averaging $10,110 per year); fellowships with full tuition reimbursements available and unspecified assistantships also available. *Faculty research:* Algorithms, computer architectures. *Unit head:* Dr. Wilson Rivera, Professor, 787-832-4040 Ext. 5217, E-mail: wilson.riveragallego@upr.edu.
Website: http://www.cisephd.ece.uprm.edu.

University of Puerto Rico, Río Piedras Campus, Graduate School of Information Sciences and Technologies, San Juan, PR 00931-3300. Offers administration of academic libraries (PMC); administration of public libraries (PMC); administration of special libraries (PMC); consultant in information services (PMC); documents and files administration (Post-Graduate Certificate); electronic information resources analyst (Post-Graduate Certificate); information science (MIS); librarianship and information services (MLS); school librarian (Post-Graduate Certificate); school librarian distance education mode (Post-Graduate Certificate); specialist in legal information (PMC). *Accreditation:* ALA. Part-time programs available. *Degree requirements:* For master's, comprehensive exam, thesis, portfolio. *Entrance requirements:* For master's, PAEG, GRE, interview, minimum GPA of 3.0, 3 letters of recommendation; for other advanced degree, PAEG, GRE, minimum GPA of 3.0, IST master's degree. *Faculty research:* Investigating the users needs and preferences for a specialized environmental library.

University of South Africa, College of Human Sciences, Pretoria, South Africa. Offers adult education (M Ed); African languages (MA, PhD); African politics (MA, PhD); Afrikaans (MA, PhD); ancient history (MA, PhD); ancient Near Eastern studies (MA, PhD); anthropology (MA, PhD); applied linguistics (MA); Arabic (MA, PhD); archaeology (MA); art history (MA); Biblical archaeology (MA); Biblical studies (M Th, D Th, PhD); Christian spirituality (M Th, D Th); church history (M Th, D Th); classical studies (MA, PhD); clinical psychology (MA); communication (MA, PhD); comparative education (M Ed, Ed D); consulting psychology (D Admin, D Com, PhD); curriculum studies (M Ed, Ed D); development studies (M Admin, MA, D Admin, PhD); didactics (M Ed, Ed D); education (M Tech); education management (M Ed, Ed D); educational psychology (M Ed); English (MA); environmental education (M Ed); French (MA, PhD); German (MA, PhD); Greek (MA); guidance and counseling (M Ed); health studies (MA, PhD), including health sciences education (MA), health services management (MA), medical and surgical nursing science (critical care general) (MA), midwifery and neonatal nursing science (MA), trauma and emergency care (MA); history (MA, PhD); history of education (Ed D); inclusive education (M Ed, Ed D); information and communications technology policy and regulation (MA); information science (MA, MIS, PhD); international politics (MA, PhD); Islamic studies (MA, PhD); Italian (MA, PhD); Judaica (MA, PhD); linguistics (MA, PhD); mathematical education (M Ed); mathematics education (MA); missiology (M Th, D Th); modern Hebrew (MA, PhD); musicology (MA, MMus, D Mus, PhD); natural science education (M Ed); New Testament (M Th, D Th); Old Testament (D Th); pastoral therapy (M Th, D Th); philosophy (MA); philosophy of education (M Ed, Ed D); politics (MA, PhD); Portuguese (MA, PhD); practical theology (M Th, D Th); psychology (MA, MS, PhD); psychology of education (M Ed, Ed D); public health (MA); religious studies (MA, D Th, PhD); Romance languages (MA); Russian (MA, PhD); Semitic languages (MA, PhD); social behavior studies in HIV/AIDS (MA); social science (mental health) (MA); social science in development studies (MA); social science in psychology (MA); social science in social work (MA); social science in sociology (MA); social work (MSW, DSW, PhD); socio-education (M Ed, Ed D); sociolinguistics (MA); sociology (MA, PhD); Spanish (MA, PhD); systematic theology (M Th, D Th); TESOL (teaching English to speakers of other languages) (MA); theological ethics (M Th, D Th); theory of literature (MA, PhD); urban ministries (D Th); urban ministry (M Th).

University of South Carolina Upstate, Graduate Programs, Spartanburg, SC 29303-4999. Offers early childhood education (M Ed); elementary education (M Ed);

informatics (MS); special education: visual impairment (M Ed). *Accreditation:* NCATE. Part-time and evening/weekend programs available. *Faculty:* 15 full-time (11 women), 6 part-time/adjunct (4 women). *Students:* 11 full-time (8 women), 164 part-time (137 women); includes 39 minority (33 Black or African American, non-Hispanic/Latino; 2 American Indian or Alaska Native, non-Hispanic/Latino; 4 Asian, non-Hispanic/Latino). Average age 38. In 2014, 11 master's awarded. *Degree requirements:* For master's, professional portfolio. *Entrance requirements:* For master's, GRE General Test or MAT, interview, minimum undergraduate GPA of 2.5, teaching certificate, 2 letters of recommendation. *Application deadline:* Applications are processed on a rolling basis. Application fee: $40. *Expenses:* Tuition, state resident: full-time $12,024; part-time $501 per semester hour. Tuition, nonresident: full-time $25,770; part-time $1073.75 per semester hour. *Financial support:* Institutionally sponsored loans and institutional work-study available. Financial award application deadline: 7/15; financial award applicants required to submit FAFSA. *Faculty research:* Promoting university diversity awareness, rough and tumble play, social justice education, American Indian literatures and cultures, diversity and multicultural education, science teaching strategy. *Unit head:* Dr. Tina Herzberg, Director of Graduate Programs, 864-503-5572, Fax: 864-503-5573, E-mail: therzberg@uscupstate.edu. *Application contact:* Donette Stewart, Associate Vice Chancellor for Enrollment Services, 864-503-5280, E-mail: dstewart@uscupstate.edu.
Website: http://www.uscupstate.edu/graduate/.

University of South Florida, College of Arts and Sciences, School of Information, Tampa, FL 33620-9951. Offers MS. *Accreditation:* ALA. Part-time and evening/weekend programs available. Postbaccalaureate distance learning degree programs offered (minimal on-campus study). *Faculty:* 11 full-time (7 women), 1 (woman) part-time/adjunct. *Students:* 68 full-time (59 women), 150 part-time (124 women); includes 45 minority (15 Black or African American, non-Hispanic/Latino; 1 American Indian or Alaska Native, non-Hispanic/Latino; 4 Asian, non-Hispanic/Latino; 22 Hispanic/Latino; 3 Two or more races, non-Hispanic/Latino), 2 international. Average age 35. 98 applicants, 73% accepted, 41 enrolled. In 2014, 117 master's awarded. *Degree requirements:* For master's, comprehensive exam, thesis optional. *Entrance requirements:* For master's, minimum GPA of 3.25 in upper-division course work, 3.5 in a completed master's degree program, or GRE; statement of purpose and goals, academic writing sample, three letters of recommendation. Additional exam requirements/recommendations for international students: Required—TOEFL (minimum score 550 paper-based; 79 iBT) or IELTS (minimum score 6.5). *Application deadline:* For fall admission, 6/1 for domestic students, 1/2 for international students; for spring admission, 10/15 for domestic students, 6/1 for international students. Applications are processed on a rolling basis. Application fee: $30. Electronic applications accepted. *Financial support:* Unspecified assistantships available. Financial award application deadline: 6/30. *Faculty research:* Youth services in libraries, community engagement and libraries, information architecture, biomedical informatics, health informatics. *Total annual research expenditures:* $49,361. *Unit head:* Dr. Jim Andrews, Director and Associate Professor, 813-974-2108, Fax: 813-974-6840, E-mail: jimandrews@usf.edu. *Application contact:* Dr. Diane Austin, Assistant Director, 813-974-6364, Fax: 813-974-6840, E-mail: dianeaustin@usf.edu.
Website: http://si.usf.edu/.

The University of Tennessee, Graduate School, College of Communication and Information, School of Information Sciences, Knoxville, TN 37996. Offers MS, PhD. *Accreditation:* ALA (one or more programs are accredited). Part-time and evening/weekend programs available. Postbaccalaureate distance learning degree programs offered (no on-campus study). *Degree requirements:* For master's, 42 semester hours; written comprehensive exam, online e-portfolio, or thesis; for doctorate, thesis/dissertation or alternative. *Entrance requirements:* For master's, GRE General Test, minimum GPA of 2.7; for doctorate, GRE General Test (minimum scores at or above the 50th percentile on the 3 components, taken within the past five years), master's degree; minimum undergraduate GPA of 3.0, graduate 3.5; recommendation letters from at least three former instructors or professional supervisors; personal statement; interview. Additional exam requirements/recommendations for international students: Required—TOEFL. Electronic applications accepted.

The University of Texas at El Paso, Graduate School, College of Engineering, Department of Computer Science, El Paso, TX 79968-0001. Offers computer science (MS, PhD); information technology (MSIT). Part-time and evening/weekend programs available. *Degree requirements:* For master's, thesis optional; for doctorate, thesis/dissertation. *Entrance requirements:* For master's, GRE, minimum GPA of 3.0; for doctorate, GRE, statement of purpose, letters of reference. Additional exam requirements/recommendations for international students: Required—TOEFL; Recommended—IELTS. Electronic applications accepted.

The University of Texas at San Antonio, College of Business, Department of Information Systems and Cyber Security, San Antonio, TX 78249-0617. Offers cyber security (MSIT); information technology (MS, PhD), including cyber security (MS); management of technology (MBA). Part-time and evening/weekend programs available. *Faculty:* 9 full-time (2 women), 3 part-time/adjunct (0 women). *Students:* 33 full-time (8 women), 75 part-time (21 women); includes 26 minority (1 Black or African American, non-Hispanic/Latino; 1 American Indian or Alaska Native, non-Hispanic/Latino; 3 Asian, non-Hispanic/Latino; 18 Hispanic/Latino; 1 Native Hawaiian or other Pacific Islander, non-Hispanic/Latino; 2 Two or more races, non-Hispanic/Latino), 22 international. Average age 31. 107 applicants, 56% accepted, 33 enrolled. In 2014, 33 master's, 3 doctorates awarded. *Degree requirements:* For master's, comprehensive exam (for some programs), thesis optional; for doctorate, comprehensive exam, thesis/dissertation. *Entrance requirements:* For master's and doctorate, GMAT/GRE, TOEFL/IELTS, official transcripts, statement of purpose, letters of recommendation. Additional exam requirements/recommendations for international students: Required—TOEFL (minimum score 550 paper-based; 79 iBT), IELTS (minimum score 6.5). *Application deadline:* For fall admission, 7/1 for domestic students, 4/1 for international students; for spring admission, 11/1 for domestic students, 9/1 for international students. Applications are processed on a rolling basis. Application fee: $45 ($80 for international students). Electronic applications accepted. *Expenses:* Expenses: Contact institution. *Financial support:* In 2014–15, 15 students received support, including 1 fellowship with full tuition reimbursement available (averaging $25,000 per year), 10 research assistantships with full and partial tuition reimbursements available (averaging $9,000 per year), 12 teaching assistantships with full and partial tuition reimbursements available (averaging $9,000 per year); scholarships/grants, health care benefits, and unspecified assistantships also available. Support available to part-time students. Financial award application deadline: 2/15. *Faculty research:* Cyber security, digital forensics, economics of information systems, information systems privacy, information technology adoption. *Total annual research expenditures:* $1.5 million. *Unit head:* Dr. Yoris A. Au, Chair/Associate Professor, 210-458-6337, Fax: 210-458-6305, E-mail: yoris.au@utsa.edu. *Application contact:* Graduate Advisor of Record.
Website: http://business.utsa.edu/directory/index.aspx?DepID=16.

University of the Sacred Heart, Graduate Programs, Department of Business Administration, Program in Information Technology, San Juan, PR 00914-0383. Offers Certificate.

University of Washington, Graduate School, The Information School, Seattle, WA 98195. Offers information management (MSIM); information science (PhD); library and information science (MLIS). *Accreditation:* ALA (one or more programs are accredited). Part-time and evening/weekend programs available. Postbaccalaureate distance learning degree programs offered (minimal on-campus study). *Faculty:* 35 full-time (19 women), 22 part-time/adjunct (12 women). *Students:* 342 full-time (208 women), 253 part-time (194 women); includes 126 minority (19 Black or African American, non-Hispanic/Latino; 8 American Indian or Alaska Native, non-Hispanic/Latino; 49 Asian, non-Hispanic/Latino; 46 Hispanic/Latino; 4 Native Hawaiian or other Pacific Islander, non-Hispanic/Latino), 154 international. Average age 32. 1,324 applicants, 37% accepted, 251 enrolled. In 2014, 222 master's, 7 doctorates awarded. Terminal master's awarded for partial completion of doctoral program. *Degree requirements:* For master's, comprehensive exam (for some programs), thesis optional, capstone project; for doctorate, comprehensive exam, thesis/dissertation. *Entrance requirements:* For master's, GRE General Test, GMAT; for doctorate, GRE General Test. Additional exam requirements/recommendations for international students: Required—TOEFL (minimum score 580 paper-based; 92 iBT), IELTS (minimum score 7). *Application deadline:* For fall admission, 12/1 priority date for domestic and international students. Application fee: $85. Electronic applications accepted. *Expenses:* Expenses: Contact institution. *Financial support:* In 2014–15, 56 students received support, including 1 fellowship with full tuition reimbursement available (averaging $6,651 per year), 27 research assistantships with full tuition reimbursements available (averaging $19,418 per year), 27 teaching assistantships with full tuition reimbursements available (averaging $19,521 per year); career-related internships or fieldwork, Federal Work-Study, institutionally sponsored loans, scholarships/grants, health care benefits, tuition waivers (full and partial), and assistantships (11 awards averaging $16,614) also available. Support available to part-time students. Financial award application deadline: 1/15; financial award applicants required to submit FAFSA. *Faculty research:* Human/computer interaction, information policy and ethics, knowledge organization, information literacy and access, data science, information assurance and cyber security, digital youth, information architecture, project management, systems analyst, user experience design. *Total annual research expenditures:* $5.2 million. *Unit head:* Dr. Harry Bruce, Dean, 206-616-0985, E-mail: harryb@uw.edu. *Application contact:* Kari Brothers, Admissions Counselor, 206-616-5541, Fax: 206-616-3152, E-mail: kari683@uw.edu.
Website: http://ischool.uw.edu/.

University of Waterloo, Graduate Studies, Faculty of Engineering, Department of Management Sciences, Waterloo, ON N2L 3G1, Canada. Offers applied operations research (MA Sc, MMS, PhD); information systems (MA Sc, MMS, PhD); management of technology (MA Sc, MMS, PhD). Part-time programs available. Postbaccalaureate distance learning degree programs offered (no on-campus study). *Degree requirements:* For master's, research paper or thesis; for doctorate, comprehensive exam, thesis/dissertation. *Entrance requirements:* For master's, GMAT or GRE, honors degree, minimum B average, resume; for doctorate, GMAT or GRE, master's degree, minimum A- average, resumé. Additional exam requirements/recommendations for international students: Required—TOEFL, TWE. *Faculty research:* Operations research, manufacturing systems, scheduling, information systems.

University of Wisconsin–Parkside, School of Business and Technology, Program in Computer and Information Systems, Kenosha, WI 53141-2000. Offers MSCIS. *Entrance requirements:* For master's, GRE General Test or GMAT, 3 letters of recommendation, minimum GPA of 3.0. *Faculty research:* Distributed systems, data bases, natural language processing, event-driven systems.

University of Wisconsin–Stout, Graduate School, College of Technology, Engineering, and Management, Program in Information and Communication Technologies, Menomonie, WI 54751. Offers MS. Part-time programs available. Postbaccalaureate distance learning degree programs offered (minimal on-campus study). *Degree requirements:* For master's, thesis. *Entrance requirements:* For master's, minimum GPA of 2.75. Additional exam requirements/recommendations for international students: Required—TOEFL (minimum score 500 paper-based; 61 iBT). Electronic applications accepted.

Western Governors University, College of Information Technology, Salt Lake City, UT 84107. Offers information security and assurance (MS); information technology (MS). Postbaccalaureate distance learning degree programs offered. *Degree requirements:* For master's, capstone project.

Youngstown State University, Graduate School, College of Science, Technology, Engineering and Mathematics, Department of Computer Science and Information Systems, Youngstown, OH 44555-0001. Offers computing and information systems (MCIS). Part-time programs available. *Degree requirements:* For master's, thesis or capstone project. *Entrance requirements:* For master's, GRE or GMAT. Additional exam requirements/recommendations for international students: Required—TOEFL (minimum score 550 paper-based). *Faculty research:* Networking, computational science, graphics and visualization, database and data mining, biometrics, artificial intelligence, online learning environments.

Internet Engineering

Hofstra University, School of Engineering and Applied Science, Hempstead, NY 11549. Offers computer science (MS), including cybersecurity, Web engineering. Part-time and evening/weekend programs available. Postbaccalaureate distance learning degree programs offered (no on-campus study). *Faculty:* 7 full-time (2 women), 3 part-time/adjunct. *Students:* 13 full-time (3 women), 17 part-time (3 women); includes 4 minority (all Asian, non-Hispanic/Latino), 8 international. Average age 30. 27 applicants, 59% accepted, 12 enrolled. In 2014, 6 master's awarded. *Degree requirements:* For master's, thesis optional, 30 credits, 3.0 GPA. *Entrance requirements:* For master's, GRE, Minimum GPA of 3.0. Additional exam requirements/recommendations for international students: Required—TOEFL (minimum score 550 paper-based; 80 iBT). *Application deadline:* Applications are processed on a rolling basis. Application fee: $70 ($75 for international students). Electronic applications accepted. *Expenses:* *Tuition:* Full-time $20,610; part-time $1145 per credit hour. *Required fees:* $970; $165 per term. Tuition and fees vary according to program. *Financial support:* In 2014–15, 10 students received support,

including 4 fellowships with full and partial tuition reimbursements available (averaging $4,300 per year), 1 research assistantship with full and partial tuition reimbursement available (averaging $8,147 per year); Federal Work-Study, institutionally sponsored loans, scholarships/grants, tuition waivers (full and partial), and unspecified assistantships also available. Support available to part-time students. Financial award applicants required to submit FAFSA. *Faculty research:* Semantic web, software engineering, data mining and machine learning, programming languages, cybersecurity. *Unit head:* Dr. Sina Rabbany, Acting Dean, 516-463-6672, E-mail: eggsyr@hofstra.edu. *Application contact:* Sunil Samuel, Assistant Vice President of Admissions, 516-463-4723, Fax: 516-463-4664, E-mail: graduateadmission@hofstra.edu.
Website: http://www.hofstra.edu/academics/colleges/seas/.

New Jersey Institute of Technology, Newark College of Engineering, Newark, NJ 07102. Offers biomedical engineering (MS, PhD); chemical engineering (MS, PhD); computer engineering (MS, PhD); electrical engineering (MS, PhD); engineering management (MS); healthcare systems management (MS); industrial engineering (MS, PhD); Internet engineering (MS); manufacturing engineering (MS); mechanical engineering (MS, PhD); occupational safety and health engineering (MS); pharmaceutical bioprocessing (MS); pharmaceutical engineering (MS); pharmaceutical systems management (MS); power and energy systems (MS); telecommunications (MS); transportation (MS, PhD). Part-time and evening/weekend programs available. Terminal master's awarded for partial completion of doctoral program. *Degree requirements:* For master's, thesis optional; for doctorate, thesis/dissertation. *Entrance requirements:* For master's, GRE General Test; for doctorate, GRE General Test, minimum graduate GPA of 3.5. Additional exam requirements/recommendations for international students: Required—TOEFL (minimum score 550 paper-based; 79 iBT). Electronic applications accepted.

University of Denver, University College, Denver, CO 80208. Offers geographic information systems (Certificate); global affairs (Certificate), including translation studies, world history and culture; information and communications technology (MCIS), including geographic information systems, information systems security, project management (MCIS, Certificate), software design and programming, technology management, telecommunications technology, Web design and development; leadership and organizations (Certificate), including human capital in organizations, philanthropic leadership, project management (MCIS, Certificate), strategic innovation and change; organizational and professional communication (MPS), including alternative dispute resolution, organizational communication, organizational development and training, public relations and marketing; security management (MAS, Certificate), including emergency planning and response, information security (MAS), organizational security. Part-time and evening/weekend programs available. Postbaccalaureate distance learning degree programs offered (no on-campus study). *Faculty:* 8 full-time (4 women), 133 part-time/adjunct (46 women). *Students:* 54 full-time (21 women), 1,327 part-time (775 women); includes 272 minority (106 Black or African American, non-Hispanic/Latino; 6 American Indian or Alaska Native, non-Hispanic/Latino; 26 Asian, non-Hispanic/Latino; 108 Hispanic/Latino; 1 Native Hawaiian or other Pacific Islander, non-Hispanic/Latino; 25 Two or more races, non-Hispanic/Latino), 116 international. Average age 35. 768 applicants, 95% accepted, 620 enrolled. In 2014, 391 master's, 196 other advanced degrees awarded. *Degree requirements:* For master's, capstone project. *Entrance requirements:* For master's, transcripts, two letters of recommendation, personal statement, resume. Additional exam requirements/recommendations for international students: Required—TOEFL (minimum score 550 paper-based; 80 iBT). *Application deadline:* For fall admission, 6/21 priority date for domestic students, 5/1 priority date for international students; for winter admission, 9/14 priority date for domestic students, 9/19 priority date for international students; for spring admission, 1/11 for domestic students, 12/12 for international students; for summer admission, 3/29 priority date for domestic students, 3/6 priority date for international students. Applications are processed on a rolling basis. Application fee: $75. Electronic applications accepted. *Expenses:* Expenses: $959 per credit hour. *Financial support:* In 2014–15, 19 students received support. Applicants required to submit FAFSA. *Unit head:* Dr. Michael McGuire, Interim Dean, 303-871-3518, E-mail: mmcguire@du.edu. *Application contact:* Information Contact, 303-871-2291, E-mail: ucoladm@du.edu.
Website: http://www.universitycollege.du.edu/.

University of Georgia, Terry College of Business, Program in Internet Technology, Athens, GA 30602. Offers MIT. Postbaccalaureate distance learning degree programs offered (no on-campus study). *Degree requirements:* For master's, capstone project.

University of San Francisco, College of Arts and Sciences, Web Science Program, San Francisco, CA 94117-1080. Offers MS. *Faculty:* 8 full-time (4 women). *Students:* 4 full-time (1 woman), 1 international. Average age 28. 1 applicant. In 2014, 4 master's awarded. *Application deadline:* For fall admission, 3/1 for domestic students; for spring admission, 10/15 for domestic students. *Expenses: Tuition:* Full-time $21,762; part-time $1209 per credit hour. Tuition and fees vary according to degree level, campus/location and program. *Financial support:* In 2014–15, 1 student received support. *Unit head:* Dr. Sophie Engle, Graduate Director, 415-422-6530, Fax: 415-422-5800. *Application contact:* Mark Landerghini, Graduate Adviser, 415-422-5101, E-mail: asgraduate@usfca.edu.
Website: http://www1.cs.usfca.edu/grad/msws/.

Wilmington University, College of Technology, New Castle, DE 19720-6491. Offers geographic information systems (MS); information assurance (MS); information systems technologies (MS); Internet/Web design (MS); management and management information systems (MS). Part-time and evening/weekend programs available. *Faculty:* 5 full-time (2 women), 53 part-time/adjunct (14 women). *Students:* 674 full-time (197 women), 131 part-time (55 women); includes 48 minority (35 Black or African American, non-Hispanic/Latino; 3 American Indian or Alaska Native, non-Hispanic/Latino; 6 Asian, non-Hispanic/Latino; 4 Hispanic/Latino), 708 international. Average age 27. 679 applicants, 100% accepted, 423 enrolled. In 2014, 102 master's awarded. *Entrance requirements:* Additional exam requirements/recommendations for international students: Required—TOEFL (minimum score 500 paper-based). *Application deadline:* Applications are processed on a rolling basis. Application fee: $35. Electronic applications accepted. *Unit head:* Dr. Edward L. Guthrie, Dean, 302-356-6870. *Application contact:* Laura Morris, Director of Admissions, 877-967-5464, E-mail: infocenter@wilmu.edu.
Website: http://www.wilmu.edu/technology/.

Medical Informatics

Arizona State University at the Tempe campus, College of Health Solutions, Department of Biomedical Informatics, Phoenix, AZ 85004. Offers MS, PhD. Terminal master's awarded for partial completion of doctoral program. *Degree requirements:* For master's, interactive Program of Study (iPOS) submitted before completing 50 percent of required credit hours; for doctorate, comprehensive exam, thesis/dissertation, interactive Program of Study (iPOS) submitted before completing 50 percent of required credit hours. *Entrance requirements:* For master's, GRE or MCAT, bachelor's degree with minimum GPA of 3.25 in computer science, biology, physiology, nursing, statistics, engineering, related fields, or unrelated fields with appropriate academic backgrounds; resume/curriculum vitae; statement of purpose; 3 letters of recommendation; all official transcripts; for doctorate, GRE or MCAT, bachelor's degree with minimum GPA of 3.5 in computer science, biology, physiology, nursing, statistics, engineering, related fields, or unrelated fields with appropriate academic backgrounds; resume/curriculum vitae; statement of purpose; 3 letters of recommendation; all official transcripts. Additional exam requirements/recommendations for international students: Required—TOEFL (minimum score 550 paper-based; 83 iBT), IELTS (minimum score 6.5). Electronic applications accepted.

Armstrong State University, School of Graduate Studies, Program in Health Services Administration, Savannah, GA 31419-1997. Offers clinical informatics (Certificate); health services administration (MHSA). *Accreditation:* CAHME; CEPH. Part-time and evening/weekend programs available. *Faculty:* 5 full-time (3 women), 2 part-time/adjunct (1 woman). *Students:* 24 full-time (16 women), 11 part-time (9 women); includes 9 minority (4 Black or African American, non-Hispanic/Latino; 2 Asian, non-Hispanic/Latino; 3 Hispanic/Latino), 3 international. Average age 31. 22 applicants, 73% accepted, 12 enrolled. In 2014, 15 master's awarded. *Degree requirements:* For master's, comprehensive exam, thesis optional, capstone project and internship, administration practicum, or research practicum. *Entrance requirements:* For master's, GMAT or GRE General Test, MAT, minimum GPA of 2.8, letter of intent, letters of recommendation. Additional exam requirements/recommendations for international students: Required—TOEFL (minimum score 523 paper-based). *Application deadline:* For fall admission, 6/1 priority date for domestic students, 5/1 priority date for international students; for spring admission, 11/15 priority date for domestic students, 9/15 priority date for international students; for summer admission, 4/15 for domestic students, 9/15 for international students. Applications are processed on a rolling basis. Application fee: $30. Electronic applications accepted. *Expenses:* Expenses: Contact institution. *Financial support:* In 2014–15, research assistantships with full tuition reimbursements (averaging $5,000 per year) were awarded; career-related internships or fieldwork, Federal Work-Study, scholarships/grants, tuition waivers (full), and unspecified assistantships also available. Support available to part-time students. Financial award applicants required to submit FAFSA. *Faculty research:* Health administration, community health, health education. *Unit head:* Dr. Robert LeFavi, Interim Department Head, 912-344-3208, Fax: 912-344-3490, E-mail: robert.lefavi@armstrong.edu. *Application contact:* Kathy Ingram, Associate Director of Graduate/Adult and Nontraditional Students, 912-344-2503, Fax: 912-344-3417, E-mail: graduate@armstrong.edu.
Website: http://www.armstrong.edu/Health_Professions/Health_Sciences/healthsciences_master_of_health_services_administration.

Brandeis University, Rabb School of Continuing Studies, Division of Graduate Professional Studies, Master of Science in Health and Medical Informatics Program, Waltham, MA 02454-9110. Offers MS. Part-time programs available. Postbaccalaureate distance learning degree programs offered (no on-campus study). *Faculty:* 2 full-time (1 woman), 36 part-time/adjunct (13 women). *Students:* 2 full-time (both women), 29 part-time (15 women); includes 13 minority (6 Black or African American, non-Hispanic/Latino; 5 Asian, non-Hispanic/Latino; 2 Hispanic/Latino). Average age 35. 16 applicants, 100% accepted, 12 enrolled. In 2014, 9 master's awarded. *Entrance requirements:* For master's, four-year bachelor's degree from regionally-accredited U.S. institution or equivalent; official transcript(s) from every college or university attended; resume or curriculum vitae; statement of goals; letter of recommendation. Additional exam requirements/recommendations for international students: Required—TOEFL (minimum scores: 600 paper-based, 100 iBT), IELTS (7), or PTE (68). *Application deadline:* For fall admission, 8/11 priority date for domestic and international students; for winter admission, 11/15 for domestic students; for spring admission, 12/15 priority date for domestic and international students; for summer admission, 4/14 priority date for domestic and international students. Applications are processed on a rolling basis. Application fee: $50. Electronic applications accepted. *Unit head:* Arthur Harvey, Chair, 781-736-8787, Fax: 781-736-3420, E-mail: aharv0001@brandeis.edu. *Application contact:* Frances Stearns, Director of Admissions and Recruitment, 781-736-8785, Fax: 781-736-3420, E-mail: fstearns@brandeis.edu.
Website: http://www.brandeis.edu/gps.

Cambridge College, School of Management, Cambridge, MA 02138-5304. Offers business negotiation and conflict resolution (M Mgt); general business (M Mgt); health care informatics (M Mgt); health care management (M Mgt); leadership in human and organizational dynamics (M Mgt); non-profit and public organization management (M Mgt); small business development (M Mgt); technology management (M Mgt). Part-time and evening/weekend programs available. *Degree requirements:* For master's, thesis, seminars. *Entrance requirements:* For master's, resume, 2 professional references. Additional exam requirements/recommendations for international students: Required—TOEFL (minimum score 550 paper-based; 79 iBT), Michigan English Language Assessment Battery (minimum score 85); Recommended—IELTS (minimum score 6). Electronic applications accepted. *Expenses:* Contact institution. *Faculty research:* Negotiation, mediation and conflict resolution; leadership; management of diverse organizations; case studies and simulation methodologies for management education, digital as a second language: social networking for digital immigrants, non-profit and public management.

Columbia University, College of Dental Medicine and Graduate School of Arts and Sciences, Programs in Dental Specialties, New York, NY 10027. Offers advanced education in general dentistry (Certificate); biomedical informatics (MA, PhD); endodontics (Certificate); orthodontics (MS, Certificate); periodontics (MS, Certificate); prosthodontics (MS, Certificate); science education (MA). *Degree requirements:* For master's, thesis, presentation of seminar. *Entrance requirements:* For master's, GRE General Test, DDS or equivalent. *Expenses:* Contact institution. *Faculty research:* Analysis of growth/form, pulpal microcirculation, implants, microbiology of oral environment, calcified tissues.

Columbia University, College of Physicians and Surgeons, Department of Biomedical Informatics, New York, NY 10032. Offers M Phil, MA, PhD, MD/PhD. *Degree requirements:* For doctorate, thesis/dissertation. *Entrance requirements:* For master's and doctorate, GRE General Test, knowledge of computational techniques. Additional exam requirements/recommendations for international students: Required—TOEFL.

Medical Informatics

Electronic applications accepted. *Faculty research:* Bioinformatics, bioimaging, clinical informatics, public health informatics.

Dalhousie University, Faculty of Computer Science, Halifax, NS B3H 1W5, Canada. Offers computational biology and bioinformatics (M Sc); computer science (MA Sc, MC Sc, PhD); electronic commerce (MEC); health informatics (MHI). *Degree requirements:* For master's, thesis (for some programs); for doctorate, thesis/dissertation. *Entrance requirements:* Additional exam requirements/recommendations for international students: Required—1 of 5 approved tests: TOEFL, IELTS, CANTEST, CAEL, Michigan English Language Assessment Battery. Electronic applications accepted.

Excelsior College, School of Health Sciences, Albany, NY 12203-5159. Offers health care informatics (Certificate); health professions education (MSHS); public health (MSHS). Part-time and evening/weekend programs available. Postbaccalaureate distance learning degree programs offered (no on-campus study). *Faculty:* 10 part-time/adjunct (8 women). *Students:* 217 part-time (151 women); includes 104 minority (65 Black or African American, non-Hispanic/Latino; 8 Asian, non-Hispanic/Latino; 26 Hispanic/Latino; 5 Native Hawaiian or other Pacific Islander, non-Hispanic/Latino), 2 international. Average age 39. *Entrance requirements:* For degree, bachelor's degree in applicable field. *Application deadline:* Applications are processed on a rolling basis. Application fee: $110. Electronic applications accepted. *Expenses: Tuition:* Part-time $620 per credit hour. *Financial support:* Scholarships/grants available. Support available to part-time students. *Unit head:* Dr. Deborah Sopczyk, Dean, 518-464-8500, Fax: 518-464-8777, E-mail: informatics@excelsior.edu. *Application contact:* Laura Goff, Director of Advisement and Evaluation, 518-464-8500, Fax: 518-464-8777, E-mail: lgoff@excelsior.edu.

Grand Valley State University, Padnos College of Engineering and Computing, Medical and Bioinformatics Program, Allendale, MI 49401-9403. Offers MS. Part-time and evening/weekend programs available. *Students:* 15 full-time (7 women), 8 part-time (5 women); includes 5 minority (2 Asian, non-Hispanic/Latino; 3 Hispanic/Latino), 12 international. Average age 29. 17 applicants, 100% accepted, 10 enrolled. In 2014, 3 master's awarded. *Degree requirements:* For master's, thesis or alternative. Application fee: $30. *Expenses:* Tuition, state resident: full-time $10,602; part-time $589 per credit hour. Tuition, nonresident: full-time $14,022; part-time $779 per credit hour. Tuition and fees vary according to degree level and program. *Financial support:* In 2014–15, 8 students received support, including 2 fellowships (averaging $1,610 per year), 7 research assistantships with full and partial tuition reimbursements available (averaging $7,390 per year); career-related internships or fieldwork, tuition waivers (full), and unspecified assistantships also available. *Faculty research:* Biomedical informatics, information visualization, data mining, high-performance computing, computational biology. *Unit head:* Paul Leidig, Director, 616-331-2308, Fax: 616-331-2106, E-mail: leidigp@gvsu.edu. *Application contact:* Dr. David Elrod, Coordinator, 616-331-8643, E-mail: elrod@gvsu.edu.

Johns Hopkins University, School of Medicine, Division of Health Sciences Informatics, Baltimore, MD 21218-2699. Offers applied health sciences informatics (MS); clinical informatics (Certificate); health sciences informatics (PhD); health sciences informatics research (MS). *Degree requirements:* For master's, thesis, publications, practica. *Entrance requirements:* Additional exam requirements/recommendations for international students: Recommended—TOEFL. Electronic applications accepted. *Faculty research:* Decision modeling, consumer health informatics, digital libraries, data standards, patient safety.

Marymount University, School of Business Administration, Program in Information Technology, Arlington, VA 22207-4299. Offers computer security and information assurance (Certificate); health care informatics (Certificate); information technology (MS, Certificate); information technology project management and technology leadership (Certificate). Part-time and evening/weekend programs available. *Faculty:* 6 full-time (3 women), 7 part-time/adjunct (1 woman). *Students:* 34 full-time (15 women), 30 part-time (11 women); includes 21 minority (14 Black or African American, non-Hispanic/Latino; 4 Asian, non-Hispanic/Latino; 3 Hispanic/Latino), 28 international. Average age 30. 53 applicants, 96% accepted, 31 enrolled. In 2014, 36 master's, 13 other advanced degrees awarded. *Degree requirements:* For master's, thesis or alternative. *Entrance requirements:* For master's, interview, resume, bachelor's degree in computer-related field or degree in another subject with a post-baccalaureate certificate in a computer-related field; for Certificate, resume. Additional exam requirements/recommendations for international students: Required—TOEFL (minimum score 600 paper-based; 96 iBT), IELTS (minimum score 6.5). *Application deadline:* For fall admission, 7/15 priority date for domestic students, 7/1 for international students; for spring admission, 11/15 priority date for domestic students, 11/15 for international students. Applications are processed on a rolling basis. Application fee: $40. Electronic applications accepted. *Expenses:* Expenses: Contact institution. *Financial support:* In 2014–15, 5 students received support, including 1 research assistantship with full and partial tuition reimbursement available, 1 teaching assistantship with full and partial tuition reimbursement available; career-related internships or fieldwork, Federal Work-Study, scholarships/grants, and unspecified assistantships also available. Support available to part-time students. Financial award applicants required to submit FAFSA. *Unit head:* Dr. Diane Murphy, Chair, 703-284-5958, Fax: 703-527-3830, E-mail: diane.murphy@marymount.edu. *Application contact:* Francesca Reed, Director, Graduate Admissions, 703-284-5901, Fax: 703-527-3815, E-mail: grad.admissions@marymount.edu.
Website: http://www.marymount.edu/Academics/School-of-Business-Administration/Graduate-Programs/Information-Technology-(M-S-).

Medical College of Wisconsin, Graduate School of Biomedical Sciences, Program in Medical Informatics, Milwaukee, WI 53226-0509. Offers MS. Program offered jointly with Milwaukee School of Engineering. Part-time and evening/weekend programs available. *Degree requirements:* For master's, thesis or alternative. *Entrance requirements:* For master's, GRE, official transcripts, three letters of recommendation. Additional exam requirements/recommendations for international students: Required—TOEFL. *Faculty research:* Computer science.

Middle Tennessee State University, College of Graduate Studies, College of Basic and Applied Sciences, Program in Professional Science, Murfreesboro, TN 37132. Offers actuarial sciences (MS); biostatistics (MS); biotechnology (MS); engineering management (MS); health care informatics (MS). Part-time and evening/weekend programs available. Postbaccalaureate distance learning degree programs offered. *Degree requirements:* For master's, comprehensive exam. *Entrance requirements:* For master's, GRE. Additional exam requirements/recommendations for international students: Required—TOEFL (minimum score 525 paper-based; 71 iBT) or IELTS (minimum score 6). *Faculty research:* Biotechnology, biostatistics, informatics.

Milwaukee School of Engineering, Rader School of Business, Program in Medical Informatics, Milwaukee, WI 53202-3109. Offers MS. Part-time and evening/weekend programs available. *Faculty:* 1 (woman) full-time, 2 part-time/adjunct (1 woman). *Students:* 3 full-time (0 women), 6 part-time (4 women). Average age 33. 8 applicants, 50% accepted, 3 enrolled. In 2014, 7 master's awarded. *Degree requirements:* For master's, thesis, capstone course, research project. *Entrance requirements:* For master's, GRE General Test or GMAT (with percentiles that average 60% or better), 3 letters of recommendation, minimum GPA of 3.0, personal essay, transcripts. Additional exam requirements/recommendations for international students: Required—TOEFL (minimum score 79 iBT), IELTS (minimum score 6.5). *Application deadline:* Applications are processed on a rolling basis. Application fee: $0. Electronic applications accepted. *Expenses: Tuition:* Part-time $732 per credit. *Financial support:* In 2014–15, 1 student received support. Career-related internships or fieldwork, institutionally sponsored loans, scholarships/grants, and tuition waivers (full) available. Financial award application deadline: 3/15; financial award applicants required to submit FAFSA. *Faculty research:* Information technology, databases. *Unit head:* Katie McCarthy, Program Director, 414-277-7279, Fax: 414-277-7279, E-mail: mccarthk@msoe.edu. *Application contact:* Ian Dahlinghaus, Graduate Admissions Counselor, 414-277-7208, E-mail: dahlinghaus@msoe.edu.
Website: http://www.msoe.edu/community/academics/business/page/1323/medical-informatics-overview.

See Display on page 58 and Close-Up on page 83.

National University, Academic Affairs, School of Health and Human Services, La Jolla, CA 92037-1011. Offers clinical affairs (MS); clinical informatics (Certificate); clinical regulatory affairs (MS); health and life science analytics (MS); health coaching (Certificate); health informatics (MS); healthcare administration (MHA); nurse anesthesia (MS); nursing (MS), including forensic nursing, nursing administration, nursing informatics; nursing administration (Certificate); nursing informatics (Certificate); nursing practice (DNP); public health (MPH), including health promotion, healthcare administration, mental health. Part-time and evening/weekend programs available. Postbaccalaureate distance learning degree programs offered (no on-campus study). *Faculty:* 26 full-time (14 women), 29 part-time/adjunct (21 women). *Students:* 302 full-time (232 women), 95 part-time (66 women); includes 282 minority (89 Black or African American, non-Hispanic/Latino; 1 American Indian or Alaska Native, non-Hispanic/Latino; 87 Asian, non-Hispanic/Latino; 76 Hispanic/Latino; 7 Native Hawaiian or other Pacific Islander, non-Hispanic/Latino; 22 Two or more races, non-Hispanic/Latino), 21 international. Average age 32. In 2014, 53 master's awarded. *Degree requirements:* For master's, thesis (for some programs). *Entrance requirements:* For master's, interview, minimum GPA of 2.5. Additional exam requirements/recommendations for international students: Required—TOEFL (minimum score 550 paper-based; 79 iBT), IELTS (minimum score 6). *Application deadline:* Applications are processed on a rolling basis. Application fee: $60 ($65 for international students). Electronic applications accepted. *Expenses: Tuition:* Full-time $14,184; part-time $1773 per course. *Financial support:* Career-related internships or fieldwork, institutionally sponsored loans, scholarships/grants, and tuition waivers (partial) available. Support available to part-time students. Financial award application deadline: 6/30; financial award applicants required to submit FAFSA. *Faculty research:* Nursing education, obesity prevention, workforce diversity. *Unit head:* School of Health and Human Services, 800-628-8648, E-mail: shhs@nu.edu. *Application contact:* Frank Rojas, Vice President for Enrollment Services, 800-628-8648, E-mail: advisor@nu.edu.
Website: http://www.nu.edu/OurPrograms/SchoolOfHealthAndHumanServices.html.

Northwestern University, Feinberg School of Medicine and Interdepartmental Programs, Integrated Graduate Programs in the Life Sciences, Chicago, IL 60611. Offers biostatistics (PhD); epidemiology (PhD); health and biomedical informatics (PhD); health services and outcomes research (PhD); healthcare quality and patient safety (PhD); translational outcomes in science (PhD). *Degree requirements:* For doctorate, comprehensive exam, thesis/dissertation, written and oral qualifying exams. *Entrance requirements:* For doctorate, GRE General Test. Additional exam requirements/recommendations for international students: Required—TOEFL (minimum score 600 paper-based). Electronic applications accepted.

Northwestern University, School of Professional Studies, Program in Information Systems, Evanston, IL 60208. Offers analytics and business intelligence (MS); database and Internet technologies (MS); information systems (MS); information systems management (MS); information systems security (MS); medical informatics (MS); software project management and development (MS).

Northwestern University, School of Professional Studies, Program in Medical Informatics, Evanston, IL 60208. Offers MS. Postbaccalaureate distance learning degree programs offered.

Nova Southeastern University, College of Osteopathic Medicine, Fort Lauderdale, FL 33328. Offers biomedical informatics (MS, Graduate Certificate), including biomedical informatics (MS), clinical informatics (Graduate Certificate), public health informatics (Graduate Certificate); disaster and emergency preparedness (MS); osteopathic medicine (DO); public health (MPH). *Accreditation:* AOsA. *Faculty:* 107 full-time (55 women), 1,235 part-time/adjunct (297 women). *Students:* 1,027 full-time (436 women), 189 part-time (124 women); includes 560 minority (92 Black or African American, non-Hispanic/Latino; 260 Asian, non-Hispanic/Latino; 174 Hispanic/Latino; 1 Native Hawaiian or other Pacific Islander, non-Hispanic/Latino; 33 Two or more races, non-Hispanic/Latino), 45 international. Average age 28. 4,012 applicants, 12% accepted, 246 enrolled. In 2014, 75 master's, 237 doctorates, 4 other advanced degrees awarded. *Entrance requirements:* For master's, GRE, licensed healthcare professional or GRE; for doctorate, MCAT, biology, chemistry, organic chemistry, physics (all with labs), and English. *Application deadline:* For fall admission, 1/15 for domestic students. Applications are processed on a rolling basis. Application fee: $50. Electronic applications accepted. *Expenses:* Expenses: Contact institution. *Financial support:* In 2014–15, 39 students received support, including 24 fellowships (averaging $45,593 per year); research assistantships, teaching assistantships, Federal Work-Study, and scholarships/grants also available. Financial award application deadline: 6/1; financial award applicants required to submit FAFSA. *Faculty research:* Teaching strategies, simulated patient use, HIV/AIDS education, minority health issues, managed care education. *Unit head:* Elaine M. Wallace, DO, Dean, 954-262-1407, E-mail: ewallace@nova.edu. *Application contact:* Monica Sanchez, Admissions Counselor, College of Osteopathic Medicine, 954-262-1110, Fax: 954-262-2282, E-mail: mh1156@nova.edu.
Website: http://www.medicine.nova.edu/.

Oregon Health & Science University, School of Medicine, Graduate Programs in Medicine, Department of Medical Informatics and Clinical Epidemiology, Portland, OR 97239-3098. Offers clinical informatics (MS, PhD, Certificate); computational biology (MS, PhD); health information management (Certificate). Part-time programs available. Postbaccalaureate distance learning degree programs offered (minimal on-campus study). *Faculty:* 12 full-time (6 women), 15 part-time/adjunct (7 women). *Students:* 32 full-time (12 women), 92 part-time (41 women); includes 43 minority (7 Black or African American, non-Hispanic/Latino; 26 Asian, non-Hispanic/Latino; 5 Hispanic/Latino; 5 Two or more races, non-Hispanic/Latino), 3 international. Average age 39. 111 applicants, 64% accepted, 52 enrolled. In 2014, 28 master's, 2 doctorates, 25 other advanced degrees awarded. Terminal master's awarded for partial completion of doctoral program. *Degree requirements:* For master's, thesis optional, thesis or capstone project; for doctorate, comprehensive exam, thesis/dissertation, qualifying exam. *Entrance requirements:* For master's and doctorate, GRE General Test (minimum scores: 153 Verbal/148 Quantitative/4.5 Analytical), coursework in computer programming, human

anatomy and physiology. Additional exam requirements/recommendations for international students: Required—IELTS or TOEFL. *Application deadline:* For fall admission, 12/1 for domestic students; for winter admission, 11/1 for domestic students; for spring admission, 2/1 for domestic students. Applications are processed on a rolling basis. Application fee: $70. Electronic applications accepted. *Expenses:* Expenses: Contact institution. *Financial support:* Fellowships with full tuition reimbursements, research assistantships, Federal Work-Study, institutionally sponsored loans, scholarships/grants, health care benefits, and full tuition and stipends (for PhD students) available. Financial award application deadline: 3/1; financial award applicants required to submit FAFSA. *Faculty research:* Clinical informatics, computational biology, health information management, genomics, data analytics. *Unit head:* Dr. Allison Fryer, Associate Dean for Graduate Studies, 503-494-6222, Fax: 503-494-3400, E-mail: somgrad@ohsu.edu. *Application contact:* Lauren Ludwig, Administrative Coordinator, 503-494-2252, E-mail: informat@ohsu.edu.
Website: http://www.ohsu.edu/dmice/.

Rochester Institute of Technology, Graduate Enrollment Services, Golisano College of Computing and Information Sciences, Information Science and Technologies Department, Program in Medical Informatics, Rochester, NY 14623-5603. Offers MS. Part-time programs available. *Students:* 1 full-time (0 women), 3 part-time (0 women). Average age 36. 14 applicants, 29% accepted, 2 enrolled. In 2014, 3 master's awarded. *Degree requirements:* For master's, thesis or alternative, capstone. *Entrance requirements:* Additional exam requirements/recommendations for international students: Required—TOEFL (minimum score 570 paper-based; 88 iBT). *Application deadline:* Applications are processed on a rolling basis. Application fee: $60. Electronic applications accepted. *Expenses: Tuition:* Full-time $38,688; part-time $1612 per credit hour. *Required fees:* $260. *Financial support:* Applicants required to submit FAFSA. *Faculty research:* Electronic health record development, database systems, clinical systems integration, Web applications for medicine, management, public health. *Unit head:* Dr. Peter Lutz, Graduate Program Director, E-mail: phlics@rit.edu. *Application contact:* Diane Ellison, Assistant Vice President, Graduate Enrollment Services, 585-475-2229, Fax: 585-475-7164, E-mail: gradinfo@rit.edu.
Website: http://www.ist.rit.edu/degrees/graduate/ms-in-mi/overview.php.

Rutgers, The State University of New Jersey, Newark, School of Health Related Professions, Department of Health Informatics, Program in Biomedical Informatics, Newark, NJ 07102. Offers MS, PhD, DMD/MS, MD/MS. Part-time and evening/weekend programs available. Postbaccalaureate distance learning degree programs offered (minimal on-campus study). *Degree requirements:* For master's, thesis; for doctorate, comprehensive exam, thesis/dissertation. *Entrance requirements:* For master's, BS, transcript of highest degree, statement of research interests, curriculum vitae, basic understanding of database concepts and calculus, 3 reference letters; for doctorate, master's degree, transcripts of highest degree, statement of research interests, curriculum vitae, basic understanding of database concepts and calculus, 3 reference letters. Additional exam requirements/recommendations for international students: Required—TOEFL. Electronic applications accepted.

Rutgers, The State University of New Jersey, Newark, School of Health Related Professions, Department of Health Informatics, Program in Health Care Informatics, Newark, NJ 07102. Offers Certificate. Part-time and evening/weekend programs available. Postbaccalaureate distance learning degree programs offered (minimal on-campus study). *Entrance requirements:* For degree, all transcripts, basic proficiency in programming language, BS, 3 reference letters. Additional exam requirements/recommendations for international students: Required—TOEFL (minimum score 500 paper-based; 79 iBT). Electronic applications accepted.

Stanford University, School of Medicine, Graduate Programs in Medicine, Biomedical Informatics Program, Stanford, CA 94305-9991. Offers MS, PhD. Terminal master's awarded for partial completion of doctoral program. *Degree requirements:* For master's, thesis; for doctorate, thesis/dissertation. *Entrance requirements:* For doctorate, GRE or MCAT. Additional exam requirements/recommendations for international students: Required—TOEFL. Electronic applications accepted. *Expenses: Tuition:* Full-time $44,184; part-time $982 per credit hour. *Required fees:* $191.

University at Buffalo, the State University of New York, Graduate School, School of Medicine and Biomedical Sciences, Program in Medical and Health Informatics, Buffalo, NY 14260. Offers Certificate. Part-time programs available. *Faculty:* 4 part-time/adjunct (0 women). *Students:* 4 part-time (2 women). Average age 35. 1 applicant. In 2014, 1 Certificate awarded. *Degree requirements:* For Certificate, 24 credit hours of coursework (18 required courses, 6 electives). *Entrance requirements:* For degree, all previous college/university transcripts; 2 letters of recommendation; personal letter with career objectives. Additional exam requirements/recommendations for international students: Required—TOEFL (minimum score 600 paper-based). *Application deadline:* For fall admission, 8/15 priority date for domestic students, 7/15 for international students. Application fee: $50. *Faculty research:* Integrated information systems planning and evaluation, management of knowledge-based information resources, scholarly communication in the health sciences, the economic value of health information, electronic health records, natural language understanding, ontologies, telemedicine/telehealth systems of healthcare, quality management information systems, implementation and evaluation of electronic health record systems, ethical and social issues in informatics. *Unit head:* Dr. Michael E. Cain, Dean, 716-829-3955, Fax: 716-829-3395, E-mail: mcain@buffalo.edu. *Application contact:* Elizabeth A. White, Staff Associate, 716-829-3399, Fax: 716-829-2437, E-mail: bethw@buffalo.edu.
Website: http://www.smbs.buffalo.edu/medinformatics/.

The University of Arizona, College of Nursing, Tucson, AZ 85721. Offers health care informatics (Certificate); nurse practitioner (MS, Certificate); nursing (DNP, PhD); rural health (Certificate). *Accreditation:* AACN. Part-time programs available. Postbaccalaureate distance learning degree programs offered (minimal on-campus study). Terminal master's awarded for partial completion of doctoral program. *Degree requirements:* For master's, thesis optional; for doctorate, comprehensive exam, thesis/dissertation. *Entrance requirements:* For master's, BSN, eligibility for RN license; for doctorate, BSN; for Certificate, GRE General Test, Arizona RN license, BSN, minimum GPA of 3.0. Additional exam requirements/recommendations for international students: Required—TOEFL (minimum score 550 paper-based; 79 iBT). Electronic applications accepted. *Expenses:* Contact institution. *Faculty research:* Vulnerable populations, injury mechanisms and biobehavioral responses, health care systems, informatics, rural health.

University of California, Davis, Graduate Studies, Graduate Group in Health Informatics, Davis, CA 95616. Offers MS. *Entrance requirements:* Additional exam requirements/recommendations for international students: Required—TOEFL (minimum score 550 paper-based).

University of Colorado Denver, College of Nursing, Aurora, CO 80045. Offers adult clinical nurse specialist (MS); adult nurse practitioner (MS); family nurse practitioner (MS); family psychiatric mental health nurse practitioner (MS); health care informatics (MS); nurse-midwifery (MS); nursing (DNP, PhD); nursing leadership and health care systems (MS); pediatric nurse practitioner (MS); special studies (MS); women's health (MS); MS/PhD. *Accreditation:* ACNM/ACME (one or more programs are accredited). Part-time and evening/weekend programs available. Postbaccalaureate distance learning degree programs offered (minimal on-campus study). *Faculty:* 97 full-time (89 women), 47 part-time/adjunct (43 women). *Students:* 342 full-time (321 women), 141 part-time (124 women); includes 83 minority (17 Black or African American, non-Hispanic/Latino; 2 American Indian or Alaska Native, non-Hispanic/Latino; 13 Asian, non-Hispanic/Latino; 36 Hispanic/Latino; 2 Native Hawaiian or other Pacific Islander, non-Hispanic/Latino; 13 Two or more races, non-Hispanic/Latino), 5 international. Average age 36. 268 applicants, 51% accepted, 113 enrolled. In 2014, 119 master's, 38 doctorates awarded. Terminal master's awarded for partial completion of doctoral program. *Degree requirements:* For master's, thesis optional; for doctorate, comprehensive exam, thesis/dissertation, 42 credits of coursework. *Entrance requirements:* For master's, GRE if cumulative undergraduate GPA is less than 3.0, undergraduate nursing degree from NLNAC- or CCNE-accredited school or university; completion of research and statistics courses with minimum grade of C; copy of current and unencumbered nursing license; for doctorate, GRE, bachelor's and/or master's degrees in nursing from NLN- or CCNE-accredited institution; portfolio; minimum undergraduate GPA of 3.0, graduate 3.5; graduate-level intermediate statistics and master's-level nursing theory courses with minimum B grade; interview. Additional exam requirements/recommendations for international students: Required—TOEFL (minimum score 560 paper-based; 83 iBT). *Application deadline:* For fall admission, 2/15 for domestic students, 1/15 for international students; for spring admission, 7/1 for domestic students, 6/1 for international students. Application fee: $50 ($75 for international students). Electronic applications accepted. *Expenses:* Expenses: Contact institution. *Financial support:* In 2014–15, 111 students received support. Fellowships, research assistantships, teaching assistantships, Federal Work-Study, institutionally sponsored loans, scholarships/grants, traineeships, and unspecified assistantships available. Support available to part-time students. Financial award application deadline: 4/1; financial award applicants required to submit FAFSA. *Faculty research:* Biological and behavioral phenomena in pregnancy and postpartum; patterns of glycemia during the insulin resistance of pregnancy; obesity, gestational diabetes, and relationship to neonatal adiposity; men's awareness and knowledge of male breast cancer; cognitive-behavioral therapy for chronic insomnia after breast cancer treatment; massage therapy for the treatment of tension-type headaches. *Total annual research expenditures:* $5.9 million. *Unit head:* Dr. Sarah Thompson, Dean, 303-724-1679, E-mail: sarah.a.thompson@ucdenver.edu. *Application contact:* Judy Campbell, Graduate Programs Coordinator, 303-724-8503, E-mail: judy.campbell@ucdenver.edu.
Website: http://www.ucdenver.edu/academics/colleges/nursing/Pages/default.aspx.

University of Illinois at Urbana–Champaign, Graduate College, Graduate School of Library and Information Science, Champaign, IL 61820. Offers bioinformatics (MS); digital libraries (CAS); library and information science (MS, PhD, CAS). *Accreditation:* ALA (one or more programs are accredited). Part-time programs available. Postbaccalaureate distance learning degree programs offered (minimal on-campus study). *Students:* 283 (208 women). *Entrance requirements:* For degree, master's degree in library and information science or related field with minimum GPA of 3.0. Application fee: $70 ($90 for international students). *Unit head:* Allen Renear, Interim Dean, 217-265-5216, Fax: 217-244-3302, E-mail: renear@illinois.edu. *Application contact:* Penny Ames, Graduate Contact, 217-333-7197, E-mail: pames@illinois.edu.
Website: http://www.lis.illinois.edu.

The University of Kansas, University of Kansas Medical Center, School of Nursing, Kansas City, KS 66160. Offers adult/gerontological clinical nurse specialist (PMC); adult/gerontological nurse practitioner (PMC); clinical research management (PMC); health care informatics (PMC); health professions educator (PMC); nurse midwife (PMC); nursing (MS, DNP, PhD); organizational leadership (PMC); psychiatric/mental health nurse practitioner (PMC); public health nursing (PMC). *Accreditation:* AACN; ACNM/ACME. Part-time programs available. Postbaccalaureate distance learning degree programs offered (minimal on-campus study). *Faculty:* 60. *Students:* 47 full-time (40 women), 320 part-time (298 women); includes 56 minority (24 Black or African American, non-Hispanic/Latino; 11 Asian, non-Hispanic/Latino; 15 Hispanic/Latino; 1 Native Hawaiian or other Pacific Islander, non-Hispanic/Latino; 5 Two or more races, non-Hispanic/Latino), 1 international. Average age 38. 117 applicants, 98% accepted, 81 enrolled. In 2014, 82 master's, 16 doctorates, 14 other advanced degrees awarded. Terminal master's awarded for partial completion of doctoral program. *Degree requirements:* For master's, comprehensive exam, thesis (for some programs), general oral exam; for doctorate, variable foreign language requirement, comprehensive exam, thesis/dissertation or alternative, comprehensive oral exam (for DNP); comprehensive written and oral exam (for PhD); PhD includes three publication option. *Entrance requirements:* For master's, bachelor's degree in nursing, minimum GPA of 3.0, 1 year of clinical experience, RN license in KS and MO; for doctorate, GRE General Test (Required for PhD only), bachelor's degree in nursing, minimum GPA of 3.5, RN license in KS and MO. Additional exam requirements/recommendations for international students: Required—TOEFL. *Application deadline:* For fall admission, 4/1 for domestic and international students; for spring admission, 9/1 for domestic and international students. Application fee: $60. Electronic applications accepted. *Financial support:* Research assistantships with full and partial tuition reimbursements, teaching assistantships with full and partial tuition reimbursements, scholarships/grants, and traineeships available. Financial award application deadline: 3/1; financial award applicants required to submit FAFSA. *Faculty research:* Breastfeeding practices of teen mothers, national database of nursing quality indicators, caregiving of families of patients using technology in the home, simulation in nursing education, diaphragm fatigue. *Total annual research expenditures:* $6.3 million. *Unit head:* Dr. Karen L. Miller, Dean, 913-588-1601, Fax: 913-588-1660, E-mail: kmiller@kumc.edu. *Application contact:* Dr. Pamela K. Barnes, Associate Dean, Student Affairs, 913-588-1619, Fax: 913-588-1615, E-mail: pbarnes2@kumc.edu.
Website: http://nursing.kumc.edu.

University of Nebraska at Omaha, Graduate Studies, College of Information Science and Technology, Department of Information Systems and Quantitative Analysis, Omaha, NE 68182. Offers biomedical informatics (MS, PhD); information assurance (MS, Certificate); information technology (PhD); management information systems (MS); project management (Certificate); systems analysis and design (Certificate). Part-time and evening/weekend programs available. *Faculty:* 25 full-time (8 women). *Students:* 137 full-time (50 women), 125 part-time (31 women); includes 36 minority (14 Black or African American, non-Hispanic/Latino; 1 American Indian or Alaska Native, non-Hispanic/Latino; 15 Asian, non-Hispanic/Latino; 2 Hispanic/Latino; 4 Two or more races, non-Hispanic/Latino), 143 international. Average age 29. 404 applicants, 50% accepted, 101 enrolled. In 2014, 46 master's, 3 doctorates, 21 other advanced degrees awarded. *Degree requirements:* For master's, comprehensive exam, thesis (for some programs); for doctorate, comprehensive exam, thesis/dissertation. *Entrance requirements:* For master's, GRE General Test, minimum GPA of 3.0, 3 letters of recommendation, writing sample, resume, official transcripts; for doctorate, GMAT or GRE General Test, minimum GPA of 3.0, 3 letters of recommendation, writing sample, resume, official transcripts; for Certificate, minimum GPA of 3.0, official transcripts. Additional exam requirements/recommendations for international students: Required—TOEFL, IELTS, PTE. *Application deadline:* For fall admission, 2/15 for domestic and international students; for spring admission, 9/15 for domestic and international students; for summer admission, 4/1 for domestic and international students. Applications are processed on a rolling basis. Application fee: $45. Electronic applications accepted. *Financial support:* In 2014–15, 35 students received support, including 28 research assistantships with tuition reimbursements available, 7 teaching assistantships with tuition reimbursements available; fellowships, career-related internships or fieldwork, Federal Work-Study, scholarships/grants, tuition waivers (partial), and unspecified assistantships also available. Financial award application deadline: 3/1; financial award applicants required to submit FAFSA. *Unit head:* Dr. Peter Wolcott, Chairperson, 402-554-2341, E-mail: graduate@unomaha.edu. *Application contact:* Dr. Leah Pietron, Graduate Program Chair, 402-554-2341, E-mail: graduate@unomaha.edu.

University of Phoenix–Phoenix Campus, College of Health Sciences and Nursing, Tempe, AZ 85282-2371. Offers family nurse practitioner (MSN, Certificate); gerontology health care (Certificate); health care education (MSN, Certificate); health care informatics (Certificate); informatics (MSN); nursing (MSN); MSN/MHA. Evening/weekend programs available. Postbaccalaureate distance learning degree programs offered. *Entrance requirements:* Additional exam requirements/recommendations for international students: Required—TOEFL, TOEIC (Test of English as an International Communication), Berlitz Online English Proficiency Exam, PTE, or IELTS. Electronic applications accepted. *Expenses:* Contact institution.

The University of Tennessee at Chattanooga, School of Nursing, Chattanooga, TN 37403. Offers administration (MSN); certified nurse anesthetist (Post-Master's Certificate); education (MSN); family nurse practitioner (MSN, Post-Master's Certificate); health care informatics (Post-Master's Certificate); nurse anesthesia (MSN); nurse education (Post-Master's Certificate); nursing (DNP). *Accreditation:* AACN; AANA/CANAEP (one or more programs are accredited). *Faculty:* 9 full-time (7 women), 2 part-time/adjunct (1 woman). *Students:* 72 full-time (39 women), 53 part-time (43 women); includes 11 minority (6 Black or African American, non-Hispanic/Latino; 1 Asian, non-Hispanic/Latino; 3 Hispanic/Latino; 1 Two or more races, non-Hispanic/Latino). Average age 33. 3 applicants, 100% accepted, 1 enrolled. In 2014, 35 master's, 10 doctorates, 2 other advanced degrees awarded. *Degree requirements:* For master's, thesis optional, qualifying exams, professional project; for Post-Master's Certificate, thesis or alternative, practicum, seminar. *Entrance requirements:* For master's, GRE General Test, MAT, BSN, minimum GPA of 3.0, eligibility for Tennessee RN license, 1 year of direct patient care experience; for Post-Master's Certificate, GRE General Test, MAT, MSN, minimum GPA of 3.0, eligibility for Tennessee RN license, one year of direct patient care experience. Additional exam requirements/recommendations for international students: Required—TOEFL (minimum score 550 paper-based; 79 iBT), IELTS (minimum score 6). *Application deadline:* For fall admission, 6/13 priority date for domestic students, 6/1 for international students; for spring admission, 10/15 priority date for domestic students, 10/1 for international students. Applications are processed on a rolling basis. Application fee: $30 ($35 for international students). Electronic applications accepted. *Expenses:* Tuition, state resident: full-time $7708; part-time $428 per credit hour. Tuition, nonresident: full-time $23,826; part-time $1323 per credit hour. *Required fees:* $1708; $252 per credit hour. *Financial support:* Career-related internships or fieldwork and scholarships/grants available. Support available to part-time students. *Faculty research:* Diabetes in women, health care for elderly, alternative medicine, hypertension, nurse anesthesia. *Total annual research expenditures:* $3.4 million. *Unit head:* Dr. Chris Smith, Interim Director, 423-425-1741, Fax: 423-425-4668, E-mail: chris-smith@utc.edu. *Application contact:* Dr. J. Randy Walker, Interim Dean of Graduate Studies, 423-425-4478, Fax: 423-425-5223, E-mail: randy-walker@utc.edu.
Website: http://www.utc.edu/Academic/Nursing/.

University of Washington, Graduate School, School of Medicine, Graduate Programs in Medicine, Department of Medical Education and Biomedical Informatics, Division of Biomedical and Health Informatics, Seattle, WA 98195. Offers MS, PhD. *Entrance requirements:* For master's and doctorate, GRE General Test, minimum GPA of 3.0; previous undergraduate course work in biology, computer programming, and mathematics. Additional exam requirements/recommendations for international students: Required—TOEFL (minimum score 580 paper-based; 70 iBT). Electronic applications accepted. *Faculty research:* Bio-clinical informatics, information retrieval, human-computer interaction, knowledge-based systems, telehealth.

University of Wisconsin–Milwaukee, Graduate School, College of Engineering and Applied Science, Program in Biomedical and Health Informatics, Milwaukee, WI 53201-0413. Offers PhD. *Degree requirements:* For doctorate, comprehensive exam, thesis/dissertation. *Entrance requirements:* For doctorate, GRE, GMAT or MCAT. Additional exam requirements/recommendations for international students: Required—TOEFL (minimum score 600 paper-based; 79 iBT), IELTS (minimum score 6.5).

Modeling and Simulation

Academy of Art University, Graduate Program, School of Animation and Visual Effects, San Francisco, CA 94105-3410. Offers 3D animation (MFA); 3D modeling (MFA); storyboarding (MFA); traditional animation (MFA); visual effects (MFA). Part-time programs available. Postbaccalaureate distance learning degree programs offered (no on-campus study). *Faculty:* 22 full-time (5 women), 71 part-time/adjunct (16 women). *Students:* 383 full-time (168 women), 206 part-time (77 women); includes 94 minority (24 Black or African American, non-Hispanic/Latino; 3 American Indian or Alaska Native, non-Hispanic/Latino; 30 Asian, non-Hispanic/Latino; 30 Hispanic/Latino; 2 Native Hawaiian or other Pacific Islander, non-Hispanic/Latino; 5 Two or more races, non-Hispanic/Latino), 353 international. Average age 29. 165 applicants, 100% accepted, 87 enrolled. In 2014, 202 master's awarded. *Degree requirements:* For master's, final review. *Entrance requirements:* For master's, statement of intent; resume; portfolio/reel; official college transcripts. *Application deadline:* Applications are processed on a rolling basis. Application fee: $100. Electronic applications accepted. *Expenses:* Tuition: Part-time $910 per unit. *Financial support:* Career-related internships or fieldwork and Federal Work-Study available. Support available to part-time students. Financial award application deadline: 8/10; financial award applicants required to submit FAFSA. *Unit head:* 800-544-ARTS, E-mail: info@academyart.edu. *Application contact:* 800-544-ARTS, E-mail: info@academyart.edu.
Website: http://www.academyart.edu/animation-school/index.html.

Arizona State University at the Tempe campus, Ira A. Fulton Schools of Engineering, ASU Engineering Online Programs, Tempe, AZ 85287. Offers construction (MS); embedded systems (M Eng); enterprise systems innovation and management (MSE); modeling and simulation (M Eng); quality and reliability engineering (M Eng); software engineering (MSE); systems engineering (M Eng).

Arizona State University at the Tempe campus, Ira A. Fulton Schools of Engineering, The Polytechnic School, Department of Engineering, Mesa, AZ 85212. Offers simulation, modeling, and applied cognitive science (PhD). Part-time programs available. *Degree requirements:* For doctorate, comprehensive exam, thesis/dissertation, interactive Program of Study (iPOS) submitted before completing 50 percent of required credit hours. *Entrance requirements:* For doctorate, GRE, master's degree in psychology, engineering, cognitive science, or computer science; 3 letters of recommendation; statement of research interests. Additional exam requirements/recommendations for international students: Required—TOEFL, IELTS, or PTE. Electronic applications accepted. *Faculty research:* Software process and automated workflow, software architecture, dotal technologies, relational database systems, embedded systems.

Carnegie Mellon University, Carnegie Institute of Technology, Department of Civil and Environmental Engineering, Pittsburgh, PA 15213. Offers advanced infrastructure systems (MS, PhD); advanced infrastructure systems technology development and application (MS); air quality engineering and science (MS); civil and environmental engineering (MS, PhD); civil and environmental engineering/engineering and public policy (PhD); civil engineering (MS, PhD); computational mechanics (MS, PhD); computational modeling and monitoring for resilient structural and material systems (MS); energy infrastructure systems (MS); environmental engineering (MS, PhD); environmental management and science (MS, PhD); IT-based sustainable global infrastructure and construction management (MS); sustainability and green design (MS); water quality engineering and science (MS). Part-time programs available. *Faculty:* 21 full-time (5 women), 12 part-time/adjunct (3 women). *Students:* 229 full-time (99 women), 31 part-time (11 women); includes 18 minority (4 Black or African American, non-Hispanic/Latino; 13 Asian, non-Hispanic/Latino; 1 Hispanic/Latino), 193 international. Average age 26. 590 applicants, 68% accepted, 124 enrolled. In 2014, 85 master's, 11 doctorates awarded. Terminal master's awarded for partial completion of doctoral program. *Degree requirements:* For master's, thesis optional; for doctorate, comprehensive exam, thesis/dissertation, two-part qualifying exam, public defense of dissertation. *Entrance requirements:* For master's, GRE General Test, BS in engineering, science or mathematics; for doctorate, GRE General Test, BS or MS in engineering, science or mathematics. Additional exam requirements/recommendations for international students: Required—TOEFL (minimum score 84 iBT) or IELTS. *Application deadline:* For fall admission, 1/5 priority date for domestic and international students; for spring admission, 9/15 priority date for domestic and international students.

Application fee: $65. Electronic applications accepted. *Financial support:* In 2014–15, 169 students received support. Fellowships with full and partial tuition reimbursements available, research assistantships with full and partial tuition reimbursements available, scholarships/grants, tuition waivers (full and partial), unspecified assistantships, and service assistantships available. Financial award application deadline: 1/5. *Faculty research:* Advanced infrastructure systems; environmental engineering, sustainability, and science; mechanics, materials, and computing. *Total annual research expenditures:* $4.9 million. *Unit head:* Dr. David A. Dzombak, Head, 412-268-2941, Fax: 412-268-7813, E-mail: dzombak@cmu.edu. *Application contact:* Melissa L. Brown, Director of Graduate Admissions & Recruiting, 412-268-8762, Fax: 412-268-7813, E-mail: mlb2@andrew.cmu.edu.
Website: http://www.cmu.edu/cee/.

Columbus State University, Graduate Studies, D. Abbott Turner College of Business and Computer Science, Columbus, GA 31907-5645. Offers applied computer science (MS); business administration (MBA); information systems security (Certificate); modeling and simulation (Certificate); organizational leadership (MS). *Accreditation:* AACSB. *Faculty:* 9 full-time (3 women), 2 part-time/adjunct (1 woman). *Students:* 86 full-time (21 women), 134 part-time (47 women); includes 68 minority (37 Black or African American, non-Hispanic/Latino; 2 American Indian or Alaska Native, non-Hispanic/Latino; 15 Asian, non-Hispanic/Latino; 10 Hispanic/Latino; 4 Two or more races, non-Hispanic/Latino), 12 international. Average age 32. 149 applicants, 51% accepted, 49 enrolled. In 2014, 141 master's awarded. *Entrance requirements:* For master's, GMAT, GRE, minimum undergraduate GPA of 2.75, letters of recommendation. Additional exam requirements/recommendations for international students: Required—TOEFL (minimum score 550 paper-based; 79 iBT). *Application deadline:* For fall admission, 6/30 for domestic students, 5/1 for international students; for spring admission, 11/1 for domestic and international students; for summer admission, 3/1 for domestic and international students. Applications are processed on a rolling basis. Application fee: $50. Electronic applications accepted. *Financial support:* In 2014–15, 66 students received support, including 16 research assistantships (averaging $3,000 per year). Financial award application deadline: 5/1; financial award applicants required to submit FAFSA. *Unit head:* Dr. Linda U. Hadley, Dean, 706-507-8153, Fax: 706-568-2184, E-mail: hadley_linda@columbusstate.edu. *Application contact:* Kristin Williams, Director of International and Graduate Recruitment, 706-507-8848, Fax: 706-568-5091, E-mail: thornton_katie@colstate.edu.
Website: http://turner.columbusstate.edu/.

Louisiana Tech University, Graduate School, College of Engineering and Science, Department of Physics, Ruston, LA 71272. Offers applied physics (MS); computational analysis and modeling (PhD); engineering physics (PhD). Part-time programs available. *Degree requirements:* For master's, thesis or alternative; for doctorate, thesis/dissertation. *Entrance requirements:* For master's, GRE General Test, minimum GPA of 3.0 in last 60 hours. Additional exam requirements/recommendations for international students: Required—TOEFL. *Faculty research:* Experimental high energy physics, laser/optics, computational physics, quantum gravity.

Naval Postgraduate School, Departments and Academic Groups, Department of Computer Science, Monterey, CA 93943. Offers computer science (MS, PhD); identity management and cyber security (MA); modeling of virtual environments and simulations (MS, PhD); software engineering (MS, PhD). Program only open to commissioned officers of the United States and friendly nations and selected United States federal civilian employees. Part-time programs available. Postbaccalaureate distance learning degree programs offered (minimal on-campus study). *Degree requirements:* For master's, thesis; for doctorate, thesis/dissertation.

Old Dominion University, College of Arts and Letters, Graduate Program in International Studies, Norfolk, VA 23529. Offers conflict and cooperation (MA, PhD); interdependence and transnationalism (MA, PhD); international cultural studies (MA, PhD); international political economy and development (MA, PhD); modeling and simulation (MA, PhD); U.S. foreign policy and international relations (MA, PhD). Part-time programs available. *Faculty:* 18 full-time (4 women). *Students:* 41 full-time (14 women), 46 part-time (23 women); includes 11 minority (5 Black or African American, non-Hispanic/Latino; 1 Asian, non-Hispanic/Latino; 2 Hispanic/Latino; 3 Two or more

races, non-Hispanic/Latino), 24 international. Average age 35. 99 applicants, 54% accepted, 34 enrolled. In 2014, 10 master's, 9 doctorates awarded. Terminal master's awarded for partial completion of doctoral program. *Degree requirements:* For master's, one foreign language, comprehensive exam, thesis optional; for doctorate, one foreign language, comprehensive exam, thesis/dissertation. *Entrance requirements:* For master's, GRE General Test, sample of written work, 2 letters of recommendation; for doctorate, GRE General Test, sample of written work, 3 letters of recommendation. Additional exam requirements/recommendations for international students: Required—TOEFL (minimum score 570 paper-based). *Application deadline:* For fall admission, 1/15 for domestic and international students; for spring admission, 10/15 for domestic and international students. Application fee: $50. Electronic applications accepted. *Expenses:* Tuition, state resident: full-time $10,488; part-time $437 per credit. Tuition, nonresident: full-time $26,136; part-time $1089 per credit. *Required fees:* $64 per semester. One-time fee: $50. *Financial support:* In 2014–15, 20 students received support, including 2 fellowships (averaging $13,000 per year), 5 research assistantships with tuition reimbursements available (averaging $15,000 per year), 7 teaching assistantships with tuition reimbursements available (averaging $15,000 per year); career-related internships or fieldwork, institutionally sponsored loans, scholarships/grants, and unspecified assistantships also available. Support available to part-time students. Financial award application deadline: 2/15; financial award applicants required to submit FAFSA. *Faculty research:* U.S. foreign policy, international security, Transatlantic and Transpacific relations, transnational issues, international political economy and development. *Total annual research expenditures:* $330,391. *Unit head:* Dr. Regina Karp, Graduate Program Director, 757-683-5700, Fax: 757-683-5701, E-mail: rkarp@odu.edu. *Application contact:* Dr. David C. Earnest, Associate Dean, 757-683-6077, Fax: 757-683-5746, E-mail: dearnest@odu.edu.
Website: http://www.al.odu.edu/gpis/.

Old Dominion University, Frank Batten College of Engineering and Technology, Program in Modeling and Simulation, Norfolk, VA 23529. Offers ME, MS, D Eng, PhD. Part-time and evening/weekend programs available. Postbaccalaureate distance learning degree programs offered (no on-campus study). *Faculty:* 10 full-time (1 woman). *Students:* 11 full-time (2 women), 64 part-time (15 women); includes 17 minority (7 Black or African American, non-Hispanic/Latino; 4 Asian, non-Hispanic/Latino; 5 Hispanic/Latino; 1 Two or more races, non-Hispanic/Latino), 23 international. Average age 34. 38 applicants, 100% accepted, 21 enrolled. In 2014, 15 master's, 2 doctorates awarded. Terminal master's awarded for partial completion of doctoral program. *Degree requirements:* For master's, comprehensive exam (for some programs), thesis (for some programs); for doctorate, comprehensive exam, thesis/dissertation, candidacy exam. *Entrance requirements:* For master's, GRE, proficiency in calculus, calculus-based statistics, and computer science; for doctorate, GRE, graduate-level proficiency in calculus, calculus-based statistics, and computer science. Additional exam requirements/recommendations for international students: Required—TOEFL (minimum score 550 paper-based; 79 iBT). *Application deadline:* For fall admission, 6/1 for domestic students, 4/15 priority date for international students; for spring admission, 11/1 for domestic students, 10/1 for international students. Applications are processed on a rolling basis. Application fee: $50. Electronic applications accepted. *Expenses:* Tuition, state resident: full-time $10,488; part-time $437 per credit. Tuition, nonresident: full-time $26,136; part-time $1089 per credit. *Required fees:* $64 per semester. One-time fee: $50. *Financial support:* In 2014–15, 18 students received support, including 2 fellowships with full tuition reimbursements available (averaging $16,000 per year), 16 research assistantships with full tuition reimbursements available (averaging $18,000 per year); career-related internships or fieldwork, scholarships/grants, and unspecified assistantships also available. Financial award application deadline: 4/15; financial award applicants required to submit FAFSA. *Faculty research:* Distributed simulation and interoperability, medical modeling and simulation, transportation modeling and simulation, human factors, discrete event systems. *Total annual research expenditures:* $3.6 million. *Unit head:* Dr. Rick McKenzie, Department Chair, 757-683-5590, Fax: 757-683-3200, E-mail: rdmckenz@odu.edu. *Application contact:* Dr. Linda Vahala, Associate Dean, 757-683-3789, Fax: 757-683-4898, E-mail: lvahala@odu.edu.
Website: http://eng.odu.edu/msve.

Philadelphia University, School of Engineering and Textiles, Program in Modeling, Simulation and Data Analytics, Philadelphia, PA 19144. Offers MS. Postbaccalaureate distance learning degree programs offered (no on-campus study).

Portland State University, Graduate Studies, College of Liberal Arts and Sciences, Systems Science Program, Portland, OR 97207-0751. Offers computational intelligence (Certificate); computer modeling and simulation (Certificate); systems science (MS); systems science/anthropology (PhD); systems science/business administration (PhD); systems science/civil engineering (PhD); systems science/economics (PhD); systems science/engineering management (PhD); systems science/general (PhD); systems science/mathematical sciences (PhD); systems science/mechanical engineering (PhD); systems science/psychology (PhD); systems science/sociology (PhD). *Faculty:* 2 full-time (0 women), 1 part-time/adjunct (0 women). *Students:* 6 full-time (2 women), 29 part-time (8 women); includes 6 minority (1 Black or African American, non-Hispanic/Latino; 1 American Indian or Alaska Native, non-Hispanic/Latino; 1 Asian, non-Hispanic/Latino; 3 Hispanic/Latino). Average age 41. 32 applicants, 19% accepted, 6 enrolled. In 2014, 10 master's, 3 doctorates awarded. *Degree requirements:* For master's, comprehensive exam (for some programs), thesis optional; for doctorate, variable foreign language requirement, comprehensive exam (for some programs), thesis/dissertation. *Entrance requirements:* For master's, GRE/GMAT scores are recommended but not required., GPA 3.0 for undergraduate or 3.0 for graduate work, 2 letters of recommendation, and statement of interest; for doctorate, GMAT, GRE General Test, GPA requirement is 3.0 for undergraduate and 3.25 for graduate, 2 letters of recommendation and statement of interest. Additional exam requirements/recommendations for international students: Required—TOEFL (minimum score 550 paper-based; 80 iBT). *Application deadline:* For fall admission, 1/15 for domestic and international students; for spring admission, 11/1 for domestic students. Application fee: $50. Electronic applications accepted. *Expenses:* Tuition, state resident: part-time $222 per credit. Tuition, nonresident: part-time $527 per credit. *Required fees:* $22 per contact hour. $100 per quarter. Tuition and fees vary according to program. *Financial support:* In 2014–15, 1 research assistantship with full and partial tuition reimbursement (averaging $2,358 per year) was awarded; teaching assistantships with full and partial tuition reimbursements, career-related internships or fieldwork, Federal Work-Study, scholarships/grants, and unspecified assistantships also available. Support available to part-time students. Financial award application deadline: 3/1; financial award applicants required to submit FAFSA. *Faculty research:* Systems theory and methodology, artificial intelligence neural networks, information theory, nonlinear dynamics/chaos, modeling and simulation. *Total annual research expenditures:* $137,833. *Unit head:* Prof. Wayne Wakeland, PhD, Chair, 503-725-4975, E-mail: wakeland@pdx.edu.
Website: http://www.pdx.edu/sysc/.

Stevens Institute of Technology, Graduate School, Charles V. Schaefer Jr. School of Engineering, Department of Civil, Environmental, and Ocean Engineering, Program in Civil Engineering, Hoboken, NJ 07030. Offers civil engineering (PhD); geotechnical engineering (Certificate); geotechnical/geoenvironmental engineering (M Eng, Engr); hydrologic modeling (M Eng); stormwater management (M Eng); structural engineering (M Eng, Engr); water resources engineering (M Eng). *Degree requirements:* For master's, thesis optional; for doctorate, variable foreign language requirement, thesis/dissertation; for other advanced degree, project or thesis. *Entrance requirements:* For doctorate, GRE. Additional exam requirements/recommendations for international students: Required—TOEFL. Electronic applications accepted.

Trent University, Graduate Studies, Program in Applications of Modeling in the Natural and Social Sciences, Peterborough, ON K9J 7B8, Canada. Offers applications of modeling in the natural and social sciences (MA); biology (M Sc, PhD); chemistry (M Sc); computer studies (M Sc); geography (M Sc, PhD); physics (M Sc). Part-time programs available. *Degree requirements:* For master's, thesis. *Entrance requirements:* For master's, honours degree. *Faculty research:* Computation of heat transfer, atmospheric physics, statistical mechanics, stress and coping, evolutionary ecology.

Université Laval, Faculty of Administrative Sciences, Programs in Business Administration, Québec, QC G1K 7P4, Canada. Offers accounting (MBA); agri-food management (MBA); electronic business (MBA, Diploma); factory management and logistics (MBA); finance (MBA); firm management (MBA); geomatic management (MBA); information technology management (MBA); international management (MBA); management (MBA); management accounting (MBA, Diploma); marketing (MBA); modeling and organizational decision (MBA); occupational health and safety management (MBA); pharmacy management (MBA); social and environmental responsibility (MBA); technological entrepreneurship (Diploma). *Accreditation:* AACSB. Part-time and evening/weekend programs available. Postbaccalaureate distance learning degree programs offered (no on-campus study). *Entrance requirements:* For master's and Diploma, knowledge of French and English. Electronic applications accepted.

University at Buffalo, the State University of New York, Graduate School, College of Arts and Sciences, Department of Geography, Buffalo, NY 14260. Offers Canadian studies (Certificate); earth systems science (MA, MS); economic geography and business geographics (MS); environmental modeling and analysis (MA); geographic information science (MA, MS); geography (MA, PhD); GIS and environmental analysis (Certificate); health geography (MS); international trade (MA); transportation and business geographics (MA); urban and regional analysis (MA). Part-time programs available. *Faculty:* 18 full-time (9 women), 1 part-time/adjunct (0 women). *Students:* 87 full-time (37 women), 26 part-time (8 women); includes 78 minority (1 Black or African American, non-Hispanic/Latino; 74 Asian, non-Hispanic/Latino; 3 Hispanic/Latino). Average age 29. 167 applicants, 44% accepted, 32 enrolled. In 2014, 24 master's, 6 doctorates awarded. Terminal master's awarded for partial completion of doctoral program. *Degree requirements:* For master's, thesis (for some programs), project or portfolio; for doctorate, thesis/dissertation. *Entrance requirements:* For master's, GRE General Test, minimum GPA of 2.9; for doctorate, GRE General Test, minimum GPA of 3.0. Additional exam requirements/recommendations for international students: Required—TOEFL (minimum score 550 paper-based; 79 iBT). *Application deadline:* For fall admission, 5/1 priority date for domestic students, 3/10 priority date for international students; for spring admission, 11/1 priority date for domestic students, 9/1 priority date for international students. Applications are processed on a rolling basis. Application fee: $75. Electronic applications accepted. *Financial support:* In 2014–15, 13 students received support, including 8 fellowships with full tuition reimbursements available (averaging $5,500 per year), 13 teaching assistantships with full tuition reimbursements available (averaging $13,800 per year); research assistantships with full tuition reimbursements available, career-related internships or fieldwork, Federal Work-Study, institutionally sponsored loans, traineeships, health care benefits, and unspecified assistantships also available. Financial award application deadline: 1/10. *Faculty research:* International business and world trade, geographic information systems and cartography, transportation, urban and regional analysis, physical and environmental geography. *Total annual research expenditures:* $2.6 million. *Unit head:* Dr. Sharmistha Bagchi-Sen, Chairman, 716-645-0473, Fax: 716-645-2329, E-mail: geosbs@buffalo.edu. *Application contact:* Betsy Crooks, Graduate Secretary, 716-645-0471, Fax: 716-645-2329, E-mail: babraham@buffalo.edu.
Website: http://www.geog.buffalo.edu/.

The University of Alabama in Huntsville, School of Graduate Studies, College of Science, Department of Computer Science, Huntsville, AL 35899. Offers computer science (MS, PhD); information assurance (MS); modeling and simulation (MS, PhD); software engineering (MSSE, Certificate). Part-time and evening/weekend programs available. Postbaccalaureate distance learning degree programs offered (minimal on-campus study). *Degree requirements:* For master's, comprehensive exam, thesis or alternative, oral and written exams; for doctorate, comprehensive exam, thesis/dissertation, oral and written exams. *Entrance requirements:* For master's, doctorate, and Certificate, GRE General Test, minimum GPA of 3.0. Additional exam requirements/recommendations for international students: Required—TOEFL (minimum score 550 paper-based; 80 iBT), IELTS (minimum score 6.5). Electronic applications accepted. *Faculty research:* Information assurance and cyber security, modeling and simulation, data science, computer graphics and visualization, multimedia systems.

The University of Alabama in Huntsville, School of Graduate Studies, Interdisciplinary Studies, Interdisciplinary Program of Modeling and Simulation, Huntsville, AL 35899. Offers MS, PhD, Certificate. Part-time and evening/weekend programs available. Postbaccalaureate distance learning degree programs offered (minimal on-campus study). *Degree requirements:* For master's, comprehensive exam, thesis or alternative, 24 hours of course work plus 6 hour thesis; for doctorate, comprehensive exam, 54 hours of course work plus 18 hour dissertation. *Entrance requirements:* For master's, doctorate, and Certificate, GRE General Test, minimum GPA of 3.0. Additional exam requirements/recommendations for international students: Required—TOEFL (minimum score 500 paper-based; 80 iBT), IELTS (minimum score 6.5). Electronic applications accepted. *Faculty research:* Simulation interoperability and composability, discrete event simulation, mathematical modeling and analysis, system-level modeling, technical team performance.

University of California, San Diego, Graduate Division, Department of Structural Engineering, La Jolla, CA 92093. Offers computational neuroscience (PhD); structural engineering (MS, PhD); structural health monitoring, prognosis, and validated simulations (MS). PhD in engineering sciences offered jointly with San Diego State University. *Students:* 166 full-time (33 women), 3 part-time (0 women); includes 48 minority (1 Black or African American, non-Hispanic/Latino; 1 American Indian or Alaska Native, non-Hispanic/Latino; 32 Asian, non-Hispanic/Latino; 14 Hispanic/Latino), 74 international. 381 applicants, 52% accepted, 84 enrolled. In 2014, 66 master's, 6 doctorates awarded. *Degree requirements:* For master's, comprehensive exam or thesis; for doctorate, comprehensive exam, thesis/dissertation, 1-quarter teaching assistantship. *Entrance requirements:* For master's and doctorate, GRE General Test. Additional exam requirements/recommendations for international students: Required—TOEFL (minimum score 550 paper-based; 80 iBT), IELTS (minimum score 7). *Application deadline:* For fall admission, 12/15 for domestic students. Application fee: $90 ($110 for international students). Electronic applications accepted. *Expenses:* Tuition, state resident: full-time $11,220; part-time $5610 per quarter. Tuition, nonresident: full-time $26,322; part-time $13,161 per quarter. *Required fees:* $570 per

quarter. Tuition and fees vary according to program. *Financial support:* Fellowships, research assistantships, teaching assistantships, scholarships/grants, and readerships available. Financial award application deadline: 3/2; financial award applicants required to submit FAFSA. *Faculty research:* Geotechnical, marine/offshore engineering; structural design and analysis; structural materials; computational mechanics; solid mechanics. *Unit head:* J. Enrique Luco, Chair, 858-534-4338, E-mail: jeluco@ucsd.edu. *Application contact:* Yvonne C. Wilson, Graduate Coordinator, 858-822-1421, E-mail: ywilson@ucsd.edu.
Website: http://www.structures.ucsd.edu/.

University of Central Florida, College of Education and Human Performance, Department of Educational and Human Sciences, Program in Instructional Design and Technology, Orlando, FL 32816. Offers instructional design and technology (MA); instructional design for simulations (Certificate). *Students:* 7 full-time (4 women), 40 part-time (23 women); includes 10 minority (6 Black or African American, non-Hispanic/Latino; 1 Asian, non-Hispanic/Latino; 2 Hispanic/Latino; 1 Two or more races, non-Hispanic/Latino). Average age 35. 27 applicants, 93% accepted, 21 enrolled. In 2014, 21 master's, 11 other advanced degrees awarded. Application fee: $30. Electronic applications accepted. *Expenses:* Tuition, state resident: part-time $288.16 per credit hour. Tuition, nonresident: part-time $1073.31 per credit hour. *Unit head:* Dr. Atsusi Hirumi, Program Coordinator, 407-823-1760, E-mail: atsusi.hirumi@ucf.edu. *Application contact:* Barbara Rodriguez Lamas, Director, Admissions and Student Services, 407-823-2766, Fax: 407-823-6442, E-mail: gradadmissions@ucf.edu.

University of Central Florida, College of Graduate Studies, Program in Modeling and Simulation, Orlando, FL 32816. Offers MS, PhD, Certificate. *Students:* 49 full-time (15 women), 61 part-time (11 women); includes 27 minority (4 Black or African American, non-Hispanic/Latino; 5 Asian, non-Hispanic/Latino; 17 Hispanic/Latino; 1 Native Hawaiian or other Pacific Islander, non-Hispanic/Latino), 15 international. Average age 35. 52 applicants, 69% accepted, 23 enrolled. In 2014, 29 master's, 10 doctorates, 13 other advanced degrees awarded. *Expenses:* Tuition, state resident: part-time $288.16 per credit hour. Tuition, nonresident: part-time $1073.31 per credit hour. *Financial support:* In 2014–15, 29 students received support, including 11 fellowships with partial tuition reimbursements available (averaging $3,600 per year), 28 research assistantships with partial tuition reimbursements available (averaging $12,500 per year), 1 teaching assistantship with partial tuition reimbursement available (averaging $25,100 per year). *Unit head:* Dr. J. Peter Kincaid, Program Director, 407-882-1330, E-mail: pkincaid@ist.ucf.edu. *Application contact:* Barbara Rodriguez Lamas, Director, Admissions and Student Services, 407-823-2766, Fax: 407-823-6442, E-mail: gradadmissions@ucf.edu.
Website: http://www.ist.ucf.edu/.

The University of Manchester, School of Chemical Engineering and Analytical Science, Manchester, United Kingdom. Offers biocatalysis (M Phil, PhD); chemical engineering (M Phil, PhD); chemical engineering and analytical science (M Phil, D Eng, PhD); colloids, crystals, interfaces and materials (M Phil, PhD); environment and sustainable technology (M Phil, PhD); instrumentation (M Phil, PhD); multi-scale modeling (M Phil, PhD); process integration (M Phil, PhD); systems biology (M Phil, PhD).

University of Pittsburgh, Dietrich School of Arts and Sciences, Program in Computational Modeling and Simulation, Pittsburgh, PA 15260. Offers bioengineering (PhD); biological science (PhD); civil and environmental engineering (PhD); computer science (PhD); economics (PhD); industrial engineering (PhD); mathematics (PhD); mechanical engineering and materials science (PhD); physics and astronomy (PhD); psychology (PhD); statistics (PhD). Part-time programs available. *Faculty:* 4 full-time (0 women). *Students:* 5 full-time (2 women), 1 part-time (0 women), 5 international. Average age 22. 14 applicants, 14% accepted, 2 enrolled. *Degree requirements:* For doctorate, comprehensive exam, thesis/dissertation, preliminary exam. *Entrance requirements:* For doctorate, GRE, statement of purpose, transcripts for all college-level institutions attended, three letters of reference. Additional exam requirements/

recommendations for international students: Required—TOEFL (minimum score 90 iBT), IELTS (minimum score 7). *Application deadline:* For fall admission, 2/21 for domestic and international students. Applications are processed on a rolling basis. Application fee: $0 ($50 for international students). Electronic applications accepted. *Expenses:* Tuition, state resident: full-time $20,742; part-time $838 per credit. Tuition, nonresident: full-time $33,960; part-time $1389 per credit. *Required fees:* $800; $205 per term. Tuition and fees vary according to program. *Financial support:* In 2014–15, 5 students received support, including 3 fellowships with tuition reimbursements available (averaging $25,500 per year), 2 research assistantships with tuition reimbursements available (averaging $26,000 per year). *Unit head:* Kathleen Blee, Associate Dean, Graduate Studies and Research, 412-624-3939, Fax: 412-624-6855. *Application contact:* Dave R. Carmen, Administrative Secretary, 412-624-6094, Fax: 412-624-6855, E-mail: drc41@pitt.edu.
Website: http://cmsp.pitt.edu/.

University of Southern California, Graduate School, Viterbi School of Engineering, Department of Computer Science, Los Angeles, CA 90089. Offers computer networks (MS); computer science (MS, PhD); computer security (MS); game development (MS); high performance computing and simulations (MS); human language technology (MS); intelligent robotics (MS); multimedia and creative technologies (MS); software engineering (MS). Part-time and evening/weekend programs available. Postbaccalaureate distance learning degree programs offered (no on-campus study). *Entrance requirements:* For master's and doctorate, GRE General Test. Additional exam requirements/recommendations for international students: Required—TOEFL. Electronic applications accepted. *Faculty research:* Databases, computer graphics and computer vision, software engineering, networks and security, robotics, multimedia and virtual reality.

Virginia Commonwealth University, Graduate School, College of Humanities and Sciences, Department of Statistical Sciences and Operations Research, Richmond, VA 23284-9005. Offers operations research (MS); statistics (MS); systems modeling and analysis (PhD). *Entrance requirements:* For master's, GRE General Test, 30 undergraduate credits in mathematics, statistics, or operations research, including calculus I and II, multivariate calculus, linear algebra, probability and statistics. Additional exam requirements/recommendations for international students: Required—TOEFL (minimum score 600 paper-based; 100 iBT); Recommended—IELTS (minimum score 6.5). Electronic applications accepted.

Worcester Polytechnic Institute, Graduate Studies and Research, Programs in Interdisciplinary Studies, Worcester, MA 01609-2280. Offers bioscience administration (MS); impact engineering (MS); manufacturing engineering management (MS); power systems management (MS); social science (PhD); systems modeling (MS). Part-time and evening/weekend programs available. *Faculty:* 1 part-time/adjunct (0 women). *Students:* 2 full-time (0 women), 74 part-time (15 women); includes 18 minority (3 Black or African American, non-Hispanic/Latino; 7 Asian, non-Hispanic/Latino; 3 Hispanic/Latino; 5 Two or more races, non-Hispanic/Latino), 5 international. 37 applicants, 97% accepted, 29 enrolled. In 2014, 10 master's, 1 doctorate awarded. *Degree requirements:* For master's, thesis; for doctorate, comprehensive exam, thesis/dissertation. *Entrance requirements:* For master's and doctorate, 3 letters of recommendation. Additional exam requirements/recommendations for international students: Required—TOEFL (minimum score 563 paper-based; 84 iBT), IELTS (minimum score 7). *Application deadline:* For fall admission, 1/1 priority date for domestic students, 1/1 for international students; for spring admission, 10/1 priority date for domestic students, 10/1 for international students. Application fee: $70. *Financial support:* Institutionally sponsored loans, scholarships/grants, and unspecified assistantships available. Financial award application deadline: 1/1; financial award applicants required to submit FAFSA. *Unit head:* Dr. Fred J. Looft, Head, 508-831-5231, Fax: 508-831-5491, E-mail: fjlooft@wpi.edu. *Application contact:* Lynne Dougherty, Administrative Assistant, 508-831-5301, Fax: 508-831-5717, E-mail: grad@wpi.edu.

Software Engineering

American Public University System, AMU/APU Graduate Programs, Charles Town, WV 25414. Offers accounting (MBA, MS); criminal justice (MA), including business administration, emergency and disaster management, general (MA, MS); educational leadership (M Ed); emergency and disaster management (MA); entrepreneurship (MBA); environmental policy and management (MS), including environmental planning, environmental sustainability, fish and wildlife management, general (MA, MS), global environmental management; finance (MBA); general (MBA); global business management (MBA); history (MA), including American history, ancient and classical history, European history, global history, public history; homeland security (MA), including business administration, counter-terrorism studies, criminal justice, cyber, emergency management and public health, intelligence studies, transportation security; homeland security resource allocation (MBA); humanities (MA); information technology (MS), including digital forensics, enterprise software development, information assurance and security, IT project management; information technology management (MBA); intelligence studies (MA), including criminal intelligence, cyber, general (MA, MS), homeland security, intelligence analysis, intelligence collection, intelligence management, intelligence operations, terrorism studies; international relations and conflict resolution (MA), including comparative and security issues, conflict resolution, international and transnational security issues, peacekeeping; legal studies (MA); management (MA), including defense management, general (MA, MS), human resource management, organizational leadership, public administration; marketing (MBA); military history (MA), including American military history, American Revolution, civil war, war since 1945, World War II; military studies (MA), including joint warfare, strategic leadership; national security studies (MA), including general (MA, MS), homeland security, regional security studies, security and intelligence analysis, terrorism studies; nonprofit management (MBA); political science (MA), including American politics and government, comparative government and development, general (MA, MS), international relations, public policy; psychology (MA); public administration (MPA), including disaster management, environmental policy, health policy, human resources, national security, organizational management, security management; public health (MPH); reverse logistics management (MA); school counseling (M Ed); security management (MA); space studies (MS), including aerospace science, general (MA, MS), planetary science; sports and health sciences (MS); teaching (M Ed), including curriculum and instruction for elementary teachers, elementary reading, English language learners, instructional leadership, online learning, special education; transportation and logistics management (MA), including general (MA, MS), maritime engineering management, reverse logistics management. Programs offered via distance learning only. Part-time and evening/weekend programs available. Postbaccalaureate

distance learning degree programs offered (no on-campus study). *Faculty:* 426 full-time (236 women), 1,864 part-time/adjunct (880 women). *Students:* 475 full-time (215 women), 10,067 part-time (4,085 women); includes 3,462 minority (1,863 Black or African American, non-Hispanic/Latino; 74 American Indian or Alaska Native, non-Hispanic/Latino; 273 Asian, non-Hispanic/Latino; 831 Hispanic/Latino; 78 Native Hawaiian or other Pacific Islander, non-Hispanic/Latino; 343 Two or more races, non-Hispanic/Latino), 131 international. Average age 36. In 2014, 3,740 master's awarded. *Degree requirements:* For master's, comprehensive exam or practicum. *Entrance requirements:* For master's, official transcript showing earned bachelor's degree from institution accredited by recognized accrediting body. Additional exam requirements/recommendations for international students: Required—TOEFL (minimum score 550 paper-based), IELTS (minimum score 6.5). *Application deadline:* Applications are processed on a rolling basis. Application fee: $0. Electronic applications accepted. *Financial support:* Applicants required to submit FAFSA. *Faculty research:* Military history, criminal justice, management performance, national security. *Unit head:* Dr. Karan Powell, Executive Vice President and Provost, 877-468-6268, Fax: 304-724-3780. *Application contact:* Terry Grant, Vice President of Enrollment Management, 877-468-6268, Fax: 304-724-3780, E-mail: info@apus.edu.
Website: http://www.apus.edu.

Arizona State University at the Tempe campus, Ira A. Fulton Schools of Engineering, ASU Engineering Online Programs, Tempe, AZ 85287. Offers construction (MS); embedded systems (M Eng); enterprise systems innovation and management (MSE); modeling and simulation (M Eng); quality and reliability engineering (M Eng); software engineering (MSE); systems engineering (M Eng).

Arizona State University at the Tempe campus, Ira A. Fulton Schools of Engineering, School of Computing, Informatics, and Decision Systems Engineering, Tempe, AZ 85287-8809. Offers computer engineering (MS, PhD); computer science (MCS, MS, PhD); industrial engineering (MS, PhD); software engineering (MS). Part-time and evening/weekend programs available. Postbaccalaureate distance learning degree programs offered (minimal on-campus study). Terminal master's awarded for partial completion of doctoral program. *Degree requirements:* For master's, comprehensive exam (for some programs), portfolio (MCS); interactive Program of Study (iPOS) submitted before completing 50 percent of required credit hours; for doctorate, comprehensive exam, thesis/dissertation, interactive Program of Study (iPOS) submitted before completing 50 percent of required credit hours. *Entrance requirements:* For master's, GRE, minimum GPA of 3.0 or equivalent in last 2 years of work leading to bachelor's degree; for doctorate, GRE, minimum GPA of 3.0 in last 2 years of work leading to bachelor's degree. Additional exam requirements/recommendations for international students: Required—TOEFL, IELTS, or PTE. Electronic applications accepted. *Expenses:* Contact institution. *Faculty research:* Artificial intelligence, cyberphysical and embedded systems, health informatics, information assurance and security, information management/multimedia/visualization, network science, personalized learning/educational games, production logistics, software and systems engineering, statistical modeling and data mining.

Auburn University, Graduate School, Ginn College of Engineering, Department of Computer Science and Software Engineering, Auburn University, AL 36849. Offers MS, MSWE, PhD. Part-time programs available. *Faculty:* 18 full-time (3 women). *Students:* 70 full-time (17 women), 54 part-time (13 women); includes 15 minority (10 Black or African American, non-Hispanic/Latino; 5 Asian, non-Hispanic/Latino), 50 international. Average age 30. 198 applicants, 34% accepted, 21 enrolled. In 2014, 26 master's, 9 doctorates awarded. *Degree requirements:* For master's, thesis (for some programs); for doctorate, thesis/dissertation. *Entrance requirements:* For master's and doctorate, GRE General Test, GRE Subject Test. *Application deadline:* For fall admission, 7/7 for domestic students; for spring admission, 11/24 for domestic students. Applications are processed on a rolling basis. Application fee: $50 ($60 for international students). Electronic applications accepted. *Expenses:* Tuition, state resident: full-time $8586; part-time $477 per credit hour. Tuition, nonresident: full-time $25,758; part-time $1431 per credit hour. *Required fees:* $804 per semester. Tuition and fees vary according to degree level and program. *Financial support:* Research assistantships, teaching assistantships, and Federal Work-Study available. Support available to part-time students. Financial award application deadline: 3/15; financial award applicants required to submit FAFSA. *Faculty research:* Parallelizable, scalable software translations; graphical representations of algorithms, structures, and processes; graph drawing. *Total annual research expenditures:* $400,000. *Unit head:* Dr. Kai Chang, Chair, 334-844-6310. *Application contact:* Dr. George Flowers, Dean of the Graduate School, 334-844-2125.
Website: http://www.eng.auburn.edu/department/cse/.

Bowling Green State University, Graduate College, College of Arts and Sciences, Department of Computer Science, Bowling Green, OH 43403. Offers computer science (MS), including operations research, parallel and distributed computing, software engineering. Part-time programs available. *Degree requirements:* For master's, thesis or alternative. *Entrance requirements:* For master's, GRE General Test. Additional exam requirements/recommendations for international students: Required—TOEFL. Electronic applications accepted. *Faculty research:* Artificial intelligence, real time and concurrent programming languages, behavioral aspects of computing, network protocols.

Brandeis University, Rabb School of Continuing Studies, Division of Graduate Professional Studies, Master of Software Engineering Program, Waltham, MA 02454-9110. Offers MSE. Part-time programs available. Postbaccalaureate distance learning degree programs offered (no on-campus study). *Faculty:* 2 full-time (1 woman), 36 part-time/adjunct (13 women). *Students:* 52 part-time (15 women); includes 8 minority (1 Black or African American, non-Hispanic/Latino; 7 Asian, non-Hispanic/Latino). Average age 35. 14 applicants, 100% accepted, 12 enrolled. In 2014, 18 master's awarded. *Entrance requirements:* For master's, four-year bachelor's degree from regionally-accredited U.S. institution or equivalent; official transcript(s) from every college or university attended; resume or curriculum vitae; statement of goals; letter of recommendation. Additional exam requirements/recommendations for international students: Required—TOEFL (minimum scores: 600 paper-based, 100 iBT), IELTS (7), or PTE (68). *Application deadline:* For fall admission, 8/11 priority date for domestic and international students; for winter admission, 11/15 for domestic students; for spring admission, 12/15 priority date for domestic and international students; for summer admission, 4/14 priority date for domestic and international students. Applications are processed on a rolling basis. Application fee: $50. Electronic applications accepted. *Unit head:* Dr. Aline Yurik, Program Chair, 781-736-8787, Fax: 781-736-3420, E-mail: ayurik@brandeis.edu. *Application contact:* Frances Stearns, Associate Director of Admissions and Student Services, 781-736-8785, Fax: 781-736-3420, E-mail: fstearns@brandeis.edu.
Website: http://www.brandeis.edu/gps.

California State University, Fullerton, Graduate Studies, College of Engineering and Computer Science, Department of Computer Science, Fullerton, CA 92834-9480. Offers computer science (MS); software engineering (MS). Part-time programs available. Postbaccalaureate distance learning degree programs offered. *Students:* 164 full-time (49 women), 376 part-time (96 women); includes 130 minority (11 Black or African American, non-Hispanic/Latino; 84 Asian, non-Hispanic/Latino; 28 Hispanic/Latino; 7 Two or more races, non-Hispanic/Latino), 354 international. Average age 27. 1,060 applicants, 39% accepted, 216 enrolled. In 2014, 138 master's awarded. *Degree requirements:* For master's, comprehensive exam, project or thesis. *Entrance requirements:* For master's, GRE General Test, minimum undergraduate GPA of 2.5. Application fee: $55. *Financial support:* Career-related internships or fieldwork, Federal Work-Study, institutionally sponsored loans, and scholarships/grants available. Support available to part-time students. Financial award application deadline: 3/1; financial award applicants required to submit FAFSA. *Faculty research:* Software engineering, development of computer networks. *Unit head:* Dr. Shawn Wang, Chair, 657-278-7258. *Application contact:* Admissions/Applications, 657-278-2371.

California State University, Northridge, Graduate Studies, College of Engineering and Computer Science, Department of Computer Science, Northridge, CA 91330. Offers computer science (MS); software engineering (MS). Part-time and evening/weekend programs available. *Students:* 46 full-time (10 women), 36 part-time (8 women); includes 20 minority (1 Black or African American, non-Hispanic/Latino; 7 Asian, non-Hispanic/Latino; 9 Hispanic/Latino; 3 Two or more races, non-Hispanic/Latino), 14 international. Average age 30. *Degree requirements:* For master's, thesis. *Entrance requirements:* For master's, GRE General Test, minimum GPA of 2.5. Additional exam requirements/recommendations for international students: Required—TOEFL. *Application deadline:* For fall admission, 11/30 for domestic students. Application fee: $55. *Expenses:* Required fees: $12,402. *Financial support:* Application deadline: 3/1. *Faculty research:* Radar data processing. *Unit head:* Rick Covington, Chair, 818-677-3398.
Website: http://www.csun.edu/computerscience/.

California State University, Sacramento, Office of Graduate Studies, College of Engineering and Computer Science, Department of Computer Science, Sacramento, CA 95819. Offers computer science (MS); software engineering (MS). Part-time and evening/weekend programs available. *Degree requirements:* For master's, thesis or comprehensive exam; writing proficiency exam. *Entrance requirements:* For master's, GRE. Additional exam requirements/recommendations for international students: Required—TOEFL. Electronic applications accepted.

Carnegie Mellon University, Carnegie Institute of Technology, Information Networking Institute, Pittsburgh, PA 15213. Offers information networking (MS); information security (MS); information technology - information security (MS); information technology - mobility (MS); information technology - software management (MS). *Degree requirements:* For master's, thesis optional. *Entrance requirements:* For master's, GRE

General Test, bachelor's degree in computer science, computer engineering, or electrical engineering, or related technology degree; programming skills (C/C++ fluency for some programs). Additional exam requirements/recommendations for international students: Required—TOEFL. *Faculty research:* Computer forensics and incident response; dependable systems, embedded systems, mobile systems, and sensor networks; computer and information networks, network and information security, human and socio-economic factors in secure system design; wireless sensor networks, survivable embedded systems, signal processing/compression; strategic management, international strategic management, group dynamics and decision-making structures, simulated competitive environments.

Carnegie Mellon University, School of Computer Science, Software Engineering Program, Pittsburgh, PA 15213-3891. Offers MSE, PhD. *Entrance requirements:* For master's, GRE General Test, GRE Subject Test (computer science), 2 years of experience in large-scale software development project.

Carnegie Mellon University, Tepper School of Business, Pittsburgh, PA 15213-3891. Offers accounting (PhD); business management and software engineering (MBMSE); business technologies (PhD); civil engineering and industrial management (MS); computational finance (MSCF); economics (PhD); environmental engineering and management (MEEM); financial economics (PhD); industrial administration (MBA), including administration and public management; marketing (PhD); mathematical finance (PhD); operations management (PhD); operations research (PhD); organizational behavior and theory (PhD); production and operations management (PhD); public policy and management (MS, MSED); software engineering and business management (MS); JD/MS; JD/MSIA; M Div/MS; MOM/MSIA; MSCF/MSIA. JD/MSIA offered jointly with University of Pittsburgh. Part-time programs available. Terminal master's awarded for partial completion of doctoral program. *Degree requirements:* For doctorate, thesis/dissertation. *Entrance requirements:* For master's, GMAT. Additional exam requirements/recommendations for international students: Required—TOEFL. *Expenses:* Contact institution.

Carroll University, Program in Software Engineering, Waukesha, WI 53186-5593. Offers MSE. Part-time and evening/weekend programs available. *Degree requirements:* For master's, professional experience, capstone project. *Entrance requirements:* For master's, BA or BS, 2 years professional experience. Additional exam requirements/recommendations for international students: Required—TOEFL. Electronic applications accepted. *Faculty research:* Networking, artificial intelligence, virtual reality, effective teaching of software design, computer science pedagogy.

Cleveland State University, College of Graduate Studies, Fenn College of Engineering, Department of Electrical and Computer Engineering, Cleveland, OH 44115. Offers electrical engineering (MS, D Eng); software engineering (MS). Part-time and evening/weekend programs available. *Faculty:* 15 full-time (2 women), 1 part-time/adjunct (0 women). *Students:* 65 full-time (10 women), 211 part-time (39 women); includes 14 minority (3 Black or African American, non-Hispanic/Latino; 6 Asian, non-Hispanic/Latino; 2 Hispanic/Latino; 3 Two or more races, non-Hispanic/Latino), 216 international. Average age 25. 633 applicants, 40% accepted, 74 enrolled. In 2014, 71 master's, 2 doctorates awarded. Terminal master's awarded for partial completion of doctoral program. *Degree requirements:* For master's, thesis optional; for doctorate, comprehensive exam, thesis/dissertation, qualifying and candidacy exams. *Entrance requirements:* For master's, GRE General Test (minimum score 650 quantitative), minimum GPA of 2.75; for doctorate, GRE General Test (minimum quantitative score in 80th percentile), minimum GPA of 3.25. Additional exam requirements/recommendations for international students: Required—TOEFL (minimum score 535 paper-based; 65 iBT) or IELTS (minimum score 6.0). *Application deadline:* For fall admission, 7/15 priority date for domestic students, 5/5 for international students. Applications are processed on a rolling basis. Application fee: $30. *Expenses:* Expenses: Contact institution. *Financial support:* In 2014–15, 31 students received support, including 23 research assistantships with full and partial tuition reimbursements available (averaging $4,242 per year), 8 teaching assistantships with full and partial tuition reimbursements available (averaging $4,242 per year); career-related internships or fieldwork, scholarships/grants, and unspecified assistantships also available. *Faculty research:* Computer networks, computer security and privacy, mobile computing, distributed computing, software engineering, knowledge-based control systems, artificial intelligence, digital communications, MEMS, sensors, power systems, power electronics. *Total annual research expenditures:* $484,362. *Unit head:* Dr. Chansu Yu, Chairperson, 216-687-2584, Fax: 216-687-5405, E-mail: f.xiong@csuohio.edu. *Application contact:* Deborah L. Brown, Interim Assistant Director, Graduate Admissions, 216-523-7572, Fax: 216-687-9214, E-mail: d.l.brown@csuohio.edu.
Website: http://www.csuohio.edu/ece.

Colorado Technical University Colorado Springs, Graduate Studies, Program in Computer Science, Colorado Springs, CO 80907-3896. Offers computer science (DCS); computer systems security (MSCS); database systems (MSCS); software engineering (MSCS). Part-time and evening/weekend programs available. Postbaccalaureate distance learning degree programs offered. *Degree requirements:* For master's, thesis or alternative; for doctorate, thesis/dissertation. *Entrance requirements:* For doctorate, minimum graduate GPA of 3.0, 5 years of related work experience. *Faculty research:* Software engineering, systems engineering.

Colorado Technical University Denver South, Program in Computer Science, Aurora, CO 80014. Offers computer systems security (MSCS); database systems (MSCS); software engineering (MSCS). Part-time and evening/weekend programs available. *Degree requirements:* For master's, thesis or alternative. *Entrance requirements:* For master's, minimum undergraduate GPA of 3.0, resume.

Concordia University, School of Graduate Studies, Faculty of Engineering and Computer Science, Department of Computer Science and Software Engineering, Montréal, QC H3G 1M8, Canada. Offers computer science (M App Comp Sc, M Comp Sc, PhD, Diploma); software engineering (MA Sc). *Degree requirements:* For master's, one foreign language, thesis optional; for doctorate, one foreign language, comprehensive exam, thesis/dissertation. *Faculty research:* Computer systems and applications, mathematics of computation, pattern recognition, artificial intelligence and robotics.

Concordia University, School of Graduate Studies, Faculty of Engineering and Computer Science, Department of Mechanical and Industrial Engineering, Montréal, QC H3G 1M8, Canada. Offers composites (M Eng); industrial engineering (M Eng, MA Sc); mechanical engineering (M Eng, MA Sc, PhD, Certificate); software systems for industrial engineering (Certificate). M Eng in composites program offered jointly with École Polytechnique de Montréal. *Degree requirements:* For master's, variable foreign language requirement, thesis or alternative; for doctorate, comprehensive exam, thesis/dissertation. *Faculty research:* Mechanical systems, fluid control systems, thermofluids engineering and robotics, industrial control systems.

DePaul University, College of Computing and Digital Media, Chicago, IL 60604. Offers animation (MA, MFA); business information technology (MS); cinema (MFA); cinema production (MS); computational finance (MS); computer and information sciences (PhD); computer game development (MS); computer information and network security (MS); computer science (MS); e-commerce technology (MS); health informatics (MS); human-

Software Engineering

computer interaction (MS); information systems (MS); information technology project management (MS); network engineering and management (MS); predictive analytics (MS); screenwriting (MFA); software engineering (MS); JD/MS. Part-time and evening/weekend programs available. Postbaccalaureate distance learning degree programs offered (no on-campus study). *Degree requirements:* For master's, thesis (for some programs); for doctorate, comprehensive exam, thesis/dissertation. *Entrance requirements:* For master's, GRE or GMAT (for MS in computational finance only), bachelor's degree, resume (MS in predictive analytics only), IT experience (MS in information technology project management only), portfolio review (all MFA programs and MA in animation); for doctorate, GRE, master's degree in computer science. Additional exam requirements/recommendations for international students: Required—TOEFL (minimum score 590 paper-based; 80 iBT), IELTS (minimum score 6.5), PTE (minimum score 53). Electronic applications accepted. *Expenses:* Contact institution. *Faculty research:* Data mining, computer science, human-computer interaction, security, animation and film.

Drexel University, College of Engineering, Department of Electrical and Computer Engineering, Program in Software Engineering, Philadelphia, PA 19104-2875. Offers MSSE. *Entrance requirements:* For master's, GRE. Additional exam requirements/recommendations for international students: Required—TOEFL. Electronic applications accepted.

East Carolina University, Graduate School, College of Engineering and Technology, Department of Computer Science, Greenville, NC 27858-4353. Offers computer science (MS); software engineering (MS). Part-time and evening/weekend programs available. *Degree requirements:* For master's, comprehensive exam, thesis or alternative. *Entrance requirements:* For master's, GRE General Test. Additional exam requirements/recommendations for international students: Required—TOEFL. Electronic applications accepted. *Expenses:* Tuition, state resident: full-time $4223. Tuition, nonresident: full-time $16,540. *Required fees:* $2184. *Faculty research:* Software development, software engineering, artificial intelligence, bioinformatics, cryptography.

Embry-Riddle Aeronautical University–Daytona, Department of Electrical, Computer, Software and Systems Engineering, Daytona Beach, FL 32114-3900. Offers cybersecurity engineering (MS); electrical and computer engineering (MSECE); software engineering (MSE); unmanned and autonomous systems engineering (MSUASE). MS in unmanned and autonomous systems engineering held jointly with Department of Electrical, Computer, Software and Systems Engineering. Part-time and evening/weekend programs available. *Faculty:* 13 full-time (0 women), 1 (woman) part-time/adjunct. *Students:* 56 full-time (15 women), 8 part-time (0 women); includes 6 minority (4 Black or African American, non-Hispanic/Latino; 1 Asian, non-Hispanic/Latino; 1 Hispanic/Latino), 41 international. Average age 25. 46 applicants, 61% accepted, 23 enrolled. In 2014, 16 master's awarded. *Degree requirements:* For master's, thesis or alternative, MS UASE students are required to complete a two-semester capstone project. *Entrance requirements:* For master's, Applicants to the MSE program are strongly encouraged to complete the GRE for this degree program; Applicants to the MSUASE program must complete the GRE; For consideration of fellowship and assistantship award programs offered by the Department of Computing, GRE scores are required., minimum CGPA of 3.0; course work in computer science. Additional exam requirements/recommendations for international students: Required—TOEFL (minimum score 550 paper-based; 79 iBT). *Application deadline:* For fall admission, 6/1 priority date for domestic and international students; for spring admission, 11/1 priority date for domestic students, 10/1 priority date for international students. Applications are processed on a rolling basis. Application fee: $50. Electronic applications accepted. *Expenses: Tuition:* Full-time $15,360; part-time $1280 per credit hour. *Required fees:* $1334. *Financial support:* In 2014–15, 24 students received support. Research assistantships with full and partial tuition reimbursements available, teaching assistantships with full and partial tuition reimbursements available, career-related internships or fieldwork, and unspecified assistantships available. Financial award application deadline: 4/15. *Faculty research:* Cybersecurity and assured systems engineering, radar, unmanned and autonomous systems, modeling and simulation, cyber-physical systems. *Unit head:* Dr. Timothy Wilson, Professor of Electrical and Computer Engineering and Chair, ECSSE Dept., 386-226-6994, E-mail: timothy.wilson@erau.edu. *Application contact:* International and Graduate Admissions, 800-388-3728, Fax: 386-226-7070, E-mail: graduate.admissions@erau.edu.
Website: http://daytonabeach.erau.edu/college-engineering/electrical-computer-software-systems/index.html.

Fairfield University, School of Engineering, Fairfield, CT 06824. Offers automated manufacturing (CAS); database management (CAS); electrical and computer engineering (MS); information security (CAS); management of technology (MS); mechanical engineering (MS); network technology (CAS); software engineering (MS); Web application development (CAS). Part-time and evening/weekend programs available. *Faculty:* 4 full-time (1 woman), 18 part-time/adjunct (5 women). *Students:* 193 full-time (50 women), 69 part-time (11 women); includes 20 minority (4 Black or African American, non-Hispanic/Latino; 6 Asian, non-Hispanic/Latino; 10 Hispanic/Latino), 199 international. Average age 27. 516 applicants, 64% accepted, 124 enrolled. In 2014, 38 master's awarded. *Degree requirements:* For master's, thesis, capstone course. *Entrance requirements:* For master's, interview, minimum GPA of 2.8, resume, 2 recommendations. Additional exam requirements/recommendations for international students: Required—TOEFL (minimum score 550 paper-based; 80 iBT) or IELTS (minimum score 6.5). *Application deadline:* For fall admission, 5/15 for international students; for spring admission, 10/15 for international students. Applications are processed on a rolling basis. Application fee: $60. Electronic applications accepted. *Expenses:* Expenses: $750 per credit hour. *Financial support:* In 2014–15, 30 students received support. Scholarships/grants and unspecified assistantships available. Financial award applicants required to submit FAFSA. *Faculty research:* Ocean dynamics modeling, thermo fluids, Web/mobile software applications, microwaves/electromagnetics, micro/nano manufacturing. *Unit head:* Dr. Bruce Berdanier, Dean, 203-254-4147, Fax: 203-254-4013, E-mail: bberdanier@fairfield.edu. *Application contact:* Marianne Gumpper, Director of Graduate and Continuing Studies Admission, 203-254-4184, Fax: 203-254-4073, E-mail: gradadmis@fairfield.edu.
Website: http://www.fairfield.edu/academics/schoolscollegescenters/schoolofengineering/graduateprograms/.

Florida Agricultural and Mechanical University, Division of Graduate Studies, Research, and Continuing Education, College of Science and Technology, Department of Computer Information Sciences, Tallahassee, FL 32307-3200. Offers software engineering (MS). *Entrance requirements:* Additional exam requirements/recommendations for international students: Required—TOEFL.

Florida Institute of Technology, Graduate Programs, Extended Studies Division, Melbourne, FL 32901-6975. Offers acquisition and contract management (MS); aerospace engineering (MS); business administration (MBA, DBA); computer information systems (MS); computer science (MS); electrical engineering (MS); engineering management (MS); human resources management (MS); logistics management (MS), including humanitarian and disaster relief logistics; management (MS), including acquisition and contract management, e-business, human resources management, information systems, logistics management, management, transportation management; material acquisition management (MS); mechanical engineering (MS); operations research (MS); project management (MS), including information systems, operations research; public administration (MPA); quality management (MS); software engineering (MS); space systems (MS); space systems management (MS); supply chain management (MS); systems management (MS), including information systems, operations research; technology management (MS). Part-time and evening/weekend programs available. Postbaccalaureate distance learning degree programs offered (no on-campus study). *Faculty:* 7 full-time (1 woman), 112 part-time/adjunct (29 women). *Students:* 98 full-time (45 women), 975 part-time (396 women); includes 440 minority (292 Black or African American, non-Hispanic/Latino; 13 American Indian or Alaska Native, non-Hispanic/Latino; 32 Asian, non-Hispanic/Latino; 79 Hispanic/Latino; 1 Native Hawaiian or other Pacific Islander, non-Hispanic/Latino; 23 Two or more races, non-Hispanic/Latino), 4 international. Average age 37. 807 applicants, 56% accepted, 258 enrolled. In 2014, 457 master's awarded. *Degree requirements:* For master's, comprehensive exam (for some programs), capstone course. *Entrance requirements:* For master's, GMAT or resume showing 8 years of supervised experience, minimum GPA of 3.0, 2 letters of recommendation, resume. Additional exam requirements/recommendations for international students: Required—TOEFL (minimum score 550 paper-based; 79 iBT). *Application deadline:* For fall admission, 4/1 for international students; for spring admission, 9/30 for international students. Applications are processed on a rolling basis. Electronic applications accepted. *Expenses:* Expenses: Contact institution. *Financial support:* Application deadline: 3/1; applicants required to submit FAFSA. *Unit head:* Dr. Theodore R. Richardson, III, Senior Associate Dean, 321-674-8123, Fax: 321-674-7597, E-mail: trichardson@fit.edu. *Application contact:* Carolyn Farrior, Director of Graduate Admissions, Online Learning and Off-Campus Programs, 321-674-7118, Fax: 321-674-8216, E-mail: cfarrior@fit.edu.
Website: http://es.fit.edu.

Gannon University, School of Graduate Studies, College of Engineering and Business, School of Engineering and Computer Science, Program in Electrical and Computer Engineering, Erie, PA 16541-0001. Offers MSEE, MSES. Part-time and evening/weekend programs available. *Degree requirements:* For master's, thesis (for some programs), oral exam (for some programs), design project (for some programs). *Entrance requirements:* For master's, GRE or GMAT, bachelor's degree in electrical or computer engineering, minimum GPA of 2.5, transcripts, 3 letters of recommendation. Additional exam requirements/recommendations for international students: Required—TOEFL (minimum score 79 iBT). Electronic applications accepted.

Gannon University, School of Graduate Studies, College of Engineering and Business, School of Engineering and Computer Science, Program in Software Engineering, Erie, PA 16541-0001. Offers MSCIS. Part-time and evening/weekend programs available. *Entrance requirements:* Additional exam requirements/recommendations for international students: Required—TOEFL (minimum score 79 iBT). Electronic applications accepted.

George Mason University, Volgenau School of Engineering, Department of Computer Science, Fairfax, VA 22030. Offers computer science (MS, PhD, Certificate); information security and assurance (MS); information systems (MS); software engineering (MS). MS programs offered jointly with Old Dominion University, University of Virginia, Virginia Commonwealth University, and Virginia Polytechnic Institute and State University. *Faculty:* 46 full-time (10 women), 17 part-time/adjunct (1 woman). *Students:* 236 full-time (68 women), 246 part-time (50 women); includes 77 minority (13 Black or African American, non-Hispanic/Latino; 48 Asian, non-Hispanic/Latino; 11 Hispanic/Latino; 5 Two or more races, non-Hispanic/Latino), 231 international. Average age 29. 874 applicants, 42% accepted, 119 enrolled. In 2014, 171 master's, 8 doctorates, 22 other advanced degrees awarded. *Degree requirements:* For master's, thesis optional; for doctorate, comprehensive exam, thesis/dissertation. *Entrance requirements:* For master's, GRE, proof of financial support; 2 official college transcripts; resume; self-evaluation form; official bank statement; photocopy of passport; 3 letters of recommendation; baccalaureate degree related to computer science; minimum GPA of 3.0 in last 2 years of undergraduate work; 1 year beyond 1st-year calculus; personal goals statement; for doctorate, GRE, personal goals statement; 2 official copies of transcripts; self-evaluation form; 3 letters of recommendation; photocopy of passport; proof of financial support; official bank statement; resume; 4-year baccalaureate degree with strong background in computer science. Additional exam requirements/recommendations for international students: Required—TOEFL (minimum score 575 paper-based; 80 iBT), IELTS (minimum score 6.5), PTE. *Application deadline:* For fall admission, 1/15 priority date for domestic students; for spring admission, 8/15 priority date for domestic students. Application fee: $65 ($80 for international students). Electronic applications accepted. *Expenses:* Expenses: Contact institution. *Financial support:* In 2014–15, 113 students received support, including 1 fellowship (averaging $9,302 per year), 46 research assistantships (averaging $19,727 per year), 67 teaching assistantships (averaging $14,678 per year); career-related internships or fieldwork, Federal Work-Study, scholarships/grants, unspecified assistantships, and health care benefits (for full-time research or teaching assistantship recipients) also available. Support available to part-time students. Financial award application deadline: 3/1; financial award applicants required to submit FAFSA. *Faculty research:* Artificial intelligence, image processing/graphics, parallel/distributed systems, software engineering systems. *Total annual research expenditures:* $3.4 million. *Unit head:* Sanjeev Setia, Chair, 703-993-4098, Fax: 703-993-1710, E-mail: setia@gmu.edu. *Application contact:* Michele Pieper, Office Manager, 703-993-9483, Fax: 703-993-1710, E-mail: mpieper@gmu.edu.
Website: http://cs.gmu.edu/.

Grand Valley State University, Padnos College of Engineering and Computing, School of Computing and Information Systems, Allendale, MI 49401-9403. Offers computer information systems (MS), including databases, distributed systems, management of information systems, object-oriented systems, software engineering. Part-time and evening/weekend programs available. *Faculty:* 8 full-time (0 women). *Students:* 26 full-time (10 women), 57 part-time (12 women); includes 10 minority (7 Asian, non-Hispanic/Latino; 3 Hispanic/Latino), 21 international. Average age 32. 44 applicants, 82% accepted, 18 enrolled. In 2014, 29 master's awarded. *Degree requirements:* For master's, thesis or alternative. *Entrance requirements:* For master's, GMAT or GRE General Test. Additional exam requirements/recommendations for international students: Required—TOEFL. *Application deadline:* For fall admission, 6/1 for international students; for winter admission, 9/1 for international students. Applications are processed on a rolling basis. Application fee: $30. Electronic applications accepted. *Expenses:* Tuition, state resident: full-time $10,602; part-time $589 per credit hour. Tuition, nonresident: full-time $14,022; part-time $779 per credit hour. Tuition and fees vary according to degree level and program. *Financial support:* In 2014–15, 17 students received support, including 10 fellowships (averaging $1,856 per year), 7 research assistantships with full and partial tuition reimbursements available (averaging $10,134 per year). *Faculty research:* Object technology, distributed computing, information systems management database, software engineering. *Unit head:* Paul Leidig, Director, 616-331-2038, Fax: 616-331-2106, E-mail: leidigp@gvsu.edu. *Application contact:* D.

Robert Adams, Graduate Program Chair, 616-331-3885, Fax: 616-331-2106, E-mail: adams@cis.gvsu.edu.
Website: http://www.cis.gvsu.edu/.

Illinois Institute of Technology, Graduate College, Armour College of Engineering, Department of Electrical and Computer Engineering, Chicago, IL 60616. Offers biomedical imaging and signals (MAS); computer engineering (MS, PhD); electrical engineering (MS, PhD); electricity markets (MAS); network engineering (MAS); power engineering (MAS); telecommunications and software engineering (MAS); vlsi and microelectronics (MAS); MS/MS. Part-time and evening/weekend programs available. Postbaccalaureate distance learning degree programs offered (minimal on-campus study). *Faculty:* 27 full-time (4 women), 3 part-time/adjunct (0 women). *Students:* 439 full-time (84 women), 90 part-time (11 women); includes 13 minority (11 Asian, non-Hispanic/Latino; 2 Hispanic/Latino), 476 international. Average age 26. 2,461 applicants, 39% accepted, 206 enrolled. In 2014, 155 master's, 7 doctorates awarded. Terminal master's awarded for partial completion of doctoral program. *Degree requirements:* For master's, comprehensive exam (for some programs), thesis (for some programs); for doctorate, comprehensive exam, thesis/dissertation. *Entrance requirements:* For master's and doctorate, GRE General Test (minimum score 1100 Quantitative and Verbal, 3.5 Analytical Writing), minimum undergraduate GPA of 3.0. Additional exam requirements/recommendations for international students: Required—TOEFL (minimum score 550 paper-based; 80 iBT); Recommended—IELTS (minimum score 5.5). *Application deadline:* For fall admission, 5/1 for domestic and international students; for spring admission, 10/15 for domestic and international students. Applications are processed on a rolling basis. Application fee: $50. Electronic applications accepted. *Expenses: Tuition:* Full-time $22,500; part-time $1250 per credit hour. *Required fees:* $30 per course. $260 per semester. One-time fee: $235. Tuition and fees vary according to course load and program. *Financial support:* Fellowships with full and partial tuition reimbursements, research assistantships with full and partial tuition reimbursements, teaching assistantships with full and partial tuition reimbursements, career-related internships or fieldwork, Federal Work-Study, institutionally sponsored loans, scholarships/grants, health care benefits, tuition waivers (full), and unspecified assistantships available. Support available to part-time students. Financial award applicants required to submit FAFSA. *Faculty research:* Communication systems, wireless networks, computer systems, computer networks, wireless security, cloud computing and micro-electronics; electromagnetics and electronics; power and control systems; signal and image processing. *Unit head:* Dr. Ashfaq Khokhar, Chair & Professor of Electrical and Computer Engineering, 312-567-5780, Fax: 312-567-8976, E-mail: ashfaq@iit.edu. *Application contact:* Rishab Malhotra, Director, Graduate Admission, 866-472-3448, Fax: 312-567-3138, E-mail: inquiry.grad@iit.edu.
Website: http://www.ece.iit.edu.

Illinois Institute of Technology, Graduate College, College of Science, Department of Computer Science, Chicago, IL 60616. Offers business (MCS); computational intelligence (MCS); computer networking and communications (MCS); computer science (MCS, MS, PhD); cyber-physical systems (MCS); data analytics (MCS); data science (MAS); database systems (MCS); distributed and cloud computing (MCS); education (MCS); finance (MCS); information security and assurance (MCS); software engineering (MCS); telecommunications and software engineering (MAS); MS/MAS. Part-time and evening/weekend programs available. Postbaccalaureate distance learning degree programs offered (no on-campus study). *Faculty:* 29 full-time (5 women), 8 part-time/adjunct (1 woman). *Students:* 432 full-time (108 women), 117 part-time (27 women); includes 11 minority (3 Black or African American, non-Hispanic/Latino; 7 Asian, non-Hispanic/Latino; 1 Two or more races, non-Hispanic/Latino), 495 international. Average age 26. 2,573 applicants, 42% accepted, 244 enrolled. In 2014, 164 master's, 2 doctorates awarded. Terminal master's awarded for partial completion of doctoral program. *Degree requirements:* For master's, thesis optional; for doctorate, comprehensive exam, thesis/dissertation. *Entrance requirements:* For master's, MS GRE General Test (minimum scores: 298 Quantitative and Verbal, 3.0 Analytical Writing); MAS GRE General Test (minimum scores: 292 Quantitative and Verbal, 2.5 Analytical Writing), minimum undergraduate GPA of 3.0; for doctorate, GRE General Test (minimum scores: 304 Quantitative and Verbal, 3.5 Analytical Writing), minimum undergraduate GPA of 3.0. Additional exam requirements/recommendations for international students: Required—TOEFL (minimum score 523 paper-based; 70 iBT). *Application deadline:* For fall admission, 5/1 for domestic and international students; for spring admission, 10/15 for domestic and international students. Applications are processed on a rolling basis. Application fee: $50. Electronic applications accepted. *Expenses: Tuition:* Full-time $22,500; part-time $1250 per credit hour. *Required fees:* $30 per course. $260 per semester. One-time fee: $235. Tuition and fees vary according to course load and program. *Financial support:* Fellowships with partial tuition reimbursements, research assistantships with full and partial tuition reimbursements, teaching assistantships with full and partial tuition reimbursements, career-related internships or fieldwork, Federal Work-Study, institutionally sponsored loans, scholarships/grants, traineeships, health care benefits, tuition waivers (partial), and unspecified assistantships available. Support available to part-time students. Financial award applicants required to submit FAFSA. *Faculty research:* Parallel and distributed processing, high-performance computing, computational linguistics, information retrieval, data mining, grid computing. *Unit head:* Dr. Eunice Santos, Chair/Professor, 312-567-5150, E-mail: eunice.santos@iit.edu. *Application contact:* Rishab Malhotra, Director, Graduate Admission, 866-472-3448, Fax: 312-567-3138, E-mail: inquiry.grad@iit.edu.
Website: http://www.iit.edu/csl/cs/.

Instituto Tecnologico de Santo Domingo, Graduate School, Area of Engineering, Santo Domingo, Dominican Republic. Offers construction administration (MS, Certificate); data telecommunications (M Eng, MS, Certificate); industrial engineering (M Eng, Certificate); industrial management (M Mgmt); information technology (Certificate); maintenance engineering (M Eng); occupational hazard prevention (M Mgmt); production management (Certificate); quantitative methods (Certificate); sanitary and environmental engineering (M Eng); structural engineering (M Eng); systems engineering and electronic data processing (Certificate); transportation (Certificate).

International Technological University, Program in Software Engineering, San Jose, CA 95113. Offers MSSE. Part-time and evening/weekend programs available. *Faculty:* 5 full-time (1 woman), 11 part-time/adjunct (2 women). *Students:* 484 full-time (236 women), 206 part-time (111 women); includes 6 minority (all Asian, non-Hispanic/Latino), 683 international. Average age 28. 209 applicants, 81% accepted, 106 enrolled. In 2014, 114 master's awarded. *Degree requirements:* For master's, thesis or alternative, capstone project. *Entrance requirements:* Additional exam requirements/recommendations for international students: Required—TOEFL, IELTS. *Application deadline:* For fall admission, 8/1 priority date for domestic students, 8/1 for international students; for winter admission, 12/31 priority date for domestic students; for spring admission, 12/1 priority date for domestic students, 12/1 for international students; for summer admission, 4/1 for domestic and international students. Applications are processed on a rolling basis. Application fee: $80. Electronic applications accepted. *Expenses: Tuition:* Full-time $13,500; part-time $500 per credit. *Required fees:* $265 per trimester. *Unit head:* Dr. Cornel Pokorny, Department Chairman, 888-488-4968. *Application contact:* Mary Tran, Admissions Manager, 888-488-4968, E-mail: admissions@itu.edu.

Jacksonville State University, College of Graduate Studies and Continuing Education, College of Arts and Sciences, Program in Computer Systems and Software Design, Jacksonville, AL 36265-1602. Offers MS. Part-time and evening/weekend programs available. *Faculty:* 11 full-time (5 women). *Students:* 1 (woman) full-time, 13 part-time (3 women); includes 1 minority (Hispanic/Latino), 3 international. Average age 30. 11 applicants, 45% accepted, 3 enrolled. In 2014, 13 master's awarded. *Degree requirements:* For master's, comprehensive exam, thesis (for some programs). *Entrance requirements:* Additional exam requirements/recommendations for international students: Required—TOEFL (minimum score 500 paper-based; 61 iBT). *Application deadline:* Applications are processed on a rolling basis. Application fee: $35. Electronic applications accepted. *Financial support:* In 2014–15, 5 students received support, including 3 teaching assistantships. Support available to part-time students. Financial award application deadline: 4/1; financial award applicants required to submit FAFSA. *Unit head:* Dr. Donnie Ford, Head, 256-782-5242, E-mail: dford@jsu.edu. *Application contact:* Dr. Jean Pugliese, Associate Dean, 256-782-8278, Fax: 256-782-5321, E-mail: pugliese@jsu.edu.

Loyola University Chicago, Graduate School, Department of Computer Science, Chicago, IL 60660. Offers computer science (MS); information technology (MS); software engineering (MS); software technology (MS). Part-time and evening/weekend programs available. *Faculty:* 10 full-time (1 woman), 10 part-time/adjunct (2 women). *Students:* 86 full-time (30 women), 40 part-time (16 women); includes 24 minority (8 Black or African American, non-Hispanic/Latino; 10 Asian, non-Hispanic/Latino; 6 Hispanic/Latino), 45 international. Average age 29. 218 applicants, 45% accepted, 60 enrolled. In 2014, 46 master's awarded. *Degree requirements:* For master's, thesis optional, ten courses; thesis (for computer science). *Entrance requirements:* For master's, 3 letters of recommendation, transcripts, statement of purpose. Additional exam requirements/recommendations for international students: Required—TOEFL (minimum score 550 paper-based; 79 iBT) or IELTS (minimum score 6.5). *Application deadline:* For fall admission, 8/10 for domestic students, 5/15 for international students; for spring admission, 12/20 for domestic students, 9/15 for international students. Applications are processed on a rolling basis. Electronic applications accepted. Application fee is waived when completed online. *Expenses: Tuition:* Full-time $17,370; part-time $965 per credit. *Required fees:* $138 per semester. *Financial support:* In 2014–15, 20 students received support, including 1 fellowship (averaging $3,000 per year), 16 teaching assistantships with partial tuition reimbursements available (averaging $4,000 per year); career-related internships or fieldwork, Federal Work-Study, scholarships/grants, tuition waivers (partial), and unspecified assistantships also available. Financial award application deadline: 3/15. *Faculty research:* Software engineering, high performance computing, algorithms and complexity, parallel and distributed computing, databases and computer networks. *Total annual research expenditures:* $22,000. *Unit head:* Dr. Chandra Sekharan, Chair, 312-915-7985, Fax: 312-915-7998, E-mail: csekhar@luc.edu. *Application contact:* Cecilia Murphy, Graduate Program Secretary, 312-915-7990, Fax: 312-915-7998, E-mail: gradinfo-cs@luc.edu.
Website: http://cs.luc.edu.

Loyola University Maryland, Graduate Programs, Loyola College of Arts and Sciences, Department of Computer Science and Software Engineering, Baltimore, MD 21210-2699. Offers computer science (MS); software engineering (MS). Part-time programs available. *Entrance requirements:* For master's, essay, letter of recommendation, transcripts, resume. Additional exam requirements/recommendations for international students: Required—TOEFL. Electronic applications accepted.

Marist College, Graduate Programs, School of Computer Science and Mathematics, Poughkeepsie, NY 12601-1387. Offers computer science/software development (MS); information systems (MS, Adv C); technology management (MS). Part-time and evening/weekend programs available. Postbaccalaureate distance learning degree programs offered (minimal on-campus study). *Entrance requirements:* For master's, resume. Additional exam requirements/recommendations for international students: Required—TOEFL (minimum score 550 paper-based; 80 iBT); Recommended—IELTS (minimum score 6.5). Electronic applications accepted. *Faculty research:* Data quality, artificial intelligence, imaging, analysis of algorithms, distributed systems and applications.

McMaster University, School of Graduate Studies, Faculty of Engineering, Department of Computing and Software, Hamilton, ON L8S 4M2, Canada. Offers computer science (M Sc, PhD); software engineering (M Eng, MA Sc, PhD). Part-time programs available. *Degree requirements:* For master's, thesis. *Entrance requirements:* Additional exam requirements/recommendations for international students: Required—TOEFL (minimum score 550 paper-based). *Faculty research:* Software engineering; theory of non-sequential systems; parallel and distributed computing; artificial intelligence; complexity, design, and analysis of algorithms; combinatorial computing, especially applications to molecular biology.

Mercer University, Graduate Studies, Macon Campus, School of Engineering, Macon, GA 31207. Offers biomedical engineering (MSE); computer engineering (MSE); electrical engineering (MSE); engineering management (MSE); environmental engineering (MSE); environmental systems (MS); mechanical engineering (MSE); software engineering (MSE); software systems (MS); technical communications management (MS); technical management (MS). Part-time and evening/weekend programs available. Postbaccalaureate distance learning degree programs offered (no on-campus study). *Faculty:* 20 full-time (6 women), 2 part-time/adjunct (0 women). *Students:* 10 full-time (4 women), 75 part-time (16 women); includes 10 minority (5 Black or African American, non-Hispanic/Latino; 4 Asian, non-Hispanic/Latino; 1 Hispanic/Latino), 4 international. Average age 42. In 2014, 70 master's awarded. *Degree requirements:* For master's, thesis or alternative. *Entrance requirements:* For master's, minimum undergraduate GPA of 3.0. Additional exam requirements/recommendations for international students: Required—TOEFL (minimum score 550 paper-based; 80 iBT). *Application deadline:* For fall admission, 4/1 priority date for domestic and international students; for spring admission, 11/1 priority date for domestic and international students. Applications are processed on a rolling basis. Application fee: $75. *Expenses:* Expenses: Contact institution. *Financial support:* Federal Work-Study available. *Unit head:* Dr. Wade H. Shaw, Dean, 478-301-2459, Fax: 478-301-5593, E-mail: shaw_wh@mercer.edu. *Application contact:* Dr. Richard O. Mines, Program Director, 478-301-2347, Fax: 478-301-5433, E-mail: mines_ro@mercer.edu.
Website: http://engineering.mercer.edu/.

Monmouth University, The Graduate School, Department of Computer Science, West Long Branch, NJ 07764-1898. Offers computer science (MS); computer science software design and development (Certificate); information systems (MS). Part-time and evening/weekend programs available. *Faculty:* 4 full-time (2 women), 6 part-time/adjunct (0 women). *Students:* 56 full-time (21 women), 21 part-time (9 women); includes 4 minority (1 Black or African American, non-Hispanic/Latino; 2 Hispanic/Latino; 1 Two or more races, non-Hispanic/Latino), 63 international. Average age 25. 238 applicants, 55% accepted, 39 enrolled. In 2014, 14 master's awarded. *Degree requirements:* For

master's, thesis (for some programs), practicum. *Entrance requirements:* For master's, minimum GPA of 3.0 in major, 2.75 overall; two letters of recommendation; calculus I and II with minimum C grade; two semesters of computer programming courses within the past five years with minimum B grade; IS-minimum 2.75 overall GPA, 3.0 in major, UG degree in major that requires substantial component of software development and/or business adm; for Certificate, minimum GPA of 3.0 in major, 2.75 overall; two letters of recommendation; calculus I and II with minimum C grade; two semesters of computer programming courses within the past five years with minimum B grade. Additional exam requirements/recommendations for international students: Required—TOEFL (minimum score 550 paper-based, 79 iBT), IELTS (minimum score 6), Michigan English Language Assessment Battery (minimum score 77) or Certificate of Advanced English (minimum score B2). *Application deadline:* For fall admission, 7/15 priority date for domestic students, 6/1 for international students; for spring admission, 11/15 priority date for domestic students, 11/1 for international students. Applications are processed on a rolling basis. Application fee: $50. Electronic applications accepted. *Expenses: Tuition:* Full-time $18,072; part-time $1004 per credit. *Required fees:* $157 per semester. *Financial support:* In 2014–15, 64 students received support, including 64 fellowships (averaging $3,184 per year), 23 research assistantships (averaging $5,888 per year); career-related internships or fieldwork, scholarships/grants, and unspecified assistantships also available. Support available to part-time students. Financial award application deadline: 3/1; financial award applicants required to submit FAFSA. *Faculty research:* Databases, natural language processing, protocols, performance analysis, communications networks (systems), cybersecurity. *Unit head:* Dr. Cui Yu, Program Director, 732-571-4460, Fax: 732-263-5202, E-mail: cyu@monmouth.edu. *Application contact:* Andrea Thompson, Graduate Admission Counselor, 732-571-3452, Fax: 732-263-5123, E-mail: gradadm@monmouth.edu.
Website: http://www.monmouth.edu/academics/CSSE/mscs.asp.

Monmouth University, The Graduate School, Department of Computer Science and Software Engineering, West Long Branch, NJ 07764-1898. Offers software development (Certificate); software engineering (MS, Certificate). Part-time and evening/weekend programs available. *Faculty:* 5 full-time (1 woman), 1 part-time/adjunct (0 women). *Students:* 22 full-time (3 women), 16 part-time (6 women); includes 6 minority (1 Black or African American, non-Hispanic/Latino; 4 Asian, non-Hispanic/Latino; 1 Hispanic/Latino), 17 international. Average age 26. 56 applicants, 77% accepted, 16 enrolled. In 2014, 8 master's awarded. *Degree requirements:* For master's, thesis or alternative, practicum. *Entrance requirements:* For master's and Certificate, bachelor's degree in software engineering, computer science, computer engineering or other engineering-related discipline; minimum GPA of 3.0 in major, 2.5 overall; completed course work in computer programming, data structures and algorithms, and software engineering. Additional exam requirements/recommendations for international students: Required—TOEFL (minimum score 550 paper-based; 79 iBT), IELTS (minimum score 6), TOEFL (minimum score 550 paper-based, 79 iBT), IELTS (minimum score 6), Michigan English Language Assessment Battery (minimum score 77) or Certificate of Advanced English (minimum score B2). *Application deadline:* For fall admission, 7/15 priority date for domestic students, 6/1 for international students; for spring admission, 11/15 priority date for domestic students, 11/1 for international students. Applications are processed on a rolling basis. Application fee: $50. Electronic applications accepted. *Expenses:* Expenses: Contact institution. *Financial support:* In 2014–15, 35 students received support, including 25 fellowships (averaging $3,698 per year), 9 research assistantships (averaging $6,545 per year); career-related internships or fieldwork, scholarships/grants, and unspecified assistantships also available. Support available to part-time students. Financial award applicants required to submit FAFSA. *Faculty research:* Conceptual structures, real time software, business rules, project management, software related to homeland security. *Unit head:* Dr. Daniela Rosca, Program Director, 732-571-4459, Fax: 732-263-5253, E-mail: drosca@monmouth.edu. *Application contact:* Andrea Thompson, Graduate Admission Counselor, 732-571-3452, Fax: 732-263-5123, E-mail: gradadm@monmouth.edu.
Website: http://www.monmouth.edu/graduate_se.

National University, Academic Affairs, School of Engineering and Computing, La Jolla, CA 92037-1011. Offers computer science (MS), including advanced computing, database engineering, software engineering; cyber security and information assurance (MS), including computer forensics, ethical hacking and penetration testing, health information assurance, information assurance and security; data analytics (MS); engineering management (MS), including enterprise architecture, project management, systems engineering, technology management; environmental engineering (MS); homeland security and emergency management (MS); management information systems (MS); project management (Certificate); sustainability management (MS); wireless communications (MS). Part-time and evening/weekend programs available. Postbaccalaureate distance learning degree programs offered (no on-campus study). *Faculty:* 24 full-time (5 women), 21 part-time/adjunct (5 women). *Students:* 275 full-time (72 women), 86 part-time (24 women); includes 147 minority (41 Black or African American, non-Hispanic/Latino; 48 Asian, non-Hispanic/Latino; 37 Hispanic/Latino; 7 Native Hawaiian or other Pacific Islander, non-Hispanic/Latino; 14 Two or more races, non-Hispanic/Latino), 95 international. Average age 33. In 2014, 281 master's awarded. *Degree requirements:* For master's, thesis (for some programs). *Entrance requirements:* For master's, interview, minimum GPA of 2.5. Additional exam requirements/recommendations for international students: Required—TOEFL (minimum score 550 paper-based; 79 iBT), IELTS (minimum score 6). *Application deadline:* Applications are processed on a rolling basis. Application fee: $60 ($65 for international students). Electronic applications accepted. *Expenses: Tuition:* Full-time $14,184; part-time $1773 per course. *Financial support:* Career-related internships or fieldwork, institutionally sponsored loans, scholarships/grants, and tuition waivers (partial) available. Support available to part-time students. Financial award application deadline: 6/30; financial award applicants required to submit FAFSA. *Faculty research:* Educational technology, scholarships in science. *Unit head:* School of Engineering and Computing, 800-628-8648, E-mail: soec@nu.edu. *Application contact:* Frank Rojas, Vice President for Enrollment Services, 800-628-8648, E-mail: advisor@nu.edu.
Website: http://www.nu.edu/OurPrograms/SchoolOfEngineeringAndTechnology.html.

Naval Postgraduate School, Departments and Academic Groups, Department of Computer Science, Monterey, CA 93943. Offers computer science (MS, PhD); identity management and cyber security (MA); modeling of virtual environments and simulations (MS, PhD); software engineering (MS, PhD). Program only open to commissioned officers of the United States and friendly nations and selected United States federal civilian employees. Part-time programs available. Postbaccalaureate distance learning degree programs offered (minimal on-campus study). *Degree requirements:* For master's, thesis; for doctorate, thesis/dissertation.

New Jersey Institute of Technology, College of Computing Science, Newark, NJ 07102. Offers computer science (MS, PhD), including bioinformatics (MS), computer science, computing and business (MS), cyber security and privacy (MS), software engineering (MS); information systems (MS, PhD), including business and information systems (MS), emergency management and business continuity (MS), information systems; information technology administration and security (MS). Part-time and evening/weekend programs available. Terminal master's awarded for partial completion of doctoral program. *Degree requirements:* For master's, thesis optional; for doctorate, thesis/dissertation. *Entrance requirements:* For master's, GRE General Test; for doctorate, GRE General Test, minimum graduate GPA of 3.5. Additional exam requirements/recommendations for international students: Required—TOEFL (minimum score 550 paper-based; 79 iBT). Electronic applications accepted. *Faculty research:* Computer systems, communications and networking, artificial intelligence, database engineering, systems analysis.

New York University, Polytechnic School of Engineering, Department of Computer Science and Engineering, Major in Software Engineering, New York, NY 10012-1019. Offers Graduate Certificate. *Students:* 2 part-time (0 women); includes 1 minority (Asian, non-Hispanic/Latino). Average age 31. 1 applicant. *Application deadline:* For fall admission, 2/15 priority date for domestic and international students; for spring admission, 11/1 priority date for domestic and international students. Applications are processed on a rolling basis. Application fee: $75. Electronic applications accepted. *Unit head:* Dr. Nasir Memon, Head, 718-260-3970, E-mail: memon@nyu.edu. *Application contact:* Raymond Lutzky, Director, Graduate Enrollment Management, 718-637-5984, Fax: 718-260-3624, E-mail: rlutzky@poly.edu.
Website: http://www.poly.edu/cis/graduate/certificates/.

North Dakota State University, College of Graduate and Interdisciplinary Studies, College of Science and Mathematics, Department of Computer Science, Program in Software Engineering, Fargo, ND 58108. Offers MS, PhD, Certificate. Part-time programs available. Postbaccalaureate distance learning degree programs offered (minimal on-campus study). Terminal master's awarded for partial completion of doctoral program. *Degree requirements:* For master's, comprehensive exam, thesis optional; for doctorate, thesis/dissertation, qualifying exam. *Entrance requirements:* For master's and doctorate, minimum GPA of 3.0 in software engineering or related field. Additional exam requirements/recommendations for international students: Required—TOEFL (minimum score 550 paper-based; 79 iBT). Electronic applications accepted. *Faculty research:* Data knowledge and engineering requirements, formal methods for software, software measurement and mobile agents, software development process.

Northern Kentucky University, Office of Graduate Programs, College of Informatics, Department of Computer Science, Highland Heights, KY 41099. Offers computer science (MSCS); geographic information systems (Certificate); secure software engineering (Certificate). Part-time and evening/weekend programs available. *Faculty:* 6 full-time (0 women), 2 part-time/adjunct (0 women). *Students:* 5 full-time (1 woman), 21 part-time (4 women); includes 4 minority (1 Black or African American, non-Hispanic/Latino; 2 Asian, non-Hispanic/Latino; 1 Two or more races, non-Hispanic/Latino), 2 international. Average age 29. 33 applicants, 42% accepted, 8 enrolled. In 2014, 11 master's awarded. *Degree requirements:* For master's, thesis optional. *Entrance requirements:* For master's, GRE, minimum GPA of 3.0, at least 4 semesters of undergraduate study in computer science including intermediate computer programming and data structures, one year of calculus, one course in discrete mathematics. Additional exam requirements/recommendations for international students: Required—TOEFL (minimum score 550 paper-based; 79 iBT); Recommended—IELTS (minimum score 6.5). *Application deadline:* For fall admission, 8/1 for domestic students, 6/1 for international students; for spring admission, 12/1 for domestic students, 10/1 for international students; for summer admission, 5/1 for domestic students, 3/1 for international students. Applications are processed on a rolling basis. Application fee: $40. Electronic applications accepted. *Expenses: Tuition, area resident:* Part-time $518 per credit hour. Tuition, state resident: part-time $630 per credit hour. Tuition, nonresident: part-time $797 per credit hour. *Required fees:* $192 per semester. Tuition and fees vary according to course load, degree level, campus/location, program and reciprocity agreements. *Financial support:* In 2014–15, 4 students received support. Scholarships/grants and unspecified assistantships available. Financial award applicants required to submit FAFSA. *Faculty research:* Data privacy, data mining, wireless security, secure software engineering, secure networking. *Unit head:* Dr. Jeff Ward, Interim Director, 859-572-1453, E-mail: wardj1@nku.edu. *Application contact:* Alison Swanson, Graduate Admissions Coordinator, 859-572-6971, E-mail: swansona1@nku.edu.
Website: http://informatics.nku.edu/departments/computer-science.html.

Northwestern University, School of Professional Studies, Program in Information Systems, Evanston, IL 60208. Offers analytics and business intelligence (MS); database and Internet technologies (MS); information systems (MS); information systems management (MS); information systems security (MS); medical informatics (MS); software project management and development (MS).

Nova Southeastern University, College of Engineering and Computing, Fort Lauderdale, FL 33314-7796. Offers computer science (MS, PhD); information assurance (PhD); information security (MS); information systems (PhD); information technology (MS); management information systems (MS); software engineering (MS). Part-time and evening/weekend programs available. Postbaccalaureate distance learning degree programs offered (minimal on-campus study). *Faculty:* 20 full-time (6 women), 24 part-time/adjunct (3 women). *Students:* 106 full-time (35 women), 758 part-time (227 women); includes 417 minority (183 Black or African American, non-Hispanic/Latino; 2 American Indian or Alaska Native, non-Hispanic/Latino; 59 Asian, non-Hispanic/Latino; 159 Hispanic/Latino; 14 Two or more races, non-Hispanic/Latino), 90 international. Average age 40. 390 applicants, 74% accepted. In 2014, 146 master's, 67 doctorates awarded. Terminal master's awarded for partial completion of doctoral program. *Degree requirements:* For master's, thesis optional; for doctorate, thesis/dissertation. *Entrance requirements:* For master's, minimum undergraduate GPA of 2.5; 3.0 in major; for doctorate, master's degree, minimum graduate GPA of 3.25. Additional exam requirements/recommendations for international students: Required—TOEFL (minimum score 80 iBT), IELTS (minimum score 6). *Application deadline:* Applications are processed on a rolling basis. Application fee: $50. Electronic applications accepted. *Expenses:* Expenses: $675/credit hour (for MS), $975 (for PhD). *Financial support:* Application deadline: 5/1; applicants required to submit FAFSA. *Faculty research:* Artificial intelligence, database management, human-computer interaction, distance education, information security. *Unit head:* Dr. Eric S. Ackerman, Dean, 954-262-2000, Fax: 954-262-2752, E-mail: esa@nova.edu. *Application contact:* Nancy Ruidiaz, Director, Admissions, 954-262-2026, Fax: 954-262-2752, E-mail: azoulayn@nova.edu.
Website: http://scis.nova.edu.

Oakland University, Graduate Study and Lifelong Learning, School of Engineering and Computer Science, Department of Computer Science and Engineering, Rochester, MI 48309-4401. Offers computer science (MS); embedded systems (MS); information systems engineering (MS); software engineering (MS). Part-time and evening/weekend programs available. *Entrance requirements:* For master's, minimum GPA of 3.0. Electronic applications accepted. *Expenses:* Contact institution. *Faculty research:* Urinary continence index for prediction of urinary incontinence in older women.

Pace University, Seidenberg School of Computer Science and Information Systems, New York, NY 10038. Offers computer science (MS); computing science (DPS); information systems (MS); Internet technology (MS); large computing systems (Certificate); network administration (Certificate); security and information assurance (Certificate); software development and engineering (MS, Certificate);

telecommunications (Certificate); telecommunications systems and networks (MS). Part-time and evening/weekend programs available. *Faculty:* 26 full-time (7 women), 7 part-time/adjunct (2 women). *Students:* 167 full-time (57 women), 324 part-time (90 women); includes 182 minority (83 Black or African American, non-Hispanic/Latino; 1 American Indian or Alaska Native, non-Hispanic/Latino; 46 Asian, non-Hispanic/Latino; 47 Hispanic/Latino; 5 Two or more races, non-Hispanic/Latino), 132 international. Average age 35. 441 applicants, 84% accepted, 157 enrolled. In 2014, 115 master's, 7 doctorates, 9 other advanced degrees awarded. *Degree requirements:* For master's, thesis or alternative, capstone course; for doctorate, comprehensive exam (for some programs), thesis/dissertation. *Entrance requirements:* For master's, GRE General Test. Additional exam requirements/recommendations for international students: Required—TOEFL. *Application deadline:* For fall admission, 8/1 priority date for domestic students, 6/1 for international students; for spring admission, 12/1 for domestic students, 10/1 for international students. Applications are processed on a rolling basis. Application fee: $70. Electronic applications accepted. *Expenses:* Expenses: Contact institution. *Financial support:* Research assistantships and career-related internships or fieldwork available. Support available to part-time students. Financial award applicants required to submit FAFSA. *Faculty research:* Computer security and forensics, cybersecurity, telehealth, mobile computing, distributed teams, robotics. *Total annual research expenditures:* $685,824. *Unit head:* Dr. Amar Gupta, Dean, Seidenberg School of Computer Science and Information Systems, 914-773-3750, Fax: 914-773-3533, E-mail: agupta@pace.edu. *Application contact:* Susan Ford-Goldschein, Director of Graduate Admissions, 914-422-4283, Fax: 914-422-4287, E-mail: gradwp@pace.edu.
Website: http://www.pace.edu/seidenberg.

Penn State Great Valley, Graduate Studies, Engineering Division, Malvern, PA 19355-1488. Offers engineering management (MEM); software engineering (MSE); systems engineering (M Eng). *Unit head:* Dr. Craig S. Edelbrock, Chancellor, 610-648-3202 Ext. 610, Fax: 610-889-1334, E-mail: cse1@psu.edu. *Application contact:* JoAnn Kelly, Director of Admissions, 610-648-3315, Fax: 610-725-5296, E-mail: jek2@psu.edu.
Website: http://www.sgps.psu.edu/Academics/Degrees/31884.htm.

Portland State University, Graduate Studies, Maseeh College of Engineering and Computer Science, Department of Computer Science, Portland, OR 97207-0751. Offers computer science (MS, PhD); software engineering (MSE). Part-time programs available. *Faculty:* 25 full-time (5 women), 5 part-time/adjunct (0 women). *Students:* 84 full-time (31 women), 50 part-time (18 women); includes 15 minority (1 Black or African American, non-Hispanic/Latino; 10 Asian, non-Hispanic/Latino; 1 Hispanic/Latino; 3 Two or more races, non-Hispanic/Latino), 73 international. Average age 30. 231 applicants, 27% accepted, 36 enrolled. In 2014, 35 master's, 5 doctorates awarded. *Degree requirements:* For master's, thesis or alternative; for doctorate, comprehensive exam, thesis/dissertation. *Entrance requirements:* For master's, GRE scores are required. The minimum for acceptance as an MS student is 60th percentile in Quantitative and 25th percentile in Verbal., 3.0 or equivalent GPA, 2 letters of recommendation and a personal statement; for doctorate, GRE scores are required. The minimum for acceptance is above 60th percentile in Quantitative and 25th percentile in Verbal., MS in computer science or allied field. Additional exam requirements/recommendations for international students: Required—TOEFL (minimum score 550 paper-based). *Application deadline:* For fall admission, 3/1 for domestic and international students; for winter admission, 5/15 for domestic and international students; for spring admission, 11/1 for domestic students, 10/1 for international students. Applications are processed on a rolling basis. Application fee: $50. *Expenses:* Tuition, state resident: part-time $222 per credit. Tuition, nonresident: part-time $527 per credit. *Required fees:* $22 per contact hour. $100 per quarter. Tuition and fees vary according to program. *Financial support:* In 2014–15, 18 research assistantships with full and partial tuition reimbursements (averaging $8,688 per year), 18 teaching assistantships with full and partial tuition reimbursements (averaging $6,231 per year) were awarded; career-related internships or fieldwork, Federal Work-Study, scholarships/grants, tuition waivers (partial), and unspecified assistantships also available. Support available to part-time students. Financial award application deadline: 3/1; financial award applicants required to submit FAFSA. *Faculty research:* Formal methods, database systems, parallel programming environments, computer security, software tools. *Total annual research expenditures:* $2 million. *Unit head:* Dr. Warren Harrison, Chair, 503-725-3108, Fax: 503-725-3211, E-mail: warren@cs.pdx.edu. *Application contact:* Sara Smith, Graduate Coordinator, 503-725-4036, Fax: 503-725-3211, E-mail: gc@cs.pdx.edu.
Website: http://www.pdx.edu/computer-science/.

Regis University, College for Professional Studies, School of Computer and Information Sciences, Denver, CO 80221-1099. Offers database development (Certificate); enterprise Java software development (Certificate); enterprise resource planning (Certificate); executive information technology (Certificate); information assurance (M Sc); information technology management (M Sc); software engineering (Certificate); software engineering and database technologies (M Sc); storage area networks (Certificate); systems engineering (M Sc, Certificate). Part-time and evening/weekend programs available. Postbaccalaureate distance learning degree programs offered (no on-campus study). *Faculty:* 8 full-time (3 women), 46 part-time/adjunct (9 women). *Students:* 254 full-time (69 women), 221 part-time (59 women); includes 159 minority (57 Black or African American, non-Hispanic/Latino; 4 American Indian or Alaska Native, non-Hispanic/Latino; 39 Asian, non-Hispanic/Latino; 49 Hispanic/Latino; 1 Native Hawaiian or other Pacific Islander, non-Hispanic/Latino; 9 Two or more races, non-Hispanic/Latino), 22 international. Average age 38. 204 applicants, 87% accepted, 128 enrolled. In 2014, 176 master's awarded. *Degree requirements:* For master's, thesis (for some programs), final research project. *Entrance requirements:* For master's, official transcript reflecting baccalaureate degree awarded from regionally-accredited college or university, 2 years of related experience, resume, interview. Additional exam requirements/recommendations for international students: Required—TOEFL (minimum score 550 paper-based; 82 iBT). *Application deadline:* For fall admission, 8/13 for domestic students, 7/13 for international students; for winter admission, 10/8 for domestic students, 9/8 for international students; for spring admission, 12/17 for domestic students, 11/17 for international students. Applications are processed on a rolling basis. Application fee: $75. Electronic applications accepted. *Expenses:* Expenses: $710 per credit hour (for M Sc). *Financial support:* In 2014–15, 16 students received support. Federal Work-Study and scholarships/grants available. Financial award application deadline: 4/15; financial award applicants required to submit FAFSA. *Faculty research:* Information policy, knowledge management, software architectures. *Unit head:* Donald Archer, Interim Dean, 303-458-4335, E-mail: archer@regis.edu. *Application contact:* Sarah Engel, Director of Admissions, 303-458-4900, Fax: 303-964-5534, E-mail: regisadm@regis.edu.
Website: http://regis.edu/CCIS.aspx.

Rochester Institute of Technology, Graduate Enrollment Services, Golisano College of Computing and Information Sciences, Software Engineering Department, MS Program in Software Engineering, Rochester, NY 14623-5608. Offers MS. Part-time programs available. *Students:* 41 full-time (12 women), 10 part-time (1 woman); includes 1 minority (Asian, non-Hispanic/Latino), 41 international. Average age 26. 114 applicants, 59% accepted, 22 enrolled. In 2014, 6 master's awarded. *Degree requirements:* For master's, thesis or alternative. *Entrance requirements:* For master's,

GRE and TOEFL, IELTS, or PTE for non-native English speakers, Recommended minimum GPA of 3.0. Additional exam requirements/recommendations for international students: Required—PTE (minimum score 58), TOEFL (minimum score 550 paper-based; 79 iBT) or IELTS (minimum score 6.5). *Application deadline:* For fall admission, 2/15 priority date for domestic and international students; for spring admission, 12/15 priority date for domestic and international students. Applications are processed on a rolling basis. Application fee: $60. Electronic applications accepted. *Expenses:* Expenses: $1,673 per credit hour. *Financial support:* In 2014–15, 14 students received support. Research assistantships with partial tuition reimbursements available, teaching assistantships with partial tuition reimbursements available, career-related internships or fieldwork, Federal Work-Study, institutionally sponsored loans, scholarships/grants, and unspecified assistantships available. Support available to part-time students. Financial award application deadline: 4/15; financial award applicants required to submit FAFSA. *Faculty research:* Software engineering education, software architecture and design, architectural styles and design patterns, mathematical foundations of software engineering, object-oriented software development, augmented and virtual reality systems, engineering of real-time and embedded software systems, concurrent systems, distributed systems, data communications and networking, programming environments and tools, computer graphics, computer vision. *Unit head:* Dr. Stephanie Ludi, Graduate Program Director, 585-475-7407, E-mail: segrad@se.rit.edu. *Application contact:* Diane Ellison, Associate Vice President, Graduate Enrollment Services, 585-475-2229, Fax: 585-475-7164, E-mail: gradinfo@rit.edu.
Website: http://www.se.rit.edu/.

Rose-Hulman Institute of Technology, Faculty of Engineering and Applied Sciences, Department of Computer Science and Software Engineering, Terre Haute, IN 47803-3999. Offers software engineering (MS). Part-time programs available. *Faculty:* 16 full-time (0 women). *Students:* 3 part-time (0 women). Average age 36. 6 applicants, 83% accepted, 1 enrolled. In 2014, 1 master's awarded. *Degree requirements:* For master's, thesis. *Entrance requirements:* For master's, GRE, minimum GPA of 3.0. Additional exam requirements/recommendations for international students: Required—TOEFL (minimum score 580 paper-based; 92 iBT). *Application deadline:* For fall admission, 2/1 priority date for domestic students. Applications are processed on a rolling basis. Application fee: $0. *Expenses:* Tuition: Full-time $40,449. *Financial support:* Fellowships with full and partial tuition reimbursements, research assistantships with full and partial tuition reimbursements, and tuition waivers (full and partial) available. *Faculty research:* Software architecture, software project management, programming languages, database systems, computer graphics. *Total annual research expenditures:* $18,259. *Unit head:* Dr. Cary Laxer, Chairman, 812-877-8429, Fax: 812-872-6060, E-mail: laxer@rose-hulman.edu. *Application contact:* Dr. Azad Siahmakoun, Associate Dean of the Faculty, 812-877-8400, Fax: 812-877-8061, E-mail: siahmako@rose-hulman.edu.
Website: http://www.rose-hulman.edu/academics/academic-departments/computer-science-software-engineering.aspx.

Royal Military College of Canada, Division of Graduate Studies and Research, Engineering Division, Department of Electrical and Computer Engineering, Kingston, ON K7K 7B4, Canada. Offers computer engineering (M Eng, PhD); electrical engineering (M Eng, PhD); software engineering (M Eng, PhD). *Degree requirements:* For master's, thesis; for doctorate, comprehensive exam, thesis/dissertation. *Entrance requirements:* For master's, honours degree with second-class standing in the appropriate field; for doctorate, master's degree. Electronic applications accepted.

St. Mary's University, Graduate School, Department of Engineering, Program in Software Engineering, San Antonio, TX 78228-8507. Offers MS. Part-time programs available. *Faculty:* 1 full-time (0 women), 2 part-time/adjunct (0 women). *Students:* 3 full-time (0 women), 6 part-time (2 women); includes 2 minority (both Hispanic/Latino), 3 international. Average age 30. 6 applicants, 17% accepted. In 2014, 2 master's awarded. *Degree requirements:* For master's, comprehensive exam. *Entrance requirements:* For master's, GRE, Have a bachelor's degree in Software Engineering, Computer Science, Computer Engineering or a closely related discipline. Have a minimum Grade Point Average (GPA) of 3.00 (A = 4.00) for their bachelor's degrees. Have a minimum GRE quantitative score of 148. Additional exam requirements/recommendations for international students: Required—TOEFL (minimum score 550 paper-based; 80 iBT), IELTS (minimum score 6.5). *Application deadline:* Applications are processed on a rolling basis. Application fee: $0. Electronic applications accepted. *Expenses:* Tuition: Full-time $15,070; part-time $800 per credit hour. *Required fees:* $156 per semester. *Financial support:* Career-related internships or fieldwork, Federal Work-Study, institutionally sponsored loans, scholarships/grants, and health care benefits available. Financial award application deadline: 3/31; financial award applicants required to submit FAFSA. *Unit head:* Dr. Djaffer Ibaroudene, Director, 210-431-2050, E-mail: dibaroudene@stmarytx.edu.
Website: https://www.stmarytx.edu/academics/set/graduate/software-engineering/.

San Jose State University, Graduate Studies and Research, Charles W. Davidson College of Engineering, Department of Computer Engineering, San Jose, CA 95192-0001. Offers computer engineering (MS); software engineering (MS). *Degree requirements:* For master's, comprehensive exam, thesis. *Entrance requirements:* For master's, GRE General Test. Electronic applications accepted. *Faculty research:* Robotics, database management systems, computer networks.

Santa Clara University, School of Engineering, Santa Clara, CA 95053. Offers analog circuit design (Certificate); applied mathematics (MS); ASIC design and test (Certificate); bioengineering (MS); civil engineering (MS); computer science and engineering (MS, PhD); controls (Certificate); digital signal processing (Certificate); dynamics (Certificate); electrical engineering (MS, PhD); engineering (Engineer); engineering management (MS); fundamentals of electrical engineering (Certificate); information assurance (Certificate); materials engineering (Certificate); mechanical design analysis (Certificate); mechanical engineering (MS, PhD); mechatronics systems engineering (Certificate); microwave and antennas (Certificate); networking (Certificate); renewable energy (Certificate); software engineering (Certificate); sustainable energy (MS); technology jump-start (Certificate); thermofluids (Certificate). Part-time and evening/weekend programs available. *Faculty:* 59 full-time (23 women), 80 part-time/adjunct (14 women). *Students:* 584 full-time (239 women), 353 part-time (102 women); includes 224 minority (7 Black or African American, non-Hispanic/Latino; 144 Asian, non-Hispanic/Latino; 50 Hispanic/Latino; 2 Native Hawaiian or other Pacific Islander, non-Hispanic/Latino; 21 Two or more races, non-Hispanic/Latino), 548 international. Average age 27. 1,248 applicants, 51% accepted, 375 enrolled. In 2014, 283 master's, 5 doctorates, 1 other advanced degree awarded. *Degree requirements:* For master's, thesis (for some programs); for doctorate, thesis/dissertation; for other advanced degree, thesis. *Entrance requirements:* For master's, GRE, transcript; for doctorate, GRE, master's degree or equivalent; for other advanced degree, master's degree, published paper. Additional exam requirements/recommendations for international students: Required—TOEFL (minimum score 550 paper-based; 79 iBT). *Application deadline:* For fall admission, 8/1 for domestic students, 7/15 for international students; for winter admission, 10/28 for domestic students, 9/23 for international students; for spring admission, 2/25 for domestic students, 1/21 for international students. Applications are processed on a rolling basis. Application fee: $60. Electronic

applications accepted. *Expenses:* Expenses: Contact institution. *Financial support:* In 2014–15, 94 students received support. Fellowships with full and partial tuition reimbursements available, research assistantships with full and partial tuition reimbursements available, teaching assistantships with full tuition reimbursements available, career-related internships or fieldwork, Federal Work-Study, institutionally sponsored loans, and scholarships/grants available. Support available to part-time students. Financial award application deadline: 3/2; financial award applicants required to submit FAFSA. *Faculty research:* Video encoding, nanostructures, robotics, microfluidics, water resources. *Total annual research expenditures:* $1.6 million. *Unit head:* Dr. Alex Zecevic, Associate Dean for Graduate Studies, 408-554-2394, E-mail: azecevic@scu.edu. *Application contact:* Stacey Tinker, Director of Enrollment Management, 408-554-4748, Fax: 408-554-4323, E-mail: stinker@scu.edu.
Website: http://www.scu.edu/engineering/graduate/.

Seattle University, College of Science and Engineering, Program in Software Engineering, Seattle, WA 98122-1090. Offers MSE. Part-time and evening/weekend programs available. *Faculty:* 8 full-time (3 women), 2 part-time/adjunct (0 women). *Students:* 10 full-time (all women), 14 part-time (5 women); includes 7 minority (6 Asian, non-Hispanic/Latino; 1 Hispanic/Latino), 9 international. Average age 32. 13 applicants, 38% accepted, 4 enrolled. In 2014, 11 master's awarded. *Degree requirements:* For master's, thesis. *Entrance requirements:* For master's, GRE General Test, minimum GPA of 3.0; 2 years of related work experience; letter noting working knowledge of at least one programming language, such as C++, Java or C#; professional autobiography; 2 recommendations. Additional exam requirements/recommendations for international students: Required—TOEFL (minimum score 580 paper-based). *Application deadline:* For fall admission, 7/20 for domestic students, 4/1 for international students; for winter admission, 11/20 for domestic students, 9/1 for international students; for spring admission, 2/20 for domestic students, 12/1 for international students. Application fee: $55. Electronic applications accepted. *Financial support:* In 2014–15, 3 students received support. Career-related internships or fieldwork and Federal Work-Study available. Support available to part-time students. Financial award applicants required to submit FAFSA. *Unit head:* Dr. Richard LeBlanc, Chair, 206-296-5510, Fax: 206-296-5518, E-mail: leblanc@seattleu.edu. *Application contact:* Janet Shandley, Associate Dean of Graduate Admissions, 206-296-5900, Fax: 206-298-5656, E-mail: grad_admissions@seattleu.edu.
Website: http://www.seattleu.edu/scieng/comsci/Default.aspx?id-59076.

Southern Methodist University, Bobby B. Lyle School of Engineering, Department of Computer Science and Engineering, Dallas, TX 75275-0122. Offers computer engineering (MS, PhD); computer science (MS, PhD); security engineering (MS); software engineering (MS, DE). Part-time and evening/weekend programs available. Postbaccalaureate distance learning degree programs offered (no on-campus study). Terminal master's awarded for partial completion of doctoral program. *Degree requirements:* For master's, thesis optional; for doctorate, thesis/dissertation, oral and written qualifying exams, oral final exam (PhD). *Entrance requirements:* For master's, GRE General Test, minimum GPA of 3.0 in last 2 years; bachelor's degree in engineering, mathematics, or sciences; for doctorate, preliminary counseling exam (PhD), minimum GPA of 3.0, bachelor's degree in related field, MA (for DE). Additional exam requirements/recommendations for international students: Required—TOEFL (minimum score 550 paper-based). *Faculty research:* Trusted and high performance network computing, software engineering and management, knowledge engineering and management, computer arithmetic, computer architecture and CAD.

Southern Polytechnic State University, School of Computing and Software Engineering, Department of Computer Science and Software Engineering, Marietta, GA 30060-2896. Offers computer science (MS, Graduate Transition Certificate); software engineering (MSSWE, Graduate Certificate); software engineering fundamentals (Postbaccalaureate Certificate). Part-time and evening/weekend programs available. Postbaccalaureate distance learning degree programs offered (no on-campus study). *Degree requirements:* For master's, thesis optional, capstone (software engineering). *Entrance requirements:* For master's, GRE (recommended). Additional exam requirements/recommendations for international students: Required—TOEFL (minimum score 550 paper-based; 79 iBT), IELTS (minimum score 6.5). Electronic applications accepted. *Faculty research:* Image processing and artificial intelligence, distributed computing, telemedicine applications, enterprise architectures, databases, software requirements engineering, software quality and metrics, usability, parallel and distributed computing, information security.

Stevens Institute of Technology, Graduate School, Charles V. Schaefer Jr. School of Engineering, Department of Computer Science, Hoboken, NJ 07030. Offers computer graphics (Certificate); computer science (MS, PhD); computer systems (Certificate); database management systems (Certificate); distributed systems (Certificate); elements of computer science (Certificate); enterprise computing (Certificate); enterprise security and information assurance (Certificate); health informatics (Certificate); multimedia experience and management (Certificate); networks and systems administration (Certificate); security and privacy (Certificate); service oriented computing (Certificate); software design (Certificate); theoretical computer science (Certificate). Part-time and evening/weekend programs available. Terminal master's awarded for partial completion of doctoral program. *Degree requirements:* For master's, thesis optional; for doctorate, variable foreign language requirement, comprehensive exam, thesis/dissertation. *Entrance requirements:* For master's and doctorate, GRE, minimum GPA of 3.0. Additional exam requirements/recommendations for international students: Required—TOEFL. Electronic applications accepted. *Faculty research:* Semantics, reliability theory, programming language, cyber security.

Stevens Institute of Technology, Graduate School, School of Systems and Enterprises, Program in Software Engineering, Hoboken, NJ 07030. Offers MS. *Entrance requirements:* Additional exam requirements/recommendations for international students: Required—TOEFL.

Stony Brook University, State University of New York, Graduate School, College of Engineering and Applied Sciences, Department of Computer Science, Stony Brook, NY 11794. Offers computer science (MS, PhD); information systems (Certificate); information systems engineering (MS); software engineering (Certificate). *Faculty:* 46 full-time (8 women), 1 part-time/adjunct (0 women). *Students:* 417 full-time (79 women), 76 part-time (13 women); includes 22 minority (1 Black or African American, non-Hispanic/Latino; 18 Asian, non-Hispanic/Latino; 3 Hispanic/Latino), 450 international. Average age 25. 2,476 applicants, 23% accepted, 214 enrolled. In 2014, 131 master's, 15 doctorates awarded. *Degree requirements:* For master's, thesis or alternative; for doctorate, comprehensive exam, thesis/dissertation. *Entrance requirements:* For master's and doctorate, GRE General Test. Additional exam requirements/recommendations for international students: Required—TOEFL. *Application deadline:* For fall admission, 1/15 for domestic students; for spring admission, 10/1 for domestic students. Application fee: $100. *Expenses:* Tuition, state resident: full-time $10,370; part-time $432 per credit. Tuition, nonresident: full-time $20,190; part-time $841 per credit. *Required fees:* $1431. *Financial support:* In 2014–15, 12 fellowships, 92 research assistantships, 46 teaching assistantships were awarded. *Faculty research:* Artificial intelligence, computer architecture, database management systems, VLSI, operating systems. *Total annual research expenditures:* $6.6 million. *Unit head:* Prof. Arie Kauffman, Chairman, 631-632-8428, Fax: 631-632-8334, E-mail: arie.kaufman@stonybrook.edu. *Application contact:* Cynthia Scalzo, Coordinator, 631-632-1521, Fax: 631-632-8334, E-mail: graduate@cs.stonybrook.edu.
Website: http://www.cs.sunysb.edu/.

Stratford University, School of Graduate Studies, Falls Church, VA 22043. Offers accounting (MS); business administration (IMBA, MBA); enterprise business management (MS); entrepreneurial management (MS); information assurance (MS); information systems (MS); software engineering (MS); telecommunications (MS). Part-time and evening/weekend programs available. Postbaccalaureate distance learning degree programs offered (no on-campus study). *Degree requirements:* For master's, comprehensive exam, capstone project. *Entrance requirements:* For master's, GRE or GMAT, baccalaureate degree. Additional exam requirements/recommendations for international students: Required—TOEFL (minimum score 79 iBT) or IELTS (6.5). Electronic applications accepted.

Strayer University, Graduate Studies, Washington, DC 20005-2603. Offers accounting (MS); acquisition (MBA); business administration (MBA); communications technology (MS); educational management (M Ed); finance (MBA); health services administration (MHSA); hospitality and tourism management (MBA); human resource management (MBA); information systems (MS), including computer security management, decision support system management, enterprise resource management, network management, software engineering management, systems development management; management (MBA); management information systems (MS); marketing (MBA); professional accounting (MS), including accounting information systems, controllership, taxation; public administration (MPA); supply chain management (MBA); technology in education (M Ed). Programs also offered at campus locations in Birmingham, AL; Chamblee, GA; Cobb County, GA; Morrow, GA; White Marsh, MD; Charleston, SC; Columbia, SC; Greensboro, NC; Greenville, SC; Lexington, KY; Louisville, KY; Nashville, TN; North Raleigh, NC; Washington, DC. Part-time and evening/weekend programs available. Postbaccalaureate distance learning degree programs offered (minimal on-campus study). *Degree requirements:* For master's, thesis. *Entrance requirements:* For master's, GMAT, GRE General Test, bachelor's degree from an accredited college or university, minimum undergraduate GPA of 2.75. Electronic applications accepted.

Tennessee Technological University, College of Graduate Studies, College of Engineering, Department of Computer Science, Cookeville, TN 38505. Offers computer software and scientific applications (MS); Internet-based computing (MS). Part-time programs available. *Students:* 8 full-time (0 women), 6 part-time (1 woman), 6 international. 125 applicants, 10% accepted, 7 enrolled. In 2014, 8 master's awarded. *Degree requirements:* For master's, thesis or alternative. *Entrance requirements:* For master's, GRE. Additional exam requirements/recommendations for international students: Required—TOEFL (minimum score 550 paper-based; 79 iBT), IELTS (minimum score 5.5), PTE (minimum score 53), or TOEIC (Test of English as an International Communication). *Application deadline:* For fall admission, 8/1 for domestic students, 5/1 for international students; for spring admission, 12/1 for domestic students, 10/1 for international students. Applications are processed on a rolling basis. Application fee: $35 ($40 for international students). Electronic applications accepted. *Expenses:* Tuition, state resident: full-time $9783; part-time $492 per credit hour. Tuition, nonresident: full-time $24,071; part-time $1179 per credit hour. *Financial support:* In 2014–15, 4 research assistantships (averaging $7,500 per year), 3 teaching assistantships (averaging $7,500 per year) were awarded. Financial award application deadline: 4/1. *Unit head:* Dr. Doug Talbert, Interim Chairperson, 931-372-3691, Fax: 931-372-3686, E-mail: dtalbert@tntech.edu. *Application contact:* Shelia K. Kendrick, Coordinator of Graduate Studies, 931-372-3808, Fax: 931-372-3497, E-mail: skendrick@tntech.edu.

Texas State University, The Graduate College, College of Science and Engineering, Department of Computer Science, Program in Software Engineering, San Marcos, TX 78666. Offers MS. *Faculty:* 4 full-time (1 woman). *Students:* 9 full-time (3 women), 5 part-time (0 women), 8 international. Average age 27. 23 applicants, 48% accepted, 6 enrolled. In 2014, 4 master's awarded. *Degree requirements:* For master's, comprehensive exam, thesis (for some programs). *Entrance requirements:* For master's, GRE General Test (preferred minimum score of 286 with no less than 140 on the verbal section and 148 on the quantitative section), baccalaureate degree from regionally-accredited university with minimum GPA of 2.75 on last 60 undergraduate semester hours. Additional exam requirements/recommendations for international students: Required—TOEFL (minimum score 550 paper-based; 78 iBT). *Application deadline:* For fall admission, 2/15 priority date for domestic and international students; for spring admission, 10/15 for domestic students, 10/1 for international students; for summer admission, 4/15 for domestic students, 3/15 for international students. Applications are processed on a rolling basis. Application fee: $40 ($90 for international students). Electronic applications accepted. *Expenses:* Expenses: $8,834 (tuition and fees combined). *Financial support:* In 2014–15, 4 students received support, including 1 teaching assistantship (averaging $12,464 per year); research assistantships, Federal Work-Study, institutionally sponsored loans, scholarships/grants, health care benefits, and unspecified assistantships also available. Support available to part-time students. Financial award application deadline: 4/1; financial award applicants required to submit FAFSA. *Unit head:* Dr. Wuxu Peng, Graduate Advisor, 512-245-3874, Fax: 512-245-8750, E-mail: wp01@txstate.edu. *Application contact:* Dr. Andrea Golato, Dean of the Graduate College, 512-245-2581, E-mail: gradcollege@txstate.edu.
Website: http://www.gradcollege.txstate.edu/soen.html.

Texas Tech University, Graduate School, Edward E. Whitacre Jr. College of Engineering, Department of Computer Science, Lubbock, TX 79409-3104. Offers computer science (MS, PhD); software engineering (MS). Part-time programs available. Postbaccalaureate distance learning degree programs offered (minimal on-campus study). *Faculty:* 16 full-time (3 women). *Students:* 97 full-time (26 women), 33 part-time (6 women); includes 6 minority (1 Asian, non-Hispanic/Latino; 4 Hispanic/Latino; 1 Two or more races, non-Hispanic/Latino), 95 international. Average age 27. 451 applicants, 47% accepted, 53 enrolled. In 2014, 23 master's, 6 doctorates awarded. Terminal master's awarded for partial completion of doctoral program. *Degree requirements:* For master's, comprehensive exam, thesis (for some programs); for doctorate, comprehensive exam, thesis/dissertation. *Entrance requirements:* For master's and doctorate, GRE (Verbal and Quantitative). Additional exam requirements/recommendations for international students: Required—TOEFL (minimum score 550 paper-based; 79 iBT). *Application deadline:* For fall admission, 6/1 priority date for domestic students, 1/15 priority date for international students; for spring admission, 9/1 priority date for domestic students, 6/15 priority date for international students. Applications are processed on a rolling basis. Application fee: $60. Electronic applications accepted. *Expenses:* Tuition, state resident: full-time $6310; part-time $262.92 per credit hour. Tuition, nonresident: full-time $14,998; part-time $624.92 per credit hour. *Required fees:* $2701; $36.50 per credit. $912.50 per semester. Tuition and fees vary according to course load. *Financial support:* In 2014–15, 58 students received support, including 58 fellowships (averaging $1,818 per year), 1 research assistantship (averaging $26,004 per year), 11 teaching assistantships (averaging $20,625 per year); scholarships/grants, tuition waivers (partial), and unspecified assistantships also available. Financial award application deadline: 4/15; financial award applicants required to submit FAFSA. *Faculty research:* High performance and parallel computing; cyber security and data science; software engineering (quality assurance, testing, design specification); artificial intelligence (intelligent systems, knowledge representation); mobile and computer networks. *Total annual research expenditures:* $748,066. *Unit head:* Dr. Rattikorn Hewett, Professor and Chair, 806-742-3527, Fax: 806-742-3519, E-mail: rattikorn.hewett@ttu.edu. *Application contact:* Jessica Lunsford, Staff Graduate Advisor, 806-742-3527, Fax: 806-742-3519, E-mail: jessica.lunsford@ttu.edu. Website: http://www.cs.ttu.edu/.

Towson University, Program in Applied Information Technology, Towson, MD 21252-0001. Offers applied information technology (MS, D Sc); database management systems (Postbaccalaureate Certificate); information security and assurance (Postbaccalaureate Certificate); information systems management (Postbaccalaureate Certificate); Internet applications development (Postbaccalaureate Certificate); networking technologies (Postbaccalaureate Certificate); software engineering (Postbaccalaureate Certificate). *Students:* 132 full-time (44 women), 219 part-time (73 women); includes 118 minority (71 Black or African American, non-Hispanic/Latino; 1 American Indian or Alaska Native, non-Hispanic/Latino; 23 Asian, non-Hispanic/Latino; 12 Hispanic/Latino; 2 Native Hawaiian or other Pacific Islander, non-Hispanic/Latino; 9 Two or more races, non-Hispanic/Latino), 85 international. *Entrance requirements:* For master's and Postbaccalaureate Certificate, bachelor's degree, minimum GPA of 3.0; for doctorate, master's degree in computer science, information systems, information technology, or closely-related areas; minimum GPA of 3.0; 2 letters of recommendation; resume. Additional exam requirements/recommendations for international students: Required—TOEFL. *Application deadline:* Applications are processed on a rolling basis. Application fee: $45. Electronic applications accepted. *Unit head:* Dr. Suranjan Chakraborty, Graduate Program Director, 410-704-4769, E-mail: schakraborty@towson.edu. *Application contact:* Alicia Arkell-Kleis, Information Contact, 410-704-6004, E-mail: grads@towson.edu. Website: http://grad.towson.edu/program/master/ait-ms/.

Université Laval, Faculty of Sciences and Engineering, Program in Software Engineering, Québec, QC G1K 7P4, Canada. Offers Diploma. Part-time programs available. *Entrance requirements:* For degree, knowledge of French. Electronic applications accepted.

The University of Alabama in Huntsville, School of Graduate Studies, College of Engineering, Department of Electrical and Computer Engineering, Huntsville, AL 35899. Offers computer engineering (MSE, PhD); electrical engineering (MSE, PhD), including optics and photonics technology (MSE), opto-electronics (MSE); information assurance (MS); optical science and engineering (PhD); optics and photonics (MSE); software engineering (MSSE). Part-time and evening/weekend programs available. *Degree requirements:* For master's, comprehensive exam, thesis or alternative, oral and written exams; for doctorate, comprehensive exam, thesis/dissertation, oral and written exams. *Entrance requirements:* For master's, GRE General Test, appropriate bachelor's degree, minimum GPA of 3.0; for doctorate, GRE General Test, minimum GPA of 3.0. Additional exam requirements/recommendations for international students: Required—TOEFL (minimum score 500 paper-based; 80 iBT), IELTS (minimum score 6.5). Electronic applications accepted. *Faculty research:* Advanced computer architecture and systems, fault tolerant computing and verification, computational electro-magnetics, nano-photonics and plasmonics, micro electro-mechanical (MEMS) systems.

The University of Alabama in Huntsville, School of Graduate Studies, College of Science, Department of Computer Science, Huntsville, AL 35899. Offers computer science (MS, PhD); information assurance (MS); modeling and simulation (MS, PhD); software engineering (MSSE, Certificate). Part-time and evening/weekend programs available. Postbaccalaureate distance learning degree programs offered (minimal on-campus study). *Degree requirements:* For master's, comprehensive exam, thesis or alternative, oral and written exams; for doctorate, comprehensive exam, thesis/dissertation, oral and written exams. *Entrance requirements:* For master's, doctorate, and Certificate, GRE General Test, minimum GPA of 3.0. Additional exam requirements/recommendations for international students: Required—TOEFL (minimum score 550 paper-based; 80 iBT), IELTS (minimum score 6.5). Electronic applications accepted. *Faculty research:* Information assurance and cyber security, modeling and simulation, data science, computer graphics and visualization, multimedia systems.

The University of British Columbia, Faculty of Applied Science, Program in Software Systems, Vancouver, BC V6T 1Z1, Canada. Offers MSS. *Degree requirements:* For master's, internship. *Entrance requirements:* For master's, bachelor's degree in science, engineering, business or technology (non-computer science). Additional exam requirements/recommendations for international students: Required—TOEFL (minimum score 600 paper-based; 100 iBT), IELTS (minimum score 6.5). Electronic applications accepted. *Expenses:* Contact institution.

University of Calgary, Faculty of Graduate Studies, Faculty of Science, Department of Computer Science, Calgary, AB T2N 1N4, Canada. Offers computer science (M Sc, PhD); software engineering (M Sc). Part-time programs available. *Degree requirements:* For master's, comprehensive exam (for some programs), thesis (for some programs); for doctorate, thesis/dissertation, oral and written departmental exam. *Entrance requirements:* For master's, bachelor's degree in computer science; for doctorate, M Sc in computer science. Additional exam requirements/recommendations for international students: Required—TOEFL (minimum score 600 paper-based); Recommended—TWE. Electronic applications accepted. *Faculty research:* Visual and interactive computing, quantum computing and cryptography, evolutionary software engineering, distributed systems and algorithms.

University of Colorado Colorado Springs, College of Engineering and Applied Science, Program in General Engineering, Colorado Springs, CO 80933-7150. Offers energy engineering (ME); engineering management (ME); information assurance (ME); software engineering (ME); space operations (ME); systems engineering (ME). Part-time and evening/weekend programs available. Postbaccalaureate distance learning degree programs offered (minimal on-campus study). *Faculty:* 2 full-time (0 women), 8 part-time/adjunct (2 women). *Students:* 15 full-time (2 women), 159 part-time (30 women); includes 29 minority (3 Black or African American, non-Hispanic/Latino; 1 American Indian or Alaska Native, non-Hispanic/Latino; 10 Asian, non-Hispanic/Latino; 12 Hispanic/Latino; 3 Two or more races, non-Hispanic/Latino), 63 international. Average age 36. 113 applicants, 65% accepted, 39 enrolled. In 2014, 29 master's, 6 doctorates awarded. *Degree requirements:* For master's, thesis, portfolio, or project; for doctorate, comprehensive exam, thesis/dissertation. *Entrance requirements:* For master's, GRE (minimum score of 148 new grading scale on quantitative portion if GPA is less than 3.0); for doctorate, GRE (minimum score of 148 new grading scale on the quantitative portion if the applicant has not graduated from a program of recognized standing), minimum GPA of 3.3 in the bachelor or master degree program attempted. Additional exam requirements/recommendations for international students: Required—TOEFL (minimum score 80 iBT), IELTS (minimum score 6). *Application deadline:* For fall admission, 6/1 for domestic and international students; for spring admission, 11/1 for domestic and international students; for summer admission, 4/15 for domestic and international students. Application fee: $60 ($100 for international students). Electronic applications accepted. *Expenses:* Expenses: Contact institution. *Financial support:* In 2014–15, 10 students received support, including 2 fellowships (averaging $6,000 per year), 16 research assistantships (averaging $11,600 per year); teaching assistantships, Federal Work-Study, and scholarships/grants also available. Support available to part-time students. Financial award application deadline: 3/1; financial award applicants required to submit FAFSA. *Total annual research expenditures:* $91,458. *Unit head:* Dr. Ramaswami Dandapani, Dean, 719-255-3543, Fax: 719-255-3542, E-mail: rdan@cas.uccs.edu. *Application contact:* Dawn House, Coordinator, 719-255-3246, E-mail: dhouse@uccs.edu.

University of Connecticut, Graduate School, School of Engineering, Department of Computer Science and Engineering, Storrs, CT 06269. Offers computer science (MS, PhD), including artificial intelligence, computer architecture, computer science, operating systems, robotics, software engineering. Terminal master's awarded for partial completion of doctoral program. *Degree requirements:* For master's, comprehensive exam, thesis or alternative; for doctorate, thesis/dissertation. *Entrance requirements:* For master's and doctorate, GRE General Test. Additional exam requirements/recommendations for international students: Required—TOEFL (minimum score 550 paper-based). Electronic applications accepted.

University of Denver, University College, Denver, CO 80208. Offers geographic information systems (Certificate); global affairs (Certificate), including translation studies, world history and culture; information and communications technology (MCIS), including geographic information systems, information systems security, project management (MCIS, Certificate), software design and programming, technology management, telecommunications technology, Web design and development; leadership and organizations (Certificate), including human capital in organizations, philanthropic leadership, project management (MCIS, Certificate), strategic innovation and change; organizational and professional communication (MPS), including alternative dispute resolution, organizational communication, organizational development and training, public relations and marketing; security management (MAS, Certificate), including emergency planning and response, information security (MAS), organizational security. Part-time and evening/weekend programs available. Postbaccalaureate distance learning degree programs offered (no on-campus study). *Faculty:* 8 full-time (4 women), 133 part-time/adjunct (46 women). *Students:* 54 full-time (21 women), 1,327 part-time (775 women); includes 272 minority (106 Black or African American, non-Hispanic/Latino; 6 American Indian or Alaska Native, non-Hispanic/Latino; 26 Asian, non-Hispanic/Latino; 108 Hispanic/Latino; 1 Native Hawaiian or other Pacific Islander, non-Hispanic/Latino; 25 Two or more races, non-Hispanic/Latino), 116 international. Average age 35. 768 applicants, 95% accepted, 620 enrolled. In 2014, 391 master's, 196 other advanced degrees awarded. *Degree requirements:* For master's, capstone project. *Entrance requirements:* For master's, transcripts, two letters of recommendation, personal statement, resume. Additional exam requirements/recommendations for international students: Required—TOEFL (minimum score 550 paper-based; 80 iBT). *Application deadline:* For fall admission, 6/21 priority date for domestic students, 5/1 priority date for international students; for winter admission, 9/14 priority date for domestic students, 9/19 priority date for international students; for spring admission, 1/11 for domestic students, 12/12 for international students; for summer admission, 3/29 priority date for domestic students, 3/6 priority date for international students. Applications are processed on a rolling basis. Application fee: $75. Electronic applications accepted. *Expenses:* Expenses: $959 per credit hour. *Financial support:* In 2014–15, 19 students received support. Applicants required to submit FAFSA. *Unit head:* Dr. Michael McGuire, Interim Dean, 303-871-3518, E-mail: mmcguire@du.edu. *Application contact:* Information Contact, 303-871-2291, E-mail: ucoladm@du.edu. Website: http://www.universitycollege.du.edu/.

University of Detroit Mercy, College of Engineering and Science, Department of Mathematics and Computer Science, Program in Computer Science, Detroit, MI 48221. Offers computer systems applications (MSCS); software engineering (MSCS). Evening/weekend programs available. *Entrance requirements:* For master's, minimum GPA of 3.0.

University of Houston–Clear Lake, School of Science and Computer Engineering, Program in Software Engineering, Houston, TX 77058-1002. Offers MS. Part-time and evening/weekend programs available. *Entrance requirements:* For master's, GRE General Test. Additional exam requirements/recommendations for international students: Required—TOEFL (minimum score 550 paper-based).

University of Management and Technology, Program in Computer Science, Arlington, VA 22209. Offers computer science (MS); information technology (AC); project management (AC); software engineering (MS). Part-time and evening/weekend programs available. Postbaccalaureate distance learning degree programs offered (no on-campus study). *Entrance requirements:* For master's, 3 recommendations, resume. Additional exam requirements/recommendations for international students: Required—TOEFL (minimum score 530 paper-based; 71 iBT). Electronic applications accepted.

University of Michigan–Dearborn, College of Engineering and Computer Science, Master of Science in Software Engineering Program, Dearborn, MI 48128. Offers MS. Part-time and evening/weekend programs available. Postbaccalaureate distance learning degree programs offered (no on-campus study). *Faculty:* 20 full-time (1 woman), 6 part-time/adjunct (0 women). *Students:* 8 full-time (3 women), 16 part-time (4 women); includes 3 minority (2 Asian, non-Hispanic/Latino; 1 Two or more races, non-Hispanic/Latino), 10 international. 25 applicants, 60% accepted, 8 enrolled. In 2014, 3 master's awarded. *Degree requirements:* For master's, thesis optional. *Entrance requirements:* For master's, bachelor's degree in mathematics, computer science or engineering, minimum GPA of 3.0. Additional exam requirements/recommendations for international students: Required—TOEFL (minimum score 560 paper-based; 84 iBT), IELTS (minimum score 6.5). *Application deadline:* For fall admission, 8/1 priority date for domestic students, 5/1 priority date for international students; for winter admission, 12/1 priority date for domestic students, 9/1 priority date for international students; for spring admission, 4/1 priority date for domestic students, 1/1 priority date for international students. Applications are processed on a rolling basis. Application fee: $60. Electronic applications accepted. *Expenses:* Tuition, state resident: full-time $12,202; part-time $707 per credit hour. Tuition, nonresident: full-time $20,980; part-time $1209 per credit hour. *Required fees:* $798; $302 per term. Tuition and fees vary according to course level, course load, degree level and program. *Financial support:* In 2014–15, 5 students received support, including 2 research assistantships (averaging $14,228 per year), 1 teaching assistantship (averaging $14,228 per year); scholarships/grants, health care benefits, and unspecified assistantships also available. Support available to part-time students. Financial award applicants required to submit FAFSA. *Faculty research:* Information systems, geometric modeling, networks, databases, data science, analytics, security, applied cryptography. *Unit head:* Dr. William I. Grosky, Chair, 313-583-6424, Fax: 313-583-6336, E-mail: wgrosky@umich.edu. *Application contact:* Leyla O. Field, Intermediate Academic Records Assistant, 313-436-9145, E-mail: leylaf@umich.edu. Website: http://umdearborn.edu/cecs/CIS/grad_prog/.

University of Minnesota, Twin Cities Campus, College of Science and Engineering, Department of Computer Science and Engineering, Program in Software Engineering, Minneapolis, MN 55455-0213. Offers MSSE. Part-time and evening/weekend programs available. *Degree requirements:* For master's, thesis optional, capstone project.

Entrance requirements: For master's, 1 year of work experience in software field; minimum undergraduate GPA of 3.0. Additional exam requirements/recommendations for international students: Required—TOEFL. Electronic applications accepted. *Faculty research:* Database systems, human-computer interaction, software development, high performance neural systems, data mining.

University of Missouri–Kansas City, School of Computing and Engineering, Kansas City, MO 64110-2499. Offers civil engineering (MS); computer and electrical engineering (PhD); computer science (MS), including bioinformatics, software engineering, telecommunications networking; computer science and informatics (PhD); computing (PhD); electrical engineering (MS); engineering (PhD); engineering and construction management (Graduate Certificate); mechanical engineering (MS); telecommunications and computer networking (PhD). PhD (interdisciplinary) offered through the School of Graduate Studies. Part-time programs available. *Faculty:* 39 full-time (5 women), 26 part-time/adjunct (3 women). *Students:* 500 full-time (143 women), 136 part-time (28 women); includes 18 minority (5 Black or African American, non-Hispanic/Latino; 8 Asian, non-Hispanic/Latino; 4 Hispanic/Latino; 1 Two or more races, non-Hispanic/Latino), 551 international. Average age 24. 1,924 applicants, 39% accepted, 200 enrolled. In 2014, 124 master's, 1 other advanced degree awarded. *Degree requirements:* For doctorate, thesis/dissertation. *Entrance requirements:* For master's, GRE General Test, minimum GPA of 3.0, 3 letters of recommendation from professors; for doctorate, GRE General Test, minimum GPA of 3.5. Additional exam requirements/recommendations for international students: Required—TOEFL (minimum score 550 paper-based; 80 iBT). *Application deadline:* For fall admission, 1/15 priority date for domestic students, 1/15 for international students. Applications are processed on a rolling basis. Application fee: $45 ($50 for international students). *Financial support:* In 2014–15, 34 research assistantships with partial tuition reimbursements (averaging $15,602 per year), 24 teaching assistantships with partial tuition reimbursements (averaging $15,090 per year) were awarded; career-related internships or fieldwork, Federal Work-Study, scholarships/grants, tuition waivers (partial), and unspecified assistantships also available. Support available to part-time students. Financial award application deadline: 3/1; financial award applicants required to submit FAFSA. *Faculty research:* Algorithms, bioinformatics and medical informatics, biomechanics/biomaterials, civil engineering materials, networking and telecommunications, thermal science. *Unit head:* Dr. Kevin Z. Truman, Dean, 816-235-2399, Fax: 816-235-5159. *Application contact:* 816-235-2399, Fax: 816-235-5159.
Website: http://sce.umkc.edu/.

University of Nebraska at Omaha, Graduate Studies, College of Information Science and Technology, Department of Computer Science, Omaha, NE 68182. Offers artificial intelligence (Certificate); communication networks (Certificate); computer science (MA, MS); software engineering (Certificate); systems and architecture (Certificate). Part-time and evening/weekend programs available. *Faculty:* 17 full-time (3 women). *Students:* 58 full-time (18 women), 51 part-time (16 women); includes 6 minority (1 Black or African American, non-Hispanic/Latino; 3 Asian, non-Hispanic/Latino; 1 Hispanic/Latino; 1 Two or more races, non-Hispanic/Latino), 80 international. Average age 26. 196 applicants, 54% accepted, 50 enrolled. In 2014, 24 master's awarded. *Degree requirements:* For master's, comprehensive exam, thesis (for some programs). *Entrance requirements:* For master's, GRE General Test, minimum GPA of 3.0, prior course work in computer science, official transcripts, resume, 2 letters of recommendation; for Certificate, minimum GPA of 3.0, resume. Additional exam requirements/recommendations for international students: Required—TOEFL, IELTS, PTE. *Application deadline:* For fall admission, 7/1 priority date for domestic students; for spring admission, 11/1 priority date for domestic and international students; for summer admission, 3/1 for domestic and international students. Applications are processed on a rolling basis. Application fee: $45. Electronic applications accepted. *Financial support:* In 2014–15, 6 students received support, including 6 research assistantships with tuition reimbursements available; teaching assistantships with tuition reimbursements available, Federal Work-Study, institutionally sponsored loans, scholarships/grants, tuition waivers (full), and unspecified assistantships also available. Support available to part-time students. Financial award application deadline: 3/1; financial award applicants required to submit FAFSA. *Unit head:* Dr. Qiuming Zhu, Chairperson, 402-554-2341, E-mail: graduate@unomaha.edu. *Application contact:* Dr. Jong-Hoon Youn, Graduate Program Chair, 402-554-2341, E-mail: graduate@unomaha.edu.

University of New Hampshire, Graduate School Manchester Campus, Manchester, NH 03101. Offers business administration (MBA); counseling (M Ed); education (M Ed, MAT); educational administration and supervision (M Ed, Ed S); information technology (MS); management of technology (MS); public administration (MPA); public health (MPH, Certificate); social work (MSW); software systems engineering (Certificate). Part-time and evening/weekend programs available. *Students:* 1 (woman) full-time, 14 part-time (0 women); includes 1 minority (Hispanic/Latino), 4 international. Average age 34. 11 applicants, 64% accepted, 5 enrolled. *Degree requirements:* For master's, thesis or alternative. *Entrance requirements:* Additional exam requirements/recommendations for international students: Required—TOEFL (minimum score 550 paper-based; 80 iBT). *Application deadline:* For fall admission, 6/1 for domestic students, 4/1 for international students; for spring admission, 12/1 for domestic students. Applications are processed on a rolling basis. Application fee: $65. Electronic applications accepted. *Expenses:* Tuition, state resident: full-time $13,500; part-time $750 per credit hour. Tuition, nonresident: full-time $26,460; part-time $1110 per credit hour. *Required fees:* $1788; $447 per semester. *Financial support:* Fellowships, research assistantships, teaching assistantships, Federal Work-Study, scholarships/grants, health care benefits, and unspecified assistantships available. Support available to part-time students. Financial award application deadline: 3/1; financial award applicants required to submit FAFSA. *Unit head:* Candice Morey, Director, 603-641-4313, E-mail: unhm.gradcenter@unh.edu. *Application contact:* Graduate Admissions Office, 603-862-3000, Fax: 603-862-0275, E-mail: grad.school@unh.edu.
Website: http://www.gradschool.unh.edu/manchester/.

University of New Haven, Graduate School, Tagliatela College of Engineering, Program in Computer and Information Science, West Haven, CT 06516-1916. Offers computer and information science (MS); computer programming (Certificate); computer systems (MS); database and information systems (MS); network systems (MS); software engineering and development (MS). Part-time and evening/weekend programs available. *Degree requirements:* For master's, thesis or alternative. *Entrance requirements:* Additional exam requirements/recommendations for international students: Required—TOEFL (minimum score 75 iBT), IELTS, PTE (minimum score 50). Electronic applications accepted. Application fee is waived when completed online.

University of North Florida, College of Computing, Engineering, and Construction, School of Computing, Jacksonville, FL 32224. Offers computer science (MS); information systems (MS); software engineering (MS). Part-time programs available. *Faculty:* 13 full-time (2 women). *Students:* 27 full-time (12 women), 48 part-time (13 women); includes 17 minority (5 Black or African American, non-Hispanic/Latino; 8 Asian, non-Hispanic/Latino; 2 Hispanic/Latino; 2 Two or more races, non-Hispanic/Latino), 18 international. Average age 30. 73 applicants, 37% accepted, 17 enrolled. In 2014, 6 master's awarded. *Degree requirements:* For master's, thesis. *Entrance requirements:* For master's, GRE General Test, minimum GPA of 3.0 in last 60 hours of course work. Additional exam requirements/recommendations for international students: Required—TOEFL (minimum score 500 paper-based; 61 iBT). *Application deadline:* For fall admission, 7/1 for domestic students, 5/1 for international students; for spring admission, 11/1 for domestic students, 10/1 for international students. Application fee: $30. Electronic applications accepted. *Expenses:* Tuition, state resident: full-time $9794; part-time $408.10 per credit hour. Tuition, nonresident: full-time $22,383; part-time $932.61 per credit hour. *Required fees:* $2047; $85.29 per credit hour. Tuition and fees vary according to course load and program. *Financial support:* In 2014–15, 11 students received support, including 4 research assistantships (averaging $1,238 per year); teaching assistantships, Federal Work-Study, scholarships/grants, and unspecified assistantships also available. Financial award application deadline: 4/1; financial award applicants required to submit FAFSA. *Total annual research expenditures:* $94,179. *Unit head:* Dr. Asai Asaithambi, Dean, 904-620-2985, E-mail: asai.asaithambi@unf.edu. *Application contact:* Dr. Amanda Pascale, Director, The Graduate School, 904-620-1360, Fax: 904-620-1362, E-mail: graduateschool@unf.edu.
Website: http://www.unf.edu/ccec/computing/.

University of Regina, Faculty of Graduate Studies and Research, Faculty of Engineering and Applied Science, Program in Software Systems Engineering, Regina, SK S4S 0A2, Canada. Offers M Eng, MA Sc. Part-time programs available. *Faculty:* 39 full-time (7 women), 24 part-time/adjunct (0 women). *Students:* 12 full-time (0 women), 4 part-time (1 woman). 49 applicants, 18% accepted. In 2014, 5 master's awarded. *Degree requirements:* For master's, comprehensive exam, thesis, project, report. *Entrance requirements:* Additional exam requirements/recommendations for international students: Required—TOEFL (minimum score 550 paper-based; 80 iBT), IELTS (minimum score 6.5), PTE (minimum score 59). *Application deadline:* For fall admission, 3/31 for domestic and international students; for winter admission, 7/31 for domestic and international students; for spring admission, 11/30 for domestic and international students. Application fee: $100. Electronic applications accepted. *Expenses:* Expenses: $2,588.85 per semester of full time study (M Eng); $1,633.35 (for MA Sc); $1,755.60 (for PhD). *Financial support:* In 2014–15, 3 fellowships (averaging $6,000 per year), 4 teaching assistantships (averaging $2,427 per year) were awarded; research assistantships, career-related internships or fieldwork, and scholarships/grants also available. Financial award application deadline: 6/15. *Faculty research:* Software design and development, network computing, multimedia communication, computational theories to real-life programming techniques, embedded systems construction. *Unit head:* Dr. Raphael Idem, Associate Dean, Research and Graduate Studies, 306-585-4470, Fax: 306-585-4855, E-mail: raphael.idem@uregina.ca. *Application contact:* Dr. Christine Chan, Graduate Coordinator, 306-585-5225, Fax: 306-585-4855, E-mail: christine.chan@uregina.ca.
Website: http://www.uregina.ca/engineering/.

University of St. Thomas, Graduate Studies, Graduate Programs in Software, Saint Paul, MN 55105. Offers advanced studies in software engineering (Certificate); big data (Certificate); business analysis (Certificate); computer security (Certificate); information systems (Certificate); information technology (MS); software design and development (Certificate); software engineering (MS); software management (MS); software systems (MSS); MS/MBA. Part-time and evening/weekend programs available. *Degree requirements:* For master's, thesis optional. *Entrance requirements:* For master's, bachelor's degree earned in U.S. or equivalent international degree. Additional exam requirements/recommendations for international students: Required—TOEFL (minimum score 80 iBT). Electronic applications accepted. *Expenses:* Contact institution. *Faculty research:* Data mining, distributed databases, computer security, big data.

University of St. Thomas, Graduate Studies, School of Engineering, St. Paul, MN 55105-1096. Offers electrical engineering (MS); manufacturing engineering and operations (MS); manufacturing systems (Certificate); mechanical engineering (MS); medical device development (Certificate); regulatory science (MS); software engineering (MS); software management (MS); systems engineering (MS); technology leadership (Certificate); technology management (MS). *Accreditation:* ABET (one or more programs are accredited). *Entrance requirements:* For master's, resume, official transcripts. Additional exam requirements/recommendations for international students: Required—TOEFL (minimum score 550 paper-based). Electronic applications accepted. *Expenses:* Contact institution.

The University of Scranton, College of Graduate and Continuing Education, Program in Software Engineering, Scranton, PA 18510. Offers MS. Part-time and evening/weekend programs available. *Faculty:* 8 full-time (0 women). *Students:* 8 full-time (0 women), 3 part-time (0 women); includes 1 minority (Two or more races, non-Hispanic/Latino), 3 international. Average age 26. 51 applicants, 20% accepted. In 2014, 6 master's awarded. *Degree requirements:* For master's, thesis, capstone experience. *Entrance requirements:* For master's, GMAT or GRE, minimum GPA of 3.0. Additional exam requirements/recommendations for international students: Required—TOEFL (minimum score 500 paper-based), IELTS (minimum score 5.5). *Application deadline:* For fall admission, 3/1 priority date for domestic students. Applications are processed on a rolling basis. Application fee: $0. *Financial support:* In 2014–15, 6 students received support, including 6 teaching assistantships with full tuition reimbursements available (averaging $8,800 per year); fellowships, career-related internships or fieldwork, Federal Work-Study, and unspecified assistantships also available. Support available to part-time students. Financial award application deadline: 3/1. *Faculty research:* Database, parallel and distributed systems, computer network, real time systems. *Unit head:* Dr. Yaodong Bi, Director, 570-941-6108, Fax: 570-941-4250, E-mail: biy1@scranton.edu. *Application contact:* Joseph M. Roback, Director of Admissions, 570-941-4385, Fax: 570-941-5928, E-mail: robackj2@scranton.edu.
Website: http://www.cs.uofs.edu/.

University of South Carolina, The Graduate School, College of Engineering and Computing, Department of Computer Science and Engineering, Columbia, SC 29208. Offers computer science and engineering (ME, MS, PhD); software engineering (MS). Part-time and evening/weekend programs available. Postbaccalaureate distance learning degree programs offered (minimal on-campus study). *Degree requirements:* For master's, comprehensive exam, thesis (for some programs); for doctorate, comprehensive exam, thesis/dissertation. *Entrance requirements:* For master's and doctorate, GRE General Test. Additional exam requirements/recommendations for international students: Required—TOEFL (minimum score 570 paper-based). Electronic applications accepted. *Faculty research:* Computer security, computer vision, artificial intelligence, multiagent systems, bioinformatics.

University of Southern California, Graduate School, Viterbi School of Engineering, Department of Computer Science, Los Angeles, CA 90089. Offers computer networks (MS); computer science (MS, PhD); computer security (MS); game development (MS); high performance computing and simulations (MS); human language technology (MS); intelligent robotics (MS); multimedia and creative technologies (MS); software engineering (MS). Part-time and evening/weekend programs available. Postbaccalaureate distance learning degree programs offered (no on-campus study). *Entrance requirements:* For master's and doctorate, GRE General Test. Additional exam requirements/recommendations for international students: Required—TOEFL. Electronic applications accepted. *Faculty research:* Databases, computer graphics and computer vision, software engineering, networks and security, robotics, multimedia and virtual reality.

University of Southern Maine, School of Applied Science, Engineering, and Technology, Department of Computer Science, Portland, ME 04104-9300. Offers computer science (MS); software systems (CGS). Part-time programs available. *Faculty:* 1 full-time, 1 part-time/adjunct (0 women). *Students:* 6 full-time (2 women), 5 part-time; includes 1 minority (Asian, non-Hispanic/Latino). Average age 37. 14 applicants, 71% accepted, 7 enrolled. In 2014, 5 master's, 1 other advanced degree awarded. *Degree requirements:* For master's, thesis. *Entrance requirements:* For master's, GRE General Test, minimum GPA of 3.0. Additional exam requirements/recommendations for international students: Required—TOEFL. *Application deadline:* For fall admission, 3/1 priority date for domestic students; for spring admission, 10/1 for domestic students. Application fee: $65. Electronic applications accepted. *Expenses: Tuition, area resident:* Full-time $6840; part-time $380 per credit hour. Tuition, state resident: full-time $10,260; part-time $570 per credit hour. Tuition, nonresident: full-time $18,468; part-time $1026 per credit hour. *Required fees:* $830; $83 per credit hour. Tuition and fees vary according to course load and program. *Financial support:* Research assistantships, teaching assistantships, and Federal Work-Study available. Support available to part-time students. Financial award application deadline: 4/1; financial award applicants required to submit FAFSA. *Faculty research:* Software engineering, database systems, formal methods, object-oriented technology, artificial intelligence, bioinformatics, data analysis and data mining, health information systems. *Unit head:* Dr. Saud Alagic, Director, 207-780-4841, Fax: 207-780-4933, E-mail: alagic@usm.maine.edu. *Application contact:* Mary Sloan, Assistant Dean of Graduate Studies and Director of Graduate Admissions, 207-780-4812, Fax: 207-780-4969, E-mail: gradstudies@usm.maine.edu.
Website: http://www.usm.maine.edu/cos.

The University of Texas at Arlington, Graduate School, College of Engineering, Department of Computer Science and Engineering, Arlington, TX 76019. Offers computer engineering (MS, PhD); computer science (MS, PhD); mathematical sciences, computer science (PhD); software engineering (MS). Part-time programs available. Postbaccalaureate distance learning degree programs offered (minimal on-campus study). Terminal master's awarded for partial completion of doctoral program. *Degree requirements:* For master's, comprehensive exam (for some programs), thesis; for doctorate, comprehensive exam, thesis/dissertation. *Entrance requirements:* For master's, GRE General Test, minimum GPA of 3.0 (3.2 in computer science-related classes); for doctorate, GRE General Test, minimum GPA of 3.5. Additional exam requirements/recommendations for international students: Required—TOEFL (minimum score 550 paper-based; 92 iBT), IELTS (minimum score 6.5). *Faculty research:* Algorithms, homeland security, mobile pervasive computing, high performance computing bioinformation.

The University of Texas at Dallas, Erik Jonsson School of Engineering and Computer Science, Department of Computer Science, Richardson, TX 75080. Offers computer science (MS, PhD); software engineering (MS, PhD). Part-time and evening/weekend programs available. *Faculty:* 47 full-time (7 women), 11 part-time/adjunct (2 women). *Students:* 990 full-time (269 women), 273 part-time (75 women); includes 59 minority (6 Black or African American, non-Hispanic/Latino; 39 Asian, non-Hispanic/Latino; 10 Hispanic/Latino; 4 Two or more races, non-Hispanic/Latino), 1,111 international. Average age 26. 2,985 applicants, 39% accepted, 505 enrolled. In 2014, 315 master's, 28 doctorates awarded. *Degree requirements:* For master's, thesis optional; for doctorate, comprehensive exam, thesis/dissertation. *Entrance requirements:* For master's, GRE General Test, minimum GPA of 3.0 in undergraduate course work, 3.3 in quantitative course work; for doctorate, GRE General Test, minimum GPA of 3.5. Additional exam requirements/recommendations for international students: Required—TOEFL (minimum score 550 paper-based). *Application deadline:* For fall admission, 7/15 for domestic students, 5/1 priority date for international students; for spring admission, 11/15 for domestic students, 9/1 priority date for international students. Applications are processed on a rolling basis. Application fee: $50 ($100 for international students). Electronic applications accepted. *Expenses:* Tuition, state resident: full-time $11,940; part-time $663 per credit. Tuition, nonresident: full-time $22,282; part-time $1238 per credit. *Financial support:* In 2014–15, 240 students received support, including 13 fellowships with partial tuition reimbursements available (averaging $8,300 per year), 71 research assistantships with partial tuition reimbursements available (averaging $17,442 per year), 66 teaching assistantships with partial tuition reimbursements available (averaging $16,650 per year); career-related internships or fieldwork, Federal Work-Study, institutionally sponsored loans, and scholarships/grants also available. Support available to part-time students. Financial award application deadline: 4/30; financial award applicants required to submit FAFSA. *Faculty research:* AI-based automated software synthesis and testing, quality of service in computer networks, wireless networks, cloud computing and IT security, speech recognition. *Unit head:* Dr. Gopal Gupta, Department Head, 972-883-4107, Fax: 972-883-2399, E-mail: gupta@utdallas.edu. *Application contact:* Dr. Balaji Raghavachari, Associate Department Head/Director of Graduate Studies, 972-883-2136, Fax: 972-883-2399, E-mail: gradecs@utdallas.edu.
Website: http://cs.utdallas.edu/.

The University of Texas at El Paso, Graduate School, College of Engineering, El Paso, TX 79968-0001. Offers biomedical engineering (PhD); civil engineering (MEENE, MS, MSENE, PhD, Certificate), including civil engineering (MS), civil engineering (PhD), construction management (MS, Certificate), environmental engineering (MEENE, MSENE); computer science (MS, MSIT, PhD), including computer science (MS, PhD), information technology (MSIT); education engineering (M Eng); electrical and computer engineering (MS, PhD), including computer engineering (MS), electrical and computer engineering (PhD), electrical engineering (MS); industrial engineering (MS, Certificate), including industrial engineering (MS), manufacturing engineering (MS), systems engineering; mechanical engineering (MS, PhD), including environmental science and engineering (PhD), mechanical engineering (MS); metallurgical and materials engineering (MS, PhD), including materials science and engineering (PhD), metallurgical and materials engineering (MS); software engineering (M Eng). Part-time and evening/weekend programs available. *Degree requirements:* For master's, thesis optional; for doctorate, thesis/dissertation. *Entrance requirements:* For master's, GRE, minimum GPA of 3.0, letters of reference; for doctorate, GRE, statement of purpose, letters of reference. Additional exam requirements/recommendations for international students: Required—TOEFL; Recommended—IELTS. Electronic applications accepted. *Expenses:* Contact institution.

University of Utah, Graduate School, David Eccles School of Business, Department of Operations and Information Systems, Salt Lake City, UT 84112. Offers information systems (MS, Graduate Certificate), including business intelligence and analytics, IT security, product and process management, software and systems architecture. Part-time and evening/weekend programs available. *Faculty:* 11 full-time (4 women), 6 part-time/adjunct (0 women). *Students:* 77 full-time (18 women), 63 part-time (7 women); includes 19 minority (2 Black or African American, non-Hispanic/Latino; 5 Asian, non-Hispanic/Latino; 10 Hispanic/Latino; 2 Two or more races, non-Hispanic/Latino), 27 international. Average age 31. 148 applicants, 72% accepted, 71 enrolled. In 2014, 63

master's awarded. *Degree requirements:* For master's, capstone project. *Entrance requirements:* For master's, GMAT/GRE, minimum undergraduate GPA of 3.0. Additional exam requirements/recommendations for international students: Required—TOEFL (minimum score 550 paper-based; 80 iBT), IELTS (minimum score 6.5). *Application deadline:* For fall admission, 7/28 for domestic students, 3/1 for international students; for spring admission, 12/7 for domestic students, 8/16 for international students. Applications are processed on a rolling basis. Application fee: $55 ($65 for international students). Electronic applications accepted. *Expenses:* Expenses: Contact institution. *Financial support:* In 2014–15, 5 students received support, including 3 fellowships with partial tuition reimbursements available (averaging $5,160 per year), 2 teaching assistantships with partial tuition reimbursements available (averaging $5,160 per year); tuition waivers (partial) and unspecified assistantships also available. Financial award application deadline: 4/14; financial award applicants required to submit FAFSA. *Faculty research:* Business intelligence and analytics, software and system architecture, product and process management, IT security, Web and data mining, applications and management of IT in healthcare. *Unit head:* Bradden Blair, Director of the MSIS Program, 801-587-9489, Fax: 801-581-3666, E-mail: b.blair@business.utah.edu. *Application contact:* Andrea Miller, Director of Admissions, 801-585-7366, Fax: 801-581-3666, E-mail: andrea.miller@business.utah.edu.
Website: http://msis.business.utah.edu.

University of Washington, Bothell, Program in Computing and Software Systems, Bothell, WA 98011-8246. Offers MS. Part-time and evening/weekend programs available. *Degree requirements:* For master's, comprehensive exam (for some programs), thesis optional. *Entrance requirements:* For master's, GRE. Additional exam requirements/recommendations for international students: Required—TOEFL (minimum score 580 paper-based; 92 iBT) or IELTS (minimum score 7). Electronic applications accepted. *Expenses:* Contact institution. *Faculty research:* Computer science, software engineering, computer graphics, parallel and distributed systems, computer vision.

University of Washington, Tacoma, Graduate Programs, Program in Computing and Software Systems, Tacoma, WA 98402-3100. Offers MS. Part-time programs available. *Degree requirements:* For master's, capstone project/thesis or 15 credits elective coursework. *Entrance requirements:* For master's, GRE, personal statement, resume, transcripts, 3 recommendations. Additional exam requirements/recommendations for international students: Required—TOEFL (minimum score 580 paper-based; 92 iBT), IELTS (minimum score 7). Electronic applications accepted. *Faculty research:* Data stream analysis, formal methods, data mining, robotic systems, software development processes.

University of Waterloo, Graduate Studies, Faculty of Engineering, Department of Electrical and Computer Engineering, Waterloo, ON N2L 3G1, Canada. Offers electrical and computer engineering (M Eng, MA Sc, PhD); electrical and computer engineering (software engineering) (MA Sc). Part-time programs available. *Degree requirements:* For master's, research paper or thesis; for doctorate, comprehensive exam, thesis/dissertation. *Entrance requirements:* For master's, honors degree, minimum B+ average; for doctorate, master's degree, minimum A- average. Additional exam requirements/recommendations for international students: Required—TOEFL (minimum score 550 paper-based), TWE (minimum score 4). Electronic applications accepted. *Faculty research:* Communications, computers, systems and control, silicon devices, power engineering.

University of Waterloo, Graduate Studies, Faculty of Mathematics, David R. Cheriton School of Computer Science, Waterloo, ON N2L 3G1, Canada. Offers computer science (M Math, PhD); software engineering (M Math); statistics and computing (M Math). Part-time programs available. *Degree requirements:* For master's, research paper or thesis; for doctorate, comprehensive exam, thesis/dissertation. *Entrance requirements:* For master's, honors degree in field, minimum B+ average; for doctorate, master's degree, minimum B+ average. *Faculty research:* Computer graphics, artificial intelligence, algorithms and complexity, distributed computing and networks, software engineering.

University of West Florida, College of Arts and Sciences: Sciences, Department of Computer Science, Pensacola, FL 32514-5750. Offers computer science (MS); database systems (MS); software engineering (MS). Part-time and evening/weekend programs available. *Degree requirements:* For master's, thesis optional. *Entrance requirements:* For master's, GRE, MAT, or GMAT, official transcripts; minimum undergraduate GPA of 3.0; letter of intent; three letters of recommendation. Additional exam requirements/recommendations for international students: Required—TOEFL (minimum score 550 paper-based).

University of West Florida, College of Professional Studies, Department of Research and Advanced Studies, Pensacola, FL 32514-5750. Offers administration (MSA), including acquisition and contract administration, biomedical/pharmaceutical, criminal justice administration, database administration, education leadership, healthcare administration, human performance technology, leadership, nursing administration, public administration, software engineering and administration; college student personnel administration (M Ed), including college personnel administration, guidance and counseling; curriculum and instruction (M Ed, Ed S); educational leadership (M Ed); middle and secondary level education and ESOL (M Ed). Part-time and evening/weekend programs available. *Entrance requirements:* For master's, GRE or MAT, official transcripts; minimum undergraduate GPA of 3.0; letter of intent; three letters of recommendation; resume. Additional exam requirements/recommendations for international students: Required—TOEFL (minimum score 550 paper-based).

University of West Florida, College of Professional Studies, Program in Administration, Pensacola, FL 32514-5750. Offers acquisition and contract administration (MSA); database administration (MSA); health care administration (MSA); human performance technology (MSA); leadership (MSA); public administration (MSA); software engineering administration (MSA). Part-time and evening/weekend programs available. Postbaccalaureate distance learning degree programs offered (no on-campus study). *Entrance requirements:* For master's, GRE General Test, letter of intent, names of references. Additional exam requirements/recommendations for international students: Required—TOEFL (minimum score 550 paper-based).

University of Wisconsin–La Crosse, Graduate Studies, College of Science and Health, Department of Computer Science, La Crosse, WI 54601-3742. Offers software engineering (MSE). Part-time programs available. *Faculty:* 11 full-time (1 woman). *Students:* 31 full-time (11 women), 7 part-time (0 women), 26 international. Average age 25. 33 applicants, 73% accepted, 17 enrolled. In 2014, 15 master's awarded. *Degree requirements:* For master's, thesis. *Entrance requirements:* Additional exam requirements/recommendations for international students: Recommended—TOEFL (minimum score 550 paper-based; 79 iBT), IELTS (minimum score 6). *Application deadline:* For fall admission, 5/1 priority date for domestic and international students; for spring admission, 11/1 priority date for domestic and international students. Applications are processed on a rolling basis. Electronic applications accepted. *Financial support:* Research assistantships with partial tuition reimbursements, Federal Work-Study, scholarships/grants, health care benefits, and tuition waivers (partial) available. Support available to part-time students. *Unit head:* Dr. Kasi Periyasamy, Software Engineering Program Director, 608-785-6823, E-mail: periyasa.kas2@uwlax.edu. *Application*

contact: Brandon Schaller, Senior Graduate Student Status Examiner, 608-785-8941, E-mail: admissions@uwlax.edu.
Website: http://www.cs.uwlax.edu/index.php/graduate-program.

Villanova University, Graduate School of Liberal Arts and Sciences, Department of Computing Sciences, Villanova, PA 19085-1699. Offers computer science (MS); software engineering (MS). Part-time and evening/weekend programs available. *Students:* 116 full-time (56 women), 21 part-time (3 women); includes 5 minority (2 Asian, non-Hispanic/Latino; 1 Hispanic/Latino; 1 Native Hawaiian or other Pacific Islander, non-Hispanic/Latino; 1 Two or more races, non-Hispanic/Latino), 102 international. Average age 27. 75 applicants, 64% accepted, 35 enrolled. In 2014, 32 master's awarded. *Degree requirements:* For master's, thesis optional, independent study project. *Entrance requirements:* For master's, GRE, minimum GPA of 3.0, 3 recommendation letters. Additional exam requirements/recommendations for international students: Required—TOEFL. *Application deadline:* For fall admission, 5/1 priority date for international students; for spring admission, 11/15 priority date for international students. Applications are processed on a rolling basis. Application fee: $50. Electronic applications accepted. *Financial support:* Research assistantships, scholarships/grants, and unspecified assistantships available. Financial award applicants required to submit FAFSA. *Unit head:* Dr. Vijay Geholt, Chair, 610-519-5843.
Website: http://www1.villanova.edu/villanova/artsci/computerscience/graduate.html.

Virginia Polytechnic Institute and State University, VT Online, Blacksburg, VA 24061. Offers advanced transportation systems (Certificate); aerospace engineering (MS); agricultural and life sciences (MSLFS); business information systems (Graduate Certificate); career and technical education (MS); civil engineering (MS); computer engineering (M Eng, MS); decision support systems (Graduate Certificate); eLearning leadership (MA); electrical engineering (M Eng, MS); engineering administration (MEA); environmental engineering (Certificate); environmental politics and policy (Graduate Certificate); environmental sciences and engineering (MS); foundations of political analysis (Graduate Certificate); health product risk management (Graduate Certificate); industrial and systems engineering (MS); information policy and society (Graduate Certificate); information security (Graduate Certificate); information technology (MIT); instructional technology (MA); integrative STEM education (MA Ed); liberal arts (Graduate Certificate); life sciences: health product risk management (MS); natural resources (MNR, Graduate Certificate); networking (Graduate Certificate); nonprofit and nongovernmental organization management (Graduate Certificate); ocean engineering (MS); political science (MA); security studies (Graduate Certificate); software development (Graduate Certificate). *Expenses:* Tuition, state resident: full-time $11,656; part-time $647.50 per credit hour. Tuition, nonresident: full-time $23,351; part-time $1297.25 per credit hour. *Required fees:* $2533; $465.75 per semester. Tuition and fees vary according to course load, campus/location and program.

West Virginia University, College of Engineering and Mineral Resources, Lane Department of Computer Science and Electrical Engineering, Program in Software Engineering, Morgantown, WV 26506. Offers MSSE. *Entrance requirements:* For master's, GRE or work experience.

Widener University, Graduate Programs in Engineering, Program in Computer and Software Engineering, Chester, PA 19013-5792. Offers M Eng. Part-time and evening/weekend programs available. *Degree requirements:* For master's, thesis optional. *Faculty research:* Computer and software engineering, computer network fault-tolerant computing, optical computing.

Winthrop University, College of Business Administration, Program in Software Project Management, Rock Hill, SC 29733. Offers software development (MS); software project management (Certificate). *Entrance requirements:* For master's, GMAT.

Systems Science

Arizona State University at the Tempe campus, College of Liberal Arts and Sciences, School of Life Sciences, Tempe, AZ 85287-4601. Offers animal behavior (PhD); applied ethics (biomedical and health ethics) (MA); biology (MS, PhD), including biology, biology and society, complex adaptive systems science (PhD), plant biology and conservation (MS); environmental life sciences (PhD); evolutionary biology (PhD); history and philosophy of science (PhD); human and social dimensions of science and technology (PhD); microbiology (PhD); molecular and cellular biology (PhD); neuroscience (PhD). Terminal master's awarded for partial completion of doctoral program. *Degree requirements:* For master's, thesis (for some programs), interactive Program of Study (iPOS) submitted before completing 50 percent of required credit hours; for doctorate, variable foreign language requirement, comprehensive exam, thesis/dissertation, interactive Program of Study (iPOS) submitted before completing 50 percent of required credit hours. *Entrance requirements:* For master's and doctorate, GRE, minimum GPA of 3.0 or equivalent in last 2 years of work leading to bachelor's degree. Additional exam requirements/recommendations for international students: Required—TOEFL (minimum score 600 paper-based; 100 iBT). Electronic applications accepted.

Arizona State University at the Tempe campus, Ira A. Fulton Schools of Engineering, ASU Engineering Online Programs, Tempe, AZ 85287. Offers construction (MS); embedded systems (M Eng); enterprise systems innovation and management (MSE); modeling and simulation (M Eng); quality and reliability engineering (M Eng); software engineering (MSE); systems engineering (M Eng).

Binghamton University, State University of New York, Graduate School, Thomas J. Watson School of Engineering and Applied Science, Department of Systems Science and Industrial Engineering, Vestal, NY 13850. Offers executive health systems (MS); industrial and systems engineering (M Eng); systems science and industrial engineering (MS, PhD). MS in executive health systems also offered in Manhattan. Part-time and evening/weekend programs available. *Faculty:* 18 full-time (4 women), 6 part-time/adjunct (1 woman). *Students:* 172 full-time (56 women), 84 part-time (20 women); includes 39 minority (11 Black or African American, non-Hispanic/Latino; 15 Asian, non-Hispanic/Latino; 13 Hispanic/Latino), 158 international. Average age 27. 321 applicants, 94% accepted, 119 enrolled. In 2014, 69 master's, 16 doctorates awarded. Terminal master's awarded for partial completion of doctoral program. *Degree requirements:* For master's, thesis; for doctorate, thesis/dissertation. *Entrance requirements:* For master's and doctorate, GRE General Test. Additional exam requirements/recommendations for international students: Required—TOEFL (minimum score 550 paper-based; 80 iBT). *Application deadline:* For fall admission, 4/15 priority date for domestic students, 1/15 priority date for international students; for spring admission, 11/1 for domestic students, 10/1 priority date for international students. Applications are processed on a rolling basis. Application fee: $75. Electronic applications accepted. *Expenses:* Expenses: $5,435 resident; $11,105 non-resident. *Financial support:* In 2014–15, 77 students received support, including 1 fellowship with full tuition reimbursement available (averaging $10,000 per year), 45 research assistantships with full tuition reimbursements available (averaging $16,500 per year), 13 teaching assistantships with full tuition reimbursements available (averaging $16,500 per year); career-related internships or fieldwork, Federal Work-Study, institutionally sponsored loans, scholarships/grants, health care benefits, tuition waivers (full and partial), and unspecified assistantships also available. Financial award application deadline: 2/15; financial award applicants required to submit FAFSA. *Faculty research:* Problem restructuring, protein modeling. *Unit head:* Ellen Tilden, Coordinator of Graduate Studies, 607-777-2873, E-mail: etilden@binghamton.edu. *Application contact:* Kishan Zuber, Recruiting and Admissions Coordinator, 607-777-2151, Fax: 607-777-2501, E-mail: kzuber@binghamton.edu.
Website: http://www.ssie.binghamton.edu.

Carleton University, Faculty of Graduate Studies, Faculty of Engineering and Design, Ottawa-Carleton Institute for Electrical Engineering, Department of Systems and Computer Engineering, Program in Information and Systems Science, Ottawa, ON K1S 5B6, Canada. Offers M Sc.

Carleton University, Faculty of Graduate Studies, Faculty of Science, Information and Systems Science Program, Ottawa, ON K1S 5B6, Canada. Offers M Sc. *Degree requirements:* For master's, thesis optional. *Entrance requirements:* For master's, honors degree. Additional exam requirements/recommendations for international students: Required—TOEFL. *Faculty research:* Software engineering, real-time and microprocessor programming, computer communications.

Carleton University, Faculty of Graduate Studies, Faculty of Science, School of Computer Science, Ottawa, ON K1S 5B6, Canada. Offers computer science (MCS, PhD); information and system science (M Sc). MCS and PhD programs offered jointly with University of Ottawa. Part-time programs available. *Degree requirements:* For master's, thesis optional, project; for doctorate, comprehensive exam, thesis/dissertation. *Entrance requirements:* For master's, honors degree. Additional exam requirements/recommendations for international students: Required—TOEFL. *Faculty research:* Programming systems, theory of computing, computer applications, computer systems.

Claremont Graduate University, Graduate Programs, Center for Information Systems and Technology, Claremont, CA 91711-6160. Offers electronic commerce (MS, PhD); health information management (MS); information systems (Certificate); knowledge management (MS, PhD); systems development (MS, PhD); telecommunications and networking (MS, PhD); MBA/MS. Part-time programs available. *Faculty:* 5 full-time (0 women), 2 part-time/adjunct (0 women). *Students:* 60 full-time (21 women), 65 part-time (22 women); includes 26 minority (5 Black or African American, non-Hispanic/Latino; 1 American Indian or Alaska Native, non-Hispanic/Latino; 15 Asian, non-Hispanic/Latino; 4 Hispanic/Latino; 1 Two or more races, non-Hispanic/Latino), 65 international. Average age 36. In 2014, 17 master's, 1 doctorate awarded. *Degree requirements:* For doctorate, comprehensive exam, thesis/dissertation, portfolio. *Entrance requirements:* For master's and doctorate, GMAT, GRE General Test. Additional exam requirements/recommendations for international students: Required—TOEFL (minimum score 550 paper-based; 80 iBT). *Application deadline:* For fall admission, 2/1 priority date for domestic and international students. Applications are processed on a rolling basis. Application fee: $80. Electronic applications accepted. *Expenses: Tuition:* Full-time $41,784; part-time $1741 per credit. *Required fees:* $600; $300 per semester. *Financial support:* Fellowships, research assistantships, teaching assistantships, Federal Work-Study, institutionally sponsored loans, and scholarships/grants available. Support available to part-time students. Financial award application deadline: 2/15; financial award applicants required to submit FAFSA. *Faculty research:* Man-machine interaction, organizational aspects of computing, implementation of information systems, information systems practice. *Unit head:* Tom Horan, Dean, 909-607-9302, Fax: 909-621-8564, E-mail: tom.horan@cgu.edu. *Application contact:* Leah Litwack, Administrative Assistant, 909-621-8209, E-mail: leah.litwack@cgu.edu.
Website: http://www.cgu.edu/pages/153.asp.

Eastern Illinois University, Graduate School, Lumpkin College of Business and Applied Sciences, School of Technology, Charleston, IL 61920. Offers computer technology (Certificate); quality systems (Certificate); technology (MS); technology security (Certificate); work performance improvement (Certificate); MS/MBA; MS/MS. Part-time and evening/weekend programs available. *Faculty:* 28. *Students:* 133 full-time (43 women), 68 part-time (39 women); includes 17 minority (11 Black or African American, non-Hispanic/Latino; 2 Asian, non-Hispanic/Latino; 2 Hispanic/Latino; 2 Two or more races, non-Hispanic/Latino), 124 international. Average age 28. 449 applicants, 31% accepted, 58 enrolled. In 2014, 61 master's awarded. *Application deadline:* For fall admission, 3/31 priority date for domestic students. Applications are processed on a rolling basis. Application fee: $30. *Expenses:* Tuition, state resident: full-time $3113; part-time $283 per credit hour. Tuition, nonresident: full-time $7469; part-time $679 per credit hour. *Required fees:* $2287; $96 per credit hour. Tuition and fees vary according to course load. *Financial support:* In 2014–15, 107 students received support, including 7 research assistantships with tuition reimbursements available, 6 teaching assistantships with tuition reimbursements available. *Unit head:* Austin Cheney, Chair, 217-581-3226, Fax: 217-581-6607, E-mail: acheney@eiu.edu. *Application contact:* Peter Ping Liu, Coordinator, 217-581-6267, Fax: 217-581-6607, E-mail: pliu@eiu.edu.
Website: http://www.eiu.edu/tech/.

Fairleigh Dickinson University, Metropolitan Campus, University College: Arts, Sciences, and Professional Studies, Program in Systems Science, Teaneck, NJ 07666-1914. Offers MS. *Entrance requirements:* For master's, GRE General Test.

Hood College, Graduate School, Program in Management of Information Technology, Frederick, MD 21701-8575. Offers MS. Part-time and evening/weekend programs available. *Degree requirements:* For master's, thesis. *Entrance requirements:* For master's, minimum GPA of 2.75. Additional exam requirements/recommendations for international students: Required—TOEFL (minimum score 575 paper-based; 89 iBT), IELTS (minimum score 6.5). Electronic applications accepted. Application fee is waived when completed online. *Faculty research:* Systems engineering, parallel distributed computing, strategy, business ethics, entrepreneurship.

Louisiana State University and Agricultural & Mechanical College, Graduate School, College of Engineering, Division of Computer Science, Baton Rouge, LA 70803. Offers computer science (MSSS, PhD); systems science (MSSS). Part-time programs available. *Faculty:* 18 full-time (2 women). *Students:* 68 full-time (10 women), 16 part-time (2 women); includes 6 minority (2 Black or African American, non-Hispanic/Latino; 1 American Indian or Alaska Native, non-Hispanic/Latino; 3 Asian, non-Hispanic/Latino),

56 international. Average age 30. 154 applicants, 45% accepted, 17 enrolled. In 2014, 29 master's, 9 doctorates awarded. Terminal master's awarded for partial completion of doctoral program. *Degree requirements:* For master's, thesis; for doctorate, thesis/dissertation. *Entrance requirements:* For master's and doctorate, GRE General Test, minimum GPA of 3.0. Additional exam requirements/recommendations for international students: Required—TOEFL (minimum score 550 paper-based; 79 iBT), IELTS (minimum score 6.5), or PTE (minimum score 59). *Application deadline:* For fall admission, 1/1 priority date for domestic students, 5/15 for international students; for spring admission, 10/15 for domestic and international students; for summer admission, 5/15 for domestic students. Applications are processed on a rolling basis. Application fee: $50 ($70 for international students). Electronic applications accepted. *Financial support:* In 2014–15, 71 students received support, including 1 fellowship with full tuition reimbursement available (averaging $9,575 per year), 22 research assistantships with full and partial tuition reimbursements available (averaging $17,323 per year), 34 teaching assistantships with full and partial tuition reimbursements available (averaging $15,335 per year); Federal Work-Study, institutionally sponsored loans, health care benefits, and unspecified assistantships also available. Financial award application deadline: 2/1; financial award applicants required to submit FAFSA. *Faculty research:* Robotics, artificial intelligence, algorithms, database software engineering, high-performance computing. *Total annual research expenditures:* $2.3 million. *Unit head:* Dr. Bijaya S. Karki, Interim Chair, 225-578-1495, Fax: 225-578-1465, E-mail: bbkarki@lsu.edu. *Application contact:* Dr. Seung-John Park, Graduate Coordinator, 225-578-3179, Fax: 225-578-1465, E-mail: sjpark@lsu.edu.
Website: http://www.cse.lsu.edu/.

Louisiana State University in Shreveport, College of Arts and Sciences, Program in Computer Systems Technology, Shreveport, LA 71115-2399. Offers MS. Part-time and evening/weekend programs available. *Students:* 6 full-time (2 women), 4 part-time (0 women); includes 3 minority (1 Asian, non-Hispanic/Latino; 2 Hispanic/Latino), 2 international. Average age 31. 13 applicants, 100% accepted, 4 enrolled. In 2014, 12 master's awarded. *Degree requirements:* For master's, comprehensive exam (for some programs), thesis or alternative. *Entrance requirements:* For master's, GRE, programming course in high-level language, interview. Additional exam requirements/recommendations for international students: Required—TOEFL (minimum score 550 paper-based; 80 iBT). *Application deadline:* For fall admission, 6/30 for domestic and international students; for spring admission, 11/30 for domestic and international students; for summer admission, 4/30 for domestic and international students. Applications are processed on a rolling basis. Application fee: $20 ($30 for international students). Electronic applications accepted. *Expenses:* Tuition, state resident: full-time $5234; part-time $290.80 per credit hour. Tuition, nonresident: full-time $16,774; part-time $879.61 per credit hour. *Required fees:* $52.28 per credit hour. *Financial support:* In 2014–15, 2 research assistantships (averaging $5,000 per year) were awarded. *Unit head:* Dr. Krishna Agarwal, Program Director, 318-795-4283, Fax: 318-795-2419, E-mail: krishna.agarwal@lsus.edu. *Application contact:* Kimberly Thornton, Director of Admissions, 318-795-2405, Fax: 318-797-5286, E-mail: kimberly.thornton@lsus.edu.

Miami University, College of Engineering and Computing, Department of Computer Science and Software Engineering, Oxford, OH 45056. Offers computer science (MCS). *Students:* 16 full-time (4 women), 8 part-time (4 women); includes 2 minority (1 Asian, non-Hispanic/Latino; 1 Two or more races, non-Hispanic/Latino), 14 international. Average age 24. In 2014, 8 master's awarded. *Entrance requirements:* For master's, GRE, personal statement; sample of computer code; three letters of recommendation. Additional exam requirements/recommendations for international students: Recommended—TOEFL (minimum score 80 iBT), IELTS (minimum score 6.5), TSE (minimum score 54). *Application deadline:* For fall admission, 2/1 for domestic and international students. Application fee: $50. Electronic applications accepted. *Expenses:* Tuition, state resident: full-time $12,887; part-time $537 per credit hour. Tuition, nonresident: full-time $28,449; part-time $1186 per credit hour. *Required fees:* $530; $24 per credit hour. $30 per quarter. Part-time tuition and fees vary according to course load and program. *Financial support:* Fellowships with full and partial tuition reimbursements, research assistantships with full and partial tuition reimbursements, and teaching assistantships with full and partial tuition reimbursements available. Financial award application deadline: 2/1; financial award applicants required to submit FAFSA. *Unit head:* Dr. James Kiper, Chair, 513-529-0340, E-mail: kiperjd@miamioh.edu. *Application contact:* Graduate Director, 513-529-0340, E-mail: cecgrad@miamioh.edu.
Website: http://miamioh.edu/cec/academics/departments/cse/.

New Jersey Institute of Technology, College of Computing Science, Newark, NJ 07102. Offers computer science (MS, PhD), including bioinformatics (MS), computer science, computing and business (MS), cyber security and privacy (MS), software engineering (MS); information systems (MS, PhD), including business and information systems (MS), emergency management and business continuity (MS), information systems; information technology administration and security (MS). Part-time and evening/weekend programs available. Terminal master's awarded for partial completion of doctoral program. *Degree requirements:* For master's, thesis optional; for doctorate, thesis/dissertation. *Entrance requirements:* For master's, GRE General Test; for doctorate, GRE General Test, minimum graduate GPA of 3.5. Additional exam requirements/recommendations for international students: Required—TOEFL (minimum score 550 paper-based; 79 iBT). Electronic applications accepted. *Faculty research:* Computer systems, communications and networking, artificial intelligence, database engineering, systems analysis.

Oakland University, Graduate Study and Lifelong Learning, School of Engineering and Computer Science, Department of Computer Science and Engineering, Rochester, MI 48309-4401. Offers computer science (MS); embedded systems (MS); information systems engineering (MS); software engineering (MS). Part-time and evening/weekend programs available. *Entrance requirements:* For master's, minimum GPA of 3.0. Electronic applications accepted. *Expenses:* Contact institution. *Faculty research:* Urinary continence index for prediction of urinary incontinence in older women.

Portland State University, Graduate Studies, College of Liberal Arts and Sciences, Systems Science Program, Portland, OR 97207-0751. Offers computational intelligence (Certificate); computer modeling and simulation (Certificate); systems science (MS); systems science/anthropology (PhD); systems science/business administration (PhD); systems science/civil engineering (PhD); systems science/economics (PhD); systems science/engineering management (PhD); systems science/general (PhD); systems science/mathematical sciences (PhD); systems science/mechanical engineering (PhD); systems science/psychology (PhD); systems science/sociology (PhD). *Faculty:* 2 full-time (0 women), 1 part-time/adjunct (0 women). *Students:* 6 full-time (2 women), 29 part-time (8 women); includes 6 minority (1 Black or African American, non-Hispanic/Latino; 1 American Indian or Alaska Native, non-Hispanic/Latino; 1 Asian, non-Hispanic/Latino; 3 Hispanic/Latino). Average age 41. 32 applicants, 19% accepted, 6 enrolled. In 2014, 10 master's, 3 doctorates awarded. *Degree requirements:* For master's, comprehensive exam (for some programs), thesis optional; for doctorate, variable foreign language requirement, comprehensive exam (for some programs), thesis/dissertation. *Entrance requirements:* For master's, GRE/GMAT scores are recommended but not required. GPA 3.0 for undergraduate or 3.0 for graduate work, 2 letters of recommendation, and

statement of interest; for doctorate, GMAT, GRE General Test, GPA requirement is 3.0 for undergraduate and 3.25 for graduate, 2 letters of recommendation and statement of interest. Additional exam requirements/recommendations for international students: Required—TOEFL (minimum score 550 paper-based; 80 iBT). *Application deadline:* For fall admission, 1/15 for domestic and international students; for spring admission, 11/1 for domestic students. Application fee: $50. Electronic applications accepted. *Expenses:* Tuition, state resident: part-time $222 per credit. Tuition, nonresident: part-time $527 per credit. *Required fees:* $22 per contact hour. $100 per quarter. Tuition and fees vary according to program. *Financial support:* In 2014–15, 1 research assistantship with full and partial tuition reimbursement (averaging $2,358 per year) was awarded; teaching assistantships with full and partial tuition reimbursements, career-related internships or fieldwork, Federal Work-Study, scholarships/grants, and unspecified assistantships also available. Support available to part-time students. Financial award application deadline: 3/1; financial award applicants required to submit FAFSA. *Faculty research:* Systems theory and methodology, artificial intelligence neural networks, information theory, nonlinear dynamics/chaos, modeling and simulation. *Total annual research expenditures:* $137,833. *Unit head:* Prof. Wayne Wakeland, PhD, Chair, 503-725-4975, E-mail: wakeland@pdx.edu.
Website: http://www.pdx.edu/sysc/.

Portland State University, Graduate Studies, Maseeh College of Engineering and Computer Science, Department of Engineering and Technology Management, Portland, OR 97207-0751. Offers engineering and technology management (M Eng); engineering management (MS); manufacturing engineering (ME); manufacturing management (M Eng); systems science/engineering management (PhD); MS/MBA; MS/MS. Part-time and evening/weekend programs available. *Faculty:* 6 full-time (1 woman), 8 part-time/adjunct (2 women). *Students:* 62 full-time (20 women), 63 part-time (18 women); includes 21 minority (3 Black or African American, non-Hispanic/Latino; 1 American Indian or Alaska Native, non-Hispanic/Latino; 12 Asian, non-Hispanic/Latino; 4 Hispanic/Latino; 1 Two or more races, non-Hispanic/Latino), 68 international. Average age 36. 90 applicants, 67% accepted, 31 enrolled. In 2014, 27 master's, 5 doctorates awarded. *Degree requirements:* For master's, thesis optional; for doctorate, one foreign language, comprehensive exam, thesis/dissertation, oral and written exams. *Entrance requirements:* For master's, GRE optional, 2.75 undergraduate or 3.0 graduate (at least 12 credits), minimum 4 years of experience in engineering or related discipline, 3 letters of recommendation and background in probability/statistics, differential equations, computer programming and linear algebra; for doctorate, GRE General Test, 1100 for the sum of verbal and quantitative, or verbal and analytical., minimum GPA of 3.0 undergraduate or 3.25 graduate. Additional exam requirements/recommendations for international students: Required—TOEFL (minimum score 550 paper-based; 80 iBT). *Application deadline:* For fall admission, 4/1 for domestic students, 3/1 for international students; for winter admission, 9/1 for domestic students, 7/1 for international students; for spring admission, 11/1 for domestic students, 9/1 for international students; for summer admission, 2/1 for domestic students, 12/1 for international students. Application fee: $50. Electronic applications accepted. *Expenses:* Tuition, state resident: part-time $222 per credit. Tuition, nonresident: part-time $527 per credit. *Required fees:* $22 per contact hour. $100 per quarter. Tuition and fees vary according to program. *Financial support:* In 2014–15, 7 research assistantships with full and partial tuition reimbursements (averaging $1,913 per year), 8 teaching assistantships with full and partial tuition reimbursements (averaging $2,823 per year) were awarded; career-related internships or fieldwork, Federal Work-Study, scholarships/grants, and unspecified assistantships also available. Support available to part-time students. Financial award application deadline: 3/1; financial award applicants required to submit FAFSA. *Faculty research:* Scheduling, hierarchical decision modeling, operations research, knowledge-based information systems. *Total annual research expenditures:* $318,571. *Unit head:* Dr. Tim Anderson, Chair, 503-725-4668, Fax: 503-725-4667, E-mail: tim.anderson@pdx.edu. *Application contact:* Shawn Wall, Department Manager, 503-725-4660, Fax: 503-547-8887, E-mail: info@etm.pdx.edu.
Website: http://www.pdx.edu/engineering-technology-management/.

Rensselaer at Hartford, Department of Engineering, Program in Computer and Systems Engineering, Hartford, CT 06120-2991. Offers ME. *Entrance requirements:* For master's, GRE.

Southern Methodist University, Bobby B. Lyle School of Engineering, Department of Engineering Management, Information, and Systems, Dallas, TX 75275. Offers engineering management (MSEM, DE); information engineering and management (MSIEM); operations research (MS, PhD); systems engineering (MS, PhD). Part-time and evening/weekend programs available. Postbaccalaureate distance learning degree programs offered. Terminal master's awarded for partial completion of doctoral program. *Degree requirements:* For master's, thesis optional; for doctorate, thesis/dissertation, oral and written qualifying exams. *Entrance requirements:* For master's, minimum GPA of 3.0 in last 2 years; bachelor's degree in engineering, mathematics, sciences, or technical area; for doctorate, GRE General Test (operations research, engineering management), bachelor's degree in related field. Additional exam requirements/recommendations for international students: Required—TOEFL. *Faculty research:* Telecommunications, decision systems, information engineering, operations research, software.

Stevens Institute of Technology, Graduate School, Charles V. Schaefer Jr. School of Engineering, Department of Mechanical Engineering, Program in Integrated Product Development, Hoboken, NJ 07030. Offers armament engineering (M Eng); computer and electrical engineering (M Eng); manufacturing technologies (M Eng); systems reliability and design (M Eng).

Stevens Institute of Technology, Graduate School, School of Systems and Enterprises, Program in Enterprise Systems, Hoboken, NJ 07030. Offers MS, PhD.

Strayer University, Graduate Studies, Washington, DC 20005-2603. Offers accounting (MS); acquisition (MBA); business administration (MBA); communications technology (MS); educational management (M Ed); finance (MBA); health services administration (MHSA); hospitality and tourism management (MBA); human resource management (MBA); information systems (MS), including computer security management, decision support system management, enterprise resource management, network management, software engineering management, systems development management; management (MBA); management information systems (MS); marketing (MBA); professional accounting (MS), including accounting information systems, controllership, taxation; public administration (MPA); supply chain management (MBA); technology in education (M Ed). Programs also offered at campus locations in Birmingham, AL; Chamblee, GA; Cobb County, GA; Morrow, GA; White Marsh, MD; Charleston, SC; Columbia, SC; Greensboro, NC; Greenville, SC; Lexington, KY; Louisville, KY; Nashville, TN; North Raleigh, NC; Washington, DC. Part-time and evening/weekend programs available. Postbaccalaureate distance learning degree programs offered (minimal on-campus study). *Degree requirements:* For master's, thesis. *Entrance requirements:* For master's, GMAT, GRE General Test, bachelor's degree from an accredited college or university, minimum undergraduate GPA of 2.75. Electronic applications accepted.

Universidad Autonoma de Guadalajara, Graduate Programs, Guadalajara, Mexico. Offers administrative law and justice (LL M); advertising and corporate communications

Systems Science

(MA); architecture (M Arch); business (MBA); computational science (MCC); education (Ed M, Ed D); English-Spanish translation (MA); entrepreneurship and management (MBA); integrated management of digital animation (MA); international business (MIB); international corporate law (LL M); internet technologies (MS); manufacturing systems (MMS); occupational health (MS); philosophy (MA, PhD); power electronics (MS); quality systems (MQS); renewable energy (MS); social evaluation of projects (MBA); strategic market research (MBA); tax law (MA); teaching mathematics (MA).

University of Ottawa, Faculty of Graduate and Postdoctoral Studies, Interdisciplinary Programs, Ottawa, ON K1N 6N5, Canada. Offers e-business (Certificate); e-commerce (Certificate); finance (Certificate); health services and policies research (Diploma); population health (PhD); population health risk assessment and management (Certificate); public management and governance (Certificate); systems science (Certificate).

University of Ottawa, Faculty of Graduate and Postdoctoral Studies, Systems Science Program, Ottawa, ON K1N 6N5, Canada. Offers M Sc, M Sys Sc, Certificate. Part-time and evening/weekend programs available. *Degree requirements:* For master's and Certificate, thesis optional. *Entrance requirements:* For master's, bachelor's degree or equivalent, minimum B average; for Certificate, honors degree or equivalent, minimum B average. Additional exam requirements/recommendations for international students: Recommended—TOEFL. Electronic applications accepted. *Faculty research:* Software engineering, communication systems, information systems, production management, corporate managerial modeling.

Worcester Polytechnic Institute, Graduate Studies and Research, Department of Social Science and Policy Studies, Worcester, MA 01609-2280. Offers interdisciplinary social science (PhD); system dynamics (MS, Graduate Certificate). Part-time and evening/weekend programs available. Postbaccalaureate distance learning degree programs offered (no on-campus study). *Faculty:* 5 full-time (2 women), 2 part-time/adjunct (0 women). *Students:* 2 full-time (1 woman), 13 part-time (2 women); includes 2 minority (1 Black or African American, non-Hispanic/Latino; 1 Hispanic/Latino), 3 international. 8 applicants, 75% accepted, 6 enrolled. In 2014, 2 master's awarded. *Entrance requirements:* For master's and doctorate, GRE General Test, 3 letters of recommendation, statement of purpose. Additional exam requirements/recommendations for international students: Required—TOEFL (minimum score 563 paper-based; 84 iBT), IELTS (minimum score 7). *Application deadline:* For fall admission, 1/1 priority date for domestic students, 1/1 for international students; for spring admission, 10/1 priority date for domestic students, 10/1 for international students. Applications are processed on a rolling basis. Application fee: $70. Electronic applications accepted. *Financial support:* Research assistantships, teaching assistantships, career-related internships or fieldwork, institutionally sponsored loans, scholarships/grants, and unspecified assistantships available. Financial award application deadline: 1/1; financial award applicants required to submit FAFSA. *Unit head:* Dr. James K. Doyle, Head, 508-831-5296, Fax: 508-831-5896, E-mail: doyle@wpi.edu. *Application contact:* Dr. Oleg Pavlov, Graduate Coordinator, 508-831-5296, Fax: 508-831-5896, E-mail: opavlov@wpi.edu.
Website: http://www.wpi.edu/academics/ssps.

CLARKSON UNIVERSITY
Information Technology Program

Programs of Study

The Master of Science in information technology (IT) program offers an interdisciplinary, broad-based curriculum for this professional degree. Students take courses from a range of disciplines that include math and computer science, electrical and computer engineering, technical communications, and management information systems. The one-year program has a practical orientation that emphasizes hands-on learning and real-world experience in collaborative projects.

The master's degree in IT program comprises a minimum of 30 credit hours, which include one course treating modern object-oriented design in a language such as C++, one course treating the principles of computing and telecommunication systems, one course in the management of technology, three courses in application of information technology, and 6 credits of project work. Additional credits can include course or project work. Through course selection and project work, students can focus on areas in IT they find compelling.

Students in this program develop a broad base of competencies in hardware, operating systems, programming, computer applications, and the management of technology. At the same time, they can choose to explore specific application areas through elective classes and project work. Projects focus on real-world problems that provide experience directly applicable to IT in an organizational setting.

Clarkson provides access to some of the latest equipment and software. Individuals can install and run multiple operating systems (UNIX/Linux, Microsoft Windows, VMware), manage Web servers, create storefront CGIs, and administer databases.

The academic year consists of two semesters of fifteen weeks each. There is no formal summer session for graduate classes, but many students complete their projects during this time.

Students can also opt to complete their degree in 1½ years, taking 10 credits each semester.

Financial Aid

Partial-tuition assistantships are available for all full-time students who are accepted. This includes up to 30 percent off the cost of tuition until degree requirements are met. This assistantship is merit-based.

Cost of Study

Tuition for graduate work is $1457 per credit hour for 2015–16. Fees are about $590 per year.

Living and Housing Costs

Estimated living expenses off campus are approximately $14,000 a year, which includes rent, food, books, clothing, recreation, and miscellaneous expenses. Most graduate students live off campus, as on-campus housing is very limited.

Student Group

There are approximately 600 total graduate students and 3,200 undergraduates.

Location

Clarkson is located in Potsdam, a quintessential college town, nestled in the foothills of the northern Adirondack region of New York. The beautiful northeast corner of the state is the home of the 6-million-acre Adirondack Park. Within 2 hours of the campus are Lake Placid and the cosmopolitan Canadian cities of Montreal and Ottawa.

The University

Founded in 1896, Clarkson stands out among America's private nationally ranked research institutions because of its dynamic collaborative learning environment, innovative degree and research programs, and unmatched track record for producing leaders and innovators.

Clarkson is New York State's highest-ranked small research institution. The University attracts 3,000 enterprising students from diverse backgrounds (including some 400 graduate students) who thrive in rigorous programs in engineering, arts, sciences, business, and health sciences.

Applying

Although there is a rolling admission policy, the recommended application deadlines are May 1 for the fall semester and December 1 for the spring semester for U.S. applicants. International applicants are encouraged to apply by April 15 for the fall semester and October 1 for the spring semester. Students who apply by January 30 for the fall semester receive priority for assistantships and other financial aid. Prospective students may submit an online application using a credit card. Study may begin in August or January. Scores on the General Test of the GRE are required for all applications. TOEFL scores must be submitted by all applicants for whom English is a second language.

Correspondence and Information

Information Technology
Graduate School
Clarkson University
Box 5802
Potsdam, New York 13699-5802
United States
Phone: 315-268-3802
Fax: 315-268-3989
E-mail: sciencegrad@clarkson.edu
　　　horn@clarkson.edu
Website: http://www.clarkson.edu/graduate

The Faculty

Fifteen full-time regular faculty members and 2 full-time regular instructors from the four departments participate in the graduate information technology program. The disciplines that compose the IT program include math and computer science, electrical and computer engineering, technical communications, and management information systems.

SAMPLE INFORMATION TECHNOLOGY PROJECTS

Virtual Computing Lab: Prototyping a Clarkson Cloud

Adviser: Wm. Dennis Horn

This project implemented a virtual computing lab (VCL) that will replace the current PC labs on campus. The purpose of this project was to make it easier for the Office of Information Technology to manage the campus PC labs and eventually make VCL available to students using a PC from anywhere on the Internet. Software used was Citrix XenDesktop 4 on Windows Server 2008R2 and the Citrix XenServer, run on a Dell Equallogic PS6000XVS Storage Array, which provides intelligent tiered storage among traditional SAS drives and solid state drives.

Academic Metric Management System

Adviser: Boris Jukic

This project was the Web design and front-end development of the Clarkson Academic Metric Management system, designed to help the Clarkson University business faculty manage the data from the compliant standards of learning set forth by the AACSB–The Association to Advance Collegiate Schools of Business. Previously, M.B.A. professors had to find a way to create and maintain metric data on their classes, but it was difficult to keep track of this data and remain organized. Written as an ITMS project, this web interface is essentially free to Clarkson and will allow the Clarkson University business faculty to maintain the necessary metric data with ease and in an organized fashion.

Web Analysis Tools for TAD Study

Adviser: Philip K. Hopke

This project analyzed the requirements, designed, implemented, and documented a Web interface for a TAD Study at Clarkson University to manage large volumes of data, maintain inventory, organize scheduling processes, etc. This project characterizes the efficiency of an air cleaner developed by a Syracuse company to reduce asthma attacks in children by providing a healthy environment. Different air quality instruments are installed in the subject's bedroom to determine the efficiency of the air cleaner in providing a healthy environment by reducing the levels of particles, VOCs, CO, etc. Subjects are tested for different biomarkers of inflammation such as nitrate levels and forced expiratory volume, using instruments such as RTubes and peak flow meters. Heart rate is also monitored during sleep.

Web-Based System for Teaching Controller Performance Assessment

Adviser: Dr. Raghunathan Rengasamy

This project includes the development of a C++ interface for communicating, with an experiment for controlling the level of liquid in multiple tanks. Matlab is used to control the liquid level by opening and closing valves that regulate the flow into the various tanks. A module written in C++ is integrated with a Web server for displaying real time on the Web data from the experiment. The system allows for a two-way communication so that commands from the Web can be directly fed to the experimental system. The complete site contains a calendar, software for user registration, authentication, and other resources.

Calculation Models for Particle Transport, Deposition, and Removal

Adviser: Professor Goodarz Ahmadi

This project uses Java to create calculation models for the NSF Combined Research-Curriculum Development for Particle Transport, Deposition and Removal. A sequence of calculation models written in the Java programming language has been developed. These models are used on a series of Web-based engineering courses as interactive illustrations and support for exercises. They are carried out via Web pages using HTML and Java applets.

Documentation of Cisco Routers and Switches

Adviser: Professor Jeanna Matthews

This project documents the configuration of Cisco Routers and Switches in Clarkson University's Cisco-ITL laboratory. The document includes basic router configuration, password recovery, Cisco switches in the ITL, IOS commands, upgrading router IOSes, making network cables, and so forth. The document will enable future students to maintain the equipment, set up experiments and classes, and update the hardware and software.

The Northern New York Schools Computer Survey Project

Adviser: Professor Donna Mosier, SUNY Potsdam

Secondary schools in the United States and Canada are investing a significant part of their budgets in computing technologies. This project attempts to use an online survey tool to determine the application of that technology in terms of equipment, infrastructure, connectivity, technological support, and student and teacher training. The survey is being offered to about 140 schools in upstate New York. For the survey the candidate designed seven online forms each with a corresponding CGI. The Perl/CGIs write to a flat database. After submitting all seven forms, a school district is granted password entry into the survey results pages. This software includes numerous programs analyzing survey results.

Windmill Research Project

Adviser: Professor Kenneth Visser

Every 10 seconds, sensors at the Windmill Site (Potsdam, New York, Airport) record data on wind speed at 18 meters, 12 meters, and 6 meters; wind direction at 18 meters and 6 meters; and the temperature, relative humidity, and pressure. This project reduces the massive amount of raw data to human-interpretable form by creating an HTML interface that allows researchers to select time intervals of minutes, hours, days, weeks, and months and graph changes over periods of days, months, and years. Perl/CGI is used to crunch the data in less than a second and graph it, using the Perl GD.pm module, in PNG format. Graphs are scaled to fit on the screen, and multiple graphs can be placed in a single display for comparison.

Thin Films Instructional Design

Adviser: Professor Ian Suni

In the past Clarkson has been successful at producing and distributing interactive instruction on the latest in Thin Films research via CD technology. This project teaches the latest research concepts using Web media. Thin Film production involves dynamic mechanical and electro-chemical processes at the molecular level. Graduate-level instruction in the latest techniques requires dynamic illustration. Instruction is carried out via Web pages using HTML, animated gifs, JavaScript, Flash, and Perl/CGI. Lessons include quizzes with remediation.

COLUMBIA UNIVERSITY
Department of Computer Science

 For more information, visit http://petersons.to/columbiacompsci

Programs of Study

The doctoral program of the Department of Computer Science is geared toward the exceptional student. The faculty believes that the best way to learn how to do research is by doing it; therefore, starting in their first semester, students conduct joint research with faculty members. In addition to conducting research they also prepare themselves for the Ph.D. comprehensive examinations, which test breadth in computer science. The primary educational goal is to prepare students for research and teaching careers either in universities or in industry.

Current research areas include artificial intelligence, collaborative work, computational biology, computational complexity, computational learning theory, computer architecture, computer-aided design of digital systems, databases, digital libraries, distributed computing, graphics, HCI, digital system design, mobile and wearable computing, multimedia, natural-language processing, networking, network management, operating systems, parallel processing, robotics, security, software engineering, user interfaces, virtual and augmented reality, vision, and Web technologies.

The Department also offers the Master of Science degree in computer science. This program can be completed within three semesters of full-time classwork. Completing the optional thesis generally stretches the program to two years. The M.S. degree can also be earned through part-time study. An interdepartmental M.S. degree in computer engineering is also offered between the computer science and electrical engineering departments. A dual-degree program in the Columbia School of Journalism and Computer Science is also offered.

Research Facilities

The Department has well-equipped lab areas for research in computer graphics, computer-aided digital design, computer vision, databases and digital libraries, data mining and knowledge discovery, distributed systems, mobile and wearable computing, virtual and augmented reality, natural-language processing, networking, operating systems, programming systems, robotics, user interfaces, and real-time multimedia.

The departmental computing infrastructure consists of a data center for computational, storage and VoIP services, one large student laboratory, featuring 18 Mac minis and 33 Linux towers each with 2 Nehalem processors, 8 cores, and 24GB memory; a remote Linux cluster with 10 servers each with 2 Xeon processors and 4GB memory; and a number of computing facilities for individual research labs. The data center houses 14TB of Network Appliance file servers and a compute cluster consisting of a Linux cloud with 32 servers, each with 2 Nehalem processors, 8 cores, and 24GB memory. This cloud can support approximately 5000 VMware instances. Additional computing facilities include 8 Intel Linux servers with 8 processors and 34GB memory each, a 3Com VoIP system, and departmental load-balanced Web cluster with 6 servers and business process servers; two online backup servers, each with 40TB capacity; and supporting servers that provide print services, LDAP, DHCP, DNS, tape backup, and software distribution to the department. The data center is internally connected via Gigabit Ethernet and accesses the Internet and Internet2 via the campus fiber network. The University provides 802.11b coverage for most of the campus.

The research infrastructure has approximately 1,000 servers including many Dell, HP, and Silicon Mechanics with Tesla GPU; it also includes hundreds of workstations from Apple, Dell, HP, and other PC manufacturers. The labs for research in image processing, vision, graphics, and robotics contain specialized equipment such as Baxter Research Robot, PR2 mobile robot manipulator, Stäubli RX 60L robot arm, Kinova MICO arm, custom-built overhead XYZ gantry robot, Toshiba FMA manipulator, Barrett Technology robotic hand, 2 RWI Pioneer mobile robots, 1 Evolution ER1 robot, 1 RWI ATRV-2 mobile robot with RTK GPS, Leica HDS-500 and HDS-3000 100-meter range scanners, and real-time imaging boards.

Financial Aid

Most doctoral students and a few master's students receive graduate research assistantships. The stipend for 2014–15 was $3,201 per month for the academic year. In addition, graduate research assistants receive full tuition exemption. A limited number of teaching assistantships are available to doctoral students.

Cost of Study

Tuition and fees totaled approximately $51,300 for the M.S. program and $41,048 for the Ph.D. program for the 2014–15 academic year.

Living and Housing Costs

In 2014–15, apartments in University-owned buildings cost $911–$1,527 and up per month. Rooms are also available at International House; these cost $943–$2,447 and up per month.

Student Group

There are 146 Ph.D. students in the Department. A large proportion of Columbia University's student body is at the graduate level; of the 24,870 students, 18,933 are in the graduate or professional schools.

Location

New York City is the intellectual, artistic, cultural, gastronomic, corporate, financial, and media center of the United States, and perhaps of the world. The city is renowned for its theaters, museums, libraries, restaurants, opera, and music. Inexpensive student tickets for cultural and sporting events are frequently available, and the museums are open to students at very modest cost or are free. The ethnic variety of the city adds to its appeal. The city is bordered by uncongested areas of great beauty that provide varied types of recreation, such as hiking, camping, skiing, and ocean and lake swimming. There are superb beaches on Long Island and in New Jersey, while to the north lie the Catskill, Green, Berkshire, and Adirondack mountains. Close at hand is the beautiful Hudson River valley.

The University

Columbia University was established as King's College in 1754. Today it consists of sixteen schools and faculties and is one of the leading universities in the world. The University draws students from many countries. The high caliber of the students and faculty makes it an intellectually stimulating place to be. Columbia University is located on Morningside Heights, close to Lincoln Center for the Performing Arts, Greenwich Village, Central Park, and midtown Manhattan. Columbia athletic teams compete in the Ivy League.

Applying

For maximum consideration for admission to the doctoral program, students should submit the required application materials before December 15 for the fall term and before October 1 for the spring term. Applicants must submit official applications, transcripts, at least three recommendation letters, and an application fee. The Graduate Record Examinations are required for all computer science graduate applicants. The deadlines for applications to the master's program are February 15 for fall admission and October 1 for spring admission.

Program information can be found at http://www.cs.columbia.edu. Further details on admission and online application for the M.S. program are on the website at http://www.cs.columbia.edu/education/admissions#msadmissions and for the Ph.D. program at http://www.cs.columbia.edu/education/admissions#phd.

Correspondence and Information

Fu Foundation School of Engineering and Applied Science
Department of Computer Science
450 Computer Science Building
Mail Code 0401
Columbia University
1214 Amsterdam Avenue
New York, New York 10027-7003
Phone: 212-939-7000
Website: http://www.cs.columbia.edu/education/admissions

Columbia University

THE FACULTY AND THEIR RESEARCH

Alfred V. Aho, Lawrence Gussman Professor. Programming languages, compilers, software, quantum computing.

Peter K. Allen, Professor. Robotics, computer vision, 3-D modeling.

Alexandr Andoni, Associate Professor. Algorithmic foundations of massive datasets, algorithms with sublinear space (streaming) and time (property testing), high-dimensional geometry, metric embeddings, theoretical machine learning.

Peter Belhumeur, Professor. Computer vision, biometrics, face recognition, computational photography, computer graphics, biological species identification.

Steven M. Bellovin, Professor. Internet security, computer security, privacy, information technology policy.

Allison Bishop, Assistant Professor. Cryptography, complexity theory, distributed algorithms, harmonic analysis.

Adam H. Cannon, Senior Lecturer in Discipline. Machine learning, statistical pattern recognition, computer science education.

Luca Carloni, Associate Professor. System-on-chip platforms, embedded systems, multi-core architectures, cyber-physical systems, computer-aided design.

Augustin Chaintreau, Assistant Professor. Networked algorithms, social networks, mobile computing, stochastic networks.

Shih-Fu Chang, Richard Dicker Professor. Multimedia, computer vision, machine learning, signal processing, information retrieval, visual search.

Xi Chen, Assistant Professor. Algorithmic game theory and economics, computational complexity theory.

Michael Collins, Vikram S. Pandit Professor. Natural language processing and machine learning.

Stephen A. Edwards, Associate Professor. Embedded systems, domain-specific languages, compilers, hardware-software codesign, computer-aided design.

Steven K. Feiner, Professor. Human-computer interaction, augmented reality and virtual environments, 3-D user interfaces, knowledge-based design of graphics and multimedia, mobile and wearable computing, computer games, health-management user interfaces, information visualization.

Roxana Geambasu, Assistant Professor. Software systems, security, privacy.

Luis Gravano, Professor. Databases, information retrieval, Web search.

Eitan Grinspun, Associate Professor. Computer graphics, geometry processing, computational mechanics, scientific computing, discrete differential geometry.

Jonathan L. Gross, Professor of Computer Science, Mathematics, and Mathematical Statistics. Computational aspects of topological graph theory and knot theory, enumerative analysis, and combinatorial models; applications to network layouts on higher-order surfaces and to interactive computer graphics of weaves and links.

Julia Hirschberg, Professor. Natural-language processing, spoken language processing, spoken dialogue systems, deceptive speech.

Daniel Hsu, Assistant Professor. Algorithmic statistics, machine learning, privacy.

Tony Jebara, Associate Professor. Machine learning, social networks, graphs, vision, spatio-temporal modeling.

Gail E. Kaiser, Professor. Software engineering and software systems, focusing on software reliability, privacy and security, and social software engineering.

John R. Kender, Professor. Computer vision, video understanding, visual user interfaces, medical image processing, artificial intelligence.

Angelos D. Keromytis, Associate Professor. Computer and network security.

Martha A. Kim, Assistant Professor. Computer architecture, hardware systems, hardware/software interaction, parallel hardware and software systems.

Jae Woo Lee, Lecturer in Discipline. Computer science education, networks, software engineering, cloud computing.

Tal G. Malkin, Associate Professor. Cryptography, information and network security, foundations of computer science, computational complexity, distributed computation, randomness in computation.

Kathleen R. McKeown, Henry and Gertrude Rothschild Professor. Artificial intelligence, natural-language processing, language generation, multimedia explanation, text summarization, user interfaces, user modeling, digital libraries.

Vishal Misra, Associate Professor. Networking, modeling and performance evaluation, Internet economics.

Shree K. Nayar, T. C. Chang Professor. Computer vision, computational imaging, computer graphics, robotics, human-computer interfaces.

Jason Nieh, Professor. Operating systems, distributed systems, mobile computing, thin-client computing, performance evaluation.

Steven M. Nowick, Professor. Asynchronous and mixed-timing digital circuits and systems, computer-aided design, networks-on-chip, interconnection networks for parallel processors, low-power digital design.

Dana Pe'er, Associate Professor. Computational biology, machine learning, biological networks, genomics and systems biology.

Itsik Pe'er, Associate Professor. Computational biology, genomics, medical and population genetics, isolated and admixed populations, analysis of heritable variation in cancer.

Kenneth A. Ross, Professor. Databases, query optimization, declarative languages for database systems, genetics, architecture-sensitive software design.

Dan Rubenstein, Associate Professor. Computer networks, network robustness and security, multimedia networking, performance evaluation, algorithms, low-power networking.

Henning G. Schulzrinne, Julian Clarence Levi Professor. Computer networks, multimedia systems, mobile and wireless systems, ubiquitous and pervasive computing.

Rocco A. Servedio, Associate Professor. Computational learning theory, computational complexity theory, randomness in computation, combinatorics.

Simha Sethumadhavan, Associate Professor. Computer architecture, hardware security.

Clifford Stein, Professor. Algorithms, combinatorial optimization, scheduling, network algorithms.

Salvatore J. Stolfo, Professor. Computer security, intrusion detection systems, parallel computing, artificial intelligence, machine learning.

Joseph F. Traub, Edwin Howard Armstrong Professor. Quantum computing, computational complexity, information-based complexity, financial computations.

Eugene Wu, Assistant Professor. Databases, data analysis, interactive data visualization, data cleaning.

Junfeng Yang, Assistant Professor. Operating systems, software reliability, programming languages, security, distributed systems, software engineering.

Mihalis Yannakakis, Percy K. and Vida L. W. Hudson Professor. Algorithms, complexity theory, combinatorial optimization, databases, testing and verification.

Changxi Zheng, Assistant Professor. Computer graphics, physically-based multi-sensory animation, physically-based sound rendering, scientific computing, robotics.

UNIVERSITY OF MICHIGAN
School of Information

Programs of Study

The University of Michigan School of Information (UMSI) is dedicated to studying information and all of its functions, from how it is created and collected to how it is preserved and accessed. The program accepts those just embarking on careers in information science as well as seasoned scholars looking to enhance their research skills. There is a strong interdisciplinary emphasis at the school, and students come from as many as 100 different majors.

The program emphasizes an academic knowledge base and research methods that train students to use information to effect positive changes. *U.S. News & World Report* consistently ranks the University of Michigan School of Information among the top 10 in archival and preservation programs, digital librarianship, and information systems.

Students work side by side with faculty members researching and creating new ways of improving access to information and developing new uses for it in society, education, and the marketplace. Active research faculty grants include the study of relevant technological advances and their relationship to information. Major initiatives include in-depth studies into virtual collaboration, the impact of deploying large-scale electronic health records systems, usability challenges in smart homes, and social media sentiment analysis, among others.

The University of Michigan School of Information prepares students for careers in the field of information at Web/software design firms, large IT organizations, consulting firms, archives and records repositories, library systems, government, and museums.

Master of Science in Information (M.S.I.): This degree program requires students to complete 48 credits in information management, research methods, cognate classes, and practical engagement courses. All students must take two core foundation courses: SI 500: Information in Social Systems: Collections, Flows, and Processing; and SI 501: Contextual Inquiry and Project Management. Students must also take a third core technology/programming course, though it may be waived in lieu of other project work.

M.S.I. Specialization Options: Students may choose to focus their studies in one or more areas, including archives and records management, human-computer interaction, information analysis and retrieval, information economics for management, library and information science, preservation of information, school and library media, or social computing. Students may also elect a tailored program according to their career interests.

Master of Health Informatics (M.H.I.): Conducted jointly with the School of Public Health, the School of Information offers a Master of Health Informatics degree program. One of the fastest-growing fields in the nation, health informatics develops innovative ways to put information and knowledge to use in promoting health and improving health care. Because clinical, consumer and public health fields are converging, students are required to acquire knowledge relevant to each of these areas. Defining features of the program include strengths in consumer informatics, population health applications, and system-related human and organizational issues.

The M.H.I. degree is 52 credits and takes 2 years (4 semesters) of full-time work on campus to complete. Students can attend part time and typically complete the program in three to four years. Requirements include 37–38 credits of core course work, 14–15 credits of elective course work, and 400 hours of internship.

Ph.D. in Information: Doctoral students in the School of Information are trained for research careers in academia or industry, focused on innovative information processes and technologies that affect classrooms, business, and society as a whole. Academic milestones for the doctoral degree in information include a pre-candidacy research project, a field preliminary exam, teaching requirements, and a successful defense of the student's final dissertation.

Doctoral program students complete a minimum of 24 hours of study in residence at the University of Michigan's Ann Arbor campus. Students must maintain full-time status and must complete their course work within seven years, although most students graduate in four or five years.

Dual-Degree Programs: The University of Michigan has developed six different programs that grant dual degrees in conjunction with the Master of Science in Information. The M.S.I. can be paired with an M.B.A. from the Ross School of Business, an M.P.P. from the Ford School of Public Policy, a J.D. from the Law School, an M.S.W. from the School of Social Work, or an M.S.N. from the School of Nursing. Degree requirements and length of study vary according to each dual-degree program's requirements. When students pursue degrees combined with Master of Science in Information degrees, the total number of credits required is less than the requirements for each degree if earned separately.

Research Facilities

The School of Information has a beautiful home in North Quad, along with the Department of Screen Arts and Cultures, the Department of Communication Studies, the Language Resource Center, and the Sweetland Writing Center. Features of this facility include the high-tech Media Gateway and 2435 NQ which support students, faculty, and staff working with multimedia, network, and communication technologies. The complex also provides classrooms, academic studios, research labs, and offices. Within North Quad, UMSI has four dedicated classrooms, all with state-of-the-art audiovisual technology. North Quad also offers many spaces to facilitate meetings or to exchange ideas. There are several UMSI project meeting rooms and a number of collaborative work spaces, such as the Media Gateway and Space 2435, which include video-teleconferences and electronic media sharing and editing.

An array of resources that support the School of Information and other users is available within the Graduate Library collection. The library maintains more than 65,000 volumes and 450 current journal titles covering all aspects of the School of Information academic programs. In addition, the University Library also provides access to a vast number of electronic and print resources such as OCLC FirstSearch, ProQuest, ISI Web of Science, JSTOR, Wilson Indexes, and dozens more, many including full-text content. In particular, library and information science resources such as Library Literature, LISA, ERIC, INSPEC, and many full-text journals may also be accessed across campus or from home. The library in the Duderstadt Center on North Campus specializes in engineering and computer science materials.

Financial Aid

There are many resources available to assist master's students with funding, including UMSI scholarships, UMSI diversity scholarships, and GSI/GSRA opportunities. In addition, there are two unique funded opportunities available: the Joyce Bonk Assistantship and the University Library Associates program.

UMSI master's students (new and continuing) have also been successful when applying for external funding. In recent years, awards received by UMSI students have included American Library Association Spectrum Scholarships, ARMA International Educational Foundation Scholarships, Association for Women in Computing Scholarships, Society of American Archivist Scholarships, and more. All external tuition scholarship awards are eligible for matching funds from UMSI, up to a maximum of $10,000 and subject to availability of funds.

The U-M Office of Financial Aid has information on federal programs for aid for U.S. citizens. The University also provides funding information for international students.

Most students also choose to work part-time while in the program, for both a source of funding and an opportunity for professional experience.

Cost of Study

Graduate tuition and fees in the School of Information for the 2015–16 academic year are $10,319 for Michigan residents and $20,884 per term for non-Michigan residents. Ph.D. students are guaranteed a minimum of four years of funding, including tuition and a stipend, contingent on their academic progress.

Living and Housing Costs

There are many options for housing both on and off campus that range from co-ops to rooms in houses to freestanding apartments. A new University graduate student residence is slated to open in 2015. Housing information is provided to admitted students in the summer before they begin the program. Housing costs for the academic year are estimated at $14,248.

Student Outcomes

There are more than 7,800 alumni from the University of Michigan School of Information; many are leaders and experts in the field and in their communities. Recent graduates of the School of Information work for top organizations including Google, Facebook, the Federal Trade Commission, the Library of Congress, and Microsoft Corporation. Between 97 and 100 percent of new alumni have found employment or are pursuing additional education within one year of graduation.

Location

Ann Arbor is a vibrant college town with many restaurants, musical venues, museums, bars, and theaters to explore. There is a multitude of recreational activities for its students and residents, with over 1,900 acres of parks in the city, as well as golfing, ice skating, and canoeing facilities. Residents of Ann Arbor also enjoy the city's diverse cultural scene, evident in the many museums, galleries, theaters, and music venues. Ann Arbor is frequently ranked as one of the top cities in America by many media organizations, including CNNMoney, The Huffington Post, *Kiplinger*, and *USA Today*.

The University and The School

The University was founded in 1817 as the Catholepistemiad, or University of Michigania. In 1821, it was officially renamed the University of Michigan. Originally located in Detroit, the institution's home moved to Ann Arbor in 1837. One of the original buildings on the Ann Arbor campus still stands and is used today as the President's house.

The University has grown to include nineteen schools and colleges, covering the liberal arts and sciences as well as most professions. The fall 2014 enrollment of undergraduate, graduate, and professional students was 43,525. According to the latest national data, the U-M spends more on research—$1.32 billion in FY2014—than any other U.S. public university.

University Of Michigan

The School of Information was chartered in 1996, but the school has had several other incarnations since its origin as the University of Michigan Department of Library Science in 1926. The department evolved to meet the needs of each new generation. In 1948, the department ended its undergraduate program, replaced the bachelor's degree in library science with a master's degree, and introduced a Ph.D. program. In 1969, the Department of Library Science became the School of Library Science. In 1986, the name was changed again, to the School of Information and Library Science.

Toward the end of the twentieth century, as the pace of change quickened in the information field, the School of Information was founded, taking on a new identity and mission: to prepare socially engaged information professionals, and to create people-centered knowledge, systems and institutions for the Information Age.

Correspondence and Information

School of Information
University of Michigan
MSI Admissions
3360 North Quad
105 South State Street
Ann Arbor, Michigan 48109-1285
Phone: 734-763-2285
Fax: 734-615-3587
E-mail: umsi.admissions@umich.edu
Website: umsi.info/pgpedu

THE FACULTY AND AREAS OF RESEARCH

Mark S. Ackerman, George Herbert Mead Collegiate Professor; Ph.D., MIT. Computer-supported cooperative work, expertise networks, organizational memory.

Eytan Adar, Associate Professor; Ph.D., Washington. Network science, Web re-visitation, network visualization.

Julia Adler-Milstein, Assistant Professor; Ph.D., Harvard. Health informatics and management, health information exchanges, impact of electronic health records on healthcare delivery.

Ceren Budak, Assistant Professor; Ph.D., California, Santa Barbara. Information analysis and retrieval, computational social science.

Yan Chen, Daniel Kahneman Collegiate Professor; Ph.D., Caltech. Economics, incentive-centered design, contributions to public goods.

Kevyn Collins-Thompson, Associate Professor; Ph.D., Carnegie Mellon. Information retrieval, text mining, natural language processing, machine learning.

Paul Conway, Associate Professor; Ph.D., Michigan. Archives and records management, digitization and representation of visual and textual archives, modeling the use of digital archives in the visual studies and the humanities.

Tawanna Dillahunt, Assistant Professor; Ph.D., Carnegie Mellon. Human-computer interaction, ubiquitous computing, social computing.

Paul N. Edwards, Professor; Ph.D., California, Santa Cruz. Science and technology studies and history, computer models of climate and Earth systems, knowledge infrastructure.

Nicole Ellison, Associate Professor; Ph.D., USC. Computer-supported cooperative work and communications; social computing, relationship formation and maintenance via social network sites.

Thomas Finholt, Interim Dean, Professor; Ph.D., Carnegie Mellon. Computer-supported cooperative work, cyberinfrastructure, scientific collaboration via virtual organizations.

Barry Fishman, Arthur F Thurnau Professor; Ph.D., Northwestern. Learning science, teacher learning, learning technologies.

Margaret Hedstrom, Robert M Warner Collegiate Professor; Ph.D., Wisconsin. Archives and records management, sustainable digital data preservation, science and big data.

John L. King, William Warner Bishop Collegiate Professor; Ph.D., California, Irvine. Public policy and computer science, requirement development for information systems design and implementation, organizational and institutional influences on information technology development.

Predrag "Pedja" Klasnja, Assistant Professor; Ph.D., Washington. Human-computer interaction, ubiquitous computing for chronic disease management, health informatics.

Erin L. Krupka, Assistant Professor; Ph.D., Carnegie Mellon. Economics and social psychology, effect of social and environmental factors on behavior, how social norms modify self-interest.

Carl Lagoze, Associate Professor; Ph.D., Cornell. Library and information science; digital libraries, metadata, and sociotechnical infrastructure for scholarly communication; scientific collaboration.

Cliff Lampe, Associate Professor; Ph.D., Michigan. Computer-supported cooperative work and communication studies, social computing, outcomes of participating in social network sites.

Silvia Lindtner, Assistant Professor; Ph.D., California, Irvine. DIY "maker" and open source culture, IT development in urban China, global processes of work and labor.

Karen Markey, Professor; Ph.D., Syracuse. Library and information science, subject searching, visual persuasion, gaming for teaching information literacy.

Qiaozhu Mei, Associate Professor; Ph.D., Illinois. Computer science; information retrieval; text, Web, and social data mining.

Markus Mobius, Associate Professor; Ph.D., MIT. Economics of social networks, belief formations in labor market outcomes.

Mark W. Newman, Associate Professor; Ph.D., California, Berkeley. Human-computer interaction, ubiquitous computing, end-user programming.

Sile O'Modhrain, Associate Professor; Ph.D., Stanford. Human-computer interaction, haptic output interfaces, movement as interaction design.

Stephen Oney, Assistant Professor; Ph.D., Carnegie-Mellon. Human-computer interaction, software engineering, programming environments.

Joyojeet Pal, Assistant Professor; Ph.D., California, Berkeley. Information and communication technology for development, assistive technology, computer-aided learning.

Casey Pierce, Assistant Professor; Ph.D., Northwestern. Organizational communication and technology, knowledge management in organizations.

Sile O'Modhrain, Associate Professor; Ph.D., Stanford. Human-computer interaction, haptic output interfaces, movement as interaction design.

Dragomir Radev, Professor; Ph.D., Columbia. Computer science, natural language processing, information retrieval.

Paul Resnick, Michael D. Cohen Collegiate Professor; Ph.D., MIT. Computer science, economics, and social psychology; social computing; reputation and recommender systems.

Soo Young Rieh, Associate Professor; Ph.D., Rutgers. Library and information science, credibility and cognitive authority judgment, human information behavior.

Lionel Robert, Assistant Professor; Ph.D., Indiana. Management information systems, diversity and team performance, collaboration technology.

Daniel Romero, Assistant Professor; Ph.D., Cornell. Social and information networks, network evolution, information diffusion, user interactions on Web.

Tanya Rosenblat, Associate Professor; Ph.D., MIT. Experimental economics, trust and altruism in social networks.

Christian Sandvig, Associate Professor; Ph.D., Stanford. Infrastructure studies, socio-technical systems, social computing, information policy.

Sarita Yardi Schoenebeck, Assistant Professor; Ph.D., Georgia Tech. Computer-supported cooperative work, social computing, youth and digital media.

Charles Severance, Clinical Associate Professor; Ph.D., Michigan State. Computer science and education; open educational resources; online learning, teaching, and collaboration systems.

Stephanie Teasley, Research Professor; Ph.D., Pittsburgh. Computer-supported cooperative work and learning science, collaboration and learning technologies, learning analytics.

Kentaro Toyama, W.K. Kellogg Professor of Community Information, Associate Professor; Ph.D., Yale. Information and communication technologies, international development (ICTD).

Douglas E. Van Houweling, Professor; Ph.D., Indiana. Public policy and management, information systems management and planning, large-scale network management.

Tiffany C.E. Veinot, Associate Professor; Ph.D., Western Ontario. Health informatics and library and information science; health information behavior within marginalized communities; social studies of health information technologies, policy, and practice.

Elizabeth Yakel, Associate Dean for Research and Faculty Affairs, Professor; Ph.D., Michigan. Archives and records management, access to digital archives, Web 2.0 and cultural heritage institutions, archival metrics and evaluation.

North Quad, home of the School of Information, on the central campus of the University of Michigan.

Section 9
Electrical and Computer Engineering

This section contains a directory of institutions offering graduate work in electrical and computer engineering, followed by an in-depth entry submitted by an institution that chose to prepare a detailed program description. Additional information about programs listed in the directory but not augmented by an in-depth entry may be obtained by writing directly to the dean of a graduate school or chair of a department at the address given in the directory.

For programs offering related work, see also in this book *Computer Science and Information Technology, Energy and Power Engineering, Engineering and Applied Sciences, Industrial Engineering,* and *Mechanical Engineering and Mechanics.* In another guide in this series:

Graduate Programs in the Physical Sciences, Mathematics, Agricultural Sciences, the Environment & Natural Resources
See *Mathematical Sciences* and *Physics*

CONTENTS

Program Directories

Display and Close-Up

Computer Engineering

Air Force Institute of Technology, Graduate School of Engineering and Management, Department of Electrical and Computer Engineering, Dayton, OH 45433-7765. Offers computer engineering (MS, PhD); computer systems/science (MS); electrical engineering (MS, PhD); electro-optics (MS, PhD). *Accreditation:* ABET (one or more programs are accredited). Part-time programs available. *Degree requirements:* For master's, thesis; for doctorate, thesis/dissertation. *Entrance requirements:* For master's and doctorate, GRE General Test, minimum GPA of 3.0, U.S. citizenship. *Faculty research:* Remote sensing, information survivability, microelectronics, computer networks, artificial intelligence.

American University of Beirut, Graduate Programs, Faculty of Engineering and Architecture, Beirut, Lebanon. Offers applied energy (ME); civil engineering (PhD); electrical and computer engineering (PhD); engineering management (MEM); environmental and water resources (ME); environmental technology (MSES); mechanical engineering (ME, PhD); urban design (MUD); urban planning and policy (MUPP). Part-time programs available. *Faculty:* 93 full-time (18 women), 3 part-time/adjunct (1 woman). *Students:* 268 full-time (111 women), 58 part-time (27 women). Average age 26. 225 applicants, 68% accepted, 79 enrolled. In 2014, 114 master's, 9 doctorates awarded. Terminal master's awarded for partial completion of doctoral program. *Degree requirements:* For master's, one foreign language, comprehensive exam, thesis (for some programs); for doctorate, one foreign language, comprehensive exam, thesis/dissertation, publications. *Entrance requirements:* For master's, letters of recommendation; for doctorate, GRE, letters of recommendation, master's degree, transcripts, curriculum vitae, interview. Additional exam requirements/recommendations for international students: Required—TOEFL (minimum score 600 paper-based; 100 iBT), IELTS (minimum score 7.5). *Application deadline:* For fall admission, 2/5 priority date for domestic and international students; for spring admission, 11/1 priority date for domestic students, 11/1 for international students. Application fee: $50. Electronic applications accepted. *Expenses:* Tuition: Full-time $15,462; part-time $859 per credit. Required fees: $692. Tuition and fees vary according to course load and program. *Financial support:* In 2014–15, 190 students received support, including 2 fellowships with full tuition reimbursements available (averaging $24,800 per year), 64 research assistantships with full tuition reimbursements available (averaging $24,800 per year), 124 teaching assistantships with full tuition reimbursements available (averaging $9,800 per year); career-related internships or fieldwork, institutionally sponsored loans, scholarships/grants, health care benefits, and unspecified assistantships also available. *Total annual research expenditures:* $1.5 million. *Unit head:* Prof. Makram T. Suidan, Dean, 961-1350000 Ext. 3400, Fax: 961-1744462, E-mail: msuidan@aub.edu.lb. *Application contact:* Dr. Salim Kanaan, Director, Admissions Office, 961-1350000 Ext. 2594, Fax: 961-1750775, E-mail: sk00@aub.edu.lb.
Website: http://staff.aub.edu.lb/~webfea.

American University of Sharjah, Graduate Programs, Sharjah, United Arab Emirates. Offers accounting (MS); business (EMBA, MBA); chemical engineering (MS Ch E); civil engineering (MSCE); computer engineering (MS); electrical engineering (MSEE); engineering systems management (MS); mathematics (MS); mechanical engineering (MSME); mechatronics engineering (MS); teaching English to speakers of other languages (MA); translation and interpreting (MA); urban planning (MUP). Part-time and evening/weekend programs available. *Degree requirements:* For master's, thesis (for some programs). *Entrance requirements:* For master's, GMAT (for MBA). Additional exam requirements/recommendations for international students: Required—TOEFL (minimum score 550 paper-based; 80 iBT), TWE (minimum score 5); Recommended—IELTS (minimum score 6.5). Electronic applications accepted. *Faculty research:* Water pollution, management and waste water treatment, energy and sustainability, air pollution, Islamic finance, family business and small and medium enterprises.

Arizona State University at the Tempe campus, Ira A. Fulton Schools of Engineering, School of Computing, Informatics, and Decision Systems Engineering, Tempe, AZ 85287-8809. Offers computer engineering (MS, PhD); computer science (MCS, MS, PhD); industrial engineering (MS, PhD); software engineering (MS). Part-time and evening/weekend programs available. Postbaccalaureate distance learning degree programs offered (minimal on-campus study). Terminal master's awarded for partial completion of doctoral program. *Degree requirements:* For master's, comprehensive exam (for some programs), portfolio (MCS); interactive Program of Study (iPOS) submitted before completing 50 percent of required credit hours; for doctorate, comprehensive exam, thesis/dissertation, interactive Program of Study (iPOS) submitted before completing 50 percent of required credit hours. *Entrance requirements:* For master's, GRE, minimum GPA of 3.0 or equivalent in last 2 years of work leading to bachelor's degree; for doctorate, GRE, minimum GPA of 3.0 in last 2 years of work leading to bachelor's degree. Additional exam requirements/recommendations for international students: Required—TOEFL, IELTS, or PTE. Electronic applications accepted. *Expenses:* Contact institution. *Faculty research:* Artificial intelligence, cyberphysical and embedded systems, health informatics, information assurance and security, information management/multimedia/visualization, network science, personalized learning/educational games, production logistics, software and systems engineering, statistical modeling and data mining.

Auburn University, Graduate School, Ginn College of Engineering, Department of Electrical and Computer Engineering, Auburn University, AL 36849. Offers MEE, MS, PhD. Part-time programs available. *Faculty:* 27 full-time (2 women), 4 part-time/adjunct (1 woman). *Students:* 158 full-time (40 women), 38 part-time (6 women); includes 5 minority (2 Black or African American, non-Hispanic/Latino; 1 American Indian or Alaska Native, non-Hispanic/Latino; 1 Asian, non-Hispanic/Latino; 1 Hispanic/Latino), 154 international. Average age 25. 412 applicants, 56% accepted, 59 enrolled. In 2014, 21 master's, 18 doctorates awarded. *Degree requirements:* For master's, comprehensive exam, thesis (for some programs); for doctorate, thesis/dissertation. *Entrance requirements:* For master's and doctorate, GRE General Test, GRE Subject Test. *Application deadline:* For fall admission, 7/7 for domestic students; for spring admission, 11/24 for domestic students. Applications are processed on a rolling basis. Application fee: $50 ($60 for international students). Electronic applications accepted. *Expenses:* Tuition, state resident: full-time $8586; part-time $477 per credit hour. Tuition, nonresident: full-time $25,758; part-time $1431 per credit hour. Required fees: $804 per semester. Tuition and fees vary according to degree level and program. *Financial support:* Fellowships, research assistantships, teaching assistantships, and Federal Work-Study available. Support available to part-time students. Financial award application deadline: 3/15; financial award applicants required to submit FAFSA. *Faculty research:* Power systems, energy conversion, electronics, electromagnetics, digital systems. *Unit head:* Dr. Mark Nelms, Head, 334-844-1830. *Application contact:* Dr. George Flowers, Dean of the Graduate School, 334-844-2125.
Website: http://www.eng.auburn.edu/department/ee/.

Baylor University, Graduate School, School of Engineering and Computer Science, Department of Electrical and Computer Engineering, Waco, TX 76798. Offers MS, PhD.

Entrance requirements: Additional exam requirements/recommendations for international students: Required—TOEFL. Electronic applications accepted. *Faculty research:* Applied electromagnetics, power energy, communications, systems.

Boise State University, College of Engineering, Department of Electrical and Computer Engineering, Boise, ID 83725-0399. Offers computer engineering (M Engr, MS); electrical and computer engineering (PhD); electrical engineering (M Engr, MS). Part-time and evening/weekend programs available. *Faculty:* 14 full-time, 2 part-time/adjunct. *Students:* 28 full-time (4 women), 26 part-time (2 women); includes 9 minority (2 Black or African American, non-Hispanic/Latino; 6 Asian, non-Hispanic/Latino; 1 Two or more races, non-Hispanic/Latino), 13 international. 47 applicants, 51% accepted, 11 enrolled. In 2014, 18 master's, 1 doctorate awarded. *Degree requirements:* For master's, thesis. *Entrance requirements:* For master's, GRE General Test, minimum GPA of 3.0. Additional exam requirements/recommendations for international students: Required—TOEFL. *Application deadline:* Applications are processed on a rolling basis. Application fee: $55. Electronic applications accepted. *Expenses:* Tuition, state resident: part-time $331 per credit hour. Tuition, nonresident: part-time $531 per credit hour. *Financial support:* In 2014–15, 23 students received support, including 20 research assistantships, 2 teaching assistantships. Financial award application deadline: 3/1; financial award applicants required to submit FAFSA. *Unit head:* Dr. Nader Rafia, Department Chair, 208-426-3711, E-mail: nrafia@boisestate.edu. *Application contact:* Linda Platt, Office Services Supervisor, Graduate Admission and Degree Services, 208-426-1074, Fax: 208-426-2789, E-mail: lplatt@boisestate.edu.
Website: http://coen.boisestate.edu/ece/prospective-graduate/.

Boston University, College of Engineering, Department of Electrical and Computer Engineering, Boston, MA 02215. Offers electrical engineering (M Eng); photonics (MS). Part-time programs available. *Faculty:* 40 full-time (3 women), 5 part-time/adjunct (0 women). *Students:* 260 full-time (71 women), 60 part-time (14 women); includes 37 minority (1 Black or African American, non-Hispanic/Latino; 1 American Indian or Alaska Native, non-Hispanic/Latino; 23 Asian, non-Hispanic/Latino; 10 Hispanic/Latino; 2 Two or more races, non-Hispanic/Latino), 224 international. Average age 25. 1,121 applicants, 27% accepted, 158 enrolled. In 2014, 109 master's, 12 doctorates awarded. Terminal master's awarded for partial completion of doctoral program. *Degree requirements:* For master's, thesis (for some programs); for doctorate, comprehensive exam, thesis/dissertation. *Entrance requirements:* For master's and doctorate, GRE General Test. Additional exam requirements/recommendations for international students: Required—TOEFL (minimum score 550 paper-based; 84 iBT), IELTS (minimum score 7). *Application deadline:* For fall admission, 3/15 for domestic and international students; for spring admission, 10/1 for domestic and international students. Applications are processed on a rolling basis. Application fee: $80. Electronic applications accepted. *Expenses:* Tuition: Full-time $45,686; part-time $1428 per credit hour. Required fees: $660; $60 per semester. Tuition and fees vary according to program. *Financial support:* In 2014–15, 100 students received support, including 8 fellowships with full tuition reimbursements available (averaging $28,950 per year), 82 research assistantships with full tuition reimbursements available (averaging $19,300 per year), 18 teaching assistantships with full tuition reimbursements available (averaging $19,300 per year); career-related internships or fieldwork, Federal Work-Study, scholarships/grants, and tuition waivers (partial) also available. Financial award application deadline: 1/15; financial award applicants required to submit FAFSA. *Faculty research:* Communications and computer networks; signal, image, video, and multimedia processing; solid-state materials, devices, and photonics; systems, control, and reliable computing; VLSI, computer engineering and high-performance computing. *Unit head:* Dr. William C. Karl, Interim Chairman, 617-353-9880, Fax: 617-353-6440, E-mail: wckarl@bu.edu. *Application contact:* Dr. Solomon Eisenberg, Senior Associate Dean of Academic Programs, 617-353-9760, Fax: 617-353-0259, E-mail: enggrad@bu.edu.
Website: http://www.bu.edu/ece/.

Boston University, Metropolitan College, Department of Computer Science, Boston, MA 02215. Offers computer information systems (MS), including computer networks, database management and business intelligence, health informatics, IT project management, security, Web application development; computer networks (Certificate); digital forensics (Certificate); health informatics (Certificate); information technology project management (Certificate); software engineering in health care systems (Certificate); telecommunications (MS), including security. Part-time and evening/weekend programs available. Postbaccalaureate distance learning degree programs offered (no on-campus study). *Faculty:* 13 full-time (3 women), 43 part-time/adjunct (3 women). *Students:* 76 full-time (22 women), 768 part-time (188 women); includes 251 minority (68 Black or African American, non-Hispanic/Latino; 1 American Indian or Alaska Native, non-Hispanic/Latino; 117 Asian, non-Hispanic/Latino; 57 Hispanic/Latino; 2 Native Hawaiian or other Pacific Islander, non-Hispanic/Latino; 6 Two or more races, non-Hispanic/Latino), 130 international. Average age 34. 463 applicants, 79% accepted, 248 enrolled. In 2014, 222 master's, 25 other advanced degrees awarded. *Degree requirements:* For master's, thesis optional. *Entrance requirements:* For master's and Certificate, official transcripts from regionally-accredited bachelor's degree program, 3 letters of recommendation, professional resume, personal statement. Additional exam requirements/recommendations for international students: Required—TOEFL (minimum score 84 iBT), IELTS. *Application deadline:* For fall admission, 6/1 priority date for international students; for spring admission, 10/1 priority date for international students. Applications are processed on a rolling basis. Application fee: $80. Electronic applications accepted. *Expenses:* Expenses: $800 per credit part-time; student services fees: $60 per semester; technology fee of $60 per credit (for online courses). *Financial support:* In 2014–15, 11 research assistantships (averaging $8,400 per year) were awarded; unspecified assistantships also available. Support available to part-time students. Financial award applicants required to submit FAFSA. *Faculty research:* Medical informatics, Web technologies, telecom and networks, security and forensics, software engineering, programming languages, multimedia and artificial intelligence (AI), information systems and IT project management. *Unit head:* Dr. Anatoly Temkin, Chairman, 617-353-2566, Fax: 617-353-2367, E-mail: csinfo@bu.edu. *Application contact:* Lesley Moreau, Academic Program Coordinator, 617-353-2566, Fax: 617-353-2367, E-mail: metcs@bu.edu.
Website: http://www.bu.edu/csmet/.

Brigham Young University, Graduate Studies, Ira A. Fulton College of Engineering and Technology, Department of Electrical and Computer Engineering, Provo, UT 84602. Offers MS, PhD. *Faculty:* 23 full-time (0 women). *Students:* 69 full-time (5 women); includes 7 minority (6 Asian, non-Hispanic/Latino; 1 Hispanic/Latino), 15 international. Average age 27. 56 applicants, 75% accepted, 24 enrolled. In 2014, 25 master's, 2 doctorates awarded. *Degree requirements:* For master's, thesis; for doctorate, comprehensive exam, thesis/dissertation. *Entrance requirements:* For master's and doctorate, GRE General Test, minimum GPA of 3.2 in last 60 hours of course work.

Additional exam requirements/recommendations for international students: Required—TOEFL (minimum score 580 paper-based; 85 iBT). *Application deadline:* For fall admission, 1/15 for domestic and international students; for winter admission, 8/15 for domestic and international students. Application fee: $50. Electronic applications accepted. *Expenses: Tuition:* Full-time $6310; part-time $371 per credit hour. Tuition and fees vary according to program and student's religious affiliation. *Financial support:* In 2014–15, 4 students received support, including 4 fellowships with full tuition reimbursements available (averaging $17,400 per year), 41 research assistantships with full tuition reimbursements available (averaging $21,000 per year), 6 teaching assistantships with full tuition reimbursements available (averaging $19,000 per year); scholarships/grants also available. Financial award application deadline: 5/15; financial award applicants required to submit FAFSA. *Faculty research:* Microwave earth remote sensing, configurable computing and embedded systems, MEMS semiconductors, integrated electro-optics, multiple-agent intelligent coordinated control systems for unmanned air vehicles. *Total annual research expenditures:* $2.7 million. *Unit head:* Dr. Brent E. Nelson, Chair, 801-422-4012, Fax: 801-422-0201, E-mail: nelson@ee.byu.edu. *Application contact:* Janalyn L. Mergist, Graduate Secretary, 801-422-4013, Fax: 801-422-0201, E-mail: janalyn@ee.byu.edu.
Website: http://www.ee.byu.edu/.

Brown University, Graduate School, School of Engineering, Program in Electrical Sciences and Computer Engineering, Providence, RI 02912. Offers Sc M, PhD. *Degree requirements:* For doctorate, thesis/dissertation, preliminary exam.

California State University, Chico, Office of Graduate Studies, College of Engineering, Computer Science, and Technology, Electrical and Computer Engineering Department, Option in Computer Engineering, Chico, CA 95929-0722. Offers MS. *Students:* 2 full-time (0 women), 2 part-time (0 women); includes 1 minority (Hispanic/Latino), 3 international. Average age 27. 15 applicants, 40% accepted, 3 enrolled. In 2014, 2 master's awarded. *Degree requirements:* For master's, comprehensive exam, thesis or project plan. *Entrance requirements:* For master's, GRE General Test, 2 letters of recommendation, statement of purpose, resume. Additional exam requirements/recommendations for international students: Required—TOEFL (minimum score 550 paper-based; 80 iBT), IELTS (minimum score 6.8), PTE (minimum score 59). *Application deadline:* For fall admission, 3/1 priority date for domestic students, 3/1 for international students; for spring admission, 9/15 priority date for domestic students, 9/15 for international students. Applications are processed on a rolling basis. Application fee: $55. Electronic applications accepted. *Expenses: Tuition,* state resident: full-time $7002. Tuition, nonresident: full-time $18,162. *Required fees:* $1530. Tuition and fees vary according to program. *Financial support:* Career-related internships or fieldwork, scholarships/grants, and traineeships available. *Unit head:* Dr. Ben Juliano, Interim Dean, 530-898-5343, Fax: 530-898-4070, E-mail: elce@csuchico.edu. *Application contact:* Judy L. Rice, Graduate Admissions Coordinator, 530-898-5416, Fax: 530-898-3342, E-mail: jlrice@csuchico.edu.
Website: http://catalog.csuchico.edu/viewer/12/ENGR/ELCENONEMS.html.

California State University, Long Beach, Graduate Studies, College of Engineering, Department of Computer Engineering and Computer Science, Long Beach, CA 90840. Offers computer engineering (MSCS); computer science (MSCS). Part-time programs available. *Degree requirements:* For master's, thesis or alternative. *Entrance requirements:* Additional exam requirements/recommendations for international students: Required—TOEFL. Electronic applications accepted. *Faculty research:* Artificial intelligence, software engineering, computer simulation and modeling, user-interface design, networking.

Carnegie Mellon University, Carnegie Institute of Technology, Department of Electrical and Computer Engineering, Pittsburgh, PA 15213-3891. Offers MS, PhD. Part-time programs available. *Degree requirements:* For master's, thesis; for doctorate, thesis/dissertation, qualifying exam, teaching experience. *Entrance requirements:* For master's and doctorate, GRE General Test. Additional exam requirements/recommendations for international students: Required—TOEFL. *Faculty research:* Computer-aided design, solid-state devices, VLSI, processing, robotics and controls, signal processing, data systems storage.

Case Western Reserve University, School of Graduate Studies, Case School of Engineering, Department of Electrical Engineering and Computer Science, Cleveland, OH 44106. Offers computer engineering (MS, PhD); computing and information sciences (MS, PhD); electrical engineering (MS, PhD); systems and control engineering (MS, PhD). Part-time and evening/weekend programs available. Postbaccalaureate distance learning degree programs offered (minimal on-campus study). *Faculty:* 33 full-time (3 women). *Students:* 158 full-time (35 women), 18 part-time (5 women); includes 5 minority (1 Black or African American, non-Hispanic/Latino; 3 Asian, non-Hispanic/Latino; 1 Hispanic/Latino), 122 international. In 2014, 37 master's, 11 doctorates awarded. Terminal master's awarded for partial completion of doctoral program. *Degree requirements:* For master's, thesis; for doctorate, thesis/dissertation, qualifying exam, teaching experience. *Entrance requirements:* For master's and doctorate, GRE General Test. Additional exam requirements/recommendations for international students: Required—TOEFL. *Application deadline:* For fall admission, 2/1 for domestic students; for spring admission, 11/1 for domestic students. Applications are processed on a rolling basis. Application fee: $50. *Financial support:* In 2014–15, 51 research assistantships with full and partial tuition reimbursements, 10 teaching assistantships were awarded; fellowships with full and partial tuition reimbursements, career-related internships or fieldwork, Federal Work-Study, and institutionally sponsored loans also available. Support available to part-time students. Financial award application deadline: 3/1; financial award applicants required to submit FAFSA. *Faculty research:* Micro/nano systems; robotics and haptics, applied artificial intelligence; automation, computer-aided design and testing of digital systems. *Total annual research expenditures:* $6 million. *Unit head:* Dr. Kenneth Loparo, Department Chair, 216-368-4115, E-mail: kal4@case.edu. *Application contact:* Kimberly Yurchick, Student Affairs Specialist, 216-368-2920, Fax: 216-368-2801, E-mail: ksy4@case.edu.
Website: http://eecs.cwru.edu/.

Clarkson University, Graduate School, Wallace H. Coulter School of Engineering, Department of Electrical and Computer Engineering, Potsdam, NY 13699. Offers electrical and computer engineering (PhD); electrical engineering (ME, MS). Part-time programs available. *Faculty:* 17 full-time (3 women), 4 part-time/adjunct (1 woman). *Students:* 40 full-time (6 women), 3 part-time (0 women); includes 4 minority (1 Asian, non-Hispanic/Latino; 3 Hispanic/Latino), 22 international. Average age 29. 50 applicants, 60% accepted, 7 enrolled. In 2014, 14 master's, 2 doctorates awarded. Terminal master's awarded for partial completion of doctoral program. *Degree requirements:* For master's, thesis (for MS); project (for ME); for doctorate, comprehensive exam, thesis/dissertation, departmental qualifying exam. *Entrance requirements:* For master's and doctorate, GRE, transcripts of all college coursework, resume, personal statement, three letters of recommendation. Additional exam requirements/recommendations for international students: Required—TOEFL (minimum score 550 paper-based; 80 iBT), IELTS (minimum score 6.5). *Application deadline:* For fall admission, 1/30 priority date for domestic and international students; for spring admission, 9/1 priority date for domestic and international students. Applications are processed on a rolling basis. Application fee: $25 ($35 for international students).

Electronic applications accepted. *Expenses: Tuition:* Full-time $16,680; part-time $1390 per credit. *Required fees:* $295 per semester. *Financial support:* In 2014–15, 31 students received support, including 2 fellowships with full tuition reimbursements available (averaging $24,029 per year), 15 research assistantships with full tuition reimbursements available (averaging $24,029 per year), 7 teaching assistantships with full tuition reimbursements available (averaging $24,029 per year); scholarships/grants, tuition waivers (partial), and unspecified assistantships also available. *Faculty research:* Under water imaging, polymer insulation, bioelectronic tongue, integrated circuits, biometric identification. *Total annual research expenditures:* $1.2 million. *Unit head:* Dr. William Jemison, Dean/Chair, 315-268-6511, Fax: 315-268-7600, E-mail: wjemison@clarkson.edu. *Application contact:* Kelly Sharlow, Assistant to the Dean, 315-268-7929, Fax: 315-268-4494, E-mail: ksharlow@clarkson.edu.
Website: http://www.clarkson.edu/ece/.

Clemson University, Graduate School, College of Engineering and Science, Department of Electrical and Computer Engineering, Program in Computer Engineering, Clemson, SC 29634. Offers MS, PhD. *Students:* 52 full-time (7 women), 2 part-time (1 woman); includes 1 minority (Two or more races, non-Hispanic/Latino), 40 international. Average age 26. 162 applicants, 26% accepted, 27 enrolled. In 2014, 11 master's, 3 doctorates awarded. *Degree requirements:* For master's, thesis or alternative; for doctorate, thesis/dissertation, departmental qualifying exam. *Entrance requirements:* For master's and doctorate, GRE General Test. Additional exam requirements/recommendations for international students: Required—TOEFL. *Application deadline:* Applications are processed on a rolling basis. Application fee: $70 ($80 for international students). Electronic applications accepted. *Financial support:* In 2014–15, 28 students received support, including 2 fellowships with full and partial tuition reimbursements available (averaging $2,500 per year), 23 research assistantships with partial tuition reimbursements available (averaging $18,889 per year), 5 teaching assistantships with partial tuition reimbursements available (averaging $25,958 per year); career-related internships or fieldwork, institutionally sponsored loans, scholarships/grants, health care benefits, and unspecified assistantships also available. Support available to part-time students. Financial award applicants required to submit FAFSA. *Faculty research:* Interface applications, software development, multisystem communications, artificial intelligence, robotics. *Unit head:* Dr. Darren Dawson, Chair, 864-656-5249, Fax: 864-656-5917, E-mail: ddarren@clemson.edu. *Application contact:* Dr. Daniel Noneaker, Coordinator, 864-656-0100, Fax: 864-656-5917, E-mail: ece-grad-program@ces.clemson.edu.
Website: http://www.clemson.edu/ces/departments/ece/index.html.

Colorado Technical University Colorado Springs, Graduate Studies, Program in Computer Engineering, Colorado Springs, CO 80907-3896. Offers MSCE. Part-time and evening/weekend programs available. Postbaccalaureate distance learning degree programs offered. *Degree requirements:* For master's, thesis or alternative.

Colorado Technical University Denver South, Program in Computer Engineering, Aurora, CO 80014. Offers MS.

Columbia University, Fu Foundation School of Engineering and Applied Science, Department of Electrical Engineering, New York, NY 10027. Offers computer engineering (MS); electrical engineering (MS, Eng Sc D, PhD). PhD offered through the Graduate School of Arts and Sciences. Part-time programs available. Postbaccalaureate distance learning degree programs offered (no on-campus study). *Faculty:* 28 full-time (2 women), 40 part-time/adjunct (1 woman). *Students:* 342 full-time (76 women), 208 part-time (45 women); includes 50 minority (4 Black or African American, non-Hispanic/Latino; 37 Asian, non-Hispanic/Latino; 4 Hispanic/Latino; 5 Two or more races, non-Hispanic/Latino), 455 international. 1,559 applicants, 37% accepted, 230 enrolled. In 2014, 195 master's, 17 doctorates awarded. *Degree requirements:* For doctorate, thesis/dissertation, qualifying exam. *Entrance requirements:* For master's and doctorate, GRE General Test. Additional exam requirements/recommendations for international students: Required—TOEFL, IELTS, PTE. *Application deadline:* For fall admission, 12/15 priority date for domestic and international students; for spring admission, 10/1 priority date for domestic and international students. Application fee: $85. Electronic applications accepted. *Financial support:* In 2014–15, 109 students received support, including 17 fellowships with full tuition reimbursements available (averaging $32,447 per year), 67 research assistantships with full tuition reimbursements available (averaging $32,447 per year), 25 teaching assistantships with full tuition reimbursements available (averaging $32,447 per year); career-related internships or fieldwork, traineeships, and health care benefits also available. Financial award application deadline: 12/15; financial award applicants required to submit FAFSA. *Faculty research:* Media informatics and signal processing, integrated circuits and cyberphysical systems, communications systems and networking, nanoscale electronics and photonics, systems biology and neuroengineering. *Unit head:* Dr. Keren Bergman, Professor and Chair, 212-854-1744, Fax: 212-932-9421, E-mail: bergman@ee.columbia.edu. *Application contact:* Dr. Zoran Kostic, Associate Professor of Professional Practice/Director of the MS in Electrical Engineering Program, 212-851-0269, Fax: 212-932-9421, E-mail: zk2172@columbia.edu.
Website: http://www.ee.columbia.edu/.

Concordia University, School of Graduate Studies, Faculty of Engineering and Computer Science, Department of Electrical and Computer Engineering, Montréal, QC H3G 1M8, Canada. Offers M Eng, MA Sc, PhD. *Degree requirements:* For master's, thesis optional; for doctorate, comprehensive exam, thesis/dissertation. *Faculty research:* Computer communications and protocols, circuits and systems, graph theory, VLSI systems, microelectronics.

Cornell University, Graduate School, Graduate Fields of Engineering, Field of Electrical and Computer Engineering, Ithaca, NY 14853. Offers computer engineering (M Eng, PhD); electrical engineering (M Eng, PhD); electrical systems (M Eng, PhD); electrophysics (M Eng, PhD). *Degree requirements:* For doctorate, comprehensive exam, thesis/dissertation. *Entrance requirements:* For master's, GRE General Test, 2 letters of recommendation; for doctorate, GRE General Test, 3 letters of recommendation. Additional exam requirements/recommendations for international students: Required—TOEFL (minimum score 600 paper-based; 77 iBT). Electronic applications accepted. *Faculty research:* Communications, information theory, signal processing and power control, computer engineering, microelectromechanical systems and nanotechnology.

Dalhousie University, Faculty of Engineering, Department of Electrical and Computer Engineering, Halifax, NS B3J 1Z1, Canada. Offers M Eng, MA Sc, PhD. *Degree requirements:* For master's, thesis; for doctorate, thesis/dissertation. *Entrance requirements:* Additional exam requirements/recommendations for international students: Required—TOEFL, IELTS, CANTEST, CAEL, or Michigan English Language Assessment Battery. Electronic applications accepted. *Faculty research:* Communications, computer engineering, power engineering, electronics, systems engineering.

Dartmouth College, Thayer School of Engineering, Program in Computer Engineering, Hanover, NH 03755. Offers MS, PhD. *Degree requirements:* For master's, thesis; for doctorate, thesis/dissertation, candidacy oral exam. *Entrance requirements:* For master's and doctorate, GRE General Test. *Application deadline:* For fall admission, 1/1

priority date for domestic students. Application fee: $45. *Financial support:* Fellowships, research assistantships, teaching assistantships, career-related internships or fieldwork, Federal Work-Study, institutionally sponsored loans, and tuition waivers (full and partial) available. Financial award application deadline: 1/15. *Faculty research:* Analog VLSI, electromagnetic fields and waves, electronic instrumentation, microelectromechanical systems, optics, lasers and non-linear optics, power electronics and integrated power converters, networking, parallel and distributed computing, simulation, VLSI design and testing, wireless networking. *Unit head:* Dr. Joseph J. Helbie, Dean, 603-646-2238, Fax: 603-646-2580, E-mail: joseph.j.helbie@dartmouth.edu. *Application contact:* Candace S. Potter, Graduate Admissions Administrator, 603-646-3844, Fax: 603-646-1620, E-mail: candace.s.potter@dartmouth.edu.
Website: http://engineering.dartmouth.edu/.

Drexel University, College of Engineering, Department of Electrical and Computer Engineering, Program in Computer Engineering, Philadelphia, PA 19104-2875. Offers MS. Part-time and evening/weekend programs available. *Degree requirements:* For master's, thesis (for some programs). Electronic applications accepted.

Duke University, Graduate School, Pratt School of Engineering, Department of Electrical and Computer Engineering, Durham, NC 27708. Offers MS, PhD, JD/MS. *Faculty:* 28 full-time. *Students:* 225 full-time (51 women); includes 19 minority (3 Black or African American, non-Hispanic/Latino; 9 Asian, non-Hispanic/Latino; 7 Hispanic/Latino), 148 international. 679 applicants, 27% accepted, 65 enrolled. In 2014, 48 master's, 26 doctorates awarded. Terminal master's awarded for partial completion of doctoral program. *Degree requirements:* For doctorate, thesis/dissertation. *Entrance requirements:* For master's and doctorate, GRE General Test. Additional exam requirements/recommendations for international students: Required—TOEFL (minimum score 90 iBT), IELTS (minimum score 7). *Application deadline:* For fall admission, 12/8 priority date for domestic and international students; for spring admission, 10/15 for domestic students. Application fee: $80. Electronic applications accepted. *Expenses: Tuition:* Full-time $45,760; part-time $2765 per credit. *Required fees:* $978. Full-time tuition and fees vary according to program. *Financial support:* Fellowships, research assistantships, and Federal Work-Study available. Financial award application deadline: 12/8. *Faculty research:* Architecture and networking; biological applications circuits and systems; nanosystems, devices and materials; quantum computing and photonics; sensing and signals visualization; waves and metamaterials. *Unit head:* Krishnendu Chakrabarty, Director of Graduate Studies, 919-660-5245, Fax: 919-660-5293. *Application contact:* Duke Graduate School Admissions, 919-684-3913, Fax: 919-684-2277, E-mail: grad-admissions@duke.edu.
Website: http://www.ece.duke.edu/grad.

See Display on page 374 and Close-Up on page 397.

Duke University, Graduate School, Pratt School of Engineering, Master of Engineering Program, Durham, NC 27708-0271. Offers biomedical engineering (M Eng); civil engineering (M Eng); electrical and computer engineering (M Eng); environmental engineering (M Eng); materials science and engineering (M Eng); mechanical engineering (M Eng); photonics and optical sciences (M Eng). Part-time programs available. *Students:* 45 full-time (17 women); includes 5 minority (1 Black or African American, non-Hispanic/Latino; 2 Asian, non-Hispanic/Latino; 2 Hispanic/Latino), 23 international. Average age 24. 285 applicants, 43% accepted, 45 enrolled. In 2014, 45 master's awarded. *Entrance requirements:* For master's, GRE General Test, resume, 3 letters of recommendation, statement of purpose, transcripts. Additional exam requirements/recommendations for international students: Required—TOEFL. *Application deadline:* For fall admission, 6/15 for domestic students, 2/15 for international students; for spring admission, 11/1 for domestic students, 9/1 for international students. Application fee: $75. *Expenses: Tuition:* Full-time $45,760; part-time $2765 per credit. *Required fees:* $978. Full-time tuition and fees vary according to program. *Financial support:* Merit scholarships/grants available. *Unit head:* Dr. Bradley A. Fox, Executive Director, 919-660-5455, Fax: 919-660-5456. *Application contact:* Susan Brown, Assistant Director of Admissions, 919-660-8451, Fax: 919-660-5456, E-mail: susan.brown@duke.edu.
Website: http://meng.pratt.duke.edu/.

East Carolina University, Graduate School, College of Engineering and Technology, Greenville, NC 27858-4353. Offers MCM, MS, PhD, Certificate. Part-time programs available. *Degree requirements:* For master's, comprehensive exam. *Application deadline:* For fall admission, 6/1 priority date for domestic students. Applications are processed on a rolling basis. Application fee: $50. *Expenses:* Tuition, state resident: full-time $4223. Tuition, nonresident: full-time $16,540. *Required fees:* $2184. *Financial support:* Fellowships, research assistantships, teaching assistantships, and Federal Work-Study available. Support available to part-time students. Financial award application deadline: 6/1. *Unit head:* Dr. David White, Dean, 252-328-9604. *Application contact:* Dean of Graduate School, 252-328-6012, Fax: 252-328-6071, E-mail: gradschool@ecu.edu.
Website: http://www.ecu.edu/tecs/.

École Polytechnique de Montréal, Graduate Programs, Department of Electrical and Computer Engineering, Montréal, QC H3C 3A7, Canada. Offers automation (M Eng, M Sc A, PhD); computer science (M Eng, M Sc A, PhD); electrical engineering (DESS); electrotechnology (M Eng, M Sc A, PhD); microelectronics (M Eng, M Sc A, PhD); microwave technology (M Eng, M Sc A, PhD). Part-time and evening/weekend programs available. *Degree requirements:* For master's, one foreign language, thesis; for doctorate, one foreign language, thesis/dissertation. *Entrance requirements:* For master's, minimum GPA of 2.75; for doctorate, minimum GPA of 3.0. *Faculty research:* Microwaves, telecommunications, software engineering.

Embry-Riddle Aeronautical University–Daytona, Department of Electrical, Computer, Software and Systems Engineering, Daytona Beach, FL 32114-3900. Offers cybersecurity engineering (MS); electrical and computer engineering (MSECE); software engineering (MSE); unmanned and autonomous systems engineering (MSUASE). MS in unmanned and autonomous systems engineering held jointly with Department of Electrical, Computer, Software and Systems Engineering. Part-time and evening/weekend programs available. *Faculty:* 13 full-time (0 women), 1 (woman) part-time/adjunct. *Students:* 56 full-time (15 women), 8 part-time (0 women); includes 6 minority (4 Black or African American, non-Hispanic/Latino; 1 Asian, non-Hispanic/Latino; 1 Hispanic/Latino), 41 international. Average age 25. 46 applicants, 61% accepted, 23 enrolled. In 2014, 16 master's awarded. *Degree requirements:* For master's, thesis or alternative, MS UASE students are required to complete a two-semester capstone project. *Entrance requirements:* For master's, Applicants to the MSE program are strongly encouraged to complete the GRE for this degree program; Applicants to the MSUASE program must complete the GRE; For consideration of fellowship and assistantship award programs offered by the Department of Computing, GRE scores are required., minimum CGPA of 3.0; course work in computer science. Additional exam requirements/recommendations for international students: Required—TOEFL (minimum score 550 paper-based; 79 iBT). *Application deadline:* For fall admission, 6/1 priority date for domestic and international students; for spring admission, 11/1 priority date for domestic students, 10/1 priority date for international students. Applications are processed on a rolling basis. Application fee: $50. Electronic applications accepted. *Expenses: Tuition:* Full-time $15,360; part-time $1280 per credit hour. *Required fees:* $1334. *Financial support:* In 2014–15, 24 students received support. Research assistantships with full and partial tuition reimbursements available, teaching assistantships with full and partial tuition reimbursements available, career-related internships or fieldwork, and unspecified assistantships available. Financial award application deadline: 4/15. *Faculty research:* Cybersecurity and assured systems engineering, radar, unmanned and autonomous systems, modeling and simulation, cyber-physical systems. *Unit head:* Dr. Timothy Wilson, Professor of Electrical and Computer Engineering and Chair, ECSSE Dept., 386-226-6994, E-mail: timothy.wilson@erau.edu. *Application contact:* International and Graduate Admissions, 800-388-3728, Fax: 386-226-7070, E-mail: graduate.admissions@erau.edu.
Website: http://daytonabeach.erau.edu/college-engineering/electrical-computer-software-systems/index.html.

Fairfield University, School of Engineering, Fairfield, CT 06824. Offers automated manufacturing (CAS); database management (CAS); electrical and computer engineering (MS); information security (CAS); management of technology (MS); mechanical engineering (MS); network technology (CAS); software engineering (MS); Web application development (CAS). Part-time and evening/weekend programs available. *Faculty:* 4 full-time (1 woman), 18 part-time/adjunct (5 women). *Students:* 193 full-time (50 women), 69 part-time (11 women); includes 20 minority (4 Black or African American, non-Hispanic/Latino; 6 Asian, non-Hispanic/Latino; 10 Hispanic/Latino), 199 international. Average age 27. 516 applicants, 64% accepted, 124 enrolled. In 2014, 38 master's awarded. *Degree requirements:* For master's, thesis, capstone course. *Entrance requirements:* For master's, interview, minimum GPA of 2.8, resume, 2 recommendations. Additional exam requirements/recommendations for international students: Required—TOEFL (minimum score 550 paper-based; 80 iBT) or IELTS (minimum score 6.5). *Application deadline:* For fall admission, 5/15 for international students; for spring admission, 10/15 for international students. Applications are processed on a rolling basis. Application fee: $60. Electronic applications accepted. *Expenses:* Expenses: $750 per credit hour. *Financial support:* In 2014–15, 30 students received support. Scholarships/grants and unspecified assistantships available. Financial award applicants required to submit FAFSA. *Faculty research:* Ocean dynamics modeling, thermo fluids, Web/mobile software applications, microwaves/electromagnetics, micro/nano manufacturing. *Unit head:* Dr. Bruce Berdanier, Dean, 203-254-4147, Fax: 203-254-4013, E-mail: bberdanier@fairfield.edu. *Application contact:* Marianne Gumpper, Director of Graduate and Continuing Studies Admission, 203-254-4184, Fax: 203-254-4073, E-mail: gradadmis@fairfield.edu.
Website: http://www.fairfield.edu/academics/schoolscollegescenters/schoolofengineering/graduateprograms/.

Fairleigh Dickinson University, Metropolitan Campus, University College: Arts, Sciences, and Professional Studies, School of Computer Sciences and Engineering, Program in Computer Engineering, Teaneck, NJ 07666-1914. Offers MS.

Florida Atlantic University, College of Engineering and Computer Science, Department of Computer and Electrical Engineering and Computer Science, Boca Raton, FL 33431-0991. Offers bioengineering (MS); computer engineering (MS, PhD); computer science (MS, PhD); electrical engineering (MS, PhD); information technology and management (MS). Part-time and evening/weekend programs available. Terminal master's awarded for partial completion of doctoral program. *Degree requirements:* For master's, thesis optional; for doctorate, thesis/dissertation, qualifying exam. *Entrance requirements:* For master's, GRE General Test, minimum GPA of 3.0; for doctorate, GRE General Test, master's degree, minimum GPA of 3.5. Additional exam requirements/recommendations for international students: Required—TOEFL (minimum score 500 paper-based; 61 iBT), IELTS (minimum score 6). *Expenses:* Tuition, state resident: full-time $7396; part-time $369.82 per credit hour. Tuition, nonresident: full-time $19,392; part-time $1024.81 per credit hour. Tuition and fees vary according to course load. *Faculty research:* VLSI and neural networks, communication networks, software engineering, computer architecture, multimedia and video processing.

Florida International University, College of Engineering and Computing, Department of Electrical and Computer Engineering, Program in Computer Engineering, Miami, FL 33175. Offers MS. Part-time and evening/weekend programs available. *Degree requirements:* For master's, thesis optional. *Entrance requirements:* For master's, minimum GPA of 3.0, resume, 3 letters of recommendation, letter of intent. Additional exam requirements/recommendations for international students: Required—TOEFL (minimum score 550 paper-based; 80 iBT). Electronic applications accepted.

George Mason University, Volgenau School of Engineering, Department of Electrical and Computer Engineering, Fairfax, VA 22030. Offers computer engineering (MS); computer forensics (MS); electrical and computer engineering (PhD, Certificate); electrical engineering (MS); telecommunications (MS). MS programs offered jointly with Old Dominion University, University of Virginia, Virginia Commonwealth University, and Virginia Polytechnic Institute and State University. *Faculty:* 31 full-time (4 women), 41 part-time/adjunct (5 women). *Students:* 258 full-time (77 women), 275 part-time (51 women); includes 113 minority (33 Black or African American, non-Hispanic/Latino; 54 Asian, non-Hispanic/Latino; 17 Hispanic/Latino; 1 Native Hawaiian or other Pacific Islander, non-Hispanic/Latino; 8 Two or more races, non-Hispanic/Latino), 237 international. Average age 30. 554 applicants, 69% accepted, 158 enrolled. In 2014, 153 master's, 4 doctorates, 24 other advanced degrees awarded. *Degree requirements:* For master's, thesis optional; for doctorate, comprehensive exam, thesis or scholarly paper. *Entrance requirements:* For master's, GRE, personal goals statement; 2 official copies of transcripts; self-evaluation form; 3 letters of recommendation; resume; official bank statement; photocopy of passport; proof of financial support; for doctorate, GRE (waived for GMU electrical and computer engineering master's graduates with minimum GPA of 3.0), personal goals statement; 2 official copies of transcripts; self-evaluation form; 3 letters of recommendation; resume; official bank statement; photocopy of passport; proof of financial support. Additional exam requirements/recommendations for international students: Required—TOEFL (minimum score 575 paper-based; 80 iBT), IELTS (minimum score 6.5), PTE. *Application deadline:* For fall admission, 1/15 priority date for domestic students; for spring admission, 8/15 priority date for domestic students. Applications are processed on a rolling basis. Application fee: $65 ($80 for international students). Electronic applications accepted. *Expenses:* Expenses: Contact institution. *Financial support:* In 2014–15, 68 students received support, including 33 research assistantships with full and partial tuition reimbursements available (averaging $18,359 per year), 38 teaching assistantships with full and partial tuition reimbursements available (averaging $11,521 per year); career-related internships or fieldwork, Federal Work-Study, scholarships/grants, unspecified assistantships, and health care benefits (for full-time research or teaching assistantship recipients) also available. Support available to part-time students. Financial award application deadline: 3/1; financial award applicants required to submit FAFSA. *Faculty research:* Communication networks, signal processing, system failure diagnosis, multiprocessors, material processing using microwave energy. *Total annual research expenditures:* $2.3 million. *Unit head:* Andre Manitius, Chair, 703-993-1570, Fax: 703-993-1601, E-mail: amanitiu@gmu.edu. *Application contact:* Jammie Chang, Academic Program Coordinator, 703-993-1570, Fax: 703-993-1601, E-mail: jchangn@gmu.edu.
Website: http://ece.gmu.edu/.

The George Washington University, School of Engineering and Applied Science, Department of Electrical and Computer Engineering, Washington, DC 20052. Offers electrical engineering (MS, PhD); telecommunication and computers (MS). Part-time and evening/weekend programs available. *Faculty:* 28 full-time (2 women), 18 part-time/adjunct (0 women). *Students:* 126 full-time (31 women), 68 part-time (14 women); includes 19 minority (6 Black or African American, non-Hispanic/Latino; 8 Asian, non-Hispanic/Latino; 5 Hispanic/Latino), 148 international. Average age 27. 536 applicants, 55% accepted, 62 enrolled. In 2014, 98 master's, 7 doctorates, 2 other advanced degrees awarded. *Degree requirements:* For master's, thesis optional; for doctorate, comprehensive exam, thesis/dissertation, dissertation defense, qualifying exam. *Entrance requirements:* For master's, appropriate bachelor's degree, minimum GPA of 3.0; for doctorate, GRE (if highest earned degree is BS), appropriate bachelor's or master's degree, minimum GPA of 3.3; for other advanced degree, appropriate master's degree, minimum GPA of 3.0. Additional exam requirements/recommendations for international students: Required—TOEFL or The George Washington University English as a Foreign Language Test. *Application deadline:* For fall admission, 3/1 priority date for domestic students; for spring admission, 10/1 for domestic students. Applications are processed on a rolling basis. Application fee: $75. *Financial support:* In 2014–15, 39 students received support. Fellowships with tuition reimbursements available, research assistantships, teaching assistantships with tuition reimbursements available, career-related internships or fieldwork, and institutionally sponsored loans available. Financial award application deadline: 3/1; financial award applicants required to submit FAFSA. *Faculty research:* Computer graphics, multimedia systems. *Unit head:* Mona Zaghloul, Chair, 202-994-9380, E-mail: zaghloul@gwu.edu. *Application contact:* Adina Lav, Marketing, Recruiting and Admissions, 202-994-5827, Fax: 202-994-0909, E-mail: engineering@gwu.edu.
Website: http://www.ece.gwu.edu/.

Georgia Institute of Technology, Graduate Studies, College of Engineering, School of Electrical and Computer Engineering, Atlanta, GA 30332-0001. Offers MS, PhD. Part-time programs available. Postbaccalaureate distance learning degree programs offered (minimal on-campus study). *Students:* 1,024 full-time (177 women), 302 part-time (31 women); includes 169 minority (27 Black or African American, non-Hispanic/Latino; 1 American Indian or Alaska Native, non-Hispanic/Latino; 100 Asian, non-Hispanic/Latino; 29 Hispanic/Latino; 12 Two or more races, non-Hispanic/Latino), 857 international. Average age 25. 2,399 applicants, 30% accepted, 409 enrolled. In 2014, 335 master's, 99 doctorates awarded. Terminal master's awarded for partial completion of doctoral program. *Degree requirements:* For master's, thesis optional; for doctorate, comprehensive exam, thesis/dissertation. *Entrance requirements:* For master's, GRE General Test, http://www.ece.gatech.edu/academics/graduate/apply.html#masters; for doctorate, GRE General Test, http://www.ece.gatech.edu/academics/graduate/apply.html#phd. Additional exam requirements/recommendations for international students: Required—TOEFL (minimum score 550 paper-based; 79 iBT). *Application deadline:* For fall admission, 12/1 for domestic and international students; for spring admission, 8/1 for domestic students, 7/1 for international students; for summer admission, 12/1 for domestic and international students. Applications are processed on a rolling basis. Application fee: $75. Electronic applications accepted. *Expenses:* Expenses: $490 per credit hour in-state/out-of-state tuition plus fees of $651 per term (for MS Shanghai); $5,880 in-state/out-of-state tuition plus fees of $651 per term (for MS Shenzhen). *Financial support:* Fellowships, research assistantships, teaching assistantships, career-related internships or fieldwork, Federal Work-Study, institutionally sponsored loans, tuition waivers (partial), and unspecified assistantships available. Support available to part-time students. Financial award application deadline: 5/1. *Faculty research:* Telecommunications, computer systems, microelectronics, optical engineering, digital signal processing. *Total annual research expenditures:* $30.5 million. *Unit head:* George Riley, Director, 404-894-4767, E-mail: george.riley@ece.gatech.edu. *Application contact:* Jacqueline Trappier, Graduate Coordinator, 404-385-1141, E-mail: jacqueline.trappier@ece.gatech.edu.
Website: http://www.ece.gatech.edu.

Grand Valley State University, Padnos College of Engineering and Computing, School of Engineering, Allendale, MI 49401-9403. Offers electrical and computer engineering (MSE); manufacturing operations (MSE); mechanical engineering (MSE); product design and manufacturing engineering (MSE). Part-time and evening/weekend programs available. *Faculty:* 15 full-time (2 women). *Students:* 29 full-time (6 women), 30 part-time (5 women); includes 4 minority (1 Asian, non-Hispanic/Latino; 3 Hispanic/Latino), 23 international. Average age 28. 66 applicants, 73% accepted, 23 enrolled. In 2014, 14 master's awarded. *Degree requirements:* For master's, project or thesis. *Entrance requirements:* For master's, engineering degree, minimum GPA of 3.0. Additional exam requirements/recommendations for international students: Required—TOEFL. *Application deadline:* Applications are processed on a rolling basis. Application fee: $30. Electronic applications accepted. *Expenses:* Tuition, state resident: full-time $10,602; part-time $589 per credit hour. Tuition, nonresident: full-time $14,022; part-time $779 per credit hour. Tuition and fees vary according to degree level and program. *Financial support:* In 2014–15, 31 students received support, including 10 fellowships (averaging $3,049 per year), 25 research assistantships with full tuition reimbursements available (averaging $10,237 per year); career-related internships or fieldwork, Federal Work-Study, institutionally sponsored loans, scholarships/grants, and unspecified assistantships also available. *Faculty research:* Digital signal processing, computer aided design, computer aided manufacturing, manufacturing simulation, biomechanics, product design. *Total annual research expenditures:* $300,000. *Unit head:* Dr. Charles Standridge, Acting Director, 616-331-6750, Fax: 616-331-7215, E-mail: standric@gvsu.edu. *Application contact:* Dr. Pranod Chaphalkar, Graduate Director, 616-331-6843, Fax: 616-331-7215, E-mail: chaphalp@gvsu.edu.
Website: http://www.engineer.gvsu.edu/.

Illinois Institute of Technology, Graduate College, Armour College of Engineering, Department of Electrical and Computer Engineering, Chicago, IL 60616. Offers biomedical imaging and signals (MAS); computer engineering (MS, PhD); electrical engineering (MS, PhD); electricity markets (MAS); network engineering (MAS); power engineering (MAS); telecommunications and software engineering (MAS); vlsi and microelectronics (MAS); MS/MS. Part-time and evening/weekend programs available. Postbaccalaureate distance learning degree programs offered (minimal on-campus study). *Faculty:* 27 full-time (4 women), 3 part-time/adjunct (0 women). *Students:* 439 full-time (84 women), 90 part-time (11 women); includes 13 minority (11 Asian, non-Hispanic/Latino; 2 Hispanic/Latino), 476 international. Average age 26. 2,461 applicants, 39% accepted, 206 enrolled. In 2014, 155 master's, 7 doctorates awarded. Terminal master's awarded for partial completion of doctoral program. *Degree requirements:* For master's, comprehensive exam (for some programs), thesis (for some programs); for doctorate, comprehensive exam, thesis/dissertation. *Entrance requirements:* For master's and doctorate, GRE General Test (minimum score 1100 Quantitative and Verbal, 3.5 Analytical Writing), minimum undergraduate GPA of 3.0. Additional exam requirements/recommendations for international students: Required—TOEFL (minimum score 550 paper-based; 80 iBT); Recommended—IELTS (minimum score 5.5). *Application deadline:* For fall admission, 5/1 for domestic and international students; for spring admission, 10/15 for domestic and international students. Applications are processed on a rolling basis. Application fee: $50. Electronic applications accepted.

Expenses: Tuition: Full-time $22,500; part-time $1250 per credit hour. *Required fees:* $30 per course. $260 per semester. One-time fee: $235. Tuition and fees vary according to course load and program. *Financial support:* Fellowships with full and partial tuition reimbursements, research assistantships with full and partial tuition reimbursements, teaching assistantships with full and partial tuition reimbursements, career-related internships or fieldwork, Federal Work-Study, institutionally sponsored loans, scholarships/grants, health care benefits, tuition waivers (full), and unspecified assistantships available. Support available to part-time students. Financial award applicants required to submit FAFSA. *Faculty research:* Communication systems, wireless networks, computer systems, computer networks, wireless security, cloud computing and micro-electronics; electromagnetics and electronics; power and control systems; signal and image processing. *Unit head:* Dr. Ashfaq Khokhar, Chair & Professor of Electrical and Computer Engineering, 312-567-5780, Fax: 312-567-8976, E-mail: ashfaq@iit.edu. *Application contact:* Rishab Malhotra, Director, Graduate Admission, 866-472-3448, Fax: 312-567-3138, E-mail: inquiry.grad@iit.edu.
Website: http://www.ece.iit.edu.

Indiana State University, College of Graduate and Professional Studies, College of Technology, Department of Electronics and Computer Technology, Terre Haute, IN 47809. Offers MS. *Degree requirements:* For master's, thesis or alternative. *Entrance requirements:* For master's, bachelor's degree in industrial technology or related field. Additional exam requirements/recommendations for international students: Required—TOEFL. Electronic applications accepted.

Indiana University–Purdue University Fort Wayne, College of Engineering, Technology, and Computer Science, Department of Engineering, Fort Wayne, IN 46805-1499. Offers civil engineering (MSE); computer engineering (MSE); electrical engineering (MSE); mechanical engineering (MSE); systems engineering (MSE). Part-time programs available. *Faculty:* 21 full-time (2 women). *Students:* 4 full-time (1 woman), 15 part-time (1 woman); includes 3 minority (2 Black or African American, non-Hispanic/Latino; 1 Asian, non-Hispanic/Latino), 2 international. Average age 30. 13 applicants, 100% accepted, 10 enrolled. In 2014, 17 master's awarded. *Entrance requirements:* For master's, minimum GPA of 3.0, bachelor's degree in engineering discipline. Additional exam requirements/recommendations for international students: Required—TOEFL (minimum score 550 paper-based; 79 iBT); Recommended—TWE. *Application deadline:* For fall admission, 7/15 priority date for domestic students, 5/15 priority date for international students; for spring admission, 12/1 priority date for domestic students, 10/15 priority date for international students. Applications are processed on a rolling basis. Application fee: $55 ($60 for international students). Electronic applications accepted. *Financial support:* In 2014–15, 3 research assistantships with partial tuition reimbursements (averaging $13,522 per year), 1 teaching assistantship with partial tuition reimbursement (averaging $13,522 per year) were awarded. Financial award application deadline: 3/1; financial award applicants required to submit FAFSA. *Faculty research:* Continuous space language model, sensor networks, wireless cloud architecture. *Total annual research expenditures:* $841,333. *Unit head:* Dr. Nashwan Younis, Chair, 260-481-6887, Fax: 260-481-6281, E-mail: younis@engr.ipfw.edu. *Application contact:* Dr. Abdullah Eroglu, Program Director/Professor, 260-481-0273, Fax: 260-481-5734, E-mail: eroglua@ipfw.edu.
Website: http://www.ipfw.edu/engr.

Indiana University–Purdue University Indianapolis, School of Engineering and Technology, Department of Electrical Engineering, Indianapolis, IN 46202. Offers biomedical engineering (MS, PhD); electrical and computer engineering (MS, PhD); engineering (interdisciplinary) (MSE). *Students:* 64 full-time (15 women), 74 part-time (14 women); includes 13 minority (2 Black or African American, non-Hispanic/Latino; 9 Asian, non-Hispanic/Latino; 2 Hispanic/Latino), 95 international. Average age 27. 147 applicants, 63% accepted, 41 enrolled. In 2014, 27 master's awarded. Application fee: $55 ($65 for international students). *Unit head:* Brian King, Acting Chair, 317-274-9723. *Application contact:* Valerie Diemer, Graduate Program, 317-278-4960, Fax: 317-278-1671, E-mail: grad@engr.iupui.edu.
Website: http://www.engr.iupui.edu/departments/ece/.

Instituto Tecnológico y de Estudios Superiores de Monterrey, Campus Chihuahua, Graduate Programs, Chihuahua, Mexico. Offers computer systems engineering (Ingeniero); electrical engineering (Ingeniero); electromechanical engineering (Ingeniero); electronic engineering (Ingeniero); engineering administration (MEA); industrial engineering (MIE, Ingeniero); international trade (MIT); mechanical engineering (Ingeniero).

International Technological University, Program in Computer Engineering, San Jose, CA 95113. Offers MSCE. Part-time and evening/weekend programs available. *Students:* 121 full-time (35 women), 45 part-time (16 women), all international. Average age 27. 72 applicants, 76% accepted, 31 enrolled. In 2014, 19 master's awarded. *Degree requirements:* For master's, thesis or alternative, capstone project. *Entrance requirements:* Additional exam requirements/recommendations for international students: Required—TOEFL, IELTS. *Application deadline:* For fall admission, 8/1 for domestic and international students; for winter admission, 12/31 for domestic students; for spring admission, 4/1 for domestic students, 8/1 for international students; for summer admission, 12/1 for domestic and international students. Applications are processed on a rolling basis. Application fee: $80. Electronic applications accepted. *Expenses:* Tuition: Full-time $13,500; part-time $500 per credit. *Required fees:* $265 per trimester. *Unit head:* Dr. May Huang, Chairman of Electrical Engineering, 888-488-4968. *Application contact:* Mary Tran, Admissions Manager, 888-488-4968, E-mail: admissions@itu.edu.
Website: http://www.itu.edu/.

Iowa State University of Science and Technology, Department of Electrical and Computer Engineering, Ames, IA 50011. Offers computer engineering (M Eng, MS, PhD); electrical engineering (M Eng, MS, PhD). *Degree requirements:* For master's, thesis or alternative; for doctorate, thesis/dissertation. *Entrance requirements:* For master's and doctorate, GRE General Test. Additional exam requirements/recommendations for international students: Required—TOEFL (minimum score 570 paper-based; 79 iBT), IELTS (minimum score 6.5). Electronic applications accepted.

Iowa State University of Science and Technology, Program in Computer Engineering, Ames, IA 50011. Offers M Eng, MS, PhD. *Entrance requirements:* For master's and doctorate, GRE. Additional exam requirements/recommendations for international students: Required—TOEFL (minimum score 570 paper-based; 79 iBT), IELTS (minimum score 6.5). Electronic applications accepted.

Johns Hopkins University, Engineering Program for Professionals, Part-time Program in Electrical and Computer Engineering, Baltimore, MD 21218-2699. Offers MS, Post-Master's Certificate. Part-time and evening/weekend programs available. Electronic applications accepted.

Johns Hopkins University, G. W. C. Whiting School of Engineering, Department of Electrical and Computer Engineering, Baltimore, MD 21218-2699. Offers MSE, PhD. Terminal master's awarded for partial completion of doctoral program. *Degree requirements:* For master's, thesis optional; for doctorate, thesis/dissertation, qualifying and oral exams, seminar. *Entrance requirements:* For master's and doctorate, GRE General Test, transcripts, 3 letters of recommendation, statement of purpose. Additional exam requirements/recommendations for international students: Required—TOEFL (minimum score 600 paper-based; 100 iBT). Electronic applications accepted. *Faculty research:* Computer engineering, systems and control, language and speech processing, photonics and optoelectronics, signal and image processing.

Kansas State University, Graduate School, College of Engineering, Department of Electrical and Computer Engineering, Manhattan, KS 66506. Offers electrical engineering (MS), including bioengineering, communication systems, design of computer systems, electrical engineering, energy and power systems, integrated circuits and devices, real time embedded systems, renewable energy, signal processing. Part-time and evening/weekend programs available. Postbaccalaureate distance learning degree programs offered (no on-campus study). *Faculty:* 21 full-time (4 women), 1 (woman) part-time/adjunct. *Students:* 38 full-time (8 women), 45 part-time (6 women); includes 13 minority (4 Black or African American, non-Hispanic/Latino; 8 Asian, non-Hispanic/Latino; 1 Hispanic/Latino), 37 international. Average age 28. 126 applicants, 29% accepted, 14 enrolled. In 2014, 22 master's, 5 doctorates awarded. *Degree requirements:* For master's, thesis or alternative, final exam; for doctorate, thesis/dissertation, final exam, preliminary exams. *Entrance requirements:* For master's, GRE General Test, bachelor's degree in electrical engineering or computer science, minimum GPA of 3.0; for doctorate, GRE General Test. Additional exam requirements/recommendations for international students: Required—TOEFL (minimum score 600 paper-based; 85 iBT). *Application deadline:* For fall admission, 1/1 priority date for domestic and international students; for spring admission, 8/1 priority date for domestic and international students. Applications are processed on a rolling basis. Application fee: $50 ($75 for international students). Electronic applications accepted. *Financial support:* In 2014–15, 40 students received support, including 22 research assistantships with tuition reimbursements available (averaging $12,100 per year), 18 teaching assistantships with full tuition reimbursements available (averaging $12,220 per year); career-related internships or fieldwork, institutionally sponsored loans, and scholarships/grants also available. Support available to part-time students. Financial award application deadline: 3/1; financial award applicants required to submit FAFSA. *Faculty research:* Energy systems and renewable energy, computer systems and real time embedded systems, communication systems and signal processing, integrated circuits and devices, bioengineering. *Total annual research expenditures:* $1.3 million. *Unit head:* Dr. Don Gruenbacher, Head, 785-532-5600, Fax: 785-532-1188, E-mail: grue@k-state.edu. *Application contact:* Dr. Andrew Rys, Graduate Program Director, 785-532-4665, Fax: 785-532-1188, E-mail: andrys@k-state.edu.
Website: http://www.ece.k-state.edu/.

Lakehead University, Graduate Studies, Faculty of Engineering, Thunder Bay, ON P7B 5E1, Canada. Offers control engineering (M Sc Engr); electrical/computer engineering (M Sc Engr); environmental engineering (M Sc Engr). Part-time programs available. *Degree requirements:* For master's, thesis. *Entrance requirements:* For master's, bachelor's degree in chemical, electrical or mechanical engineering, minimum B average. Additional exam requirements/recommendations for international students: Required—TOEFL. *Faculty research:* Pulp and paper, adaptive/process control, robust/interactive learning control, vibration control.

Lawrence Technological University, College of Engineering, Southfield, MI 48075-1058. Offers architectural engineering (MS); automotive engineering (MS); civil engineering (MA, MS, PhD); construction engineering management (MA); electrical and computer engineering (MS); engineering management (MEM); industrial engineering (MS); manufacturing systems (ME, DE); mechanical engineering (MS, DE); mechatronic systems engineering (MS). Part-time and evening/weekend programs available. *Faculty:* 24 full-time (5 women), 15 part-time/adjunct (0 women). *Students:* 16 full-time (6 women), 478 part-time (71 women); includes 295 minority (15 Black or African American, non-Hispanic/Latino; 271 Asian, non-Hispanic/Latino; 7 Hispanic/Latino; 2 Two or more races, non-Hispanic/Latino), 38 international. Average age 27. 1,786 applicants, 40% accepted, 218 enrolled. In 2014, 106 master's awarded. *Degree requirements:* For master's, thesis (for some programs). *Entrance requirements:* Additional exam requirements/recommendations for international students: Required—TOEFL (minimum score 550 paper-based; 79 iBT). *Application deadline:* For fall admission, 8/1 priority date for domestic students, 5/29 for international students; for spring admission, 12/1 priority date for domestic students, 10/15 for international students. Applications are processed on a rolling basis. Application fee: $50. Electronic applications accepted. *Expenses: Tuition:* Full-time $14,700; part-time $1050 per credit hour. *Required fees:* $150. One-time fee: $150 part-time. *Financial support:* In 2014–15, 31 students received support, including 8 research assistantships (averaging $9,338 per year); Federal Work-Study and institutionally sponsored loans also available. Support available to part-time students. Financial award application deadline: 4/1; financial award applicants required to submit FAFSA. *Faculty research:* Advanced composite materials in bridges, strengthening existing bridges with carbon and glass fiber sheets, development of drive shafts using composite materials. *Unit head:* Dr. Nabil Grace, Dean, 248-204-2500, Fax: 248-204-2509, E-mail: engrdean@ltu.edu. *Application contact:* Jane Rohrback, Director of Admissions, 248-204-3160, Fax: 248-204-2228, E-mail: admissions@ltu.edu.
Website: http://www.ltu.edu/engineering/index.asp.

Lehigh University, P.C. Rossin College of Engineering and Applied Science, Department of Computer Science and Engineering, Bethlehem, PA 18015. Offers computer engineering (M Eng, MS, PhD); computer science (M Eng, MS, PhD); MBA/E. Part-time programs available. *Faculty:* 12 full-time (2 women), 1 (woman) part-time/adjunct. *Students:* 57 full-time (8 women), 6 part-time (0 women); includes 6 minority (4 Asian, non-Hispanic/Latino; 2 Two or more races, non-Hispanic/Latino), 40 international. Average age 25. 252 applicants, 22% accepted, 21 enrolled. In 2014, 18 master's, 6 doctorates awarded. *Degree requirements:* For master's, oral presentation of thesis; for doctorate, thesis/dissertation, qualifying, general, and oral exams. *Entrance requirements:* For master's, GRE General Test, minimum GPA of 3.0; for doctorate, GRE General Test, minimum GPA of 3.5. Additional exam requirements/recommendations for international students: Required—TOEFL (minimum score 550 paper-based; 79 iBT). *Application deadline:* For fall admission, 4/1 for domestic and international students; for spring admission, 11/1 for domestic and international students. Applications are processed on a rolling basis. Application fee: $75. Electronic applications accepted. *Expenses:* Expenses: $1,340 per credit. *Financial support:* In 2014–15, 19 students received support, including 2 fellowships with full tuition reimbursements available (averaging $19,920 per year), 6 research assistantships with full tuition reimbursements available (averaging $18,920 per year), 5 teaching assistantships with full tuition reimbursements available (averaging $20,490 per year). Financial award application deadline: 1/15. *Faculty research:* Artificial intelligence, networking-pattern recognition, multimedia e-learning/data mining/Web search, mobile robotics, bioinformatics, computer vision. *Total annual research expenditures:* $1.3 million. *Unit head:* Dr. Hank Korth, Interim Chair, 610-758-5782, Fax: 610-758-4096, E-mail: hfk2@lehigh.edu. *Application contact:* Heidi Wegrzyn, Graduate Coordinator, 610-758-3065, Fax: 610-758-4096, E-mail: hew207@lehigh.edu.
Website: http://www.cse.lehigh.edu/.

Lehigh University, P.C. Rossin College of Engineering and Applied Science, Department of Electrical and Computer Engineering, Bethlehem, PA 18015. Offers electrical engineering (MS, PhD); wireless network engineering (MS). Part-time programs available. *Faculty:* 19 full-time (3 women). *Students:* 38 full-time (4 women), 16 part-time (5 women); includes 1 minority (Black or African American, non-Hispanic/Latino), 46 international. Average age 27. 608 applicants, 4% accepted, 12 enrolled. In 2014, 13 master's, 4 doctorates awarded. Terminal master's awarded for partial completion of doctoral program. *Degree requirements:* For master's, thesis optional; for doctorate, thesis/dissertation, qualifying or comprehensive exam for all 1st year PhD's; general exam 7 months or more prior to completion/dissertation defense. *Entrance requirements:* For master's and doctorate, GRE General Test, BS in field or related field. Additional exam requirements/recommendations for international students: Required—TOEFL (minimum score 79 iBT). *Application deadline:* For fall admission, 1/15 priority date for domestic and international students; for spring admission, 11/1 for domestic and international students. Application fee: $75. Electronic applications accepted. *Expenses:* Expenses: $1,340 per credit hour. *Financial support:* In 2014–15, 42 students received support, including 5 fellowships with full tuition reimbursements available (averaging $19,920 per year), 29 research assistantships with full tuition reimbursements available (averaging $19,917 per year), 6 teaching assistantships with full tuition reimbursements available (averaging $20,484 per year); career-related internships or fieldwork, Federal Work-Study, institutionally sponsored loans, scholarships/grants, and tuition waivers (full and partial) also available. Support available to part-time students. Financial award application deadline: 1/15. *Faculty research:* Nanostructures/nanodevices, terahertz generation, analog devices, mixed mode design and signal circuits, optoelectronic sensors, micro-fabrication technology and design, packaging/reliability of microsensors, coding and networking information theory, radio frequency, wireless and optical wireless communication, wireless networks. *Total annual research expenditures:* $2 million. *Unit head:* Dr. Filbert J. Bartoli, Chair, 610-758-4069, Fax: 610-758-6279, E-mail: fjb205@lehigh.edu. *Application contact:* Diane Hubinsky, Graduate Coordinator, 610-758-4072, Fax: 610-758-6279, E-mail: dih2@lehigh.edu.
Website: http://www.ece.lehigh.edu/.

Louisiana State University and Agricultural & Mechanical College, Graduate School, College of Engineering, Division of Electrical and Computer Engineering, Baton Rouge, LA 70803. Offers MSEE, PhD. *Faculty:* 23 full-time (1 woman), 1 part-time/adjunct (0 women). *Students:* 107 full-time (16 women), 3 part-time (1 woman); includes 4 minority (1 Black or African American, non-Hispanic/Latino; 3 Asian, non-Hispanic/Latino), 96 international. Average age 27. 251 applicants, 55% accepted, 16 enrolled. In 2014, 23 master's, 8 doctorates awarded. Terminal master's awarded for partial completion of doctoral program. *Degree requirements:* For master's, thesis optional; for doctorate, thesis/dissertation. *Entrance requirements:* For master's, GRE General Test, minimum GPA of 3.0; for doctorate, GRE General Test, minimum GPA of 3.5. Additional exam requirements/recommendations for international students: Required—TOEFL (minimum score 550 paper-based; 79 IBT), IELTS (minimum score 6.5), or PTE (minimum score 59). *Application deadline:* For fall admission, 1/1 priority date for domestic students, 5/15 for international students; for spring admission, 10/15 for domestic and international students; for summer admission, 5/15 for domestic and international students. Applications are processed on a rolling basis. Application fee: $50 ($70 for international students). Electronic applications accepted. *Financial support:* In 2014–15, 102 students received support, including 3 fellowships with full and partial tuition reimbursements available (averaging $29,125 per year), 50 research assistantships with full and partial tuition reimbursements available (averaging $15,318 per year), 43 teaching assistantships with full and partial tuition reimbursements available (averaging $12,949 per year); Federal Work-Study, institutionally sponsored loans, health care benefits, tuition waivers (full and partial), and unspecified assistantships also available. Financial award application deadline: 2/28; financial award applicants required to submit FAFSA. *Faculty research:* Computer engineering, electronics, control systems and signal processing, communications. *Total annual research expenditures:* $2.3 million. *Unit head:* Dr. Jerry Trahan, Interim Chair, 225-578-5241, Fax: 225-578-5200, E-mail: jtrahan@lsu.edu. *Application contact:* Dr. Ramachandran Vaidyanathan, Graduate Adviser, 225-578-5238, Fax: 225-578-5200, E-mail: vaidy@lsu.edu.
Website: http://www.ece.lsu.edu/.

Manhattan College, Graduate Programs, School of Engineering, Program in Computer Engineering, Riverdale, NY 10471. Offers MS. Part-time and evening/weekend programs available. *Faculty:* 3 full-time (1 woman). *Students:* 6 full-time (1 woman), 1 (woman) part-time. Average age 26. 9 applicants, 22% accepted, 2 enrolled. In 2014, 4 master's awarded. *Degree requirements:* For master's, thesis or alternative. *Entrance requirements:* For master's, GRE (recommended), minimum GPA of 3.0. Additional exam requirements/recommendations for international students: Required—TOEFL (minimum score 550 paper-based; 80 iBT), IELTS (minimum score 6). *Application deadline:* For fall admission, 8/10 priority date for domestic students, 8/10 for international students; for spring admission, 1/7 for domestic and international students. Applications are processed on a rolling basis. Application fee: $60. *Financial support:* In 2014–15, 1 student received support, including 1 teaching assistantship with partial tuition reimbursement available (averaging $5,000 per year); fellowships, research assistantships, career-related internships or fieldwork, Federal Work-Study, scholarships/grants, and unspecified assistantships also available. Support available to part-time students. Financial award application deadline: 2/1. *Unit head:* Dr. George Giakos, Chairperson, 718-862-7154, Fax: 718-862-7162, E-mail: george.giakos@manhattan.edu. *Application contact:* Bobbie Moore, Information Contact, 718-862-7153, Fax: 718-862-7162, E-mail: ece@manhattan.edu.
Website: http://www.engineering.manhattan.edu.

Marquette University, Graduate School, Opus College of Engineering, Department of Electrical and Computer Engineering, Milwaukee, WI 53201-1881. Offers digital signal processing (Certificate); electric machines, drives, and controls (Certificate); electrical and computer engineering (MS, PhD); microwaves and antennas (Certificate); sensors and smart systems (Certificate). Part-time and evening/weekend programs available. Terminal master's awarded for partial completion of doctoral program. *Degree requirements:* For master's, comprehensive exam (for some programs), thesis optional; for doctorate, thesis/dissertation, dissertation defense, qualifying exam. *Entrance requirements:* For master's, GRE General Test (recommended), official transcripts from all current and previous colleges/universities except Marquette, three letters of recommendation; for doctorate, GRE General Test, minimum GPA of 3.0, official transcripts from all current and previous colleges/universities except Marquette, three letters of recommendation, statement of purpose, submission of any English language publications authored by applicant (strongly recommended). Additional exam requirements/recommendations for international students: Required—TOEFL (minimum score 530 paper-based). Electronic applications accepted. *Faculty research:* Electric machines, drives, and controls; applied solid-state electronics; computers and signal processing; microwaves and antennas; solid state devices and acoustic wave sensors.

Massachusetts Institute of Technology, School of Engineering, Department of Electrical Engineering and Computer Science, Cambridge, MA 02139. Offers computer science (PhD, Sc D, ECS); computer science and engineering (PhD, Sc D); electrical engineering (PhD, Sc D, EE); electrical engineering and computer science (M Eng, SM, PhD, Sc D); SM/MBA. *Faculty:* 120 full-time (19 women). *Students:* 795 full-time (185 women), 4 part-time (0 women); includes 193 minority (13 Black or African American, non-Hispanic/Latino; 2 American Indian or Alaska Native, non-Hispanic/Latino; 119 Asian, non-Hispanic/Latino; 40 Hispanic/Latino; 19 Two or more races, non-Hispanic/Latino), 390 international. Average age 26. 2,971 applicants, 13% accepted, 277 enrolled. In 2014, 219 master's, 101 doctorates, 4 other advanced degrees awarded. Terminal master's awarded for partial completion of doctoral program. *Degree requirements:* For master's and other advanced degree, thesis; for doctorate, comprehensive exam, thesis/dissertation. *Entrance requirements:* Additional exam requirements/recommendations for international students: Required—TOEFL (minimum score 100 iBT), IELTS (minimum score 7). *Application deadline:* For fall admission, 12/15 for domestic and international students. Application fee: $75. Electronic applications accepted. *Expenses:* Tuition: Full-time $44,720; part-time $699 per unit. *Required fees:* $296. *Financial support:* In 2014–15, 743 students received support, including 124 fellowships (averaging $36,900 per year), 493 research assistantships (averaging $34,100 per year), 142 teaching assistantships (averaging $34,800 per year); Federal Work-Study, institutionally sponsored loans, scholarships/grants, traineeships, health care benefits, and unspecified assistantships also available. Financial award application deadline: 4/15; financial award applicants required to submit FAFSA. *Faculty research:* Information systems, circuits, biomedical sciences and engineering, computer science: artificial intelligence, systems, theory. *Total annual research expenditures:* $112 million. *Unit head:* Prof. Anantha P. Chandrakasan, Department Head, 617-253-4600. *Application contact:* Graduate Admissions, 617-253-4603, Fax: 617-258-7354, E-mail: grad-ap@eecs.mit.edu. Website: http://www.eecs.mit.edu/.

McGill University, Faculty of Graduate and Postdoctoral Studies, Faculty of Engineering, Department of Electrical and Computer Engineering, Montréal, QC H3A 2T5, Canada. Offers M Eng, PhD.

Memorial University of Newfoundland, School of Graduate Studies, Faculty of Engineering and Applied Science, St. John's, NL A1C 5S7, Canada. Offers civil engineering (M Eng, PhD); electrical and computer engineering (M Eng, PhD); mechanical engineering (M Eng, PhD); ocean and naval architecture engineering (M Eng, PhD). Part-time programs available. *Degree requirements:* For master's, thesis; for doctorate, comprehensive exam, thesis/dissertation, oral thesis defense. *Entrance requirements:* For master's, 2nd class degree; for doctorate, master's degree in engineering. Electronic applications accepted. *Faculty research:* Engineering analysis, environmental and hydrotechnical studies, manufacturing and robotics, mechanics, structures and materials.

Memorial University of Newfoundland, School of Graduate Studies, Interdisciplinary Program in Computer Engineering, St. John's, NL A1C 5S7, Canada. Offers MA Sc. *Degree requirements:* For master's, project course. *Entrance requirements:* For master's, 2nd class engineering degree.

Mercer University, Graduate Studies, Macon Campus, School of Engineering, Macon, GA 31207. Offers biomedical engineering (MSE); computer engineering (MSE); electrical engineering (MSE); engineering management (MSE); environmental engineering (MSE); environmental systems (MS); mechanical engineering (MSE); software engineering (MSE); software systems (MS); technical communications management (MS); technical management (MS). Part-time and evening/weekend programs available. Postbaccalaureate distance learning degree programs offered (no on-campus study). *Faculty:* 20 full-time (6 women), 2 part-time/adjunct (0 women). *Students:* 10 full-time (4 women), 75 part-time (16 women); includes 10 minority (5 Black or African American, non-Hispanic/Latino; 4 Asian, non-Hispanic/Latino; 1 Hispanic/Latino), 4 international. Average age 42. In 2014, 70 master's awarded. *Degree requirements:* For master's, thesis or alternative. *Entrance requirements:* For master's, minimum undergraduate GPA of 3.0. Additional exam requirements/recommendations for international students: Required—TOEFL (minimum score 550 paper-based; 80 iBT). *Application deadline:* For fall admission, 4/1 priority date for domestic and international students; for spring admission, 11/1 priority date for domestic and international students. Applications are processed on a rolling basis. Application fee: $75. *Expenses:* Expenses: Contact institution. *Financial support:* Federal Work-Study available. *Unit head:* Dr. Wade H. Shaw, Dean, 478-301-2459, Fax: 478-301-5593, E-mail: shaw_wh@mercer.edu. *Application contact:* Dr. Richard O. Mines, Program Director, 478-301-2347, Fax: 478-301-5433, E-mail: mines_ro@mercer.edu. Website: http://engineering.mercer.edu/.

Michigan Technological University, Graduate School, College of Engineering, Department of Electrical and Computer Engineering, Houghton, MI 49931. Offers advanced electric power engineering (Graduate Certificate); computer engineering (MS, PhD); electrical engineering (MS, PhD). Part-time programs available. Postbaccalaureate distance learning degree programs offered (minimal on-campus study). *Faculty:* 29 full-time, 8 part-time/adjunct. *Students:* 203 full-time, 70 part-time; includes 13 minority (4 Black or African American, non-Hispanic/Latino; 4 Asian, non-Hispanic/Latino; 5 Hispanic/Latino), 217 international. Average age 27. 1,168 applicants, 36% accepted, 78 enrolled. In 2014, 65 master's, 7 doctorates, 17 other advanced degrees awarded. Terminal master's awarded for partial completion of doctoral program. *Degree requirements:* For master's, comprehensive exam (for some programs), thesis (for some programs); for doctorate, comprehensive exam, thesis/dissertation. *Entrance requirements:* For master's and doctorate, GRE, statement of purpose, official transcripts, 2 letters of recommendation; for Graduate Certificate, statement of purpose, official transcripts. Additional exam requirements/recommendations for international students: Required—TOEFL (recommended score 100 iBT) or IELTS. *Application deadline:* For fall admission, 2/15 priority date for domestic and international students; for spring admission, 8/15 priority date for domestic and international students. Applications are processed on a rolling basis. Electronic applications accepted. *Expenses:* Expenses: Contact institution. *Financial support:* In 2014–15, 156 students received support, including 7 fellowships with full and partial tuition reimbursements available (averaging $13,824 per year), 31 research assistantships with full and partial tuition reimbursements available (averaging $13,824 per year), 22 teaching assistantships with full and partial tuition reimbursements available (averaging $13,824 per year); career-related internships or fieldwork, Federal Work-Study, scholarships/grants, health care benefits, unspecified assistantships, and cooperative program also available. Financial award applicants required to submit FAFSA. *Faculty research:* Information systems (signal processing and communications), solid-state electronics, power and energy systems, computer engineering, electro-physics. *Total annual research expenditures:* $1.8 million. *Unit head:* Dr. Daniel R. Fuhrmann, Department Chair, 906-487-2550, Fax: 906-487-2949, E-mail: fuhrmann@mtu.edu. *Application contact:* Lisa Rouleau, Business Manager/Technical Communications Specialist, 906-487-2550, Fax: 906-487-2949, E-mail: mlkamppi@mtu.edu. Website: http://www.mtu.edu/ece/.

Michigan Technological University, Graduate School, Interdisciplinary Programs, Houghton, MI 49931. Offers atmospheric sciences (PhD); biochemistry and molecular biology (PhD); computational science and engineering (PhD); environmental engineering (PhD); interdisciplinary studies (M Ed, MS, Graduate Certificate). Part-time programs available. *Faculty:* 6 full-time, 3 part-time/adjunct. *Students:* 46 full-time (20

women), 6 part-time (3 women); includes 2 minority (1 Asian, non-Hispanic/Latino; 1 Two or more races, non-Hispanic/Latino), 35 international. Average age 30. 239 applicants, 16% accepted, 9 enrolled. In 2014, 4 doctorates awarded. Terminal master's awarded for partial completion of doctoral program. *Degree requirements:* For master's, comprehensive exam (for some programs), thesis (for some programs); for doctorate, comprehensive exam, thesis/dissertation. *Entrance requirements:* For master's, doctorate, and Graduate Certificate, GRE, statement of purpose, official transcripts, 2-3 letters of recommendation. Additional exam requirements/recommendations for international students: Required—TOEFL or IELTS. *Application deadline:* Applications are processed on a rolling basis. Electronic applications accepted. *Expenses:* Tuition, state resident: full-time $14,769; part-time $820.50 per credit. Tuition, nonresident: full-time $14,769; part-time $820.50 per credit. *Required fees:* $248; $248 per year. Tuition and fees vary according to course load and program. *Financial support:* In 2014–15, 42 students received support, including 6 fellowships with full and partial tuition reimbursements available (averaging $13,824 per year), 25 research assistantships with full and partial tuition reimbursements available (averaging $13,824 per year), 4 teaching assistantships with full and partial tuition reimbursements available (averaging $13,824 per year); career-related internships or fieldwork, Federal Work-Study, scholarships/grants, health care benefits, unspecified assistantships, and cooperative program also available. Financial award applicants required to submit FAFSA. *Faculty research:* Big data, atmospheric sciences, bioinformatics and systems biology, molecular dynamics. *Unit head:* Dr. Jacqueline E. Huntoon, Dean, 906-487-2327, Fax: 906-487-2284, E-mail: jeh@mtu.edu. *Application contact:* Carol T. Wingerson, Administrative Aide, 906-487-2328, Fax: 906-487-2284, E-mail: gradadms@mtu.edu.

Mississippi State University, Bagley College of Engineering, Department of Electrical and Computer Engineering, Mississippi State, MS 39762. Offers computer engineering (MS, PhD); electrical engineering (MS, PhD). Part-time programs available. Postbaccalaureate distance learning degree programs offered (minimal on-campus study). *Faculty:* 60 full-time (5 women), 4 part-time/adjunct (0 women). *Students:* 59 full-time (10 women), 39 part-time (3 women); includes 18 minority (7 Black or African American, non-Hispanic/Latino; 7 Asian, non-Hispanic/Latino; 3 Hispanic/Latino; 1 Two or more races, non-Hispanic/Latino), 45 international. Average age 33. 164 applicants, 38% accepted, 23 enrolled. In 2014, 6 master's, 12 doctorates awarded. Terminal master's awarded for partial completion of doctoral program. *Degree requirements:* For master's, comprehensive exam, thesis optional; for doctorate, comprehensive exam, thesis/dissertation, written exam, oral preliminary exam. *Entrance requirements:* For master's, GRE (for graduates from program not accredited by EAC/ABET), minimum GPA of 3.0 on BS; for doctorate, GRE (for graduates from program not accredited by EAC/ABET), minimum GPA of 3.5 on BS or MS. Additional exam requirements/recommendations for international students: Required—TOEFL (minimum score 550 paper-based; 79 iBT); Recommended—IELTS (minimum score 6.5). *Application deadline:* For fall admission, 7/1 for domestic students, 5/1 for international students; for spring admission, 11/1 for domestic students, 9/1 for international students. Applications are processed on a rolling basis. Application fee: $60. Electronic applications accepted. *Expenses:* Tuition, state resident: full-time $7140; part-time $783 per credit hour. Tuition, nonresident: full-time $18,478; part-time $2043 per credit hour. *Financial support:* In 2014–15, 19 research assistantships with full tuition reimbursements (averaging $17,720 per year), 19 teaching assistantships with full tuition reimbursements (averaging $15,184 per year) were awarded; Federal Work-Study, institutionally sponsored loans, scholarships/grants, and unspecified assistantships also available. Financial award application deadline: 4/1; financial award applicants required to submit FAFSA. *Faculty research:* Digital computing, power, controls, communication systems, microelectronics. *Total annual research expenditures:* $9 million. *Unit head:* Dr. Nicholas H. Younan, Jr., Professor and Department Head, 662-325-3912, Fax: 662-325-2298, E-mail: ece-head@ece.msstate.edu. *Application contact:* Dr. James E. Fowler, Professor/Interim Graduate Program Director, 662-325-3640, Fax: 662-325-2298, E-mail: fowler@ece.msstate.edu. Website: http://www.ece.msstate.edu/.

Missouri University of Science and Technology, Graduate School, School of Engineering, Department of Electrical and Computer Engineering, Rolla, MO 65409. Offers computer engineering (MS, DE, PhD); electrical engineering (MS, DE, PhD). Part-time and evening/weekend programs available. Terminal master's awarded for partial completion of doctoral program. *Degree requirements:* For master's, thesis optional; for doctorate, comprehensive exam, thesis/dissertation, departmental qualifying exam. *Entrance requirements:* For master's, GRE General Test (minimum score 1100 verbal and quantitative, writing 4.5); for doctorate, GRE General Test (minimum score: verbal and quantitative 1100, writing 3.5). Additional exam requirements/recommendations for international students: Required—TOEFL. Electronic applications accepted. *Faculty research:* Power systems, computer/communication networks, intelligent control/robotics, robust control, nanotechnologies.

Montana State University, The Graduate School, College of Engineering, Department of Electrical and Computer Engineering, Bozeman, MT 59717. Offers electrical engineering (MS); engineering (PhD), including electrical and computer engineering option. Part-time programs available. *Degree requirements:* For master's, comprehensive exam, thesis (for some programs); for doctorate, comprehensive exam, thesis/dissertation. *Entrance requirements:* For master's, GRE, BS in electrical or computer engineering or related field; for doctorate, GRE, MS in electrical or computer engineering or related field. Additional exam requirements/recommendations for international students: Required—TOEFL (minimum score 550 paper-based). Electronic applications accepted. *Faculty research:* Optics and optoelectronics, communications and signal processing, microfabrication, complex systems and control, energy systems.

Naval Postgraduate School, Departments and Academic Groups, Department of Electrical and Computer Engineering, Monterey, CA 93943-5216. Offers computer engineering (MS); electrical engineer (EE); electrical engineering (PhD); engineering acoustics (MS); engineering science (MS). Program only open to commissioned officers of the United States and friendly nations and selected United States federal civilian employees. *Accreditation:* ABET (one or more programs are accredited). Part-time programs available. Postbaccalaureate distance learning degree programs offered (minimal on-campus study). *Degree requirements:* For master's and EE, thesis (for some programs), capstone project or research/dissertation paper (for some programs); for doctorate, thesis/dissertation. *Faculty research:* Theory and design of digital communication systems; behavior modeling for detection, identification, prediction and reaction in artificial intelligence (AI) systems solutions; waveform design for target class discrimination with closed-loop radar; iterative technique for system identification with adaptive signal design.

New Jersey Institute of Technology, Newark College of Engineering, Newark, NJ 07102. Offers biomedical engineering (MS, PhD); chemical engineering (MS, PhD); computer engineering (MS, PhD); electrical engineering (MS, PhD); engineering management (MS); healthcare systems management (MS); industrial engineering (MS, PhD); Internet engineering (MS); manufacturing engineering (MS); mechanical engineering (MS, PhD); occupational safety and health engineering (MS); pharmaceutical bioprocessing (MS); pharmaceutical engineering (MS); pharmaceutical systems management (MS); power and energy systems (MS); telecommunications

(MS); transportation (MS, PhD). Part-time and evening/weekend programs available. Terminal master's awarded for partial completion of doctoral program. *Degree requirements:* For master's, thesis optional; for doctorate, thesis/dissertation. *Entrance requirements:* For master's, GRE General Test; for doctorate, GRE General Test, minimum graduate GPA of 3.5. Additional exam requirements/recommendations for international students: Required—TOEFL (minimum score 550 paper-based; 79 iBT). Electronic applications accepted.

New Mexico State University, College of Engineering, Klipsch School of Electrical and Computer Engineering, Las Cruces, NM 88003-8001. Offers MSEE, PhD, Graduate Certificate. Part-time and evening/weekend programs available. Postbaccalaureate distance learning degree programs offered (no on-campus study). *Faculty:* 17 full-time (1 woman), 1 part-time/adjunct (0 women). *Students:* 97 full-time (14 women), 54 part-time (4 women); includes 38 minority (2 American Indian or Alaska Native, non-Hispanic/Latino; 34 Hispanic/Latino; 2 Two or more races, non-Hispanic/Latino), 82 international. Average age 29. 168 applicants, 56% accepted, 30 enrolled. In 2014, 24 master's, 9 doctorates awarded. Terminal master's awarded for partial completion of doctoral program. *Degree requirements:* For master's, thesis (for some programs), final oral or written exam; for doctorate, comprehensive exam, thesis/dissertation. *Entrance requirements:* For master's, GRE, minimum GPA of 3.0; for doctorate, departmental qualifying exam, minimum GPA of 3.0. Additional exam requirements/recommendations for international students: Required—TOEFL (minimum score 550 paper-based; 79 iBT), IELTS (minimum score 6.5). *Application deadline:* For fall admission, 3/1 priority date for domestic and international students; for spring admission, 8/1 priority date for domestic and international students. Applications are processed on a rolling basis. Application fee: $40 ($50 for international students). Electronic applications accepted. *Expenses:* Tuition, state resident: full-time $3969; part-time $220.50 per credit hour. Tuition, nonresident: full-time $13,838; part-time $768.80 per credit hour. *Required fees:* $853; $47.40 per credit hour. *Financial support:* In 2014–15, 91 students received support, including 1 fellowship (averaging $3,970 per year), 25 research assistantships (averaging $13,922 per year), 31 teaching assistantships (averaging $11,005 per year); career-related internships or fieldwork, Federal Work-Study, scholarships/grants, traineeships, health care benefits, and unspecified assistantships also available. Support available to part-time students. Financial award application deadline: 3/1. *Faculty research:* Image and digital signal processing, energy systems, wireless communications, analog and mixed-signal VLSI design, electro-optics. *Total annual research expenditures:* $2.5 million. *Unit head:* Dr. Satishkuma Ranade, Academic Department Head, 575-646-3115, Fax: 575-646-1435, E-mail: sranade@nmsu.edu. *Application contact:* 575-646-3115, Fax: 575-646-1435, E-mail: eceoffice@nmsu.edu. Website: http://ece.nmsu.edu.

New York Institute of Technology, School of Engineering and Computing Sciences, Department of Electrical Engineering, Old Westbury, NY 11568-8000. Offers electrical and computer engineering (MS). Part-time and evening/weekend programs available. *Degree requirements:* For master's, project. *Entrance requirements:* For master's, GRE General Test (if QPA less than 2.85), BS in electrical engineering or related field, minimum QPA of 2.85. Additional exam requirements/recommendations for international students: Required—TOEFL (minimum score 550 paper-based; 79 iBT), IELTS (minimum score 6). Electronic applications accepted. *Faculty research:* Detection of physical node capture in wireless sensor networks, intelligent networks for health monitoring, technology to patients with Parkinson's disease, assistive technologies.

New York University, Polytechnic School of Engineering, Department of Electrical and Computer Engineering, Major in Computer Engineering, New York, NY 10012-1019. Offers MS, Certificate. Postbaccalaureate distance learning degree programs offered (no on-campus study). *Students:* 105 full-time (23 women), 20 part-time (2 women); includes 3 minority (2 Asian, non-Hispanic/Latino; 1 Two or more races, non-Hispanic/Latino), 114 international. Average age 24. 281 applicants, 42% accepted, 36 enrolled. In 2014, 36 master's awarded. *Degree requirements:* For master's, comprehensive exam (for some programs), thesis (for some programs). *Entrance requirements:* For master's, BS in electrical engineering. Additional exam requirements/recommendations for international students: Required—TOEFL (minimum score 550 paper-based; 80 iBT); Recommended—IELTS (minimum score 6.5). *Application deadline:* For fall admission, 2/15 priority date for domestic and international students; for spring admission, 11/1 priority date for domestic and international students. Applications are processed on a rolling basis. Application fee: $75. Electronic applications accepted. *Financial support:* Applicants required to submit FAFSA. *Unit head:* Prof. Ramesh Karri, Program Director, 718-260-3596, E-mail: rkarri@nyu.edu. *Application contact:* Raymond Lutzky, Director, Graduate Enrollment Management, 718-637-5984, Fax: 718-260-3624, E-mail: rlutzky@poly.edu.

Norfolk State University, School of Graduate Studies, School of Science and Technology, Program in Electronics Engineering, Norfolk, VA 23504. Offers MS.

North Carolina Agricultural and Technical State University, School of Graduate Studies, College of Engineering, Department of Electrical and Computer Engineering, Greensboro, NC 27411. Offers electrical engineering (MSEE, PhD), including communications and signal processing, computer engineering, electronic and optical materials and devices, power systems and control. Part-time programs available. *Degree requirements:* For master's, project, thesis defense; for doctorate, thesis/dissertation. *Entrance requirements:* For master's, GRE General Test, GRE Subject Test, minimum GPA of 2.8; for doctorate, GRE General Test, minimum GPA of 3.0. *Faculty research:* Semiconductor compounds, VLSI design, image processing, optical systems and devices, fault-tolerant computing.

North Carolina State University, Graduate School, College of Engineering, Department of Electrical and Computer Engineering, Program in Computer Engineering, Raleigh, NC 27695. Offers MS, PhD. *Degree requirements:* For master's, thesis (for some programs); for doctorate, thesis/dissertation. *Entrance requirements:* For master's and doctorate, GRE. Additional exam requirements/recommendations for international students: Required—TOEFL (minimum score 575 paper-based). Electronic applications accepted. *Faculty research:* Computer architecture, parallel processing, embedded computer systems, VLSI design, computer networking performance and control.

North Dakota State University, College of Graduate and Interdisciplinary Studies, College of Engineering and Architecture, Department of Electrical and Computer Engineering, Fargo, ND 58108. Offers MS, PhD. Part-time programs available. Terminal master's awarded for partial completion of doctoral program. *Degree requirements:* For master's, comprehensive exam, thesis; for doctorate, comprehensive exam, thesis/dissertation. *Entrance requirements:* Additional exam requirements/recommendations for international students: Required—TOEFL (minimum score 525 paper-based; 71 iBT). Electronic applications accepted. *Faculty research:* Computers, power and control systems, microwaves, communications and signal processing, bioengineering.

Northeastern University, College of Engineering, Boston, MA 02115-5096. Offers bioengineering (PhD); chemical engineering (MS, PhD); civil engineering (MS, PhD); computer engineering (PhD); computer systems engineering (MS); electrical and computer engineering (MS); electrical and engineering leadership (MS); electrical engineering (PhD); energy systems (MS); engineering leadership (Certificate); engineering management (MRTP); industrial engineering (MS, PhD); information assurance (PhD); information systems (MS); interdisciplinary (PhD); mechanical engineering (MS, PhD); operations research (MS); telecommunication systems management (MS). Part-time programs available. *Expenses:* Contact institution.

Northwestern Polytechnic University, School of Engineering, Fremont, CA 94539-7482. Offers computer science (MS); computer systems engineering (MS); electrical engineering (MS). Part-time and evening/weekend programs available. *Degree requirements:* For master's, thesis optional. *Entrance requirements:* For master's, minimum GPA of 3.0. Additional exam requirements/recommendations for international students: Required—TOEFL (minimum score 550 paper-based; 79 iBT). *Faculty research:* Computer networking, database design, Internet technology, software engineering, digital signal processing.

Northwestern University, McCormick School of Engineering and Applied Science, Department of Electrical Engineering and Computer Science, Evanston, IL 60208. Offers electrical engineering, computer engineering, and computer science (MS, PhD); information technology (MS). MS and PhD admissions and degrees offered through The Graduate School. Part-time programs available. *Faculty:* 47 full-time (3 women). *Students:* 301 full-time (61 women), 57 part-time (11 women); includes 27 minority (3 Black or African American, non-Hispanic/Latino; 13 Asian, non-Hispanic/Latino; 9 Hispanic/Latino; 2 Two or more races, non-Hispanic/Latino), 299 international. Average age 26. 1,544 applicants, 24% accepted, 123 enrolled. In 2014, 42 master's, 27 doctorates awarded. Terminal master's awarded for partial completion of doctoral program. *Degree requirements:* For master's, comprehensive exam (for some programs), thesis optional; for doctorate, comprehensive exam, thesis/dissertation. *Entrance requirements:* For master's and doctorate, GRE General Test. Additional exam requirements/recommendations for international students: Required—TOEFL (minimum score 577 paper-based; 90 iBT) or IELTS (minimum score of 7.0). *Application deadline:* For fall admission, 12/31 for domestic and international students; for winter admission, 11/15 for domestic students, 11/1 for international students; for spring admission, 2/15 for domestic students, 2/1 for international students. Application fee: $95. Electronic applications accepted. *Financial support:* Fellowships with full tuition reimbursements, research assistantships with full tuition reimbursements, teaching assistantships with full tuition reimbursements, career-related internships or fieldwork, institutionally sponsored loans, health care benefits, and unspecified assistantships available. Financial award application deadline: 1/15; financial award applicants required to submit FAFSA. *Faculty research:* Solid state and photonics; computing, algorithms, and applications; computer engineering and systems; cognitive systems; graphics and interactive media; signals and systems. *Total annual research expenditures:* $14.7 million. *Unit head:* Dr. Alan Sahakian, Chair, 847-491-7007, Fax: 847-491-4455, E-mail: sahakian@ece.northwestern.edu. *Application contact:* Dr. Allen Taflove, Director of Graduate Admissions, 847-491-4127, Fax: 847-491-4455, E-mail: taflove@ece.northwestern.edu. Website: http://www.eecs.northwestern.edu/.

Oakland University, Graduate Study and Lifelong Learning, School of Engineering and Computer Science, Department of Computer Science and Engineering, Rochester, MI 48309-4401. Offers computer science (MS); embedded systems (MS); information systems engineering (MS); software engineering (MS). Part-time and evening/weekend programs available. *Entrance requirements:* For master's, minimum GPA of 3.0. Electronic applications accepted. *Expenses:* Contact institution. *Faculty research:* Urinary continence index for prediction of urinary incontinence in older women.

Oakland University, Graduate Study and Lifelong Learning, School of Engineering and Computer Science, Department of Electrical and Computer Engineering, Rochester, MI 48309-4401. Offers MS. Part-time and evening/weekend programs available. *Entrance requirements:* For master's, minimum GPA of 3.0. Additional exam requirements/recommendations for international students: Required—TOEFL (minimum score 550 paper-based). Electronic applications accepted. *Expenses:* Contact institution. *Faculty research:* Reliable peripheral nerve interfaces.

The Ohio State University, Graduate School, College of Engineering, Department of Computer Science and Engineering, Columbus, OH 43210. Offers computer science and engineering (MS, PhD). *Faculty:* 43. *Students:* 321 full-time (55 women), 17 part-time (3 women); includes 8 minority (2 Black or African American, non-Hispanic/Latino; 4 Asian, non-Hispanic/Latino; 1 Hispanic/Latino; 1 Two or more races, non-Hispanic/Latino), 293 international. Average age 26. In 2014, 93 master's, 26 doctorates awarded. *Degree requirements:* For master's, thesis optional; for doctorate, thesis/dissertation. *Entrance requirements:* For master's and doctorate, GRE (minimum score Quantitative 750 old, 159 new, Verbal 500 old, 155 new, Analytical Writing 3.0); GRE CS subject test is strongly recommended for those whose undergraduate degree is not in computer science. Additional exam requirements/recommendations for international students: Required—TOEFL (minimum score 550 paper-based; 79 iBT), Michigan English Language Assessment Battery (minimum score 82); Recommended—IELTS (minimum score 7). *Application deadline:* For fall admission, 12/13 priority date for domestic students, 11/30 priority date for international students; for winter admission, 12/1 for domestic students, 11/1 for international students; for spring admission, 10/15 priority date for domestic and international students. Applications are processed on a rolling basis. Application fee: $60 ($70 for international students). Electronic applications accepted. *Financial support:* Fellowships with tuition reimbursements, research assistantships with tuition reimbursements, teaching assistantships with tuition reimbursements, career-related internships or fieldwork, Federal Work-Study, institutionally sponsored loans, unspecified assistantships, and administrative assistantships available. Support available to part-time students. Financial award application deadline: 1/15. *Unit head:* Dr. Xiadong Zhang, Chair, 614-292-2770, E-mail: zhang.574@osu.edu. *Application contact:* Graduate and Professional Admissions, 614-292-9444, Fax: 614-292-3895, E-mail: gpadmissions@osu.edu. Website: http://www.cse.osu.edu.

The Ohio State University, Graduate School, College of Engineering, Department of Electrical and Computer Engineering, Columbus, OH 43210. Offers electrical and computer engineering (MS, PhD); electrical engineering (MS, PhD). Part-time programs available. *Faculty:* 56. *Students:* 436 full-time (90 women), 29 part-time (7 women); includes 30 minority (5 Black or African American, non-Hispanic/Latino; 18 Asian, non-Hispanic/Latino; 3 Hispanic/Latino; 4 Two or more races, non-Hispanic/Latino), 342 international. Average age 26. In 2014, 120 master's, 27 doctorates awarded. Terminal master's awarded for partial completion of doctoral program. *Degree requirements:* For master's, thesis optional; for doctorate, thesis/dissertation. *Entrance requirements:* For master's, GRE General Test (for all graduates of foreign universities and for applicants if undergraduate GPA below 3.2); for doctorate, GRE General Test (for all graduates of foreign universities and for applicants if graduate work GPA is below 3.5). Additional exam requirements/recommendations for international students: Required—TOEFL (minimum score 580 paper-based; 92 iBT), TSE recommended; Recommended—IELTS (minimum score 7.5). *Application deadline:* For fall admission, 12/1 priority date for domestic and international students; for winter admission, 12/1 for domestic students, 11/1 for international students; for spring admission, 3/1 for domestic students, 2/1 for international students. Applications are processed on a rolling basis. Application fee: $60 ($70 for international students). Electronic applications accepted. *Financial support:* Fellowships with full tuition reimbursements, research assistantships with full tuition reimbursements, teaching assistantships with full tuition reimbursements, career-related

internships or fieldwork, Federal Work-Study, institutionally sponsored loans, scholarships/grants, traineeships, health care benefits, and unspecified assistantships available. Support available to part-time students. *Unit head:* Dr. Joel T. Johnson, Chair, 614-292-1563, E-mail: johnson.1374@osu.edu. *Application contact:* Electrical and Computer Engineering Graduate Program, 614-292-2572, Fax: 614-292-7596, E-mail: ecegrad@ece.osu.edu.
Website: http://ece.osu.edu/.

Oklahoma State University, College of Engineering, Architecture and Technology, School of Electrical and Computer Engineering, Stillwater, OK 74078. Offers MS, PhD. Postbaccalaureate distance learning degree programs offered. *Faculty:* 24 full-time (1 woman), 1 part-time/adjunct (0 women). *Students:* 149 full-time (48 women), 86 part-time (15 women); includes 16 minority (1 Black or African American, non-Hispanic/Latino; 1 American Indian or Alaska Native, non-Hispanic/Latino; 4 Asian, non-Hispanic/Latino; 4 Hispanic/Latino; 6 Two or more races, non-Hispanic/Latino), 182 international. Average age 26. 627 applicants, 24% accepted, 64 enrolled. In 2014, 59 master's, 9 doctorates awarded. *Degree requirements:* For master's, thesis or alternative; for doctorate, comprehensive exam, thesis/dissertation. *Entrance requirements:* For master's and doctorate, GRE or GMAT. Additional exam requirements/recommendations for international students: Required—TOEFL (minimum score 550 paper-based; 79 iBT). *Application deadline:* For fall admission, 3/1 priority date for international students; for spring admission, 8/1 priority date for international students. Applications are processed on a rolling basis. Application fee: $40 ($75 for international students). Electronic applications accepted. *Expenses:* Tuition, state resident: full-time $4488; part-time $187 per credit hour. Tuition, nonresident: full-time $18,360; part-time $765 per credit hour. *Required fees:* $2413; $100.55 per credit hour. Tuition and fees vary according to campus/location. *Financial support:* In 2014–15, 46 research assistantships (averaging $15,357 per year), 28 teaching assistantships (averaging $14,057 per year) were awarded; career-related internships or fieldwork, Federal Work-Study, scholarships/grants, health care benefits, tuition waivers (partial), and unspecified assistantships also available. Support available to part-time students. Financial award application deadline: 3/1; financial award applicants required to submit FAFSA. *Unit head:* Dr. James C. West, Interim Department Head, 405-744-5151, Fax: 405-744-9198, E-mail: jwest@okstate.edu.
Website: http://www.ece.okstate.edu.

Old Dominion University, Frank Batten College of Engineering and Technology, Program in Electrical and Computer Engineering, Norfolk, VA 23529. Offers ME, MS, PhD. Part-time programs available. Postbaccalaureate distance learning degree programs offered (minimal on-campus study). *Faculty:* 21 full-time (1 woman), 2 part-time/adjunct (both women). *Students:* 37 full-time (10 women), 65 part-time (11 women); includes 21 minority (6 Black or African American, non-Hispanic/Latino; 1 American Indian or Alaska Native, non-Hispanic/Latino; 7 Asian, non-Hispanic/Latino; 5 Hispanic/Latino; 1 Native Hawaiian or other Pacific Islander, non-Hispanic/Latino; 1 Two or more races, non-Hispanic/Latino), 47 international. Average age 30. 144 applicants, 62% accepted, 16 enrolled. In 2014, 18 master's, 8 doctorates awarded. *Degree requirements:* For master's, comprehensive exam (for some programs), thesis (for some programs); for doctorate, thesis/dissertation, candidacy exam, diagnostic exam. *Entrance requirements:* For master's, GRE, two letters of recommendation; for doctorate, GRE, three letters of recommendation, resume, personal statement of objective. Additional exam requirements/recommendations for international students: Required—TOEFL (minimum score 550 paper-based; 79 iBT). *Application deadline:* For fall admission, 6/1 for domestic students, 4/15 for international students; for spring admission, 11/1 for domestic students, 10/1 for international students. Applications are processed on a rolling basis. Application fee: $50. Electronic applications accepted. *Expenses:* Tuition, state resident: full-time $10,488; part-time $437 per credit. Tuition, nonresident: full-time $26,136; part-time $1089 per credit. *Required fees:* $64 per semester. One-time fee: $50. *Financial support:* In 2014–15, 2 fellowships with full tuition reimbursements (averaging $17,500 per year), 24 research assistantships with full and partial tuition reimbursements (averaging $15,000 per year), 25 teaching assistantships with full and partial tuition reimbursements (averaging $15,000 per year) were awarded; career-related internships or fieldwork, Federal Work-Study, scholarships/grants, tuition waivers (full), and unspecified assistantships also available. Support available to part-time students. Financial award application deadline: 2/15; financial award applicants required to submit FAFSA. *Faculty research:* Signal and image processing biomedical and target detection applications, renewal energy applications including the development of high efficiency solar cells, nanotechnology and nanoscale thin film techniques, ultrafast (femtosecond) laser applications, linear and nonlinear systems theory. *Total annual research expenditures:* $3 million. *Unit head:* Dr. Dimitrie Popescu, Graduate Program Director, 757-683-5414, Fax: 757-683-3220, E-mail: ecegpd@odu.edu. *Application contact:* Linda Marshall, Senior Secretary, 757-683-3741, Fax: 757-683-3220, E-mail: lmarshal@odu.edu.
Website: http://eng.odu.edu/ece/.

Oregon Health & Science University, School of Medicine, Graduate Programs in Medicine, Department of Computer Science and Engineering, Portland, OR 97239-3098. Offers computer science and engineering (MS, PhD); electrical engineering (MS, PhD). Part-time programs available. *Faculty:* 7 full-time (2 women), 1 part-time/adjunct (0 women). *Students:* 18 full-time (8 women), 10 international. Average age 32. 10 applicants, 60% accepted, 5 enrolled. In 2014, 1 master's, 3 doctorates awarded. Terminal master's awarded for partial completion of doctoral program. *Degree requirements:* For master's, thesis (for some programs); for doctorate, comprehensive exam, thesis/dissertation, qualifying exam. *Entrance requirements:* For master's and doctorate, GRE General Test (minimum scores: 153 Verbal/148 Quantitative/4.5 Analytical). Additional exam requirements/recommendations for international students: Required—IELTS or TOEFL. *Application deadline:* For fall admission, 7/15 for domestic students, 5/15 for international students; for winter admission, 10/15 for domestic students, 9/15 for international students; for spring admission, 1/15 for domestic students, 12/15 for international students. Applications are processed on a rolling basis. Application fee: $70. Electronic applications accepted. *Financial support:* Health care benefits, tuition waivers (full), and full tuition and stipends (for PhD students) available. *Faculty research:* Natural language processing, speech signal processing, computational biology, autism spectrum disorders, hearing and speaking disorders. *Unit head:* Dr. Peter Heeman, Program Director, 503-748-1635, E-mail: cseedept@csee.ogi.edu. *Application contact:* Pat Dickerson, Administrative Coordinator, 503-748-1635, E-mail: cseedept@csee.ogi.edu.

Oregon State University, College of Engineering, Program in Electrical and Computer Engineering, Corvallis, OR 97331. Offers M Eng, MS, PhD. *Faculty:* 49 full-time (7 women), 2 part-time/adjunct (both women). *Students:* 170 full-time (26 women), 19 part-time (5 women); includes 10 minority (8 Asian, non-Hispanic/Latino; 1 Hispanic/Latino; 1 Two or more races, non-Hispanic/Latino), 139 international. Average age 28. 500 applicants, 19% accepted, 65 enrolled. In 2014, 44 master's, 20 doctorates awarded. *Entrance requirements:* For master's and doctorate, GRE. Additional exam requirements/recommendations for international students: Required—TOEFL (minimum score 600 paper-based; 80 iBT), IELTS (minimum score 7). *Application deadline:* For fall admission, 1/15 for domestic students. Application fee: $60. *Expenses:* Expenses:

$15,359 full-time resident tuition and fees; $23,405 non-resident. *Unit head:* Bella Bose, Professor/Interim School Head, 541-737-5573. *Application contact:* Graduate Coordinator, 541-737-7234, Fax: 541-737-1300, E-mail: eecs.gradinfo@oregonstate.edu.
Website: http://eecs.oregonstate.edu/current-students/graduate/ece-program.

Penn State University Park, Graduate School, College of Engineering, Department of Computer Science and Engineering, University Park, PA 16802. Offers M Eng, MS, PhD. *Unit head:* Dr. Amr S. Elnashai, Dean, 814-865-7537, Fax: 814-863-4749, E-mail: ase2@psu.edu. *Application contact:* Lori A. Stania, Director, Graduate Student Services, 814-867-5278, Fax: 814-863-4627, E-mail: gswww@psu.edu.
Website: http://www.cse.psu.edu/.

Polytechnic University of Puerto Rico, Graduate School, Hato Rey, PR 00919. Offers business administration (MBA), including computer information systems, general management, management of information systems, management of international enterprises; civil engineering (ME, MS); computer engineering (ME, MS); computer science (MCS, MS); electrical engineering (ME, MS); engineering management (MEM); environmental management (MEM); landscape architecture (M Land Arch); manufacturing competitiveness (MMC, MS); manufacturing engineering (ME, MS); mechanical engineering (M Mech E). Part-time and evening/weekend programs available. *Entrance requirements:* For master's, 3 letters of recommendation.

Portland State University, Graduate Studies, Maseeh College of Engineering and Computer Science, Department of Electrical and Computer Engineering, Portland, OR 97207-0751. Offers M Eng, MS, PhD. Part-time and evening/weekend programs available. *Faculty:* 22 full-time (3 women), 4 part-time/adjunct (1 woman). *Students:* 217 full-time (53 women), 112 part-time (19 women); includes 33 minority (7 Black or African American, non-Hispanic/Latino; 1 American Indian or Alaska Native, non-Hispanic/Latino; 21 Asian, non-Hispanic/Latino; 3 Hispanic/Latino; 1 Native Hawaiian or other Pacific Islander, non-Hispanic/Latino), 207 international. Average age 29. 515 applicants, 38% accepted, 116 enrolled. In 2014, 93 master's awarded. *Degree requirements:* For master's, variable foreign language requirement, oral exam; for doctorate, one foreign language, comprehensive exam, thesis/dissertation, oral and written exams. *Entrance requirements:* For master's, GRE, Incoming students must have a 2.5 GPA for conditional admission and a 2.75 GPA for regular admission. We normally expect students to have at least a 3.0 undergraduate GPA; for doctorate, GRE General Test, GRE Subject Test, Master's degree in electrical engineering or a related field, 3 reference letters, statement of purpose and a writing sample. Additional exam requirements/recommendations for international students: Required—TOEFL (minimum score 550 paper-based; 80 iBT). *Application deadline:* For fall admission, 2/1 for domestic and international students; for winter admission, 8/15 for domestic and international students; for spring admission, 11/1 for domestic and international students. Application fee: $50. *Expenses:* Tuition, state resident: part-time $222 per credit. Tuition, nonresident: part-time $527 per credit. *Required fees:* $22 per contact hour. $100 per quarter. Tuition and fees vary according to program. *Financial support:* In 2014–15, 10 research assistantships with full and partial tuition reimbursements (averaging $7,253 per year), 14 teaching assistantships with full and partial tuition reimbursements (averaging $2,768 per year) were awarded; career-related internships or fieldwork, Federal Work-Study, scholarships/grants, and unspecified assistantships also available. Support available to part-time students. Financial award application deadline: 3/1; financial award applicants required to submit FAFSA. *Faculty research:* Optics and laser systems, design automation, VLSI design, computer systems, power electronics. *Total annual research expenditures:* $1.5 million. *Unit head:* Dr. James McNames, Chair, 503-725-5390, Fax: 503-725-3807, E-mail: mcnames@ece.pdx.edu. *Application contact:* Eliza Conlin, Graduate Coordinator, 503-725-3002, Fax: 503-725-3807, E-mail: kelleyg@ece.pdx.edu.
Website: http://www.pdx.edu/ece/.

Purdue University, College of Engineering, School of Electrical and Computer Engineering, West Lafayette, IN 47907-2035. Offers MS, MSE, MSECE, PhD. MS and PhD degree programs in biomedical engineering offered jointly with School of Mechanical Engineering and School of Chemical Engineering. Part-time programs available. Postbaccalaureate distance learning degree programs offered (no on-campus study). Terminal master's awarded for partial completion of doctoral program. *Entrance requirements:* For master's and doctorate, GRE General Test, minimum GPA of 3.25. Additional exam requirements/recommendations for international students: Required—TOEFL (minimum score 550 paper-based; 77 iBT). Electronic applications accepted. *Faculty research:* Automatic controls; biomedical imaging; computer engineering; communications, networking signal and image processing; fields and optics.

Purdue University Calumet, Graduate Studies Office, School of Engineering, Mathematics, and Science, Department of Engineering, Hammond, IN 46323-2094. Offers computer engineering (MSE); electrical engineering (MSE); engineering (MS); mechanical engineering (MSE). Evening/weekend programs available. *Entrance requirements:* Additional exam requirements/recommendations for international students: Required—TOEFL.

Queen's University at Kingston, School of Graduate Studies, Faculty of Applied Science, Department of Electrical and Computer Engineering, Kingston, ON K7L 3N6, Canada. Offers M Eng, M Sc, M Sc Eng, PhD. Part-time programs available. *Degree requirements:* For master's, thesis optional; for doctorate, comprehensive exam, thesis/dissertation. *Entrance requirements:* Additional exam requirements/recommendations for international students: Required—TOEFL (minimum score 580 paper-based). *Faculty research:* Communications and signal processing systems, computer engineering systems.

Rensselaer at Hartford, Department of Engineering, Program in Computer and Systems Engineering, Hartford, CT 06120-2991. Offers ME. *Entrance requirements:* For master's, GRE.

Rensselaer Polytechnic Institute, Graduate School, School of Engineering, Program in Computer and Systems Engineering, Troy, NY 12180-3590. Offers M Eng, MS, D Eng, PhD. *Faculty:* 12 full-time (2 women), 2 part-time/adjunct (1 woman). *Students:* 14 full-time (4 women), 2 part-time (0 women), 12 international. Average age 28. 50 applicants, 12% accepted, 5 enrolled. In 2014, 4 master's, 1 doctorate awarded. Terminal master's awarded for partial completion of doctoral program. *Degree requirements:* For master's, thesis (for some programs); for doctorate, thesis/dissertation. *Entrance requirements:* For master's and doctorate, GRE. Additional exam requirements/recommendations for international students: Required—TOEFL (minimum score 570 paper-based; 88 iBT), IELTS (minimum score 6.5), PTE (minimum score 60). *Application deadline:* For fall admission, 1/1 priority date for domestic and international students; for spring admission, 8/15 priority date for domestic and international students. Applications are processed on a rolling basis. Application fee: $75. Electronic applications accepted. *Expenses:* Tuition: Full-time $46,700; part-time $1945 per credit. Tuition and fees vary according to course load. *Financial support:* In 2014–15, 11 students received support, including research assistantships (averaging $18,500 per year), teaching assistantships (averaging $18,500 per year); fellowships also available. Financial award application deadline: 1/1. *Faculty research:* Communications, information, and signals and systems; computer engineering, hardware, and

architecture; computer networking; control, robotics, and automation; energy sources and systems; image science: computer vision, image processing, and geographic information science; microelectronics, photonics, VLSI, and mixed-signal design; plasma science and electromagnetics. *Total annual research expenditures:* $1.9 million. *Unit head:* Dr. Ken Vastola, Graduate Program Director, 518-576-6074, E-mail: gpd@ecse.rpi.edu. *Application contact:* Office of Graduate Admissions, 518-276-6216, E-mail: gradadmissions@rpi.edu.
Website: http://www.ecse.rpi.edu/.

Rice University, Graduate Programs, George R. Brown School of Engineering, Department of Electrical and Computer Engineering, Houston, TX 77251-1892. Offers bioengineering (MS, PhD); circuits, controls, and communication systems (MS, PhD); computer science and engineering (MS, PhD); electrical engineering (MEE); lasers, microwaves, and solid-state electronics (MS, PhD); MBA/MEE. Part-time programs available. *Degree requirements:* For master's, thesis (for some programs); for doctorate, thesis/dissertation. *Entrance requirements:* For master's and doctorate, GRE General Test, GRE Subject Test, minimum GPA of 3.0. Additional exam requirements/recommendations for international students: Required—TOEFL (minimum score 600 paper-based; 90 iBT). Electronic applications accepted. *Faculty research:* Physical electronics, systems, computer engineering, bioengineering.

Rice University, Graduate Programs, George R. Brown School of Engineering, Program in Computational Science and Engineering, Houston, TX 77251-1892. Offers MCSE.

Rochester Institute of Technology, Graduate Enrollment Services, Kate Gleason College of Engineering, Computer Engineering Department, MS Program in Computer Engineering, Rochester, NY 14623-5603. Offers MS. Part-time programs available. *Students:* 45 full-time (4 women), 13 part-time (2 women); includes 6 minority (3 Black or African American, non-Hispanic/Latino; 2 Asian, non-Hispanic/Latino; 1 Hispanic/Latino), 30 international. Average age 24. 167 applicants, 34% accepted, 25 enrolled. In 2014, 19 master's awarded. *Degree requirements:* For master's, thesis. *Entrance requirements:* For master's, GRE and TOEFL, IELTS, or PTE for non-native English speakers, Recommended minimum GPA of 3.0. Additional exam requirements/recommendations for international students: Required—PTE (minimum score 58), TOEFL (minimum score 550 paper-based; 79 iBT) or IELTS (minimum score 6.5). *Application deadline:* For fall admission, 2/15 priority date for domestic students, 2/15 for international students; for spring admission, 12/15 priority date for domestic and international students. Applications are processed on a rolling basis. Application fee: $60. Electronic applications accepted. *Expenses:* Expenses: $1,673 per credit hour. *Financial support:* In 2014–15, 55 students received support. Research assistantships with partial tuition reimbursements available, teaching assistantships with partial tuition reimbursements available, career-related internships or fieldwork, Federal Work-Study, institutionally sponsored loans, scholarships/grants, and unspecified assistantships available. Support available to part-time students. Financial award applicants required to submit FAFSA. *Faculty research:* Computer architecture; integrated circuits and systems; networks and security; computer vision and machine intelligence; signal processing, control and embedded systems. *Unit head:* Dr. Dhireesha Kudithipudi, Graduate Program Director, 585-475-5085, E-mail: dxkeec@rit.edu. *Application contact:* Diane Ellison, Associate Vice President, Graduate Enrollment Services, 585-475-2229, Fax: 585-475-7164, E-mail: gradinfo@rit.edu.
Website: http://www.rit.edu/kgcoe/computerengineering/program/graduate-ms/overview.

Rose-Hulman Institute of Technology, Faculty of Engineering and Applied Sciences, Department of Electrical and Computer Engineering, Terre Haute, IN 47803-3999. Offers electrical and computer engineering (M Eng); electrical engineering (MS); systems engineering and management (MS). Part-time programs available. Postbaccalaureate distance learning degree programs offered (minimal on-campus study). *Faculty:* 19 full-time (3 women), 1 (woman) part-time/adjunct. *Students:* 16 full-time (4 women), 6 part-time (0 women); includes 2 minority (both Asian, non-Hispanic/Latino), 16 international. Average age 24. 28 applicants, 93% accepted, 11 enrolled. In 2014, 14 master's awarded. *Degree requirements:* For master's, thesis (for some programs). *Entrance requirements:* For master's, GRE, minimum GPA of 3.0. Additional exam requirements/recommendations for international students: Required—TOEFL (minimum score 580 paper-based; 92 iBT). *Application deadline:* For fall admission, 2/1 priority date for domestic students. Applications are processed on a rolling basis. Application fee: $0. *Expenses: Tuition:* Full-time $40,449. *Financial support:* In 2014–15, 21 students received support. Fellowships with full and partial tuition reimbursements available, research assistantships with full and partial tuition reimbursements available, institutionally sponsored loans, scholarships/grants, and tuition waivers (full and partial) available. *Faculty research:* VLSI, power systems, analog electronics, communications, electromagnetics. *Total annual research expenditures:* $20,179. *Unit head:* Dr. Robert Throne, Chairman, 812-877-8414, Fax: 812-877-8895, E-mail: robert.d.throne@rose-hulman.edu. *Application contact:* Dr. Azad Siahmakoun, Associate Dean of the Faculty, 812-877-8400, Fax: 812-877-8061, E-mail: siahmako@rose-hulman.edu.
Website: http://www.rose-hulman.edu/academics/academic-departments/electrical-computer-engineering.aspx.

Royal Military College of Canada, Division of Graduate Studies and Research, Engineering Division, Department of Electrical and Computer Engineering, Kingston, ON K7K 7B4, Canada. Offers computer engineering (M Eng, PhD); electrical engineering (M Eng, PhD); software engineering (M Eng, PhD). *Degree requirements:* For master's, thesis; for doctorate, comprehensive exam, thesis/dissertation. *Entrance requirements:* For master's, honours degree with second-class standing in the appropriate field; for doctorate, master's degree. Electronic applications accepted.

Rutgers, The State University of New Jersey, New Brunswick, Graduate School-New Brunswick, Department of Electrical and Computer Engineering, Piscataway, NJ 08854-8097. Offers communications and solid-state electronics (MS, PhD); computer engineering (MS, PhD); control systems (MS, PhD); digital signal processing (MS, PhD). Part-time programs available. Terminal master's awarded for partial completion of doctoral program. *Degree requirements:* For master's, thesis or alternative; for doctorate, thesis/dissertation. *Entrance requirements:* For master's and doctorate, GRE General Test. Additional exam requirements/recommendations for international students: Required—TOEFL. Electronic applications accepted. *Faculty research:* Communication and information processing, wireless information networks, micro-vacuum devices, machine vision, VLSI design.

St. Mary's University, Graduate School, Department of Engineering, Program in Computer Engineering, San Antonio, TX 78228-8507. Offers MS. *Faculty:* 2 full-time (0 women). *Students:* 2 full-time (1 woman), 3 part-time (1 woman); includes 4 minority (all Hispanic/Latino), 1 international. Average age 30. 11 applicants, 9% accepted, 1 enrolled. *Entrance requirements:* For master's, GRE, Have a bachelor's degree in Computer Engineering, Electrical Engineering or a closely related discipline. Have a minimum Grade Point Average (GPA) of 3.00 (A = 4.00) for their bachelor's degrees. Have a minimum GRE quantitative score of 148. Additional exam requirements/recommendations for international students: Required—TOEFL (minimum score 550 paper-based; 80 iBT), IELTS (minimum score 6.5). *Application deadline:* Applications are processed on a rolling basis. Electronic applications accepted. Application fee is waived when completed online. *Expenses: Tuition:* Full-time $15,070; part-time $800 per credit hour. *Required fees:* $156 per semester. *Financial support:* In 2014–15, 1 research assistantship (averaging $21,600 per year) was awarded; stipend for 9 months also available. Financial award application deadline: 3/31; financial award applicants required to submit FAFSA. *Faculty research:* Computer architecture, parallel processing, computer security, computer networking. *Unit head:* Dr. Djaffer Ibaroudene, Graduate Program Director, 210-431-2050, E-mail: dibaroudene@stmarytx.edu. *Application contact:* Dean of the Graduate School.

San Jose State University, Graduate Studies and Research, Charles W. Davidson College of Engineering, Department of Computer Engineering, San Jose, CA 95192-0001. Offers computer engineering (MS); software engineering (MS). *Degree requirements:* For master's, comprehensive exam, thesis. *Entrance requirements:* For master's, GRE General Test. Electronic applications accepted. *Faculty research:* Robotics, database management systems, computer networks.

Santa Clara University, School of Engineering, Santa Clara, CA 95053. Offers analog circuit design (Certificate); applied mathematics (MS); ASIC design and test (Certificate); bioengineering (MS); civil engineering (MS); computer science and engineering (MS, PhD); controls (Certificate); digital signal processing (Certificate); dynamics (Certificate); electrical engineering (MS, PhD); engineering (Engineer); engineering management (MS); fundamentals of electrical engineering (Certificate); information assurance (Certificate); materials engineering (Certificate); mechanical design analysis (Certificate); mechanical engineering (MS, PhD); mechatronics systems engineering (Certificate); microwave and antennas (Certificate); networking (Certificate); renewable energy (Certificate); software engineering (Certificate); sustainable energy (MS); technology jump-start (Certificate); thermofluids (Certificate). Part-time and evening/weekend programs available. *Faculty:* 59 full-time (23 women), 80 part-time/adjunct (14 women). *Students:* 584 full-time (239 women), 353 part-time (102 women); includes 224 minority (7 Black or African American, non-Hispanic/Latino; 144 Asian, non-Hispanic/Latino; 50 Hispanic/Latino; 2 Native Hawaiian or other Pacific Islander, non-Hispanic/Latino; 21 Two or more races, non-Hispanic/Latino), 548 international. Average age 27. 1,248 applicants, 51% accepted, 375 enrolled. In 2014, 283 master's, 5 doctorates, 1 other advanced degree awarded. *Degree requirements:* For master's, thesis (for some programs); for doctorate, thesis/dissertation; for other advanced degree, thesis. *Entrance requirements:* For master's, GRE, transcript; for doctorate, GRE, master's degree or equivalent; for other advanced degree, master's degree, published paper. Additional exam requirements/recommendations for international students: Required—TOEFL (minimum score 550 paper-based; 79 iBT). *Application deadline:* For fall admission, 8/1 for domestic students, 7/15 for international students; for winter admission, 10/28 for domestic students, 9/23 for international students; for spring admission, 2/25 for domestic students, 1/21 for international students. Applications are processed on a rolling basis. Application fee: $60. Electronic applications accepted. *Expenses:* Expenses: Contact institution. *Financial support:* In 2014–15, 94 students received support. Fellowships with full and partial tuition reimbursements available, research assistantships with full and partial tuition reimbursements available, teaching assistantships with full tuition reimbursements available, career-related internships or fieldwork, Federal Work-Study, institutionally sponsored loans, and scholarships/grants available. Support available to part-time students. Financial award application deadline: 3/2; financial award applicants required to submit FAFSA. *Faculty research:* Video encoding, nanostructures, robotics, microfluidics, water resources. *Total annual research expenditures:* $1.6 million. *Unit head:* Dr. Alex Zecevic, Associate Dean for Graduate Studies, 408-554-2394, E-mail: azecevic@scu.edu. *Application contact:* Stacey Tinker, Director of Enrollment Management, 408-554-4748, Fax: 408-554-4323, E-mail: stinker@scu.edu.
Website: http://www.scu.edu/engineering/graduate/.

Silicon Valley University, Graduate Programs, San Jose, CA 95131. Offers business administration (MBA); computer engineering (MSCE); computer science (MSCS). *Degree requirements:* For master's, project (MSCS).

Southern Illinois University Carbondale, Graduate School, College of Engineering, Department of Electrical and Computer Engineering, Carbondale, IL 62901-4701. Offers MS, PhD. *Faculty:* 15 full-time (1 woman), 1 part-time/adjunct (0 women). *Students:* 191 full-time (44 women), 55 part-time (10 women); includes 5 minority (2 Black or African American, non-Hispanic/Latino; 2 Asian, non-Hispanic/Latino; 1 Hispanic/Latino), 223 international. 481 applicants, 45% accepted, 60 enrolled. In 2014, 42 master's, 12 doctorates awarded. *Degree requirements:* For master's, comprehensive exam, thesis. *Entrance requirements:* For master's, minimum GPA of 2.7. Additional exam requirements/recommendations for international students: Required—TOEFL. *Application deadline:* Applications are processed on a rolling basis. Application fee: $50. *Expenses:* Tuition, state resident: full-time $10,176; part-time $1153 per credit. Tuition, nonresident: full-time $20,814; part-time $1744 per credit. *Required fees:* $7092; $394 per credit. $2364 per semester. *Financial support:* In 2014–15, 21 students received support, including 6 research assistantships with full tuition reimbursements available; fellowships with full tuition reimbursements available, teaching assistantships with full tuition reimbursements available, Federal Work-Study, institutionally sponsored loans, and tuition waivers (full) also available. Support available to part-time students. Financial award application deadline: 1/15. *Faculty research:* Circuits and power systems, communications and signal processing, controls and systems, electromagnetics and optics, electronics instrumentation and bioengineering. *Total annual research expenditures:* $254,257. *Unit head:* Dr. Spyros Tragoudas, Chair, 618-536-2364, E-mail: trag@siu.edu. *Application contact:* Lisa Short, Office Manager, 618-453-2110, E-mail: ecedept@siu.edu.

Southern Methodist University, Bobby B. Lyle School of Engineering, Department of Computer Science and Engineering, Dallas, TX 75275-0122. Offers computer engineering (MS, PhD); computer science (MS, PhD); security engineering (MS); software engineering (MS, DE). Part-time and evening/weekend programs available. Postbaccalaureate distance learning degree programs offered (no on-campus study). Terminal master's awarded for partial completion of doctoral program. *Degree requirements:* For master's, thesis optional; for doctorate, thesis/dissertation, oral and written qualifying exams, oral final exam (PhD). *Entrance requirements:* For master's, GRE General Test, minimum GPA of 3.0 in last 2 years; bachelor's degree in engineering, mathematics, or sciences; for doctorate, preliminary counseling exam (PhD), minimum GPA of 3.0, bachelor's degree in related field, MA (for DE). Additional exam requirements/recommendations for international students: Required—TOEFL (minimum score 550 paper-based). *Faculty research:* Trusted and high performance network computing, software engineering and management, knowledge engineering and management, computer arithmetic, computer architecture and CAD.

Southern Polytechnic State University, School of Engineering Technology and Management, Department of Electrical and Computer Engineering Technology, Marietta, GA 30060-2896. Offers electrical engineering technology (MS). Part-time and evening/weekend programs available. *Degree requirements:* For master's, thesis. *Entrance requirements:* For master's, GRE (minimum scores: 147 Verbal, 147 Quantitative, 3.5 Analytical), minimum GPA of 2.7. Additional exam requirements/

recommendations for international students: Required—TOEFL (minimum score 550 paper-based; 79 iBT), IELTS (minimum score 6.5). Electronic applications accepted. *Faculty research:* Analog and digital communications, computer networking, analog and low power electronics design, control systems and digital signal processing, instrumentation (medical and industrial), biomedical signal analysis, biomedical imaging, renewable energy systems, electronics, power distribution, power electronics.

Stevens Institute of Technology, Graduate School, Charles V. Schaefer Jr. School of Engineering, Department of Electrical and Computer Engineering, Program in Computer Engineering, Hoboken, NJ 07030. Offers computer engineering (PhD); computer systems (M Eng); data communications and networks (M Eng); digital signal processing (Certificate); digital systems design (M Eng); engineered software systems (M Eng); image processing and multimedia (M Eng); information system security (M Eng); information systems (M Eng); real-time and embedded systems (Certificate). Part-time and evening/weekend programs available. Terminal master's awarded for partial completion of doctoral program. *Degree requirements:* For doctorate, thesis/dissertation. *Entrance requirements:* For master's, doctorate, and Certificate, GRE. Additional exam requirements/recommendations for international students: Required—TOEFL. Electronic applications accepted.

Stevens Institute of Technology, Graduate School, Charles V. Schaefer Jr. School of Engineering, Department of Mechanical Engineering, Program in Integrated Product Development, Hoboken, NJ 07030. Offers armament engineering (M Eng); computer and electrical engineering (M Eng); manufacturing technologies (M Eng); systems reliability and design (M Eng).

Stony Brook University, State University of New York, Graduate School, College of Engineering and Applied Sciences, Department of Electrical and Computer Engineering, Program in Computer Engineering, Stony Brook, NY 11794. Offers MS, PhD. *Students:* 29 full-time (2 women), 6 part-time (3 women); includes 3 minority (1 Black or African American, non-Hispanic/Latino; 2 Asian, non-Hispanic/Latino), 26 international. Average age 26. 261 applicants, 31% accepted, 17 enrolled. In 2014, 24 master's, 2 doctorates awarded. *Entrance requirements:* For master's, GRE; for doctorate, GRE, statement of purpose, resume, three recommendation letters. Additional exam requirements/recommendations for international students: Required—TOEFL. *Application deadline:* For fall admission, 1/15 for domestic students; for spring admission, 10/1 for domestic students. Application fee: $100. *Expenses:* Tuition, state resident: full-time $10,370; part-time $432 per credit. Tuition, nonresident: full-time $20,190; part-time $841 per credit. *Required fees:* $1431. *Financial support:* Research assistantships and teaching assistantships available. *Unit head:* Dr. Serge Luryi, Chair, 631-632-8420. *Application contact:* Susan Hayden, Coordinator, 631-632-8400, Fax: 631-632-8494, E-mail: susan.hayden@stonybrook.edu.

Syracuse University, L. C. Smith College of Engineering and Computer Science, Program in Computer Engineering, Syracuse, NY 13244. Offers MS, CE. Part-time programs available. *Students:* 191 full-time (54 women), 16 part-time (1 woman); includes 8 minority (4 Black or African American, non-Hispanic/Latino; 2 Asian, non-Hispanic/Latino; 1 Hispanic/Latino; 1 Native Hawaiian or other Pacific Islander, non-Hispanic/Latino), 189 international. Average age 24. 247 applicants, 47% accepted, 46 enrolled. In 2014, 93 master's awarded. *Degree requirements:* For master's, comprehensive exam (for some programs), thesis (for some programs); for CE, comprehensive exam, thesis. *Entrance requirements:* For master's, GRE General Test. Additional exam requirements/recommendations for international students: Required—TOEFL (minimum score 100 iBT). *Application deadline:* For fall admission, 6/1 priority date for domestic and international students; for spring admission, 11/15 priority date for domestic students, 10/15 priority date for international students. Applications are processed on a rolling basis. Application fee: $75. Electronic applications accepted. *Expenses: Tuition:* Part-time $1341 per credit. *Required fees:* $1341 per credit. *Financial support:* Fellowships with full tuition reimbursements, research assistantships with full and partial tuition reimbursements, teaching assistantships with full and partial tuition reimbursements, and tuition waivers (partial) available. Financial award application deadline: 1/1; financial award applicants required to submit FAFSA. *Faculty research:* Hardware, software, computer applications. *Unit head:* Dr. Qinru Qiu,, Qinru Qiu, 4-133 Center for Science and Technology, 315-443- 1836, Fax 315-443-2583; qiqiu@syr.edu., 315-443-1836, E-mail: qiqiu@syr.edu. *Application contact:* Brenda Flowers, Administrative Assistant II, 315-443-2369, Fax: 315-443-2369, E-mail: topgrads@syr.edu.
Website: http://lcs.syr.edu/.

Syracuse University, L. C. Smith College of Engineering and Computer Science, Program in Electrical and Computer Engineering, Syracuse, NY 13244. Offers PhD. Part-time programs available. *Students:* 76 full-time (15 women), 16 part-time (3 women); includes 3 minority (1 Black or African American, non-Hispanic/Latino; 2 Asian, non-Hispanic/Latino), 75 international. Average age 29. 78 applicants, 18% accepted, 13 enrolled. In 2014, 12 doctorates awarded. *Degree requirements:* For doctorate, comprehensive exam, thesis/dissertation. *Entrance requirements:* For doctorate, GRE General Test. Additional exam requirements/recommendations for international students: Required—TOEFL (minimum score 100 iBT). *Application deadline:* For fall admission, 7/1 priority date for domestic students, 6/1 priority date for international students. Applications are processed on a rolling basis. Application fee: $75. Electronic applications accepted. *Expenses: Tuition:* Part-time $1341 per credit. *Required fees:* $1341 per credit. *Financial support:* Fellowships with full tuition reimbursements, research assistantships with full and partial tuition reimbursements, and teaching assistantships with full and partial tuition reimbursements available. Financial award application deadline: 1/1. *Unit head:* Dr. Chilukuri Mohan, Chair, 315-443-2583, E-mail: mohan@syr.edu. *Application contact:* Brenda Flowers, Information Contact, 315-443-4408, Fax: 315-443-2583, E-mail: bflowers@syr.edu.
Website: http://lcs.syr.edu/.

Tennessee State University, The School of Graduate Studies and Research, College of Engineering, Nashville, TN 37209-1561. Offers biomedical engineering (ME); civil engineering (ME); computer and information systems engineering (MS, PhD); electrical engineering (ME); environmental engineering (ME); manufacturing engineering (ME); mathematical sciences (MS); mechanical engineering (ME). Part-time and evening/weekend programs available. *Degree requirements:* For master's, project; for doctorate, comprehensive exam, thesis/dissertation. *Entrance requirements:* For doctorate, minimum GPA of 3.3. *Faculty research:* Robotics, intelligent systems, human-computer interaction software systems, biomedical engineering, signal/image processing, probabilistic design, intelligent manufacturing, cooperative mobile robots, condition based maintenance, sensor fusion.

Texas A&M University, College of Engineering, Department of Electrical and Computer Engineering, College Station, TX 77843. Offers computer engineering (M Eng, MS, PhD); electrical engineering (M Eng, MS, PhD). *Faculty:* 64. *Students:* 628 full-time (102 women), 96 part-time (14 women); includes 40 minority (8 Black or African American, non-Hispanic/Latino; 1 American Indian or Alaska Native, non-Hispanic/Latino; 12 Asian, non-Hispanic/Latino; 16 Hispanic/Latino; 1 Native Hawaiian or other Pacific Islander, non-Hispanic/Latino; 2 Two or more races, non-Hispanic/Latino), 624 international. Average age 27. 2,211 applicants, 26% accepted, 242 enrolled. In 2014, 107 master's, 45 doctorates awarded. *Degree requirements:* For master's, thesis (MS); for doctorate, thesis/dissertation. *Entrance requirements:* For master's and doctorate, GRE General Test. Additional exam requirements/recommendations for international students: Required—TOEFL. Application fee: $50 ($90 for international students). *Expenses:* Tuition, state resident: full-time $4078; part-time $226.55 per credit hour. Tuition, nonresident: full-time $10,594; part-time $577.55 per credit hour. *Required fees:* $2813; $237.70 per credit hour. $278.50 per semester. Tuition and fees vary according to degree level and student level. *Financial support:* In 2014–15, 479 students received support, including 30 fellowships with full and partial tuition reimbursements available (averaging $13,748 per year), 195 research assistantships with full and partial tuition reimbursements available (averaging $6,484 per year), 111 teaching assistantships with full and partial tuition reimbursements available (averaging $4,036 per year); career-related internships or fieldwork, institutionally sponsored loans, scholarships/grants, traineeships, health care benefits, tuition waivers (full and partial), and unspecified assistantships also available. Support available to part-time students. Financial award application deadline: 4/1; financial award applicants required to submit FAFSA. *Faculty research:* Solid-state, electric power systems, and communications engineering. *Unit head:* Dr. Miroslav M. Begovic, Department Head, 979-862-1553, E-mail: begovic@ece.tamu.edu. *Application contact:* Dr. Krishna Narayanan, Director of Graduate Studies, 979-862-2691, E-mail: krn@ece.tamu.edu.
Website: http://engineering.tamu.edu/electrical/.

The University of Akron, Graduate School, College of Engineering, Department of Electrical and Computer Engineering, Akron, OH 44325. Offers electrical engineering (MS); engineering (PhD). Evening/weekend programs available. *Faculty:* 15 full-time (1 woman), 6 part-time/adjunct (1 woman). *Students:* 58 full-time (7 women), 9 part-time (4 women); includes 2 minority (1 Asian, non-Hispanic/Latino; 1 Two or more races, non-Hispanic/Latino), 54 international. Average age 27. 154 applicants, 31% accepted, 10 enrolled. In 2014, 19 master's, 2 doctorates awarded. *Degree requirements:* For master's, oral comprehensive exam or thesis; for doctorate, one foreign language, thesis/dissertation, candidacy exam, qualifying exam. *Entrance requirements:* For master's, GRE, minimum GPA of 2.75, three letters of recommendation, statement of purpose; for doctorate, GRE, minimum GPA of 3.0 with bachelor's degree, 3.5 with master's degree; three letters of recommendation; statement of purpose. Additional exam requirements/recommendations for international students: Required—TOEFL (minimum score 550 paper-based; 79 iBT), IELTS (minimum score 6.5). *Application deadline:* Applications are processed on a rolling basis. Application fee: $45 ($70 for international students). Electronic applications accepted. *Expenses:* Tuition, state resident: full-time $7578; part-time $421 per credit hour. Tuition, nonresident: full-time $12,977; part-time $721 per credit hour. *Required fees:* $1388; $35 per credit hour. Tuition and fees vary according to course load. *Financial support:* In 2014–15, 42 research assistantships with full tuition reimbursements, 14 teaching assistantships with full tuition reimbursements were awarded. *Faculty research:* Computational electromagnetics and nondestructive testing, control systems, sensors and actuators applications and networks, alternative energy systems and hybrid vehicles, analog integrated circuit (IC) design, embedded systems. *Total annual research expenditures:* $1.7 million. *Unit head:* Dr. Abbas Omar, Chair, 330-972-7483, E-mail: aomar@uakron.edu. *Application contact:* Dr. Shivakumar Sastry, Graduate Director, 330-972-7646, E-mail: ssastry@uakron.edu.
Website: http://www.uakron.edu/engineering/ECE/.

The University of Alabama, Graduate School, College of Engineering, Department of Electrical and Computer Engineering, Tuscaloosa, AL 35487-0286. Offers electrical engineering (MS, PhD). Part-time programs available. Postbaccalaureate distance learning degree programs offered (minimal on-campus study). *Faculty:* 18 full-time (4 women). *Students:* 44 full-time (5 women), 8 part-time (0 women); includes 4 minority (2 Asian, non-Hispanic/Latino; 2 Hispanic/Latino), 38 international. Average age 28. 94 applicants, 46% accepted, 14 enrolled. In 2014, 9 master's, 5 doctorates awarded. *Degree requirements:* For master's, thesis or alternative; for doctorate, one foreign language, comprehensive exam, thesis/dissertation. *Entrance requirements:* For master's, GRE (for students from non ABET-accredited schools), minimum GPA of 3.0 in last 60 hours of course work or overall; for doctorate, GRE (for students from non ABET-accredited schools), minimum GPA of 3.0 overall. Additional exam requirements/recommendations for international students: Required—TOEFL (minimum score 550 paper-based). *Application deadline:* For fall admission, 7/1 priority date for domestic students, 1/15 priority date for international students; for spring admission, 11/1 priority date for domestic students, 6/1 priority date for international students. Applications are processed on a rolling basis. Application fee: $50 ($60 for international students). Electronic applications accepted. *Expenses:* Tuition, state resident: full-time $9826. Tuition, nonresident: full-time $24,950. *Financial support:* In 2014–15, 1 fellowship with full tuition reimbursement (averaging $15,000 per year), 14 research assistantships with full tuition reimbursements (averaging $14,000 per year), 6 teaching assistantships with full tuition reimbursements (averaging $11,025 per year) were awarded; health care benefits and unspecified assistantships also available. *Faculty research:* Devices and materials, electromechanical systems, embedded systems. *Total annual research expenditures:* $1.8 million. *Unit head:* Dr. D. Jeff Jackson, Department Head, 205-348-2919, Fax: 205-348-6959, E-mail: jjackson@eng.ua.edu. *Application contact:* Dr. Tim Haskew, Graduate Program Director, 205-348-1766, Fax: 205-348-6959, E-mail: thaskew@eng.ua.edu.
Website: http://ece.eng.ua.edu.

The University of Alabama at Birmingham, School of Engineering, Program in Computer Engineering, Birmingham, AL 35294. Offers PhD. Program offered jointly with The University of Alabama in Huntsville. *Students:* 9 full-time (0 women), 6 part-time (0 women); includes 5 minority (3 Black or African American, non-Hispanic/Latino; 1 Asian, non-Hispanic/Latino; 1 Hispanic/Latino), 9 international. Average age 31. In 2014, 2 doctorates awarded. *Degree requirements:* For doctorate, comprehensive exam, thesis/dissertation. *Entrance requirements:* Additional exam requirements/recommendations for international students: Required—TOEFL, TWE. *Expenses:* Tuition, state resident: full-time $7090; part-time $370 per credit hour. Tuition, nonresident: full-time $16,072; part-time $869 per credit hour. Full-time tuition and fees vary according to course load and program. *Unit head:* Dr. Sandra Muhammad, Graduate Program Director, 205-934-8440, E-mail: smuhamma@uab.edu. *Application contact:* Susan Noblitt Banks, Director of Graduate School Operations, 205-934-8227, Fax: 205-934-8413, E-mail: gradschool@uab.edu.
Website: http://www.uab.edu/engineering/home/departments-research/ece/grad#phd.

The University of Alabama in Huntsville, School of Graduate Studies, College of Engineering, Department of Electrical and Computer Engineering, Huntsville, AL 35899. Offers computer engineering (MSE, PhD); electrical engineering (MSE, PhD), including optics and photonics technology (MSE), opto-electronics (MSE); information assurance (MS); optical science and engineering (PhD); optics and photonics (MSE); software engineering (MSSE). Part-time and evening/weekend programs available. *Degree requirements:* For master's, comprehensive exam, thesis or alternative, oral and written exams; for doctorate, comprehensive exam, thesis/dissertation, oral and written exams. *Entrance requirements:* For master's, GRE General Test, appropriate bachelor's degree, minimum GPA of 3.0; for doctorate, GRE General Test, minimum GPA of 3.0. Additional exam requirements/recommendations for international students: Required—TOEFL (minimum score 500 paper-based; 80 iBT), IELTS (minimum score 6.5). Electronic applications accepted. *Faculty research:* Advanced computer architecture and systems, fault tolerant computing and verification, computational electro-magnetics, nano-photonics and plasmonics, micro electro-mechanical (MEMS) systems.

The University of Alabama in Huntsville, School of Graduate Studies, Interdisciplinary Studies, Interdisciplinary Program in Information Assurance and Security, Huntsville, AL 35899. Offers computer engineering (MS), including computer science; information systems (Certificate). Part-time and evening/weekend programs available. *Degree requirements:* For master's, comprehensive exam, thesis. *Entrance requirements:* For master's, GRE General Test, minimum GPA of 3.0; for Certificate, GMAT, minimum GPA of 3.0. Additional exam requirements/recommendations for international students: Required—TOEFL (minimum score 550 paper-based; 80 iBT), IELTS (minimum score 6.5). Electronic applications accepted. *Faculty research:* Service discovery, enterprise security, security metrics, cryptography, network security.

University of Alberta, Faculty of Graduate Studies and Research, Department of Electrical and Computer Engineering, Edmonton, AB T6G 2E1, Canada. Offers communications (M Eng, M Sc, PhD); computer engineering (M Eng, M Sc, PhD); electromagnetics (M Eng, M Sc, PhD); nanotechnology and microdevices (M Eng, M Sc, PhD); power/power electronics (M Eng, M Sc, PhD); systems (M Eng, M Sc, PhD). Terminal master's awarded for partial completion of doctoral program. *Degree requirements:* For master's, thesis; for doctorate, thesis/dissertation. *Entrance requirements:* Additional exam requirements/recommendations for international students: Required—TOEFL. Electronic applications accepted. *Faculty research:* Controls, communications, microelectronics, electromagnetics.

The University of Arizona, College of Engineering, Department of Electrical and Computer Engineering, Tucson, AZ 85721. Offers M Eng, MS, PhD. Part-time programs available. *Degree requirements:* For master's, thesis (for some programs); for doctorate, thesis/dissertation. *Entrance requirements:* For master's, GRE General Test, 3 letters of recommendation, statement of purpose; for doctorate, GRE General Test, master's degree in related field, 3 letters of recommendation, statement of purpose. Additional exam requirements/recommendations for international students: Required—TOEFL (minimum score 550 paper-based; 79 iBT). Electronic applications accepted. *Faculty research:* Communication systems, control systems, signal processing, computer-aided logic.

University of Arkansas, Graduate School, College of Engineering, Department of Computer Science and Computer Engineering, Program in Computer Engineering, Fayetteville, AR 72701-1201. Offers MS Cmp E, MSE, PhD. *Degree requirements:* For master's, thesis optional; for doctorate, one foreign language, thesis/dissertation. Electronic applications accepted.

University of Bridgeport, School of Engineering, Departments of Computer Science and Computer Engineering, Bridgeport, CT 06604. Offers computer engineering (MS); computer science (MS); computer science and engineering (PhD). *Degree requirements:* For master's, thesis optional; for doctorate, comprehensive exam, thesis/dissertation. *Entrance requirements:* Additional exam requirements/recommendations for international students: Recommended—TOEFL (minimum score 550 paper-based; 80 iBT), IELTS (minimum score 6.5). Electronic applications accepted. *Expenses:* Contact institution.

The University of British Columbia, Faculty of Applied Science, Department of Electrical and Computer Engineering, Vancouver, BC V6T 1Z4, Canada. Offers M Eng, MA Sc, PhD. Part-time programs available. *Degree requirements:* For master's, thesis (for some programs); for doctorate, thesis/dissertation. *Entrance requirements:* Additional exam requirements/recommendations for international students: Required—TOEFL (minimum score 600 paper-based; 100 iBT), IELTS (minimum score 7). Electronic applications accepted. *Faculty research:* Applied electromagnetics, biomedical engineering, communications and signal processing, computer and software engineering, power engineering, robotics, solid-state, systems and control.

University of Calgary, Faculty of Graduate Studies, Schulich School of Engineering, Department of Electrical and Computer Engineering, Calgary, AB T2N 1N4, Canada. Offers M Eng, M Sc, PhD. Part-time programs available. *Degree requirements:* For master's, thesis (for M Sc); for doctorate, thesis/dissertation, candidacy exam. *Entrance requirements:* For master's, minimum GPA of 3.0; for doctorate, minimum GPA of 3.5. Additional exam requirements/recommendations for international students: Required—TOEFL (minimum score 550 paper-based; 80 iBT) or IELTS (minimum score 7). Electronic applications accepted. *Faculty research:* Biomedical and bioelectrics, telecommunications and signal processing, software and computer engineering, power and control, microelectronics and instrumentation.

University of California, Davis, College of Engineering, Program in Electrical and Computer Engineering, Davis, CA 95616. Offers MS, PhD. Terminal master's awarded for partial completion of doctoral program. *Degree requirements:* For master's, comprehensive exam (for some programs), thesis (for some programs); for doctorate, thesis/dissertation, preliminary and qualifying exams, thesis defense. *Entrance requirements:* For master's, GRE General Test, minimum GPA of 3.2; for doctorate, GRE, minimum graduate GPA of 3.5. Additional exam requirements/recommendations for international students: Required—TOEFL (minimum score 550 paper-based). Electronic applications accepted.

University of California, Riverside, Graduate Division, Department of Computer Science and Engineering, Computer Engineering Program, Riverside, CA 92521. Offers MS. Part-time programs available. *Degree requirements:* For master's, comprehensive exam, thesis or alternative, 36 total units. *Entrance requirements:* For master's, GRE General Test (minimum score of 1100 or 300 for new format), minimum GPA of 3.2 in junior/senior years of undergraduate study (last two years). Additional exam requirements/recommendations for international students: Required—TOEFL (minimum score 550 paper-based; 80 iBT). Electronic applications accepted. *Expenses:* Tuition, state resident: full-time $5399. Tuition, nonresident: full-time $10,433.

University of California, San Diego, Graduate Division, Department of Computer Science and Engineering, La Jolla, CA 92093. Offers computer engineering (MS, PhD); computer science (MS, PhD). *Students:* 338 full-time (58 women), 22 part-time (4 women); includes 60 minority (4 Black or African American, non-Hispanic/Latino; 50 Asian, non-Hispanic/Latino; 6 Hispanic/Latino), 219 international. 2,663 applicants, 13% accepted, 121 enrolled. In 2014, 75 master's, 24 doctorates awarded. *Degree requirements:* For master's, comprehensive exam (for some programs), thesis (for some programs), comprehensive exam or thesis; for doctorate, comprehensive exam, thesis/dissertation, 1-quarter teaching assistantship. *Entrance requirements:* For master's and doctorate, GRE General Test, GRE Subject Test (recommended). Additional exam requirements/recommendations for international students: Required—TOEFL (minimum score 550 paper-based; 80 iBT), IELTS. *Application deadline:* For fall admission, 12/14 for domestic students. Application fee: $90 ($110 for international students). Electronic applications accepted. *Expenses:* Tuition, state resident: full-time $11,220; part-time $5610 per quarter. Tuition, nonresident: full-time $26,322; part-time $13,161 per quarter. *Required fees:* $570 per quarter. Tuition and fees vary according to program. *Financial support:* Fellowships, research assistantships, teaching assistantships, career-related internships or fieldwork, and scholarships/grants available. Financial award applicants required to submit FAFSA. *Faculty research:* Algorithms and complexity; artificial intelligence and machine learning, bioinformatics, computer architecture, computer graphics, computer vision, databases, embedded systems and software, high-performance computing, programming languages and compilers, security and cryptography, software engineering, systems and networking, ubiquitous computing, VLSI/CAD. *Unit head:* Rajesh Gupta, Chair, 858-822-4391, E-mail: gupta@cs.ucsd.edu. *Application contact:* Julie Connor, Graduate Coordinator, 858-534-3622, E-mail: gradinfo@cs.ucsd.edu.
Website: http://cse.ucsd.edu.

University of California, San Diego, Graduate Division, Department of Electrical and Computer Engineering, La Jolla, CA 92093. Offers applied ocean science (MS, PhD); applied physics (MS, PhD); communication theory and systems (MS, PhD); computer engineering (MS, PhD); electronic circuits and systems (MS, PhD); intelligent systems, robotics and control (MS, PhD); medical devices and systems (MS, PhD); nanoscale devices and systems (MS, PhD); photonics (MS, PhD); signal and image processing (MS, PhD). *Students:* 435 full-time (81 women), 43 part-time (8 women); includes 78 minority (2 Black or African American, non-Hispanic/Latino; 1 American Indian or Alaska Native, non-Hispanic/Latino; 69 Asian, non-Hispanic/Latino; 6 Hispanic/Latino), 306 international. 2,710 applicants, 18% accepted, 177 enrolled. In 2014, 109 master's, 50 doctorates awarded. *Degree requirements:* For master's, thesis or written exam; for doctorate, comprehensive exam, thesis/dissertation. *Entrance requirements:* For master's and doctorate, GRE General Test, minimum GPA of 3.0. Additional exam requirements/recommendations for international students: Required—TOEFL (minimum score 550 paper-based; 80 iBT), IELTS. *Application deadline:* For fall admission, 12/15 for domestic students. Application fee: $90 ($110 for international students). Electronic applications accepted. *Expenses:* Tuition, state resident: full-time $11,220; part-time $5610 per quarter. Tuition, nonresident: full-time $26,322; part-time $13,161 per quarter. *Required fees:* $570 per quarter. Tuition and fees vary according to program. *Financial support:* Fellowships, research assistantships, teaching assistantships, scholarships/grants, and unspecified assistantships available. Financial award applicants required to submit FAFSA. *Faculty research:* Applied ocean science; applied physics; communication theory and systems; computer engineering; electronic circuits and systems; intelligent systems, robotics and control; medical devices and systems; nanoscale devices and systems; photonics; signal and image processing. *Unit head:* Truong Nguyen, Chair, 858-822-5554, E-mail: nguyent@ece.ucsd.edu. *Application contact:* Shana Slebioda, Graduate Coordinator, 858-822-2513, E-mail: ecegradapps@ece.ucsd.edu.
Website: http://ece.ucsd.edu/.

University of California, Santa Barbara, Graduate Division, College of Engineering, Department of Computer Science, Santa Barbara, CA 93106-5110. Offers cognitive science (PhD); computational science and engineering (PhD); computer science (MS, PhD); technology and society (PhD). Terminal master's awarded for partial completion of doctoral program. *Degree requirements:* For master's, comprehensive exam (for some programs), thesis (for some programs), project (for some programs); for doctorate, thesis/dissertation. *Entrance requirements:* For master's and doctorate, GRE. Additional exam requirements/recommendations for international students: Required—TOEFL (minimum score 600 paper-based; 100 iBT), IELTS (minimum score 7). Electronic applications accepted. *Faculty research:* Bioinformatics, cloud computing, computer architecture, computational science and engineering, database and information systems, foundations and algorithms, intelligent and interactive systems, programming languages, quantum computing, software engineering and security.

University of California, Santa Barbara, Graduate Division, College of Engineering, Department of Electrical and Computer Engineering, Santa Barbara, CA 93106-2014. Offers communications, control and signal processing (MS, PhD); computer engineering (MS, PhD); electronics and photonics (MS, PhD); MS/PhD. *Degree requirements:* For master's, comprehensive exam, thesis; for doctorate, thesis/dissertation. *Entrance requirements:* For master's and doctorate, GRE General Test. Additional exam requirements/recommendations for international students: Required—TOEFL (minimum score 550 paper-based; 80 iBT), IELTS (minimum score 7). Electronic applications accepted. *Faculty research:* Communications, signal processing, computer engineering, control, electronics and photonics.

University of California, Santa Barbara, Graduate Division, College of Engineering, Department of Mechanical Engineering, Santa Barbara, CA 93106-5070. Offers computational science and engineering (MS, PhD); mechanical engineering (MS, PhD); MS/PhD. Terminal master's awarded for partial completion of doctoral program. *Degree requirements:* For master's, thesis; for doctorate, comprehensive exam, thesis/dissertation. *Entrance requirements:* For master's and doctorate, GRE. Additional exam requirements/recommendations for international students: Required—TOEFL (minimum score 550 paper-based; 80 iBT), IELTS (minimum score 7). Electronic applications accepted. *Faculty research:* Micro/nanoscale technology; bioengineering and systems biology; computational science and engineering; dynamics systems, controls and robotics; thermofluid sciences; solid mechanics, materials, and structures.

University of California, Santa Barbara, Graduate Division, College of Letters and Sciences, Division of Mathematics, Life, and Physical Sciences, Department of Ecology, Evolution, and Marine Biology, Santa Barbara, CA 93106-9620. Offers computational science and engineering (MA); computational sciences and engineering (PhD); ecology, evolution, and marine biology (MA, PhD); MA/PhD. *Degree requirements:* For master's, comprehensive exam (for some programs), thesis (for some programs); for doctorate, comprehensive exam, thesis/dissertation. *Entrance requirements:* For master's and doctorate, GRE General Test. Additional exam requirements/recommendations for international students: Required—TOEFL (minimum score 550 paper-based; 80 iBT), IELTS. Electronic applications accepted. *Faculty research:* Community ecology, evolution, marine biology, population genetics, stream ecology.

University of California, Santa Cruz, Division of Graduate Studies, Jack Baskin School of Engineering, Program in Computer Engineering, Santa Cruz, CA 95064. Offers computer engineering (MS, PhD); network engineering (MS). Part-time programs available. Terminal master's awarded for partial completion of doctoral program. *Degree requirements:* For master's, thesis; for doctorate, comprehensive exam, thesis/dissertation, oral qualifying exams. *Entrance requirements:* For master's and doctorate, GRE General Test, GRE Subject Test. Additional exam requirements/recommendations for international students: Required—TOEFL (minimum score 570 paper-based; 89 iBT); Recommended—IELTS (minimum score 8). Electronic applications accepted. *Faculty research:* Computer-aided design of digital systems, networks, robotics and control, sensing and interaction.

University of Central Florida, College of Engineering and Computer Science, Department of Electrical Engineering and Computer Science, Orlando, FL 32816. Offers computer engineering (MS Cp E, PhD); computer science (MS, PhD), including computer science, digital forensics (MS); electrical engineering (MSEE, PhD, Certificate), including electrical engineering (MSEE, PhD), electronic circuits (Certificate). Part-time and evening/weekend programs available. *Faculty:* 39 full-time (7

women), 11 part-time/adjunct (0 women). *Students:* 402 full-time (87 women), 204 part-time (32 women); includes 88 minority (16 Black or African American, non-Hispanic/Latino; 28 Asian, non-Hispanic/Latino; 41 Hispanic/Latino; 3 Two or more races, non-Hispanic/Latino), 306 international. Average age 30. 734 applicants, 74% accepted, 185 enrolled. In 2014, 134 master's, 36 doctorates awarded. *Degree requirements:* For master's, thesis or alternative; for doctorate, thesis/dissertation, departmental qualifying exam, candidacy exam. *Entrance requirements:* For master's, GRE General Test, minimum GPA of 3.0 in last 60 hours; for doctorate, GRE General Test, minimum GPA of 3.5 in last 60 hours. Additional exam requirements/recommendations for international students: Required—TOEFL. *Application deadline:* For fall admission, 7/15 priority date for domestic students; for spring admission, 12/1 priority date for domestic students. Application fee: $30. Electronic applications accepted. *Expenses:* Tuition, state resident: part-time $288.16 per credit hour. Tuition, nonresident: part-time $1073.31 per credit hour. *Financial support:* In 2014–15, 191 students received support, including 55 fellowships with partial tuition reimbursements available (averaging $5,800 per year), 119 research assistantships with partial tuition reimbursements available (averaging $10,600 per year), 86 teaching assistantships with partial tuition reimbursements available (averaging $10,100 per year); career-related internships or fieldwork, Federal Work-Study, institutionally sponsored loans, tuition waivers (partial), and unspecified assistantships also available. Financial award application deadline: 3/1; financial award applicants required to submit FAFSA. *Faculty research:* Communication theory, solid-state devices, electromagnetics, electro-optics, digital signal processing. *Unit head:* Dr. Zhihua Qu, Chair, 407-823-5976, Fax: 407-823-5835, E-mail: qu@ucf.edu. *Application contact:* Barbara Rodriguez Lamas, Director, Admissions and Student Services, 407-823-2766, Fax: 407-823-6442, E-mail: gradadmissions@ucf.edu.
Website: http://web.eecs.ucf.edu/.

University of Cincinnati, Graduate School, College of Engineering and Applied Science, Department of Electrical and Computer Engineering and Computer Science, Program in Computer Engineering, Cincinnati, OH 45221. Offers MS. *Degree requirements:* For master's, thesis. *Entrance requirements:* For master's, GRE General Test. Additional exam requirements/recommendations for international students: Required—TOEFL (minimum score 550 paper-based). Electronic applications accepted. *Faculty research:* Digital signal processing, large-scale systems, picture processing.

University of Cincinnati, Graduate School, College of Engineering and Applied Science, Department of Electrical and Computer Engineering and Computer Science, Program in Computer Science and Engineering, Cincinnati, OH 45221. Offers PhD. *Degree requirements:* For doctorate, thesis/dissertation. *Entrance requirements:* For doctorate, GRE General Test. Additional exam requirements/recommendations for international students: Required—TOEFL.

University of Colorado Boulder, Graduate School, College of Engineering and Applied Science, Department of Electrical, Computer and Energy Engineering, Boulder, CO 80309. Offers ME, MS, PhD. *Faculty:* 32 full-time (4 women). *Students:* 205 full-time (37 women), 74 part-time (8 women); includes 24 minority (1 Black or African American, non-Hispanic/Latino; 12 Asian, non-Hispanic/Latino; 9 Hispanic/Latino; 2 Two or more races, non-Hispanic/Latino), 150 international. Average age 27. 830 applicants, 32% accepted, 86 enrolled. In 2014, 82 master's, 18 doctorates awarded. Terminal master's awarded for partial completion of doctoral program. *Degree requirements:* For master's, thesis or alternative; for doctorate, one foreign language, thesis/dissertation, departmental qualifying exam. *Entrance requirements:* For master's, GRE General Test, minimum undergraduate GPA of 3.0; for doctorate, GRE General Test, minimum undergraduate GPA of 3.5. *Application deadline:* For fall admission, 1/15 for domestic and international students; for spring admission, 9/1 for domestic and international students. Applications are processed on a rolling basis. Application fee: $50 ($70 for international students). Electronic applications accepted. *Financial support:* In 2014–15, 388 students received support, including 35 fellowships (averaging $14,187 per year), 85 research assistantships with full and partial tuition reimbursements available (averaging $34,633 per year), 25 teaching assistantships with full and partial tuition reimbursements available (averaging $21,307 per year); institutionally sponsored loans, scholarships/grants, health care benefits, and unspecified assistantships also available. Financial award application deadline: 1/15; financial award applicants required to submit FAFSA. *Faculty research:* Electrical engineering/electronics, signal processing, electromagnetic propagation, electromagnetics. *Total annual research expenditures:* $9.9 million.
Website: http://ecee.colorado.edu.

University of Dayton, Department of Electrical and Computer Engineering, Dayton, OH 45469. Offers MSEE, DE, PhD. Part-time and evening/weekend programs available. *Faculty:* 16 full-time (0 women), 12 part-time/adjunct (2 women). *Students:* 220 full-time (43 women), 35 part-time (4 women); includes 11 minority (3 Black or African American, non-Hispanic/Latino; 5 Asian, non-Hispanic/Latino; 1 Hispanic/Latino; 2 Two or more races, non-Hispanic/Latino), 199 international. Average age 27. 495 applicants, 40% accepted, 66 enrolled. In 2014, 61 master's, 6 doctorates awarded. *Degree requirements:* For master's, thesis optional; for doctorate, variable foreign language requirement, thesis/dissertation, departmental qualifying exam. *Entrance requirements:* Additional exam requirements/recommendations for international students: Required—TOEFL (minimum score 550 paper-based; 80 iBT). *Application deadline:* For fall admission, 8/1 for domestic students, 5/1 priority date for international students; for winter admission, 7/1 for international students; for spring admission, 11/1 priority date for international students. Applications are processed on a rolling basis. Application fee: $0 ($50 for international students). Electronic applications accepted. *Expenses:* Tuition: Full-time $10,176; part-time $848 per credit. *Required fees:* $25; $25 per course. Part-time tuition and fees vary according to course level, course load, degree level and program. *Financial support:* In 2014–15, 1 fellowship (averaging $27,500 per year), 32 research assistantships with full tuition reimbursements (averaging $12,500 per year), 21 teaching assistantships with full tuition reimbursements (averaging $10,065 per year) were awarded; institutionally sponsored loans, health care benefits, and unspecified assistantships also available. Financial award application deadline: 3/1; financial award applicants required to submit FAFSA. *Faculty research:* Electrical engineering, video processing, leaky wave antenna. *Total annual research expenditures:* $1.1 million. *Unit head:* Dr. Guru Subramanyam, Chair, 937-229-3188, Fax: 937-229-4529, E-mail: gsubramanyam1@udayton.edu. *Application contact:* E-mail: graduateadmission@udayton.edu.
Website: https://www.udayton.edu/engineering/departments/electrical_and_computer/index.php.

University of Delaware, College of Engineering, Department of Electrical and Computer Engineering, Newark, DE 19716. Offers MSECE, PhD. Part-time programs available. Postbaccalaureate distance learning degree programs offered (no on-campus study). Terminal master's awarded for partial completion of doctoral program. *Degree requirements:* For master's, thesis optional; for doctorate, thesis/dissertation. *Entrance requirements:* For master's, GRE General Test; for doctorate, GRE General Test, qualifying exam. Additional exam requirements/recommendations for international students: Required—TOEFL. Electronic applications accepted. *Faculty research:* HIV evolution during dynamic therapy, compressive sensing in imaging, sensor, networks,

and UWB radios, computer network time synchronization, silicon spintronics, devices and imaging in the high-terahertz band.

University of Denver, Daniel Felix Ritchie School of Engineering and Computer Science, Department of Electrical and Computer Engineering, Denver, CO 80208. Offers computer engineering (MS); electrical and computer engineering (PhD); electrical engineering (MS); engineering (MS); mechatronic systems engineering (MS, PhD). Part-time and evening/weekend programs available. *Faculty:* 11 full-time (1 woman), 1 part-time/adjunct (0 women). *Students:* 5 full-time (1 woman), 94 part-time (14 women); includes 13 minority (1 Black or African American, non-Hispanic/Latino; 2 Asian, non-Hispanic/Latino; 6 Hispanic/Latino; 4 Two or more races, non-Hispanic/Latino), 41 international. Average age 28. 104 applicants, 74% accepted, 20 enrolled. In 2014, 35 master's, 7 doctorates awarded. Terminal master's awarded for partial completion of doctoral program. *Degree requirements:* For master's, thesis optional, proficiency in high- or low-level computer language; for doctorate, comprehensive exam, thesis/dissertation, proficiency in high- or low-level computer language. *Entrance requirements:* For master's, GRE General Test, bachelor's degree, transcripts, personal statement, resume or curriculum vitae, three letters of recommendation; for doctorate, GRE General Test, master's degree, transcripts, personal statement, resume or curriculum vitae, three letters of recommendation. Additional exam requirements/recommendations for international students: Required—TOEFL (minimum score 550 paper-based; 80 iBT). *Application deadline:* For fall admission, 2/1 priority date for domestic and international students. Applications are processed on a rolling basis. Application fee: $65. Electronic applications accepted. *Expenses:* Expenses: $1,199 per credit hour. *Financial support:* In 2014–15, 42 students received support, including 12 research assistantships with full and partial tuition reimbursements available (averaging $12,047 per year), 16 teaching assistantships with full and partial tuition reimbursements available (averaging $13,375 per year); Federal Work-Study, scholarships/grants, and unspecified assistantships also available. Financial award application deadline: 2/15; financial award applicants required to submit FAFSA. *Faculty research:* Energy and power, microelectromechanical systems (MEMS), unmanned systems, image processing/pattern recognition. *Unit head:* Dr. Kimon Valavanis, Chair, 303-871-2586, Fax: 303-871-2194, E-mail: kimon.valavanis@du.edu. *Application contact:* Crystal Harris, Administrative Assistant to the Chair, 303-871-6618, Fax: 303-871-2194, E-mail: crystal.harris@du.edu.
Website: http://www.du.edu/rsecs/departments/ece/index.html.

University of Detroit Mercy, College of Engineering and Science, Department of Electrical and Computer Engineering, Detroit, MI 48221. Offers computer engineering (ME, DE); mechatronics systems (ME, DE); signals and systems (ME, DE). Evening/weekend programs available. *Degree requirements:* For doctorate, thesis/dissertation. *Faculty research:* Electromagnetics, computer architecture, systems.

University of Florida, Graduate School, College of Engineering and College of Liberal Arts and Sciences, Department of Computer and Information Science and Engineering, Gainesville, FL 32611. Offers computer engineering (ME, MS, PhD); computer science (MS); digital arts and sciences (MS). Part-time programs available. Postbaccalaureate distance learning degree programs offered (minimal on-campus study). *Faculty:* 42 full-time (6 women), 32 part-time/adjunct (4 women). *Students:* 364 full-time (91 women), 90 part-time (9 women); includes 30 minority (8 Black or African American, non-Hispanic/Latino; 1 American Indian or Alaska Native, non-Hispanic/Latino; 12 Asian, non-Hispanic/Latino; 9 Hispanic/Latino), 370 international. 2,043 applicants, 22% accepted, 156 enrolled. In 2014, 218 master's, 18 doctorates awarded. Terminal master's awarded for partial completion of doctoral program. *Degree requirements:* For master's, comprehensive exam, thesis optional; for doctorate, comprehensive exam, thesis/dissertation. *Entrance requirements:* For master's and doctorate, minimum GPA of 3.0. Additional exam requirements/recommendations for international students: Required—TOEFL (minimum score 550 paper-based; 80 iBT), IELTS (minimum score 6). *Application deadline:* For fall admission, 12/15 priority date for domestic students, 2/1 for international students; for spring admission, 9/1 for domestic and international students. Applications are processed on a rolling basis. Application fee: $30. Electronic applications accepted. *Financial support:* Unspecified assistantships available. Financial award application deadline: 2/1; financial award applicants required to submit FAFSA. *Faculty research:* Computer systems and computer networking; high-performance computing and algorithm; database and machine learning; computer graphics, vision, and intelligent systems; human center computing and digital art. *Unit head:* Paul Gader, PhD, Chair, 352-392-1527, Fax: 352-392-1220, E-mail: pgader@cise.ufl.edu. *Application contact:* Jih-Kwon Peir, PhD, Graduate Coordinator, 352-505-1573, Fax: 352-392-1220, E-mail: peir@cise.ufl.edu.
Website: http://www.cise.ufl.edu/.

University of Florida, Graduate School, College of Engineering, Department of Electrical and Computer Engineering, Gainesville, FL 32611. Offers ME, MS, PhD, JD/MS, MSM/MS. Part-time programs available. Postbaccalaureate distance learning degree programs offered. *Faculty:* 47 full-time (3 women), 7 part-time/adjunct (1 woman). *Students:* 424 full-time (93 women), 76 part-time (11 women); includes 59 minority (11 Black or African American, non-Hispanic/Latino; 2 American Indian or Alaska Native, non-Hispanic/Latino; 22 Asian, non-Hispanic/Latino; 24 Hispanic/Latino), 352 international. 1,571 applicants, 37% accepted, 183 enrolled. In 2014, 219 master's, 42 doctorates awarded. Terminal master's awarded for partial completion of doctoral program. *Degree requirements:* For master's, comprehensive exam (for some programs), thesis (for some programs); for doctorate, comprehensive exam, thesis/dissertation. *Entrance requirements:* For master's, minimum GPA of 3.0; for doctorate, minimum GPA of 3.5. Additional exam requirements/recommendations for international students: Required—TOEFL (minimum score 550 paper-based; 80 iBT), IELTS (minimum score 6). *Application deadline:* For fall admission, 1/15 priority date for domestic students, 1/15 for international students. Applications are processed on a rolling basis. Application fee: $30. Electronic applications accepted. *Financial support:* Unspecified assistantships available. Financial award application deadline: 1/15; financial award applicants required to submit FAFSA. *Faculty research:* Computer engineering, devices, electromagnetics and energy systems, electronics and signals and systems. *Unit head:* John G. Harris, PhD, Chair, 352-392-0913, Fax: 352-392-8671, E-mail: harris@ece.ufl.edu. *Application contact:* Gijs Bosman, PhD, Professor and Graduate Coordinator, 352-392-0910, Fax: 352-392-8671, E-mail: bosman@ece.ufl.edu.
Website: http://www.ece.ufl.edu/.

University of Houston–Clear Lake, School of Science and Computer Engineering, Program in Computer Engineering, Houston, TX 77058-1002. Offers MS. Part-time and evening/weekend programs available. *Entrance requirements:* For master's, GRE General Test. Additional exam requirements/recommendations for international students: Required—TOEFL (minimum score 550 paper-based).

University of Idaho, College of Graduate Studies, College of Engineering, Department of Electrical and Computer Engineering, Moscow, ID 83844-1023. Offers computer engineering (M Engr, MS); electrical engineering (M Engr, MS, PhD). *Faculty:* 12 full-time, 3 part-time/adjunct. *Students:* 27 full-time, 83 part-time. Average age 35. In 2014, 27 master's, 7 doctorates awarded. *Degree requirements:* For master's, thesis; for doctorate, thesis/dissertation. *Entrance requirements:* For master's, minimum GPA of

2.8; for doctorate, minimum undergraduate GPA of 2.8, 3.0 graduate. *Application deadline:* For fall admission, 8/1 for domestic students; for spring admission, 12/15 for domestic students. Applications are processed on a rolling basis. Application fee: $60. Electronic applications accepted. *Expenses:* Tuition, state resident: full-time $4784; part-time $280.50 per credit hour. Tuition, nonresident: full-time $18,314; part-time $957.50 per credit hour. *Required fees:* $2000; $58.50 per credit hour. Tuition and fees vary according to program. *Financial support:* Fellowships, research assistantships, teaching assistantships, career-related internships or fieldwork, and Federal Work-Study available. Financial award applicants required to submit FAFSA. *Faculty research:* Microelectronics, laser electrophotography, intelligent systems research, advanced transportation technologies. *Unit head:* Dr. Fred Barlow, Chair, 208-885-6554, E-mail: info@ece.uidaho.edu. *Application contact:* Sean Scoggin, Graduate Recruitment Coordinator, 208-885-4001, Fax: 208-885-4406, E-mail: graduateadmissions@uidaho.edu.
Website: http://www.uidaho.edu/engr/ece/.

University of Illinois at Urbana–Champaign, Graduate College, College of Engineering, Department of Electrical and Computer Engineering, Champaign, IL 61820. Offers MS, PhD, MS/MBA. *Students:* 535 (79 women). Application fee: $70 ($90 for international students). *Unit head:* William H. Sanders, Head, 217-333-2301, Fax: 217-244-7075, E-mail: whs@illinois.edu. *Application contact:* Laurie A. Fisher, Administrative Aide, 217-333-9709, Fax: 217-333-8582, E-mail: fisher2@illinois.edu.
Website: http://www.ece.illinois.edu/.

The University of Iowa, Graduate College, College of Engineering, Department of Electrical and Computer Engineering, Iowa City, IA 52242-1316. Offers MS, PhD. Part-time programs available. *Faculty:* 16 full-time (4 women), 5 part-time/adjunct (0 women). *Students:* 67 full-time (12 women); includes 9 minority (1 Black or African American, non-Hispanic/Latino; 3 Asian, non-Hispanic/Latino; 5 Hispanic/Latino), 41 international. Average age 27. 115 applicants, 10% accepted, 6 enrolled. In 2014, 5 master's, 7 doctorates awarded. *Degree requirements:* For master's, comprehensive exam, thesis optional; for doctorate, comprehensive exam, thesis/dissertation, qualifying exam. *Entrance requirements:* For master's and doctorate, GRE. Additional exam requirements/recommendations for international students: Required—TOEFL (minimum score 550 paper-based; 81 iBT). *Application deadline:* For fall admission, 2/1 priority date for domestic students, 2/1 for international students; for spring admission, 12/1 for domestic students; for summer admission, 4/15 for domestic students. Applications are processed on a rolling basis. Application fee: $60 ($100 for international students). Electronic applications accepted. *Financial support:* In 2014–15, 3 fellowships with full tuition reimbursements, 40 research assistantships with full and partial tuition reimbursements (averaging $18,080 per year), 11 teaching assistantships with full tuition reimbursements (averaging $18,080 per year) were awarded; scholarships/grants and unspecified assistantships also available. Financial award application deadline: 2/1; financial award applicants required to submit FAFSA. *Faculty research:* Applied optics and nanotechnology, compressive sensing, computational genomics, database management systems, large-scale intelligent and control systems, medical image processing, VLSI design and test. *Total annual research expenditures:* $5.8 million. *Unit head:* Dr. Er-Wei Bai, Department Executive Officer, 319-335-5949, Fax: 319-335-6028, E-mail: er-wei-bai@uiowa.edu. *Application contact:* Cathy Kern, Secretary, 319-335-5197, Fax: 319-335-6028, E-mail: ece@engineering.uiowa.edu.
Website: http://www.engineering.uiowa.edu/ece.

The University of Kansas, Graduate Studies, School of Engineering, Program in Computer Engineering, Lawrence, KS 66045. Offers MS. Part-time programs available. *Faculty:* 33 full-time, 1 part-time/adjunct. *Students:* 13 full-time (2 women), 2 part-time (0 women); includes 2 minority (1 Asian, non-Hispanic/Latino; 1 Hispanic/Latino), 9 international. Average age 25. 25 applicants, 40% accepted, 6 enrolled. In 2014, 2 master's awarded. *Degree requirements:* For master's, thesis optional, exam. *Entrance requirements:* For master's, GRE, minimum GPA of 3.0. Additional exam requirements/recommendations for international students: Required—TOEFL (minimum score 600 paper-based; 100 iBT). *Application deadline:* For fall admission, 3/1 priority date for domestic students, 3/1 for international students; for spring admission, 10/1 priority date for domestic students, 10/1 for international students. Applications are processed on a rolling basis. Application fee: $55 ($65 for international students). Electronic applications accepted. *Financial support:* Fellowships with full and partial tuition reimbursements, research assistantships with full and partial tuition reimbursements, teaching assistantships with full and partial tuition reimbursements, career-related internships or fieldwork, scholarships/grants, and unspecified assistantships available. Financial award application deadline: 1/1. *Faculty research:* Communication systems and networking, computer systems design, interactive intelligent systems, radar systems and remote sensing, bioinformatics. *Unit head:* James Stiles, Associate Chair for Graduate Studies, 785-864-8803, E-mail: jstiles@eecs.ku.edu. *Application contact:* Pam Shadoin, Graduate Admissions Contact, 785-864-4487, E-mail: pshadoin@ku.edu.
Website: http://www.eecs.ku.edu/.

University of Louisiana at Lafayette, College of Engineering, Center for Advanced Computer Studies, Lafayette, LA 70504. Offers computer engineering (MS, PhD); computer science (MS, PhD). Part-time programs available. Terminal master's awarded for partial completion of doctoral program. *Degree requirements:* For master's, thesis or alternative; for doctorate, comprehensive exam, thesis/dissertation, final oral exam. *Entrance requirements:* For master's, GRE General Test, minimum GPA of 2.75; for doctorate, GRE General Test, minimum GPA of 3.0. Additional exam requirements/recommendations for international students: Required—TOEFL. Electronic applications accepted.

University of Louisiana at Lafayette, College of Engineering, Department of Electrical and Computer Engineering, Lafayette, LA 70504. Offers computer engineering (MS, PhD); telecommunications (MSTC). *Degree requirements:* For master's, thesis or alternative; for doctorate, comprehensive exam, thesis/dissertation, final oral exam. *Entrance requirements:* For master's, GRE General Test, minimum GPA of 2.75. Additional exam requirements/recommendations for international students: Required—TOEFL (minimum score 550 paper-based). Electronic applications accepted.

University of Louisville, J. B. Speed School of Engineering, Department of Computer Engineering and Computer Science, Louisville, KY 40292-0001. Offers computer engineering and computer science (M Eng, MS); computer science and engineering (PhD); data mining (Certificate); network and information security (Certificate). *Accreditation:* ABET (one or more programs are accredited). Part-time programs available. Postbaccalaureate distance learning degree programs offered (no on-campus study). *Students:* 77 full-time (22 women), 68 part-time (14 women); includes 17 minority (8 Black or African American, non-Hispanic/Latino; 6 Asian, non-Hispanic/Latino; 2 Hispanic/Latino; 1 Two or more races, non-Hispanic/Latino), 51 international. Average age 29. 92 applicants, 54% accepted, 29 enrolled. In 2014, 8 master's, 3 doctorates, 6 other advanced degrees awarded. Terminal master's awarded for partial completion of doctoral program. *Degree requirements:* For master's, comprehensive exam (for some programs), thesis optional, minimum GPA of 3.0; for doctorate, comprehensive exam, thesis/dissertation, minimum GPA of 3.0. *Entrance requirements:* For master's and doctorate, GRE, letters of recommendation, final official transcripts; for Certificate, undergraduate degree. Additional exam requirements/recommendations for international students: Required—TOEFL (minimum score 80 iBT) or IELTS. *Application deadline:* For fall admission, 6/15 for domestic students, 5/1 priority date for international students; for spring admission, 11/22 for domestic students, 11/1 priority date for international students; for summer admission, 3/31 for domestic students, 4/1 priority date for international students. Application fee: $60. Electronic applications accepted. *Expenses:* Tuition, state resident: full-time $11,326; part-time $630 per credit hour. Tuition, nonresident: full-time $23,568; part-time $1311 per credit hour. *Required fees:* $196. Tuition and fees vary according to program and reciprocity agreements. *Financial support:* Fellowships with full tuition reimbursements, research assistantships with full tuition reimbursements, and teaching assistantships with full tuition reimbursements available. Financial award application deadline: 2/3. *Faculty research:* Software systems engineering, information security and forensics, multimedia and vision, mobile and distributed computing, intelligent systems. *Total annual research expenditures:* $1.3 million. *Unit head:* Dr. Adel S. Elmaghraby, Chair, 502-852-6304, Fax: 502-852-4713, E-mail: adel@louisville.edu. *Application contact:* Dr. Michael Harris, Director of Academic Programs, J. B. Speed School of Engineering, 502-852-6278, Fax: 502-852-6294, E-mail: mharris@louisville.edu.
Website: http://louisville.edu/speed/computer.

University of Louisville, J. B. Speed School of Engineering, Department of Electrical and Computer Engineering, Louisville, KY 40292-0001. Offers M Eng, MS, PhD. *Accreditation:* ABET (one or more programs are accredited). Part-time programs available. *Students:* 66 full-time (8 women), 26 part-time (5 women); includes 12 minority (4 Black or African American, non-Hispanic/Latino; 4 Asian, non-Hispanic/Latino; 4 Hispanic/Latino), 37 international. Average age 27. 64 applicants, 48% accepted, 14 enrolled. In 2014, 14 master's, 6 doctorates awarded. Terminal master's awarded for partial completion of doctoral program. *Degree requirements:* For master's, comprehensive exam (for some programs), thesis or alternative; for doctorate, comprehensive exam, thesis/dissertation, minimum GPA of 3.0. *Entrance requirements:* For master's and doctorate, GRE General Test. Additional exam requirements/recommendations for international students: Required—TOEFL (minimum score 550 paper-based; 80 iBT), IELTS (minimum score 6.5). *Application deadline:* For fall admission, 5/1 priority date for domestic and international students; for spring admission, 11/1 priority date for domestic and international students. Applications are processed on a rolling basis. Application fee: $60. Electronic applications accepted. *Expenses:* Tuition, state resident: full-time $11,326; part-time $630 per credit hour. Tuition, nonresident: full-time $23,568; part-time $1311 per credit hour. *Required fees:* $196. Tuition and fees vary according to program and reciprocity agreements. *Financial support:* In 2014–15, 16 students received support, including 4 fellowships with full tuition reimbursements available (averaging $20,000 per year), 4 research assistantships with full tuition reimbursements available (averaging $21,000 per year), 8 teaching assistantships with full tuition reimbursements available (averaging $20,000 per year). Financial award application deadline: 1/25; financial award applicants required to submit FAFSA. *Faculty research:* Nanotechnology; microfabrication; computer engineering; control, communication and signal processing; electronic devices and systems. *Total annual research expenditures:* $5.8 million. *Unit head:* James H. Graham, Acting Chair, 502-852-6289, Fax: 502-852-6807, E-mail: jhgrah01@louisville.edu. *Application contact:* Dr. Michael Day, Associate Dean, 502-852-6195, Fax: 502-852-7294, E-mail: day@louisville.edu.
Website: http://www.louisville.edu/speed/electrical/.

University of Maine, Graduate School, College of Engineering, Department of Electrical and Computer Engineering, Orono, ME 04469. Offers computer engineering (MS); electrical engineering (MS, PhD). Part-time programs available. *Faculty:* 12 full-time (1 woman), 4 part-time/adjunct (0 women). *Students:* 22 full-time (3 women), 1 (woman) part-time; includes 1 minority (Hispanic/Latino), 11 international. Average age 27. 32 applicants, 47% accepted, 6 enrolled. In 2014, 4 master's, 2 doctorates awarded. Terminal master's awarded for partial completion of doctoral program. *Degree requirements:* For master's, thesis (for some programs); for doctorate, comprehensive exam, thesis/dissertation. *Entrance requirements:* For master's and doctorate, GRE General Test. Additional exam requirements/recommendations for international students: Required—TOEFL. *Application deadline:* For fall admission, 2/1 for domestic students. Applications are processed on a rolling basis. Application fee: $65. Electronic applications accepted. *Expenses:* Tuition, state resident: part-time $658 per credit hour. Tuition, nonresident: part-time $1550 per credit hour. *Financial support:* In 2014–15, 16 students received support, including 1 fellowship, 10 research assistantships with full tuition reimbursements available (averaging $14,600 per year), 4 teaching assistantships with full tuition reimbursements available (averaging $14,600 per year); Federal Work-Study, institutionally sponsored loans, and tuition waivers (full and partial) also available. Financial award application deadline: 3/1. *Faculty research:* Microwave acoustic sensors, semiconductor devices and fabrication, high performance computing, instrumentation and industrial automation, wireless communication. *Total annual research expenditures:* $959,995. *Unit head:* Dr. Donald Hummels, Chair, 207-581-2244. *Application contact:* Scott G. Delcourt, Assistant Vice President for Graduate Studies and Senior Associate Dean, 207-581-3291, Fax: 207-581-3232, E-mail: graduate@maine.edu.
Website: http://www.ece.umaine.edu/.

University of Manitoba, Faculty of Graduate Studies, Faculty of Engineering, Department of Electrical and Computer Engineering, Winnipeg, MB R3T 2N2, Canada. Offers M Eng, M Sc, PhD. *Degree requirements:* For master's, thesis; for doctorate, thesis/dissertation.

University of Maryland, Baltimore County, The Graduate School, College of Engineering and Information Technology, Department of Computer Science and Electrical Engineering, Program in Computer Engineering, Baltimore, MD 21250. Offers MS, PhD. Part-time programs available. *Students:* 22 full-time (5 women), 10 part-time (1 woman); includes 3 minority (1 Black or African American, non-Hispanic/Latino; 1 Asian, non-Hispanic/Latino; 1 Hispanic/Latino), 19 international. Average age 28. 38 applicants, 68% accepted, 10 enrolled. In 2014, 5 master's, 1 doctorate awarded. *Degree requirements:* For master's, comprehensive exam (for some programs), thesis or alternative; for doctorate, comprehensive exam, thesis/dissertation. *Entrance requirements:* For master's, GRE General Test, strong background in computer engineering, computer science, and math courses; for doctorate, GRE General Test, MS in computer science (strongly recommended); strong background in computer engineering, computer science, and mathematics courses. Additional exam requirements/recommendations for international students: Required—TOEFL (minimum score 550 paper-based; 80 iBT). *Application deadline:* For fall admission, 6/1 for domestic students, 1/1 for international students; for spring admission, 11/1 for domestic students, 6/1 for international students. Applications are processed on a rolling basis. Application fee: $70. Electronic applications accepted. *Expenses:* Tuition, state resident: part-time $557. Tuition, nonresident: part-time $922. *Required fees:* $122 per semester. One-time fee: $200 part-time. *Financial support:* In 2014–15, 2 research assistantships with full tuition reimbursements (averaging $18,000 per year), 13 teaching assistantships with full tuition reimbursements (averaging $18,000 per year) were awarded; career-related internships or fieldwork, Federal Work-Study, scholarships/grants, health care benefits, tuition waivers (partial), and unspecified

assistantships also available. Support available to part-time students. Financial award application deadline: 6/30; financial award applicants required to submit FAFSA. *Faculty research:* Communication and signal processing, photonics and micro electronics, sensor systems, signal processing architectures, VLSI design and test. *Unit head:* Dr. Gary Carter, Professor and Chair, 410-455-3500, Fax: 410-455-3969, E-mail: carter@cs.umbc.edu. *Application contact:* Dr. Curtis Menyuk, Professor and Graduate Program Director, 410-455-3500, Fax: 410-455-3969, E-mail: menyuk@umbc.edu.
Website: http://www.cs.umbc.edu/.

University of Maryland, College Park, Academic Affairs, A. James Clark School of Engineering, Department of Electrical and Computer Engineering, College Park, MD 20742. Offers electrical and computer engineering (M Eng, MS, PhD); electrical engineering (MS, PhD); telecommunications (MS). Part-time and evening/weekend programs available. Postbaccalaureate distance learning degree programs offered. *Degree requirements:* For master's, thesis optional; for doctorate, thesis/dissertation, oral exam, qualifying exam. *Entrance requirements:* For master's and doctorate, GRE General Test, 3 letters of recommendation. Electronic applications accepted. *Faculty research:* Communications and control, electrophysics, micro-electronics, robotics, computer engineering.

University of Massachusetts Amherst, Graduate School, College of Engineering, Department of Electrical and Computer Engineering, Amherst, MA 01003. Offers MSECE, PhD. Part-time programs available. *Faculty:* 45 full-time (2 women). *Students:* 228 full-time (65 women), 10 part-time (3 women); includes 6 minority (2 Black or African American, non-Hispanic/Latino; 4 Asian, non-Hispanic/Latino), 204 international. Average age 25. 1,074 applicants, 23% accepted, 71 enrolled. In 2014, 70 master's, 13 doctorates awarded. Terminal master's awarded for partial completion of doctoral program. *Degree requirements:* For master's, thesis or alternative; for doctorate, comprehensive exam, thesis/dissertation. *Entrance requirements:* For master's and doctorate, GRE General Test. Additional exam requirements/recommendations for international students: Required—TOEFL (minimum score 550 paper-based; 80 iBT), IELTS (minimum score 6.5). *Application deadline:* For fall admission, 1/15 for domestic and international students; for spring admission, 10/1 for domestic and international students. Applications are processed on a rolling basis. Application fee: $75. Electronic applications accepted. *Expenses:* Tuition, state resident: full-time $1980; part-time $110 per credit. Tuition, nonresident: full-time $14,644; part-time $414 per credit. *Required fees:* $11,417. One-time fee: $357. *Financial support:* Fellowships with full and partial tuition reimbursements, research assistantships with full and partial tuition reimbursements, teaching assistantships with full and partial tuition reimbursements, career-related internships or fieldwork, Federal Work-Study, scholarships/grants, traineeships, health care benefits, tuition waivers (full and partial), and unspecified assistantships available. Support available to part-time students. Financial award application deadline: 1/15. *Unit head:* Dr. C. Mani Krishna, Graduate Program Director, 413-545-4583, Fax: 413-545-4611, E-mail: ecegrad@ecs.umass.edu. *Application contact:* Lindsay DeSantis, Supervisor of Admissions, 413-545-0722, Fax: 413-577-0010, E-mail: gradadm@grad.umass.edu.
Website: http://ece.umass.edu/.

University of Massachusetts Dartmouth, Graduate School, College of Engineering, Department of Electrical and Computer Engineering, North Dartmouth, MA 02747-2300. Offers acoustics (Postbaccalaureate Certificate); communications (Postbaccalaureate Certificate); computer engineering (MS, PhD); computer systems engineering (Postbaccalaureate Certificate); digital signal processing (Postbaccalaureate Certificate); electrical engineering (MS, PhD); electrical engineering systems (Postbaccalaureate Certificate). Part-time programs available. *Faculty:* 16 full-time (3 women). *Students:* 47 full-time (15 women), 38 part-time (2 women); includes 8 minority (1 Black or African American, non-Hispanic/Latino; 4 Asian, non-Hispanic/Latino; 2 Hispanic/Latino; 1 Two or more races, non-Hispanic/Latino), 45 international. Average age 27. 127 applicants, 60% accepted, 26 enrolled. In 2014, 9 master's, 4 doctorates, 1 other advanced degree awarded. *Degree requirements:* For master's, thesis or project; for doctorate, comprehensive exam, thesis/dissertation. *Entrance requirements:* For master's, GRE (UMass Dartmouth electrical/computer engineering bachelor's degree recipients are exempt), statement of purpose (minimum of 300 words), resume, 3 letters of recommendation, official transcripts; for doctorate, GRE, statement of purpose (minimum of 300 words), resume, 3 letters of recommendation, official transcripts; for Postbaccalaureate Certificate, statement of purpose (minimum of 300 words), resume, official transcripts. Additional exam requirements/recommendations for international students: Required—TOEFL (minimum score 533 paper-based; 72 iBT), IELTS (minimum score 6). *Application deadline:* For fall admission, 2/15 priority date for domestic students, 1/15 priority date for international students; for spring admission, 11/1 priority date for domestic students, 10/1 priority date for international students. Applications are processed on a rolling basis. Application fee: $60. Electronic applications accepted. *Expenses:* Tuition, state resident: full-time $2071; part-time $86.29 per credit. Tuition, nonresident: full-time $8099; part-time $337.46 per credit. *Required fees:* $16,520; $712.33 per credit. Tuition and fees vary according to course load and reciprocity agreements. *Financial support:* In 2014–15, 2 fellowships with full and partial tuition reimbursements (averaging $14,337 per year), 13 research assistantships with full and partial tuition reimbursements (averaging $12,775 per year), 11 teaching assistantships with full and partial tuition reimbursements (averaging $12,273 per year) were awarded; Federal Work-Study and unspecified assistantships also available. Support available to part-time students. Financial award application deadline: 3/1; financial award applicants required to submit FAFSA. *Faculty research:* Computer engineering, cyber security, acoustics, signals and systems, electromagnetics, electronics and solid-state devices, marine systems, photonics. *Total annual research expenditures:* $2.5 million. *Unit head:* Dr. Karen Payton, Graduate Program Director, 508-999-8434, Fax: 508-999-8489, E-mail: kpayton@umassd.edu. *Application contact:* Steven Briggs, Director of Marketing and Recruitment for Graduate Studies, 508-999-8604, Fax: 508-999-8183, E-mail: graduate@umassd.edu.
Website: http://www.umassd.edu/engineering/ece/.

University of Massachusetts Lowell, Francis College of Engineering, Department of Electrical and Computer Engineering, Program in Computer Engineering, Lowell, MA 01854. Offers MS Eng. *Degree requirements:* For master's, thesis optional.

University of Memphis, Graduate School, Herff College of Engineering, Department of Electrical and Computer Engineering, Memphis, TN 38152. Offers automatic control systems (MS); biomedical systems (MS); communications and propagation systems (MS); computer engineering (PhD); electrical engineering (PhD); engineering computer systems (MS). *Faculty:* 10 full-time (1 woman), 2 part-time/adjunct (0 women). *Students:* 27 full-time (10 women), 9 part-time (2 women); includes 10 minority (6 Black or African American, non-Hispanic/Latino; 2 Asian, non-Hispanic/Latino; 1 Hispanic/Latino; 1 Two or more races, non-Hispanic/Latino), 21 international. Average age 28. 22 applicants, 95% accepted, 14 enrolled. In 2014, 21 master's awarded. *Degree requirements:* For master's, comprehensive exam, thesis or alternative. *Entrance requirements:* For master's, GRE General Test or MAT, minimum undergraduate GPA of 2.5. *Application deadline:* For fall admission, 8/1 for domestic students; for spring admission, 12/1 for domestic students. Application fee: $35 ($60 for international students). *Financial support:* In 2014–15, 4 students received support. Research assistantships, teaching assistantships, career-related internships or fieldwork, Federal Work-Study, scholarships/grants, and unspecified assistantships available. Financial award application deadline: 2/15; financial award applicants required to submit FAFSA. *Faculty research:* Image processing, imaging sensors, biomedical systems, intelligent systems. *Unit head:* Dr. David Russomanno, Chair/Professor, 901-678-2175, Fax: 901-678-5469, E-mail: russmnn@memphis.edu. *Application contact:* Dr. Steven T. Griffin, Coordinator of Graduate Studies, 901-678-5268, Fax: 901-678-5469, E-mail: stgriffn@memphis.edu.
Website: http://www.memphis.edu/eece/.

University of Memphis, Graduate School, Herff College of Engineering, Department of Engineering Technology, Memphis, TN 38152. Offers computer engineering technology (MS); electronics engineering technology (MS). Part-time and evening/weekend programs available. *Faculty:* 2 full-time (0 women). *Students:* 2 full-time (0 women), 9 part-time (2 women); includes 8 minority (6 Black or African American, non-Hispanic/Latino; 1 Hispanic/Latino; 1 Two or more races, non-Hispanic/Latino). Average age 37. 4 applicants, 75% accepted. In 2014, 5 master's awarded. *Degree requirements:* For master's, comprehensive exam, thesis optional. *Entrance requirements:* For master's, GRE General Test, minimum undergraduate GPA of 2.5. *Application deadline:* For fall admission, 8/1 for domestic students; for spring admission, 12/1 for domestic students. Applications are processed on a rolling basis. Application fee: $25 ($50 for international students). Electronic applications accepted. *Financial support:* In 2014–15, 5 students received support. Research assistantships with full tuition reimbursements available, career-related internships or fieldwork, Federal Work-Study, scholarships/grants, and unspecified assistantships available. Financial award application deadline: 2/15; financial award applicants required to submit FAFSA. *Faculty research:* Teacher education services-technology education; flexible manufacturing control systems; embedded, dedicated, and real-time computer systems; network, Internet, and Web-based programming; analog and digital electronic communication systems. *Unit head:* Deborah J. Hochstein, Chairman, 901-678-2225, Fax: 901-678-5145, E-mail: dhochstn@memphis.edu. *Application contact:* Carl R. Williams, Coordinator of Graduate Studies, 901-678-3296, Fax: 901-678-5145, E-mail: crwillia@memphis.edu.
Website: http://www.memphis.edu/et/index.php.

University of Miami, Graduate School, College of Engineering, Department of Electrical and Computer Engineering, Coral Gables, FL 33124. Offers MSECE, PhD. Part-time programs available. *Degree requirements:* For master's, thesis (for some programs); for doctorate, comprehensive exam, thesis/dissertation, dissertation proposal defense. *Entrance requirements:* For master's, GRE General Test, minimum GPA of 3.0; for doctorate, GRE General Test, minimum undergraduate GPA of 3.3, graduate 3.5. Additional exam requirements/recommendations for international students: Required—TOEFL (minimum score 550 paper-based; 59 iBT), IELTS (minimum score 7). Electronic applications accepted. *Faculty research:* Computer network, image processing, database systems, digital signal processing, machine intelligence.

University of Michigan, College of Engineering, Department of Computer Science and Engineering, Ann Arbor, MI 48109. Offers MS, MSE, PhD. *Students:* 284 full-time (44 women), 4 part-time (2 women). 1,451 applicants, 17% accepted, 90 enrolled. In 2014, 70 master's, 19 doctorates awarded. *Faculty research:* Solid state electronics and optics; communications, control, signal process; sensors and integrated circuitry; software systems; artificial intelligence; hardware systems. *Total annual research expenditures:* $22.5 million. *Unit head:* Prof. Marios Papaefthymiou, Interim Chair, 734-764-8504, Fax: 734-763-1503, E-mail: marios@umich.edu. *Application contact:* Dawn Freysinger, Graduate Programs Coordinator, 734-647-1807, Fax: 734-763-1503, E-mail: dawnf@umich.edu.
Website: http://eecs.umich.edu/cse/.

University of Michigan–Dearborn, College of Engineering and Computer Science, MSE Program in Computer Engineering, Dearborn, MI 48128. Offers MSE. Postbaccalaureate distance learning degree programs offered (no on-campus study). *Faculty:* 20 full-time (1 woman), 11 part-time/adjunct (0 women). *Students:* 2 full-time (1 woman), 28 part-time (3 women); includes 6 minority (1 Black or African American, non-Hispanic/Latino; 3 Asian, non-Hispanic/Latino; 2 Hispanic/Latino), 6 international. 25 applicants, 52% accepted, 11 enrolled. In 2014, 16 master's awarded. *Degree requirements:* For master's, thesis optional. *Entrance requirements:* For master's, bachelor's degree in electrical and/or computer engineering with minimum overall GPA of 3.0. Additional exam requirements/recommendations for international students: Required—TOEFL (minimum score 560 paper-based; 84 iBT), IELTS (minimum score 6.5). *Application deadline:* For fall admission, 8/1 for domestic students, 5/1 for international students; for winter admission, 12/1 for domestic students, 9/1 for international students; for spring admission, 4/1 for domestic students, 1/1 for international students. Applications are processed on a rolling basis. Application fee: $60. Electronic applications accepted. *Expenses:* Tuition, state resident: full-time $12,202; part-time $707 per credit hour. Tuition, nonresident: full-time $20,980; part-time $1209 per credit hour. *Required fees:* $798; $302 per term. Tuition and fees vary according to course level, course load, degree level and program. *Financial support:* In 2014–15, 3 students received support. Scholarships/grants and unspecified assistantships available. Support available to part-time students. Financial award applicants required to submit FAFSA. *Faculty research:* Vehicle electronics, wireless communication, pattern recognition and machine intelligence, machine vision, fuzzy systems, smart systems. *Unit head:* Dr. YiLu Murphey, Chair, 313-593-5028, Fax: 313-583-6336, E-mail: yilu@umich.edu. *Application contact:* Michael Patrick Hicks, Intermediate Academic Records Assistant, 313-593-5420, Fax: 313-583-6336, E-mail: ece-grad@umd.umich.edu.
Website: http://umdearborn.edu/cecs/ECE/grad_prog/index.php.

University of Minnesota, Duluth, Graduate School, Swenson College of Science and Engineering, Department of Electrical and Computer Engineering, Duluth, MN 55812-2496. Offers MSECE. Part-time programs available. *Degree requirements:* For master's, thesis. *Entrance requirements:* Additional exam requirements/recommendations for international students: Recommended—TOEFL, IELTS, TWE. *Faculty research:* Biomedical instrumentation, transportation systems, computer hardware and software, signal processing, optical communications.

University of Minnesota, Twin Cities Campus, College of Science and Engineering, Department of Computer Science and Engineering, Minneapolis, MN 55455-0213. Offers computer science (MCS, MS, PhD); data science (MS); software engineering (MSSE). Part-time programs available. Terminal master's awarded for partial completion of doctoral program. *Degree requirements:* For doctorate, thesis/dissertation. *Entrance requirements:* For master's and doctorate, GRE General Test. Additional exam requirements/recommendations for international students: Required—TOEFL. Electronic applications accepted. *Faculty research:* Computer architecture, bioinformatics and computational biology, data mining, graphics and visualization, high performance computing, human-computer interaction, networks, software systems, theory, artificial intelligence.

University of Minnesota, Twin Cities Campus, College of Science and Engineering, Department of Electrical and Computer Engineering, Minneapolis, MN 55455-0213. Offers MSEE, PhD. Part-time programs available. *Degree requirements:* For master's, thesis or alternative; for doctorate, thesis/dissertation. *Entrance requirements:* Additional exam requirements/recommendations for international students: Required—TOEFL (minimum score 550 paper-based). Electronic applications accepted. *Faculty research:* Signal processing, micro and nano structures, computers, controls, power electronics.

University of Missouri–Kansas City, School of Computing and Engineering, Kansas City, MO 64110-2499. Offers civil engineering (MS); computer and electrical engineering (PhD); computer science (MS), including bioinformatics, software engineering, telecommunications networking; computer science and informatics (PhD); computing (PhD); electrical engineering (MS); engineering (PhD); engineering and construction management (Graduate Certificate); mechanical engineering (MS); telecommunications and computer networking (PhD). PhD (interdisciplinary) offered through the School of Graduate Studies. Part-time programs available. *Faculty:* 39 full-time (5 women), 26 part-time/adjunct (3 women). *Students:* 500 full-time (143 women), 136 part-time (28 women); includes 18 minority (5 Black or African American, non-Hispanic/Latino; 8 Asian, non-Hispanic/Latino; 4 Hispanic/Latino; 1 Two or more races, non-Hispanic/Latino), 551 international. Average age 24. 1,924 applicants, 39% accepted, 200 enrolled. In 2014, 124 master's, 1 other advanced degree awarded. *Degree requirements:* For doctorate, thesis/dissertation. *Entrance requirements:* For master's, GRE General Test, minimum GPA of 3.0, 3 letters of recommendation from professors; for doctorate, GRE General Test, minimum GPA of 3.5. Additional exam requirements/recommendations for international students: Required—TOEFL (minimum score 550 paper-based; 80 iBT). *Application deadline:* For fall admission, 1/15 priority date for domestic students, 1/15 for international students. Applications are processed on a rolling basis. Application fee: $45 ($50 for international students). *Financial support:* In 2014–15, 34 research assistantships with partial tuition reimbursements (averaging $15,602 per year), 24 teaching assistantships with partial tuition reimbursements (averaging $15,090 per year) were awarded; career-related internships or fieldwork, Federal Work-Study, scholarships/grants, tuition waivers (partial), and unspecified assistantships also available. Support available to part-time students. Financial award application deadline: 3/1; financial award applicants required to submit FAFSA. *Faculty research:* Algorithms, bioinformatics and medical informatics, biomechanics/biomaterials, civil engineering materials, networking and telecommunications, thermal science. *Unit head:* Dr. Kevin Z. Truman, Dean, 816-235-2399, Fax: 816-235-5159. *Application contact:* 816-235-2399, Fax: 816-235-5159.
Website: http://sce.umkc.edu/.

University of Nebraska–Lincoln, Graduate College, College of Arts and Sciences and College of Engineering, Department of Computer Science and Engineering, Lincoln, NE 68588. Offers bioinformatics (MS, PhD); computer engineering (MS, PhD); computer science (MS, PhD); information technology (PhD). *Degree requirements:* For master's, thesis optional; for doctorate, comprehensive exam, thesis/dissertation. *Entrance requirements:* For master's and doctorate, GRE General Test. Additional exam requirements/recommendations for international students: Required—TOEFL (minimum score 600 paper-based). Electronic applications accepted. *Faculty research:* Software engineering, geo- and bio-informatics, scientific computation, secure communication.

University of Nevada, Las Vegas, Graduate College, Howard R. Hughes College of Engineering, Department of Electrical and Computer Engineering, Las Vegas, NV 89154-4026. Offers MS, PhD, MS/MS, MS/PhD. Part-time programs available. *Faculty:* 17 full-time (2 women). *Students:* 39 full-time (6 women), 8 part-time (1 woman); includes 9 minority (1 Black or African American, non-Hispanic/Latino; 4 Asian, non-Hispanic/Latino; 3 Hispanic/Latino; 1 Two or more races, non-Hispanic/Latino), 28 international. Average age 30. 31 applicants, 45% accepted, 8 enrolled. In 2014, 12 master's, 4 doctorates awarded. *Degree requirements:* For master's, comprehensive exam, thesis, project; for doctorate, comprehensive exam, thesis/dissertation. *Entrance requirements:* Additional exam requirements/recommendations for international students: Required—TOEFL (minimum score 550 paper-based; 80 iBT), IELTS (minimum score 7). *Application deadline:* For fall admission, 2/1 for domestic students, 5/1 for international students; for spring admission, 10/1 for domestic and international students. Application fee: $60 ($95 for international students). Electronic applications accepted. *Financial support:* In 2014–15, 45 students received support, including 17 research assistantships with partial tuition reimbursements available (averaging $13,888 per year), 28 teaching assistantships with partial tuition reimbursements available (averaging $14,192 per year); institutionally sponsored loans, scholarships/grants, health care benefits, tuition waivers (full), and unspecified assistantships also available. Financial award application deadline: 3/1. *Faculty research:* Computer engineering, power engineering, semiconductor and nanotechnology, electronics and VLSI, telecommunications and control. *Total annual research expenditures:* $1.2 million. *Unit head:* Dr. Peter Stubberud, Chair/Professor, 702-895-0869, E-mail: peter.stubberud@unlv.edu. *Application contact:* Graduate College Admissions Evaluator, 702-895-3320, Fax: 702-895-4180, E-mail: gradcollege@unlv.edu.
Website: http://ece.unlv.edu/.

University of Nevada, Reno, Graduate School, College of Engineering, Department of Computer Science and Engineering, Reno, NV 89557. Offers MS, PhD. Terminal master's awarded for partial completion of doctoral program. *Degree requirements:* For master's, thesis optional; for doctorate, thesis/dissertation. *Entrance requirements:* For master's, GRE General Test, minimum GPA of 2.75; for doctorate, GRE General Test, minimum GPA of 3.0. Additional exam requirements/recommendations for international students: Required—TOEFL (minimum score 500 paper-based; 61 iBT), IELTS (minimum score 6). Electronic applications accepted. *Faculty research:* Evolutionary computing systems, computer vision/virtual reality, software engineering.

University of New Brunswick Fredericton, School of Graduate Studies, Faculty of Engineering, Department of Electrical and Computer Engineering, Fredericton, NB E3B 5A3, Canada. Offers M Eng, M Sc E, PhD. Part-time programs available. *Faculty:* 13 full-time (3 women), 16 part-time/adjunct (1 woman). *Students:* 50 full-time (7 women), 10 part-time (3 women). 45 applicants, 44% accepted. In 2014, 11 master's, 6 doctorates awarded. *Degree requirements:* For master's, thesis, research proposal; 10 courses (for M Eng); for doctorate, comprehensive exam, thesis/dissertation, research proposal. *Entrance requirements:* For master's, minimum GPA of 3.3; references; for doctorate, M Sc; minimum GPA of 3.3; previous transcripts; references. Additional exam requirements/recommendations for international students: Required—TOEFL (minimum score 580 paper-based; 93 iBT), IELTS (minimum score 7), TWE (minimum score 4). *Application deadline:* Applications are processed on a rolling basis. Application fee: $50 Canadian dollars. Electronic applications accepted. *Financial support:* In 2014–15, 142 fellowships, 78 research assistantships, 64 teaching assistantships were awarded. *Faculty research:* Biomedical engineering, communications, robotics and control systems, electromagnetic systems, embedded systems, optical fiber systems, sustainable energy and power systems, power electronics, image and signal processing, software systems, electronics and digital systems. *Unit head:* Dr. Maryhelen Stevenson, Director of Graduate Studies, 504-447-3147, Fax: 504-453-3589, E-mail: stevenso@unb.ca. *Application contact:* Shelley Cormier, Graduate Secretary, 506-452-6142, Fax: 506-453-3589, E-mail: scormier@unb.ca.
Website: http://go.unb.ca/gradprograms.

University of New Haven, Graduate School, Tagliatela College of Engineering, Program in Electrical Engineering, West Haven, CT 06516-1916. Offers control systems (MS); digital signal processing and communication (MS); electrical and computer engineering (MS); electrical engineering (MS). Part-time and evening/weekend programs available. *Degree requirements:* For master's, thesis or alternative. *Entrance requirements:* For master's, bachelor's degree in electrical engineering. Additional exam requirements/recommendations for international students: Required—TOEFL (minimum score 75 iBT), IELTS, PTE (minimum score 50). Electronic applications accepted. Application fee is waived when completed online.

University of New Haven, Graduate School, Tagliatela College of Engineering, Program in Network Systems, West Haven, CT 06516-1916. Offers MS. Part-time and evening/weekend programs available. *Degree requirements:* For master's, project. *Entrance requirements:* Additional exam requirements/recommendations for international students: Required—TOEFL (minimum score 75 iBT), IELTS, PTE (minimum score 50). Electronic applications accepted. Application fee is waived when completed online.

University of New Mexico, Graduate School, School of Engineering, Programs in Computer Engineering, Albuquerque, NM 87131-2039. Offers MS, PhD. Part-time and evening/weekend programs available. Postbaccalaureate distance learning degree programs offered (minimal on-campus study). *Faculty:* 10 full-time (2 women). *Students:* 23 full-time (4 women), 16 part-time (1 woman); includes 5 minority (1 Black or African American, non-Hispanic/Latino; 4 Hispanic/Latino), 18 international. Average age 30. 38 applicants, 29% accepted, 9 enrolled. In 2014, 14 master's, 7 doctorates awarded. Terminal master's awarded for partial completion of doctoral program. *Degree requirements:* For master's, thesis; for doctorate, comprehensive exam, thesis/dissertation. *Entrance requirements:* For master's, GRE General Test, minimum GPA of 3.0; for doctorate, GRE General Test, minimum GPA of 3.5. Additional exam requirements/recommendations for international students: Required—TOEFL (minimum score 550 paper-based; 79 iBT). *Application deadline:* For fall admission, 6/15 for domestic students, 2/15 for international students; for spring admission, 11/1 for domestic students, 6/15 for international students. Application fee: $50. Electronic applications accepted. *Financial support:* In 2014–15, 30 students received support, including 1 fellowship with tuition reimbursement available (averaging $3,000 per year), 23 research assistantships with tuition reimbursements available (averaging $13,883 per year), 3 teaching assistantships with tuition reimbursements available (averaging $9,861 per year); scholarships/grants, health care benefits, and unspecified assistantships also available. Financial award application deadline: 2/15; financial award applicants required to submit FAFSA. *Faculty research:* Bioengineering, computational intelligence, computer architecture and VLSI design, computer graphics and vision, computer networks and systems, image processing. *Unit head:* Dr. Chaouki T. Abdallah, Chair, 505-277-0298, Fax: 505-277-1439, E-mail: chaouki@ece.unm.edu. *Application contact:* Elmyra Grelle, Coordinator, 505-277-2600, Fax: 505-277-1439, E-mail: egrelle@ece.unm.edu.
Website: http://www.ece.unm.edu/.

The University of North Carolina at Charlotte, The William States Lee College of Engineering, Department of Electrical and Computer Engineering, Charlotte, NC 28223-0001. Offers electrical engineering (MSEE, PhD). Part-time and evening/weekend programs available. *Faculty:* 27 full-time (2 women). *Students:* 218 full-time (41 women), 47 part-time (11 women); includes 13 minority (7 Black or African American, non-Hispanic/Latino; 2 Asian, non-Hispanic/Latino; 2 Hispanic/Latino; 2 Two or more races, non-Hispanic/Latino), 227 international. Average age 25. 963 applicants, 39% accepted, 109 enrolled. In 2014, 69 master's, 10 doctorates awarded. Terminal master's awarded for partial completion of doctoral program. *Degree requirements:* For master's, thesis or project; for doctorate, thesis/dissertation. *Entrance requirements:* For master's, GRE General Test, minimum GPA of 3.0 in undergraduate major, 2.75 overall; for doctorate, GRE General Test, 3 letters of reference. Additional exam requirements/recommendations for international students: Required—TOEFL (minimum score 557 paper-based; 83 iBT). *Application deadline:* For fall admission, 5/1 for domestic and international students; for spring admission, 10/1 for domestic and international students. Applications are processed on a rolling basis. Application fee: $75. Electronic applications accepted. *Expenses:* Tuition, state resident: full-time $4008. Tuition, nonresident: full-time $16,295. *Required fees:* $2755. Tuition and fees vary according to course load and program. *Financial support:* In 2014–15, 66 students received support, including 1 fellowship (averaging $48,000 per year), 36 research assistantships (averaging $9,180 per year), 29 teaching assistantships (averaging $5,754 per year); career-related internships or fieldwork, institutionally sponsored loans, scholarships/grants, and unspecified assistantships also available. Support available to part-time students. Financial award application deadline: 4/1; financial award applicants required to submit FAFSA. *Faculty research:* Communication, control, and signal processing; devices, circuits, and systems; energy and sustainability; high performance embedded computing; power systems. *Total annual research expenditures:* $1.6 million. *Unit head:* Dr. Ian Ferguson, Chair, 704-687-8404, Fax: 704-687-4762, E-mail: ianf@uncc.edu. *Application contact:* Kathy B. Giddings, Director of Graduate Admissions, 704-687-5503, Fax: 704-687-1668, E-mail: gradadm@uncc.edu.
Website: http://coe.uncc.edu/students/prospective/graduate.htm.

University of North Texas, Robert B. Toulouse School of Graduate Studies, Denton, TX 76203-5459. Offers accounting (MS); applied anthropology (MA, MS); applied behavior analysis (Certificate); applied geography (MA); applied technology and performance improvement (M Ed, MS); art education (MA); art history (MA); art museum education (Certificate); arts leadership (Certificate); audiology (Au D); behavior analysis (MS); behavioral science (PhD); biochemistry and molecular biology (MS); biology (MA, MS); biomedical engineering (MS); business analysis (MS); chemistry (MS); clinical health psychology (PhD); communication studies (MA, MS); computer engineering (MS); computer science (MS); counseling (M Ed, MS), including clinical mental health counseling (MS), college and university counseling, elementary school counseling, secondary school counseling; creative writing (MA); criminal justice (MS); curriculum and instruction (M Ed); decision sciences (MBA); design (MA, MFA), including fashion design (MFA), innovation studies, interior design (MFA); early childhood studies (MS); economics (MS); educational leadership (M Ed, Ed D); educational psychology (MS, PhD), including family studies (MS), gifted and talented (MS), human development (MS), learning and cognition (MS), research, measurement and evaluation (MS); electrical engineering (MS); emergency management (MPA); engineering technology (MS); English (MA); English as a second language (MA); environmental science (MS); finance (MBA, MS); financial management (MPA); French (MA); health services management (MBA); higher education (M Ed, Ed D); history (MA, MS); hospitality management (MS); human resources management (MPA); information science (MS); information systems (PhD); information technologies (MBA); interdisciplinary studies (MA, MS); international studies (MA); international sustainable tourism (MS); jazz studies (MM); journalism (MA, MJ, Graduate Certificate), including interactive and virtual digital communication (Graduate Certificate), narrative journalism (Graduate Certificate), public relations (Graduate Certificate); kinesiology (MS); linguistics (MA); local government management (MPA); logistics (PhD); logistics and supply chain management (MBA); long-term care, senior housing, and aging services (MA); management (PhD); marketing

(MBA); mathematics (MA, MS); mechanical and energy engineering (MS, PhD); music (MA), including ethnomusicology, music theory, musicology, performance; music composition (PhD); music education (MM Ed, PhD); nonprofit management (MPA); operations and supply chain management (MBA); performance (MM, DMA); philosophy (MA); political science (MA); professional and technical communication (MA); radio, television and film (MA, MFA); rehabilitation counseling (Certificate); sociology (MA); Spanish (MA); special education (M Ed); speech-language pathology (MA); strategic management (MBA); studio art (MFA); teaching (M Ed); MBA/MS. Part-time and evening/weekend programs available. Postbaccalaureate distance learning degree programs offered. *Faculty:* 651 full-time (215 women), 233 part-time/adjunct (139 women). *Students:* 3,040 full-time (1,598 women), 3,401 part-time (2,097 women); includes 1,740 minority (533 Black or African American, non-Hispanic/Latino; 15 American Indian or Alaska Native, non-Hispanic/Latino; 286 Asian, non-Hispanic/Latino; 746 Hispanic/Latino; 3 Native Hawaiian or other Pacific Islander, non-Hispanic/Latino; 157 Two or more races, non-Hispanic/Latino), 1,145 international. Terminal master's awarded for partial completion of doctoral program. *Degree requirements:* For master's, variable foreign language requirement, comprehensive exam (for some programs), thesis (for some programs); for doctorate, variable foreign language requirement, comprehensive exam (for some programs), thesis/dissertation; for other advanced degree, variable foreign language requirement, comprehensive exam (for some programs). *Entrance requirements:* For master's and doctorate, GRE, GMAT. Additional exam requirements/recommendations for international students: Required—TOEFL (minimum score 550 paper-based; 79 iBT). *Application deadline:* For fall admission, 7/15 for domestic students, 3/15 for international students; for spring admission, 11/15 for domestic students, 9/15 for international students; for summer admission, 5/1 for domestic students. Applications are processed on a rolling basis. Application fee: $60. Electronic applications accepted. *Expenses:* Tuition, state resident: full-time $5450; part-time $3633 per year. Tuition, nonresident: full-time $11,966; part-time $7977 per year. *Required fees:* $1301; $398 per credit hour. $685 per semester. Tuition and fees vary according to program and reciprocity agreements. *Financial support:* Fellowships with partial tuition reimbursements, research assistantships with partial tuition reimbursements, teaching assistantships, career-related internships or fieldwork, Federal Work-Study, institutionally sponsored loans, scholarships/grants, health care benefits, and library assistantships available. Support available to part-time students. Financial award applicants required to submit FAFSA. *Unit head:* Mark Wardell, Dean, 940-565-2383, E-mail: mark.wardell@unt.edu. *Application contact:* Toulouse School of Graduate Studies, 940-565-2383, Fax: 940-565-2141, E-mail: gradsch@unt.edu.
Website: http://tsgs.unt.edu/.

University of Notre Dame, Graduate School, College of Engineering, Department of Computer Science and Engineering, Notre Dame, IN 46556. Offers MSCSE, PhD. Terminal master's awarded for partial completion of doctoral program. *Degree requirements:* For master's, comprehensive exam; for doctorate, thesis/dissertation, candidacy exam. *Entrance requirements:* For master's and doctorate, GRE General Test. Additional exam requirements/recommendations for international students: Required—TOEFL (minimum score 600 paper-based; 80 iBT). Electronic applications accepted. *Faculty research:* Algorithms and theory of computer science, artificial intelligence, behavior-based robotics, biometrics, computer vision.

University of Oklahoma, Gallogly College of Engineering, School of Electrical and Computer Engineering, Program in Electrical and Computer Engineering, Norman, OK 73019. Offers MS, PhD. Part-time programs available. *Students:* 102 full-time (19 women), 35 part-time (8 women); includes 16 minority (2 Black or African American, non-Hispanic/Latino; 1 American Indian or Alaska Native, non-Hispanic/Latino; 4 Asian, non-Hispanic/Latino; 5 Hispanic/Latino; 1 Native Hawaiian or other Pacific Islander, non-Hispanic/Latino; 3 Two or more races, non-Hispanic/Latino), 83 international. Average age 28. 137 applicants, 32% accepted, 22 enrolled. In 2014, 23 master's, 10 doctorates awarded. Terminal master's awarded for partial completion of doctoral program. *Degree requirements:* For master's, comprehensive exam (for some programs), thesis (for some programs); for doctorate, thesis/dissertation, general exam. *Entrance requirements:* For master's and doctorate, GRE, minimum GPA of 3.0. Additional exam requirements/ recommendations for international students: Required—TOEFL (minimum score 79 iBT). *Application deadline:* For fall admission, 4/1 for domestic students, 3/1 for international students; for spring admission, 11/1 for domestic students, 10/1 for international students. Application fee: $50 ($100 for international students). Electronic applications accepted. *Expenses:* Tuition, state resident: full-time $4394; part-time $183.10 per credit hour. Tuition, nonresident: full-time $16,970; part-time $707.10 per credit hour. *Required fees:* $2892; $109.95 per credit hour. $126.50 per semester. *Financial support:* In 2014–15, 119 students received support, including 2 fellowships with full tuition reimbursements available (averaging $2,500 per year); career-related internships or fieldwork, scholarships/grants, health care benefits, and unspecified assistantships also available. Financial award application deadline: 6/1; financial award applicants required to submit FAFSA. *Faculty research:* Biomedical imaging, radar engineering, semiconductor devices, intelligent transportation systems, signals and systems. *Unit head:* Dr. J.R. Cruz, Director, 405-325-8131, Fax: 405-325-7066, E-mail: jcruz@ou.edu. *Application contact:* Lisa Wilkins, Graduate Program Assistant, 405-325-4285, Fax: 405-325-7066, E-mail: lwikins@ou.edu.
Website: http://ece.ou.edu.

University of Ottawa, Faculty of Graduate and Postdoctoral Studies, Faculty of Engineering, Ottawa-Carleton Institute for Electrical and Computer Engineering, Ottawa, ON K1N 6N5, Canada. Offers M Eng, MA Sc, PhD. *Degree requirements:* For master's, thesis or alternative, project; for doctorate, comprehensive exam, thesis/dissertation. *Entrance requirements:* For master's, honors degree or equivalent, minimum B average; for doctorate, minimum A- average. Electronic applications accepted. *Faculty research:* CAD, distributed systems.

University of Pittsburgh, Swanson School of Engineering, Computer Engineering Program, Pittsburgh, PA 15260. Offers MS, PhD. *Faculty:* 15 full-time (2 women). *Students:* 7 full-time (0 women); includes 2 minority (both Black or African American, non-Hispanic/Latino), 3 international. Average age 27. 147 applicants, 1% accepted, 1 enrolled. In 2014, 1 master's, 2 doctorates awarded. Terminal master's awarded for partial completion of doctoral program. *Degree requirements:* For master's, thesis; for doctorate, comprehensive exam, thesis/dissertation, preliminary exams. *Entrance requirements:* For master's and doctorate, GRE General Test. Additional exam requirements/recommendations for international students: Required—TOEFL (minimum score 90 iBT). *Application deadline:* For fall admission, 1/15 priority date for domestic and international students. Applications are processed on a rolling basis. Application fee: $50. Electronic applications accepted. *Expenses:* Tuition, state resident: full-time $20,742; part-time $838 per credit. Tuition, nonresident: full-time $33,960; part-time $1389 per credit. *Required fees:* $800; $205 per term. Tuition and fees vary according to program. *Financial support:* In 2014–15, fellowships (averaging $18,700 per year), 1 research assistantship with full tuition reimbursement (averaging $17,900 per year), 1 teaching assistantship with full tuition reimbursement (averaging $16,300 per year) were awarded; health care benefits also available. Support available to part-time students. Financial award application deadline: 1/15. *Faculty research:* Computer architecture, high performance parallel and distributed systems, electronic design automation,

reconfigurable computing systems and wireless networks. *Unit head:* Dr. Donald M. Chiarulli, Co-Director, 412-624-8839, Fax: 412-624-5249, E-mail: don@cs.pitt.edu. *Application contact:* Keena M. Walker, Graduate Secretary, 412-624-8495, Fax: 412-624-8854, E-mail: keena@cs.pitt.edu.
Website: http://www.engineering.pitt.edu/computer/.

University of Puerto Rico, Mayagüez Campus, Graduate Studies, College of Engineering, Department of Electrical and Computer Engineering, Mayagüez, PR 00681-9000. Offers computer engineering (ME, MS); computing and information sciences and engineering (PhD); electrical engineering (ME, MS). Part-time programs available. *Faculty:* 43 full-time (5 women). *Students:* 70 full-time (8 women), 7 part-time (0 women). 36 applicants, 83% accepted, 18 enrolled. In 2014, 13 master's awarded. *Degree requirements:* For master's, comprehensive exam, thesis; for doctorate, comprehensive exam, thesis/dissertation. *Entrance requirements:* For master's, proficiency in English and Spanish, BS in electrical or computer engineering or equivalent, minimum GPA of 3.0; for doctorate, GRE. *Application deadline:* For fall admission, 2/15 for domestic and international students; for spring admission, 9/15 for domestic and international students. Applications are processed on a rolling basis. Application fee: $25. *Expenses:* Tuition, area resident: Full-time $2466; part-time $822 per credit. *International tuition:* $6371 full-time. *Required fees:* $1095; $1095 per year. Tuition and fees vary according to course level, course load and reciprocity agreements. *Financial support:* In 2014–15, 54 students received support, including 32 research assistantships (averaging $7,499 per year), 32 teaching assistantships (averaging $7,614 per year); fellowships with full tuition reimbursements available, Federal Work-Study, institutionally sponsored loans, and unspecified assistantships also available. *Faculty research:* Microcomputer interfacing, control systems, power systems, electronics. *Unit head:* Dr. Pedro Rivera, Chairperson, 787-832-4040 Ext. 3821, E-mail: p.rivera@upr.edu. *Application contact:* Sandra Montalvo, Administrative Staff, 787-832-4040 Ext. 3094, Fax: 787-831-7564, E-mail: sandra@ece.uprm.edu.
Website: http://www.ece.uprm.edu.

University of Regina, Faculty of Graduate Studies and Research, Faculty of Engineering and Applied Science, Program in Electronic Systems Engineering, Regina, SK S4S 0A2, Canada. Offers M Eng, MA Sc, PhD. Part-time programs available. *Faculty:* 39 full-time (7 women), 24 part-time/adjunct (0 women). *Students:* 45 full-time (10 women), 1 part-time (0 women). 161 applicants, 32% accepted. In 2014, 15 master's awarded. *Degree requirements:* For master's, thesis, project, report; for doctorate, thesis/dissertation. *Entrance requirements:* For doctorate, master's degree. Additional exam requirements/recommendations for international students: Required—TOEFL (minimum score 550 paper-based; 80 iBT), IELTS (minimum score 6.5), PTE (minimum score 59). *Application deadline:* For fall admission, 3/31 for domestic and international students; for winter admission, 7/31 for domestic and international students; for spring admission, 11/30 for domestic and international students. Application fee: $100. Electronic applications accepted. *Expenses: Expenses:* $2,588.85 per semester of full time study (M Eng); $1,633.35 (for MA Sc); $1,755.60 (for PhD). *Financial support:* In 2014–15, 8 fellowships (averaging $6,250 per year), 8 teaching assistantships (averaging $2,457 per year) were awarded; research assistantships, career-related internships or fieldwork, and scholarships/grants also available. Financial award application deadline: 6/15. *Faculty research:* Local area networks, digital and data communications systems design, telecommunications and computer networks, image processing, radio frequency (RF) and microwave engineering. *Unit head:* Dr. Rapahel Idem, Associate Dean, Research and Graduate Studies, 306-585-4470, Fax: 306-585-4855, E-mail: raphael.idem@uregina.ca. *Application contact:* Dr. Lei Zhang, Graduate Coordinator, 306-337-2588, Fax: 306-585-4855, E-mail: lei.zhang@uregina.ca.
Website: http://www.uregina.ca/engineering/.

University of Rhode Island, Graduate School, College of Engineering, Department of Electrical, Computer and Biomedical Engineering, Kingston, RI 02881. Offers MS, PhD, Graduate Certificate. Part-time programs available. *Faculty:* 20 full-time (2 women). *Students:* 30 full-time (6 women), 25 part-time (4 women); includes 4 minority (1 Black or African American, non-Hispanic/Latino; 2 Asian, non-Hispanic/Latino; 1 Hispanic/Latino), 23 international. In 2014, 18 master's, 2 doctorates awarded. *Degree requirements:* For master's, comprehensive exam (for some programs), thesis optional; for doctorate, comprehensive exam, thesis/dissertation. *Entrance requirements:* For master's and doctorate, GRE, 2 letters of recommendation (3 for international applicants). Additional exam requirements/recommendations for international students: Required—TOEFL (minimum score 550 paper-based). *Application deadline:* For fall admission, 7/15 for domestic students, 2/1 for international students; for spring admission, 11/15 for domestic students, 7/15 for international students. Application fee: $65. Electronic applications accepted. *Expenses:* Tuition, state resident: full-time $11,532; part-time $641 per credit. Tuition, nonresident: full-time $23,606; part-time $1311 per credit. *Required fees:* $1442; $39 per credit. $35 per semester. One-time fee: $155. *Financial support:* In 2014–15, 6 research assistantships with full and partial tuition reimbursements (averaging $8,108 per year), 4 teaching assistantships with full and partial tuition reimbursements (averaging $8,093 per year) were awarded. Financial award application deadline: 7/15; financial award applicants required to submit FAFSA. *Faculty research:* Biomedical instrumentation, cardiac physiology and computational modeling, analog/digital CMOS circuits, neural-machine interface, digital circuit design and VLSI testing. *Total annual research expenditures:* $2.2 million. *Unit head:* Dr. Godi Fischer, Chair, 401-874-5879, Fax: 401-782-6422, E-mail: fischer@ele.uri.edu. *Application contact:* Dr. Frederick J. Vetter, Graduate Director, 401-874-5141, Fax: 401-874-6422, E-mail: fred@uri.edu.
Website: http://www.ele.uri.edu/.

University of Rochester, Hajim School of Engineering and Applied Sciences, Department of Electrical and Computer Engineering, Rochester, NY 14627. Offers MS, PhD. *Faculty:* 20 full-time (1 woman). *Students:* 140 full-time (35 women), 3 part-time (1 woman); includes 8 minority (3 Black or African American, non-Hispanic/Latino; 3 Asian, non-Hispanic/Latino; 2 Hispanic/Latino), 115 international. 605 applicants, 36% accepted, 45 enrolled. In 2014, 53 master's, 15 doctorates awarded. Terminal master's awarded for partial completion of doctoral program. *Degree requirements:* For master's, comprehensive exam; for doctorate, thesis/dissertation, preliminary and oral exams. *Entrance requirements:* For master's and doctorate, GRE. Additional exam requirements/recommendations for international students: Required—TOEFL. *Application deadline:* For fall admission, 1/15 for domestic students. Application fee: $60. *Expenses: Tuition:* Full-time $46,150; part-time $1442 per credit hour. *Required fees:* $504. *Financial support:* Fellowships, research assistantships, teaching assistantships, and tuition waivers (full and partial) available. Financial award application deadline: 2/1. *Faculty research:* Bio-informatics, communications, digital audio, image processing, medical imaging. *Unit head:* Mark Bocko, Chair, 585-275-4879. *Application contact:* Barbara Dick, Administrative Assistant/Academic Coordinator, 585-275-5719.
Website: http://www.ece.rochester.edu/graduate/index.html.

University of Rochester, Hajim School of Engineering and Applied Sciences, Master of Science in Technical Entrepreneurship and Management Program, Rochester, NY 14642. Offers biomedical engineering (MS); chemical engineering (MS); computer science (MS); electrical and computer engineering (MS); energy and the environment

(MS); materials science (MS); mechanical engineering (MS); optics (MS). Program offered in collaboration with the Simon School of Business. Part-time programs available. *Students:* 36 full-time (12 women), 7 part-time (1 woman); includes 3 minority (2 Hispanic/Latino; 1 Two or more races, non-Hispanic/Latino), 33 international. Average age 24. 152 applicants, 68% accepted, 27 enrolled. In 2014, 28 master's awarded. *Degree requirements:* For master's, comprehensive exam. *Entrance requirements:* For master's, GRE or GMAT, 3 letters of recommendation; personal statement; official transcript; bachelor's degree (or equivalent for international students) in engineering, science, or mathematics. Additional exam requirements/recommendations for international students: Required—TOEFL or IELTS. *Application deadline:* For fall admission, 2/1 for domestic and international students. Applications are processed on a rolling basis. Application fee: $60. Electronic applications accepted. *Expenses: Tuition:* Full-time $46,150; part-time $1442 per credit hour. *Required fees:* $504. *Financial support:* Career-related internships or fieldwork and scholarships/grants available. Financial award application deadline: 2/1. *Faculty research:* High efficiency solar cells, macromolecular self-assembly, digital signal processing, memory hierarchy management, molecular and physical mechanisms in cell migration, optical imaging systems. *Unit head:* Duncan T. Moore, Vice Provost for Entrepreneurship, 585-275-5248, Fax: 585-473-6745, E-mail: moore@optics.rochester.edu. *Application contact:* Andrea M. Galati, Executive Director, 585-276-3407, Fax: 585-276-2357, E-mail: andrea.galati@rochester.edu.
Website: http://www.rochester.edu/team.

University of South Carolina, The Graduate School, College of Engineering and Computing, Department of Computer Science and Engineering, Columbia, SC 29208. Offers computer science and engineering (ME, MS, PhD); software engineering (MS). Part-time and evening/weekend programs available. Postbaccalaureate distance learning degree programs offered (minimal on-campus study). *Degree requirements:* For master's, comprehensive exam, thesis (for some programs); for doctorate, comprehensive exam, thesis/dissertation. *Entrance requirements:* For master's and doctorate, GRE General Test. Additional exam requirements/recommendations for international students: Required—TOEFL (minimum score 570 paper-based). Electronic applications accepted. *Faculty research:* Computer security, computer vision, artificial intelligence, multiagent systems, bioinformatics.

University of Southern California, Graduate School, Viterbi School of Engineering, Department of Computer Science, Los Angeles, CA 90089. Offers computer networks (MS); computer science (MS, PhD); computer security (MS); game development (MS); high performance computing and simulations (MS); human language technology (MS); intelligent robotics (MS); multimedia and creative technologies (MS); software engineering (MS). Part-time and evening/weekend programs available. Postbaccalaureate distance learning degree programs offered (no on-campus study). *Entrance requirements:* For master's and doctorate, GRE General Test. Additional exam requirements/recommendations for international students: Required—TOEFL. Electronic applications accepted. *Faculty research:* Databases, computer graphics and computer vision, software engineering, networks and security, robotics, multimedia and virtual reality.

University of Southern California, Graduate School, Viterbi School of Engineering, Ming Hsieh Department of Electrical Engineering, Los Angeles, CA 90089. Offers computer engineering (MS, PhD); electric power (MS); electrical engineering (MS, PhD, Engr); engineering technology commercialization (Graduate Certificate); multimedia and creative technologies (MS); telecommunications (MS); VLSI design (MS); wireless health technology (MS). Part-time programs available. Postbaccalaureate distance learning degree programs offered (no on-campus study). Terminal master's awarded for partial completion of doctoral program. *Degree requirements:* For master's, thesis optional; for doctorate, thesis/dissertation. *Entrance requirements:* For master's and doctorate, GRE General Test. Additional exam requirements/recommendations for international students: Recommended—TOEFL. Electronic applications accepted. *Faculty research:* Communications, computer engineering and networks, control systems, integrated circuits and systems, electromagnetics and energy conversion, micro electro-mechanical systems and nanotechnology, photonics and quantum electronics, plasma research, signal and image processing.

University of South Florida, College of Engineering, Department of Computer Science and Engineering, Tampa, FL 33620-9951. Offers computer engineering (MSCP); computer science (MSCS); computer science and engineering (PhD). Part-time programs available. *Faculty:* 18 full-time (3 women). *Students:* 116 full-time (29 women), 30 part-time (7 women); includes 15 minority (2 Black or African American, non-Hispanic/Latino; 5 Asian, non-Hispanic/Latino; 8 Hispanic/Latino), 91 international. Average age 27. 504 applicants, 27% accepted, 45 enrolled. In 2014, 30 master's, 7 doctorates awarded. Terminal master's awarded for partial completion of doctoral program. *Degree requirements:* For master's, comprehensive exam, thesis or alternative; for doctorate, comprehensive exam, thesis/dissertation, teaching of at least one undergraduate computer science and engineering course. *Entrance requirements:* For master's, GRE General Test, minimum GPA of 3.0 in last 60 hours of coursework, three letters of recommendation, statement of purpose; for doctorate, GRE General Test, minimum GPA of 3.0 in last 60 hours of coursework, three letters of recommendation, statement of purpose that includes three areas of research interest. Additional exam requirements/recommendations for international students: Required—TOEFL (minimum score 550 paper-based; 79 iBT) or IELTS (minimum score 6.5). *Application deadline:* For fall admission, 2/15 for domestic students, 1/2 for international students; for spring admission, 10/15 for domestic students, 6/1 for international students. Application fee: $30. Electronic applications accepted. *Financial support:* In 2014–15, 65 students received support, including 30 research assistantships with tuition reimbursements available (averaging $14,942 per year), 35 teaching assistantships with tuition reimbursements available (averaging $14,003 per year); unspecified assistantships also available. Financial award application deadline: 1/1; financial award applicants required to submit FAFSA. *Faculty research:* Artificial intelligence/intelligence systems; computational biology and bioinformatics; computer vision and pattern recognition; databases; distributed systems; graphics; information systems (networks) and location-aware information systems; robotics (biomorphic robotics and robot perception and action); software security; VLSI, computer architecture, and parallel processing. *Total annual research expenditures:* $1.4 million. *Unit head:* Dr. Lawrence Hall, Professor and Department Chair, 813-974-4195, Fax: 813-974-5094, E-mail: hall@cse.usf.edu. *Application contact:* Dr. Srivinas Katkoori, Associate Professor and Graduate Program Director, 813-974-5737, Fax: 813-974-5094, E-mail: katkoori@cse.usf.edu.
Website: http://www.cse.usf.edu/.

The University of Tennessee, Graduate School, College of Engineering, Department of Electrical Engineering and Computer Science, Program in Computer Engineering, Knoxville, TN 37966. Offers MS, PhD. Part-time programs available. *Faculty:* 10 full-time (2 women). *Students:* 28 full-time (4 women), 11 part-time (1 woman); includes 2 minority (both Asian, non-Hispanic/Latino), 24 international. Average age 27. 108 applicants, 13% accepted, 11 enrolled. In 2014, 7 master's, 4 doctorates awarded. *Degree requirements:* For master's, thesis or alternative; for doctorate, comprehensive exam, thesis/dissertation. *Entrance requirements:* For master's, GRE General Test (for MS students pursuing research thesis), minimum GPA of 2.7 (for U.S. degree holders), 3.0 (for international degree holders); 3 references; personal statement; for doctorate, GRE General Test (for all PhD candidates), minimum GPA of 3.0 on previous graduate course work; 3 references; personal statement. Additional exam requirements/recommendations for international students: Required—TOEFL (minimum score 550 paper-based). *Application deadline:* For fall admission, 2/1 priority date for domestic and international students; for spring admission, 6/15 for domestic and international students. Applications are processed on a rolling basis. Application fee: $35. Electronic applications accepted. *Financial support:* In 2014–15, 28 students received support, including 15 research assistantships with full tuition reimbursements available (averaging $21,455 per year), 11 teaching assistantships with full tuition reimbursements available (averaging $17,873 per year); fellowships with full tuition reimbursements available, career-related internships or fieldwork, Federal Work-Study, institutionally sponsored loans, health care benefits, and unspecified assistantships also available. Financial award application deadline: 2/1; financial award applicants required to submit FAFSA. *Unit head:* Dr. Leon Tolbert, Head, 865-974-3461, Fax: 865-974-5483, E-mail: tolbert@utk.edu. *Application contact:* Dr. Lynne E. Parker, Associate Head, 865-974-4394, Fax: 865-974-5483, E-mail: parker@eecs.utk.edu.
Website: http://www.eecs.utk.edu.

The University of Texas at Arlington, Graduate School, College of Engineering, Department of Computer Science and Engineering, Arlington, TX 76019. Offers computer engineering (MS, PhD); computer science (MS, PhD); mathematical sciences, computer science (PhD); software engineering (MS). Part-time programs available. Postbaccalaureate distance learning degree programs offered (minimal on-campus study). Terminal master's awarded for partial completion of doctoral program. *Degree requirements:* For master's, comprehensive exam (for some programs), thesis; for doctorate, comprehensive exam, thesis/dissertation. *Entrance requirements:* For master's, GRE General Test, minimum GPA of 3.0 (3.2 in computer science-related classes); for doctorate, GRE General Test, minimum GPA of 3.5. Additional exam requirements/recommendations for international students: Required—TOEFL (minimum score 550 paper-based; 92 iBT), IELTS (minimum score 6.5). *Faculty research:* Algorithms, homeland security, mobile pervasive computing, high performance computing bioinformation.

The University of Texas at Austin, Graduate School, Cockrell School of Engineering, Department of Electrical and Computer Engineering, Austin, TX 78712-1111. Offers MS, PhD. Part-time programs available. *Entrance requirements:* For master's, GRE General Test, minimum GPA of 3.3 in upper-division course work; for doctorate, GRE General Test. Electronic applications accepted.

The University of Texas at Dallas, Erik Jonsson School of Engineering and Computer Science, Department of Electrical Engineering, Richardson, TX 75080. Offers computer engineering (MS, PhD); electrical engineering (MSEE, PhD); systems engineering and management (MS); telecommunications engineering (MSTE, PhD). Part-time and evening/weekend programs available. *Faculty:* 51 full-time (4 women), 5 part-time/adjunct (1 woman). *Students:* 756 full-time (186 women), 288 part-time (83 women); includes 89 minority (14 Black or African American, non-Hispanic/Latino; 44 Asian, non-Hispanic/Latino; 24 Hispanic/Latino; 7 Two or more races, non-Hispanic/Latino), 870 international. Average age 26. 3,191 applicants, 30% accepted, 363 enrolled. In 2014, 250 master's, 31 doctorates awarded. *Degree requirements:* For master's, thesis or major design project; for doctorate, thesis/dissertation. *Entrance requirements:* For master's, GRE General Test, minimum GPA of 3.0 in related bachelor's degree; for doctorate, GRE General Test, minimum GPA of 3.5. Additional exam requirements/recommendations for international students: Required—TOEFL (minimum score 550 paper-based). *Application deadline:* For fall admission, 7/15 for domestic students, 5/1 priority date for international students; for spring admission, 11/15 for domestic students, 9/1 priority date for international students. Applications are processed on a rolling basis. Application fee: $50 ($100 for international students). Electronic applications accepted. *Expenses:* Tuition, state resident: full-time $11,940; part-time $663 per credit. Tuition, nonresident: full-time $22,282; part-time $1238 per credit. *Financial support:* In 2014–15, 269 students received support, including 13 fellowships with partial tuition reimbursements available (averaging $5,598 per year), 129 research assistantships with partial tuition reimbursements available (averaging $17,609 per year), 80 teaching assistantships with partial tuition reimbursements available (averaging $17,480 per year); Federal Work-Study, institutionally sponsored loans, scholarships/grants, unspecified assistantships, and cooperative positions also available. Support available to part-time students. Financial award application deadline: 4/30; financial award applicants required to submit FAFSA. *Faculty research:* Semiconductor device manufacturing, photonics devices and systems, signal processing and language technology, nano-fabrication, energy efficient digital systems. *Unit head:* Dr. James L. Coleman, Department Head, 972-883-6755, Fax: 972-883-2710, E-mail: james.coleman@utdallas.edu. *Application contact:* Patricia Williams, Degree Plan Evaluator, 972-883-4315, Fax: 972-883-2710, E-mail: gradeeadvisors@utdallas.edu.
Website: http://www.ee.utdallas.edu.

The University of Texas at El Paso, Graduate School, College of Engineering, Department of Electrical and Computer Engineering, El Paso, TX 79968-0001. Offers computer engineering (MS); electrical and computer engineering (PhD); electrical engineering (MS). Part-time and evening/weekend programs available. Terminal master's awarded for partial completion of doctoral program. *Degree requirements:* For master's, thesis optional; for doctorate, thesis/dissertation. *Entrance requirements:* For master's, GRE General Test, minimum GPA of 3.0; for doctorate, GRE General Test, minimum graduate GPA of 3.0. Additional exam requirements/recommendations for international students: Required—TOEFL. Electronic applications accepted. *Faculty research:* Signal and image processing, computer architecture, fiber optics, computational electromagnetics, electronic displays and thin films.

The University of Texas at San Antonio, College of Engineering, Department of Electrical and Computer Engineering, San Antonio, TX 78249-0617. Offers advanced materials engineering (MS); computer engineering (MS); electrical engineering (MSEE, PhD). Part-time programs available. *Faculty:* 24 full-time (3 women), 1 part-time/adjunct (0 women). *Students:* 210 full-time (58 women), 101 part-time (21 women); includes 47 minority (3 Black or African American, non-Hispanic/Latino; 11 Asian, non-Hispanic/Latino; 28 Hispanic/Latino; 5 Two or more races, non-Hispanic/Latino), 218 international. Average age 26. 450 applicants, 86% accepted, 128 enrolled. In 2014, 45 master's, 8 doctorates awarded. Terminal master's awarded for partial completion of doctoral program. *Degree requirements:* For master's, comprehensive exam, thesis (for some programs); for doctorate, comprehensive exam, thesis/dissertation. *Entrance requirements:* For master's, GRE General Test, bachelor's degree in electrical or computer engineering from ABET-accredited institution of higher education or related field; minimum GPA of 3.0 on the last 60 semester credit hours of undergraduate studies; for doctorate, GRE General Test, master's degree or minimum GPA of 3.3 in last 60 semester credit hours of undergraduate level coursework in electrical engineering; statement of purpose. Additional exam requirements/recommendations for international students: Required—TOEFL (minimum score 550 paper-based; 79 iBT), IELTS (minimum score 6.5). *Application deadline:* For fall admission, 7/1 for domestic students, 4/1 for international students; for spring admission, 11/1 for domestic students,

9/1 for international students. Applications are processed on a rolling basis. Application fee: $45 ($80 for international students). Electronic applications accepted. *Expenses:* Tuition, state resident: full-time $4671; part-time $260 per credit hour. Tuition, nonresident: full-time $18,022; part-time $1001 per credit hour. *Financial support:* Unspecified assistantships available. Financial award application deadline: 3/31. *Faculty research:* Computer engineering, digital signal processing, systems and controls, communications, electronics materials and devices, electric power engineering. *Unit head:* Dr. Daniel Pack, Department Chair/Professor, 210-458-7076, Fax: 210-458-5947, E-mail: electrical.engineering@utsa.edu. *Application contact:* Graduate Advisor of Record, E-mail: graduate.ece@utsa.edu.
Website: http://ece.utsa.edu/.

University of Toronto, School of Graduate Studies, Faculty of Applied Science and Engineering, Department of Electrical and Computer Engineering, Toronto, ON M5S 2J7, Canada. Offers M Eng, MA Sc, PhD. Part-time programs available. *Degree requirements:* For master's, thesis (for some programs), oral thesis defense (MA Sc); for doctorate, thesis/dissertation, qualifying exam, thesis defense. *Entrance requirements:* For master's, four-year degree in electrical or computer engineering, minimum B average, 2 letters of reference; for doctorate, minimum B+ average, MA Sc in electrical or computer engineering, 2 letters of reference. Additional exam requirements/recommendations for international students: Required—TOEFL (minimum score 580 paper-based; 93 iBT). Electronic applications accepted.

The University of Tulsa, Graduate School, College of Engineering and Natural Sciences, Program in Computer Engineering, Tulsa, OK 74104. Offers PhD. Program jointly offered by the Department of Electrical and Computer Engineering and the Tandy School of Computer Science. *Faculty:* 11 full-time (1 woman). *Students:* 2 full-time (0 women). Average age 28. 2 applicants, 50% accepted, 1 enrolled. In 2014, 2 doctorates awarded. *Entrance requirements:* For doctorate, GRE General Test, baccalaureate or master's degree from accredited institutions in the United States or from recognized institution in another country; minimum GPA of 3.5 undergraduate, 3.0 graduate; letter of intent; three references. Additional exam requirements/recommendations for international students: Required—TOEFL (minimum score 550 paper-based; 80 iBT). *Application deadline:* For fall admission, 2/1 priority date for domestic and international students. Applications are processed on a rolling basis. Application fee: $55. Electronic applications accepted. *Expenses: Tuition:* Full-time $20,160; part-time $1120 per credit hour. *Required fees:* $6 per credit hour. Tuition and fees vary according to course level and course load. *Financial support:* Research assistantships, teaching assistantships, career-related internships or fieldwork, institutionally sponsored loans, health care benefits, and unspecified assistantships available. *Faculty research:* Integrated circuits, transistors, analog circuitry, operating systems, applications and user interfaces, embedded devices. *Unit head:* Dr. James Sorem, Dean, 918-631-2288, E-mail: james-sorem@utulsa.edu. *Application contact:* Dr. Sujeet Shenoi, Advisor, 918-631-3269, Fax: 918-631-2156, E-mail: sujeet@utulsa.edu.
Website: http://engineering.utulsa.edu/academics/electrical-and-computer-engineering/.

University of Victoria, Faculty of Graduate Studies, Faculty of Engineering, Department of Electrical and Computer Engineering, Victoria, BC V8W 2Y2, Canada. Offers M Eng, MA Sc, PhD. *Degree requirements:* For master's, thesis; for doctorate, thesis/dissertation, candidacy exam. *Entrance requirements:* For master's, GRE (recommended), bachelor's degree in engineering; for doctorate, GRE (recommended), master's degree. Additional exam requirements/recommendations for international students: Required—TOEFL (minimum score 575 paper-based), IELTS (minimum score 7). Electronic applications accepted. *Faculty research:* Communications and computers; electromagnetics, microwaves, and optics; electronics; power systems, signal processing, and control.

University of Virginia, School of Engineering and Applied Science, Department of Electrical and Computer Engineering, Program in Computer Engineering, Charlottesville, VA 22903. Offers ME, MS, PhD. Postbaccalaureate distance learning degree programs offered (no on-campus study). *Students:* 30 full-time (6 women); includes 1 minority (Black or African American, non-Hispanic/Latino), 20 international. Average age 25. 98 applicants, 12% accepted, 11 enrolled. In 2014, 5 doctorates awarded. Terminal master's awarded for partial completion of doctoral program. *Degree requirements:* For master's, thesis (for some programs); for doctorate, comprehensive exam, thesis/dissertation. *Entrance requirements:* For master's, GRE General Test, 3 letters of recommendation; for doctorate, GRE General Test, 3 letters of recommendation; essay. Additional exam requirements/recommendations for international students: Required—TOEFL (minimum score 650 paper-based; 90 iBT), IELTS (minimum score 7). *Application deadline:* For fall admission, 8/1 for domestic students, 4/1 for international students; for winter admission, 12/1 for domestic students, 8/1 for international students; for spring admission, 5/1 for domestic students, 1/1 for international students. Applications are processed on a rolling basis. Application fee: $60. Electronic applications accepted. *Expenses:* Tuition, state resident: full-time $14,164; part-time $349 per credit hour. Tuition, nonresident: full-time $23,722; part-time $1300 per credit hour. *Required fees:* $2514. *Financial support:* Fellowships, research assistantships, and teaching assistantships available. Financial award application deadline: 1/15; financial award applicants required to submit FAFSA. *Faculty research:* Computer architecture, VLSI, switching theory, operating systems, real-time and embedded systems, compiler, software systems and software engineering, fault-tolerant computing and reliability engineering. *Unit head:* Joanne Bechta Dugan, Director, 434-924-3198, Fax: 434-924-8818, E-mail: compe@virginia.edu. *Application contact:* Pamela M. Morris, Associate Dean for Research and Graduate Programs, 434-243-7683, Fax: 434-982-3044, E-mail: pamela@virginia.edu.
Website: http://www.cpe.virginia.edu/grads/.

University of Washington, Bothell, Program in Computing and Software Systems, Bothell, WA 98011-8246. Offers MS. Part-time and evening/weekend programs available. *Degree requirements:* For master's, comprehensive exam (for some programs), thesis optional. *Entrance requirements:* For master's, GRE. Additional exam requirements/recommendations for international students: Required—TOEFL (minimum score 580 paper-based; 92 iBT) or IELTS (minimum score 7). Electronic applications accepted. *Expenses:* Contact institution. *Faculty research:* Computer science, software engineering, computer graphics, parallel and distributed systems, computer vision.

University of Washington, Tacoma, Graduate Programs, Program in Computing and Software Systems, Tacoma, WA 98402-3100. Offers MS. Part-time programs available. *Degree requirements:* For master's, capstone project/thesis or 15 credits elective coursework. *Entrance requirements:* For master's, GRE, personal statement, resume, transcripts, 3 recommendations. Additional exam requirements/recommendations for international students: Required—TOEFL (minimum score 580 paper-based; 92 iBT), IELTS (minimum score 7). Electronic applications accepted. *Faculty research:* Data stream analysis, formal methods, data mining, robotic systems, software development processes.

University of Waterloo, Graduate Studies, Faculty of Engineering, Department of Electrical and Computer Engineering, Waterloo, ON N2L 3G1, Canada. Offers electrical and computer engineering (M Eng, MA Sc, PhD); electrical and computer engineering

(software engineering) (MA Sc). Part-time programs available. *Degree requirements:* For master's, research paper or thesis; for doctorate, comprehensive exam, thesis/dissertation. *Entrance requirements:* For master's, honors degree, minimum B+ average; for doctorate, master's degree, minimum A- average. Additional exam requirements/recommendations for international students: Required—TOEFL (minimum score 550 paper-based), TWE (minimum score 4). Electronic applications accepted. *Faculty research:* Communications, computers, systems and control, silicon devices, power engineering.

The University of Western Ontario, Faculty of Graduate Studies, Physical Sciences Division, Faculty of Engineering, London, ON N6A 5B8, Canada. Offers chemical and biochemical engineering (ME Sc, PhD); civil and environmental engineering (M Eng, ME Sc, PhD); electrical and computer engineering (M Eng, ME Sc, PhD); mechanical and materials engineering (M Eng, ME Sc, PhD). Part-time programs available. Terminal master's awarded for partial completion of doctoral program. *Degree requirements:* For master's, thesis; for doctorate, thesis/dissertation. *Entrance requirements:* For master's, minimum B average; for doctorate, minimum B+ average. *Faculty research:* Wind, geotechnical, chemical reactor engineering, applied electrostatics, biochemical engineering.

University of Wisconsin–Milwaukee, Graduate School, College of Engineering and Applied Science, Program in Engineering, Milwaukee, WI 53201-0413. Offers civil engineering (MS); electrical and computer engineering (MS); energy engineering (Certificate); engineering (PhD); engineering management (MS); engineering mechanics (MS); ergonomics (Certificate); industrial and management engineering (MS); manufacturing engineering (MS); materials engineering (MS); mechanical engineering (MS); MUP/MS. Part-time programs available. *Degree requirements:* For master's, comprehensive exam (for some programs), thesis or alternative; for doctorate, comprehensive exam, thesis/dissertation, internship. *Entrance requirements:* For master's, GRE, minimum GPA of 2.75; for doctorate, GRE, minimum GPA of 3.5. Additional exam requirements/recommendations for international students: Required—TOEFL (minimum score 550 paper-based; 79 iBT), IELTS (minimum score 6.5).

Villanova University, College of Engineering, Department of Electrical and Computer Engineering, Program in Computer Engineering, Villanova, PA 19085-1699. Offers computer architectures (Certificate); computer engineering (MSCPE); intelligent control systems (Certificate). Part-time and evening/weekend programs available. *Degree requirements:* For master's, thesis optional. *Entrance requirements:* For master's, GRE General Test (for applicants with degrees from foreign universities), BEE, minimum GPA of 3.0. Additional exam requirements/recommendations for international students: Required—TOEFL (minimum score 600 paper-based; 100 iBT). Electronic applications accepted. *Faculty research:* Expert systems, computer vision, neural networks, image processing, computer architectures.

Virginia Polytechnic Institute and State University, Graduate School, College of Engineering, Blacksburg, VA 24061. Offers aerospace engineering (ME, MS, PhD); biological systems engineering (ME, MS, PhD); biomedical engineering (MS, PhD); chemical engineering (ME, MS, PhD); civil engineering (ME, MS, PhD); computer engineering (ME, MS, PhD); computer science (MS, PhD); electrical engineering (ME, PhD); engineering education (PhD); engineering mechanics (ME, MS, PhD); environmental engineering (MS); environmental science and engineering (MS); industrial and systems engineering (ME, MS, PhD); materials science and engineering (ME, MS, PhD); mechanical engineering (ME, MS, PhD); mining and minerals engineering (PhD); mining engineering (ME, MS); nuclear engineering (MS, PhD); ocean engineering (MS); systems engineering (ME, MS). *Accreditation:* ABET (one or more programs are accredited). *Faculty:* 356 full-time (60 women), 3 part-time/adjunct (1 woman). *Students:* 1,700 full-time (398 women), 345 part-time (58 women); includes 213 minority (43 Black or African American, non-Hispanic/Latino; 1 American Indian or Alaska Native, non-Hispanic/Latino; 87 Asian, non-Hispanic/Latino; 58 Hispanic/Latino; 1 Native Hawaiian or other Pacific Islander, non-Hispanic/Latino; 23 Two or more races, non-Hispanic/Latino), 1,079 international. Average age 27. 5,228 applicants, 18% accepted, 471 enrolled. In 2014, 438 master's, 211 doctorates awarded. *Degree requirements:* For master's, comprehensive exam (for some programs), thesis (for some programs); for doctorate, comprehensive exam (for some programs), thesis/dissertation (for some programs). *Entrance requirements:* For master's and doctorate, GRE/GMAT (may vary by department). Additional exam requirements/recommendations for international students: Required—TOEFL (minimum score 550 paper-based). *Application deadline:* For fall admission, 8/1 for domestic students, 4/1 for international students; for spring admission, 1/1 for domestic students, 9/1 for international students. Applications are processed on a rolling basis. Application fee: $75. Electronic applications accepted. *Expenses:* Tuition, state resident: full-time $11,656; part-time $647.50 per credit hour. Tuition, nonresident: full-time $23,351; part-time $1297.25 per credit hour. *Required fees:* $2533; $465.75 per semester. Tuition and fees vary according to course load, campus/location and program. *Financial support:* In 2014–15, 148 fellowships with full tuition reimbursements (averaging $8,031 per year), 855 research assistantships with full tuition reimbursements (averaging $22,855 per year), 288 teaching assistantships with full tuition reimbursements (averaging $20,291 per year) were awarded. Financial award application deadline: 3/1; financial award applicants required to submit FAFSA. *Total annual research expenditures:* $90.5 million. *Unit head:* Dr. Richard C. Benson, Dean, 540-231-9752, Fax: 540-231-3031, E-mail: deaneng@vt.edu. *Application contact:* Linda Perkins, Executive Assistant, 540-231-9752, Fax: 540-231-3031, E-mail: lperkins@vt.edu.
Website: http://www.eng.vt.edu/.

Virginia Polytechnic Institute and State University, VT Online, Blacksburg, VA 24061. Offers advanced transportation systems (Certificate); aerospace engineering (MS); agricultural and life sciences (MSLFS); business information systems (Graduate Certificate); career and technical education (MS); civil engineering (MS); computer engineering (M Eng, MS); decision support systems (Graduate Certificate); eLearning leadership (MA); electrical engineering (M Eng, MS); engineering administration (MEA); environmental engineering (Certificate); environmental politics and policy (Graduate Certificate); environmental sciences and engineering (MS); foundations of political analysis (Graduate Certificate); health product risk management (Graduate Certificate); industrial and systems engineering (MS); information policy and society (Graduate Certificate); information security (Graduate Certificate); information technology (MIT); instructional technology (MA); integrative STEM education (MA Ed); liberal arts (Graduate Certificate); life sciences: health product risk management (MS); natural resources (MNR, Graduate Certificate); networking (Graduate Certificate); nonprofit and nongovernmental organization management (Graduate Certificate); ocean engineering (MS); political science (MA); security studies (Graduate Certificate); software development (Graduate Certificate). *Expenses:* Tuition, state resident: full-time $11,656; part-time $647.50 per credit hour. Tuition, nonresident: full-time $23,351; part-time $1297.25 per credit hour. *Required fees:* $2533; $465.75 per semester. Tuition and fees vary according to course load, campus/location and program.

Washington State University, Voiland College of Engineering and Architecture, School of Electrical Engineering and Computer Science, Pullman, WA 99164-2752. Offers computer engineering (MS); computer science (MS); electrical engineering (MS); electrical engineering and computer science (PhD); electrical power engineering (MS).

MS programs in computer engineering, computer science and electrical engineering also offered at Tri-Cities campus; MS in electrical power engineering offered at the Global (online) campus. Part-time programs available. *Faculty:* 51 full-time (4 women), 4 part-time/adjunct (0 women). *Students:* 122 full-time (29 women), 49 part-time (12 women); includes 13 minority (1 Black or African American, non-Hispanic/Latino; 8 Asian, non-Hispanic/Latino; 3 Hispanic/Latino; 1 Native Hawaiian or other Pacific Islander, non-Hispanic/Latino), 108 international. Average age 28. 451 applicants, 16% accepted, 44 enrolled. In 2014, 24 master's, 11 doctorates awarded. *Degree requirements:* For master's, comprehensive exam (for some programs), thesis or alternative; for doctorate, comprehensive exam, thesis/dissertation. *Entrance requirements:* For master's and doctorate, GRE General Test, minimum GPA of 3.0, 3 letters of recommendation, statement of purpose, transcripts. Additional exam requirements/recommendations for international students: Required—TOEFL (minimum score 580 paper-based). *Application deadline:* For fall admission, 1/10 priority date for domestic students, 3/1 priority date for international students; for spring admission, 7/1 priority date for domestic and international students. Applications are processed on a rolling basis. Application fee: $75. *Expenses:* Tuition, state resident: full-time $11,768. Tuition, nonresident: full-time $25,200. *Required fees:* $960. Tuition and fees vary according to program. *Financial support:* In 2014–15, 74 students received support, including 5 fellowships (averaging $2,500 per year), 72 research assistantships with full and partial tuition reimbursements available (averaging $12,843 per year), 24 teaching assistantships with full and partial tuition reimbursements available (averaging $13,981 per year); career-related internships or fieldwork, Federal Work-Study, institutionally sponsored loans, tuition waivers (partial), and teaching associateships also available. Financial award application deadline: 4/1; financial award applicants required to submit FAFSA. *Faculty research:* Software engineering, networks, distributed computing, computer engineering, electrophysics, artificial intelligence, bioinformatics and computational biology, computer graphics, communications, control systems, signal processing, power systems, microelectronics, algorithms. *Total annual research expenditures:* $7.3 million. *Unit head:* Dr. Behrooz Shirazi, Chair/Director, 509-335-8148, Fax: 509-335-3818. *Application contact:* Sidra S. Gleason, Graduate Student Advisor, 509-335-6636, Fax: 509-335-1949, E-mail: gradsch@wsu.edu.
Website: http://www.eecs.wsu.edu/.

Washington University in St. Louis, School of Engineering and Applied Science, Department of Computer Science and Engineering, St. Louis, MO 63130-4899. Offers computer engineering (MS, PhD); computer science (MS, PhD); computer science and engineering (M Eng). Part-time programs available. Terminal master's awarded for partial completion of doctoral program. *Degree requirements:* For master's, thesis optional; for doctorate, thesis/dissertation. *Entrance requirements:* For doctorate, GRE General Test. Additional exam requirements/recommendations for international students: Required—TOEFL. Electronic applications accepted. *Faculty research:* Artificial intelligence, computational genomics, computer and systems architecture, media and machines, networking and communication, software systems.

Wayne State University, College of Engineering, Department of Electrical and Computer Engineering, Program in Computer Engineering, Detroit, MI 48202. Offers MS, PhD. *Students:* 34 full-time (6 women), 6 part-time (1 woman); includes 3 minority (2 Asian, non-Hispanic/Latino; 1 Hispanic/Latino), 34 international. Average age 27. 141 applicants, 40% accepted, 15 enrolled. In 2014, 5 master's, 6 doctorates awarded. *Degree requirements:* For master's, thesis optional; for doctorate, thesis/dissertation. *Entrance requirements:* For master's, BS from ABET-accredited college or university, or GRE, publications, and/or inventions. Additional exam requirements/recommendations for international students: Required—TOEFL (minimum score 550 paper-based; 79 iBT), TWE (minimum score 5.5), Michigan English Language Assessment Battery (minimum score 85); Recommended—IELTS (minimum score 6.5). *Application deadline:* For fall admission, 6/1 priority date for domestic students, 5/1 priority date for international students; for winter admission, 10/1 priority date for domestic students, 9/1 priority date for international students; for spring admission, 2/1 priority date for domestic students, 1/1 priority date for international students. Applications are processed on a rolling basis. Application fee: $0. Electronic applications accepted. *Expenses:* Expenses: Contact institution. *Financial support:* In 2014–15, 22 students received support. Fellowships with tuition reimbursements available, research assistantships with tuition reimbursements available, teaching assistantships with tuition reimbursements available, scholarships/grants, health care benefits, and unspecified assistantships available. Financial award application deadline: 3/31; financial award applicants required to submit FAFSA. *Faculty research:* Neural networks, parallel processing, pattern recognition, VLSI, computer architecture. *Unit head:* Dr. Cheng-Zhong Xu, Department Chair, 313-577-3856, E-mail: czxu@wayne.edu. *Application contact:* Dr. Nabil J. Sarhan, Graduate Program Director, 313-577-3920, E-mail: nabil@ece.eng.wayne.edu.
Website: http://engineering.wayne.edu/ece/.

Western Michigan University, Graduate College, College of Engineering and Applied Sciences, Department of Electrical and Computer Engineering, Kalamazoo, MI 49008. Offers computer engineering (MSE); electrical and computer engineering (PhD); electrical engineering (MSE). Part-time programs available. *Degree requirements:* For master's, thesis optional. *Application deadline:* For fall admission, 2/15 for domestic students. *Financial support:* Application deadline: 2/15. *Application contact:* Admissions and Orientation, 269-387-2000, Fax: 269-387-2096.

West Virginia University, College of Engineering and Mineral Resources, Lane Department of Computer Science and Electrical Engineering, Program in Computer Engineering, Morgantown, WV 26506. Offers PhD. *Degree requirements:* For doctorate, comprehensive exam, thesis/dissertation. *Entrance requirements:* For doctorate, GRE General Test, minimum GPA of 3.0, letters of recommendation. Additional exam requirements/recommendations for international students: Required—TOEFL. *Faculty research:* Software engineering, microprocessor applications, microelectronic systems, fault tolerance, advanced computer architectures and networks.

Wichita State University, Graduate School, College of Engineering, Department of Electrical Engineering and Computer Science, Wichita, KS 67260. Offers computer networking (MS); computer science (MS); electrical engineering (MS); electrical engineering and computer science (PhD). Part-time and evening/weekend programs available. *Unit head:* Dr. John Watkins, Chair, 316-978-3156, Fax: 316-978-5408, E-mail: john.watkins@wichita.edu. *Application contact:* Jordan Oleson, Admissions Coordinator, 316-978-3095, Fax: 316-978-3253, E-mail: jordan.oleson@wichita.edu.
Website: http://www.wichita.edu/eecs.

Widener University, Graduate Programs in Engineering, Program in Computer and Software Engineering, Chester, PA 19013-5792. Offers M Eng. Part-time and evening/weekend programs available. *Degree requirements:* For master's, thesis optional. *Faculty research:* Computer and software engineering, computer network fault-tolerant computing, optical computing.

Worcester Polytechnic Institute, Graduate Studies and Research, Department of Electrical and Computer Engineering, Worcester, MA 01609-2280. Offers electrical and computer engineering (Advanced Certificate, Graduate Certificate); electrical engineering (M Eng, MS, PhD). Part-time and evening/weekend programs available. *Faculty:* 17 full-time (0 women), 20 part-time/adjunct (2 women). *Students:* 184 full-time (37 women), 116 part-time (17 women); includes 30 minority (4 Black or African American, non-Hispanic/Latino; 17 Asian, non-Hispanic/Latino; 6 Hispanic/Latino; 3 Two or more races, non-Hispanic/Latino), 159 international. 707 applicants, 35% accepted, 90 enrolled. In 2014, 73 master's, 9 doctorates awarded. Terminal master's awarded for partial completion of doctoral program. *Degree requirements:* For master's, thesis optional; for doctorate, comprehensive exam, thesis/dissertation. *Entrance requirements:* For master's, GRE, 3 letters of recommendation; for doctorate, GRE, 3 letters of recommendation, statement of purpose. Additional exam requirements/recommendations for international students: Required—TOEFL (minimum score 563 paper-based; 84 iBT), IELTS (minimum score 7). *Application deadline:* For fall admission, 1/1 priority date for domestic students, 1/1 for international students; for spring admission, 10/1 priority date for domestic students, 10/1 for international students. Applications are processed on a rolling basis. Application fee: $70. Electronic applications accepted. *Financial support:* Research assistantships, teaching assistantships, career-related internships or fieldwork, institutionally sponsored loans, scholarships/grants, and unspecified assistantships available. Financial award application deadline: 1/1; financial award applicants required to submit FAFSA. *Unit head:* Dr. Yehia Massoud, Department Head, 508-831-5231, Fax: 508-831-5491, E-mail: massoud@wpi.edu. *Application contact:* Dr. Kaveh Pahlavan, Graduate Coordinator, 508-831-5231, Fax: 508-831-5491, E-mail: kaveh@wpi.edu.
Website: http://www.wpi.edu/academics/ece.

Wright State University, School of Graduate Studies, College of Engineering and Computer Science, Department of Computer Science and Engineering, Computer Engineering Program, Dayton, OH 45435. Offers MSCE. *Degree requirements:* For master's, thesis optional. *Entrance requirements:* For master's, GRE General Test, minimum GPA of 3.0 in major, 2.7 overall. Additional exam requirements/recommendations for international students: Required—TOEFL. *Faculty research:* Networking and digital communications, parallel and concurrent computing, robotics and control, computer vision, optical computing.

Wright State University, School of Graduate Studies, College of Engineering and Computer Science, Department of Computer Science and Engineering, Program in Computer Science and Engineering, Dayton, OH 45435. Offers PhD. *Degree requirements:* For doctorate, thesis/dissertation, candidacy and general exams. *Entrance requirements:* For doctorate, GRE General Test, minimum GPA of 3.3. Additional exam requirements/recommendations for international students: Required—TOEFL.

Youngstown State University, Graduate School, College of Science, Technology, Engineering and Mathematics, Department of Electrical and Computer Engineering, Youngstown, OH 44555-0001. Offers computer engineering (MSE); electrical engineering (MSE). Part-time and evening/weekend programs available. *Degree requirements:* For master's, thesis optional. *Entrance requirements:* For master's, minimum GPA of 2.75 in field. Additional exam requirements/recommendations for international students: Required—TOEFL. *Faculty research:* Computer-aided design, power systems, electromagnetic energy conversion, sensors, control systems.

Electrical Engineering

Air Force Institute of Technology, Graduate School of Engineering and Management, Department of Electrical and Computer Engineering, Dayton, OH 45433-7765. Offers computer engineering (MS, PhD); computer systems/science (MS); electrical engineering (MS, PhD); electro-optics (MS, PhD). *Accreditation:* ABET (one or more programs are accredited). Part-time programs available. *Degree requirements:* For master's, thesis; for doctorate, thesis/dissertation. *Entrance requirements:* For master's and doctorate, GRE General Test, minimum GPA of 3.0, U.S. citizenship. *Faculty research:* Remote sensing, information survivability, microelectronics, computer networks, artificial intelligence.

Alfred University, Graduate School, New York State College of Ceramics, Kazuo Inamori School of Engineering, Alfred, NY 14802. Offers biomaterials engineering (MS); ceramic engineering (MS); ceramics (PhD); electrical engineering (MS); glass science (MS, PhD); materials science and engineering (MS, PhD); mechanical engineering (MS). Part-time programs available. *Degree requirements:* For master's, thesis; for doctorate, thesis/dissertation. *Entrance requirements:* Additional exam requirements/recommendations for international students: Required—TOEFL (minimum score 590 paper-based; 90 iBT), IELTS (minimum score 6.5). Electronic applications accepted. *Expenses:* Contact institution. *Faculty research:* X-ray diffraction, biomaterials and polymers, thin-film processing, electronic and optical ceramics, solid-state chemistry.

American University of Beirut, Graduate Programs, Faculty of Engineering and Architecture, Beirut, Lebanon. Offers applied energy (ME); civil engineering (PhD); electrical and computer engineering (PhD); engineering management (MEM); environmental and water resources (ME); environmental technology (MSES); mechanical engineering (ME, PhD); urban design (MUD); urban planning and policy (MUPP). Part-time programs available. *Faculty:* 93 full-time (18 women), 3 part-time/adjunct (1 woman). *Students:* 268 full-time (111 women), 58 part-time (27 women). Average age 26. 225 applicants, 68% accepted, 79 enrolled. In 2014, 114 master's, 9 doctorates awarded. Terminal master's awarded for partial completion of doctoral program. *Degree requirements:* For master's, one foreign language, comprehensive exam, thesis (for some programs); for doctorate, one foreign language, comprehensive exam, thesis/dissertation, publications. *Entrance requirements:* For master's, letters of recommendation; for doctorate, GRE, letters of recommendation, master's degree, transcripts, curriculum vitae, interview. Additional exam requirements/recommendations for international students: Required—TOEFL (minimum score 600 paper-based; 100 iBT), IELTS (minimum score 7.5). *Application deadline:* For fall admission, 2/5 priority date for domestic and international students; for spring admission, 11/1 priority date for domestic students, 11/1 for international students. Application fee: $50. Electronic applications accepted. *Expenses: Tuition:* Full-time $15,462; part-time $859 per credit. *Required fees:* $692. Tuition and fees vary according to course load and program. *Financial support:* In 2014–15, 190 students received support, including 2 fellowships with full tuition reimbursements available (averaging $24,800 per year), 64 research assistantships with full tuition reimbursements available (averaging $24,800 per year),

124 teaching assistantships with full tuition reimbursements available (averaging $9,800 per year); career-related internships or fieldwork, institutionally sponsored loans, scholarships/grants, health care benefits, and unspecified assistantships also available. *Total annual research expenditures:* $1.5 million. *Unit head:* Prof. Makram T. Suidan, Dean, 961-1350000 Ext. 3400, Fax: 961-1744462, E-mail: msuidan@aub.edu.lb. *Application contact:* Dr. Salim Kanaan, Director, Admissions Office, 961-1350000 Ext. 2594, Fax: 961-1750775, E-mail: sk00@aub.edu.lb.
Website: http://staff.aub.edu.lb/~webfea.

American University of Sharjah, Graduate Programs, Sharjah, United Arab Emirates. Offers accounting (MS); business (EMBA, MBA); chemical engineering (MS Ch E); civil engineering (MSCE); computer engineering (MS); electrical engineering (MSEE); engineering systems management (MS); mathematics (MS); mechanical engineering (MSME); mechatronics engineering (MS); teaching English to speakers of other languages (MA); translation and interpreting (MA); urban planning (MUP). Part-time and evening/weekend programs available. *Degree requirements:* For master's, thesis (for some programs). *Entrance requirements:* For master's, GMAT (for MBA). Additional exam requirements/recommendations for international students: Required—TOEFL (minimum score 550 paper-based; 80 iBT), TWE (minimum score 5); Recommended—IELTS (minimum score 6.5). Electronic applications accepted. *Faculty research:* Water pollution, management and waste water treatment, energy and sustainability, air pollution, Islamic finance, family business and small and medium enterprises.

Arizona State University at the Tempe campus, Ira A. Fulton Schools of Engineering, School of Electrical, Computer and Energy Engineering, Tempe, AZ 85287-5706. Offers electrical engineering (MS, MSE, PhD); nuclear power generation (Graduate Certificate). Part-time and evening/weekend programs available. Postbaccalaureate distance learning degree programs offered (minimal on-campus study). Terminal master's awarded for partial completion of doctoral program. *Degree requirements:* For master's, thesis and defense (MS); comprehensive exams (MSE); interactive Program of Study (iPOS) submitted before completing 50 percent of required credit hours; for doctorate, comprehensive exam, thesis/dissertation, interactive Program of Study (iPOS) submitted before completing 50 percent of required credit hours. *Entrance requirements:* For master's, GRE, minimum GPA of 3.0 in last 2 years of work leading to bachelor's degree, 3.5 if from non-ABET accredited school; for doctorate, GRE, master's degree with minimum GPA of 3.5 or 3.6 in last 2 years of ABET-accredited undergraduate program. Additional exam requirements/recommendations for international students: Required—TOEFL, IELTS, or PTE. Electronic applications accepted. *Expenses:* Contact institution. *Faculty research:* Power and energy systems, signal processing and communications, solid state devices and modeling, wireless communications and circuits, photovoltaics, biosignatures discovery automation, flexible electronics, nanostructures.

Auburn University, Graduate School, Ginn College of Engineering, Department of Electrical and Computer Engineering, Auburn University, AL 36849. Offers MEE, MS, PhD. Part-time programs available. *Faculty:* 27 full-time (2 women), 4 part-time/adjunct (1 woman). *Students:* 158 full-time (40 women), 38 part-time (6 women); includes 5 minority (2 Black or African American, non-Hispanic/Latino; 1 American Indian or Alaska Native, non-Hispanic/Latino; 1 Asian, non-Hispanic/Latino; 1 Hispanic/Latino), 154 international. Average age 25. 412 applicants, 56% accepted, 59 enrolled. In 2014, 21 master's, 18 doctorates awarded. *Degree requirements:* For master's, comprehensive exam, thesis (for some programs); for doctorate, thesis/dissertation. *Entrance requirements:* For master's and doctorate, GRE General Test, GRE Subject Test. *Application deadline:* For fall admission, 7/7 for domestic students; for spring admission, 11/24 for domestic students. Applications are processed on a rolling basis. Application fee: $50 ($60 for international students). Electronic applications accepted. *Expenses:* Tuition, state resident: full-time $8586; part-time $477 per credit hour. Tuition, nonresident: full-time $25,758; part-time $1431 per credit hour. *Required fees:* $804 per semester. Tuition and fees vary according to degree level and program. *Financial support:* Fellowships, research assistantships, teaching assistantships, and Federal Work-Study available. Support available to part-time students. Financial award application deadline: 3/15; financial award applicants required to submit FAFSA. *Faculty research:* Power systems, energy conversion, electronics, electromagnetics, digital systems. *Unit head:* Dr. Mark Nelms, Head, 334-844-1830. *Application contact:* Dr. George Flowers, Dean of the Graduate School, 334-844-2125.
Website: http://www.eng.auburn.edu/department/ee/.

Baylor University, Graduate School, School of Engineering and Computer Science, Department of Electrical and Computer Engineering, Waco, TX 76798. Offers MS, PhD. *Entrance requirements:* Additional exam requirements/recommendations for international students: Required—TOEFL. Electronic applications accepted. *Faculty research:* Applied electromagnetics, power energy, communications, systems.

Binghamton University, State University of New York, Graduate School, Thomas J. Watson School of Engineering and Applied Science, Department of Electrical and Computer Engineering, Vestal, NY 13850. Offers M Eng, MS, PhD. Part-time and evening/weekend programs available. *Faculty:* 19 full-time (1 woman), 5 part-time/adjunct (1 woman). *Students:* 115 full-time (17 women), 101 part-time (11 women); includes 24 minority (3 Black or African American, non-Hispanic/Latino; 15 Asian, non-Hispanic/Latino; 4 Hispanic/Latino; 2 Native Hawaiian or other Pacific Islander, non-Hispanic/Latino), 139 international. Average age 27. 470 applicants, 56% accepted, 80 enrolled. In 2014, 54 master's, 6 doctorates awarded. *Degree requirements:* For master's, thesis (for some programs); for doctorate, comprehensive exam, thesis/dissertation. *Entrance requirements:* For master's and doctorate, GRE General Test. Additional exam requirements/recommendations for international students: Required—TOEFL (minimum score 550 paper-based; 80 iBT). *Application deadline:* For fall admission, 4/15 priority date for domestic students, 1/15 priority date for international students; for spring admission, 11/1 for domestic students, 10/1 priority date for international students. Applications are processed on a rolling basis. Application fee: $75. Electronic applications accepted. *Expenses:* Expenses: $5,435 resident; $11,105 non-resident. *Financial support:* In 2014–15, 51 students received support, including 28 research assistantships with full tuition reimbursements available (averaging $16,500 per year), 21 teaching assistantships with full tuition reimbursements available (averaging $16,500 per year); career-related internships or fieldwork, Federal Work-Study, institutionally sponsored loans, scholarships/grants, health care benefits, tuition waivers (full and partial), and unspecified assistantships also available. Financial award application deadline: 2/15; financial award applicants required to submit FAFSA. *Unit head:* Ellen Tilden, Coordinator of Graduate Programs, 607-777-2873, E-mail: etilden@binghamton.edu. *Application contact:* Kishan Zuber, Recruiting and Admissions Coordinator, 607-777-2151, Fax: 607-777-2501, E-mail: kzuber@binghamton.edu.

Boise State University, College of Engineering, Department of Electrical and Computer Engineering, Boise, ID 83725-0399. Offers computer engineering (M Engr, MS); electrical and computer engineering (PhD); electrical engineering (M Engr, MS). Part-time and evening/weekend programs available. *Faculty:* 14 full-time, 2 part-time/adjunct. *Students:* 28 full-time (4 women), 26 part-time (2 women); includes 9 minority (2 Black or African American, non-Hispanic/Latino; 6 Asian, non-Hispanic/Latino; 1 Two or more races, non-Hispanic/Latino), 13 international. 47 applicants, 51% accepted, 11 enrolled. In 2014, 18 master's, 1 doctorate awarded. *Degree requirements:* For master's, thesis. *Entrance requirements:* For master's, GRE General Test, minimum GPA of 3.0. Additional exam requirements/recommendations for international students: Required—TOEFL. *Application deadline:* Applications are processed on a rolling basis. Application fee: $55. Electronic applications accepted. *Expenses:* Tuition, state resident: part-time $331 per credit hour. Tuition, nonresident: part-time $531 per credit hour. *Financial support:* In 2014–15, 23 students received support, including 20 research assistantships, 2 teaching assistantships. Financial award application deadline: 3/1; financial award applicants required to submit FAFSA. *Unit head:* Dr. Nader Rafia, Department Chair, 208-426-3711, E-mail: nrafia@boisestate.edu. *Application contact:* Linda Platt, Office Services Supervisor, Graduate Admission and Degree Services, 208-426-1074, Fax: 208-426-2789, E-mail: lplatt@boisestate.edu.
Website: http://coen.boisestate.edu/ece/prospective-graduate/.

Boston University, College of Engineering, Department of Electrical and Computer Engineering, Boston, MA 02215. Offers electrical engineering (M Eng); photonics (MS). Part-time programs available. *Faculty:* 40 full-time (3 women), 5 part-time/adjunct (0 women). *Students:* 260 full-time (71 women), 60 part-time (14 women); includes 37 minority (1 Black or African American, non-Hispanic/Latino; 1 American Indian or Alaska Native, non-Hispanic/Latino; 23 Asian, non-Hispanic/Latino; 10 Hispanic/Latino; 2 Two or more races, non-Hispanic/Latino), 224 international. Average age 25. 1,121 applicants, 27% accepted, 158 enrolled. In 2014, 109 master's, 12 doctorates awarded. Terminal master's awarded for partial completion of doctoral program. *Degree requirements:* For master's, thesis (for some programs); for doctorate, comprehensive exam, thesis/dissertation. *Entrance requirements:* For master's and doctorate, GRE General Test. Additional exam requirements/recommendations for international students: Required—TOEFL (minimum score 550 paper-based; 84 iBT), IELTS (minimum score 7). *Application deadline:* For fall admission, 3/15 for domestic and international students; for spring admission, 10/1 for domestic and international students. Applications are processed on a rolling basis. Application fee: $80. Electronic applications accepted. *Expenses: Tuition:* Full-time $45,686; part-time $1428 per credit hour. *Required fees:* $660; $60 per semester. Tuition and fees vary according to program. *Financial support:* In 2014–15, 100 students received support, including 8 fellowships with full tuition reimbursements available (averaging $28,950 per year), 82 research assistantships with full tuition reimbursements available (averaging $19,300 per year), 18 teaching assistantships with full tuition reimbursements available (averaging $19,300 per year); career-related internships or fieldwork, Federal Work-Study, scholarships/grants, and tuition waivers (partial) also available. Financial award application deadline: 1/15; financial award applicants required to submit FAFSA. *Faculty research:* Communications and computer networks; signal, image, video, and multimedia processing; solid-state materials, devices, and photonics; systems, control, and reliable computing; VLSI, computer engineering and high-performance computing. *Unit head:* Dr. William C. Karl, Interim Chairman, 617-353-9880, Fax: 617-353-6440, E-mail: wckarl@bu.edu. *Application contact:* Dr. Solomon Eisenberg, Senior Associate Dean of Academic Programs, 617-353-9760, Fax: 617-353-0259, E-mail: enggrad@bu.edu.
Website: http://www.bu.edu/ece/.

Bradley University, Graduate School, College of Engineering and Technology, Department of Electrical and Computer Engineering, Peoria, IL 61625-0002. Offers MSEE. Part-time and evening/weekend programs available. *Faculty:* 9 full-time (0 women), 1 part-time/adjunct (0 women). *Students:* 26 full-time (12 women), 18 part-time (9 women), 41 international. 194 applicants, 34% accepted, 22 enrolled. In 2014, 14 master's awarded. *Degree requirements:* For master's, comprehensive exam. *Entrance requirements:* For master's, GRE, minimum GPA of 3.0. Additional exam requirements/recommendations for international students: Required—TOEFL (minimum score 550 paper-based; 79 iBT), IELTS (minimum score 6.5). *Application deadline:* For fall admission, 5/15 priority date for domestic and international students; for spring admission, 10/15 priority date for domestic and international students. Applications are processed on a rolling basis. Application fee: $40 ($50 for international students). Electronic applications accepted. *Expenses: Tuition:* Full-time $14,580; part-time $810 per credit. *Required fees:* $224. Full-time tuition and fees vary according to course load. *Financial support:* In 2014–15, 15 research assistantships with full and partial tuition reimbursements were awarded; teaching assistantships, scholarships/grants, tuition waivers (partial), and unspecified assistantships also available. Support available to part-time students. Financial award application deadline: 4/1. *Unit head:* In Soo Ahn, Department Chair, 309-677-2734, E-mail: isa@bradley.edu. *Application contact:* Kayla Carroll, Director of International Admissions and Student Services, 309-677-2375, E-mail: klcarroll@fsmail.bradley.edu.

Brigham Young University, Graduate Studies, Ira A. Fulton College of Engineering and Technology, Department of Electrical and Computer Engineering, Provo, UT 84602. Offers MS, PhD. *Faculty:* 23 full-time (0 women). *Students:* 69 full-time (5 women); includes 7 minority (6 Asian, non-Hispanic/Latino; 1 Hispanic/Latino), 15 international. Average age 27. 56 applicants, 75% accepted, 24 enrolled. In 2014, 25 master's, 2 doctorates awarded. *Degree requirements:* For master's, thesis; for doctorate, comprehensive exam, thesis/dissertation. *Entrance requirements:* For master's and doctorate, GRE General Test, minimum GPA of 3.2 in last 60 hours of course work. Additional exam requirements/recommendations for international students: Required—TOEFL (minimum score 580 paper-based; 85 iBT). *Application deadline:* For fall admission, 1/15 for domestic and international students; for winter admission, 8/15 for domestic and international students. Application fee: $50. Electronic applications accepted. *Expenses: Tuition:* Full-time $6310; part-time $371 per credit hour. Tuition and fees vary according to program and student's religious affiliation. *Financial support:* In 2014–15, 4 students received support, including 4 fellowships with full tuition reimbursements available (averaging $17,400 per year), 41 research assistantships with full tuition reimbursements available (averaging $21,000 per year), 6 teaching assistantships with full tuition reimbursements available (averaging $19,000 per year); scholarships/grants also available. Financial award application deadline: 5/15; financial award applicants required to submit FAFSA. *Faculty research:* Microwave earth remote sensing, configurable computing and embedded systems, MEMS semiconductors, integrated electro-optics, multiple-agent intelligent coordinated control systems for unmanned air vehicles. *Total annual research expenditures:* $2.7 million. *Unit head:* Dr. Brent E. Nelson, Chair, 801-422-4012, Fax: 801-422-0201, E-mail: nelson@ee.byu.edu. *Application contact:* Janalyn L. Mergist, Graduate Secretary, 801-422-4013, Fax: 801-422-0201, E-mail: janalyn@ee.byu.edu.
Website: http://www.ee.byu.edu/.

Brown University, Graduate School, School of Engineering, Program in Electrical Sciences and Computer Engineering, Providence, RI 02912. Offers Sc M, PhD. *Degree requirements:* For doctorate, thesis/dissertation, preliminary exam.

Bucknell University, Graduate Studies, College of Engineering, Department of Electrical Engineering, Lewisburg, PA 17837. Offers MSEE. Part-time programs available. *Degree requirements:* For master's, thesis. *Entrance requirements:* For master's, GRE General Test, minimum GPA of 3.0. Additional exam requirements/recommendations for international students: Required—TOEFL (minimum score 600 paper-based).

Electrical Engineering

California Institute of Technology, Division of Engineering and Applied Science, Option in Electrical Engineering, Pasadena, CA 91125-0001. Offers MS, PhD, Engr. *Degree requirements:* For doctorate, thesis/dissertation. Electronic applications accepted. *Faculty research:* Solid-state electronics, power electronics, communications, controls, submillimeter-wave integrated circuits.

California Polytechnic State University, San Luis Obispo, College of Engineering, Department of Electrical Engineering, San Luis Obispo, CA 93407. Offers MS. Part-time programs available. *Faculty:* 15 full-time (4 women). *Students:* 53 full-time (9 women), 11 part-time (0 women); includes 22 minority (1 Black or African American, non-Hispanic/Latino; 8 Asian, non-Hispanic/Latino; 10 Hispanic/Latino; 3 Two or more races, non-Hispanic/Latino), 10 international. Average age 24. 62 applicants, 52% accepted, 23 enrolled. In 2014, 27 master's awarded. *Degree requirements:* For master's, comprehensive exam (for some programs), thesis (for some programs). *Application deadline:* For fall admission, 4/1 for domestic and international students; for winter admission, 11/1 for domestic students, 6/30 for international students; for spring admission, 2/1 for domestic students. Applications are processed on a rolling basis. Application fee: $55. Electronic applications accepted. *Expenses:* Tuition, state resident: full-time $6738; part-time $3906 per year. Tuition, nonresident: full-time $15,666; part-time $8370 per year. *Required fees:* $3447; $1001 per quarter. One-time fee: $3447 full-time; $3003 part-time. *Financial support:* Fellowships, research assistantships, teaching assistantships, career-related internships or fieldwork, Federal Work-Study, scholarships/grants, and unspecified assistantships available. Support available to part-time students. Financial award application deadline: 3/2; financial award applicants required to submit FAFSA. *Faculty research:* Communications, systems design and analysis, control systems, electronic devices, microprocessors. *Unit head:* Dr. Jane Zhang, Graduate Coordinator, 805-756-7528, Fax: 805-756-1458, E-mail: jzhang@calpoly.edu. *Application contact:* Dr. James Maraviglia, Associate Vice Provost for Marketing and Enrollment Development, 805-756-2311, Fax: 805-756-5400, E-mail: admissions@calpoly.edu.
Website: http://www.ee.calpoly.edu/.

California State Polytechnic University, Pomona, Program in Electrical Engineering, Pomona, CA 91768-2557. Offers MSEE. *Students:* 21 full-time (5 women), 78 part-time (10 women); includes 46 minority (1 Black or African American, non-Hispanic/Latino; 1 American Indian or Alaska Native, non-Hispanic/Latino; 30 Asian, non-Hispanic/Latino; 13 Hispanic/Latino; 1 Two or more races, non-Hispanic/Latino), 20 international. Average age 26. 114 applicants, 58% accepted, 39 enrolled. In 2014, 14 master's awarded. *Application deadline:* Applications are processed on a rolling basis. Application fee: $55. Electronic applications accepted. *Expenses:* Tuition, state resident: full-time $6738. Tuition, nonresident: full-time $12,300. *Required fees:* $1400. *Unit head:* Dr. Halima M. El Naga, Graduate Coordinator, 909-869-2515, Fax: 909-869-4687, E-mail: helnaga@cpp.edu.
Website: http://www.cpp.edu/~ece/msee.

California State University, Chico, Office of Graduate Studies, College of Engineering, Computer Science, and Technology, Electrical and Computer Engineering Department, Option in Electronic Engineering, Chico, CA 95929-0722. Offers MS. *Students:* 12 full-time (2 women), 7 part-time (0 women); includes 1 minority (Hispanic/Latino), 17 international. Average age 23. 67 applicants, 64% accepted, 11 enrolled. In 2014, 9 master's awarded. *Degree requirements:* For master's, thesis or project plan. *Entrance requirements:* For master's, GRE General Test, 2 letters of recommendation, statement of purpose, resume. Additional exam requirements/recommendations for international students: Required—TOEFL (minimum score 550 paper-based; 80 iBT), IELTS (minimum score 6.5), PTE (minimum score 59). *Application deadline:* For fall admission, 3/1 priority date for domestic students, 3/1 for international students; for spring admission, 9/15 priority date for domestic students, 9/15 for international students. Application fee: $55. Electronic applications accepted. *Expenses:* Tuition, state resident: full-time $7002. Tuition, nonresident: full-time $18,162. *Required fees:* $1530. Tuition and fees vary according to program. *Unit head:* Dr. Larry L. Wear, Interim Chair, 530-898-5343, Fax: 530-898-4956, E-mail: elce@csuchico.edu. *Application contact:* Judy L. Rice, Graduate Admissions Coordinator, 530-898-5416, Fax: 530-898-3342, E-mail: jlrice@csuchico.edu.
Website: https://catalog.csuchico.edu/viewer/12/ENGR/ELCENONEMS.html.

California State University, Fresno, Division of Graduate Studies, College of Engineering and Computer Science, Program in Electrical Engineering, Fresno, CA 93740-8027. Offers MS. Offered at Edwards Air Force Base. Part-time and evening/weekend programs available. *Degree requirements:* For master's, thesis or alternative. *Entrance requirements:* For master's, GRE General Test, minimum GPA of 2.7. Additional exam requirements/recommendations for international students: Required—TOEFL. Electronic applications accepted. *Faculty research:* Research in electromagnetic devices.

California State University, Fullerton, Graduate Studies, College of Engineering and Computer Science, Department of Electrical Engineering, Fullerton, CA 92834-9480. Offers electrical engineering (MS); systems engineering (MS). Part-time programs available. *Students:* 126 full-time (24 women), 168 part-time (37 women); includes 33 minority (4 Black or African American, non-Hispanic/Latino; 20 Asian, non-Hispanic/Latino; 7 Hispanic/Latino; 2 Two or more races, non-Hispanic/Latino), 238 international. Average age 24. 513 applicants, 78% accepted, 164 enrolled. In 2014, 35 master's awarded. *Degree requirements:* For master's, comprehensive exam, project or thesis. *Entrance requirements:* For master's, GRE General Test, GRE Subject Test, minimum undergraduate GPA of 2.5, 3.0 graduate. Application fee: $55. *Financial support:* Career-related internships or fieldwork, Federal Work-Study, institutionally sponsored loans, and scholarships/grants available. Support available to part-time students. Financial award application deadline: 3/1; financial award applicants required to submit FAFSA. *Unit head:* Dr. Mostafa Shiva, Chair, 657-278-3013. *Application contact:* Admissions/Applications, 657-278-2371.

California State University, Long Beach, Graduate Studies, College of Engineering, Department of Electrical Engineering, Long Beach, CA 90840. Offers MSEE. Part-time programs available. *Degree requirements:* For master's, comprehensive exam or thesis. *Entrance requirements:* Additional exam requirements/recommendations for international students: Required—TOEFL. Electronic applications accepted. *Faculty research:* Health care systems, VLSI, communications, CAD/CAM.

California State University, Los Angeles, Graduate Studies, College of Engineering, Computer Science, and Technology, Department of Electrical and Computer Engineering, Los Angeles, CA 90032-8530. Offers electrical engineering (MS). Part-time and evening/weekend programs available. *Degree requirements:* For master's, comprehensive exam or thesis. *Entrance requirements:* For master's, GRE General Test, GRE Subject Test. Additional exam requirements/recommendations for international students: Required—TOEFL (minimum score 550 paper-based). Electronic applications accepted. *Expenses:* Tuition, state resident: full-time $6738; part-time $3609 per year. Tuition, nonresident: full-time $15,666; part-time $8073 per year. Tuition and fees vary according to course load, degree level and program.

California State University, Northridge, Graduate Studies, College of Engineering and Computer Science, Department of Electrical and Computer Engineering, Northridge, CA

91330. Offers electrical engineering (MS). Part-time and evening/weekend programs available. *Students:* 87 full-time (17 women), 80 part-time (20 women); includes 18 minority (7 Asian, non-Hispanic/Latino; 8 Hispanic/Latino; 1 Native Hawaiian or other Pacific Islander, non-Hispanic/Latino; 2 Two or more races, non-Hispanic/Latino), 105 international. Average age 27. *Degree requirements:* For master's, thesis or alternative. *Entrance requirements:* For master's, GRE General Test, minimum GPA of 2.75. Additional exam requirements/recommendations for international students: Required—TOEFL. *Application deadline:* For fall admission, 11/30 for domestic students. Application fee: $55. *Expenses: Required fees:* $12,402. *Financial support:* Application deadline: 3/1. *Faculty research:* Reflector antenna study. *Unit head:* Dr. Ali Amini, Chair, 818-677-2190, E-mail: ece@csun.edu. *Application contact:* Dr. Ali Amini, Graduate Coordinator, 818-677-2190, E-mail: ece@csun.edu.
Website: http://www.ecs.csun.edu/ece/index.html.

California State University, Sacramento, Office of Graduate Studies, College of Engineering and Computer Science, Department of Electrical and Electronic Engineering, Sacramento, CA 95819. Offers MS. Part-time and evening/weekend programs available. *Degree requirements:* For master's, thesis or comprehensive exam, writing proficiency exam. *Entrance requirements:* Additional exam requirements/recommendations for international students: Required—TOEFL. Electronic applications accepted.

Capitol Technology University, Graduate Programs, Laurel, MD 20708-9759. Offers business administration (MBA); computer science (MS); electrical engineering (MS); information and telecommunications systems management (MS); information architecture (MS); network security (MS). Part-time and evening/weekend programs available. Postbaccalaureate distance learning degree programs offered (no on-campus study). *Entrance requirements:* For master's, minimum GPA of 3.0. Electronic applications accepted.

Carleton University, Faculty of Graduate Studies, Faculty of Engineering and Design, Ottawa-Carleton Institute for Electrical Engineering, Department of Electronics, Ottawa, ON K1S 5B6, Canada. Offers electrical engineering (M Eng, MA Sc, PhD). *Degree requirements:* For master's, thesis optional; for doctorate, comprehensive exam, thesis/dissertation. *Entrance requirements:* For master's, honors degree; for doctorate, MA Sc or M Eng. Additional exam requirements/recommendations for international students: Required—TOEFL.

Carleton University, Faculty of Graduate Studies, Faculty of Engineering and Design, Ottawa-Carleton Institute for Electrical Engineering, Department of Systems and Computer Engineering, Ottawa, ON K1S 5B6, Canada. Offers electrical engineering (MA Sc, PhD); information and systems science (M Sc); technology innovation management (M Eng, MA Sc). PhD program offered jointly with University of Ottawa. *Degree requirements:* For master's, thesis optional. *Entrance requirements:* For master's, honors degree. Additional exam requirements/recommendations for international students: Required—TOEFL. *Faculty research:* Design manufacturing management; network design, protocols, and performance; software engineering; wireless and satellite communications.

Carnegie Mellon University, Carnegie Institute of Technology, Department of Electrical and Computer Engineering, Pittsburgh, PA 15213-3891. Offers MS, PhD. Part-time programs available. *Degree requirements:* For master's, thesis; for doctorate, thesis/dissertation, qualifying exam, teaching experience. *Entrance requirements:* For master's and doctorate, GRE General Test. Additional exam requirements/recommendations for international students: Required—TOEFL. *Faculty research:* Computer-aided design, solid-state devices, VLSI, processing, robotics and controls, signal processing, data systems storage.

Case Western Reserve University, School of Graduate Studies, Case School of Engineering, Department of Electrical Engineering and Computer Science, Cleveland, OH 44106. Offers computer engineering (MS, PhD); computing and information sciences (MS, PhD); electrical engineering (MS, PhD); systems and control engineering (MS, PhD). Part-time and evening/weekend programs available. Postbaccalaureate distance learning degree programs offered (minimal on-campus study). *Faculty:* 33 full-time (3 women). *Students:* 158 full-time (35 women), 18 part-time (5 women); includes 5 minority (1 Black or African American, non-Hispanic/Latino; 3 Asian, non-Hispanic/Latino; 1 Hispanic/Latino), 122 international. In 2014, 37 master's, 11 doctorates awarded. Terminal master's awarded for partial completion of doctoral program. *Degree requirements:* For master's, thesis; for doctorate, thesis/dissertation, qualifying exam, teaching experience. *Entrance requirements:* For master's and doctorate, GRE General Test. Additional exam requirements/recommendations for international students: Required—TOEFL. *Application deadline:* For fall admission, 2/1 for domestic students; for spring admission, 11/1 for domestic students. Applications are processed on a rolling basis. Application fee: $50. *Financial support:* In 2014–15, 51 research assistantships with full and partial tuition reimbursements, 10 teaching assistantships were awarded; fellowships with full and partial tuition reimbursements, career-related internships or fieldwork, Federal Work-Study, and institutionally sponsored loans also available. Support available to part-time students. Financial award application deadline: 3/1; financial award applicants required to submit FAFSA. *Faculty research:* Micro/nano systems; robotics and haptics, applied artificial intelligence; automation, computer-aided design and testing of digital systems. *Total annual research expenditures:* $6 million. *Unit head:* Dr. Kenneth Loparo, Department Chair, 216-368-4115, E-mail: kal4@case.edu. *Application contact:* Kimberly Yurchick, Student Affairs Specialist, 216-368-2920, Fax: 216-368-2801, E-mail: ksy4@case.edu.
Website: http://eecs.cwru.edu/.

The Catholic University of America, School of Engineering, Department of Electrical Engineering and Computer Science, Washington, DC 20064. Offers MEE, MSCS, PhD. Part-time programs available. *Faculty:* 12 full-time (2 women), 9 part-time/adjunct (3 women). *Students:* 13 full-time (5 women), 44 part-time (8 women); includes 9 minority (3 Black or African American, non-Hispanic/Latino; 3 Asian, non-Hispanic/Latino; 2 Hispanic/Latino; 1 Two or more races, non-Hispanic/Latino), 30 international. Average age 33. 56 applicants, 52% accepted, 13 enrolled. In 2014, 16 master's, 5 doctorates awarded. *Degree requirements:* For master's, thesis or alternative; for doctorate, comprehensive exam, thesis/dissertation, oral exams. *Entrance requirements:* For master's and doctorate, statement of purpose, official copies of academic transcripts, three letters of recommendation. Additional exam requirements/recommendations for international students: Required—TOEFL (minimum score 580 paper-based). *Application deadline:* For fall admission, 7/15 priority date for domestic students, 7/1 for international students; for spring admission, 11/15 priority date for domestic students, 11/1 for international students. Applications are processed on a rolling basis. Application fee: $55. Electronic applications accepted. *Expenses:* Expenses: Contact institution. *Financial support:* Fellowships, research assistantships, teaching assistantships, Federal Work-Study, scholarships/grants, tuition waivers (full and partial), and unspecified assistantships available. Financial award application deadline: 2/1; financial award applicants required to submit FAFSA. *Faculty research:* Signal and image processing, computer communications, robotics, intelligent controls, bioelectromagnetics. *Total annual research expenditures:* $216,563. *Unit head:* Dr. Ozlem Kilic, Chair, 202-319-5879, Fax: 202-319-5195, E-mail: regalia@cua.edu.

Application contact: Director of Graduate Admissions, 202-319-5057, Fax: 202-319-6533, E-mail: cua-admissions@cua.edu.
Website: http://eecs.cua.edu/.

City College of the City University of New York, Graduate School, Grove School of Engineering, Department of Electrical Engineering, New York, NY 10031-9198. Offers ME, MS, PhD. PhD program offered jointly with Graduate School and University Center of the City University of New York. Part-time programs available. *Degree requirements:* For master's, thesis optional; for doctorate, one foreign language, comprehensive exam, thesis/dissertation. *Entrance requirements:* For master's and doctorate, GRE General Test. Additional exam requirements/recommendations for international students: Required—TOEFL (minimum score 500 paper-based; 61 iBT). *Faculty research:* Optical electronics, microwaves, communication, signal processing, control systems.

Clarkson University, Graduate School, Wallace H. Coulter School of Engineering, Department of Electrical and Computer Engineering, Potsdam, NY 13699. Offers electrical and computer engineering (PhD); electrical engineering (ME, MS). Part-time programs available. *Faculty:* 17 full-time (3 women), 4 part-time/adjunct (1 woman). *Students:* 40 full-time (6 women), 3 part-time (0 women); includes 4 minority (1 Asian, non-Hispanic/Latino; 3 Hispanic/Latino), 22 international. Average age 29. 50 applicants, 60% accepted, 7 enrolled. In 2014, 14 master's, 2 doctorates awarded. Terminal master's awarded for partial completion of doctoral program. *Degree requirements:* For master's, thesis (for MS); project (for ME); for doctorate, comprehensive exam, thesis/dissertation, departmental qualifying exam. *Entrance requirements:* For master's and doctorate, GRE, transcripts of all college coursework, resume, personal statement, three letters of recommendation. Additional exam requirements/recommendations for international students: Required—TOEFL (minimum score 550 paper-based; 80 iBT), IELTS (minimum score 6.5). *Application deadline:* For fall admission, 1/30 priority date for domestic and international students; for spring admission, 9/1 priority date for domestic and international students. Applications are processed on a rolling basis. Application fee: $25 ($35 for international students). Electronic applications accepted. *Expenses: Tuition:* Full-time $16,680; part-time $1390 per credit. *Required fees:* $295 per semester. *Financial support:* In 2014–15, 31 students received support, including 2 fellowships with full tuition reimbursements available (averaging $24,029 per year), 15 research assistantships with full tuition reimbursements available (averaging $24,029 per year), 7 teaching assistantships with full tuition reimbursements available (averaging $24,029 per year); scholarships/grants, tuition waivers (partial), and unspecified assistantships also available. *Faculty research:* Under water imaging, polymer insulation, bioelectronic tongue, integrated circuits, biometric identification. *Total annual research expenditures:* $1.2 million. *Unit head:* Dr. William Jemison, Dean/Chair, 315-268-6511, Fax: 315-268-7600, E-mail: wjemison@clarkson.edu. *Application contact:* Kelly Sharlow, Assistant to the Dean, 315-268-7929, Fax: 315-268-4494, E-mail: ksharlow@clarkson.edu.
Website: http://www.clarkson.edu/ece/.

Clemson University, Graduate School, College of Engineering and Science, Department of Electrical and Computer Engineering, Program in Electrical Engineering, Clemson, SC 29634. Offers M Engr, MS, PhD. *Students:* 124 full-time (30 women), 12 part-time (3 women); includes 9 minority (2 Black or African American, non-Hispanic/Latino; 3 Asian, non-Hispanic/Latino; 3 Hispanic/Latino; 1 Two or more races, non-Hispanic/Latino), 101 international. Average age 26. 670 applicants, 17% accepted, 70 enrolled. In 2014, 25 master's, 12 doctorates awarded. *Degree requirements:* For master's, thesis or alternative; for doctorate, thesis/dissertation, departmental qualifying exam. *Entrance requirements:* For master's, GRE General Test (for MS); for doctorate, GRE General Test. Additional exam requirements/recommendations for international students: Required—TOEFL. *Application deadline:* For fall admission, 6/1 for domestic students, 4/15 for international students; for spring admission, 9/15 for international students. Applications are processed on a rolling basis. Application fee: $70 ($80 for international students). Electronic applications accepted. *Financial support:* In 2014–15, 72 students received support, including 19 fellowships with full and partial tuition reimbursements available (averaging $5,579 per year), 47 research assistantships with partial tuition reimbursements available (averaging $18,381 per year), 21 teaching assistantships with partial tuition reimbursements available (averaging $21,615 per year); career-related internships or fieldwork, institutionally sponsored loans, scholarships/grants, health care benefits, and unspecified assistantships also available. Support available to part-time students. Financial award applicants required to submit FAFSA. *Faculty research:* Microelectronics, robotics, signal processing/communications, power systems, control. *Unit head:* Dr. Darren Dawson, Chair, 864-656-5249, Fax: 864-656-5917, E-mail: ddarren@clemson.edu. *Application contact:* Dr. Daniel Noneaker, Coordinator, 864-656-0100, Fax: 864-656-5917, E-mail: ece-grad-program@ces.clemson.edu.
Website: http://www.clemson.edu/ces/departments/ece/index.html.

Cleveland State University, College of Graduate Studies, Fenn College of Engineering, Department of Electrical and Computer Engineering, Cleveland, OH 44115. Offers electrical engineering (MS, D Eng); software engineering (MS). Part-time and evening/weekend programs available. *Faculty:* 15 full-time (2 women), 1 part-time/adjunct (0 women). *Students:* 65 full-time (10 women), 211 part-time (39 women); includes 14 minority (3 Black or African American, non-Hispanic/Latino; 6 Asian, non-Hispanic/Latino; 2 Hispanic/Latino; 3 Two or more races, non-Hispanic/Latino), 216 international. Average age 25. 633 applicants, 40% accepted, 74 enrolled. In 2014, 71 master's, 2 doctorates awarded. Terminal master's awarded for partial completion of doctoral program. *Degree requirements:* For master's, thesis optional; for doctorate, comprehensive exam, thesis/dissertation, qualifying and candidacy exams. *Entrance requirements:* For master's, GRE General Test (minimum score 650 quantitative), minimum GPA of 2.75; for doctorate, GRE General Test (minimum quantitative score in 80th percentile), minimum GPA of 3.25. Additional exam requirements/recommendations for international students: Required—TOEFL (minimum score 535 paper-based; 65 iBT) or IELTS (minimum score 6.0). *Application deadline:* For fall admission, 7/15 priority date for domestic students, 5/5 for international students. Applications are processed on a rolling basis. Application fee: $30. *Expenses:* Expenses: Contact institution. *Financial support:* In 2014–15, 31 students received support, including 23 research assistantships with full and partial tuition reimbursements available (averaging $4,242 per year), 8 teaching assistantships with full and partial tuition reimbursements available (averaging $4,242 per year); career-related internships or fieldwork, scholarships/grants, and unspecified assistantships also available. *Faculty research:* Computer networks, computer security and privacy, mobile computing, distributed computing, software engineering, knowledge-based control systems, artificial intelligence, digital communications, MEMS, sensors, power systems, power electronics. *Total annual research expenditures:* $484,362. *Unit head:* Dr. Chansu Yu, Chairperson, 216-687-2584, Fax: 216-687-5405, E-mail: f.xiong@csuohio.edu. *Application contact:* Deborah L. Brown, Interim Assistant Director, Graduate Admissions, 216-523-7572, Fax: 216-687-9214, E-mail: d.l.brown@csuohio.edu.
Website: http://www.csuohio.edu/ece.

Colorado School of Mines, Graduate School, Department of Electrical Engineering and Computer Science, Golden, CO 80401. Offers computer science (MS, PhD); electrical engineering (MS, PhD). Part-time programs available. *Faculty:* 22 full-time (5

women), 8 part-time/adjunct (2 women). *Students:* 60 full-time (9 women), 22 part-time (3 women); includes 7 minority (1 Black or African American, non-Hispanic/Latino; 2 Asian, non-Hispanic/Latino; 3 Hispanic/Latino; 1 Two or more races, non-Hispanic/Latino), 31 international. Average age 30. 122 applicants, 58% accepted, 26 enrolled. In 2014, 43 master's, 9 doctorates awarded. *Degree requirements:* For master's, thesis (for some programs); for doctorate, comprehensive exam, thesis/dissertation. *Entrance requirements:* For master's and doctorate, GRE General Test. Additional exam requirements/recommendations for international students: Required—TOEFL (minimum score 550 paper-based; 80 iBT). *Application deadline:* For fall admission, 12/15 priority date for domestic and international students; for spring admission, 9/1 priority date for domestic and international students. Application fee: $50 ($70 for international students). Electronic applications accepted. *Financial support:* In 2014–15, 36 students received support, including 4 fellowships (averaging $21,120 per year), 19 research assistantships (averaging $21,120 per year), 7 teaching assistantships (averaging $21,120 per year); career-related internships or fieldwork, Federal Work-Study, institutionally sponsored loans, scholarships/grants, health care benefits, and unspecified assistantships also available. Financial award application deadline: 12/15; financial award applicants required to submit FAFSA. *Total annual research expenditures:* $1.4 million. *Unit head:* Dr. Randy Haupt, Head, 303-273-3721, E-mail: rhaupt@mines.edu. *Application contact:* Lori Sisneros, Graduate Program Administrator, 303-384-3658, E-mail: sisneros@mines.edu.
Website: http://eecs.mines.edu/.

Colorado State University, Graduate School, College of Engineering, Department of Electrical and Computer Engineering, Fort Collins, CO 80523-1373. Offers electrical engineering (MEE, MS, PhD). Part-time programs available. Postbaccalaureate distance learning degree programs offered (no on-campus study). *Faculty:* 25 full-time (4 women), 1 part-time/adjunct (0 women). *Students:* 117 full-time (28 women), 132 part-time (24 women); includes 12 minority (5 Asian, non-Hispanic/Latino; 4 Hispanic/Latino; 3 Two or more races, non-Hispanic/Latino), 181 international. Average age 29. 305 applicants, 55% accepted, 63 enrolled. In 2014, 34 master's, 9 doctorates awarded. Terminal master's awarded for partial completion of doctoral program. *Degree requirements:* For master's, comprehensive exam (for some programs), thesis (for some programs), final exam; for doctorate, comprehensive exam, thesis/dissertation, qualifying, preliminary, and final exams. *Entrance requirements:* For master's, GRE General Test, minimum GPA of 3.5, BA/BS from ABET-accredited institution, 3 letters of recommendation; for doctorate, GRE General Test, minimum GPA of 3.5, transcripts, 3 letters of recommendation, statement of purpose. Additional exam requirements/recommendations for international students: Required—TOEFL, IELTS. *Application deadline:* For fall admission, 2/1 for domestic and international students; for spring admission, 9/1 for domestic and international students. Applications are processed on a rolling basis. Application fee: $50. Electronic applications accepted. *Expenses:* Tuition, state resident: full-time $9348; part-time $519 per credit. Tuition, nonresident: full-time $22,916; part-time $1273 per credit. *Required fees:* $1584. *Financial support:* In 2014–15, 60 students received support, including 5 fellowships with tuition reimbursements available (averaging $42,669 per year), 44 research assistantships with full tuition reimbursements available (averaging $16,738 per year), 11 teaching assistantships with full tuition reimbursements available (averaging $8,727 per year); career-related internships or fieldwork, scholarships/grants, traineeships, health care benefits, and unspecified assistantships also available. Financial award application deadline: 2/1. *Faculty research:* Biomedical engineering, systems (communications and signal processing controls and robotics), computer engineering, electric power and energy systems, lasers/optics and electromagnetics/remote sensing. *Total annual research expenditures:* $13.2 million. *Unit head:* Dr. Anthony A. Maciejewski, Department Head, 970-491-6600, Fax: 970-491-2249, E-mail: aam@engr.colostate.edu. *Application contact:* Karen Ungerer, Coordinator, 970-491-0500, Fax: 970-491-2249, E-mail: karen.ungerer@colostate.edu.
Website: http://www.engr.colostate.edu/ece/.

Colorado Technical University Colorado Springs, Graduate Studies, Program in Electrical Engineering, Colorado Springs, CO 80907-3896. Offers MSEE. Part-time and evening/weekend programs available. Postbaccalaureate distance learning degree programs offered. *Degree requirements:* For master's, thesis or alternative. *Faculty research:* Electronic systems design, communication systems design.

Colorado Technical University Denver South, Program in Electrical Engineering, Aurora, CO 80014. Offers MS.

Columbia University, Fu Foundation School of Engineering and Applied Science, Department of Electrical Engineering, New York, NY 10027. Offers computer engineering (MS); electrical engineering (MS, Eng Sc D, PhD). PhD offered through the Graduate School of Arts and Sciences. Part-time programs available. Postbaccalaureate distance learning degree programs offered (no on-campus study). *Faculty:* 28 full-time (2 women), 40 part-time/adjunct (1 woman). *Students:* 342 full-time (76 women), 208 part-time (45 women); includes 50 minority (4 Black or African American, non-Hispanic/Latino; 37 Asian, non-Hispanic/Latino; 4 Hispanic/Latino; 5 Two or more races, non-Hispanic/Latino), 455 international. 1,559 applicants, 37% accepted, 230 enrolled. In 2014, 195 master's, 17 doctorates awarded. *Degree requirements:* For doctorate, thesis/dissertation, qualifying exam. *Entrance requirements:* For master's and doctorate, GRE General Test. Additional exam requirements/recommendations for international students: Required—TOEFL, IELTS, PTE. *Application deadline:* For fall admission, 12/15 priority date for domestic and international students; for spring admission, 10/1 priority date for domestic and international students. Application fee: $85. Electronic applications accepted. *Financial support:* In 2014–15, 109 students received support, including 17 fellowships with full tuition reimbursements available (averaging $32,447 per year), 67 research assistantships with full tuition reimbursements available (averaging $32,447 per year), 25 teaching assistantships with full tuition reimbursements available (averaging $32,447 per year); career-related internships or fieldwork, traineeships, and health care benefits also available. Financial award application deadline: 12/15; financial award applicants required to submit FAFSA. *Faculty research:* Media informatics and signal processing, integrated circuits and cyberphysical systems, communications systems and networking, nanoscale electronics and photonics, systems biology and neuroengineering. *Unit head:* Dr. Keren Bergman, Professor and Chair, 212-854-1744, Fax: 212-932-9421, E-mail: bergman@ee.columbia.edu. *Application contact:* Dr. Zoran Kostic, Associate Professor of Professional Practice/Director of the MS in Electrical Engineering Program, 212-851-0269, Fax: 212-932-9421, E-mail: zk2172@columbia.edu.
Website: http://www.ee.columbia.edu/.

Concordia University, School of Graduate Studies, Faculty of Engineering and Computer Science, Department of Electrical and Computer Engineering, Montréal, QC H3G 1M8, Canada. Offers M Eng, MA Sc, PhD. *Degree requirements:* For master's, thesis optional; for doctorate, comprehensive exam, thesis/dissertation. *Faculty research:* Computer communications and protocols, circuits and systems, graph theory, VLSI systems, microelectronics.

Cooper Union for the Advancement of Science and Art, Albert Nerken School of Engineering, New York, NY 10003-7120. Offers chemical engineering (ME); civil engineering (ME); electrical engineering (ME); mechanical engineering (ME). Part-time

Electrical Engineering

programs available. *Faculty:* 27 full-time (1 woman), 15 part-time/adjunct (2 women). *Students:* 45 full-time (10 women), 20 part-time (4 women); includes 24 minority (3 Black or African American, non-Hispanic/Latino; 15 Asian, non-Hispanic/Latino; 4 Hispanic/Latino; 2 Two or more races, non-Hispanic/Latino), 4 international. Average age 23. 86 applicants, 71% accepted, 44 enrolled. In 2014, 22 master's awarded. *Degree requirements:* For master's, thesis (for some programs). *Entrance requirements:* For master's, BE or BS in engineering discipline, high school and college transcripts, two letters of recommendation, resume. Additional exam requirements/recommendations for international students: Required—TOEFL (minimum score 600 paper-based; 100 iBT). *Application deadline:* For fall admission, 4/1 for domestic and international students. Application fee: $70. Electronic applications accepted. *Expenses: Tuition:* Full-time $39,600; part-time $1173 per credit. *Required fees:* $925 per semester. One-time fee: $250. *Financial support:* In 2014–15, 65 students received support, including 4 fellowships with full and partial tuition reimbursements available (averaging $11,000 per year); career-related internships or fieldwork, Federal Work-Study, tuition waivers (full and partial), and tuition scholarships offered to exceptional students also available. Support available to part-time students. Financial award application deadline: 5/1; financial award applicants required to submit FAFSA. *Faculty research:* Civil infrastructure, imaging and sensing technology, biomedical engineering, encryption technology, process engineering. *Unit head:* Dr. Teresa Dahlberg, Dean of Engineering, 212-353-4285, E-mail: dahlberg@cooper.edu. *Application contact:* Student Contact, 212-353-4120, E-mail: admissions@cooper.edu.
Website: http://cooper.edu/engineering.

Cornell University, Graduate School, Graduate Fields of Engineering, Field of Electrical and Computer Engineering, Ithaca, NY 14853. Offers computer engineering (M Eng, PhD); electrical engineering (M Eng, PhD); electrical systems (M Eng, PhD); electrophysics (M Eng, PhD). *Degree requirements:* For doctorate, comprehensive exam, thesis/dissertation. *Entrance requirements:* For master's, GRE General Test, 2 letters of recommendation; for doctorate, GRE General Test, 3 letters of recommendation. Additional exam requirements/recommendations for international students: Required—TOEFL (minimum score 600 paper-based; 77 iBT). Electronic applications accepted. *Faculty research:* Communications, information theory, signal processing and power control, computer engineering, microelectromechanical systems and nanotechnology.

Dalhousie University, Faculty of Engineering, Department of Electrical and Computer Engineering, Halifax, NS B3J 1Z1, Canada. Offers M Eng, MA Sc, PhD. *Degree requirements:* For master's, thesis; for doctorate, thesis/dissertation. *Entrance requirements:* Additional exam requirements/recommendations for international students: Required—TOEFL, IELTS, CANTEST, CAEL, or Michigan English Language Assessment Battery. Electronic applications accepted. *Faculty research:* Communications, computer engineering, power engineering, electronics, systems engineering.

DeVry University, Graduate Programs, Downers Grove, IL 60515. Offers accounting and financial management (MAFM); business administration (MBA); education (MS); educational technology (MS); electrical engineering (MS); human resources management (MHRM); information systems management (MISM); network and communications management (MNCM); project management (MPM); public administration (MPA).

Drexel University, College of Engineering, Department of Electrical and Computer Engineering, Program in Electrical Engineering, Philadelphia, PA 19104-2875. Offers MSEE. Part-time and evening/weekend programs available. Terminal master's awarded for partial completion of doctoral program. *Degree requirements:* For master's, thesis (for some programs). Electronic applications accepted.

Duke University, Graduate School, Pratt School of Engineering, Department of Electrical and Computer Engineering, Durham, NC 27708. Offers MS, PhD, JD/MS. *Faculty:* 28 full-time. *Students:* 225 full-time (51 women); includes 19 minority (3 Black or African American, non-Hispanic/Latino; 9 Asian, non-Hispanic/Latino; 7 Hispanic/Latino), 148 international. 679 applicants, 27% accepted, 65 enrolled. In 2014, 48 master's, 26 doctorates awarded. Terminal master's awarded for partial completion of doctoral program. *Degree requirements:* For doctorate, thesis/dissertation. *Entrance requirements:* For master's and doctorate, GRE General Test. Additional exam requirements/recommendations for international students: Required—TOEFL (minimum score 90 iBT), IELTS (minimum score 7). *Application deadline:* For fall admission, 12/8 priority date for domestic and international students; for spring admission, 10/15 for domestic students. Application fee: $80. Electronic applications accepted. *Expenses: Tuition:* Full-time $45,760; part-time $2765 per credit. *Required fees:* $978. Full-time tuition and fees vary according to program. *Financial support:* Fellowships, research assistantships, and Federal Work-Study available. Financial award application deadline: 12/8. *Faculty research:* Architecture and networking; biological applications circuits and systems; nanosystems, devices and materials; quantum computing and photonics; sensing and signals visualization; waves and metamaterials. *Unit head:* Krishnendu Chakrabarty, Director of Graduate Studies, 919-660-5245, Fax: 919-660-5293. *Application contact:* Duke Graduate School Admissions, 919-684-3913, Fax: 919-684-2277, E-mail: grad-admissions@duke.edu.
Website: http://www.ece.duke.edu/grad.

See Display on this page and Close-Up on page 397.

Duke University, Graduate School, Pratt School of Engineering, Master of Engineering Program, Durham, NC 27708-0271. Offers biomedical engineering (M Eng); civil engineering (M Eng); electrical and computer engineering (M Eng); environmental engineering (M Eng); materials science and engineering (M Eng); mechanical engineering (M Eng); photonics and optical sciences (M Eng). Part-time programs available. *Students:* 45 full-time (17 women); includes 5 minority (1 Black or African American, non-Hispanic/Latino; 2 Asian, non-Hispanic/Latino; 2 Hispanic/Latino), 23 international. Average age 24. 285 applicants, 43% accepted, 45 enrolled. In 2014, 45 master's awarded. *Entrance requirements:* For master's, GRE General Test, resume, 3 letters of recommendation, statement of purpose, transcripts. Additional exam requirements/recommendations for international students: Required—TOEFL. *Application deadline:* For fall admission, 6/15 for domestic students, 2/15 for international students; for spring admission, 11/1 for domestic students, 9/1 for international students. Application fee: $75. *Expenses: Tuition:* Full-time $45,760; part-time $2765 per credit. *Required fees:* $978. Full-time tuition and fees vary according to program. *Financial support:* Merit scholarships/grants available. *Unit head:* Dr. Bradley A. Fox, Executive Director, 919-660-5455, Fax: 919-660-5456. *Application contact:* Susan Brown, Assistant Director of Admissions, 919-660-8451, Fax: 919-660-5456, E-mail: susan.brown@duke.edu.
Website: http://meng.pratt.duke.edu/.

École Polytechnique de Montréal, Graduate Programs, Department of Electrical and Computer Engineering, Montréal, QC H3C 3A7, Canada. Offers automation (M Eng, M Sc A, PhD); computer science (M Eng, M Sc A, PhD); electrical engineering (DESS); electrotechnology (M Eng, M Sc A, PhD); microelectronics (M Eng, M Sc A, PhD); microwave technology (M Eng, M Sc A, PhD). Part-time and evening/weekend programs available. *Degree requirements:* For master's, one foreign language, thesis;

for doctorate, one foreign language, thesis/dissertation. *Entrance requirements:* For master's, minimum GPA of 2.75; for doctorate, minimum GPA of 3.0. *Faculty research:* Microwaves, telecommunications, software engineering.

Embry-Riddle Aeronautical University–Daytona, Department of Electrical, Computer, Software and Systems Engineering, Daytona Beach, FL 32114-3900. Offers cybersecurity engineering (MS); electrical and computer engineering (MSECE); software engineering (MSE); unmanned and autonomous systems engineering (MSUASE). MS in unmanned and autonomous systems engineering held jointly with Department of Electrical, Computer, Software and Systems Engineering. Part-time and evening/weekend programs available. *Faculty:* 13 full-time (0 women), 1 (woman) part-time/adjunct. *Students:* 56 full-time (15 women), 8 part-time (0 women); includes 6 minority (4 Black or African American, non-Hispanic/Latino; 1 Asian, non-Hispanic/Latino; 1 Hispanic/Latino), 41 international. Average age 25. 46 applicants, 61% accepted, 23 enrolled. In 2014, 16 master's awarded. *Degree requirements:* For master's, thesis or alternative, MS UASE students are required to complete a two-semester capstone project. *Entrance requirements:* For master's, Applicants to the MSE program are strongly encouraged to complete the GRE for this degree program; Applicants to the MSUASE program must complete the GRE; For consideration of fellowship and assistantship award programs offered by the Department of Computing, GRE scores are required., minimum CGPA of 3.0; course work in computer science. Additional exam requirements/recommendations for international students: Required—TOEFL (minimum score 550 paper-based; 79 iBT). *Application deadline:* For fall admission, 6/1 priority date for domestic and international students; for spring admission, 11/1 priority date for domestic students, 10/1 priority date for international students. Applications are processed on a rolling basis. Application fee: $50. Electronic applications accepted. *Expenses: Tuition:* Full-time $15,360; part-time $1280 per credit hour. *Required fees:* $1334. *Financial support:* In 2014–15, 24 students received support. Research assistantships with full and partial tuition reimbursements available, teaching assistantships with full and partial tuition reimbursements available, career-related internships or fieldwork, and unspecified assistantships available. Financial award application deadline: 4/15. *Faculty research:* Cybersecurity and assured systems engineering, radar, unmanned and autonomous systems, modeling and simulation, cyber-physical systems. *Unit head:* Dr. Timothy Wilson, Professor of Electrical and Computer Engineering and Chair, ECSSE Dept., 386-226-6994, E-mail: timothy.wilson@erau.edu. *Application contact:* International and Graduate Admissions, 800-388-3728, Fax: 386-226-7070, E-mail: graduate.admissions@erau.edu. Website: http://daytonabeach.erau.edu/college-engineering/electrical-computer-software-systems/index.html.

Fairfield University, School of Engineering, Fairfield, CT 06824. Offers automated manufacturing (CAS); database management (CAS); electrical and computer engineering (MS); information security (CAS); management of technology (MS); mechanical engineering (MS); network technology (CAS); software engineering (MS); Web application development (CAS). Part-time and evening/weekend programs available. *Faculty:* 4 full-time (1 woman), 18 part-time/adjunct (5 women). *Students:* 193 full-time (50 women), 69 part-time (11 women); includes 20 minority (4 Black or African American, non-Hispanic/Latino; 6 Asian, non-Hispanic/Latino; 10 Hispanic/Latino), 199 international. Average age 27. 516 applicants, 64% accepted, 124 enrolled. In 2014, 38 master's awarded. *Degree requirements:* For master's, thesis, capstone course. *Entrance requirements:* For master's, interview, minimum GPA of 2.8, resume, 2 recommendations. Additional exam requirements/recommendations for international students: Required—TOEFL (minimum score 550 paper-based; 80 iBT) or IELTS (minimum score 6.5). *Application deadline:* For fall admission, 5/15 for international students; for spring admission, 10/15 for international students. Applications are processed on a rolling basis. Application fee: $60. Electronic applications accepted. *Expenses:* Expenses: $750 per credit hour. *Financial support:* In 2014–15, 30 students received support. Scholarships/grants and unspecified assistantships available. Financial award applicants required to submit FAFSA. *Faculty research:* Ocean dynamics modeling, thermo fluids, Web/mobile software applications, microwaves/electromagnetics, micro/nano manufacturing. *Unit head:* Dr. Bruce Berdanier, Dean, 203-254-4147, Fax: 203-254-4013, E-mail: bberdanier@fairfield.edu. *Application contact:* Marianne Gumpper, Director of Graduate and Continuing Studies Admission, 203-254-4184, Fax: 203-254-4073, E-mail: gradadmis@fairfield.edu. Website: http://www.fairfield.edu/academics/schoolscollegescenters/schoolofengineering/graduateprograms/.

Fairleigh Dickinson University, Metropolitan Campus, University College: Arts, Sciences, and Professional Studies, School of Computer Sciences and Engineering, Program in Electrical Engineering, Teaneck, NJ 07666-1914. Offers MSEE. *Entrance requirements:* For master's, GRE General Test.

Florida Agricultural and Mechanical University, Division of Graduate Studies, Research, and Continuing Education, FAMU-FSU College of Engineering, Department of Electrical and Computer Engineering, Tallahassee, FL 32307-3200. Offers electrical engineering (MS, PhD). *Degree requirements:* For master's, comprehensive exam, thesis, conference paper; for doctorate, comprehensive exam, thesis/dissertation, publishable paper. *Entrance requirements:* For master's, GRE General Test, minimum GPA of 3.0; for doctorate, minimum GPA of 3.3. Additional exam requirements/recommendations for international students: Required—TOEFL (minimum score 550 paper-based). *Faculty research:* Electromagnetics, computer security, advanced power systems, sensor systems.

Florida Atlantic University, College of Engineering and Computer Science, Department of Computer and Electrical Engineering and Computer Science, Boca Raton, FL 33431-0991. Offers bioengineering (MS); computer engineering (MS, PhD); computer science (MS, PhD); electrical engineering (MS, PhD); information technology and management (MS). Part-time and evening/weekend programs available. Terminal master's awarded for partial completion of doctoral program. *Degree requirements:* For master's, thesis optional; for doctorate, thesis/dissertation, qualifying exam. *Entrance requirements:* For master's, GRE General Test, minimum GPA of 3.0; for doctorate, GRE General Test, master's degree, minimum GPA of 3.5. Additional exam requirements/recommendations for international students: Required—TOEFL (minimum score 500 paper-based; 61 iBT), IELTS (minimum score 6). *Expenses:* Tuition, state resident: full-time $7396; part-time $369.82 per credit hour. Tuition, nonresident: full-time $19,392; part-time $1024.81 per credit hour. Tuition and fees vary according to course load. *Faculty research:* VLSI and neural networks, communication networks, software engineering, computer architecture, multimedia and video processing.

Florida Institute of Technology, Graduate Programs, College of Engineering, Program in Electrical Engineering, Melbourne, FL 32901-6975. Offers MS, PhD. Part-time and evening/weekend programs available. *Students:* 128 full-time (24 women), 40 part-time (5 women); includes 10 minority (7 Asian, non-Hispanic/Latino; 2 Hispanic/Latino; 1 Two or more races, non-Hispanic/Latino), 139 international. Average age 27. 578 applicants, 68% accepted, 50 enrolled. In 2014, 34 master's, 5 doctorates awarded. *Degree requirements:* For master's, comprehensive exam (for some programs), thesis or final exam, faculty-supervised specialized research; for doctorate, comprehensive exam, thesis/dissertation, significant original research, publication in professional journal of conference proceedings, minimum 48 credit hours after master's degree. *Entrance*

requirements: For master's, minimum GPA of 3.0, bachelor's degree from an ABET-accredited program; for doctorate, 3 letters of recommendation, resume, minimum GPA of 3.2, statement of objectives, on-campus interview (highly recommended). Additional exam requirements/recommendations for international students: Required—TOEFL (minimum score 550 paper-based; 79 iBT). *Application deadline:* For fall admission, 4/1 for international students; for spring admission, 9/30 for international students. Applications are processed on a rolling basis. Electronic applications accepted. *Expenses: Tuition:* Part-time $1179 per credit hour. Tuition and fees vary according to campus/location. *Financial support:* Career-related internships or fieldwork, institutionally sponsored loans, tuition waivers (partial), unspecified assistantships, and tuition remissions available. Support available to part-time students. Financial award application deadline: 3/1; financial award applicants required to submit FAFSA. *Faculty research:* Electro-optics, electromagnetics, microelectronics, communications, computer architecture, neural networks. *Unit head:* Dr. Samuel P. Kozaitis, Department Head, 321-674-8060, Fax: 321-674-8192, E-mail: kozaitis@fit.edu. *Application contact:* Cheryl A. Brown, Associate Director of Graduate Admissions, 321-674-7581, Fax: 321-723-9468, E-mail: cbrown@fit.edu. Website: http://coe.fit.edu/ee/.

Florida Institute of Technology, Graduate Programs, Extended Studies Division, Melbourne, FL 32901-6975. Offers acquisition and contract management (MS); aerospace engineering (MS); business administration (MBA, DBA); computer information systems (MS); computer science (MS); electrical engineering (MS); engineering management (MS); human resources management (MS); logistics management (MS), including humanitarian and disaster relief logistics; management (MS), including acquisition and contract management, e-business, human resources management, information systems, logistics management, management, transportation management; material acquisition management (MS); mechanical engineering (MS); operations research (MS); project management (MS), including information systems, operations research; public administration (MPA); quality management (MS); software engineering (MS); space systems (MS); space systems management (MS); supply chain management (MS); systems management (MS), including information systems, operations research; technology management (MS). Part-time and evening/weekend programs available. Postbaccalaureate distance learning degree programs offered (no on-campus study). *Faculty:* 7 full-time (1 woman), 112 part-time/adjunct (29 women). *Students:* 98 full-time (45 women), 975 part-time (396 women); includes 440 minority (292 Black or African American, non-Hispanic/Latino; 13 American Indian or Alaska Native, non-Hispanic/Latino; 32 Asian, non-Hispanic/Latino; 79 Hispanic/Latino; 1 Native Hawaiian or other Pacific Islander, non-Hispanic/Latino; 23 Two or more races, non-Hispanic/Latino), 4 international. Average age 37. 807 applicants, 56% accepted, 258 enrolled. In 2014, 457 master's awarded. *Degree requirements:* For master's, comprehensive exam (for some programs), capstone course. *Entrance requirements:* For master's, GMAT or resume showing 8 years of supervised experience, minimum GPA of 3.0, 2 letters of recommendation, resume. Additional exam requirements/recommendations for international students: Required—TOEFL (minimum score 550 paper-based; 79 iBT). *Application deadline:* For fall admission, 4/1 for international students; for spring admission, 9/30 for international students. Applications are processed on a rolling basis. Electronic applications accepted. *Expenses:* Expenses: Contact institution. *Financial support:* Application deadline: 3/1; applicants required to submit FAFSA. *Unit head:* Dr. Theodore R. Richardson, III, Senior Associate Dean, 321-674-8123, Fax: 321-674-7597, E-mail: trichardson@fit.edu. *Application contact:* Carolyn Farrior, Director of Graduate Admissions, Online Learning and Off-Campus Programs, 321-674-7118, Fax: 321-674-8216, E-mail: cfarrior@fit.edu. Website: http://es.fit.edu.

Florida International University, College of Engineering and Computing, Department of Electrical and Computer Engineering, Program in Electrical Engineering, Miami, FL 33175. Offers MS, PhD. Part-time and evening/weekend programs available. Terminal master's awarded for partial completion of doctoral program. *Degree requirements:* For master's, thesis optional; for doctorate, comprehensive exam, thesis/dissertation. *Entrance requirements:* For master's, minimum undergraduate GPA of 3.0 in upper-level coursework, resume, letters of recommendation, letter of intent; for doctorate, GRE General Test, minimum graduate GPA of 3.3, resume, master's degree, letters of recommendation, letter of intent. Additional exam requirements/recommendations for international students: Required—TOEFL (minimum score 550 paper-based; 80 iBT). Electronic applications accepted.

Florida State University, The Graduate School, FAMU-FSU College of Engineering, Department of Electrical and Computer Engineering, Tallahassee, FL 32310. Offers electrical engineering (MS, PhD). Part-time programs available. *Degree requirements:* For master's, thesis; for doctorate, comprehensive exam, thesis/dissertation, preliminary exam, qualifying exam. *Entrance requirements:* For master's, GRE General Test, minimum GPA of 3.0, BS in electrical engineering; for doctorate, GRE General Test, minimum graduate GPA of 3.3, MS in electrical engineering. Additional exam requirements/recommendations for international students: Required—TOEFL (minimum score 550 paper-based; 80 iBT). Electronic applications accepted. *Expenses:* Tuition, state resident: part-time $403.51 per credit hour. Tuition, nonresident: part-time $1004.85 per credit hour. *Required fees:* $75.81 per credit hour. One-time fee: $20 part-time. Tuition and fees vary according to campus/location. *Faculty research:* Electromagnetics, digital signal processing, computer systems, image processing, laser optics.

Gannon University, School of Graduate Studies, College of Engineering and Business, School of Engineering and Computer Science, Program in Electrical and Computer Engineering, Erie, PA 16541-0001. Offers MSEE, MSES. Part-time and evening/weekend programs available. *Degree requirements:* For master's, thesis (for some programs), oral exam (for some programs), design project (for some programs). *Entrance requirements:* For master's, GRE or GMAT, bachelor's degree in electrical or computer engineering, minimum GPA of 2.5, transcripts, 3 letters of recommendation. Additional exam requirements/recommendations for international students: Required—TOEFL (minimum score 79 iBT). Electronic applications accepted.

George Mason University, Volgenau School of Engineering, Department of Electrical and Computer Engineering, Fairfax, VA 22030. Offers computer engineering (MS); computer forensics (MS); electrical and computer engineering (PhD, Certificate); electrical engineering (MS); telecommunications (MS). MS programs offered jointly with Old Dominion University, University of Virginia, Virginia Commonwealth University, and Virginia Polytechnic Institute and State University. *Faculty:* 31 full-time (4 women), 41 part-time/adjunct (5 women). *Students:* 258 full-time (77 women), 275 part-time (51 women); includes 113 minority (33 Black or African American, non-Hispanic/Latino; 54 Asian, non-Hispanic/Latino; 17 Hispanic/Latino; 1 Native Hawaiian or other Pacific Islander, non-Hispanic/Latino; 8 Two or more races, non-Hispanic/Latino), 237 international. Average age 30. 554 applicants, 69% accepted, 158 enrolled. In 2014, 153 master's, 4 doctorates, 24 other advanced degrees awarded. *Degree requirements:* For master's, thesis optional; for doctorate, comprehensive exam, thesis or scholarly paper. *Entrance requirements:* For master's, GRE, personal goals statement; 2 official copies of transcripts; self-evaluation form; 3 letters of recommendation; resume; official bank statement; photocopy of passport; proof of financial support; for doctorate, GRE (waived

for GMU electrical and computer engineering master's graduates with minimum GPA of 3.0), personal goals statement; 2 official copies of transcripts; self-evaluation form; 3 letters of recommendation; resume; official bank statement; photocopy of passport; proof of financial support. Additional exam requirements/recommendations for international students: Required—TOEFL (minimum score 575 paper-based; 80 iBT), IELTS (minimum score 6.5), PTE. *Application deadline:* For fall admission, 1/15 priority date for domestic students; for spring admission, 8/15 priority date for domestic students. Applications are processed on a rolling basis. Application fee: $65 ($80 for international students). Electronic applications accepted. *Expenses:* Expenses: Contact institution. *Financial support:* In 2014–15, 68 students received support, including 33 research assistantships with full and partial tuition reimbursements available (averaging $18,359 per year), 38 teaching assistantships with full and partial tuition reimbursements available (averaging $11,521 per year); career-related internships or fieldwork, Federal Work-Study, scholarships/grants, unspecified assistantships, and health care benefits (for full-time research or teaching assistantship recipients) also available. Support available to part-time students. Financial award application deadline: 3/1; financial award applicants required to submit FAFSA. *Faculty research:* Communication networks, signal processing, system failure diagnosis, multiprocessors, material processing using microwave energy. *Total annual research expenditures:* $2.3 million. *Unit head:* Andre Manitius, Chair, 703-993-1570, Fax: 703-993-1601, E-mail: amanitiu@gmu.edu. *Application contact:* Jammie Chang, Academic Program Coordinator, 703-993-1570, Fax: 703-993-1601, E-mail: jchangn@gmu.edu.
Website: http://ece.gmu.edu/.

The George Washington University, School of Engineering and Applied Science, Department of Electrical and Computer Engineering, Washington, DC 20052. Offers electrical engineering (MS, PhD); telecommunication and computers (MS). Part-time and evening/weekend programs available. *Faculty:* 28 full-time (2 women), 18 part-time/adjunct (0 women). *Students:* 126 full-time (31 women), 68 part-time (14 women); includes 19 minority (6 Black or African American, non-Hispanic/Latino; 8 Asian, non-Hispanic/Latino; 5 Hispanic/Latino), 148 international. Average age 27. 536 applicants, 55% accepted, 62 enrolled. In 2014, 98 master's, 7 doctorates, 2 other advanced degrees awarded. *Degree requirements:* For master's, thesis optional; for doctorate, comprehensive exam, thesis/dissertation, dissertation defense, qualifying exam. *Entrance requirements:* For master's, appropriate bachelor's degree, minimum GPA of 3.0; for doctorate, GRE (if highest earned degree is BS), appropriate bachelor's or master's degree, minimum GPA of 3.3; for other advanced degree, appropriate master's degree, minimum GPA of 3.0. Additional exam requirements/recommendations for international students: Required—TOEFL or The George Washington University English as a Foreign Language Test. *Application deadline:* For fall admission, 3/1 priority date for domestic students; for spring admission, 10/1 for domestic students. Applications are processed on a rolling basis. Application fee: $75. *Financial support:* In 2014–15, 39 students received support. Fellowships with tuition reimbursements available, research assistantships, teaching assistantships with tuition reimbursements available, career-related internships or fieldwork, and institutionally sponsored loans available. Financial award application deadline: 3/1; financial award applicants required to submit FAFSA. *Faculty research:* Computer graphics, multimedia systems. *Unit head:* Mona Zaghloul, Chair, 202-994-9380, E-mail: zaghloul@gwu.edu. *Application contact:* Adina Lav, Marketing, Recruiting and Admissions, 202-994-5827, Fax: 202-994-0909, E-mail: engineering@gwu.edu.
Website: http://www.ece.gwu.edu/.

Georgia Institute of Technology, Graduate Studies, College of Engineering, School of Electrical and Computer Engineering, Atlanta, GA 30332-0001. Offers MS, PhD. Part-time programs available. Postbaccalaureate distance learning degree programs offered (minimal on-campus study). *Students:* 1,024 full-time (177 women), 302 part-time (31 women); includes 169 minority (27 Black or African American, non-Hispanic/Latino; 1 American Indian or Alaska Native, non-Hispanic/Latino; 100 Asian, non-Hispanic/Latino; 29 Hispanic/Latino; 12 Two or more races, non-Hispanic/Latino), 857 international. Average age 25. 2,399 applicants, 30% accepted, 409 enrolled. In 2014, 335 master's, 99 doctorates awarded. Terminal master's awarded for partial completion of doctoral program. *Degree requirements:* For master's, thesis optional; for doctorate, comprehensive exam, thesis/dissertation. *Entrance requirements:* For master's, GRE General Test, http://www.ece.gatech.edu/academics/graduate/apply.html#masters; for doctorate, GRE General Test, http://www.ece.gatech.edu/academics/graduate/apply.html#phd. Additional exam requirements/recommendations for international students: Required—TOEFL (minimum score 550 paper-based; 79 iBT). *Application deadline:* For fall admission, 12/1 for domestic and international students; for spring admission, 8/1 for domestic students, 7/1 for international students; for summer admission, 12/1 for domestic and international students. Applications are processed on a rolling basis. Application fee: $75. Electronic applications accepted. *Expenses:* Expenses: $490 per credit hour in-state/out-of-state tuition plus fees of $651 per term (for MS Shanghai); $5,880 in-state/out-of-state tuition plus fees of $651 per term (for MS Shenzhen). *Financial support:* Fellowships, research assistantships, teaching assistantships, career-related internships or fieldwork, Federal Work-Study, institutionally sponsored loans, tuition waivers (partial), and unspecified assistantships available. Support available to part-time students. Financial award application deadline: 5/1. *Faculty research:* Telecommunications, computer systems, microelectronics, optical engineering, digital signal processing. *Total annual research expenditures:* $30.5 million. *Unit head:* George Riley, Director, 404-894-4767, E-mail: george.riley@ece.gatech.edu. *Application contact:* Jacqueline Trappier, Graduate Coordinator, 404-385-1141, E-mail: jacqueline.trappier@ece.gatech.edu.
Website: http://www.ece.gatech.edu.

Georgia Southern University, Jack N. Averitt College of Graduate Studies, Allen E. Paulson College of Engineering and Information Technology, Program in Engineering/Electrical and Electronic Systems, Statesboro, GA 30460. Offers MSAE. *Students:* 4 full-time (0 women); includes 1 minority (Hispanic/Latino), 2 international. Average age 24. 4 applicants, 75% accepted, 3 enrolled. *Degree requirements:* For master's, thesis optional. *Entrance requirements:* For master's, GPA 2.75. Additional exam requirements/recommendations for international students: Required—TOEFL (minimum score 80 iBT). *Application deadline:* For fall admission, 2/1 for domestic students; for spring admission, 10/1 for domestic students. Application fee: $50. *Expenses:* Tuition, state resident: full-time $7236; part-time $277 per semester hour. Tuition, nonresident: full-time $27,118; part-time $1105 per semester hour. *Required fees:* $2092. *Financial support:* In 2014–15, 4 students received support. *Unit head:* Dr. Frank Goforth, Program Chair, 912-478-7583, E-mail: fgoforth@georgiasouthern.edu.

The Graduate Center, City University of New York, Graduate Studies, Program in Engineering, New York, NY 10016-4039. Offers biomedical engineering (PhD); chemical engineering (PhD); civil engineering (PhD); electrical engineering (PhD); mechanical engineering (PhD). *Degree requirements:* For doctorate, thesis/dissertation. *Entrance requirements:* For doctorate, GRE General Test. Additional exam requirements/recommendations for international students: Required—TOEFL. Electronic applications accepted.

Grand Valley State University, Padnos College of Engineering and Computing, School of Engineering, Allendale, MI 49401-9403. Offers electrical and computer engineering (MSE); manufacturing operations (MSE); mechanical engineering (MSE); product design and manufacturing engineering (MSE). Part-time and evening/weekend programs available. *Faculty:* 15 full-time (2 women). *Students:* 29 full-time (6 women), 30 part-time (5 women); includes 4 minority (1 Asian, non-Hispanic/Latino; 3 Hispanic/Latino), 23 international. Average age 28. 66 applicants, 73% accepted, 23 enrolled. In 2014, 14 master's awarded. *Degree requirements:* For master's, project or thesis. *Entrance requirements:* For master's, engineering degree, minimum GPA of 3.0. Additional exam requirements/recommendations for international students: Required—TOEFL. *Application deadline:* Applications are processed on a rolling basis. Application fee: $30. Electronic applications accepted. *Expenses:* Tuition, state resident: full-time $10,602; part-time $589 per credit hour. Tuition, nonresident: full-time $14,022; part-time $779 per credit hour. Tuition and fees vary according to degree level and program. *Financial support:* In 2014–15, 31 students received support, including 10 fellowships (averaging $3,049 per year), 25 research assistantships with full tuition reimbursements available (averaging $10,237 per year); career-related internships or fieldwork, Federal Work-Study, institutionally sponsored loans, scholarships/grants, and unspecified assistantships also available. *Faculty research:* Digital signal processing, computer aided design, computer aided manufacturing, manufacturing simulation, biomechanics, product design. *Total annual research expenditures:* $300,000. *Unit head:* Dr. Charles Standridge, Acting Director, 616-331-6750, Fax: 616-331-7215, E-mail: standric@gvsu.edu. *Application contact:* Dr. Pranod Chaphalkar, Graduate Director, 616-331-6843, Fax: 616-331-7215, E-mail: chaphalp@gvsu.edu.
Website: http://www.engineer.gvsu.edu/.

Howard University, College of Engineering, Architecture, and Computer Sciences, School of Engineering and Computer Science, Department of Electrical Engineering, Washington, DC 20059-0002. Offers M Eng, PhD. Offered through the Graduate School of Arts and Sciences. Part-time programs available. *Degree requirements:* For master's, thesis (for some programs), qualifying exam; for doctorate, thesis/dissertation, preliminary exam. *Entrance requirements:* For master's, GRE General Test, bachelor's degree in electrical engineering, minimum GPA of 3.0; for doctorate, GRE General Test, minimum GPA of 3.0. Additional exam requirements/recommendations for international students: Required—TOEFL. Electronic applications accepted. *Faculty research:* Solid-state electronics, antennas and microwaves, communications and signal processing, controls and power systems, nanotechnology.

Illinois Institute of Technology, Graduate College, Armour College of Engineering, Department of Electrical and Computer Engineering, Chicago, IL 60616. Offers biomedical imaging and signals (MAS); computer engineering (MS, PhD); electrical engineering (MS, PhD); electricity markets (MAS); network engineering (MAS); power engineering (MAS); telecommunications and software engineering (MAS); vlsi and microelectronics (MAS); MS/MS. Part-time and evening/weekend programs available. Postbaccalaureate distance learning degree programs offered (minimal on-campus study). *Faculty:* 27 full-time (4 women), 3 part-time/adjunct (0 women). *Students:* 439 full-time (84 women), 90 part-time (11 women); includes 13 minority (11 Asian, non-Hispanic/Latino; 2 Hispanic/Latino), 476 international. Average age 26. 2,461 applicants, 39% accepted, 206 enrolled. In 2014, 155 master's, 7 doctorates awarded. Terminal master's awarded for partial completion of doctoral program. *Degree requirements:* For master's, comprehensive exam (for some programs), thesis (for some programs); for doctorate, comprehensive exam, thesis/dissertation. *Entrance requirements:* For master's and doctorate, GRE General Test (minimum score 1100 Quantitative and Verbal, 3.5 Analytical Writing), minimum undergraduate GPA of 3.0. Additional exam requirements/recommendations for international students: Required—TOEFL (minimum score 550 paper-based; 80 iBT); Recommended—IELTS (minimum score 5.5). *Application deadline:* For fall admission, 5/1 for domestic and international students; for spring admission, 10/15 for domestic and international students. Applications are processed on a rolling basis. Application fee: $50. Electronic applications accepted. *Expenses: Tuition:* Full-time $22,500; part-time $1250 per credit hour. *Required fees:* $30 per course. $260 per semester. One-time fee: $235. Tuition and fees vary according to course load and program. *Financial support:* Fellowships with full and partial tuition reimbursements, research assistantships with full and partial tuition reimbursements, teaching assistantships with full and partial tuition reimbursements, career-related internships or fieldwork, Federal Work-Study, institutionally sponsored loans, scholarships/grants, health care benefits, tuition waivers (full), and unspecified assistantships available. Support available to part-time students. Financial award applicants required to submit FAFSA. *Faculty research:* Communication systems, wireless networks, computer systems, computer networks, wireless security, cloud computing and micro-electronics; electromagnetics and electronics; power and control systems; signal and image processing. *Unit head:* Dr. Ashfaq Khokhar, Chair & Professor of Electrical and Computer Engineering, 312-567-5780, Fax: 312-567-8976, E-mail: ashfaq@iit.edu. *Application contact:* Rishab Malhotra, Director, Graduate Admission, 866-472-3448, Fax: 312-567-3138, E-mail: inquiry.grad@iit.edu.
Website: http://www.ece.iit.edu.

Indiana University–Purdue University Fort Wayne, College of Engineering, Technology, and Computer Science, Department of Engineering, Fort Wayne, IN 46805-1499. Offers civil engineering (MSE); computer engineering (MSE); electrical engineering (MSE); mechanical engineering (MSE); systems engineering (MSE). Part-time programs available. *Faculty:* 21 full-time (2 women). *Students:* 4 full-time (1 woman), 15 part-time (1 woman); includes 3 minority (2 Black or African American, non-Hispanic/Latino; 1 Asian, non-Hispanic/Latino), 2 international. Average age 30. 13 applicants, 100% accepted, 10 enrolled. In 2014, 17 master's awarded. *Entrance requirements:* For master's, minimum GPA of 3.0, bachelor's degree in engineering discipline. Additional exam requirements/recommendations for international students: Required—TOEFL (minimum score 550 paper-based; 79 iBT); Recommended—TWE. *Application deadline:* For fall admission, 7/15 priority date for domestic students, 5/15 priority date for international students; for spring admission, 12/1 priority date for domestic students, 10/15 priority date for international students. Applications are processed on a rolling basis. Application fee: $55 ($60 for international students). Electronic applications accepted. *Financial support:* In 2014–15, 3 research assistantships with partial tuition reimbursements (averaging $13,522 per year), 1 teaching assistantship with partial tuition reimbursement (averaging $13,522 per year) were awarded. Financial award application deadline: 3/1; financial award applicants required to submit FAFSA. *Faculty research:* Continuous space language model, sensor networks, wireless cloud architecture. *Total annual research expenditures:* $841,333. *Unit head:* Dr. Nashwan Younis, Chair, 260-481-6887, Fax: 260-481-6281, E-mail: younis@engr.ipfw.edu. *Application contact:* Dr. Abdullah Eroglu, Program Director/Professor, 260-481-0273, Fax: 260-481-5734, E-mail: eroglua@ipfw.edu.
Website: http://www.ipfw.edu/engr.

Indiana University–Purdue University Indianapolis, School of Engineering and Technology, Department of Electrical Engineering, Indianapolis, IN 46202. Offers biomedical engineering (MS, PhD); electrical and computer engineering (MS, PhD); engineering (interdisciplinary) (MSE). *Students:* 64 full-time (15 women), 74 part-time (14 women); includes 13 minority (2 Black or African American, non-Hispanic/Latino; 9 Asian, non-Hispanic/Latino; 2 Hispanic/Latino), 95 international. Average age 27. 147 applicants, 63% accepted, 41 enrolled. In 2014, 27 master's awarded. Application fee:

$55 ($65 for international students). *Unit head:* Brian King, Acting Chair, 317-274-9723. *Application contact:* Valerie Diemer, Graduate Program, 317-278-4960, Fax: 317-278-1671, E-mail: grad@engr.iupui.edu.
Website: http://www.engr.iupui.edu/departments/ece/.

Instituto Tecnológico y de Estudios Superiores de Monterrey, Campus Chihuahua, Graduate Programs, Chihuahua, Mexico. Offers computer systems engineering (Ingeniero); electrical engineering (Ingeniero); electromechanical engineering (Ingeniero); electronic engineering (Ingeniero); engineering administration (MEA); industrial engineering (MIE, Ingeniero); international trade (MIT); mechanical engineering (Ingeniero).

Instituto Tecnológico y de Estudios Superiores de Monterrey, Campus Monterrey, Graduate and Research Division, Programs in Engineering, Monterrey, Mexico. Offers applied statistics (M Eng); artificial intelligence (PhD); automation engineering (M Eng); chemical engineering (M Eng); civil engineering (M Eng); electrical engineering (M Eng); electronic engineering (M Eng); environmental engineering (M Eng); industrial engineering (M Eng, PhD); manufacturing engineering (M Eng); mechanical engineering (M Eng); systems and quality engineering (M Eng). M Eng program offered jointly with University of Waterloo; PhD in industrial engineering with Texas A&M University. Part-time and evening/weekend programs available. Terminal master's awarded for partial completion of doctoral program. *Degree requirements:* For master's, one foreign language, thesis; for doctorate, one foreign language, thesis/dissertation. *Entrance requirements:* For master's, EXADEP; for doctorate, GRE, master's degree in related field. Additional exam requirements/recommendations for international students: Required—TOEFL. *Faculty research:* Flexible manufacturing cells, materials, statistical methods, environmental prevention, control and evaluation.

International Technological University, Program in Electrical Engineering, San Jose, CA 95113. Offers MSEE, PhD. Part-time and evening/weekend programs available. *Faculty:* 5 full-time (1 woman), 2 part-time/adjunct (0 women). *Students:* 29 full-time (7 women), 4 part-time (1 woman), all international. Average age 27. 26 applicants, 88% accepted, 12 enrolled. In 2014, 7 master's awarded. *Degree requirements:* For master's, thesis or capstone project; for doctorate, comprehensive exam, thesis/dissertation. *Entrance requirements:* For master's, 3 semesters of calculus, minimum GPA of 2.5. Additional exam requirements/recommendations for international students: Required—TOEFL, IELTS. *Application deadline:* For fall admission, 8/1 priority date for domestic students, 8/1 for international students; for winter admission, 12/31 priority date for domestic students; for spring admission, 12/1 priority date for domestic students, 12/1 for international students; for summer admission, 4/1 for domestic and international students. Applications are processed on a rolling basis. Application fee: $80. Electronic applications accepted. *Expenses: Tuition:* Full-time $13,500; part-time $500 per credit. *Required fees:* $265 per trimester. *Unit head:* Dr. May Huang, Department Chair, 888-488-4968. *Application contact:* Mary Tran, Admissions Manager, 888-488-4968, E-mail: admissions@itu.edu.

Iowa State University of Science and Technology, Department of Electrical and Computer Engineering, Ames, IA 50011. Offers computer engineering (M Eng, MS, PhD); electrical engineering (M Eng, MS, PhD). *Degree requirements:* For master's, thesis or alternative; for doctorate, thesis/dissertation. *Entrance requirements:* For master's and doctorate, GRE General Test. Additional exam requirements/recommendations for international students: Required—TOEFL (minimum score 570 paper-based; 79 iBT), IELTS (minimum score 6.5). Electronic applications accepted.

Johns Hopkins University, Engineering Program for Professionals, Part-time Program in Electrical and Computer Engineering, Baltimore, MD 21218-2699. Offers MS, Post-Master's Certificate. Part-time and evening/weekend programs available. Electronic applications accepted.

Johns Hopkins University, G. W. C. Whiting School of Engineering, Department of Electrical and Computer Engineering, Baltimore, MD 21218-2699. Offers MSE, PhD. Terminal master's awarded for partial completion of doctoral program. *Degree requirements:* For master's, thesis optional; for doctorate, thesis/dissertation, qualifying and oral exams, seminar. *Entrance requirements:* For master's and doctorate, GRE General Test, transcripts, 3 letters of recommendation, statement of purpose. Additional exam requirements/recommendations for international students: Required—TOEFL (minimum score 600 paper-based; 100 iBT). Electronic applications accepted. *Faculty research:* Computer engineering, systems and control, language and speech processing, photonics and optoelectronics, signal and image processing.

Kansas State University, Graduate School, College of Engineering, Department of Electrical and Computer Engineering, Manhattan, KS 66506. Offers electrical engineering (MS), including bioengineering, communication systems, design of computer systems, electrical engineering, energy and power systems, integrated circuits and devices, real time embedded systems, renewable energy, signal processing. Part-time and evening/weekend programs available. Postbaccalaureate distance learning degree programs offered (no on-campus study). *Faculty:* 21 full-time (4 women), 1 (woman) part-time/adjunct. *Students:* 38 full-time (8 women), 45 part-time (6 women); includes 13 minority (4 Black or African American, non-Hispanic/Latino; 8 Asian, non-Hispanic/Latino; 1 Hispanic/Latino), 37 international. Average age 28. 126 applicants, 29% accepted, 14 enrolled. In 2014, 22 master's, 5 doctorates awarded. *Degree requirements:* For master's, thesis or alternative, final exam; for doctorate, thesis/dissertation, final exam, preliminary exams. *Entrance requirements:* For master's, GRE General Test, bachelor's degree in electrical engineering or computer science, minimum GPA of 3.0; for doctorate, GRE General Test. Additional exam requirements/recommendations for international students: Required—TOEFL (minimum score 600 paper-based; 85 iBT). *Application deadline:* For fall admission, 1/1 priority date for domestic and international students; for spring admission, 8/1 priority date for domestic and international students. Applications are processed on a rolling basis. Application fee: $50 ($75 for international students). Electronic applications accepted. *Financial support:* In 2014–15, 40 students received support, including 22 research assistantships with tuition reimbursements available (averaging $12,100 per year), 18 teaching assistantships with full tuition reimbursements available (averaging $12,220 per year); career-related internships or fieldwork, institutionally sponsored loans, and scholarships/grants also available. Support available to part-time students. Financial award application deadline: 3/1; financial award applicants required to submit FAFSA. *Faculty research:* Energy systems and renewable energy, computer systems and real time embedded systems, communication systems and signal processing, integrated circuits and devices, bioengineering. *Total annual research expenditures:* $1.3 million. *Unit head:* Dr. Don Gruenbacher, Head, 785-532-5600, Fax: 785-532-1188, E-mail: grue@k-state.edu. *Application contact:* Dr. Andrew Rys, Graduate Program Director, 785-532-4665, Fax: 785-532-1188, E-mail: andrys@k-state.edu.
Website: http://www.ece.k-state.edu/.

Kettering University, Graduate School, Electrical and Computer Engineering Department, Flint, MI 48504. Offers engineering (MS). Part-time and evening/weekend programs available. Postbaccalaureate distance learning degree programs offered (no on-campus study). *Degree requirements:* For master's, thesis optional. *Entrance requirements:* Additional exam requirements/recommendations for international students: Required—TOEFL (minimum score 550 paper-based; 79 iBT). Electronic applications accepted. *Faculty research:* Electric power trains, batteries, motor control, haptics.

Lakehead University, Graduate Studies, Faculty of Engineering, Thunder Bay, ON P7B 5E1, Canada. Offers control engineering (M Sc Engr); electrical/computer engineering (M Sc Engr); environmental engineering (M Sc Engr). Part-time programs available. *Degree requirements:* For master's, thesis. *Entrance requirements:* For master's, bachelor's degree in chemical, electrical or mechanical engineering, minimum B average. Additional exam requirements/recommendations for international students: Required—TOEFL. *Faculty research:* Pulp and paper, adaptive/process control, robust/interactive learning control, vibration control.

Lamar University, College of Graduate Studies, College of Engineering, Department of Electrical Engineering, Beaumont, TX 77710. Offers ME, MES, DE. Part-time programs available. *Faculty:* 7 full-time (0 women). *Students:* 43 full-time (9 women), 28 part-time (5 women); includes 1 minority (Hispanic/Latino), 69 international. Average age 24. 398 applicants, 36% accepted, 71 enrolled. In 2014, 17 master's, 3 doctorates awarded. *Degree requirements:* For master's, thesis (for some programs); for doctorate, thesis/dissertation. *Entrance requirements:* For master's and doctorate, GRE General Test. Additional exam requirements/recommendations for international students: Required—TOEFL (minimum score 550 paper-based; 79 iBT), IELTS (minimum score 6.5). *Application deadline:* For fall admission, 8/10 for domestic students, 7/1 for international students; for spring admission, 1/5 for domestic students, 12/1 for international students. Applications are processed on a rolling basis. Application fee: $25 ($50 for international students). *Expenses:* Tuition, state resident: full-time $5724; part-time $1908 per semester. Tuition, nonresident: full-time $12,240; part-time $4080 per semester. *Required fees:* $1940; $318 per credit hour. *Financial support:* In 2014–15, 2 fellowships with partial tuition reimbursements (averaging $6,000 per year), 20 research assistantships with partial tuition reimbursements (averaging $6,000 per year), 2 teaching assistantships with partial tuition reimbursements (averaging $4,500 per year) were awarded; tuition waivers (partial) also available. Financial award application deadline: 4/1. *Faculty research:* Video processing, photonics, VLSI design, computer networking. *Unit head:* Dr. Harley Ross Myler, Chair, 409-880-8746, Fax: 409-880-8121. *Application contact:* Melissa Gallien, Director, Admissions and Academic Services, 409-880-8888, Fax: 409-880-7419, E-mail: gradmissions@lamar.edu.
Website: http://engineering.lamar.edu/electrical.

Lawrence Technological University, College of Engineering, Southfield, MI 48075-1058. Offers architectural engineering (MS); automotive engineering (MS); civil engineering (MA, MS, PhD); construction engineering management (MA); electrical and computer engineering (MS); engineering management (MEM); industrial engineering (MS); manufacturing systems (ME, DE); mechanical engineering (MS, DE); mechatronic systems engineering (MS). Part-time and evening/weekend programs available. *Faculty:* 24 full-time (5 women), 15 part-time/adjunct (0 women). *Students:* 16 full-time (6 women), 478 part-time (71 women); includes 295 minority (15 Black or African American, non-Hispanic/Latino; 271 Asian, non-Hispanic/Latino; 7 Hispanic/Latino; 2 Two or more races, non-Hispanic/Latino), 38 international. Average age 27. 1,786 applicants, 40% accepted, 218 enrolled. In 2014, 106 master's awarded. *Degree requirements:* For master's, thesis (for some programs). *Entrance requirements:* Additional exam requirements/recommendations for international students: Required—TOEFL (minimum score 550 paper-based; 79 iBT). *Application deadline:* For fall admission, 8/1 priority date for domestic students, 5/29 for international students; for spring admission, 12/1 priority date for domestic students, 10/15 for international students. Applications are processed on a rolling basis. Application fee: $50. Electronic applications accepted. *Expenses: Tuition:* Full-time $14,700; part-time $1050 per credit hour. *Required fees:* $150. One-time fee: $150 part-time. *Financial support:* In 2014–15, 31 students received support, including 8 research assistantships (averaging $9,338 per year); Federal Work-Study and institutionally sponsored loans also available. Support available to part-time students. Financial award application deadline: 4/1; financial award applicants required to submit FAFSA. *Faculty research:* Advanced composite materials in bridges, strengthening existing bridges with carbon and glass fiber sheets, development of drive shafts using composite materials. *Unit head:* Dr. Nabil Grace, Dean, 248-204-2500, Fax: 248-204-2509, E-mail: engrdean@ltu.edu. *Application contact:* Jane Rohrback, Director of Admissions, 248-204-3160, Fax: 248-204-2228, E-mail: admissions@ltu.edu.
Website: http://www.ltu.edu/engineering/index.asp.

Lehigh University, P.C. Rossin College of Engineering and Applied Science, Department of Electrical and Computer Engineering, Bethlehem, PA 18015. Offers electrical engineering (MS, PhD); wireless network engineering (MS). Part-time programs available. *Faculty:* 19 full-time (3 women). *Students:* 38 full-time (4 women), 16 part-time (5 women); includes 1 minority (Black or African American, non-Hispanic/Latino), 46 international. Average age 27. 608 applicants, 4% accepted, 12 enrolled. In 2014, 13 master's, 4 doctorates awarded. Terminal master's awarded for partial completion of doctoral program. *Degree requirements:* For master's, thesis optional; for doctorate, thesis/dissertation, qualifying or comprehensive exam for all 1st year PhD's; general exam 7 months or more prior to completion/dissertation defense. *Entrance requirements:* For master's and doctorate, GRE General Test, BS in field or related field. Additional exam requirements/recommendations for international students: Required—TOEFL (minimum score 79 iBT). *Application deadline:* For fall admission, 1/15 priority date for domestic and international students; for spring admission, 11/1 for domestic and international students. Application fee: $75. Electronic applications accepted. *Expenses:* Expenses: $1,340 per credit hour. *Financial support:* In 2014–15, 42 students received support, including 5 fellowships with full tuition reimbursements available (averaging $19,920 per year), 29 research assistantships with full tuition reimbursements available (averaging $19,917 per year), 6 teaching assistantships with full tuition reimbursements available (averaging $20,484 per year); career-related internships or fieldwork, Federal Work-Study, institutionally sponsored loans, scholarships/grants, and tuition waivers (full and partial) also available. Support available to part-time students. Financial award application deadline: 1/15. *Faculty research:* Nanostructures/nanodevices, terahertz generation, analog devices, mixed mode design and signal circuits, optoelectronic sensors, micro-fabrication technology and design, packaging/reliability of microsensors, coding and networking information theory, radio frequency, wireless and optical wireless communication, wireless networks. *Total annual research expenditures:* $2 million. *Unit head:* Dr. Filbert J. Bartoli, Chair, 610-758-4069, Fax: 610-758-6279, E-mail: fjb205@lehigh.edu. *Application contact:* Diane Hubinsky, Graduate Coordinator, 610-758-4072, Fax: 610-758-6279, E-mail: dih2@lehigh.edu.
Website: http://www.ece.lehigh.edu/.

Louisiana State University and Agricultural & Mechanical College, Graduate School, College of Engineering, Division of Electrical and Computer Engineering, Baton Rouge, LA 70803. Offers MSEE, PhD. *Faculty:* 23 full-time (1 woman), 1 part-time/adjunct (0 women). *Students:* 107 full-time (16 women), 3 part-time (1 woman); includes 4 minority (1 Black or African American, non-Hispanic/Latino; 3 Asian, non-Hispanic/Latino), 96 international. Average age 27. 251 applicants, 55% accepted, 16 enrolled. In 2014, 23 master's, 8 doctorates awarded. Terminal master's awarded for partial completion of doctoral program. *Degree requirements:* For master's, thesis optional; for doctorate, thesis/dissertation. *Entrance requirements:* For master's, GRE General Test,

minimum GPA of 3.0; for doctorate, GRE General Test, minimum GPA of 3.5. Additional exam requirements/recommendations for international students: Required—TOEFL (minimum score 550 paper-based; 79 IBT), IELTS (minimum score 6.5), or PTE (minimum score 59). *Application deadline:* For fall admission, 1/1 priority date for domestic students, 5/15 for international students; for spring admission, 10/15 for domestic and international students; for summer admission, 5/15 for domestic and international students. Applications are processed on a rolling basis. Application fee: $50 ($70 for international students). Electronic applications accepted. *Financial support:* In 2014–15, 102 students received support, including 3 fellowships with full and partial tuition reimbursements available (averaging $29,125 per year), 50 research assistantships with full and partial tuition reimbursements available (averaging $15,318 per year), 43 teaching assistantships with full and partial tuition reimbursements available (averaging $12,949 per year); Federal Work-Study, institutionally sponsored loans, health care benefits, tuition waivers (full and partial), and unspecified assistantships also available. Financial award application deadline: 2/28; financial award applicants required to submit FAFSA. *Faculty research:* Computer engineering, electronics, control systems and signal processing, communications. *Total annual research expenditures:* $2.3 million. *Unit head:* Dr. Jerry Trahan, Interim Chair, 225-578-5241, Fax: 225-578-5200, E-mail: jtrahan@lsu.edu. *Application contact:* Dr. Ramachandran Vaidyanathan, Graduate Adviser, 225-578-5238, Fax: 225-578-5200, E-mail: vaidy@lsu.edu.
Website: http://www.ece.lsu.edu/.

Louisiana Tech University, Graduate School, College of Engineering and Science, Department of Electrical Engineering, Ruston, LA 71272. Offers MS, PhD. Part-time programs available. Terminal master's awarded for partial completion of doctoral program. *Degree requirements:* For master's, thesis; for doctorate, thesis/dissertation. *Entrance requirements:* For master's, GRE General Test, minimum GPA of 3.0 in last 60 hours; for doctorate, minimum graduate GPA of 3.25 (with MS) or GRE General Test. Additional exam requirements/recommendations for international students: Required—TOEFL. *Faculty research:* Communications, computers and microprocessors, electrical and power systems, pattern recognition, robotics.

Manhattan College, Graduate Programs, School of Engineering, Program in Electrical Engineering, Riverdale, NY 10471. Offers MS. Part-time and evening/weekend programs available. *Faculty:* 7 full-time (0 women). *Students:* 8 full-time (0 women), 13 part-time (2 women); includes 3 minority (2 Asian, non-Hispanic/Latino; 1 Hispanic/Latino). Average age 26. 21 applicants, 71% accepted, 8 enrolled. In 2014, 4 master's awarded. *Degree requirements:* For master's, thesis or alternative. *Entrance requirements:* For master's, GRE (recommended), minimum GPA of 3.0. Additional exam requirements/recommendations for international students: Required—TOEFL (minimum score 550 paper-based; 80 iBT), IELTS (minimum score 6). *Application deadline:* For fall admission, 8/10 priority date for domestic students, 8/10 for international students; for spring admission, 1/7 for domestic and international students. Applications are processed on a rolling basis. Application fee: $60. *Financial support:* In 2014–15, 4 students received support, including 4 teaching assistantships with partial tuition reimbursements available (averaging $8,750 per year); career-related internships or fieldwork, Federal Work-Study, scholarships/grants, unspecified assistantships, and laboratory assistantships also available. Support available to part-time students. Financial award application deadline: 2/1. *Faculty research:* Multimedia tools, neural networks, robotic control systems, magnetic resonance imaging, telemedicine, computer-based instruction. *Unit head:* Dr. George Giakos, Chairperson, 718-862-7154, Fax: 718-862-7162, E-mail: george.giakos@manhattan.edu. *Application contact:* Bobbie Moore, Information Contact, 718-862-7153, Fax: 718-862-7162, E-mail: ece@manhattan.edu.
Website: http://www.engineering.manhattan.edu.

Marquette University, Graduate School, Opus College of Engineering, Department of Electrical and Computer Engineering, Milwaukee, WI 53201-1881. Offers digital signal processing (Certificate); electric machines, drives, and controls (Certificate); electrical and computer engineering (MS, PhD); microwaves and antennas (Certificate); sensors and smart systems (Certificate). Part-time and evening/weekend programs available. Terminal master's awarded for partial completion of doctoral program. *Degree requirements:* For master's, comprehensive exam (for some programs), thesis optional; for doctorate, thesis/dissertation, dissertation defense, qualifying exam. *Entrance requirements:* For master's, GRE General Test (recommended), official transcripts from all current and previous colleges/universities except Marquette, three letters of recommendation; for doctorate, GRE General Test, minimum GPA of 3.0, official transcripts from all current and previous colleges/universities except Marquette, three letters of recommendation, statement of purpose, submission of any English language publications authored by applicant (strongly recommended). Additional exam requirements/recommendations for international students: Required—TOEFL (minimum score 530 paper-based). Electronic applications accepted. *Faculty research:* Electric machines, drives, and controls; applied solid-state electronics; computers and signal processing; microwaves and antennas; solid state devices and acoustic wave sensors.

Massachusetts Institute of Technology, School of Engineering, Department of Electrical Engineering and Computer Science, Cambridge, MA 02139. Offers computer science (PhD, Sc D, ECS); computer science and engineering (PhD, Sc D); electrical engineering (PhD, Sc D, EE); electrical engineering and computer science (M Eng, SM, PhD, Sc D); SM/MBA. *Faculty:* 120 full-time (19 women). *Students:* 795 full-time (185 women), 4 part-time (0 women); includes 193 minority (13 Black or African American, non-Hispanic/Latino; 2 American Indian or Alaska Native, non-Hispanic/Latino; 119 Asian, non-Hispanic/Latino; 40 Hispanic/Latino; 19 Two or more races, non-Hispanic/Latino), 390 international. Average age 26. 2,971 applicants, 13% accepted, 277 enrolled. In 2014, 219 master's, 101 doctorates, 4 other advanced degrees awarded. Terminal master's awarded for partial completion of doctoral program. *Degree requirements:* For master's and other advanced degree, thesis; for doctorate, comprehensive exam, thesis/dissertation. *Entrance requirements:* Additional exam requirements/recommendations for international students: Required—TOEFL (minimum score 100 iBT), IELTS (minimum score 7). *Application deadline:* For fall admission, 12/15 for domestic and international students. Application fee: $75. Electronic applications accepted. *Expenses: Tuition:* Full-time $44,720; part-time $699 per unit. *Required fees:* $296. *Financial support:* In 2014–15, 743 students received support, including 124 fellowships (averaging $36,900 per year), 493 research assistantships (averaging $34,100 per year), 142 teaching assistantships (averaging $34,800 per year); Federal Work-Study, institutionally sponsored loans, scholarships/grants, traineeships, health care benefits, and unspecified assistantships also available. Financial award application deadline: 4/15; financial award applicants required to submit FAFSA. *Faculty research:* Information systems, circuits, biomedical sciences and engineering, computer science: artificial intelligence, systems, theory. *Total annual research expenditures:* $112 million. *Unit head:* Prof. Anantha P. Chandrakasan, Department Head, 617-253-4600. *Application contact:* Graduate Admissions, 617-253-4603, Fax: 617-258-7354, E-mail: grad-ap@eecs.mit.edu.
Website: http://www.eecs.mit.edu/.

McGill University, Faculty of Graduate and Postdoctoral Studies, Faculty of Engineering, Department of Electrical and Computer Engineering, Montréal, QC H3A 2T5, Canada. Offers M Eng, PhD.

McMaster University, School of Graduate Studies, Faculty of Engineering, Department of Electrical and Computer Engineering, Hamilton, ON L8S 4M2, Canada. Offers electrical engineering (M Eng, MA Sc, PhD). *Degree requirements:* For master's, thesis; for doctorate, comprehensive exam, thesis/dissertation. *Entrance requirements:* Additional exam requirements/recommendations for international students: Required—TOEFL (minimum score 550 paper-based). *Faculty research:* Robust and blind adaptive filtering, topics in statistical signal processing, local and metropolitan area networks, smart antennas, embedded wireless communications.

McNeese State University, Doré School of Graduate Studies, College of Engineering and Engineering Technology, Department of Engineering, Master of Engineering Program, Lake Charles, LA 70609. Offers chemical engineering (M Eng); civil engineering (M Eng); electrical engineering (M Eng); engineering management (M Eng); mechanical engineering (M Eng). Part-time and evening/weekend programs available. *Degree requirements:* For master's, thesis or alternative. *Entrance requirements:* For master's, GRE, baccalaureate degree, minimum overall GPA of 3.0. Additional exam requirements/recommendations for international students: Required—TOEFL (minimum score 560 paper-based; 83 iBT).

Memorial University of Newfoundland, School of Graduate Studies, Faculty of Engineering and Applied Science, St. John's, NL A1C 5S7, Canada. Offers civil engineering (M Eng, PhD); electrical and computer engineering (M Eng, PhD); mechanical engineering (M Eng, PhD); ocean and naval architecture engineering (M Eng, PhD). Part-time programs available. *Degree requirements:* For master's, thesis; for doctorate, comprehensive exam, thesis/dissertation, oral thesis defense. *Entrance requirements:* For master's, 2nd class degree; for doctorate, master's degree in engineering. Electronic applications accepted. *Faculty research:* Engineering analysis, environmental and hydrotechnical studies, manufacturing and robotics, mechanics, structures and materials.

Mercer University, Graduate Studies, Macon Campus, School of Engineering, Macon, GA 31207. Offers biomedical engineering (MSE); computer engineering (MSE); electrical engineering (MSE); engineering management (MSE); environmental engineering (MSE); environmental systems (MS); mechanical engineering (MSE); software engineering (MSE); software systems (MS); technical communications management (MS); technical management (MS). Part-time and evening/weekend programs available. Postbaccalaureate distance learning degree programs offered (no on-campus study). *Faculty:* 20 full-time (6 women), 2 part-time/adjunct (0 women). *Students:* 10 full-time (4 women), 75 part-time (16 women); includes 10 minority (5 Black or African American, non-Hispanic/Latino; 4 Asian, non-Hispanic/Latino; 1 Hispanic/Latino), 4 international. Average age 42. In 2014, 70 master's awarded. *Degree requirements:* For master's, thesis or alternative. *Entrance requirements:* For master's, minimum undergraduate GPA of 3.0. Additional exam requirements/recommendations for international students: Required—TOEFL (minimum score 550 paper-based; 80 iBT). *Application deadline:* For fall admission, 4/1 priority date for domestic and international students; for spring admission, 11/1 priority date for domestic and international students. Applications are processed on a rolling basis. Application fee: $75. *Expenses:* Expenses: Contact institution. *Financial support:* Federal Work-Study available. *Unit head:* Dr. Wade H. Shaw, Dean, 478-301-2459, Fax: 478-301-5593, E-mail: shaw_wh@mercer.edu. *Application contact:* Dr. Richard O. Mines, Program Director, 478-301-2347, Fax: 478-301-5433, E-mail: mines_ro@mercer.edu.
Website: http://engineering.mercer.edu/.

Michigan State University, The Graduate School, College of Engineering, Department of Electrical and Computer Engineering, East Lansing, MI 48824. Offers electrical engineering (MS, PhD). *Entrance requirements:* Additional exam requirements/recommendations for international students: Required—TOEFL. Electronic applications accepted.

Michigan Technological University, Graduate School, College of Engineering, Department of Electrical and Computer Engineering, Houghton, MI 49931. Offers advanced electric power engineering (Graduate Certificate); computer engineering (MS, PhD); electrical engineering (MS, PhD). Part-time programs available. Postbaccalaureate distance learning degree programs offered (minimal on-campus study). *Faculty:* 29 full-time, 8 part-time/adjunct. *Students:* 203 full-time, 70 part-time; includes 13 minority (4 Black or African American, non-Hispanic/Latino; 4 Asian, non-Hispanic/Latino; 5 Hispanic/Latino), 217 international. Average age 27. 1,168 applicants, 36% accepted, 78 enrolled. In 2014, 65 master's, 7 doctorates, 17 other advanced degrees awarded. Terminal master's awarded for partial completion of doctoral program. *Degree requirements:* For master's, comprehensive exam (for some programs), thesis (for some programs); for doctorate, comprehensive exam, thesis/dissertation. *Entrance requirements:* For master's and doctorate, GRE, statement of purpose, official transcripts, 2 letters of recommendation; for Graduate Certificate, statement of purpose, official transcripts. Additional exam requirements/recommendations for international students: Required—TOEFL (recommended score 100 iBT) or IELTS. *Application deadline:* For fall admission, 2/15 priority date for domestic and international students; for spring admission, 8/15 priority date for domestic and international students. Applications are processed on a rolling basis. Electronic applications accepted. *Expenses:* Expenses: Contact institution. *Financial support:* In 2014–15, 156 students received support, including 7 fellowships with full and partial tuition reimbursements available (averaging $13,824 per year), 31 research assistantships with full and partial tuition reimbursements available (averaging $13,824 per year), 22 teaching assistantships with full and partial tuition reimbursements available (averaging $13,824 per year); career-related internships or fieldwork, Federal Work-Study, scholarships/grants, health care benefits, unspecified assistantships, and cooperative program also available. Financial award applicants required to submit FAFSA. *Faculty research:* Information systems (signal processing and communications), solid-state electronics, power and energy systems, computer engineering, electro-physics. *Total annual research expenditures:* $1.8 million. *Unit head:* Dr. Daniel R. Fuhrmann, Department Chair, 906-487-2550, Fax: 906-487-2949, E-mail: fuhrmann@mtu.edu. *Application contact:* Lisa Rouleau, Business Manager/Technical Communications Specialist, 906-487-2550, Fax: 906-487-2949, E-mail: mlkamppi@mtu.edu.
Website: http://www.mtu.edu/ece/.

Minnesota State University Mankato, College of Graduate Studies, College of Science, Engineering and Technology, Department of Electrical and Computer Engineering and Technology, Mankato, MN 56001. Offers MSE. *Students:* 36 full-time (9 women), 17 part-time (3 women). *Degree requirements:* For master's, comprehensive exam, thesis. *Entrance requirements:* For master's, GRE General Test, minimum GPA of 3.0 during previous 2 years. Additional exam requirements/recommendations for international students: Required—TOEFL (minimum score 550 paper-based; 80 iBT). *Application deadline:* For fall admission, 7/1 priority date for domestic students; for spring admission, 11/1 for domestic students. Applications are processed on a rolling basis. Application fee: $40. Electronic applications accepted. *Financial support:*

Research assistantships with full tuition reimbursements, teaching assistantships with full tuition reimbursements, and unspecified assistantships available. Financial award application deadline: 3/15. *Unit head:* Dr. Han-Way Huang, Graduate Coordinator, 507-389-1121. *Application contact:* 507-389-2321, E-mail: grad@mnsu.edu.
Website: http://cset.mnsu.edu/ecet/.

Mississippi State University, Bagley College of Engineering, Department of Electrical and Computer Engineering, Mississippi State, MS 39762. Offers computer engineering (MS, PhD); electrical engineering (MS, PhD). Part-time programs available. Postbaccalaureate distance learning degree programs offered (minimal on-campus study). *Faculty:* 60 full-time (5 women), 4 part-time/adjunct (0 women). *Students:* 59 full-time (10 women), 39 part-time (3 women); includes 18 minority (7 Black or African American, non-Hispanic/Latino; 7 Asian, non-Hispanic/Latino; 3 Hispanic/Latino; 1 Two or more races, non-Hispanic/Latino), 45 international. Average age 33. 164 applicants, 38% accepted, 23 enrolled. In 2014, 6 master's, 12 doctorates awarded. Terminal master's awarded for partial completion of doctoral program. *Degree requirements:* For master's, comprehensive exam, thesis optional; for doctorate, comprehensive exam, thesis/dissertation, written exam, oral preliminary exam. *Entrance requirements:* For master's, GRE (for graduates from program not accredited by EAC/ABET), minimum GPA of 3.0 on BS; for doctorate, GRE (for graduates from program not accredited by EAC/ABET), minimum GPA of 3.5 on BS or MS. Additional exam requirements/recommendations for international students: Required—TOEFL (minimum score 550 paper-based; 79 iBT); Recommended—IELTS (minimum score 6.5). *Application deadline:* For fall admission, 7/1 for domestic students, 5/1 for international students; for spring admission, 11/1 for domestic students, 9/1 for international students. Applications are processed on a rolling basis. Application fee: $60. Electronic applications accepted. *Expenses:* Tuition, state resident: full-time $7140; part-time $783 per credit hour. Tuition, nonresident: full-time $18,478; part-time $2043 per credit hour. *Financial support:* In 2014–15, 19 research assistantships with full tuition reimbursements (averaging $17,720 per year), 19 teaching assistantships with full tuition reimbursements (averaging $15,184 per year) were awarded; Federal Work-Study, institutionally sponsored loans, scholarships/grants, and unspecified assistantships also available. Financial award application deadline: 4/1; financial award applicants required to submit FAFSA. *Faculty research:* Digital computing, power, controls, communication systems, microelectronics. *Total annual research expenditures:* $9 million. *Unit head:* Dr. Nicholas H. Younan, Jr., Professor and Department Head, 662-325-3912, Fax: 662-325-2298, E-mail: ece-head@ece.msstate.edu. *Application contact:* Dr. James E. Fowler, Professor/Interim Graduate Program Director, 662-325-3640, Fax: 662-325-2298, E-mail: fowler@ece.msstate.edu.
Website: http://www.ece.msstate.edu/.

Missouri University of Science and Technology, Graduate School, School of Engineering, Department of Electrical and Computer Engineering, Rolla, MO 65409. Offers computer engineering (MS, DE, PhD); electrical engineering (MS, DE, PhD). Part-time and evening/weekend programs available. Terminal master's awarded for partial completion of doctoral program. *Degree requirements:* For master's, thesis optional; for doctorate, comprehensive exam, thesis/dissertation, departmental qualifying exam. *Entrance requirements:* For master's, GRE General Test (minimum score 1100 verbal and quantitative, writing 4.5); for doctorate, GRE General Test (minimum score: verbal and quantitative 1100, writing 3.5). Additional exam requirements/recommendations for international students: Required—TOEFL. Electronic applications accepted. *Faculty research:* Power systems, computer/communication networks, intelligent control/robotics, robust control, nanotechnologies.

Montana State University, The Graduate School, College of Engineering, Department of Electrical and Computer Engineering, Bozeman, MT 59717. Offers electrical engineering (MS); engineering (PhD), including electrical and computer engineering option. Part-time programs available. *Degree requirements:* For master's, comprehensive exam, thesis (for some programs); for doctorate, comprehensive exam, thesis/dissertation. *Entrance requirements:* For master's, GRE, BS in electrical or computer engineering or related field; for doctorate, GRE, MS in electrical or computer engineering or related field. Additional exam requirements/recommendations for international students: Required—TOEFL (minimum score 550 paper-based). Electronic applications accepted. *Faculty research:* Optics and optoelectonics, communications and signal processing, microfabrication, complex systems and control, energy systems.

Montana Tech of The University of Montana, Graduate School, Electrical Engineering Program, Butte, MT 59701-8997. Offers MS. Part-time programs available. *Degree requirements:* For master's, comprehensive exam (for some programs), thesis optional. *Entrance requirements:* For master's, minimum GPA of 3.0. Additional exam requirements/recommendations for international students: Required—TOEFL (minimum score 525 paper-based; 71 iBT). Electronic applications accepted. *Expenses:* Tuition, state resident: full-time $5802; part-time $241 per credit. Tuition, nonresident: full-time $15,895; part-time $662 per credit. *Required fees:* $1516; $414 per credit. $207 per semester. One-time fee: $30. *Faculty research:* Energy grid modernization, battery diagnostics instrumentation, wind turbine research, improving energy efficiency.

Morgan State University, School of Graduate Studies, Clarence M. Mitchell, Jr. School of Engineering, Baltimore, MD 21251. Offers civil engineering (M Eng, D Eng); electrical and computer engineering (M Eng, MS, D Eng); industrial and systems engineering (M Eng, D Eng); transportation (MS). Part-time and evening/weekend programs available. *Degree requirements:* For master's, thesis, comprehensive exam or equivalent; for doctorate, thesis/dissertation, comprehensive exam or equivalent. *Entrance requirements:* For master's, GRE, minimum undergraduate GPA of 2.5; for doctorate, GRE, minimum GPA of 3.0. Additional exam requirements/recommendations for international students: Required—TOEFL (minimum score 550 paper-based).

Naval Postgraduate School, Departments and Academic Groups, Department of Electrical and Computer Engineering, Monterey, CA 93943-5216. Offers computer engineering (MS); electrical engineer (EE); electrical engineering (PhD); engineering acoustics (MS); engineering science (MS). Program only open to commissioned officers of the United States and friendly nations and selected United States federal civilian employees. *Accreditation:* ABET (one or more programs are accredited). Part-time programs available. Postbaccalaureate distance learning degree programs offered (minimal on-campus study). *Degree requirements:* For master's and EE, thesis (for some programs), capstone project or research/dissertation paper (for some programs); for doctorate, thesis/dissertation. *Faculty research:* Theory and design of digital communication systems; behavior modeling for detection, identification, prediction and reaction in artificial intelligence (AI) systems solutions; waveform design for target class discrimination with closed-loop radar; iterative technique for system identification with adaptive signal design.

Naval Postgraduate School, Departments and Academic Groups, Space Systems Academic Group, Monterey, CA 93943. Offers applied physics (MS); astronautical engineering (MS); computer science (MS); electrical engineering (MS); mechanical engineering (MS); space systems (Engr); space systems operations (MS). Program only open to commissioned officers of the United States and friendly nations and selected United States federal civilian employees. Part-time programs available. *Degree requirements:* For master's and Engr, thesis; for doctorate, thesis/dissertation. *Faculty research:* Military applications for space; space reconnaissance and remote sensing; radiation-hardened electronics for space; design, construction and operations of small satellites; satellite communications systems.

Naval Postgraduate School, Departments and Academic Groups, Undersea Warfare Academic Group, Monterey, CA 93943. Offers applied mathematics (MS); applied physics (MS); applied science (MS), including acoustics, operations research, physical oceanography, signal processing; electrical engineering (MS); engineering acoustics (MS, PhD); engineering science (MS), including electrical engineering, mechanical engineering; mechanical engineer (ME); mechanical engineering (MS, MSME); meteorology (MS); operations research (MS); physical oceanography (MS). Program only open to commissioned officers of the United States and friendly nations and selected United States federal civilian employees. Part-time programs available. *Degree requirements:* For master's, thesis. *Faculty research:* Unmanned/autonomous vehicles, sea mines and countermeasures, submarine warfare in the twentieth and twenty-first centuries.

New Jersey Institute of Technology, Newark College of Engineering, Newark, NJ 07102. Offers biomedical engineering (MS, PhD); chemical engineering (MS, PhD); computer engineering (MS, PhD); electrical engineering (MS, PhD); engineering management (MS); healthcare systems management (MS); industrial engineering (MS, PhD); Internet engineering (MS); manufacturing engineering (MS); mechanical engineering (MS, PhD); occupational safety and health engineering (MS); pharmaceutical bioprocessing (MS); pharmaceutical engineering (MS); pharmaceutical systems management (MS); power and energy systems (MS); telecommunications (MS); transportation (MS, PhD). Part-time and evening/weekend programs available. Terminal master's awarded for partial completion of doctoral program. *Degree requirements:* For master's, thesis optional; for doctorate, thesis/dissertation. *Entrance requirements:* For master's, GRE General Test; for doctorate, GRE General Test, minimum graduate GPA of 3.5. Additional exam requirements/recommendations for international students: Required—TOEFL (minimum score 550 paper-based; 79 iBT). Electronic applications accepted.

New Mexico Institute of Mining and Technology, Graduate Studies, Department of Electrical Engineering, Socorro, NM 87801. Offers MS. *Entrance requirements:* Additional exam requirements/recommendations for international students: Required—TOEFL (minimum score 540 paper-based). Electronic applications accepted.

New Mexico State University, College of Engineering, Klipsch School of Electrical and Computer Engineering, Las Cruces, NM 88003-8001. Offers MSEE, PhD, Graduate Certificate. Part-time and evening/weekend programs available. Postbaccalaureate distance learning degree programs offered (no on-campus study). *Faculty:* 17 full-time (1 woman), 1 part-time/adjunct (0 women). *Students:* 97 full-time (14 women), 54 part-time (4 women); includes 38 minority (2 American Indian or Alaska Native, non-Hispanic/Latino; 34 Hispanic/Latino; 2 Two or more races, non-Hispanic/Latino), 82 international. Average age 29. 168 applicants, 56% accepted, 30 enrolled. In 2014, 24 master's, 9 doctorates awarded. Terminal master's awarded for partial completion of doctoral program. *Degree requirements:* For master's, thesis (for some programs), final oral or written exam; for doctorate, comprehensive exam, thesis/dissertation. *Entrance requirements:* For master's, GRE, minimum GPA of 3.0; for doctorate, departmental qualifying exam, minimum GPA of 3.0. Additional exam requirements/recommendations for international students: Required—TOEFL (minimum score 550 paper-based; 79 iBT), IELTS (minimum score 6.5). *Application deadline:* For fall admission, 3/1 priority date for domestic and international students; for spring admission, 8/1 priority date for domestic and international students. Applications are processed on a rolling basis. Application fee: $40 ($50 for international students). Electronic applications accepted. *Expenses:* Tuition, state resident: full-time $3969; part-time $220.50 per credit hour. Tuition, nonresident: full-time $13,838; part-time $768.80 per credit hour. *Required fees:* $853; $47.40 per credit hour. *Financial support:* In 2014–15, 91 students received support, including 1 fellowship (averaging $3,970 per year), 25 research assistantships (averaging $13,922 per year), 31 teaching assistantships (averaging $11,005 per year); career-related internships or fieldwork, Federal Work-Study, scholarships/grants, traineeships, health care benefits, and unspecified assistantships also available. Support available to part-time students. Financial award application deadline: 3/1. *Faculty research:* Image and digital signal processing, energy systems, wireless communications, analog and mixed-signal VLSI design, electro-optics. *Total annual research expenditures:* $2.5 million. *Unit head:* Dr. Satishkuma Ranade, Academic Department Head, 575-646-3115, Fax: 575-646-1435, E-mail: sranade@nmsu.edu. *Application contact:* 575-646-3115, Fax: 575-646-1435, E-mail: eceoffice@nmsu.edu.
Website: http://ece.nmsu.edu.

New York Institute of Technology, School of Engineering and Computing Sciences, Department of Electrical Engineering, Old Westbury, NY 11568-8000. Offers electrical and computer engineering (MS). Part-time and evening/weekend programs available. *Degree requirements:* For master's, project. *Entrance requirements:* For master's, GRE General Test (if QPA less than 2.85), BS in electrical engineering or related field, minimum QPA of 2.85. Additional exam requirements/recommendations for international students: Required—TOEFL (minimum score 550 paper-based; 79 iBT), IELTS (minimum score 6). Electronic applications accepted. *Faculty research:* Detection of physical node capture in wireless sensor networks, intelligent networks for health monitoring, technology to patients with Parkinson's disease, assistive technologies.

New York University, Polytechnic School of Engineering, Department of Electrical and Computer Engineering, Major in Electrical Engineering, New York, NY 10012-1019. Offers MS, PhD. Part-time and evening/weekend programs available. Postbaccalaureate distance learning degree programs offered (no on-campus study). *Students:* 437 full-time (63 women), 71 part-time (13 women); includes 43 minority (7 Black or African American, non-Hispanic/Latino; 30 Asian, non-Hispanic/Latino; 5 Hispanic/Latino; 1 Two or more races, non-Hispanic/Latino), 426 international. Average age 25. 1,522 applicants, 38% accepted, 239 enrolled. In 2014, 203 master's, 21 doctorates awarded. *Degree requirements:* For master's, comprehensive exam (for some programs), thesis (for some programs); for doctorate, comprehensive exam, thesis/dissertation, qualifying exam. *Entrance requirements:* For master's, BS in electrical engineering; for doctorate, MS in electrical engineering. Additional exam requirements/recommendations for international students: Required—TOEFL (minimum score 550 paper-based; 80 iBT); Recommended—IELTS (minimum score 6.5). *Application deadline:* For fall admission, 2/15 priority date for domestic and international students; for spring admission, 11/1 priority date for domestic and international students. Applications are processed on a rolling basis. Application fee: $75. Electronic applications accepted. *Financial support:* Fellowships, research assistantships, teaching assistantships, institutionally sponsored loans, scholarships/grants, and unspecified assistantships available. Support available to part-time students. Financial award applicants required to submit FAFSA. *Unit head:* Prof. Yao Wang, Program Director, 718-260-3469, E-mail: yw523@nyu.edu. *Application contact:* Raymond Lutzky, Director of Graduate Enrollment Management, 718-637-5984, Fax: 718-260-3624, E-mail: rlutzky@poly.edu.

Norfolk State University, School of Graduate Studies, School of Science and Technology, Program in Electronics Engineering, Norfolk, VA 23504. Offers MS.

Electrical Engineering

North Carolina Agricultural and Technical State University, School of Graduate Studies, College of Engineering, Department of Electrical and Computer Engineering, Greensboro, NC 27411. Offers electrical engineering (MSEE, PhD), including communications and signal processing, computer engineering, electronic and optical materials and devices, power systems and control. Part-time programs available. *Degree requirements:* For master's, project, thesis defense; for doctorate, thesis/dissertation. *Entrance requirements:* For master's, GRE General Test, GRE Subject Test, minimum GPA of 2.8; for doctorate, GRE General Test, minimum GPA of 3.0. *Faculty research:* Semiconductor compounds, VLSI design, image processing, optical systems and devices, fault-tolerant computing.

North Carolina Agricultural and Technical State University, School of Graduate Studies, School of Technology, Department of Electronics, Computer, and Information Technology, Greensboro, NC 27411. Offers electronics and computer technology (MSIT, MSTM); information technology (MSIT, MSTM).

North Carolina State University, Graduate School, College of Engineering, Department of Electrical and Computer Engineering, Program in Electrical Engineering, Raleigh, NC 27695. Offers MS, PhD. *Degree requirements:* For master's, thesis (for some programs); for doctorate, thesis/dissertation. *Entrance requirements:* For master's and doctorate, GRE. Additional exam requirements/recommendations for international students: Required—TOEFL (minimum score 575 paper-based). Electronic applications accepted. *Faculty research:* Microwave devices, wireless communications, nanoelectronics and photonics, robotic and mechatronics, power electronics.

North Dakota State University, College of Graduate and Interdisciplinary Studies, College of Engineering and Architecture, Department of Electrical and Computer Engineering, Fargo, ND 58108. Offers MS, PhD. Part-time programs available. Terminal master's awarded for partial completion of doctoral program. *Degree requirements:* For master's, comprehensive exam, thesis; for doctorate, comprehensive exam, thesis/dissertation. *Entrance requirements:* Additional exam requirements/recommendations for international students: Required—TOEFL (minimum score 525 paper-based; 71 iBT). Electronic applications accepted. *Faculty research:* Computers, power and control systems, microwaves, communications and signal processing, bioengineering.

Northeastern University, College of Engineering, Boston, MA 02115-5096. Offers bioengineering (PhD); chemical engineering (MS, PhD); civil engineering (MS, PhD); computer engineering (PhD); computer systems engineering (MS); electrical and computer engineering (MS); electrical and engineering leadership (MS); electrical engineering (PhD); energy systems (MS); engineering leadership (Certificate); engineering management (MRTP); industrial engineering (MS, PhD); information assurance (PhD); information systems (MS); interdisciplinary (PhD); mechanical engineering (MS, PhD); operations research (MS); telecommunication systems management (MS). Part-time programs available. *Expenses:* Contact institution.

Northern Arizona University, Graduate College, College of Engineering, Forestry and Natural Sciences, Programs in Engineering, Flagstaff, AZ 86011. Offers civil and environmental engineering (M Eng); civil engineering (MSE); computer science (MSE); electrical engineering (M Eng, MSE); engineering (M Eng, MSE); environmental engineering (M Eng, MSE); mechanical engineering (M Eng, MSE). Part-time programs available. Postbaccalaureate distance learning degree programs offered (no on-campus study). *Degree requirements:* For master's, thesis. *Entrance requirements:* For master's, GRE General Test. Additional exam requirements/recommendations for international students: Required—TOEFL (minimum score 550 paper-based; 80 iBT), IELTS (minimum score 7). Electronic applications accepted.

Northern Illinois University, Graduate School, College of Engineering and Engineering Technology, Department of Electrical Engineering, De Kalb, IL 60115-2854. Offers MS. Part-time and evening/weekend programs available. *Faculty:* 9 full-time (0 women). *Students:* 37 full-time (11 women), 24 part-time (4 women); includes 3 minority (all Asian, non-Hispanic/Latino), 51 international. Average age 24. 321 applicants, 35% accepted, 25 enrolled. In 2014, 19 master's awarded. *Degree requirements:* For master's, comprehensive exam, thesis optional. *Entrance requirements:* For master's, GRE General Test, minimum GPA of 2.75. Additional exam requirements/recommendations for international students: Required—TOEFL (minimum score 550 paper-based). *Application deadline:* For fall admission, 6/1 for domestic students, 5/1 for international students; for spring admission, 11/1 for domestic students, 10/1 for international students. Applications are processed on a rolling basis. Application fee: $40. Electronic applications accepted. *Financial support:* In 2014–15, 4 research assistantships with full tuition reimbursements, 15 teaching assistantships with full tuition reimbursements were awarded; fellowships with full tuition reimbursements, career-related internships or fieldwork, Federal Work-Study, scholarships/grants, tuition waivers (full), and staff assistantships also available. Support available to part-time students. Financial award applicants required to submit FAFSA. *Faculty research:* Digital signal processing, optics, nano-electronic devices, VLSI. *Unit head:* Dr. Ibrahim Abdel-Motaleb, Chair, 815-753-1290, Fax: 815-753-1289, E-mail: ibrahim@niu.edu. *Application contact:* Graduate School Office, 815-753-0395, E-mail: gradsch@niu.edu.
Website: http://www.niu.edu/ee/.

Northwestern Polytechnic University, School of Engineering, Fremont, CA 94539-7482. Offers computer science (MS); computer systems engineering (MS); electrical engineering (MS). Part-time and evening/weekend programs available. *Degree requirements:* For master's, thesis optional. *Entrance requirements:* For master's, minimum GPA of 3.0. Additional exam requirements/recommendations for international students: Required—TOEFL (minimum score 550 paper-based; 79 iBT). *Faculty research:* Computer networking, database design, Internet technology, software engineering, digital signal processing.

Northwestern University, McCormick School of Engineering and Applied Science, Department of Electrical Engineering and Computer Science, Evanston, IL 60208. Offers electrical engineering, computer engineering, and computer science (MS, PhD); information technology (MS). MS and PhD admissions and degrees offered through The Graduate School. Part-time programs available. *Faculty:* 47 full-time (3 women). *Students:* 301 full-time (61 women), 57 part-time (11 women); includes 27 minority (3 Black or African American, non-Hispanic/Latino; 13 Asian, non-Hispanic/Latino; 9 Hispanic/Latino; 2 Two or more races, non-Hispanic/Latino), 299 international. Average age 26. 1,544 applicants, 24% accepted, 123 enrolled. In 2014, 42 master's, 27 doctorates awarded. Terminal master's awarded for partial completion of doctoral program. *Degree requirements:* For master's, comprehensive exam (for some programs), thesis optional; for doctorate, comprehensive exam, thesis/dissertation. *Entrance requirements:* For master's and doctorate, GRE General Test. Additional exam requirements/recommendations for international students: Required—TOEFL (minimum score 577 paper-based; 90 iBT) or IELTS (minimum score of 7.0). *Application deadline:* For fall admission, 12/31 for domestic and international students; for winter admission, 11/15 for domestic students, 11/1 for international students; for spring admission, 2/15 for domestic students, 2/1 for international students. Application fee: $95. Electronic applications accepted. *Financial support:* Fellowships with full tuition reimbursements, research assistantships with full tuition reimbursements, teaching assistantships with full tuition reimbursements, career-related internships or fieldwork, institutionally sponsored loans, health care benefits, and unspecified assistantships available. Financial award application deadline: 1/15; financial award applicants required to submit FAFSA. *Faculty research:* Solid state and photonics; computing, algorithms, and applications; computer engineering and systems; cognitive systems; graphics and interactive media; signals and systems. *Total annual research expenditures:* $14.7 million. *Unit head:* Dr. Alan Sahakian, Chair, 847-491-7007, Fax: 847-491-4455, E-mail: sahakian@ece.northwestern.edu. *Application contact:* Dr. Allen Taflove, Director of Graduate Admissions, 847-491-4127, Fax: 847-491-4455, E-mail: taflove@ece.northwestern.edu.
Website: http://www.eecs.northwestern.edu/.

Oakland University, Graduate Study and Lifelong Learning, School of Engineering and Computer Science, Department of Electrical and Computer Engineering, Rochester, MI 48309-4401. Offers MS. Part-time and evening/weekend programs available. *Entrance requirements:* For master's, minimum GPA of 3.0. Additional exam requirements/recommendations for international students: Required—TOEFL (minimum score 550 paper-based). Electronic applications accepted. *Expenses:* Contact institution. *Faculty research:* Reliable peripheral nerve interfaces.

The Ohio State University, Graduate School, College of Engineering, Department of Electrical and Computer Engineering, Columbus, OH 43210. Offers electrical and computer engineering (MS, PhD); electrical engineering (MS, PhD). Part-time programs available. *Faculty:* 56. *Students:* 436 full-time (90 women), 29 part-time (7 women); includes 30 minority (5 Black or African American, non-Hispanic/Latino; 18 Asian, non-Hispanic/Latino; 3 Hispanic/Latino; 4 Two or more races, non-Hispanic/Latino), 342 international. Average age 26. In 2014, 120 master's, 27 doctorates awarded. Terminal master's awarded for partial completion of doctoral program. *Degree requirements:* For master's, thesis optional; for doctorate, thesis/dissertation. *Entrance requirements:* For master's, GRE General Test (for all graduates of foreign universities and for applicants if undergraduate GPA below 3.2); for doctorate, GRE General Test (for all graduates of foreign universities and for applicants if graduate work GPA is below 3.5). Additional exam requirements/recommendations for international students: Required—TOEFL (minimum score 580 paper-based; 92 iBT), TSE recommended; Recommended—IELTS (minimum score 7.5). *Application deadline:* For fall admission, 12/1 priority date for domestic and international students; for winter admission, 12/1 for domestic students, 11/1 for international students; for spring admission, 3/1 for domestic students, 2/1 for international students. Applications are processed on a rolling basis. Application fee: $60 ($70 for international students). Electronic applications accepted. *Financial support:* Fellowships with full tuition reimbursements, research assistantships with full tuition reimbursements, teaching assistantships with full tuition reimbursements, career-related internships or fieldwork, Federal Work-Study, institutionally sponsored loans, scholarships/grants, traineeships, health care benefits, and unspecified assistantships available. Support available to part-time students. *Unit head:* Dr. Joel T. Johnson, Chair, 614-292-1563, E-mail: johnson.1374@osu.edu. *Application contact:* Electrical and Computer Engineering Graduate Program, 614-292-2572, Fax: 614-292-7596, E-mail: ecegrad@ece.osu.edu.
Website: http://ece.osu.edu/.

Ohio University, Graduate College, Russ College of Engineering and Technology, School of Electrical Engineering and Computer Science, Athens, OH 45701-2979. Offers computer science (MS); electrical engineering (MS); electrical engineering and computer science (PhD). *Degree requirements:* For master's, comprehensive exam (for some programs), thesis; for doctorate, comprehensive exam, thesis/dissertation, qualifying exams. *Entrance requirements:* For master's, GRE, BSEE or BSCS, minimum GPA of 3.0; for doctorate, GRE, MSEE or MSCS, minimum GPA of 3.0. Additional exam requirements/recommendations for international students: Required—TOEFL (minimum score 550 paper-based; 80 iBT) or IELTS (minimum score 6.5). Electronic applications accepted. *Faculty research:* Avionics, networking/communications, intelligent distribution, real-time computing, control systems, optical properties of semiconductors.

Oklahoma State University, College of Engineering, Architecture and Technology, School of Electrical and Computer Engineering, Stillwater, OK 74078. Offers MS, PhD. Postbaccalaureate distance learning degree programs offered. *Faculty:* 24 full-time (1 woman), 1 part-time/adjunct (0 women). *Students:* 149 full-time (48 women), 86 part-time (15 women); includes 16 minority (1 Black or African American, non-Hispanic/Latino; 1 American Indian or Alaska Native, non-Hispanic/Latino; 4 Asian, non-Hispanic/Latino; 4 Hispanic/Latino; 6 Two or more races, non-Hispanic/Latino), 182 international. Average age 26. 627 applicants, 24% accepted, 64 enrolled. In 2014, 59 master's, 9 doctorates awarded. *Degree requirements:* For master's, thesis or alternative; for doctorate, comprehensive exam, thesis/dissertation. *Entrance requirements:* For master's and doctorate, GRE or GMAT. Additional exam requirements/recommendations for international students: Required—TOEFL (minimum score 550 paper-based; 79 iBT). *Application deadline:* For fall admission, 3/1 priority date for international students; for spring admission, 8/1 priority date for international students. Applications are processed on a rolling basis. Application fee: $40 ($75 for international students). Electronic applications accepted. *Expenses:* Tuition, state resident: full-time $4488; part-time $187 per credit hour. Tuition, nonresident: full-time $18,360; part-time $765 per credit hour. *Required fees:* $2413; $100.55 per credit hour. Tuition and fees vary according to campus/location. *Financial support:* In 2014–15, 46 research assistantships (averaging $15,357 per year), 28 teaching assistantships (averaging $14,057 per year) were awarded; career-related internships or fieldwork, Federal Work-Study, scholarships/grants, health care benefits, tuition waivers (partial), and unspecified assistantships also available. Support available to part-time students. Financial award application deadline: 3/1; financial award applicants required to submit FAFSA. *Unit head:* Dr. James C. West, Interim Department Head, 405-744-5151, Fax: 405-744-9198, E-mail: jwest@okstate.edu.
Website: http://www.ece.okstate.edu.

Old Dominion University, Frank Batten College of Engineering and Technology, Program in Electrical and Computer Engineering, Norfolk, VA 23529. Offers ME, MS, PhD. Part-time programs available. Postbaccalaureate distance learning degree programs offered (minimal on-campus study). *Faculty:* 21 full-time (1 woman), 2 part-time/adjunct (both women). *Students:* 37 full-time (10 women), 65 part-time (11 women); includes 21 minority (6 Black or African American, non-Hispanic/Latino; 1 American Indian or Alaska Native, non-Hispanic/Latino; 7 Asian, non-Hispanic/Latino; 5 Hispanic/Latino; 1 Native Hawaiian or other Pacific Islander, non-Hispanic/Latino; 1 Two or more races, non-Hispanic/Latino), 47 international. Average age 30. 144 applicants, 62% accepted, 16 enrolled. In 2014, 18 master's, 8 doctorates awarded. *Degree requirements:* For master's, comprehensive exam (for some programs), thesis (for some programs); for doctorate, thesis/dissertation, candidacy exam, diagnostic exam. *Entrance requirements:* For master's, GRE, two letters of recommendation; for doctorate, GRE, three letters of recommendation, resume, personal statement of objective. Additional exam requirements/recommendations for international students: Required—TOEFL (minimum score 550 paper-based; 79 iBT). *Application deadline:* For fall admission, 6/1 for domestic students, 4/15 for international students; for spring admission, 11/1 for domestic students, 10/1 for international students. Applications are processed on a rolling basis. Application fee: $50. Electronic applications accepted. *Expenses:* Tuition, state resident: full-time $10,488; part-time $437 per credit. Tuition, nonresident: full-time $26,136; part-time $1089 per credit. *Required fees:* $64 per semester. One-time fee: $50. *Financial support:* In 2014–15, 2 fellowships with full

tuition reimbursements (averaging $17,500 per year), 24 research assistantships with full and partial tuition reimbursements (averaging $15,000 per year), 25 teaching assistantships with full and partial tuition reimbursements (averaging $15,000 per year) were awarded; career-related internships or fieldwork, Federal Work-Study, scholarships/grants, tuition waivers (full), and unspecified assistantships also available. Support available to part-time students. Financial award application deadline: 2/15; financial award applicants required to submit FAFSA. *Faculty research:* Signal and image processing biomedical and target detection applications, renewal energy applications including the development of high efficiency solar cells, nanotechnology and nanoscale thin film techniques, ultrafast (femtosecond) laser applications, linear and nonlinear systems theory. *Total annual research expenditures:* $3 million. *Unit head:* Dr. Dimitrie Popescu, Graduate Program Director, 757-683-5414, Fax: 757-683-3220, E-mail: ecegpd@odu.edu. *Application contact:* Linda Marshall, Senior Secretary, 757-683-3741, Fax: 757-683-3220, E-mail: lmarshal@odu.edu.
Website: http://eng.odu.edu/ece/.

Oregon Health & Science University, School of Medicine, Graduate Programs in Medicine, Department of Computer Science and Engineering, Portland, OR 97239-3098. Offers computer science and engineering (MS, PhD); electrical engineering (MS, PhD). Part-time programs available. *Faculty:* 7 full-time (2 women), 1 part-time/adjunct (0 women). *Students:* 18 full-time (8 women), 10 international. Average age 32. 10 applicants, 60% accepted, 5 enrolled. In 2014, 1 master's, 3 doctorates awarded. Terminal master's awarded for partial completion of doctoral program. *Degree requirements:* For master's, thesis (for some programs); for doctorate, comprehensive exam, thesis/dissertation, qualifying exam. *Entrance requirements:* For master's and doctorate, GRE General Test (minimum scores: 153 Verbal/148 Quantitative/4.5 Analytical). Additional exam requirements/recommendations for international students: Required—IELTS or TOEFL. *Application deadline:* For fall admission, 7/15 for domestic students, 5/15 for international students; for winter admission, 10/15 for domestic students, 9/15 for international students; for spring admission, 1/15 for domestic students, 12/15 for international students. Applications are processed on a rolling basis. Application fee: $70. Electronic applications accepted. *Financial support:* Health care benefits, tuition waivers (full), and full tuition and stipends (for PhD students) available. *Faculty research:* Natural language processing, speech signal processing, computational biology, autism spectrum disorders, hearing and speaking disorders. *Unit head:* Dr. Peter Heeman, Program Director, 503-748-1635, E-mail: cseedept@csee.ogi.edu. *Application contact:* Pat Dickerson, Administrative Coordinator, 503-748-1635, E-mail: cseedept@csee.ogi.edu.

Oregon State University, College of Engineering, Program in Electrical and Computer Engineering, Corvallis, OR 97331. Offers M Eng, MS, PhD. *Faculty:* 49 full-time (7 women), 2 part-time/adjunct (both women). *Students:* 170 full-time (26 women), 19 part-time (5 women); includes 10 minority (8 Asian, non-Hispanic/Latino; 1 Hispanic/Latino; 1 Two or more races, non-Hispanic/Latino), 139 international. Average age 28. 500 applicants, 19% accepted, 65 enrolled. In 2014, 44 master's, 20 doctorates awarded. *Entrance requirements:* For master's and doctorate, GRE. Additional exam requirements/recommendations for international students: Required—TOEFL (minimum score 600 paper-based; 80 iBT), IELTS (minimum score 7). *Application deadline:* For fall admission, 1/15 for domestic students. Application fee: $60. *Expenses:* Expenses: $15,359 full-time resident tuition and fees; $23,405 non-resident. *Unit head:* Bella Bose, Professor/Interim School Head, 541-737-5573. *Application contact:* Graduate Coordinator, 541-737-7234, Fax: 541-737-1300, E-mail: eecs.gradinfo@oregonstate.edu.
Website: http://eecs.oregonstate.edu/current-students/graduate/ece-program.

Penn State Harrisburg, Graduate School, School of Science, Engineering and Technology, Middletown, PA 17057-4898. Offers computer science (MS); electrical engineering (M Eng, MS); engineering management (MPS); engineering science (M Eng); environmental engineering (M Eng); structural engineering (Certificate). Part-time and evening/weekend programs available. *Unit head:* Dr. Mukund S. Kulkarni, Chancellor, 717-948-6105, Fax: 717-948-6452, E-mail: msk5@psu.edu. *Application contact:* Robert W. Coffman, Jr., Director of Enrollment Management, Admissions, 717-948-6250, Fax: 717-948-6325, E-mail: ric1@psu.edu.
Website: http://harrisburg.psu.edu/science-engineering-technology.

Penn State University Park, Graduate School, College of Engineering, Department of Electrical Engineering, University Park, PA 16802. Offers M Eng, MS, PhD. *Unit head:* Dr. Amr S. Elnashai, Dean, 814-865-7537, Fax: 814-863-4749, E-mail: ase2@psu.edu. *Application contact:* Lori A. Stania, Director, Graduate Student Services, 814-867-5278, Fax: 814-863-4627, E-mail: gswww@psu.edu.
Website: http://www.ee.psu.edu/.

Polytechnic University of Puerto Rico, Graduate School, Hato Rey, PR 00919. Offers business administration (MBA), including computer information systems, general management, management of information systems, management of international enterprises; civil engineering (ME, MS); computer engineering (ME, MS); computer science (MCS, MS); electrical engineering (ME, MS); engineering management (MEM); environmental management (MEM); landscape architecture (M Land Arch); manufacturing competitiveness (MMC, MS); manufacturing engineering (ME, MS); mechanical engineering (M Mech E). Part-time and evening/weekend programs available. *Entrance requirements:* For master's, 3 letters of recommendation.

Portland State University, Graduate Studies, Maseeh College of Engineering and Computer Science, Department of Electrical and Computer Engineering, Portland, OR 97207-0751. Offers M Eng, MS, PhD. Part-time and evening/weekend programs available. *Faculty:* 22 full-time (3 women), 4 part-time/adjunct (1 woman). *Students:* 217 full-time (53 women), 112 part-time (19 women); includes 33 minority (7 Black or African American, non-Hispanic/Latino; 1 American Indian or Alaska Native, non-Hispanic/Latino; 21 Asian, non-Hispanic/Latino; 3 Hispanic/Latino; 1 Native Hawaiian or other Pacific Islander, non-Hispanic/Latino), 207 international. Average age 29. 515 applicants, 38% accepted, 116 enrolled. In 2014, 93 master's awarded. *Degree requirements:* For master's, variable foreign language requirement, oral exam; for doctorate, one foreign language, comprehensive exam, thesis/dissertation, oral and written exams. *Entrance requirements:* For master's, GRE, Incoming students must have a 2.5 GPA for conditional admission and a 2.75 GPA for regular admission. We normally expect students to have at least a 3.0 undergraduate GPA; for doctorate, GRE General Test, GRE Subject Test, Master's degree in electrical engineering or a related field, 3 reference letters, statement of purpose and a writing sample. Additional exam requirements/recommendations for international students: Required—TOEFL (minimum score 550 paper-based; 80 iBT). *Application deadline:* For fall admission, 2/1 for domestic and international students; for winter admission, 8/15 for domestic and international students; for spring admission, 11/1 for domestic and international students. Application fee: $50. *Expenses:* Tuition, state resident: part-time $222 per credit. Tuition, nonresident: part-time $527 per credit. *Required fees:* $22 per contact hour. $100 per quarter. Tuition and fees vary according to program. *Financial support:* In 2014–15, 10 research assistantships with full and partial tuition reimbursements (averaging $7,253 per year), 14 teaching assistantships with full and partial tuition reimbursements (averaging $2,768 per year) were awarded; career-related internships or fieldwork, Federal Work-Study, scholarships/grants, and unspecified assistantships

also available. Support available to part-time students. Financial award application deadline: 3/1; financial award applicants required to submit FAFSA. *Faculty research:* Optics and laser systems, design automation, VLSI design, computer systems, power electronics. *Total annual research expenditures:* $1.5 million. *Unit head:* Dr. James McNames, Chair, 503-725-5390, Fax: 503-725-3807, E-mail: mcnames@ece.pdx.edu. *Application contact:* Eliza Conlin, Graduate Coordinator, 503-725-3002, Fax: 503-725-3807, E-mail: kelleyg@ece.pdx.edu.
Website: http://www.pdx.edu/ece/.

Prairie View A&M University, College of Engineering, Prairie View, TX 77446-0519. Offers computer information systems (MSCIS); computer science (MSCS); electrical engineering (MSEE, PhDEE); engineering (MS Engr). Part-time and evening/weekend programs available. *Faculty:* 29 full-time (5 women), 1 (woman) part-time/adjunct. *Students:* 113 full-time (46 women), 55 part-time (23 women); includes 72 minority (49 Black or African American, non-Hispanic/Latino; 1 American Indian or Alaska Native, non-Hispanic/Latino; 18 Asian, non-Hispanic/Latino; 3 Hispanic/Latino; 1 Two or more races, non-Hispanic/Latino), 73 international. Average age 32. 106 applicants, 98% accepted, 64 enrolled. In 2014, 37 master's, 5 doctorates awarded. *Degree requirements:* For master's, thesis (for some programs); for doctorate, comprehensive exam, thesis/dissertation. *Entrance requirements:* For master's, GRE General Test (minimum score of 900), bachelor's degree in engineering from ABET-accredited institution; for doctorate, minimum GPA of 3.0. Additional exam requirements/recommendations for international students: Required—TOEFL (minimum score 550 paper-based; 79 iBT). *Application deadline:* For fall admission, 7/1 priority date for domestic students, 6/1 priority date for international students; for spring admission, 11/1 priority date for domestic students, 10/1 priority date for international students; for summer admission, 3/1 priority date for domestic students, 2/1 priority date for international students. Application fee: $50. Electronic applications accepted. *Expenses:* Expenses: $6,686 tuition and fees. *Financial support:* In 2014–15, 14 research assistantships with partial tuition reimbursements (averaging $8,000 per year), 14 teaching assistantships with partial tuition reimbursements (averaging $7,500 per year) were awarded; career-related internships or fieldwork, institutionally sponsored loans, scholarships/grants, health care benefits, tuition waivers (partial), and unspecified assistantships also available. Financial award application deadline: 3/1; financial award applicants required to submit FAFSA. *Faculty research:* Applied radiation research, thermal science, computational fluid dynamics, analog mixed signal, aerial space battlefield. *Unit head:* Dr. Kendall T. Harris, Dean, 936-261-9956, Fax: 936-261-9869, E-mail: tharris@pvamu.edu. *Application contact:* Pauline Walker, Administrative Assistant II, Research and Graduate Studies, 936-261-3521, Fax: 936-261-3529, E-mail: pmwalker@pvamu.edu.

Princeton University, Graduate School, School of Engineering and Applied Science, Department of Electrical Engineering, Princeton, NJ 08544-1019. Offers M Eng, PhD. Terminal master's awarded for partial completion of doctoral program. *Degree requirements:* For doctorate, thesis/dissertation, general exam. *Entrance requirements:* For master's, GRE General Test, 3 letters of recommendation; for doctorate, GRE General Test, official transcript(s), 3 letters of recommendation, personal statement. Additional exam requirements/recommendations for international students: Required—TOEFL. Electronic applications accepted. *Faculty research:* Computer engineering, electronic materials and devices, information sciences and systems, optics and optical electronics.

Purdue University, College of Engineering, School of Electrical and Computer Engineering, West Lafayette, IN 47907-2035. Offers MS, MSE, MSECE, PhD. MS and PhD degree programs in biomedical engineering offered jointly with School of Mechanical Engineering and School of Chemical Engineering. Part-time programs available. Postbaccalaureate distance learning degree programs offered (no on-campus study). Terminal master's awarded for partial completion of doctoral program. *Entrance requirements:* For master's and doctorate, GRE General Test, minimum GPA of 3.25. Additional exam requirements/recommendations for international students: Required—TOEFL (minimum score 550 paper-based; 77 iBT). Electronic applications accepted. *Faculty research:* Automatic controls; biomedical imaging; computer engineering; communications, networking signal and image processing; fields and optics.

Purdue University Calumet, Graduate Studies Office, School of Engineering, Mathematics, and Science, Department of Engineering, Hammond, IN 46323-2094. Offers computer engineering (MSE); electrical engineering (MSE); engineering (MS); mechanical engineering (MSE). Evening/weekend programs available. *Entrance requirements:* Additional exam requirements/recommendations for international students: Required—TOEFL.

Queen's University at Kingston, School of Graduate Studies, Faculty of Applied Science, Department of Electrical and Computer Engineering, Kingston, ON K7L 3N6, Canada. Offers M Eng, M Sc, M Sc Eng, PhD. Part-time programs available. *Degree requirements:* For master's, thesis optional; for doctorate, comprehensive exam, thesis/dissertation. *Entrance requirements:* Additional exam requirements/recommendations for international students: Required—TOEFL (minimum score 580 paper-based). *Faculty research:* Communications and signal processing systems, computer engineering systems.

Rensselaer at Hartford, Department of Engineering, Program in Electrical Engineering, Hartford, CT 06120-2991. Offers ME, MS. Part-time and evening/weekend programs available. *Degree requirements:* For master's, thesis optional. *Entrance requirements:* For master's, GRE. Additional exam requirements/recommendations for international students: Required—TOEFL (minimum score 600 paper-based; 100 iBT).

Rensselaer Polytechnic Institute, Graduate School, School of Engineering, Program in Electrical Engineering, Troy, NY 12180-3590. Offers M Eng, MS, D Eng, PhD. *Faculty:* 44 full-time (11 women), 9 part-time/adjunct (1 woman). *Students:* 93 full-time (14 women), 9 part-time (1 woman); includes 5 minority (2 Black or African American, non-Hispanic/Latino; 2 Asian, non-Hispanic/Latino; 1 Two or more races, non-Hispanic/Latino), 78 international. Average age 27. 464 applicants, 13% accepted, 30 enrolled. In 2014, 24 master's, 14 doctorates awarded. Terminal master's awarded for partial completion of doctoral program. *Degree requirements:* For master's, thesis (for some programs); for doctorate, thesis/dissertation. *Entrance requirements:* For master's and doctorate, GRE. Additional exam requirements/recommendations for international students: Required—TOEFL (minimum score 570 paper-based; 88 iBT), IELTS (minimum score 6.5), PTE (minimum score 60). *Application deadline:* For fall admission, 1/1 priority date for domestic and international students; for spring admission, 8/15 priority date for domestic and international students. Applications are processed on a rolling basis. Application fee: $75. Electronic applications accepted. *Expenses:* Tuition: Full-time $46,700; part-time $1945 per credit. Tuition and fees vary according to course load. *Financial support:* In 2014–15, 72 students received support, including research assistantships (averaging $18,500 per year), teaching assistantships (averaging $18,500 per year); fellowships also available. Financial award application deadline: 1/1. *Faculty research:* Communications, information, and signals and systems; computer engineering, hardware, and architecture; computer networking; control, robotics, and automation; energy sources and systems; image science: computer vision, image processing, and geographic information science; microelectronics, photonics, VLSI, and mixed-signal design; plasma science and electromagnetics. *Total annual research*

expenditures: $7.3 million. *Unit head:* Dr. Ken Vastola, Graduate Program Director, 518-276-6074, E-mail: gpd@ecse.rpi.edu. *Application contact:* Office of Graduate Admissions, 518-276-6216, E-mail: gradadmissions@rpi.edu.
Website: http://www.ecse.rpi.edu/.

Rice University, Graduate Programs, George R. Brown School of Engineering, Department of Electrical and Computer Engineering, Houston, TX 77251-1892. Offers bioengineering (MS, PhD); circuits, controls, and communication systems (MS, PhD); computer science and engineering (MS, PhD); electrical engineering (MEE); lasers, microwaves, and solid-state electronics (MS, PhD); MBA/MEE. Part-time programs available. *Degree requirements:* For master's, thesis (for some programs); for doctorate, thesis/dissertation. *Entrance requirements:* For master's and doctorate, GRE General Test, GRE Subject Test, minimum GPA of 3.0. Additional exam requirements/recommendations for international students: Required—TOEFL (minimum score 600 paper-based; 90 iBT). Electronic applications accepted. *Faculty research:* Physical electronics, systems, computer engineering, bioengineering.

Rochester Institute of Technology, Graduate Enrollment Services, Kate Gleason College of Engineering, Electrical and Microelectronic Engineering Department, MS Program in Electrical Engineering, Rochester, NY 14623-5603. Offers MS. Part-time programs available. *Students:* 151 full-time (32 women), 73 part-time (10 women); includes 12 minority (1 Black or African American, non-Hispanic/Latino; 8 Asian, non-Hispanic/Latino; 2 Hispanic/Latino; 1 Two or more races, non-Hispanic/Latino), 170 international. Average age 24. 509 applicants, 54% accepted, 79 enrolled. In 2014, 69 master's awarded. *Degree requirements:* For master's, thesis or alternative. *Entrance requirements:* For master's, GRE and TOEFL, IELTS, or PTE for non-native English speakers, baccalaureate degree from accredited university in engineering or related field, official transcripts, minimum GPA of 3.0, two letters of reference. Additional exam requirements/recommendations for international students: Required—TOEFL, PTE (minimum score 58), TOEFL (minimum score 550 paper-based; 79 iBT) or IELTS (minimum score 6.5). *Application deadline:* For fall admission, 2/15 priority date for domestic and international students; for spring admission, 12/15 priority date for domestic and international students. Applications are processed on a rolling basis. Application fee: $60. Electronic applications accepted. *Expenses:* Expenses: $1,673 per credit hour. *Financial support:* In 2014–15, 110 students received support. Research assistantships with partial tuition reimbursements available, teaching assistantships with partial tuition reimbursements available, career-related internships or fieldwork, Federal Work-Study, institutionally sponsored loans, scholarships/grants, and unspecified assistantships available. Support available to part-time students. Financial award applicants required to submit FAFSA. *Faculty research:* Analog and RF; digital and computer systems; image, video, and computer vision; multi-agent bio-robotics; robotics and control systems; wireless communication. *Unit head:* Dr. Jayanti Venkatraman, Graduate Program Director, 585-475-2143, E-mail: jnveee@rit.edu. *Application contact:* Diane Ellison, Associate Vice President, Graduate Enrollment Services, 585-475-2229, Fax: 585-475-7164, E-mail: gradinfo@rit.edu.
Website: https://www.rit.edu/kgcoe/electrical/graduate-ms/overview.

Rochester Institute of Technology, Graduate Enrollment Services, Kate Gleason College of Engineering, Electrical and Microelectronic Engineering Department, MS Program in Microelectronic Engineering, Rochester, NY 14623-5603. Offers MS. Part-time programs available. *Students:* 12 full-time (4 women), 3 part-time, 9 international. Average age 23. 32 applicants, 38% accepted, 4 enrolled. In 2014, 6 master's awarded. *Degree requirements:* For master's, thesis. *Entrance requirements:* For master's, GRE and TOEFL, IELTS, or PTE for non-native English speakers, Recommended minimum GPA of 3.0. Additional exam requirements/recommendations for international students: Required—PTE (minimum score 58), TOEFL (minimum score 550 paper-based; 79 iBT) or IELTS (minimum score 6.5). *Application deadline:* For fall admission, 2/15 priority date for domestic and international students; for winter admission, 10/15 for domestic and international students; for spring admission, 12/15 priority date for domestic and international students. Applications are processed on a rolling basis. Application fee: $60. Electronic applications accepted. *Expenses:* Expenses: $1,673 per credit hour. *Financial support:* In 2014–15, 13 students received support. Research assistantships with partial tuition reimbursements available, teaching assistantships with partial tuition reimbursements available, career-related internships or fieldwork, Federal Work-Study, institutionally sponsored loans, scholarships/grants, and unspecified assistantships available. Support available to part-time students. Financial award applicants required to submit FAFSA. *Faculty research:* Electromagnetics, microelectromechanical systems (MEMS) and microfluidics. *Unit head:* Dr. Robert Pearson, Graduate Program Director, 585-475-2923, Fax: 585-475-5845, E-mail: robert.pearson@rit.edu. *Application contact:* Diane Ellison, Associate Vice President, Graduate Enrollment Services, 585-475-2229, Fax: 585-475-7164, E-mail: gradinfo@rit.edu.
Website: https://www.rit.edu/kgcoe/eme/meMS.

Rose-Hulman Institute of Technology, Faculty of Engineering and Applied Sciences, Department of Electrical and Computer Engineering, Terre Haute, IN 47803-3999. Offers electrical and computer engineering (M Eng); electrical engineering (MS); systems engineering and management (MS). Part-time programs available. Postbaccalaureate distance learning degree programs offered (minimal on-campus study). *Faculty:* 19 full-time (3 women), 1 (woman) part-time/adjunct. *Students:* 16 full-time (4 women), 6 part-time (0 women); includes 2 minority (both Asian, non-Hispanic/Latino), 16 international. Average age 24. 28 applicants, 93% accepted, 11 enrolled. In 2014, 14 master's awarded. *Degree requirements:* For master's, thesis (for some programs). *Entrance requirements:* For master's, GRE, minimum GPA of 3.0. Additional exam requirements/recommendations for international students: Required—TOEFL (minimum score 580 paper-based; 92 iBT). *Application deadline:* For fall admission, 2/1 priority date for domestic students. Applications are processed on a rolling basis. Application fee: $0. *Expenses: Tuition:* Full-time $40,449. *Financial support:* In 2014–15, 21 students received support. Fellowships with full and partial tuition reimbursements available, research assistantships with full and partial tuition reimbursements available, institutionally sponsored loans, scholarships/grants, and tuition waivers (full and partial) available. *Faculty research:* VLSI, power systems, analog electronics, communications, electromagnetics. *Total annual research expenditures:* $20,179. *Unit head:* Dr. Robert Throne, Chairman, 812-877-8414, Fax: 812-877-8895, E-mail: robert.d.throne@rose-hulman.edu. *Application contact:* Dr. Azad Siahmakoun, Associate Dean of the Faculty, 812-877-8400, Fax: 812-877-8061, E-mail: siahmako@rose-hulman.edu.
Website: http://www.rose-hulman.edu/academics/academic-departments/electrical-computer-engineering.aspx.

Rowan University, Graduate School, College of Engineering, Department of Electrical Engineering, Glassboro, NJ 08028-1701. Offers MS. *Faculty:* 5 full-time (1 woman). *Students:* 16 full-time (3 women), 12 part-time (1 woman); includes 3 minority (all Asian, non-Hispanic/Latino), 5 international. Average age 28. 10 applicants, 100% accepted, 8 enrolled. In 2014, 21 master's awarded. *Application deadline:* For fall admission, 8/1 for domestic students, 5/1 for international students; for spring admission, 11/1 for domestic and international students; for summer admission, 4/1 for domestic students, 2/15 for international students. Applications are processed on a rolling basis. Application fee: $65. Electronic applications accepted. *Expenses: Tuition, area resident:* Part-time $648 per credit. Tuition, state resident: part-time $648 per credit. Tuition, nonresident: part-time $648 per credit. *Required fees:* $145 per credit. Tuition and fees vary according to degree level, campus/location, program and student level. *Unit head:* Dr. Steve Chin, Dean, 856-256-5301. *Application contact:* Dr. Ralph Dusseau, Program Adviser, 856-256-5332.

Royal Military College of Canada, Division of Graduate Studies and Research, Engineering Division, Department of Electrical and Computer Engineering, Kingston, ON K7K 7B4, Canada. Offers computer engineering (M Eng, PhD); electrical engineering (M Eng, PhD); software engineering (M Eng, PhD). *Degree requirements:* For master's, thesis; for doctorate, comprehensive exam, thesis/dissertation. *Entrance requirements:* For master's, honours degree with second-class standing in the appropriate field; for doctorate, master's degree. Electronic applications accepted.

Rutgers, The State University of New Jersey, New Brunswick, Graduate School-New Brunswick, Department of Electrical and Computer Engineering, Piscataway, NJ 08854-8097. Offers communications and solid-state electronics (MS, PhD); computer engineering (MS, PhD); control systems (MS, PhD); digital signal processing (MS, PhD). Part-time programs available. Terminal master's awarded for partial completion of doctoral program. *Degree requirements:* For master's, thesis or alternative; for doctorate, thesis/dissertation. *Entrance requirements:* For master's and doctorate, GRE General Test. Additional exam requirements/recommendations for international students: Required—TOEFL. Electronic applications accepted. *Faculty research:* Communication and information processing, wireless information networks, micro-vacuum devices, machine vision, VLSI design.

St. Cloud State University, School of Graduate Studies, College of Science and Engineering, Department of Electrical and Computer Engineering, St. Cloud, MN 56301-4498. Offers electrical engineering (MS). *Degree requirements:* For master's, thesis or alternative. *Entrance requirements:* For master's, GRE General Test, minimum GPA of 2.75. Additional exam requirements/recommendations for international students: Required—Michigan English Language Assessment Battery; Recommended—TOEFL (minimum score 550 paper-based), IELTS (minimum score 6.5). Electronic applications accepted.

St. Mary's University, Graduate School, Department of Engineering, Program in Electrical Engineering, San Antonio, TX 78228-8507. Offers MS. Part-time programs available. *Faculty:* 2 full-time (0 women). *Students:* 4 full-time (0 women), 3 part-time (0 women); includes 1 minority (Hispanic/Latino), 4 international. Average age 32. 23 applicants, 22% accepted, 1 enrolled. In 2014, 1 master's awarded. *Degree requirements:* For master's, comprehensive exam. *Entrance requirements:* For master's, GRE, Have a bachelor's degree in Electrical Engineering, Computer Engineering or a closely related discipline. Have a minimum Grade Point Average (GPA) of 3.00 (A = 4.00) for their bachelor's degrees. Have a minimum GRE quantitative score of 148. Additional exam requirements/recommendations for international students: Required—TOEFL (minimum score 550 paper-based; 80 iBT), IELTS (minimum score 6.5). *Application deadline:* Applications are processed on a rolling basis. Application fee: $0. Electronic applications accepted. *Expenses: Tuition:* Full-time $15,070; part-time $800 per credit hour. *Required fees:* $156 per semester. *Financial support:* In 2014–15, 1 research assistantship (averaging $21,600 per year) was awarded; career-related internships or fieldwork, Federal Work-Study, institutionally sponsored loans, scholarships/grants, health care benefits, and stipend for 9 months also available. Financial award application deadline: 3/31; financial award applicants required to submit FAFSA. *Faculty research:* Digital signal processing, image processing, wireless communication, neural networks, pattern recognition. *Unit head:* Dr. Djaffer Ibaroudene, Graduate Program Director, 210-431-2050, E-mail: dibaroudene@stmarytx.edu.
Website: https://www.stmarytx.edu/academics/set/graduate/electrical-engineering/.

San Diego State University, Graduate and Research Affairs, College of Engineering, Department of Electrical and Computer Engineering, San Diego, CA 92182. Offers electrical engineering (MS). Evening/weekend programs available. *Entrance requirements:* For master's, GRE General Test. Additional exam requirements/recommendations for international students: Required—TOEFL. Electronic applications accepted. *Faculty research:* Ultra-high speed integral circuits and systems, naval command control and ocean surveillance, signal processing and analysis.

San Jose State University, Graduate Studies and Research, Charles W. Davidson College of Engineering, Department of Electrical Engineering, San Jose, CA 95192-0001. Offers MS. *Degree requirements:* For master's, thesis. *Entrance requirements:* For master's, GRE General Test. Electronic applications accepted.

Santa Clara University, School of Engineering, Santa Clara, CA 95053. Offers analog circuit design (Certificate); applied mathematics (MS); ASIC design and test (Certificate); bioengineering (MS); civil engineering (MS); computer science and engineering (MS, PhD); controls (Certificate); digital signal processing (Certificate); dynamics (Certificate); electrical engineering (MS, PhD); engineering (Engineer); engineering management (MS); fundamentals of electrical engineering (Certificate); information assurance (Certificate); materials engineering (Certificate); mechanical design analysis (Certificate); mechanical engineering (MS, PhD); mechatronics systems engineering (Certificate); microwave and antennas (Certificate); networking (Certificate); renewable energy (Certificate); software engineering (Certificate); sustainable energy (MS); technology jump-start (Certificate); thermofluids (Certificate). Part-time and evening/weekend programs available. *Faculty:* 59 full-time (23 women), 80 part-time/adjunct (14 women). *Students:* 584 full-time (239 women), 353 part-time (102 women); includes 224 minority (7 Black or African American, non-Hispanic/Latino; 144 Asian, non-Hispanic/Latino; 50 Hispanic/Latino; 2 Native Hawaiian or other Pacific Islander, non-Hispanic/Latino; 21 Two or more races, non-Hispanic/Latino), 548 international. Average age 27. 1,248 applicants, 51% accepted, 375 enrolled. In 2014, 283 master's, 5 doctorates, 1 other advanced degree awarded. *Degree requirements:* For master's, thesis (for some programs); for doctorate, thesis/dissertation; for other advanced degree, thesis. *Entrance requirements:* For master's, GRE, transcript; for doctorate, GRE, master's degree or equivalent; for other advanced degree, master's degree, published paper. Additional exam requirements/recommendations for international students: Required—TOEFL (minimum score 550 paper-based; 79 iBT). *Application deadline:* For fall admission, 8/1 for domestic students, 7/15 for international students; for winter admission, 10/28 for domestic students, 9/23 for international students; for spring admission, 2/25 for domestic students, 1/21 for international students. Applications are processed on a rolling basis. Application fee: $60. Electronic applications accepted. *Expenses:* Expenses: Contact institution. *Financial support:* In 2014–15, 94 students received support. Fellowships with full and partial tuition reimbursements available, research assistantships with full and partial tuition reimbursements available, teaching assistantships with full tuition reimbursements available, career-related internships or fieldwork, Federal Work-Study, institutionally sponsored loans, and scholarships/grants available. Support available to part-time students. Financial award application deadline: 3/2; financial award applicants required to submit FAFSA. *Faculty research:* Video encoding, nanostructures, robotics, microfluidics, water resources. *Total annual research expenditures:* $1.6 million. *Unit head:* Dr. Alex Zecevic, Associate Dean for Graduate Studies, 408-554-2394, E-mail:

azecevic@scu.edu. *Application contact:* Stacey Tinker, Director of Enrollment Management, 408-554-4748, Fax: 408-554-4323, E-mail: stinker@scu.edu.
Website: http://www.scu.edu/engineering/graduate/.

South Dakota School of Mines and Technology, Graduate Division, Program in Electrical Engineering, Rapid City, SD 57701-3995. Offers MS. Part-time programs available. *Faculty:* 7 full-time (1 woman), 2 part-time/adjunct (0 women). *Students:* 13 full-time (5 women), 5 part-time (0 women), 15 international. Average age 26. 35 applicants, 46% accepted, 8 enrolled. In 2014, 2 master's awarded. *Degree requirements:* For master's, thesis. *Entrance requirements:* Additional exam requirements/recommendations for international students: Required—TOEFL (minimum score 520 paper-based; 68 iBT), TWE. *Application deadline:* For fall admission, 7/1 priority date for domestic students, 4/1 for international students; for spring admission, 11/1 for domestic students, 9/1 for international students. Applications are processed on a rolling basis. Application fee: $35. Electronic applications accepted. *Expenses:* Tuition, state resident: full-time $5050; part-time $210.40 per credit hour. Tuition, nonresident: full-time $11,290; part-time $470.30 per credit hour. *Required fees:* $4680. *Financial support:* In 2014–15, 3 fellowships (averaging $3,158 per year), 6 research assistantships with partial tuition reimbursements (averaging $5,396 per year), 6 teaching assistantships with partial tuition reimbursements (averaging $3,475 per year) were awarded; Federal Work-Study and institutionally sponsored loans also available. Support available to part-time students. Financial award application deadline: 5/15. *Faculty research:* Semiconductors, systems, digital systems, computers, superconductivity. *Total annual research expenditures:* $230,328. *Unit head:* Scott Rausch, Department Head and Professor, 605-394-1220, E-mail: scott.rausch@sdsmt.edu. *Application contact:* Rachel Howard, Office of Graduate Education, 605-355-3468, Fax: 605-394-1767, E-mail: rachel.howard@sdsmt.edu.
Website: http://www.sdsmt.edu/Academics/Departments/Electrical-and-Computer-Engineering/Graduate-Education/.

South Dakota State University, Graduate School, College of Engineering, Department of Electrical Engineering and Computer Science, Brookings, SD 57007. Offers electrical engineering (PhD); engineering (MS). Part-time programs available. *Degree requirements:* For master's, thesis (for some programs), oral exam; for doctorate, comprehensive exam, thesis/dissertation, oral exam. *Entrance requirements:* For master's and doctorate, GRE. Additional exam requirements/recommendations for international students: Required—TOEFL (minimum score 575 paper-based). *Faculty research:* Image processing, communications, power systems, electronic materials and devices, nanotechnology, photovoltaics.

Southern Illinois University Carbondale, Graduate School, College of Engineering, Department of Electrical and Computer Engineering, Carbondale, IL 62901-4701. Offers MS, PhD. *Faculty:* 15 full-time (1 woman), 1 part-time/adjunct (0 women). *Students:* 191 full-time (44 women), 55 part-time (10 women); includes 5 minority (2 Black or African American, non-Hispanic/Latino; 2 Asian, non-Hispanic/Latino; 1 Hispanic/Latino), 223 international. 481 applicants, 45% accepted, 60 enrolled. In 2014, 42 master's, 12 doctorates awarded. *Degree requirements:* For master's, comprehensive exam, thesis. *Entrance requirements:* For master's, minimum GPA of 2.7. Additional exam requirements/recommendations for international students: Required—TOEFL. *Application deadline:* Applications are processed on a rolling basis. Application fee: $50. *Expenses:* Tuition, state resident: full-time $10,176; part-time $1153 per credit. Tuition, nonresident: full-time $20,814; part-time $1744 per credit. *Required fees:* $7092; $394 per credit. $2364 per semester. *Financial support:* In 2014–15, 21 students received support, including 6 research assistantships with full tuition reimbursements available; fellowships with full tuition reimbursements available, teaching assistantships with full tuition reimbursements available, Federal Work-Study, institutionally sponsored loans, and tuition waivers (full) also available. Support available to part-time students. Financial award application deadline: 1/15. *Faculty research:* Circuits and power systems, communications and signal processing, controls and systems, electromagnetics and optics, electronics instrumentation and bioengineering. *Total annual research expenditures:* $254,257. *Unit head:* Dr. Spyros Tragoudas, Chair, 618-536-2364, E-mail: trag@siu.edu. *Application contact:* Lisa Short, Office Manager, 618-453-2110, E-mail: ecedept@siu.edu.

Southern Illinois University Edwardsville, Graduate School, School of Engineering, Department of Electrical and Computer Engineering, Edwardsville, IL 62026-0001. Offers electrical engineering (MS). Part-time and evening/weekend programs available. *Faculty:* 9 full-time (0 women). *Students:* 67 full-time (27 women), 40 part-time (10 women); includes 7 minority (2 Black or African American, non-Hispanic/Latino; 3 Asian, non-Hispanic/Latino; 2 Hispanic/Latino), 78 international. 263 applicants, 41% accepted. In 2014, 29 master's awarded. *Degree requirements:* For master's, thesis (for some programs), research paper, final exam. *Entrance requirements:* For master's, minimum undergraduate GPA of 2.75 in engineering, mathematics, and science courses. Additional exam requirements/recommendations for international students: Required—TOEFL (minimum score 550 paper-based; 79 iBT), IELTS (minimum score 6.5). *Application deadline:* For fall admission, 7/24 for domestic students, 7/15 for international students; for spring admission, 12/11 for domestic students, 11/15 for international students; for summer admission, 4/29 for domestic students, 4/15 for international students. Applications are processed on a rolling basis. Application fee: $30. Electronic applications accepted. *Expenses:* Tuition, state resident: full-time $5026. Tuition, nonresident: full-time $12,566. *International tuition:* $25,136 full-time. *Required fees:* $1682. Tuition and fees vary according to course load, campus/location and program. *Financial support:* In 2014–15, 28 students received support, including 1 fellowship with full tuition reimbursement available (averaging $8,370 per year), 9 research assistantships with full tuition reimbursements available, 18 teaching assistantships with full tuition reimbursements available; institutionally sponsored loans, scholarships/grants, and unspecified assistantships also available. Financial award application deadline: 3/1; financial award applicants required to submit FAFSA. *Unit head:* Dr. Oktay Alkin, Chair, 618-650-2524, E-mail: oalkin@siue.edu. *Application contact:* Melissa K Mace, Assistant Director of Admissions for Graduate and International Recruitment, 618-650-2756, Fax: 618-650-3618, E-mail: mmace@siue.edu.
Website: http://www.siue.edu/engineering/ece/.

Southern Methodist University, Bobby B. Lyle School of Engineering, Department of Electrical Engineering, Dallas, TX 75275-0338. Offers applied science (MS); electrical engineering (MSEE, PhD); telecommunications (MS). Part-time and evening/weekend programs available. Postbaccalaureate distance learning degree programs offered (no on-campus study). Terminal master's awarded for partial completion of doctoral program. *Degree requirements:* For master's, thesis optional; for doctorate, thesis/dissertation, oral and written qualifying exams, oral final exam. *Entrance requirements:* For master's, GRE General Test, minimum GPA of 3.0 in last 2 years; bachelor's degree in engineering, mathematics, or sciences; for doctorate, preliminary counseling exam, minimum GPA of 3.0, bachelor's degree in related field. Additional exam requirements/recommendations for international students: Required—TOEFL. Electronic applications accepted. *Faculty research:* Mobile communications, optical communications, digital signal processing, photonics.

Southern Polytechnic State University, School of Engineering Technology and Management, Department of Electrical and Computer Engineering Technology, Marietta, GA 30060-2896. Offers electrical engineering technology (MS). Part-time and evening/weekend programs available. *Degree requirements:* For master's, thesis. *Entrance requirements:* For master's, GRE (minimum scores: 147 Verbal, 147 Quantitative, 3.5 Analytical), minimum GPA of 2.7. Additional exam requirements/recommendations for international students: Required—TOEFL (minimum score 550 paper-based; 79 iBT), IELTS (minimum score 6.5). Electronic applications accepted. *Faculty research:* Analog and digital communications, computer networking, analog and low power electronics design, control systems and digital signal processing, instrumentation (medical and industrial), biomedical signal analysis, biomedical imaging, renewable energy systems, electronics, power distribution, power electronics.

Stanford University, School of Engineering, Department of Electrical Engineering, Stanford, CA 94305-9991. Offers MS, PhD. Terminal master's awarded for partial completion of doctoral program. *Degree requirements:* For doctorate, thesis/dissertation. *Entrance requirements:* For master's and doctorate, GRE General Test. Additional exam requirements/recommendations for international students: Required—TOEFL. Electronic applications accepted. *Expenses: Tuition:* Full-time $44,184; part-time $982 per credit hour. *Required fees:* $191.

State University of New York at New Paltz, Graduate School, School of Science and Engineering, Department of Electrical and Computer Engineering, New Paltz, NY 12561. Offers electrical engineering (MS). Part-time and evening/weekend programs available. *Faculty:* 10 full-time (1 woman), 5 part-time/adjunct (0 women). *Students:* 98 full-time (23 women), 36 part-time (7 women); includes 2 minority (1 Black or African American, non-Hispanic/Latino; 1 Asian, non-Hispanic/Latino), 127 international. Average age 23. 248 applicants, 68% accepted, 53 enrolled. In 2014, 12 master's awarded. *Degree requirements:* For master's, comprehensive exam, thesis optional. *Entrance requirements:* For master's, minimum GPA of 3.0. Additional exam requirements/recommendations for international students: Required—TOEFL (minimum score 550 paper-based; 80 iBT), IELTS (minimum score 6.5). *Application deadline:* For fall admission, 5/15 for domestic and international students; for spring admission, 11/15 for domestic and international students. Applications are processed on a rolling basis. Application fee: $50. Electronic applications accepted. *Financial support:* In 2014–15, 11 fellowships with partial tuition reimbursements, 2 research assistantships with partial tuition reimbursements (averaging $5,000 per year) were awarded. *Unit head:* Dr. Baback Izadi, Chair, 845-257-3823, E-mail: engr@newpaltz.edu. *Application contact:* Prof. Damodaran Radhakrishnan, Graduate Coordinator, 845-257-3772, E-mail: damu@newpaltz.edu.
Website: http://www.engr.newpaltz.edu/.

Stevens Institute of Technology, Graduate School, Charles V. Schaefer Jr. School of Engineering, Department of Electrical and Computer Engineering, Program in Electrical Engineering, Hoboken, NJ 07030. Offers computer architecture and digital systems (M Eng); electrical engineering (PhD); microelectronics and photonics science and technology (M Eng); signal processing for communications (M Eng); telecommunications systems engineering (M Eng); wireless communications (M Eng, Certificate). *Degree requirements:* For master's, thesis optional; for doctorate, variable foreign language requirement, thesis/dissertation. *Entrance requirements:* For master's, doctorate, and Certificate, GRE. Additional exam requirements/recommendations for international students: Required—TOEFL. Electronic applications accepted.

Stevens Institute of Technology, Graduate School, Charles V. Schaefer Jr. School of Engineering, Department of Mechanical Engineering, Program in Integrated Product Development, Hoboken, NJ 07030. Offers armament engineering (M Eng); computer and electrical engineering (M Eng); manufacturing technologies (M Eng); systems reliability and design (M Eng).

Stevens Institute of Technology, Graduate School, Charles V. Schaefer Jr. School of Engineering, Interdisciplinary Program in Microelectronics and Photonics, Hoboken, NJ 07030. Offers Certificate.

Stony Brook University, State University of New York, Graduate School, College of Engineering and Applied Sciences, Department of Electrical and Computer Engineering, Program in Electrical Engineering, Stony Brook, NY 11794. Offers MS, PhD. *Students:* 99 full-time (21 women), 26 part-time (9 women); includes 11 minority (1 Black or African American, non-Hispanic/Latino; 9 Asian, non-Hispanic/Latino; 1 Two or more races, non-Hispanic/Latino), 97 international. 659 applicants, 29% accepted, 40 enrolled. In 2014, 67 master's, 8 doctorates awarded. *Entrance requirements:* For doctorate, GRE, two official transcripts, letters of recommendation. Additional exam requirements/recommendations for international students: Required—TOEFL (minimum score 90 iBT). *Application deadline:* For fall admission, 1/15 for domestic students; for spring admission, 10/1 for domestic students. Application fee: $100. *Expenses:* Tuition, state resident: full-time $10,370; part-time $432 per credit. Tuition, nonresident: full-time $20,190; part-time $841 per credit. *Required fees:* $1431. *Financial support:* Research assistantships and teaching assistantships available. *Unit head:* Dr. Serge Luryi, Chairman, 631-632-8420, Fax: 631-632-8494, E-mail: arie.kaufman@stonybrook.edu. *Application contact:* Susan Hayden, Coordinator, 631-632-8400, Fax: 631-632-8494, E-mail: susan.hayden@stonybrook.edu.

Syracuse University, L. C. Smith College of Engineering and Computer Science, Program in Electrical and Computer Engineering, Syracuse, NY 13244. Offers PhD. Part-time programs available. *Students:* 76 full-time (15 women), 16 part-time (3 women); includes 3 minority (1 Black or African American, non-Hispanic/Latino; 2 Asian, non-Hispanic/Latino), 75 international. Average age 29. 78 applicants, 18% accepted, 13 enrolled. In 2014, 12 doctorates awarded. *Degree requirements:* For doctorate, comprehensive exam, thesis/dissertation. *Entrance requirements:* For doctorate, GRE General Test. Additional exam requirements/recommendations for international students: Required—TOEFL (minimum score 100 iBT). *Application deadline:* For fall admission, 7/1 priority date for domestic students, 6/1 priority date for international students. Applications are processed on a rolling basis. Application fee: $75. Electronic applications accepted. *Expenses: Tuition:* Part-time $1341 per credit. *Required fees:* $1341 per credit. *Financial support:* Fellowships with full tuition reimbursements, research assistantships with full and partial tuition reimbursements, and teaching assistantships with full and partial tuition reimbursements available. Financial award application deadline: 1/1. *Unit head:* Dr. Chilukuri Mohan, Chair, 315-443-2583, E-mail: mohan@syr.edu. *Application contact:* Brenda Flowers, Information Contact, 315-443-4408, Fax: 315-443-2583, E-mail: bflowers@syr.edu.
Website: http://lcs.syr.edu/.

Syracuse University, L. C. Smith College of Engineering and Computer Science, Program in Electrical Engineering, Syracuse, NY 13244. Offers MS, EE. Part-time programs available. *Students:* 129 full-time (34 women), 21 part-time (1 woman); includes 10 minority (3 Black or African American, non-Hispanic/Latino; 1 American Indian or Alaska Native, non-Hispanic/Latino; 5 Asian, non-Hispanic/Latino; 1 Hispanic/Latino), 126 international. Average age 24. 837 applicants, 32% accepted, 68 enrolled. In 2014, 48 master's awarded. *Degree requirements:* For master's, thesis optional. *Entrance requirements:* For master's, GRE General Test. Additional exam requirements/recommendations for international students: Required—TOEFL (minimum score 100

iBT). *Application deadline:* For fall admission, 7/1 priority date for domestic students, 6/1 priority date for international students. Applications are processed on a rolling basis. Application fee: $75. Electronic applications accepted. *Expenses: Tuition:* Part-time $1341 per credit. *Required fees:* $1341 per credit. *Financial support:* Fellowships with full tuition reimbursements, research assistantships with full and partial tuition reimbursements, teaching assistantships with full and partial tuition reimbursements, scholarships/grants, and tuition waivers (partial) available. Financial award application deadline: 1/1; financial award applicants required to submit FAFSA. *Faculty research:* Electromagnetics, electronic devices, systems. *Unit head:* Dr. Prasanta Ghosh, Program Director, 315-443-4440, Fax: 315-443-2583, E-mail: pkghosh@syr.edu.. *Application contact:* Brenda Flowers, Administrative Specialist, 314-443-4408, E-mail: bflowers@syr.edu.
Website: http://lcs.syr.edu.

Syracuse University, L. C. Smith College of Engineering and Computer Science, Program in Microwave Engineering, Syracuse, NY 13244. Offers CAS. Part-time programs available. *Degree requirements:* For CAS, thesis. *Entrance requirements:* For degree, GRE General Test. Additional exam requirements/recommendations for international students: Required—TOEFL (minimum score 100 iBT). *Application deadline:* For fall admission, 7/1 priority date for domestic students, 6/1 priority date for international students. Applications are processed on a rolling basis. Application fee: $75. Electronic applications accepted. *Expenses: Tuition:* Part-time $1341 per credit. *Required fees:* $1341 per credit. *Faculty research:* Software engineering, parallel and high-performance computing, computer aided design and architectures, coding theory, neural networks. *Application contact:* Brenda Flowers, Information Contact, 315-443-4408, E-mail: bflowers@syr.edu.
Website: http://lcs.syr.edu/.

Temple University, College of Engineering, Department of Electrical and Computer Engineering, Philadelphia, PA 19122-6096. Offers electrical engineering (MSEE); engineering (PhD). Part-time and evening/weekend programs available. *Faculty:* 14 full-time (3 women), 11 part-time/adjunct (3 women). *Students:* 24 full-time (10 women), 7 part-time (2 women); includes 4 minority (all Asian, non-Hispanic/Latino), 20 international. 66 applicants, 48% accepted, 10 enrolled. In 2014, 13 master's awarded. Terminal master's awarded for partial completion of doctoral program. *Degree requirements:* For master's, thesis optional; for doctorate, thesis/dissertation, preliminary exam, dissertation proposal and defense. *Entrance requirements:* For master's, GRE General Test, minimum GPA of 3.0; BS in engineering from ABET-accredited or equivalent institution; resume; goals statement; three letters of reference; official transcripts; for doctorate, GRE General Test, minimum GPA of 3.0; MS in engineering from ABET-accredited or equivalent institution (preferred); resume; goals statement; three letters of reference; official transcripts. Additional exam requirements/recommendations for international students: Required—TOEFL (minimum score 550 paper-based; 79 iBT), IELTS (minimum score 6.5). *Application deadline:* For fall admission, 3/1 priority date for domestic and international students; for spring admission, 11/1 priority date for domestic students, 8/1 priority date for international students. Applications are processed on a rolling basis. Application fee: $60. Electronic applications accepted. *Expenses:* Expenses: $913 per credit hour in-state; $1,210 per credit hour out-of-state. *Financial support:* Fellowships with full and partial tuition reimbursements, research assistantships with full and partial tuition reimbursements, teaching assistantships with full and partial tuition reimbursements, Federal Work-Study, institutionally sponsored loans, scholarships/grants, health care benefits, and unspecified assistantships available. Financial award application deadline: 3/1; financial award applicants required to submit FAFSA. *Faculty research:* Embedded systems and system-on-a-chip design, intelligent interactive multimedia, intrusion detection, multisensor fusion, speaker identification, speech processing, visualization and fault detection in multicasting networks. *Unit head:* Dr. Saroj Biswas, Acting Chair, 215-204-8403, Fax: 215-204-6936, E-mail: sbiswas@temple.edu. *Application contact:* Mojan Arshad, Assistant Coordinator, Graduate Studies, 215-204-7800, Fax: 215-204-6936, E-mail: gradengr@temple.edu.
Website: http://engineering.temple.edu/department/electrical-computer-engineering.

Tennessee State University, The School of Graduate Studies and Research, College of Engineering, Nashville, TN 37209-1561. Offers biomedical engineering (ME); civil engineering (ME); computer and information systems engineering (MS, PhD); electrical engineering (ME); environmental engineering (ME); manufacturing engineering (ME); mathematical sciences (MS); mechanical engineering (ME). Part-time and evening/weekend programs available. *Degree requirements:* For master's, project; for doctorate, comprehensive exam, thesis/dissertation. *Entrance requirements:* For doctorate, minimum GPA of 3.3. *Faculty research:* Robotics, intelligent systems, human-computer interaction software systems, biomedical engineering, signal/image processing, probabilistic design, intelligent manufacturing, cooperative mobile robots, condition based maintenance, sensor fusion.

Tennessee Technological University, College of Graduate Studies, College of Engineering, Department of Electrical and Computer Engineering, Cookeville, TN 38505. Offers MS. Part-time programs available. *Faculty:* 19 full-time (0 women). *Students:* 13 full-time (2 women), 8 part-time (0 women); includes 1 minority (Two or more races, non-Hispanic/Latino), 15 international. Average age 27. 144 applicants, 25% accepted, 5 enrolled. In 2014, 11 master's awarded. *Degree requirements:* For master's, thesis. *Entrance requirements:* For master's, GRE. Additional exam requirements/recommendations for international students: Required—TOEFL (minimum score 550 paper-based; 79 iBT), IELTS (minimum score 5.5), PTE (minimum score 53), or TOEIC (Test of English as an International Communication). *Application deadline:* For fall admission, 8/1 for domestic students, 5/1 for international students; for spring admission, 12/1 for domestic students, 10/1 for international students. Applications are processed on a rolling basis. Application fee: $35 ($40 for international students). Electronic applications accepted. *Expenses:* Tuition, state resident: full-time $9783; part-time $492 per credit hour. Tuition, nonresident: full-time $24,071; part-time $1179 per credit hour. *Financial support:* In 2014–15, 1 fellowship (averaging $8,000 per year), 9 research assistantships (averaging $7,650 per year), 15 teaching assistantships (averaging $7,500 per year) were awarded; career-related internships or fieldwork also available. Financial award application deadline: 4/1. *Faculty research:* Control, digital, and power systems. *Unit head:* Dr. R. Wayne Johnson, Chairperson, 931-372-3397, Fax: 931-372-3436, E-mail: wjohnson@tntech.edu. *Application contact:* Shelia K. Kendrick, Coordinator of Graduate Studies, 931-372-3808, Fax: 931-372-3497, E-mail: skendrick@tntech.edu.

Texas A&M University, College of Engineering, Department of Electrical and Computer Engineering, College Station, TX 77843. Offers computer engineering (M Eng, MS, PhD); electrical engineering (M Eng, MS, PhD). *Faculty:* 64. *Students:* 628 full-time (102 women), 96 part-time (14 women); includes 40 minority (8 Black or African American, non-Hispanic/Latino; 1 American Indian or Alaska Native, non-Hispanic/Latino; 12 Asian, non-Hispanic/Latino; 16 Hispanic/Latino; 1 Native Hawaiian or other Pacific Islander, non-Hispanic/Latino; 2 Two or more races, non-Hispanic/Latino), 624 international. Average age 27. 2,211 applicants, 26% accepted, 242 enrolled. In 2014, 107 master's, 45 doctorates awarded. *Degree requirements:* For master's, thesis (MS); for doctorate, thesis/dissertation. *Entrance requirements:* For master's and doctorate, GRE General Test. Additional exam requirements/recommendations for international students: Required—TOEFL. Application fee: $50 ($90 for international students). *Expenses:* Tuition, state resident: full-time $4078; part-time $226.55 per credit hour. Tuition, nonresident: full-time $10,594; part-time $577.55 per credit hour. *Required fees:* $2813; $237.70 per credit hour. $278.50 per semester. Tuition and fees vary according to degree level and student level. *Financial support:* In 2014–15, 479 students received support, including 30 fellowships with full and partial tuition reimbursements available (averaging $13,748 per year), 195 research assistantships with full and partial tuition reimbursements available (averaging $6,484 per year), 111 teaching assistantships with full and partial tuition reimbursements available (averaging $4,036 per year); career-related internships or fieldwork, institutionally sponsored loans, scholarships/grants, traineeships, health care benefits, tuition waivers (full and partial), and unspecified assistantships also available. Support available to part-time students. Financial award application deadline: 4/1; financial award applicants required to submit FAFSA. *Faculty research:* Solid-state, electric power systems, and communications engineering. *Unit head:* Dr. Miroslav M. Begovic, Department Head, 979-862-1553, E-mail: begovic@ece.tamu.edu. *Application contact:* Dr. Krishna Narayanan, Director of Graduate Studies, 979-862-2691, E-mail: krn@ece.tamu.edu.
Website: http://engineering.tamu.edu/electrical/.

Texas A&M University–Kingsville, College of Graduate Studies, College of Engineering, Department of Electrical Engineering and Computer Science, Program in Electrical Engineering, Kingsville, TX 78363. Offers ME, MS. *Students:* 357 full-time (74 women), 70 part-time (19 women); includes 5 minority (2 Black or African American, non-Hispanic/Latino; 2 Asian, non-Hispanic/Latino; 1 Hispanic/Latino), 421 international. Average age 23. 738 applicants, 91% accepted, 209 enrolled. In 2014, 78 master's awarded. *Degree requirements:* For master's, variable foreign language requirement, comprehensive exam, thesis (for some programs). *Entrance requirements:* For master's, GRE, MAT, GMAT, minimum score of 145 quantitative GRE revised score, minimum score of 800 (Q+V) old GRE. Additional exam requirements/recommendations for international students: Required—TOEFL (minimum score 550 paper-based; 79 iBT). *Application deadline:* For fall admission, 8/15 for domestic students, 6/1 for international students; for spring admission, 12/15 for domestic students, 10/1 for international students; for summer admission, 5/15 for domestic students, 4/1 for international students. Applications are processed on a rolling basis. Application fee: $35 ($50 for international students). Electronic applications accepted. *Financial support:* In 2014–15, 78 students received support, including 2 research assistantships (averaging $1,440 per year), 22 teaching assistantships (averaging $1,396 per year); career-related internships or fieldwork, Federal Work-Study, institutionally sponsored loans, scholarships/grants, health care benefits, tuition waivers (full and partial), and unspecified assistantships also available. Support available to part-time students. Financial award application deadline: 5/15; financial award applicants required to submit FAFSA. *Unit head:* Dr. Rajab Challoo, Coordinator, 361-593-2628, E-mail: rajab.challoo@tamuk.edu. *Application contact:* Dr. Mohamed Abdelrahman, Dean of Graduate Studies, 361-593-2809, E-mail: mohamed.abdelrahman@tamuk.edu.

Texas Tech University, Graduate School, Edward E. Whitacre Jr. College of Engineering, Department of Electrical and Computer Engineering, Lubbock, TX 79409-3102. Offers electrical engineering (MSEE, PhD). Part-time programs available. *Faculty:* 24 full-time (4 women), 4 part-time/adjunct (1 woman). *Students:* 194 full-time (47 women), 29 part-time (2 women); includes 15 minority (3 Black or African American, non-Hispanic/Latino; 3 Asian, non-Hispanic/Latino; 7 Hispanic/Latino; 2 Two or more races, non-Hispanic/Latino), 156 international. Average age 26. 570 applicants, 33% accepted, 98 enrolled. In 2014, 39 master's, 14 doctorates awarded. *Degree requirements:* For master's, comprehensive exam, thesis (for some programs); for doctorate, comprehensive exam, thesis/dissertation. *Entrance requirements:* For master's and doctorate, GRE (Verbal and Quantitative), minimum GPA of 3.0, statement of purpose, 3 letters of recommendation, resume. Additional exam requirements/recommendations for international students: Required—TOEFL (minimum score 550 paper-based; 79 iBT). *Application deadline:* For fall admission, 6/1 priority date for domestic students, 1/15 priority date for international students; for spring admission, 9/1 priority date for domestic students, 6/15 priority date for international students. Applications are processed on a rolling basis. Application fee: $60. Electronic applications accepted. *Expenses:* Tuition, state resident: full-time $6310; part-time $262.92 per credit hour. Tuition, nonresident: full-time $14,998; part-time $624.92 per credit hour. *Required fees:* $2701; $36.50 per credit. $912.50 per semester. Tuition and fees vary according to course load. *Financial support:* In 2014–15, 199 students received support, including 195 fellowships (averaging $2,832 per year), 17 research assistantships (averaging $25,050 per year), 10 teaching assistantships (averaging $18,563 per year); scholarships/grants, tuition waivers (partial), and unspecified assistantships also available. Financial award application deadline: 4/15; financial award applicants required to submit FAFSA. *Faculty research:* Pulsed power and power electronics (wide band-gap power semiconductors, nano-photonics and nano-technology), neural imaging and image analysis (signal processing, renewable power systems integration and smart grid technology), cyber security. *Total annual research expenditures:* $1.7 million. *Unit head:* Dr. Michael Giesselmann, Chair, 806-742-3533, E-mail: michael.giesselmann@ttu.edu. *Application contact:* Jackie Charlebois, Supervisor, Graduate Admissions, 806-742-3533, Fax: 806-742-1245, E-mail: jackie.charlebois@ttu.edu.
Website: http://www.depts.ttu.edu/ece/.

Tufts University, Graduate School of Arts and Sciences, Graduate Certificate Programs, Microwave and Wireless Engineering Program, Medford, MA 02155. Offers Certificate. Part-time and evening/weekend programs available. Electronic applications accepted. *Expenses: Tuition:* Full-time $45,590; part-time $1161 per credit hour. *Required fees:* $782. Full-time tuition and fees vary according to degree level, program and student level. Part-time tuition and fees vary according to course load.

Tufts University, School of Engineering, Department of Electrical and Computer Engineering, Medford, MA 02155. Offers bioengineering (ME, MS), including signals and systems; electrical engineering (MS, PhD). Part-time programs available. *Faculty:* 17 full-time (3 women), 3 part-time/adjunct. *Students:* 64 full-time (20 women), 11 part-time (3 women); includes 7 minority (4 Asian, non-Hispanic/Latino; 1 Hispanic/Latino; 2 Two or more races, non-Hispanic/Latino), 53 international. Average age 27. 203 applicants, 33% accepted, 21 enrolled. In 2014, 16 master's, 6 doctorates awarded. Terminal master's awarded for partial completion of doctoral program. *Degree requirements:* For master's, thesis or alternative; for doctorate, thesis/dissertation. *Entrance requirements:* For master's and doctorate, GRE General Test. Additional exam requirements/recommendations for international students: Required—TOEFL (minimum score 550 paper-based; 80 iBT), IELTS (minimum score 6.5). *Application deadline:* For fall admission, 1/15 priority date for domestic students, 1/15 for international students; for spring admission, 9/15 for domestic and international students. Applications are processed on a rolling basis. Application fee: $75. Electronic applications accepted. *Expenses: Tuition:* Full-time $45,590; part-time $1161 per credit hour. *Required fees:* $782. Full-time tuition and fees vary according to degree level, program and student level. Part-time tuition and fees vary according to course load. *Financial support:*

Fellowships with full tuition reimbursements, research assistantships with full and partial tuition reimbursements, teaching assistantships with full and partial tuition reimbursements, Federal Work-Study, scholarships/grants, tuition waivers (partial), and unspecified assistantships available. Financial award application deadline: 5/15; financial award applicants required to submit FAFSA. *Faculty research:* Communication theory, networks, protocol, and transmission technology; simulation and modeling; digital processing technology; image and signal processing for security and medical applications; integrated circuits and VLSI. *Unit head:* Dr. Eric Miller, Graduate Program Director. *Application contact:* Office of Graduate Admissions, 617-627-3395, E-mail: gradadmissions@tufts.edu.
Website: http://engineering.tufts.edu/ece/.

Tuskegee University, Graduate Programs, College of Engineering, Department of Electrical Engineering, Tuskegee, AL 36088. Offers MSEE. *Degree requirements:* For master's, thesis or alternative. *Entrance requirements:* For master's, GRE General Test, GRE Subject Test. Additional exam requirements/recommendations for international students: Required—TOEFL (minimum score 500 paper-based). *Expenses: Tuition:* Full-time $18,560; part-time $1542 per credit hour. *Required fees:* $2910; $1455 per semester. *Faculty research:* Photovoltaic insulation, automatic guidance and control, wind energy.

Union Graduate College, School of Engineering and Computer Science, Schenectady, NY 12308-3107. Offers computer science (MS); electrical engineering (MS); engineering and management systems (MS); mechanical engineering (MS). Part-time and evening/weekend programs available. *Degree requirements:* For master's, capstone course. *Entrance requirements:* For master's, minimum GPA of 3.0, letters of recommendation. Additional exam requirements/recommendations for international students: Required—TOEFL (minimum score 550 paper-based). Electronic applications accepted. *Expenses:* Contact institution.

Universidad de las Américas Puebla, Division of Graduate Studies, School of Engineering, Program in Electronic Engineering, Puebla, Mexico. Offers MS. Part-time and evening/weekend programs available. *Faculty research:* Telecommunications, data processing, digital systems.

Université de Moncton, Faculty of Engineering, Program in Electrical Engineering, Moncton, NB E1A 3E9, Canada. Offers M Sc A. *Degree requirements:* For master's, thesis, proficiency in French. *Faculty research:* Telecommunications, electronics and instrumentation, analog and digital electronics, electronic control of machines, energy systems, electronic design.

Université de Sherbrooke, Faculty of Engineering, Department of Electrical Engineering and Computer Engineering, Sherbrooke, QC J1K 2R1, Canada. Offers electrical engineering (M Sc A, PhD). *Degree requirements:* For master's, one foreign language, thesis; for doctorate, comprehensive exam, thesis/dissertation. *Entrance requirements:* For master's, bachelor's degree in engineering or equivalent. Electronic applications accepted. *Faculty research:* Minielectronics, biomedical engineering, digital signal prolonging and telecommunications, software engineering and artificial intelligence.

Université du Québec à Trois-Rivières, Graduate Programs, Program in Electrical Engineering, Trois-Rivières, QC G9A 5H7, Canada. Offers M Sc A, PhD. Part-time programs available. *Degree requirements:* For master's, thesis; for doctorate, thesis/dissertation. *Entrance requirements:* For master's, appropriate bachelor's degree, proficiency in French; for doctorate, appropriate master's degree, proficiency in French. *Faculty research:* Industrial electronics.

Université Laval, Faculty of Sciences and Engineering, Department of Electrical and Computer Engineering, Programs in Electrical Engineering, Québec, QC G1K 7P4, Canada. Offers M Sc, PhD. Terminal master's awarded for partial completion of doctoral program. *Degree requirements:* For master's, thesis (for some programs); for doctorate, thesis/dissertation. *Entrance requirements:* For master's and doctorate, knowledge of French and English. Electronic applications accepted.

University at Buffalo, the State University of New York, Graduate School, School of Engineering and Applied Sciences, Department of Electrical Engineering, Buffalo, NY 14260. Offers ME, MS, PhD. Part-time programs available. *Faculty:* 28 full-time (4 women), 3 part-time/adjunct (0 women). *Students:* 391 full-time (91 women), 16 part-time (0 women); includes 12 minority (4 Black or African American, non-Hispanic/Latino; 1 American Indian or Alaska Native, non-Hispanic/Latino; 2 Asian, non-Hispanic/Latino; 3 Hispanic/Latino; 2 Two or more races, non-Hispanic/Latino), 364 international. Average age 25. 1,388 applicants, 35% accepted, 154 enrolled. In 2014, 114 master's, 9 doctorates awarded. Terminal master's awarded for partial completion of doctoral program. *Degree requirements:* For master's, comprehensive exam (for some programs), thesis or exam; for doctorate, comprehensive exam, thesis/dissertation. *Entrance requirements:* For master's and doctorate, GRE General Test. Additional exam requirements/recommendations for international students: Required—TOEFL (minimum score 550 paper-based; 79 iBT). *Application deadline:* For fall admission, 2/1 priority date for domestic and international students; for spring admission, 10/1 priority date for domestic and international students. Applications are processed on a rolling basis. Application fee: $75. Electronic applications accepted. *Financial support:* In 2014–15, 79 students received support, including 3 fellowships with full and partial tuition reimbursements available (averaging $24,000 per year), 38 research assistantships with full and partial tuition reimbursements available (averaging $20,340 per year), 42 teaching assistantships with full and partial tuition reimbursements available (averaging $21,763 per year); career-related internships or fieldwork, Federal Work-Study, institutionally sponsored loans, tuition waivers (full and partial), and unspecified assistantships also available. Financial award application deadline: 2/1; financial award applicants required to submit FAFSA. *Faculty research:* High power electronics and plasmas, electronic materials signal and image processing, photonics and communications, optics, nanoelectronics. *Total annual research expenditures:* $8 million. *Unit head:* Dr. Stella N. Batalama, Chairman, 716-645-3115, Fax: 716-645-3656, E-mail: batalama@buffalo.edu. *Application contact:* Dr. Leslie Ying, Director of Graduate Admissions, 716-645-1609, Fax: 716-645-3656, E-mail: eegradapply@buffalo.edu.
Website: http://www.ee.buffalo.edu/.

The University of Akron, Graduate School, College of Engineering, Department of Electrical and Computer Engineering, Akron, OH 44325. Offers electrical engineering (MS); engineering (PhD). Evening/weekend programs available. *Faculty:* 15 full-time (1 woman), 6 part-time/adjunct (1 woman). *Students:* 58 full-time (7 women), 9 part-time (4 women); includes 2 minority (1 Asian, non-Hispanic/Latino; 1 Two or more races, non-Hispanic/Latino), 54 international. Average age 27. 154 applicants, 31% accepted, 10 enrolled. In 2014, 19 master's, 2 doctorates awarded. *Degree requirements:* For master's, oral comprehensive exam or thesis; for doctorate, one foreign language, thesis/dissertation, candidacy exam, qualifying exam. *Entrance requirements:* For master's, GRE, minimum GPA of 2.75, three letters of recommendation, statement of purpose; for doctorate, GRE, minimum GPA of 3.0 with bachelor's degree, 3.5 with master's degree; three letters of recommendation; statement of purpose. Additional exam requirements/recommendations for international students: Required—TOEFL (minimum score 550 paper-based; 79 iBT), IELTS (minimum score 6.5). *Application deadline:* Applications are processed on a rolling basis. Application fee: $45 ($70 for

international students). Electronic applications accepted. *Expenses:* Tuition, state resident: full-time $7578; part-time $421 per credit hour. Tuition, nonresident: full-time $12,977; part-time $721 per credit hour. *Required fees:* $1388; $35 per credit hour. Tuition and fees vary according to course load. *Financial support:* In 2014–15, 42 research assistantships with full tuition reimbursements, 14 teaching assistantships with full tuition reimbursements were awarded. *Faculty research:* Computational electromagnetics and nondestructive testing, control systems, sensors and actuators applications and networks, alternative energy systems and hybrid vehicles, analog integrated circuit (IC) design, embedded systems. *Total annual research expenditures:* $1.7 million. *Unit head:* Dr. Abbas Omar, Chair, 330-972-7483, E-mail: aomar@uakron.edu. *Application contact:* Dr. Shivakumar Sastry, Graduate Director, 330-972-7646, E-mail: ssastry@uakron.edu.
Website: http://www.uakron.edu/engineering/ECE/.

The University of Alabama, Graduate School, College of Engineering, Department of Electrical and Computer Engineering, Tuscaloosa, AL 35487-0286. Offers electrical engineering (MS, PhD). Part-time programs available. Postbaccalaureate distance learning degree programs offered (minimal on-campus study). *Faculty:* 18 full-time (4 women). *Students:* 44 full-time (5 women), 8 part-time (0 women); includes 4 minority (2 Asian, non-Hispanic/Latino; 2 Hispanic/Latino), 38 international. Average age 28. 94 applicants, 46% accepted, 14 enrolled. In 2014, 9 master's, 5 doctorates awarded. *Degree requirements:* For master's, thesis or alternative; for doctorate, one foreign language, comprehensive exam, thesis/dissertation. *Entrance requirements:* For master's, GRE (for students from non ABET-accredited schools), minimum GPA of 3.0 in last 60 hours of course work or overall; for doctorate, GRE (for students from non ABET-accredited schools), minimum GPA of 3.0 overall. Additional exam requirements/recommendations for international students: Required—TOEFL (minimum score 550 paper-based). *Application deadline:* For fall admission, 7/1 priority date for domestic students, 1/15 priority date for international students; for spring admission, 11/1 priority date for domestic students, 6/1 priority date for international students. Applications are processed on a rolling basis. Application fee: $50 ($60 for international students). Electronic applications accepted. *Expenses:* Tuition, state resident: full-time $9826. Tuition, nonresident: full-time $24,950. *Financial support:* In 2014–15, 1 fellowship with full tuition reimbursement (averaging $15,000 per year), 14 research assistantships with full tuition reimbursements (averaging $14,000 per year), 6 teaching assistantships with full tuition reimbursements (averaging $11,025 per year) were awarded; health care benefits and unspecified assistantships also available. *Faculty research:* Devices and materials, electromechanical systems, embedded systems. *Total annual research expenditures:* $1.8 million. *Unit head:* Dr. D. Jeff Jackson, Department Head, 205-348-2919, Fax: 205-348-6959, E-mail: jjackson@eng.ua.edu. *Application contact:* Dr. Tim Haskew, Graduate Program Director, 205-348-1766, Fax: 205-348-6959, E-mail: thaskew@eng.ua.edu.
Website: http://ece.eng.ua.edu.

The University of Alabama at Birmingham, School of Engineering, Program in Electrical Engineering, Birmingham, AL 35294. Offers MSEE. *Students:* 10 full-time (2 women), 12 part-time (2 women); includes 3 minority (1 Asian, non-Hispanic/Latino; 1 Hispanic/Latino; 1 Two or more races, non-Hispanic/Latino), 9 international. Average age 29. In 2014, 3 master's awarded. *Degree requirements:* For master's, thesis (for some programs). *Entrance requirements:* For master's, GRE, minimum GPA of 3.0 in all junior and senior electrical and computer engineering and mathematics courses attempted, letters of evaluation. Additional exam requirements/recommendations for international students: Required—TOEFL. *Expenses:* Tuition, state resident: full-time $7090; part-time $370 per credit hour. Tuition, nonresident: full-time $16,072; part-time $869 per credit hour. Full-time tuition and fees vary according to course load and program. *Financial support:* Research assistantships available. *Unit head:* Dr. Mohammad Haider, Program Director, 205-934-8440, Fax: 205-975-3337, E-mail: mrhaider@uab.edu. *Application contact:* Susan Noblitt Banks, Director of Graduate School Operations, 205-934-8227, Fax: 205-934-8413, E-mail: gradschool@uab.edu.
Website: https://www.uab.edu/engineering/home/graduate#msee.

The University of Alabama in Huntsville, School of Graduate Studies, College of Engineering, Department of Electrical and Computer Engineering, Huntsville, AL 35899. Offers computer engineering (MSE, PhD); electrical engineering (MSE, PhD), including optics and photonics technology (MSE), opto-electronics (MSE); information assurance (MS); optical science and engineering (PhD); optics and photonics (MSE); software engineering (MSSE). Part-time and evening/weekend programs available. *Degree requirements:* For master's, comprehensive exam, thesis or alternative, oral and written exams; for doctorate, comprehensive exam, thesis/dissertation, oral and written exams. *Entrance requirements:* For master's, GRE General Test, appropriate bachelor's degree, minimum GPA of 3.0; for doctorate, GRE General Test, minimum GPA of 3.0. Additional exam requirements/recommendations for international students: Required—TOEFL (minimum score 500 paper-based; 80 iBT), IELTS (minimum score 6.5). Electronic applications accepted. *Faculty research:* Advanced computer architecture and systems, fault tolerant computing and verification, computational electro-magnetics, nano-photonics and plasmonics, micro electro-mechanical (MEMS) systems.

University of Alaska Fairbanks, College of Engineering and Mines, Department of Electrical and Computer Engineering, Fairbanks, AK 99775-5915. Offers electrical engineering (MEE, MS). Part-time programs available. *Faculty:* 8 full-time (1 woman). *Students:* 12 full-time (3 women), 3 part-time (0 women); includes 2 minority (1 Hispanic/Latino; 1 Two or more races, non-Hispanic/Latino), 4 international. Average age 28. 11 applicants, 64% accepted, 6 enrolled. In 2014, 5 master's awarded. *Degree requirements:* For master's, comprehensive exam. *Entrance requirements:* For master's, GRE General Test, bachelor's degree from accredited institution with minimum cumulative undergraduate and major GPA of 3.0. Additional exam requirements/recommendations for international students: Required—TOEFL (minimum score 550 paper-based; 79 iBT), IELTS (minimum score 6.5). *Application deadline:* For fall admission, 6/1 for domestic students, 3/1 for international students; for spring admission, 10/15 for domestic students, 9/1 for international students. Applications are processed on a rolling basis. Application fee: $60. Electronic applications accepted. *Expenses:* Tuition, state resident: full-time $7614; part-time $423 per credit. Tuition, nonresident: full-time $15,552; part-time $864 per credit. Tuition and fees vary according to course level, course load and reciprocity agreements. *Financial support:* In 2014–15, 3 research assistantships with full tuition reimbursements (averaging $10,445 per year), 7 teaching assistantships with full tuition reimbursements (averaging $7,302 per year) were awarded; fellowships with full tuition reimbursements, career-related internships or fieldwork, Federal Work-Study, scholarships/grants, health care benefits, and unspecified assistantships also available. Support available to part-time students. Financial award application deadline: 7/1; financial award applicants required to submit FAFSA. *Faculty research:* Geomagnetically-induced currents in power lines, electromagnetic wave propagation, laser radar systems, bioinformatics, distributed sensor networks. *Unit head:* Dr. Charles Mayer, Chair, 907-474-7137, Fax: 907-474-5135, E-mail: uaf-cem-ece-dept@alaska.edu. *Application contact:* Mary Kreta, Director of Admissions, 907-474-7500, Fax: 907-474-7097, E-mail: admissions@uaf.edu.
Website: http://cem.uaf.edu/ece/.

Electrical Engineering

University of Alberta, Faculty of Graduate Studies and Research, Department of Electrical and Computer Engineering, Edmonton, AB T6G 2E1, Canada. Offers communications (M Eng, M Sc, PhD); computer engineering (M Eng, M Sc, PhD); electromagnetics (M Eng, M Sc, PhD); nanotechnology and microdevices (M Eng, M Sc, PhD); power/power electronics (M Eng, M Sc, PhD); systems (M Eng, M Sc, PhD). Terminal master's awarded for partial completion of doctoral program. *Degree requirements:* For master's, thesis; for doctorate, thesis/dissertation. *Entrance requirements:* Additional exam requirements/recommendations for international students: Required—TOEFL. Electronic applications accepted. *Faculty research:* Controls, communications, microelectronics, electromagnetics.

The University of Arizona, College of Engineering, Department of Electrical and Computer Engineering, Tucson, AZ 85721. Offers M Eng, MS, PhD. Part-time programs available. *Degree requirements:* For master's, thesis (for some programs); for doctorate, thesis/dissertation. *Entrance requirements:* For master's, GRE General Test, 3 letters of recommendation, statement of purpose; for doctorate, GRE General Test, master's degree in related field, 3 letters of recommendation, statement of purpose. Additional exam requirements/recommendations for international students: Required—TOEFL (minimum score 550 paper-based; 79 iBT). Electronic applications accepted. *Faculty research:* Communication systems, control systems, signal processing, computer-aided logic.

University of Arkansas, Graduate School, College of Engineering, Department of Electrical Engineering, Fayetteville, AR 72701-1201. Offers electrical engineering (MSEE, PhD); telecommunications engineering (MS Tc E). *Degree requirements:* For master's, thesis optional; for doctorate, one foreign language, thesis/dissertation. *Entrance requirements:* For master's and doctorate, GRE General Test. Electronic applications accepted.

University of Bridgeport, School of Engineering, Department of Electrical Engineering, Bridgeport, CT 06604. Offers MS. Part-time and evening/weekend programs available. Terminal master's awarded for partial completion of doctoral program. *Degree requirements:* For master's, thesis optional. *Entrance requirements:* Additional exam requirements/recommendations for international students: Recommended—TOEFL (minimum score 550 paper-based; 80 iBT), IELTS (minimum score 6.5). Electronic applications accepted. *Expenses:* Contact institution.

The University of British Columbia, Faculty of Applied Science, Department of Electrical and Computer Engineering, Vancouver, BC V6T 1Z4, Canada. Offers M Eng, MA Sc, PhD. Part-time programs available. *Degree requirements:* For master's, thesis (for some programs); for doctorate, thesis/dissertation. *Entrance requirements:* Additional exam requirements/recommendations for international students: Required—TOEFL (minimum score 600 paper-based; 100 iBT), IELTS (minimum score 7). Electronic applications accepted. *Faculty research:* Applied electromagnetics, biomedical engineering, communications and signal processing, computer and software engineering, power engineering, robotics, solid-state, systems and control.

University of Calgary, Faculty of Graduate Studies, Schulich School of Engineering, Department of Electrical and Computer Engineering, Calgary, AB T2N 1N4, Canada. Offers M Eng, M Sc, PhD. Part-time programs available. *Degree requirements:* For master's, thesis (for M Sc); for doctorate, thesis/dissertation, candidacy exam. *Entrance requirements:* For master's, minimum GPA of 3.0; for doctorate, minimum GPA of 3.5. Additional exam requirements/recommendations for international students: Required—TOEFL (minimum score 550 paper-based; 80 iBT) or IELTS (minimum score 7). Electronic applications accepted. *Faculty research:* Biomedical and bioelectrics, telecommunications and signal processing, software and computer engineering, power and control, microelectronics and instrumentation.

University of California, Berkeley, Graduate Division, College of Engineering, Department of Electrical Engineering and Computer Sciences, Berkeley, CA 94720-1500. Offers computer science (MS, PhD); electrical engineering (MS, PhD). *Degree requirements:* For master's, comprehensive exam or thesis; for doctorate, thesis/dissertation, qualifying exam. *Entrance requirements:* For master's and doctorate, GRE General Test, minimum GPA of 3.0, 3 letters of recommendation. Additional exam requirements/recommendations for international students: Required—TOEFL. Electronic applications accepted.

University of California, Davis, College of Engineering, Program in Electrical and Computer Engineering, Davis, CA 95616. Offers MS, PhD. Terminal master's awarded for partial completion of doctoral program. *Degree requirements:* For master's, comprehensive exam (for some programs), thesis (for some programs); for doctorate, thesis/dissertation, preliminary and qualifying exams, thesis defense. *Entrance requirements:* For master's, GRE General Test, minimum GPA of 3.2; for doctorate, GRE, minimum graduate GPA of 3.5. Additional exam requirements/recommendations for international students: Required—TOEFL (minimum score 550 paper-based). Electronic applications accepted.

University of California, Irvine, Henry Samueli School of Engineering, Department of Electrical Engineering and Computer Science, Irvine, CA 92697. Offers electrical engineering and computer science (MS, PhD); networked systems (MS, PhD). Part-time programs available. *Students:* 322 full-time (84 women), 29 part-time (4 women); includes 25 minority (23 Asian, non-Hispanic/Latino; 1 Hispanic/Latino; 1 Two or more races, non-Hispanic/Latino), 292 international. Average age 27. 2,452 applicants, 14% accepted, 139 enrolled. In 2014, 74 master's, 25 doctorates awarded. Terminal master's awarded for partial completion of doctoral program. *Degree requirements:* For doctorate, thesis/dissertation. *Entrance requirements:* For master's and doctorate, GRE General Test, minimum GPA of 3.0, 3 letters of recommendation. Additional exam requirements/recommendations for international students: Required—TOEFL (minimum score 550 paper-based). *Application deadline:* For fall admission, 1/15 priority date for domestic students, 1/15 for international students. Applications are processed on a rolling basis. Application fee: $90 ($110 for international students). Electronic applications accepted. *Financial support:* Fellowships, research assistantships with full tuition reimbursements, teaching assistantships, institutionally sponsored loans, traineeships, health care benefits, and unspecified assistantships available. Financial award application deadline: 3/1; financial award applicants required to submit FAFSA. *Faculty research:* Optics and electronic devices and circuits, signal processing, communications, machine vision, power electronics. *Unit head:* Prof. K. Kumar Wickramasinghe, Chair, 949-824-2213, E-mail: hkwick@uci.edu. *Application contact:* Jean Bennett, Director of Graduate Student Affairs, 949-824-6475, Fax: 949-824-8200, E-mail: jean.bennett@uci.edu. Website: http://www.eng.uci.edu/dept/eecs.

University of California, Los Angeles, Graduate Division, Henry Samueli School of Engineering and Applied Science, Department of Electrical Engineering, Los Angeles, CA 90095-1594. Offers MS, PhD. *Faculty:* 45 full-time (7 women), 17 part-time/adjunct (0 women). *Students:* 487 full-time (81 women); includes 62 minority (1 Black or African American, non-Hispanic/Latino; 48 Asian, non-Hispanic/Latino; 10 Hispanic/Latino; 3 Two or more races, non-Hispanic/Latino), 376 international. 2,032 applicants, 20% accepted, 182 enrolled. In 2014, 176 master's, 39 doctorates awarded. *Degree requirements:* For master's, comprehensive exam or thesis; for doctorate, thesis/dissertation, qualifying exams. *Entrance requirements:* For master's, GRE General Test, minimum GPA of 3.0; for doctorate, GRE General Test, minimum GPA of 3.25.

Additional exam requirements/recommendations for international students: Required—TOEFL (minimum score 560 paper-based; 87 iBT), IELTS (minimum score 7). *Application deadline:* For fall admission, 12/15 for domestic and international students. Application fee: $80 ($100 for international students). Electronic applications accepted. *Financial support:* In 2014–15, 206 fellowships, 373 research assistantships, 118 teaching assistantships were awarded; career-related internships or fieldwork, Federal Work-Study, institutionally sponsored loans, and tuition waivers (full and partial) also available. Financial award application deadline: 12/15; financial award applicants required to submit FAFSA. *Faculty research:* Circuits and embedded systems, physical and wave electronics, signals and systems. *Total annual research expenditures:* $17.8 million. *Unit head:* Dr. Gregory Pottie, Chair, 310-825-8150, E-mail: pottie@ee.ucla.edu. *Application contact:* Mandy Smith, Student Affairs Officer, 310-825-9383, E-mail: msmith@seas.ucla.edu.
Website: http://www.ee.ucla.edu/.

University of California, Merced, Graduate Division, School of Engineering, Merced, CA 95343. Offers biological engineering and small scale technologies (MS, PhD); electrical engineering and computer science (MS, PhD); environmental systems (MS, PhD); mechanical engineering (MS); mechanical engineering and applied mechanics (PhD). *Faculty:* 38 full-time (6 women), 1 part-time/adjunct (0 women). *Students:* 128 full-time (36 women), 2 part-time (0 women); includes 21 minority (1 Black or African American, non-Hispanic/Latino; 11 Asian, non-Hispanic/Latino; 6 Hispanic/Latino; 3 Two or more races, non-Hispanic/Latino), 72 international. Average age 28. 230 applicants, 39% accepted, 38 enrolled. In 2014, 5 master's, 18 doctorates awarded. *Degree requirements:* For master's, variable foreign language requirement, comprehensive exam, thesis (for some programs); for doctorate, variable foreign language requirement, comprehensive exam, thesis/dissertation. *Entrance requirements:* For master's and doctorate, GRE. Additional exam requirements/recommendations for international students: Required—TOEFL (minimum score 550 paper-based; 68 iBT); Recommended—IELTS. Application fee: $80 ($100 for international students). *Expenses:* Tuition, state resident: full-time $11,220; part-time $2805 per semester. *Required fees:* $1940; $970 per semester hour. *Financial support:* In 2014–15, 19 fellowships with full and partial tuition reimbursements (averaging $6,683 per year) were awarded; scholarships/grants also available. *Faculty research:* Artificial intelligence, biomedical imaging, thermal science, ecology, nanotechnology. *Unit head:* Dr. Erik Rolland, Interim Dean, 209-228-4296, Fax: 209-228-4047, E-mail: erolland@ucmerced.edu. *Application contact:* Tsu Ya, Graduate Admissions and Academic Services Manager, 209-228-4521, Fax: 209-228-6906, E-mail: tya@ucmerced.edu.

University of California, Riverside, Graduate Division, Department of Electrical Engineering, Riverside, CA 92521-0102. Offers electrical engineering (MS, PhD), including computer engineering (MS), control and robotics, intelligent systems, nano-materials, devices and circuits, signal processing and communications. Terminal master's awarded for partial completion of doctoral program. *Degree requirements:* For master's, thesis optional; for doctorate, thesis/dissertation, qualifying exams. *Entrance requirements:* For master's and doctorate, GRE General Test, minimum GPA of 3.25. Additional exam requirements/recommendations for international students: Required—TOEFL (minimum score 550 paper-based; 80 iBT). Electronic applications accepted. *Expenses:* Tuition, state resident: full-time $5399. Tuition, nonresident: full-time $10,433. *Faculty research:* Solid state devices, integrated circuits, signal processing.

University of California, San Diego, Graduate Division, Department of Electrical and Computer Engineering, La Jolla, CA 92093. Offers applied ocean science (MS, PhD); applied physics (MS, PhD); communication theory and systems (MS, PhD); computer engineering (MS, PhD); electronic circuits and systems (MS, PhD); intelligent systems, robotics and control (MS, PhD); medical devices and systems (MS, PhD); nanoscale devices and systems (MS, PhD); photonics (MS, PhD); signal and image processing (MS, PhD). *Students:* 435 full-time (81 women), 43 part-time (8 women); includes 78 minority (2 Black or African American, non-Hispanic/Latino; 1 American Indian or Alaska Native, non-Hispanic/Latino; 69 Asian, non-Hispanic/Latino; 6 Hispanic/Latino), 306 international. 2,710 applicants, 18% accepted, 177 enrolled. In 2014, 109 master's, 50 doctorates awarded. *Degree requirements:* For master's, thesis or written exam; for doctorate, comprehensive exam, thesis/dissertation. *Entrance requirements:* For master's and doctorate, GRE General Test, minimum GPA of 3.0. Additional exam requirements/recommendations for international students: Required—TOEFL (minimum score 550 paper-based; 80 iBT), IELTS. *Application deadline:* For fall admission, 12/15 for domestic students. Application fee: $90 ($110 for international students). Electronic applications accepted. *Expenses:* Tuition, state resident: full-time $11,220; part-time $5610 per quarter. Tuition, nonresident: full-time $26,322; part-time $13,161 per quarter. *Required fees:* $570 per quarter. Tuition and fees vary according to program. *Financial support:* Fellowships, research assistantships, teaching assistantships, scholarships/grants, and unspecified assistantships available. Financial award applicants required to submit FAFSA. *Faculty research:* Applied ocean science; applied physics; communication theory and systems; computer engineering; electronic circuits and systems; intelligent systems, robotics and control; medical devices and systems; nanoscale devices and systems; photonics; signal and image processing. *Unit head:* Truong Nguyen, Chair, 858-822-5554, E-mail: nguyent@ece.ucsd.edu. *Application contact:* Shana Slebioda, Graduate Coordinator, 858-822-2513, E-mail: ecegradapps@ece.ucsd.edu.
Website: http://ece.ucsd.edu/.

University of California, Santa Barbara, Graduate Division, College of Engineering, Department of Electrical and Computer Engineering, Santa Barbara, CA 93106-2014. Offers communications, control and signal processing (MS, PhD); computer engineering (MS, PhD); electronics and photonics (MS, PhD); MS/PhD. *Degree requirements:* For master's, comprehensive exam, thesis; for doctorate, thesis/dissertation. *Entrance requirements:* For master's and doctorate, GRE General Test. Additional exam requirements/recommendations for international students: Required—TOEFL (minimum score 550 paper-based; 80 iBT), IELTS (minimum score 7). Electronic applications accepted. *Faculty research:* Communications, signal processing, computer engineering, control, electronics and photonics.

University of California, Santa Cruz, Division of Graduate Studies, Jack Baskin School of Engineering, Department of Electrical Engineering, Santa Cruz, CA 95064. Offers MS, PhD. *Degree requirements:* For master's, thesis; for doctorate, thesis/dissertation, qualifying exam. *Entrance requirements:* For master's and doctorate, GRE General Test. Additional exam requirements/recommendations for international students: Required—TOEFL (minimum score 570 paper-based; 89 iBT); Recommended—IELTS (minimum score 8). Electronic applications accepted. *Faculty research:* Photonics and electronics, signal processing and communications, remote sensing, nanotechnology.

University of Central Florida, College of Engineering and Computer Science, Department of Electrical Engineering and Computer Science, Program in Electrical Engineering, Orlando, FL 32816. Offers electrical engineering (MSEE, PhD); electronic circuits (Certificate). Part-time and evening/weekend programs available. *Students:* 155 full-time (26 women), 52 part-time (6 women); includes 21 minority (4 Black or African American, non-Hispanic/Latino; 6 Asian, non-Hispanic/Latino; 11 Hispanic/Latino), 125 international. Average age 29. 293 applicants, 76% accepted, 55 enrolled. In 2014, 34

master's, 22 doctorates awarded. *Degree requirements:* For master's, thesis or alternative; for doctorate, thesis/dissertation, departmental qualifying exam, candidacy exam. *Entrance requirements:* For master's, GRE General Test, minimum GPA of 3.0 in last 60 hours; for doctorate, GRE General Test, minimum GPA of 3.5 in last 60 hours. Additional exam requirements/recommendations for international students: Required—TOEFL. *Application deadline:* For fall admission, 7/15 priority date for domestic students; for spring admission, 12/1 priority date for domestic students. Application fee: $30. Electronic applications accepted. *Expenses:* Tuition, state resident: part-time $288.16 per credit hour. Tuition, nonresident: part-time $1073.31 per credit hour. *Financial support:* In 2014–15, 82 students received support, including 30 fellowships with partial tuition reimbursements available (averaging $5,800 per year), 62 research assistantships with partial tuition reimbursements available (averaging $10,900 per year), 27 teaching assistantships with partial tuition reimbursements available (averaging $8,600 per year); tuition waivers (partial) also available. *Unit head:* Dr. Zhihua Qu, Interim Chair, 407-823-5976, Fax: 407-823-5835, E-mail: qu@ucf.edu. *Application contact:* Barbara Rodriguez Lamas, Director, Admissions and Student Services, 407-823-2766, Fax: 407-823-6442, E-mail: gradadmissions@ucf.edu.
Website: http://web.eecs.ucf.edu/.

University of Central Oklahoma, The Jackson College of Graduate Studies, College of Mathematics and Science, Department of Engineering and Physics, Edmond, OK 73034-5209. Offers biomedical engineering (MS); electrical engineering (MS); mechanical systems (MS); physics (MS). Part-time programs available. *Degree requirements:* For master's, thesis optional. *Entrance requirements:* For master's, GRE, 24 hours of course work in physics or equivalent, mathematics through differential equations, minimum GPA of 2.75 overall and 3.0 in last 60 hours attempted. Additional exam requirements/recommendations for international students: Required—TOEFL (minimum score 550 paper-based). Electronic applications accepted.

University of Cincinnati, Graduate School, College of Engineering and Applied Science, Department of Electrical and Computer Engineering and Computer Science, Program in Electrical Engineering, Cincinnati, OH 45221. Offers MS, PhD. *Degree requirements:* For master's, thesis; for doctorate, thesis/dissertation. *Entrance requirements:* For master's and doctorate, GRE General Test. Additional exam requirements/recommendations for international students: Required—TOEFL (minimum score 550 paper-based). *Faculty research:* Integrated circuits and optical devices, charge-coupled devices, photosensitive devices.

University of Colorado Boulder, Graduate School, College of Engineering and Applied Science, Department of Electrical, Computer and Energy Engineering, Boulder, CO 80309. Offers ME, MS, PhD. *Faculty:* 32 full-time (4 women). *Students:* 205 full-time (37 women), 74 part-time (8 women); includes 24 minority (1 Black or African American, non-Hispanic/Latino; 12 Asian, non-Hispanic/Latino; 9 Hispanic/Latino; 2 Two or more races, non-Hispanic/Latino), 150 international. Average age 27. 830 applicants, 32% accepted, 86 enrolled. In 2014, 82 master's, 18 doctorates awarded. Terminal master's awarded for partial completion of doctoral program. *Degree requirements:* For master's, thesis or alternative; for doctorate, one foreign language, thesis/dissertation, departmental qualifying exam. *Entrance requirements:* For master's, GRE General Test, minimum undergraduate GPA of 3.0; for doctorate, GRE General Test, minimum undergraduate GPA of 3.5. *Application deadline:* For fall admission, 1/15 for domestic and international students; for spring admission, 9/1 for domestic and international students. Applications are processed on a rolling basis. Application fee: $50 ($70 for international students). Electronic applications accepted. *Financial support:* In 2014–15, 388 students received support, including 35 fellowships (averaging $14,187 per year), 85 research assistantships with full and partial tuition reimbursements available (averaging $34,633 per year), 25 teaching assistantships with full and partial tuition reimbursements available (averaging $21,307 per year); institutionally sponsored loans, scholarships/grants, health care benefits, and unspecified assistantships also available. Financial award application deadline: 1/15; financial award applicants required to submit FAFSA. *Faculty research:* Electrical engineering/electronics, signal processing, electromagnetic propagation, electromagnetics. *Total annual research expenditures:* $9.9 million.
Website: http://ecee.colorado.edu.

University of Colorado Colorado Springs, College of Engineering and Applied Science, Department of Electrical and Computer Engineering, Colorado Springs, CO 80933-7150. Offers electrical engineering (MS). Part-time and evening/weekend programs available. *Faculty:* 8 full-time (1 woman), 10 part-time/adjunct (2 women). *Students:* 3 full-time (0 women), 47 part-time (4 women); includes 5 minority (4 Asian, non-Hispanic/Latino; 1 Hispanic/Latino), 25 international. Average age 28. 65 applicants, 69% accepted, 14 enrolled. In 2014, 16 master's awarded. *Degree requirements:* For master's, thesis (for some programs), final oral exam (for non-thesis option). *Entrance requirements:* For master's, GRE scores: for the Computer Science Department, the GRE is required with a score of at least 148 on the quantitative portion; for the Electrical & Computer Engineering Department, the GRE is required with a minimum of 1200 combined score on verbal and quantitative; for the Mechanical & Aerospace Engineering Department, the GRE is required., minimum GPA of 3.0, BS or course work in electrical engineering. Additional exam requirements/recommendations for international students: Required—TOEFL (minimum score 550 paper-based; 78 iBT), IELTS (minimum score 6). *Application deadline:* For fall admission, 4/1 for domestic and international students; for spring admission, 10/1 for domestic and international students. Applications are processed on a rolling basis. Application fee: $60 ($100 for international students). *Expenses:* Tuition, state resident: full-time $9900; part-time $1892 per course. Tuition, nonresident: full-time $18,792; part-time $3375 per course. One-time fee: $100. Tuition and fees vary according to course load, program and reciprocity agreements. *Financial support:* In 2014–15, 8 students received support, including 2 research assistantships (averaging $12,000 per year); fellowships, teaching assistantships, career-related internships or fieldwork, Federal Work-Study, and scholarships/grants also available. Support available to part-time students. Financial award application deadline: 3/1; financial award applicants required to submit FAFSA. *Faculty research:* Micro heater array development, testing and testable design of digital and analog circuits, boards, and systems, linear and nonlinear adaptive filtering; dynamic system modeling, state estimation and control, computer architecture and design, wireless communication systems, DSP algorithm development for communication systems, sensor networks, statistical signal processing, real-time digital signal processing, microwave and RF systems, traveling-wave tubes. *Total annual research expenditures:* $1 million. *Unit head:* Dr. T. S. Kalkur, Chair, 719-255-3147, Fax: 719-255-3589. *Application contact:* Eva Wynhorst, Program Assistant, 719-255-3548, Fax: 719-255-3589, E-mail: ewynhors@uccs.edu.
Website: http://www.uccs.edu/~ece/.

University of Colorado Denver, College of Engineering and Applied Science, Department of Electrical Engineering, Denver, CO 80217. Offers MS, EASPh D. Part-time and evening/weekend programs available. *Faculty:* 11 full-time (1 woman). *Students:* 117 full-time (27 women), 31 part-time (1 woman); includes 12 minority (3 Black or African American, non-Hispanic/Latino; 4 Asian, non-Hispanic/Latino; 3 Hispanic/Latino; 1 Native Hawaiian or other Pacific Islander, non-Hispanic/Latino; 1 Two or more races, non-Hispanic/Latino), 114 international. Average age 27. 412 applicants, 59% accepted, 68 enrolled. In 2014, 26 master's awarded. *Degree requirements:* For master's, thesis or project, 30 credit hours; for doctorate, dissertation, 60 credit hours beyond master's work (30 of which are for dissertation research). *Entrance requirements:* For master's and doctorate, GRE, three letters of recommendation, personal statement. Additional exam requirements/recommendations for international students: Required—TOEFL (minimum score 550 paper-based; 80 iBT), TOEFL (minimum score 600 paper-based) for EAS PhD; Recommended—IELTS (minimum score 6.8). *Application deadline:* For fall admission, 5/1 for domestic students, 4/15 for international students; for spring admission, 10/1 for domestic students, 9/15 for international students. Application fee: $50 ($75 for international students). Electronic applications accepted. *Expenses:* Expenses: Contact institution. *Financial support:* In 2014–15, 2 students received support. Fellowships, research assistantships, teaching assistantships, career-related internships or fieldwork, Federal Work-Study, institutionally sponsored loans, scholarships/grants, traineeships, and unspecified assistantships available. Financial award application deadline: 4/1; financial award applicants required to submit FAFSA. *Faculty research:* Communication and signal processing, embedded systems, electromagnetic fields and matter, energy and power systems, photonics and biomedical imaging. *Unit head:* Dr. Stephen Gedney, Chair, 303-352-3744, E-mail: stephen.gedney@ucdenver.edu. *Application contact:* Annie Bennett, Program Assistant, 303-556-4718, E-mail: annie.bennett@ucdenver.edu.
Website: http://www.ucdenver.edu/academics/colleges/Engineering/Programs/Electrical-Engineering/Pages/ElectricalEngineering.aspx.

University of Colorado Denver, College of Engineering and Applied Science, Master of Engineering Program, Denver, CO 80217-3364. Offers civil engineering (M Eng), including civil engineering, geographic information systems, transportation systems; electrical engineering (M Eng); mechanical engineering (M Eng). Part-time programs available. *Students:* 30 full-time (9 women), 20 part-time (7 women); includes 3 minority (1 Black or African American, non-Hispanic/Latino; 2 Hispanic/Latino), 8 international. Average age 34. 35 applicants, 83% accepted, 15 enrolled. In 2014, 14 master's awarded. *Degree requirements:* For master's, comprehensive exam, 27 credit hours of course work, 3 credit hours of report or thesis work. *Entrance requirements:* For master's, GRE (for those with GPA below 2.75), transcripts, references, statement of purpose. Additional exam requirements/recommendations for international students: Required—TOEFL (minimum score 537 paper-based; 75 iBT); Recommended—IELTS (minimum score 6.5). *Application deadline:* For fall admission, 4/1 for domestic students, 3/1 for international students; for spring admission, 10/1 for domestic students, 9/15 for international students. Applications are processed on a rolling basis. Application fee: $50 ($75 for international students). Electronic applications accepted. *Expenses:* Expenses: Contact institution. *Financial support:* In 2014–15, 4 students received support. Fellowships, research assistantships, teaching assistantships, Federal Work-Study, institutionally sponsored loans, scholarships/grants, traineeships, and unspecified assistantships available. Financial award application deadline: 4/1; financial award applicants required to submit FAFSA. *Faculty research:* Civil, electrical and mechanical engineering. *Unit head:* 303-556-2870, Fax: 303-556-2511, E-mail: engineering@ucdenver.edu. *Application contact:* Graduate School Admissions, 303-556-2704, E-mail: admissions@ucdenver.edu.
Website: http://www.ucdenver.edu/academics/colleges/Engineering/admissions/Masters/Pages/MastersAdmissions.aspx.

University of Connecticut, Graduate School, School of Engineering, Department of Electrical and Computer Engineering, Field of Electrical Engineering, Storrs, CT 06269. Offers MS, PhD. Terminal master's awarded for partial completion of doctoral program. *Degree requirements:* For master's, comprehensive exam; for doctorate, thesis/dissertation. *Entrance requirements:* For master's and doctorate, GRE General Test. Additional exam requirements/recommendations for international students: Required—TOEFL (minimum score 550 paper-based). Electronic applications accepted.

University of Dayton, Department of Electrical and Computer Engineering, Dayton, OH 45469. Offers MSEE, DE, PhD. Part-time and evening/weekend programs available. *Faculty:* 16 full-time (0 women), 12 part-time/adjunct (2 women). *Students:* 220 full-time (43 women), 35 part-time (4 women); includes 11 minority (3 Black or African American, non-Hispanic/Latino; 5 Asian, non-Hispanic/Latino; 1 Hispanic/Latino; 2 Two or more races, non-Hispanic/Latino), 199 international. Average age 27. 495 applicants, 40% accepted, 66 enrolled. In 2014, 61 master's, 6 doctorates awarded. *Degree requirements:* For master's, thesis optional; for doctorate, variable foreign language requirement, thesis/dissertation, departmental qualifying exam. *Entrance requirements:* Additional exam requirements/recommendations for international students: Required—TOEFL (minimum score 550 paper-based; 80 iBT). *Application deadline:* For fall admission, 8/1 for domestic students, 5/1 priority date for international students; for winter admission, 7/1 for international students; for spring admission, 11/1 priority date for international students. Applications are processed on a rolling basis. Application fee: $0 ($50 for international students). Electronic applications accepted. *Expenses:* Tuition: Full-time $10,176; part-time $848 per credit. *Required fees:* $25; $25 per course. Part-time tuition and fees vary according to course level, course load, degree level and program. *Financial support:* In 2014–15, 1 fellowship (averaging $27,500 per year), 32 research assistantships with full tuition reimbursements (averaging $12,500 per year), 21 teaching assistantships with full tuition reimbursements (averaging $10,065 per year) were awarded; institutionally sponsored loans, health care benefits, and unspecified assistantships also available. Financial award application deadline: 3/1; financial award applicants required to submit FAFSA. *Faculty research:* Electrical engineering, video processing, leaky wave antenna. *Total annual research expenditures:* $1.1 million. *Unit head:* Dr. Guru Subramanyam, Chair, 937-229-3188, Fax: 937-229-4529, E-mail: gsubramanyam1@udayton.edu. *Application contact:* E-mail: graduateadmission@udayton.edu.
Website: https://www.udayton.edu/engineering/departments/electrical_and_computer/index.php.

University of Delaware, College of Engineering, Department of Electrical and Computer Engineering, Newark, DE 19716. Offers MSECE, PhD. Part-time programs available. Postbaccalaureate distance learning degree programs offered (no on-campus study). Terminal master's awarded for partial completion of doctoral program. *Degree requirements:* For master's, thesis optional; for doctorate, thesis/dissertation. *Entrance requirements:* For master's, GRE General Test; for doctorate, GRE General Test, qualifying exam. Additional exam requirements/recommendations for international students: Required—TOEFL. Electronic applications accepted. *Faculty research:* HIV evolution during dynamic therapy, compressive sensing in imaging, sensor, networks, and UWB radios, computer network time synchronization, silicon spintronics, devices and imaging in the high-terahertz band.

University of Denver, Daniel Felix Ritchie School of Engineering and Computer Science, Department of Electrical and Computer Engineering, Denver, CO 80208. Offers computer engineering (MS); electrical and computer engineering (PhD); electrical engineering (MS); engineering (MS); mechatronic systems engineering (MS, PhD). Part-time and evening/weekend programs available. *Faculty:* 11 full-time (1 woman), 1 part-time/adjunct (0 women). *Students:* 5 full-time (1 woman), 94 part-time (14 women); includes 13 minority (1 Black or African American, non-Hispanic/Latino; 2 Asian, non-Hispanic/Latino; 6 Hispanic/Latino; 4 Two or more races, non-Hispanic/Latino), 41

international. Average age 28. 104 applicants, 74% accepted, 20 enrolled. In 2014, 35 master's, 7 doctorates awarded. Terminal master's awarded for partial completion of doctoral program. *Degree requirements:* For master's, thesis optional, proficiency in high- or low-level computer language; for doctorate, comprehensive exam, thesis/dissertation, proficiency in high- or low-level computer language. *Entrance requirements:* For master's, GRE General Test, bachelor's degree, transcripts, personal statement, resume or curriculum vitae, three letters of recommendation; for doctorate, GRE General Test, master's degree, transcripts, personal statement, resume or curriculum vitae, three letters of recommendation. Additional exam requirements/recommendations for international students: Required—TOEFL (minimum score 550 paper-based; 80 iBT). *Application deadline:* For fall admission, 2/1 priority date for domestic and international students. Applications are processed on a rolling basis. Application fee: $65. Electronic applications accepted. *Expenses:* Expenses: $1,199 per credit hour. *Financial support:* In 2014–15, 42 students received support, including 12 research assistantships with full and partial tuition reimbursements available (averaging $12,047 per year), 16 teaching assistantships with full and partial tuition reimbursements available (averaging $13,375 per year); Federal Work-Study, scholarships/grants, and unspecified assistantships also available. Financial award application deadline: 2/15; financial award applicants required to submit FAFSA. *Faculty research:* Energy and power, microelectromechanical systems (MEMS), unmanned systems, image processing/pattern recognition. *Unit head:* Dr. Kimon Valavanis, Chair, 303-871-2586, Fax: 303-871-2194, E-mail: kimon.valavanis@du.edu. *Application contact:* Crystal Harris, Administrative Assistant to the Chair, 303-871-6618, Fax: 303-871-2194, E-mail: crystal.harris@du.edu.
Website: http://www.du.edu/rsecs/departments/ece/index.html.

University of Detroit Mercy, College of Engineering and Science, Department of Electrical and Computer Engineering, Detroit, MI 48221. Offers computer engineering (ME, DE); mechatronics systems (ME, DE); signals and systems (ME, DE). Evening/weekend programs available. *Degree requirements:* For doctorate, thesis/dissertation. *Faculty research:* Electromagnetics, computer architecture, systems.

University of Florida, Graduate School, College of Engineering, Department of Electrical and Computer Engineering, Gainesville, FL 32611. Offers ME, MS, PhD, JD/MS, MSM/MS. Part-time programs available. Postbaccalaureate distance learning degree programs offered. *Faculty:* 47 full-time (3 women), 7 part-time/adjunct (1 woman). *Students:* 424 full-time (93 women), 76 part-time (11 women); includes 59 minority (11 Black or African American, non-Hispanic/Latino; 2 American Indian or Alaska Native, non-Hispanic/Latino; 22 Asian, non-Hispanic/Latino; 24 Hispanic/Latino), 352 international. 1,571 applicants, 37% accepted, 183 enrolled. In 2014, 219 master's, 42 doctorates awarded. Terminal master's awarded for partial completion of doctoral program. *Degree requirements:* For master's, comprehensive exam (for some programs), thesis (for some programs); for doctorate, comprehensive exam, thesis/dissertation. *Entrance requirements:* For master's, minimum GPA of 3.0; for doctorate, minimum GPA of 3.5. Additional exam requirements/recommendations for international students: Required—TOEFL (minimum score 550 paper-based; 80 iBT), IELTS (minimum score 6). *Application deadline:* For fall admission, 1/15 priority date for domestic students, 1/15 for international students. Applications are processed on a rolling basis. Application fee: $30. Electronic applications accepted. *Financial support:* Unspecified assistantships available. Financial award application deadline: 1/15; financial award applicants required to submit FAFSA. *Faculty research:* Computer engineering, devices, electromagnetics and energy systems, electronics and signals and systems. *Unit head:* John G. Harris, PhD, Chair, 352-392-0913, Fax: 352-392-8671, E-mail: harris@ece.ufl.edu. *Application contact:* Gijs Bosman, PhD, Professor and Graduate Coordinator, 352-392-0910, Fax: 352-392-8671, E-mail: bosman@ece.ufl.edu.
Website: http://www.ece.ufl.edu/.

University of Hawaii at Manoa, Graduate Division, College of Engineering, Department of Electrical Engineering, Honolulu, HI 96822. Offers MS, PhD. Part-time programs available. *Degree requirements:* For master's, comprehensive exam, thesis; for doctorate, comprehensive exam, thesis/dissertation. *Entrance requirements:* For master's and doctorate, GRE General Test. Additional exam requirements/recommendations for international students: Required—TOEFL (minimum score 540 paper-based; 76 iBT), IELTS (minimum score 5). *Faculty research:* Computers and artificial intelligence, communication and networking, control theory, physical electronics, VLSI design, micromillimeter waves.

University of Houston, Cullen College of Engineering, Department of Electrical and Computer Engineering, Houston, TX 77204. Offers electrical engineering (MEE, MSEE, PhD). Part-time programs available. Terminal master's awarded for partial completion of doctoral program. *Degree requirements:* For master's, thesis (for some programs); for doctorate, comprehensive exam, thesis/dissertation. *Entrance requirements:* For master's and doctorate, GRE General Test. Additional exam requirements/recommendations for international students: Required—TOEFL (minimum score 580 paper-based; 92 iBT). Electronic applications accepted. *Faculty research:* Applied electromagnetics and microelectronics, signal and image processing, biomedical engineering, geophysical applications, control engineering.

University of Idaho, College of Graduate Studies, College of Engineering, Department of Electrical and Computer Engineering, Moscow, ID 83844-1023. Offers computer engineering (M Engr, MS); electrical engineering (M Engr, MS, PhD). *Faculty:* 12 full-time, 3 part-time/adjunct. *Students:* 27 full-time, 83 part-time. Average age 35. In 2014, 27 master's, 7 doctorates awarded. *Degree requirements:* For master's, thesis; for doctorate, thesis/dissertation. *Entrance requirements:* For master's, minimum GPA of 2.8; for doctorate, minimum undergraduate GPA of 2.8, 3.0 graduate. *Application deadline:* For fall admission, 8/1 for domestic students; for spring admission, 12/15 for domestic students. Applications are processed on a rolling basis. Application fee: $60. Electronic applications accepted. *Expenses:* Tuition, state resident: full-time $4784; part-time $280.50 per credit hour. Tuition, nonresident: full-time $18,314; part-time $957.50 per credit hour. *Required fees:* $2000; $58.50 per credit hour. Tuition and fees vary according to program. *Financial support:* Fellowships, research assistantships, teaching assistantships, career-related internships or fieldwork, and Federal Work-Study available. Financial award applicants required to submit FAFSA. *Faculty research:* Microelectronics, laser electrophotography, intelligent systems research, advanced transportation technologies. *Unit head:* Dr. Fred Barlow, Chair, 208-885-6554, E-mail: info@ece.uidaho.edu. *Application contact:* Sean Scoggin, Graduate Recruitment Coordinator, 208-885-4001, Fax: 208-885-4406, E-mail: graduateadmissions@uidaho.edu.
Website: http://www.uidaho.edu/engr/ece/.

University of Illinois at Urbana–Champaign, Graduate College, College of Engineering, Department of Electrical and Computer Engineering, Champaign, IL 61820. Offers MS, PhD, MS/MBA. *Students:* 535 (79 women). Application fee: $70 ($90 for international students). *Unit head:* William H. Sanders, Head, 217-333-2301, Fax: 217-244-7075, E-mail: whs@illinois.edu. *Application contact:* Laurie A. Fisher, Administrative Aide, 217-333-9709, Fax: 217-333-8582, E-mail: fisher2@illinois.edu.
Website: http://www.ece.illinois.edu/.

The University of Iowa, Graduate College, College of Engineering, Department of Electrical and Computer Engineering, Iowa City, IA 52242-1316. Offers MS, PhD. Part-time programs available. *Faculty:* 16 full-time (4 women), 5 part-time/adjunct (0 women). *Students:* 67 full-time (12 women); includes 9 minority (1 Black or African American, non-Hispanic/Latino; 3 Asian, non-Hispanic/Latino; 5 Hispanic/Latino), 41 international. Average age 27. 115 applicants, 10% accepted, 6 enrolled. In 2014, 5 master's, 7 doctorates awarded. *Degree requirements:* For master's, comprehensive exam, thesis optional; for doctorate, comprehensive exam, thesis/dissertation, qualifying exam. *Entrance requirements:* For master's and doctorate, GRE. Additional exam requirements/recommendations for international students: Required—TOEFL (minimum score 550 paper-based; 81 iBT). *Application deadline:* For fall admission, 2/1 priority date for domestic students, 2/1 for international students; for spring admission, 12/1 for domestic students; for summer admission, 4/15 for domestic students. Applications are processed on a rolling basis. Application fee: $60 ($100 for international students). Electronic applications accepted. *Financial support:* In 2014–15, 3 fellowships with full tuition reimbursements, 40 research assistantships with full and partial tuition reimbursements (averaging $18,080 per year), 11 teaching assistantships with full tuition reimbursements (averaging $18,080 per year) were awarded; scholarships/grants and unspecified assistantships also available. Financial award application deadline: 2/1; financial award applicants required to submit FAFSA. *Faculty research:* Applied optics and nanotechnology, compressive sensing, computational genomics, database management systems, large-scale intelligent and control systems, medical image processing, VLSI design and test. *Total annual research expenditures:* $5.8 million. *Unit head:* Dr. Er-Wei Bai, Department Executive Officer, 319-335-5949, Fax: 319-335-6028, E-mail: er-wei-bai@uiowa.edu. *Application contact:* Cathy Kern, Secretary, 319-335-5197, Fax: 319-335-6028, E-mail: ece@engineering.uiowa.edu.
Website: http://www.engineering.uiowa.edu/ece.

The University of Kansas, Graduate Studies, School of Engineering, Program in Electrical Engineering, Lawrence, KS 66045. Offers MS, DE, PhD. Part-time programs available. *Faculty:* 33 full-time, 1 part-time/adjunct. *Students:* 74 full-time (21 women), 14 part-time (2 women); includes 4 minority (1 Black or African American, non-Hispanic/Latino; 2 Asian, non-Hispanic/Latino; 1 Hispanic/Latino), 60 international. Average age 26. 108 applicants, 66% accepted, 24 enrolled. In 2014, 12 master's, 6 doctorates awarded. Terminal master's awarded for partial completion of doctoral program. *Degree requirements:* For master's, thesis optional, exam; for doctorate, one foreign language, comprehensive exam, thesis/dissertation, qualifying exams. *Entrance requirements:* For master's, GRE, minimum GPA of 3.0; for doctorate, GRE, minimum GPA of 3.5. Additional exam requirements/recommendations for international students: Required—TOEFL (minimum score 600 paper-based; 100 iBT). *Application deadline:* For fall admission, 3/1 priority date for domestic students, 3/1 for international students; for spring admission, 10/1 priority date for domestic students, 10/1 for international students. Applications are processed on a rolling basis. Application fee: $55 ($65 for international students). Electronic applications accepted. *Financial support:* Fellowships with full and partial tuition reimbursements, research assistantships with full and partial tuition reimbursements, teaching assistantships with full and partial tuition reimbursements, career-related internships or fieldwork, scholarships/grants, and unspecified assistantships available. Financial award application deadline: 1/1. *Faculty research:* Communication systems and networking, computer systems design, radar systems and remote sensing. *Unit head:* James Stiles, Associate Chair for Graduate Studies, 785-864-8803, E-mail: jstilles@eecs.ku.edu. *Application contact:* Pam Shadoin, Graduate Admissions Contact, 785-864-4487, E-mail: pshadoin@ku.edu.
Website: http://www.eecs.ku.edu/prospective_students/graduate/masters#electrical_engineering.

University of Kentucky, Graduate School, College of Engineering, Program in Electrical Engineering, Lexington, KY 40506-0032. Offers MSEE, PhD. *Degree requirements:* For master's, comprehensive exam, thesis optional; for doctorate, one foreign language, comprehensive exam, thesis/dissertation. *Entrance requirements:* For master's, GRE General Test, minimum undergraduate GPA of 2.75; for doctorate, GRE General Test, minimum undergraduate GPA of 3.0. Additional exam requirements/recommendations for international students: Required—TOEFL (minimum score 550 paper-based). Electronic applications accepted. *Faculty research:* Signal processing, systems, and control; electromagnetic field theory; power electronics and machines; computer engineering and VLSI; materials and devices.

University of Louisville, J. B. Speed School of Engineering, Department of Electrical and Computer Engineering, Louisville, KY 40292-0001. Offers M Eng, MS, PhD. *Accreditation:* ABET (one or more programs are accredited). Part-time programs available. *Students:* 66 full-time (8 women), 26 part-time (5 women); includes 12 minority (4 Black or African American, non-Hispanic/Latino; 4 Asian, non-Hispanic/Latino; 4 Hispanic/Latino), 37 international. Average age 27. 64 applicants, 48% accepted, 14 enrolled. In 2014, 14 master's, 6 doctorates awarded. Terminal master's awarded for partial completion of doctoral program. *Degree requirements:* For master's, comprehensive exam (for some programs), thesis or alternative; for doctorate, comprehensive exam, thesis/dissertation, minimum GPA of 3.0. *Entrance requirements:* For master's and doctorate, GRE General Test. Additional exam requirements/recommendations for international students: Required—TOEFL (minimum score 550 paper-based; 80 iBT), IELTS (minimum score 6.5). *Application deadline:* For fall admission, 5/1 priority date for domestic and international students; for spring admission, 11/1 priority date for domestic and international students. Applications are processed on a rolling basis. Application fee: $60. Electronic applications accepted. *Expenses:* Tuition, state resident: full-time $11,326; part-time $630 per credit hour. Tuition, nonresident: full-time $23,568; part-time $1311 per credit hour. *Required fees:* $196. Tuition and fees vary according to program and reciprocity agreements. *Financial support:* In 2014–15, 16 students received support, including 4 fellowships with full tuition reimbursements available (averaging $20,000 per year), 4 research assistantships with full tuition reimbursements available (averaging $21,000 per year), 8 teaching assistantships with full tuition reimbursements available (averaging $20,000 per year). Financial award application deadline: 1/25; financial award applicants required to submit FAFSA. *Faculty research:* Nanotechnology; microfabrication; computer engineering; control, communication and signal processing; electronic devices and systems. *Total annual research expenditures:* $5.8 million. *Unit head:* James H. Graham, Acting Chair, 502-852-6289, Fax: 502-852-6807, E-mail: jhgrah01@louisville.edu. *Application contact:* Dr. Michael Day, Associate Dean, 502-852-6195, Fax: 502-852-7294, E-mail: day@louisville.edu.
Website: http://www.louisville.edu/speed/electrical/.

University of Maine, Graduate School, College of Engineering, Department of Electrical and Computer Engineering, Orono, ME 04469. Offers computer engineering (MS); electrical engineering (MS, PhD). Part-time programs available. *Faculty:* 12 full-time (1 woman), 4 part-time/adjunct (0 women). *Students:* 22 full-time (3 women), 1 (woman) part-time; includes 1 minority (Hispanic/Latino), 11 international. Average age 27. 32 applicants, 47% accepted, 6 enrolled. In 2014, 4 master's, 2 doctorates awarded. Terminal master's awarded for partial completion of doctoral program. *Degree requirements:* For master's, thesis (for some programs); for doctorate, comprehensive exam, thesis/dissertation. *Entrance requirements:* For master's and doctorate, GRE

General Test. Additional exam requirements/recommendations for international students: Required—TOEFL. *Application deadline:* For fall admission, 2/1 for domestic students. Applications are processed on a rolling basis. Application fee: $65. Electronic applications accepted. *Expenses:* Tuition, state resident: part-time $658 per credit hour. Tuition, nonresident: part-time $1550 per credit hour. *Financial support:* In 2014–15, 16 students received support, including 1 fellowship, 10 research assistantships with full tuition reimbursements available (averaging $14,600 per year), 4 teaching assistantships with full tuition reimbursements available (averaging $14,600 per year); Federal Work-Study, institutionally sponsored loans, and tuition waivers (full and partial) also available. Financial award application deadline: 3/1. *Faculty research:* Microwave acoustic sensors, semiconductor devices and fabrication, high performance computing, instrumentation and industrial automation, wireless communication. *Total annual research expenditures:* $959,995. *Unit head:* Dr. Donald Hummels, Chair, 207-581-2244. *Application contact:* Scott G. Delcourt, Assistant Vice President for Graduate Studies and Senior Associate Dean, 207-581-3291, Fax: 207-581-3232, E-mail: graduate@maine.edu.
Website: http://www.ece.umaine.edu/.

The University of Manchester, School of Electrical and Electronic Engineering, Manchester, United Kingdom. Offers M Phil, PhD.

University of Manitoba, Faculty of Graduate Studies, Faculty of Engineering, Department of Electrical and Computer Engineering, Winnipeg, MB R3T 2N2, Canada. Offers M Eng, M Sc, PhD. *Degree requirements:* For master's, thesis; for doctorate, thesis/dissertation.

University of Maryland, Baltimore County, The Graduate School, College of Engineering and Information Technology, Department of Computer Science and Electrical Engineering, Program in Electrical Engineering, Baltimore, MD 21250. Offers MS, PhD. Part-time programs available. *Students:* 37 full-time (9 women), 13 part-time (2 women); includes 6 minority (4 Black or African American, non-Hispanic/Latino; 1 Asian, non-Hispanic/Latino; 1 Hispanic/Latino), 25 international. Average age 29. 96 applicants, 43% accepted, 11 enrolled. In 2014, 6 master's, 8 doctorates awarded. *Degree requirements:* For master's, thesis optional; for doctorate, comprehensive exam, thesis/dissertation. *Entrance requirements:* For master's and doctorate, GRE General Test, BS from ABET-accredited undergraduate program in electrical engineering or strong background in computer science, mathematics, physics, or other areas of engineering or science. Additional exam requirements/recommendations for international students: Required—TOEFL (minimum score 550 paper-based; 80 iBT). *Application deadline:* For fall admission, 6/1 for domestic students, 1/1 for international students; for spring admission, 11/1 for domestic students, 6/1 for international students. Applications are processed on a rolling basis. Application fee: $70. Electronic applications accepted. *Expenses:* Tuition, state resident: part-time $557. Tuition, nonresident: part-time $922. *Required fees:* $122 per semester. One-time fee: $200 part-time. *Financial support:* In 2014–15, fellowships with full tuition reimbursements (averaging $18,000 per year), 17 research assistantships with full tuition reimbursements (averaging $18,000 per year), 7 teaching assistantships with full tuition reimbursements (averaging $16,000 per year) were awarded; career-related internships or fieldwork, Federal Work-Study, scholarships/grants, health care benefits, tuition waivers (partial), and unspecified assistantships also available. Support available to part-time students. Financial award application deadline: 6/30; financial award applicants required to submit FAFSA. *Faculty research:* Communication and signal processing, photonics and micro electronics, sensor systems, signal processing architectures, VLSI design and test. *Unit head:* Dr. Gary Carter, Professor and Chair, 410-455-3500, Fax: 410-455-3969, E-mail: carter@cs.umbc.edu. *Application contact:* Dr. Curtis Menyuk, Professor and Graduate Program Director, 410-455-3500, Fax: 410-455-3969, E-mail: menyuk@umbc.edu.
Website: http://www.cs.umbc.edu/.

University of Maryland, College Park, Academic Affairs, A. James Clark School of Engineering, Department of Electrical and Computer Engineering, Electrical Engineering Program, College Park, MD 20742. Offers MS, PhD. *Degree requirements:* For master's, thesis or alternative; for doctorate, thesis/dissertation, oral exam, qualifying exam. *Entrance requirements:* For master's and doctorate, GRE General Test, minimum GPA of 3.0. Electronic applications accepted.

University of Massachusetts Amherst, Graduate School, College of Engineering, Department of Electrical and Computer Engineering, Amherst, MA 01003. Offers MSECE, PhD. Part-time programs available. *Faculty:* 45 full-time (2 women). *Students:* 228 full-time (65 women), 10 part-time (3 women); includes 6 minority (2 Black or African American, non-Hispanic/Latino; 4 Asian, non-Hispanic/Latino), 204 international. Average age 25. 1,074 applicants, 23% accepted, 71 enrolled. In 2014, 70 master's, 13 doctorates awarded. Terminal master's awarded for partial completion of doctoral program. *Degree requirements:* For master's, thesis or alternative; for doctorate, comprehensive exam, thesis/dissertation. *Entrance requirements:* For master's and doctorate, GRE General Test. Additional exam requirements/recommendations for international students: Required—TOEFL (minimum score 550 paper-based; 80 iBT), IELTS (minimum score 6.5). *Application deadline:* For fall admission, 1/15 for domestic and international students; for spring admission, 10/1 for domestic and international students. Applications are processed on a rolling basis. Application fee: $75. Electronic applications accepted. *Expenses:* Tuition, state resident: full-time $1980; part-time $110 per credit. Tuition, nonresident: full-time $14,644; part-time $414 per credit. *Required fees:* $11,417. One-time fee: $357. *Financial support:* Fellowships with full and partial tuition reimbursements, research assistantships with full and partial tuition reimbursements, teaching assistantships with full and partial tuition reimbursements, career-related internships or fieldwork, Federal Work-Study, scholarships/grants, traineeships, health care benefits, tuition waivers (full and partial), and unspecified assistantships available. Support available to part-time students. Financial award application deadline: 1/15. *Unit head:* Dr. C. Mani Krishna, Graduate Program Director, 413-545-4583, Fax: 413-545-4611, E-mail: ecegrad@ecs.umass.edu. *Application contact:* Lindsay DeSantis, Supervisor of Admissions, 413-545-0722, Fax: 413-577-0010, E-mail: gradadm@grad.umass.edu.
Website: http://ece.umass.edu/.

University of Massachusetts Dartmouth, Graduate School, College of Engineering, Department of Electrical and Computer Engineering, North Dartmouth, MA 02747-2300. Offers acoustics (Postbaccalaureate Certificate); communications (Postbaccalaureate Certificate); computer engineering (MS, PhD); computer systems engineering (Postbaccalaureate Certificate); digital signal processing (Postbaccalaureate Certificate); electrical engineering (MS, PhD); electrical engineering systems (Postbaccalaureate Certificate). Part-time programs available. *Faculty:* 16 full-time (3 women). *Students:* 47 full-time (15 women), 38 part-time (2 women); includes 8 minority (1 Black or African American, non-Hispanic/Latino; 4 Asian, non-Hispanic/Latino; 2 Hispanic/Latino; 1 Two or more races, non-Hispanic/Latino), 45 international. Average age 27. 127 applicants, 60% accepted, 26 enrolled. In 2014, 9 master's, 4 doctorates, 1 other advanced degree awarded. *Degree requirements:* For master's, thesis or project; for doctorate, comprehensive exam, thesis/dissertation. *Entrance requirements:* For master's, GRE (UMass Dartmouth electrical/computer engineering bachelor's degree

recipients are exempt), statement of purpose (minimum of 300 words), resume, 3 letters of recommendation, official transcripts; for doctorate, GRE, statement of purpose (minimum of 300 words), resume, 3 letters of recommendation, official transcripts; for Postbaccalaureate Certificate, statement of purpose (minimum of 300 words), resume, official transcripts. Additional exam requirements/recommendations for international students: Required—TOEFL (minimum score 533 paper-based; 72 iBT), IELTS (minimum score 6). *Application deadline:* For fall admission, 2/15 priority date for domestic students, 1/15 priority date for international students; for spring admission, 11/1 priority date for domestic students, 10/1 priority date for international students. Applications are processed on a rolling basis. Application fee: $60. Electronic applications accepted. *Expenses:* Tuition, state resident: full-time $2071; part-time $86.29 per credit. Tuition, nonresident: full-time $8099; part-time $337.46 per credit. *Required fees:* $16,520; $712.33 per credit. Tuition and fees vary according to course load and reciprocity agreements. *Financial support:* In 2014–15, 2 fellowships with full and partial tuition reimbursements (averaging $14,337 per year), 13 research assistantships with full and partial tuition reimbursements (averaging $12,775 per year), 11 teaching assistantships with full and partial tuition reimbursements (averaging $12,273 per year) were awarded; Federal Work-Study and unspecified assistantships also available. Support available to part-time students. Financial award application deadline: 3/1; financial award applicants required to submit FAFSA. *Faculty research:* Computer engineering, cyber security, acoustics, signals and systems, electromagnetics, electronics and solid-state devices, marine systems, photonics. *Total annual research expenditures:* $2.5 million. *Unit head:* Dr. Karen Payton, Graduate Program Director, 508-999-8434, Fax: 508-999-8489, E-mail: kpayton@umassd.edu. *Application contact:* Steven Briggs, Director of Marketing and Recruitment for Graduate Studies, 508-999-8604, Fax: 508-999-8183, E-mail: graduate@umassd.edu.
Website: http://www.umassd.edu/engineering/ece/.

University of Massachusetts Lowell, Francis College of Engineering, Department of Electrical and Computer Engineering, Program in Electrical Engineering, Lowell, MA 01854. Offers MS Eng, D Eng. Part-time and evening/weekend programs available. Terminal master's awarded for partial completion of doctoral program. *Degree requirements:* For master's, thesis; for doctorate, 2 foreign languages, thesis/dissertation. *Entrance requirements:* For master's and doctorate, GRE General Test.

University of Memphis, Graduate School, Herff College of Engineering, Department of Electrical and Computer Engineering, Memphis, TN 38152. Offers automatic control systems (MS); biomedical systems (MS); communications and propagation systems (MS); computer engineering (PhD); electrical engineering (PhD); engineering computer systems (MS). *Faculty:* 10 full-time (1 woman), 2 part-time/adjunct (0 women). *Students:* 27 full-time (10 women), 9 part-time (2 women); includes 10 minority (6 Black or African American, non-Hispanic/Latino; 2 Asian, non-Hispanic/Latino; 1 Hispanic/Latino; 1 Two or more races, non-Hispanic/Latino), 21 international. Average age 28. 22 applicants, 95% accepted, 14 enrolled. In 2014, 21 master's awarded. *Degree requirements:* For master's, comprehensive exam, thesis or alternative. *Entrance requirements:* For master's, GRE General Test or MAT, minimum undergraduate GPA of 2.5. *Application deadline:* For fall admission, 8/1 for domestic students; for spring admission, 12/1 for domestic students. Application fee: $35 ($60 for international students). *Financial support:* In 2014–15, 4 students received support. Research assistantships, teaching assistantships, career-related internships or fieldwork, Federal Work-Study, scholarships/grants, and unspecified assistantships available. Financial award application deadline: 2/15; financial award applicants required to submit FAFSA. *Faculty research:* Image processing, imaging sensors, biomedical systems, intelligent systems. *Unit head:* Dr. David Russomanno, Chair/Professor, 901-678-2175, Fax: 901-678-5469, E-mail: russmnn@memphis.edu. *Application contact:* Dr. Steven T. Griffin, Coordinator of Graduate Studies, 901-678-5268, Fax: 901-678-5469, E-mail: stgriffn@memphis.edu.
Website: http://www.memphis.edu/eece/.

University of Miami, Graduate School, College of Engineering, Department of Electrical and Computer Engineering, Coral Gables, FL 33124. Offers MSECE, PhD. Part-time programs available. *Degree requirements:* For master's, thesis (for some programs); for doctorate, comprehensive exam, thesis/dissertation, dissertation proposal defense. *Entrance requirements:* For master's, GRE General Test, minimum GPA of 3.0; for doctorate, GRE General Test, minimum undergraduate GPA of 3.3, graduate 3.5. Additional exam requirements/recommendations for international students: Required—TOEFL (minimum score 550 paper-based; 59 iBT), IELTS (minimum score 7). Electronic applications accepted. *Faculty research:* Computer network, image processing, database systems, digital signal processing, machine intelligence.

University of Michigan, College of Engineering, Department of Electrical Engineering and Computer Science, Ann Arbor, MI 48109. Offers MS, MSE, PhD. *Students:* 598 full-time (96 women), 9 part-time (2 women). 1,997 applicants, 26% accepted, 241 enrolled. In 2014, 199 master's, 49 doctorates awarded. *Faculty research:* Solid state electronics and optics; communications, control, signal process; sensors and integrated circuitry; software systems; artificial intelligence; hardware systems. *Total annual research expenditures:* $39.3 million. *Unit head:* Prof. Khalil Najafi, Department Chair, 734-647-7010, Fax: 734-647-7009, E-mail: najafi@umich.edu. *Application contact:* Steven Pejuan, Graduate Coordinator, 734-647-1758, Fax: 734-763-1503, E-mail: spejuan@umich.edu.
Website: http://www.eecs.umich.edu.

University of Michigan–Dearborn, College of Engineering and Computer Science, MSE Program in Electrical Engineering, Dearborn, MI 48128. Offers MSE. Part-time and evening/weekend programs available. Postbaccalaureate distance learning degree programs offered (no on-campus study). *Faculty:* 20 full-time (1 woman), 11 part-time/adjunct (0 women). *Students:* 57 full-time (18 women), 104 part-time (23 women); includes 16 minority (3 Black or African American, non-Hispanic/Latino; 11 Asian, non-Hispanic/Latino; 2 Hispanic/Latino), 92 international. 114 applicants, 66% accepted, 46 enrolled. In 2014, 34 master's awarded. *Degree requirements:* For master's, thesis optional. *Entrance requirements:* For master's, bachelor's degree in electrical and/or computer engineering with minimum overall GPA of 3.0. Additional exam requirements/recommendations for international students: Required—TOEFL (minimum score 560 paper-based; 84 iBT), IELTS (minimum score 6.5). *Application deadline:* For fall admission, 8/1 for domestic students, 5/1 for international students; for winter admission, 12/1 for domestic students, 9/1 for international students; for spring admission, 4/1 for domestic students, 1/1 for international students. Applications are processed on a rolling basis. Application fee: $60. Electronic applications accepted. *Expenses:* Tuition, state resident: full-time $12,202; part-time $707 per credit hour. Tuition, nonresident: full-time $20,980; part-time $1209 per credit hour. *Required fees:* $798; $302 per term. Tuition and fees vary according to course level, course load, degree level and program. *Financial support:* In 2014–15, 63 students received support. Scholarships/grants and unspecified assistantships available. Support available to part-time students. Financial award applicants required to submit FAFSA. *Faculty research:* Vehicle electronics, machine intelligence, machine vision, wireless communications, fuzzy systems, sensor networks, nanoelectronics. *Unit head:* Dr. YiLu Murphey, Chair, 313-593-5028, Fax: 313-583-6336, E-mail: yilu@umich.edu. *Application contact:* Michael Patrick Hicks,

Electrical Engineering

Intermediate Academic Records Assistant, 313-593-5420, Fax: 313-583-6336, E-mail: ece-grad@umd.umich.edu. Website: http://umdearborn.edu/cecs/ECE/grad_prog/index.php.

University of Minnesota, Duluth, Graduate School, Swenson College of Science and Engineering, Department of Electrical and Computer Engineering, Duluth, MN 55812-2496. Offers MSECE. Part-time programs available. *Degree requirements:* For master's, thesis. *Entrance requirements:* Additional exam requirements/recommendations for international students: Recommended—TOEFL, IELTS, TWE. *Faculty research:* Biomedical instrumentation, transportation systems, computer hardware and software, signal processing, optical communications.

University of Minnesota, Twin Cities Campus, College of Science and Engineering, Department of Electrical and Computer Engineering, Minneapolis, MN 55455-0213. Offers MSEE, PhD. Part-time programs available. *Degree requirements:* For master's, thesis or alternative; for doctorate, thesis/dissertation. *Entrance requirements:* Additional exam requirements/recommendations for international students: Required—TOEFL (minimum score 550 paper-based). Electronic applications accepted. *Faculty research:* Signal processing, micro and nano structures, computers, controls, power electronics.

University of Missouri, Office of Research and Graduate Studies, College of Engineering, Department of Electrical and Computer Engineering, Columbia, MO 65211. Offers MS, PhD. *Faculty:* 26 full-time (4 women), 3 part-time/adjunct (0 women). *Students:* 75 full-time (16 women), 80 part-time (14 women); includes 5 minority (1 Black or African American, non-Hispanic/Latino; 2 Asian, non-Hispanic/Latino; 1 Hispanic/Latino; 1 Two or more races, non-Hispanic/Latino), 128 international. Average age 27. 207 applicants, 36% accepted, 33 enrolled. In 2014, 23 master's, 7 doctorates awarded. *Degree requirements:* For master's, thesis or alternative; for doctorate, thesis/dissertation. *Entrance requirements:* For master's, GRE General Test, minimum GPA of 3.0; for doctorate, GRE General Test, GRE Subject Test, minimum GPA of 3.0. Additional exam requirements/recommendations for international students: Required—TOEFL (minimum score 550 paper-based; 80 iBT). *Application deadline:* For fall admission, 2/15 priority date for domestic and international students; for winter admission, 9/1 priority date for domestic and international students. Applications are processed on a rolling basis. Application fee: $55 ($75 for international students). Electronic applications accepted. *Financial support:* Fellowships, research assistantships, teaching assistantships, institutionally sponsored loans, scholarships/grants, traineeships, health care benefits, and unspecified assistantships available. Support available to part-time students. *Faculty research:* Communication and signal processing, physical electronics, intelligent systems, systems modeling and control, nano and micro electronics, digital/computer systems. *Unit head:* Dr. Scott Kovaleski, Interim Director, 573-882-6387, E-mail: kovaleskis@missouri.edu. *Application contact:* Shirley Holdmeier, Academic Advisor, 573-882-4436, E-mail: holdmeiers@missouri.edu.
Website: http://engineering.missouri.edu/ece/degree-programs/.

University of Missouri–Kansas City, School of Computing and Engineering, Kansas City, MO 64110-2499. Offers civil engineering (MS); computer and electrical engineering (PhD); computer science (MS), including bioinformatics, software engineering, telecommunications networking; computer science and informatics (PhD); computing (PhD); electrical engineering (MS); engineering (PhD); engineering and construction management (Graduate Certificate); mechanical engineering (MS); telecommunications and computer networking (PhD). PhD (interdisciplinary) offered through the School of Graduate Studies. Part-time programs available. *Faculty:* 39 full-time (5 women), 26 part-time/adjunct (3 women). *Students:* 500 full-time (143 women), 136 part-time (28 women); includes 18 minority (5 Black or African American, non-Hispanic/Latino; 8 Asian, non-Hispanic/Latino; 4 Hispanic/Latino; 1 Two or more races, non-Hispanic/Latino), 551 international. Average age 24. 1,924 applicants, 39% accepted, 200 enrolled. In 2014, 124 master's, 1 other advanced degree awarded. *Degree requirements:* For doctorate, thesis/dissertation. *Entrance requirements:* For master's, GRE General Test, minimum GPA of 3.0, 3 letters of recommendation from professors; for doctorate, GRE General Test, minimum GPA of 3.5. Additional exam requirements/recommendations for international students: Required—TOEFL (minimum score 550 paper-based; 80 iBT). *Application deadline:* For fall admission, 1/15 priority date for domestic students, 1/15 for international students. Applications are processed on a rolling basis. Application fee: $45 ($50 for international students). *Financial support:* In 2014–15, 34 research assistantships with partial tuition reimbursements (averaging $15,602 per year), 24 teaching assistantships with partial tuition reimbursements (averaging $15,090 per year) were awarded; career-related internships or fieldwork, Federal Work-Study, scholarships/grants, tuition waivers (partial), and unspecified assistantships also available. Support available to part-time students. Financial award application deadline: 3/1; financial award applicants required to submit FAFSA. *Faculty research:* Algorithms, bioinformatics and medical informatics, biomechanics/biomaterials, civil engineering materials, networking and telecommunications, thermal science. *Unit head:* Dr. Kevin Z. Truman, Dean, 816-235-2399, Fax: 816-235-5159. *Application contact:* 816-235-2399, Fax: 816-235-5159.
Website: http://sce.umkc.edu/.

University of Nebraska–Lincoln, Graduate College, College of Engineering, Department of Electrical Engineering, Lincoln, NE 68588. Offers MS, PhD. *Degree requirements:* For master's, thesis optional; for doctorate, comprehensive exam, thesis/dissertation. *Entrance requirements:* For master's and doctorate, GRE General Test. Additional exam requirements/recommendations for international students: Required—TOEFL (minimum score 550 paper-based). Electronic applications accepted. *Faculty research:* Electromagnetics, communications, biomedical digital signal processing, electrical breakdown of gases, optical properties of microelectronic materials.

University of Nevada, Las Vegas, Graduate College, Howard R. Hughes College of Engineering, Department of Electrical and Computer Engineering, Las Vegas, NV 89154-4026. Offers MS, PhD, MS/MS, MS/PhD. Part-time programs available. *Faculty:* 17 full-time (2 women). *Students:* 39 full-time (6 women), 8 part-time (1 woman); includes 9 minority (1 Black or African American, non-Hispanic/Latino; 4 Asian, non-Hispanic/Latino; 3 Hispanic/Latino; 1 Two or more races, non-Hispanic/Latino), 28 international. Average age 30. 31 applicants, 45% accepted, 8 enrolled. In 2014, 12 master's, 4 doctorates awarded. *Degree requirements:* For master's, comprehensive exam, thesis, project; for doctorate, comprehensive exam, thesis/dissertation. *Entrance requirements:* Additional exam requirements/recommendations for international students: Required—TOEFL (minimum score 550 paper-based; 80 iBT), IELTS (minimum score 7). *Application deadline:* For fall admission, 2/1 for domestic students, 5/1 for international students; for spring admission, 10/1 for domestic and international students. Application fee: $60 ($95 for international students). Electronic applications accepted. *Financial support:* In 2014–15, 45 students received support, including 17 research assistantships with partial tuition reimbursements available (averaging $13,888 per year), 28 teaching assistantships with partial tuition reimbursements available (averaging $14,192 per year); institutionally sponsored loans, scholarships/grants, health care benefits, tuition waivers (full), and unspecified assistantships also available. Financial award application deadline: 3/1. *Faculty research:* Computer engineering, power engineering, semiconductor and nanotechnology, electronics and VLSI,

telecommunications and control. *Total annual research expenditures:* $1.2 million. *Unit head:* Dr. Peter Stubberud, Chair/Professor, 702-895-0869, E-mail: peter.stubberud@unlv.edu. *Application contact:* Graduate College Admissions Evaluator, 702-895-3320, Fax: 702-895-4180, E-mail: gradcollege@unlv.edu.
Website: http://ece.unlv.edu/.

University of Nevada, Reno, Graduate School, College of Engineering, Department of Electrical Engineering, Reno, NV 89557. Offers MS, PhD. Terminal master's awarded for partial completion of doctoral program. *Degree requirements:* For master's, thesis optional; for doctorate, thesis/dissertation. *Entrance requirements:* For master's, GRE General Test, minimum GPA of 2.75; for doctorate, GRE General Test, minimum GPA of 3.0. Additional exam requirements/recommendations for international students: Required—TOEFL (minimum score 500 paper-based; 61 iBT), IELTS (minimum score 6). Electronic applications accepted. *Faculty research:* Acoustics, neural networking, synthetic aperture radar simulation, optical fiber communications and sensors.

University of New Brunswick Fredericton, School of Graduate Studies, Faculty of Engineering, Department of Electrical and Computer Engineering, Fredericton, NB E3B 5A3, Canada. Offers M Eng, M Sc E, PhD. Part-time programs available. *Faculty:* 13 full-time (3 women), 16 part-time/adjunct (1 woman). *Students:* 50 full-time (7 women), 10 part-time (3 women). 45 applicants, 44% accepted. In 2014, 11 master's, 6 doctorates awarded. *Degree requirements:* For master's, thesis, research proposal; 10 courses (for M Eng); for doctorate, comprehensive exam, thesis/dissertation, research proposal. *Entrance requirements:* For master's, minimum GPA of 3.3; references; for doctorate, M Sc; minimum GPA of 3.3; previous transcripts; references. Additional exam requirements/recommendations for international students: Required—TOEFL (minimum score 580 paper-based; 93 iBT), IELTS (minimum score 7), TWE (minimum score 4). *Application deadline:* Applications are processed on a rolling basis. Application fee: $50 Canadian dollars. Electronic applications accepted. *Financial support:* In 2014–15, 142 fellowships, 78 research assistantships, 64 teaching assistantships were awarded. *Faculty research:* Biomedical engineering, communications, robotics and control systems, electromagnetic systems, embedded systems, optical fiber systems, sustainable energy and power systems, power electronics, image and signal processing, software systems, electronics and digital systems. *Unit head:* Dr. Maryhelen Stevenson, Director of Graduate Studies, 504-447-3147, Fax: 504-453-3589, E-mail: stevenso@unb.ca. *Application contact:* Shelley Cormier, Graduate Secretary, 506-452-6142, Fax: 506-453-3589, E-mail: scormier@unb.ca.
Website: http://go.unb.ca/gradprograms.

University of New Hampshire, Graduate School, College of Engineering and Physical Sciences, Department of Electrical and Computer Engineering, Durham, NH 03824. Offers M Engr, MS, PhD. Part-time and evening/weekend programs available. *Faculty:* 10 full-time (0 women). *Students:* 17 full-time (2 women), 18 part-time (3 women); includes 7 minority (5 Asian, non-Hispanic/Latino; 2 Hispanic/Latino), 10 international. Average age 25. 33 applicants, 58% accepted, 9 enrolled. In 2014, 11 master's awarded. *Degree requirements:* For master's, thesis or alternative; for doctorate, thesis/dissertation. *Entrance requirements:* For master's and doctorate, GRE (for non-U.S. university bachelor's degree holders). Additional exam requirements/recommendations for international students: Required—TOEFL (minimum score 550 paper-based; 80 iBT). *Application deadline:* For fall admission, 4/1 priority date for domestic students, 4/1 for international students; for spring admission, 12/1 for domestic students. Applications are processed on a rolling basis. Application fee: $65. Electronic applications accepted. *Expenses:* Tuition, state resident: full-time $13,500; part-time $750 per credit hour. Tuition, nonresident: full-time $26,460; part-time $1110 per credit hour. *Required fees:* $1788; $447 per semester. *Financial support:* In 2014–15, 18 students received support, including 7 research assistantships, 9 teaching assistantships; fellowships, Federal Work-Study, scholarships/grants, and tuition waivers (full and partial) also available. Support available to part-time students. Financial award application deadline: 2/15. *Faculty research:* Biomedical engineering, communications systems and information theory, digital systems, illumination engineering. *Unit head:* John LaCourse, III, Chairperson, 603-862-1324. *Application contact:* Kathryn Reynolds, Administrative Assistant, 603-862-1358, E-mail: ece.dept@unh.edu.
Website: http://www.ece.unh.edu/.

University of New Haven, Graduate School, Tagliatela College of Engineering, Program in Electrical Engineering, West Haven, CT 06516-1916. Offers control systems (MS); digital signal processing and communication (MS); electrical and computer engineering (MS); electrical engineering (MS). Part-time and evening/weekend programs available. *Degree requirements:* For master's, thesis or alternative. *Entrance requirements:* For master's, bachelor's degree in electrical engineering. Additional exam requirements/recommendations for international students: Required—TOEFL (minimum score 75 iBT), IELTS, PTE (minimum score 50). Electronic applications accepted. Application fee is waived when completed online.

University of New Mexico, Graduate School, School of Engineering, Programs in Electrical Engineering, Albuquerque, NM 87131-2039. Offers MS, PhD. Part-time and evening/weekend programs available. Postbaccalaureate distance learning degree programs offered (minimal on-campus study). *Faculty:* 16 full-time (2 women), 2 part-time/adjunct (0 women). *Students:* 42 full-time (7 women), 36 part-time (6 women); includes 25 minority (8 Asian, non-Hispanic/Latino; 17 Hispanic/Latino), 24 international. Average age 29. 144 applicants, 28% accepted, 22 enrolled. In 2014, 31 master's, 11 doctorates awarded. Terminal master's awarded for partial completion of doctoral program. *Degree requirements:* For master's, thesis; for doctorate, comprehensive exam, thesis/dissertation. *Entrance requirements:* For master's, GRE General Test, minimum GPA of 3.0; for doctorate, GRE General Test, minimum GPA of 3.5. Additional exam requirements/recommendations for international students: Required—TOEFL (minimum score 550 paper-based; 79 iBT). *Application deadline:* For fall admission, 6/15 for domestic students, 2/15 for international students; for spring admission, 11/1 for domestic students, 6/15 for international students. Application fee: $50. Electronic applications accepted. *Financial support:* In 2014–15, 1 fellowship with tuition reimbursement (averaging $20,000 per year), 72 research assistantships with tuition reimbursements (averaging $16,805 per year), 1 teaching assistantship with tuition reimbursement (averaging $14,791 per year) were awarded; scholarships/grants, health care benefits, and unspecified assistantships also available. *Faculty research:* Applied electromagnetics, biomedical engineering, communications, image processing, microelectronics, optoelectronics, signal processing, systems and controls. *Unit head:* Dr. Chaouki T. Abdallah, Chair, 505-277-0298, Fax: 505-277-1439, E-mail: chaouki@ece.unm.edu. *Application contact:* Elmyra Grelle, Coordinator, 505-277-2600, Fax: 505-277-1439, E-mail: egrelle@ece.unm.edu.
Website: http://www.ece.unm.edu/.

The University of North Carolina at Charlotte, The William States Lee College of Engineering, Department of Electrical and Computer Engineering, Charlotte, NC 28223-0001. Offers electrical engineering (MSEE, PhD). Part-time and evening/weekend programs available. *Faculty:* 27 full-time (2 women). *Students:* 218 full-time (41 women), 47 part-time (11 women); includes 13 minority (7 Black or African American, non-Hispanic/Latino; 2 Asian, non-Hispanic/Latino; 2 Hispanic/Latino; 2 Two or more races, non-Hispanic/Latino), 227 international. Average age 25. 963 applicants, 39% accepted, 109 enrolled. In 2014, 69 master's, 10 doctorates awarded. Terminal master's awarded

for partial completion of doctoral program. *Degree requirements:* For master's, thesis or project; for doctorate, thesis/dissertation. *Entrance requirements:* For master's, GRE General Test, minimum GPA of 3.0 in undergraduate major, 2.75 overall; for doctorate, GRE General Test, 3 letters of reference. Additional exam requirements/recommendations for international students: Required—TOEFL (minimum score 557 paper-based; 83 iBT). *Application deadline:* For fall admission, 5/1 for domestic and international students; for spring admission, 10/1 for domestic and international students. Applications are processed on a rolling basis. Application fee: $75. Electronic applications accepted. *Expenses:* Tuition, state resident: full-time $4008. Tuition, nonresident: full-time $16,295. *Required fees:* $2755. Tuition and fees vary according to course load and program. *Financial support:* In 2014–15, 66 students received support, including 1 fellowship (averaging $48,000 per year), 36 research assistantships (averaging $9,180 per year), 29 teaching assistantships (averaging $5,754 per year); career-related internships or fieldwork, institutionally sponsored loans, scholarships/grants, and unspecified assistantships also available. Support available to part-time students. Financial award application deadline: 4/1; financial award applicants required to submit FAFSA. *Faculty research:* Communication, control, and signal processing; devices, circuits, and systems; energy and sustainability; high performance embedded computing; power systems. *Total annual research expenditures:* $1.6 million. *Unit head:* Dr. Ian Ferguson, Chair, 704-687-8404, Fax: 704-687-4762, E-mail: ianf@uncc.edu. *Application contact:* Kathy B. Giddings, Director of Graduate Admissions, 704-687-5503, Fax: 704-687-1668, E-mail: gradadm@uncc.edu.
Website: http://coe.uncc.edu/students/prospective/graduate.htm.

University of North Dakota, Graduate School, School of Engineering and Mines, Department of Electrical Engineering, Grand Forks, ND 58202. Offers M Engr, MS. Part-time programs available. *Degree requirements:* For master's, comprehensive exam, thesis or alternative. *Entrance requirements:* For master's, GRE General Test, minimum GPA of 3.0 (MS), 2.5 (M Engr). Additional exam requirements/recommendations for international students: Required—TOEFL (minimum score 550 paper-based; 79 iBT), IELTS (minimum score 6.5). Electronic applications accepted. *Faculty research:* Controls and robotics, signal processing, energy conversion, microwaves, computer engineering.

University of North Florida, College of Computing, Engineering, and Construction, School of Engineering, Jacksonville, FL 32224. Offers MSCE, MSEE, MSME. Part-time programs available. *Faculty:* 17 full-time (1 woman), 1 part-time/adjunct (0 women). *Students:* 9 full-time (2 women), 22 part-time (7 women); includes 8 minority (1 Black or African American, non-Hispanic/Latino; 4 Asian, non-Hispanic/Latino; 2 Hispanic/Latino; 1 Two or more races, non-Hispanic/Latino), 4 international. Average age 28. 60 applicants, 28% accepted, 8 enrolled. In 2014, 14 master's awarded. *Application deadline:* For fall admission, 7/1 for domestic students, 5/1 for international students; for spring admission, 11/1 for domestic students, 10/1 for international students. Application fee: $30. *Expenses:* Tuition, state resident: full-time $9794; part-time $408.10 per credit hour. Tuition, nonresident: full-time $22,383; part-time $932.61 per credit hour. *Required fees:* $2047; $85.29 per credit hour. Tuition and fees vary according to course load and program. *Financial support:* In 2014–15, 16 students received support, including 2 research assistantships (averaging $2,775 per year); teaching assistantships, Federal Work-Study, scholarships/grants, tuition waivers, and unspecified assistantships also available. Financial award application deadline: 4/1; financial award applicants required to submit FAFSA. *Total annual research expenditures:* $863,034. *Unit head:* Dr. Murat Tiryakioglu, Associate Dean, 904-620-2504, E-mail: m.tiryakioglu@unf.edu. *Application contact:* Dr. Amanda Pascale, Director, The Graduate School, 904-320-1360, Fax: 904-620-1362, E-mail: graduateschool@unf.edu.
Website: http://www.unf.edu/ccec/engineering/.

University of North Texas, Robert B. Toulouse School of Graduate Studies, Denton, TX 76203-5459. Offers accounting (MS); applied anthropology (MA, MS); applied behavior analysis (Certificate); applied geography (MA); applied technology and performance improvement (M Ed, MS); art education (MA); art history (MA); art museum education (Certificate); arts leadership (Certificate); audiology (Au D); behavior analysis (MS); behavioral science (PhD); biochemistry and molecular biology (MS); biology (MA, MS); biomedical engineering (MS); business analysis (MS); chemistry (MS); clinical health psychology (PhD); communication studies (MA, MS); computer engineering (MS); computer science (MS); counseling (M Ed, MS), including clinical mental health counseling (MS), college and university counseling, elementary school counseling, secondary school counseling; creative writing (MA); criminal justice (MS); curriculum and instruction (M Ed); decision sciences (MBA); design (MA, MFA), including fashion design (MFA), innovation studies, interior design (MFA); early childhood studies (MS); economics (MS); educational leadership (M Ed, Ed D); educational psychology (MS, PhD), including family studies (MS), gifted and talented (MS), human development (MS), learning and cognition (MS), research, measurement and evaluation (MS); electrical engineering (MS); emergency management (MPA); engineering technology (MS); English (MA); English as a second language (MA); environmental science (MS); finance (MBA, MS); financial management (MPA); French (MA); health services management (MBA); higher education (M Ed, Ed D); history (MA, MS); hospitality management (MS); human resources management (MPA); information science (MS); information systems (PhD); information technologies (MBA); interdisciplinary studies (MA, MS); international studies (MA); international sustainable tourism (MS); jazz studies (MM); journalism (MA, MJ, Graduate Certificate), including interactive and virtual digital communication (Graduate Certificate), narrative journalism (Graduate Certificate), public relations (Graduate Certificate); kinesiology (MS); linguistics (MA); local government management (MPA); logistics (PhD); logistics and supply chain management (MBA); long-term care, senior housing, and aging services (MA); management (PhD); marketing (MBA); mathematics (MA, MS); mechanical and energy engineering (MS, PhD); music (MA), including ethnomusicology, music theory, musicology, performance; music composition (PhD); music education (MM Ed, PhD); nonprofit management (MPA); operations and supply chain management (MBA); performance (MM, DMA); philosophy (MA); political science (MA); professional and technical communication (MA); radio, television and film (MA, MFA); rehabilitation counseling (Certificate); sociology (MA); Spanish (MA); special education (M Ed); speech-language pathology (MA); strategic management (MBA); studio art (MFA); teaching (M Ed); MBA/MS. Part-time and evening/weekend programs available. Postbaccalaureate distance learning degree programs offered. *Faculty:* 651 full-time (215 women), 233 part-time/adjunct (139 women). *Students:* 3,040 full-time (1,598 women), 3,401 part-time (2,097 women); includes 1,740 minority (533 Black or African American, non-Hispanic/Latino; 15 American Indian or Alaska Native, non-Hispanic/Latino; 286 Asian, non-Hispanic/Latino; 746 Hispanic/Latino; 3 Native Hawaiian or other Pacific Islander, non-Hispanic/Latino; 157 Two or more races, non-Hispanic/Latino), 1,145 international. Terminal master's awarded for partial completion of doctoral program. *Degree requirements:* For master's, variable foreign language requirement, comprehensive exam (for some programs), thesis (for some programs); for doctorate, variable foreign language requirement, comprehensive exam (for some programs), thesis/dissertation; for other advanced degree, variable foreign language requirement, comprehensive exam (for some programs). *Entrance requirements:* For master's and doctorate, GRE, GMAT. Additional exam requirements/recommendations for international students: Required—TOEFL (minimum score 550 paper-based; 79 iBT). *Application deadline:* For fall admission, 7/15 for domestic students, 3/15 for international students; for spring admission, 11/15 for domestic students, 9/15 for international students; for summer admission, 5/1 for domestic students. Applications are processed on a rolling basis. Application fee: $60. Electronic applications accepted. *Expenses:* Tuition, state resident: full-time $5450; part-time $3633 per year. Tuition, nonresident: full-time $11,966; part-time $7977 per year. *Required fees:* $1301; $398 per credit hour. $685 per semester. Tuition and fees vary according to program and reciprocity agreements. *Financial support:* Fellowships with partial tuition reimbursements, research assistantships with partial tuition reimbursements, teaching assistantships, career-related internships or fieldwork, Federal Work-Study, institutionally sponsored loans, scholarships/grants, health care benefits, and library assistantships available. Support available to part-time students. Financial award applicants required to submit FAFSA. *Unit head:* Mark Wardell, Dean, 940-565-2383, E-mail: mark.wardell@unt.edu. *Application contact:* Toulouse School of Graduate Studies, 940-565-2383, Fax: 940-565-2141, E-mail: gradsch@unt.edu.
Website: http://tsgs.unt.edu/.

University of Notre Dame, Graduate School, College of Engineering, Department of Electrical Engineering, Notre Dame, IN 46556. Offers MSEE, PhD. Terminal master's awarded for partial completion of doctoral program. *Degree requirements:* For master's, comprehensive exam; for doctorate, thesis/dissertation, candidacy exam. *Entrance requirements:* For master's and doctorate, GRE General Test. Additional exam requirements/recommendations for international students: Required—TOEFL (minimum score 600 paper-based; 80 iBT). Electronic applications accepted. *Faculty research:* Electronic properties of materials and devices, signal and imaging processing, communication theory, control theory and applications, optoelectronics.

University of Oklahoma, Gallogly College of Engineering, School of Electrical and Computer Engineering, Program in Electrical and Computer Engineering, Norman, OK 73019. Offers MS, PhD. Part-time programs available. *Students:* 102 full-time (19 women), 35 part-time (8 women); includes 16 minority (2 Black or African American, non-Hispanic/Latino; 1 American Indian or Alaska Native, non-Hispanic/Latino; 4 Asian, non-Hispanic/Latino; 5 Hispanic/Latino; 1 Native Hawaiian or other Pacific Islander, non-Hispanic/Latino; 3 Two or more races, non-Hispanic/Latino), 83 international. Average age 28. 137 applicants, 32% accepted, 22 enrolled. In 2014, 23 master's, 10 doctorates awarded. Terminal master's awarded for partial completion of doctoral program. *Degree requirements:* For master's, comprehensive exam (for some programs), thesis (for some programs); for doctorate, thesis/dissertation, general exam. *Entrance requirements:* For master's and doctorate, GRE, minimum GPA of 3.0. Additional exam requirements/recommendations for international students: Required—TOEFL (minimum score 79 iBT). *Application deadline:* For fall admission, 4/1 for domestic students, 3/1 for international students; for spring admission, 11/1 for domestic students, 10/1 for international students. Application fee: $50 ($100 for international students). Electronic applications accepted. *Expenses:* Tuition, state resident: full-time $4394; part-time $183.10 per credit hour. Tuition, nonresident: full-time $16,970; part-time $707.10 per credit hour. *Required fees:* $2892; $109.95 per credit hour. $126.50 per semester. *Financial support:* In 2014–15, 119 students received support, including 2 fellowships with full tuition reimbursements available (averaging $2,500 per year); career-related internships or fieldwork, scholarships/grants, health care benefits, and unspecified assistantships also available. Financial award application deadline: 6/1; financial award applicants required to submit FAFSA. *Faculty research:* Biomedical imaging, radar engineering, semiconductor devices, intelligent transportation systems, signals and systems. *Unit head:* Dr. J.R. Cruz, Director, 405-325-8131, Fax: 405-325-7066, E-mail: jcruz@ou.edu. *Application contact:* Lisa Wilkins, Graduate Program Assistant, 405-325-4285, Fax: 405-325-7066, E-mail: lwikins@ou.edu.
Website: http://ece.ou.edu.

University of Ottawa, Faculty of Graduate and Postdoctoral Studies, Faculty of Engineering, Ottawa-Carleton Institute for Electrical and Computer Engineering, Ottawa, ON K1N 6N5, Canada. Offers M Eng, MA Sc, PhD. *Degree requirements:* For master's, thesis or alternative, project; for doctorate, comprehensive exam, thesis/dissertation. *Entrance requirements:* For master's, honors degree or equivalent, minimum B average; for doctorate, minimum A- average. Electronic applications accepted. *Faculty research:* CAD, distributed systems.

University of Pennsylvania, School of Engineering and Applied Science, Department of Electrical and Systems Engineering, Philadelphia, PA 19104. Offers MSE, PhD. Part-time programs available. *Faculty:* 25 full-time (2 women), 6 part-time/adjunct (0 women). *Students:* 223 full-time (67 women), 27 part-time (8 women); includes 12 minority (2 Black or African American, non-Hispanic/Latino; 8 Asian, non-Hispanic/Latino; 1 Hispanic/Latino; 1 Two or more races, non-Hispanic/Latino), 201 international. 1,164 applicants, 31% accepted, 155 enrolled. In 2014, 104 master's, 6 doctorates awarded. Terminal master's awarded for partial completion of doctoral program. *Degree requirements:* For master's, thesis optional; for doctorate, comprehensive exam, thesis/dissertation. *Entrance requirements:* For master's and doctorate, GRE General Test. Additional exam requirements/recommendations for international students: Required—TOEFL. *Application deadline:* For fall admission, 6/1 priority date for domestic students, 5/1 priority date for international students; for spring admission, 11/1 priority date for domestic students, 10/1 priority date for international students. Applications are processed on a rolling basis. Application fee: $70. Electronic applications accepted. *Financial support:* Fellowships, research assistantships, teaching assistantships, institutionally sponsored loans, scholarships/grants, traineeships, health care benefits, and unspecified assistantships available. *Faculty research:* Electro-optics, microwave and millimeter-wave optics, solid-state and chemical electronics, electromagnetic propagation, telecommunications. *Unit head:* Eduardo D. Glandt, Dean, 215-898-7244, E-mail: seasdean@seas.upenn.edu. *Application contact:* School of Engineering and Applied Science Graduate Admissions, 215-898-4542, E-mail: gradstudies@seas.upenn.edu.
Website: http://www.seas.upenn.edu.

University of Pittsburgh, Swanson School of Engineering, Program in Electrical Engineering, Pittsburgh, PA 15260. Offers MSEE, PhD. Part-time programs available. Postbaccalaureate distance learning degree programs offered. *Faculty:* 20 full-time (2 women), 11 part-time/adjunct (3 women). *Students:* 115 full-time (26 women), 55 part-time (6 women); includes 13 minority (6 Black or African American, non-Hispanic/Latino; 4 Asian, non-Hispanic/Latino; 3 Hispanic/Latino), 99 international. 1,007 applicants, 14% accepted, 53 enrolled. In 2014, 45 master's, 10 doctorates awarded. Terminal master's awarded for partial completion of doctoral program. *Degree requirements:* For master's, thesis optional; for doctorate, comprehensive exam, thesis/dissertation, final oral exams. *Entrance requirements:* For master's and doctorate, GRE General Test, minimum GPA of 3.0. Additional exam requirements/recommendations for international students: Required—TOEFL (minimum score 550 paper-based; 80 iBT). *Application deadline:* For fall admission, 3/1 priority date for domestic and international students; for spring admission, 7/1 priority date for domestic and international students. Applications are processed on a rolling basis. Application fee: $50. Electronic applications accepted. *Expenses:* Tuition, state resident: full-time $20,742; part-time $838 per credit. Tuition, nonresident: full-time $33,960; part-time $1389 per credit. *Required fees:* $800; $205 per term. Tuition and fees vary according to program. *Financial support:* In 2014–15, 74 students received support, including 5 fellowships with full tuition reimbursements available (averaging $29,376 per year), 42 research assistantships with full tuition reimbursements available (averaging $25,056 per year), 27 teaching assistantships with full tuition reimbursements available (averaging $25,692 per year); scholarships/grants and tuition waivers (full and partial) also available. Financial award application deadline: 4/15. *Faculty research:* Computer engineering, image processing, signal processing, electro-optic devices, controls/power. *Total annual research expenditures:* $8.7 million. *Unit head:* Dr. William Stanchina, Chairman, 412-624-8000, Fax: 412-624-8003, E-mail: wstasnchina@engr.bitt.edu. *Application contact:* Dr. Mahmoud El Nokali, Graduate Coordinator, 412-624-8001, Fax: 412-624-8003, E-mail: men@pitt.edu.

University of Portland, School of Engineering, Portland, OR 97203-5798. Offers biomedical engineering (MBME); civil engineering (ME); computer science (ME); electrical engineering (ME); mechanical engineering (ME). Part-time and evening/weekend programs available. *Faculty:* 10 full-time (2 women), 1 part-time/adjunct (0 women). *Students:* 4 full-time (1 woman), 2 part-time (0 women); includes 1 minority (Two or more races, non-Hispanic/Latino), 1 international. Average age 27. In 2014, 2 master's awarded. *Degree requirements:* For master's, thesis optional. *Entrance requirements:* For master's, GRE General Test, minimum GPA of 3.0, 3 letters of recommendation, resume, statement of goals, official transcripts. Additional exam requirements/recommendations for international students: Required—TOEFL (minimum score 550 paper-based; 80 iBT), IELTS (minimum score 7). *Application deadline:* For fall admission, 7/15 priority date for domestic and international students; for spring admission, 12/15 priority date for domestic and international students. Applications are processed on a rolling basis. Application fee: $50. *Expenses:* Expenses: Contact institution. *Financial support:* Career-related internships or fieldwork, Federal Work-Study, and scholarships/grants available. Support available to part-time students. Financial award application deadline: 3/1; financial award applicants required to submit FAFSA. *Unit head:* Dr. Sharon Jones, Dean, 503-943-8169, E-mail: joness@up.edu. *Application contact:* Allison Able, Graduate Program Coordinator, 503-943-7107, Fax: 503-943-7315, E-mail: able@up.edu.
Website: http://engineering.up.edu/default.aspx?cid-6464&pid-2432.

University of Puerto Rico, Mayagüez Campus, Graduate Studies, College of Engineering, Department of Electrical and Computer Engineering, Mayagüez, PR 00681-9000. Offers computer engineering (ME, MS); computing and information sciences and engineering (PhD); electrical engineering (ME, MS). Part-time programs available. *Faculty:* 43 full-time (5 women). *Students:* 70 full-time (8 women), 7 part-time (0 women). 36 applicants, 83% accepted, 18 enrolled. In 2014, 13 master's awarded. *Degree requirements:* For master's, comprehensive exam, thesis; for doctorate, comprehensive exam, thesis/dissertation. *Entrance requirements:* For master's, proficiency in English and Spanish, BS in electrical or computer engineering or equivalent, minimum GPA of 3.0; for doctorate, GRE. *Application deadline:* For fall admission, 2/15 for domestic and international students; for spring admission, 9/15 for domestic and international students. Applications are processed on a rolling basis. Application fee: $25. *Expenses: Tuition, area resident:* Full-time $2466; part-time $822 per credit. *International tuition:* $6371 full-time. *Required fees:* $1095; $1095 per year. Tuition and fees vary according to course level, course load and reciprocity agreements. *Financial support:* In 2014–15, 54 students received support, including 32 research assistantships (averaging $7,499 per year), 32 teaching assistantships (averaging $7,614 per year); fellowships with full tuition reimbursements available, Federal Work-Study, institutionally sponsored loans, and unspecified assistantships also available. *Faculty research:* Microcomputer interfacing, control systems, power systems, electronics. *Unit head:* Dr. Pedro Rivera, Chairperson, 787-832-4040 Ext. 3821, E-mail: p.rivera@upr.edu. *Application contact:* Sandra Montalvo, Administrative Staff, 787-832-4040 Ext. 3094, Fax: 787-831-7564, E-mail: sandra@ece.uprm.edu.
Website: http://www.ece.uprm.edu.

University of Rhode Island, Graduate School, College of Engineering, Department of Electrical, Computer and Biomedical Engineering, Kingston, RI 02881. Offers MS, PhD, Graduate Certificate. Part-time programs available. *Faculty:* 20 full-time (2 women). *Students:* 30 full-time (6 women), 25 part-time (4 women); includes 4 minority (1 Black or African American, non-Hispanic/Latino; 2 Asian, non-Hispanic/Latino; 1 Hispanic/Latino), 23 international. In 2014, 18 master's, 2 doctorates awarded. *Degree requirements:* For master's, comprehensive exam (for some programs), thesis optional; for doctorate, comprehensive exam, thesis/dissertation. *Entrance requirements:* For master's and doctorate, GRE, 2 letters of recommendation (3 for international applicants). Additional exam requirements/recommendations for international students: Required—TOEFL (minimum score 550 paper-based). *Application deadline:* For fall admission, 7/15 for domestic students, 2/1 for international students; for spring admission, 11/15 for domestic students, 7/15 for international students. Application fee: $65. Electronic applications accepted. *Expenses:* Tuition, state resident: full-time $11,532; part-time $641 per credit. Tuition, nonresident: full-time $23,606; part-time $1311 per credit. *Required fees:* $1442; $39 per credit. $35 per semester. One-time fee: $155. *Financial support:* In 2014–15, 6 research assistantships with full and partial tuition reimbursements (averaging $8,108 per year), 4 teaching assistantships with full and partial tuition reimbursements (averaging $8,093 per year) were awarded. Financial award application deadline: 7/15; financial award applicants required to submit FAFSA. *Faculty research:* Biomedical instrumentation, cardiac physiology and computational modeling, analog/digital CMOS circuits, neural-machine interface, digital circuit design and VLSI testing. *Total annual research expenditures:* $2.2 million. *Unit head:* Dr. Godi Fischer, Chair, 401-874-5879, Fax: 401-782-6422, E-mail: fischer@ele.uri.edu. *Application contact:* Dr. Frederick J. Vetter, Graduate Director, 401-874-5141, Fax: 401-874-6422, E-mail: fred@uri.edu.
Website: http://www.ele.uri.edu/.

University of Rochester, Hajim School of Engineering and Applied Sciences, Department of Electrical and Computer Engineering, Rochester, NY 14627. Offers MS, PhD. *Faculty:* 20 full-time (1 woman). *Students:* 140 full-time (35 women), 3 part-time (1 woman); includes 8 minority (3 Black or African American, non-Hispanic/Latino; 3 Asian, non-Hispanic/Latino; 2 Hispanic/Latino), 115 international. 605 applicants, 36% accepted, 45 enrolled. In 2014, 53 master's, 15 doctorates awarded. Terminal master's awarded for partial completion of doctoral program. *Degree requirements:* For master's, comprehensive exam; for doctorate, thesis/dissertation, preliminary and oral exams. *Entrance requirements:* For master's and doctorate, GRE. Additional exam requirements/recommendations for international students: Required—TOEFL. *Application deadline:* For fall admission, 1/15 for domestic students. Application fee: $60. *Expenses: Tuition:* Full-time $46,150; part-time $1442 per credit hour. *Required fees:* $504. *Financial support:* Fellowships, research assistantships, teaching assistantships, and tuition waivers (full and partial) available. Financial award application deadline: 2/1. *Faculty research:* Bio-informatics, communications, digital audio, image processing, medical imaging. *Unit head:* Mark Bocko, Chair, 585-275-4879. *Application contact:* Barbara Dick, Administrative Assistant/Academic Coordinator, 585-275-5719.
Website: http://www.ece.rochester.edu/graduate/index.html.

University of Rochester, Hajim School of Engineering and Applied Sciences, Master of Science in Technical Entrepreneurship and Management Program, Rochester, NY 14642. Offers biomedical engineering (MS); chemical engineering (MS); computer science (MS); electrical and computer engineering (MS); energy and the environment (MS); materials science (MS); mechanical engineering (MS); optics (MS). Program offered in collaboration with the Simon School of Business. Part-time programs available. *Students:* 36 full-time (12 women), 7 part-time (1 woman); includes 3 minority (2 Hispanic/Latino; 1 Two or more races, non-Hispanic/Latino), 33 international. Average age 24. 152 applicants, 68% accepted, 27 enrolled. In 2014, 28 master's awarded. *Degree requirements:* For master's, comprehensive exam. *Entrance requirements:* For master's, GRE or GMAT, 3 letters of recommendation; personal statement; official transcript; bachelor's degree (or equivalent for international students) in engineering, science, or mathematics. Additional exam requirements/recommendations for international students: Required—TOEFL or IELTS. *Application deadline:* For fall admission, 2/1 for domestic and international students. Applications are processed on a rolling basis. Application fee: $60. Electronic applications accepted. *Expenses: Tuition:* Full-time $46,150; part-time $1442 per credit hour. *Required fees:* $504. *Financial support:* Career-related internships or fieldwork and scholarships/grants available. Financial award application deadline: 2/1. *Faculty research:* High efficiency solar cells, macromolecular self-assembly, digital signal processing, memory hierarchy management, molecular and physical mechanisms in cell migration, optical imaging systems. *Unit head:* Duncan T. Moore, Vice Provost for Entrepreneurship, 585-275-5248, Fax: 585-473-6745, E-mail: moore@optics.rochester.edu. *Application contact:* Andrea M. Galati, Executive Director, 585-276-3407, Fax: 585-276-2357, E-mail: andrea.galati@rochester.edu.
Website: http://www.rochester.edu/team.

University of St. Thomas, Graduate Studies, School of Engineering, St. Paul, MN 55105-1096. Offers electrical engineering (MS); manufacturing engineering and operations (MS); manufacturing systems (Certificate); mechanical engineering (MS); medical device development (Certificate); regulatory science (MS); software engineering (MS); software management (MS); systems engineering (MS); technology leadership (Certificate); technology management (MS). *Accreditation:* ABET (one or more programs are accredited). *Entrance requirements:* For master's, resume, official transcripts. Additional exam requirements/recommendations for international students: Required—TOEFL (minimum score 550 paper-based). Electronic applications accepted. *Expenses:* Contact institution.

University of Saskatchewan, College of Graduate Studies and Research, College of Engineering, Electrical Engineering Program, Saskatoon, SK S7N 5A9, Canada. Offers M Eng, M Sc, PhD, PGD. Part-time programs available. *Degree requirements:* For master's, thesis (for some programs), 30 credits (for M Eng); thesis and 12 credits (for MS); for doctorate, comprehensive exam, thesis/dissertation, qualifying exam, 18 credits; for PGD, 30 credits. *Entrance requirements:* For master's and doctorate, GRE. Additional exam requirements/recommendations for international students: Required—TOEFL, TOEFL (minimum iBT score of 80), IELTS (6.5), CanTEST (4.5), or PTE (59). Electronic applications accepted. *Faculty research:* Artificial neural networks and fuzzy logic, biomedical microdevices, computer engineering, control systems, digital signal processing, electrical machines and power magnetics, embedded systems, high aspect ratio micro patterning, instrumentation and microprocessor applications, multimedia and video signal processing, optoelectronics and photonics, power system protection and control, power system reliability economics, renewable energy applications, thin films.

University of South Carolina, The Graduate School, College of Engineering and Computing, Department of Electrical Engineering, Columbia, SC 29208. Offers ME, MS, PhD. Part-time and evening/weekend programs available. Postbaccalaureate distance learning degree programs offered (minimal on-campus study). *Degree requirements:* For master's, comprehensive exam, thesis (for some programs); for doctorate, comprehensive exam, thesis/dissertation, qualifying exam. *Entrance requirements:* For master's and doctorate, GRE General Test. Additional exam requirements/recommendations for international students: Required—TOEFL (minimum score 570 paper-based; 88 iBT). Electronic applications accepted. *Faculty research:* Microelectronics, photonics, wireless communications, signal integrity, energy and control systems.

University of Southern California, Graduate School, Viterbi School of Engineering, Ming Hsieh Department of Electrical Engineering, Los Angeles, CA 90089. Offers computer engineering (MS, PhD); electric power (MS); electrical engineering (MS, PhD, Engr); engineering technology commercialization (Graduate Certificate); multimedia and creative technologies (MS); telecommunications (MS); VLSI design (MS); wireless health technology (MS). Part-time programs available. Postbaccalaureate distance learning degree programs offered (no on-campus study). Terminal master's awarded for partial completion of doctoral program. *Degree requirements:* For master's, thesis optional; for doctorate, thesis/dissertation. *Entrance requirements:* For master's and doctorate, GRE General Test. Additional exam requirements/recommendations for international students: Recommended—TOEFL. Electronic applications accepted. *Faculty research:* Communications, computer engineering and networks, control systems, integrated circuits and systems, electromagnetics and energy conversion, micro electro-mechanical systems and nanotechnology, photonics and quantum electronics, plasma research, signal and image processing.

University of South Florida, College of Engineering, Department of Electrical Engineering, Tampa, FL 33620-9951. Offers MSEE, PhD. Part-time programs available. Postbaccalaureate distance learning degree programs offered (no on-campus study). *Faculty:* 26 full-time (3 women), 2 part-time/adjunct (0 women). *Students:* 232 full-time (55 women), 77 part-time (10 women); includes 36 minority (10 Black or African American, non-Hispanic/Latino; 11 Asian, non-Hispanic/Latino; 12 Hispanic/Latino; 1 Native Hawaiian or other Pacific Islander, non-Hispanic/Latino; 2 Two or more races, non-Hispanic/Latino), 225 international. Average age 27. 520 applicants, 59% accepted, 99 enrolled. In 2014, 50 master's, 13 doctorates awarded. Terminal master's awarded for partial completion of doctoral program. *Degree requirements:* For master's, comprehensive exam, thesis or alternative; for doctorate, comprehensive exam, thesis/dissertation. *Entrance requirements:* For master's, minimum GPA of 3.0 in last 60 hours of coursework, three letters of recommendation; for doctorate, GRE General Test (minimum preferred scores of 60th percentile quantitative and 29th percentile verbal), minimum GPA of 3.0 in last 60 hours of coursework, three letters of recommendation, statement of purpose. Additional exam requirements/recommendations for international students: Required—TOEFL (minimum score 550 paper-based; 79 iBT) or IELTS (minimum score 6.5). *Application deadline:* For fall admission, 2/15 for domestic students, 1/2 for international students; for spring admission, 10/15 for domestic students, 6/1 for international students. Application fee: $30. Electronic applications accepted. *Financial support:* In 2014–15, 98 students received support, including 57 research assistantships (averaging $12,357 per year), 41 teaching assistantships with tuition reimbursements available (averaging $13,528 per year). Financial award applicants required to submit FAFSA. *Faculty research:* Wireless communication and signal processing, surface science, wireless and microwave information systems (WAMI), in vivo Wireless Information Networking (iWINLAB), personalized interactive experiences (PIE), Smart Grid power systems, defense and intelligence. *Total annual research expenditures:* $2.8 million. *Unit head:* Dr. Thomas Weller, Professor and Department Chair, 813-974-2740, E-mail: weller@usf.edu. *Application contact:* Dr.

Andrew Hoff, Associate Professor and Graduate Program Director, 813-974-4958, Fax: 813-974-5250, E-mail: hoff@usf.edu.
Website: http://ee.eng.usf.edu/.

University of South Florida, University College/Distance Education, Tampa, FL 33620-9951. *Unit head:* Kathy Barnes, Interdisciplinary Programs Coordinator, 813-974-8031, Fax: 813-974-7061, E-mail: barnesk@usf.edu. *Application contact:* Karen Tylinski, Metro Initiatives, 813-974-9943, Fax: 813-974-7061, E-mail: ktylinsk@usf.edu.
Website: http://www.usf.edu/innovative-education/.

The University of Tennessee, Graduate School, College of Engineering, Department of Electrical Engineering and Computer Science, Program in Electrical Engineering, Knoxville, TN 37966. Offers MS, PhD. Part-time programs available. *Faculty:* 28 full-time (4 women), 9 part-time/adjunct (0 women). *Students:* 111 full-time (23 women), 15 part-time (1 woman); includes 6 minority (1 Black or African American, non-Hispanic/Latino; 3 Asian, non-Hispanic/Latino; 2 Two or more races, non-Hispanic/Latino), 91 international. Average age 28. 408 applicants, 10% accepted, 28 enrolled. In 2014, 24 master's, 11 doctorates awarded. *Degree requirements:* For master's, thesis or alternative; for doctorate, comprehensive exam, thesis/dissertation. *Entrance requirements:* For master's, GRE General Test (for MS students pursuing research thesis), minimum GPA of 2.7 (for U.S. degree holders), 3.0 (for international degree holders); 3 references; personal statement; for doctorate, GRE General Test (for all PhD candidates), minimum GPA of 3.0 on previous graduate coursework; 3 references; personal statement. Additional exam requirements/recommendations for international students: Required—TOEFL (minimum score 550 paper-based). *Application deadline:* For fall admission, 2/1 priority date for domestic and international students; for spring admission, 6/15 for domestic and international students. Applications are processed on a rolling basis. Application fee: $35. Electronic applications accepted. *Financial support:* In 2014–15, 104 students received support, including 62 research assistantships with full tuition reimbursements available (averaging $21,294 per year), 30 teaching assistantships with full tuition reimbursements available (averaging $20,285 per year); fellowships with full tuition reimbursements available, career-related internships or fieldwork, Federal Work-Study, institutionally sponsored loans, health care benefits, and unspecified assistantships also available. Financial award application deadline: 2/1; financial award applicants required to submit FAFSA. *Unit head:* Dr. Leon Tolbert, Head, 865-974-3461, Fax: 865-974-5483, E-mail: tolbert@utk.edu. *Application contact:* Dr. Lynne E. Parker, Associate Head, 865-974-4394, Fax: 865-974-5483, E-mail: parker@eecs.utk.edu.
Website: http://www.eecs.utk.edu.

The University of Tennessee at Chattanooga, Program in Engineering, Chattanooga, TN 37403. Offers chemical engineering (MS Engr); civil engineering (MS Engr); computational engineering (MS Engr); electrical engineering (MS Engr); industrial engineering (MS Engr); mechanical engineering (MS Engr). Part-time and evening/weekend programs available. *Faculty:* 20 full-time (3 women), 3 part-time/adjunct (0 women). *Students:* 42 full-time (7 women), 41 part-time (5 women); includes 6 minority (2 Black or African American, non-Hispanic/Latino; 1 Asian, non-Hispanic/Latino; 2 Hispanic/Latino; 1 Two or more races, non-Hispanic/Latino), 30 international. Average age 29. 96 applicants, 32% accepted, 17 enrolled. In 2014, 29 master's awarded. *Degree requirements:* For master's, comprehensive exam, thesis or alternative, engineering project. *Entrance requirements:* For master's, GRE General Test, minimum undergraduate GPA of 2.5 or 3.0 in last 30 hours of coursework. Additional exam requirements/recommendations for international students: Required—TOEFL (minimum score 550 paper-based; 79 iBT), IELTS (minimum score 6). *Application deadline:* For fall admission, 6/13 priority date for domestic students, 6/1 for international students; for spring admission, 10/15 priority date for domestic students, 10/1 for international students. Applications are processed on a rolling basis. Application fee: $30 ($35 for international students). Electronic applications accepted. *Expenses:* Tuition, state resident: full-time $7708; part-time $428 per credit hour. Tuition, nonresident: full-time $23,826; part-time $1323 per credit hour. *Required fees:* $1708; $252 per credit hour. *Financial support:* In 2014–15, 24 research assistantships with tuition reimbursements (averaging $7,669 per year), 7 teaching assistantships with tuition reimbursements (averaging $5,735 per year) were awarded; career-related internships or fieldwork, scholarships/grants, and unspecified assistantships also available. Support available to part-time students. *Faculty research:* Quality control and reliability engineering, financial management, thermal science, energy conservation, structural analysis. *Total annual research expenditures:* $1.6 million. *Unit head:* Dr. William Sutton, Dean, 423-425-2256, Fax: 423-425-5229, E-mail: will-sutton@utc.edu. *Application contact:* Dr. J. Randy Walker, Interim Dean of Graduate Studies, 423-425-4478, Fax: 423-425-5223, E-mail: randy-walker@utc.edu.
Website: http://www.utc.edu/Departments/engrcs/ms_engr.php.

The University of Texas at Arlington, Graduate School, College of Engineering, Department of Electrical Engineering, Arlington, TX 76019. Offers M Engr, MS, PhD. Part-time and evening/weekend programs available. Postbaccalaureate distance learning degree programs offered (no on-campus study). Terminal master's awarded for partial completion of doctoral program. *Degree requirements:* For master's, thesis optional; for doctorate, comprehensive exam, thesis/dissertation, written diagnostic exam. *Entrance requirements:* For master's, GRE General Test, minimum GPA of 3.25; for doctorate, GRE General Test, minimum GPA of 3.5. Additional exam requirements/recommendations for international students: Required—TOEFL (minimum score 560 paper-based); Recommended—TWE (minimum score 4). *Faculty research:* Nanotech and microelectromechanical systems (MEMS), digital image processing, telecommunications and optics, energy systems and power electronics, VLSI and semiconductors.

The University of Texas at Austin, Graduate School, Cockrell School of Engineering, Department of Electrical and Computer Engineering, Austin, TX 78712-1111. Offers MS, PhD. Part-time programs available. *Entrance requirements:* For master's, GRE General Test, minimum GPA of 3.3 in upper-division course work; for doctorate, GRE General Test. Electronic applications accepted.

The University of Texas at Dallas, Erik Jonsson School of Engineering and Computer Science, Department of Electrical Engineering, Richardson, TX 75080. Offers computer engineering (MS, PhD); electrical engineering (MSEE, PhD); systems engineering and management (MS); telecommunications engineering (MSTE, PhD). Part-time and evening/weekend programs available. *Faculty:* 51 full-time (4 women), 5 part-time/adjunct (1 woman). *Students:* 756 full-time (186 women), 288 part-time (83 women); includes 89 minority (14 Black or African American, non-Hispanic/Latino; 44 Asian, non-Hispanic/Latino; 24 Hispanic/Latino; 7 Two or more races, non-Hispanic/Latino), 870 international. Average age 26. 3,191 applicants, 30% accepted, 363 enrolled. In 2014, 250 master's, 31 doctorates awarded. *Degree requirements:* For master's, thesis or major design project; for doctorate, thesis/dissertation. *Entrance requirements:* For master's, GRE General Test, minimum GPA of 3.0 in related bachelor's degree; for doctorate, GRE General Test, minimum GPA of 3.5. Additional exam requirements/recommendations for international students: Required—TOEFL (minimum score 550 paper-based). *Application deadline:* For fall admission, 7/15 for domestic students, 5/1 priority date for international students; for spring admission, 11/15 for domestic students, 9/1 priority date for international students. Applications are processed on a rolling basis. Application fee: $50 ($100 for international students). Electronic applications accepted. *Expenses:* Tuition, state resident: full-time $11,940; part-time $663 per credit. Tuition, nonresident: full-time $22,282; part-time $1238 per credit. *Financial support:* In 2014–15, 269 students received support, including 13 fellowships with partial tuition reimbursements available (averaging $5,598 per year), 129 research assistantships with partial tuition reimbursements available (averaging $17,609 per year), 80 teaching assistantships with partial tuition reimbursements available (averaging $17,480 per year); Federal Work-Study, institutionally sponsored loans, scholarships/grants, unspecified assistantships, and cooperative positions also available. Support available to part-time students. Financial award application deadline: 4/30; financial award applicants required to submit FAFSA. *Faculty research:* Semiconductor device manufacturing, photonics devices and systems, signal processing and language technology, nano-fabrication, energy efficient digital systems. *Unit head:* Dr. James L. Coleman, Department Head, 972-883-6755, Fax: 972-883-2710, E-mail: james.coleman@utdallas.edu. *Application contact:* Patricia Williams, Degree Plan Evaluator, 972-883-4315, Fax: 972-883-2710, E-mail: gradeeadvisors@utdallas.edu.
Website: http://www.ee.utdallas.edu.

The University of Texas at El Paso, Graduate School, College of Engineering, Department of Electrical and Computer Engineering, El Paso, TX 79968-0001. Offers computer engineering (MS); electrical and computer engineering (PhD); electrical engineering (MS). Part-time and evening/weekend programs available. Terminal master's awarded for partial completion of doctoral program. *Degree requirements:* For master's, thesis optional; for doctorate, thesis/dissertation. *Entrance requirements:* For master's, GRE General Test, minimum GPA of 3.0; for doctorate, GRE General Test, minimum graduate GPA of 3.0. Additional exam requirements/recommendations for international students: Required—TOEFL. Electronic applications accepted. *Faculty research:* Signal and image processing, computer architecture, fiber optics, computational electromagnetics, electronic displays and thin films.

The University of Texas at San Antonio, College of Engineering, Department of Electrical and Computer Engineering, San Antonio, TX 78249-0617. Offers advanced materials engineering (MS); computer engineering (MS); electrical engineering (MSEE, PhD). Part-time programs available. *Faculty:* 24 full-time (3 women), 1 part-time/adjunct (0 women). *Students:* 210 full-time (58 women), 101 part-time (21 women); includes 47 minority (3 Black or African American, non-Hispanic/Latino; 11 Asian, non-Hispanic/Latino; 28 Hispanic/Latino; 5 Two or more races, non-Hispanic/Latino), 218 international. Average age 26. 450 applicants, 86% accepted, 128 enrolled. In 2014, 45 master's, 8 doctorates awarded. Terminal master's awarded for partial completion of doctoral program. *Degree requirements:* For master's, comprehensive exam, thesis (for some programs); for doctorate, comprehensive exam, thesis/dissertation. *Entrance requirements:* For master's, GRE General Test, bachelor's degree in electrical or computer engineering from ABET-accredited institution of higher education or related field; minimum GPA of 3.0 on the last 60 semester credit hours of undergraduate studies; for doctorate, GRE General Test, master's degree or minimum GPA of 3.3 in last 60 semester credit hours of undergraduate level coursework in electrical engineering; statement of purpose. Additional exam requirements/recommendations for international students: Required—TOEFL (minimum score 550 paper-based; 79 iBT), IELTS (minimum score 6.5). *Application deadline:* For fall admission, 7/1 for domestic students, 4/1 for international students; for spring admission, 11/1 for domestic students, 9/1 for international students. Applications are processed on a rolling basis. Application fee: $45 ($80 for international students). Electronic applications accepted. *Expenses:* Tuition, state resident: full-time $4671; part-time $260 per credit hour. Tuition, nonresident: full-time $18,022; part-time $1001 per credit hour. *Financial support:* Unspecified assistantships available. Financial award application deadline: 3/31. *Faculty research:* Computer engineering, digital signal processing, systems and controls, communications, electronics materials and devices, electric power engineering. *Unit head:* Dr. Daniel Pack, Department Chair/Professor, 210-458-7076, Fax: 210-458-5947, E-mail: electrical.engineering@utsa.edu. *Application contact:* Graduate Advisor of Record, E-mail: graduate.ece@utsa.edu.
Website: http://ece.utsa.edu/.

The University of Texas at Tyler, College of Engineering and Computer Science, Department of Electrical Engineering, Tyler, TX 75799-0001. Offers MS. Part-time and evening/weekend programs available. *Degree requirements:* For master's, comprehensive exam (for some programs). *Entrance requirements:* For master's, GRE General Test, bachelor's degree in electrical engineering. Additional exam requirements/recommendations for international students: Required—TOEFL. *Faculty research:* Electronics, digital sign processing, real time systems electromagnetic fields, semiconductor modeling.

The University of Texas–Pan American, College of Engineering and Computer Science, Department of Electrical Engineering, Edinburg, TX 78539. Offers MS. *Expenses:* Tuition, state resident: full-time $4187; part-time $232.60 per credit hour. Tuition, nonresident: full-time $10,857; part-time $603.16 per credit hour. *Required fees:* $782; $27.50 per credit hour. $143.35 per semester.

University of the District of Columbia, School of Engineering and Applied Science, Department of Electrical and Computer Engineering, Washington, DC 20008-1175. Offers electrical engineering (MS).

The University of Toledo, College of Graduate Studies, College of Engineering, Department of Electrical Engineering and Computer Science, Toledo, OH 43606-3390. Offers computer science (MS, PhD); electrical engineering (MS, PhD). Part-time and evening/weekend programs available. *Degree requirements:* For master's, thesis or alternative; for doctorate, thesis/dissertation, qualifying exam. *Entrance requirements:* For master's, GRE General Test, minimum GPA of 3.0; for doctorate, GRE General Test, minimum GPA of 3.3. Additional exam requirements/recommendations for international students: Required—TOEFL (minimum score 550 paper-based; 80 iBT). Electronic applications accepted. *Faculty research:* Communication and signal processing, high performance computing systems, intelligent systems, power electronics and energy systems, RF and microwave systems, sensors and medical devices, solid state devices.

University of Toronto, School of Graduate Studies, Faculty of Applied Science and Engineering, Department of Electrical and Computer Engineering, Toronto, ON M5S 2J7, Canada. Offers M Eng, MA Sc, PhD. Part-time programs available. *Degree requirements:* For master's, thesis (for some programs), oral thesis defense (MA Sc); for doctorate, thesis/dissertation, qualifying exam, thesis defense. *Entrance requirements:* For master's, four-year degree in electrical or computer engineering, minimum B average, 2 letters of reference; for doctorate, minimum B+ average, MA Sc in electrical or computer engineering, 2 letters of reference. Additional exam requirements/recommendations for international students: Required—TOEFL (minimum score 580 paper-based; 93 iBT). Electronic applications accepted.

The University of Tulsa, Graduate School, College of Engineering and Natural Sciences, Department of Electrical and Computer Engineering, Tulsa, OK 74104-3189. Offers ME, MSE, PhD. Part-time programs available. *Faculty:* 6 full-time (0 women). *Students:* 9 full-time (2 women), 2 part-time (0 women), 5 international. Average age 25. 21 applicants, 33% accepted, 1 enrolled. In 2014, 4 master's awarded. Terminal

master's awarded for partial completion of doctoral program. *Degree requirements:* For master's, comprehensive exam (for some programs), design report (ME), thesis (MS). *Entrance requirements:* For master's, GRE General Test. Additional exam requirements/recommendations for international students: Required—TOEFL (minimum score 550 paper-based; 80 iBT), IELTS (minimum score 6). *Application deadline:* Applications are processed on a rolling basis. Application fee: $55. Electronic applications accepted. *Expenses: Tuition:* Full-time $20,160; part-time $1120 per credit hour. *Required fees:* $6 per credit hour. Tuition and fees vary according to course level and course load. *Financial support:* In 2014–15, 7 students received support, including 1 research assistantship with full and partial tuition reimbursement available (averaging $15,338 per year), 6 teaching assistantships with full and partial tuition reimbursements available (averaging $12,092 per year); fellowships with full and partial tuition reimbursements available, career-related internships or fieldwork, Federal Work-Study, scholarships/grants, health care benefits, tuition waivers (full and partial), and unspecified assistantships also available. Support available to part-time students. Financial award application deadline: 2/1; financial award applicants required to submit FAFSA. *Faculty research:* VLSI microprocessors, intelligent systems, electromagnetics, intrusion detection systems, digital electronics. *Total annual research expenditures:* $320,447. *Unit head:* Dr. Kaveh Ashenayi, Chairperson, 918-631-3278, Fax: 918-631-3344, E-mail: kash@utulsa.edu. *Application contact:* Dr. Heng-Ming Tai, Adviser, 918-631-3271, Fax: 918-631-3344, E-mail: tai@utulsa.edu.
Website: http://engineering.utulsa.edu/academics/electrical-and-computer-engineering/.

University of Utah, Graduate School, College of Engineering, Department of Electrical and Computer Engineering, Salt Lake City, UT 84112. Offers electrical engineering (ME, MS, PhD); MS/MBA. Part-time programs available. *Faculty:* 30 full-time (3 women), 11 part-time/adjunct (1 woman). *Students:* 175 full-time (26 women), 20 part-time (1 woman); includes 10 minority (1 Black or African American, non-Hispanic/Latino; 6 Asian, non-Hispanic/Latino; 1 Hispanic/Latino; 2 Two or more races, non-Hispanic/Latino), 115 international. Average age 28. 496 applicants, 40% accepted, 57 enrolled. In 2014, 37 master's, 9 doctorates awarded. Terminal master's awarded for partial completion of doctoral program. *Degree requirements:* For master's, comprehensive exam (for some programs), thesis (for some programs); for doctorate, comprehensive exam, thesis/dissertation. *Entrance requirements:* For master's, GRE General Test, minimum GPA of 3.2; for doctorate, GRE General Test, minimum GPA of 3.5. Additional exam requirements/recommendations for international students: Required—TOEFL (minimum score 600 paper-based; 100 iBT); Recommended—IELTS (minimum score 7.5). *Application deadline:* For fall admission, 1/15 for domestic and international students; for spring admission, 10/1 for domestic students. Application fee: $10 ($25 for international students). *Expenses:* Expenses: Contact institution. *Financial support:* In 2014–15, 2 students received support, including 2 fellowships with full tuition reimbursements available (averaging $30,000 per year), 65 research assistantships with full tuition reimbursements available (averaging $22,000 per year), 26 teaching assistantships with full tuition reimbursements available (averaging $19,000 per year); Federal Work-Study, institutionally sponsored loans, health care benefits, and unspecified assistantships also available. Financial award application deadline: 1/15; financial award applicants required to submit FAFSA. *Faculty research:* Semiconductors, VLSI design, control systems, electromagnetics and applied optics, communication theory and digital signal processing, power systems. *Total annual research expenditures:* $4.7 million. *Unit head:* Dr. Gianluca Lazzi, Chair, 801-581-6941, Fax: 801-581-5281, E-mail: lazzi@utah.edu. *Application contact:* Holly Cox, Administrative Manager, 801-581-3843, Fax: 801-581-5281, E-mail: h.cox@utah.edu.
Website: http://www.ece.utah.edu/.

University of Vermont, Graduate College, College of Engineering and Mathematics, Department of Electrical Engineering, Burlington, VT 05405. Offers MS, PhD. *Degree requirements:* For master's, thesis or alternative; for doctorate, one foreign language, thesis/dissertation. *Entrance requirements:* For master's, GRE General Test. Additional exam requirements/recommendations for international students: Required—TOEFL (minimum score 550 paper-based; 80 iBT). Electronic applications accepted.

University of Victoria, Faculty of Graduate Studies, Faculty of Engineering, Department of Electrical and Computer Engineering, Victoria, BC V8W 2Y2, Canada. Offers M Eng, MA Sc, PhD. *Degree requirements:* For master's, thesis; for doctorate, thesis/dissertation, candidacy exam. *Entrance requirements:* For master's, GRE (recommended), bachelor's degree in engineering; for doctorate, GRE (recommended), master's degree. Additional exam requirements/recommendations for international students: Required—TOEFL (minimum score 575 paper-based), IELTS (minimum score 7). Electronic applications accepted. *Faculty research:* Communications and computers; electromagnetics, microwaves, and optics; electronics; power systems, signal processing, and control.

University of Virginia, School of Engineering and Applied Science, Department of Electrical and Computer Engineering, Program in Electrical Engineering, Charlottesville, VA 22903. Offers ME, MS, PhD. *Students:* 85 full-time (20 women), 8 part-time (0 women); includes 13 minority (3 Black or African American, non-Hispanic/Latino; 6 Asian, non-Hispanic/Latino; 2 Hispanic/Latino; 2 Two or more races, non-Hispanic/Latino), 58 international. Average age 27. 398 applicants, 8% accepted, 20 enrolled. In 2014, 10 master's, 18 doctorates awarded. *Degree requirements:* For doctorate, thesis/dissertation. *Entrance requirements:* For master's, GRE General Test, 3 letters of recommendation; for doctorate, GRE General Test, 3 letters of recommendation; essay. Additional exam requirements/recommendations for international students: Required—TOEFL (minimum score 650 paper-based; 100 iBT), IELTS (minimum score 7). *Application deadline:* For fall admission, 8/1 for domestic students, 1/15 for international students; for winter admission, 12/1 for domestic students, 8/1 for international students; for spring admission, 5/1 for domestic students. Applications are processed on a rolling basis. Application fee: $60. Electronic applications accepted. *Expenses:* Tuition, state resident: full-time $14,164; part-time $349 per credit hour. Tuition, nonresident: full-time $23,722; part-time $1300 per credit hour. *Required fees:* $2514. *Financial support:* Fellowships, research assistantships, and teaching assistantships available. Financial award application deadline: 1/15; financial award applicants required to submit FAFSA. *Unit head:* John C. Lach, Chair, 434-924-3960, Fax: 434-924-8818, E-mail: jlach@virginia.edu. *Application contact:* Graduate Program Director, 434-924-3960, Fax: 434-924-8818, E-mail: eceinfo@virginia.edu.
Website: http://www.ece.virginia.edu/curriculum/grads/ee.html.

University of Washington, Graduate School, College of Engineering, Department of Electrical Engineering, Seattle, WA 98195-2500. Offers electrical engineering (MS, PhD); electrical engineering and nanotechnology (PhD). Part-time programs available. Postbaccalaureate distance learning degree programs offered (no on-campus study). *Faculty:* 37 full-time (5 women). *Students:* 233 full-time (50 women), 115 part-time (14 women). Average age 28. 1,318 applicants, 17% accepted, 118 enrolled. In 2014, 72 master's, 30 doctorates awarded. Terminal master's awarded for partial completion of doctoral program. *Degree requirements:* For master's, thesis optional; for doctorate, thesis/dissertation, qualifying, general, and final exams. *Entrance requirements:* For master's, GRE General Test (recommended minimum Quantitative score of 160), GPA of 3.5 recommended; resume or curriculum vitae, statement of purpose, 3 letters of recommendation, undergraduate and graduate transcripts; for doctorate, GRE General Test (recommended minimum Quantitative score of 160), GPA of 3.5 recommended, resume or curriculum vitae, statement of purpose, 3 letters of recommendation, undergraduate and graduate transcripts. Additional exam requirements/recommendations for international students: Required—TOEFL (minimum score 600 paper-based; 92 iBT); Recommended—IELTS (minimum score 7). *Application deadline:* For fall admission, 12/15 for domestic and international students. Applications are processed on a rolling basis. Application fee: $85. Electronic applications accepted. *Expenses:* Expenses: Contact institution. *Financial support:* In 2014–15, 199 students received support, including 15 fellowships with full tuition reimbursements available, 122 research assistantships with full tuition reimbursements available, 62 teaching assistantships with full tuition reimbursements available; career-related internships or fieldwork, Federal Work-Study, and institutionally sponsored loans also available. Financial award application deadline: 1/1; financial award applicants required to submit FAFSA. *Faculty research:* Smart grid, advanced wireless networks and communications, nanotechnology, biorobotics, signal processing and compression. *Total annual research expenditures:* $18.5 million. *Unit head:* Dr. Radha Poovendran, Professor/Chair, 206-543-6515, Fax: 206-543-3842, E-mail: chair@ee.washington.edu. *Application contact:* Brenda Larson, Lead Graduate Program Academic Counselor, 206-616-1351, Fax: 206-543-3842, E-mail: brenda@ee.washington.edu.
Website: http://www.ee.washington.edu/.

University of Waterloo, Graduate Studies, Faculty of Engineering, Department of Electrical and Computer Engineering, Waterloo, ON N2L 3G1, Canada. Offers electrical and computer engineering (M Eng, MA Sc, PhD); electrical and computer engineering (software engineering) (MA Sc). Part-time programs available. *Degree requirements:* For master's, research paper or thesis; for doctorate, comprehensive exam, thesis/dissertation. *Entrance requirements:* For master's, honors degree, minimum B+ average; for doctorate, master's degree, minimum A- average. Additional exam requirements/recommendations for international students: Required—TOEFL (minimum score 550 paper-based), TWE (minimum score 4). Electronic applications accepted. *Faculty research:* Communications, computers, systems and control, silicon devices, power engineering.

The University of Western Ontario, Faculty of Graduate Studies, Physical Sciences Division, Faculty of Engineering, London, ON N6A 5B8, Canada. Offers chemical and biochemical engineering (ME Sc, PhD); civil and environmental engineering (M Eng, ME Sc, PhD); electrical and computer engineering (M Eng, ME Sc, PhD); mechanical and materials engineering (M Eng, ME Sc, PhD). Part-time programs available. Terminal master's awarded for partial completion of doctoral program. *Degree requirements:* For master's, thesis; for doctorate, thesis/dissertation. *Entrance requirements:* For master's, minimum B average; for doctorate, minimum B+ average. *Faculty research:* Wind, geotechnical, chemical reactor engineering, applied electrostatics, biochemical engineering.

University of Windsor, Faculty of Graduate Studies, Faculty of Engineering, Department of Electrical and Computer Engineering, Windsor, ON N9B 3P4, Canada. Offers electrical engineering (M Eng, MA Sc, PhD). Part-time programs available. *Degree requirements:* For master's, thesis; for doctorate, comprehensive exam, thesis/dissertation. *Entrance requirements:* For master's, minimum B average; for doctorate, master's degree, minimum B+ average. Additional exam requirements/recommendations for international students: Required—TOEFL (minimum score 600 paper-based). Electronic applications accepted. *Faculty research:* Systems, signals, power.

University of Wisconsin–Madison, Graduate School, College of Engineering, Department of Electrical and Computer Engineering, Madison, WI 53706. Offers electrical engineering (MS, PhD). Part-time programs available. Postbaccalaureate distance learning degree programs offered (minimal on-campus study). Terminal master's awarded for partial completion of doctoral program. *Degree requirements:* For master's, thesis or alternative; for doctorate, thesis/dissertation, exam. *Entrance requirements:* For master's and doctorate, GRE General Test. Additional exam requirements/recommendations for international students: Required—TOEFL (minimum score 550 paper-based; 92 iBT), IELTS. Electronic applications accepted. *Expenses:* Tuition, state resident: full-time $10,723; part-time $745 per credit. Tuition, nonresident: full-time $24,054; part-time $1578 per credit. *Required fees:* $374 per semester. Tuition and fees vary according to course load, program and reciprocity agreements. *Faculty research:* Microelectronics, computer architecture, power electronics and systems, communications, signal processing.

University of Wisconsin–Milwaukee, Graduate School, College of Engineering and Applied Science, Program in Engineering, Milwaukee, WI 53201-0413. Offers civil engineering (MS); electrical and computer engineering (MS); energy engineering (Certificate); engineering (PhD); engineering management (MS); engineering mechanics (MS); ergonomics (Certificate); industrial and management engineering (MS); manufacturing engineering (MS); materials engineering (MS); mechanical engineering (MS); MUP/MS. Part-time programs available. *Degree requirements:* For master's, comprehensive exam (for some programs), thesis or alternative; for doctorate, comprehensive exam, thesis/dissertation, internship. *Entrance requirements:* For master's, GRE, minimum GPA of 2.75; for doctorate, GRE, minimum GPA of 3.5. Additional exam requirements/recommendations for international students: Required—TOEFL (minimum score 550 paper-based; 79 iBT), IELTS (minimum score 6.5).

University of Wyoming, College of Engineering and Applied Sciences, Department of Electrical and Computer Engineering, Laramie, WY 82071. Offers electrical engineering (MS, PhD). Part-time programs available. *Degree requirements:* For master's, thesis (for some programs); for doctorate, comprehensive exam, thesis/dissertation, dissertation proposal/presentation. *Entrance requirements:* For master's, GRE General Test, minimum undergraduate GPA of 3.0; for doctorate, GRE General Test, minimum GPA of 3.0. Additional exam requirements/recommendations for international students: Required—TOEFL (minimum score 550 paper-based; 79 iBT). Electronic applications accepted. *Faculty research:* Robotics and controls, signal and image processing, power electronics, power systems, computer networks, wind energy.

Utah State University, School of Graduate Studies, College of Engineering, Department of Electrical and Computer Engineering, Logan, UT 84322. Offers electrical engineering (ME, MS, PhD). Part-time programs available. *Degree requirements:* For master's, thesis (for some programs); for doctorate, comprehensive exam, thesis/dissertation. *Entrance requirements:* For master's, GRE General Test, minimum GPA of 3.0, BS in electrical engineering, 3 recommendation letters; for doctorate, GRE General Test, minimum GPA of 3.0, MS in electrical engineering, 3 recommendation letters. Additional exam requirements/recommendations for international students: Required—TOEFL. Electronic applications accepted. *Faculty research:* Parallel processing, networking, control systems, digital signal processing, communications.

Vanderbilt University, School of Engineering, Department of Electrical Engineering and Computer Science, Program in Electrical Engineering, Nashville, TN 37240-1001. Offers M Eng, MS, PhD. MS and PhD offered through the Graduate School. Part-time programs available. Terminal master's awarded for partial completion of doctoral program. *Degree requirements:* For master's, thesis; for doctorate, comprehensive exam, thesis/dissertation. *Entrance requirements:* For master's and doctorate, GRE General Test, 3 letters of recommendation. Additional exam requirements/recommendations for international students: Required—TOEFL. Electronic applications accepted. *Expenses: Tuition:* Full-time $42,768; part-time $1782 per credit hour. *Required fees:* $422. One-time fee: $30 full-time. *Faculty research:* Robotics, microelectronics, signal and image processing, VLSI, solid-state sensors, radiation effects and reliability.

Villanova University, College of Engineering, Department of Electrical and Computer Engineering, Program in Electrical Engineering, Villanova, PA 19085-1699. Offers electric power systems (Certificate); electrical engineering (MSEE); electro mechanical systems (Certificate); high frequency systems (Certificate); intelligent control systems (Certificate); wireless and digital communications (Certificate). Part-time and evening/weekend programs available. *Degree requirements:* For master's, thesis optional. *Entrance requirements:* For master's, GRE General Test (for applicants with degrees from foreign universities), BEE, minimum GPA of 3.0. Additional exam requirements/recommendations for international students: Required—TOEFL (minimum score 600 paper-based; 100 iBT). *Faculty research:* Signal processing, communications, antennas, devices.

Virginia Commonwealth University, Graduate School, School of Engineering, Department of Electrical and Computer Engineering, Richmond, VA 23284-9005. Offers electrical engineering (MS, PhD). *Entrance requirements:* For master's and doctorate, GRE. Additional exam requirements/recommendations for international students: Required—TOEFL (minimum score 600 paper-based; 100 iBT). Electronic applications accepted.

Virginia Polytechnic Institute and State University, Graduate School, College of Engineering, Blacksburg, VA 24061. Offers aerospace engineering (ME, MS, PhD); biological systems engineering (ME, MS, PhD); biomedical engineering (MS, PhD); chemical engineering (ME, MS, PhD); civil engineering (ME, MS, PhD); computer engineering (ME, MS, PhD); computer science (MS, PhD); electrical engineering (ME, PhD); engineering education (PhD); engineering mechanics (ME, MS, PhD); environmental engineering (MS); environmental science and engineering (MS); industrial and systems engineering (ME, MS, PhD); materials science and engineering (ME, MS, PhD); mechanical engineering (ME, MS, PhD); mining and minerals engineering (PhD); mining engineering (ME, MS); nuclear engineering (MS, PhD); ocean engineering (MS); systems engineering (ME, MS). *Accreditation:* ABET (one or more programs are accredited). *Faculty:* 356 full-time (60 women), 3 part-time/adjunct (1 woman). *Students:* 1,700 full-time (398 women), 345 part-time (58 women); includes 213 minority (43 Black or African American, non-Hispanic/Latino; 1 American Indian or Alaska Native, non-Hispanic/Latino; 87 Asian, non-Hispanic/Latino; 58 Hispanic/Latino; 1 Native Hawaiian or other Pacific Islander, non-Hispanic/Latino; 23 Two or more races, non-Hispanic/Latino), 1,079 international. Average age 27. 5,228 applicants, 18% accepted, 471 enrolled. In 2014, 438 master's, 211 doctorates awarded. *Degree requirements:* For master's, comprehensive exam (for some programs), thesis (for some programs); for doctorate, comprehensive exam (for some programs), thesis/dissertation (for some programs). *Entrance requirements:* For master's and doctorate, GRE/GMAT (may vary by department). Additional exam requirements/recommendations for international students: Required—TOEFL (minimum score 550 paper-based). *Application deadline:* For fall admission, 8/1 for domestic students, 4/1 for international students; for spring admission, 1/1 for domestic students, 9/1 for international students. Applications are processed on a rolling basis. Application fee: $75. Electronic applications accepted. *Expenses:* Tuition, state resident: full-time $11,656; part-time $647.50 per credit hour. Tuition, nonresident: full-time $23,351; part-time $1297.25 per credit hour. *Required fees:* $2533; $465.75 per semester. Tuition and fees vary according to course load, campus/location and program. *Financial support:* In 2014–15, 148 fellowships with full tuition reimbursements (averaging $8,031 per year), 855 research assistantships with full tuition reimbursements (averaging $22,855 per year), 288 teaching assistantships with full tuition reimbursements (averaging $20,291 per year) were awarded. Financial award application deadline: 3/1; financial award applicants required to submit FAFSA. *Total annual research expenditures:* $90.5 million. *Unit head:* Dr. Richard C. Benson, Dean, 540-231-9752, Fax: 540-231-3031, E-mail: deaneng@vt.edu. *Application contact:* Linda Perkins, Executive Assistant, 540-231-9752, Fax: 540-231-3031, E-mail: lperkins@vt.edu.
Website: http://www.eng.vt.edu/.

Virginia Polytechnic Institute and State University, VT Online, Blacksburg, VA 24061. Offers advanced transportation systems (Certificate); aerospace engineering (MS); agricultural and life sciences (MSLFS); business information systems (Graduate Certificate); career and technical education (MS); civil engineering (MS); computer engineering (M Eng, MS); decision support systems (Graduate Certificate); eLearning leadership (MA); electrical engineering (M Eng, MS); engineering administration (MEA); environmental engineering (Certificate); environmental politics and policy (Graduate Certificate); environmental sciences and engineering (MS); foundations of political analysis (Graduate Certificate); health product risk management (Graduate Certificate); industrial and systems engineering (MS); information policy and society (Graduate Certificate); information security (Graduate Certificate); information technology (MIT); instructional technology (MA); integrative STEM education (MA Ed); liberal arts (Graduate Certificate); life sciences: health product risk management (MS); natural resources (MNR, Graduate Certificate); networking (Graduate Certificate); nonprofit and nongovernmental organization management (Graduate Certificate); ocean engineering (MS); political science (MA); security studies (Graduate Certificate); software development (Graduate Certificate). *Expenses:* Tuition, state resident: full-time $11,656; part-time $647.50 per credit hour. Tuition, nonresident: full-time $23,351; part-time $1297.25 per credit hour. *Required fees:* $2533; $465.75 per semester. Tuition and fees vary according to course load, campus/location and program.

Washington State University, Voiland College of Engineering and Architecture, School of Electrical Engineering and Computer Science, Pullman, WA 99164-2752. Offers computer engineering (MS); computer science (MS); electrical engineering (MS); electrical engineering and computer science (PhD); electrical power engineering (MS). MS programs in computer engineering, computer science and electrical engineering also offered at Tri-Cities campus; MS in electrical power engineering offered at the Global (online) campus. Part-time programs available. *Faculty:* 51 full-time (4 women), 4 part-time/adjunct (0 women). *Students:* 122 full-time (29 women), 49 part-time (12 women); includes 13 minority (1 Black or African American, non-Hispanic/Latino; 8 Asian, non-Hispanic/Latino; 3 Hispanic/Latino; 1 Native Hawaiian or other Pacific Islander, non-Hispanic/Latino), 108 international. Average age 28. 451 applicants, 16% accepted, 44 enrolled. In 2014, 24 master's, 11 doctorates awarded. *Degree requirements:* For master's, comprehensive exam (for some programs), thesis or alternative; for doctorate, comprehensive exam, thesis/dissertation. *Entrance requirements:* For master's and doctorate, GRE General Test, minimum GPA of 3.0, 3 letters of recommendation, statement of purpose, transcripts. Additional exam requirements/recommendations for international students: Required—TOEFL (minimum score 580 paper-based). *Application deadline:* For fall admission, 1/10 priority date for domestic students, 3/1 priority date for international students; for spring admission, 7/1

priority date for domestic and international students. Applications are processed on a rolling basis. Application fee: $75. *Expenses:* Tuition, state resident: full-time $11,768. Tuition, nonresident: full-time $25,200. *Required fees:* $960. Tuition and fees vary according to program. *Financial support:* In 2014–15, 74 students received support, including 5 fellowships (averaging $2,500 per year), 72 research assistantships with full and partial tuition reimbursements available (averaging $12,843 per year), 24 teaching assistantships with full and partial tuition reimbursements available (averaging $13,981 per year); career-related internships or fieldwork, Federal Work-Study, institutionally sponsored loans, tuition waivers (partial), and teaching associateships also available. Financial award application deadline: 4/1; financial award applicants required to submit FAFSA. *Faculty research:* Software engineering, networks, distributed computing, computer engineering, electrophysics, artificial intelligence, bioinformatics and computational biology, computer graphics, communications, control systems, signal processing, power systems, microelectronics, algorithms. *Total annual research expenditures:* $7.3 million. *Unit head:* Dr. Behrooz Shirazi, Chair/Director, 509-335-8148, Fax: 509-335-3818. *Application contact:* Sidra S. Gleason, Graduate Student Advisor, 509-335-6636, Fax: 509-335-1949, E-mail: gradsch@wsu.edu.
Website: http://www.eecs.wsu.edu/.

Wayne State University, College of Engineering, Department of Electrical and Computer Engineering, Program in Electrical Engineering, Detroit, MI 48202. Offers MS, PhD. *Students:* 110 full-time (20 women), 27 part-time (2 women); includes 8 minority (2 Black or African American, non-Hispanic/Latino; 6 Asian, non-Hispanic/Latino), 111 international. Average age 26. 487 applicants, 47% accepted, 50 enrolled. In 2014, 12 master's, 11 doctorates awarded. *Degree requirements:* For master's, thesis optional; for doctorate, thesis/dissertation. *Entrance requirements:* For master's, BS from an ABET-accredited college or university, or GRE, publications, and/or inventions. Additional exam requirements/recommendations for international students: Required—TOEFL (minimum score 550 paper-based; 79 iBT), TWE (minimum score 5.5), Michigan English Language Assessment Battery (minimum score 85); Recommended—IELTS (minimum score 6.5). *Application deadline:* For fall admission, 6/1 priority date for domestic students, 5/1 priority date for international students; for winter admission, 10/1 priority date for domestic students, 9/1 priority date for international students; for spring admission, 2/1 priority date for domestic students, 1/1 priority date for international students. Applications are processed on a rolling basis. Application fee: $0. Electronic applications accepted. *Expenses:* Expenses: Contact institution. *Financial support:* In 2014–15, 58 students received support. Fellowships with tuition reimbursements available, research assistantships with tuition reimbursements available, teaching assistantships with tuition reimbursements available, scholarships/grants, health care benefits, and unspecified assistantships available. Support available to part-time students. Financial award application deadline: 3/31; financial award applicants required to submit FAFSA. *Faculty research:* Biomedical systems, control systems, solid state materials, optical materials, hybrid vehicle. *Unit head:* Dr. Cheng-Zhong Xu, Department Chair, 313-577-3856, E-mail: czxu@wayne.edu. *Application contact:* Emily Reetz, Electrical and Computer Engineering Academic Advisor, 313-577-2692, E-mail: ereetz@wayne.edu.
Website: http://engineering.wayne.edu/ece/.

Western Michigan University, Graduate College, College of Engineering and Applied Sciences, Department of Electrical and Computer Engineering, Kalamazoo, MI 49008. Offers computer engineering (MSE); electrical and computer engineering (PhD); electrical engineering (MSE). Part-time programs available. *Degree requirements:* For master's, thesis optional. *Application deadline:* For fall admission, 2/15 for domestic students. *Financial support:* Application deadline: 2/15. *Application contact:* Admissions and Orientation, 269-387-2000, Fax: 269-387-2096.

Western New England University, College of Engineering, Department of Electrical Engineering, Springfield, MA 01119. Offers MSEE. Part-time and evening/weekend programs available. *Students:* 18 part-time (1 woman); includes 3 minority (all Black or African American, non-Hispanic/Latino), 4 international. Average age 28. In 2014, 3 master's awarded. *Degree requirements:* For master's, comprehensive exam, thesis optional. *Entrance requirements:* For master's, official transcript, bachelor's degree in engineering or related field, two recommendations, resume. Additional exam requirements/recommendations for international students: Required—TOEFL (minimum score 79 iBT). *Application deadline:* Applications are processed on a rolling basis. Application fee: $30. Electronic applications accepted. *Financial support:* Application deadline: 4/15; applicants required to submit FAFSA. *Faculty research:* Superconductors, microwave cooking, computer voice output, digital filters, computer engineering. *Unit head:* Dr. James J. Moriarty, Chair, 413-782-1725, E-mail: jmoriart@wne.edu. *Application contact:* Matthew Fox, Director of Recruiting and Marketing for Adult Learners, 413-782-1517, Fax: 413-782-1779, E-mail: study@wne.edu.
Website: http://www1.wne.edu/engineering/index.cfm?selection-doc.8531.

West Virginia University, College of Engineering and Mineral Resources, Lane Department of Computer Science and Electrical Engineering, Program in Electrical Engineering, Morgantown, WV 26506. Offers MSEE, PhD. Terminal master's awarded for partial completion of doctoral program. *Degree requirements:* For master's, thesis or alternative; for doctorate, comprehensive exam, thesis/dissertation. *Entrance requirements:* For master's and doctorate, GRE General Test, minimum GPA of 3.0, letters of recommendation. Additional exam requirements/recommendations for international students: Required—TOEFL. *Faculty research:* Power and control systems, communications and signal processing, electromechanical systems, microelectronics and photonics.

Wichita State University, Graduate School, College of Engineering, Department of Electrical Engineering and Computer Science, Wichita, KS 67260. Offers computer networking (MS); computer science (MS); electrical engineering (MS); electrical engineering and computer science (PhD). Part-time and evening/weekend programs available. *Unit head:* Dr. John Watkins, Chair, 316-978-3156, Fax: 316-978-5408, E-mail: john.watkins@wichita.edu. *Application contact:* Jordan Oleson, Admissions Coordinator, 316-978-3095, Fax: 316-978-3253, E-mail: jordan.oleson@wichita.edu.
Website: http://www.wichita.edu/eecs.

Wilkes University, College of Graduate and Professional Studies, College of Science and Engineering, Department of Electrical Engineering and Physics, Wilkes-Barre, PA 18766-0002. Offers bioengineering (MS); electrical engineering (MSEE). Part-time programs available. *Students:* 18 full-time (6 women), 10 part-time (4 women); includes 4 minority (1 Black or African American, non-Hispanic/Latino; 2 Asian, non-Hispanic/Latino; 1 Hispanic/Latino), 7 international. Average age 26. In 2014, 2 master's awarded. *Entrance requirements:* For master's, GRE General Test. Additional exam requirements/recommendations for international students: Required—TOEFL (minimum score 550 paper-based; 79 iBT). *Application deadline:* Applications are processed on a rolling basis. Application fee: $45 ($65 for international students). Electronic applications accepted. *Financial support:* Federal Work-Study and unspecified assistantships available. Financial award application deadline: 3/1; financial award applicants required to submit FAFSA. *Unit head:* Dr. Terese Wignot, Interim Dean, 570-408-4600, Fax: 570-408-7846, E-mail: terese.wignot@wilkes.edu. *Application contact:* Joanne Thomas,

Electrical Engineering

Director of Graduate Enrollment, 570-408-4234, Fax: 570-408-7846, E-mail: joanne.thomas1@wilkes.edu.
Website: http://www.wilkes.edu/academics/colleges/science-and-engineering/engineering-physics/electrical-engineering-physics/index.aspx.

Worcester Polytechnic Institute, Graduate Studies and Research, Department of Electrical and Computer Engineering, Worcester, MA 01609-2280. Offers electrical and computer engineering (Advanced Certificate, Graduate Certificate); electrical engineering (M Eng, MS, PhD). Part-time and evening/weekend programs available. *Faculty:* 17 full-time (0 women), 20 part-time/adjunct (2 women). *Students:* 184 full-time (37 women), 116 part-time (17 women); includes 30 minority (4 Black or African American, non-Hispanic/Latino; 17 Asian, non-Hispanic/Latino; 6 Hispanic/Latino; 3 Two or more races, non-Hispanic/Latino), 159 international. 707 applicants, 35% accepted, 90 enrolled. In 2014, 73 master's, 9 doctorates awarded. Terminal master's awarded for partial completion of doctoral program. *Degree requirements:* For master's, thesis optional; for doctorate, comprehensive exam, thesis/dissertation. *Entrance requirements:* For master's, GRE, 3 letters of recommendation; for doctorate, GRE, 3 letters of recommendation, statement of purpose. Additional exam requirements/recommendations for international students: Required—TOEFL (minimum score 563 paper-based; 84 iBT), IELTS (minimum score 7). *Application deadline:* For fall admission, 1/1 priority date for domestic students, 1/1 for international students; for spring admission, 10/1 priority date for domestic students, 10/1 for international students. Applications are processed on a rolling basis. Application fee: $70. Electronic applications accepted. *Financial support:* Research assistantships, teaching assistantships, career-related internships or fieldwork, institutionally sponsored loans, scholarships/grants, and unspecified assistantships available. Financial award application deadline: 1/1; financial award applicants required to submit FAFSA. *Unit head:* Dr. Yehia Massoud, Department Head, 508-831-5231, Fax: 508-831-5491,

E-mail: massoud@wpi.edu. *Application contact:* Dr. Kaveh Pahlavan, Graduate Coordinator, 508-831-5231, Fax: 508-831-5491, E-mail: kaveh@wpi.edu.
Website: http://www.wpi.edu/academics/ece.

Wright State University, School of Graduate Studies, College of Engineering and Computer Science, Programs in Engineering, Program in Electrical Engineering, Dayton, OH 45435. Offers MSE. Part-time and evening/weekend programs available. *Degree requirements:* For master's, thesis or course option alternative. *Entrance requirements:* Additional exam requirements/recommendations for international students: Required—TOEFL. *Faculty research:* Robotics, circuit design, power electronics, image processing, communication systems.

Yale University, Graduate School of Arts and Sciences, School of Engineering and Applied Science, Department of Electrical Engineering, New Haven, CT 06520. Offers MS, PhD. Terminal master's awarded for partial completion of doctoral program. *Degree requirements:* For doctorate, thesis/dissertation, exam. *Entrance requirements:* For master's and doctorate, GRE General Test. Additional exam requirements/recommendations for international students: Required—TOEFL. *Faculty research:* Signal processing, control, and communications; digital systems and computer engineering; microelectronics and photonics; nanotechnology; computers, sensors, and networking.

Youngstown State University, Graduate School, College of Science, Technology, Engineering and Mathematics, Department of Electrical and Computer Engineering, Youngstown, OH 44555-0001. Offers computer engineering (MSE); electrical engineering (MSE). Part-time and evening/weekend programs available. *Degree requirements:* For master's, thesis optional. *Entrance requirements:* For master's, minimum GPA of 2.75 in field. Additional exam requirements/recommendations for international students: Required—TOEFL. *Faculty research:* Computer-aided design, power systems, electromagnetic energy conversion, sensors, control systems.

DUKE UNIVERSITY
Department of Electrical and Computer Engineering

Duke
DEPARTMENT OF
Electrical & Computer
Engineering

Programs of Study

Graduate study in the Department of Electrical and Computer Engineering (ECE) is intended to prepare students for leadership roles in academia, industry, and government that require creative technical problem-solving skills. The Department offers both Ph.D. and M.S. degree programs, with opportunities for study in a broad spectrum of areas within the disciplines of electrical and computer engineering. Research and course offerings in the Department are organized into four areas of specialization: computer engineering; information physics; microelectronics, photonics, and nanotechnology; and signal and information processing. Interdisciplinary programs are also available that connect the above programs with those in other engineering departments and computer science, the natural sciences, and the Medical School. Students in the Department may also be involved in research conducted in one of the Duke centers, e.g., the Fitzpatrick Institute for Photonics or the Center for Metamaterials and Intregrated Plasmonics. Under a reciprocal agreement with neighboring universities, a student may elect to enroll in some courses offered at the University of North Carolina at Chapel Hill and North Carolina State University in Raleigh. Since an important criterion for admitting new students is the match between student and faculty research interests, prospective students are encouraged to indicate in which Departmental specialization areas they are interested when applying.

Research Facilities

The ECE department currently occupies approximately 47,000 square feet in two buildings: the Fitzpatrick Center for Interdisciplinary Engineering, Medicine and Applied Sciences (FCIEMAS) and Hudson Hall. CIEMAS houses cross-disciplinary activities involving the Pratt School and its partners in the fields of bioengineering, photonics, microsystems integration, sensing and simulation, and materials science and materials engineering. This comprehensive facility provides extensive fabrication and test laboratories, Departmental offices, teaching labs, and other lab support spaces as well as direct access to a café. In addition, the Shared Materials Instrumentation Facility (SMiF), a state-of-the-art clean room for nanotechnology research, is housed on its main floor. Hudson Hall is the oldest of the buildings in the engineering complex. It was built in 1948 when the Engineering School moved to Duke's West Campus and was known as Old Red. An annex was built onto the back of the building in 1972, and in 1992, the building was expanded again and renamed Hudson Hall to honor Fitzgerald S. (Jerry) Hudson E'46. Hudson Hall is home to all four departments in the Pratt School of Engineering, as well as the school's laboratories, computing facilities, offices, and classrooms.

Financial Aid

Financial support is available for the majority of Ph.D. students. Graduate fellowships for the first two semesters of study provide a stipend, registration fees, and full tuition. Beyond this initial period, most students receive research assistantships funded by faculty research grants, which, together with financial aid, cover their full registration fees, tuition, and stipend until completion of the Ph.D. degree.

Cost of Study

For the 2015–16 academic year, tuition for Ph.D. and master's students is $47,590. The Graduate School estimates the cost of room, board, local transportation, and personal and miscellaneous costs to be approximately $2,012/month in 2015–16.

Living and Housing Costs

Duke has a limited number of residential apartment facilities available to graduate students through an application process. These furnished apartments are available for continuous occupancy throughout the calendar year. Academic-year rates in central campus apartments begin at approximately $8,222 per person. There are also a wide variety of options for off-campus housing near campus and in the greater Durham area.

Student Group

In the 2015–16 academic year a total of 251 students are enrolled, of whom 168 are doctoral students and 83 are master's students.

Location

Located in the rolling central Piedmont area of North Carolina, the Duke University campus is widely regarded as one of the most beautiful in the nation. The four-season climate is mild, but winter skiing is available in the North Carolina mountains a few hours' drive to the west, and ocean recreation is a similar distance away to the east. Duke is readily accessible by Interstates 85 and 40 and from Raleigh-Durham International Airport, which is about a 20-minute drive from the campus via Interstate 40 and the Durham expressway.

The University and The Department

Trinity College, founded in 1859, was selected by James B. Duke as the major recipient of a 1924 endowment that enabled a university to be organized around the college and to be named for Washington B. Duke, the family patriarch. A department of engineering was established at Trinity College in 1910, and the Department of Electrical Engineering was formed in 1920. Its name changed to the Department of Electrical and Computer Engineering in 1996. Duke University remains a privately supported university, with more than 14,000 students in degree programs.

Applying

Admission to the Department is based on a review of previous education and experience, the applicant's statement of intent, letters of evaluation, standardized test scores (GRE and TOEFL), and grade point average. The application deadline for spring admission (Ph.D. only) is October 15. December 8 is the priority deadline for submission of Ph.D. applications for admission and financial award for the fall semester. January 31 is the priority deadline for submission of all M.S. applications for admission.

Correspondence and Information

Andrew D. Hilton
Assistant Professor of the Practice and Managing Director of Graduate
  Studies
Department of Electrical and Computer Engineering
Pratt School of Engineering, Box 90291
Duke University
Durham, North Carolina 27708-0291
Phone: 919-660-5245
E-mail: dgs@ee.duke.edu
Website: http://www.ee.duke.edu

THE FACULTY AND THEIR RESEARCH

John A. Board, Bass Fellow and Associate Professor of ECE and Computer Science; D.Phil., Oxford. High performance scientific computing and simulation, novel computer architectures, cluster computing and parallel processing, ubiquitous computing.

David J. Brady, Bass Fellow and Michael J. Fitzpatrick Professor; Ph.D., Caltech. Computational optical sensor systems, hyperspectral microscopy, Raman spectroscopy for tissue chemometrics, optical coherence sensors and infrared spectral filters.

Martin A. Brooke, Associate Professor; Ph.D., USC. Integrated analog CMOS circuit design, integrated nanoscale systems, mixed signal VLSI design, sensing and sensor systems, optical imaging and communications, analog and power electronics, electronic circuit assembly and testing.

April S. Brown, John Cocke Professor; D.Sc., Cornell. Nanomaterial manufacturing and characterization, sensing and sensor systems, nanoscale/microscale computing systems, integrated nanoscale systems.

Robert Calderbank, Charles S. Snyder Professor of Computer Science and Professor of ECE and Math; Ph.D., Caltech. Computer engineering, computer architecture, information theory.

Lawrence Carin, Duke Vice Provost for Research and Professor of ECE; Ph.D., Maryland, College Park, Homeland security, sensing and sensor systems, signal processing, land mine detection.

Krishnendu Chakrabarty, William H. Younger Professor and Executive Director of Graduate Studies; Ph.D., Michigan. Computer engineering, nanoscale/microscale computing systems, self-assembled computer architecture, micro-electronic mechanical machines, failure analysis, integrated nanoscale systems, microsystems.

Leslie M. Collins, Professor; Ph.D., Michigan. Sensing and sensor systems, homeland security, land mine detection, neural prosthesis, geophysics, signal processing.

Steven A. Cummer, Professor; Ph.D., Stanford. Geophysics, photonics, atmospheric science, metamaterials, electromagnetics.

Duke University

Chris Dwyer, Associate Professor; Ph.D., North Carolina at Chapel Hill. Self-assembled computer architecture, nanoscale/microscale computing systems, nanomaterial manufacturing and characterization, computer engineering, biological computing, computer architecture, nanoscience, materials.

Richard B. Fair, Lord-Chandran Professor; Ph.D., Duke. Computer engineering, sensing and sensor systems, electronic devices, integrated nanoscale systems, medical diagnostics, microsystems, semiconductors.

Aaron D. Franklin, Associate Professor; Ph.D., Purdue. Low-dimensional nanoelectronics, carbon nanotube (CNT) transistors, device scaling, transport studies, advanced integration approaches.

Michael E. Gehm, Associate Professor; Ph.D., Duke. Computational sensor systems, spectroscopy, spectral imaging, computational mass spectrometry, adaptive sensors, mmW and THz imaging, rapid prototyping of optical components, general optical physics.

Joel A. Greenberg, Assistant Research Professor; Ph.D., Duke. Atomic, molecular, and optical physics; nonlinear dynamics and complex systems.

Jeffrey T. Glass, Professor and Hogg Family Director, Engineering Management and Entrepreneurship; Ph.D., Virginia. Micro-electronic mechanical machines, engineering management, entrepreneurship, social entrepreneurship, sensing and sensor systems, materials.

Michael R. Gustafson, Associate Professor of the Practice; Ph.D., Duke. Engineering education, electronic circuit assembly and testing, electronic devices.

Kris Hauser, Associate Professor; Ph.D., Stanford. Robot motion planning and control, semiautonomous robots, integrating perception and planning, automated vehicle collision avoidance, robotic manipulation, robot-assisted medicine, legged locomotion.

Andrew D. Hilton, Assistant Professor of the Practice and Co-Director of Graduate Studies; Ph.D., Pennsylvania. Processor micro-architecture, latency tolerance, energy efficient computation, architectural simulation and sampling methodologies, architectural support for security.

Lisa G. Huettel, Professor of the Practice, Associate Chair, and Director of Undergraduate Studies; Ph.D., Duke. Sensing and sensor systems, engineering education, signal processing, distributed systems.

William T. Joines, Professor; Ph.D., Duke. Photonics, electromagnetics, electromagnetic field and wave interactions with materials and structures.

Nan M. Jokerst, J. A. Jones Professor; Ph.D., USC. Photonics, sensing and sensor systems, nanomaterial manufacturing and characterization, semiconductors, integrated nanoscale systems, microsystems.

Tom Katsouleas, Dean and Professor; Ph.D., Physics, UCLA. Use of plasmas as novel particle accelerators and light sources.

Jungsang Kim, Professor; Ph.D., Stanford. Photonics, micro-electronic mechanical machines, sensing and sensor systems, semiconductors, quantum information, integrated nanoscale systems.

George D. Konidaris, Assistant Professor of Computer Science and Electrical and Computer Engineering; Ph.D., UMass-Amherst. Reinforcement learning, mobile manipulation, intelligent robotics, effective learning, planning for control in unstructured environments.

Jeffrey L. Krolik, Professor; Ph.D., Toronto (Canada). Sensing and sensor systems, signal processing, acoustics, medical imaging, homeland security, electromagnetics, antennas.

Benjamin C. Lee, Nortel Networks Assistant Professor; Ph.D., Harvard. Scalable technologies, power-efficient computer architectures, high-performance applications.

Xuejun Liao, Assistant Research Professor; Ph.D., Xidian University, Xi'an (China). Pattern recognition and machine learning, bioinformatics, signal processing.

Qing H. Liu, Professor; Ph.D., Illinois at Urbana-Champaign. Electromagnetics, antennas, medical imaging, photonics, acoustics, computational electromagnetics.

Daniel L. Marks, Associate Research Professor; Ph.D., Illinois at Urbana-Champaign. Imaging and spectroscopy.

Hisham Z. Massoud, Professor; Ph.D., Stanford. Nanomaterial manufacturing and characterization, nanoscale/microscale computing systems, computer engineering, engineering education, electronic devices, manufacturing, semiconductors, microsystems.

Maiken H. Mikkelsen, Assistant Professor; Ph.D., California, Santa Barbara. Nanophysics, experimental condensed matter physics, spintronics, nanophotonics, and quantum information science.

James Morizio, Assistant Research Professor; Ph.D., Duke. Computer engineering, nanoscale/microscale computing systems, biological computing, mixed signal VLSI design, integrated analog CMOS circuit design.

Loren W. Nolte, Professor; Ph.D., Michigan. Sensing and sensor systems, medical imaging, signal processing.

Douglas P. Nowacek, Repass-Rodgers University Associate Professor of Conservation Technology and Associate Professor of ECE; Ph.D., MIT/Woods Hole Oceanographic Institution. Acoustics, micro-electronic mechanical machines.

Willie J. Padilla, Professor; Ph.D., California, San Diego. Experimental condensed matter physics, infrared, optical and magneto-optical properties of novel materials, fourier transform, terahertz time domain spectroscopy.

Miroslav Pajic, Assistant Professor; Ph.D., Pennsylvania. Design and analysis of cyber-physical systems, real-time and embedded systems, distributed/networked control systems, high-confidence medical device systems.

Henry D. Pfister, Associate Professor; Ph.D., California, San Diego. Information theory, channel coding, and iterative information processing with applications in wireless communications, data storage, and signal processing.

Galen Reeves, Assistant Professor of ECE and Statistical Science; Ph.D., Berkeley. Signal processing, statistics, information theory, machine learning, compressive sensing.

Guillermo Sapiro, Edmund T. Pratt, Jr. School Professor; D.Sc., Technion, Haifa (Israel). Image and video processing, computer graphics, computational vision, biomedical imaging, cryotomography of viruses.

David R. Smith, William Bevan Professor; Ph.D., California, San Diego. Photonics, metamaterials, electromagnetic, plasmonics.

Daniel J. Sorin, Associate Professor; Ph.D., Wisconsin–Madison. Computer engineering, computer architecture, fault tolerance, reliability.

Adrienne D. Stiff-Roberts, Associate Professor; Ph.D., Michigan. Nanomaterial manufacturing and characterization, semiconductor photonic devices, photonics, nanoscience.

Kishor S. Trivedi; Hudson Professor of ECE and Professor of Computer Science; Ph.D., Illinois at Urbana-Champaign. Computer engineering, failure analysis, fault tolerance, reliability, computer architecture.

Yaroslav A. Urzhumov, Assistant Research Professor; Ph.D., Texas at Austin. Numerical simulation of metamaterials and plasmonic nanosystems.

Gary A. Ybarra, Professor of the Practice; Ph.D., North Carolina State. Engineering education, K–12 education in science and mathematics, medical imaging.

ECE Student, Duke Pratt School of Engineering.

Hudson Hall, Duke Pratt School of Engineering.

Section 10
Energy and Power Engineering

This section contains a directory of institutions offering graduate work in energy and power engineering. Additional information about programs listed in the directory may be obtained by writing directly to the dean of a graduate school or chair of a department at the address given in the directory.

For programs offering related work, see also in this book *Computer Science and Information Technology, Engineering and Applied Sciences, Industrial Engineering,* and *Mechanical Engineering and Mechanics.* In another guide in this series:

Graduate Programs in the Physical Sciences, Mathematics, Agricultural Sciences, the Environment & Natural Resources
See *Physics* and *Mathematical Sciences*

CONTENTS

Program Directories

Energy and Power Engineering

Appalachian State University, Cratis D. Williams Graduate School, Department of Technology, Boone, NC 28608. Offers appropriate technology (MS); renewable energy engineering (MS). Part-time programs available. *Degree requirements:* For master's, comprehensive exam, thesis optional. *Entrance requirements:* For master's, GRE General Test, 3 letters of recommendation. Additional exam requirements/recommendations for international students: Required—TOEFL (minimum score 550 paper-based; 79 iBT), IELTS (minimum score 6.5). Electronic applications accepted. *Faculty research:* Wind power, biofuels, green construction, solar energy production.

Arizona State University at the Tempe campus, Ira A. Fulton Schools of Engineering, School for Engineering of Matter, Transport and Energy, Tempe, AZ 85281. Offers aerospace engineering (MS, PhD); chemical engineering (MS, PhD); materials science and engineering (MS, PhD); mechanical engineering (MS, PhD); solar energy engineering and commercialization (PSM). Part-time and evening/weekend programs available. Postbaccalaureate distance learning degree programs offered (minimal on-campus study). Terminal master's awarded for partial completion of doctoral program. *Degree requirements:* For master's, thesis and oral defense (MS); applied project or comprehensive exam (MSE); interactive Program of Study (iPOS) submitted before completing 50 percent of required credit hours; for doctorate, comprehensive exam, thesis/dissertation, interactive Program of Study (iPOS) submitted before completing 50 percent of required credit hours. *Entrance requirements:* For master's, GRE, minimum GPA of 3.0 or equivalent in last 2 years of work leading to bachelor's degree; for doctorate, GRE, minimum GPA of 3.0 in last 2 years of work leading to bachelor's degree. Additional exam requirements/recommendations for international students: Required—TOEFL, IELTS, or PTE. Electronic applications accepted. *Expenses:* Contact institution. *Faculty research:* Electronic materials and packaging, materials for energy (batteries), adaptive/intelligent materials and structures, multiscale fluid mechanics, membranes, therapeutics and bioseparations, flexible structures, nanostructured materials, and micro/nano transport.

Carnegie Mellon University, Carnegie Institute of Technology, Department of Civil and Environmental Engineering, Pittsburgh, PA 15213. Offers advanced infrastructure systems (MS, PhD); advanced infrastructure systems technology development and application (MS); air quality engineering and science (MS); civil and environmental engineering (MS, PhD); civil and environmental engineering/engineering and public policy (PhD); civil engineering (MS, PhD); computational mechanics (MS, PhD); computational modeling and monitoring for resilient structural and material systems (MS); energy infrastructure systems (MS); environmental engineering (MS, PhD); environmental management and science (MS, PhD); IT-based sustainable global infrastructure and construction management (MS); sustainability and green design (MS); water quality engineering and science (MS). Part-time programs available. *Faculty:* 21 full-time (5 women), 12 part-time/adjunct (3 women). *Students:* 229 full-time (99 women), 31 part-time (11 women); includes 18 minority (4 Black or African American, non-Hispanic/Latino; 13 Asian, non-Hispanic/Latino; 1 Hispanic/Latino), 193 international. Average age 26. 590 applicants, 68% accepted, 124 enrolled. In 2014, 85 master's, 11 doctorates awarded. Terminal master's awarded for partial completion of doctoral program. *Degree requirements:* For master's, thesis optional; for doctorate, comprehensive exam, thesis/dissertation, two-part qualifying exam, public defense of dissertation. *Entrance requirements:* For master's, GRE General Test, BS in engineering, science or mathematics; for doctorate, GRE General Test, BS or MS in engineering, science or mathematics. Additional exam requirements/recommendations for international students: Required—TOEFL (minimum score 84 iBT) or IELTS. *Application deadline:* For fall admission, 1/5 priority date for domestic and international students; for spring admission, 9/15 priority date for domestic and international students. Application fee: $65. Electronic applications accepted. *Financial support:* In 2014–15, 169 students received support. Fellowships with full and partial tuition reimbursements available, research assistantships with full and partial tuition reimbursements available, scholarships/grants, tuition waivers (full and partial), unspecified assistantships, and service assistantships available. Financial award application deadline: 1/5. *Faculty research:* Advanced infrastructure systems; environmental engineering, sustainability, and science; mechanics, materials, and computing. *Total annual research expenditures:* $4.9 million. *Unit head:* Dr. David A. Dzombak, Head, 412-268-2941, Fax: 412-268-7813, E-mail: dzombak@cmu.edu. *Application contact:* Melissa L. Brown, Director of Graduate Admissions & Recruiting, 412-268-8762, Fax: 412-268-7813, E-mail: mlb2@andrew.cmu.edu.
Website: http://www.cmu.edu/cee/.

Carnegie Mellon University, Mellon College of Science, Department of Chemistry, Pittsburgh, PA 15213-3891. Offers atmospheric chemistry (PhD); bioinorganic chemistry (PhD); bioorganic chemistry and chemical biology (PhD); biophysical chemistry (PhD); catalysis (PhD); green and environmental chemistry (PhD); materials and nanoscience (PhD); renewable energy (PhD); sensors, probes, and imaging (PhD); spectroscopy and single molecule analysis (PhD); theoretical and computational chemistry (PhD). Part-time programs available. Terminal master's awarded for partial completion of doctoral program. *Degree requirements:* For doctorate, thesis/dissertation, departmental qualifying and oral exams, teaching experience. *Entrance requirements:* For doctorate, GRE General Test, GRE Subject Test. Additional exam requirements/recommendations for international students: Required—TOEFL. Electronic applications accepted. *Faculty research:* Physical and theoretical chemistry, chemical synthesis, biophysical/bioinorganic chemistry.

Cornell University, Graduate School, Graduate Fields of Agriculture and Life Sciences and Graduate Fields of Engineering, Field of Biological and Environmental Engineering, Ithaca, NY 14853-0001. Offers bioenergy and integrated energy systems (M Eng, MPS, MS, PhD); biological engineering (M Eng, MPS, MS, PhD); bioprocess engineering (M Eng, MPS, MS, PhD); ecohydrology (M Eng, MPS, MS, PhD); environmental engineering (M Eng, MPS, MS, PhD); environmental management (MPS); food engineering (M Eng, MPS, MS, PhD); industrial biotechnology (M Eng, MPS, MS, PhD); nanobiotechnology (M Eng, MPS, MS, PhD); sustainable systems (M Eng, MPS, MS, PhD); synthetic biology (MS); syntheticbiology (M Eng, MPS, PhD). Terminal master's awarded for partial completion of doctoral program. *Degree requirements:* For master's, thesis (MS); for doctorate, comprehensive exam, thesis/dissertation. *Entrance requirements:* For master's, letters of recommendation (3 for MS, 2 for M Eng and MPS); for doctorate, GRE General Test, 3 letters of recommendation. Additional exam requirements/recommendations for international students: Required—TOEFL (minimum score 550 paper-based; 77 iBT). Electronic applications accepted. *Faculty research:* Biological and food engineering, environmental, soil and water engineering, international agricultural engineering, structures and controlled environments, machine systems and energy.

Florida State University, The Graduate School, FAMU-FSU College of Engineering, Department of Mechanical Engineering, Tallahassee, FL 32310-6046. Offers mechanical engineering (MS, PhD); sustainable energy (MS). Part-time programs available. Terminal master's awarded for partial completion of doctoral program. *Degree requirements:* For master's, thesis optional, 30 credit hours (24 coursework, 6 research); for doctorate, thesis/dissertation, 45 credit hours (21 coursework, 24 research). *Entrance requirements:* For master's and doctorate, GRE General Test (minimum scores: Verbal 150, Quantitative 155), minimum GPA of 3.0, official transcripts, resume, personal statement, 3 letters of recommendation. Additional exam requirements/recommendations for international students: Required—TOEFL (minimum score 550 paper-based; 80 iBT), IELTS (minimum score 6.5), Michigan English Language Assessment Battery (minimum score 77). Electronic applications accepted. *Expenses:* Tuition, state resident: part-time $403.51 per credit hour. Tuition, nonresident: part-time $1004.85 per credit hour. *Required fees:* $75.81 per credit hour. One-time fee: $20 part-time. Tuition and fees vary according to campus/location. *Faculty research:* Aero-propulsion, superconductivity, smart materials, nanomaterials, intelligent robotic systems, robotic locomotion, sustainable energy.

Georgia Southern University, Jack N. Averitt College of Graduate Studies, Allen E. Paulson College of Engineering and Information Technology, Department of Mechanical Engineering, Program in Engineering/Energy Science, Statesboro, GA 30460. Offers MSAE. Part-time programs available. *Students:* 4 full-time (0 women), 3 part-time (0 women); includes 1 minority (Black or African American, non-Hispanic/Latino), 4 international. Average age 27. 8 applicants, 75% accepted, 2 enrolled. In 2014, 3 master's awarded. *Degree requirements:* For master's, thesis optional. *Entrance requirements:* Additional exam requirements/recommendations for international students: Required—TOEFL (minimum score 80 iBT). *Application deadline:* For fall admission, 3/1 priority date for domestic students; for spring admission, 11/1 for domestic students. Application fee: $50. *Expenses:* Tuition, state resident: full-time $7236; part-time $277 per semester hour. Tuition, nonresident: full-time $27,118; part-time $1105 per semester hour. *Required fees:* $2092. *Financial support:* In 2014–15, 4 students received support. Unspecified assistantships available. *Faculty research:* Renewable energy and engines, biomechatronics, digital surface imaging, smart materials, nanocomposite material science. *Unit head:* Dr. Frank Goforth, Chair, 912-478-7583, Fax: 912-478-1455, E-mail: fgoforth@georgiasouthern.edu.

Instituto Tecnologico de Santo Domingo, Graduate School, Area of Basic And Environmental Sciences, Santo Domingo, Dominican Republic. Offers environmental science (M En S), including environmental education, environmental management, marine resources, natural resources management; mathematics (MS, PhD); renewable energy technology (MS, Certificate).

Kansas State University, Graduate School, College of Engineering, Department of Electrical and Computer Engineering, Manhattan, KS 66506. Offers electrical engineering (MS), including bioengineering, communication systems, design of computer systems, electrical engineering, energy and power systems, integrated circuits and devices, real time embedded systems, renewable energy, signal processing. Part-time and evening/weekend programs available. Postbaccalaureate distance learning degree programs offered (no on-campus study). *Faculty:* 21 full-time (4 women), 1 (woman) part-time/adjunct. *Students:* 38 full-time (8 women), 45 part-time (6 women); includes 13 minority (4 Black or African American, non-Hispanic/Latino; 8 Asian, non-Hispanic/Latino; 1 Hispanic/Latino), 37 international. Average age 28. 126 applicants, 29% accepted, 14 enrolled. In 2014, 22 master's, 5 doctorates awarded. *Degree requirements:* For master's, thesis or alternative, final exam; for doctorate, thesis/dissertation, final exam, preliminary exams. *Entrance requirements:* For master's, GRE General Test, bachelor's degree in electrical engineering or computer science, minimum GPA of 3.0; for doctorate, GRE General Test. Additional exam requirements/recommendations for international students: Required—TOEFL (minimum score 600 paper-based; 85 iBT). *Application deadline:* For fall admission, 1/1 priority date for domestic and international students; for spring admission, 8/1 priority date for domestic and international students. Applications are processed on a rolling basis. Application fee: $50 ($75 for international students). Electronic applications accepted. *Financial support:* In 2014–15, 40 students received support, including 22 research assistantships with tuition reimbursements available (averaging $12,100 per year), 18 teaching assistantships with full tuition reimbursements available (averaging $12,220 per year); career-related internships or fieldwork, institutionally sponsored loans, and scholarships/grants also available. Support available to part-time students. Financial award application deadline: 3/1; financial award applicants required to submit FAFSA. *Faculty research:* Energy systems and renewable energy, computer systems and real time embedded systems, communication systems and signal processing, integrated circuits and devices, bioengineering. *Total annual research expenditures:* $1.3 million. *Unit head:* Dr. Don Gruenbacher, Head, 785-532-5600, Fax: 785-532-1188, E-mail: grue@k-state.edu. *Application contact:* Dr. Andrew Rys, Graduate Program Director, 785-532-4665, Fax: 785-532-1188, E-mail: andrys@k-state.edu.
Website: http://www.ece.k-state.edu/.

Lehigh University, P.C. Rossin College of Engineering and Applied Science, Program in Energy Systems Engineering, Bethlehem, PA 18015. Offers M Eng. Part-time programs available. *Faculty:* 1 (woman) full-time. *Students:* 14 full-time (4 women), 1 (woman) part-time; includes 1 minority (Asian, non-Hispanic/Latino), 6 international. Average age 25. 35 applicants, 89% accepted, 6 enrolled. In 2014, 15 master's awarded. *Entrance requirements:* For master's, GRE. Additional exam requirements/recommendations for international students: Required—TOEFL (minimum score 79 iBT). *Application deadline:* For fall admission, 5/15 for domestic and international students. Applications are processed on a rolling basis. Application fee: $75. Electronic applications accepted. *Financial support:* In 2014–15, 10 students received support. Scholarships/grants available. Financial award application deadline: 1/15. *Unit head:* Martha Dodge, Director, 610-758-3529, E-mail: mds482@lehigh.edu. *Application contact:* Eileen Kaplan, Coordinator, 610-758-3650, E-mail: inesei@lehigh.edu.
Website: http://www.lehigh.edu/esei.

New Jersey Institute of Technology, Newark College of Engineering, Newark, NJ 07102. Offers biomedical engineering (MS, PhD); chemical engineering (MS, PhD); computer engineering (MS, PhD); electrical engineering (MS, PhD); engineering management (MS); healthcare systems management (MS); industrial engineering (MS, PhD); Internet engineering (MS); manufacturing engineering (MS); mechanical engineering (MS, PhD); occupational safety and health engineering (MS); pharmaceutical bioprocessing (MS); pharmaceutical engineering (MS); pharmaceutical systems management (MS); power and energy systems (MS); telecommunications (MS); transportation (MS, PhD). Part-time and evening/weekend programs available. Terminal master's awarded for partial completion of doctoral program. *Degree requirements:* For master's, thesis optional; for doctorate, thesis/dissertation. *Entrance requirements:* For master's, GRE General Test; for doctorate, GRE General Test, minimum graduate GPA of 3.5. Additional exam requirements/recommendations for international students: Required—TOEFL (minimum score 550 paper-based; 79 iBT). Electronic applications accepted.

New York Institute of Technology, School of Engineering and Computing Sciences, Department of Energy Management, Old Westbury, NY 11568-8000. Offers energy management (MS); energy technology (Advanced Certificate); environmental management (Advanced Certificate); facilities management (Advanced Certificate); infrastructure security management (Advanced Certificate). Part-time and evening/weekend programs available. Postbaccalaureate distance learning degree programs offered (minimal on-campus study). *Degree requirements:* For master's, comprehensive exam, thesis or alternative. *Entrance requirements:* For master's, minimum QPA of 2.85. Additional exam requirements/recommendations for international students: Required—TOEFL (minimum score 550 paper-based; 79 iBT), IELTS (minimum score 6). Electronic applications accepted.

North Carolina Agricultural and Technical State University, School of Graduate Studies, College of Engineering, Department of Electrical and Computer Engineering, Greensboro, NC 27411. Offers electrical engineering (MSEE, PhD), including communications and signal processing, computer engineering, electronic and optical materials and devices, power systems and control. Part-time programs available. *Degree requirements:* For master's, project, thesis defense; for doctorate, thesis/dissertation. *Entrance requirements:* For master's, GRE General Test, GRE Subject Test, minimum GPA of 2.8; for doctorate, GRE General Test, minimum GPA of 3.0. *Faculty research:* Semiconductor compounds, VLSI design, image processing, optical systems and devices, fault-tolerant computing.

Northeastern University, College of Engineering, Boston, MA 02115-5096. Offers bioengineering (PhD); chemical engineering (MS, PhD); civil engineering (MS, PhD); computer engineering (PhD); computer systems engineering (MS); electrical and computer engineering (MS); electrical and engineering leadership (MS); electrical engineering (PhD); energy systems (MS); engineering leadership (Certificate); engineering management (MRTP); industrial engineering (MS, PhD); information assurance (PhD); information systems (MS); interdisciplinary (PhD); mechanical engineering (MS, PhD); operations research (MS); telecommunication systems management (MS). Part-time programs available. *Expenses:* Contact institution.

Saginaw Valley State University, College of Science, Engineering, and Technology, University Center, MI 48710. Offers energy and materials (MS). Part-time and evening/weekend programs available. *Faculty:* 2 full-time (0 women), 3 part-time/adjunct (1 woman). *Students:* 2 full-time (0 women), 5 part-time (1 woman); includes 1 minority (Black or African American, non-Hispanic/Latino), 3 international. Average age 30. 12 applicants, 58% accepted, 4 enrolled. In 2014, 1 master's awarded. *Degree requirements:* For master's, field project or thesis work. *Entrance requirements:* For master's, minimum GPA of 3.0. Additional exam requirements/recommendations for international students: Required—TOEFL (minimum score 550 paper-based; 79 iBT). *Application deadline:* For fall admission, 7/15 for international students; for winter admission, 11/15 for international students; for spring admission, 4/15 for international students. Applications are processed on a rolling basis. Application fee: $30 ($90 for international students). Electronic applications accepted. *Expenses:* Tuition, state resident: full-time $8957; part-time $497.60 per credit hour. Tuition, nonresident: full-time $17,081; part-time $948.95 per credit hour. *Required fees:* $263; $14.60 per credit hour. Tuition and fees vary according to degree level. *Financial support:* Federal Work-Study and scholarships/grants available. Support available to part-time students. Financial award application deadline: 4/1; financial award applicants required to submit FAFSA. *Unit head:* Dr. Robert Tuttle, Program Coordinator, 989-964-4144, Fax: 989-964-2717. *Application contact:* Jenna Briggs, Director, Graduate and International Admissions, 989-964-6096, Fax: 989-964-2788, E-mail: gradadm@svsu.edu.
Website: http://www.svsu.edu/collegeofscienceengineeringtechnology/.

San Francisco State University, Division of Graduate Studies, College of Science and Engineering, School of Engineering, San Francisco, CA 94132-1722. Offers energy systems (MS); structural/earthquake engineering (MS). Part-time programs available. *Application deadline:* Applications are processed on a rolling basis. Electronic applications accepted. *Expenses:* Tuition, state resident: full-time $6738. Tuition, nonresident: full-time $17,898; part-time $372 per credit hour. *Required fees:* $498 per semester. *Unit head:* Dr. Wenshen Pong, Director, 415-338-7738, Fax: 415-338-0525, E-mail: wspong@sfsu.edu. *Application contact:* Dr. Hamid Shahnasser, Graduate Coordinator, 415-338-2124, Fax: 415-338-0525, E-mail: hamid@sfsu.edu.
Website: http://engineering.sfsu.edu/.

Santa Clara University, School of Engineering, Santa Clara, CA 95053. Offers analog circuit design (Certificate); applied mathematics (MS); ASIC design and test (Certificate); bioengineering (MS); civil engineering (MS); computer science and engineering (MS, PhD); controls (Certificate); digital signal processing (Certificate); dynamics (Certificate); electrical engineering (MS, PhD); engineering (Engineer); engineering management (MS); fundamentals of electrical engineering (Certificate); information assurance (Certificate); materials engineering (Certificate); mechanical design analysis (Certificate); mechanical engineering (MS, PhD); mechatronics systems engineering (Certificate); microwave and antennas (Certificate); networking (Certificate); renewable energy (Certificate); software engineering (Certificate); sustainable energy (MS); technology jump-start (Certificate); thermofluids (Certificate). Part-time and evening/weekend programs available. *Faculty:* 59 full-time (23 women), 80 part-time/adjunct (14 women). *Students:* 584 full-time (239 women), 353 part-time (102 women); includes 224 minority (7 Black or African American, non-Hispanic/Latino; 144 Asian, non-Hispanic/Latino; 50 Hispanic/Latino; 2 Native Hawaiian or other Pacific Islander, non-Hispanic/Latino; 21 Two or more races, non-Hispanic/Latino), 548 international. Average age 27. 1,248 applicants, 51% accepted, 375 enrolled. In 2014, 283 master's, 5 doctorates, 1 other advanced degree awarded. *Degree requirements:* For master's, thesis (for some programs); for doctorate, thesis/dissertation; for other advanced degree, thesis. *Entrance requirements:* For master's, GRE, transcript; for doctorate, GRE, master's degree or equivalent; for other advanced degree, master's degree, published paper. Additional exam requirements/recommendations for international students: Required—TOEFL (minimum score 550 paper-based; 79 iBT). *Application deadline:* For fall admission, 8/1 for domestic students, 7/15 for international students; for winter admission, 10/28 for domestic students, 9/23 for international students; for spring admission, 2/25 for domestic students, 1/21 for international students. Applications are processed on a rolling basis. Application fee: $60. Electronic applications accepted. *Expenses:* Expenses: Contact institution. *Financial support:* In 2014–15, 94 students received support. Fellowships with full and partial tuition reimbursements available, research assistantships with full and partial tuition reimbursements available, teaching assistantships with full tuition reimbursements available, career-related internships or fieldwork, Federal Work-Study, institutionally sponsored loans, and scholarships/grants available. Support available to part-time students. Financial award application deadline: 3/2; financial award applicants required to submit FAFSA. *Faculty research:* Video encoding, nanostructures, robotics, microfluidics, water resources. *Total annual research expenditures:* $1.6 million. *Unit head:* Dr. Alex Zecevic, Associate Dean for Graduate Studies, 408-554-2394, E-mail: azecevic@scu.edu. *Application contact:* Stacey Tinker, Director of Enrollment Management, 408-554-4748, Fax: 408-554-4323, E-mail: stinker@scu.edu.
Website: http://www.scu.edu/engineering/graduate/.

Stanford University, School of Engineering, Department of Civil and Environmental Engineering, Stanford, CA 94305-9991. Offers atmosphere and energy (MS, PhD); construction (MS), including construction engineering and management, design-construction integration, sustainable design and construction; environmental engineering and science (MS, PhD, Eng); environmental fluid mechanics and hydrology (PhD); geomechanics (MS); structural engineering (MS). Terminal master's awarded for partial completion of doctoral program. *Degree requirements:* For doctorate, thesis/dissertation, qualifying exam; for Eng, thesis. *Entrance requirements:* For master's, doctorate, and Eng, GRE General Test. Additional exam requirements/recommendations for international students: Required—TOEFL. Electronic applications accepted. *Expenses: Tuition:* Full-time $44,184; part-time $982 per credit hour. *Required fees:* $,191.

Syracuse University, L. C. Smith College of Engineering and Computer Science, Program in Energy Systems Engineering, Syracuse, NY 13244. Offers MS. Part-time programs available. *Students:* 8 full-time (1 woman), 8 international. Average age 23. 33 applicants, 64% accepted, 5 enrolled. *Entrance requirements:* For master's, GRE, BS. *Application deadline:* For fall admission, 7/1 priority date for domestic students, 6/1 priority date for international students; for spring admission, 11/15 priority date for domestic students, 10/15 priority date for international students. Applications are processed on a rolling basis. Application fee: $75. Electronic applications accepted. *Expenses: Tuition:* Part-time $1341 per credit. *Required fees:* $1341 per credit. *Unit head:* Dr. H. Ezzat Khalifa, Program Contact, 315-443-1286, E-mail: hekhalif@syr.edu. *Application contact:* Kathleen Joyce, Assistant Dean, 315-443-2219, E-mail: topgrads@syr.edu.
Website: http://eng-cs.syr.edu/.

Texas A&M University–Kingsville, College of Graduate Studies, College of Engineering, Program in Sustainable Energy Systems Engineering, Kingsville, TX 78363. Offers PhD. *Degree requirements:* For doctorate, variable foreign language requirement, comprehensive exam, thesis/dissertation (for some programs). *Entrance requirements:* For doctorate, GRE, MAT, GMAT, bachelor's or master's degree in engineering or science, curriculum vitae, official transcripts, statement of purpose, three letters of recommendation. Additional exam requirements/recommendations for international students: Required—TOEFL (minimum score 550 paper-based; 79 iBT). *Application deadline:* For fall admission, 8/15 for domestic students, 6/1 for international students; for spring admission, 12/15 for domestic students, 10/1 for international students; for summer admission, 5/15 for domestic students, 4/1 for international students. Applications are processed on a rolling basis. Application fee: $35 ($50 for international students). Electronic applications accepted. *Financial support:* Career-related internships or fieldwork, Federal Work-Study, institutionally sponsored loans, scholarships/grants, health care benefits, tuition waivers (full and partial), and unspecified assistantships available. Support available to part-time students. Financial award application deadline: 5/1; financial award applicants required to submit FAFSA. *Unit head:* Dr. Stephan Nix, Dean, 361-593-4857, E-mail: stephan.nix@tamuk.edu. *Application contact:* Dr. Mohamed Abdelrahman, Dean, College of Graduate Studies, 361-593-2809, E-mail: mohamed.abdelrahman@tamuk.edu.

Texas Tech University, Graduate School, Interdisciplinary Programs, Lubbock, TX 79409-1030. Offers arid land studies (MS); biotechnology (MS); heritage management (MS); interdisciplinary studies (MA, MS); museum science (MA); wind science and engineering (PhD); JD/MS. Part-time programs available. *Faculty:* 4 full-time (3 women). *Students:* 112 full-time (70 women), 122 part-time (70 women); includes 71 minority (20 Black or African American, non-Hispanic/Latino; 1 American Indian or Alaska Native, non-Hispanic/Latino; 4 Asian, non-Hispanic/Latino; 40 Hispanic/Latino; 6 Two or more races, non-Hispanic/Latino), 43 international. Average age 30. 172 applicants, 65% accepted, 70 enrolled. In 2014, 56 master's, 4 doctorates awarded. Terminal master's awarded for partial completion of doctoral program. *Degree requirements:* For master's, comprehensive exam (for some programs), thesis (for some programs); for doctorate, comprehensive exam, thesis/dissertation (for some programs). *Entrance requirements:* Additional exam requirements/recommendations for international students: Required—TOEFL (minimum score 550 paper-based; 79 iBT). *Application deadline:* For fall admission, 6/1 priority date for domestic students, 1/15 priority date for international students; for spring admission, 9/1 priority date for domestic students, 6/15 priority date for international students. Applications are processed on a rolling basis. Application fee: $60. Electronic applications accepted. *Expenses:* Tuition, state resident: full-time $6310; part-time $262.92 per credit hour. Tuition, nonresident: full-time $14,998; part-time $624.92 per credit hour. *Required fees:* $2701; $36.50 per credit. $912.50 per semester. Tuition and fees vary according to course load. *Financial support:* In 2014–15, 201 students received support, including 196 fellowships (averaging $2,655 per year), 5 research assistantships (averaging $12,144 per year), 2 teaching assistantships (averaging $7,785 per year); scholarships/grants and unspecified assistantships also available. Financial award application deadline: 4/15; financial award applicants required to submit FAFSA. *Total annual research expenditures:* $241,842. *Unit head:* Dr. Mark Sheridan, Vice Provost for Graduate and Postdoctoral Affairs/Dean of the Graduate School, 806-742-2787, Fax: 806-742-1746, E-mail: mark.sheridan@ttu.edu. *Application contact:* Shannon Samson, Coordinator of Graduate School Recruitment, 806-834-5201, Fax: 806-742-1746, E-mail: gradschool@ttu.edu.
Website: http://www.depts.ttu.edu/gradschool/about/INDS/index.php.

Universidad Autonoma de Guadalajara, Graduate Programs, Guadalajara, Mexico. Offers administrative law and justice (LL M); advertising and corporate communications (MA); architecture (M Arch); business (MBA); computational science (MCC); education (Ed M, Ed D); English-Spanish translation (MA); entrepreneurship and management (MBA); integrated management of digital animation (MA); international business (MIB); international corporate law (LL M); internet technologies (MS); manufacturing systems (MMS); occupational health (MS); philosophy (MA, PhD); power electronics (MS); quality systems (MQS); renewable energy (MS); social evaluation of projects (MBA); strategic market research (MBA); tax law (MA); teaching mathematics (MA).

University of Alberta, Faculty of Graduate Studies and Research, Department of Electrical and Computer Engineering, Edmonton, AB T6G 2E1, Canada. Offers communications (M Eng, M Sc, PhD); computer engineering (M Eng, M Sc, PhD); electromagnetics (M Eng, M Sc, PhD); nanotechnology and microdevices (M Eng, M Sc, PhD); power/power electronics (M Eng, M Sc, PhD); systems (M Eng, M Sc, PhD). Terminal master's awarded for partial completion of doctoral program. *Degree requirements:* For master's, thesis; for doctorate, thesis/dissertation. *Entrance requirements:* Additional exam requirements/recommendations for international students: Required—TOEFL. Electronic applications accepted. *Faculty research:* Controls, communications, microelectronics, electromagnetics.

University of Calgary, Faculty of Graduate Studies, Schulich School of Engineering, Department of Chemical and Petroleum Engineering, Calgary, AB T2N 1N4, Canada. Offers chemical engineering (M Eng, M Sc, PhD); energy and environment engineering (M Eng, M Sc, PhD); energy and environmental systems (M Eng, M Sc, PhD); environmental engineering (M Eng, M Sc, PhD); petroleum engineering (M Eng, M Sc, PhD); reservoir characterization (M Eng, M Sc). Part-time programs available. *Degree requirements:* For master's, thesis (for some programs); for doctorate, comprehensive exam, thesis/dissertation, candidacy exam. *Entrance requirements:* For master's, minimum GPA of 3.0 or equivalent; for doctorate, minimum GPA of 3.5 or equivalent. Additional exam requirements/recommendations for international students: Required—TOEFL (minimum score 550 paper-based; 80 iBT), IELTS (minimum score 7). Electronic applications accepted. *Faculty research:* Environmental engineering, biomedical engineering modeling, simulation and control, petroleum recovery and reservoir engineering, phase equilibria and transport properties.

University of Calgary, Faculty of Graduate Studies, Schulich School of Engineering, Department of Civil Engineering, Calgary, AB T2N 1N4, Canada. Offers avalanche mechanics (M Sc, PhD); civil engineering (M Eng, M Sc, PhD); energy and environment engineering (M Eng, M Sc, PhD); environmental engineering (M Eng, M Sc, PhD); geotechnical engineering (M Eng, M Sc, PhD); materials science (M Eng, M Sc, PhD); project management (M Eng, M Sc, PhD); structures and solid mechanics (M Eng, M Sc, PhD); transportation engineering (M Eng, M Sc, PhD); water resources (M Eng, M Sc, PhD). Part-time programs available. *Degree requirements:* For master's, thesis; for doctorate, thesis/dissertation, written and oral candidacy exam. *Entrance requirements:* For master's, minimum GPA of 3.0; for doctorate, minimum GPA of 3.5. Additional exam requirements/recommendations for international students: Required—TOEFL (minimum score 580 paper-based; 93 iBT), IELTS (minimum score 7). Electronic applications accepted. *Faculty research:* Geotechnical engineering, energy and environment, transportation, project management, structures and solid mechanics.

University of Colorado Colorado Springs, College of Engineering and Applied Science, Program in General Engineering, Colorado Springs, CO 80933-7150. Offers energy engineering (ME); engineering management (ME); information assurance (ME); software engineering (ME); space operations (ME); systems engineering (ME). Part-time and evening/weekend programs available. Postbaccalaureate distance learning degree programs offered (minimal on-campus study). *Faculty:* 2 full-time (0 women), 8 part-time/adjunct (2 women). *Students:* 15 full-time (2 women), 159 part-time (30 women); includes 29 minority (3 Black or African American, non-Hispanic/Latino; 1 American Indian or Alaska Native, non-Hispanic/Latino; 10 Asian, non-Hispanic/Latino; 12 Hispanic/Latino; 3 Two or more races, non-Hispanic/Latino), 63 international. Average age 36. 113 applicants, 65% accepted, 39 enrolled. In 2014, 29 master's, 6 doctorates awarded. *Degree requirements:* For master's, thesis, portfolio, or project; for doctorate, comprehensive exam, thesis/dissertation. *Entrance requirements:* For master's, GRE (minimum score of 148 new grading scale on quantitative portion if GPA is less than 3.0); for doctorate, GRE (minimum score of 148 new grading scale on the quantitative portion if the applicant has not graduated from a program of recognized standing), minimum GPA of 3.3 in the bachelor or master degree program attempted. Additional exam requirements/recommendations for international students: Required—TOEFL (minimum score 80 iBT), IELTS (minimum score 6). *Application deadline:* For fall admission, 6/1 for domestic and international students; for spring admission, 11/1 for domestic and international students; for summer admission, 4/15 for domestic and international students. Application fee: $60 ($100 for international students). Electronic applications accepted. *Expenses:* Expenses: Contact institution. *Financial support:* In 2014–15, 10 students received support, including 2 fellowships (averaging $6,000 per year), 16 research assistantships (averaging $11,600 per year); teaching assistantships, Federal Work-Study, and scholarships/grants also available. Support available to part-time students. Financial award application deadline: 3/1; financial award applicants required to submit FAFSA. *Total annual research expenditures:* $91,458. *Unit head:* Dr. Ramaswami Dandapani, Dean, 719-255-3543, Fax: 719-255-3542, E-mail: rdan@cas.uccs.edu. *Application contact:* Dawn House, Coordinator, 719-255-3246, E-mail: dhouse@uccs.edu.

University of Illinois at Urbana–Champaign, Graduate College, College of Engineering, Department of Nuclear, Plasma, and Radiological Engineering, Urbana, IL 61801. Offers energy systems (M Eng); nuclear, plasma, and radiological engineering (MS, PhD). *Students:* 72 (5 women). Terminal master's awarded for partial completion of doctoral program. *Application deadline:* For fall admission, 1/15 for domestic and international students. Application fee: $70 ($90 for international students). *Unit head:* James F. Stubbins, Professor/Department Head, 217-333-2295, Fax: 217-333-2906, E-mail: jstubbin@illinois.edu. *Application contact:* Becky J. Meline, Admissions and Records Officer, 217-333-3598, Fax: 217-333-2906, E-mail: bmeline@illinois.edu.
Website: http://npre.illinois.edu/.

The University of Iowa, Graduate College, College of Engineering, Department of Mechanical Engineering, Iowa City, IA 52242-1316. Offers energy systems (MS, PhD); engineering design (MS, PhD); fluid dynamics (MS, PhD); materials and manufacturing (MS, PhD); wind energy (MS, PhD). *Faculty:* 14 full-time (1 woman). *Students:* 50 full-time (5 women); includes 1 minority (Black or African American, non-Hispanic/Latino), 34 international. Average age 28. 68 applicants, 19% accepted, 4 enrolled. In 2014, 9 master's, 7 doctorates awarded. Terminal master's awarded for partial completion of doctoral program. *Degree requirements:* For master's, oral exam or thesis; for doctorate, comprehensive exam, thesis/dissertation. *Entrance requirements:* For master's and doctorate, GRE. Additional exam requirements/recommendations for international students: Required—TOEFL (minimum score 600 paper-based; 100 iBT). *Application deadline:* For fall admission, 1/15 for domestic and international students; for spring admission, 9/1 for domestic and international students; for summer admission, 1/15 for domestic and international students. Application fee: $60 ($100 for international students). Electronic applications accepted. *Financial support:* In 2014–15, 3 fellowships with partial tuition reimbursements (averaging $19,933 per year), 36 research assistantships with full tuition reimbursements (averaging $20,823 per year), 21 teaching assistantships with full tuition reimbursements (averaging $6,457 per year) were awarded; traineeships and unspecified assistantships also available. Financial award applicants required to submit FAFSA. *Faculty research:* Computer simulation methodology, biomechanics, metal casting, dynamics, laser processing, system reliability, ship hydrodynamics, solid mechanics, fluid dynamics, energy, human modeling and nano technology. *Total annual research expenditures:* $9.8 million. *Unit head:* Dr. Andrew Kusiak, Departmental Executive Officer, 319-335-5934, Fax: 319-335-5669, E-mail: andrew-kusiak@uiowa.edu. *Application contact:* Andrea Flaherty, Academic Program Specialist, 319-335-5939, Fax: 319-335-5669, E-mail: mech_eng@engineering.uiowa.edu.
Website: http://www.engineering.uiowa.edu/mie.

University of Massachusetts Lowell, Francis College of Engineering, Program in Energy Engineering, Lowell, MA 01854. Offers MS Eng, D Eng, PhD. *Degree requirements:* For master's, thesis optional. *Entrance requirements:* For master's, GRE General Test. Additional exam requirements/recommendations for international students: Required—TOEFL.

University of Memphis, Graduate School, Herff College of Engineering, Department of Mechanical Engineering, Memphis, TN 38152. Offers industrial engineering (MS); power systems (MS). Part-time programs available. *Faculty:* 5 full-time (0 women). *Students:* 8 full-time (1 woman), 4 part-time (0 women); includes 4 minority (3 Black or African American, non-Hispanic/Latino; 1 Asian, non-Hispanic/Latino), 5 international. Average age 25. 14 applicants, 79% accepted, 4 enrolled. In 2014, 7 master's awarded. Terminal master's awarded for partial completion of doctoral program. *Degree requirements:* For master's, comprehensive exam, thesis; for doctorate, comprehensive exam, thesis/dissertation. *Entrance requirements:* For master's, GRE General Test, BS in mechanical engineering, minimum undergraduate GPA of 3.0. *Application deadline:* For fall admission, 8/1 for domestic students; for spring admission, 12/1 for domestic students. Application fee: $35 ($60 for international students). *Financial support:* In 2014–15, 6 students received support. Fellowships with full tuition reimbursements available, research assistantships with full tuition reimbursements available, teaching assistantships with full tuition reimbursements available, career-related internships or fieldwork, Federal Work-Study, scholarships/grants, and unspecified assistantships available. Financial award application deadline: 2/15; financial award applicants required to submit FAFSA. *Faculty research:* Computational fluid dynamics, computational mechanics, integrated design, nondestructive testing, operations research. *Unit head:* Dr. John I. Hochstein, Chair, 901-678-2173, Fax: 901-678-5459, E-mail: jhochste@memphis.edu. *Application contact:* Dr. Teong Tan, Graduate Studies Coordinator, 901-678-3264, Fax: 901-678-5459, E-mail: ttan@memphis.edu.
Website: http://www.me.memphis.edu/.

University of Michigan, College of Engineering, Interpro Programs in Engineering, Ann Arbor, MI 48109. Offers automotive engineering (M Eng); design science (PhD); energy systems engineering (MS); financial engineering (MS); global automotive and manufacturing engineering (M Eng); manufacturing engineering (M Eng, D Eng); pharmaceutical engineering (M Eng); robotics and autonomous vehicles (M Eng); MBA/M Eng; MSE/MS. Part-time programs available. Postbaccalaureate distance learning degree programs offered (no on-campus study). *Students:* 187 full-time (46 women), 250 part-time (40 women). 364 applicants, 2% accepted, 3 enrolled. In 2014, 171 master's, 1 doctorate awarded. Terminal master's awarded for partial completion of doctoral program. *Degree requirements:* For master's, capstone project; for doctorate, thesis/dissertation. *Entrance requirements:* For master's, GRE; for doctorate, GRE, 2 years of work experience. Additional exam requirements/recommendations for international students: Required—TOEFL (minimum score 560 paper-based). *Application deadline:* Applications are processed on a rolling basis. Electronic applications accepted. *Financial support:* Fellowships, research assistantships with full tuition reimbursements, teaching assistantships with full tuition reimbursements, career-related internships or fieldwork, scholarships/grants, and unspecified assistantships available. Financial award application deadline: 2/15; financial award applicants required to submit FAFSA. *Faculty research:* Automotive engineering, design science, energy systems engineering, engineering sustainable systems, financial engineering, global automotive and manufacturing engineering, integrated microsystems, manufacturing engineering, pharmaceutical engineering, robotics and autonomous vehicles. *Total annual research expenditures:* $263,643. *Unit head:* Prof. Panos Papalambros, Director, 734-647-8401, Fax: 734-647-0079, E-mail: pyp@umich.edu. *Application contact:* Patti Mackmiller, Program Manager, 734-764-3071, Fax: 734-647-2243, E-mail: pmackmil@umich.edu.
Website: http://www.isd.engin.umich.edu.

University of Michigan–Dearborn, College of Engineering and Computer Science, MSE Program in Energy Systems Engineering, Dearborn, MI 48128. Offers MSE. Part-time and evening/weekend programs available. *Faculty:* 1 full-time (0 women). *Students:* 1 full-time (0 women), 7 part-time (0 women), 2 international. 12 applicants, 33% accepted, 1 enrolled. In 2014, 5 master's awarded. *Entrance requirements:* Additional exam requirements/recommendations for international students: Required—TOEFL (minimum score 560 paper-based; 84 iBT), IELTS (minimum score 6.5). *Application deadline:* For fall admission, 8/1 for domestic students, 5/1 for international students; for winter admission, 12/1 for domestic students, 9/1 for international students; for spring admission, 4/1 for domestic students, 1/1 for international students. Applications are processed on a rolling basis. Application fee: $60. Electronic applications accepted. *Expenses:* Tuition, state resident: full-time $12,202; part-time $707 per credit hour. Tuition, nonresident: full-time $20,980; part-time $1209 per credit hour. *Required fees:* $798; $302 per term. Tuition and fees vary according to course level, course load, degree level and program. *Financial support:* In 2014–15, 1 student received support. Scholarships/grants and unspecified assistantships available. Support available to part-time students. Financial award application deadline: 4/1; financial award applicants required to submit FAFSA. *Unit head:* Dr. Pankaj K. Mallick, Director/Professor, 313-593-5119, Fax: 313-593-5386, E-mail: pkm@umich.edu. *Application contact:* Sherry Boyd, Intermediate Administrative Assistant, 313-593-5582, Fax: 313-593-5386, E-mail: idpgrad@umd.umich.edu.
Website: http://umdearborn.edu/cecs/IDP/mse_ese/index.php.

The University of North Carolina at Charlotte, The William States Lee College of Engineering, Department of Engineering Technology and Construction Management, Charlotte, NC 28223-0001. Offers applied energy and electromechanical systems (MS); construction and facilities management (MS); fire protection and administration (MS). *Faculty:* 26 full-time (5 women). *Students:* 30 full-time (6 women), 15 part-time (1 woman); includes 7 minority (3 Black or African American, non-Hispanic/Latino; 1 American Indian or Alaska Native, non-Hispanic/Latino; 1 Asian, non-Hispanic/Latino; 1 Hispanic/Latino; 1 Two or more races, non-Hispanic/Latino), 13 international. Average age 27. 69 applicants, 78% accepted, 27 enrolled. In 2014, 8 master's awarded. *Degree requirements:* For master's, comprehensive exam, thesis optional. *Entrance requirements:* Additional exam requirements/recommendations for international students: Required—TOEFL (minimum score 557 paper-based; 83 iBT). *Application deadline:* For fall admission, 5/1 for domestic and international students; for spring admission, 10/1 for domestic and international students. Application fee: $75. Electronic applications accepted. *Expenses:* Tuition, state resident: full-time $4008. Tuition, nonresident: full-time $16,295. *Required fees:* $2755. Tuition and fees vary according to course load and program. *Financial support:* In 2014–15, 24 students received support, including 22 research assistantships (averaging $6,665 per year), 2 teaching assistantships (averaging $14,250 per year); career-related internships or fieldwork, institutionally sponsored loans, scholarships/grants, and unspecified assistantships also available. Support available to part-time students. Financial award application deadline: 4/1; financial award applicants required to submit FAFSA. *Total annual research expenditures:* $1.1 million. *Unit head:* Dr. Cheng Liu, Chair Emeritus, 704-687-2474, E-mail: liu@uncc.edu. *Application contact:* Kathy B. Giddings, Director of Graduate Admissions, 704-687-5503, Fax: 704-687-1668, E-mail: gradadm@uncc.edu.
Website: http://et.uncc.edu/.

The University of North Carolina at Charlotte, The William States Lee College of Engineering, Department of Systems Engineering and Engineering Management, Charlotte, NC 28223-0001. Offers energy analytics (Graduate Certificate); engineering management (MSEM); engineering science (MS); infrastructure and environmental systems (PhD); Lean Six Sigma (Graduate Certificate); logistics and supply chains (Graduate Certificate); systems analytics (Graduate Certificate). Part-time and evening/weekend programs available. Postbaccalaureate distance learning degree programs offered. *Faculty:* 7 full-time (2 women), 1 part-time/adjunct (0 women). *Students:* 33 full-time (8 women), 47 part-time (14 women); includes 15 minority (9 Black or African American, non-Hispanic/Latino; 3 Asian, non-Hispanic/Latino; 3 Hispanic/Latino), 33 international. Average age 29. 146 applicants, 51% accepted, 42 enrolled. In 2014, 19 master's awarded. *Degree requirements:* For master's, thesis or alternative, project. *Entrance requirements:* For master's, GRE or GMAT, letters of recommendation. Additional exam requirements/recommendations for international students: Required—

TOEFL (minimum score 557 paper-based; 83 iBT). *Application deadline:* For fall admission, 5/1 priority date for domestic students, 5/1 for international students; for spring admission, 10/1 priority date for domestic students, 10/1 for international students. Application fee: $75. Electronic applications accepted. *Expenses:* Tuition, state resident: full-time $4008. Tuition, nonresident: full-time $16,295. *Required fees:* $2755. Tuition and fees vary according to course load and program. *Financial support:* In 2014–15, 5 students received support, including 3 research assistantships (averaging $5,317 per year), 2 teaching assistantships (averaging $3,125 per year); career-related internships or fieldwork, institutionally sponsored loans, scholarships/grants, and unspecified assistantships also available. Support available to part-time students. Financial award application deadline: 4/1; financial award applicants required to submit FAFSA. *Faculty research:* Sustainable material and renewable technology; thermal analysis; large scale optimization; project risk management; supply chains; leans systems; global product innovation; quality and reliability analysis and management; productivity and project management; business forecasting, market analyses and feasibility studies. *Total annual research expenditures:* $106,777. *Unit head:* Dr. Robert E. Johnson, Dean, 704-687-8242, Fax: 704-687-2352, E-mail: robejohn@uncc.edu. *Application contact:* Kathy B. Giddings, Director of Graduate Admissions, 704-687-5503, Fax: 704-687-1668, E-mail: gradadm@uncc.edu.
Website: http://seem.uncc.edu/.

University of North Texas, Robert B. Toulouse School of Graduate Studies, Denton, TX 76203-5459. Offers accounting (MS); applied anthropology (MA, MS); applied behavior analysis (Certificate); applied geography (MA); applied technology and performance improvement (M Ed, MS); art education (MA); art history (MA); art museum education (Certificate); arts leadership (Certificate); audiology (Au D); behavior analysis (MS); behavioral science (PhD); biochemistry and molecular biology (MS); biology (MA, MS); biomedical engineering (MS); business analysis (MS); chemistry (MS); clinical health psychology (PhD); communication studies (MA, MS); computer engineering (MS); computer science (MS); counseling (M Ed, MS), including clinical mental health counseling (MS), college and university counseling, elementary school counseling, secondary school counseling; creative writing (MA); criminal justice (MS); curriculum and instruction (M Ed); decision sciences (MBA); design (MA, MFA), including fashion design (MFA), innovation studies, interior design (MFA), early childhood studies (MS); economics (MS); educational leadership (M Ed, Ed D); educational psychology (MS, PhD), including family studies (MS), gifted and talented (MS), human development (MS), learning and cognition (MS), research, measurement and evaluation (MS); electrical engineering (MS); emergency management (MPA); engineering technology (MS); English (MA); English as a second language (MA); environmental science (MS); finance (MBA, MS); financial management (MPA); French (MA); health services management (MBA); higher education (M Ed, Ed D); history (MA, MS); hospitality management (MS); human resources management (MPA); information science (MS); information systems (PhD); information technologies (MBA); interdisciplinary studies (MA, MS); international studies (MA); international sustainable tourism (MS); jazz studies (MM); journalism (MA, MJ, Graduate Certificate), including interactive and virtual digital communication (Graduate Certificate), narrative journalism (Graduate Certificate), public relations (Graduate Certificate); kinesiology (MS); linguistics (MA); local government management (MPA); logistics (PhD); logistics and supply chain management (MBA); long-term care, senior housing, and aging services (MA); management (PhD); marketing (MBA); mathematics (MA, MS); mechanical and energy engineering (MS, PhD); music (MA), including ethnomusicology, music theory, musicology, performance; music composition (PhD); music education (MM Ed, PhD); nonprofit management (MPA); operations and supply chain management (MBA); performance (MM, DMA); philosophy (MA); political science (MA); professional and technical communication (MA); radio, television and film (MA, MFA); rehabilitation counseling (Certificate); sociology (MA); Spanish (MA); special education (M Ed); speech-language pathology (MA); strategic management (MBA); studio art (MFA); teaching (M Ed); MBA/MS. Part-time and evening/weekend programs available. Postbaccalaureate distance learning degree programs offered. *Faculty:* 651 full-time (215 women), 233 part-time/adjunct (139 women). *Students:* 3,040 full-time (1,598 women), 3,401 part-time (2,097 women); includes 1,740 minority (533 Black or African American, non-Hispanic/Latino; 15 American Indian or Alaska Native, non-Hispanic/Latino; 286 Asian, non-Hispanic/Latino; 746 Hispanic/Latino; 3 Native Hawaiian or other Pacific Islander, non-Hispanic/Latino; 157 Two or more races, non-Hispanic/Latino), 1,145 international. Terminal master's awarded for partial completion of doctoral program. *Degree requirements:* For master's, variable foreign language requirement, comprehensive exam (for some programs), thesis (for some programs); for doctorate, variable foreign language requirement, comprehensive exam (for some programs), thesis/dissertation; for other advanced degree, variable foreign language requirement, comprehensive exam (for some programs). *Entrance requirements:* For master's and doctorate, GRE, GMAT. Additional exam requirements/recommendations for international students: Required—TOEFL (minimum score 550 paper-based; 79 iBT). *Application deadline:* For fall admission, 7/15 for domestic students, 3/15 for international students; for spring admission, 11/15 for domestic students, 9/15 for international students; for summer admission, 5/1 for domestic students. Applications are processed on a rolling basis. Application fee: $60. Electronic applications accepted. *Expenses:* Tuition, state resident: full-time $5450; part-time $3633 per year. Tuition, nonresident: full-time $11,966; part-time $7977 per year. *Required fees:* $1301; $398 per credit hour. $685 per semester. Tuition and fees vary according to program and reciprocity agreements. *Financial support:* Fellowships with partial tuition reimbursements, research assistantships with partial tuition reimbursements, teaching assistantships, career-related internships or fieldwork, Federal Work-Study, institutionally sponsored loans, scholarships/grants, health care benefits, and library assistantships available. Support available to part-time students. Financial award applicants required to submit FAFSA. *Unit head:* Mark Wardell, Dean, 940-565-2383, E-mail: mark.wardell@unt.edu. *Application contact:* Toulouse School of Graduate Studies, 940-565-2383, Fax: 940-565-2141, E-mail: gradsch@unt.edu.
Website: http://tsgs.unt.edu/.

University of Rochester, Hajim School of Engineering and Applied Sciences, Program in Alternative Energy, Rochester, NY 14627. Offers MS. *Students:* 6 full-time (1 woman), 1 part-time (0 women); includes 1 minority (Hispanic/Latino), 5 international. 19 applicants, 84% accepted, 3 enrolled. In 2014, 8 master's awarded. *Entrance requirements:* For master's, GRE. Additional exam requirements/recommendations for international students: Required—TOEFL. *Application deadline:* For fall admission, 1/15 for domestic students. Application fee: $60. Electronic applications accepted. *Expenses:* Tuition: Full-time $46,150; part-time $1442 per credit hour. *Required fees:* $504. *Faculty research:* Solar cells, fuel dells, biofuels, nuclear fusion, nanotechnology. *Unit head:* Matthew Yates, Chairman, 585-273-2335. *Application contact:* Gina Eagan, Coordinator, 585-275-4913.
Website: http://www.che.rochester.edu/graduate/index.html.

The University of Tennessee, Graduate School, College of Engineering, Bredesen Center for Interdisciplinary Research and Graduate Education, Knoxville, TN 37966. Offers energy science and engineering (PhD). *Students:* 43 full-time (12 women); includes 4 minority (1 Black or African American, non-Hispanic/Latino; 1 Asian, non-Hispanic/Latino; 2 Two or more races, non-Hispanic/Latino), 9 international. Average age 27. 73 applicants, 42% accepted, 29 enrolled. In 2014, 2 doctorates awarded.

Degree requirements: For doctorate, comprehensive exam, thesis/dissertation, qualifying examination. *Entrance requirements:* For doctorate, GRE General Test, research interest letter, resume/curriculum vitae, 3 letters of recommendation. Additional exam requirements/recommendations for international students: Required—TOEFL (minimum score 550 paper-based). *Application deadline:* For fall admission, 1/31 for domestic and international students. Applications are processed on a rolling basis. Application fee: $35. Electronic applications accepted. *Financial support:* In 2014–15, 43 students received support, including 43 fellowships with full tuition reimbursements available (averaging $28,000 per year); health care benefits also available. Financial award application deadline: 1/31. *Faculty research:* Biomass processing for biofuels, cellulosic ethanol, and lignin repurposing; applied photosynthesis; nuclear fusion, reactor design and modeling; design and distribution of wind power; development of photovoltaic materials; fuel cell and battery design for energy conversion and storage; development of next generation SMART grid systems and novel grid management tools; climate change modeling, environmental, and planetary sciences as they relate to energy usage. *Unit head:* Dr. Lee Riedinger, Director, 865-974-7999, Fax: 865-974-9482, E-mail: lrieding@utk.edu. *Application contact:* 865-974-7999, Fax: 865-974-9482, E-mail: cire@utk.edu.
Website: http://bredesencenter.utk.edu/.

The University of Tennessee at Chattanooga, Department of Engineering Management, Chattanooga, TN 37403. Offers engineering management (MS); fundamentals of engineering management (Graduate Certificate); leadership and ethics (Graduate Certificate); logistics and supply chain management (Graduate Certificate); nuclear engineering (Graduate Certificate); power system protection (Graduate Certificate); power systems management (Graduate Certificate); project and value management (Graduate Certificate); quality management (Graduate Certificate); sustainable electric energy (Graduate Certificate). Postbaccalaureate distance learning degree programs offered (no on-campus study). *Faculty:* 5 full-time (1 woman). *Students:* 14 full-time (5 women), 67 part-time (14 women); includes 24 minority (13 Black or African American, non-Hispanic/Latino; 6 Asian, non-Hispanic/Latino; 4 Hispanic/Latino; 1 Two or more races, non-Hispanic/Latino), 6 international. Average age 31. 31 applicants, 45% accepted, 10 enrolled. In 2014, 31 master's, 17 other advanced degrees awarded. *Degree requirements:* For master's, thesis. *Entrance requirements:* For master's, GRE General Test, letters of recommendation; minimum undergraduate GPA of 2.5 overall or 3.0 in senior year. Additional exam requirements/recommendations for international students: Required—TOEFL (minimum score 550 paper-based; 79 iBT), IELTS (minimum score 6). *Application deadline:* For fall admission, 6/13 priority date for domestic students, 6/1 for international students; for spring admission, 10/15 priority date for domestic students, 10/1 for international students. Applications are processed on a rolling basis. Application fee: $30 ($35 for international students). Electronic applications accepted. *Expenses:* Tuition, state resident: full-time $7708; part-time $428 per credit hour. Tuition, nonresident: full-time $23,826; part-time $1323 per credit hour. *Required fees:* $1708; $252 per credit hour. *Financial support:* In 2014–15, 5 research assistantships (averaging $6,528 per year), 3 teaching assistantships (averaging $6,781 per year) were awarded; career-related internships or fieldwork, scholarships/grants, and unspecified assistantships also available. Support available to part-time students. Financial award applicants required to submit FAFSA. *Faculty research:* Plant layout design, lean manufacturing, Six Sigma, value management, product development. *Unit head:* Dr. Neslihan Alp, Department Head, 423-425-4032, Fax: 423-425-5229, E-mail: neslihan-alp@utc.edu. *Application contact:* Dr. J. Randy Walker, Interim Dean of Graduate Studies, 423-425-4478, Fax: 423-425-5223, E-mail: randy-walker@utc.edu.
Website: http://www.utc.edu/Departments/engrcs/engm/index.php.

Washington State University, Voiland College of Engineering and Architecture, School of Electrical Engineering and Computer Science, Pullman, WA 99164-2752. Offers computer engineering (MS); computer science (MS); electrical engineering (MS); electrical engineering and computer science (PhD); electrical power engineering (MS). MS programs in computer engineering, computer science and electrical engineering also offered at Tri-Cities campus; MS in electrical power engineering offered at the Global (online) campus. Part-time programs available. *Faculty:* 51 full-time (4 women), 4 part-time/adjunct (0 women). *Students:* 122 full-time (29 women), 49 part-time (12 women); includes 13 minority (1 Black or African American, non-Hispanic/Latino; 8 Asian, non-Hispanic/Latino; 3 Hispanic/Latino; 1 Native Hawaiian or other Pacific Islander, non-Hispanic/Latino), 108 international. Average age 28. 451 applicants, 16% accepted, 44 enrolled. In 2014, 24 master's, 11 doctorates awarded. *Degree requirements:* For master's, comprehensive exam (for some programs), thesis or alternative; for doctorate, comprehensive exam, thesis/dissertation. *Entrance requirements:* For master's and doctorate, GRE General Test, minimum GPA of 3.0, 3 letters of recommendation, statement of purpose, transcripts. Additional exam requirements/recommendations for international students: Required—TOEFL (minimum score 580 paper-based). *Application deadline:* For fall admission, 1/10 priority date for domestic students, 3/1 priority date for international students; for spring admission, 7/1 priority date for domestic and international students. Applications are processed on a rolling basis. Application fee: $75. *Expenses:* Tuition, state resident: full-time $11,768. Tuition, nonresident: full-time $25,200. *Required fees:* $960. Tuition and fees vary according to program. *Financial support:* In 2014–15, 74 students received support, including 5 fellowships (averaging $2,500 per year), 72 research assistantships with full and partial tuition reimbursements available (averaging $12,843 per year), 24 teaching assistantships with full and partial tuition reimbursements available (averaging $13,981 per year); career-related internships or fieldwork, Federal Work-Study, institutionally sponsored loans, tuition waivers (partial), and teaching associateships also available. Financial award application deadline: 4/1; financial award applicants required to submit FAFSA. *Faculty research:* Software engineering, networks, distributed computing, computer engineering, electrophysics, artificial intelligence, bioinformatics and computational biology, computer graphics, communications, control systems, signal processing, power systems, microelectronics, algorithms. *Total annual research expenditures:* $7.3 million. *Unit head:* Dr. Behrooz Shirazi, Chair/Director, 509-335-8148, Fax: 509-335-3818. *Application contact:* Sidra S. Gleason, Graduate Student Advisor, 509-335-6636, Fax: 509-335-1949, E-mail: gradsch@wsu.edu.
Website: http://www.eecs.wsu.edu/.

Wayne State University, College of Engineering, Alternative Energy Technology Program, Detroit, MI 48202. Offers MS, Graduate Certificate. *Students:* 6 part-time (0 women); includes 2 minority (both Asian, non-Hispanic/Latino), 1 international. Average age 31. 25 applicants, 40% accepted, 2 enrolled. In 2014, 1 master's awarded. *Degree requirements:* For master's, thesis optional. *Entrance requirements:* For master's, bachelor's degree in engineering; minimum GPA of 3.0 or significant professional experience; for Graduate Certificate, bachelor's degree in engineering. Additional exam requirements/recommendations for international students: Required—TOEFL (minimum score 550 paper-based; 79 iBT), Michigan English Language Assessment Battery (minimum score 85); Recommended—IELTS (minimum score 6.5). *Application deadline:* For fall admission, 6/1 priority date for domestic students, 5/1 priority date for international students; for winter admission, 10/1 priority date for domestic students, 9/1 priority date for international students; for spring admission, 2/1 priority date for domestic students, 1/1 priority date for international students; for summer admission, 2/1 priority

date for domestic students, 1/1 priority date for international students. Applications are processed on a rolling basis. Application fee: $0. Electronic applications accepted. *Expenses:* Expenses: Contact institution. *Financial support:* Scholarships/grants available. Support available to part-time students. Financial award application deadline: 3/31; financial award applicants required to submit FAFSA. *Unit head:* Dr. Simon Ng, Professor and Program Director, 313-577-3805, E-mail: fotouhi@wayne.edu. *Application contact:* E-mail: aet@wayne.edu.
Website: http://engineering.wayne.edu/aet/.

Worcester Polytechnic Institute, Graduate Studies and Research, Programs in Interdisciplinary Studies, Worcester, MA 01609-2280. Offers bioscience administration (MS); impact engineering (MS); manufacturing engineering management (MS); power systems management (MS); social science (PhD); systems modeling (MS). Part-time and evening/weekend programs available. *Faculty:* 1 part-time/adjunct (0 women). *Students:* 2 full-time (0 women), 74 part-time (15 women); includes 18 minority (3 Black or African American, non-Hispanic/Latino; 7 Asian, non-Hispanic/Latino; 3 Hispanic/Latino; 5 Two or more races, non-Hispanic/Latino), 5 international. 37 applicants, 97% accepted, 29 enrolled. In 2014, 10 master's, 1 doctorate awarded. *Degree requirements:* For master's, thesis; for doctorate, comprehensive exam, thesis/dissertation. *Entrance requirements:* For master's and doctorate, 3 letters of recommendation. Additional exam requirements/recommendations for international students: Required—TOEFL (minimum score 563 paper-based; 84 iBT), IELTS (minimum score 7). *Application deadline:* For fall admission, 1/1 priority date for domestic students, 1/1 for international students; for spring admission, 10/1 priority date for domestic students, 10/1 for international students. Application fee: $70. *Financial support:* Institutionally sponsored loans, scholarships/grants, and unspecified assistantships available. Financial award application deadline: 1/1; financial award applicants required to submit FAFSA. *Unit head:* Dr. Fred J. Looft, Head, 508-831-5231, Fax: 508-831-5491, E-mail: fjlooft@wpi.edu. *Application contact:* Lynne Dougherty, Administrative Assistant, 508-831-5301, Fax: 508-831-5717, E-mail: grad@wpi.edu.

Nuclear Engineering

Air Force Institute of Technology, Graduate School of Engineering and Management, Department of Engineering Physics, Dayton, OH 45433-7765. Offers applied physics (MS, PhD); electro-optics (MS, PhD); materials science (PhD); nuclear engineering (MS, PhD); space physics (MS). Part-time programs available. *Degree requirements:* For master's, thesis; for doctorate, thesis/dissertation. *Entrance requirements:* For master's and doctorate, GRE General Test, minimum GPA of 3.0, U.S. citizenship. *Faculty research:* High-energy lasers, space physics, nuclear weapon effects, semiconductor physics.

Arizona State University at the Tempe campus, Ira A. Fulton Schools of Engineering, School of Electrical, Computer and Energy Engineering, Tempe, AZ 85287-5706. Offers electrical engineering (MS, MSE, PhD); nuclear power generation (Graduate Certificate). Part-time and evening/weekend programs available. Postbaccalaureate distance learning degree programs offered (minimal on-campus study). Terminal master's awarded for partial completion of doctoral program. *Degree requirements:* For master's, thesis and defense (MS); comprehensive exams (MSE); interactive Program of Study (iPOS) submitted before completing 50 percent of required credit hours; for doctorate, comprehensive exam, thesis/dissertation, interactive Program of Study (iPOS) submitted before completing 50 percent of required credit hours. *Entrance requirements:* For master's, GRE, minimum GPA of 3.0 in last 2 years of work leading to bachelor's degree, 3.5 if from non-ABET accredited school; for doctorate, GRE, master's degree with minimum GPA of 3.5 or 3.6 in last 2 years of ABET-accredited undergraduate program. Additional exam requirements/recommendations for international students: Required—TOEFL, IELTS, or PTE. Electronic applications accepted. *Expenses:* Contact institution. *Faculty research:* Power and energy systems, signal processing and communications, solid state devices and modeling, wireless communications and circuits, photovoltaics, biosignatures discovery automation, flexible electronics, nanostructures.

Colorado School of Mines, Graduate School, Department of Physics, Golden, CO 80401. Offers applied physics (MS, PhD); materials science (MS, PhD); nuclear engineering (ME, MS, PhD). Part-time programs available. *Faculty:* 35 full-time (5 women), 9 part-time/adjunct (1 woman). *Students:* 60 full-time (17 women), 12 part-time (2 women); includes 6 minority (2 Asian, non-Hispanic/Latino; 4 Hispanic/Latino), 14 international. Average age 28. 100 applicants, 22% accepted, 11 enrolled. In 2014, 10 master's, 8 doctorates awarded. *Degree requirements:* For master's, thesis (for some programs); for doctorate, comprehensive exam, thesis/dissertation. *Entrance requirements:* For master's and doctorate, GRE General Test, GRE Subject Test. Additional exam requirements/recommendations for international students: Required—TOEFL (minimum score 550 paper-based; 80 iBT). *Application deadline:* For fall admission, 12/15 priority date for domestic and international students; for spring admission, 9/1 priority date for domestic and international students. Application fee: $50 ($70 for international students). Electronic applications accepted. *Financial support:* In 2014–15, 49 students received support, including 1 fellowship with full tuition reimbursement available (averaging $21,120 per year), 35 research assistantships with full tuition reimbursements available (averaging $21,120 per year), 12 teaching assistantships with full tuition reimbursements available (averaging $21,120 per year); scholarships/grants, health care benefits, and unspecified assistantships also available. Financial award application deadline: 12/15; financial award applicants required to submit FAFSA. *Faculty research:* Light scattering, low-energy nuclear physics, high fusion plasma diagnostics, laser operations, mathematical physics. *Total annual research expenditures:* $7.6 million. *Unit head:* Dr. Jeff Squier, Head, 303-273-2385, Fax: 303-273-3919, E-mail: jsquier@mines.edu. *Application contact:* Dr. David Wood, Professor, 303-273-3853, Fax: 303-273-3919, E-mail: dwood@mines.edu.
Website: http://physics.mines.edu.

École Polytechnique de Montréal, Graduate Programs, Institute of Nuclear Engineering, Montréal, QC H3C 3A7, Canada. Offers nuclear engineering (M Eng, PhD, DESS); nuclear engineering, socio-economics of energy (M Sc A). *Degree requirements:* For master's, one foreign language, thesis; for doctorate, one foreign language, thesis/dissertation. *Entrance requirements:* For master's, minimum GPA of 2.75; for doctorate, minimum GPA of 3.0. *Faculty research:* Nuclear technology, thermohydraulics.

Georgia Institute of Technology, Graduate Studies, College of Engineering, George W. Woodruff School of Mechanical Engineering, Nuclear and Radiological Engineering and Medical Physics Programs, Atlanta, GA 30332-0001. Offers medical physics (MS); nuclear and radiological engineering (PhD); nuclear engineering (MS). Part-time programs available. Postbaccalaureate distance learning degree programs offered. *Students:* 75 full-time (14 women), 23 part-time (5 women); includes 25 minority (5 Black or African American, non-Hispanic/Latino; 7 Asian, non-Hispanic/Latino; 7 Hispanic/Latino; 6 Two or more races, non-Hispanic/Latino), 7 international. Average age 26. 153 applicants, 54% accepted, 26 enrolled. In 2014, 11 master's, 7 doctorates awarded. Terminal master's awarded for partial completion of doctoral program. *Degree requirements:* For master's, thesis optional; for doctorate, comprehensive exam, thesis/dissertation. *Entrance requirements:* For master's and doctorate, GRE General Test, minimum GPA of 3.0. Additional exam requirements/recommendations for international students: Required—TOEFL (minimum score 580 paper-based; 94 iBT). *Application deadline:* For fall admission, 2/1 priority date for domestic and international students; for spring admission, 10/1 priority date for domestic and international students; for summer admission, 2/1 for domestic and international students. Applications are processed on a rolling basis. Application fee: $75. Electronic applications accepted. *Expenses:* Tuition, state resident: full-time $12,344; part-time $515 per credit hour. Tuition, nonresident: full-time $27,600; part-time $1150 per credit hour. *Required fees:* $1196 per term. Part-time tuition and fees vary according to course load. *Financial support:* Fellowships, research assistantships with tuition reimbursements, teaching assistantships with tuition reimbursements, career-related internships or fieldwork, Federal Work-Study, institutionally sponsored loans, traineeships, tuition waivers (partial), and unspecified assistantships available. Support available to part-time students. Financial award application deadline: 5/1. *Faculty research:* Reactor physics, nuclear materials, plasma physics, radiation detection, radiological assessment. *Unit head:* Farzad Rahnema, Director, 404-894-3731, E-mail: farzad.rahnema@nre.gatech.edu. *Application contact:* Wayne Whiteman, Graduate Coordinator, 404-894-3204, E-mail: wayne.whiteman@me.gatech.edu.
Website: http://www.nre.gatech.edu.

Idaho State University, Office of Graduate Studies, College of Science and Engineering, Nuclear Engineering and Health Physics Department, Pocatello, ID 83209. Offers nuclear science and engineering (MS, PhD). Part-time programs available. *Degree requirements:* For master's, comprehensive exam (for some programs), thesis, seminar; for doctorate, comprehensive exam, thesis/dissertation, oral and written exams at the end of 1st year. *Entrance requirements:* For master's, GRE; for doctorate, master's degree in engineering, physics, geosciences, math, etc.; 3 letters of recommendation. Additional exam requirements/recommendations for international students: Required—TOEFL (minimum score 550 paper-based; 80 iBT). Electronic applications accepted.

Kansas State University, Graduate School, College of Engineering, Department of Mechanical and Nuclear Engineering, Manhattan, KS 66506. Offers mechanical engineering (MS); nuclear engineering (PhD). *Faculty:* 22 full-time (3 women). *Students:* 17 full-time (1 woman), 15 part-time (2 women); includes 6 minority (3 Asian, non-Hispanic/Latino; 3 Hispanic/Latino), 19 international. Average age 27. 66 applicants, 44% accepted, 22 enrolled. In 2014, 20 master's, 3 doctorates awarded. *Degree requirements:* For master's, thesis optional; for doctorate, comprehensive exam, thesis/dissertation. *Entrance requirements:* For master's, GRE General Test; for doctorate, GRE General Test, master's degree in mechanical engineering; minimum GPA of 3.0 overall or last 60 hours in calculus-based engineering or related program. Additional exam requirements/recommendations for international students: Required—TOEFL (minimum score 550 paper-based; 79 iBT). *Application deadline:* For fall and spring admission, 12/1 priority date for domestic and international students. Applications are processed on a rolling basis. Application fee: $50 ($75 for international students). Electronic applications accepted. *Financial support:* In 2014–15, 20 research assistantships (averaging $22,700 per year), 17 teaching assistantships with full and partial tuition reimbursements (averaging $21,000 per year) were awarded; career-related internships or fieldwork, institutionally sponsored loans, and scholarships/grants also available. Support available to part-time students. Financial award application deadline: 3/1; financial award applicants required to submit FAFSA. *Faculty research:* Radiation detection and protection, heat and mass transfer, machine design, control systems, nuclear reactor physics and engineering. *Total annual research expenditures:* $1.5 million. *Unit head:* Dr. William Dunn, Head, 785-532-5610, Fax: 785-532-7057, E-mail: dunn@k-state.edu. *Application contact:* Dr. Steve Eckels, Graduate Program Director, 785-532-5610, Fax: 785-532-7057, E-mail: eckels@k-state.edu.
Website: http://www.mne.k-state.edu/.

Massachusetts Institute of Technology, School of Engineering, Department of Nuclear Science and Engineering, Cambridge, MA 02139. Offers SM, PhD, Sc D, NE. *Faculty:* 16 full-time (3 women). *Students:* 111 full-time (22 women); includes 7 minority (1 Black or African American, non-Hispanic/Latino; 1 American Indian or Alaska Native, non-Hispanic/Latino; 3 Asian, non-Hispanic/Latino; 1 Hispanic/Latino; 1 Two or more races, non-Hispanic/Latino), 51 international. Average age 26. 150 applicants, 35% accepted, 38 enrolled. In 2014, 13 master's, 22 doctorates awarded. Terminal master's awarded for partial completion of doctoral program. *Degree requirements:* For master's and NE, thesis; for doctorate, comprehensive exam, thesis/dissertation. *Entrance requirements:* For master's, doctorate, and NE, GRE General Test. Additional exam requirements/recommendations for international students: Required—TOEFL (minimum score 577 paper-based; 90 iBT), IELTS (minimum score 7). *Application deadline:* For fall and spring admission, 12/15 for domestic and international students. Application fee: $75. Electronic applications accepted. *Expenses: Tuition:* Full-time $44,720; part-time $699 per unit. *Required fees:* $296. *Financial support:* In 2014–15, 101 students received support, including 35 fellowships (averaging $33,300 per year), 62 research assistantships (averaging $33,400 per year), 6 teaching assistantships (averaging $34,600 per year); Federal Work-Study, institutionally sponsored loans, scholarships/grants, health care benefits, and unspecified assistantships also available. Financial award application deadline: 4/15; financial award applicants required to submit FAFSA. *Faculty research:* Advanced fission reactor engineering and innovation; nuclear fuel cycle technology and economics; plasma physics and fusion engineering; advanced computation and simulation; materials in extreme environments; radiation sources, detection, and measurement; quantum engineering; nuclear systems engineering, design, management and policy. *Total annual research expenditures:* $17.7 million. *Unit head:* Prof. Richard Lester, Department Head, 617-253-7522, E-mail: nse-info@mit.edu. *Application contact:* Academic Programs Administrator, 617-253-3814, Fax: 617-258-7437.
Website: http://web.mit.edu/nse/.

McMaster University, School of Graduate Studies, Faculty of Engineering, Department of Engineering Physics, Hamilton, ON L8S 4M2, Canada. Offers engineering physics (M Eng, MA Sc, PhD); nuclear engineering (PhD). *Degree requirements:* For master's, thesis or alternative; for doctorate, comprehensive exam, thesis/dissertation. *Entrance requirements:* For master's, minimum B average in engineering, mathematics, or physical sciences. Additional exam requirements/recommendations for international students: Required—TOEFL (minimum score 550 paper-based). *Faculty research:* Non-thermal plasmas for pollution control and electrostatic precipitation, bulk and thin film luminescent materials, devices and systems for optical fiber communications, physics and applications of III-V materials and devices, defect spectroscopy in semiconductors.

Missouri University of Science and Technology, Graduate School, Department of Mining and Nuclear Engineering, Rolla, MO 65409. Offers mining engineering (MS, DE, PhD); nuclear engineering (MS, DE, PhD). *Degree requirements:* For master's, thesis optional; for doctorate, comprehensive exam. *Entrance requirements:* For master's, GRE (minimum score 600 quantitative, 3 writing); for doctorate, GRE (minimum score: quantitative 600, writing 3.5). Additional exam requirements/recommendations for international students: Required—TOEFL (minimum score 550 paper-based). *Faculty research:* Mine health and safety, nuclear radiation transport, modeling of mining operations, radiation effects, blasting.

North Carolina State University, Graduate School, College of Engineering, Department of Nuclear Engineering, Raleigh, NC 27695. Offers MNE, MS, PhD. *Degree requirements:* For master's, thesis (for some programs); for doctorate, thesis/dissertation. *Entrance requirements:* For master's, bachelor's degree in engineering or GRE; for doctorate, engineering degree or GRE. Electronic applications accepted. *Faculty research:* Computational reactor engineering, plasma applications, waste management, materials, radiation applications and measurement.

The Ohio State University, Graduate School, College of Engineering, Department of Mechanical and Aerospace Engineering, Program in Nuclear Engineering, Columbus, OH 43210. Offers MS, PhD. *Faculty:* 9. *Students:* 39 full-time (8 women); includes 1 minority (Asian, non-Hispanic/Latino), 13 international. Average age 25. In 2014, 5 master's, 5 doctorates awarded. *Degree requirements:* For master's, thesis optional; for doctorate, thesis/dissertation. *Entrance requirements:* For master's and doctorate, GRE. Additional exam requirements/recommendations for international students: Required—TOEFL (minimum score 550 paper-based; 79 iBT), Michigan English Language Assessment Battery (minimum score 82); Recommended—IELTS (minimum score 7). *Application deadline:* For fall admission, 11/30 priority date for domestic and international students; for winter admission, 12/1 for domestic students, 11/1 for international students; for spring admission, 10/1 for domestic and international students. Applications are processed on a rolling basis. Application fee: $60 ($70 for international students). Electronic applications accepted. *Financial support:* Fellowships with tuition reimbursements, research assistantships with tuition reimbursements, teaching assistantships with tuition reimbursements, career-related internships or fieldwork, Federal Work-Study, and institutionally sponsored loans available. Support available to part-time students. *Unit head:* Dr. Tunc Aldemir, Graduate Studies Committee Chair, 614-292-4627, E-mail: aldemir.1@osu.edu. *Application contact:* Janeen Sands, Graduate Programs Coordinator, 614-247-6605, Fax: 614-292-5746, E-mail: maegradadmissions@osu.edu.
Website: http://nuclear.osu.edu.

Oregon State University, College of Engineering, Program in Nuclear Engineering, Corvallis, OR 97331. Offers M Eng, MS, PhD. *Faculty:* 11 full-time (3 women), 2 part-time/adjunct (both women). *Students:* 36 full-time (3 women), 4 part-time (0 women); includes 2 minority (1 Hispanic/Latino; 1 Two or more races, non-Hispanic/Latino), 7 international. Average age 26. 59 applicants, 27% accepted, 10 enrolled. In 2014, 9 master's, 3 doctorates awarded. *Entrance requirements:* For master's and doctorate, GRE. Additional exam requirements/recommendations for international students: Required—TOEFL (minimum score 80 iBT), IELTS (minimum score 6.5). *Application deadline:* For fall admission, 8/1 for domestic and international students. Application fee: $60. *Expenses:* Expenses: $15,359 full-time resident tuition and fees; $23,405 non-resident. *Unit head:* Dr. Kathryn Higley, Department Head/Professor, 541-737-7063, E-mail: kathryn.higley@oregonstate.edu. *Application contact:* Heidi Braly, Graduate Student Liaison, 541-737-7062, E-mail: heidi.braly@oregonstate.edu.
Website: http://ne.oregonstate.edu/nuclear-engineering-program.

Penn State University Park, Graduate School, College of Engineering, Department of Mechanical and Nuclear Engineering, University Park, PA 16802. Offers mechanical engineering (PhD); nuclear engineering (PhD). *Unit head:* Dr. Amr S. Elnashai, Dean, 814-865-7537, Fax: 814-863-4749, E-mail: ase2@psu.edu. *Application contact:* Lori A. Stania, Director, Graduate Student Services, 814-867-5278, Fax: 814-863-4627, E-mail: gswww@psu.edu.
Website: http://www.mne.psu.edu/.

Purdue University, College of Engineering, School of Nuclear Engineering, West Lafayette, IN 47907-2017. Offers MS, MSNE, PhD. Part-time programs available. Terminal master's awarded for partial completion of doctoral program. *Entrance requirements:* For master's and doctorate, GRE General Test, minimum GPA of 3.0. Additional exam requirements/recommendations for international students: Required—TOEFL (minimum score 550 paper-based; 77 iBT); Recommended—TWE. Electronic applications accepted. *Faculty research:* Nuclear reactor safety, thermal hydraulics, fusion technology, reactor materials, reactor physics.

Rensselaer Polytechnic Institute, Graduate School, School of Engineering, Program in Nuclear Engineering, Troy, NY 12180-3590. Offers M Eng, MS, D Eng, PhD. *Faculty:* 42 full-time (5 women), 7 part-time/adjunct (0 women). *Students:* 25 full-time (5 women), 1 part-time (0 women); includes 2 minority (1 Black or African American, non-Hispanic/Latino; 1 Hispanic/Latino), 6 international. Average age 26. 43 applicants, 35% accepted, 2 enrolled. In 2014, 2 master's, 6 doctorates awarded. Terminal master's awarded for partial completion of doctoral program. *Degree requirements:* For master's, thesis (for some programs); for doctorate, thesis/dissertation. *Entrance requirements:* For master's and doctorate, GRE. Additional exam requirements/recommendations for international students: Required—TOEFL (minimum score 600 paper-based; 100 iBT), IELTS (minimum score 7), PTE (minimum score 68). *Application deadline:* For fall admission, 1/1 priority date for domestic and international students; for spring admission, 8/15 priority date for domestic and international students. Applications are processed on a rolling basis. Application fee: $75. Electronic applications accepted. *Expenses:* Tuition: Full-time $46,700; part-time $1945 per credit. Tuition and fees vary according to course load. *Financial support:* In 2014–15, 11 students received support, including research assistantships (averaging $18,500 per year), teaching assistantships (averaging $18,500 per year); fellowships also available. Financial award application deadline: 1/1. *Faculty research:* Design, dynamics and vibrations, fissions systems and radiation transport, fluid mechanics (computational, theoretical, and experimental), heat transfer and energy conversion, manufacturing, medical imaging and health physics, multiscale/computational modeling, nanostructured materials and properties, nuclear physics/nuclear reactor, propulsion. *Total annual research expenditures:* $3.5 million. *Unit head:* Dr. Theo Borca-Tasciuc, Graduate Program Director, 518-276-2627, E-mail: borcat@rpi.edu. *Application contact:* Office of Graduate Admissions, 518-276-6216, E-mail: gradadmissions@rpi.edu.
Website: http://mane.rpi.edu/academics.

Royal Military College of Canada, Division of Graduate Studies and Research, Engineering Division, Program in Nuclear Engineering, Kingston, ON K7K 7B4, Canada. Offers M Eng, MA Sc, PhD. *Degree requirements:* For master's, thesis; for doctorate, comprehensive exam, thesis/dissertation. *Entrance requirements:* For master's, honours degree with second-class standing; for doctorate, master's degree. Electronic applications accepted.

Royal Military College of Canada, Division of Graduate Studies and Research, Engineering Division, Program in Nuclear Science, Kingston, ON K7K 7B4, Canada. Offers M Sc, PhD. *Degree requirements:* For master's, thesis; for doctorate, comprehensive exam, thesis/dissertation. *Entrance requirements:* For master's, honour's degree with second-class standing; for doctorate, master's degree. Electronic applications accepted.

Texas A&M University, College of Engineering, Department of Nuclear Engineering, College Station, TX 77843. Offers health physics (MS); nuclear engineering (M Eng, MS, PhD). *Faculty:* 19. *Students:* 125 full-time (18 women), 30 part-time (5 women); includes 35 minority (5 Black or African American, non-Hispanic/Latino; 1 American Indian or Alaska Native, non-Hispanic/Latino; 5 Asian, non-Hispanic/Latino; 22 Hispanic/Latino; 2 Two or more races, non-Hispanic/Latino), 31 international. Average age 27. 121 applicants, 56% accepted, 32 enrolled. In 2014, 22 master's, 8 doctorates awarded. *Degree requirements:* For master's, thesis or alternative; for doctorate, thesis/dissertation, departmental qualifying exams. *Entrance requirements:* For master's and doctorate, GRE General Test, 3 letters of recommendation. Additional exam requirements/recommendations for international students: Required—TOEFL. *Application deadline:* For fall admission, 3/1 for domestic and international students; for spring admission, 8/1 for domestic and international students. Applications are processed on a rolling basis. Application fee: $50 ($90 for international students). Electronic applications accepted. *Expenses:* Tuition, state resident: full-time $4078; part-time $226.55 per credit hour. Tuition, nonresident: full-time $10,594; part-time $577.55 per credit hour. *Required fees:* $2813; $237.70 per credit hour. $278.50 per semester. Tuition and fees vary according to degree level and student level. *Financial support:* In 2014–15, 128 students received support, including 19 fellowships with full and partial tuition reimbursements available (averaging $26,061 per year), 74 research assistantships with full and partial tuition reimbursements available (averaging $9,175 per year), 20 teaching assistantships with full and partial tuition reimbursements available (averaging $7,239 per year); career-related internships or fieldwork, institutionally sponsored loans, scholarships/grants, traineeships, health care benefits, tuition waivers (full and partial), and unspecified assistantships also available. Support available to part-time students. Financial award application deadline: 4/1; financial award applicants required to submit FAFSA. *Unit head:* Dr. Yassin A. Hassan, Head, 979-845-7090, E-mail: y-hassan@tamu.edu. *Application contact:* Robb Jenson, Graduate Program Coordinator, 979-458-2072, E-mail: robb.jenson@tamu.edu.
Website: https://engineering.tamu.edu/nuclear.

University of California, Berkeley, Graduate Division, College of Engineering, Department of Nuclear Engineering, Berkeley, CA 94720-1730. Offers M Eng, MS, D Eng, PhD. *Degree requirements:* For master's, project or thesis; for doctorate, thesis/dissertation, oral exam. *Entrance requirements:* For master's and doctorate, GRE General Test, minimum GPA of 3.0, 3 letters of recommendation. Additional exam requirements/recommendations for international students: Required—TOEFL. *Faculty research:* Applied nuclear reactions and instrumentation, fission reactor engineering, fusion reactor technology, nuclear waste and materials management, radiation protection and environmental effects.

University of Cincinnati, Graduate School, College of Engineering and Applied Science, Department of Mechanical and Materials Engineering, Cincinnati, OH 45221. Offers industrial engineering (PhD); mechanical engineering (MS, PhD); nuclear engineering (PhD); MBA/MS. Part-time and evening/weekend programs available. Terminal master's awarded for partial completion of doctoral program. *Degree requirements:* For doctorate, thesis/dissertation. *Entrance requirements:* For master's and doctorate, GRE General Test. Additional exam requirements/recommendations for international students: Required—TOEFL (minimum score 575 paper-based). Electronic applications accepted.

University of Florida, Graduate School, College of Engineering, Department of Materials Science and Engineering, Nuclear Engineering Program, Gainesville, FL 32611. Offers imaging science and technology (PhD); nuclear engineering sciences (ME, MS, PhD). Part-time programs available. *Faculty:* 4 full-time (1 woman). *Students:* 28 full-time (4 women), 5 part-time (2 women); includes 12 minority (1 Black or African American, non-Hispanic/Latino; 2 Asian, non-Hispanic/Latino; 9 Hispanic/Latino), 7 international. 30 applicants, 43% accepted, 6 enrolled. In 2014, 6 master's, 1 doctorate awarded. Terminal master's awarded for partial completion of doctoral program. *Degree requirements:* For master's, comprehensive exam, thesis; for doctorate, comprehensive exam, thesis/dissertation. *Entrance requirements:* For master's and doctorate, minimum GPA of 3.0. Additional exam requirements/recommendations for international students: Required—TOEFL (minimum score 550 paper-based; 80 iBT), IELTS (minimum score 6). *Application deadline:* For fall admission, 7/1 priority date for domestic students, 5/1 for international students; for spring admission, 11/1 for domestic students, 9/1 for international students. Applications are processed on a rolling basis. Application fee: $30. Electronic applications accepted. *Financial support:* Institutionally sponsored loans and unspecified assistantships available. Financial award application deadline: 3/1; financial award applicants required to submit FAFSA. *Faculty research:* Nuclear materials, radiation detection, thermal hydraulics, reactor physics and transport, generation 4 reactor technology. *Unit head:* Simon R. Phillpot, PhD, Director of Nuclear Engineering Program, 352-392-8112, Fax: 352-392-3380, E-mail: sphil@mse.ufl.edu. *Application contact:* Dr. Jack Mecholsky, Jr., Professor and Graduate Coordinator, 352-846-3306, Fax: 352-392-3380, E-mail: jmech@mse.ufl.edu.
Website: http://www.nuceng.ufl.edu/.

University of Idaho, College of Graduate Studies, College of Engineering, Department of Engineering, Moscow, ID 83844-1011. Offers environmental engineering (M Engr, MS); nuclear engineering (M Engr, MS, PhD); technology management (MS). *Faculty:* 4 full-time, 2 part-time/adjunct. *Students:* 1 full-time, 12 part-time. Average age 44. In 2014, 5 master's awarded. *Application deadline:* Applications are processed on a rolling basis. Application fee: $60. Electronic applications accepted. *Expenses:* Tuition, state resident: full-time $4784; part-time $280.50 per credit hour. Tuition, nonresident: full-time $18,314; part-time $957.50 per credit hour. *Required fees:* $2000; $58.50 per credit hour. Tuition and fees vary according to program. *Financial support:* Applicants required to submit FAFSA. *Unit head:* Dr. Larry Stauffer, Interim Dean, 208-885-6479. *Application contact:* Stephanie Thomas, Graduate Recruitment Coordinator, 208-885-4001, Fax: 208-885-4406, E-mail: gadms@uidaho.edu.
Website: http://www.uidaho.edu/engr/.

University of Illinois at Urbana–Champaign, Graduate College, College of Engineering, Department of Nuclear, Plasma, and Radiological Engineering, Urbana, IL 61801. Offers energy systems (M Eng); nuclear, plasma, and radiological engineering (MS, PhD). *Students:* 72 (5 women). Terminal master's awarded for partial completion of doctoral program. *Application deadline:* For fall admission, 1/15 for domestic and international students. Application fee: $70 ($90 for international students). *Unit head:* James F. Stubbins, Professor/Department Head, 217-333-2295, Fax: 217-333-2906,

E-mail: jstubbin@illinois.edu. *Application contact:* Becky J. Meline, Admissions and Records Officer, 217-333-3598, Fax: 217-333-2906, E-mail: bmeline@illinois.edu.
Website: http://npre.illinois.edu/.

The University of Manchester, School of Mechanical, Aerospace and Civil Engineering, Manchester, United Kingdom. Offers advanced manufacturing technology (M Ent); aerospace engineering (M Phil, M Sc, PhD); civil engineering (M Phil, M Sc, PhD); environmental engineering (M Phil, PhD); management of projects (M Phil, M Sc, PhD); mechanical engineering (M Phil, M Sc, PhD); mechanical engineering design (M Ent); nuclear engineering (M Phil, D Eng, PhD).

University of Maryland, College Park, Academic Affairs, A. James Clark School of Engineering, Department of Materials Science and Engineering, Nuclear Engineering Program, College Park, MD 20742. Offers ME, MS, PhD. Part-time and evening/weekend programs available. Postbaccalaureate distance learning degree programs offered. *Degree requirements:* For master's, thesis optional; for doctorate, variable foreign language requirement, thesis/dissertation, oral exam. *Entrance requirements:* For master's and doctorate, GRE General Test, minimum GPA of 3.0. Additional exam requirements/recommendations for international students: Required—TOEFL. Electronic applications accepted. *Faculty research:* Reliability and risk assessment, heat transfer and two-phase flow, reactor safety analysis, nuclear reactor, radiation/polymers.

University of Massachusetts Lowell, Francis College of Engineering, Program in Energy Engineering, Lowell, MA 01854. Offers MS Eng, D Eng, PhD. *Degree requirements:* For master's, thesis optional. *Entrance requirements:* For master's, GRE General Test. Additional exam requirements/recommendations for international students: Required—TOEFL.

University of Michigan, College of Engineering, Department of Nuclear Engineering and Radiological Sciences, Ann Arbor, MI 48109. Offers nuclear engineering (Nuc E); nuclear engineering and radiological sciences (MSE, PhD); nuclear science (MS, PhD). *Students:* 124 full-time (16 women). 151 applicants, 49% accepted, 39 enrolled. In 2014, 19 master's, 20 doctorates awarded. Terminal master's awarded for partial completion of doctoral program. *Degree requirements:* For master's, thesis optional; for doctorate, thesis/dissertation, oral defense of dissertation, preliminary exams. *Entrance requirements:* For master's and doctorate, GRE General Test. Additional exam requirements/recommendations for international students: Required—TOEFL (minimum score 560 paper-based). *Application deadline:* Applications are processed on a rolling basis. Electronic applications accepted. *Financial support:* Fellowships, research assistantships, teaching assistantships, career-related internships or fieldwork, institutionally sponsored loans, scholarships/grants, traineeships, health care benefits, and unspecified assistantships available. *Faculty research:* Radiation safety, environmental sciences, medical physics, fission systems and radiation transport, materials, plasmas and fusion, radiation measurements and imaging. *Total annual research expenditures:* $14.2 million. *Unit head:* Dr. Ronald Gilgenbach, Chair, 734-763-1261, Fax: 734-763-4540, E-mail: rongilg@umich.edu. *Application contact:* Peggy Jo Gramer, Graduate Program Coordinator, 734-615-8810, Fax: 734-763-4540, E-mail: ners-grad-admissions@umich.edu.
Website: http://www.engin.umich.edu/ners.

University of Missouri, Office of Research and Graduate Studies, College of Engineering, Nuclear Engineering Program, Columbia, MO 65211. Offers environmental and regulatory compliance (MS, PhD); materials (PhD); medical physics (MS); nuclear engineering (Certificate); nuclear safeguards science and technology (Certificate); thermal hydraulics (MS, PhD). *Faculty:* 5 full-time (0 women). *Students:* 36 full-time (6 women), 9 part-time (6 women); includes 3 minority (2 Asian, non-Hispanic/Latino; 1 Hispanic/Latino), 12 international. Average age 30. 42 applicants, 17% accepted, 5 enrolled. In 2014, 15 master's, 11 doctorates, 6 other advanced degrees awarded. *Degree requirements:* For master's, research project; for doctorate, thesis/dissertation. *Entrance requirements:* For master's and doctorate, GRE General Test. Additional exam requirements/recommendations for international students: Required—TOEFL (minimum score 500 paper-based; 61 iBT). *Application deadline:* For fall admission, 3/1 priority date for domestic and international students; for winter admission, 10/1 priority date for domestic students, 9/1 priority date for international students. Application fee: $55 ($75 for international students). Electronic applications accepted. *Financial support:* Fellowships with full and partial tuition reimbursements, research assistantships with full and partial tuition reimbursements, teaching assistantships with full and partial tuition reimbursements, institutionally sponsored loans, scholarships/grants, health care benefits, and unspecified assistantships available. Support available to part-time students. *Faculty research:* Nuclear materials management, aerosol mechanics, reactor safety analysis, nuclear energy conversion, reactor physics, reactor design, nondestructive testing and measurement, radiative heat transfer, neutron spectrometry, neutron and gamma ray transport, neutron activation analysis, nuclear waste management, nuclear plasma research, health physics, magnetic resonance imaging, radiation therapy and alternative and renewable energy concepts. *Unit head:* Dr. John M. Gahl, Director, 573-882-5345, E-mail: gahlj@missouri.edu.
Website: http://engineering.missouri.edu/nuclear/.

University of Nevada, Las Vegas, Graduate College, Howard R. Hughes College of Engineering, Department of Mechanical Engineering, Las Vegas, NV 89154-4027. Offers biomedical engineering (MS); materials and nuclear engineering (MS); mechanical engineering (MS); nuclear criticality safety engineering (Certificate). Part-time programs available. *Faculty:* 13 full-time (0 women), 1 (woman) part-time/adjunct. *Students:* 33 full-time (13 women), 13 part-time (3 women); includes 8 minority (1 Asian, non-Hispanic/Latino; 2 Hispanic/Latino; 5 Two or more races, non-Hispanic/Latino), 12 international. Average age 29. 43 applicants, 51% accepted, 11 enrolled. In 2014, 9 master's, 6 doctorates, 3 other advanced degrees awarded. *Degree requirements:* For master's, comprehensive exam, thesis (for some programs), project; for doctorate, comprehensive exam, thesis/dissertation. *Entrance requirements:* For master's, doctorate, and Certificate, GRE General Test. Additional exam requirements/recommendations for international students: Required—TOEFL (minimum score 550 paper-based; 80 iBT), IELTS (minimum score 7). *Application deadline:* For fall admission, 8/1 for domestic students, 5/1 for international students; for spring admission, 12/1 for domestic students, 10/1 for international students. Application fee: $60 ($95 for international students). Electronic applications accepted. *Financial support:* In 2014–15, 33 students received support, including 6 research assistantships with partial tuition reimbursements available (averaging $15,198 per year), 27 teaching assistantships with partial tuition reimbursements available (averaging $14,029 per year); institutionally sponsored loans, scholarships/grants, health care benefits, and unspecified assistantships also available. Financial award application deadline: 3/1. *Faculty research:* Dynamics and control systems; energy systems including renewable and nuclear; computational fluid and solid mechanics; structures, materials and manufacturing; vibrations and acoustics. *Total annual research expenditures:* $1.9 million. *Unit head:* Dr. Brendan O'Toole, Chair/Professor, 702-895-3885, Fax: 702-895-3936, E-mail: brendan.otoole@unlv.edu. *Application contact:* Graduate College Admissions Evaluator, 702-895-3320, Fax: 702-895-4180, E-mail: gradcollege@unlv.edu.
Website: http://me.unlv.edu/.

University of New Mexico, Graduate School, School of Engineering, Program in Nuclear Engineering, Albuquerque, NM 87131-2039. Offers MS, PhD. Part-time programs available. Postbaccalaureate distance learning degree programs offered (no on-campus study). *Faculty:* 15 full-time (3 women), 5 part-time/adjunct (1 woman). *Students:* 16 full-time (2 women), 33 part-time (8 women); includes 11 minority (1 Asian, non-Hispanic/Latino; 9 Hispanic/Latino; 1 Two or more races, non-Hispanic/Latino), 1 international. Average age 32. 187 applicants, 36% accepted, 37 enrolled. In 2014, 6 master's, 4 doctorates awarded. Terminal master's awarded for partial completion of doctoral program. *Degree requirements:* For master's, thesis (for some programs); for doctorate, comprehensive exam, thesis/dissertation. *Entrance requirements:* For master's, GRE General Test, minimum GPA of 3.0, 3 letters of recommendation, letter of intent; for doctorate, GRE General Test, 3 letters of recommendation, letter of intent. Additional exam requirements/recommendations for international students: Required—TOEFL. *Application deadline:* For fall admission, 1/15 priority date for domestic students, 3/1 for international students; for spring admission, 7/15 priority date for domestic students, 8/1 for international students. Application fee: $50. Electronic applications accepted. *Financial support:* In 2014–15, 21 students received support, including 22 research assistantships with full tuition reimbursements available (averaging $24,000 per year); scholarships/grants, health care benefits, and tuition waivers (full) also available. Financial award application deadline: 3/1; financial award applicants required to submit FAFSA. *Faculty research:* Plasma science, space power, thermal hydraulics, radiation measurement and protection, fusion plasma measurements, medical physics, nuclear criticality safety, radiation measurements and protection, radiation transport modeling and simulation, Monte Carlo methods. *Total annual research expenditures:* $1 million. *Unit head:* Dr. Anil Prinja, Associate Chair, 505-277-5431, Fax: 505-277-5433, E-mail: tward@unm.edu. *Application contact:* Jocelyn White, Coordinator/Program Advisor, 505-277-5606, Fax: 505-277-5433, E-mail: jowhite@unm.edu.
Website: http://www-chne.unm.edu/nucleargraduate.html.

University of South Carolina, The Graduate School, College of Engineering and Computing, Department of Nuclear Engineering, Columbia, SC 29208. Offers ME, MS, PhD. Part-time and evening/weekend programs available. Postbaccalaureate distance learning degree programs offered. *Degree requirements:* For master's, thesis (for some programs); for doctorate, thesis/dissertation. *Entrance requirements:* For master's and doctorate, GRE General Test. Additional exam requirements/recommendations for international students: Required—TOEFL (minimum score 600 paper-based; 100 iBT). Electronic applications accepted.

The University of Tennessee, Graduate School, College of Engineering, Department of Nuclear Engineering, Program in Nuclear Engineering, Knoxville, TN 37966. Offers MS, PhD. Part-time programs available. *Faculty:* 32 full-time (4 women), 11 part-time/adjunct (0 women). *Students:* 100 full-time (14 women), 23 part-time (3 women); includes 9 minority (3 Black or African American, non-Hispanic/Latino; 2 Asian, non-Hispanic/Latino; 1 Hispanic/Latino; 3 Two or more races, non-Hispanic/Latino), 14 international. Average age 31. 148 applicants, 72% accepted, 62 enrolled. In 2014, 24 master's, 12 doctorates awarded. *Degree requirements:* For master's, thesis or alternative; for doctorate, comprehensive exam, thesis/dissertation. *Entrance requirements:* For master's, GRE General Test (for MS students pursuing research thesis), minimum GPA of 2.7 (for U.S. degree holders), 3.0 (for international degree holders); for doctorate, GRE General Test (for all PhD candidates), minimum GPA of 3.0 on previous graduate course work. Additional exam requirements/recommendations for international students: Required—TOEFL (minimum score 550 paper-based). *Application deadline:* For fall admission, 2/1 priority date for domestic and international students; for spring admission, 6/15 for domestic students, 5/15 for international students. Applications are processed on a rolling basis. Application fee: $35. Electronic applications accepted. *Financial support:* In 2014–15, 88 students received support, including 56 research assistantships with full tuition reimbursements available (averaging $25,630 per year), 15 teaching assistantships with full tuition reimbursements available (averaging $21,263 per year); fellowships with full tuition reimbursements available, career-related internships or fieldwork, Federal Work-Study, institutionally sponsored loans, health care benefits, and unspecified assistantships also available. Financial award application deadline: 2/1; financial award applicants required to submit FAFSA. *Faculty research:* Heat transfer and fluid dynamics; instrumentation, sensors and controls; nuclear materials and nuclear security; radiological engineering; reactor system design and safety. *Unit head:* Dr. J. Wesley Hines, Head, 865-974-2525, Fax: 865-974-0668, E-mail: jhines2@utk.edu. *Application contact:* Dr. Masood Parang, Associate Dean of Student Affairs, 865-974-2454, Fax: 865-974-9871, E-mail: mparang@utk.edu.

The University of Tennessee at Chattanooga, Department of Engineering Management, Chattanooga, TN 37403. Offers engineering management (MS); fundamentals of engineering management (Graduate Certificate); leadership and ethics (Graduate Certificate); logistics and supply chain management (Graduate Certificate); nuclear engineering (Graduate Certificate); power system protection (Graduate Certificate); power systems management (Graduate Certificate); project and value management (Graduate Certificate); quality management (Graduate Certificate); sustainable electric energy (Graduate Certificate). Postbaccalaureate distance learning degree programs offered (no on-campus study). *Faculty:* 5 full-time (1 woman). *Students:* 14 full-time (5 women), 67 part-time (14 women); includes 24 minority (13 Black or African American, non-Hispanic/Latino; 6 Asian, non-Hispanic/Latino; 4 Hispanic/Latino; 1 Two or more races, non-Hispanic/Latino), 6 international. Average age 31. 31 applicants, 45% accepted, 10 enrolled. In 2014, 31 master's, 17 other advanced degrees awarded. *Degree requirements:* For master's, thesis. *Entrance requirements:* For master's, GRE General Test, letters of recommendation; minimum undergraduate GPA of 2.5 overall or 3.0 in senior year. Additional exam requirements/recommendations for international students: Required—TOEFL (minimum score 550 paper-based; 79 iBT), IELTS (minimum score 6). *Application deadline:* For fall admission, 6/13 priority date for domestic students, 6/1 for international students; for spring admission, 10/15 priority date for domestic students, 10/1 for international students. Applications are processed on a rolling basis. Application fee: $30 ($35 for international students). Electronic applications accepted. *Expenses:* Tuition, state resident: full-time $7708; part-time $428 per credit hour. Tuition, nonresident: full-time $23,826; part-time $1323 per credit hour. *Required fees:* $1708; $252 per credit hour. *Financial support:* In 2014–15, 5 research assistantships (averaging $6,528 per year), 3 teaching assistantships (averaging $6,781 per year) were awarded; career-related internships or fieldwork, scholarships/grants, and unspecified assistantships also available. Support available to part-time students. Financial award applicants required to submit FAFSA. *Faculty research:* Plant layout design, lean manufacturing, Six Sigma, value management, product development. *Unit head:* Dr. Neslihan Alp, Department Head, 423-425-4032, Fax: 423-425-5229, E-mail: neslihan-alp@utc.edu. *Application contact:* Dr. J. Randy Walker, Interim Dean of Graduate Studies, 423-425-4478, Fax: 423-425-5223, E-mail: randy-walker@utc.edu.
Website: http://www.utc.edu/Departments/engrcs/engm/index.php.

University of Utah, Graduate School, College of Engineering, Department of Civil and Environmental Engineering, Program in Nuclear Engineering, Salt Lake City, UT 84112.

Offers MS, PhD. Part-time programs available. *Students:* 15 full-time (4 women), 6 part-time (1 woman); includes 3 minority (1 Black or African American, non-Hispanic/Latino; 2 Two or more races, non-Hispanic/Latino), 4 international. Average age 31. 18 applicants, 56% accepted, 8 enrolled. In 2014, 4 master's, 1 doctorate awarded. Terminal master's awarded for partial completion of doctoral program. *Degree requirements:* For master's, comprehensive exam, thesis (for some programs); for doctorate, comprehensive exam, thesis/dissertation, qualifying exam. *Entrance requirements:* For master's and doctorate, GRE General Test, minimum GPA of 3.0. Additional exam requirements/recommendations for international students: Required—TOEFL (minimum score 550 paper-based; 80 iBT). *Application deadline:* For fall admission, 1/15 for domestic students, 12/15 for international students; for spring admission, 10/1 for domestic and international students. Applications are processed on a rolling basis. Application fee: $10 ($25 for international students). Electronic applications accepted. *Expenses:* Expenses: Contact institution. *Financial support:* In 2014–15, 17 students received support, including 9 fellowships with full tuition reimbursements available (averaging $22,000 per year), 7 research assistantships with full tuition reimbursements available (averaging $21,438 per year), 1 teaching assistantship with full tuition reimbursement available (averaging $21,068 per year); career-related internships or fieldwork, institutionally sponsored loans, scholarships/grants, traineeships, health care benefits, and unspecified assistantships also available. Support available to part-time students. Financial award application deadline: 12/15; financial award applicants required to submit FAFSA. *Faculty research:* Dosimetry, material damage, energy, forensics. *Unit head:* Dr. Michael Barber, Interim Chair, 801-581-6931, Fax: 801-585-5477, E-mail: barber@civil.utah.edu. *Application contact:* Bonnie Ogden, Academic Advisor, 801-581-6678, Fax: 801-585-5477, E-mail: bonnie.ogden@utah.edu.
Website: http://www.nuclear.utah.edu/.

University of Wisconsin–Madison, Graduate School, College of Engineering, Department of Engineering Physics, Madison, WI 53706. Offers engineering mechanics (MS, PhD); nuclear engineering and engineering physics (MS, PhD). Part-time programs available. Postbaccalaureate distance learning degree programs offered (minimal on-campus study). *Faculty:* 21 full-time (1 woman), 8 part-time/adjunct (4 women). *Students:* 123 full-time (20 women), 9 part-time (0 women); includes 17 minority (3 Black or African American, non-Hispanic/Latino; 1 American Indian or Alaska Native, non-Hispanic/Latino; 6 Asian, non-Hispanic/Latino; 5 Hispanic/Latino; 2 Two or more races, non-Hispanic/Latino), 25 international. Average age 26. 221 applicants, 47% accepted, 48 enrolled. In 2014, 36 master's, 11 doctorates awarded. Terminal master's awarded for partial completion of doctoral program. *Degree requirements:* For master's, thesis optional; for doctorate, thesis/dissertation. *Entrance requirements:* For master's and doctorate, GRE General Test, minimum GPA of 3.0 in last 60 hours, appropriate bachelor's degree. Additional exam requirements/recommendations for international students: Required—TOEFL (minimum score 600 paper-based). *Application deadline:* For fall admission, 1/1 priority date for domestic and international students. Applications are processed on a rolling basis. Application fee: $56. Electronic applications accepted. *Expenses:* Tuition, state resident: full-time $10,723; part-time $745 per credit. Tuition, nonresident: full-time $24,054; part-time $1578 per credit. *Required fees:* $374 per semester. Tuition and fees vary according to course load, program and reciprocity agreements. *Financial support:* In 2014–15, 74 students received support, including 21 fellowships with full tuition reimbursements available (averaging $25,101 per year), 89 research assistantships with full tuition reimbursements available (averaging $21,224 per year), 16 teaching assistantships with full tuition reimbursements available (averaging $14,326 per year); career-related internships or fieldwork, Federal Work-Study, institutionally sponsored loans, unspecified assistantships, and project assistantships also available. Support available

to part-time students. Financial award application deadline: 1/15. *Faculty research:* Fission reactor engineering and safety, plasma physics and fusion technology, plasma processing and ion implantation, nanotechnology, engineering mechanics and astronautics. *Total annual research expenditures:* $16.3 million. *Unit head:* Dr. Doug Henderson, Chair, 608-263-0391, Fax: 608-263-7451, E-mail: henderson@engr.wisc.edu. *Application contact:* Betsy A. Wood, Graduate Coordinator, 608-263-7038, Fax: 608-263-7451, E-mail: betsy.wood@wisc.edu.
Website: http://www.engr.wisc.edu/ep/.

Virginia Commonwealth University, Graduate School, School of Engineering, Department of Mechanical and Nuclear Engineering, Richmond, VA 23284-9005. Offers MS, PhD. *Entrance requirements:* For master's and doctorate, GRE. Additional exam requirements/recommendations for international students: Required—TOEFL (minimum score 600 paper-based; 100 iBT). Electronic applications accepted.

Virginia Polytechnic Institute and State University, Graduate School, College of Engineering, Blacksburg, VA 24061. Offers aerospace engineering (ME, MS, PhD); biological systems engineering (ME, MS, PhD); biomedical engineering (MS, PhD); chemical engineering (ME, MS, PhD); civil engineering (ME, MS, PhD); computer engineering (ME, MS, PhD); computer science (MS, PhD); electrical engineering (ME, PhD); engineering education (PhD); engineering mechanics (ME, MS, PhD); environmental engineering (MS); environmental science and engineering (MS); industrial and systems engineering (ME, MS, PhD); materials science and engineering (ME, MS, PhD); mechanical engineering (ME, MS, PhD); mining and minerals engineering (PhD); mining engineering (ME, MS); nuclear engineering (MS, PhD); ocean engineering (MS); systems engineering (ME, MS). *Accreditation:* ABET (one or more programs are accredited). *Faculty:* 356 full-time (60 women), 3 part-time/adjunct (1 woman). *Students:* 1,700 full-time (398 women), 345 part-time (58 women); includes 213 minority (43 Black or African American, non-Hispanic/Latino; 1 American Indian or Alaska Native, non-Hispanic/Latino; 87 Asian, non-Hispanic/Latino; 58 Hispanic/Latino; 1 Native Hawaiian or other Pacific Islander, non-Hispanic/Latino; 23 Two or more races, non-Hispanic/Latino), 1,079 international. Average age 27. 5,228 applicants, 18% accepted, 471 enrolled. In 2014, 438 master's, 211 doctorates awarded. *Degree requirements:* For master's, comprehensive exam (for some programs), thesis (for some programs); for doctorate, comprehensive exam (for some programs), thesis/dissertation (for some programs). *Entrance requirements:* For master's and doctorate, GRE/GMAT (may vary by department). Additional exam requirements/recommendations for international students: Required—TOEFL (minimum score 550 paper-based). *Application deadline:* For fall admission, 8/1 for domestic students, 4/1 for international students; for spring admission, 1/1 for domestic students, 9/1 for international students. Applications are processed on a rolling basis. Application fee: $75. Electronic applications accepted. *Expenses:* Tuition, state resident: full-time $11,656; part-time $647.50 per credit hour. Tuition, nonresident: full-time $23,351; part-time $1297.25 per credit hour. *Required fees:* $2533; $465.75 per semester. Tuition and fees vary according to course load, campus/location and program. *Financial support:* In 2014–15, 148 fellowships with full tuition reimbursements (averaging $8,031 per year), 855 research assistantships with full tuition reimbursements (averaging $22,855 per year), 288 teaching assistantships with full tuition reimbursements (averaging $20,291 per year) were awarded. Financial award application deadline: 3/1; financial award applicants required to submit FAFSA. *Total annual research expenditures:* $90.5 million. *Unit head:* Dr. Richard C. Benson, Dean, 540-231-9752, Fax: 540-231-3031, E-mail: deaneng@vt.edu. *Application contact:* Linda Perkins, Executive Assistant, 540-231-9752, Fax: 540-231-3031, E-mail: lperkins@vt.edu.
Website: http://www.eng.vt.edu/.

Section 11
Engineering Design

This section contains a directory of institutions offering graduate work in engineering design. Additional information about programs listed in the directory may be obtained by writing directly to the dean of a graduate school or chair of a department at the address given in the directory.

For programs offering related work, see also in this book *Aerospace/Aeronautical Engineering; Agricultural Engineering and Bioengineering; Biomedical Engineering and Biotechnology; Computer Science and Information Technology; Electrical and Computer Engineering; Energy and Power Engineering; Engineering and Applied Sciences; Industrial Engineering; Management of Engineering and Technology;* and *Mechanical Engineering and Mechanics.* In another guide in this series:

Graduate Programs in the Biological/Biomedical Sciences & Health-Related Medical Professions
See *Biological and Biomedical Sciences*

CONTENTS

Program Directory

Engineering Design

Northwestern University, McCormick School of Engineering and Applied Science, Segal Design Institute, MS in Engineering Design and Innovation Program, Evanston, IL 60208. Offers MS. *Faculty:* 9 full-time (4 women). *Students:* 27 full-time (18 women); includes 6 minority (2 Asian, non-Hispanic/Latino; 2 Hispanic/Latino; 2 Two or more races, non-Hispanic/Latino), 3 international. Average age 23. 57 applicants, 49% accepted, 13 enrolled. In 2014, 13 master's awarded. *Entrance requirements:* For master's, GRE General Test, 2 letters of recommendation. Additional exam requirements/recommendations for international students: Required—TOEFL (minimum score 550 paper-based; 80 iBT) or IELTS (minimum score 7). *Application deadline:* For fall admission, 1/15 priority date for domestic and international students. Applications are processed on a rolling basis. Application fee: $95. Electronic applications accepted. *Financial support:* Career-related internships or fieldwork, institutionally sponsored loans, health care benefits, and unspecified assistantships available. Financial award application deadline: 1/15; financial award applicants required to submit FAFSA. *Unit head:* Greg Holderfield, Director, 847-491-2987, Fax: 847-491-2603, E-mail: g-holderfield@northwestern.edu. *Application contact:* Amy O'Keefe, Associate Director, 847-467-4275, Fax: 847-491-2603, E-mail: amy.okeefe@northwestern.edu. Website: http://segal.northwestern.edu/programs/graduate/engineering-design-innovation/index.html.

Penn State University Park, Graduate School, College of Engineering, School of Engineering Design, Technology, and Professional Programs, University Park, PA 16802. Offers engineering design (M Eng, MS). *Degree requirements:* For master's, thesis (MS); internship or scholarly paper (M Eng). *Unit head:* Dr. Amr S. Elnashai, Dean, 814-865-7537, Fax: 814-863-4749, E-mail: ase2@psu.edu. *Application contact:* Lori A. Stania, Director, Graduate Student Services, 814-867-5278, Fax: 814-863-4627, E-mail: gswww@psu.edu.
Website: http://www.sedtapp.psu.edu/.

San Diego State University, Graduate and Research Affairs, College of Engineering, Department of Mechanical Engineering, San Diego, CA 92182. Offers engineering sciences and applied mechanics (PhD); manufacture and design (MS); mechanical engineering (MS). PhD offered jointly with University of California, San Diego and Department of Aerospace Engineering and Engineering Mechanics. Evening/weekend programs available. *Degree requirements:* For master's, comprehensive exam (for some programs), thesis (for some programs); for doctorate, thesis/dissertation. *Entrance requirements:* For master's, GRE General Test; for doctorate, GRE, 3 letters of recommendation. Additional exam requirements/recommendations for international students: Required—TOEFL. Electronic applications accepted. *Faculty research:* Energy analysis and diagnosis, seawater pump design, space-related research.

Santa Clara University, School of Engineering, Santa Clara, CA 95053. Offers analog circuit design (Certificate); applied mathematics (MS); ASIC design and test (Certificate); bioengineering (MS); civil engineering (MS); computer science and engineering (MS, PhD); controls (Certificate); digital signal processing (Certificate); dynamics (Certificate); electrical engineering (MS, PhD); engineering (Engineer); engineering management (MS); fundamentals of electrical engineering (Certificate); information assurance (Certificate); materials engineering (Certificate); mechanical design analysis (Certificate); mechanical engineering (MS, PhD); mechatronics systems engineering (Certificate); microwave and antennas (Certificate); networking (Certificate); renewable energy (Certificate); software engineering (Certificate); sustainable energy (MS); technology jump-start (Certificate); thermofluids (Certificate). Part-time and evening/weekend programs available. *Faculty:* 59 full-time (23 women), 80 part-time/adjunct (14 women). *Students:* 584 full-time (239 women), 353 part-time (102 women); includes 224 minority (7 Black or African American, non-Hispanic/Latino; 144 Asian, non-Hispanic/Latino; 50 Hispanic/Latino; 2 Native Hawaiian or other Pacific Islander, non-Hispanic/Latino; 21 Two or more races, non-Hispanic/Latino), 548 international. Average age 27. 1,248 applicants, 51% accepted, 375 enrolled. In 2014, 283 master's, 5 doctorates, 1 other advanced degree awarded. *Degree requirements:* For master's, thesis (for some programs); for doctorate, thesis/dissertation; for other advanced degree, thesis. *Entrance requirements:* For master's, GRE, transcript; for doctorate, GRE, master's degree or equivalent; for other advanced degree, master's degree, published paper. Additional exam requirements/recommendations for international students: Required—TOEFL (minimum score 550 paper-based; 79 iBT). *Application deadline:* For fall admission, 8/1 for domestic students, 7/15 for international students; for winter admission, 10/28 for domestic students, 9/23 for international students; for spring admission, 2/25 for domestic students, 1/21 for international students. Applications are processed on a rolling basis. Application fee: $60. Electronic applications accepted. *Expenses:* Expenses: Contact institution. *Financial support:* In 2014–15, 94 students received support. Fellowships with full and partial tuition reimbursements available, research assistantships with full and partial tuition reimbursements available, teaching assistantships with full tuition reimbursements available, career-related internships or fieldwork, Federal Work-Study, institutionally sponsored loans, and scholarships/grants available. Support available to part-time students. Financial award application deadline: 3/2; financial award applicants required to submit FAFSA. *Faculty research:* Video encoding, nanostructures, robotics, microfluidics, water resources. *Total annual research expenditures:* $1.6 million. *Unit head:* Dr. Alex Zecevic, Associate Dean for Graduate Studies, 408-554-2394, E-mail: azecevic@scu.edu. *Application contact:* Stacey Tinker, Director of Enrollment Management, 408-554-4748, Fax: 408-554-4323, E-mail: stinker@scu.edu. Website: http://www.scu.edu/engineering/graduate/.

Stanford University, School of Engineering, Department of Mechanical Engineering, Program in Product Design, Stanford, CA 94305-9991. Offers MS. *Entrance requirements:* For master's, GRE General Test, undergraduate degree in engineering, math or sciences. Additional exam requirements/recommendations for international students: Required—TOEFL. *Expenses: Tuition:* Full-time $44,184; part-time $982 per credit hour. *Required fees:* $191.

Stevens Institute of Technology, Graduate School, Charles V. Schaefer Jr. School of Engineering, Department of Mechanical Engineering, Program in Product Architecture and Engineering, Hoboken, NJ 07030. Offers M Eng.

The University of Alabama at Birmingham, School of Engineering, Program in Mechanical Engineering, Birmingham, AL 35294. Offers mechanical engineering (MSME); research/design (MSME); technology/engineering management (MSME). *Students:* 8 full-time (1 woman), 16 part-time (1 woman); includes 2 minority (1 Black or African American, non-Hispanic/Latino; 1 Asian, non-Hispanic/Latino), 8 international. Average age 27. In 2014, 5 master's awarded. *Degree requirements:* For master's, thesis (for some programs). *Entrance requirements:* For master's, GRE (minimum 50th percentile ranking on Quantitative Reasoning and Verbal Reasoning sections), minimum B-level scholarship overall or over the last 60 semester hours of earned credit. Additional exam requirements/recommendations for international students: Required—TOEFL (minimum score 80 iBT). *Application deadline:* For fall admission, 7/1 for domestic students; for spring admission, 11/1 for domestic students; for summer admission, 4/1 for domestic students. Electronic applications accepted. *Expenses:* Tuition, state resident: full-time $7090; part-time $370 per credit hour. Tuition, nonresident: full-time $16,072; part-time $869 per credit hour. Full-time tuition and fees vary according to course load and program. *Financial support:* Research assistantships available. *Unit head:* Dr. David Littlefield, Graduate Program Director, 205-934-8460, E-mail: littlefield@uab.edu. *Application contact:* Susan Noblitt Banks, Director of Graduate School Operations, 205-934-8227, Fax: 205-934-8413, E-mail: gradschool@uab.edu.
Website: http://www.uab.edu/engineering/home/departments-research/me/graduate.

Worcester Polytechnic Institute, Graduate Studies and Research, School of Business, Worcester, MA 01609-2280. Offers information technology (MS), including information security management; management (Graduate Certificate); marketing and technological innovation (MS); operations design and leadership (MS); technology (MBA, MS). *Accreditation:* AACSB. Part-time and evening/weekend programs available. Postbaccalaureate distance learning degree programs offered (minimal on-campus study). *Faculty:* 17 full-time (10 women), 20 part-time/adjunct (2 women). *Students:* 184 full-time (120 women), 231 part-time (76 women); includes 37 minority (4 Black or African American, non-Hispanic/Latino; 19 Asian, non-Hispanic/Latino; 11 Hispanic/Latino; 3 Two or more races, non-Hispanic/Latino), 174 international. 656 applicants, 64% accepted, 147 enrolled. In 2014, 165 master's awarded. *Degree requirements:* For master's, thesis optional. *Entrance requirements:* For master's, GMAT (MBA); GMAT or GRE General Test (MS), statement of purpose, 3 letters of recommendation, resume; for Graduate Certificate, GMAT or GRE General Test, statement of purpose, 3 letters of recommendation. Additional exam requirements/recommendations for international students: Required—TOEFL (minimum score 563 paper-based; 84 iBT), IELTS (minimum score 7). *Application deadline:* For fall admission, 6/1 priority date for domestic and international students; for spring admission, 11/1 priority date for domestic students, 10/1 priority date for international students. Applications are processed on a rolling basis. Application fee: $70. Electronic applications accepted. *Financial support:* Career-related internships or fieldwork, institutionally sponsored loans, scholarships/grants, and unspecified assistantships available. Financial award application deadline: 6/1; financial award applicants required to submit FAFSA. *Unit head:* Dr. Paul Mack, Dean, 508-831-4665, Fax: 508-831-4665, E-mail: biz@wpi.edu. *Application contact:* Eileen Dagostino, Recruiting Operations Coordinator, 508-831-4665, Fax: 508-831-5720, E-mail: edag@wpi.edu.
Website: http://www.wpi.edu/academics/business/about.html.

Section 12
Engineering Physics

This section contains a directory of institutions offering graduate work in engineering physics. Additional information about programs listed in the directory may be obtained by writing directly to the dean of a graduate school or chair of a department at the address given in the directory.

For programs offering related work, see also in this book *Electrical and Computer Engineering, Energy and Power Engineering (Nuclear Engineering), Engineering and Applied Sciences,* and *Materials Sciences and Engineering.* In the other guides in this series:

Graduate Programs in the Biological/Biomedical Sciences & Health-Related Medical Professions
See *Biophysics* and *Health Sciences (Medical Physics)*

Graduate Programs in the Physical Sciences, Mathematics, Agricultural Sciences, the Environment & Natural Resources
See *Physics*

CONTENTS

v

Engineering Physics

Air Force Institute of Technology, Graduate School of Engineering and Management, Department of Engineering Physics, Dayton, OH 45433-7765. Offers applied physics (MS, PhD); electro-optics (MS, PhD); materials science (PhD); nuclear engineering (MS, PhD); space physics (MS). Part-time programs available. *Degree requirements:* For master's, thesis; for doctorate, thesis/dissertation. *Entrance requirements:* For master's and doctorate, GRE General Test, minimum GPA of 3.0, U.S. citizenship. *Faculty research:* High-energy lasers, space physics, nuclear weapon effects, semiconductor physics.

Appalachian State University, Cratis D. Williams Graduate School, Department of Physics and Astronomy, Boone, NC 28608. Offers engineering physics (MS), including systems and lab automation. Part-time programs available. *Degree requirements:* For master's, comprehensive exam, thesis optional. *Entrance requirements:* For master's, GRE General Test, 3 letters of recommendation. Additional exam requirements/recommendations for international students: Required—TOEFL (minimum score 570 paper-based; 79 iBT), IELTS (minimum score 6.5). Electronic applications accepted. *Faculty research:* Raman spectroscopy, applied electrostatics, scanning tunneling microscope/atomic force microscope (STM/AFM), stellar spectroscopy and photometry, surface physics, remote sensing.

Cornell University, Graduate School, Graduate Fields of Engineering, Field of Applied Physics, Ithaca, NY 14853-0001. Offers applied physics (PhD); engineering physics (M Eng). *Degree requirements:* For doctorate, comprehensive exam, thesis/dissertation, written exams. *Entrance requirements:* For master's, GRE General Test, 3 letters of recommendation; for doctorate, GRE General Test, GRE Subject Test (physics), GRE Writing Assessment, 3 letters of recommendation. Additional exam requirements/recommendations for international students: Required—TOEFL (minimum score 600 paper-based; 77 iBT). Electronic applications accepted. *Faculty research:* Quantum and nonlinear optics, plasma physics, solid state physics, condensed matter physics and nanotechnology, electron and X-ray spectroscopy.

École Polytechnique de Montréal, Graduate Programs, Department of Engineering Physics, Montréal, QC H3C 3A7, Canada. Offers optical engineering (M Eng, M Sc A, PhD); solid-state physics and engineering (M Eng, M Sc A, PhD). Part-time programs available. *Degree requirements:* For master's, one foreign language, thesis; for doctorate, one foreign language, thesis/dissertation. *Entrance requirements:* For master's, minimum GPA of 2.75; for doctorate, minimum GPA of 3.0. *Faculty research:* Optics, thin-film physics, laser spectroscopy, plasmas, photonic devices.

Embry-Riddle Aeronautical University–Daytona, Department of Physical Sciences, Daytona Beach, FL 32114-3900. Offers engineering physics (MS, PhD). Part-time and evening/weekend programs available. *Faculty:* 9 full-time (0 women), 1 part-time/adjunct (0 women). *Students:* 33 full-time (8 women), 2 part-time (1 woman); includes 5 minority (1 Asian, non-Hispanic/Latino; 2 Hispanic/Latino; 2 Two or more races, non-Hispanic/Latino), 12 international. Average age 25. 37 applicants, 49% accepted, 13 enrolled. In 2014, 6 master's, 3 doctorates awarded. *Degree requirements:* For master's, thesis optional; for doctorate, comprehensive exam, thesis/dissertation. *Entrance requirements:* For master's, Required to submit GRE scores from the General Test., Applicants for admission to the MSEP program must possess a baccalaureate degree in engineering, physics, chemistry, or mathematics; minimum CGPA of 3.00; for doctorate, GRE [minimum (verbal plus quantitative) score of 1200 in the old scale and 310 in the new scale, obtained within the previous two years of the application], bachelor's or master's degree in physics, engineering, or related field; minimum CGPA of 3.2 required for both the bachelor's and master's degrees; statement of goals (2-5 pages), 3 letters of recommendation. Additional exam requirements/recommendations for international students: Required—TOEFL (minimum score 550 paper-based; 79 iBT), TOEFL (minimum score 600 paper-based, 105 iBT) for PhD. *Application deadline:* For fall admission, 6/1 priority date for domestic students, 5/1 priority date for international students; for spring admission, 11/1 priority date for domestic students, 10/1 priority date for international students. Applications are processed on a rolling basis. Application fee: $50. Electronic applications accepted. *Expenses: Tuition:* Full-time $15,360; part-time $1280 per credit hour. *Required fees:* $1334. *Financial support:* In 2014–15, 2 students received support. Research assistantships with full and partial tuition reimbursements available, teaching assistantships with full and partial tuition reimbursements available, career-related internships or fieldwork, and unspecified assistantships available. Financial award application deadline: 4/15. *Faculty research:* Aeronomy/upper atmospheric physics, space physics, spacecraft instrumentation, spacecraft systems engineering, spacecraft power and thermal control. *Unit head:* Terry Oswalt, PhD, Professor of Engineering Physics and Chair, Department of Physical Sciences, 386-226-6100, E-mail: Terry.Oswalt@erau.edu. *Application contact:* International and Graduate Admissions, 386-226-6176, Fax: 386-226-7070, E-mail: graduate.admissions@erau.edu.
Website: http://daytonabeach.erau.edu/coas/physical-sciences/graduate-degrees/index.html.

George Mason University, College of Science, School of Physics, Astronomy and Computational Sciences, Fairfax, VA 22030. Offers applied and engineering physics (MS); computational science (MS); computational science and informatics (PhD); computational techniques and applications (Certificate); physics (PhD). *Faculty:* 51 full-time (11 women), 13 part-time/adjunct (1 woman). *Students:* 57 full-time (14 women), 82 part-time (15 women); includes 27 minority (8 Black or African American, non-Hispanic/Latino; 8 Asian, non-Hispanic/Latino; 8 Hispanic/Latino; 1 Native Hawaiian or other Pacific Islander, non-Hispanic/Latino; 2 Two or more races, non-Hispanic/Latino), 23 international. Average age 36. 102 applicants, 45% accepted, 21 enrolled. In 2014, 14 master's, 14 doctorates, 2 other advanced degrees awarded. *Degree requirements:* For master's, thesis optional; for doctorate, comprehensive exam, thesis/dissertation. *Entrance requirements:* For master's and doctorate, GRE, baccalaureate degree in related field with minimum GPA of 3.0 in last 60 credit hours; 3 letters of recommendation; expanded goals statement; resume; 2 copies of official transcripts. Additional exam requirements/recommendations for international students: Required—TOEFL (minimum score 570 paper-based; 80 iBT), IELTS (minimum score 6.5), PTE. *Application deadline:* For fall admission, 4/15 priority date for domestic students; for spring admission, 11/15 priority date for domestic students. Application fee: $65 ($80 for international students). Electronic applications accepted. *Expenses:* Tuition, state resident: full-time $9794; part-time $408 per credit hour. Tuition, nonresident: full-time $26,978; part-time $1124 per credit hour. *Required fees:* $2820; $118 per credit hour. Tuition and fees vary according to course load and program. *Financial support:* In 2014–15, 39 students received support, including 1 fellowship (averaging $8,000 per year), 25 research assistantships with full and partial tuition reimbursements available (averaging $18,871 per year), 14 teaching assistantships with full and partial tuition reimbursements available (averaging $15,157 per year); career-related internships or fieldwork, Federal Work-Study, scholarships/grants, unspecified assistantships, and health care benefits (for full-time research or teaching assistantship recipients) also

available. Support available to part-time students. Financial award application deadline: 3/1; financial award applicants required to submit FAFSA. *Faculty research:* Particle and nuclear physics; computational statistics; astronomy, astrophysics, and space and planetary science; astronomy and physics education; atomic physics; biophysics and neuroscience; optical physics; fundamental theoretical studies; multidimensional data analysis. *Total annual research expenditures:* $4.1 million. *Unit head:* Chi Yang, Acting Director, 703-993-4077, Fax: 703-993-1269, E-mail: cyang@gmu.edu. *Application contact:* Dr. Paul So, Graduate Advisor, 703-993-4377, Fax: 703-993-1269, E-mail: paso@gmu.edu.
Website: http://spacs.gmu.edu/.

Louisiana Tech University, Graduate School, College of Engineering and Science, Department of Physics, Ruston, LA 71272. Offers applied physics (MS); computational analysis and modeling (PhD); engineering physics (PhD). Part-time programs available. *Degree requirements:* For master's, thesis or alternative; for doctorate, thesis/dissertation. *Entrance requirements:* For master's, GRE General Test, minimum GPA of 3.0 in last 60 hours. Additional exam requirements/recommendations for international students: Required—TOEFL. *Faculty research:* Experimental high energy physics, laser/optics, computational physics, quantum gravity.

McMaster University, School of Graduate Studies, Faculty of Engineering, Department of Engineering Physics, Hamilton, ON L8S 4M2, Canada. Offers engineering physics (M Eng, MA Sc, PhD); nuclear engineering (PhD). *Degree requirements:* For master's, thesis or alternative; for doctorate, comprehensive exam, thesis/dissertation. *Entrance requirements:* For master's, minimum B average in engineering, mathematics, or physical sciences. Additional exam requirements/recommendations for international students: Required—TOEFL (minimum score 550 paper-based). *Faculty research:* Non-thermal plasmas for pollution control and electrostatic precipitation, bulk and thin film luminescent materials, devices and systems for optical fiber communications, physics and applications of III-V materials and devices, defect spectroscopy in semiconductors.

Michigan Technological University, Graduate School, College of Sciences and Arts, Department of Physics, Houghton, MI 49931. Offers engineering physics (PhD); physics (MS, PhD). Part-time programs available. *Faculty:* 26 full-time, 5 part-time/adjunct. *Students:* 32 full-time, 1 part-time; includes 1 minority (Black or African American, non-Hispanic/Latino), 23 international. Average age 29. 128 applicants, 9% accepted, 6 enrolled. In 2014, 5 master's, 2 doctorates awarded. Terminal master's awarded for partial completion of doctoral program. *Degree requirements:* For master's, comprehensive exam (for some programs), thesis (for some programs); for doctorate, comprehensive exam, thesis/dissertation, qualifying exam, research proposal. *Entrance requirements:* For master's and doctorate, GRE (recommended minimum quantitative score of 156 and analytical score of 3.0), statement of purpose, official transcripts, 3 letters of recommendation. Additional exam requirements/recommendations for international students: Required—TOEFL (recommended score 88 iBT) or IELTS. *Application deadline:* For fall admission, 3/1 priority date for domestic students, 1/15 priority date for international students; for spring admission, 10/1 priority date for domestic students, 9/1 priority date for international students. Applications are processed on a rolling basis. Electronic applications accepted. *Expenses:* Tuition, state resident: full-time $14,769; part-time $820.50 per credit. Tuition, nonresident: full-time $14,769; part-time $820.50 per credit. *Required fees:* $248; $248 per year. Tuition and fees vary according to course load and program. *Financial support:* In 2014–15, 31 students received support, including 1 fellowship with full and partial tuition reimbursement available (averaging $13,824 per year), 10 research assistantships with full and partial tuition reimbursements available (averaging $13,824 per year), 19 teaching assistantships with full and partial tuition reimbursements available (averaging $13,824 per year); career-related internships or fieldwork, Federal Work-Study, scholarships/grants, health care benefits, unspecified assistantships, and cooperative program also available. Financial award applicants required to submit FAFSA. *Faculty research:* Atmospheric physics, astrophysics, biophysics, materials physics, atomic/molecular physics. *Total annual research expenditures:* $1.9 million. *Unit head:* Dr. Ravindra Pandey, Chair, 906-487-2086, Fax: 906-487-2933, E-mail: physics@mtu.edu. *Application contact:* Taana Kallianen, Office Assistant 4, 906-487-2087, Fax: 906-487-2933, E-mail: taana@mtu.edu.
Website: http://www.phy.mtu.edu/.

Rensselaer Polytechnic Institute, Graduate School, School of Engineering, Program in Engineering Physics, Troy, NY 12180-3590. Offers MS, PhD. Part-time programs available. *Faculty:* 4 full-time (1 woman), 1 (woman) part-time/adjunct. *Students:* 1 full-time (0 women). Average age 28. 4 applicants, 25% accepted. Terminal master's awarded for partial completion of doctoral program. *Degree requirements:* For master's, thesis (for some programs); for doctorate, thesis/dissertation. *Entrance requirements:* For master's and doctorate, GRE. Additional exam requirements/recommendations for international students: Required—TOEFL (minimum score 600 paper-based; 100 iBT), IELTS (minimum score 7), PTE (minimum score 68). *Application deadline:* For fall admission, 1/1 priority date for domestic and international students; for spring admission, 8/15 priority date for domestic and international students. Applications are processed on a rolling basis. Application fee: $75. Electronic applications accepted. *Expenses: Tuition:* Full-time $46,700; part-time $1945 per credit. Tuition and fees vary according to course load. *Financial support:* In 2014–15, 1 student received support, including fellowships (averaging $18,500 per year), research assistantships (averaging $18,500 per year), teaching assistantships (averaging $18,500 per year). Financial award application deadline: 1/1. *Faculty research:* Applied radiation, radiation transport, medical physics, multiphase phenomena, sonoluminescence, fusion plasma engineering. *Total annual research expenditures:* $1.1 million. *Unit head:* Dr. Theo Borca-Tasciuc, Graduate Program Director, 518-276-2627, E-mail: borcat@rpi.edu. *Application contact:* Graduate Admissions, 518-276-6216, E-mail: gradadmissions@rpi.edu.
Website: http://www.rpi.edu/dept/mane.

Stevens Institute of Technology, Graduate School, Charles V. Schaefer Jr. School of Engineering, Department of Physics and Engineering Physics, Hoboken, NJ 07030. Offers applied optics (Certificate); engineering physics (M Eng); microdevices and microsystems (Certificate); physics (MS, PhD); plasma and surface physics (Certificate). Part-time and evening/weekend programs available. Terminal master's awarded for partial completion of doctoral program. *Degree requirements:* For master's, thesis optional; for doctorate, thesis/dissertation. *Entrance requirements:* For master's and doctorate, GRE. Additional exam requirements/recommendations for international students: Required—TOEFL. Electronic applications accepted. *Faculty research:* Laser spectroscopy, physical kinetics, semiconductor-device physics, condensed-matter theory.

University of California, San Diego, Graduate Division, Department of Mechanical and Aerospace Engineering, Program in Engineering Physics, La Jolla, CA 92093. Offers

MS, PhD. *Students:* 18 full-time (6 women), 2 part-time (0 women); includes 1 minority (Black or African American, non-Hispanic/Latino), 10 international. 23 applicants, 48% accepted, 1 enrolled. In 2014, 2 master's awarded. *Degree requirements:* For master's, comprehensive exam or thesis; for doctorate, comprehensive exam, thesis/dissertation. *Entrance requirements:* For master's and doctorate, GRE General Test, minimum GPA of 3.0. Additional exam requirements/recommendations for international students: Required—TOEFL (minimum score 550 paper-based; 80 iBT), IELTS (minimum score 7). *Application deadline:* For fall admission, 12/15 for domestic students, 1/2 for international students. Application fee: $90 ($110 for international students). Electronic applications accepted. *Expenses:* Tuition, state resident: full-time $11,220; part-time $5610 per quarter. Tuition, nonresident: full-time $26,322; part-time $13,161 per quarter. *Required fees:* $570 per quarter. Tuition and fees vary according to program. *Financial support:* Fellowships, research assistantships, teaching assistantships, scholarships/grants, and unspecified assistantships available. Financial award application deadline: 1/2; financial award applicants required to submit FAFSA. *Faculty research:* Experimental, theoretical, and computational programs addressing turbulent flows; mechanics of two-phase flow; rheology of suspensions; laminar and turbulent combustion; chemical kinetics of combustion systems. *Unit head:* Vitali Nesterenko, Chair, 858-534-0113, E-mail: mae-chair-l@ucsd.edu. *Application contact:* Linda McKamey, Graduate Coordinator, 858-534-4065, E-mail: mae-gradadm-l@ucsd.edu. Website: http://maeweb.ucsd.edu/.

University of Central Oklahoma, The Jackson College of Graduate Studies, College of Mathematics and Science, Department of Engineering and Physics, Edmond, OK 73034-5209. Offers biomedical engineering (MS); electrical engineering (MS); mechanical systems (MS); physics (MS). Part-time programs available. *Degree requirements:* For master's, thesis optional. *Entrance requirements:* For master's, GRE, 24 hours of course work in physics or equivalent, mathematics through differential equations, minimum GPA of 2.75 overall and 3.0 in last 60 hours attempted. Additional exam requirements/recommendations for international students: Required—TOEFL (minimum score 550 paper-based). Electronic applications accepted.

University of Maine, Graduate School, College of Liberal Arts and Sciences, Department of Physics and Astronomy, Orono, ME 04469. Offers engineering physics (ME); physics (MS, PhD). *Faculty:* 13 full-time (1 woman), 1 part-time/adjunct (0 women). *Students:* 47 full-time (11 women), 9 part-time (6 women); includes 6 minority (1 American Indian or Alaska Native, non-Hispanic/Latino; 3 Asian, non-Hispanic/Latino; 1 Hispanic/Latino; 1 Two or more races, non-Hispanic/Latino), 2 international. Average age 29. 43 applicants, 21% accepted, 9 enrolled. In 2014, 1 master's, 5 doctorates awarded. Terminal master's awarded for partial completion of doctoral program. *Degree requirements:* For master's, thesis; for doctorate, comprehensive exam, thesis/dissertation. *Entrance requirements:* For master's, GRE General Test, GRE Subject Test; for doctorate, GRE General Test. Additional exam requirements/recommendations for international students: Required—TOEFL. *Application deadline:* For fall admission, 1/15 priority date for domestic students. Applications are processed on a rolling basis. Application fee: $65. Electronic applications accepted. *Expenses:* Tuition, state resident: part-time $658 per credit hour. Tuition, nonresident: part-time $1550 per credit hour. *Financial support:* In 2014–15, 31 students received support, including 5 research assistantships with full tuition reimbursements available (averaging $14,600 per year), 26 teaching assistantships with full tuition reimbursements available (averaging $14,600 per year); tuition waivers (full and partial) also available. Financial award application deadline: 3/1. *Faculty research:* Physics education research, experimental and theoretical biophysics, surface/nano physics, extragalactic astrophysics, environmental/nuclear physics, thermal/statistical physics theory. Total annual research expenditures: $4.7 million. *Unit head:* Dr. David Batuski, Chair, 207-581-1015, Fax: 207-581-3410. *Application contact:* Scott G. Delcourt, Associate Dean of the Graduate School, 207-581-3291, Fax: 207-581-3232, E-mail: graduate@maine.edu. Website: http://www.physics.umaine.edu/.

University of Oklahoma, Gallogly College of Engineering, Department of Engineering Physics, Norman, OK 73019. Offers MS, PhD. *Students:* 2 full-time (0 women), 2 part-time (0 women), 3 international. Average age 25. Terminal master's awarded for partial completion of doctoral program. *Degree requirements:* For master's, thesis or alternative, departmental qualifying exam; for doctorate, thesis/dissertation, comprehensive, departmental qualifying, oral, and written exams. *Entrance requirements:* For master's and doctorate, GRE General Test, GRE Subject Test (physics), previous course work in physics. Additional exam requirements/recommendations for international students: Required—TOEFL (minimum score 100 iBT). *Application deadline:* For fall admission, 3/1 for domestic and international students; for spring admission, 10/1 for domestic students, 9/1 for international students. Applications are processed on a rolling basis. Application fee: $50 ($100 for international students). Electronic applications accepted. *Expenses:* Tuition, state resident: full-time $4394; part-time $183.10 per credit hour. Tuition, nonresident: full-time $16,970; part-time $707.10 per credit hour. *Required fees:* $2892; $109.95 per credit hour. $126.50 per semester. *Financial support:* In 2014–15, 4 students received support. Scholarships/grants, health care benefits, tuition waivers (full), and unspecified assistantships available. Financial award application deadline: 6/1; financial award applicants required to submit FAFSA. *Faculty research:* Nanoscience, ultra cold atoms, high energy physics. *Unit head:* Dr. Mike Santos, Director, 405-325-3961, E-mail: msantos@ou.edu. Website: http://www.ou.edu/content/coe/ephysics/grad.html.

University of Saskatchewan, College of Graduate Studies and Research, College of Arts and Science, Department of Physics and Engineering Physics, Saskatoon, SK S7N 5A2, Canada. Offers M Sc, PhD. *Degree requirements:* For master's, thesis; for doctorate, comprehensive exam (for some programs), thesis/dissertation. *Entrance requirements:* Additional exam requirements/recommendations for international

students: Required—TOEFL (minimum score 80 iBT); Recommended—IELTS (minimum score 6.5). Electronic applications accepted.

The University of Tulsa, Graduate School, College of Engineering and Natural Sciences, Department of Physics and Engineering Physics, Program in Engineering Physics, Tulsa, OK 74104-3189. Offers MS. Part-time programs available. *Students:* 3 applicants, 33% accepted. In 2014, 1 master's awarded. *Degree requirements:* For master's, thesis. *Entrance requirements:* For master's, GRE General Test. Additional exam requirements/recommendations for international students: Required—TOEFL (minimum score 550 paper-based; 80 iBT), IELTS (minimum score 6). *Application deadline:* Applications are processed on a rolling basis. Application fee: $55. Electronic applications accepted. *Expenses: Tuition:* Full-time $20,160; part-time $1120 per credit hour. *Required fees:* $6 per credit hour. Tuition and fees vary according to course level and course load. *Financial support:* Fellowships, research assistantships, teaching assistantships, career-related internships or fieldwork, Federal Work-Study, scholarships/grants, health care benefits, tuition waivers (full and partial), and unspecified assistantships available. Support available to part-time students. *Faculty research:* Nanotechnology, theoretical plasma physics/fusion, condensed matter, laser spectroscopy, optics and optical applications for environmental applications. *Unit head:* Dr. George Miller, Program Chair, 918-631-3021, Fax: 918-631-2995, E-mail: george-miller@utulsa.edu. *Application contact:* Dr. Scott Holmstrom, Advisor, 918-631-3031, Fax: 918-631-2995, E-mail: scott-holmstrom@utulsa.edu.

University of Virginia, School of Engineering and Applied Science, Program in Engineering Physics, Charlottesville, VA 22903. Offers MEP, MS, PhD. Postbaccalaureate distance learning degree programs offered (no on-campus study). *Students:* 14 full-time (6 women); includes 1 minority (Asian, non-Hispanic/Latino), 3 international. Average age 28. 27 applicants, 22% accepted, 1 enrolled. In 2014, 6 master's, 1 doctorate awarded. *Degree requirements:* For master's, comprehensive exam; for doctorate, comprehensive exam, thesis/dissertation. *Entrance requirements:* For master's and doctorate, GRE General Test, 3 recommendations. Additional exam requirements/recommendations for international students: Required—TOEFL. *Application deadline:* For fall admission, 1/15 for domestic and international students. Applications are processed on a rolling basis. Application fee: $60. Electronic applications accepted. *Expenses:* Tuition, state resident: full-time $14,164; part-time $349 per credit hour. Tuition, nonresident: full-time $23,722; part-time $1300 per credit hour. *Required fees:* $2514. *Financial support:* Fellowships, research assistantships, and teaching assistantships available. Financial award application deadline: 2/1; financial award applicants required to submit FAFSA. *Faculty research:* Continuum and rarefied gas dynamics, ultracentrifuge isotope enrichment, solid-state physics, atmospheric physics, atomic collisions. *Unit head:* Petra Reinke, Co-Chair, 434-924-7237, Fax: 434-982-5660, E-mail: pr6e@virginia.edu. *Application contact:* Kimberly Ann Fitzhugh-Higgins, Graduate Student Coordinator, 434-982-5641, Fax: 434-982-5660, E-mail: kaf5r@virginia.edu. Website: http://www.virginia.edu/ep/.

University of Wisconsin–Madison, Graduate School, College of Engineering, Department of Engineering Physics, Madison, WI 53706. Offers engineering mechanics (MS, PhD); nuclear engineering and engineering physics (MS, PhD). Part-time programs available. Postbaccalaureate distance learning degree programs offered (minimal on-campus study). *Faculty:* 21 full-time (1 woman), 8 part-time/adjunct (4 women). *Students:* 123 full-time (20 women), 9 part-time (0 women); includes 17 minority (3 Black or African American, non-Hispanic/Latino; 1 American Indian or Alaska Native, non-Hispanic/Latino; 6 Asian, non-Hispanic/Latino; 5 Hispanic/Latino; 2 Two or more races, non-Hispanic/Latino), 25 international. Average age 26. 221 applicants, 47% accepted, 48 enrolled. In 2014, 36 master's, 11 doctorates awarded. Terminal master's awarded for partial completion of doctoral program. *Degree requirements:* For master's, thesis optional; for doctorate, thesis/dissertation. *Entrance requirements:* For master's and doctorate, GRE General Test, minimum GPA of 3.0 in last 60 hours, appropriate bachelor's degree. Additional exam requirements/recommendations for international students: Required—TOEFL (minimum score 600 paper-based). *Application deadline:* For fall admission, 1/1 priority date for domestic and international students. Applications are processed on a rolling basis. Application fee: $56. Electronic applications accepted. *Expenses:* Tuition, state resident: full-time $10,723; part-time $745 per credit. Tuition, nonresident: full-time $24,054; part-time $1578 per credit. *Required fees:* $374 per semester. Tuition and fees vary according to course load, program and reciprocity agreements. *Financial support:* In 2014–15, 74 students received support, including 21 fellowships with full tuition reimbursements available (averaging $25,101 per year), 89 research assistantships with full tuition reimbursements available (averaging $21,224 per year), 16 teaching assistantships with full tuition reimbursements available (averaging $14,326 per year); career-related internships or fieldwork, Federal Work-Study, institutionally sponsored loans, unspecified assistantships, and project assistantships also available. Support available to part-time students. Financial award application deadline: 1/15. *Faculty research:* Fission reactor engineering and safety, plasma physics and fusion technology, plasma processing and ion implantation, nanotechnology, engineering mechanics and astronautics. Total annual research expenditures: $16.3 million. *Unit head:* Dr. Doug Henderson, Chair, 608-263-0391, Fax: 608-263-7451, E-mail: henderson@engr.wisc.edu. *Application contact:* Betsy A. Wood, Graduate Coordinator, 608-263-7038, Fax: 608-263-7451, E-mail: betsy.wood@wisc.edu. Website: http://www.engr.wisc.edu/ep/.

Yale University, Graduate School of Arts and Sciences, School of Engineering and Applied Science, Department of Applied Physics, New Haven, CT 06520. Offers MS, PhD. Terminal master's awarded for partial completion of doctoral program. *Degree requirements:* For doctorate, thesis/dissertation, area exam. *Entrance requirements:* For master's and doctorate, GRE General Test. Additional exam requirements/recommendations for international students: Required—TOEFL. *Faculty research:* Condensed-matter physics, optical physics, materials science.

Section 13
Geological, Mineral/Mining, and Petroleum Engineering

This section contains a directory of institutions offering graduate work in geological, mineral/mining, and petroleum engineering. Additional information about programs listed in the directory may be obtained by writing directly to the dean of a graduate school or chair of a department at the address given in the directory.

For programs offering related work, see also in this book *Chemical Engineering, Civil and Environmental Engineering, Electrical and Computer Engineering, Energy and Power Engineering, Engineering and Applied Sciences, Management of Engineering and Technology,* and *Materials Sciences and Engineering.* In another guide in this series:

Graduate Programs in the Physical Sciences, Mathematics, Agricultural Sciences, the Environment & Natural Resources
See *Geosciences* and *Marine Sciences and Oceanography*

CONTENTS

Program Directories

Geological Engineering

Arizona State University at the Tempe campus, College of Liberal Arts and Sciences, School of Earth and Space Exploration, Tempe, AZ 85287-1404. Offers astrophysics (MS, PhD); exploration systems design (PhD); geological sciences (MS, PhD). PhD in exploration systems design is offered in collaboration with the Ira A. Fulton School of Engineering. Terminal master's awarded for partial completion of doctoral program. *Degree requirements:* For master's, thesis, interactive Program of Study (iPOS) submitted before completing 50 percent of required credit hours; for doctorate, thesis/dissertation, interactive Program of Study (iPOS) submitted before completing 50 percent of required credit hours. *Entrance requirements:* For master's and doctorate, GRE, minimum GPA of 3.0 or equivalent in last 2 years of work leading to bachelor's degree. Additional exam requirements/recommendations for international students: Required—TOEFL, IELTS, or PTE. Electronic applications accepted.

Colorado School of Mines, Graduate School, Department of Geology and Geological Engineering, Golden, CO 80401. Offers geochemistry (MS, PMS, PhD); geological engineering (ME, MS, PhD); geology (MS, PhD). Part-time programs available. *Faculty:* 27 full-time (11 women), 7 part-time/adjunct (4 women). *Students:* 148 full-time (46 women), 33 part-time (9 women); includes 15 minority (2 American Indian or Alaska Native, non-Hispanic/Latino; 2 Asian, non-Hispanic/Latino; 10 Hispanic/Latino; 1 Two or more races, non-Hispanic/Latino), 32 international. Average age 31. 371 applicants, 35% accepted, 64 enrolled. In 2014, 45 master's, 10 doctorates awarded. *Degree requirements:* For master's, thesis (for some programs); for doctorate, comprehensive exam, thesis/dissertation. *Entrance requirements:* For master's and doctorate, GRE General Test. Additional exam requirements/recommendations for international students: Required—TOEFL (minimum score 550 paper-based; 80 iBT). *Application deadline:* For fall admission, 12/15 priority date for domestic and international students; for spring admission, 9/1 priority date for domestic and international students. Application fee: $50 ($70 for international students). Electronic applications accepted. *Financial support:* In 2014–15, 105 students received support, including 18 fellowships with full tuition reimbursements available (averaging $21,120 per year), 63 research assistantships with full tuition reimbursements available (averaging $21,120 per year), 16 teaching assistantships with full tuition reimbursements available (averaging $21,120 per year); scholarships/grants, health care benefits, and unspecified assistantships also available. Financial award application deadline: 12/15; financial award applicants required to submit FAFSA. *Faculty research:* Predictive sediment modeling, petrophysics, aquifer-contaminant flow modeling, water-rock interactions, geotechnical engineering. *Total annual research expenditures:* $3.6 million. *Unit head:* Dr. Paul Santi, Head, 303-273-3108, Fax: 303-273-3800, E-mail: psanti@mines.edu. *Application contact:* Dr. Christian Shorey, Lecturer, 303-273-3556, Fax: 303-273-3800, E-mail: cshorey@mines.edu.
Website: http://geology.mines.edu.

Colorado School of Mines, Graduate School, Department of Geophysics, Golden, CO 80401-1887. Offers geophysical engineering (ME, MS, PhD); geophysics (MS, PhD); hydrology (MS, PhD); mineral exploration and mining geosciences (PMS). Part-time programs available. *Faculty:* 16 full-time (1 woman), 3 part-time/adjunct (0 women). *Students:* 84 full-time (26 women), 5 part-time (1 woman); includes 11 minority (2 Black or African American, non-Hispanic/Latino; 1 American Indian or Alaska Native, non-Hispanic/Latino; 2 Asian, non-Hispanic/Latino; 6 Hispanic/Latino), 46 international. Average age 32. 170 applicants, 29% accepted, 32 enrolled. In 2014, 19 master's, 5 doctorates awarded. *Degree requirements:* For master's, thesis (for some programs); for doctorate, one foreign language, comprehensive exam, thesis/dissertation, oral exams. *Entrance requirements:* For master's and doctorate, GRE General Test. Additional exam requirements/recommendations for international students: Required—TOEFL (minimum score 550 paper-based; 80 iBT). *Application deadline:* For fall admission, 12/15 priority date for domestic and international students; for spring admission, 9/1 priority date for domestic students, 9/1 for international students. Application fee: $50 ($70 for international students). Electronic applications accepted. *Financial support:* In 2014–15, 67 students received support, including 3 fellowships with full tuition reimbursements available (averaging $21,120 per year), 60 research assistantships with full tuition reimbursements available (averaging $21,120 per year), 4 teaching assistantships with full tuition reimbursements available (averaging $21,120 per year); scholarships/grants, health care benefits, and unspecified assistantships also available. Financial award application deadline: 12/15; financial award applicants required to submit FAFSA. *Faculty research:* Seismic exploration, gravity and geomagnetic fields, electrical mapping and sounding, bore hole measurements, environmental physics. *Total annual research expenditures:* $5.9 million. *Unit head:* Dr. Terence K. Young, Head, 303-273-3454, Fax: 303-273-3478, E-mail: tkyoung@mines.edu. *Application contact:* Michelle Szobody, Program Assistant, 303-273-3935, Fax: 303-273-3478, E-mail: mszobody@mines.edu.
Website: http://geophysics.mines.edu.

Michigan Technological University, Graduate School, College of Engineering, Department of Geological and Mining Engineering and Sciences, Houghton, MI 49931. Offers geological engineering (MS, PhD); geology (MS, PhD); geophysics (MS, PhD); mining engineering (MS, PhD). Part-time programs available. *Faculty:* 25 full-time, 31 part-time/adjunct. *Students:* 68 full-time (31 women), 15 part-time (8 women); includes 5 minority (1 Black or African American, non-Hispanic/Latino; 1 Asian, non-Hispanic/Latino; 2 Hispanic/Latino; 1 Two or more races, non-Hispanic/Latino), 39 international. Average age 28. 208 applicants, 28% accepted, 26 enrolled. In 2014, 12 master's, 3 doctorates awarded. Terminal master's awarded for partial completion of doctoral program. *Degree requirements:* For master's, comprehensive exam (for some programs), thesis (for some programs); for doctorate, comprehensive exam, thesis/dissertation. *Entrance requirements:* For master's and doctorate, GRE, statement of purpose, official transcripts, 3 letters of recommendation. Additional exam requirements/recommendations for international students: Required—TOEFL (recommended score 79 iBT) or IELTS. *Application deadline:* For fall admission, 2/1 priority date for domestic and international students. Applications are processed on a rolling basis. Electronic applications accepted. *Expenses:* Tuition, state resident: full-time $14,769; part-time $820.50 per credit. Tuition, nonresident: full-time $14,769; part-time $820.50 per credit. *Required fees:* $248; $248 per year. Tuition and fees vary according to course load and program. *Financial support:* In 2014–15, 53 students received support, including 9 fellowships with full and partial tuition reimbursements available (averaging $13,824 per year), 15 research assistantships with full and partial tuition reimbursements available (averaging $13,824 per year), 7 teaching assistantships with full and partial tuition reimbursements available (averaging $13,824 per year); career-related internships or fieldwork, Federal Work-Study, scholarships/grants, health care benefits, unspecified assistantships, and cooperative program also available. Financial award applicants required to submit FAFSA. *Faculty research:* Volcanic hazards and volcanic clouds, oil and gas exploration and development, groundwater measurement and modeling, geophysics, environmental paleomagnetism. *Total annual research expenditures:* $1.8 million. *Unit head:* Dr. John S. Gierke, Chair, 906-487-2535, Fax: 906-487-3371, E-mail: jsgierke@mtu.edu. *Application contact:* Amie S. Ledgerwood, Assistant to the Dean, 906-487-2531, Fax: 906-487-3371, E-mail: asledger@mtu.edu.
Website: http://www.mtu.edu/geo/.

Missouri University of Science and Technology, Graduate School, Department of Geological Sciences and Engineering, Rolla, MO 65409. Offers geological engineering (MS, DE, PhD); geology and geophysics (MS, PhD), including geochemistry, geology, geophysics, groundwater and environmental geology; petroleum engineering (MS, DE, PhD). Part-time programs available. *Degree requirements:* For master's, thesis optional; for doctorate, comprehensive exam, thesis/dissertation. *Entrance requirements:* For master's, GRE General Test (minimum score 600 quantitative, writing 3.5), minimum GPA of 3.0 in last 4 semesters; for doctorate, GRE General Test (minimum: Q 600, GRE WR 3.5). Additional exam requirements/recommendations for international students: Required—TOEFL. Electronic applications accepted. *Faculty research:* Digital image processing and geographic information systems, mineralogy, igneous and sedimentary petrology-geochemistry, sedimentology groundwater hydrology and contaminant transport.

Montana Tech of The University of Montana, Graduate School, Geosciences Programs, Butte, MT 59701-8997. Offers geochemistry (MS); geological engineering (MS); geology (MS); geophysical engineering (MS); hydrogeological engineering (MS); hydrogeology (MS). Part-time programs available. *Degree requirements:* For master's, comprehensive exam (for some programs), thesis (for some programs). *Entrance requirements:* For master's, GRE General Test, minimum GPA of 3.0. Additional exam requirements/recommendations for international students: Required—TOEFL (minimum score 525 paper-based; 71 iBT). Electronic applications accepted. *Expenses:* Tuition, state resident: full-time $5802; part-time $241 per credit. Tuition, nonresident: full-time $15,895; part-time $662 per credit. *Required fees:* $1516; $414 per credit. $207 per semester. One-time fee: $30. *Faculty research:* Water resource development, seismic processing, petroleum reservoir characterization, environmental geochemistry, geologic mapping.

New Mexico State University, College of Engineering, Department of Civil and Geological Engineering, Las Cruces, NM 88003-8001. Offers MS Env E, MSCE, PhD. Part-time programs available. Postbaccalaureate distance learning degree programs offered (minimal on-campus study). *Faculty:* 14 full-time (3 women). *Students:* 58 full-time (17 women), 19 part-time (3 women); includes 22 minority (2 Black or African American, non-Hispanic/Latino; 3 American Indian or Alaska Native, non-Hispanic/Latino; 1 Asian, non-Hispanic/Latino; 15 Hispanic/Latino; 1 Two or more races, non-Hispanic/Latino), 36 international. Average age 30. 74 applicants, 41% accepted, 16 enrolled. In 2014, 14 master's awarded. *Degree requirements:* For master's, thesis (for some programs); for doctorate, comprehensive exam (for some programs), thesis/dissertation, qualifying exam. *Entrance requirements:* For master's and doctorate, BS in engineering, minimum GPA of 3.0. Additional exam requirements/recommendations for international students: Required—TOEFL (minimum score 550 paper-based; 79 iBT), IELTS (minimum score 6.5). *Application deadline:* For fall admission, 4/1 priority date for domestic and international students; for spring admission, 9/1 priority date for domestic and international students. Applications are processed on a rolling basis. Application fee: $40 ($50 for international students). Electronic applications accepted. *Expenses:* Tuition, state resident: full-time $3969; part-time $220.50 per credit hour. Tuition, nonresident: full-time $13,838; part-time $768.80 per credit hour. *Required fees:* $853; $47.40 per credit hour. *Financial support:* In 2014–15, 59 students received support, including 8 fellowships (averaging $2,510 per year), 24 research assistantships (averaging $12,168 per year), 27 teaching assistantships (averaging $9,444 per year); career-related internships or fieldwork, Federal Work-Study, scholarships/grants, traineeships, health care benefits, and unspecified assistantships also available. Support available to part-time students. Financial award application deadline: 3/1. *Faculty research:* Structural engineering, water resources engineering, environmental engineering, geotechnical engineering, transportation. *Total annual research expenditures:* $2.1 million. *Unit head:* Dr. Peter T. Martin, Head, 575-646-3801, E-mail: wales@nmsu.edu. *Application contact:* 575-646-3801, E-mail: civil@nmsu.edu.
Website: http://ce.nmsu.edu.

South Dakota School of Mines and Technology, Graduate Division, Department of Geology and Geological Engineering, Rapid City, SD 57701-3995. Offers geology and geological engineering (MS, PhD); paleontology (MS). Part-time programs available. *Faculty:* 9 full-time (4 women), 3 part-time/adjunct (0 women). *Students:* 29 full-time (11 women), 12 part-time (5 women); includes 3 minority (2 Hispanic/Latino; 1 Two or more races, non-Hispanic/Latino). Average age 29. 66 applicants, 29% accepted, 11 enrolled. In 2014, 12 master's, 3 doctorates awarded. *Degree requirements:* For master's, thesis; for doctorate, thesis/dissertation. *Entrance requirements:* For master's and doctorate, GRE General Test, GRE Subject Test. Additional exam requirements/recommendations for international students: Required—TOEFL (minimum score 520 paper-based; 68 iBT), TWE. *Application deadline:* For fall admission, 7/1 priority date for domestic students, 4/1 for international students; for spring admission, 11/1 for domestic students, 9/1 for international students. Applications are processed on a rolling basis. Application fee: $35. Electronic applications accepted. *Expenses:* Tuition, state resident: full-time $5050; part-time $210.40 per credit hour. Tuition, nonresident: full-time $11,290; part-time $470.30 per credit hour. *Required fees:* $4680. *Financial support:* In 2014–15, 10 fellowships (averaging $2,480 per year), 12 research assistantships with partial tuition reimbursements (averaging $13,144 per year), 18 teaching assistantships with partial tuition reimbursements (averaging $4,633 per year) were awarded; Federal Work-Study and institutionally sponsored loans also available. Support available to part-time students. Financial award application deadline: 5/15. *Faculty research:* Contaminants in soil, nitrate leaching, environmental changes, fracture formations, greenhouse effect. *Total annual research expenditures:* $387,027. *Unit head:* Dr. Laurie Anderson, Chair, 605-394-1290, E-mail: laurie.anderson@sdsmt.edu. *Application contact:* Rachel Howard, Office of Graduate Education, 605-355-3468, Fax: 605-394-1767, E-mail: rachel.howard@sdsmt.edu.

The University of Akron, Graduate School, Buchtel College of Arts and Sciences, Department of Geosciences, Akron, OH 44325. Offers earth science (MS); engineering geology (MS); environmental geology (MS); geology (MS); geophysics (MS). Part-time programs available. *Faculty:* 10 full-time (2 women), 2 part-time/adjunct (0 women). *Students:* 15 full-time (5 women), 1 part-time (0 women), 1 international. Average age 25. 22 applicants, 59% accepted, 7 enrolled. In 2014, 8 master's awarded. *Degree requirements:* For master's, comprehensive exam, thesis, seminar, proficiency exam. *Entrance requirements:* For master's, minimum GPA of 2.75, three letters of recommendation, statement of purpose. Additional exam requirements/recommendations for international students: Required—TOEFL (minimum score 550 paper-based; 79 iBT). *Application deadline:* Applications are processed on a rolling basis. Application fee: $45 ($70 for international students). Electronic applications accepted. *Expenses:* Tuition, state resident: full-time $7578; part-time $421 per credit

hour. Tuition, nonresident: full-time $12,977; part-time $721 per credit hour. *Required fees:* $1388; $35 per credit hour. Tuition and fees vary according to course load. *Financial support:* In 2014–15, 14 teaching assistantships with full tuition reimbursements were awarded. *Faculty research:* Terrestrial environmental change, karst hydrogeology, lacustrine paleoenvironments, environmental magnetism and geophysics. *Total annual research expenditures:* $480,927. *Unit head:* Dr. James McManus, Chair, 330-972-7991, E-mail: jmcmanus@uakron.edu. *Application contact:* Dr. LaVerne Friberg, Director of Graduate Studies, 330-972-8046, E-mail: lfribe1@uakron.edu.
Website: http://www.uakron.edu/geology/.

University of Alaska Anchorage, School of Engineering, Program in Arctic Engineering, Anchorage, AK 99508. Offers MS. Part-time and evening/weekend programs available. *Degree requirements:* For master's, thesis or alternative, engineering project report. *Entrance requirements:* For master's, bachelor's degree in engineering. Additional exam requirements/recommendations for international students: Required—TOEFL (minimum score 550 paper-based). *Faculty research:* Load-bearing ice, control of drifting snow, permafrost and foundations, frozen ground engineering.

University of Alaska Fairbanks, College of Engineering and Mines, Department of Mining and Geological Engineering, Fairbanks, AK 99775-5800. Offers geological engineering (MS); mineral preparation engineering (MS); mining engineering (MS). Part-time programs available. *Faculty:* 8 full-time (1 woman). *Students:* 9 full-time (2 women); includes 1 minority (Two or more races, non-Hispanic/Latino), 7 international. Average age 30. 11 applicants, 55% accepted, 5 enrolled. In 2014, 4 master's awarded. *Degree requirements:* For master's, comprehensive exam, oral defense of project or thesis. *Entrance requirements:* For master's, GRE General Test (for geological engineering), bachelor's degree from accredited institution with minimum cumulative undergraduate and major GPA of 3.0. Additional exam requirements/recommendations for international students: Required—TOEFL (minimum score 550 paper-based; 79 iBT), IELTS (minimum score 6.5). *Application deadline:* For fall admission, 6/1 for domestic students, 3/1 for international students; for spring admission, 10/15 for domestic students, 9/1 for international students. Applications are processed on a rolling basis. Application fee: $60. Electronic applications accepted. *Expenses:* Tuition, state resident: full-time $7614; part-time $423 per credit. Tuition, nonresident: full-time $15,552; part-time $864 per credit. Tuition and fees vary according to course level, course load and reciprocity agreements. *Financial support:* In 2014–15, 5 research assistantships with full tuition reimbursements (averaging $5,794 per year), 5 teaching assistantships with full tuition reimbursements (averaging $6,207 per year) were awarded; fellowships with full tuition reimbursements, career-related internships or fieldwork, Federal Work-Study, scholarships/grants, health care benefits, and unspecified assistantships also available. Support available to part-time students. Financial award application deadline: 7/1; financial award applicants required to submit FAFSA. *Faculty research:* Underground mining in permafrost, testing of ultra clean diesel, slope stability, fractal and mathematical morphology, soil and rock mechanics. *Unit head:* Dr. Rajive Ganguli, Chair, 907-474-7388, Fax: 907-474-6635, E-mail: uaf-cemmingeo-dept@alaska.edu. *Application contact:* Mary Kreta, Director of Admissions, 907-474-7500, Fax: 907-474-7097, E-mail: admissions@uaf.edu.
Website: http://cem.uaf.edu/mingeo.

The University of Arizona, College of Engineering, Department of Mining and Geological Engineering, Tucson, AZ 85721. Offers mining and geological engineering (M Eng, MS, PhD); mining engineering (Certificate), including mine health and safety, mine information and production technology, rock mechanics. Part-time programs available. Postbaccalaureate distance learning degree programs offered (minimal on-campus study). *Degree requirements:* For master's, thesis; for doctorate, thesis/dissertation. *Entrance requirements:* For master's, GRE General Test, 3 letters of recommendation; for doctorate, GRE General Test, 3 letters of recommendation, statements of purpose. Additional exam requirements/recommendations for international students: Required—TOEFL (minimum score 550 paper-based; 79 iBT). Electronic applications accepted. *Faculty research:* Geomechanics, mineral processing, information technology, automation, geosensing.

The University of British Columbia, Faculty of Science, Department of Earth, Ocean and Atmospheric Sciences, Vancouver, BC V6T 1Z4, Canada. Offers atmospheric science (M Sc, PhD); geological engineering (M Eng, MA Sc, PhD); geological sciences (M Sc, PhD); geophysics (M Sc, MA Sc, PhD); oceanography (M Sc, PhD). *Degree requirements:* For master's, one foreign language, thesis (for some programs); for doctorate, one foreign language, comprehensive exam, thesis/dissertation. *Entrance requirements:* Additional exam requirements/recommendations for international students: Required—TOEFL (minimum score 600 paper-based; 100 iBT). *Faculty research:* Oceans and atmosphere, environmental earth science, hydro geology, mineral deposits, geophysics.

University of Hawaii at Manoa, Graduate Division, School of Ocean and Earth Science and Technology, Department of Geology and Geophysics, Honolulu, HI 96822. Offers high-pressure geophysics and geochemistry (MS, PhD); hydrogeology and engineering geology (MS, PhD); marine geology and geophysics (MS, PhD); planetary geosciences and remote sensing (MS, PhD); seismology and solid-earth geophysics (MS, PhD); volcanology, petrology, and geochemistry (MS, PhD). Part-time programs available. Terminal master's awarded for partial completion of doctoral program. *Degree requirements:* For master's, thesis optional; for doctorate, comprehensive exam, thesis/dissertation. *Entrance requirements:* For master's and doctorate, GRE General Test, minimum GPA of 3.0. Additional exam requirements/recommendations for international students: Required—TOEFL (minimum score 580 paper-based; 92 iBT), IELTS (minimum score 5).

University of Idaho, College of Graduate Studies, College of Engineering, Department of Civil Engineering, Moscow, ID 83844-1022. Offers civil engineering (M Engr, MS, PhD); engineering management (M Engr); geological engineering (MS). *Faculty:* 13 full-time, 3 part-time/adjunct. *Students:* 24 full-time, 86 part-time. Average age 37. In 2014, 25 master's, 3 doctorates awarded. *Degree requirements:* For master's, thesis; for doctorate, thesis/dissertation. *Entrance requirements:* For master's, minimum GPA of 2.8; for doctorate, minimum undergraduate GPA of 2.8, 3.0 graduate. *Application deadline:* For fall admission, 8/1 for domestic students; for spring admission, 12/15 for domestic students. Applications are processed on a rolling basis. Application fee: $60. Electronic applications accepted. *Expenses:* Tuition, state resident: full-time $4784; part-time $280.50 per credit hour. Tuition, nonresident: full-time $18,314; part-time $957.50 per credit hour. *Required fees:* $2000; $58.50 per credit hour. Tuition and fees vary according to program. *Financial support:* Fellowships, research assistantships, teaching assistantships, and career-related internships or fieldwork available. Financial award applicants required to submit FAFSA. *Faculty research:* Water resources systems, structural analysis and design, soil mechanics, transportation technology. *Unit head:* Richard J. Nielsen, Chair, 208-885-6782, E-mail: civilengr@uidaho.edu. *Application contact:* Sean Scoggin, Graduate Recruitment Coordinator, 208-885-4001, Fax: 208-885-4406, E-mail: graduateadmissions@uidaho.edu.
Website: http://www.uidaho.edu/engr/ce/.

University of Minnesota, Twin Cities Campus, College of Science and Engineering, Department of Civil, Environmental, and Geo-Engineering, Minneapolis, MN 55455-0213. Offers civil engineering (MCE, MS, PhD); geological engineering (M Geo E, MS); stream restoration science and engineering (Certificate). Part-time programs available. *Degree requirements:* For master's, thesis optional; for doctorate, thesis/dissertation. *Entrance requirements:* For master's and doctorate, GRE General Test. Additional exam requirements/recommendations for international students: Required—TOEFL. Electronic applications accepted. *Faculty research:* Environmental engineering, geomechanics, structural engineering, transportation, water resources.

University of Nevada, Reno, Graduate School, College of Science, Mackay School of Earth Sciences and Engineering, Department of Geological Sciences and Engineering, Program in Geological Engineering, Reno, NV 89557. Offers MS, PhD. Terminal master's awarded for partial completion of doctoral program. *Degree requirements:* For master's, thesis optional; for doctorate, thesis/dissertation. *Entrance requirements:* For master's and doctorate, GRE General Test, minimum GPA of 2.75. Additional exam requirements/recommendations for international students: Required—TOEFL (minimum score 500 paper-based; 61 iBT), IELTS (minimum score 6). Electronic applications accepted. *Faculty research:* Reclamation, remediation, restoration.

University of North Dakota, Graduate School, School of Engineering and Mines, Department of Geological Engineering, Grand Forks, ND 58202. Offers M Engr, MS. *Degree requirements:* For master's, thesis. *Entrance requirements:* For master's, GRE General Test. Additional exam requirements/recommendations for international students: Required—TOEFL (minimum score 550 paper-based; 79 iBT), IELTS (minimum score 6.5). Electronic applications accepted.

University of Oklahoma, Mewbourne College of Earth and Energy, Mewbourne School of Petroleum and Geological Engineering, Program in Geological Engineering, Norman, OK 73019. Offers MS, PhD. Part-time programs available. *Students:* 1 full-time (0 women), all international. Average age 29. 7 applicants, 14% accepted, 1 enrolled. Terminal master's awarded for partial completion of doctoral program. *Degree requirements:* For master's, variable foreign language requirement, comprehensive exam (for some programs), thesis (for some programs); for doctorate, variable foreign language requirement, comprehensive exam, thesis/dissertation. *Entrance requirements:* For master's, GRE, 3 letters of reference, statement of purpose, resume/curriculum vitae, minimum GPA of 3.2; for doctorate, GRE, statement of purpose, 3 letters of reference, resume/curriculum vitae, minimum GPA of 3.2. Additional exam requirements/recommendations for international students: Required—TOEFL (minimum score 79 iBT). *Application deadline:* For fall admission, 4/1 for domestic students, 3/1 for international students; for spring admission, 10/1 for domestic students, 9/1 for international students. Application fee: $50 ($100 for international students). Electronic applications accepted. *Expenses:* Tuition, state resident: full-time $4394; part-time $183.10 per credit hour. Tuition, nonresident: full-time $16,970; part-time $707.10 per credit hour. *Required fees:* $2892; $109.95 per credit hour. $126.50 per semester. *Financial support:* Unspecified assistantships available. Financial award application deadline: 6/1; financial award applicants required to submit FAFSA. *Faculty research:* Geomechanics applied to petroleum and geothermal reservoir development, reaction fluid flow in fractures. *Unit head:* Dr. Deepak Devegowda, Associate Professor and Graduate Liaison, 405-325-3081, Fax: 405-325-7477, E-mail: deepak.devegowda@ou.edu. *Application contact:* Sheriee Parnell, Graduate Programs Coordinator, 405-325-6821, Fax: 405-325-7477, E-mail: sheriee@ou.edu.
Website: http://mpge.ou.edu.

University of Saskatchewan, College of Graduate Studies and Research, College of Engineering, Civil and Geological Engineering Program, Saskatoon, SK S7N 5A9, Canada. Offers M Eng, M Sc, PhD. Part-time programs available. *Degree requirements:* For master's, thesis (for some programs), 30 credits (for M Eng); thesis and 12 credits (for MS); for doctorate, comprehensive exam, thesis/dissertation, qualifying exam, 18 credits. *Entrance requirements:* For master's, GRE, minimum GPA of 5.0 on an 8.0 scale; for doctorate, GRE. Additional exam requirements/recommendations for international students: Required—TOEFL, TOEFL (minimum iBT score of 80), IELTS (6.5), CanTEST (4.5), or PTE (59). Electronic applications accepted. *Faculty research:* Geotechnical/geo-environmental engineering, structural engineering, water resources engineering, civil engineering materials, environmental/sanitary engineering, hydrogeology, rock mechanics and mining, transportation engineering.

University of Utah, Graduate School, College of Mines and Earth Sciences, Department of Geology and Geophysics, Salt Lake City, UT 84112. Offers environmental engineering (ME, MS, PhD); geological engineering (ME, MS, PhD); geology (MS, PhD); geophysics (MS, PhD). *Faculty:* 23 full-time (5 women), 9 part-time/adjunct (3 women). *Students:* 50 full-time (20 women), 36 part-time (18 women); includes 6 minority (1 Black or African American, non-Hispanic/Latino; 1 American Indian or Alaska Native, non-Hispanic/Latino; 4 Hispanic/Latino), 17 international. Average age 29. 228 applicants, 14% accepted, 22 enrolled. In 2014, 26 master's, 5 doctorates awarded. Terminal master's awarded for partial completion of doctoral program. *Degree requirements:* For master's, comprehensive exam, thesis; for doctorate, thesis/dissertation, qualifying exam (written and oral). *Entrance requirements:* For master's and doctorate, GRE General Test, minimum GPA of 3.25. Additional exam requirements/recommendations for international students: Required—TOEFL (minimum score 500 paper-based; 61 iBT). *Application deadline:* For fall admission, 1/15 priority date for domestic and international students. Application fee: $55 ($65 for international students). Electronic applications accepted. *Financial support:* In 2014–15, 62 students received support, including 14 fellowships with full tuition reimbursements available (averaging $17,500 per year), 32 research assistantships with full tuition reimbursements available (averaging $23,000 per year), 16 teaching assistantships with full tuition reimbursements available (averaging $17,500 per year); career-related internships or fieldwork, institutionally sponsored loans, scholarships/grants, unspecified assistantships, and stipends also available. Financial award application deadline: 1/15; financial award applicants required to submit FAFSA. *Faculty research:* Igneous, metamorphic, and sedimentary petrology; stratigraphy; paleoclimatology; hydrology; seismology. *Total annual research expenditures:* $4.1 million. *Unit head:* Dr. John Bartley, Chair, 801-585-1670, Fax: 801-581-7065, E-mail: john.bartley@utah.edu. *Application contact:* Dr. Gabriel J. Bowen, Director of Graduate Studies, 801-585-7925, Fax: 801-581-7065, E-mail: gabe.bowen@utah.edu.
Website: http://www.earth.utah.edu/.

University of Wisconsin–Madison, Graduate School, College of Engineering, Geological Engineering Program, Madison, WI 53706. Offers MS, PhD. Part-time programs available. *Degree requirements:* For doctorate, thesis/dissertation. *Entrance requirements:* For master's and doctorate, GRE. Additional exam requirements/recommendations for international students: Required—TOEFL (minimum score 550 paper-based; 92 iBT). Electronic applications accepted. *Expenses:* Tuition, state resident: full-time $10,723; part-time $745 per credit. Tuition, nonresident: full-time $24,054; part-time $1578 per credit. *Required fees:* $374 per semester. Tuition and fees vary according to course load, program and reciprocity agreements. *Faculty research:* Constitutive models for geomaterials, rock fracture, in situ stress determination, environmental geotechnics, site remediation.

Mineral/Mining Engineering

Colorado School of Mines, Graduate School, Department of Geophysics, Golden, CO 80401-1887. Offers geophysical engineering (ME, MS, PhD); geophysics (MS, PhD); hydrology (MS, PhD); mineral exploration and mining geosciences (PMS). Part-time programs available. *Faculty:* 16 full-time (1 woman), 3 part-time/adjunct (0 women). *Students:* 84 full-time (26 women), 5 part-time (1 woman); includes 11 minority (2 Black or African American, non-Hispanic/Latino; 1 American Indian or Alaska Native, non-Hispanic/Latino; 2 Asian, non-Hispanic/Latino; 6 Hispanic/Latino), 46 international. Average age 32. 170 applicants, 29% accepted, 32 enrolled. In 2014, 19 master's, 5 doctorates awarded. *Degree requirements:* For master's, thesis (for some programs); for doctorate, one foreign language, comprehensive exam, thesis/dissertation, oral exams. *Entrance requirements:* For master's and doctorate, GRE General Test. Additional exam requirements/recommendations for international students: Required—TOEFL (minimum score 550 paper-based; 80 iBT). *Application deadline:* For fall admission, 12/15 priority date for domestic and international students; for spring admission, 9/1 priority date for domestic students, 9/1 for international students. Application fee: $50 ($70 for international students). Electronic applications accepted. *Financial support:* In 2014–15, 67 students received support, including 3 fellowships with full tuition reimbursements available (averaging $21,120 per year), 60 research assistantships with full tuition reimbursements available (averaging $21,120 per year), 4 teaching assistantships with full tuition reimbursements available (averaging $21,120 per year); scholarships/grants, health care benefits, and unspecified assistantships also available. Financial award application deadline: 12/15; financial award applicants required to submit FAFSA. *Faculty research:* Seismic exploration, gravity and geomagnetic fields, electrical mapping and sounding, bore hole measurements, environmental physics. *Total annual research expenditures:* $5.9 million. *Unit head:* Dr. Terence K. Young, Head, 303-273-3454, Fax: 303-273-3478, E-mail: tkyoung@mines.edu. *Application contact:* Michelle Szobody, Program Assistant, 303-273-3935, Fax: 303-273-3478, E-mail: mszobody@mines.edu.
Website: http://geophysics.mines.edu.

Colorado School of Mines, Graduate School, Department of Mining Engineering, Golden, CO 80401. Offers engineer of mines (ME); mining and earth systems engineering (MS); mining engineering (PhD); underground construction and tunneling (MS, PhD). Part-time programs available. *Faculty:* 13 full-time (2 women), 10 part-time/adjunct (2 women). *Students:* 33 full-time (3 women), 9 part-time (1 woman); includes 2 minority (1 Black or African American, non-Hispanic/Latino; 1 Hispanic/Latino), 22 international. Average age 33. 44 applicants, 82% accepted, 14 enrolled. In 2014, 12 master's, 4 doctorates awarded. *Degree requirements:* For master's, thesis (for some programs); for doctorate, one foreign language, comprehensive exam, thesis/dissertation. *Entrance requirements:* For master's and doctorate, GRE General Test. Additional exam requirements/recommendations for international students: Required—TOEFL (minimum score 550 paper-based; 80 iBT). *Application deadline:* For fall admission, 12/15 priority date for domestic and international students; for spring admission, 9/1 priority date for domestic and international students. Application fee: $50 ($70 for international students). Electronic applications accepted. *Financial support:* In 2014–15, 17 students received support, including 4 fellowships with full tuition reimbursements available (averaging $21,120 per year), 6 research assistantships with full tuition reimbursements available (averaging $21,120 per year), 7 teaching assistantships with full tuition reimbursements available (averaging $21,120 per year); scholarships/grants, health care benefits, and unspecified assistantships also available. Financial award application deadline: 12/15; financial award applicants required to submit FAFSA. *Faculty research:* Mine evaluation and planning, geostatistics, mining robotics, water jet cutting, rock mechanics. *Total annual research expenditures:* $4.7 million. *Unit head:* Dr. Priscella Nelson, Head, 303-273-2606, E-mail: pnelson@mines.edu. *Application contact:* Melanie Barnhart, Program Assistant, 303-273-3768, E-mail: barnhart@mines.edu.
Website: http://mining.mines.edu.

Dalhousie University, Faculty of Engineering, Department of Mineral Resource Engineering, Halifax, NS B3J 1Z1, Canada. Offers mineral resource engineering (M Eng, MA Sc, PhD). *Degree requirements:* For master's, thesis; for doctorate, thesis/dissertation. *Entrance requirements:* Additional exam requirements/recommendations for international students: Required—TOEFL, IELTS, CANTEST, CAEL, or Michigan English Language Assessment Battery. Electronic applications accepted. *Faculty research:* Mining technology, environmental impact, petroleum engineering, mine waste management, rock mechanics.

Laurentian University, School of Graduate Studies and Research, Programme in Geology (Earth Sciences), Sudbury, ON P3E 2C6, Canada. Offers geology (M Sc); mineral deposits and precambrian geology (PhD); mineral exploration (M Sc). Part-time programs available. *Degree requirements:* For master's, thesis. *Entrance requirements:* For master's, honors degree with second class or better. *Faculty research:* Localization and metallogenesis of Ni-Cu-(PGE) sulfide mineralization in the Thompson Nickel Belt, mapping lithology and ore-grade and monitoring dissolved organic carbon in lakes using remote sensing, global reefs, volcanic effects on VMS deposits.

Laurentian University, School of Graduate Studies and Research, School of Engineering, Sudbury, ON P3E 2C6, Canada. Offers mineral resources engineering (M Eng, MA Sc); natural resources engineering (PhD). Part-time programs available. *Faculty research:* Mining engineering, rock mechanics (tunneling, rockbursts, rock support), metallurgy (mineral processing, hydro and pyrometallurgy), simulations and remote mining, simulations and scheduling.

McGill University, Faculty of Graduate and Postdoctoral Studies, Faculty of Engineering, Department of Mining and Materials Engineering, Montréal, QC H3A 2T5, Canada. Offers materials engineering (M Eng, PhD); mining engineering (M Eng, M Sc, PhD, Diploma).

Michigan Technological University, Graduate School, College of Engineering, Department of Geological and Mining Engineering and Sciences, Houghton, MI 49931. Offers geological engineering (MS, PhD); geology (MS, PhD); geophysics (MS, PhD); mining engineering (MS, PhD). Part-time programs available. *Faculty:* 25 full-time, 31 part-time/adjunct. *Students:* 68 full-time (31 women), 15 part-time (8 women); includes 5 minority (1 Black or African American, non-Hispanic/Latino; 1 Asian, non-Hispanic/Latino; 2 Hispanic/Latino; 1 Two or more races, non-Hispanic/Latino), 39 international. Average age 28. 208 applicants, 28% accepted, 26 enrolled. In 2014, 12 master's, 3 doctorates awarded. Terminal master's awarded for partial completion of doctoral program. *Degree requirements:* For master's, comprehensive exam (for some programs), thesis (for some programs); for doctorate, comprehensive exam, thesis/dissertation. *Entrance requirements:* For master's and doctorate, GRE, statement of purpose, official transcripts, 3 letters of recommendation. Additional exam requirements/recommendations for international students: Required—TOEFL (recommended score 79 iBT) or IELTS. *Application deadline:* For fall admission, 2/1 priority date for domestic and international students. Applications are processed on a rolling basis. Electronic

applications accepted. *Expenses:* Tuition, state resident: full-time $14,769; part-time $820.50 per credit. Tuition, nonresident: full-time $14,769; part-time $820.50 per credit. *Required fees:* $248; $248 per year. Tuition and fees vary according to course load and program. *Financial support:* In 2014–15, 53 students received support, including 9 fellowships with full and partial tuition reimbursements available (averaging $13,824 per year), 15 research assistantships with full and partial tuition reimbursements available (averaging $13,824 per year), 7 teaching assistantships with full and partial tuition reimbursements available (averaging $13,824 per year); career-related internships or fieldwork, Federal Work-Study, scholarships/grants, health care benefits, unspecified assistantships, and cooperative program also available. Financial award applicants required to submit FAFSA. *Faculty research:* Volcanic hazards and volcanic clouds, oil and gas exploration and development, groundwater measurement and modeling, geophysics, environmental paleomagnetism. *Total annual research expenditures:* $1.8 million. *Unit head:* Dr. John S. Gierke, Chair, 906-487-2535, Fax: 906-487-3371, E-mail: jsgierke@mtu.edu. *Application contact:* Amie S. Ledgerwood, Assistant to the Dean, 906-487-2531, Fax: 906-487-3371, E-mail: asledger@mtu.edu.
Website: http://www.mtu.edu/geo/.

Missouri University of Science and Technology, Graduate School, Department of Mining and Nuclear Engineering, Rolla, MO 65409. Offers mining engineering (MS, DE, PhD); nuclear engineering (MS, DE, PhD). *Degree requirements:* For master's, thesis optional; for doctorate, comprehensive exam. *Entrance requirements:* For master's, GRE (minimum score 600 quantitative, 3 writing); for doctorate, GRE (minimum score: quantitative 600, writing 3.5). Additional exam requirements/recommendations for international students: Required—TOEFL (minimum score 550 paper-based). *Faculty research:* Mine health and safety, nuclear radiation transport, modeling of mining operations, radiation effects, blasting.

Montana Tech of The University of Montana, Graduate School, Metallurgical/Mineral Processing Engineering Programs, Butte, MT 59701-8997. Offers MS. Part-time programs available. *Degree requirements:* For master's, comprehensive exam (for some programs), thesis optional. *Entrance requirements:* For master's, GRE General Test, minimum GPA of 3.0. Additional exam requirements/recommendations for international students: Required—TOEFL (minimum score 525 paper-based; 71 iBT). Electronic applications accepted. *Expenses:* Tuition, state resident: full-time $5802; part-time $241 per credit. Tuition, nonresident: full-time $15,895; part-time $662 per credit. *Required fees:* $1516; $414 per credit. $207 per semester. One-time fee: $30. *Faculty research:* Stabilizing hazardous waste, decontamination of metals by melt refining, ultraviolet enhancement of stabilization reactions, extractive metallurgy, fuel cells.

Montana Tech of The University of Montana, Graduate School, Mining Engineering Program, Butte, MT 59701-8997. Offers MS. Part-time programs available. *Degree requirements:* For master's, thesis optional. *Entrance requirements:* For master's, minimum GPA of 3.0. Additional exam requirements/recommendations for international students: Required—TOEFL (minimum score 525 paper-based; 71 iBT). Electronic applications accepted. *Expenses:* Tuition, state resident: full-time $5802; part-time $241 per credit. Tuition, nonresident: full-time $15,895; part-time $662 per credit. *Required fees:* $1516; $414 per credit. $207 per semester. One-time fee: $30. *Faculty research:* Geostatistics, geomechanics, mine planning, economic models, equipment selection.

New Mexico Institute of Mining and Technology, Graduate Studies, Department of Mineral Engineering, Socorro, NM 87801. Offers MS. *Degree requirements:* For master's, thesis. *Entrance requirements:* Additional exam requirements/recommendations for international students: Required—TOEFL (minimum score 540 paper-based). *Faculty research:* Drilling and blasting, geological engineering, mine design, applied mineral exploration, rock mechanics.

Penn State University Park, Graduate School, College of Earth and Mineral Sciences, Department of Energy and Mineral Engineering, University Park, PA 16802. Offers MS, PhD. *Unit head:* Dr. William E. Easterling, III, Dean, 814-865-7482, Fax: 814-863-7708, E-mail: wee2@psu.edu. *Application contact:* Lori A. Stania, Director, Graduate Student Services, 814-867-5278, Fax: 814-863-4627, E-mail: gswww@psu.edu.
Website: http://www.eme.psu.edu/.

Queen's University at Kingston, School of Graduate Studies, Faculty of Applied Science, Department of Mining Engineering, Kingston, ON K7L 3N6, Canada. Offers M Eng, M Sc, M Sc Eng, PhD. Part-time programs available. *Degree requirements:* For master's, thesis optional; for doctorate, comprehensive exam, thesis/dissertation. *Entrance requirements:* Additional exam requirements/recommendations for international students: Required—TOEFL (minimum score 550 paper-based). Electronic applications accepted. *Faculty research:* Rock mechanics, drilling, ventilation/environmental control, gold extraction.

South Dakota School of Mines and Technology, Graduate Division, Department of Mining Engineering and Management, Rapid City, SD 57701-3995. Offers mining engineering (MS). Part-time programs available. *Faculty:* 3 full-time (1 woman), 2 part-time/adjunct (1 woman). *Students:* 2 full-time (1 woman), 6 part-time (2 women); includes 2 minority (both Asian, non-Hispanic/Latino), 1 international. Average age 31. 9 applicants, 44% accepted, 4 enrolled. *Entrance requirements:* For master's, GRE General Test. Additional exam requirements/recommendations for international students: Required—TOEFL (minimum score 520 paper-based; 68 iBT), TWE. *Application deadline:* For fall admission, 7/1 priority date for domestic students, 4/1 for international students; for spring admission, 11/10 for domestic students, 9/1 for international students. Applications are processed on a rolling basis. Application fee: $35. Electronic applications accepted. *Expenses:* Tuition, state resident: full-time $5050; part-time $210.40 per credit hour. Tuition, nonresident: full-time $11,290; part-time $470.30 per credit hour. *Required fees:* $4680. *Financial support:* In 2014–15, 4 research assistantships with full and partial tuition reimbursements (averaging $13,448 per year), 3 teaching assistantships with full and partial tuition reimbursements (averaging $5,793 per year) were awarded; fellowships also available. Financial award application deadline: 5/15. *Total annual research expenditures:* $196,853. *Unit head:* Dr. Lance A. Roberts, Head, 605-394-1973, E-mail: lance.roberts@sdsmt.edu. *Application contact:* Dr. Charles A. Kliche, Program Director, 605-394-1972, E-mail: charles.kliche@sdsmt.edu.
Website: http://www.sdsmt.edu/Academics/Departments/Mining-Engineering-and-Management/Mining-Engineering-and-Management/.

Southern Illinois University Carbondale, Graduate School, College of Engineering, Department of Mining and Mineral Resources Engineering, Carbondale, IL 62901-4701. Offers MS. *Faculty:* 3 full-time (0 women), 1 part-time/adjunct (0 women). *Students:* 12 full-time (1 woman), 4 part-time (1 woman); includes 1 minority (Asian, non-Hispanic/Latino), 13 international. Average age 25. 14 applicants, 21% accepted, 2 enrolled. In 2014, 1 master's awarded. *Degree requirements:* For master's, comprehensive exam, thesis. *Entrance requirements:* For master's, minimum GPA of 2.7. Additional exam requirements/recommendations for international students: Required—TOEFL.

Application deadline: Applications are processed on a rolling basis. Application fee: $50. *Expenses:* Tuition, state resident: full-time $10,176; part-time $1153 per credit. Tuition, nonresident: full-time $20,814; part-time $1744 per credit. *Required fees:* $7092; $394 per credit. $2364 per semester. *Financial support:* Fellowships with full tuition reimbursements, research assistantships with full tuition reimbursements, teaching assistantships with full tuition reimbursements, Federal Work-Study, institutionally sponsored loans, and tuition waivers (full) available. Support available to part-time students. Financial award application deadline: 3/1. *Faculty research:* Rock mechanics and ground control, mine subsidence, mine systems analysis, fine coal cleaning, surface mine reclamation. *Total annual research expenditures:* $1.7 million. *Unit head:* Dr. Rasit Koc, Chairperson, 618-536-2396, E-mail: kocr@siu.edu. *Application contact:* Diane Gasa, Administrative Clerk, 618-536-6637, E-mail: lyall@siu.edu.

Université du Québec en Abitibi-Témiscamingue, Graduate Programs, Program in Engineering, Rouyn-Noranda, QC J9X 5E4, Canada. Offers engineering (ME); mineral engineering (ME); mining engineering (DESS).

Université Laval, Faculty of Sciences and Engineering, Department of Mining, Metallurgical and Materials Engineering, Programs in Mining Engineering, Québec, QC G1K 7P4, Canada. Offers M Sc, PhD. Terminal master's awarded for partial completion of doctoral program. *Degree requirements:* For master's, thesis; for doctorate, comprehensive exam, thesis/dissertation. *Entrance requirements:* For master's and doctorate, knowledge of French and English. Electronic applications accepted.

University of Alaska Fairbanks, College of Engineering and Mines, Department of Mining and Geological Engineering, Program in Mineral Preparation Engineering, Fairbanks, AK 99775. Offers MS. Part-time programs available. *Students:* 1 full-time (0 women), all international. Average age 37. 1 applicant. *Degree requirements:* For master's, comprehensive exam, oral defense of project or thesis. *Entrance requirements:* For master's, bachelor's degree from accredited institution with minimum cumulative undergraduate and major GPA of 3.0. Additional exam requirements/recommendations for international students: Required—TOEFL (minimum score 550 paper-based; 79 iBT), IELTS (minimum score 6.5). *Application deadline:* For fall admission, 6/1 for domestic students, 3/1 for international students; for spring admission, 10/15 for domestic students, 9/1 for international students. Applications are processed on a rolling basis. Application fee: $60. Electronic applications accepted. *Expenses:* Tuition, state resident: full-time $7614; part-time $423 per credit. Tuition, nonresident: full-time $15,552; part-time $864 per credit. Tuition and fees vary according to course level, course load and reciprocity agreements. *Financial support:* In 2014–15, 1 research assistantship with full tuition reimbursement (averaging $2,392 per year) was awarded; fellowships with full tuition reimbursements, teaching assistantships with full tuition reimbursements, career-related internships or fieldwork, Federal Work-Study, scholarships/grants, health care benefits, and unspecified assistantships also available. Support available to part-time students. Financial award application deadline: 7/1; financial award applicants required to submit FAFSA. *Faculty research:* Washability of coal, microbial mining, mineral leaching, pollution control technology, concentration of target minerals. *Unit head:* Dr. Rajive Ganguli, Department Chair, 907-474-7388, Fax: 907-474-6635, E-mail: cem.mingeo@alaska.edu. *Application contact:* Mary Kreta, Director of Admissions, 907-474-7500, Fax: 907-474-7097, E-mail: admissions@uaf.edu.
Website: http://cem.uaf.edu/mingeo.

University of Alberta, Faculty of Graduate Studies and Research, Department of Civil and Environmental Engineering, Edmonton, AB T6G 2E1, Canada. Offers construction engineering and management (M Eng, M Sc, PhD); environmental engineering (M Eng, M Sc, PhD); environmental science (M Sc, PhD); geoenvironmental engineering (M Eng, M Sc, PhD); geotechnical engineering (M Eng, M Sc, PhD); mining engineering (M Eng, M Sc, PhD); petroleum engineering (M Eng, M Sc, PhD); structural engineering (M Eng, M Sc, PhD); water resources (M Eng, M Sc, PhD). Part-time programs available. Postbaccalaureate distance learning degree programs offered (minimal on-campus study). *Degree requirements:* For master's, thesis (for some programs); for doctorate, thesis/dissertation. *Entrance requirements:* For master's, minimum GPA of 3.0 in last 2 years of undergraduate studies; for doctorate, minimum GPA of 3.0. Additional exam requirements/recommendations for international students: Required—TOEFL (minimum score 550 paper-based). Electronic applications accepted. *Faculty research:* Mining.

The University of Arizona, College of Engineering, Department of Mining and Geological Engineering, Tucson, AZ 85721. Offers mining and geological engineering (M Eng, MS, PhD); mining engineering (Certificate), including mine health and safety, mine information and production technology, rock mechanics. Part-time programs available. Postbaccalaureate distance learning degree programs offered (minimal on-campus study). *Degree requirements:* For master's, thesis; for doctorate, thesis/dissertation. *Entrance requirements:* For master's, GRE General Test, 3 letters of recommendation; for doctorate, GRE General Test, 3 letters of recommendation, statements of purpose. Additional exam requirements/recommendations for international students: Required—TOEFL (minimum score 550 paper-based; 79 iBT). Electronic applications accepted. *Faculty research:* Geomechanics, mineral processing, information technology, automation, geosensing.

The University of British Columbia, Faculty of Applied Science, Program in Mining Engineering, Vancouver, BC V6T 1Z4, Canada. Offers M Eng, MA Sc, PhD. *Degree requirements:* For master's, thesis; for doctorate, thesis/dissertation. *Entrance requirements:* Additional exam requirements/recommendations for international students: Required—TOEFL (minimum score 80 iBT), IELTS. *Faculty research:* Advanced mining methods and automation, rock mechanics, mine economics, operations research, mine waste management, environmental aspects of mining, process control, fine particle processing, surface chemistry.

University of Kentucky, Graduate School, College of Engineering, Program in Mining Engineering, Lexington, KY 40506-0032. Offers MME, MS Min, PhD. *Degree requirements:* For master's, comprehensive exam, thesis optional; for doctorate, one foreign language, comprehensive exam, thesis/dissertation. *Entrance requirements:* For master's, GRE General Test, minimum undergraduate GPA of 2.75; for doctorate, GRE General Test, minimum undergraduate GPA of 3.0. Additional exam requirements/recommendations for international students: Required—TOEFL (minimum score 550 paper-based). Electronic applications accepted. *Faculty research:* Benefication of fine and ultrafine particles, operation research in mining and mineral processing, land reclamation.

University of Nevada, Reno, Graduate School, College of Science, Mackay School of Earth Sciences and Engineering, Department of Mining Engineering, Reno, NV 89557. Offers MS. *Degree requirements:* For master's, thesis optional. *Entrance requirements:* For master's, GRE, minimum GPA of 2.75. Additional exam requirements/recommendations for international students: Required—TOEFL (minimum score 500 paper-based; 61 iBT), IELTS (minimum score 6). Electronic applications accepted. *Faculty research:* Mine ventilation, rock mechanics, mine design.

University of North Dakota, Graduate School, School of Engineering and Mines, Department of Civil Engineering, Grand Forks, ND 58202. Offers civil engineering (M Engr); sanitary engineering (M Engr), including soils and structures engineering, surface mining engineering. Part-time programs available. *Degree requirements:* For master's, comprehensive exam, thesis or alternative. *Entrance requirements:* For master's, GRE General Test, minimum GPA of 2.5. Additional exam requirements/recommendations for international students: Required—TOEFL (minimum score 550 paper-based; 79 iBT), IELTS (minimum score 6.5). Electronic applications accepted. *Faculty research:* Soil-structures, environmental-water resources.

The University of Texas at Austin, Graduate School, Cockrell School of Engineering, Department of Petroleum and Geosystems Engineering, Program in Energy and Earth Resources, Austin, TX 78712-1111. Offers MA. *Degree requirements:* For master's, thesis, seminar. *Entrance requirements:* For master's, GRE General Test. Additional exam requirements/recommendations for international students: Required—TOEFL. Electronic applications accepted.

University of Utah, Graduate School, College of Mines and Earth Sciences, Department of Mining Engineering, Salt Lake City, UT 84112. Offers ME, MS, PhD. Part-time programs available. *Faculty:* 14 full-time (4 women), 3 part-time/adjunct (0 women). *Students:* 14 full-time (4 women), 3 part-time (0 women); includes 2 minority (1 Asian, non-Hispanic/Latino; 1 Hispanic/Latino), 9 international. Average age 30. 24 applicants, 21% accepted, 3 enrolled. In 2014, 2 master's, 1 doctorate awarded. *Degree requirements:* For master's, comprehensive exam (for some programs), thesis (for some programs); for doctorate, one foreign language, comprehensive exam, thesis/dissertation. *Entrance requirements:* For master's, minimum undergraduate GPA of 3.0; for doctorate, GRE General Test, minimum undergraduate GPA of 3.0. Additional exam requirements/recommendations for international students: Required—TOEFL (minimum score 550 paper-based; 80 iBT). *Application deadline:* For fall admission, 4/1 for domestic and international students; for spring admission, 11/1 priority date for domestic students, 11/1 for international students. Application fee: $55 ($65 for international students). Electronic applications accepted. *Financial support:* In 2014–15, 5 students received support, including 4 fellowships with full and partial tuition reimbursements available (averaging $19,000 per year), 4 research assistantships with full and partial tuition reimbursements available (averaging $19,000 per year), 1 teaching assistantship with full and partial tuition reimbursement available (averaging $19,000 per year); career-related internships or fieldwork and institutionally sponsored loans also available. Support available to part-time students. Financial award application deadline: 2/15. *Faculty research:* Blasting, underground coal mine design and operations, rock mechanics, mine ventilation, 2-D and 3-D visualization, mine automation, mine safety. *Total annual research expenditures:* $324,354. *Unit head:* Dr. Michael Gordon Nelson, Chair, 801-585-3064, Fax: 801-585-5410, E-mail: mike.nelson@utah.edu. *Application contact:* Pam Hofmann, Administrative Manager, 801-581-7198, Fax: 801-585-5410, E-mail: pam.hofmann@utah.edu.
Website: http://www.mining.utah.edu/.

Virginia Polytechnic Institute and State University, Graduate School, College of Engineering, Blacksburg, VA 24061. Offers aerospace engineering (ME, MS, PhD); biological systems engineering (ME, MS, PhD); biomedical engineering (MS, PhD); chemical engineering (ME, MS, PhD); civil engineering (ME, MS, PhD); computer engineering (ME, MS, PhD); computer science (MS, PhD); electrical engineering (ME, PhD); engineering education (PhD); engineering mechanics (ME, MS, PhD); environmental engineering (MS); environmental science and engineering (MS); industrial and systems engineering (ME, MS, PhD); materials science and engineering (ME, MS, PhD); mechanical engineering (ME, MS, PhD); mining and minerals engineering (PhD); mining engineering (ME, MS); nuclear engineering (MS, PhD); ocean engineering (MS); systems engineering (ME, MS). *Accreditation:* ABET (one or more programs are accredited). *Faculty:* 356 full-time (60 women), 3 part-time/adjunct (1 woman). *Students:* 1,700 full-time (398 women), 345 part-time (58 women); includes 213 minority (43 Black or African American, non-Hispanic/Latino; 1 American Indian or Alaska Native, non-Hispanic/Latino; 87 Asian, non-Hispanic/Latino; 58 Hispanic/Latino; 1 Native Hawaiian or other Pacific Islander, non-Hispanic/Latino; 23 Two or more races, non-Hispanic/Latino), 1,079 international. Average age 27. 5,228 applicants, 18% accepted, 471 enrolled. In 2014, 438 master's, 211 doctorates awarded. *Degree requirements:* For master's, comprehensive exam (for some programs), thesis (for some programs); for doctorate, comprehensive exam (for some programs), thesis/dissertation (for some programs). *Entrance requirements:* For master's and doctorate, GRE/GMAT (may vary by department). Additional exam requirements/recommendations for international students: Required—TOEFL (minimum score 550 paper-based). *Application deadline:* For fall admission, 8/1 for domestic students, 4/1 for international students; for spring admission, 1/1 for domestic students, 9/1 for international students. Applications are processed on a rolling basis. Application fee: $75. Electronic applications accepted. *Expenses:* Tuition, state resident: full-time $11,656; part-time $647.50 per credit hour. Tuition, nonresident: full-time $23,351; part-time $1297.25 per credit hour. *Required fees:* $2533; $465.75 per semester. Tuition and fees vary according to course load, campus/location and program. *Financial support:* In 2014–15, 148 fellowships with full tuition reimbursements (averaging $8,031 per year), 855 research assistantships with full tuition reimbursements (averaging $22,855 per year), 288 teaching assistantships with full tuition reimbursements (averaging $20,291 per year) were awarded. Financial award application deadline: 3/1; financial award applicants required to submit FAFSA. *Total annual research expenditures:* $90.5 million. *Unit head:* Dr. Richard C. Benson, Dean, 540-231-9752, Fax: 540-231-3031, E-mail: deaneng@vt.edu. *Application contact:* Linda Perkins, Executive Assistant, 540-231-9752, Fax: 540-231-3031, E-mail: lperkins@vt.edu.
Website: http://www.eng.vt.edu/.

West Virginia University, College of Engineering and Mineral Resources, Department of Mining Engineering, Morgantown, WV 26506. Offers MS Min E, PhD. Part-time programs available. *Degree requirements:* For master's, thesis; for doctorate, comprehensive exam, thesis/dissertation. *Entrance requirements:* For master's, minimum GPA of 3.0; for doctorate, GRE General Test, MS in mineral engineering, minimum GPA of 3.5. Additional exam requirements/recommendations for international students: Required—TOEFL. *Faculty research:* Mine safety.

Petroleum Engineering

Colorado School of Mines, Graduate School, Department of Petroleum Engineering, Golden, CO 80401. Offers petroleum engineering (ME, MS, PhD); petroleum reservoir systems (PMS). Part-time programs available. *Faculty:* 15 full-time (4 women), 7 part-time/adjunct (3 women). *Students:* 103 full-time (17 women), 5 part-time (2 women); includes 5 minority (3 Black or African American, non-Hispanic/Latino; 1 Asian, non-Hispanic/Latino; 1 Hispanic/Latino), 81 international. Average age 29. 351 applicants, 13% accepted, 24 enrolled. In 2014, 20 master's, 3 doctorates awarded. *Degree requirements:* For master's, thesis (for some programs); for doctorate, comprehensive exam, thesis/dissertation. *Entrance requirements:* For master's and doctorate, GRE General Test. Additional exam requirements/recommendations for international students: Required—TOEFL (minimum score 550 paper-based; 80 iBT). *Application deadline:* For fall admission, 12/15 priority date for domestic and international students; for spring admission, 9/1 priority date for domestic and international students. Application fee: $50 ($70 for international students). Electronic applications accepted. *Financial support:* In 2014–15, 75 students received support, including fellowships with full tuition reimbursements available (averaging $21,120 per year), 50 research assistantships with full tuition reimbursements available (averaging $21,120 per year), 25 teaching assistantships with full tuition reimbursements available (averaging $21,120 per year); career-related internships or fieldwork, scholarships/grants, health care benefits, and unspecified assistantships also available. Financial award application deadline: 12/15; financial award applicants required to submit FAFSA. *Faculty research:* Dynamic rock mechanics, deflagration theory, geostatistics, geochemistry, petrophysics. *Total annual research expenditures:* $3.1 million. *Unit head:* Dr. Erdal Ozkan, Head, 303-273-3188, Fax: 303-273-3189, E-mail: eozkan@mines.edu. *Application contact:* Denise Winn-Bower, Program Assistant, 303-273-3945, Fax: 303-273-3189, E-mail: dwinnbow@mines.edu.
Website: http://petroleum.mines.edu.

Louisiana State University and Agricultural & Mechanical College, Graduate School, College of Engineering, Department of Petroleum Engineering, Baton Rouge, LA 70803. Offers MS Pet E, PhD. *Faculty:* 10 full-time (1 woman), 1 part-time/adjunct (0 women). *Students:* 61 full-time (10 women), 4 part-time (0 women); includes 11 minority (3 Black or African American, non-Hispanic/Latino; 5 Asian, non-Hispanic/Latino; 3 Hispanic/Latino), 43 international. Average age 29. 340 applicants, 6% accepted, 13 enrolled. In 2014, 17 master's, 5 doctorates awarded. *Degree requirements:* For master's, thesis or alternative; for doctorate, thesis/dissertation, exam. *Entrance requirements:* For master's and doctorate, GRE General Test, minimum GPA of 3.0. Additional exam requirements/recommendations for international students: Required— TOEFL (minimum score 550 paper-based; 79 iBT), IELTS (minimum score 6.5), or PTE (minimum score 59). *Application deadline:* For fall admission, 1/1 priority date for domestic students, 5/15 for international students; for spring admission, 10/15 for domestic and international students; for summer admission, 5/15 for domestic students, 5/10 for international students. Applications are processed on a rolling basis. Application fee: $50 ($70 for international students). Electronic applications accepted. *Financial support:* In 2014–15, 58 students received support, including 27 research assistantships with full and partial tuition reimbursements available (averaging $13,052 per year), 19 teaching assistantships with full and partial tuition reimbursements available (averaging $10,242 per year); fellowships, Federal Work-Study, institutionally sponsored loans, health care benefits, and unspecified assistantships also available. Financial award applicants required to submit FAFSA. *Faculty research:* Rock properties, well logging, production engineering, drilling, reservoir engineering. *Total annual research expenditures:* $1.9 million. *Unit head:* Dr. Karsten Thompson, Chair, 225-578-5215, Fax: 225-578-6039, E-mail: karsten@lsu.edu. *Application contact:* Dr. Andrew Wojtanowicz, Graduate Adviser, 225-578-6049, Fax: 225-578-6039, E-mail: awojtan@lsu.edu.
Website: http://www.pete.lsu.edu/.

Missouri University of Science and Technology, Graduate School, Department of Geological Sciences and Engineering, Rolla, MO 65409. Offers geological engineering (MS, DE, PhD); geology and geophysics (MS, PhD), including geochemistry, geology, geophysics, groundwater and environmental geology; petroleum engineering (MS, DE, PhD). Part-time programs available. *Degree requirements:* For master's, thesis optional; for doctorate, comprehensive exam, thesis/dissertation. *Entrance requirements:* For master's, GRE General Test (minimum score 600 quantitative, writing 3.5), minimum GPA of 3.0 in last 4 semesters; for doctorate, GRE General Test (minimum: Q 600, GRE WR 3.5). Additional exam requirements/recommendations for international students: Required—TOEFL. Electronic applications accepted. *Faculty research:* Digital image processing and geographic information systems, mineralogy, igneous and sedimentary petrology-geochemistry, sedimentology groundwater hydrology and contaminant transport.

Montana Tech of The University of Montana, Graduate School, Department of Petroleum Engineering, Butte, MT 59701-8997. Offers MS. Part-time and evening/weekend programs available. *Degree requirements:* For master's, comprehensive exam, thesis optional. *Entrance requirements:* For master's, minimum GPA of 3.0. Additional exam requirements/recommendations for international students: Required— TOEFL (minimum score 525 paper-based; 71 iBT). Electronic applications accepted. *Expenses:* Tuition, state resident: full-time $5802; part-time $241 per credit. Tuition, nonresident: full-time $15,895; part-time $662 per credit. *Required fees:* $1516; $414 per credit. $207 per semester. One-time fee: $30. *Faculty research:* Reservoir characterization, simulations, near well bore problems, environmental waste.

New Mexico Institute of Mining and Technology, Graduate Studies, Program in Petroleum Engineering, Socorro, NM 87801. Offers MS, PhD. *Degree requirements:* For master's, thesis optional; for doctorate, thesis/dissertation. *Entrance requirements:* For master's, GRE General Test; for doctorate, GRE General Test, GRE Subject Test. Additional exam requirements/recommendations for international students: Required— TOEFL (minimum score 540 paper-based). *Faculty research:* Enhanced recovery processes, drilling and production, reservoir evaluation, produced water management, wettability and phase behavior.

Stanford University, School of Earth Sciences, Department of Energy Resources Engineering, Stanford, CA 94305-9991. Offers energy resources engineering (MS, PhD, Eng); petroleum engineering (MS, PhD). Terminal master's awarded for partial completion of doctoral program. *Degree requirements:* For doctorate, thesis/dissertation; for Eng, thesis. *Entrance requirements:* For master's, doctorate, and Eng, GRE General Test. Additional exam requirements/recommendations for international students: Required—TOEFL. Electronic applications accepted. *Expenses: Tuition:* Full-time $44,184; part-time $982 per credit hour. *Required fees:* $191.

Texas A&M University, College of Engineering, Department of Petroleum Engineering, College Station, TX 77843. Offers M Eng, MS, PhD. Part-time programs available. Postbaccalaureate distance learning degree programs offered (no on-campus study). *Faculty:* 32. *Students:* 261 full-time (66 women), 181 part-time (29 women); includes 68 minority (11 Black or African American, non-Hispanic/Latino; 2 American Indian or Alaska Native, non-Hispanic/Latino; 23 Asian, non-Hispanic/Latino; 28 Hispanic/Latino; 4 Two or more races, non-Hispanic/Latino), 238 international. Average age 29. 719 applicants, 18% accepted, 96 enrolled. In 2014, 78 master's, 17 doctorates awarded. *Degree requirements:* For master's, comprehensive exam, thesis (MS); for doctorate, comprehensive exam, thesis/dissertation. *Entrance requirements:* For master's and doctorate, GRE General Test. Additional exam requirements/recommendations for international students: Required—TOEFL (minimum score 550 paper-based). *Application deadline:* Applications are processed on a rolling basis. Application fee: $50 ($90 for international students). Electronic applications accepted. *Expenses:* Tuition, state resident: full-time $4078; part-time $226.55 per credit hour. Tuition, nonresident: full-time $10,594; part-time $577.55 per credit hour. *Required fees:* $2813; $237.70 per credit hour. $278.50 per semester. Tuition and fees vary according to degree level and student level. *Financial support:* In 2014–15, 268 students received support, including 7 fellowships with full and partial tuition reimbursements available (averaging $19,325 per year), 148 research assistantships with full and partial tuition reimbursements available (averaging $7,269 per year), 40 teaching assistantships with full and partial tuition reimbursements available (averaging $6,004 per year); career-related internships or fieldwork, institutionally sponsored loans, scholarships/grants, traineeships, health care benefits, tuition waivers (full and partial), and unspecified assistantships also available. Support available to part-time students. Financial award application deadline: 3/1; financial award applicants required to submit FAFSA. *Faculty research:* Drilling and well stimulation, well completions and well performance, reservoir modeling and reservoir description, reservoir simulation, improved/enhanced recovery. *Unit head:* Dr. A. Daniel Hill, Department Head, 979-845-2244, E-mail: dan.hill@pe.tamu.edu. *Application contact:* Graduate Advisor, 979-847-9095, E-mail: graduate_program@pe.tamu.edu.
Website: http://engineering.tamu.edu/petroleum.

Texas A&M University–Kingsville, College of Graduate Studies, College of Engineering, Wayne H. King Department of Chemical and Natural Gas Engineering, Program in Natural Gas Engineering, Kingsville, TX 78363. Offers ME, MS. *Students:* 35 full-time (5 women), 8 part-time (0 women); includes 3 minority (2 Black or African American, non-Hispanic/Latino; 1 Hispanic/Latino), 38 international. Average age 28. 40 applicants, 65% accepted, 10 enrolled. In 2014, 12 master's awarded. *Degree requirements:* For master's, variable foreign language requirement, comprehensive exam, thesis (for some programs). *Entrance requirements:* For master's, GRE, MAT, GMAT, minimum GPA of 2.7, minimum GRE quantitative score of 150, minimum GRE verbal score 145. Additional exam requirements/recommendations for international students: Required—TOEFL (minimum score 550 paper-based; 79 iBT). *Application deadline:* For fall admission, 8/15 for domestic students, 6/1 for international students; for spring admission, 12/15 for domestic students, 10/1 for international students; for summer admission, 5/15 for domestic students, 4/1 for international students. Applications are processed on a rolling basis. Application fee: $35 ($50 for international students). Electronic applications accepted. *Financial support:* In 2014–15, 15 students received support, including 2 teaching assistantships (averaging $3,247 per year); career-related internships or fieldwork, Federal Work-Study, institutionally sponsored loans, scholarships/grants, health care benefits, tuition waivers (full and partial), and unspecified assistantships also available. Support available to part-time students. Financial award application deadline: 5/15; financial award applicants required to submit FAFSA. *Unit head:* Dr. Ali A. Pilehvari, Graduate Coordinator, 361-593-2089, Fax: 361-593-2106, E-mail: ali.pilehvari@tamuk.edu. *Application contact:* Dr. Mohamed Abdelrahman, Dean, College of Graduate Studies, 361-593-2809, E-mail: mohamed.abdelrahman@tamuk.edu.

Texas Tech University, Graduate School, Edward E. Whitacre Jr. College of Engineering, Bob L. Herd Department of Petroleum Engineering, Lubbock, TX 79409-3111. Offers MSPE, PhD. Part-time programs available. *Faculty:* 11 full-time (0 women), 1 part-time/adjunct (0 women). *Students:* 53 full-time (9 women), 8 part-time (1 woman); includes 1 minority (Black or African American, non-Hispanic/Latino), 55 international. Average age 29. 371 applicants, 12% accepted, 11 enrolled. In 2014, 28 master's, 7 doctorates awarded. *Degree requirements:* For master's, comprehensive exam, thesis (for some programs); for doctorate, comprehensive exam, thesis/dissertation, qualifying exam, proposal defense exam. *Entrance requirements:* For master's, GRE (Verbal and Quantitative), Graduate Certificate in petroleum engineering (for non-petroleum students); for doctorate, GRE (Verbal and Quantitative). Additional exam requirements/recommendations for international students: Required—TOEFL (minimum score 550 paper-based; 79 iBT), IELTS (minimum score 6.5). *Application deadline:* For fall admission, 6/1 priority date for domestic students, 1/15 priority date for international students; for spring admission, 9/1 priority date for domestic students, 6/15 priority date for international students. Applications are processed on a rolling basis. Application fee: $60. Electronic applications accepted. *Expenses:* Tuition, state resident: full-time $6310; part-time $262.92 per credit hour. Tuition, nonresident: full-time $14,998; part-time $624.92 per credit hour. *Required fees:* $2701; $36.50 per credit. $912.50 per semester. Tuition and fees vary according to course load. *Financial support:* In 2014–15, 36 students received support, including 35 fellowships (averaging $1,454 per year), 1 research assistantship (averaging $27,500 per year), 18 teaching assistantships (averaging $20,625 per year); scholarships/grants, tuition waivers (partial), and unspecified assistantships also available. Financial award application deadline: 5/22; financial award applicants required to submit FAFSA. *Faculty research:* Development of conventional/unconventional oil and gas resources; enhanced oil recovery processes; oil and gas reserves definitions and economics; drilling and completion practices; production engineering and stimulation including latest in hydraulic fracturing technology. *Total annual research expenditures:* $229,212. *Unit head:* Dr. Marshall C. Watson, Chair, 806-742-1801, Fax: 806-742-3502, E-mail: marshall.watson@ttu.edu. *Application contact:* Dr. Habib K. Menouar, Graduate Advisor, 806-834-3452, Fax: 806-742-3502, E-mail: habib.menouar@ttu.edu.
Website: http://www.pe.ttu.edu/.

University of Alaska Fairbanks, College of Engineering and Mines, Department of Petroleum Engineering, Fairbanks, AK 99775. Offers MS. Part-time programs available. *Faculty:* 5 full-time (0 women). *Students:* 21 full-time (4 women), 13 part-time (3 women), 21 international. Average age 27. 84 applicants, 12% accepted, 7 enrolled. In 2014, 4 master's awarded. *Degree requirements:* For master's, comprehensive exam, oral defense of project or thesis. *Entrance requirements:* For master's, bachelor's degree in engineering or the natural sciences with minimum cumulative undergraduate and major GPA of 3.0. Additional exam requirements/recommendations for international students: Required—TOEFL (minimum score 550 paper-based; 79 iBT), IELTS (minimum score 6.5). *Application deadline:* For fall admission, 6/1 for domestic students, 3/1 for international students; for spring admission, 10/15 for domestic students, 9/1 for international students. Applications are processed on a rolling basis. Application fee: $60. Electronic applications accepted. *Expenses:* Tuition, state resident: full-time $7614; part-time $423 per credit. Tuition, nonresident: full-time $15,552; part-time $864

per credit. Tuition and fees vary according to course level, course load and reciprocity agreements. *Financial support:* In 2014–15, 6 research assistantships with full tuition reimbursements (averaging $4,209 per year), 7 teaching assistantships with full tuition reimbursements (averaging $5,998 per year) were awarded; fellowships with full tuition reimbursements, career-related internships or fieldwork, Federal Work-Study, scholarships/grants, health care benefits, and unspecified assistantships also available. Support available to part-time students. Financial award application deadline: 7/1; financial award applicants required to submit FAFSA. *Faculty research:* Gas-to-liquid transportation hydraulics and issues, carbon sequestration, enhanced oil recovery, reservoir engineering, coal bed methane. *Unit head:* Dr. Abhijit Dandekar, Chair, 907-474-7734, Fax: 907-474-5912, E-mail: uaf-pete-dept@alaska.edu. *Application contact:* Mary Kreta, Director of Admissions, 907-474-7500, Fax: 907-474-7097, E-mail: admissions@uaf.edu.
Website: http://cem.uaf.edu/pete/.

University of Alberta, Faculty of Graduate Studies and Research, Department of Civil and Environmental Engineering, Edmonton, AB T6G 2E1, Canada. Offers construction engineering and management (M Eng, M Sc, PhD); environmental engineering (M Eng, M Sc, PhD); environmental science (M Sc, PhD); geoenvironmental engineering (M Eng, M Sc, PhD); geotechnical engineering (M Eng, M Sc, PhD); mining engineering (M Eng, M Sc, PhD); petroleum engineering (M Eng, M Sc, PhD); structural engineering (M Eng, M Sc, PhD); water resources (M Eng, M Sc, PhD). Part-time programs available. Postbaccalaureate distance learning degree programs offered (minimal on-campus study). *Degree requirements:* For master's, thesis (for some programs); for doctorate, thesis/dissertation. *Entrance requirements:* For master's, minimum GPA of 3.0 in last 2 years of undergraduate studies; for doctorate, minimum GPA of 3.0. Additional exam requirements/recommendations for international students: Required—TOEFL (minimum score 550 paper-based). Electronic applications accepted. *Faculty research:* Mining.

University of Calgary, Faculty of Graduate Studies, Schulich School of Engineering, Department of Chemical and Petroleum Engineering, Calgary, AB T2N 1N4, Canada. Offers chemical engineering (M Eng, M Sc, PhD); energy and environment engineering (M Eng, M Sc, PhD); energy and environmental systems (M Eng, M Sc, PhD); environmental engineering (M Eng, M Sc, PhD); petroleum engineering (M Eng, M Sc, PhD); reservoir characterization (M Eng, M Sc). Part-time programs available. *Degree requirements:* For master's, thesis (for some programs); for doctorate, comprehensive exam, thesis/dissertation, candidacy exam. *Entrance requirements:* For master's, minimum GPA of 3.0 or equivalent; for doctorate, minimum GPA of 3.5 or equivalent. Additional exam requirements/recommendations for international students: Required—TOEFL (minimum score 550 paper-based; 80 iBT), IELTS (minimum score 7). Electronic applications accepted. *Faculty research:* Environmental engineering, biomedical engineering modeling, simulation and control, petroleum recovery and reservoir engineering, phase equilibria and transport properties.

University of Houston, Cullen College of Engineering, Department of Chemical and Biomolecular Engineering, Houston, TX 77204. Offers chemical engineering (MCHE, PhD); petroleum engineering (M Pet E). Part-time programs available. Terminal master's awarded for partial completion of doctoral program. *Entrance requirements:* For master's and doctorate, GRE General Test. Additional exam requirements/recommendations for international students: Required—TOEFL (minimum score 550 paper-based; 79 iBT), IELTS (minimum score 6.5). *Faculty research:* Chemical engineering.

The University of Kansas, Graduate Studies, School of Engineering, Program in Chemical and Petroleum Engineering, Lawrence, KS 66045. Offers MS, PhD. *Faculty:* 19 full-time, 4 part-time/adjunct. *Students:* 29 full-time (8 women), 1 part-time (0 women); includes 1 minority (American Indian or Alaska Native, non-Hispanic/Latino), 19 international. Average age 28. 58 applicants, 26% accepted, 5 enrolled. In 2014, 3 doctorates awarded. *Degree requirements:* For master's, thesis (for some programs), exam; for doctorate, comprehensive exam, thesis/dissertation, qualifying exams. *Entrance requirements:* For master's, GRE General Test, minimum GPA of 3.0; for doctorate, GRE General Test, minimum GPA of 3.5. Additional exam requirements/recommendations for international students: Required—TOEFL. *Application deadline:* For fall admission, 1/10 priority date for domestic students, 1/10 for international students; for spring admission, 6/10 priority date for domestic students, 6/10 for international students. Applications are processed on a rolling basis. Application fee: $55 ($65 for international students). Electronic applications accepted. *Financial support:* Fellowships, research assistantships with full and partial tuition reimbursements, teaching assistantships with full and partial tuition reimbursements, career-related internships or fieldwork, Federal Work-Study, scholarships/grants, traineeships, and unspecified assistantships available. Financial award application deadline: 4/1; financial award applicants required to submit FAFSA. *Faculty research:* Enhanced oil recovery, catalysis and kinetics, electrochemical engineering, biomedical engineering, semiconductor materials processing. *Unit head:* Laurence Weatherley, Chair, 785-864-3553, E-mail: lweather@ku.edu. *Application contact:* Carol Miner, Graduate Program Assistant, 785-864-2900, E-mail: cminer@ku.edu.
Website: http://www.cpe.engr.ku.edu.

The University of Kansas, Graduate Studies, School of Engineering, Program in Petroleum Engineering, Lawrence, KS 66045. Offers MS. *Faculty:* 19 full-time, 4 part-time/adjunct. *Students:* 10 full-time (2 women), 2 part-time; includes 1 minority (Two or more races, non-Hispanic/Latino), 7 international. Average age 28. 99 applicants, 15% accepted, 7 enrolled. *Unit head:* Laurence Weatherley, Dean, 785-864-3553, E-mail: lweather@ku.edu. *Application contact:* Carol Miner, Graduate Secretary, 785-864-2900, E-mail: cminer@ku.edu.
Website: http://www.cpe.engr.ku.edu/petro.html.

University of Louisiana at Lafayette, College of Engineering, Department of Petroleum Engineering, Lafayette, LA 70504. Offers MSE. Evening/weekend programs available. *Degree requirements:* For master's, comprehensive exam, thesis or alternative. *Entrance requirements:* For master's, GRE General Test, minimum GPA of 2.85. Electronic applications accepted.

University of Oklahoma, Mewbourne College of Earth and Energy, Mewbourne School of Petroleum and Geological Engineering, Program in Natural Gas Engineering and Management, Norman, OK 73019. Offers MS. Part-time programs available. *Students:* 16 full-time (6 women), 4 part-time (0 women); includes 1 minority (Hispanic/Latino), 17 international. Average age 27. 15 applicants, 60% accepted, 7 enrolled. In 2014, 3 master's awarded. Terminal master's awarded for partial completion of doctoral program. *Degree requirements:* For master's, variable foreign language requirement, comprehensive exam (for some programs), thesis (for some programs). *Entrance requirements:* For master's, GRE, 3 letters of reference, statement of purpose, resume/curriculum vitae, minimum GPA of 3.2. Additional exam requirements/recommendations for international students: Required—TOEFL (minimum score 79 iBT). *Application deadline:* For fall admission, 4/1 for domestic students, 3/1 for international students; for spring admission, 10/1 for domestic students, 9/1 for international students. Application fee: $50 ($100 for international students). Electronic applications accepted. *Expenses:* Tuition, state resident: full-time $4394; part-time $183.10 per credit hour. Tuition, nonresident: full-time $16,970; part-time $707.10 per credit hour. *Required fees:* $2892; $109.95 per credit hour. $126.50 per semester. *Financial support:* In 2014–15, 14 students received support. Unspecified assistantships available. Financial award application deadline: 6/1; financial award applicants required to submit FAFSA. *Faculty research:* Natural gas processing, field production technology, oil/gas project management. *Unit head:* Dr. Suresh Sharma, Director, 405-325-5928, Fax: 405-325-7477, E-mail: ssharma@ou.edu. *Application contact:* Sheriee Parnell, Graduate Programs Coordinator, 405-325-6821, Fax: 405-325-7477, E-mail: sheriee@ou.edu.
Website: http://mpge.ou.edu.

University of Oklahoma, Mewbourne College of Earth and Energy, Mewbourne School of Petroleum and Geological Engineering, Program in Petroleum Engineering, Norman, OK 73019. Offers MS, PhD. Part-time programs available. *Students:* 79 full-time (15 women), 23 part-time (4 women); includes 4 minority (1 Black or African American, non-Hispanic/Latino; 1 American Indian or Alaska Native, non-Hispanic/Latino; 2 Asian, non-Hispanic/Latino), 92 international. Average age 27. 349 applicants, 10% accepted, 33 enrolled. In 2014, 17 master's, 2 doctorates awarded. Terminal master's awarded for partial completion of doctoral program. *Degree requirements:* For master's, variable foreign language requirement, comprehensive exam (for some programs), thesis (for some programs); for doctorate, variable foreign language requirement, comprehensive exam, thesis/dissertation. *Entrance requirements:* For master's, GRE General Test, bachelor's degree, 3 letters of reference, statement of purpose, resume/curriculum vitae, minimum GPA of 3.2; for doctorate, GRE General Test, BS/MS, statement of purpose, 3 references, resume/curriculum vitae, minimum GPA of 3.2. Additional exam requirements/recommendations for international students: Required—TOEFL (minimum score 79 iBT). *Application deadline:* For fall admission, 4/1 for domestic students, 3/1 for international students; for spring admission, 10/1 for domestic students, 9/1 for international students. Application fee: $50 ($100 for international students). Electronic applications accepted. *Expenses:* Tuition, state resident: full-time $4394; part-time $183.10 per credit hour. Tuition, nonresident: full-time $16,970; part-time $707.10 per credit hour. *Required fees:* $2892; $109.95 per credit hour. $126.50 per semester. *Financial support:* In 2014–15, 89 students received support. Unspecified assistantships available. Financial award application deadline: 6/1; financial award applicants required to submit FAFSA. *Faculty research:* Unconventional oil, reservoir, oil and gas processing, flow assurance and mitigation in reservoirs. *Unit head:* Dr. Deepak Devegowda, Associate Professor and Graduate Liaison, 405-325-3081, Fax: 405-325-7477, E-mail: deepak.devegowda@ou.edu. *Application contact:* Sheriee Parnell, Graduate Programs Coordinator, 405-325-6821, Fax: 405-325-7477, E-mail: sheriee@ou.edu.
Website: http://mpge.ou.edu/.

University of Pittsburgh, Swanson School of Engineering, Department of Chemical and Petroleum Engineering, Pittsburgh, PA 15260. Offers petroleum engineering (MSPE); MS Ch E/MSPE. Part-time programs available. Postbaccalaureate distance learning degree programs offered. *Faculty:* 21 full-time (4 women), 28 part-time/adjunct (2 women). *Students:* 84 full-time (25 women), 7 part-time (0 women); includes 11 minority (3 Black or African American, non-Hispanic/Latino; 4 Asian, non-Hispanic/Latino; 1 Hispanic/Latino; 3 Two or more races, non-Hispanic/Latino), 51 international. 337 applicants, 38% accepted, 41 enrolled. In 2014, 9 master's, 5 doctorates awarded. *Degree requirements:* For master's, thesis; for doctorate, comprehensive exam, thesis/dissertation, final oral exams. *Entrance requirements:* For master's and doctorate, GRE General Test, minimum GPA of 3.0. Additional exam requirements/recommendations for international students: Required—TOEFL (minimum score 550 paper-based; 80 iBT). *Application deadline:* For fall admission, 3/1 priority date for domestic and international students; for spring admission, 7/1 priority date for domestic and international students. Applications are processed on a rolling basis. Application fee: $50. Electronic applications accepted. *Expenses:* Tuition, state resident: full-time $20,742; part-time $838 per credit. Tuition, nonresident: full-time $33,960; part-time $1389 per credit. *Required fees:* $800; $205 per term. Tuition and fees vary according to program. *Financial support:* In 2014–15, 52 students received support, including 6 fellowships with full tuition reimbursements available (averaging $29,376 per year), 21 research assistantships with full tuition reimbursements available (averaging $27,000 per year), 25 teaching assistantships with full tuition reimbursements available (averaging $26,004 per year); scholarships/grants, traineeships, and tuition waivers (full and partial) also available. Financial award application deadline: 4/15. *Faculty research:* Biotechnology, polymers, catalysis, energy and environment, computational modeling. *Total annual research expenditures:* $8.6 million. *Unit head:* Dr. Steven R. Little, Chairman, 412-624-9614, Fax: 412-624-9639, E-mail: srlittle@pitt.edu. *Application contact:* Dr. Joseph John McCarthy, Professor/Graduate Coordinator, 412-624-7362, Fax: 412-624-9639, E-mail: jjmcc@pitt.edu.
Website: http://www.engineering.pitt.edu/Chemical/.

University of Regina, Faculty of Graduate Studies and Research, Faculty of Engineering and Applied Science, Program in Petroleum Systems Engineering, Regina, SK S4S 0A2, Canada. Offers M Eng, MA Sc, PhD. Part-time programs available. *Faculty:* 39 full-time (7 women), 24 part-time/adjunct (0 women). *Students:* 60 full-time (15 women), 1 part-time (0 women). 198 applicants, 10% accepted. In 2014, 13 master's, 6 doctorates awarded. *Degree requirements:* For master's, thesis, project, report; for doctorate, thesis/dissertation. *Entrance requirements:* For doctorate, master's degree. Additional exam requirements/recommendations for international students: Required—TOEFL (minimum score 550 paper-based; 80 iBT), IELTS (minimum score 6.5), PTE (minimum score 59). *Application deadline:* For fall admission, 3/31 for domestic and international students; for winter admission, 7/31 for domestic and international students; for spring admission, 11/30 for domestic and international students. Application fee: $100. Electronic applications accepted. *Expenses:* Expenses: $2,588.85 per semester of full time study (M Eng); $1,633.35 (for MA Sc); $1,755.60 (for PhD). *Financial support:* In 2014–15, 10 fellowships (averaging $6,500 per year), 10 teaching assistantships (averaging $2,475 per year) were awarded; research assistantships, career-related internships or fieldwork, and scholarships/grants also available. Financial award application deadline: 6/15. *Faculty research:* Enhanced oil recovery, production engineering, reservoir engineering, surface thermodynamics, geostatistics. *Unit head:* Dr. Raphael Idem, Associate Dean, Research and Graduate Studies, 306-337-3287, Fax: 306-585-4855, E-mail: raphael.idem@uregina.ca. *Application contact:* Dr. Fanhua (Bill) Zeng, Program Chair/Graduate Coordinator, 306-337-2526, Fax: 306-585-4855, E-mail: fanhua.zeng@uregina.ca.
Website: http://www.uregina.ca/engineering/.

University of Southern California, Graduate School, Viterbi School of Engineering, Mork Family Department of Chemical Engineering and Materials Science, Los Angeles, CA 90089. Offers chemical engineering (MS, PhD, Engr); geoscience technologies (MS); materials engineering (MS); materials science (MS, PhD, Engr); petroleum engineering (MS, PhD, Engr); smart oilfield technologies (MS, Graduate Certificate). Terminal master's awarded for partial completion of doctoral program. *Degree requirements:* For master's, thesis optional; for doctorate, thesis/dissertation. *Entrance requirements:* For master's and doctorate, GRE General Test. Additional exam requirements/recommendations for international students: Recommended—TOEFL. Electronic applications accepted. *Expenses:* Contact institution. *Faculty research:* Heterogeneous materials and porous media, statistical mechanics, molecular simulation, polymer science and engineering, advanced materials, reaction engineering

Petroleum Engineering

and catalysis, membrane processes and separation, biochemical engineering, cell culture, bioreactor modeling, petroleum engineering.

The University of Texas at Austin, Graduate School, Cockrell School of Engineering, Department of Petroleum and Geosystems Engineering, Austin, TX 78712-1111. Offers energy and earth resources (MA); petroleum engineering (MS, PhD). Evening/weekend programs available. Postbaccalaureate distance learning degree programs offered (no on-campus study). *Entrance requirements:* For master's and doctorate, GRE General Test. Electronic applications accepted.

The University of Tulsa, Graduate School, College of Engineering and Natural Sciences, McDougall School of Petroleum Engineering, Tulsa, OK 74104-3189. Offers ME, MSE, PhD. Part-time programs available. *Faculty:* 13 full-time (0 women). *Students:* 87 full-time (18 women), 20 part-time (3 women); includes 3 minority (1 Asian, non-Hispanic/Latino; 2 Hispanic/Latino), 102 international. Average age 29. 419 applicants, 14% accepted, 34 enrolled. In 2014, 18 master's, 4 doctorates awarded. Terminal master's awarded for partial completion of doctoral program. *Degree requirements:* For master's, thesis (MSE); for doctorate, one foreign language, comprehensive exam, thesis/dissertation. *Entrance requirements:* For master's and doctorate, GRE General Test. Additional exam requirements/recommendations for international students: Required—TOEFL (minimum score 550 paper-based; 80 iBT), IELTS (minimum score 6). *Application deadline:* Applications are processed on a rolling basis. Application fee: $55. Electronic applications accepted. *Expenses: Tuition:* Full-time $20,160; part-time $1120 per credit hour. *Required fees:* $6 per credit hour. Tuition and fees vary according to course level and course load. *Financial support:* In 2014–15, 80 students received support, including 23 fellowships with full and partial tuition reimbursements available (averaging $4,062 per year), 68 research assistantships with full and partial tuition reimbursements available (averaging $12,458 per year), 20 teaching assistantships with full and partial tuition reimbursements available (averaging $10,067 per year); career-related internships or fieldwork, Federal Work-Study, scholarships/grants, health care benefits, tuition waivers (full and partial), and unspecified assistantships also available. Support available to part-time students. Financial award application deadline: 2/1; financial award applicants required to submit FAFSA. *Faculty research:* Artificial lift, drilling, multiphase flow in pipes, separation technology, horizontal well technology, reservoir characterization, well testing, reservoir simulation, unconventional natural gas. *Total annual research expenditures:* $6.5 million. *Unit head:* Dr. Mohan Kelkar, Chairperson, 918-631-3036, Fax: 915-631-2059, E-mail: mohan@utulsa.edu. *Application contact:* Dr. Rami Younis, Adviser, 918-631-2426, Fax: 918-631-5142, E-mail: rami-younis@utulsa.edu.
Website: http://engineering.utulsa.edu/academics/petroleum-engineering/.

University of Utah, Graduate School, College of Engineering, Department of Chemical Engineering, Salt Lake City, UT 84112-5820. Offers chemical engineering (MS, PhD); petroleum engineering (MS); MS/MBA. Part-time and evening/weekend programs available. Postbaccalaureate distance learning degree programs offered (minimal on-campus study). *Faculty:* 13 full-time (1 woman), 10 part-time/adjunct (1 woman). *Students:* 76 full-time (15 women), 23 part-time (2 women); includes 12 minority (4 Black or African American, non-Hispanic/Latino; 2 Asian, non-Hispanic/Latino; 5 Hispanic/Latino; 1 Native Hawaiian or other Pacific Islander, non-Hispanic/Latino), 41 international. Average age 30. 201 applicants, 30% accepted, 28 enrolled. In 2014, 6 master's, 7 doctorates awarded. *Degree requirements:* For master's, comprehensive exam, thesis (for some programs); for doctorate, comprehensive exam, thesis/dissertation. *Entrance requirements:* For master's, GRE General Test, minimum GPA of 3.0; for doctorate, GRE General Test, minimum GPA of 3.0, degree or course work in chemical engineering. Additional exam requirements/recommendations for international students: Required—TOEFL (minimum score 550 paper-based; 80 iBT), IELTS (minimum score 6.5). *Application deadline:* For fall admission, 1/15 priority date for domestic and international students; for spring admission, 10/1 priority date for domestic and international students; for summer admission, 2/1 priority date for domestic and international students. Applications are processed on a rolling basis. Application fee: $0 ($15 for international students). Electronic applications accepted. Application fee is waived when completed online. *Expenses:* Expenses: Contact institution. *Financial support:* In 2014–15, 5 fellowships with full tuition reimbursements (averaging $25,450 per year), 41 research assistantships with full tuition reimbursements (averaging $24,444 per year), 6 teaching assistantships (averaging $6,848 per year) were awarded; Federal Work-Study, institutionally sponsored loans, scholarships/grants, and unspecified assistantships also available. Financial award application deadline: 4/1; financial award applicants required to submit FAFSA. *Faculty research:* Drug delivery, fossil fuel and biomass combustion and gasification, oil and gas reservoir characteristics and management, multi-scale simulation, micro-scale synthesis. *Unit head:* Dr. Milind D. Deo, Chair, 801-581-6915, Fax: 801-585-9291, E-mail: milind.deo@utah.edu. *Application contact:* Rachelle L. Reed, Graduate Coordinator, 801-587-3610, Fax: 801-585-9291, E-mail: rachelle@chemeng.utah.edu.
Website: http://www.che.utah.edu/.

University of Wyoming, College of Engineering and Applied Sciences, Department of Chemical and Petroleum Engineering, Program in Petroleum Engineering, Laramie, WY 82071. Offers MS, PhD. Part-time programs available. Terminal master's awarded for partial completion of doctoral program. *Degree requirements:* For master's, thesis; for doctorate, thesis/dissertation. *Entrance requirements:* For master's and doctorate, GRE General Test, minimum GPA of 3.0. Additional exam requirements/recommendations for international students: Required—TOEFL (minimum score 600 paper-based). Electronic applications accepted. *Faculty research:* Oil recovery methods, oil production, coal bed methane.

West Virginia University, College of Engineering and Mineral Resources, Department of Petroleum and Natural Gas Engineering, Morgantown, WV 26506. Offers MSPNGE, PhD. Part-time programs available. *Degree requirements:* For master's, thesis; for doctorate, thesis/dissertation. *Entrance requirements:* For master's, minimum GPA of 3.0, BS or equivalent in petroleum or natural gas engineering; for doctorate, minimum GPA of 3.0, BS or MS in petroleum engineering from an ABET accredited or an internationally recognized petroleum engineering program or equivalent. Additional exam requirements/recommendations for international students: Required—TOEFL. *Faculty research:* Gas reservoir engineering, well logging, environment artificial intelligence.

Section 14
Industrial Engineering

This section contains a directory of institutions offering graduate work in industrial engineering. Additional information about programs listed in the directory may be obtained by writing directly to the dean of a graduate school or chair of a department at the address given in the directory.

For programs offering related work, see also in this book *Computer Science and Information Technology, Electrical and Computer Engineering, Energy and Power Engineering, Engineering and Applied Sciences,* and *Management of Engineering and Technology.* In the other guides in this series:

Graduate Programs in the Physical Sciences, Mathematics, Agricultural Sciences, the Environment & Natural Resources
See *Mathematical Sciences*

Graduate Programs in Business, Education, Information Studies, Law & Social Work
See *Business Administration and Management*

CONTENTS

Program Directories

Automotive Engineering

Clemson University, Graduate School, College of Engineering and Science, Department of Automotive Engineering, Greenville, SC 29634. Offers MS, PhD. *Faculty:* 15 full-time (2 women), 2 part-time/adjunct (0 women). *Students:* 193 full-time (22 women), 11 part-time (0 women); includes 8 minority (2 Black or African American, non-Hispanic/Latino; 1 Asian, non-Hispanic/Latino; 3 Hispanic/Latino; 2 Two or more races, non-Hispanic/Latino), 163 international. Average age 26. 589 applicants, 18% accepted, 76 enrolled. In 2014, 72 master's, 5 doctorates awarded. Terminal master's awarded for partial completion of doctoral program. *Degree requirements:* For master's, one foreign language, internship; for doctorate, one foreign language, comprehensive exam, thesis/dissertation. *Entrance requirements:* For master's, GRE, BS in engineering, math or applied science; two years of post-bachelor's experience (preferred); for doctorate, GRE, MS in engineering, math, or applied science and/or two years of post-bachelor's experience (preferred). Additional exam requirements/recommendations for international students: Required—TOEFL. *Application deadline:* For fall admission, 1/15 priority date for domestic and international students; for spring admission, 9/15 for domestic and international students. Applications are processed on a rolling basis. Application fee: $80 ($90 for international students). Electronic applications accepted. *Expenses:* Expenses: Contact institution. *Financial support:* In 2014–15, 62 students received support, including 28 fellowships with partial tuition reimbursements available (averaging $5,571 per year), 37 research assistantships with partial tuition reimbursements available (averaging $19,298 per year), 14 teaching assistantships with partial tuition reimbursements available (averaging $17,500 per year); career-related internships or fieldwork, scholarships/grants, and unspecified assistantships also available. Financial award application deadline: 2/1. *Faculty research:* Advanced powertrains, automotive systems integration, human factors, manufacturing and materials, vehicle performance, vehicle-to-vehicle and vehicle-infrastructure integration, vehicular electronics. *Total annual research expenditures:* $3.3 million. *Unit head:* Prof. Imtiaz Haque, Chair, 864-283-7212, E-mail: sih@clemson.edu. *Application contact:* Prof. Laine Mears, Graduate Coordinator, 864-283-7229, E-mail: mears@clemson.edu.
Website: http://www.grad.clemson.edu/programs/automotive-engineering/.

College for Creative Studies, Graduate Programs, Detroit, MI 48202-4034. Offers interdisciplinary design (MFA); transportation design (MFA).

Lawrence Technological University, College of Engineering, Southfield, MI 48075-1058. Offers architectural engineering (MS); automotive engineering (MS); civil engineering (MA, MS, PhD); construction engineering management (MA); electrical and computer engineering (MS); engineering management (MEM); industrial engineering (MS); manufacturing systems (ME, DE); mechanical engineering (MS, DE); mechatronic systems engineering (MS). Part-time and evening/weekend programs available. *Faculty:* 24 full-time (5 women), 15 part-time/adjunct (0 women). *Students:* 16 full-time (6 women), 478 part-time (71 women); includes 295 minority (15 Black or African American, non-Hispanic/Latino; 271 Asian, non-Hispanic/Latino; 7 Hispanic/Latino; 2 Two or more races, non-Hispanic/Latino), 38 international. Average age 27. 1,786 applicants, 40% accepted, 218 enrolled. In 2014, 106 master's awarded. *Degree requirements:* For master's, thesis (for some programs). *Entrance requirements:* Additional exam requirements/recommendations for international students: Required—TOEFL (minimum score 550 paper-based; 79 iBT). *Application deadline:* For fall admission, 8/1 priority date for domestic students, 5/29 for international students; for spring admission, 12/1 priority date for domestic students, 10/15 for international students. Applications are processed on a rolling basis. Application fee: $50. Electronic applications accepted. *Expenses: Tuition:* Full-time $14,700; part-time $1050 per credit hour. *Required fees:* $150. One-time fee: $150 part-time. *Financial support:* In 2014–15, 31 students received support, including 8 research assistantships (averaging $9,338 per year); Federal Work-Study and institutionally sponsored loans also available. Support available to part-time students. Financial award application deadline: 4/1; financial award applicants required to submit FAFSA. *Faculty research:* Advanced composite materials in bridges, strengthening existing bridges with carbon and glass fiber sheets, development of drive shafts using composite materials. *Unit head:* Dr. Nabil Grace, Dean, 248-204-2500, Fax: 248-204-2509, E-mail: engrdean@ltu.edu. *Application contact:* Jane Rohrback, Director of Admissions, 248-204-3160, Fax: 248-204-2228, E-mail: admissions@ltu.edu.
Website: http://www.ltu.edu/engineering/index.asp.

Michigan Technological University, Graduate School, College of Engineering, Department of Mechanical Engineering-Engineering Mechanics, Houghton, MI 49931. Offers engineering mechanics (MS); hybrid electric drive vehicle engineering (Graduate Certificate); mechanical engineering (MS); mechanical engineering-engineering mechanics (PhD). Part-time programs available. Postbaccalaureate distance learning degree programs offered (minimal on-campus study). *Faculty:* 63 full-time, 38 part-time/adjunct. *Students:* 243 full-time, 85 part-time; includes 11 minority (3 Black or African American, non-Hispanic/Latino; 4 Asian, non-Hispanic/Latino; 3 Hispanic/Latino; 1 Two or more races, non-Hispanic/Latino), 250 international. Average age 27. 1,421 applicants, 23% accepted, 95 enrolled. In 2014, 106 master's, 16 doctorates, 12 other advanced degrees awarded. Terminal master's awarded for partial completion of doctoral program. *Degree requirements:* For master's, comprehensive exam (for some programs), thesis (for some programs); for doctorate, comprehensive exam, thesis/dissertation. *Entrance requirements:* For master's, GRE (Michigan Tech students exempt - recommended for external funding opportunities), statement of purpose, official transcripts, 2 letters of recommendation, resume/curriculum vitae; for doctorate, GRE (Michigan Tech students exempt - recommended for external funding opportunities), MS (preferred), statement of purpose, official transcripts, 2 letters of recommendation, resume/curriculum vitae; for Graduate Certificate, statement of purpose, official transcripts, BS in engineering. Additional exam requirements/recommendations for international students: Required—TOEFL (minimum score 90 iBT) or IELTS. *Application deadline:* For fall admission, 3/1 priority date for domestic and international students; for spring admission, 8/1 priority date for domestic and international students. Applications are processed on a rolling basis. Electronic applications accepted. *Expenses:* Expenses: Contact institution. *Financial support:* In 2014–15, 182 students received support, including 16 fellowships with full and partial tuition reimbursements available (averaging $13,824 per year), 33 research assistantships with full and partial tuition reimbursements available (averaging $13,824 per year), 28 teaching assistantships with full and partial tuition reimbursements available (averaging $13,824 per year); career-related internships or fieldwork, Federal Work-Study, scholarships/grants, health care benefits, unspecified assistantships, and cooperative program also available. Financial award applicants required to submit FAFSA. *Faculty research:* Design and dynamic systems, energy-thermofluids, manufacturing, solid mechanics, sustainability. *Total annual research expenditures:* $3.7 million. *Unit head:* Dr. William W. Predebon, Chair, 906-487-2551, Fax: 906-487-2822, E-mail: wwpredeb@mtu.edu. *Application contact:* Jillian Isaacson, Office Assistant, 906-487-3611, Fax: 906-487-2822, E-mail: jillian@mtu.edu.
Website: http://www.mtu.edu/mechanical/.

Minnesota State University Mankato, College of Graduate Studies, College of Science, Engineering and Technology, Department of Automotive and Manufacturing Engineering Technology, Mankato, MN 56001. Offers manufacturing engineering technology (MS). *Students:* 2 full-time (0 women), 11 part-time (0 women). *Degree requirements:* For master's, comprehensive exam, thesis. *Entrance requirements:* For master's, GRE General Test (if GPA less than 3.0), minimum GPA of 3.0 during previous 2 years. Additional exam requirements/recommendations for international students: Required—TOEFL. *Application deadline:* For fall admission, 7/1 priority date for domestic students; for spring admission, 11/1 for domestic students. Applications are processed on a rolling basis. Application fee: $40. Electronic applications accepted. *Financial support:* Research assistantships with full tuition reimbursements, teaching assistantships with full tuition reimbursements, and unspecified assistantships available. Financial award application deadline: 3/15; financial award applicants required to submit FAFSA. *Unit head:* Dr. Bruce Jones, Graduate Coordinator, 507-389-6700. *Application contact:* 507-389-2321, E-mail: grad@mnsu.edu.

University of Michigan, College of Engineering, Interpro Programs in Engineering, Ann Arbor, MI 48109. Offers automotive engineering (M Eng); design science (PhD); energy systems engineering (MS); financial engineering (MS); global automotive and manufacturing engineering (M Eng); manufacturing engineering (M Eng, D Eng); pharmaceutical engineering (M Eng); robotics and autonomous vehicles (M Eng); MBA/M Eng; MSE/MS. Part-time programs available. Postbaccalaureate distance learning degree programs offered (no on-campus study). *Students:* 187 full-time (46 women), 250 part-time (40 women). 364 applicants, 2% accepted, 3 enrolled. In 2014, 171 master's, 1 doctorate awarded. Terminal master's awarded for partial completion of doctoral program. *Degree requirements:* For master's, capstone project; for doctorate, thesis/dissertation. *Entrance requirements:* For master's, GRE; for doctorate, GRE, 2 years of work experience. Additional exam requirements/recommendations for international students: Required—TOEFL (minimum score 560 paper-based). *Application deadline:* Applications are processed on a rolling basis. Electronic applications accepted. *Financial support:* Fellowships, research assistantships with full tuition reimbursements, teaching assistantships with full tuition reimbursements, career-related internships or fieldwork, scholarships/grants, and unspecified assistantships available. Financial award application deadline: 2/15; financial award applicants required to submit FAFSA. *Faculty research:* Automotive engineering, design science, energy systems engineering, engineering sustainable systems, financial engineering, global automotive and manufacturing engineering, integrated microsystems, manufacturing engineering, pharmaceutical engineering, robotics and autonomous vehicles. *Total annual research expenditures:* $263,643. *Unit head:* Prof. Panos Papalambros, Director, 734-647-8401, Fax: 734-647-0079, E-mail: pyp@umich.edu. *Application contact:* Patti Mackmiller, Program Manager, 734-764-3071, Fax: 734-647-2243, E-mail: pmackmil@umich.edu.
Website: http://www.isd.engin.umich.edu.

University of Michigan–Dearborn, College of Engineering and Computer Science, MSE Program in Automotive Systems Engineering, Dearborn, MI 48128. Offers MSE. Part-time and evening/weekend programs available. Postbaccalaureate distance learning degree programs offered. *Faculty:* 1 full-time (0 women). *Students:* 80 full-time (2 women), 52 part-time (3 women); includes 7 minority (4 Asian, non-Hispanic/Latino; 3 Hispanic/Latino), 104 international. 193 applicants, 52% accepted, 64 enrolled. In 2014, 28 master's awarded. *Degree requirements:* For master's, thesis optional. *Entrance requirements:* For master's, BS or equivalent degree in engineering from ABET-accredited program with minimum cumulative GPA of 3.0. Additional exam requirements/recommendations for international students: Required—TOEFL (minimum score 560 paper-based; 84 iBT), IELTS (minimum score 6.5). *Application deadline:* For fall admission, 8/1 priority date for domestic students, 5/1 for international students; for winter admission, 12/1 priority date for domestic students, 9/1 for international students; for spring admission, 4/1 priority date for domestic students, 1/1 for international students. Applications are processed on a rolling basis. Application fee: $60. Electronic applications accepted. *Expenses:* Tuition, state resident: full-time $12,202; part-time $707 per credit hour. Tuition, nonresident: full-time $20,980; part-time $1209 per credit hour. *Required fees:* $798; $302 per term. Tuition and fees vary according to course level, course load, degree level and program. *Financial support:* In 2014–15, 81 students received support, including 1 research assistantship with full tuition reimbursement available (averaging $21,156 per year); scholarships/grants and unspecified assistantships also available. Financial award application deadline: 4/1; financial award applicants required to submit FAFSA. *Faculty research:* Performance of lightweight automotive materials, stamping, hydroforming, tailor-welded blanking, automotive composites processing and design, thermoplastic matrix composites, injection molding. *Unit head:* Dr. Pankaj K. Mallick, Director/Professor, 313-593-5119, Fax: 313-593-5386, E-mail: pkm@umich.edu. *Application contact:* Sherry Boyd, Intermediate Administrative Assistant, 313-593-5582, Fax: 313-593-5386, E-mail: idpgrad@umd.umich.edu.
Website: http://umdearborn.edu/cecs/IDP/mse_ase/index.php.

University of Michigan–Dearborn, College of Engineering and Computer Science, PhD Program in Automotive Systems Engineering, Dearborn, MI 48128. Offers PhD. Part-time and evening/weekend programs available. *Faculty:* 1 full-time (0 women). *Students:* 14 part-time (2 women), 12 international. 16 applicants, 44% accepted, 3 enrolled. In 2014, 1 doctorate awarded. *Degree requirements:* For doctorate, thesis/dissertation. *Entrance requirements:* For doctorate, GRE. Additional exam requirements/recommendations for international students: Required—TOEFL (minimum score 560 paper-based; 84 iBT). *Application deadline:* For fall admission, 1/15 priority date for domestic and international students; for winter admission, 4/15 priority date for domestic and international students. Application fee: $60. Electronic applications accepted. *Expenses:* Tuition, state resident: full-time $12,202; part-time $707 per credit hour. Tuition, nonresident: full-time $20,980; part-time $1209 per credit hour. *Required fees:* $798; $302 per term. Tuition and fees vary according to course level, course load, degree level and program. *Financial support:* In 2014–15, 3 research assistantships with full tuition reimbursements (averaging $26,500 per year) were awarded; scholarships/grants and unspecified assistantships also available. Financial award applicants required to submit FAFSA. *Unit head:* Dr. Pankaj K. Mallick, Director/Professor, 313-593-5119, Fax: 313-593-5386, E-mail: pkm@umich.edu. *Application contact:* Sherry Boyd, Intermediate Administrative Assistant, 313-593-5582, Fax: 313-593-5386, E-mail: idpgrad@umd.umich.edu.
Website: http://www.engin.umd.umich.edu/IDP/phd_ase/.

Wayne State University, College of Engineering, Program in Electric-Drive Vehicle Engineering, Detroit, MI 48202. Offers MS, Graduate Certificate. *Students:* 14 full-time

(0 women), 13 part-time (2 women); includes 5 minority (1 Black or African American, non-Hispanic/Latino; 3 Asian, non-Hispanic/Latino; 1 Hispanic/Latino), 12 international. Average age 30. 42 applicants, 62% accepted, 5 enrolled. In 2014, 7 master's, 2 other advanced degrees awarded. *Degree requirements:* For master's, thesis optional. *Entrance requirements:* For master's, bachelor's degree in engineering from accredited institution with minimum GPA of 3.0 or enrollment in EVE Graduate Certificate program; for Graduate Certificate, bachelor's degree in engineering from accredited institution with minimum GPA of 2.7. Additional exam requirements/recommendations for international students: Required—TOEFL (minimum score 550 paper-based; 79 iBT), TWE (minimum score 5.5), Michigan English Language Assessment Battery (minimum score 85); Recommended—IELTS (minimum score 6.5). *Application deadline:* For fall admission, 6/1 priority date for domestic students, 5/1 priority date for international students; for winter admission, 10/1 priority date for domestic students, 9/1 priority date for international students; for spring admission, 2/1 priority date for domestic students, 1/1 priority date for international students. Applications are processed on a rolling basis. Application fee: $0. Electronic applications accepted. *Expenses:* Expenses: Contact institution. *Financial support:* In 2014–15, 5 students received support. Scholarships/grants available. Financial award application deadline: 3/31; financial award applicants required to submit FAFSA. *Unit head:* Dr. Simon Ng, Program Director, 313-577-3805, E-mail: sng@wayne.edu. *Application contact:* Andrea Eidenberg, Academic Services Officer, 313-577-3716, E-mail: aeisen@eng.wayne.edu.
Website: http://engineering.wayne.edu/eve/index.php.

Industrial/Management Engineering

American University of Armenia, Graduate Programs, Yerevan, Armenia. Offers business administration (MBA); computer and information science (MS), including business management, design and manufacturing, energy (ME, MS), industrial engineering and systems management; economics (MS); industrial engineering and systems management (ME), including business, computer aided design/manufacturing, energy (ME, MS), information technology; law (LL M); political science and international affairs (MPSIA); public health (MPH); teaching English as a foreign language (MA). Part-time and evening/weekend programs available. *Degree requirements:* For master's, thesis (for some programs), capstone/project. *Entrance requirements:* For master's, GRE, GMAT, or LSAT. Additional exam requirements/recommendations for international students: Recommended—TOEFL (minimum score 79 iBT), IELTS (minimum score 6.5). *Faculty research:* Microfinance, finance (rural/development, international, corporate), firm life cycle theory, TESOL, language proficiency testing, public policy, administrative law, economic development, cryptography, artificial intelligence, energy efficiency/renewable energy, computer-aided design/manufacturing, health financing, tuberculosis control, mother/child health, preventive ophthalmology, post-earthquake psychopathological investigations, tobacco control, environmental health risk assessments.

Arizona State University at the Tempe campus, Ira A. Fulton Schools of Engineering, School of Computing, Informatics, and Decision Systems Engineering, Tempe, AZ 85287-8809. Offers computer engineering (MS, PhD); computer science (MCS, MS, PhD); industrial engineering (MS, PhD); software engineering (MS). Part-time and evening/weekend programs available. Postbaccalaureate distance learning degree programs offered (minimal on-campus study). Terminal master's awarded for partial completion of doctoral program. *Degree requirements:* For master's, comprehensive exam (for some programs), portfolio (MCS); interactive Program of Study (iPOS) submitted before completing 50 percent of required credit hours; for doctorate, comprehensive exam, thesis/dissertation, interactive Program of Study (iPOS) submitted before completing 50 percent of required credit hours. *Entrance requirements:* For master's, GRE, minimum GPA of 3.0 or equivalent in last 2 years of work leading to bachelor's degree; for doctorate, GRE, minimum GPA of 3.0 in last 2 years of work leading to bachelor's degree. Additional exam requirements/recommendations for international students: Required—TOEFL, IELTS, or PTE. Electronic applications accepted. *Expenses:* Contact institution. *Faculty research:* Artificial intelligence, cyberphysical and embedded systems, health informatics, information assurance and security, information management/multimedia/visualization, network science, personalized learning/educational games, production logistics, software and systems engineering, statistical modeling and data mining.

Auburn University, Graduate School, Ginn College of Engineering, Department of Industrial and Systems Engineering, Auburn University, AL 36849. Offers MISE, MS, PhD, Graduate Certificate. Part-time programs available. *Faculty:* 12 full-time (1 woman), 1 part-time/adjunct (0 women). *Students:* 84 full-time (16 women), 39 part-time (11 women); includes 9 minority (5 Black or African American, non-Hispanic/Latino; 1 Asian, non-Hispanic/Latino; 3 Hispanic/Latino), 76 international. Average age 29. 212 applicants, 66% accepted, 30 enrolled. In 2014, 43 master's, 8 doctorates, 12 other advanced degrees awarded. *Degree requirements:* For master's, thesis (MS); for doctorate, thesis/dissertation. *Entrance requirements:* For master's and doctorate, GRE General Test. *Application deadline:* For fall admission, 7/7 for domestic students; for spring admission, 11/24 for domestic students. Applications are processed on a rolling basis. Application fee: $50 ($60 for international students). *Expenses:* Tuition, state resident: full-time $8586; part-time $477 per credit hour. Tuition, nonresident: full-time $25,758; part-time $1431 per credit hour. *Required fees:* $804 per semester. Tuition and fees vary according to degree level and program. *Financial support:* Fellowships, research assistantships, teaching assistantships, and Federal Work-Study available. Support available to part-time students. Financial award application deadline: 3/15; financial award applicants required to submit FAFSA. *Unit head:* Dr. Jorge Valenzuela, Chair, 334-844-1400. *Application contact:* Dr. George Flowers, Dean of the Graduate School, 334-844-2125.
Website: http://www.eng.auburn.edu/department/ie.

Binghamton University, State University of New York, Graduate School, Thomas J. Watson School of Engineering and Applied Science, Department of Systems Science and Industrial Engineering, Vestal, NY 13850. Offers executive health systems (MS); industrial and systems engineering (M Eng); systems science and industrial engineering (MS, PhD). MS in executive health systems also offered in Manhattan. Part-time and evening/weekend programs available. *Faculty:* 18 full-time (4 women), 6 part-time/adjunct (1 woman). *Students:* 172 full-time (56 women), 84 part-time (20 women); includes 39 minority (11 Black or African American, non-Hispanic/Latino; 15 Asian, non-Hispanic/Latino; 13 Hispanic/Latino), 158 international. Average age 27. 321 applicants, 94% accepted, 119 enrolled. In 2014, 69 master's, 16 doctorates awarded. Terminal master's awarded for partial completion of doctoral program. *Degree requirements:* For master's, thesis; for doctorate, thesis/dissertation. *Entrance requirements:* For master's and doctorate, GRE General Test. Additional exam requirements/recommendations for international students: Required—TOEFL (minimum score 550 paper-based; 80 iBT). *Application deadline:* For fall admission, 4/15 priority date for domestic students, 1/15 priority date for international students; for spring admission, 11/1 for domestic students, 10/1 priority date for international students. Applications are processed on a rolling basis. Application fee: $75. Electronic applications accepted. *Expenses:* Expenses: $5,435 resident; $11,105 non-resident. *Financial support:* In 2014–15, 77 students received support, including 1 fellowship with full tuition reimbursement available (averaging $10,000 per year), 45 research assistantships with full tuition reimbursements available (averaging $16,500 per year), 13 teaching assistantships with full tuition reimbursements available (averaging $16,500 per year); career-related internships or fieldwork, Federal Work-Study, institutionally sponsored loans, scholarships/grants, health care benefits, tuition waivers (full and partial), and unspecified assistantships also available. Financial award application deadline: 2/15; financial award applicants required to submit FAFSA. *Faculty research:* Problem restructuring, protein modeling. *Unit head:* Ellen Tilden, Coordinator of Graduate Studies, 607-777-2873, E-mail: etilden@binghamton.edu. *Application contact:* Kishan Zuber, Recruiting and Admissions Coordinator, 607-777-2151, Fax: 607-777-2501, E-mail: kzuber@binghamton.edu.
Website: http://www.ssie.binghamton.edu.

Bradley University, Graduate School, College of Engineering and Technology, Department of Industrial and Manufacturing Engineering and Technology, Peoria, IL 61625-0002. Offers industrial engineering (MS); manufacturing engineering (MS). Part-time and evening/weekend programs available. *Faculty:* 10 full-time (1 woman). *Students:* 18 full-time (4 women), 25 part-time (5 women); includes 1 minority (Black or African American, non-Hispanic/Latino), 35 international. 103 applicants, 30% accepted, 19 enrolled. In 2014, 10 master's awarded. *Degree requirements:* For master's, comprehensive exam, project. *Entrance requirements:* Additional exam requirements/recommendations for international students: Required—TOEFL (minimum score 550 paper-based; 79 iBT), IELTS (minimum score 6.5). *Application deadline:* For fall admission, 5/15 priority date for domestic and international students; for spring admission, 10/15 priority date for domestic and international students. Applications are processed on a rolling basis. Application fee: $40 ($50 for international students). Electronic applications accepted. *Expenses: Tuition:* Full-time $14,580; part-time $810 per credit. *Required fees:* $224. Full-time tuition and fees vary according to course load. *Financial support:* In 2014–15, 6 research assistantships with full and partial tuition reimbursements (averaging $10,130 per year) were awarded; scholarships/grants, tuition waivers (partial), and unspecified assistantships also available. Support available to part-time students. Financial award application deadline: 4/1. *Unit head:* Dr. Joseph Chen, Department Chair, 309-677-2740, E-mail: jchen@bradley.edu. *Application contact:* Kayla Carroll, Director of International Admission and Student Services, 309-677-2375, E-mail: klcarroll@fsmail.bradley.edu.

Buffalo State College, State University of New York, The Graduate School, Faculty of Applied Science and Education, Department of Technology, Program in Industrial Technology, Buffalo, NY 14222-1095. Offers MS. *Degree requirements:* For master's, thesis or project. *Entrance requirements:* For master's, minimum GPA of 2.5. Additional exam requirements/recommendations for international students: Required—TOEFL (minimum score 550 paper-based).

California Polytechnic State University, San Luis Obispo, College of Engineering, Department of Industrial Engineering, San Luis Obispo, CA 93407. Offers MS. Part-time programs available. *Faculty:* 3 full-time (1 woman). *Students:* 4 full-time (1 woman), 2 part-time (0 women); includes 2 minority (both Asian, non-Hispanic/Latino), 2 international. Average age 25. 20 applicants, 10% accepted, 1 enrolled. In 2014, 5 master's awarded. *Degree requirements:* For master's, comprehensive exam (for some programs), thesis (for some programs). *Application deadline:* For fall admission, 4/1 for domestic and international students; for winter admission, 11/1 for domestic students, 6/30 for international students; for spring admission, 2/1 for domestic students. Applications are processed on a rolling basis. Application fee: $55. Electronic applications accepted. *Expenses:* Tuition, state resident: full-time $6738; part-time $3906 per year. Tuition, nonresident: full-time $15,666; part-time $8370 per year. *Required fees:* $3447; $1001 per quarter. One-time fee: $3447 full-time; $3003 part-time. *Financial support:* Fellowships, research assistantships, teaching assistantships, career-related internships or fieldwork, Federal Work-Study, institutionally sponsored loans, and scholarships/grants available. Support available to part-time students. Financial award application deadline: 3/2; financial award applicants required to submit FAFSA. *Faculty research:* Operations research, simulation, project management, supply chain and logistics, quality engineering. *Unit head:* Dr. Jon Pan, Graduate Coordinator, 805-756-2540, Fax: 805-756-5439, E-mail: pan@calpoly.edu. *Application contact:* Dr. James Maraviglia, Associate Vice Provost for Marketing and Enrollment Development, 805-756-2311, Fax: 805-756-5400, E-mail: admissions@calpoly.edu.
Website: http://www.ime.calpoly.edu/programs/graduate/.

California State University, East Bay, Office of Academic Programs and Graduate Studies, College of Business and Economics, MBA Program, Hayward, CA 94542-3000. Offers accounting/finance (MBA); entrepreneurship (MBA); global innovators (MBA); human resources and organizational behavior (MBA); information technology management (MBA); marketing management (MBA); operations and supply chain management (MBA); strategy and international business (MBA). Part-time and evening/weekend programs available. *Degree requirements:* For master's, comprehensive exam or thesis. *Entrance requirements:* For master's, GMAT (minimum 20th percentile verbal and quantitative section), bachelor's degree, minimum GPA of 2.75. Additional exam requirements/recommendations for international students: Required—TOEFL (minimum score 550 paper-based; 79 iBT). *Application deadline:* For fall admission, 6/30 for domestic and international students. Applications are processed on a rolling basis. Application fee: $55. Electronic applications accepted. *Expenses:* Expenses: Contact institution. *Financial support:* Career-related internships or fieldwork, Federal Work-Study, institutionally sponsored loans, and scholarships/grants available. Support available to part-time students. Financial award application deadline: 3/2; financial award applicants required to submit FAFSA. *Unit head:* Xinjian Lu, Associate Dean, 510-855-3290, E-mail: xinjian.lu@csueastbay.edu. *Application contact:* Dr. Donna Wiley, Interim Associate Vice President for Academic Programs and Graduate Studies, 510-885-3716, Fax: 510-885-4777, E-mail: donna.wiley@csueastbay.edu.
Website: http://www20.csueastbay.edu/ecat/graduate-chapters/g-buad.html#mba.

California State University, Fresno, Division of Graduate Studies, College of Agricultural Sciences and Technology, Department of Industrial Technology, Fresno, CA

93740-8027. Offers MS. Part-time and evening/weekend programs available. *Degree requirements:* For master's, comprehensive exam (for some programs), thesis (for some programs). *Entrance requirements:* For master's, GRE General Test, minimum GPA of 2.5. Additional exam requirements/recommendations for international students: Required—TOEFL. Electronic applications accepted. *Faculty research:* Fuels/pollution, energy, outdoor storage methods.

California State University, Northridge, Graduate Studies, College of Engineering and Computer Science, Department of Manufacturing Systems Engineering and Management, Northridge, CA 91330. Offers engineering automation (MS); engineering management (MS); manufacturing systems engineering (MS); materials engineering (MS). Postbaccalaureate distance learning degree programs offered. *Students:* 180 full-time (38 women), 56 part-time (15 women); includes 24 minority (11 Asian, non-Hispanic/Latino; 8 Hispanic/Latino; 5 Two or more races, non-Hispanic/Latino), 172 international. Average age 26. *Entrance requirements:* For master's, GRE (if cumulative undergraduate GPA less than 3.0). *Application deadline:* For fall admission, 3/30 for domestic students; for spring admission, 9/30 for domestic students. Application fee: $55. *Expenses: Required fees:* $12,402. *Unit head:* Kang Chang, Acting Chair, 818-677-2167.
Website: http://www.csun.edu/~msem/.

Central Washington University, Graduate Studies and Research, College of Education and Professional Studies, Department of Industrial and Engineering Technology, Ellensburg, WA 98926. Offers engineering technology (MS). Part-time programs available. *Degree requirements:* For master's, thesis or alternative. *Entrance requirements:* For master's, minimum GPA of 3.0. Additional exam requirements/recommendations for international students: Required—TOEFL (minimum score 550 paper-based; 79 iBT), IELTS (minimum score 6.5). Electronic applications accepted.

Clemson University, Graduate School, College of Engineering and Science, Department of Industrial Engineering, Clemson, SC 29634. Offers M Eng, MS, PhD. Part-time programs available. Postbaccalaureate distance learning degree programs offered (no on-campus study). *Faculty:* 13 full-time (3 women), 3 part-time/adjunct (1 woman). *Students:* 106 full-time (23 women), 125 part-time (30 women); includes 20 minority (6 Black or African American, non-Hispanic/Latino; 1 American Indian or Alaska Native, non-Hispanic/Latino; 4 Asian, non-Hispanic/Latino; 7 Hispanic/Latino; 2 Two or more races, non-Hispanic/Latino), 109 international. Average age 30. 417 applicants, 49% accepted, 129 enrolled. In 2014, 63 master's, 9 doctorates awarded. Terminal master's awarded for partial completion of doctoral program. *Degree requirements:* For master's, thesis or alternative; for doctorate, comprehensive exam, thesis/dissertation. *Entrance requirements:* Additional exam requirements/recommendations for international students: Required—TOEFL. *Application deadline:* For fall admission, 4/15 for domestic students, 1/15 for international students. Applications are processed on a rolling basis. Application fee: $70 ($80 for international students). Electronic applications accepted. *Financial support:* In 2014–15, 33 students received support, including 2 fellowships with full and partial tuition reimbursements available (averaging $5,000 per year), 19 research assistantships with partial tuition reimbursements available (averaging $20,724 per year), 14 teaching assistantships with partial tuition reimbursements available (averaging $19,031 per year); career-related internships or fieldwork, institutionally sponsored loans, scholarships/grants, health care benefits, and unspecified assistantships also available. Support available to part-time students. Financial award applicants required to submit FAFSA. *Faculty research:* System optimization, health care engineering, human factors and safety, human-computer interaction, quality. *Total annual research expenditures:* $915,420. *Unit head:* Dr. Scott Mason, Interim Department Chair, 864-656-5645, E-mail: mason@clemson.edu. *Application contact:* Kevin M. Taaffe, Graduate Coordinator, 864-656-0291, E-mail: taaffe@clemson.edu.
Website: http://www.clemson.edu/ces/departments/ie/index.html.

Cleveland State University, College of Graduate Studies, Fenn College of Engineering, Department of Industrial and Manufacturing Engineering, Cleveland, OH 44115. Offers industrial engineering (MS, D Eng). Part-time programs available. *Faculty:* 5 full-time (0 women), 2 part-time/adjunct (0 women). *Students:* 4 full-time (0 women), 8 part-time (3 women); includes 2 minority (1 Black or African American, non-Hispanic/Latino; 1 Asian, non-Hispanic/Latino), 4 international. Average age 29. 19 applicants, 21% accepted. In 2014, 4 master's awarded. Terminal master's awarded for partial completion of doctoral program. *Degree requirements:* For master's, thesis or alternative; for doctorate, thesis/dissertation, candidacy and qualifying exams. *Entrance requirements:* For master's, GRE General Test, minimum GPA of 2.75; for doctorate, GRE General Test, minimum GPA of 3.25. Additional exam requirements/recommendations for international students: Required—TOEFL (minimum score 525 paper-based). *Application deadline:* For fall admission, 7/15 priority date for domestic students, 6/1 priority date for international students; for spring admission, 11/1 priority date for international students. Applications are processed on a rolling basis. Application fee: $30. *Expenses:* Tuition, state resident: full-time $9566; part-time $531 per credit hour. Tuition, nonresident: full-time $17,980; part-time $999 per credit hour. *Required fees:* $25 per semester. Tuition and fees vary according to degree level and program. *Financial support:* In 2014–15, 4 research assistantships with full and partial tuition reimbursements (averaging $3,550 per year), 2 teaching assistantships with tuition reimbursements (averaging $3,725 per year) were awarded; fellowships, career-related internships or fieldwork, institutionally sponsored loans, tuition waivers (partial), and unspecified assistantships also available. Support available to part-time students. *Faculty research:* Modeling of manufacturing systems, statistical process control, computerized production planning and facilities design, cellular manufacturing, artificial intelligence and sensors. *Unit head:* Dr. Joseph A. Svestka, Chairperson, 216-687-4662, Fax: 216-687-9330, E-mail: j.svestka@csuohio.edu. *Application contact:* Shirley A. Love, Administrative Services Coordinator, 216-687-2044, Fax: 216-687-9330, E-mail: s.love@csuohio.edu.
Website: http://www.csuohio.edu/engineering/ime/.

Colorado State University–Pueblo, College of Education, Engineering and Professional Studies, Department of Engineering, Pueblo, CO 81001-4901. Offers industrial and systems engineering (MS). *Degree requirements:* For master's, thesis optional. *Entrance requirements:* For master's, GRE General Test. Additional exam requirements/recommendations for international students: Required—TOEFL (minimum score 500 paper-based). *Faculty research:* Nanotechnology, applied operations, research transportation, decision analysis.

Columbia University, Fu Foundation School of Engineering and Applied Science, Department of Industrial Engineering and Operations Research, New York, NY 10027. Offers financial engineering (MS); industrial engineering and operations research (MS, Eng Sc D, PhD); management science and engineering (MS); MS/MBA. Part-time and evening/weekend programs available. Postbaccalaureate distance learning degree programs offered (no on-campus study). *Faculty:* 22 full-time (3 women), 50 part-time/adjunct (2 women). *Students:* 417 full-time (152 women), 258 part-time (95 women); includes 37 minority (27 Asian, non-Hispanic/Latino; 7 Hispanic/Latino; 3 Two or more races, non-Hispanic/Latino), 598 international. 2,369 applicants, 27% accepted, 364 enrolled. In 2014, 331 master's, 13 doctorates awarded. *Degree requirements:* For doctorate, thesis/dissertation, oral and written qualifying exams. *Entrance requirements:* For master's and doctorate, GRE General Test. Additional exam requirements/recommendations for international students: Required—TOEFL, IELTS, PTE. *Application deadline:* For fall admission, 12/15 priority date for domestic and international students; for spring admission, 10/1 priority date for domestic and international students. Application fee: $85. Electronic applications accepted. *Financial support:* In 2014–15, 49 students received support, including 1 fellowship with full tuition reimbursement available (averaging $25,000 per year), 24 research assistantships with full tuition reimbursements available (averaging $21,485 per year), 23 teaching assistantships with full tuition reimbursements available (averaging $21,485 per year); health care benefits and funding for travel to conferences also available. Financial award application deadline: 12/15; financial award applicants required to submit FAFSA. *Faculty research:* Applied probability and optimization; financial engineering, modeling risk including credit risk and systemic risk, asset allocation, portfolio execution, behavioral finance, agent-based model in finance; revenue management; management and optimization of service systems, call centers, capacity allocation in healthcare systems, inventory control for vaccines; energy, smart grids, demand shaping, managing renewable energy sources, energy-aware scheduling. *Unit head:* Dr. Garud N. Iyengar, Professor and Department Chair, Industrial Engineering and Operations Research, 212-854-4594, Fax: 212-854-8103, E-mail: garud@ieor.columbia.edu. *Application contact:* Adina Berrios Brooks, Associate Director, Graduate Admissions and Student Affairs, 212-854-1934, Fax: 212-854-8103, E-mail: admit@ieor.columbia.edu.
Website: http://www.ieor.columbia.edu/.

Concordia University, School of Graduate Studies, Faculty of Engineering and Computer Science, Department of Mechanical and Industrial Engineering, Montréal, QC H3G 1M8, Canada. Offers composites (M Eng); industrial engineering (M Eng, MA Sc); mechanical engineering (M Eng, MA Sc, PhD, Certificate); software systems for industrial engineering (Certificate). M Eng in composites program offered jointly with École Polytechnique de Montréal. *Degree requirements:* For master's, variable foreign language requirement, thesis or alternative; for doctorate, comprehensive exam, thesis/dissertation. *Faculty research:* Mechanical systems, fluid control systems, thermofluids engineering and robotics, industrial control systems.

Cornell University, Graduate School, Graduate Fields of Agriculture and Life Sciences and Graduate Fields of Engineering, Field of Biological and Environmental Engineering, Ithaca, NY 14853-0001. Offers bioenergy and integrated energy systems (M Eng, MPS, MS, PhD); biological engineering (M Eng, MPS, MS, PhD); bioprocess engineering (M Eng, MPS, MS, PhD); ecohydrology (M Eng, MPS, MS, PhD); environmental engineering (M Eng, MPS, MS, PhD); environmental management (MPS); food engineering (M Eng, MPS, MS, PhD); industrial biotechnology (M Eng, MPS, MS, PhD); nanobiotechnology (M Eng, MPS, MS, PhD); sustainable systems (M Eng, MPS, MS, PhD); synthetic biology (MS); syntheticbiology (M Eng, MPS, PhD). Terminal master's awarded for partial completion of doctoral program. *Degree requirements:* For master's, thesis (MS); for doctorate, comprehensive exam, thesis/dissertation. *Entrance requirements:* For master's, letters of recommendation (3 for MS, 2 for M Eng and MPS); for doctorate, GRE General Test, 3 letters of recommendation. Additional exam requirements/recommendations for international students: Required—TOEFL (minimum score 550 paper-based; 77 iBT). Electronic applications accepted. *Faculty research:* Biological and food engineering, environmental, soil and water engineering, international agricultural engineering, structures and controlled environments, machine systems and energy.

Cornell University, Graduate School, Graduate Fields of Engineering, Field of Operations Research and Information Engineering, Ithaca, NY 14853. Offers applied probability and statistics (PhD); manufacturing systems engineering (PhD); mathematical programming (PhD); operations research and industrial engineering (M Eng). *Degree requirements:* For doctorate, comprehensive exam, thesis/dissertation. *Entrance requirements:* For master's and doctorate, GRE General Test, 3 letters of recommendation. Additional exam requirements/recommendations for international students: Required—TOEFL (minimum score 600 paper-based; 100 iBT). Electronic applications accepted. *Faculty research:* Mathematical programming and combinatorial optimization, statistics, stochastic processes, mathematical finance, simulation, manufacturing, e-commerce.

Dalhousie University, Faculty of Engineering, Department of Industrial Engineering, Halifax, NS B3J 2X4, Canada. Offers M Eng, MA Sc, PhD. *Degree requirements:* For master's, thesis; for doctorate, thesis/dissertation. *Entrance requirements:* Additional exam requirements/recommendations for international students: Required—TOEFL, IELTS, CANTEST, CAEL, or Michigan English Language Assessment Battery. Electronic applications accepted. *Faculty research:* Industrial ergonomics, operations research, production manufacturing systems, scheduling stochastic models.

Eastern Kentucky University, The Graduate School, College of Business and Technology, Department of Technology, Program in Industrial Technology, Richmond, KY 40475-3102. Offers MS. Part-time programs available. *Entrance requirements:* For master's, GRE General Test, minimum GPA of 2.5. *Faculty research:* Quality control, dental implants, manufacturing technology.

École Polytechnique de Montréal, Graduate Programs, Department of Mathematics and Industrial Engineering, Montréal, QC H3C 3A7, Canada. Offers ergonomy (M Eng, M Sc A, DESS); mathematical method in CA engineering (M Eng, M Sc A, PhD); operational research (M Eng, M Sc A, PhD); production (M Eng, M Sc A); technology management (M Eng, M Sc A). DESS program offered jointly with HEC Montreal and Université de Montréal. Part-time programs available. *Degree requirements:* For master's, one foreign language, thesis. *Entrance requirements:* For master's, minimum GPA of 2.75. *Faculty research:* Use of computers in organizations.

Florida Agricultural and Mechanical University, Division of Graduate Studies, Research, and Continuing Education, FAMU-FSU College of Engineering, Department of Industrial and Manufacturing Engineering, Tallahassee, FL 32307-3200. Offers industrial engineering (MS, PhD). *Degree requirements:* For master's, thesis optional. *Entrance requirements:* For master's, GRE General Test, minimum GPA of 3.0. Additional exam requirements/recommendations for international students: Required—TOEFL (minimum score 550 paper-based). *Faculty research:* Design for environmentally conscious manufacturing, affordable composite manufacturing, integrated product and process design, precision machining research.

Florida State University, The Graduate School, FAMU-FSU College of Engineering, Department of Industrial and Manufacturing Engineering, Tallahassee, FL 32310. Offers industrial engineering (MS, PhD). *Degree requirements:* For master's, thesis, proposal presentation, progress presentation, defense presentation; for doctorate, thesis/dissertation, preliminary exam, proposal exam, defense exam. *Entrance requirements:* For master's, GRE General Test (minimum new score of 146 Verbal and 155 Quantitative), minimum GPA of 3.0; for doctorate, GRE General Test (minimum new score of 146 Verbal and 155 Quantitative), minimum GPA of 3.0 (without MS in industrial engineering), 3.4 (with MS in industrial engineering). Additional exam requirements/recommendations for international students: Required—TOEFL (minimum score 550 paper-based; 80 iBT); Recommended—IELTS (minimum score 6.5). Electronic applications accepted. *Expenses:* Tuition, state resident: part-time $403.51 per credit hour. Tuition, nonresident: part-time $1004.85 per credit hour. *Required fees:* $75.81

per credit hour. One-time fee: $20 part-time. Tuition and fees vary according to campus/location. *Faculty research:* Precision manufacturing, composite manufacturing, green manufacturing, applied optimization, simulation.

Georgia Institute of Technology, Graduate Studies, College of Engineering, School of Industrial and Systems Engineering, Program in Industrial and Systems Engineering, Atlanta, GA 30332-0001. Offers industrial engineering (MS, PhD). Part-time programs available. Postbaccalaureate distance learning degree programs offered. *Students:* 105 full-time (21 women), 22 part-time (11 women); includes 13 minority (6 Asian, non-Hispanic/Latino; 4 Hispanic/Latino; 3 Two or more races, non-Hispanic/Latino), 100 international. Average age 24. 507 applicants, 17% accepted, 41 enrolled. In 2014, 61 master's, 21 doctorates awarded. Terminal master's awarded for partial completion of doctoral program. *Degree requirements:* For master's, thesis optional; for doctorate, comprehensive exam, thesis/dissertation. *Entrance requirements:* For master's, GRE General Test, http://www.isye.gatech.edu/academics/masters/ms-industrial-engineering/admissions; for doctorate, GRE General Test, http://www.isye.gatech.edu/academics/doctoral/phd-industrial-engineering/admissions. Additional exam requirements/recommendations for international students: Required—TOEFL (minimum score 550 paper-based; 79 iBT). *Application deadline:* For fall admission, 12/15 priority date for domestic and international students; for spring admission, 2/1 for domestic and international students. Applications are processed on a rolling basis. Application fee: $75. Electronic applications accepted. *Expenses:* Tuition, state resident: full-time $12,344; part-time $515 per credit hour. Tuition, nonresident: full-time $27,600; part-time $1150 per credit hour. *Required fees:* $1196 per term. Part-time tuition and fees vary according to course load. *Financial support:* Fellowships, research assistantships, teaching assistantships, career-related internships or fieldwork, Federal Work-Study, institutionally sponsored loans, tuition waivers (partial), and unspecified assistantships available. Support available to part-time students. Financial award application deadline: 5/1. *Faculty research:* Computer-integrated manufacturing systems, materials handling systems, production and distribution. *Unit head:* Alan Erera, Director, 404-385-0358, E-mail: alan.erera@isye.gatech.edu. *Application contact:* Pam Morrison, Graduate Coordinator, 404-894-4289, E-mail: pam.morrison@isye.gatech.edu.
Website: http://www.isye.gatech.edu.

Illinois State University, Graduate School, College of Applied Science and Technology, Department of Technology, Normal, IL 61790-2200. Offers MS. *Degree requirements:* For master's, thesis or alternative. *Entrance requirements:* For master's, GRE General Test, minimum GPA of 2.8. *Faculty research:* National Center for Engineering and Technology Education, Illinois Manufacturing Extension Center Field Office hosting, model for the professional development of K-12 technology education teachers, Illinois State University Illinois Mathematics and Science Partnership, Illinois University council for career and technical education.

Indiana State University, College of Graduate and Professional Studies, College of Technology, Program in Industrial Technology, Terre Haute, IN 47809. Offers MS. *Entrance requirements:* For master's, bachelor's degree in industrial technology or related field. Additional exam requirements/recommendations for international students: Required—TOEFL. Electronic applications accepted.

Indiana University–Purdue University Fort Wayne, College of Engineering, Technology, and Computer Science, Program in Technology, Fort Wayne, IN 46805-1499. Offers industrial technology/manufacturing (MS); information technology/advanced computer applications (MS). Part-time programs available. *Faculty:* 14 full-time (5 women). *Students:* 4 full-time (2 women), 8 part-time (2 women); includes 3 minority (2 Black or African American, non-Hispanic/Latino; 1 American Indian or Alaska Native, non-Hispanic/Latino), 4 international. Average age 34. 7 applicants, 100% accepted, 5 enrolled. In 2014, 11 master's awarded. *Entrance requirements:* For master's, minimum GPA of 3.0. Additional exam requirements/recommendations for international students: Required—TOEFL (minimum score 550 paper-based; 79 iBT), TWE. *Application deadline:* For fall admission, 7/15 for domestic students, 5/15 for international students; for spring admission, 12/1 for domestic students, 10/15 for international students. Applications are processed on a rolling basis. Application fee: $55 ($60 for international students). Electronic applications accepted. *Financial support:* In 2014–15, 2 teaching assistantships with partial tuition reimbursements (averaging $13,522 per year) were awarded; career-related internships or fieldwork, scholarships/grants, and unspecified assistantships also available. Support available to part-time students. Financial award application deadline: 3/1; financial award applicants required to submit FAFSA. *Unit head:* Dr. Max Yen, Dean, 260-481-6839, Fax: 260-481-5734, E-mail: yens@ipfw.edu. *Application contact:* Dr. Ali Alavizadeh, Director, 260-481-0234, Fax: 260-481-5734, E-mail: alavizaa@ipfw.edu.
Website: http://www.ipfw.edu/etcs.

Instituto Tecnologico de Santo Domingo, Graduate School, Area of Engineering, Santo Domingo, Dominican Republic. Offers construction administration (MS, Certificate); data telecommunications (M Eng, MS, Certificate); industrial engineering (M Eng, Certificate); industrial management (M Mgmt); information technology (Certificate); maintenance engineering (M Eng); occupational hazard prevention (M Mgmt); production management (Certificate); quantitative methods (Certificate); sanitary and environmental engineering (M Eng); structural engineering (M Eng); systems engineering and electronic data processing (Certificate); transportation (Certificate).

Instituto Tecnológico y de Estudios Superiores de Monterrey, Campus Chihuahua, Graduate Programs, Chihuahua, Mexico. Offers computer systems engineering (Ingeniero); electrical engineering (Ingeniero); electromechanical engineering (Ingeniero); electronic engineering (Ingeniero); engineering administration (MEA); industrial engineering (MIE, Ingeniero); international trade (MIT); mechanical engineering (Ingeniero).

Instituto Tecnológico y de Estudios Superiores de Monterrey, Campus Ciudad de México, Virtual University Division, Ciudad de Mexico, Mexico. Offers administration of information technologies (MA); computer sciences (MA); education (MA, PhD); educational technology (MA); environmental engineering (MA); environmental systems (MA); humanistic studies (MA); industrial engineering (MA); international business for Latin America (MA); quality systems (MA); quality systems and productivity (MA). Part-time and evening/weekend programs available. Postbaccalaureate distance learning degree programs offered (minimal on-campus study). *Entrance requirements:* For master's and doctorate, Instituto entrance exam. Additional exam requirements/recommendations for international students: Required—TOEFL.

Instituto Tecnológico y de Estudios Superiores de Monterrey, Campus Laguna, Graduate School, Torreón, Mexico. Offers business administration (MBA); industrial engineering (MIE); management information systems (MS). Part-time programs available. *Entrance requirements:* For master's, GMAT. *Faculty research:* Computer communications from home to the university.

Instituto Tecnológico y de Estudios Superiores de Monterrey, Campus Monterrey, Graduate and Research Division, Programs in Engineering, Monterrey, Mexico. Offers applied statistics (M Eng); artificial intelligence (PhD); automation engineering (M Eng); chemical engineering (M Eng); civil engineering (M Eng); electrical engineering (M Eng); electronic engineering (M Eng); environmental engineering (M Eng); industrial engineering (M Eng, PhD); manufacturing engineering (M Eng); mechanical engineering (M Eng); systems and quality engineering (M Eng). M Eng program offered jointly with University of Waterloo; PhD in industrial engineering with Texas A&M University. Part-time and evening/weekend programs available. Terminal master's awarded for partial completion of doctoral program. *Degree requirements:* For master's, one foreign language, thesis; for doctorate, one foreign language, thesis/dissertation. *Entrance requirements:* For master's, EXADEP; for doctorate, GRE, master's degree in related field. Additional exam requirements/recommendations for international students: Required—TOEFL. *Faculty research:* Flexible manufacturing cells, materials, statistical methods, environmental prevention, control and evaluation.

Iowa State University of Science and Technology, Department of Industrial and Manufacturing Systems Engineering, Ames, IA 50011. Offers industrial engineering (M Eng, MS, PhD); operations research (MS); systems engineering (M Eng). *Degree requirements:* For master's, thesis or alternative; for doctorate, thesis/dissertation. *Entrance requirements:* For master's and doctorate, GRE General Test. Additional exam requirements/recommendations for international students: Required—TOEFL (minimum score 550 paper-based; 79 iBT), IELTS (minimum score 6.5). Electronic applications accepted. *Faculty research:* Economic modeling, valuation techniques, robotics, digital controls, systems reliability.

Kansas State University, Graduate School, College of Engineering, Department of Industrial and Manufacturing Systems Engineering, Manhattan, KS 66506. Offers engineering management (MEM); industrial engineering (MS); operations research (MS). Part-time programs available. Postbaccalaureate distance learning degree programs offered (no on-campus study). *Faculty:* 10 full-time (2 women), 1 part-time/adjunct (0 women). *Students:* 26 full-time (8 women), 58 part-time (9 women); includes 11 minority (5 Black or African American, non-Hispanic/Latino; 2 Asian, non-Hispanic/Latino; 1 Hispanic/Latino; 1 Native Hawaiian or other Pacific Islander, non-Hispanic/Latino; 2 Two or more races, non-Hispanic/Latino), 16 international. Average age 29. 61 applicants, 46% accepted, 13 enrolled. In 2014, 26 master's, 4 doctorates awarded. *Degree requirements:* For master's, thesis or alternative; for doctorate, thesis/dissertation. *Entrance requirements:* For master's, GRE General Test (minimum score of 750 old version, 159 new format on Quantitative portion of exam), bachelor's degree in engineering, mathematics, or physical science; for doctorate, GRE General Test (minimum score of 770 old version, 164 new format on Quantitative portion of exam), master's degree in engineering or industrial manufacturing. Additional exam requirements/recommendations for international students: Required—PTE (minimum score 58), TOEFL (minimum score 550 paper-based; 79 iBT) or IELTS (minimum score 6.5). *Application deadline:* For fall admission, 6/1 priority date for domestic students, 12/1 priority date for international students; for spring admission, 11/1 priority date for domestic students, 8/1 priority date for international students. Applications are processed on a rolling basis. Application fee: $50 ($75 for international students). Electronic applications accepted. *Financial support:* In 2014–15, 12 research assistantships (averaging $12,442 per year), 9 teaching assistantships with full tuition reimbursements (averaging $14,111 per year) were awarded; Federal Work-Study, institutionally sponsored loans, and scholarships/grants also available. Support available to part-time students. Financial award application deadline: 3/1; financial award applicants required to submit FAFSA. *Faculty research:* Industrial engineering, ergonomics, healthcare systems engineering, manufacturing processes, operations research, engineering management. *Total annual research expenditures:* $2.6 million. *Unit head:* Dr. Bradley Kramer, Head, 785-532-5606, Fax: 785-532-3738, E-mail: bradleyk@k-state.edu. *Application contact:* Dr. David Ben-Arieh, Chair of Graduate Committee, 785-532-5606, Fax: 785-532-3738, E-mail: imse@k-state.edu.
Website: http://www.imse.k-state.edu/.

Lamar University, College of Graduate Studies, College of Engineering, Department of Industrial Engineering, Beaumont, TX 77710. Offers engineering management (MEM); industrial engineering (ME, MES, DE). *Faculty:* 7 full-time (1 woman). *Students:* 83 full-time (10 women), 14 part-time (4 women); includes 3 minority (2 Black or African American, non-Hispanic/Latino; 1 Asian, non-Hispanic/Latino), 89 international. Average age 26. 161 applicants, 71% accepted, 53 enrolled. In 2014, 6 master's, 4 doctorates awarded. *Degree requirements:* For doctorate, thesis/dissertation. *Entrance requirements:* For master's and doctorate, GRE General Test. Additional exam requirements/recommendations for international students: Required—TOEFL (minimum score 550 paper-based; 79 iBT), IELTS (minimum score 6.5). *Application deadline:* For fall admission, 8/10 for domestic students, 7/1 for international students; for spring admission, 1/5 for domestic students, 12/1 for international students. Applications are processed on a rolling basis. Application fee: $25 ($50 for international students). *Expenses:* Tuition, state resident: full-time $5724; part-time $1908 per semester. Tuition, nonresident: full-time $12,240; part-time $4080 per semester. *Required fees:* $1940; $318 per credit hour. *Financial support:* In 2014–15, 2 fellowships (averaging $6,000 per year), 4 research assistantships (averaging $1,000 per year), 2 teaching assistantships (averaging $4,500 per year) were awarded. Financial award application deadline: 4/1. *Faculty research:* Process simulation, total quality management, ergonomics and safety, scheduling. *Unit head:* Dr. Brian Craig, Chair, 409-880-8804, Fax: 409-880-8121. *Application contact:* Melissa Gallien, Director, Admissions and Academic Services, 409-880-8888, Fax: 409-880-7419, E-mail: gradmissions@lamar.edu.
Website: http://engineering.lamar.edu/industrial.

Lawrence Technological University, College of Engineering, Southfield, MI 48075-1058. Offers architectural engineering (MS); automotive engineering (MS); civil engineering (MA, MS, PhD); construction engineering management (MA); electrical and computer engineering (MS); engineering management (MEM); industrial engineering (MS); manufacturing systems (ME, DE); mechanical engineering (MS, DE); mechatronic systems engineering (MS). Part-time and evening/weekend programs available. *Faculty:* 24 full-time (5 women), 15 part-time/adjunct (0 women). *Students:* 16 full-time (6 women), 478 part-time (71 women); includes 295 minority (15 Black or African American, non-Hispanic/Latino; 271 Asian, non-Hispanic/Latino; 7 Hispanic/Latino; 2 Two or more races, non-Hispanic/Latino), 38 international. Average age 27. 1,786 applicants, 40% accepted, 218 enrolled. In 2014, 106 master's awarded. *Degree requirements:* For master's, thesis (for some programs). *Entrance requirements:* Additional exam requirements/recommendations for international students: Required—TOEFL (minimum score 550 paper-based; 79 iBT). *Application deadline:* For fall admission, 8/1 priority date for domestic students, 5/29 for international students; for spring admission, 12/1 priority date for domestic students, 10/15 for international students. Applications are processed on a rolling basis. Application fee: $50. Electronic applications accepted. *Expenses: Tuition:* Full-time $14,700; part-time $1050 per credit hour. *Required fees:* $150. One-time fee: $150 part-time. *Financial support:* In 2014–15, 31 students received support, including 8 research assistantships (averaging $9,338 per year); Federal Work-Study and institutionally sponsored loans also available. Support available to part-time students. Financial award application deadline: 4/1; financial award applicants required to submit FAFSA. *Faculty research:* Advanced composite materials in bridges, strengthening existing bridges with carbon and glass fiber sheets, development of drive shafts using composite materials. *Unit head:* Dr. Nabil Grace, Dean, 248-204-2500, Fax: 248-204-2509, E-mail: engrdean@ltu.edu.

Industrial/Management Engineering

Application contact: Jane Rohrback, Director of Admissions, 248-204-3160, Fax: 248-204-2228, E-mail: admissions@ltu.edu. Website: http://www.ltu.edu/engineering/index.asp.

Lehigh University, P.C. Rossin College of Engineering and Applied Science, Department of Industrial and Systems Engineering, Bethlehem, PA 18015. Offers analytical finance (MS); healthcare systems engineering (M Eng); industrial and systems engineering (M Eng, MS); industrial engineering (PhD); management science and engineering (M Eng, MS); MBA/E. Part-time programs available. Postbaccalaureate distance learning degree programs offered (no on-campus study). *Faculty:* 16 full-time (2 women), 4 part-time/adjunct (1 woman). *Students:* 91 full-time (24 women), 14 part-time (4 women); includes 2 minority (both Asian, non-Hispanic/Latino, 93 international. Average age 25. 351 applicants, 20% accepted, 38 enrolled. In 2014, 39 master's, 3 doctorates awarded. *Degree requirements:* For master's, thesis (MS); project (M Eng); for doctorate, comprehensive exam, thesis/dissertation. *Entrance requirements:* For master's and doctorate, GRE General Test. Additional exam requirements/recommendations for international students: Required—TOEFL (minimum score 550 paper-based; 79 iBT). *Application deadline:* For fall admission, 7/15 for domestic and international students; for spring admission, 12/1 for domestic and international students. Applications are processed on a rolling basis. Application fee: $75. Electronic applications accepted. *Expenses:* Expenses: $1,340 per credit hour. *Financial support:* In 2014–15, 25 students received support, including 2 fellowships with full tuition reimbursements available (averaging $17,460 per year), 13 research assistantships with full tuition reimbursements available (averaging $15,300 per year), 10 teaching assistantships with full tuition reimbursements available (averaging $18,360 per year); career-related internships or fieldwork, scholarships/grants, tuition waivers, and unspecified assistantships also available. Financial award application deadline: 1/15. *Faculty research:* Mathematical optimization; logistics and service systems, stochastic processes and simulation; computational optimization and high performance computing; financial engineering and robust optimization. *Total annual research expenditures:* $2 million. *Unit head:* Dr. Tamas Terlaky, Chair, 610-758-4050, Fax: 610-758-4886, E-mail: terlaky@lehigh.edu. *Application contact:* Rita Frey, Graduate Coordinator, 610-758-4051, Fax: 610-758-4886, E-mail: ise@lehigh.edu. Website: http://www.lehigh.edu/ise.

Louisiana Tech University, Graduate School, College of Engineering and Science, Department of Industrial Engineering, Ruston, LA 71272. Offers engineering and technology management (MS); industrial engineering (MS).

Mississippi State University, Bagley College of Engineering, Department of Industrial and Systems Engineering, Mississippi State, MS 39762. Offers industrial and systems engineering (PhD); industrial engineering (MS). Part-time programs available. Postbaccalaureate distance learning degree programs offered (no on-campus study). *Faculty:* 9 full-time (2 women). *Students:* 19 full-time (4 women), 59 part-time (13 women); includes 15 minority (6 Black or African American, non-Hispanic/Latino; 3 Asian, non-Hispanic/Latino; 5 Hispanic/Latino; 1 Native Hawaiian or other Pacific Islander, non-Hispanic/Latino), 13 international. Average age 36. 106 applicants, 34% accepted, 23 enrolled. In 2014, 8 master's, 4 doctorates awarded. *Degree requirements:* For master's, comprehensive exam (for some programs), thesis optional, comprehensive oral or written exam; for doctorate, comprehensive exam, thesis/dissertation, candidacy exam. *Entrance requirements:* For master's, GRE (for graduates from program not accredited by EAC/ABET), minimum GPA of 3.0 on junior and senior years; for doctorate, GRE (for graduates from program not accredited by EAC/ABET), minimum GPA of 3.5 on master's degree and junior and senior years of BS. Additional exam requirements/recommendations for international students: Required—TOEFL (minimum score 550 paper-based; 79 iBT); Recommended—IELTS (minimum score 6.5). *Application deadline:* For fall admission, 7/1 for domestic students, 5/1 for international students; for spring admission, 11/1 for domestic students, 9/1 for international students. Applications are processed on a rolling basis. Application fee: $60. *Expenses:* Tuition, state resident: full-time $7140; part-time $783 per credit hour. Tuition, nonresident: full-time $18,478; part-time $2043 per credit hour. *Financial support:* In 2014–15, 9 research assistantships with full tuition reimbursements (averaging $15,844 per year), 1 teaching assistantship (averaging $13,500 per year) were awarded; Federal Work-Study, institutionally sponsored loans, and unspecified assistantships also available. Financial award application deadline: 4/1; financial award applicants required to submit FAFSA. *Faculty research:* Operations research, ergonomics, production systems, management systems, transportation. *Unit head:* Dr. John Usher, Professor/Department Head/Graduate Coordinator, 662-325-7624, Fax: 662-325-7618, E-mail: usher@ise.msstate.edu. *Application contact:* Dr. Kari Babski-Reeves, Associate Professor and Graduate Coordinator, 662-325-1677, Fax: 662-325-7618, E-mail: kari@ise.msstate.edu. Website: http://www.ise.msstate.edu/.

Montana State University, The Graduate School, College of Engineering, Department of Mechanical and Industrial Engineering, Bozeman, MT 59717. Offers engineering (PhD), including industrial engineering, mechanical engineering; industrial and management engineering (MS); mechanical engineering (MS). Part-time programs available. *Degree requirements:* For master's, comprehensive exam, thesis, oral exams; for doctorate, comprehensive exam, thesis/dissertation, qualifying exam. *Entrance requirements:* For master's, GRE, official transcript, minimum GPA of 3.0, demonstrated potential for success, statement of goals, three letters of recommendation, proof of funds affidavit; for doctorate, minimum undergraduate GPA of 3.0, 3.2 graduate; three letters of recommendation; statement of objectives. Additional exam requirements/recommendations for international students: Required—TOEFL or IELTS. Electronic applications accepted. *Faculty research:* Human factors engineering, energy, design and manufacture, systems modeling, materials and structures, measurement systems.

Montana Tech of The University of Montana, Graduate School, Project Engineering and Management Program, Butte, MT 59701-8997. Offers MPEM. Part-time and evening/weekend programs available. Postbaccalaureate distance learning degree programs offered (no on-campus study). *Degree requirements:* For master's, comprehensive exam, final project presentation. *Entrance requirements:* For master's, minimum GPA of 3.0. Additional exam requirements/recommendations for international students: Required—TOEFL (minimum score 550 paper-based; 71 iBT). Electronic applications accepted. *Expenses:* Tuition, state resident: full-time $5802; part-time $241 per credit. Tuition, nonresident: full-time $15,895; part-time $662 per credit. *Required fees:* $1516; $414 per credit. $207 per semester. One-time fee: $30.

Morehead State University, Graduate Programs, College of Science and Technology, Department of Industrial and Engineering Technology, Morehead, KY 40351. Offers career and technical education (MS); engineering technology (MS). Part-time and evening/weekend programs available. *Degree requirements:* For master's, completion and defense of thesis or written and oral comprehensive exit exams. *Entrance requirements:* For master's, GRE, minimum undergraduate GPA of 3.0 in major. Additional exam requirements/recommendations for international students: Required—TOEFL (minimum score 500 paper-based). Electronic applications accepted.

Morgan State University, School of Graduate Studies, Clarence M. Mitchell, Jr. School of Engineering, Baltimore, MD 21251. Offers civil engineering (M Eng, D Eng); electrical and computer engineering (M Eng, MS, D Eng); industrial and systems engineering (M Eng, D Eng); transportation (MS). Part-time and evening/weekend programs available. *Degree requirements:* For master's, thesis, comprehensive exam or equivalent; for doctorate, thesis/dissertation, comprehensive exam or equivalent. *Entrance requirements:* For master's, GRE, minimum undergraduate GPA of 2.5; for doctorate, GRE, minimum GPA of 3.0. Additional exam requirements/recommendations for international students: Required—TOEFL (minimum score 550 paper-based).

New Jersey Institute of Technology, Newark College of Engineering, Newark, NJ 07102. Offers biomedical engineering (MS, PhD); chemical engineering (MS, PhD); computer engineering (MS, PhD); electrical engineering (MS, PhD); engineering management (MS); healthcare systems management (MS); industrial engineering (MS, PhD); Internet engineering (MS); manufacturing engineering (MS); mechanical engineering (MS, PhD); occupational safety and health engineering (MS); pharmaceutical bioprocessing (MS); pharmaceutical engineering (MS); pharmaceutical systems management (MS); power and energy systems (MS); telecommunications (MS); transportation (MS, PhD). Part-time and evening/weekend programs available. Terminal master's awarded for partial completion of doctoral program. *Degree requirements:* For master's, thesis optional; for doctorate, thesis/dissertation. *Entrance requirements:* For master's, GRE General Test; for doctorate, GRE General Test, minimum graduate GPA of 3.5. Additional exam requirements/recommendations for international students: Required—TOEFL (minimum score 550 paper-based; 79 iBT). Electronic applications accepted.

New Mexico State University, College of Engineering, Department of Industrial Engineering, Las Cruces, NM 88003-8001. Offers industrial engineering (PhD); systems engineering (Graduate Certificate). Part-time and evening/weekend programs available. Postbaccalaureate distance learning degree programs offered (no on-campus study). *Faculty:* 6 full-time (2 women). *Students:* 35 full-time (4 women), 98 part-time (24 women); includes 50 minority (10 Black or African American, non-Hispanic/Latino; 2 American Indian or Alaska Native, non-Hispanic/Latino; 7 Asian, non-Hispanic/Latino; 29 Hispanic/Latino; 2 Two or more races, non-Hispanic/Latino), 20 international. Average age 32. 100 applicants, 51% accepted, 25 enrolled. In 2014, 65 master's, 3 doctorates, 5 other advanced degrees awarded. *Degree requirements:* For master's, thesis optional; for doctorate, comprehensive exam, thesis/dissertation, qualifying exam. *Entrance requirements:* Additional exam requirements/recommendations for international students: Required—TOEFL (minimum score 550 paper-based; 79 iBT), IELTS (minimum score 6.5). *Application deadline:* For fall admission, 7/1 priority date for domestic students, 3/1 for international students; for spring admission, 11/1 for domestic students, 10/1 for international students. Applications are processed on a rolling basis. Application fee: $40 ($50 for international students). Electronic applications accepted. *Expenses:* Tuition, state resident: full-time $3969; part-time $220.50 per credit hour. Tuition, nonresident: full-time $13,838; part-time $768.80 per credit hour. *Required fees:* $853; $47.40 per credit hour. *Financial support:* In 2014–15, 21 students received support, including 5 research assistantships (averaging $12,373 per year), 7 teaching assistantships (averaging $15,446 per year); career-related internships or fieldwork, Federal Work-Study, scholarships/grants, traineeships, health care benefits, and unspecified assistantships also available. Support available to part-time students. Financial award application deadline: 3/1. *Faculty research:* Operations research, simulation, manufacturing engineering, systems engineering, applied statistics. *Total annual research expenditures:* $163,409. *Unit head:* Dr. Edward Pines, Academic Department Head, 575-646-4923, Fax: 575-646-2976, E-mail: epines@nmsu.edu. *Application contact:* 575-646-4923, Fax: 575-646-2976, E-mail: ie@nmsu.edu. Website: http://ie.nmsu.edu.

New York University, Polytechnic School of Engineering, Department of Technology Management, Major in Industrial Engineering, New York, NY 10012-1019. Offers MS. Part-time and evening/weekend programs available. Postbaccalaureate distance learning degree programs offered (no on-campus study). *Students:* 64 full-time (11 women), 19 part-time (6 women); includes 6 minority (3 Black or African American, non-Hispanic/Latino; 1 Asian, non-Hispanic/Latino; 2 Hispanic/Latino), 68 international. Average age 25. 195 applicants, 51% accepted, 42 enrolled. In 2014, 38 master's awarded. *Degree requirements:* For master's, comprehensive exam (for some programs), thesis (for some programs). *Entrance requirements:* For master's, BE or BS in engineering, physics, chemistry, mathematical sciences, or biological sciences, or MBA. Additional exam requirements/recommendations for international students: Required—TOEFL (minimum score 550 paper-based; 80 iBT); Recommended—IELTS (minimum score 6.5). *Application deadline:* For fall admission, 2/15 priority date for domestic and international students; for spring admission, 11/1 priority date for domestic and international students. Applications are processed on a rolling basis. Application fee: $75. Electronic applications accepted. *Financial support:* Institutionally sponsored loans, scholarships/grants, and unspecified assistantships available. Support available to part-time students. Financial award applicants required to submit FAFSA. *Unit head:* Prof. Mark De Lessio, Program Director, E-mail: mpdelessio@nyu.edu. *Application contact:* Raymond Lutzky, Director of Graduate Enrollment Management, 718-637-5984, Fax: 718-260-3624, E-mail: rlutzky@poly.edu.

North Carolina Agricultural and Technical State University, School of Graduate Studies, College of Engineering, Department of Industrial and Systems Engineering, Greensboro, NC 27411. Offers industrial engineering (MSIE, PhD). Part-time programs available. *Degree requirements:* For master's, thesis, project; for doctorate, thesis/dissertation. *Entrance requirements:* For master's, GRE General Test (recommended); for doctorate, GRE General Test, degree in engineering, BS in industrial engineering from ABET-accredited program with minimum cumulative credit point average of 3.7 or MS in discipline related to industrial engineering from college or university recognized by a regional or general accrediting agency with minimum cumulative GPA of 3.3. Additional exam requirements/recommendations for international students: Required—TOEFL (minimum score 550 paper-based; 79 iBT). *Faculty research:* Human-machine systems engineering, management systems engineering, operations research and systems analysis, production systems engineering.

North Carolina State University, Graduate School, College of Engineering, Edward P. Fitts Department of Industrial and Systems Engineering, Raleigh, NC 27695. Offers industrial engineering (MIE, MS, PhD). PhD offered jointly with North Carolina Agricultural and Technical State University, The University of North Carolina at Charlotte. Part-time programs available. Terminal master's awarded for partial completion of doctoral program. *Degree requirements:* For master's, thesis optional; for doctorate, thesis/dissertation. *Entrance requirements:* For master's, GRE General Test, minimum GPA of 3.0; for doctorate, GRE General Test. Additional exam requirements/recommendations for international students: Required—TOEFL. Electronic applications accepted.

North Dakota State University, College of Graduate and Interdisciplinary Studies, College of Engineering and Architecture, Department of Industrial and Manufacturing Engineering, Fargo, ND 58108. Offers industrial and manufacturing engineering (PhD); industrial engineering and management (MS); manufacturing engineering (MS). Part-time programs available. *Degree requirements:* For doctorate, comprehensive exam, thesis/dissertation. *Entrance requirements:* For master's, GRE General Test, bachelor's degree in engineering; for doctorate, GRE General Test, master's degree in engineering. Additional exam requirements/recommendations for international students: Required—TOEFL (minimum score 550 paper-based; 79 iBT), TWE (minimum score 4). Electronic applications accepted. *Faculty research:* Electronics manufacturing, quality engineering, manufacturing process science, healthcare, lean manufacturing.

Northeastern University, College of Engineering, Boston, MA 02115-5096. Offers bioengineering (PhD); chemical engineering (MS, PhD); civil engineering (MS, PhD); computer engineering (PhD); computer systems engineering (MS); electrical and computer engineering (MS); electrical and engineering leadership (MS); electrical engineering (PhD); energy systems (MS); engineering leadership (Certificate); engineering management (MRTP); industrial engineering (MS, PhD); information assurance (PhD); information systems (MS); interdisciplinary (PhD); mechanical engineering (MS, PhD); operations research (MS); telecommunication systems management (MS). Part-time programs available. *Expenses:* Contact institution.

Northern Illinois University, Graduate School, College of Engineering and Engineering Technology, Department of Industrial Engineering, De Kalb, IL 60115-2854. Offers MS. Part-time programs available. *Faculty:* 4 full-time (1 woman), 1 part-time/adjunct (0 women). *Students:* 34 full-time (6 women), 19 part-time (7 women); includes 3 minority (all Asian, non-Hispanic/Latino), 35 international. Average age 26. 87 applicants, 71% accepted, 21 enrolled. In 2014, 12 master's awarded. *Degree requirements:* For master's, comprehensive exam, thesis optional. *Entrance requirements:* For master's, GRE General Test, minimum GPA of 2.75. Additional exam requirements/recommendations for international students: Required—TOEFL (minimum score 550 paper-based). *Application deadline:* For fall admission, 6/1 for domestic students, 5/1 for international students; for spring admission, 11/1 for domestic students, 10/1 for international students. Applications are processed on a rolling basis. Application fee: $40. Electronic applications accepted. *Financial support:* In 2014–15, 9 research assistantships, 11 teaching assistantships were awarded; fellowships, Federal Work-Study, scholarships/grants, tuition waivers (full), and staff assistantships also available. Support available to part-time students. Financial award applicants required to submit FAFSA. *Faculty research:* Assembly robots, engineering ethics, quality cost models, data mining. *Unit head:* Dr. Purushothaman Damodaran, Chair, 815-753-1349, Fax: 815-753-0823. *Application contact:* Graduate School Office, 815-753-0395, E-mail: gradsch@niu.edu.
Website: http://www.niu.edu/isye.

Northwestern University, McCormick School of Engineering and Applied Science, Department of Industrial Engineering and Management Sciences, Evanston, IL 60208. Offers analytics (MS); engineering management (MEM); industrial engineering and management science (MS, PhD). MS and PhD admissions and degrees offered through The Graduate School. *Faculty:* 20 full-time (2 women). *Students:* 60 full-time (22 women); includes 5 minority (1 Asian, non-Hispanic/Latino; 3 Hispanic/Latino; 1 Two or more races, non-Hispanic/Latino), 46 international. Average age 23. 209 applicants, 11% accepted, 10 enrolled. In 2014, 9 master's, 9 doctorates awarded. Terminal master's awarded for partial completion of doctoral program. *Degree requirements:* For master's, comprehensive exam; for doctorate, comprehensive exam, thesis/dissertation. *Entrance requirements:* For master's and doctorate, GRE General Test. Additional exam requirements/recommendations for international students: Required—TOEFL (minimum score 577 paper-based; 90 iBT), IELTS (minimum score 7). *Application deadline:* For fall admission, 12/31 for domestic and international students. Application fee: $95. Electronic applications accepted. *Financial support:* In 2014–15, 10 students received support. Fellowships with full tuition reimbursements available, research assistantships with full tuition reimbursements available, teaching assistantships with full tuition reimbursements available, career-related internships or fieldwork, scholarships/grants, health care benefits, and unspecified assistantships available. Financial award application deadline: 1/15. *Faculty research:* Financial engineering, healthcare engineering, humanitarian logistics, optimization, organization behavior and technology management, production and logistics, social and organizational networks, statistics for enterprise engineering, stochastic modeling and simulation. *Unit head:* Dr. Barry Nelson, Chair, 847-491-3747, Fax: 847-491-8005, E-mail: nelsonb@northwestern.edu. *Application contact:* Dr. Jeremy Staum, Admission Officer, 847-491-3383, Fax: 847-491-8005, E-mail: j-staum@northwestern.edu.
Website: http://www.iems.northwestern.edu/.

The Ohio State University, Graduate School, College of Engineering, Department of Integrated Systems Engineering, Columbus, OH 43210. Offers industrial and systems engineering (MS, PhD). *Faculty:* 18. *Students:* 81 full-time (21 women), 7 part-time (1 woman); includes 5 minority (1 Black or African American, non-Hispanic/Latino; 4 Asian, non-Hispanic/Latino), 63 international. Average age 28. In 2014, 23 master's, 8 doctorates awarded. *Degree requirements:* For master's, thesis optional; for doctorate, thesis/dissertation. *Entrance requirements:* For master's and doctorate, GRE General Test (desired minimum scores: Quantitative 166, Verbal 153, Analytical Writing 4.5). Additional exam requirements/recommendations for international students: Required—TOEFL (minimum score 550 paper-based; 79 iBT), Michigan English Language Assessment Battery (minimum score 82); Recommended—IELTS (minimum score 7). *Application deadline:* For fall admission, 12/13 priority date for domestic students, 11/30 priority date for international students; for winter admission, 12/1 for domestic students, 7/1 for international students; for spring admission, 10/1 for domestic and international students; for summer admission, 2/1 for domestic and international students. Applications are processed on a rolling basis. Application fee: $60 ($70 for international students). Electronic applications accepted. *Financial support:* Fellowships with tuition reimbursements, research assistantships with tuition reimbursements, teaching assistantships with tuition reimbursements, career-related internships or fieldwork, Federal Work-Study, institutionally sponsored loans, and unspecified assistantships available. Support available to part-time students. *Unit head:* Dr. Philip J. Smith, Chair, 614-292-4120, E-mail: smith.131@osu.edu. *Application contact:* Dr. Jerald Brevik, Graduate Studies Chair, 614-292-0177, Fax: 614-292-7852, E-mail: brevik.1@osu.edu.
Website: http://ise.osu.edu/.

Ohio University, Graduate College, Russ College of Engineering and Technology, Department of Industrial and Systems Engineering, Athens, OH 45701-2979. Offers M Eng Mgt, MS. Part-time and evening/weekend programs available. *Degree requirements:* For master's, comprehensive exam (for some programs), thesis optional, research project. *Entrance requirements:* For master's, GRE General Test. Additional exam requirements/recommendations for international students: Required—TOEFL (minimum score 550 paper-based; 80 iBT) or IELTS (minimum score 6.5). Electronic applications accepted. *Faculty research:* Software systems integration, human factors and ergonomics.

Ohio University, Graduate College, Russ College of Engineering and Technology, Program in Mechanical and Systems Engineering, Athens, OH 45701-2979. Offers industrial engineering (PhD); mechanical engineering (PhD). *Degree requirements:* For doctorate, comprehensive exam, thesis/dissertation. *Entrance requirements:* For doctorate, GRE General Test, MS in engineering or related field. Additional exam requirements/recommendations for international students: Required—TOEFL (minimum score 550 paper-based; 80 iBT) or IELTS (minimum score 6.5). Electronic applications accepted. *Faculty research:* Material processing, expert systems, environmental geotechnical manufacturing, thermal systems, robotics.

Oklahoma State University, College of Engineering, Architecture and Technology, School of Industrial Engineering and Management, Stillwater, OK 74078. Offers MS, PhD. Postbaccalaureate distance learning degree programs offered. *Faculty:* 14 full-time (3 women), 2 part-time/adjunct (1 woman). *Students:* 73 full-time (16 women), 167 part-time (23 women); includes 36 minority (8 Black or African American, non-Hispanic/Latino; 3 American Indian or Alaska Native, non-Hispanic/Latino; 6 Asian, non-Hispanic/Latino; 9 Hispanic/Latino; 1 Native Hawaiian or other Pacific Islander, non-Hispanic/Latino; 9 Two or more races, non-Hispanic/Latino), 87 international. Average age 31. 364 applicants, 20% accepted, 47 enrolled. In 2014, 78 master's, 2 doctorates awarded. *Degree requirements:* For master's, creative component or thesis; for doctorate, comprehensive exam, thesis/dissertation. *Entrance requirements:* For master's and doctorate, GRE or GMAT. Additional exam requirements/recommendations for international students: Required—TOEFL (minimum score 550 paper-based; 79 iBT). *Application deadline:* For fall admission, 3/1 priority date for international students; for spring admission, 8/1 priority date for international students. Applications are processed on a rolling basis. Application fee: $40 ($75 for international students). Electronic applications accepted. *Expenses:* Tuition, state resident: full-time $4488; part-time $187 per credit hour. Tuition, nonresident: full-time $18,360; part-time $765 per credit hour. *Required fees:* $2413; $100.55 per credit hour. Tuition and fees vary according to campus/location. *Financial support:* In 2014–15, 17 research assistantships (averaging $16,200 per year), 27 teaching assistantships (averaging $16,512 per year) were awarded; career-related internships or fieldwork, Federal Work-Study, scholarships/grants, health care benefits, tuition waivers (partial), and unspecified assistantships also available. Support available to part-time students. Financial award application deadline: 3/1; financial award applicants required to submit FAFSA. *Unit head:* Dr. Sunderesh Heragu, Head, 405-744-6055, Fax: 405-744-4654, E-mail: sunderesh.heragu@okstate.edu. *Application contact:* Dr. Manjunath Kamath, Director of Graduate Program, 405-744-6055, Fax: 405-744-4654, E-mail: m.kamath@okstate.edu.
Website: http://iem.okstate.edu/.

Oregon State University, College of Engineering, Program in Industrial Engineering, Corvallis, OR 97331. Offers M Eng, MS, PhD. Postbaccalaureate distance learning degree programs offered (no on-campus study). *Faculty:* 45 full-time (7 women), 1 part-time/adjunct (0 women). *Students:* 56 full-time (11 women), 11 part-time (2 women); includes 3 minority (1 Asian, non-Hispanic/Latino; 1 Hispanic/Latino; 1 Two or more races, non-Hispanic/Latino), 43 international. Average age 28. 133 applicants, 32% accepted, 27 enrolled. In 2014, 17 master's, 6 doctorates awarded. *Entrance requirements:* For master's and doctorate, GRE. Additional exam requirements/recommendations for international students: Required—TOEFL (minimum score 80 iBT), IELTS (minimum score 6.5). *Application deadline:* For fall admission, 8/1 for domestic students, 4/1 for international students; for winter admission, 12/1 for domestic students, 7/1 for international students; for spring admission, 2/1 for domestic students, 10/1 for international students; for summer admission, 5/1 for domestic students, 1/1 for international students. Application fee: $60. *Expenses:* Expenses: $15,359 full-time resident tuition and fees; $23,405 non-resident. *Financial support:* Application deadline: 1/15. *Unit head:* Dr. Robert Stone, Professor and School Head, 541-737-3638. *Application contact:* Jean Robinson, Graduate Records Specialist, 541-737-9191, Fax: 541-737-2600, E-mail: jean.robinson@oregonstate.edu.
Website: http://mime.oregonstate.edu/academics/grad/ie.

Penn State University Park, Graduate School, College of Engineering, Department of Industrial and Manufacturing Engineering, University Park, PA 16802. Offers industrial engineering (M Eng, PhD). *Unit head:* Dr. Amr S. Elnashai, Dean, 814-865-7537, Fax: 814-863-4749, E-mail: ase2@psu.edu. *Application contact:* Lori A. Stania, Director, Graduate Student Services, 814-867-5278, Fax: 814-863-4627, E-mail: gswww@psu.edu.
Website: http://www.ie.psu.edu/.

Purdue University, College of Engineering, School of Industrial Engineering, West Lafayette, IN 47907-2023. Offers MS, MSIE, PhD. Part-time programs available. Postbaccalaureate distance learning degree programs offered (no on-campus study). Terminal master's awarded for partial completion of doctoral program. *Entrance requirements:* For master's and doctorate, GRE General Test, minimum GPA of 3.0. Additional exam requirements/recommendations for international students: Required—TOEFL (minimum score 570 paper-based); Recommended—TWE. Electronic applications accepted. *Faculty research:* Precision manufacturing process, computer-aided manufacturing, computer-aided process planning, knowledge-based systems, combinatorics.

Rensselaer Polytechnic Institute, Graduate School, School of Engineering, Program in Decision Sciences and Engineering Systems, Troy, NY 12180-3590. Offers PhD. *Faculty:* 21 full-time (4 women), 4 part-time/adjunct (1 woman). *Students:* 14 full-time (5 women); includes 1 minority (Asian, non-Hispanic/Latino), 9 international. Average age 29. 23 applicants, 48% accepted, 6 enrolled. In 2014, 2 doctorates awarded. Terminal master's awarded for partial completion of doctoral program. *Degree requirements:* For doctorate, thesis/dissertation. *Entrance requirements:* For doctorate, GRE. Additional exam requirements/recommendations for international students: Required—TOEFL (minimum score 570 paper-based; 88 iBT), IELTS (minimum score 6.5), PTE (minimum score 60). *Application deadline:* For fall admission, 1/1 priority date for domestic students, 1/1 for international students; for spring admission, 8/15 for domestic and international students. Applications are processed on a rolling basis. Application fee: $75. Electronic applications accepted. *Expenses:* Tuition: Full-time $46,700; part-time $1945 per credit. Tuition and fees vary according to course load. *Financial support:* In 2014–15, 13 students received support, including research assistantships (averaging $18,500 per year), teaching assistantships (averaging $18,500 per year); fellowships also available. Financial award application deadline: 1/1. *Faculty research:* Agent-based modeling, computational optimization, data mining, decision analysis, decision technologies, human factors engineering, logistics, network optimization and analysis, scheduling, simulation modeling, statistical analysis, stochastic programming. *Total annual research expenditures:* $69,998. *Unit head:* Dr. David Mendonca, Graduate Program Director, 518-276-4222, E-mail: mondod@rpi.edu. *Application contact:* Office of Graduate Admissions, 518-276-6216, E-mail: gradadmissions@rpi.edu.
Website: http://ise.rpi.edu/.

Rensselaer Polytechnic Institute, Graduate School, School of Engineering, Program in Industrial and Management Engineering, Troy, NY 12180-3590. Offers M Eng, MS. Part-time programs available. *Faculty:* 4 full-time (0 women), 1 part-time/adjunct (0 women). *Students:* 2 full-time (0 women), 1 part-time (0 women); includes 1 minority (Hispanic/Latino), 1 international. Average age 26. 52 applicants, 15% accepted, 3 enrolled. In 2014, 3 master's awarded. *Degree requirements:* For master's, thesis (for some programs). *Entrance requirements:* For master's, GRE. Additional exam requirements/recommendations for international students: Required—TOEFL (minimum score 570 paper-based; 88 iBT), IELTS (minimum score 6.5), PTE (minimum score 60). *Application deadline:* For fall admission, 1/1 priority date for domestic and international students; for spring admission, 8/15 priority date for domestic and international students. Applications are processed on a rolling basis. Application fee: $75. Electronic applications accepted. *Expenses:* Tuition: Full-time $46,700; part-time $1945 per credit. Tuition and fees vary according to course load. *Financial support:* In 2014–15, 2

students received support, including teaching assistantships (averaging $18,500 per year). Financial award application deadline: 1/1. *Faculty research:* Bayesian decision systems; database systems; decision technologies for adaptive supply chains; maritime safety systems; materials flow logistics; network optimization, simulated based optimization; social networks/data mining, soft computing/computational optimization; statistical forecasting/exploratory data analysis; stochastic processes in supply chains. *Total annual research expenditures:* $284,550. *Unit head:* Dr. Bill Foley, Graduate Program Director, 518-276-2886, E-mail: foleyw@rpi.edu. *Application contact:* Office of Graduate Admissions, 518-276-6216, E-mail: gradadmissions@rpi.edu.
Website: http://ise.rpi.edu/.

Rochester Institute of Technology, Graduate Enrollment Services, Kate Gleason College of Engineering, Industrial and Systems Engineering Department, ME Program in Industrial and Systems Engineering, Rochester, NY 14623-5603. Offers ME. *Students:* 11 full-time (2 women), 2 part-time, 10 international. Average age 26. 76 applicants, 25% accepted, 7 enrolled. In 2014, 13 master's awarded. *Degree requirements:* For master's, thesis or alternative, Capstone Project. *Entrance requirements:* For master's, TOEFL, IELTS, or PTE for non-native English speakers, Recommended minimum GPA of 3.0. Additional exam requirements/recommendations for international students: Required—PTE (minimum score 58), TOEFL (minimum score 550 paper-based; 79 iBT) or IELTS (minimum score 6.5). *Application deadline:* For fall admission, 2/15 priority date for domestic and international students; for spring admission, 12/15 priority date for domestic and international students. Applications are processed on a rolling basis. Electronic applications accepted. *Expenses:* Expenses: $1,673 per credit hour. *Financial support:* In 2014–15, 7 students received support. Research assistantships with partial tuition reimbursements available, teaching assistantships with partial tuition reimbursements available, career-related internships or fieldwork, Federal Work-Study, institutionally sponsored loans, scholarships/grants, and unspecified assistantships available. Support available to part-time students. *Faculty research:* Advanced manufacturing, engineering education, ergonomics and human factors, healthcare delivery systems, operations research and simulation, systems engineering, production and logistics, sustainable engineering. *Unit head:* Dr. Marcos Esterman, Associate Professor, 585-475-2598, E-mail: mxeeie@rit.edu. *Application contact:* Diane Ellison, Associate Vice President, Graduate Enrollment Services, 585-475-2229, Fax: 585-475-7164, E-mail: gradinfo@rit.edu.
Website: http://www.rit.edu/kgcoe/ise/program/ms-industrial-systems-engineering/master-engineering-industrial-and-systems-engineering.

Rochester Institute of Technology, Graduate Enrollment Services, Kate Gleason College of Engineering, Industrial and Systems Engineering Department, MS Program in Industrial and Systems Engineering, Rochester, NY 14623-5603. Offers MS. Part-time programs available. *Students:* 34 full-time (2 women), 10 part-time (1 woman), 38 international. Average age 24. 250 applicants, 30% accepted, 19 enrolled. In 2014, 3 master's awarded. *Degree requirements:* For master's, thesis. *Entrance requirements:* For master's, GRE and TOEFL, IELTS, or PTE for non-native English speakers, Recommended minimum GPA of 3.0. Additional exam requirements/recommendations for international students: Required—PTE (minimum score 58), TOEFL (minimum score 550 paper-based; 79 iBT) or IELTS (minimum score 6.5). *Application deadline:* For fall admission, 2/15 priority date for domestic and international students; for spring admission, 12/15 priority date for domestic and international students. Applications are processed on a rolling basis. Electronic applications accepted. *Expenses:* Expenses: $1,673 per credit hour. *Financial support:* In 2014–15, 25 students received support. Research assistantships with partial tuition reimbursements available, teaching assistantships with partial tuition reimbursements available, career-related internships or fieldwork, Federal Work-Study, institutionally sponsored loans, scholarships/grants, and unspecified assistantships available. Support available to part-time students. Financial award applicants required to submit FAFSA. *Faculty research:* Advanced manufacturing, engineering education, ergonomics and human factors, healthcare delivery systems, operations research and simulation, systems engineering, production and logistics, sustainable engineering. *Unit head:* Dr. Marcos Esterman, Associate Professor, 585-475-2598, E-mail: mxeeie@rit.edu. *Application contact:* Diane Ellison, Associate Vice President, Graduate Enrollment Services, 585-475-2229, Fax: 585-475-7164, E-mail: gradinfo@rit.edu.
Website: http://www.rit.edu/kgcoe/ise/program/master-science-degrees/master-science-industrial-and-systems-engineering.

Rutgers, The State University of New Jersey, New Brunswick, Graduate School-New Brunswick, Department of Industrial and Systems Engineering, Piscataway, NJ 08854-8097. Offers industrial and systems engineering (MS, PhD); information technology (MS); manufacturing systems engineering (MS); quality and reliability engineering (MS). Part-time and evening/weekend programs available. Terminal master's awarded for partial completion of doctoral program. *Degree requirements:* For master's, thesis or alternative, seminar; for doctorate, comprehensive exam, thesis/dissertation. *Entrance requirements:* For master's and doctorate, GRE General Test. Additional exam requirements/recommendations for international students: Required—TOEFL. *Faculty research:* Production and manufacturing systems, quality and reliability engineering, systems engineering and aviation safety.

St. Mary's University, Graduate School, Department of Engineering, Program in Industrial Engineering, San Antonio, TX 78228-8507. Offers MS. Part-time programs available. *Students:* 2 full-time (0 women), 7 part-time (1 woman); includes 2 minority (both Hispanic/Latino), 5 international. Average age 32. 17 applicants, 41% accepted. In 2014, 8 master's awarded. *Degree requirements:* For master's, comprehensive exam. *Entrance requirements:* For master's, GRE, Have a Bachelor of Science (B.S.) degree in engineering, or related areas such as the physical sciences or mathematics. Have a minimum grade point average (GPA) of 3.00. Submit a completed application form, a written statement of purpose indicating the applicant's interests and objectives, two letters of recommendation, and official transcripts. Additional exam requirements/recommendations for international students: Required—TOEFL (minimum score 550 paper-based; 80 iBT), IELTS (minimum score 6). *Application deadline:* Applications are processed on a rolling basis. Application fee: $0. Electronic applications accepted. *Expenses: Tuition:* Full-time $15,070; part-time $800 per credit hour. *Required fees:* $156 per semester. *Financial support:* Career-related internships or fieldwork, Federal Work-Study, institutionally sponsored loans, scholarships/grants, and health care benefits available. Financial award application deadline: 3/31; financial award applicants required to submit FAFSA. *Unit head:* Dr. Rafael Moras, Director, 210-431-2017, E-mail: rmoras@stmarytx.edu.
Website: https://www.stmarytx.edu/academics/set/graduate/industrial-engineering/.

San Jose State University, Graduate Studies and Research, Charles W. Davidson College of Engineering, Department of Industrial and Systems Engineering, San Jose, CA 95192-0001. Offers MS. Part-time programs available. *Degree requirements:* For master's, comprehensive exam. Electronic applications accepted.

South Dakota State University, Graduate School, College of Engineering, Department of Engineering Technology and Management, Brookings, SD 57007. Offers industrial management (MS). *Degree requirements:* For master's, comprehensive exam, thesis

(for some programs), oral exam. *Entrance requirements:* Additional exam requirements/recommendations for international students: Required—TOEFL (minimum score 575 paper-based). *Faculty research:* Query, economic development, statistical process control, foreign business plans, operations management.

Southern Illinois University Edwardsville, Graduate School, School of Engineering, Department of Mechanical and Industrial Engineering, Program in Industrial Engineering, Edwardsville, IL 62026. Offers MS. Part-time and evening/weekend programs available. *Students:* 14 full-time (2 women), 11 part-time (1 woman); includes 1 minority (Black or African American, non-Hispanic/Latino), 21 international. 55 applicants, 33% accepted. In 2014, 10 master's awarded. *Degree requirements:* For master's, thesis (for some programs), final exam. *Entrance requirements:* For master's, GRE (for applicants whose degree is from non-ABET accredited institution). Additional exam requirements/recommendations for international students: Required—TOEFL (minimum score 550 paper-based; 79 iBT), IELTS (minimum score 6.5). *Application deadline:* For fall admission, 7/24 for domestic students, 7/15 for international students; for spring admission, 12/11 for domestic students, 11/15 for international students; for summer admission, 4/29 for domestic students, 4/15 for international students. Applications are processed on a rolling basis. Application fee: $30. Electronic applications accepted. *Expenses: Tuition*, state resident: full-time $5026. Tuition, nonresident: full-time $12,566. *International tuition:* $25,136 full-time. *Required fees:* $1682. Tuition and fees vary according to course load, campus/location and program. *Financial support:* In 2014–15, 12 students received support, including 1 fellowship (averaging $8,370 per year), 4 research assistantships with full tuition reimbursements available, 7 teaching assistantships with full tuition reimbursements available; institutionally sponsored loans, scholarships/grants, and unspecified assistantships also available. Financial award application deadline: 3/1; financial award applicants required to submit FAFSA. *Unit head:* Dr. Felix Lee, Director, 618-650-2805, E-mail: hflee@siue.edu. *Application contact:* Melissa K Mace, Assistant Director of Admissions for Graduate and International Recruitment, 618-650-2756, Fax: 618-650-3618, E-mail: mmace@siue.edu.
Website: http://www.siue.edu/ENGINEER/IE/.

Southern Polytechnic State University, School of Engineering Technology and Management, Department of Industrial Engineering Technology, Marietta, GA 30060-2896. Offers quality assurance (MS, Graduate Certificate). Part-time and evening/weekend programs available. Postbaccalaureate distance learning degree programs offered (no on-campus study). *Degree requirements:* For master's and Graduate Certificate, comprehensive exam (for some programs). *Entrance requirements:* For master's, 3 reference forms, minimum GPA of 2.7, statement of purpose; for Graduate Certificate, minimum GPA of 2.7, statement of purpose. Additional exam requirements/recommendations for international students: Required—TOEFL (minimum score 550 paper-based; 79 iBT), IELTS (minimum score 6.5). Electronic applications accepted. *Faculty research:* Assessing technical and non-technical workforce skills in a two-year college; analysis of the effectiveness of using exclusively workshop-style instruction in the college algebra classroom, focused on engineering and engineering technology; the human impact potential of engineering as outreach; comparison of an introductory level undergraduate statistics course taught with traditional, hybrid, and online delivery methods; reducing TB incidence.

Stanford University, School of Engineering, Department of Management Science and Engineering, Stanford, CA 94305-9991. Offers MS, PhD. Terminal master's awarded for partial completion of doctoral program. *Degree requirements:* For doctorate, thesis/dissertation, qualification procedure. *Entrance requirements:* For master's and doctorate, GRE General Test. Additional exam requirements/recommendations for international students: Required—TOEFL. Electronic applications accepted. *Expenses: Tuition:* Full-time $44,184; part-time $982 per credit hour. *Required fees:* $191.

Texas A&M University, College of Engineering, Department of Industrial and Systems Engineering, College Station, TX 77843. Offers industrial engineering (M Eng, MS, PhD). Part-time programs available. Postbaccalaureate distance learning degree programs offered (no on-campus study). *Faculty:* 22. *Students:* 200 full-time (54 women), 54 part-time (20 women); includes 33 minority (10 Black or African American, non-Hispanic/Latino; 12 Asian, non-Hispanic/Latino; 10 Hispanic/Latino; 1 Two or more races, non-Hispanic/Latino), 196 international. Average age 26. 797 applicants, 22% accepted, 112 enrolled. In 2014, 75 master's, 5 doctorates awarded. *Degree requirements:* For master's, comprehensive exam (for some programs), thesis optional; for doctorate, comprehensive exam, thesis/dissertation. *Entrance requirements:* For master's and doctorate, GRE General Test. Additional exam requirements/recommendations for international students: Required—TOEFL. *Application deadline:* For fall admission, 3/1 priority date for domestic and international students; for spring admission, 8/1 priority date for domestic and international students. Applications are processed on a rolling basis. Application fee: $50 ($90 for international students). Electronic applications accepted. *Expenses: Tuition,* state resident: full-time $4078; part-time $226.55 per credit hour. Tuition, nonresident: full-time $10,594; part-time $577.55 per credit hour. *Required fees:* $2813; $237.70 per credit hour. $278.50 per semester. Tuition and fees vary according to degree level and student level. *Financial support:* In 2014–15, 137 students received support, including 9 fellowships with full and partial tuition reimbursements available (averaging $19,173 per year), 53 research assistantships with full and partial tuition reimbursements available (averaging $5,340 per year), 33 teaching assistantships with full and partial tuition reimbursements available (averaging $4,816 per year); career-related internships or fieldwork, institutionally sponsored loans, scholarships/grants, traineeships, health care benefits, tuition waivers (full and partial), and unspecified assistantships also available. Support available to part-time students. Financial award application deadline: 2/1; financial award applicants required to submit FAFSA. *Faculty research:* Manufacturing systems, computer integration, operations research, logistics, simulation. *Unit head:* Dr. Cesar O. Malave, Head, 979-845-5535, Fax: 979-458-4299, E-mail: malave@tamu.edu. *Application contact:* Erin Roady, Graduate Program Coordinator, 979-845-5536, Fax: 979-458-4299, E-mail: erinroady@tamu.edu.
Website: http://engineering.tamu.edu/industrial.

Texas A&M University–Kingsville, College of Graduate Studies, College of Engineering, Department of Mechanical and Industrial Engineering, Program in Industrial Engineering, Kingsville, TX 78363. Offers ME, MS. *Students:* 61 full-time (9 women), 27 part-time (4 women); includes 18 minority (7 Black or African American, non-Hispanic/Latino; 4 Asian, non-Hispanic/Latino; 7 Hispanic/Latino), 62 international. Average age 26. 144 applicants, 89% accepted, 37 enrolled. In 2014, 21 master's awarded. *Degree requirements:* For master's, variable foreign language requirement, comprehensive exam, thesis (for some programs). *Entrance requirements:* For master's, GRE (minimum overall old score of 900-1000 depending on GPA), MAT, GMAT. Additional exam requirements/recommendations for international students: Required—TOEFL (minimum score 550 paper-based; 79 iBT). *Application deadline:* For fall admission, 8/15 for domestic students, 6/1 for international students; for spring admission, 12/15 for domestic students, 10/1 for international students; for summer admission, 5/15 for domestic students, 4/1 for international students. Applications are processed on a rolling basis. Application fee: $35 ($50 for international students). Electronic applications accepted. *Financial support:* In 2014–15, 18 students received support, including 2 research assistantships (averaging $2,104 per year), 3 teaching assistantships (averaging $4,667 per year); career-related internships or fieldwork, Federal Work-Study, institutionally sponsored loans, scholarships/grants, health care benefits, tuition waivers (full and partial), and unspecified assistantships also available. Support available to part-time students. Financial award application deadline: 5/15; financial award applicants required to submit FAFSA. *Unit head:* Dr. Larry Peel, Department Chair, 361-593-2003, Fax: 361-593-4026, E-mail: larry.peel@tamuk.edu. *Application contact:* Dr. Mohamed Abdelrahman, Dean of Graduate Studies, 361-593-2809, E-mail: mohamed.abdelrahman@tamuk.edu.

Texas Southern University, School of Science and Technology, Department of Industrial Technology, Houston, TX 77004-4584. Offers MS. *Degree requirements:* For master's, comprehensive exam. *Entrance requirements:* For master's, GRE General Test, minimum GPA of 2.5. Additional exam requirements/recommendations for international students: Required—TOEFL. Electronic applications accepted.

Texas State University, The Graduate College, College of Science and Engineering, Department of Engineering Technology, San Marcos, TX 78666. Offers technology management (MST), including industrial technology. Part-time and evening/weekend programs available. *Faculty:* 8 full-time (2 women). *Degree requirements:* For master's, comprehensive exam, thesis optional. *Entrance requirements:* For master's, minimum GPA of 2.75 in last 60 hours of undergraduate work. Additional exam requirements/recommendations for international students: Required—TOEFL (minimum score 550 paper-based; 78 iBT). *Application deadline:* For fall admission, 6/15 priority date for domestic students, 6/1 priority date for international students; for spring admission, 10/15 priority date for domestic students, 10/1 priority date for international students. Applications are processed on a rolling basis. Application fee: $40 ($90 for international students). Electronic applications accepted. *Financial support:* Research assistantships, teaching assistantships, career-related internships or fieldwork, Federal Work-Study, institutionally sponsored loans, scholarships/grants, health care benefits, and unspecified assistantships available. Support available to part-time students. Financial award application deadline: 4/1; financial award applicants required to submit FAFSA. *Unit head:* Dr. Andy Batey, Chair, 512-245-2137, Fax: 512-245-3052, E-mail: ab08@txstate.edu. *Application contact:* Dr. Andrea Golato, Dean of the Graduate College, 512-245-2581, E-mail: gradcollege@txstate.edu.
Website: http://www.txstate.edu/technology/.

Texas Tech University, Graduate School, Edward E. Whitacre Jr. College of Engineering, Department of Industrial Engineering, Lubbock, TX 79409-3061. Offers industrial engineering (MSIE, PhD); systems and engineering management (MSSEM, PhD). Part-time programs available. Postbaccalaureate distance learning degree programs offered (minimal on-campus study). *Faculty:* 14 full-time (2 women), 1 part-time/adjunct (0 women). *Students:* 79 full-time (17 women), 64 part-time (14 women); includes 15 minority (5 Black or African American, non-Hispanic/Latino; 1 American Indian or Alaska Native, non-Hispanic/Latino; 2 Asian, non-Hispanic/Latino; 6 Hispanic/Latino; 1 Two or more races, non-Hispanic/Latino), 80 international. Average age 32. 275 applicants, 55% accepted, 58 enrolled. In 2014, 17 master's, 7 doctorates awarded. Terminal master's awarded for partial completion of doctoral program. *Degree requirements:* For master's, comprehensive exam, thesis optional; for doctorate, comprehensive exam, thesis/dissertation. *Entrance requirements:* For master's, GRE (Verbal and Quantitative); for doctorate, GRE (Verbal and Quantitative), MS. Additional exam requirements/recommendations for international students: Required—TOEFL (minimum score 550 paper-based; 79 iBT). *Application deadline:* For fall admission, 6/1 priority date for domestic students, 1/15 priority date for international students; for spring admission, 9/1 priority date for domestic students, 6/15 priority date for international students. Applications are processed on a rolling basis. Application fee: $60. Electronic applications accepted. *Expenses:* Tuition, state resident: full-time $6310; part-time $262.92 per credit hour. Tuition, nonresident: full-time $14,998; part-time $624.92 per credit hour. *Required fees:* $2701; $36.50 per credit. $912.50 per semester. Tuition and fees vary according to course load. *Financial support:* In 2014–15, 57 students received support, including 55 fellowships (averaging $3,146 per year), 5 research assistantships (averaging $26,747 per year), 13 teaching assistantships (averaging $20,625 per year); scholarships/grants, tuition waivers (partial), and unspecified assistantships also available. Financial award application deadline: 2/1; financial award applicants required to submit FAFSA. *Faculty research:* Engineering management, operations research, manufacturing, ergonomics, quality. *Total annual research expenditures:* $614,109. *Unit head:* Dr. Hong-Chao Zhang, Interim Chair, 806-742-3543, E-mail: hong-chao.zhang@ttu.edu. *Application contact:* Dr. Simon Hsiang, Professor, 806-742-3543, Fax: 806-742-3411, E-mail: simon.hsiang@ttu.edu.
Website: http://www.ie.ttu.edu/.

Universidad de las Américas Puebla, Division of Graduate Studies, School of Engineering, Program in Industrial Engineering, Puebla, Mexico. Offers industrial engineering (MS); production management (M Adm). Part-time and evening/weekend programs available. *Degree requirements:* For master's, one foreign language, thesis. *Faculty research:* Textile industry, quality control.

Université de Moncton, Faculty of Engineering, Program in Industrial Engineering, Moncton, NB E1A 3E9, Canada. Offers M Sc A. *Degree requirements:* For master's, thesis, proficiency in French. *Faculty research:* Production systems, optimization, simulation and expert systems, modeling and warehousing systems, quality control.

Université du Québec à Trois-Rivières, Graduate Programs, Program in Industrial Engineering, Trois-Rivières, QC G9A 5H7, Canada. Offers M Sc, DESS. *Entrance requirements:* For degree, appropriate bachelor's degree, proficiency in French. *Faculty research:* Production.

Université Laval, Faculty of Sciences and Engineering, Programs in Industrial Engineering, Québec, QC G1K 7P4, Canada. Offers Diploma. Part-time programs available. *Entrance requirements:* For degree, knowledge of French. Electronic applications accepted.

University at Buffalo, the State University of New York, Graduate School, School of Engineering and Applied Sciences, Department of Industrial and Systems Engineering, Buffalo, NY 14260. Offers ME, MS, PhD. Part-time programs available. Postbaccalaureate distance learning degree programs offered (minimal on-campus study). *Faculty:* 16 full-time (3 women), 1 part-time/adjunct (0 women). *Students:* 213 full-time (57 women), 12 part-time (2 women); includes 8 minority (2 Black or African American, non-Hispanic/Latino; 1 American Indian or Alaska Native, non-Hispanic/Latino; 2 Asian, non-Hispanic/Latino; 2 Hispanic/Latino; 1 Two or more races, non-Hispanic/Latino), 191 international. Average age 26. 1,030 applicants, 21% accepted, 55 enrolled. In 2014, 83 master's, 12 doctorates awarded. Terminal master's awarded for partial completion of doctoral program. *Degree requirements:* For master's, comprehensive exam (for some programs), thesis or alternative; for doctorate, thesis/dissertation. *Entrance requirements:* For master's and doctorate, GRE General Test. Additional exam requirements/recommendations for international students: Required—TOEFL (minimum score 550 paper-based; 79 iBT). *Application deadline:* For fall admission, 2/1 priority date for domestic and international students; for spring admission, 10/1 priority date for domestic and international students. Applications are processed on a rolling basis. Application fee: $75. Electronic applications accepted.

Financial support: In 2014–15, 60 students received support, including 11 fellowships with full and partial tuition reimbursements available (averaging $27,816 per year), 32 research assistantships with full and partial tuition reimbursements available (averaging $21,816 per year), 15 teaching assistantships with full and partial tuition reimbursements available (averaging $21,763 per year); Federal Work-Study, institutionally sponsored loans, tuition waivers (full and partial), and unspecified assistantships also available. Financial award application deadline: 2/1; financial award applicants required to submit FAFSA. *Faculty research:* Ergonomics, operations research, production systems, human factors. *Total annual research expenditures:* $7.6 million. *Unit head:* Dr. Ann Bisantz, Chairman, 716-645-2357, Fax: 716-645-3302, E-mail: bisantz@buffalo.edu. *Application contact:* Dr. Li Lin, Director of Graduate Studies, 716-645-4713, Fax: 716-645-3302, E-mail: iegrad@buffalo.edu.
Website: http://www.ise.buffalo.edu/index.php.

The University of Alabama in Huntsville, School of Graduate Studies, College of Engineering, Department of Industrial and Systems Engineering and Engineering Management, Huntsville, AL 35899. Offers engineering management (PhD); industrial and systems engineering (MSE, PhD); industrial engineering (MSE, PhD); operations research (MSOR); systems engineering (MSE). Part-time and evening/weekend programs available. Postbaccalaureate distance learning degree programs offered (minimal on-campus study). *Degree requirements:* For master's, comprehensive exam, thesis or alternative, oral and written exams; for doctorate, comprehensive exam, thesis/dissertation, oral and written exams. *Entrance requirements:* For master's and doctorate, GRE General Test, minimum GPA of 3.0. Additional exam requirements/recommendations for international students: Required—TOEFL (minimum score 500 paper-based; 80 iBT), IELTS (minimum score 6.5). Electronic applications accepted. *Faculty research:* Systems engineering process, electronic manufacturing, heuristic manufacturing, teams and team development.

The University of Arizona, College of Engineering, Department of Systems and Industrial Engineering, Program in Industrial Engineering, Tucson, AZ 85721. Offers MS. Part-time programs available. Postbaccalaureate distance learning degree programs offered. *Entrance requirements:* Additional exam requirements/recommendations for international students: Required—TOEFL (minimum score 575 paper-based; 80 iBT). Electronic applications accepted. *Faculty research:* Operations research, manufacturing systems, quality and reliability, statistical/engineering design.

The University of Arizona, College of Engineering, Department of Systems and Industrial Engineering, Program in Systems and Industrial Engineering, Tucson, AZ 85721. Offers MS, PhD. Postbaccalaureate distance learning degree programs offered. *Degree requirements:* For doctorate, thesis/dissertation. *Entrance requirements:* For master's, GRE General Test (minimum score: 500 Verbal, 700 Quantitative), 3 letters of recommendation, letter of intent; for doctorate, GRE General Test (minimum score: 500 Verbal, 750 Quantitative), 3 letters of recommendation, letter of intent. Additional exam requirements/recommendations for international students: Required—TOEFL (minimum score 575 paper-based; 80 iBT). Electronic applications accepted. *Faculty research:* Optimization, systems theory, logistics, transportation, embedded systems.

University of Arkansas, Graduate School, College of Engineering, Department of Industrial Engineering, Program in Industrial Engineering, Fayetteville, AR 72701-1201. Offers MSE, MSIE, PhD. *Degree requirements:* For master's, thesis optional; for doctorate, one foreign language, thesis/dissertation. Electronic applications accepted.

University of California, Berkeley, Graduate Division, College of Engineering, Department of Industrial Engineering and Operations Research, Berkeley, CA 94720-1500. Offers M Eng, MS, D Eng, PhD. *Degree requirements:* For master's, comprehensive exam or thesis (MS); for doctorate, thesis/dissertation, qualifying exam. *Entrance requirements:* For master's and doctorate, GRE General Test, minimum GPA of 3.0, 3 letters of recommendation. *Faculty research:* Mathematical programming, robotics and manufacturing, linear and nonlinear optimization, production planning and scheduling, queuing theory.

University of Central Florida, College of Engineering and Computer Science, Department of Industrial Engineering and Management Systems, Orlando, FL 32816. Offers MSIE, PhD, Certificate. Part-time and evening/weekend programs available. *Faculty:* 15 full-time (3 women), 2 part-time/adjunct (0 women). *Students:* 87 full-time (25 women), 163 part-time (46 women); includes 75 minority (15 Black or African American, non-Hispanic/Latino; 14 Asian, non-Hispanic/Latino; 41 Hispanic/Latino; 5 Two or more races, non-Hispanic/Latino), 59 international. Average age 32. 209 applicants, 61% accepted, 77 enrolled. In 2014, 104 master's, 20 doctorates, 25 other advanced degrees awarded. *Degree requirements:* For master's, thesis; for doctorate, thesis/dissertation, departmental qualifying exam, candidacy exam. *Entrance requirements:* For master's, GRE General Test, minimum GPA of 3.0 in last 60 hours of course work; for doctorate, minimum GPA of 3.5 in last 60 hours of course work. Additional exam requirements/recommendations for international students: Required—TOEFL. *Application deadline:* For fall admission, 7/15 priority date for domestic students; for spring admission, 12/1 priority date for domestic students. Application fee: $30. Electronic applications accepted. *Expenses:* Tuition, state resident: part-time $288.16 per credit hour. Tuition, nonresident: part-time $1073.31 per credit hour. *Financial support:* In 2014–15, 20 students received support, including 12 fellowships with partial tuition reimbursements available (averaging $3,700 per year), 6 research assistantships with partial tuition reimbursements available (averaging $10,000 per year), 9 teaching assistantships with partial tuition reimbursements available (averaging $10,100 per year); career-related internships or fieldwork, Federal Work-Study, institutionally sponsored loans, tuition waivers (partial), and unspecified assistantships also available. Financial award application deadline: 3/1; financial award applicants required to submit FAFSA. *Unit head:* Dr. Waldemar Karwowski, Chair, 407-823-0042, E-mail: wkar@ucf.edu. *Application contact:* Barbara Rodriguez Lamas, Director, Admissions and Student Services, 407-823-2766, Fax: 407-823-6442, E-mail: gradadmissions@ucf.edu.
Website: http://iems.ucf.edu/.

University of Cincinnati, Graduate School, College of Engineering and Applied Science, Department of Mechanical and Materials Engineering, Cincinnati, OH 45221. Offers industrial engineering (PhD); mechanical engineering (MS, PhD); nuclear engineering (PhD); MBA/MS. Part-time and evening/weekend programs available. Terminal master's awarded for partial completion of doctoral program. *Degree requirements:* For doctorate, thesis/dissertation. *Entrance requirements:* For master's and doctorate, GRE General Test. Additional exam requirements/recommendations for international students: Required—TOEFL (minimum score 575 paper-based). Electronic applications accepted.

University of Florida, Graduate School, College of Engineering, Department of Industrial and Systems Engineering, Gainesville, FL 32611. Offers ME, MS, PhD, Engr. Part-time and evening/weekend programs available. Postbaccalaureate distance learning degree programs offered (minimal on-campus study). *Faculty:* 13 full-time (1 woman), 1 part-time/adjunct (0 women). *Students:* 62 full-time (19 women), 113 part-time (26 women); includes 30 minority (8 Black or African American, non-Hispanic/Latino; 1 American Indian or Alaska Native, non-Hispanic/Latino; 7 Asian, non-Hispanic/Latino; 14 Hispanic/Latino), 63 international. 595 applicants, 24% accepted, 71 enrolled.

In 2014, 136 master's, 14 doctorates, 1 other advanced degree awarded. Terminal master's awarded for partial completion of doctoral program. *Degree requirements:* For master's, thesis (for some programs); for doctorate, comprehensive exam (for some programs), thesis/dissertation (for some programs). *Entrance requirements:* For master's and doctorate, minimum GPA of 3.0; for Engr, GRE General Test. Additional exam requirements/recommendations for international students: Required—TOEFL (minimum score 550 paper-based; 80 iBT), IELTS (minimum score 6). *Application deadline:* For fall admission, 12/31 priority date for domestic students, 2/1 for international students; for spring admission, 8/31 for domestic students, 8/1 for international students. Applications are processed on a rolling basis. Application fee: $30. Electronic applications accepted. *Financial support:* Career-related internships or fieldwork, Federal Work-Study, and unspecified assistantships available. Financial award application deadline: 1/15; financial award applicants required to submit FAFSA. *Faculty research:* Operations research; financial engineering; logistics and supply chain management; energy, healthcare, and transportation applications of operations research. *Unit head:* Joseph Geunes, Professor and Interim Chair, 352-392-1464 Ext. 2020, Fax: 352-392-3537, E-mail: geunes@ise.ufl.edu. *Application contact:* Office of Admissions, 352-392-1365, E-mail: webrequests@admissions.ufl.edu.
Website: http://www.ise.ufl.edu/.

University of Houston, Cullen College of Engineering, Department of Industrial Engineering, Houston, TX 77204. Offers MIE, PhD. Part-time programs available. Terminal master's awarded for partial completion of doctoral program. *Degree requirements:* For master's, thesis (for some programs); for doctorate, thesis/dissertation, departmental qualifying exam. *Entrance requirements:* For master's and doctorate, GRE General Test. Additional exam requirements/recommendations for international students: Required—TOEFL; Recommended—IELTS. Electronic applications accepted.

University of Illinois at Chicago, Graduate College, College of Engineering, Department of Mechanical and Industrial Engineering, Program in Industrial Engineering, Chicago, IL 60607-7128. Offers industrial engineering (MS); industrial engineering and operations research (PhD). Part-time programs available. *Students:* 82 full-time (15 women), 5 part-time (1 woman); includes 10 minority (2 Asian, non-Hispanic/Latino; 8 Hispanic/Latino), 76 international. Average age 25. 321 applicants, 58% accepted, 53 enrolled. In 2014, 15 master's, 4 doctorates awarded. *Degree requirements:* For doctorate, thesis/dissertation. *Entrance requirements:* For doctorate, GRE General Test, minimum GPA of 2.75. Additional exam requirements/recommendations for international students: Required—TOEFL. *Application deadline:* For fall admission, 5/15 for domestic students, 2/15 for international students; for spring admission, 11/1 for domestic students, 7/15 for international students. Applications are processed on a rolling basis. Application fee: $60. Electronic applications accepted. *Expenses:* Expenses: $17,602 in-state; $29,600 out-of-state. *Financial support:* Fellowships with full tuition reimbursements, research assistantships with full tuition reimbursements, teaching assistantships with full tuition reimbursements, Federal Work-Study, scholarships/grants, traineeships, tuition waivers (full), and unspecified assistantships available. Financial award application deadline: 3/1; financial award applicants required to submit FAFSA. *Faculty research:* Manufacturing information systems and manufacturing control, supply chain, logistics, optimization quality control, haptics and virtual reality, industrial automation, safety and reliability engineering, diagnostics, prognostics, controls and statistical modeling. *Unit head:* Prof. Farzad Mashayek, Head, 312-996-6122, E-mail: mashayek@uic.edu.
Website: http://catalog.uic.edu/gcat/colleges-schools/engineering/ie/.

University of Illinois at Urbana–Champaign, Graduate College, College of Engineering, Department of Industrial and Enterprise Systems Engineering, Urbana, IL 61801. Offers industrial engineering (MS, PhD); systems and entrepreneurial engineering (MS, PhD); MBA/MS. *Faculty:* 22 full-time (7 women), 4 part-time/adjunct (0 women). *Students:* 73 (15 women); includes 2 minority (both Asian, non-Hispanic/Latino), 50 international. 296 applicants, 13% accepted, 19 enrolled. In 2014, 6 master's, 6 doctorates awarded. Application fee: $70 ($90 for international students). *Unit head:* Rakesh Nagi, Head, 217-333-2731. *Application contact:* Holly Michelle Kizer, Graduate Programs Coordinator, 217-333-2730, Fax: 217-244-5705, E-mail: tippy6@illinois.edu.
Website: http://ise.illinois.edu/.

University of Illinois at Urbana–Champaign, Graduate College, College of Engineering, Department of Mechanical Science and Engineering, Champaign, IL 61820. Offers mechanical engineering (MS, PhD); theoretical and applied mechanics (MS, PhD). Terminal master's awarded for partial completion of doctoral program. *Entrance requirements:* Additional exam requirements/recommendations for international students: Required—TOEFL (minimum score 613 paper-based; 103 iBT), IELTS (minimum score 7). *Application deadline:* For fall admission, 1/4 for domestic students; for spring admission, 10/1 for domestic students. Application fee: $70 ($90 for international students). *Financial support:* Application deadline: 12/15. *Unit head:* Placid Mathew Ferreira, Head, 217-333-0639, Fax: 217-244-6534, E-mail: pferreir@illinois.edu. *Application contact:* Katrina Hagler, Assistant Director of Graduate Recruiting and Admissions, 217-244-3416, Fax: 217-244-6534, E-mail: kkappes2@illinois.edu.
Website: http://mechanical.illinois.edu/.

The University of Iowa, Graduate College, College of Engineering, Department of Industrial Engineering, Iowa City, IA 52242-1316. Offers engineering design and manufacturing (MS, PhD); healthcare systems (MS, PhD); human factors (MS, PhD); information and engineering management (MS, PhD); operations research (MS, PhD); wind energy (MS, PhD). *Faculty:* 8 full-time (1 woman). *Students:* 19 full-time (3 women); includes 1 minority (Asian, non-Hispanic/Latino), 10 international. Average age 28. 59 applicants, 12% accepted, 3 enrolled. In 2014, 1 master's, 4 doctorates awarded. Terminal master's awarded for partial completion of doctoral program. *Degree requirements:* For master's, thesis optional, exam; for doctorate, comprehensive exam, thesis/dissertation, final defense exam. *Entrance requirements:* For master's and doctorate, GRE General Test. Additional exam requirements/recommendations for international students: Required—TOEFL (minimum score 600 paper-based; 100 iBT). *Application deadline:* For fall admission, 7/15 for domestic students, 4/15 for international students; for spring admission, 12/1 for domestic students, 10/1 for international students; for summer admission, 4/15 for domestic students, 3/1 for international students. Applications are processed on a rolling basis. Application fee: $60 ($100 for international students). Electronic applications accepted. *Financial support:* In 2014–15, 4 fellowships with partial tuition reimbursements (averaging $20,619 per year), 16 research assistantships with full tuition reimbursements (averaging $18,131 per year), 5 teaching assistantships with full tuition reimbursements (averaging $5,424 per year) were awarded; career-related internships or fieldwork, scholarships/grants, and unspecified assistantships also available. Support available to part-time students. Financial award applicants required to submit FAFSA. *Faculty research:* Operations research, informatics, human factors engineering, healthcare systems, biomanufacturing, manufacturing systems, renewable energy, human-machine interactions. *Total annual research expenditures:* $3.5 million. *Unit head:* Dr. Andrew Kusiak, Department Executive Officer, 319-335-5934, Fax: 319-335-5669, E-mail: andrew-kusiak@uiowa.edu. *Application contact:* Andrea Flaherty, Academic Program Specialist, 319-335-5939, Fax: 319-335-5669, E-mail: indeng@engineering.uiowa.edu.
Website: http://www.engineering.uiowa.edu/mie.

University of Louisville, J. B. Speed School of Engineering, Department of Industrial Engineering, Louisville, KY 40292-0001. Offers engineering management (M Eng); industrial engineering (M Eng, MS, PhD); logistics and distribution (Certificate). *Accreditation:* ABET (one or more programs are accredited). Part-time programs available. *Students:* 104 full-time (27 women), 118 part-time (20 women); includes 25 minority (7 Black or African American, non-Hispanic/Latino; 7 Asian, non-Hispanic/Latino; 7 Hispanic/Latino; 4 Two or more races, non-Hispanic/Latino), 97 international. Average age 29. 109 applicants, 70% accepted, 41 enrolled. In 2014, 16 master's, 10 doctorates awarded. Terminal master's awarded for partial completion of doctoral program. *Degree requirements:* For master's, comprehensive exam (for some programs), thesis or alternative; for doctorate, comprehensive exam, thesis/dissertation, minimum GPA of 3.0. *Entrance requirements:* For master's and doctorate, GRE General Test. Additional exam requirements/recommendations for international students: Required—TOEFL (minimum score 550 paper-based; 80 iBT), IELTS (minimum score 6.5). *Application deadline:* For fall admission, 5/1 priority date for domestic and international students; for spring admission, 11/1 priority date for domestic and international students. Applications are processed on a rolling basis. Application fee: $60. Electronic applications accepted. *Expenses:* Tuition, state resident: full-time $11,326; part-time $630 per credit hour. Tuition, nonresident: full-time $23,568; part-time $1311 per credit hour. *Required fees:* $196. Tuition and fees vary according to program and reciprocity agreements. *Financial support:* In 2014–15, 7 fellowships with full tuition reimbursements (averaging $20,000 per year), 2 research assistantships with full tuition reimbursements (averaging $20,000 per year), 6 teaching assistantships with full tuition reimbursements (averaging $20,000 per year) were awarded. Financial award application deadline: 1/25; financial award applicants required to submit FAFSA. *Faculty research:* Optimization, computer simulation, logistics and distribution, ergonomics and human factors, advanced manufacturing process. *Total annual research expenditures:* $748,000. *Unit head:* Dr. John S. Usher, Chair, 502-852-6342, Fax: 502-852-5633, E-mail: usher@louisville.edu. *Application contact:* Dr. Michael Day, Associate Dean, 502-852-6195, Fax: 502-852-7294, E-mail: day@louisville.edu.
Website: http://www.louisville.edu/speed/industrial/.

University of Manitoba, Faculty of Graduate Studies, Faculty of Engineering, Department of Mechanical and Manufacturing Engineering, Winnipeg, MB R3T 2N2, Canada. Offers M Eng, M Sc, PhD. *Degree requirements:* For master's, thesis; for doctorate, thesis/dissertation.

University of Massachusetts Amherst, Graduate School, College of Engineering, Department of Mechanical and Industrial Engineering, Amherst, MA 01003. Offers industrial engineering and operations research (MS, PhD); mechanical engineering (MSME, PhD). Part-time programs available. *Faculty:* 29 full-time (4 women). *Students:* 90 full-time (20 women), 29 part-time (6 women); includes 12 minority (2 Black or African American, non-Hispanic/Latino; 1 American Indian or Alaska Native, non-Hispanic/Latino; 4 Asian, non-Hispanic/Latino; 3 Hispanic/Latino; 2 Two or more races, non-Hispanic/Latino), 65 international. Average age 28. 411 applicants, 31% accepted, 33 enrolled. In 2014, 27 master's, 7 doctorates awarded. Terminal master's awarded for partial completion of doctoral program. *Degree requirements:* For master's, thesis or alternative; for doctorate, comprehensive exam, thesis/dissertation. *Entrance requirements:* For master's and doctorate, GRE General Test. Additional exam requirements/recommendations for international students: Required—TOEFL (minimum score 550 paper-based; 80 iBT), IELTS (minimum score 6.5). *Application deadline:* For fall admission, 1/15 for domestic and international students; for spring admission, 10/1 for domestic and international students. Applications are processed on a rolling basis. Application fee: $75. Electronic applications accepted. *Expenses:* Tuition, state resident: full-time $1980; part-time $110 per credit. Tuition, nonresident: full-time $14,644; part-time $414 per credit. *Required fees:* $11,417. One-time fee: $357. *Financial support:* Fellowships with full and partial tuition reimbursements, research assistantships with full and partial tuition reimbursements, teaching assistantships with full and partial tuition reimbursements, career-related internships or fieldwork, Federal Work-Study, scholarships/grants, traineeships, health care benefits, tuition waivers (full and partial), and unspecified assistantships available. Support available to part-time students. Financial award application deadline: 1/15. *Unit head:* Dr. David Schmidt, Graduate Program Director, 413-545-3827, Fax: 413-545-1027. *Application contact:* Lindsay DeSantis, Supervisor of Admissions, 413-545-0722, Fax: 413-577-0100, E-mail: gradadm@grad.umass.edu.
Website: http://mie.umass.edu/.

University of Massachusetts Dartmouth, Graduate School, College of Engineering, Department of Mechanical Engineering, North Dartmouth, MA 02747-2300. Offers industrial and systems engineering (MS); mechanical engineering (MS). Part-time programs available. *Faculty:* 11 full-time (1 woman). *Students:* 8 full-time (1 woman), 11 part-time (0 women); includes 1 minority (Asian, non-Hispanic/Latino), 9 international. Average age 26. 30 applicants, 60% accepted, 2 enrolled. In 2014, 10 master's awarded. *Degree requirements:* For master's, comprehensive exam, thesis or project. *Entrance requirements:* For master's, GRE (UMass Dartmouth mechanical engineering bachelor's degree recipients are exempt), statement of purpose (minimum of 300 words), resume, 3 letters of recommendation, official transcripts. Additional exam requirements/recommendations for international students: Required—TOEFL (minimum score 533 paper-based; 72 iBT), IELTS (minimum score 6). *Application deadline:* For fall admission, 2/15 priority date for domestic students, 1/15 priority date for international students; for spring admission, 11/15 priority date for domestic students, 10/15 priority date for international students. Applications are processed on a rolling basis. Application fee: $60. Electronic applications accepted. *Expenses:* Tuition, state resident: full-time $2071; part-time $86.29 per credit. Tuition, nonresident: full-time $8099; part-time $337.46 per credit. *Required fees:* $16,520; $712.33 per credit. Tuition and fees vary according to course load and reciprocity agreements. *Financial support:* In 2014–15, 1 research assistantship with full tuition reimbursement (averaging $5,718 per year), 3 teaching assistantships with full tuition reimbursements (averaging $10,000 per year) were awarded; Federal Work-Study and unspecified assistantships also available. Support available to part-time students. Financial award application deadline: 3/1; financial award applicants required to submit FAFSA. *Faculty research:* Biopreservation, renewable energy, fluid structure interaction, buoyant flows, high performance heat exchanges, mechanics of biomaterials, composite materials, computational mechanics. *Total annual research expenditures:* $1.2 million. *Unit head:* John Rice, Graduate Program Director, 508-999-8498, Fax: 508-999-8881, E-mail: jrice@umassd.edu. *Application contact:* Steven Briggs, Director of Marketing and Recruitment for Graduate Studies, 508-999-8604, Fax: 508-999-8183, E-mail: graduate@umassd.edu.
Website: http://www.umassd.edu/engineering/mne/.

University of Massachusetts Dartmouth, Graduate School, College of Engineering, Program in Engineering and Applied Science, North Dartmouth, MA 02747-2300. Offers applied mechanics and materials (PhD); computational science and engineering (PhD); computer science and information systems (PhD); industrial and systems engineering (PhD). Part-time programs available. *Students:* 21 full-time (6 women), 1 (woman) part-

time; includes 2 minority (1 Black or African American, non-Hispanic/Latino; 1 Two or more races, non-Hispanic/Latino), 12 international. Average age 30. 23 applicants, 65% accepted, 5 enrolled. In 2014, 1 doctorate awarded. *Degree requirements:* For doctorate, comprehensive exam, thesis/dissertation. *Entrance requirements:* For doctorate, GRE, statement of purpose (minimum of 300 words), resume, 3 letters of recommendation, official transcripts. Additional exam requirements/recommendations for international students: Required—TOEFL (minimum score 550 paper-based; 79 iBT). *Application deadline:* For fall admission, 2/15 priority date for domestic students, 1/15 priority date for international students; for spring admission, 11/15 priority date for domestic students, 10/15 priority date for international students. Applications are processed on a rolling basis. Application fee: $60. Electronic applications accepted. *Expenses:* Tuition, state resident: full-time $2071; part-time $86.29 per credit. Tuition, nonresident: full-time $8099; part-time $337.46 per credit. *Required fees:* $16,520; $712.33 per credit. Tuition and fees vary according to course load and reciprocity agreements. *Financial support:* In 2014–15, 8 fellowships with full tuition reimbursements (averaging $16,577 per year), 8 research assistantships with full tuition reimbursements (averaging $13,627 per year), 5 teaching assistantships with full tuition reimbursements (averaging $12,400 per year) were awarded; Federal Work-Study and unspecified assistantships also available. Support available to part-time students. Financial award application deadline: 3/1; financial award applicants required to submit FAFSA. *Faculty research:* Tissue/cell engineering, biotransport sensors/networks, marine systems biomimetic materials, composite/polymeric materials, resilient infrastructure robotics, renewable energy. *Total annual research expenditures:* $1.7 million. *Unit head:* Gaurav Khanna, Graduate Program Director, 508-910-6605, Fax: 508-999-9115, E-mail: gkhanna@umassd.edu. *Application contact:* Steven Briggs, Director of Marketing and Recruitment for Graduate Studies, 508-999-8604, Fax: 508-999-8183, E-mail: graduate@umassd.edu.
Website: http://www.umassd.edu/engineering/graduate/doctoraldegreeprograms/egrandappliedsciencephd/.

University of Massachusetts Lowell, College of Health Sciences, Department of Work Environment, Lowell, MA 01854. Offers cleaner production and pollution prevention (MS, Sc D); environmental risk assessment (Certificate); epidemiology (MS, Sc D); ergonomics and safety (MS, Sc D); identification and control of ergonomic hazards (Certificate); job stress and healthy job redesign (Certificate); occupational and environmental hygiene (MS, Sc D); radiological health physics and general work environment protection (Certificate); work environment policy (MS, Sc D). *Accreditation:* ABET (one or more programs are accredited). Part-time programs available. Terminal master's awarded for partial completion of doctoral program. *Degree requirements:* For master's, thesis optional; for doctorate, thesis/dissertation. *Entrance requirements:* For master's and doctorate, GRE General Test. Additional exam requirements/recommendations for international students: Required—TOEFL.

University of Memphis, Graduate School, Herff College of Engineering, Department of Mechanical Engineering, Memphis, TN 38152. Offers industrial engineering (MS); power systems (MS). Part-time programs available. *Faculty:* 5 full-time (0 women). *Students:* 8 full-time (1 woman), 4 part-time (0 women); includes 4 minority (3 Black or African American, non-Hispanic/Latino; 1 Asian, non-Hispanic/Latino), 5 international. Average age 25. 14 applicants, 79% accepted, 4 enrolled. In 2014, 7 master's awarded. Terminal master's awarded for partial completion of doctoral program. *Degree requirements:* For master's, comprehensive exam, thesis; for doctorate, comprehensive exam, thesis/dissertation. *Entrance requirements:* For master's, GRE General Test, BS in mechanical engineering, minimum undergraduate GPA of 3.0. *Application deadline:* For fall admission, 8/1 for domestic students; for spring admission, 12/1 for domestic students. Application fee: $35 ($60 for international students). *Financial support:* In 2014–15, 6 students received support. Fellowships with full tuition reimbursements available, research assistantships with full tuition reimbursements available, teaching assistantships with full tuition reimbursements available, career-related internships or fieldwork, Federal Work-Study, scholarships/grants, and unspecified assistantships available. Financial award application deadline: 2/15; financial award applicants required to submit FAFSA. *Faculty research:* Computational fluid dynamics, computational mechanics, integrated design, nondestructive testing, operations research. *Unit head:* Dr. John I. Hochstein, Chair, 901-678-2173, Fax: 901-678-5459, E-mail: jhochste@memphis.edu. *Application contact:* Dr. Teong Tan, Graduate Studies Coordinator, 901-678-3264, Fax: 901-678-5459, E-mail: ttan@memphis.edu.
Website: http://www.me.memphis.edu/.

University of Miami, Graduate School, College of Engineering, Department of Industrial Engineering, Coral Gables, FL 33124. Offers environmental health and safety (MS); ergonomics (PhD); industrial engineering (MSIE, PhD); management of technology (MS); occupational ergonomics and safety (MS, MSOES), including environmental health and safety (MS), occupational ergonomics and safety (MSOES); MBA/MSIE. Part-time programs available. *Degree requirements:* For master's, thesis (for some programs); for doctorate, comprehensive exam, thesis/dissertation. *Entrance requirements:* For master's and doctorate, GRE General Test, minimum GPA of 3.0. Additional exam requirements/recommendations for international students: Required—TOEFL (minimum score 550 paper-based). *Faculty research:* Logistics, supply chain management, industrial applications of biomechanics and ergonomics, technology management, back pain, aging, operations research, manufacturing, safety, human reliability, energy assessment.

University of Michigan, College of Engineering, Department of Industrial and Operations Engineering, Ann Arbor, MI 48109. Offers MS, MSE, PhD, MBA/MS, MBA/MSE. *Accreditation:* ABET. Part-time programs available. *Students:* 153 full-time (50 women), 17 part-time (4 women). 564 applicants, 33% accepted, 93 enrolled. In 2014, 103 master's, 13 doctorates awarded. Terminal master's awarded for partial completion of doctoral program. *Degree requirements:* For doctorate, oral defense of dissertation, preliminary exams, qualifying exam. *Entrance requirements:* For master's, GRE General Test, minimum GPA of 3.2; for doctorate, GRE General Test, minimum GPA of 3.5. Additional exam requirements/recommendations for international students: Required—TOEFL. *Application deadline:* Applications are processed on a rolling basis. Electronic applications accepted. *Financial support:* Fellowships, research assistantships, teaching assistantships, Federal Work-Study, institutionally sponsored loans, scholarships/grants, traineeships, health care benefits, and unspecified assistantships available. Financial award applicants required to submit FAFSA. *Faculty research:* Production/distribution/logistics, financial engineering and enterprise systems, ergonomics (physical and cognitive), stochastic processes, linear and nonlinear optimization, operations research. *Total annual research expenditures:* $3.9 million. *Unit head:* Mark Daskin, Department Chair, 734-764-9422, Fax: 734-764-3451, E-mail: msdaskin@umich.edu. *Application contact:* Matt Irelan, Graduate Student Advisor/Program Coordinator, 734-764-6480, Fax: 734-764-3451, E-mail: mirelan@umich.edu.
Website: http://ioe.engin.umich.edu/.

University of Michigan–Dearborn, College of Engineering and Computer Science, MSE Program in Industrial and Systems Engineering, Dearborn, MI 48128. Offers MSE. Part-time and evening/weekend programs available. Postbaccalaureate distance learning degree programs offered (no on-campus study). *Faculty:* 14 full-time (1 woman), 7 part-time/adjunct (1 woman). *Students:* 21 full-time (9 women), 29 part-time (14 women); includes 6 minority (3 Asian, non-Hispanic/Latino; 2 Hispanic/Latino; 1 Two or more races, non-Hispanic/Latino), 26 international. 77 applicants, 73% accepted, 25 enrolled. In 2014, 14 master's awarded. *Entrance requirements:* For master's, bachelor's degree in engineering, a physical science, computer science, or applied mathematics. Additional exam requirements/recommendations for international students: Required—TOEFL (minimum score 560 paper-based; 84 iBT), IELTS (minimum score 6.5). *Application deadline:* For fall admission, 8/1 for domestic students, 5/1 for international students; for winter admission, 12/1 for domestic students, 9/1 for international students; for spring admission, 4/1 for domestic students, 1/1 for international students. Applications are processed on a rolling basis. Application fee: $60. Electronic applications accepted. *Expenses:* Tuition, state resident: full-time $12,202; part-time $707 per credit hour. Tuition, nonresident: full-time $20,980; part-time $1209 per credit hour. *Required fees:* $798; $302 per term. Tuition and fees vary according to course level, course load, degree level and program. *Financial support:* In 2014–15, 7 students received support. Scholarships/grants available. Support available to part-time students. Financial award applicants required to submit FAFSA. *Faculty research:* Integrated design and manufacturing, operations research and decision science, human factors and ergonomics. *Unit head:* Dr. Armen Zakarian, Chair, 313-593-5361, Fax: 313-593-3692, E-mail: zakarian@umich.edu. *Application contact:* Joey W. Woods, Graduate Program Assistant, 313-593-5361, Fax: 313-593-3692, E-mail: jwwoods@umd.umich.edu.
Website: http://umdearborn.edu/cecs/IMSE/grad_prog/index.php.

University of Minnesota, Twin Cities Campus, College of Science and Engineering, Department of Industrial and Systems Engineering, Minneapolis, MN 55455-0213. Offers MS, PhD. Part-time programs available. *Degree requirements:* For doctorate, thesis/dissertation. *Entrance requirements:* For master's, GRE General Test, minimum GPA of 3.0; for doctorate, GRE General Test. Additional exam requirements/recommendations for international students: Required—TOEFL. Electronic applications accepted. *Faculty research:* Operations research, supply chains and logistics, health care, revenue management, transportation, service and manufacturing operations.

University of Missouri, Office of Research and Graduate Studies, College of Engineering, Department of Industrial and Manufacturing Systems Engineering, Columbia, MO 65211. Offers MS, PhD. *Faculty:* 11 full-time (2 women). *Students:* 20 full-time (7 women), 15 part-time (6 women); includes 2 minority (both Two or more races, non-Hispanic/Latino), 32 international. Average age 26. 72 applicants, 36% accepted, 7 enrolled. In 2014, 10 master's, 2 doctorates awarded. *Degree requirements:* For master's, thesis or alternative; for doctorate, thesis/dissertation. *Entrance requirements:* For master's and doctorate, GRE General Test, minimum GPA of 3.0. Additional exam requirements/recommendations for international students: Required—TOEFL (minimum score 550 paper-based; 80 iBT). *Application deadline:* For fall admission, 3/1 priority date for domestic and international students; for winter admission, 9/15 priority date for domestic and international students. Applications are processed on a rolling basis. Application fee: $55 ($75 for international students). Electronic applications accepted. *Financial support:* Fellowships, research assistantships, teaching assistantships, institutionally sponsored loans, traineeships, health care benefits, and unspecified assistantships available. Support available to part-time students. *Faculty research:* Logistics systems analysis and design, supply chain modeling, material flow design and improvement, intelligent systems. *Unit head:* Dr. Luis Occena, Department Chair, 573-882-9566, E-mail: occenal@missouri.edu. *Application contact:* Nicole Theberge, Administrative Associate I, 573-882-9540, E-mail: thebergen@missouri.edu.
Website: http://engineering.missouri.edu/imse/degree-programs/.

University of Nebraska–Lincoln, Graduate College, College of Engineering, Department of Industrial and Management Systems Engineering, Lincoln, NE 68588. Offers engineering management (M Eng); industrial and management systems engineering (MS, PhD); manufacturing systems engineering (MS). Postbaccalaureate distance learning degree programs offered. *Degree requirements:* For master's, thesis optional; for doctorate, comprehensive exam, thesis/dissertation. *Entrance requirements:* For master's and doctorate, GRE. Additional exam requirements/recommendations for international students: Required—TOEFL (minimum score 525 paper-based). Electronic applications accepted. *Faculty research:* Ergonomics, occupational safety, quality control, industrial packaging, facility design.

University of New Haven, Graduate School, Tagliatela College of Engineering, Program in Industrial Engineering, West Haven, CT 06516-1916. Offers industrial engineering (MSIE); lean/Six Sigma (Certificate); quality engineering (Certificate); MBA/MSIE. Part-time and evening/weekend programs available. *Degree requirements:* For master's, project. *Entrance requirements:* For master's, bachelor's degree in engineering. Additional exam requirements/recommendations for international students: Required—TOEFL (minimum score 75 iBT), IELTS, PTE (minimum score 50). Electronic applications accepted. Application fee is waived when completed online.

University of Oklahoma, Gallogly College of Engineering, School of Industrial and Systems Engineering, Norman, OK 73019. Offers MS, PhD. Part-time programs available. *Faculty:* 12 full-time (3 women). *Students:* 35 full-time (11 women), 27 part-time (6 women); includes 6 minority (2 Black or African American, non-Hispanic/Latino; 2 American Indian or Alaska Native, non-Hispanic/Latino; 1 Hispanic/Latino; 1 Two or more races, non-Hispanic/Latino), 40 international. Average age 28. 135 applicants, 39% accepted, 23 enrolled. In 2014, 13 master's awarded. *Degree requirements:* For master's, comprehensive exam (for some programs), thesis (for some programs); for doctorate, comprehensive exam, thesis/dissertation. *Entrance requirements:* For master's and doctorate, GRE. Additional exam requirements/recommendations for international students: Required—TOEFL (minimum score 79 iBT). *Application deadline:* For fall admission, 6/1 for domestic students, 4/1 for international students; for spring admission, 11/1 for domestic students, 9/1 for international students. Application fee: $50 ($100 for international students). Electronic applications accepted. *Expenses:* Tuition, state resident: full-time $4394; part-time $183.10 per credit hour. Tuition, nonresident: full-time $16,970; part-time $707.10 per credit hour. *Required fees:* $2892; $109.95 per credit hour. $126.50 per semester. *Financial support:* In 2014–15, 30 students received support, including 1 fellowship with full tuition reimbursement available (averaging $2,500 per year), 4 research assistantships with partial tuition reimbursements available (averaging $12,788 per year), 11 teaching assistantships with partial tuition reimbursements available (averaging $13,261 per year); unspecified assistantships also available. Financial award application deadline: 6/1; financial award applicants required to submit FAFSA. *Faculty research:* Human factors, design and manufacturing, logistics, supply chain management, optimization. *Total annual research expenditures:* $473,193. *Unit head:* Dr. Randa Shehab, Director and Professor, 405-325-3721, Fax: 405-325-7555, E-mail: rlshehab@ou.edu. *Application contact:* Jenn Covington, Student Services Coordinator, 405-325-3721, Fax: 405-325-7555, E-mail: jcovington@ou.edu.
Website: http://www.ou.edu/coe/ise.html.

University of Pittsburgh, Dietrich School of Arts and Sciences, Program in Computational Modeling and Simulation, Pittsburgh, PA 15260. Offers bioengineering (PhD); biological science (PhD); civil and environmental engineering (PhD); computer science (PhD); economics (PhD); industrial engineering (PhD); mathematics (PhD);

mechanical engineering and materials science (PhD); physics and astronomy (PhD); psychology (PhD); statistics (PhD). Part-time programs available. *Faculty:* 4 full-time (0 women). *Students:* 5 full-time (2 women), 1 part-time (0 women), 5 international. Average age 22. 14 applicants, 14% accepted, 2 enrolled. *Degree requirements:* For doctorate, comprehensive exam, thesis/dissertation, preliminary exam. *Entrance requirements:* For doctorate, GRE, statement of purpose, transcripts for all college-level institutions attended, three letters of reference. Additional exam requirements/recommendations for international students: Required—TOEFL (minimum score 90 iBT), IELTS (minimum score 7). *Application deadline:* For fall admission, 2/21 for domestic and international students. Applications are processed on a rolling basis. Application fee: $0 ($50 for international students). Electronic applications accepted. *Expenses:* Tuition, state resident: full-time $20,742; part-time $838 per credit. Tuition, nonresident: full-time $33,960; part-time $1389 per credit. *Required fees:* $800; $205 per term. Tuition and fees vary according to program. *Financial support:* In 2014–15, 5 students received support, including 3 fellowships with tuition reimbursements available (averaging $25,500 per year), 2 research assistantships with tuition reimbursements available (averaging $26,000 per year). *Unit head:* Kathleen Blee, Associate Dean, Graduate Studies and Research, 412-624-3939, Fax: 412-624-6855. *Application contact:* Dave R. Carmen, Administrative Secretary, 412-624-6094, Fax: 412-624-6855, E-mail: drc41@pitt.edu.
Website: http://cmsp.pitt.edu/.

University of Pittsburgh, Swanson School of Engineering, Department of Industrial Engineering, Pittsburgh, PA 15260. Offers MSIE, PhD. Part-time programs available. Postbaccalaureate distance learning degree programs offered. *Faculty:* 13 full-time (2 women), 11 part-time/adjunct (3 women). *Students:* 86 full-time (26 women), 27 part-time (8 women); includes 8 minority (2 Black or African American, non-Hispanic/Latino; 2 Asian, non-Hispanic/Latino; 3 Hispanic/Latino; 1 Two or more races, non-Hispanic/Latino), 81 international. 409 applicants, 33% accepted, 33 enrolled. In 2014, 54 master's, 4 doctorates awarded. Terminal master's awarded for partial completion of doctoral program. *Degree requirements:* For master's, thesis optional; for doctorate, comprehensive exam, thesis/dissertation, final oral exams. *Entrance requirements:* For master's and doctorate, GRE General Test, minimum GPA of 3.0. Additional exam requirements/recommendations for international students: Required—TOEFL (minimum score 550 paper-based; 80 iBT). *Application deadline:* For fall admission, 3/1 priority date for domestic and international students; for spring admission, 7/1 priority date for domestic and international students. Applications are processed on a rolling basis. Application fee: $50. Electronic applications accepted. *Expenses:* Tuition, state resident: full-time $20,742; part-time $838 per credit. Tuition, nonresident: full-time $33,960; part-time $1389 per credit. *Required fees:* $800; $205 per term. Tuition and fees vary according to program. *Financial support:* In 2014–15, 41 students received support, including 3 fellowships with full tuition reimbursements available (averaging $29,376 per year), 16 research assistantships with full tuition reimbursements available (averaging $26,484 per year), 22 teaching assistantships with full tuition reimbursements available (averaging $26,484 per year); scholarships/grants and tuition waivers (full and partial) also available. Financial award application deadline: 4/15. *Faculty research:* Operations research, engineering management, computational intelligence, manufacturing, information systems. *Total annual research expenditures:* $4.6 million. *Unit head:* Dr. Bopaya Bidanda, Chairman, 412-624-9830, Fax: 412-624-9831. *Application contact:* Dr. Jayant Rajgopal, Graduate Coordinator, 412-624-9840, Fax: 412-624-9831, E-mail: rajgopal@pitt.edu.

University of Puerto Rico, Mayagüez Campus, Graduate Studies, College of Engineering, Department of Industrial Engineering, Mayagüez, PR 00681-9000. Offers ME, MS. Part-time programs available. *Faculty:* 12 full-time (6 women), 3 part-time/adjunct (2 women). *Students:* 29 full-time (13 women), 9 part-time (4 women). 18 applicants, 94% accepted, 16 enrolled. In 2014, 7 master's awarded. *Degree requirements:* For master's, comprehensive exam, thesis, project. *Entrance requirements:* For master's, minimum GPA of 2.5; proficiency in English and Spanish; BS in engineering. Additional exam requirements/recommendations for international students: Required—TOEFL. *Application deadline:* For fall admission, 2/15 for domestic and international students; for spring admission, 9/15 for domestic and international students. Applications are processed on a rolling basis. Application fee: $25. *Expenses: Tuition, area resident:* Full-time $2466; part-time $822 per credit. *International tuition:* $6371 full-time. *Required fees:* $1095; $1095 per year. Tuition and fees vary according to course level, course load and reciprocity agreements. *Financial support:* In 2014–15, 24 students received support, including 13 research assistantships (averaging $6,826 per year), 17 teaching assistantships (averaging $4,262 per year); fellowships with full tuition reimbursements available, Federal Work-Study, institutionally sponsored loans, and unspecified assistantships also available. *Unit head:* Dr. Viviana Cesani, Chairperson, 787-265-3819, Fax: 787-265-3820, E-mail: viviana.cesani@upr.edu.
Website: http://ininweb.uprm.edu.

University of Regina, Faculty of Graduate Studies and Research, Faculty of Engineering and Applied Science, Program in Industrial Systems Engineering, Regina, SK S4S 0A2, Canada. Offers M Eng, MA Sc, PhD. Part-time programs available. *Faculty:* 39 full-time (7 women), 24 part-time/adjunct (0 women). *Students:* 47 full-time (14 women), 6 part-time (0 women). 126 applicants, 30% accepted. In 2014, 17 master's, 2 doctorates awarded. *Degree requirements:* For master's, thesis, project, report; for doctorate, thesis/dissertation. *Entrance requirements:* For doctorate, master's degree. Additional exam requirements/recommendations for international students: Required—TOEFL (minimum score 550 paper-based; 80 iBT), IELTS (minimum score 6.5), PTE (minimum score 59). *Application deadline:* For fall admission, 3/31 for domestic and international students; for winter admission, 7/31 for domestic and international students; for spring admission, 11/30 for domestic and international students. Application fee: $100. Electronic applications accepted. *Expenses:* Expenses: $2,588.85 per semester of full time study (M Eng); $1,633.35 (for MA Sc); $1,755.60 (for PhD). *Financial support:* In 2014–15, 7 fellowships (averaging $6,429 per year), 15 teaching assistantships (averaging $2,475 per year) were awarded; research assistantships, career-related internships or fieldwork, and scholarships/grants also available. Financial award application deadline: 6/15. *Faculty research:* Stochastic systems simulation, metallurgy of welding, computer-aided engineering, finite element method of engineering systems, manufacturing systems. *Unit head:* Dr. Raphael Idem, Associate Dean, Research and Graduate Studies, 306-337-2696, Fax: 306-585-4855, E-mail: raphael.idem@uregina.ca. *Application contact:* Dr. Rene Mayorga, Graduate Coordinator, 306-585-4726, Fax: 306-585-4822, E-mail: rene.mayorga@uregina.ca.
Website: http://www.uregina.ca/engineering/.

University of Southern California, Graduate School, Viterbi School of Engineering, Daniel J. Epstein Department of Industrial and Systems Engineering, Los Angeles, CA 90089. Offers digital supply chain management (MS); engineering management (MS); engineering technology communication (Graduate Certificate); health systems operations (Graduate Certificate); industrial and systems engineering (MS, PhD, Engr); manufacturing engineering (MS); operations research engineering (MS); optimization and supply chain management (Graduate Certificate); product development engineering (MS); safety systems and security (MS); systems architecting and engineering (MS, Graduate Certificate); systems safety and security (Graduate Certificate); transportation systems (Graduate Certificate); MS/MBA. Part-time and evening/weekend programs available. Postbaccalaureate distance learning degree programs offered (no on-campus study). Terminal master's awarded for partial completion of doctoral program. *Degree requirements:* For master's, thesis optional; for doctorate, thesis/dissertation. *Entrance requirements:* For master's and doctorate, GRE General Test. Additional exam requirements/recommendations for international students: Recommended—TOEFL. Electronic applications accepted. *Faculty research:* Health systems, music cognition and retrieval, transportation and logistics, manufacturing and automation, engineering systems design, risk and economic analysis.

University of South Florida, College of Engineering, Department of Industrial and Management Systems Engineering, Tampa, FL 33620-9951. Offers engineering management (MSEM); industrial engineering (MSIE, PhD); information technology (MSIT). Part-time programs available. Postbaccalaureate distance learning degree programs offered (minimal on-campus study). *Faculty:* 12 full-time (3 women). *Students:* 69 full-time (23 women), 83 part-time (19 women); includes 32 minority (6 Black or African American, non-Hispanic/Latino; 7 Asian, non-Hispanic/Latino; 16 Hispanic/Latino; 3 Two or more races, non-Hispanic/Latino), 60 international. Average age 30. 271 applicants, 45% accepted, 34 enrolled. In 2014, 71 master's, 6 doctorates awarded. Terminal master's awarded for partial completion of doctoral program. *Degree requirements:* For master's, comprehensive exam, thesis (for some programs); for doctorate, comprehensive exam, thesis/dissertation, 2 tools of research as specified by dissertation committee. *Entrance requirements:* For master's, GRE General Test, BS in engineering (or equivalent) with minimum GPA of 3.0 in last 60 hours of coursework, letter of recommendation, resume; for doctorate, GRE General Test, minimum GPA of 3.0 in last 60 hours of undergraduate/graduate coursework, three letters of recommendation, statement of purpose, strong background in scientific and engineering principles. Additional exam requirements/recommendations for international students: Required—TOEFL (minimum score 550 paper-based; 79 iBT) or IELTS (minimum score 6.5). *Application deadline:* For fall admission, 2/15 for domestic students, 1/2 for international students; for spring admission, 10/15 for domestic students, 6/1 for international students. Application fee: $30. Electronic applications accepted. *Financial support:* In 2014–15, 31 students received support, including 20 research assistantships with partial tuition reimbursements available (averaging $16,748 per year), 11 teaching assistantships with partial tuition reimbursements available (averaging $15,000 per year); tuition waivers (partial) also available. Financial award applicants required to submit FAFSA. *Faculty research:* Healthcare, healthcare systems, public health policies, energy and environment, manufacturing, logistics, transportation. *Total annual research expenditures:* $224,800. *Unit head:* Dr. Tapas K. Das, Professor and Department Chair, 813-974-5585, Fax: 813-974-5953, E-mail: das@usf.edu. *Application contact:* Dr. Alex Savachkin, Associate Professor and Graduate Director, 813-974-5577, Fax: 813-974-5953, E-mail: alexs@usf.edu.
Website: http://imse.eng.usf.edu.

University of South Florida, University College/Distance Education, Tampa, FL 33620-9951. *Unit head:* Kathy Barnes, Interdisciplinary Programs Coordinator, 813-974-8031, Fax: 813-974-7061, E-mail: barnesk@usf.edu. *Application contact:* Karen Tylinski, Metro Initiatives, 813-974-9943, Fax: 813-974-7061, E-mail: ktylinsk@usf.edu.
Website: http://www.usf.edu/innovative-education/.

The University of Tennessee, Graduate School, College of Engineering, Department of Industrial and Systems Engineering, Knoxville, TN 37966. Offers engineering management (MS); industrial engineering (MS, PhD); reliability and maintainability engineering (MS); MS/MBA. Part-time programs available. Postbaccalaureate distance learning degree programs offered (minimal on-campus study). *Faculty:* 12 full-time (2 women), 11 part-time/adjunct (1 woman). *Students:* 68 full-time (15 women), 58 part-time (12 women); includes 15 minority (6 Black or African American, non-Hispanic/Latino; 6 Asian, non-Hispanic/Latino; 1 Hispanic/Latino; 2 Two or more races, non-Hispanic/Latino), 40 international. Average age 37. 116 applicants, 63% accepted, 37 enrolled. In 2014, 55 master's, 4 doctorates awarded. *Degree requirements:* For master's, thesis or alternative; for doctorate, comprehensive exam, thesis/dissertation. *Entrance requirements:* For master's, GRE General Test (for MS students pursuing research thesis), minimum GPA of 2.7 (for U.S. degree holders), 3.0 (for international degree holders); for doctorate, GRE General Test (for all PhD candidates), minimum GPA of 3.0 on previous graduate course work. Additional exam requirements/recommendations for international students: Required—TOEFL (minimum score 550 paper-based). *Application deadline:* For fall admission, 2/1 priority date for domestic and international students; for spring admission, 6/15 for domestic and international students. Applications are processed on a rolling basis. Application fee: $35. Electronic applications accepted. *Financial support:* In 2014–15, 41 students received support, including 3 fellowships with full tuition reimbursements available (averaging $25,164 per year), 22 research assistantships with full tuition reimbursements available (averaging $18,763 per year), 13 teaching assistantships with full tuition reimbursements available (averaging $19,241 per year); career-related internships or fieldwork, Federal Work-Study, institutionally sponsored loans, health care benefits, and unspecified assistantships also available. Financial award application deadline: 2/1; financial award applicants required to submit FAFSA. *Faculty research:* Defense-oriented supply chain modeling; dependability and reliability of large computer networks; design of lean, reliable systems; new product development; operations research in the automotive industry. *Total annual research expenditures:* $1.4 million. *Unit head:* Dr. John Kobza, Department Head, 865-974-3333, Fax: 865-974-0588, E-mail: jkobza@utk.edu. *Application contact:* Dr. Alberto Garcia-Diaz, Professor, 865-974-7647, E-mail: agd@utk.edu.
Website: http://www.engr.utk.edu/ie/.

The University of Tennessee, The University of Tennessee Space Institute, Tullahoma, TN 37388. Offers aerospace engineering (MS, PhD); biomedical engineering (MS, PhD); engineering science (MS, PhD); industrial and systems engineering/engineering management (MS, PhD); mechanical engineering (MS, PhD); physics (MS, PhD). Part-time programs available. Postbaccalaureate distance learning degree programs offered. *Faculty:* 19 full-time (3 women), 4 part-time/adjunct. *Students:* 31 full-time (6 women), 82 part-time (11 women); includes 10 minority (6 Black or African American, non-Hispanic/Latino; 1 American Indian or Alaska Native, non-Hispanic/Latino; 2 Asian, non-Hispanic/Latino; 1 Hispanic/Latino), 11 international. 60 applicants, 55% accepted, 22 enrolled. In 2014, 25 master's, 5 doctorates awarded. Terminal master's awarded for partial completion of doctoral program. *Degree requirements:* For doctorate, one foreign language, thesis/dissertation. *Entrance requirements:* Additional exam requirements/recommendations for international students: Required—TOEFL (minimum score 550 paper-based; 80 iBT), IELTS (minimum score 6.5). *Application deadline:* For fall admission, 2/1 for international students; for spring admission, 6/15 for international students. Applications are processed on a rolling basis. Application fee: $60. Electronic applications accepted. *Financial support:* In 2014–15, 6 fellowships with full tuition reimbursements (averaging $2,451 per year), 24 research assistantships with full tuition reimbursements (averaging $20,244 per year) were awarded; career-related internships or fieldwork, Federal Work-Study, institutionally sponsored loans, health care benefits, and unspecified assistantships also available. *Faculty research:* Fluid mechanics/aerodynamics, chemical and electric propulsion and laser diagnostics,

computational mechanics and simulations, carbon fiber production and composite materials. *Total annual research expenditures:* $1.8 million. *Unit head:* Dr. Charles Johnson, Associate Executive Director, 931-393-7318, Fax: 931-393-7211, E-mail: cjohnson@utsi.edu. *Application contact:* Dee Merriman, Director, 931-393-7213, Fax: 931-393-7211, E-mail: dmerrima@utsi.edu.
Website: http://www.utsi.edu/.

The University of Tennessee at Chattanooga, Program in Engineering, Chattanooga, TN 37403. Offers chemical engineering (MS Engr); civil engineering (MS Engr); computational engineering (MS Engr); electrical engineering (MS Engr); industrial engineering (MS Engr); mechanical engineering (MS Engr). Part-time and evening/weekend programs available. *Faculty:* 20 full-time (3 women), 3 part-time/adjunct (0 women). *Students:* 42 full-time (7 women), 41 part-time (5 women); includes 6 minority (2 Black or African American, non-Hispanic/Latino; 1 Asian, non-Hispanic/Latino; 2 Hispanic/Latino; 1 Two or more races, non-Hispanic/Latino), 30 international. Average age 29. 96 applicants, 32% accepted, 17 enrolled. In 2014, 29 master's awarded. *Degree requirements:* For master's, comprehensive exam, thesis or alternative, engineering project. *Entrance requirements:* For master's, GRE General Test, minimum undergraduate GPA of 2.5 or 3.0 in last 30 hours of coursework. Additional exam requirements/recommendations for international students: Required—TOEFL (minimum score 550 paper-based; 79 iBT), IELTS (minimum score 6). *Application deadline:* For fall admission, 6/13 priority date for domestic students, 6/1 for international students; for spring admission, 10/15 priority date for domestic students, 10/1 for international students. Applications are processed on a rolling basis. Application fee: $30 ($35 for international students). Electronic applications accepted. *Expenses:* Tuition, state resident: full-time $7708; part-time $428 per credit hour. Tuition, nonresident: full-time $23,826; part-time $1323 per credit hour. *Required fees:* $1708; $252 per credit hour. *Financial support:* In 2014–15, 24 research assistantships with tuition reimbursements (averaging $7,669 per year), 7 teaching assistantships with tuition reimbursements (averaging $5,735 per year) were awarded; career-related internships or fieldwork, scholarships/grants, and unspecified assistantships also available. Support available to part-time students. *Faculty research:* Quality control and reliability engineering, financial management, thermal science, energy conservation, structural analysis. *Total annual research expenditures:* $1.6 million. *Unit head:* Dr. William Sutton, Dean, 423-425-2256, Fax: 423-425-5229, E-mail: will-sutton@utc.edu. *Application contact:* Dr. J. Randy Walker, Interim Dean of Graduate Studies, 423-425-4478, Fax: 423-425-5223, E-mail: randy-walker@utc.edu.
Website: http://www.utc.edu/Departments/engrcs/ms_engr.php.

The University of Texas at Arlington, Graduate School, College of Engineering, Department of Industrial and Manufacturing Systems Engineering, Arlington, TX 76019. Offers engineering management (MS); industrial engineering (MS, PhD); logistics (MS); systems engineering (MS). Part-time and evening/weekend programs available. Postbaccalaureate distance learning degree programs offered (no on-campus study). Terminal master's awarded for partial completion of doctoral program. *Degree requirements:* For master's, comprehensive exam, thesis optional; for doctorate, comprehensive exam, thesis/dissertation. *Entrance requirements:* For master's and doctorate, GRE General Test, minimum GPA of 3.0. Additional exam requirements/recommendations for international students: Required—TOEFL (minimum score 550 paper-based). *Faculty research:* Manufacturing, healthcare logistics, environmental systems, operations research, statistics.

The University of Texas at Austin, Graduate School, Cockrell School of Engineering, Department of Mechanical Engineering, Program in Operations Research and Industrial Engineering, Austin, TX 78712-1111. Offers MS, PhD. *Entrance requirements:* For master's and doctorate, GRE General Test. Additional exam requirements/recommendations for international students: Required—TOEFL.

The University of Texas at El Paso, Graduate School, College of Engineering, Department of Industrial Engineering, El Paso, TX 79968-0001. Offers industrial engineering (MS); manufacturing engineering (MS); systems engineering (MS, Certificate). Part-time and evening/weekend programs available. *Degree requirements:* For master's, thesis optional. *Entrance requirements:* For master's, GRE General Test, minimum GPA of 3.0 in major. Additional exam requirements/recommendations for international students: Required—TOEFL. Electronic applications accepted. *Faculty research:* Computer vision, automated inspection, simulation and modeling.

The University of Toledo, College of Graduate Studies, College of Engineering, Department of Mechanical, Industrial, and Manufacturing Engineering, Toledo, OH 43606-3390. Offers industrial engineering (MS, PhD); mechanical engineering (MS, PhD). Part-time programs available. Postbaccalaureate distance learning degree programs offered (minimal on-campus study). *Degree requirements:* For master's, thesis optional; for doctorate, thesis/dissertation, qualifying exam. *Entrance requirements:* For master's, GRE General Test, minimum GPA of 3.0; for doctorate, GRE General Test, minimum GPA of 3.3. Additional exam requirements/recommendations for international students: Required—TOEFL (minimum score 550 paper-based; 80 iBT). Electronic applications accepted. *Faculty research:* Computational and experimental thermal sciences, manufacturing process and systems, mechanics, materials, design, quality and management engineering systems.

University of Toronto, School of Graduate Studies, Faculty of Applied Science and Engineering, Department of Mechanical and Industrial Engineering, Toronto, ON M5S 2J7, Canada. Offers M Eng, MA Sc, PhD. Part-time programs available. *Degree requirements:* For master's, thesis (for some programs), oral exam/thesis defense (MA Sc); for doctorate, thesis/dissertation, thesis defense, qualifying examination. *Entrance requirements:* For master's, GRE (recommended), minimum B+ average in last 2 years of undergraduate study, 2 letters of reference, resume, Canadian citizenship or permanent residency (M Eng); for doctorate, GRE (recommended), minimum B+ average, 2 letters of reference, resume. Additional exam requirements/recommendations for international students: Required—TOEFL (minimum score 580 paper-based), Michigan English Language Assessment Battery (minimum score 85), IELTS (minimum score 7), or COPE (minimum score 4). Electronic applications accepted.

University of Washington, Graduate School, College of Engineering, Department of Industrial and Systems Engineering, Seattle, WA 98195-2650. Offers MISE, MS, PhD. Part-time programs available. Postbaccalaureate distance learning degree programs offered (no on-campus study). *Faculty:* 9 full-time (5 women). *Students:* 59 full-time (30 women), 35 part-time (10 women). Average age 28. 287 applicants, 41% accepted, 47 enrolled. In 2014, 11 master's, 4 doctorates awarded. Terminal master's awarded for partial completion of doctoral program. *Degree requirements:* For master's, thesis optional; for doctorate, comprehensive exam, thesis/dissertation, qualifying, general, and final exams. *Entrance requirements:* For master's, GRE General Test, minimum GPA of 3.0; bachelor's degree in engineering, math, or science; transcripts; letters of recommendation; resume; statement of objectives; for doctorate, GRE General Test, minimum GPA of 3.0; transcripts; letters of recommendation; resume; statement of objectives. Additional exam requirements/recommendations for international students: Required—TOEFL (minimum score 580 paper-based; 92 iBT); Recommended—IELTS (minimum score 7). *Application deadline:* For fall admission, 1/1 priority date for

domestic students, 1/1 for international students. Applications are processed on a rolling basis. Application fee: $85. Electronic applications accepted. *Expenses:* Expenses: Contact institution. *Financial support:* In 2014–15, 28 students received support, including 2 fellowships, 18 research assistantships with full tuition reimbursements available, 8 teaching assistantships with full tuition reimbursements available; career-related internships or fieldwork, scholarships/grants, traineeships, and tuition waivers (full) also available. Financial award application deadline: 2/1; financial award applicants required to submit FAFSA. *Faculty research:* Manufacturing, systems engineering and integration, optimization, human factors, virtual reality, quality and reliability, large-scale assembly, supply chain management, health systems engineering. *Total annual research expenditures:* $1.7 million. *Unit head:* Dr. Linda Ng Boyle, Professor/Chair, 206-543-1427, Fax: 206-685-3072, E-mail: linda@uw.edu. *Application contact:* Jennifer W. Tsai, Academic Counselor, 206-543-5041, Fax: 206-685-3072, E-mail: ieadvise@uw.edu.
Website: http://depts.washington.edu/ie/.

University of Windsor, Faculty of Graduate Studies, Faculty of Engineering, Department of Industrial and Manufacturing Systems Engineering, Windsor, ON N9B 3P4, Canada. Offers industrial engineering (M Eng, MA Sc); manufacturing systems engineering (PhD). Part-time programs available. *Degree requirements:* For master's, thesis; for doctorate, comprehensive exam, thesis/dissertation. *Entrance requirements:* For master's, minimum B average; for doctorate, master's degree, minimum B average. Additional exam requirements/recommendations for international students: Required—TOEFL (minimum score 560 paper-based). Electronic applications accepted. *Faculty research:* Human factors, operations research.

University of Wisconsin–Madison, Graduate School, College of Engineering, Department of Industrial and Systems Engineering, Madison, WI 53706. Offers MS, PhD. Part-time programs available. *Faculty:* 17 full-time (5 women), 18 part-time/adjunct (5 women). *Students:* 108 full-time (40 women), 14 part-time (5 women); includes 6 minority (2 Black or African American, non-Hispanic/Latino; 1 American Indian or Alaska Native, non-Hispanic/Latino; 3 Asian, non-Hispanic/Latino), 102 international. Average age 27. 505 applicants, 29% accepted, 53 enrolled. In 2014, 41 master's, 8 doctorates awarded. Terminal master's awarded for partial completion of doctoral program. *Degree requirements:* For master's, thesis optional; for doctorate, comprehensive exam, thesis/dissertation. *Entrance requirements:* For master's, GRE General Test, minimum GPA of 3.0, BS in engineering or equivalent, course work in computer programming and statistics; for doctorate, GRE General Test, minimum GPA of 3.0. Additional exam requirements/recommendations for international students: Required—IELTS (minimum score 6); Recommended—TOEFL (minimum score 550 paper-based; 80 iBT). *Application deadline:* For fall admission, 1/15 priority date for domestic and international students; for spring admission, 10/1 priority date for domestic and international students. Application fee: $56. Electronic applications accepted. *Expenses:* Tuition, state resident: full-time $10,723; part-time $745 per credit. Tuition, nonresident: full-time $24,054; part-time $1578 per credit. *Required fees:* $374 per semester. Tuition and fees vary according to course load, program and reciprocity agreements. *Financial support:* In 2014–15, 94 students received support, including 1 fellowship with full tuition reimbursement available (averaging $23,376 per year), 44 research assistantships with full tuition reimbursements available (averaging $41,616 per year), 30 teaching assistantships with full tuition reimbursements available (averaging $29,492 per year); career-related internships or fieldwork, Federal Work-Study, institutionally sponsored loans, scholarships/grants, traineeships, health care benefits, and unspecified assistantships also available. *Faculty research:* Human factors and ergonomics, manufacturing and production systems, health systems engineering, decision science/operations research, quality engineering. *Total annual research expenditures:* $11.5 million. *Unit head:* Dr. Vicki M. Bier, Chair, 608-262-2064, Fax: 608-262-8454, E-mail: bier@engr.wisc.edu. *Application contact:* Deidre Vincevineus, Graduate Admissions Coordinator, 608-265-1452, Fax: 608-890-2204, E-mail: vincevineus@wisc.edu.
Website: http://www.engr.wisc.edu/isye.html.

University of Wisconsin–Milwaukee, Graduate School, College of Engineering and Applied Science, Program in Engineering, Milwaukee, WI 53201-0413. Offers civil engineering (MS); electrical and computer engineering (MS); energy engineering (Certificate); engineering (PhD); engineering management (MS); engineering mechanics (MS); ergonomics (Certificate); industrial and management engineering (MS); manufacturing engineering (MS); materials engineering (MS); mechanical engineering (MS); MUP/MS. Part-time programs available. *Degree requirements:* For master's, comprehensive exam (for some programs), thesis or alternative; for doctorate, comprehensive exam, thesis/dissertation, internship. *Entrance requirements:* For master's, GRE, minimum GPA of 2.75; for doctorate, GRE, minimum GPA of 3.5. Additional exam requirements/recommendations for international students: Required—TOEFL (minimum score 550 paper-based; 79 iBT), IELTS (minimum score 6.5).

University of Wisconsin–Stout, Graduate School, College of Technology, Engineering, and Management, MS Program in Risk Control, Menomonie, WI 54751. Offers MS. Part-time programs available. *Degree requirements:* For master's, thesis. *Entrance requirements:* For master's, minimum GPA of 3.0. Additional exam requirements/recommendations for international students: Required—TOEFL (minimum score 500 paper-based; 61 iBT). Electronic applications accepted. *Faculty research:* Environmental microbiology, water supply safety, facilities planning, industrial ventilation, bioterrorist.

Virginia Polytechnic Institute and State University, Graduate School, College of Engineering, Blacksburg, VA 24061. Offers aerospace engineering (ME, MS, PhD); biological systems engineering (ME, MS, PhD); biomedical engineering (MS, PhD); chemical engineering (ME, MS, PhD); civil engineering (ME, MS, PhD); computer engineering (ME, MS, PhD); computer science (MS, PhD); electrical engineering (ME, PhD); engineering education (PhD); engineering mechanics (ME, MS, PhD); environmental engineering (MS); environmental science and engineering (MS); industrial and systems engineering (ME, MS, PhD); materials science and engineering (ME, MS, PhD); mechanical engineering (ME, MS, PhD); mining and minerals engineering (PhD); mining engineering (ME, MS); nuclear engineering (MS, PhD); ocean engineering (MS); systems engineering (ME, MS). *Accreditation:* ABET (one or more programs are accredited). *Faculty:* 356 full-time (60 women), 3 part-time/adjunct (1 woman). *Students:* 1,700 full-time (398 women), 345 part-time (58 women); includes 213 minority (43 Black or African American, non-Hispanic/Latino; 1 American Indian or Alaska Native, non-Hispanic/Latino; 87 Asian, non-Hispanic/Latino; 58 Hispanic/Latino; 1 Native Hawaiian or other Pacific Islander, non-Hispanic/Latino; 23 Two or more races, non-Hispanic/Latino), 1,079 international. Average age 27. 5,228 applicants, 18% accepted, 471 enrolled. In 2014, 438 master's, 211 doctorates awarded. *Degree requirements:* For master's, comprehensive exam (for some programs), thesis (for some programs); for doctorate, comprehensive exam (for some programs), thesis/dissertation (for some programs). *Entrance requirements:* For master's and doctorate, GRE/GMAT (may vary by department). Additional exam requirements/recommendations for international students: Required—TOEFL (minimum score 550 paper-based). *Application deadline:* For fall admission, 8/1 for domestic students, 4/1 for international students; for spring admission, 1/1 for domestic students, 9/1 for international students. Applications are processed on a rolling basis. Application fee: $75. Electronic

applications accepted. *Expenses:* Tuition, state resident: full-time $11,656; part-time $647.50 per credit hour. Tuition, nonresident: full-time $23,351; part-time $1297.25 per credit hour. *Required fees:* $2533; $465.75 per semester. Tuition and fees vary according to course load, campus/location and program. *Financial support:* In 2014–15, 148 fellowships with full tuition reimbursements (averaging $8,031 per year), 855 research assistantships with full tuition reimbursements (averaging $22,855 per year), 288 teaching assistantships with full tuition reimbursements (averaging $20,291 per year) were awarded. Financial award application deadline: 3/1; financial award applicants required to submit FAFSA. *Total annual research expenditures:* $90.5 million. *Unit head:* Dr. Richard C. Benson, Dean, 540-231-9752, Fax: 540-231-3031, E-mail: deaneng@vt.edu. *Application contact:* Linda Perkins, Executive Assistant, 540-231-9752, Fax: 540-231-3031, E-mail: lperkins@vt.edu.
Website: http://www.eng.vt.edu/.

Virginia Polytechnic Institute and State University, VT Online, Blacksburg, VA 24061. Offers advanced transportation systems (Certificate); aerospace engineering (MS); agricultural and life sciences (MSLFS); business information systems (Graduate Certificate); career and technical education (MS); civil engineering (MS); computer engineering (M Eng, MS); decision support systems (Graduate Certificate); eLearning leadership (MA); electrical engineering (M Eng, MS); engineering administration (MEA); environmental engineering (Certificate); environmental politics and policy (Graduate Certificate); environmental sciences and engineering (MS); foundations of political analysis (Graduate Certificate); health product risk management (Graduate Certificate); industrial and systems engineering (MS); information policy and society (Graduate Certificate); information security (Graduate Certificate); information technology (MIT); instructional technology (MA); integrative STEM education (MA Ed); liberal arts (Graduate Certificate); life sciences: health product risk management (MS); natural resources (MNR, Graduate Certificate); networking (Graduate Certificate); nonprofit and nongovernmental organization management (Graduate Certificate); ocean engineering (MS); political science (MA); security studies (Graduate Certificate); software development (Graduate Certificate). *Expenses:* Tuition, state resident: full-time $11,656; part-time $647.50 per credit hour. Tuition, nonresident: full-time $23,351; part-time $1297.25 per credit hour. *Required fees:* $2533; $465.75 per semester. Tuition and fees vary according to course load, campus/location and program.

Wayne State University, College of Engineering, Department of Industrial and Systems Engineering, Program in Industrial Engineering, Detroit, MI 48202. Offers MS, PhD. *Students:* 136 full-time (15 women), 52 part-time (13 women); includes 16 minority (7 Black or African American, non-Hispanic/Latino; 6 Asian, non-Hispanic/Latino; 3 Two or more races, non-Hispanic/Latino), 133 international. Average age 28. 455 applicants, 61% accepted, 72 enrolled. In 2014, 24 master's, 6 doctorates awarded. *Degree requirements:* For master's, thesis optional; for doctorate, thesis/dissertation, preliminary exam, written and oral exam, oral dissertation defense. *Entrance requirements:* For master's, baccalaureate degree in engineering from an ABET-accredited institution, minimum undergraduate upper-division GPA of 2.8; for doctorate, GRE, minimum GPA of 3.5 in MS in industrial engineering or operations research; undergraduate major or specialized work in the proposed doctoral major field. Additional exam requirements/recommendations for international students: Required—TOEFL (minimum score 550 paper-based; 79 iBT), TWE (minimum score 5.5), Michigan English Language Assessment Battery (minimum score 85); Recommended—IELTS (minimum score 6.5). *Application deadline:* For fall admission, 6/1 priority date for domestic students, 5/1 priority date for international students; for winter admission, 10/1 priority date for domestic students, 9/1 priority date for international students; for spring admission, 2/1 priority date for domestic students, 1/1 priority date for international students. Applications are processed on a rolling basis. Application fee: $0. Electronic applications accepted. *Expenses:* Expenses: Contact institution. *Financial support:* In 2014–15, 52 students received support. Fellowships with tuition reimbursements available, research assistantships with tuition reimbursements available, teaching assistantships with tuition reimbursements available, scholarships/grants, health care benefits, and unspecified assistantships available. Support available to part-time students. Financial award application deadline: 3/31; financial award applicants required to submit FAFSA. *Faculty research:* Healthcare systems engineering, product design and development, quality and reliability engineering, supply chain management and logistics. *Unit head:* Dr. Leslie Monplaisir, Associate Professor/Chair, 313-577-1645, Fax: 313-577-8833, E-mail: ad5365@wayne.edu. *Application contact:* Dr. Kyoung-Yun Kim, Associate Professor and MS Program Officer, 313-577-4396, Fax: 313-577-8833, E-mail: kykim@eng.wayne.edu.
Website: http://engineering.wayne.edu/ise/.

Western Carolina University, Graduate School, Kimmel School of Construction Management and Technology, Department of Engineering and Technology, Cullowhee, NC 28723. Offers MS. Part-time programs available. *Degree requirements:* For master's, comprehensive exam. *Entrance requirements:* For master's, GRE, appropriate undergraduate degree with minimum GPA of 3.0, 3 letters of recommendation. Additional exam requirements/recommendations for international students: Required—TOEFL (minimum score 550 paper-based; 79 iBT). *Faculty research:* Electrophysiology, 3D graphics, digital signal processing, CAM and advanced machining, fluid power, polymer science, wireless communication.

Western Michigan University, Graduate College, College of Engineering and Applied Sciences, Department of Industrial and Entrepreneurial Engineering and Engineering Management, Kalamazoo, MI 49008. Offers engineering management (MS); industrial engineering (MSE, PhD). *Degree requirements:* For master's, thesis optional. *Application deadline:* For fall admission, 2/15 for domestic students. *Financial support:* Application deadline: 2/15. *Application contact:* Admissions and Orientation, 269-387-2000, Fax: 269-387-2096.

West Virginia University, College of Engineering and Mineral Resources, Department of Industrial and Management Systems Engineering, Program in Industrial Engineering, Morgantown, WV 26506. Offers engineering (MSE); industrial engineering (MSIE, PhD). Part-time programs available. *Degree requirements:* For master's, thesis or alternative; for doctorate, comprehensive exam, thesis/dissertation. *Entrance requirements:* For master's, GRE General Test, minimum GPA of 3.0 Regular; 2.75 Provisional; for doctorate, GRE General Test, minimum GPA of 3.5. Additional exam requirements/recommendations for international students: Required—TOEFL (minimum score 550 paper-based; 80 iBT). Electronic applications accepted. *Faculty research:* Production planning and control, quality control, robotics and CIMS, ergonomics, castings.

Wichita State University, Graduate School, College of Engineering, Department of Industrial and Manufacturing Engineering, Wichita, KS 67260. Offers engineering management (MEM); industrial engineering (MS, PhD). Part-time programs available. In 2014, 37 master's, 3 doctorates awarded. *Entrance requirements:* Additional exam requirements/recommendations for international students: Required—TOEFL. *Financial support:* Teaching assistantships available. *Unit head:* Dr. Krishna Krishnan, Chair, 316-978-3425, Fax: 316-978-3742, E-mail: krishna.krishnan@wichita.edu. *Application contact:* Jordan Oleson, Admissions Coordinator, 316-978-3095, Fax: 316-978-3253, E-mail: jordan.oleson@wichita.edu.
Website: http://www.wichita.edu/ime.

Youngstown State University, Graduate School, College of Science, Technology, Engineering and Mathematics, Department of Industrial and Systems Engineering, Youngstown, OH 44555-0001. Offers MSE.

Manufacturing Engineering

American University of Armenia, Graduate Programs, Yerevan, Armenia. Offers business administration (MBA); computer and information science (MS), including business management, design and manufacturing, energy (ME, MS), industrial engineering and systems management; economics (MS); industrial engineering and systems management (ME), including business, computer aided design/manufacturing, energy (ME, MS), information technology; law (LL M); political science and international affairs (MPSIA); public health (MPH); teaching English as a foreign language (MA). Part-time and evening/weekend programs available. *Degree requirements:* For master's, thesis (for some programs), capstone/project. *Entrance requirements:* For master's, GRE, GMAT, or LSAT. Additional exam requirements/recommendations for international students: Recommended—TOEFL (minimum score 79 iBT), IELTS (minimum score 6.5). *Faculty research:* Microfinance, finance (rural/development, international, corporate), firm life cycle theory, TESOL, language proficiency testing, public policy, administrative law, economic development, cryptography, artificial intelligence, energy efficiency/renewable energy, computer-aided design/manufacturing, health financing, tuberculosis control, mother/child health, preventive ophthalmology, post-earthquake psychopathological investigations, tobacco control, environmental health risk assessments.

Arizona State University at the Tempe campus, Ira A. Fulton Schools of Engineering, The Polytechnic School, Program in Engineering Technology, Mesa, AZ 85212. Offers manufacturing engineering technology (MS). Part-time and evening/weekend programs available. *Degree requirements:* For master's, thesis or applied project and oral defense, final examination, interactive Program of Study (iPOS) submitted before completing 50 percent of required credit hours. *Entrance requirements:* For master's, bachelor's degree with minimum of 30 credit hours or equivalent in a technology area including course work applicable to the concentration being sought and minimum of 16 credit hours of math and science; industrial experience beyond bachelor's degree (recommended). Additional exam requirements/recommendations for international students: Required—TOEFL, IELTS, or PTE. Electronic applications accepted. *Faculty research:* Manufacturing modeling and simulation &ITsmart&RO and composite materials, optimization of turbine engines, machinability and manufacturing processes design, fuel cells and other alternative energy sources.

Boston University, College of Engineering, Department of Mechanical Engineering, Boston, MA 02215. Offers manufacturing engineering (MS); mechanical engineering (MS, PhD); mechanical engineering with engineering practice (MS); MS/MBA. Part-time programs available. Postbaccalaureate distance learning degree programs offered (no on-campus study). *Faculty:* 38 full-time (5 women), 1 part-time/adjunct (0 women). *Students:* 129 full-time (22 women), 22 part-time (4 women); includes 15 minority (1 Black or African American, non-Hispanic/Latino; 8 Asian, non-Hispanic/Latino; 5 Hispanic/Latino; 1 Two or more races, non-Hispanic/Latino), 56 international. Average age 26. 502 applicants, 34% accepted, 73 enrolled. In 2014, 44 master's, 10 doctorates awarded. Terminal master's awarded for partial completion of doctoral program. *Degree requirements:* For master's, thesis (for some programs); for doctorate, comprehensive exam, thesis/dissertation. *Entrance requirements:* For master's and doctorate, GRE General Test. Additional exam requirements/recommendations for international students: Required—TOEFL (minimum score 550 paper-based; 84 iBT), IELTS (minimum score 7). *Application deadline:* For fall admission, 3/15 for domestic and international students; for spring admission, 10/1 for domestic and international students. Application fee: $80. Electronic applications accepted. *Expenses: Tuition:* Full-time $45,686; part-time $1428 per credit hour. *Required fees:* $660; $60 per semester. Tuition and fees vary according to program. *Financial support:* In 2014–15, 50 students received support, including 13 fellowships with full tuition reimbursements available (averaging $28,950 per year), 41 research assistantships with full tuition reimbursements available (averaging $19,300 per year), 19 teaching assistantships with full tuition reimbursements available (averaging $19,300 per year); career-related internships or fieldwork, Federal Work-Study, scholarships/grants, and tuition waivers (partial) also available. Financial award application deadline: 1/15; financial award applicants required to submit FAFSA. *Faculty research:* Acoustics, ultrasound, and vibrations; biomechanics; dynamics, control, and robotics; energy and thermofluid sciences; MEMS and nanotechnology. *Total annual research expenditures:* $11 million. *Unit head:* Dr. Alice White, Chairperson, 617-353-2814, Fax: 617-353-5866, E-mail: aew1@bu.edu. *Application contact:* Dr. Solomon Eisenberg, Senior Associate Dean of Academic Programs, 617-353-9760, Fax: 617-353-0259, E-mail: enggrad@bu.edu.
Website: http://www.bu.edu/me/.

Bowling Green State University, Graduate College, College of Technology, Department of Technology Systems, Bowling Green, OH 43403. Offers construction management (MIT); manufacturing technology (MIT). Part-time programs available. *Degree requirements:* For master's, thesis or alternative. *Entrance requirements:* For master's, GRE General Test. Additional exam requirements/recommendations for international students: Required—TOEFL. Electronic applications accepted.

Bradley University, Graduate School, College of Engineering and Technology, Department of Industrial and Manufacturing Engineering and Technology, Peoria, IL 61625-0002. Offers industrial engineering (MS); manufacturing engineering (MS). Part-time and evening/weekend programs available. *Faculty:* 10 full-time (1 woman). *Students:* 18 full-time (4 women), 25 part-time (5 women); includes 1 minority (Black or African American, non-Hispanic/Latino), 35 international. 103 applicants, 30% accepted, 19 enrolled. In 2014, 10 master's awarded. *Degree requirements:* For master's, comprehensive exam, project. *Entrance requirements:* Additional exam requirements/recommendations for international students: Required—TOEFL (minimum score 550 paper-based; 79 iBT), IELTS (minimum score 6.5). *Application deadline:* For fall admission, 5/15 priority date for domestic and international students; for spring admission, 10/15 priority date for domestic and international students. Applications are processed on a rolling basis. Application fee: $40 ($50 for international students). Electronic applications accepted. *Expenses: Tuition:* Full-time $14,580; part-time $810 per credit. *Required fees:* $224. Full-time tuition and fees vary according to course load. *Financial support:* In 2014–15, 6 research assistantships with full and partial tuition reimbursements (averaging $10,130 per year) were awarded; scholarships/grants, tuition waivers (partial), and unspecified assistantships also available. Support available to part-time students. Financial award application deadline: 4/1. *Unit head:* Dr. Joseph Chen, Department Chair, 309-677-2740, E-mail: jchen@bradley.edu. *Application contact:* Kayla Carroll, Director of International Admission and Student Services, 309-677-2375, E-mail: klcarroll@fsmail.bradley.edu.

California State University, Northridge, Graduate Studies, College of Engineering and Computer Science, Department of Manufacturing Systems Engineering and Management, Northridge, CA 91330. Offers engineering automation (MS); engineering management (MS); manufacturing systems engineering (MS); materials engineering (MS). Postbaccalaureate distance learning degree programs offered. *Students:* 180 full-time (38 women), 56 part-time (15 women); includes 24 minority (11 Asian, non-Hispanic/Latino; 8 Hispanic/Latino; 5 Two or more races, non-Hispanic/Latino), 172 international. Average age 26. *Entrance requirements:* For master's, GRE (if cumulative undergraduate GPA less than 3.0). *Application deadline:* For fall admission, 3/30 for domestic students; for spring admission, 9/30 for domestic students. Application fee: $55. *Expenses: Required fees:* $12,402. *Unit head:* Kang Chang, Acting Chair, 818-677-2167.

Website: http://www.csun.edu/~msem/.

Clemson University, Graduate School, College of Agriculture, Forestry and Life Sciences, Department of Food, Nutrition and Packaging Sciences, Program of Packaging Science, Clemson, SC 29634. Offers MS. *Faculty:* 7 full-time (2 women), 1 part-time/adjunct (0 women). *Students:* 10 full-time (3 women), 5 part-time (1 woman); includes 2 minority (1 Black or African American, non-Hispanic/Latino; 1 Two or more races, non-Hispanic/Latino). Average age 25. 18 applicants, 28% accepted, 5 enrolled. In 2014, 2 master's awarded. *Entrance requirements:* For master's, GRE General Test. *Application deadline:* For fall admission, 4/15 for international students; for spring admission, 9/15 for international students. Applications are processed on a rolling basis. Application fee: $70 ($80 for international students). Electronic applications accepted. *Expenses:* Expenses: Contact institution. *Financial support:* In 2014–15, 8 students received support, including 4 research assistantships with partial tuition reimbursements available (averaging $12,021 per year), 4 teaching assistantships with partial tuition reimbursements available (averaging $18,667 per year); fellowships with full and partial tuition reimbursements available, career-related internships or fieldwork, institutionally sponsored loans, scholarships/grants, health care benefits, and unspecified assistantships also available. Support available to part-time students. *Total annual research expenditures:* $143,855. *Unit head:* Dr. Anthony Pometto, III, Department Chair, 864-656-4382, Fax: 864-656-0331, E-mail: pometto@clemson.edu. *Application contact:* Dr. Ron Thomas, Coordinator, 864-656-5697, Fax: 864-656-4395, E-mail: rthms@clemson.edu.

Website: http://www.clemson.edu/cafls/departments/fnps/graduate/pkg_sci_ms.html.

Cornell University, Graduate School, Graduate Fields of Engineering, Field of Operations Research and Information Engineering, Ithaca, NY 14853. Offers applied probability and statistics (PhD); manufacturing systems engineering (PhD); mathematical programming (PhD); operations research and industrial engineering (M Eng). *Degree requirements:* For doctorate, comprehensive exam, thesis/dissertation. *Entrance requirements:* For master's and doctorate, GRE General Test, 3 letters of recommendation. Additional exam requirements/recommendations for international students: Required—TOEFL (minimum score 600 paper-based; 100 iBT). Electronic applications accepted. *Faculty research:* Mathematical programming and combinatorial optimization, statistics, stochastic processes, mathematical finance, simulation, manufacturing, e-commerce.

Eastern Kentucky University, The Graduate School, College of Business and Technology, Department of Technology, Richmond, KY 40475-3102. Offers industrial education (MS), including occupational training and development, technical administration, technology education; industrial technology (MS). Part-time and evening/weekend programs available. *Entrance requirements:* For master's, GRE General Test, minimum GPA of 2.5. *Faculty research:* Lunar excavation, computer networking, integrating academic and vocational education.

East Tennessee State University, School of Graduate Studies, College of Business and Technology, Department of Engineering Technology, Surveying and Digital Media, Johnson City, TN 37614. Offers MS, Postbaccalaureate Certificate. Part-time programs available. *Faculty:* 17 full-time (3 women). *Students:* 18 full-time (2 women), 10 part-time (2 women); includes 1 minority (Black or African American, non-Hispanic/Latino), 8 international. Average age 32. 51 applicants, 41% accepted, 12 enrolled. In 2014, 14 master's awarded. *Degree requirements:* For master's, comprehensive exam, thesis optional, capstone. *Entrance requirements:* For master's, bachelor's degree in technical or related area, minimum GPA of 3.0; for Postbaccalaureate Certificate, minimum GPA of 2.5, three letters of recommendation. Additional exam requirements/recommendations for international students: Required—TOEFL (minimum score 550 paper-based; 79 iBT). *Application deadline:* For fall admission, 6/1 for domestic students, 4/30 for international students; for spring admission, 11/1 for domestic students, 9/30 for international students. Application fee: $35 ($45 for international students). Electronic applications accepted. *Financial support:* In 2014–15, 16 students received support, including 14 research assistantships with full tuition reimbursements available (averaging $6,000 per year); career-related internships or fieldwork, institutionally sponsored loans, scholarships/grants, and unspecified assistantships also available. Financial award application deadline: 7/1; financial award applicants required to submit FAFSA. *Faculty research:* Computer-integrated manufacturing, alternative energy, sustainability, CAD/CAM, organizational change. *Unit head:* Dr. Keith V. Johnson, Chair, 423-439-7822, Fax: 423-439-7750, E-mail: johnsonk@etsu.edu. *Application contact:* Kimberly Brockman, Graduate Specialist, 423-439-6165, Fax: 423-439-5624, E-mail: brockmank@etsu.edu.

Website: http://applieddesign.etsu.edu/.

Fairfield University, School of Engineering, Fairfield, CT 06824. Offers automated manufacturing (CAS); database management (CAS); electrical and computer engineering (MS); information security (CAS); management of technology (MS); mechanical engineering (MS); network technology (CAS); software engineering (MS); Web application development (CAS). Part-time and evening/weekend programs available. *Faculty:* 4 full-time (1 woman), 18 part-time/adjunct (5 women). *Students:* 193 full-time (50 women), 69 part-time (11 women); includes 20 minority (4 Black or African American, non-Hispanic/Latino; 6 Asian, non-Hispanic/Latino; 10 Hispanic/Latino), 199 international. Average age 27. 516 applicants, 64% accepted, 124 enrolled. In 2014, 38 master's awarded. *Degree requirements:* For master's, thesis, capstone course. *Entrance requirements:* For master's, interview, minimum GPA of 2.8, resume, 2 recommendations. Additional exam requirements/recommendations for international students: Required—TOEFL (minimum score 550 paper-based; 80 iBT) or IELTS (minimum score 6.5). *Application deadline:* For fall admission, 5/15 for international

students; for spring admission, 10/15 for international students. Applications are processed on a rolling basis. Application fee: $60. Electronic applications accepted. *Expenses:* Expenses: $750 per credit hour. *Financial support:* In 2014–15, 30 students received support. Scholarships/grants and unspecified assistantships available. Financial award applicants required to submit FAFSA. *Faculty research:* Ocean dynamics modeling, thermo fluids, Web/mobile software applications, microwaves/electromagnetics, micro/nano manufacturing. *Unit head:* Dr. Bruce Berdanier, Dean, 203-254-4147, Fax: 203-254-4013, E-mail: bberdanier@fairfield.edu. *Application contact:* Marianne Gumpper, Director of Graduate and Continuing Studies Admission, 203-254-4184, Fax: 203-254-4073, E-mail: gradadmis@fairfield.edu.

Website: http://www.fairfield.edu/academics/schoolscollegescenters/schoolofengineering/graduateprograms/.

Florida State University, The Graduate School, FAMU-FSU College of Engineering, Department of Industrial and Manufacturing Engineering, Tallahassee, FL 32310. Offers industrial engineering (MS, PhD). *Degree requirements:* For master's, thesis, proposal presentation, progress presentation, defense presentation; for doctorate, thesis/dissertation, preliminary exam, proposal exam, defense exam. *Entrance requirements:* For master's, GRE General Test (minimum new score of 146 Verbal and 155 Quantitative), minimum GPA of 3.0; for doctorate, GRE General Test (minimum new score of 146 Verbal and 155 Quantitative), minimum GPA of 3.0 (without MS in industrial engineering), 3.4 (with MS in industrial engineering). Additional exam requirements/recommendations for international students: Required—TOEFL (minimum score 550 paper-based; 80 iBT); Recommended—IELTS (minimum score 6.5). Electronic applications accepted. *Expenses:* Tuition, state resident: part-time $403.51 per credit hour. Tuition, nonresident: part-time $1004.85 per credit hour. *Required fees:* $75.81 per credit hour. One-time fee: $20 part-time. Tuition and fees vary according to campus/location. *Faculty research:* Precision manufacturing, composite manufacturing, green manufacturing, applied optimization, simulation.

Georgia Southern University, Jack N. Averitt College of Graduate Studies, Allen E. Paulson College of Engineering and Information Technology, Department of Mechanical Engineering, Program in Engineering and Manufacturing Management, Statesboro, GA 30460. Offers Graduate Certificate. *Students:* 1 full-time (0 women), 2 part-time (1 woman); all minorities (all Hispanic/Latino). Average age 53. *Entrance requirements:* Additional exam requirements/recommendations for international students: Required—TOEFL (minimum score 80 iBT). *Application deadline:* For fall admission, 3/1 priority date for domestic students. Application fee: $50. *Expenses:* Tuition, state resident: full-time $7236; part-time $277 per semester hour. Tuition, nonresident: full-time $27,118; part-time $1105 per semester hour. *Required fees:* $2092. *Financial support:* Research assistantships, teaching assistantships, Federal Work-Study, scholarships/grants, and tuition waivers available. *Unit head:* Dr. Mohammad S. Davoud, Chair, 912-478-0540, Fax: 912-478-1455, E-mail: mdavoud@georgiasouthern.edu.

Grand Valley State University, Padnos College of Engineering and Computing, School of Engineering, Allendale, MI 49401-9403. Offers electrical and computer engineering (MSE); manufacturing operations (MSE); mechanical engineering (MSE); product design and manufacturing engineering (MSE). Part-time and evening/weekend programs available. *Faculty:* 15 full-time (2 women). *Students:* 29 full-time (6 women), 30 part-time (5 women); includes 4 minority (1 Asian, non-Hispanic/Latino; 3 Hispanic/Latino), 23 international. Average age 28. 66 applicants, 73% accepted, 23 enrolled. In 2014, 14 master's awarded. *Degree requirements:* For master's, project or thesis. *Entrance requirements:* For master's, engineering degree, minimum GPA of 3.0. Additional exam requirements/recommendations for international students: Required—TOEFL. *Application deadline:* Applications are processed on a rolling basis. Application fee: $30. Electronic applications accepted. *Expenses:* Tuition, state resident: full-time $10,602; part-time $589 per credit hour. Tuition, nonresident: full-time $14,022; part-time $779 per credit hour. Tuition and fees vary according to degree level and program. *Financial support:* In 2014–15, 31 students received support, including 10 fellowships (averaging $3,049 per year), 25 research assistantships with full tuition reimbursements available (averaging $10,237 per year); career-related internships or fieldwork, Federal Work-Study, institutionally sponsored loans, scholarships/grants, and unspecified assistantships also available. *Faculty research:* Digital signal processing, computer aided design, computer aided manufacturing, manufacturing simulation, biomechanics, product design. *Total annual research expenditures:* $300,000. *Unit head:* Dr. Charles Standridge, Acting Director, 616-331-6750, Fax: 616-331-7215, E-mail: standric@gvsu.edu. *Application contact:* Dr. Pranod Chaphalkar, Graduate Director, 616-331-6843, Fax: 616-331-7215, E-mail: chaphalp@gvsu.edu.

Website: http://www.engineer.gvsu.edu/.

Illinois Institute of Technology, Graduate College, Armour College of Engineering, Department of Mechanical, Materials and Aerospace Engineering, Chicago, IL 60616. Offers manufacturing engineering (MAS, MS); materials science and engineering (MAS, MS, PhD); mechanical and aerospace engineering (MAS, MS, PhD), including economics (MS), energy (MS), environment (MS). Part-time and evening/weekend programs available. Postbaccalaureate distance learning degree programs offered (minimal on-campus study). *Faculty:* 29 full-time (3 women), 10 part-time/adjunct (2 women). *Students:* 187 full-time (35 women), 27 part-time (3 women); includes 8 minority (2 Black or African American, non-Hispanic/Latino; 4 Asian, non-Hispanic/Latino; 2 Hispanic/Latino), 168 international. Average age 26. 1,562 applicants, 31% accepted, 76 enrolled. In 2014, 74 master's, 7 doctorates awarded. Terminal master's awarded for partial completion of doctoral program. *Degree requirements:* For master's, comprehensive exam (for some programs), thesis (for some programs); for doctorate, comprehensive exam, thesis/dissertation. *Entrance requirements:* For master's and doctorate, GRE General Test (minimum score 1000 Quantitative and Verbal, 3.0 Analytical Writing), minimum undergraduate GPA of 3.0. Additional exam requirements/recommendations for international students: Required—TOEFL (minimum score 550 paper-based; 80 iBT). *Application deadline:* For fall admission, 5/1 for domestic and international students; for spring admission, 10/15 for domestic and international students. Applications are processed on a rolling basis. Application fee: $50. Electronic applications accepted. *Expenses: Tuition:* Full-time $22,500; part-time $1250 per credit hour. *Required fees:* $30 per course. $260 per semester. One-time fee: $235. Tuition and fees vary according to course load and program. *Financial support:* Fellowships with full and partial tuition reimbursements, research assistantships with full and partial tuition reimbursements, teaching assistantships with full and partial tuition reimbursements, Federal Work-Study, institutionally sponsored loans, scholarships/grants, health care benefits, tuition waivers, and unspecified assistantships available. Support available to part-time students. Financial award applicants required to submit FAFSA. *Faculty research:* Fluid dynamics, metallurgical and materials engineering, solids and structures, computational mechanics, computer added design and manufacturing, thermal sciences, dynamic analysis and control of complex systems. *Unit head:* Dr. Keith Bowman, Chair of the Department of Mechanical, Materials and Aerospace Engineering & Duchossois Leadership Professor of Materials Engineering, 312-567-3175, Fax: 312-567-7230, E-mail: keith.bowman@iit.edu. *Application contact:* Rishab Malhotra, Director, Graduate Admission, 866-472-3448, Fax: 312-567-3138, E-mail: inquiry.grad@iit.edu.

Website: http://www.mmae.iit.edu.

Manufacturing Engineering

Instituto Tecnológico y de Estudios Superiores de Monterrey, Campus Monterrey, Graduate and Research Division, Programs in Engineering, Monterrey, Mexico. Offers applied statistics (M Eng); artificial intelligence (PhD); automation engineering (M Eng); chemical engineering (M Eng); civil engineering (M Eng); electrical engineering (M Eng); electronic engineering (M Eng); environmental engineering (M Eng); industrial engineering (M Eng, PhD); manufacturing engineering (M Eng); mechanical engineering (M Eng); systems and quality engineering (M Eng). M Eng program offered jointly with University of Waterloo; PhD in industrial engineering with Texas A&M University. Part-time and evening/weekend programs available. Terminal master's awarded for partial completion of doctoral program. *Degree requirements:* For master's, one foreign language, thesis; for doctorate, one foreign language, thesis/dissertation. *Entrance requirements:* For master's, EXADEP; for doctorate, GRE, master's degree in related field. Additional exam requirements/recommendations for international students: Required—TOEFL. *Faculty research:* Flexible manufacturing cells, materials, statistical methods, environmental prevention, control and evaluation.

Kansas State University, Graduate School, College of Engineering, Department of Industrial and Manufacturing Systems Engineering, Manhattan, KS 66506. Offers engineering management (MEM); industrial engineering (MS); operations research (MS). Part-time programs available. Postbaccalaureate distance learning degree programs offered (no on-campus study). *Faculty:* 10 full-time (2 women), 1 part-time/adjunct (0 women). *Students:* 26 full-time (8 women), 58 part-time (9 women); includes 11 minority (5 Black or African American, non-Hispanic/Latino; 2 Asian, non-Hispanic/Latino; 1 Hispanic/Latino; 1 Native Hawaiian or other Pacific Islander, non-Hispanic/Latino; 2 Two or more races, non-Hispanic/Latino), 16 international. Average age 29. 61 applicants, 46% accepted, 13 enrolled. In 2014, 26 master's, 4 doctorates awarded. *Degree requirements:* For master's, thesis or alternative; for doctorate, thesis/dissertation. *Entrance requirements:* For master's, GRE General Test (minimum score of 750 old version, 159 new format on Quantitative portion of exam), bachelor's degree in engineering, mathematics, or physical science; for doctorate, GRE General Test (minimum score of 770 old version, 164 new format on Quantitative portion of exam), master's degree in engineering or industrial manufacturing. Additional exam requirements/recommendations for international students: Required—PTE (minimum score 58), TOEFL (minimum score 550 paper-based; 79 iBT) or IELTS (minimum score 6.5). *Application deadline:* For fall admission, 6/1 priority date for domestic students, 12/1 priority date for international students; for spring admission, 11/1 priority date for domestic students, 8/1 priority date for international students. Applications are processed on a rolling basis. Application fee: $50 ($75 for international students). Electronic applications accepted. *Financial support:* In 2014–15, 12 research assistantships (averaging $12,442 per year), 9 teaching assistantships with full tuition reimbursements (averaging $14,111 per year) were awarded; Federal Work-Study, institutionally sponsored loans, and scholarships/grants also available. Support available to part-time students. Financial award application deadline: 3/1; financial award applicants required to submit FAFSA. *Faculty research:* Industrial engineering, ergonomics, healthcare systems engineering, manufacturing processes, operations research, engineering management. *Total annual research expenditures:* $2.6 million. *Unit head:* Dr. Bradley Kramer, Head, 785-532-5606, Fax: 785-532-3738, E-mail: bradleyk@k-state.edu. *Application contact:* Dr. David Ben-Arieh, Chair of Graduate Committee, 785-532-5606, Fax: 785-532-3738, E-mail: imse@k-state.edu.
Website: http://www.imse.k-state.edu/.

Kettering University, Graduate School, Department of Industrial and Manufacturing Engineering, Flint, MI 48504. Offers engineering (MS). Part-time and evening/weekend programs available. Postbaccalaureate distance learning degree programs offered (no on-campus study). *Degree requirements:* For master's, thesis optional. *Entrance requirements:* Additional exam requirements/recommendations for international students: Required—TOEFL (minimum score 550 paper-based; 79 iBT). Electronic applications accepted. *Faculty research:* Failure analysis, gestural controls.

Lawrence Technological University, College of Engineering, Southfield, MI 48075-1058. Offers architectural engineering (MS); automotive engineering (MS); civil engineering (MA, MS, PhD); construction engineering management (MA); electrical and computer engineering (MS); engineering management (MEM); industrial engineering (MS); manufacturing systems (ME, DE); mechanical engineering (MS, DE); mechatronic systems engineering (MS). Part-time and evening/weekend programs available. *Faculty:* 24 full-time (5 women), 15 part-time/adjunct (0 women). *Students:* 16 full-time (6 women), 478 part-time (71 women); includes 295 minority (15 Black or African American, non-Hispanic/Latino; 271 Asian, non-Hispanic/Latino; 7 Hispanic/Latino; 2 Two or more races, non-Hispanic/Latino), 38 international. Average age 27. 1,786 applicants, 40% accepted, 218 enrolled. In 2014, 106 master's awarded. *Degree requirements:* For master's, thesis (for some programs). *Entrance requirements:* Additional exam requirements/recommendations for international students: Required—TOEFL (minimum score 550 paper-based; 79 iBT). *Application deadline:* For fall admission, 8/1 priority date for domestic students, 5/29 for international students; for spring admission, 12/1 priority date for domestic students, 10/15 for international students. Applications are processed on a rolling basis. Application fee: $50. Electronic applications accepted. *Expenses: Tuition:* Full-time $14,700; part-time $1050 per credit hour. *Required fees:* $150. One-time fee: $150 part-time. *Financial support:* In 2014–15, 31 students received support, including 8 research assistantships (averaging $9,338 per year); Federal Work-Study and institutionally sponsored loans also available. Support available to part-time students. Financial award application deadline: 4/1; financial award applicants required to submit FAFSA. *Faculty research:* Advanced composite materials in bridges, strengthening existing bridges with carbon and glass fiber sheets, development of drive shafts using composite materials. *Unit head:* Dr. Nabil Grace, Dean, 248-204-2500, Fax: 248-204-2509, E-mail: engrdean@ltu.edu. *Application contact:* Jane Rohrback, Director of Admissions, 248-204-3160, Fax: 248-204-2228, E-mail: admissions@ltu.edu.
Website: http://www.ltu.edu/engineering/index.asp.

Lehigh University, P.C. Rossin College of Engineering and Applied Science, Program in Manufacturing Systems Engineering, Bethlehem, PA 18015. Offers MS, MBA/E. Part-time and evening/weekend programs available. Postbaccalaureate distance learning degree programs offered (no on-campus study). *Faculty:* 3 full-time (0 women). *Students:* 2 full-time (1 woman), 18 part-time (7 women); includes 4 minority (1 Black or African American, non-Hispanic/Latino; 2 Asian, non-Hispanic/Latino; 1 Hispanic/Latino), 1 international. Average age 31. 13 applicants, 62% accepted, 3 enrolled. In 2014, 11 master's awarded. *Degree requirements:* For master's, comprehensive exam, project or thesis. *Entrance requirements:* For master's, GRE General Test, minimum GPA of 2.75. Additional exam requirements/recommendations for international students: Required—TOEFL (minimum score 620 paper-based; 85 iBT). *Application deadline:* For fall admission, 7/15 priority date for domestic students, 7/15 for international students; for spring admission, 12/1 priority date for domestic students, 12/1 for international students. Applications are processed on a rolling basis. Application fee: $75. Electronic applications accepted. *Faculty research:* Manufacturing systems design, development, and implementation; accounting and management; agile/lean systems; supply chain issues; sustainable systems design; product design. *Unit head:* Dr. Keith M. Gardiner, Director, 610-758-5070, Fax: 610-758-6527, E-mail: kg03@lehigh.edu. *Application contact:* Carolyn C. Jones, Graduate Coordinator, 610-758-5157, Fax: 610-758-6527, E-mail: ccj1@lehigh.edu.
Website: https://mse.lehigh.edu/.

Massachusetts Institute of Technology, School of Engineering, Department of Mechanical Engineering, Cambridge, MA 02139. Offers manufacturing (M Eng); mechanical engineering (SM, PhD, Sc D, Mech E); naval architecture and marine engineering (SM, PhD, Sc D); naval engineering (Naval E); ocean engineering (SM, PhD, Sc D); oceanographic engineering (SM, PhD, Sc D); SM/MBA. *Faculty:* 70 full-time (8 women). *Students:* 549 full-time (140 women); includes 98 minority (8 Black or African American, non-Hispanic/Latino; 1 American Indian or Alaska Native, non-Hispanic/Latino; 47 Asian, non-Hispanic/Latino; 28 Hispanic/Latino; 14 Two or more races, non-Hispanic/Latino), 252 international. Average age 27. 1,409 applicants, 19% accepted, 200 enrolled. In 2014, 166 master's, 60 doctorates, 9 other advanced degrees awarded. Terminal master's awarded for partial completion of doctoral program. *Degree requirements:* For master's and other advanced degree, thesis; for doctorate, comprehensive exam, thesis/dissertation, a minor program of study in a field different from that of the major. *Entrance requirements:* For master's, doctorate, and other advanced degree, GRE General Test. Additional exam requirements/recommendations for international students: Required—TOEFL (minimum score 577 paper-based; 90 iBT), IELTS (minimum score 7). *Application deadline:* For fall and spring admission, 12/15 for domestic and international students. Application fee: $75. Electronic applications accepted. *Expenses: Tuition:* Full-time $44,720; part-time $699 per unit. *Required fees:* $296. *Financial support:* In 2014–15, 459 students received support, including 102 fellowships (averaging $32,900 per year), 338 research assistantships (averaging $33,600 per year), 50 teaching assistantships (averaging $36,700 per year); Federal Work-Study, institutionally sponsored loans, scholarships/grants, traineeships, health care benefits, and unspecified assistantships also available. Financial award application deadline: 4/15; financial award applicants required to submit FAFSA. *Faculty research:* Mechanics: modeling, experimentation and computation; design, manufacturing, and product development; controls, instrumentation, and robotics; energy science and engineering; ocean science and engineering; bioengineering; micro- and nano-engineering. *Total annual research expenditures:* $64 million. *Unit head:* Gang Chen, Department Head, 617-253-2201, Fax: 617-258-6156, E-mail: mehq@mit.edu. *Application contact:* Graduate Office, 617-253-2291, Fax: 617-258-5802, E-mail: megradoffice@mit.edu.
Website: http://meche.mit.edu/.

Michigan State University, The Graduate School, College of Agriculture and Natural Resources, School of Packaging, East Lansing, MI 48824. Offers MS, PhD. *Entrance requirements:* Additional exam requirements/recommendations for international students: Required—TOEFL. Electronic applications accepted.

Minnesota State University Mankato, College of Graduate Studies, College of Science, Engineering and Technology, Department of Automotive and Manufacturing Engineering Technology, Mankato, MN 56001. Offers manufacturing engineering technology (MS). *Students:* 2 full-time (0 women), 11 part-time (0 women). *Degree requirements:* For master's, comprehensive exam, thesis. *Entrance requirements:* For master's, GRE General Test (if GPA less than 3.0), minimum GPA of 3.0 during previous 2 years. Additional exam requirements/recommendations for international students: Required—TOEFL. *Application deadline:* For fall admission, 7/1 priority date for domestic students; for spring admission, 11/1 for domestic students. Applications are processed on a rolling basis. Application fee: $40. Electronic applications accepted. *Financial support:* Research assistantships with full tuition reimbursements, teaching assistantships with full tuition reimbursements, and unspecified assistantships available. Financial award application deadline: 3/15; financial award applicants required to submit FAFSA. *Unit head:* Dr. Bruce Jones, Graduate Coordinator, 507-389-6700. *Application contact:* 507-389-2321, E-mail: grad@mnsu.edu.

Missouri University of Science and Technology, Graduate School, Department of Engineering Management and Systems Engineering, Rolla, MO 65409. Offers engineering management (MS, DE, PhD); manufacturing engineering (M Eng, MS); systems engineering (MS, PhD). *Degree requirements:* For master's, thesis optional; for doctorate, comprehensive exam. *Entrance requirements:* For master's, GRE (minimum score 1150 verbal and quantitative, 4.5 writing); for doctorate, GRE (minimum score: 1100 verbal and quantitative, 3.5 writing). Additional exam requirements/recommendations for international students: Required—TOEFL (minimum score 580 paper-based). *Faculty research:* Management of technology, industrial engineering, manufacturing engineering, packaging engineering, quality engineering.

New Jersey Institute of Technology, Newark College of Engineering, Newark, NJ 07102. Offers biomedical engineering (MS, PhD); chemical engineering (MS, PhD); computer engineering (MS, PhD); electrical engineering (MS, PhD); engineering management (MS); healthcare systems management (MS); industrial engineering (MS, PhD); Internet engineering (MS); manufacturing engineering (MS); mechanical engineering (MS, PhD); occupational safety and health engineering (MS); pharmaceutical bioprocessing (MS); pharmaceutical engineering (MS); pharmaceutical systems management (MS); power and energy systems (MS); telecommunications (MS); transportation (MS, PhD). Part-time and evening/weekend programs available. Terminal master's awarded for partial completion of doctoral program. *Degree requirements:* For master's, thesis optional; for doctorate, thesis/dissertation. *Entrance requirements:* For master's, GRE General Test; for doctorate, GRE General Test, minimum graduate GPA of 3.5. Additional exam requirements/recommendations for international students: Required—TOEFL (minimum score 550 paper-based; 79 iBT). Electronic applications accepted.

New York University, Polytechnic School of Engineering, Department of Technology Management, Major in Manufacturing Engineering, New York, NY 10012-1019. Offers MS. Part-time and evening/weekend programs available. Postbaccalaureate distance learning degree programs offered (no on-campus study). *Students:* 7 full-time (1 woman), 3 part-time (1 woman), 7 international. Average age 26. 31 applicants, 55% accepted, 7 enrolled. In 2014, 6 master's awarded. *Degree requirements:* For master's, comprehensive exam (for some programs), thesis (for some programs). *Entrance requirements:* For master's, BE or BS in engineering, physics, chemistry, mathematical sciences, or biological sciences, or MBA. Additional exam requirements/recommendations for international students: Required—TOEFL (minimum score 550 paper-based; 80 iBT); Recommended—IELTS (minimum score 6.5). *Application deadline:* For fall admission, 2/15 priority date for domestic and international students; for spring admission, 11/1 priority date for domestic and international students. Applications are processed on a rolling basis. Application fee: $75. Electronic applications accepted. *Financial support:* Institutionally sponsored loans, scholarships/grants, and unspecified assistantships available. Support available to part-time students. Financial award applicants required to submit FAFSA. *Unit head:* Prof. Mark De Lessio, Program Director, E-mail: mpdelessio@nyu.edu. *Application contact:* Raymond Lutzky, Director, Graduate Enrollment Management, 718-637-5984, Fax: 718-260-3624, E-mail: rlutzky@poly.edu.

North Carolina State University, Graduate School, College of Engineering, Integrated Manufacturing Systems Engineering Institute, Raleigh, NC 27695. Offers MIMS. Part-time programs available. *Degree requirements:* For master's, thesis optional. *Entrance requirements:* For master's, GRE. Additional exam requirements/recommendations for international students: Required—TOEFL. Electronic applications accepted. *Faculty research:* Mechatronics, manufacturing systems modeling, systems integration product and process engineering, logistics.

North Dakota State University, College of Graduate and Interdisciplinary Studies, College of Engineering and Architecture, Department of Industrial and Manufacturing Engineering, Fargo, ND 58108. Offers industrial and manufacturing engineering (PhD); industrial engineering and management (MS); manufacturing engineering (MS). Part-time programs available. *Degree requirements:* For doctorate, comprehensive exam, thesis/dissertation. *Entrance requirements:* For master's, GRE General Test, bachelor's degree in engineering; for doctorate, GRE General Test, master's degree in engineering. Additional exam requirements/recommendations for international students: Required—TOEFL (minimum score 550 paper-based; 79 iBT), TWE (minimum score 4). Electronic applications accepted. *Faculty research:* Electronics manufacturing, quality engineering, manufacturing process science, healthcare, lean manufacturing.

Oregon Institute of Technology, Program in Manufacturing Engineering Technology, Klamath Falls, OR 97601-8801. Offers MS. Part-time programs available. Postbaccalaureate distance learning degree programs offered (minimal on-campus study). *Degree requirements:* For master's, one foreign language, project. *Entrance requirements:* For master's, GRE General Test. Electronic applications accepted.

Polytechnic University of Puerto Rico, Graduate School, Hato Rey, PR 00919. Offers business administration (MBA), including computer information systems, general management, management of information systems, management of international enterprises; civil engineering (ME, MS); computer engineering (ME, MS); computer science (MCS, MS); electrical engineering (ME, MS); engineering management (MEM); environmental management (MEM); landscape architecture (M Land Arch); manufacturing competitiveness (MMC, MS); manufacturing engineering (ME, MS); mechanical engineering (M Mech E). Part-time and evening/weekend programs available. *Entrance requirements:* For master's, 3 letters of recommendation.

Portland State University, Graduate Studies, Maseeh College of Engineering and Computer Science, Department of Engineering and Technology Management, Portland, OR 97207-0751. Offers engineering and technology management (M Eng); engineering management (MS); manufacturing engineering (ME); manufacturing management (M Eng); systems science/engineering management (PhD); MS/MBA; MS/MS. Part-time and evening/weekend programs available. *Faculty:* 6 full-time (1 woman), 8 part-time/adjunct (2 women). *Students:* 62 full-time (20 women), 63 part-time (18 women); includes 21 minority (3 Black or African American, non-Hispanic/Latino; 1 American Indian or Alaska Native, non-Hispanic/Latino; 12 Asian, non-Hispanic/Latino; 4 Hispanic/Latino; 1 Two or more races, non-Hispanic/Latino), 68 international. Average age 36. 90 applicants, 67% accepted, 31 enrolled. In 2014, 27 master's, 5 doctorates awarded. *Degree requirements:* For master's, thesis optional; for doctorate, one foreign language, comprehensive exam, thesis/dissertation, oral and written exams. *Entrance requirements:* For master's, GRE optional, 2.75 undergraduate or 3.0 graduate (at least 12 credits), minimum 4 years of experience in engineering or related discipline, 3 letters of recommendation and background in probability/statistics, differential equations, computer programming and linear algebra; for doctorate, GRE General Test, 1100 for the sum of verbal and quantitative, or verbal and analytical., minimum GPA of 3.0 undergraduate or 3.25 graduate. Additional exam requirements/recommendations for international students: Required—TOEFL (minimum score 550 paper-based; 80 iBT). *Application deadline:* For fall admission, 4/1 for domestic students, 3/1 for international students; for winter admission, 9/1 for domestic students, 7/1 for international students; for spring admission, 11/1 for domestic students, 9/1 for international students; for summer admission, 2/1 for domestic students, 12/1 for international students. Application fee: $50. Electronic applications accepted. *Expenses:* Tuition, state resident: part-time $222 per credit. Tuition, nonresident: part-time $527 per credit. *Required fees:* $22 per contact hour. $100 per quarter. Tuition and fees vary according to program. *Financial support:* In 2014–15, 7 research assistantships with full and partial tuition reimbursements (averaging $1,913 per year), 8 teaching assistantships with full and partial tuition reimbursements (averaging $2,823 per year) were awarded; career-related internships or fieldwork, Federal Work-Study, scholarships/grants, and unspecified assistantships also available. Support available to part-time students. Financial award application deadline: 3/1; financial award applicants required to submit FAFSA. *Faculty research:* Scheduling, hierarchical decision modeling, operations research, knowledge-based information systems. *Total annual research expenditures:* $318,571. *Unit head:* Dr. Tim Anderson, Chair, 503-725-4668, Fax: 503-725-4667, E-mail: tim.anderson@pdx.edu. *Application contact:* Shawn Wall, Department Manager, 503-725-4660, Fax: 503-547-8887, E-mail: info@etm.pdx.edu.
Website: http://www.pdx.edu/engineering-technology-management/.

Rochester Institute of Technology, Graduate Enrollment Services, College of Applied Science and Technology, School of Engineering Technology, MS Program in Manufacturing and Mechanical Systems Integration, Rochester, NY 14623-5604. Offers MS. Part-time and evening/weekend programs available. *Students:* 39 full-time (8 women), 6 part-time (1 woman); includes 1 minority (Asian, non-Hispanic/Latino), 34 international. Average age 24. 62 applicants, 66% accepted, 23 enrolled. In 2014, 10 master's awarded. *Degree requirements:* For master's, thesis (for some programs). *Entrance requirements:* For master's, GRE, and TOEFL, IELTS, or PTE for non-native English speakers, Recommended minimum GPA of 3.0. Additional exam requirements/recommendations for international students: Required—PTE (minimum score 58), TOEFL (minimum score 550 paper-based; 79 iBT) or IELTS (minimum score 6.5). *Application deadline:* For fall admission, 2/15 priority date for domestic and international students; for winter admission, 11/1 for domestic and international students; for spring admission, 12/15 priority date for domestic and international students. Applications are processed on a rolling basis. Application fee: $60. Electronic applications accepted. *Expenses:* Expenses: $1,673 per credit hour. *Financial support:* In 2014–15, 18 students received support. Research assistantships with partial tuition reimbursements available, teaching assistantships with partial tuition reimbursements available, career-related internships or fieldwork, Federal Work-Study, institutionally sponsored loans, scholarships/grants, and unspecified assistantships available. Support available to part-time students. Financial award application deadline: 2/15; financial award applicants required to submit FAFSA. *Faculty research:* Product development, electronics packaging, automated manufacturing, quality and systems management. *Unit head:* Dr. S. Manian Ramkumar, Program Chair, 585-475-6081, E-mail: smrmet@rit.edu. *Application contact:* Diane Ellison, Associate Vice President, Graduate Enrollment Services, 585-475-2229, Fax: 585-475-7164, E-mail: gradinfo@rit.edu.
Website: http://www.rit.edu/cast/mmet/graduate-programs/ms-in-manufacturing-and-mechanical-systems-integration.

Rochester Institute of Technology, Graduate Enrollment Services, College of Applied Science and Technology, School of Engineering Technology, MS Program in Packaging Science, Rochester, NY 14623-5604. Offers MS. Part-time programs available. *Students:* 36 full-time (10 women), 9 part-time (1 woman); includes 2 minority (both Black or African American, non-Hispanic/Latino), 39 international. Average age 25. 32 applicants, 59% accepted, 17 enrolled. In 2014, 13 master's awarded. *Degree

requirements: For master's, thesis or alternative, thesis or project. *Entrance requirements:* For master's, TOEFL, IELTS, or PTE for non-native English speakers, Recommended minimum GPA of 3.0. Additional exam requirements/recommendations for international students: Required—PTE (minimum score 58), TOEFL (minimum score 550 paper-based; 79 iBT) or IELTS (minimum score 6.5). *Application deadline:* For fall admission, 2/15 priority date for domestic and international students; for spring admission, 12/15 priority date for domestic and international students. Applications are processed on a rolling basis. Application fee: $60. Electronic applications accepted. *Expenses:* Expenses: $1,673 per credit hour. *Financial support:* In 2014–15, 20 students received support. Research assistantships with partial tuition reimbursements available, teaching assistantships with partial tuition reimbursements available, career-related internships or fieldwork, Federal Work-Study, institutionally sponsored loans, scholarships/grants, and unspecified assistantships available. Support available to part-time students. Financial award applicants required to submit FAFSA. *Faculty research:* Sustainable packaging, food packaging and distribution, packaging structures and design. *Unit head:* Deanna Jacobs, Chair, 585-475-6801, E-mail: dmjipk@rit.edu. *Application contact:* Diane Ellison, Associate Vice President, Graduate Enrollment Services, 585-475-2229, Fax: 585-475-7164, E-mail: gradinfo@rit.edu.
Website: http://www.rit.edu/cast/packaging/ms-packaging-science.

Rochester Institute of Technology, Graduate Enrollment Services, Kate Gleason College of Engineering, Electrical and Microelectronic Engineering Department, ME Program in Microelectronic Manufacturing Engineering, Rochester, NY 14623-5603. Offers ME. Part-time programs available. Postbaccalaureate distance learning degree programs offered (no on-campus study). *Students:* 4 full-time (2 women), 4 part-time (2 women); includes 3 minority (2 Black or African American, non-Hispanic/Latino; 1 Asian, non-Hispanic/Latino), 2 international. Average age 29. 20 applicants, 35% accepted, 4 enrolled. In 2014, 4 master's awarded. *Degree requirements:* For master's, thesis or alternative. *Entrance requirements:* For master's, TOEFL, IELTS, or PTE for non-native English speakers, Recommended minimum GPA of 3.0. Additional exam requirements/recommendations for international students: Required—PTE (minimum score 58), TOEFL (minimum score 550 paper-based; 79 iBT) or IELTS (minimum score 6.5). *Application deadline:* For fall admission, 2/15 for domestic and international students. Applications are processed on a rolling basis. Application fee: $60. Electronic applications accepted. *Expenses:* Expenses: $1,673 per credit hour. *Financial support:* In 2014–15, 4 students received support. Research assistantships with partial tuition reimbursements available, teaching assistantships with partial tuition reimbursements available, career-related internships or fieldwork, Federal Work-Study, institutionally sponsored loans, scholarships/grants, and unspecified assistantships available. Support available to part-time students. Financial award applicants required to submit FAFSA. *Faculty research:* Semiconductor modeling; analog integrated circuits; thin-film transistors; signal/image processing, digital communications, and control; semiconductor devices, processes and electrical characterization; phase adaptive optics, nano/microlithography and design of experiments. *Unit head:* Dr. Robert Pearson, Graduate Program Director, 585-475-2923, Fax: 585-475-5845, E-mail: robert.pearson@rit.edu. *Application contact:* Diane Ellison, Associate Vice President, Graduate Enrollment Services, 585-475-2229, Fax: 585-475-7164, E-mail: gradinfo@rit.edu.
Website: http://www.rit.edu/kgcoe/eme/meME.

Rochester Institute of Technology, Graduate Enrollment Services, Kate Gleason College of Engineering, Industrial and Systems Engineering Department, Rochester, NY 14623-5603. Offers engineering management (ME); industrial and systems engineering (ME, MS); sustainable engineering (ME, MS). Part-time programs available. *Students:* 78 full-time (23 women), 19 part-time (5 women); includes 2 minority (1 Black or African American, non-Hispanic/Latino; 1 Hispanic/Latino), 64 international. Average age 24. 528 applicants, 29% accepted, 53 enrolled. In 2014, 50 master's awarded. *Degree requirements:* For master's, thesis (for some programs). *Entrance requirements:* For master's, GRE and TOEFL, IELTS, or PTE for non-native English speakers, Recommended minimum GPA of 3.0. Additional exam requirements/recommendations for international students: Required—PTE (minimum score 58), TOEFL (minimum score 550 paper-based; 79 iBT) or IELTS (minimum score 6.5). *Application deadline:* For fall admission, 2/15 priority date for domestic and international students; for spring admission, 12/15 priority date for domestic and international students. Applications are processed on a rolling basis. Application fee: $60. Electronic applications accepted. *Expenses:* Expenses: $1,673 per credit hour. *Financial support:* In 2014–15, 64 students received support. Research assistantships with full and partial tuition reimbursements available, teaching assistantships with partial tuition reimbursements available, career-related internships or fieldwork, Federal Work-Study, institutionally sponsored loans, scholarships/grants, tuition waivers (partial), and unspecified assistantships available. Support available to part-time students. Financial award applicants required to submit FAFSA. *Faculty research:* Advanced manufacturing, engineering education, ergonomics and human factors, healthcare delivery systems, operations research and simulation, production and logistics, sustainable engineering. *Unit head:* Dr. Scott Grasman, Department Head, 585-475-2598, Fax: 585-475-2520, E-mail: ise@rit.edu. *Application contact:* Diane Ellison, Associate Vice President, Graduate Enrollment Services, 585-475-2229, Fax: 585-475-7164, E-mail: gradinfo@rit.edu.
Website: http://www.rit.edu/kgcoe/ise/.

Southern Methodist University, Bobby B. Lyle School of Engineering, Department of Mechanical Engineering, Dallas, TX 75205. Offers manufacturing systems management (MS); mechanical engineering (MSME, PhD); packaging of electronic and optical devices (MS). Part-time and evening/weekend programs available. Postbaccalaureate distance learning degree programs offered (no on-campus study). Terminal master's awarded for partial completion of doctoral program. *Degree requirements:* For master's, thesis optional; for doctorate, thesis/dissertation, oral and written qualifying exams, oral final exam. *Entrance requirements:* For master's, GRE General Test, minimum GPA of 3.0 in last 2 years; bachelor's degree in engineering, mathematics, or sciences; for doctorate, preliminary counseling exam, minimum graduate GPA of 3.0, bachelor's degree in related field. Additional exam requirements/recommendations for international students: Required—TOEFL. *Faculty research:* Design, systems, and controls; thermal and fluid sciences.

Stevens Institute of Technology, Graduate School, Charles V. Schaefer Jr. School of Engineering, Department of Mechanical Engineering, Program in Integrated Product Development, Hoboken, NJ 07030. Offers armament engineering (M Eng); computer and electrical engineering (M Eng); manufacturing technologies (M Eng); systems reliability and design (M Eng).

Tennessee State University, The School of Graduate Studies and Research, College of Engineering, Nashville, TN 37209-1561. Offers biomedical engineering (ME); civil engineering (ME); computer and information systems engineering (MS, PhD); electrical engineering (ME); environmental engineering (ME); manufacturing engineering (ME); mathematical sciences (MS); mechanical engineering (ME). Part-time and evening/weekend programs available. *Degree requirements:* For master's, project; for doctorate, comprehensive exam, thesis/dissertation. *Entrance requirements:* For doctorate, minimum GPA of 3.3. *Faculty research:* Robotics, intelligent systems, human-computer

Manufacturing Engineering

interaction software systems, biomedical engineering, signal/image processing, probabilistic design, intelligent manufacturing, cooperative mobile robots, condition based maintenance, sensor fusion.

Texas A&M University, College of Engineering, Department of Engineering Technology and Industrial Distribution, College Station, TX 77843. Offers industrial distribution (MID). *Faculty:* 13. *Students:* 123 full-time (18 women), 1 part-time (0 women); includes 36 minority (9 Black or African American, non-Hispanic/Latino; 2 American Indian or Alaska Native, non-Hispanic/Latino; 2 Asian, non-Hispanic/Latino; 21 Hispanic/Latino; 1 Native Hawaiian or other Pacific Islander, non-Hispanic/Latino; 1 Two or more races, non-Hispanic/Latino), 2 international. Average age 36. 63 applicants, 100% accepted, 55 enrolled. In 2014, 35 master's awarded. *Entrance requirements:* Additional exam requirements/recommendations for international students: Required—TOEFL. *Application deadline:* For fall admission, 3/1 priority date for domestic and international students; for spring admission, 8/1 priority date for domestic and international students. Applications are processed on a rolling basis. Application fee: $50 ($90 for international students). Electronic applications accepted. *Expenses:* Tuition, state resident: full-time $4078; part-time $226.55 per credit hour. Tuition, nonresident: full-time $10,594; part-time $577.55 per credit hour. *Required fees:* $2813; $237.70 per credit hour. $278.50 per semester. Tuition and fees vary according to degree level and student level. *Financial support:* In 2014–15, 74 students received support. Application deadline: 2/1. *Unit head:* Dr. Reza Langari, Department Head, 979-862-4945, E-mail: rlangari@tamu.edu. *Application contact:* Graduate Admissions, 979-458-0427, E-mail: graduate-admissions@tamu.edu.
Website: http://engineering.tamu.edu/etid.

Texas State University, The Graduate College, College of Science and Engineering, Program in Engineering, San Marcos, TX 78666. Offers manufacturing engineering (MS). *Faculty:* 15 full-time (2 women), 1 part-time/adjunct (0 women). *Degree requirements:* For master's, comprehensive exam, thesis (for some programs). *Entrance requirements:* For master's, GRE (minimum preferred scores of 285 overall, 135 verbal, 150 quantitative), baccalaureate degree from regionally-accredited university in engineering, computer science, physics, technology, or closely-related field with minimum GPA of 3.0 on last 60 undergraduate semester hours. Additional exam requirements/recommendations for international students: Required—TOEFL (minimum score 78 iBT), IELTS (minimum score 6.5). *Application deadline:* For fall admission, 2/15 priority date for domestic students, 2/1 priority date for international students. Electronic applications accepted. *Unit head:* Dr. Vishu Viswanathan, Graduate Advisor, 512-245-1826, E-mail: v_v42@txstate.edu. *Application contact:* Dr. Andrea Golato, Dean of Graduate School, 512-245-2581, Fax: 512-245-8365, E-mail: gradcollege@txstate.edu.
Website: http://www.engineering.txstate.edu/.

Tufts University, Graduate School of Arts and Sciences, Graduate Certificate Programs, Manufacturing Engineering Program, Medford, MA 02155. Offers Certificate. Part-time and evening/weekend programs available. Electronic applications accepted. *Expenses: Tuition:* Full-time $45,590; part-time $1161 per credit hour. *Required fees:* $782. Full-time tuition and fees vary according to degree level, program and student level. Part-time tuition and fees vary according to course load.

Universidad Autonoma de Guadalajara, Graduate Programs, Guadalajara, Mexico. Offers administrative law and justice (LL M); advertising and corporate communications (MA); architecture (M Arch); business (MBA); computational science (MCC); education (Ed M, Ed D); English-Spanish translation (MA); entrepreneurship and management (MBA); integrated management of digital animation (MA); international business (MIB); international corporate law (LL M); internet technologies (MS); manufacturing systems (MMS); occupational health (MS); philosophy (MA, PhD); power electronics (MS); quality systems (MQS); renewable energy (MS); social evaluation of projects (MBA); strategic market research (MBA); tax law (MA); teaching mathematics (MA).

Universidad de las Américas Puebla, Division of Graduate Studies, School of Engineering, Program in Manufacturing Administration, Puebla, Mexico. Offers MS. *Faculty research:* Operations research, construction.

University of Calgary, Faculty of Graduate Studies, Schulich School of Engineering, Department of Mechanical and Manufacturing Engineering, Calgary, AB T2N 1N4, Canada. Offers M Eng, M Sc, PhD. Part-time programs available. *Degree requirements:* For master's, thesis (for some programs); for doctorate, thesis/dissertation, candidacy exam. *Entrance requirements:* For master's, minimum GPA of 3.0; for doctorate, minimum GPA of 3.3. Additional exam requirements/recommendations for international students: Required—TOEFL (minimum score 550 paper-based; 80 iBT), IELTS (minimum score 7). *Faculty research:* Thermofluids, solid mechanics, materials, biomechanics, manufacturing.

University of California, Irvine, Henry Samueli School of Engineering, Program in Materials and Manufacturing Technology, Irvine, CA 92697. Offers engineering (MS, PhD). Part-time programs available. *Students:* 26 full-time (7 women), 3 part-time (1 woman); includes 10 minority (9 Asian, non-Hispanic/Latino; 1 Two or more races, non-Hispanic/Latino), 18 international. Average age 27. 33 applicants, 67% accepted, 11 enrolled. In 2014, 6 master's, 2 doctorates awarded. *Entrance requirements:* For master's and doctorate, GRE General Test, 3 letters of recommendation, minimum GPA of 3.0. Additional exam requirements/recommendations for international students: Required—TOEFL (minimum score 550 paper-based). *Application deadline:* For fall admission, 1/15 priority date for domestic students, 1/15 for international students. Applications are processed on a rolling basis. Application fee: $90 ($110 for international students). Electronic applications accepted. *Financial support:* Fellowships with tuition reimbursements, research assistantships with full tuition reimbursements, teaching assistantships with tuition reimbursements, institutionally sponsored loans, traineeships, health care benefits, and unspecified assistantships available. Financial award application deadline: 3/1; financial award applicants required to submit FAFSA. *Faculty research:* Advanced materials, microelectronic and photonic devices and packaging, biomedical devices, MEMS, thin film materials, nanotechnology. *Unit head:* Gregory N. Washington, Dean, 949-824-4333, Fax: 949-824-8200, E-mail: engineering@uci.edu. *Application contact:* Nadia Ortiz, Assistant Director of Graduate Student Affairs, 949-824-3562, Fax: 949-824-9096, E-mail: nortiz@uci.edu.
Website: http://www.eng.uci.edu/.

University of California, Los Angeles, Graduate Division, Henry Samueli School of Engineering and Applied Science, Department of Mechanical and Aerospace Engineering, Program in Manufacturing Engineering, Los Angeles, CA 90095-1597. Offers MS. *Faculty:* 31 full-time (2 women), 6 part-time/adjunct (0 women). *Students:* 10 applicants. *Degree requirements:* For master's, comprehensive exam or thesis. *Entrance requirements:* For master's, GRE General Test, minimum GPA of 3.0. Additional exam requirements/recommendations for international students: Required—TOEFL (minimum score 560 paper-based; 87 iBT), IELTS (minimum score 7). *Application deadline:* For fall admission, 12/15 for domestic and international students; for winter admission, 10/1 for domestic students; for spring admission, 12/31 for domestic students. Application fee: $80 ($100 for international students). Electronic applications accepted. *Financial support:* Fellowships, research assistantships, teaching assistantships, Federal Work-Study, institutionally sponsored loans, and tuition waivers (full and partial) available. Financial award application deadline: 12/15; financial

award applicants required to submit FAFSA. *Unit head:* Dr. Tsu-Chin Tsao, Chair, 310-206-2819, E-mail: ttsao@seas.ucla.edu. *Application contact:* Angie Castillo, Student Affairs Officer, 310-825-7793, Fax: 310-206-4830, E-mail: angie@seas.ucla.edu.
Website: http://www.mae.ucla.edu/.

The University of Iowa, Graduate College, College of Engineering, Department of Industrial Engineering, Iowa City, IA 52242-1316. Offers engineering design and manufacturing (MS, PhD); healthcare systems (MS, PhD); human factors (MS, PhD); information and engineering management (MS, PhD); operations research (MS, PhD); wind energy (MS, PhD). *Faculty:* 8 full-time (1 woman). *Students:* 19 full-time (3 women); includes 1 minority (Asian, non-Hispanic/Latino), 10 international. Average age 28. 59 applicants, 12% accepted, 3 enrolled. In 2014, 1 master's, 4 doctorates awarded. Terminal master's awarded for partial completion of doctoral program. *Degree requirements:* For master's, thesis optional, exam; for doctorate, comprehensive exam, thesis/dissertation, final defense exam. *Entrance requirements:* For master's and doctorate, GRE General Test. Additional exam requirements/recommendations for international students: Required—TOEFL (minimum score 600 paper-based; 100 iBT). *Application deadline:* For fall admission, 7/15 for domestic students, 4/15 for international students; for spring admission, 12/1 for domestic students, 10/1 for international students; for summer admission, 4/15 for domestic students, 3/1 for international students. Applications are processed on a rolling basis. Application fee: $60 ($100 for international students). Electronic applications accepted. *Financial support:* In 2014–15, 4 fellowships with partial tuition reimbursements (averaging $20,619 per year), 16 research assistantships with full tuition reimbursements (averaging $18,131 per year), 5 teaching assistantships with full tuition reimbursements (averaging $5,424 per year) were awarded; career-related internships or fieldwork, scholarships/grants, and unspecified assistantships also available. Support available to part-time students. Financial award applicants required to submit FAFSA. *Faculty research:* Operations research, informatics, human factors engineering, healthcare systems, biomanufacturing, manufacturing systems, renewable energy, human-machine interactions. *Total annual research expenditures:* $3.5 million. *Unit head:* Dr. Andrew Kusiak, Department Executive Officer, 319-335-5934, Fax: 319-335-5669, E-mail: andrew-kusiak@uiowa.edu. *Application contact:* Andrea Flaherty, Academic Program Specialist, 319-335-5939, Fax: 319-335-5669, E-mail: indeng@engineering.uiowa.edu.
Website: http://www.engineering.uiowa.edu/mie.

The University of Iowa, Graduate College, College of Engineering, Department of Mechanical Engineering, Iowa City, IA 52242-1316. Offers energy systems (MS, PhD); engineering design (MS, PhD); fluid dynamics (MS, PhD); materials and manufacturing (MS, PhD); wind energy (MS, PhD). *Faculty:* 14 full-time (1 woman). *Students:* 50 full-time (5 women); includes 1 minority (Black or African American, non-Hispanic/Latino), 34 international. Average age 28. 68 applicants, 19% accepted, 4 enrolled. In 2014, 9 master's, 7 doctorates awarded. Terminal master's awarded for partial completion of doctoral program. *Degree requirements:* For master's, oral exam or thesis; for doctorate, comprehensive exam, thesis/dissertation. *Entrance requirements:* For master's and doctorate, GRE. Additional exam requirements/recommendations for international students: Required—TOEFL (minimum score 600 paper-based; 100 iBT). *Application deadline:* For fall admission, 1/15 for domestic and international students; for spring admission, 9/1 for domestic and international students; for summer admission, 1/15 for domestic and international students. Application fee: $60 ($100 for international students). Electronic applications accepted. *Financial support:* In 2014–15, 3 fellowships with partial tuition reimbursements (averaging $19,933 per year), 36 research assistantships with full tuition reimbursements (averaging $20,823 per year), 21 teaching assistantships with full tuition reimbursements (averaging $6,457 per year) were awarded; traineeships and unspecified assistantships also available. Financial award applicants required to submit FAFSA. *Faculty research:* Computer simulation methodology, biomechanics, metal casting, dynamics, laser processing, system reliability, ship hydrodynamics, solid mechanics, fluid dynamics, energy, human modeling and nano technology. *Total annual research expenditures:* $9.8 million. *Unit head:* Dr. Andrew Kusiak, Departmental Executive Officer, 319-335-5934, Fax: 319-335-5669, E-mail: andrew-kusiak@uiowa.edu. *Application contact:* Andrea Flaherty, Academic Program Specialist, 319-335-5939, Fax: 319-335-5669, E-mail: mech_eng@engineering.uiowa.edu.
Website: http://www.engineering.uiowa.edu/mie.

University of Kentucky, Graduate School, College of Engineering, Program in Manufacturing Systems Engineering, Lexington, KY 40506-0032. Offers MSMSE. *Degree requirements:* For master's, comprehensive exam. *Entrance requirements:* For master's, GRE General Test, minimum undergraduate GPA of 2.75. Additional exam requirements/recommendations for international students: Required—TOEFL (minimum score 550 paper-based). Electronic applications accepted. *Faculty research:* Manufacturing processes and equipment, manufacturing systems and control, computer-aided design and manufacturing, automation in manufacturing, electric manufacturing and packaging.

University of Manitoba, Faculty of Graduate Studies, Faculty of Engineering, Department of Mechanical and Manufacturing Engineering, Winnipeg, MB R3T 2N2, Canada. Offers M Eng, M Sc, PhD. *Degree requirements:* For master's, thesis; for doctorate, thesis/dissertation.

University of Maryland, College Park, Academic Affairs, A. James Clark School of Engineering, Department of Mechanical Engineering, College Park, MD 20742. Offers electronic packaging and reliability (MS, PhD); manufacturing and design (MS, PhD); mechanics and materials (MS, PhD); reliability engineering (M Eng, MS, PhD); thermal and fluid sciences (MS, PhD). Part-time and evening/weekend programs available. Postbaccalaureate distance learning degree programs offered. *Degree requirements:* For master's, thesis optional; for doctorate, thesis/dissertation, qualifying exam. *Entrance requirements:* For master's, GRE General Test, 3 letters of recommendation; for doctorate, GRE General Test, minimum GPA of 3.0. Additional exam requirements/recommendations for international students: Required—TOEFL. Electronic applications accepted. *Faculty research:* Injection molding, electronic packaging, fluid mechanics, product engineering.

University of Michigan, College of Engineering, Interpro Programs in Engineering, Ann Arbor, MI 48109. Offers automotive engineering (M Eng); design science (PhD); energy systems engineering (MS); financial engineering (MS); global automotive and manufacturing engineering (M Eng); manufacturing engineering (M Eng, D Eng); pharmaceutical engineering (M Eng); robotics and autonomous vehicles (M Eng); MBA/M Eng; MSE/MS. Part-time programs available. Postbaccalaureate distance learning degree programs offered (no on-campus study). *Students:* 187 full-time (46 women), 250 part-time (40 women). 364 applicants, 2% accepted, 3 enrolled. In 2014, 171 master's, 1 doctorate awarded. Terminal master's awarded for partial completion of doctoral program. *Degree requirements:* For master's, capstone project; for doctorate, thesis/dissertation. *Entrance requirements:* For master's, GRE; for doctorate, GRE, 2 years of work experience. Additional exam requirements/recommendations for international students: Required—TOEFL (minimum score 560 paper-based). *Application deadline:* Applications are processed on a rolling basis. Electronic applications accepted. *Financial support:* Fellowships, research assistantships with full tuition reimbursements, teaching assistantships with full tuition reimbursements, career-

related internships or fieldwork, scholarships/grants, and unspecified assistantships available. Financial award application deadline: 2/15; financial award applicants required to submit FAFSA. *Faculty research:* Automotive engineering, design science, energy systems engineering, engineering sustainable systems, financial engineering, global automotive and manufacturing engineering, integrated microsystems, manufacturing engineering, pharmaceutical engineering, robotics and autonomous vehicles. *Total annual research expenditures:* $263,643. *Unit head:* Prof. Panos Papalambros, Director, 734-647-8401, Fax: 734-647-0079, E-mail: pyp@umich.edu. *Application contact:* Patti Mackmiller, Program Manager, 734-764-3071, Fax: 734-647-2243, E-mail: pmackmil@umich.edu.
Website: http://www.isd.engin.umich.edu.

University of Michigan–Dearborn, College of Engineering and Computer Science, MSE Program in Manufacturing Systems Engineering, Dearborn, MI 48128. Offers MSE. Part-time and evening/weekend programs available. *Faculty:* 1 full-time (0 women). *Students:* 4 full-time (1 woman), 5 part-time (1 woman); includes 2 minority (1 Black or African American, non-Hispanic/Latino; 1 Hispanic/Latino), 6 international. 18 applicants, 61% accepted, 5 enrolled. In 2014, 4 master's awarded. *Degree requirements:* For master's, thesis optional. *Entrance requirements:* For master's, BS in engineering or a physical science from accredited program with minimum B average. Additional exam requirements/recommendations for international students: Required—TOEFL (minimum score 560 paper-based; 84 iBT); Recommended—IELTS (minimum score 6.5). *Application deadline:* For fall admission, 8/1 priority date for domestic students, 5/1 priority date for international students; for winter admission, 12/1 priority date for domestic students, 9/1 priority date for international students; for spring admission, 4/1 priority date for domestic students, 1/1 priority date for international students. Applications are processed on a rolling basis. Application fee: $60. Electronic applications accepted. *Expenses:* Tuition, state resident: full-time $12,202; part-time $707 per credit hour. Tuition, nonresident: full-time $20,980; part-time $1209 per credit hour. *Required fees:* $798; $302 per term. Tuition and fees vary according to course level, course load, degree level and program. *Financial support:* In 2014–15, 1 student received support. Scholarships/grants and unspecified assistantships available. Support available to part-time students. Financial award application deadline: 4/1; financial award applicants required to submit FAFSA. *Faculty research:* Toolwear metrology, paper handling, grinding wheel imbalance, machine mission. *Unit head:* Dr. Pankaj K. Mallick, Director/Professor, 313-593-5119, Fax: 313-593-5386, E-mail: pkm@umich.edu. *Application contact:* Sherry Boyd, Intermediate Administrative Assistant, 313-593-5582, Fax: 313-593-5386, E-mail: idpgrad@umd.umich.edu.
Website: http://umdearborn.edu/cecs/IDP/mse_mse/index.php.

University of Missouri, Office of Research and Graduate Studies, College of Engineering, Department of Industrial and Manufacturing Systems Engineering, Columbia, MO 65211. Offers MS, PhD. *Faculty:* 11 full-time (2 women). *Students:* 20 full-time (7 women), 15 part-time (6 women); includes 2 minority (both Two or more races, non-Hispanic/Latino), 32 international. Average age 26. 72 applicants, 36% accepted, 7 enrolled. In 2014, 10 master's, 2 doctorates awarded. *Degree requirements:* For master's, thesis or alternative; for doctorate, thesis/dissertation. *Entrance requirements:* For master's and doctorate, GRE General Test, minimum GPA of 3.0. Additional exam requirements/recommendations for international students: Required—TOEFL (minimum score 550 paper-based; 80 iBT). *Application deadline:* For fall admission, 3/1 priority date for domestic and international students; for winter admission, 9/15 priority date for domestic and international students. Applications are processed on a rolling basis. Application fee: $55 ($75 for international students). Electronic applications accepted. *Financial support:* Fellowships, research assistantships, teaching assistantships, institutionally sponsored loans, traineeships, health care benefits, and unspecified assistantships available. Support available to part-time students. *Faculty research:* Logistics systems analysis and design, supply chain modeling, material flow design and improvement, intelligent systems. *Unit head:* Dr. Luis Occena, Department Chair, 573-882-9566, E-mail: occenal@missouri.edu. *Application contact:* Nicole Theberge, Administrative Associate I, 573-882-9540, E-mail: thebergen@missouri.edu.
Website: http://engineering.missouri.edu/imse/degree-programs/.

University of Nebraska–Lincoln, Graduate College, College of Engineering, Department of Industrial and Management Systems Engineering, Lincoln, NE 68588. Offers engineering management (M Eng); industrial and management systems engineering (MS, PhD); manufacturing systems engineering (MS). Postbaccalaureate distance learning degree programs offered. *Degree requirements:* For master's, thesis optional; for doctorate, comprehensive exam, thesis/dissertation. *Entrance requirements:* For master's and doctorate, GRE. Additional exam requirements/recommendations for international students: Required—TOEFL (minimum score 525 paper-based). Electronic applications accepted. *Faculty research:* Ergonomics, occupational safety, quality control, industrial packaging, facility design.

University of New Mexico, Graduate School, School of Engineering, Manufacturing Engineering Program, Albuquerque, NM 87131. Offers MEME, MBA/MEME. Part-time programs available. *Faculty:* 1 full-time (0 women). *Students:* 3 full-time (0 women), 2 part-time (0 women); includes 3 minority (1 Black or African American, non-Hispanic/Latino; 2 Hispanic/Latino), 2 international. Average age 28. 4 applicants. In 2014, 5 master's awarded. *Degree requirements:* For master's, 500 hours of relevant industry experience (paid or unpaid). *Entrance requirements:* For master's, GRE General Test (minimum combined score: 300), minimum GPA of 3.0. Additional exam requirements/recommendations for international students: Required—TOEFL (minimum score 550 paper-based; 79 iBT). *Application deadline:* For fall admission, 7/30 priority date for domestic students, 3/1 for international students; for spring admission, 11/30 priority date for domestic students, 8/1 for international students. Application fee: $50. Electronic applications accepted. *Financial support:* In 2014–15, 2 students received support, including 1 teaching assistantship (averaging $5,045 per year); career-related internships or fieldwork and health care benefits also available. Support available to part-time students. Financial award application deadline: 3/1; financial award applicants required to submit FAFSA. *Faculty research:* Robotics, automation control and machine vision, microsystems and microgrippers, semiconductor manufacturing and metrology, cross-training and operations of technicians and engineers. *Total annual research expenditures:* $1.1 million. *Unit head:* Dr. John E. Wood, Director, 505-272-7000, Fax: 505-272-7152, E-mail: jw@unm.edu. *Application contact:* Arden L. Ballantine, Information Contact, 505-272-7000, Fax: 505-272-7152, E-mail: aballant@unm.edu.
Website: http://www.mfg.unm.edu/.

University of St. Thomas, Graduate Studies, School of Engineering, St. Paul, MN 55105-1096. Offers electrical engineering (MS); manufacturing engineering and operations (MS); manufacturing systems (Certificate); mechanical engineering (MS); medical device development (Certificate); regulatory science (MS); software engineering (MS); software management (MS); systems engineering (MS); technology leadership (Certificate); technology management (MS). *Accreditation:* ABET (one or more programs are accredited). *Entrance requirements:* For master's, resume, official transcripts. Additional exam requirements/recommendations for international students: Required—TOEFL (minimum score 550 paper-based). Electronic applications accepted. *Expenses:* Contact institution.

University of Southern California, Graduate School, Viterbi School of Engineering, Daniel J. Epstein Department of Industrial and Systems Engineering, Los Angeles, CA 90089. Offers digital supply chain management (MS); engineering management (MS); engineering technology communication (Graduate Certificate); health systems operations (Graduate Certificate); industrial and systems engineering (MS, PhD, Engr); manufacturing engineering (MS); operations research engineering (MS); optimization and supply chain management (Graduate Certificate); product development engineering (MS); safety systems and security (MS); systems architecting and engineering (MS, Graduate Certificate); systems safety and security (Graduate Certificate); transportation systems (Graduate Certificate); MS/MBA. Part-time and evening/weekend programs available. Postbaccalaureate distance learning degree programs offered (no on-campus study). Terminal master's awarded for partial completion of doctoral program. *Degree requirements:* For master's, thesis optional; for doctorate, thesis/dissertation. *Entrance requirements:* For master's and doctorate, GRE General Test. Additional exam requirements/recommendations for international students: Recommended—TOEFL. Electronic applications accepted. *Faculty research:* Health systems, music cognition and retrieval, transportation and logistics, manufacturing and automation, engineering systems design, risk and economic analysis.

The University of Texas at El Paso, Graduate School, College of Engineering, Department of Industrial Engineering, El Paso, TX 79968-0001. Offers industrial engineering (MS); manufacturing engineering (MS); systems engineering (MS, Certificate). Part-time and evening/weekend programs available. *Degree requirements:* For master's, thesis optional. *Entrance requirements:* For master's, GRE General Test, minimum GPA of 3.0 in major. Additional exam requirements/recommendations for international students: Required—TOEFL. Electronic applications accepted. *Faculty research:* Computer vision, automated inspection, simulation and modeling.

The University of Texas at San Antonio, College of Engineering, Department of Mechanical Engineering, San Antonio, TX 78249-0617. Offers advanced manufacturing and enterprise engineering (MS); mechanical engineering (MS, PhD). Part-time and evening/weekend programs available. *Faculty:* 19 full-time (2 women), 5 part-time/adjunct (0 women). *Students:* 67 full-time (10 women), 43 part-time (7 women); includes 39 minority (4 Black or African American, non-Hispanic/Latino; 6 Asian, non-Hispanic/Latino; 24 Hispanic/Latino; 5 Two or more races, non-Hispanic/Latino), 44 international. Average age 28. 143 applicants, 73% accepted, 36 enrolled. In 2014, 20 master's, 2 doctorates awarded. Terminal master's awarded for partial completion of doctoral program. *Degree requirements:* For master's, comprehensive exam, thesis; for doctorate, comprehensive exam, thesis/dissertation. *Entrance requirements:* For master's, GRE General Test, bachelor's degree in mechanical engineering or related field from accredited institution of higher education; for doctorate, GRE General Test, master's degree in mechanical engineering or exceptionally outstanding undergraduate record in mechanical engineering or related field, minimum GPA of 3.33. Additional exam requirements/recommendations for international students: Required—TOEFL (minimum score 550 paper-based; 79 iBT), IELTS (minimum score 6.5). *Application deadline:* For fall admission, 7/1 for domestic students, 4/1 for international students; for spring admission, 11/1 for domestic students, 9/1 for international students. Applications are processed on a rolling basis. Application fee: $45 ($80 for international students). Electronic applications accepted. *Expenses:* Expenses: Contact institution. *Financial support:* In 2014–15, 25 students received support, including 10 fellowships with partial tuition reimbursements available (averaging $25,000 per year), 8 research assistantships (averaging $15,665 per year), 27 teaching assistantships (averaging $10,000 per year); career-related internships or fieldwork and unspecified assistantships also available. Financial award application deadline: 10/1. *Faculty research:* Mechanics and materials, advanced manufacturing, wind turbine, computational fluid dynamics, robotics, biomechanics, wind energy. *Total annual research expenditures:* $1.7 million. *Unit head:* Dr. Hai-Chao Han, Department Chair/Professor. *Application contact:* Dr. Frank Chen, Professor/Graduate Advisor of Record, 210-458-5382, E-mail: ff.chen@utsa.edu.
Website: http://engineering.utsa.edu/me/.

The University of Texas–Pan American, College of Engineering and Computer Science, Department of Manufacturing Engineering, Edinburg, TX 78539. Offers engineering management (MS); manufacturing engineering (MS); systems engineering (MS). *Expenses:* Tuition, state resident: full-time $4187; part-time $232.60 per credit hour. Tuition, nonresident: full-time $10,857; part-time $603.16 per credit hour. *Required fees:* $782; $27.50 per credit hour. $143.35 per semester.

University of Toronto, School of Graduate Studies, Advanced Design and Manufacturing Institute, Toronto, ON M5S 2J7, Canada. Offers M Eng. Program offered jointly with McMaster University, Queen's University, and The University of Western Ontario; available only to Canadian citizens and permanent residents of Canada. Part-time programs available. *Entrance requirements:* For master's, honours bachelor's degree in engineering with grades equivalent to a mid-B or better. Additional exam requirements/recommendations for international students: Required—TOEFL (minimum score 580 paper-based; 93 iBT), TWE (minimum score 4). Electronic applications accepted.

University of Windsor, Faculty of Graduate Studies, Faculty of Engineering, Department of Industrial and Manufacturing Systems Engineering, Windsor, ON N9B 3P4, Canada. Offers industrial engineering (M Eng, MA Sc); manufacturing systems engineering (PhD). Part-time programs available. *Degree requirements:* For master's, thesis; for doctorate, comprehensive exam, thesis/dissertation. *Entrance requirements:* For master's, minimum B average; for doctorate, master's degree, minimum B average. Additional exam requirements/recommendations for international students: Required—TOEFL (minimum score 560 paper-based). Electronic applications accepted. *Faculty research:* Human factors, operations research.

University of Wisconsin–Madison, Graduate School, College of Engineering, Manufacturing Systems Engineering Program, Madison, WI 53706. Offers MS. Part-time programs available. *Faculty:* 29 part-time/adjunct (2 women). *Students:* 38 full-time (7 women), 5 part-time (0 women); includes 1 minority (Native Hawaiian or other Pacific Islander, non-Hispanic/Latino), 37 international. Average age 27. 83 applicants, 36% accepted, 18 enrolled. In 2014, 11 master's awarded. *Degree requirements:* For master's, thesis (for some programs), independent research projects. *Entrance requirements:* For master's, GRE General Test, 2 years of work experience in manufacturing. Additional exam requirements/recommendations for international students: Required—TOEFL (minimum score 550 paper-based; 80 iBT). *Application deadline:* For fall admission, 2/1 for domestic and international students; for spring admission, 9/1 for domestic and international students; for summer admission, 3/1 for domestic and international students. Application fee: $56. Electronic applications accepted. *Expenses:* Tuition, state resident: full-time $10,723; part-time $745 per credit. Tuition, nonresident: full-time $24,054; part-time $1578 per credit. *Required fees:* $374 per semester. Tuition and fees vary according to course load, program and reciprocity agreements. *Financial support:* In 2014–15, 4 students received support, including fellowships with full tuition reimbursements available (averaging $16,500 per year), 2 research assistantships with full tuition reimbursements available (averaging $41,616 per year), 2 teaching assistantships with full tuition reimbursements available (averaging $29,492 per year); career-related internships or fieldwork, institutionally sponsored

loans, health care benefits, and unspecified assistantships also available. Financial award application deadline: 5/31. *Faculty research:* Advanced manufacturing, computer-aided manufacturing, rapid prototyping, lead time reduction, quick response manufacturing. *Unit head:* Prof. Frank E. Pfefferkorn, Director, 608-263-2668, E-mail: mse@engr.wisc.edu. *Application contact:* Theresa J. Pillar-Groesbeck, Student Status Examiner, 608-263-3955, E-mail: mse@engr.wisc.edu.
Website: http://www.engr.wisc.edu/msep.html.

University of Wisconsin–Milwaukee, Graduate School, College of Engineering and Applied Science, Program in Engineering, Milwaukee, WI 53201-0413. Offers civil engineering (MS); electrical and computer engineering (MS); energy engineering (Certificate); engineering (PhD); engineering management (MS); engineering mechanics (MS); ergonomics (Certificate); industrial and management engineering (MS); manufacturing engineering (MS); materials engineering (MS); mechanical engineering (MS); MUP/MS. Part-time programs available. *Degree requirements:* For master's, comprehensive exam (for some programs), thesis or alternative; for doctorate, comprehensive exam, thesis/dissertation, internship. *Entrance requirements:* For master's, GRE, minimum GPA of 2.75; for doctorate, GRE, minimum GPA of 3.5. Additional exam requirements/recommendations for international students: Required—TOEFL (minimum score 550 paper-based; 79 iBT), IELTS (minimum score 6.5).

University of Wisconsin–Stout, Graduate School, College of Technology, Engineering, and Management, Program in Manufacturing Engineering, Menomonie, WI 54751. Offers MS. Postbaccalaureate distance learning degree programs offered (minimal on-campus study). *Degree requirements:* For master's, thesis. *Entrance requirements:* For master's, minimum GPA of 3.0. Additional exam requirements/recommendations for international students: Required—TOEFL (minimum score 500 paper-based; 61 iBT). Electronic applications accepted. *Faculty research:* General ceramics patents, metal matrix composites, solidification processing, high temperature processing.

Villanova University, College of Engineering, Department of Mechanical Engineering, Villanova, PA 19085-1699. Offers electro-mechanical systems (Certificate); machinery dynamics (Certificate); mechanical engineering (MSME); nonlinear dynamics and control (Certificate); thermofluid systems (Certificate). Part-time and evening/weekend programs available. Postbaccalaureate distance learning degree programs offered (no on-campus study). *Degree requirements:* For master's, thesis optional. *Entrance requirements:* For master's, GRE General Test (for applicants with degrees from foreign universities), BME, minimum GPA of 3.0. Additional exam requirements/recommendations for international students: Required—TOEFL (minimum score 600 paper-based; 100 iBT). Electronic applications accepted. *Faculty research:* Composite materials, power plant systems, fluid mechanics, automated manufacturing, dynamic analysis.

Wayne State University, College of Engineering, Department of Industrial and Systems Engineering, Program in Manufacturing Engineering, Detroit, MI 48202. Offers MS. *Students:* 10 full-time (1 woman), 5 part-time (2 women); includes 2 minority (1 Black or African American, non-Hispanic/Latino; 1 Asian, non-Hispanic/Latino), 9 international. Average age 27. 49 applicants, 53% accepted, 7 enrolled. In 2014, 3 master's awarded. *Degree requirements:* For master's, thesis optional. *Entrance requirements:* For master's, minimum undergraduate upper-division GPA of 2.8, baccalaureate degree in engineering from ABET-accredited institution. Additional exam requirements/recommendations for international students: Required—TOEFL (minimum score 550 paper-based; 79 iBT), TWE (minimum score 5.5), Michigan English Language Assessment Battery (minimum score 85); Recommended—IELTS (minimum score 6.5). *Application deadline:* For fall admission, 6/1 priority date for domestic students, 5/1 priority date for international students; for winter admission, 10/1 priority date for domestic students, 9/1 priority date for international students; for spring admission, 2/1 priority date for domestic students, 1/1 priority date for international students. Applications are processed on a rolling basis. Application fee: $0. Electronic applications accepted. *Expenses:* Expenses: Contact institution. *Financial support:* In 2014–15, 4 students received support. Fellowships with tuition reimbursements available, research assistantships with tuition reimbursements available, teaching assistantships with tuition reimbursements available, scholarships/grants, health care benefits, and unspecified assistantships available. Financial award application deadline: 3/31; financial award applicants required to submit FAFSA. *Faculty research:* Healthcare systems engineering, product design and development, quality and reliability engineering, supply chain management and logistics. *Unit head:* Dr. Leslie Monplaisir, Associate Professor/Chair, 313-577-1645, Fax: 313-577-8833, E-mail: ad5365@wayne.edu. *Application contact:* Dr. Kyoung-Yun Kim, Associate Professor and MS Program Officer, 313-577-4396, Fax: 313-577-8833, E-mail: kykim@eng.wayne.edu.
Website: http://engineering.wayne.edu/ise/masters/manufacturing.php.

Western Illinois University, School of Graduate Studies, College of Business and Technology, Department of Engineering Technology, Macomb, IL 61455-1390. Offers manufacturing engineering systems (MS). Part-time programs available. *Students:* 11 full-time (3 women), 2 part-time (1 woman); includes 1 minority (Black or African American, non-Hispanic/Latino), 9 international. Average age 27. 15 applicants, 80% accepted, 8 enrolled. In 2014, 4 master's awarded. *Degree requirements:* For master's, thesis or alternative. *Entrance requirements:* Additional exam requirements/recommendations for international students: Required—TOEFL (minimum score 550 paper-based; 80 iBT). *Application deadline:* Applications are processed on a rolling basis. Application fee: $30. Electronic applications accepted. *Financial support:* In 2014–15, 5 students received support, including 2 teaching assistantships with full tuition reimbursements available (averaging $8,688 per year). Financial award applicants required to submit FAFSA. *Unit head:* Dr. Ray Diéz, Chairperson, 309-298-1091. *Application contact:* Dr. Nancy Parsons, Associate Provost and Director of Graduate Studies, 309-298-1806, Fax: 309-298-2345, E-mail: grad-office@wiu.edu.
Website: http://wiu.edu/engrtech.

Western Michigan University, Graduate College, College of Engineering and Applied Sciences, Department of Engineering Design, Manufacturing, and Management Systems, Kalamazoo, MI 49008. Offers MS. *Application deadline:* For fall admission, 2/15 for domestic students. *Financial support:* Application deadline: 2/15. *Application contact:* Admissions and Orientation, 269-387-2000, Fax: 269-387-2096.

Western New England University, College of Engineering, Master's Program in Engineering Management, Springfield, MA 01119. Offers business and engineering information systems (MSEM); general engineering management (MSEM); production and manufacturing systems (MSEM); quality engineering (MSEM); MSEM/MBA. Part-time and evening/weekend programs available. Postbaccalaureate distance learning degree programs offered (no on-campus study). *Students:* 45 part-time (6 women); includes 4 minority (1 Black or African American, non-Hispanic/Latino; 1 Asian, non-Hispanic/Latino; 1 Hispanic/Latino; 1 Two or more races, non-Hispanic/Latino), 3 international. Average age 31. In 2014, 30 master's awarded. *Degree requirements:* For master's, thesis optional. *Entrance requirements:* For master's, official transcript, bachelor's degree in engineering or related field, two recommendations, resume. Additional exam requirements/recommendations for international students: Required—TOEFL (minimum score 79 iBT). *Application deadline:* Applications are processed on a rolling basis. Application fee: $30. Electronic applications accepted. *Financial support:* Application deadline: 4/15; applicants required to submit FAFSA. *Unit head:* Dr. S. Hossein Cheraghi, Dean, 413-782-1285, E-mail: cheraghi@wne.edu. *Application contact:* Matthew Fox, Director of Recruiting and Marketing for Adult Learners, 413-782-1517, Fax: 413-782-1777, E-mail: study@wne.edu.
Website: http://www1.wne.edu/engineering/index.cfm?selection-doc.9104.

Wichita State University, Graduate School, College of Engineering, Department of Industrial and Manufacturing Engineering, Wichita, KS 67260. Offers engineering management (MEM); industrial engineering (MS, PhD). Part-time programs available. In 2014, 37 master's, 3 doctorates awarded. *Entrance requirements:* Additional exam requirements/recommendations for international students: Required—TOEFL. *Financial support:* Teaching assistantships available. *Unit head:* Dr. Krishna Krishnan, Chair, 316-978-3425, Fax: 316-978-3742, E-mail: krishna.krishnan@wichita.edu. *Application contact:* Jordan Oleson, Admissions Coordinator, 316-978-3095, Fax: 316-978-3253, E-mail: jordan.oleson@wichita.edu.
Website: http://www.wichita.edu/ime.

Worcester Polytechnic Institute, Graduate Studies and Research, Department of Mechanical Engineering, Program in Manufacturing Engineering, Worcester, MA 01609-2280. Offers MS, PhD. Part-time and evening/weekend programs available. *Students:* 13 full-time (3 women), 18 part-time (2 women); includes 10 minority (2 Black or African American, non-Hispanic/Latino; 2 Asian, non-Hispanic/Latino; 6 Hispanic/Latino), 7 international. 34 applicants, 76% accepted, 11 enrolled. In 2014, 6 master's, 2 doctorates awarded. *Degree requirements:* For master's, thesis optional; for doctorate, comprehensive exam, thesis/dissertation, research proposal. *Entrance requirements:* For master's and doctorate, GRE (recommended), 3 letters of recommendation. Additional exam requirements/recommendations for international students: Required—TOEFL (minimum score 563 paper-based; 84 iBT), IELTS (minimum score 7). *Application deadline:* For fall admission, 1/1 priority date for domestic and international students; for spring admission, 10/1 priority date for domestic and international students. Applications are processed on a rolling basis. Application fee: $70. Electronic applications accepted. *Financial support:* Research assistantships, teaching assistantships, career-related internships or fieldwork, institutionally sponsored loans, scholarships/grants, and unspecified assistantships available. Financial award application deadline: 1/1; financial award applicants required to submit FAFSA. *Unit head:* Dr. Kevin Rong, Director, 508-831-6088, Fax: 508-831-5673, E-mail: rong@wpi.edu. *Application contact:* GlorieAnn Minnich, Graduate Secretary, 508-831-6088, Fax: 508-831-5673, E-mail: gkminnich@wpi.edu.
Website: http://www.wpi.edu/academics/mfe.

Worcester Polytechnic Institute, Graduate Studies and Research, Programs in Interdisciplinary Studies, Worcester, MA 01609-2280. Offers bioscience administration (MS); impact engineering (MS); manufacturing engineering management (MS); power systems management (MS); social science (PhD); systems modeling (MS). Part-time and evening/weekend programs available. *Faculty:* 1 part-time/adjunct (0 women). *Students:* 2 full-time (0 women), 74 part-time (15 women); includes 18 minority (3 Black or African American, non-Hispanic/Latino; 7 Asian, non-Hispanic/Latino; 3 Hispanic/Latino; 5 Two or more races, non-Hispanic/Latino), 5 international. 37 applicants, 97% accepted, 29 enrolled. In 2014, 10 master's, 1 doctorate awarded. *Degree requirements:* For master's, thesis; for doctorate, comprehensive exam, thesis/dissertation. *Entrance requirements:* For master's and doctorate, 3 letters of recommendation. Additional exam requirements/recommendations for international students: Required—TOEFL (minimum score 563 paper-based; 84 iBT), IELTS (minimum score 7). *Application deadline:* For fall admission, 1/1 priority date for domestic students, 1/1 for international students; for spring admission, 10/1 priority date for domestic students, 10/1 for international students. Application fee: $70. *Financial support:* Institutionally sponsored loans, scholarships/grants, and unspecified assistantships available. Financial award application deadline: 1/1; financial award applicants required to submit FAFSA. *Unit head:* Dr. Fred J. Looft, Head, 508-831-5231, Fax: 508-831-5491, E-mail: fjlooft@wpi.edu. *Application contact:* Lynne Dougherty, Administrative Assistant, 508-831-5301, Fax: 508-831-5717, E-mail: grad@wpi.edu.

Pharmaceutical Engineering

New Jersey Institute of Technology, Newark College of Engineering, Newark, NJ 07102. Offers biomedical engineering (MS, PhD); chemical engineering (MS, PhD); computer engineering (MS, PhD); electrical engineering (MS, PhD); engineering management (MS); healthcare systems management (MS); industrial engineering (MS, PhD); Internet engineering (MS); manufacturing engineering (MS); mechanical engineering (MS, PhD); occupational safety and health engineering (MS); pharmaceutical bioprocessing (MS); pharmaceutical engineering (MS); pharmaceutical systems management (MS); power and energy systems (MS); telecommunications (MS); transportation (MS, PhD). Part-time and evening/weekend programs available. Terminal master's awarded for partial completion of doctoral program. *Degree requirements:* For master's, thesis optional; for doctorate, thesis/dissertation. *Entrance requirements:* For master's, GRE General Test; for doctorate, GRE General Test, minimum graduate GPA of 3.5. Additional exam requirements/recommendations for international students: Required—TOEFL (minimum score 550 paper-based; 79 iBT). Electronic applications accepted.

University of Michigan, College of Engineering, Interpro Programs in Engineering, Ann Arbor, MI 48109. Offers automotive engineering (M Eng); design science (PhD); energy systems engineering (MS); financial engineering (MS); global automotive and manufacturing engineering (M Eng); manufacturing engineering (M Eng, D Eng); pharmaceutical engineering (M Eng); robotics and autonomous vehicles (M Eng); MBA/M Eng; MSE/MS. Part-time programs available. Postbaccalaureate distance learning degree programs offered (no on-campus study). *Students:* 187 full-time (46 women), 250 part-time (40 women). 364 applicants, 2% accepted, 3 enrolled. In 2014, 171 master's, 1 doctorate awarded. Terminal master's awarded for partial completion of doctoral program. *Degree requirements:* For master's, capstone project; for doctorate, thesis/dissertation. *Entrance requirements:* For master's, GRE; for doctorate, GRE, 2

years of work experience. Additional exam requirements/recommendations for international students: Required—TOEFL (minimum score 560 paper-based). *Application deadline:* Applications are processed on a rolling basis. Electronic applications accepted. *Financial support:* Fellowships, research assistantships with full tuition reimbursements, teaching assistantships with full tuition reimbursements, career-related internships or fieldwork, scholarships/grants, and unspecified assistantships available. Financial award application deadline: 2/15; financial award applicants required to submit FAFSA. *Faculty research:* Automotive engineering, design science, energy systems engineering, engineering sustainable systems, financial engineering, global automotive and manufacturing engineering, integrated microsystems, manufacturing engineering, pharmaceutical engineering, robotics and autonomous vehicles. *Total annual research expenditures:* $263,643. *Unit head:* Prof. Panos Papalambros, Director, 734-647-8401, Fax: 734-647-0079, E-mail: pyp@umich.edu. *Application contact:* Patti Mackmiller, Program Manager, 734-764-3071, Fax: 734-647-2243, E-mail: pmackmil@umich.edu.
Website: http://www.isd.engin.umich.edu.

Reliability Engineering

Arizona State University at the Tempe campus, Ira A. Fulton Schools of Engineering, ASU Engineering Online Programs, Tempe, AZ 85287. Offers construction (MS); embedded systems (M Eng); enterprise systems innovation and management (MSE); modeling and simulation (M Eng); quality and reliability engineering (M Eng); software engineering (MSE); systems engineering (M Eng).

University of Maryland, College Park, Academic Affairs, A. James Clark School of Engineering, Department of Mechanical Engineering, Reliability Engineering Program, College Park, MD 20742. Offers M Eng, MS, PhD. Part-time and evening/weekend programs available. Postbaccalaureate distance learning degree programs offered. *Degree requirements:* For master's, thesis optional; for doctorate, thesis/dissertation. *Entrance requirements:* For master's, GRE General Test, 3 letters of recommendation; for doctorate, GRE General Test, minimum GPA of 3.0. Additional exam requirements/recommendations for international students: Required—TOEFL. Electronic applications accepted. *Faculty research:* Electron linear acceleration, x-ray and imaging.

The University of Tennessee, Graduate School, College of Engineering, Department of Chemical and Biomolecular Engineering, Knoxville, TN 37996. Offers chemical engineering (MS, PhD); reliability and maintainability engineering (MS); MS/MBA. Part-time programs available. *Faculty:* 30 full-time (0 women). *Students:* 54 full-time (16 women), 2 part-time (0 women); includes 7 minority (1 Black or African American, non-Hispanic/Latino; 1 Asian, non-Hispanic/Latino; 2 Hispanic/Latino; 3 Two or more races, non-Hispanic/Latino), 24 international. Average age 26. 104 applicants, 29% accepted, 14 enrolled. In 2014, 11 master's, 10 doctorates awarded. *Degree requirements:* For master's, thesis or alternative; for doctorate, comprehensive exam, thesis/dissertation. *Entrance requirements:* For master's, GRE General Test (for MS students pursuing research thesis), minimum GPA of 2.7 (for U.S. degree holders), 3.0 (for international degree holders); for doctorate, GRE General Test (for all PhD candidates), minimum GPA of 3.0 on previous graduate course work. Additional exam requirements/recommendations for international students: Required—TOEFL (minimum score 550 paper-based). *Application deadline:* For fall admission, 2/1 priority date for domestic and international students; for spring admission, 6/15 for domestic and international students. Applications are processed on a rolling basis. Application fee: $35. Electronic applications accepted. *Financial support:* In 2014–15, 50 students received support, including 3 fellowships (averaging $25,333 per year), 29 research assistantships with full tuition reimbursements available (averaging $24,097 per year), 18 teaching assistantships with full tuition reimbursements available (averaging $24,033 per year); career-related internships or fieldwork, Federal Work-Study, institutionally sponsored loans, health care benefits, and unspecified assistantships also available. Financial award application deadline: 2/1; financial award applicants required to submit FAFSA. *Faculty research:* Bio-fuels; engineering of soft, functional and structural materials; fuel cells and energy storage devices; molecular and cellular bioengineering; molecular modeling and simulations. *Total annual research expenditures:* $4 million. *Unit head:* Dr. Bamin Khomami, Head, 865-974-2421, Fax: 865-974-7076, E-mail: bkhomami@utk.edu. *Application contact:* Dr. Paul Frymier, Graduate Program Coordinator, 865-974-4961, Fax: 865-974-7076, E-mail: pdf@utk.edu.
Website: http://www.engr.utk.edu/cbe/.

The University of Tennessee, Graduate School, College of Engineering, Department of Electrical Engineering and Computer Science, Knoxville, TN 37966. Offers computer engineering (MS, PhD); computer science (MS, PhD); electrical engineering (MS, PhD); reliability and maintainability engineering (MS); MS/MBA. Part-time programs available. *Faculty:* 70 full-time (11 women), 14 part-time/adjunct (4 women). *Students:* 182 full-time (38 women), 44 part-time (4 women); includes 16 minority (2 Black or African American, non-Hispanic/Latino; 9 Asian, non-Hispanic/Latino; 2 Hispanic/Latino; 3 Two or more races, non-Hispanic/Latino), 138 international. Average age 28. 681 applicants, 12% accepted, 52 enrolled. In 2014, 42 master's, 18 doctorates awarded. *Degree requirements:* For master's, thesis or alternative; for doctorate, comprehensive exam, thesis/dissertation. *Entrance requirements:* For master's, GRE General Test (for MS students pursuing research thesis), minimum GPA of 2.7 (for U.S. degree holders), 3.0 (for international degree holders); 3 references; personal statement; for doctorate, GRE General Test (for all PhD candidates), minimum GPA of 3.0 on previous graduate course work; 3 references; personal statement. Additional exam requirements/recommendations for international students: Required—TOEFL (minimum score 550 paper-based). *Application deadline:* For fall admission, 2/1 priority date for domestic and international students; for spring admission, 6/15 for domestic and international students. Applications are processed on a rolling basis. Application fee: $35. Electronic applications accepted. *Financial support:* In 2014–15, 172 students received support, including 37 fellowships with full tuition reimbursements available (averaging $6,660 per year), 92 research assistantships with full tuition reimbursements available (averaging $21,659 per year), 61 teaching assistantships with full tuition reimbursements available (averaging $19,037 per year); career-related internships or fieldwork, Federal Work-Study, institutionally sponsored loans, health care benefits, and unspecified assistantships also available. Financial award application deadline: 2/1; financial award applicants required to submit FAFSA. *Faculty research:* Artificial intelligence and visualization; microelectronics, mixed-signal electronics, VLSI, embedded systems; scientific and distributed computing; computer vision, robotics, and image processing; power electronics, power systems, communications. *Total annual research expenditures:* $13.8 million. *Unit head:* Dr. Kevin Tomsovic, Head, 865-974-3461, Fax: 865-974-5483, E-mail: tomsovic@eecs.utk.edu. *Application contact:* Dr. Lynne E. Parker, Associate Head, 865-974-4394, Fax: 865-974-5483, E-mail: parker@eecs.utk.edu.
Website: http://www.eecs.utk.edu.

The University of Tennessee, Graduate School, College of Engineering, Department of Industrial and Systems Engineering, Knoxville, TN 37966. Offers engineering management (MS); industrial engineering (MS, PhD); reliability and maintainability engineering (MS); MS/MBA. Part-time programs available. Postbaccalaureate distance learning degree programs offered (minimal on-campus study). *Faculty:* 12 full-time (2 women), 11 part-time/adjunct (1 woman). *Students:* 68 full-time (15 women), 58 part-time (12 women); includes 15 minority (6 Black or African American, non-Hispanic/Latino; 6 Asian, non-Hispanic/Latino; 1 Hispanic/Latino; 2 Two or more races, non-Hispanic/Latino), 40 international. Average age 37. 116 applicants, 63% accepted, 37 enrolled. In 2014, 55 master's, 4 doctorates awarded. *Degree requirements:* For master's, thesis or alternative; for doctorate, comprehensive exam, thesis/dissertation. *Entrance requirements:* For master's, GRE General Test (for MS students pursuing research thesis), minimum GPA of 2.7 (for U.S. degree holders), 3.0 (for international degree holders); for doctorate, GRE General Test (for all PhD candidates), minimum GPA of 3.0 on previous graduate course work. Additional exam requirements/recommendations for international students: Required—TOEFL (minimum score 550 paper-based). *Application deadline:* For fall admission, 2/1 priority date for domestic and international students; for spring admission, 6/15 for domestic and international students. Applications are processed on a rolling basis. Application fee: $35. Electronic applications accepted. *Financial support:* In 2014–15, 41 students received support, including 3 fellowships with full tuition reimbursements available (averaging $25,164 per year), 22 research assistantships with full tuition reimbursements available (averaging $18,763 per year), 13 teaching assistantships with full tuition reimbursements available (averaging $19,241 per year); career-related internships or fieldwork, Federal Work-Study, institutionally sponsored loans, health care benefits, and unspecified assistantships also available. Financial award application deadline: 2/1; financial award applicants required to submit FAFSA. *Faculty research:* Defense-oriented supply chain modeling; dependability and reliability of large computer networks; design of lean, reliable systems; new product development; operations research in the automotive industry. *Total annual research expenditures:* $1.4 million. *Unit head:* Dr. John Kobza, Department Head, 865-974-3333, Fax: 865-974-0588, E-mail: jkobza@utk.edu. *Application contact:* Dr. Alberto Garcia-Diaz, Professor, 865-974-7647, E-mail: agd@utk.edu.
Website: http://www.engr.utk.edu/ie/.

The University of Tennessee, Graduate School, College of Engineering, Department of Materials Science and Engineering, Knoxville, TN 37996-2200. Offers materials science and engineering (MS, PhD); polymer engineering (MS, PhD); reliability and maintainability engineering (MS); MS/MBA. Part-time programs available. *Faculty:* 32 full-time (4 women), 7 part-time/adjunct (1 woman). *Students:* 86 full-time (20 women), 6 part-time (1 woman); includes 6 minority (1 Black or African American, non-Hispanic/Latino; 2 Asian, non-Hispanic/Latino; 2 Hispanic/Latino; 1 Two or more races, non-Hispanic/Latino), 50 international. Average age 29. 154 applicants, 19% accepted, 22 enrolled. In 2014, 6 master's, 16 doctorates awarded. *Degree requirements:* For master's, thesis or alternative; for doctorate, comprehensive exam, thesis/dissertation. *Entrance requirements:* For master's, GRE General Test (for MS students pursuing research thesis), minimum GPA of 2.7 (for U.S. degree holders), 3.0 (for international degree holders); 3 references; for doctorate, GRE General Test (for all PhD candidates), minimum GPA of 3.0 on previous graduate course work; 3 references. Additional exam requirements/recommendations for international students: Required—TOEFL (minimum score 550 paper-based). *Application deadline:* For fall admission, 2/1 priority date for domestic and international students; for spring admission, 6/15 for domestic and international students. Applications are processed on a rolling basis. Application fee: $35. Electronic applications accepted. *Financial support:* In 2014–15, 80 students received support, including 3 fellowships with full tuition reimbursements available (averaging $9,096 per year), 59 research assistantships with full tuition reimbursements available (averaging $21,077 per year), 19 teaching assistantships with full tuition reimbursements available (averaging $22,829 per year); career-related internships or fieldwork, Federal Work-Study, institutionally sponsored loans, health care benefits, and unspecified assistantships also available. Financial award application deadline: 2/1; financial award applicants required to submit FAFSA. *Faculty research:* Biomaterials; functional materials electronic, magnetic and optical; high temperature materials; mechanical behavior of materials; neutron materials science. *Total annual research expenditures:* $9.1 million. *Unit head:* Dr. Kurt Sickafus, Head, 865-974-4858, Fax: 865-974-4115, E-mail: kurt@utk.edu. *Application contact:* Dr. Roberto S. Benson, Associate Head, 865-974-5347, Fax: 865-974-4115, E-mail: rbenson1@utk.edu.
Website: http://www.engr.utk.edu/mse.

The University of Tennessee, Graduate School, College of Engineering, Department of Nuclear Engineering, Program in Reliability and Maintainability Engineering, Knoxville, TN 37966. Offers MS. *Students:* 2 full-time (0 women), 13 part-time (0 women); includes 2 minority (1 Hispanic/Latino; 1 Two or more races, non-Hispanic/Latino), 1 international. Average age 34. 6 applicants, 50% accepted, 3 enrolled. In 2014, 2 master's awarded. *Degree requirements:* For master's, thesis or alternative. *Entrance requirements:* For master's, GRE General Test (for MS students pursuing research thesis), minimum GPA of 2.7 (for U.S. degree holders), 3.0 (for international degree holders). Additional exam requirements/recommendations for international students: Required—TOEFL (minimum score 550 paper-based). *Application deadline:* For fall admission, 2/1 priority date for domestic and international students; for spring admission, 6/15 for domestic and international students. Applications are processed on a rolling basis. Application fee: $35. Electronic applications accepted. *Financial support:* Career-related internships or fieldwork, Federal Work-Study, institutionally sponsored loans, health care benefits, and unspecified assistantships available. Financial award application deadline: 2/1; financial award applicants required to submit FAFSA. *Unit head:* Dr. J. Wesley Hines, Head, 865-974-2525, Fax: 865-974-0668, E-mail: jhines2@utk.edu. *Application contact:* Dr. Masood Parang, Associate Dean of Student Affairs, 865-974-2454, Fax: 865-974-9871, E-mail: mparang@utk.edu.
Website: http://www.engr.utk.edu/rme/.

Safety Engineering

Embry-Riddle Aeronautical University–Prescott, Department of Behavioral and Safety Sciences, Prescott, AZ 86301-3720. Offers MSSS. Part-time programs available. *Faculty:* 3 full-time (0 women), 3 part-time/adjunct (all women). *Students:* 24 full-time (4 women), 11 part-time (3 women); includes 10 minority (1 Black or African American, non-Hispanic/Latino; 5 Hispanic/Latino; 4 Two or more races, non-Hispanic/Latino), 7 international. Average age 31. 17 applicants, 65% accepted, 7 enrolled. In 2014, 12 master's awarded. *Degree requirements:* For master's, thesis optional, research project or thesis. *Entrance requirements:* Additional exam requirements/recommendations for international students: Required—TOEFL (minimum score 550 paper-based; 79 iBT). *Application deadline:* For fall admission, 6/1 priority date for domestic students, 5/1 priority date for international students; for spring admission, 11/1 priority date for domestic students, 10/1 priority date for international students. Applications are processed on a rolling basis. Application fee: $50. Electronic applications accepted. *Expenses: Tuition:* Full-time $15,360; part-time $1280 per credit hour. *Required fees:* $1034. *Financial support:* In 2014–15, 5 students received support. Research assistantships with full and partial tuition reimbursements available, career-related internships or fieldwork, and unspecified assistantships available. Financial award application deadline: 4/15. *Faculty research:* Service quality in aviation, engineering psychology, accident investigation and analysis, occupational safety/biomechanics, crash management/response/survivability. *Unit head:* Erin E. Bowen, PhD, Department Chair and Associate Professor Safety Science, 928-777-6960, E-mail: erin.bowen@erau.edu. *Application contact:* Graduate Admissions, 928-777-6600, E-mail: prescottgradinfo@erau.edu.
Website: http://prescott.erau.edu/college-arts-sciences/safety-science/index.html.

Florida Institute of Technology, Graduate Programs, College of Aeronautics, Program in Applied Aviation Safety, Melbourne, FL 32901-6975. Offers MSA. *Students:* 7 full-time (0 women); includes 2 minority (1 Black or African American, non-Hispanic/Latino; 1 Hispanic/Latino), 4 international. Average age 26. 15 applicants, 53% accepted, 1 enrolled. In 2014, 5 master's awarded. *Degree requirements:* For master's, comprehensive exam (for some programs), thesis or alternative, capstone, 30 credit hours. *Entrance requirements:* For master's, letter of recommendation, resume, statement of objectives. *Expenses: Tuition:* Part-time $1179 per credit hour. Tuition and fees vary according to campus/location. *Unit head:* Dr. Korhan Oyman, Dean, 321-674-8971, E-mail: koyman@fit.edu. *Application contact:* Cheryl A. Brown, Associate Director of Graduate Admissions, 321-674-7581, Fax: 321-723-9468, E-mail: cbrown@fit.edu.
Website: http://www.fit.edu/programs/8205/msa-aviation-applied-aviation-safety#.VUDm_k10ypo.

Indiana University Bloomington, School of Public Health, Department of Applied Health Science, Bloomington, IN 47405. Offers behavioral, social, and community health (MPH); family health (MPH); health behavior (PhD); nutrition science (MS); professional health education (MPH); public health administration (MPH); safety management (MS); school and college health education (MS). *Accreditation:* CEPH (one or more programs are accredited). *Faculty:* 30 full-time (19 women). *Students:* 93 full-time (60 women), 17 part-time (6 women); includes 29 minority (12 Black or African American, non-Hispanic/Latino; 5 Asian, non-Hispanic/Latino; 7 Hispanic/Latino; 5 Two or more races, non-Hispanic/Latino), 18 international. Average age 30. 148 applicants, 68% accepted, 63 enrolled. In 2014, 36 master's, 10 doctorates awarded. *Degree requirements:* For master's, thesis optional; for doctorate, comprehensive exam, thesis/dissertation. *Entrance requirements:* For master's, GRE (for MS in nutrition science), 3 recommendations; for doctorate, GRE, 3 recommendations. Additional exam requirements/recommendations for international students: Required—TOEFL (minimum score 550 paper-based; 80 iBT). *Application deadline:* For fall admission, 2/1 priority date for domestic students, 12/1 priority date for international students; for spring admission, 11/15 priority date for domestic students, 9/1 priority date for international students. Application fee: $55 ($65 for international students). Electronic applications accepted. *Financial support:* Fellowships, research assistantships with full and partial tuition reimbursements, teaching assistantships with full and partial tuition reimbursements, career-related internships or fieldwork, Federal Work-Study, institutionally sponsored loans, scholarships/grants, health care benefits, tuition waivers (partial), unspecified assistantships, and fee remissions available. Financial award application deadline: 3/1; financial award applicants required to submit FAFSA. *Faculty research:* Cancer education, HIV/AIDS and drug education, public health, parent-child interactions, safety education, obesity, public health policy, public health administration, school health, health education, human development, nutrition, human sexuality, chronic disease, early childhood health. *Total annual research expenditures:* $1.4 million. *Unit head:* Dr. David K. Lohrmann, Chair, 812-856-5101, Fax: 812-855-3936, E-mail: dlohrman@indiana.edu. *Application contact:* Dr. Susan Middlestadt, Associate Professor and Graduate Coordinator, 812-856-5768, Fax: 812-855-3936, E-mail: semiddle@indiana.edu.
Website: http://www.publichealth.indiana.edu/departments/applied-health-science/index.shtml.

Murray State University, College of Health Sciences and Human Services, Program in Occupational Safety and Health, Murray, KY 42071. Offers environmental science (MS); industrial hygiene (MS); safety management (MS). *Accreditation:* ABET. Part-time programs available. *Degree requirements:* For master's, comprehensive exam, thesis optional, professional internship. Electronic applications accepted. *Faculty research:* Light effects on plant growth, ergonomics, toxic effects of pets' pesticides, traffic safety.

New Jersey Institute of Technology, Newark College of Engineering, Newark, NJ 07102. Offers biomedical engineering (MS, PhD); chemical engineering (MS, PhD); computer engineering (MS, PhD); electrical engineering (MS, PhD); engineering management (MS); healthcare systems management (MS); industrial engineering (MS, PhD); Internet engineering (MS); manufacturing engineering (MS); mechanical engineering (MS, PhD); occupational safety and health engineering (MS); pharmaceutical bioprocessing (MS); pharmaceutical engineering (MS); pharmaceutical systems management (MS); power and energy systems (MS); telecommunications (MS); transportation (MS, PhD). Part-time and evening/weekend programs available. Terminal master's awarded for partial completion of doctoral program. *Degree requirements:* For master's, thesis optional; for doctorate, thesis/dissertation. *Entrance requirements:* For master's, GRE General Test; for doctorate, GRE General Test, minimum graduate GPA of 3.5. Additional exam requirements/recommendations for international students: Required—TOEFL (minimum score 550 paper-based; 79 iBT). Electronic applications accepted.

Rochester Institute of Technology, Graduate Enrollment Services, College of Applied Science and Technology, School of Engineering Technology, MS Program in Environmental, Health and Safety Management, Rochester, NY 14623-5604. Offers MS. Part-time programs available. Postbaccalaureate distance learning degree programs offered (no on-campus study). *Students:* 16 full-time (7 women), 15 part-time (2 women); includes 5 minority (2 Black or African American, non-Hispanic/Latino; 1 Asian, non-Hispanic/Latino; 2 Hispanic/Latino), 9 international. Average age 31. 53 applicants, 34% accepted, 8 enrolled. In 2014, 27 master's awarded. *Degree requirements:* For master's, thesis or alternative. *Entrance requirements:* For master's, TOEFL, IELTS, or PTE for non-native English speakers, Recommended minimum GPA of 3.0. Additional exam requirements/recommendations for international students: Required—PTE (minimum score 58), TOEFL (minimum score 550 paper-based; 79 iBT) or IELTS (minimum score 6.5). *Application deadline:* Applications are processed on a rolling basis. Application fee: $60. Electronic applications accepted. *Expenses:* Expenses: $1,673 per credit hour. *Financial support:* In 2014–15, 22 students received support. Research assistantships with partial tuition reimbursements available, teaching assistantships with partial tuition reimbursements available, career-related internships or fieldwork, Federal Work-Study, institutionally sponsored loans, scholarships/grants, and unspecified assistantships available. Support available to part-time students. Financial award applicants required to submit FAFSA. *Faculty research:* Air emissions, wastewater, solid and hazardous waste, occupational safety and occupational health (industrial hygiene), integrated environmental, health and safety management systems in industry. *Unit head:* Joseph Rosenbeck, Graduate Program Director, 585-475-6469, E-mail: jmrcem@rit.edu. *Application contact:* Diane Ellison, Associate Vice President, Graduate Enrollment Services, 585-475-2229, Fax: 585-475-7164, E-mail: gradinfo@rit.edu.
Website: http://www.rit.edu/cast/cetems/ms-environmental-health-safety-management.

The University of Alabama at Birmingham, School of Engineering, Program in Engineering, Birmingham, AL 35294. Offers advanced safety engineering and management (M Eng); construction engineering management (M Eng); information engineering management (M Eng). Part-time programs available. Postbaccalaureate distance learning degree programs offered (no on-campus study). *Students:* 14 full-time (4 women), 237 part-time (44 women); includes 91 minority (71 Black or African American, non-Hispanic/Latino; 1 American Indian or Alaska Native, non-Hispanic/Latino; 3 Asian, non-Hispanic/Latino; 8 Hispanic/Latino; 8 Two or more races, non-Hispanic/Latino), 6 international. Average age 38. In 2014, 90 master's awarded. *Entrance requirements:* Additional exam requirements/recommendations for international students: Required—TOEFL. *Expenses:* Tuition, state resident: full-time $7090; part-time $370 per credit hour. Tuition, nonresident: full-time $16,072; part-time $869 per credit hour. Full-time tuition and fees vary according to course load and program. *Unit head:* Dr. J. Iwan Alexander, Dean, 205-934-8400, Fax: 205-934-8437, E-mail: ialex@uab.edu. *Application contact:* Susan Noblitt Banks, Director of Graduate School Operations, 205-934-8227, Fax: 205-934-8413, E-mail: gradschool@uab.edu.
Website: http://www.uab.edu/engineering/home/professional-programs.

University of Minnesota, Duluth, Graduate School, Swenson College of Science and Engineering, Department of Mechanical and Industrial Engineering, Duluth, MN 55812-2496. Offers engineering management (MSEM); environmental health and safety (MEHS). Part-time and evening/weekend programs available. Postbaccalaureate distance learning degree programs offered (no on-campus study). *Degree requirements:* For master's, comprehensive exam, thesis or alternative, capstone design project (MSEM), field project (MEHS). *Entrance requirements:* For master's, GRE (MEHS), interview (MEHS), letters of recommendation. Additional exam requirements/recommendations for international students: Required—TOEFL (minimum score 550 paper-based). *Faculty research:* Transportation, ergonomics, toxicology, supply chain management, automation and robotics.

University of Southern California, Graduate School, Viterbi School of Engineering, Daniel J. Epstein Department of Industrial and Systems Engineering, Los Angeles, CA 90089. Offers digital supply chain management (MS); engineering management (MS); engineering technology communication (Graduate Certificate); health systems operations (Graduate Certificate); industrial and systems engineering (MS, PhD, Engr); manufacturing engineering (MS); operations research engineering (MS); optimization and supply chain management (Graduate Certificate); product development engineering (MS); safety systems and security (MS); systems architecting and engineering (MS, Graduate Certificate); systems safety and security (Graduate Certificate); transportation systems (Graduate Certificate); MS/MBA. Part-time and evening/weekend programs available. Postbaccalaureate distance learning degree programs offered (no on-campus study). Terminal master's awarded for partial completion of doctoral program. *Degree requirements:* For master's, thesis optional; for doctorate, thesis/dissertation. *Entrance requirements:* For master's and doctorate, GRE General Test. Additional exam requirements/recommendations for international students: Recommended—TOEFL. Electronic applications accepted. *Faculty research:* Health systems, music cognition and retrieval, transportation and logistics, manufacturing and automation, engineering systems design, risk and economic analysis.

West Virginia University, College of Engineering and Mineral Resources, Department of Industrial and Management Systems Engineering, Program in Safety Management, Morgantown, WV 26506. Offers MS. *Accreditation:* ABET. *Degree requirements:* For master's, comprehensive exam, thesis optional. *Entrance requirements:* For master's, minimum GPA of 3.0 for regular admission; 2.75 for provisional. Additional exam requirements/recommendations for international students: Required—TOEFL (minimum score 550 paper-based; 80 iBT). Electronic applications accepted.

Systems Engineering

Air Force Institute of Technology, Graduate School of Engineering and Management, Department of Aeronautics and Astronautics, Dayton, OH 45433-7765. Offers aeronautical engineering (MS, PhD); astronautical engineering (MS, PhD); materials science (MS, PhD); space operations (MS); systems engineering (MS, PhD). *Accreditation:* ABET (one or more programs are accredited). Part-time programs available. *Degree requirements:* For master's, thesis; for doctorate, thesis/dissertation.

Entrance requirements: For master's and doctorate, GRE General Test, minimum GPA of 3.0, U.S. citizenship. *Faculty research:* Computational fluid dynamics, experimental aerodynamics, computational structural mechanics, experimental structural mechanics, aircraft and spacecraft stability and control.

Arizona State University at the Tempe campus, Ira A. Fulton Schools of Engineering, ASU Engineering Online Programs, Tempe, AZ 85287. Offers construction (MS); embedded systems (M Eng); enterprise systems innovation and management (MSE); modeling and simulation (M Eng); quality and reliability engineering (M Eng); software engineering (MSE); systems engineering (M Eng).

Auburn University, Graduate School, Ginn College of Engineering, Department of Industrial and Systems Engineering, Auburn University, AL 36849. Offers MISE, MS, PhD, Graduate Certificate. Part-time programs available. *Faculty:* 12 full-time (1 woman), 1 part-time/adjunct (0 women). *Students:* 84 full-time (16 women), 39 part-time (11 women); includes 9 minority (5 Black or African American, non-Hispanic/Latino; 1 Asian, non-Hispanic/Latino; 3 Hispanic/Latino), 76 international. Average age 29. 212 applicants, 66% accepted, 30 enrolled. In 2014, 43 master's, 8 doctorates, 12 other advanced degrees awarded. *Degree requirements:* For master's, thesis (MS); for doctorate, thesis/dissertation. *Entrance requirements:* For master's and doctorate, GRE General Test. *Application deadline:* For fall admission, 7/7 for domestic students; for spring admission, 11/24 for domestic students. Applications are processed on a rolling basis. Application fee: $50 ($60 for international students). *Expenses:* Tuition, state resident: full-time $8586; part-time $477 per credit hour. Tuition, nonresident: full-time $25,758; part-time $1431 per credit hour. *Required fees:* $804 per semester. Tuition and fees vary according to degree level and program. *Financial support:* Fellowships, research assistantships, teaching assistantships, and Federal Work-Study available. Support available to part-time students. Financial award application deadline: 3/15; financial award applicants required to submit FAFSA. *Unit head:* Dr. Jorge Valenzuela, Chair, 334-844-1400. *Application contact:* Dr. George Flowers, Dean of the Graduate School, 334-844-2125.
Website: http://www.eng.auburn.edu/department/ie.

Boston University, College of Engineering, Division of Systems Engineering, Boston, MA 02215. Offers engineering practice option (M Eng); systems engineering (PhD). Part-time programs available. *Students:* 42 full-time (16 women), 5 part-time (1 woman); includes 5 minority (3 Asian, non-Hispanic/Latino; 2 Two or more races, non-Hispanic/Latino), 35 international. Average age 26. 213 applicants, 25% accepted, 17 enrolled. In 2014, 21 master's, 6 doctorates awarded. Terminal master's awarded for partial completion of doctoral program. *Degree requirements:* For master's, thesis (for some programs); for doctorate, comprehensive exam, thesis/dissertation. *Entrance requirements:* For master's and doctorate, GRE General Test. Additional exam requirements/recommendations for international students: Required—TOEFL (minimum score 550 paper-based; 84 iBT), IELTS (minimum score 7). *Application deadline:* For fall admission, 3/15 for domestic and international students; for spring admission, 10/1 for domestic and international students. Application fee: $80. Electronic applications accepted. *Expenses:* Tuition: Full-time $45,686; part-time $1428 per credit hour. *Required fees:* $660; $60 per semester. Tuition and fees vary according to program. *Financial support:* In 2014–15, 29 students received support, including 7 fellowships with full tuition reimbursements available (averaging $28,950 per year), 17 research assistantships with full tuition reimbursements available (averaging $19,300 per year), 3 teaching assistantships with full tuition reimbursements available (averaging $19,300 per year); career-related internships or fieldwork, Federal Work-Study, scholarships/grants, and tuition waivers (partial) also available. Financial award application deadline: 1/15; financial award applicants required to submit FAFSA. *Faculty research:* Communication, network, sensing, and information systems; control systems, automation, and robotics; discrete event, queuing, hybrid, and complex systems; optimization and algorithms; production, service, distribution, and energy systems. *Unit head:* Dr. Christos Cassandras, Division Head, 617-353-7154, Fax: 617-353-5548, E-mail: cgc@bu.edu. *Application contact:* Dr. Solomon Eisenberg, Senior Associate Dean of Academic Programs, 617-353-9760, Fax: 617-353-0259, E-mail: enggrad@bu.edu.
Website: http://www.bu.edu/se/.

California Institute of Technology, Division of Engineering and Applied Science, Option in Control and Dynamical Systems, Pasadena, CA 91125-0001. Offers MS, PhD. *Degree requirements:* For doctorate, thesis/dissertation. *Faculty research:* Robustness, multivariable and nonlinear systems, optimal control, decentralized control, modeling and system identification for robust control.

California State University, Fullerton, Graduate Studies, College of Engineering and Computer Science, Department of Electrical Engineering, Fullerton, CA 92834-9480. Offers electrical engineering (MS); systems engineering (MS). Part-time programs available. *Students:* 126 full-time (24 women), 168 part-time (37 women); includes 33 minority (4 Black or African American, non-Hispanic/Latino; 20 Asian, non-Hispanic/Latino; 7 Hispanic/Latino; 2 Two or more races, non-Hispanic/Latino), 238 international. Average age 24. 513 applicants, 78% accepted, 164 enrolled. In 2014, 35 master's awarded. *Degree requirements:* For master's, comprehensive exam, project or thesis. *Entrance requirements:* For master's, GRE General Test, GRE Subject Test, minimum undergraduate GPA of 2.5, 3.0 graduate. Application fee: $55. *Financial support:* Career-related internships or fieldwork, Federal Work-Study, institutionally sponsored loans, and scholarships/grants available. Support available to part-time students. Financial award application deadline: 3/1; financial award applicants required to submit FAFSA. *Unit head:* Dr. Mostafa Shiva, Chair, 657-278-3013. *Application contact:* Admissions/Applications, 657-278-2371.

California State University, Northridge, Graduate Studies, College of Engineering and Computer Science, Department of Manufacturing Systems Engineering and Management, Northridge, CA 91330. Offers engineering automation (MS); engineering management (MS); manufacturing systems engineering (MS); materials engineering (MS). Postbaccalaureate distance learning degree programs offered. *Students:* 180 full-time (38 women), 56 part-time (15 women); includes 24 minority (11 Asian, non-Hispanic/Latino; 8 Hispanic/Latino; 5 Two or more races, non-Hispanic/Latino), 172 international. Average age 26. *Entrance requirements:* For master's, GRE (if cumulative undergraduate GPA less than 3.0). *Application deadline:* For fall admission, 3/30 for domestic students; for spring admission, 9/30 for domestic students. Application fee: $55. *Expenses: Required fees:* $12,402. *Unit head:* Kang Chang, Acting Chair, 818-677-2167.
Website: http://www.csun.edu/~msem/.

Carleton University, Faculty of Graduate Studies, Faculty of Engineering and Design, Ottawa-Carleton Institute for Electrical Engineering, Department of Systems and Computer Engineering, Ottawa, ON K1S 5B6, Canada. Offers electrical engineering (MA Sc, PhD); information and systems science (M Sc); technology innovation management (M Eng, MA Sc). PhD program offered jointly with University of Ottawa. *Degree requirements:* For master's, thesis optional. *Entrance requirements:* For master's, honors degree. Additional exam requirements/recommendations for international students: Required—TOEFL. *Faculty research:* Design manufacturing

management; network design, protocols, and performance; software engineering; wireless and satellite communications.

Carnegie Mellon University, Carnegie Institute of Technology, Information Networking Institute, Pittsburgh, PA 15213. Offers information networking (MS); information security (MS); information technology - information security (MS); information technology - mobility (MS); information technology - software management (MS). *Degree requirements:* For master's, thesis optional. *Entrance requirements:* For master's, GRE General Test, bachelor's degree in computer science, computer engineering, or electrical engineering, or related technology degree; programming skills (C/C++ fluency for some programs). Additional exam requirements/recommendations for international students: Required—TOEFL. *Faculty research:* Computer forensics and incident response; dependable systems, embedded systems, mobile systems, and sensor networks; computer and information networks, network and information security, human and socio-economic factors in secure system design; wireless sensor networks, survivable embedded systems, signal processing/compression; strategic management, international strategic management, group dynamics and decision-making structures, simulated competitive environments.

Case Western Reserve University, School of Graduate Studies, Case School of Engineering, Department of Electrical Engineering and Computer Science, Cleveland, OH 44106. Offers computer engineering (MS, PhD); computing and information sciences (MS, PhD); electrical engineering (MS, PhD); systems and control engineering (MS, PhD). Part-time and evening/weekend programs available. Postbaccalaureate distance learning degree programs offered (minimal on-campus study). *Faculty:* 33 full-time (3 women). *Students:* 158 full-time (35 women), 18 part-time (5 women); includes 5 minority (1 Black or African American, non-Hispanic/Latino; 3 Asian, non-Hispanic/Latino; 1 Hispanic/Latino), 122 international. In 2014, 37 master's, 11 doctorates awarded. Terminal master's awarded for partial completion of doctoral program. *Degree requirements:* For master's, thesis; for doctorate, thesis/dissertation, qualifying exam, teaching experience. *Entrance requirements:* For master's and doctorate, GRE General Test. Additional exam requirements/recommendations for international students: Required—TOEFL. *Application deadline:* For fall admission, 2/1 for domestic students; for spring admission, 11/1 for domestic students. Applications are processed on a rolling basis. Application fee: $50. *Financial support:* In 2014–15, 51 research assistantships with full and partial tuition reimbursements, 10 teaching assistantships were awarded; fellowships with full and partial tuition reimbursements, career-related internships or fieldwork, Federal Work-Study, and institutionally sponsored loans also available. Support available to part-time students. Financial award application deadline: 3/1; financial award applicants required to submit FAFSA. *Faculty research:* Micro/nano systems; robotics and haptics, applied artificial intelligence; automation, computer-aided design and testing of digital systems. *Total annual research expenditures:* $6 million. *Unit head:* Dr. Kenneth Loparo, Department Chair, 216-368-4115, E-mail: kal4@case.edu. *Application contact:* Kimberly Yurchick, Student Affairs Specialist, 216-368-2920, Fax: 216-368-2801, E-mail: ksy4@case.edu.
Website: http://eecs.cwru.edu/.

Colorado State University–Pueblo, College of Education, Engineering and Professional Studies, Department of Engineering, Pueblo, CO 81001-4901. Offers industrial and systems engineering (MS). *Degree requirements:* For master's, thesis optional. *Entrance requirements:* For master's, GRE General Test. Additional exam requirements/recommendations for international students: Required—TOEFL (minimum score 500 paper-based). *Faculty research:* Nanotechnology, applied operations, research transportation, decision analysis.

Colorado Technical University Colorado Springs, Graduate Studies, Program in Systems Engineering, Colorado Springs, CO 80907-3896. Offers MS.

Colorado Technical University Denver South, Program in Systems Engineering, Aurora, CO 80014. Offers MS.

Concordia University, School of Graduate Studies, Faculty of Engineering and Computer Science, Concordia Institute for Information Systems Engineering (CIISE), Montréal, QC H3G 1M8, Canada. Offers 3D graphics and game development (Certificate); information systems security (M Eng, MA Sc); quality systems engineering (M Eng, MA Sc); service engineering and network management (Certificate).

Cornell University, Graduate School, Graduate Fields of Engineering, Field of Systems Engineering, Ithaca, NY 14853-0001. Offers M Eng. *Degree requirements:* For master's, thesis. *Entrance requirements:* For master's, GRE General Test. Additional exam requirements/recommendations for international students: Required—TOEFL (minimum score 600 paper-based; 77 iBT). *Faculty research:* Space systems, systems engineering of mechanical and aerospace systems, multi-echelon inventory theory, math modeling of complex systems, chain supply integration.

Embry-Riddle Aeronautical University–Daytona, Department of Aerospace Engineering, Daytona Beach, FL 32114-3900. Offers aerospace engineering (MAE, MSAE, PhD); unmanned and autonomous systems engineering (MS). Part-time programs available. *Faculty:* 20 full-time (2 women), 3 part-time/adjunct (0 women). *Students:* 146 full-time (24 women), 15 part-time (3 women); includes 11 minority (1 Black or African American, non-Hispanic/Latino; 4 Asian, non-Hispanic/Latino; 4 Hispanic/Latino; 2 Two or more races, non-Hispanic/Latino), 114 international. Average age 24. 174 applicants, 47% accepted, 47 enrolled. In 2014, 37 master's awarded. *Degree requirements:* For master's, thesis; for doctorate, comprehensive exam, thesis/dissertation. *Entrance requirements:* For master's, BS in Aeronautical or Aerospace Engineering, or equivalent; minimum CGPA of 3.0; for doctorate, Graduate Record Examination (GRE), a Masters or Bachelor degree in aerospace engineering or closely related engineering discipline; minimum Masters cumulative grade point average (CGPA) of 3.5. Additional exam requirements/recommendations for international students: Required—TOEFL (minimum score 550 paper-based; 79 iBT). *Application deadline:* For fall admission, 1/15 priority date for domestic students, 12/15 priority date for international students; for spring admission, 6/15 priority date for domestic and international students. Applications are processed on a rolling basis. Application fee: $50. Electronic applications accepted. *Expenses: Tuition:* Full-time $15,360; part-time $1280 per credit hour. *Required fees:* $1334. *Financial support:* In 2014–15, 44 students received support, including research assistantships with full and partial tuition reimbursements available (averaging $7,500 per year); career-related internships or fieldwork and unspecified assistantships also available. Financial award application deadline: 1/15. *Faculty research:* Aeroacoustic modeling, rotorcraft aerodynamics, flow control, airbreathing hypersonic and rocket propulsion, autonomous unpiloted air and ground vehicles, aircraft and spacecraft guidance, navigation and control, aeroelasticity, composites, nanomaterials, smart materials, structural health monitoring, computational structural mechanics and design optimization. *Unit head:* Dr. Anastasios Lyrintzis, Distinguished Professor and Chair, Aerospace Engineering, 386-226-7007, Fax: 386-226-6747, E-mail: lyrintzi@erau.edu. *Application contact:* International and Graduate Admissions, 386-226-6176, E-mail: graduate.admissions@erau.edu.
Website: http://daytonabeach.erau.edu/college-engineering/aerospace/index.html.

Embry-Riddle Aeronautical University–Daytona, Department of Electrical, Computer, Software and Systems Engineering, Daytona Beach, FL 32114-3900. Offers

cybersecurity engineering (MS); electrical and computer engineering (MSECE); software engineering (MSE); unmanned and autonomous systems engineering (MSUASE). MS in unmanned and autonomous systems engineering held jointly with Department of Electrical, Computer, Software and Systems Engineering. Part-time and evening/weekend programs available. *Faculty:* 13 full-time (0 women), 1 (woman) part-time/adjunct. *Students:* 56 full-time (15 women), 8 part-time (0 women); includes 6 minority (4 Black or African American, non-Hispanic/Latino; 1 Asian, non-Hispanic/Latino; 1 Hispanic/Latino), 41 international. Average age 25. 46 applicants, 61% accepted, 23 enrolled. In 2014, 16 master's awarded. *Degree requirements:* For master's, thesis or alternative, MS UASE students are required to complete a two-semester capstone project. *Entrance requirements:* For master's, Applicants to the MSE program are strongly encouraged to complete the GRE for this degree program; Applicants to the MSUASE program must complete the GRE; For consideration of fellowship and assistantship award programs offered by the Department of Computing, GRE scores are required., minimum CGPA of 3.0; course work in computer science. Additional exam requirements/recommendations for international students: Required—TOEFL (minimum score 550 paper-based; 79 iBT). *Application deadline:* For fall admission, 6/1 priority date for domestic and international students; for spring admission, 11/1 priority date for domestic students, 10/1 priority date for international students. Applications are processed on a rolling basis. Application fee: $50. Electronic applications accepted. *Expenses: Tuition:* Full-time $15,360; part-time $1280 per credit hour. *Required fees:* $1334. *Financial support:* In 2014–15, 24 students received support. Research assistantships with full and partial tuition reimbursements available, teaching assistantships with full and partial tuition reimbursements available, career-related internships or fieldwork, and unspecified assistantships available. Financial award application deadline: 4/15. *Faculty research:* Cybersecurity and assured systems engineering, radar, unmanned and autonomous systems, modeling and simulation, cyber-physical systems. *Unit head:* Dr. Timothy Wilson, Professor of Electrical and Computer Engineering and Chair, ECSSE Dept., 386-226-6994, E-mail: timothy.wilson@erau.edu. *Application contact:* International and Graduate Admissions, 800-388-3728, Fax: 386-226-7070, E-mail: graduate.admissions@erau.edu.
Website: http://daytonabeach.erau.edu/college-engineering/electrical-computer-software-systems/index.html.

Embry-Riddle Aeronautical University–Daytona, Department of Human Factors, Daytona Beach, FL 32114-3900. Offers human factors (PhD); human factors engineering (MSHFS); systems engineering (MSHFS). Part-time and evening/weekend programs available. *Faculty:* 7 full-time (4 women), 1 part-time/adjunct (0 women). *Students:* 28 full-time (23 women), 10 part-time (4 women); includes 9 minority (4 Black or African American, non-Hispanic/Latino; 1 Asian, non-Hispanic/Latino; 4 Two or more races, non-Hispanic/Latino), 4 international. Average age 27. 32 applicants, 59% accepted, 18 enrolled. In 2014, 55 master's awarded. *Degree requirements:* For master's, thesis. *Entrance requirements:* Additional exam requirements/recommendations for international students: Required—TOEFL (minimum score 550 paper-based; 79 iBT). *Application deadline:* For fall admission, 6/1 priority date for domestic students, 5/1 priority date for international students; for spring admission, 11/1 priority date for domestic students, 10/1 priority date for international students. Applications are processed on a rolling basis. Application fee: $50. Electronic applications accepted. *Expenses: Tuition:* Full-time $15,360; part-time $1280 per credit hour. *Required fees:* $1334. *Financial support:* In 2014–15, 12 students received support. Research assistantships with full and partial tuition reimbursements available, teaching assistantships with full and partial tuition reimbursements available, career-related internships or fieldwork, and unspecified assistantships available. Financial award application deadline: 4/15. *Faculty research:* Healthcare human factors, game-based learning, aerospace physiology, aerospace psychology, teamwork and team training. *Unit head:* Scott Shappell, PhD, Professor and Chair, Department of Human Factors, 386-226-7744, E-mail: scott.shappell@erau.edu. *Application contact:* International and Graduate Admissions, 386-226-6176, Fax: 386-226-7070, E-mail: graduate.admissions@erau.edu.
Website: http://daytonabeach.erau.edu/college-arts-sciences/human-factors/index.html.

Embry-Riddle Aeronautical University–Worldwide, College of Aeronautics, Daytona Beach, FL 32114-3900. Offers aeronautical science (MAS); human factors (MS); occupational safety management (MS); systems engineering (M Sys E); unmanned systems (MS). Part-time and evening/weekend programs available. Postbaccalaureate distance learning degree programs offered (no on-campus study). *Faculty:* 34 full-time (4 women), 189 part-time/adjunct (23 women). *Students:* 1,151 full-time (188 women), 1,227 part-time (191 women); includes 498 minority (198 Black or African American, non-Hispanic/Latino; 7 American Indian or Alaska Native, non-Hispanic/Latino; 66 Asian, non-Hispanic/Latino; 92 Hispanic/Latino; 4 Native Hawaiian or other Pacific Islander, non-Hispanic/Latino; 131 Two or more races, non-Hispanic/Latino), 109 international. Average age 37. In 2014, 882 master's awarded. *Degree requirements:* For master's, comprehensive exam (for some programs), thesis or alternative, thesis or capstone project. *Entrance requirements:* Additional exam requirements/recommendations for international students: Recommended—TOEFL (minimum score 550 paper-based; 79 iBT). *Application deadline:* Applications are processed on a rolling basis. Application fee: $50. Electronic applications accepted. *Expenses: Tuition:* Full-time $6720; part-time $560 per credit hour. *Financial support:* In 2014–15, 385 students received support. Career-related internships or fieldwork available. *Faculty research:* Aerodynamics statistical design and educational development. *Unit head:* Dr. Ian McAndrew, Department Chair, Department of Aeronautics, Graduate Studies, E-mail: ian.mcandrew@erau.edu. *Application contact:* Admissions, 800-522-6787, E-mail: worldwide@erau.edu.
Website: http://worldwide.erau.edu/degrees-programs/colleges/aeronautics/department-of-graduate-studies/index.html.

Florida Institute of Technology, Graduate Programs, College of Engineering, Program in Systems Engineering, Melbourne, FL 32901-6975. Offers MS, PhD. Part-time and evening/weekend programs available. *Students:* 15 full-time (2 women), 17 part-time (4 women); includes 6 minority (1 Black or African American, non-Hispanic/Latino; 3 Asian, non-Hispanic/Latino; 2 Hispanic/Latino), 17 international. Average age 32. 34 applicants, 47% accepted, 8 enrolled. In 2014, 28 master's, 1 doctorate awarded. *Degree requirements:* For master's, comprehensive exam (for some programs), portfolio of competencies and summary of career relevance, thesis or final exam, capstone design project; for doctorate, comprehensive exam, thesis/dissertation, one journal paper in review, 48 credits hours past master's degree, complete and present one conference paper at recognized conference. *Entrance requirements:* For master's, GRE General Test (if GPA less than 3.0), minimum GPA of 3.0, 2 letters of recommendation, resume, bachelor's degree in engineering from ABET-accredited program, statement of objectives; for doctorate, GRE, minimum GPA of 3.5, 3 letters of recommendation, resume, statement of objectives. Additional exam requirements/recommendations for international students: Required—TOEFL (minimum score 550 paper-based; 79 iBT). *Application deadline:* For fall admission, 4/1 for international students; for spring admission, 9/30 for international students. Applications are processed on a rolling basis. Electronic applications accepted. *Expenses: Tuition:* Part-time $1179 per credit hour. Tuition and fees vary according to campus/location. *Financial support:* Career-related internships or fieldwork, institutionally sponsored loans, unspecified assistantships, and tuition remissions available. Support available to part-time students. Financial award application deadline: 3/1; financial award applicants required to submit FAFSA. *Faculty research:* System/software engineering, simulation and analytical modeling, project management, multimedia tools, quality. *Unit head:* Dr. Muzaffar A. Shaikh, Department Head, 321-674-7132, Fax: 321-674-7136, E-mail: mshaikh@fit.edu. *Application contact:* Cheryl A. Brown, Associate Director of Graduate Admissions, 321-674-7581, Fax: 321-723-9468, E-mail: cbrown@fit.edu.
Website: http://coe.fit.edu/se/.

George Mason University, Volgenau School of Engineering, Department of Systems Engineering and Operations Research, Fairfax, VA 22030. Offers operations research (MS); systems engineering (MS); systems engineering and operations research (PhD, Certificate). MS programs offered jointly with Old Dominion University, University of Virginia, Virginia Commonwealth University, and Virginia Polytechnic Institute and State University. *Faculty:* 18 full-time (5 women), 13 part-time/adjunct (2 women). *Students:* 42 full-time (8 women), 98 part-time (16 women); includes 27 minority (4 Black or African American, non-Hispanic/Latino; 12 Asian, non-Hispanic/Latino; 7 Hispanic/Latino; 4 Two or more races, non-Hispanic/Latino), 18 international. Average age 32. 134 applicants, 66% accepted, 37 enrolled. In 2014, 61 master's, 6 doctorates, 12 other advanced degrees awarded. *Degree requirements:* For master's, thesis optional; for doctorate, comprehensive exam, thesis/dissertation, qualifying exams. *Entrance requirements:* For master's, GRE General Test, BS in related field; minimum GPA of 3.0; 3 letters of recommendation; 2 official transcripts; expanded goals statement; proof of financial support; photocopy of passport; official bank statement; multivariable calculus, applied probability, statistics and a computer language course; self evaluation form; for doctorate, GRE, MS with minimum GPA of 3.5; BS with minimum GPA of 3.0 in systems or operational research; 2 official transcripts; 3 letters of recommendation; resume; expanded goals statement; self evaluation form; photocopy of passport; official bank statement; proof of financial support; for Certificate, personal goals statement; 2 official transcripts; self-evaluation form; letter of recommendation; resume; official bank statement; photocopy of passport; proof of financial support; baccalaureate degree in related field. Additional exam requirements/recommendations for international students: Required—TOEFL (minimum score 575 paper-based; 80 iBT), IELTS (minimum score 6.5), PTE. *Application deadline:* For fall admission, 1/15 priority date for domestic students; for spring admission, 8/15 priority date for domestic students. Application fee: $65 ($80 for international students). Electronic applications accepted. *Expenses:* Expenses: Contact institution. *Financial support:* In 2014–15, 13 students received support, including 6 research assistantships with full and partial tuition reimbursements available (averaging $19,974 per year), 7 teaching assistantships with full and partial tuition reimbursements available (averaging $12,909 per year); career-related internships or fieldwork, Federal Work-Study, scholarships/grants, unspecified assistantships, and health care benefits (for full-time research or teaching assistantship recipients) also available. Support available to part-time students. Financial award application deadline: 3/1; financial award applicants required to submit FAFSA. *Faculty research:* Requirements engineering, signal processing, systems architecture, data fusion. *Total annual research expenditures:* $603,678. *Unit head:* Ariela Sofer, Chair, 703-993-1692, Fax: 703-993-1521, E-mail: asofer@gmu.edu. *Application contact:* Angel Manzo, Program Specialist, 703-993-1636, Fax: 703-993-1521, E-mail: amanzo@gmu.edu.
Website: http://seor.gmu.edu.

Georgetown University, Graduate School of Arts and Sciences, School of Continuing Studies, Washington, DC 20057. Offers American studies (MALS); Catholic studies (MALS); classical civilizations (MALS); emergency and disaster management (MPS); ethics and the professions (MALS); hospitality management (MPS); human resources management (MPS); humanities (MALS); individualized study (MALS); international affairs (MALS); Islam and Muslim-Christian relations (MALS); journalism (MPS); liberal studies (DLS); literature and society (MALS); medieval and early modern European studies (MALS); public relations and corporate communications (MPS); real estate (MPS); religious studies (MALS); social and public policy (MALS); sports industry management (MPS); systems engineering management (MPS); technology management (MPS); the theory and practice of American democracy (MALS); urban and regional planning (MPS); visual culture (MALS). MPS in systems engineering management offered jointly with Stevens Institute of Technology. *Entrance requirements:* Additional exam requirements/recommendations for international students: Required—TOEFL.

The George Washington University, School of Engineering and Applied Science, Department of Engineering Management and Systems Engineering, Washington, DC 20052. Offers system engineering (PhD). Part-time and evening/weekend programs available. *Faculty:* 18 full-time (3 women), 87 part-time/adjunct (9 women). *Students:* 87 full-time (34 women), 799 part-time (212 women); includes 300 minority (161 Black or African American, non-Hispanic/Latino; 4 American Indian or Alaska Native, non-Hispanic/Latino; 95 Asian, non-Hispanic/Latino; 32 Hispanic/Latino; 5 Native Hawaiian or other Pacific Islander, non-Hispanic/Latino; 3 Two or more races, non-Hispanic/Latino), 54 international. Average age 37. 491 applicants, 66% accepted, 181 enrolled. In 2014, 413 master's, 21 doctorates, 118 other advanced degrees awarded. *Degree requirements:* For master's, thesis optional; for doctorate, one foreign language, thesis/dissertation, final and qualifying exams, submission of articles; for other advanced degree, professional project. *Entrance requirements:* For master's, appropriate bachelor's degree, minimum GPA of 2.7, second-semester calculus; for doctorate, appropriate master's degree, minimum GPA of 3.5, 2 letters of recommendation; for other advanced degree, appropriate master's degree, minimum GPA of 3.4. Additional exam requirements/recommendations for international students: Required—TOEFL or The George Washington University English as a Foreign Language Test. *Application deadline:* For fall admission, 3/1 for domestic students; for spring admission, 10/1 for domestic students. Applications are processed on a rolling basis. Application fee: $75. *Financial support:* In 2014–15, 35 students received support. Fellowships with tuition reimbursements available, research assistantships, teaching assistantships with tuition reimbursements available, career-related internships or fieldwork, and institutionally sponsored loans available. Financial award application deadline: 3/1; financial award applicants required to submit FAFSA. *Faculty research:* Artificial intelligence and expert systems, human factors engineering and systems analysis. *Total annual research expenditures:* $421,800. *Unit head:* Dr. Thomas Mazzuchi, Chair, 202-994-7424, Fax: 202-994-0245, E-mail: mazzu@gwu.edu. *Application contact:* Adina Lav, Marketing, Recruiting and Admissions, 202-994-5827, Fax: 202-994-0909, E-mail: engineering@gwu.edu.
Website: http://www.emse.gwu.edu/.

Georgia Institute of Technology, Graduate Studies, College of Engineering, Professional Master's in Applied Systems Engineering Program, Atlanta, GA 30332-0001. Offers PMS. Part-time programs available. *Students:* 53 part-time (6 women); includes 16 minority (5 Black or African American, non-Hispanic/Latino; 1 American Indian or Alaska Native, non-Hispanic/Latino; 5 Asian, non-Hispanic/Latino; 4 Hispanic/Latino; 1 Two or more races, non-Hispanic/Latino), 3 international. Average age 32. 41

applicants, 78% accepted, 22 enrolled. In 2014, 26 master's awarded. *Degree requirements:* For master's, capstone project. *Entrance requirements:* For master's, https://pe.gatech.edu/degrees/pmase/admission-requirements. Additional exam requirements/recommendations for international students: Required—TOEFL (minimum score 550 paper-based; 79 iBT). *Application deadline:* For fall admission, 5/1 for domestic and international students. Applications are processed on a rolling basis. Application fee: $75. Electronic applications accepted. *Expenses:* Tuition, state resident: full-time $12,344; part-time $515 per credit hour. Tuition, nonresident: full-time $27,600; part-time $1150 per credit hour. *Required fees:* $1196 per term. Part-time tuition and fees vary according to course load. *Financial support:* Fellowships, research assistantships, teaching assistantships, career-related internships or fieldwork, Federal Work-Study, institutionally sponsored loans, tuition waivers (partial), and unspecified assistantships available. Support available to part-time students. Financial award application deadline: 5/1. *Unit head:* Carlee Bishop, Director, 404-407-6335, E-mail: carlee.bishop@gtri.gatech.edu. *Application contact:* Rose Jacobsen, Graduate Coordinator, 404-407-7129, E-mail: rose.jacobsen@gtri.gatech.edu.
Website: https://pe.gatech.edu/degrees/pmase.

Georgia Southern University, Jack N. Averitt College of Graduate Studies, Allen E. Paulson College of Engineering and Information Technology, Program in Engineering/Electrical and Electronic Systems, Statesboro, GA 30460. Offers MSAE. *Students:* 4 full-time (0 women); includes 1 minority (Hispanic/Latino), 2 international. Average age 24. 4 applicants, 75% accepted, 3 enrolled. *Degree requirements:* For master's, thesis optional. *Entrance requirements:* For master's, GPA 2.75. Additional exam requirements/recommendations for international students: Required—TOEFL (minimum score 80 iBT). *Application deadline:* For fall admission, 2/1 for domestic students; for spring admission, 10/1 for domestic students. Application fee: $50. *Expenses:* Tuition, state resident: full-time $7236; part-time $277 per semester hour. Tuition, nonresident: full-time $27,118; part-time $1105 per semester hour. *Required fees:* $2092. *Financial support:* In 2014–15, 4 students received support. *Unit head:* Dr. Frank Goforth, Program Chair, 912-478-7583, E-mail: fgoforth@georgiasouthern.edu.

Harrisburg University of Science and Technology, Program in Information Systems Engineering and Management, Harrisburg, PA 17101. Offers digital government (MS); digital health (MS); entrepreneurship (MS). Part-time programs available. *Degree requirements:* For master's, comprehensive exam, thesis optional. *Entrance requirements:* For master's, baccalaureate degree. Additional exam requirements/recommendations for international students: Required—TOEFL (minimum score 520 paper-based; 80 iBT). Electronic applications accepted.

Indiana University–Purdue University Fort Wayne, College of Engineering, Technology, and Computer Science, Department of Engineering, Fort Wayne, IN 46805-1499. Offers civil engineering (MSE); computer engineering (MSE); electrical engineering (MSE); mechanical engineering (MSE); systems engineering (MSE). Part-time programs available. *Faculty:* 21 full-time (2 women). *Students:* 4 full-time (1 woman), 15 part-time (1 woman); includes 3 minority (2 Black or African American, non-Hispanic/Latino; 1 Asian, non-Hispanic/Latino), 2 international. Average age 30. 13 applicants, 100% accepted, 10 enrolled. In 2014, 17 master's awarded. *Entrance requirements:* For master's, minimum GPA of 3.0, bachelor's degree in engineering discipline. Additional exam requirements/recommendations for international students: Required—TOEFL (minimum score 550 paper-based; 79 iBT); Recommended—TWE. *Application deadline:* For fall admission, 7/15 priority date for domestic students, 5/15 priority date for international students; for spring admission, 12/1 priority date for domestic students, 10/15 priority date for international students. Applications are processed on a rolling basis. Application fee: $55 ($60 for international students). Electronic applications accepted. *Financial support:* In 2014–15, 3 research assistantships with partial tuition reimbursements (averaging $13,522 per year), 1 teaching assistantship with partial tuition reimbursement (averaging $13,522 per year) were awarded. Financial award application deadline: 3/1; financial award applicants required to submit FAFSA. *Faculty research:* Continuous space language model, sensor networks, wireless cloud architecture. *Total annual research expenditures:* $841,333. *Unit head:* Dr. Nashwan Younis, Chair, 260-481-6887, Fax: 260-481-6281, E-mail: younis@engr.ipfw.edu. *Application contact:* Dr. Abdullah Eroglu, Program Director/Professor, 260-481-0273, Fax: 260-481-5734, E-mail: eroglua@ipfw.edu.
Website: http://www.ipfw.edu/engr.

Instituto Tecnológico y de Estudios Superiores de Monterrey, Campus Chihuahua, Graduate Programs, Chihuahua, Mexico. Offers computer systems engineering (Ingeniero); electrical engineering (Ingeniero); electromechanical engineering (Ingeniero); electronic engineering (Ingeniero); engineering administration (MEA); industrial engineering (MIE, Ingeniero); international trade (MIT); mechanical engineering (Ingeniero).

Instituto Tecnológico y de Estudios Superiores de Monterrey, Campus Monterrey, Graduate and Research Division, Programs in Engineering, Monterrey, Mexico. Offers applied statistics (M Eng); artificial intelligence (PhD); automation engineering (M Eng); chemical engineering (M Eng); civil engineering (M Eng); electrical engineering (M Eng); electronic engineering (M Eng); environmental engineering (M Eng); industrial engineering (M Eng, PhD); manufacturing engineering (M Eng); mechanical engineering (M Eng); systems and quality engineering (M Eng). M Eng program offered jointly with University of Waterloo; PhD in industrial engineering with Texas A&M University. Part-time and evening/weekend programs available. Terminal master's awarded for partial completion of doctoral program. *Degree requirements:* For master's, one foreign language, thesis; for doctorate, one foreign language, thesis/dissertation. *Entrance requirements:* For master's, EXADEP; for doctorate, GRE, master's degree in related field. Additional exam requirements/recommendations for international students: Required—TOEFL. *Faculty research:* Flexible manufacturing cells, materials, statistical methods, environmental prevention, control and evaluation.

Iowa State University of Science and Technology, Program in Systems Engineering, Ames, IA 50011. Offers M Eng. *Entrance requirements:* Additional exam requirements/recommendations for international students: Required—TOEFL (minimum score 550 paper-based; 79 iBT), IELTS (minimum score 6.5). Electronic applications accepted.

Johns Hopkins University, Engineering Program for Professionals, Part-time Program in Systems Engineering, Baltimore, MD 21218-2699. Offers MS, Graduate Certificate, Post-Master's Certificate. Part-time and evening/weekend programs available. Postbaccalaureate distance learning degree programs offered (no on-campus study). Electronic applications accepted.

Lehigh University, P.C. Rossin College of Engineering and Applied Science, Department of Industrial and Systems Engineering, Bethlehem, PA 18015. Offers analytical finance (MS); healthcare systems engineering (M Eng); industrial and systems engineering (M Eng, MS); industrial engineering (PhD); management science and engineering (M Eng, MS); MBA/E. Part-time programs available. Postbaccalaureate distance learning degree programs offered (no on-campus study). *Faculty:* 16 full-time (2 women), 4 part-time/adjunct (1 woman). *Students:* 91 full-time (24 women), 14 part-time (4 women); includes 2 minority (both Asian, non-Hispanic/Latino), 93 international. Average age 25. 351 applicants, 20% accepted, 38 enrolled. In 2014, 39 master's, 3 doctorates awarded. *Degree requirements:* For master's, thesis (MS); project (M Eng); for doctorate, comprehensive exam, thesis/dissertation. *Entrance requirements:* For master's and doctorate, GRE General Test. Additional exam requirements/recommendations for international students: Required—TOEFL (minimum score 550 paper-based; 79 iBT). *Application deadline:* For fall admission, 7/15 for domestic and international students; for spring admission, 12/1 for domestic and international students. Applications are processed on a rolling basis. Application fee: $75. Electronic applications accepted. *Expenses:* Expenses: $1,340 per credit hour. *Financial support:* In 2014–15, 25 students received support, including 2 fellowships with full tuition reimbursements available (averaging $17,460 per year), 13 research assistantships with full tuition reimbursements available (averaging $15,300 per year), 10 teaching assistantships with full tuition reimbursements available (averaging $18,360 per year); career-related internships or fieldwork, scholarships/grants, tuition waivers, and unspecified assistantships also available. Financial award application deadline: 1/15. *Faculty research:* Mathematical optimization; logistics and service systems, stochastic processes and simulation; computational optimization and high performance computing; financial engineering and robust optimization. *Total annual research expenditures:* $2 million. *Unit head:* Dr. Tamas Terlaky, Chair, 610-758-4050, Fax: 610-758-4886, E-mail: terlaky@lehigh.edu. *Application contact:* Rita Frey, Graduate Coordinator, 610-758-4051, Fax: 610-758-4886, E-mail: ise@lehigh.edu.
Website: http://www.lehigh.edu/ise.

Lehigh University, P.C. Rossin College of Engineering and Applied Science, Program in Manufacturing Systems Engineering, Bethlehem, PA 18015. Offers MS, MBA/E. Part-time and evening/weekend programs available. Postbaccalaureate distance learning degree programs offered (no on-campus study). *Faculty:* 3 full-time (0 women). *Students:* 2 full-time (1 woman), 18 part-time (7 women); includes 4 minority (1 Black or African American, non-Hispanic/Latino; 2 Asian, non-Hispanic/Latino; 1 Hispanic/Latino), 1 international. Average age 31. 13 applicants, 62% accepted, 3 enrolled. In 2014, 11 master's awarded. *Degree requirements:* For master's, comprehensive exam, project or thesis. *Entrance requirements:* For master's, GRE General Test, minimum GPA of 2.75. Additional exam requirements/recommendations for international students: Required—TOEFL (minimum score 620 paper-based; 85 iBT). *Application deadline:* For fall admission, 7/15 priority date for domestic students, 7/15 for international students; for spring admission, 12/1 priority date for domestic students, 12/1 for international students. Applications are processed on a rolling basis. Application fee: $75. Electronic applications accepted. *Faculty research:* Manufacturing systems design, development, and implementation; accounting and management; agile/lean systems; supply chain issues; sustainable systems design; product design. *Unit head:* Dr. Keith M. Gardiner, Director, 610-758-5070, Fax: 610-758-6527, E-mail: kg03@lehigh.edu. *Application contact:* Carolyn C. Jones, Graduate Coordinator, 610-758-5157, Fax: 610-758-6527, E-mail: ccj1@lehigh.edu.
Website: https://mse.lehigh.edu/.

Loyola Marymount University, College of Business Administration, MBA/MS Program in Systems Engineering, Los Angeles, CA 90045. Offers MBA/MS. Part-time programs available. *Entrance requirements:* Additional exam requirements/recommendations for international students: Required—TOEFL (minimum score 600 paper-based; 100 iBT). Electronic applications accepted. *Expenses:* Contact institution.

Loyola Marymount University, College of Science and Engineering, Department of Systems Engineering and Engineering Management, Program in System Engineering Leadership, Los Angeles, CA 90045-2659. Offers MS/MBA. *Entrance requirements:* Additional exam requirements/recommendations for international students: Required—TOEFL (minimum score 600 paper-based; 100 iBT). Electronic applications accepted.

Loyola Marymount University, College of Science and Engineering, Department of Systems Engineering and Engineering Management, Program in Systems Engineering, Los Angeles, CA 90045. Offers MS. *Degree requirements:* For master's, thesis. *Entrance requirements:* For master's, personal statement, resume, letters of recommendation. Additional exam requirements/recommendations for international students: Required—TOEFL (minimum score 550 paper-based; 80 iBT). Electronic applications accepted.

Massachusetts Institute of Technology, School of Engineering, Engineering Systems Division, Cambridge, MA 02139. Offers engineering and management (SM); engineering systems (SM, PhD); logistics (M Eng); technology and policy (SM); technology, management and policy (PhD); SM/MBA. *Faculty:* 19 full-time (5 women). *Students:* 327 full-time (106 women); includes 53 minority (7 Black or African American, non-Hispanic/Latino; 28 Asian, non-Hispanic/Latino; 15 Hispanic/Latino; 3 Two or more races, non-Hispanic/Latino), 141 international. Average age 31. 1,143 applicants, 32% accepted, 254 enrolled. In 2014, 158 master's, 9 doctorates awarded. *Degree requirements:* For master's, thesis; for doctorate, comprehensive exam, thesis/dissertation. *Entrance requirements:* Additional exam requirements/recommendations for international students: Required—IELTS. *Application deadline:* For fall admission, 12/15 for domestic and international students. Application fee: $75. Electronic applications accepted. *Expenses:* Expenses: Contact institution. *Financial support:* In 2014–15, 213 students received support, including 39 fellowships (averaging $35,000 per year), 102 research assistantships (averaging $33,200 per year), 18 teaching assistantships (averaging $31,400 per year); Federal Work-Study, institutionally sponsored loans, scholarships/grants, traineeships, health care benefits, and unspecified assistantships also available. Financial award application deadline: 4/15; financial award applicants required to submit FAFSA. *Faculty research:* Critical infrastructures, extended enterprises, energy and sustainability, health care delivery, humans and technology, uncertainty and dynamics, design and implementation, networks and flows, policy and standards. *Total annual research expenditures:* $14.4 million. *Unit head:* Munther A. Dahleh, Acting Director, 617-258-8773, E-mail: esdinquiries@mit.edu. *Application contact:* Graduate Admissions, 617-253-1182, E-mail: esdgrad@mit.edu.
Website: http://esd.mit.edu/.

Mississippi State University, Bagley College of Engineering, Department of Industrial and Systems Engineering, Mississippi State, MS 39762. Offers industrial and systems engineering (PhD); industrial engineering (MS). Part-time programs available. Postbaccalaureate distance learning degree programs offered (no on-campus study). *Faculty:* 9 full-time (2 women). *Students:* 19 full-time (4 women), 59 part-time (13 women); includes 15 minority (6 Black or African American, non-Hispanic/Latino; 3 Asian, non-Hispanic/Latino; 5 Hispanic/Latino; 1 Native Hawaiian or other Pacific Islander, non-Hispanic/Latino), 13 international. Average age 36. 106 applicants, 34% accepted, 23 enrolled. In 2014, 8 master's, 4 doctorates awarded. *Degree requirements:* For master's, comprehensive exam (for some programs), thesis optional, comprehensive oral or written exam; for doctorate, comprehensive exam, thesis/dissertation, candidacy exam. *Entrance requirements:* For master's, GRE (for graduates from program not accredited by EAC/ABET), minimum GPA of 3.0 on junior and senior years; for doctorate, GRE (for graduates from program not accredited by EAC/ABET), minimum GPA of 3.5 on master's degree and junior and senior years of BS. Additional exam requirements/recommendations for international students: Required—TOEFL (minimum score 550 paper-based; 79 iBT); Recommended—IELTS (minimum score 6.5). *Application deadline:* For fall admission, 7/1 for domestic students, 5/1 for international students; for spring admission, 11/1 for domestic students, 9/1 for

international students. Applications are processed on a rolling basis. Application fee: $60. *Expenses:* Tuition, state resident: full-time $7140; part-time $783 per credit hour. Tuition, nonresident: full-time $18,478; part-time $2043 per credit hour. *Financial support:* In 2014–15, 9 research assistantships with full tuition reimbursements (averaging $15,844 per year), 1 teaching assistantship (averaging $13,500 per year) were awarded; Federal Work-Study, institutionally sponsored loans, and unspecified assistantships also available. Financial award application deadline: 4/1; financial award applicants required to submit FAFSA. *Faculty research:* Operations research, ergonomics, production systems, management systems, transportation. *Unit head:* Dr. John Usher, Professor/Department Head/Graduate Coordinator, 662-325-7624, Fax: 662-325-7618, E-mail: usher@ise.msstate.edu. *Application contact:* Dr. Kari Babski-Reeves, Associate Professor and Graduate Coordinator, 662-325-1677, Fax: 662-325-7618, E-mail: kari@ise.msstate.edu.
Website: http://www.ise.msstate.edu/.

Missouri University of Science and Technology, Graduate School, Department of Engineering Management and Systems Engineering, Rolla, MO 65409. Offers engineering management (MS, DE, PhD); manufacturing engineering (M Eng, MS); systems engineering (MS, PhD). *Degree requirements:* For master's, thesis optional; for doctorate, comprehensive exam. *Entrance requirements:* For master's, GRE (minimum score 1150 verbal and quantitative, 4.5 writing); for doctorate, GRE (minimum score: 1100 verbal and quantitative, 3.5 writing). Additional exam requirements/recommendations for international students: Required—TOEFL (minimum score 580 paper-based). *Faculty research:* Management of technology, industrial engineering, manufacturing engineering, packaging engineering, quality engineering.

National University, Academic Affairs, School of Engineering and Computing, La Jolla, CA 92037-1011. Offers computer science (MS), including advanced computing, database engineering, software engineering; cyber security and information assurance (MS), including computer forensics, ethical hacking and penetration testing, health information assurance, information assurance and security; data analytics (MS); engineering management (MS), including enterprise architecture, project management, systems engineering, technology management; environmental engineering (MS); homeland security and emergency management (MS); management information systems (MS); project management (Certificate); sustainability management (MS); wireless communications (MS). Part-time and evening/weekend programs available. Postbaccalaureate distance learning degree programs offered (no on-campus study). *Faculty:* 24 full-time (5 women), 21 part-time/adjunct (5 women). *Students:* 275 full-time (72 women), 86 part-time (24 women); includes 147 minority (41 Black or African American, non-Hispanic/Latino; 48 Asian, non-Hispanic/Latino; 37 Hispanic/Latino; 7 Native Hawaiian or other Pacific Islander, non-Hispanic/Latino; 14 Two or more races, non-Hispanic/Latino), 95 international. Average age 33. In 2014, 281 master's awarded. *Degree requirements:* For master's, thesis (for some programs). *Entrance requirements:* For master's, interview, minimum GPA of 2.5. Additional exam requirements/recommendations for international students: Required—TOEFL (minimum score 550 paper-based; 79 iBT), IELTS (minimum score 6). *Application deadline:* Applications are processed on a rolling basis. Application fee: $60 ($65 for international students). Electronic applications accepted. *Expenses: Tuition:* Full-time $14,184; part-time $1773 per course. *Financial support:* Career-related internships or fieldwork, institutionally sponsored loans, scholarships/grants, and tuition waivers (partial) available. Support available to part-time students. Financial award application deadline: 6/30; financial award applicants required to submit FAFSA. *Faculty research:* Educational technology, scholarships in science. *Unit head:* School of Engineering and Computing, 800-628-8648, E-mail: soec@nu.edu. *Application contact:* Frank Rojas, Vice President for Enrollment Services, 800-628-8648, E-mail: advisor@nu.edu.
Website: http://www.nu.edu/OurPrograms/SchoolOfEngineeringAndTechnology.html.

Naval Postgraduate School, Departments and Academic Groups, Department of Systems Engineering, Monterey, CA 93943. Offers engineering systems (MS); product development (MS); systems engineering (MS, PhD, Certificate); systems engineering analysis (MS, PhD); systems engineering management (MS, PhD). Program only open to commissioned officers of the United States and friendly nations and selected United States federal civilian employees. Part-time programs available. *Degree requirements:* For master's, thesis (for some programs), internal project, capstone project, or research/dissertation paper (for some programs); for doctorate, thesis/dissertation (for some programs), internal project, capstone project, or research/dissertation paper (for some programs). *Faculty research:* Net-centric enterprise systems/services, artificial intelligence (AI) systems engineering, unconventional weapons of mass destruction, complex systems engineering, risk-benefit analysis.

New Mexico Institute of Mining and Technology, Graduate Studies, Program in Mechanical Engineering, Socorro, NM 87801. Offers explosives engineering (MS); fluid and thermal sciences (MS); mechatronics systems engineering (MS); solid mechanics (MS). *Degree requirements:* For master's, thesis (for some programs). *Entrance requirements:* For master's, GRE General Test. Additional exam requirements/recommendations for international students: Required—TOEFL (minimum score 540 paper-based). *Faculty research:* Vibrations, fluid-structure interactions.

New Mexico State University, College of Engineering, Department of Industrial Engineering, Las Cruces, NM 88003-8001. Offers industrial engineering (PhD); systems engineering (Graduate Certificate). Part-time and evening/weekend programs available. Postbaccalaureate distance learning degree programs offered (no on-campus study). *Faculty:* 6 full-time (2 women). *Students:* 35 full-time (4 women), 98 part-time (24 women); includes 50 minority (10 Black or African American, non-Hispanic/Latino; 2 American Indian or Alaska Native, non-Hispanic/Latino; 7 Asian, non-Hispanic/Latino; 29 Hispanic/Latino; 2 Two or more races, non-Hispanic/Latino), 20 international. Average age 32. 100 applicants, 51% accepted, 25 enrolled. In 2014, 65 master's, 3 doctorates, 5 other advanced degrees awarded. *Degree requirements:* For master's, thesis optional; for doctorate, comprehensive exam, thesis/dissertation, qualifying exam. *Entrance requirements:* Additional exam requirements/recommendations for international students: Required—TOEFL (minimum score 550 paper-based; 79 iBT), IELTS (minimum score 6.5). *Application deadline:* For fall admission, 7/1 priority date for domestic students, 3/1 for international students; for spring admission, 11/1 for domestic students, 10/1 for international students. Applications are processed on a rolling basis. Application fee: $40 ($50 for international students). Electronic applications accepted. *Expenses:* Tuition, state resident: full-time $3969; part-time $220.50 per credit hour. Tuition, nonresident: full-time $13,838; part-time $768.80 per credit hour. *Required fees:* $853; $47.40 per credit hour. *Financial support:* In 2014–15, 21 students received support, including 5 research assistantships (averaging $12,373 per year), 7 teaching assistantships (averaging $15,446 per year); career-related internships or fieldwork, Federal Work-Study, scholarships/grants, traineeships, health care benefits, and unspecified assistantships also available. Support available to part-time students. Financial award application deadline: 3/1. *Faculty research:* Operations research, simulation, manufacturing engineering, systems engineering, applied statistics. *Total annual research expenditures:* $163,409. *Unit head:* Dr. Edward Pines, Academic Department Head, 575-646-4923, Fax: 575-646-2976, E-mail: epines@nmsu.edu. *Application contact:* 575-646-4923, Fax: 575-646-2976, E-mail: ie@nmsu.edu.
Website: http://ie.nmsu.edu.

New York University, Polytechnic School of Engineering, Department of Electrical and Computer Engineering, Major in Systems Engineering, New York, NY 10012-1019. Offers MS. Part-time and evening/weekend programs available. Postbaccalaureate distance learning degree programs offered (no on-campus study). *Students:* 8 full-time (4 women), 8 part-time (2 women); includes 2 minority (1 Asian, non-Hispanic/Latino; 1 Two or more races, non-Hispanic/Latino), 5 international. Average age 29. 33 applicants, 30% accepted, 4 enrolled. In 2014, 4 master's awarded. *Degree requirements:* For master's, comprehensive exam (for some programs), thesis (for some programs). *Entrance requirements:* For master's, BS in electrical engineering. Additional exam requirements/recommendations for international students: Required—TOEFL (minimum score 550 paper-based; 80 iBT); Recommended—IELTS (minimum score 6.5). *Application deadline:* For fall admission, 2/15 priority date for domestic and international students; for spring admission, 11/1 priority date for domestic and international students. Applications are processed on a rolling basis. Application fee: $75. Electronic applications accepted. *Financial support:* Fellowships, research assistantships, teaching assistantships, institutionally sponsored loans, scholarships/grants, and unspecified assistantships available. Support available to part-time students. Financial award applicants required to submit FAFSA. *Unit head:* Dr. Shivendra Panwar, Department Chair, 718-260-3740, E-mail: panwar@nyu.edu. *Application contact:* Raymond Lutzky, Director, Graduate Enrollment Management, 718-637-5984, Fax: 718-260-3624, E-mail: rlutzky@poly.edu.

North Carolina Agricultural and Technical State University, School of Graduate Studies, College of Engineering, Department of Industrial and Systems Engineering, Greensboro, NC 27411. Offers industrial engineering (MSIE, PhD). Part-time programs available. *Degree requirements:* For master's, thesis, project; for doctorate, thesis/dissertation. *Entrance requirements:* For master's, GRE General Test (recommended); for doctorate, GRE General Test, degree in engineering, BS in industrial engineering from ABET-accredited program with minimum cumulative credit point average of 3.7 or MS in discipline related to industrial engineering from college or university recognized by a regional or general accrediting agency with minimum cumulative GPA of 3.3. Additional exam requirements/recommendations for international students: Required—TOEFL (minimum score 550 paper-based; 79 iBT). *Faculty research:* Human-machine systems engineering, management systems engineering, operations research and systems analysis, production systems engineering.

Northeastern University, College of Engineering, Boston, MA 02115-5096. Offers bioengineering (PhD); chemical engineering (MS, PhD); civil engineering (MS, PhD); computer engineering (PhD); computer systems engineering (MS); electrical and computer engineering (MS); electrical and engineering leadership (MS); electrical engineering (PhD); energy systems (MS); engineering leadership (Certificate); engineering management (MRTP); industrial engineering (MS, PhD); information assurance (PhD); information systems (MS); interdisciplinary (PhD); mechanical engineering (MS, PhD); operations research (MS); telecommunication systems management (MS). Part-time programs available. *Expenses:* Contact institution.

Oakland University, Graduate Study and Lifelong Learning, School of Engineering and Computer Science, Department of Computer Science and Engineering, Rochester, MI 48309-4401. Offers computer science (MS); embedded systems (MS); information systems engineering (MS); software engineering (MS). Part-time and evening/weekend programs available. *Entrance requirements:* For master's, minimum GPA of 3.0. Electronic applications accepted. *Expenses:* Contact institution. *Faculty research:* Urinary continence index for prediction of urinary incontinence in older women.

Oakland University, Graduate Study and Lifelong Learning, School of Engineering and Computer Science, Department of Industrial and Systems Engineering, Program in Systems Engineering, Rochester, MI 48309-4401. Offers MS, PhD. *Degree requirements:* For doctorate, thesis/dissertation. *Entrance requirements:* For master's and doctorate, minimum GPA of 3.0. Additional exam requirements/recommendations for international students: Required—TOEFL (minimum score 550 paper-based). Electronic applications accepted. *Expenses:* Contact institution.

The Ohio State University, Graduate School, College of Engineering, Department of Integrated Systems Engineering, Columbus, OH 43210. Offers industrial and systems engineering (MS, PhD). *Faculty:* 18. *Students:* 81 full-time (21 women), 7 part-time (1 woman); includes 5 minority (1 Black or African American, non-Hispanic/Latino; 4 Asian, non-Hispanic/Latino), 63 international. Average age 28. In 2014, 23 master's, 8 doctorates awarded. *Degree requirements:* For master's, thesis optional; for doctorate, thesis/dissertation. *Entrance requirements:* For master's and doctorate, GRE General Test (desired minimum scores: Quantitative 166, Verbal 153, Analytical Writing 4.5). Additional exam requirements/recommendations for international students: Required—TOEFL (minimum score 550 paper-based; 79 iBT), Michigan English Language Assessment Battery (minimum score 82); Recommended—IELTS (minimum score 7). *Application deadline:* For fall admission, 12/13 priority date for domestic students, 11/30 priority date for international students; for winter admission, 12/1 for domestic students, 7/1 for international students; for spring admission, 10/1 for domestic and international students; for summer admission, 2/1 for domestic and international students. Applications are processed on a rolling basis. Application fee: $60 ($70 for international students). Electronic applications accepted. *Financial support:* Fellowships with tuition reimbursements, research assistantships with tuition reimbursements, teaching assistantships with tuition reimbursements, career-related internships or fieldwork, Federal Work-Study, institutionally sponsored loans, and unspecified assistantships available. Support available to part-time students. *Unit head:* Dr. Philip J. Smith, Chair, 614-292-4120, E-mail: smith.131@osu.edu. *Application contact:* Dr. Jerald Brevik, Graduate Studies Chair, 614-292-0177, Fax: 614-292-7852, E-mail: brevik.1@osu.edu.
Website: http://ise.osu.edu/.

Ohio University, Graduate College, Russ College of Engineering and Technology, Department of Industrial and Systems Engineering, Athens, OH 45701-2979. Offers M Eng Mgt, MS. Part-time and evening/weekend programs available. *Degree requirements:* For master's, comprehensive exam (for some programs), thesis optional, research project. *Entrance requirements:* For master's, GRE General Test. Additional exam requirements/recommendations for international students: Required—TOEFL (minimum score 550 paper-based; 80 iBT) or IELTS (minimum score 6.5). Electronic applications accepted. *Faculty research:* Software systems integration, human factors and ergonomics.

Old Dominion University, Frank Batten College of Engineering and Technology, Program in Engineering Management and Systems Engineering, Norfolk, VA 23529. Offers D Eng. Part-time and evening/weekend programs available. Postbaccalaureate distance learning degree programs offered (no on-campus study). *Faculty:* 14 full-time (2 women), 12 part-time/adjunct (2 women). *Students:* 2 full-time (both women), 11 part-time (2 women); includes 4 minority (1 Black or African American, non-Hispanic/Latino; 1 American Indian or Alaska Native, non-Hispanic/Latino; 2 Hispanic/Latino). Average age 43. 3 applicants, 67% accepted, 2 enrolled. In 2014, 1 doctorate awarded. *Degree requirements:* For doctorate, thesis/dissertation, candidacy exam, project. *Entrance requirements:* For doctorate, GRE, resume, letters of recommendation, minimum GPA of 3.0, interview. Additional exam requirements/recommendations for international students: Required—TOEFL (minimum score 550 paper-based; 79 iBT). *Application deadline:* For fall admission, 6/1 priority date for domestic students, 4/15 for international

students; for spring admission, 11/1 priority date for domestic students, 2/1 for international students. Applications are processed on a rolling basis. Application fee: $50. Electronic applications accepted. *Expenses:* Tuition, state resident: full-time $10,488; part-time $437 per credit. Tuition, nonresident: full-time $26,136; part-time $1089 per credit. *Required fees:* $64 per semester. One-time fee: $50. *Financial support:* In 2014–15, research assistantships with full and partial tuition reimbursements (averaging $20,000 per year), teaching assistantships with full and partial tuition reimbursements (averaging $20,000 per year) were awarded; fellowships, career-related internships or fieldwork, and tuition waivers also available. Support available to part-time students. Financial award application deadline: 2/15; financial award applicants required to submit FAFSA. *Faculty research:* Project management, systems engineering, modeling and simulation, virtual collaboration environments, multidisciplinary designs. *Total annual research expenditures:* $729,085. *Unit head:* Dr. Adrian Gheorghe, Department Chair, 757-683-4558, Fax: 757-683-5640, E-mail: enmagpd@odu.edu. *Application contact:* Dr. Andres Sousa-Poza, Graduate Program Director, 757-683-4734, Fax: 757-683-5640, E-mail: enmagpd@odu.edu.
Website: http://eng.odu.edu/enma/.

Old Dominion University, Frank Batten College of Engineering and Technology, Program in Systems Engineering, Norfolk, VA 23529. Offers ME. Part-time and evening/weekend programs available. Postbaccalaureate distance learning degree programs offered (no on-campus study). *Faculty:* 14 full-time (2 women), 12 part-time/adjunct (2 women). *Students:* 5 full-time (1 woman), 50 part-time (14 women); includes 22 minority (11 Black or African American, non-Hispanic/Latino; 3 Asian, non-Hispanic/Latino; 5 Hispanic/Latino; 3 Two or more races, non-Hispanic/Latino), 3 international. Average age 34. 16 applicants, 81% accepted, 11 enrolled. In 2014, 14 master's awarded. *Degree requirements:* For master's, comprehensive exam, project. *Entrance requirements:* For master's, GRE, minimum GPA of 3.0. Additional exam requirements/recommendations for international students: Required—TOEFL (minimum score 550 paper-based; 79 iBT). *Application deadline:* For fall admission, 6/1 priority date for domestic students, 4/15 for international students; for spring admission, 11/1 priority date for domestic students, 2/1 for international students. Applications are processed on a rolling basis. Application fee: $50. Electronic applications accepted. *Expenses:* Tuition, state resident: full-time $10,488; part-time $437 per credit. Tuition, nonresident: full-time $26,136; part-time $1089 per credit. *Required fees:* $64 per semester. One-time fee: $50. *Financial support:* In 2014–15, research assistantships with partial tuition reimbursements (averaging $20,000 per year), teaching assistantships with partial tuition reimbursements (averaging $20,000 per year) were awarded; fellowships, career-related internships or fieldwork, scholarships/grants, and tuition waivers (partial) also available. Support available to part-time students. Financial award application deadline: 2/15; financial award applicants required to submit FAFSA. *Faculty research:* System of systems engineering, complex systems, optimization. *Total annual research expenditures:* $729,085. *Unit head:* Dr. Adrian Gheorghe, Chair, 757-683-4558, Fax: 757-683-5640, E-mail: agheorgh@odu.edu. *Application contact:* Dr. Ariel Pinto, Graduate Program Director, 757-683-4218, Fax: 757-683-5640, E-mail: enmagpd@odu.edu.
Website: http://eng.odu.edu/enma/academics/systemsengr.shtml.

Penn State Great Valley, Graduate Studies, Engineering Division, Malvern, PA 19355-1488. Offers engineering management (MEM); software engineering (MSE); systems engineering (M Eng). *Unit head:* Dr. Craig S. Edelbrock, Chancellor, 610-648-3202 Ext. 610, Fax: 610-889-1334, E-mail: cse1@psu.edu. *Application contact:* JoAnn Kelly, Director of Admissions, 610-648-3315, Fax: 610-725-5296, E-mail: jek2@psu.edu.
Website: http://www.sgps.psu.edu/Academics/Degrees/31884.htm.

Regis University, College for Professional Studies, School of Computer and Information Sciences, Denver, CO 80221-1099. Offers database development (Certificate); enterprise Java software development (Certificate); enterprise resource planning (Certificate); executive information technology (Certificate); information assurance (M Sc); information technology management (M Sc); software engineering (Certificate); software engineering and database technologies (M Sc); storage area networks (Certificate); systems engineering (M Sc, Certificate). Part-time and evening/weekend programs available. Postbaccalaureate distance learning degree programs offered (no on-campus study). *Faculty:* 8 full-time (3 women), 46 part-time/adjunct (9 women). *Students:* 254 full-time (69 women), 221 part-time (59 women); includes 159 minority (57 Black or African American, non-Hispanic/Latino; 4 American Indian or Alaska Native, non-Hispanic/Latino; 39 Asian, non-Hispanic/Latino; 49 Hispanic/Latino; 1 Native Hawaiian or other Pacific Islander, non-Hispanic/Latino; 9 Two or more races, non-Hispanic/Latino), 22 international. Average age 38. 204 applicants, 87% accepted, 128 enrolled. In 2014, 176 master's awarded. *Degree requirements:* For master's, thesis (for some programs), final research project. *Entrance requirements:* For master's, official transcript reflecting baccalaureate degree awarded from regionally-accredited college or university, 2 years of related experience, resume, interview. Additional exam requirements/recommendations for international students: Required—TOEFL (minimum score 550 paper-based; 82 iBT). *Application deadline:* For fall admission, 8/13 for domestic students, 7/13 for international students; for winter admission, 10/8 for domestic students, 9/8 for international students; for spring admission, 12/17 for domestic students, 11/17 for international students. Applications are processed on a rolling basis. Application fee: $75. Electronic applications accepted. *Expenses:* Expenses: $710 per credit hour (for M Sc). *Financial support:* In 2014–15, 16 students received support. Federal Work-Study and scholarships/grants available. Financial award application deadline: 4/15; financial award applicants required to submit FAFSA. *Faculty research:* Information policy, knowledge management, software architectures. *Unit head:* Donald Archer, Interim Dean, 303-458-4335, E-mail: archer@regis.edu. *Application contact:* Sarah Engel, Director of Admissions, 303-458-4900, Fax: 303-964-5534, E-mail: regisadm@regis.edu.
Website: http://regis.edu/CCIS.aspx.

Rensselaer Polytechnic Institute, Graduate School, School of Engineering, Program in Computer and Systems Engineering, Troy, NY 12180-3590. Offers M Eng, MS, D Eng, PhD. *Faculty:* 12 full-time (2 women), 2 part-time/adjunct (1 woman). *Students:* 14 full-time (4 women), 2 part-time (0 women), 12 international. Average age 28. 50 applicants, 12% accepted, 5 enrolled. In 2014, 4 master's, 1 doctorate awarded. Terminal master's awarded for partial completion of doctoral program. *Degree requirements:* For master's, thesis (for some programs); for doctorate, thesis/dissertation. *Entrance requirements:* For master's and doctorate, GRE. Additional exam requirements/recommendations for international students: Required—TOEFL (minimum score 570 paper-based; 88 iBT), IELTS (minimum score 6.5), PTE (minimum score 60). *Application deadline:* For fall admission, 1/1 priority date for domestic and international students; for spring admission, 8/15 priority date for domestic and international students. Applications are processed on a rolling basis. Application fee: $75. Electronic applications accepted. *Expenses: Tuition:* Full-time $46,700; part-time $1945 per credit. Tuition and fees vary according to course load. *Financial support:* In 2014–15, 11 students received support, including research assistantships (averaging $18,500 per year), teaching assistantships (averaging $18,500 per year); fellowships also available. Financial award application deadline: 1/1. *Faculty research:* Communications, information, and signals and systems; computer engineering, hardware, and architecture; computer networking; control, robotics, and automation; energy sources and systems; image science: computer vision, image processing, and geographic information science; microelectronics, photonics, VLSI, and mixed-signal design; plasma science and electromagnetics. *Total annual research expenditures:* $1.9 million. *Unit head:* Dr. Ken Vastola, Graduate Program Director, 518-576-6074, E-mail: gpd@ecse.rpi.edu. *Application contact:* Office of Graduate Admissions, 518-276-6216, E-mail: gradadmissions@rpi.edu.
Website: http://www.ecse.rpi.edu/.

Rensselaer Polytechnic Institute, Graduate School, School of Engineering, Program in Decision Sciences and Engineering Systems, Troy, NY 12180-3590. Offers PhD. *Faculty:* 21 full-time (4 women), 4 part-time/adjunct (1 woman). *Students:* 14 full-time (5 women); includes 1 minority (Asian, non-Hispanic/Latino), 9 international. Average age 29. 23 applicants, 48% accepted, 6 enrolled. In 2014, 2 doctorates awarded. Terminal master's awarded for partial completion of doctoral program. *Degree requirements:* For doctorate, thesis/dissertation. *Entrance requirements:* For doctorate, GRE. Additional exam requirements/recommendations for international students: Required—TOEFL (minimum score 570 paper-based; 88 iBT), IELTS (minimum score 6.5), PTE (minimum score 60). *Application deadline:* For fall admission, 1/1 priority date for domestic students, 1/1 for international students; for spring admission, 8/15 for domestic and international students. Applications are processed on a rolling basis. Application fee: $75. Electronic applications accepted. *Expenses: Tuition:* Full-time $46,700; part-time $1945 per credit. Tuition and fees vary according to course load. *Financial support:* In 2014–15, 13 students received support, including research assistantships (averaging $18,500 per year), teaching assistantships (averaging $18,500 per year); fellowships also available. Financial award application deadline: 1/1. *Faculty research:* Agent-based modeling, computational optimization, data mining, decision analysis, decision technologies, human factors engineering, logistics, network optimization and analysis, scheduling, simulation modeling, statistical analysis, stochastic programming. *Total annual research expenditures:* $69,998. *Unit head:* Dr. David Mendonca, Graduate Program Director, 518-276-4222, E-mail: mondod@rpi.edu. *Application contact:* Office of Graduate Admissions, 518-276-6216, E-mail: gradadmissions@rpi.edu.
Website: http://ise.rpi.edu/.

Rensselaer Polytechnic Institute, Graduate School, School of Engineering, Program in Systems Engineering and Technology Management, Troy, NY 12180-3590. Offers M Eng. Part-time programs available. *Faculty:* 8 full-time (3 women), 4 part-time/adjunct (1 woman). *Students:* 7 applicants, 14% accepted, 1 enrolled. In 2014, 1 master's awarded. *Degree requirements:* For master's, thesis (for some programs). *Entrance requirements:* For master's, GRE. Additional exam requirements/recommendations for international students: Required—TOEFL (minimum score 570 paper-based; 88 iBT), IELTS (minimum score 6.5), PTE (minimum score 60). *Application deadline:* For fall admission, 1/1 priority date for domestic and international students; for spring admission, 8/15 priority date for domestic and international students. Applications are processed on a rolling basis. Application fee: $75. Electronic applications accepted. *Expenses: Tuition:* Full-time $46,700; part-time $1945 per credit. Tuition and fees vary according to course load. *Financial support:* Career-related internships or fieldwork and institutionally sponsored loans available. Financial award application deadline: 1/1. *Total annual research expenditures:* $600,900. *Unit head:* Dr. Bill Foley, Graduate Program Director, 518-276-4009, E-mail: foleyw@rpi.edu. *Application contact:* Graduate Admissions, 518-276-6216, E-mail: gradadmissions@rpi.edu.

Rochester Institute of Technology, Graduate Enrollment Services, Kate Gleason College of Engineering, Design, Development and Manufacturing Department, MS Program in Product Development, Rochester, NY 14623-5603. Offers MS. Part-time and evening/weekend programs available. Postbaccalaureate distance learning degree programs offered. *Students:* 39 part-time (4 women); includes 2 minority (1 Black or African American, non-Hispanic/Latino; 1 Hispanic/Latino), 1 international. Average age 35. 23 applicants, 74% accepted, 16 enrolled. In 2014, 13 master's awarded. *Degree requirements:* For master's, capstone project. *Entrance requirements:* For master's, TOEFL, IELTS, or PTE for non-native English speakers, undergraduate degree in engineering or related field, minimum GPA of 3.0, 2 years of experience in product development. Additional exam requirements/recommendations for international students: Required—PTE (minimum score 58), TOEFL (minimum score 550 paper-based; 79 iBT) or IELTS (minimum score 6.5). *Application deadline:* For fall admission, 2/15 for domestic and international students. Applications are processed on a rolling basis. Application fee: $60. Electronic applications accepted. *Expenses:* Expenses: $1,673 per credit hour. *Financial support:* Institutionally sponsored loans and scholarships/grants available. Support available to part-time students. Financial award applicants required to submit FAFSA. *Faculty research:* Platform element dynamics in a multi-product development environment, applying self-organizing principles to product development in a globally-distributed environment, collaborative design and development to accelerate durable goods design and manufacturing. *Unit head:* Mark Smith, Graduate Program Director, 585-475-7971, Fax: 585-475-4080, E-mail: mpdmail@rit.edu. *Application contact:* Diane Ellison, Associate Vice President, Graduate Enrollment Services, 585-475-2229, Fax: 585-475-7164, E-mail: gradinfo@rit.edu.
Website: https://www.rit.edu/kgcoe/mpd/.

Rochester Institute of Technology, Graduate Enrollment Services, Kate Gleason College of Engineering, Industrial and Systems Engineering Department, ME Program in Industrial and Systems Engineering, Rochester, NY 14623-5603. Offers ME. *Students:* 11 full-time (2 women), 2 part-time, 10 international. Average age 26. 76 applicants, 25% accepted, 7 enrolled. In 2014, 13 master's awarded. *Degree requirements:* For master's, thesis or alternative, Capstone Project. *Entrance requirements:* For master's, TOEFL, IELTS, or PTE for non-native English speakers, Recommended minimum GPA of 3.0. Additional exam requirements/recommendations for international students: Required—PTE (minimum score 58), TOEFL (minimum score 550 paper-based; 79 iBT) or IELTS (minimum score 6.5). *Application deadline:* For fall admission, 2/15 priority date for domestic and international students; for spring admission, 12/15 priority date for domestic and international students. Applications are processed on a rolling basis. Electronic applications accepted. *Expenses:* Expenses: $1,673 per credit hour. *Financial support:* In 2014–15, 7 students received support. Research assistantships with partial tuition reimbursements available, teaching assistantships with partial tuition reimbursements available, career-related internships or fieldwork, Federal Work-Study, institutionally sponsored loans, scholarships/grants, and unspecified assistantships available. Support available to part-time students. *Faculty research:* Advanced manufacturing, engineering education, ergonomics and human factors, healthcare delivery systems, operations research and simulation, systems engineering, production and logistics, sustainable engineering. *Unit head:* Dr. Marcos Esterman, Associate Professor, 585-475-2598, E-mail: mxeeie@rit.edu. *Application contact:* Diane Ellison, Associate Vice President, Graduate Enrollment Services, 585-475-2229, Fax: 585-475-7164, E-mail: gradinfo@rit.edu.
Website: http://www.rit.edu/kgcoe/ise/program/ms-industrial-systems-engineering/master-engineering-industrial-and-systems-engineering.

Rochester Institute of Technology, Graduate Enrollment Services, Kate Gleason College of Engineering, Industrial and Systems Engineering Department, MS Program

in Industrial and Systems Engineering, Rochester, NY 14623-5603. Offers MS. Part-time programs available. *Students:* 34 full-time (2 women), 10 part-time (1 woman), 38 international. Average age 24. 250 applicants, 30% accepted, 19 enrolled. In 2014, 3 master's awarded. *Degree requirements:* For master's, thesis. *Entrance requirements:* For master's, GRE and TOEFL, IELTS, or PTE for non-native English speakers, Recommended minimum GPA of 3.0. Additional exam requirements/recommendations for international students: Required—PTE (minimum score 58), TOEFL (minimum score 550 paper-based; 79 iBT) or IELTS (minimum score 6.5). *Application deadline:* For fall admission, 2/15 priority date for domestic and international students; for spring admission, 12/15 priority date for domestic and international students. Applications are processed on a rolling basis. Electronic applications accepted. *Expenses:* Expenses: $1,673 per credit hour. *Financial support:* In 2014–15, 25 students received support. Research assistantships with partial tuition reimbursements available, teaching assistantships with partial tuition reimbursements available, career-related internships or fieldwork, Federal Work-Study, institutionally sponsored loans, scholarships/grants, and unspecified assistantships available. Support available to part-time students. Financial award applicants required to submit FAFSA. *Faculty research:* Advanced manufacturing, engineering education, ergonomics and human factors, healthcare delivery systems, operations research and simulation, systems engineering, production and logistics, sustainable engineering. *Unit head:* Dr. Marcos Esterman, Associate Professor, 585-475-2598, E-mail: mxeeie@rit.edu. *Application contact:* Diane Ellison, Associate Vice President, Graduate Enrollment Services, 585-475-2229, Fax: 585-475-7164, E-mail: gradinfo@rit.edu.
Website: http://www.rit.edu/kgcoe/ise/program/master-science-degrees/master-science-industrial-and-systems-engineering.

Rochester Institute of Technology, Graduate Enrollment Services, Kate Gleason College of Engineering, Microsystems Engineering Department, PhD Program in Microsystems Engineering, Rochester, NY 14623-5603. Offers PhD. Part-time programs available. *Students:* 37 full-time (4 women), 3 part-time (2 women); includes 1 minority (Asian, non-Hispanic/Latino), 23 international. Average age 29. 38 applicants, 21% accepted, 7 enrolled. In 2014, 9 doctorates awarded. *Degree requirements:* For doctorate, comprehensive exam, thesis/dissertation. *Entrance requirements:* For doctorate, GRE and TOEFL, IELTS, or PTE for non-native English speakers, Recommended minimum GPA of 3.0. Additional exam requirements/recommendations for international students: Required—PTE (minimum score 58), TOEFL (minimum score 550 paper-based; 79 iBT) or IELTS (minimum score 6.5). *Application deadline:* For fall admission, 1/15 priority date for domestic and international students. Applications are processed on a rolling basis. Electronic applications accepted. *Expenses:* Expenses: $1,673 per credit hour. *Financial support:* In 2014–15, 1 student received support. Fellowships, research assistantships with full and partial tuition reimbursements available, teaching assistantships with full and partial tuition reimbursements available, career-related internships or fieldwork, Federal Work-Study, institutionally sponsored loans, scholarships/grants, health care benefits, and unspecified assistantships available. Support available to part-time students. Financial award applicants required to submit FAFSA. *Faculty research:* Advanced micro- and nano-electronics, photovoltaics, microfluidics, compound semiconductor materials, integrated photonics, thin film devices, MEMS, direct-printed electronics, nanopatterning, biomedical microsystems. *Unit head:* Dr. Bruce Smith, Director, 585-475-2058, E-mail: bwsemc@rit.edu. *Application contact:* Diane Ellison, Associate Vice President, Graduate Enrollment Services, 585-475-2229, Fax: 585-475-7164, E-mail: gradinfo@rit.edu.
Website: http://www.rit.edu/kgcoe/program/microsystems-engineering.

Rose-Hulman Institute of Technology, Faculty of Engineering and Applied Sciences, Department of Electrical and Computer Engineering, Terre Haute, IN 47803-3999. Offers electrical and computer engineering (M Eng); electrical engineering (MS); systems engineering and management (MS). Part-time programs available. Postbaccalaureate distance learning degree programs offered (minimal on-campus study). *Faculty:* 19 full-time (3 women), 1 (woman) part-time/adjunct. *Students:* 16 full-time (4 women), 6 part-time (0 women); includes 2 minority (both Asian, non-Hispanic/Latino), 16 international. Average age 24. 28 applicants, 93% accepted, 11 enrolled. In 2014, 14 master's awarded. *Degree requirements:* For master's, thesis (for some programs). *Entrance requirements:* For master's, GRE, minimum GPA of 3.0. Additional exam requirements/recommendations for international students: Required—TOEFL (minimum score 580 paper-based; 92 iBT). *Application deadline:* For fall admission, 2/1 priority date for domestic students. Applications are processed on a rolling basis. Application fee: $0. *Expenses: Tuition:* Full-time $40,449. *Financial support:* In 2014–15, 21 students received support. Fellowships with full and partial tuition reimbursements available, research assistantships with full and partial tuition reimbursements available, institutionally sponsored loans, scholarships/grants, and tuition waivers (full and partial) available. *Faculty research:* VLSI, power systems, analog electronics, communications, electromagnetics. *Total annual research expenditures:* $20,179. *Unit head:* Dr. Robert Throne, Chairman, 812-877-8414, Fax: 812-877-8895, E-mail: robert.d.throne@rose-hulman.edu. *Application contact:* Dr. Azad Siahmakoun, Associate Dean of the Faculty, 812-877-8400, Fax: 812-877-8061, E-mail: siahmako@rose-hulman.edu.
Website: http://www.rose-hulman.edu/academics/academic-departments/electrical-computer-engineering.aspx.

Rutgers, The State University of New Jersey, New Brunswick, Graduate School-New Brunswick, Department of Industrial and Systems Engineering, Piscataway, NJ 08854-8097. Offers industrial and systems engineering (MS, PhD); information technology (MS); manufacturing systems engineering (MS); quality and reliability engineering (MS). Part-time and evening/weekend programs available. Terminal master's awarded for partial completion of doctoral program. *Degree requirements:* For master's, thesis or alternative, seminar; for doctorate, comprehensive exam, thesis/dissertation. *Entrance requirements:* For master's and doctorate, GRE General Test. Additional exam requirements/recommendations for international students: Required—TOEFL. *Faculty research:* Production and manufacturing systems, quality and reliability engineering, systems engineering and aviation safety.

San Jose State University, Graduate Studies and Research, Charles W. Davidson College of Engineering, Department of Industrial and Systems Engineering, San Jose, CA 95192-0001. Offers MS. Part-time programs available. *Degree requirements:* For master's, comprehensive exam. Electronic applications accepted.

Simon Fraser University, Office of Graduate Studies, Faculty of Applied Sciences, School of Mechatronic Systems Engineering, Burnaby, BC V5A 1S6, Canada. Offers MA Sc, PhD. *Degree requirements:* For master's, one foreign language, thesis; for doctorate, one foreign language, comprehensive exam, thesis/dissertation. *Entrance requirements:* Additional exam requirements/recommendations for international students: Required—TOEFL (minimum score 580 paper-based; 93 iBT), IELTS (minimum score 7), TWE (minimum score 5). Electronic applications accepted. *Faculty research:* Intelligent systems and smart materials, micro-electro mechanical systems (MEMS), biomedical engineering, thermal engineering, alternative energy.

Southern Methodist University, Bobby B. Lyle School of Engineering, Department of Engineering Management, Information, and Systems, Dallas, TX 75275. Offers engineering management (MSEM, DE); information engineering and management (MSIEM); operations research (MS, PhD); systems engineering (MS, PhD). Part-time and evening/weekend programs available. Postbaccalaureate distance learning degree programs offered. Terminal master's awarded for partial completion of doctoral program. *Degree requirements:* For master's, thesis optional; for doctorate, thesis/dissertation, oral and written qualifying exams. *Entrance requirements:* For master's, minimum GPA of 3.0 in last 2 years; bachelor's degree in engineering, mathematics, sciences, or technical area; for doctorate, GRE General Test (operations research, engineering management), bachelor's degree in related field. Additional exam requirements/recommendations for international students: Required—TOEFL. *Faculty research:* Telecommunications, decision systems, information engineering, operations research, software.

Southern Methodist University, Bobby B. Lyle School of Engineering, Program in Datacenter Systems Engineering, Dallas, TX 75275. Offers MS. Part-time programs available. Postbaccalaureate distance learning degree programs offered (no on-campus study). *Entrance requirements:* For master's, BS in one of the engineering disciplines, computer science, one of the quantitative sciences or mathematics; minimum of two years of college-level mathematics including one year of college-level calculus.

Southern Polytechnic State University, School of Engineering, Department of Mechanical and Systems Engineering, Marietta, GA 30060-2896. Offers systems engineering (MS, Graduate Certificate). Part-time and evening/weekend programs available. Postbaccalaureate distance learning degree programs offered (no on-campus study). *Degree requirements:* For master's, thesis optional. *Entrance requirements:* For master's, GRE. Additional exam requirements/recommendations for international students: Required—TOEFL (minimum score 550 paper-based; 79 iBT), IELTS (minimum score 6.5). Electronic applications accepted. *Faculty research:* Supply chain and logistics reliability, maintainability system analysis, design optimization, engineering education.

Stevens Institute of Technology, Graduate School, School of Systems and Enterprises, Program in Systems Engineering, Hoboken, NJ 07030. Offers agile systems and enterprises (Certificate); systems and supportability engineering (Certificate); systems engineering (M Eng, PhD); systems engineering management (Certificate).

Stony Brook University, State University of New York, Graduate School, College of Engineering and Applied Sciences, Department of Computer Science, Program in Information Systems Engineering, Stony Brook, NY 11794. Offers MS. *Entrance requirements:* Additional exam requirements/recommendations for international students: Required—TOEFL. *Expenses:* Tuition, state resident: full-time $10,370; part-time $432 per credit. Tuition, nonresident: full-time $20,190; part-time $841 per credit. *Required fees:* $1431. *Unit head:* Prof. Arie Kauffman, Chair, 631-632-8470, Fax: 631-632-8334, E-mail: arie.kaufman@stonybrook.edu. *Application contact:* Lourdes Hartwell, Graduate Program Admissions Administrator, 631-632-8470, Fax: 631-632-8334, E-mail: graduate@cs.sunysb.edu.

Syracuse University, L. C. Smith College of Engineering and Computer Science, Program in Systems Assurance, Syracuse, NY 13244. Offers CAS. Part-time programs available. *Students:* 1 applicant, 100% accepted. *Entrance requirements:* For degree, GRE General Test. *Expenses: Tuition:* Part-time $1341 per credit. *Required fees:* $1341 per credit. *Unit head:* Tom Lumpkin, Program Contact, 315-443-3164, E-mail: lumpkin@syr.edu. *Application contact:* Kathleen Joyce, Assistant Dean, 314-443-2219, E-mail: topgrads@syr.edu.
Website: http://lcs.syr.edu.

Tennessee State University, The School of Graduate Studies and Research, College of Engineering, Nashville, TN 37209-1561. Offers biomedical engineering (ME); civil engineering (ME); computer and information systems engineering (MS, PhD); electrical engineering (ME); environmental engineering (ME); manufacturing engineering (ME); mathematical sciences (MS); mechanical engineering (ME). Part-time and evening/weekend programs available. *Degree requirements:* For master's, project; for doctorate, comprehensive exam, thesis/dissertation. *Entrance requirements:* For doctorate, minimum GPA of 3.3. *Faculty research:* Robotics, intelligent systems, human-computer interaction software systems, biomedical engineering, signal/image processing, probabilistic design, intelligent manufacturing, cooperative mobile robots, condition based maintenance, sensor fusion.

Texas A&M University–Kingsville, College of Graduate Studies, College of Engineering, Program in Sustainable Energy Systems Engineering, Kingsville, TX 78363. Offers PhD. *Degree requirements:* For doctorate, variable foreign language requirement, comprehensive exam, thesis/dissertation (for some programs). *Entrance requirements:* For doctorate, GRE, MAT, GMAT, bachelor's or master's degree in engineering or science, curriculum vitae, official transcripts, statement of purpose, three letters of recommendation. Additional exam requirements/recommendations for international students: Required—TOEFL (minimum score 550 paper-based; 79 iBT). *Application deadline:* For fall admission, 8/15 for domestic students, 6/1 for international students; for spring admission, 12/15 for domestic students, 10/1 for international students; for summer admission, 5/15 for domestic students, 4/1 for international students. Applications are processed on a rolling basis. Application fee: $35 ($50 for international students). Electronic applications accepted. *Financial support:* Career-related internships or fieldwork, Federal Work-Study, institutionally sponsored loans, scholarships/grants, health care benefits, tuition waivers (full and partial), and unspecified assistantships available. Support available to part-time students. Financial award application deadline: 5/1; financial award applicants required to submit FAFSA. *Unit head:* Dr. Stephan Nix, Dean, 361-593-4857, E-mail: stephan.nix@tamuk.edu. *Application contact:* Dr. Mohamed Abdelrahman, Dean, College of Graduate Studies, 361-593-2809, E-mail: mohamed.abdelrahman@tamuk.edu.

Texas Tech University, Graduate School, Edward E. Whitacre Jr. College of Engineering, Department of Industrial Engineering, Lubbock, TX 79409-3061. Offers industrial engineering (MSIE, PhD); systems and engineering management (MSSEM, PhD). Part-time programs available. Postbaccalaureate distance learning degree programs offered (minimal on-campus study). *Faculty:* 14 full-time (2 women), 1 part-time/adjunct (0 women). *Students:* 79 full-time (17 women), 64 part-time (14 women); includes 15 minority (5 Black or African American, non-Hispanic/Latino; 1 American Indian or Alaska Native, non-Hispanic/Latino; 2 Asian, non-Hispanic/Latino; 6 Hispanic/Latino; 1 Two or more races, non-Hispanic/Latino), 80 international. Average age 32. 275 applicants, 55% accepted, 58 enrolled. In 2014, 17 master's, 7 doctorates awarded. Terminal master's awarded for partial completion of doctoral program. *Degree requirements:* For master's, comprehensive exam, thesis optional; for doctorate, comprehensive exam, thesis/dissertation. *Entrance requirements:* For master's, GRE (Verbal and Quantitative); for doctorate, GRE (Verbal and Quantitative), MS. Additional exam requirements/recommendations for international students: Required—TOEFL (minimum score 550 paper-based; 79 iBT). *Application deadline:* For fall admission, 6/1 priority date for domestic students, 1/15 priority date for international students; for spring admission, 9/1 priority date for domestic students, 6/15 priority date for international students. Applications are processed on a rolling basis. Application fee: $60. Electronic applications accepted. *Expenses:* Tuition, state resident: full-time $6310; part-time $262.92 per credit hour. Tuition, nonresident: full-time $14,998; part-time $624.92 per

credit hour. *Required fees:* $2701; $36.50 per credit. $912.50 per semester. Tuition and fees vary according to course load. *Financial support:* In 2014–15, 57 students received support, including 55 fellowships (averaging $3,146 per year), 5 research assistantships (averaging $26,747 per year), 13 teaching assistantships (averaging $20,625 per year); scholarships/grants, tuition waivers (partial), and unspecified assistantships also available. Financial award application deadline: 2/1; financial award applicants required to submit FAFSA. *Faculty research:* Engineering management, operations research, manufacturing, ergonomics, quality. *Total annual research expenditures:* $614,109. *Unit head:* Dr. Hong-Chao Zhang, Interim Chair, 806-742-3543, E-mail: hong-chao.zhang@ttu.edu. *Application contact:* Dr. Simon Hsiang, Professor, 806-742-3543, Fax: 806-742-3411, E-mail: simon.hsiang@ttu.edu.
Website: http://www.ie.ttu.edu/.

The University of Alabama in Huntsville, School of Graduate Studies, College of Engineering, Department of Industrial and Systems Engineering and Engineering Management, Huntsville, AL 35899. Offers engineering management (PhD); industrial and systems engineering (MSE, PhD); industrial engineering (MSE, PhD); operations research (MSOR); systems engineering (MSE). Part-time and evening/weekend programs available. Postbaccalaureate distance learning degree programs offered (minimal on-campus study). *Degree requirements:* For master's, comprehensive exam, thesis or alternative, oral and written exams; for doctorate, comprehensive exam, thesis/dissertation, oral and written exams. *Entrance requirements:* For master's and doctorate, GRE General Test, minimum GPA of 3.0. Additional exam requirements/recommendations for international students: Required—TOEFL (minimum score 500 paper-based; 80 iBT), IELTS (minimum score 6.5). Electronic applications accepted. *Faculty research:* Systems engineering process, electronic manufacturing, heuristic manufacturing, teams and team development.

University of Alberta, Faculty of Graduate Studies and Research, Department of Electrical and Computer Engineering, Edmonton, AB T6G 2E1, Canada. Offers communications (M Eng, M Sc, PhD); computer engineering (M Eng, M Sc, PhD); electromagnetics (M Eng, M Sc, PhD); nanotechnology and microdevices (M Eng, M Sc, PhD); power/power electronics (M Eng, M Sc, PhD); systems (M Eng, M Sc, PhD). Terminal master's awarded for partial completion of doctoral program. *Degree requirements:* For master's, thesis; for doctorate, thesis/dissertation. *Entrance requirements:* Additional exam requirements/recommendations for international students: Required—TOEFL. Electronic applications accepted. *Faculty research:* Controls, communications, microelectronics, electromagnetics.

The University of Arizona, College of Engineering, Department of Systems and Industrial Engineering, Program in Systems and Industrial Engineering, Tucson, AZ 85721. Offers MS, PhD. Postbaccalaureate distance learning degree programs offered. *Degree requirements:* For doctorate, thesis/dissertation. *Entrance requirements:* For master's, GRE General Test (minimum score: 500 Verbal, 700 Quantitative), 3 letters of recommendation, letter of intent; for doctorate, GRE General Test (minimum score: 500 Verbal, 750 Quantitative), 3 letters of recommendation, letter of intent. Additional exam requirements/recommendations for international students: Required—TOEFL (minimum score 575 paper-based; 80 iBT). Electronic applications accepted. *Faculty research:* Optimization, systems theory, logistics, transportation, embedded systems.

The University of Arizona, College of Engineering, Department of Systems and Industrial Engineering, Program in Systems Engineering, Tucson, AZ 85721. Offers MS, PhD. Part-time programs available. *Entrance requirements:* For master's, GRE General Test (minimum score: 500 Verbal, 700 Quantitative), 3 letters of recommendation, letter of intent; for doctorate, GRE General Test (minimum score: 500 Verbal, 750 Quantitative), minimum GPA of 3.5, 3 letters of recommendation, letter of intent. Additional exam requirements/recommendations for international students: Required—TOEFL (minimum score 575 paper-based; 80 iBT). Electronic applications accepted. *Faculty research:* Man/machine systems, optimal control, algorithmic probability.

University of Arkansas at Little Rock, Graduate School, George W. Donaghey College of Engineering and Information Technology, Department of Systems Engineering, Little Rock, AR 72204-1099. Offers MS, PhD, Graduate Certificate. *Expenses:* Tuition, state resident: full-time $6000; part-time $300 per credit hour. Tuition, nonresident: full-time $13,800; part-time $690 per credit hour. *Required fees:* $1126; $603 per term. One-time fee: $40 full-time. *Unit head:* Dr. Mary L. Good, Dean, 501-569-3333, E-mail: mlgood@ualr.edu.
Website: http://ualr.edu/systemsengineering/.

University of California, Merced, Graduate Division, School of Engineering, Merced, CA 95343. Offers biological engineering and small scale technologies (MS, PhD); electrical engineering and computer science (MS, PhD); environmental systems (MS, PhD); mechanical engineering (MS); mechanical engineering and applied mechanics (PhD). *Faculty:* 38 full-time (6 women), 1 part-time/adjunct (0 women). *Students:* 128 full-time (36 women), 2 part-time (0 women); includes 21 minority (1 Black or African American, non-Hispanic/Latino; 11 Asian, non-Hispanic/Latino; 6 Hispanic/Latino; 3 Two or more races, non-Hispanic/Latino), 72 international. Average age 28. 230 applicants, 39% accepted, 38 enrolled. In 2014, 5 master's, 18 doctorates awarded. *Degree requirements:* For master's, variable foreign language requirement, comprehensive exam, thesis (for some programs); for doctorate, variable foreign language requirement, comprehensive exam, thesis/dissertation. *Entrance requirements:* For master's and doctorate, GRE. Additional exam requirements/recommendations for international students: Required—TOEFL (minimum score 550 paper-based; 68 iBT); Recommended—IELTS. Application fee: $80 ($100 for international students). *Expenses:* Tuition, state resident: full-time $11,220; part-time $2805 per semester. *Required fees:* $1940; $970 per semester hour. *Financial support:* In 2014–15, 19 fellowships with full and partial tuition reimbursements (averaging $6,683 per year) were awarded; scholarships/grants also available. *Faculty research:* Artificial intelligence, biomedical imaging, thermal science, ecology, nanotechnology. *Unit head:* Dr. Erik Rolland, Interim Dean, 209-228-4296, Fax: 209-228-4047, E-mail: erolland@ucmerced.edu. *Application contact:* Tsu Ya, Graduate Admissions and Academic Services Manager, 209-228-4521, Fax: 209-228-6906, E-mail: tya@ucmerced.edu.

University of Colorado Colorado Springs, College of Engineering and Applied Science, Program in General Engineering, Colorado Springs, CO 80933-7150. Offers energy engineering (ME); engineering management (ME); information assurance (ME); software engineering (ME); space operations (ME); systems engineering (ME). Part-time and evening/weekend programs available. Postbaccalaureate distance learning degree programs offered (minimal on-campus study). *Faculty:* 2 full-time (0 women), 8 part-time/adjunct (2 women). *Students:* 15 full-time (2 women), 159 part-time (30 women); includes 29 minority (3 Black or African American, non-Hispanic/Latino; 1 American Indian or Alaska Native, non-Hispanic/Latino; 10 Asian, non-Hispanic/Latino; 12 Hispanic/Latino; 3 Two or more races, non-Hispanic/Latino), 63 international. Average age 36. 113 applicants, 65% accepted, 39 enrolled. In 2014, 29 master's, 6 doctorates awarded. *Degree requirements:* For master's, thesis, portfolio, or project; for doctorate, comprehensive exam, thesis/dissertation. *Entrance requirements:* For master's, GRE (minimum score of 148 new grading scale on quantitative portion if GPA is less than 3.0); for doctorate, GRE (minimum score of 148 new grading scale on the quantitative portion if the applicant has not graduated from a program of recognized standing), minimum GPA of 3.3 in the bachelor or master degree program attempted. Additional exam requirements/recommendations for international students: Required—TOEFL (minimum score 80 iBT), IELTS (minimum score 6). *Application deadline:* For fall admission, 6/1 for domestic and international students; for spring admission, 11/1 for domestic and international students; for summer admission, 4/15 for domestic and international students. Application fee: $60 ($100 for international students). Electronic applications accepted. *Expenses:* Expenses: Contact institution. *Financial support:* In 2014–15, 10 students received support, including 2 fellowships (averaging $6,000 per year), 16 research assistantships (averaging $11,600 per year); teaching assistantships, Federal Work-Study, and scholarships/grants also available. Support available to part-time students. Financial award application deadline: 3/1; financial award applicants required to submit FAFSA. *Total annual research expenditures:* $91,458. *Unit head:* Dr. Ramaswami Dandapani, Dean, 719-255-3543, Fax: 719-255-3542, E-mail: rdan@cas.uccs.edu. *Application contact:* Dawn House, Coordinator, 719-255-3246, E-mail: dhouse@uccs.edu.

University of Florida, Graduate School, College of Engineering, Department of Industrial and Systems Engineering, Gainesville, FL 32611. Offers ME, MS, PhD, Engr. Part-time and evening/weekend programs available. Postbaccalaureate distance learning degree programs offered (minimal on-campus study). *Faculty:* 13 full-time (1 woman), 1 part-time/adjunct (0 women). *Students:* 62 full-time (19 women), 113 part-time (26 women); includes 30 minority (8 Black or African American, non-Hispanic/Latino; 1 American Indian or Alaska Native, non-Hispanic/Latino; 7 Asian, non-Hispanic/Latino; 14 Hispanic/Latino), 63 international. 595 applicants, 24% accepted, 71 enrolled. In 2014, 136 master's, 14 doctorates, 1 other advanced degree awarded. Terminal master's awarded for partial completion of doctoral program. *Degree requirements:* For master's, thesis (for some programs); for doctorate, comprehensive exam (for some programs), thesis/dissertation (for some programs). *Entrance requirements:* For master's and doctorate, minimum GPA of 3.0; for Engr, GRE General Test. Additional exam requirements/recommendations for international students: Required—TOEFL (minimum score 550 paper-based; 80 iBT), IELTS (minimum score 6). *Application deadline:* For fall admission, 12/31 priority date for domestic students, 2/1 for international students; for spring admission, 8/31 for domestic students, 8/1 for international students. Applications are processed on a rolling basis. Application fee: $30. Electronic applications accepted. *Financial support:* Career-related internships or fieldwork, Federal Work-Study, and unspecified assistantships available. Financial award application deadline: 1/15; financial award applicants required to submit FAFSA. *Faculty research:* Operations research; financial engineering; logistics and supply chain management; energy, healthcare, and transportation applications of operations research. *Unit head:* Joseph Geunes, Professor and Interim Chair, 352-392-1464 Ext. 2020, Fax: 352-392-3537, E-mail: geunes@ise.ufl.edu. *Application contact:* Office of Admissions, 352-392-1365, E-mail: webrequests@admissions.ufl.edu.
Website: http://www.ise.ufl.edu/.

University of Houston–Clear Lake, School of Science and Computer Engineering, Program in System Engineering, Houston, TX 77058-1002. Offers MS. *Entrance requirements:* Additional exam requirements/recommendations for international students: Required—TOEFL (minimum score 550 paper-based).

University of Illinois at Urbana–Champaign, Graduate College, College of Engineering, Department of Industrial and Enterprise Systems Engineering, Urbana, IL 61801. Offers industrial engineering (MS, PhD); systems and entrepreneurial engineering (MS, PhD); MBA/MS. *Faculty:* 22 full-time (7 women), 4 part-time/adjunct (0 women). *Students:* 73 (15 women); includes 2 minority (both Asian, non-Hispanic/Latino), 50 international. 296 applicants, 13% accepted, 19 enrolled. In 2014, 6 master's, 6 doctorates awarded. Application fee: $70 ($90 for international students). *Unit head:* Rakesh Nagi, Head, 217-333-2731. *Application contact:* Holly Michelle Kizer, Graduate Programs Coordinator, 217-333-2730, Fax: 217-244-5705, E-mail: tippy6@illinois.edu.
Website: http://ise.illinois.edu/.

University of Maryland, Baltimore County, The Graduate School, Program in Systems Engineering, Baltimore, MD 21250. Offers MS, Postbaccalaureate Certificate. Part-time programs available. *Students:* 6 full-time (0 women), 52 part-time (12 women); includes 22 minority (12 Black or African American, non-Hispanic/Latino; 7 Asian, non-Hispanic/Latino; 3 Hispanic/Latino), 4 international. Average age 33. 36 applicants, 81% accepted, 18 enrolled. In 2014, 12 master's, 2 other advanced degrees awarded. *Degree requirements:* For master's, comprehensive exam (for some programs), thesis optional. *Entrance requirements:* Additional exam requirements/recommendations for international students: Required—TOEFL (minimum score 550 paper-based; 80 iBT), GRE General Test. *Application deadline:* For fall admission, 7/1 for domestic and international students; for spring admission, 12/1 for domestic and international students. Applications are processed on a rolling basis. Application fee: $70. Electronic applications accepted. *Expenses:* Tuition, state resident: part-time $557. Tuition, nonresident: part-time $922. *Required fees:* $122 per semester. One-time fee: $200 part-time. *Financial support:* In 2014–15, 1 research assistantship (averaging $20,000 per year) was awarded; career-related internships or fieldwork, Federal Work-Study, scholarships/grants, health care benefits, tuition waivers (partial), and unspecified assistantships also available. Support available to part-time students. Financial award application deadline: 6/30; financial award applicants required to submit FAFSA. *Faculty research:* Systems architecture design, modeling and simulation, design and risk analysis, system integrations test, management and engineering projects. *Unit head:* Dr. Julia M. Ross, Dean, College of Engineering and Information Technology, 410-455-3270, Fax: 410-455-3559, E-mail: jross@umbc.edu. *Application contact:* Dr. Thomas M. Moore, Lecturer/Graduate Program Director, E-mail: mooretg@umbc.edu.
Website: http://www.umbc.edu/gradschool/gradcatalog/programs/sys_eng.html.

University of Maryland, College Park, Academic Affairs, A. James Clark School of Engineering, Systems Engineering Program, College Park, MD 20742. Offers M Eng, MS. Part-time and evening/weekend programs available. *Degree requirements:* For master's, thesis optional. *Entrance requirements:* For master's, GRE General Test, minimum GPA of 3.0. Electronic applications accepted. *Faculty research:* Automation, computer, information, manufacturing, and process systems.

University of Massachusetts Dartmouth, Graduate School, College of Engineering, Department of Mechanical Engineering, North Dartmouth, MA 02747-2300. Offers industrial and systems engineering (MS); mechanical engineering (MS). Part-time programs available. *Faculty:* 11 full-time (1 woman). *Students:* 8 full-time (1 woman), 11 part-time (0 women); includes 1 minority (Asian, non-Hispanic/Latino), 9 international. Average age 26. 30 applicants, 60% accepted, 2 enrolled. In 2014, 10 master's awarded. *Degree requirements:* For master's, comprehensive exam, thesis or project. *Entrance requirements:* For master's, GRE (UMass Dartmouth mechanical engineering bachelor's degree recipients are exempt), statement of purpose (minimum of 300 words), resume, 3 letters of recommendation, official transcripts. Additional exam requirements/recommendations for international students: Required—TOEFL (minimum score 533 paper-based; 72 iBT), IELTS (minimum score 6). *Application deadline:* For fall admission, 2/15 priority date for domestic students, 1/15 priority date for international students; for spring admission, 11/15 priority date for domestic students, 10/15 priority date for international students. Applications are processed on a rolling basis. Application

fee: $60. Electronic applications accepted. *Expenses:* Tuition, state resident: full-time $2071; part-time $86.29 per credit. Tuition, nonresident: full-time $8099; part-time $337.46 per credit. *Required fees:* $16,520; $712.33 per credit. Tuition and fees vary according to course load and reciprocity agreements. *Financial support:* In 2014–15, 1 research assistantship with full tuition reimbursement (averaging $5,718 per year), 3 teaching assistantships with full tuition reimbursements (averaging $10,000 per year) were awarded; Federal Work-Study and unspecified assistantships also available. Support available to part-time students. Financial award application deadline: 3/1; financial award applicants required to submit FAFSA. *Faculty research:* Biopreservation, renewable energy, fluid structure interaction, buoyant flows, high performance heat exchanges, mechanics of biomaterials, composite materials, computational mechanics. *Total annual research expenditures:* $1.2 million. *Unit head:* John Rice, Graduate Program Director, 508-999-8498, Fax: 508-999-8881, E-mail: jrice@umassd.edu. *Application contact:* Steven Briggs, Director of Marketing and Recruitment for Graduate Studies, 508-999-8604, Fax: 508-999-8183, E-mail: graduate@umassd.edu.
Website: http://www.umassd.edu/engineering/mne/.

University of Massachusetts Dartmouth, Graduate School, College of Engineering, Program in Engineering and Applied Science, North Dartmouth, MA 02747-2300. Offers applied mechanics and materials (PhD); computational science and engineering (PhD); computer science and information systems (PhD); industrial and systems engineering (PhD). Part-time programs available. *Students:* 21 full-time (6 women), 1 (woman) part-time; includes 2 minority (1 Black or African American, non-Hispanic/Latino; 1 Two or more races, non-Hispanic/Latino), 12 international. Average age 30. 23 applicants, 65% accepted, 5 enrolled. In 2014, 1 doctorate awarded. *Degree requirements:* For doctorate, comprehensive exam, thesis/dissertation. *Entrance requirements:* For doctorate, GRE, statement of purpose (minimum of 300 words), resume, 3 letters of recommendation, official transcripts. Additional exam requirements/recommendations for international students: Required—TOEFL (minimum score 550 paper-based; 79 iBT). *Application deadline:* For fall admission, 2/15 priority date for domestic students, 1/15 priority date for international students; for spring admission, 11/15 priority date for domestic students, 10/15 priority date for international students. Applications are processed on a rolling basis. Application fee: $60. Electronic applications accepted. *Expenses:* Tuition, state resident: full-time $2071; part-time $86.29 per credit. Tuition, nonresident: full-time $8099; part-time $337.46 per credit. *Required fees:* $16,520; $712.33 per credit. Tuition and fees vary according to course load and reciprocity agreements. *Financial support:* In 2014–15, 8 fellowships with full tuition reimbursements (averaging $16,577 per year), 8 research assistantships with full tuition reimbursements (averaging $13,627 per year), 5 teaching assistantships with full tuition reimbursements (averaging $12,400 per year) were awarded; Federal Work-Study and unspecified assistantships also available. Support available to part-time students. Financial award application deadline: 3/1; financial award applicants required to submit FAFSA. *Faculty research:* Tissue/cell engineering, biotransport sensors/networks, marine systems biomimetic materials, composite/polymeric materials, resilient infrastructure robotics, renewable energy. *Total annual research expenditures:* $1.7 million. *Unit head:* Gaurav Khanna, Graduate Program Director, 508-910-6605, Fax: 508-999-9115, E-mail: gkhanna@umassd.edu. *Application contact:* Steven Briggs, Director of Marketing and Recruitment for Graduate Studies, 508-999-8604, Fax: 508-999-8183, E-mail: graduate@umassd.edu.
Website: http://www.umassd.edu/engineering/graduate/doctoraldegreeprograms/egrandappliedsciencephd/.

University of Michigan–Dearborn, College of Engineering and Computer Science, MSE Program in Industrial and Systems Engineering, Dearborn, MI 48128. Offers MSE. Part-time and evening/weekend programs available. Postbaccalaureate distance learning degree programs offered (no on-campus study). *Faculty:* 14 full-time (1 woman), 7 part-time/adjunct (1 woman). *Students:* 21 full-time (9 women), 29 part-time (14 women); includes 6 minority (3 Asian, non-Hispanic/Latino; 2 Hispanic/Latino; 1 Two or more races, non-Hispanic/Latino), 26 international. 77 applicants, 73% accepted, 25 enrolled. In 2014, 14 master's awarded. *Entrance requirements:* For master's, bachelor's degree in engineering, a physical science, computer science, or applied mathematics. Additional exam requirements/recommendations for international students: Required—TOEFL (minimum score 560 paper-based; 84 iBT), IELTS (minimum score 6.5). *Application deadline:* For fall admission, 8/1 for domestic students, 5/1 for international students; for winter admission, 12/1 for domestic students, 9/1 for international students; for spring admission, 4/1 for domestic students, 1/1 for international students. Applications are processed on a rolling basis. Application fee: $60. Electronic applications accepted. *Expenses:* Tuition, state resident: full-time $12,202; part-time $707 per credit hour. Tuition, nonresident: full-time $20,980; part-time $1209 per credit hour. *Required fees:* $798; $302 per term. Tuition and fees vary according to course level, course load, degree level and program. *Financial support:* In 2014–15, 7 students received support. Scholarships/grants available. Support available to part-time students. Financial award applicants required to submit FAFSA. *Faculty research:* Integrated design and manufacturing, operations research and decision science, human factors and ergonomics. *Unit head:* Dr. Armen Zakarian, Chair, 313-593-5361, Fax: 313-593-3692, E-mail: zakarian@umich.edu. *Application contact:* Joey W. Woods, Graduate Program Assistant, 313-593-5361, Fax: 313-593-3692, E-mail: jwwoods@umd.umich.edu.
Website: http://umdearborn.edu/cecs/IMSE/grad_prog/index.php.

University of Michigan–Dearborn, College of Engineering and Computer Science, PhD Program in Information Systems Engineering, Dearborn, MI 48128. Offers PhD. Part-time and evening/weekend programs available. *Faculty:* 1 full-time (0 women). *Students:* 2 full-time (0 women), 6 part-time (0 women); includes 2 minority (1 Asian, non-Hispanic/Latino; 1 Two or more races, non-Hispanic/Latino), 3 international. 16 applicants, 13% accepted, 1 enrolled. In 2014, 1 doctorate awarded. *Degree requirements:* For doctorate, thesis/dissertation. *Entrance requirements:* For doctorate, GRE. Additional exam requirements/recommendations for international students: Required—TOEFL (minimum score 560 paper-based; 84 iBT). *Application deadline:* For fall admission, 1/15 priority date for domestic and international students; for winter admission, 4/15 priority date for domestic and international students. Application fee: $60. Electronic applications accepted. *Expenses:* Tuition, state resident: full-time $12,202; part-time $707 per credit hour. Tuition, nonresident: full-time $20,980; part-time $1209 per credit hour. *Required fees:* $798; $302 per term. Tuition and fees vary according to course level, course load, degree level and program. *Financial support:* In 2014–15, 1 research assistantship (averaging $26,500 per year) was awarded; scholarships/grants and unspecified assistantships also available. Financial award applicants required to submit FAFSA. *Unit head:* Dr. Pankaj K. Mallick, Director/Professor, 313-593-5119, Fax: 313-593-5386, E-mail: pkm@umich.edu. *Application contact:* Sherry Boyd, Intermediate Administrative Assistant, 313-593-5582, Fax: 313-593-5386, E-mail: idpgrad@umd.umich.edu.
Website: http://umdearborn.edu/cecs/IDP/phd_ise/index.php.

University of Nebraska at Omaha, Graduate Studies, College of Information Science and Technology, Department of Computer Science, Omaha, NE 68182. Offers artificial intelligence (Certificate); communication networks (Certificate); computer science (MA, MS); software engineering (Certificate); systems and architecture (Certificate). Part-time and evening/weekend programs available. *Faculty:* 17 full-time (3 women). *Students:* 58 full-time (18 women), 51 part-time (16 women); includes 6 minority (1 Black or African American, non-Hispanic/Latino; 3 Asian, non-Hispanic/Latino; 1 Hispanic/Latino; 1 Two or more races, non-Hispanic/Latino), 80 international. Average age 26. 196 applicants, 54% accepted, 50 enrolled. In 2014, 24 master's awarded. *Degree requirements:* For master's, comprehensive exam, thesis (for some programs). *Entrance requirements:* For master's, GRE General Test, minimum GPA of 3.0, prior course work in computer science, official transcripts, resume, 2 letters of recommendation; for Certificate, minimum GPA of 3.0, resume. Additional exam requirements/recommendations for international students: Required—TOEFL, IELTS, PTE. *Application deadline:* For fall admission, 7/1 priority date for domestic students; for spring admission, 11/1 priority date for domestic and international students; for summer admission, 3/1 for domestic and international students. Applications are processed on a rolling basis. Application fee: $45. Electronic applications accepted. *Financial support:* In 2014–15, 6 students received support, including 6 research assistantships with tuition reimbursements available; teaching assistantships with tuition reimbursements available, Federal Work-Study, institutionally sponsored loans, scholarships/grants, tuition waivers (full), and unspecified assistantships also available. Support available to part-time students. Financial award application deadline: 3/1; financial award applicants required to submit FAFSA. *Unit head:* Dr. Qiuming Zhu, Chairperson, 402-554-2341, E-mail: graduate@unomaha.edu. *Application contact:* Dr. Jong-Hoon Youn, Graduate Program Chair, 402-554-2341, E-mail: graduate@unomaha.edu.

University of New Haven, Graduate School, Tagliatela College of Engineering, Program in Computer and Information Science, West Haven, CT 06516-1916. Offers computer and information science (MS); computer programming (Certificate); computer systems (MS); database and information systems (MS); network systems (MS); software engineering and development (MS). Part-time and evening/weekend programs available. *Degree requirements:* For master's, thesis or alternative. *Entrance requirements:* Additional exam requirements/recommendations for international students: Required—TOEFL (minimum score 75 iBT), IELTS, PTE (minimum score 50). Electronic applications accepted. Application fee is waived when completed online.

University of New Mexico, Graduate School, School of Engineering, Program in Nanoscience and Microsystems Engineering, Albuquerque, NM 87131. Offers MS, PhD. Part-time programs available. *Students:* 30 full-time (10 women), 24 part-time (4 women); includes 19 minority (2 Black or African American, non-Hispanic/Latino; 3 Asian, non-Hispanic/Latino; 11 Hispanic/Latino; 3 Two or more races, non-Hispanic/Latino), 2 international. Average age 33. 18 applicants, 39% accepted, 1 enrolled. In 2014, 6 master's, 5 doctorates awarded. *Degree requirements:* For master's, comprehensive exam, thesis; for doctorate, comprehensive exam, thesis/dissertation. *Entrance requirements:* For master's and doctorate, GRE. Additional exam requirements/recommendations for international students: Required—TOEFL. *Application deadline:* For fall admission, 7/30 for domestic students, 2/1 for international students; for spring admission, 11/30 for domestic students, 6/1 for international students. Applications are processed on a rolling basis. Application fee: $50. Electronic applications accepted. *Financial support:* In 2014–15, 48 students received support, including 39 research assistantships with full tuition reimbursements available (averaging $17,556 per year), 9 teaching assistantships with full tuition reimbursements available (averaging $7,505 per year). *Unit head:* Dr. Abhaya Datye, Professor, 505-277-0477, Fax: 505-277-1024, E-mail: datye@unm.edu. *Application contact:* Heather Elizabeth Armstrong, Program Specialist, 505-277-6824, Fax: 505-277-1024, E-mail: heathera@unm.edu.
Website: http://nsms.unm.edu.

The University of North Carolina at Charlotte, The William States Lee College of Engineering, Department of Civil and Environmental Engineering, Charlotte, NC 28223-0001. Offers civil engineering (MSCE); infrastructure and environmental systems (PhD), including infrastructure and environmental systems design. Part-time and evening/weekend programs available. *Faculty:* 24 full-time (4 women). *Students:* 58 full-time (17 women), 44 part-time (13 women); includes 15 minority (8 Black or African American, non-Hispanic/Latino; 2 Asian, non-Hispanic/Latino; 5 Hispanic/Latino), 35 international. Average age 29. 105 applicants, 49% accepted, 22 enrolled. In 2014, 18 master's, 3 doctorates awarded. Terminal master's awarded for partial completion of doctoral program. *Degree requirements:* For master's, thesis or project; for doctorate, comprehensive exam, thesis/dissertation. *Entrance requirements:* For master's, GRE General Test, minimum GPA of 3.0 in undergraduate major, 2.75 overall; for doctorate, GRE General Test, minimum undergraduate GPA of 3.2, graduate 3.5; three letters of recommendation. Additional exam requirements/recommendations for international students: Required—TOEFL (minimum score 557 paper-based; 83 iBT). *Application deadline:* For fall admission, 5/1 priority date for domestic students, 5/1 for international students; for spring admission, 10/1 priority date for domestic students, 10/1 for international students. Applications are processed on a rolling basis. Application fee: $75. Electronic applications accepted. *Expenses:* Tuition, state resident: full-time $4008. Tuition, nonresident: full-time $16,295. *Required fees:* $2755. Tuition and fees vary according to course load and program. *Financial support:* In 2014–15, 37 students received support, including 1 fellowship (averaging $23,545 per year), 24 research assistantships (averaging $7,949 per year), 12 teaching assistantships (averaging $4,663 per year); career-related internships or fieldwork, institutionally sponsored loans, scholarships/grants, and unspecified assistantships also available. Support available to part-time students. Financial award application deadline: 4/1; financial award applicants required to submit FAFSA. *Faculty research:* Structural analysis and design, civil design for sustainability, structural materials, transportation engineering, geotechnical engineering, environmental management, water resources. *Total annual research expenditures:* $973,550. *Unit head:* Dr. John L. Daniels, Chair, 704-687-1219, Fax: 704-687-6953, E-mail: jodaniels@uncc.edu. *Application contact:* Kathy B. Giddings, Director of Graduate Admissions, 704-687-5503, Fax: 704-687-1668, E-mail: gradadm@uncc.edu.
Website: https://cee.uncc.edu/graduate-program.

The University of North Carolina at Charlotte, The William States Lee College of Engineering, Department of Systems Engineering and Engineering Management, Charlotte, NC 28223-0001. Offers energy analytics (Graduate Certificate); engineering management (MSEM); engineering science (MS); infrastructure and environmental systems (PhD); Lean Six Sigma (Graduate Certificate); logistics and supply chains (Graduate Certificate); systems analytics (Graduate Certificate). Part-time and evening/weekend programs available. Postbaccalaureate distance learning degree programs offered. *Faculty:* 7 full-time (2 women), 1 part-time/adjunct (0 women). *Students:* 33 full-time (8 women), 47 part-time (14 women); includes 15 minority (9 Black or African American, non-Hispanic/Latino; 3 Asian, non-Hispanic/Latino; 3 Hispanic/Latino), 33 international. Average age 29. 146 applicants, 51% accepted, 42 enrolled. In 2014, 19 master's awarded. *Degree requirements:* For master's, thesis or alternative, project. *Entrance requirements:* For master's, GRE or GMAT, letters of recommendation. Additional exam requirements/recommendations for international students: Required—TOEFL (minimum score 557 paper-based; 83 iBT). *Application deadline:* For fall admission, 5/1 priority date for domestic students, 5/1 for international students; for spring admission, 10/1 priority date for domestic students, 10/1 for international

students. Application fee: $75. Electronic applications accepted. *Expenses:* Tuition, state resident: full-time $4008. Tuition, nonresident: full-time $16,295. *Required fees:* $2755. Tuition and fees vary according to course load and program. *Financial support:* In 2014–15, 5 students received support, including 3 research assistantships (averaging $5,317 per year), 2 teaching assistantships (averaging $3,125 per year); career-related internships or fieldwork, institutionally sponsored loans, scholarships/grants, and unspecified assistantships also available. Support available to part-time students. Financial award application deadline: 4/1; financial award applicants required to submit FAFSA. *Faculty research:* Sustainable material and renewable technology; thermal analysis; large scale optimization; project risk management; supply chains; leans systems; global product innovation; quality and reliability analysis and management; productivity and project management; business forecasting, market analyses and feasibility studies. *Total annual research expenditures:* $106,777. *Unit head:* Dr. Robert E. Johnson, Dean, 704-687-8242, Fax: 704-687-2352, E-mail: robejohn@uncc.edu. *Application contact:* Kathy B. Giddings, Director of Graduate Admissions, 704-687-5503, Fax: 704-687-1668, E-mail: gradadm@uncc.edu.
Website: http://seem.uncc.edu/.

University of Pennsylvania, School of Engineering and Applied Science, Department of Electrical and Systems Engineering, Philadelphia, PA 19104. Offers MSE, PhD. Part-time programs available. *Faculty:* 25 full-time (2 women), 6 part-time/adjunct (0 women). *Students:* 223 full-time (67 women), 27 part-time (8 women); includes 12 minority (2 Black or African American, non-Hispanic/Latino; 8 Asian, non-Hispanic/Latino; 1 Hispanic/Latino; 1 Two or more races, non-Hispanic/Latino), 201 international. 1,164 applicants, 31% accepted, 155 enrolled. In 2014, 104 master's, 6 doctorates awarded. Terminal master's awarded for partial completion of doctoral program. *Degree requirements:* For master's, thesis optional; for doctorate, comprehensive exam, thesis/dissertation. *Entrance requirements:* For master's and doctorate, GRE General Test. Additional exam requirements/recommendations for international students: Required—TOEFL. *Application deadline:* For fall admission, 6/1 priority date for domestic students, 5/1 priority date for international students; for spring admission, 11/1 priority date for domestic students, 10/1 priority date for international students. Applications are processed on a rolling basis. Application fee: $70. Electronic applications accepted. *Financial support:* Fellowships, research assistantships, teaching assistantships, institutionally sponsored loans, scholarships/grants, traineeships, health care benefits, and unspecified assistantships available. *Faculty research:* Electro-optics, microwave and millimeter-wave optics, solid-state and chemical electronics, electromagnetic propagation, telecommunications. *Unit head:* Eduardo D. Glandt, Dean, 215-898-7244, E-mail: seasdean@seas.upenn.edu. *Application contact:* School of Engineering and Applied Science Graduate Admissions, 215-898-4542, E-mail: gradstudies@seas.upenn.edu.
Website: http://www.seas.upenn.edu.

University of Regina, Faculty of Graduate Studies and Research, Faculty of Engineering and Applied Science, Program in Industrial Systems Engineering, Regina, SK S4S 0A2, Canada. Offers M Eng, MA Sc, PhD. Part-time programs available. *Faculty:* 39 full-time (7 women), 24 part-time/adjunct (0 women). *Students:* 47 full-time (14 women), 6 part-time (0 women). 126 applicants, 30% accepted. In 2014, 17 master's, 2 doctorates awarded. *Degree requirements:* For master's, thesis, project, report; for doctorate, thesis/dissertation. *Entrance requirements:* For doctorate, master's degree. Additional exam requirements/recommendations for international students: Required—TOEFL (minimum score 550 paper-based; 80 iBT), IELTS (minimum score 6.5), PTE (minimum score 59). *Application deadline:* For fall admission, 3/31 for domestic and international students; for winter admission, 7/31 for domestic and international students; for spring admission, 11/30 for domestic and international students. Application fee: $100. Electronic applications accepted. *Expenses:* Expenses: $2,588.85 per semester of full time study (M Eng); $1,633.35 (for MA Sc); $1,755.60 (for PhD). *Financial support:* In 2014–15, 7 fellowships (averaging $6,429 per year), 15 teaching assistantships (averaging $2,475 per year) were awarded; research assistantships, career-related internships or fieldwork, and scholarships/grants also available. Financial award application deadline: 6/15. *Faculty research:* Stochastic systems simulation, metallurgy of welding, computer-aided engineering, finite element method of engineering systems, manufacturing systems. *Unit head:* Dr. Raphael Idem, Associate Dean, Research and Graduate Studies, 306-337-2696, Fax: 306-585-4855, E-mail: raphael.idem@uregina.ca. *Application contact:* Dr. Rene Mayorga, Graduate Coordinator, 306-585-4726, Fax: 306-585-4822, E-mail: rene.mayorga@uregina.ca.
Website: http://www.uregina.ca/engineering/.

University of Regina, Faculty of Graduate Studies and Research, Faculty of Engineering and Applied Science, Program in Petroleum Systems Engineering, Regina, SK S4S 0A2, Canada. Offers M Eng, MA Sc, PhD. Part-time programs available. *Faculty:* 39 full-time (7 women), 24 part-time/adjunct (0 women). *Students:* 60 full-time (15 women), 1 part-time (0 women). 198 applicants, 10% accepted. In 2014, 13 master's, 6 doctorates awarded. *Degree requirements:* For master's, thesis, project, report; for doctorate, thesis/dissertation. *Entrance requirements:* For doctorate, master's degree. Additional exam requirements/recommendations for international students: Required—TOEFL (minimum score 550 paper-based; 80 iBT), IELTS (minimum score 6.5), PTE (minimum score 59). *Application deadline:* For fall admission, 3/31 for domestic and international students; for winter admission, 7/31 for domestic and international students; for spring admission, 11/30 for domestic and international students. Application fee: $100. Electronic applications accepted. *Expenses:* Expenses: $2,588.85 per semester of full time study (M Eng); $1,633.35 (for MA Sc); $1,755.60 (for PhD). *Financial support:* In 2014–15, 10 fellowships (averaging $6,500 per year), 10 teaching assistantships (averaging $2,475 per year) were awarded; research assistantships, career-related internships or fieldwork, and scholarships/grants also available. Financial award application deadline: 6/15. *Faculty research:* Enhanced oil recovery, production engineering, reservoir engineering, surface thermodynamics, geostatistics. *Unit head:* Dr. Raphael Idem, Associate Dean, Research and Graduate Studies, 306-337-3287, Fax: 306-585-4855, E-mail: raphael.idem@uregina.ca. *Application contact:* Dr. Fanhua (Bill) Zeng, Program Chair/Graduate Coordinator, 306-337-2526, Fax: 306-585-4855, E-mail: fanhua.zeng@uregina.ca.
Website: http://www.uregina.ca/engineering/.

University of Regina, Faculty of Graduate Studies and Research, Faculty of Engineering and Applied Science, Program in Process Systems Engineering, Regina, SK S4S 0A2, Canada. Offers M Eng, MA Sc. Part-time programs available. *Faculty:* 39 full-time (7 women), 24 part-time/adjunct (0 women). *Students:* 22 full-time (6 women), 1 part-time (0 women). 57 applicants, 32% accepted. In 2014, 7 master's awarded. *Degree requirements:* For master's, thesis, project, report. *Entrance requirements:* Additional exam requirements/recommendations for international students: Required—TOEFL (minimum score 550 paper-based; 80 iBT), IELTS (minimum score 6.5), PTE (minimum score 59). *Application deadline:* For fall admission, 3/31 for domestic and international students; for winter admission, 7/31 for domestic and international students; for spring admission, 11/30 for domestic and international students. Application fee: $100. Electronic applications accepted. *Expenses:* Expenses: $2,588.85 per semester of full time study (M Eng); $1,633.35 (for MA Sc); $1,755.60 (for PhD). *Financial support:* In 2014–15, 2 teaching assistantships (averaging $2,427 per

year) were awarded; fellowships, research assistantships, career-related internships or fieldwork, and scholarships/grants also available. Financial award application deadline: 6/15. *Faculty research:* Membrane separation technologies, advanced reaction engineering, advanced transport phenomena, advanced heat transfer, advanced mass transfer. *Unit head:* Dr. Raphael Idem, Associate Dean, Research and Graduate Studies, 306-585-4470, Fax: 306-585-4855, E-mail: raphael.idem@uregina.ca. *Application contact:* Dr. Hussameldin Ibrahim, Graduate Coordinator, 306-337-3347, Fax: 306-585-4855, E-mail: hussameldin.ibrahim@uregina.ca.
Website: http://www.uregina.ca/engineering/.

University of St. Thomas, Graduate Studies, School of Engineering, St. Paul, MN 55105-1096. Offers electrical engineering (MS); manufacturing engineering and operations (MS); manufacturing systems (Certificate); mechanical engineering (MS); medical device development (Certificate); regulatory science (MS); software engineering (MS); software management (MS); systems engineering (MS); technology leadership (Certificate); technology management (MS). *Accreditation:* ABET (one or more programs are accredited). *Entrance requirements:* For master's, resume, official transcripts. Additional exam requirements/recommendations for international students: Required—TOEFL (minimum score 550 paper-based). Electronic applications accepted. *Expenses:* Contact institution.

University of South Alabama, College of Engineering, Program in Systems Engineering, Mobile, AL 36688. Offers D Sc. *Students:* 6 full-time (1 woman), 1 part-time (0 women), 1 international. Average age 34. 3 applicants, 33% accepted, 1 enrolled. *Degree requirements:* For doctorate, thesis/dissertation, qualifying examination. *Entrance requirements:* For doctorate, GRE, MS in engineering, minimum graduate GPA of 3.0. Additional exam requirements/recommendations for international students: Required—TOEFL (minimum score 525 paper-based; 71 iBT). *Application deadline:* For fall admission, 7/15 for domestic students. Application fee: $35. Electronic applications accepted. *Expenses:* Expenses: Contact institution. *Financial support:* Fellowships, research assistantships, teaching assistantships, career-related internships or fieldwork, Federal Work-Study, institutionally sponsored loans, scholarships/grants, and unspecified assistantships available. Support available to part-time students. Financial award application deadline: 5/1; financial award applicants required to submit FAFSA. *Unit head:* Dr. John Steadham, Dean, College of Engineering, 251-460-6140, Fax: 251-460-6343, E-mail: engineering@southalabama.edu. *Application contact:* Henry Lester, Instructor, 251-460-7993, Fax: 251-460-6343, E-mail: hlester@southalabama.edu.
Website: http://www.southalabama.edu/colleges/engineering/dsc-se/index.html.

University of Southern California, Graduate School, Viterbi School of Engineering, Daniel J. Epstein Department of Industrial and Systems Engineering, Los Angeles, CA 90089. Offers digital supply chain management (MS); engineering management (MS); engineering technology communication (Graduate Certificate); health systems operations (Graduate Certificate); industrial and systems engineering (MS, PhD, Engr); manufacturing engineering (MS); operations research engineering (MS); optimization and supply chain management (Graduate Certificate); product development engineering (MS); safety systems and security (MS); systems architecting and engineering (MS, Graduate Certificate); systems safety and security (Graduate Certificate); transportation systems (Graduate Certificate); MS/MBA. Part-time and evening/weekend programs available. Postbaccalaureate distance learning degree programs offered (no on-campus study). Terminal master's awarded for partial completion of doctoral program. *Degree requirements:* For master's, thesis optional; for doctorate, thesis/dissertation. *Entrance requirements:* For master's and doctorate, GRE General Test. Additional exam requirements/recommendations for international students: Recommended—TOEFL. Electronic applications accepted. *Faculty research:* Health systems, music cognition and retrieval, transportation and logistics, manufacturing and automation, engineering systems design, risk and economic analysis.

University of South Florida, University College/Distance Education, Tampa, FL 33620-9951. *Unit head:* Kathy Barnes, Interdisciplinary Programs Coordinator, 813-974-8031, Fax: 813-974-7061, E-mail: barnesk@usf.edu. *Application contact:* Karen Tylinski, Metro Initiatives, 813-974-9943, Fax: 813-974-7061, E-mail: ktylinsk@usf.edu.
Website: http://www.usf.edu/innovative-education/.

The University of Texas at Arlington, Graduate School, College of Engineering, Department of Industrial and Manufacturing Systems Engineering, Program in Systems Engineering, Arlington, TX 76019. Offers MS.

The University of Texas at Dallas, Erik Jonsson School of Engineering and Computer Science, Department of Electrical Engineering, Richardson, TX 75080. Offers computer engineering (MS, PhD); electrical engineering (MSEE, PhD); systems engineering and management (MS); telecommunications engineering (MSTE, PhD). Part-time and evening/weekend programs available. *Faculty:* 51 full-time (4 women), 5 part-time/adjunct (1 woman). *Students:* 756 full-time (186 women), 288 part-time (83 women); includes 89 minority (14 Black or African American, non-Hispanic/Latino; 44 Asian, non-Hispanic/Latino; 24 Hispanic/Latino; 7 Two or more races, non-Hispanic/Latino), 870 international. Average age 26. 3,191 applicants, 30% accepted, 363 enrolled. In 2014, 250 master's, 31 doctorates awarded. *Degree requirements:* For master's, thesis or major design project; for doctorate, thesis/dissertation. *Entrance requirements:* For master's, GRE General Test, minimum GPA of 3.0 in related bachelor's degree; for doctorate, GRE General Test, minimum GPA of 3.5. Additional exam requirements/recommendations for international students: Required—TOEFL (minimum score 550 paper-based). *Application deadline:* For fall admission, 7/15 for domestic students, 5/1 priority date for international students; for spring admission, 11/15 for domestic students, 9/1 priority date for international students. Applications are processed on a rolling basis. Application fee: $50 ($100 for international students). Electronic applications accepted. *Expenses:* Tuition, state resident: full-time $11,940; part-time $663 per credit. Tuition, nonresident: full-time $22,282; part-time $1238 per credit. *Financial support:* In 2014–15, 269 students received support, including 13 fellowships with partial tuition reimbursements available (averaging $5,598 per year), 129 research assistantships with partial tuition reimbursements available (averaging $17,609 per year), 80 teaching assistantships with partial tuition reimbursements available (averaging $17,480 per year); Federal Work-Study, institutionally sponsored loans, scholarships/grants, unspecified assistantships, and cooperative positions also available. Support available to part-time students. Financial award application deadline: 4/30; financial award applicants required to submit FAFSA. *Faculty research:* Semiconductor device manufacturing, photonics devices and systems, signal processing and language technology, nano-fabrication, energy efficient digital systems. *Unit head:* Dr. James L. Coleman, Department Head, 972-883-6755, Fax: 972-883-2710, E-mail: james.coleman@utdallas.edu. *Application contact:* Patricia Williams, Degree Plan Evaluator, 972-883-4315, Fax: 972-883-2710, E-mail: gradeeadvisors@utdallas.edu.
Website: http://www.ee.utdallas.edu.

The University of Texas at Dallas, Erik Jonsson School of Engineering and Computer Science, Department of Mechanical Engineering, Richardson, TX 75080. Offers mechanical engineering (PhD); mechanical systems engineering (MSME); microelectromechanical systems (MSME). Part-time and evening/weekend programs available. *Faculty:* 15 full-time (2 women), 2 part-time/adjunct (0 women). *Students:* 132 full-time (14 women), 18 part-time (4 women); includes 14 minority (2 Black or African

Systems Engineering

American, non-Hispanic/Latino; 4 Asian, non-Hispanic/Latino; 7 Hispanic/Latino; 1 Two or more races, non-Hispanic/Latino), 111 international. Average age 25. 327 applicants, 49% accepted, 76 enrolled. In 2014, 19 master's awarded. *Degree requirements:* For master's, thesis or major design project; for doctorate, comprehensive exam, thesis/dissertation, final exam, research project, qualifying exam. *Entrance requirements:* For master's, GRE General Test, minimum GPA of 3.0 in related bachelor's degree; for doctorate, GRE, essay. Additional exam requirements/recommendations for international students: Required—TOEFL (minimum score 550 paper-based). *Application deadline:* For fall admission, 7/15 for domestic students, 5/1 priority date for international students; for spring admission, 11/15 for domestic students, 9/1 priority date for international students. Applications are processed on a rolling basis. Application fee: $50 ($100 for international students). Electronic applications accepted. *Expenses:* Tuition, state resident: full-time $11,940; part-time $663 per credit. Tuition, nonresident: full-time $22,282; part-time $1238 per credit. *Financial support:* In 2014–15, 59 students received support, including 3 fellowships (averaging $15,000 per year), 25 research assistantships with partial tuition reimbursements available (averaging $16,650 per year), 22 teaching assistantships with partial tuition reimbursements available (averaging $16,650 per year); career-related internships or fieldwork, Federal Work-Study, institutionally sponsored loans, scholarships/grants, and unspecified assistantships also available. Support available to part-time students. Financial award application deadline: 4/30; financial award applicants required to submit FAFSA. *Faculty research:* Nano-materials and nano-electronic devices, biomedical devices, nonlinear systems and controls, semiconductor and oxide surfaces, flexible electronics. *Unit head:* Dr. Mario Rotea, Department Head, 972-883-2720, Fax: 972-883-2813, E-mail: rotea@utdallas.edu. *Application contact:* Dr. Hongbing Lu, Associate Department Head, 972-883-4647, Fax: 972-883-2813, E-mail: megrad@utdallas.edu.
Website: http://me.utdallas.edu.

The University of Texas at El Paso, Graduate School, College of Engineering, Department of Industrial Engineering, El Paso, TX 79968-0001. Offers industrial engineering (MS); manufacturing engineering (MS); systems engineering (MS, Certificate). Part-time and evening/weekend programs available. *Degree requirements:* For master's, thesis optional. *Entrance requirements:* For master's, GRE General Test, minimum GPA of 3.0 in major. Additional exam requirements/recommendations for international students: Required—TOEFL. Electronic applications accepted. *Faculty research:* Computer vision, automated inspection, simulation and modeling.

The University of Texas–Pan American, College of Engineering and Computer Science, Department of Manufacturing Engineering, Edinburg, TX 78539. Offers engineering management (MS); manufacturing engineering (MS); systems engineering (MS). *Expenses:* Tuition, state resident: full-time $4187; part-time $232.60 per credit hour. Tuition, nonresident: full-time $10,857; part-time $603.16 per credit hour. *Required fees:* $782; $27.50 per credit hour. $143.35 per semester.

University of Utah, Graduate School, David Eccles School of Business, Department of Operations and Information Systems, Salt Lake City, UT 84112. Offers information systems (MS, Graduate Certificate), including business intelligence and analytics, IT security, product and process management, software and systems architecture. Part-time and evening/weekend programs available. *Faculty:* 11 full-time (4 women), 6 part-time/adjunct (0 women). *Students:* 77 full-time (18 women), 63 part-time (7 women); includes 19 minority (2 Black or African American, non-Hispanic/Latino; 5 Asian, non-Hispanic/Latino; 10 Hispanic/Latino; 2 Two or more races, non-Hispanic/Latino), 27 international. Average age 31. 148 applicants, 72% accepted, 71 enrolled. In 2014, 63 master's awarded. *Degree requirements:* For master's, capstone project. *Entrance requirements:* For master's, GMAT/GRE, minimum undergraduate GPA of 3.0. Additional exam requirements/recommendations for international students: Required—TOEFL (minimum score 550 paper-based; 80 iBT), IELTS (minimum score 6.5). *Application deadline:* For fall admission, 7/28 for domestic students, 3/1 for international students; for spring admission, 12/7 for domestic students, 8/16 for international students. Applications are processed on a rolling basis. Application fee: $55 ($65 for international students). Electronic applications accepted. *Expenses:* Expenses: Contact institution. *Financial support:* In 2014–15, 5 students received support, including 3 fellowships with partial tuition reimbursements available (averaging $5,160 per year), 2 teaching assistantships with partial tuition reimbursements available (averaging $5,160 per year); tuition waivers (partial) and unspecified assistantships also available. Financial award application deadline: 4/14; financial award applicants required to submit FAFSA. *Faculty research:* Business intelligence and analytics, software and system architecture, product and process management, IT security, Web and data mining, applications and management of IT in healthcare. *Unit head:* Bradden Blair, Director of the MSIS Program, 801-587-9489, Fax: 801-581-3666, E-mail: b.blair@business.utah.edu. *Application contact:* Andrea Miller, Director of Admissions, 801-585-7366, Fax: 801-581-3666, E-mail: andrea.miller@business.utah.edu.
Website: http://msis.business.utah.edu.

University of Virginia, School of Engineering and Applied Science, Department of Systems and Information Engineering, Charlottesville, VA 22903. Offers ME, MS, PhD, ME/MBA. Postbaccalaureate distance learning degree programs offered (no on-campus study). *Faculty:* 19 full-time (2 women). *Students:* 71 full-time (16 women), 7 part-time (1 woman); includes 13 minority (2 Black or African American, non-Hispanic/Latino; 5 Asian, non-Hispanic/Latino; 5 Hispanic/Latino; 1 Two or more races, non-Hispanic/Latino), 37 international. Average age 28. 141 applicants, 35% accepted, 20 enrolled. In 2014, 45 master's, 13 doctorates awarded. *Degree requirements:* For master's, comprehensive exam (for some programs); for doctorate, comprehensive exam, thesis/dissertation. *Entrance requirements:* For master's, GRE General Test, 3 letters of recommendation; for doctorate, GRE General Test, 3 letters of recommendation; essay. Additional exam requirements/recommendations for international students: Required—TOEFL (minimum score 650 paper-based; 90 iBT), IELTS (minimum score 7). *Application deadline:* For fall admission, 8/1 for domestic students, 4/1 for international students; for winter admission, 12/1 for domestic students, 8/1 for international students; for spring admission, 5/1 for domestic students, 1/1 for international students. Applications are processed on a rolling basis. Application fee: $60. Electronic applications accepted. *Expenses:* Tuition, state resident: full-time $14,164; part-time $349 per credit hour. Tuition, nonresident: full-time $23,722; part-time $1300 per credit hour. *Required fees:* $2514. *Financial support:* Fellowships, research assistantships, and teaching assistantships available. Financial award application deadline: 1/15; financial award applicants required to submit FAFSA. *Faculty research:* Systems integration, human factors, computational statistics and simulation, risk and decision analysis, optimization and control. *Unit head:* Barry Horowitz, Chair, 434-924-5393, Fax: 434-982-2972, E-mail: bh8e@virginia.edu. *Application contact:* Jayne Weber, Coordinator, 434-924-6473, Fax: 434-982-2972, E-mail: jef2f@virginia.edu.
Website: http://www.sys.virginia.edu/.

University of Waterloo, Graduate Studies, Faculty of Engineering, Department of Systems Design Engineering, Waterloo, ON N2L 3G1, Canada. Offers M Eng, MA Sc, PhD. Part-time programs available. *Degree requirements:* For master's, research project or thesis; for doctorate, comprehensive exam, thesis/dissertation. *Entrance requirements:* For master's, honors degree, minimum B average, resumé; for doctorate, master's degree, minimum A- average. Additional exam requirements/recommendations

for international students: Required—TOEFL, TWE. Electronic applications accepted. *Faculty research:* Ergonomics, human factors and biomedical engineering, modeling and simulation, pattern analysis, machine intelligence and robotics.

University of Wisconsin–Madison, Graduate School, College of Engineering, Department of Industrial and Systems Engineering, Madison, WI 53706. Offers MS, PhD. Part-time programs available. *Faculty:* 17 full-time (5 women), 18 part-time/adjunct (5 women). *Students:* 108 full-time (40 women), 14 part-time (5 women); includes 6 minority (2 Black or African American, non-Hispanic/Latino; 1 American Indian or Alaska Native, non-Hispanic/Latino; 3 Asian, non-Hispanic/Latino), 102 international. Average age 27. 505 applicants, 29% accepted, 53 enrolled. In 2014, 41 master's, 8 doctorates awarded. Terminal master's awarded for partial completion of doctoral program. *Degree requirements:* For master's, thesis optional; for doctorate, comprehensive exam, thesis/dissertation. *Entrance requirements:* For master's, GRE General Test, minimum GPA of 3.0, BS in engineering or equivalent, course work in computer programming and statistics; for doctorate, GRE General Test, minimum GPA of 3.0. Additional exam requirements/recommendations for international students: Required—IELTS (minimum score 6); Recommended—TOEFL (minimum score 550 paper-based; 80 iBT). *Application deadline:* For fall admission, 1/15 priority date for domestic and international students; for spring admission, 10/1 priority date for domestic and international students. Application fee: $56. Electronic applications accepted. *Expenses:* Tuition, state resident: full-time $10,723; part-time $745 per credit. Tuition, nonresident: full-time $24,054; part-time $1578 per credit. *Required fees:* $374 per semester. Tuition and fees vary according to course load, program and reciprocity agreements. *Financial support:* In 2014–15, 94 students received support, including 1 fellowship with full tuition reimbursement available (averaging $23,376 per year), 44 research assistantships with full tuition reimbursements available (averaging $41,616 per year), 30 teaching assistantships with full tuition reimbursements available (averaging $29,492 per year); career-related internships or fieldwork, Federal Work-Study, institutionally sponsored loans, scholarships/grants, traineeships, health care benefits, and unspecified assistantships also available. *Faculty research:* Human factors and ergonomics, manufacturing and production systems, health systems engineering, decision science/operations research, quality engineering. *Total annual research expenditures:* $11.5 million. *Unit head:* Dr. Vicki M. Bier, Chair, 608-262-2064, Fax: 608-262-8454, E-mail: bier@engr.wisc.edu. *Application contact:* Deidre Vincevineus, Graduate Admissions Coordinator, 608-265-1452, Fax: 608-890-2204, E-mail: vincevineus@wisc.edu.
Website: http://www.engr.wisc.edu/isye.html.

Virginia Polytechnic Institute and State University, Graduate School, College of Engineering, Blacksburg, VA 24061. Offers aerospace engineering (ME, MS, PhD); biological systems engineering (ME, MS, PhD); biomedical engineering (MS, PhD); chemical engineering (ME, MS, PhD); civil engineering (ME, MS, PhD); computer engineering (ME, MS, PhD); computer science (MS, PhD); electrical engineering (ME, PhD); engineering education (PhD); engineering mechanics (ME, MS, PhD); environmental engineering (MS); environmental science and engineering (MS); industrial and systems engineering (ME, MS, PhD); materials science and engineering (ME, MS, PhD); mechanical engineering (ME, MS, PhD); mining and minerals engineering (PhD); mining engineering (ME, MS); nuclear engineering (MS, PhD); ocean engineering (MS); systems engineering (ME, MS). *Accreditation:* ABET (one or more programs are accredited). *Faculty:* 356 full-time (60 women), 3 part-time/adjunct (1 woman). *Students:* 1,700 full-time (398 women), 345 part-time (58 women); includes 213 minority (43 Black or African American, non-Hispanic/Latino; 1 American Indian or Alaska Native, non-Hispanic/Latino; 87 Asian, non-Hispanic/Latino; 58 Hispanic/Latino; 1 Native Hawaiian or other Pacific Islander, non-Hispanic/Latino; 23 Two or more races, non-Hispanic/Latino), 1,079 international. Average age 27. 5,228 applicants, 18% accepted, 471 enrolled. In 2014, 438 master's, 211 doctorates awarded. *Degree requirements:* For master's, comprehensive exam (for some programs), thesis (for some programs); for doctorate, comprehensive exam (for some programs), thesis/dissertation (for some programs). *Entrance requirements:* For master's and doctorate, GRE/GMAT (may vary by department). Additional exam requirements/recommendations for international students: Required—TOEFL (minimum score 550 paper-based). *Application deadline:* For fall admission, 8/1 for domestic students, 4/1 for international students; for spring admission, 1/1 for domestic students, 9/1 for international students. Applications are processed on a rolling basis. Application fee: $75. Electronic applications accepted. *Expenses:* Tuition, state resident: full-time $11,656; part-time $647.50 per credit hour. Tuition, nonresident: full-time $23,351; part-time $1297.25 per credit hour. *Required fees:* $2533; $465.75 per semester. Tuition and fees vary according to course load, campus/location and program. *Financial support:* In 2014–15, 148 fellowships with full tuition reimbursements (averaging $8,031 per year), 855 research assistantships with full tuition reimbursements (averaging $22,855 per year), 288 teaching assistantships with full tuition reimbursements (averaging $20,291 per year) were awarded. Financial award application deadline: 3/1; financial award applicants required to submit FAFSA. *Total annual research expenditures:* $90.5 million. *Unit head:* Dr. Richard C. Benson, Dean, 540-231-9752, Fax: 540-231-3031, E-mail: deaneng@vt.edu. *Application contact:* Linda Perkins, Executive Assistant, 540-231-9752, Fax: 540-231-3031, E-mail: lperkins@vt.edu.
Website: http://www.eng.vt.edu/.

Virginia Polytechnic Institute and State University, VT Online, Blacksburg, VA 24061. Offers advanced transportation systems (Certificate); aerospace engineering (MS); agricultural and life sciences (MSLFS); business information systems (Graduate Certificate); career and technical education (MS); civil engineering (MS); computer engineering (M Eng, MS); decision support systems (Graduate Certificate); eLearning leadership (MA); electrical engineering (M Eng, MS); engineering administration (MEA); environmental engineering (Certificate); environmental politics and policy (Graduate Certificate); environmental sciences and engineering (MS); foundations of political analysis (Graduate Certificate); health product risk management (Graduate Certificate); industrial and systems engineering (MS); information policy and society (Graduate Certificate); information security (Graduate Certificate); information technology (MIT); instructional technology (MA); integrative STEM education (MA Ed); liberal arts (Graduate Certificate); life sciences: health product risk management (MS); natural resources (MNR, Graduate Certificate); networking (Graduate Certificate); nonprofit and nongovernmental organization management (Graduate Certificate); ocean engineering (MS); political science (MA); security studies (Graduate Certificate); software development (Graduate Certificate). *Expenses:* Tuition, state resident: full-time $11,656; part-time $647.50 per credit hour. Tuition, nonresident: full-time $23,351; part-time $1297.25 per credit hour. *Required fees:* $2533; $465.75 per semester. Tuition and fees vary according to course load, campus/location and program.

Wayne State University, College of Engineering, Department of Industrial and Systems Engineering, Detroit, MI 48202. Offers engineering management (MS, Certificate); industrial engineering (MS, PhD); manufacturing engineering (MS); systems engineering (Certificate). *Students:* 165 full-time (20 women), 100 part-time (28 women); includes 44 minority (19 Black or African American, non-Hispanic/Latino; 18 Asian, non-Hispanic/Latino; 3 Hispanic/Latino; 4 Two or more races, non-Hispanic/Latino), 148 international. Average age 30. 588 applicants, 53% accepted, 87 enrolled. In 2014, 48 master's, 6 doctorates awarded. *Degree requirements:* For master's, thesis (for some programs); for doctorate, thesis/dissertation. *Entrance requirements:* For master's, BS from ABET-accredited institution; for doctorate, MS in industrial engineering or operations research with minimum graduate GPA of 3.5; for Certificate, BS in engineering or other technical field from an ABET-accredited institution, full-time work experience as a practicing engineering or technical leader. Additional exam requirements/recommendations for international students: Required—TOEFL (minimum score 550 paper-based; 79 iBT), TWE (minimum score 5.5), Michigan English Language Assessment Battery (minimum score 85); Recommended—IELTS (minimum score 6.5). *Application deadline:* For fall admission, 6/1 priority date for domestic students, 5/1 priority date for international students; for winter admission, 10/1 priority date for domestic students, 9/1 priority date for international students; for spring admission, 2/1 priority date for domestic students, 1/1 priority date for international students. Applications are processed on a rolling basis. Application fee: $0. Electronic applications accepted. *Expenses:* Expenses: Contact institution. *Financial support:* In 2014–15, 104 students received support, including 2 fellowships with tuition reimbursements available (averaging $18,321 per year), 10 research assistantships with tuition reimbursements available (averaging $20,829 per year), 14 teaching assistantships with tuition reimbursements available (averaging $19,043 per year); scholarships/grants, health care benefits, tuition waivers (full), and unspecified assistantships also available. Financial award application deadline: 3/31; financial award applicants required to submit FAFSA. *Faculty research:* Healthcare systems engineering, product design and development, quality and reliability engineering, supply chain management and logistics. *Total annual research expenditures:* $3.7 million. *Unit head:* Dr. Leslie Monplaisir, Associate Professor/Chair, 313-577-1645, Fax: 313-577-8833, E-mail: ad5365@eng.wayne.edu. *Application contact:* Dr. Ratna Babu Chinnam, Graduate Program Officer, 313-577-4846, E-mail: ratna.chinnam@wayne.edu. Website: http://engineering.wayne.edu/ise/.

Western International University, Graduate Programs in Business, Master of Science Program in Information System Engineering, Phoenix, AZ 85021-2718. Offers MS. Part-time and evening/weekend programs available. Postbaccalaureate distance learning degree programs offered (no on-campus study). *Entrance requirements:* For master's, minimum GPA of 2.75. Additional exam requirements/recommendations for international students: Required—TOEFL (minimum score 550 paper-based; 79 iBT), TWE (minimum score 5), or IELTS. Electronic applications accepted.

Worcester Polytechnic Institute, Graduate Studies and Research, Program in Systems Engineering, Worcester, MA 01609-2280. Offers MS, Graduate Certificate. Postbaccalaureate distance learning degree programs offered (no on-campus study). *Students:* 180 part-time (22 women); includes 26 minority (2 Black or African American, non-Hispanic/Latino; 1 American Indian or Alaska Native, non-Hispanic/Latino; 9 Asian, non-Hispanic/Latino; 4 Hispanic/Latino; 10 Two or more races, non-Hispanic/Latino), 3 international. 60 applicants, 78% accepted, 38 enrolled. In 2014, 49 master's awarded. *Entrance requirements:* For master's, 3 letters of recommendation. Additional exam requirements/recommendations for international students: Required—TOEFL (minimum score 563 paper-based; 84 iBT). *Application deadline:* For fall admission, 1/1 for domestic and international students; for spring admission, 10/1 for domestic and international students. Application fee: $70. *Unit head:* Don Gelosh, Director, E-mail: dsgelosh@wpi.edu. *Application contact:* Lynne Dougherty, Administrative Assistant, 508-831-5301, Fax: 508-831-5717, E-mail: grad@wpi.edu. Website: http://cpe.wpi.edu/online/systems.html.

Section 15
Management of Engineering and Technology

This section contains a directory of institutions offering graduate work in management of engineering and technology. Additional information about programs listed in the directory may be obtained by writing directly to the dean of a graduate school or chair of a department at the address given in the directory.

For programs offering related work, in the other guides in this series:

Graduate Programs in the Humanities, Arts & Social Sciences
See *Applied Arts and Design, Architecture, Economics,* and *Sociology, Anthropology, and Archaeology*

Graduate Programs in the Biological/Biomedical Sciences & Health-Related Medical Professions
See *Biophysics (Radiation Biology); Ecology, Environmental Biology, and Evolutionary Biology;* and *Health Services (Health Services Management and Hospital Administration)*

Graduate Programs in Business, Education, Information Studies, Law & Social Work
'See *Business Administration and Management* and *Law*

CONTENTS

Program Directories

Display and Close-Up

See:

Construction Management

The American University in Dubai, Graduate Programs, Dubai, United Arab Emirates. Offers construction management (MS); education (M Ed); finance (MBA); generalist (MBA); marketing (MBA). Part-time and evening/weekend programs available. *Degree requirements:* For master's, thesis optional. *Entrance requirements:* For master's, GMAT (for MBA); GRE (for M Ed and MS), minimum undergraduate GPA of 3.0, official transcripts, two reference forms, curriculum vitae/resume, statement of career objectives, work experience. Additional exam requirements/recommendations for international students: Required—TOEFL (minimum score 550 paper-based; 79 iBT). Electronic applications accepted.

Arizona State University at the Tempe campus, Ira A. Fulton Schools of Engineering, ASU Engineering Online Programs, Tempe, AZ 85287. Offers construction (MS); embedded systems (M Eng); enterprise systems innovation and management (MSE); modeling and simulation (M Eng); quality and reliability engineering (M Eng); software engineering (MSE); systems engineering (M Eng).

Arizona State University at the Tempe campus, Ira A. Fulton Schools of Engineering, School of Sustainable Engineering and the Built Environment, Tempe, AZ 85287-5306. Offers civil, environmental and sustainable engineering (MS, MSE, PhD); construction engineering (MSE); construction management (MS, PhD). Part-time and evening/weekend programs available. Postbaccalaureate distance learning degree programs offered (minimal on-campus study). Terminal master's awarded for partial completion of doctoral program. *Degree requirements:* For master's, thesis optional, comprehensive exams (MSE); interactive Program of Study (iPOS) submitted before completing 50 percent of required credit hours; for doctorate, comprehensive exam, thesis/dissertation, interactive Program of Study (iPOS) submitted before completing 50 percent of required credit hours. *Entrance requirements:* For master's, GRE, minimum GPA of 3.0 or equivalent in last 2 years of work leading to bachelor's degree; for doctorate, GRE, minimum GPA of 3.0 in last 2 years of work leading to bachelor's degree, 3.2 in all graduate-level coursework with master's degree; 3 letters of recommendation; resume/curriculum vitae; letter of intent; thesis (if applicable); statement of research interests. Additional exam requirements/recommendations for international students: Required—TOEFL, IELTS, or PTE. Electronic applications accepted. *Expenses:* Contact institution. *Faculty research:* Water purification, transportation (safety and materials), construction management, environmental biotechnology, environmental nanotechnology, earth systems engineering and management, SMART innovations, project performance metrics, and underground infrastructure.

Auburn University, Graduate School, College of Architecture, Design, and Construction, Department of Building Science, Auburn University, AL 36849. Offers building construction (MBC); construction management (MBC); integrated design and construction (MIDC). *Faculty:* 17 full-time (1 woman), 2 part-time/adjunct (1 woman). *Students:* 25 full-time (4 women), 47 part-time (13 women); includes 9 minority (3 Black or African American, non-Hispanic/Latino; 2 Asian, non-Hispanic/Latino; 4 Hispanic/Latino), 4 international. Average age 33. 84 applicants, 85% accepted, 52 enrolled. In 2014, 36 master's awarded. *Entrance requirements:* For master's, GRE General Test. *Application deadline:* For fall admission, 7/7 for domestic students; for spring admission, 11/24 for domestic students. Applications are processed on a rolling basis. Application fee: $50 ($60 for international students). Electronic applications accepted. *Expenses:* Tuition, state resident: full-time $8586; part-time $477 per credit hour. Tuition, nonresident: full-time $25,758; part-time $1431 per credit hour. *Required fees:* $804 per semester. Tuition and fees vary according to degree level and program. *Financial support:* Application deadline: 3/15; applicants required to submit FAFSA. *Unit head:* Dr. Richard Burt, Head, 334-844-5260. *Application contact:* Dr. George Flowers, Dean of the Graduate School, 334-844-2125.
Website: http://cadc.auburn.edu/bsci/Pages/default.aspx.

Bowling Green State University, Graduate College, College of Technology, Department of Technology Systems, Bowling Green, OH 43403. Offers construction management (MIT); manufacturing technology (MIT). Part-time programs available. *Degree requirements:* For master's, thesis or alternative. *Entrance requirements:* For master's, GRE General Test. Additional exam requirements/recommendations for international students: Required—TOEFL. Electronic applications accepted.

Brigham Young University, Graduate Studies, Ira A. Fulton College of Engineering and Technology, School of Technology, Provo, UT 84602-1001. Offers construction management (MS); information technology (MS); manufacturing systems (MS); technology and engineering education (MS). *Faculty:* 27 full-time (0 women). *Students:* 40 full-time (4 women); includes 6 minority (3 Asian, non-Hispanic/Latino; 2 Hispanic/Latino; 1 Native Hawaiian or other Pacific Islander, non-Hispanic/Latino), 1 international. Average age 30. 19 applicants, 63% accepted, 12 enrolled. In 2014, 12 master's awarded. *Degree requirements:* For master's, thesis. *Entrance requirements:* For master's, GRE General Test; GMAT or GRE (for construction management emphasis), minimum GPA of 3.0 in last 60 hours of course work. Additional exam requirements/recommendations for international students: Required—TOEFL (minimum score 580 paper-based; 85 iBT). *Application deadline:* For fall admission, 2/15 for domestic and international students; for winter admission, 9/10 for domestic students, 9/15 for international students; for spring admission, 2/15 for domestic and international students; for summer admission, 2/15 for domestic students. Application fee: $50. Electronic applications accepted. *Expenses: Tuition:* Full-time $6310; part-time $371 per credit hour. Tuition and fees vary according to program and student's religious affiliation. *Financial support:* In 2014–15, 40 students received support, including 17 research assistantships (averaging $4,305 per year), 18 teaching assistantships (averaging $4,257 per year); scholarships/grants also available. *Faculty research:* Information assurance and security, HEI and databases, manufacturing materials, processes and systems, innovation in construction management scheduling and delivery methods. *Total annual research expenditures:* $534,164. *Unit head:* Richard E. Fry, Director, 801-422-4445, Fax: 801-422-0490, E-mail: rfry@byu.edu. *Application contact:* Barry M. Lunt, Graduate Coordinator, 801-422-2264, Fax: 801-422-0490, E-mail: sotadminasst@byu.edu.
Website: http://www.et.byu.edu/sot/.

California Baptist University, Program in Business Administration, Riverside, CA 92504-3206. Offers accounting (MBA); construction management (MBA); healthcare management (MBA); management (MBA). *Accreditation:* ACBSP. Part-time and evening/weekend programs available. Postbaccalaureate distance learning degree programs offered (minimal on-campus study). *Faculty:* 19 full-time (4 women), 3 part-time/adjunct (1 woman). *Students:* 31 full-time (13 women), 87 part-time (39 women); includes 61 minority (11 Black or African American, non-Hispanic/Latino; 1 American Indian or Alaska Native, non-Hispanic/Latino; 10 Asian, non-Hispanic/Latino; 36 Hispanic/Latino; 3 Two or more races, non-Hispanic/Latino), 8 international. Average age 30. 119 applicants, 60% accepted, 43 enrolled. In 2014, 54 master's awarded. *Degree requirements:* For master's, interdisciplinary capstone project. *Entrance requirements:* For master's, GMAT, minimum GPA of 2.5; two recommendations;

comprehensive essay; resume; interview. Additional exam requirements/recommendations for international students: Required—TOEFL (minimum score 80 iBT). *Application deadline:* For fall admission, 8/1 priority date for domestic students, 7/1 for international students; for spring admission, 12/1 priority date for domestic students, 11/1 for international students. Applications are processed on a rolling basis. Application fee: $45. Electronic applications accepted. *Expenses:* Expenses: Contact institution. *Financial support:* Institutionally sponsored loans available. Financial award applicants required to submit CSS PROFILE or FAFSA. *Faculty research:* Behavioral economics, economic indicators, marketing ethics, international business, microfinance. *Unit head:* Dr. Franco Gandolfi, Dean, School of Business, 951-343-4968, Fax: 951-343-4361, E-mail: fgandolfi@calbaptist.edu. *Application contact:* Dr. Keanon Alderson, Director, Business Administration Program, 951-343-4768, E-mail: kalderson@calbaptist.edu.
Website: http://www.calbaptist.edu/mba/about/.

California State University, East Bay, Office of Academic Programs and Graduate Studies, College of Science, School of Engineering, Program in Construction Management, Hayward, CA 94542-3000. Offers MS. *Degree requirements:* For master's, comprehensive exam (for some programs), research project or exam. *Entrance requirements:* For master's, GRE or GMAT, baccalaureate degree from accredited university with minimum overall GPA of 2.5; relevant work experience; college algebra and trigonometry or equivalent level math courses; personal statement; resume; two letters of recommendation. Additional exam requirements/recommendations for international students: Required—TOEFL (minimum score 550 paper-based; 79 iBT). *Application deadline:* For fall admission, 6/30 for domestic and international students. Applications are processed on a rolling basis. Application fee: $55. Electronic applications accepted. *Expenses:* Tuition, state resident: full-time $7830; part-time $1302 per credit hour. Tuition, nonresident: full-time $16,368. *Required fees:* $327 per quarter. Tuition and fees vary according to course load and program. *Financial support:* Federal Work-Study and institutionally sponsored loans available. Support available to part-time students. Financial award application deadline: 3/2; financial award applicants required to submit FAFSA. *Unit head:* Dr. Saeid Motavalli, Department Chair/Graduate Advisor, 510-885-4481, E-mail: saeid.motavalli@csueastbay.edu. *Application contact:* Dr. Donna Wiley, Interim Associate Vice President for Academic Programs and Graduate Studies, 510-885-3716, Fax: 510-885-4777, E-mail: donna.wiley@csueastbay.edu.
Website: http://www20.csueastbay.edu/csci/departments/engineering/.

Carnegie Mellon University, Carnegie Institute of Technology, Department of Civil and Environmental Engineering, Pittsburgh, PA 15213. Offers advanced infrastructure systems (MS, PhD); advanced infrastructure systems technology development and application (MS); air quality engineering and science (MS); civil and environmental engineering (MS, PhD); civil and environmental engineering/engineering and public policy (PhD); civil engineering (MS, PhD); computational mechanics (MS, PhD); computational modeling and monitoring for resilient structural and material systems (MS); energy infrastructure systems (MS); environmental engineering (MS, PhD); environmental management and science (MS, PhD); IT-based sustainable global infrastructure and construction management (MS); sustainability and green design (MS); water quality engineering and science (MS). Part-time programs available. *Faculty:* 21 full-time (5 women), 12 part-time/adjunct (3 women). *Students:* 229 full-time (99 women), 31 part-time (11 women); includes 18 minority (4 Black or African American, non-Hispanic/Latino; 13 Asian, non-Hispanic/Latino; 1 Hispanic/Latino), 193 international. Average age 26. 590 applicants, 68% accepted, 124 enrolled. In 2014, 85 master's, 11 doctorates awarded. Terminal master's awarded for partial completion of doctoral program. *Degree requirements:* For master's, thesis optional; for doctorate, comprehensive exam, thesis/dissertation, two-part qualifying exam, public defense of dissertation. *Entrance requirements:* For master's, GRE General Test, BS in engineering, science or mathematics; for doctorate, GRE General Test, BS or MS in engineering, science or mathematics. Additional exam requirements/recommendations for international students: Required—TOEFL (minimum score 84 iBT) or IELTS. *Application deadline:* For fall admission, 1/5 priority date for domestic and international students; for spring admission, 9/15 priority date for domestic and international students. Application fee: $65. Electronic applications accepted. *Financial support:* In 2014–15, 169 students received support. Fellowships with full and partial tuition reimbursements available, research assistantships with full and partial tuition reimbursements available, scholarships/grants, tuition waivers (full and partial), unspecified assistantships, and service assistantships available. Financial award application deadline: 1/5. *Faculty research:* Advanced infrastructure systems; environmental engineering, sustainability, and science; mechanics, materials, and computing. *Total annual research expenditures:* $4.9 million. *Unit head:* Dr. David A. Dzombak, Head, 412-268-2941, Fax: 412-268-7813, E-mail: dzombak@cmu.edu. *Application contact:* Melissa L. Brown, Director of Graduate Admissions & Recruiting, 412-268-8762, Fax: 412-268-7813, E-mail: mlb2@andrew.cmu.edu.
Website: http://www.cmu.edu/cee/.

Carnegie Mellon University, College of Fine Arts, School of Architecture, Pittsburgh, PA 15213-3891. Offers architecture (MSA); architecture, engineering, and construction management (PhD); building performance and diagnostics (MS, PhD); computational design (MS, PhD); engineering construction management (MSA); tangible interaction design (MTID); urban design (MUD). Terminal master's awarded for partial completion of doctoral program. *Degree requirements:* For doctorate, thesis/dissertation. *Entrance requirements:* For master's and doctorate, GRE General Test. Additional exam requirements/recommendations for international students: Required—TOEFL.

Central Connecticut State University, School of Graduate Studies, School of Engineering, Science and Technology, Department of Manufacturing and Construction Management, New Britain, CT 06050-4010. Offers construction management (MS, Certificate); lean manufacturing and Six Sigma (Certificate); supply chain and logistics (Certificate); technology management (MS). Part-time and evening/weekend programs available. *Faculty:* 9 full-time (1 woman), 3 part-time/adjunct (0 women). *Students:* 32 full-time (9 women), 96 part-time (27 women); includes 25 minority (13 Black or African American, non-Hispanic/Latino; 1 American Indian or Alaska Native, non-Hispanic/Latino; 7 Asian, non-Hispanic/Latino; 4 Hispanic/Latino), 18 international. Average age 32. 90 applicants, 66% accepted, 41 enrolled. In 2014, 38 master's, 5 other advanced degrees awarded. *Degree requirements:* For master's, comprehensive exam, thesis or alternative; for Certificate, qualifying exam. *Entrance requirements:* For master's, minimum undergraduate GPA of 2.7. Additional exam requirements/recommendations for international students: Required—TOEFL (minimum score 550 paper-based; 79 iBT). *Application deadline:* For fall admission, 6/1 for domestic students, 5/1 for international students; for spring admission, 11/1 for domestic and international students. Applications are processed on a rolling basis. Application fee: $50. Electronic applications accepted. *Expenses: Tuition, area resident:* Full-time $5730; part-time $534 per credit. Tuition, state resident: full-time $8596; part-time $534 per credit. Tuition,

nonresident: full-time $15,964; part-time $548 per credit. *Required fees:* $4211; $215 per credit. *Financial support:* In 2014–15, 6 students received support, including 5 research assistantships; career-related internships or fieldwork, Federal Work-Study, scholarships/grants, and unspecified assistantships also available. Support available to part-time students. Financial award application deadline: 3/1; financial award applicants required to submit FAFSA. *Faculty research:* All aspects of middle management, technical supervision in the workplace. *Unit head:* Dr. Jacob Kovel, Chair, 860-832-1830, E-mail: kovelj@ccsu.edu. *Application contact:* Patricia Gardner, Associate Director of Graduate Studies, 860-832-2350, Fax: 860-832-2362, E-mail: graduateadmissions@ccsu.edu.
Website: http://web.ccsu.edu/set/academics/programs/manufacturingConstruction/.

Clemson University, Graduate School, College of Architecture, Arts, and Humanities, Department of Construction Science and Management, Clemson, SC 29634. Offers MCSM. Part-time programs available. Postbaccalaureate distance learning degree programs offered (no on-campus study). *Faculty:* 8 full-time (2 women), 1 part-time/adjunct (0 women). *Students:* 16 full-time (3 women), 12 part-time (0 women), 10 international. Average age 30. 54 applicants, 46% accepted, 15 enrolled. In 2014, 2 master's awarded. *Degree requirements:* For master's, comprehensive exam, thesis optional. *Entrance requirements:* For master's, GRE General Test, one year of construction experience, current resume. Additional exam requirements/recommendations for international students: Required—TOEFL (minimum score 80 iBT). *Application deadline:* For fall admission, 3/1 for domestic and international students; for spring admission, 10/1 for domestic and international students. Application fee: $70 ($80 for international students). Electronic applications accepted. *Financial support:* Teaching assistantships with partial tuition reimbursements, career-related internships or fieldwork, institutionally sponsored loans, scholarships/grants, health care benefits, and unspecified assistantships available. Support available to part-time students. Financial award applicants required to submit FAFSA. *Faculty research:* Construction best practices, productivity improvement, women's issues in construction, construction project management. *Total annual research expenditures:* $21,217. *Unit head:* Dr. Roger Liska, Chair and Professor, 864-656-0181, E-mail: riggor@clemson.edu. *Application contact:* Dr. Shima Clarke, Professor and Graduate Coordinator, 864-656-4498, E-mail: shimac@clemson.edu.
Website: http://www.clemson.edu/caah/csm/.

Colorado State University, Graduate School, College of Health and Human Sciences, Department of Construction Management, Fort Collins, CO 80523-1584. Offers MS. Part-time and evening/weekend programs available. *Faculty:* 10 full-time (2 women). *Students:* 14 full-time (3 women), 14 part-time (4 women); includes 1 minority (Hispanic/Latino), 13 international. Average age 32. 43 applicants, 72% accepted, 9 enrolled. In 2014, 6 master's awarded. *Degree requirements:* For master's, thesis (for some programs), S- professional paper, R- submit article for journal or proceedings with faculty advisor. *Entrance requirements:* For master's, GRE, CSU requires undergraduate GPA of 3.0 for Track I Admission. If GPA is below 3.0 then may qualify for Track II with five years professional experience. Additional exam requirements/recommendations for international students: Required—TOEFL (minimum score 550 paper-based; 80 iBT), IELTS (minimum score 6.5). *Application deadline:* For fall admission, 2/1 for domestic and international students; for spring admission, 1/1 for domestic and international students. Applications are processed on a rolling basis. Application fee: $50. Electronic applications accepted. *Expenses:* Tuition, state resident: full-time $9348; part-time $519 per credit. Tuition, nonresident: full-time $22,916; part-time $1273 per credit. *Required fees:* $1584. *Financial support:* In 2014–15, 9 students received support, including 4 research assistantships with tuition reimbursements available (averaging $11,487 per year), 5 teaching assistantships with full tuition reimbursements available (averaging $10,941 per year); fellowships with tuition reimbursements available, scholarships/grants, and unspecified assistantships also available. Financial award application deadline: 3/1; financial award applicants required to submit FAFSA. *Faculty research:* Sustainability, transportation, infrastructure, productivity and workforce development. *Total annual research expenditures:* $244,862. *Unit head:* Dr. Mostafa M. Khattab, Department Head, 970-491-6808, Fax: 970-491-2473, E-mail: mostafa.khattab@colostate.edu. *Application contact:* Terry Richardson, Graduate Program Advisor, 970-491-7353, Fax: 970-491-2473, E-mail: terry.richardson@colostate.edu.
Website: http://www.cm.chhs.colostate.edu/.

Columbia University, Fu Foundation School of Engineering and Applied Science, Department of Civil Engineering and Engineering Mechanics, New York, NY 10027. Offers civil engineering (MS, Eng Sc D, PhD); construction engineering and management (MS); engineering mechanics (MS, Eng Sc D, PhD). Part-time programs available. Postbaccalaureate distance learning degree programs offered (no on-campus study). *Faculty:* 19 full-time (4 women), 27 part-time/adjunct (2 women). *Students:* 153 full-time (40 women), 100 part-time (27 women); includes 19 minority (1 Black or African American, non-Hispanic/Latino; 11 Asian, non-Hispanic/Latino; 6 Hispanic/Latino; 1 Two or more races, non-Hispanic/Latino), 194 international. 504 applicants, 38% accepted, 110 enrolled. In 2014, 131 master's, 7 doctorates awarded. Terminal master's awarded for partial completion of doctoral program. *Degree requirements:* For doctorate, thesis/dissertation, qualifying exam. *Entrance requirements:* For master's and doctorate, GRE General Test. Additional exam requirements/recommendations for international students: Required—TOEFL, IELTS, PTE. *Application deadline:* For fall admission, 12/15 priority date for domestic and international students; for spring admission, 10/1 priority date for domestic and international students. Application fee: $85. Electronic applications accepted. *Financial support:* In 2014–15, 44 students received support, including 13 fellowships with full tuition reimbursements available (averaging $27,500 per year), 18 research assistantships with full tuition reimbursements available (averaging $32,448 per year), 13 teaching assistantships with full tuition reimbursements available (averaging $32,448 per year); health care benefits also available. Financial award application deadline: 12/15; financial award applicants required to submit FAFSA. *Faculty research:* Structural dynamics, structural health and monitoring, fatigue and fracture mechanics, geo-environmental engineering, multiscale science and engineering. *Unit head:* Dr. George Deodatis, Professor and Chair, Civil Engineering and Engineering Mechanics, 212-854-6267, E-mail: deodatis@civil.columbia.edu. *Application contact:* Scott Kelly, Graduate Admissions and Student Affairs, 212-854-3219, E-mail: kelly@civil.columbia.edu.
Website: http://www.civil.columbia.edu/.

Columbia University, School of Continuing Education, Program in Construction Administration, New York, NY 10027. Offers MS. Part-time and evening/weekend programs available. *Degree requirements:* For master's, minimum GPA of 3.0 or internship. *Entrance requirements:* For master's, bachelor's degree, minimum GPA of 3.0. Additional exam requirements/recommendations for international students: Recommended—TOEFL. Electronic applications accepted.

Drexel University, Goodwin College of Professional Studies, School of Technology and Professional Studies, Philadelphia, PA 19104-2875. Offers construction management (MS); creativity and innovation (MS); engineering technology (MS); food science (MS); hospitality management (MS); professional studies: creativity studies (MS); professional studies: e-learning leadership (MS); professional studies: homeland security management (MS); project management (MS); property management (MS); sport management (MS). Part-time and evening/weekend programs available. *Entrance requirements:* Additional exam requirements/recommendations for international students: Required—TOEFL, IELTS. Electronic applications accepted. Application fee is waived when completed online.

East Carolina University, Graduate School, College of Engineering and Technology, Department of Construction Management, Greenville, NC 27858-4353. Offers MCM. *Expenses:* Tuition, state resident: full-time $4223. Tuition, nonresident: full-time $16,540. *Required fees:* $2184.

Eastern Michigan University, Graduate School, College of Technology, School of Visual and Built Environments, Programs in Construction Management, Ypsilanti, MI 48197. Offers MS. Part-time and evening/weekend programs available. Postbaccalaureate distance learning degree programs offered (minimal on-campus study). *Students:* 14 full-time (2 women), 10 part-time (2 women); includes 5 minority (all Black or African American, non-Hispanic/Latino), 11 international. Average age 30. 32 applicants, 53% accepted, 10 enrolled. In 2014, 9 master's awarded. *Entrance requirements:* Additional exam requirements/recommendations for international students: Required—TOEFL. *Application deadline:* Applications are processed on a rolling basis. Application fee: $45. *Financial support:* Fellowships, research assistantships with full tuition reimbursements, teaching assistantships with full tuition reimbursements, career-related internships or fieldwork, Federal Work-Study, institutionally sponsored loans, scholarships/grants, tuition waivers (partial), and unspecified assistantships available. Support available to part-time students. Financial award applicants required to submit FAFSA. *Application contact:* Dr. Williiam Moylan, Program Coordinator, 734-487-1940, Fax: 734-487-8755, E-mail: william.moylan@emich.edu.

Florida International University, College of Engineering and Computing, School of Construction, Miami, FL 33175. Offers construction management (MS, PMS). Part-time and evening/weekend programs available. *Degree requirements:* For master's, thesis optional. *Entrance requirements:* For master's, minimum GPA of 3.0 in upper-level course work. Additional exam requirements/recommendations for international students: Required—TOEFL (minimum score 550 paper-based; 80 iBT). Electronic applications accepted. *Faculty research:* Information technology, construction organizations, contracts and partnerships in construction, construction education, concrete technology.

Harrisburg University of Science and Technology, Program in Project Management, Harrisburg, PA 17101. Offers construction services (MS); governmental services (MS); information technology (MS). Part-time and evening/weekend programs available. *Entrance requirements:* For master's, BS, BBA. Additional exam requirements/recommendations for international students: Required—TOEFL (minimum score 520 paper-based; 80 iBT). Electronic applications accepted.

Illinois Institute of Technology, Graduate College, Armour College of Engineering, Department of Civil, Architectural and Environmental Engineering, Chicago, IL 60616. Offers architectural engineering (M Arch E); civil engineering (MS, PhD), including architectural engineering (MS), construction engineering and management (MS), geoenvironmental engineering (MS), geotechnical engineering (MS), structural engineering (MS), transportation engineering (MS); construction engineering and management (MCEM); environmental engineering (M Env E, MS, PhD); geoenvironmental engineering (M Geoenv E); geotechnical engineering (MGE); infrastructure engineering and management (MPW); structural engineering (MSE); transportation engineering (M Trans E). Part-time and evening/weekend programs available. Postbaccalaureate distance learning degree programs offered (minimal on-campus study). *Faculty:* 12 full-time (1 woman), 15 part-time/adjunct (1 woman). *Students:* 165 full-time (48 women), 54 part-time (11 women); includes 31 minority (2 Black or African American, non-Hispanic/Latino; 21 Asian, non-Hispanic/Latino; 7 Hispanic/Latino; 1 Native Hawaiian or other Pacific Islander, non-Hispanic/Latino), 157 international. Average age 29. 1,039 applicants, 42% accepted, 82 enrolled. In 2014, 94 master's, 7 doctorates awarded. Terminal master's awarded for partial completion of doctoral program. *Degree requirements:* For master's, thesis (for some programs); for doctorate, comprehensive exam, thesis/dissertation. *Entrance requirements:* For master's, GRE General Test (minimum score 900 Quantitative and Verbal, 2.5 Analytical Writing), minimum undergraduate GPA of 3.0; for doctorate, GRE General Test (minimum score 1000 Quantitative and Verbal, 3.0 Analytical Writing), minimum undergraduate GPA of 3.0. Additional exam requirements/recommendations for international students: Required—TOEFL (minimum score 550 paper-based; 80 iBT). *Application deadline:* For fall admission, 5/1 for domestic and international students; for spring admission, 10/15 for domestic and international students. Applications are processed on a rolling basis. Application fee: $50. Electronic applications accepted. *Expenses: Tuition:* Full-time $22,500; part-time $1250 per credit hour. *Required fees:* $30 per course. $260 per semester. One-time fee: $235. Tuition and fees vary according to course load and program. *Financial support:* Fellowships with full and partial tuition reimbursements, research assistantships with full and partial tuition reimbursements, teaching assistantships with full and partial tuition reimbursements, Federal Work-Study, institutionally sponsored loans, scholarships/grants, health care benefits, tuition waivers (partial), and unspecified assistantships available. Support available to part-time students. Financial award applicants required to submit FAFSA. *Faculty research:* Structural, architectural, geotechnical and geoenvironmental engineering; construction engineering and management; transportation engineering; environmental engineering and public works. *Unit head:* Dr. Gongkang Fu, Professor and Chairman, 312-567-3540, Fax: 312-567-3519, E-mail: gfu2@iit.edu. *Application contact:* Rishab Malhotra, Director, Graduate Admission, 866-472-3448, Fax: 312-567-3138, E-mail: inquiry.grad@iit.edu.
Website: http://engineering.iit.edu/caee.

Instituto Tecnologico de Santo Domingo, Graduate School, Area of Engineering, Santo Domingo, Dominican Republic. Offers construction administration (MS, Certificate); data telecommunications (M Eng, MS, Certificate); industrial engineering (M Eng, Certificate); industrial management (M Mgmt); information technology (Certificate); maintenance engineering (M Eng); occupational hazard prevention (M Mgmt); production management (Certificate); quantitative methods (Certificate); sanitary and environmental engineering (M Eng); structural engineering (M Eng); systems engineering and electronic data processing (Certificate); transportation (Certificate).

Louisiana State University and Agricultural & Mechanical College, Graduate School, College of Engineering, Department of Construction Management, Baton Rouge, LA 70803. Offers MS, PhD. *Faculty:* 9 full-time (2 women). *Students:* 9 full-time (1 woman), 50 part-time (7 women); includes 11 minority (6 Black or African American, non-Hispanic/Latino; 1 Asian, non-Hispanic/Latino; 3 Hispanic/Latino; 1 Two or more races, non-Hispanic/Latino), 4 international. Average age 34. 38 applicants, 58% accepted, 12 enrolled. In 2014, 6 master's awarded. Terminal master's awarded for partial completion of doctoral program. *Degree requirements:* For master's, thesis; for doctorate, thesis/dissertation. *Entrance requirements:* For master's and doctorate, GRE General Test, minimum GPA of 3.0. Additional exam requirements/recommendations for international students: Required—TOEFL (minimum score 550 paper-based; 79 IBT),

IELTS (minimum score 6.5), or PTE (minimum score 59). *Application deadline:* For fall admission, 1/1 priority date for domestic students, 5/15 for international students; for spring admission, 10/15 for domestic and international students; for summer admission, 5/15 for domestic and international students. Applications are processed on a rolling basis. Application fee: $50 ($70 for international students). Electronic applications accepted. *Financial support:* In 2014–15, 7 students received support, including 2 research assistantships with partial tuition reimbursements available (averaging $10,800 per year); fellowships, teaching assistantships with partial tuition reimbursements available, Federal Work-Study, institutionally sponsored loans, health care benefits, and unspecified assistantships also available. Financial award application deadline: 5/1; financial award applicants required to submit FAFSA. *Faculty research:* Ergonomics and occupational health, information technology, production systems, supply management, construction safety and methods. *Total annual research expenditures:* $742,090. *Unit head:* Dr. Charles Berryman, Chair, 225-578-5112, Fax: 225-578-5109, E-mail: cberryman@lsumail.net. *Application contact:* Dr. Marwa Hassan, Associate Dean for Research and Graduate Studies, 225-578-9189, Fax: 225-578-5109, E-mail: marwa@lsu.edu.
Website: http://www.cm.lsu.edu/.

Marquette University, Graduate School, Opus College of Engineering, Department of Civil, Construction and Environmental Engineering, Milwaukee, WI 53201-1881. Offers construction engineering and management (MS, PhD, Certificate); environmental engineering (MS, PhD); structural design (Certificate); structural engineering and structural mechanics (MS, PhD); transportation (Certificate); transportation engineering and materials (MS, PhD); waste and wastewater treatment processes (Certificate); water resources engineering (Certificate). Part-time and evening/weekend programs available. Terminal master's awarded for partial completion of doctoral program. *Degree requirements:* For master's, comprehensive exam (for some programs), thesis or alternative; for doctorate, thesis/dissertation. *Entrance requirements:* For master's, GRE General Test (recommended), minimum GPA of 3.0, official transcripts from all current and previous colleges/universities except Marquette, three letters of recommendation; for doctorate, GRE General Test, minimum GPA of 3.0, official transcripts from all current and previous colleges/universities except Marquette, three letters of recommendation, brief statement of purpose, submission of any English language publications authored by applicant (strongly recommended). Additional exam requirements/recommendations for international students: Required—TOEFL (minimum score 530 paper-based). Electronic applications accepted. *Faculty research:* Highway safety, highway performance, and intelligent transportation systems; surface mount technology; watershed management.

Michigan State University, The Graduate School, College of Agriculture and Natural Resources and College of Social Science, School of Planning, Design and Construction, East Lansing, MI 48824. Offers construction management (MS, PhD); environmental design (MA); interior design and facilities management (MA); international planning studies (MIPS); urban and regional planning (MURP). *Degree requirements:* For master's, thesis or alternative. *Entrance requirements:* Additional exam requirements/recommendations for international students: Required—TOEFL. Electronic applications accepted.

Milwaukee School of Engineering, Rader School of Business, Program in Construction and Business Management, Milwaukee, WI 53202-3109. Offers MS. Evening/weekend programs available. Postbaccalaureate distance learning degree programs offered (minimal on-campus study). *Faculty:* 1 full-time (0 women), 2 part-time/adjunct (0 women). *Students:* 2 full-time (1 woman), 5 part-time (0 women); includes 1 minority (Black or African American, non-Hispanic/Latino), 2 international. Average age 30. 6 applicants, 50% accepted, 2 enrolled. In 2014, 6 master's awarded. *Degree requirements:* For master's, thesis, capstone project. *Entrance requirements:* For master's, GRE or GMAT if GPA is less than 2.8, BS in related field, official transcripts, two letters of recommendation, personal essay. Additional exam requirements/recommendations for international students: Required—TOEFL (minimum score 90 iBT), IELTS (minimum score 6.5). *Application deadline:* Applications are processed on a rolling basis. Application fee: $0. Electronic applications accepted. *Expenses: Tuition:* Part-time $732 per credit. *Financial support:* In 2014–15, 1 student received support. Career-related internships or fieldwork, institutionally sponsored loans, scholarships/grants, and tuition waivers (full) available. Financial award application deadline: 3/15; financial award applicants required to submit FAFSA. *Unit head:* Gene Wright, Director, 414-277-2286, Fax: 414-277-7479, E-mail: wright@msoe.edu. *Application contact:* Ian Dahlinghaus, Graduate Admissions Counselor, 414-277-7208, E-mail: dahlinghaus@msoe.edu.
Website: http://www.msoe.edu/community/academics/business/page/1296/construction-and-business-management-overview.

See Display on page 58 and Close-Up on page 83.

Missouri State University, Graduate College, College of Business Administration, Department of Technology and Construction Management, Springfield, MO 65897. Offers MS. Part-time programs available. *Faculty:* 4 full-time (0 women), 2 part-time/adjunct (1 woman). *Students:* 11 full-time (3 women), 68 part-time (18 women); includes 17 minority (6 Black or African American, non-Hispanic/Latino; 1 American Indian or Alaska Native, non-Hispanic/Latino; 3 Asian, non-Hispanic/Latino; 5 Hispanic/Latino; 2 Two or more races, non-Hispanic/Latino), 2 international. Average age 35. 35 applicants, 94% accepted, 22 enrolled. In 2014, 37 master's awarded. *Degree requirements:* For master's, thesis or alternative. *Entrance requirements:* For master's, GRE or GMAT, minimum GPA of 2.75. Additional exam requirements/recommendations for international students: Required—TOEFL (minimum score 550 paper-based; 79 iBT). *Application deadline:* For fall admission, 7/20 for domestic students, 5/1 for international students; for spring admission, 12/20 for domestic students, 9/1 for international students. Applications are processed on a rolling basis. Application fee: $35 ($50 for international students). Electronic applications accepted. *Expenses:* Tuition, state resident: full-time $2250; part-time $250 per credit hour. Tuition, nonresident: full-time $4509; part-time $501 per credit hour. Tuition and fees vary according to course level, course load and program. *Financial support:* Federal Work-Study, institutionally sponsored loans, scholarships/grants, and unspecified assistantships available. Financial award application deadline: 3/31; financial award applicants required to submit FAFSA. *Unit head:* Dr. Richard N Callahan, Department Head, 417-836-5121, Fax: 417-836-8556, E-mail: indmgt@missouristate.edu. *Application contact:* Misty Stewart, Coordinator of Graduate Admissions and Recruitment, 417-836-6079, Fax: 417-836-6200, E-mail: mistystewart@missouristate.edu.
Website: http://tcm.missouristate.edu/.

New England Institute of Technology, Program in Construction Management, East Greenwich, RI 02818. Offers MS. Part-time and evening/weekend programs available. Postbaccalaureate distance learning degree programs offered. *Application deadline:* Applications are processed on a rolling basis. Application fee: $25. Electronic applications accepted. *Unit head:* James Jessup, Director of Admissions, 401-467-7744 Ext. 3339, Fax: 401-886-0868, E-mail: jjessup@neit.edu. *Application contact:* James Jessup, Director of Admissions, 401-467-7744 Ext. 3339, Fax: 401-886-0868, E-mail: jjessup@neit.edu.
Website: http://www.neit.edu/Programs/Masters-Degree-Programs/Construction-Management-Masters-Degree.

NewSchool of Architecture and Design, Program in Construction Management, San Diego, CA 92101-6634. Offers MCM. Part-time programs available. Postbaccalaureate distance learning degree programs offered (no on-campus study). *Degree requirements:* For master's, thesis. *Entrance requirements:* For master's, GRE/GMAT. Additional exam requirements/recommendations for international students: Required—TOEFL, IELTS. Electronic applications accepted.

New York University, Polytechnic School of Engineering, Department of Civil and Urban Engineering, Major in Construction Management, New York, NY 10012-1019. Offers MS. *Students:* 35 full-time (9 women), 38 part-time (8 women); includes 16 minority (5 Black or African American, non-Hispanic/Latino; 5 Asian, non-Hispanic/Latino; 6 Hispanic/Latino), 33 international. Average age 29. 176 applicants, 50% accepted, 32 enrolled. In 2014, 25 master's awarded. *Degree requirements:* For master's, comprehensive exam (for some programs), thesis (for some programs). *Entrance requirements:* Additional exam requirements/recommendations for international students: Required—TOEFL (minimum score 550 paper-based; 80 iBT); Recommended—IELTS (minimum score 6.5). *Application deadline:* For fall admission, 2/15 priority date for domestic and international students; for spring admission, 11/1 priority date for domestic and international students. Applications are processed on a rolling basis. Application fee: $75. Electronic applications accepted. *Financial support:* Institutionally sponsored loans, scholarships/grants, and unspecified assistantships available. Support available to part-time students. *Unit head:* Dr. Fletcher Graffis, Head, 718-260-3713, E-mail: griffis@nyu.edu. *Application contact:* Raymond Lutzky, Director, Graduate Enrollment Management, 718-637-5984, Fax: 718-260-3624, E-mail: rlutzky@poly.edu.

New York University, Polytechnic School of Engineering, Department of Technology Management, New York, NY 10012-1019. Offers construction management (Advanced Certificate); electronic business management (Advanced Certificate); entrepreneurship (Advanced Certificate); human resources management (Advanced Certificate); industrial engineering (MS); information management (Advanced Certificate); management (MS); management of technology (MS); manufacturing engineering (MS); organizational behavior (MS, Advanced Certificate); project management (Advanced Certificate); technology management (MBA, PhD, Advanced Certificate); telecommunications management (Advanced Certificate). Part-time and evening/weekend programs available. *Faculty:* 11 full-time (2 women), 43 part-time/adjunct (1 woman). *Students:* 294 full-time (126 women), 102 part-time (38 women); includes 42 minority (5 Black or African American, non-Hispanic/Latino; 1 American Indian or Alaska Native, non-Hispanic/Latino; 26 Asian, non-Hispanic/Latino; 9 Hispanic/Latino; 1 Two or more races, non-Hispanic/Latino), 301 international. Average age 26. 843 applicants, 48% accepted, 165 enrolled. In 2014, 193 master's awarded. *Degree requirements:* For master's, comprehensive exam (for some programs), thesis (for some programs); for doctorate, comprehensive exam, thesis/dissertation. *Entrance requirements:* For master's, GMAT, minimum B average in undergraduate course work. Additional exam requirements/recommendations for international students: Required—TOEFL (minimum score 550 paper-based; 80 iBT); Recommended—IELTS (minimum score 6.5). *Application deadline:* For fall admission, 2/15 priority date for domestic and international students; for spring admission, 11/1 priority date for domestic and international students. Applications are processed on a rolling basis. Application fee: $75. Electronic applications accepted. *Financial support:* In 2014–15, 1 fellowship (averaging $26,400 per year) was awarded; research assistantships, teaching assistantships, institutionally sponsored loans, scholarships/grants, and unspecified assistantships also available. Support available to part-time students. *Faculty research:* Global innovation and research and development strategy, managing emerging technologies, technology and development, service design and innovation, tech entrepreneurship and commercialization, sustainable and clean-tech innovation, impacts of information technology upon individuals, organizations and society. *Total annual research expenditures:* $271,808. *Unit head:* Prof. Bharadwaj Rao, Head, 718-260-3617, Fax: 718-260-3874, E-mail: bharat.rao@nyu.edu. *Application contact:* Raymond Lutzky, Director of Graduate Enrollment Management, 718-637-5984, Fax: 718-260-3624, E-mail: rlutzky@poly.edu.
Website: http://www.poly.edu/academics/departments/technology/.

New York University, School of Continuing and Professional Studies, Schack Institute of Real Estate, Program in Construction Management, New York, NY 10012-1019. Offers MS, Advanced Certificate. Part-time and evening/weekend programs available. *Faculty:* 3 full-time (1 woman), 16 part-time/adjunct (1 woman). *Students:* 11 full-time (3 women), 57 part-time (15 women); includes 16 minority (5 Black or African American, non-Hispanic/Latino; 6 Asian, non-Hispanic/Latino; 5 Hispanic/Latino), 17 international. Average age 30. 65 applicants, 42% accepted, 12 enrolled. In 2014, 29 master's, 5 other advanced degrees awarded. *Degree requirements:* For master's, thesis, capstone project. *Entrance requirements:* For master's, GRE or GMAT only upon request, bachelor's degree, resume with relevant professional work, internship or volunteer experience, two letters of recommendation, statement of purpose. Additional exam requirements/recommendations for international students: Required—TOEFL (minimum score 600 paper-based; 100 iBT), IELTS (minimum score 7). *Application deadline:* For fall admission, 2/1 priority date for domestic and international students; for spring admission, 10/15 priority date for domestic students, 8/15 priority date for international students. Applications are processed on a rolling basis. Application fee: $150. Electronic applications accepted. *Financial support:* In 2014–15, 17 students received support, including 15 fellowships (averaging $1,239 per year); Federal Work-Study and scholarships/grants also available. Support available to part-time students. Financial award application deadline: 4/1; financial award applicants required to submit FAFSA. *Unit head:* Rosemary Scanlon, Divisional Dean. *Application contact:* Office of Admissions, 212-998-7100, E-mail: sps.gradadmissions@nyu.edu.
Website: http://www.sps.nyu.edu/areas-of-study/real-estate/graduate-programs/.

North Carolina Agricultural and Technical State University, School of Graduate Studies, School of Technology, Department of Construction Management and Occupational Safety and Health, Greensboro, NC 27411. Offers construction management (MSTM); environmental and occupational safety (MSTM); occupational safety and health (MSTM).

North Dakota State University, College of Graduate and Interdisciplinary Studies, College of Engineering and Architecture, Department of Construction Management and Engineering, Fargo, ND 58108. Offers construction management (MS). *Entrance requirements:* Additional exam requirements/recommendations for international students: Required—TOEFL (minimum score 525 paper-based; 71 iBT). Electronic applications accepted.

Norwich University, College of Graduate and Continuing Studies, Master of Business Administration Program, Northfield, VT 05663. Offers construction management (MBA); finance (MBA); organizational leadership (MBA); project management (MBA); supply chain management and logistics (MBA). *Accreditation:* ACBSP. Evening/weekend

programs available. Postbaccalaureate distance learning degree programs offered (minimal on-campus study). *Faculty:* 2 full-time (1 woman), 13 part-time/adjunct (4 women). *Students:* 193 full-time (54 women); includes 41 minority (23 Black or African American, non-Hispanic/Latino; 1 American Indian or Alaska Native, non-Hispanic/Latino; 10 Asian, non-Hispanic/Latino; 4 Hispanic/Latino; 1 Native Hawaiian or other Pacific Islander, non-Hispanic/Latino; 2 Two or more races, non-Hispanic/Latino). Average age 35. 133 applicants, 100% accepted, 90 enrolled. In 2014, 86 master's awarded. *Degree requirements:* For master's, comprehensive exam, thesis optional. *Entrance requirements:* For master's, minimum undergraduate GPA of 2.75. Additional exam requirements/recommendations for international students: Required—TOEFL (minimum score 550 paper-based; 80 iBT), IELTS (minimum score 6.5). *Application deadline:* For fall admission, 8/8 for domestic and international students; for winter admission, 11/7 for domestic and international students; for spring admission, 2/16 for domestic and international students; for summer admission, 5/18 for domestic and international students. Applications are processed on a rolling basis. Electronic applications accepted. *Expenses:* Expenses: Contact institution. *Financial support:* In 2014–15, 114 students received support. Scholarships/grants available. Financial award applicants required to submit FAFSA. *Unit head:* Dr. Jose Cordova, Program Director, 802-485-2567, Fax: 802-485-2533, E-mail: jcordova@norwich.edu. *Application contact:* Toni Raftery, Associate Program Director, 802-485-3292, Fax: 802-485-2533, E-mail: traftery@norwich.edu.
Website: http://online.norwich.edu/degree-programs/masters/master-business-administration/overview.

Norwich University, College of Graduate and Continuing Studies, Master of Civil Engineering Program, Northfield, VT 05663. Offers construction management engineering (MCE); environmental/water resources engineering (MCE); geotechnical engineering (MCE); structural engineering (MCE). Evening/weekend programs available. Postbaccalaureate distance learning degree programs offered (minimal on-campus study). *Faculty:* 14 part-time/adjunct (2 women). *Students:* 111 full-time (17 women); includes 28 minority (16 Black or African American, non-Hispanic/Latino; 2 American Indian or Alaska Native, non-Hispanic/Latino; 7 Asian, non-Hispanic/Latino; 3 Hispanic/Latino). Average age 36. 61 applicants, 100% accepted, 42 enrolled. In 2014, 57 master's awarded. *Entrance requirements:* For master's, minimum undergraduate GPA of 2.75. Additional exam requirements/recommendations for international students: Required—TOEFL (minimum score 550 paper-based; 80 iBT), IELTS (minimum score 6.5). *Application deadline:* For fall admission, 8/8 for domestic and international students; for spring admission, 2/16 for domestic and international students. Applications are processed on a rolling basis. Electronic applications accepted. *Expenses:* Expenses: Contact institution. *Financial support:* In 2014–15, 27 students received support. Scholarships/grants available. Financial award applicants required to submit FAFSA. *Unit head:* Dr. Thomas Descoteaux, Program Director, 802-485-2730, Fax: 802-485-2533, E-mail: tdescote@norwich.edu. *Application contact:* Rija Ramahatra, Associate Program Director, 802-485-2892, Fax: 802-485-2533, E-mail: ramahatr@norwich.edu.
Website: http://online.norwich.edu/degree-programs/masters/master-civil-engineering/overview.

Philadelphia University, College of Architecture and the Built Environment, Program in Construction Management, Philadelphia, PA 19144. Offers MS.

Polytechnic University of Puerto Rico, Miami Campus, Graduate School, Miami, FL 33166. Offers accounting (MBA); business administration (MBA); construction management (MEM); environmental management (MEM); finance (MBA); human resources management (MBA); logistics and supply chain management (MBA); management of international enterprises (MBA); manufacturing management (MEM); marketing management (MBA); project management (MBA). Part-time and evening/weekend programs available. Postbaccalaureate distance learning degree programs offered (no on-campus study). *Entrance requirements:* For master's, minimum GPA of 3.0. Electronic applications accepted.

Polytechnic University of Puerto Rico, Orlando Campus, Graduate School, Winter Park, FL 32792. Offers accounting (MBA); business administration (MBA); construction management (MEM); engineering management (MEM); environmental management (MEM); finance (MBA); human resources management (MBA); management of international enterprises (MBA); management of technology (MBA); manufacturing management (MEM). Part-time and evening/weekend programs available. Postbaccalaureate distance learning degree programs offered (no on-campus study). *Entrance requirements:* For master's, minimum GPA of 3.0. Additional exam requirements/recommendations for international students: Recommended—TOEFL. Electronic applications accepted.

Purdue University, Graduate School, College of Technology, Department of Building Construction Management, West Lafayette, IN 47907. Offers MS. Postbaccalaureate distance learning degree programs offered (no on-campus study). *Entrance requirements:* For master's, GRE, BS/BA with minimum GPA of 3.0. Additional exam requirements/recommendations for international students: Required—TOEFL (minimum score 550 paper-based; 77 iBT); Recommended—TWE. Electronic applications accepted.

Roger Williams University, School of Engineering, Computing and Construction Management, Bristol, RI 02809. Offers construction management (MSCM). *Faculty:* 1 full-time (0 women), 1 part-time/adjunct (0 women). *Students:* 5 part-time (2 women). Average age 24. In 2014, 5 master's awarded. *Entrance requirements:* Additional exam requirements/recommendations for international students: Required—TOEFL (minimum score 85 iBT). *Expenses: Tuition:* Full-time $7362; part-time $2454 per course. Tuition and fees vary according to course load, campus/location and program. *Unit head:* Robert Potter, Dean, 401-254-3498, E-mail: bobpotter@rwu.edu. *Application contact:* Jamie Grenon, Director of Graduate Admissions, 401-254-6000, E-mail: gradadmit@rwu.edu.
Website: http://www.rwu.edu/academics/schools/seccm/.

South Dakota School of Mines and Technology, Graduate Division, Program in Construction Engineering Management, Rapid City, SD 57701-3995. Offers MS. Part-time and evening/weekend programs available. Postbaccalaureate distance learning degree programs offered. *Faculty:* 11 full-time (2 women), 3 part-time/adjunct (1 woman). *Students:* 4 full-time (0 women), 8 part-time (2 women); includes 2 minority (1 American Indian or Alaska Native, non-Hispanic/Latino; 1 Hispanic/Latino). Average age 32. 12 applicants, 42% accepted, 3 enrolled. In 2014, 10 master's awarded. *Entrance requirements:* For master's, GRE General Test. Additional exam requirements/recommendations for international students: Required—TOEFL (minimum score 520 paper-based; 68 iBT). *Application deadline:* For fall admission, 7/1 for domestic students, 4/1 for international students; for spring admission, 11/1 for domestic students, 9/1 for international students. Applications are processed on a rolling basis. Application fee: $35. Electronic applications accepted. *Expenses:* Tuition, state resident: full-time $5050; part-time $210.40 per credit hour. Tuition, nonresident: full-time $11,290; part-time $470.30 per credit hour. *Required fees:* $4680. *Financial support:* Application deadline: 5/15. *Unit head:* Clifford Bienert, Coordinator, 605-394-1694, E-mail:

clifford.bienert@sdsmt.edu. *Application contact:* Rachel Howard, Office of Graduate Education, 605-355-3468, Fax: 605-394-1767, E-mail: rachel.howard@sdsmt.edu.
Website: http://graded.sdsmt.edu/academics/programs/cm/.

Southern Polytechnic State University, School of Architecture and Construction Management, Department of Construction Management, Marietta, GA 30060. Offers MS. Part-time and evening/weekend programs available. *Degree requirements:* For master's, comprehensive exam, thesis or alternative. *Entrance requirements:* For master's, GMAT or GRE, 3 reference forms, minimum GPA of 2.75. Additional exam requirements/recommendations for international students: Required—TOEFL (minimum score 550 paper-based; 79 iBT), IELTS (minimum score 6.5). Electronic applications accepted. *Faculty research:* Environmental construction and green building techniques, risk management, bidding strategies in construction, construction worker safety, building automation and performance measurements.

State University of New York College of Environmental Science and Forestry, Department of Sustainable Construction Management and Engineering, Syracuse, NY 13210-2779. Offers construction management (MPS, MS, PhD); sustainable construction (MPS, MS, PhD); wood science (MPS, MS, PhD). *Degree requirements:* For master's, thesis (for some programs); for doctorate, comprehensive exam, thesis/dissertation. *Entrance requirements:* For master's and doctorate, GRE General Test, minimum GPA of 3.0. Additional exam requirements/recommendations for international students: Required—TOEFL (minimum score 550 paper-based; 80 iBT), IELTS (minimum score 6).

Stevens Institute of Technology, Graduate School, Charles V. Schaefer Jr. School of Engineering, Department of Civil, Environmental, and Ocean Engineering, Program in Construction Management, Hoboken, NJ 07030. Offers construction accounting/estimating (Certificate); construction engineering (Certificate); construction law/disputes (Certificate); construction management (MS); construction/quality management (Certificate). *Degree requirements:* For master's, thesis optional. *Entrance requirements:* For master's, GMAT, GRE General Test. Additional exam requirements/recommendations for international students: Required—TOEFL. Electronic applications accepted.

Texas A&M University, College of Architecture, Department of Construction Science, College Station, TX 77843. Offers construction management (MS). *Faculty:* 16. *Students:* 84 full-time (19 women), 11 part-time (3 women); includes 9 minority (3 Black or African American, non-Hispanic/Latino; 2 Asian, non-Hispanic/Latino; 4 Hispanic/Latino), 77 international. Average age 26. 123 applicants, 74% accepted, 48 enrolled. In 2014, 28 master's awarded. *Degree requirements:* For master's, comprehensive exam. *Entrance requirements:* For master's, GRE General Test, 3 recommendation letters, resume, statement of research interest, minimum undergraduate GPA of 3.0 in last 60 hours of applicant's undergraduate degree. Additional exam requirements/recommendations for international students: Required—TOEFL. *Application deadline:* For fall admission, 3/15 for domestic and international students. Applications are processed on a rolling basis. Application fee: $50 ($90 for international students). Electronic applications accepted. *Expenses:* Tuition, state resident: full-time $4078; part-time $226.55 per credit hour. Tuition, nonresident: full-time $10,594; part-time $577.55 per credit hour. *Required fees:* $2813; $237.70 per credit hour. $278.50 per semester. Tuition and fees vary according to degree level and student level. *Financial support:* In 2014–15, 70 students received support, including 9 fellowships with full and partial tuition reimbursements available (averaging $3,333 per year), 14 research assistantships with full and partial tuition reimbursements available (averaging $2,277 per year), 6 teaching assistantships with full and partial tuition reimbursements available (averaging $1,876 per year); career-related internships or fieldwork, institutionally sponsored loans, scholarships/grants, traineeships, health care benefits, tuition waivers (full and partial), and unspecified assistantships also available. Support available to part-time students. Financial award application deadline: 4/1; financial award applicants required to submit FAFSA. *Faculty research:* Advanced project management, construction operation, construction productivity and labor, facility management, information technology in construction, law and risk management, sustainability. *Unit head:* Prof. Joe Horlen, Head, 979-458-3477, E-mail: jhorlen@tamu.edu. *Application contact:* Dr. Sarel Lavy, Graduate Program Coordinator, 979-845-0632, E-mail: slavy@arch.tamu.edu.
Website: http://cosc.arch.tamu.edu/.

Universidad de las Américas Puebla, Division of Graduate Studies, School of Engineering, Program in Construction Management, Puebla, Mexico. Offers M Adm. Part-time and evening/weekend programs available. *Degree requirements:* For master's, one foreign language, thesis. *Faculty research:* Building structures, budget, project management.

University of Alaska Fairbanks, College of Engineering and Mines, Department of Civil and Environmental Engineering, Fairbanks, AK 99775-5900. Offers arctic engineering (MS); civil engineering (MCE, MS); design and construction management (Graduate Certificate); engineering and science management (MS), including engineering management, science management; environmental engineering (MS, PhD); environmental quality science (MS), including environmental contaminants, environmental science and management, water supply and waste treatment. Part-time programs available. *Faculty:* 10 full-time (2 women). *Students:* 14 full-time (7 women), 8 part-time (2 women); includes 4 minority (1 Black or African American, non-Hispanic/Latino; 1 American Indian or Alaska Native, non-Hispanic/Latino; 1 Hispanic/Latino; 1 Two or more races, non-Hispanic/Latino), 5 international. Average age 30. 19 applicants, 37% accepted, 5 enrolled. In 2014, 3 master's, 1 other advanced degree awarded. *Degree requirements:* For master's, comprehensive exam, thesis (for some programs), oral defense of project or thesis; for doctorate, comprehensive exam, thesis/dissertation. *Entrance requirements:* For master's, bachelor's degree from accredited institution with minimum cumulative undergraduate and major GPA of 3.0. Additional exam requirements/recommendations for international students: Required—TOEFL, IELTS. *Application deadline:* For fall admission, 6/1 for domestic students, 3/1 for international students; for spring admission, 10/15 for domestic students, 9/1 for international students. Applications are processed on a rolling basis. Application fee: $60. Electronic applications accepted. *Expenses:* Tuition, state resident: full-time $7614; part-time $423 per credit. Tuition, nonresident: full-time $15,552; part-time $864 per credit. Tuition and fees vary according to course level, course load and reciprocity agreements. *Financial support:* In 2014–15, 7 research assistantships with full tuition reimbursements (averaging $8,189 per year), 6 teaching assistantships with full tuition reimbursements (averaging $5,809 per year) were awarded; fellowships with full tuition reimbursements, career-related internships or fieldwork, Federal Work-Study, scholarships/grants, health care benefits, and unspecified assistantships also available. Support available to part-time students. Financial award application deadline: 7/1; financial award applicants required to submit FAFSA. *Faculty research:* Soils, structures, culvert thawing with solar power, pavement drainage, contaminant hydrogeology. *Unit head:* Dr. Robert Perkins, Department Chair, 907-474-7241, Fax: 907-474-6087, E-mail: fycee@uaf.edu. *Application contact:* Mary Kreta, Director of Admissions, 907-474-7500, Fax: 907-474-7097, E-mail: admissions@uaf.edu.
Website: http://cem.uaf.edu/cee.

Construction Management

University of Arkansas at Little Rock, Graduate School, George W. Donughey College of Engineering and Information Technology, Department of Construction Management and Civil and Construction Engineering, Little Rock, AR 72204-1099. Offers construction management (MS). *Expenses:* Tuition, state resident: full-time $6000; part-time $300 per credit hour. Tuition, nonresident: full-time $13,800; part-time $690 per credit hour. *Required fees:* $1126; $603 per term. One-time fee: $40 full-time. *Unit head:* Mike Tramel, Chairperson, 501-569-8229, E-mail: jmtramel@ualr.edu.
Website: http://ualr.edu/constructionmanagement/.

University of California, Berkeley, UC Berkeley Extension, Certificate Programs in Engineering, Construction and Facilities Management, Berkeley, CA 94720-1500. Offers construction management (Certificate); HVAC (Certificate); integrated circuit design and techniques (online) (Certificate). Postbaccalaureate distance learning degree programs offered.

University of Denver, Daniels College of Business, Franklin L. Burns School of Real Estate and Construction Management, Denver, CO 80208. Offers IMBA, MBA, MS. Part-time and evening/weekend programs available. *Faculty:* 8 full-time (1 woman), 2 part-time/adjunct (0 women). *Students:* 12 full-time (2 women), 68 part-time (22 women); includes 15 minority (7 Black or African American, non-Hispanic/Latino; 5 Hispanic/Latino; 3 Two or more races, non-Hispanic/Latino), 13 international. Average age 35. 70 applicants, 77% accepted, 26 enrolled. In 2014, 26 master's awarded. *Entrance requirements:* For master's, GRE General Test or GMAT, bachelor's degree, transcripts, essays, resume, interview. Additional exam requirements/recommendations for international students: Required—TOEFL (minimum score 570 paper-based; 88 iBT). *Application deadline:* For fall admission, 11/15 priority date for domestic and international students; for spring admission, 10/1 priority date for domestic and international students. Applications are processed on a rolling basis. Application fee: $100. Electronic applications accepted. *Expenses:* Expenses: $1,199 per credit hour. *Financial support:* In 2014–15, 42 students received support, including 6 teaching assistantships with full and partial tuition reimbursements available (averaging $1,464 per year); career-related internships or fieldwork, Federal Work-Study, institutionally sponsored loans, scholarships/grants, and unspecified assistantships also available. Support available to part-time students. Financial award application deadline: 2/15; financial award applicants required to submit FAFSA. *Unit head:* Dr. Barbara Jackson, Director, 303-871-3470, E-mail: barbara.jackson@du.edu. *Application contact:* Terese Allred, Graduate Admissions Coordinator, 303-871-7629, E-mail: terese.allred@du.edu.
Website: http://daniels.du.edu/masters-degrees/real-estate-construction-management/.

University of Florida, Graduate School, College of Design, Construction and Planning, Doctoral Program in Design, Construction and Planning, Gainesville, FL 32611. Offers construction management (PhD); design, construction and planning (PhD); interior design (PhD); landscape architecture (PhD); urban and regional planning (PhD). *Students:* 79 full-time (32 women), 21 part-time (7 women); includes 12 minority (4 Black or African American, non-Hispanic/Latino; 1 American Indian or Alaska Native, non-Hispanic/Latino; 4 Asian, non-Hispanic/Latino; 3 Hispanic/Latino), 51 international. 92 applicants, 25% accepted, 14 enrolled. In 2014, 18 doctorates awarded. *Degree requirements:* For doctorate, thesis/dissertation. *Entrance requirements:* For doctorate, GRE General Test, minimum GPA of 3.0. Additional exam requirements/recommendations for international students: Required—TOEFL (minimum score 550 paper-based; 80 iBT), IELTS (minimum score 6). *Application deadline:* For fall admission, 2/1 for domestic and international students. Applications are processed on a rolling basis. Application fee: $30. Electronic applications accepted. *Financial support:* Unspecified assistantships available. Financial award applicants required to submit FAFSA. *Faculty research:* Architecture, building construction, urban and regional planning. *Unit head:* Zhong-Ren Peng, PhD, Professor/Director, 352-392-0997 Ext. 429, Fax: 352-392-3308, E-mail: zpeng@ufl.edu. *Application contact:* Zhong-Ren Peng, PhD, Professor/Director, 352-392-0997 Ext. 429, Fax: 352-392-3308, E-mail: zpeng@ufl.edu.
Website: http://www.dcp.ufl.edu/docprogram/.

University of Florida, Graduate School, College of Design, Construction and Planning, M.E. Rinker, Sr. School of Construction Management, Gainesville, FL 32611. Offers fire and emergency services (MFES); international construction management (MICM). Part-time programs available. Postbaccalaureate distance learning degree programs offered. *Faculty:* 13 full-time (0 women). *Students:* 46 full-time (16 women), 11 part-time (4 women); includes 11 minority (1 Black or African American, non-Hispanic/Latino; 1 American Indian or Alaska Native, non-Hispanic/Latino; 2 Asian, non-Hispanic/Latino; 7 Hispanic/Latino), 23 international. 66 applicants, 88% accepted, 20 enrolled. In 2014, 37 master's awarded. *Degree requirements:* For master's, thesis. *Entrance requirements:* For master's, GRE General Test, minimum GPA of 3.0. Additional exam requirements/recommendations for international students: Required—TOEFL (minimum score 550 paper-based; 80 iBT), IELTS (minimum score 6). *Application deadline:* Applications are processed on a rolling basis. Application fee: $30. Electronic applications accepted. *Financial support:* Career-related internships or fieldwork and unspecified assistantships available. Financial award applicants required to submit FAFSA. *Faculty research:* Safety, affordable housing, construction management, environmental issues, sustainable construction. *Unit head:* Dr. Robert J. Ries, Interim Director, 352-273-1155, Fax: 352-392-9606, E-mail: rriesi@ufl.edu. *Application contact:* Dr. R. Edward Minchin, Director of Master's Programs, 352-273-1153, Fax: 352-392-7266, E-mail: minch@ufl.edu.
Website: http://www.bcn.ufl.edu/.

University of Houston, College of Technology, Department of Engineering Technology, Houston, TX 77204. Offers construction management (MS); engineering technology (MS); network communications (M Tech). Part-time programs available. *Degree requirements:* For master's, project or thesis (most programs). *Entrance requirements:* For master's, GRE. Additional exam requirements/recommendations for international students: Required—TOEFL (minimum score 550 paper-based; 79 iBT). Electronic applications accepted.

The University of Kansas, Graduate Studies, School of Engineering, Program in Construction Management, Lawrence, KS 66045. Offers MCM. Part-time and evening/weekend programs available. *Faculty:* 25 full-time, 8 part-time/adjunct. *Students:* 1 (woman) full-time, 4 part-time (3 women); includes 2 minority (1 Black or African American, non-Hispanic/Latino; 1 Two or more races, non-Hispanic/Latino). Average age 31. 8 applicants, 25% accepted, 2 enrolled. *Degree requirements:* For master's, thesis or alternative, exam. *Entrance requirements:* For master's, GRE. Additional exam requirements/recommendations for international students: Required—TOEFL. *Application deadline:* For fall admission, 7/1 priority date for domestic students, 3/1 priority date for international students; for spring admission, 12/1 priority date for domestic students, 8/15 priority date for international students. Applications are processed on a rolling basis. Application fee: $55 ($65 for international students). Electronic applications accepted. *Financial support:* Career-related internships or fieldwork available. Financial award application deadline: 2/7. *Faculty research:* Construction engineering, construction management. *Unit head:* David Darwin, Chair, 785-864-3827, Fax: 785-864-5631, E-mail: daved@ku.edu. *Application contact:* Susan Scott, Administrative Assistant, 785-864-3826, E-mail: sbscott@ku.edu.
Website: http://ceae.ku.edu/overview-6.

University of New Mexico, Graduate School, School of Engineering, Program in Civil Engineering, Albuquerque, NM 87131-0001. Offers civil engineering (M Eng, MSCE); construction management (MCM); engineering (PhD). Part-time programs available. *Faculty:* 11 full-time (2 women), 4 part-time/adjunct (1 woman). *Students:* 26 full-time (9 women), 28 part-time (14 women); includes 15 minority (1 American Indian or Alaska Native, non-Hispanic/Latino; 13 Hispanic/Latino; 1 Two or more races, non-Hispanic/Latino), 11 international. Average age 28. 72 applicants, 39% accepted, 17 enrolled. In 2014, 20 master's, 4 doctorates awarded. Terminal master's awarded for partial completion of doctoral program. *Degree requirements:* For master's, comprehensive exam, thesis (for some programs); for doctorate, comprehensive exam, thesis/dissertation. *Entrance requirements:* For master's, GRE General Test (for MSCE and M Eng); GRE or GMAT (for MCM), minimum GPA of 3.0; for doctorate, GRE General Test, minimum GPA of 3.0. Additional exam requirements/recommendations for international students: Required—TOEFL (minimum score 550 paper-based; 80 iBT), IELTS (minimum score 6.5). *Application deadline:* For fall admission, 7/15 for domestic students, 3/1 for international students; for spring admission, 11/10 for domestic students, 8/1 for international students. Applications are processed on a rolling basis. Application fee: $50. Electronic applications accepted. *Financial support:* In 2014–15, research assistantships with full and partial tuition reimbursements (averaging $19,944 per year), teaching assistantships with full and partial tuition reimbursements (averaging $15,000 per year) were awarded; scholarships/grants, health care benefits, and unspecified assistantships also available. Support available to part-time students. Financial award application deadline: 3/1; financial award applicants required to submit FAFSA. *Faculty research:* Integrating design and construction, project delivery methods, sustainable design and construction, leadership and management in construction, project management and project supervision, production management and improvement. *Total annual research expenditures:* $2.6 million. *Unit head:* Dr. John C. Stormont, Chair, 505-277-2722, Fax: 505-277-1988, E-mail: jcstorm@unm.edu. *Application contact:* Missy Garoza, Professional Academic Advisor, 505-277-2722, Fax: 505-277-1988, E-mail: civil@unm.edu.
Website: http://civil.unm.edu.

University of New Mexico, Graduate School, School of Engineering, Program in Construction Management, Albuquerque, NM 87131. Offers MCM. Part-time programs available. *Faculty:* 2 full-time (0 women). *Students:* 1 (woman) full-time, 1 part-time (0 women); includes 1 minority (Hispanic/Latino). Average age 30. 12 applicants, 17% accepted, 1 enrolled. In 2014, 2 master's awarded. *Degree requirements:* For master's, comprehensive exam, thesis optional. *Entrance requirements:* For master's, GMAT (minimum score 500) or GRE (minimum score 294 combined verbal and quantitative), minimum GPA of 3.0; courses in statistics, elements of calculus, engineering economy, and construction contracting. Additional exam requirements/recommendations for international students: Required—TOEFL (minimum score 550 paper-based; 80 iBT), IELTS (minimum score 6.5). *Application deadline:* For fall admission, 7/15 for domestic students, 3/1 for international students; for spring admission, 11/10 for domestic students, 8/1 for international students. Applications are processed on a rolling basis. Application fee: $50. Electronic applications accepted. *Financial support:* In 2014–15, 2 students received support. Scholarships/grants, health care benefits, and unspecified assistantships available. Support available to part-time students. Financial award application deadline: 3/1; financial award applicants required to submit FAFSA. *Faculty research:* Applied industry research and training, integration of the design/construction continuum, leadership in project management, life-cycle costing, production management and productivity management, project delivery methods, sustainable asset management, sustainable design and construction. *Total annual research expenditures:* $2.6 million. *Unit head:* Dr. John C. Stormont, Chair, 505-277-2722, Fax: 505-277-1988, E-mail: jcstorm@unm.edu. *Application contact:* Missy Garoza, Professional Academic Advisor, 505-277-2722, Fax: 505-277-1988, E-mail: civil@unm.edu.
Website: http://civil.unm.edu.

The University of North Carolina at Charlotte, The William States Lee College of Engineering, Department of Engineering Technology and Construction Management, Charlotte, NC 28223-0001. Offers applied energy and electromechanical systems (MS); construction and facilities management (MS); fire protection and administration (MS). *Faculty:* 26 full-time (5 women). *Students:* 30 full-time (6 women), 15 part-time (1 woman); includes 7 minority (3 Black or African American, non-Hispanic/Latino; 1 American Indian or Alaska Native, non-Hispanic/Latino; 1 Asian, non-Hispanic/Latino; 1 Hispanic/Latino; 1 Two or more races, non-Hispanic/Latino), 13 international. Average age 27. 69 applicants, 78% accepted, 27 enrolled. In 2014, 8 master's awarded. *Degree requirements:* For master's, comprehensive exam, thesis optional. *Entrance requirements:* Additional exam requirements/recommendations for international students: Required—TOEFL (minimum score 557 paper-based; 83 iBT). *Application deadline:* For fall admission, 5/1 for domestic and international students; for spring admission, 10/1 for domestic and international students. Application fee: $75. Electronic applications accepted. *Expenses:* Tuition, state resident: full-time $4008. Tuition, nonresident: full-time $16,295. *Required fees:* $2755. Tuition and fees vary according to course load and program. *Financial support:* In 2014–15, 24 students received support, including 22 research assistantships (averaging $6,665 per year), 2 teaching assistantships (averaging $14,250 per year); career-related internships or fieldwork, institutionally sponsored loans, scholarships/grants, and unspecified assistantships also available. Support available to part-time students. Financial award application deadline: 4/1; financial award applicants required to submit FAFSA. *Total annual research expenditures:* $1.1 million. *Unit head:* Dr. Cheng Liu, Chair Emeritus, 704-687-2474, E-mail: liu@uncc.edu. *Application contact:* Kathy B. Giddings, Director of Graduate Admissions, 704-687-5503, Fax: 704-687-1668, E-mail: gradadm@uncc.edu.
Website: http://et.uncc.edu/.

University of North Florida, Coggin College of Business, MBA Program, Jacksonville, FL 32224. Offers accounting (MBA); construction management (MBA); e-commerce (MBA); economics (MBA); finance (MBA); human resource management (MBA); international business (MBA); logistics (MBA); management applications (MBA). *Accreditation:* AACSB. Part-time and evening/weekend programs available. *Faculty:* 19 full-time (5 women), 1 part-time/adjunct (0 women). *Students:* 96 full-time (38 women), 189 part-time (70 women); includes 48 minority (18 Black or African American, non-Hispanic/Latino; 9 Asian, non-Hispanic/Latino; 14 Hispanic/Latino; 7 Two or more races, non-Hispanic/Latino), 29 international. Average age 29. 208 applicants, 36% accepted, 51 enrolled. In 2014, 121 master's awarded. *Entrance requirements:* For master's, GMAT or GRE, U.S. bachelor's degree from regionally-accredited university or equivalent foreign degree. Additional exam requirements/recommendations for international students: Required—TOEFL (minimum score 550 paper-based; 79 iBT). *Application deadline:* For fall admission, 7/1 priority date for domestic students, 5/1 for international students; for spring admission, 11/1 priority date for domestic students, 10/1 for international students. Application fee: $30. *Expenses:* Tuition, state resident: full-time $9794; part-time $408.10 per credit hour. Tuition, nonresident: full-time $22,383; part-time $932.61 per credit hour. *Required fees:* $2047; $85.29 per credit hour. Tuition and fees vary according to course load and program. *Financial support:* In 2014–15, 35 students received support, including 1 research assistantship (averaging $2,340 per year); teaching assistantships, Federal Work-Study, and tuition waivers (partial) also available. Support available to part-time students. Financial award application deadline: 4/1; financial award applicants required to submit FAFSA. *Faculty research:* Performance measures, costing, and inventory issues in logistics and supply chain management; inter-organizational systems; international management and marketing practices; e-commerce; organizational learning and socialization processes. *Total annual research expenditures:* $3,750. *Application contact:* Cheryl Campbell, Graduate Advisor, 904-620-2575, Fax: 904-620-2832, E-mail: coggin.students@unf.edu. Website: http://www.unf.edu/graduateschool/academics/programs/MBA.aspx.

University of Oklahoma, College of Architecture, Division of Construction Administration, Norman, OK 73019. Offers MS. Part-time and evening/weekend programs available. *Faculty:* 1 full-time (0 women). *Students:* 1 full-time (0 women), 1 part-time (0 women), 1 international. Average age 33. 6 applicants, 33% accepted, 1 enrolled. In 2014, 4 master's awarded. Terminal master's awarded for partial completion of doctoral program. *Degree requirements:* For master's, final project or thesis. *Entrance requirements:* Additional exam requirements/recommendations for international students: Required—TOEFL (minimum score 79 iBT). *Application deadline:* For fall admission, 4/30 for domestic and international students. Application fee: $50 ($100 for international students). Electronic applications accepted. *Expenses:* Tuition, state resident: full-time $4394; part-time $183.10 per credit hour. Tuition, nonresident: full-time $16,970; part-time $707.10 per credit hour. *Required fees:* $2892; $109.95 per credit hour. $126.50 per semester. *Financial support:* In 2014–15, 2 students received support, including 2 research assistantships (averaging $10,372 per year); scholarships/grants and unspecified assistantships also available. Financial award application deadline: 6/1; financial award applicants required to submit FAFSA. *Faculty research:* Construction, safety, sustainability, earthen construction, education. *Unit head:* Tammy McCoen, Acting Associate Professor, 405-325-4131, E-mail: tammymccoen@ou.edu. *Application contact:* Lisa Holliday, Graduate Liaison, 405-325-9464, E-mail: lisaholliday@ou.edu.
Website: http://cns.ou.edu/.

University of Southern California, Graduate School, Viterbi School of Engineering, Sonny Astani Department of Civil Engineering, Los Angeles, CA 90089. Offers applied mechanics (MS); civil engineering (MS, PhD); computer-aided engineering (ME, Graduate Certificate); construction management (MCM); engineering technology commercialization (Graduate Certificate); environmental engineering (MS, PhD); environmental quality management (ME); structural design (ME); sustainable cities (Graduate Certificate); transportation systems (MS, Graduate Certificate); water and waste management (MS). Part-time and evening/weekend programs available. Terminal master's awarded for partial completion of doctoral program. *Degree requirements:* For master's, thesis optional; for doctorate, thesis/dissertation. *Entrance requirements:* For master's and doctorate, GRE General Test. Additional exam requirements/recommendations for international students: Recommended—TOEFL. Electronic applications accepted. *Faculty research:* Geotechnical engineering, transportation engineering, structural engineering, construction management, environmental engineering, water resources.

The University of Texas at Arlington, Graduate School, College of Engineering, Department of Civil Engineering, Arlington, TX 76019. Offers civil engineering (M Engr, MS, PhD); construction management (MCM). Part-time and evening/weekend programs available. Postbaccalaureate distance learning degree programs offered (minimal on-campus study). Terminal master's awarded for partial completion of doctoral program. *Degree requirements:* For master's, comprehensive exam, thesis (for some programs), oral and written exams; for doctorate, comprehensive exam, thesis/dissertation, oral and written defense of dissertation. *Entrance requirements:* For master's, GRE General Test, minimum GPA of 3.0 in last 60 hours of undergraduate course work; for doctorate, GRE General Test, minimum GPA of 3.5. Additional exam requirements/recommendations for international students: Required—TOEFL. Electronic applications accepted. *Faculty research:* Environmental and water resources structures, geotechnical, transportation.

The University of Texas at El Paso, Graduate School, College of Engineering, Department of Civil Engineering, El Paso, TX 79968-0001. Offers civil engineering (MS, PhD); construction management (MS, Certificate); environmental engineering (MEENE, MSENE). Part-time and evening/weekend programs available. *Degree requirements:* For master's, comprehensive exam, thesis optional; for doctorate, comprehensive exam, thesis/dissertation. *Entrance requirements:* For master's, GRE, minimum GPA of 3.0; for doctorate, GRE. Additional exam requirements/recommendations for international students: Required—TOEFL. Electronic applications accepted. *Faculty research:* Non-destructive testing for geotechnical and pavement applications, transportation systems, wastewater treatment systems, air quality, linear and non-linear modeling of structures, structural reliability.

University of Washington, Graduate School, College of Built Environments, Department of Construction Management, Seattle, WA 98195. Offers MSCM. Part-time and evening/weekend programs available. *Degree requirements:* For master's, thesis or alternative. *Entrance requirements:* For master's, GRE General Test, minimum GPA of 3.0. Additional exam requirements/recommendations for international students: Required—TOEFL. Electronic applications accepted. *Faculty research:* Business practices, delivery methods, materials, productivity.

Virginia Polytechnic Institute and State University, Graduate School, College of Architecture and Urban Studies, Blacksburg, VA 24061. Offers architecture (MS Arch); architecture and design research (PhD); building/construction science and management (MS); creative technologies (MFA); environmental design and planning (PhD); landscape architecture (MLA); planning, governance, and globalization (PhD); public administration (MPA); public administration/public affairs (PhD, Certificate); public and

international affairs (MPIA); urban and regional planning (MURP); MS/MA. *Accreditation:* ASLA (one or more programs are accredited). *Faculty:* 133 full-time (54 women), 2 part-time/adjunct (1 woman). *Students:* 316 full-time (166 women), 237 part-time (108 women); includes 104 minority (46 Black or African American, non-Hispanic/Latino; 1 American Indian or Alaska Native, non-Hispanic/Latino; 20 Asian, non-Hispanic/Latino; 21 Hispanic/Latino; 16 Two or more races, non-Hispanic/Latino), 108 international. Average age 32. 609 applicants, 50% accepted, 108 enrolled. In 2014, 155 master's, 29 doctorates awarded. *Degree requirements:* For master's, comprehensive exam (for some programs), thesis (for some programs); for doctorate, comprehensive exam (for some programs), thesis/dissertation (for some programs). *Entrance requirements:* For master's and doctorate, GRE/GMAT (may vary by department). Additional exam requirements/recommendations for international students: Required—TOEFL (minimum score 550 paper-based). *Application deadline:* For fall admission, 8/1 for domestic students, 4/1 for international students; for spring admission, 1/1 for domestic students, 9/1 for international students. Applications are processed on a rolling basis. Application fee: $75. Electronic applications accepted. *Expenses:* Tuition, state resident: full-time $11,656; part-time $647.50 per credit hour. Tuition, nonresident: full-time $23,351; part-time $1297.25 per credit hour. *Required fees:* $2533; $465.75 per semester. Tuition and fees vary according to course load, campus/location and program. *Financial support:* In 2014–15, 13 research assistantships with full tuition reimbursements (averaging $20,302 per year), 44 teaching assistantships with full tuition reimbursements (averaging $19,484 per year) were awarded. Financial award application deadline: 3/1; financial award applicants required to submit FAFSA. *Total annual research expenditures:* $3.2 million. *Unit head:* Dr. A. J. Davis, Dean, 540-231-6416, Fax: 540-231-6332, E-mail: davisa@vt.edu. *Application contact:* Christine Mattsson-Coon, Executive Assistant, 540-231-6416, Fax: 540-231-6332, E-mail: cmattsso@vt.edu.
Website: http://www.caus.vt.edu/.

Wentworth Institute of Technology, Construction Management Program, Boston, MA 02115-5998. Offers MS. Part-time and evening/weekend programs available. Postbaccalaureate distance learning degree programs offered (no on-campus study). *Faculty:* 8 full-time (3 women), 6 part-time/adjunct (2 women). *Students:* 82 part-time (15 women); includes 14 minority (3 Black or African American, non-Hispanic/Latino; 2 Asian, non-Hispanic/Latino; 4 Hispanic/Latino; 5 Two or more races, non-Hispanic/Latino). Average age 32. 102 applicants, 49% accepted, 50 enrolled. In 2014, 24 master's awarded. *Degree requirements:* For master's, thesis optional, Capstone. *Entrance requirements:* For master's, two recommendations from employer, current resume, bachelor's degree in construction management or a bachelor's degree with competencies in construction and a Statement of Purpose. Additional exam requirements/recommendations for international students: Required—TOEFL (minimum score 525 paper-based). *Application deadline:* For fall admission, 7/15 for domestic students, 5/1 for international students; for spring admission, 12/15 for domestic students. Applications are processed on a rolling basis. Application fee: $50. Electronic applications accepted. *Expenses:* Expenses: Contact institution. *Financial support:* Institutionally sponsored loans available. Financial award application deadline: 5/1; financial award applicants required to submit FAFSA. *Unit head:* Philip Hammond, Director of Graduate Programs, 617-989-4594, Fax: 617-989-4399, E-mail: hammondp1@wit.edu.
Website: http://www.wit.edu/ccev/mscm/.

Western Carolina University, Graduate School, Kimmel School of Construction Management and Technology, Department of Construction Management, Cullowhee, NC 28723. Offers MCM. Part-time and evening/weekend programs available. Postbaccalaureate distance learning degree programs offered. *Entrance requirements:* For master's, GRE or GMAT, appropriate undergraduate degree, resume, letters of recommendation, work experience. Additional exam requirements/recommendations for international students: Required—TOEFL (minimum score 550 paper-based; 79 iBT). *Faculty research:* Hazardous waste management, energy management and conservation, engineering materials, refrigeration and air conditioning systems.

Worcester Polytechnic Institute, Graduate Studies and Research, Department of Civil and Environmental Engineering, Worcester, MA 01609-2280. Offers civil and environmental engineering (Advanced Certificate, Graduate Certificate); civil engineering (ME, MS, PhD); construction project management (MS); environmental engineering (M Eng, MS); master builder (M Eng). Part-time and evening/weekend programs available. Postbaccalaureate distance learning degree programs offered (no on-campus study). *Faculty:* 27 full-time (1 woman), 24 part-time/adjunct (3 women). *Students:* 36 full-time (14 women), 13 part-time (5 women); includes 4 minority (1 Hispanic/Latino; 3 Two or more races, non-Hispanic/Latino), 20 international. 160 applicants, 65% accepted, 26 enrolled. In 2014, 30 master's, 1 doctorate awarded. *Degree requirements:* For master's, thesis optional; for doctorate, comprehensive exam, thesis/dissertation. *Entrance requirements:* For master's and doctorate, GRE (recommended), 3 letters of recommendation. Additional exam requirements/recommendations for international students: Required—TOEFL (minimum score 563 paper-based; 84 iBT), IELTS (minimum score 7). *Application deadline:* For fall admission, 1/1 priority date for domestic and international students; for spring admission, 10/1 priority date for domestic and international students. Applications are processed on a rolling basis. Application fee: $70. Electronic applications accepted. *Financial support:* Research assistantships, teaching assistantships, career-related internships or fieldwork, institutionally sponsored loans, scholarships/grants, and unspecified assistantships available. Financial award application deadline: 1/1; financial award applicants required to submit FAFSA. *Unit head:* Dr. Tahar El-Korchi, Interim Head, 508-831-5530, Fax: 508-831-5808, E-mail: tek@wpi.edu. *Application contact:* Dr. Rajib Mallick, Graduate Coordinator, 508-831-5530, Fax: 508-831-5808, E-mail: rajib@wpi.edu.
Website: http://www.wpi.edu/academics/cee.

Energy Management and Policy

American University of Armenia, Graduate Programs, Yerevan, Armenia. Offers business administration (MBA); computer and information science (MS), including business management, design and manufacturing, energy (ME, MS), industrial engineering and systems management; economics (MS); industrial engineering and systems management (ME), including business, computer aided design/manufacturing, energy (ME, MS), information technology; law (LL M); political science and international affairs (MPSIA); public health (MPH); teaching English as a foreign language (MA). Part-time and evening/weekend programs available. *Degree requirements:* For master's, thesis (for some programs), capstone/project. *Entrance requirements:* For master's, GRE, GMAT, or LSAT. Additional exam requirements/recommendations for international

students: Recommended—TOEFL (minimum score 79 iBT), IELTS (minimum score 6.5). *Faculty research:* Microfinance, finance (rural/development, international, corporate), firm life cycle theory, TESOL, language proficiency testing, public policy, administrative law, economic development, cryptography, artificial intelligence, energy efficiency/renewable energy, computer-aided design/manufacturing, health financing, tuberculosis control, mother/child health, preventive ophthalmology, post-earthquake psychopathological investigations, tobacco control, environmental health risk assessments.

Boston University, Graduate School of Arts and Sciences, Department of Earth and Environment, Boston, MA 02215. Offers earth sciences (MA, PhD); energy and

environmental analysis (MA); environmental remote sensing and GIS (MA); geography and environment (MA, PhD); global development policy (MA); international relations and environmental policy (MA). *Students:* 67 full-time (31 women), 5 part-time (2 women); includes 6 minority (4 Asian, non-Hispanic/Latino; 2 Hispanic/Latino), 19 international. Average age 29. 213 applicants, 34% accepted, 16 enrolled. In 2014, 1 master's, 4 doctorates awarded. *Degree requirements:* For master's, comprehensive exam (for some programs), thesis (for some programs); for doctorate, comprehensive exam, thesis/dissertation. *Entrance requirements:* For master's and doctorate, GRE, 3 letters of recommendation, official transcripts, personal statement. Additional exam requirements/recommendations for international students: Required—TOEFL (minimum score 550 paper-based; 84 iBT). *Application deadline:* For fall admission, 1/31 for domestic and international students; for winter admission, 11/1 for domestic and international students. Application fee: $80. Electronic applications accepted. *Expenses: Tuition:* Full-time $45,686; part-time $1428 per credit hour. *Required fees:* $660; $60 per semester. Tuition and fees vary according to program. *Financial support:* In 2014–15, 59 students received support, including 2 fellowships with full tuition reimbursements available (averaging $20,500 per year), 25 research assistantships with full tuition reimbursements available (averaging $20,500 per year), 19 teaching assistantships with full tuition reimbursements available (averaging $20,500 per year); Federal Work-Study, scholarships/grants, traineeships, and health care benefits also available. Financial award application deadline: 1/31. *Faculty research:* Biogeosciences, climate and surface processes; energy, environment and society; geographical sciences; geology, geochemistry and geophysics. *Unit head:* Curtis Woodcock, Chair, 617-353-5746, E-mail: curtis@bu.edu. *Application contact:* Nora Watson, Graduate Program Coordinator, 617-353-2529, Fax: 617-353-8399, E-mail: norala31@bu.edu.
Website: http://www.bu.edu/earth/.

Duke University, The Fuqua School of Business, The Duke MBA Cross Continent Program, Durham, NC 27708-0586. Offers business administration (MBA); energy and the environment (MBA); entrepreneurship and innovation (MBA); finance (MBA); health sector management (Certificate); marketing (MBA); strategy (MBA). *Faculty:* 89 full-time (16 women), 51 part-time/adjunct (10 women). *Students:* 223 full-time (73 women); includes 50 minority (9 Black or African American, non-Hispanic/Latino; 34 Asian, non-Hispanic/Latino; 6 Hispanic/Latino; 1 Native Hawaiian or other Pacific Islander, non-Hispanic/Latino), 57 international. Average age 31. In 2014, 115 master's awarded. *Degree requirements:* For master's, one foreign language. *Entrance requirements:* For master's, GMAT or GRE, transcripts, essays, resume, recommendation letters, interview. Additional exam requirements/recommendations for international students: Required—TOEFL, IELTS, PTE. *Application deadline:* For fall admission, 10/15 for domestic and international students; for winter admission, 2/11 for domestic and international students; for spring admission, 5/6 for domestic and international students; for summer admission, 6/3 for domestic and international students. Application fee: $225. Electronic applications accepted. *Expenses:* Expenses: Contact institution. *Financial support:* In 2014–15, 46 students received support. Institutionally sponsored loans and scholarships/grants available. Financial award applicants required to submit FAFSA. *Unit head:* John Gallagher, Associate Dean for Executive MBA Programs, 919-660-7641, E-mail: johng@duke.edu. *Application contact:* Liz Riley Hargrove, Associate Dean for Admissions, 919-660-7705, Fax: 919-681-8026, E-mail: admissions-info@fuqua.duke.edu.
Website: http://www.fuqua.duke.edu/programs/duke_mba/cross_continent/.

Duke University, The Fuqua School of Business, The Duke MBA Daytime Program, Durham, NC 27708-0586. Offers academic excellence in finance (Certificate); business administration (MBA); decision sciences (MBA); energy and environment (MBA); energy finance (MBA); entrepreneurship and innovation (MBA); finance (MBA); financial analysis (MBA); health sector management (Certificate); leadership and ethics (MBA); management (MBA); marketing (MBA); operations management (MBA); social entrepreneurship (MBA); strategy (MBA). *Faculty:* 89 full-time (16 women), 51 part-time/adjunct (10 women). *Students:* 889 full-time (295 women); includes 171 minority (28 Black or African American, non-Hispanic/Latino; 90 Asian, non-Hispanic/Latino; 45 Hispanic/Latino; 2 Native Hawaiian or other Pacific Islander, non-Hispanic/Latino; 6 Two or more races, non-Hispanic/Latino), 346 international. Average age 29. In 2014, 433 master's awarded. *Entrance requirements:* For master's, GMAT or GRE, transcripts, essays, resume, recommendation letters, interview. Additional exam requirements/recommendations for international students: Required—TOEFL, IELTS, PTE. *Application deadline:* For fall admission, 9/17 for domestic and international students; for winter admission, 10/20 for domestic and international students; for spring admission, 1/5 for domestic and international students; for summer admission, 3/19 for domestic and international students. Application fee: $225. Electronic applications accepted. *Expenses:* Expenses: $58,000 (first-year tuition). *Financial support:* In 2014–15, 373 students received support. Institutionally sponsored loans and scholarships/grants available. Financial award applicants required to submit FAFSA. *Unit head:* Russ Morgan, Associate Dean for the Daytime MBA Program, 919-660-2931, Fax: 919-684-8742, E-mail: ruskin.morgan@duke.edu. *Application contact:* Liz Riley Hargrove, Associate Dean for Admissions, 919-660-7705, Fax: 919-681-8026, E-mail: admissions-info@fuqua.duke.edu.
Website: http://www.fuqua.duke.edu/daytime-mba/.

Duke University, The Fuqua School of Business, The Duke MBA Global Executive Program, Durham, NC 27708-0586. Offers business administration (MBA); energy and the environment (MBA); entrepreneurship and innovation (MBA); finance (MBA); health sector management (Certificate); marketing (MBA); strategy (MBA). *Faculty:* 89 full-time (16 women), 51 part-time/adjunct (10 women). *Students:* 36 full-time (6 women); includes 9 minority (3 Black or African American, non-Hispanic/Latino; 4 Asian, non-Hispanic/Latino; 2 Hispanic/Latino), 9 international. Average age 40. In 2014, 49 master's awarded. *Entrance requirements:* For master's, transcripts, essays, resume, recommendation letters, interview. Additional exam requirements/recommendations for international students: Required—TOEFL, IELTS, PTE. *Application deadline:* For fall admission, 9/3 for domestic and international students; for winter admission, 10/15 for domestic and international students; for spring admission, 12/2 for domestic and international students; for summer admission, 1/12 for domestic and international students. Application fee: $225. Electronic applications accepted. *Expenses:* Expenses: Contact institution. *Financial support:* In 2014–15, 10 students received support. Institutionally sponsored loans and scholarships/grants available. Financial award applicants required to submit FAFSA. *Unit head:* John Gallagher, Associate Dean for Executive MBA Programs, 919-660-7728, E-mail: johng@duke.edu. *Application contact:* Liz Riley Hargrove, Associate Dean for Admissions, 919-660-7705, Fax: 919-681-8026, E-mail: admissions-info@fuqua.duke.edu.
Website: http://www.fuqua.duke.edu/programs/duke_mba/global-executive/.

Duke University, The Fuqua School of Business, Weekend Executive MBA Program, Durham, NC 27708-0586. Offers business administration (MBA); energy and environment (MBA); entrepreneurship and innovation (MBA); finance (MBA); health sector management (Certificate); marketing (MBA); strategy (MBA). *Faculty:* 89 full-time (16 women), 51 part-time/adjunct (10 women). *Students:* 181 full-time (28 women); includes 70 minority (10 Black or African American, non-Hispanic/Latino; 50 Asian, non-Hispanic/Latino; 9 Hispanic/Latino; 1 Two or more races, non-Hispanic/Latino), 33 international. Average age 36. In 2014, 93 master's awarded. *Degree requirements:* For master's, one foreign language. *Entrance requirements:* For master's, GMAT or GRE, waiver available, transcripts, essays, resume, recommendation letters, interview. Additional exam requirements/recommendations for international students: Required—TOEFL, IELTS, PTE. *Application deadline:* For fall admission, 9/3 for domestic and international students; for winter admission, 10/15 for domestic and international students; for spring admission, 2/11 for domestic and international students; for summer admission, 4/1 for domestic and international students. Application fee: $225. Electronic applications accepted. *Expenses:* Expenses: Contact institution. *Financial support:* In 2014–15, 13 students received support. Institutionally sponsored loans and scholarships/grants available. Financial award applicants required to submit FAFSA. *Unit head:* John Gallagher, Associate Dean for Executive MBA Programs, 919-660-7728, E-mail: johng@duke.edu. *Application contact:* Liz Riley Hargrove, Associate Dean for Admissions, 919-660-7705, Fax: 919-681-8026, E-mail: admissions-info@fuqua.duke.edu.
Website: http://www.fuqua.duke.edu/programs/duke_mba/weekend_executive/.

Eastern Illinois University, Graduate School, Lumpkin College of Business and Applied Sciences, School of Technology, Program in Sustainable Energy, Charleston, IL 61920. Offers MS, MS/MBA, MS/MS. Part-time and evening/weekend programs available. *Faculty:* 28. *Students:* 14 full-time (4 women), 2 part-time (both women), 13 international. Average age 27. 31 applicants, 65% accepted, 11 enrolled. In 2014, 4 master's awarded. *Degree requirements:* For master's, comprehensive exam. *Entrance requirements:* For master's, GMAT or GRE. Additional exam requirements/recommendations for international students: Required—TOEFL (minimum score 500 paper-based; 61 iBT), IELTS (minimum score 6). *Application deadline:* For fall admission, 5/15 for domestic and international students; for spring admission, 10/15 for domestic and international students. Applications are processed on a rolling basis. Application fee: $30. Electronic applications accepted. *Expenses:* Tuition, state resident: full-time $3113; part-time $283 per credit hour. Tuition, nonresident: full-time $7469; part-time $679 per credit hour. *Required fees:* $2287; $96 per credit hour. Tuition and fees vary according to course load. *Financial support:* In 2014–15, 18 students received support, including 5 research assistantships with full tuition reimbursements available (averaging $7,830 per year); career-related internships or fieldwork, Federal Work-Study, and unspecified assistantships also available. Support available to part-time students. Financial award application deadline: 3/1; financial award applicants required to submit FAFSA. *Unit head:* Peter Ping Liu, Graduate Coordinator, 217-581-6267, Fax: 217-581-6607, E-mail: pliu@eiu.edu.
Website: http://www.eiu.edu/sustainable/.

Franklin Pierce University, Graduate and Professional Studies, Rindge, NH 03461-0060. Offers curriculum and instruction (M Ed); emerging network technologies (Graduate Certificate); energy and sustainability studies (MBA); health administration (MBA, Graduate Certificate); human resource management (MBA, Graduate Certificate); information technology (MBA); information technology management (MS); leadership (MBA); nursing (MS); physical therapy (DPT); physician assistant studies (MPAS); special education (M Ed); sports management (MBA). *Accreditation:* APTA. Part-time programs available. Postbaccalaureate distance learning degree programs offered (no on-campus study). *Faculty:* 18 full-time (11 women), 96 part-time/adjunct (57 women). *Students:* 357 full-time (207 women), 185 part-time (123 women); includes 31 minority (9 Black or African American, non-Hispanic/Latino; 4 American Indian or Alaska Native, non-Hispanic/Latino; 17 Asian, non-Hispanic/Latino; 1 Native Hawaiian or other Pacific Islander, non-Hispanic/Latino), 19 international. Average age 38. In 2014, 118 master's, 66 doctorates awarded. *Degree requirements:* For master's, concentrated original research projects; student teaching; fieldwork and/or internship; leadership project; PRAXIS I and II (for M Ed); for doctorate, concentrated original research projects, clinical fieldwork and/or internship, leadership project. *Entrance requirements:* For master's, minimum GPA of 2.5, 3 letters of recommendation; competencies in accounting, economics, statistics, and computer skills through life experience or undergraduate coursework (for MBA); certification/e-portfolio, minimum C grade in all education courses (for M Ed); license to practice as RN (for MS in nursing); for doctorate, GRE, BA/BS, 3 letters of recommendation, personal mission statement, interview, writing sample, minimum cumulative GPA of 2.8, master's degree (for DA); 80 hours of observation/work in PT settings, completion of anatomy, chemistry, physics, and statistics, minimum GPA of 3.0 (for DPT). Additional exam requirements/recommendations for international students: Required—TOEFL (minimum score 550 paper-based; 61 iBT). *Application deadline:* Applications are processed on a rolling basis. Application fee: $0. Electronic applications accepted. *Expenses: Tuition:* Part-time $645 per credit. *Required fees:* $100 per term. One-time fee: $200 part-time. Tuition and fees vary according to degree level and program. *Financial support:* In 2014–15, 125 students received support, including 32 teaching assistantships with full and partial tuition reimbursements available (averaging $8,000 per year); career-related internships or fieldwork and unspecified assistantships also available. Support available to part-time students. Financial award applicants required to submit FAFSA. *Faculty research:* Evidence-based practice in sports physical therapy, human resource management in economic crisis, leadership in nursing, innovation in sports facility management, differentiated learning and understanding by design. *Unit head:* Dr. Maria Altobello, Interim Dean of Graduate and Professional Studies, 603-647-3530, Fax: 603-229-4580, E-mail: altobellom@franklinpierce.edu. *Application contact:* Graduate Studies, 800-437-0048, Fax: 603-626-4815, E-mail: cgps@franklinpierce.edu.
Website: http://www.franklinpierce.edu/academics/gradstudies/index.htm.

George Mason University, College of Humanities and Social Sciences, Interdisciplinary Studies Program, Fairfax, VA 22030. Offers community college teaching (MAIS); computational social science (MAIS); energy and sustainability (MAIS); film and video studies (MAIS); folklore studies (MAIS); higher education administration (MAIS); neuroethics (MAIS); religion, culture and values (MAIS); social entrepreneurship (MAIS); war and military in society (MAIS); women and gender studies (MAIS). *Faculty:* 11 full-time (3 women), 4 part-time/adjunct (all women). *Students:* 22 full-time (3 women), 87 part-time (51 women); includes 31 minority (21 Black or African American, non-Hispanic/Latino; 2 Asian, non-Hispanic/Latino; 6 Hispanic/Latino; 2 Two or more races, non-Hispanic/Latino), 6 international. Average age 32. 75 applicants, 75% accepted, 28 enrolled. In 2014, 31 master's awarded. *Degree requirements:* For master's, project or thesis. *Entrance requirements:* For master's, 3 letters of recommendation; writing sample; official transcript; resume. Additional exam requirements/recommendations for international students: Required—TOEFL (minimum score 570 paper-based; 80 iBT), IELTS (minimum score 6.5), PTE. *Application deadline:* For fall admission, 3/1 priority date for domestic students; for spring admission, 10/15 for domestic students. Application fee: $65 ($80 for international students). Electronic applications accepted. *Expenses:* Tuition, state resident: full-time $9794; part-time $408 per credit hour. Tuition, nonresident: full-time $26,978; part-time $1124 per credit hour. *Required fees:* $2820; $118 per credit hour. Tuition and fees vary according to course load and program. *Financial support:* In 2014–15, 10 students received support, including 1 fellowship (averaging $6,935 per year), 2 research assistantships with full and partial tuition reimbursements available (averaging $6,499 per year), 8 teaching assistantships with full and partial tuition reimbursements available (averaging $8,271 per year); career-related internships or fieldwork, Federal Work-Study, scholarships/

grants, unspecified assistantships, and health care benefits (for full-time research or teaching assistantship recipients) also available. Support available to part-time students. Financial award application deadline: 3/1; financial award applicants required to submit FAFSA. *Faculty research:* Combined English and folklore, religious and cultural studies (Christianity and Muslim society). *Unit head:* Meredith H. Lair, Director, 703-993-2159, Fax: 703-993-1251, E-mail: mlair@gmu.edu. *Application contact:* Lisa Struckmeyer, Administrative Coordinator, 703-993-8762, Fax: 703-993-5585, E-mail: lstruckm@gmu.edu.
Website: http://mais.gmu.edu.

Holy Names University, Graduate Division, Department of Business, Oakland, CA 94619-1699. Offers energy and environment management (MBA); finance (MBA); management and leadership (MBA); marketing (MBA); sports management (MBA). Part-time and evening/weekend programs available. *Faculty:* 8. *Students:* 18 full-time (12 women), 18 part-time (6 women); includes 23 minority (9 Black or African American, non-Hispanic/Latino; 6 Asian, non-Hispanic/Latino; 7 Hispanic/Latino; 1 Two or more races, non-Hispanic/Latino), 7 international. Average age 31. 37 applicants, 51% accepted, 12 enrolled. In 2014, 26 master's awarded. *Entrance requirements:* For master's, minimum undergraduate GPA of 2.6 overall, 3.0 in major; two recommendations (letter or form) from previous professors or current or previous work supervisors; 1-3 page personal statement; resume. Additional exam requirements/recommendations for international students: Required—TOEFL (minimum score 550 paper-based; 79 iBT). *Application deadline:* For fall admission, 8/1 priority date for domestic students, 7/15 for international students; for spring admission, 12/1 priority date for domestic students, 12/1 for international students; for summer admission, 5/1 priority date for domestic students, 5/1 for international students. Applications are processed on a rolling basis. Application fee: $65. Electronic applications accepted. Application fee is waived when completed online. *Financial support:* Career-related internships or fieldwork, Federal Work-Study, scholarships/grants, and unspecified assistantships available. Support available to part-time students. Financial award application deadline: 3/2; financial award applicants required to submit FAFSA. *Faculty research:* Business ethics, sustainable economics, accounting models, cross-cultural management, diversity in organizations. *Unit head:* Russell Jacobus, MBA Program Director, 510-436-1622, E-mail: jacobus@hnu.edu. *Application contact:* 800-430-1321, Fax: 510-436-1325, E-mail: graduateadmissions@hnu.edu.
Website: http://www.hnu.edu.

Indiana University Bloomington, School of Public and Environmental Affairs, Environmental Science Programs, Bloomington, IN 47405. Offers applied ecology (MSES); energy (MSES); environmental chemistry, toxicology, and risk assessment (MSES); environmental science (PhD); hazardous materials management (Certificate); specialized environmental science (MSES); water resources (MSES); JD/MSES; MSES/MA; MSES/MPA; MSES/MS. Part-time programs available. Terminal master's awarded for partial completion of doctoral program. *Degree requirements:* For master's, capstone or thesis; internship; for doctorate, comprehensive exam, thesis/dissertation. *Entrance requirements:* For master's, GRE General Test or GMAT, official transcripts, 3 letters of recommendation, resume, personal statement; for doctorate, GRE General Test or LSAT, official transcripts, 3 letters of recommendation, resume or curriculum vitae, statement of purpose. Additional exam requirements/recommendations for international students: Required—TOEFL (minimum score 600 paper-based; 96 iBT); Recommended—IELTS (minimum score 7). Electronic applications accepted. *Faculty research:* Applied ecology, bio-geochemistry, toxicology, wetlands ecology, environmental microbiology, forest ecology, environmental chemistry.

Indiana University Bloomington, School of Public and Environmental Affairs, Public Affairs Programs, Bloomington, IN 47405. Offers economic development (MPA); energy (MPA); environmental policy (PhD); environmental policy and natural resource management (MPA); information systems (MPA); international development (MPA); local government management (MPA); nonprofit management (MPA, Certificate); policy analysis (MPA); public budgeting and financial management (Certificate); public finance (PhD); public financial administration (MPA); public management (MPA, PhD, Certificate); public policy analysis (PhD); social entrepreneurship (Certificate); specialized public affairs (MPA); sustainability and sustainable development (MPA); JD/MPA; MPA/MA; MPA/MIS; MPA/MLS; MSES/MPA. *Accreditation:* NASPAA (one or more programs are accredited). Part-time programs available. *Degree requirements:* For master's, capstone, internship; for doctorate, comprehensive exam, thesis/dissertation. *Entrance requirements:* For master's, GRE General Test or GMAT, official transcripts, 3 letters of recommendation, resume, personal statement; for doctorate, GRE General Test, official transcripts, 3 letters of recommendation, statement of purpose. Additional exam requirements/recommendations for international students: Required—TOEFL (minimum score 600 paper-based; 96 iBT); Recommended—IELTS (minimum score 7). Electronic applications accepted. *Faculty research:* International development, environmental policy and resource management, policy analysis, public finance, public management, urban management, nonprofit management, energy policy, social policy, public finance.

Instituto Tecnologico de Santo Domingo, Graduate School, Area of Basic And Environmental Sciences, Santo Domingo, Dominican Republic. Offers environmental science (M En S), including environmental education, environmental management, marine resources, natural resources management; mathematics (MS, PhD); renewable energy technology (MS, Certificate).

Johns Hopkins University, Zanvyl Krieger School of Arts and Sciences, Advanced Academic Programs, Program in Environmental Sciences and Policy, Washington, DC 20036. Offers energy policy and climate (MS); environmental sciences (MS); geographic information systems (MS, Certificate). Part-time and evening/weekend programs available. Postbaccalaureate distance learning degree programs offered (minimal on-campus study). *Degree requirements:* For master's, thesis (for some programs). *Entrance requirements:* For master's, minimum GPA of 3.0, coursework in chemistry and calculus. Additional exam requirements/recommendations for international students: Required—TOEFL (minimum score 100 iBT). Electronic applications accepted.

Kansas State University, Graduate School, College of Engineering, Department of Electrical and Computer Engineering, Manhattan, KS 66506. Offers electrical engineering (MS), including bioengineering, communication systems, design of computer systems, electrical engineering, energy and power systems, integrated circuits and devices, real time embedded systems, renewable energy, signal processing. Part-time and evening/weekend programs available. Postbaccalaureate distance learning degree programs offered (no on-campus study). *Faculty:* 21 full-time (4 women), 1 (woman) part-time/adjunct. *Students:* 38 full-time (8 women), 45 part-time (6 women); includes 13 minority (4 Black or African American, non-Hispanic/Latino; 8 Asian, non-Hispanic/Latino; 1 Hispanic/Latino), 37 international. Average age 28. 126 applicants, 29% accepted, 14 enrolled. In 2014, 22 master's, 5 doctorates awarded. *Degree requirements:* For master's, thesis or alternative, final exam; for doctorate, thesis/dissertation, final exam, preliminary exams. *Entrance requirements:* For master's, GRE General Test, bachelor's degree in electrical engineering or computer science, minimum GPA of 3.0; for doctorate, GRE General Test. Additional exam requirements/recommendations for international students: Required—TOEFL (minimum score 600

paper-based; 85 iBT). *Application deadline:* For fall admission, 1/1 priority date for domestic and international students; for spring admission, 8/1 priority date for domestic and international students. Applications are processed on a rolling basis. Application fee: $50 ($75 for international students). Electronic applications accepted. *Financial support:* In 2014–15, 40 students received support, including 22 research assistantships with tuition reimbursements available (averaging $12,100 per year), 18 teaching assistantships with full tuition reimbursements available (averaging $12,220 per year); career-related internships or fieldwork, institutionally sponsored loans, and scholarships/grants also available. Support available to part-time students. Financial award application deadline: 3/1; financial award applicants required to submit FAFSA. *Faculty research:* Energy systems and renewable energy, computer systems and real time embedded systems, communication systems and signal processing, integrated circuits and devices, bioengineering. *Total annual research expenditures:* $1.3 million. *Unit head:* Dr. Don Gruenbacher, Head, 785-532-5600, Fax: 785-532-1188, E-mail: grue@k-state.edu. *Application contact:* Dr. Andrew Rys, Graduate Program Director, 785-532-4665, Fax: 785-532-1188, E-mail: andrys@k-state.edu.
Website: http://www.ece.k-state.edu/.

Michigan Technological University, Graduate School, College of Sciences and Arts, Department of Social Sciences, Houghton, MI 49931. Offers environmental and energy policy (MS, PhD); industrial archaeology (MS); industrial heritage and archeology (PhD). Part-time programs available. *Faculty:* 29 full-time (12 women), 13 part-time/adjunct (4 women). *Students:* 29 full-time (14 women), 18 part-time (6 women); includes 8 minority (1 Black or African American, non-Hispanic/Latino; 1 American Indian or Alaska Native, non-Hispanic/Latino; 4 Asian, non-Hispanic/Latino; 1 Hispanic/Latino; 1 Two or more races, non-Hispanic/Latino), 10 international. Average age 33. 57 applicants, 32% accepted, 10 enrolled. In 2014, 9 master's awarded. Terminal master's awarded for partial completion of doctoral program. *Degree requirements:* For master's, comprehensive exam (for some programs), thesis (for some programs); for doctorate, comprehensive exam, thesis/dissertation. *Entrance requirements:* For master's and doctorate, GRE, statement of purpose, official transcripts, 3 letters of recommendation, writing sample, resume/curriculum vitae. Additional exam requirements/recommendations for international students: Required—TOEFL (recommended score 100 iBT) or IELTS. *Application deadline:* For fall admission, 2/1 priority date for domestic and international students. Applications are processed on a rolling basis. Electronic applications accepted. *Expenses:* Tuition, state resident: full-time $14,769; part-time $820.50 per credit. Tuition, nonresident: full-time $14,769; part-time $820.50 per credit. *Required fees:* $248; $248 per year. Tuition and fees vary according to course load and program. *Financial support:* In 2014–15, 35 students received support, including 3 fellowships with full and partial tuition reimbursements available (averaging $13,824 per year), 10 research assistantships with full and partial tuition reimbursements available (averaging $13,824 per year), 12 teaching assistantships with full and partial tuition reimbursements available (averaging $13,824 per year); career-related internships or fieldwork, Federal Work-Study, scholarships/grants, health care benefits, unspecified assistantships, and cooperative program also available. Financial award applicants required to submit FAFSA. *Faculty research:* Industrial archeology of early American industry, mining history, environmental and energy policy, land-use policy, environmental decision-making. *Total annual research expenditures:* $746,653. *Unit head:* Dr. Patrick E. Martin, Chair, 906-487-2070, Fax: 906-487-2284, E-mail: pemartin@mtu.edu. *Application contact:* Amy Spahn, Office Assistant, 906-487-2113, Fax: 906-487-2284, E-mail: gradadms@mtu.edu.
Website: http://www.social.mtu.edu/.

New York Institute of Technology, School of Engineering and Computing Sciences, Department of Energy Management, Old Westbury, NY 11568-8000. Offers energy management (MS); energy technology (Advanced Certificate); environmental management (Advanced Certificate); facilities management (Advanced Certificate); infrastructure security management (Advanced Certificate). Part-time and evening/weekend programs available. Postbaccalaureate distance learning degree programs offered (minimal on-campus study). *Degree requirements:* For master's, comprehensive exam, thesis or alternative. *Entrance requirements:* For master's, minimum QPA of 2.85. Additional exam requirements/recommendations for international students: Required—TOEFL (minimum score 550 paper-based; 79 iBT), IELTS (minimum score 6). Electronic applications accepted.

New York University, School of Continuing and Professional Studies, Center for Global Affairs, New York, NY 10012-1019. Offers global affairs (MS), including environment/energy policy, human rights and international law, international development and humanitarian assistance, international relations, peace building, private sector, transnational security; global energy (Advanced Certificate); peacebuilding (Advanced Certificate); transnational security (Advanced Certificate). Part-time and evening/weekend programs available. *Faculty:* 11 full-time (6 women), 32 part-time/adjunct (14 women). *Students:* 156 full-time (105 women), 136 part-time (86 women); includes 79 minority (24 Black or African American, non-Hispanic/Latino; 17 Asian, non-Hispanic/Latino; 37 Hispanic/Latino; 1 Two or more races, non-Hispanic/Latino), 66 international. Average age 28. 357 applicants, 72% accepted, 98 enrolled. In 2014, 144 master's awarded. *Degree requirements:* For master's, thesis. *Entrance requirements:* For master's, GRE or GMAT only upon request, bachelor's degree, resume with relevant professional work, internship or volunteer experience, two letters of recommendation, statement of purpose. Additional exam requirements/recommendations for international students: Required—TOEFL (minimum score 600 paper-based; 100 iBT), IELTS (minimum score 7). *Application deadline:* For fall admission, 2/1 priority date for domestic and international students; for spring admission, 10/15 priority date for domestic students, 8/15 priority date for international students. Applications are processed on a rolling basis. Application fee: $150. Electronic applications accepted. *Financial support:* In 2014–15, 99 students received support, including 95 fellowships (averaging $2,218 per year); Federal Work-Study and scholarships/grants also available. Support available to part-time students. Financial award application deadline: 4/1; financial award applicants required to submit FAFSA. *Unit head:* Vera Jelinek, Divisional Dean and Clinical Associate Professor, 212-992-8380. *Application contact:* Office of Admissions, 212-998-7100, E-mail: sps.gradadmissions@nyu.edu.
Website: http://www.sps.nyu.edu/academics/departments/global-affairs.html.

Oklahoma Baptist University, Program in Business Administration, Shawnee, OK 74804. Offers business administration (MBA); energy management (MBA). *Accreditation:* ACBSP. Postbaccalaureate distance learning degree programs offered (no on-campus study).

Oklahoma City University, Meinders School of Business, Program in Energy Legal Studies, Oklahoma City, OK 73106-1402. Offers MS. Part-time and evening/weekend programs available. Postbaccalaureate distance learning degree programs offered (no on-campus study). *Faculty:* 5 full-time (1 woman), 2 part-time/adjunct (1 woman). *Students:* 2 full-time (1 woman), 58 part-time (25 women); includes 11 minority (3 American Indian or Alaska Native, non-Hispanic/Latino; 2 Asian, non-Hispanic/Latino; 3 Hispanic/Latino; 3 Two or more races, non-Hispanic/Latino). Average age 32. 17 applicants, 100% accepted, 17 enrolled. In 2014, 18 master's awarded. *Entrance requirements:* For master's, GRE/GMAT, bachelor's degree from accredited institution, minimum GPA of 3.0, essay, recommendation letters, professional resume. Additional exam requirements/recommendations for international students: Required—TOEFL (minimum score 550 paper-based; 80 iBT). *Application deadline:* Applications are processed on a rolling basis. Application fee: $50. Electronic applications accepted. *Expenses: Tuition:* Part-time $936 per credit hour. *Required fees:* $115 per credit hour. One-time fee: $250. Tuition and fees vary according to course load, degree level, program and student's religious affiliation. *Financial support:* In 2014–15, 60 students received support. Career-related internships or fieldwork, Federal Work-Study, institutionally sponsored loans, scholarships/grants, and tuition waivers available. Support available to part-time students. Financial award applicants required to submit FAFSA. *Unit head:* Dr. Steve Agee, Dean, 405-208-5275, Fax: 405-208-5008, E-mail: sagee@okcu.edu. *Application contact:* Michael Harrington, Director of Graduate Admission, 800-633-7242, Fax: 405-208-5356, E-mail: gadmissions@okcu.edu.

Oklahoma City University, Meinders School of Business, Program in Energy Management, Oklahoma City, OK 73106-1402. Offers MS. Part-time and evening/weekend programs available. Postbaccalaureate distance learning degree programs offered (no on-campus study). *Faculty:* 5 full-time (1 woman), 2 part-time/adjunct (1 woman). *Students:* 4 full-time (0 women), 65 part-time (10 women); includes 8 minority (3 Black or African American, non-Hispanic/Latino; 2 Asian, non-Hispanic/Latino; 3 Hispanic/Latino). Average age 33. 36 applicants, 86% accepted, 20 enrolled. In 2014, 12 master's awarded. *Entrance requirements:* For master's, GRE/GMAT, bachelor's degree from accredited institution, minimum GPA of 3.0, essay, recommendation letters, resume. Additional exam requirements/recommendations for international students: Required—TOEFL (minimum score 550 paper-based; 80 iBT). *Application deadline:* Applications are processed on a rolling basis. Application fee: $50. Electronic applications accepted. *Expenses: Tuition:* Part-time $936 per credit hour. *Required fees:* $115 per credit hour. One-time fee: $250. Tuition and fees vary according to course load, degree level, program and student's religious affiliation. *Financial support:* In 2014–15, 67 students received support. Career-related internships or fieldwork, Federal Work-Study, institutionally sponsored loans, scholarships/grants, and tuition waivers available. Support available to part-time students. Financial award applicants required to submit FAFSA. *Unit head:* Dr. Steve Agee, Dean, 405-208-5275, Fax: 405-208-5008, E-mail: sagee@okcu.edu. *Application contact:* Michael Harrington, Director, Graduate Admissions, 800-633-7242, Fax: 405-208-5356, E-mail: gadmissions@okcu.edu.

Samford University, Howard College of Arts and Sciences, Birmingham, AL 35229. Offers energy management and policy (MSEM); JD/MSEM. Part-time and evening/weekend programs available. *Faculty:* 8 full-time (2 women), 4 part-time/adjunct (0 women). *Students:* 23 full-time (7 women); 4 part-time (2 women); includes 5 minority (all Black or African American, non-Hispanic/Latino), 15 international. Average age 27. 20 applicants, 80% accepted, 11 enrolled. In 2014, 33 master's awarded. *Entrance requirements:* For master's, GRE General Test (minimum score 295 combined) or MAT (minimum score 396), minimum GPA of 2.5 with 3 years of work experience or 3.0 for a recent college graduate. Additional exam requirements/recommendations for international students: Required—TOEFL (minimum score 90 iBT); Recommended—IELTS (minimum score 6.5). *Application deadline:* For fall admission, 8/1 for domestic and international students; for winter admission, 12/1 for domestic and international students; for spring admission, 12/1 for domestic and international students; for summer admission, 5/1 for domestic and international students. Applications are processed on a rolling basis. Application fee: $35. *Expenses: Tuition:* Full-time $11,904; part-time $744 per credit hour. *Required fees:* $500. Tuition and fees vary according to course load, degree level and student level. *Financial support:* In 2014–15, 2 students received support. Application deadline: 3/1; applicants required to submit FAFSA. *Faculty research:* Mosquito fish as an environmental model for pollutants, PCB contamination, environmental epidemiology and toxicology, geographic information systems, geology and natural resource management, energy management, chemical and biological analysis of water, aquatic biomonitoring. *Application contact:* Dr. Ronald N. Hunsinger, Professor/Chair, Biological and Environmental Sciences, 205-726-2944, Fax: 205-726-2479, E-mail: rnhunsin@samford.edu.
Website: http://howard.samford.edu/.

Santa Clara University, School of Engineering, Santa Clara, CA 95053. Offers analog circuit design (Certificate); applied mathematics (MS); ASIC design and test (Certificate); bioengineering (MS); civil engineering (MS); computer science and engineering (MS, PhD); controls (Certificate); digital signal processing (Certificate); dynamics (Certificate); electrical engineering (MS, PhD); engineering (Engineer); engineering management (MS); fundamentals of electrical engineering (Certificate); information assurance (Certificate); materials engineering (Certificate); mechanical design analysis (Certificate); mechanical engineering (MS, PhD); mechatronics systems engineering (Certificate); microwave and antennas (Certificate); networking (Certificate); renewable energy (Certificate); software engineering (Certificate); sustainable energy (MS); technology jump-start (Certificate); thermofluids (Certificate). Part-time and evening/weekend programs available. *Faculty:* 59 full-time (23 women), 80 part-time/adjunct (14 women). *Students:* 584 full-time (239 women), 353 part-time (102 women); includes 224 minority (7 Black or African American, non-Hispanic/Latino; 144 Asian, non-Hispanic/Latino; 50 Hispanic/Latino; 2 Native Hawaiian or other Pacific Islander, non-Hispanic/Latino; 21 Two or more races, non-Hispanic/Latino), 548 international. Average age 27. 1,248 applicants, 51% accepted, 375 enrolled. In 2014, 283 master's, 5 doctorates, 1 other advanced degree awarded. *Degree requirements:* For master's, thesis (for some programs); for doctorate, thesis/dissertation; for other advanced degree, thesis. *Entrance requirements:* For master's, GRE, transcript; for doctorate, GRE, master's degree or equivalent; for other advanced degree, master's degree, published paper. Additional exam requirements/recommendations for international students: Required—TOEFL (minimum score 550 paper-based; 79 iBT). *Application deadline:* For fall admission, 8/1 for domestic students, 7/15 for international students; for winter admission, 10/28 for domestic students, 9/23 for international students; for spring admission, 2/25 for domestic students, 1/21 for international students. Applications are processed on a rolling basis. Application fee: $60. Electronic applications accepted. *Expenses:* Expenses: Contact institution. *Financial support:* In 2014–15, 94 students received support. Fellowships with full and partial tuition reimbursements available, research assistantships with full and partial tuition reimbursements available, teaching assistantships with full tuition reimbursements available, career-related internships or fieldwork, Federal Work-Study, institutionally sponsored loans, and scholarships/grants available. Support available to part-time students. Financial award application deadline: 3/2; financial award applicants required to submit FAFSA. *Faculty research:* Video encoding, nanostructures, robotics, microfluidics, water resources. *Total annual research expenditures:* $1.6 million. *Unit head:* Dr. Alex Zecevic, Associate Dean for Graduate Studies, 408-554-2394, E-mail: azecevic@scu.edu. *Application contact:* Stacey Tinker, Director of Enrollment Management, 408-554-4748, Fax: 408-554-4323, E-mail: stinker@scu.edu.
Website: http://www.scu.edu/engineering/graduate/.

Texas Christian University, Neeley School of Business, MBA for Energy Professionals Program, Fort Worth, TX 76129-0002. Offers MBA. Part-time and evening/weekend programs available. *Students:* 44 full-time (10 women), 4 part-time (2 women); includes 7 minority (all Hispanic/Latino), 2 international. Average age 30. 47 applicants, 96% accepted, 36 enrolled. *Degree requirements:* For master's, comprehensive exam. *Entrance requirements:* For master's, GMAT, minimum of 3 years' work experience in field. Additional exam requirements/recommendations for international students: Required—TOEFL (minimum score 100 iBT); Recommended—IELTS. *Application deadline:* For fall admission, 11/1 priority date for domestic and international students; for winter admission, 1/15 priority date for domestic and international students; for spring admission, 3/1 priority date for domestic students, 3/1 for international students; for summer admission, 4/15 for domestic students, 4/14 for international students. Application fee: $100. Application fee is waived when completed online. *Expenses: Tuition:* Full-time $22,860; part-time $1270 per credit hour. *Unit head:* Ann Bluntzer, Director of Specialized Graduate Programs, 817-257-4643, Fax: 817-257-6431, E-mail: a.bluntzer@tcu.edu. *Application contact:* Anita Unger, Admissions, TCU Graduate Studies Office, 817-257-7515, Fax: 817-257-7484, E-mail: frogmail@tcu.edu.
Website: http://www.neeley.tcu.edu/energymba/.

Tulane University, A. B. Freeman School of Business, New Orleans, LA 70118-5669. Offers analytics (MBA); banking and financial services (M Fin); energy (M Acct, M Fin, MBA); entrepreneurship (MBA); finance (MBA, PhD); finance supporting (M Acct); international business (MBA); international management (MBA); management (MMG); marketing (MBA); strategic management and leadership (MBA); the business of energy (MME); JD/M Acct; JD/MBA; MBA/M Acc; MBA/MA; MBA/MD; MBA/ME; MBA/MPH. *Accreditation:* AACSB. Part-time and evening/weekend programs available. *Faculty:* 54 full-time (17 women), 52 part-time/adjunct (11 women). *Students:* 575 full-time (293 women), 261 part-time (107 women); includes 87 minority (33 Black or African American, non-Hispanic/Latino; 4 American Indian or Alaska Native, non-Hispanic/Latino; 17 Asian, non-Hispanic/Latino; 31 Hispanic/Latino; 2 Two or more races, non-Hispanic/Latino), 493 international. Average age 28. 1,719 applicants, 80% accepted, 600 enrolled. In 2014, 707 master's, 1 doctorate awarded. Terminal master's awarded for partial completion of doctoral program. *Degree requirements:* For master's, one foreign language, comprehensive exam (for some programs); for doctorate, one foreign language, comprehensive exam, thesis/dissertation. *Entrance requirements:* For master's, GMAT, Interview; for doctorate, GMAT or GRE, Interview. Additional exam requirements/recommendations for international students: Required—TOEFL (minimum score 610 paper-based, 102 iBT) or IELTS (minimum score 7.0). *Application deadline:* For fall admission, 11/1 priority date for domestic and international students; for winter admission, 1/5 for domestic and international students; for spring admission, 3/1 priority date for domestic and international students; for summer admission, 5/4 for domestic students. Application fee: $125. Electronic applications accepted. *Expenses:* Expenses: Cost of attendance is available on each program's website at http://freeman.tulane.edu/programs/. *Financial support:* In 2014–15, 153 students received support. Fellowships with full and partial tuition reimbursements available, research assistantships, teaching assistantships, career-related internships or fieldwork, Federal Work-Study, tuition waivers (full and partial), and unspecified assistantships available. Support available to part-time students. Financial award application deadline: 4/15; financial award applicants required to submit FAFSA. *Faculty research:* Corporate finance, managerial accounting and financial reporting, platform and management strategies, consumer behavior and decision making, organizational behavior. *Unit head:* Ira Solomon, PhD, Dean, 504-865-5407, Fax: 504-865-5491, E-mail: businessdean@tulane.edu. *Application contact:* Melissa Booth, Director of Graduate Admissions and Financial Aid, 800-223-5402, E-mail: freeman.admissions@tulane.edu.
Website: http://www.freeman.tulane.edu.

Université du Québec, Institut National de la Recherche Scientifique, Graduate Programs, Research Center–Energy Materials Telecommunications, Varennes, QC J3X 1S2, Canada. Offers energy and materials science (M Sc, PhD); telecommunications (M Sc, PhD). Part-time programs available. *Faculty:* 39 full-time. *Students:* 177 full-time (50 women), 7 part-time (1 woman), 123 international. Average age 30. 51 applicants, 84% accepted, 33 enrolled. In 2014, 16 master's, 16 doctorates awarded. *Degree requirements:* For master's, thesis (for some programs); for doctorate, thesis/dissertation. *Entrance requirements:* For master's, appropriate bachelor's degree, proficiency in French; for doctorate, appropriate master's degree, proficiency in French. *Application deadline:* For fall admission, 3/30 for domestic and international students; for winter admission, 11/1 for domestic and international students; for spring admission, 3/1 for domestic and international students. Application fee: $45. Electronic applications accepted. *Financial support:* In 2014–15, fellowships (averaging $16,500 per year) were awarded; research assistantships also available. *Faculty research:* New energy sources, plasmas, telecommunications, advanced materials ultrafast photonics. *Unit head:* Federico Rosei, Director, 450-228-6905, E-mail: rosei@emt.inrs.ca. *Application contact:* Sylvie Richard, Registrar, 418-654-2518, Fax: 418-654-3858, E-mail: sylvie.richard@adm.inrs.ca.
Website: http://www.emt.inrs.ca/emt.

University of Calgary, Faculty of Graduate Studies, Schulich School of Engineering, Department of Chemical and Petroleum Engineering, Calgary, AB T2N 1N4, Canada. Offers chemical engineering (M Eng, M Sc, PhD); energy and environment engineering (M Eng, M Sc, PhD); energy and environmental systems (M Eng, M Sc, PhD); environmental engineering (M Eng, M Sc, PhD); petroleum engineering (M Eng, M Sc, PhD); reservoir characterization (M Eng, M Sc). Part-time programs available. *Degree requirements:* For master's, thesis (for some programs); for doctorate, comprehensive exam, thesis/dissertation, candidacy exam. *Entrance requirements:* For master's, minimum GPA of 3.0 or equivalent; for doctorate, minimum GPA of 3.5 or equivalent. Additional exam requirements/recommendations for international students: Required—TOEFL (minimum score 550 paper-based; 80 iBT), IELTS (minimum score 7). Electronic applications accepted. *Faculty research:* Environmental engineering, biomedical engineering modeling, simulation and control, petroleum recovery and reservoir engineering, phase equilibria and transport properties.

University of California, Berkeley, Graduate Division, Group in Energy and Resources, Berkeley, CA 94720-1500. Offers MA, MS, PhD. *Degree requirements:* For master's, project or thesis; for doctorate, one foreign language, thesis/dissertation, qualifying exam. *Entrance requirements:* For master's and doctorate, GRE General Test, minimum GPA of 3.0, 3 letters of recommendation. *Faculty research:* Technical, economic, environmental, and institutional aspects of energy conservation in residential and commercial buildings; international patterns of energy use; renewable energy sources; assessment of valuation of energy and environmental resources pricing.

University of Colorado Denver, Business School, Program in Global Energy Management, Denver, CO 80217. Offers MS. Postbaccalaureate distance learning degree programs offered (minimal on-campus study). *Students:* 70 full-time (19 women), 3 part-time (1 woman); includes 13 minority (3 Black or African American, non-Hispanic/Latino; 1 Asian, non-Hispanic/Latino; 6 Hispanic/Latino; 3 Two or more races, non-Hispanic/Latino), 4 international. Average age 33. 34 applicants, 82% accepted, 19 enrolled. In 2014, 43 master's awarded. *Degree requirements:* For master's, 36 semester credit hours. *Entrance requirements:* For master's, GMAT if less than three years of experience in the energy industry (waived for students already holding a graduate degree), minimum of 5 years' experience in energy industry; resume; letters of recommendation; essays. Additional exam requirements/recommendations for international students: Required—TOEFL (minimum score 525 paper-based; 71 iBT); Recommended—IELTS (minimum score 6). *Application deadline:* For fall admission, 6/1

for domestic and international students; for winter admission, 12/1 for domestic and international students; for spring admission, 12/1 for domestic and international students. Application fee: $50 ($75 for international students). Electronic applications accepted. *Expenses:* Expenses: Contact institution. *Financial support:* Fellowships, research assistantships, teaching assistantships, Federal Work-Study, institutionally sponsored loans, scholarships/grants, and traineeships available. Financial award application deadline: 4/1; financial award applicants required to submit FAFSA. *Unit head:* Wayne Cascio, Chair in Global Leadership Management, 303-315-8434, E-mail: wayne.cascio@ucdenver.edu. *Application contact:* Michele Motley, Graduate Advisor, Global Energy Management Program, 303-315-8066, E-mail: michelle.motley@ucdenver.edu.
Website: http://www.ucdenver.edu/academics/colleges/business/degrees/ms/gem/Pages/Overview.aspx.

University of Delaware, Center for Energy and Environmental Policy, Newark, DE 19716. Offers energy and environmental policy (MA, MEEP, PhD); urban affairs and public policy (PhD), including technology, environment, and society. *Degree requirements:* For master's, analytical paper or thesis; for doctorate, comprehensive exam, thesis/dissertation. *Entrance requirements:* For master's, GRE General Test, minimum GPA of 3.0; for doctorate, GRE General Test, minimum GPA of 3.5. Additional exam requirements/recommendations for international students: Required—TOEFL. Electronic applications accepted. *Faculty research:* Sustainable development, renewable energy, climate change, environmental policy, environmental justice, disaster policy.

University of Illinois at Urbana–Champaign, Graduate College, College of Agricultural, Consumer and Environmental Sciences, Program in Bioenergy, Champaign, IL 61820. Offers PSM. Applications accepted for Fall semester only. *Students:* 17 (2 women). Application fee: $70 ($90 for international students). *Unit head:* Hans Blaschek, Director, 217-244-9270, E-mail: blascheck@illinois.edu. *Application contact:* Ann Jones, Education and Project Coordinator, 217-244-0731, E-mail: acjones3@illinois.edu.
Website: http://www.bioenergy.illinois.edu/.

University of Mary, Gary Tharaldson School of Business, Bismarck, ND 58504-9652. Offers business administration (MBA); energy management (MBA, MS); executive (MBA, MS); health care (MBA, MS); human resource management (MBA); project management (MBA, MPM). Part-time and evening/weekend programs available. *Faculty:* 5 full-time (4 women), 50 part-time/adjunct (23 women). *Students:* 130 full-time (67 women), 189 part-time (105 women); includes 59 minority (22 Black or African American, non-Hispanic/Latino; 12 American Indian or Alaska Native, non-Hispanic/Latino; 11 Asian, non-Hispanic/Latino; 10 Hispanic/Latino; 1 Native Hawaiian or other Pacific Islander, non-Hispanic/Latino; 3 Two or more races, non-Hispanic/Latino), 20 international. Average age 40. In 2014, 249 master's awarded. *Entrance requirements:* For master's, minimum GPA of 2.5. Additional exam requirements/recommendations for international students: Required—TOEFL (minimum score 550 paper-based; 80 iBT). *Application deadline:* Applications are processed on a rolling basis. Application fee: $45. Electronic applications accepted. *Expenses: Tuition:* Full-time $4772; part-time $530.25 per credit hour. *Required fees:* $20 per credit hour. Tuition and fees vary according to degree level and program. *Financial support:* Application deadline: 8/1; applicants required to submit FAFSA. *Unit head:* Dr. James Long, Chair of Graduate and Distance Education, 701-355-8093, Fax: 701-255-7687, E-mail: jdlong@umary.edu. *Application contact:* 701-355-8128, Fax: 701-255-7687, E-mail: admissions@umary.edu.
Website: http://www.umary.edu/academics/schools/business.php.

University of Phoenix–Bay Area Campus, School of Business, San Jose, CA 95134-1805. Offers accountancy (MS); accounting (MBA); business administration (MBA, DBA); energy management (MBA); global management (MBA); health care management (MBA); human resource management (MBA); human resources management (MM); management (MM); marketing (MBA); organizational leadership (DM); project management (MBA); public administration (MPA); technology management (MBA). Evening/weekend programs available. Postbaccalaureate distance learning degree programs offered (no on-campus study). *Degree requirements:* For master's, thesis (for some programs). *Entrance requirements:* For master's, minimum undergraduate GPA of 3.0, 3 years of work experience. Additional exam requirements/recommendations for international students: Required—TOEFL (minimum score 550 paper-based; 79 iBT). Electronic applications accepted.

University of Phoenix–Milwaukee Campus, School of Business, Milwaukee, WI 53224. Offers accounting (MBA); business administration (MBA); energy management (MBA); global management (MBA); health care management (MBA); human resource management (MBA); management (MM); marketing (MBA); project management (MBA); technology management (MBA). Evening/weekend programs available. Postbaccalaureate distance learning degree programs offered. *Entrance requirements:* Additional exam requirements/recommendations for international students: Required—TOEFL, TOEIC (Test of English as an International Communication), Berlitz Online English Proficiency Exam, PTE, or IELTS. Electronic applications accepted. *Expenses:* Contact institution.

University of Phoenix–Online Campus, School of Business, Phoenix, AZ 85034-7209. Offers accountancy (MS); accounting (MBA, Certificate); business administration (MBA); energy management (MBA); global management (MBA); health care management (MBA); human resource management (MBA, Certificate); human resources management (MM); management (MM); marketing (MBA, Certificate); project management (MBA, Certificate); public administration (MBA, MM); technology management (MBA). Evening/weekend programs available. Postbaccalaureate distance learning degree programs offered. *Entrance requirements:* Additional exam requirements/recommendations for international students: Required—TOEFL, TOEIC (Test of English as an International Communication), Berlitz Online English Proficiency Exam, PTE, or IELTS. Electronic applications accepted. *Expenses:* Contact institution.

University of Phoenix–Phoenix Campus, School of Business, Tempe, AZ 85282-2371. Offers accounting (MBA, MS, Certificate); business administration (MBA); energy management (MBA); global management (MBA); health care management (MBA); human resource management (MBA, Certificate); management (MM); marketing (MBA); project management (MBA); technology management (MBA). Evening/weekend programs available. Postbaccalaureate distance learning degree programs offered. *Entrance requirements:* Additional exam requirements/recommendations for international students: Required—TOEFL, TOEIC (Test of English as an International Communication), Berlitz Online English Proficiency Exam, PTE, or IELTS. Electronic applications accepted. *Expenses:* Contact institution.

University of Phoenix–Puerto Rico Campus, School of Business, Guaynabo, PR 00968. Offers accounting (MBA); energy management (MBA); global management (MBA); human resource management (MBA); marketing (MBA); project management (MBA); small business administration (MBA). Evening/weekend programs available. *Degree requirements:* For master's, thesis (for some programs). *Entrance requirements:* For master's, minimum undergraduate GPA of 3.0, 3 years work experience. Additional exam requirements/recommendations for international students: Required—TOEFL (minimum score 550 paper-based; 79 iBT). Electronic applications accepted.

University of Phoenix–Southern California Campus, School of Business, Costa Mesa, CA 92626. Offers accounting (MBA); business administration (MBA); energy management (MBA); global management (MBA); health care management (MBA); human resource management (MBA); management (MM); marketing (MBA); project management (MBA); technology management (MBA). Evening/weekend programs available. Postbaccalaureate distance learning degree programs offered. *Entrance requirements:* Additional exam requirements/recommendations for international students: Required—TOEFL, TOEIC (Test of English as an International Communication), Berlitz Online English Proficiency Exam, PTE, or IELTS. Electronic applications accepted. *Expenses:* Contact institution.

University of Pittsburgh, Graduate School of Public and International Affairs, Master of Public Administration Program, Pittsburgh, PA 15260. Offers energy and environment (MPA); governance and international public management (MPA); policy research and analysis (MPA); public and nonprofit management (MPA); urban affairs and planning (MPA); JD/MPA; MPA/MID; MPA/MPIA; MPH/MPA; MSIS/MPA; MSW/MPA. Part-time and evening/weekend programs available. *Faculty:* 32 full-time (12 women), 13 part-time/adjunct (5 women). *Students:* 99 full-time (69 women), 15 part-time (10 women); includes 8 minority (5 Black or African American, non-Hispanic/Latino; 1 Asian, non-Hispanic/Latino; 1 Hispanic/Latino; 1 Two or more races, non-Hispanic/Latino), 52 international. Average age 26. 273 applicants, 70% accepted, 51 enrolled. In 2014, 50 master's awarded. *Degree requirements:* For master's, thesis optional, internship, capstone seminar. *Entrance requirements:* For master's, GRE General Test or GMAT, 2 letters of recommendation, resume; undergraduate transcripts, personal statement. Additional exam requirements/recommendations for international students: Required—TOEFL (minimum score 550 paper-based; 80 iBT); Recommended—IELTS (minimum score 7), TWE (minimum score 4). *Application deadline:* For fall admission, 2/1 for domestic students, 1/15 for international students; for spring admission, 11/1 for domestic students, 8/1 for international students. Application fee: $50. Electronic applications accepted. *Expenses:* Tuition, state resident: full-time $20,742; part-time $838 per credit. Tuition, nonresident: full-time $33,960; part-time $1389 per credit. *Required fees:* $800; $205 per term. Tuition and fees vary according to program. *Financial support:* In 2014–15, 17 students received support, including 3 fellowships (averaging $13,980 per year); scholarships/grants, unspecified assistantships, and student employment also available. Financial award application deadline: 2/1. *Faculty research:* Urban management, regional development, disaster response management, public program evaluation, comparative regional governance, nonprofit management, health policy, environmental policy, strategic management, human resources management. Total annual research expenditures: $640,844. *Unit head:* Dr. David Y. Miller, Director, 412-648-7606, Fax: 412-648-2605, E-mail: dymiller@pitt.edu. *Application contact:* Elizabeth A. Hruby, Graduate Enrollment Counselor, 412-648-7640, Fax: 412-648-7641, E-mail: eah44@pitt.edu.
Website: http://www.gspia.pitt.edu/.

University of Rochester, Hajim School of Engineering and Applied Sciences, Master of Science in Technical Entrepreneurship and Management Program, Rochester, NY 14642. Offers biomedical engineering (MS); chemical engineering (MS); computer science (MS); electrical and computer engineering (MS); energy and the environment (MS); materials science (MS); mechanical engineering (MS); optics (MS). Program offered in collaboration with the Simon School of Business. Part-time programs available. *Students:* 36 full-time (12 women), 7 part-time (1 woman); includes 3 minority (2 Hispanic/Latino; 1 Two or more races, non-Hispanic/Latino), 33 international. Average age 24. 152 applicants, 68% accepted, 27 enrolled. In 2014, 28 master's awarded. *Degree requirements:* For master's, comprehensive exam. *Entrance requirements:* For master's, GRE or GMAT, 3 letters of recommendation; personal statement; official transcript; bachelor's degree (or equivalent for international students) in engineering, science, or mathematics. Additional exam requirements/recommendations for international students: Required—TOEFL or IELTS. *Application deadline:* For fall admission, 2/1 for domestic and international students. Applications are processed on a rolling basis. Application fee: $60. Electronic applications accepted. *Expenses: Tuition:* Full-time $46,150; part-time $1442 per credit hour. *Required fees:* $504. *Financial support:* Career-related internships or fieldwork and scholarships/grants available. Financial award application deadline: 2/1. *Faculty research:* High efficiency solar cells, macromolecular self-assembly, digital signal processing, memory hierarchy management, molecular and physical mechanisms in cell migration, optical imaging systems. *Unit head:* Duncan T. Moore, Vice Provost for Entrepreneurship, 585-275-5248, Fax: 585-473-6745, E-mail: moore@optics.rochester.edu. *Application contact:* Andrea M. Galati, Executive Director, 585-276-3407, Fax: 585-276-2357, E-mail: andrea.galati@rochester.edu.
Website: http://www.rochester.edu/team.

The University of Tulsa, Graduate School, Collins College of Business, Master of Business Administration Program, Tulsa, OK 74104-3189. Offers accounting (MBA); business administration (MBA); energy management (MBA); finance (MBA); international business (MBA); management information systems (MBA); taxation (MBA); JD/MBA; MBA/MSCS; MBA/MSF. Accreditation: AACSB. Part-time and evening/weekend programs available. *Faculty:* 32 full-time (6 women). *Students:* 47 full-time (19 women), 31 part-time (11 women); includes 12 minority (1 Black or African American, non-Hispanic/Latino; 4 American Indian or Alaska Native, non-Hispanic/Latino; 2 Asian, non-Hispanic/Latino; 3 Hispanic/Latino; 2 Two or more races, non-Hispanic/Latino), 13 international. Average age 27. 61 applicants, 61% accepted, 29 enrolled. In 2014, 42 master's awarded. *Entrance requirements:* For master's, GMAT. Additional exam requirements/recommendations for international students: Required—TOEFL (minimum score 577 paper-based; 91 iBT), IELTS (minimum score 6.5). *Application deadline:* Applications are processed on a rolling basis. Application fee: $55. Electronic applications accepted. *Expenses: Tuition:* Full-time $20,160; part-time $1120 per credit hour. *Required fees:* $6 per credit hour. Tuition and fees vary according to course level and course load. *Financial support:* In 2014–15, 29 students received support, including 29 teaching assistantships with full and partial tuition reimbursements available (averaging $9,543 per year); fellowships, research assistantships, career-related internships or fieldwork, institutionally sponsored loans, scholarships/grants, health care benefits, tuition waivers (full and partial), and unspecified assistantships also available. Support available to part-time students. Financial award application deadline: 2/1; financial award applicants required to submit FAFSA. *Faculty research:* Accounting, energy management, finance, international business, management information systems, taxation. *Unit head:* Dr. Linda Nichols, Associate Dean of the Collins College of Business, 918-631-2242, Fax: 918-631-2142, E-mail: linda-nichols@utulsa.edu. *Application contact:* Information Contact, 918-631-2242, E-mail: graduate-business@utulsa.edu.

The University of Tulsa, Graduate School, Collins College of Business, Online Program in Energy Business, Tulsa, OK 74104-3189. Offers MEB. Part-time and evening/weekend programs available. Postbaccalaureate distance learning degree programs offered (no on-campus study). *Students:* 134 part-time (32 women); includes 14 minority (4 Black or African American, non-Hispanic/Latino; 5 American Indian or Alaska Native, non-Hispanic/Latino; 3 Hispanic/Latino; 2 Two or more races, non-Hispanic/Latino), 1 international. Average age 33. 66 applicants, 94% accepted, 49 enrolled. In 2014, 23 master's awarded. *Degree requirements:* For master's, thesis optional. *Entrance requirements:* For master's, GMAT. Additional exam requirements/recommendations for international students: Required—TOEFL (minimum score 577 paper-based; 91 iBT), IELTS (minimum score 6.5). *Application deadline:* For fall admission, 7/1 for domestic students. Applications are processed on a rolling basis. Application fee: $55. Electronic applications accepted. *Expenses: Tuition:* Full-time $20,160; part-time $1120 per credit hour. *Required fees:* $6 per credit hour. Tuition and fees vary according to course level and course load. *Financial support:* Fellowships with full and partial tuition reimbursements, career-related internships or fieldwork, Federal Work-Study, institutionally sponsored loans, scholarships/grants, health care benefits, and tuition waivers available. Support available to part-time students. *Unit head:* Dr. Linda Nichols, Associate Dean, 918-631-2242, Fax: 918-631-2142. *Application contact:* Ashley Chapa, Marketing Manager, 918-631-2680, Fax: 918-631-2142, E-mail: graduate-business@utulsa.edu.

Vermont Law School, Graduate and Professional Programs, Environmental Law Center, South Royalton, VT 05068-0096. Offers energy law (LL M); energy regulation and law (MERL); environmental law (LL M); environmental law and policy (MELP); food and agriculture law (LL M); food and agriculture law and policy (MFALP); JD/MELP; JD/MERL; JD/MFALP. Part-time programs available. Postbaccalaureate distance learning degree programs offered. *Entrance requirements:* Additional exam requirements/recommendations for international students: Required—TOEFL. *Application deadline:* For fall admission, 3/1 priority date for domestic students. Applications are processed on a rolling basis. Application fee: $60. *Expenses: Tuition:* Full-time $47,135. *Financial support:* Fellowships with full tuition reimbursements, career-related internships or fieldwork, Federal Work-Study, institutionally sponsored loans, scholarships/grants, and tuition waivers (partial) available. Support available to part-time students. Financial award application deadline: 3/1; financial award applicants required to submit FAFSA. *Faculty research:* Environment and technology; takings; international environmental law; interaction among science, law, and environmental policy; air pollution. *Unit head:* Marc B. Mihaly, Dean, 802-831-1237, Fax: 802-763-2490. *Application contact:* John D. Miller, Jr., Associate Dean of Enrollment and Marketing, 802-831-1239, Fax: 802-831-1174, E-mail: admiss@vermontlaw.edu.
Website: http://www.vermontlaw.edu/Academics/degrees/masters.

Waynesburg University, Graduate and Professional Studies, Canonsburg, PA 15370. Offers business (MBA), including energy management, finance, health systems, human resources, leadership, market development; counseling (MA), including addictions counseling, clinical mental health; education (M Ed, MAT), including autism (M Ed); curriculum and instruction (M Ed), educational leadership (M Ed), online teaching (M Ed); nursing (MSN), including administration, education, informatics; nursing practice (DNP); special education (M Ed); technology (M Ed); MSN/MBA. *Accreditation:* AACN. Part-time and evening/weekend programs available. *Degree requirements:* For doctorate, thesis/dissertation. *Entrance requirements:* Additional exam requirements/recommendations for international students: Required—TOEFL. Electronic applications accepted.

Engineering Management

Air Force Institute of Technology, Graduate School of Engineering and Management, Department of Systems and Engineering Management, Dayton, OH 45433-7765. Offers cost analysis (MS); environmental and engineering management (MS); environmental engineering science (MS); information resource/systems management (MS). *Accreditation:* ABET. Part-time programs available. *Degree requirements:* For master's, thesis. *Entrance requirements:* For master's, GRE, GMAT, minimum GPA of 3.0.

American University of Beirut, Graduate Programs, Faculty of Engineering and Architecture, Beirut, Lebanon. Offers applied energy (ME); civil engineering (PhD); electrical and computer engineering (PhD); engineering management (MEM); environmental and water resources (ME); environmental technology (MSES); mechanical engineering (ME, PhD); urban design (MUD); urban planning and policy (MUPP). Part-time programs available. *Faculty:* 93 full-time (18 women), 3 part-time/adjunct (1 woman). *Students:* 268 full-time (111 women), 58 part-time (27 women). Average age 26. 225 applicants, 68% accepted, 79 enrolled. In 2014, 114 master's, 9 doctorates awarded. Terminal master's awarded for partial completion of doctoral program. *Degree requirements:* For master's, one foreign language, comprehensive exam, thesis (for some programs); for doctorate, one foreign language, comprehensive exam, thesis/dissertation, publications. *Entrance requirements:* For master's, letters of recommendation; for doctorate, GRE, letters of recommendation, master's degree, transcripts, curriculum vitae, interview. Additional exam requirements/recommendations for international students: Required—TOEFL (minimum score 600 paper-based; 100 iBT), IELTS (minimum score 7.5). *Application deadline:* For fall admission, 2/5 priority date for domestic and international students; for spring admission, 11/1 priority date for domestic students, 11/1 for international students. Application fee: $50. Electronic applications accepted. *Expenses: Tuition:* Full-time $15,462; part-time $859 per credit. *Required fees:* $692. Tuition and fees vary according to course load and program. *Financial support:* In 2014–15, 190 students received support, including 2 fellowships with full tuition reimbursements available (averaging $24,800 per year), 64 research assistantships with full tuition reimbursements available (averaging $24,800 per year), 124 teaching assistantships with full tuition reimbursements available (averaging $9,800 per year); career-related internships or fieldwork, institutionally sponsored loans, scholarships/grants, health care benefits, and unspecified assistantships also available. *Total annual research expenditures:* $1.5 million. *Unit head:* Prof. Makram T. Suidan, Dean, 961-1350000 Ext. 3400, Fax: 961-1744462, E-mail: msuidan@aub.edu.lb. *Application contact:* Dr. Salim Kanaan, Director, Admissions Office, 961-1350000 Ext. 2594, Fax: 961-1750775, E-mail: sk00@aub.edu.lb.
Website: http://staff.aub.edu.lb/~webfea.

American University of Sharjah, Graduate Programs, Sharjah, United Arab Emirates. Offers accounting (MS); business (EMBA, MBA); chemical engineering (MS Ch E); civil engineering (MSCE); computer engineering (MS); electrical engineering (MSEE); engineering systems management (MS); mathematics (MS); mechanical engineering (MSME); mechatronics engineering (MS); teaching English to speakers of other languages (MA); translation and interpreting (MA); urban planning (MUP). Part-time and evening/weekend programs available. *Degree requirements:* For master's, thesis (for some programs). *Entrance requirements:* For master's, GMAT (for MBA). Additional exam requirements/recommendations for international students: Required—TOEFL (minimum score 550 paper-based; 80 iBT), TWE (minimum score 5); Recommended—IELTS (minimum score 6.5). Electronic applications accepted. *Faculty research:* Water pollution, management and waste water treatment, energy and sustainability, air pollution, Islamic finance, family business and small and medium enterprises.

Arkansas State University, Graduate School, College of Engineering, State University, AR 72467. Offers MEM, MS Eng. Part-time programs available. *Faculty:* 7 full-time (0 women). *Students:* 22 full-time (6 women), 9 part-time (0 women); includes 1 minority (Black or African American, non-Hispanic/Latino), 28 international. Average age 25. 91 applicants, 49% accepted, 25 enrolled. In 2014, 7 master's awarded. *Degree requirements:* For master's, comprehensive exam. *Entrance requirements:* For master's, GRE, appropriate bachelor's degree, official transcript, letters of recommendation, resume, immunization records. Additional exam requirements/recommendations for international students: Required—TOEFL (minimum score 550 paper-based; 79 iBT), IELTS (minimum score 6), PTE (minimum score 56). *Application deadline:* For fall admission, 6/1 for domestic and international students; for spring admission, 10/15 for domestic and international students. Applications are processed on a rolling basis. Application fee: $30 ($40 for international students). Electronic applications accepted. *Expenses:* Expenses: Contact institution. *Financial support:* In 2014–15, 7 students received support. Career-related internships or fieldwork, scholarships/grants, and unspecified assistantships available. Financial award application deadline: 7/1; financial award applicants required to submit FAFSA. *Unit head:* Dr. Paul Mixon, Interim Dean, 870-972-2088, Fax: 870-972-3539, E-mail: pmixon@astate.edu. *Application contact:* Vickey Ring, Graduate Admissions Coordinator, 870-972-3029, Fax: 870-972-3857, E-mail: vickeyring@astate.edu.
Website: http://www.astate.edu/college/engineering/index.dot.

California Maritime Academy, Graduate Studies, Vallejo, CA 94590. Offers transportation and engineering management (MS), including engineering management, humanitarian disaster management, transportation. Postbaccalaureate distance learning degree programs offered (no on-campus study). *Faculty:* 14 part-time/adjunct (2 women). *Students:* 50 full-time (7 women); includes 12 minority (3 Black or African American, non-Hispanic/Latino; 4 Asian, non-Hispanic/Latino; 4 Hispanic/Latino; 1 Native Hawaiian or other Pacific Islander, non-Hispanic/Latino), 3 international. 36 applicants, 97% accepted, 35 enrolled. In 2014, 14 master's awarded. *Degree requirements:* For master's, capstone course and project. *Entrance requirements:* For master's, equivalent of four-year U.S. bachelor's degree with minimum GPA of 2.5 during last two years (60 semester units or 90 quarter units) of coursework in degree program; five years of professional experience or GMAT/GRE. Additional exam requirements/recommendations for international students: Required—TOEFL (minimum score 550 paper-based). *Application deadline:* Applications are processed on a rolling basis. Application fee: $55. Electronic applications accepted. *Unit head:* Dr. Jim Burns, Dean, Graduate Studies. *Application contact:* Kathy Arnold, Program Coordinator, 707-654-1271, Fax: 707-654-1158, E-mail: karnold@csum.edu.
Website: http://www.csum.edu/web/industry/graduate-studies.

California National University for Advanced Studies, College of Quality and Engineering Management, Northridge, CA 91325. Offers MEM. Part-time programs available. *Entrance requirements:* For master's, minimum GPA of 3.0.

California State Polytechnic University, Pomona, Program in Engineering Management, Pomona, CA 91768-2557. Offers MS. *Students:* 5 full-time (0 women), 24 part-time (7 women); includes 19 minority (2 Black or African American, non-Hispanic/Latino; 10 Asian, non-Hispanic/Latino; 7 Hispanic/Latino), 5 international. Average age 25. 40 applicants, 25% accepted, 7 enrolled. In 2014, 13 master's awarded. *Degree requirements:* For master's, thesis or project. *Application deadline:* Applications are processed on a rolling basis. Application fee: $55. Electronic applications accepted. *Expenses:* Tuition, state resident: full-time $6738. Tuition, nonresident: full-time $12,300. *Required fees:* $1400. *Unit head:* Dr. Abdul B. Sadat, Chair/Graduate Coordinator, 909-869-2555, Fax: 909-869-2564, E-mail: absadat@cpp.edu.
Website: http://www.cpp.edu/~ime/msem.htm.

California State University, East Bay, Office of Academic Programs and Graduate Studies, College of Science, School of Engineering, Program in Engineering Management, Hayward, CA 94542-3000. Offers MS. *Degree requirements:* For master's, comprehensive exam (for some programs), research project or exam. *Entrance requirements:* For master's, GRE or GMAT, minimum GPA of 2.5; personal statement, two letters of recommendation, resume; college algebra/trigonometry or equivalent. Additional exam requirements/recommendations for international students: Required—TOEFL (minimum score 550 paper-based). *Application deadline:* For fall admission, 6/30 for domestic and international students. Application fee: $55. Electronic applications accepted. *Expenses:* Tuition, state resident: full-time $7830; part-time $1302 per credit hour. Tuition, nonresident: full-time $16,368. *Required fees:* $327 per quarter. Tuition and fees vary according to course load and program. *Financial support:* Federal Work-Study and institutionally sponsored loans available. Support available to part-time students. Financial award application deadline: 3/2; financial award applicants required to submit FAFSA. *Unit head:* Dr. Saeid Motavalli, Department Chair/Graduate Advisor, 510-885-4481, E-mail: saeid.motavalli@csueastbay.edu. *Application contact:* Dr. Donna Wiley, Interim Associate Vice President for Academic Programs and Graduate Studies, 510-885-3716, Fax: 510-885-4777, E-mail: donna.wiley@csueastbay.edu.
Website: http://www20.csueastbay.edu/csci/departments/engineering/.

California State University, Long Beach, Graduate Studies, College of Engineering, Department of Mechanical and Aerospace Engineering, Long Beach, CA 90840. Offers aerospace engineering (MSAE); engineering and industrial applied mathematics (PhD); interdisciplinary engineering (MSE); management engineering (MSE); mechanical engineering (MSME). Part-time programs available. *Entrance requirements:* Additional exam requirements/recommendations for international students: Required—TOEFL. Electronic applications accepted. *Faculty research:* Unsteady turbulent flows, solar energy, energy conversion, CAD/CAM, computer-assisted instruction.

California State University, Northridge, Graduate Studies, College of Engineering and Computer Science, Department of Manufacturing Systems Engineering and Management, Northridge, CA 91330. Offers engineering automation (MS); engineering management (MS); manufacturing systems engineering (MS); materials engineering (MS). Postbaccalaureate distance learning degree programs offered. *Students:* 180 full-time (38 women), 56 part-time (15 women); includes 24 minority (11 Asian, non-Hispanic/Latino; 8 Hispanic/Latino; 5 Two or more races, non-Hispanic/Latino), 172 international. Average age 26. *Entrance requirements:* For master's, GRE (if cumulative undergraduate GPA less than 3.0). *Application deadline:* For fall admission, 3/30 for domestic students; for spring admission, 9/30 for domestic students. Application fee:

$55. *Expenses: Required fees:* $12,402. *Unit head:* Kang Chang, Acting Chair, 818-677-2167.
Website: http://www.csun.edu/~msem/.

Case Western Reserve University, School of Graduate Studies, Case School of Engineering, The Institute for Management and Engineering, Cleveland, OH 44106. Offers MEM. *Students:* 33 full-time (8 women), 1 part-time (0 women); includes 7 minority (2 Black or African American, non-Hispanic/Latino; 5 Asian, non-Hispanic/Latino), 16 international. In 2014, 51 master's awarded. *Entrance requirements:* Additional exam requirements/recommendations for international students: Required—TOEFL, IELTS (minimum score 7.5). *Application deadline:* For fall admission, 5/1 for domestic students, 2/1 for international students. *Financial support:* In 2014–15, 33 fellowships (averaging $12,696 per year) were awarded; scholarships/grants also available. *Unit head:* Laura Marshall, Interim Executive Director, 216-368-5762, Fax: 216-368-0144, E-mail: laura.marshall@case.edu. *Application contact:* Ramona David, Program Assistant, 216-368-0596, Fax: 216-368-0144, E-mail: rxd47@cwru.edu.
Website: http://www.mem.case.edu.

The Catholic University of America, School of Engineering, Program in Engineering Management, Washington, DC 20064. Offers MSE, Certificate. Part-time programs available. *Faculty:* 5 part-time/adjunct (0 women). *Students:* 25 full-time (7 women), 10 part-time (6 women); includes 3 minority (1 Black or African American, non-Hispanic/Latino; 1 Asian, non-Hispanic/Latino; 1 Hispanic/Latino), 25 international. Average age 29. 45 applicants, 80% accepted, 17 enrolled. In 2014, 22 master's awarded. *Degree requirements:* For master's, thesis optional. *Entrance requirements:* For master's and Certificate, statement of purpose, official copies of academic transcripts, three letters of recommendation. Additional exam requirements/recommendations for international students: Required—TOEFL (minimum score 580 paper-based). *Application deadline:* For fall admission, 7/15 priority date for domestic students, 7/1 for international students; for spring admission, 11/15 priority date for domestic students, 11/1 for international students. Applications are processed on a rolling basis. Application fee: $55. Electronic applications accepted. *Expenses:* Expenses: Contact institution. *Financial support:* Fellowships, research assistantships, teaching assistantships, Federal Work-Study, scholarships/grants, tuition waivers (full and partial), and unspecified assistantships available. Financial award application deadline: 2/1; financial award applicants required to submit FAFSA. *Faculty research:* Engineering management and organization, project and systems engineering management, technology management. *Unit head:* Jeffrey E. Giangiuli, Director, 202-319-5191, Fax: 202-319-6860, E-mail: giangiuli@cua.edu. *Application contact:* Director of Graduate Admissions, 202-319-5057, Fax: 202-319-6533, E-mail: cua-admissions@cua.edu.
Website: http://engrmgmt.cua.edu/.

Central Michigan University, Central Michigan University Global Campus, Program in Administration, Mount Pleasant, MI 48859. Offers acquisitions administration (MSA, Certificate); engineering management administration (MSA, Certificate); general administration (MSA, Certificate); health services administration (MSA, Certificate); human resources administration (MSA, Certificate); information resource management (MSA); information resource management administration (Certificate); international administration (MSA, Certificate); leadership (MSA, Certificate); philanthropy and fundraising administration (MSA, Certificate); public administration (MSA, Certificate); recreation and park administration (MSA); research administration (MSA, Certificate). Part-time and evening/weekend programs available. Postbaccalaureate distance learning degree programs offered (no on-campus study). *Students:* Average age 38. *Entrance requirements:* For master's, minimum GPA of 2.7 in major. *Application deadline:* Applications are processed on a rolling basis. Application fee: $50. Electronic applications accepted. *Financial support:* Scholarships/grants available. Support available to part-time students. Financial award applicants required to submit FAFSA. *Unit head:* Dr. Patricia Chase, Director, 989-774-6525, E-mail: chase1pb@cmich.edu. *Application contact:* 877-268-4636, E-mail: cmuglobal@cmich.edu.

The Citadel, The Military College of South Carolina, Citadel Graduate College, Engineering Leadership and Program Management Department, Charleston, SC 29409. Offers technical project management (MS). Part-time and evening/weekend programs available. *Entrance requirements:* For master's, GRE or GMAT, evidence of a minimum of one year of professional experience, or permission from department head; two letters of reference; resume detailing previous work. Additional exam requirements/recommendations for international students: Required—TOEFL (minimum score 550 paper-based; 79 iBT). Electronic applications accepted.

Clarkson University, Graduate School, Program in Engineering Management, Potsdam, NY 13699. Offers MS. Part-time and evening/weekend programs available. Postbaccalaureate distance learning degree programs offered (minimal on-campus study). *Students:* 90 part-time (21 women); includes 12 minority (2 Black or African American, non-Hispanic/Latino; 3 Asian, non-Hispanic/Latino; 5 Hispanic/Latino; 2 Two or more races, non-Hispanic/Latino), 1 international. Average age 32. 80 applicants, 60% accepted, 28 enrolled. In 2014, 3 master's awarded. *Entrance requirements:* For master's, GMAT or GRE, transcripts of all college coursework, resume, personal statement, three letters of recommendation. Additional exam requirements/recommendations for international students: Required—TOEFL (minimum score 550 paper-based; 80 iBT), IELTS (minimum score 6.5). *Application deadline:* For fall admission, 1/30 priority date for domestic and international students; for spring admission, 9/1 priority date for domestic and international students. Applications are processed on a rolling basis. Application fee: $25 ($35 for international students). Electronic applications accepted. *Expenses: Tuition:* Full-time $16,680; part-time $1390 per credit. *Required fees:* $295 per semester. *Financial support:* In 2014–15, 52 students received support. Scholarships/grants available. *Unit head:* Dr. Timothy Sugrue, President/CEO, 845-838-1600, Fax: 845-838-6613, E-mail: sugrue@clarkson.edu. *Application contact:* Michael Walsh, Director of Academic Programs, 845-838-1600 Ext. 13, Fax: 845-838-6613, E-mail: mwalsh@clarkson.edu.
Website: http://www.clarkson.edu/business/em_ms/.

Colorado School of Mines, Graduate School, Division of Economics and Business, Golden, CO 80401. Offers engineering and technology management (MS); mineral economics (PhD); operations research and engineering (PhD). Part-time programs available. *Faculty:* 11 full-time (3 women), 24 part-time/adjunct (4 women). *Students:* 114 full-time (21 women), 22 part-time (5 women); includes 17 minority (3 Black or African American, non-Hispanic/Latino; 4 Asian, non-Hispanic/Latino; 8 Hispanic/Latino; 2 Two or more races, non-Hispanic/Latino), 36 international. Average age 30. 172 applicants, 66% accepted, 62 enrolled. In 2014, 60 master's, 4 doctorates awarded. *Degree requirements:* For master's, thesis (for some programs); for doctorate, comprehensive exam, thesis/dissertation. *Entrance requirements:* For master's and doctorate, GRE General Test. Additional exam requirements/recommendations for international students: Required—TOEFL (minimum score 550 paper-based; 80 iBT). *Application deadline:* For fall admission, 12/15 priority date for domestic and international students; for spring admission, 9/1 priority date for domestic and international students. Application fee: $50 ($70 for international students). Electronic applications accepted. *Financial support:* In 2014–15, 45 students received support, including 4 fellowships with full tuition reimbursements available (averaging $21,120 per year), 8 research assistantships with full tuition reimbursements available (averaging $21,120 per year), 23 teaching assistantships with full tuition reimbursements available (averaging $21,120 per year); scholarships/grants, health care benefits, and unspecified assistantships also available. Financial award application deadline: 1/15; financial award applicants required to submit FAFSA. *Faculty research:* International trade, resource and environmental economics, energy economics, operations research. *Total annual research expenditures:* $371,588. *Unit head:* Dr. Michael Walls, Interim Director, 303-273-3492, Fax: 303-273-3416, E-mail: mwalls@mines.edu. *Application contact:* Kathleen Martin, Program Assistant, 303-273-3482, Fax: 303-273-3416, E-mail: kmartin@mines.edu.
Website: http://econbus.mines.edu.

Cornell University, Graduate School, Graduate Fields of Engineering, Field of Civil and Environmental Engineering, Ithaca, NY 14853-0001. Offers engineering management (M Eng, MS, PhD); environmental engineering (M Eng, MS, PhD); environmental fluid mechanics and hydrology (M Eng, MS, PhD); environmental systems engineering (M Eng, MS, PhD); geotechnical engineering (M Eng, MS, PhD); remote sensing (M Eng, MS, PhD); structural engineering (M Eng, MS, PhD); structural mechanics (M Eng, MS); transportation engineering (MS, PhD); transportation systems engineering (M Eng); water resource systems (M Eng, MS, PhD). Terminal master's awarded for partial completion of doctoral program. *Degree requirements:* For master's, thesis (MS); for doctorate, comprehensive exam, thesis/dissertation. *Entrance requirements:* For master's and doctorate, GRE General Test (recommended), 2 letters of recommendation. Additional exam requirements/recommendations for international students: Required—TOEFL (minimum score 600 paper-based; 77 iBT). Electronic applications accepted. *Faculty research:* Environmental engineering, geotechnical engineering, remote sensing, environmental fluid mechanics and hydrology, structural engineering.

Dallas Baptist University, College of Business, Business Administration Program, Dallas, TX 75211-9299. Offers accounting (MBA); business communication (MBA); conflict resolution management (MBA); entrepreneurship (MBA); finance (MBA); health care management (MBA); international business (MBA); leading the non-profit organization (MBA); management (MBA); management information systems (MBA); marketing (MBA); project management (MBA); technology and engineering (MBA). *Accreditation:* ACBSP. Part-time and evening/weekend programs available. *Entrance requirements:* For master's, GMAT, minimum GPA of 3.0. Additional exam requirements/recommendations for international students: Required—TOEFL, IELTS. Electronic applications accepted. *Expenses: Tuition:* Full-time $14,130; part-time $785 per credit hour. *Required fees:* $200 per semester. Tuition and fees vary according to course level and course load. *Faculty research:* Sports management, services marketing, retailing, strategic management, financial planning/investments.

Dartmouth College, Thayer School of Engineering, Program in Engineering Management, Hanover, NH 03755. Offers MEM. Program offered in conjunction with Tuck School of Business. *Degree requirements:* For master's, capstone experience. *Entrance requirements:* For master's, GRE General Test. Additional exam requirements/recommendations for international students: Required—TOEFL. *Application deadline:* For fall admission, 1/1 priority date for domestic students. Applications are processed on a rolling basis. Application fee: $45. *Expenses:* Expenses: $16,040 per term. *Financial support:* Fellowships, teaching assistantships, career-related internships or fieldwork, Federal Work-Study, institutionally sponsored loans, scholarships/grants, health care benefits, and tuition waivers (full and partial) available. Financial award application deadline: 1/15; financial award applicants required to submit CSS PROFILE. *Unit head:* Benoit Cushman-Roisin, Director, 603-646-9075, Fax: 603-646-2580, E-mail: benoit.cushman.roisin@dartmouth.edu. *Application contact:* Candace S. Potter, Graduate Admissions and Financial Aid Administrator, 603-646-3844, Fax: 603-646-1620, E-mail: candace.s.potter@dartmouth.edu.
Website: http://engineering.dartmouth.edu/academics/graduate/mem.

Drexel University, College of Engineering, Program in Engineering Management, Philadelphia, PA 19104-2875. Offers MS, Certificate. Part-time and evening/weekend programs available. Postbaccalaureate distance learning degree programs offered (no on-campus study). *Degree requirements:* For master's, thesis optional. *Entrance requirements:* For master's, minimum GPA of 3.0. Additional exam requirements/recommendations for international students: Required—TOEFL. Electronic applications accepted. *Faculty research:* Quality, operations research and management, ergonomics, applied statistics.

Duke University, Graduate School, Pratt School of Engineering, Distributed Master of Engineering Management Program (d-MEMP), Durham, NC 27708-0271. Offers MEM. Part-time and evening/weekend programs available. Postbaccalaureate distance learning degree programs offered (minimal on-campus study). *Faculty:* 15 full-time (5 women), 12 part-time/adjunct (1 woman). *Students:* 25 part-time (7 women); includes 3 minority (1 Black or African American, non-Hispanic/Latino; 1 Asian, non-Hispanic/Latino; 1 Hispanic/Latino), 2 international. Average age 26. 59 applicants, 66% accepted, 25 enrolled. *Entrance requirements:* For master's, GRE General Test, resume, 3 letters of recommendation, statement of purpose, transcripts. Additional exam requirements/recommendations for international students: Required—TOEFL. *Application deadline:* For fall admission, 6/15 for domestic students. Application fee: $75. Electronic applications accepted. *Expenses:* Expenses: Contact institution. *Faculty research:* Entrepreneurship, innovation and product development, project management, operations and supply chain management, financial engineering. *Unit head:* Dr. Bradley A. Fox, Executive Director, Professional Master's Programs, 919-660-5516, Fax: 919-660-5456, E-mail: brad.fox@duke.edu. *Application contact:* Susan Brown, Assistant Director of Admissions, 919-660-8451, Fax: 919-660-5456, E-mail: susan.brown@duke.edu.
Website: http://memp.pratt.duke.edu/distance.

Duke University, Graduate School, Pratt School of Engineering, Master of Engineering Management Program, Durham, NC 27708-0271. Offers MEM. Part-time programs available. Postbaccalaureate distance learning degree programs offered. *Faculty:* 15 full-time (5 women), 12 part-time/adjunct (1 woman). *Students:* 161 full-time (59 women), 1 (woman) part-time; includes 21 minority (5 Black or African American, non-Hispanic/Latino; 2 American Indian or Alaska Native, non-Hispanic/Latino; 8 Asian, non-Hispanic/Latino; 5 Hispanic/Latino; 1 Native Hawaiian or other Pacific Islander, non-Hispanic/Latino), 126 international. Average age 24. 693 applicants, 44% accepted, 162 enrolled. In 2014, 143 master's awarded. *Entrance requirements:* For master's, GRE General Test, resume, 3 letters of recommendation, statement of purpose, transcripts. Additional exam requirements/recommendations for international students: Required—TOEFL. *Application deadline:* For fall admission, 6/15 for domestic students, 3/15 for international students; for spring admission, 11/1 for domestic students, 9/1 for international students. Application fee: $75. Electronic applications accepted. *Expenses:* Expenses: Contact institution. *Financial support:* Merit scholarships available. *Faculty research:* Entrepreneurship, innovation and product development, project management, operations and supply chain management, financial engineering. *Unit head:* Dr. Bradley A. Fox, Executive Director, 919-660-5455, Fax: 919-660-5456, E-mail: brad.fox@duke.edu. *Application contact:* Susan Brown, Assistant Director of Admissions, 919-660-8451, E-mail: Susan.Brown@duke.edu.
Website: http://memp.pratt.duke.edu/.

Engineering Management

Eastern Michigan University, Graduate School, College of Technology, School of Engineering Technology, Program in Engineering Management, Ypsilanti, MI 48197. Offers MS. Part-time and evening/weekend programs available. Postbaccalaureate distance learning degree programs offered (minimal on-campus study). *Students:* 19 full-time (8 women), 67 part-time (10 women); includes 11 minority (6 Black or African American, non-Hispanic/Latino; 1 American Indian or Alaska Native, non-Hispanic/Latino; 3 Asian, non-Hispanic/Latino; 1 Hispanic/Latino), 17 international. Average age 32. 66 applicants, 56% accepted, 17 enrolled. In 2014, 32 master's awarded. *Entrance requirements:* Additional exam requirements/recommendations for international students: Required—TOEFL. *Application deadline:* Applications are processed on a rolling basis. Application fee: $45. *Financial support:* Fellowships, research assistantships with full tuition reimbursements, teaching assistantships with full tuition reimbursements, career-related internships or fieldwork, Federal Work-Study, institutionally sponsored loans, scholarships/grants, tuition waivers (partial), and unspecified assistantships available. Support available to part-time students. Financial award applicants required to submit FAFSA. *Application contact:* Dr. Bryan Booker, Program Coordinator, 734-487-2040, Fax: 734-487-8755, E-mail: bbooker1@emich.edu.

Embry-Riddle Aeronautical University–Worldwide, College of Business, Daytona Beach, FL 32114-3900. Offers aviation (MBAA); engineering management (MSEM); leadership (MSL); logistics and supply chain management (MSLSCM); management (MSM); project management (MSPM). Part-time and evening/weekend programs available. Postbaccalaureate distance learning degree programs offered (no on-campus study). *Faculty:* 31 full-time (9 women), 160 part-time/adjunct (43 women). *Students:* 1,131 full-time (272 women), 1,036 part-time (219 women); includes 551 minority (235 Black or African American, non-Hispanic/Latino; 13 American Indian or Alaska Native, non-Hispanic/Latino; 72 Asian, non-Hispanic/Latino; 97 Hispanic/Latino; 5 Native Hawaiian or other Pacific Islander, non-Hispanic/Latino; 129 Two or more races, non-Hispanic/Latino), 80 international. Average age 37. In 2014, 585 master's awarded. *Degree requirements:* For master's, comprehensive exam (for some programs), thesis (for some programs). *Entrance requirements:* Additional exam requirements/recommendations for international students: Required—TOEFL (minimum score 550 paper-based; 79 iBT). *Application deadline:* Applications are processed on a rolling basis. Application fee: $50. Electronic applications accepted. *Expenses: Tuition:* Full-time $6720; part-time $560 per credit hour. *Financial support:* In 2014–15, 338 students received support. Scholarships/grants available. *Unit head:* Bobby McMasters, EdD, Interim Dean, Worldwide College of Business. *Application contact:* Admissions, 800-522-6787, E-mail: worldwide@erau.edu.
Website: http://worldwide.erau.edu/degrees-programs/colleges/business/department-of-business-admin/index.html.

Florida Institute of Technology, Graduate Programs, Extended Studies Division, Melbourne, FL 32901-6975. Offers acquisition and contract management (MS); aerospace engineering (MS); business administration (MBA, DBA); computer information systems (MS); computer science (MS); electrical engineering (MS); engineering management (MS); human resources management (MS); logistics management (MS), including humanitarian and disaster relief logistics; management (MS), including acquisition and contract management, e-business, human resources management, information systems, logistics management, management, transportation management; material acquisition management (MS); mechanical engineering (MS); operations research (MS); project management (MS), including information systems, operations research; public administration (MPA); quality management (MS); software engineering (MS); space systems (MS); space systems management (MS); supply chain management (MS); systems management (MS), including information systems, operations research; technology management (MS). Part-time and evening/weekend programs available. Postbaccalaureate distance learning degree programs offered (no on-campus study). *Faculty:* 7 full-time (1 woman), 112 part-time/adjunct (29 women). *Students:* 98 full-time (45 women), 975 part-time (396 women); includes 440 minority (292 Black or African American, non-Hispanic/Latino; 13 American Indian or Alaska Native, non-Hispanic/Latino; 32 Asian, non-Hispanic/Latino; 79 Hispanic/Latino; 1 Native Hawaiian or other Pacific Islander, non-Hispanic/Latino; 23 Two or more races, non-Hispanic/Latino), 4 international. Average age 37. 807 applicants, 56% accepted, 258 enrolled. In 2014, 457 master's awarded. *Degree requirements:* For master's, comprehensive exam (for some programs), capstone course. *Entrance requirements:* For master's, GMAT or resume showing 8 years of supervised experience, minimum GPA of 3.0, 2 letters of recommendation, resume. Additional exam requirements/recommendations for international students: Required—TOEFL (minimum score 550 paper-based; 79 iBT). *Application deadline:* For fall admission, 4/1 for international students; for spring admission, 9/30 for international students. Applications are processed on a rolling basis. Electronic applications accepted. *Expenses:* Expenses: Contact institution. *Financial support:* Application deadline: 3/1; applicants required to submit FAFSA. *Unit head:* Dr. Theodore R. Richardson, III, Senior Associate Dean, 321-674-8123, Fax: 321-674-7597, E-mail: trichardson@fit.edu. *Application contact:* Carolyn Farrior, Director of Graduate Admissions, Online Learning and Off-Campus Programs, 321-674-7118, Fax: 321-674-8216, E-mail: cfarrior@fit.edu.
Website: http://es.fit.edu.

Gannon University, School of Graduate Studies, College of Engineering and Business, School of Engineering and Computer Science, Program in Engineering Management, Erie, PA 16541-0001. Offers MSEM. Part-time and evening/weekend programs available. *Degree requirements:* For master's, comprehensive exam, thesis. *Entrance requirements:* For master's, GRE or GMAT, bachelor's degree in engineering, minimum GPA of 2.5, transcripts, 3 letters of recommendation. Additional exam requirements/recommendations for international students: Required—TOEFL (minimum score 79 iBT). Electronic applications accepted.

The George Washington University, School of Engineering and Applied Science, Department of Engineering Management and Systems Engineering, Washington, DC 20052. Offers system engineering (PhD). Part-time and evening/weekend programs available. *Faculty:* 18 full-time (3 women), 87 part-time/adjunct (9 women). *Students:* 87 full-time (34 women), 799 part-time (212 women); includes 300 minority (161 Black or African American, non-Hispanic/Latino; 4 American Indian or Alaska Native, non-Hispanic/Latino; 95 Asian, non-Hispanic/Latino; 32 Hispanic/Latino; 5 Native Hawaiian or other Pacific Islander, non-Hispanic/Latino; 3 Two or more races, non-Hispanic/Latino), 54 international. Average age 37. 491 applicants, 66% accepted, 181 enrolled. In 2014, 413 master's, 21 doctorates, 118 other advanced degrees awarded. *Degree requirements:* For master's, thesis optional; for doctorate, one foreign language, thesis/dissertation, final and qualifying exams, submission of articles; for other advanced degree, professional project. *Entrance requirements:* For master's, appropriate bachelor's degree, minimum GPA of 2.7, second-semester calculus; for doctorate, appropriate master's degree, minimum GPA of 3.5, 2 letters of recommendation; for other advanced degree, appropriate master's degree, minimum GPA of 3.4. Additional exam requirements/recommendations for international students: Required—TOEFL or The George Washington University English as a Foreign Language Test. *Application deadline:* For fall admission, 3/1 for domestic students; for spring admission, 10/1 for domestic students. Applications are processed on a rolling basis. Application fee: $75. *Financial support:* In 2014–15, 35 students received support. Fellowships with tuition reimbursements available, research assistantships, teaching assistantships with tuition reimbursements available, career-related internships or fieldwork, and institutionally sponsored loans available. Financial award application deadline: 3/1; financial award applicants required to submit FAFSA. *Faculty research:* Artificial intelligence and expert systems, human factors engineering and systems analysis. *Total annual research expenditures:* $421,800. *Unit head:* Dr. Thomas Mazzuchi, Chair, 202-994-7424, Fax: 202-994-0245, E-mail: mazzu@gwu.edu. *Application contact:* Adina Lav, Marketing, Recruiting and Admissions, 202-994-5827, Fax: 202-994-0909, E-mail: engineering@gwu.edu.
Website: http://www.emse.gwu.edu/.

Georgia Southern University, Jack N. Averitt College of Graduate Studies, Allen E. Paulson College of Engineering and Information Technology, Department of Mechanical Engineering, Program in Engineering/Engineering Management, Statesboro, GA 30460. Offers MSAE. *Students:* 14 full-time (2 women), 14 part-time (3 women); includes 10 minority (4 Black or African American, non-Hispanic/Latino; 1 Asian, non-Hispanic/Latino; 4 Hispanic/Latino; 1 Two or more races, non-Hispanic/Latino), 3 international. Average age 28. 6 applicants, 83% accepted, 4 enrolled. In 2014, 4 master's awarded. *Degree requirements:* For master's, thesis optional. *Entrance requirements:* Additional exam requirements/recommendations for international students: Required—TOEFL (minimum score 80 iBT). *Application deadline:* For fall admission, 3/1 priority date for domestic students; for spring admission, 11/1 for domestic students. Application fee: $50. *Expenses:* Tuition, state resident: full-time $7236; part-time $277 per semester hour. Tuition, nonresident: full-time $27,118; part-time $1105 per semester hour. *Required fees:* $2092. *Financial support:* In 2014–15, 13 students received support. Unspecified assistantships available. *Faculty research:* Business intelligence, data mining and analytics, e-commerce, industrial economics, business continuity and disaster recovery. *Unit head:* Dr. Frank Goforth, Chair, 912-478-7583, Fax: 912-478-1455, E-mail: fgoforth@georgiasouthern.edu.

Instituto Tecnológico y de Estudios Superiores de Monterrey, Campus Chihuahua, Graduate Programs, Chihuahua, Mexico. Offers computer systems engineering (Ingeniero); electrical engineering (Ingeniero); electromechanical engineering (Ingeniero); electronic engineering (Ingeniero); engineering administration (MEA); industrial engineering (MIE, Ingeniero); international trade (MIT); mechanical engineering (Ingeniero).

International Technological University, Program in Engineering Management, San Jose, CA 95113. Offers MSEM. Part-time and evening/weekend programs available. *Faculty:* 2 full-time (1 woman), 1 part-time/adjunct (0 women). *Students:* 312 full-time (137 women), 131 part-time (57 women); includes 1 minority (Asian, non-Hispanic/Latino), 442 international. Average age 28. 110 applicants, 87% accepted, 56 enrolled. In 2014, 34 master's awarded. *Degree requirements:* For master's, thesis or capstone project. *Entrance requirements:* Additional exam requirements/recommendations for international students: Required—TOEFL, IELTS. *Application deadline:* For fall admission, 8/1 for domestic and international students; for spring admission, 12/1 for domestic and international students; for summer admission, 4/1 for domestic and international students. Applications are processed on a rolling basis. Application fee: $80. Electronic applications accepted. *Expenses: Tuition:* Full-time $13,500; part-time $500 per credit. *Required fees:* $265 per trimester. *Unit head:* Dr. Barbara Hecker, 888-488-4968. *Application contact:* Mary Tran, Admissions Manager, 888-488-4968, E-mail: admissions@itu.edu.

Johns Hopkins University, G. W. C. Whiting School of Engineering, Master of Science in Engineering Management Program, Baltimore, MD 21218-2699. Offers biomaterials (MSEM); civil engineering (MSEM); communications science (MSEM); computer science (MSEM); environmental systems analysis, economics and public policy (MSEM); fluid mechanics (MSEM); materials science and engineering (MSEM); mechanical engineering (MSEM); mechanics and materials (MSEM); nanobiotechnology (MSEM); nanomaterials and nanotechnology (MSEM); operations research (MSEM); probability and statistics (MSEM); smart product and device design (MSEM). *Entrance requirements:* For master's, GRE, 3 letters of recommendation, resume. Additional exam requirements/recommendations for international students: Required—TOEFL (minimum score 600 paper-based; 100 iBT) or IELTS (minimum score 7). Electronic applications accepted.

Kansas State University, Graduate School, College of Engineering, Department of Industrial and Manufacturing Systems Engineering, Manhattan, KS 66506. Offers engineering management (MEM); industrial engineering (MS); operations research (MS). Part-time programs available. Postbaccalaureate distance learning degree programs offered (no on-campus study). *Faculty:* 10 full-time (2 women), 1 part-time/adjunct (0 women). *Students:* 26 full-time (8 women), 58 part-time (9 women); includes 11 minority (5 Black or African American, non-Hispanic/Latino; 2 Asian, non-Hispanic/Latino; 1 Hispanic/Latino; 1 Native Hawaiian or other Pacific Islander, non-Hispanic/Latino; 2 Two or more races, non-Hispanic/Latino), 16 international. Average age 29. 61 applicants, 46% accepted, 13 enrolled. In 2014, 26 master's, 4 doctorates awarded. *Degree requirements:* For master's, thesis or alternative; for doctorate, thesis/dissertation. *Entrance requirements:* For master's, GRE General Test (minimum score of 750 old version, 159 new format on Quantitative portion of exam), bachelor's degree in engineering, mathematics, or physical science; for doctorate, GRE General Test (minimum score of 770 old version, 164 new format on Quantitative portion of exam), master's degree in engineering or industrial manufacturing. Additional exam requirements/recommendations for international students: Required—PTE (minimum score 58), TOEFL (minimum score 550 paper-based; 79 iBT) or IELTS (minimum score 6.5). *Application deadline:* For fall admission, 6/1 priority date for domestic students, 12/1 priority date for international students; for spring admission, 11/1 priority date for domestic students, 8/1 priority date for international students. Applications are processed on a rolling basis. Application fee: $50 ($75 for international students). Electronic applications accepted. *Financial support:* In 2014–15, 12 research assistantships (averaging $12,442 per year), 9 teaching assistantships with full tuition reimbursements (averaging $14,111 per year) were awarded; Federal Work-Study, institutionally sponsored loans, and scholarships/grants also available. Support available to part-time students. Financial award application deadline: 3/1; financial award applicants required to submit FAFSA. *Faculty research:* Industrial engineering, ergonomics, healthcare systems engineering, manufacturing processes, operations research, engineering management. *Total annual research expenditures:* $2.6 million. *Unit head:* Dr. Bradley Kramer, Head, 785-532-5606, Fax: 785-532-3738, E-mail: bradleyk@k-state.edu. *Application contact:* Dr. David Ben-Arieh, Chair of Graduate Committee, 785-532-5606, Fax: 785-532-3738, E-mail: imse@k-state.edu.
Website: http://www.imse.k-state.edu/.

Kettering University, Graduate School, Department of Business, Flint, MI 48504. Offers MBA, MS. *Accreditation:* ACBSP. Part-time and evening/weekend programs available. Postbaccalaureate distance learning degree programs offered (no on-campus study). *Entrance requirements:* Additional exam requirements/recommendations for international students: Required—TOEFL (minimum score 550 paper-based; 79 iBT). Electronic applications accepted.

Lamar University, College of Graduate Studies, College of Engineering, Department of Industrial Engineering, Beaumont, TX 77710. Offers engineering management (MEM); industrial engineering (ME, MES, DE). *Faculty:* 7 full-time (1 woman). *Students:* 83 full-time (10 women), 14 part-time (4 women); includes 3 minority (2 Black or African American, non-Hispanic/Latino; 1 Asian, non-Hispanic/Latino), 89 international. Average age 26. 161 applicants, 71% accepted, 53 enrolled. In 2014, 6 master's, 4 doctorates awarded. *Degree requirements:* For doctorate, thesis/dissertation. *Entrance requirements:* For master's and doctorate, GRE General Test. Additional exam requirements/recommendations for international students: Required—TOEFL (minimum score 550 paper-based; 79 iBT), IELTS (minimum score 6.5). *Application deadline:* For fall admission, 8/10 for domestic students, 7/1 for international students; for spring admission, 1/5 for domestic students, 12/1 for international students. Applications are processed on a rolling basis. Application fee: $25 ($50 for international students). *Expenses:* Tuition, state resident: full-time $5724; part-time $1908 per semester. Tuition, nonresident: full-time $12,240; part-time $4080 per semester. *Required fees:* $1940; $318 per credit hour. *Financial support:* In 2014–15, 2 fellowships (averaging $6,000 per year), 4 research assistantships (averaging $1,000 per year), 2 teaching assistantships (averaging $4,500 per year) were awarded. Financial award application deadline: 4/1. *Faculty research:* Process simulation, total quality management, ergonomics and safety, scheduling. *Unit head:* Dr. Brian Craig, Chair, 409-880-8804, Fax: 409-880-8121. *Application contact:* Melissa Gallien, Director, Admissions and Academic Services, 409-880-8888, Fax: 409-880-7419, E-mail: gradmissions@lamar.edu.
Website: http://engineering.lamar.edu/industrial.

Lawrence Technological University, College of Engineering, Southfield, MI 48075-1058. Offers architectural engineering (MS); automotive engineering (MS); civil engineering (MA, MS, PhD); construction engineering management (MA); electrical and computer engineering (MS); engineering management (MEM); industrial engineering (MS); manufacturing systems (ME, DE); mechanical engineering (MS, DE); mechatronic systems engineering (MS). Part-time and evening/weekend programs available. *Faculty:* 24 full-time (5 women), 15 part-time/adjunct (0 women). *Students:* 16 full-time (6 women), 478 part-time (71 women); includes 295 minority (15 Black or African American, non-Hispanic/Latino; 271 Asian, non-Hispanic/Latino; 7 Hispanic/Latino; 2 Two or more races, non-Hispanic/Latino), 38 international. Average age 27. 1,786 applicants, 40% accepted, 218 enrolled. In 2014, 106 master's awarded. *Degree requirements:* For master's, thesis (for some programs). *Entrance requirements:* Additional exam requirements/recommendations for international students: Required—TOEFL (minimum score 550 paper-based; 79 iBT). *Application deadline:* For fall admission, 8/1 priority date for domestic students, 5/29 for international students; for spring admission, 12/1 priority date for domestic students, 10/15 for international students. Applications are processed on a rolling basis. Application fee: $50. Electronic applications accepted. *Expenses: Tuition:* Full-time $14,700; part-time $1050 per credit hour. *Required fees:* $150. One-time fee: $150 part-time. *Financial support:* In 2014–15, 31 students received support, including 8 research assistantships (averaging $9,338 per year); Federal Work-Study and institutionally sponsored loans also available. Support available to part-time students. Financial award application deadline: 4/1; financial award applicants required to submit FAFSA. *Faculty research:* Advanced composite materials in bridges, strengthening existing bridges with carbon and glass fiber sheets, development of drive shafts using composite materials. *Unit head:* Dr. Nabil Grace, Dean, 248-204-2500, Fax: 248-204-2509, E-mail: engrdean@ltu.edu. *Application contact:* Jane Rohrback, Director of Admissions, 248-204-3160, Fax: 248-204-2228, E-mail: admissions@ltu.edu.
Website: http://www.ltu.edu/engineering/index.asp.

Lehigh University, P.C. Rossin College of Engineering and Applied Science, Department of Industrial and Systems Engineering, Bethlehem, PA 18015. Offers analytical finance (MS); healthcare systems engineering (M Eng); industrial and systems engineering (M Eng, MS); industrial engineering (PhD); management science and engineering (M Eng, MS); MBA/E. Part-time programs available. Postbaccalaureate distance learning degree programs offered (no on-campus study). *Faculty:* 16 full-time (2 women), 4 part-time/adjunct (1 woman). *Students:* 91 full-time (24 women), 14 part-time (4 women); includes 2 minority (both Asian, non-Hispanic/Latino), 93 international. Average age 25. 351 applicants, 20% accepted, 38 enrolled. In 2014, 39 master's, 3 doctorates awarded. *Degree requirements:* For master's, thesis (MS); project (M Eng); for doctorate, comprehensive exam, thesis/dissertation. *Entrance requirements:* For master's and doctorate, GRE General Test. Additional exam requirements/recommendations for international students: Required—TOEFL (minimum score 550 paper-based; 79 iBT). *Application deadline:* For fall admission, 7/15 for domestic and international students; for spring admission, 12/1 for domestic and international students. Applications are processed on a rolling basis. Application fee: $75. Electronic applications accepted. *Expenses:* Expenses: $1,340 per credit hour. *Financial support:* In 2014–15, 25 students received support, including 2 fellowships with full tuition reimbursements available (averaging $17,460 per year), 13 research assistantships with full tuition reimbursements available (averaging $15,300 per year), 10 teaching assistantships with full tuition reimbursements available (averaging $18,360 per year); career-related internships or fieldwork, scholarships/grants, tuition waivers, and unspecified assistantships also available. Financial award application deadline: 1/15. *Faculty research:* Mathematical optimization; logistics and service systems, stochastic processes and simulation; computational optimization and high performance computing; financial engineering and robust optimization. *Total annual research expenditures:* $2 million. *Unit head:* Dr. Tamas Terlaky, Chair, 610-758-4050, Fax: 610-758-4886, E-mail: terlaky@lehigh.edu. *Application contact:* Rita Frey, Graduate Coordinator, 610-758-4051, Fax: 610-758-4886, E-mail: ise@lehigh.edu.
Website: http://www.lehigh.edu/ise.

LeTourneau University, Graduate Programs, Longview, TX 75607-7001. Offers business administration (MBA); counseling (MA); curriculum and instruction (M Ed); education administration (M Ed); engineering (ME, MS); engineering management (MEM); health care administration (MS); marriage and family therapy (MA); psychology (MA); strategic leadership (MSL); teacher leadership (M Ed); teaching and learning (M Ed). Part-time programs available. Postbaccalaureate distance learning degree programs offered (no on-campus study). *Faculty:* 14 full-time (4 women), 41 part-time/adjunct (18 women). *Students:* 58 full-time (37 women), 359 part-time (289 women); includes 140 minority (78 Black or African American, non-Hispanic/Latino; 2 American Indian or Alaska Native, non-Hispanic/Latino; 4 Asian, non-Hispanic/Latino; 40 Hispanic/Latino; 16 Two or more races, non-Hispanic/Latino), 11 international. Average age 38. 199 applicants, 73% accepted, 130 enrolled. In 2014, 139 master's awarded. *Degree requirements:* For master's, thesis (for some programs). *Entrance requirements:* For master's, GRE (for engineering and psychology programs). Additional exam requirements/recommendations for international students: Required—TOEFL. *Application deadline:* For fall admission, 8/22 for domestic students, 8/29 for international students; for winter admission, 10/10 for domestic students; for spring admission, 1/2 for domestic students, 1/10 for international students; for summer admission, 5/1 for domestic and international students. Applications are processed on a rolling basis. Electronic applications accepted. Application fee is waived when completed online. *Financial support:* In 2014–15, 11 students received support,

including 16 research assistantships (averaging $11,621 per year); institutionally sponsored loans and unspecified assistantships also available. Financial award applicants required to submit FAFSA. *Application contact:* Chris Fontaine, Assistant Vice President for Global Campus Admissions, 903-233-4312, E-mail: chrisfontaine@letu.edu.
Website: http://www.letu.edu.

Lipscomb University, Program in Engineering Management, Nashville, TN 37204-3951. Offers MS. Part-time programs available. *Faculty:* 1 full-time (0 women), 2 part-time/adjunct (0 women). *Students:* 4 full-time (0 women), 6 part-time (2 women); includes 3 minority (all Black or African American, non-Hispanic/Latino). Average age 29. 9 applicants, 89% accepted, 5 enrolled. In 2014, 5 master's awarded. *Degree requirements:* For master's, capstone project. *Entrance requirements:* For master's, GRE (minimum scores 154 Verbal, 166 Quantitative, 3.6 Writing), 2 references, resume. Additional exam requirements/recommendations for international students: Required—TOEFL (minimum score 570 paper-based; 80 iBT). *Application deadline:* Applications are processed on a rolling basis. Application fee: $50 ($75 for international students). Electronic applications accepted. *Expenses:* Expenses: $1,225 per credit hour. *Financial support:* Applicants required to submit FAFSA. *Unit head:* David Davidson, Director, 615-966-5071, E-mail: david.davidson@lipscomb.edu. *Application contact:* Jenni Jones, Enrollment Manager, 615-966-5039, E-mail: jenni.jones@lipscomb.edu.
Website: http://www.lipscomb.edu/engineering/graduate-programs.

Louisiana Tech University, Graduate School, College of Engineering and Science, Department of Industrial Engineering, Ruston, LA 71272. Offers engineering and technology management (MS); industrial engineering (MS).

Loyola Marymount University, College of Science and Engineering, Department of Systems Engineering and Engineering Management, Program in System Engineering Leadership, Los Angeles, CA 90045-2659. Offers MS/MBA. *Entrance requirements:* Additional exam requirements/recommendations for international students: Required—TOEFL (minimum score 600 paper-based; 100 iBT). Electronic applications accepted.

Marquette University, Graduate School, Opus College of Engineering, Department of Mechanical Engineering, Milwaukee, WI 53201-1881. Offers engineering innovation (Certificate); engineering management (MSEM); mechanical engineering (MS, PhD); new product and process development (Certificate). Part-time and evening/weekend programs available. Terminal master's awarded for partial completion of doctoral program. *Degree requirements:* For master's, comprehensive exam, thesis (for some programs); for doctorate, comprehensive exam, thesis/dissertation, qualifying exam. *Entrance requirements:* For master's, GRE General Test, minimum GPA of 3.0, official transcripts from all current and previous colleges/universities except Marquette, three letters of recommendation; for doctorate, GRE General Test, minimum GPA of 3.0, official transcripts from all current and previous colleges/universities except Marquette, three letters of recommendation, statement of purpose, copies of any published work. Additional exam requirements/recommendations for international students: Required—TOEFL (minimum score 530 paper-based). Electronic applications accepted. *Faculty research:* Computer-integrated manufacturing, energy conversion, simulation modeling and optimization, applied mechanics, metallurgy.

Marshall University, Academic Affairs Division, College of Information Technology and Engineering, Weisbert Division of Engineering, Huntington, WV 25755. Offers engineering management (MSE); environmental engineering (MSE); mechanical engineering (MS); transportation and infrastructure engineering (MSE). Part-time and evening/weekend programs available. *Students:* 30 full-time (5 women), 28 part-time (7 women); includes 3 minority (all Black or African American, non-Hispanic/Latino), 22 international. Average age 29. In 2014, 11 master's awarded. *Degree requirements:* For master's, final project, oral exam. *Entrance requirements:* For master's, GMAT or GRE General Test, minimum undergraduate GPA of 2.75. Application fee: $40. *Financial support:* Tuition waivers (full) available. Support available to part-time students. Financial award application deadline: 8/1; financial award applicants required to submit FAFSA. *Unit head:* Dr. William Pierson, Chair, 304-696-2695, E-mail: pierson@marshall.edu. *Application contact:* Information Contact, 304-746-1900, Fax: 304-746-1902, E-mail: services@marshall.edu.
Website: http://www.marshall.edu/cite/.

Massachusetts Institute of Technology, School of Engineering, Engineering Systems Division, Cambridge, MA 02139. Offers engineering and management (SM); engineering systems* (SM, PhD); logistics (M Eng); technology and policy (SM); technology, management and policy (PhD); SM/MBA. *Faculty:* 19 full-time (5 women). *Students:* 327 full-time (106 women); includes 53 minority (7 Black or African American, non-Hispanic/Latino; 28 Asian, non-Hispanic/Latino; 15 Hispanic/Latino; 3 Two or more races, non-Hispanic/Latino), 141 international. Average age 31. 1,143 applicants, 32% accepted, 254 enrolled. In 2014, 158 master's, 9 doctorates awarded. *Degree requirements:* For master's, thesis; for doctorate, comprehensive exam, thesis/dissertation. *Entrance requirements:* Additional exam requirements/recommendations for international students: Required—IELTS. *Application deadline:* For fall admission, 12/15 for domestic and international students. Application fee: $75. Electronic applications accepted. *Expenses:* Expenses: Contact institution. *Financial support:* In 2014–15, 213 students received support, including 39 fellowships (averaging $35,000 per year), 102 research assistantships (averaging $33,200 per year), 18 teaching assistantships (averaging $31,400 per year); Federal Work-Study, institutionally sponsored loans, scholarships/grants, traineeships, health care benefits, and unspecified assistantships also available. Financial award application deadline: 4/15; financial award applicants required to submit FAFSA. *Faculty research:* Critical infrastructures, extended enterprises, energy and sustainability, health care delivery, humans and technology, uncertainty and dynamics, design and implementation, networks and flows, policy and standards. *Total annual research expenditures:* $14.4 million. *Unit head:* Munther A. Dahleh, Acting Director, 617-258-8773, E-mail: esdinquiries@mit.edu. *Application contact:* Graduate Admissions, 617-253-1182, E-mail: esdgrad@mit.edu.
Website: http://esd.mit.edu/.

McNeese State University, Doré School of Graduate Studies, College of Engineering and Engineering Technology, Department of Engineering, Master of Engineering Program, Lake Charles, LA 70609. Offers chemical engineering (M Eng); civil engineering (M Eng); electrical engineering (M Eng); engineering management (M Eng); mechanical engineering (M Eng). Part-time and evening/weekend programs available. *Degree requirements:* For master's, thesis or alternative. *Entrance requirements:* For master's, GRE, baccalaureate degree, minimum overall GPA of 3.0. Additional exam requirements/recommendations for international students: Required—TOEFL (minimum score 560 paper-based; 83 iBT).

Mercer University, Graduate Studies, Macon Campus, School of Engineering, Macon, GA 31207. Offers biomedical engineering (MSE); computer engineering (MSE); electrical engineering (MSE); engineering management (MSE); environmental engineering (MSE); environmental systems (MS); mechanical engineering (MSE); software engineering (MSE); software systems (MS); technical communications management (MS); technical management (MS). Part-time and evening/weekend programs available. Postbaccalaureate distance learning degree programs offered (no

on-campus study). *Faculty:* 20 full-time (6 women), 2 part-time/adjunct (0 women). *Students:* 10 full-time (4 women), 75 part-time (16 women); includes 10 minority (5 Black or African American, non-Hispanic/Latino; 4 Asian, non-Hispanic/Latino; 1 Hispanic/Latino), 4 international. Average age 42. In 2014, 70 master's awarded. *Degree requirements:* For master's, thesis or alternative. *Entrance requirements:* For master's, minimum undergraduate GPA of 3.0. Additional exam requirements/recommendations for international students: Required—TOEFL (minimum score 550 paper-based; 80 iBT). *Application deadline:* For fall admission, 4/1 priority date for domestic and international students; for spring admission, 11/1 priority date for domestic and international students. Applications are processed on a rolling basis. Application fee: $75. *Expenses:* Expenses: Contact institution. *Financial support:* Federal Work-Study available. *Unit head:* Dr. Wade H. Shaw, Dean, 478-301-2459, Fax: 478-301-5593, E-mail: shaw_wh@mercer.edu. *Application contact:* Dr. Richard O. Mines, Program Director, 478-301-2347, Fax: 478-301-5433, E-mail: mines_ro@mercer.edu.
Website: http://engineering.mercer.edu/.

Merrimack College, School of Science and Engineering, North Andover, MA 01845-5800. Offers mechanical engineering (MS), including engineering management. Part-time programs available. *Faculty:* 4 full-time (0 women), 1 part-time/adjunct (0 women). *Students:* 13 full-time (3 women), 3 part-time (0 women); includes 1 minority (Two or more races, non-Hispanic/Latino), 1 international. Average age 27. 22 applicants, 59% accepted, 8 enrolled. In 2014, 5 master's awarded. *Degree requirements:* For master's, variable foreign language requirement, comprehensive exam, thesis optional. *Entrance requirements:* For master's, official college transcripts, resume, personal statement, 2 recommendations. Additional exam requirements/recommendations for international students: Required—TOEFL (minimum score 84 iBT), IELTS (minimum score 6.5), PTE (minimum score 56). *Application deadline:* For fall admission, 8/15 for domestic and international students; for winter admission, 12/1 for domestic students, 11/15 for international students; for spring admission, 1/10 for domestic and international students. Applications are processed on a rolling basis. Application fee: $0. Electronic applications accepted. *Expenses:* Expenses: Contact institution. *Financial support:* Career-related internships or fieldwork, scholarships/grants, and health care benefits available. Support available to part-time students. Financial award application deadline: 5/1; financial award applicants required to submit FAFSA. *Application contact:* Rachael Tampone, Graduate Admission Counselor, 978-837-5196, E-mail: tamponer@merrimack.edu.
Website: http://www.merrimack.edu/academics/graduate/engineering/.

Middle Tennessee State University, College of Graduate Studies, College of Basic and Applied Sciences, Program in Professional Science, Murfreesboro, TN 37132. Offers actuarial sciences (MS); biostatistics (MS); biotechnology (MS); engineering management (MS); health care informatics (MS). Part-time and evening/weekend programs available. Postbaccalaureate distance learning degree programs offered. *Degree requirements:* For master's, comprehensive exam. *Entrance requirements:* For master's, GRE. Additional exam requirements/recommendations for international students: Required—TOEFL (minimum score 525 paper-based; 71 iBT) or IELTS (minimum score 6). *Faculty research:* Biotechnology, biostatistics, informatics.

Milwaukee School of Engineering, Rader School of Business, Program in Engineering Management, Milwaukee, WI 53202-3109. Offers MS. Part-time and evening/weekend programs available. *Faculty:* 2 full-time (1 woman), 8 part-time/adjunct (4 women). *Students:* 9 full-time (2 women), 45 part-time (6 women); includes 8 minority (2 Black or African American, non-Hispanic/Latino; 6 Hispanic/Latino), 2 international. Average age 32. 35 applicants, 57% accepted, 12 enrolled. In 2014, 37 master's awarded. *Degree requirements:* For master's, thesis, thesis defense or capstone project. *Entrance requirements:* For master's, GRE General Test or GMAT if undergraduate GPA less than 2.8, BS in engineering, engineering technology, science, business, management, or related area; 2 letters of recommendation. Additional exam requirements/recommendations for international students: Required—TOEFL (minimum score 90 iBT), IELTS (minimum score 6.5). *Application deadline:* Applications are processed on a rolling basis. Application fee: $0. Electronic applications accepted. *Expenses: Tuition:* Part-time $732 per credit. *Financial support:* In 2014–15, 15 students received support. Career-related internships or fieldwork, institutionally sponsored loans, scholarships/grants, traineeships, and tuition waivers (partial) available. Financial award application deadline: 3/15; financial award applicants required to submit FAFSA. *Faculty research:* Operations, project management, quality marketing. *Unit head:* Gene Wright, Director, 414-277-2286, Fax: 414-277-2487, E-mail: wright@msoe.edu. *Application contact:* Ian Dahlinghaus, Graduate Program Associate, 414-277-7208, E-mail: dahlinghaus@msoe.edu.
Website: http://www.msoe.edu/community/academics/business/page/1300/engineering-management-overview.

See Display on page 58 and Close-Up on page 83.

Milwaukee School of Engineering, Rader School of Business, Program in STEM Leadership, Milwaukee, WI 53202-3109. Offers MBA. Part-time programs available. *Students:* 1 applicant, 100% accepted. *Entrance requirements:* For master's, GRE or GMAT if GPA is below 3.0, official transcripts, two letters of recommendation, personal essay, minimum GPA of 3.0. Additional exam requirements/recommendations for international students: Required—TOEFL (minimum score 90 iBT), IELTS (minimum score 6.5). *Application deadline:* Applications are processed on a rolling basis. Electronic applications accepted. Application fee is waived when completed online. *Expenses: Tuition:* Part-time $732 per credit. *Financial support:* Institutionally sponsored loans available. Financial award application deadline: 3/15; financial award applicants required to submit FAFSA. *Unit head:* Dr. Kathy S. Faggiani, Director, 414-277-2711, E-mail: faggiani@msoe.edu. *Application contact:* Ian Dahlinghaus, Graduate Program Associate, 414-277-7208, E-mail: dahlinghaus@msoe.edu.
Website: http://www.msoe.edu/community/academics/business/page/2450/master-of-business-administration-in-stem-leadership-overview.

Missouri University of Science and Technology, Graduate School, Department of Engineering Management and Systems Engineering, Rolla, MO 65409. Offers engineering management (MS, DE, PhD); manufacturing engineering (M Eng, MS); systems engineering (MS, PhD). *Degree requirements:* For master's, thesis optional; for doctorate, comprehensive exam. *Entrance requirements:* For master's, GRE (minimum score 1150 verbal and quantitative, 4.5 writing); for doctorate, GRE (minimum score: 1100 verbal and quantitative, 3.5 writing). Additional exam requirements/recommendations for international students: Required—TOEFL (minimum score 580 paper-based). *Faculty research:* Management of technology, industrial engineering, manufacturing engineering, packaging engineering, quality engineering.

National University, Academic Affairs, School of Engineering and Computing, La Jolla, CA 92037-1011. Offers computer science (MS), including advanced computing, database engineering, software engineering; cyber security and information assurance (MS), including computer forensics, ethical hacking and penetration testing, health information assurance, information assurance and security; data analytics (MS); engineering management (MS), including enterprise architecture, project management, systems engineering, technology management; environmental engineering (MS); homeland security and emergency management (MS); management information systems (MS); project management (Certificate); sustainability management (MS); wireless communications (MS). Part-time and evening/weekend programs available. Postbaccalaureate distance learning degree programs offered (no on-campus study). *Faculty:* 24 full-time (5 women), 21 part-time/adjunct (5 women). *Students:* 275 full-time (72 women), 86 part-time (24 women); includes 147 minority (41 Black or African American, non-Hispanic/Latino; 48 Asian, non-Hispanic/Latino; 37 Hispanic/Latino; 7 Native Hawaiian or other Pacific Islander, non-Hispanic/Latino; 14 Two or more races, non-Hispanic/Latino), 95 international. Average age 33. In 2014, 281 master's awarded. *Degree requirements:* For master's, thesis (for some programs). *Entrance requirements:* For master's, interview, minimum GPA of 2.5. Additional exam requirements/recommendations for international students: Required—TOEFL (minimum score 550 paper-based; 79 iBT), IELTS (minimum score 6). *Application deadline:* Applications are processed on a rolling basis. Application fee: $60 ($65 for international students). Electronic applications accepted. *Expenses: Tuition:* Full-time $14,184; part-time $1773 per course. *Financial support:* Career-related internships or fieldwork, institutionally sponsored loans, scholarships/grants, and tuition waivers (partial) available. Support available to part-time students. Financial award application deadline: 6/30; financial award applicants required to submit FAFSA. *Faculty research:* Educational technology, scholarships in science. *Unit head:* School of Engineering and Computing, 800-628-8648, E-mail: soec@nu.edu. *Application contact:* Frank Rojas, Vice President for Enrollment Services, 800-628-8648, E-mail: advisor@nu.edu.
Website: http://www.nu.edu/OurPrograms/SchoolOfEngineeringAndTechnology.html.

Naval Postgraduate School, Departments and Academic Groups, Department of Systems Engineering, Monterey, CA 93943. Offers engineering systems (MS); product development (MS); systems engineering (MS, PhD, Certificate); systems engineering analysis (MS, PhD); systems engineering management (MS, PhD). Program only open to commissioned officers of the United States and friendly nations and selected United States federal civilian employees. Part-time programs available. *Degree requirements:* For master's, thesis (for some programs), internal project, capstone project, or research/dissertation paper (for some programs); for doctorate, thesis/dissertation (for some programs), internal project, capstone project, or research/dissertation paper (for some programs). *Faculty research:* Net-centric enterprise systems/services, artificial intelligence (AI) systems engineering, unconventional weapons of mass destruction, complex systems engineering, risk-benefit analysis.

New Jersey Institute of Technology, Newark College of Engineering, Newark, NJ 07102. Offers biomedical engineering (MS, PhD); chemical engineering (MS, PhD); computer engineering (MS, PhD); electrical engineering (MS, PhD); engineering management (MS); healthcare systems management (MS); industrial engineering (MS, PhD); Internet engineering (MS); manufacturing engineering (MS); mechanical engineering (MS, PhD); occupational safety and health engineering (MS); pharmaceutical bioprocessing (MS); pharmaceutical engineering (MS); pharmaceutical systems management (MS); power and energy systems (MS); telecommunications (MS); transportation (MS, PhD). Part-time and evening/weekend programs available. Terminal master's awarded for partial completion of doctoral program. *Degree requirements:* For master's, thesis optional; for doctorate, thesis/dissertation. *Entrance requirements:* For master's, GRE General Test; for doctorate, GRE General Test, minimum graduate GPA of 3.5. Additional exam requirements/recommendations for international students: Required—TOEFL (minimum score 550 paper-based; 79 iBT). Electronic applications accepted.

New Mexico Institute of Mining and Technology, Graduate Studies, Department of Management, Socorro, NM 87801. Offers engineering management (MEM). Part-time programs available.

Northeastern University, College of Engineering, Boston, MA 02115-5096. Offers bioengineering (PhD); chemical engineering (MS, PhD); civil engineering (MS, PhD); computer engineering (PhD); computer systems engineering (MS); electrical and computer engineering (MS); electrical and engineering leadership (MS); electrical engineering (PhD); energy systems (MS); engineering leadership (Certificate); engineering management (MRTP); industrial engineering (MS, PhD); information assurance (PhD); information systems (MS); interdisciplinary (PhD); mechanical engineering (MS, PhD); operations research (MS); telecommunication systems management (MS). Part-time programs available. *Expenses:* Contact institution.

Northwestern University, McCormick School of Engineering and Applied Science, Department of Industrial Engineering and Management Sciences, Master's in Engineering Management Program, Evanston, IL 60208. Offers MEM. Part-time and evening/weekend programs available. *Faculty:* 9 full-time (0 women), 8 part-time/adjunct (1 woman). *Students:* 61 full-time (22 women), 69 part-time (12 women); includes 41 minority (15 Black or African American, non-Hispanic/Latino; 22 Asian, non-Hispanic/Latino; 3 Hispanic/Latino; 1 Two or more races, non-Hispanic/Latino), 38 international. Average age 34. 315 applicants, 42% accepted, 94 enrolled. In 2014, 89 master's awarded. *Entrance requirements:* For master's, 3 years of work experience. Additional exam requirements/recommendations for international students: Required—TOEFL (minimum score 550 paper-based; 80 iBT), IELTS (minimum score 7). *Application deadline:* For fall admission, 8/15 priority date for domestic students, 7/1 priority date for international students; for winter admission, 11/15 priority date for domestic students, 11/1 priority date for international students; for spring admission, 2/15 priority date for domestic students, 2/1 priority date for international students. Applications are processed on a rolling basis. Application fee: $50. Electronic applications accepted. *Expenses:* Expenses: Contact institution. *Financial support:* Institutionally sponsored loans available. Financial award application deadline: 12/31; financial award applicants required to submit FAFSA. *Unit head:* Dr. Mark Werwath, Director, 847-491-4696, Fax: 847-491-5980, E-mail: m-werwath@northwestern.edu. *Application contact:* Diane Kessler, Associate Director, 847-491-2281, Fax: 847-491-5980, E-mail: dkessler@northwestern.edu.
Website: http://www.mem.northwestern.edu/.

Northwestern University, McCormick School of Engineering and Applied Science, MMM Program, Evanston, IL 60208. Offers MBA/MEM. *Unit head:* Dr. Julio Ottino, Dean, 847-491-5220, E-mail: jm-ottino@northwestern.edu. *Application contact:* Dr. Bruce Alan Lindvall, Assistant Dean for Graduate Studies, 847-491-4547, Fax: 847-491-5341, E-mail: b-lindvall@northwestern.edu.
Website: http://www.mmm.northwestern.edu/.

Oakland University, Graduate Study and Lifelong Learning, School of Engineering and Computer Science, Department of Industrial and Systems Engineering, Program in Engineering Management, Rochester, MI 48309-4401. Offers MS. *Entrance requirements:* Additional exam requirements/recommendations for international students: Required—TOEFL (minimum score 550 paper-based). Electronic applications accepted. *Expenses:* Contact institution.

Old Dominion University, Frank Batten College of Engineering and Technology, Program in Engineering Management, Norfolk, VA 23529. Offers MEM, MS, PhD. Part-time and evening/weekend programs available. Postbaccalaureate distance learning degree programs offered (no on-campus study). *Faculty:* 14 full-time (2 women), 12 part-time/adjunct (2 women). *Students:* 46 full-time (14 women), 243 part-time (42 women); includes 60 minority (27 Black or African American, non-Hispanic/Latino; 1

American Indian or Alaska Native, non-Hispanic/Latino; 11 Asian, non-Hispanic/Latino; 12 Hispanic/Latino; 3 Native Hawaiian or other Pacific Islander, non-Hispanic/Latino; 6 Two or more races, non-Hispanic/Latino), 42 international. Average age 32. 176 applicants, 78% accepted, 107 enrolled. In 2014, 138 master's, 11 doctorates awarded. *Degree requirements:* For master's, comprehensive exam, thesis optional, project; for doctorate, thesis/dissertation, candidacy exam. *Entrance requirements:* For master's, GRE, minimum GPA of 3.0; for doctorate, GRE, resume, letters of recommendation, minimum GPA of 3.0. Additional exam requirements/recommendations for international students: Required—TOEFL (minimum score 550 paper-based; 79 iBT). *Application deadline:* For fall admission, 6/1 priority date for domestic students, 4/15 for international students; for spring admission, 11/1 priority date for domestic students, 2/1 for international students. Applications are processed on a rolling basis. Application fee: $50. Electronic applications accepted. *Expenses:* Tuition, state resident: full-time $10,488; part-time $437 per credit. Tuition, nonresident: full-time $26,136; part-time $1089 per credit. *Required fees:* $64 per semester. One-time fee: $50. *Financial support:* In 2014–15, research assistantships with full and partial tuition reimbursements (averaging $20,000 per year), teaching assistantships with full and partial tuition reimbursements (averaging $20,000 per year) were awarded; fellowships, career-related internships or fieldwork, scholarships/grants, and tuition waivers (partial) also available. Support available to part-time students. Financial award application deadline: 2/15; financial award applicants required to submit FAFSA. *Faculty research:* Project management, systems engineering, modeling and simulation, virtual collaborative environments, multidisciplinary designs. *Total annual research expenditures:* $729,085. *Unit head:* Dr. Adrian Gheorghe, Chair, 757-683-4558, Fax: 757-683-5640, E-mail: agheorgh@odu.edu. *Application contact:* Dr. Ariel Pinto, Graduate Program Director, 757-683-4218, Fax: 757-683-5640, E-mail: enmagpd@odu.edu.
Website: http://eng.odu.edu/enma/.

Old Dominion University, Frank Batten College of Engineering and Technology, Program in Engineering Management and Systems Engineering, Norfolk, VA 23529. Offers D Eng. Part-time and evening/weekend programs available. Postbaccalaureate distance learning degree programs offered (no on-campus study). *Faculty:* 14 full-time (2 women), 12 part-time/adjunct (2 women). *Students:* 2 full-time (both women), 11 part-time (2 women); includes 4 minority (1 Black or African American, non-Hispanic/Latino; 1 American Indian or Alaska Native, non-Hispanic/Latino; 2 Hispanic/Latino). Average age 43. 3 applicants, 67% accepted, 2 enrolled. In 2014, 1 doctorate awarded. *Degree requirements:* For doctorate, thesis/dissertation, candidacy exam, project. *Entrance requirements:* For doctorate, GRE, resume, letters of recommendation, minimum GPA of 3.0, interview. Additional exam requirements/recommendations for international students: Required—TOEFL (minimum score 550 paper-based; 79 iBT). *Application deadline:* For fall admission, 6/1 priority date for domestic students, 4/15 for international students; for spring admission, 11/1 priority date for domestic students, 2/1 for international students. Applications are processed on a rolling basis. Application fee: $50. Electronic applications accepted. *Expenses:* Tuition, state resident: full-time $10,488; part-time $437 per credit. Tuition, nonresident: full-time $26,136; part-time $1089 per credit. *Required fees:* $64 per semester. One-time fee: $50. *Financial support:* In 2014–15, research assistantships with full and partial tuition reimbursements (averaging $20,000 per year), teaching assistantships with full and partial tuition reimbursements (averaging $20,000 per year) were awarded; fellowships, career-related internships or fieldwork, and tuition waivers also available. Support available to part-time students. Financial award application deadline: 2/15; financial award applicants required to submit FAFSA. *Faculty research:* Project management, systems engineering, modeling and simulation, virtual collaboration environments, multidisciplinary designs. *Total annual research expenditures:* $729,085. *Unit head:* Dr. Adrian Gheorghe, Department Chair, 757-683-4558, Fax: 757-683-5640, E-mail: enmagpd@odu.edu. *Application contact:* Dr. Andres Sousa-Poza, Graduate Program Director, 757-683-4734, Fax: 757-683-5640, E-mail: enmagpd@odu.edu.
Website: http://eng.odu.edu/enma/.

Penn State Great Valley, Graduate Studies, Engineering Division, Malvern, PA 19355-1488. Offers engineering management (MEM); software engineering (MSE); systems engineering (M Eng). *Unit head:* Dr. Craig S. Edelbrock, Chancellor, 610-648-3202 Ext. 610, Fax: 610-889-1334, E-mail: cse1@psu.edu. *Application contact:* JoAnn Kelly, Director of Admissions, 610-648-3315, Fax: 610-725-5296, E-mail: jek2@psu.edu.
Website: http://www.sgps.psu.edu/Academics/Degrees/31884.htm.

Penn State Harrisburg, Graduate School, School of Science, Engineering and Technology, Middletown, PA 17057-4898. Offers computer science (MS); electrical engineering (M Eng, MS); engineering management (MPS); engineering science (M Eng); environmental engineering (M Eng); structural engineering (Certificate). Part-time and evening/weekend programs available. *Unit head:* Dr. Mukund S. Kulkarni, Chancellor, 717-948-6105, Fax: 717-948-6452, E-mail: msk5@psu.edu. *Application contact:* Robert W. Coffman, Jr., Director of Enrollment Management, Admissions, 717-948-6250, Fax: 717-948-6325, E-mail: ric1@psu.edu.
Website: http://harrisburg.psu.edu/science-engineering-technology.

Point Park University, School of Arts and Sciences, Department of Natural Science and Engineering Technology, Pittsburgh, PA 15222-1984. Offers engineering management (MS); environmental studies (MS). Part-time and evening/weekend programs available. *Degree requirements:* For master's, comprehensive exam (for some programs), thesis or alternative. *Entrance requirements:* For master's, minimum QPA of 2.75, 2 letters of recommendation, minimum B average in engineering technology or a related field, official undergraduate transcript, statement of intent, resume. Additional exam requirements/recommendations for international students: Required—TOEFL. Electronic applications accepted.

Polytechnic University of Puerto Rico, Graduate School, Hato Rey, PR 00919. Offers business administration (MBA), including computer information systems, general management, management of information systems, management of international enterprises; civil engineering (ME, MS); computer engineering (ME, MS); computer science (MCS, MS); electrical engineering (ME, MS); engineering management (MEM); environmental management (MEM); landscape architecture (M Land Arch); manufacturing competitiveness (MMC, MS); manufacturing engineering (ME, MS); mechanical engineering (M Mech E). Part-time and evening/weekend programs available. *Entrance requirements:* For master's, 3 letters of recommendation.

Polytechnic University of Puerto Rico, Orlando Campus, Graduate School, Winter Park, FL 32792. Offers accounting (MBA); business administration (MBA); construction management (MEM); engineering management (MEM); environmental management (MEM); finance (MBA); human resources management (MBA); management of international enterprises (MBA); management of technology (MBA); manufacturing management (MEM). Part-time and evening/weekend programs available. Postbaccalaureate distance learning degree programs offered (no on-campus study). *Entrance requirements:* For master's, minimum GPA of 3.0. Additional exam requirements/recommendations for international students: Recommended—TOEFL. Electronic applications accepted.

Portland State University, Graduate Studies, College of Liberal Arts and Sciences, Systems Science Program, Portland, OR 97207-0751. Offers computational intelligence (Certificate); computer modeling and simulation (Certificate); systems science (MS); systems science/anthropology (PhD); systems science/business administration (PhD); systems science/civil engineering (PhD); systems science/economics (PhD); systems science/engineering management (PhD); systems science/general (PhD); systems science/mathematical sciences (PhD); systems science/mechanical engineering (PhD); systems science/psychology (PhD); systems science/sociology (PhD). *Faculty:* 2 full-time (0 women), 1 part-time/adjunct (0 women). *Students:* 6 full-time (2 women), 29 part-time (8 women); includes 6 minority (1 Black or African American, non-Hispanic/Latino; 1 American Indian or Alaska Native, non-Hispanic/Latino; 1 Asian, non-Hispanic/Latino; 3 Hispanic/Latino). Average age 41. 32 applicants, 19% accepted, 6 enrolled. In 2014, 10 master's, 3 doctorates awarded. *Degree requirements:* For master's, comprehensive exam (for some programs), thesis optional; for doctorate, variable foreign language requirement, comprehensive exam (for some programs), thesis/dissertation. *Entrance requirements:* For master's, GRE/GMAT scores are recommended but not required., GPA 3.0 for undergraduate or 3.0 for graduate work, 2 letters of recommendation, and statement of interest; for doctorate, GMAT, GRE General Test, GPA requirement is 3.0 for undergraduate and 3.25 for graduate, 2 letters of recommendation and statement of interest. Additional exam requirements/recommendations for international students: Required—TOEFL (minimum score 550 paper-based; 80 iBT). *Application deadline:* For fall admission, 1/15 for domestic and international students; for spring admission, 11/1 for domestic students. Application fee: $50. Electronic applications accepted. *Expenses:* Tuition, state resident: part-time $222 per credit. Tuition, nonresident: part-time $527 per credit. *Required fees:* $22 per contact hour. $100 per quarter. Tuition and fees vary according to program. *Financial support:* In 2014–15, 1 research assistantship with full and partial tuition reimbursement (averaging $2,358 per year) was awarded; teaching assistantships with full and partial tuition reimbursements, career-related internships or fieldwork, Federal Work-Study, scholarships/grants, and unspecified assistantships also available. Support available to part-time students. Financial award application deadline: 3/1; financial award applicants required to submit FAFSA. *Faculty research:* Systems theory and methodology, artificial intelligence neural networks, information theory, nonlinear dynamics/chaos, modeling and simulation. *Total annual research expenditures:* $137,833. *Unit head:* Prof. Wayne Wakeland, PhD, Chair, 503-725-4975, E-mail: wakeland@pdx.edu.
Website: http://www.pdx.edu/sysc/.

Portland State University, Graduate Studies, Maseeh College of Engineering and Computer Science, Department of Civil and Environmental Engineering, Portland, OR 97207-0751. Offers civil and environmental engineering (M Eng, MS, PhD); civil and environmental engineering management (M Eng); environmental sciences and resources (PhD); systems science (PhD). Part-time and evening/weekend programs available. *Faculty:* 16 full-time (3 women), 1 part-time/adjunct (0 women). *Students:* 71 full-time (18 women), 42 part-time (6 women); includes 9 minority (4 Black or African American, non-Hispanic/Latino; 1 Asian, non-Hispanic/Latino; 2 Hispanic/Latino; 2 Two or more races, non-Hispanic/Latino), 45 international. Average age 31. 119 applicants, 54% accepted, 29 enrolled. In 2014, 29 master's, 3 doctorates awarded. *Degree requirements:* For master's, comprehensive exam (for some programs), thesis (for some programs); for doctorate, one foreign language, comprehensive exam, thesis/dissertation, oral and written exams. *Entrance requirements:* For master's, B.S degree in an engineering field, science, or closely related area with a minimum GPA of 3.00; for doctorate, M.S. degree in an engineering field, science, or closely related area. Additional exam requirements/recommendations for international students: Required—TOEFL (minimum score 550 paper-based). *Application deadline:* For fall admission, 1/4 priority date for domestic and international students; for winter admission, 9/1 for domestic and international students; for spring admission, 11/1 for domestic and international students. Applications are processed on a rolling basis. Application fee: $50. *Expenses:* Tuition, state resident: part-time $222 per credit. Tuition, nonresident: part-time $527 per credit. *Required fees:* $22 per contact hour. $100 per quarter. Tuition and fees vary according to program. *Financial support:* In 2014–15, 15 research assistantships with full and partial tuition reimbursements (averaging $6,105 per year), 12 teaching assistantships with full and partial tuition reimbursements (averaging $2,471 per year) were awarded; career-related internships or fieldwork, Federal Work-Study, scholarships/grants, and unspecified assistantships also available. Support available to part-time students. Financial award application deadline: 3/1; financial award applicants required to submit FAFSA. *Faculty research:* Structures, water resources, geotechnical engineering, environmental engineering, transportation. *Total annual research expenditures:* $3.1 million. *Unit head:* Dr. Chris Monsere, Acting Chair, 503-725-9746, Fax: 503-725-4298, E-mail: monserec@cecs.pdx.edu. *Application contact:* Ariel Lewis, Department Manager, 503-725-4244, Fax: 503-725-4298, E-mail: ariel.lewis@pdx.edu.
Website: http://www.pdx.edu/cee/.

Portland State University, Graduate Studies, Maseeh College of Engineering and Computer Science, Department of Engineering and Technology Management, Portland, OR 97207-0751. Offers engineering and technology management (M Eng); engineering management (MS); manufacturing engineering (ME); manufacturing management (M Eng); systems science/engineering management (PhD); MS/MBA; MS/MS. Part-time and evening/weekend programs available. *Faculty:* 6 full-time (1 woman), 8 part-time/adjunct (2 women). *Students:* 62 full-time (20 women), 63 part-time (18 women); includes 21 minority (3 Black or African American, non-Hispanic/Latino; 1 American Indian or Alaska Native, non-Hispanic/Latino; 12 Asian, non-Hispanic/Latino; 4 Hispanic/Latino; 1 Two or more races, non-Hispanic/Latino), 68 international. Average age 36. 90 applicants, 67% accepted, 31 enrolled. In 2014, 27 master's, 5 doctorates awarded. *Degree requirements:* For master's, thesis optional; for doctorate, one foreign language, comprehensive exam, thesis/dissertation, oral and written exams. *Entrance requirements:* For master's, GRE optional, 2.75 undergraduate or 3.0 graduate (at least 12 credits), minimum 4 years of experience in engineering or related discipline, 3 letters of recommendation and background in probability/statistics, differential equations, computer programming and linear algebra; for doctorate, GRE General Test, 1100 for the sum of verbal and quantitative, or verbal and analytical., minimum GPA of 3.0 undergraduate or 3.25 graduate. Additional exam requirements/recommendations for international students: Required—TOEFL (minimum score 550 paper-based; 80 iBT). *Application deadline:* For fall admission, 4/1 for domestic students, 3/1 for international students; for winter admission, 9/1 for domestic students, 7/1 for international students; for spring admission, 11/1 for domestic students, 9/1 for international students; for summer admission, 2/1 for domestic students, 12/1 for international students. Application fee: $50. Electronic applications accepted. *Expenses:* Tuition, state resident: part-time $222 per credit. Tuition, nonresident: part-time $527 per credit. *Required fees:* $22 per contact hour. $100 per quarter. Tuition and fees vary according to program. *Financial support:* In 2014–15, 7 research assistantships with full and partial tuition reimbursements (averaging $1,913 per year), 8 teaching assistantships with full and partial tuition reimbursements (averaging $2,823 per year) were awarded; career-related internships or fieldwork, Federal Work-Study, scholarships/grants, and unspecified assistantships also available. Support available to part-time students. Financial award application deadline: 3/1; financial award applicants required to submit FAFSA. *Faculty research:* Scheduling, hierarchical decision modeling, operations research, knowledge-based information systems. *Total annual research expenditures:* $318,571. *Unit head:* Dr. Tim Anderson, Chair, 503-725-4668, Fax: 503-725-4667,

E-mail: tim.anderson@pdx.edu. *Application contact:* Shawn Wall, Department Manager, 503-725-4660, Fax: 503-547-8887, E-mail: info@etm.pdx.edu.
Website: http://www.pdx.edu/engineering-technology-management/.

Rensselaer Polytechnic Institute, Graduate School, Lally School of Management, Troy, NY 12180-3590. Offers MBA, MS, PhD, MS/MBA. *Accreditation:* AACSB. Part-time and evening/weekend programs available. *Faculty:* 151 full-time (30 women), 29 part-time/adjunct (11 women). *Students:* 77 full-time (35 women), 22 part-time (15 women); includes 8 minority (2 Black or African American, non-Hispanic/Latino; 3 Asian, non-Hispanic/Latino; 3 Two or more races, non-Hispanic/Latino), 75 international. Average age 31. 760 applicants, 34% accepted, 91 enrolled. In 2014, 140 master's, 4 doctorates awarded. *Degree requirements:* For doctorate, thesis/dissertation. *Entrance requirements:* For master's and doctorate, GMAT or GRE. Additional exam requirements/recommendations for international students: Required—TOEFL (minimum score 570 paper-based; 88 iBT), IELTS (minimum score 6.5), PTE (minimum score 60). *Application deadline:* For fall admission, 1/1 priority date for domestic and international students; for spring admission, 8/15 priority date for domestic and international students. Applications are processed on a rolling basis. Application fee: $75. Electronic applications accepted. *Expenses: Tuition:* Full-time $46,700; part-time $1945 per credit. Tuition and fees vary according to course load. *Financial support:* In 2014–15, 90 students received support, including research assistantships (averaging $18,500 per year), teaching assistantships (averaging $18,500 per year); fellowships and scholarships/grants also available. Financial award application deadline: 1/1; financial award applicants required to submit FAFSA. *Faculty research:* Business analytics, quantitative finance and risk analytics, management, supply chain management, technology commercialization and entrepreneurship. *Total annual research expenditures:* $986,905. *Unit head:* Dr. Gina O'Connor, Associate Dean, Lally School of Management, 518-276-6842, E-mail: oconng@rpi.edu. *Application contact:* Office of Graduate Admissions, 518-276-6216, E-mail: gradadmissions@rpi.edu.
Website: http://lallyschool.rpi.edu/.

Robert Morris University, Graduate Studies, School of Engineering, Mathematics and Science, Moon Township, PA 15108-1189. Offers engineering management (MS). Part-time and evening/weekend programs available. *Faculty:* 7 full-time (0 women). *Students:* 42 part-time (4 women); includes 4 minority (all Black or African American, non-Hispanic/Latino), 9 international. Average age 30. 45 applicants, 38% accepted, 15 enrolled. In 2014, 32 master's awarded. *Entrance requirements:* For master's, letters of recommendation. Additional exam requirements/recommendations for international students: Required—TOEFL (minimum score 550 paper-based; 79 iBT). *Application deadline:* For fall admission, 7/1 priority date for domestic and international students; for spring admission, 11/1 priority date for domestic and international students. Applications are processed on a rolling basis. Application fee: $35. Electronic applications accepted. *Expenses:* Expenses: Contact institution. *Financial support:* Federal Work-Study, institutionally sponsored loans, and unspecified assistantships available. Financial award application deadline: 5/1; financial award applicants required to submit FAFSA. *Unit head:* Dr. Maria V. Kalevitch, Dean, 412-397-4020, Fax: 412-397-2472, E-mail: kalevitch@rmu.edu.
Website: http://www.rmu.edu/web/cms/schools/sems/.

Rochester Institute of Technology, Graduate Enrollment Services, Kate Gleason College of Engineering, Design, Development and Manufacturing Department, MS Program in Product Development, Rochester, NY 14623-5603. Offers MS. Part-time and evening/weekend programs available. Postbaccalaureate distance learning degree programs offered. *Students:* 39 part-time (4 women); includes 2 minority (1 Black or African American, non-Hispanic/Latino; 1 Hispanic/Latino), 1 international. Average age 35. 23 applicants, 74% accepted, 16 enrolled. In 2014, 13 master's awarded. *Degree requirements:* For master's, capstone project. *Entrance requirements:* For master's, TOEFL, IELTS, or PTE for non-native English speakers, undergraduate degree in engineering or related field, minimum GPA of 3.0, 2 years of experience in product development. Additional exam requirements/recommendations for international students: Required—PTE (minimum score 58), TOEFL (minimum score 550 paper-based; 79 iBT) or IELTS (minimum score 6.5). *Application deadline:* For fall admission, 2/15 for domestic and international students. Applications are processed on a rolling basis. Application fee: $60. Electronic applications accepted. *Expenses:* Expenses: $1,673 per credit hour. *Financial support:* Institutionally sponsored loans and scholarships/grants available. Support available to part-time students. Financial award applicants required to submit FAFSA. *Faculty research:* Platform element dynamics in a multi-product development environment, applying self-organizing principles to product development in a globally-distributed environment, collaborative design and development to accelerate durable goods design and manufacturing. *Unit head:* Mark Smith, Graduate Program Director, 585-475-7971, Fax: 585-475-4080, E-mail: mpdmail@rit.edu. *Application contact:* Diane Ellison, Associate Vice President, Graduate Enrollment Services, 585-475-2229, Fax: 585-475-7164, E-mail: gradinfo@rit.edu.
Website: https://www.rit.edu/kgcoe/mpd/.

Rochester Institute of Technology, Graduate Enrollment Services, Kate Gleason College of Engineering, Industrial and Systems Engineering Department, ME Program in Engineering Management, Rochester, NY 14623-5603. Offers ME. Part-time programs available. *Students:* 21 full-time (13 women), 3 part-time (2 women); includes 1 minority (Hispanic/Latino), 10 international. Average age 24. 174 applicants, 29% accepted, 20 enrolled. In 2014, 31 master's awarded. *Degree requirements:* For master's, Capstone. *Entrance requirements:* For master's, TOEFL, IELTS, or PTE for non-native English speakers, Recommended minimum GPA of 3.0. Additional exam requirements/recommendations for international students: Required—PTE (minimum score 58), TOEFL (minimum score 550 paper-based; 79 iBT) or IELTS (minimum score 6.5). *Application deadline:* For fall admission, 2/15 priority date for domestic and international students; for spring admission, 12/15 priority date for domestic and international students. Applications are processed on a rolling basis. Electronic applications accepted. *Expenses:* Expenses: $1,673 per credit hour. *Financial support:* In 2014–15, 20 students received support. Research assistantships with partial tuition reimbursements available, teaching assistantships with partial tuition reimbursements available, career-related internships or fieldwork, Federal Work-Study, institutionally sponsored loans, scholarships/grants, and unspecified assistantships available. Support available to part-time students. Financial award applicants required to submit FAFSA. *Faculty research:* Advanced manufacturing, engineering education, ergonomics and human factors, healthcare delivery systems, operations research and simulation, systems engineering, production and logistics, sustainable engineering. *Unit head:* Dr. Marcos Esterman, Associate Professor, 585-475-2598, E-mail: mxeeie@rit.edu. *Application contact:* Diane Ellison, Associate Vice President, Graduate Enrollment Services, 585-475-2229, Fax: 585-475-7164, E-mail: gradinfo@rit.edu.
Website: http://www.rit.edu/kgcoe/ise/program/master-engineering-degrees/master-engineering-engineering-management.

Rose-Hulman Institute of Technology, Faculty of Engineering and Applied Sciences, Department of Engineering Management, Terre Haute, IN 47803-3999. Offers M Eng, MS. Part-time and evening/weekend programs available. Postbaccalaureate distance learning degree programs offered (minimal on-campus study). *Faculty:* 5 full-time (1 woman), 2 part-time/adjunct (0 women). *Students:* 31 full-time (13 women), 9 part-time (7 women); includes 3 minority (1 Black or African American, non-Hispanic/Latino; 1 American Indian or Alaska Native, non-Hispanic/Latino; 1 Two or more races, non-Hispanic/Latino), 17 international. Average age 25. 46 applicants, 78% accepted, 24 enrolled. In 2014, 21 master's awarded. *Degree requirements:* For master's, integrated project. *Entrance requirements:* For master's, GRE, minimum GPA of 3.0. Additional exam requirements/recommendations for international students: Required—TOEFL (minimum score 580 paper-based; 92 iBT). *Application deadline:* For fall admission, 2/1 priority date for domestic students. Applications are processed on a rolling basis. Application fee: $0. *Expenses: Tuition:* Full-time $40,449. *Financial support:* In 2014–15, 30 students received support. Fellowships with full and partial tuition reimbursements available available. *Faculty research:* Systems engineering, technical entrepreneurship, project management, organizational development and management, manufacturing and supply chain, marketing and new product development. *Unit head:* Dr. Craig Downing, Chairman, 812-877-8822, Fax: 812-877-8878, E-mail: craig.downing@rose-hulman.edu. *Application contact:* Dr. Azad Siahmakoun, Associate Dean of the Faculty, 812-877-8400, Fax: 812-877-8061, E-mail: siahmako@rose-hulman.edu.
Website: http://www.rose-hulman.edu/academics/academic-departments/engineering-management.aspx.

St. Cloud State University, School of Graduate Studies, College of Science and Engineering, Program in Engineering Management, St. Cloud, MN 56301-4498. Offers MEM. *Degree requirements:* For master's, thesis or alternative. *Entrance requirements:* For master's, GRE General Test, minimum GPA of 2.75. Additional exam requirements/recommendations for international students: Required—Michigan English Language Assessment Battery; Recommended—TOEFL (minimum score 550 paper-based), IELTS (minimum score 6.5). Electronic applications accepted.

Saint Martin's University, Office of Graduate Studies, Program in Engineering Management, Lacey, WA 98503. Offers M Eng Mgt. Part-time and evening/weekend programs available. *Faculty:* 1 full-time (0 women), 1 part-time/adjunct (0 women). *Students:* 8 full-time (3 women), 5 part-time (0 women); includes 3 minority (2 Black or African American, non-Hispanic/Latino; 1 Asian, non-Hispanic/Latino), 7 international. Average age 29. 11 applicants, 73% accepted, 3 enrolled. In 2014, 4 master's awarded. *Degree requirements:* For master's, comprehensive exam (for some programs), thesis optional. *Entrance requirements:* For master's, engineering license examination, minimum GPA of 2.8. Additional exam requirements/recommendations for international students: Required—TOEFL (minimum score 550 paper-based; 79 iBT); Recommended—IELTS (minimum score 6.5). *Application deadline:* For fall admission, 4/1 priority date for domestic and international students; for spring admission, 11/1 priority date for domestic and international students. Applications are processed on a rolling basis. Application fee: $50. Electronic applications accepted. *Expenses: Tuition:* Part-time $1045 per credit. *Financial support:* Fellowships, research assistantships, and Federal Work-Study available. Support available to part-time students. Financial award application deadline: 3/1; financial award applicants required to submit FAFSA. *Faculty research:* Highway safety management, transportation, hydraulics, database structure. *Unit head:* Bill Phillips, Director, 360-438-4320, Fax: 560-438-4522, E-mail: bphillips@stmartin.edu. *Application contact:* Bailey Craft, Assistant Director for Graduate Recruitment, 360-412-6142, E-mail: gradstudies@stmartin.edu.
Website: http://www.stmartin.edu/GradStudies/MEM/.

St. Mary's University, Graduate School, Department of Engineering, Program in Engineering Systems Management, San Antonio, TX 78228-8507. Offers MS. Part-time programs available. Postbaccalaureate distance learning degree programs offered (no on-campus study). *Students:* 12 full-time (4 women), 10 part-time (4 women); includes 7 minority (1 Black or African American, non-Hispanic/Latino; 6 Hispanic/Latino), 13 international. Average age 30. 20 applicants, 40% accepted, 6 enrolled. In 2014, 29 master's awarded. *Degree requirements:* For master's, comprehensive exam. *Entrance requirements:* For master's, GRE, Have a Bachelor of Science (B.S.) degree in engineering, or related areas such as the physical sciences or mathematics. Have a minimum grade point average (GPA) of 3.00. A completed application form, a written statement of purpose indicating the applicant's interests and objectives, two letters of recommendation, and official transcripts. Additional exam requirements/recommendations for international students: Required—TOEFL (minimum score 550 paper-based; 80 iBT), IELTS (minimum score 6). *Application deadline:* Applications are processed on a rolling basis. Application fee: $0. Electronic applications accepted. *Expenses: Tuition:* Full-time $15,070; part-time $800 per credit hour. *Required fees:* $156 per semester. *Financial support:* Career-related internships or fieldwork, Federal Work-Study, institutionally sponsored loans, scholarships/grants, and health care benefits available. Financial award application deadline: 3/31; financial award applicants required to submit FAFSA. *Unit head:* Dr. Rafael Moras, Director, 210-431-2017, E-mail: rmoras@stmarytx.edu.
Website: https://www.stmarytx.edu/academics/set/graduate/engineering-systems-management/.

Santa Clara University, School of Engineering, Santa Clara, CA 95053. Offers analog circuit design (Certificate); applied mathematics (MS); ASIC design and test (Certificate); bioengineering (MS); civil engineering (MS); computer science and engineering (MS, PhD); controls (Certificate); digital signal processing (Certificate); dynamics (Certificate); electrical engineering (MS, PhD); engineering (Engineer); engineering management (MS); fundamentals of electrical engineering (Certificate); information assurance (Certificate); materials engineering (Certificate); mechanical design analysis (Certificate); mechanical engineering (MS, PhD); mechatronics systems engineering (Certificate); microwave and antennas (Certificate); networking (Certificate); renewable energy (Certificate); software engineering (Certificate); sustainable energy (MS); technology jump-start (Certificate); thermofluids (Certificate). Part-time and evening/weekend programs available. *Faculty:* 59 full-time (23 women), 80 part-time/adjunct (14 women). *Students:* 584 full-time (239 women), 353 part-time (102 women); includes 224 minority (7 Black or African American, non-Hispanic/Latino; 144 Asian, non-Hispanic/Latino; 50 Hispanic/Latino; 2 Native Hawaiian or other Pacific Islander, non-Hispanic/Latino; 21 Two or more races, non-Hispanic/Latino), 548 international. Average age 27. 1,248 applicants, 51% accepted, 375 enrolled. In 2014, 283 master's, 5 doctorates, 1 other advanced degree awarded. *Degree requirements:* For master's, thesis (for some programs); for doctorate, thesis/dissertation; for other advanced degree, thesis. *Entrance requirements:* For master's, GRE, transcript; for doctorate, GRE, master's degree or equivalent; for other advanced degree, master's degree, published paper. Additional exam requirements/recommendations for international students: Required—TOEFL (minimum score 550 paper-based; 79 iBT). *Application deadline:* For fall admission, 8/1 for domestic students, 7/15 for international students; for winter admission, 10/28 for domestic students, 9/23 for international students; for spring admission, 2/25 for domestic students, 1/21 for international students. Applications are processed on a rolling basis. Application fee: $60. Electronic applications accepted. *Expenses:* Expenses: Contact institution. *Financial support:* In 2014–15, 94 students received support. Fellowships with full and partial tuition reimbursements available, research assistantships with full and partial tuition reimbursements available, teaching assistantships with full tuition reimbursements available, career-related internships or fieldwork, Federal Work-Study, institutionally sponsored loans, and scholarships/grants available. Support available to part-time students. Financial award application deadline: 3/2; financial award applicants required to submit FAFSA. *Faculty research:* Video encoding, nanostructures, robotics, microfluidics, water resources. *Total annual research expenditures:* $1.6 million. *Unit head:* Dr. Alex Zecevic, Associate Dean for Graduate Studies, 408-554-2394, E-mail: azecevic@scu.edu. *Application contact:* Stacey Tinker, Director of Enrollment Management, 408-554-4748, Fax: 408-554-4323, E-mail: stinker@scu.edu. Website: http://www.scu.edu/engineering/graduate/.

South Dakota School of Mines and Technology, Graduate Division, Program in Construction Engineering Management, Rapid City, SD 57701-3995. Offers MS. Part-time and evening/weekend programs available. Postbaccalaureate distance learning degree programs offered. *Faculty:* 11 full-time (2 women), 3 part-time/adjunct (1 woman). *Students:* 4 full-time (0 women), 8 part-time (2 women); includes 2 minority (1 American Indian or Alaska Native, non-Hispanic/Latino; 1 Hispanic/Latino). Average age 32. 12 applicants, 42% accepted, 3 enrolled. In 2014, 10 master's awarded. *Entrance requirements:* For master's, GRE General Test. Additional exam requirements/recommendations for international students: Required—TOEFL (minimum score 520 paper-based; 68 iBT). *Application deadline:* For fall admission, 7/1 for domestic students, 4/1 for international students; for spring admission, 11/1 for domestic students, 9/1 for international students. Applications are processed on a rolling basis. Application fee: $35. Electronic applications accepted. *Expenses:* Tuition, state resident: full-time $5050; part-time $210.40 per credit hour.. Tuition, nonresident: full-time $11,290; part-time $470.30 per credit hour. *Required fees:* $4680. *Financial support:* Application deadline: 5/15. *Unit head:* Clifford Bienert, Coordinator, 605-394-1694, E-mail: clifford.bienert@sdsmt.edu. *Application contact:* Rachel Howard, Office of Graduate Education, 605-355-3468, Fax: 605-394-1767, E-mail: rachel.howard@sdsmt.edu. Website: http://graded.sdsmt.edu/academics/programs/cm/.

South Dakota School of Mines and Technology, Graduate Division, Program in Engineering Management, Rapid City, SD 57701-3995. Offers MS. Program offered jointly with The University of South Dakota. Part-time programs available. Postbaccalaureate distance learning degree programs offered (no on-campus study). *Faculty:* 11 full-time (3 women), 3 part-time/adjunct (1 woman). *Students:* 12 full-time (1 woman), 33 part-time (8 women); includes 4 minority (1 American Indian or Alaska Native, non-Hispanic/Latino; 3 Hispanic/Latino), 4 international. Average age 30. 26 applicants, 62% accepted, 13 enrolled. In 2014, 16 master's awarded. *Entrance requirements:* For master's, GMAT. Additional exam requirements/recommendations for international students: Required—TOEFL, TWE. *Application deadline:* For fall admission, 7/1 priority date for domestic students, 4/1 for international students; for spring admission, 11/1 for domestic students, 9/1 for international students. Applications are processed on a rolling basis. Application fee: $35. Electronic applications accepted. *Expenses:* Tuition, state resident: full-time $5050; part-time $210.40 per credit hour. Tuition, nonresident: full-time $11,290; part-time $470.30 per credit hour. *Required fees:* $4680. *Financial support:* In 2014–15, 2 students received support, including 5 research assistantships with partial tuition reimbursements available (averaging $7,368 per year), 4 teaching assistantships with partial tuition reimbursements available (averaging $3,374 per year); fellowships, Federal Work-Study, and institutionally sponsored loans also available. Support available to part-time students. Financial award application deadline: 5/15. *Total annual research expenditures:* $84,822. *Unit head:* Dr. Stuart D. Kellogg, Director, 605-394-1271, E-mail: stuart.kellogg@sdsmt.edu. *Application contact:* Rachel Howard, Office of Graduate Education, 605-355-3468, Fax: 605-394-1767, E-mail: rachel.howard@sdsmt.edu. Website: http://www.sdsmt.edu/Academics/Departments/Industrial-Engineering/Graduate-Education/Engineering-Management-MS/.

Southern Illinois University Carbondale, Graduate School, College of Engineering, Program in Quality Engineering Management, Carbondale, IL 62901-4701. Offers MS. *Faculty:* 11 full-time (1 woman). *Students:* 27 full-time (6 women), 37 part-time (5 women); includes 12 minority (8 Black or African American, non-Hispanic/Latino; 1 American Indian or Alaska Native, non-Hispanic/Latino; 1 Asian, non-Hispanic/Latino; 2 Hispanic/Latino), 13 international. Average age 25. 45 applicants, 60% accepted, 19 enrolled. In 2014; 20 master's awarded. *Degree requirements:* For master's, comprehensive exam, thesis. *Entrance requirements:* For master's, minimum GPA of 2.7. Additional exam requirements/recommendations for international students: Required—TOEFL. *Application deadline:* Applications are processed on a rolling basis. Application fee: $50. *Expenses:* Tuition, state resident: full-time $10,176; part-time $1153 per credit. Tuition, nonresident: full-time $20,814; part-time $1744 per credit. *Required fees:* $7092; $394 per credit. $2364 per semester. *Financial support:* In 2014–15, 1 fellowship with full tuition reimbursement, 3 research assistantships with full tuition reimbursements, 9 teaching assistantships with full tuition reimbursements were awarded; tuition waivers (full) also available. Financial award application deadline: 7/1. *Faculty research:* Computer-aided manufacturing, robotics, quality assurance. *Total annual research expenditures:* $205,198. *Unit head:* Dr. Mandara Savage, Interim Chair, 618-536-3396. *Application contact:* Jeanne Baker, Administrative Clerk, 618-536-3396, E-mail: jeanne@engr.siu.edu.

Southern Methodist University, Bobby B. Lyle School of Engineering, Department of Engineering Management, Information, and Systems, Dallas, TX 75275. Offers engineering management (MSEM, DE); information engineering and management (MSIEM); operations research (MS, PhD); systems engineering (MS, PhD). Part-time and evening/weekend programs available. Postbaccalaureate distance learning degree programs offered. Terminal master's awarded for partial completion of doctoral program. *Degree requirements:* For master's, thesis optional; for doctorate, thesis/dissertation, oral and written qualifying exams. *Entrance requirements:* For master's, minimum GPA of 3.0 in last 2 years; bachelor's degree in engineering, mathematics, sciences, or technical area; for doctorate, GRE General Test (operations research, engineering management), bachelor's degree in related field. Additional exam requirements/recommendations for international students: Required—TOEFL. *Faculty research:* Telecommunications, decision systems, information engineering, operations research, software.

Stanford University, School of Engineering, Department of Management Science and Engineering, Stanford, CA 94305-9991. Offers MS, PhD. Terminal master's awarded for partial completion of doctoral program. *Degree requirements:* For doctorate, thesis/dissertation, qualification procedure. *Entrance requirements:* For master's and doctorate, GRE General Test. Additional exam requirements/recommendations for international students: Required—TOEFL. Electronic applications accepted. *Expenses: Tuition:* Full-time $44,184; part-time $982 per credit hour. *Required fees:* $191.

Stevens Institute of Technology, Graduate School, School of Systems and Enterprises, Program in Engineering Management, Hoboken, NJ 07030. Offers M Eng, PhD.

Stevens Institute of Technology, Graduate School, Wesley J. Howe School of Technology Management, Program in Business Administration, Hoboken, NJ 07030. Offers engineering management (MBA); financial engineering (MBA); information management (MBA); information technology in financial services (MBA); information

technology in the pharmaceutical industry (MBA); information technology outsourcing (MBA); pharmaceutical management (MBA); project management (MBA); technology management (MBA); telecommunications management (MBA).

Syracuse University, L. C. Smith College of Engineering and Computer Science, Program in Engineering Management, Syracuse, NY 13244. Offers MS. Part-time programs available. *Students:* 49 full-time (14 women), 9 part-time (4 women); includes 3 minority (1 Black or African American, non-Hispanic/Latino; 1 Asian, non-Hispanic/Latino; 1 Two or more races, non-Hispanic/Latino), 45 international. Average age 25. 194 applicants, 44% accepted, 15 enrolled. In 2014, 27 master's awarded. *Entrance requirements:* Additional exam requirements/recommendations for international students: Required—TOEFL (minimum score 100 iBT). *Application deadline:* For fall admission, 7/1 priority date for domestic students, 6/1 priority date for international students. Applications are processed on a rolling basis. Application fee: $75. Electronic applications accepted. *Expenses:* Tuition: Part-time $1341 per credit. *Required fees:* $1341 per credit. *Financial support:* Fellowships, research assistantships, and teaching assistantships available. Financial award application deadline: 1/1. *Unit head:* Fred Carranti, Program Director, 315-443-4346, E-mail: carranti@syr.edu. *Application contact:* Kathy Datthyn-Madigan, Information Contact, 315-443-4367, E-mail: kjdatthy@syr.edu. Website: http://lcs.syr.edu/.

Tarleton State University, College of Graduate Studies, College of Science and Technology, Department of Engineering Technology, Stephenville, TX 76402. Offers MS. Part-time and evening/weekend programs available. *Degree requirements:* For master's, comprehensive exam, thesis optional. *Entrance requirements:* For master's, GRE General Test, minimum GPA of 3.0. Additional exam requirements/recommendations for international students: Required—TOEFL (minimum score 550 paper-based; 80 iBT). Electronic applications accepted.

Temple University, College of Engineering, Program in Engineering Management, Philadelphia, PA 19122-6096. Offers MS, Certificate. Program jointly offered with Fox School of Business and Management. Part-time and evening/weekend programs available. *Faculty:* 1 full-time (0 women), 1 part-time/adjunct (0 women). *Students:* 3 full-time (1 woman), 3 part-time (1 woman); includes 1 minority (Black or African American, non-Hispanic/Latino), 2 international. Average age 26. 16 applicants, 69% accepted, 6 enrolled. *Entrance requirements:* For master's, GRE, minimum GPA of 3.0; BS in engineering from ABET-accredited or equivalent institution or related degree; resume; goals statement; three letters of reference; official transcripts. Additional exam requirements/recommendations for international students: Required—TOEFL (minimum score 550 paper-based; 79 iBT), IELTS (minimum score 6.5). *Application deadline:* For fall admission, 3/1 priority date for domestic and international students; for spring admission, 11/1 priority date for domestic students, 8/1 priority date for international students. Applications are processed on a rolling basis. Application fee: $60. Electronic applications accepted. *Expenses:* Expenses: $913 per credit hour in-state; $1,210 per credit hour out-of-state. *Financial support:* Application deadline: 3/1; applicants required to submit FAFSA. *Application contact:* Mojan Arshad, Assistant Coordinator, Graduate Studies, 215-204-7800, Fax: 215-204-6936, E-mail: gradengr@temple.edu. Website: http://engineering.temple.edu/department/engineering-management.

Texas Tech University, Graduate School, Edward E. Whitacre Jr. College of Engineering, Department of Industrial Engineering, Lubbock, TX 79409-3061. Offers industrial engineering (MSIE, PhD); systems and engineering management (MSSEM, PhD). Part-time programs available. Postbaccalaureate distance learning degree programs offered (minimal on-campus study). *Faculty:* 14 full-time (2 women), 1 part-time/adjunct (0 women). *Students:* 79 full-time (17 women), 64 part-time (14 women); includes 15 minority (5 Black or African American, non-Hispanic/Latino; 1 American Indian or Alaska Native, non-Hispanic/Latino; 2 Asian, non-Hispanic/Latino; 6 Hispanic/Latino; 1 Two or more races, non-Hispanic/Latino), 80 international. Average age 32. 275 applicants, 55% accepted, 58 enrolled. In 2014, 17 master's, 7 doctorates awarded. Terminal master's awarded for partial completion of doctoral program. *Degree requirements:* For master's, comprehensive exam, thesis optional; for doctorate, comprehensive exam, thesis/dissertation. *Entrance requirements:* For master's, GRE (Verbal and Quantitative); for doctorate, GRE (Verbal and Quantitative), MS. Additional exam requirements/recommendations for international students: Required—TOEFL (minimum score 550 paper-based; 79 iBT). *Application deadline:* For fall admission, 6/1 priority date for domestic students, 1/15 priority date for international students; for spring admission, 9/1 priority date for domestic students, 6/15 priority date for international students. Applications are processed on a rolling basis. Application fee: $60. Electronic applications accepted. *Expenses:* Tuition, state resident: full-time $6310; part-time $262.92 per credit hour. Tuition, nonresident: full-time $14,998; part-time $624.92 per credit hour. *Required fees:* $2701; $36.50 per credit. $912.50 per semester. Tuition and fees vary according to course load. *Financial support:* In 2014–15, 57 students received support, including 55 fellowships (averaging $3,146 per year), 5 research assistantships (averaging $26,747 per year), 13 teaching assistantships (averaging $20,625 per year); scholarships/grants, tuition waivers (partial), and unspecified assistantships also available. Financial award application deadline: 2/1; financial award applicants required to submit FAFSA. *Faculty research:* Engineering management, operations research, manufacturing, ergonomics, quality. *Total annual research expenditures:* $614,109. *Unit head:* Dr. Hong-Chao Zhang, Interim Chair, 806-742-3543, E-mail: hong-chao.zhang@ttu.edu. *Application contact:* Dr. Simon Hsiang, Professor, 806-742-3543, Fax: 806-742-3411, E-mail: simon.hsiang@ttu.edu. Website: http://www.ie.ttu.edu/.

Trine University, Allen School of Engineering and Technology, Angola, IN 46703-1764. Offers civil engineering (ME); engineering management (MS). Part-time and evening/weekend programs available. *Students:* 2 full-time (0 women). In 2014, 4 master's awarded. *Degree requirements:* For master's, comprehensive exam, thesis. *Entrance requirements:* Additional exam requirements/recommendations for international students: Required—TOEFL. *Application deadline:* For fall admission, 6/30 for domestic students. Application fee: $100. *Expenses: Tuition:* Full-time $12,000; part-time $670 per credit hour. Tuition and fees vary according to degree level, campus/location, program and student level. *Financial support:* Career-related internships or fieldwork and traineeships available. Financial award application deadline: 3/1; financial award applicants required to submit FAFSA. *Faculty research:* CAD, computer numerical control, parametric modeling, megatronics. *Unit head:* Dr. VK Sharma, Dean, Allen School of Engineering and Technology, 260-665-4432, E-mail: sharmavk@trine.edu. *Application contact:* Dr. Earl D. Brooks, II, President, 260-665-4101, E-mail: brookse@trine.edu.

Tufts University, School of Engineering, The Gordon Institute, Medford, MA 02155. Offers MSEM. Part-time programs available. *Faculty:* 3 full-time (2 women), 19 part-time/adjunct (7 women). *Students:* 125 full-time (30 women), 40 part-time (5 women); includes 36 minority (4 Black or African American, non-Hispanic/Latino; 19 Asian, non-Hispanic/Latino; 8 Hispanic/Latino; 5 Two or more races, non-Hispanic/Latino), 13 international. Average age 32. 118 applicants, 62% accepted, 62 enrolled. In 2014, 65 master's awarded. *Entrance requirements:* Additional exam requirements/recommendations for international students: Required—TOEFL (minimum score 550 paper-based; 80 iBT), IELTS (minimum score 6.5). *Application deadline:* For fall

admission, 3/15 priority date for domestic students, 1/15 for international students. Applications are processed on a rolling basis. Application fee: $75. Electronic applications accepted. *Expenses:* Expenses: Contact institution. *Faculty research:* Engineering management, engineering leadership. *Unit head:* Nancy Buczko, Graduate Program Director. *Application contact:* Carla Eberle, Admissions Manager, 617-627-3395, E-mail: tgi@tufts.edu.
Website: http://gordon.tufts.edu/.

Union Graduate College, School of Engineering and Computer Science, Schenectady, NY 12308-3107. Offers computer science (MS); electrical engineering (MS); engineering and management systems (MS); mechanical engineering (MS). Part-time and evening/weekend programs available. *Degree requirements:* For master's, capstone course. *Entrance requirements:* For master's, minimum GPA of 3.0, letters of recommendation. Additional exam requirements/recommendations for international students: Required—TOEFL (minimum score 550 paper-based). Electronic applications accepted. *Expenses:* Contact institution.

Université de Sherbrooke, Faculty of Engineering, Programs in Engineering Management, Sherbrooke, QC J1K 2R1, Canada. Offers M Eng, Diploma. Part-time and evening/weekend programs available. *Entrance requirements:* For master's and Diploma, bachelor's degree in engineering, 1 year of practical experience. Electronic applications accepted.

The University of Alabama at Birmingham, School of Engineering, Program in Materials Engineering, Birmingham, AL 35294. Offers MS Mt E, PhD. PhD offered jointly with The University of Alabama (Tuscaloosa). *Students:* 24 full-time (4 women), 7 part-time (0 women); includes 8 minority (4 Black or African American, non-Hispanic/Latino; 3 Asian, non-Hispanic/Latino; 1 Hispanic/Latino), 13 international. Average age 28. In 2014, 6 master's, 1 doctorate awarded. *Degree requirements:* For master's, comprehensive exam, thesis (for some programs), project/thesis; for doctorate, comprehensive exam, thesis/dissertation. *Entrance requirements:* For master's and doctorate, GRE General Test (minimum quantitative score of 148/170 [600/800 on the old scale], verbal score of 153/180 [500/800 on the old scale], and 3/6 on the analytical writing), minimum GPA of 3.0 on all undergraduate degree major courses attempted. Additional exam requirements/recommendations for international students: Required—TOEFL (minimum score 80 iBT), TWE (minimum score 3.5). Application fee: $0 ($60 for international students). Electronic applications accepted. *Expenses:* Tuition, state resident: full-time $7090; part-time $370 per credit hour. Tuition, nonresident: full-time $16,072; part-time $869 per credit hour. Full-time tuition and fees vary according to course load and program. *Financial support:* Fellowships with full and partial tuition reimbursements, research assistantships with full tuition reimbursements, career-related internships or fieldwork, Federal Work-Study, and institutionally sponsored loans available. Support available to part-time students. *Faculty research:* Casting metallurgy, microgravity solidification, thin film techniques, ceramics/glass processing, biomedical materials processing. *Unit head:* Dr. Uday Vaidya, Graduate Program Director, 205-934-9199, E-mail: uvaidya@uab.edu. *Application contact:* Susan Noblitt Banks, Director of Graduate School Operations, 205-934-8227, Fax: 205-934-8413, E-mail: gradschool@uab.edu.
Website: https://www.uab.edu/engineering/home/departments-research/mse/grad.

The University of Alabama at Birmingham, School of Engineering, Program in Mechanical Engineering, Birmingham, AL 35294. Offers mechanical engineering (MSME); research/design (MSME); technology/engineering management (MSME). *Students:* 8 full-time (1 woman), 16 part-time (1 woman); includes 2 minority (1 Black or African American, non-Hispanic/Latino; 1 Asian, non-Hispanic/Latino), 8 international. Average age 27. In 2014, 5 master's awarded. *Degree requirements:* For master's, thesis (for some programs). *Entrance requirements:* For master's, GRE (minimum 50th percentile ranking on Quantitative Reasoning and Verbal Reasoning sections), minimum B-level scholarship overall or over the last 60 semester hours of earned credit. Additional exam requirements/recommendations for international students: Required—TOEFL (minimum score 80 iBT). *Application deadline:* For fall admission, 7/1 for domestic students; for spring admission, 11/1 for domestic students; for summer admission, 4/1 for domestic students. Electronic applications accepted. *Expenses:* Tuition, state resident: full-time $7090; part-time $370 per credit hour. Tuition, nonresident: full-time $16,072; part-time $869 per credit hour. Full-time tuition and fees vary according to course load and program. *Financial support:* Research assistantships available. *Unit head:* Dr. David Littlefield, Graduate Program Director, 205-934-8460, E-mail: littlefield@uab.edu. *Application contact:* Susan Noblitt Banks, Director of Graduate School Operations, 205-934-8227, Fax: 205-934-8413, E-mail: gradschool@uab.edu.
Website: http://www.uab.edu/engineering/home/departments-research/me/graduate.

University of Alaska Anchorage, School of Engineering, Program in Engineering Management, Anchorage, AK 99508. Offers MS. Part-time and evening/weekend programs available. *Degree requirements:* For master's, comprehensive exam (for some programs), thesis optional. *Entrance requirements:* For master's, BS in engineering or science, work experience in engineering or science. Additional exam requirements/recommendations for international students: Required—TOEFL (minimum score 550 paper-based). *Faculty research:* Engineering economy, long-range forecasting, multicriteria design making, project management process and training.

University of Alaska Anchorage, School of Engineering, Program in Science Management, Anchorage, AK 99508. Offers MS. Part-time and evening/weekend programs available. *Degree requirements:* For master's, comprehensive exam (for some programs), thesis (for some programs). *Entrance requirements:* For master's, GRE General Test, BS in engineering or scientific field. Additional exam requirements/recommendations for international students: Required—TOEFL (minimum score 550 paper-based). *Faculty research:* Engineering economy, long-range forecasting, multicriteria decision making, project management process and training.

University of Alaska Fairbanks, College of Engineering and Mines, Department of Civil and Environmental Engineering, Engineering and Science Management Program, Fairbanks, AK 99775. Offers science management (MS). Part-time programs available. *Students:* 1 (woman) full-time, 4 part-time (1 woman); includes 2 minority (1 American Indian or Alaska Native, non-Hispanic/Latino; 1 Hispanic/Latino). Average age 38. 2 applicants, 50% accepted, 1 enrolled. *Degree requirements:* For master's, comprehensive exam, thesis or alternative, project, oral defense of project. *Entrance requirements:* For master's, bachelor's degree from accredited institution with minimum cumulative undergraduate and major GPA of 3.0, on-the-job experience (recommended). Additional exam requirements/recommendations for international students: Required—TOEFL (minimum score 550 paper-based; 79 iBT), IELTS (minimum score 6.5). *Application deadline:* For fall admission, 6/1 for domestic students, 3/1 for international students; for spring admission, 10/15 for domestic students, 9/1 for international students. Applications are processed on a rolling basis. Application fee: $60. Electronic applications accepted. *Expenses:* Tuition, state resident: full-time $7614; part-time $423 per credit. Tuition, nonresident: full-time $15,552; part-time $864 per credit. Tuition and fees vary according to course level, course load and reciprocity agreements. *Financial support:* In 2014–15, 1 teaching assistantship (averaging $7,302 per year) was awarded; fellowships, research assistantships, career-related internships or fieldwork, Federal Work-Study, scholarships/grants, health care benefits, and unspecified assistantships also available. Support available to part-time students. Financial award application deadline: 7/1; financial award applicants required to submit FAFSA. *Faculty research:* Traffic studies, decision analysis, application of optimization, transportation safety. *Unit head:* Dr. Robert Perkins, Program Coordinator, 907-474-7241, Fax: 907-474-6087, E-mail: fycee@uaf.edu. *Application contact:* Mary Kreta, Director of Admissions, 907-474-7500, Fax: 907-474-7097, E-mail: admissions@uaf.edu.
Website: http://cem.uaf.edu/cee/esm.aspx.

University of Alberta, Faculty of Graduate Studies and Research, Department of Mechanical Engineering, Edmonton, AB T6G 2E1, Canada. Offers engineering management (M Eng); mechanical engineering (M Eng, M Sc, PhD); MBA/M Eng. Part-time programs available. *Degree requirements:* For master's, thesis; for doctorate, thesis/dissertation. *Entrance requirements:* For master's and doctorate, minimum GPA of 7.0 on a 9.0 scale. Additional exam requirements/recommendations for international students: Required—TOEFL (minimum score 580 paper-based). *Faculty research:* Combustion and environmental issues, advanced materials, computational fluid dynamics, biomedical, acoustics and vibrations.

University of California, Berkeley, Graduate Division, College of Engineering, Department of Civil and Environmental Engineering, Berkeley, CA 94720-1500. Offers engineering and project management (M Eng, MS, D Eng, PhD); environmental engineering (M Eng, MS, D Eng, PhD); geoengineering (M Eng, MS, D Eng, PhD); structural engineering, mechanics and materials (M Eng, MS, D Eng, PhD); transportation engineering (M Eng, MS, D Eng, PhD); M Arch/MS; MCP/MS; MPP/MS. *Degree requirements:* For master's, comprehensive exam or thesis (MS); for doctorate, thesis/dissertation, qualifying exam. *Entrance requirements:* For master's, GRE General Test, minimum GPA of 3.0, 3 letters of recommendation; for doctorate, GRE General Test, minimum GPA of 3.5, 3 letters of recommendation. Additional exam requirements/recommendations for international students: Required—TOEFL (minimum score 570 paper-based). Electronic applications accepted.

University of California, Irvine, Henry Samueli School of Engineering, Program in Engineering Management, Irvine, CA 92697. Offers MS. Program offered jointly with the Paul Merage School of Business. *Students:* 19 full-time (6 women); includes 5 minority (2 Asian, non-Hispanic/Latino; 2 Hispanic/Latino; 1 Two or more races, non-Hispanic/Latino), 13 international. Average age 25. 194 applicants, 26% accepted, 18 enrolled. In 2014, 9 master's awarded. *Application deadline:* For fall admission, 1/15 priority date for domestic students. Applications are processed on a rolling basis. Application fee: $90 ($110 for international students). *Unit head:* John LaRue, Graduate Advisor, 949-824-6737, E-mail: jclarue@uci.edu. *Application contact:* Jean Bennett, Director of Graduate Student Affairs, 949-824-6475, Fax: 949-824-8200, E-mail: jean.bennett@uci.edu.
Website: http://www.eng.uci.edu/admissions/graduate/programs-and-concentrations/engineering-management.

University of Colorado Boulder, Graduate School, College of Engineering and Applied Science, Engineering Management Program, Boulder, CO 80309. Offers operations and logistics (ME); quality and process (ME); research and development (ME). *Students:* 74 full-time (17 women), 110 part-time (28 women); includes 40 minority (8 Black or African American, non-Hispanic/Latino; 1 American Indian or Alaska Native, non-Hispanic/Latino; 12 Asian, non-Hispanic/Latino; 13 Hispanic/Latino; 6 Two or more races, non-Hispanic/Latino), 7 international. Average age 34. 66 applicants, 65% accepted, 35 enrolled. *Entrance requirements:* For master's, minimum undergraduate GPA of 3.0. *Application deadline:* For fall admission, 3/15 for domestic students, 1/15 for international students; for spring admission, 10/15 for domestic students, 8/5 for international students. Application fee: $50 ($70 for international students). Electronic applications accepted. *Financial support:* In 2014–15, 39 students received support, including 11 fellowships (averaging $2,760 per year); institutionally sponsored loans, scholarships/grants, health care benefits, and unspecified assistantships also available. Financial award applicants required to submit FAFSA. *Faculty research:* Quality and process, research and development, operations and logistics.
Website: http://engineeringanywhere.colorado.edu/emp.

University of Colorado Colorado Springs, College of Engineering and Applied Science, Program in General Engineering, Colorado Springs, CO 80933-7150. Offers energy engineering (ME); engineering management (ME); information assurance (ME); software engineering (ME); space operations (ME); systems engineering (ME). Part-time and evening/weekend programs available. Postbaccalaureate distance learning degree programs offered (minimal on-campus study). *Faculty:* 2 full-time (0 women), 8 part-time/adjunct (2 women). *Students:* 15 full-time (2 women), 159 part-time (30 women); includes 29 minority (3 Black or African American, non-Hispanic/Latino; 1 American Indian or Alaska Native, non-Hispanic/Latino; 10 Asian, non-Hispanic/Latino; 12 Hispanic/Latino; 3 Two or more races, non-Hispanic/Latino), 63 international. Average age 36. 113 applicants, 65% accepted, 39 enrolled. In 2014, 29 master's, 6 doctorates awarded. *Degree requirements:* For master's, thesis, portfolio, or project; for doctorate, comprehensive exam, thesis/dissertation. *Entrance requirements:* For master's, GRE (minimum score of 148 new grading scale on quantitative portion if GPA is less than 3.0); for doctorate, GRE (minimum score of 148 new grading scale on the quantitative portion if the applicant has not graduated from a program of recognized standing), minimum GPA of 3.3 in the bachelor or master degree program attempted. Additional exam requirements/recommendations for international students: Required—TOEFL (minimum score 80 iBT), IELTS (minimum score 6). *Application deadline:* For fall admission, 6/1 for domestic and international students; for spring admission, 11/1 for domestic and international students; for summer admission, 4/15 for domestic and international students. Application fee: $60 ($100 for international students). Electronic applications accepted. *Expenses:* Expenses: Contact institution. *Financial support:* In 2014–15, 10 students received support, including 2 fellowships (averaging $6,000 per year), 16 research assistantships (averaging $11,600 per year); teaching assistantships, Federal Work-Study, and scholarships/grants also available. Support available to part-time students. Financial award application deadline: 3/1; financial award applicants required to submit FAFSA. *Total annual research expenditures:* $91,458. *Unit head:* Dr. Ramaswami Dandapani, Dean, 719-255-3543, Fax: 719-255-3542, E-mail: rdan@cas.uccs.edu. *Application contact:* Dawn House, Coordinator, 719-255-3246, E-mail: dhouse@uccs.edu.

University of Dayton, Department of Engineering Management and Systems, Dayton, OH 45469. Offers engineering management (MSEM); management science (MSMS). Part-time and evening/weekend programs available. Postbaccalaureate distance learning degree programs offered (no on-campus study). *Faculty:* 4 full-time (1 woman), 13 part-time/adjunct (2 women). *Students:* 85 full-time (18 women), 31 part-time (8 women); includes 10 minority (7 Black or African American, non-Hispanic/Latino; 2 Asian, non-Hispanic/Latino; 1 Hispanic/Latino), 56 international. Average age 29. 186 applicants, 55% accepted, 35 enrolled. In 2014, 37 master's awarded. *Degree requirements:* For master's, thesis or alternative, 7 core courses/5 electives (for MSEM); 4 core courses/8 electives (for MSMS). *Entrance requirements:* For master's, undergraduate degree from accredited program in engineering, engineering technology,

math or science with minimum GPA of 3.0 (for engineering management); undergraduate degree with at least three semesters of analytic geometry and calculus, linear algebra background, and minimum GPA of 3.0 (for management science). Additional exam requirements/recommendations for international students: Required—TOEFL (minimum score 550 paper-based; 80 iBT). *Application deadline:* For fall admission, 8/1 for domestic students, 5/1 priority date for international students; for winter admission, 7/1 for international students; for spring admission, 11/1 priority date for international students; for summer admission, 3/1 for international students. Applications are processed on a rolling basis. Application fee: $0. Electronic applications accepted. *Expenses: Tuition:* Full-time $10,176; part-time $848 per credit. *Required fees:* $25; $25 per course. Part-time tuition and fees vary according to course level, course load, degree level and program. *Financial support:* Application deadline: 3/1; applicants required to submit FAFSA. *Faculty research:* Modeling and simulation analysis, statistical experimental design, reliability and maintainability, operations research modeling, engineering education. *Total annual research expenditures:* $70,621. *Unit head:* Dr. Edward Mykytka, Chair, 937-229-2238, E-mail: emykytka1@udayton.edu. *Application contact:* 937-229-4462, E-mail: graduateadmission@udayton.edu.
Website: http://www.udayton.edu/engineering/departments/engineering_management_and_systems.

University of Denver, Daniel Felix Ritchie School of Engineering and Computer Science, Department of Mechanical and Materials Engineering, Denver, CO 80208. Offers bioengineering (MS); engineering (MS, PhD); engineering/management (MS); materials science (MS, PhD); mechanical engineering (MS, PhD); nanoscale science and engineering (MS, PhD). Part-time programs available. *Faculty:* 10 full-time (1 woman), 1 (woman) part-time/adjunct. *Students:* 4 full-time (2 women), 44 part-time (12 women); includes 6 minority (1 Black or African American, non-Hispanic/Latino; 3 Asian, non-Hispanic/Latino; 1 Hispanic/Latino; 1 Two or more races, non-Hispanic/Latino), 20 international. Average age 29. 67 applicants, 88% accepted, 16 enrolled. In 2014, 7 master's, 1 doctorate awarded. Terminal master's awarded for partial completion of doctoral program. *Degree requirements:* For master's, thesis optional; for doctorate, comprehensive exam, thesis/dissertation. *Entrance requirements:* For master's, GRE General Test, bachelor's degree, transcripts, personal statement, resume or curriculum vitae, two letters of recommendation; for doctorate, GRE General Test, master's degree, transcripts, personal statement, resume or curriculum vitae, two letters of recommendation. Additional exam requirements/recommendations for international students: Required—TOEFL (minimum score 550 paper-based; 80 iBT). *Application deadline:* For fall admission, 2/1 priority date for domestic and international students. Applications are processed on a rolling basis. Application fee: $65. Electronic applications accepted. *Expenses:* Expenses: $1,199 per credit hour. *Financial support:* In 2014–15, 24 students received support, including 17 research assistantships with full and partial tuition reimbursements available (averaging $12,842 per year), 17 teaching assistantships with full and partial tuition reimbursements available (averaging $9,975 per year); Federal Work-Study, institutionally sponsored loans, scholarships/grants, health care benefits, and unspecified assistantships also available. Financial award application deadline: 2/15; financial award applicants required to submit FAFSA. *Faculty research:* Aerosols, biomechanics, composite materials, photo optics, drug delivery. *Unit head:* Dr. Matt Gordon, Chair, 303-871-3580, Fax: 303-871-4450, E-mail: matthew.gordon@du.edu. *Application contact:* Yvonne Petitt, Assistant to the Chair, 303-871-2107, Fax: 303-871-4450, E-mail: yvonne.petitt@du.edu.
Website: http://www.du.edu/rsecs/departments/mme/index.html.

University of Detroit Mercy, College of Engineering and Science, Program in Engineering Management, Detroit, MI 48221. Offers M Eng Mgt. Evening/weekend programs available. *Degree requirements:* For master's, thesis or alternative.

University of Idaho, College of Graduate Studies, College of Engineering, Department of Civil Engineering, Moscow, ID 83844-1022. Offers civil engineering (M Engr, MS, PhD); engineering management (M Engr); geological engineering (MS). *Faculty:* 13 full-time, 3 part-time/adjunct. *Students:* 24 full-time, 86 part-time. Average age 37. In 2014, 25 master's, 3 doctorates awarded. *Degree requirements:* For master's, thesis; for doctorate, thesis/dissertation. *Entrance requirements:* For master's, minimum GPA of 2.8; for doctorate, minimum undergraduate GPA of 2.8, 3.0 graduate. *Application deadline:* For fall admission, 8/1 for domestic students; for spring admission, 12/15 for domestic students. Applications are processed on a rolling basis. Application fee: $60. Electronic applications accepted. *Expenses:* Tuition, state resident: full-time $4784; part-time $280.50 per credit hour. Tuition, nonresident: full-time $18,314; part-time $957.50 per credit hour. *Required fees:* $2000; $58.50 per credit hour. Tuition and fees vary according to program. *Financial support:* Fellowships, research assistantships, teaching assistantships, and career-related internships or fieldwork available. Financial award applicants required to submit FAFSA. *Faculty research:* Water resources systems, structural analysis and design, soil mechanics, transportation technology. *Unit head:* Richard J. Nielsen, Chair, 208-885-6782, E-mail: civilengr@uidaho.edu. *Application contact:* Sean Scoggin, Graduate Recruitment Coordinator, 208-885-4001, Fax: 208-885-4406, E-mail: graduateadmissions@uidaho.edu.
Website: http://www.uidaho.edu/engr/ce/.

The University of Kansas, Graduate Studies, School of Engineering, Program in Engineering Management, Overland Park, KS 66213. Offers MS. Part-time and evening/weekend programs available. Postbaccalaureate distance learning degree programs offered (no on-campus study). *Faculty:* 9 part-time/adjunct. *Students:* 10 full-time (4 women), 95 part-time (18 women); includes 14 minority (7 Black or African American, non-Hispanic/Latino; 4 Asian, non-Hispanic/Latino; 1 Hispanic/Latino; 2 Two or more races, non-Hispanic/Latino), 15 international. Average age 31. 51 applicants, 80% accepted, 31 enrolled. In 2014, 49 master's awarded. *Degree requirements:* For master's, exam. *Entrance requirements:* For master's, minimum GPA of 3.0, 2 years of industrial experience. Additional exam requirements/recommendations for international students: Required—TOEFL (minimum score 600 paper-based; 100 iBT). *Application deadline:* Applications are processed on a rolling basis. Application fee: $55 ($65 for international students). Electronic applications accepted. *Faculty research:* Project management, systems analysis, high performance teams, manufacturing systems, strategic analysis. *Unit head:* Herbert R. Tuttle, Director, 913-897-8561, E-mail: htuttle@ku.edu. *Application contact:* Parveen Mozaffar, Academic Services Coordinator, 913-897-8560, E-mail: emgt@ku.edu.
Website: http://emgt.ku.edu/.

University of Louisiana at Lafayette, College of Engineering, Department of Engineering and Technology Management, Lafayette, LA 70504. Offers MSET. Part-time and evening/weekend programs available. *Degree requirements:* For master's, comprehensive exam, thesis or alternative. *Entrance requirements:* For master's, GRE General Test, minimum GPA of 2.85. Additional exam requirements/recommendations for international students: Required—TOEFL (minimum score 550 paper-based). Electronic applications accepted. *Faculty research:* Mathematical programming, production management forecasting.

University of Louisville, J. B. Speed School of Engineering, Department of Industrial Engineering, Louisville, KY 40292-0001. Offers engineering management (M Eng); industrial engineering (M Eng, MS, PhD); logistics and distribution (Certificate). *Accreditation:* ABET (one or more programs are accredited). Part-time programs available. *Students:* 104 full-time (27 women), 118 part-time (20 women); includes 25 minority (7 Black or African American, non-Hispanic/Latino; 7 Asian, non-Hispanic/Latino; 7 Hispanic/Latino; 4 Two or more races, non-Hispanic/Latino), 97 international. Average age 29. 109 applicants, 70% accepted, 41 enrolled. In 2014, 16 master's, 10 doctorates awarded. Terminal master's awarded for partial completion of doctoral program. *Degree requirements:* For master's, comprehensive exam (for some programs), thesis or alternative; for doctorate, comprehensive exam, thesis/dissertation, minimum GPA of 3.0. *Entrance requirements:* For master's and doctorate, GRE General Test. Additional exam requirements/recommendations for international students: Required—TOEFL (minimum score 550 paper-based; 80 iBT), IELTS (minimum score 6.5). *Application deadline:* For fall admission, 5/1 priority date for domestic and international students; for spring admission, 11/1 priority date for domestic and international students. Applications are processed on a rolling basis. Application fee: $60. Electronic applications accepted. *Expenses:* Tuition, state resident: full-time $11,326; part-time $630 per credit hour. Tuition, nonresident: full-time $23,568; part-time $1311 per credit hour. *Required fees:* $196. Tuition and fees vary according to program and reciprocity agreements. *Financial support:* In 2014–15, 7 fellowships with full tuition reimbursements (averaging $20,000 per year), 2 research assistantships with full tuition reimbursements (averaging $20,000 per year), 6 teaching assistantships with full tuition reimbursements (averaging $20,000 per year) were awarded. Financial award application deadline: 1/25; financial award applicants required to submit FAFSA. *Faculty research:* Optimization, computer simulation, logistics and distribution, ergonomics and human factors, advanced manufacturing process. *Total annual research expenditures:* $748,000. *Unit head:* Dr. John S. Usher, Chair, 502-852-6342, Fax: 502-852-5633, E-mail: usher@louisville.edu. *Application contact:* Dr. Michael Day, Associate Dean, 502-852-6195, Fax: 502-852-7294, E-mail: day@louisville.edu.
Website: http://www.louisville.edu/speed/industrial/.

University of Management and Technology, Program in Engineering Management, Arlington, VA 22209. Offers MS.

The University of Manchester, School of Mechanical, Aerospace and Civil Engineering, Manchester, United Kingdom. Offers advanced manufacturing technology (M Ent); aerospace engineering (M Phil, M Sc, PhD); civil engineering (M Phil, M Sc, PhD); environmental engineering (M Phil, PhD); management of projects (M Phil, M Sc, PhD); mechanical engineering (M Phil, M Sc, PhD); mechanical engineering design (M Ent); nuclear engineering (M Phil, D Eng, PhD).

University of Maryland, Baltimore County, The Graduate School, Program in Engineering Management, Baltimore, MD 21250. Offers MS, Postbaccalaureate Certificate. Part-time programs available. *Students:* 23 full-time (11 women), 72 part-time (13 women); includes 29 minority (15 Black or African American, non-Hispanic/Latino; 8 Asian, non-Hispanic/Latino; 5 Hispanic/Latino; 1 Two or more races, non-Hispanic/Latino), 19 international. Average age 31. 76 applicants, 61% accepted, 30 enrolled. In 2014, 26 master's, 11 other advanced degrees awarded. *Degree requirements:* For master's, comprehensive exam (for some programs), thesis optional. *Entrance requirements:* For master's, BS in engineering, computer science, mathematics, physics, chemistry, or other physical sciences; two letters of recommendation (for international students). Additional exam requirements/recommendations for international students: Required—TOEFL (minimum score 550 paper-based; 80 iBT), GRE General Test. *Application deadline:* For fall admission, 7/1 for domestic and international students; for spring admission, 12/1 for domestic and international students. Applications are processed on a rolling basis. Application fee: $70. Electronic applications accepted. *Expenses:* Tuition, state resident: part-time $557. Tuition, nonresident: part-time $922. *Required fees:* $122 per semester. One-time fee: $200 part-time. *Financial support:* Career-related internships or fieldwork, Federal Work-Study, scholarships/grants, health care benefits, and unspecified assistantships available. Support available to part-time students. Financial award application deadline: 6/30; financial award applicants required to submit FAFSA. *Faculty research:* Regulatory engineering, environmental engineering, systems engineering, advanced manufacturing, chemical engineering. *Unit head:* Dr. Julia M. Ross, Dean of College of Engineering and Information Technology, 410-455-3270, Fax: 410-455-3559, E-mail: jross@umbc.edu. *Application contact:* Dr. Thomas M. Moore, Lecturer/Graduate Program Director, E-mail: mooretg@umbc.edu.

University of Michigan–Dearborn, College of Engineering and Computer Science, MS Program in Engineering Management, Dearborn, MI 48128. Offers MS. Part-time and evening/weekend programs available. Postbaccalaureate distance learning degree programs offered (no on-campus study). *Faculty:* 14 full-time (1 woman), 7 part-time/adjunct (1 woman). *Students:* 6 full-time (3 women), 65 part-time (15 women); includes 10 minority (2 Black or African American, non-Hispanic/Latino; 6 Asian, non-Hispanic/Latino; 2 Hispanic/Latino), 8 international. 55 applicants, 45% accepted, 13 enrolled. In 2014, 22 master's awarded. *Entrance requirements:* Additional exam requirements/recommendations for international students: Required—TOEFL (minimum score 560 paper-based; 84 iBT), IELTS (minimum score 6.5). *Application deadline:* For fall admission, 8/1 for domestic students, 5/1 for international students; for winter admission, 12/1 for domestic students, 9/1 for international students; for spring admission, 4/1 for domestic students, 1/1 for international students. Applications are processed on a rolling basis. Application fee: $60. Electronic applications accepted. *Expenses:* Tuition, state resident: full-time $12,202; part-time $707 per credit hour. Tuition, nonresident: full-time $20,980; part-time $1209 per credit hour. *Required fees:* $798; $302 per term. Tuition and fees vary according to course level, course load, degree level and program. *Financial support:* In 2014–15, 3 students received support. Scholarships/grants and unspecified assistantships available. Support available to part-time students. Financial award applicants required to submit FAFSA. *Faculty research:* Integrated design and manufacturing, operations research and decision science, human factors and ergonomics. *Unit head:* Dr. Armen Zakarian, Chair, 313-593-5361, Fax: 313-593-3692, E-mail: zakarian@umich.edu. *Application contact:* Joey W. Woods, Graduate Program Assistant, 313-593-5361, Fax: 313-593-3692, E-mail: jwwoods@umd.umich.edu.
Website: http://umdearborn.edu/cecs/IMSE/grad_prog/index.php.

University of Minnesota, Duluth, Graduate School, Swenson College of Science and Engineering, Department of Mechanical and Industrial Engineering, Duluth, MN 55812-2496. Offers engineering management (MSEM); environmental health and safety (MEHS). Part-time and evening/weekend programs available. Postbaccalaureate distance learning degree programs offered (no on-campus study). *Degree requirements:* For master's, comprehensive exam, thesis or alternative, capstone design project (MSEM), field project (MEHS). *Entrance requirements:* For master's, GRE (MEHS), interview (MEHS), letters of recommendation. Additional exam requirements/recommendations for international students: Required—TOEFL (minimum score 550 paper-based). *Faculty research:* Transportation, ergonomics, toxicology, supply chain management, automation and robotics.

University of Missouri–Kansas City, School of Computing and Engineering, Kansas City, MO 64110-2499. Offers civil engineering (MS); computer and electrical engineering (PhD); computer science (MS), including bioinformatics, software engineering, telecommunications networking; computer science and informatics (PhD); computing (PhD); electrical engineering (MS); engineering (PhD); engineering and construction

management (Graduate Certificate); mechanical engineering (MS); telecommunications and computer networking (PhD). PhD (interdisciplinary) offered through the School of Graduate Studies. Part-time programs available. *Faculty:* 39 full-time (5 women), 26 part-time/adjunct (3 women). *Students:* 500 full-time (143 women), 136 part-time (28 women); includes 18 minority (5 Black or African American, non-Hispanic/Latino; 8 Asian, non-Hispanic/Latino; 4 Hispanic/Latino; 1 Two or more races, non-Hispanic/Latino), 551 international. Average age 24. 1,924 applicants, 39% accepted, 200 enrolled. In 2014, 124 master's, 1 other advanced degree awarded. *Degree requirements:* For doctorate, thesis/dissertation. *Entrance requirements:* For master's, GRE General Test, minimum GPA of 3.0, 3 letters of recommendation from professors; for doctorate, GRE General Test, minimum GPA of 3.5. Additional exam requirements/recommendations for international students: Required—TOEFL (minimum score 550 paper-based; 80 iBT). *Application deadline:* For fall admission, 1/15 priority date for domestic students, 1/15 for international students. Applications are processed on a rolling basis. Application fee: $45 ($50 for international students). *Financial support:* In 2014–15, 34 research assistantships with partial tuition reimbursements (averaging $15,602 per year), 24 teaching assistantships with partial tuition reimbursements (averaging $15,090 per year) were awarded; career-related internships or fieldwork, Federal Work-Study, scholarships/grants, tuition waivers (partial), and unspecified assistantships also available. Support available to part-time students. Financial award application deadline: 3/1; financial award applicants required to submit FAFSA. *Faculty research:* Algorithms, bioinformatics and medical informatics, biomechanics/biomaterials, civil engineering materials, networking and telecommunications, thermal science. *Unit head:* Dr. Kevin Z. Truman, Dean, 816-235-2399, Fax: 816-235-5159. *Application contact:* 816-235-2399, Fax: 816-235-5159.
Website: http://sce.umkc.edu/.

University of Nebraska–Lincoln, Graduate College, College of Engineering, Department of Industrial and Management Systems Engineering, Lincoln, NE 68588. Offers engineering management (M Eng); industrial and management systems engineering (MS, PhD); manufacturing systems engineering (MS). Postbaccalaureate distance learning degree programs offered. *Degree requirements:* For master's, thesis optional; for doctorate, comprehensive exam, thesis/dissertation. *Entrance requirements:* For master's and doctorate, GRE. Additional exam requirements/recommendations for international students: Required—TOEFL (minimum score 525 paper-based). Electronic applications accepted. *Faculty research:* Ergonomics, occupational safety, quality control, industrial packaging, facility design.

University of New Brunswick Fredericton, School of Graduate Studies, Faculty of Business Administration, Fredericton, NB E3B 5A3, Canada. Offers business administration (MBA); engineering management (MBA); entrepreneurship (MBA); sports and recreation management (MBA); MBA/LL B. Part-time programs available. *Faculty:* 22 full-time (3 women), 4 part-time/adjunct (1 woman). *Students:* 33 full-time (13 women), 38 part-time (12 women), 1 international. In 2014, 54 master's awarded. *Degree requirements:* For master's, thesis optional. *Entrance requirements:* For master's, GMAT (minimum score 550), minimum GPA of 3.0; 3-5 years of work experience; 3 letters of reference with at least one academic reference. Additional exam requirements/recommendations for international students: Required—TOEFL (minimum score 580 paper-based; 92 iBT) or IELTS (minimum score 7). *Application deadline:* For fall admission, 10/31 priority date for domestic and international students; for spring admission, 3/31 priority date for domestic and international students. Application fee: $50 Canadian dollars. Electronic applications accepted. *Financial support:* In 2014–15, 6 fellowships, 3 research assistantships (averaging $4,500 per year), 22 teaching assistantships (averaging $2,250 per year) were awarded. *Faculty research:* Entrepreneurship, finance, law, sport and recreation management, engineering management. *Unit head:* Dr. Donglei Du, Director of Graduate Studies, 506-458-7353, Fax: 506-453-3561, E-mail: ddu@unb.ca. *Application contact:* Marilyn Davis, Acting Graduate Secretary, 506-453-4766, Fax: 506-453-3561, E-mail: mbacontact@unb.ca.
Website: http://go.unb.ca/gradprograms.

University of New Haven, Graduate School, Tagliatela College of Engineering, Program in Engineering and Operations Management, West Haven, CT 06516-1916. Offers engineering and operations management (MS); engineering management (MS); Lean/Six Sigma (Certificate). *Entrance requirements:* Additional exam requirements/recommendations for international students: Required—TOEFL (minimum score 75 iBT), IELTS, PTE (minimum score 50). Electronic applications accepted. Application fee is waived when completed online.

University of New Orleans, Graduate School, College of Engineering, Program in Engineering Management, New Orleans, LA 70148. Offers MS. *Degree requirements:* For master's, thesis optional. *Entrance requirements:* For master's, GRE General Test, minimum GPA of 3.0. Additional exam requirements/recommendations for international students: Required—TOEFL (minimum score 550 paper-based; 79 iBT). Electronic applications accepted.

The University of North Carolina at Charlotte, The William States Lee College of Engineering, Department of Systems Engineering and Engineering Management, Charlotte, NC 28223-0001. Offers energy analytics (Graduate Certificate); engineering management (MSEM); engineering science (MS); infrastructure and environmental systems (PhD); Lean Six Sigma (Graduate Certificate); logistics and supply chains (Graduate Certificate); systems analytics (Graduate Certificate). Part-time and evening/weekend programs available. Postbaccalaureate distance learning degree programs offered. *Faculty:* 7 full-time (2 women), 1 part-time/adjunct (0 women). *Students:* 33 full-time (8 women), 47 part-time (14 women); includes 15 minority (9 Black or African American, non-Hispanic/Latino; 3 Asian, non-Hispanic/Latino; 3 Hispanic/Latino), 33 international. Average age 29. 146 applicants, 51% accepted, 42 enrolled. In 2014, 19 master's awarded. *Degree requirements:* For master's, thesis or alternative, project. *Entrance requirements:* For master's, GRE or GMAT, letters of recommendation. Additional exam requirements/recommendations for international students: Required—TOEFL (minimum score 557 paper-based; 83 iBT). *Application deadline:* For fall admission, 5/1 priority date for domestic students, 5/1 for international students; for spring admission, 10/1 priority date for domestic students, 10/1 for international students. Application fee: $75. Electronic applications accepted. *Expenses:* Tuition, state resident: full-time $4008. Tuition, nonresident: full-time $16,295. *Required fees:* $2755. Tuition and fees vary according to course load and program. *Financial support:* In 2014–15, 5 students received support, including 3 research assistantships (averaging $5,317 per year), 2 teaching assistantships (averaging $3,125 per year); career-related internships or fieldwork, institutionally sponsored loans, scholarships/grants, and unspecified assistantships also available. Support available to part-time students. Financial award application deadline: 4/1; financial award applicants required to submit FAFSA. *Faculty research:* Sustainable material and renewable technology; thermal analysis; large scale optimization; project risk management; supply chains; leans systems; global product innovation; quality and reliability analysis and management; productivity and project management; business forecasting, market analyses and feasibility studies. *Total annual research expenditures:* $106,777. *Unit head:* Dr. Robert E. Johnson, Dean, 704-687-8242, Fax: 704-687-2352, E-mail: robejohn@uncc.edu. *Application contact:* Kathy B. Giddings, Director of Graduate Admissions, 704-687-5503, Fax: 704-687-1668, E-mail: gradadm@uncc.edu.
Website: http://seem.uncc.edu/.

University of Ottawa, Faculty of Graduate and Postdoctoral Studies, Faculty of Engineering, Engineering Management Program, Ottawa, ON K1N 6N5, Canada. Offers engineering management (M Eng); information technology (Certificate); project management (Certificate). *Degree requirements:* For master's, thesis or alternative. *Entrance requirements:* For master's and Certificate, honors degree or equivalent, minimum B average. Electronic applications accepted.

University of Regina, Faculty of Graduate Studies and Research, Kenneth Levene Graduate School of Business, Program in Business Administration, Regina, SK S4S 0A2, Canada. Offers business foundations (PGD); engineering management (MBA); executive business administration (EMBA); general management (MBA); international business (MBA); leadership (M Admin); organizational leadership (Master's Certificate); project management (Master's Certificate). Part-time and evening/weekend programs available. *Faculty:* 42 full-time (13 women), 6 part-time/adjunct (0 women). *Students:* 66 full-time (31 women), 51 part-time (29 women). 79 applicants, 32% accepted. In 2014, 67 master's, 23 other advanced degrees awarded. *Degree requirements:* For master's, project (for some programs). *Entrance requirements:* For master's, GMAT, three years of relevant work experience, four-year undergraduate degree; for other advanced degree, GMAT (for PGD), four-year undergraduate degree and two years of relevant work experience (for Master's Certificate); three years' work experience (for PGD). Additional exam requirements/recommendations for international students: Required—TOEFL (minimum score 580 paper-based; 80 iBT), IELTS (minimum score 6.5), PTE (minimum score 59). *Application deadline:* Applications are processed on a rolling basis. Application fee: $100. Electronic applications accepted. *Expenses:* Expenses: $4,958.85 per semester full-time (for M Admin); $6,293.85 (for MBA); $3,281.85 (for Post-Graduate Diploma). *Financial support:* In 2014–15, 3 fellowships (averaging $6,000 per year), 1 research assistantship (averaging $5,500 per year), 6 teaching assistantships (averaging $2,427 per year) were awarded; career-related internships or fieldwork and scholarships/grants also available. Financial award application deadline: 6/15. *Faculty research:* Business policy and strategy, production and operations management, human behavior in organizations, financial management, social issues in business. *Unit head:* Dr. Andrew Gaudes, Dean, 306-585-4162, Fax: 306-585-5361, E-mail: andrew.gaudes@uregina.ca. *Application contact:* Steve Wield, Manager, Graduate Programs, 306-337-8463, Fax: 306-585-5361, E-mail: steve.wield@uregina.ca.
Website: http://www.uregina.ca/business/levene/.

University of St. Thomas, Graduate Studies, School of Engineering, St. Paul, MN 55105-1096. Offers electrical engineering (MS); manufacturing engineering and operations (MS); manufacturing systems (Certificate); mechanical engineering (MS); medical device development (Certificate); regulatory science (MS); software engineering (MS); software management (MS); systems engineering (MS); technology leadership (Certificate); technology management (MS). *Accreditation:* ABET (one or more programs are accredited). *Entrance requirements:* For master's, resume, official transcripts. Additional exam requirements/recommendations for international students: Required—TOEFL (minimum score 550 paper-based). Electronic applications accepted. *Expenses:* Contact institution.

University of Southern California, Graduate School, Viterbi School of Engineering, Daniel J. Epstein Department of Industrial and Systems Engineering, Los Angeles, CA 90089. Offers digital supply chain management (MS); engineering management (MS); engineering technology communication (Graduate Certificate); health systems operations (Graduate Certificate); industrial and systems engineering (MS, PhD, Engr); manufacturing engineering (MS); operations research engineering (MS); optimization and supply chain management (Graduate Certificate); product development engineering (MS); safety systems and security (MS); systems architecting and engineering (MS, Graduate Certificate); systems safety and security (Graduate Certificate); transportation systems (Graduate Certificate); MS/MBA. Part-time and evening/weekend programs available. Postbaccalaureate distance learning degree programs offered (no on-campus study). Terminal master's awarded for partial completion of doctoral program. *Degree requirements:* For master's, thesis optional; for doctorate, thesis/dissertation. *Entrance requirements:* For master's and doctorate, GRE General Test. Additional exam requirements/recommendations for international students: Recommended—TOEFL. Electronic applications accepted. *Faculty research:* Health systems, music cognition and retrieval, transportation and logistics, manufacturing and automation, engineering systems design, risk and economic analysis.

University of Southern California, Graduate School, Viterbi School of Engineering, Department of Aerospace and Mechanical Engineering, Los Angeles, CA 90089. Offers aerospace and mechanical engineering: computational fluid and solid mechanics (MS); aerospace and mechanical engineering: dynamics and control (MS); aerospace engineering (MS, PhD, Engr), including aerospace engineering (PhD, Engr); green technologies (MS); mechanical engineering (MS, PhD, Engr), including energy conversion (MS), mechanical engineering (PhD, Engr), nuclear power (MS); product development engineering (MS). Part-time and evening/weekend programs available. Postbaccalaureate distance learning degree programs offered (no on-campus study). Terminal master's awarded for partial completion of doctoral program. *Degree requirements:* For master's, thesis optional; for doctorate, thesis/dissertation. *Entrance requirements:* For master's, doctorate, and Engr, GRE General Test. Additional exam requirements/recommendations for international students: Recommended—TOEFL. Electronic applications accepted. *Faculty research:* Mechanics and materials, aerodynamics of air/ground vehicles, gas dynamics, aerosols, astronautics and space science, geophysical and microgravity flows, planetary physics, power MEMs and MEMS vacuum pumps, heat transfer and combustion.

University of South Florida, College of Engineering, Department of Industrial and Management Systems Engineering, Tampa, FL 33620-9951. Offers engineering management (MSEM); industrial engineering (MSIE, PhD); information technology (MSIT). Part-time programs available. Postbaccalaureate distance learning degree programs offered (minimal on-campus study). *Faculty:* 12 full-time (3 women). *Students:* 69 full-time (23 women), 83 part-time (19 women); includes 32 minority (6 Black or African American, non-Hispanic/Latino; 7 Asian, non-Hispanic/Latino; 16 Hispanic/Latino; 3 Two or more races, non-Hispanic/Latino), 60 international. Average age 30. 271 applicants, 45% accepted, 34 enrolled. In 2014, 71 master's, 6 doctorates awarded. Terminal master's awarded for partial completion of doctoral program. *Degree requirements:* For master's, comprehensive exam, thesis (for some programs); for doctorate, comprehensive exam, thesis/dissertation, 2 tools of research as specified by dissertation committee. *Entrance requirements:* For master's, GRE General Test, BS in engineering (or equivalent) with minimum GPA of 3.0 in last 60 hours of coursework, letter of recommendation, resume; for doctorate, GRE General Test, minimum GPA of 3.0 in last 60 hours of undergraduate/graduate coursework, three letters of recommendation, statement of purpose, strong background in scientific and engineering principles. Additional exam requirements/recommendations for international students: Required—TOEFL (minimum score 550 paper-based; 79 iBT) or IELTS (minimum score 6.5). *Application deadline:* For fall admission, 2/15 for domestic students, 1/2 for

international students; for spring admission, 10/15 for domestic students, 6/1 for international students. Application fee: $30. Electronic applications accepted. *Financial support:* In 2014–15, 31 students received support, including 20 research assistantships with partial tuition reimbursements available (averaging $16,748 per year), 11 teaching assistantships with partial tuition reimbursements available (averaging $15,000 per year); tuition waivers (partial) also available. Financial award applicants required to submit FAFSA. *Faculty research:* Healthcare, healthcare systems, public health policies, energy and environment, manufacturing, logistics, transportation. *Total annual research expenditures:* $224,800. *Unit head:* Dr. Tapas K. Das, Professor and Department Chair, 813-974-5585, Fax: 813-974-5953, E-mail: das@usf.edu. *Application contact:* Dr. Alex Savachkin, Associate Professor and Graduate Director, 813-974-5577, Fax: 813-974-5953, E-mail: alexs@usf.edu.
Website: http://imse.eng.usf.edu.

The University of Tennessee, Graduate School, College of Engineering, Department of Industrial and Systems Engineering, Knoxville, TN 37966. Offers engineering management (MS); industrial engineering (MS, PhD); reliability and maintainability engineering (MS); MS/MBA. Part-time programs available. Postbaccalaureate distance learning degree programs offered (minimal on-campus study). *Faculty:* 12 full-time (2 women), 11 part-time/adjunct (1 woman). *Students:* 68 full-time (15 women), 58 part-time (12 women); includes 15 minority (6 Black or African American, non-Hispanic/Latino; 6 Asian, non-Hispanic/Latino; 1 Hispanic/Latino; 2 Two or more races, non-Hispanic/Latino), 40 international. Average age 37. 116 applicants, 63% accepted, 37 enrolled. In 2014, 55 master's, 4 doctorates awarded. *Degree requirements:* For master's, thesis or alternative; for doctorate, comprehensive exam, thesis/dissertation. *Entrance requirements:* For master's, GRE General Test (for MS students pursuing research thesis), minimum GPA of 2.7 (for U.S. degree holders), 3.0 (for international degree holders); for doctorate, GRE General Test (for all PhD candidates), minimum GPA of 3.0 on previous graduate course work. Additional exam requirements/recommendations for international students: Required—TOEFL (minimum score 550 paper-based). *Application deadline:* For fall admission, 2/1 priority date for domestic and international students; for spring admission, 6/15 for domestic and international students. Applications are processed on a rolling basis. Application fee: $35. Electronic applications accepted. *Financial support:* In 2014–15, 41 students received support, including 3 fellowships with full tuition reimbursements available (averaging $25,164 per year), 22 research assistantships with full tuition reimbursements available (averaging $18,763 per year), 13 teaching assistantships with full tuition reimbursements available (averaging $19,241 per year); career-related internships or fieldwork, Federal Work-Study, institutionally sponsored loans, health care benefits, and unspecified assistantships also available. Financial award application deadline: 2/1; financial award applicants required to submit FAFSA. *Faculty research:* Defense-oriented supply chain modeling; dependability and reliability of large computer networks; design of lean, reliable systems; new product development; operations research in the automotive industry. *Total annual research expenditures:* $1.4 million. *Unit head:* Dr. John Kobza, Department Head, 865-974-3333, Fax: 865-974-0588, E-mail: jkobza@utk.edu. *Application contact:* Dr. Alberto Garcia-Diaz, Professor, 865-974-7647, E-mail: agd@utk.edu.
Website: http://www.engr.utk.edu/ie/.

The University of Tennessee, The University of Tennessee Space Institute, Tullahoma, TN 37388. Offers aerospace engineering (MS, PhD); biomedical engineering (MS, PhD); engineering science (MS, PhD); industrial and systems engineering/engineering management (MS, PhD); mechanical engineering (MS, PhD); physics (MS, PhD). Part-time programs available. Postbaccalaureate distance learning degree programs offered. *Faculty:* 19 full-time (3 women), 4 part-time/adjunct. *Students:* 31 full-time (6 women), 82 part-time (11 women); includes 10 minority (6 Black or African American, non-Hispanic/Latino; 1 American Indian or Alaska Native, non-Hispanic/Latino; 2 Asian, non-Hispanic/Latino; 1 Hispanic/Latino), 11 international. 60 applicants, 55% accepted, 22 enrolled. In 2014, 25 master's, 5 doctorates awarded. Terminal master's awarded for partial completion of doctoral program. *Degree requirements:* For doctorate, one foreign language, thesis/dissertation. *Entrance requirements:* Additional exam requirements/recommendations for international students: Required—TOEFL (minimum score 550 paper-based; 80 iBT), IELTS (minimum score 6.5). *Application deadline:* For fall admission, 2/1 for international students; for spring admission, 6/15 for international students. Applications are processed on a rolling basis. Application fee: $60. Electronic applications accepted. *Financial support:* In 2014–15, 6 fellowships with full tuition reimbursements (averaging $2,451 per year), 24 research assistantships with full tuition reimbursements (averaging $20,244 per year) were awarded; career-related internships or fieldwork, Federal Work-Study, institutionally sponsored loans, health care benefits, and unspecified assistantships also available. *Faculty research:* Fluid mechanics/aerodynamics, chemical and electric propulsion and laser diagnostics, computational mechanics and simulations, carbon fiber production and composite materials. *Total annual research expenditures:* $1.8 million. *Unit head:* Dr. Charles Johnson, Associate Executive Director, 931-393-7318, Fax: 931-393-7211, E-mail: cjohnson@utsi.edu. *Application contact:* Dee Merriman, Director, 931-393-7213, Fax: 931-393-7211, E-mail: dmerrima@utsi.edu.
Website: http://www.utsi.edu/.

The University of Tennessee at Chattanooga, Department of Engineering Management, Chattanooga, TN 37403. Offers engineering management (MS); fundamentals of engineering management (Graduate Certificate); leadership and ethics (Graduate Certificate); logistics and supply chain management (Graduate Certificate); nuclear engineering (Graduate Certificate); power system protection (Graduate Certificate); power systems management (Graduate Certificate); project and value management (Graduate Certificate); quality management (Graduate Certificate); sustainable electric energy (Graduate Certificate). Postbaccalaureate distance learning degree programs offered (no on-campus study). *Faculty:* 5 full-time (1 woman). *Students:* 14 full-time (5 women), 67 part-time (14 women); includes 24 minority (13 Black or African American, non-Hispanic/Latino; 6 Asian, non-Hispanic/Latino; 4 Hispanic/Latino; 1 Two or more races, non-Hispanic/Latino), 6 international. Average age 31. 31 applicants, 45% accepted, 10 enrolled. In 2014, 31 master's, 17 other advanced degrees awarded. *Degree requirements:* For master's, thesis. *Entrance requirements:* For master's, GRE General Test, letters of recommendation; minimum undergraduate GPA of 2.5 overall or 3.0 in senior year. Additional exam requirements/recommendations for international students: Required—TOEFL (minimum score 550 paper-based; 79 iBT), IELTS (minimum score 6). *Application deadline:* For fall admission, 6/13 priority date for domestic students, 6/1 for international students; for spring admission, 10/15 priority date for domestic students, 10/1 for international students. Applications are processed on a rolling basis. Application fee: $30 ($35 for international students). Electronic applications accepted. *Expenses:* Tuition, state resident: full-time $7708; part-time $428 per credit hour. Tuition, nonresident: full-time $23,826; part-time $1323 per credit hour. *Required fees:* $1708; $252 per credit hour. *Financial support:* In 2014–15, 5 research assistantships (averaging $6,528 per year), 3 teaching assistantships (averaging $6,781 per year) were awarded; career-related internships or fieldwork, scholarships/grants, and unspecified assistantships also available. Support available to part-time students. Financial award applicants required to submit FAFSA. *Faculty research:* Plant layout design, lean manufacturing, Six Sigma, value management, product development. *Unit head:* Dr. Neslihan Alp, Department Head, 423-425-4032, Fax: 423-425-5229, E-mail: neslihan-alp@utc.edu. *Application contact:* Dr. J. Randy Walker, Interim Dean of Graduate Studies, 423-425-4478, Fax: 423-425-5223, E-mail: randy-walker@utc.edu.
Website: http://www.utc.edu/Departments/engrcs/engm/index.php.

The University of Texas at Arlington, Graduate School, College of Engineering, Department of Industrial and Manufacturing Systems Engineering, Program in Engineering Management, Arlington, TX 76019. Offers MS. Part-time and evening/weekend programs available. Postbaccalaureate distance learning degree programs offered (minimal on-campus study). *Degree requirements:* For master's, comprehensive exam, thesis optional. *Entrance requirements:* For master's, GRE, 3 years of full-time work experience, minimum GPA of 3.0. Additional exam requirements/recommendations for international students: Required—TOEFL (minimum score 550 paper-based).

The University of Texas–Pan American, College of Engineering and Computer Science, Department of Manufacturing Engineering, Edinburg, TX 78539. Offers engineering management (MS); manufacturing engineering (MS); systems engineering (MS). *Expenses:* Tuition, state resident: full-time $4187; part-time $232.60 per credit hour. Tuition, nonresident: full-time $10,857; part-time $603.16 per credit hour. *Required fees:* $782; $27.50 per credit hour. $143.35 per semester.

University of Waterloo, Graduate Studies, Faculty of Engineering, Department of Management Sciences, Waterloo, ON N2L 3G1, Canada. Offers applied operations research (MA Sc, MMS, PhD); information systems (MA Sc, MMS, PhD); management of technology (MA Sc, MMS, PhD). Part-time programs available. Postbaccalaureate distance learning degree programs offered (no on-campus study). *Degree requirements:* For master's, research paper or thesis; for doctorate, comprehensive exam, thesis/dissertation. *Entrance requirements:* For master's, GMAT or GRE, honors degree, minimum B average, resume; for doctorate, GMAT or GRE, master's degree, minimum A- average, resumé. Additional exam requirements/recommendations for international students: Required—TOEFL, TWE. *Faculty research:* Operations research, manufacturing systems, scheduling, information systems.

University of Wisconsin–Milwaukee, Graduate School, College of Engineering and Applied Science, Program in Engineering, Milwaukee, WI 53201-0413. Offers civil engineering (MS); electrical and computer engineering (MS); energy engineering (Certificate); engineering (PhD); engineering management (MS); engineering mechanics (MS); ergonomics (Certificate); industrial and management engineering (MS); manufacturing engineering (MS); materials engineering (MS); mechanical engineering (MS); MUP/MS. Part-time programs available. *Degree requirements:* For master's, comprehensive exam (for some programs), thesis or alternative; for doctorate, comprehensive exam, thesis/dissertation, internship. *Entrance requirements:* For master's, GRE, minimum GPA of 2.75; for doctorate, GRE, minimum GPA of 3.5. Additional exam requirements/recommendations for international students: Required—TOEFL (minimum score 550 paper-based; 79 iBT), IELTS (minimum score 6.5).

Valparaiso University, Graduate School, College of Business, Valparaiso, IN 46383. Offers business administration (MBA); business intelligence (Certificate); engineering management (Certificate); entrepreneurship (Certificate); finance (Certificate); general business (Certificate); management (Certificate); marketing (Certificate); sustainability (Certificate); JD/MBA; MSN/MBA. *Accreditation:* AACSB. Part-time and evening/weekend programs available. Postbaccalaureate distance learning degree programs offered (minimal on-campus study). *Faculty:* 10 part-time/adjunct (2 women). *Students:* 26 full-time (8 women), 32 part-time (11 women); includes 4 minority (1 Black or African American, non-Hispanic/Latino; 3 Asian, non-Hispanic/Latino), 2 international. Average age 33. In 2014, 28 master's awarded. *Entrance requirements:* For master's, GMAT, GRE, minimum GPA of 3.0. Additional exam requirements/recommendations for international students: Required—TOEFL (minimum score 550 paper-based; 80 iBT), IELTS (minimum score 6). *Application deadline:* Applications are processed on a rolling basis. Application fee: $30 ($50 for international students). Electronic applications accepted. *Expenses:* Expenses: $833 per credit hour. *Financial support:* Available to part-time students. Applicants required to submit FAFSA. *Unit head:* Bruce MacLean, Director of Graduate Programs in Management, 219-465-7952, Fax: 219-464-5789, E-mail: bruce.maclean@valpo.edu. *Application contact:* Cindy Scanlan, Assistant Director of Graduate Programs in Management, 219-465-7952, Fax: 219-464-5789, E-mail: cindy.scanlan@valpo.edu.
Website: http://www.valpo.edu/mba/.

Virginia Polytechnic Institute and State University, VT Online, Blacksburg, VA 24061. Offers advanced transportation systems (Certificate); aerospace engineering (MS); agricultural and life sciences (MSLFS); business information systems (Graduate Certificate); career and technical education (MS); civil engineering (MS); computer engineering (M Eng, MS); decision support systems (Graduate Certificate); eLearning leadership (MA); electrical engineering (M Eng, MS); engineering administration (MEA); environmental engineering (Certificate); environmental politics and policy (Graduate Certificate); environmental sciences and engineering (MS); foundations of political analysis (Graduate Certificate); health product risk management (Graduate Certificate); industrial and systems engineering (MS); information policy and society (Graduate Certificate); information security (Graduate Certificate); information technology (MIT); instructional technology (MA); integrative STEM education (MA Ed); liberal arts (Graduate Certificate); life sciences: health product risk management (MS); natural resources (MNR, Graduate Certificate); networking (Graduate Certificate); nonprofit and nongovernmental organization management (Graduate Certificate); ocean engineering (MS); political science (MA); security studies (Graduate Certificate); software development (Graduate Certificate). *Expenses:* Tuition, state resident: full-time $11,656; part-time $647.50 per credit hour. Tuition, nonresident: full-time $23,351; part-time $1297.25 per credit hour. *Required fees:* $2533; $465.75 per semester. Tuition and fees vary according to course load, campus/location and program.

Washington State University, Voiland College of Engineering and Architecture, Program in Engineering and Technology Management, Pullman, WA 99164-2785. Offers METM, Certificate. Program offered through the Global (online) campus. Part-time and evening/weekend programs available. Postbaccalaureate distance learning degree programs offered (no on-campus study). *Students:* 78 part-time (15 women); includes 22 minority (6 Black or African American, non-Hispanic/Latino; 7 Asian, non-Hispanic/Latino; 6 Hispanic/Latino; 3 Two or more races, non-Hispanic/Latino), 6 international. Average age 34. 30 applicants, 73% accepted, 21 enrolled. In 2014, 19 master's, 17 Certificates awarded. *Degree requirements:* For master's, one foreign language, comprehensive exam (for some programs). *Entrance requirements:* Additional exam requirements/recommendations for international students: Required—TOEFL. *Application deadline:* For fall admission, 7/1 for domestic students, 6/1 for international students; for winter admission, 9/1 for international students; for spring admission, 10/1 for domestic students. Applications are processed on a rolling basis. Application fee: $75. Electronic applications accepted. *Expenses:* Tuition, state resident: full-time $11,768. Tuition, nonresident: full-time $25,200. *Required fees:* $960. Tuition and fees vary according to program. *Faculty research:* Constraints management, Six Sigma quality management, supply chain management, project management,

construction management, systems engineering management, manufacturing leadership. *Unit head:* Dr. John Ringo, Program Director, 509-335-5595, Fax: 509-335-7290, E-mail: ringo@wsu.edu. *Application contact:* Patti Elshafei, Program Support Supervisor, 509-335-0125, Fax: 509-335-4725, E-mail: etm@wsu.edu.
Website: http://etm.wsu.edu/.

Wayne State University, College of Engineering, Department of Industrial and Systems Engineering, Program in Engineering Management, Detroit, MI 48202. Offers MS, Certificate. *Students:* 19 full-time (4 women), 44 part-time (14 women); includes 17 minority (7 Black or African American, non-Hispanic/Latino; 7 Asian, non-Hispanic/Latino; 3 Hispanic/Latino), 6 international. Average age 34. 111 applicants, 16% accepted, 8 enrolled. In 2014, 21 master's awarded. *Degree requirements:* For master's, thesis optional. *Entrance requirements:* For master's, undergraduate degree from accredited institution with minimum GPA of 3.0 in upper-division coursework; practicing engineer or technical leader with undergraduate degree from accredited engineering program; two years of full-time work experience or currently working full-time in U.S. in an engineering-related job; for Certificate, undergraduate degree from accredited institution with minimum GPA of 3.0 in upper-division coursework; practicing engineer or technical leader with undergraduate degree from accredited engineering program; one year of full-time work experience or currently working full-time in U.S. in an engineering-related job. Additional exam requirements/recommendations for international students: Required—TOEFL (minimum score 550 paper-based; 79 iBT), TWE (minimum score 5.5), Michigan English Language Assessment Battery (minimum score 85); Recommended—IELTS (minimum score 6.5). *Application deadline:* For fall admission, 6/1 priority date for domestic students, 5/1 priority date for international students; for winter admission, 10/1 priority date for domestic students, 9/1 priority date for international students; for spring admission, 2/1 priority date for domestic students, 1/1 priority date for international students. Applications are processed on a rolling basis. Application fee: $0. Electronic applications accepted. *Expenses:* Expenses: Contact institution. *Financial support:* In 2014–15, 48 students received support. Fellowships with tuition reimbursements available, research assistantships with tuition reimbursements available, teaching assistantships with tuition reimbursements available, career-related internships or fieldwork, scholarships/grants, and unspecified assistantships available. Support available to part-time students. Financial award application deadline: 3/31; financial award applicants required to submit FAFSA. *Faculty research:* Healthcare systems engineering, product design and development, quality and reliability engineering, supply chain management and logistics. *Unit head:* Dr. Leslie Monplaisir, Associate Professor/Chair, 313-577-1645, Fax: 313-577-8833, E-mail: ad5365@wayne.edu. *Application contact:* Dr. Kenneth Chelst, Director, 313-577-3857, E-mail: kchelst@wayne.edu.
Website: http://engineering.wayne.edu/ise/.

Webster University, College of Arts and Sciences, Department of Biological Sciences, Program in Science Management and Leadership, St. Louis, MO 63119-3194. Offers MS. *Entrance requirements:* Additional exam requirements/recommendations for international students: Required—TOEFL.

Western Michigan University, Graduate College, College of Engineering and Applied Sciences, Department of Industrial and Entrepreneurial Engineering and Engineering Management, Kalamazoo, MI 49008. Offers engineering management (MS); industrial engineering (MSE, PhD). *Degree requirements:* For master's, thesis optional. *Application deadline:* For fall admission, 2/15 for domestic students. *Financial support:* Application deadline: 2/15. *Application contact:* Admissions and Orientation, 269-387-2000, Fax: 269-387-2096.

Western New England University, College of Engineering, Master's Program in Engineering Management, Springfield, MA 01119. Offers business and engineering information systems (MSEM); general engineering management (MSEM); production and manufacturing systems (MSEM); quality engineering (MSEM); MSEM/MBA. Part-time and evening/weekend programs available. Postbaccalaureate distance learning degree programs offered (no on-campus study). *Students:* 45 part-time (6 women); includes 4 minority (1 Black or African American, non-Hispanic/Latino; 1 Asian, non-Hispanic/Latino; 1 Hispanic/Latino; 1 Two or more races, non-Hispanic/Latino), 3 international. Average age 31. In 2014, 30 master's awarded. *Degree requirements:* For master's, thesis optional. *Entrance requirements:* For master's, official transcript, bachelor's degree in engineering or related field, two recommendations, resume. Additional exam requirements/recommendations for international students: Required—TOEFL (minimum score 79 iBT). *Application deadline:* Applications are processed on a rolling basis. Application fee: $30. Electronic applications accepted. *Financial support:* Application deadline: 4/15; applicants required to submit FAFSA. *Unit head:* Dr. S. Hossein Cheraghi, Dean, 413-782-1285, E-mail: cheraghi@wne.edu. *Application contact:* Matthew Fox, Director of Recruiting and Marketing for Adult Learners, 413-782-1517, Fax: 413-782-1777, E-mail: study@wne.edu.
Website: http://www1.wne.edu/engineering/index.cfm?selection-doc.9104.

Western New England University, College of Engineering, PhD Program in Engineering Management, Springfield, MA 01119. Offers PhD. Part-time and evening/weekend programs available. *Students:* 14 part-time (5 women); includes 4 minority (2 Asian, non-Hispanic/Latino; 1 Hispanic/Latino; 1 Two or more races, non-Hispanic/Latino), 5 international. Average age 33. *Degree requirements:* For doctorate, comprehensive exam, thesis/dissertation. *Entrance requirements:* For doctorate, GRE, official transcript, bachelor's or master's degree in engineering or related field, two letters of recommendation, minimum GPA of 3.5. Additional exam requirements/recommendations for international students: Required—TOEFL (minimum score 550 paper-based; 79 iBT). *Application deadline:* For fall admission, 1/15 priority date for domestic students. Applications are processed on a rolling basis. Application fee: $30. Electronic applications accepted. *Financial support:* Fellowships with full and partial tuition reimbursements available. Financial award application deadline: 4/15; financial award applicants required to submit FAFSA. *Unit head:* Dr. S. Hossein Cheraghi, Dean, 413-782-1285, E-mail: cheraghi@wne.edu. *Application contact:* Matthew Fox, Director of Recruiting and Marketing for Adult Learners, 413-782-1517, Fax: 413-782-1777, E-mail: study@wne.edu.
Website: http://www1.wne.edu/engineering/index.cfm?selection-doc.9183.

Wichita State University, Graduate School, College of Engineering, Department of Industrial and Manufacturing Engineering, Wichita, KS 67260. Offers engineering management (MEM); industrial engineering (MS, PhD). Part-time programs available. In 2014, 37 master's, 3 doctorates awarded. *Entrance requirements:* Additional exam requirements/recommendations for international students: Required—TOEFL. *Financial support:* Teaching assistantships available. *Unit head:* Dr. Krishna Krishnan, Chair, 316-978-3425, Fax: 316-978-3742, E-mail: krishna.krishnan@wichita.edu. *Application contact:* Jordan Oleson, Admissions Coordinator, 316-978-3095, Fax: 316-978-3253, E-mail: jordan.oleson@wichita.edu.
Website: http://www.wichita.edu/ime.

Widener University, Graduate Programs in Engineering, Program in Engineering Management, Chester, PA 19013-5792. Offers M Eng. Part-time and evening/weekend programs available. *Degree requirements:* For master's, thesis optional.

Wilkes University, College of Graduate and Professional Studies, College of Science and Engineering, Department of Mechanical Engineering and Engineering Management, Wilkes-Barre, PA 18766-0002. Offers engineering management (MS); mechanical engineering (MS). *Students:* 14 full-time (0 women), 14 part-time (0 women); includes 4 minority (1 Black or African American, non-Hispanic/Latino; 1 Asian, non-Hispanic/Latino; 1 Hispanic/Latino; 1 Two or more races, non-Hispanic/Latino), 14 international. Average age 31. In 2014, 21 master's awarded. *Unit head:* Dr. Terese Wignot, Interim Dean, 570-408-6000, Fax: 570-408-7860, E-mail: terese.wignot@wilkes.edu. *Application contact:* Joanne Thomas, Director of Graduate Enrollment, 570-408-4234, Fax: 570-408-7846, E-mail: joanne.thomas1@wilkes.edu.
Website: http://www.wilkes.edu/academics/colleges/science-and-engineering/mechanical-engineering-engineering-management-applied-and-engineering-sciences/index..

Ergonomics and Human Factors

Arizona State University at the Tempe campus, Ira A. Fulton Schools of Engineering, The Polytechnic School, Programs in Technology Management, Mesa, AZ 85212. Offers aviation management and human factors (MS); environmental technology management (MS); global technology and development (MS); graphic information technology (MS); management of technology (MS). Part-time and evening/weekend programs available. Postbaccalaureate distance learning degree programs offered (minimal on-campus study). *Degree requirements:* For master's, thesis or applied project and oral defense; interactive Program of Study (iPOS) submitted before completing 50 percent of required credit hours. *Entrance requirements:* For master's, GRE, minimum GPA of 3.0 or equivalent in last 2 years of work leading to bachelor's degree. Additional exam requirements/recommendations for international students: Required—TOEFL, IELTS, or PTE. Electronic applications accepted. *Faculty research:* Digital imaging, digital publishing, Internet development/e-commerce, information aviation human factors, pilot selection, databases, multimedia, commercial digital photography, digital workflow, computer graphics modeling and animation, information design, sociotechnology, visual and technical literacy, environmental management, quality management, project management, industrial ethics, hazardous materials, environmental chemistry.

Bentley University, Graduate School of Business, Program in Human Factors in Information Design, Waltham, MA 02452-4705. Offers MSHFID. Part-time and evening/weekend programs available. Postbaccalaureate distance learning degree programs offered (minimal on-campus study). *Faculty:* 85 full-time (28 women), 26 part-time/adjunct (9 women). *Students:* 20 full-time (17 women), 83 part-time (54 women); includes 21 minority (2 Black or African American, non-Hispanic/Latino; 11 Asian, non-Hispanic/Latino; 5 Hispanic/Latino; 3 Two or more races, non-Hispanic/Latino), 12 international. Average age 35. 65 applicants, 88% accepted, 30 enrolled. In 2014, 41 master's awarded. *Entrance requirements:* For master's, GMAT or GRE General Test. Additional exam requirements/recommendations for international students: Required—TOEFL (minimum score 600 paper-based; 100 iBT) or IELTS (minimum score 7). *Application deadline:* For fall admission, 12/1 priority date for domestic and international students; for spring admission, 10/1 for domestic and international students. Applications are processed on a rolling basis. Application fee: $50. Electronic applications accepted. *Expenses: Tuition:* Full-time $31,320. *Required fees:* $437. *Financial support:* In 2014–15, 14 students received support. Scholarships/grants available. Financial award application deadline: 6/1; financial award applicants required to submit CSS PROFILE or FAFSA. *Faculty research:* Usability engineering, ethnography, human-computer interaction, project management, user experience. *Unit head:* Dr. William M. Gribbons, Director, 781-891-2926, E-mail: wgribbons@bentley.edu. *Application contact:* Sharon Hill, Director of Graduate Admissions, 781-891-2108, Fax: 781-891-2464, E-mail: bentleygraduateadmissions@bentley.edu.
Website: http://www.bentley.edu/graduate/ms-programs/hfid.

California State University, Long Beach, Graduate Studies, College of Liberal Arts, Department of Psychology, Long Beach, CA 90840. Offers human factors (MS); industrial/organizational psychology (MS); psychology (MA). Part-time and evening/weekend programs available. *Degree requirements:* For master's, comprehensive exam, thesis. *Entrance requirements:* For master's, GRE General Test, GRE Subject Test. Electronic applications accepted. *Faculty research:* Physiological psychology, social and personality psychology, community-clinical psychology, industrial-organizational psychology, developmental psychology.

California State University, Northridge, Graduate Studies, College of Social and Behavioral Sciences, Department of Psychology, Northridge, CA 91330. Offers clinical psychology (MA); general-experimental psychology (MA); human factors and applied experimental psychology (MA). *Students:* 46 full-time (32 women), 16 part-time (10 women); includes 27 minority (3 Black or African American, non-Hispanic/Latino; 2 Asian, non-Hispanic/Latino; 20 Hispanic/Latino; 2 Two or more races, non-Hispanic/Latino). Average age 26. *Degree requirements:* For master's, thesis. *Entrance requirements:* For master's, GRE General Test, GRE Subject Test, minimum GPA of 3.0, letters of recommendation. Additional exam requirements/recommendations for international students: Required—TOEFL. *Application deadline:* For fall admission, 11/30 for domestic students. Application fee: $55. *Expenses: Required fees:* $12,402. *Financial support:* Application deadline: 3/1. *Unit head:* Jill Razani, Chair, 818-677-3506.
Website: http://www.csun.edu/csbs/departments/psychology/index.html.

The Catholic University of America, School of Arts and Sciences, Department of Psychology, Washington, DC 20064. Offers applied experimental psychology (PhD); clinical psychology (PhD); general psychology (MA); human factors (MA); MA/JD. *Accreditation:* APA (one or more programs are accredited). Part-time programs available. *Faculty:* 13 full-time (6 women), 7 part-time/adjunct (2 women). *Students:* 37 full-time (26 women), 42 part-time (33 women); includes 17 minority (1 Black or African American, non-Hispanic/Latino; 3 Asian, non-Hispanic/Latino; 7 Hispanic/Latino; 6 Two or more races, non-Hispanic/Latino), 3 international. Average age 28. 263 applicants, 14% accepted, 19 enrolled. In 2014, 19 master's, 6 doctorates awarded. *Degree requirements:* For master's, comprehensive exam, thesis (for some programs); for

doctorate, comprehensive exam, thesis/dissertation. *Entrance requirements:* For master's, GRE General Test, statement of purpose, official copies of academic transcripts, three letters of recommendation; for doctorate, GRE General Test, GRE Subject Test, statement of purpose, official copies of academic transcripts, three letters of recommendation. Additional exam requirements/recommendations for international students: Required—TOEFL (minimum score 580 paper-based). *Application deadline:* For fall admission, 7/15 priority date for domestic students, 7/1 for international students; for spring admission, 11/15 priority date for domestic students, 11/1 for international students. Applications are processed on a rolling basis. Application fee: $55. Electronic applications accepted. *Expenses: Tuition:* Full-time $40,200; part-time $1600 per credit hour. *Required fees:* $400; $195 per semester. One-time fee: $425. *Financial support:* Fellowships, research assistantships, teaching assistantships, Federal Work-Study, scholarships/grants, tuition waivers (full and partial), and unspecified assistantships available. Financial award application deadline: 2/1; financial award applicants required to submit FAFSA. *Faculty research:* Clinical psychology, applied cognitive science, psychopathology, cognitive neuroscience, psychotherapy. *Total annual research expenditures:* $1.2 million. *Unit head:* Dr. Marc M. Sebrechts, Chair, 202-319-5750, Fax: 202-319-6263, E-mail: sebrechts@cua.edu. *Application contact:* Director of Graduate Admissions, 202-319-5057, Fax: 202-319-6533, E-mail: cua-admissions@cua.edu.
Website: http://psychology.cua.edu/.

Clemson University, Graduate School, College of Business and Behavioral Science, Department of Psychology, Program in Human Factors Psychology, Clemson, SC 29634. Offers PhD. *Students:* 15 full-time (8 women), 2 part-time (0 women); includes 2 minority (both Two or more races, non-Hispanic/Latino). Average age 28. 37 applicants, 14% accepted, 4 enrolled. In 2014, 2 doctorates awarded. *Degree requirements:* For doctorate, thesis/dissertation. *Entrance requirements:* For doctorate, GRE General Test. Additional exam requirements/recommendations for international students: Required—TOEFL. *Application deadline:* For fall admission, 1/15 for domestic students. Applications are processed on a rolling basis. Application fee: $70 ($80 for international students). Electronic applications accepted. *Expenses:* Expenses: Contact institution. *Financial support:* In 2014–15, 14 students received support, including 6 fellowships with full and partial tuition reimbursements available (averaging $5,000 per year), 14 teaching assistantships with partial tuition reimbursements available (averaging $20,000 per year); research assistantships with partial tuition reimbursements available, career-related internships or fieldwork, institutionally sponsored loans, scholarships/grants, health care benefits, and unspecified assistantships also available. Support available to part-time students. *Faculty research:* Transportation safety, human factors in health care, human-computer interaction, ergonomics, vision and visual performance. *Unit head:* Dr. Patrick Raymark, Chair, 864-656-4715, Fax: 864-656-0358, E-mail: praymar@clemson.edu. *Application contact:* Dr. Lee Gugerty, Professor, 864-656-4467, Fax: 864-656-0358, E-mail: gugerty@clemson.edu.
Website: http://www.clemson.edu/psych.

Cornell University, Graduate School, Graduate Fields of Human Ecology, Field of Design and Environmental Analysis, Ithaca, NY 14853. Offers applied research in human-environment relations (MS); facilities planning and management (MS); housing and design (MS); human factors and ergonomics (MS); human-environment relations (MS); interior design (MA, MPS). *Degree requirements:* For master's, thesis. *Entrance requirements:* For master's, GRE General Test, portfolio or slides of recent work; bachelor's degree in interior design, architecture or related design discipline; 2 letters of recommendation. Additional exam requirements/recommendations for international students: Required—TOEFL (minimum score 600 paper-based; 105 iBT). Electronic applications accepted. *Faculty research:* Facility planning and management, environmental psychology, housing, interior design, ergonomics and human factors.

Embry-Riddle Aeronautical University–Daytona, Department of Human Factors, Daytona Beach, FL 32114-3900. Offers human factors (PhD); human factors engineering (MSHFS); systems engineering (MSHFS). Part-time and evening/weekend programs available. *Faculty:* 7 full-time (4 women), 1 part-time/adjunct (0 women). *Students:* 28 full-time (23 women), 10 part-time (4 women); includes 9 minority (4 Black or African American, non-Hispanic/Latino; 1 Asian, non-Hispanic/Latino; 4 Two or more races, non-Hispanic/Latino), 4 international. Average age 27. 32 applicants, 59% accepted, 18 enrolled. In 2014, 55 master's awarded. *Degree requirements:* For master's, thesis. *Entrance requirements:* Additional exam requirements/recommendations for international students: Required—TOEFL (minimum score 550 paper-based; 79 iBT). *Application deadline:* For fall admission, 6/1 priority date for domestic students, 5/1 priority date for international students; for spring admission, 11/1 priority date for domestic students, 10/1 priority date for international students. Applications are processed on a rolling basis. Application fee: $50. Electronic applications accepted. *Expenses: Tuition:* Full-time $15,360; part-time $1280 per credit hour. *Required fees:* $1334. *Financial support:* In 2014–15, 12 students received support. Research assistantships with full and partial tuition reimbursements available, teaching assistantships with full and partial tuition reimbursements available, career-related internships or fieldwork, and unspecified assistantships available. Financial award application deadline: 4/15. *Faculty research:* Healthcare human factors, game-based learning, aerospace physiology, aerospace psychology, teamwork and team training. *Unit head:* Scott Shappell, PhD, Professor and Chair, Department of Human Factors, 386-226-7744, E-mail: scott.shappell@erau.edu. *Application contact:* International and Graduate Admissions, 386-226-6176, Fax: 386-226-7070, E-mail: graduate.admissions@erau.edu.
Website: http://daytonabeach.erau.edu/college-arts-sciences/human-factors/index.html.

Florida Institute of Technology, Graduate Programs, College of Aeronautics, Program in Aviation Human Factors, Melbourne, FL 32901-6975. Offers MS. *Students:* 8 full-time (2 women), 1 international. Average age 24. 12 applicants, 50% accepted, 3 enrolled. In 2014, 4 master's awarded. *Degree requirements:* For master's, comprehensive exam, thesis, 36 credit hours. *Entrance requirements:* For master's, GRE General Test, 3 letters of recommendation, statement of objectives, resume. *Application deadline:* Applications are processed on a rolling basis. Electronic applications accepted. *Expenses: Tuition:* Part-time $1179 per credit hour. Tuition and fees vary according to campus/location. *Unit head:* Dr. Korhan Oyman, Dean, 321-674-8971, Fax: 321-674-8059, E-mail: koyman@fit.edu. *Application contact:* Cheryl A. Brown, Associate Director of Graduate Admissions, 321-674-7581, Fax: 321-723-9468, E-mail: cbrown@fit.edu.
Website: http://www.fit.edu/programs/8229/ms-aviation-human-factors#.VT_URE10ypo.

Florida Institute of Technology, Graduate Programs, College of Aeronautics, Program in Human Factors in Aeronautics, Melbourne, FL 32901-6975. Offers MS. Postbaccalaureate distance learning degree programs offered (no on-campus study). In 2014, 11 master's awarded. *Degree requirements:* For master's, thesis or capstone project. *Entrance requirements:* For master's, letter of recommednation, resume, statement of objectives. *Application deadline:* Applications are processed on a rolling basis. Electronic applications accepted. *Expenses: Tuition:* Part-time $1179 per credit hour. Tuition and fees vary according to campus/location. *Unit head:* Dr. Korhan Oyman, Dean, 321-674-8971, E-mail: koyman@fit.edu. *Application contact:* Cheryl A. Brown, Associate Director of Graduate Admissions, 321-674-7581, Fax: 321-723-9468, E-mail: cbrown@fit.edu.
Website: http://coa.fit.edu/programs/human-factors.php.

Florida Institute of Technology, Graduate Programs, School of Human-Centered Design, Innovation and Art, Melbourne, FL 32901-6975. Offers MS, PhD. Part-time and evening/weekend programs available. *Students:* 11 full-time (5 women), 3 part-time (1 woman); includes 2 minority (both Black or African American, non-Hispanic/Latino), 7 international. Average age 32. 18 applicants, 67% accepted, 6 enrolled. In 2014, 3 doctorates awarded. *Degree requirements:* For master's, comprehensive exam (for some programs), thesis or final exam, professional oriented project; for doctorate, comprehensive exam, thesis/dissertation, publication in journal. *Entrance requirements:* For master's, GRE (minimum score of 1100), undergraduate degree with minimum cumulative GPA of 3.2; three letters of recommendation; statement of objectives, resume; for doctorate, GRE, master's degree with minimum cumulative GPA of 3.2; transcripts; three letters of recommendation; statement of objectives, resume. Additional exam requirements/recommendations for international students: Required—TOEFL (minimum score 600 paper-based; 100 iBT). *Application deadline:* For fall admission, 4/1 for international students; for spring admission, 9/30 for international students. Applications are processed on a rolling basis. Electronic applications accepted. *Expenses: Tuition:* Part-time $1179 per credit hour. Tuition and fees vary according to campus/location. *Financial support:* In 2014–15, 2 research assistantships were awarded; career-related internships or fieldwork, institutionally sponsored loans, tuition waivers (partial), unspecified assistantships, and tuition remissions also available. Support available to part-time students. Financial award application deadline: 3/1; financial award applicants required to submit FAFSA. *Faculty research:* Cognitive engineering, advanced interaction media, complexity analysis in human-centered design, life-critical systems, human-centered organization design and management, modeling and simulation. *Unit head:* Dr. Guy Boy, Director, 321-674-7631, Fax: 321-984-8461, E-mail: gboy@fit.edu. *Application contact:* Cheryl A. Brown, Associate Director of Graduate Admissions, 321-674-7581, Fax: 321-723-9468, E-mail: cbrown@fit.edu.
Website: http://research.fit.edu/hcdi/.

Georgia Institute of Technology, Graduate Studies, College of Computing, Program in Human-Centered Computing, Atlanta, GA 30332-0001. Offers PhD. Part-time programs available. *Students:* 33 full-time (15 women), 7 part-time (2 women); includes 9 minority (3 Black or African American, non-Hispanic/Latino; 2 Asian, non-Hispanic/Latino; 3 Hispanic/Latino; 1 Two or more races, non-Hispanic/Latino), 5 international. Average age 29. 74 applicants, 20% accepted, 4 enrolled. In 2014, 1 doctorate awarded. *Degree requirements:* For doctorate, comprehensive exam, thesis/dissertation, research project, teaching requirement. *Entrance requirements:* For doctorate, GRE General Test, http://www.ic.gatech.edu/future/phdhcc/admissions. Additional exam requirements/recommendations for international students: Required—TOEFL (minimum score 600 paper-based; 100 iBT). *Application deadline:* For fall admission, 12/15 for domestic and international students. Applications are processed on a rolling basis. Application fee: $75. Electronic applications accepted. *Expenses:* Tuition, state resident: full-time $12,344; part-time $515 per credit hour. Tuition, nonresident: full-time $27,600; part-time $1150 per credit hour. *Required fees:* $1196 per term. Part-time tuition and fees vary according to course load. *Financial support:* Fellowships, research assistantships, teaching assistantships, career-related internships or fieldwork, Federal Work-Study, institutionally sponsored loans, tuition waivers (partial), and unspecified assistantships available. Support available to part-time students. Financial award application deadline: 5/1. *Unit head:* Gregory Abowd, Director, 404-385-5055, E-mail: abowd@gatech.edu. *Application contact:* Jessica Celestine, Graduate Coordinator, 404-385-7205, E-mail: jcelesti@cc.gatech.edu.
Website: http://www.ic.gatech.edu/future/phdhcc.

Indiana University Bloomington, School of Public Health, Department of Kinesiology, Bloomington, IN 47405. Offers applied sport science (MS); athletic administration/sport management (MS); athletic training (MS); biomechanics (MS); ergonomics (MS); exercise physiology (MS); human performance (PhD), including biomechanics, exercise physiology, motor learning/control, sport management; motor learning/control (MS); physical activity (MPH); physical activity, fitness and wellness (MS). Part-time programs available. *Faculty:* 26 full-time (9 women). *Students:* 100 full-time (35 women), 15 part-time (5 women); includes 13 minority (5 Black or African American, non-Hispanic/Latino; 2 American Indian or Alaska Native, non-Hispanic/Latino; 2 Asian, non-Hispanic/Latino; 2 Hispanic/Latino; 2 Two or more races, non-Hispanic/Latino), 27 international. Average age 28. 188 applicants, 46% accepted, 39 enrolled. In 2014, 45 master's, 5 doctorates awarded. Terminal master's awarded for partial completion of doctoral program. *Degree requirements:* For master's, thesis optional; for doctorate, variable foreign language requirement, comprehensive exam, thesis/dissertation. *Entrance requirements:* For master's, GRE General Test, minimum GPA of 2.8; for doctorate, GRE General Test, minimum graduate GPA of 3.5, undergraduate 3.0. Additional exam requirements/recommendations for international students: Required—TOEFL (minimum score 80 iBT). *Application deadline:* For fall admission, 1/1 priority date for international students; for spring admission, 9/1 priority date for international students. Applications are processed on a rolling basis. Application fee: $55 ($65 for international students). *Financial support:* Fellowships, research assistantships with full tuition reimbursements, teaching assistantships with full tuition reimbursements, career-related internships or fieldwork, Federal Work-Study, institutionally sponsored loans, scholarships/grants, health care benefits, tuition waivers (partial), unspecified assistantships, and fee remissions available. Support available to part-time students. Financial award application deadline: 3/1; financial award applicants required to submit FAFSA. *Faculty research:* Exercise physiology and biochemistry, sports biomechanics, human motor control, adaptation of fitness and exercise to special populations. *Unit head:* Dr. David M. Koceja, Chairperson, 812-855-5523, Fax: 812-855-3193, E-mail: koceja@indiana.edu. *Application contact:* Kristine M. Wasson, Administrative Assistant for Graduate Studies, 812-855-5523, Fax: 812-855-3193, E-mail: ktanksle@indiana.edu.
Website: http://www.publichealth.indiana.edu/departments/kinesiology/index.shtml.

Michigan Technological University, Graduate School, College of Sciences and Arts, Department of Cognitive and Learning Sciences, Houghton, MI 49931. Offers applied cognitive science and human factors (PhD); applied science education (MS). Part-time programs available. Postbaccalaureate distance learning degree programs offered (minimal on-campus study). *Faculty:* 15 full-time (5 women), 6 part-time/adjunct (2 women). *Students:* 16 full-time (11 women), 29 part-time (18 women); includes 7 minority (1 Black or African American, non-Hispanic/Latino; 1 American Indian or Alaska Native, non-Hispanic/Latino; 1 Asian, non-Hispanic/Latino; 4 Two or more races, non-Hispanic/Latino), 7 international. Average age 35. 36 applicants, 19% accepted, 5 enrolled. In 2014, 3 master's awarded. Terminal master's awarded for partial completion of doctoral program. *Degree requirements:* For master's, comprehensive exam (for some programs), thesis (for some programs); for doctorate, comprehensive exam, thesis/dissertation, applied internship experience. *Entrance requirements:* For master's, GRE (applied cognitive science and human factors program only), statement of purpose, official transcripts, 3 letters of recommendation, resume/curriculum vitae; for doctorate,

GRE, statement of purpose, official transcripts, 3 letters of recommendation, resume/ curriculum vitae. Additional exam requirements/recommendations for international students: Required—TOEFL (recommended score 90 iBT) or IELTS. *Application deadline:* For fall admission, 2/15 priority date for domestic and international students. Applications are processed on a rolling basis. Electronic applications accepted. *Expenses:* Tuition, state resident: full-time $14,769; part-time $820.50 per credit. Tuition, nonresident: full-time $14,769; part-time $820.50 per credit. *Required fees:* $248; $248 per year. Tuition and fees vary according to course load and program. *Financial support:* In 2014–15, 23 students received support, including 7 research assistantships with full and partial tuition reimbursements available (averaging $13,824 per year), 3 teaching assistantships (averaging $13,824 per year); career-related internships or fieldwork, Federal Work-Study, scholarships/grants, health care benefits, unspecified assistantships, and adjunct instructor positions also available. Financial award applicants required to submit FAFSA. *Faculty research:* Cognitive engineering and decision-making, human-centered design, individual differences in human performance, STEM education. *Total annual research expenditures:* $280,705. *Unit head:* Dr. Susan L. Amato-Henderson, Chair, 906-487-2536, Fax: 906-487-2468, E-mail: slamato@mtu.edu. *Application contact:* Carol T. Wingerson, Senior Staff Assistant, 906-487-2327, Fax: 906-487-2463, E-mail: gradadms@mtu.edu.
Website: http://cls.mtu.edu/.

Missouri Western State University, Program in Applied Science, St. Joseph, MO 64507-2294. Offers chemistry (MAS); engineering technology management (MAS); human factors and usability testing (MAS); industrial life science (MAS); information technology management (MAS); sport and fitness management (MAS). Part-time programs available. *Students:* 42 full-time (14 women), 34 part-time (10 women); includes 6 minority (5 Black or African American, non-Hispanic/Latino; 1 Asian, non-Hispanic/Latino), 25 international. Average age 28. 40 applicants, 100% accepted, 26 enrolled. In 2014, 16 master's awarded. *Entrance requirements:* Additional exam requirements/recommendations for international students: Recommended—TOEFL (minimum score 70 iBT), IELTS (minimum score 6). *Application deadline:* For fall admission, 7/15 for domestic and international students; for spring admission, 11/1 for domestic students, 10/15 for international students; for summer admission, 4/29 for domestic students. Applications are processed on a rolling basis. Application fee: $45 ($50 for international students). Electronic applications accepted. *Expenses:* Tuition, state resident: full-time $5506; part-time $305.91 per credit hour. Tuition, nonresident: full-time $10,075; part-time $559.71 per credit hour. *Required fees:* $504; $99 per credit hour. $176 per semester. Tuition and fees vary according to course load and program. *Financial support:* Scholarships/grants and unspecified assistantships available. Support available to part-time students. *Unit head:* Dr. Benjamin D. Caldwell, Dean of the Graduate School, 816-271-4394, Fax: 816-271-4525, E-mail: graduate@missouriwestern.edu.

New York University, Graduate School of Arts and Science, Department of Environmental Medicine, New York, NY 10012-1019. Offers environmental health sciences (MS, PhD), including biostatistics (PhD), environmental hygiene (MS), epidemiology (PhD), ergonomics and biomechanics (PhD), exposure assessment and health effects (PhD), molecular toxicology/carcinogenesis (PhD), toxicology. Part-time programs available. *Faculty:* 26 full-time (7 women). *Students:* 65 full-time (35 women), 9 part-time (5 women); includes 18 minority (1 Black or African American, non-Hispanic/Latino; 8 Asian, non-Hispanic/Latino; 8 Hispanic/Latino; 1 Two or more races, non-Hispanic/Latino), 27 international. Average age 30. 79 applicants, 44% accepted, 20 enrolled. In 2014, 8 master's, 6 doctorates awarded. Terminal master's awarded for partial completion of doctoral program. *Degree requirements:* For master's, thesis or alternative; for doctorate, one foreign language, thesis/dissertation, oral and written exams. *Entrance requirements:* For master's and doctorate, GRE General Test, minimum GPA of 3.0; bachelor's degree in biological, physical, or engineering science. Additional exam requirements/recommendations for international students: Required—TOEFL. *Application deadline:* For fall admission, 12/18 for domestic and international students. Application fee: $100. *Financial support:* Fellowships with tuition reimbursements, teaching assistantships with tuition reimbursements, career-related internships or fieldwork, Federal Work-Study, institutionally sponsored loans, and health care benefits available. Financial award application deadline: 12/18; financial award applicants required to submit FAFSA. *Unit head:* Dr. Max Costa, Chair, 845-731-3661, Fax: 845-351-4510, E-mail: ehs@env.med.nyu.edu. *Application contact:* Dr. Jerome J. Solomon, Director of Graduate Studies, 845-731-3661, Fax: 845-351-4510, E-mail: ehs@env.med.nyu.edu.
Website: http://environmental-medicine.med.nyu.edu/.

North Carolina State University, Graduate School, College of Humanities and Social Sciences, Department of Psychology, Raleigh, NC 27695. Offers developmental psychology (PhD); ergonomics and experimental psychology (PhD); industrial/organizational psychology (PhD); psychology in the public interest (PhD); school psychology (PhD). *Accreditation:* APA. *Degree requirements:* For doctorate, comprehensive exam, thesis/dissertation. *Entrance requirements:* For doctorate, GRE General Test, GRE Subject Test (industrial/organizational psychology), MAT (recommended), minimum GPA of 3.0 in major. Electronic applications accepted. *Faculty research:* Cognitive and social development (human factors, families, the workplace, community issues and health, aging).

Old Dominion University, College of Sciences, Doctoral Program in Psychology, Norfolk, VA 23529. Offers applied experimental psychology (PhD); human factors psychology (PhD). *Faculty:* 22 full-time (7 women). *Students:* 35 full-time (16 women), 17 part-time (13 women); includes 8 minority (3 Black or African American, non-Hispanic/Latino; 5 Hispanic/Latino), 3 international. Average age 27. 82 applicants, 30% accepted, 7 enrolled. In 2014, 5 doctorates awarded. *Degree requirements:* For doctorate, thesis/dissertation, candidacy exam. *Entrance requirements:* For doctorate, GRE General Test, GRE Subject Test, 3 recommendation letters. Additional exam requirements/recommendations for international students: Required—TOEFL. *Application deadline:* For winter admission, 1/5 for domestic and international students. Application fee: $50. Electronic applications accepted. *Expenses:* Tuition, state resident: full-time $10,488; part-time $437 per credit. Tuition, nonresident: full-time $26,136; part-time $1089 per credit. *Required fees:* $64 per semester. One-time fee: $50. *Financial support:* In 2014–15, 42 students received support, including 4 research assistantships with full tuition reimbursements available (averaging $17,500 per year), 38 teaching assistantships with full tuition reimbursements available (averaging $17,500 per year). Financial award application deadline: 1/15. *Faculty research:* Human factors, industrial psychology, organizational psychology, applied experimental (health, developmental, quantitative). *Total annual research expenditures:* $978,563. *Unit head:* Dr. Bryan E. Porter, Graduate Program Director, 757-683-4458, Fax: 757-683-5087, E-mail: bporter@odu.edu. *Application contact:* William Heffelfinger, Director of Graduate Admissions, 757-683-5554, Fax: 757-683-3255, E-mail: gradadmit@odu.edu.
Website: http://sci.odu.edu/psychology/.

Purdue University, Graduate School, College of Health and Human Sciences, School of Health Sciences, West Lafayette, IN 47907. Offers health physics (MS, PhD); medical physics (MS, PhD); occupational and environmental health science (MS, PhD), including aerosol deposition and lung disease, ergonomics, exposure and risk assessment, indoor air quality and bioaerosols (PhD), liver/lung toxicology; radiation biology (PhD); toxicology (PhD); MS/PhD. Part-time programs available. *Degree requirements:* For master's, thesis optional; for doctorate, one foreign language, thesis/dissertation. *Entrance requirements:* For master's and doctorate, GRE General Test, minimum undergraduate GPA of 3.0 or equivalent. Additional exam requirements/recommendations for international students: Required—TOEFL (minimum score 550 paper-based; 77 iBT); Recommended—TWE. Electronic applications accepted. *Faculty research:* Environmental toxicology, industrial hygiene, radiation dosimetry.

Tufts University, School of Engineering, Department of Mechanical Engineering, Medford, MA 02155. Offers bioengineering (ME, MS), including bioinformatics, biomechanical systems and devices, signals and systems; bioinformatics (MS); human factors (MS); mechanical engineering (ME, MS, PhD). Part-time programs available. *Faculty:* 15 full-time (1 woman), 7 part-time/adjunct (1 woman). *Students:* 35 full-time (12 women), 23 part-time (11 women); includes 11 minority (3 Black or African American, non-Hispanic/Latino; 1 American Indian or Alaska Native, non-Hispanic/Latino; 3 Asian, non-Hispanic/Latino; 2 Hispanic/Latino; 2 Two or more races, non-Hispanic/Latino), 14 international. Average age 27. 112 applicants, 47% accepted, 16 enrolled. In 2014, 18 master's, 6 doctorates awarded. Terminal master's awarded for partial completion of doctoral program. *Degree requirements:* For master's, thesis; for doctorate, thesis/dissertation. *Entrance requirements:* For master's and doctorate, GRE General Test. Additional exam requirements/recommendations for international students: Required—TOEFL (minimum score 550 paper-based; 80 iBT), IELTS (minimum score 6.5). *Application deadline:* For fall admission, 1/15 priority date for domestic students, 1/15 for international students; for spring admission, 9/15 for domestic and international students. Applications are processed on a rolling basis. Application fee: $75. Electronic applications accepted. *Expenses:* *Tuition:* Full-time $45,590; part-time $1161 per credit hour. *Required fees:* $782. Full-time tuition and fees vary according to degree level, program and student level. Part-time tuition and fees vary according to course load. *Financial support:* Fellowships with full tuition reimbursements, research assistantships with full and partial tuition reimbursements, teaching assistantships with full and partial tuition reimbursements, Federal Work-Study, scholarships/grants, tuition waivers (partial), and unspecified assistantships available. Financial award application deadline: 5/15; financial award applicants required to submit FAFSA. *Faculty research:* Applied mechanics, biomaterials, controls/robotics, design/systems, human factors. *Unit head:* Dr. Robert C. White, Graduate Program Director. *Application contact:* Office of Graduate Admissions, 617-627-3395, E-mail: gradadmissions@tufts.edu.
Website: http://engineering.tufts.edu/me.

Université de Montréal, Faculty of Medicine, Programs in Ergonomics, Montréal, QC H3C 3J7, Canada. Offers occupational therapy (DESS). Program offered jointly with École Polytechnique de Montréal.

Université du Québec à Montréal, Graduate Programs, Program in Ergonomics in Occupational Health and Safety, Montréal, QC H3C 3P8, Canada. Offers Diploma. Part-time programs available. *Entrance requirements:* For degree, appropriate bachelor's degree or equivalent, proficiency in French.

The University of Alabama, Graduate School, College of Human Environmental Sciences, Program in Human Environmental Science, Tuscaloosa, AL 35487. Offers interactive technology (MS); quality management (MS); restaurant and meeting management (MS); rural community health (MS); sport management (MS). Part-time and evening/weekend programs available. Postbaccalaureate distance learning degree programs offered (no on-campus study). *Faculty:* 1 full-time (0 women). *Students:* 66 full-time (39 women), 97 part-time (46 women); includes 46 minority (33 Black or African American, non-Hispanic/Latino; 2 Asian, non-Hispanic/Latino; 5 Hispanic/Latino; 6 Two or more races, non-Hispanic/Latino), 1 international. Average age 33. 109 applicants, 70% accepted, 66 enrolled. In 2014, 94 master's awarded. *Degree requirements:* For master's, comprehensive exam. *Entrance requirements:* For master's, GRE (for some specializations), minimum GPA of 3.0. Additional exam requirements/recommendations for international students: Required—TOEFL. *Application deadline:* For fall admission, 7/1 for domestic students; for spring admission, 11/1 for domestic students; for summer admission, 4/15 for domestic students. Applications are processed on a rolling basis. Application fee: $50 ($60 for international students). Electronic applications accepted. *Expenses:* Tuition, state resident: full-time $9826. Tuition, nonresident: full-time $24,950. *Financial support:* In 2014–15, 2 teaching assistantships with full tuition reimbursements were awarded. Financial award application deadline: 7/1. *Faculty research:* Rural health, hospitality management, sport management, interactive technology, consumer quality management, environmental health and safety. *Unit head:* Dr. Milla D. Boschung, Dean, 205-348-6250, Fax: 205-348-1786, E-mail: mboschun@ches.ua.edu. *Application contact:* Dr. Stuart Usdan, Associate Dean, 205-348-6150, Fax: 205-348-3789, E-mail: susdan@ches.ua.edu.
Website: http://www.ches.ua.edu/programs-of-study.html.

University of Cincinnati, Graduate School, College of Medicine, Graduate Programs in Biomedical Sciences, Department of Environmental Health, Cincinnati, OH 45221. Offers environmental and industrial hygiene (MS, PhD); environmental and occupational medicine (MS); environmental genetics and molecular toxicology (MS, PhD); epidemiology and biostatistics (MS, PhD); occupational safety and ergonomics (MS, PhD). *Accreditation:* ABET (one or more programs are accredited). *Faculty:* 26 full-time (10 women). *Students:* 39 full-time (16 women), 34 part-time (18 women); includes 11 minority (4 Black or African American, non-Hispanic/Latino; 4 Asian, non-Hispanic/Latino; 3 Hispanic/Latino), 22 international. 136 applicants, 28% accepted. In 2014, 12 master's, 8 doctorates awarded. Terminal master's awarded for partial completion of doctoral program. *Degree requirements:* For master's, thesis; for doctorate, thesis/dissertation, qualifying exam. *Entrance requirements:* For master's, GRE General Test, bachelor's degree in science; for doctorate, GRE General Test. Additional exam requirements/recommendations for international students: Required—TOEFL (minimum score 600 paper-based; 100 iBT). *Application deadline:* For fall admission, 3/1 priority date for domestic and international students. Applications are processed on a rolling basis. Application fee: $40. Electronic applications accepted. *Financial support:* In 2014–15, 69 students received support, including research assistantships with full tuition reimbursements available (averaging $17,850 per year); career-related internships or fieldwork, scholarships/grants, traineeships, tuition waivers (partial), and unspecified assistantships also available. Financial award application deadline: 5/1. *Faculty research:* Carcinogens and mutagenesis, pulmonary studies, reproduction and development. *Total annual research expenditures:* $16.9 million. *Unit head:* Dr. Shuk-Mei Ho, Chairman, 513-558-5701, Fax: 513-558-4397, E-mail: hosm@ucmail.uc.edu. *Application contact:* Stephanie W. Starkey, Graduate Program Coordinator, 513-558-5704, Fax: 513-558-5457, E-mail: stephanie.starkey@uc.edu.
Website: http://www.med.uc.edu/.

The University of Iowa, Graduate College, College of Engineering, Department of Industrial Engineering, Iowa City, IA 52242-1316. Offers engineering design and manufacturing (MS, PhD); healthcare systems (MS, PhD); human factors (MS, PhD); information and engineering management (MS, PhD); operations research (MS, PhD); wind energy (MS, PhD). *Faculty:* 8 full-time (1 woman). *Students:* 19 full-time (3 women); includes 1 minority (Asian, non-Hispanic/Latino), 10 international. Average age

28. 59 applicants, 12% accepted, 3 enrolled. In 2014, 1 master's, 4 doctorates awarded. Terminal master's awarded for partial completion of doctoral program. *Degree requirements:* For master's, thesis optional, exam; for doctorate, comprehensive exam, thesis/dissertation, final defense exam. *Entrance requirements:* For master's and doctorate, GRE General Test. Additional exam requirements/recommendations for international students: Required—TOEFL (minimum score 600 paper-based; 100 iBT). *Application deadline:* For fall admission, 7/15 for domestic students, 4/15 for international students; for spring admission, 12/1 for domestic students, 10/1 for international students; for summer admission, 4/15 for domestic students, 3/1 for international students. Applications are processed on a rolling basis. Application fee: $60 ($100 for international students). Electronic applications accepted. *Financial support:* In 2014–15, 4 fellowships with partial tuition reimbursements (averaging $20,619 per year), 16 research assistantships with full tuition reimbursements (averaging $18,131 per year), 5 teaching assistantships with full tuition reimbursements (averaging $5,424 per year) were awarded; career-related internships or fieldwork, scholarships/grants, and unspecified assistantships also available. Support available to part-time students. Financial award applicants required to submit FAFSA. *Faculty research:* Operations research, informatics, human factors engineering, healthcare systems, biomanufacturing, manufacturing systems, renewable energy, human-machine interactions. *Total annual research expenditures:* $3.5 million. *Unit head:* Dr. Andrew Kusiak, Department Executive Officer, 319-335-5934, Fax: 319-335-5669, E-mail: andrew-kusiak@uiowa.edu. *Application contact:* Andrea Flaherty, Academic Program Specialist, 319-335-5939, Fax: 319-335-5669, E-mail: indeng@engineering.uiowa.edu.
Website: http://www.engineering.uiowa.edu/mie.

The University of Iowa, Graduate College, College of Public Health, Department of Occupational and Environmental Health, Iowa City, IA 52242-1316. Offers agricultural safety and health (MS, PhD); ergonomics (MPH); industrial hygiene (MS, PhD); occupational and environmental health (MPH, MS, PhD, Certificate); MS/MA; MS/MS. *Accreditation:* ABET (one or more programs are accredited); CEPH. *Degree requirements:* For master's, thesis optional, exam; for doctorate, comprehensive exam, thesis/dissertation. *Entrance requirements:* For master's and doctorate, GRE General Test, minimum GPA of 3.0. Additional exam requirements/recommendations for international students: Required—TOEFL (minimum score 600 paper-based; 100 iBT). Electronic applications accepted.

University of Massachusetts Lowell, College of Health Sciences, Department of Work Environment, Lowell, MA 01854. Offers cleaner production and pollution prevention (MS, Sc D); environmental risk assessment (Certificate); epidemiology (MS, Sc D); ergonomics and safety (MS, Sc D); identification and control of ergonomic hazards (Certificate); job stress and healthy job redesign (Certificate); occupational and environmental hygiene (MS, Sc D); radiological health physics and general work environment protection (Certificate); work environment policy (MS, Sc D). *Accreditation:* ABET (one or more programs are accredited). Part-time programs available. Terminal master's awarded for partial completion of doctoral program. *Degree requirements:* For master's, thesis optional; for doctorate, thesis/dissertation. *Entrance requirements:* For master's and doctorate, GRE General Test. Additional exam requirements/recommendations for international students: Required—TOEFL.

University of Miami, Graduate School, College of Engineering, Department of Industrial Engineering, Program in Occupational Ergonomics and Safety, Coral Gables, FL 33124. Offers environmental health and safety (MS); occupational ergonomics and safety (MSOES). Part-time programs available. *Degree requirements:* For master's, thesis optional. *Entrance requirements:* For master's, GRE General Test, minimum GPA of 3.0. Additional exam requirements/recommendations for international students: Required—TOEFL (minimum score 550 paper-based). Electronic applications accepted. *Faculty research:* Noise, heat stress, water pollution.

University of Wisconsin–Milwaukee, Graduate School, College of Engineering and Applied Science, Program in Engineering, Milwaukee, WI 53201-0413. Offers civil engineering (MS); electrical and computer engineering (MS); energy engineering (Certificate); engineering (PhD); engineering management (MS); engineering mechanics (MS); ergonomics (Certificate); industrial and management engineering (MS); manufacturing engineering (MS); materials engineering (MS); mechanical engineering (MS); MUP/MS. Part-time programs available. *Degree requirements:* For master's, comprehensive exam (for some programs), thesis or alternative; for doctorate, comprehensive exam, thesis/dissertation, internship. *Entrance requirements:* For master's, GRE, minimum GPA of 2.75; for doctorate, GRE, minimum GPA of 3.5. Additional exam requirements/recommendations for international students: Required—TOEFL (minimum score 550 paper-based; 79 iBT), IELTS (minimum score 6.5).

University of Wisconsin–Milwaukee, Graduate School, College of Health Sciences, Department of Occupational Science and Technology, Milwaukee, WI 53201-0413. Offers ergonomics (Certificate); occupational therapy (MS); therapeutic recreation (Certificate). *Accreditation:* AOTA. *Degree requirements:* For master's, thesis or alternative. *Entrance requirements:* Additional exam requirements/recommendations for international students: Required—TOEFL (minimum score 550 paper-based; 79 iBT), IELTS (minimum score 6.5).

Wright State University, School of Graduate Studies, College of Engineering and Computer Science, Programs in Engineering, Program in Biomedical and Human Factors Engineering, Dayton, OH 45435. Offers biomedical engineering (MSE); human factors engineering (MSE). Part-time programs available. *Degree requirements:* For master's, thesis or course option alternative. *Entrance requirements:* Additional exam requirements/recommendations for international students: Required—TOEFL. *Faculty research:* Medical imaging, functional electrical stimulation, implantable aids, man-machine interfaces, expert systems.

Wright State University, School of Graduate Studies, College of Science and Mathematics, Department of Psychology, Program in Human Factors and Industrial/Organizational Psychology, Dayton, OH 45435. Offers MS, PhD. *Degree requirements:* For master's, thesis; for doctorate, thesis/dissertation.

Management of Technology

Air Force Institute of Technology, Graduate School of Engineering and Management, Department of Operational Sciences, Dayton, OH 45433-7765. Offers logistics management (MS); operations research (MS, PhD); space operations (MS). Part-time programs available. *Degree requirements:* For master's, thesis; for doctorate, thesis/dissertation. *Entrance requirements:* For doctorate, GRE General Test, minimum GPA of 3.0, U.S. citizenship. *Faculty research:* Optimization, simulation, combat modeling and analysis, reliability and maintainability, resource scheduling.

Arizona State University at the Tempe campus, Ira A. Fulton Schools of Engineering, The Polytechnic School, Programs in Technology Management, Mesa, AZ 85212. Offers aviation management and human factors (MS); environmental technology management (MS); global technology and development (MS); graphic information technology (MS); management of technology (MS). Part-time and evening/weekend programs available. Postbaccalaureate distance learning degree programs offered (minimal on-campus study). *Degree requirements:* For master's, thesis or applied project and oral defense; interactive Program of Study (iPOS) submitted before completing 50 percent of required credit hours. *Entrance requirements:* For master's, GRE, minimum GPA of 3.0 or equivalent in last 2 years of work leading to bachelor's degree. Additional exam requirements/recommendations for international students: Required—TOEFL, IELTS, or PTE. Electronic applications accepted. *Faculty research:* Digital imaging, digital publishing, Internet development/e-commerce, information aviation human factors, pilot selection, databases, multimedia, commercial digital photography, digital workflow, computer graphics modeling and animation, information design, sociotechnology, visual and technical literacy, environmental management, quality management, project management, industrial ethics, hazardous materials, environmental chemistry.

Athabasca University, Centre for Innovative Management, St. Albert, AB T8N 1B4, Canada. Offers business administration (MBA); information technology management (MBA), including policing concentration; management (GDM); project management (MBA, GDM). Part-time and evening/weekend programs available. Postbaccalaureate distance learning degree programs offered (no on-campus study). *Degree requirements:* For master's, thesis or alternative, applied project. *Entrance requirements:* For master's, 3-8 years of managerial experience, 3 years with undergraduate degree, 5 years managerial experience with professional designation, 8-10 years management experience (on exception). Electronic applications accepted. *Expenses:* Contact institution. *Faculty research:* Human resources, project management, operations research, information technology management, corporate stewardship, energy management.

Boston University, Metropolitan College, Department of Administrative Sciences, Boston, MA 02215. Offers banking and financial services management (MSM); business continuity in emergency management (MSM); financial economics (MSAS); innovation and technology (MSAS); insurance management (MSM); international marketing management (MSM); project management (MS). *Accreditation:* AACSB. Part-time and evening/weekend programs available. Postbaccalaureate distance learning degree programs offered (no on-campus study). *Faculty:* 15 full-time (3 women), 22 part-time/adjunct (3 women). *Students:* 214 full-time (111 women), 619 part-time (325 women); includes 146 minority (52 Black or African American, non-Hispanic/Latino; 1 American Indian or Alaska Native, non-Hispanic/Latino; 38 Asian, non-Hispanic/Latino; 43 Hispanic/Latino; 2 Native Hawaiian or other Pacific Islander, non-Hispanic/Latino; 10 Two or more races, non-Hispanic/Latino), 268 international. Average age 32. 593 applicants, 69% accepted, 260 enrolled. In 2014, 163 master's awarded. *Degree requirements:* For master's, thesis optional. *Entrance requirements:* For master's, 1 year of work experience, minimum GPA of 3.0. Additional exam requirements/recommendations for international students: Required—TOEFL (minimum score 84 iBT). *Application deadline:* Applications are processed on a rolling basis. Application fee: $80. Electronic applications accepted. *Expenses:* Expenses: $800 per credit part-time; student services fees: $60 per semester; technology fee of $60 per credit (for online courses). *Financial support:* In 2014–15, 15 students received support, including 14 research assistantships (averaging $8,400 per year); career-related internships or fieldwork, Federal Work-Study, and unspecified assistantships also available. *Faculty research:* International business, innovative process. *Unit head:* Dr. John Sullivan, Chair, 617-353-3016, E-mail: adminsc@bu.edu. *Application contact:* Fiona Niven, Administrative Sciences Department, 617-353-3016, E-mail: adminsc@bu.edu.
Website: http://www.bu.edu/met/academic-community/departments/administrative-sciences/.

California Lutheran University, Graduate Studies, School of Management, Thousand Oaks, CA 91360-2787. Offers business (IMBA); computer science (MS); econometrics (MBA); economics (MS); entrepreneurship (MBA, Certificate); finance (MBA, Certificate); financial planning (MBA, Certificate); information systems and technology (MS); information technology management (MBA, Certificate); international business (MBA, Certificate); management and organization behavior (MBA); management and organizational behavior (Certificate); marketing (MBA, Certificate); microeconomics (MBA); nonprofit and social enterprise (MBA). Part-time and evening/weekend programs available. Postbaccalaureate distance learning degree programs offered (no on-campus study). *Faculty:* 35 full-time (13 women), 44 part-time/adjunct (13 women). *Students:* 385 full-time (171 women), 256 part-time (109 women); includes 118 minority (15 Black or African American, non-Hispanic/Latino; 2 American Indian or Alaska Native, non-Hispanic/Latino; 25 Asian, non-Hispanic/Latino; 65 Hispanic/Latino; 1 Native Hawaiian or other Pacific Islander, non-Hispanic/Latino; 10 Two or more races, non-Hispanic/Latino), 320 international. Average age 32. 620 applicants, 69% accepted, 120 enrolled. In 2014, 317 master's awarded. *Entrance requirements:* For master's, GMAT, interview, minimum GPA of 3.0. *Application deadline:* Applications are processed on a rolling basis. Application fee: $50. *Expenses:* Expenses: Contact institution. *Unit head:* Dr. Gerhard Apfelthaler, Dean, 805-493-3360. *Application contact:* 805-493-3325, Fax: 805-493-3861, E-mail: clugrad@callutheran.edu.
Website: http://www.callutheran.edu/business/.

California State University, Los Angeles, Graduate Studies, College of Engineering, Computer Science, and Technology, Department of Technology, Los Angeles, CA 90032-8530. Offers industrial and technical studies (MA). Part-time and evening/weekend programs available. *Entrance requirements:* For master's, minimum GPA of 2.5. Additional exam requirements/recommendations for international students: Required—TOEFL (minimum score 550 paper-based). *Expenses:* Tuition, state resident: full-time $6738; part-time $3609 per year. Tuition, nonresident: full-time $15,666; part-time $8073 per year. Tuition and fees vary according to course load, degree level and program.

Cambridge College, School of Management, Cambridge, MA 02138-5304. Offers business negotiation and conflict resolution (M Mgt); general business (M Mgt); health care informatics (M Mgt); health care management (M Mgt); leadership in human and organizational dynamics (M Mgt); non-profit and public organization management (M Mgt); small business development (M Mgt); technology management (M Mgt). Part-time and evening/weekend programs available. *Degree requirements:* For master's, thesis, seminars. *Entrance requirements:* For master's, resume, 2 professional references. Additional exam requirements/recommendations for international students: Required—TOEFL (minimum score 550 paper-based; 79 iBT), Michigan English Language Assessment Battery (minimum score 85); Recommended—IELTS (minimum score 6). Electronic applications accepted. *Expenses:* Contact institution. *Faculty research:* Negotiation, mediation and conflict resolution; leadership; management of diverse organizations; case studies and simulation methodologies for management education, digital as a second language: social networking for digital immigrants, non-profit and public management.

Capella University, School of Business and Technology, Doctoral Programs in Technology, Minneapolis, MN 55402. Offers general information technology (PhD); global operations and supply chain management (DBA); information assurance and security (PhD); information technology education (PhD); information technology management (DBA, PhD).

Capella University, School of Business and Technology, Master's Programs in Technology, Minneapolis, MN 55402. Offers enterprise software architecture (MS); general information systems and technology management (MS); global operations and supply chain management (MBA); information assurance and security (MS); information technology management (MBA); network management (MS).

Carleton University, Faculty of Graduate Studies, Faculty of Engineering and Design, Ottawa-Carleton Institute for Electrical Engineering, Department of Systems and Computer Engineering, Program in Technology Innovation Management, Ottawa, ON K1S 5B6, Canada. Offers M Eng, MA Sc. *Degree requirements:* For master's, thesis optional. *Entrance requirements:* For master's, honors degree. Additional exam requirements/recommendations for international students: Required—TOEFL.

Central Connecticut State University, School of Graduate Studies, School of Engineering, Science and Technology, Department of Manufacturing and Construction Management, New Britain, CT 06050-4010. Offers construction management (MS, Certificate); lean manufacturing and Six Sigma (Certificate); supply chain and logistics (Certificate); technology management (MS). Part-time and evening/weekend programs available. *Faculty:* 9 full-time (1 woman), 3 part-time/adjunct (0 women). *Students:* 32 full-time (9 women), 96 part-time (27 women); includes 25 minority (13 Black or African American, non-Hispanic/Latino; 1 American Indian or Alaska Native, non-Hispanic/Latino; 7 Asian, non-Hispanic/Latino; 4 Hispanic/Latino), 18 international. Average age 32. 90 applicants, 66% accepted, 41 enrolled. In 2014, 38 master's, 5 other advanced degrees awarded. *Degree requirements:* For master's, comprehensive exam, thesis or alternative; for Certificate, qualifying exam. *Entrance requirements:* For master's, minimum undergraduate GPA of 2.7. Additional exam requirements/recommendations for international students: Required—TOEFL (minimum score 550 paper-based; 79 iBT). *Application deadline:* For fall admission, 6/1 for domestic students, 5/1 for international students; for spring admission, 11/1 for domestic and international students. Applications are processed on a rolling basis. Application fee: $50. Electronic applications accepted. *Expenses: Tuition, area resident:* Full-time $5730; part-time $534 per credit. Tuition, state resident: full-time $8596; part-time $534 per credit. Tuition, nonresident: full-time $15,964; part-time $548 per credit. *Required fees:* $4211; $215 per credit. *Financial support:* In 2014–15, 6 students received support, including 5 research assistantships; career-related internships or fieldwork, Federal Work-Study, scholarships/grants, and unspecified assistantships also available. Support available to part-time students. Financial award application deadline: 3/1; financial award applicants required to submit FAFSA. *Faculty research:* All aspects of middle management, technical supervision in the workplace. *Unit head:* Dr. Jacob Kovel, Chair, 860-832-1830, E-mail: kovelj@ccsu.edu. *Application contact:* Patricia Gardner, Associate Director of Graduate Studies, 860-832-2350, Fax: 860-832-2362, E-mail: graduateadmissions@ccsu.edu.
Website: http://web.ccsu.edu/set/academics/programs/manufacturingConstruction/.

Champlain College, Graduate Studies, Burlington, VT 05402-0670. Offers business (MBA); digital forensic management (MS); digital forensic science (MS); early childhood education (M Ed); emergent media (MFA, MS); health care administration (MS); law (MS); managing innovation and information technology (MS); mediation and applied conflict studies (MS). MS in emergent media program held in Shanghai. Part-time programs available. Postbaccalaureate distance learning degree programs offered (no on-campus study). *Degree requirements:* For master's, capstone project. *Entrance requirements:* Additional exam requirements/recommendations for international students: Required—TOEFL (minimum score 550 paper-based; 80 iBT). Electronic applications accepted.

City University of Seattle, Graduate Division, School of Management, Seattle, WA 98121. Offers accounting (Certificate); change leadership (MBA, Certificate); computer systems (MS); finance (Certificate); financial management (MBA); general management (MBA); general management-Europe (MBA); global marketing (MBA); human resources management (Certificate); individualized study (MBA); information security (MS); information systems (MBA); leadership (MA); marketing (MBA, Certificate); project management (MBA, MS, Certificate); sustainable business (Certificate); technology management (MBA, Certificate). Part-time and evening/weekend programs available. Postbaccalaureate distance learning degree programs offered (no on-campus study). *Faculty:* 4 full-time (1 woman), 168 part-time/adjunct (63 women). *Students:* 445 full-time (227 women), 249 part-time (130 women); includes 115 minority (42 Black or African American, non-Hispanic/Latino; 3 American Indian or Alaska Native, non-Hispanic/Latino; 41 Asian, non-Hispanic/Latino; 22 Hispanic/Latino; 4 Native Hawaiian or other Pacific Islander, non-Hispanic/Latino; 3 Two or more races, non-Hispanic/Latino), 227 international. Average age 33. 127 applicants, 100% accepted, 127 enrolled. In 2014, 200 master's, 15 other advanced degrees awarded. *Degree requirements:* For master's, comprehensive exam (for some programs), thesis (for some programs). *Entrance requirements:* For master's, baccalaureate degree or equivalent from an accredited or otherwise recognized institution. Additional exam requirements/recommendations for international students: Required—TOEFL (minimum score 567 paper-based; 87 iBT); Recommended—IELTS. *Application deadline:* For fall admission, 9/1 for international students; for winter admission, 12/1 for international students; for spring admission, 3/1 for international students. Applications are processed on a rolling basis. Application fee: $50. Electronic applications accepted. *Expenses: Tuition:* Full-time $30,000; part-time $600 per credit. One-time fee: $50. Tuition and fees vary according to degree level and program. *Financial support:* In 2014–15, 47 students received support. Federal Work-Study and scholarships/grants available. Support available to part-time students. Financial award applicants required to submit FAFSA. *Unit head:* Dr. Kurt Kirstein, Dean, 206-239-4860 Ext. 5456, E-mail: kdkirstein@cityu.edu. *Application contact:* 888-422-4898, Fax: 425-709-5363, E-mail: info@cityu.edu.

Coleman University, Program in Business and Technology Management, San Diego, CA 92123. Offers MS. Evening/weekend programs available. Postbaccalaureate distance learning degree programs offered (no on-campus study). *Entrance requirements:* For master's, bachelor's degree, minimum GPA of 3.0. Additional exam requirements/recommendations for international students: Required—TOEFL (minimum score 500 paper-based).

Colorado School of Mines, Graduate School, Division of Economics and Business, Golden, CO 80401. Offers engineering and technology management (MS); mineral economics (PhD); operations research and engineering (PhD). Part-time programs available. *Faculty:* 11 full-time (3 women), 24 part-time/adjunct (4 women). *Students:* 114 full-time (21 women), 22 part-time (5 women); includes 17 minority (3 Black or African American, non-Hispanic/Latino; 4 Asian, non-Hispanic/Latino; 8 Hispanic/Latino; 2 Two or more races, non-Hispanic/Latino), 36 international. Average age 30. 172 applicants, 66% accepted, 62 enrolled. In 2014, 60 master's, 4 doctorates awarded. *Degree requirements:* For master's, thesis (for some programs); for doctorate, comprehensive exam, thesis/dissertation. *Entrance requirements:* For master's and doctorate, GRE General Test. Additional exam requirements/recommendations for international students: Required—TOEFL (minimum score 550 paper-based; 80 iBT). *Application deadline:* For fall admission, 12/15 priority date for domestic and international students; for spring admission, 9/1 priority date for domestic and international students. Application fee: $50 ($70 for international students). Electronic applications accepted. *Financial support:* In 2014–15, 45 students received support, including 4 fellowships with full tuition reimbursements available (averaging $21,120 per year), 8 research assistantships with full tuition reimbursements available (averaging $21,120 per year), 23 teaching assistantships with full tuition reimbursements available (averaging $21,120 per year); scholarships/grants, health care benefits, and unspecified assistantships also available. Financial award application deadline: 1/15; financial award applicants required to submit FAFSA. *Faculty research:* International trade, resource and environmental economics, energy economics, operations research. *Total annual research expenditures:* $371,588. *Unit head:* Dr. Michael Walls, Interim Director, 303-273-3492, Fax: 303-273-3416, E-mail: mwalls@mines.edu. *Application contact:* Kathleen Martin, Program Assistant, 303-273-3482, Fax: 303-273-3416, E-mail: kmartin@mines.edu.
Website: http://econbus.mines.edu.

Colorado Technical University Colorado Springs, Graduate Studies, Program in Management, Colorado Springs, CO 80907-3896. Offers accounting (MBA, MSA); business administration (MBA); finance (MBA); human resources management (MBA); logistics/supply chain management (MBA); management (DM); marketing (MBA); mediation and dispute resolution (MBA); operations management (MBA); project management (MBA); technology management (MBA). Part-time and evening/weekend programs available. Postbaccalaureate distance learning degree programs offered. *Degree requirements:* For master's, thesis or alternative; for doctorate, thesis/dissertation. *Entrance requirements:* For doctorate, minimum graduate GPA of 3.0, 5 years of related work experience. *Faculty research:* Sexual harassment, performance evaluation, critical thinking.

Colorado Technical University Denver South, Programs in Business Administration and Management, Aurora, CO 80014. Offers accounting (MBA); business administration (MBA); business administration and management (EMBA); finance (MBA); human resource management (MBA); marketing (MBA); mediation and dispute resolution (MBA); operations management (MBA); project management (MBA); technology management (MBA). Part-time and evening/weekend programs available. *Degree requirements:* For master's, thesis or alternative. *Entrance requirements:* For master's, minimum undergraduate GPA of 3.0, resume.

Columbia University, School of Continuing Education, Program in Technology Management, New York, NY 10027. Offers Exec MS. Part-time and evening/weekend programs available. *Entrance requirements:* For master's, minimum undergraduate GPA of 3.0. Additional exam requirements/recommendations for international students: Required—American Language Program placement test. Electronic applications accepted. *Faculty research:* Information systems, management.

Dallas Baptist University, College of Business, Business Administration Program, Dallas, TX 75211-9299. Offers accounting (MBA); business communication (MBA); conflict resolution management (MBA); entrepreneurship (MBA); finance (MBA); health care management (MBA); international business (MBA); leading the non-profit organization (MBA); management (MBA); management information systems (MBA); marketing (MBA); project management (MBA); technology and engineering (MBA). *Accreditation:* ACBSP. Part-time and evening/weekend programs available. *Entrance requirements:* For master's, GMAT, minimum GPA of 3.0. Additional exam requirements/recommendations for international students: Required—TOEFL, IELTS. Electronic applications accepted. *Expenses: Tuition:* Full-time $14,130; part-time $785 per credit hour. *Required fees:* $200 per semester. Tuition and fees vary according to course level and course load. *Faculty research:* Sports management, services marketing, retailing, strategic management, financial planning/investments.

DePaul University, College of Computing and Digital Media, Chicago, IL 60604. Offers animation (MA, MFA); business information technology (MS); cinema (MFA); cinema production (MS); computational finance (MS); computer and information sciences (PhD); computer game development (MS); computer information and network security (MS); computer science (MS); e-commerce technology (MS); health informatics (MS); human-computer interaction (MS); information systems (MS); information technology project management (MS); network engineering and management (MS); predictive analytics (MS); screenwriting (MFA); software engineering (MS); JD/MS. Part-time and evening/weekend programs available. Postbaccalaureate distance learning degree programs offered (no on-campus study). *Degree requirements:* For master's, thesis (for some programs); for doctorate, comprehensive exam, thesis/dissertation. *Entrance requirements:* For master's, GRE or GMAT (for MS in computational finance only), bachelor's degree, resume (MS in predictive analytics only), IT experience (MS in information technology project management only), portfolio review (all MFA programs and MA in animation); for doctorate, GRE, master's degree in computer science. Additional exam requirements/recommendations for international students: Required—TOEFL (minimum score 590 paper-based; 80 iBT), IELTS (minimum score 6.5), PTE (minimum score 53). Electronic applications accepted. *Expenses:* Contact institution. *Faculty research:* Data mining, computer science, human-computer interaction, security, animation and film.

East Carolina University, Graduate School, College of Engineering and Technology, Department of Technology Systems, Greenville, NC 27858-4353. Offers computer network professional (Certificate); information assurance (Certificate); Lean Six Sigma Black Belt (Certificate); network technology (MS), including computer networking management, digital communications technology, information security, Web technologies; occupational safety (MS); technology management (PhD); technology systems (MS), including industrial distribution and logistics, manufacturing systems, performance improvement, quality systems; Website developer (Certificate). *Entrance requirements:* For master's and Certificate, GRE General Test or MAT, minimum GPA of 2.5; for doctorate, GRE General Test, related work experience. *Expenses:* Tuition, state resident: full-time $4223. Tuition, nonresident: full-time $16,540. *Required fees:* $2184.

Eastern Michigan University, Graduate School, College of Technology, Program in Technology, Ypsilanti, MI 48197. Offers PhD. Part-time and evening/weekend programs available. *Students:* 10 full-time (6 women), 55 part-time (22 women); includes 11 minority (6 Black or African American, non-Hispanic/Latino; 2 Asian, non-Hispanic/Latino; 3 Hispanic/Latino), 19 international. Average age 41. 53 applicants, 53% accepted, 16 enrolled. In 2014, 5 doctorates awarded. *Degree requirements:* For doctorate, comprehensive exam, thesis/dissertation. *Entrance requirements:* For doctorate, GRE. Additional exam requirements/recommendations for international students: Required—TOEFL. *Application deadline:* For fall admission, 2/15 for domestic and international students; for winter admission, 10/15 for domestic and international students. Applications are processed on a rolling basis. Application fee: $45. *Financial support:* Fellowships, research assistantships with full and partial tuition reimbursements, teaching assistantships with full and partial tuition reimbursements, career-related internships or fieldwork, Federal Work-Study, institutionally sponsored loans, scholarships/grants, tuition waivers (partial), and unspecified assistantships available. Support available to part-time students. Financial award applicants required to submit FAFSA. *Application contact:* Tracy Rush-Byers, Program Associate, 734-487-2338, Fax: 734-487-0843, E-mail: trushbye@emich.edu.

École Polytechnique de Montréal, Graduate Programs, Department of Mathematics and Industrial Engineering, Montréal, QC H3C 3A7, Canada. Offers ergonomy (M Eng, M Sc A, DESS); mathematical method in CA engineering (M Eng, M Sc A, PhD); operational research (M Eng, M Sc A, PhD); production (M Eng, M Sc A); technology management (M Eng, M Sc A). DESS program offered jointly with HEC Montreal and Université de Montréal. Part-time programs available. *Degree requirements:* For master's, one foreign language, thesis. *Entrance requirements:* For master's, minimum GPA of 2.75. *Faculty research:* Use of computers in organizations.

Excelsior College, School of Business and Technology, Albany, NY 12203-5159. Offers business administration (MBA); cybersecurity (MS); cybersecurity management (MBA, Graduate Certificate); health care management (MBA); human performance technology (MBA); leadership (MBA); social media management (MBA); technology management (MBA). Part-time and evening/weekend programs available. Postbaccalaureate distance learning degree programs offered (no on-campus study). *Faculty:* 34 part-time/adjunct (14 women). *Students:* 1,469 part-time (447 women); includes 605 minority (318 Black or African American, non-Hispanic/Latino; 7 American Indian or Alaska Native, non-Hispanic/Latino; 50 Asian, non-Hispanic/Latino; 165 Hispanic/Latino; 8 Native Hawaiian or other Pacific Islander, non-Hispanic/Latino; 57 Two or more races, non-Hispanic/Latino), 12 international. Average age 38. In 2014, 108 master's awarded. *Application deadline:* Applications are processed on a rolling basis. Application fee: $110. *Expenses:* Tuition: Part-time $620 per credit hour. *Financial support:* Scholarships/grants available. *Unit head:* Dr. Karl Lawrence, Dean, 888-647-2388. *Application contact:* Admissions, 888-647-2388 Ext. 133, Fax: 518-464-8777, E-mail: admissions@excelsior.edu.

Fairfield University, School of Engineering, Fairfield, CT 06824. Offers automated manufacturing (CAS); database management (CAS); electrical and computer engineering (MS); information security (CAS); management of technology (MS); mechanical engineering (MS); network technology (CAS); software engineering (MS); Web application development (CAS). Part-time and evening/weekend programs available. *Faculty:* 4 full-time (1 woman), 18 part-time/adjunct (5 women). *Students:* 193 full-time (50 women), 69 part-time (11 women); includes 20 minority (4 Black or African American, non-Hispanic/Latino; 6 Asian, non-Hispanic/Latino; 10 Hispanic/Latino), 199 international. Average age 27. 516 applicants, 64% accepted, 124 enrolled. In 2014, 38 master's awarded. *Degree requirements:* For master's, thesis, capstone course. *Entrance requirements:* For master's, interview, minimum GPA of 2.8, resume, 2 recommendations. Additional exam requirements/recommendations for international students: Required—TOEFL (minimum score 550 paper-based; 80 iBT) or IELTS (minimum score 6.5). *Application deadline:* For fall admission, 5/15 for international students; for spring admission, 10/15 for international students. Applications are processed on a rolling basis. Application fee: $60. Electronic applications accepted. *Expenses:* Expenses: $750 per credit hour. *Financial support:* In 2014–15, 30 students received support. Scholarships/grants and unspecified assistantships available. Financial award applicants required to submit FAFSA. *Faculty research:* Ocean dynamics modeling, thermo fluids, Web/mobile software applications, microwaves/ electromagnetics, micro/nano manufacturing. *Unit head:* Dr. Bruce Berdanier, Dean, 203-254-4147, Fax: 203-254-4013, E-mail: bberdanier@fairfield.edu. *Application contact:* Marianne Gumpper, Director of Graduate and Continuing Studies Admission, 203-254-4184, Fax: 203-254-4073, E-mail: gradadmis@fairfield.edu. Website: http://www.fairfield.edu/academics/schoolscollegescenters/ schoolofengineering/graduateprograms/.

Fairleigh Dickinson University, College at Florham, Silberman College of Business, Departments of Management, Marketing, and Entrepreneurial Studies, Program in Management, Madison, NJ 07940-1099. Offers evolving technology (Certificate); management (MBA); MBA/MA.

Florida Institute of Technology, Graduate Programs, Extended Studies Division, Melbourne, FL 32901-6975. Offers acquisition and contract management (MS); aerospace engineering (MS); business administration (MBA, DBA); computer information systems (MS); computer science (MS); electrical engineering (MS); engineering management (MS); human resources management (MS); logistics management (MS), including humanitarian and disaster relief logistics; management (MS), including acquisition and contract management, e-business, human resources management, information systems, logistics management, management, transportation management; material acquisition management (MS); mechanical engineering (MS); operations research (MS); project management (MS), including information systems, operations research; public administration (MPA); quality management (MS); software engineering (MS); space systems (MS); space systems management (MS); supply chain management (MS); systems management (MS), including information systems, operations research; technology management (MS). Part-time and evening/weekend programs available. Postbaccalaureate distance learning degree programs offered (no on-campus study). *Faculty:* 7 full-time (1 woman), 112 part-time/adjunct (29 women). *Students:* 98 full-time (45 women), 975 part-time (396 women); includes 440 minority (292 Black or African American, non-Hispanic/Latino; 13 American Indian or Alaska Native, non-Hispanic/Latino; 32 Asian, non-Hispanic/Latino; 79 Hispanic/Latino; 1 Native Hawaiian or other Pacific Islander, non-Hispanic/Latino; 23 Two or more races, non-Hispanic/Latino), 4 international. Average age 37. 807 applicants, 56% accepted, 258 enrolled. In 2014, 457 master's awarded. *Degree requirements:* For master's, comprehensive exam (for some programs), capstone course. *Entrance requirements:* For master's, GMAT or resume showing 8 years of supervised experience, minimum GPA of 3.0, 2 letters of recommendation, resume. Additional exam requirements/ recommendations for international students: Required—TOEFL (minimum score 550 paper-based; 79 iBT). *Application deadline:* For fall admission, 4/1 for international students; for spring admission, 9/30 for international students. Applications are processed on a rolling basis. Electronic applications accepted. *Expenses:* Expenses: Contact institution. *Financial support:* *Application deadline:* 3/1; applicants required to submit FAFSA. *Unit head:* Dr. Theodore R. Richardson, III, Senior Associate Dean, 321-674-8123, Fax: 321-674-7597, E-mail: trichardson@fit.edu. *Application contact:* Carolyn Farrior, Director of Graduate Admissions, Online Learning and Off-Campus Programs, 321-674-7118, Fax: 321-674-8216, E-mail: cfarrior@fit.edu. Website: http://es.fit.edu.

George Mason University, School of Business, Program in Technology Management, Fairfax, VA 22030. Offers MS. *Faculty:* 4 full-time (0 women). *Students:* 18 full-time (5 women); includes 6 minority (3 Black or African American, non-Hispanic/Latino; 3 Asian, non-Hispanic/Latino), 1 international. Average age 43. 1 applicant. In 2014, 19 master's awarded. *Entrance requirements:* For master's, GMAT/GRE, resume; official transcripts; 2 professional letters of recommendation; professional essay; expanded goals

statement; interview. Additional exam requirements/recommendations for international students: Required—TOEFL (minimum score 570 paper-based; 80 iBT), IELTS (minimum score 6.5), PTE. *Application deadline:* For spring admission, 10/1 priority date for domestic students. Application fee: $65 ($80 for international students). Electronic applications accepted. *Expenses:* Expenses: Contact institution. *Financial support:* Application deadline: 3/1; applicants required to submit FAFSA. *Faculty research:* Leadership careers in technology-oriented businesses, achieving success in the technology marketplace, emphasizing technology leadership and management, technology innovation, commercialization, methods and approaches of systems thinking. *Unit head:* J. P. Auffret, Director, 703-993-5641, Fax: 703-993-1778, E-mail: jauffret@gmu.edu. *Application contact:* Nancy Doernhoefer, Program Coordinator, 703-993-4128, Fax: 703-993-1778, E-mail: ndoernho@gmu.edu. Website: http://business.gmu.edu/masters-in-technology-management/.

Georgetown University, Graduate School of Arts and Sciences, School of Continuing Studies, Washington, DC 20057. Offers American studies (MALS); Catholic studies (MALS); classical civilizations (MALS); emergency and disaster management (MPS); ethics and the professions (MALS); hospitality management (MPS); human resources management (MPS); humanities (MALS); individualized study (MALS); international affairs (MALS); Islam and Muslim-Christian relations (MALS); journalism (MPS); liberal studies (DLS); literature and society (MALS); medieval and early modern European studies (MALS); public relations and corporate communications (MPS); real estate (MPS); religious studies (MALS); social and public policy (MALS); sports industry management (MPS); systems engineering management (MPS); technology management (MPS); the theory and practice of American democracy (MALS); urban and regional planning (MPS); visual culture (MALS). MPS in systems engineering management offered jointly with Stevens Institute of Technology. *Entrance requirements:* Additional exam requirements/recommendations for international students: Required—TOEFL.

The George Washington University, School of Business, Department of Information Systems and Technology Management, Washington, DC 20052. Offers information and decision systems (PhD); information systems (MSIST); information systems development (MSIST); information systems management (MBA); information systems project management (MSIST); management information systems (MSIST); management of science, technology, and innovation (MBA, PhD). Programs also offered in Ashburn and Arlington, VA. Part-time and evening/weekend programs available. Postbaccalaureate distance learning degree programs offered (no on-campus study). *Faculty:* 9 full-time (2 women). *Students:* 125 full-time (50 women), 100 part-time (30 women); includes 58 minority (22 Black or African American, non-Hispanic/Latino; 21 Asian, non-Hispanic/Latino; 13 Hispanic/Latino; 2 Two or more races, non-Hispanic/ Latino), 105 international. Average age 30. 401 applicants, 56% accepted, 96 enrolled. In 2014, 95 master's awarded. *Entrance requirements:* For master's, GMAT. Additional exam requirements/recommendations for international students: Required—TOEFL. *Application deadline:* For fall admission, 4/1 priority date for domestic students; for spring admission, 10/1 for domestic students. Applications are processed on a rolling basis. Application fee: $75. *Financial support:* In 2014–15, 35 students received support. Fellowships, teaching assistantships, career-related internships or fieldwork, Federal Work-Study, institutionally sponsored loans, and tuition waivers available. Financial award application deadline: 4/1. *Faculty research:* Expert systems, decision support systems. *Unit head:* Subhasish Dasgupta, Chair, 202-994-7408, E-mail: dasgupta@gwu.edu. *Application contact:* Christopher Storer, Executive Director, Graduate Admissions, 202-994-1212, E-mail: gwmba@gwu.edu.

Golden Gate University, Ageno School of Business, San Francisco, CA 94105-2968. Offers accounting (MBA); business administration (EMBA, MBA, PMBA, DBA); finance (MBA, MS, Certificate); financial planning (MS, Certificate); healthcare information systems (Certificate); human resource management (MBA, MS); human resources management (Certificate); information systems (MS); information technology (MBA); information technology management (Certificate); integrated marketing and communications (MS, Certificate); international business (MBA); management (MBA); marketing (MBA, MS, Certificate); operations supply chain management (Certificate); psychology (MA, Certificate); public administration (EMPA); public relations (MS, Certificate); technical market analysis (Certificate); JD/MBA. Part-time and evening/ weekend programs available. *Degree requirements:* For doctorate, thesis/dissertation, qualifying examination. *Entrance requirements:* For master's, GMAT (MBA), minimum GPA of 2.5 (MS). Additional exam requirements/recommendations for international students: Required—TOEFL (minimum score 550 paper-based; 79 iBT). Electronic applications accepted. *Expenses:* Contact institution.

Harding University, Paul R. Carter College of Business Administration, Searcy, AR 72149-0001. Offers health care management (MBA); information technology management (MBA); international business (MBA); leadership and organizational management (MBA). *Accreditation:* ACBSP. Part-time and evening/weekend programs available. Postbaccalaureate distance learning degree programs offered (no on-campus study). *Faculty:* 26 part-time/adjunct (6 women). *Students:* 50 full-time (29 women), 117 part-time (53 women); includes 22 minority (17 Black or African American, non-Hispanic/ Latino; 5 Asian, non-Hispanic/Latino), 24 international. Average age 34. 45 applicants, 98% accepted, 44 enrolled. In 2014, 87 master's awarded. *Degree requirements:* For master's, portfolio. *Entrance requirements:* For master's, GMAT (minimum score of 500) or GRE (minimum score of 300), minimum GPA of 3.0, 2 letters of recommendation, resume, 3 essays, all official transcripts. Additional exam requirements/ recommendations for international students: Required—TOEFL (minimum score 550 paper-based; 79 iBT). *Application deadline:* For fall admission, 8/1 priority date for domestic and international students; for spring admission, 12/1 priority date for domestic and international students. Applications are processed on a rolling basis. Application fee: $40. *Expenses:* Tuition: Full-time $12,096; part-time $672 per credit hour. *Required fees:* $432; $24 per credit hour. Tuition and fees vary according to course load and degree level. *Financial support:* Unspecified assistantships available. Financial award application deadline: 7/30; financial award applicants required to submit FAFSA. *Unit head:* Glen Metheny, Director of Graduate Studies, 501-279-5851, Fax: 501-279-4805, E-mail: gmetheny@harding.edu. *Application contact:* Melanie Kiihnl, Recruiting Manager/Director of Marketing, 501-279-4523, Fax: 501-279-4805, E-mail: mba@ harding.edu. Website: http://www.harding.edu/mba.

Harrisburg University of Science and Technology, Program in Project Management, Harrisburg, PA 17101. Offers construction services (MS); governmental services (MS); information technology (MS). Part-time and evening/weekend programs available. *Entrance requirements:* For master's, BS, BBA. Additional exam requirements/ recommendations for international students: Required—TOEFL (minimum score 520 paper-based; 80 iBT). Electronic applications accepted.

Harvard University, Graduate School of Arts and Sciences, Program in Information, Technology and Management, Cambridge, MA 02138. Offers PhD.

Harvard University, Harvard Business School, Doctoral Programs in Management, Boston, MA 02163. Offers accounting and management (DBA); business economics (PhD); health policy management (PhD); management (DBA); marketing (DBA);

Management of Technology

organizational behavior (PhD); science, technology and management (PhD); strategy (DBA); technology and operations management (DBA). *Degree requirements:* For doctorate, comprehensive exam (for some programs), thesis/dissertation. *Entrance requirements:* For doctorate, GRE General Test or GMAT. Additional exam requirements/recommendations for international students: Required—TOEFL.

Herzing University Online, Program in Business Administration, Milwaukee, WI 53203. Offers accounting (MBA); business administration (MBA); business management (MBA); healthcare management (MBA); human resources (MBA); marketing (MBA); project management (MBA); technology management (MBA). Postbaccalaureate distance learning degree programs offered (no on-campus study).

Idaho State University, Office of Graduate Studies, College of Technology, Department of Human Resource Training and Development, Pocatello, ID 83209-8380. Offers MTD. Part-time and evening/weekend programs available. *Degree requirements:* For master's, comprehensive exam, thesis optional, statistical procedures. *Entrance requirements:* For master's, GRE or MAT, minimum GPA of 3.0 in upper-division courses. Additional exam requirements/recommendations for international students: Required—TOEFL (minimum score 550 paper-based; 80 iBT). Electronic applications accepted. *Faculty research:* Learning styles, instructional methodology, leadership administration.

Illinois State University, Graduate School, College of Applied Science and Technology, Department of Technology, Normal, IL 61790-2200. Offers MS. *Degree requirements:* For master's, thesis or alternative. *Entrance requirements:* For master's, GRE General Test, minimum GPA of 2.8. *Faculty research:* National Center for Engineering and Technology Education, Illinois Manufacturing Extension Center Field Office hosting, model for the professional development of K-12 technology education teachers, Illinois State University Illinois Mathematics and Science Partnership, Illinois University council for career and technical education.

Indiana State University, College of Graduate and Professional Studies, Program in Technology Management, Terre Haute, IN 47809. Offers PhD. Postbaccalaureate distance learning degree programs offered (minimal on-campus study). *Degree requirements:* For doctorate, thesis/dissertation. *Entrance requirements:* For doctorate, GRE or GMAT, minimum graduate GPA of 3.5, 6000 hours of occupational experience. Electronic applications accepted. *Faculty research:* Production management, quality control, human resource development, construction project management, lean manufacturing.

Instituto Centroamericano de Administración de Empresas, Graduate Programs, La Garita, Costa Rica. Offers agribusiness management (MIAM); business administration (EMBA); finance (MBA); real estate management (MGREM); sustainable development (MBA); technology (MBA). *Degree requirements:* For master's, comprehensive exam, essay. *Entrance requirements:* For master's, GMAT or GRE General Test, fluency in Spanish, interview, letters of recommendation, minimum 1 year of work experience. Additional exam requirements/recommendations for international students: Recommended—TOEFL. Electronic applications accepted. *Faculty research:* Competitiveness, production.

Instituto Tecnológico y de Estudios Superiores de Monterrey, Campus Cuernavaca, Programs in Information Science, Temixco, Mexico. Offers administration of information technology (MATI); computer science (MCC, DCC); information technology (MTI).

Instituto Tecnológico y de Estudios Superiores de Monterrey, Campus Irapuato, Graduate Programs, Irapuato, Mexico. Offers administration (MBA); administration of information technology (MAIT); administration of telecommunications (MAT); architecture (M Arch); computer science (MCS); education (M Ed); educational administration (MEA); educational innovation and technology (DEIT); educational technology (MET); electronic commerce (MBA); environmental administration and planning (MEAP); environmental systems (MES); finances (MBA); humanistic studies (MHS); international management for Latin American executives (MIMLAE); library and information science (MLIS); manufacturing quality management (MMQM); marketing research (MBA).

Iona College, Hagan School of Business, Department of Information Systems, New Rochelle, NY 10801-1890. Offers business continuity and risk management (AC); information systems (PMC). Part-time and evening/weekend programs available. *Faculty:* 7 full-time (0 women), 2 part-time/adjunct (0 women). *Students:* 7 full-time (1 woman), 20 part-time (10 women); includes 5 minority (1 Black or African American, non-Hispanic/Latino; 4 Hispanic/Latino), 1 international. Average age 28. 6 applicants, 83% accepted, 4 enrolled. In 2014, 14 master's, 13 other advanced degrees awarded. *Entrance requirements:* For master's, GMAT, 2 letters of recommendation, minimum GPA of 3.0; for other advanced degree, GMAT, minimum GPA of 3.0. Additional exam requirements/recommendations for international students: Required—TOEFL (minimum score 550 paper-based; 80 iBT), IELTS (minimum score 6.5). *Application deadline:* For fall admission, 8/15 priority date for domestic students, 8/1 priority date for international students; for winter admission, 11/15 priority date for domestic students, 11/1 priority date for international students; for spring admission, 2/15 priority date for domestic students, 2/1 priority date for international students; for summer admission, 5/15 priority date for domestic students, 5/1 priority date for international students. Applications are processed on a rolling basis. Application fee: $50. Electronic applications accepted. *Expenses:* Expenses: Contact institution. *Financial support:* In 2014–15, 1 student received support. Scholarships/grants, tuition waivers (partial), and unspecified assistantships available. Support available to part-time students. Financial award application deadline: 4/15; financial award applicants required to submit FAFSA. *Faculty research:* Fuzzy sets, risk management, computer security, competence set analysis, investment strategies. *Unit head:* Dr. Robert Richardson, Chairman, 914-637-7726, E-mail: rrichardson@iona.edu. *Application contact:* Katelyn Brunck, Director of MBA Admissions, 914-633-2451, Fax: 914-633-2277, E-mail: kbrunck@iona.edu. Website: http://www.iona.edu/Academics/Hagan-School-of-Business/Departments/Information-Systems/Graduate-Programs.aspx.

Johns Hopkins University, Engineering Program for Professionals, Part-time Program in Technical Management, Baltimore, MD 21218-2699. Offers MS, Graduate Certificate, Post-Master's Certificate. Part-time and evening/weekend programs available. Electronic applications accepted.

Kansas State University, Graduate School, College of Technology and Aviation, Salina, KS 67401-8196. Offers MT. *Faculty:* 4 full-time (1 woman), 1 part-time/adjunct (0 women). *Students:* 2 full-time (1 woman), 5 part-time (1 woman); includes 2 minority (1 Black or African American, non-Hispanic/Latino; 1 Hispanic/Latino), 2 international. Average age 37. 4 applicants, 100% accepted, 3 enrolled. In 2014, 1 master's awarded. *Entrance requirements:* For master's, GRE. Additional exam requirements/recommendations for international students: Required—TOEFL (minimum score 550 paper-based; 79 iBT), IELTS (minimum score 6.5), TWE, or PTE. *Application deadline:* For fall admission, 3/1 for domestic students, 1/1 for international students; for spring admission, 10/1 for domestic students, 8/1 for international students. Application fee: $50 ($75 for international students). Electronic applications accepted. *Total annual research expenditures:* $12.4 million. *Unit head:* Dr. Verna Fitzsimmons, Dean, 785-

826-2601, E-mail: vfitzsimmons@ksu.edu. *Application contact:* Dr. Patricia E. Ackerman, Graduate Program Director, 785-826-2904, E-mail: salgrad@k-state.edu.

La Salle University, School of Arts and Sciences, Program in Information Technology Leadership, Philadelphia, PA 19141-1199. Offers information technology leadership (MS); software project leadership (Certificate). Postbaccalaureate distance learning degree programs offered (minimal on-campus study). *Degree requirements:* For master's, capstone course. *Entrance requirements:* For master's, GRE, GMAT, or MAT, two letters of recommendation; background in computer science or equivalent other training; professional resume; interview; for Certificate, two letters of recommendation; background in computer science or equivalent other training; professional resume; interview. Additional exam requirements/recommendations for international students: Required—TOEFL. Electronic applications accepted. Application fee is waived when completed online.

Lewis University, College of Business, Graduate School of Management, Program in Business Administration, Romeoville, IL 60446. Offers accounting (MBA); custom elective option (MBA); e-business (MBA); finance (MBA); healthcare management (MBA); human resources management (MBA); international business (MBA); management information systems (MBA); marketing (MBA); project management (MBA); technology and operations management (MBA). Part-time and evening/weekend programs available. *Students:* 104 full-time (61 women), 226 part-time (123 women); includes 128 minority (63 Black or African American, non-Hispanic/Latino; 3 American Indian or Alaska Native, non-Hispanic/Latino; 6 Asian, non-Hispanic/Latino; 50 Hispanic/Latino; 6 Two or more races, non-Hispanic/Latino), 17 international. Average age 31. In 2014, 99 master's awarded. *Entrance requirements:* For master's, interview, bachelor's degree, resume, 2 recommendations. Additional exam requirements/recommendations for international students: Required—TOEFL (minimum score 550 paper-based). *Application deadline:* For fall admission, 8/15 priority date for domestic students, 5/1 priority date for international students; for spring admission, 11/15 priority date for international students. Applications are processed on a rolling basis. Application fee: $40. Electronic applications accepted. *Financial support:* Career-related internships or fieldwork, Federal Work-Study, scholarships/grants, and unspecified assistantships available. Financial award application deadline: 5/1; financial award applicants required to submit FAFSA. *Unit head:* Dr. Maureen Culleeney, Academic Program Director, 815-838-0500 Ext. 5631, E-mail: culleema@lewisu.edu. *Application contact:* Michele Ryan, Director of Admission, 815-838-0500 Ext. 5384, E-mail: gsm@lewisu.edu.

Liberty University, School of Business, Lynchburg, VA 24515. Offers accounting (MBA, MS, DBA); business administration (MBA); criminal justice (MBA); cyber security (MS); executive leadership (MA); healthcare (MBA); human resources (DBA); information systems (MS), including information assurance, technology management; international business (MBA, DBA); leadership (MBA, DBA); marketing (MBA, MS, DBA), including digital marketing and advertising (MS), project management (MS), public relations (MS), sports marketing and media (MS); project management (MBA, DBA); public administration (MBA); public relations (MBA). Part-time programs available. Postbaccalaureate distance learning degree programs offered (minimal on-campus study). *Students:* 1,520 full-time (813 women), 4,179 part-time (1,982 women); includes 1,402 minority (1,110 Black or African American, non-Hispanic/Latino; 30 American Indian or Alaska Native, non-Hispanic/Latino; 82 Asian, non-Hispanic/Latino; 59 Hispanic/Latino; 7 Native Hawaiian or other Pacific Islander, non-Hispanic/Latino; 114 Two or more races, non-Hispanic/Latino), 119 international. Average age 35. 5,645 applicants, 49% accepted, 1445 enrolled. In 2014, 1,474 master's, 63 other advanced degrees awarded. *Entrance requirements:* For master's, minimum undergraduate GPA of 3.0, 15 hours of upper-level business courses. Additional exam requirements/recommendations for international students: Required—TOEFL (minimum score 600 paper-based; 100 iBT). *Application deadline:* Applications are processed on a rolling basis. Application fee: $50. Electronic applications accepted. *Expenses:* Expenses: Contact institution. *Unit head:* Dr. Scott Hicks, Dean, 434-592-4808, Fax: 434-582-2366, E-mail: smhicks@liberty.edu. *Application contact:* Jay Bridge, Director of Graduate Admissions, 800-424-9595, Fax: 800-628-7977, E-mail: gradadmissions@liberty.edu. Website: http://www.liberty.edu/academics/business/index.cfm?PID-149.

Lipscomb University, College of Computing and Technology, Nashville, TN 37204-3951. Offers information technology (MS), including data science. Part-time and evening/weekend programs available. *Faculty:* 5 full-time (2 women), 8 part-time/adjunct (5 women). *Students:* 11 full-time (4 women), 11 part-time (2 women); includes 3 minority (2 Black or African American, non-Hispanic/Latino; 1 Asian, non-Hispanic/Latino), 1 international. Average age 39. In 2014, 33 master's awarded. *Degree requirements:* For master's, capstone project. *Entrance requirements:* For master's, GRE, 2 references, transcripts, resume, personal statement. Additional exam requirements/recommendations for international students: Required—TOEFL (minimum score 570 paper-based; 80 iBT). *Application deadline:* Applications are processed on a rolling basis. Application fee: $50 ($75 for international students). Electronic applications accepted. *Expenses:* Expenses: $1,225 per credit hour. *Financial support:* Scholarships/grants and employer agreements available. Financial award applicants required to submit FAFSA. *Unit head:* Dr. Fortune S. Mhlanga, Director, 615-966-5073, E-mail: fortune.mhlanga@lipscomb.edu. *Application contact:* Finn Breland, Enrollment Management Specialist, 615-966-1193, E-mail: finn.breland@lipscomb.edu. Website: http://www.lipscomb.edu/technology/.

Marist College, Graduate Programs, School of Computer Science and Mathematics, Poughkeepsie, NY 12601-1387. Offers computer science/software development (MS); information systems (MS, Adv C); technology management (MS). Part-time and evening/weekend programs available. Postbaccalaureate distance learning degree programs offered (minimal on-campus study). *Entrance requirements:* For master's, resume. Additional exam requirements/recommendations for international students: Required—TOEFL (minimum score 550 paper-based; 80 iBT); Recommended—IELTS (minimum score 6.5). Electronic applications accepted. *Faculty research:* Data quality, artificial intelligence, imaging, analysis of algorithms, distributed systems and applications.

Marist College, Graduate Programs, School of Management and School of Computer Science and Mathematics, Program in Technology Management, Poughkeepsie, NY 12601-1387. Offers MS. Part-time and evening/weekend programs available. Postbaccalaureate distance learning degree programs offered (minimal on-campus study). *Entrance requirements:* For master's, GMAT or GRE, minimum undergraduate GPA of 3.0, 2 letters of recommendation, resume, professional experience. Additional exam requirements/recommendations for international students: Required—TOEFL (minimum score 550 paper-based; 80 iBT); Recommended—IELTS (minimum score 6.5). Electronic applications accepted.

Marquette University, Graduate School, Opus College of Engineering, Department of Biomedical Engineering, Milwaukee, WI 53201-1881. Offers biocomputing (ME); bioimaging (ME); bioinstrumentation (ME); bioinstrumentation/computers (MS, PhD); biomechanics (ME); biomechanics/biomaterials (MS, PhD); biorehabilitation (ME); functional imaging (PhD); healthcare technologies management (MS); rehabilitation bioengineering (PhD); systems physiology (MS, PhD). Part-time and evening/weekend programs available. Terminal master's awarded for partial completion of doctoral program. *Degree requirements:* For master's, comprehensive exam, thesis; for doctorate, comprehensive exam, thesis/dissertation, dissertation defense, qualifying exam. *Entrance requirements:* For master's, GRE General Test, minimum GPA of 3.0, official transcripts from all current and previous colleges/universities except Marquette, three letters of recommendation, brief statement of purpose that includes proposed area of research specialization, interview with program director (for ME), one year of post-baccalaureate professional work experience; for doctorate, GRE General Test, minimum GPA of 3.0, official transcripts from all current and previous colleges/universities except Marquette, three letters of recommendation, brief statement of purpose that includes proposed area of research specialization. Additional exam requirements/recommendations for international students: Required—TOEFL (minimum score 530 paper-based). Electronic applications accepted. *Faculty research:* Cell and organ physiology, signal processing, gait analysis, orthopedic rehabilitation engineering, telemedicine.

Marshall University, Academic Affairs Division, College of Information Technology and Engineering, Division of Applied Science and Technology, Program in Technology Management, Huntington, WV 25755. Offers MS. Part-time and evening/weekend programs available. *Students:* 16 full-time (2 women), 23 part-time (1 woman); includes 2 minority (both Black or African American, non-Hispanic/Latino), 12 international. Average age 33. In 2014, 10 master's awarded. *Degree requirements:* For master's, final project, oral exam. *Entrance requirements:* For master's, GRE General Test or GMAT, minimum undergraduate GPA of 2.5. Application fee: $40. *Financial support:* Tuition waivers (full) available. Support available to part-time students. Financial award application deadline: 8/1; financial award applicants required to submit FAFSA. *Unit head:* Dr. Tracy Christofero, Program Coordinator, 304-746-2078, E-mail: christofero@marshall.edu. *Application contact:* Information Contact, 304-746-1900, Fax: 304-746-1902, E-mail: services@marshall.edu.
Website: http://www.marshall.edu/cite/.

Mercer University, Graduate Studies, Macon Campus, School of Engineering, Macon, GA 31207. Offers biomedical engineering (MSE); computer engineering (MSE); electrical engineering (MSE); engineering management (MSE); environmental engineering (MSE); environmental systems (MS); mechanical engineering (MSE); software engineering (MSE); software systems (MS); technical communications management (MS); technical management (MS). Part-time and evening/weekend programs available. Postbaccalaureate distance learning degree programs offered (no on-campus study). *Faculty:* 20 full-time (6 women), 2 part-time/adjunct (0 women). *Students:* 10 full-time (4 women), 75 part-time (16 women); includes 10 minority (5 Black or African American, non-Hispanic/Latino; 4 Asian, non-Hispanic/Latino; 1 Hispanic/Latino), 4 international. Average age 42. In 2014, 70 master's awarded. *Degree requirements:* For master's, thesis or alternative. *Entrance requirements:* For master's, minimum undergraduate GPA of 3.0. Additional exam requirements/recommendations for international students: Required—TOEFL (minimum score 550 paper-based; 80 iBT). *Application deadline:* For fall admission, 4/1 priority date for domestic and international students; for spring admission, 11/1 priority date for domestic and international students. Applications are processed on a rolling basis. Application fee: $75. *Expenses:* Expenses: Contact institution. *Financial support:* Federal Work-Study available. *Unit head:* Dr. Wade H. Shaw, Dean, 478-301-2459, Fax: 478-301-5593, E-mail: shaw_wh@mercer.edu. *Application contact:* Dr. Richard O. Mines, Program Director, 478-301-2347, Fax: 478-301-5433, E-mail: mines_ro@mercer.edu.
Website: http://engineering.mercer.edu/.

Murray State University, College of Science, Engineering and Technology, Program in Management of Technology, Murray, KY 42071. Offers MS. Part-time and evening/weekend programs available. *Degree requirements:* For master's, comprehensive exam. *Entrance requirements:* Additional exam requirements/recommendations for international students: Required—TOEFL or IELTS. *Faculty research:* Environmental, hydrology, groundworks.

National University, Academic Affairs, School of Engineering and Computing, La Jolla, CA 92037-1011. Offers computer science (MS), including advanced computing, database engineering, software engineering; cyber security and information assurance (MS), including computer forensics, ethical hacking and penetration testing, health information assurance, information assurance and security; data analytics (MS); engineering management (MS), including enterprise architecture, project management, systems engineering, technology management; environmental engineering (MS); homeland security and emergency management (MS); management information systems (MS); project management (Certificate); sustainability management (MS); wireless communications (MS). Part-time and evening/weekend programs available. Postbaccalaureate distance learning degree programs offered (no on-campus study). *Faculty:* 24 full-time (5 women), 21 part-time/adjunct (5 women). *Students:* 275 full-time (72 women), 86 part-time (24 women); includes 147 minority (41 Black or African American, non-Hispanic/Latino; 48 Asian, non-Hispanic/Latino; 37 Hispanic/Latino; 7 Native Hawaiian or other Pacific Islander, non-Hispanic/Latino; 14 Two or more races, non-Hispanic/Latino), 95 international. Average age 33. In 2014, 281 master's awarded. *Degree requirements:* For master's, thesis (for some programs). *Entrance requirements:* For master's, interview, minimum GPA of 2.5. Additional exam requirements/recommendations for international students: Required—TOEFL (minimum score 550 paper-based; 79 iBT), IELTS (minimum score 6). *Application deadline:* Applications are processed on a rolling basis. Application fee: $60 ($65 for international students). Electronic applications accepted. *Expenses: Tuition:* Full-time $14,184; part-time $1773 per course. *Financial support:* Career-related internships or fieldwork, institutionally sponsored loans, scholarships/grants, and tuition waivers (partial) available. Support available to part-time students. Financial award application deadline: 6/30; financial award applicants required to submit FAFSA. *Faculty research:* Educational technology, scholarships in science. *Unit head:* School of Engineering and Computing, 800-628-8648, E-mail: soec@nu.edu. *Application contact:* Frank Rojas, Vice President for Enrollment Services, 800-628-8648, E-mail: advisor@nu.edu.
Website: http://www.nu.edu/OurPrograms/SchoolOfEngineeringAndTechnology.html.

New York University, Polytechnic School of Engineering, Department of Finance and Risk Engineering, New York, NY 10012-1019. Offers financial engineering (MS, Advanced Certificate), including capital markets (MS), computational finance (MS), financial technology (MS); financial technology management (Advanced Certificate); organizational behavior (Advanced Certificate); risk management (Advanced Certificate); technology management (Advanced Certificate). MS program also offered in Manhattan. Part-time and evening/weekend programs available. *Faculty:* 9 full-time (4 women), 13 part-time/adjunct (4 women). *Students:* 270 full-time (80 women), 39 part-time (9 women); includes 19 minority (5 Black or African American, non-Hispanic/Latino; 11 Asian, non-Hispanic/Latino; 2 Hispanic/Latino; 1 Two or more races, non-Hispanic/Latino), 279 international. Average age 25. 782 applicants, 23% accepted, 163 enrolled. In 2014, 125 master's awarded. *Degree requirements:* For master's, comprehensive exam (for some programs), thesis (for some programs). *Entrance requirements:* For master's, GMAT, minimum B average in undergraduate course work. Additional exam requirements/recommendations for international students: Required—TOEFL (minimum score 550 paper-based; 80 iBT); Recommended—IELTS (minimum score 6.5). *Application deadline:* For fall admission, 2/15 priority date for domestic and international

students; for spring admission, 11/1 priority date for domestic and international students. Applications are processed on a rolling basis. Application fee: $75. Electronic applications accepted. *Financial support:* Institutionally sponsored loans, scholarships/grants, and unspecified assistantships available. Support available to part-time students. Financial award applicants required to submit FAFSA. *Faculty research:* Optimal control theory, general modeling and analysis, risk parity optimality, a new algorithmic approach to entangled political economy. *Total annual research expenditures:* $387,325. *Unit head:* Dr. Charles S. Tapiero, Department Chair, 718-260-3653, Fax: 718-260-3874, E-mail: cst262@nyu.edu. *Application contact:* Raymond Lutzky, Director, Graduate Enrollment Management, 718-637-5984, Fax: 718-260-3624, E-mail: rlutzky@poly.edu.

New York University, Polytechnic School of Engineering, Department of Technology Management, Major in Management of Technology, New York, NY 10012-1019. Offers MS. Program also offered in Manhattan. *Students:* 131 full-time (56 women), 43 part-time (13 women); includes 13 minority (2 Black or African American, non-Hispanic/Latino; 10 Asian, non-Hispanic/Latino; 1 Hispanic/Latino), 142 international. Average age 27. 335 applicants, 51% accepted, 67 enrolled. In 2014, 66 master's awarded. *Degree requirements:* For master's, comprehensive exam (for some programs), thesis (for some programs). *Entrance requirements:* For master's, GMAT, minimum B average in undergraduate course work. Additional exam requirements/recommendations for international students: Required—TOEFL (minimum score 550 paper-based; 80 iBT); Recommended—IELTS (minimum score 6.5). *Application deadline:* For fall admission, 2/15 priority date for domestic and international students; for spring admission, 11/1 priority date for domestic and international students. Applications are processed on a rolling basis. Application fee: $75. Electronic applications accepted. *Financial support:* Institutionally sponsored loans, scholarships/grants, and unspecified assistantships available. Support available to part-time students. Financial award applicants required to submit FAFSA. *Unit head:* Dr. Joseph Nadan, Program Director, 718-260-4025, E-mail: jnadan@nyu.edu. *Application contact:* Raymond Lutzky, Director of Graduate Enrollment Management, 718-637-5984, Fax: 718-260-3624, E-mail: rlutzky@poly.edu.

New York University, Polytechnic School of Engineering, Department of Technology Management, Major in Technology Management, New York, NY 10012-1019. Offers MBA, PhD. *Students:* 5 full-time (2 women); includes 2 minority (1 Asian, non-Hispanic/Latino; 1 Hispanic/Latino), 1 international. Average age 31. 37 applicants, 3% accepted, 1 enrolled. *Entrance requirements:* Additional exam requirements/recommendations for international students: Required—TOEFL (minimum score 550 paper-based; 80 iBT); Recommended—IELTS (minimum score 6.5). *Application deadline:* For fall admission, 2/15 priority date for domestic and international students; for spring admission, 11/1 priority date for domestic and international students. Applications are processed on a rolling basis. Application fee: $75. Electronic applications accepted. *Financial support:* Institutionally sponsored loans, scholarships/grants, and unspecified assistantships available. Support available to part-time students. *Unit head:* Prof. Bharadwaj Rao, Head, 718-260-3617, Fax: 718-260-3874, E-mail: bharat.rao@nyu.edu. *Application contact:* Raymond Lutzky, Director, Graduate Enrollment Management, 718-637-5984, Fax: 718-260-3624, E-mail: rlutzky@poly.edu.

North Carolina Agricultural and Technical State University, School of Graduate Studies, School of Technology, Department of Manufacturing Systems, Greensboro, NC 27411. Offers manufacturing (MSTM). Part-time and evening/weekend programs available. *Degree requirements:* For master's, comprehensive exam, thesis or alternative, qualifying exam. *Entrance requirements:* For master's, GRE General Test, minimum GPA of 3.0.

North Carolina State University, Graduate School, College of Textiles, Program in Textile Technology Management, Raleigh, NC 27695. Offers PhD. *Degree requirements:* For doctorate, one foreign language, thesis/dissertation, cumulative exams. *Entrance requirements:* For doctorate, GRE or GMAT. Electronic applications accepted. *Faculty research:* Niche markets, supply chain, globalization, logistics.

Northern Kentucky University, Office of Graduate Programs, College of Informatics, Program in Computer Information Technology, Highland Heights, KY 41099. Offers MSCIT. Part-time and evening/weekend programs available. *Faculty:* 5 full-time (1 woman), 3 part-time/adjunct (1 woman). *Students:* 20 full-time (7 women), 39 part-time (9 women); includes 8 minority (4 Black or African American, non-Hispanic/Latino; 1 Asian, non-Hispanic/Latino; 2 Hispanic/Latino; 1 Two or more races, non-Hispanic/Latino), 14 international. Average age 33. In 2014, 19 master's awarded. *Degree requirements:* For master's, comprehensive exam (for some programs), thesis or alternative. *Entrance requirements:* For master's, GRE (waived for undergraduates with GPA greater than 3.0 from a STEM discipline), resume, transcripts. Additional exam requirements/recommendations for international students: Required—TOEFL (minimum score 79 iBT); Recommended—IELTS (minimum score 6.5). *Application deadline:* For fall admission, 8/1 for domestic students, 6/1 for international students; for spring admission, 12/1 for domestic students, 10/1 for international students; for summer admission, 5/1 for domestic students, 3/1 for international students. Applications are processed on a rolling basis. Application fee: $40. Electronic applications accepted. *Expenses: Tuition, area resident:* Part-time $518 per credit hour. Tuition, state resident: part-time $630 per credit hour. Tuition, nonresident: part-time $797 per credit hour. *Required fees:* $192 per semester. Tuition and fees vary according to course load, degree level, campus/location, program and reciprocity agreements. *Financial support:* In 2014–15, 15 students received support. Scholarships/grants and unspecified assistantships available. Financial award applicants required to submit FAFSA. *Faculty research:* Data privacy, security, cloud computing, social networks, intrusion detection. *Unit head:* Dr. Traian Marius Truta, Director, 859-572-7551, E-mail: trutat1@nku.edu. *Application contact:* Alison Swanson, Graduate Admissions Coordinator, 859-572-6971, E-mail: swansona1@nku.edu.
Website: http://informatics.nku.edu/departments/computer-science/programs/mscit.html.

Notre Dame de Namur University, Division of Academic Affairs, School of Business and Management, Program in Business Administration, Belmont, CA 94002-1908. Offers business administration (MBA); entrepreneurship (MBA); finance (MBA); human resource management (MBA); marketing (MBA); media and promotion (MBA); technology and operations management (MBA). *Accreditation:* ACBSP. Part-time and evening/weekend programs available. *Entrance requirements:* For master's, minimum GPA of 2.5. Additional exam requirements/recommendations for international students: Required—TOEFL (minimum score 550 paper-based; 79 iBT). Electronic applications accepted.

Old Dominion University, Strome College of Business, MBA Program, Norfolk, VA 23529. Offers business and economic forecasting (MBA); financial analysis and valuation (MBA); health sciences administration (MBA); information technology and enterprise integration (MBA); international business (MBA); maritime and port management (MBA); public administration (MBA). *Accreditation:* AACSB. Part-time and evening/weekend programs available. Postbaccalaureate distance learning degree programs offered (no on-campus study). *Faculty:* 83 full-time (19 women), 5 part-time/adjunct (2 women). *Students:* 37 full-time (24 women), 86 part-time (40 women); includes 22 minority (9 Black or African American, non-Hispanic/Latino; 5 Asian, non-Hispanic/Latino; 2 Hispanic/Latino; 6 Two or more races, non-Hispanic/Latino), 13

international. Average age 29. 200 applicants, 37% accepted, 54 enrolled. In 2014, 61 degrees awarded. *Entrance requirements:* For master's, GMAT, GRE, letter of reference, resume, essay. Additional exam requirements/recommendations for international students: Required—TOEFL (minimum score 550 paper-based; 80 iBT). *Application deadline:* For fall admission, 6/1 priority date for domestic students, 4/15 priority date for international students; for spring admission, 11/1 priority date for domestic students, 10/1 priority date for international students; for summer admission, 3/1 priority date for domestic students, 2/1 priority date for international students. Applications are processed on a rolling basis. Application fee: $50. Electronic applications accepted. *Expenses:* Expenses: Contact institution. *Financial support:* In 2014–15, 47 students received support, including 94 research assistantships with partial tuition reimbursements available (averaging $8,900 per year); career-related internships or fieldwork, scholarships/grants, and unspecified assistantships also available. Support available to part-time students. Financial award application deadline: 2/15; financial award applicants required to submit FAFSA. *Faculty research:* International business, buyer behavior, financial markets, strategy, operations research, maritime and transportation economics. *Unit head:* Dr. Kiran Karaude, Graduate Program Director, 757-683-3585, Fax: 757-683-5750, E-mail: mbainfo@odu.edu. *Application contact:* Sandi Phillips, MBA Program Assistant, 757-683-3585, Fax: 757-683-5750, E-mail: mbainfo@odu.edu.
Website: http://www.odu.edu/mba/.

Pacific States University, College of Business, Los Angeles, CA 90006. Offers accounting (MBA); finance (MBA); international business (MBA, DBA); management of information technology (MBA); real estate management (MBA). Part-time and evening/weekend programs available. Postbaccalaureate distance learning degree programs offered (no on-campus study). *Degree requirements:* For doctorate, comprehensive exam, thesis/dissertation. *Entrance requirements:* For master's, minimum undergraduate GPA of 2.5 during last 90 hours of course work. Additional exam requirements/recommendations for international students: Required—TOEFL (minimum score 500 paper-based; 61 iBT), IELTS (minimum score 5.5).

Polytechnic University of Puerto Rico, Graduate School, Hato Rey, PR 00919. Offers business administration (MBA), including computer information systems, general management, management of information systems, management of international enterprises; civil engineering (ME, MS); computer engineering (ME, MS); computer science (MCS, MS); electrical engineering (ME, MS); engineering management (MEM); environmental management (MEM); landscape architecture (M Land Arch); manufacturing competitiveness (MMC, MS); manufacturing engineering (ME, MS); mechanical engineering (M Mech E). Part-time and evening/weekend programs available. *Entrance requirements:* For master's, 3 letters of recommendation.

Polytechnic University of Puerto Rico, Orlando Campus, Graduate School, Winter Park, FL 32792. Offers accounting (MBA); business administration (MBA); construction management (MEM); engineering management (MEM); environmental management (MEM); finance (MBA); human resources management (MBA); management of international enterprises (MBA); management of technology (MBA); manufacturing management (MEM). Part-time and evening/weekend programs available. Postbaccalaureate distance learning degree programs offered (no on-campus study). *Entrance requirements:* For master's, minimum GPA of 3.0. Additional exam requirements/recommendations for international students: Recommended—TOEFL. Electronic applications accepted.

Portland State University, Graduate Studies, Maseeh College of Engineering and Computer Science, Department of Engineering and Technology Management, Portland, OR 97207-0751. Offers engineering and technology management (M Eng); engineering management (MS); manufacturing engineering (ME); manufacturing management (M Eng); systems science/engineering management (PhD); MS/MBA; MS/MS. Part-time and evening/weekend programs available. *Faculty:* 6 full-time (1 woman), 8 part-time/adjunct (2 women). *Students:* 62 full-time (20 women), 63 part-time (18 women); includes 21 minority (3 Black or African American, non-Hispanic/Latino; 1 American Indian or Alaska Native, non-Hispanic/Latino; 12 Asian, non-Hispanic/Latino; 4 Hispanic/Latino; 1 Two or more races, non-Hispanic/Latino), 68 international. Average age 36. 90 applicants, 67% accepted, 31 enrolled. In 2014, 27 master's, 5 doctorates awarded. *Degree requirements:* For master's, thesis optional; for doctorate, one foreign language, comprehensive exam, thesis/dissertation, oral and written exams. *Entrance requirements:* For master's, GRE optional, 2.75 undergraduate or 3.0 graduate (at least 12 credits), minimum 4 years of experience in engineering or related discipline, 3 letters of recommendation and background in probability/statistics, differential equations, computer programming and linear algebra; for doctorate, GRE General Test, 1100 for the sum of verbal and quantitative, or verbal and analytical., minimum GPA of 3.0 undergraduate or 3.25 graduate. Additional exam requirements/recommendations for international students: Required—TOEFL (minimum score 550 paper-based; 80 iBT). *Application deadline:* For fall admission, 4/1 for domestic students, 3/1 for international students; for winter admission, 9/1 for domestic students, 7/1 for international students; for spring admission, 11/1 for domestic students, 9/1 for international students; for summer admission, 2/1 for domestic students, 12/1 for international students. Application fee: $50. Electronic applications accepted. *Expenses:* Tuition, state resident: part-time $222 per credit. Tuition, nonresident: part-time $527 per credit. *Required fees:* $22 per contact hour. $100 per quarter. Tuition and fees vary according to program. *Financial support:* In 2014–15, 7 research assistantships with full and partial tuition reimbursements (averaging $1,913 per year), 8 teaching assistantships with full and partial tuition reimbursements (averaging $2,823 per year) were awarded; career-related internships or fieldwork, Federal Work-Study, scholarships/grants, and unspecified assistantships also available. Support available to part-time students. Financial award application deadline: 3/1; financial award applicants required to submit FAFSA. *Faculty research:* Scheduling, hierarchical decision modeling, operations research, knowledge-based information systems. *Total annual research expenditures:* $318,571. *Unit head:* Dr. Tim Anderson, Chair, 503-725-4668, Fax: 503-725-4667, E-mail: tim.anderson@pdx.edu. *Application contact:* Shawn Wall, Department Manager, 503-725-4660, Fax: 503-547-8887, E-mail: info@etm.pdx.edu.
Website: http://www.pdx.edu/engineering-technology-management/.

Purdue University, Graduate School, College of Technology, Department of Technology Leadership and Innovation, West Lafayette, IN 47907. Offers leadership (MS, PhD); organizational leadership (MS); technology innovation (MS). Part-time and evening/weekend programs available. Postbaccalaureate distance learning degree programs offered (minimal on-campus study). *Entrance requirements:* For master's, GRE General Test, minimum GPA of 3.0. Additional exam requirements/recommendations for international students: Required—TOEFL (minimum score 550 paper-based; 77 iBT); Recommended—TWE. Electronic applications accepted.

Rensselaer Polytechnic Institute, Graduate School, Lally School of Management, Program in Management, Troy, NY 12180-3590. Offers MBA, MS, PhD. Part-time programs available. *Faculty:* 69 full-time (15 women), 10 part-time/adjunct (3 women). *Students:* 55 full-time (26 women), 10 part-time (6 women); includes 6 minority (2 Black or African American, non-Hispanic/Latino; 3 Asian, non-Hispanic/Latino; 1 Two or more races, non-Hispanic/Latino), 50 international. Average age 32. 240 applicants, 43% accepted, 28 enrolled. In 2014, 63 master's, 4 doctorates awarded. *Degree requirements:* For doctorate, thesis/dissertation. *Entrance requirements:* For master's and doctorate, GMAT or GRE. Additional exam requirements/recommendations for international students: Required—TOEFL (minimum score 570 paper-based; 88 iBT), IELTS (minimum score 6.5), PTE (minimum score 60), TOEFL (minimum score 600 paper-based; 100 iBT), IELTS (minimum score 7.0), or PTE (minimum score 68) for PhD. *Application deadline:* For fall admission, 1/1 priority date for domestic and international students; for spring admission, 8/15 priority date for domestic and international students. Applications are processed on a rolling basis. Application fee: $75. Electronic applications accepted. *Expenses: Tuition:* Full-time $46,700; part-time $1945 per credit. Tuition and fees vary according to course load. *Financial support:* In 2014–15, 56 students received support, including research assistantships (averaging $18,500 per year), teaching assistantships (averaging $18,500 per year); fellowships and scholarships/grants also available. Financial award application deadline: 1/1; financial award applicants required to submit FAFSA. *Faculty research:* Business analytics; finance, financial engineering and risk analytics; innovation and technological entrepreneurship; management; management of information systems; new product development and marketing; supply chain management; technology commercialization and entrepreneurship; accounting; information systems; marketing; operations management; organization behavior; strategic management. *Total annual research expenditures:* $863,236. *Unit head:* Dr. Gina O'Connor, Associate Dean, Lally School of Management, 518-276-6842, E-mail: oconng@rpi.edu. *Application contact:* Office of Graduate Admissions, 518-276-6216, E-mail: gradadmissions@rpi.edu.
Website: http://lallyschool.rpi.edu/academics/ms_management.html.

Rollins College, Crummer Graduate School of Business, Winter Park, FL 32789-4499. Offers business administration (EDBA); entrepreneurship (MBA); finance (MBA); international business (MBA); management (MBA); marketing (MBA); operations and technology management (MBA). *Accreditation:* AACSB. Part-time and evening/weekend programs available. Postbaccalaureate distance learning degree programs offered (minimal on-campus study). *Faculty:* 20 full-time (2 women), 6 part-time/adjunct (5 women). *Students:* 187 full-time (82 women), 135 part-time (50 women); includes 76 minority (15 Black or African American, non-Hispanic/Latino; 22 Asian, non-Hispanic/Latino; 35 Hispanic/Latino; 4 Two or more races, non-Hispanic/Latino), 21 international. Average age 30. 348 applicants, 50% accepted, 132 enrolled. In 2014, 139 master's awarded. *Degree requirements:* For master's, minimum GPA of 2.85; for doctorate, thesis/dissertation, minimum GPA of 3.0. *Entrance requirements:* For master's, GMAT or GRE, official transcripts, two letters of recommendation, essay, current resume/curriculum vitae, interview; for doctorate, official transcripts, two letters of recommendation, essays, current resume/curriculum vitae, interview with EDBA academic committee. Additional exam requirements/recommendations for international students: Required—TOEFL (minimum score 100 iBT) or IELTS (minimum score 7). *Application deadline:* Applications are processed on a rolling basis. Application fee: $50. Electronic applications accepted. *Expenses:* Expenses: Contact institution. *Financial support:* In 2014–15, 114 students received support. Federal Work-Study and scholarships/grants available. Support available to part-time students. Financial award applicants required to submit FAFSA. *Faculty research:* Sustainability, world financial markets, international business, market research, strategic marketing. *Unit head:* Tom McEvoy, Dean, 407-646-2249, Fax: 407-646-1550, E-mail: tmcevoy@rollins.edu. *Application contact:* Jennifer L. Cox, Admissions Coordinator, 407-646-2405, Fax: 407-646-1550, E-mail: mbaadmissions@rollins.edu.
Website: http://www.rollins.edu/mba/.

Rutgers, The State University of New Jersey, Newark, Rutgers Business School–Newark and New Brunswick, Doctoral Programs in Management, Newark, NJ 07102. Offers accounting (PhD); accounting information systems (PhD); economics (PhD); finance (PhD); individualized study (PhD); information technology (PhD); international business (PhD); management science (PhD); marketing science (PhD); organizational management (PhD); science, technology and management (PhD); supply chain management (PhD). *Degree requirements:* For doctorate, comprehensive exam, thesis/dissertation. *Entrance requirements:* For doctorate, GRE or GMAT. Additional exam requirements/recommendations for international students: Required—TOEFL (minimum score 550 paper-based; 79 iBT). Electronic applications accepted.

St. Ambrose University, College of Arts and Sciences, Program in Information Technology Management, Davenport, IA 52803-2898. Offers MSITM. Part-time programs available. *Degree requirements:* For master's, thesis (for some programs), practica. *Entrance requirements:* For master's, GRE or GMAT, minimum GPA of 2.8. Additional exam requirements/recommendations for international students: Required—TOEFL. Electronic applications accepted.

Seton Hall University, Stillman School of Business, Programs in Business Administration, South Orange, NJ 07079-2697. Offers accounting (MBA); finance (MBA); information technology management (MBA); international business (MBA); management (MBA); marketing (MBA); sport management (MBA); supply chain management (MBA). Part-time and evening/weekend programs available. *Faculty:* 21 full-time (7 women), 15 part-time/adjunct (2 women). *Students:* 35 full-time (13 women), 135 part-time (38 women); includes 15 minority (3 Black or African American, non-Hispanic/Latino; 1 American Indian or Alaska Native, non-Hispanic/Latino; 5 Hispanic/Latino; 6 Native Hawaiian or other Pacific Islander, non-Hispanic/Latino). Average age 29. 292 applicants, 42% accepted, 94 enrolled. In 2014, 118 master's awarded. *Degree requirements:* For master's, 20 hours of community service (Social Responsibility Project). *Entrance requirements:* For master's, GMAT, GRE or CPA, advanced degree from AACSB institution, MS in a business discipline, professional degree (MD, JD, PhD, DVM, DDS, etc.), minimum undergraduate GPA of 3.0. Additional exam requirements/recommendations for international students: Required—TOEFL (minimum score 102 iBT), IELTS or PTE. *Application deadline:* For fall admission, 5/31 priority date for domestic students, 3/31 priority date for international students; for spring admission, 10/31 priority date for domestic students, 9/30 priority date for international students. Applications are processed on a rolling basis. Application fee: $75. Electronic applications accepted. *Financial support:* In 2014–15, 24 students received support, including research assistantships with full tuition reimbursements available (averaging $24,687 per year); career-related internships or fieldwork, Federal Work-Study, scholarships/grants, and unspecified assistantships also available. Support available to part-time students. Financial award application deadline: 6/30; financial award applicants required to submit FAFSA. *Faculty research:* Sport, hedge funds, international business, legal issues, disclosure and branding. *Unit head:* Dr. Joyce Strawser, Dean, 973-761-9013, Fax: 973-761-9217, E-mail: joyce.strawser@shu.edu. *Application contact:* Catherine Bianchi, Director of Graduate Admissions, 973-761-9262, Fax: 973-761-9208, E-mail: catherine.bianchi@shu.edu.
Website: http://www.shu.edu/academics/business.

Simon Fraser University, Office of Graduate Studies, Faculty of Business Administration, Vancouver, BC V6C 1W6, Canada. Offers business administration (EMBA, PhD, Graduate Diploma); finance (M Sc); management of technology (MBA); management of technology/biotechnology (MBA). *Accreditation:* AACSB. Postbaccalaureate distance learning degree programs offered. *Degree requirements:* For master's, thesis (for some programs); for doctorate, comprehensive exam, thesis/dissertation. *Entrance requirements:* For master's, GMAT, minimum GPA of 3.0 (on scale of 4.33), or 3.33 based on last 60 credits of undergraduate courses; for doctorate, minimum GPA of 3.5 (on scale of 4.33); for Graduate Diploma, minimum GPA of 2.5 (on scale of 4.33), or 2.67 based on the last 60 credits of undergraduate courses. Additional exam requirements/recommendations for international students: Recommended— TOEFL (minimum score 580 paper-based; 93 iBT), IELTS (minimum score 7), TWE (minimum score 5). *Expenses:* Contact institution. *Faculty research:* Accounting, management and organizational studies, technology and operations management, finance, international business.

South Dakota School of Mines and Technology, Graduate Division, Program in Engineering Management, Rapid City, SD 57701-3995. Offers MS. Program offered jointly with The University of South Dakota. Part-time programs available. Postbaccalaureate distance learning degree programs offered (no on-campus study). *Faculty:* 11 full-time (3 women), 3 part-time/adjunct (1 woman). *Students:* 12 full-time (1 woman), 33 part-time (8 women); includes 4 minority (1 American Indian or Alaska Native, non-Hispanic/Latino; 3 Hispanic/Latino), 4 international. Average age 30. 26 applicants, 62% accepted, 13 enrolled. In 2014, 16 master's awarded. *Entrance requirements:* For master's, GMAT. Additional exam requirements/recommendations for international students: Required—TOEFL, TWE. *Application deadline:* For fall admission, 7/1 priority date for domestic students, 4/1 for international students; for spring admission, 11/1 for domestic students, 9/1 for international students. Applications are processed on a rolling basis. Application fee: $35. Electronic applications accepted. *Expenses:* Tuition, state resident: full-time $5050; part-time $210.40 per credit hour. Tuition, nonresident: full-time $11,290; part-time $470.30 per credit hour. *Required fees:* $4680. *Financial support:* In 2014–15, 2 students received support, including 5 research assistantships with partial tuition reimbursements available (averaging $7,368 per year), 4 teaching assistantships with partial tuition reimbursements available (averaging $3,374 per year); fellowships, Federal Work-Study, and institutionally sponsored loans also available. Support available to part-time students. Financial award application deadline: 5/15. *Total annual research expenditures:* $84,822. *Unit head:* Dr. Stuart D. Kellogg, Director, 605-394-1271, E-mail: stuart.kellogg@sdsmt.edu. *Application contact:* Rachel Howard, Office of Graduate Education, 605-355-3468, Fax: 605-394-1767, E-mail: rachel.howard@sdsmt.edu.
Website: http://www.sdsmt.edu/Academics/Departments/Industrial-Engineering/Graduate-Education/Engineering-Management-MS/.

Southeast Missouri State University, School of Graduate Studies, Department of Polytechnic Studies, Cape Girardeau, MO 63701-4799. Offers technology management (MS). Part-time and evening/weekend programs available. Postbaccalaureate distance learning degree programs offered (no on-campus study). *Faculty:* 13 full-time (3 women). *Students:* 90 full-time (21 women), 18 part-time (2 women); includes 4 minority (all Black or African American, non-Hispanic/Latino), 93 international. Average age 26. 219 applicants, 42% accepted, 28 enrolled. In 2014, 26 master's awarded. *Degree requirements:* For master's, comprehensive exam (for some programs), thesis or alternative. *Entrance requirements:* Additional exam requirements/recommendations for international students: Required—TOEFL (minimum score 550 paper-based; 79 iBT), IELTS (minimum score 6), PTE (minimum score 53). *Application deadline:* For fall admission, 8/1 for domestic students, 5/1 for international students; for spring admission, 11/1 for domestic students, 10/1 for international students. Applications are processed on a rolling basis. Application fee: $30 ($40 for international students). Electronic applications accepted. *Expenses:* Tuition, state resident: full-time $5256; part-time $292 per credit hour. Tuition, nonresident: full-time $9288; part-time $516 per credit hour. *Financial support:* In 2014–15, 91 students received support. Career-related internships or fieldwork, Federal Work-Study, scholarships/grants, traineeships, tuition waivers (full), and unspecified assistantships available. Financial award application deadline: 6/30; financial award applicants required to submit FAFSA. *Faculty research:* Cybersecurity, mechanical engineering, electrical engineering, industrial systems, networking. *Total annual research expenditures:* $25,000. *Unit head:* Dr. Brad Deken, Department Chair, 573-651-2104, Fax: 573-986-6174, E-mail: bdeken@semo.edu. *Application contact:* Dr. Khaled Bawahen, Graduate Coordinator, 573-986-7478, Fax: 573-986-6174, E-mail: kbawaneh@semo.edu.
Website: http://www.semo.edu/polytech/.

Southern Polytechnic State University, School of Engineering Technology and Management, Department of Business Administration, Marietta, GA 30060-2896. Offers accounting (MBA, MSA); business administration (Graduate Transition Certificate); finance (MBA); general (MBA); management (MBA); management information systems (MBA); marketing (MBA); operations and technology management (MBA). *Accreditation:* ACBSP. Part-time and evening/weekend programs available. Postbaccalaureate distance learning degree programs offered (no on-campus study). *Degree requirements:* For master's, comprehensive exam (for some programs), capstone course and major field exam (for MBA); 30 semester hours of course work (for MSA). *Entrance requirements:* For master's, GMAT or GRE, letters of recommendation, statement of purpose, resume, minimum GPA of 2.75 or undergraduate degree in business with up to 6 transition courses; undergraduate degree in accounting from regionally-accredited school (for MSA). Additional exam requirements/recommendations for international students: Required—TOEFL (minimum score 550 paper-based; 79 iBT), IELTS (minimum score 6.5). Electronic applications accepted. *Faculty research:* Ethics, virtual reality, sustainability, management of technology, quality management, capacity planning, human-computer interaction/interface, enterprise integration planning, economic impact of educational institutions, behavioral accounting, accounting ethics, taxation, information security, visualization simulation, human-computer interaction, supply chain, logistics, economics.

State University of New York Polytechnic Institute, Program in Business Administration in Technology Management, Utica, NY 13504-3050. Offers accounting and finance (MBA); business management (MBA); health services management (MBA); human resource management (MBA); marketing management (MBA). Part-time programs available. Postbaccalaureate distance learning degree programs offered (no on-campus study). *Degree requirements:* For master's, capstone course. *Entrance requirements:* For master's, GMAT, resume, one letter of reference. Additional exam requirements/recommendations for international students: Required—TOEFL (minimum score 550 paper-based; 79 iBT), IELTS (minimum score 6.5). Electronic applications accepted. *Faculty research:* Technology management, writing schools, leadership, new products.

Stevens Institute of Technology, Graduate School, Wesley J. Howe School of Technology Management, Doctoral Program in Technology Management, Hoboken, NJ 07030. Offers information management (PhD); technology management (PhD); telecommunications management (PhD). Part-time and evening/weekend programs available. Postbaccalaureate distance learning degree programs offered (minimal on-campus study). *Entrance requirements:* Additional exam requirements/recommendations for international students: Required—TOEFL. Electronic applications accepted.

Stevens Institute of Technology, Graduate School, Wesley J. Howe School of Technology Management, Program in Business Administration for Experienced Professionals, Hoboken, NJ 07030. Offers technology management (EMBA).

Stevens Institute of Technology, Graduate School, Wesley J. Howe School of Technology Management, Program in Management, Hoboken, NJ 07030. Offers general management (MS); global innovation management (MS); human resource management (MS); information management (MS); project management (MS); technology commercialization (MS); technology management (MS). Part-time programs available. *Degree requirements:* For master's, thesis optional. *Entrance requirements:* For master's, GMAT, GRE General Test. Additional exam requirements/recommendations for international students: Required—TOEFL. Electronic applications accepted. *Faculty research:* Industrial economics.

Stevens Institute of Technology, Graduate School, Wesley J. Howe School of Technology Management, Program in Technology Management for Experienced Professionals, Hoboken, NJ 07030. Offers EMTM, MS, Certificate. Part-time and evening/weekend programs available. Postbaccalaureate distance learning degree programs offered. *Entrance requirements:* For master's, GMAT, GRE General Test. Additional exam requirements/recommendations for international students: Required—TOEFL. Electronic applications accepted. *Expenses:* Contact institution.

Stevens Institute of Technology, Graduate School, Wesley J. Howe School of Technology Management, Program in Telecommunications Management, Hoboken, NJ 07030. Offers business (MS); global innovation management (MS); management of wireless networks (MS); online security, technology and business (MS); project management (MS); technical management (MS); telecommunications management (PhD, Certificate). *Degree requirements:* For master's, thesis optional; for doctorate, thesis/dissertation. *Entrance requirements:* For master's and doctorate, GMAT, GRE General Test. Additional exam requirements/recommendations for international students: Required—TOEFL. Electronic applications accepted.

Stevenson University, Program in Business and Technology Management, Owings Mills, MD 21117. Offers MS. *Faculty:* 1 full-time (0 women), 12 part-time/adjunct (3 women). *Students:* 38 full-time (19 women), 116 part-time (60 women); includes 69 minority (57 Black or African American, non-Hispanic/Latino; 1 American Indian or Alaska Native, non-Hispanic/Latino; 11 Asian, non-Hispanic/Latino). Average age 31. 110 applicants, 70% accepted, 41 enrolled. In 2014, 45 master's awarded. *Degree requirements:* For master's, capstone course. *Entrance requirements:* Additional exam requirements/recommendations for international students: Required—TOEFL (minimum score 550 paper-based), IELTS (minimum score 6.5). *Application deadline:* Applications are processed on a rolling basis. Application fee: $0. Electronic applications accepted. *Expenses:* Expenses: $645 per credit, $125 fee. *Unit head:* Steven Engorn, Coordinator, 443-352-4220, Fax: 443-394-0538, E-mail: sengorn@stevenson.edu. *Application contact:* Tonia Cristino, Assistant Director, Recruitment and Admissions, 443-352-4058, Fax: 443-394-0538, E-mail: tcristino@stevenson.edu.
Website: http://www.stevenson.edu.

Stony Brook University, State University of New York, Graduate School, College of Business, Program in Technology Management, Stony Brook, NY 11794. Offers MS. Program conducted mostly in Korea. Evening/weekend programs available. Postbaccalaureate distance learning degree programs offered. *Students:* 24 applicants, 4% accepted. In 2014, 1 master's awarded. *Entrance requirements:* For master's, GMAT or GRE General Test, 3 years of work experience, minimum GPA of 3.0, letters of recommendation. Additional exam requirements/recommendations for international students: Required—TOEFL (minimum score 550 paper-based). Application fee: $100. *Expenses:* Tuition, state resident: full-time $10,370; part-time $432 per credit. Tuition, nonresident: full-time $20,190; part-time $841 per credit. *Required fees:* $1431. *Unit head:* Dr. Manuel London, Dean, 631-632-7171, Fax: 631-632-8181, E-mail: manuel.london@stonybrook.edu. *Application contact:* 631-632-7171, Fax: 631-632-8181, E-mail: OSS@stonybrook.edu.
Website: http://www.stonybrook.edu/commcms/business/outreach/mstm.html.

Stony Brook University, State University of New York, Graduate School, College of Engineering and Applied Sciences, Department of Technology and Society, Program in Global Operations Management, Stony Brook, NY 11794. Offers MS. Postbaccalaureate distance learning degree programs offered. *Entrance requirements:* For master's, https://www.grad.stonybrook.edu/ProspectiveStudents/faq.shtml. Additional exam requirements/recommendations for international students: Required—TOEFL, IELTS. *Application deadline:* For fall admission, 2/1 for domestic students; for spring admission, 10/1 for domestic students. Electronic applications accepted. *Expenses:* Tuition, state resident: full-time $10,370; part-time $432 per credit. Tuition, nonresident: full-time $20,190; part-time $841 per credit. *Required fees:* $1431. *Unit head:* Dr. David Ferguson, Chairman, 631-632-8770, E-mail: david.ferguson@stonybrook.edu. *Application contact:* Dr. Sheldon Reaven, Graduate Director, 631-632-8765, Fax: 631-632-7809, E-mail: sheldon.raven@sunysb.edu.
Website: http://www.stonybrook.edu/est/graduate/elearn.shtml.

Texas State University, The Graduate College, College of Science and Engineering, Department of Engineering Technology, Program in Technology Management, San Marcos, TX 78666. Offers MS, MST. Part-time and evening/weekend programs available. *Faculty:* 11 full-time (2 women). *Students:* 23 full-time (6 women), 25 part-time (3 women); includes 6 minority (1 Black or African American, non-Hispanic/Latino; 1 Asian, non-Hispanic/Latino; 4 Hispanic/Latino), 19 international. Average age 30. 38 applicants, 71% accepted, 14 enrolled. In 2014, 12 master's awarded. *Degree requirements:* For master's, comprehensive exam, thesis optional. *Entrance requirements:* For master's, baccalaureate degree from regionally-accredited university with minimum GPA of 2.75 on last 60 undergraduate semester hours. Additional exam requirements/recommendations for international students: Required—TOEFL (minimum score 550 paper-based; 78 iBT). *Application deadline:* For fall admission, 2/1 priority date for domestic and international students; for spring admission, 10/15 for domestic students, 10/1 for international students; for summer admission, 4/15 for domestic students, 3/15 for international students. Applications are processed on a rolling basis. Application fee: $40 ($90 for international students). Electronic applications accepted. *Expenses:* Expenses: $8,834 (tuition and fees combined). *Financial support:* In 2014–15, 15 students received support, including 4 research assistantships (averaging $11,838 per year), 9 teaching assistantships (averaging $11,398 per year); career-related internships or fieldwork, Federal Work-Study, and institutionally sponsored loans also available. Support available to part-time students. Financial award application deadline: 4/1; financial award applicants required to submit FAFSA. *Faculty research:* Pavement preservation, property of materials, assembly tolerance. *Total annual research expenditures:* $158,087. *Unit head:* Dr. Andy Batey, Graduate Advisor, 512-245-2137, E-mail: ab08@txstate.edu. *Application contact:* Dr. Andrea Golato, Dean of the Graduate College, 512-245-2581, E-mail: gradcollege@txstate.edu.
Website: http://www.txstate.edu/technology/.

Towson University, Program in e-Business and Technology Management, Towson, MD 21252-0001. Offers project, program and portfolio management (Postbaccalaureate Certificate); supply chain management (MS, Postbaccalaureate Certificate). *Students:* 4 full-time (2 women), 29 part-time (11 women); includes 12 minority (10 Black or African American, non-Hispanic/Latino; 1 Asian, non-Hispanic/Latino; 1 Hispanic/Latino), 5 international. *Entrance requirements:* For master's and Postbaccalaureate Certificate, GRE or GMAT, bachelor's degree in relevant field and/or three years of post-bachelor's

experience working in supply chain related areas; minimum cumulative GPA of 3.0; resume; 1-2 page statement; 2 reference letters. Additional exam requirements/recommendations for international students: Required—TOEFL (minimum score 550 paper-based). *Application deadline:* Applications are processed on a rolling basis. Application fee: $45. Electronic applications accepted. *Unit head:* Dr. Chaodong Hang, Director, 410-704-4658, E-mail: chan@towson.edu. *Application contact:* Jennifer Bethke, Information Contact, 410-704-6004, E-mail: grads@towson.edu.
Website: http://web.towson.edu/cbe/ebusiness/grad.html.

Trevecca Nazarene University, Graduate Business Programs, Nashville, TN 37210-2877. Offers business administration (MBA); healthcare administration (Certificate); information technology (MBA, MS, Certificate); management (MSM); management and leadership (Certificate); project management (Certificate). Evening/weekend programs available. Postbaccalaureate distance learning degree programs offered. *Faculty:* 7 full-time (1 woman), 8 part-time/adjunct (3 women). *Students:* 117 full-time (72 women), 13 part-time (3 women); includes 48 minority (41 Black or African American, non-Hispanic/Latino; 3 Asian, non-Hispanic/Latino; 3 Hispanic/Latino; 1 Two or more races, non-Hispanic/Latino), 1 international. Average age 33. In 2014, 44 master's awarded. *Entrance requirements:* For master's, minimum GPA of 2.75, resume, official transcript from regionally-accredited institution, minimum math grade of C, minimum English composition grade of C; undergraduate computing degree (for MS). Additional exam requirements/recommendations for international students: Required—TOEFL (minimum score 550 paper-based; 80 iBT). *Application deadline:* Applications are processed on a rolling basis. Application fee: $25. *Expenses:* Expenses: Contact institution. *Financial support:* Applicants required to submit FAFSA. *Unit head:* Dr. Rick Mann, Director of Graduate and Professional Programs for School of Business, 615-248-1529, E-mail: management@trevecca.edu. *Application contact:* 615-248-1529, E-mail: cll@trevecca.edu.
Website: http://trevecca.edu/academics/program/management or trevecca.edu/academics/program/master-of-business-administration.

University at Albany, State University of New York, School of Business, MBA Programs, Albany, NY 12222. Offers business administration (MBA); human resource information systems (MBA); information technology management (MBA); JD/MBA. Part-time and evening/weekend programs available. *Degree requirements:* For master's, thesis (for some programs), field project. *Entrance requirements:* For master's, GMAT. Additional exam requirements/recommendations for international students: Required—TOEFL (minimum score 600 paper-based; 100 iBT); Recommended—IELTS. Electronic applications accepted. *Faculty research:* Cyber security, entrepreneurship, human resource information systems, information technology management, finance, marketing.

University of Advancing Technology, Master of Science Program in Technology, Tempe, AZ 85283-1042. Offers advancing computer science (MS); emerging technologies (MS); game production and management (MS); information assurance (MS); technology leadership (MS). *Degree requirements:* For master's, project or thesis. *Entrance requirements:* Additional exam requirements/recommendations for international students: Required—TOEFL (minimum score 550 paper-based). Electronic applications accepted. *Faculty research:* Artificial intelligence, fractals, organizational management.

The University of Akron, Graduate School, College of Business Administration, Department of Management, Akron, OH 44325. Offers global technological innovation (MBA); healthcare management (MBA); information systems management (MSM); leadership and organizational change (MBA); management (MBA); supply chain management (MBA); technological innovation (MSM); JD/MSM. *Accreditation:* AACSB. Part-time and evening/weekend programs available. *Faculty:* 18 full-time (4 women), 14 part-time/adjunct (4 women). *Students:* 105 full-time (40 women), 89 part-time (31 women); includes 12 minority (2 Black or African American, non-Hispanic/Latino; 6 Asian, non-Hispanic/Latino; 3 Hispanic/Latino; 1 Two or more races, non-Hispanic/Latino), 75 international. Average age 28. 159 applicants, 79% accepted, 70 enrolled. In 2014, 64 master's awarded. *Entrance requirements:* For master's, GMAT, minimum GPA of 2.75, two letters of recommendation, statement of purpose, resume. Additional exam requirements/recommendations for international students: Required—TOEFL (minimum score 550 paper-based; 79 iBT), IELTS (minimum score 6.5). *Application deadline:* For fall admission, 7/15 for domestic and international students; for spring admission, 11/15 for domestic and international students; for summer admission, 4/15 for domestic and international students. Application fee: $45 ($75 for international students). Electronic applications accepted. *Expenses:* Tuition, state resident: full-time $7578; part-time $421 per credit hour. Tuition, nonresident: full-time $12,977; part-time $721 per credit hour. *Required fees:* $1388; $35 per credit hour. Tuition and fees vary according to course load. *Financial support:* In 2014–15, 30 teaching assistantships with full tuition reimbursements were awarded; career-related internships or fieldwork, Federal Work-Study, and unspecified assistantships also available. *Faculty research:* Human resource management, innovation, entrepreneurship, technology management and technology transfer, artificial intelligence and belief functions. *Unit head:* Dr. Steve Ash, Interim Chair, 330-972-6086, E-mail: ash@uakron.edu. *Application contact:* Dr. William Hauser, Director of Graduate Business Programs, 330-972-7043, Fax: 330-972-6588, E-mail: whauser@uakron.edu.
Website: http://www.uakron.edu/cba/departments/management/.

The University of Alabama in Huntsville, School of Graduate Studies, College of Business Administration, Programs in Business and Management, Huntsville, AL 35899. Offers federal contracting and procurement management (Certificate); management (MBA), including acquisition management, entrepreneurship, federal contract accounting, finance, human resource management, logistics and supply chain management, marketing, project management; supply chain management (Certificate); technology and innovation management (Certificate). *Accreditation:* AACSB. Part-time and evening/weekend programs available. *Degree requirements:* For master's, comprehensive exam, thesis or alternative. *Entrance requirements:* For master's, GMAT (minimum score 500), minimum AACSB index of 1080. Additional exam requirements/recommendations for international students: Required—TOEFL (minimum score 550 paper-based; 80 iBT), IELTS (minimum score 6.5). Electronic applications accepted. *Faculty research:* Supply chain management, management of research and development, international marketing and branding, organizational behavior and human resource management, social networks and computational economics.

University of Bridgeport, School of Engineering, Department of Technology Management, Bridgeport, CT 06604. Offers MS. *Degree requirements:* For master's, thesis optional. *Entrance requirements:* Additional exam requirements/recommendations for international students: Recommended—TOEFL (minimum score 550 paper-based; 80 iBT), IELTS (minimum score 6.5). Electronic applications accepted. *Expenses:* Contact institution. *Faculty research:* CAD/CAM.

University of California, Santa Barbara, Graduate Division, College of Engineering, Program in Technology Management, Santa Barbara, CA 93106-2014. Offers MTM.

University of California, Santa Cruz, Division of Graduate Studies, Jack Baskin School of Engineering, Department of Technology and Information Management, Santa Cruz, CA 95064. Offers MS, PhD. Terminal master's awarded for partial completion of doctoral program. *Degree requirements:* For master's, thesis, 2 seminars; for doctorate, thesis/dissertation, 2 seminars. *Entrance requirements:* For master's and doctorate, GRE General Test; GRE Subject Test preferably in computer science, engineering, physics, or mathematics (highly recommended), minimum GPA of 3.5. Additional exam requirements/recommendations for international students: Required—TOEFL (minimum score 570 paper-based; 89 iBT); Recommended—IELTS (minimum score 8). Electronic applications accepted. *Faculty research:* Integration of information systems, technology, and business management.

University of Central Missouri, The Graduate School, Warrensburg, MO 64093. Offers accountancy (MA); accounting (MBA); applied mathematics (MS); aviation safety (MA); biology (MS); business administration (MBA); career and technical education leadership (MS); college student personnel administration (MS); communication (MA); computer science (MS); counseling (MS); criminal justice (MS); educational leadership (Ed D); educational technology (MS); elementary and early childhood education (MSE); English (MA); environmental studies (MA); finance (MBA); history (MA); human services/educational technology (Ed S); human services/learning resources (Ed S); human services/professional counseling (Ed S); industrial hygiene (MS); industrial management (MS); information systems (MBA); information technology (MS); kinesiology (MS); library science and information services (MS); literacy education (MSE); marketing (MBA); mathematics (MS); music (MA); occupational safety management (MS); psychology (MS); rural family nursing (MS); school administration (MSE); social gerontology (MS); sociology (MA); special education (MSE); speech language pathology (MS); superintendency (Ed S); teaching (MAT); teaching English as a second language (MA); technology (MS); technology management (PhD); theatre (MA). Part-time programs available. *Faculty:* 314 full-time (137 women), 24 part-time/adjunct (14 women). *Students:* 1,624 full-time (542 women), 1,773 part-time (1,055 women); includes 194 minority (104 Black or African American, non-Hispanic/Latino; 6 American Indian or Alaska Native, non-Hispanic/Latino; 23 Asian, non-Hispanic/Latino; 41 Hispanic/Latino; 3 Native Hawaiian or other Pacific Islander, non-Hispanic/Latino; 17 Two or more races, non-Hispanic/Latino), 1,592 international. Average age 31. 2,800 applicants, 63% accepted, 1223 enrolled. In 2014, 796 master's, 81 other advanced degrees awarded. *Degree requirements:* For master's and Ed S, comprehensive exam (for some programs), thesis (for some programs). *Entrance requirements:* Additional exam requirements/recommendations for international students: Required—TOEFL (minimum score 550 paper-based; 79 iBT). *Application deadline:* For fall admission, 6/1 for domestic students; for spring admission, 10/1 for domestic and international students. Applications are processed on a rolling basis. Application fee: $30 ($75 for international students). Electronic applications accepted. *Expenses:* Tuition, state resident: full-time $6630; part-time $276.25 per credit hour. Tuition, nonresident: full-time $13,260; part-time $552.50 per credit hour. *Required fees:* $29 per credit hour. Tuition and fees vary according to campus/location. *Financial support:* In 2014–15, 118 students received support, including 271 research assistantships with full and partial tuition reimbursements available (averaging $7,500 per year), 109 teaching assistantships with full and partial tuition reimbursements available (averaging $7,500 per year); career-related internships or fieldwork, Federal Work-Study, scholarships/grants, and administrative and laboratory assistantships also available. Support available to part-time students. Financial award application deadline: 3/1; financial award applicants required to submit FAFSA. *Unit head:* Tina Church-Hockett, Director of Graduate School and International Admissions, 660-543-4621, Fax: 660-543-4778, E-mail: church@ucmo.edu. *Application contact:* Brittany Lawrence, Graduate Student Services Coordinator, 660-543-4621, Fax: 660-543-4778, E-mail: gradinfo@ucmo.edu.
Website: http://www.ucmo.edu/graduate/.

University of Colorado Denver, Business School, Master of Business Administration Program, Denver, CO 80217. Offers bioinnovation and entrepreneurship (MBA); business intelligence (MBA); business strategy (MBA); business to business marketing (MBA); business to consumer marketing (MBA); change management (MBA); corporate financial management (MBA); enterprise technology management (MBA); entrepreneurship (MBA); health administration (MBA), including financial management, health administration, health information technologies, international health management and policy; human resources management (MBA); international business (MBA); investment management (MBA); managing for sustainability (MBA); sports and entertainment management (MBA). *Accreditation:* AACSB. Part-time and evening/weekend programs available. Postbaccalaureate distance learning degree programs offered (no on-campus study). *Students:* 542 full-time (207 women), 139 part-time (50 women); includes 86 minority (15 Black or African American, non-Hispanic/Latino; 1 American Indian or Alaska Native, non-Hispanic/Latino; 29 Asian, non-Hispanic/Latino; 34 Hispanic/Latino; 7 Two or more races, non-Hispanic/Latino), 32 international. Average age 33. 324 applicants, 68% accepted, 163 enrolled. In 2014, 278 master's awarded. *Degree requirements:* For master's, 48 semester hours, including 30 of core courses, 3 in international business, and 15 in electives from over 50 other graduate business courses. *Entrance requirements:* For master's, GMAT, resume, official transcripts, essay, two letters of recommendation, financial statements (for international applicants). Additional exam requirements/recommendations for international students: Required—TOEFL (minimum score 560 paper-based; 83 iBT); Recommended—IELTS (minimum score 6.5). *Application deadline:* For fall admission, 4/15 priority date for domestic students, 3/15 priority date for international students; for spring admission, 10/15 priority date for domestic students, 9/15 priority date for international students; for summer admission, 2/15 priority date for domestic students, 1/15 priority date for international students. Applications are processed on a rolling basis. Application fee: $50 ($75 for international students). Electronic applications accepted. *Expenses:* Expenses: Contact institution. *Financial support:* In 2014–15, 73 students received support. Fellowships, research assistantships, teaching assistantships, Federal Work-Study, institutionally sponsored loans, scholarships/grants, traineeships, and unspecified assistantships available. Financial award application deadline: 4/1; financial award applicants required to submit FAFSA. *Faculty research:* Marketing, management, entrepreneurship, finance, health administration. *Unit head:* Woodrow Eckard, MBA Director, 303-315-8470, E-mail: woody.eckard@ucdenver.edu. *Application contact:* Shelly Townley, Admissions Director, Graduate Programs, 303-315-8202, E-mail: shelly.townley@ucdenver.edu.
Website: http://www.ucdenver.edu/academics/colleges/business/degrees/mba/Pages/MBA.aspx.

University of Colorado Denver, Business School, Program in Information Systems, Denver, CO 80217. Offers accounting and information systems audit and control (MS); business intelligence systems (MS); digital health entrepreneurship (MS); enterprise risk management (MS); enterprise technology management (MS); geographic information systems (MS); health information technology (MS); technology innovation and entrepreneurship (MS); Web and mobile computing (MS). Part-time and evening/weekend programs available. Postbaccalaureate distance learning degree programs offered (no on-campus study). *Students:* 72 full-time (22 women), 29 part-time (9 women); includes 18 minority (2 Black or African American, non-Hispanic/Latino; 12 Asian, non-Hispanic/Latino; 3 Hispanic/Latino; 1 Two or more races, non-Hispanic/Latino), 31 international. Average age 31. 81 applicants, 75% accepted, 24 enrolled. In 2014, 21 master's awarded. *Degree requirements:* For master's, 30 credit hours. *Entrance requirements:* For master's, GMAT, resume, essay, two letters of recommendation, financial statements (for international applicants). Additional exam

requirements/recommendations for international students: Required—TOEFL (minimum score 525 paper-based; 71 iBT); Recommended—IELTS (minimum score 6.5). *Application deadline:* For fall admission, 4/15 priority date for domestic students, 3/15 priority date for international students; for spring admission, 10/15 priority date for domestic students, 9/15 priority date for international students; for summer admission, 2/15 priority date for domestic students, 1/15 priority date for international students. Applications are processed on a rolling basis. Application fee: $50 ($75 for international students). Electronic applications accepted. *Expenses:* Expenses: Contact institution. *Financial support:* In 2014–15, 21 students received support. Fellowships, research assistantships, teaching assistantships, Federal Work-Study, institutionally sponsored loans, scholarships/grants, and traineeships available. Financial award application deadline: 4/1; financial award applicants required to submit FAFSA. *Faculty research:* Human-computer interaction, expert systems, database management, electronic commerce, object-oriented software development. *Unit head:* Dr. Jahangir Karimi, Director of Information Systems Programs, 303-315-8430, E-mail: jahangir.karimi@ ucdenver.edu. *Application contact:* Shelly Townley, Admissions Director, Graduate Programs, 303-315-8202, E-mail: shelly.townley@ucdenver.edu.
Website: http://www.ucdenver.edu/academics/colleges/business/degrees/ms/IS/Pages/Information-Systems.aspx.

University of Colorado Denver, Business School, Program in Management and Organization, Denver, CO 80217. Offers business strategy (MS); change and innovation (MS); enterprise technology management (MS); entrepreneurship and innovation (MS); global management (MS); leadership (MS); managing for sustainability (MS); managing human resources (MS); sports and entertainment management (MS). *Accreditation:* AACSB. Part-time and evening/weekend programs available. Postbaccalaureate distance learning degree programs offered (no on-campus study). *Students:* 25 full-time (15 women), 13 part-time (6 women); includes 3 minority (1 Black or African American, non-Hispanic/Latino; 1 Hispanic/Latino; 1 Two or more races, non-Hispanic/Latino), 4 international. Average age 30. 32 applicants, 50% accepted, 4 enrolled. In 2014, 18 master's awarded. *Degree requirements:* For master's, 30 semester hours (12 of required courses, 12 of management electives, and 6 of free electives). *Entrance requirements:* For master's, GMAT, resume, two letters of recommendation, essay, financial statements (for international applicants). Additional exam requirements/recommendations for international students: Required—TOEFL (minimum score 525 paper-based; 71 iBT); Recommended—IELTS (minimum score 6.5). *Application deadline:* For fall admission, 4/15 priority date for domestic students, 3/15 priority date for international students; for spring admission, 10/15 priority date for domestic students, 9/15 priority date for international students; for summer admission, 2/15 priority date for domestic students, 1/15 priority date for international students. Applications are processed on a rolling basis. Application fee: $50 ($75 for international students). Electronic applications accepted. *Expenses:* Expenses: Contact institution. *Financial support:* In 2014–15, 5 students received support. Fellowships, research assistantships, teaching assistantships, Federal Work-Study, institutionally sponsored loans, scholarships/grants, and traineeships available. Financial award application deadline: 4/1; financial award applicants required to submit FAFSA. *Faculty research:* Human resource management, management of catastrophe, turnaround strategies. *Unit head:* Dr. Kenneth Bettenhausen, Associate Professor/Director of MS in Management, 303-315-8425, E-mail: kenneth.bettenhausen@ucdenver.edu. *Application contact:* Shelly Townley, Admissions Director, Graduate Programs, 303-315-8202, E-mail: shelly.townley@ucdenver.edu.
Website: http://www.ucdenver.edu/academics/colleges/business/degrees/ms/management/Pages/Management.aspx.

University of Dallas, Graduate School of Management, Irving, TX 75062-4736. Offers accounting (MBA, MM, MS); business management (MBA, MM); corporate finance (MBA, MM); financial services (MBA); global business (MBA, MM); health services management (MBA, MM); human resource management (MBA, MM); information assurance (MBA, MM, MS); information technology (MBA, MM, MS); information technology service management (MBA, MM, MS); marketing management (MBA, MM); organization development (MBA, MM); project management (MBA, MM); sports and entertainment management (MBA, MM); strategic leadership (MBA, MM); supply chain management (MBA); supply chain management and market logistics (MM). *Accreditation:* ACBSP. Part-time and evening/weekend programs available. Postbaccalaureate distance learning degree programs offered (no on-campus study). *Entrance requirements:* Additional exam requirements/recommendations for international students: Required—TOEFL. Electronic applications accepted. *Expenses:* Contact institution.

University of Delaware, Alfred Lerner College of Business and Economics, Department of Accounting and Management Information Systems and Department of Electrical and Computer Engineering, Program in Information Systems and Technology Management, Newark, DE 19716. Offers MS. Part-time and evening/weekend programs available. *Entrance requirements:* For master's, GRE or GMAT, 2 letters of recommendation, resume, minimum GPA of 2.75. Additional exam requirements/recommendations for international students: Required—TOEFL (minimum score 600 paper-based). *Faculty research:* Security, developer trust, XML.

University of Denver, University College, Denver, CO 80208. Offers geographic information systems (Certificate); global affairs (Certificate), including translation studies, world history and culture; information and communications technology (MCIS), including geographic information systems, information systems security, project management (MCIS, Certificate), software design and programming, technology management, telecommunications technology, Web design and development; leadership and organizations (Certificate), including human capital in organizations, philanthropic leadership, project management (MCIS, Certificate), strategic innovation and change; organizational and professional communication (MPS), including alternative dispute resolution, organizational communication, organizational development and training, public relations and marketing; security management (MAS, Certificate), including emergency planning and response, information security (MAS), organizational security. Part-time and evening/weekend programs available. Postbaccalaureate distance learning degree programs offered (no on-campus study). *Faculty:* 8 full-time (4 women), 133 part-time/adjunct (46 women). *Students:* 54 full-time (21 women), 1,327 part-time (775 women); includes 272 minority (106 Black or African American, non-Hispanic/Latino; 6 American Indian or Alaska Native, non-Hispanic/Latino; 26 Asian, non-Hispanic/Latino; 108 Hispanic/Latino; 1 Native Hawaiian or other Pacific Islander, non-Hispanic/Latino; 25 Two or more races, non-Hispanic/Latino), 116 international. Average age 35. 768 applicants, 95% accepted, 620 enrolled. In 2014, 391 master's, 196 other advanced degrees awarded. *Degree requirements:* For master's, capstone project. *Entrance requirements:* For master's, transcripts, two letters of recommendation, personal statement, resume. Additional exam requirements/recommendations for international students: Required—TOEFL (minimum score 550 paper-based; 80 iBT). *Application deadline:* For fall admission, 6/21 priority date for domestic students, 5/1 priority date for international students; for winter admission, 9/14 priority date for domestic students, 9/19 priority date for international students; for spring admission, 1/11 for domestic students, 12/12 for international students; for summer admission, 3/29 priority date for domestic students, 3/6 priority date for international

students. Applications are processed on a rolling basis. Application fee: $75. Electronic applications accepted. *Expenses:* Expenses: $959 per credit hour. *Financial support:* In 2014–15, 19 students received support. Applicants required to submit FAFSA. *Unit head:* Dr. Michael McGuire, Interim Dean, 303-871-3518, E-mail: mmcguire@du.edu. *Application contact:* Information Contact, 303-871-2291, E-mail: ucoladm@du.edu.
Website: http://www.universitycollege.du.edu/.

University of Idaho, College of Graduate Studies, College of Engineering, Department of Engineering, Moscow, ID 83844-1011. Offers environmental engineering (M Engr, MS); nuclear engineering (M Engr, MS, PhD); technology management (MS). *Faculty:* 4 full-time, 2 part-time/adjunct. *Students:* 1 full-time, 12 part-time. Average age 44. In 2014, 5 master's awarded. *Application deadline:* Applications are processed on a rolling basis. Application fee: $60. Electronic applications accepted. *Expenses:* Tuition, state resident: full-time $4784; part-time $280.50 per credit hour. Tuition, nonresident: full-time $18,314; part-time $957.50 per credit hour. *Required fees:* $2000; $58.50 per credit hour. Tuition and fees vary according to program. *Financial support:* Applicants required to submit FAFSA. *Unit head:* Dr. Larry Stauffer, Interim Dean, 208-885-6479. *Application contact:* Stephanie Thomas, Graduate Recruitment Coordinator, 208-885-4001, Fax: 208-885-4406, E-mail: gadms@uidaho.edu.
Website: http://www.uidaho.edu/engr/.

University of Illinois at Urbana–Champaign, Graduate College, College of Agricultural, Consumer and Environmental Sciences, Department of Agricultural and Biological Engineering, Champaign, IL 61820. Offers agricultural and biological engineering (MS, PhD); technical systems management (MS, PSM). *Students:* 75 full-time (23 women). Application fee: $70 ($90 for international students). *Unit head:* Kuan Chong Ting, Head, 217-333-3570, Fax: 217-244-0323, E-mail: kcting@illinois.edu. *Application contact:* Jana R. Lenz, Office Administrator, 217-324-1654, Fax: 217-244-0323, E-mail: janalenz@illinois.edu.
Website: http://abe.illinois.edu.

University of Illinois at Urbana–Champaign, Graduate College, College of Business, Department of Business Administration, Champaign, IL 61820. Offers business administration (MS, PhD); technology management (MS). *Accreditation:* AACSB. *Students:* 194 (93 women). Application fee: $70 ($90 for international students). *Expenses:* Expenses: Contact institution. *Unit head:* Aric P. Rindfleisch, Interim Head, 217-333-4240, Fax: 217-244-7969, E-mail: aric@illinois.edu. *Application contact:* Diana K. Gonzalez, Coordinator of Graduate Programs, 217-300-8484, Fax: 217-244-7969, E-mail: dgonzal2@illinois.edu.
Website: http://www.business.illinois.edu/ba/.

University of Maryland University College, The Graduate School, Program in Technology Management, Adelphi, MD 20783. Offers MS, Certificate. Part-time and evening/weekend programs available. Postbaccalaureate distance learning degree programs offered (no on-campus study). *Students:* 5 full-time (2 women), 358 part-time (168 women); includes 200 minority (148 Black or African American, non-Hispanic/Latino; 18 Asian, non-Hispanic/Latino; 24 Hispanic/Latino; 2 Native Hawaiian or other Pacific Islander, non-Hispanic/Latino; 8 Two or more races, non-Hispanic/Latino), 3 international. Average age 37. 78 applicants, 100% accepted, 36 enrolled. In 2014, 117 master's, 58 other advanced degrees awarded. *Degree requirements:* For master's, thesis or alternative, capstone course. *Application deadline:* Applications are processed on a rolling basis. Application fee: $50. Electronic applications accepted. *Financial support:* Federal Work-Study and scholarships/grants available. Support available to part-time students. Financial award application deadline: 6/1; financial award applicants required to submit FAFSA. *Unit head:* Dr. Garth MacKenzie, Chair, 240-684-2400, Fax: 240-684-2401, E-mail: garth.mackenzie@umuc.edu. *Application contact:* Coordinator, Graduate Admissions, 800-888-8682, Fax: 240-684-2151, E-mail: newgrad@umuc.edu.
Website: http://www.umuc.edu/academic-programs/masters-degrees/technology-management.cfm.

University of Miami, Graduate School, College of Engineering, Department of Industrial Engineering, Coral Gables, FL 33124. Offers environmental health and safety (MS); ergonomics (PhD); industrial engineering (MSIE, PhD); management of technology (MS); occupational ergonomics and safety (MS, MSOES), including environmental health and safety (MS), occupational ergonomics and safety (MSOES); MBA/MSIE. Part-time programs available. *Degree requirements:* For master's, thesis (for some programs); for doctorate, comprehensive exam, thesis/dissertation. *Entrance requirements:* For master's and doctorate, GRE General Test, minimum GPA of 3.0. Additional exam requirements/recommendations for international students: Required—TOEFL (minimum score 550 paper-based). *Faculty research:* Logistics, supply chain management, industrial applications of biomechanics and ergonomics, technology management, back pain, aging, operations research, manufacturing, safety, human reliability, energy assessment.

University of Minnesota, Twin Cities Campus, College of Science and Engineering, Technological Leadership Institute, Program in Management of Technology, Minneapolis, MN 55455-0213. Offers MSMOT. Evening/weekend programs available. *Degree requirements:* For master's, thesis, capstone project. *Entrance requirements:* For master's, 5 years of work experience in high-tech company, preferably in Twin Cities area; demonstrated technological leadership ability. Additional exam requirements/recommendations for international students: Required—TOEFL (minimum score 580 paper-based; 90 iBT). Electronic applications accepted. *Expenses:* Contact institution. *Faculty research:* Operations management, strategic management, technology foresight, marketing, business analysis.

University of New Mexico, Robert O. Anderson Graduate School of Management, Department of Finance, International, Technology and Entrepreneurship, Albuquerque, NM 87131-1221. Offers entrepreneurship (MBA); finance (MBA); international management (MBA); international management in Latin America (MBA); management of technology (MBA). Part-time and evening/weekend programs available. *Faculty:* 14 full-time (2 women), 5 part-time/adjunct (0 women). In 2014, 73 master's awarded. *Entrance requirements:* For master's, GMAT or GRE, minimum GPA of 3.0 on last 60 hours of coursework. Additional exam requirements/recommendations for international students: Required—TOEFL (minimum score 550 paper-based; 79 iBT). *Application deadline:* For fall admission, 4/1 priority date for domestic and international students; for spring admission, 10/1 priority date for domestic and international students. Applications are processed on a rolling basis. Application fee: $50. Electronic applications accepted. *Expenses:* Expenses: Contact institution. *Financial support:* Fellowships, research assistantships, career-related internships or fieldwork, Federal Work-Study, scholarships/grants, and unspecified assistantships available. Support available to part-time students. Financial award application deadline: 6/1; financial award applicants required to submit FAFSA. *Faculty research:* Corporate finance, investments, management in Latin America, management of technology, entrepreneurship. *Unit head:* Dr. Sul Kassicieh, Chair, 505-277-6471, Fax: 505-277-7108, E-mail: sul@ unm.edu. *Application contact:* Tracy Wilkey, Manager, Academic Advisement, 505-277-3290, Fax: 505-277-8436, E-mail: andersonadvising@unm.edu.
Website: http://mba.mgt.unm.edu/default.asp.

University of North Dakota, Graduate School, College of Business and Public Administration, Department of Technology, Grand Forks, ND 58202. Offers MST. Part-time programs available. *Degree requirements:* For master's, comprehensive exam (for some programs), thesis optional. *Entrance requirements:* For master's, minimum GPA of 2.75. Additional exam requirements/recommendations for international students: Required—TOEFL (minimum score 550 paper-based; 76 iBT), IELTS (minimum score 6.5). Electronic applications accepted.

University of Pennsylvania, School of Engineering and Applied Science, Executive Master's in Technology Management Program, Philadelphia, PA 19104. Offers MSE. Program offered jointly with the Wharton School. Part-time and evening/weekend programs available. In 2014, 39 master's awarded. *Application deadline:* For fall admission, 4/1 priority date for domestic students. Application fee: $70. *Unit head:* Eduardo D. Glandt, Dean, 215-898-7244, E-mail: seasdean@seas.upenn.edu. *Application contact:* School of Engineering and Applied Science Graduate Admissions, 215-898-4542, E-mail: gradstudies@seas.upenn.edu.
Website: http://www.emtm.upenn.edu.

University of Phoenix–Atlanta Campus, College of Information Systems and Technology, Sandy Springs, GA 30350-4153. Offers information systems (MIS); technology management (MBA). Evening/weekend programs available. *Degree requirements:* For master's, thesis (for some programs). *Entrance requirements:* For master's, 3 years of work experience, minimum undergraduate GPA of 3.0. Additional exam requirements/recommendations for international students: Required—TOEFL (minimum score 550 paper-based; 79 iBT). Electronic applications accepted.

University of Phoenix–Augusta Campus, College of Information Systems and Technology, Augusta, GA 30909-4583. Offers information systems (MIS); technology management (MBA).

University of Phoenix–Austin Campus, College of Information Systems and Technology, Austin, TX 78759. Offers information systems (MIS); technology management (MBA).

University of Phoenix–Bay Area Campus, School of Business, San Jose, CA 95134-1805. Offers accountancy (MS); accounting (MBA); business administration (MBA, DBA); energy management (MBA); global management (MBA); health care management (MBA); human resource management (MBA); human resources management (MM); management (MM); marketing (MBA); organizational leadership (DM); project management (MBA); public administration (MPA); technology management (MBA). Evening/weekend programs available. Postbaccalaureate distance learning degree programs offered (no on-campus study). *Degree requirements:* For master's, thesis (for some programs). *Entrance requirements:* For master's, minimum undergraduate GPA of 3.0, 3 years of work experience. Additional exam requirements/recommendations for international students: Required—TOEFL (minimum score 550 paper-based; 79 iBT). Electronic applications accepted.

University of Phoenix–Birmingham Campus, College of Information Systems and Technology, Birmingham, AL 35242. Offers information systems (MIS); technology management (MBA).

University of Phoenix–Boston Campus, College of Information Systems and Technology, Braintree, MA 02184. Offers technology management (MBA). Evening/weekend programs available. *Degree requirements:* For master's, thesis (for some programs). *Entrance requirements:* For master's, minimum GPA of 3.0, 3 years of work experience. Additional exam requirements/recommendations for international students: Required—TOEFL (minimum score 550 paper-based; 79 iBT). Electronic applications accepted.

University of Phoenix–Central Valley Campus, College of Information Systems and Technology, Fresno, CA 93720-1562. Offers information systems (MIS); technology management (MBA).

University of Phoenix–Charlotte Campus, College of Information Systems and Technology, Charlotte, NC 28273-3409. Offers information systems (MIS); information systems management (MISM); technology management (MBA). Evening/weekend programs available. *Degree requirements:* For master's, thesis (for some programs). *Entrance requirements:* For master's, minimum undergraduate GPA of 3.0, 3 years work experience. Additional exam requirements/recommendations for international students: Required—TOEFL (minimum score 550 paper-based; 79 iBT). Electronic applications accepted.

University of Phoenix–Chicago Campus, College of Information Systems and Technology, Schaumburg, IL 60173-4399. Offers e-business (MBA); information systems (MIS); management (MM); technology management (MBA). Evening/weekend programs available. *Degree requirements:* For master's, thesis (for some programs). *Entrance requirements:* For master's, 3 years of work experience, minimum undergraduate GPA of 3.0. Additional exam requirements/recommendations for international students: Required—TOEFL (minimum score 550 paper-based; 79 iBT). Electronic applications accepted.

University of Phoenix–Cleveland Campus, College of Information Systems and Technology, Beachwood, OH 44122. Offers information management (MIS); technology management (MBA). Evening/weekend programs available. Postbaccalaureate distance learning degree programs offered (no on-campus study). *Degree requirements:* For master's, thesis (for some programs). *Entrance requirements:* For master's, minimum undergraduate GPA of 3.0, 3 years of work experience. Additional exam requirements/recommendations for international students: Required—TOEFL (minimum score 550 paper-based; 79 iBT). Electronic applications accepted.

University of Phoenix–Colorado Campus, College of Information Systems and Technology, Lone Tree, CO 80124-5453. Offers e-business (MBA); management (MIS); technology management (MBA). Evening/weekend programs available. Postbaccalaureate distance learning degree programs offered. *Degree requirements:* For master's, thesis (for some programs). *Entrance requirements:* For master's, minimum undergraduate GPA of 3.0, 3 years of work experience. Additional exam requirements/recommendations for international students: Required—TOEFL (minimum score 550 paper-based; 79 iBT). Electronic applications accepted.

University of Phoenix–Colorado Springs Downtown Campus, College of Information Systems and Technology, Colorado Springs, CO 80903. Offers technology management (MBA). Evening/weekend programs available. *Degree requirements:* For master's, thesis (for some programs). *Entrance requirements:* For master's, minimum undergraduate GPA of 3.0, 3 years of work experience. Additional exam requirements/recommendations for international students: Required—TOEFL (minimum score 550 paper-based; 79 iBT). Electronic applications accepted.

University of Phoenix–Columbia Campus, College of Information Systems and Technology, Columbia, SC 29223. Offers technology management (MBA).

University of Phoenix–Columbus Georgia Campus, College of Information Systems and Technology, Columbus, GA 31909. Offers e-business (MBA); information systems (MIS); technology management (MBA). Evening/weekend programs available. Postbaccalaureate distance learning degree programs offered. *Degree requirements:* For master's, thesis (for some programs). *Entrance requirements:* For master's, minimum undergraduate GPA of 3.0, 3 years of work experience. Additional exam requirements/recommendations for international students: Required—TOEFL (minimum score 550 paper-based; 79 iBT). Electronic applications accepted.

University of Phoenix–Dallas Campus, College of Information Systems and Technology, Dallas, TX 75251. Offers e-business (MBA); information systems (MIS); technology management (MBA). Evening/weekend programs available. *Degree requirements:* For master's, thesis (for some programs). *Entrance requirements:* For master's, minimum undergraduate GPA of 3.0, 3 years of work experience. Additional exam requirements/recommendations for international students: Required—TOEFL (minimum score 550 paper-based; 79 iBT). Electronic applications accepted.

University of Phoenix–Des Moines Campus, College of Information Systems and Technology, Des Moines, IA 50309. Offers information systems (MIS); technology management (MBA). Postbaccalaureate distance learning degree programs offered.

University of Phoenix–Hawaii Campus, College of Information Systems and Technology, Honolulu, HI 96813-4317. Offers information systems (MIS); technology management (MBA). Evening/weekend programs available. *Degree requirements:* For master's, thesis (for some programs). *Entrance requirements:* For master's, minimum undergraduate GPA of 3.0, 3 years of work experience. Additional exam requirements/recommendations for international students: Required—TOEFL (minimum score 550 paper-based; 79 iBT). Electronic applications accepted.

University of Phoenix–Houston Campus, College of Information Systems and Technology, Houston, TX 77079-2004. Offers e-business (MBA); information systems (MIS); technology management (MBA). Evening/weekend programs available. Postbaccalaureate distance learning degree programs offered. *Degree requirements:* For master's, comprehensive exam (for some programs), thesis. *Entrance requirements:* For master's, minimum undergraduate GPA of 3.0, 3 years of work experience. Additional exam requirements/recommendations for international students: Required—TOEFL (minimum score 550 paper-based; 79 iBT). Electronic applications accepted.

University of Phoenix–Idaho Campus, College of Information Systems and Technology, Meridian, ID 83642-5114. Offers information systems (MIS); technology management (MBA). Evening/weekend programs available. *Degree requirements:* For master's, thesis (for some programs). *Entrance requirements:* For master's, minimum undergraduate GPA of 3.0, 3 years of work experience. Additional exam requirements/recommendations for international students: Required—TOEFL (minimum score 550 paper-based). Electronic applications accepted.

University of Phoenix–Indianapolis Campus, College of Information Systems and Technology, Indianapolis, IN 46250-932. Offers information systems (MIS); technology management (MBA). Evening/weekend programs available. *Degree requirements:* For master's, thesis (for some programs). *Entrance requirements:* For master's, minimum undergraduate GPA of 3.0, 3 years of work experience. Additional exam requirements/recommendations for international students: Required—TOEFL (minimum score 550 paper-based). Electronic applications accepted.

University of Phoenix–Jersey City Campus, College of Information Systems and Technology, Jersey City, NJ 07310. Offers information systems (MIS); technology management (MBA). Postbaccalaureate distance learning degree programs offered.

University of Phoenix–Kansas City Campus, College of Information Systems and Technology, Kansas City, MO 64131. Offers management (MIS); technology management (MBA). Evening/weekend programs available. *Degree requirements:* For master's, thesis (for some programs). *Entrance requirements:* For master's, minimum undergraduate GPA of 3.0, 3 years of work experience. Additional exam requirements/recommendations for international students: Required—TOEFL (minimum score 550 paper-based). Electronic applications accepted.

University of Phoenix–Las Vegas Campus, College of Information Systems and Technology, Las Vegas, NV 89135. Offers information systems (MIS); technology management (MBA). Evening/weekend programs available. *Degree requirements:* For master's, thesis (for some programs). *Entrance requirements:* For master's, minimum undergraduate GPA of 3.0, 3 years of work experience. Additional exam requirements/recommendations for international students: Required—TOEFL (minimum score 550 paper-based; 79 iBT). Electronic applications accepted.

University of Phoenix–Maryland Campus, School of Business, Columbia, MD 21045-5424. Offers business administration (MBA); global management (MBA); technology management (MBA). Evening/weekend programs available. Postbaccalaureate distance learning degree programs offered. *Entrance requirements:* Additional exam requirements/recommendations for international students: Required—TOEFL, TOEIC (Test of English as an International Communication), Berlitz Online English Proficiency Exam, PTE, or IELTS. Electronic applications accepted. *Expenses:* Contact institution.

University of Phoenix–Memphis Campus, College of Information Systems and Technology, Cordova, TN 38018. Offers information systems (MIS); technology management (MBA).

University of Phoenix–Minneapolis/St. Paul Campus, College of Information Systems and Technology, St. Louis Park, MN 55426. Offers technology management (MBA).

University of Phoenix–Nashville Campus, College of Information Systems and Technology, Nashville, TN 37214-5048. Offers technology management (MBA). Evening/weekend programs available. *Degree requirements:* For master's, thesis (for some programs). *Entrance requirements:* For master's, 3 years of work experience, minimum undergraduate GPA of 3.0. Additional exam requirements/recommendations for international students: Required—TOEFL (minimum score 550 paper-based; 79 iBT). Electronic applications accepted.

University of Phoenix–New Mexico Campus, College of Information Systems and Technology, Albuquerque, NM 87113-1570. Offers e-business (MBA); information systems (MS); technology management (MBA). Evening/weekend programs available. *Degree requirements:* For master's, thesis (for some programs). *Entrance requirements:* For master's, minimum undergraduate GPA of 3.0, 3 years of work experience. Additional exam requirements/recommendations for international students: Required—TOEFL (minimum score 550 paper-based; 79 iBT). Electronic applications accepted.

University of Phoenix–Oklahoma City Campus, College of Information Systems and Technology, Oklahoma City, OK 73116-8244. Offers e-business (MBA); technology management (MBA). Evening/weekend programs available. *Degree requirements:* For master's, thesis (for some programs). *Entrance requirements:* For master's, minimum undergraduate GPA of 3.0, 3 years of work experience. Additional exam requirements/recommendations for international students: Required—TOEFL (minimum score 550 paper-based; 79 iBT). Electronic applications accepted.

University of Phoenix–Online Campus, School of Business, Phoenix, AZ 85034-7209. Offers accountancy (MS); accounting (MBA, Certificate); business administration (MBA); energy management (MBA); global management (MBA); health care management (MBA); human resource management (MBA, Certificate); human resources management (MM); management (MM); marketing (MBA, Certificate); project management (MBA, Certificate); public administration (MBA, MM); technology management (MBA). Evening/weekend programs available. Postbaccalaureate distance learning degree programs offered. *Entrance requirements:* Additional exam requirements/recommendations for international students: Required—TOEFL, TOEIC (Test of English as an International Communication), Berlitz Online English Proficiency Exam, PTE, or IELTS. Electronic applications accepted. *Expenses:* Contact institution.

University of Phoenix–Oregon Campus, College of Information Systems and Technology, Tigard, OR 97223. Offers information systems (MIS); technology management (MBA). Evening/weekend programs available. *Degree requirements:* For master's, thesis (for some programs). *Entrance requirements:* For master's, minimum undergraduate GPA of 2.5, 3 years work experience. Additional exam requirements/recommendations for international students: Required—TOEFL (minimum score 550 paper-based; 79 iBT). Electronic applications accepted.

University of Phoenix–Philadelphia Campus, College of Information Systems and Technology, Wayne, PA 19087-2121. Offers information systems (MIS); technology management (MBA). Evening/weekend programs available. *Degree requirements:* For master's, thesis (for some programs). *Entrance requirements:* For master's, 3 years of work experience, minimum undergraduate GPA of 3.0. Additional exam requirements/recommendations for international students: Required—TOEFL (minimum score 550 paper-based; 79 iBT). Electronic applications accepted.

University of Phoenix–Phoenix Campus, School of Business, Tempe, AZ 85282-2371. Offers accounting (MBA, MS, Certificate); business administration (MBA); energy management (MBA); global management (MBA); health care management (MBA); human resource management (MBA, Certificate); management (MM); marketing (MBA); project management (MBA); technology management (MBA). Evening/weekend programs available. Postbaccalaureate distance learning degree programs offered. *Entrance requirements:* Additional exam requirements/recommendations for international students: Required—TOEFL, TOEIC (Test of English as an International Communication), Berlitz Online English Proficiency Exam, PTE, or IELTS. Electronic applications accepted. *Expenses:* Contact institution.

University of Phoenix–Puerto Rico Campus, College of Information Systems and Technology, Guaynabo, PR 00968. Offers technology management (MBA). Evening/weekend programs available. *Degree requirements:* For master's, thesis (for some programs). *Entrance requirements:* For master's, minimum undergraduate GPA of 3.0, 3 years of work experience. Additional exam requirements/recommendations for international students: Required—TOEFL (minimum score 550 paper-based; 79 iBT). Electronic applications accepted.

University of Phoenix–Richmond-Virginia Beach Campus, College of Information Systems and Technology, Glen Allen, VA 23060. Offers information systems (MIS); technology management (MBA). Evening/weekend programs available. *Degree requirements:* For master's, thesis (for some programs). *Entrance requirements:* For master's, minimum undergraduate GPA of 3.0, 3 years work experience. Additional exam requirements/recommendations for international students: Required—TOEFL (minimum score 500 paper-based; 79 iBT). Electronic applications accepted.

University of Phoenix–Sacramento Valley Campus, College of Information Systems and Technology, Sacramento, CA 95833-3632. Offers management (MIS); technology management (MBA). Evening/weekend programs available. *Degree requirements:* For master's, thesis (for some programs). *Entrance requirements:* For master's, minimum undergraduate GPA of 3.0, 3 years work experience. Additional exam requirements/recommendations for international students: Required—TOEFL (minimum score 550 paper-based; 79 iBT). Electronic applications accepted.

University of Phoenix–San Antonio Campus, College of Information Systems and Technology, San Antonio, TX 78230. Offers information systems (MIS); technology management (MBA).

University of Phoenix–San Diego Campus, College of Information Systems and Technology, San Diego, CA 92123. Offers management (MIS); technology management (MBA). Evening/weekend programs available. *Degree requirements:* For master's, thesis (for some programs). *Entrance requirements:* For master's, minimum undergraduate GPA of 3.0, 3 years work experience. Additional exam requirements/recommendations for international students: Required—TOEFL (minimum score 550 paper-based; 79 iBT). Electronic applications accepted.

University of Phoenix–Savannah Campus, College of Information Systems and Technology, Savannah, GA 31405-7400. Offers information systems and technology (MIS); technology management (MBA).

University of Phoenix–Southern Arizona Campus, College of Information Systems and Technology, Tucson, AZ 85711. Offers information systems (MIS); technology management (MBA). Evening/weekend programs available. *Degree requirements:* For master's, thesis (for some programs). *Entrance requirements:* For master's, minimum undergraduate GPA of 3.0, 3 years of work experience. Additional exam requirements/recommendations for international students: Required—TOEFL (minimum score 550 paper-based; 79 iBT). Electronic applications accepted.

University of Phoenix–Southern California Campus, School of Business, Costa Mesa, CA 92626. Offers accounting (MBA); business administration (MBA); energy management (MBA); global management (MBA); health care management (MBA); human resource management (MBA); management (MM); marketing (MBA); project management (MBA); technology management (MBA). Evening/weekend programs available. Postbaccalaureate distance learning degree programs offered. *Entrance requirements:* Additional exam requirements/recommendations for international students: Required—TOEFL, TOEIC (Test of English as an International Communication), Berlitz Online English Proficiency Exam, PTE, or IELTS. Electronic applications accepted. *Expenses:* Contact institution.

University of Phoenix–Utah Campus, School of Business, Salt Lake City, UT 84123-4617. Offers accounting (MBA); business administration (MBA); global management (MBA); human resource management (MBA, MM); management (MM); marketing (MBA); technology management (MBA). Evening/weekend programs available. *Degree requirements:* For master's, thesis (for some programs). *Entrance requirements:* For master's, minimum undergraduate GPA of 3.0, 3 years of work experience. Additional exam requirements/recommendations for international students: Required—TOEFL (minimum score 550 paper-based; 79 iBT). Electronic applications accepted.

University of Portland, Dr. Robert B. Pamplin, Jr. School of Business, Portland, OR 97203-5798. Offers entrepreneurship (MBA); finance (MBA, MS); health care management (MBA); marketing (MBA); nonprofit management (EMBA); operations and technology management (MBA, MS); sustainability (MBA). *Accreditation:* AACSB. Part-time and evening/weekend programs available. *Faculty:* 26 full-time (5 women), 8 part-time/adjunct (1 woman). *Students:* 50 full-time (18 women), 83 part-time (37 women); includes 25 minority (2 Black or African American, non-Hispanic/Latino; 12 Asian, non-Hispanic/Latino; 4 Hispanic/Latino; 7 Two or more races, non-Hispanic/Latino), 20 international. Average age 31. In 2014, 67 master's awarded. *Entrance requirements:* For master's, GMAT, minimum GPA of 3.0, resume, 2 letters of recommendation. Additional exam requirements/recommendations for international students: Required—TOEFL (minimum score 570 paper-based; 89 iBT), IELTS (minimum score 7). *Application deadline:* For fall admission, 7/15 priority date for domestic and international students; for spring admission, 12/15 priority date for domestic and international students. Applications are processed on a rolling basis. Application fee: $50. *Expenses:* Expenses: Contact institution. *Financial support:* Federal Work-Study, scholarships/grants, and tuition waivers (partial) available. Support available to part-time students. Financial award application deadline: 3/1; financial award applicants required to submit FAFSA. *Unit head:* Melissa McCarthy, Director, 503-943-7224, E-mail: mba-up@up.edu.
Website: http://business.up.edu/mba/default.aspx?cid-1179&pid-6450.

University of St. Thomas, Graduate Studies, School of Engineering, St. Paul, MN 55105-1096. Offers electrical engineering (MS); manufacturing engineering and operations (MS); manufacturing systems (Certificate); mechanical engineering (MS); medical device development (Certificate); regulatory science (MS); software engineering (MS); software management (MS); systems engineering (MS); technology leadership (Certificate); technology management (MS). *Accreditation:* ABET (one or more programs are accredited). *Entrance requirements:* For master's, resume, official transcripts. Additional exam requirements/recommendations for international students: Required—TOEFL (minimum score 550 paper-based). Electronic applications accepted. *Expenses:* Contact institution.

University of South Florida, University College/Distance Education, Tampa, FL 33620-9951. *Unit head:* Kathy Barnes, Interdisciplinary Programs Coordinator, 813-974-8031, Fax: 813-974-7061, E-mail: barnesk@usf.edu. *Application contact:* Karen Tylinski, Metro Initiatives, 813-974-9943, Fax: 813-974-7061, E-mail: ktylinsk@usf.edu.
Website: http://www.usf.edu/innovative-education/.

The University of Texas at Dallas, Naveen Jindal School of Management, Program in Information Systems and Operations Management, Richardson, TX 75080. Offers business analytics (MS); information technology and management (MS); supply chain management (MS). Part-time and evening/weekend programs available. *Faculty:* 30 full-time (3 women), 13 part-time/adjunct (4 women). *Students:* 882 full-time (339 women), 287 part-time (120 women); includes 85 minority (22 Black or African American, non-Hispanic/Latino; 55 Asian, non-Hispanic/Latino; 4 Hispanic/Latino; 4 Two or more races, non-Hispanic/Latino), 1,008 international. Average age 26. 1,956 applicants, 52% accepted, 546 enrolled. In 2014, 403 master's awarded. *Degree requirements:* For master's, thesis optional. *Entrance requirements:* For master's, GMAT. Additional exam requirements/recommendations for international students: Required—TOEFL (minimum score 550 paper-based). *Application deadline:* For fall admission, 7/15 for domestic students, 5/1 priority date for international students; for spring admission, 11/15 for domestic students, 9/1 priority date for international students. Applications are processed on a rolling basis. Application fee: $50 ($100 for international students). Electronic applications accepted. *Expenses:* Tuition, state resident: full-time $11,940; part-time $663 per credit. Tuition, nonresident: full-time $22,282; part-time $1238 per credit. *Financial support:* In 2014–15, 204 students received support, including 4 research assistantships with partial tuition reimbursements available (averaging $14,000 per year), 24 teaching assistantships with partial tuition reimbursements available (averaging $10,050 per year); career-related internships or fieldwork, Federal Work-Study, institutionally sponsored loans, scholarships/grants, and unspecified assistantships also available. Support available to part-time students. Financial award application deadline: 4/30; financial award applicants required to submit FAFSA. *Faculty research:* Technology marketing, measuring information work productivity, electronic commerce, decision support systems, data quality. *Unit head:* Dr. Milind Dawande, Area Coordinator, 972-883-2793, E-mail: milind@utdallas.edu. *Application contact:* Dr. Ozalp Ozer, PhD Area Coordinator, 972-883-2316, E-mail: oozer@utdallas.edu.
Website: http://jindal.utdallas.edu/isom/.

The University of Texas at San Antonio, College of Business, Department of Information Systems and Cyber Security, San Antonio, TX 78249-0617. Offers cyber security (MSIT); information technology (MS, PhD), including cyber security (MS); management of technology (MBA). Part-time and evening/weekend programs available. *Faculty:* 9 full-time (2 women), 3 part-time/adjunct (0 women). *Students:* 33 full-time (8 women), 75 part-time (21 women); includes 26 minority (1 Black or African American, non-Hispanic/Latino; 1 American Indian or Alaska Native, non-Hispanic/Latino; 3 Asian, non-Hispanic/Latino; 18 Hispanic/Latino; 1 Native Hawaiian or other Pacific Islander, non-Hispanic/Latino; 2 Two or more races, non-Hispanic/Latino), 22 international. Average age 31. 107 applicants, 56% accepted, 33 enrolled. In 2014, 33 master's, 3 doctorates awarded. *Degree requirements:* For master's, comprehensive exam (for some programs), thesis optional; for doctorate, comprehensive exam, thesis/dissertation. *Entrance requirements:* For master's and doctorate, GMAT/GRE, TOEFL/IELTS, official transcripts, statement of purpose, letters of recommendation. Additional exam requirements/recommendations for international students: Required—TOEFL (minimum score 550 paper-based; 79 iBT), IELTS (minimum score 6.5). *Application deadline:* For fall admission, 7/1 for domestic students, 4/1 for international students; for spring admission, 11/1 for domestic students, 9/1 for international students. Applications are processed on a rolling basis. Application fee: $45 ($80 for international students). Electronic applications accepted. *Expenses:* Expenses: Contact institution. *Financial support:* In 2014–15, 15 students received support, including 1 fellowship with full tuition reimbursement available (averaging $25,000 per year), 10 research assistantships with full and partial tuition reimbursements available (averaging $9,000 per year), 12 teaching assistantships with full and partial tuition reimbursements available (averaging $9,000 per year); scholarships/grants, health care benefits, and unspecified assistantships also available. Support available to part-time students. Financial award application deadline: 2/15. *Faculty research:* Cyber security, digital forensics, economics of information systems, information systems privacy, information technology adoption. *Total annual research expenditures:* $1.5 million. *Unit head:* Dr. Yoris A. Au, Chair/Associate Professor, 210-458-6337, Fax: 210-458-6305, E-mail: yoris.au@utsa.edu. *Application contact:* Graduate Advisor of Record.
Website: http://business.utsa.edu/directory/index.aspx?DepID=16.

University of Toronto, Faculty of Medicine, Program in Management of Innovation, Toronto, ON M5S 2J7, Canada. Offers MMI. *Entrance requirements:* For master's, GMAT, minimum B+ average, 2 reference letters, resume/curriculum vitae. Additional exam requirements/recommendations for international students: Required—TOEFL (minimum score 580 paper-based; 93 iBT), TWE (minimum score 5). Electronic applications accepted.

University of Washington, Graduate School, Michael G. Foster School of Business, Seattle, WA 98195-3200. Offers auditing and assurance (MP Acc); business administration (MBA, PhD); executive business administration (MBA); global executive business administration (MBA); taxation (MP Acc); technology management (MBA); JD/MBA; MBA/MAIS; MBA/MHA. *Accreditation:* AACSB. Part-time and evening/weekend programs available. *Faculty:* 101 full-time (26 women), 56 part-time/adjunct (25 women). *Students:* 400 full-time (144 women), 558 part-time (173 women); includes 261 minority (18 Black or African American, non-Hispanic/Latino; 5 American Indian or Alaska Native, non-Hispanic/Latino; 201 Asian, non-Hispanic/Latino; 22 Hispanic/Latino; 6 Native Hawaiian or other Pacific Islander, non-Hispanic/Latino; 9 Two or more races, non-Hispanic/Latino), 95 international. Average age 32. 2,857 applicants, 21% accepted, 429 enrolled. In 2014, 506 master's, 8 doctorates awarded. Terminal master's awarded for partial completion of doctoral program. *Degree requirements:* For doctorate, comprehensive exam, thesis/dissertation. *Entrance requirements:* For master's and doctorate, GMAT, GRE. Additional exam requirements/recommendations for

international students: Required—TOEFL (minimum score 600 paper-based; 100 iBT). *Application deadline:* For fall admission, 3/15 for domestic students, 1/15 for international students. Application fee: $85. Electronic applications accepted. *Expenses:* Expenses: Contact institution. *Financial support:* Fellowships with partial tuition reimbursements, research assistantships with partial tuition reimbursements, teaching assistantships with partial tuition reimbursements, Federal Work-Study, institutionally sponsored loans, and scholarships/grants available. Financial award application deadline: 2/28; financial award applicants required to submit FAFSA. *Faculty research:* Finance, marketing, organizational behavior, information technology, strategy. *Unit head:* Dr. James Jiambalvo, Dean, 206-543-4750. *Application contact:* Erin Town, Director of Admissions, 206-543-4661, Fax: 206-616-7351, E-mail: mba@uw.edu.
Website: http://www.foster.washington.edu/.

University of Waterloo, Graduate Studies, Centre for Business, Entrepreneurship and Technology, Waterloo, ON N2L 3G1, Canada. Offers MBET. *Entrance requirements:* For master's, honors degree. Additional exam requirements/recommendations for international students: Required—TOEFL (minimum score 550 paper-based), TWE. Electronic applications accepted.

University of Waterloo, Graduate Studies, Faculty of Engineering, Department of Management Sciences, Waterloo, ON N2L 3G1, Canada. Offers applied operations research (MA Sc, MMS, PhD); information systems (MA Sc, MMS, PhD); management of technology (MA Sc, MMS, PhD). Part-time programs available. Postbaccalaureate distance learning degree programs offered (no on-campus study). *Degree requirements:* For master's, research paper or thesis; for doctorate, comprehensive exam, thesis/dissertation. *Entrance requirements:* For master's, GMAT or GRE, honors degree, minimum B average, resume; for doctorate, GMAT or GRE, master's degree, minimum A- average, resumé. Additional exam requirements/recommendations for international students: Required—TOEFL, TWE. *Faculty research:* Operations research, manufacturing systems, scheduling, information systems.

University of Wisconsin–Madison, Graduate School, Wisconsin School of Business, Wisconsin Full-Time MBA Program, Madison, WI 53706. Offers applied security analysis (MBA); arts administration (MBA); brand and product management (MBA); corporate finance and investment banking (MBA); marketing research (MBA); operations and technology management (MBA); real estate (MBA); risk management and insurance (MBA); strategic human resource management (MBA); supply chain management (MBA). *Faculty:* 55 full-time (9 women), 13 part-time/adjunct (4 women). *Students:* 199 full-time (72 women); includes 30 minority (11 Black or African American, non-Hispanic/Latino; 1 American Indian or Alaska Native, non-Hispanic/Latino; 3 Asian, non-Hispanic/Latino; 12 Hispanic/Latino; 3 Two or more races, non-Hispanic/Latino), 39 international. Average age 28. 473 applicants, 29% accepted, 100 enrolled. In 2014, 92 master's awarded. *Entrance requirements:* For master's, GMAT or GRE, bachelor's or equivalent degree, 2 years of work experience, essay, one letter of recommendation, resume. Additional exam requirements/recommendations for international students: Required—TOEFL (minimum score 100 iBT), IELTS (minimum score 7.5). *Application deadline:* For fall admission, 11/4 for domestic and international students; for winter admission, 2/3 for domestic and international students; for spring admission, 4/28 for domestic students, 4/2 for international students. Applications are processed on a rolling basis. Application fee: $56. Electronic applications accepted. *Expenses:* Expenses: Contact institution. *Financial support:* In 2014–15, 157 students received support, including 10 fellowships with full tuition reimbursements available (averaging $37,956 per year), 82 research assistantships with full tuition reimbursements available (averaging $28,175 per year), 50 teaching assistantships with full tuition reimbursements available (averaging $28,175 per year); scholarships/grants, health care benefits, and unspecified assistantships also available. Financial award application deadline: 4/28; financial award applicants required to submit FAFSA. *Faculty research:* Market consequences of International Financial Reporting Standards (IFRS), inter-firm relationships and strategic partnerships, application of Bayesian statistical methods and applied probability models to understanding individuals' behaviors in the context of customer relationship management (CRM) applications, liquidity provision and the structure of financial markets, strategic management of global startups. *Unit head:* Prof. Ella Mae Matsumura, Associate Dean Full-time MBA Program, 608-262-9731, E-mail: ematsumura@bus.wisc.edu. *Application contact:* Betsy Kacizak, Director of Admissions and Recruiting, Full-time MBA Program, 608-262-4000, E-mail: mlewitzke@bus.wisc.edu.
Website: http://www.bus.wisc.edu/mba.

University of Wisconsin–Stout, Graduate School, College of Technology, Engineering, and Management, Program in Technology Management, Menomonie, WI 54751. Offers MS. Part-time programs available. *Degree requirements:* For master's, thesis. *Entrance requirements:* For master's, minimum GPA of 2.75. Additional exam requirements/recommendations for international students: Required—TOEFL (minimum score 500 paper-based; 61 iBT). Electronic applications accepted. *Faculty research:* Miniature engines, solid modeling, packaging, lean manufacturing, supply chain management.

University of Wisconsin–Whitewater, School of Graduate Studies, College of Business and Economics, Program in Business Administration, Whitewater, WI 53190-1790. Offers finance (MBA); human resource management (MBA); information technology management (MBA); international business (MBA); management (MBA); marketing (MBA); operations and supply chain management (MBA). *Accreditation:* AACSB. Part-time and evening/weekend programs available. Postbaccalaureate distance learning degree programs offered (no on-campus study). *Entrance requirements:* For master's, GMAT or GRE, minimum AACSB index of 1000, minimum GPA of 2.75. Additional exam requirements/recommendations for international students: Required—TOEFL (minimum score 550 paper-based; 80 iBT), IELTS (minimum score 6). Electronic applications accepted. *Faculty research:* Interface between social institutions and individual behavior, technology and innovation management, occupational mental health, workplace deviance and workplace romance.

Washington State University, Voiland College of Engineering and Architecture, Program in Engineering and Technology Management, Pullman, WA 99164-2785. Offers METM, Certificate. Program offered through the Global (online) campus. Part-time and evening/weekend programs available. Postbaccalaureate distance learning degree programs offered (no on-campus study). *Students:* 78 part-time (15 women); includes 22 minority (6 Black or African American, non-Hispanic/Latino; 7 Asian, non-Hispanic/Latino; 6 Hispanic/Latino; 3 Two or more races, non-Hispanic/Latino), 6 international. Average age 34. 30 applicants, 73% accepted, 21 enrolled. In 2014, 19 master's, 17 Certificates awarded. *Degree requirements:* For master's, one foreign language, comprehensive exam (for some programs). *Entrance requirements:* Additional exam requirements/recommendations for international students: Required—TOEFL. *Application deadline:* For fall admission, 7/1 for domestic students, 6/1 for international students; for winter admission, 9/1 for international students; for spring admission, 10/1 for domestic students. Applications are processed on a rolling basis. Application fee: $75. Electronic applications accepted. *Expenses:* Tuition, state resident: full-time $11,768. Tuition, nonresident: full-time $25,200. *Required fees:* $960. Tuition and fees vary according to program. *Faculty research:* Constraints management, Six Sigma quality management, supply chain management, project management, construction management, systems engineering management, manufacturing leadership. *Unit head:* Dr. John Ringo, Program Director, 509-335-5595, Fax: 509-335-7290, E-mail: ringo@wsu.edu. *Application contact:* Patti Elshafei, Program Support Supervisor, 509-335-0125, Fax: 509-335-4725, E-mail: etm@wsu.edu.
Website: http://etm.wsu.edu/.

Wentworth Institute of Technology, Program in Technology Management–Online, Boston, MA 02115-5998. Offers MS. Part-time and evening/weekend programs available. Postbaccalaureate distance learning degree programs offered (no on-campus study). *Faculty:* 1 full-time, 3 part-time/adjunct. *Students:* Average age 32. 42 applicants, 60% accepted, 25 enrolled. *Degree requirements:* For master's, thesis optional, Capstone. *Entrance requirements:* For master's, resume, official transcripts, two professional recommendations, BA or BS, one year of professional experience in a technical role and/or technical organization and a statement of purpose. Additional exam requirements/recommendations for international students: Required—TOEFL (minimum score 525 paper-based). *Application deadline:* For fall admission, 7/15 for domestic and international students; for spring admission, 12/15 for domestic and international students. Applications are processed on a rolling basis. Application fee: $50. Electronic applications accepted. *Financial support:* Application deadline: 5/1; applicants required to submit FAFSA. *Unit head:* Philip Hammond, Director of graduate Programs, 617-989-4594, Fax: 617-989-4399, E-mail: hammondp1@wit.edu.

Western Kentucky University, Graduate Studies, Ogden College of Science and Engineering, Department of Architectural and Manufacturing Sciences, Bowling Green, KY 42101. Offers technology management (MS).

Westminster College, The Bill and Vieve Gore School of Business, Salt Lake City, UT 84105-3697. Offers accountancy (M Acc); business administration (MBA, Certificate); technology management (MBATM). *Accreditation:* ACBSP. Part-time and evening/weekend programs available. Postbaccalaureate distance learning degree programs offered (minimal on-campus study). *Faculty:* 27 full-time (8 women), 8 part-time/adjunct (4 women). *Students:* 220 full-time (78 women), 133 part-time (41 women); includes 76 minority (6 Black or African American, non-Hispanic/Latino; 2 American Indian or Alaska Native, non-Hispanic/Latino; 38 Asian, non-Hispanic/Latino; 27 Hispanic/Latino; 1 Native Hawaiian or other Pacific Islander, non-Hispanic/Latino; 2 Two or more races, non-Hispanic/Latino), 18 international. Average age 33. 162 applicants, 73% accepted, 60 enrolled. In 2014, 201 master's, 26 other advanced degrees awarded. *Entrance requirements:* For master's, GMAT, 2 professional recommendations, employer letter of support, personal resume, essay, official transcripts. Additional exam requirements/recommendations for international students: Required—TOEFL (minimum score 600 paper-based; 100 iBT), IELTS (minimum score 7.5). *Application deadline:* For fall admission, 9/30 for domestic students, 5/31 for international students; for spring admission, 1/1 for domestic students; for summer admission, 5/1 for domestic students. Application fee: $50. Electronic applications accepted. *Expenses:* Expenses: Contact institution. *Financial support:* In 2014–15, 94 students received support. Career-related internships or fieldwork, scholarships/grants, unspecified assistantships, and tuition reimbursements, tuition remission available. Support available to part-time students. Financial award applicants required to submit FAFSA. *Faculty research:* Innovation and entrepreneurship, business strategy and change, financial analysis and capital budgeting, leadership development, knowledge management. *Unit head:* Preston Chiaro, Dean, Gore School of Business, 801-832-2600, Fax: 801-832-3106, E-mail: pchiaro@westminstercollege.edu. *Application contact:* Dr. John Baworowsky, Vice President of Enrollment Management, 801-832-2200, Fax: 801-832-3101, E-mail: admission@westminstercollege.edu.
Website: http://www.westminstercollege.edu/mba/.

Wilfrid Laurier University, Faculty of Graduate and Postdoctoral Studies, School of Business and Economics, Department of Business, Waterloo, ON N2L 3C5, Canada. Offers accounting (PhD); finance (M Fin); financial economics (PhD); marketing (PhD); operations and supply chain management (PhD); organizational behavior and human resource management (M Sc); organizational behaviour and human resource management (PhD); supply chain management (M Sc); technology management (EMTM). *Accreditation:* AACSB. Part-time and evening/weekend programs available. *Degree requirements:* For master's, thesis optional; for doctorate, comprehensive exam, thesis/dissertation. *Entrance requirements:* For master's, GMAT, 4-year honors degree with minimum B+ average; for doctorate, GMAT, master's degree, minimum B+ average. Additional exam requirements/recommendations for international students: Required—TOEFL (minimum score 89 iBT). Electronic applications accepted. *Faculty research:* Financial economics, management and organizational behavior, operations and supply chain management.

Operations Research

Air Force Institute of Technology, Graduate School of Engineering and Management, Department of Operational Sciences, Dayton, OH 45433-7765. Offers logistics management (MS); operations research (MS, PhD); space operations (MS). Part-time programs available. *Degree requirements:* For master's, thesis; for doctorate, thesis/dissertation. *Entrance requirements:* For doctorate, GRE General Test, minimum GPA of 3.0, U.S. citizenship. *Faculty research:* Optimization, simulation, combat modeling and analysis, reliability and maintainability, resource scheduling.

Bowling Green State University, Graduate College, College of Arts and Sciences, Department of Computer Science, Bowling Green, OH 43403. Offers computer science (MS), including operations research, parallel and distributed computing, software engineering. Part-time programs available. *Degree requirements:* For master's, thesis or alternative. *Entrance requirements:* For master's, GRE General Test. Additional exam requirements/recommendations for international students: Required—TOEFL. Electronic applications accepted. *Faculty research:* Artificial intelligence, real time and concurrent programming languages, behavioral aspects of computing, network protocols.

Capella University, School of Business and Technology, Master's Programs in Business, Minneapolis, MN 55402. Offers accounting (MBA); business analysis (MS);

business intelligence (MBA); entrepreneurship (MBA); finance (MBA); general business administration (MBA); general human resource management (MS); general leadership (MS); health care management (MBA); human resource management (MBA); marketing (MBA); project management (MBA, MS).

Carnegie Mellon University, Tepper School of Business, Program in Operations Research, Pittsburgh, PA 15213-3891. Offers PhD. *Degree requirements:* For doctorate, thesis/dissertation. *Entrance requirements:* For doctorate, GMAT or GRE General Test.

Case Western Reserve University, Weatherhead School of Management, Department of Operations, Cleveland, OH 44106. Offers operations and supply chain management (MSM); operations research (PhD); MBA/MSM. Part-time programs available. *Degree requirements:* For doctorate, thesis/dissertation. *Entrance requirements:* For master's, GRE General Test; for doctorate, GMAT, GRE General Test. *Faculty research:* Mathematical finance, mathematical programming, scheduling, stochastic optimization, environmental/energy models.

The Catholic University of America, School of Business and Economics, Washington, DC 20064. Offers accounting (MS); business analysis (MS); integral economic development management (MA); integral economic development policy (MA); international political economics (MA). Part-time programs available. *Faculty:* 21 full-time (7 women), 25 part-time/adjunct (4 women). *Students:* 56 full-time (37 women), 13 part-time (6 women); includes 23 minority (11 Black or African American, non-Hispanic/Latino; 5 Asian, non-Hispanic/Latino; 7 Hispanic/Latino), 21 international. Average age 27. 92 applicants, 64% accepted, 40 enrolled. In 2014, 30 master's awarded. *Degree requirements:* For master's, comprehensive exam. *Entrance requirements:* For master's, GRE General Test, statement of purpose, official copies of academic transcripts, three letters of recommendation. Additional exam requirements/recommendations for international students: Required—TOEFL (minimum score 580 paper-based). *Application deadline:* For fall admission, 7/15 priority date for domestic students, 7/1 for international students; for spring admission, 11/15 priority date for domestic students, 11/1 for international students. Applications are processed on a rolling basis. Application fee: $55. Electronic applications accepted. *Expenses: Tuition:* Full-time $40,200; part-time $1600 per credit hour. *Required fees:* $400; $195 per semester. One-time fee: $425. *Financial support:* Fellowships, research assistantships, teaching assistantships, Federal Work-Study, scholarships/grants, tuition waivers (full and partial), and unspecified assistantships available. Financial award application deadline: 2/1; financial award applicants required to submit FAFSA. *Faculty research:* Integrity of the marketing process, economics of energy and the environment, emerging markets, social change, international finance and economic development. *Total annual research expenditures:* $105,784. *Unit head:* Dr. Andrew V. Abela, Chair, 202-319-5235, Fax: 202-319-4426, E-mail: abela@cua.edu. *Application contact:* Director of Graduate Admissions, 202-319-5057, Fax: 202-319-6533, E-mail: cua-admissions@cua.edu.
Website: http://business.cua.edu/.

Claremont Graduate University, Graduate Programs, Institute of Mathematical Sciences, Claremont, CA 91711-6160. Offers computational and systems biology (PhD); computational mathematics and numerical analysis (MA, MS); computational science (PhD); engineering and industrial applied mathematics (PhD); mathematics (PhD); operations research and statistics (MA, MS); physical applied mathematics (MA, MS); pure mathematics (MA, MS); scientific computing (MA, MS); systems and control theory (MA, MS). Part-time programs available. *Faculty:* 6 full-time (1 woman), 2 part-time/adjunct (0 women). *Students:* 40 full-time (14 women), 34 part-time (14 women); includes 20 minority (4 Black or African American, non-Hispanic/Latino; 8 Asian, non-Hispanic/Latino; 7 Hispanic/Latino; 1 Two or more races, non-Hispanic/Latino), 28 international. Average age 32. In 2014, 30 master's, 13 doctorates awarded. Terminal master's awarded for partial completion of doctoral program. *Entrance requirements:* For master's and doctorate, GRE General Test. Additional exam requirements/recommendations for international students: Required—TOEFL (minimum score 550 paper-based; 80 iBT). *Application deadline:* For fall admission, 2/1 priority date for domestic and international students. Applications are processed on a rolling basis. Application fee: $80. Electronic applications accepted. *Expenses: Tuition:* Full-time $41,784; part-time $1741 per credit. *Required fees:* $600; $300 per semester. *Financial support:* Fellowships, research assistantships, Federal Work-Study, institutionally sponsored loans, scholarships/grants, and tuition waivers (full and partial) available. Support available to part-time students. Financial award application deadline: 2/15; financial award applicants required to submit FAFSA. *Unit head:* Allon Percus, Director, 909-607-0744, E-mail: allon.percus@cgu.edu. *Application contact:* Charlotte Ballesteros, Coordinator, 909-621-8080, Fax: 909-607-8261, E-mail: charlotte.ballesteros@cgu.edu.
Website: http://www.cgu.edu/pages/168.asp.

Clemson University, Graduate School, College of Engineering and Science, Department of Mathematical Sciences, Clemson, SC 29634. Offers applied and pure analysis (MS, PhD); computational mathematics (MS, PhD); operations research (MS, PhD); statistics (MS, PhD). Part-time programs available. *Faculty:* 76 full-time (32 women), 11 part-time/adjunct (7 women). *Students:* 115 full-time (44 women), 5 part-time (2 women); includes 5 minority (1 Black or African American, non-Hispanic/Latino; 1 American Indian or Alaska Native, non-Hispanic/Latino; 1 Asian, non-Hispanic/Latino; 2 Two or more races, non-Hispanic/Latino), 59 international. Average age 27. 174 applicants, 56% accepted, 19 enrolled. In 2014, 31 master's, 14 doctorates awarded. *Degree requirements:* For master's, final project or thesis; for doctorate, comprehensive exam, thesis/dissertation, 3 qualifying exams. *Entrance requirements:* For master's and doctorate, GRE General Test, General Subject Test (mathematics). Additional exam requirements/recommendations for international students: Required—TOEFL. *Application deadline:* For fall admission, 1/15 priority date for domestic and international students; for spring admission, 10/1 priority date for domestic students, 9/15 priority date for international students. Applications are processed on a rolling basis. Application fee: $70 ($80 for international students). Electronic applications accepted. *Financial support:* In 2014–15, 101 students received support, including 4 fellowships with full and partial tuition reimbursements available (averaging $5,000 per year), 7 research assistantships with partial tuition reimbursements available (averaging $21,619 per year), 94 teaching assistantships with partial tuition reimbursements available (averaging $20,835 per year); career-related internships or fieldwork, institutionally sponsored loans, scholarships/grants, health care benefits, and unspecified assistantships also available. Support available to part-time students. Financial award application deadline: 4/15. *Faculty research:* Applied and computational analysis, cryptography, discrete mathematics, optimization, statistics. *Total annual research expenditures:* $811,214. *Unit head:* Prof. James B. Coykendall, Chair, 864-656-0862, Fax: 864-656-5230, E-mail: jcoyken@clemson.edu. *Application contact:* Prof. Kevin L. James, Graduate Coordinator, 864-656-1516, Fax: 864-656-5230, E-mail: mthgrad@clemson.edu.
Website: http://www.clemson.edu/ces/departments/math/index.html.

The College of William and Mary, Faculty of Arts and Sciences, Department of Computer Science, Program in Computational Operations Research, Williamsburg, VA 23187-8795. Offers MS. Part-time programs available. *Faculty:* 8 full-time (3 women), 1 part-time/adjunct (0 women). *Students:* 21 full-time (8 women), 1 (woman) part-time; includes 1 minority (Black or African American, non-Hispanic/Latino), 3 international. Average age 25. 24 applicants, 92% accepted, 13 enrolled. In 2014, 15 master's awarded. *Degree requirements:* For master's, research project. *Entrance requirements:* For master's, GRE General Test, minimum GPA of 3.0. Additional exam requirements/recommendations for international students: Required—TOEFL. *Application deadline:* For fall admission, 3/1 priority date for domestic students, 3/15 priority date for international students; for spring admission, 11/1 for domestic and international students. Applications are processed on a rolling basis. Application fee: $45. Electronic applications accepted. *Financial support:* In 2014–15, 13 students received support, including 6 fellowships (averaging $9,000 per year), 7 teaching assistantships with full tuition reimbursements available (averaging $13,500 per year); scholarships/grants, tuition waivers (full), and unspecified assistantships also available. Financial award application deadline: 3/1; financial award applicants required to submit FAFSA. *Faculty research:* Metaheuristics, reliability, optimization, statistics, networks. *Unit head:* Dr. Rex Kincaid, Professor, 757-221-2038, Fax: 757-221-1717, E-mail: rrkinc@math.wm.edu. *Application contact:* Vanessa Godwin, Administrative Director, 757-221-3455, Fax: 757-221-1717, E-mail: cor@cs.wm.edu.
Website: http://www.wm.edu/as/mathematics/graduate/cor/index.php.

Colorado School of Mines, Graduate School, Division of Economics and Business, Golden, CO 80401. Offers engineering and technology management (MS); mineral economics (PhD); operations research and engineering (PhD). Part-time programs available. *Faculty:* 11 full-time (3 women), 24 part-time/adjunct (4 women). *Students:* 114 full-time (21 women), 22 part-time (5 women); includes 17 minority (3 Black or African American, non-Hispanic/Latino; 4 Asian, non-Hispanic/Latino; 8 Hispanic/Latino; 2 Two or more races, non-Hispanic/Latino), 36 international. Average age 30. 172 applicants, 66% accepted, 62 enrolled. In 2014, 60 master's, 4 doctorates awarded. *Degree requirements:* For master's, thesis (for some programs); for doctorate, comprehensive exam, thesis/dissertation. *Entrance requirements:* For master's and doctorate, GRE General Test. Additional exam requirements/recommendations for international students: Required—TOEFL (minimum score 550 paper-based; 80 iBT). *Application deadline:* For fall admission, 12/15 priority date for domestic and international students; for spring admission, 9/1 priority date for domestic and international students. Application fee: $50 ($70 for international students). Electronic applications accepted. *Financial support:* In 2014–15, 45 students received support, including 4 fellowships with full tuition reimbursements available (averaging $21,120 per year), 8 research assistantships with full tuition reimbursements available (averaging $21,120 per year), 23 teaching assistantships with full tuition reimbursements available (averaging $21,120 per year); scholarships/grants, health care benefits, and unspecified assistantships also available. Financial award application deadline: 1/15; financial award applicants required to submit FAFSA. *Faculty research:* International trade, resource and environmental economics, energy economics, operations research. *Total annual research expenditures:* $371,588. *Unit head:* Dr. Michael Walls, Interim Director, 303-273-3492, Fax: 303-273-3416, E-mail: mwalls@mines.edu. *Application contact:* Kathleen Martin, Program Assistant, 303-273-3482, Fax: 303-273-3416, E-mail: kmartin@mines.edu.
Website: http://econbus.mines.edu.

Columbia University, Fu Foundation School of Engineering and Applied Science, Department of Industrial Engineering and Operations Research, New York, NY 10027. Offers financial engineering (MS); industrial engineering and operations research (MS, Eng Sc D, PhD); management science and engineering (MS); MS/MBA. Part-time and evening/weekend programs available. Postbaccalaureate distance learning degree programs offered (no on-campus study). *Faculty:* 22 full-time (3 women), 50 part-time/adjunct (2 women). *Students:* 417 full-time (152 women), 258 part-time (95 women); includes 37 minority (27 Asian, non-Hispanic/Latino; 7 Hispanic/Latino; 3 Two or more races, non-Hispanic/Latino), 598 international. 2,369 applicants, 27% accepted, 364 enrolled. In 2014, 331 master's, 13 doctorates awarded. *Degree requirements:* For doctorate, thesis/dissertation, oral and written qualifying exams. *Entrance requirements:* For master's and doctorate, GRE General Test. Additional exam requirements/recommendations for international students: Required—TOEFL, IELTS, PTE. *Application deadline:* For fall admission, 12/15 priority date for domestic and international students; for spring admission, 10/1 priority date for domestic and international students. Application fee: $85. Electronic applications accepted. *Financial support:* In 2014–15, 49 students received support, including 1 fellowship with full tuition reimbursement available (averaging $25,000 per year), 24 research assistantships with full tuition reimbursements available (averaging $21,485 per year), 23 teaching assistantships with full tuition reimbursements available (averaging $21,485 per year); health care benefits and funding for travel to conferences also available. Financial award application deadline: 12/15; financial award applicants required to submit FAFSA. *Faculty research:* Applied probability and optimization; financial engineering, modeling risk including credit risk and systemic risk, asset allocation, portfolio execution, behavioral finance, agent-based model in finance; revenue management; management and optimization of service systems, call centers, capacity allocation in healthcare systems, inventory control for vaccines; energy, smart grids, demand shaping, managing renewable energy sources, energy-aware scheduling. *Unit head:* Dr. Garud N. Iyengar, Professor and Department Chair, Industrial Engineering and Operations Research, 212-854-4594, Fax: 212-854-8103, E-mail: garud@ieor.columbia.edu. *Application contact:* Adina Berrios Brooks, Associate Director, Graduate Admissions and Student Affairs, 212-854-1934, Fax: 212-854-8103, E-mail: admit@ieor.columbia.edu.
Website: http://www.ieor.columbia.edu/.

Cornell University, Graduate School, Graduate Fields of Engineering, Field of Operations Research and Information Engineering, Ithaca, NY 14853. Offers applied probability and statistics (PhD); manufacturing systems engineering (PhD); mathematical programming (PhD); operations research and industrial engineering (M Eng). *Degree requirements:* For doctorate, comprehensive exam, thesis/dissertation. *Entrance requirements:* For master's and doctorate, GRE General Test, 3 letters of recommendation. Additional exam requirements/recommendations for international students: Required—TOEFL (minimum score 600 paper-based; 100 iBT). Electronic applications accepted. *Faculty research:* Mathematical programming and combinatorial optimization, statistics, stochastic processes, mathematical finance, simulation, manufacturing, e-commerce.

École Polytechnique de Montréal, Graduate Programs, Department of Mathematics and Industrial Engineering, Montréal, QC H3C 3A7, Canada. Offers ergonomy (M Eng, M Sc A, DESS); mathematical method in CA engineering (M Eng, M Sc A, PhD); operational research (M Eng, M Sc A, PhD); production (M Eng, M Sc A); technology management (M Eng, M Sc A). DESS program offered jointly with HEC Montreal and Université de Montréal. Part-time programs available. *Degree requirements:* For master's, one foreign language, thesis. *Entrance requirements:* For master's, minimum GPA of 2.75. *Faculty research:* Use of computers in organizations.

Florida Institute of Technology, Graduate Programs, Extended Studies Division, Melbourne, FL 32901-6975. Offers acquisition and contract management (MS); aerospace engineering (MS); business administration (MBA, DBA); computer information systems (MS); computer science (MS); electrical engineering (MS); engineering management (MS); human resources management (MS); logistics management (MS), including humanitarian and disaster relief logistics; management (MS), including acquisition and contract management, e-business, human resources

management, information systems, logistics management, management, transportation management; material acquisition management (MS); mechanical engineering (MS); operations research (MS); project management (MS), including information systems, operations research; public administration (MPA); quality management (MS); software engineering (MS); space systems (MS); space systems management (MS); supply chain management (MS); systems management (MS), including information systems, operations research; technology management (MS). Part-time and evening/weekend programs available. Postbaccalaureate distance learning degree programs offered (no on-campus study). *Faculty:* 7 full-time (1 woman), 112 part-time/adjunct (29 women). *Students:* 98 full-time (45 women), 975 part-time (396 women); includes 440 minority (292 Black or African American, non-Hispanic/Latino; 13 American Indian or Alaska Native, non-Hispanic/Latino; 32 Asian, non-Hispanic/Latino; 79 Hispanic/Latino; 1 Native Hawaiian or other Pacific Islander, non-Hispanic/Latino; 23 Two or more races, non-Hispanic/Latino), 4 international. Average age 37. 807 applicants, 56% accepted, 258 enrolled. In 2014, 457 master's awarded. *Degree requirements:* For master's, comprehensive exam (for some programs), capstone course. *Entrance requirements:* For master's, GMAT or resume showing 8 years of supervised experience, minimum GPA of 3.0, 2 letters of recommendation, resume. Additional exam requirements/recommendations for international students: Required—TOEFL (minimum score 550 paper-based; 79 iBT). *Application deadline:* For fall admission, 4/1 for international students; for spring admission, 9/30 for international students. Applications are processed on a rolling basis. Electronic applications accepted. *Expenses:* Expenses: Contact institution. *Financial support:* Application deadline: 3/1; applicants required to submit FAFSA. *Unit head:* Dr. Theodore R. Richardson, III, Senior Associate Dean, 321-674-8123, Fax: 321-674-7597, E-mail: trichardson@fit.edu. *Application contact:* Carolyn Farrior, Director of Graduate Admissions, Online Learning and Off-Campus Programs, 321-674-7118, Fax: 321-674-8216, E-mail: cfarrior@fit.edu.
Website: http://es.fit.edu.

George Mason University, Volgenau School of Engineering, Department of Systems Engineering and Operations Research, Fairfax, VA 22030. Offers operations research (MS); systems engineering (MS); systems engineering and operations research (PhD, Certificate). MS programs offered jointly with Old Dominion University, University of Virginia, Virginia Commonwealth University, and Virginia Polytechnic Institute and State University. *Faculty:* 18 full-time (5 women), 13 part-time/adjunct (2 women). *Students:* 42 full-time (8 women), 98 part-time (16 women); includes 27 minority (4 Black or African American, non-Hispanic/Latino; 12 Asian, non-Hispanic/Latino; 7 Hispanic/Latino; 4 Two or more races, non-Hispanic/Latino), 18 international. Average age 32. 134 applicants, 66% accepted, 37 enrolled. In 2014, 61 master's, 6 doctorates, 12 other advanced degrees awarded. *Degree requirements:* For master's, thesis optional; for doctorate, comprehensive exam, thesis/dissertation, qualifying exams. *Entrance requirements:* For master's, GRE General Test, BS in related field; minimum GPA of 3.0; 3 letters of recommendation; 2 official transcripts; expanded goals statement; proof of financial support; photocopy of passport; official bank statement; multivariable calculus, applied probability, statistics and a computer language course; self evaluation form; for doctorate, GRE, MS with minimum GPA of 3.5; BS with minimum GPA of 3.0 in systems or operational research; 2 official transcripts; 3 letters of recommendation; resume; expanded goals statement; self evaluation form; photocopy of passport; official bank statement; proof of financial support; for Certificate, personal goals statement; 2 official transcripts; self-evaluation form; letter of recommendation; resume; official bank statement; photocopy of passport; proof of financial support; baccalaureate degree in related field. Additional exam requirements/recommendations for international students: Required—TOEFL (minimum score 575 paper-based; 80 iBT), IELTS (minimum score 6.5), PTE. *Application deadline:* For fall admission, 1/15 priority date for domestic students; for spring admission, 8/15 priority date for domestic students. Application fee: $65 ($80 for international students). Electronic applications accepted. *Expenses:* Expenses: Contact institution. *Financial support:* In 2014–15, 13 students received support, including 6 research assistantships with full and partial tuition reimbursements available (averaging $19,974 per year), 7 teaching assistantships with full and partial tuition reimbursements available (averaging $12,909 per year); career-related internships or fieldwork, Federal Work-Study, scholarships/grants, unspecified assistantships, and health care benefits (for full-time research or teaching assistantship recipients) also available. Support available to part-time students. Financial award application deadline: 3/1; financial award applicants required to submit FAFSA. *Faculty research:* Requirements engineering, signal processing, systems architecture, data fusion. *Total annual research expenditures:* $603,678. *Unit head:* Ariela Sofer, Chair, 703-993-1692, Fax: 703-993-1521, E-mail: asofer@gmu.edu. *Application contact:* Angel Manzo, Program Specialist, 703-993-1636, Fax: 703-993-1521, E-mail: amanzo@gmu.edu.
Website: http://seor.gmu.edu.

Georgia Institute of Technology, Graduate Studies, College of Engineering, School of Industrial and Systems Engineering, Program in Operations Research, Atlanta, GA 30332-0001. Offers MS, PhD. Part-time programs available. Postbaccalaureate distance learning degree programs offered. *Students:* 70 full-time (14 women), 16 part-time (6 women); includes 6 minority (1 Black or African American, non-Hispanic/Latino; 2 Asian, non-Hispanic/Latino; 2 Hispanic/Latino; 1 Two or more races, non-Hispanic/Latino), 57 international. Average age 26. 193 applicants, 40% accepted, 23 enrolled. In 2014, 36 master's, 3 doctorates awarded. *Degree requirements:* For doctorate, comprehensive exam. *Entrance requirements:* For master's, GRE General Test, http://www.isye.gatech.edu/academics/masters/ms-operations-research/admissions; for doctorate, GRE General Test, http://www.isye.gatech.edu/academics/doctoral/phd-operations-research/admissions. Additional exam requirements/recommendations for international students: Required—TOEFL (minimum score 550 paper-based; 79 iBT). *Application deadline:* For fall admission, 12/15 for domestic and international students; for spring admission, 2/1 for domestic and international students. Applications are processed on a rolling basis. Application fee: $75. Electronic applications accepted. *Expenses:* Tuition, state resident: full-time $12,344; part-time $515 per credit hour. Tuition, nonresident: full-time $27,600; part-time $1150 per credit hour. *Required fees:* $1196 per term. Part-time tuition and fees vary according to course load. *Financial support:* Fellowships, research assistantships, teaching assistantships, career-related internships or fieldwork, Federal Work-Study, institutionally sponsored loans, tuition waivers (partial), and unspecified assistantships available. Support available to part-time students. Financial award application deadline: 5/1. *Faculty research:* Linear and nonlinear deterministic models in operations research, mathematical statistics, design of experiments. *Unit head:* Alan Erera, Director, 404-385-0358, E-mail: alan.erera@isye.gatech.edu. *Application contact:* Pam Morrison, Graduate Coordinator, 404-894-4289, E-mail: pam.morrison@isye.gatech.edu.
Website: http://www.isye.gatech.edu.

Georgia State University, J. Mack Robinson College of Business, Department of Managerial Sciences, Atlanta, GA 30302-3083. Offers business analysis (MBA, MS); entrepreneurship (MBA); human resources management (MBA, MS); operations management (MBA, MS); organization behavior/human resource management (PhD); organization management (MBA); organizational change (MS); strategic management (PhD). *Accreditation:* AACSB. Part-time and evening/weekend programs available. *Faculty:* 15 full-time (5 women). *Students:* 36 full-time (21 women), 28 part-time (16 women); includes 22 minority (17 Black or African American, non-Hispanic/Latino; 3 Asian, non-Hispanic/Latino; 1 Hispanic/Latino; 1 Two or more races, non-Hispanic/Latino), 24 international. Average age 31. 102 applicants, 25% accepted, 18 enrolled. In 2014, 25 master's awarded. *Degree requirements:* For doctorate, comprehensive exam, thesis/dissertation. *Entrance requirements:* For master's, GRE or GMAT, transcripts from all institutions attended, resume, essays; for doctorate, GMAT, three letters of recommendation, personal statement, transcripts from all institutions attended, resume. Additional exam requirements/recommendations for international students: Required—TOEFL (minimum score 610 paper-based; 101 iBT), IELTS (minimum score 7). *Application deadline:* For fall admission, 5/1 priority date for domestic students, 2/1 priority date for international students; for spring admission, 9/15 priority date for domestic students, 4/1 priority date for international students. Applications are processed on a rolling basis. Application fee: $50. Electronic applications accepted. *Expenses:* Tuition, state resident: full-time $6516; part-time $362 per credit hour. Tuition, nonresident: full-time $22,014; part-time $1223 per credit hour. *Required fees:* $2128 per semester. Tuition and fees vary according to course load and program. *Financial support:* Research assistantships, teaching assistantships, scholarships/grants, tuition waivers, and unspecified assistantships available. *Faculty research:* Entrepreneurship and innovation; strategy process; workplace interactions, relationships, and processes; leadership and culture; supply chain management. *Unit head:* Dr. Pamela S. Barr, Interim Chair, 404-413-7525, Fax: 404-413-7571. *Application contact:* Toby McChesney, Assistant Dean for Graduate Recruiting and Student Services, 404-413-7167, Fax: 404-413-7162, E-mail: rcbgradadmissions@gsu.edu.
Website: http://mgmt.robinson.gsu.edu/.

HEC Montreal, School of Business Administration, Master of Science Programs in Administration, Program in Business Analytics, Montréal, QC H3T 2A7, Canada. Offers M Sc. All courses are given in French. *Students:* 11 full-time (5 women), 1 (woman) part-time. 8 applicants, 63% accepted, 3 enrolled. In 2014, 1 master's awarded. *Degree requirements:* For master's, one foreign language, thesis. *Entrance requirements:* For master's, Test de francais international (TFI) with minimum score of 850 (for those who have never studied in French), BBA, undergraduate degree in another field, degree deemed equivalent by program director and minimum GPA of 3.0 on 4.3 scale. *Application deadline:* For fall admission, 3/15 for domestic and international students; for winter admission, 9/15 for domestic and international students. Application fee: $83. Electronic applications accepted. *Financial support:* Research assistantships, teaching assistantships, and scholarships/grants available. Financial award application deadline: 9/2. *Unit head:* Dr. Anne Bourhis, Director, 514-340-6873, Fax: 514-340-6880, E-mail: anne.bourhis@hec.ca. *Application contact:* Marianne de Moura, Administrative Director, 514-340-7106, Fax: 514-340-6411, E-mail: marianne.de-moura@hec.ca.
Website: http://www.hec.ca/programmes_formations/msc/options/analytique_affaires/index.html.

Idaho State University, Office of Graduate Studies, College of Science and Engineering, Mechanical Engineering Department, Pocatello, ID 83209-8060. Offers measurement and control engineering (MS); mechanical engineering (MS). Part-time programs available. *Degree requirements:* For master's, comprehensive exam (for some programs), 2 semesters of seminar; thesis or project. *Entrance requirements:* For master's, GRE. Additional exam requirements/recommendations for international students: Required—TOEFL (minimum score 550 paper-based; 80 iBT). Electronic applications accepted. *Faculty research:* Modeling and identification of biomedical systems, intelligent systems and adaptive control, active flow control of turbo machinery, validation of advanced computational codes for thermal fluid interactions, development of methodologies for the assessment of passive safety system performance in advanced reactors, alternative energy research (wind, solar, hydrogen).

Indiana University–Purdue University Fort Wayne, College of Arts and Sciences, Department of Mathematical Sciences, Fort Wayne, IN 46805-1499. Offers applied mathematics (MS); applied statistics (Certificate); mathematics (MS); operations research (MS); teaching (MAT). Part-time and evening/weekend programs available. *Faculty:* 18 full-time (5 women). *Students:* 3 full-time (0 women), 9 part-time (5 women), 2 international. Average age 31. 5 applicants, 100% accepted, 5 enrolled. In 2014, 4 master's, 1 other advanced degree awarded. *Entrance requirements:* For master's, minimum GPA of 3.0, major or minor in mathematics, three letters of recommendation. Additional exam requirements/recommendations for international students: Required—TOEFL (minimum score 550 paper-based; 79 iBT); Recommended—TWE. *Application deadline:* For fall admission, 8/1 priority date for domestic students, 7/1 priority date for international students; for spring admission, 12/1 for domestic students, 10/1 for international students. Applications are processed on a rolling basis. Application fee: $55 ($60 for international students). Electronic applications accepted. *Financial support:* In 2014–15, 7 teaching assistantships with partial tuition reimbursements (averaging $13,522 per year) were awarded; scholarships/grants and unspecified assistantships also available. Support available to part-time students. Financial award application deadline: 3/1; financial award applicants required to submit FAFSA. *Faculty research:* Eves' Theorem, paired-placements for student teaching, holomorphic maps. *Total annual research expenditures:* $33,250. *Unit head:* Dr. Peter Dragnev, Interim Chair/Professor, 260-481-6382, Fax: 260-481-0155, E-mail: dragnevp@ipfw.edu. *Application contact:* Dr. W. Douglas Weakley, Director of Graduate Studies, 260-481-6233, Fax: 260-481-0155, E-mail: weakley@ipfw.edu.
Website: http://www.ipfw.edu/math/.

Iowa State University of Science and Technology, Department of Industrial and Manufacturing Systems Engineering, Ames, IA 50011. Offers industrial engineering (M Eng, MS, PhD); operations research (MS); systems engineering (M Eng). *Degree requirements:* For master's, thesis or alternative; for doctorate, thesis/dissertation. *Entrance requirements:* For master's and doctorate, GRE General Test. Additional exam requirements/recommendations for international students: Required—TOEFL (minimum score 550 paper-based; 79 iBT), IELTS (minimum score 6.5). Electronic applications accepted. *Faculty research:* Economic modeling, valuation techniques, robotics, digital controls, systems reliability.

Johns Hopkins University, G. W. C. Whiting School of Engineering, Department of Applied Mathematics and Statistics, Baltimore, MD 21218-2699. Offers computational medicine (PhD); discrete mathematics (MA, MSE, PhD); financial mathematics (MSE); operations research/optimization (MA, MSE, PhD); statistics/probability (MA, MSE, PhD). Terminal master's awarded for partial completion of doctoral program. *Degree requirements:* For master's, thesis (for some programs); for doctorate, thesis/dissertation, oral exam, introductory exam. *Entrance requirements:* For master's and doctorate, GRE General Test, GRE Subject Test. Additional exam requirements/recommendations for international students: Required—TOEFL (minimum score 600 paper-based; 100 iBT). Electronic applications accepted. *Faculty research:* Discrete mathematics, probability, statistics, optimization and operations research, scientific computation, financial mathematics.

Johns Hopkins University, G. W. C. Whiting School of Engineering, Master of Science in Engineering Management Program, Baltimore, MD 21218-2699. Offers biomaterials (MSEM); civil engineering (MSEM); communications science (MSEM); computer science (MSEM); environmental systems analysis, economics and public policy (MSEM); fluid mechanics (MSEM); materials science and engineering (MSEM);

mechanical engineering (MSEM); mechanics and materials (MSEM); nano-biotechnology (MSEM); nanomaterials and nanotechnology (MSEM); operations research (MSEM); probability and statistics (MSEM); smart product and device design (MSEM). *Entrance requirements:* For master's, GRE, 3 letters of recommendation, resume. Additional exam requirements/recommendations for international students: Required—TOEFL (minimum score 600 paper-based; 100 iBT) or IELTS (minimum score 7). Electronic applications accepted.

Kansas State University, Graduate School, College of Engineering, Department of Industrial and Manufacturing Systems Engineering, Manhattan, KS 66506. Offers engineering management (MEM); industrial engineering (MS); operations research (MS). Part-time programs available. Postbaccalaureate distance learning degree programs offered (no on-campus study). *Faculty:* 10 full-time (2 women), 1 part-time/adjunct (0 women). *Students:* 26 full-time (8 women), 58 part-time (9 women); includes 11 minority (5 Black or African American, non-Hispanic/Latino; 2 Asian, non-Hispanic/Latino; 1 Hispanic/Latino; 1 Native Hawaiian or other Pacific Islander, non-Hispanic/Latino; 2 Two or more races, non-Hispanic/Latino), 16 international. Average age 29. 61 applicants, 46% accepted, 13 enrolled. In 2014, 26 master's, 4 doctorates awarded. *Degree requirements:* For master's, thesis or alternative; for doctorate, thesis/dissertation. *Entrance requirements:* For master's, GRE General Test (minimum score of 750 old version, 159 new format on Quantitative portion of exam), bachelor's degree in engineering, mathematics, or physical science; for doctorate, GRE General Test (minimum score of 770 old version, 164 new format on Quantitative portion of exam), master's degree in engineering or industrial manufacturing. Additional exam requirements/recommendations for international students: Required—PTE (minimum score 58), TOEFL (minimum score 550 paper-based; 79 iBT) or IELTS (minimum score 6.5). *Application deadline:* For fall admission, 6/1 priority date for domestic students, 12/1 priority date for international students; for spring admission, 11/1 priority date for domestic students, 8/1 priority date for international students. Applications are processed on a rolling basis. Application fee: $50 ($75 for international students). Electronic applications accepted. *Financial support:* In 2014–15, 12 research assistantships (averaging $12,442 per year), 9 teaching assistantships with full tuition reimbursements (averaging $14,111 per year) were awarded; Federal Work-Study, institutionally sponsored loans, and scholarships/grants also available. Support available to part-time students. Financial award application deadline: 3/1; financial award applicants required to submit FAFSA. *Faculty research:* Industrial engineering, ergonomics, healthcare systems engineering, manufacturing processes, operations research, engineering management. *Total annual research expenditures:* $2.6 million. *Unit head:* Dr. Bradley Kramer, Head, 785-532-5606, Fax: 785-532-3738, E-mail: bradleyk@k-state.edu. *Application contact:* Dr. David Ben-Arieh, Chair of Graduate Committee, 785-532-5606, Fax: 785-532-3738, E-mail: imse@k-state.edu. Website: http://www.imse.k-state.edu/.

Massachusetts Institute of Technology, Operations Research Center, Cambridge, MA 02139. Offers SM, PhD. *Faculty:* 47 full-time (9 women), 3 part-time/adjunct (0 women). *Students:* 83 full-time (15 women), 1 part-time (0 women); includes 6 minority (5 Asian, non-Hispanic/Latino; 1 Hispanic/Latino), 49 international. Average age 26. 328 applicants, 9% accepted, 26 enrolled. In 2014, 7 master's, 6 doctorates awarded. Terminal master's awarded for partial completion of doctoral program. *Degree requirements:* For master's, thesis; for doctorate, comprehensive exam, thesis/dissertation, Hands-on-Experience requirement. *Entrance requirements:* For master's and doctorate, GRE General Test. Additional exam requirements/recommendations for international students: Required—TOEFL (minimum score 100 iBT), IELTS (minimum score 7). *Application deadline:* For fall admission, 12/15 for domestic and international students. Application fee: $75. Electronic applications accepted. *Expenses:* Tuition: Full-time $44,720; part-time $699 per unit. *Required fees:* $296. *Financial support:* In 2014–15, 77 students received support, including 13 fellowships (averaging $35,300 per year), 56 research assistantships (averaging $32,700 per year), 8 teaching assistantships (averaging $36,600 per year); Federal Work-Study, institutionally sponsored loans, scholarships/grants, health care benefits, and unspecified assistantships also available. Financial award application deadline: 4/15; financial award applicants required to submit FAFSA. *Faculty research:* Probability, mathematical programming, statistics, stochastic processes, business analytics. *Unit head:* Dr. Dimitris J. Bertsimas, Co-Director, 617-253-3601, Fax: 617-258-9214, E-mail: orc-www@mit.edu. *Application contact:* Laura A. Rose, Graduate Admissions Coordinator, 617-253-9303, Fax: 617-258-9214, E-mail: lrose@mit.edu.
Website: http://web.mit.edu/orc/www/.

Naval Postgraduate School, Departments and Academic Groups, Department of Operations Research, Monterey, CA 93943. Offers applied science (MS), including operations research; cost estimating analysis (MS); human systems integration (MS); operations research (MS, PhD); systems analysis (MS). Program only open to commissioned officers of the United States and friendly nations and selected United States federal civilian employees. Part-time programs available. *Degree requirements:* For master's, thesis (for some programs); for doctorate, thesis/dissertation. *Faculty research:* Next generation network science, performance analysis of ground solider mobile ad-hoc networks, irregular warfare methods and tools, human social cultural behavior modeling, large-scale optimization.

Naval Postgraduate School, Departments and Academic Groups, Undersea Warfare Academic Group, Monterey, CA 93943. Offers applied mathematics (MS); applied physics (MS); applied science (MS), including acoustics, operations research, physical oceanography, signal processing; electrical engineering (MS); engineering acoustics (MS, PhD); engineering science (MS), including electrical engineering, mechanical engineering; mechanical engineer (ME); mechanical engineering (MS, MSME); meteorology (MS); operations research (MS); physical oceanography (MS). Program only open to commissioned officers of the United States and friendly nations and selected United States federal civilian employees. Part-time programs available. *Degree requirements:* For master's, thesis. *Faculty research:* Unmanned/autonomous vehicles, sea mines and countermeasures, submarine warfare in the twentieth and twenty-first centuries.

New Mexico Institute of Mining and Technology, Graduate Studies, Department of Mathematics, Socorro, NM 87801. Offers applied and industrial mathematics (PhD); industrial mathematics (MS); mathematics (MS); operations research and statistics (MS). *Degree requirements:* For master's, thesis optional; for doctorate, thesis/dissertation. *Entrance requirements:* For master's, GRE General Test. Additional exam requirements/recommendations for international students: Required—TOEFL (minimum score 540 paper-based). *Faculty research:* Applied mathematics, differential equations, industrial mathematics, numerical analysis, stochastic processes.

North Carolina State University, Graduate School, College of Engineering and College of Physical and Mathematical Sciences, Program in Operations Research, Raleigh, NC 27695. Offers MOR, MS, PhD. Part-time programs available. *Degree requirements:* For master's, thesis (for some programs), thesis (MS); for doctorate, thesis/dissertation, comprehensive oral and written exams. *Entrance requirements:* For master's, GRE General Test, minimum GPA of 2.7; for doctorate, GRE General Test, minimum GPA of 3.0. Additional exam requirements/recommendations for international students: Required—TOEFL. Electronic applications accepted. *Faculty research:*

Queuing analysis, simulation, inventory theory, supply chain management, mathematical programming.

North Carolina State University, Graduate School, Institute for Advanced Analytics, Raleigh, NC 27695. Offers analytics (MS). *Entrance requirements:* For master's, GRE General Test. Additional exam requirements/recommendations for international students: Required—TOEFL. Electronic applications accepted.

North Dakota State University, College of Graduate and Interdisciplinary Studies, College of Science and Mathematics, Department of Computer Science, Fargo, ND 58108. Offers computer science (MS, PhD); digital enterprise (Certificate); operations research (MS); software engineering (MS, PhD, Certificate). Part-time programs available. *Degree requirements:* For master's, comprehensive exam, thesis optional; for doctorate, thesis/dissertation, qualifying exam. *Entrance requirements:* For master's, minimum GPA of 3.0, BS in computer science or related field; for doctorate, minimum GPA of 3.25, MS in computer science or related field. Additional exam requirements/recommendations for international students: Required—TOEFL (minimum score 550 paper-based; 79 iBT). Electronic applications accepted. *Faculty research:* Networking, software engineering, artificial intelligence, database, programming languages.

Northeastern University, College of Engineering, Boston, MA 02115-5096. Offers bioengineering (PhD); chemical engineering (MS, PhD); civil engineering (MS, PhD); computer engineering (PhD); computer systems engineering (MS); electrical and computer engineering (MS); electrical and engineering leadership (MS); electrical engineering (PhD); energy systems (MS); engineering leadership (Certificate); engineering management (MRTP); industrial engineering (MS, PhD); information assurance (PhD); information systems (MS); interdisciplinary (PhD); mechanical engineering (MS, PhD); operations research (MS); telecommunication systems management (MS). Part-time programs available. *Expenses:* Contact institution.

Northeastern University, College of Science, Department of Mathematics, Boston, MA 02115-5096. Offers applied mathematics (MS); mathematics (MS, PhD); operations research (MSOR). Part-time programs available. Terminal master's awarded for partial completion of doctoral program. *Degree requirements:* For master's, thesis (for some programs), 32 credit hours; for doctorate, one foreign language, comprehensive exam, thesis/dissertation, qualifying exams. *Entrance requirements:* For master's and doctorate, GRE Subject Test, GRE General Test. Additional exam requirements/recommendations for international students: Required—TOEFL (minimum score 100 iBT). Electronic applications accepted. *Faculty research:* Algebra and singularities, combinatorics, topology, probability and statistics, geometric analysis and partial differential equations.

The Ohio State University, Graduate School, Max M. Fisher College of Business, Program in Business Operational Excellence, Columbus, OH 43210. Offers MBOE. Postbaccalaureate distance learning degree programs offered (minimal on-campus study). *Students:* 44 full-time (20 women); includes 6 minority (4 Black or African American, non-Hispanic/Latino; 2 Two or more races, non-Hispanic/Latino), 2 international. Average age 41. In 2014, 35 master's awarded. *Entrance requirements:* For master's, GMAT if undergraduate GPA is below a 3.0, bachelor's degree from accredited university; at least 3-5 years of successful work experience in which managing processes are part of the job; recommendation by an executive sponsor. Additional exam requirements/recommendations for international students: Required—TOEFL (minimum score 550 paper-based; 79 iBT), Michigan English Language Assessment Battery (minimum score 82); Recommended—IELTS (minimum score 7). *Application deadline:* For fall admission, 10/1 for domestic and international students. *Unit head:* Peter Ward, Chair, 614-292-5294, E-mail: ward.1@osu.edu. *Application contact:* Graduate and Professional Admissions, 614-292-9444, Fax: 614-292-3895, E-mail: gpadmissions@osu.edu.
Website: http://fisher.osu.edu/mboe.

Princeton University, Graduate School, School of Engineering and Applied Science, Department of Operations Research and Financial Engineering, Princeton, NJ 08544-1019. Offers M Eng, MSE, PhD. Terminal master's awarded for partial completion of doctoral program. *Degree requirements:* For master's, thesis (MSE); for doctorate, thesis/dissertation, general exam. *Entrance requirements:* For master's and doctorate, GRE General Test, official transcript(s), 3 letters of recommendation, personal statement. Additional exam requirements/recommendations for international students: Required—TOEFL. Electronic applications accepted. *Faculty research:* Applied and computational mathematics; financial mathematics; optimization, queuing theory, and machine learning; statistics and stochastic analysis; transportation and logistics.

Rutgers, The State University of New Jersey, New Brunswick, Graduate School-New Brunswick, Program in Operations Research, Piscataway, NJ 08854-8097. Offers PhD. Part-time programs available. *Degree requirements:* For doctorate, comprehensive exam, thesis/dissertation, qualifying exam. *Entrance requirements:* For doctorate, GRE General Test, GRE Subject Test. Electronic applications accepted. *Faculty research:* Mathematical programming, combinatorial optimization, graph theory, stochastic modeling, queuing theory.

Simon Fraser University, Office of Graduate Studies, Faculty of Science, Department of Mathematics, Burnaby, BC V5A 1S6, Canada. Offers applied and computational mathematics (M Sc, PhD); mathematics (M Sc, PhD); operations research (M Sc, PhD). *Degree requirements:* For master's, thesis or alternative; for doctorate, comprehensive exam, thesis/dissertation. *Entrance requirements:* For master's, GRE General Test, GRE Subject Test (mathematics), minimum GPA of 3.0 (on scale of 4.33), or 3.33 based on last 60 credits of undergraduate courses; for doctorate, GRE General Test, GRE Subject Test (mathematics), minimum GPA of 3.5 (on scale of 4.33). Additional exam requirements/recommendations for international students: Recommended—TOEFL (minimum score 580 paper-based; 93 iBT), IELTS (minimum score 7), TWE (minimum score 5). Electronic applications accepted. *Faculty research:* Computer algebra, discrete mathematics, fluid dynamics, nonlinear partial differential equations and variation methods, numerical analysis and scientific computing.

Southern Illinois University Edwardsville, Graduate School, College of Arts and Sciences, Department of Mathematics and Statistics, Program in Statistics and Operations Research, Edwardsville, IL 62026. Offers MS. Part-time programs available. *Students:* 4 full-time (3 women), 10 part-time (7 women); includes 4 minority (all Black or African American, non-Hispanic/Latino), 2 international. 8 applicants, 50% accepted. In 2014, 11 master's awarded. *Degree requirements:* For master's, thesis (for some programs), special project. *Entrance requirements:* Additional exam requirements/recommendations for international students: Required—TOEFL (minimum score 550 paper-based, 79 iBT), IELTS (minimum score 6.5), Michigan Test of English Language Proficiency or PTE. *Application deadline:* For fall admission, 7/18 for domestic students, 6/1 for international students; for spring admission, 12/12 for domestic students, 10/1 for international students; for summer admission, 4/24 for domestic students, 3/1 for international students. Applications are processed on a rolling basis. Application fee: $30. Electronic applications accepted. *Expenses:* Tuition, state resident: full-time $5026. Tuition, nonresident: full-time $12,566. *International tuition:* $25,136 full-time. *Required fees:* $1682. Tuition and fees vary according to course load, campus/location and program. *Financial support:* Institutionally sponsored loans, scholarships/grants, and unspecified assistantships available. *Unit head:* Dr. Myung Sin Song, Program

Director, 618-650-2580, E-mail: msong@siue.edu. *Application contact:* Melissa K. Mace, Assistant Director of Graduate and International Recruitment, 618-650-2756, Fax: 618-650-3618, E-mail: mmace@siue.edu.
Website: http://www.siue.edu/artsandsciences/math/.

Southern Methodist University, Bobby B. Lyle School of Engineering, Department of Engineering Management, Information, and Systems, Dallas, TX 75275. Offers engineering management (MSEM, DE); information engineering and management (MSIEM); operations research (MS, PhD); systems engineering (MS, PhD). Part-time and evening/weekend programs available. Postbaccalaureate distance learning degree programs offered. Terminal master's awarded for partial completion of doctoral program. *Degree requirements:* For master's, thesis optional; for doctorate, thesis/dissertation, oral and written qualifying exams. *Entrance requirements:* For master's, minimum GPA of 3.0 in last 2 years; bachelor's degree in engineering, mathematics, sciences, or technical area; for doctorate, GRE General Test (operations research, engineering management), bachelor's degree in related field. Additional exam requirements/recommendations for international students: Required—TOEFL. *Faculty research:* Telecommunications, decision systems, information engineering, operations research, software.

Texas Tech University, Graduate School, Rawls College of Business Administration, Lubbock, TX 79409-2101. Offers accounting (MSA, PhD), including audit/financial reporting (MSA), taxation (MSA); business statistics (MS, PhD); finance (MS, PhD); general business (MBA); health organization management (MBA); healthcare management (MS); management (PhD); management information systems (MS, PhD); marketing (PhD); production and operations management (PhD); STEM (MBA); JD/MBA; JD/MSA; MBA/M Arch; MBA/MD; MBA/MS; MBA/Pharm D. *Accreditation:* AACSB; CAHME (one or more programs are accredited). Part-time and evening/weekend programs available. *Faculty:* 67 full-time (8 women). *Students:* 920 full-time (327 women); includes 163 minority (27 Black or African American, non-Hispanic/Latino; 6 American Indian or Alaska Native, non-Hispanic/Latino; 46 Asian, non-Hispanic/Latino; 72 Hispanic/Latino; 12 Two or more races, non-Hispanic/Latino), 210 international. Average age 28. 701 applicants, 57% accepted, 283 enrolled. In 2014, 320 master's, 10 doctorates awarded. Terminal master's awarded for partial completion of doctoral program. *Degree requirements:* For master's, capstone course; for doctorate, comprehensive exam, thesis/dissertation, qualifying exams. *Entrance requirements:* For master's and doctorate, GMAT, holistic review of academic credentials. Additional exam requirements/recommendations for international students: Required—TOEFL (minimum score 550 paper-based; 79 iBT). *Application deadline:* For fall admission, 7/1 priority date for domestic students, 1/15 for international students; for spring admission, 11/1 priority date for domestic students, 6/15 for international students. Applications are processed on a rolling basis. Application fee: $60. Electronic applications accepted. *Expenses:* Expenses: Contact institution. *Financial support:* In 2014–15, 142 students received support, including 25 research assistantships (averaging $22,725 per year), 27 teaching assistantships (averaging $22,725 per year); fellowships, career-related internships or fieldwork, Federal Work-Study, scholarships/grants, health care benefits, and unspecified assistantships also available. Financial award applicants required to submit FAFSA. *Faculty research:* Governmental and nonprofit accounting, securities and options futures, statistical analysis and design, leadership, consumer behavior. *Unit head:* Dr. Lance Nail, Dean, 806-742-3188, Fax: 806-742-1092, E-mail: lance.nail@ttu.edu. *Application contact:* Chathry Kumarapathiranalage, Applications Manager, Graduate and Professional Programs, 806-742-3184, Fax: 806-742-3958, E-mail: rawlsgrad@ttu.edu.
Website: http://grad.ba.ttu.edu.

The University of Alabama in Huntsville, School of Graduate Studies, College of Engineering, Department of Industrial and Systems Engineering and Engineering Management, Huntsville, AL 35899. Offers engineering management (PhD); industrial and systems engineering (MSE, PhD); industrial engineering (MSE, PhD); operations research (MSOR); systems engineering (MSE). Part-time and evening/weekend programs available. Postbaccalaureate distance learning degree programs offered (minimal on-campus study). *Degree requirements:* For master's, comprehensive exam, thesis or alternative, oral and written exams; for doctorate, comprehensive exam, thesis/dissertation, oral and written exams. *Entrance requirements:* For master's and doctorate, GRE General Test, minimum GPA of 3.0. Additional exam requirements/recommendations for international students: Required—TOEFL (minimum score 500 paper-based; 80 iBT), IELTS (minimum score 6.5). Electronic applications accepted. *Faculty research:* Systems engineering process, electronic manufacturing, heuristic manufacturing, teams and team development.

University of Arkansas, Graduate School, College of Engineering, Department of Industrial Engineering, Fayetteville, AR 72701-1201. Offers industrial engineering (MSE, MSIE, PhD); operations management (MS); operations research (MSE, MSOR). *Degree requirements:* For master's, thesis optional; for doctorate, one foreign language, thesis/dissertation. Electronic applications accepted.

The University of British Columbia, Sauder School of Business, Master of Management in Operations Research, Vancouver, BC V6T 1Z1, Canada. Offers MM. *Degree requirements:* For master's, course work and industry project. *Entrance requirements:* For master's, GMAT or GRE, strong quantitative or analytical background, bachelor's degree or recognized equivalent from an accredited university-level institution, minimum of B+ average in undergraduate upper-level course work. Additional exam requirements/recommendations for international students: Required—TOEFL, IELTS or Michigan English Language Assessment Battery. Electronic applications accepted. *Expenses:* Contact institution. *Faculty research:* Operations and logistics.

University of California, Berkeley, Graduate Division, College of Engineering, Department of Industrial Engineering and Operations Research, Berkeley, CA 94720-1500. Offers M Eng, MS, D Eng, PhD. *Degree requirements:* For master's, comprehensive exam or thesis (MS); for doctorate, thesis/dissertation, qualifying exam. *Entrance requirements:* For master's and doctorate, GRE General Test, minimum GPA of 3.0, 3 letters of recommendation. *Faculty research:* Mathematical programming, robotics and manufacturing, linear and nonlinear optimization, production planning and scheduling, queuing theory.

University of Colorado Boulder, Graduate School, College of Engineering and Applied Science, Engineering Management Program, Boulder, CO 80309. Offers operations and logistics (ME); quality and process (ME); research and development (ME). *Students:* 74 full-time (17 women), 110 part-time (28 women); includes 40 minority (8 Black or African American, non-Hispanic/Latino; 1 American Indian or Alaska Native, non-Hispanic/Latino; 12 Asian, non-Hispanic/Latino; 13 Hispanic/Latino; 6 Two or more races, non-Hispanic/Latino), 7 international. Average age 34. 66 applicants, 65% accepted, 35 enrolled. *Entrance requirements:* For master's, minimum undergraduate GPA of 3.0. *Application deadline:* For fall admission, 3/15 for domestic students, 1/15 for international students; for spring admission, 10/15 for domestic students, 8/5 for international students. Application fee: $50 ($70 for international students). Electronic applications accepted. *Financial support:* In 2014–15, 39 students received support, including 11 fellowships (averaging $2,760 per year); institutionally sponsored loans, scholarships/grants, health care benefits, and unspecified assistantships also available. Financial award applicants required to submit FAFSA. *Faculty research:* Quality and process, research and development, operations and logistics.
Website: http://engineeringanywhere.colorado.edu/emp.

University of Colorado Denver, College of Liberal Arts and Sciences, Department of Mathematical and Statistical Sciences, Denver, CO 80217. Offers applied mathematics (MS, PhD), including applied mathematics, applied probability (MS), applied statistics (MS), computational biology, computational mathematics (PhD), discrete mathematics, finite geometry (PhD), mathematics education (PhD), mathematics of engineering and science (MS), numerical analysis, operations research (MS), optimization and operations research (PhD), probability (PhD), statistics (PhD). Part-time programs available. *Faculty:* 17 full-time (5 women), 1 part-time/adjunct (0 women). *Students:* 47 full-time (15 women), 7 part-time (2 women); includes 8 minority (2 Black or African American, non-Hispanic/Latino; 3 Asian, non-Hispanic/Latino; 3 Hispanic/Latino), 15 international. Average age 29. 70 applicants, 71% accepted, 15 enrolled. In 2014, 7 master's, 4 doctorates awarded. *Degree requirements:* For master's, comprehensive exam, thesis optional, 30 hours of course work with minimum GPA of 3.0; for doctorate, comprehensive exam, thesis/dissertation, 42 hours of course work with minimum GPA of 3.25. *Entrance requirements:* For master's, GRE General Test; GRE Subject Test in math (recommended), 30 hours of course work in mathematics (24 of which must be upper-division mathematics), bachelor's degree with minimum GPA of 3.0; for doctorate, GRE General Test; GRE Subject Test in math (recommended), 30 hours of course work in mathematics (24 of which must be upper-division mathematics), master's degree with minimum GPA of 3.25. Additional exam requirements/recommendations for international students: Required—TOEFL (minimum score 537 paper-based; 75 iBT); Recommended—IELTS (minimum score 6.5). *Application deadline:* For fall admission, 4/1 for domestic and international students; for spring admission, 10/1 for domestic and international students; for summer admission, 4/1 for domestic and international students. Application fee: $50 ($75 for international students). Electronic applications accepted. *Financial support:* In 2014–15, 34 students received support. Fellowships with partial tuition reimbursements available, research assistantships with full tuition reimbursements available, teaching assistantships with full tuition reimbursements available, Federal Work-Study, institutionally sponsored loans, scholarships/grants, and traineeships available. Financial award application deadline: 4/1; financial award applicants required to submit FAFSA. *Faculty research:* Computational mathematics, computational biology, discrete mathematics and geometry, probability and statistics, optimization. *Unit head:* Dr. Jan Mandel, Professor and Chair, 303-315-1703, E-mail: jan.mandel@ucdenver.edu. *Application contact:* Julie Blunck, Graduate Program Assistant, 303-315-1743, E-mail: julie.blunck@ucdenver.edu.
Website: http://www.ucdenver.edu/academics/colleges/CLAS/Departments/math/Pages/MathStats.aspx.

University of Delaware, College of Agriculture and Natural Resources, Department of Food and Resource Economics, Operations Research Program, Newark, DE 19716. Offers MS. Part-time programs available. *Degree requirements:* For master's, thesis, oral exam. *Entrance requirements:* For master's, GRE General Test, 3 letters of recommendation, program language/s, engineering calculus. Additional exam requirements/recommendations for international students: Required—TOEFL. Electronic applications accepted. *Faculty research:* Simulation and modeling-production scheduling and optimization, agricultural production and resource economics, transportation engineering, statistical quality control.

University of Illinois at Chicago, Graduate College, College of Engineering, Department of Mechanical and Industrial Engineering, Program in Industrial Engineering, Chicago, IL 60607-7128. Offers industrial engineering (MS); industrial engineering and operations research (PhD). Part-time programs available. *Students:* 82 full-time (15 women), 5 part-time (1 woman); includes 10 minority (2 Asian, non-Hispanic/Latino; 8 Hispanic/Latino), 76 international. Average age 25. 321 applicants, 58% accepted, 53 enrolled. In 2014, 15 master's, 4 doctorates awarded. *Degree requirements:* For doctorate, thesis/dissertation. *Entrance requirements:* For doctorate, GRE General Test, minimum GPA of 2.75. Additional exam requirements/recommendations for international students: Required—TOEFL. *Application deadline:* For fall admission, 5/15 for domestic students, 2/15 for international students; for spring admission, 11/1 for domestic students, 7/15 for international students. Applications are processed on a rolling basis. Application fee: $60. Electronic applications accepted. *Expenses:* Expenses: $17,602 in-state; $29,600 out-of-state. *Financial support:* Fellowships with full tuition reimbursements, research assistantships with full tuition reimbursements, teaching assistantships with full tuition reimbursements, Federal Work-Study, scholarships/grants, traineeships, tuition waivers (full), and unspecified assistantships available. Financial award application deadline: 3/1; financial award applicants required to submit FAFSA. *Faculty research:* Manufacturing information systems and manufacturing control, supply chain, logistics, optimization quality control, haptics and virtual reality, industrial automation, safety and reliability engineering, diagnostics, prognostics, controls and statistical modeling. *Unit head:* Prof. Farzad Mashayek, Head, 312-996-6122, E-mail: mashayek@uic.edu.
Website: http://catalog.uic.edu/gcat/colleges-schools/engineering/ie/.

The University of Iowa, Graduate College, College of Engineering, Department of Industrial Engineering, Iowa City, IA 52242-1316. Offers engineering design and manufacturing (MS, PhD); healthcare systems (MS, PhD); human factors (MS, PhD); information and engineering management (MS, PhD); operations research (MS, PhD); wind energy (MS, PhD). *Faculty:* 8 full-time (1 woman). *Students:* 19 full-time (3 women); includes 1 minority (Asian, non-Hispanic/Latino), 10 international. Average age 28. 59 applicants, 12% accepted, 3 enrolled. In 2014, 1 master's, 4 doctorates awarded. Terminal master's awarded for partial completion of doctoral program. *Degree requirements:* For master's, thesis optional, exam; for doctorate, comprehensive exam, thesis/dissertation, final defense exam. *Entrance requirements:* For master's and doctorate, GRE General Test. Additional exam requirements/recommendations for international students: Required—TOEFL (minimum score 600 paper-based; 100 iBT). *Application deadline:* For fall admission, 7/15 for domestic students, 4/15 for international students; for spring admission, 12/1 for domestic students, 10/1 for international students; for summer admission, 4/15 for domestic students, 3/1 for international students. Applications are processed on a rolling basis. Application fee: $60 ($100 for international students). Electronic applications accepted. *Financial support:* In 2014–15, 4 fellowships with partial tuition reimbursements (averaging $20,619 per year), 16 research assistantships with full tuition reimbursements (averaging $18,131 per year), 5 teaching assistantships with full tuition reimbursements (averaging $5,424 per year) were awarded; career-related internships or fieldwork, scholarships/grants, and unspecified assistantships also available. Support available to part-time students. Financial award applicants required to submit FAFSA. *Faculty research:* Operations research, informatics, human factors engineering, healthcare systems, biomanufacturing, manufacturing systems, renewable energy, human-machine interactions. *Total annual research expenditures:* $3.5 million. *Unit head:* Dr. Andrew Kusiak, Department Executive Officer, 319-335-5934, Fax: 319-335-5669, E-mail:

andrew-kusiak@uiowa.edu. *Application contact:* Andrea Flaherty, Academic Program Specialist, 319-335-5939, Fax: 319-335-5669, E-mail: indeng@engineering.uiowa.edu. Website: http://www.engineering.uiowa.edu/mie.

University of Massachusetts Amherst, Graduate School, College of Engineering, Department of Mechanical and Industrial Engineering, Amherst, MA 01003. Offers industrial engineering and operations research (MS, PhD); mechanical engineering (MSME, PhD). Part-time programs available. *Faculty:* 29 full-time (4 women). *Students:* 90 full-time (20 women), 29 part-time (6 women); includes 12 minority (2 Black or African American, non-Hispanic/Latino; 1 American Indian or Alaska Native, non-Hispanic/Latino; 4 Asian, non-Hispanic/Latino; 3 Hispanic/Latino; 2 Two or more races, non-Hispanic/Latino), 65 international. Average age 28. 411 applicants, 31% accepted, 33 enrolled. In 2014, 27 master's, 7 doctorates awarded. Terminal master's awarded for partial completion of doctoral program. *Degree requirements:* For master's, thesis or alternative; for doctorate, comprehensive exam, thesis/dissertation. *Entrance requirements:* For master's and doctorate, GRE General Test. Additional exam requirements/recommendations for international students: Required—TOEFL (minimum score 550 paper-based; 80 iBT), IELTS (minimum score 6.5). *Application deadline:* For fall admission, 1/15 for domestic and international students; for spring admission, 10/1 for domestic and international students. Applications are processed on a rolling basis. Application fee: $75. Electronic applications accepted. *Expenses:* Tuition, state resident: full-time $1980; part-time $110 per credit. Tuition, nonresident: full-time $14,644; part-time $414 per credit. *Required fees:* $11,417. One-time fee: $357. *Financial support:* Fellowships with full and partial tuition reimbursements, research assistantships with full and partial tuition reimbursements, teaching assistantships with full and partial tuition reimbursements, career-related internships or fieldwork, Federal Work-Study, scholarships/grants, traineeships, health care benefits, tuition waivers (full and partial), and unspecified assistantships available. Support available to part-time students. Financial award application deadline: 1/15. *Unit head:* Dr. David Schmidt, Graduate Program Director, 413-545-3827, Fax: 413-545-1027. *Application contact:* Lindsay DeSantis, Supervisor of Admissions, 413-545-0722, Fax: 413-577-0100, E-mail: gradadm@grad.umass.edu. Website: http://mie.umass.edu/.

University of Michigan, College of Engineering, Department of Industrial and Operations Engineering, Ann Arbor, MI 48109. Offers MS, MSE, PhD, MBA/MS, MBA/MSE. *Accreditation:* ABET. Part-time programs available. *Students:* 153 full-time (50 women), 17 part-time (4 women). 564 applicants, 33% accepted, 93 enrolled. In 2014, 103 master's, 13 doctorates awarded. Terminal master's awarded for partial completion of doctoral program. *Degree requirements:* For doctorate, oral defense of dissertation, preliminary exams, qualifying exam. *Entrance requirements:* For master's, GRE General Test, minimum GPA of 3.2; for doctorate, GRE General Test, minimum GPA of 3.5. Additional exam requirements/recommendations for international students: Required—TOEFL. *Application deadline:* Applications are processed on a rolling basis. Electronic applications accepted. *Financial support:* Fellowships, research assistantships, teaching assistantships, Federal Work-Study, institutionally sponsored loans, scholarships/grants, traineeships, health care benefits, and unspecified assistantships available. Financial award applicants required to submit FAFSA. *Faculty research:* Production/distribution/logistics, financial engineering and enterprise systems, ergonomics (physical and cognitive), stochastic processes, linear and nonlinear optimization, operations research. *Total annual research expenditures:* $3.9 million. *Unit head:* Mark Daskin, Department Chair, 734-764-9422, Fax: 734-764-3451, E-mail:

msdaskin@umich.edu. *Application contact:* Matt Irelan, Graduate Student Advisor/Program Coordinator, 734-764-6480, Fax: 734-764-3451, E-mail: mirelan@umich.edu. Website: http://ioe.engin.umich.edu/.

The University of North Carolina at Chapel Hill, Graduate School, College of Arts and Sciences, Department of Operations Research, Chapel Hill, NC 27599. Offers MS, PhD. *Degree requirements:* For master's, comprehensive exam; for doctorate, comprehensive exam, thesis/dissertation. *Entrance requirements:* For master's and doctorate, GRE General Test, minimum GPA of 3.0.

University of Southern California, Graduate School, Viterbi School of Engineering, Daniel J. Epstein Department of Industrial and Systems Engineering, Los Angeles, CA 90089. Offers digital supply chain management (MS); engineering management (MS); engineering technology communication (Graduate Certificate); health systems operations (Graduate Certificate); industrial and systems engineering (MS, PhD, Engr); manufacturing engineering (MS); operations research engineering (MS); optimization and supply chain management (Graduate Certificate); product development engineering (MS); safety systems and security (MS); systems architecting and engineering (MS, Graduate Certificate); systems safety and security (Graduate Certificate); transportation systems (Graduate Certificate); MS/MBA. Part-time and evening/weekend programs available. Postbaccalaureate distance learning degree programs offered (no on-campus study). Terminal master's awarded for partial completion of doctoral program. *Degree requirements:* For master's, thesis optional; for doctorate, thesis/dissertation. *Entrance requirements:* For master's and doctorate, GRE General Test. Additional exam requirements/recommendations for international students: Recommended—TOEFL. Electronic applications accepted. *Faculty research:* Health systems, music cognition and retrieval, transportation and logistics, manufacturing and automation, engineering systems design, risk and economic analysis.

The University of Texas at Austin, Graduate School, Cockrell School of Engineering, Department of Mechanical Engineering, Program in Operations Research and Industrial Engineering, Austin, TX 78712-1111. Offers MS, PhD. *Entrance requirements:* For master's and doctorate, GRE General Test. Additional exam requirements/recommendations for international students: Required—TOEFL.

University of Waterloo, Graduate Studies, Faculty of Engineering, Department of Management Sciences, Waterloo, ON N2L 3G1, Canada. Offers applied operations research (MA Sc, MMS, PhD); information systems (MA Sc, MMS, PhD); management of technology (MA Sc, MMS, PhD). Part-time programs available. Postbaccalaureate distance learning degree programs offered (no on-campus study). *Degree requirements:* For master's, research paper or thesis; for doctorate, comprehensive exam, thesis/dissertation. *Entrance requirements:* For master's, GMAT or GRE, honors degree, minimum B average, resume; for doctorate, GMAT or GRE, master's degree, minimum A- average, resumé. Additional exam requirements/recommendations for international students: Required—TOEFL, TWE. *Faculty research:* Operations research, manufacturing systems, scheduling, information systems.

Virginia Commonwealth University, Graduate School, College of Humanities and Sciences, Department of Statistical Sciences and Operations Research, Richmond, VA 23284-9005. Offers operations research (MS); statistics (MS); systems modeling and analysis (PhD). *Entrance requirements:* For master's, GRE General Test, 30 undergraduate credits in mathematics, statistics, or operations research, including calculus I and II, multivariate calculus, linear algebra, probability and statistics. Additional exam requirements/recommendations for international students: Required—TOEFL (minimum score 600 paper-based; 100 iBT); Recommended—IELTS (minimum score 6.5). Electronic applications accepted.

Technology and Public Policy

Arizona State University at the Tempe campus, College of Liberal Arts and Sciences, Program in Science and Technology Policy, Tempe, AZ 85287-6505. Offers MS. Fall admission only. *Degree requirements:* For master's, thesis or alternative, internship, applied project, interactive Program of Study (iPOS) submitted before completing 50 percent of required credit hours. *Entrance requirements:* For master's, GRE, bachelor's degree (or equivalent) or graduate degree from regionally-accredited college or university or of recognized standing; minimum GPA of 3.0 or equivalent in last 2 years of work leading to bachelor's degree; 3 letters of recommendation; personal statement; current resume. Additional exam requirements/recommendations for international students: Required—TOEFL, IELTS, or PTE. Electronic applications accepted. *Expenses:* Contact institution.

Carnegie Mellon University, Carnegie Institute of Technology, Department of Civil and Environmental Engineering, Pittsburgh, PA 15213. Offers advanced infrastructure systems (MS, PhD); advanced infrastructure systems technology development and application (MS); air quality engineering and science (MS); civil and environmental engineering (MS, PhD); civil and environmental engineering/engineering and public policy (PhD); civil engineering (MS, PhD); computational mechanics (MS, PhD); computational modeling and monitoring for resilient structural and material systems (MS); energy infrastructure systems (MS); environmental engineering (MS, PhD); environmental management and science (MS, PhD); IT-based sustainable global infrastructure and construction management (MS); sustainability and green design (MS); water quality engineering and science (MS). Part-time programs available. *Faculty:* 21 full-time (5 women), 12 part-time/adjunct (3 women). *Students:* 229 full-time (99 women), 31 part-time (11 women); includes 18 minority (4 Black or African American, non-Hispanic/Latino; 13 Asian, non-Hispanic/Latino; 1 Hispanic/Latino), 193 international. Average age 26. 590 applicants, 68% accepted, 124 enrolled. In 2014, 85 master's, 11 doctorates awarded. Terminal master's awarded for partial completion of doctoral program. *Degree requirements:* For master's, thesis optional; for doctorate, comprehensive exam, thesis/dissertation, two-part qualifying exam, public defense of dissertation. *Entrance requirements:* For master's, GRE General Test, BS in engineering, science or mathematics; for doctorate, GRE General Test, BS or MS in engineering, science or mathematics. Additional exam requirements/recommendations for international students: Required—TOEFL (minimum score 84 iBT) or IELTS. *Application deadline:* For fall admission, 1/5 priority date for domestic and international students; for spring admission, 9/15 priority date for domestic and international students. Application fee: $65. Electronic applications accepted. *Financial support:* In 2014–15, 169 students received support. Fellowships with full and partial tuition reimbursements available, research assistantships with full and partial tuition reimbursements available, scholarships/grants, tuition waivers (full and partial), unspecified assistantships, and service assistantships available. Financial award application deadline: 1/5. *Faculty research:* Advanced infrastructure systems; environmental engineering, sustainability, and science; mechanics, materials, and computing. *Total annual research expenditures:* $4.9 million. *Unit head:* Dr. David A. Dzombak, Head, 412-268-2941, Fax: 412-268-7813, E-mail: dzombak@cmu.edu. *Application contact:* Melissa L. Brown, Director of

Graduate Admissions & Recruiting, 412-268-8762, Fax: 412-268-7813, E-mail: mlb2@andrew.cmu.edu. Website: http://www.cmu.edu/cee/.

Carnegie Mellon University, Carnegie Institute of Technology, Department of Engineering and Public Policy, Pittsburgh, PA 15213-3891. Offers PhD. *Degree requirements:* For doctorate, thesis/dissertation. *Entrance requirements:* For doctorate, GRE General Test, BS in physical sciences or engineering. Additional exam requirements/recommendations for international students: Required—TOEFL. *Faculty research:* Issues in energy and environmental policy, IT and telecommunications policy, risk analysis and communication, management of technological innovation, security and engineered civil systems.

Eastern Michigan University, Graduate School, College of Technology, School of Technology and Professional Services Management, Programs in Technology Studies, Ypsilanti, MI 48197. Offers interdisciplinary technology (MLS); technology studies (MS). Part-time and evening/weekend programs available. Postbaccalaureate distance learning degree programs offered (minimal on-campus study). *Students:* 13 full-time (2 women), 91 part-time (10 women); includes 17 minority (11 Black or African American, non-Hispanic/Latino; 1 Asian, non-Hispanic/Latino; 5 Two or more races, non-Hispanic/Latino), 1 international. Average age 37. 44 applicants, 73% accepted, 21 enrolled. In 2014, 36 master's awarded. *Degree requirements:* For master's, thesis optional. *Entrance requirements:* For master's, GRE General Test, minimum GPA of 2.6. Additional exam requirements/recommendations for international students: Required—TOEFL. *Application deadline:* Applications are processed on a rolling basis. Application fee: $45. *Financial support:* Fellowships, research assistantships with full tuition reimbursements, teaching assistantships with full tuition reimbursements, career-related internships or fieldwork, Federal Work-Study, institutionally sponsored loans, scholarships/grants, tuition waivers (partial), and unspecified assistantships available. Support available to part-time students. Financial award applicants required to submit FAFSA. *Application contact:* Dr. Denise Pilato, Program Coordinator, 734-487-1161, Fax: 734-487-7690, E-mail: denise.pilato@emich.edu.

The George Washington University, Elliott School of International Affairs, Program in International Science and Technology Policy, Washington, DC 20052. Offers MA, Graduate Certificate. Part-time programs available. *Students:* 18 full-time (7 women), 13 part-time (4 women); includes 8 minority (1 Asian, non-Hispanic/Latino; 4 Hispanic/Latino; 3 Two or more races, non-Hispanic/Latino), 2 international. Average age 28. 31 applicants, 11 enrolled. In 2014, 13 master's, 2 other advanced degrees awarded. *Degree requirements:* For master's, one foreign language, capstone project. *Entrance requirements:* For master's, GRE General Test. Additional exam requirements/recommendations for international students: Required—TOEFL (minimum score 100 iBT), IELTS (minimum score 7). *Application deadline:* For fall admission, 1/15 priority date for domestic and international students; for spring admission, 10/1 for domestic students. Application fee: $75. Electronic applications accepted. *Financial support:* In 2014–15, 15 students received support. Fellowships with partial tuition reimbursements

available, Federal Work-Study, and scholarships/grants available. Financial award application deadline: 1/15; financial award applicants required to submit FAFSA. *Faculty research:* Science policy, space policy, risk assessment, technology transfer, energy policy. *Unit head:* Prof. Allison Macfarlane, Director, 202-994-7292, E-mail: cistp@gwu.edu. *Application contact:* Nicole A. Campbell, Director of Graduate Admissions, 202-994-7050, Fax: 202-994-9537, E-mail: esiagrad@gwu.edu.
Website: http://elliott.gwu.edu/international-science-and-technology-policy.

Massachusetts Institute of Technology, School of Engineering, Engineering Systems Division, Cambridge, MA 02139. Offers engineering and management (SM); engineering systems (SM, PhD); logistics (M Eng); technology and policy (SM); technology, management and policy (PhD); SM/MBA. *Faculty:* 19 full-time (5 women). *Students:* 327 full-time (106 women); includes 53 minority (7 Black or African American, non-Hispanic/Latino; 28 Asian, non-Hispanic/Latino; 15 Hispanic/Latino; 3 Two or more races, non-Hispanic/Latino), 141 international. Average age 31. 1,143 applicants, 32% accepted, 254 enrolled. In 2014, 158 master's, 9 doctorates awarded. *Degree requirements:* For master's, thesis; for doctorate, comprehensive exam, thesis/dissertation. *Entrance requirements:* Additional exam requirements/recommendations for international students: Required—IELTS. *Application deadline:* For fall admission, 12/15 for domestic and international students. Application fee: $75. Electronic applications accepted. *Expenses:* Expenses: Contact institution. *Financial support:* In 2014–15, 213 students received support, including 39 fellowships (averaging $35,000 per year), 102 research assistantships (averaging $33,200 per year), 18 teaching assistantships (averaging $31,400 per year); Federal Work-Study, institutionally sponsored loans, scholarships/grants, traineeships, health care benefits, and unspecified assistantships also available. Financial award application deadline: 4/15; financial award applicants required to submit FAFSA. *Faculty research:* Critical infrastructures, extended enterprises, energy and sustainability, health care delivery, humans and technology, uncertainty and dynamics, design and implementation, networks and flows, policy and standards. *Total annual research expenditures:* $14.4 million. *Unit head:* Munther A. Dahleh, Acting Director, 617-258-8773, E-mail: esdinquiries@mit.edu. *Application contact:* Graduate Admissions, 617-253-1182, E-mail: esdgrad@mit.edu.
Website: http://esd.mit.edu/.

Massachusetts Institute of Technology, School of Humanities, Arts, and Social Sciences, Program in Science, Technology, and Society, Cambridge, MA 02139. Offers history, anthropology, and science, technology and society (PhD). *Faculty:* 11 full-time (6 women). *Students:* 31 full-time (23 women); includes 7 minority (1 Black or African American, non-Hispanic/Latino; 2 American Indian or Alaska Native, non-Hispanic/Latino; 3 Asian, non-Hispanic/Latino; 1 Hispanic/Latino), 7 international. Average age 31. 145 applicants, 7% accepted, 3 enrolled. In 2014, 6 doctorates awarded. *Degree requirements:* For doctorate, comprehensive exam, thesis/dissertation. *Entrance requirements:* For doctorate, GRE General Test. Additional exam requirements/recommendations for international students: Required—TOEFL (minimum score 577 paper-based; 90 iBT), IELTS (minimum score 7). *Application deadline:* For fall admission, 12/15 for domestic and international students. Application fee: $75. Electronic applications accepted. *Expenses: Tuition:* Full-time $44,720; part-time $699 per unit. *Required fees:* $296. *Financial support:* In 2014–15, 29 students received support, including 19 fellowships (averaging $32,800 per year), 2 research assistantships (averaging $35,800 per year), 7 teaching assistantships (averaging $36,600 per year); Federal Work-Study, institutionally sponsored loans, scholarships/grants, health care benefits, and unspecified assistantships also available. Financial award application deadline: 4/15; financial award applicants required to submit FAFSA. *Faculty research:* History of science; history of technology; sociology of science and technology; anthropology of science and technology; science, technology, and society. *Total annual research expenditures:* $64,000. *Unit head:* Prof. David Kaiser, Program Director, 617-253-4062, Fax: 617-258-8118, E-mail: stsprogram@mit.edu. *Application contact:* Academic Administrator, 617-253-9759, Fax: 617-258-8118, E-mail: hasts@mit.edu.
Website: http://web.mit.edu/sts/.

Rensselaer Polytechnic Institute, Graduate School, School of Humanities, Arts, and Social Sciences, Program in Science and Technology Studies, Troy, NY 12180-3590. Offers MS, PhD. *Faculty:* 20 full-time (10 women). *Students:* 25 full-time (9 women), 3 part-time (1 woman); includes 5 minority (1 Black or African American, non-Hispanic/Latino; 2 Hispanic/Latino; 2 Two or more races, non-Hispanic/Latino), 4 international. Average age 32. 24 applicants, 33% accepted, 3 enrolled. In 2014, 3 master's, 1 doctorate awarded. Terminal master's awarded for partial completion of doctoral program. *Degree requirements:* For master's, thesis (for some programs); for doctorate, comprehensive exam, thesis/dissertation. *Entrance requirements:* For master's and doctorate, GRE. Additional exam requirements/recommendations for international students: Required—TOEFL (minimum score 600 paper-based; 100 iBT), IELTS (minimum score 7), PTE (minimum score 68). *Application deadline:* For fall admission, 1/1 priority date for domestic and international students; for spring admission, 8/15 priority date for domestic and international students. Applications are processed on a rolling basis. Application fee: $75. Electronic applications accepted. *Expenses: Tuition:* Full-time $46,700; part-time $1945 per credit. Tuition and fees vary according to course load. *Financial support:* In 2014–15, 25 students received support, including research assistantships (averaging $18,500 per year), teaching assistantships (averaging $18,500 per year); fellowships also available. Financial award application deadline: 1/1. *Faculty research:* Policy studies, science studies, technology studies. *Total annual research expenditures:* $5,000. *Unit head:* Dr. Abby Kinchy, Graduate Program Director, 518-276-6980, E-mail: kincha@rpi.edu. *Application contact:* Office of Graduate Admissions, 518-276-6216, E-mail: gradadmissions@rpi.edu.
Website: http://www.sts.rpi.edu/pl/graduate-programs-sts.

Rochester Institute of Technology, Graduate Enrollment Services, College of Liberal Arts, Department of Public Policy, MS Program in Science, Technology and Public Policy, Rochester, NY 14623-5604. Offers MS. Part-time programs available. *Students:* 4 full-time (1 woman), 2 part-time (1 woman), 1 international. Average age 28. 4 applicants, 50% accepted. In 2014, 2 master's awarded. *Degree requirements:* For master's, thesis. *Entrance requirements:* For master's, GRE and TOEFL, IELTS, or PTE for non-native English speakers, Recommended minimum GPA of 3.0. Additional exam requirements/recommendations for international students: Required—TOEFL (minimum score 570 paper-based; 88 iBT), PTE (minimum score 58), TOEFL (minimum score 550 paper-based; 79 iBT) or IELTS (minimum score 6.5). *Application deadline:* For fall admission, 2/15 priority date for domestic and international students; for spring admission, 12/15 priority date for domestic and international students. Applications are processed on a rolling basis. Electronic applications accepted. *Expenses:* Expenses: $1,673 per credit hour. *Financial support:* In 2014–15, 4 students received support. Research assistantships with partial tuition reimbursements available, teaching assistantships with partial tuition reimbursements available, career-related internships or fieldwork, Federal Work-Study, institutionally sponsored loans, scholarships/grants, and unspecified assistantships available. Support available to part-time students. *Faculty research:* Environmental policy, information and communications policy, energy policy, biotechnology policy. *Unit head:* Franz Foltz, Graduate Program Director, 585-475-5368, E-mail: fafgsh@rit.edu. *Application contact:* Diane Ellison, Associate Vice President, Graduate Enrollment Services, 585-475-2229, Fax: 585-475-7164, E-mail: gradinfo@rit.edu.
Website: http://www.rit.edu/cla/publicpolicy/academics/science-technology-and-public-policy-ms.

St. Cloud State University, School of Graduate Studies, College of Science and Engineering, Department of Environmental and Technological Studies, St. Cloud, MN 56301-4498. Offers MS. *Degree requirements:* For master's, thesis or alternative. *Entrance requirements:* For master's, minimum GPA of 2.75. Additional exam requirements/recommendations for international students: Required—TOEFL (minimum score 550 paper-based), Michigan English Language Assessment Battery; Recommended—IELTS (minimum score 6.5). Electronic applications accepted.

Stony Brook University, State University of New York, Graduate School, College of Engineering and Applied Sciences, Department of Technology and Society, Program in Technology, Policy, and Innovation, Stony Brook, NY 11794-3760. Offers PhD. Part-time programs available. *Students:* 17 full-time (5 women), 6 part-time (3 women); includes 7 minority (3 Black or African American, non-Hispanic/Latino; 3 Asian, non-Hispanic/Latino; 1 Hispanic/Latino), 8 international. Average age 28. 17 applicants, 35% accepted, 5 enrolled. *Degree requirements:* For doctorate, comprehensive exam, thesis/dissertation, qualifying examination, preliminary examination. *Entrance requirements:* For doctorate, GRE General Test, minimum undergraduate GPA of 3.0, CV. Additional exam requirements/recommendations for international students: Required—TOEFL. *Application deadline:* For fall admission, 1/5 for domestic and international students; for spring admission, 10/1 for domestic students. Application fee: $100. *Expenses:* Tuition, state resident: full-time $10,370; part-time $432 per credit. Tuition, nonresident: full-time $20,190; part-time $841 per credit. *Required fees:* $1431. *Unit head:* Dr. David Ferguson, Chair, 631-632-8770, Fax: 631-632-7809, E-mail: david.ferguson@stonybrook.edu. *Application contact:* Dr. Sheldon Reaven, Graduate Director, 631-632-8768, Fax: 631-632-7809.
Website: http://www.stonybrook.edu/est/graduate/phd.shtml.

University of Minnesota, Twin Cities Campus, Graduate School, Hubert H. Humphrey School of Public Affairs, Program in Science, Technology, and Environmental Policy, Minneapolis, MN 55455. Offers MS, JD/MS. Part-time programs available. *Students:* 3 full-time (2 women), 1 international. Average age 25. 15 applicants, 67% accepted, 3 enrolled. In 2014, 12 master's awarded. *Degree requirements:* For master's, thesis. *Entrance requirements:* For master's, GRE General Test, undergraduate training in the biological or physical sciences or engineering, minimum undergraduate GPA of 3.0. Additional exam requirements/recommendations for international students: Required—TOEFL (minimum score 600 paper-based; 100 iBT), IELTS (minimum score 7). *Application deadline:* For fall admission, 4/1 for domestic and international students. Applications are processed on a rolling basis. Application fee: $75 ($95 for international students). Electronic applications accepted. *Expenses:* Expenses: State resident full-time: $17,603 per year, nonresident full-time: $25,417 per year (6-16 credits per semester). *Financial support:* In 2014–15, 4 students received support, including fellowships with full and partial tuition reimbursements available (averaging $15,000 per year); career-related internships or fieldwork, Federal Work-Study, scholarships/grants, health care benefits, tuition waivers (full and partial), and unspecified assistantships also available. Financial award application deadline: 1/15. *Faculty research:* Economics, history, philosophy, and politics of science and technology; organization and management of science and technology. *Unit head:* Laura Bloomberg, Associate Dean, 612-625-0608, Fax: 612-626-0002, E-mail: bloom004@umn.edu. *Application contact:* Amy Luitjens, Director of Admissions, 612-626-7229, Fax: 612-626-0002, E-mail: luitjens@umn.edu.
Website: http://www.hhh.umn.edu/degrees/ms_step/.

University of South Africa, College of Human Sciences, Pretoria, South Africa. Offers adult education (M Ed); African languages (MA, PhD); African politics (MA, PhD); Afrikaans (MA, PhD); ancient history (MA, PhD); ancient Near Eastern studies (MA, PhD); anthropology (MA, PhD); applied linguistics (MA); Arabic (MA, PhD); archaeology (MA); art history (MA); Biblical archaeology (MA); Biblical studies (M Th, D Th, PhD); Christian spirituality (M Th, D Th); church history (M Th, D Th); classical studies (MA, PhD); clinical psychology (MA); communication (MA, PhD); comparative education (M Ed, Ed D); consulting psychology (D Admin, D Com, PhD); curriculum studies (M Ed, Ed D); development studies (M Admin, MA, D Admin, PhD); didactics (M Ed, Ed D); education (M Tech); education management (M Ed, Ed D); educational psychology (M Ed); English (MA); environmental education (M Ed); French (MA, PhD); German (MA, PhD); Greek (MA); guidance and counseling (M Ed); health studies (MA, PhD), including health sciences education (MA), health services management (MA), medical and surgical nursing science (critical care general) (MA), midwifery and neonatal nursing science (MA), trauma and emergency care (MA); history (MA, PhD); history of education (Ed D); inclusive education (M Ed, Ed D); information and communications technology policy and regulation (MA); information science (MA, MIS, PhD); international politics (MA, PhD); Islamic studies (MA, PhD); Italian (MA, PhD); Judaica (MA, PhD); linguistics (MA, PhD); mathematical education (M Ed); mathematics education (MA); missiology (M Th, D Th); modern Hebrew (MA, PhD); musicology (MA, MMus, D Mus, PhD); natural science education (M Ed); New Testament (M Th, D Th); Old Testament (D Th); pastoral therapy (M Th, D Th); philosophy (MA); philosophy of education (M Ed, Ed D); politics (MA, PhD); Portuguese (MA, PhD); practical theology (M Th, D Th); psychology (MA, MS, PhD); psychology of education (M Ed, Ed D); public health (MA); religious studies (MA, D Th, PhD); Romance languages (MA); Russian (MA, PhD); Semitic languages (MA, PhD); social behavior studies in HIV/AIDS (MA); social science (mental health) (MA); social science in development studies (MA); social science in psychology (MA); social science in social work (MA); social science in sociology (MA); social work (MSW, DSW, PhD); socio-education (M Ed, Ed D); sociolinguistics (MA); sociology (MA, PhD); Spanish (MA, PhD); systematic theology (M Th, D Th); TESOL (teaching English to speakers of other languages) (MA); theological ethics (M Th, D Th); theory of literature (MA, PhD); urban ministries (D Th); urban ministry (M Th).

The University of Texas at Austin, Graduate School, McCombs School of Business, Program in Technology Commercialization, Austin, TX 78712-1111. Offers MS. Twelve-month program, beginning in May, with classes held every other Friday and Saturday. Evening/weekend programs available. Postbaccalaureate distance learning degree programs offered (no on-campus study). *Degree requirements:* For master's, year-long global teaming project. *Entrance requirements:* For master's, GRE General Test or GMAT. Additional exam requirements/recommendations for international students: Required—TOEFL (minimum score 550 paper-based; 79 iBT). Electronic applications accepted. *Expenses:* Contact institution. *Faculty research:* Technology transfer; entrepreneurship; commercialization; research, development and innovation.

Section 16
Materials Sciences and Engineering

This section contains a directory of institutions offering graduate work in materials sciences and engineering, followed by an in-depth entry submitted by an institution that chose to prepare a detailed program description. Additional information about programs listed in the directory but not augmented by an in-depth entry may be obtained by writing directly to the dean of a graduate school or chair of a department at the address given in the directory.

For programs offering related work, see also in this book *Agricultural Engineering and Bioengineering, Biomedical Engineering and Biotechnology, Engineering and Applied Sciences,* and *Geological, Mineral/Mining, and Petroleum Engineering.* In another guide in this series:
Graduate Programs in the Physical Sciences, Mathematics, Agricultural Sciences, the Environment & Natural Resources
See *Chemistry* and *Geosciences*

CONTENTS

Program Directories

Ceramic Sciences and Engineering

Alfred University, Graduate School, New York State College of Ceramics, Kazuo Inamori School of Engineering, Alfred, NY 14802. Offers biomaterials engineering (MS); ceramic engineering (MS); ceramics (PhD); electrical engineering (MS); glass science (MS, PhD); materials science and engineering (MS, PhD); mechanical engineering (MS). Part-time programs available. *Degree requirements:* For master's, thesis; for doctorate, thesis/dissertation. *Entrance requirements:* Additional exam requirements/recommendations for international students: Required—TOEFL (minimum score 590 paper-based; 90 iBT), IELTS (minimum score 6.5). Electronic applications accepted. *Expenses:* Contact institution. *Faculty research:* X-ray diffraction, biomaterials and polymers, thin-film processing, electronic and optical ceramics, solid-state chemistry.

Missouri University of Science and Technology, Graduate School, Department of Materials Science and Engineering, Rolla, MO 65409. Offers ceramic engineering (MS, DE, PhD); metallurgical engineering (MS, PhD). *Degree requirements:* For master's, thesis optional; for doctorate, comprehensive exam. *Entrance requirements:* For master's, GRE (minimum combined score 1100, 600 verbal, 3.5 writing); for doctorate, GRE (minimum score: quantitative 600, writing 3.5). Additional exam requirements/recommendations for international students: Required—TOEFL (minimum score 570 paper-based).

Electronic Materials

Colorado School of Mines, Graduate School, Department of Metallurgical and Materials Engineering, Golden, CO 80401-1887. Offers materials science (MS, PhD); metallurgical and materials engineering (ME, MS, PhD). Part-time programs available. *Faculty:* 25 full-time (2 women), 12 part-time/adjunct (0 women). *Students:* 112 full-time (33 women), 12 part-time (2 women); includes 9 minority (3 Asian, non-Hispanic/Latino; 4 Hispanic/Latino; 2 Two or more races, non-Hispanic/Latino), 38 international. Average age 29. 207 applicants, 23% accepted, 35 enrolled. In 2014, 31 master's, 17 doctorates awarded. *Degree requirements:* For master's, thesis (for some programs); for doctorate, comprehensive exam, thesis/dissertation. *Entrance requirements:* For master's and doctorate, GRE General Test. Additional exam requirements/recommendations for international students: Required—TOEFL (minimum score 550 paper-based; 80 iBT). *Application deadline:* For fall admission, 12/15 priority date for domestic and international students; for spring admission, 9/1 priority date for domestic and international students. Application fee: $50 ($70 for international students). Electronic applications accepted. *Financial support:* In 2014–15, 88 students received support, including 5 fellowships with full tuition reimbursements available (averaging $21,120 per year), 69 research assistantships with full tuition reimbursements available (averaging $21,120 per year), 11 teaching assistantships with full tuition reimbursements available (averaging $21,120 per year); scholarships/grants, health care benefits, and unspecified assistantships also available. Financial award application deadline: 12/15; financial award applicants required to submit FAFSA. *Total annual research expenditures:* $7.4 million. *Unit head:* Dr. Ivar Reimanis, Interim Head, 303-273-3549, E-mail: ireimani@mines.edu. *Application contact:* Kelly Hummel, Program Assistant, 303-273-3660, Fax: 303-273-3795, E-mail: khummel@mines.edu.
Website: http://metallurgy.mines.edu.

Princeton University, Princeton Institute for the Science and Technology of Materials (PRISM), Princeton, NJ 08544-1019. Offers materials (PhD).

University of Arkansas, Graduate School, Interdisciplinary Program in Microelectronics and Photonics, Fayetteville, AR 72701-1201. Offers MS, PhD. *Degree requirements:* For doctorate, thesis/dissertation. Electronic applications accepted.

Materials Engineering

Arizona State University at the Tempe campus, Ira A. Fulton Schools of Engineering, School for Engineering of Matter, Transport and Energy, Tempe, AZ 85281. Offers aerospace engineering (MS, PhD); chemical engineering (MS, PhD); materials science and engineering (MS, PhD); mechanical engineering (MS, PhD); solar energy engineering and commercialization (PSM). Part-time and evening/weekend programs available. Postbaccalaureate distance learning degree programs offered (minimal on-campus study). Terminal master's awarded for partial completion of doctoral program. *Degree requirements:* For master's, thesis and oral defense (MS); applied project or comprehensive exam (MSE); interactive Program of Study (iPOS) submitted before completing 50 percent of required credit hours; for doctorate, comprehensive exam, thesis/dissertation, interactive Program of Study (iPOS) submitted before completing 50 percent of required credit hours. *Entrance requirements:* For master's, GRE, minimum GPA of 3.0 or equivalent in last 2 years of work leading to bachelor's degree; for doctorate, GRE, minimum GPA of 3.0 in last 2 years of work leading to bachelor's degree. Additional exam requirements/recommendations for international students: Required—TOEFL, IELTS, or PTE. Electronic applications accepted. *Expenses:* Contact institution. *Faculty research:* Electronic materials and packaging, materials for energy (batteries), adaptive/intelligent materials and structures, multiscale fluid mechanics, membranes, therapeutics and bioseparations, flexible structures, nanostructured materials, and micro/nano transport.

Auburn University, Graduate School, Ginn College of Engineering, Department of Mechanical Engineering, Program in Materials Engineering, Auburn University, AL 36849. Offers M Mtl E, MS, PhD. *Faculty:* 29 full-time (0 women), 1 part-time/adjunct (0 women). *Students:* 15 full-time (7 women), 14 part-time (5 women); includes 2 minority (1 Black or African American, non-Hispanic/Latino; 1 Asian, non-Hispanic/Latino), 17 international. Average age 28. 54 applicants, 54% accepted, 3 enrolled. In 2014, 4 master's, 6 doctorates awarded. *Degree requirements:* For master's, thesis (MS), oral exam; for doctorate, one foreign language, thesis/dissertation. *Entrance requirements:* For master's and doctorate, GRE General Test. *Application deadline:* For fall admission, 7/7 for domestic students; for spring admission, 11/24 for domestic students. Applications are processed on a rolling basis. Application fee: $50 ($60 for international students). Electronic applications accepted. *Expenses:* Tuition, state resident: full-time $8586; part-time $477 per credit hour. Tuition, nonresident: full-time $25,758; part-time $1431 per credit hour. *Required fees:* $804 per semester. Tuition and fees vary according to degree level and program. *Financial support:* Fellowships, research assistantships, teaching assistantships, and Federal Work-Study available. Support available to part-time students. Financial award application deadline: 3/15; financial award applicants required to submit FAFSA. *Faculty research:* Smart materials. *Unit head:* Dr. Bryan Chin, Head, 334-844-3322. *Application contact:* Dr. George Flowers, Dean of the Graduate School, 334-844-2125.

Binghamton University, State University of New York, Graduate School, Thomas J. Watson School of Engineering and Applied Science and School of Arts and Sciences, Materials Science and Engineering Program, Vestal, NY 13850. Offers MS, PhD. *Faculty:* 3 full-time (0 women). *Students:* 14 full-time (1 woman), 31 part-time (16 women); includes 2 minority (both Asian, non-Hispanic/Latino), 36 international. Average age 27. 74 applicants, 58% accepted, 14 enrolled. In 2014, 2 master's, 3 doctorates awarded. *Degree requirements:* For master's, thesis; for doctorate, comprehensive exam, thesis/dissertation. *Entrance requirements:* For master's and doctorate, GRE General Test. Additional exam requirements/recommendations for international students: Required—TOEFL (minimum score 550 paper-based; 80 iBT). Application fee: $75. *Expenses:* Expenses: $5,435 resident; $11,105 non-resident. *Financial support:* In 2014–15, 32 students received support, including 21 research assistantships with full tuition reimbursements available (averaging $17,500 per year), 10 teaching assistantships with full tuition reimbursements available (averaging $17,500 per year); career-related internships or fieldwork, Federal Work-Study, institutionally sponsored loans, scholarships/grants, health care benefits, tuition waivers (full and partial), and unspecified assistantships also available. Financial award application deadline: 2/15; financial award applicants required to submit FAFSA. *Unit head:* Ellen Tilden, Coordinator of Graduate Programs, 607-777-2873, E-mail: etilden@binghamton.edu. *Application contact:* Kishan Zuber, Recruiting and Admissions Coordinator, 607-777-2151, Fax: 607-777-2501, E-mail: kzuber@binghamton.edu.
Website: http://materials.binghamton.edu/materials/.

Boise State University, College of Engineering, Department of Materials Science and Engineering, Boise, ID 83725-0399. Offers M Engr, MS, PhD. *Faculty:* 18 full-time, 12 part-time/adjunct. *Students:* 21 full-time (4 women), 19 part-time (2 women); includes 3 minority (all Asian, non-Hispanic/Latino), 3 international. 30 applicants, 77% accepted, 13 enrolled. In 2014, 7 master's awarded. *Application deadline:* For fall admission, 3/1 priority date for domestic students; for spring admission, 10/1 priority date for domestic students. Application fee: $55. *Expenses:* Tuition, state resident: part-time $331 per credit hour. Tuition, nonresident: part-time $531 per credit hour. *Financial support:* In 2014–15, 20 students received support, including 20 research assistantships. *Unit head:* Dr. Peter Mullner, Department Chair, 208-426-5136, E-mail: petermullner@boisestate.edu. *Application contact:* Linda Platt, Office Services Supervisor, Graduate Admission and Degree Services, 208-426-1074, Fax: 208-426-2789, E-mail: lplatt@boisestate.edu.
Website: http://coen.boisestate.edu/mse/degreeprograms/.

Boston University, College of Engineering, Division of Materials Science and Engineering, Boston, MA 02215. Offers materials science and engineering (MS). Part-time programs available. *Students:* 50 full-time (15 women), 10 part-time (4 women); includes 4 minority (3 Asian, non-Hispanic/Latino; 1 Hispanic/Latino), 42 international. Average age 25. 208 applicants, 34% accepted, 29 enrolled. In 2014, 4 master's, 5 doctorates awarded. Terminal master's awarded for partial completion of doctoral program. *Degree requirements:* For master's, thesis (for some programs); for doctorate, comprehensive exam, thesis/dissertation. *Entrance requirements:* For master's and doctorate, GRE General Test. Additional exam requirements/recommendations for international students: Required—TOEFL (minimum score 550 paper-based; 84 iBT), IELTS (minimum score 7). *Application deadline:* For fall admission, 3/15 for domestic and international students; for spring admission, 10/1 for domestic and international students. Application fee: $80. Electronic applications accepted. *Expenses: Tuition:* Full-time $45,686; part-time $1428 per credit hour. *Required fees:* $660; $60 per semester. Tuition and fees vary according to program. *Financial support:* In 2014–15, 23 students received support, including 2 fellowships with full tuition reimbursements available (averaging $28,950 per year), 15 research assistantships with full tuition reimbursements available (averaging $19,300 per year), 4 teaching assistantships with full tuition reimbursements available (averaging $19,300 per year); career-related internships or fieldwork, Federal Work-Study, scholarships/grants, and tuition waivers (partial) also available. Financial award application deadline: 1/15; financial award applicants required to submit FAFSA. *Faculty research:* Biomaterials, electronic and photonic materials, materials for energy and environment, nanomaterials. *Unit head:* Dr. David Bishop, Division Head, 617-353-8899, Fax: 617-353-5548, E-mail: djb1@bu.edu. *Application contact:* Dr. Solomon Eisenberg, Senior Associate Dean of Academic Programs, 617-353-9760, Fax: 617-353-0259, E-mail: enggrad@bu.edu.
Website: http://www.bu.edu/mse/.

California State University, Northridge, Graduate Studies, College of Engineering and Computer Science, Department of Manufacturing Systems Engineering and Management, Northridge, CA 91330. Offers engineering automation (MS); engineering management (MS); manufacturing systems engineering (MS); materials engineering (MS). Postbaccalaureate distance learning degree programs offered. *Students:* 180 full-time (38 women), 56 part-time (15 women); includes 24 minority (11 Asian, non-Hispanic/Latino; 8 Hispanic/Latino; 5 Two or more races, non-Hispanic/Latino), 172 international. Average age 26. *Entrance requirements:* For master's, GRE (if cumulative undergraduate GPA less than 3.0). *Application deadline:* For fall admission, 3/30 for

domestic students; for spring admission, 9/30 for domestic students. Application fee: $55. *Expenses: Required fees:* $12,402. *Unit head:* Kang Chang, Acting Chair, 818-677-2167.
Website: http://www.csun.edu/~msem/.

Carleton University, Faculty of Graduate Studies, Faculty of Engineering and Design, Department of Mechanical and Aerospace Engineering, Ottawa, ON K1S 5B6, Canada. Offers aerospace engineering (M Eng, MA Sc, PhD); materials engineering (M Eng, MA Sc); mechanical engineering (M Eng, MA Sc, PhD). *Degree requirements:* For master's, thesis optional; for doctorate, thesis/dissertation. *Entrance requirements:* For master's, honors degree; for doctorate, MA Sc or M Eng. Additional exam requirements/recommendations for international students: Required—TOEFL. *Faculty research:* Thermal fluids engineering, heat transfer, vehicle engineering.

Carnegie Mellon University, Carnegie Institute of Technology, Department of Materials Science and Engineering, Pittsburgh, PA 15213-3891. Offers MS, PhD. Part-time programs available. Terminal master's awarded for partial completion of doctoral program. *Degree requirements:* For master's, exam; for doctorate, thesis/dissertation, qualifying exam. *Entrance requirements:* For master's and doctorate, GRE General Test. Additional exam requirements/recommendations for international students: Required—TOEFL. *Faculty research:* Materials characterization, process metallurgy, high strength alloys, growth kinetics, ceramics.

Case Western Reserve University, School of Graduate Studies, Case School of Engineering, Department of Materials Science and Engineering, Cleveland, OH 44106. Offers materials science and engineering (MS, PhD). Part-time programs available. Postbaccalaureate distance learning degree programs offered (no on-campus study). *Faculty:* 13 full-time (1 woman). *Students:* 34 full-time (13 women), 5 part-time (1 woman); includes 3 minority (1 Black or African American, non-Hispanic/Latino; 1 Asian, non-Hispanic/Latino; 1 Hispanic/Latino), 21 international. In 2014, 6 master's, 5 doctorates awarded. Terminal master's awarded for partial completion of doctoral program. *Degree requirements:* For master's, thesis (for some programs); for doctorate, thesis/dissertation, qualifying exam, teaching experience. *Entrance requirements:* For master's and doctorate, GRE General Test. Additional exam requirements/recommendations for international students: Required—TOEFL. *Application deadline:* For fall admission, 2/15 priority date for domestic students; for spring admission, 9/15 for domestic students. Applications are processed on a rolling basis. Application fee: $50. *Financial support:* In 2014–15, 30 research assistantships with full and partial tuition reimbursements were awarded; fellowships with full and partial tuition reimbursements and teaching assistantships also available. Financial award application deadline: 4/30; financial award applicants required to submit FAFSA. *Faculty research:* Surface hardening of steels and other alloys, chemistry and structure of surfaces, microstructural and mechanical property characterization, materials for energy applications, thermodynamics and kinetics of materials, performance and reliability of materials. *Total annual research expenditures:* $5.3 million. *Unit head:* Dr. James D. McGuffin-Cawley, Department Chair, 216-368-6482, Fax: 216-368-4224, E-mail: emse.info@case.edu. *Application contact:* Theresa Claytor, Student Affairs Coordinator, 216-368-8555, Fax: 216-368-8555, E-mail: esme.info@case.edu.
Website: http://dmseg5.case.edu.

The Catholic University of America, School of Engineering, Department of Materials Science and Engineering, Washington, DC 20064. Offers MS. Part-time programs available. *Students:* 8 full-time (5 women), 2 part-time (1 woman); includes 2 minority (both Black or African American, non-Hispanic/Latino), 8 international. Average age 29. 10 applicants, 100% accepted, 4 enrolled. In 2014, 5 master's awarded. *Degree requirements:* For master's, thesis optional. *Entrance requirements:* For master's, GRE (minimum score 1250), minimum GPA of 3.0, statement of purpose, official copies of academic transcripts. Additional exam requirements/recommendations for international students: Required—TOEFL (minimum score 580 paper-based). *Application deadline:* For fall admission, 7/15 for domestic students, 7/1 for international students; for spring admission, 11/15 for domestic students, 11/1 for international students. Applications are processed on a rolling basis. Application fee: $55. Electronic applications accepted. *Expenses: Tuition:* Full-time $40,200; part-time $1600 per credit hour. *Required fees:* $400; $195 per semester. One-time fee: $425. *Financial support:* Fellowships, research assistantships, teaching assistantships, Federal Work-Study, scholarships/grants, tuition waivers (full and partial), and unspecified assistantships available. Financial award application deadline: 2/1; financial award applicants required to submit FAFSA. *Faculty research:* Nanotechnology, biomaterials, magnetic and optical materials, glass, ceramics, and metallurgy processing and instrumentation. *Unit head:* Dr. Biprodas Dutta, Director, 202-319-5535, Fax: 202-319-4469, E-mail: duttab@cua.edu. *Application contact:* Director of Graduate Admissions, 202-319-5057, Fax: 202-319-6533, E-mail: cua-admissions@cua.edu.
Website: http://materialsscience.cua.edu/.

Clarkson University, Graduate School, Wallace H. Coulter School of Engineering, Program in Materials Science and Engineering, Potsdam, NY 13699. Offers PhD. Part-time programs available. *Students:* 10 full-time (2 women), 5 international. Average age 27. 18 applicants, 61% accepted, 4 enrolled. In 2014, 1 doctorate awarded. *Degree requirements:* For doctorate, comprehensive exam, thesis/dissertation, departmental qualifying exam. *Entrance requirements:* For doctorate, GRE, transcripts of all college coursework, resume, personal statement, three letters of recommendation. Additional exam requirements/recommendations for international students: Required—TOEFL (minimum score 550 paper-based; 80 iBT), IELTS (minimum score 6.5). *Application deadline:* For fall admission, 1/30 priority date for domestic and international students; for spring admission, 9/1 priority date for domestic and international students. Applications are processed on a rolling basis. Application fee: $25 ($35 for international students). Electronic applications accepted. *Expenses: Tuition:* Full-time $16,680; part-time $1390 per credit. *Required fees:* $295 per semester. *Financial support:* In 2014–15, 10 students received support, including 2 fellowships with full tuition reimbursements available (averaging $24,029 per year), 2 research assistantships with full tuition reimbursements available (averaging $24,029 per year), 1 teaching assistantship with full tuition reimbursement available (averaging $24,029 per year); scholarships/grants, tuition waivers (partial), and unspecified assistantships also available. *Unit head:* Dr. Marilyn Freeman, Chair, 315-268-2316, Fax: 315-268-4494, E-mail: mfreeman@clarkson.edu. *Application contact:* Kelly Sharlow, Assistant to the Dean, 315-268-7929, Fax: 315-268-4494, E-mail: ksharlow@clarkson.edu.
Website: http://www.clarkson.edu/engineering/graduate/mat_sci_eng_phd/.

Clemson University, Graduate School, College of Engineering and Science, Department of Materials Science and Engineering, Clemson, SC 29634. Offers MS, PhD. Part-time programs available. *Faculty:* 15 full-time (1 woman), 4 part-time/adjunct (2 women). *Students:* 55 full-time (13 women), 7 part-time (3 women); includes 2 minority (1 Black or African American, non-Hispanic/Latino; 1 Two or more races, non-Hispanic/Latino), 26 international. Average age 26. 162 applicants, 35% accepted, 19 enrolled. In 2014, 4 master's, 8 doctorates awarded. Terminal master's awarded for partial completion of doctoral program. *Degree requirements:* For master's, thesis; for doctorate, comprehensive exam, thesis/dissertation. *Entrance requirements:* For master's and doctorate, GRE General Test. Additional exam requirements/recommendations for international students: Required—TOEFL. *Application deadline:* For fall admission, 2/1 priority date for domestic students; for spring admission, 9/1 priority date for domestic students. Applications are processed on a rolling basis. Application fee: $70 ($80 for international students). Electronic applications accepted. *Financial support:* In 2014–15, 31 students received support, including 2 fellowships with full and partial tuition reimbursements available (averaging $1,000 per year), 31 research assistantships with partial tuition reimbursements available (averaging $21,668 per year); teaching assistantships with partial tuition reimbursements available, career-related internships or fieldwork, institutionally sponsored loans, scholarships/grants, health care benefits, and unspecified assistantships also available. Support available to part-time students. Financial award applicants required to submit FAFSA. *Total annual research expenditures:* $2 million. *Unit head:* Dr. Rajendra K. Bordia, Chair of the Department of Materials Science and Engineering, 864-656-3311, Fax: 864-656-5973, E-mail: rbordia@clemson.edu. *Application contact:* Heather L. Cox, Program Manager, 864-656-1512, Fax: 864-656-5973, E-mail: hlcox@clemson.edu.
Website: http://www.clemson.edu/mse/.

Colorado School of Mines, Graduate School, Department of Metallurgical and Materials Engineering, Golden, CO 80401-1887. Offers materials science (MS, PhD); metallurgical and materials engineering (ME, MS, PhD). Part-time programs available. *Faculty:* 25 full-time (2 women), 12 part-time/adjunct (0 women). *Students:* 112 full-time (33 women), 12 part-time (2 women); includes 9 minority (3 Asian, non-Hispanic/Latino; 4 Hispanic/Latino; 2 Two or more races, non-Hispanic/Latino), 38 international. Average age 29. 207 applicants, 23% accepted, 35 enrolled. In 2014, 31 master's, 17 doctorates awarded. *Degree requirements:* For master's, thesis (for some programs); for doctorate, comprehensive exam, thesis/dissertation. *Entrance requirements:* For master's and doctorate, GRE General Test. Additional exam requirements/recommendations for international students: Required—TOEFL (minimum score 550 paper-based; 80 iBT). *Application deadline:* For fall admission, 12/15 priority date for domestic and international students; for spring admission, 9/1 priority date for domestic and international students. Application fee: $50 ($70 for international students). Electronic applications accepted. *Financial support:* In 2014–15, 88 students received support, including 5 fellowships with full tuition reimbursements available (averaging $21,120 per year), 69 research assistantships with full tuition reimbursements available (averaging $21,120 per year), 11 teaching assistantships with full tuition reimbursements available (averaging $21,120 per year); scholarships/grants, health care benefits, and unspecified assistantships also available. Financial award application deadline: 12/15; financial award applicants required to submit FAFSA. *Total annual research expenditures:* $7.4 million. *Unit head:* Dr. Ivar Reimanis, Interim Head, 303-273-3549, E-mail: ireimani@mines.edu. *Application contact:* Kelly Hummel, Program Assistant, 303-273-3660, Fax: 303-273-3795, E-mail: khummel@mines.edu.
Website: http://metallurgy.mines.edu.

Columbia University, Fu Foundation School of Engineering and Applied Science, Department of Applied Physics and Applied Mathematics, New York, NY 10027. Offers applied physics (Eng Sc D); applied physics and applied mathematics (MS, PhD); materials science and engineering (MS, Eng Sc D, PhD); medical physics (MS). Part-time programs available. Postbaccalaureate distance learning degree programs offered (no on-campus study). *Faculty:* 34 full-time (4 women), 33 part-time/adjunct (4 women). *Students:* 130 full-time (31 women), 26 part-time (8 women); includes 21 minority (17 Asian, non-Hispanic/Latino; 3 Hispanic/Latino; 1 Two or more races, non-Hispanic/Latino), 97 international. 439 applicants, 30% accepted, 59 enrolled. In 2014, 49 master's, 10 doctorates awarded. Terminal master's awarded for partial completion of doctoral program. *Degree requirements:* For master's, comprehensive exam; for doctorate, thesis/dissertation, qualifying exam. *Entrance requirements:* For master's, GRE General Test, GRE Subject Test (strongly recommended); for doctorate, GRE General Test, GRE Subject Test (applied physics). Additional exam requirements/recommendations for international students: Required—TOEFL, IELTS, PTE. *Application deadline:* For fall admission, 12/15 priority date for domestic and international students; for spring admission, 10/1 priority date for domestic and international students. Application fee: $85. Electronic applications accepted. *Financial support:* In 2014–15, 60 students received support, including 1 fellowship with full tuition reimbursement available (averaging $37,500 per year), 42 research assistantships with full tuition reimbursements available (averaging $33,781 per year), 17 teaching assistantships with full tuition reimbursements available (averaging $33,781 per year); health care benefits also available. Financial award application deadline: 12/15; financial award applicants required to submit FAFSA. *Faculty research:* Plasma physics and fusion energy; optical and laser physics; atmospheric, oceanic and earth physics; applied mathematics; solid state science and processing of materials, their properties, and their structure; medical physics. *Unit head:* Dr. I. Cevdet Noyan, Professor and Chair, Applied Physics and Applied Mathematics, 212-854-8919, E-mail: seasinfo.apam@columbia.edu. *Application contact:* Montserrat Fernandez-Pinkley, Student Services Coordinator, 212-854-4457, Fax: 212-854-8257, E-mail: mf2157@columbia.edu.
Website: http://www.apam.columbia.edu/.

Cornell University, Graduate School, Graduate Fields of Engineering, Field of Materials Science and Engineering, Ithaca, NY 14853. Offers materials engineering (M Eng, PhD); materials science (M Eng, PhD). *Degree requirements:* For doctorate, comprehensive exam, thesis/dissertation. *Entrance requirements:* For master's and doctorate, GRE General Test, 3 letters of recommendation. Additional exam requirements/recommendations for international students: Required—TOEFL (minimum score 550 paper-based; 77 iBT). Electronic applications accepted. *Faculty research:* Ceramics, complex fluids, glass, metals, polymers semiconductors.

Dalhousie University, Faculty of Engineering, Department of Materials Engineering, Halifax, NS B3H 1Z1, Canada. Offers M Eng, MA Sc, PhD. *Degree requirements:* For master's, thesis; for doctorate, thesis/dissertation. *Entrance requirements:* Additional exam requirements/recommendations for international students: Required—TOEFL, IELTS, CANTEST, CAEL, or Michigan English Language Assessment Battery. Electronic applications accepted. *Faculty research:* Ceramic and metal matrix composites, electron microscopy, electrolysis in molten salt, fracture mechanics, electronic materials.

Dartmouth College, Thayer School of Engineering, Program in Materials Sciences and Engineering, Hanover, NH 03755. Offers MS, PhD. *Degree requirements:* For master's, thesis; for doctorate, thesis/dissertation, candidacy oral exam. *Entrance requirements:* For master's and doctorate, GRE General Test. *Application deadline:* For fall admission, 1/1 priority date for domestic students. Application fee: $45. *Financial support:* Fellowships, research assistantships, teaching assistantships, career-related internships or fieldwork, Federal Work-Study, institutionally sponsored loans, and tuition waivers (full and partial) available. Financial award application deadline: 1/15. *Faculty research:* Electronic and magnetic materials, microstructural evolution, biomaterials and nanostructures, laser-material interactions, nano composites. *Total annual research expenditures:* $3.2 million. *Unit head:* Dr. Joseph J. Helbie, Dean, 603-646-2238, Fax: 603-646-2580, E-mail: joseph.j.helbie@dartmouth.edu. *Application contact:* Candace S. Potter, Graduate Admissions Administrator, 603-646-3844, Fax: 603-646-1620, E-mail: candace.s.potter@dartmouth.edu.
Website: http://engineering.dartmouth.edu/.

Materials Engineering

Drexel University, College of Engineering, Department of Materials Engineering, Philadelphia, PA 19104-2875. Offers MS, PhD. Part-time and evening/weekend programs available. Terminal master's awarded for partial completion of doctoral program. *Degree requirements:* For master's, thesis or alternative; for doctorate, thesis/dissertation. *Entrance requirements:* For master's, minimum GPA of 3.0; for doctorate, minimum GPA of 3.0, MS. Additional exam requirements/recommendations for international students: Required—TOEFL. Electronic applications accepted. *Faculty research:* Composite science; polymer and biomedical engineering; solidification; near net shape processing, including powder metallurgy.

Duke University, Graduate School, Pratt School of Engineering, Master of Engineering Program, Durham, NC 27708-0271. Offers biomedical engineering (M Eng); civil engineering (M Eng); electrical and computer engineering (M Eng); environmental engineering (M Eng); materials science and engineering (M Eng); mechanical engineering (M Eng); photonics and optical sciences (M Eng). Part-time programs available. *Students:* 45 full-time (17 women); includes 5 minority (1 Black or African American, non-Hispanic/Latino; 2 Asian, non-Hispanic/Latino; 2 Hispanic/Latino), 23 international. Average age 24. 285 applicants, 43% accepted, 45 enrolled. In 2014, 45 master's awarded. *Entrance requirements:* For master's, GRE General Test, resume, 3 letters of recommendation, statement of purpose, transcripts. Additional exam requirements/recommendations for international students: Required—TOEFL. *Application deadline:* For fall admission, 6/15 for domestic students, 2/15 for international students; for spring admission, 11/1 for domestic students, 9/1 for international students. Application fee: $75. *Expenses: Tuition:* Full-time $45,760; part-time $2765 per credit. *Required fees:* $978. Full-time tuition and fees vary according to program. *Financial support:* Merit scholarships/grants available. *Unit head:* Dr. Bradley A. Fox, Executive Director, 919-660-5455, Fax: 919-660-5456. *Application contact:* Susan Brown, Assistant Director of Admissions, 919-660-8451, Fax: 919-660-5456, E-mail: susan.brown@duke.edu.
Website: http://meng.pratt.duke.edu/.

Florida International University, College of Engineering and Computing, Department of Mechanical and Materials Engineering, Materials Science and Engineering Program, Miami, FL 33175. Offers MS, PhD. Part-time and evening/weekend programs available. Terminal master's awarded for partial completion of doctoral program. *Degree requirements:* For master's, thesis or alternative; for doctorate, comprehensive exam, thesis/dissertation. *Entrance requirements:* For master's, GRE, 3 letters of recommendation, minimum undergraduate GPA of 3.0 in upper-level course work; for doctorate, GRE, minimum GPA of 3.0, 3 letters of recommendation, letter of intent. Additional exam requirements/recommendations for international students: Required—TOEFL (minimum score 550 paper-based; 80 iBT). Electronic applications accepted.

Florida State University, The Graduate School, Materials Science and Engineering Program, Tallahassee, FL 32310. Offers MS, PhD. *Faculty:* 37 full-time (6 women). *Students:* 17 full-time (3 women), 1 part-time (0 women); includes 2 minority (both Hispanic/Latino), 9 international. Average age 26. 51 applicants, 18% accepted, 2 enrolled. In 2014, 2 master's, 1 doctorate awarded. Terminal master's awarded for partial completion of doctoral program. *Degree requirements:* For master's, thesis; for doctorate, comprehensive exam, thesis/dissertation. *Entrance requirements:* For master's and doctorate, GRE General Test (minimum new format 55th percentile Verbal, 75th percentile Quantitative, old version 1100 combined Verbal and Quantitative), minimum GPA of 3.0, 3 letters of recommendation. Additional exam requirements/recommendations for international students: Required—TOEFL (minimum score 80 iBT). *Application deadline:* For fall admission, 5/1 for domestic and international students; for spring admission, 9/1 for domestic and international students; for summer admission, 1/1 for domestic and international students. Applications are processed on a rolling basis. Application fee: $30. Electronic applications accepted. *Expenses:* Tuition, state resident: part-time $403.51 per credit hour. Tuition, nonresident: part-time $1004.85 per credit hour. *Required fees:* $75.81 per credit hour. One-time fee: $20 part-time. Tuition and fees vary according to campus/location. *Financial support:* In 2014–15, 17 students received support, including 17 research assistantships with full tuition reimbursements available (averaging $21,990 per year); partial payment of required health insurance also available. Financial award application deadline: 12/15. *Faculty research:* Magnetism and magnetic materials, composites, superconductors, polymers, computations, nanotechnology. *Unit head:* Prof. Eric Hellstrom, Director, 850-645-7489, Fax: 850-645-7754, E-mail: hellstrom@asc.magnet.fsu.edu. *Application contact:* Judy Gardner, Admissions Coordinator, 850-645-8980, Fax: 850-645-9123, E-mail: jdgardner@fsu.edu.
Website: http://materials.fsu.edu.

Georgia Institute of Technology, Graduate Studies, College of Engineering, School of Materials Science and Engineering, Atlanta, GA 30332-0001. Offers MS, PhD. Part-time programs available. *Students:* 159 full-time (31 women), 13 part-time (4 women); includes 27 minority (4 Black or African American, non-Hispanic/Latino; 15 Asian, non-Hispanic/Latino; 4 Hispanic/Latino; 4 Two or more races, non-Hispanic/Latino), 84 international. Average age 26. 381 applicants, 26% accepted, 35 enrolled. In 2014, 14 master's, 23 doctorates awarded. Terminal master's awarded for partial completion of doctoral program. *Degree requirements:* For master's, thesis optional; for doctorate, comprehensive exam, thesis/dissertation, teaching assignment. *Entrance requirements:* For master's and doctorate, GRE General Test, http://www.mse.gatech.edu/academics/app-requirements. Additional exam requirements/recommendations for international students: Required—TOEFL (minimum score 620 paper-based; 105 iBT). *Application deadline:* For fall admission, 12/15 priority date for domestic students, 12/15 for international students; for spring admission, 10/1 for domestic students; for summer admission, 2/1 for domestic students. Applications are processed on a rolling basis. Application fee: $75. Electronic applications accepted. *Expenses:* Tuition, state resident: full-time $12,344; part-time $515 per credit hour. Tuition, nonresident: full-time $27,600; part-time $1150 per credit hour. *Required fees:* $1196 per term. Part-time tuition and fees vary according to course load. *Financial support:* Fellowships with tuition reimbursements, research assistantships with tuition reimbursements, teaching assistantships, career-related internships or fieldwork, Federal Work-Study, institutionally sponsored loans, traineeships, tuition waivers (partial), and unspecified assistantships available. Support available to part-time students. Financial award application deadline: 5/1. *Faculty research:* Nanomaterials, biomaterials, computational materials science, mechanical behavior, advanced engineering materials. *Total annual research expenditures:* $10.4 million. *Unit head:* David Bucknall, Director, 404-894-2535, E-mail: david.bucknall@mse.gatech.edu. *Application contact:* Susan Bowman, Graduate Coordinator, 404-894-8414, E-mail: susan.bowman@mse.gatech.edu.
Website: http://www.mse.gatech.edu.

Illinois Institute of Technology, Graduate College, Armour College of Engineering, Department of Mechanical, Materials and Aerospace Engineering, Chicago, IL 60616. Offers manufacturing engineering (MAS, MS); materials science and engineering (MAS, MS, PhD); mechanical and aerospace engineering (MAS, MS, PhD), including economics (MS), energy (MS), environment (MS). Part-time and evening/weekend programs available. Postbaccalaureate distance learning degree programs offered (minimal on-campus study). *Faculty:* 29 full-time (3 women), 10 part-time/adjunct (2 women). *Students:* 187 full-time (35 women), 27 part-time (3 women); includes 8 minority (2 Black or African American, non-Hispanic/Latino; 4 Asian, non-Hispanic/Latino; 2 Hispanic/Latino), 168 international. Average age 26. 1,562 applicants, 31% accepted, 76 enrolled. In 2014, 74 master's, 7 doctorates awarded. Terminal master's awarded for partial completion of doctoral program. *Degree requirements:* For master's, comprehensive exam (for some programs), thesis (for some programs); for doctorate, comprehensive exam, thesis/dissertation. *Entrance requirements:* For master's and doctorate, GRE General Test (minimum score 1000 Quantitative and Verbal, 3.0 Analytical Writing), minimum undergraduate GPA of 3.0. Additional exam requirements/recommendations for international students: Required—TOEFL (minimum score 550 paper-based; 80 iBT). *Application deadline:* For fall admission, 5/1 for domestic and international students; for spring admission, 10/15 for domestic and international students. Applications are processed on a rolling basis. Application fee: $50. Electronic applications accepted. *Expenses: Tuition:* Full-time $22,500; part-time $1250 per credit hour. *Required fees:* $30 per course. $260 per semester. One-time fee: $235. Tuition and fees vary according to course load and program. *Financial support:* Fellowships with full and partial tuition reimbursements, research assistantships with full and partial tuition reimbursements, teaching assistantships with full and partial tuition reimbursements, Federal Work-Study, institutionally sponsored loans, scholarships/grants, health care benefits, tuition waivers, and unspecified assistantships available. Support available to part-time students. Financial award applicants required to submit FAFSA. *Faculty research:* Fluid dynamics, metallurgical and materials engineering, solids and structures, computational mechanics, computer added design and manufacturing, thermal sciences, dynamic analysis and control of complex systems. *Unit head:* Dr. Keith Bowman, Chair of the Department of Mechanical, Materials and Aerospace Engineering & Duchossois Leadership Professor of Materials Engineering, 312-567-3175, Fax: 312-567-7230, E-mail: keith.bowman@iit.edu. *Application contact:* Rishab Malhotra, Director, Graduate Admission, 866-472-3448, Fax: 312-567-3138, E-mail: inquiry.grad@iit.edu.
Website: http://www.mmae.iit.edu.

Instituto Tecnológico y de Estudios Superiores de Monterrey, Campus Estado de México, Professional and Graduate Division, Estado de Mexico, Mexico. Offers administration of information technologies (MITA); architecture (M Arch); business administration (GMBA, MBA); computer sciences (MCS, PhD); education (M Ed); educational institution administration (MAD); educational technology and innovation (PhD); electronic commerce (MEC); environmental systems (MS); finance (MAF); humanistic studies (MHS); information sciences and knowledge management (MISKM); information systems (MS); manufacturing systems (MS); marketing (MEM); quality systems and productivity (MS); science and materials engineering (PhD); telecommunications management (MTM). Part-time programs available. Postbaccalaureate distance learning degree programs offered (minimal on-campus study). *Degree requirements:* For master's, one foreign language, thesis (for some programs); for doctorate, one foreign language, thesis/dissertation. *Entrance requirements:* For master's, E-PAEP 500, interview; for doctorate, E-PAEP 500, research proposal. Additional exam requirements/recommendations for international students: Required—TOEFL (minimum score 550 paper-based). *Faculty research:* Surface treatments by plasmas, mechanical properties, robotics, graphical computing, mechatronics security protocols.

Iowa State University of Science and Technology, Department of Materials Science and Engineering, Ames, IA 50011. Offers MS, PhD. *Entrance requirements:* For master's and doctorate, GRE General Test. Additional exam requirements/recommendations for international students: Required—TOEFL (minimum score 550 paper-based; 79 iBT), IELTS (minimum score 6.5). Electronic applications accepted.

Johns Hopkins University, Engineering Program for Professionals, Part-time Program in Materials Science and Engineering, Baltimore, MD 21218-2699. Offers M Mat SE, MSE. Part-time and evening/weekend programs available. Electronic applications accepted.

Johns Hopkins University, G. W. C. Whiting School of Engineering, Department of Materials Science and Engineering, Baltimore, MD 21218-2699. Offers M Mat SE, MSE, PhD. Part-time and evening/weekend programs available. Terminal master's awarded for partial completion of doctoral program. *Degree requirements:* For master's, thesis, oral exam; for doctorate, thesis/dissertation, oral exam, thesis defense. *Entrance requirements:* For master's and doctorate, GRE General Test. Additional exam requirements/recommendations for international students: Required—TOEFL (minimum score 600 paper-based). Electronic applications accepted. *Faculty research:* Thin films, nanomaterials, biomaterials, materials characterization, electronic materials.

Johns Hopkins University, G. W. C. Whiting School of Engineering, Master of Science in Engineering Management Program, Baltimore, MD 21218-2699. Offers biomaterials (MSEM); civil engineering (MSEM); communications science (MSEM); computer science (MSEM); environmental systems analysis, economics and public policy (MSEM); fluid mechanics (MSEM); materials science and engineering (MSEM); mechanical engineering (MSEM); mechanics and materials (MSEM); nano-biotechnology (MSEM); nanomaterials and nanotechnology (MSEM); operations research (MSEM); probability and statistics (MSEM); smart product and device design (MSEM). *Entrance requirements:* For master's, GRE, 3 letters of recommendation, resume. Additional exam requirements/recommendations for international students: Required—TOEFL (minimum score 600 paper-based; 100 iBT) or IELTS (minimum score 7). Electronic applications accepted.

Lehigh University, P.C. Rossin College of Engineering and Applied Science, Department of Materials Science and Engineering, Bethlehem, PA 18015. Offers materials science and engineering (M Eng, MS, PhD); photonics (MS); polymer science/engineering (M Eng, MS, PhD); MBA/E. Part-time programs available. *Faculty:* 14 full-time (3 women), 1 part-time/adjunct (0 women). *Students:* 28 full-time (9 women), 8 part-time (0 women); includes 3 minority (2 Asian, non-Hispanic/Latino; 1 Two or more races, non-Hispanic/Latino), 15 international. Average age 27. 238 applicants, 3% accepted, 4 enrolled. In 2014, 3 master's, 5 doctorates awarded. *Degree requirements:* For master's, thesis; for doctorate, comprehensive exam, thesis/dissertation. *Entrance requirements:* For master's and doctorate, GRE General Test. Additional exam requirements/recommendations for international students: Required—TOEFL (minimum score 487 paper-based; 85 iBT). *Application deadline:* For fall admission, 1/15 priority date for domestic students, 1/15 for international students; for spring admission, 12/1 priority date for domestic students, 12/1 for international students. Applications are processed on a rolling basis. Application fee: $75. Electronic applications accepted. *Financial support:* In 2014–15, 26 students received support, including 3 fellowships with full and partial tuition reimbursements available (averaging $19,920 per year), 22 research assistantships with full and partial tuition reimbursements available (averaging $25,550 per year), 6 teaching assistantships with full and partial tuition reimbursements available (averaging $20,490 per year); career-related internships or fieldwork, Federal Work-Study, institutionally sponsored loans, scholarships/grants, and unspecified assistantships also available. Support available to part-time students. Financial award application deadline: 1/15. *Faculty research:* Metals, ceramics, crystals, polymers, fatigue crack propagation, biomaterials. *Total annual research expenditures:* $4.2 million. *Unit head:* Dr. Helen Chan, Chairperson, 610-758-5554, Fax: 610-758-4244,

E-mail: hmc0@lehigh.edu. *Application contact:* Lisa Carreras Arechiga, Graduate Administrative Coordinator, 610-758-4222, Fax: 610-758-4244, E-mail: lia4@lehigh.edu.
Website: http://www.lehigh.edu/~inmatsci/.

Massachusetts Institute of Technology, School of Engineering, Department of Civil and Environmental Engineering, Cambridge, MA 02139. Offers biological oceanography (PhD, Sc D); chemical oceanography (PhD, Sc D); civil and environmental engineering (M Eng, SM, PhD, Sc D); civil and environmental systems (PhD, Sc D); civil engineering (PhD, Sc D, CE); coastal engineering (PhD, Sc D); construction engineering and management (PhD, Sc D); environmental biology (PhD, Sc D); environmental chemistry (PhD, Sc D); environmental engineering (PhD, Sc D); environmental fluid mechanics (PhD, Sc D); geotechnical and geoenvironmental engineering (PhD, Sc D); hydrology (PhD, Sc D); information technology (PhD, Sc D); oceanographic engineering (PhD, Sc D); structures and materials (PhD, Sc D); transportation (PhD, Sc D); SM/MBA. *Faculty:* 34 full-time (8 women), 1 part-time/adjunct (0 women). *Students:* 216 full-time (82 women); includes 25 minority (1 Black or African American, non-Hispanic/Latino; 10 Asian, non-Hispanic/Latino; 8 Hispanic/Latino; 6 Two or more races, non-Hispanic/Latino), 117 international. Average age 26. 565 applicants, 22% accepted, 85 enrolled. In 2014, 76 master's, 18 doctorates awarded. *Degree requirements:* For master's and CE, thesis; for doctorate, comprehensive exam, thesis/dissertation. *Entrance requirements:* For master's and doctorate, GRE General Test. Additional exam requirements/recommendations for international students: Required—TOEFL (minimum score 577 paper-based; 100 iBT), IELTS (minimum score 7). *Application deadline:* For fall admission, 12/15 for domestic and international students. Application fee: $75. Electronic applications accepted. *Expenses: Tuition:* Full-time $44,720; part-time $699 per unit. *Required fees:* $296. *Financial support:* In 2014–15, 170 students received support, including 32 fellowships (averaging $32,800 per year), 132 research assistantships (averaging $33,800 per year), 13 teaching assistantships (averaging $32,900 per year); Federal Work-Study, institutionally sponsored loans, scholarships/grants, traineeships, health care benefits, and unspecified assistantships also available. Financial award application deadline: 4/15; financial award applicants required to submit FAFSA. *Faculty research:* Environmental chemistry, environmental fluid mechanics and coastal engineering, environmental microbiology, geotechnical engineering and geomechanics, hydrology and hydroclimatology, infrastructure systems, mechanics of materials and structures, transportation systems. *Total annual research expenditures:* $22.9 million. *Unit head:* Prof. Markus Buehler, Department Head, 617-324-6488. *Application contact:* Graduate Admissions Coordinator, 617-253-7119, E-mail: cee-admissions@mit.edu.
Website: http://cee.mit.edu/.

Massachusetts Institute of Technology, School of Engineering, Department of Materials Science and Engineering, Cambridge, MA 02139. Offers archaeological materials (PhD, Sc D); materials engineering (Mat E); materials science and engineering (SM, PhD, Sc D). *Faculty:* 30 full-time (10 women). *Students:* 199 full-time (47 women); includes 35 minority (2 Black or African American, non-Hispanic/Latino; 23 Asian, non-Hispanic/Latino; 5 Hispanic/Latino; 5 Two or more races, non-Hispanic/Latino), 109 international. Average age 26. 406 applicants, 14% accepted, 34 enrolled. In 2014, 8 master's, 35 doctorates awarded. *Degree requirements:* For master's, thesis; for doctorate, comprehensive exam, thesis/dissertation. *Entrance requirements:* For master's, doctorate, and Mat E, GRE General Test. Additional exam requirements/recommendations for international students: Required—IELTS (minimum score 7). *Application deadline:* For fall admission, 12/15 for domestic and international students. Application fee: $75. Electronic applications accepted. *Expenses: Tuition:* Full-time $44,720; part-time $699 per unit. *Required fees:* $296. *Financial support:* In 2014–15, 178 students received support, including 44 fellowships (averaging $29,400 per year), 134 research assistantships (averaging $33,400 per year), 13 teaching assistantships (averaging $36,400 per year); Federal Work-Study, institutionally sponsored loans, scholarships/grants, traineeships, health care benefits, and unspecified assistantships also available. Financial award application deadline: 4/15; financial award applicants required to submit FAFSA. *Faculty research:* Thermodynamics and kinetics of materials; structure, processing and properties of materials; electronic, structural and biological materials engineering; computational materials science; materials in energy, medicine, nanotechnology and the environment. *Total annual research expenditures:* $26.5 million. *Unit head:* Prof. Christopher Schuh, Department Head, 617-253-3300, Fax: 617-252-1775. *Application contact:* Prof. Christopher Schuh, Department Head, 617-253-3300, Fax: 617-252-1775.
Website: http://dmse.mit.edu/.

McGill University, Faculty of Graduate and Postdoctoral Studies, Faculty of Engineering, Department of Civil Engineering and Applied Mechanics, Montréal, QC H3A 2T5, Canada. Offers environmental engineering (M Eng, M Sc, PhD); fluid mechanics (M Sc); fluid mechanics and hydraulic engineering (M Eng, PhD); materials engineering (M Eng, PhD); rehabilitation of urban infrastructure (M Eng, PhD); soil behavior (M Eng, PhD); soil mechanics and foundations (M Eng, PhD); structures and structural mechanics (M Eng, PhD); water resources (M Sc); water resources engineering (M Eng, PhD).

McGill University, Faculty of Graduate and Postdoctoral Studies, Faculty of Engineering, Department of Mining and Materials Engineering, Montréal, QC H3A 2T5, Canada. Offers materials engineering (M Eng, PhD); mining engineering (M Eng, M Sc, PhD, Diploma).

McMaster University, School of Graduate Studies, Faculty of Engineering, Department of Materials Science and Engineering, Hamilton, ON L8S 4M2, Canada. Offers materials engineering (M Eng, MA Sc, PhD); materials science (M Eng, PhD). *Degree requirements:* For master's, thesis; for doctorate, comprehensive exam, thesis/dissertation. *Entrance requirements:* Additional exam requirements/recommendations for international students: Required—TOEFL (minimum score 550 paper-based). *Faculty research:* Localized corrosion of metals and alloys, electron microscopy, polymer synthesis and characterization, polymer reaction kinetics and engineering, polymer process modeling.

Michigan State University, The Graduate School, College of Engineering, Department of Chemical Engineering and Materials Science, East Lansing, MI 48824. Offers chemical engineering (MS, PhD); materials science and engineering (MS, PhD). *Entrance requirements:* Additional exam requirements/recommendations for international students: Required—TOEFL. Electronic applications accepted.

Michigan Technological University, Graduate School, College of Engineering, Department of Materials Science and Engineering, Houghton, MI 49931. Offers MS, PhD. Part-time programs available. *Faculty:* 19 full-time, 10 part-time/adjunct. *Students:* 33 full-time (9 women); includes 1 minority (Two or more races, non-Hispanic/Latino), 16 international. Average age 28. 234 applicants, 16% accepted, 8 enrolled. In 2014, 1 master's, 5 doctorates awarded. Terminal master's awarded for partial completion of doctoral program. *Degree requirements:* For master's, comprehensive exam (for some programs), thesis (for some programs); for doctorate, comprehensive exam, thesis/dissertation. *Entrance requirements:* For master's and doctorate, GRE (domestic students from ABET-accredited programs exempt), statement of purpose, official transcripts, 3 letters of recommendation. Additional exam requirements/recommendations for international students: Required—TOEFL (recommended score 79 iBT) or IELTS. *Application deadline:* For fall admission, 2/1 priority date for domestic and international students; for spring admission, 8/15 priority date for domestic and international students. Applications are processed on a rolling basis. Electronic applications accepted. *Expenses:* Expenses: Contact institution. *Financial support:* In 2014–15, 26 students received support, including 2 fellowships with full and partial tuition reimbursements available (averaging $13,824 per year), 22 research assistantships with full and partial tuition reimbursements available (averaging $13,824 per year), 1 teaching assistantship with full and partial tuition reimbursement available (averaging $13,824 per year); career-related internships or fieldwork, Federal Work-Study, scholarships/grants, health care benefits, unspecified assistantships, and cooperative program also available. Financial award applicants required to submit FAFSA. *Faculty research:* Structure/property/processing relationships, microstructural characterization, alloy design, electronic/magnetic/photonic materials, materials and manufacturing processes. *Total annual research expenditures:* $1.3 million. *Unit head:* Dr. Stephen L. Kampe, Chair, 906-487-2036, Fax: 906-487-2934, E-mail: kampe@mtu.edu. *Application contact:* Stephen A. Hackney, Associate Department Chair for Graduate Studies, 906-487-2170, Fax: 906-487-2934, E-mail: hackney@mtu.edu.
Website: http://www.mtu.edu/materials/.

New Jersey Institute of Technology, College of Science and Liberal Arts, Newark, NJ 07102. Offers applied mathematics (MS); applied physics (M Sc, PhD); applied statistics (MS); biology (MS, PhD); biostatistics (MS); chemistry (MS, PhD); computational biology (MS); environmental science (MS, PhD); history (MA, MAT); materials science and engineering (MS, PhD); mathematical and computational finance (MS); mathematics science (PhD); pharmaceutical chemistry (MS); professional and technical communications (MS). Part-time and evening/weekend programs available. Terminal master's awarded for partial completion of doctoral program. *Degree requirements:* For master's, thesis optional; for doctorate, thesis/dissertation. *Entrance requirements:* For master's, GRE General Test; for doctorate, GRE General Test, minimum graduate GPA of 3.5. Additional exam requirements/recommendations for international students: Required—TOEFL (minimum score 550 paper-based; 79 iBT). Electronic applications accepted.

New Mexico Institute of Mining and Technology, Graduate Studies, Department of Materials Engineering, Socorro, NM 87801. Offers MS, PhD. *Degree requirements:* For master's, thesis; for doctorate, thesis/dissertation. *Entrance requirements:* For master's, GRE General Test; for doctorate, GRE General Test, GRE Subject Test. Additional exam requirements/recommendations for international students: Required—TOEFL (minimum score 540 paper-based). *Faculty research:* Thin films, ceramics, damage studies from radiation, corrosion shock.

North Carolina State University, Graduate School, College of Engineering, Department of Materials Science and Engineering, Raleigh, NC 27695. Offers MMSE, MS, PhD. PhD offered jointly with The University of North Carolina at Charlotte. *Degree requirements:* For master's, thesis; for doctorate, thesis/dissertation. Electronic applications accepted. *Faculty research:* Processing and properties of wide band gap semiconductors, ferroelectric thin-film materials, ductility of nanocrystalline materials, computational materials science, defects in silicon-based devices.

Northwestern University, McCormick School of Engineering and Applied Science, Department of Materials Science and Engineering, Evanston, IL 60208. Offers integrated computational materials engineering (Certificate); materials science and engineering (MS, PhD). Admissions and degrees offered through The Graduate School. Part-time programs available. *Faculty:* 25 full-time (4 women). *Students:* 204 full-time (64 women), 10 part-time (5 women); includes 38 minority (2 Black or African American, non-Hispanic/Latino; 1 American Indian or Alaska Native, non-Hispanic/Latino; 19 Asian, non-Hispanic/Latino; 10 Hispanic/Latino; 6 Two or more races, non-Hispanic/Latino), 97 international. Average age 26. 737 applicants, 18% accepted, 59 enrolled. In 2014, 15 master's, 33 doctorates awarded. Terminal master's awarded for partial completion of doctoral program. *Degree requirements:* For master's, thesis, oral thesis defense; for doctorate, comprehensive exam, thesis/dissertation, oral defense of dissertation, preliminary evaluation, qualifying exam. *Entrance requirements:* For master's and doctorate, GRE General Test. Additional exam requirements/recommendations for international students: Required—TOEFL (minimum score 577 paper-based; 90 iBT) or IELTS (minimum score 7). *Application deadline:* For fall admission, 12/31 for domestic and international students. Application fee: $75. Electronic applications accepted. *Financial support:* Fellowships with full tuition reimbursements, research assistantships with full tuition reimbursements, teaching assistantships with full tuition reimbursements, career-related internships or fieldwork, institutionally sponsored loans, health care benefits, and unspecified assistantships available. Financial award application deadline: 1/15; financial award applicants required to submit FAFSA. *Faculty research:* Art conservation science; biomaterials; ceramics; composites; energy; magnetic materials; materials for electronics and photonics; materials synthesis and processing; materials theory, computation, and design; metals; nanomaterials; polymers, self-assembly, and surfaces and interfaces. *Total annual research expenditures:* $31.4 million. *Unit head:* Dr. Michael Bedzyk, Chair, 847-491-3570, Fax: 847-491-7820, E-mail: bedzyk@northwestern.edu. *Application contact:* Dr. Chris Wolverton, Admissions Officer, 847-497-0593, Fax: 847-491-7820, E-mail: c-wolverton@northwestern.edu.
Website: http://www.matsci.northwestern.edu/.

The Ohio State University, Graduate School, College of Engineering, Department of Materials Science and Engineering, Columbus, OH 43210. Offers materials science and engineering (MS, PhD); welding engineering (MS, PhD). *Faculty:* 34. *Students:* 132 full-time (23 women), 31 part-time (6 women); includes 13 minority (1 Black or African American, non-Hispanic/Latino; 4 Asian, non-Hispanic/Latino; 7 Hispanic/Latino; 1 Two or more races, non-Hispanic/Latino), 55 international. Average age 27. In 2014, 38 master's, 16 doctorates awarded. *Degree requirements:* For master's, thesis; for doctorate, thesis/dissertation. *Entrance requirements:* For master's and doctorate, GRE (for graduates of foreign universities and holders of non-engineering degrees). Additional exam requirements/recommendations for international students: Required—TOEFL (minimum score 550 paper-based; 79 iBT), Michigan English Language Assessment Battery (minimum score 82); Recommended—IELTS (minimum score 7). *Application deadline:* For fall admission, 12/13 priority date for domestic students, 11/30 priority date for international students; for winter admission, 12/1 for domestic students, 11/1 for international students; for spring admission, 12/14 for domestic students, 11/12 for international students; for summer admission, 5/15 for domestic students, 4/14 for international students. Applications are processed on a rolling basis. Application fee: $60 ($70 for international students). Electronic applications accepted. *Financial support:* Fellowships with tuition reimbursements, research assistantships with tuition reimbursements, teaching assistantships, career-related internships or fieldwork, scholarships/grants, and unspecified assistantships available. *Faculty research:* Computational materials modeling, biomaterials, metallurgy, ceramics, advanced alloys/composites. *Total annual research expenditures:* $10 million. *Unit head:* Dr. Michael Mills, Interim Chair, E-mail: mills.108@osu.edu. *Application contact:* Mark Cooper, Graduate Studies Coordinator, 614-292-7280, Fax: 614-292-1357, E-mail: mse@osu.edu.
Website: http://mse.osu.edu/.

Materials Engineering

Penn State University Park, Graduate School, Intercollege Graduate Programs, Intercollege Graduate Program in Materials Science and Engineering, University Park, PA 16802. Offers MS, PhD. *Financial support:* Fellowships available. *Unit head:* Dr. Regina Vasilatos-Younken, Interim Dean, 814-865-2516, Fax: 814-863-4627, E-mail: rxv@psu.edu. *Application contact:* Lori A. Stania, Director, Graduate Student Services, 814-867-5278, Fax: 814-863-4627, E-mail: gswww@psu.edu.

Purdue University, College of Engineering, School of Materials Engineering, West Lafayette, IN 47907. Offers MSMSE, PhD. Part-time programs available. *Entrance requirements:* For master's and doctorate, minimum GPA of 3.0. Additional exam requirements/recommendations for international students: Required—TOEFL (minimum score 550 paper-based; 77 iBT); Recommended—TWE. Electronic applications accepted. *Faculty research:* Electronic behavior, mechanical behavior, thermodynamics, kinetics, phase transformations.

Rensselaer Polytechnic Institute, Graduate School, School of Engineering, Program in Materials Science and Engineering, Troy, NY 12180. Offers M Eng, MS, D Eng, PhD. *Faculty:* 37 full-time (9 women), 3 part-time/adjunct (2 women). *Students:* 57 full-time (13 women), 4 part-time (1 woman); includes 5 minority (3 Hispanic/Latino; 2 Two or more races, non-Hispanic/Latino), 29 international. Average age 26. 185 applicants, 18% accepted, 18 enrolled. In 2014, 7 master's, 9 doctorates awarded. Terminal master's awarded for partial completion of doctoral program. *Degree requirements:* For master's, thesis; for doctorate, comprehensive exam, thesis/dissertation. *Entrance requirements:* For master's and doctorate, GRE. Additional exam requirements/recommendations for international students: Required—TOEFL (minimum score 600 paper-based; 100 iBT), IELTS (minimum score 7), PTE (minimum score 68). *Application deadline:* For fall admission, 1/1 priority date for domestic and international students; for spring admission, 8/15 priority date for domestic and international students. Applications are processed on a rolling basis. Application fee: $75. Electronic applications accepted. *Expenses:* Tuition: Full-time $46,700; part-time $1945 per credit. Tuition and fees vary according to course load. *Financial support:* In 2014–15, 40 students received support, including research assistantships with full tuition reimbursements available (averaging $18,500 per year), teaching assistantships with full tuition reimbursements available (averaging $18,500 per year); fellowships also available. Financial award application deadline: 1/1. *Faculty research:* Advanced processing and synthesis, composites, computational materials, corrosion/electrochemical materials, electronic materials, glasses/ceramics, materials characterization, materials for energy, materials/biology interface, metals, nanomaterials, polymeric materials. *Total annual research expenditures:* $2 million. *Unit head:* Dr. Pawel Keblinski, Graduate Program Director, 518-276-6858, E-mail: keblip@rpi.edu. *Application contact:* Office of Graduate Admissions, 518-276-6216, E-mail: gradadmissions@rpi.edu. Website: http://www.mse.rpi.edu/.

Rochester Institute of Technology, Graduate Enrollment Services, College of Science, School of Chemistry and Materials Science, Rochester, NY 14623-5603. Offers MS. Part-time programs available. *Students:* 24 full-time (7 women), 14 part-time (7 women); includes 2 minority (1 Asian, non-Hispanic/Latino; 1 Hispanic/Latino), 13 international. Average age 25. 72 applicants, 46% accepted, 8 enrolled. In 2014, 6 master's awarded. *Degree requirements:* For master's, thesis or alternative. *Entrance requirements:* For master's, TOEFL, IELTS, or PTE for non-native English speakers, GRE for some programs, recommended minimum GPA of 3.0. Additional exam requirements/recommendations for international students: Required—PTE (minimum score 58), TOEFL (minimum score 550 paper-based; 79 iBT) or IELTS (minimum score 6.5). *Application deadline:* For fall admission, 2/15 priority date for domestic and international students; for spring admission, 12/15 priority date for domestic and international students. Applications are processed on a rolling basis. Electronic applications accepted. *Expenses:* Expenses: $1,673 per credit hour. *Financial support:* In 2014–15, 24 students received support. Research assistantships with partial tuition reimbursements available, teaching assistantships with partial tuition reimbursements available, career-related internships or fieldwork, Federal Work-Study, institutionally sponsored loans, scholarships/grants, and unspecified assistantships available. Support available to part-time students. Financial award applicants required to submit FAFSA. *Faculty research:* Organic chemistry, analytical chemistry, inorganic chemistry, physical chemistry, polymer chemistry, materials science, and biochemistry; polymer engineering, chemistry, and physics; nanomaterials; electronic materials; metallurgy; nonlinear phenomena; electronic properties of molecular crystals; experimental low temperature physics; large scale computations; parallel processing; superconductivity. *Unit head:* Dr. Paul Craig, Head, 585-475-2497, E-mail: science@rit.edu. *Application contact:* Diane Ellison, Associate Vice President, Graduate Enrollment Services, 585-475-2229, Fax: 585-475-7164, E-mail: gradinfo@rit.edu. Website: https://www.rit.edu/cos/scms/.

Rutgers, The State University of New Jersey, New Brunswick, Graduate School-New Brunswick, Program in Materials Science and Engineering, Piscataway, NJ 08854-8097. Offers MS, PhD. Part-time programs available. *Degree requirements:* For master's, thesis; for doctorate, comprehensive exam, thesis/dissertation. *Entrance requirements:* For master's and doctorate, GRE General Test. Additional exam requirements/recommendations for international students: Recommended—TOEFL. Electronic applications accepted. *Faculty research:* Ceramic processing, nanostructured materials, electrical and structural ceramics, fiber optics.

Saginaw Valley State University, College of Science, Engineering, and Technology, University Center, MI 48710. Offers energy and materials (MS). Part-time and evening/weekend programs available. *Faculty:* 2 full-time (0 women), 3 part-time/adjunct (1 woman). *Students:* 2 full-time (0 women), 5 part-time (1 woman); includes 1 minority (Black or African American, non-Hispanic/Latino), 3 international. Average age 30. 12 applicants, 58% accepted, 4 enrolled. In 2014, 1 master's awarded. *Degree requirements:* For master's, field project or thesis work. *Entrance requirements:* For master's, minimum GPA of 3.0. Additional exam requirements/recommendations for international students: Required—TOEFL (minimum score 550 paper-based; 79 iBT). *Application deadline:* For fall admission, 7/15 for international students; for winter admission, 11/15 for international students; for spring admission, 4/15 for international students. Applications are processed on a rolling basis. Application fee: $30 ($90 for international students). Electronic applications accepted. *Expenses:* Tuition, state resident: full-time $8957; part-time $497.60 per credit hour. Tuition, nonresident: full-time $17,081; part-time $948.95 per credit hour. *Required fees:* $263; $14.60 per credit hour. Tuition and fees vary according to degree level. *Financial support:* Federal Work-Study and scholarships/grants available. Support available to part-time students. Financial award application deadline: 4/1; financial award applicants required to submit FAFSA. *Unit head:* Dr. Robert Tuttle, Program Coordinator, 989-964-4144, Fax: 989-964-2717. *Application contact:* Jenna Briggs, Director, Graduate and International Admissions, 989-964-6096, Fax: 989-964-2788, E-mail: gradadm@svsu.edu. Website: http://www.svsu.edu/collegeofscienceengineeringtechnology/.

San Jose State University, Graduate Studies and Research, Charles W. Davidson College of Engineering, Department of Chemical and Materials Engineering, Program in Materials Engineering, San Jose, CA 95192-0001. Offers MS. Part-time programs available. *Degree requirements:* For master's, thesis or alternative. *Entrance requirements:* For master's, GRE. Additional exam requirements/recommendations for international students: Required—TOEFL. Electronic applications accepted. *Faculty research:* Electronic materials, thin films, electron microscopy, fiber composites, polymeric materials.

Santa Clara University, School of Engineering, Santa Clara, CA 95053. Offers analog circuit design (Certificate); applied mathematics (MS); ASIC design and test (Certificate); bioengineering (MS); civil engineering (MS); computer science and engineering (MS, PhD); controls (Certificate); digital signal processing (Certificate); dynamics (Certificate); electrical engineering (MS, PhD); engineering (Engineer); engineering management (MS); fundamentals of electrical engineering (Certificate); information assurance (Certificate); materials engineering (Certificate); mechanical design analysis (Certificate); mechanical engineering (MS, PhD); mechatronics systems engineering (Certificate); microwave and antennas (Certificate); networking (Certificate); renewable energy (Certificate); software engineering (Certificate); sustainable energy (MS); technology jump-start (Certificate); thermofluids (Certificate). Part-time and evening/weekend programs available. *Faculty:* 59 full-time (23 women), 80 part-time/adjunct (14 women). *Students:* 584 full-time (239 women), 353 part-time (102 women); includes 224 minority (7 Black or African American, non-Hispanic/Latino; 144 Asian, non-Hispanic/Latino; 50 Hispanic/Latino; 2 Native Hawaiian or other Pacific Islander, non-Hispanic/Latino; 21 Two or more races, non-Hispanic/Latino), 548 international. Average age 27. 1,248 applicants, 51% accepted, 375 enrolled. In 2014, 283 master's, 5 doctorates, 1 other advanced degree awarded. *Degree requirements:* For master's, thesis (for some programs); for doctorate, thesis/dissertation; for other advanced degree, thesis. *Entrance requirements:* For master's, GRE, transcript; for doctorate, GRE, master's degree or equivalent; for other advanced degree, master's degree, published paper. Additional exam requirements/recommendations for international students: Required—TOEFL (minimum score 550 paper-based; 79 iBT). *Application deadline:* For fall admission, 8/1 for domestic students, 7/15 for international students; for winter admission, 10/28 for domestic students, 9/23 for international students; for spring admission, 2/25 for domestic students, 1/21 for international students. Applications are processed on a rolling basis. Application fee: $60. Electronic applications accepted. *Expenses:* Expenses: Contact institution. *Financial support:* In 2014–15, 94 students received support. Fellowships with full and partial tuition reimbursements available, research assistantships with full and partial tuition reimbursements available, teaching assistantships with full tuition reimbursements available, career-related internships or fieldwork, Federal Work-Study, institutionally sponsored loans, and scholarships/grants available. Support available to part-time students. Financial award application deadline: 3/2; financial award applicants required to submit FAFSA. *Faculty research:* Video encoding, nanostructures, robotics, microfluidics, water resources. *Total annual research expenditures:* $1.6 million. *Unit head:* Dr. Alex Zecevic, Associate Dean for Graduate Studies, 408-554-2394, E-mail: azecevic@scu.edu. *Application contact:* Stacey Tinker, Director of Enrollment Management, 408-554-4748, Fax: 408-554-4323, E-mail: stinker@scu.edu. Website: http://www.scu.edu/engineering/graduate/.

South Dakota School of Mines and Technology, Graduate Division, Doctoral Program in Materials Engineering and Science, Rapid City, SD 57701-3995. Offers PhD. Part-time programs available. *Faculty:* 7 full-time (0 women), 1 part-time/adjunct (0 women). *Students:* 5 full-time (1 woman), 7 part-time (0 women); includes 1 minority (Asian, non-Hispanic/Latino), 5 international. Average age 33. 9 applicants, 44% accepted, 4 enrolled. In 2014, 5 doctorates awarded. *Degree requirements:* For doctorate, thesis/dissertation. *Entrance requirements:* For doctorate, GRE General Test, minimum graduate GPA of 3.0, 3 letters of recommendation. Additional exam requirements/recommendations for international students: Required—TOEFL (minimum score 520 paper-based; 68 iBT), TWE. *Application deadline:* For fall admission, 7/1 priority date for domestic students, 4/1 for international students; for spring admission, 11/1 for domestic students, 9/1 for international students. Applications are processed on a rolling basis. Application fee: $35. Electronic applications accepted. *Expenses:* Tuition, state resident: full-time $5050; part-time $210.40 per credit hour. Tuition, nonresident: full-time $11,290; part-time $470.30 per credit hour. *Required fees:* $4680. *Financial support:* In 2014–15, 1 fellowship (averaging $5,000 per year), 16 research assistantships with partial tuition reimbursements (averaging $7,722 per year), 1 teaching assistantship with partial tuition reimbursement (averaging $14,000 per year) were awarded; Federal Work-Study and institutionally sponsored loans also available. Support available to part-time students. Financial award application deadline: 5/15. *Faculty research:* Thermophysical properties of solids, development of multiphase materials and composites, concrete technology, electronic polymer materials. *Total annual research expenditures:* $3 million. *Unit head:* Dr. Jon J. Keller, Coordinator, 605-394-2343, E-mail: jon.keller@sdsmt.edu. *Application contact:* Rachel Howard, Office of Graduate Education, 605-355-3468, Fax: 605-394-1767, E-mail: rachel.howard@sdsmt.edu. Website: http://www.sdsmt.edu/Academics/Departments/Mechanical-Engineering/Graduate-Education/Mechanical-Engineering-PhD/.

South Dakota School of Mines and Technology, Graduate Division, Master's Program in Materials Engineering and Science, Rapid City, SD 57701-3995. Offers MS. *Faculty:* 7 full-time (0 women), 1 part-time/adjunct (0 women). *Students:* 14 full-time (4 women), 5 part-time (0 women), 6 international. Average age 27. 15 applicants, 47% accepted, 6 enrolled. In 2014, 5 master's awarded. *Degree requirements:* For master's, thesis (for some programs). *Entrance requirements:* For master's, GRE General Test. Additional exam requirements/recommendations for international students: Required—TOEFL (minimum score 520 paper-based; 68 iBT), TWE. *Application deadline:* For fall admission, 7/1 priority date for domestic students, 4/1 for international students; for spring admission, 11/1 for domestic students, 9/1 for international students. Applications are processed on a rolling basis. Application fee: $35. Electronic applications accepted. *Expenses:* Tuition, state resident: full-time $5050; part-time $210.40 per credit hour. Tuition, nonresident: full-time $11,290; part-time $470.30 per credit hour. *Required fees:* $4680. *Financial support:* In 2014–15, 4 fellowships (averaging $4,738 per year), 21 research assistantships with partial tuition reimbursements (averaging $8,307 per year), 8 teaching assistantships with partial tuition reimbursements (averaging $6,208 per year) were awarded. Financial award application deadline: 5/15. *Unit head:* Dr. Jon J. Keller, Coordinator, 605-394-2343, E-mail: jon.keller@sdsmt.edu. *Application contact:* Rachel Howard, Office of Graduate Education, 605-355-3468, Fax: 605-394-1767, E-mail: rachel.howard@sdsmt.edu. Website: http://www.sdsmt.edu/Academics/Departments/Materials-and-Metallurgical-Engineering/Graduate-Education/.

Southern Methodist University, Dedman College of Humanities and Sciences, Department of Chemistry, Dallas, TX 75275-0314. Offers chemistry (MS, PhD); materials science and engineering (MS, PhD). Terminal master's awarded for partial completion of doctoral program. *Degree requirements:* For master's, thesis; for doctorate, comprehensive exam, thesis/dissertation. *Entrance requirements:* For master's, GRE General Test, bachelor's degree in chemistry, minimum GPA of 3.0; for doctorate, GRE General Test, bachelor's degree in chemistry or closely-related field, minimum GPA of 3.0. Additional exam requirements/recommendations for international students: Required—TOEFL (minimum score 550 paper-based; 80 iBT). Electronic applications accepted. *Faculty research:* Materials/polymer, medicinal/bioorganic, theoretical and computational, organic/inorganic/organometallic synthesis, inorganic polymer chemistry.

Stanford University, School of Engineering, Department of Materials Science and Engineering, Stanford, CA 94305-9991. Offers MS, PhD. Terminal master's awarded for partial completion of doctoral program. *Degree requirements:* For doctorate, thesis/dissertation. *Entrance requirements:* For master's and doctorate, GRE General Test. Additional exam requirements/recommendations for international students: Required—TOEFL. Electronic applications accepted. *Expenses: Tuition:* Full-time $44,184; part-time $982 per credit hour. *Required fees:* $191.

Stevens Institute of Technology, Graduate School, Charles V. Schaefer Jr. School of Engineering, Department of Chemical Engineering and Materials Science, Program in Materials Science, Hoboken, NJ 07030. Offers M Eng, PhD.

Stony Brook University, State University of New York, Graduate School, College of Engineering and Applied Sciences, Department of Materials Science and Engineering, Stony Brook, NY 11794. Offers MS, PhD. *Faculty:* 17 full-time (6 women), 9 part-time/adjunct (1 woman). *Students:* 128 full-time (43 women), 21 part-time (11 women); includes 10 minority (3 Black or African American, non-Hispanic/Latino; 5 Asian, non-Hispanic/Latino; 1 Hispanic/Latino; 1 Two or more races, non-Hispanic/Latino), 100 international. Average age 26. 231 applicants, 46% accepted, 47 enrolled. In 2014, 39 master's, 12 doctorates awarded. *Degree requirements:* For master's, thesis or alternative; for doctorate, comprehensive exam, thesis/dissertation. *Entrance requirements:* For master's and doctorate, GRE General Test, minimum undergraduate GPA of 3.0. Additional exam requirements/recommendations for international students: Required—TOEFL. *Application deadline:* For fall admission, 1/15 for domestic students; for spring admission, 10/1 for domestic students. Application fee: $100. *Expenses:* Tuition, state resident: full-time $10,370; part-time $432 per credit. Tuition, nonresident: full-time $20,190; part-time $841 per credit. *Required fees:* $1431. *Financial support:* In 2014–15, 5 fellowships, 48 research assistantships, 12 teaching assistantships were awarded. *Faculty research:* Electronic materials, biomaterials, synchrotron topography. *Total annual research expenditures:* $3 million. *Unit head:* Dr. Michael Dudley, Chairman, 631-632-8484, Fax: 631-632-8052, E-mail: michael.dudley@stonybrook.edu. *Application contact:* Shauntae Smith, Coordinator, 631-632-4986, Fax: 631-632-8052, E-mail: shauntae.smith@stonybrook.edu.
Website: http://www.matscieng.sunysb.edu/.

Texas A&M University, College of Engineering, Department of Materials Science and Engineering, College Station, TX 77843. Offers M Eng, MS, PhD. *Faculty:* 9. *Students:* 86 full-time (18 women), 13 part-time (3 women); includes 8 minority (2 Black or African American, non-Hispanic/Latino; 3 Asian, non-Hispanic/Latino; 1 Hispanic/Latino; 2 Two or more races, non-Hispanic/Latino), 65 international. Average age 29. 121 applicants, 37% accepted, 17 enrolled. In 2014, 6 master's, 13 doctorates awarded. *Degree requirements:* For master's, thesis (MS); for doctorate, thesis/dissertation. *Entrance requirements:* For master's and doctorate, GRE General Test. Additional exam requirements/recommendations for international students: Required—TOEFL. Application fee: $50 ($90 for international students). *Expenses:* Tuition, state resident: full-time $4078; part-time $226.55 per credit hour. Tuition, nonresident: full-time $10,594; part-time $577.55 per credit hour. *Required fees:* $2813; $237.70 per credit hour. $278.50 per semester. Tuition and fees vary according to degree level and student level. *Financial support:* In 2014–15, 98 students received support, including 6 fellowships with full and partial tuition reimbursements available (averaging $20,633 per year), 69 research assistantships with full and partial tuition reimbursements available (averaging $7,178 per year), 10 teaching assistantships with full and partial tuition reimbursements available (averaging $6,298 per year); career-related internships or fieldwork, institutionally sponsored loans, scholarships/grants, traineeships, health care benefits, tuition waivers (full and partial), and unspecified assistantships also available. Support available to part-time students. Financial award application deadline: 4/15; financial award applicants required to submit FAFSA. *Faculty research:* Innovative design methods, pavement distress characterization, materials property, characterization and modeling recyclable materials. *Unit head:* Ibrahim Karaman, Department Head, 979-862-3923, E-mail: ikaraman@tamu.edu. *Application contact:* Mildan Radovic, Associate Department Head, 979-845-5114, E-mail: mradovic@tamu.edu.
Website: http://engineering.tamu.edu/materials.

Texas State University, The Graduate College, College of Science and Engineering, Material Science, Engineering, and Commercialization Program, San Marcos, TX 78666. Offers PhD. *Faculty:* 16 full-time (4 women). *Students:* 27 full-time (5 women), 3 part-time (0 women); includes 5 minority (2 Asian, non-Hispanic/Latino; 2 Hispanic/Latino; 1 Two or more races, non-Hispanic/Latino), 17 international. Average age 31. 25 applicants, 64% accepted, 10 enrolled. In 2014, 3 doctorates awarded. *Degree requirements:* For doctorate, comprehensive exam, thesis/dissertation. *Entrance requirements:* For doctorate, baccalaureate degree from regionally-accredited college or university; master's degree from regionally-accredited college or university in biology, chemistry, engineering, materials science, physics, technology, or closely-related field with minimum GPA of 3.5. Additional exam requirements/recommendations for international students: Required—TOEFL (minimum score 550 paper-based; 78 iBT); Recommended—IELTS (minimum score 6.5). *Application deadline:* For fall admission, 6/15 for domestic students, 6/1 for international students; for spring admission, 11/30 for domestic students, 10/1 for international students. Application fee: $40 ($90 for international students). Electronic applications accepted. *Expenses:* Expenses: $8,834 (tuition and fees combined). *Financial support:* In 2014–15, 14 students received support, including 7 research assistantships (averaging $30,186 per year), 19 teaching assistantships (averaging $32,000 per year). Financial award applicants required to submit FAFSA. *Faculty research:* Heterointegration, high operability, photoconductivity, water bonding systems, semiconductor research, next generation systems. *Total annual research expenditures:* $1.5 million. *Unit head:* Dr. Thomas Myers, Program Director, 512-245-1839, E-mail: tm33@txstate.edu. *Application contact:* Dr. Andrea Golato, Dean of Graduate School, 512-245-2581, Fax: 512-245-8365, E-mail: gradcollege@txstate.edu.
Website: http://www.msec.txstate.edu/.

Tuskegee University, Graduate Programs, College of Engineering, Department of Materials Science and Engineering, Tuskegee, AL 36088. Offers PhD. *Entrance requirements:* Additional exam requirements/recommendations for international students: Required—TOEFL (minimum score 500 paper-based). *Expenses: Tuition:* Full-time $18,560; part-time $1542 per credit hour. *Required fees:* $2910; $1455 per semester.

The University of Alabama, Graduate School, College of Engineering, Department of Metallurgical and Materials Engineering, Tuscaloosa, AL 35487. Offers MS Met E, PhD. PhD offered jointly with The University of Alabama at Birmingham. *Faculty:* 10 full-time (3 women). *Students:* 21 full-time (4 women), 1 part-time (0 women); includes 3 minority (2 Black or African American, non-Hispanic/Latino; 1 Asian, non-Hispanic/Latino), 9 international. Average age 26. 29 applicants, 41% accepted, 5 enrolled. In 2014, 3 master's, 5 doctorates awarded. *Degree requirements:* For master's, thesis or alternative; for doctorate, thesis/dissertation. *Entrance requirements:* For master's, GRE General Test, minimum GPA of 3.0 in last 60 hours; for doctorate, GRE General Test, minimum graduate GPA of 3.0, graduate degree. Additional exam requirements/recommendations for international students: Required—TOEFL (minimum score 550 paper-based). *Application deadline:* For fall admission, 7/1 for domestic students, 5/1 priority date for international students. Applications are processed on a rolling basis. Application fee: $50 ($60 for international students). Electronic applications accepted. *Expenses:* Tuition, state resident: full-time $9826. Tuition, nonresident: full-time $24,950. *Financial support:* In 2014–15, 3 fellowships (averaging $15,000 per year), 14 research assistantships (averaging $14,700 per year), 6 teaching assistantships (averaging $12,250 per year) were awarded; Federal Work-Study and unspecified assistantships also available. *Faculty research:* Thermodynamics, molten metals processing, casting and solidification, mechanical properties of materials, thin films and nanostructures, electrochemistry, corrosion and alloy development. *Total annual research expenditures:* $1.6 million. *Unit head:* Dr. Viola L. Acoff, Head/Professor, 205-348-2080, Fax: 205-348-2164, E-mail: vacoff@eng.ua.edu. *Application contact:* Dr. Greg B. Thompson, Associate Professor, 205-348-1589, Fax: 205-348-2164, E-mail: sgupta@eng.ua.edu.
Website: http://www.eng.ua.edu/~mtedept/.

The University of Alabama at Birmingham, School of Engineering, Program in Materials Engineering, Birmingham, AL 35294. Offers MS Mt E, PhD. PhD offered jointly with The University of Alabama (Tuscaloosa). *Students:* 24 full-time (4 women), 7 part-time (0 women); includes 8 minority (4 Black or African American, non-Hispanic/Latino; 3 Asian, non-Hispanic/Latino; 1 Hispanic/Latino), 13 international. Average age 28. In 2014, 6 master's, 1 doctorate awarded. *Degree requirements:* For master's, comprehensive exam, thesis (for some programs), project/thesis; for doctorate, comprehensive exam, thesis/dissertation. *Entrance requirements:* For master's and doctorate, GRE General Test (minimum quantitative score of 148/170 [600/800 on the old scale], verbal score of 153/180 [500/800 on the old scale], and 3/6 on the analytical writing), minimum GPA of 3.0 on all undergraduate degree major courses attempted. Additional exam requirements/recommendations for international students: Required—TOEFL (minimum score 80 iBT), TWE (minimum score 3.5). Application fee: $0 ($60 for international students). Electronic applications accepted. *Expenses:* Tuition, state resident: full-time $7090; part-time $370 per credit hour. Tuition, nonresident: full-time $16,072; part-time $869 per credit hour. Full-time tuition and fees vary according to course load and program. *Financial support:* Fellowships with full and partial tuition reimbursements, research assistantships with full tuition reimbursements, career-related internships or fieldwork, Federal Work-Study, and institutionally sponsored loans available. Support available to part-time students. *Faculty research:* Casting metallurgy, microgravity solidification, thin film techniques, ceramics/glass processing, biomedical materials processing. *Unit head:* Dr. Uday Vaidya, Graduate Program Director, 205-934-9199, E-mail: uvaidya@uab.edu. *Application contact:* Susan Noblitt Banks, Director of Graduate School Operations, 205-934-8227, Fax: 205-934-8413, E-mail: gradschool@uab.edu.
Website: https://www.uab.edu/engineering/home/departments-research/mse/grad.

University of Alberta, Faculty of Graduate Studies and Research, Department of Chemical and Materials Engineering, Edmonton, AB T6G 2E1, Canada. Offers chemical engineering (M Eng, M Sc, PhD); materials engineering (M Eng, M Sc, PhD); process control (M Eng, M Sc, PhD); welding (M Eng). Part-time programs available. Postbaccalaureate distance learning degree programs offered (minimal on-campus study). Terminal master's awarded for partial completion of doctoral program. *Degree requirements:* For master's, thesis; for doctorate, thesis/dissertation. *Faculty research:* Advanced materials and polymers, catalytic and reaction engineering, mineral processing, physical metallurgy, fluid mechanics.

The University of Arizona, College of Engineering, Department of Materials Science and Engineering, Tucson, AZ 85721. Offers MS, PhD. Part-time programs available. *Degree requirements:* For master's, thesis (for some programs); for doctorate, comprehensive exam, thesis/dissertation. *Entrance requirements:* For master's and doctorate, GRE General Test, 3 letters of recommendation, statement of purpose. Additional exam requirements/recommendations for international students: Required—TOEFL (minimum score 550 paper-based; 79 iBT). Electronic applications accepted. *Faculty research:* High-technology ceramics, optical materials, electronic materials, chemical metallurgy, science of materials.

The University of British Columbia, Faculty of Applied Science, Department of Materials Engineering, Vancouver, BC V6T 1Z1, Canada. Offers materials and metallurgy (M Sc, PhD); metals and materials engineering (MA Sc, PhD). *Degree requirements:* For master's, comprehensive exam, thesis; for doctorate, comprehensive exam, thesis/dissertation. *Entrance requirements:* Additional exam requirements/recommendations for international students: Required—TOEFL (minimum score 560 paper-based; 83 iBT). Electronic applications accepted. *Faculty research:* Electroslag melting, mathematical modeling, solidification and hydrometallurgy.

University of California, Berkeley, Graduate Division, College of Engineering, Department of Materials Science and Engineering, Berkeley, CA 94720-1500. Offers engineering (M Eng, MS, D Eng, PhD); engineering science (M Eng, MS, PhD). *Degree requirements:* For master's, comprehensive exam or thesis (MS); for doctorate, comprehensive exam, thesis/dissertation, qualifying exam. *Entrance requirements:* For master's and doctorate, GRE General Test, minimum GPA of 3.0, 3 letters of recommendation. Additional exam requirements/recommendations for international students: Required—TOEFL. *Faculty research:* Ceramics, biomaterials, structural, electronic, magnetic and optical materials.

University of California, Davis, College of Engineering, Program in Materials Science and Engineering, Davis, CA 95616. Offers MS, PhD. Terminal master's awarded for partial completion of doctoral program. *Degree requirements:* For master's, comprehensive exam (for some programs), thesis (for some programs); for doctorate, comprehensive exam, thesis/dissertation. *Entrance requirements:* Additional exam requirements/recommendations for international students: Required—TOEFL (minimum score 550 paper-based).

University of California, Irvine, Henry Samueli School of Engineering, Department of Chemical Engineering and Materials Science, Irvine, CA 92697. Offers chemical and biochemical engineering (MS, PhD); materials science and engineering (MS, PhD). Part-time programs available. *Students:* 132 full-time (48 women), 8 part-time (1 woman); includes 45 minority (2 Black or African American, non-Hispanic/Latino; 31 Asian, non-Hispanic/Latino; 7 Hispanic/Latino; 1 Native Hawaiian or other Pacific Islander, non-Hispanic/Latino; 4 Two or more races, non-Hispanic/Latino), 48 international. Average age 26. 549 applicants, 32% accepted, 55 enrolled. In 2014, 29 master's, 11 doctorates awarded. Terminal master's awarded for partial completion of doctoral program. *Degree requirements:* For doctorate, thesis/dissertation. *Entrance requirements:* For master's and doctorate, GRE General Test, minimum GPA of 3.0, 3 letters of recommendation. Additional exam requirements/recommendations for international students: Required—TOEFL (minimum score 550 paper-based). *Application deadline:* For fall admission, 1/15 priority date for domestic students, 1/15 for international students. Applications are processed on a rolling basis. Application fee: $90 ($110 for international students). Electronic applications accepted. *Financial support:* Fellowships with tuition reimbursements, research assistantships with full

tuition reimbursements, teaching assistantships with tuition reimbursements, institutionally sponsored loans, traineeships, health care benefits, and unspecified assistantships available. Financial award application deadline: 3/1; financial award applicants required to submit FAFSA. *Faculty research:* Molecular biotechnology, nano-bio-materials, biophotonics, synthesis, superplasticity and mechanical behavior, characterization of advanced and nanostructural materials. *Unit head:* Prof. Vasan Venugopalan, Chair, 949-824-5802, Fax: 949-824-2541, E-mail: vvenugop@uci.edu. *Application contact:* Grace Hai-Chin Chau, Academic Program and Graduate Admission Coordinator, 949-824-3887, Fax: 949-824-2541, E-mail: chaug@uci.edu.
Website: http://www.eng.uci.edu/dept/chems.

University of California, Irvine, Henry Samueli School of Engineering, Program in Materials and Manufacturing Technology, Irvine, CA 92697. Offers engineering (MS, PhD). Part-time programs available. *Students:* 26 full-time (7 women), 3 part-time (1 woman); includes 10 minority (9 Asian, non-Hispanic/Latino; 1 Two or more races, non-Hispanic/Latino), 18 international. Average age 27. 33 applicants, 67% accepted, 11 enrolled. In 2014, 6 master's, 2 doctorates awarded. *Entrance requirements:* For master's and doctorate, GRE General Test, 3 letters of recommendation, minimum GPA of 3.0. Additional exam requirements/recommendations for international students: Required—TOEFL (minimum score 550 paper-based). *Application deadline:* For fall admission, 1/15 priority date for domestic students, 1/15 for international students. Applications are processed on a rolling basis. Application fee: $90 ($110 for international students). Electronic applications accepted. *Financial support:* Fellowships with tuition reimbursements, research assistantships with full tuition reimbursements, teaching assistantships with tuition reimbursements, institutionally sponsored loans, traineeships, health care benefits, and unspecified assistantships available. Financial award application deadline: 3/1; financial award applicants required to submit FAFSA. *Faculty research:* Advanced materials, microelectronic and photonic devices and packaging, biomedical devices, MEMS, thin film materials, nanotechnology. *Unit head:* Gregory N. Washington, Dean, 949-824-4333, Fax: 949-824-8200, E-mail: engineering@uci.edu. *Application contact:* Nadia Ortiz, Assistant Director of Graduate Student Affairs, 949-824-3562, Fax: 949-824-9096, E-mail: nortiz@uci.edu.
Website: http://www.eng.uci.edu/.

University of California, Los Angeles, Graduate Division, Henry Samueli School of Engineering and Applied Science, Department of Materials Science and Engineering, Los Angeles, CA 90095-1595. Offers MS, PhD. *Faculty:* 14 full-time (2 women), 2 part-time/adjunct (0 women). *Students:* 161 full-time (39 women); includes 35 minority (1 Black or African American, non-Hispanic/Latino; 21 Asian, non-Hispanic/Latino; 9 Hispanic/Latino; 4 Two or more races, non-Hispanic/Latino), 93 international. 334 applicants, 50% accepted, 59 enrolled. In 2014, 22 master's, 16 doctorates awarded. *Degree requirements:* For master's, comprehensive exam or thesis; for doctorate, thesis/dissertation, qualifying exams. *Entrance requirements:* For master's, GRE General Test, minimum GPA of 3.0; for doctorate, GRE General Test, minimum GPA of 3.25. Additional exam requirements/recommendations for international students: Required—TOEFL (minimum score 560 paper-based; 87 iBT), IELTS (minimum score 7). *Application deadline:* For fall admission, 12/15 for domestic and international students. Application fee: $80 ($100 for international students). Electronic applications accepted. *Financial support:* In 2014–15, 78 fellowships, 192 research assistantships, 39 teaching assistantships were awarded; Federal Work-Study, institutionally sponsored loans, and tuition waivers (full and partial) also available. Financial award application deadline: 1/15; financial award applicants required to submit FAFSA. *Faculty research:* Ceramics and ceramic processing, electronic and optical materials, structural materials. *Total annual research expenditures:* $8.4 million. *Unit head:* Dr. Dwight C. Streit, Chair, 310-825-7011, E-mail: streit@ucla.edu. *Application contact:* Patti Barrera, Student Affairs Officer, 310-825-8916, Fax: 310-206-7353, E-mail: patti@seas.ucla.edu.
Website: http://www.mse.ucla.edu.

University of California, Riverside, Graduate Division, Materials Science and Engineering Program, Riverside, CA 92521. Offers MS, PhD. *Entrance requirements:* For master's and doctorate, GRE. Additional exam requirements/recommendations for international students: Required—TOEFL (minimum score 550 paper-based; 80 iBT). Electronic applications accepted. *Expenses:* Tuition, state resident: full-time $5399. Tuition, nonresident: full-time $10,433.

University of California, Santa Barbara, Graduate Division, College of Engineering, Department of Materials, Santa Barbara, CA 93106-5050. Offers MS, PhD, MS/PhD. Terminal master's awarded for partial completion of doctoral program. *Degree requirements:* For master's, variable foreign language requirement, comprehensive exam, thesis; for doctorate, variable foreign language requirement, comprehensive exam, thesis/dissertation. *Entrance requirements:* For master's and doctorate, GRE General Test. Additional exam requirements/recommendations for international students: Required—TOEFL (minimum score 600 paper-based; 100 iBT), IELTS (minimum score 7). Electronic applications accepted. *Faculty research:* Electronic and photonic materials, inorganic materials, macromolecular and biomolecular materials, structural materials.

University of Central Florida, College of Engineering and Computer Science, Department of Materials Science and Engineering, Orlando, FL 32816. Offers MSMSE, PhD. *Students:* 43 full-time (14 women), 8 part-time (1 woman); includes 6 minority (2 Asian, non-Hispanic/Latino; 1 Hispanic/Latino; 3 Two or more races, non-Hispanic/Latino), 28 international. Average age 28. 86 applicants, 28% accepted, 9 enrolled. In 2014, 12 master's, 4 doctorates awarded. *Degree requirements:* For master's, thesis or alternative; for doctorate, thesis/dissertation, candidacy exam, departmental qualifying exam. *Application deadline:* For fall admission, 7/15 priority date for domestic students; for spring admission, 12/1 priority date for domestic students. Application fee: $30. Electronic applications accepted. *Expenses:* Tuition, state resident: part-time $288.16 per credit hour. Tuition, nonresident: part-time $1073.31 per credit hour. *Financial support:* In 2014–15, 34 students received support, including 13 fellowships with tuition reimbursements available (averaging $2,000 per year), 32 research assistantships (averaging $11,000 per year), 2 teaching assistantships (averaging $12,800 per year). *Unit head:* Dr. Sudipta Seal, Interim Chair, 407-823-5277, E-mail: sseal@ucf.edu. *Application contact:* Barbara Rodriguez Lamas, Director, Admissions and Student Services, 407-823-2766, Fax: 407-823-6442, E-mail: gradadmissions@ucf.edu.
Website: http://mse.ucf.edu/.

University of Cincinnati, Graduate School, College of Engineering and Applied Science, Department of Chemical and Materials Engineering, Program in Materials Science and Engineering, Cincinnati, OH 45221. Offers MS, PhD. Evening/weekend programs available. *Degree requirements:* For master's, thesis optional; for doctorate, one foreign language, comprehensive exam, thesis/dissertation, oral English proficiency exam. *Entrance requirements:* For master's and doctorate, GRE General Test, BS in related field, minimum undergraduate GPA of 3.0. Additional exam requirements/recommendations for international students: Required—TOEFL. Electronic applications accepted. *Faculty research:* Polymer characterization, surface analysis, and adhesion; mechanical behavior of high-temperature materials; composites; electrochemistry of materials.

University of Connecticut, Graduate School, School of Engineering, Department of Metallurgy and Materials Engineering, Storrs, CT 06269. Offers MS, PhD. Terminal master's awarded for partial completion of doctoral program. *Degree requirements:* For master's, comprehensive exam, thesis or alternative; for doctorate, thesis/dissertation. *Entrance requirements:* For master's and doctorate, GRE General Test, GRE Subject Test. Additional exam requirements/recommendations for international students: Required—TOEFL (minimum score 550 paper-based). Electronic applications accepted. *Faculty research:* Microsegregation and coarsening, fatigue crack, electron-dislocation interaction.

University of Dayton, Department of Materials Engineering, Dayton, OH 45469. Offers MS Mat E, DE, PhD. Part-time and evening/weekend programs available. *Faculty:* 2 full-time (0 women), 9 part-time/adjunct (0 women). *Students:* 61 full-time (17 women), 11 part-time (3 women); includes 7 minority (4 Black or African American, non-Hispanic/Latino; 2 Asian, non-Hispanic/Latino; 1 Hispanic/Latino), 28 international. Average age 31. 115 applicants, 48% accepted, 18 enrolled. In 2014, 45 master's, 3 doctorates awarded. *Degree requirements:* For master's, thesis optional; for doctorate, variable foreign language requirement, thesis/dissertation, departmental qualifying exam. *Entrance requirements:* Additional exam requirements/recommendations for international students: Required—TOEFL (minimum score 550 paper-based; 80 iBT). *Application deadline:* For fall admission, 8/1 priority date for domestic students, 5/1 priority date for international students; for winter admission, 7/1 for international students; for spring admission, 11/1 priority date for international students. Applications are processed on a rolling basis. Application fee: $0 ($50 for international students). Electronic applications accepted. *Expenses: Tuition:* Full-time $10,176; part-time $848 per credit. *Required fees:* $25; $25 per course. Part-time tuition and fees vary according to course level, course load, degree level and program. *Financial support:* In 2014–15, 5 research assistantships with full tuition reimbursements (averaging $12,412 per year) were awarded; institutionally sponsored loans, scholarships/grants, health care benefits, and unspecified assistantships also available. Support available to part-time students. Financial award application deadline: 3/1; financial award applicants required to submit FAFSA. *Faculty research:* Ultra-fine microstructure by rapid hot-compaction of Armstrong Process Titanium Powder, diffusion during synthesis of titanium alloys by means of power metallurgy. *Total annual research expenditures:* $37,397. *Unit head:* Dr. Charles Browning, Chair and Interim Graduate Program Director, 937-229-2679, E-mail: cbrowning1@udayton.edu.
Website: https://www.udayton.edu/engineering/departments/chemical_and_materials/index.php.

University of Delaware, College of Engineering, Department of Materials Science and Engineering, Newark, DE 19716. Offers MMSE, PhD. Terminal master's awarded for partial completion of doctoral program. *Degree requirements:* For master's, thesis; for doctorate, thesis/dissertation. *Entrance requirements:* For master's and doctorate, GRE General Test, 3 letters of recommendation, minimum GPA of 3.2. Additional exam requirements/recommendations for international students: Required—TOEFL. Electronic applications accepted. *Faculty research:* Thin films and self assembly, drug delivery and tissue engineering, biomaterials and nanocomposites, semiconductor and oxide interfaces, electronic and magnetic materials.

University of Denver, Daniel Felix Ritchie School of Engineering and Computer Science, Department of Mechanical and Materials Engineering, Denver, CO 80208. Offers bioengineering (MS); engineering (MS, PhD); engineering/management (MS); materials science (MS, PhD); mechanical engineering (MS, PhD); nanoscale science and engineering (MS, PhD). Part-time programs available. *Faculty:* 10 full-time (1 woman), 1 (woman) part-time/adjunct. *Students:* 4 full-time (2 women), 44 part-time (12 women); includes 6 minority (1 Black or African American, non-Hispanic/Latino; 3 Asian, non-Hispanic/Latino; 1 Hispanic/Latino; 1 Two or more races, non-Hispanic/Latino), 20 international. Average age 29. 67 applicants, 88% accepted, 16 enrolled. In 2014, 7 master's, 1 doctorate awarded. Terminal master's awarded for partial completion of doctoral program. *Degree requirements:* For master's, thesis optional; for doctorate, comprehensive exam, thesis/dissertation. *Entrance requirements:* For master's, GRE General Test, bachelor's degree, transcripts, personal statement, resume or curriculum vitae, two letters of recommendation; for doctorate, GRE General Test, master's degree, transcripts, personal statement, resume or curriculum vitae, two letters of recommendation. Additional exam requirements/recommendations for international students: Required—TOEFL (minimum score 550 paper-based; 80 iBT). *Application deadline:* For fall admission, 2/1 priority date for domestic and international students. Applications are processed on a rolling basis. Application fee: $65. Electronic applications accepted. *Expenses:* Expenses: $1,199 per credit hour. *Financial support:* In 2014–15, 24 students received support, including 17 research assistantships with full and partial tuition reimbursements available (averaging $12,842 per year), 17 teaching assistantships with full and partial tuition reimbursements available (averaging $9,975 per year); Federal Work-Study, institutionally sponsored loans, scholarships/grants, health care benefits, and unspecified assistantships also available. Financial award application deadline: 2/15; financial award applicants required to submit FAFSA. *Faculty research:* Aerosols, biomechanics, composite materials, photo optics, drug delivery. *Unit head:* Dr. Matt Gordon, Chair, 303-871-3580, Fax: 303-871-4450, E-mail: matthew.gordon@du.edu. *Application contact:* Yvonne Petitt, Assistant to the Chair, 303-871-2107, Fax: 303-871-4450, E-mail: yvonne.petitt@du.edu.
Website: http://www.du.edu/rsecs/departments/mme/index.html.

University of Florida, Graduate School, College of Engineering, Department of Materials Science and Engineering, Gainesville, FL 32611. Offers material science and engineering (MS), including clinical and translational science; nuclear engineering (ME, PhD), including imaging science and technology (PhD), nuclear engineering sciences (ME, MS, PhD); nuclear engineering (MS), including nuclear engineering sciences (ME, MS, PhD); JD/MS. Part-time programs available. Postbaccalaureate distance learning degree programs offered. *Faculty:* 32 full-time (5 women), 32 part-time/adjunct (9 women). *Students:* 251 full-time (65 women), 36 part-time (12 women); includes 42 minority (7 Black or African American, non-Hispanic/Latino; 18 Asian, non-Hispanic/Latino; 17 Hispanic/Latino), 144 international. 502 applicants, 54% accepted, 61 enrolled. In 2014, 64 master's, 25 doctorates awarded. Terminal master's awarded for partial completion of doctoral program. *Degree requirements:* For master's, comprehensive exam, thesis; for doctorate, comprehensive exam, thesis/dissertation; for Engr, thesis optional. *Entrance requirements:* For master's and doctorate, minimum GPA of 3.0; for Engr, GRE General Test. Additional exam requirements/recommendations for international students: Required—TOEFL (minimum score 550 paper-based; 80 iBT), IELTS (minimum score 6). *Application deadline:* For fall admission, 7/1 priority date for domestic students, 5/1 for international students; for spring admission, 11/1 for domestic students, 9/1 for international students. Applications are processed on a rolling basis. Application fee: $30. Electronic applications accepted. *Financial support:* Applicants required to submit FAFSA. *Faculty research:* Polymeric system, biomaterials and biomimetics; inorganic and organic electronic materials; functional ceramic materials for energy systems and microelectronic applications; advanced metallic systems for aerospace, transportation and biological applications; nuclear materials. *Unit head:* Simon R. Phillpot, PhD, Chair, 352-846-3782, Fax: 352-392-7219, E-mail: sphil@mse.ufl.edu. *Application contact:* Dr. Jack Mecholsky, Jr., Graduate Coordinator, 352-846-3306, Fax: 352-846-1182, E-mail: jmech@mse.ufl.edu.
Website: http://www.mse.ufl.edu/.

University of Illinois at Chicago, Graduate College, College of Engineering, Department of Civil and Materials Engineering, Chicago, IL 60607-7128. Offers MS, PhD. Evening/weekend programs available. *Faculty:* 17 full-time (2 women), 5 part-time/adjunct (0 women). *Students:* 74 full-time (15 women), 30 part-time (6 women); includes 12 minority (7 Asian, non-Hispanic/Latino; 5 Hispanic/Latino), 61 international. Average age 30. 285 applicants, 54% accepted, 26 enrolled. In 2014, 20 master's, 4 doctorates awarded. *Degree requirements:* For master's, thesis (for some programs); for doctorate, thesis/dissertation, preliminary and qualifying exams. *Entrance requirements:* For master's and doctorate, GRE General Test, minimum GPA of 3.0. Additional exam requirements/recommendations for international students: Required—TOEFL. *Application deadline:* For fall admission, 5/15 for domestic students, 3/15 for international students; for spring admission, 11/1 for domestic students, 7/15 for international students. Applications are processed on a rolling basis. Application fee: $60. Electronic applications accepted. *Expenses:* Expenses: $17,602 in-state; $29,600 out-of-state. *Financial support:* Fellowships with full tuition reimbursements, research assistantships with full tuition reimbursements, teaching assistantships with full tuition reimbursements, Federal Work-Study, and tuition waivers (full) available. Financial award application deadline: 3/1; financial award applicants required to submit FAFSA. *Faculty research:* Integrated fiber optic, acoustic emission and MEMS-based sensors development; monitoring the state of repaired and strengthened structures; development of weigh-in-motion (WIM) systems; image processing techniques for characterization of concrete entrained air bubble systems. *Total annual research expenditures:* $1.8 million. *Unit head:* Prof. Farhad Ansaru, Head, 312-996-3428, Fax: 312-996-2426. *Application contact:* J. Ernesto Indacochea, Director of Graduate Studies, 312-996-5283, E-mail: jeindaco@uic.edu.
Website: http://www.uic.edu/depts/cme/.

University of Illinois at Urbana–Champaign, Graduate College, College of Engineering, Department of Materials Science and Engineering, Champaign, IL 61820. Offers M Eng, MS, PhD, MS/MBA, PhD/MBA. *Students:* 189 (52 women). Application fee: $70 ($90 for international students). *Unit head:* David G. Cahill, Head, 217-333-6753, Fax: 217-244-1631, E-mail: d-cahill@illinois.edu. *Application contact:* Michelle L. Malloch, Office Support Associate, 217-333-8517, Fax: 217-333-2736, E-mail: malloch@illinois.edu.
Website: http://www.matse.illinois.edu/.

The University of Iowa, Graduate College, College of Engineering, Department of Mechanical Engineering, Iowa City, IA 52242-1316. Offers energy systems (MS, PhD); engineering design (MS, PhD); fluid dynamics (MS, PhD); materials and manufacturing (MS, PhD); wind energy (MS, PhD). *Faculty:* 14 full-time (1 woman). *Students:* 50 full-time (5 women); includes 1 minority (Black or African American, non-Hispanic/Latino), 34 international. Average age 28. 68 applicants, 19% accepted, 4 enrolled. In 2014, 9 master's, 7 doctorates awarded. Terminal master's awarded for partial completion of doctoral program. *Degree requirements:* For master's, oral exam or thesis; for doctorate, comprehensive exam, thesis/dissertation. *Entrance requirements:* For master's and doctorate, GRE. Additional exam requirements/recommendations for international students: Required—TOEFL (minimum score 600 paper-based; 100 iBT). *Application deadline:* For fall admission, 1/15 for domestic and international students; for spring admission, 9/1 for domestic and international students; for summer admission, 1/15 for domestic and international students. Application fee: $60 ($100 for international students). Electronic applications accepted. *Financial support:* In 2014–15, 3 fellowships with partial tuition reimbursements (averaging $19,933 per year), 36 research assistantships with full tuition reimbursements (averaging $20,823 per year), 21 teaching assistantships with full tuition reimbursements (averaging $6,457 per year) were awarded; traineeships and unspecified assistantships also available. Financial award applicants required to submit FAFSA. *Faculty research:* Computer simulation methodology, biomechanics, metal casting, dynamics, laser processing, system reliability, ship hydrodynamics, solid mechanics, fluid dynamics, energy, human modeling and nano technology. *Total annual research expenditures:* $9.8 million. *Unit head:* Dr. Andrew Kusiak, Departmental Executive Officer, 319-335-5934, Fax: 319-335-5669, E-mail: andrew-kusiak@uiowa.edu. *Application contact:* Andrea Flaherty, Academic Program Specialist, 319-335-5939, Fax: 319-335-5669, E-mail: mech_eng@engineering.uiowa.edu.
Website: http://www.engineering.uiowa.edu/mie.

University of Kentucky, Graduate School, College of Engineering, Program in Materials Science and Engineering, Lexington, KY 40506-0032. Offers MS, PhD. *Degree requirements:* For master's, comprehensive exam, thesis optional; for doctorate, comprehensive exam, thesis/dissertation. *Entrance requirements:* For master's, GRE General Test, minimum undergraduate GPA of 2.75; for doctorate, GRE General Test, minimum undergraduate GPA of 3.0. Additional exam requirements/recommendations for international students: Required—TOEFL (minimum score 550 paper-based). Electronic applications accepted. *Faculty research:* Physical and mechanical metallurgy, computational material engineering, polymers and composites, high-temperature ceramics, powder metallurgy.

University of Maryland, College Park, Academic Affairs, A. James Clark School of Engineering, Department of Materials Science and Engineering, Materials Science and Engineering Program, College Park, MD 20742. Offers MS, PhD. Part-time and evening/weekend programs available. Postbaccalaureate distance learning degree programs offered. *Degree requirements:* For master's, comprehensive exam, thesis optional, research paper; for doctorate, thesis/dissertation, oral exam. *Entrance requirements:* For master's and doctorate, GRE General Test, minimum B+ average in undergraduate course work. Additional exam requirements/recommendations for international students: Required—TOEFL. Electronic applications accepted.

University of Maryland, College Park, Academic Affairs, A. James Clark School of Engineering, Department of Mechanical Engineering, College Park, MD 20742. Offers electronic packaging and reliability (MS, PhD); manufacturing and design (MS, PhD); mechanics and materials (MS, PhD); reliability engineering (M Eng, MS, PhD); thermal and fluid sciences (MS, PhD). Part-time and evening/weekend programs available. Postbaccalaureate distance learning degree programs offered. *Degree requirements:* For master's, thesis optional; for doctorate, thesis/dissertation, qualifying exam. *Entrance requirements:* For master's, GRE General Test, 3 letters of recommendation; for doctorate, GRE General Test, minimum GPA of 3.0. Additional exam requirements/recommendations for international students: Required—TOEFL. Electronic applications accepted. *Faculty research:* Injection molding, electronic packaging, fluid mechanics, product engineering.

University of Massachusetts Lowell, Francis College of Engineering, Department of Plastics Engineering, Lowell, MA 01854. Offers elastomers (Graduate Certificate); medical plastics design and manufacturing (Graduate Certificate); plastics design (Graduate Certificate); plastics engineering (MS Eng, D Eng, PhD), including coatings and adhesives (MS Eng), plastics materials (MS Eng), plastics processing (MS Eng), product design (MS Eng); plastics engineering fundamentals (Graduate Certificate); plastics materials (Graduate Certificate); plastics processing (Graduate Certificate); polymer science/plastics engineering (PhD). Part-time programs available. Terminal master's awarded for partial completion of doctoral program. *Degree requirements:* For master's, thesis optional; for doctorate, comprehensive exam, thesis/dissertation.

Entrance requirements: For master's and doctorate, GRE General Test. Additional exam requirements/recommendations for international students: Required—TOEFL.

University of Michigan, College of Engineering, Department of Materials Science and Engineering, Ann Arbor, MI 48109. Offers MS, PhD. Part-time programs available. *Students:* 162 full-time (46 women), 2 part-time (0 women). 508 applicants, 18% accepted, 34 enrolled. In 2014, 36 master's, 28 doctorates awarded. *Degree requirements:* For master's, thesis, oral defense of thesis; for doctorate, thesis/dissertation, oral defense of dissertation, written exam. *Entrance requirements:* For master's, GRE General Test, minimum GPA of 3.0 in related field; for doctorate, GRE General Test, minimum GPA of 3.0 in related field, master's degree. Additional exam requirements/recommendations for international students: Required—TOEFL. *Application deadline:* Applications are processed on a rolling basis. Electronic applications accepted. *Financial support:* Fellowships, research assistantships, and teaching assistantships available. Financial award applicants required to submit FAFSA. *Faculty research:* Soft materials (polymers, biomaterials), computational materials science, structural materials, electronic and optical materials, nanocomposite materials. *Total annual research expenditures:* $17.6 million. *Unit head:* Amit Misra, Department Chair, 734-764-7799, Fax: 734-763-4788, E-mail: amitmis@umich.edu. *Application contact:* Renee Hilgendorf, Graduate Program Coordinator, 734-763-9790, Fax: 734-763-4788, E-mail: reneeh@umich.edu.
Website: http://www.mse.engin.umich.edu.

University of Minnesota, Twin Cities Campus, College of Science and Engineering, Department of Chemical Engineering and Materials Science, Program in Materials Science and Engineering, Minneapolis, MN 55455-0132. Offers M Mat SE, MS Mat SE, PhD. Part-time programs available. Terminal master's awarded for partial completion of doctoral program. *Degree requirements:* For master's, thesis; for doctorate, thesis/dissertation. *Entrance requirements:* For master's and doctorate, GRE General Test. Additional exam requirements/recommendations for international students: Required—TOEFL. Electronic applications accepted. *Faculty research:* Ceramics and metals; coating processes and interfacial engineering; crystal growth and design; polymers; electronic, photonic and magnetic materials.

University of Nebraska–Lincoln, Graduate College, College of Engineering, Department of Mechanical and Materials Engineering, Lincoln, NE 68588-0526. Offers biomedical engineering (PhD); engineering mechanics (MS); materials engineering (PhD); mechanical engineering (MS), including materials science engineering, metallurgical engineering; mechanical engineering and applied mechanics (PhD); MS/MS. MS/MS offered with University of Rouen-France. *Degree requirements:* For master's, thesis optional; for doctorate, comprehensive exam, thesis/dissertation. *Entrance requirements:* For master's and doctorate, GRE General Test. Additional exam requirements/recommendations for international students: Required—TOEFL (minimum score 550 paper-based). Electronic applications accepted. *Faculty research:* Medical robotics, rehabilitation dynamics, and design; combustion, fluid mechanics, and heat transfer; nano-materials, manufacturing, and devices; fiber, tissue, bio-polymer, and adaptive composites; blast, impact, fracture, and failure; electro-active and magnetic materials and devices; functional materials, design, and added manufacturing; materials characterization, modeling, and computational simulation.

University of Nevada, Las Vegas, Graduate College, Howard R. Hughes College of Engineering, Department of Mechanical Engineering, Las Vegas, NV 89154-4027. Offers biomedical engineering (MS); materials and nuclear engineering (MS); mechanical engineering (MS); nuclear criticality safety engineering (Certificate). Part-time programs available. *Faculty:* 13 full-time (0 women), 1 (woman) part-time/adjunct. *Students:* 33 full-time (13 women), 13 part-time (3 women); includes 8 minority (1 Asian, non-Hispanic/Latino; 2 Hispanic/Latino; 5 Two or more races, non-Hispanic/Latino), 12 international. Average age 29. 43 applicants, 51% accepted, 11 enrolled. In 2014, 9 master's, 6 doctorates, 3 other advanced degrees awarded. *Degree requirements:* For master's, comprehensive exam, thesis (for some programs), project; for doctorate, comprehensive exam, thesis/dissertation. *Entrance requirements:* For master's, doctorate, and Certificate, GRE General Test. Additional exam requirements/recommendations for international students: Required—TOEFL (minimum score 550 paper-based; 80 iBT), IELTS (minimum score 7). *Application deadline:* For fall admission, 8/1 for domestic students, 5/1 for international students; for spring admission, 12/1 for domestic students, 10/1 for international students. Application fee: $60 ($95 for international students). Electronic applications accepted. *Financial support:* In 2014–15, 33 students received support, including 6 research assistantships with partial tuition reimbursements available (averaging $15,198 per year), 27 teaching assistantships with partial tuition reimbursements available (averaging $14,029 per year); institutionally sponsored loans, scholarships/grants, health care benefits, and unspecified assistantships also available. Financial award application deadline: 3/1. *Faculty research:* Dynamics and control systems; energy systems including renewable and nuclear; computational fluid and solid mechanics; structures, materials and manufacturing; vibrations and acoustics. *Total annual research expenditures:* $1.9 million. *Unit head:* Dr. Brendan O'Toole, Chair/Professor, 702-895-3885, Fax: 702-895-3936, E-mail: brendan.otoole@unlv.edu. *Application contact:* Graduate College Admissions Evaluator, 702-895-3320, Fax: 702-895-4180, E-mail: gradcollege@unlv.edu.
Website: http://me.unlv.edu/.

University of Nevada, Reno, Graduate School, College of Engineering, Department of Chemical and Materials Engineering, Program in Materials Science and Engineering, Reno, NV 89557. Offers MS, PhD. Terminal master's awarded for partial completion of doctoral program. *Degree requirements:* For master's, thesis; for doctorate, one foreign language, thesis/dissertation. *Entrance requirements:* For master's, minimum GPA of 2.75; for doctorate, GRE, minimum GPA of 3.0. Additional exam requirements/recommendations for international students: Required—TOEFL (minimum score 500 paper-based; 61 iBT), IELTS (minimum score 6). Electronic applications accepted. *Faculty research:* Hydrometallurgy, applied surface chemistry, mineral processing, mineral bioprocessing, ceramics.

University of Pennsylvania, School of Engineering and Applied Science, Department of Materials Science and Engineering, Philadelphia, PA 19104. Offers MSE, PhD, MSE/MBA. Part-time programs available. *Faculty:* 14 full-time (3 women), 1 part-time/adjunct (0 women). *Students:* 146 full-time (43 women), 14 part-time (3 women); includes 13 minority (9 Asian, non-Hispanic/Latino; 3 Hispanic/Latino; 1 Two or more races, non-Hispanic/Latino), 117 international. 568 applicants, 23% accepted, 66 enrolled. In 2014, 57 master's, 6 doctorates awarded. Terminal master's awarded for partial completion of doctoral program. *Degree requirements:* For master's, thesis; for doctorate, thesis/dissertation. *Entrance requirements:* Additional exam requirements/recommendations for international students: Required—TOEFL. *Application deadline:* For fall admission, 6/1 priority date for domestic students, 5/1 priority date for international students; for spring admission, 11/1 priority date for domestic students, 10/1 priority date for international students. Applications are processed on a rolling basis. Application fee: $70. Electronic applications accepted. *Financial support:* Fellowships, research assistantships, teaching assistantships, institutionally sponsored loans, scholarships/grants, traineeships, health care benefits, and unspecified assistantships available. *Faculty research:* Advanced metallic, ceramic, and polymeric materials for device

applications; micromechanics and structure of interfaces; thin film electronic materials; physics and chemistry of solids. *Unit head:* Eduardo D. Glandt, Dean, 215-898-7244, E-mail: seasdean@seas.upenn.edu. *Application contact:* School of Engineering and Applied Science Graduate Admissions, 215-898-4542, E-mail: gradstudies@seas.upenn.edu.
Website: http://www.mse.seas.upenn.edu.

University of Southern California, Graduate School, Viterbi School of Engineering, Mork Family Department of Chemical Engineering and Materials Science, Los Angeles, CA 90089. Offers chemical engineering (MS, PhD, Engr); geoscience technologies (MS); materials engineering (MS); materials science (MS, PhD, Engr); petroleum engineering (MS, PhD, Engr); smart oilfield technologies (MS, Graduate Certificate). Terminal master's awarded for partial completion of doctoral program. *Degree requirements:* For master's, thesis optional; for doctorate, thesis/dissertation. *Entrance requirements:* For master's and doctorate, GRE General Test. Additional exam requirements/recommendations for international students: Recommended—TOEFL. Electronic applications accepted. *Expenses:* Contact institution. *Faculty research:* Heterogeneous materials and porous media, statistical mechanics, molecular simulation, polymer science and engineering, advanced materials, reaction engineering and catalysis, membrane processes and separation, biochemical engineering, cell culture, bioreactor modeling, petroleum engineering.

University of South Florida, College of Arts and Sciences, Department of Physics, Tampa, FL 33620-9951. Offers applied physics (MS, PhD); atmospheric physics (MS); atomic and molecular physics (MS); laser physics (MS); materials physics (MS); materials science and engineering (MSE); medical physics (MS); optical physics (MS); semiconductor physics (MS); solid state physics (MS). MSE offered jointly with College of Engineering. Part-time programs available. *Faculty:* 24 full-time (3 women). *Students:* 71 full-time (15 women), 7 part-time (0 women); includes 13 minority (2 Black or African American, non-Hispanic/Latino; 11 Hispanic/Latino), 37 international. Average age 31. 96 applicants, 23% accepted, 12 enrolled. In 2014, 8 master's, 9 doctorates awarded. *Degree requirements:* For master's, comprehensive exam, thesis optional; for doctorate, comprehensive exam, thesis/dissertation. *Entrance requirements:* For master's and doctorate, GRE General Test; GRE Subject Test in physics (recommended), minimum GPA of 3.0, three letters of recommendation, statement of purpose. Additional exam requirements/recommendations for international students: Required—TOEFL (minimum score 550 paper-based; 79 iBT) or IELTS (minimum score 6.5). *Application deadline:* For fall admission, 2/15 priority date for domestic students, 1/2 for international students; for spring admission, 9/1 for domestic students, 7/1 for international students. Applications are processed on a rolling basis. Application fee: $30. Electronic applications accepted. *Financial support:* In 2014–15, 70 students received support, including 27 research assistantships with tuition reimbursements available (averaging $15,272 per year), 43 teaching assistantships with tuition reimbursements available (averaging $16,267 per year); unspecified assistantships also available. *Faculty research:* The molecular organization of collagen, lipid rafts in biological membranes, the formation of Alzheimer plaques, the role of cellular ion pumps in wound healing, carbon nanotubes as biological detectors, optical imaging of neuronal activity, three-dimensional imaging of intact tissues, motility of cancer cells, the optical detection of pathogens in water. *Total annual research expenditures:* $3 million. *Unit head:* Dr. Pritish Mukherjee, Professor and Chairperson, 813-974-3293, Fax: 813-974-5813, E-mail: pritish@usf.edu. *Application contact:* Dr. Lilia Woods, Professor and Graduate Program Director, 813-974-2862, Fax: 813-974-5813, E-mail: lmwoods@usf.edu.
Website: http://physics.usf.edu/.

University of South Florida, College of Engineering, Department of Civil and Environmental Engineering, Tampa, FL 33620-9951. Offers civil engineering (MCE, MSCE, PhD), including environmental engineering (MSES, PhD), geotechnical engineering (MCE, MSCE, MSES, PhD), interdisciplinary transportation (MSCE), materials engineering and science, structural engineering, transportation engineering, water resources; engineering science (MSES), including environmental engineering (MSES, PhD), geotechnical engineering (MCE, MSCE, MSES, PhD); environmental engineering (MEVE, MSEV, PhD). Part-time programs available. *Faculty:* 19 full-time (5 women). *Students:* 97 full-time (35 women), 83 part-time (25 women); includes 41 minority (6 Black or African American, non-Hispanic/Latino; 1 American Indian or Alaska Native, non-Hispanic/Latino; 3 Asian, non-Hispanic/Latino; 25 Hispanic/Latino; 6 Two or more races, non-Hispanic/Latino), 39 international. Average age 30. 229 applicants, 51% accepted, 43 enrolled. In 2014, 68 master's, 9 doctorates awarded. Terminal master's awarded for partial completion of doctoral program. *Degree requirements:* For master's, comprehensive exam, thesis (for some programs); for doctorate, comprehensive exam, thesis/dissertation. *Entrance requirements:* For master's, GRE General Test (preferred minimum scores of 20th percentile verbal, 50th percentile quantitative, and 10th percentile in analytical writing), minimum GPA of 3.0 in major, two letters of reference, statement of purpose; for doctorate, GRE General Test (preferred minimum scores of 45th percentile verbal, 65th percentile quantitative, and 50th percentile in analytical writing), three letters of recommendation, statement of purpose, resume. Additional exam requirements/recommendations for international students: Required—TOEFL (minimum score 550 paper-based; 79 iBT) or IELTS (minimum score 6.5). *Application deadline:* For fall admission, 2/15 for domestic students, 1/2 priority date for international students; for spring admission, 10/15 for domestic students, 6/1 priority date for international students. Application fee: $30. Electronic applications accepted. *Financial support:* In 2014–15, 65 students received support, including 44 research assistantships (averaging $14,123 per year), 21 teaching assistantships with tuition reimbursements available (averaging $15,329 per year). *Faculty research:* Environmental and water resources engineering, geotechnics and geoenvironmental systems, structures and materials systems, transportation systems. *Total annual research expenditures:* $3.3 million. *Unit head:* Dr. Manjriker Gunaratne, Professor and Department Chair, 813-974-5818, Fax: 813-974-2957, E-mail: gunaratn@usf.edu. *Application contact:* Dr. Sarina J. Ergas, Professor and Graduate Program Coordinator, 813-974-1119, Fax: 813-974-2957, E-mail: sergas@usf.edu.
Website: http://ce.eng.usf.edu/.

University of South Florida, College of Engineering, Interdisciplinary Programs in Engineering, Tampa, FL 33620-9951. Offers engineering science (PhD); materials science and engineering (MSMSE). *Degree requirements:* For master's, comprehensive exam, thesis (for some programs); for doctorate, comprehensive exam, thesis/dissertation. *Entrance requirements:* For master's, GRE General Test, minimum GPA of 3.0 in last 60 hours of coursework; for doctorate, GRE General Test, minimum GPA of 3.3 in last 60 hours of coursework. Additional exam requirements/recommendations for international students: Required—TOEFL (minimum score 550 paper-based; 79 iBT). *Faculty research:* Biomedical engineering and sustainability, particularly in water resources and energy; electrical engineering; civil/environmental engineering; industrial/management systems engineering; chemical engineering; computer science and engineering; mechanical engineering. *Unit head:* Dr. Robert Bishop, Dean, 813-974-3864, Fax: 813-974-5094, E-mail: robertbishop@usf.edu. *Application contact:* Dr. Rafael Perez, Associate Dean for Academic Affairs, 813-974-3934, Fax: 813-974-5094, E-mail: perez@usf.edu.
Website: http://www2.eng.usf.edu/.

University of South Florida, University College/Distance Education, Tampa, FL 33620-9951. *Unit head:* Kathy Barnes, Interdisciplinary Programs Coordinator, 813-974-8031, Fax: 813-974-7061, E-mail: barnesk@usf.edu. *Application contact:* Karen Tylinski, Metro Initiatives, 813-974-9943, Fax: 813-974-7061, E-mail: ktylinsk@usf.edu.
Website: http://www.usf.edu/innovative-education/.

The University of Tennessee, Graduate School, College of Engineering, Department of Materials Science and Engineering, Program in Materials Science and Engineering, Knoxville, TN 37996. Offers MS, PhD. *Faculty:* 27 full-time (3 women), 7 part-time/adjunct (1 woman). *Students:* 85 full-time (20 women), 6 part-time (1 woman); includes 6 minority (1 Black or African American, non-Hispanic/Latino; 2 Asian, non-Hispanic/Latino; 2 Hispanic/Latino; 1 Two or more races, non-Hispanic/Latino), 49 international. Average age 29. 154 applicants, 19% accepted, 22 enrolled. In 2014, 6 master's, 12 doctorates awarded. *Degree requirements:* For master's, thesis or alternative; for doctorate, comprehensive exam, thesis/dissertation. *Entrance requirements:* For master's, GRE General Test (for MS students pursuing research thesis), minimum GPA of 2.7 (for U.S. degree holders), 3.0 (for international degree holders); 3 references; for doctorate, GRE General Test (for all PhD candidates), minimum GPA of 3.0 on previous graduate course work; 3 references. Additional exam requirements/recommendations for international students: Required—TOEFL (minimum score 550 paper-based). *Application deadline:* For fall admission, 2/1 priority date for domestic and international students; for spring admission, 6/15 for domestic and international students. Applications are processed on a rolling basis. Application fee: $35. Electronic applications accepted. *Financial support:* In 2014–15, 79 students received support, including 58 research assistantships with full tuition reimbursements available (averaging $21,092 per year), 19 teaching assistantships with full tuition reimbursements available (averaging $22,829 per year); fellowships with full tuition reimbursements available, career-related internships or fieldwork, Federal Work-Study, institutionally sponsored loans, health care benefits, and unspecified assistantships also available. Financial award application deadline: 2/1; financial award applicants required to submit FAFSA. *Faculty research:* Biomaterials; functional materials electronic, magnetic and optical; high temperature materials; mechanical behavior of materials; neutron materials science. *Unit head:* Dr. Kurt Sickafus, Head, 865-974-4858, Fax: 865-974-4115, E-mail: kurt@utk.edu. *Application contact:* Dr. Roberto S. Benson, Associate Head, 865-974-5347, Fax: 865-974-4115, E-mail: rbenson1@utk.edu.
Website: http://www.engr.utk.edu/mse.

The University of Texas at Arlington, Graduate School, College of Engineering, Department of Materials Science and Engineering, Arlington, TX 76019. Offers M Engr, MS, PhD. Terminal master's awarded for partial completion of doctoral program. *Degree requirements:* For master's, comprehensive exam (for some programs), thesis optional; for doctorate, comprehensive exam, thesis/dissertation optional. *Entrance requirements:* For master's, GRE General Test, minimum GPA of 3.0; for doctorate, GRE General Test, minimum GPA of 3.5. Additional exam requirements/recommendations for international students: Required—TOEFL (minimum score 550 paper-based; 79 iBT), IELTS. *Faculty research:* Electronic materials, conductive polymer, composites biomaterial, structural materials.

The University of Texas at Austin, Graduate School, Cockrell School of Engineering, Program in Materials Science and Engineering, Austin, TX 78712-1111. Offers MS, PhD. Part-time programs available. *Degree requirements:* For master's, thesis (for some programs); for doctorate, thesis/dissertation. *Entrance requirements:* For master's and doctorate, GRE General Test. Additional exam requirements/recommendations for international students: Required—TOEFL (minimum score 550 paper-based). Electronic applications accepted.

The University of Texas at Dallas, Erik Jonsson School of Engineering and Computer Science, Department of Materials Science and Engineering, Richardson, TX 75080. Offers MS, PhD. Part-time and evening/weekend programs available. *Faculty:* 14 full-time (2 women). *Students:* 55 full-time (18 women), 3 part-time (2 women); includes 9 minority (2 Black or African American, non-Hispanic/Latino; 2 Asian, non-Hispanic/Latino; 4 Hispanic/Latino; 1 Two or more races, non-Hispanic/Latino), 39 international. Average age 27. 118 applicants, 25% accepted, 13 enrolled. In 2014, 9 master's, 11 doctorates awarded. *Degree requirements:* For master's, thesis or major design project; for doctorate, thesis/dissertation. *Entrance requirements:* For master's, GRE General Test, minimum GPA of 3.0 in related bachelor's degree; for doctorate, GRE General Test, minimum GPA of 3.5. Additional exam requirements/recommendations for international students: Required—TOEFL (minimum score 550 paper-based). *Application deadline:* For fall admission, 7/15 for domestic students, 5/1 priority date for international students; for spring admission, 11/15 for domestic students, 9/1 priority date for international students. Applications are processed on a rolling basis. Application fee: $50 ($100 for international students). Electronic applications accepted. *Expenses:* Tuition, state resident: full-time $11,940; part-time $663 per credit. Tuition, nonresident: full-time $22,282; part-time $1238 per credit. *Financial support:* In 2014–15, 55 students received support, including 1 fellowship (averaging $28,600 per year), 52 research assistantships with partial tuition reimbursements available (averaging $19,500 per year); teaching assistantships with partial tuition reimbursements available, career-related internships or fieldwork, Federal Work-Study, institutionally sponsored loans, scholarships/grants, and unspecified assistantships also available. Support available to part-time students. Financial award application deadline: 4/30; financial award applicants required to submit FAFSA. *Faculty research:* Graphene-based semiconducting materials, neuro-inspired computational paradigms, electronic materials with emphasis on dielectrics, energy harvesting (photovoltaics, lithium-ion batteries), biosensors and hydrogen storage materials. *Unit head:* Dr. Yves Chabal, Department Head, 972-883-5751, Fax: 972-883-5725, E-mail: chabal@utdallas.edu. *Application contact:* Dr. Julia Hsu, Associate Department Head, 972-883-5789, Fax: 972-883-5725, E-mail: jwhsu@utdallas.edu.
Website: http://mse.utdallas.edu/.

The University of Texas at El Paso, Graduate School, College of Engineering, Department of Metallurgical and Materials Engineering, El Paso, TX 79968-0001. Offers materials science and engineering (PhD); metallurgical and materials engineering (MS). Part-time and evening/weekend programs available. *Degree requirements:* For master's, thesis. *Entrance requirements:* For master's, GRE General Test. Additional exam requirements/recommendations for international students: Required—TOEFL. Electronic applications accepted.

The University of Texas at El Paso, Graduate School, Interdisciplinary Program in Materials Science and Engineering, El Paso, TX 79968-0001. Offers PhD. Part-time and evening/weekend programs available. *Degree requirements:* For doctorate, thesis/dissertation. *Entrance requirements:* For doctorate, GRE, letters of recommendation. Additional exam requirements/recommendations for international students: Required—TOEFL; Recommended—IELTS. Electronic applications accepted.

The University of Texas at San Antonio, College of Engineering, Department of Electrical and Computer Engineering, San Antonio, TX 78249-0617. Offers advanced materials engineering (MS); computer engineering (MS); electrical engineering (MSEE, PhD). Part-time programs available. *Faculty:* 24 full-time (3 women), 1 part-time/adjunct (0 women). *Students:* 210 full-time (58 women), 101 part-time (21 women); includes 47 minority (3 Black or African American, non-Hispanic/Latino; 11 Asian, non-Hispanic/

Latino; 28 Hispanic/Latino; 5 Two or more races, non-Hispanic/Latino), 218 international. Average age 26. 450 applicants, 86% accepted, 128 enrolled. In 2014, 45 master's, 8 doctorates awarded. Terminal master's awarded for partial completion of doctoral program. *Degree requirements:* For master's, comprehensive exam, thesis (for some programs); for doctorate, comprehensive exam, thesis/dissertation. *Entrance requirements:* For master's, GRE General Test, bachelor's degree in electrical or computer engineering from ABET-accredited institution of higher education or related field; minimum GPA of 3.0 on the last 60 semester credit hours of undergraduate studies; for doctorate, GRE General Test, master's degree or minimum GPA of 3.3 in last 60 semester credit hours of undergraduate level coursework in electrical engineering; statement of purpose. Additional exam requirements/recommendations for international students: Required—TOEFL (minimum score 550 paper-based; 79 iBT), IELTS (minimum score 6.5). *Application deadline:* For fall admission, 7/1 for domestic students, 4/1 for international students; for spring admission, 11/1 for domestic students, 9/1 for international students. Applications are processed on a rolling basis. Application fee: $45 ($80 for international students). Electronic applications accepted. *Expenses:* Tuition, state resident: full-time $4671; part-time $260 per credit hour. Tuition, nonresident: full-time $18,022; part-time $1001 per credit hour. *Financial support:* Unspecified assistantships available. Financial award application deadline: 3/31. *Faculty research:* Computer engineering, digital signal processing, systems and controls, communications, electronics materials and devices, electric power engineering. *Unit head:* Dr. Daniel Pack, Department Chair/Professor, 210-458-7076, Fax: 210-458-5947, E-mail: electrical.engineering@utsa.edu. *Application contact:* Graduate Advisor of Record, E-mail: graduate.ece@utsa.edu.
Website: http://ece.utsa.edu/.

University of Toronto, School of Graduate Studies, Faculty of Applied Science and Engineering, Department of Materials Science and Engineering, Toronto, ON M5S 2J7, Canada. Offers M Eng, MA Sc, PhD. Part-time programs available. *Degree requirements:* For master's, thesis (for some programs), oral presentation/thesis defense (MA Sc), qualifying exam; for doctorate, thesis/dissertation. *Entrance requirements:* For master's, BA Sc or B Sc in materials science and engineering, 2 letters of reference; for doctorate, MA Sc or equivalent, 2 letters of reference, minimum B+ average in last 2 years. Additional exam requirements/recommendations for international students: Required—TOEFL (minimum score 580 paper-based), TWE (minimum score 4). Electronic applications accepted.

University of Utah, Graduate School, College of Engineering, Department of Materials Science and Engineering, Salt Lake City, UT 84112. Offers MS, PhD. *Faculty:* 8 full-time (0 women), 2 part-time/adjunct (1 woman). *Students:* 34 full-time (8 women), 5 part-time (1 woman); includes 2 minority (both Asian, non-Hispanic/Latino), 21 international. Average age 28. 69 applicants, 22% accepted, 10 enrolled. In 2014, 2 master's, 5 doctorates awarded. *Degree requirements:* For master's, thesis; for doctorate, thesis/ dissertation. *Entrance requirements:* For master's and doctorate, GRE General Test, minimum GPA of 3.0. Additional exam requirements/recommendations for international students: Required—TOEFL (minimum score 570 paper-based; 88 iBT), IELTS (minimum score 7). *Application deadline:* For fall admission, 1/15 for domestic students, 12/15 for international students. Application fee: $0 ($15 for international students). Electronic applications accepted. *Expenses:* Expenses: Contact institution. *Financial support:* In 2014–15, 2 students received support, including 5 fellowships with full tuition reimbursements available (averaging $26,780 per year), 34 research assistantships with full tuition reimbursements available (averaging $23,000 per year); teaching assistantships with full tuition reimbursements available also available. Financial award application deadline: 2/5; financial award applicants required to submit FAFSA. *Faculty research:* Solid oxide fuel cells, computational nanostructures, solar cells, nanosensors, batteries: renewable energy. *Total annual research expenditures:* $3.3 million. *Unit head:* Dr. Feng Liu, Chair, 801-581-6863, Fax: 801-581-4816, E-mail: fliu@ eng.utah.edu. *Application contact:* Ashley Quimby, Academic Advisor, 801-581-6863, Fax: 801-581-4816, E-mail: ashley.quimby@utah.edu.
Website: http://www.mse.utah.edu/.

University of Washington, Graduate School, College of Engineering, Department of Materials Science and Engineering, Seattle, WA 98195-2120. Offers applied materials science and engineering (MS); materials science and engineering (MS, PhD). Part-time programs available. *Faculty:* 13 full-time (2 women). *Students:* 88 full-time (24 women), 9 part-time (4 women). Average age 27. 322 applicants, 37% accepted, 41 enrolled. In 2014, 19 master's, 10 doctorates awarded. Terminal master's awarded for partial completion of doctoral program. *Degree requirements:* For master's, comprehensive exam, thesis optional, final presentation; for doctorate, comprehensive exam, thesis/ dissertation, qualifying evaluation, general and final exams. *Entrance requirements:* For master's and doctorate, GRE General Test, minimum GPA of 3.0. Additional exam requirements/recommendations for international students: Required—TOEFL (minimum score 580 paper-based; 92 iBT); Recommended—IELTS (minimum score 7). *Application deadline:* For fall admission, 12/15 for domestic and international students. Applications are processed on a rolling basis. Application fee: $85. Electronic applications accepted. *Expenses:* Expenses: Contact institution. *Financial support:* In 2014–15, 34 students received support, including 2 fellowships with full tuition reimbursements available, 21 research assistantships with full tuition reimbursements available, 11 teaching assistantships with full tuition reimbursements available; career-related internships or fieldwork, Federal Work-Study, institutionally sponsored loans, scholarships/grants, health care benefits, unspecified assistantships, and stipend supplements also available. Financial award application deadline: 1/15; financial award applicants required to submit FAFSA. *Faculty research:* Synthesis/structure/property and processing, biomaterials and biomimetics, materials chemistry and characterization, optical and electronic materials. *Total annual research expenditures:* $6.4 million. *Unit head:* Dr. Alex Jen, Professor/Chair, 206-543-2600, Fax: 206-543-3100, E-mail: ajen@ uw.edu. *Application contact:* Karen Wetterhahn, Academic Counselor, 206-543-2740, Fax: 206-543-3100, E-mail: karenlw@uw.edu.
Website: http://depts.washington.edu/mse/.

The University of Western Ontario, Faculty of Graduate Studies, Physical Sciences Division, Faculty of Engineering, London, ON N6A 5B8, Canada. Offers chemical and biochemical engineering (ME Sc, PhD); civil and environmental engineering (M Eng, ME Sc, PhD); electrical and computer engineering (M Eng, ME Sc, PhD); mechanical and materials engineering (M Eng, ME Sc, PhD). Part-time programs available. Terminal master's awarded for partial completion of doctoral program. *Degree requirements:* For master's, thesis; for doctorate, thesis/dissertation. *Entrance requirements:* For master's, minimum B average; for doctorate, minimum B+ average. *Faculty research:* Wind, geotechnical, chemical reactor engineering, applied electrostatics, biochemical engineering.

University of Windsor, Faculty of Graduate Studies, Faculty of Engineering, Department of Mechanical, Automotive, and Materials Engineering, Windsor, ON N9B 3P4, Canada. Offers engineering materials (M Eng, MA Sc, PhD); mechanical engineering (M Eng, MA Sc, PhD). Part-time programs available. *Degree requirements:* For master's, thesis; for doctorate, comprehensive exam, thesis/dissertation. *Entrance requirements:* For master's, minimum B average; for doctorate, master's degree, minimum B average. Additional exam requirements/recommendations for international

students: Required—TOEFL (minimum score 600 paper-based). Electronic applications accepted. *Faculty research:* Thermofluids, applied mechanics, materials engineering.

University of Wisconsin–Madison, Graduate School, College of Engineering, Department of Materials Science and Engineering, Madison, WI 53706. Offers materials engineering (MS, PhD). Part-time programs available. *Faculty:* 13 full-time (3 women). *Students:* 11 full-time (2 women); includes 8 minority (all Asian, non-Hispanic/Latino), 1 international. Average age 25. 156 applicants, 2% accepted, 3 enrolled. Terminal master's awarded for partial completion of doctoral program. *Degree requirements:* For master's, thesis; for doctorate, comprehensive exam, thesis/dissertation. *Entrance requirements:* For master's and doctorate, GRE General Test. Additional exam requirements/recommendations for international students: Required—TOEFL (minimum score 580 paper-based). *Application deadline:* For fall admission, 1/1 priority date for domestic and international students; for spring admission, 10/15 priority date for domestic and international students. Applications are processed on a rolling basis. Application fee: $9. Electronic applications accepted. *Expenses:* Tuition, state resident: full-time $10,723; part-time $745 per credit. Tuition, nonresident: full-time $24,054; part-time $1578 per credit. *Required fees:* $374 per semester. Tuition and fees vary according to course load, program and reciprocity agreements. *Financial support:* In 2014–15, 1 fellowship with tuition reimbursement (averaging $32,000 per year), 4 research assistantships with tuition reimbursements (averaging $20,400 per year), 1 teaching assistantship with tuition reimbursement (averaging $27,600 per year) were awarded. Financial award application deadline: 1/15. *Faculty research:* Materials characterization, electronic materials, metallurgy, computational materials science, nanotechnology. *Total annual research expenditures:* $16.3 million. *Unit head:* Dr. Donald S. Stone, Chair, 608-262-8791, Fax: 608-262-8353, E-mail: stone@ engr.wisc.edu. *Application contact:* Lynn J. Neis, University Services Program Associate, 608-262-3732, Fax: 608-262-8353, E-mail: lynn@engr.wisc.edu.
Website: http://www.engr.wisc.edu/mse/.

University of Wisconsin–Milwaukee, Graduate School, College of Engineering and Applied Science, Program in Engineering, Milwaukee, WI 53201-0413. Offers civil engineering (MS); electrical and computer engineering (MS); energy engineering (Certificate); engineering (PhD); engineering management (MS); engineering mechanics (MS); ergonomics (Certificate); industrial and management engineering (MS); manufacturing engineering (MS); materials engineering (MS); mechanical engineering (MS); MUP/MS. Part-time programs available. *Degree requirements:* For master's, comprehensive exam (for some programs), thesis or alternative; for doctorate, comprehensive exam, thesis/dissertation, internship. *Entrance requirements:* For master's, GRE, minimum GPA of 2.75; for doctorate, GRE, minimum GPA of 3.5. Additional exam requirements/recommendations for international students: Required—TOEFL (minimum score 550 paper-based; 79 iBT), IELTS (minimum score 6.5).

Virginia Polytechnic Institute and State University, Graduate School, College of Engineering, Blacksburg, VA 24061. Offers aerospace engineering (ME, MS, PhD); biological systems engineering (ME, MS, PhD); biomedical engineering (MS, PhD); chemical engineering (ME, MS, PhD); civil engineering (ME, MS, PhD); computer engineering (ME, MS, PhD); computer science (MS, PhD); electrical engineering (ME, PhD); engineering education (PhD); engineering mechanics (ME, MS, PhD); environmental engineering (MS); environmental science and engineering (MS); industrial and systems engineering (ME, MS, PhD); materials science and engineering (ME, MS, PhD); mechanical engineering (ME, MS, PhD); mining and minerals engineering (PhD); mining engineering (ME, MS); nuclear engineering (MS, PhD); ocean engineering (MS); systems engineering (ME, MS). *Accreditation:* ABET (one or more programs are accredited). *Faculty:* 356 full-time (60 women), 3 part-time/adjunct (1 woman). *Students:* 1,700 full-time (398 women), 345 part-time (58 women); includes 213 minority (43 Black or African American, non-Hispanic/Latino; 1 American Indian or Alaska Native, non-Hispanic/Latino; 87 Asian, non-Hispanic/Latino; 58 Hispanic/Latino; 1 Native Hawaiian or other Pacific Islander, non-Hispanic/Latino; 23 Two or more races, non-Hispanic/Latino), 1,079 international. Average age 27. 5,228 applicants, 18% accepted, 471 enrolled. In 2014, 438 master's, 211 doctorates awarded. *Degree requirements:* For master's, comprehensive exam (for some programs), thesis (for some programs); for doctorate, comprehensive exam (for some programs), thesis/dissertation (for some programs). *Entrance requirements:* For master's and doctorate, GRE/GMAT (may vary by department). Additional exam requirements/recommendations for international students: Required—TOEFL (minimum score 550 paper-based). *Application deadline:* For fall admission, 8/1 for domestic students, 4/1 for international students; for spring admission, 1/1 for domestic students, 9/1 for international students. Applications are processed on a rolling basis. Application fee: $75. Electronic applications accepted. *Expenses:* Tuition, state resident: full-time $11,656; part-time $647.50 per credit hour. Tuition, nonresident: full-time $23,351; part-time $1297.25 per credit hour. *Required fees:* $2533; $465.75 per semester. Tuition and fees vary according to course load, campus/location and program. *Financial support:* In 2014–15, 148 fellowships with full tuition reimbursements (averaging $8,031 per year), 855 research assistantships with full tuition reimbursements (averaging $22,855 per year), 288 teaching assistantships with full tuition reimbursements (averaging $20,291 per year) were awarded. Financial award application deadline: 3/1; financial award applicants required to submit FAFSA. *Total annual research expenditures:* $90.5 million. *Unit head:* Dr. Richard C. Benson, Dean, 540-231-9752, Fax: 540-231-3031, E-mail: deaneng@vt.edu. *Application contact:* Linda Perkins, Executive Assistant, 540-231-9752, Fax: 540-231-3031, E-mail: lperkins@vt.edu.
Website: http://www.eng.vt.edu/.

Washington State University, Voiland College of Engineering and Architecture, School of Mechanical and Materials Engineering, Pullman, WA 99164-2920. Offers materials science and engineering (MS, PhD); mechanical engineering (MS, PhD). MS programs also offered at Tri-Cities campus. Part-time programs available. *Faculty:* 29 full-time (4 women), 3 part-time/adjunct (1 woman). *Students:* 79 full-time (12 women), 27 part-time (4 women); includes 5 minority (2 Black or African American, non-Hispanic/Latino; 2 Asian, non-Hispanic/Latino; 1 Hispanic/Latino), 60 international. Average age 29. 169 applicants, 37% accepted, 39 enrolled. In 2014, 23 master's, 7 doctorates awarded. Terminal master's awarded for partial completion of doctoral program. *Degree requirements:* For master's, comprehensive exam, thesis; for doctorate, comprehensive exam, thesis/dissertation, preliminary exam. *Entrance requirements:* For master's, GRE, bachelor's degree, minimum GPA of 3.0, resume, statement of purpose, 3 letters of recommendation, official transcripts, Student Interest Profile form; for doctorate, GRE, bachelor's degree, minimum GPA of 3.4, resume, statement of purpose, 3 letters of recommendation, official transcripts, Student Interest Profile form. Additional exam requirements/recommendations for international students: Required—TOEFL (minimum score 500 paper-based), IELTS. *Application deadline:* For fall admission, 1/10 priority date for domestic and international students; for spring admission, 7/1 priority date for domestic and international students. Applications are processed on a rolling basis. Application fee: $75. Electronic applications accepted. *Expenses:* Tuition, state resident: full-time $11,768. Tuition, nonresident: full-time $25,200. *Required fees:* $960. Tuition and fees vary according to program. *Financial support:* In 2014–15, 94 students received support, including 3 fellowships with full tuition reimbursements available (averaging $38,200 per year), 22 research assistantships with full tuition reimbursements available (averaging $13,883 per year), 32 teaching assistantships with

full tuition reimbursements available (averaging $13,862 per year); career-related internships or fieldwork, scholarships/grants, health care benefits, and unspecified assistantships also available. Financial award application deadline: 4/1; financial award applicants required to submit FAFSA. *Faculty research:* Multiscale modeling and characterization of materials; advanced energy; bioengineering; engineering education and curricular innovation; modeling and visualization in the areas of product realization, materials, and processes. *Total annual research expenditures:* $4.4 million. *Unit head:* Dr. Michael Kessler, Director, 509-335-8654, Fax: 509-335-4662, E-mail: michael.kessler@wsu.edu. *Application contact:* Graduate School Admissions, 800-GRADWSU, Fax: 509-335-1949, E-mail: gradsch@wsu.edu.
Website: http://www.mme.wsu.edu/.

Worcester Polytechnic Institute, Graduate Studies and Research, Department of Mechanical Engineering, Program in Materials Science and Engineering, Worcester, MA 01609-2280. Offers MS, PhD. Part-time and evening/weekend programs available. *Students:* 71 full-time (23 women), 10 part-time (5 women); includes 8 minority (2 Asian, non-Hispanic/Latino; 2 Hispanic/Latino; 4 Two or more races, non-Hispanic/Latino), 58 international. 151 applicants, 76% accepted, 38 enrolled. In 2014, 35 master's, 4 doctorates awarded. *Degree requirements:* For master's, thesis; for doctorate, comprehensive exam, thesis/dissertation. *Entrance requirements:* For master's and doctorate, GRE (recommended), 3 letters of recommendation. Additional exam requirements/recommendations for international students: Required—TOEFL (minimum score 563 paper-based; 84 iBT), IELTS (minimum score 7). *Application deadline:* For fall admission, 1/1 priority date for domestic students, 1/1 for international students; for spring admission, 10/1 priority date for domestic students, 10/1 for international students. Applications are processed on a rolling basis. Application fee: $70. Electronic applications accepted. *Financial support:* Research assistantships, teaching assistantships, career-related internships or fieldwork, institutionally sponsored loans, scholarships/grants, and unspecified assistantships available. Financial award application deadline: 1/1; financial award applicants required to submit FAFSA. *Unit head:* Dr. Richard D. Sisson, Jr., Director, 508-831-5633, Fax: 508-831-5178, E-mail: sisson@wpi.edu. *Application contact:* Rita Shilansky, Graduate Secretary, 508-831-5633, Fax: 508-831-5178, E-mail: rita@wpi.edu.
Website: http://www.wpi.edu/academics/mte.

Wright State University, School of Graduate Studies, College of Engineering and Computer Science, Programs in Engineering, Program in Mechanical and Materials Engineering, Dayton, OH 45435. Offers materials science and engineering (MSE); mechanical engineering (MSE). *Degree requirements:* For master's, thesis or course option alternative. *Entrance requirements:* Additional exam requirements/recommendations for international students: Required—TOEFL.

Materials Sciences

Air Force Institute of Technology, Graduate School of Engineering and Management, Department of Aeronautics and Astronautics, Dayton, OH 45433-7765. Offers aeronautical engineering (MS, PhD); astronautical engineering (MS, PhD); materials science (MS, PhD); space operations (MS); systems engineering (MS, PhD). *Accreditation:* ABET (one or more programs are accredited). Part-time programs available. *Degree requirements:* For master's, thesis; for doctorate, thesis/dissertation. *Entrance requirements:* For master's and doctorate, GRE General Test, minimum GPA of 3.0, U.S. citizenship. *Faculty research:* Computational fluid dynamics, experimental aerodynamics, computational structural mechanics, experimental structural mechanics, aircraft and spacecraft stability and control.

Air Force Institute of Technology, Graduate School of Engineering and Management, Department of Engineering Physics, Dayton, OH 45433-7765. Offers applied physics (MS, PhD); electro-optics (MS, PhD); materials science (PhD); nuclear engineering (MS, PhD); space physics (MS). Part-time programs available. *Degree requirements:* For master's, thesis; for doctorate, thesis/dissertation. *Entrance requirements:* For master's and doctorate, GRE General Test, minimum GPA of 3.0, U.S. citizenship. *Faculty research:* High-energy lasers, space physics, nuclear weapon effects, semiconductor physics.

Alabama Agricultural and Mechanical University, School of Graduate Studies, School of Arts and Sciences, Department of Physics, Huntsville, AL 35811. Offers physics (MS, PhD), including applied physics (PhD), materials science (PhD), optics/lasers (PhD). Part-time and evening/weekend programs available. *Degree requirements:* For doctorate, thesis/dissertation. *Entrance requirements:* For master's and doctorate, GRE General Test. Additional exam requirements/recommendations for international students: Required—TOEFL (minimum score 500 paper-based; 61 iBT). Electronic applications accepted.

Alfred University, Graduate School, New York State College of Ceramics, Kazuo Inamori School of Engineering, Alfred, NY 14802. Offers biomaterials engineering (MS); ceramic engineering (MS); ceramics (PhD); electrical engineering (MS); glass science (MS, PhD); materials science and engineering (MS, PhD); mechanical engineering (MS). Part-time programs available. *Degree requirements:* For master's, thesis; for doctorate, thesis/dissertation. *Entrance requirements:* Additional exam requirements/recommendations for international students: Required—TOEFL (minimum score 590 paper-based; 90 iBT), IELTS (minimum score 6.5). Electronic applications accepted. *Expenses:* Contact institution. *Faculty research:* X-ray diffraction, biomaterials and polymers, thin-film processing, electronic and optical ceramics, solid-state chemistry.

Arizona State University at the Tempe campus, Ira A. Fulton Schools of Engineering, School for Engineering of Matter, Transport and Energy, Tempe, AZ 85281. Offers aerospace engineering (MS, PhD); chemical engineering (MS, PhD); materials science and engineering (MS, PhD); mechanical engineering (MS, PhD); solar energy engineering and commercialization (PSM). Part-time and evening/weekend programs available. Postbaccalaureate distance learning degree programs offered (minimal on-campus study). Terminal master's awarded for partial completion of doctoral program. *Degree requirements:* For master's, thesis and oral defense (MS); applied project or comprehensive exam (MSE); interactive Program of Study (iPOS) submitted before completing 50 percent of required credit hours; for doctorate, comprehensive exam, thesis/dissertation, interactive Program of Study (iPOS) submitted before completing 50 percent of required credit hours. *Entrance requirements:* For master's, GRE, minimum GPA of 3.0 or equivalent in last 2 years of work leading to bachelor's degree; for doctorate, GRE, minimum GPA of 3.0 in last 2 years of work leading to bachelor's degree. Additional exam requirements/recommendations for international students: Required—TOEFL, IELTS, or PTE. Electronic applications accepted. *Expenses:* Contact institution. *Faculty research:* Electronic materials and packaging, materials for energy (batteries), adaptive/intelligent materials and structures, multiscale fluid mechanics, membranes, therapeutics and bioseparations, flexible structures, nanostructured materials, and micro/nano transport.

Binghamton University, State University of New York, Graduate School, Thomas J. Watson School of Engineering and Applied Science and School of Arts and Sciences, Materials Science and Engineering Program, Vestal, NY 13850. Offers MS, PhD. *Faculty:* 3 full-time (0 women). *Students:* 14 full-time (1 woman), 31 part-time (16 women); includes 2 minority (both Asian, non-Hispanic/Latino), 36 international. Average age 27. 74 applicants, 58% accepted, 14 enrolled. In 2014, 2 master's, 3 doctorates awarded. *Degree requirements:* For master's, thesis; for doctorate, comprehensive exam, thesis/dissertation. *Entrance requirements:* For master's and doctorate, GRE General Test. Additional exam requirements/recommendations for international students: Required—TOEFL (minimum score 550 paper-based; 80 iBT). Application fee: $75. *Expenses:* Expenses: $5,435 resident; $11,105 non-resident. *Financial support:* In 2014–15, 32 students received support, including 21 research assistantships with full tuition reimbursements available (averaging $17,500 per year), 10 teaching assistantships with full tuition reimbursements available (averaging $17,500 per year); career-related internships or fieldwork, Federal Work-Study, institutionally sponsored loans, scholarships/grants, health care benefits, tuition waivers (full and partial), and unspecified assistantships also available. Financial award application deadline: 2/15; financial award applicants required to submit FAFSA. *Unit head:* Ellen Tilden, Coordinator of Graduate Programs, 607-777-2873, E-mail: etilden@binghamton.edu. *Application contact:* Kishan Zuber, Recruiting and Admissions Coordinator, 607-777-2151, Fax: 607-777-2501, E-mail: kzuber@binghamton.edu.
Website: http://materials.binghamton.edu/materials/.

Boston University, College of Engineering, Division of Materials Science and Engineering, Boston, MA 02215. Offers materials science and engineering (MS). Part-time programs available. *Students:* 50 full-time (15 women), 10 part-time (4 women); includes 4 minority (3 Asian, non-Hispanic/Latino; 1 Hispanic/Latino), 42 international. Average age 25. 208 applicants, 34% accepted, 29 enrolled. In 2014, 4 master's, 5 doctorates awarded. Terminal master's awarded for partial completion of doctoral program. *Degree requirements:* For master's, thesis (for some programs); for doctorate, comprehensive exam, thesis/dissertation. *Entrance requirements:* For master's and doctorate, GRE General Test. Additional exam requirements/recommendations for international students: Required—TOEFL (minimum score 550 paper-based; 84 iBT), IELTS (minimum score 7). *Application deadline:* For fall admission, 3/15 for domestic and international students; for spring admission, 10/1 for domestic and international students. Application fee: $80. Electronic applications accepted. *Expenses: Tuition:* Full-time $45,686; part-time $1428 per credit hour. *Required fees:* $660; $60 per semester. Tuition and fees vary according to program. *Financial support:* In 2014–15, 23 students received support, including 2 fellowships with full tuition reimbursements available (averaging $28,950 per year), 15 research assistantships with full tuition reimbursements available (averaging $19,300 per year), 4 teaching assistantships with full tuition reimbursements available (averaging $19,300 per year); career-related internships or fieldwork, Federal Work-Study, scholarships/grants, and tuition waivers (partial) also available. Financial award application deadline: 1/15; financial award applicants required to submit FAFSA. *Faculty research:* Biomaterials, electronic and photonic materials, materials for energy and environment, nanomaterials. *Unit head:* Dr. David Bishop, Division Head, 617-353-8899, Fax: 617-353-5548, E-mail: djb1@bu.edu. *Application contact:* Dr. Solomon Eisenberg, Senior Associate Dean of Academic Programs, 617-353-9760, Fax: 617-353-0259, E-mail: enggrad@bu.edu.
Website: http://www.bu.edu/mse/.

Brown University, Graduate School, School of Engineering, Program in Materials Science and Engineering, Providence, RI 02912. Offers Sc M, PhD. *Degree requirements:* For doctorate, thesis/dissertation, preliminary exam.

California Institute of Technology, Division of Engineering and Applied Science, Option in Materials Science, Pasadena, CA 91125-0001. Offers MS, PhD. *Degree requirements:* For doctorate, thesis/dissertation. *Faculty research:* Mechanical properties, physical properties, kinetics of phase transformations, metastable phases, transmission electron microscopy.

Carnegie Mellon University, Carnegie Institute of Technology, Department of Materials Science and Engineering, Pittsburgh, PA 15213-3891. Offers MS, PhD. Part-time programs available. Terminal master's awarded for partial completion of doctoral program. *Degree requirements:* For master's, exam; for doctorate, thesis/dissertation, qualifying exam. *Entrance requirements:* For master's and doctorate, GRE General Test. Additional exam requirements/recommendations for international students: Required—TOEFL. *Faculty research:* Materials characterization, process metallurgy, high strength alloys, growth kinetics, ceramics.

Case Western Reserve University, School of Graduate Studies, Case School of Engineering, Department of Materials Science and Engineering, Cleveland, OH 44106. Offers materials science and engineering (MS, PhD). Part-time programs available. Postbaccalaureate distance learning degree programs offered (no on-campus study). *Faculty:* 13 full-time (1 woman). *Students:* 34 full-time (13 women), 5 part-time (1 woman); includes 3 minority (1 Black or African American, non-Hispanic/Latino; 1 Asian, non-Hispanic/Latino; 1 Hispanic/Latino), 21 international. In 2014, 6 master's, 5 doctorates awarded. Terminal master's awarded for partial completion of doctoral program. *Degree requirements:* For master's, thesis (for some programs); for doctorate, thesis/dissertation, qualifying exam, teaching experience. *Entrance requirements:* For master's and doctorate, GRE General Test. Additional exam requirements/recommendations for international students: Required—TOEFL. *Application deadline:* For fall admission, 2/15 priority date for domestic students; for spring admission, 9/15 for domestic students. Applications are processed on a rolling basis. Application fee: $50. *Financial support:* In 2014–15, 30 research assistantships with full and partial tuition reimbursements were awarded; fellowships with full and partial tuition reimbursements and teaching assistantships also available. Financial award application deadline: 4/30; financial award applicants required to submit FAFSA. *Faculty research:* Surface hardening of steels and other alloys, chemistry and structure of surfaces, microstructural and mechanical property characterization, materials for energy applications, thermodynamics and kinetics of materials, performance and reliability of materials. *Total annual research expenditures:* $5.3 million. *Unit head:* Dr. James D. McGuffin-Cawley, Department Chair, 216-368-6482, Fax: 216-368-4224, E-mail: emse.info@case.edu. *Application contact:* Theresa Claytor, Student Affairs Coordinator, 216-368-8555, Fax: 216-368-8555, E-mail: esme.info@case.edu.
Website: http://dmseg5.case.edu.

The Catholic University of America, School of Engineering, Department of Materials Science and Engineering, Washington, DC 20064. Offers MS. Part-time programs

available. *Students:* 8 full-time (5 women), 2 part-time (1 woman); includes 2 minority (both Black or African American, non-Hispanic/Latino), 8 international. Average age 29. 10 applicants, 100% accepted, 4 enrolled. In 2014, 5 master's awarded. *Degree requirements:* For master's, thesis optional. *Entrance requirements:* For master's, GRE (minimum score 1250), minimum GPA of 3.0, statement of purpose, official copies of academic transcripts. Additional exam requirements/recommendations for international students: Required—TOEFL (minimum score 580 paper-based). *Application deadline:* For fall admission, 7/15 for domestic students, 7/1 for international students; for spring admission, 11/15 for domestic students, 11/1 for international students. Applications are processed on a rolling basis. Application fee: $55. Electronic applications accepted. *Expenses: Tuition:* Full-time $40,200; part-time $1600 per credit hour. *Required fees:* $400; $195 per semester. One-time fee: $425. *Financial support:* Fellowships, research assistantships, teaching assistantships, Federal Work-Study, scholarships/grants, tuition waivers (full and partial), and unspecified assistantships available. Financial award application deadline: 2/1; financial award applicants required to submit FAFSA. *Faculty research:* Nanotechnology, biomaterials, magnetic and optical materials, glass, ceramics, and metallurgy processing and instrumentation. *Unit head:* Dr. Biprodas Dutta, Director, 202-319-5535, Fax: 202-319-4469, E-mail: duttab@cua.edu. *Application contact:* Director of Graduate Admissions, 202-319-5057, Fax: 202-319-6533, E-mail: cua-admissions@cua.edu.
Website: http://materialsscience.cua.edu/.

Central Michigan University, College of Graduate Studies, College of Science and Technology, Department of Physics, Program in the Science of Advanced Materials, Mount Pleasant, MI 48859. Offers PhD. *Degree requirements:* For doctorate, comprehensive exam, thesis/dissertation. *Entrance requirements:* For doctorate, GRE. Electronic applications accepted. *Faculty research:* Electronic properties of nanomaterials, polymers for energy and for environmental applications, inorganic materials synthesis, magnetic properties from first-principles, and nano devices for biomedical applications and environmental remediation.

Clarkson University, Graduate School, Wallace H. Coulter School of Engineering, Program in Materials Science and Engineering, Potsdam, NY 13699. Offers PhD. Part-time programs available. *Students:* 10 full-time (2 women), 5 international. Average age 27. 18 applicants, 61% accepted, 4 enrolled. In 2014, 1 doctorate awarded. *Degree requirements:* For doctorate, comprehensive exam, thesis/dissertation, departmental qualifying exam. *Entrance requirements:* For doctorate, GRE, transcripts of all college coursework, resume, personal statement, three letters of recommendation. Additional exam requirements/recommendations for international students: Required—TOEFL (minimum score 550 paper-based; 80 iBT), IELTS (minimum score 6.5). *Application deadline:* For fall admission, 1/30 priority date for domestic and international students; for spring admission, 9/1 priority date for domestic and international students. Applications are processed on a rolling basis. Application fee: $25 ($35 for international students). Electronic applications accepted. *Expenses: Tuition:* Full-time $16,680; part-time $1390 per credit. *Required fees:* $295 per semester. *Financial support:* In 2014–15, 10 students received support, including 2 fellowships with full tuition reimbursements available (averaging $24,029 per year), 2 research assistantships with full tuition reimbursements available (averaging $24,029 per year), 1 teaching assistantship with full tuition reimbursement available (averaging $24,029 per year); scholarships/grants, tuition waivers (partial), and unspecified assistantships also available. *Unit head:* Dr. Marilyn Freeman, Chair, 315-268-2316, Fax: 315-268-4494, E-mail: mfreeman@clarkson.edu. *Application contact:* Kelly Sharlow, Assistant to the Dean, 315-268-7929, Fax: 315-268-4494, E-mail: ksharlow@clarkson.edu.
Website: http://www.clarkson.edu/engineering/graduate/mat_sci_eng_phd/.

Clemson University, Graduate School, College of Engineering and Science, Department of Materials Science and Engineering, Clemson, SC 29634. Offers MS, PhD. Part-time programs available. *Faculty:* 15 full-time (1 woman), 4 part-time/adjunct (2 women). *Students:* 55 full-time (13 women), 7 part-time (3 women); includes 2 minority (1 Black or African American, non-Hispanic/Latino; 1 Two or more races, non-Hispanic/Latino), 26 international. Average age 26. 162 applicants, 35% accepted, 19 enrolled. In 2014, 4 master's, 8 doctorates awarded. Terminal master's awarded for partial completion of doctoral program. *Degree requirements:* For master's, thesis; for doctorate, comprehensive exam, thesis/dissertation. *Entrance requirements:* For master's and doctorate, GRE General Test. Additional exam requirements/recommendations for international students: Required—TOEFL. *Application deadline:* For fall admission, 2/1 priority date for domestic students; for spring admission, 9/1 priority date for domestic students. Applications are processed on a rolling basis. Application fee: $70 ($80 for international students). Electronic applications accepted. *Financial support:* In 2014–15, 31 students received support, including 2 fellowships with full and partial tuition reimbursements available (averaging $1,000 per year), 31 research assistantships with partial tuition reimbursements available (averaging $21,668 per year); teaching assistantships with partial tuition reimbursements available, career-related internships or fieldwork, institutionally sponsored loans, scholarships/grants, health care benefits, and unspecified assistantships also available. Support available to part-time students. Financial award applicants required to submit FAFSA. *Total annual research expenditures:* $2 million. *Unit head:* Dr. Rajendra K. Bordia, Chair of the Department of Materials Science and Engineering, 864-656-3311, Fax: 864-656-5973, E-mail: rbordia@clemson.edu. *Application contact:* Heather L. Cox, Program Manager, 864-656-1512, Fax: 864-656-5973, E-mail: hlcox@clemson.edu.
Website: http://www.clemson.edu/mse/.

Colorado School of Mines, Graduate School, Department of Metallurgical and Materials Engineering, Golden, CO 80401-1887. Offers materials science (MS, PhD); metallurgical and materials engineering (ME, MS, PhD). Part-time programs available. *Faculty:* 25 full-time (2 women), 12 part-time/adjunct (0 women). *Students:* 112 full-time (33 women), 12 part-time (2 women); includes 9 minority (3 Asian, non-Hispanic/Latino; 4 Hispanic/Latino; 2 Two or more races, non-Hispanic/Latino), 38 international. Average age 29. 207 applicants, 23% accepted, 35 enrolled. In 2014, 31 master's, 17 doctorates awarded. *Degree requirements:* For master's, thesis (for some programs); for doctorate, comprehensive exam, thesis/dissertation. *Entrance requirements:* For master's and doctorate, GRE General Test. Additional exam requirements/recommendations for international students: Required—TOEFL (minimum score 550 paper-based; 80 iBT). *Application deadline:* For fall admission, 12/15 priority date for domestic and international students; for spring admission, 9/1 priority date for domestic and international students. Application fee: $50 ($70 for international students). Electronic applications accepted. *Financial support:* In 2014–15, 88 students received support, including 5 fellowships with full tuition reimbursements available (averaging $21,120 per year), 69 research assistantships with full tuition reimbursements available (averaging $21,120 per year), 11 teaching assistantships with full tuition reimbursements available (averaging $21,120 per year); scholarships/grants, health care benefits, and unspecified assistantships also available. Financial award application deadline: 12/15; financial award applicants required to submit FAFSA. *Total annual research expenditures:* $7.4 million. *Unit head:* Dr. Ivar Reimanis, Interim Head, 303-273-3549, E-mail: ireimani@mines.edu. *Application contact:* Kelly Hummel, Program Assistant, 303-273-3660, Fax: 303-273-3795, E-mail: khummel@mines.edu.
Website: http://metallurgy.mines.edu.

Columbia University, Fu Foundation School of Engineering and Applied Science, Department of Applied Physics and Applied Mathematics, New York, NY 10027. Offers applied physics (Eng Sc D); applied physics and applied mathematics (MS, PhD); materials science and engineering (MS, Eng Sc D, PhD); medical physics (MS). Part-time programs available. Postbaccalaureate distance learning degree programs offered (no on-campus study). *Faculty:* 34 full-time (4 women), 33 part-time/adjunct (4 women). *Students:* 130 full-time (31 women), 26 part-time (8 women); includes 21 minority (17 Asian, non-Hispanic/Latino; 3 Hispanic/Latino; 1 Two or more races, non-Hispanic/Latino), 97 international. 439 applicants, 30% accepted, 59 enrolled. In 2014, 49 master's, 10 doctorates awarded. Terminal master's awarded for partial completion of doctoral program. *Degree requirements:* For master's, comprehensive exam; for doctorate, thesis/dissertation, qualifying exam. *Entrance requirements:* For master's, GRE General Test, GRE Subject Test (strongly recommended); for doctorate, GRE General Test, GRE Subject Test (applied physics). Additional exam requirements/recommendations for international students: Required—TOEFL, IELTS, PTE. *Application deadline:* For fall admission, 12/15 priority date for domestic and international students; for spring admission, 10/1 priority date for domestic and international students. Application fee: $85. Electronic applications accepted. *Financial support:* In 2014–15, 60 students received support, including 1 fellowship with full tuition reimbursement available (averaging $37,500 per year), 42 research assistantships with full tuition reimbursements available (averaging $33,781 per year), 17 teaching assistantships with full tuition reimbursements available (averaging $33,781 per year); health care benefits also available. Financial award application deadline: 12/15; financial award applicants required to submit FAFSA. *Faculty research:* Plasma physics and fusion energy; optical and laser physics; atmospheric, oceanic and earth physics; applied mathematics; solid state science and processing of materials, their properties, and their structure; medical physics. *Unit head:* Dr. I. Cevdet Noyan, Professor and Chair, Applied Physics and Applied Mathematics, 212-854-8919, E-mail: seasinfo.apam@columbia.edu. *Application contact:* Montserrat Fernandez-Pinkley, Student Services Coordinator, 212-854-4457, Fax: 212-854-8257, E-mail: mf2157@columbia.edu.
Website: http://www.apam.columbia.edu/.

Cornell University, Graduate School, Graduate Fields of Engineering, Field of Materials Science and Engineering, Ithaca, NY 14853. Offers materials engineering (M Eng, PhD); materials science (M Eng, PhD). *Degree requirements:* For doctorate, comprehensive exam, thesis/dissertation. *Entrance requirements:* For master's and doctorate, GRE General Test, 3 letters of recommendation. Additional exam requirements/recommendations for international students: Required—TOEFL (minimum score 550 paper-based; 77 iBT). Electronic applications accepted. *Faculty research:* Ceramics, complex fluids, glass, metals, polymers semiconductors.

Dartmouth College, Thayer School of Engineering, Program in Materials Sciences and Engineering, Hanover, NH 03755. Offers MS, PhD. *Degree requirements:* For master's, thesis; for doctorate, thesis/dissertation, candidacy oral exam. *Entrance requirements:* For master's and doctorate, GRE General Test. *Application deadline:* For fall admission, 1/1 priority date for domestic students. Application fee: $45. *Financial support:* Fellowships, research assistantships, teaching assistantships, career-related internships or fieldwork, Federal Work-Study, institutionally sponsored loans, and tuition waivers (full and partial) available. Financial award application deadline: 1/15. *Faculty research:* Electronic and magnetic materials, microstructural evolution, biomaterials and nanostructures, laser-material interactions, nano composites. *Total annual research expenditures:* $3.2 million. *Unit head:* Dr. Joseph J. Helbie, Dean, 603-646-2238, Fax: 603-646-2580, E-mail: joseph.j.helbie@dartmouth.edu. *Application contact:* Candace S. Potter, Graduate Admissions Administrator, 603-646-3844, Fax: 603-646-1620, E-mail: candace.s.potter@dartmouth.edu.
Website: http://engineering.dartmouth.edu/.

Duke University, Graduate School, Pratt School of Engineering, Department of Mechanical Engineering and Materials Science, Durham, NC 27708. Offers materials science (MS, PhD); mechanical engineering (MS, PhD); JD/MS. *Faculty:* 25 full-time. *Students:* 83 full-time (21 women); includes 11 minority (3 Black or African American, non-Hispanic/Latino; 2 Asian, non-Hispanic/Latino; 6 Hispanic/Latino), 41 international. 302 applicants, 18% accepted, 23 enrolled. In 2014, 11 master's, 10 doctorates awarded. Terminal master's awarded for partial completion of doctoral program. *Degree requirements:* For master's, thesis optional; for doctorate, thesis/dissertation. *Entrance requirements:* For master's and doctorate, GRE General Test. Additional exam requirements/recommendations for international students: Required—TOEFL (minimum score 90 iBT), IELTS (minimum score 7). *Application deadline:* For fall admission, 12/8 priority date for domestic and international students; for spring admission, 10/15 for domestic students. Application fee: $80. Electronic applications accepted. *Expenses: Tuition:* Full-time $45,760; part-time $2765 per credit. *Required fees:* $978. Full-time tuition and fees vary according to program. *Financial support:* Fellowships, research assistantships, teaching assistantships, and Federal Work-Study available. Financial award application deadline: 12/8. *Unit head:* Brian Mann, Director of Graduate Studies, 919-660-5310, Fax: 919-660-8963, E-mail: kparrish@duke.edu. *Application contact:* Kathy Parrish, -, Fax: -, E-mail: grad-admissions@duke.edu.
Website: http://www.mems.duke.edu/grad.

Duke University, Graduate School, Pratt School of Engineering, Master of Engineering Program, Durham, NC 27708-0271. Offers biomedical engineering (M Eng); civil engineering (M Eng); electrical and computer engineering (M Eng); environmental engineering (M Eng); materials science and engineering (M Eng); mechanical engineering (M Eng); photonics and optical sciences (M Eng). Part-time programs available. *Students:* 45 full-time (17 women); includes 5 minority (1 Black or African American, non-Hispanic/Latino; 2 Asian, non-Hispanic/Latino; 2 Hispanic/Latino), 23 international. Average age 24. 285 applicants, 43% accepted, 45 enrolled. In 2014, 45 master's awarded. *Entrance requirements:* For master's, GRE General Test, resume, 3 letters of recommendation, statement of purpose, transcripts. Additional exam requirements/recommendations for international students: Required—TOEFL. *Application deadline:* For fall admission, 6/15 for domestic students, 2/15 for international students; for spring admission, 11/1 for domestic students, 9/1 for international students. Application fee: $75. *Expenses: Tuition:* Full-time $45,760; part-time $2765 per credit. *Required fees:* $978. Full-time tuition and fees vary according to program. *Financial support:* Merit scholarships/grants available. *Unit head:* Dr. Bradley A. Fox, Executive Director, 919-660-5455, Fax: 919-660-5456. *Application contact:* Susan Brown, Assistant Director of Admissions, 919-660-8451, Fax: 919-660-5456, E-mail: susan.brown@duke.edu.
Website: http://meng.pratt.duke.edu/.

Florida International University, College of Engineering and Computing, Department of Mechanical and Materials Engineering, Materials Science and Engineering Program, Miami, FL 33175. Offers MS, PhD. Part-time and evening/weekend programs available. Terminal master's awarded for partial completion of doctoral program. *Degree requirements:* For master's, thesis or alternative; for doctorate, comprehensive exam, thesis/dissertation. *Entrance requirements:* For master's, GRE, 3 letters of recommendation, minimum undergraduate GPA of 3.0 in upper-level course work; for doctorate, GRE, minimum GPA of 3.0, 3 letters of recommendation, letter of intent.

Additional exam requirements/recommendations for international students: Required—TOEFL (minimum score 550 paper-based; 80 iBT). Electronic applications accepted.

Florida State University, The Graduate School, College of Arts and Sciences, Department of Chemistry and Biochemistry, Tallahassee, FL 32306-4390. Offers analytical chemistry (MS, PhD); biochemistry (MS, PhD); inorganic chemistry (MS, PhD); materials chemistry (PhD); organic chemistry (MS, PhD); physical chemistry (MS, PhD). *Faculty:* 42 full-time (5 women), 4 part-time/adjunct (2 women). *Students:* 151 full-time (49 women), 4 part-time (0 women); includes 71 minority (6 Black or African American, non-Hispanic/Latino; 46 Asian, non-Hispanic/Latino; 16 Hispanic/Latino; 3 Two or more races, non-Hispanic/Latino), 50 international. Average age 26. 174 applicants, 45% accepted, 38 enrolled. In 2014, 4 master's, 17 doctorates awarded. Terminal master's awarded for partial completion of doctoral program. *Degree requirements:* For master's, comprehensive exam, thesis (for some programs); for doctorate, comprehensive exam, thesis/dissertation. *Entrance requirements:* For master's and doctorate, GRE General Test (minimum scores: 150 verbal, 151 quantitative; 1100 total on the old scale), minimum GPA of 3.1 in undergraduate course work. Additional exam requirements/recommendations for international students: Required—TOEFL (minimum score 90 iBT). *Application deadline:* For fall admission, 12/15 priority date for domestic and international students; for spring admission, 9/15 for domestic and international students. Applications are processed on a rolling basis. Application fee: $30. Electronic applications accepted. *Expenses:* Expenses: Contact institution. *Financial support:* In 2014–15, 151 students received support, including 4 fellowships with full and partial tuition reimbursements available (averaging $3,625 per year), 35 research assistantships with full tuition reimbursements available (averaging $20,000 per year), 116 teaching assistantships with full tuition reimbursements available (averaging $20,000 per year); health care benefits also available. Financial award application deadline: 12/15; financial award applicants required to submit FAFSA. *Faculty research:* Bioanalytical chemistry, including separations, microfluidics, petroleomics; materials chemistry, including magnets, polymers, catalysts, nanomaterials; spectroscopy, including NMR and EPR, ultrafast, Raman, and mass spectrometry; organic synthesis, natural products, photochemistry, and supramolecular chemistry; biochemistry, with focus on structural biology, metabolomics, and anticancer drugs. *Total annual research expenditures:* $5.8 million. *Unit head:* Dr. Timothy Logan, Chairman, 850-644-3810, Fax: 850-644-8281, E-mail: gradinfo@chem.fsu.edu. *Application contact:* Dr. Michael Shatruk, Associate Chair for Graduate Studies, 850-417-8417, Fax: 850-644-8281, E-mail: gradinfo@chem.fsu.edu.
Website: http://www.chem.fsu.edu/.

Florida State University, The Graduate School, College of Arts and Sciences, Department of Scientific Computing, Tallahassee, FL 32306-4120. Offers computational science (MS, PSM, PhD), including atmospheric science (PhD), biochemistry (PhD), biological science (PhD), computational molecular biology/bioinformatics (PSM), computational science (PhD), geological science (PhD), materials science (PhD), physics (PhD). Part-time programs available. *Faculty:* 14 full-time (2 women). *Students:* 30 full-time (5 women); includes 13 minority (1 Black or African American, non-Hispanic/Latino; 7 Asian, non-Hispanic/Latino; 4 Hispanic/Latino; 1 Two or more races, non-Hispanic/Latino). Average age 27. 28 applicants, 43% accepted, 7 enrolled. In 2014, 9 master's, 7 doctorates awarded. Terminal master's awarded for partial completion of doctoral program. *Degree requirements:* For master's, thesis (for some programs); for doctorate, comprehensive exam, thesis/dissertation. *Entrance requirements:* For master's and doctorate, GRE General Test, knowledge of at least one object-oriented computing language, 3 letters of recommendation. Additional exam requirements/recommendations for international students: Required—TOEFL (minimum score 550 paper-based; 80 iBT). *Application deadline:* For fall admission, 1/15 for domestic and international students. Application fee: $30. Electronic applications accepted. *Expenses:* Tuition, state resident: part-time $403.51 per credit hour. Tuition, nonresident: part-time $1004.85 per credit hour. *Required fees:* $75.81 per credit hour. One-time fee: $20 part-time. Tuition and fees vary according to campus/location. *Financial support:* In 2014–15, 32 students received support, including 10 research assistantships with full tuition reimbursements available (averaging $20,000 per year), 23 teaching assistantships with full tuition reimbursements available (averaging $20,000 per year); scholarships/grants and unspecified assistantships also available. Financial award application deadline: 4/15. *Faculty research:* Morphometrics, mathematical and systems biology, mining proteomic and metabolic data, computational materials research, advanced 4-D Var data-assimilation methods in dynamic meteorology and oceanography, computational fluid dynamics, astrophysics. *Unit head:* Dr. Max Gunzburger, Chair, 850-644-1010, E-mail: mgunzburger@fsu.edu. *Application contact:* Mark Howard, Academic Program Specialist, 850-644-0143, Fax: 850-644-0098, E-mail: mlhoward@fsu.edu.
Website: http://www.sc.fsu.edu.

Florida State University, The Graduate School, Materials Science and Engineering Program, Tallahassee, FL 32310. Offers MS, PhD. *Faculty:* 37 full-time (6 women). *Students:* 17 full-time (3 women), 1 part-time (0 women); includes 2 minority (both Hispanic/Latino), 9 international. Average age 26. 51 applicants, 18% accepted, 2 enrolled. In 2014, 2 master's, 1 doctorate awarded. Terminal master's awarded for partial completion of doctoral program. *Degree requirements:* For master's, thesis; for doctorate, comprehensive exam, thesis/dissertation. *Entrance requirements:* For master's and doctorate, GRE General Test (minimum new format 55th percentile Verbal, 75th percentile Quantitative, old version 1100 combined Verbal and Quantitative), minimum GPA of 3.0, 3 letters of recommendation. Additional exam requirements/recommendations for international students: Required—TOEFL (minimum score 80 iBT). *Application deadline:* For fall admission, 5/1 for domestic and international students; for spring admission, 9/1 for domestic and international students; for summer admission, 1/1 for domestic and international students. Applications are processed on a rolling basis. Application fee: $30. Electronic applications accepted. *Expenses:* Tuition, state resident: part-time $403.51 per credit hour. Tuition, nonresident: part-time $1004.85 per credit hour. *Required fees:* $75.81 per credit hour. One-time fee: $20 part-time. Tuition and fees vary according to campus/location. *Financial support:* In 2014–15, 17 students received support, including 17 research assistantships with full tuition reimbursements available (averaging $21,990 per year); partial payment of required health insurance also available. Financial award application deadline: 12/15. *Faculty research:* Magnetism and magnetic materials, composites, superconductors, polymers, computations, nanotechnology. *Unit head:* Prof. Eric Hellstrom, Director, 850-645-7489, Fax: 850-645-7754, E-mail: hellstrom@asc.magnet.fsu.edu. *Application contact:* Judy Gardner, Admissions Coordinator, 850-645-8980, Fax: 850-645-9123, E-mail: jdgardner@fsu.edu.
Website: http://materials.fsu.edu.

Georgetown University, Graduate School of Arts and Sciences, Department of Chemistry, Washington, DC 20057. Offers analytical chemistry (PhD); biochemistry (PhD); computational chemistry (PhD); inorganic chemistry (PhD); materials chemistry (PhD); organic chemistry (PhD); theoretical chemistry (PhD). Terminal master's awarded for partial completion of doctoral program. *Degree requirements:* For doctorate, comprehensive exam, thesis/dissertation. *Entrance requirements:* For doctorate, GRE General Test. Additional exam requirements/recommendations for international students: Required—TOEFL.

The George Washington University, Columbian College of Arts and Sciences, Department of Chemistry, Washington, DC 20052. Offers analytical chemistry (MS, PhD); inorganic chemistry (MS, PhD); materials science (MS, PhD); organic chemistry (MS, PhD); physical chemistry (MS, PhD). Part-time and evening/weekend programs available. *Faculty:* 17 full-time (5 women). *Students:* 19 full-time (11 women), 17 part-time (6 women); includes 1 minority (Asian, non-Hispanic/Latino), 10 international. Average age 28. 63 applicants, 6% accepted, 2 enrolled. In 2014, 4 master's, 4 doctorates awarded. Terminal master's awarded for partial completion of doctoral program. *Degree requirements:* For master's, comprehensive exam, thesis or alternative; for doctorate, thesis/dissertation, general exam. *Entrance requirements:* For master's and doctorate, GRE General Test, interview, minimum GPA of 3.0. Additional exam requirements/recommendations for international students: Required—TOEFL (minimum score 550 paper-based; 80 iBT). *Application deadline:* For fall admission, 1/15 priority date for domestic and international students; for spring admission, 9/1 priority date for domestic and international students. Applications are processed on a rolling basis. Application fee: $75. Electronic applications accepted. *Financial support:* In 2014–15, 27 students received support. Fellowships with tuition reimbursements available, research assistantships, teaching assistantships with tuition reimbursements available, Federal Work-Study, and tuition waivers available. Financial award application deadline: 1/15. *Unit head:* Dr. Michael King, Chair, 202-994-6488. *Application contact:* Information Contact, 202-994-6121, E-mail: gwchem@gwu.edu.
Website: http://chemistry.columbian.gwu.edu/.

Illinois Institute of Technology, Graduate College, Armour College of Engineering, Department of Mechanical, Materials and Aerospace Engineering, Chicago, IL 60616. Offers manufacturing engineering (MAS, MS); materials science and engineering (MAS, MS, PhD); mechanical and aerospace engineering (MAS, MS, PhD), including economics (MS), energy (MS), environment (MS). Part-time and evening/weekend programs available. Postbaccalaureate distance learning degree programs offered (minimal on-campus study). *Faculty:* 29 full-time (3 women), 10 part-time/adjunct (2 women). *Students:* 187 full-time (35 women), 27 part-time (3 women); includes 8 minority (2 Black or African American, non-Hispanic/Latino; 4 Asian, non-Hispanic/Latino; 2 Hispanic/Latino), 168 international. Average age 26. 1,562 applicants, 31% accepted, 76 enrolled. In 2014, 74 master's, 7 doctorates awarded. Terminal master's awarded for partial completion of doctoral program. *Degree requirements:* For master's, comprehensive exam (for some programs), thesis (for some programs); for doctorate, comprehensive exam, thesis/dissertation. *Entrance requirements:* For master's and doctorate, GRE General Test (minimum score 1000 Quantitative and Verbal, 3.0 Analytical Writing), minimum undergraduate GPA of 3.0. Additional exam requirements/recommendations for international students: Required—TOEFL (minimum score 550 paper-based; 80 iBT). *Application deadline:* For fall admission, 5/1 for domestic and international students; for spring admission, 10/15 for domestic and international students. Applications are processed on a rolling basis. Application fee: $50. Electronic applications accepted. *Expenses: Tuition:* Full-time $22,500; part-time $1250 per credit hour. *Required fees:* $30 per course. $260 per semester. One-time fee: $235. Tuition and fees vary according to course load and program. *Financial support:* Fellowships with full and partial tuition reimbursements, research assistantships with full and partial tuition reimbursements, teaching assistantships with full and partial tuition reimbursements, Federal Work-Study, institutionally sponsored loans, scholarships/grants, health care benefits, tuition waivers, and unspecified assistantships available. Support available to part-time students. Financial award applicants required to submit FAFSA. *Faculty research:* Fluid dynamics, metallurgical and materials engineering, solids and structures, computational mechanics, computer added design and manufacturing, thermal sciences, dynamic analysis and control of complex systems. *Unit head:* Dr. Keith Bowman, Chair of the Department of Mechanical, Materials and Aerospace Engineering & Duchossois Leadership Professor of Materials Engineering, 312-567-3175, Fax: 312-567-7230, E-mail: keith.bowman@iit.edu. *Application contact:* Rishab Malhotra, Director, Graduate Admission, 866-472-3448, Fax: 312-567-3138, E-mail: inquiry.grad@iit.edu.
Website: http://www.mmae.iit.edu.

Illinois Institute of Technology, Graduate College, College of Science, Department of Chemical Sciences, Chicago, IL 60616. Offers analytical chemistry (MAS); chemistry (MAS, MS, PhD); materials chemistry (MAS), including inorganic. Part-time and evening/weekend programs available. Postbaccalaureate distance learning degree programs offered (no on-campus study). *Faculty:* 13 full-time (4 women), 2 part-time/adjunct (1 woman). *Students:* 47 full-time (16 women), 58 part-time (32 women); includes 6 minority (1 Black or African American, non-Hispanic/Latino; 2 Asian, non-Hispanic/Latino; 2 Hispanic/Latino; 1 Two or more races, non-Hispanic/Latino), 42 international. Average age 29. 178 applicants, 40% accepted, 28 enrolled. In 2014, 22 master's, 3 doctorates awarded. Terminal master's awarded for partial completion of doctoral program. *Degree requirements:* For master's, comprehensive exam, thesis (for some programs); for doctorate, comprehensive exam, thesis/dissertation. *Entrance requirements:* For master's, GRE General Test (minimum score 300 Quantitative and Verbal, 2.5 Analytical Writing), minimum undergraduate GPA of 3.0; for doctorate, GRE General Test (minimum score 310 Quantitative and Verbal, 3.0 Analytical Writing), GRE Subject Test, minimum undergraduate GPA of 3.0; strongly encouraged to submit the subject-area GRE score (Subject No. 27); Applicants to the doctoral program in molecular biochemistry and biophysics are strongly encouraged to take one of the subject exams in biology, molecular biology, chemistry, or physics. Additional exam requirements/recommendations for international students: Required—TOEFL (minimum score 550 paper-based; 80 iBT); Recommended—IELTS. *Application deadline:* For fall admission, 5/1 for domestic and international students; for spring admission, 10/15 for domestic and international students. Applications are processed on a rolling basis. Application fee: $50. Electronic applications accepted. *Expenses: Tuition:* Full-time $22,500; part-time $1250 per credit hour. *Required fees:* $30 per course. $260 per semester. One-time fee: $235. Tuition and fees vary according to course load and program. *Financial support:* Fellowships with full and partial tuition reimbursements, research assistantships with full and partial tuition reimbursements, teaching assistantships with full and partial tuition reimbursements, Federal Work-Study, institutionally sponsored loans, scholarships/grants, health care benefits, tuition waivers (partial), and unspecified assistantships available. Support available to part-time students. Financial award applicants required to submit FAFSA. *Faculty research:* Materials science, biological chemistry, synthetic chemistry, computational chemistry, energy, sensor science and technology, scholarship of teaching and learning. *Unit head:* Dr. M. Ishaque Khan, Executive Associate Chair for Chemistry, 312-567-3431, Fax: 312-567-3494, E-mail: khan@iit.edu. *Application contact:* Rishab Malhotra, Director, Graduate Admission, 866-472-3448, Fax: 312-567-3138, E-mail: inquiry.grad@iit.edu.
Website: http://www.iit.edu/csl/che/.

Indiana University Bloomington, University Graduate School, College of Arts and Sciences, Department of Chemistry, Bloomington, IN 47405. Offers analytical chemistry (PhD); chemical biology (PhD); chemistry (MAT); inorganic chemistry (PhD); materials chemistry (PhD); organic chemistry (PhD); physical chemistry (PhD); MSES/MS. *Faculty:* 42 full-time (4 women). *Students:* 203 full-time (82 women); includes 18 minority (5 Black or African American, non-Hispanic/Latino; 5 Asian, non-Hispanic/Latino; 4 Hispanic/Latino; 4 Two or more races, non-Hispanic/Latino), 55 international. Average

age 25. 241 applicants, 51% accepted, 48 enrolled. In 2014, 4 master's, 28 doctorates awarded. Terminal master's awarded for partial completion of doctoral program. *Degree requirements:* For master's, thesis; for doctorate, thesis/dissertation. *Entrance requirements:* For master's and doctorate, GRE General Test, GRE Subject Test. Additional exam requirements/recommendations for international students: Required—TOEFL. *Application deadline:* For fall admission, 12/15 for domestic students, 12/1 for international students. Applications are processed on a rolling basis. Application fee: $55 ($65 for international students). Electronic applications accepted. *Financial support:* In 2014–15, 13 fellowships with full tuition reimbursements, 74 research assistantships with full tuition reimbursements, 118 teaching assistantships with full tuition reimbursements were awarded; Federal Work-Study and institutionally sponsored loans also available. *Faculty research:* Synthesis of complex natural products, organic reaction mechanisms, organic electrochemistry, transitive-metal chemistry, solid-state and surface chemistry. *Total annual research expenditures:* $7.7 million. *Unit head:* Dr. David Giedroc, Chairperson, 812-855-6239, E-mail: chemchair@indiana.edu. *Application contact:* Toni D. Lady, Administrative Assistant for Graduate Affairs, 812-855-2068, Fax: -, E-mail: tlady@indiana.edu.
Website: http://www.chem.indiana.edu/.

Instituto Tecnológico y de Estudios Superiores de Monterrey, Campus Estado de México, Professional and Graduate Division, Estado de Mexico, Mexico. Offers administration of information technologies (MITA); architecture (M Arch); business administration (GMBA, MBA); computer sciences (MCS, PhD); education (M Ed); educational institution administration (MAD); educational technology and innovation (PhD); electronic commerce (MEC); environmental systems (MS); finance (MAF); humanistic studies (MHS); information sciences and knowledge management (MISKM); information systems (MS); manufacturing systems (MS); marketing (MEM); quality systems and productivity (MS); science and materials engineering (PhD); telecommunications management (MTM). Part-time programs available. Postbaccalaureate distance learning degree programs offered (minimal on-campus study). *Degree requirements:* For master's, one foreign language, thesis (for some programs); for doctorate, one foreign language, thesis/dissertation. *Entrance requirements:* For master's, E-PAEP 500, interview; for doctorate, E-PAEP 500, research proposal. Additional exam requirements/recommendations for international students: Required—TOEFL (minimum score 550 paper-based). *Faculty research:* Surface treatments by plasmas, mechanical properties, robotics, graphical computing, mechatronics security protocols.

Iowa State University of Science and Technology, Department of Materials Science and Engineering, Ames, IA 50011. Offers MS, PhD. *Entrance requirements:* For master's and doctorate, GRE General Test. Additional exam requirements/recommendations for international students: Required—TOEFL (minimum score 550 paper-based; 79 iBT), IELTS (minimum score 6.5). Electronic applications accepted.

Jackson State University, Graduate School, College of Science, Engineering and Technology, Department of Technology, Jackson, MS 39217. Offers hazardous materials management (MS); technology education (MS Ed). Part-time and evening/weekend programs available. *Degree requirements:* For master's, comprehensive exam, thesis or alternative. *Entrance requirements:* For master's, GRE General Test. Additional exam requirements/recommendations for international students: Required—TOEFL (minimum score 520 paper-based; 67 iBT).

Johns Hopkins University, Engineering Program for Professionals, Part-time Program in Materials Science and Engineering, Baltimore, MD 21218-2699. Offers M Mat SE, MSE. Part-time and evening/weekend programs available. Electronic applications accepted.

Johns Hopkins University, G. W. C. Whiting School of Engineering, Department of Materials Science and Engineering, Baltimore, MD 21218-2699. Offers M Mat SE, MSE, PhD. Part-time and evening/weekend programs available. Terminal master's awarded for partial completion of doctoral program. *Degree requirements:* For master's, thesis, oral exam; for doctorate, thesis/dissertation, oral exam, thesis defense. *Entrance requirements:* For master's and doctorate, GRE General Test. Additional exam requirements/recommendations for international students: Required—TOEFL (minimum score 600 paper-based). Electronic applications accepted. *Faculty research:* Thin films, nanomaterials, biomaterials, materials characterization, electronic materials.

Johns Hopkins University, G. W. C. Whiting School of Engineering, Master of Science in Engineering Management Program, Baltimore, MD 21218-2699. Offers biomaterials (MSEM); civil engineering (MSEM); communications science (MSEM); computer science (MSEM); environmental systems analysis, economics and public policy (MSEM); fluid mechanics (MSEM); materials science and engineering (MSEM); mechanical engineering (MSEM); mechanics and materials (MSEM); nano-biotechnology (MSEM); nanomaterials and nanotechnology (MSEM); operations research (MSEM); probability and statistics (MSEM); smart product and device design (MSEM). *Entrance requirements:* For master's, GRE, 3 letters of recommendation, resume. Additional exam requirements/recommendations for international students: Required—TOEFL (minimum score 600 paper-based; 100 iBT) or IELTS (minimum score 7). Electronic applications accepted.

Lehigh University, P.C. Rossin College of Engineering and Applied Science, Department of Materials Science and Engineering, Bethlehem, PA 18015. Offers materials science and engineering (M Eng, MS, PhD); photonics (MS); polymer science/ engineering (M Eng, MS, PhD); MBA/E. Part-time programs available. *Faculty:* 14 full-time (3 women), 1 part-time/adjunct (0 women). *Students:* 28 full-time (9 women), 8 part-time (0 women); includes 3 minority (2 Asian, non-Hispanic/Latino; 1 Two or more races, non-Hispanic/Latino), 15 international. Average age 27. 238 applicants, 3% accepted, 4 enrolled. In 2014, 3 master's, 5 doctorates awarded. *Degree requirements:* For master's, thesis; for doctorate, comprehensive exam, thesis/dissertation. *Entrance requirements:* For master's and doctorate, GRE General Test. Additional exam requirements/ recommendations for international students: Required—TOEFL (minimum score 487 paper-based; 85 iBT). *Application deadline:* For fall admission, 1/15 priority date for domestic students, 1/15 for international students; for spring admission, 12/1 priority date for domestic students, 12/1 for international students. Applications are processed on a rolling basis. Application fee: $75. Electronic applications accepted. *Financial support:* In 2014–15, 26 students received support, including 3 fellowships with full and partial tuition reimbursements available (averaging $19,920 per year), 22 research assistantships with full and partial tuition reimbursements available (averaging $25,550 per year), 6 teaching assistantships with full and partial tuition reimbursements available (averaging $20,490 per year); career-related internships or fieldwork, Federal Work-Study, institutionally sponsored loans, scholarships/grants, and unspecified assistantships also available. Support available to part-time students. Financial award application deadline: 1/15. *Faculty research:* Metals, ceramics, crystals, polymers, fatigue crack propagation, biomaterials. *Total annual research expenditures:* $4.2 million. *Unit head:* Dr. Helen Chan, Chairperson, 610-758-5554, Fax: 610-758-4244, E-mail: hmc0@lehigh.edu. *Application contact:* Lisa Carreras Arechiga, Graduate Administrative Coordinator, 610-758-4222, Fax: 610-758-4244, E-mail: lia4@lehigh.edu. Website: http://www.lehigh.edu/~inmatsci/.

Massachusetts Institute of Technology, School of Engineering, Department of Materials Science and Engineering, Cambridge, MA 02139. Offers archaeological materials (PhD, Sc D); materials engineering (Mat E); materials science and engineering (SM, PhD, Sc D). *Faculty:* 30 full-time (10 women). *Students:* 199 full-time (47 women); includes 35 minority (2 Black or African American, non-Hispanic/Latino; 23 Asian, non-Hispanic/Latino; 5 Hispanic/Latino; 5 Two or more races, non-Hispanic/Latino), 109 international. Average age 26. 406 applicants, 14% accepted, 34 enrolled. In 2014, 8 master's, 35 doctorates awarded. *Degree requirements:* For master's, thesis; for doctorate, comprehensive exam, thesis/dissertation. *Entrance requirements:* For master's, doctorate, and Mat E, GRE General Test. Additional exam requirements/ recommendations for international students: Required—IELTS (minimum score 7). *Application deadline:* For fall admission, 12/15 for domestic and international students. Application fee: $75. Electronic applications accepted. *Expenses: Tuition:* Full-time $44,720; part-time $699 per unit. *Required fees:* $296. *Financial support:* In 2014–15, 178 students received support, including 44 fellowships (averaging $29,400 per year), 134 research assistantships (averaging $33,400 per year), 13 teaching assistantships (averaging $36,400 per year); Federal Work-Study, institutionally sponsored loans, scholarships/grants, traineeships, health care benefits, and unspecified assistantships also available. Financial award application deadline: 4/15; financial award applicants required to submit FAFSA. *Faculty research:* Thermodynamics and kinetics of materials; structure, processing and properties of materials; electronic, structural and biological materials engineering; computational materials science; materials in energy, medicine, nanotechnology and the environment. *Total annual research expenditures:* $26.5 million. *Unit head:* Prof. Christopher Schuh, Department Head, 617-253-3300, Fax: 617-252-1775. *Application contact:* Prof. Christopher Schuh, Department Head, 617-253-3300, Fax: 617-252-1775.
Website: http://dmse.mit.edu/.

McMaster University, School of Graduate Studies, Faculty of Engineering, Department of Materials Science and Engineering, Hamilton, ON L8S 4M2, Canada. Offers materials engineering (M Eng, MA Sc, PhD); materials science (M Eng, PhD). *Degree requirements:* For master's, thesis; for doctorate, comprehensive exam, thesis/dissertation. *Entrance requirements:* Additional exam requirements/recommendations for international students: Required—TOEFL (minimum score 550 paper-based). *Faculty research:* Localized corrosion of metals and alloys, electron microscopy, polymer synthesis and characterization, polymer reaction kinetics and engineering, polymer process modeling.

Michigan State University, The Graduate School, College of Engineering, Department of Chemical Engineering and Materials Science, East Lansing, MI 48824. Offers chemical engineering (MS, PhD); materials science and engineering (MS, PhD). *Entrance requirements:* Additional exam requirements/recommendations for international students: Required—TOEFL. Electronic applications accepted.

Missouri State University, Graduate College, College of Natural and Applied Sciences, Department of Physics, Astronomy, and Materials Science, Springfield, MO 65897. Offers materials science (MS); physics (MNAS), including physics (MNAS, MS Ed); secondary education (MS Ed), including physics (MNAS, MS Ed). Part-time programs available. *Faculty:* 9 full-time (0 women). *Students:* 12 full-time (2 women), 5 part-time (0 women), 11 international. Average age 26. 8 applicants, 88% accepted, 5 enrolled. In 2014, 10 master's awarded. *Degree requirements:* For master's, comprehensive exam, thesis. *Entrance requirements:* For master's, GRE (MS, MNAS), minimum undergraduate GPA of 3.0 (MS and MNAS), 9-12 teaching certification (MS Ed). Additional exam requirements/recommendations for international students: Required—TOEFL (minimum score 550 paper-based; 79 iBT). *Application deadline:* For fall admission, 7/20 priority date for domestic students, 5/1 for international students; for spring admission, 12/20 priority date for domestic students, 9/1 for international students. Applications are processed on a rolling basis. Application fee: $35 ($50 for international students). Electronic applications accepted. *Expenses:* Tuition, state resident: full-time $2250; part-time $250 per credit hour. Tuition, nonresident: full-time $4509; part-time $501 per credit hour. Tuition and fees vary according to course level, course load and program. *Financial support:* In 2014–15, 3 research assistantships with full tuition reimbursements (averaging $10,280 per year), 9 teaching assistantships with full tuition reimbursements (averaging $10,280 per year) were awarded; Federal Work-Study, institutionally sponsored loans, scholarships/grants, and unspecified assistantships also available. Financial award application deadline: 3/31; financial award applicants required to submit FAFSA. *Faculty research:* Nanocomposites, ferroelectricity, infrared focal plane array sensors, biosensors, pulsating stars. *Unit head:* Dr. David Cornelison, Department Head, 417-836-4467, Fax: 417-836-6226, E-mail: physics@missouristate.edu. *Application contact:* Misty Stewart, Coordinator of Graduate Recruitment, 417-836-6079, Fax: 417-836-6200, E-mail: mistystewart@missouristate.edu.
Website: http://physics.missouristate.edu/.

Montana Tech of The University of Montana, Graduate School, Program in Materials Science, Butte, MT 59701-8997. Offers PhD. *Expenses:* Tuition, state resident: full-time $5802; part-time $241 per credit. Tuition, nonresident: full-time $15,895; part-time $662 per credit. *Required fees:* $1516; $414 per credit. $207 per semester. One-time fee: $30.

New Jersey Institute of Technology, College of Science and Liberal Arts, Newark, NJ 07102. Offers applied mathematics (MS); applied physics (M Sc, PhD); applied statistics (MS); biology (MS, PhD); biostatistics (MS); chemistry (MS, PhD); computational biology (MS); environmental science (MS, PhD); history (MA, MAT); materials science and engineering (MS, PhD); mathematical and computational finance (MS); mathematics science (PhD); pharmaceutical chemistry (MS); professional and technical communications (MS). Part-time and evening/weekend programs available. Terminal master's awarded for partial completion of doctoral program. *Degree requirements:* For master's, thesis optional; for doctorate, thesis/dissertation. *Entrance requirements:* For master's, GRE General Test; for doctorate, GRE General Test, minimum graduate GPA of 3.5. Additional exam requirements/recommendations for international students: Required—TOEFL (minimum score 550 paper-based; 79 iBT). Electronic applications accepted.

Norfolk State University, School of Graduate Studies, School of Science and Technology, Department of Chemistry, Norfolk, VA 23504. Offers materials science (MS). *Entrance requirements:* Additional exam requirements/recommendations for international students: Required—TOEFL (minimum score 500 paper-based).

North Carolina State University, Graduate School, College of Engineering, Department of Materials Science and Engineering, Raleigh, NC 27695. Offers MMSE, MS, PhD. PhD offered jointly with The University of North Carolina at Charlotte. *Degree requirements:* For master's, thesis; for doctorate, thesis/dissertation. Electronic applications accepted. *Faculty research:* Processing and properties of wide band gap semiconductors, ferroelectric thin-film materials, ductility of nanocrystalline materials, computational materials science, defects in silicon-based devices.

North Dakota State University, College of Graduate and Interdisciplinary Studies, Interdisciplinary Program in Materials and Nanotechnology, Fargo, ND 58108. Offers MS, PhD. *Entrance requirements:* For doctorate, GRE General Test. Additional exam requirements/recommendations for international students: Required—TOEFL (minimum score 525 paper-based; 71 iBT).

Northwestern University, McCormick School of Engineering and Applied Science, Department of Civil and Environmental Engineering, Evanston, IL 60208-3109. Offers environmental engineering and science (MS, PhD); geotechnical engineering (MS, PhD); mechanics of materials and solids (MS, PhD); project management (MS, PhD); structural engineering and materials (MS, PhD); transportation systems analysis and planning (MS, PhD). MS and PhD admissions and degrees offered through The Graduate School. Part-time programs available. *Faculty:* 19 full-time (2 women). *Students:* 118 full-time (36 women), 5 part-time (2 women); includes 7 minority (3 Black or African American, non-Hispanic/Latino; 2 Asian, non-Hispanic/Latino; 1 Hispanic/Latino; 1 Two or more races, non-Hispanic/Latino), 95 international. Average age 24. 412 applicants, 36% accepted, 49 enrolled. In 2014, 42 master's, 10 doctorates awarded. Terminal master's awarded for partial completion of doctoral program. *Degree requirements:* For master's, thesis (for some programs); for doctorate, comprehensive exam, thesis/dissertation. *Entrance requirements:* For master's and doctorate, GRE General Test, minimum 2 letters of recommendation, transcripts from all academic institutions attended. Additional exam requirements/recommendations for international students: Required—TOEFL (minimum score 577 paper-based; 90 iBT), IELTS (minimum score 7). *Application deadline:* For fall admission, 12/31 for domestic and international students; for winter admission, 11/15 for domestic and international students; for spring admission, 1/15 for domestic and international students. Application fee: $95. Electronic applications accepted. *Financial support:* Fellowships with full tuition reimbursements, research assistantships with full tuition reimbursements, teaching assistantships with full tuition reimbursements, career-related internships or fieldwork, institutionally sponsored loans, health care benefits, and unspecified assistantships available. Financial award application deadline: 12/31; financial award applicants required to submit FAFSA. *Faculty research:* Environmental engineering and science, geotechnics, mechanics of materials and solids, structural engineering and materials, transportation systems analysis and planning. *Total annual research expenditures:* $5.8 million. *Unit head:* Dr. Jianmin Qu, Chair, 847-467-4528, Fax: 847-491-4011, E-mail: j-qu@northwestern.edu. *Application contact:* Dr. David Corr, Academic Coordinator, 847-467-0890, Fax: 847-491-4011, E-mail: d-corr@u.northwestern.edu.
Website: http://www.civil.northwestern.edu/.

Northwestern University, McCormick School of Engineering and Applied Science, Department of Materials Science and Engineering, Evanston, IL 60208. Offers integrated computational materials engineering (Certificate); materials science and engineering (MS, PhD). Admissions and degrees offered through The Graduate School. Part-time programs available. *Faculty:* 25 full-time (4 women). *Students:* 204 full-time (64 women), 10 part-time (5 women); includes 38 minority (2 Black or African American, non-Hispanic/Latino; 1 American Indian or Alaska Native, non-Hispanic/Latino; 19 Asian, non-Hispanic/Latino; 10 Hispanic/Latino; 6 Two or more races, non-Hispanic/Latino), 97 international. Average age 26. 737 applicants, 18% accepted, 59 enrolled. In 2014, 15 master's, 33 doctorates awarded. Terminal master's awarded for partial completion of doctoral program. *Degree requirements:* For master's, thesis, oral thesis defense; for doctorate, comprehensive exam, thesis/dissertation, oral defense of dissertation, preliminary evaluation, qualifying exam. *Entrance requirements:* For master's and doctorate, GRE General Test. Additional exam requirements/recommendations for international students: Required—TOEFL (minimum score 577 paper-based; 90 iBT) or IELTS (minimum score 7). *Application deadline:* For fall admission, 12/31 for domestic and international students. Application fee: $75. Electronic applications accepted. *Financial support:* Fellowships with full tuition reimbursements, research assistantships with full tuition reimbursements, teaching assistantships with full tuition reimbursements, career-related internships or fieldwork, institutionally sponsored loans, health care benefits, and unspecified assistantships available. Financial award application deadline: 1/15; financial award applicants required to submit FAFSA. *Faculty research:* Art conservation science; biomaterials; ceramics; composites; energy; magnetic materials; materials for electronics and photonics; materials synthesis and processing; materials theory, computation, and design; metals; nanomaterials; polymers, self-assembly, and surfaces and interfaces. *Total annual research expenditures:* $31.4 million. *Unit head:* Dr. Michael Bedzyk, Chair, 847-491-3570, Fax: 847-491-7820, E-mail: bedzyk@northwestern.edu. *Application contact:* Dr. Chris Wolverton, Admissions Officer, 847-497-0593, Fax: 847-491-7820, E-mail: c-wolverton@northwestern.edu.
Website: http://www.matsci.northwestern.edu/.

The Ohio State University, Graduate School, College of Engineering, Department of Materials Science and Engineering, Columbus, OH 43210. Offers materials science and engineering (MS, PhD); welding engineering (MS, PhD). *Faculty:* 34. *Students:* 132 full-time (23 women), 31 part-time (6 women); includes 13 minority (1 Black or African American, non-Hispanic/Latino; 4 Asian, non-Hispanic/Latino; 7 Hispanic/Latino; 1 Two or more races, non-Hispanic/Latino), 55 international. Average age 27. In 2014, 38 master's, 16 doctorates awarded. *Degree requirements:* For master's, thesis; for doctorate, thesis/dissertation. *Entrance requirements:* For master's and doctorate, GRE (for graduates of foreign universities and holders of non-engineering degrees). Additional exam requirements/recommendations for international students: Required—TOEFL (minimum score 550 paper-based; 79 iBT), Michigan English Language Assessment Battery (minimum score 82); Recommended—IELTS (minimum score 7). *Application deadline:* For fall admission, 12/13 priority date for domestic students, 11/30 priority date for international students; for winter admission, 12/1 for domestic students, 11/1 for international students; for spring admission, 12/14 for domestic students, 11/12 for international students; for summer admission, 5/15 for domestic students, 4/14 for international students. Applications are processed on a rolling basis. Application fee: $60 ($70 for international students). Electronic applications accepted. *Financial support:* Fellowships with tuition reimbursements, research assistantships with tuition reimbursements, teaching assistantships, career-related internships or fieldwork, scholarships/grants, and unspecified assistantships available. *Faculty research:* Computational materials modeling, biomaterials, metallurgy, ceramics, advanced alloys/composites. *Total annual research expenditures:* $10 million. *Unit head:* Dr. Michael Mills, Interim Chair, E-mail: mills.108@osu.edu. *Application contact:* Mark Cooper, Graduate Studies Coordinator, 614-292-7280, Fax: 614-292-1357, E-mail: mse@osu.edu.
Website: http://mse.osu.edu/.

Oregon State University, College of Engineering, Program in Materials Science, Corvallis, OR 97331. Offers MS, PhD. *Faculty:* 45 full-time (7 women), 1 part-time/adjunct (0 women). *Students:* 43 full-time (7 women), 6 part-time (2 women); includes 5 minority (3 Hispanic/Latino; 2 Two or more races, non-Hispanic/Latino), 19 international. Average age 29. 113 applicants, 17% accepted, 8 enrolled. In 2014, 4 master's, 3 doctorates awarded. *Degree requirements:* For master's, thesis or alternative. *Entrance requirements:* For master's and doctorate, GRE. Additional exam requirements/recommendations for international students: Required—TOEFL (minimum score 80 iBT), IELTS (minimum score 6.5). *Application deadline:* For fall admission, 8/1 for domestic students, 4/1 for international students; for winter admission, 12/1 for domestic students, 7/1 for international students; for spring admission, 2/1 for domestic students, 10/1 for international students; for summer admission, 5/1 for domestic students, 1/1 for international students. Application fee: $60. *Expenses:* Expenses: $15,359 full-time resident tuition and fees; $23,405 non-resident. *Financial support:* Fellowships, research assistantships, teaching assistantships, Federal Work-Study, and institutionally sponsored loans available. Support available to part-time students. Financial award application deadline: 1/15. *Unit head:* Dr. William Warnes, Associate Professor/Director, OSU Materials Science Graduate Program, 541-737-7016. *Application contact:* Jean Robinson, Mechanical Engineering Advisor.
Website: http://matsci.oregonstate.edu/.

Penn State University Park, Graduate School, Intercollege Graduate Programs, Intercollege Graduate Program in Materials Science and Engineering, University Park, PA 16802. Offers MS, PhD. *Financial support:* Fellowships available. *Unit head:* Dr. Regina Vasilatos-Younken, Interim Dean, 814-865-2516, Fax: 814-863-4627, E-mail: rxv@psu.edu. *Application contact:* Lori A. Stania, Director, Graduate Student Services, 814-867-5278, Fax: 814-863-4627, E-mail: gswww@psu.edu.

Princeton University, Princeton Institute for the Science and Technology of Materials (PRISM), Princeton, NJ 08544-1019. Offers materials (PhD).

Rensselaer Polytechnic Institute, Graduate School, School of Engineering, Program in Materials Science and Engineering, Troy, NY 12180. Offers M Eng, MS, D Eng, PhD. *Faculty:* 37 full-time (9 women), 3 part-time/adjunct (2 women). *Students:* 57 full-time (13 women), 4 part-time (1 woman); includes 5 minority (3 Hispanic/Latino; 2 Two or more races, non-Hispanic/Latino), 29 international. Average age 26. 185 applicants, 18% accepted, 18 enrolled. In 2014, 7 master's, 9 doctorates awarded. Terminal master's awarded for partial completion of doctoral program. *Degree requirements:* For master's, thesis; for doctorate, comprehensive exam, thesis/dissertation. *Entrance requirements:* For master's and doctorate, GRE. Additional exam requirements/recommendations for international students: Required—TOEFL (minimum score 600 paper-based; 100 iBT), IELTS (minimum score 7), PTE (minimum score 68). *Application deadline:* For fall admission, 1/1 priority date for domestic and international students; for spring admission, 8/15 priority date for domestic and international students. Applications are processed on a rolling basis. Application fee: $75. Electronic applications accepted. *Expenses: Tuition:* Full-time $46,700; part-time $1945 per credit. Tuition and fees vary according to course load. *Financial support:* In 2014–15, 40 students received support, including research assistantships with full tuition reimbursements available (averaging $18,500 per year), teaching assistantships with full tuition reimbursements available (averaging $18,500 per year); fellowships also available. Financial award application deadline: 1/1. *Faculty research:* Advanced processing and synthesis, composites, computational materials, corrosion/electrochemical materials, electronic materials, glasses/ceramics, materials characterization, materials for energy, materials/biology interface, metals, nanomaterials, polymeric materials. *Total annual research expenditures:* $2 million. *Unit head:* Dr. Pawel Keblinski, Graduate Program Director, 518-276-6858, E-mail: keblip@rpi.edu. *Application contact:* Office of Graduate Admissions, 518-276-6216, E-mail: gradadmissions@rpi.edu.
Website: http://www.mse.rpi.edu/.

Rice University, Graduate Programs, George R. Brown School of Engineering, Department of Mechanical Engineering and Materials Science, Houston, TX 77251-1892. Offers materials science (MMS, MS, PhD); mechanical engineering (MME, MS, PhD); MBA/ME. Part-time programs available. Terminal master's awarded for partial completion of doctoral program. *Degree requirements:* For master's, comprehensive exam, thesis; for doctorate, comprehensive exam, thesis/dissertation. *Entrance requirements:* For master's and doctorate, GRE General Test, minimum GPA of 3.0. Additional exam requirements/recommendations for international students: Required—TOEFL (minimum score 600 paper-based; 90 iBT), IELTS (minimum score 7). Electronic applications accepted. *Faculty research:* Heat transfer, biomedical engineering, fluid dynamics, aero-astronautics, control systems/robotics, materials science.

Rochester Institute of Technology, Graduate Enrollment Services, College of Science, School of Chemistry and Materials Science, Rochester, NY 14623-5603. Offers MS. Part-time programs available. *Students:* 24 full-time (7 women), 14 part-time (7 women); includes 2 minority (1 Asian, non-Hispanic/Latino; 1 Hispanic/Latino), 13 international. Average age 25. 72 applicants, 46% accepted, 8 enrolled. In 2014, 6 master's awarded. *Degree requirements:* For master's, thesis or alternative. *Entrance requirements:* For master's, TOEFL, IELTS, or PTE for non-native English speakers, GRE for some programs, recommended minimum GPA of 3.0. Additional exam requirements/recommendations for international students: Required—PTE (minimum score 58), TOEFL (minimum score 550 paper-based; 79 iBT) or IELTS (minimum score 6.5). *Application deadline:* For fall admission, 2/15 priority date for domestic and international students; for spring admission, 12/15 priority date for domestic and international students. Applications are processed on a rolling basis. Electronic applications accepted. *Expenses:* Expenses: $1,673 per credit hour. *Financial support:* In 2014–15, 24 students received support. Research assistantships with partial tuition reimbursements available, teaching assistantships with partial tuition reimbursements available, career-related internships or fieldwork, Federal Work-Study, institutionally sponsored loans, scholarships/grants, and unspecified assistantships available. Support available to part-time students. Financial award applicants required to submit FAFSA. *Faculty research:* Organic chemistry, analytical chemistry, inorganic chemistry, physical chemistry, polymer chemistry, materials science, and biochemistry; polymer engineering, chemistry, and physics; nanomaterials; electronic materials; metallurgy; nonlinear phenomena; electronic properties of molecular crystals; experimental low temperature physics; large scale computations; parallel processing; superconductivity. *Unit head:* Dr. Paul Craig, Head, 585-475-2497, E-mail: science@rit.edu. *Application contact:* Diane Ellison, Associate Vice President, Graduate Enrollment Services, 585-475-2229, Fax: 585-475-7164, E-mail: gradinfo@rit.edu.
Website: https://www.rit.edu/cos/scms/.

Royal Military College of Canada, Division of Graduate Studies and Research, Engineering Division, Program in Chemical and Materials Science, Kingston, ON K7K 7B4, Canada. Offers M Sc, PhD. *Degree requirements:* For master's, thesis; for doctorate, comprehensive exam, thesis/dissertation. *Entrance requirements:* For master's, honours degree with second-class standing; for doctorate, master's degree. Electronic applications accepted.

Rutgers, The State University of New Jersey, New Brunswick, Graduate School-New Brunswick, Program in Materials Science and Engineering, Piscataway, NJ 08854-8097. Offers MS, PhD. Part-time programs available. *Degree requirements:* For master's, thesis; for doctorate, comprehensive exam, thesis/dissertation. *Entrance requirements:* For master's and doctorate, GRE General Test. Additional exam requirements/recommendations for international students: Recommended—TOEFL. Electronic applications accepted. *Faculty research:* Ceramic processing, nanostructured materials, electrical and structural ceramics, fiber optics.

School of the Art Institute of Chicago, Graduate Division, Department of Fiber and Material Studies, Chicago, IL 60603-3103. Offers MFA. *Accreditation:* NASAD. *Entrance requirements:* Additional exam requirements/recommendations for international students: Required—TOEFL, IELTS.

South Dakota School of Mines and Technology, Graduate Division, Doctoral Program in Materials Engineering and Science, Rapid City, SD 57701-3995. Offers PhD. Part-time programs available. *Faculty:* 7 full-time (0 women), 1 part-time/adjunct (0 women). *Students:* 5 full-time (1 woman), 7 part-time (0 women); includes 1 minority (Asian, non-Hispanic/Latino), 5 international. Average age 33. 9 applicants, 44% accepted, 4 enrolled. In 2014, 5 doctorates awarded. *Degree requirements:* For doctorate, thesis/dissertation. *Entrance requirements:* For doctorate, GRE General Test, minimum graduate GPA of 3.0, 3 letters of recommendation. Additional exam requirements/recommendations for international students: Required—TOEFL (minimum score 520 paper-based; 68 iBT), TWE. *Application deadline:* For fall admission, 7/1 priority date for domestic students, 4/1 for international students; for spring admission, 11/1 for domestic students, 9/1 for international students. Applications are processed on a rolling basis. Application fee: $35. Electronic applications accepted. *Expenses:* Tuition, state resident: full-time $5050; part-time $210.40 per credit hour. Tuition, nonresident: full-time $11,290; part-time $470.30 per credit hour. *Required fees:* $4680. *Financial support:* In 2014–15, 1 fellowship (averaging $5,000 per year), 16 research assistantships with partial tuition reimbursements (averaging $7,722 per year), 1 teaching assistantship with partial tuition reimbursement (averaging $14,000 per year) were awarded; Federal Work-Study and institutionally sponsored loans also available. Support available to part-time students. Financial award application deadline: 5/15. *Faculty research:* Thermophysical properties of solids, development of multiphase materials and composites, concrete technology, electronic polymer materials. *Total annual research expenditures:* $3 million. *Unit head:* Dr. Jon J. Keller, Coordinator, 605-394-2343, E-mail: jon.keller@sdsmt.edu. *Application contact:* Rachel Howard, Office of Graduate Education, 605-355-3468, Fax: 605-394-1767, E-mail: rachel.howard@sdsmt.edu.
Website: http://www.sdsmt.edu/Academics/Departments/Mechanical-Engineering/Graduate-Education/Mechanical-Engineering-PhD/.

South Dakota School of Mines and Technology, Graduate Division, Master's Program in Materials Engineering and Science, Rapid City, SD 57701-3995. Offers MS. *Faculty:* 7 full-time (0 women), 1 part-time/adjunct (0 women). *Students:* 14 full-time (4 women), 5 part-time (0 women), 6 international. Average age 27. 15 applicants, 47% accepted, 6 enrolled. In 2014, 5 master's awarded. *Degree requirements:* For master's, thesis (for some programs). *Entrance requirements:* For master's, GRE General Test. Additional exam requirements/recommendations for international students: Required—TOEFL (minimum score 520 paper-based; 68 iBT), TWE. *Application deadline:* For fall admission, 7/1 priority date for domestic students, 4/1 for international students; for spring admission, 11/1 for domestic students, 9/1 for international students. Applications are processed on a rolling basis. Application fee: $35. Electronic applications accepted. *Expenses:* Tuition, state resident: full-time $5050; part-time $210.40 per credit hour. Tuition, nonresident: full-time $11,290; part-time $470.30 per credit hour. *Required fees:* $4680. *Financial support:* In 2014–15, 4 fellowships (averaging $4,738 per year), 21 research assistantships with partial tuition reimbursements (averaging $8,307 per year), 8 teaching assistantships with partial tuition reimbursements (averaging $6,208 per year) were awarded. Financial award application deadline: 5/15. *Unit head:* Dr. Jon J. Keller, Coordinator, 605-394-2343, E-mail: jon.keller@sdsmt.edu. *Application contact:* Rachel Howard, Office of Graduate Education, 605-355-3468, Fax: 605-394-1767, E-mail: rachel.howard@sdsmt.edu.
Website: http://www.sdsmt.edu/Academics/Departments/Materials-and-Metallurgical-Engineering/Graduate-Education/.

Southern Methodist University, Dedman College of Humanities and Sciences, Department of Chemistry, Dallas, TX 75275-0314. Offers chemistry (MS, PhD); materials science and engineering (MS, PhD). Terminal master's awarded for partial completion of doctoral program. *Degree requirements:* For master's, thesis; for doctorate, comprehensive exam, thesis/dissertation. *Entrance requirements:* For master's, GRE General Test, bachelor's degree in chemistry, minimum GPA of 3.0; for doctorate, GRE General Test, bachelor's degree in chemistry or closely-related field, minimum GPA of 3.0. Additional exam requirements/recommendations for international students: Required—TOEFL (minimum score 550 paper-based; 80 iBT). Electronic applications accepted. *Faculty research:* Materials/polymer, medicinal/bioorganic, theoretical and computational, organic/inorganic/organometallic synthesis, inorganic polymer chemistry.

Stanford University, School of Engineering, Department of Materials Science and Engineering, Stanford, CA 94305-9991. Offers MS, PhD. Terminal master's awarded for partial completion of doctoral program. *Degree requirements:* For doctorate, thesis/dissertation. *Entrance requirements:* For master's and doctorate, GRE General Test. Additional exam requirements/recommendations for international students: Required—TOEFL. Electronic applications accepted. *Expenses: Tuition:* Full-time $44,184; part-time $982 per credit hour. *Required fees:* $191.

State University of New York College of Environmental Science and Forestry, Department of Paper and Bioprocess Engineering, Syracuse, NY 13210-2779. Offers biomaterials engineering (MS, PhD); bioprocess engineering (MPS, MS, PhD); bioprocessing (Advanced Certificate); paper science and engineering (MPS, MS, PhD); sustainable engineering management (MPS). *Degree requirements:* For master's, thesis; for doctorate, comprehensive exam, thesis/dissertation; for Advanced Certificate, 15 credit hours. *Entrance requirements:* For master's and doctorate, GRE General Test, minimum GPA of 3.0; for Advanced Certificate, BS, calculus plus science major. Additional exam requirements/recommendations for international students: Required—TOEFL (minimum score 550 paper-based; 80 iBT), IELTS (minimum score 6). *Faculty research:* Sustainable products and processes, biorefinery, pulping and papermaking, nanocellulose, bioconversions, process control and modeling.

Stony Brook University, State University of New York, Graduate School, College of Engineering and Applied Sciences, Department of Materials Science and Engineering, Stony Brook, NY 11794. Offers MS, PhD. *Faculty:* 17 full-time (6 women), 9 part-time/adjunct (1 woman). *Students:* 128 full-time (43 women), 21 part-time (11 women); includes 10 minority (3 Black or African American, non-Hispanic/Latino; 5 Asian, non-Hispanic/Latino; 1 Hispanic/Latino; 1 Two or more races, non-Hispanic/Latino), 100 international. Average age 26. 231 applicants, 46% accepted, 47 enrolled. In 2014, 39 master's, 12 doctorates awarded. *Degree requirements:* For master's, thesis or alternative; for doctorate, comprehensive exam, thesis/dissertation. *Entrance requirements:* For master's and doctorate, GRE General Test, minimum undergraduate GPA of 3.0. Additional exam requirements/recommendations for international students: Required—TOEFL. *Application deadline:* For fall admission, 1/15 for domestic students; for spring admission, 10/1 for domestic students. Application fee: $100. *Expenses:* Tuition, state resident: full-time $10,370; part-time $432 per credit. Tuition, nonresident: full-time $20,190; part-time $841 per credit. *Required fees:* $1431. *Financial support:* In 2014–15, 5 fellowships, 48 research assistantships, 12 teaching assistantships were awarded. *Faculty research:* Electronic materials, biomaterials, synchrotron topography. *Total annual research expenditures:* $3 million. *Unit head:* Dr. Michael Dudley, Chairman, 631-632-8484, Fax: 631-632-8052, E-mail: michael.dudley@stonybrook.edu. *Application contact:* Shauntae Smith, Coordinator, 631-632-4986, Fax: 631-632-8052, E-mail: shauntae.smith@stonybrook.edu.
Website: http://www.matscieng.sunysb.edu/.

Texas A&M University, College of Engineering, Department of Materials Science and Engineering, College Station, TX 77843. Offers M Eng, MS, PhD. *Faculty:* 9. *Students:* 86 full-time (18 women), 13 part-time (3 women); includes 8 minority (2 Black or African American, non-Hispanic/Latino; 3 Asian, non-Hispanic/Latino; 1 Hispanic/Latino; 2 Two or more races, non-Hispanic/Latino), 65 international. Average age 29. 121 applicants, 37% accepted, 17 enrolled. In 2014, 6 master's, 13 doctorates awarded. *Degree requirements:* For master's, thesis (MS); for doctorate, thesis/dissertation. *Entrance requirements:* For master's and doctorate, GRE General Test. Additional exam requirements/recommendations for international students: Required—TOEFL. Application fee: $50 ($90 for international students). *Expenses:* Tuition, state resident: full-time $4078; part-time $226.55 per credit hour. Tuition, nonresident: full-time $10,594; part-time $577.55 per credit hour. *Required fees:* $2813; $237.70 per credit hour. $278.50 per semester. Tuition and fees vary according to degree level and student level. *Financial support:* In 2014–15, 98 students received support, including 6 fellowships with full and partial tuition reimbursements available (averaging $20,633 per year), 69 research assistantships with full and partial tuition reimbursements available (averaging $7,178 per year), 10 teaching assistantships with full and partial tuition reimbursements available (averaging $6,298 per year); career-related internships or fieldwork, institutionally sponsored loans, scholarships/grants, traineeships, health care benefits, tuition waivers (full and partial), and unspecified assistantships also available. Support available to part-time students. Financial award application deadline: 4/15; financial award applicants required to submit FAFSA. *Faculty research:* Innovative design methods, pavement distress characterization, materials property, characterization and modeling recyclable materials. *Unit head:* Ibrahim Karaman, Department Head, 979-862-3923, E-mail: ikaraman@tamu.edu. *Application contact:* Mildan Radovic, Associate Department Head, 979-845-5114, E-mail: mradovic@tamu.edu.
Website: http://engineering.tamu.edu/materials.

Texas State University, The Graduate College, College of Science and Engineering, Department of Physics, Program in Material Physics, San Marcos, TX 78666. Offers MS. *Faculty:* 8 full-time (1 woman), 1 part-time/adjunct (0 women). *Students:* 5 full-time (2 women), 3 international. Average age 33. 11 applicants, 18% accepted, 1 enrolled. In 2014, 2 master's awarded. *Degree requirements:* For master's, comprehensive exam, thesis. *Entrance requirements:* For master's, The Materials Physics program does not require the Graduate Record Exam (GRE). However, if applicants have a GPA below 3.0 on junior and senior level physics courses and have taken the Graduate Record Exam (GRE) prior to admission with a preferred score of 302, they may be considered for admission., baccalaureate degree from regionally-accredited university with minimum GPA of 2.75 on last 60 undergraduate semester hours. Additional exam requirements/recommendations for international students: Required—TOEFL (minimum score 550 paper-based; 78 iBT). *Application deadline:* For fall admission, 2/15 priority date for domestic and international students; for spring admission, 10/15 for domestic students, 10/1 for international students. Applications are processed on a rolling basis. Application fee: $40 ($90 for international students). Electronic applications accepted. *Expenses:* Expenses: $8,834 (tuition and fees combined). *Financial support:* In 2014–15, 3 students received support, including 1 research assistantship (averaging $9,855 per year), 3 teaching assistantships (averaging $11,589 per year); Federal Work-Study, institutionally sponsored loans, scholarships/grants, health care benefits, and unspecified assistantships also available. Support available to part-time students. Financial award application deadline: 4/1; financial award applicants required to submit FAFSA. *Unit head:* Dr. Wihelmus Geerts, Graduate Advisor, 512-245-1821, Fax: 512-245-8233, E-mail: wg06@txstate.edu. *Application contact:* Dr. Andrea Golato, Dean of Graduate School, 512-245-2581, Fax: 512-245-8365, E-mail: gradcollege@txstate.edu.
Website: http://www.mse.txstate.edu/.

Texas State University, The Graduate College, College of Science and Engineering, Material Science, Engineering, and Commercialization Program, San Marcos, TX 78666. Offers PhD. *Faculty:* 16 full-time (4 women). *Students:* 27 full-time (5 women), 3 part-time (0 women); includes 5 minority (2 Asian, non-Hispanic/Latino; 2 Hispanic/Latino; 1 Two or more races, non-Hispanic/Latino), 17 international. Average age 31. 25 applicants, 64% accepted, 10 enrolled. In 2014, 3 doctorates awarded. *Degree requirements:* For doctorate, comprehensive exam, thesis/dissertation. *Entrance requirements:* For doctorate, baccalaureate degree from regionally-accredited college or university; master's degree from regionally-accredited college or university in biology, chemistry, engineering, materials science, physics, technology, or closely-related field with minimum GPA of 3.5. Additional exam requirements/recommendations for international students: Required—TOEFL (minimum score 550 paper-based; 78 iBT); Recommended—IELTS (minimum score 6.5). *Application deadline:* For fall admission, 6/15 for domestic students, 6/1 for international students; for spring admission, 11/30 for domestic students, 10/1 for international students. Application fee: $40 ($90 for international students). Electronic applications accepted. *Expenses:* Expenses: $8,834 (tuition and fees combined). *Financial support:* In 2014–15, 14 students received support, including 7 research assistantships (averaging $30,186 per year), 19 teaching assistantships (averaging $32,000 per year). Financial award applicants required to submit FAFSA. *Faculty research:* Heterointegration, high operability, photoconductivity, water bonding systems, semiconductor research, next generation systems. *Total annual research expenditures:* $1.5 million. *Unit head:* Dr. Thomas Myers, Program Director, 512-245-1839, E-mail: tm33@txstate.edu. *Application contact:* Dr. Andrea Golato, Dean of Graduate School, 512-245-2581, Fax: 512-245-8365, E-mail: gradcollege@txstate.edu.
Website: http://www.msec.txstate.edu/.

Trent University, Graduate Studies, Program in Materials Science, Peterborough, ON K9J 7B8, Canada. Offers M Sc.

Université du Québec, Institut National de la Recherche Scientifique, Graduate Programs, Research Center–Energy Materials Telecommunications, Varennes, QC J3X 1S2, Canada. Offers energy and materials science (M Sc, PhD); telecommunications (M Sc, PhD). Part-time programs available. *Faculty:* 39 full-time. *Students:* 177 full-time (50 women), 7 part-time (1 woman), 123 international. Average age 30. 51 applicants, 84% accepted, 33 enrolled. In 2014, 16 master's, 16 doctorates awarded. *Degree requirements:* For master's, thesis (for some programs); for doctorate, thesis/dissertation. *Entrance requirements:* For master's, appropriate bachelor's degree, proficiency in French; for doctorate, appropriate master's degree, proficiency in French. *Application deadline:* For fall admission, 3/30 for domestic and international students; for winter admission, 11/1 for domestic and international students; for spring admission, 3/1 for domestic and international students. Application fee: $45. Electronic applications accepted. *Financial support:* In 2014–15, fellowships (averaging $16,500 per year) were awarded; research assistantships also available. *Faculty research:* New energy sources, plasmas, telecommunications, advanced materials ultrafast photonics. *Unit head:* Federico Rosei, Director, 450-228-6905, E-mail: rosei@emt.inrs.ca. *Application contact:* Sylvie Richard, Registrar, 418-654-2518, Fax: 418-654-3858, E-mail: sylvie.richard@adm.inrs.ca.
Website: http://www.emt.inrs.ca/emt.

The University of Alabama, Graduate School, College of Engineering and College of Arts and Sciences, Tri-Campus Materials Science PhD Program, Tuscaloosa, AL

35487. Offers PhD. Program offered jointly with The University of Alabama at Birmingham and The University of Alabama in Huntsville. *Students:* 24 full-time (6 women), 1 part-time (0 women); includes 5 minority (all Black or African American, non-Hispanic/Latino), 16 international. Average age 27. 18 applicants, 61% accepted, 6 enrolled. In 2014, 3 doctorates awarded. *Degree requirements:* For doctorate, comprehensive exam, thesis/dissertation. *Entrance requirements:* For doctorate, GRE General Test. Additional exam requirements/recommendations for international students: Required—TOEFL (minimum score 550 paper-based). *Application deadline:* For fall admission, 2/28 priority date for domestic and international students; for spring admission, 10/30 priority date for domestic students, 9/30 priority date for international students. Applications are processed on a rolling basis. Application fee: $50 ($60 for international students). Electronic applications accepted. *Expenses:* Tuition, state resident: full-time $9826. Tuition, nonresident: full-time $24,950. *Financial support:* In 2014–15, 4 research assistantships with full tuition reimbursements (averaging $19,500 per year) were awarded; career-related internships or fieldwork and unspecified assistantships also available. Financial award application deadline: 2/28. *Faculty research:* Magnetic multilayers, metals casting, molecular electronics, conducting polymers, metals physics, electrodeposition. *Unit head:* Prof. Garry Warren, Campus Coordinator, 205-348-4337, E-mail: gwarren@coe.eng.ua.edu. *Application contact:* Dr. David A. Francko, Dean, 205-348-8280, Fax: 205-348-0400, E-mail: dfrancko@ua.edu.

The University of Alabama at Birmingham, School of Engineering, Joint Materials Science PhD Program, Birmingham, AL 35294. Offers PhD. Program offered jointly with The University of Alabama (Tuscaloosa), The University of Alabama in Huntsville. *Degree requirements:* For doctorate, thesis/dissertation. *Entrance requirements:* For doctorate, GRE General Test. *Expenses:* Tuition, state resident: full-time $7090; part-time $370 per credit hour. Tuition, nonresident: full-time $16,072; part-time $869 per credit hour. Full-time tuition and fees vary according to course load and program. *Financial support:* Fellowships with full and partial tuition reimbursements, research assistantships with full tuition reimbursements, career-related internships or fieldwork, Federal Work-Study, and institutionally sponsored loans available. Support available to part-time students. Financial award application deadline: 4/1. *Faculty research:* Biocompatibility studies with biomaterials, microgravity solidification of proteins and metals, analysis of microelectronic materials, thin film analysis using transmission electron microscopy (TEM). *Unit head:* Dr. J. Barry Andrews, Chair, 205-934-8460, Fax: 205-934-8485, E-mail: barry@uab.edu. *Application contact:* Susan Noblitt Banks, Director of Graduate School Operations, 205-934-8227, Fax: 205-934-8413, E-mail: gradschool@uab.edu.

The University of Alabama in Huntsville, School of Graduate Studies, College of Engineering, Department of Chemical and Materials Engineering, Huntsville, AL 35899. Offers biotechnology science and engineering (PhD); chemical engineering (MSE); materials science (MS, PhD); mechanical engineering (PhD), including chemical engineering. Part-time and evening/weekend programs available. *Degree requirements:* For master's, comprehensive exam, thesis or alternative, oral and written exams; for doctorate, comprehensive exam, thesis/dissertation. *Entrance requirements:* For master's, GRE General Test, appropriate bachelor's degree, minimum GPA of 3.0; for doctorate, GRE General Test, minimum GPA of 3.0. Additional exam requirements/recommendations for international students: Required—TOEFL (minimum score 500 paper-based; 80 iBT), IELTS (minimum score 6.5). Electronic applications accepted. *Faculty research:* Ultrathin films for optical, sensor and biological applications; materials processing including low gravity; hypergolic reactants; computational fluid dynamics; biofuels and renewable resources.

The University of Alabama in Huntsville, School of Graduate Studies, College of Science, Department of Chemistry, Huntsville, AL 35899. Offers biotechnology science and engineering (PhD); chemistry (MS); education (MS); materials science (PhD). Part-time and evening/weekend programs available. *Degree requirements:* For master's, comprehensive exam, thesis or alternative, oral and written exams. *Entrance requirements:* For master's, GRE General Test, minimum GPA of 3.0. Additional exam requirements/recommendations for international students: Required—TOEFL (minimum score 550 paper-based; 80 iBT), IELTS (minimum score 6.5). Electronic applications accepted. *Faculty research:* Natural products drug discovery, protein biochemistry, macromolecular biophysics, polymer synthesis, surface modification and analysis of materials.

The University of Alabama in Huntsville, School of Graduate Studies, Interdisciplinary Studies, Interdisciplinary Program in Materials Science, Huntsville, AL 35899. Offers MS, PhD. PhD offered jointly with The University of Alabama (Tuscaloosa) and The University of Alabama at Birmingham. Part-time and evening/weekend programs available. *Degree requirements:* For master's, comprehensive exam, thesis or alternative, oral and written exams; for doctorate, comprehensive exam, thesis/dissertation, oral and written exams. *Entrance requirements:* For master's, GRE General Test, minimum GPA of 3.0; for doctorate, GRE General Test, bachelor's degree in engineering or physical science, minimum GPA of 3.0. Additional exam requirements/recommendations for international students: Required—TOEFL (minimum score 500 paper-based; 80 iBT), IELTS (minimum score 6.5). Electronic applications accepted. *Faculty research:* Materials structure and properties; materials processing; mechanical behavior; macromolecular materials; electronic, optical, and magnetic materials.

The University of Arizona, College of Engineering, Department of Materials Science and Engineering, Tucson, AZ 85721. Offers MS, PhD. Part-time programs available. *Degree requirements:* For master's, thesis (for some programs); for doctorate, comprehensive exam, thesis/dissertation. *Entrance requirements:* For master's and doctorate, GRE General Test, 3 letters of recommendation, statement of purpose. Additional exam requirements/recommendations for international students: Required—TOEFL (minimum score 550 paper-based; 79 iBT). Electronic applications accepted. *Faculty research:* High-technology ceramics, optical materials, electronic materials, chemical metallurgy, science of materials.

The University of British Columbia, Faculty of Applied Science, Department of Materials Engineering, Vancouver, BC V6T 1Z1, Canada. Offers materials and metallurgy (M Sc, PhD); metals and materials engineering (MA Sc, PhD). *Degree requirements:* For master's, comprehensive exam, thesis; for doctorate, comprehensive exam, thesis/dissertation. *Entrance requirements:* Additional exam requirements/recommendations for international students: Required—TOEFL (minimum score 560 paper-based; 83 iBT). Electronic applications accepted. *Faculty research:* Electroslag melting, mathematical modeling, solidification and hydrometallurgy.

University of Calgary, Faculty of Graduate Studies, Schulich School of Engineering, Department of Civil Engineering, Calgary, AB T2N 1N4, Canada. Offers avalanche mechanics (M Sc, PhD); civil engineering (M Eng, M Sc, PhD); energy and environment engineering (M Eng, M Sc, PhD); environmental engineering (M Eng, M Sc, PhD); geotechnical engineering (M Eng, M Sc, PhD); materials science (M Eng, M Sc, PhD); project management (M Eng, M Sc, PhD); structures and solid mechanics (M Eng, M Sc, PhD); transportation engineering (M Eng, M Sc, PhD); water resources (M Eng, M Sc, PhD). Part-time programs available. *Degree requirements:* For master's, thesis; for doctorate, thesis/dissertation, written and oral candidacy exam. *Entrance requirements:* For master's, minimum GPA of 3.0; for doctorate, minimum GPA of 3.5. Additional exam requirements/recommendations for international students: Required—TOEFL (minimum score 580 paper-based; 93 iBT), IELTS (minimum score 7). Electronic applications accepted. *Faculty research:* Geotechnical engineering, energy and environment, transportation, project management, structures and solid mechanics.

University of California, Berkeley, Graduate Division, College of Engineering, Department of Materials Science and Engineering, Berkeley, CA 94720-1500. Offers engineering (M Eng, MS, D Eng, PhD); engineering science (M Eng, MS, PhD). *Degree requirements:* For master's, comprehensive exam or thesis (MS); for doctorate, comprehensive exam, thesis/dissertation, qualifying exam. *Entrance requirements:* For master's and doctorate, GRE General Test, minimum GPA of 3.0, 3 letters of recommendation. Additional exam requirements/recommendations for international students: Required—TOEFL. *Faculty research:* Ceramics, biomaterials, structural, electronic, magnetic and optical materials.

University of California, Davis, College of Engineering, Program in Materials Science and Engineering, Davis, CA 95616. Offers MS, PhD. Terminal master's awarded for partial completion of doctoral program. *Degree requirements:* For master's, comprehensive exam (for some programs), thesis (for some programs); for doctorate, comprehensive exam, thesis/dissertation. *Entrance requirements:* Additional exam requirements/recommendations for international students: Required—TOEFL (minimum score 550 paper-based).

University of California, Irvine, Henry Samueli School of Engineering, Department of Chemical Engineering and Materials Science, Irvine, CA 92697. Offers chemical and biochemical engineering (MS, PhD); materials science and engineering (MS, PhD). Part-time programs available. *Students:* 132 full-time (48 women), 8 part-time (1 woman); includes 45 minority (2 Black or African American, non-Hispanic/Latino; 31 Asian, non-Hispanic/Latino; 7 Hispanic/Latino; 1 Native Hawaiian or other Pacific Islander, non-Hispanic/Latino; 4 Two or more races, non-Hispanic/Latino), 48 international. Average age 26. 549 applicants, 32% accepted, 55 enrolled. In 2014, 29 master's, 11 doctorates awarded. Terminal master's awarded for partial completion of doctoral program. *Degree requirements:* For doctorate, thesis/dissertation. *Entrance requirements:* For master's and doctorate, GRE General Test, minimum GPA of 3.0, 3 letters of recommendation. Additional exam requirements/recommendations for international students: Required—TOEFL (minimum score 550 paper-based). *Application deadline:* For fall admission, 1/15 priority date for domestic students, 1/15 for international students. Applications are processed on a rolling basis. Application fee: $90 ($110 for international students). Electronic applications accepted. *Financial support:* Fellowships with tuition reimbursements, research assistantships with full tuition reimbursements, teaching assistantships with tuition reimbursements, institutionally sponsored loans, traineeships, health care benefits, and unspecified assistantships available. Financial award application deadline: 3/1; financial award applicants required to submit FAFSA. *Faculty research:* Molecular biotechnology, nano-bio-materials, biophotonics, synthesis, superplasticity and mechanical behavior, characterization of advanced and nanostructural materials. *Unit head:* Prof. Vasan Venugopalan, Chair, 949-824-5802, Fax: 949-824-2541, E-mail: vvenugop@uci.edu. *Application contact:* Grace Hai-Chin Chau, Academic Program and Graduate Admission Coordinator, 949-824-3887, Fax: 949-824-2541, E-mail: chaug@uci.edu.
Website: http://www.eng.uci.edu/dept/chems.

University of California, Irvine, School of Physical Sciences, Department of Chemistry and Department of Physics and Astronomy, Program in Chemical and Materials Physics (CHAMP), Irvine, CA 92697. Offers MS, PhD. *Students:* 64 full-time (13 women); includes 17 minority (1 Black or African American, non-Hispanic/Latino; 1 American Indian or Alaska Native, non-Hispanic/Latino; 8 Asian, non-Hispanic/Latino; 5 Hispanic/Latino; 2 Two or more races, non-Hispanic/Latino), 12 international. Average age 27. 59 applicants, 44% accepted, 15 enrolled. In 2014, 7 master's, 7 doctorates awarded. *Degree requirements:* For doctorate, thesis/dissertation. *Entrance requirements:* For master's and doctorate, GRE General Test, GRE Subject Test, minimum GPA of 3.0. *Application deadline:* For fall admission, 1/15 priority date for domestic students, 1/15 for international students. Applications are processed on a rolling basis. Application fee: $80 ($100 for international students). Electronic applications accepted. *Financial support:* Fellowships, research assistantships with full tuition reimbursements, teaching assistantships, institutionally sponsored loans, traineeships, health care benefits, and unspecified assistantships available. Financial award application deadline: 3/1; financial award applicants required to submit FAFSA. *Unit head:* A.J. Shaka, Co-Director, 949-824-8509, E-mail: ajshaka@uci.edu. *Application contact:* Jaime M. Albano, Student Affairs Manager, 949-824-4261, Fax: 949-824-8571, E-mail: jmalbano@uci.edu.

University of California, Los Angeles, Graduate Division, Henry Samueli School of Engineering and Applied Science, Department of Materials Science and Engineering, Los Angeles, CA 90095-1595. Offers MS, PhD. *Faculty:* 14 full-time (2 women), 2 part-time/adjunct (0 women). *Students:* 161 full-time (39 women); includes 35 minority (1 Black or African American, non-Hispanic/Latino; 21 Asian, non-Hispanic/Latino; 9 Hispanic/Latino; 4 Two or more races, non-Hispanic/Latino), 93 international. 334 applicants, 50% accepted, 59 enrolled. In 2014, 22 master's, 16 doctorates awarded. *Degree requirements:* For master's, comprehensive exam or thesis; for doctorate, thesis/dissertation, qualifying exams. *Entrance requirements:* For master's, GRE General Test, minimum GPA of 3.0; for doctorate, GRE General Test, minimum GPA of 3.25. Additional exam requirements/recommendations for international students: Required—TOEFL (minimum score 560 paper-based; 87 iBT), IELTS (minimum score 7). *Application deadline:* For fall admission, 12/15 for domestic and international students. Application fee: $80 ($100 for international students). Electronic applications accepted. *Financial support:* In 2014–15, 78 fellowships, 192 research assistantships, 39 teaching assistantships were awarded; Federal Work-Study, institutionally sponsored loans, and tuition waivers (full and partial) also available. Financial award application deadline: 1/15; financial award applicants required to submit FAFSA. *Faculty research:* Ceramics and ceramic processing, electronic and optical materials, structural materials. *Total annual research expenditures:* $8.4 million. *Unit head:* Dr. Dwight C. Streit, Chair, 310-825-7011, E-mail: streit@ucla.edu. *Application contact:* Patti Barrera, Student Affairs Officer, 310-825-8916, Fax: 310-206-7353, E-mail: patti@seas.ucla.edu.
Website: http://www.mse.ucla.edu.

University of California, Riverside, Graduate Division, Materials Science and Engineering Program, Riverside, CA 92521. Offers MS, PhD. *Entrance requirements:* For master's and doctorate, GRE. Additional exam requirements/recommendations for international students: Required—TOEFL (minimum score 550 paper-based; 80 iBT). Electronic applications accepted. *Expenses:* Tuition, state resident: full-time $5399. Tuition, nonresident: full-time $10,433.

University of California, San Diego, Graduate Division, Program in Materials Science and Engineering, La Jolla, CA 92093. Offers MS, PhD. *Students:* 155 full-time (46 women), 1 part-time (0 women); includes 24 minority (2 Black or African American, non-Hispanic/Latino; 1 American Indian or Alaska Native, non-Hispanic/Latino; 14 Asian, non-Hispanic/Latino; 7 Hispanic/Latino), 113 international. 362 applicants, 39% accepted, 36 enrolled. In 2014, 16 master's, 17 doctorates awarded. *Degree requirements:* For master's, comprehensive exam (for some programs), thesis (for some programs), thesis or comprehensive exam; for doctorate, comprehensive exam, thesis/dissertation. *Entrance requirements:* For master's and doctorate, GRE General Test, minimum GPA of 3.2. Additional exam requirements/recommendations for international

students: Required—TOEFL (minimum score 550 paper-based; 80 iBT), IELTS (minimum score 7). *Application deadline:* For fall admission, 1/15 for domestic students; for winter admission, 1/15 for domestic students; for spring admission, 1/15 for domestic students. Application fee: $90 ($110 for international students). Electronic applications accepted. *Expenses:* Tuition, state resident: full-time $11,220; part-time $5610 per quarter. Tuition, nonresident: full-time $26,322; part-time $13,161 per quarter. *Required fees:* $570 per quarter. Tuition and fees vary according to program. *Financial support:* Fellowships, research assistantships, and teaching assistantships available. Financial award application deadline: 1/15; financial award applicants required to submit FAFSA. *Faculty research:* Magnetic and nano materials, structural materials, electronic materials and interfaces, biomaterials, energy materials and applications. *Unit head:* Sungho Jin, Chair, 858-534-4903, E-mail: jin@ucsd.edu. *Application contact:* Charlotte Lauve, Graduate Coordinator, 858-534-7715, E-mail: clauve@ucsd.edu.
Website: http://matsci.ucsd.edu/.

University of California, Santa Barbara, Graduate Division, College of Engineering, Department of Materials, Santa Barbara, CA 93106-5050. Offers MS, PhD, MS/PhD. Terminal master's awarded for partial completion of doctoral program. *Degree requirements:* For master's, variable foreign language requirement, comprehensive exam, thesis; for doctorate, variable foreign language requirement, comprehensive exam, thesis/dissertation. *Entrance requirements:* For master's and doctorate, GRE General Test. Additional exam requirements/recommendations for international students: Required—TOEFL (minimum score 600 paper-based; 100 iBT), IELTS (minimum score 7). Electronic applications accepted. *Faculty research:* Electronic and photonic materials, inorganic materials, macromolecular and biomolecular materials, structural materials.

University of Central Florida, College of Engineering and Computer Science, Department of Materials Science and Engineering, Orlando, FL 32816. Offers MSMSE, PhD. *Students:* 43 full-time (14 women), 8 part-time (1 woman); includes 6 minority (2 Asian, non-Hispanic/Latino; 1 Hispanic/Latino; 3 Two or more races, non-Hispanic/Latino), 28 international. Average age 28. 86 applicants, 28% accepted, 9 enrolled. In 2014, 12 master's, 4 doctorates awarded. *Degree requirements:* For master's, thesis or alternative; for doctorate, thesis/dissertation, candidacy exam, departmental qualifying exam. *Application deadline:* For fall admission, 7/15 priority date for domestic students; for spring admission, 12/1 priority date for domestic students. Application fee: $30. Electronic applications accepted. *Expenses:* Tuition, state resident: part-time $288.16 per credit hour. Tuition, nonresident: part-time $1073.31 per credit hour. *Financial support:* In 2014–15, 34 students received support, including 13 fellowships with tuition reimbursements available (averaging $2,000 per year), 32 research assistantships (averaging $11,000 per year), 2 teaching assistantships (averaging $12,800 per year). *Unit head:* Dr. Sudipta Seal, Interim Chair, 407-823-5277, E-mail: sseal@ucf.edu. *Application contact:* Barbara Rodriguez Lamas, Director, Admissions and Student Services, 407-823-2766, Fax: 407-823-6442, E-mail: gradadmissions@ucf.edu.
Website: http://mse.ucf.edu/.

University of Cincinnati, Graduate School, College of Engineering and Applied Science, Department of Chemical and Materials Engineering, Program in Materials Science and Engineering, Cincinnati, OH 45221. Offers MS, PhD. Evening/weekend programs available. *Degree requirements:* For master's, thesis optional; for doctorate, one foreign language, comprehensive exam, thesis/dissertation, oral English proficiency exam. *Entrance requirements:* For master's and doctorate, GRE General Test, BS in related field, minimum undergraduate GPA of 3.0. Additional exam requirements/recommendations for international students: Required—TOEFL. Electronic applications accepted. *Faculty research:* Polymer characterization, surface analysis, and adhesion; mechanical behavior of high-temperature materials; composites; electrochemistry of materials.

University of Connecticut, Graduate School, School of Engineering, Department of Chemical, Materials and Biomolecular Engineering, Field of Materials Science and Engineering, Storrs, CT 06269. Offers MS, PhD. Terminal master's awarded for partial completion of doctoral program. *Degree requirements:* For master's, comprehensive exam; for doctorate, thesis/dissertation. *Entrance requirements:* For master's and doctorate, GRE General Test, GRE Subject Test. Additional exam requirements/recommendations for international students: Required—TOEFL (minimum score 550 paper-based). Electronic applications accepted.

University of Connecticut, Institute of Materials Science, Storrs, CT 06269. Offers MS, PhD.

University of Delaware, College of Engineering, Department of Materials Science and Engineering, Newark, DE 19716. Offers MMSE, PhD. Terminal master's awarded for partial completion of doctoral program. *Degree requirements:* For master's, thesis; for doctorate, thesis/dissertation. *Entrance requirements:* For master's and doctorate, GRE General Test, 3 letters of recommendation, minimum GPA of 3.2. Additional exam requirements/recommendations for international students: Required—TOEFL. Electronic applications accepted. *Faculty research:* Thin films and self assembly, drug delivery and tissue engineering, biomaterials and nanocomposites, semiconductor and oxide interfaces, electronic and magnetic materials.

University of Denver, Daniel Felix Ritchie School of Engineering and Computer Science, Department of Mechanical and Materials Engineering, Denver, CO 80208. Offers bioengineering (MS); engineering (MS, PhD); engineering/management (MS); materials science (MS, PhD); mechanical engineering (MS, PhD); nanoscale science and engineering (MS, PhD). Part-time programs available. *Faculty:* 10 full-time (1 woman), 1 (woman) part-time/adjunct. *Students:* 4 full-time (2 women), 44 part-time (12 women); includes 6 minority (1 Black or African American, non-Hispanic/Latino; 3 Asian, non-Hispanic/Latino; 1 Hispanic/Latino; 1 Two or more races, non-Hispanic/Latino), 20 international. Average age 29. 67 applicants, 88% accepted, 16 enrolled. In 2014, 7 master's, 1 doctorate awarded. Terminal master's awarded for partial completion of doctoral program. *Degree requirements:* For master's, thesis optional; for doctorate, comprehensive exam, thesis/dissertation. *Entrance requirements:* For master's, GRE General Test, bachelor's degree, transcripts, personal statement, resume or curriculum vitae, two letters of recommendation; for doctorate, GRE General Test, master's degree, transcripts, personal statement, resume or curriculum vitae, two letters of recommendation. Additional exam requirements/recommendations for international students: Required—TOEFL (minimum score 550 paper-based; 80 iBT). *Application deadline:* For fall admission, 2/1 priority date for domestic and international students. Applications are processed on a rolling basis. Application fee: $65. Electronic applications accepted. *Expenses:* Expenses: $1,199 per credit hour. *Financial support:* In 2014–15, 24 students received support, including 17 research assistantships with full and partial tuition reimbursements available (averaging $12,842 per year), 17 teaching assistantships with full and partial tuition reimbursements available (averaging $9,975 per year); Federal Work-Study, institutionally sponsored loans, scholarships/grants, health care benefits, and unspecified assistantships also available. Financial award application deadline: 2/15; financial award applicants required to submit FAFSA. *Faculty research:* Aerosols, biomechanics, composite materials, photo optics, drug delivery. *Unit head:* Dr. Matt Gordon, Chair, 303-871-3580, Fax: 303-871-4450, E-mail:

matthew.gordon@du.edu. *Application contact:* Yvonne Petitt, Assistant to the Chair, 303-871-2107, Fax: 303-871-4450, E-mail: yvonne.petitt@du.edu.
Website: http://www.du.edu/rsecs/departments/mme/index.html.

University of Florida, Graduate School, College of Engineering, Department of Materials Science and Engineering, Gainesville, FL 32611. Offers material science and engineering (MS), including clinical and translational science; nuclear engineering (ME, PhD), including imaging science and technology (PhD), nuclear engineering sciences (ME, MS, PhD); nuclear engineering (MS), including nuclear engineering sciences (ME, MS, PhD); JD/MS. Part-time programs available. Postbaccalaureate distance learning degree programs offered. *Faculty:* 32 full-time (5 women), 32 part-time/adjunct (9 women). *Students:* 251 full-time (65 women), 36 part-time (12 women); includes 42 minority (7 Black or African American, non-Hispanic/Latino; 18 Asian, non-Hispanic/Latino; 17 Hispanic/Latino), 144 international. 502 applicants, 54% accepted, 61 enrolled. In 2014, 64 master's, 25 doctorates awarded. Terminal master's awarded for partial completion of doctoral program. *Degree requirements:* For master's, comprehensive exam, thesis; for doctorate, comprehensive exam, thesis/dissertation; for Engr, thesis optional. *Entrance requirements:* For master's and doctorate, minimum GPA of 3.0; for Engr, GRE General Test. Additional exam requirements/recommendations for international students: Required—TOEFL (minimum score 550 paper-based; 80 iBT), IELTS (minimum score 6). *Application deadline:* For fall admission, 7/1 priority date for domestic students, 5/1 for international students; for spring admission, 11/1 for domestic students, 9/1 for international students. Applications are processed on a rolling basis. Application fee: $30. Electronic applications accepted. *Financial support:* Applicants required to submit FAFSA. *Faculty research:* Polymeric system, biomaterials and biomimetics; inorganic and organic electronic materials; functional ceramic materials for energy systems and microelectronic applications; advanced metallic systems for aerospace, transportation and biological applications; nuclear materials. *Unit head:* Simon R. Phillpot, PhD, Chair, 352-846-3782, Fax: 352-392-7219, E-mail: sphil@mse.ufl.edu. *Application contact:* Dr. Jack Mecholsky, Jr., Graduate Coordinator, 352-846-3306, Fax: 352-846-1182, E-mail: jmech@mse.ufl.edu.
Website: http://www.mse.ufl.edu/.

University of Idaho, College of Graduate Studies, College of Engineering, Department of Chemical and Materials Engineering, Moscow, ID 83844-1021. Offers chemical engineering (M Engr, MS, PhD); materials science and engineering (MS, PhD). *Faculty:* 8 full-time. *Students:* 13 full-time, 6 part-time. Average age 32. In 2014, 7 master's, 4 doctorates awarded. *Degree requirements:* For master's, thesis; for doctorate, one foreign language, thesis/dissertation. *Entrance requirements:* For master's, GRE, minimum GPA of 2.8; for doctorate, GRE, minimum undergraduate GPA of 2.8, 3.0 graduate. *Application deadline:* For fall admission, 8/1 for domestic students; for spring admission, 12/15 for domestic students. Applications are processed on a rolling basis. Application fee: $60. Electronic applications accepted. *Expenses:* Tuition, state resident: full-time $4784; part-time $280.50 per credit hour. Tuition, nonresident: full-time $18,314; part-time $957.50 per credit hour. *Required fees:* $2000; $58.50 per credit hour. Tuition and fees vary according to program. *Financial support:* Fellowships, research assistantships, and teaching assistantships available. Financial award applicants required to submit FAFSA. *Faculty research:* Geothermal energy utilization, alcohol production from agriculture waste material, energy conservation in pulp and paper mills. *Unit head:* Dr. Eric Aston, Interim Chair, 208-885-7572, E-mail: che@uidaho.edu. *Application contact:* Sean Scoggin, Graduate Recruitment Coordinator, 208-885-4001, Fax: 208-885-4406, E-mail: graduateadmissions@uidaho.edu.
Website: http://www.uidaho.edu/engr/cme/about/materials.

University of Illinois at Urbana–Champaign, Graduate College, College of Engineering, Department of Materials Science and Engineering, Champaign, IL 61820. Offers M Eng, MS, PhD, MS/MBA, PhD/MBA. *Students:* 189 (52 women). Application fee: $70 ($90 for international students). *Unit head:* David G. Cahill, Head, 217-333-6753, Fax: 217-244-1631, E-mail: d-cahill@illinois.edu. *Application contact:* Michelle L. Malloch, Office Support Associate, 217-333-8517, Fax: 217-333-2736, E-mail: malloch@illinois.edu.
Website: http://www.matse.illinois.edu/.

University of Kentucky, Graduate School, College of Engineering, Program in Materials Science and Engineering, Lexington, KY 40506-0032. Offers MS, PhD. *Degree requirements:* For master's, comprehensive exam, thesis optional; for doctorate, comprehensive exam, thesis/dissertation. *Entrance requirements:* For master's, GRE General Test, minimum undergraduate GPA of 2.75; for doctorate, GRE General Test, minimum undergraduate GPA of 3.0. Additional exam requirements/recommendations for international students: Required—TOEFL (minimum score 550 paper-based). Electronic applications accepted. *Faculty research:* Physical and mechanical metallurgy, computational material engineering, polymers and composites, high-temperature ceramics, powder metallurgy.

The University of Manchester, School of Chemistry, Manchester, United Kingdom. Offers biological chemistry (PhD); chemistry (M Ent, M Phil, M Sc, D Ent, PhD); inorganic chemistry (PhD); materials chemistry (PhD); nanoscience (PhD); nuclear fission (PhD); organic chemistry (PhD); physical chemistry (PhD); theoretical chemistry (PhD).

The University of Manchester, School of Materials, Manchester, United Kingdom. Offers advanced aerospace materials engineering (M Sc); advanced metallic systems (PhD); biomedical materials (M Phil, M Sc, PhD); ceramics and glass (M Phil, M Sc, PhD); composite materials (M Sc, PhD); corrosion and protection (M Phil, M Sc, PhD); materials (M Phil, PhD); metallic materials (M Phil, M Sc, PhD); nanostructural materials (M Phil, M Sc, PhD); paper science (M Phil, M Sc, PhD); polymer science and engineering (M Phil, M Sc, PhD); technical textiles (M Sc); textile design, fashion and management (M Phil, M Sc, PhD); textile science and technology (M Phil, M Sc, PhD); textiles (M Phil, PhD); textiles and fashion (M Ent).

University of Maryland, College Park, Academic Affairs, A. James Clark School of Engineering, Department of Materials Science and Engineering, Materials Science and Engineering Program, College Park, MD 20742. Offers MS, PhD. Part-time and evening/weekend programs available. Postbaccalaureate distance learning degree programs offered. *Degree requirements:* For master's, comprehensive exam, thesis optional, research paper; for doctorate, thesis/dissertation, oral exam. *Entrance requirements:* For master's and doctorate, GRE General Test, minimum B+ average in undergraduate course work. Additional exam requirements/recommendations for international students: Required—TOEFL. Electronic applications accepted.

University of Michigan, College of Engineering, Department of Materials Science and Engineering, Ann Arbor, MI 48109. Offers MS, PhD. Part-time programs available. *Students:* 162 full-time (46 women), 2 part-time (0 women). 508 applicants, 18% accepted, 34 enrolled. In 2014, 36 master's, 28 doctorates awarded. *Degree requirements:* For master's, thesis, oral defense of thesis; for doctorate, thesis/dissertation, oral defense of dissertation, written exam. *Entrance requirements:* For master's, GRE General Test, minimum GPA of 3.0 in related field; for doctorate, GRE General Test, minimum GPA of 3.0 in related field, master's degree. Additional exam requirements/recommendations for international students: Required—TOEFL. *Application deadline:* Applications are processed on a rolling basis. Electronic

applications accepted. *Financial support:* Fellowships, research assistantships, and teaching assistantships available. Financial award applicants required to submit FAFSA. *Faculty research:* Soft materials (polymers, biomaterials), computational materials science, structural materials, electronic and optical materials, nanocomposite materials. *Total annual research expenditures:* $17.6 million. *Unit head:* Amit Misra, Department Chair, 734-764-7799, Fax: 734-763-4788, E-mail: amitmis@umich.edu. *Application contact:* Renee Hilgendorf, Graduate Program Coordinator, 734-763-9790, Fax: 734-763-4788, E-mail: reneeh@umich.edu.
Website: http://www.mse.engin.umich.edu.

University of Michigan, Horace H. Rackham School of Graduate Studies, College of Literature, Science, and the Arts, Department of Chemistry, Ann Arbor, MI 48109-1055. Offers analytical (PhD); chemical biology (PhD); inorganic (PhD); materials (PhD); organic (PhD); physical (PhD). *Faculty:* 40 full-time (10 women), 10 part-time/adjunct (1 woman). *Students:* 231 full-time (95 women). 555 applicants, 22% accepted, 43 enrolled. In 2014, 43 doctorates awarded. *Degree requirements:* For doctorate, comprehensive exam, thesis/dissertation, oral defense of dissertation, organic cumulative proficiency exams. *Entrance requirements:* For doctorate, GRE General Test, GRE Subject Test (recommended), 3 letters of recommendation. Additional exam requirements/recommendations for international students: Required—TOEFL (minimum score 560 paper-based; 84 iBT). *Application deadline:* For fall admission, 12/15 for domestic and international students. Applications are processed on a rolling basis. Application fee: $0 ($90 for international students). Electronic applications accepted. *Financial support:* In 2014–15, 231 students received support, including 13 fellowships with full tuition reimbursements available (averaging $29,000 per year), 78 research assistantships with full tuition reimbursements available (averaging $28,457 per year), 140 teaching assistantships with full tuition reimbursements available (averaging $28,457 per year); career-related internships or fieldwork, scholarships/grants, traineeships, health care benefits, and unspecified assistantships also available. *Faculty research:* Biological catalysis, protein engineering, chemical sensors, de novo metalloprotein design, supramolecular architecture. *Unit head:* Dr. Robert Kennedy, Hobart H. Willard Distinguished University Professor of Chemistry, Chair, 734-763-9681, Fax: 734-647-4847. *Application contact:* Elizabeth Oxford, Graduate Program Coordinator, 734-764-7278, Fax: 734-647-4865, E-mail: chemadmissions@umich.edu. Website: http://www.lsa.umich.edu/chem/.

University of Minnesota, Twin Cities Campus, College of Science and Engineering, Department of Chemical Engineering and Materials Science, Program in Materials Science and Engineering, Minneapolis, MN 55455-0132. Offers M Mat SE, MS Mat SE, PhD. Part-time programs available. Terminal master's awarded for partial completion of doctoral program. *Degree requirements:* For master's, thesis; for doctorate, thesis/dissertation. *Entrance requirements:* For master's and doctorate, GRE General Test. Additional exam requirements/recommendations for international students: Required—TOEFL. Electronic applications accepted. *Faculty research:* Ceramics and metals; coating processes and interfacial engineering; crystal growth and design; polymers; electronic, photonic and magnetic materials.

University of Mississippi Medical Center, School of Graduate Studies in the Health Sciences, Program in Biomedical Materials Science, Jackson, MS 39216-4505. Offers MS, PhD. Terminal master's awarded for partial completion of doctoral program. *Degree requirements:* For master's, thesis; for doctorate, comprehensive exam, thesis/dissertation. *Entrance requirements:* For master's, GRE, BS; for doctorate, GRE, BS, MS (preferred). Additional exam requirements/recommendations for international students: Required—TOEFL (minimum score 105 iBT). Electronic applications accepted. *Faculty research:* Tissue engineering, fatigue life prediction, metallurgy and alloy development, dental implant design and testing, ceramics, materials for dental applications.

University of Nebraska–Lincoln, Graduate College, College of Arts and Sciences, Department of Chemistry, Lincoln, NE 68588. Offers analytical chemistry (PhD); biochemistry (PhD); chemistry (MS); inorganic chemistry (PhD); materials chemistry (PhD); organic chemistry (PhD); physical chemistry (PhD). *Degree requirements:* For master's, one foreign language, thesis optional, departmental qualifying exam; for doctorate, one foreign language, comprehensive exam, thesis/dissertation, departmental qualifying exams. *Entrance requirements:* For master's and doctorate, GRE. Additional exam requirements/recommendations for international students: Required—TOEFL (minimum score 550 paper-based). Electronic applications accepted. *Faculty research:* Bioorganic and bioinorganic chemistry, biophysical and bioanalytical chemistry, structure-function of DNA and proteins, organometallics, mass spectrometry.

University of New Brunswick Fredericton, School of Graduate Studies, Faculty of Engineering, Department of Civil Engineering, Fredericton, NB E3B 5A3, Canada. Offers construction engineering and management (M Eng, M Sc E, PhD); environmental engineering (M Eng, M Sc E, PhD); environmental studies (M Eng); geotechnical engineering (M Eng, M Sc E, PhD); groundwater/hydrology (M Eng, M Sc E, PhD); materials (M Eng, M Sc E, PhD); pavements (M Eng, M Sc E, PhD); structures (M Eng, M Sc E, PhD); transportation (M Eng, M Sc E, PhD). Part-time programs available. *Faculty:* 12 full-time (1 woman), 4 part-time/adjunct (0 women). *Students:* 16 full-time (4 women), 15 part-time (5 women). In 2014, 9 master's, 3 doctorates awarded. *Degree requirements:* For master's, thesis, proposal; for doctorate, comprehensive exam, thesis/dissertation, qualifying exam; 27 credit hours of courses. *Entrance requirements:* For master's, minimum GPA of 3.0; B Sc E in civil engineering or related engineering degree; for doctorate, minimum GPA of 3.0; graduate degree in engineering or applied science. Additional exam requirements/recommendations for international students: Required—IELTS (minimum score 7.5), TWE (minimum score 4), Michigan English Language Assessment Battery (minimum score 85) or CanTest (minimum score 4.5); Recommended—TOEFL (minimum score 580 paper-based). *Application deadline:* For fall admission, 5/1 for domestic students; for winter admission, 11/1 for domestic students. Applications are processed on a rolling basis. Application fee: $50 Canadian dollars. Electronic applications accepted. *Financial support:* In 2014–15, 35 fellowships, 48 research assistantships, 35 teaching assistantships were awarded; career-related internships or fieldwork and scholarships/grants also available. *Faculty research:* Construction engineering and management; engineering materials and infrastructure renewal; highway and pavement research; structures and solid mechanics; geotechnical and geoenvironmental engineering; structure interaction; transportation and planning; environment, solid waste management; structural engineering; water and environmental engineering. *Unit head:* Dr. Kerry MacQuarrie, Director of Graduate Studies, 506-453-5121, Fax: 506-453-3568, E-mail: ktm@unb.ca. *Application contact:* Joyce Moore, Graduate Secretary, 506-452-6127, Fax: 506-453-3568, E-mail: joycem@unb.ca. Website: http://go.unb.ca/gradprograms.

University of New Hampshire, Graduate School, College of Engineering and Physical Sciences, Program in Materials Science, Durham, NH 03824. Offers MS, PhD. *Faculty:* 2 full-time (1 woman). *Students:* 5 full-time (2 women), 1 part-time (0 women); includes 1 minority (Two or more races, non-Hispanic/Latino), 4 international. Average age 28. 14 applicants. In 2014, 2 master's, 1 doctorate awarded. *Degree requirements:* For master's, thesis or alternative. *Entrance requirements:* For master's, GRE. Additional exam requirements/recommendations for international students: Required—TOEFL (minimum score 550 paper-based; 80 iBT). *Application deadline:* For fall admission, 4/1

priority date for domestic students, 4/1 for international students. Applications are processed on a rolling basis. Application fee: $65. Electronic applications accepted. *Expenses:* Tuition, state resident: full-time $13,500; part-time $750 per credit hour. Tuition, nonresident: full-time $26,460; part-time $1110 per credit hour. *Required fees:* $1788; $447 per semester. *Financial support:* In 2014–15, 4 students received support, including 2 research assistantships, 1 teaching assistantship; fellowships, Federal Work-Study, scholarships/grants, and tuition waivers (full and partial) also available. Support available to part-time students. Financial award application deadline: 2/15. *Unit head:* Dr. Glenn Miller, Chairperson, 603-862-2456. *Application contact:* Katie Makem-Boucher, Administrative Assistant, 603-862-2669, E-mail: materials.science@unh.edu. Website: http://www.unh.edu/materials-science/.

The University of North Carolina at Chapel Hill, Graduate School, College of Arts and Sciences, Curriculum in Applied Sciences and Engineering, Chapel Hill, NC 27599. Offers materials science (MS, PhD). Terminal master's awarded for partial completion of doctoral program. *Degree requirements:* For doctorate, thesis/dissertation. *Entrance requirements:* For master's, GRE General Test, minimum GPA of 3.0; for doctorate, GRE General Test. Electronic applications accepted. *Faculty research:* Scanning tunneling microscopy, magnetic resonance, carbon nanotubes, thin films, biomaterials, nano-materials, nanotechnology, polymeric materials, electronic and optic materials, tissue engineering.

University of Pennsylvania, School of Engineering and Applied Science, Department of Materials Science and Engineering, Philadelphia, PA 19104. Offers MSE, PhD, MSE/MBA. Part-time programs available. *Faculty:* 14 full-time (3 women), 1 part-time/adjunct (0 women). *Students:* 146 full-time (43 women), 14 part-time (3 women); includes 13 minority (9 Asian, non-Hispanic/Latino; 3 Hispanic/Latino; 1 Two or more races, non-Hispanic/Latino), 117 international. 568 applicants, 23% accepted, 66 enrolled. In 2014, 57 master's, 6 doctorates awarded. Terminal master's awarded for partial completion of doctoral program. *Degree requirements:* For master's, thesis; for doctorate, thesis/dissertation. *Entrance requirements:* Additional exam requirements/recommendations for international students: Required—TOEFL. *Application deadline:* For fall admission, 6/1 priority date for domestic students, 5/1 priority date for international students; for spring admission, 11/1 priority date for domestic students, 10/1 priority date for international students. Applications are processed on a rolling basis. Application fee: $70. Electronic applications accepted. *Financial support:* Fellowships, research assistantships, teaching assistantships, institutionally sponsored loans, scholarships/grants, traineeships, health care benefits, and unspecified assistantships available. *Faculty research:* Advanced metallic, ceramic, and polymeric materials for device applications; micromechanics and structure of interfaces; thin film electronic materials; physics and chemistry of solids. *Unit head:* Eduardo D. Glandt, Dean, 215-898-7244, E-mail: seasdean@seas.upenn.edu. *Application contact:* School of Engineering and Applied Science Graduate Admissions, 215-898-4542, E-mail: gradstudies@seas.upenn.edu.
Website: http://www.mse.seas.upenn.edu.

University of Pittsburgh, Dietrich School of Arts and Sciences, Program in Computational Modeling and Simulation, Pittsburgh, PA 15260. Offers bioengineering (PhD); biological science (PhD); civil and environmental engineering (PhD); computer science (PhD); economics (PhD); industrial engineering (PhD); mathematics (PhD); mechanical engineering and materials science (PhD); physics and astronomy (PhD); psychology (PhD); statistics (PhD). Part-time programs available. *Faculty:* 4 full-time (0 women). *Students:* 5 full-time (2 women), 1 part-time (0 women), 5 international. Average age 22. 14 applicants, 14% accepted, 2 enrolled. *Degree requirements:* For doctorate, comprehensive exam, thesis/dissertation, preliminary exam. *Entrance requirements:* For doctorate, GRE, statement of purpose, transcripts for all college-level institutions attended, three letters of reference. Additional exam requirements/recommendations for international students: Required—TOEFL (minimum score 90 iBT), IELTS (minimum score 7). *Application deadline:* For fall admission, 2/21 for domestic and international students. Applications are processed on a rolling basis. Application fee: $0 ($50 for international students). Electronic applications accepted. *Expenses:* Tuition, state resident: full-time $20,742; part-time $838 per credit. Tuition, nonresident: full-time $33,960; part-time $1389 per credit. *Required fees:* $800; $205 per term. Tuition and fees vary according to program. *Financial support:* In 2014–15, 5 students received support, including 3 fellowships with tuition reimbursements available (averaging $25,500 per year), 2 research assistantships with tuition reimbursements available (averaging $26,000 per year). *Unit head:* Kathleen Blee, Associate Dean, Graduate Studies and Research, 412-624-3939, Fax: 412-624-6855. *Application contact:* Dave R. Carmen, Administrative Secretary, 412-624-6094, Fax: 412-624-6855, E-mail: drc41@pitt.edu.
Website: http://cmsp.pitt.edu/.

University of Pittsburgh, Swanson School of Engineering, Department of Mechanical Engineering and Materials Science, Pittsburgh, PA 15260. Offers MSME, MSNE, PhD. Part-time programs available. Postbaccalaureate distance learning degree programs offered. *Faculty:* 28 full-time (2 women), 33 part-time/adjunct (0 women). *Students:* 153 full-time (29 women), 131 part-time (16 women); includes 12 minority (4 Black or African American, non-Hispanic/Latino; 3 Asian, non-Hispanic/Latino; 4 Hispanic/Latino; 1 Two or more races, non-Hispanic/Latino), 120 international. 639 applicants, 36% accepted, 71 enrolled. In 2014, 72 master's, 16 doctorates awarded. Terminal master's awarded for partial completion of doctoral program. *Degree requirements:* For master's, thesis optional; for doctorate, comprehensive exam, thesis/dissertation, final oral exams. *Entrance requirements:* For master's and doctorate, minimum GPA of 3.0. Additional exam requirements/recommendations for international students: Required—TOEFL (minimum score 550 paper-based; 80 iBT). *Application deadline:* For fall admission, 3/1 priority date for domestic and international students; for spring admission, 7/1 priority date for domestic and international students. Applications are processed on a rolling basis. Application fee: $50. Electronic applications accepted. *Expenses:* Tuition, state resident: full-time $20,742; part-time $838 per credit. Tuition, nonresident: full-time $33,960; part-time $1389 per credit. *Required fees:* $800; $205 per term. Tuition and fees vary according to program. *Financial support:* In 2014–15, 98 students received support, including 9 fellowships with full tuition reimbursements available (averaging $29,376 per year), 60 research assistantships with full tuition reimbursements available (averaging $24,996 per year), 29 teaching assistantships with full tuition reimbursements available (averaging $25,692 per year); scholarships/grants and tuition waivers (full and partial) also available. Financial award application deadline: 4/15. *Faculty research:* Smart materials and structure solid mechanics, computational fluid dynamics, multiphase bio-fluid dynamics, mechanical vibration analysis. *Total annual research expenditures:* $7.5 million. *Unit head:* Dr. Brian M. Gleeson, Chairman, 412-624-1185, Fax: 412-624-4846, E-mail: bgleeson@pitt.edu. *Application contact:* Dr. Qing-Ming Wang, Graduate Coordinator, 412-624-4885, Fax: 412-624-4846, E-mail: qiw4@pitt.edu.
Website: http://www.engineering.pitt.edu/MEMS/.

University of Rochester, Hajim School of Engineering and Applied Sciences, Master of Science in Technical Entrepreneurship and Management Program, Rochester, NY 14642. Offers biomedical engineering (MS); chemical engineering (MS); computer science (MS); electrical and computer engineering (MS); energy and the environment

(MS); materials science (MS); mechanical engineering (MS); optics (MS). Program offered in collaboration with the Simon School of Business. Part-time programs available. *Students:* 36 full-time (12 women), 7 part-time (1 woman); includes 3 minority (2 Hispanic/Latino; 1 Two or more races, non-Hispanic/Latino), 33 international. Average age 24. 152 applicants, 68% accepted, 27 enrolled. In 2014, 28 master's awarded. *Degree requirements:* For master's, comprehensive exam. *Entrance requirements:* For master's, GRE or GMAT, 3 letters of recommendation; personal statement; official transcript; bachelor's degree (or equivalent for international students) in engineering, science, or mathematics. Additional exam requirements/recommendations for international students: Required—TOEFL or IELTS. *Application deadline:* For fall admission, 2/1 for domestic and international students. Applications are processed on a rolling basis. Application fee: $60. Electronic applications accepted. *Expenses: Tuition:* Full-time $46,150; part-time $1442 per credit hour. *Required fees:* $504. *Financial support:* Career-related internships or fieldwork and scholarships/grants available. Financial award application deadline: 2/1. *Faculty research:* High efficiency solar cells, macromolecular self-assembly, digital signal processing, memory hierarchy management, molecular and physical mechanisms in cell migration, optical imaging systems. *Unit head:* Duncan T. Moore, Vice Provost for Entrepreneurship, 585-275-5248, Fax: 585-473-6745, E-mail: moore@optics.rochester.edu. *Application contact:* Andrea M. Galati, Executive Director, 585-276-3407, Fax: 585-276-2357, E-mail: andrea.galati@rochester.edu.
Website: http://www.rochester.edu/team.

University of Rochester, Hajim School of Engineering and Applied Sciences, Program in Materials Science, Rochester, NY 14627. Offers MS, PhD. *Students:* 38 full-time (14 women), 1 part-time (0 women); includes 3 minority (1 American Indian or Alaska Native, non-Hispanic/Latino; 1 Asian, non-Hispanic/Latino; 1 Hispanic/Latino), 29 international. 131 applicants, 28% accepted, 9 enrolled. In 2014, 12 master's, 4 doctorates awarded. Terminal master's awarded for partial completion of doctoral program. *Degree requirements:* For master's, comprehensive exam, thesis optional; for doctorate, thesis/dissertation, preliminary and qualifying exams. *Entrance requirements:* For master's and doctorate, GRE. Additional exam requirements/recommendations for international students: Required—TOEFL. *Application deadline:* For fall admission, 2/1 for domestic students. Application fee: $60. *Expenses: Tuition:* Full-time $46,150; part-time $1442 per credit hour. *Required fees:* $504. *Financial support:* Fellowships, research assistantships, teaching assistantships, and tuition waivers (full and partial) available. Financial award application deadline: 2/1. *Unit head:* Dr. Todd D. Krauss, Director, 585-275-5093. *Application contact:* Lynda McGarry, Administrative Assistant, 585-275-1626.
Website: http://www.rochester.edu/college/matsci/.

University of Southern California, Graduate School, Viterbi School of Engineering, Mork Family Department of Chemical Engineering and Materials Science, Los Angeles, CA 90089. Offers chemical engineering (MS, PhD, Engr); geoscience technologies (MS); materials engineering (MS); materials science (MS, PhD, Engr); petroleum engineering (MS, PhD, Engr); smart oilfield technologies (MS, Graduate Certificate). Terminal master's awarded for partial completion of doctoral program. *Degree requirements:* For master's, thesis optional; for doctorate, thesis/dissertation. *Entrance requirements:* For master's and doctorate, GRE General Test. Additional exam requirements/recommendations for international students: Recommended—TOEFL. Electronic applications accepted. *Expenses:* Contact institution. *Faculty research:* Heterogeneous materials and porous media, statistical mechanics, molecular simulation, polymer science and engineering, advanced materials, reaction engineering and catalysis, membrane processes and separation, biochemical engineering, cell culture, bioreactor modeling, petroleum engineering.

University of South Florida, College of Arts and Sciences, Department of Physics, Tampa, FL 33620-9951. Offers applied physics (MS, PhD); atmospheric physics (MS); atomic and molecular physics (MS); laser physics (MS); materials physics (MS); materials science and engineering (MSE); medical physics (MS); optical physics (MS); semiconductor physics (MS); solid state physics (MS). MSE offered jointly with College of Engineering. Part-time programs available. *Faculty:* 24 full-time (3 women). *Students:* 71 full-time (15 women), 7 part-time (0 women); includes 13 minority (2 Black or African American, non-Hispanic/Latino; 11 Hispanic/Latino), 37 international. Average age 31. 96 applicants, 23% accepted, 12 enrolled. In 2014, 8 master's, 9 doctorates awarded. *Degree requirements:* For master's, comprehensive exam, thesis optional; for doctorate, comprehensive exam, thesis/dissertation. *Entrance requirements:* For master's and doctorate, GRE General Test; GRE Subject Test in physics (recommended), minimum GPA of 3.0, three letters of recommendation, statement of purpose. Additional exam requirements/recommendations for international students: Required—TOEFL (minimum score 550 paper-based; 79 iBT) or IELTS (minimum score 6.5). *Application deadline:* For fall admission, 2/15 priority date for domestic students, 1/2 for international students; for spring admission, 9/1 for domestic students, 7/1 for international students. Applications are processed on a rolling basis. Application fee: $30. Electronic applications accepted. *Financial support:* In 2014–15, 70 students received support, including 27 research assistantships with tuition reimbursements available (averaging $15,272 per year), 43 teaching assistantships with tuition reimbursements available (averaging $16,267 per year); unspecified assistantships also available. *Faculty research:* The molecular organization of collagen, lipid rafts in biological membranes, the formation of Alzheimer plaques, the role of cellular ion pumps in wound healing, carbon nanotubes as biological detectors, optical imaging of neuronal activity, three-dimensional imaging of intact tissues, motility of cancer cells, the optical detection of pathogens in water. *Total annual research expenditures:* $3 million. *Unit head:* Dr. Pritish Mukherjee, Professor and Chairperson, 813-974-3293, Fax: 813-974-5813, E-mail: pritish@usf.edu. *Application contact:* Dr. Lilia Woods, Professor and Graduate Program Director, 813-974-2862, Fax: 813-974-5813, E-mail: lmwoods@usf.edu.
Website: http://physics.usf.edu/.

University of South Florida, College of Engineering, Department of Civil and Environmental Engineering, Tampa, FL 33620-9951. Offers civil engineering (MCE, MSCE, PhD), including environmental engineering (MSES, PhD), geotechnical engineering (MCE, MSCE, MSES, PhD), interdisciplinary transportation (MSCE), materials engineering and science, structural engineering, transportation engineering, water resources; engineering science (MSES), including environmental engineering (MSES, PhD), geotechnical engineering (MCE, MSCE, MSES, PhD); environmental engineering (MEVE, MSEV, PhD). Part-time programs available. *Faculty:* 19 full-time (5 women). *Students:* 97 full-time (35 women), 83 part-time (25 women); includes 41 minority (6 Black or African American, non-Hispanic/Latino; 1 American Indian or Alaska Native, non-Hispanic/Latino; 3 Asian, non-Hispanic/Latino; 25 Hispanic/Latino; 6 Two or more races, non-Hispanic/Latino), 39 international. Average age 30. 229 applicants, 51% accepted, 43 enrolled. In 2014, 68 master's, 9 doctorates awarded. Terminal master's awarded for partial completion of doctoral program. *Degree requirements:* For master's, comprehensive exam, thesis (for some programs); for doctorate, comprehensive exam, thesis/dissertation. *Entrance requirements:* For master's, GRE General Test (preferred minimum scores of 20th percentile verbal, 50th percentile quantitative, and 10th percentile in analytical writing), minimum GPA of 3.0 in major, two letters of reference, statement of purpose; for doctorate, GRE General Test (preferred minimum scores of 45th percentile verbal, 65th percentile quantitative, and 50th

percentile in analytical writing), three letters of recommendation, statement of purpose, resume. Additional exam requirements/recommendations for international students: Required—TOEFL (minimum score 550 paper-based; 79 iBT) or IELTS (minimum score 6.5). *Application deadline:* For fall admission, 2/15 for domestic students, 1/2 priority date for international students; for spring admission, 10/15 for domestic students, 6/1 priority date for international students. Application fee: $30. Electronic applications accepted. *Financial support:* In 2014–15, 65 students received support, including 44 research assistantships (averaging $14,123 per year), 21 teaching assistantships with tuition reimbursements available (averaging $15,329 per year). *Faculty research:* Environmental and water resources engineering, geotechnics and geoenvironmental systems, structures and materials systems, transportation systems. *Total annual research expenditures:* $3.3 million. *Unit head:* Dr. Manjriker Gunaratne, Professor and Department Chair, 813-974-5818, Fax: 813-974-2957, E-mail: gunaratn@usf.edu. *Application contact:* Dr. Sarina J. Ergas, Professor and Graduate Program Coordinator, 813-974-1119, Fax: 813-974-2957, E-mail: sergas@usf.edu.
Website: http://ce.eng.usf.edu/.

University of South Florida, College of Engineering, Interdisciplinary Programs in Engineering, Tampa, FL 33620-9951. Offers engineering science (PhD); materials science and engineering (MSMSE). *Degree requirements:* For master's, comprehensive exam, thesis (for some programs); for doctorate, comprehensive exam, thesis/dissertation. *Entrance requirements:* For master's, GRE General Test, minimum GPA of 3.0 in last 60 hours of coursework; for doctorate, GRE General Test, minimum GPA of 3.3 in last 60 hours of coursework. Additional exam requirements/recommendations for international students: Required—TOEFL (minimum score 550 paper-based; 79 iBT). *Faculty research:* Biomedical engineering and sustainability, particularly in water resources and energy; electrical engineering; civil/environmental engineering; industrial/management systems engineering; chemical engineering; computer science and engineering; mechanical engineering. *Unit head:* Dr. Robert Bishop, Dean, 813-974-3864, Fax: 813-974-5094, E-mail: robertbishop@usf.edu. *Application contact:* Dr. Rafael Perez, Associate Dean for Academic Affairs, 813-974-3934, Fax: 813-974-5094, E-mail: perez@usf.edu.
Website: http://www2.eng.usf.edu/.

University of South Florida, University College/Distance Education, Tampa, FL 33620-9951. *Unit head:* Kathy Barnes, Interdisciplinary Programs Coordinator, 813-974-8031, Fax: 813-974-7061, E-mail: barnesk@usf.edu. *Application contact:* Karen Tylinski, Metro Initiatives 813-974-9943, Fax: 813-974-7061, E-mail: ktylinsk@usf.edu.
Website: http://www.usf.edu/innovative-education/.

The University of Tennessee, Graduate School, College of Engineering, Department of Materials Science and Engineering, Program in Materials Science and Engineering, Knoxville, TN 37996. Offers MS, PhD. *Faculty:* 27 full-time (3 women), 7 part-time/adjunct (1 woman). *Students:* 85 full-time (20 women), 6 part-time (1 woman); includes 6 minority (1 Black or African American, non-Hispanic/Latino; 2 Asian, non-Hispanic/Latino; 2 Hispanic/Latino; 1 Two or more races, non-Hispanic/Latino), 49 international. Average age 29. 154 applicants, 19% accepted, 22 enrolled. In 2014, 6 master's, 12 doctorates awarded. *Degree requirements:* For master's, thesis or alternative; for doctorate, comprehensive exam, thesis/dissertation. *Entrance requirements:* For master's, GRE General Test (for MS students pursuing research thesis), minimum GPA of 2.7 (for U.S. degree holders), 3.0 (for international degree holders); 3 references; for doctorate, GRE General Test (for all PhD candidates), minimum GPA of 3.0 on previous graduate course work; 3 references. Additional exam requirements/recommendations for international students: Required—TOEFL (minimum score 550 paper-based). *Application deadline:* For fall admission, 2/1 priority date for domestic and international students; for spring admission, 6/15 for domestic and international students. Applications are processed on a rolling basis. Application fee: $35. Electronic applications accepted. *Financial support:* In 2014–15, 79 students received support, including 58 research assistantships with full tuition reimbursements available (averaging $21,092 per year), 19 teaching assistantships with full tuition reimbursements available (averaging $22,829 per year); fellowships with full tuition reimbursements available, career-related internships or fieldwork, Federal Work-Study, institutionally sponsored loans, health care benefits, and unspecified assistantships also available. Financial award application deadline: 2/1; financial award applicants required to submit FAFSA. *Faculty research:* Biomaterials; functional materials electronic, magnetic and optical; high temperature materials; mechanical behavior of materials; neutron materials science. *Unit head:* Dr. Kurt Sickafus, Head, 865-974-4858, Fax: 865-974-4115, E-mail: kurt@utk.edu. *Application contact:* Dr. Roberto S. Benson, Associate Head, 865-974-5347, Fax: 865-974-4115, E-mail: rbenson1@utk.edu.
Website: http://www.engr.utk.edu/mse.

The University of Texas at Arlington, Graduate School, College of Engineering, Department of Materials Science and Engineering, Arlington, TX 76019. Offers M Engr, MS, PhD. Terminal master's awarded for partial completion of doctoral program. *Degree requirements:* For master's, comprehensive exam (for some programs), thesis optional; for doctorate, comprehensive exam, thesis/dissertation optional. *Entrance requirements:* For master's, GRE General Test, minimum GPA of 3.0; for doctorate, GRE General Test, minimum GPA of 3.5. Additional exam requirements/recommendations for international students: Required—TOEFL (minimum score 550 paper-based; 79 iBT), IELTS. *Faculty research:* Electronic materials, conductive polymer, composites biomaterial, structural materials.

The University of Texas at Austin, Graduate School, Cockrell School of Engineering, Program in Materials Science and Engineering, Austin, TX 78712-1111. Offers MS, PhD. Part-time programs available. *Degree requirements:* For master's, thesis (for some programs); for doctorate, thesis/dissertation. *Entrance requirements:* For master's and doctorate, GRE General Test. Additional exam requirements/recommendations for international students: Required—TOEFL (minimum score 550 paper-based). Electronic applications accepted.

The University of Texas at Dallas, Erik Jonsson School of Engineering and Computer Science, Department of Materials Science and Engineering, Richardson, TX 75080. Offers MS, PhD. Part-time and evening/weekend programs available. *Faculty:* 14 full-time (2 women). *Students:* 55 full-time (18 women), 3 part-time (2 women); includes 9 minority (2 Black or African American, non-Hispanic/Latino; 2 Asian, non-Hispanic/Latino; 4 Hispanic/Latino; 1 Two or more races, non-Hispanic/Latino), 39 international. Average age 27. 118 applicants, 25% accepted, 13 enrolled. In 2014, 9 master's, 11 doctorates awarded. *Degree requirements:* For master's, thesis or major design project; for doctorate, thesis/dissertation. *Entrance requirements:* For master's, GRE General Test, minimum GPA of 3.0 in related bachelor's degree; for doctorate, GRE General Test, minimum GPA of 3.5. Additional exam requirements/recommendations for international students: Required—TOEFL (minimum score 550 paper-based). *Application deadline:* For fall admission, 7/15 for domestic students, 5/1 priority date for international students; for spring admission, 11/15 for domestic students, 9/1 priority date for international students. Applications are processed on a rolling basis. Application fee: $50 ($100 for international students). Electronic applications accepted. *Expenses:* Tuition, state resident: full-time $11,940; part-time $663 per credit. Tuition, nonresident: full-time $22,282; part-time $1238 per credit. *Financial support:* In 2014–15, 55 students received support, including 1 fellowship (averaging $28,600 per year), 52 research

assistantships with partial tuition reimbursements available (averaging $19,500 per year); teaching assistantships with partial tuition reimbursements available, career-related internships or fieldwork, Federal Work-Study, institutionally sponsored loans, scholarships/grants, and unspecified assistantships also available. Support available to part-time students. Financial award application deadline: 4/30; financial award applicants required to submit FAFSA. *Faculty research:* Graphene-based semiconducting materials, neuro-inspired computational paradigms, electronic materials with emphasis on dielectrics, energy harvesting (photovoltaics, lithium-ion batteries), biosensors and hydrogen storage materials. *Unit head:* Dr. Yves Chabal, Department Head, 972-883-5751, Fax: 972-883-5725, E-mail: chabal@utdallas.edu. *Application contact:* Dr. Julia Hsu, Associate Department Head, 972-883-5789, Fax: 972-883-5725, E-mail: jwhsu@utdallas.edu.
Website: http://mse.utdallas.edu/.

The University of Texas at El Paso, Graduate School, College of Engineering, Department of Metallurgical and Materials Engineering, El Paso, TX 79968-0001. Offers materials science and engineering (PhD); metallurgical and materials engineering (MS). Part-time and evening/weekend programs available. *Degree requirements:* For master's, thesis. *Entrance requirements:* For master's, GRE General Test. Additional exam requirements/recommendations for international students: Required—TOEFL. Electronic applications accepted.

The University of Texas at El Paso, Graduate School, Interdisciplinary Program in Materials Science and Engineering, El Paso, TX 79968-0001. Offers PhD. Part-time and evening/weekend programs available. *Degree requirements:* For doctorate, thesis/dissertation. *Entrance requirements:* For doctorate, GRE, letters of recommendation. Additional exam requirements/recommendations for international students: Required—TOEFL; Recommended—IELTS. Electronic applications accepted.

The University of Toledo, College of Graduate Studies, College of Natural Sciences and Mathematics, Department of Physics and Astronomy, Toledo, OH 43606-3390. Offers photovoltaics (PSM); physics (MS, PhD), including astrophysics (PhD), materials science, medical physics (PhD); MS/PhD. *Degree requirements:* For master's, thesis; for doctorate, thesis/dissertation, departmental qualifying exam. *Entrance requirements:* For master's and doctorate, GRE General Test, GRE Subject Test, minimum cumulative point-hour ratio of 2.7 for all previous academic work, three letters of recommendation, statement of purpose, transcripts from all prior institutions attended. Additional exam requirements/recommendations for international students: Required—TOEFL (minimum score 550 paper-based; 80 iBT). Electronic applications accepted. *Faculty research:* Atomic physics, solid-state physics, materials science, astrophysics.

University of Toronto, School of Graduate Studies, Faculty of Applied Science and Engineering, Department of Materials Science and Engineering, Toronto, ON M5S 2J7, Canada. Offers M Eng, MA Sc, PhD. Part-time programs available. *Degree requirements:* For master's, thesis (for some programs), oral presentation/thesis defense (MA Sc), qualifying exam; for doctorate, thesis/dissertation. *Entrance requirements:* For master's, BA Sc or B Sc in materials science and engineering, 2 letters of reference; for doctorate, MA Sc or equivalent, 2 letters of reference, minimum B+ average in last 2 years. Additional exam requirements/recommendations for international students: Required—TOEFL (minimum score 580 paper-based), TWE (minimum score 4). Electronic applications accepted.

University of Utah, Graduate School, College of Engineering, Department of Materials Science and Engineering, Salt Lake City, UT 84112. Offers MS, PhD. *Faculty:* 8 full-time (0 women), 2 part-time/adjunct (1 woman). *Students:* 34 full-time (8 women), 5 part-time (1 woman); includes 2 minority (both Asian, non-Hispanic/Latino), 21 international. Average age 28. 69 applicants, 22% accepted, 10 enrolled. In 2014, 2 master's, 5 doctorates awarded. *Degree requirements:* For master's, thesis; for doctorate, thesis/dissertation. *Entrance requirements:* For master's and doctorate, GRE General Test, minimum GPA of 3.0. Additional exam requirements/recommendations for international students: Required—TOEFL (minimum score 570 paper-based; 88 iBT), IELTS (minimum score 7). *Application deadline:* For fall admission, 1/15 for domestic students, 12/15 for international students. Application fee: $0 ($15 for international students). Electronic applications accepted. *Expenses:* Expenses: Contact institution. *Financial support:* In 2014–15, 2 students received support, including 5 fellowships with full tuition reimbursements available (averaging $26,780 per year), 34 research assistantships with full tuition reimbursements available (averaging $23,000 per year); teaching assistantships with full tuition reimbursements available also available. Financial award application deadline: 2/5; financial award applicants required to submit FAFSA. *Faculty research:* Solid oxide fuel cells, computational nanostructures, solar cells, nanosensors, batteries: renewable energy. *Total annual research expenditures:* $3.3 million. *Unit head:* Dr. Feng Liu, Chair, 801-581-6863, Fax: 801-581-4816, E-mail: fliu@eng.utah.edu. *Application contact:* Ashley Quimby, Academic Advisor, 801-581-6863, Fax: 801-581-4816, E-mail: ashley.quimby@utah.edu.
Website: http://www.mse.utah.edu/.

University of Vermont, Graduate College, College of Engineering and Mathematics, Program in Materials Science, Burlington, VT 05405. Offers MS, PhD. *Degree requirements:* For master's, thesis or alternative; for doctorate, thesis/dissertation. *Entrance requirements:* For master's and doctorate, GRE General Test. Additional exam requirements/recommendations for international students: Required—TOEFL (minimum score 550 paper-based; 80 iBT). Electronic applications accepted.

University of Virginia, School of Engineering and Applied Science, Department of Materials Science and Engineering, Charlottesville, VA 22903. Offers materials science (MMSE, MS, PhD). Part-time programs available. Postbaccalaureate distance learning degree programs offered (no on-campus study). *Faculty:* 20 full-time (2 women). *Students:* 63 full-time (17 women), 1 (woman) part-time; includes 4 minority (3 Asian, non-Hispanic/Latino; 1 Hispanic/Latino), 23 international. Average age 26. 140 applicants, 16% accepted, 13 enrolled. In 2014, 12 master's, 8 doctorates awarded. Terminal master's awarded for partial completion of doctoral program. *Degree requirements:* For master's, comprehensive exam, thesis (for some programs); for doctorate, comprehensive exam, thesis/dissertation. *Entrance requirements:* For master's and doctorate, GRE General Test, three recommendations. Additional exam requirements/recommendations for international students: Required—TOEFL. *Application deadline:* For fall admission, 1/15 for domestic and international students. Applications are processed on a rolling basis. Application fee: $60. Electronic applications accepted. *Expenses:* Tuition, state resident: full-time $14,164; part-time $349 per credit hour. Tuition, nonresident: full-time $23,722; part-time $1300 per credit hour. *Required fees:* $2514. *Financial support:* Fellowships, research assistantships, and teaching assistantships available. Financial award application deadline: 1/15; financial award applicants required to submit FAFSA. *Faculty research:* Environmental effects on material behavior, electronic materials, metals, polymers, tribology. *Unit head:* William C. Johnson, Chair, 434-982-5641, Fax: 434-982-5660, E-mail: wcj2c@virginia.edu. *Application contact:* Pamela M. Morris, Associate Dean for Research and Graduate Programs, 434-243-7683, Fax: 434-982-3044, E-mail: pamela@cs.virginia.edu.
Website: http://www.virginia.edu/ms/.

University of Washington, Graduate School, College of Engineering, Department of Materials Science and Engineering, Seattle, WA 98195-2120. Offers applied materials science and engineering (MS); materials science and engineering (MS, PhD). Part-time programs available. *Faculty:* 13 full-time (2 women). *Students:* 88 full-time (24 women), 9 part-time (4 women). Average age 27. 322 applicants, 37% accepted, 41 enrolled. In 2014, 19 master's, 10 doctorates awarded. Terminal master's awarded for partial completion of doctoral program. *Degree requirements:* For master's, comprehensive exam, thesis optional, final presentation; for doctorate, comprehensive exam, thesis/dissertation, qualifying evaluation, general and final exams. *Entrance requirements:* For master's and doctorate, GRE General Test, minimum GPA of 3.0. Additional exam requirements/recommendations for international students: Required—TOEFL (minimum score 580 paper-based; 92 iBT); Recommended—IELTS (minimum score 7). *Application deadline:* For fall admission, 12/15 for domestic and international students. Applications are processed on a rolling basis. Application fee: $85. Electronic applications accepted. *Expenses:* Expenses: Contact institution. *Financial support:* In 2014–15, 34 students received support, including 2 fellowships with full tuition reimbursements available, 21 research assistantships with full tuition reimbursements available, 11 teaching assistantships with full tuition reimbursements available; career-related internships or fieldwork, Federal Work-Study, institutionally sponsored loans, scholarships/grants, health care benefits, unspecified assistantships, and stipend supplements also available. Financial award application deadline: 1/15; financial award applicants required to submit FAFSA. *Faculty research:* Synthesis/structure/property and processing, biomaterials and biomimetics, materials chemistry and characterization, optical and electronic materials. *Total annual research expenditures:* $6.4 million. *Unit head:* Dr. Alex Jen, Professor/Chair, 206-543-2600, Fax: 206-543-3100, E-mail: ajen@uw.edu. *Application contact:* Karen Wetterhahn, Academic Counselor, 206-543-2740, Fax: 206-543-3100, E-mail: karenlw@uw.edu.
Website: http://depts.washington.edu/mse/.

University of Wisconsin–Madison, Graduate School, College of Engineering, Materials Science Program, Madison, WI 53706. Offers MS, PhD. Part-time programs available. *Faculty:* 80 full-time (14 women). *Students:* 86 full-time (17 women); includes 45 minority (1 Black or African American, non-Hispanic/Latino; 1 American Indian or Alaska Native, non-Hispanic/Latino; 39 Asian, non-Hispanic/Latino; 4 Hispanic/Latino). Average age 27. 350 applicants, 11% accepted, 9 enrolled. In 2014, 19 master's, 10 doctorates awarded. Terminal master's awarded for partial completion of doctoral program. *Degree requirements:* For master's, thesis or alternative; for doctorate, comprehensive exam, thesis/dissertation. *Entrance requirements:* For master's and doctorate, GRE General Test. Additional exam requirements/recommendations for international students: Required—TOEFL (minimum score 580 paper-based; 92 iBT). *Application deadline:* For fall admission, 4/1 for domestic and international students; for spring admission, 10/1 for domestic and international students. Applications are processed on a rolling basis. Application fee: $56. Electronic applications accepted. *Expenses:* Tuition, state resident: full-time $10,723; part-time $745 per credit. Tuition, nonresident: full-time $24,054; part-time $1578 per credit. *Required fees:* $374 per semester. Tuition and fees vary according to course load, program and reciprocity agreements. *Financial support:* In 2014–15, 9 fellowships with full tuition reimbursements (averaging $23,376 per year), 76 research assistantships with full tuition reimbursements (averaging $20,808 per year), 1 teaching assistantship with full tuition reimbursement (averaging $28,175 per year) were awarded; traineeships, health care benefits, and unspecified assistantships also available. Financial award application deadline: 1/15. *Faculty research:* Electronic materials, polymers and biomaterials, nanotechnology and nanoscience, structural and mechanical materials, magnetic and superconducting materials, ceramics, metals, computational and theoretical modeling of materials, photonics and optical materials, materials for energy or environmental technology. *Unit head:* Prof. Ray Vanderby, Jr., Director, 608-265-3032, Fax: 608-262-8353, E-mail: vanderby@ortho.wisc.edu. *Application contact:* Diana Rhoads, University Services Program Associate, 608-263-1795, Fax: 608-262-8353, E-mail: rhoads@engr.wisc.edu.
Website: http://www.engr.wisc.edu/interd/msp/.

Vanderbilt University, School of Engineering, Interdisciplinary Program in Materials Science, Nashville, TN 37240-1001. Offers M Eng, MS, PhD. Part-time programs available. Terminal master's awarded for partial completion of doctoral program. *Degree requirements:* For master's, thesis; for doctorate, thesis/dissertation. *Entrance requirements:* For master's and doctorate, GRE General Test. Electronic applications accepted. *Expenses:* *Tuition:* Full-time $42,768; part-time $1782 per credit hour. *Required fees:* $422. One-time fee: $30 full-time. *Faculty research:* Nanostructure materials, materials physics, surface and interface science, materials synthesis, biomaterials.

Virginia Polytechnic Institute and State University, Graduate School, College of Engineering, Blacksburg, VA 24061. Offers aerospace engineering (ME, MS, PhD); biological systems engineering (ME, MS, PhD); biomedical engineering (MS, PhD); chemical engineering (ME, MS, PhD); civil engineering (ME, MS, PhD); computer engineering (ME, MS, PhD); computer science (MS, PhD); electrical engineering (ME, PhD); engineering education (PhD); engineering mechanics (ME, MS, PhD); environmental engineering (MS); environmental science and engineering (MS); industrial and systems engineering (ME, MS, PhD); materials science and engineering (ME, MS, PhD); mechanical engineering (ME, MS, PhD); mining and minerals engineering (PhD); mining engineering (ME, MS); nuclear engineering (MS, PhD); ocean engineering (MS); systems engineering (ME, MS). *Accreditation:* ABET (one or more programs are accredited). *Faculty:* 356 full-time (60 women), 3 part-time/adjunct (1 woman). *Students:* 1,700 full-time (398 women), 345 part-time (58 women); includes 213 minority (43 Black or African American, non-Hispanic/Latino; 1 American Indian or Alaska Native, non-Hispanic/Latino; 87 Asian, non-Hispanic/Latino; 58 Hispanic/Latino; 1 Native Hawaiian or other Pacific Islander, non-Hispanic/Latino; 23 Two or more races, non-Hispanic/Latino), 1,079 international. Average age 27. 5,228 applicants, 18% accepted, 471 enrolled. In 2014, 438 master's, 211 doctorates awarded. *Degree requirements:* For master's, comprehensive exam (for some programs), thesis (for some programs); for doctorate, comprehensive exam (for some programs), thesis/dissertation (for some programs). *Entrance requirements:* For master's and doctorate, GRE/GMAT (may vary by department). Additional exam requirements/recommendations for international students: Required—TOEFL (minimum score 550 paper-based). *Application deadline:* For fall admission, 8/1 for domestic students, 4/1 for international students; for spring admission, 1/1 for domestic students, 9/1 for international students. Applications are processed on a rolling basis. Application fee: $75. Electronic applications accepted. *Expenses:* Tuition, state resident: full-time $11,656; part-time $647.50 per credit hour. Tuition, nonresident: full-time $23,351; part-time $1297.25 per credit hour. *Required fees:* $2533; $465.75 per semester. Tuition and fees vary according to course load, campus/location and program. *Financial support:* In 2014–15, 148 fellowships with full tuition reimbursements (averaging $8,031 per year), 855 research assistantships with full tuition reimbursements (averaging $22,855 per year), 288 teaching assistantships with full tuition reimbursements (averaging $20,291 per year) were awarded. Financial award application deadline: 3/1; financial award applicants required to submit FAFSA. *Total annual research expenditures:* $90.5 million. *Unit head:* Dr. Richard C. Benson, Dean, 540-231-9752, Fax: 540-231-3031, E-mail:

deaneng@vt.edu. *Application contact:* Linda Perkins, Executive Assistant, 540-231-9752, Fax: 540-231-3031, E-mail: lperkins@vt.edu. Website: http://www.eng.vt.edu/.

Washington State University, Voiland College of Engineering and Architecture, School of Mechanical and Materials Engineering, Pullman, WA 99164-2920. Offers materials science and engineering (MS, PhD); mechanical engineering (MS, PhD). MS programs also offered at Tri-Cities campus. Part-time programs available. *Faculty:* 29 full-time (4 women), 3 part-time/adjunct (1 woman). *Students:* 79 full-time (12 women), 27 part-time (4 women); includes 5 minority (2 Black or African American, non-Hispanic/Latino; 2 Asian, non-Hispanic/Latino; 1 Hispanic/Latino), 60 international. Average age 29. 169 applicants, 37% accepted, 39 enrolled. In 2014, 23 master's, 7 doctorates awarded. Terminal master's awarded for partial completion of doctoral program. *Degree requirements:* For master's, comprehensive exam, thesis; for doctorate, comprehensive exam, thesis/dissertation, preliminary exam. *Entrance requirements:* For master's, GRE, bachelor's degree, minimum GPA of 3.0, resume, statement of purpose, 3 letters of recommendation, official transcripts, Student Interest Profile form; for doctorate, GRE, bachelor's degree, minimum GPA of 3.4, resume, statement of purpose, 3 letters of recommendation, official transcripts, Student Interest Profile form. Additional exam requirements/recommendations for international students: Required—TOEFL (minimum score 500 paper-based), IELTS. *Application deadline:* For fall admission, 1/10 priority date for domestic and international students; for spring admission, 7/1 priority date for domestic and international students. Applications are processed on a rolling basis. Application fee: $75. Electronic applications accepted. *Expenses:* Tuition, state resident: full-time $11,768. Tuition, nonresident: full-time $25,200. *Required fees:* $960. Tuition and fees vary according to program. *Financial support:* In 2014–15, 94 students received support, including 3 fellowships with full tuition reimbursements available (averaging $38,200 per year), 22 research assistantships with full tuition reimbursements available (averaging $13,883 per year), 32 teaching assistantships with full tuition reimbursements available (averaging $13,862 per year); career-related internships or fieldwork, scholarships/grants, health care benefits, and unspecified assistantships also available. Financial award application deadline: 4/1; financial award applicants required to submit FAFSA. *Faculty research:* Multiscale modeling and characterization of materials; advanced energy; bioengineering; engineering education and curricular innovation; modeling and visualization in the areas of product realization, materials, and processes. *Total annual research expenditures:* $4.4 million. *Unit head:* Dr. Michael Kessler, Director, 509-335-8654, Fax: 509-335-4662, E-mail: michael.kessler@wsu.edu. *Application contact:* Graduate School Admissions, 800-GRADWSU, Fax: 509-335-1949, E-mail: gradsch@wsu.edu. Website: http://www.mme.wsu.edu/.

Washington University in St. Louis, School of Engineering and Applied Science, Department of Mechanical Engineering and Materials Science, St. Louis, MO 63130-4899. Offers aerospace engineering (MS, PhD); materials science (MS); mechanical engineering (M Eng, MS, PhD). Part-time programs available. Terminal master's awarded for partial completion of doctoral program. *Degree requirements:* For master's, thesis optional; for doctorate, thesis/dissertation optional. *Entrance requirements:* For master's, GRE; for doctorate, GRE General Test, departmental qualifying exam. *Faculty research:* Aerosols science and technology, applied mechanics, biomechanics and biomedical engineering, design, dynamic systems, combustion science, composite materials, materials science.

Wayne State University, College of Engineering, Department of Chemical Engineering and Materials Science, Program in Materials Science and Engineering, Detroit, MI 48202. Offers materials science and engineering (MS, PhD); polymer engineering (Graduate Certificate). Part-time programs available. *Students:* 13 full-time (5 women), 8 part-time (5 women); includes 2 minority (1 Black or African American, non-Hispanic/Latino; 1 Asian, non-Hispanic/Latino), 14 international. Average age 27. 60 applicants, 35% accepted, 7 enrolled. In 2014, 1 master's, 3 doctorates awarded. *Degree requirements:* For master's, thesis optional; for doctorate, thesis/dissertation. *Entrance requirements:* For master's, GRE (if applying for financial support), recommendations; resume; bachelor's degree in engineering or the physical scienes with minimum GPA of 3.0; for doctorate, GRE, recommendations; resume, personal statement, minimum GPA of 3.5 in MS program, or BS from accredited U.S. institution. Additional exam requirements/recommendations for international students: Required—TOEFL (minimum score 550 paper-based; 79 iBT), TWE (minimum score 5.5), Michigan English Language

Assessment Battery (minimum score 85); Recommended—IELTS (minimum score 6.5). *Application deadline:* For fall admission, 6/1 priority date for domestic students, 5/1 priority date for international students; for winter admission, 10/1 priority date for domestic students, 9/1 priority date for international students; for spring admission, 2/1 priority date for domestic students, 1/1 priority date for international students. Applications are processed on a rolling basis. Application fee: $0. Electronic applications accepted. *Expenses:* Expenses: Contact institution. *Financial support:* In 2014–15, 13 students received support. Fellowships with tuition reimbursements available, research assistantships with tuition reimbursements available, teaching assistantships with tuition reimbursements available, scholarships/grants, health care benefits, and unspecified assistantships available. Support available to part-time students. Financial award application deadline: 3/31; financial award applicants required to submit FAFSA. *Faculty research:* Polymer science, rheology, fatigue in metals, metal matrix composites, ceramics. *Unit head:* Dr. Charles Manke, Chair, 313-577-3849, Fax: 313-577-3810, E-mail: cmanke@eng.wayne.edu. *Application contact:* Dr. Guangzhao Mao, Director of Materials Science Graduate Program, 313-577-3804, E-mail: gzmao@eng.wayne.edu. Website: http://engineering.wayne.edu/che/.

Worcester Polytechnic Institute, Graduate Studies and Research, Department of Mechanical Engineering, Program in Materials Process Engineering, Worcester, MA 01609-2280. Offers MS. Part-time and evening/weekend programs available. *Students:* 1 full-time (0 women), 7 part-time (2 women), 1 international. 9 applicants, 67% accepted, 4 enrolled. *Degree requirements:* For master's, thesis optional. *Entrance requirements:* For master's, GRE (recommended), 3 letters of recommendation. Additional exam requirements/recommendations for international students: Required—TOEFL (minimum score 563 paper-based; 84 iBT). *Application deadline:* For fall admission, 1/1 priority date for domestic and international students; for spring admission, 10/1 priority date for domestic and international students. Applications are processed on a rolling basis. Application fee: $70. Electronic applications accepted. *Financial support:* Research assistantships and teaching assistantships available. Financial award application deadline: 1/1; financial award applicants required to submit FAFSA. *Unit head:* Dr. Richard D. Sisson, Jr., Director, 508-831-5633, Fax: 508-831-5178, E-mail: sisson@wpi.edu. *Application contact:* Rita Shilansky, Graduate Secretary, 508-831-5633, Fax: 508-831-5178, E-mail: rita@wpi.edu. Website: http://www.wpi.edu/academics/mpe.

Worcester Polytechnic Institute, Graduate Studies and Research, Department of Mechanical Engineering, Program in Materials Science and Engineering, Worcester, MA 01609-2280. Offers MS, PhD. Part-time and evening/weekend programs available. *Students:* 71 full-time (23 women), 10 part-time (5 women); includes 8 minority (2 Asian, non-Hispanic/Latino; 2 Hispanic/Latino; 4 Two or more races, non-Hispanic/Latino), 58 international. 151 applicants, 76% accepted, 38 enrolled. In 2014, 35 master's, 4 doctorates awarded. *Degree requirements:* For master's, thesis; for doctorate, comprehensive exam, thesis/dissertation. *Entrance requirements:* For master's and doctorate, GRE (recommended), 3 letters of recommendation. Additional exam requirements/recommendations for international students: Required—TOEFL (minimum score 563 paper-based; 84 iBT), IELTS (minimum score 7). *Application deadline:* For fall admission, 1/1 priority date for domestic students, 1/1 for international students; for spring admission, 10/1 priority date for domestic students, 10/1 for international students. Applications are processed on a rolling basis. Application fee: $70. Electronic applications accepted. *Financial support:* Research assistantships, teaching assistantships, career-related internships or fieldwork, institutionally sponsored loans, scholarships/grants, and unspecified assistantships available. Financial award application deadline: 1/1; financial award applicants required to submit FAFSA. *Unit head:* Dr. Richard D. Sisson, Jr., Director, 508-831-5633, Fax: 508-831-5178, E-mail: sisson@wpi.edu. *Application contact:* Rita Shilansky, Graduate Secretary, 508-831-5633, Fax: 508-831-5178, E-mail: rita@wpi.edu. Website: http://www.wpi.edu/academics/mte.

Wright State University, School of Graduate Studies, College of Engineering and Computer Science, Programs in Engineering, Program in Mechanical and Materials Engineering, Dayton, OH 45435. Offers materials science and engineering (MSE); mechanical engineering (MSE). *Degree requirements:* For master's, thesis or course option alternative. *Entrance requirements:* Additional exam requirements/recommendations for international students: Required—TOEFL.

Metallurgical Engineering and Metallurgy

Colorado School of Mines, Graduate School, Department of Metallurgical and Materials Engineering, Golden, CO 80401-1887. Offers materials science (MS, PhD); metallurgical and materials engineering (ME, MS, PhD). Part-time programs available. *Faculty:* 25 full-time (2 women), 12 part-time/adjunct (0 women). *Students:* 112 full-time (33 women), 12 part-time (2 women); includes 9 minority (3 Asian, non-Hispanic/Latino; 4 Hispanic/Latino; 2 Two or more races, non-Hispanic/Latino), 38 international. Average age 29. 207 applicants, 23% accepted, 35 enrolled. In 2014, 31 master's, 17 doctorates awarded. *Degree requirements:* For master's, thesis (for some programs); for doctorate, comprehensive exam, thesis/dissertation. *Entrance requirements:* For master's and doctorate, GRE General Test. Additional exam requirements/recommendations for international students: Required—TOEFL (minimum score 550 paper-based; 80 iBT). *Application deadline:* For fall admission, 12/15 priority date for domestic and international students; for spring admission, 9/1 priority date for domestic and international students. Application fee: $50 ($70 for international students). Electronic applications accepted. *Financial support:* In 2014–15, 88 students received support, including 5 fellowships with full tuition reimbursements available (averaging $21,120 per year), 69 research assistantships with full tuition reimbursements available (averaging $21,120 per year), 11 teaching assistantships with full tuition reimbursements available (averaging $21,120 per year); scholarships/grants, health care benefits, and unspecified assistantships also available. Financial award application deadline: 12/15; financial award applicants required to submit FAFSA. *Total annual research expenditures:* $7.4 million. *Unit head:* Dr. Ivar Reimanis, Interim Head, 303-273-3549, E-mail: ireimani@mines.edu. *Application contact:* Kelly Hummel, Program Assistant, 303-273-3660, Fax: 303-273-3795, E-mail: khummel@mines.edu. Website: http://metallurgy.mines.edu.

Michigan Technological University, Graduate School, College of Engineering, Department of Materials Science and Engineering, Houghton, MI 49931. Offers MS, PhD. Part-time programs available. *Faculty:* 19 full-time, 10 part-time/adjunct. *Students:* 33 full-time (9 women); includes 1 minority (Two or more races, non-Hispanic/Latino), 16 international. Average age 28. 234 applicants, 16% accepted, 8 enrolled. In 2014, 1 master's, 5 doctorates awarded. Terminal master's awarded for partial completion of doctoral program. *Degree requirements:* For master's, comprehensive exam (for some

programs), thesis (for some programs); for doctorate, comprehensive exam, thesis/dissertation. *Entrance requirements:* For master's and doctorate, GRE (domestic students from ABET-accredited programs exempt), statement of purpose, official transcripts, 3 letters of recommendation. Additional exam requirements/recommendations for international students: Required—TOEFL (recommended score 79 iBT) or IELTS. *Application deadline:* For fall admission, 2/1 priority date for domestic and international students; for spring admission, 8/15 priority date for domestic and international students. Applications are processed on a rolling basis. Electronic applications accepted. *Expenses:* Expenses: Contact institution. *Financial support:* In 2014–15, 26 students received support, including 2 fellowships with full and partial tuition reimbursements available (averaging $13,824 per year), 22 research assistantships with full and partial tuition reimbursements available (averaging $13,824 per year), 1 teaching assistantship with full and partial tuition reimbursement available (averaging $13,824 per year); career-related internships or fieldwork, Federal Work-Study, scholarships/grants, health care benefits, unspecified assistantships, and cooperative program also available. Financial award applicants required to submit FAFSA. *Faculty research:* Structure/property/processing relationships, microstructural characterization, alloy design, electronic/magnetic/photonic materials, materials and manufacturing processes. *Total annual research expenditures:* $1.3 million. *Unit head:* Dr. Stephen L. Kampe, Chair, 906-487-2036, Fax: 906-487-2934, E-mail: kampe@mtu.edu. *Application contact:* Stephen A. Hackney, Associate Department Chair for Graduate Studies, 906-487-2170, Fax: 906-487-2934, E-mail: hackney@mtu.edu. Website: http://www.mtu.edu/materials/.

Missouri University of Science and Technology, Graduate School, Department of Materials Science and Engineering, Rolla, MO 65409. Offers ceramic engineering (MS, DE, PhD); metallurgical engineering (MS, PhD). *Degree requirements:* For master's, thesis optional; for doctorate, comprehensive exam. *Entrance requirements:* For master's, GRE (minimum combined score 1100, 600 verbal, 3.5 writing); for doctorate, GRE (minimum score: quantitative 600, writing 3.5). Additional exam requirements/recommendations for international students: Required—TOEFL (minimum score 570 paper-based).

Metallurgical Engineering and Metallurgy

Montana Tech of The University of Montana, Graduate School, Metallurgical/Mineral Processing Engineering Programs, Butte, MT 59701-8997. Offers MS. Part-time programs available. *Degree requirements:* For master's, comprehensive exam (for some programs), thesis optional. *Entrance requirements:* For master's, GRE General Test, minimum GPA of 3.0. Additional exam requirements/recommendations for international students: Required—TOEFL (minimum score 525 paper-based; 71 iBT). Electronic applications accepted. *Expenses:* Tuition, state resident: full-time $5802; part-time $241 per credit. Tuition, nonresident: full-time $15,895; part-time $662 per credit. *Required fees:* $1516; $414 per credit. $207 per semester. One-time fee: $30. *Faculty research:* Stabilizing hazardous waste, decontamination of metals by melt refining, ultraviolet enhancement of stabilization reactions, extractive metallurgy, fuel cells.

The Ohio State University, Graduate School, College of Engineering, Department of Materials Science and Engineering, Program in Welding Engineering, Columbus, OH 43210. Offers MS, PhD. Postbaccalaureate distance learning degree programs offered. *Faculty:* 11. *Students:* 34 full-time (6 women), 29 part-time (6 women); includes 9 minority (1 Black or African American, non-Hispanic/Latino; 2 Asian, non-Hispanic/Latino; 5 Hispanic/Latino; 1 Two or more races, non-Hispanic/Latino), 15 international. Average age 29. In 2014, 8 master's, 3 doctorates awarded. *Degree requirements:* For master's, thesis optional; for doctorate, thesis/dissertation. *Entrance requirements:* For master's and doctorate, GRE General Test (for all international applicants and domestic applicants with undergraduate GPA less than 3.0 or with a non-ABET accredited degree). Additional exam requirements/recommendations for international students: Required—TOEFL (minimum score 550 paper-based; 79 iBT), Michigan English Language Assessment Battery (minimum score 82); Recommended—IELTS (minimum score 7). *Application deadline:* For fall admission, 12/1 priority date for domestic students, 11/30 priority date for international students; for winter admission, 12/1 for domestic students, 11/1 for international students; for spring admission, 12/14 for domestic students, 11/12 for international students; for summer admission, 5/15 for domestic students, 4/14 for international students. Applications are processed on a rolling basis. Application fee: $60 ($70 for international students). Electronic applications accepted. *Financial support:* Fellowships with tuition reimbursements, research assistantships with tuition reimbursements, teaching assistantships with tuition reimbursements, Federal Work-Study, and institutionally sponsored loans available. Support available to part-time students. *Unit head:* Dr. Antonio Ramirez Londono, Graduate Studies Committee Chair, 614-292-8662, E-mail: ramirezlondono.1@osu.edu. *Application contact:* Mark Cooper, Graduate Studies Coordinator, 614-292-7280, Fax: 614-292-1537, E-mail: cooper.73@osu.edu.
Website: http://engineering.osu.edu/graduate/welding.

Université Laval, Faculty of Sciences and Engineering, Department of Mining, Metallurgical and Materials Engineering, Programs in Metallurgical Engineering, Québec, QC G1K 7P4, Canada. Offers M Sc, PhD. Terminal master's awarded for partial completion of doctoral program. *Degree requirements:* For master's, thesis; for doctorate, comprehensive exam, thesis/dissertation. *Entrance requirements:* For master's and doctorate, knowledge of French and English. Electronic applications accepted.

The University of Alabama, Graduate School, College of Engineering, Department of Metallurgical and Materials Engineering, Tuscaloosa, AL 35487. Offers MS Met E, PhD. PhD offered jointly with The University of Alabama at Birmingham. *Faculty:* 10 full-time (3 women). *Students:* 21 full-time (4 women), 1 part-time (0 women); includes 3 minority (2 Black or African American, non-Hispanic/Latino; 1 Asian, non-Hispanic/Latino), 9 international. Average age 26. 29 applicants, 41% accepted, 5 enrolled. In 2014, 3 master's, 5 doctorates awarded. *Degree requirements:* For master's, thesis or alternative; for doctorate, thesis/dissertation. *Entrance requirements:* For master's, GRE General Test, minimum GPA of 3.0 in last 60 hours; for doctorate, GRE General Test, minimum graduate GPA of 3.0, graduate degree. Additional exam requirements/recommendations for international students: Required—TOEFL (minimum score 550 paper-based). *Application deadline:* For fall admission, 7/1 for domestic students, 5/1 priority date for international students. Applications are processed on a rolling basis. Application fee: $50 ($60 for international students). Electronic applications accepted. *Expenses:* Tuition, state resident: full-time $9826. Tuition, nonresident: full-time $24,950. *Financial support:* In 2014–15, 3 fellowships (averaging $15,000 per year), 14 research assistantships (averaging $14,700 per year), 6 teaching assistantships (averaging $12,250 per year) were awarded; Federal Work-Study and unspecified assistantships also available. *Faculty research:* Thermodynamics, molten metals processing, casting and solidification, mechanical properties of materials, thin films and nanostructures, electrochemistry, corrosion and alloy development. *Total annual research expenditures:* $1.6 million. *Unit head:* Dr. Viola L. Acoff, Head/Professor, 205-348-2080, Fax: 205-348-2164, E-mail: vacoff@eng.ua.edu. *Application contact:* Dr. Greg B. Thompson, Associate Professor, 205-348-1589, Fax: 205-348-2164, E-mail: sgupta@eng.ua.edu.
Website: http://www.eng.ua.edu/~mtedept/.

The University of British Columbia, Faculty of Applied Science, Department of Materials Engineering, Vancouver, BC V6T 1Z1, Canada. Offers materials and metallurgy (M Sc, PhD); metals and materials engineering (MA Sc, PhD). *Degree requirements:* For master's, comprehensive exam, thesis; for doctorate, comprehensive exam, thesis/dissertation. *Entrance requirements:* Additional exam requirements/recommendations for international students: Required—TOEFL (minimum score 560 paper-based; 83 iBT). Electronic applications accepted. *Faculty research:* Electroslag melting, mathematical modeling, solidification and hydrometallurgy.

University of Connecticut, Graduate School, School of Engineering, Department of Metallurgy and Materials Engineering, Storrs, CT 06269. Offers MS, PhD. Terminal master's awarded for partial completion of doctoral program. *Degree requirements:* For master's, comprehensive exam, thesis or alternative; for doctorate, thesis/dissertation. *Entrance requirements:* For master's and doctorate, GRE General Test, GRE Subject Test. Additional exam requirements/recommendations for international students: Required—TOEFL (minimum score 550 paper-based). Electronic applications accepted. *Faculty research:* Microsegregation and coarsening, fatigue crack, electron-dislocation interaction.

The University of Manchester, School of Materials, Manchester, United Kingdom. Offers advanced aerospace materials engineering (M Sc); advanced metallic systems (PhD); biomedical materials (M Phil, M Sc, PhD); ceramics and glass (M Phil, M Sc, PhD); composite materials (M Sc, PhD); corrosion and protection (M Phil, M Sc, PhD); materials (M Phil, PhD); metallic materials (M Phil, M Sc, PhD); nanostructural materials (M Phil, M Sc, PhD); paper science (M Phil, M Sc, PhD); polymer science and engineering (M Phil, M Sc, PhD); technical textiles (M Sc); textile design, fashion and management (M Phil, M Sc, PhD); textile science and technology (M Phil, M Sc, PhD); textiles (M Phil, PhD); textiles and fashion (M Ent).

University of Nebraska–Lincoln, Graduate College, College of Engineering, Department of Mechanical and Materials Engineering, Lincoln, NE 68588-0526. Offers biomedical engineering (PhD); engineering mechanics (MS); materials engineering (PhD); mechanical engineering (MS), including materials science engineering, metallurgical engineering; mechanical engineering and applied mechanics (PhD); MS/MS. MS/MS offered with University of Rouen-France. *Degree requirements:* For master's, thesis optional; for doctorate, comprehensive exam, thesis/dissertation. *Entrance requirements:* For master's and doctorate, GRE General Test. Additional exam requirements/recommendations for international students: Required—TOEFL (minimum score 550 paper-based). Electronic applications accepted. *Faculty research:* Medical robotics, rehabilitation dynamics, and design; combustion, fluid mechanics, and heat transfer; nano-materials, manufacturing, and devices; fiber, tissue, bio-polymer, and adaptive composites; blast, impact, fracture, and failure; electro-active and magnetic materials and devices; functional materials, design, and added manufacturing; materials characterization, modeling, and computational simulation.

University of Nevada, Reno, Graduate School, College of Engineering, Department of Chemical and Materials Engineering, Program in Materials Science and Engineering, Reno, NV 89557. Offers MS, PhD. Terminal master's awarded for partial completion of doctoral program. *Degree requirements:* For master's, thesis; for doctorate, one foreign language, thesis/dissertation. *Entrance requirements:* For master's, minimum GPA of 2.75; for doctorate, GRE, minimum GPA of 3.0. Additional exam requirements/recommendations for international students: Required—TOEFL (minimum score 500 paper-based; 61 iBT), IELTS (minimum score 6). Electronic applications accepted. *Faculty research:* Hydrometallurgy, applied surface chemistry, mineral processing, mineral bioprocessing, ceramics.

The University of Texas at El Paso, Graduate School, College of Engineering, Department of Metallurgical and Materials Engineering, El Paso, TX 79968-0001. Offers materials science and engineering (PhD); metallurgical and materials engineering (MS). Part-time and evening/weekend programs available. *Degree requirements:* For master's, thesis. *Entrance requirements:* For master's, GRE General Test. Additional exam requirements/recommendations for international students: Required—TOEFL. Electronic applications accepted.

University of Utah, Graduate School, College of Mines and Earth Sciences, Department of Metallurgical Engineering, Salt Lake City, UT 84112. Offers ME, MS, PhD. Part-time programs available. *Faculty:* 17 full-time (1 woman), 1 part-time/adjunct (0 women). *Students:* 42 full-time (5 women), 10 part-time (5 women); includes 2 minority (both Asian, non-Hispanic/Latino), 35 international. Average age 27. 34 applicants, 62% accepted, 8 enrolled. In 2014, 7 master's, 6 doctorates awarded. Terminal master's awarded for partial completion of doctoral program. *Degree requirements:* For master's, thesis; for doctorate, comprehensive exam, thesis/dissertation. *Entrance requirements:* For master's and doctorate, GRE General Test, minimum GPA of 3.0. Additional exam requirements/recommendations for international students: Required—TOEFL (minimum score 530 paper-based; 71 iBT) or IELTS (minimum score 5.5). *Application deadline:* For fall admission, 4/1 priority date for domestic students, 2/1 priority date for international students; for spring admission, 11/1 priority date for domestic students, 9/1 priority date for international students; for summer admission, 3/15 priority date for domestic students, 1/15 priority date for international students. Application fee: $55 ($65 for international students). Electronic applications accepted. *Financial support:* In 2014–15, 4 fellowships with full tuition reimbursements (averaging $18,000 per year), 39 research assistantships with full tuition reimbursements (averaging $19,900 per year) were awarded; institutionally sponsored loans also available. Financial award application deadline: 2/16; financial award applicants required to submit FAFSA. *Faculty research:* Physical metallurgy, mathematical modeling, mineral processing, chemical metallurgy nanoscience and technology. *Total annual research expenditures:* $4.1 million. *Unit head:* Dr. Manoranjan Misra, Chair, 801-587-9769, Fax: 801-581-4937, E-mail: mano.misra@utah.edu. *Application contact:* Sara J. Wilson, Office Manager, 801-581-6386, Fax: 801-581-4937, E-mail: sara.j.wilson@utah.edu.
Website: http://www.metallurgy.utah.edu/.

Polymer Science and Engineering

Auburn University, Graduate School, Ginn College of Engineering, Department of Polymer and Fiber Engineering, Auburn University, AL 36849. Offers MS, PhD. *Faculty:* 8 full-time (2 women). *Students:* 11 full-time (1 woman), 1 part-time (0 women), 9 international. Average age 25. 30 applicants, 60% accepted, 3 enrolled. In 2014, 4 master's, 3 doctorates awarded. *Degree requirements:* For master's, thesis optional. *Expenses:* Tuition, state resident: full-time $8586; part-time $477 per credit hour. Tuition, nonresident: full-time $25,758; part-time $1431 per credit hour. *Required fees:* $804 per semester. Tuition and fees vary according to degree level and program. *Financial support:* Unspecified assistantships available. *Unit head:* Maria Auad, Interim Head, 334-844-5452. *Application contact:* Dr. George Flowers, Dean of the Graduate School, 334-844-2125.
Website: http://www.eng.auburn.edu/programs/pfen/programs/grad/index.html.

California Polytechnic State University, San Luis Obispo, College of Science and Mathematics, Department of Chemistry and Biochemistry, San Luis Obispo, CA 93407. Offers polymers and coating science (MS). Part-time programs available. *Faculty:* 2 full-time (1 woman). *Students:* 8 full-time (5 women), 3 part-time (0 women); includes 2 minority (1 Asian, non-Hispanic/Latino; 1 Hispanic/Latino), 1 international. Average age 24. 11 applicants, 73% accepted, 5 enrolled. In 2014, 5 master's awarded. *Degree requirements:* For master's, comprehensive exam (for some programs), thesis (for some programs). *Application deadline:* For fall admission, 4/1 for domestic and international students; for winter admission, 11/1 for domestic students, 6/30 for international students; for spring admission, 2/1 for domestic students. Applications are processed on a rolling basis. Application fee: $55. Electronic applications accepted. *Expenses:* Tuition, state resident: full-time $6738; part-time $3906 per year. Tuition, nonresident: full-time $15,666; part-time $8370 per year. *Required fees:* $3447; $1001 per quarter. One-time fee: $3447 full-time; $3003 part-time. *Financial support:* Fellowships, research assistantships, career-related internships or fieldwork, Federal Work-Study, and scholarships/grants available. Support available to part-time students. Financial award application deadline: 3/2; financial award applicants required to submit FAFSA. *Faculty research:* Polymer physical chemistry and analysis, polymer synthesis, coatings formulation. *Unit head:* Dr. Ray Fernando, Graduate Coordinator, 805-756-2395, Fax: 805-756-5500, E-mail: rhfernan@calpoly.edu. *Application contact:* Dr. James

Maraviglia, Associate Vice Provost for Marketing and Enrollment Development, 805-756-2311, Fax: 805-756-5400, E-mail: admissions@calpoly.edu. Website: http://www.chemistry.calpoly.edu/.

Carnegie Mellon University, Carnegie Institute of Technology, Department of Chemical Engineering and Department of Chemistry, Program in Colloids, Polymers and Surfaces, Pittsburgh, PA 15213-3891. Offers MS. Part-time and evening/weekend programs available. *Entrance requirements:* For master's, GRE General Test, GRE Subject Test. Additional exam requirements/recommendations for international students: Required—TOEFL. *Faculty research:* Surface phenomena, polymer rheology, solubilization phenomena, colloid transport phenomena, polymer synthesis.

Case Western Reserve University, School of Graduate Studies, Case School of Engineering, Department of Macromolecular Science and Engineering, Cleveland, OH 44106. Offers MS, PhD, MD/PhD. Part-time programs available. *Faculty:* 14 full-time (2 women). *Students:* 87 full-time (26 women), 4 part-time (2 women); includes 12 minority (5 Black or African American, non-Hispanic/Latino; 3 Asian, non-Hispanic/Latino; 3 Hispanic/Latino; 1 Two or more races, non-Hispanic/Latino), 63 international. In 2014, 6 master's, 4 doctorates awarded. Terminal master's awarded for partial completion of doctoral program. *Degree requirements:* For master's, thesis; for doctorate, thesis/dissertation, qualifying exam, teaching experience. *Entrance requirements:* For master's and doctorate, GRE General Test. Additional exam requirements/recommendations for international students: Required—TOEFL. *Application deadline:* For fall admission, 2/28 priority date for domestic students; for spring admission, 10/1 priority date for domestic students. Applications are processed on a rolling basis. Application fee: $50. *Financial support:* In 2014–15, 4 fellowships, 56 research assistantships with full and partial tuition reimbursements were awarded. Financial award applicants required to submit FAFSA. *Faculty research:* Synthesis and molecular design; processing, modeling and simulation, structure-property relationships. *Total annual research expenditures:* $4.5 million. *Unit head:* Dr. David Schiraldi, Department Chair, 216-368-4243, Fax: 216-368-4202, E-mail: das44@case.edu. *Application contact:* Theresa Claytor, Student Affairs Coordinator, 216-368-8555, Fax: 216-368-8555, E-mail: theresa.claytor@case.edu. Website: http://polymers.case.edu.

The College of William and Mary, Faculty of Arts and Sciences, Department of Applied Science, Williamsburg, VA 23187-8795. Offers accelerator science (PhD); applied mathematics (PhD); applied mechanics (PhD); applied robotics (PhD); applied science (MS); interface, thin film and surface science (PhD); lasers and optics (PhD); magnetic resonance (PhD); nanotechnology (PhD); non-destructive evaluation (PhD); polymer chemistry (PhD); remote sensing (PhD). Part-time programs available. *Faculty:* 8 full-time (2 women), 2 part-time/adjunct (0 women). *Students:* 28 full-time (11 women), 5 part-time (2 women); includes 5 minority (2 Black or African American, non-Hispanic/Latino; 2 Asian, non-Hispanic/Latino; 1 Hispanic/Latino), 13 international. Average age 28. 32 applicants, 38% accepted, 7 enrolled. In 2014, 6 master's, 4 doctorates awarded. Terminal master's awarded for partial completion of doctoral program. *Degree requirements:* For master's, comprehensive exam, thesis; for doctorate, comprehensive exam, thesis/dissertation, 4 core courses. *Entrance requirements:* For master's and doctorate, GRE General Test, GRE Subject Test. Additional exam requirements/recommendations for international students: Required—TOEFL, TWE. *Application deadline:* For fall admission, 2/3 priority date for domestic students, 2/3 for international students; for spring admission, 10/15 priority date for domestic students, 10/14 for international students. Applications are processed on a rolling basis. Application fee: $45. Electronic applications accepted. *Financial support:* Fellowships, research assistantships, teaching assistantships, Federal Work-Study, health care benefits, tuition waivers (full), and unspecified assistantships available. Financial award application deadline: 4/15; financial award applicants required to submit FAFSA. *Faculty research:* Computational biology, non-destructive evaluation, neurophysiology, lasers and optics. *Total annual research expenditures:* $1.7 million. *Unit head:* Dr. Christopher Del Negro, Chair, 757-221-7808, Fax: 757-221-2050, E-mail: cadeln@wm.edu. *Application contact:* Lianne Rios Ashburne, Graduate Program Coordinator, 757-221-2563, Fax: 757-221-2050, E-mail: lrashburne@wm.edu. Website: http://www.wm.edu/as/appliedscience.

Cornell University, Graduate School, Graduate Fields of Engineering, Field of Chemical Engineering, Ithaca, NY 14853-0001. Offers advanced materials processing (M Eng, MS, PhD); applied mathematics and computational methods (M Eng, MS, PhD); biochemical engineering (M Eng, MS, PhD); chemical reaction engineering (M Eng, MS, PhD); classical and statistical thermodynamics (M Eng, MS, PhD); fluid dynamics, rheology and biorheology (M Eng, MS, PhD); heat and mass transfer (M Eng, MS, PhD); kinetics and catalysis (M Eng, MS, PhD); polymers (M Eng, MS, PhD); surface science (M Eng, MS, PhD). *Degree requirements:* For master's, thesis (MS); for doctorate, comprehensive exam, thesis/dissertation. *Entrance requirements:* For master's and doctorate, GRE General Test, 2 letters of recommendation. Additional exam requirements/recommendations for international students: Required—TOEFL (minimum score 600 paper-based; 77 iBT). Electronic applications accepted. *Faculty research:* Biochemical, biomedical and metabolic engineering; fluid and polymer dynamics; surface science and chemical kinetics; electronics materials; microchemical systems and nanotechnology.

Cornell University, Graduate School, Graduate Fields of Human Ecology, Field of Fiber Science and Apparel Design, Ithaca, NY 14853. Offers apparel design (MA, MPS); fiber science (MS, PhD); polymer science (MS, PhD); textile science (MS, PhD). *Degree requirements:* For master's, thesis (MA, MS), project paper (MPS); for doctorate, comprehensive exam, thesis/dissertation. *Entrance requirements:* For master's, GRE General Test, 2 letters of recommendation, portfolio (for functional apparel design); for doctorate, GRE General Test, 2 letters of recommendation. Additional exam requirements/recommendations for international students: Required—TOEFL (minimum score 600 paper-based; 77 iBT). Electronic applications accepted. *Faculty research:* Apparel design, consumption, mass customization, 3-D body scanning.

Eastern Michigan University, Graduate School, College of Technology, School of Engineering Technology, Programs in Polymers and Coatings Technology, Ypsilanti, MI 48197. Offers MS. Part-time and evening/weekend programs available. Postbaccalaureate distance learning degree programs offered (minimal on-campus study). *Students:* 4 full-time (2 women), 16 part-time (6 women), 13 international. Average age 28. 16 applicants, 56% accepted, 6 enrolled. In 2014, 7 master's awarded. *Degree requirements:* For master's, thesis optional. *Entrance requirements:* For master's, GRE General Test, BS in chemistry, minimum GPA of 2.6. Additional exam requirements/recommendations for international students: Required—TOEFL. *Application deadline:* Applications are processed on a rolling basis. Application fee: $45. *Financial support:* Fellowships, research assistantships with full tuition reimbursements, teaching assistantships with full tuition reimbursements, career-related internships or fieldwork, Federal Work-Study, institutionally sponsored loans, scholarships/grants, tuition waivers (partial), and unspecified assistantships available. Support available to part-time students. Financial award applicants required to submit FAFSA. *Application contact:* Dr. Vijay Mannari, Program Coordinator, 734-487-2040, Fax: 734-487-8755, E-mail: vijay.mannari@emich.edu.

Lehigh University, P.C. Rossin College of Engineering and Applied Science and College of Arts and Sciences, Center for Polymer Science and Engineering, Bethlehem,

PA 18015. Offers M Eng, MS, PhD. Part-time and evening/weekend programs available. Postbaccalaureate distance learning degree programs offered (no on-campus study). *Faculty:* 19 full-time (1 woman), 1 part-time/adjunct (0 women). *Students:* 2 full-time (1 woman), 17 part-time (2 women); includes 1 minority (Asian, non-Hispanic/Latino). Average age 31. 29 applicants, 21% accepted, 4 enrolled. In 2014, 4 master's, 3 doctorates awarded. Terminal master's awarded for partial completion of doctoral program. *Degree requirements:* For master's, thesis (for some programs); for doctorate, thesis/dissertation. *Entrance requirements:* For master's and doctorate, GRE General Test. Additional exam requirements/recommendations for international students: Required—TOEFL (minimum score 487 paper-based; 85 iBT). *Application deadline:* For fall admission, 7/15 for domestic students, 1/15 for international students; for spring admission, 12/1 for domestic and international students. Applications are processed on a rolling basis. Application fee: $75. Electronic applications accepted. *Financial support:* In 2014–15, 1 student received support, including 1 fellowship (averaging $26,500 per year), 1 research assistantship (averaging $1,000 per year). Financial award application deadline: 1/15. *Faculty research:* Polymer colloids, polymer coatings, blends and composites, polymer interfaces, emulsion polymer. *Unit head:* Dr. Raymond A. Pearson, Director, 610-758-3857, Fax: 610-758-3526, E-mail: rp02@lehigh.edu. *Application contact:* James E. Roberts, Chair, Polymer Education Committee, 610-758-4841, Fax: 610-758-6536, E-mail: jer1@lehigh.edu. Website: http://www.lehigh.edu/~inpcreng/academics/graduate/polymerscieng.html.

Lehigh University, P.C. Rossin College of Engineering and Applied Science, Department of Materials Science and Engineering, Bethlehem, PA 18015. Offers materials science and engineering (M Eng, MS, PhD); photonics (MS); polymer science/engineering (M Eng, MS, PhD); MBA/E. Part-time programs available. *Faculty:* 14 full-time (3 women), 1 part-time/adjunct (0 women). *Students:* 28 full-time (9 women), 8 part-time (0 women); includes 3 minority (2 Asian, non-Hispanic/Latino; 1 Two or more races, non-Hispanic/Latino), 15 international. Average age 27. 238 applicants, 3% accepted, 4 enrolled. In 2014, 3 master's, 5 doctorates awarded. *Degree requirements:* For master's, thesis; for doctorate, comprehensive exam, thesis/dissertation. *Entrance requirements:* For master's and doctorate, GRE General Test. Additional exam requirements/recommendations for international students: Required—TOEFL (minimum score 487 paper-based; 85 iBT). *Application deadline:* For fall admission, 1/15 priority date for domestic students, 1/15 for international students; for spring admission, 12/1 priority date for domestic students, 12/1 for international students. Applications are processed on a rolling basis. Application fee: $75. Electronic applications accepted. *Financial support:* In 2014–15, 26 students received support, including 3 fellowships with full and partial tuition reimbursements available (averaging $19,920 per year), 22 research assistantships with full and partial tuition reimbursements available (averaging $25,550 per year), 6 teaching assistantships with full and partial tuition reimbursements available (averaging $20,490 per year); career-related internships or fieldwork, Federal Work-Study, institutionally sponsored loans, scholarships/grants, and unspecified assistantships also available. Support available to part-time students. Financial award application deadline: 1/15. *Faculty research:* Metals, ceramics, crystals, polymers, fatigue crack propagation, biomaterials. *Total annual research expenditures:* $4.2 million. *Unit head:* Dr. Helen Chan, Chairperson, 610-758-5554, Fax: 610-758-4244, E-mail: hmc0@lehigh.edu. *Application contact:* Lisa Carreras Arechiga, Graduate Administrative Coordinator, 610-758-4222, Fax: 610-758-4244, E-mail: lia4@lehigh.edu. Website: http://www.lehigh.edu/~inmatsci/.

North Carolina State University, Graduate School, College of Textiles, Program in Fiber and Polymer Science, Raleigh, NC 27695. Offers PhD. *Degree requirements:* For doctorate, one foreign language, thesis/dissertation, cumulative exams. *Entrance requirements:* For doctorate, GRE. Electronic applications accepted. *Faculty research:* Polymer science, fiber mechanics, medical textiles, nanotechnology.

North Dakota State University, College of Graduate and Interdisciplinary Studies, College of Science and Mathematics, Department of Coatings and Polymeric Materials, Fargo, ND 58108. Offers MS, PhD. Part-time programs available. Terminal master's awarded for partial completion of doctoral program. *Degree requirements:* For master's, thesis, cumulative exams; for doctorate, comprehensive exam, thesis/dissertation, cumulative exams. *Entrance requirements:* For master's and doctorate, BS in chemistry or chemical engineering, minimum GPA of 3.0. Additional exam requirements/recommendations for international students: Required—TOEFL (minimum score 550 paper-based). Electronic applications accepted. *Faculty research:* Nanomaterials, combinatorial materials science.

Pittsburg State University, Graduate School, College of Arts and Sciences, Department of Chemistry, Pittsburg, KS 66762. Offers chemistry (MS); polymer chemistry (MS). *Degree requirements:* For master's, thesis or alternative.

Stevens Institute of Technology, Graduate School, Charles V. Schaefer Jr. School of Engineering, Department of Chemistry, Chemical Biology and Biomedical Engineering, Hoboken, NJ 07030. Offers analytical chemistry (PhD, Certificate); bioinformatics (PhD, Certificate); biomedical chemistry (Certificate); biomedical engineering (M Eng, Certificate); chemical biology (MS, PhD, Certificate); chemical physiology (Certificate); chemistry (MS, PhD); organic chemistry (PhD); physical chemistry (PhD); polymer chemistry (PhD, Certificate). Part-time and evening/weekend programs available. Postbaccalaureate distance learning degree programs offered (no on-campus study). Terminal master's awarded for partial completion of doctoral program. *Degree requirements:* For master's, thesis or alternative; for doctorate, one foreign language, thesis/dissertation; for Certificate, project or thesis. *Entrance requirements:* Additional exam requirements/recommendations for international students: Required—TOEFL. Electronic applications accepted. *Faculty research:* Biochemical reaction engineering, polymerization engineering, reactor design, biochemical process control and synthesis.

The University of Akron, Graduate School, College of Polymer Science and Polymer Engineering, Department of Polymer Engineering, Akron, OH 44325. Offers MS, PhD. Part-time and evening/weekend programs available. *Faculty:* 15 full-time (2 women), 4 part-time/adjunct (2 women). *Students:* 141 full-time (46 women), 16 part-time (3 women); includes 5 minority (1 Black or African American, non-Hispanic/Latino; 2 Asian, non-Hispanic/Latino; 1 Hispanic/Latino; 1 Two or more races, non-Hispanic/Latino), 126 international. Average age 25. 157 applicants, 43% accepted, 60 enrolled. In 2014, 22 master's, 16 doctorates awarded. *Degree requirements:* For master's, thesis, basic engineering exam; for doctorate, one foreign language, thesis/dissertation, candidacy exam. *Entrance requirements:* For master's and doctorate, GRE, bachelor's degree in engineering or physical science, minimum GPA of 2.75 (3.0 in last two years), three letters of recommendation, statement of purpose. Additional exam requirements/recommendations for international students: Required—TOEFL (minimum score 550 paper-based; 79 iBT), IELTS (minimum score 6.5). *Application deadline:* For fall admission, 1/15 priority date for domestic and international students. Application fee: $45 ($70 for international students). Electronic applications accepted. *Expenses:* Tuition, state resident: full-time $7578; part-time $421 per credit hour. Tuition, nonresident: full-time $12,977; part-time $721 per credit hour. *Required fees:* $1388; $35 per credit hour. Tuition and fees vary according to course load. *Financial support:* In 2014–15, 87 research assistantships with full tuition reimbursements, 2 teaching assistantships with full tuition reimbursements were awarded. *Faculty research:*

Polymer Science and Engineering

Processing and properties of multi-functional polymeric materials, nanomaterials and nanocomposites, micro and nano-scale materials processing, novel self-assembled polymeric materials for energy applications, coating materials and coating technology. *Total annual research expenditures:* $4.8 million. *Unit head:* Dr. Robert Weiss, Chair, 330-972-2581, E-mail: rweiss@uakron.edu. *Application contact:* Sarah Thorley, Coordinator of Academic Program, 330-972-8845, E-mail: sarah3@uakron.edu.
Website: http://www.uakron.edu/dpe/.

The University of Akron, Graduate School, College of Polymer Science and Polymer Engineering, Department of Polymer Science, Akron, OH 44325. Offers MS, PhD. Part-time and evening/weekend programs available. *Faculty:* 19 full-time (2 women), 1 part-time/adjunct (0 women). *Students:* 187 full-time (61 women), 9 part-time (4 women); includes 10 minority (5 Black or African American, non-Hispanic/Latino; 5 Asian, non-Hispanic/Latino), 153 international. Average age 25. 139 applicants, 47% accepted, 61 enrolled. In 2014, 32 master's, 20 doctorates awarded. Terminal master's awarded for partial completion of doctoral program. *Degree requirements:* For master's, thesis; for doctorate, one foreign language, thesis/dissertation, cumulative exam, seminars. *Entrance requirements:* For master's and doctorate, GRE, minimum GPA of 3.0, three letters of recommendation, statement of purpose. Additional exam requirements/recommendations for international students: Required—TOEFL (minimum score 550 paper-based; 79 iBT), IELTS (minimum score 6.5). *Application deadline:* For fall admission, 12/1 priority date for domestic students, 12/15 priority date for international students. Application fee: $45 ($70 for international students). Electronic applications accepted. *Expenses:* Tuition, state resident: full-time $7578; part-time $421 per credit hour. Tuition, nonresident: full-time $12,977; part-time $721 per credit hour. *Required fees:* $1388; $35 per credit hour. Tuition and fees vary according to course load. *Financial support:* In 2014–15, 1 fellowship with full tuition reimbursement, 122 research assistantships with full tuition reimbursements were awarded; scholarships/grants also available. *Faculty research:* Synthesis of polymers, structure of polymers, physical properties of polymers, engineering and technological properties of polymers, elastomers. *Total annual research expenditures:* $9.4 million. *Unit head:* Dr. Coleen Pugh, Interim Chair, 330-972-6614, E-mail: cpugh@uakron.edu. *Application contact:* Melissa Bowman, Coordinator, Academic Programs, 330-972-7532, E-mail: mb8@uakron.edu.
Website: http://www.uakron.edu/dps/.

University of Connecticut, Institute of Materials Science, Polymer Program, Storrs, CT 06269-3136. Offers polymer science and engineering (MS, PhD). Part-time programs available. Terminal master's awarded for partial completion of doctoral program. *Degree requirements:* For master's, thesis (for some programs); for doctorate, one foreign language, comprehensive exam, thesis/dissertation. *Entrance requirements:* For master's and doctorate, GRE General Test. Additional exam requirements/recommendations for international students: Required—TOEFL (minimum score 550 paper-based; 80 iBT), IELTS (minimum score 6.5). Electronic applications accepted. *Faculty research:* Nanomaterials and nanotechnology, biomaterials and sensors, synthesis, electronic/photonic materials, solar cells and fuel cells, structure and function of proteins, biodegradable polymers, molecular simulations, drug targeting and delivery.

The University of Manchester, School of Materials, Manchester, United Kingdom. Offers advanced aerospace materials engineering (M Sc); advanced metallic systems (PhD); biomedical materials (M Phil, M Sc, PhD); ceramics and glass (M Phil, M Sc, PhD); composite materials (M Sc, PhD); corrosion and protection (M Phil, M Sc, PhD); materials (M Phil, PhD); metallic materials (M Phil, M Sc, PhD); nanostructural materials (M Phil, M Sc, PhD); paper science (M Phil, M Sc, PhD); polymer science and engineering (M Phil, M Sc, PhD); technical textiles (M Sc); textile design, fashion and management (M Phil, M Sc, PhD); textile science and technology (M Phil, M Sc, PhD); textiles (M Phil, PhD); textiles and fashion (M Ent).

University of Massachusetts Amherst, Graduate School, College of Natural Sciences, Department of Polymer Science and Engineering, Amherst, MA 01003. Offers MS, PhD. *Faculty:* 16 full-time (0 women). *Students:* 102 full-time (37 women), 3 part-time (1 woman); includes 14 minority (2 Black or African American, non-Hispanic/Latino; 7 Asian, non-Hispanic/Latino; 3 Hispanic/Latino; 2 Two or more races, non-Hispanic/Latino), 49 international. Average age 26. 194 applicants, 14% accepted, 12 enrolled. In 2014, 21 master's, 15 doctorates awarded. Terminal master's awarded for partial completion of doctoral program. *Degree requirements:* For master's, thesis or alternative; for doctorate, comprehensive exam, thesis/dissertation. *Entrance requirements:* For master's and doctorate, GRE General Test. Additional exam requirements/recommendations for international students: Required—TOEFL (minimum score 550 paper-based; 80 iBT), IELTS (minimum score 6.5). *Application deadline:* For fall admission, 1/2 for domestic and international students. Applications are processed on a rolling basis. Application fee: $75. Electronic applications accepted. *Expenses:* Tuition, state resident: full-time $1980; part-time $110 per credit. Tuition, nonresident: full-time $14,644; part-time $414 per credit. *Required fees:* $11,417. One-time fee: $357. *Financial support:* Fellowships with full and partial tuition reimbursements, research assistantships with full and partial tuition reimbursements, teaching assistantships with full and partial tuition reimbursements, career-related internships or fieldwork, Federal Work-Study, scholarships/grants, traineeships, health care benefits, tuition waivers (full and partial), and unspecified assistantships available. Support available to part-time students. Financial award application deadline: 1/2. *Unit head:* Dr. Gregory Tew, Graduate Program Director, 413-577-9120, Fax: 413-545-0082. *Application contact:* Lindsay DeSantis, Supervisor of Admissions, 413-545-0722, Fax: 413-577-0010, E-mail: gradadm@grad.umass.edu.
Website: http://www.pse.umass.edu/.

University of Massachusetts Lowell, College of Sciences, Department of Chemistry, Program in Polymer Science, Lowell, MA 01854. Offers MS. *Degree requirements:* For master's, thesis. *Entrance requirements:* For master's, GRE General Test. Electronic applications accepted.

University of Massachusetts Lowell, Francis College of Engineering, Department of Plastics Engineering, Lowell, MA 01854. Offers elastomers (Graduate Certificate); medical plastics design and manufacturing (Graduate Certificate); plastics design (Graduate Certificate); plastics engineering (MS Eng, D Eng, PhD), including coatings and adhesives (MS Eng), plastics materials (MS Eng), plastics processing (MS Eng), product design (MS Eng); plastics engineering fundamentals (Graduate Certificate); plastics materials (Graduate Certificate); plastics processing (Graduate Certificate); polymer science/plastics engineering (PhD). Part-time programs available. Terminal master's awarded for partial completion of doctoral program. *Degree requirements:* For master's, thesis optional; for doctorate, comprehensive exam, thesis/dissertation. *Entrance requirements:* For master's and doctorate, GRE General Test. Additional exam requirements/recommendations for international students: Required—TOEFL.

University of Missouri–Kansas City, College of Arts and Sciences, Department of Chemistry, Kansas City, MO 64110-2499. Offers analytical chemistry (MS, PhD); inorganic chemistry (MS, PhD); organic chemistry (MS, PhD); physical chemistry (MS, PhD); polymer chemistry (MS, PhD). PhD (interdisciplinary) offered through the School of Graduate Studies. Part-time and evening/weekend programs available. *Faculty:* 14 full-time (2 women), 1 part-time/adjunct (0 women). *Students:* 2 full-time (1 woman), 4 part-time (1 woman); includes 1 minority (Black or African American, non-Hispanic/Latino), 1 international. Average age 37. 20 applicants, 50% accepted, 1 enrolled. In 2014, 4 master's awarded. *Degree requirements:* For master's, thesis (for some programs); for doctorate, thesis/dissertation. *Entrance requirements:* For master's, equivalent of American Chemical Society approved bachelor's degree in chemistry; for doctorate, GRE General Test, equivalent of American Chemical Society approved bachelor's degree in chemistry. Additional exam requirements/recommendations for international students: Required—TOEFL (minimum score 550 paper-based; 80 iBT), TWE. *Application deadline:* For fall admission, 4/15 for domestic and international students; for spring admission, 10/15 for domestic and international students. Applications are processed on a rolling basis. Application fee: $45 ($50 for international students). Electronic applications accepted. *Financial support:* In 2014–15, 5 research assistantships with partial tuition reimbursements (averaging $20,163 per year), 23 teaching assistantships with partial tuition reimbursements (averaging $19,202 per year) were awarded; Federal Work-Study, institutionally sponsored loans, and scholarships/grants also available. Support available to part-time students. Financial award application deadline: 3/1; financial award applicants required to submit FAFSA. *Faculty research:* Molecular spectroscopy, characterization and synthesis of materials and compounds, computational chemistry, natural products, drug delivery systems and anti-tumor agents. *Unit head:* Dr. Kathleen V. Kilway, Chair, 816-235-2289, Fax: 816-235-5502, E-mail: kilwayk@umkc.edu. *Application contact:* Graduate Recruiting Committee, 816-235-2272, Fax: 816-235-5502, E-mail: umkc-chemdept@umkc.edu.

University of Southern Mississippi, Graduate School, College of Science and Technology, School of Polymers and High Performance Materials, Hattiesburg, MS 39406-0001. Offers polymer science (MS); polymer science and engineering (MS, PhD), including polymer science and engineering (PhD), sports and high performance materials. Terminal master's awarded for partial completion of doctoral program. *Degree requirements:* For master's, comprehensive exam, thesis; for doctorate, comprehensive exam, thesis/dissertation, original proposal. *Entrance requirements:* For master's, GRE General Test, minimum GPA of 2.75; for doctorate, GRE General Test, minimum GPA of 3.5. Additional exam requirements/recommendations for international students: Required—TOEFL, IELTS. Electronic applications accepted. *Faculty research:* Water-soluble polymers; polymer composites; coatings; solid-state, laser-initiated polymerization.

The University of Tennessee, Graduate School, College of Engineering, Department of Materials Science and Engineering, Program in Polymer Engineering, Knoxville, TN 37996. Offers MS, PhD. *Faculty:* 5 full-time (1 woman). *Students:* 1 full-time (0 women), all international. Average age 34. In 2014, 4 doctorates awarded. *Degree requirements:* For master's, thesis or alternative; for doctorate, comprehensive exam, thesis/dissertation. *Entrance requirements:* For master's, GRE General Test (for MS students pursuing research thesis), minimum GPA of 2.7 (for U.S. degree holders), 3.0 (for international degree holders); 3 references; for doctorate, GRE General Test (for all PhD candidates), minimum GPA of 3.0 on previous graduate course work; 3 references. Additional exam requirements/recommendations for international students: Required—TOEFL (minimum score 550 paper-based). *Application deadline:* For fall admission, 2/1 priority date for domestic and international students; for spring admission, 6/15 for domestic and international students. Applications are processed on a rolling basis. Application fee: $35. Electronic applications accepted. *Financial support:* In 2014–15, 1 student received support, including 1 research assistantship with full tuition reimbursement available (averaging $20,200 per year); fellowships with full tuition reimbursements available, teaching assistantships with full tuition reimbursements available, career-related internships or fieldwork, Federal Work-Study, institutionally sponsored loans, health care benefits, and unspecified assistantships also available. Financial award application deadline: 2/1; financial award applicants required to submit FAFSA. *Faculty research:* Polymer chemistry, processing, and characterization. *Unit head:* Dr. Kurt Sickafus, Head, 865-974-4858, Fax: 865-974-4115, E-mail: kurt@utk.edu. *Application contact:* Dr. Roberto S. Benson, Associate Head, 865-974-5347, Fax: 865-974-4115, E-mail: rbenson1@utk.edu.
Website: http://www.engr.utk.edu/mse.

University of Wisconsin–Madison, Graduate School, College of Engineering, Department of Mechanical Engineering, Madison, WI 53706-1380. Offers mechanical engineering (MS, PhD); polymers (ME). Part-time programs available. Postbaccalaureate distance learning degree programs offered (no on-campus study). *Faculty:* 30 full-time (3 women), 1 part-time/adjunct (0 women). *Students:* 217 full-time (26 women), 31 part-time (0 women); includes 19 minority (1 Black or African American, non-Hispanic/Latino; 1 American Indian or Alaska Native, non-Hispanic/Latino; 9 Asian, non-Hispanic/Latino; 7 Hispanic/Latino; 1 Native Hawaiian or other Pacific Islander, non-Hispanic/Latino). Average age 27. 615 applicants, 19% accepted, 49 enrolled. In 2014, 67 master's, 10 doctorates awarded. Terminal master's awarded for partial completion of doctoral program. *Degree requirements:* For master's, thesis optional; for doctorate, thesis/dissertation, qualifying exam, preliminary exam, final oral defense. *Entrance requirements:* For master's, GRE, BS in mechanical engineering or related field, minimum GPA of 3.0 in last 60 hours of course work; for doctorate, GRE, BS in mechanical engineering or related field, minimum undergraduate GPA of 3.0 in last 60 hours of course work. Additional exam requirements/recommendations for international students: Required—TOEFL (minimum score 550 paper-based; 80 iBT). *Application deadline:* For fall admission, 8/1 for domestic students, 6/1 for international students; for spring admission, 1/1 for domestic students, 11/1 for international students; for summer admission, 5/1 for domestic students, 3/1 for international students. Applications are processed on a rolling basis. Application fee: $56. Electronic applications accepted. *Expenses:* Tuition, state resident: full-time $10,723; part-time $745 per credit. Tuition, nonresident: full-time $24,054; part-time $1578 per credit. *Required fees:* $374 per semester. Tuition and fees vary according to course load, program and reciprocity agreements. *Financial support:* In 2014–15, 150 students received support, including 6 fellowships with full tuition reimbursements available (averaging $45,000 per year), 294 research assistantships with full tuition reimbursements available (averaging $21,000 per year), 97 teaching assistantships with full tuition reimbursements available (averaging $10,500 per year); career-related internships or fieldwork, institutionally sponsored loans, scholarships/grants, traineeships, health care benefits, and unspecified assistantships also available. Financial award application deadline: 5/31. *Faculty research:* Design and manufacturing, materials processing, combustion, energy systems nanotechnology. *Total annual research expenditures:* $16 million. *Unit head:* Jaal B. Ghandhi, Chair, 608-263-1684, E-mail: ghandhi@engr.wisc.edu. *Application contact:* Theresa J. Pillar-Groesbeck, Advisor to Graduate Students, 608-263-3955, Fax: 608-890-2204, E-mail: pillar@wisc.edu.
Website: http://www.engr.wisc.edu/me/.

Wayne State University, College of Engineering, Department of Chemical Engineering and Materials Science, Program in Materials Science and Engineering, Detroit, MI 48202. Offers materials science and engineering (MS, PhD); polymer engineering (Graduate Certificate). Part-time programs available. *Students:* 13 full-time (5 women), 8 part-time (5 women); includes 2 minority (1 Black or African American, non-Hispanic/Latino; 1 Asian, non-Hispanic/Latino), 14 international. Average age 27. 60 applicants, 35% accepted, 7 enrolled. In 2014, 1 master's, 3 doctorates awarded. *Degree requirements:* For master's, thesis optional; for doctorate, thesis/dissertation. *Entrance requirements:* For master's, GRE (if applying for financial support), recommendations;

resume; bachelor's degree in engineering or the physical scienes with minimum GPA of 3.0; for doctorate, GRE, recommendations; resume, personal statement, minimum GPA of 3.5 in MS program, or BS from accredited U.S. institution. Additional exam requirements/recommendations for international students: Required—TOEFL (minimum score 550 paper-based; 79 iBT), TWE (minimum score 5.5), Michigan English Language Assessment Battery (minimum score 85); Recommended—IELTS (minimum score 6.5). *Application deadline:* For fall admission, 6/1 priority date for domestic students, 5/1 priority date for international students; for winter admission, 10/1 priority date for domestic students, 9/1 priority date for international students; for spring admission, 2/1 priority date for domestic students, 1/1 priority date for international students. Applications are processed on a rolling basis. Application fee: $0. Electronic applications accepted. *Expenses:* Expenses: Contact institution. *Financial support:* In 2014–15, 13 students received support. Fellowships with tuition reimbursements available, research assistantships with tuition reimbursements available, teaching assistantships with tuition reimbursements available, scholarships/grants, health care benefits, and unspecified assistantships available. Support available to part-time students. Financial award application deadline: 3/31; financial award applicants required to submit FAFSA. *Faculty research:* Polymer science, rheology, fatigue in metals, metal matrix composites, ceramics. *Unit head:* Dr. Charles Manke, Chair, 313-577-3849, Fax: 313-577-3810, E-mail: cmanke@eng.wayne.edu. *Application contact:* Dr. Guangzhao Mao, Director of Materials Science Graduate Program, 313-577-3804, E-mail: gzmao@eng.wayne.edu. Website: http://engineering.wayne.edu/che/.

Section 17
Mechanical Engineering and Mechanics

This section contains a directory of institutions offering graduate work in mechanical engineering and mechanics. Additional information about programs listed in the directory may be obtained by writing directly to the dean of a graduate school or chair of a department at the address given in the directory.

For programs offering related work, see also in this book *Engineering and Applied Sciences, Management of Engineering and Technology,* and *Materials Sciences and Engineering.* In another guide in this series:

Graduate Programs in the Physical Sciences, Mathematics, Agricultural Sciences, the Environment & Natural Resources
See *Geosciences* and *Physics*

CONTENTS

Program Directories

Mechanical Engineering

Alfred University, Graduate School, New York State College of Ceramics, Kazuo Inamori School of Engineering, Alfred, NY 14802. Offers biomaterials engineering (MS); ceramic engineering (MS); ceramics (PhD); electrical engineering (MS); glass science (MS, PhD); materials science and engineering (MS, PhD); mechanical engineering (MS). Part-time programs available. *Degree requirements:* For master's, thesis; for doctorate, thesis/dissertation. *Entrance requirements:* Additional exam requirements/recommendations for international students: Required—TOEFL (minimum score 590 paper-based; 90 iBT), IELTS (minimum score 6.5). Electronic applications accepted. *Expenses:* Contact institution. *Faculty research:* X-ray diffraction, biomaterials and polymers, thin-film processing, electronic and optical ceramics, solid-state chemistry.

The American University in Cairo, School of Sciences and Engineering, Department of Mechanical Engineering, Cairo, Egypt. Offers mechanical engineering (MS); product development and systems management (M Eng). Tuition and fees vary according to course load and program.

American University of Beirut, Graduate Programs, Faculty of Engineering and Architecture, Beirut, Lebanon. Offers applied energy (ME); civil engineering (PhD); electrical and computer engineering (PhD); engineering management (MEM); environmental and water resources (ME); environmental technology (MSES); mechanical engineering (ME, PhD); urban design (MUD); urban planning and policy (MUPP). Part-time programs available. *Faculty:* 93 full-time (18 women), 3 part-time/ adjunct (1 woman). *Students:* 268 full-time (111 women), 58 part-time (27 women). Average age 26. 225 applicants, 68% accepted, 79 enrolled. In 2014, 114 master's, 9 doctorates awarded. Terminal master's awarded for partial completion of doctoral program. *Degree requirements:* For master's, one foreign language, comprehensive exam, thesis (for some programs); for doctorate, one foreign language, comprehensive exam, thesis/dissertation, publications. *Entrance requirements:* For master's, letters of recommendation; for doctorate, GRE, letters of recommendation, master's degree, transcripts, curriculum vitae, interview. Additional exam requirements/recommendations for international students: Required—TOEFL (minimum score 600 paper-based; 100 iBT), IELTS (minimum score 7.5). *Application deadline:* For fall admission, 2/5 priority date for domestic and international students; for spring admission, 11/1 priority date for domestic students, 11/1 for international students. Application fee: $50. Electronic applications accepted. *Expenses: Tuition:* Full-time $15,462; part-time $859 per credit. *Required fees:* $692. Tuition and fees vary according to course load and program. *Financial support:* In 2014–15, 190 students received support, including 2 fellowships with full tuition reimbursements available (averaging $24,800 per year), 64 research assistantships with full tuition reimbursements available (averaging $24,800 per year), 124 teaching assistantships with full tuition reimbursements available (averaging $9,800 per year); career-related internships or fieldwork, institutionally sponsored loans, scholarships/grants, health care benefits, and unspecified assistantships also available. *Total annual research expenditures:* $1.5 million. *Unit head:* Prof. Makram T. Suidan, Dean, 961-1350000 Ext. 3400, Fax: 961-1744462, E-mail: msuidan@aub.edu.lb. *Application contact:* Dr. Salim Kanaan, Director, Admissions Office, 961-1350000 Ext. 2594, Fax: 961-1750775, E-mail: sk00@aub.edu.lb.
Website: http://staff.aub.edu.lb/~webfea.

American University of Sharjah, Graduate Programs, Sharjah, United Arab Emirates. Offers accounting (MS); business (EMBA, MBA); chemical engineering (MS Ch E); civil engineering (MSCE); computer engineering (MS); electrical engineering (MSEE); engineering systems management (MS); mathematics (MS); mechanical engineering (MSME); mechatronics engineering (MS); teaching English to speakers of other languages (MA); translation and interpreting (MA); urban planning (MUP). Part-time and evening/weekend programs available. *Degree requirements:* For master's, thesis (for some programs). *Entrance requirements:* For master's, GMAT (for MBA). Additional exam requirements/recommendations for international students: Required—TOEFL (minimum score 550 paper-based; 80 iBT), TWE (minimum score 5); Recommended— IELTS (minimum score 6.5). Electronic applications accepted. *Faculty research:* Water pollution, management and waste water treatment, energy and sustainability, air pollution, Islamic finance, family business and small and medium enterprises.

Arizona State University at the Tempe campus, Ira A. Fulton Schools of Engineering, The Polytechnic School, Program in Engineering Technology, Mesa, AZ 85212. Offers manufacturing engineering technology (MS). Part-time and evening/weekend programs available. *Degree requirements:* For master's, thesis or applied project and oral defense, final examination, interactive Program of Study (iPOS) submitted before completing 50 percent of required credit hours. *Entrance requirements:* For master's, bachelor's degree with minimum of 30 credit hours or equivalent in a technology area including course work applicable to the concentration being sought and minimum of 16 credit hours of math and science; industrial experience beyond bachelor's degree (recommended). Additional exam requirements/recommendations for international students: Required—TOEFL, IELTS, or PTE. Electronic applications accepted. *Faculty research:* Manufacturing modeling and simulation &ITsmart&RO and composite materials, optimization of turbine engines, machinability and manufacturing processes design, fuel cells and other alternative energy sources.

Arizona State University at the Tempe campus, Ira A. Fulton Schools of Engineering, School for Engineering of Matter, Transport and Energy, Tempe, AZ 85281. Offers aerospace engineering (MS, PhD); chemical engineering (MS, PhD); materials science and engineering (MS, PhD); mechanical engineering (MS, PhD); solar energy engineering and commercialization (PSM). Part-time and evening/weekend programs available. Postbaccalaureate distance learning degree programs offered (minimal on-campus study). Terminal master's awarded for partial completion of doctoral program. *Degree requirements:* For master's, thesis and oral defense (MS); applied project or comprehensive exam (MSE); interactive Program of Study (iPOS) submitted before completing 50 percent of required credit hours; for doctorate, comprehensive exam, thesis/dissertation, interactive Program of Study (iPOS) submitted before completing 50 percent of required credit hours. *Entrance requirements:* For master's, GRE, minimum GPA of 3.0 or equivalent in last 2 years of work leading to bachelor's degree; for doctorate, GRE, minimum GPA of 3.0 in last 2 years of work leading to bachelor's degree. Additional exam requirements/recommendations for international students: Required—TOEFL, IELTS, or PTE. Electronic applications accepted. *Expenses:* Contact institution. *Faculty research:* Electronic materials and packaging, materials for energy (batteries), adaptive/intelligent materials and structures, multiscale fluid mechanics, membranes, therapeutics and bioseparations, flexible structures, nanostructured materials, and micro/nano transport.

Auburn University, Graduate School, Ginn College of Engineering, Department of Mechanical Engineering, Auburn University, AL 36849. Offers materials engineering (M Mtl E, MS, PhD); mechanical engineering (MME, MS, PhD). Part-time programs available. *Faculty:* 29 full-time (0 women), 1 part-time/adjunct (0 women). *Students:* 91 full-time (17 women), 69 part-time (10 women); includes 9 minority (1 Black or African American, non-Hispanic/Latino; 4 Asian, non-Hispanic/Latino; 4 Hispanic/Latino), 88

international. Average age 27. 216 applicants, 57% accepted, 39 enrolled. In 2014, 22 master's, 10 doctorates awarded. *Degree requirements:* For master's, thesis (for some programs); for doctorate, one foreign language, thesis/dissertation. *Entrance requirements:* For master's and doctorate, GRE General Test. *Application deadline:* For fall admission, 7/7 for domestic students; for spring admission, 11/24 for domestic students. Applications are processed on a rolling basis. Application fee: $50 ($60 for international students). *Expenses:* Tuition, state resident: full-time $8586; part-time $477 per credit hour. Tuition, nonresident: full-time $25,758; part-time $1431 per credit hour. *Required fees:* $804 per semester. Tuition and fees vary according to degree level and program. *Financial support:* Fellowships, research assistantships, teaching assistantships, and Federal Work-Study available. Support available to part-time students. Financial award application deadline: 3/15; financial award applicants required to submit FAFSA. *Faculty research:* Engineering mechanics, experimental mechanics, engineering design, engineering acoustics, engineering optics. *Unit head:* Dr. Jeff Suhling, Chair, 334-844-3332. *Application contact:* Dr. George Flowers, Dean of the Graduate School, 334-844-2125.
Website: http://www.eng.auburn.edu/department/me/.

Baylor University, Graduate School, School of Engineering and Computer Science, Department of Mechanical Engineering, Waco, TX 76798. Offers biomedical engineering (MSBME); engineering (ME); mechanical engineering (MS). Part-time programs available. *Degree requirements:* For master's, thesis (for some programs). *Entrance requirements:* For master's, GRE. Additional exam requirements/ recommendations for international students: Required—TOEFL (minimum score 550 paper-based; 80 iBT), IELTS (minimum score 6.5), PTE (minimum score 58). Electronic applications accepted.

Binghamton University, State University of New York, Graduate School, Thomas J. Watson School of Engineering and Applied Science, Department of Mechanical Engineering, Vestal, NY 13850. Offers M Eng, MS, PhD. Part-time and evening/ weekend programs available. *Faculty:* 21 full-time (1 woman), 6 part-time/adjunct (0 women). *Students:* 68 full-time (6 women), 30 part-time (4 women); includes 9 minority (1 Black or African American, non-Hispanic/Latino; 7 Asian, non-Hispanic/Latino; 1 Native Hawaiian or other Pacific Islander, non-Hispanic/Latino), 65 international. Average age 26. 185 applicants, 69% accepted, 38 enrolled. In 2014, 18 master's, 8 doctorates awarded. *Degree requirements:* For master's, thesis (for some programs); for doctorate, comprehensive exam, thesis/dissertation. *Entrance requirements:* For master's and doctorate, GRE General Test. Additional exam requirements/ recommendations for international students: Required—TOEFL (minimum score 550 paper-based; 80 iBT). *Application deadline:* For fall admission, 4/15 priority date for domestic students, 1/15 priority date for international students; for spring admission, 11/ 1 for domestic students, 10/1 priority date for international students. Applications are processed on a rolling basis. Application fee: $75. Electronic applications accepted. *Expenses:* Expenses: $5,435 resident; $11,105 non-resident. *Financial support:* In 2014–15, 39 students received support, including 21 research assistantships with full tuition reimbursements available (averaging $16,500 per year), 15 teaching assistantships with full tuition reimbursements available (averaging $16,500 per year); career-related internships or fieldwork, Federal Work-Study, institutionally sponsored loans, scholarships/grants, health care benefits, tuition waivers (full), and unspecified assistantships also available. Financial award application deadline: 2/15; financial award applicants required to submit FAFSA. *Unit head:* Ellen Tilden, Coordinator of Graduate Studies, 607-777-2873, E-mail: etilden@binghamton.edu. *Application contact:* Kishan Zuber, Recruiting and Admissions Coordinator, 607-777-2151, Fax: 607-777-2501, E-mail: kzuber@binghamton.edu.

Boise State University, College of Engineering, Department of Mechanical and Biomedical Engineering, Boise, ID 83725-0399. Offers mechanical engineering (M Engr, MS). Part-time and evening/weekend programs available. *Faculty:* 9 full-time, 5 part-time/adjunct. *Students:* 10 full-time (4 women), 5 part-time (0 women); includes 1 minority (Two or more races, non-Hispanic/Latino). 15 applicants, 67% accepted, 5 enrolled. In 2014, 7 master's awarded. *Degree requirements:* For master's, thesis. *Entrance requirements:* For master's, GRE General Test, minimum GPA of 3.0. Additional exam requirements/recommendations for international students: Required— TOEFL. *Application deadline:* For fall admission, 7/17 priority date for domestic students; for spring admission, 12/5 priority date for domestic students. Applications are processed on a rolling basis. Application fee: $55. Electronic applications accepted. *Expenses:* Tuition, state resident: part-time $331 per credit hour. Tuition, nonresident: part-time $531 per credit hour. *Financial support:* In 2014–15, 6 students received support, including 4 research assistantships, 1 teaching assistantship. Financial award application deadline: 3/1; financial award applicants required to submit FAFSA. *Unit head:* Dr. Don Plumlee, Department Chair, 208-426-3575, E-mail: dplumlee@ boisestate.edu. *Application contact:* Dr. John Gardner, Coordinator, 208-426-5702, E-mail: jgardner@boisestate.edu.
Website: http://coen.boisestate.edu/mbe/students/graduate-students/.

Boston University, College of Engineering, Department of Mechanical Engineering, Boston, MA 02215. Offers manufacturing engineering (MS); mechanical engineering (MS, PhD); mechanical engineering with engineering practice (MS); MS/MBA. Part-time programs available. Postbaccalaureate distance learning degree programs offered (no on-campus study). *Faculty:* 38 full-time (5 women), 1 part-time/adjunct (0 women). *Students:* 129 full-time (22 women), 22 part-time (4 women); includes 15 minority (1 Black or African American, non-Hispanic/Latino; 8 Asian, non-Hispanic/Latino; 5 Hispanic/Latino; 1 Two or more races, non-Hispanic/Latino), 56 international. Average age 26. 502 applicants, 34% accepted, 73 enrolled. In 2014, 44 master's, 10 doctorates awarded. Terminal master's awarded for partial completion of doctoral program. *Degree requirements:* For master's, thesis (for some programs); for doctorate, comprehensive exam, thesis/dissertation. *Entrance requirements:* For master's and doctorate, GRE General Test. Additional exam requirements/recommendations for international students: Required—TOEFL (minimum score 550 paper-based; 84 iBT), IELTS (minimum score 7). *Application deadline:* For fall admission, 3/15 for domestic and international students; for spring admission, 10/1 for domestic and international students. Application fee: $80. Electronic applications accepted. *Expenses: Tuition:* Full-time $45,686; part-time $1428 per credit hour. *Required fees:* $660; $60 per semester. Tuition and fees vary according to program. *Financial support:* In 2014–15, 50 students received support, including 13 fellowships with full tuition reimbursements available (averaging $28,950 per year), 41 research assistantships with full tuition reimbursements available (averaging $19,300 per year), 19 teaching assistantships with full tuition reimbursements available (averaging $19,300 per year); career-related internships or fieldwork, Federal Work-Study, scholarships/grants, and tuition waivers (partial) also available. Financial award application deadline: 1/15; financial award applicants required to submit FAFSA. *Faculty research:* Acoustics, ultrasound, and vibrations; biomechanics; dynamics, control, and robotics; energy and thermofluid sciences; MEMS and nanotechnology. *Total annual research expenditures:* $11 million. *Unit head:* Dr. Alice White, Chairperson, 617-353-2814, Fax: 617-353-5866, E-mail: aew1@bu.edu. *Application contact:* Dr. Solomon Eisenberg, Senior Associate Dean of Academic Programs, 617-353-9760, Fax: 617-353-0259, E-mail: enggrad@bu.edu. Website: http://www.bu.edu/me/.

Bradley University, Graduate School, College of Engineering and Technology, Department of Mechanical Engineering, Peoria, IL 61625-0002. Offers MSME. Part-time and evening/weekend programs available. *Faculty:* 13 full-time (2 women), 1 part-time/adjunct (0 women). *Students:* 65 full-time (7 women), 39 part-time (2 women); includes 1 minority (Hispanic/Latino), 87 international. 177 applicants, 52% accepted, 49 enrolled. In 2014, 22 master's awarded. *Degree requirements:* For master's, comprehensive exam, thesis optional. *Entrance requirements:* Additional exam requirements/recommendations for international students: Required—TOEFL (minimum score 550 paper-based; 79 iBT), IELTS (minimum score 6.5). *Application deadline:* For fall admission, 5/15 priority date for domestic and international students; for spring admission, 10/15 priority date for domestic and international students. Applications are processed on a rolling basis. Application fee: $40 ($50 for international students). Electronic applications accepted. *Expenses: Tuition:* Full-time $14,580; part-time $810 per credit. *Required fees:* $224. Full-time tuition and fees vary according to course load. *Financial support:* In 2014–15, 15 research assistantships with full and partial tuition reimbursements (averaging $10,130 per year) were awarded; teaching assistantships, scholarships/grants, tuition waivers (partial), and unspecified assistantships also available. Support available to part-time students. Financial award application deadline: 4/1. *Faculty research:* Ground-coupled heat pumps, robotic end-effectors, power plant optimization. *Unit head:* Dr. Paul Mehta, Department Chairperson, 309-677-2754. *Application contact:* Kayla Carroll, Director of International Admissions and Student Services, 309-677-2375, E-mail: klcarroll@fsmail.bradley.edu.

Brigham Young University, Graduate Studies, Ira A. Fulton College of Engineering and Technology, Department of Mechanical Engineering, Provo, UT 84602. Offers MS, PhD. *Faculty:* 26 full-time (1 woman). *Students:* 111 full-time (8 women); includes 2 minority (both Asian, non-Hispanic/Latino), 5 international. Average age 27. 45 applicants, 62% accepted, 19 enrolled. In 2014, 30 master's, 4 doctorates awarded. Terminal master's awarded for partial completion of doctoral program. *Degree requirements:* For master's, thesis; for doctorate, comprehensive exam, thesis/dissertation. *Entrance requirements:* For master's and doctorate, GRE General Test, minimum GPA of 3.0 in undergraduate degree course work, 3 letters of recommendation, personal statement of intent, resume. Additional exam requirements/recommendations for international students: Required—TOEFL (minimum score 580 paper-based; 85 iBT), IELTS (minimum score 7). *Application deadline:* For fall admission, 1/15 for domestic and international students; for winter admission, 9/1 for domestic and international students; for spring admission, 1/15 for domestic and international students. Application fee: $50. Electronic applications accepted. *Expenses: Tuition:* Full-time $6310; part-time $371 per credit hour. Tuition and fees vary according to program and student's religious affiliation. *Financial support:* In 2014–15, 17 students received support, including 17 fellowships with full and partial tuition reimbursements available (averaging $5,549 per year), 9 research assistantships with full and partial tuition reimbursements available (averaging $4,442 per year), 9 teaching assistantships with full and partial tuition reimbursements available (averaging $4,442 per year); scholarships/grants also available. Financial award application deadline: 3/1; financial award applicants required to submit FAFSA. *Faculty research:* Computational and experimental fluid mechanics, dynamic and mechatronic systems and controls, product design and development, manufacturing systems and processes, materials and bio-mechanics. *Total annual research expenditures:* $4.5 million. *Unit head:* Dr. Daniel Maynes, Chair, 801-422-2625, Fax: 801-422-0516, E-mail: maynes@byu.edu. *Application contact:* Miriam Busch, Graduate Advisor, 801-422-2624, Fax: 801-422-0516, E-mail: mbusch@byu.edu. Website: http://me.byu.edu.

Brown University, Graduate School, School of Engineering, Program in Mechanics of Solids and Structures, Providence, RI 02912. Offers Sc M, PhD. *Degree requirements:* For doctorate, thesis/dissertation, preliminary exam.

Bucknell University, Graduate Studies, College of Engineering, Department of Mechanical Engineering, Lewisburg, PA 17837. Offers MSME. Part-time programs available. *Degree requirements:* For master's, thesis. *Entrance requirements:* For master's, GRE General Test, minimum GPA of 3.0. Additional exam requirements/recommendations for international students: Required—TOEFL (minimum score 600 paper-based). *Faculty research:* Heat pump performance, microprocessors in heat engine testing, computer-aided design.

California Institute of Technology, Division of Engineering and Applied Science, Option in Mechanical Engineering, Pasadena, CA 91125-0001. Offers MS, PhD, Engr. *Degree requirements:* For doctorate, thesis/dissertation. *Faculty research:* Design, mechanics, thermal and fluids engineering, jet propulsion.

California Polytechnic State University, San Luis Obispo, College of Engineering, Department of Mechanical Engineering, San Luis Obispo, CA 93407. Offers MS. Part-time programs available. *Faculty:* 15 full-time (2 women), 2 part-time/adjunct (0 women). *Students:* 38 full-time (6 women), 14 part-time (1 woman); includes 18 minority (1 Black or African American, non-Hispanic/Latino; 6 Asian, non-Hispanic/Latino; 7 Hispanic/Latino; 4 Two or more races, non-Hispanic/Latino), 3 international. Average age 24. 53 applicants, 74% accepted, 27 enrolled. In 2014, 23 master's awarded. *Degree requirements:* For master's, comprehensive exam (for some programs), thesis (for some programs). *Application deadline:* For fall admission, 1/1 for domestic and international students. Applications are processed on a rolling basis. Application fee: $55. Electronic applications accepted. *Expenses: Tuition:* state resident: full-time $6738; part-time $3906 per year. Tuition, nonresident: full-time $15,666; part-time $8370 per year. *Required fees:* $3447; $1001 per quarter. One-time fee: $3447 full-time; $3003 part-time. *Financial support:* Fellowships, research assistantships, teaching assistantships, career-related internships or fieldwork, Federal Work-Study, and scholarships/grants available. Support available to part-time students. Financial award application deadline: 3/2; financial award applicants required to submit FAFSA. *Faculty research:* Mechatronics, robotics, thermosciences, mechanics and stress analysis, composite materials. *Unit head:* Dr. Saeed Niku, Graduate Coordinator, 805-756-1376, Fax: 805-756-1137, E-mail: sniku@calpoly.edu. *Application contact:* Dr. James Maraviglia, Associate Vice Provost for Marketing and Enrollment Development, 805-756-2311, Fax: 805-756-5400, E-mail: admissions@calpoly.edu. Website: http://me.calpoly.edu.

California State Polytechnic University, Pomona, Program in Mechanical Engineering, Pomona, CA 91768-2557. Offers MS. *Students:* 6 full-time (1 woman), 49 part-time (4 women); includes 30 minority (1 Black or African American, non-Hispanic/Latino; 15 Asian, non-Hispanic/Latino; 13 Hispanic/Latino; 1 Two or more races, non-Hispanic/Latino), 9 international. Average age 26. 82 applicants, 55% accepted, 19 enrolled. In 2014, 14 master's awarded. *Application deadline:* Applications are processed on a rolling basis. Application fee: $55. Electronic applications accepted. *Expenses:* Tuition, state resident: full-time $6738. Tuition, nonresident: full-time

$12,300. *Required fees:* $1400. *Unit head:* Dr. Henry Xue, Graduate Coordinator, 909-869-4304, Fax: 909-869-4341, E-mail: hxue@cpp.edu. Website: http://www.cpp.edu/~me.

California State University, Fresno, Division of Graduate Studies, College of Engineering and Computer Science, Program in Mechanical Engineering, Fresno, CA 93740-8027. Offers MS. Offered at Edwards Air Force Base. Part-time programs available. *Degree requirements:* For master's, thesis or alternative. *Entrance requirements:* For master's, GRE General Test, minimum GPA of 2.7. Additional exam requirements/recommendations for international students: Required—TOEFL. Electronic applications accepted. *Faculty research:* Flowmeter calibration, digital camera calibration.

California State University, Fullerton, Graduate Studies, College of Engineering and Computer Science, Department of Mechanical Engineering, Fullerton, CA 92834-9480. Offers MS. Part-time programs available. *Students:* 28 full-time (1 woman), 72 part-time (6 women); includes 34 minority (19 Asian, non-Hispanic/Latino; 14 Hispanic/Latino; 1 Two or more races, non-Hispanic/Latino), 49 international. Average age 25. 169 applicants, 72% accepted, 52 enrolled. In 2014, 25 master's awarded. *Degree requirements:* For master's, comprehensive exam, project or thesis. *Entrance requirements:* For master's, minimum undergraduate GPA of 2.5. Application fee: $55. *Financial support:* Career-related internships or fieldwork, Federal Work-Study, institutionally sponsored loans, and scholarships/grants available. Support available to part-time students. Financial award application deadline: 3/1; financial award applicants required to submit FAFSA. *Unit head:* Dr. Roberta E. Rikli, Chair, 657-278-3014. *Application contact:* Admissions/Applications, 657-278-2371.

California State University, Long Beach, Graduate Studies, College of Engineering, Department of Mechanical and Aerospace Engineering, Long Beach, CA 90840. Offers aerospace engineering (MSAE); engineering and industrial applied mathematics (PhD); interdisciplinary engineering (MSE); management engineering (MSE); mechanical engineering (MSME). Part-time programs available. *Entrance requirements:* Additional exam requirements/recommendations for international students: Required—TOEFL. Electronic applications accepted. *Faculty research:* Unsteady turbulent flows, solar energy, energy conversion, CAD/CAM, computer-assisted instruction.

California State University, Los Angeles, Graduate Studies, College of Engineering, Computer Science, and Technology, Department of Mechanical Engineering, Los Angeles, CA 90032-8530. Offers MS. Part-time and evening/weekend programs available. *Degree requirements:* For master's, comprehensive exam or thesis. *Entrance requirements:* For master's, minimum GPA of 2.75. Additional exam requirements/recommendations for international students: Required—TOEFL (minimum score 550 paper-based). Electronic applications accepted. *Expenses:* Tuition, state resident: full-time $6738; part-time $3609 per year. Tuition, nonresident: full-time $15,666; part-time $8073 per year. Tuition and fees vary according to course load, degree level and program. *Faculty research:* Mechanical design, thermal systems, solar-powered vehicle.

California State University, Northridge, Graduate Studies, College of Engineering and Computer Science, Department of Mechanical Engineering, Northridge, CA 91330. Offers MS. Part-time and evening/weekend programs available. *Students:* 64 full-time (6 women), 34 part-time (3 women); includes 22 minority (5 Asian, non-Hispanic/Latino; 13 Hispanic/Latino; 2 Native Hawaiian or other Pacific Islander, non-Hispanic/Latino; 2 Two or more races, non-Hispanic/Latino), 49 international. Average age 27. *Degree requirements:* For master's, thesis or project. *Entrance requirements:* Additional exam requirements/recommendations for international students: Required—TOEFL. *Application deadline:* For fall admission, 11/30 for domestic students. Application fee: $55. *Expenses: Required fees:* $12,402. *Financial support:* Application deadline: 3/1. *Unit head:* Dr. Hamid Johari, Chair, 818-677-2187. Website: http://www.ecs.csun.edu/me/.

California State University, Sacramento, Office of Graduate Studies, College of Engineering and Computer Science, Department of Mechanical Engineering, Sacramento, CA 95819. Offers MS. Evening/weekend programs available. *Entrance requirements:* Additional exam requirements/recommendations for international students: Required—TOEFL. Electronic applications accepted.

Carleton University, Faculty of Graduate Studies, Faculty of Engineering and Design, Department of Mechanical and Aerospace Engineering, Ottawa, ON K1S 5B6, Canada. Offers aerospace engineering (M Eng, MA Sc, PhD); materials engineering (M Eng, MA Sc); mechanical engineering (M Eng, MA Sc, PhD). *Degree requirements:* For master's, thesis optional; for doctorate, thesis/dissertation. *Entrance requirements:* For master's, honors degree; for doctorate, MA Sc or M Eng. Additional exam requirements/recommendations for international students: Required—TOEFL. *Faculty research:* Thermal fluids engineering, heat transfer, vehicle engineering.

Carnegie Mellon University, Carnegie Institute of Technology, Department of Mechanical Engineering, Pittsburgh, PA 15213-3891. Offers MS, PhD. Part-time and evening/weekend programs available. Terminal master's awarded for partial completion of doctoral program. *Degree requirements:* For master's, thesis (for some programs); for doctorate, thesis/dissertation (for some programs), qualifying exam. *Entrance requirements:* For master's and doctorate, GRE General Test. Additional exam requirements/recommendations for international students: Required—TOEFL. *Faculty research:* Combustion, design, fluid, and thermal sciences; computational fluid dynamics; energy and environment; solid mechanics; systems and controls; materials and manufacturing.

Case Western Reserve University, School of Graduate Studies, Case School of Engineering, Department of Mechanical and Aerospace Engineering, Cleveland, OH 44106. Offers MS, PhD, MD/PhD. Part-time programs available. Postbaccalaureate distance learning degree programs offered (no on-campus study). *Faculty:* 14 full-time (3 women). *Students:* 84 full-time (11 women), 12 part-time (3 women); includes 10 minority (2 Black or African American, non-Hispanic/Latino; 5 Asian, non-Hispanic/Latino; 2 Hispanic/Latino; 1 Two or more races, non-Hispanic/Latino), 53 international. In 2014, 11 master's, 7 doctorates awarded. *Degree requirements:* For master's, thesis (for some programs); for doctorate, thesis/dissertation, qualifying exam, teaching experience. *Entrance requirements:* For master's and doctorate, GRE General Test. Additional exam requirements/recommendations for international students: Required—TOEFL. *Application deadline:* For fall admission, 7/1 priority date for domestic students. Applications are processed on a rolling basis. Application fee: $50. *Financial support:* In 2014–15, 5 fellowships with full and partial tuition reimbursements, 21 research assistantships with full and partial tuition reimbursements, 9 teaching assistantships were awarded; institutionally sponsored loans and tuition waivers (full and partial) also available. Financial award application deadline: 3/1; financial award applicants required to submit FAFSA. *Faculty research:* Musculoskeletal biomechanics, combustion diagnostics and computation, mechanical behavior of advanced materials and nanostructures, biorobotics. *Total annual research expenditures:* $4.1 million. *Unit head:* Dr. Robert Gao, Department Chair, 216-368-6045, Fax: 216-368-6445, E-mail: robert.gao@case.edu. *Application contact:* Carla Wilson, Student Affairs Coordinator, 216-368-4580, Fax: 216-368-3007, E-mail: cxw75@case.edu. Website: http://www.engineering.case.edu/emae.

Mechanical Engineering

The Catholic University of America, School of Engineering, Department of Mechanical Engineering, Washington, DC 20064. Offers MME, MSE, PhD. Part-time programs available. *Faculty:* 9 full-time (0 women), 6 part-time/adjunct (0 women). *Students:* 16 full-time (2 women), 14 part-time (2 women); includes 9 minority (2 Black or African American, non-Hispanic/Latino; 1 Asian, non-Hispanic/Latino; 3 Hispanic/Latino; 3 Two or more races, non-Hispanic/Latino), 7 international. Average age 29. 33 applicants, 79% accepted, 18 enrolled. In 2014, 6 master's, 1 doctorate awarded. *Degree requirements:* For master's, thesis (for some programs); for doctorate, comprehensive exam, thesis/dissertation, oral exams. *Entrance requirements:* For master's and doctorate, statement of purpose, official copies of academic transcripts, three letters of recommendation. Additional exam requirements/recommendations for international students: Required—TOEFL (minimum score 580 paper-based). *Application deadline:* For fall admission, 7/15 priority date for domestic students, 7/1 for international students; for spring admission, 11/15 priority date for domestic students, 11/1 for international students. Applications are processed on a rolling basis. Application fee: $55. Electronic applications accepted. *Expenses:* Expenses: Contact institution. *Financial support:* Fellowships, research assistantships, teaching assistantships, Federal Work-Study, scholarships/grants, tuition waivers (full and partial), and unspecified assistantships available. Financial award application deadline: 2/1; financial award applicants required to submit FAFSA. *Faculty research:* Fluid mechanics, dynamics, acoustics, computational mechanics, solar winds. *Total annual research expenditures:* $456,358. *Unit head:* Dr. Sen Nieh, Chair, 202-319-5170, Fax: 202-319-5173, E-mail: nieh@cua.edu. *Application contact:* Director of Graduate Admissions, 202-319-5057, Fax: 202-319-6533, E-mail: cua-admissions@cua.edu.
Website: http://mechanical.cua.edu/.

City College of the City University of New York, Graduate School, Grove School of Engineering, Department of Mechanical Engineering, New York, NY 10031-9198. Offers ME, MS, PhD. PhD program offered jointly with Graduate School and University Center of the City University of New York. Part-time programs available. *Degree requirements:* For master's, thesis optional; for doctorate, one foreign language, comprehensive exam, thesis/dissertation. *Entrance requirements:* For master's and doctorate, GRE General Test. Additional exam requirements/recommendations for international students: Required—TOEFL (minimum score 500 paper-based). *Faculty research:* Bio-heat and mass transfer, bone mechanics, fracture mechanics, heat transfer in computer parts, mechanisms design.

Clarkson University, Graduate School, Wallace H. Coulter School of Engineering, Department of Mechanical and Aeronautical Engineering, Potsdam, NY 13699. Offers mechanical engineering (ME, MS, PhD). Part-time programs available. *Faculty:* 33 full-time (4 women), 3 part-time/adjunct (1 woman). *Students:* 50 full-time (7 women), 1 part-time (0 women); includes 3 minority (2 Black or African American, non-Hispanic/Latino; 1 Two or more races, non-Hispanic/Latino), 24 international. Average age 28. 63 applicants, 71% accepted, 13 enrolled. In 2014, 11 master's, 4 doctorates awarded. Terminal master's awarded for partial completion of doctoral program. *Degree requirements:* For master's, thesis (for MS); project (for ME); for doctorate, comprehensive exam, thesis/dissertation, departmental qualifying exam. *Entrance requirements:* For master's and doctorate, GRE, transcripts of all college coursework, resume, personal statement, three letters of recommendation. Additional exam requirements/recommendations for international students: Required—TOEFL (minimum score 550 paper-based; 80 iBT), IELTS (minimum score 6.5). *Application deadline:* For fall admission, 1/30 priority date for domestic and international students; for spring admission, 9/1 priority date for domestic and international students. Applications are processed on a rolling basis. Application fee: $25 ($35 for international students). Electronic applications accepted. *Expenses: Tuition:* Full-time $16,680; part-time $1390 per credit. *Required fees:* $295 per semester. *Financial support:* In 2014–15, 48 students received support, including 3 fellowships with full tuition reimbursements available (averaging $24,029 per year), 14 research assistantships with full tuition reimbursements available (averaging $24,029 per year), 20 teaching assistantships with full tuition reimbursements available (averaging $24,029 per year); scholarships/grants, tuition waivers (partial), and unspecified assistantships also available. *Faculty research:* Bolt materials, UCT systems, flow fields, radiation transport, long span bridges. *Total annual research expenditures:* $1.3 million. *Unit head:* Dr. Daryush Aidun, Chair, 315-268-6586, Fax: 315-268-6695, E-mail: daidun@clarkson.edu. *Application contact:* Kelly Sharlow, Assistant to the Dean, 315-268-7929, Fax: 315-268-4494, E-mail: ksharlow@clarkson.edu.
Website: http://www.clarkson.edu/mae/.

Clemson University, Graduate School, College of Engineering and Science, Department of Mechanical Engineering, Clemson, SC 29634. Offers MS, PhD. Part-time programs available. Postbaccalaureate distance learning degree programs offered (minimal on-campus study). *Faculty:* 32 full-time (3 women), 1 part-time/adjunct (0 women). *Students:* 177 full-time (15 women), 15 part-time (3 women); includes 2 minority (both Asian, non-Hispanic/Latino), 159 international. Average age 25. 655 applicants, 34% accepted, 112 enrolled. In 2014, 47 master's, 10 doctorates awarded. Terminal master's awarded for partial completion of doctoral program. *Degree requirements:* For master's, thesis (for some programs); for doctorate, comprehensive exam, thesis/dissertation. *Entrance requirements:* For master's and doctorate, GRE General Test. Additional exam requirements/recommendations for international students: Required—TOEFL. *Application deadline:* For fall admission, 6/1 for domestic students, 2/15 for international students; for spring admission, 10/15 for domestic students, 9/15 for international students. Application fee: $70 ($80 for international students). Electronic applications accepted. *Expenses:* Expenses: Contact institution. *Financial support:* In 2014–15, 64 students received support, including 4 fellowships with partial tuition reimbursements available (averaging $2,000 per year), 30 research assistantships with full tuition reimbursements available (averaging $16,608 per year), 26 teaching assistantships with full tuition reimbursements available (averaging $16,051 per year); career-related internships or fieldwork, institutionally sponsored loans, scholarships/grants, health care benefits, and unspecified assistantships also available. Support available to part-time students. Financial award applicants required to submit FAFSA. *Faculty research:* Engineering design, thermal and fluid sciences, automated manufacturing, dynamical systems and robotics, engineering mechanics and materials. *Total annual research expenditures:* $2.2 million. *Unit head:* Dr. Melur Ramasubramanian, Chair, 864-656-5620, Fax: 864-656-4435, E-mail: rammk@clemson.edu. *Application contact:* Dr. Joshua David Summers, Director of Graduate Studies, 864-656-3295, Fax: 864-656-4435, E-mail: jsummer@clemson.edu.
Website: http://www.clemson.edu/ces/me/.

Cleveland State University, College of Graduate Studies, Fenn College of Engineering, Department of Civil and Environmental Engineering, Cleveland, OH 44115. Offers accelerated civil engineering (MS); accelerated environmental engineering (MS); civil engineering (MS, D Eng); engineering mechanics (MS); environmental engineering (MS). Part-time and evening/weekend programs available. *Faculty:* 8 full-time (2 women). *Students:* 20 full-time (0 women), 46 part-time (6 women); includes 2 minority (both Asian, non-Hispanic/Latino), 41 international. Average age 26. 113 applicants, 53% accepted, 22 enrolled. In 2014, 18 master's, 2 doctorates awarded. *Degree requirements:* For master's, project or thesis; for doctorate, comprehensive exam, thesis/dissertation, candidacy and qualifying exams. *Entrance requirements:* For master's, GRE General Test, GRE Subject Test, minimum GPA of 2.75; for doctorate, GRE General Test, GRE Subject Test, minimum GPA of 3.25. Additional exam requirements/recommendations for international students: Required—TOEFL (minimum score 525 paper-based). *Application deadline:* For fall admission, 7/15 priority date for domestic students. Applications are processed on a rolling basis. Application fee: $30. *Expenses:* Tuition, state resident: full-time $9566; part-time $531 per credit hour. Tuition, nonresident: full-time $17,980; part-time $999 per credit hour. *Required fees:* $25 per semester. Tuition and fees vary according to degree level and program. *Financial support:* In 2014–15, 9 research assistantships with full and partial tuition reimbursements (averaging $3,920 per year) were awarded; teaching assistantships with tuition reimbursements, career-related internships or fieldwork, scholarships/grants, and unspecified assistantships also available. Financial award application deadline: 9/1. *Faculty research:* Solid-waste disposal, constitutive modeling, transportation, safety engineering, concrete materials. *Total annual research expenditures:* $800,000. *Unit head:* Dr. Norbert Joseph Delatte, Chairperson, 216-687-9259, Fax: 216-687-5395, E-mail: n.delatte@csuohio.edu. *Application contact:* Deborah L. Brown, Interim Assistant Director, Graduate Admissions, 216-523-7572, Fax: 216-687-9214, E-mail: d.l.brown@csuohio.edu.
Website: http://www.csuohio.edu/engineering/civil.

Cleveland State University, College of Graduate Studies, Fenn College of Engineering, Department of Mechanical Engineering, Cleveland, OH 44115. Offers MS, D Eng. Part-time programs available. *Faculty:* 8 full-time (0 women). *Students:* 22 full-time (3 women), 62 part-time (6 women); includes 5 minority (1 Black or African American, non-Hispanic/Latino; 2 Hispanic/Latino; 2 Two or more races, non-Hispanic/Latino), 39 international. Average age 26. 272 applicants, 32% accepted, 25 enrolled. In 2014, 16 master's, 1 doctorate awarded. *Degree requirements:* For master's, project or thesis; for doctorate, thesis/dissertation, candidacy and qualifying exams. *Entrance requirements:* For master's, GRE General Test, minimum GPA of 3.0; for doctorate, GRE General Test, minimum GPA of 3.25. Additional exam requirements/recommendations for international students: Required—TOEFL (minimum score 525 paper-based). *Application deadline:* For fall admission, 7/15 priority date for domestic students; for spring admission, 12/15 priority date for domestic students. Applications are processed on a rolling basis. Application fee: $30. *Expenses:* Tuition, state resident: full-time $9566; part-time $531 per credit hour. Tuition, nonresident: full-time $17,980; part-time $999 per credit hour. *Required fees:* $25 per semester. Tuition and fees vary according to degree level and program. *Financial support:* In 2014–15, 22 students received support, including 9 research assistantships with full and partial tuition reimbursements available (averaging $3,480 per year); teaching assistantships with partial tuition reimbursements available, career-related internships or fieldwork, Federal Work-Study, institutionally sponsored loans, and unspecified assistantships also available. Support available to part-time students. *Faculty research:* Fluid piezoelectric sensors, laser-optical inspection simulation of forging and forming processes, multiphase flow and heat transfer, turbulent flows. *Unit head:* Dr. William J. Atherton, Interim Chair, 216-687-2595, Fax: 216-687-5375, E-mail: w.atherton@csuohio.edu. *Application contact:* Deborah L. Brown, Interim Assistant Director, Graduate Admissions, 216-523-7572, Fax: 216-687-9214, E-mail: d.l.brown@csuohio.edu.
Website: http://www.csuohio.edu/engineering/mce/.

Colorado School of Mines, Graduate School, Department of Mechanical Engineering, Golden, CO 80401. Offers mechanical engineering (PhD). *Faculty:* 31 full-time (5 women), 4 part-time/adjunct (0 women). *Students:* 82 full-time (17 women), 13 part-time (2 women); includes 16 minority (1 Black or African American, non-Hispanic/Latino; 1 American Indian or Alaska Native, non-Hispanic/Latino; 3 Asian, non-Hispanic/Latino; 8 Hispanic/Latino; 3 Two or more races, non-Hispanic/Latino), 11 international. Average age 28. 113 applicants, 73% accepted, 38 enrolled. In 2014, 35 master's, 3 doctorates awarded. *Degree requirements:* For master's, thesis (for some programs); for doctorate, comprehensive exam, thesis/dissertation. *Entrance requirements:* For master's and doctorate, GRE General Test. Additional exam requirements/recommendations for international students: Required—TOEFL (minimum score 550 paper-based; 80 iBT). *Application deadline:* For fall admission, 12/15 priority date for domestic and international students; for spring admission, 9/1 priority date for domestic and international students. Application fee: $50 ($70 for international students). Electronic applications accepted. *Financial support:* In 2014–15, 59 students received support, including 3 fellowships (averaging $21,120 per year), 30 research assistantships (averaging $21,120 per year), 14 teaching assistantships (averaging $21,120 per year); career-related internships or fieldwork, Federal Work-Study, institutionally sponsored loans, scholarships/grants, health care benefits, and unspecified assistantships also available. Financial award application deadline: 12/15; financial award applicants required to submit FAFSA. *Faculty research:* Biomechanics; robotics, automation, and design; solid mechanics and materials; thermal science and engineering. *Total annual research expenditures:* $2 million. *Unit head:* Dr. Gregory Jackson, Department Head, 303-273-3609, E-mail: gsjackso@mines.edu. *Application contact:* Lori Sisneros, Program Assistant, 303-273-3658, E-mail: sisneros@mines.edu.
Website: http://mechanical.mines.edu/.

Colorado State University, Graduate School, College of Engineering, Department of Mechanical Engineering, Fort Collins, CO 80523-1374. Offers ME, MS, PhD. Part-time programs available. Postbaccalaureate distance learning degree programs offered (no on-campus study). *Faculty:* 23 full-time (3 women), 1 part-time/adjunct (0 women). *Students:* 39 full-time (9 women), 51 part-time (10 women); includes 9 minority (2 Asian, non-Hispanic/Latino; 4 Hispanic/Latino; 3 Two or more races, non-Hispanic/Latino), 19 international. Average age 30. 109 applicants, 36% accepted, 22 enrolled. In 2014, 11 master's, 8 doctorates awarded. *Degree requirements:* For master's, comprehensive exam (for some programs), thesis (for some programs), oral exam; for doctorate, comprehensive exam, thesis/dissertation, preliminary exams, diagnostic exams, defense as final exam. *Entrance requirements:* For master's and doctorate, GRE, 3.0 GPA. Additional exam requirements/recommendations for international students: Required—TOEFL (minimum score 550 paper-based; 80 iBT), IELTS (minimum score 6.5). *Application deadline:* For fall admission, 4/1 for domestic and international students; for spring admission, 9/1 for domestic and international students. Application fee: $50. Electronic applications accepted. *Expenses:* Expenses: Contact institution. *Financial support:* In 2014–15, 70 students received support, including 6 fellowships with full tuition reimbursements available (averaging $48,525 per year), 43 research assistantships with full tuition reimbursements available (averaging $13,311 per year), 21 teaching assistantships with full tuition reimbursements available (averaging $11,465 per year); Federal Work-Study, scholarships/grants, traineeships, tuition waivers (full), and unspecified assistantships also available. Support available to part-time students. Financial award application deadline: 2/1. *Faculty research:* Energy, materials and manufacturing, health. *Total annual research expenditures:* $12.5 million. *Unit head:* Dr. Susan P. James, Professor and Department Head, 970-491-0924, Fax: 970-491-3827, E-mail: susan.james@engr.colostate.edu. *Application contact:* Megan Kosovski, Graduate Program Coordinator, 970-491-4268, Fax: 970-491-3827, E-mail: megan.kosovski@colostate.edu.
Website: http://www.engr.colostate.edu/me/.

Columbia University, Fu Foundation School of Engineering and Applied Science, Department of Mechanical Engineering, New York, NY 10027. Offers MS, Eng Sc D,

PhD. PhD offered through the Graduate School of Arts and Sciences. Part-time programs available. Postbaccalaureate distance learning degree programs offered (no on-campus study). *Faculty:* 15 full-time (2 women), 12 part-time/adjunct (1 woman). *Students:* 137 full-time (27 women), 77 part-time (18 women); includes 20 minority (5 Black or African American, non-Hispanic/Latino; 12 Asian, non-Hispanic/Latino; 3 Hispanic/Latino), 152 international. 606 applicants, 37% accepted, 82 enrolled. In 2014, 68 master's, 13 doctorates awarded. *Degree requirements:* For doctorate, thesis/dissertation, qualifying exam. *Entrance requirements:* For master's, GRE General Test, minimum GPA of 3.3; for doctorate, GRE General Test. Additional exam requirements/recommendations for international students: Required—TOEFL, IELTS, PTE. *Application deadline:* For fall admission, 12/15 priority date for domestic and international students; for spring admission, 10/1 priority date for domestic and international students. Application fee: $85. Electronic applications accepted. *Financial support:* In 2014–15, 93 students received support, including 25 fellowships with full tuition reimbursements available (averaging $25,833 per year), 62 research assistantships with full tuition reimbursements available (averaging $32,447 per year), 31 teaching assistantships with full tuition reimbursements available (averaging $24,335 per year). Financial award application deadline: 12/15; financial award applicants required to submit FAFSA. *Faculty research:* Musculoskeletal biomechanics; nanomechanics, nanomaterials and nanofabrication; manufacturing; optical nanostructure; biofluidic micro systems. *Unit head:* Dr. Jeffrey W. Kysar, Professor and Chair of Mechanical Engineering, 212-854-7432, Fax: 212-854-3304, E-mail: jk2079@columbia.edu. *Application contact:* Rebecca Chambers, Student Affairs Manager, 212-854-3874, Fax: 212-854-3304, E-mail: rchambers@columbia.edu.
Website: http://www.me.columbia.edu.

Concordia University, School of Graduate Studies, Faculty of Engineering and Computer Science, Department of Mechanical and Industrial Engineering, Montréal, QC H3G 1M8, Canada. Offers composites (M Eng); industrial engineering (M Eng, MA Sc); mechanical engineering (M Eng, MA Sc, PhD, Certificate); software systems for industrial engineering (Certificate). M Eng in composites program offered jointly with École Polytechnique de Montréal. *Degree requirements:* For master's, variable foreign language requirement, thesis or alternative; for doctorate, comprehensive exam, thesis/dissertation. *Faculty research:* Mechanical systems, fluid control systems, thermofluids engineering and robotics, industrial control systems.

Cooper Union for the Advancement of Science and Art, Albert Nerken School of Engineering, New York, NY 10003-7120. Offers chemical engineering (ME); civil engineering (ME); electrical engineering (ME); mechanical engineering (ME). Part-time programs available. *Faculty:* 27 full-time (1 woman), 15 part-time/adjunct (2 women). *Students:* 45 full-time (10 women), 20 part-time (4 women); includes 24 minority (3 Black or African American, non-Hispanic/Latino; 15 Asian, non-Hispanic/Latino; 4 Hispanic/Latino; 2 Two or more races, non-Hispanic/Latino), 4 international. Average age 23. 86 applicants, 71% accepted, 44 enrolled. In 2014, 22 master's awarded. *Degree requirements:* For master's, thesis (for some programs). *Entrance requirements:* For master's, BE or BS in engineering discipline, high school and college transcripts, two letters of recommendation, resume. Additional exam requirements/recommendations for international students: Required—TOEFL (minimum score 600 paper-based; 100 iBT). *Application deadline:* For fall admission, 4/1 for domestic and international students. Application fee: $70. Electronic applications accepted. *Expenses: Tuition:* Full-time $39,600; part-time $1173 per credit. *Required fees:* $925 per semester. One-time fee: $250. *Financial support:* In 2014–15, 65 students received support, including 4 fellowships with full and partial tuition reimbursements available (averaging $11,000 per year); career-related internships or fieldwork, Federal Work-Study, tuition waivers (full and partial), and tuition scholarships offered to exceptional students also available. Support available to part-time students. Financial award application deadline: 5/1; financial award applicants required to submit FAFSA. *Faculty research:* Civil infrastructure, imaging and sensing technology, biomedical engineering, encryption technology, process engineering. *Unit head:* Dr. Teresa Dahlberg, Dean of Engineering, 212-353-4285, E-mail: dahlberg@cooper.edu. *Application contact:* Student Contact, 212-353-4120, E-mail: admissions@cooper.edu.
Website: http://cooper.edu/engineering.

Cornell University, Graduate School, Graduate Fields of Engineering, Field of Mechanical Engineering, Ithaca, NY 14853-0001. Offers biomechanical engineering (M Eng, MS, PhD); combustion (M Eng, MS, PhD); energy and power systems (M Eng, MS, PhD); fluid mechanics (M Eng, MS, PhD); heat transfer (M Eng, MS, PhD); materials and manufacturing engineering (M Eng, MS, PhD); mechanical systems and design (M Eng, MS, PhD); multiphase flows (M Eng, MS, PhD). Terminal master's awarded for partial completion of doctoral program. *Degree requirements:* For master's, project (M Eng), thesis (MS); for doctorate, one foreign language, comprehensive exam, thesis/dissertation, 2 semesters of teaching experience. *Entrance requirements:* For master's and doctorate, GRE General Test, 3 letters of recommendation. Additional exam requirements/recommendations for international students: Required—TOEFL (minimum score 550 paper-based; 77 iBT). Electronic applications accepted. *Faculty research:* Combustion and heat transfer, fluid mechanics and computational fluid mechanics, system dynamics and control, biomechanics, manufacturing.

Dalhousie University, Faculty of Engineering, Department of Mechanical Engineering, Halifax, NS B3J 2X4, Canada. Offers M Eng, MA Sc, PhD. *Degree requirements:* For master's, thesis; for doctorate, thesis/dissertation. *Entrance requirements:* Additional exam requirements/recommendations for international students: Required—TOEFL, IELTS, CANTEST, CAEL, or Michigan English Language Assessment Battery. Electronic applications accepted. *Faculty research:* Fluid dynamics and energy, system dynamics, naval architecture, MEMS, space structures.

Dartmouth College, Thayer School of Engineering, Program in Mechanical Engineering, Hanover, NH 03755. Offers MS, PhD. *Degree requirements:* For master's, thesis; for doctorate, thesis/dissertation, candidacy oral exam. *Entrance requirements:* For master's and doctorate, GRE General Test. *Application deadline:* For fall admission, 1/1 priority date for domestic students. Application fee: $45. *Financial support:* Fellowships, research assistantships, teaching assistantships, career-related internships or fieldwork, Federal Work-Study, institutionally sponsored loans, and tuition waivers (full and partial) available. Financial award application deadline: 1/15. *Faculty research:* Tribology, dynamics and control systems, thermal science and energy conversion, fluid mechanics and multi-phase flow, mobile robots. *Unit head:* Dr. Joseph J. Helbie, Dean, 603-646-2238, Fax: 603-646-2580, E-mail: joseph.j.helbie@dartmouth.edu. *Application contact:* Candace S. Potter, Graduate Admissions Administrator, 603-646-3844, Fax: 603-646-1620, E-mail: candace.s.potter@dartmouth.edu.
Website: http://engineering.dartmouth.edu/.

Drexel University, College of Engineering, Department of Mechanical Engineering and Mechanics, Philadelphia, PA 19104-2875. Offers mechanical engineering (MS, PhD). Part-time and evening/weekend programs available. Terminal master's awarded for partial completion of doctoral program. *Degree requirements:* For master's, thesis optional; for doctorate, thesis/dissertation. *Entrance requirements:* For master's, minimum GPA of 3.0, BS in engineering or science; for doctorate, minimum GPA of 3.5, MS in engineering or science. Additional exam requirements/recommendations for international students: Required—TOEFL. Electronic applications accepted. *Faculty research:* Composites, dynamic systems and control, combustion and fuels, biomechanics, mechanics and thermal fluid sciences.

Duke University, Graduate School, Pratt School of Engineering, Department of Mechanical Engineering and Materials Science, Durham, NC 27708. Offers materials science (MS, PhD); mechanical engineering (MS, PhD); JD/MS. *Faculty:* 25 full-time. *Students:* 83 full-time (21 women); includes 11 minority (3 Black or African American, non-Hispanic/Latino; 2 Asian, non-Hispanic/Latino; 6 Hispanic/Latino), 41 international. 302 applicants, 18% accepted, 23 enrolled. In 2014, 11 master's, 10 doctorates awarded. Terminal master's awarded for partial completion of doctoral program. *Degree requirements:* For master's, thesis optional; for doctorate, thesis/dissertation. *Entrance requirements:* For master's and doctorate, GRE General Test. Additional exam requirements/recommendations for international students: Required—TOEFL (minimum score 90 iBT), IELTS (minimum score 7). *Application deadline:* For fall admission, 12/8 priority date for domestic and international students; for spring admission, 10/15 for domestic students. Application fee: $80. Electronic applications accepted. *Expenses: Tuition:* Full-time $45,760; part-time $2765 per credit. *Required fees:* $978. Full-time tuition and fees vary according to program. *Financial support:* Fellowships, research assistantships, teaching assistantships, and Federal Work-Study available. Financial award application deadline: 12/8. *Unit head:* Brian Mann, Director of Graduate Studies, 919-660-5310, Fax: 919-660-8963, E-mail: kparrish@duke.edu. *Application contact:* Kathy Parrish, -, Fax: -, E-mail: grad-admissions@duke.edu.
Website: http://www.mems.duke.edu/grad.

Duke University, Graduate School, Pratt School of Engineering, Master of Engineering Program, Durham, NC 27708-0271. Offers biomedical engineering (M Eng); civil engineering (M Eng); electrical and computer engineering (M Eng); environmental engineering (M Eng); materials science and engineering (M Eng); mechanical engineering (M Eng); photonics and optical sciences (M Eng). Part-time programs available. *Students:* 45 full-time (17 women); includes 5 minority (1 Black or African American, non-Hispanic/Latino; 2 Asian, non-Hispanic/Latino; 2 Hispanic/Latino), 23 international. Average age 24. 285 applicants, 43% accepted, 45 enrolled. In 2014, 45 master's awarded. *Entrance requirements:* For master's, GRE General Test, resume, 3 letters of recommendation, statement of purpose, transcripts. Additional exam requirements/recommendations for international students: Required—TOEFL. *Application deadline:* For fall admission, 6/15 for domestic students, 2/15 for international students; for spring admission, 11/1 for domestic students, 9/1 for international students. Application fee: $75. *Expenses: Tuition:* Full-time $45,760; part-time $2765 per credit. *Required fees:* $978. Full-time tuition and fees vary according to program. *Financial support:* Merit scholarships/grants available. *Unit head:* Dr. Bradley A. Fox, Executive Director, 919-660-5455, Fax: 919-660-5456. *Application contact:* Susan Brown, Assistant Director of Admissions, 919-660-8451, Fax: 919-660-5456, E-mail: susan.brown@duke.edu.
Website: http://meng.pratt.duke.edu/.

École Polytechnique de Montréal, Graduate Programs, Department of Mechanical Engineering, Montréal, QC H3C 3A7, Canada. Offers aerothermics (M Eng, M Sc A, PhD); applied mechanics (M Eng, M Sc A, PhD); tool design (M Eng, M Sc A, PhD). Part-time and evening/weekend programs available. *Degree requirements:* For master's, one foreign language, thesis; for doctorate, one foreign language, thesis/dissertation. *Entrance requirements:* For master's, minimum GPA of 2.75; for doctorate, minimum GPA of 3.0. *Faculty research:* Noise control and vibration, fatigue and creep, aerodynamics, composite materials, biomechanics, robotics.

Embry-Riddle Aeronautical University–Daytona, Department of Mechanical Engineering, Daytona Beach, FL 32114-3900. Offers MSME, PhD. Part-time and evening/weekend programs available. *Faculty:* 8 full-time (2 women), 1 part-time/adjunct (0 women). *Students:* 57 full-time (8 women), 18 part-time (3 women); includes 10 minority (5 Black or African American, non-Hispanic/Latino; 1 Asian, non-Hispanic/Latino; 4 Hispanic/Latino), 41 international. Average age 25. 72 applicants, 49% accepted, 27 enrolled. In 2014, 32 master's awarded. *Degree requirements:* For master's, thesis optional; for doctorate, comprehensive exam, thesis/dissertation. *Entrance requirements:* For master's, GRE (Not required for ERAU students), Have completed a bachelor's degree in an ABET accredited engineering program (or international equivalent) or closely related engineering discipline; minimum CGPA of 3.0; for doctorate, Have taken GRE within 5 years of application, Minimum CGPA of 3.5 on 4.0 scale; 3 letters of recommendation. Additional exam requirements/recommendations for international students: Required—TOEFL (minimum score 550 paper-based; 79 iBT). *Application deadline:* For fall admission, 6/1 priority date for domestic students, 5/1 priority date for international students; for spring admission, 11/1 priority date for domestic students, 10/1 priority date for international students. Applications are processed on a rolling basis. Application fee: $50. Electronic applications accepted. *Expenses: Tuition:* Full-time $15,360; part-time $1280 per credit hour. *Required fees:* $1334. *Financial support:* In 2014–15, 13 students received support. Research assistantships, teaching assistantships, career-related internships or fieldwork, and unspecified assistantships available. Financial award application deadline: 4/15. *Faculty research:* High-performance vehicles and vehicle dynamics, unmanned and autonomous systems, computational fluid dynamics and heat transfer, design and simulation, biomedical engineering. *Unit head:* Charles Reinholtz, PhD, Professor and Chair, Department of Mechanical Engineering, 386-323-8848, E-mail: charles.reinholtz@erau.edu. *Application contact:* International and Graduate Admissions, 386-226-6176, Fax: 386-226-7070, E-mail: graduate.admissions@erau.edu.
Website: http://daytonabeach.erau.edu/coe/degrees/graduate-degrees/mechanical-engineering/index.html.

Fairfield University, School of Engineering, Fairfield, CT 06824. Offers automated manufacturing (CAS); database management (CAS); electrical and computer engineering (MS); information security (CAS); management of technology (MS); mechanical engineering (MS); network technology (CAS); software engineering (MS); Web application development (CAS). Part-time and evening/weekend programs available. *Faculty:* 4 full-time (1 woman), 18 part-time/adjunct (5 women). *Students:* 193 full-time (50 women), 69 part-time (11 women); includes 20 minority (4 Black or African American, non-Hispanic/Latino; 6 Asian, non-Hispanic/Latino; 10 Hispanic/Latino), 199 international. Average age 27. 516 applicants, 64% accepted, 124 enrolled. In 2014, 38 master's awarded. *Degree requirements:* For master's, thesis, capstone course. *Entrance requirements:* For master's, interview, minimum GPA of 2.8, resume, 2 recommendations. Additional exam requirements/recommendations for international students: Required—TOEFL (minimum score 550 paper-based; 80 iBT) or IELTS (minimum score 6.5). *Application deadline:* For fall admission, 5/15 for international students; for spring admission, 10/15 for international students. Applications are processed on a rolling basis. Application fee: $60. Electronic applications accepted. *Expenses:* Expenses: $750 per credit hour. *Financial support:* In 2014–15, 30 students received support. Scholarships/grants and unspecified assistantships available. Financial award applicants required to submit FAFSA. *Faculty research:* Ocean dynamics modeling, thermo fluids, Web/mobile software applications, microwaves/electromagnetics, micro/nano manufacturing. *Unit head:* Dr. Bruce Berdanier, Dean,

203-254-4147, Fax: 203-254-4013, E-mail: bberdanier@fairfield.edu. *Application contact:* Marianne Gumpper, Director of Graduate and Continuing Studies Admission, 203-254-4184, Fax: 203-254-4073, E-mail: gradadmis@fairfield.edu.
Website: http://www.fairfield.edu/academics/schoolscollegescenters/schoolofengineering/graduateprograms/.

Florida Agricultural and Mechanical University, Division of Graduate Studies, Research, and Continuing Education, FAMU-FSU College of Engineering, Department of Mechanical Engineering, Tallahassee, FL 32307-3200. Offers MS, PhD. *Degree requirements:* For master's, thesis optional; for doctorate, comprehensive exam, thesis/dissertation. *Entrance requirements:* For master's, GRE General Test, minimum GPA of 3.0. Additional exam requirements/recommendations for international students: Required—TOEFL (minimum score 550 paper-based). *Faculty research:* Fluid mechanical and heat transfer, thermodynamics, dynamics and controls, mechanics and materials.

Florida Atlantic University, College of Engineering and Computer Science, Department of Ocean and Mechanical Engineering, Boca Raton, FL 33431-0991. Offers mechanical engineering (MS, PhD); ocean engineering (MS, PhD). Part-time and evening/weekend programs available. Terminal master's awarded for partial completion of doctoral program. *Degree requirements:* For master's, thesis (for some programs); for doctorate, comprehensive exam, thesis/dissertation, qualifying exam. *Entrance requirements:* For master's and doctorate, GRE General Test, minimum GPA of 3.0. Additional exam requirements/recommendations for international students: Required—TOEFL (minimum score 500 paper-based; 61 iBT), IELTS (minimum score 6). *Expenses:* Tuition, state resident: full-time $7396; part-time $369.82 per credit hour. Tuition, nonresident: full-time $19,392; part-time $1024.81 per credit hour. Tuition and fees vary according to course load. *Faculty research:* Marine materials and corrosion, ocean structures, marine vehicles, acoustics and vibrations, hydrodynamics, coastal engineering.

Florida Institute of Technology, Graduate Programs, College of Engineering, Program in Mechanical Engineering, Melbourne, FL 32901-6975. Offers MS, PhD. Part-time programs available. *Students:* 65 full-time (6 women), 16 part-time (0 women); includes 4 minority (1 Black or African American, non-Hispanic/Latino; 2 Asian, non-Hispanic/Latino; 1 Hispanic/Latino), 64 international. Average age 26. 387 applicants, 42% accepted, 25 enrolled. In 2014, 13 master's awarded. Terminal master's awarded for partial completion of doctoral program. *Degree requirements:* For master's, comprehensive exam (for some programs), thesis optional; for doctorate, comprehensive exam, thesis/dissertation, oral section of written exam, significant original research. *Entrance requirements:* For master's, GRE General Test, minimum GPA of 3.0, bachelor's degree from an ABET-accredited program, transcripts; for doctorate, GRE General Test, 3 letters of recommendation, minimum GPA of 3.2, resume, statement of objectives. Additional exam requirements/recommendations for international students: Required—TOEFL (minimum score 550 paper-based; 79 iBT). *Application deadline:* For fall admission, 4/1 for international students; for spring admission, 9/30 for international students. Applications are processed on a rolling basis. Application fee: $0. Electronic applications accepted. *Expenses: Tuition:* Part-time $1179 per credit hour. Tuition and fees vary according to campus/location. *Financial support:* Career-related internships or fieldwork, institutionally sponsored loans, tuition waivers (partial), unspecified assistantships, and tuition remissions available. Support available to part-time students. Financial award application deadline: 3/1; financial award applicants required to submit FAFSA. *Faculty research:* Dynamic systems, robotics, and controls; structures, solid mechanics, and materials; thermal-fluid sciences, optical tomography, composite/recycled materials. *Unit head:* Dr. Hamid Hefazi, Department Head, 321-674-7255, Fax: 321-674-8813, E-mail: hhefazi@fit.edu. *Application contact:* Cheryl A. Brown, Associate Director of Graduate Admissions, 321-674-7581, Fax: 321-723-9468, E-mail: cbrown@fit.edu.
Website: http://coe.fit.edu/mae/.

Florida Institute of Technology, Graduate Programs, Extended Studies Division, Melbourne, FL 32901-6975. Offers acquisition and contract management (MS); aerospace engineering (MS); business administration (MBA, DBA); computer information systems (MS); computer science (MS); electrical engineering (MS); engineering management (MS); human resources management (MS); logistics management (MS), including humanitarian and disaster relief logistics; management (MS), including acquisition and contract management, e-business, human resources management, information systems, logistics management, management, transportation management; material acquisition management (MS); mechanical engineering (MS); operations research (MS); project management (MS), including information systems, operations research; public administration (MPA); quality management (MS); software engineering (MS); space systems (MS); space systems management (MS); supply chain management (MS); systems management (MS), including information systems, operations research; technology management (MS). Part-time and evening/weekend programs available. Postbaccalaureate distance learning degree programs offered (no on-campus study). *Faculty:* 7 full-time (1 woman), 112 part-time/adjunct (29 women). *Students:* 98 full-time (45 women), 975 part-time (396 women); includes 440 minority (292 Black or African American, non-Hispanic/Latino; 13 American Indian or Alaska Native, non-Hispanic/Latino; 32 Asian, non-Hispanic/Latino; 79 Hispanic/Latino; 1 Native Hawaiian or other Pacific Islander, non-Hispanic/Latino; 23 Two or more races, non-Hispanic/Latino), 4 international. Average age 37. 807 applicants, 56% accepted, 258 enrolled. In 2014, 457 master's awarded. *Degree requirements:* For master's, comprehensive exam (for some programs), capstone course. *Entrance requirements:* For master's, GMAT or resume showing 8 years of supervised experience, minimum GPA of 3.0, 2 letters of recommendation, resume. Additional exam requirements/recommendations for international students: Required—TOEFL (minimum score 550 paper-based; 79 iBT). *Application deadline:* For fall admission, 4/1 for international students; for spring admission, 9/30 for international students. Applications are processed on a rolling basis. Electronic applications accepted. *Expenses:* Expenses: Contact institution. *Financial support:* Application deadline: 3/1; applicants required to submit FAFSA. *Unit head:* Dr. Theodore R. Richardson, III, Senior Associate Dean, 321-674-8123, Fax: 321-674-7597, E-mail: trichardson@fit.edu. *Application contact:* Carolyn Farrior, Director of Graduate Admissions, Online Learning and Off-Campus Programs, 321-674-7118, Fax: 321-674-8216, E-mail: cfarrior@fit.edu.
Website: http://es.fit.edu.

Florida International University, College of Engineering and Computing, Department of Mechanical and Materials Engineering, Mechanical Engineering Program, Miami, FL 33175. Offers MS, PhD. Part-time and evening/weekend programs available. Terminal master's awarded for partial completion of doctoral program. *Degree requirements:* For master's, thesis or alternative; for doctorate, comprehensive exam, thesis/dissertation. *Entrance requirements:* For master's, minimum undergraduate GPA of 3.0 in upper level coursework, letters of recommendation, letter of intent; for doctorate, GRE, minimum undergraduate GPA of 3.0, 3 letters of recommendation, letter of intent. Additional exam requirements/recommendations for international students: Required—TOEFL (minimum score 550 paper-based; 80 iBT). Electronic applications accepted.

Florida State University, The Graduate School, FAMU-FSU College of Engineering, Department of Mechanical Engineering, Tallahassee, FL 32310-6046. Offers mechanical engineering (MS, PhD); sustainable energy (MS). Part-time programs available. Terminal master's awarded for partial completion of doctoral program. *Degree requirements:* For master's, thesis optional, 30 credit hours (24 coursework, 6 research); for doctorate, thesis/dissertation, 45 credit hours (21 coursework, 24 research). *Entrance requirements:* For master's and doctorate, GRE General Test (minimum scores: Verbal 150, Quantitative 155), minimum GPA of 3.0, official transcripts, resume, personal statement, 3 letters of recommendation. Additional exam requirements/recommendations for international students: Required—TOEFL (minimum score 550 paper-based; 80 iBT), IELTS (minimum score 6.5), Michigan English Language Assessment Battery (minimum score 77). Electronic applications accepted. *Expenses:* Tuition, state resident: part-time $403.51 per credit hour. Tuition, nonresident: part-time $1004.85 per credit hour. *Required fees:* $75.81 per credit hour. One-time fee: $20 part-time. Tuition and fees vary according to campus/location. *Faculty research:* Aero-propulsion, superconductivity, smart materials, nanomaterials, intelligent robotic systems, robotic locomotion, sustainable energy.

Gannon University, School of Graduate Studies, College of Engineering and Business, School of Engineering and Computer Science, Program in Mechanical Engineering, Erie, PA 16541-0001. Offers MSME. Part-time and evening/weekend programs available. *Degree requirements:* For master's, comprehensive exam, thesis (for some programs), oral exam (for some programs), design project (for some programs). *Entrance requirements:* For master's, GRE or GMAT, bachelor's degree in mechanical engineering, minimum GPA of 2.5, transcript, 3 letters of recommendation. Additional exam requirements/recommendations for international students: Required—TOEFL (minimum score 79 iBT). Electronic applications accepted.

The George Washington University, School of Engineering and Applied Science, Department of Mechanical and Aerospace Engineering, Washington, DC 20052. Offers mechanical and aerospace engineering (Engr). Part-time and evening/weekend programs available. *Faculty:* 22 full-time (4 women), 15 part-time/adjunct (0 women). *Students:* 70 full-time (10 women), 64 part-time (11 women); includes 17 minority (1 Black or African American, non-Hispanic/Latino; 6 Asian, non-Hispanic/Latino; 5 Hispanic/Latino; 1 Native Hawaiian or other Pacific Islander, non-Hispanic/Latino; 4 Two or more races, non-Hispanic/Latino), 71 international. Average age 28. 265 applicants, 63% accepted, 44 enrolled. In 2014, 33 master's, 6 doctorates, 1 other advanced degree awarded. *Degree requirements:* For master's, thesis optional; for doctorate, thesis/dissertation, final and qualifying exams. *Entrance requirements:* For master's, appropriate bachelor's degree, minimum GPA of 3.0; for doctorate, GRE (if highest earned degree is BS), appropriate bachelor's or master's degree, minimum GPA of 3.4; for other advanced degree, appropriate master's degree, minimum GPA of 3.0. Additional exam requirements/recommendations for international students: Required—TOEFL or The George Washington University English as a Foreign Language Test. *Application deadline:* For fall admission, 3/1 priority date for domestic students; for spring admission, 10/1 for domestic students. Applications are processed on a rolling basis. Application fee: $75. *Financial support:* In 2014–15, 51 students received support. Fellowships with tuition reimbursements available, research assistantships, teaching assistantships with tuition reimbursements available, career-related internships or fieldwork, and institutionally sponsored loans available. Financial award application deadline: 3/1; financial award applicants required to submit FAFSA. *Unit head:* Dr. Michael Plesniak, Chairman, 202-994-6749, E-mail: maeng@gwu.edu. *Application contact:* Adina Lav, Marketing, Recruiting and Admissions, 202-994-5827, Fax: 202-994-0909, E-mail: engineering@gwu.edu.
Website: http://www.gwu.edu/graduate-programs/mechanical-and-aerospace-engineering.

Georgia Institute of Technology, Graduate Studies, College of Engineering, George W. Woodruff School of Mechanical Engineering, Program in Mechanical Engineering, Atlanta, GA 30332-0001. Offers MS, PhD. Part-time programs available. Postbaccalaureate distance learning degree programs offered. *Students:* 491 full-time (66 women), 190 part-time (37 women); includes 130 minority (12 Black or African American, non-Hispanic/Latino; 1 American Indian or Alaska Native, non-Hispanic/Latino; 71 Asian, non-Hispanic/Latino; 27 Hispanic/Latino; 1 Native Hawaiian or other Pacific Islander, non-Hispanic/Latino; 18 Two or more races, non-Hispanic/Latino), 218 international. Average age 25. 1,253 applicants, 28% accepted, 183 enrolled. In 2014, 155 master's, 31 doctorates awarded. Terminal master's awarded for partial completion of doctoral program. *Degree requirements:* For master's, thesis; for doctorate, comprehensive exam, thesis/dissertation. *Entrance requirements:* For master's and doctorate, GRE General Test, minimum GPA of 3.3. Additional exam requirements/recommendations for international students: Required—TOEFL (minimum score 580 paper-based; 94 iBT). *Application deadline:* For fall admission, 1/10 priority date for domestic and international students; for spring admission, 10/1 priority date for domestic and international students; for summer admission, 1/10 priority date for domestic students, 1/10 for international students. Applications are processed on a rolling basis. Application fee: $75. Electronic applications accepted. *Expenses:* Tuition, state resident: full-time $12,344; part-time $515 per credit hour. Tuition, nonresident: full-time $27,600; part-time $1150 per credit hour. *Required fees:* $1196 per term. Part-time tuition and fees vary according to course load. *Financial support:* Fellowships, research assistantships, teaching assistantships, career-related internships or fieldwork, Federal Work-Study, institutionally sponsored loans, tuition waivers (partial), and unspecified assistantships available. Support available to part-time students. Financial award application deadline: 5/1. *Faculty research:* Automation and mechatronics; computer-aided engineering and design; micro-electronic mechanical systems; heat transfer, combustion and energy systems; fluid mechanics. *Unit head:* Paul Neitzel, Director, 404-894-3242, E-mail: paul.neitzel@gatech.edu. *Application contact:* Wayne Whiteman, Graduate Coordinator, 404-894-3204, E-mail: wayne.whiteman@me.gatech.edu.

Georgia Southern University, Jack N. Averitt College of Graduate Studies, Allen E. Paulson College of Engineering and Information Technology, Department of Mechanical Engineering, Program in Engineering/Mechatronics, Statesboro, GA 30460. Offers MSAE. *Students:* 14 full-time (2 women), 4 part-time (0 women); includes 5 minority (2 Black or African American, non-Hispanic/Latino; 1 Asian, non-Hispanic/Latino; 2 Hispanic/Latino), 7 international. Average age 25. 12 applicants, 75% accepted, 7 enrolled. In 2014, 6 master's awarded. *Degree requirements:* For master's, thesis optional. *Entrance requirements:* Additional exam requirements/recommendations for international students: Required—TOEFL (minimum score 80 iBT). *Application deadline:* For fall admission, 3/1 priority date for domestic students; for spring admission, 11/1 priority date for domestic students. *Expenses:* Tuition, state resident: full-time $7236; part-time $277 per semester hour. Tuition, nonresident: full-time $27,118; part-time $1105 per semester hour. *Required fees:* $2092. *Financial support:* In 2014–15, 14 students received support. Unspecified assistantships available. *Faculty research:* Biomechatronics, electromagnetics, smart antennas, wireless communication systems and networks, wireless sensor and actuator networks. *Unit head:* Dr. Frank Goforth, Chair, 912-478-7583, Fax: 912-478-1455, E-mail: fgoforth@georgiasouthern.edu.

The Graduate Center, City University of New York, Graduate Studies, Program in Engineering, New York, NY 10016-4039. Offers biomedical engineering (PhD); chemical engineering (PhD); civil engineering (PhD); electrical engineering (PhD); mechanical engineering (PhD). *Degree requirements:* For doctorate, thesis/dissertation. *Entrance* *requirements:* For doctorate, GRE General Test. Additional exam requirements/recommendations for international students: Required—TOEFL. Electronic applications accepted.

Grand Valley State University, Padnos College of Engineering and Computing, School of Engineering, Allendale, MI 49401-9403. Offers electrical and computer engineering (MSE); manufacturing operations (MSE); mechanical engineering (MSE); product design and manufacturing engineering (MSE). Part-time and evening/weekend programs available. *Faculty:* 15 full-time (2 women). *Students:* 29 full-time (6 women), 30 part-time (5 women); includes 4 minority (1 Asian, non-Hispanic/Latino; 3 Hispanic/Latino), 23 international. Average age 28. 66 applicants, 73% accepted, 23 enrolled. In 2014, 14 master's awarded. *Degree requirements:* For master's, project or thesis. *Entrance requirements:* For master's, engineering degree, minimum GPA of 3.0. Additional exam requirements/recommendations for international students: Required—TOEFL. *Application deadline:* Applications are processed on a rolling basis. Application fee: $30. Electronic applications accepted. *Expenses:* Tuition, state resident: full-time $10,602; part-time $589 per credit hour. Tuition, nonresident: full-time $14,022; part-time $779 per credit hour. Tuition and fees vary according to degree level and program. *Financial support:* In 2014–15, 31 students received support, including 10 fellowships (averaging $3,049 per year), 25 research assistantships with full tuition reimbursements available (averaging $10,237 per year); career-related internships or fieldwork, Federal Work-Study, institutionally sponsored loans, scholarships/grants, and unspecified assistantships also available. *Faculty research:* Digital signal processing, computer aided design, computer aided manufacturing, manufacturing simulation, biomechanics, product design. *Total annual research expenditures:* $300,000. *Unit head:* Dr. Charles Standridge, Acting Director, 616-331-6750, Fax: 616-331-7215, E-mail: standric@gvsu.edu. *Application contact:* Dr. Pranod Chaphalkar, Graduate Director, 616-331-6843, Fax: 616-331-7215, E-mail: chaphalp@gvsu.edu.
Website: http://www.engineer.gvsu.edu/.

Howard University, College of Engineering, Architecture, and Computer Sciences, School of Engineering and Computer Science, Department of Mechanical Engineering, Washington, DC 20059-0002. Offers M Eng, PhD. *Degree requirements:* For master's, comprehensive exam, thesis; for doctorate, one foreign language, comprehensive exam, thesis/dissertation, 2 terms of residency. *Entrance requirements:* For master's and doctorate, GRE General Test, minimum GPA of 3.0. Additional exam requirements/recommendations for international students: Required—TOEFL. Electronic applications accepted. *Faculty research:* The dynamics and control of large flexible space structures, optimization of space structures.

Idaho State University, Office of Graduate Studies, College of Science and Engineering, Mechanical Engineering Department, Pocatello, ID 83209-8060. Offers measurement and control engineering (MS); mechanical engineering (MS). Part-time programs available. *Degree requirements:* For master's, comprehensive exam (for some programs), 2 semesters of seminar; thesis or project. *Entrance requirements:* For master's, GRE. Additional exam requirements/recommendations for international students: Required—TOEFL (minimum score 550 paper-based; 80 iBT). Electronic applications accepted. *Faculty research:* Modeling and identification of biomedical systems, intelligent systems and adaptive control, active flow control of turbo machinery, validation of advanced computational codes for thermal fluid interactions, development of methodologies for the assessment of passive safety system performance in advanced reactors, alternative energy research (wind, solar, hydrogen).

Illinois Institute of Technology, Graduate College, Armour College of Engineering, Department of Mechanical, Materials and Aerospace Engineering, Chicago, IL 60616. Offers manufacturing engineering (MAS, MS); materials science and engineering (MAS, MS, PhD); mechanical and aerospace engineering (MAS, MS, PhD), including economics (MS), energy (MS), environment (MS). Part-time and evening/weekend programs available. Postbaccalaureate distance learning degree programs offered (minimal on-campus study). *Faculty:* 29 full-time (3 women), 10 part-time/adjunct (2 women). *Students:* 187 full-time (35 women), 27 part-time (3 women); includes 8 minority (2 Black or African American, non-Hispanic/Latino; 4 Asian, non-Hispanic/Latino; 2 Hispanic/Latino), 168 international. Average age 26. 1,562 applicants, 31% accepted, 76 enrolled. In 2014, 74 master's, 7 doctorates awarded. Terminal master's awarded for partial completion of doctoral program. *Degree requirements:* For master's, comprehensive exam (for some programs), thesis (for some programs); for doctorate, comprehensive exam, thesis/dissertation. *Entrance requirements:* For master's and doctorate, GRE General Test (minimum score 1000 Quantitative and Verbal, 3.0 Analytical Writing), minimum undergraduate GPA of 3.0. Additional exam requirements/recommendations for international students: Required—TOEFL (minimum score 550 paper-based; 80 iBT). *Application deadline:* For fall admission, 5/1 for domestic and international students; for spring admission, 10/15 for domestic and international students. Applications are processed on a rolling basis. Application fee: $50. Electronic applications accepted. *Expenses: Tuition:* Full-time $22,500; part-time $1250 per credit hour. *Required fees:* $30 per course. $260 per semester. One-time fee: $235. Tuition and fees vary according to course load and program. *Financial support:* Fellowships with full and partial tuition reimbursements, research assistantships with full and partial tuition reimbursements, teaching assistantships with full and partial tuition reimbursements, Federal Work-Study, institutionally sponsored loans, scholarships/grants, health care benefits, tuition waivers, and unspecified assistantships available. Support available to part-time students. Financial award applicants required to submit FAFSA. *Faculty research:* Fluid dynamics, metallurgical and materials engineering, solids and structures, computational mechanics, computer added design and manufacturing, thermal sciences, dynamic analysis and control of complex systems. *Unit head:* Dr. Keith Bowman, Chair of the Department of Mechanical, Materials and Aerospace Engineering & Duchossois Leadership Professor of Materials Engineering, 312-567-3175, Fax: 312-567-7230, E-mail: keith.bowman@iit.edu. *Application contact:* Rishab Malhotra, Director, Graduate Admission, 866-472-3448, Fax: 312-567-3138, E-mail: inquiry.grad@iit.edu.
Website: http://www.mmae.iit.edu.

Indiana University–Purdue University Fort Wayne, College of Engineering, Technology, and Computer Science, Department of Engineering, Fort Wayne, IN 46805-1499. Offers civil engineering (MSE); computer engineering (MSE); electrical engineering (MSE); mechanical engineering (MSE); systems engineering (MSE). Part-time programs available. *Faculty:* 21 full-time (2 women). *Students:* 4 full-time (1 woman), 15 part-time (1 woman); includes 3 minority (2 Black or African American, non-Hispanic/Latino; 1 Asian, non-Hispanic/Latino), 2 international. Average age 30. 13 applicants, 100% accepted, 10 enrolled. In 2014, 17 master's awarded. *Entrance requirements:* For master's, minimum GPA of 3.0, bachelor's degree in engineering discipline. Additional exam requirements/recommendations for international students: Required—TOEFL (minimum score 550 paper-based; 79 iBT); Recommended—TWE. *Application deadline:* For fall admission, 7/15 priority date for domestic students, 5/15 priority date for international students; for spring admission, 12/1 priority date for domestic students, 10/15 priority date for international students. Applications are processed on a rolling basis. Application fee: $55 ($60 for international students). Electronic applications accepted. *Financial support:* In 2014–15, 3 research assistantships with partial tuition reimbursements (averaging $13,522 per year), 1

teaching assistantship with partial tuition reimbursement (averaging $13,522 per year) were awarded. Financial award application deadline: 3/1; financial award applicants required to submit FAFSA. *Faculty research:* Continuous space language model, sensor networks, wireless cloud architecture. *Total annual research expenditures:* $841,333. *Unit head:* Dr. Nashwan Younis, Chair, 260-481-6887, Fax: 260-481-6281, E-mail: younis@engr.ipfw.edu. *Application contact:* Dr. Abdullah Eroglu, Program Director/Professor, 260-481-0273, Fax: 260-481-5734, E-mail: eroglua@ipfw.edu.
Website: http://www.ipfw.edu/engr.

Indiana University–Purdue University Indianapolis, School of Engineering and Technology, Department of Mechanical Engineering, Indianapolis, IN 46202. Offers biomedical engineering (MS Bm E); computer-aided mechanical engineering (Certificate); mechanical engineering (MSME, PhD). Part-time programs available. *Students:* 57 full-time (4 women), 59 part-time (7 women); includes 7 minority (1 Black or African American, non-Hispanic/Latino; 3 Asian, non-Hispanic/Latino; 2 Hispanic/Latino; 1 Two or more races, non-Hispanic/Latino), 72 international. Average age 28. 177 applicants, 56% accepted, 47 enrolled. In 2014, 29 master's, 1 other advanced degree awarded. *Degree requirements:* For master's, thesis optional. *Entrance requirements:* For master's, GRE. Additional exam requirements/recommendations for international students: Required—TOEFL. *Application deadline:* For fall admission, 7/1 for domestic students. Application fee: $55 ($65 for international students). *Financial support:* Fellowships with tuition reimbursements, research assistantships with full and partial tuition reimbursements, and tuition waivers (full and partial) available. Financial award application deadline: 3/1. *Faculty research:* Computational fluid dynamics, heat transfer, finite-element methods, composites, biomechanics. *Unit head:* Dr. Jie Chen, Chairman, 317-274-9717. *Application contact:* Valerie Diemer, Graduate Program, 317-278-4960, Fax: 317-278-1671, E-mail: grad@engr.iupui.edu.
Website: http://www.engr.iupui.edu/me/.

Instituto Tecnológico y de Estudios Superiores de Monterrey, Campus Chihuahua, Graduate Programs, Chihuahua, Mexico. Offers computer systems engineering (Ingeniero); electrical engineering (Ingeniero); electromechanical engineering (Ingeniero); electronic engineering (Ingeniero); engineering administration (MEA); industrial engineering (MIE, Ingeniero); international trade (MIT); mechanical engineering (Ingeniero).

Instituto Tecnológico y de Estudios Superiores de Monterrey, Campus Monterrey, Graduate and Research Division, Programs in Engineering, Monterrey, Mexico. Offers applied statistics (M Eng); artificial intelligence (PhD); automation engineering (M Eng); chemical engineering (M Eng); civil engineering (M Eng); electrical engineering (M Eng); electronic engineering (M Eng); environmental engineering (M Eng); industrial engineering (M Eng, PhD); manufacturing engineering (M Eng); mechanical engineering (M Eng); systems and quality engineering (M Eng). M Eng program offered jointly with University of Waterloo; PhD in industrial engineering with Texas A&M University. Part-time and evening/weekend programs available. Terminal master's awarded for partial completion of doctoral program. *Degree requirements:* For master's, one foreign language, thesis; for doctorate, one foreign language, thesis/dissertation. *Entrance requirements:* For master's, EXADEP; for doctorate, GRE, master's degree in related field. Additional exam requirements/recommendations for international students: Required—TOEFL. *Faculty research:* Flexible manufacturing cells, materials, statistical methods, environmental prevention, control and evaluation.

Iowa State University of Science and Technology, Department of Mechanical Engineering, Ames, IA 50011. Offers mechanical engineering (M Eng, MS, PhD); systems engineering (M Eng). *Degree requirements:* For master's, thesis or alternative; for doctorate, thesis/dissertation. *Entrance requirements:* For master's and doctorate, GRE General Test, resume. Additional exam requirements/recommendations for international students: Required—TOEFL (minimum score 570 paper-based; 79 iBT), IELTS (minimum score 6.5). Electronic applications accepted.

Johns Hopkins University, Engineering Program for Professionals, Part-time Program in Mechanical Engineering, Baltimore, MD 21218-2699. Offers MME. Part-time and evening/weekend programs available. Electronic applications accepted.

Johns Hopkins University, G. W. C. Whiting School of Engineering, Department of Mechanical Engineering, Baltimore, MD 21218-2681. Offers MSE, PhD. Terminal master's awarded for partial completion of doctoral program. *Degree requirements:* For master's, thesis (for some programs); for doctorate, comprehensive exam, thesis/dissertation, oral exam. *Entrance requirements:* For master's and doctorate, GRE General Test. Additional exam requirements/recommendations for international students: Required—TOEFL or IELTS. Electronic applications accepted. *Faculty research:* Microscale/nanoscale science and engineering, computational engineering, aerospace and marine systems, robotics and human-machine interaction, energy and the environment, mechanics and materials.

Johns Hopkins University, G. W. C. Whiting School of Engineering, Master of Science in Engineering Management Program, Baltimore, MD 21218-2699. Offers biomaterials (MSEM); civil engineering (MSEM); communications science (MSEM); computer science (MSEM); environmental systems analysis, economics and public policy (MSEM); fluid mechanics (MSEM); materials science and engineering (MSEM); mechanical engineering (MSEM); mechanics and materials (MSEM); nano-biotechnology (MSEM); nanomaterials and nanotechnology (MSEM); operations research (MSEM); probability and statistics (MSEM); smart product and device design (MSEM). *Entrance requirements:* For master's, GRE, 3 letters of recommendation, resume. Additional exam requirements/recommendations for international students: Required—TOEFL (minimum score 600 paper-based; 100 iBT) or IELTS (minimum score 7). Electronic applications accepted.

Kansas State University, Graduate School, College of Engineering, Department of Mechanical and Nuclear Engineering, Manhattan, KS 66506. Offers mechanical engineering (MS); nuclear engineering (PhD). *Faculty:* 22 full-time (3 women). *Students:* 17 full-time (1 woman), 15 part-time (2 women); includes 6 minority (3 Asian, non-Hispanic/Latino; 3 Hispanic/Latino), 19 international. Average age 27. 66 applicants, 44% accepted, 22 enrolled. In 2014, 20 master's, 3 doctorates awarded. *Degree requirements:* For master's, thesis optional; for doctorate, comprehensive exam, thesis/dissertation. *Entrance requirements:* For master's, GRE General Test; for doctorate, GRE General Test, master's degree in mechanical engineering; minimum GPA of 3.0 overall or last 60 hours in calculus-based engineering or related program. Additional exam requirements/recommendations for international students: Required—TOEFL (minimum score 550 paper-based; 79 iBT). *Application deadline:* For fall and spring admission, 12/1 priority date for domestic and international students. Applications are processed on a rolling basis. Application fee: $50 ($75 for international students). Electronic applications accepted. *Financial support:* In 2014–15, 20 research assistantships (averaging $22,700 per year), 17 teaching assistantships with full and partial tuition reimbursements (averaging $21,000 per year) were awarded; career-related internships or fieldwork, institutionally sponsored loans, and scholarships/grants also available. Support available to part-time students. Financial award application deadline: 3/1; financial award applicants required to submit FAFSA. *Faculty research:* Radiation detection and protection, heat and mass transfer, machine design, control systems, nuclear reactor physics and engineering. *Total annual research expenditures:*

Mechanical Engineering

$1.5 million. *Unit head:* Dr. William Dunn, Head, 785-532-5610, Fax: 785-532-7057, E-mail: dunn@k-state.edu. *Application contact:* Dr. Steve Eckels, Graduate Program Director, 785-532-5610, Fax: 785-532-7057, E-mail: eckels@k-state.edu. Website: http://www.mne.k-state.edu/.

Kettering University, Graduate School, Mechanical Engineering Department, Flint, MI 48504. Offers engineering (MS). Part-time and evening/weekend programs available. Postbaccalaureate distance learning degree programs offered (no on-campus study). *Degree requirements:* For master's, thesis optional. *Entrance requirements:* Additional exam requirements/recommendations for international students: Required—TOEFL (minimum score 550 paper-based; 79 iBT). Electronic applications accepted. *Faculty research:* Occupant protection crash safety, biomechanics, alternative energy systems, advanced auto powertrain.

Lamar University, College of Graduate Studies, College of Engineering, Department of Mechanical Engineering, Beaumont, TX 77710. Offers ME, MES, DE. Part-time programs available. *Faculty:* 8 full-time (1 woman). *Students:* 271 full-time (38 women), 35 part-time (3 women); includes 10 minority (4 Black or African American, non-Hispanic/Latino; 3 Asian, non-Hispanic/Latino; 2 Hispanic/Latino; 1 Two or more races, non-Hispanic/Latino), 291 international. Average age 24. 336 applicants, 78% accepted, 140 enrolled. In 2014, 16 master's awarded. Terminal master's awarded for partial completion of doctoral program. *Degree requirements:* For master's, comprehensive exam (for some programs), thesis (for some programs); for doctorate, thesis/dissertation. *Entrance requirements:* For master's and doctorate, GRE General Test. Additional exam requirements/recommendations for international students: Required—TOEFL (minimum score 550 paper-based; 79 iBT), IELTS (minimum score 6.5). *Application deadline:* For fall admission, 8/1 for domestic students, 7/1 for international students; for spring admission, 1/5 for domestic students, 12/1 for international students. Applications are processed on a rolling basis. Application fee: $25 ($50 for international students). *Expenses:* Tuition, state resident: full-time $5724; part-time $1908 per semester. Tuition, nonresident: full-time $12,240; part-time $4080 per semester. *Required fees:* $1940; $318 per credit hour. *Financial support:* In 2014–15, 2 fellowships (averaging $7,200 per year), 4 research assistantships, 5 teaching assistantships were awarded; tuition waivers (partial) also available. Financial award application deadline: 4/1. *Faculty research:* Materials combustion, mechanical and multiphysics study in micro-electronics, structural instability/reliability, mechanics of micro electronics. *Unit head:* Dr. Hsing-Wei Chu, Chair, 409-880-8094, Fax: 409-880-8121. *Application contact:* Melissa Gallien, Director, Admissions and Academic Services, 409-880-8888, Fax: 409-880-7419, E-mail: gradmissions@lamar.edu. Website: http://engineering.lamar.edu/mechanical.

Lawrence Technological University, College of Engineering, Southfield, MI 48075-1058. Offers architectural engineering (MS); automotive engineering (MS); civil engineering (MA, MS, PhD); construction engineering management (MA); electrical and computer engineering (MS); engineering management (MEM); industrial engineering (MS); manufacturing systems (ME, DE); mechanical engineering (MS, DE); mechatronic systems engineering (MS). Part-time and evening/weekend programs available. *Faculty:* 24 full-time (5 women), 15 part-time/adjunct (0 women). *Students:* 16 full-time (6 women), 478 part-time (71 women); includes 295 minority (15 Black or African American, non-Hispanic/Latino; 271 Asian, non-Hispanic/Latino; 7 Hispanic/Latino; 2 Two or more races, non-Hispanic/Latino), 38 international. Average age 27. 1,786 applicants, 40% accepted, 218 enrolled. In 2014, 106 master's awarded. *Degree requirements:* For master's, thesis (for some programs). *Entrance requirements:* Additional exam requirements/recommendations for international students: Required—TOEFL (minimum score 550 paper-based; 79 iBT). *Application deadline:* For fall admission, 8/1 priority date for domestic students, 5/29 for international students; for spring admission, 12/1 priority date for domestic students, 10/15 for international students. Applications are processed on a rolling basis. Application fee: $50. Electronic applications accepted. *Expenses: Tuition:* Full-time $14,700; part-time $1050 per credit hour. *Required fees:* $150. One-time fee: $150 part-time. *Financial support:* In 2014–15, 31 students received support, including 8 research assistantships (averaging $9,338 per year); Federal Work-Study and institutionally sponsored loans also available. Support available to part-time students. Financial award application deadline: 4/1; financial award applicants required to submit FAFSA. *Faculty research:* Advanced composite materials in bridges, strengthening existing bridges with carbon and glass fiber sheets, development of drive shafts using composite materials. *Unit head:* Dr. Nabil Grace, Dean, 248-204-2500, Fax: 248-204-2509, E-mail: engrdean@ltu.edu. *Application contact:* Jane Rohrback, Director of Admissions, 248-204-3160, Fax: 248-204-2228, E-mail: admissions@ltu.edu. Website: http://www.ltu.edu/engineering/index.asp.

Lehigh University, P.C. Rossin College of Engineering and Applied Science, Department of Mechanical Engineering and Mechanics, Bethlehem, PA 18015. Offers computational engineering and mechanics (MS); mechanical engineering (M Eng, PhD); MBA/E. Part-time and evening/weekend programs available. Postbaccalaureate distance learning degree programs offered (no on-campus study). *Faculty:* 27 full-time (1 woman), 2 part-time/adjunct (1 woman). *Students:* 139 full-time (17 women), 29 part-time (4 women); includes 17 minority (3 Black or African American, non-Hispanic/Latino; 8 Asian, non-Hispanic/Latino; 5 Hispanic/Latino; 1 Two or more races, non-Hispanic/Latino), 89 international. Average age 26. 657 applicants, 18% accepted, 51 enrolled. In 2014, 50 master's, 6 doctorates awarded. Terminal master's awarded for partial completion of doctoral program. *Degree requirements:* For master's, thesis (for MS); for doctorate, thesis/dissertation, general exam. *Entrance requirements:* Additional exam requirements/recommendations for international students: Required—TOEFL (minimum score 550 paper-based; 79 iBT). *Application deadline:* For fall admission, 7/15 for domestic and international students; for spring admission, 12/1 for domestic and international students. Application fee: $75. Electronic applications accepted. *Expenses:* Expenses: $1,340 per credit hour. *Financial support:* In 2014–15, 36 students received support, including 5 fellowships with full and partial tuition reimbursements available (averaging $25,787 per year), 47 research assistantships with full and partial tuition reimbursements available (averaging $24,300 per year), 14 teaching assistantships with full and partial tuition reimbursements available (averaging $26,559 per year); unspecified assistantships and dean's doctoral assistantships also available. Financial award application deadline: 1/15. *Faculty research:* Thermofluids, dynamic systems, CAD/CAM, computational mechanics, solid mechanics. *Total annual research expenditures:* $3.1 million. *Unit head:* Dr. D. Gary Harlow, Chairman, 610-758-4102, Fax: 610-758-6224, E-mail: dgh0@lehigh.edu. *Application contact:* Jo Ann M. Casciano, Graduate Coordinator, 610-758-4107, Fax: 610-758-6224, E-mail: jmc4@lehigh.edu. Website: http://www.lehigh.edu/~inmem/.

Louisiana State University and Agricultural & Mechanical College, Graduate School, College of Engineering, Department of Mechanical and Industrial Engineering, Baton Rouge, LA 70803. Offers MSME, PhD. Part-time programs available. *Faculty:* 32 full-time (3 women), 1 part-time/adjunct (0 women). *Students:* 76 full-time (14 women), 17 part-time (1 woman); includes 4 minority (1 Asian, non-Hispanic/Latino; 2 Hispanic/Latino; 1 Two or more races, non-Hispanic/Latino), 68 international. Average age 28. 132 applicants, 31% accepted, 12 enrolled. In 2014, 23 master's, 16 doctorates awarded. Terminal master's awarded for partial completion of doctoral program. *Degree

requirements: For master's, thesis; for doctorate, thesis/dissertation. *Entrance requirements:* For master's and doctorate, GRE General Test, minimum GPA of 3.0. Additional exam requirements/recommendations for international students: Required—TOEFL (minimum score 550 paper-based; 79 iBT), IELTS (minimum score 6.5), or PTE (minimum score 59). *Application deadline:* For fall admission, 1/1 priority date for domestic students, 2/15 priority date for international students; for spring admission, 10/15 for domestic and international students; for summer admission, 5/15 for domestic and international students. Applications are processed on a rolling basis. Application fee: $50 ($70 for international students). Electronic applications accepted. *Financial support:* In 2014–15, 79 students received support, including 3 fellowships with full and partial tuition reimbursements available (averaging $15,816 per year), 42 research assistantships with partial tuition reimbursements available (averaging $19,368 per year), 30 teaching assistantships with partial tuition reimbursements available (averaging $13,016 per year); Federal Work-Study, institutionally sponsored loans, health care benefits, tuition waivers (full and partial), and unspecified assistantships also available. Financial award applicants required to submit FAFSA. *Faculty research:* Computer-aided design, thermal and fluid sciences materials engineering, fluid mechanics, combustion and microsystems engineering. *Total annual research expenditures:* $2.8 million. *Unit head:* Dr. Dimitris Nikitopoulos, Chair, 225-578-5792, E-mail: medimi@egateway.lsu.edu. *Application contact:* Dr. Sunggook Park, Graduate Adviser, 225-578-0279, Fax: 225-578-5924, E-mail: sunggook@lsu.edu. Website: http://me.lsu.edu/.

Louisiana Tech University, Graduate School, College of Engineering and Science, Department of Mechanical Engineering, Ruston, LA 71272. Offers MS, PhD. Part-time programs available. Terminal master's awarded for partial completion of doctoral program. *Degree requirements:* For master's, thesis; for doctorate, thesis/dissertation. *Entrance requirements:* For master's, GRE General Test, minimum GPA of 3.0 in last 60 hours; for doctorate, minimum graduate GPA of 3.25 (with MS) or GRE General Test. Additional exam requirements/recommendations for international students: Required—TOEFL. *Faculty research:* Engineering management, facilities planning, thermodynamics, automated manufacturing, micromanufacturing.

Loyola Marymount University, College of Science and Engineering, Department of Mechanical Engineering, Program in Mechanical Engineering, Los Angeles, CA 90045-2659. Offers MSE. *Degree requirements:* For master's, thesis or alternative. *Entrance requirements:* For master's, letters of recommendation, personal statement. Additional exam requirements/recommendations for international students: Required—TOEFL (minimum score 550 paper-based; 80 iBT). Electronic applications accepted.

Manhattan College, Graduate Programs, School of Engineering, Program in Mechanical Engineering, Riverdale, NY 10471. Offers MS. Part-time and evening/weekend programs available. *Faculty:* 7 full-time (2 women), 2 part-time/adjunct (0 women). *Students:* 26 full-time (4 women), 6 part-time (0 women); includes 1 minority (Hispanic/Latino). Average age 24. 15 applicants, 87% accepted, 10 enrolled. In 2014, 26 master's awarded. *Degree requirements:* For master's, thesis optional. *Entrance requirements:* For master's, GRE (recommended), minimum GPA of 3.0. Additional exam requirements/recommendations for international students: Required—TOEFL (minimum score 550 paper-based; 80 iBT), IELTS (minimum score 6). *Application deadline:* For fall admission, 8/10 priority date for domestic students, 8/10 for international students; for spring admission, 1/7 for domestic and international students. Applications are processed on a rolling basis. Application fee: $60. *Financial support:* In 2014–15, 8 students received support, including 7 teaching assistantships with partial tuition reimbursements available (averaging $7,000 per year); career-related internships or fieldwork, Federal Work-Study, scholarships/grants, and unspecified assistantships also available. Support available to part-time students. Financial award application deadline: 2/1. *Faculty research:* Thermal analysis of rocket thrust chambers, quality of wood, biomechanics/structural analysis of cacti, orthodontic research. *Unit head:* Dr. Bahman Litkouhi, Director, Graduate Program, 718-862-7927, Fax: 718-862-7163, E-mail: mechdept@manhattan.edu. *Application contact:* Kathy Balaj, Information Contact, 718-862-7145, Fax: 718-862-7163, E-mail: kathy.balaj@manhattan.edu. Website: http://www.engineering.manhattan.edu.

Marquette University, Graduate School, Opus College of Engineering, Department of Mechanical Engineering, Milwaukee, WI 53201-1881. Offers engineering innovation (Certificate); engineering management (MSEM); mechanical engineering (MS, PhD); new product and process development (Certificate). Part-time and evening/weekend programs available. Terminal master's awarded for partial completion of doctoral program. *Degree requirements:* For master's, comprehensive exam, thesis (for some programs); for doctorate, comprehensive exam, thesis/dissertation, qualifying exam. *Entrance requirements:* For master's, GRE General Test, minimum GPA of 3.0, official transcripts from all current and previous colleges/universities except Marquette, three letters of recommendation; for doctorate, GRE General Test, minimum GPA of 3.0, official transcripts from all current and previous colleges/universities except Marquette, three letters of recommendation, statement of purpose, copies of any published work. Additional exam requirements/recommendations for international students: Required—TOEFL (minimum score 530 paper-based). Electronic applications accepted. *Faculty research:* Computer-integrated manufacturing, energy conversion, simulation modeling and optimization, applied mechanics, metallurgy.

Marshall University, Academic Affairs Division, College of Information Technology and Engineering, Weisbert Division of Engineering, Huntington, WV 25755. Offers engineering management (MSE); environmental engineering (MSE); mechanical engineering (MS); transportation and infrastructure engineering (MSE). Part-time and evening/weekend programs available. *Students:* 30 full-time (5 women), 28 part-time (7 women); includes 3 minority (all Black or African American, non-Hispanic/Latino), 22 international. Average age 29. In 2014, 11 master's awarded. *Degree requirements:* For master's, final project, oral exam. *Entrance requirements:* For master's, GMAT or GRE General Test, minimum undergraduate GPA of 2.75. Application fee: $40. *Financial support:* Tuition waivers (full) available. Support available to part-time students. Financial award application deadline: 8/1; financial award applicants required to submit FAFSA. *Unit head:* Dr. William Pierson, Chair, 304-696-2695, E-mail: pierson@marshall.edu. *Application contact:* Information Contact, 304-746-1900, Fax: 304-746-1902, E-mail: services@marshall.edu. Website: http://www.marshall.edu/cite/.

Massachusetts Institute of Technology, School of Engineering, Department of Mechanical Engineering, Cambridge, MA 02139. Offers manufacturing (M Eng); mechanical engineering (SM, PhD, Sc D, Mech E); naval architecture and marine engineering (SM, PhD, Sc D); naval engineering (Naval E); ocean engineering (SM, PhD, Sc D); oceanographic engineering (SM, PhD, Sc D); SM/MBA. *Faculty:* 70 full-time (8 women). *Students:* 549 full-time (140 women); includes 98 minority (8 Black or African American, non-Hispanic/Latino; 1 American Indian or Alaska Native, non-Hispanic/Latino; 47 Asian, non-Hispanic/Latino; 28 Hispanic/Latino; 14 Two or more races, non-Hispanic/Latino), 252 international. Average age 27. 1,409 applicants, 19% accepted, 200 enrolled. In 2014, 166 master's, 60 doctorates, 9 other advanced degrees awarded. Terminal master's awarded for partial completion of doctoral program. *Degree requirements:* For master's and other advanced degree, thesis; for doctorate, comprehensive exam, thesis/dissertation, a minor program of study in a field different

from that of the major. *Entrance requirements:* For master's, doctorate, and other advanced degree, GRE General Test. Additional exam requirements/recommendations for international students: Required—TOEFL (minimum score 577 paper-based; 90 iBT), IELTS (minimum score 7). *Application deadline:* For fall and spring admission, 12/15 for domestic and international students. Application fee: $75. Electronic applications accepted. *Expenses: Tuition:* Full-time $44,720; part-time $699 per unit. *Required fees:* $296. *Financial support:* In 2014–15, 459 students received support, including 102 fellowships (averaging $32,900 per year), 338 research assistantships (averaging $33,600 per year), 50 teaching assistantships (averaging $36,700 per year); Federal Work-Study, institutionally sponsored loans, scholarships/grants, traineeships, health care benefits, and unspecified assistantships also available. Financial award application deadline: 4/15; financial award applicants required to submit FAFSA. *Faculty research:* Mechanics: modeling, experimentation and computation; design, manufacturing, and product development; controls, instrumentation, and robotics; energy science and engineering; ocean science and engineering; bioengineering; micro- and nano-engineering. *Total annual research expenditures:* $64 million. *Unit head:* Gang Chen, Department Head, 617-253-2201, Fax: 617-258-6156, E-mail: mehq@mit.edu. *Application contact:* Graduate Office, 617-253-2291, Fax: 617-258-5802, E-mail: megradoffice@mit.edu.
Website: http://meche.mit.edu/.

McGill University, Faculty of Graduate and Postdoctoral Studies, Faculty of Engineering, Department of Mechanical Engineering, Montréal, QC H3A 2T5, Canada. Offers aerospace (M Eng); manufacturing management (MMM); mechanical engineering (M Eng, M Sc, PhD).

McMaster University, School of Graduate Studies, Faculty of Engineering, Department of Mechanical Engineering, Hamilton, ON L8S 4M2, Canada. Offers M Eng, MA Sc, PhD. M Eng degree offered as part of the Advanced Design and Manufacturing Institute (ADMI) group collaboration with the University of Toronto, University of Western Ontario, and University of Waterloo. *Degree requirements:* For master's, thesis; for doctorate, comprehensive exam, thesis/dissertation. *Entrance requirements:* Additional exam requirements/recommendations for international students: Required—TOEFL (minimum score 550 paper-based). *Faculty research:* Manufacturing engineering, dimensional metrology, micro-fluidics, multi-phase flow and heat transfer, process modeling simulation.

McNeese State University, Doré School of Graduate Studies, College of Engineering and Engineering Technology, Department of Engineering, Master of Engineering Program, Lake Charles, LA 70609. Offers chemical engineering (M Eng); civil engineering (M Eng); electrical engineering (M Eng); engineering management (M Eng); mechanical engineering (M Eng). Part-time and evening/weekend programs available. *Degree requirements:* For master's, thesis or alternative. *Entrance requirements:* For master's, GRE, baccalaureate degree, minimum overall GPA of 3.0. Additional exam requirements/recommendations for international students: Required—TOEFL (minimum score 560 paper-based; 83 iBT).

McNeese State University, Doré School of Graduate Studies, College of Engineering and Engineering Technology, Department of Engineering, Pump Reliability Engineering Graduate Certificate Program, Lake Charles, LA 70609. Offers Graduate Certificate. *Entrance requirements:* For degree, GRE, engineering bachelor degree. Additional exam requirements/recommendations for international students: Required—TOEFL (minimum score 560 paper-based).

McNeese State University, Doré School of Graduate Studies, College of Engineering and Engineering Technology, Department of Engineering, Pump Reliability Engineering Postbaccalaureate Certificate Program, Lake Charles, LA 70609. Offers Postbaccalaureate Certificate. *Entrance requirements:* For degree, engineering bachelor degree. Additional exam requirements/recommendations for international students: Required—TOEFL (minimum score 560 paper-based).

Memorial University of Newfoundland, School of Graduate Studies, Faculty of Engineering and Applied Science, St. John's, NL A1C 5S7, Canada. Offers civil engineering (M Eng, PhD); electrical and computer engineering (M Eng, PhD); mechanical engineering (M Eng, PhD); ocean and naval architecture engineering (M Eng, PhD). Part-time programs available. *Degree requirements:* For master's, thesis; for doctorate, comprehensive exam, thesis/dissertation, oral thesis defense. *Entrance requirements:* For master's, 2nd class degree; for doctorate, master's degree in engineering. Electronic applications accepted. *Faculty research:* Engineering analysis, environmental and hydrotechnical studies, manufacturing and robotics, mechanics, structures and materials.

Mercer University, Graduate Studies, Macon Campus, School of Engineering, Macon, GA 31207. Offers biomedical engineering (MSE); computer engineering (MSE); electrical engineering (MSE); engineering management (MSE); environmental engineering (MSE); environmental systems (MS); mechanical engineering (MSE); software engineering (MSE); software systems (MS); technical communications management (MS); technical management (MS). Part-time and evening/weekend programs available. Postbaccalaureate distance learning degree programs offered (no on-campus study). *Faculty:* 20 full-time (6 women), 2 part-time/adjunct (0 women). *Students:* 10 full-time (4 women), 75 part-time (16 women); includes 10 minority (5 Black or African American, non-Hispanic/Latino; 4 Asian, non-Hispanic/Latino; 1 Hispanic/Latino), 4 international. Average age 42. In 2014, 70 master's awarded. *Degree requirements:* For master's, thesis or alternative. *Entrance requirements:* For master's, minimum undergraduate GPA of 3.0. Additional exam requirements/recommendations for international students: Required—TOEFL (minimum score 550 paper-based; 80 iBT). *Application deadline:* For fall admission, 4/1 priority date for domestic and international students; for spring admission, 11/1 priority date for domestic and international students. Applications are processed on a rolling basis. Application fee: $75. *Expenses:* Expenses: Contact institution. *Financial support:* Federal Work-Study available. *Unit head:* Dr. Wade H. Shaw, Dean, 478-301-2459, Fax: 478-301-5593, E-mail: shaw_wh@mercer.edu. *Application contact:* Dr. Richard O. Mines, Program Director, 478-301-2347, Fax: 478-301-5433, E-mail: mines_ro@mercer.edu.
Website: http://engineering.mercer.edu/.

Merrimack College, School of Science and Engineering, North Andover, MA 01845-5800. Offers mechanical engineering (MS), including engineering management. Part-time programs available. *Faculty:* 4 full-time (0 women), 1 part-time/adjunct (0 women). *Students:* 13 full-time (3 women), 3 part-time (0 women); includes 1 minority (Two or more races, non-Hispanic/Latino), 1 international. Average age 27. 22 applicants, 59% accepted, 8 enrolled. In 2014, 5 master's awarded. *Degree requirements:* For master's, variable foreign language requirement, comprehensive exam, thesis optional. *Entrance requirements:* For master's, official college transcripts, resume, personal statement, 2 recommendations. Additional exam requirements/recommendations for international students: Required—TOEFL (minimum score 84 iBT), IELTS (minimum score 6.5), PTE (minimum score 56). *Application deadline:* For fall admission, 8/15 for domestic and international students; for winter admission, 12/1 for domestic students, 11/15 for international students; for spring admission, 1/10 for domestic and international students. Applications are processed on a rolling basis. Application fee: $0. Electronic applications accepted. *Expenses:* Expenses: Contact institution. *Financial support:* Career-related internships or fieldwork, scholarships/grants, and health care benefits available. Support available to part-time students. Financial award application deadline: 5/1; financial award applicants required to submit FAFSA. *Application contact:* Rachael Tampone, Graduate Admission Counselor, 978-837-5196, E-mail: tamponer@merrimack.edu.
Website: http://www.merrimack.edu/academics/graduate/engineering/.

Michigan State University, The Graduate School, College of Engineering, Department of Mechanical Engineering, East Lansing, MI 48824. Offers engineering mechanics (MS, PhD); mechanical engineering (MS, PhD). *Entrance requirements:* For master's, GRE General Test. Additional exam requirements/recommendations for international students: Required—TOEFL. Electronic applications accepted.

Michigan Technological University, Graduate School, College of Engineering, Department of Mechanical Engineering-Engineering Mechanics, Houghton, MI 49931. Offers engineering mechanics (MS); hybrid electric drive vehicle engineering (Graduate Certificate); mechanical engineering (MS); mechanical engineering-engineering mechanics (PhD). Part-time programs available. Postbaccalaureate distance learning degree programs offered (minimal on-campus study). *Faculty:* 63 full-time, 38 part-time/adjunct. *Students:* 243 full-time, 85 part-time; includes 11 minority (3 Black or African American, non-Hispanic/Latino; 4 Asian, non-Hispanic/Latino; 3 Hispanic/Latino; 1 Two or more races, non-Hispanic/Latino), 250 international. Average age 27. 1,421 applicants, 23% accepted, 95 enrolled. In 2014, 106 master's, 16 doctorates, 12 other advanced degrees awarded. Terminal master's awarded for partial completion of doctoral program. *Degree requirements:* For master's, comprehensive exam (for some programs), thesis (for some programs); for doctorate, comprehensive exam, thesis/dissertation. *Entrance requirements:* For master's, GRE (Michigan Tech students exempt - recommended for external funding opportunities), statement of purpose, official transcripts, 2 letters of recommendation, resume/curriculum vitae; for doctorate, GRE (Michigan Tech students exempt - recommended for external funding opportunities), MS (preferred), statement of purpose, official transcripts, 2 letters of recommendation, resume/curriculum vitae; for Graduate Certificate, statement of purpose, official transcripts, BS in engineering. Additional exam requirements/recommendations for international students: Required—TOEFL (minimum score 90 iBT) or IELTS. *Application deadline:* For fall admission, 3/1 priority date for domestic and international students; for spring admission, 8/1 priority date for domestic and international students. Applications are processed on a rolling basis. Electronic applications accepted. *Expenses:* Expenses: Contact institution. *Financial support:* In 2014–15, 182 students received support, including 16 fellowships with full and partial tuition reimbursements available (averaging $13,824 per year), 33 research assistantships with full and partial tuition reimbursements available (averaging $13,824 per year), 28 teaching assistantships with full and partial tuition reimbursements available (averaging $13,824 per year); career-related internships or fieldwork, Federal Work-Study, scholarships/grants, health care benefits, unspecified assistantships, and cooperative program also available. Financial award applicants required to submit FAFSA. *Faculty research:* Design and dynamic systems, energy-thermofluids, manufacturing, solid mechanics, sustainability. *Total annual research expenditures:* $3.7 million. *Unit head:* Dr. William W. Predebon, Chair, 906-487-2551, Fax: 906-487-2822, E-mail: wwpredeb@mtu.edu. *Application contact:* Jillian Isaacson, Office Assistant, 906-487-3611, Fax: 906-487-2822, E-mail: jillian@mtu.edu.
Website: http://www.mtu.edu/mechanical/.

Mississippi State University, Bagley College of Engineering, Department of Mechanical Engineering, Mississippi State, MS 39762. Offers engineering (PhD), including mechanical engineering; mechanical engineering (MS). Part-time programs available. Postbaccalaureate distance learning degree programs offered (minimal on-campus study). *Faculty:* 22 full-time (2 women), 1 part-time/adjunct (0 women). *Students:* 67 full-time (9 women), 18 part-time (1 woman); includes 11 minority (4 Black or African American, non-Hispanic/Latino; 2 Asian, non-Hispanic/Latino; 4 Hispanic/Latino; 1 Two or more races, non-Hispanic/Latino), 22 international. Average age 27. 96 applicants, 51% accepted, 23 enrolled. In 2014, 11 master's, 8 doctorates awarded. *Degree requirements:* For master's, thesis optional, oral exam; for doctorate, thesis/dissertation, qualifying exam, preliminary exam, dissertation defense. *Entrance requirements:* For master's, GRE (for graduates from program not accredited by EAC/ABET), minimum GPA of 2.75; for doctorate, GRE, minimum GPA of 2.75. Additional exam requirements/recommendations for international students: Required—TOEFL (minimum score 550 paper-based; 79 iBT); Recommended—IELTS (minimum score 6.5). *Application deadline:* For fall admission, 7/1 for domestic students, 5/1 for international students; for spring admission, 11/1 for domestic students, 9/1 for international students. Applications are processed on a rolling basis. Application fee: $60. Electronic applications accepted. *Expenses:* Tuition, state resident: full-time $7140; part-time $783 per credit hour. Tuition, nonresident: full-time $18,478; part-time $2043 per credit hour. *Financial support:* In 2014–15, 22 research assistantships with full tuition reimbursements (averaging $14,161 per year), 2 teaching assistantships with full tuition reimbursements (averaging $15,094 per year) were awarded; career-related internships or fieldwork, Federal Work-Study, institutionally sponsored loans, scholarships/grants, and unspecified assistantships also available. Financial award application deadline: 4/1; financial award applicants required to submit FAFSA. *Faculty research:* Fatigue and fracture, heat transfer, fluid dynamics, manufacturing systems, materials. *Total annual research expenditures:* $11.6 million. *Unit head:* Dr. Pedro Mago, Professor/Head, 662-325-6602, Fax: 662-325-7223, E-mail: mago@me.msstate.edu. *Application contact:* Dr. Mark Horstemeyer, Graduate Coordinator, 662-325-3260, Fax: 662-325-7223, E-mail: graduate@me.msstate.edu.
Website: http://www.me.msstate.edu/.

Missouri University of Science and Technology, Graduate School, Department of Mechanical and Aerospace Engineering, Rolla, MO 65409. Offers aerospace engineering (MS, PhD); mechanical engineering (MS, DE, PhD). Part-time and evening/weekend programs available. Terminal master's awarded for partial completion of doctoral program. *Degree requirements:* For master's, thesis optional; for doctorate, comprehensive exam, thesis/dissertation. *Entrance requirements:* For master's, GRE General Test (minimum score 1100 verbal and quantitative, writing 3.5), minimum GPA of 3.0; for doctorate, GRE General Test (minimum score: verbal and quantitative 1100, writing 3.5), minimum GPA of 3.5. Additional exam requirements/recommendations for international students: Required—TOEFL. Electronic applications accepted. *Faculty research:* Dynamics and controls, acoustics, computational fluid dynamics, space mechanics, hypersonics.

Montana State University, The Graduate School, College of Engineering, Department of Mechanical and Industrial Engineering, Bozeman, MT 59717. Offers engineering (PhD), including industrial engineering, mechanical engineering; industrial and management engineering (MS); mechanical engineering (MS). Part-time programs available. *Degree requirements:* For master's, comprehensive exam, thesis, oral exams; for doctorate, comprehensive exam, thesis/dissertation, qualifying exam. *Entrance requirements:* For master's, GRE, official transcript, minimum GPA of 3.0, demonstrated potential for success, statement of goals, three letters of recommendation, proof of funds affidavit; for doctorate, minimum undergraduate GPA of 3.0, 3.2 graduate; three letters of recommendation; statement of objectives. Additional exam requirements/

recommendations for international students: Required—TOEFL or IELTS. Electronic applications accepted. *Faculty research:* Human factors engineering, energy, design and manufacture, systems modeling, materials and structures, measurement systems.

Naval Postgraduate School, Departments and Academic Groups, Department of Mechanical and Aerospace Engineering, Monterey, CA 93943. Offers astronautical engineer (AstE); astronautical engineering (MS); engineering science (MS), including astronautical engineering, mechanical engineering; mechanical and aerospace engineering (PhD); mechanical engineering (MS). Program only open to commissioned officers of the United States and friendly nations and selected United States federal civilian employees. *Accreditation:* ABET (one or more programs are accredited). Part-time programs available. Postbaccalaureate distance learning degree programs offered. *Degree requirements:* For master's, thesis (for some programs), capstone or research/dissertation paper (for some programs); for doctorate, thesis/dissertation; for AstE, thesis. *Faculty research:* Sensors and actuators, new materials and methods, mechanics of materials, laser and material interaction, energy harvesting and storage.

Naval Postgraduate School, Departments and Academic Groups, Space Systems Academic Group, Monterey, CA 93943. Offers applied physics (MS); astronautical engineering (MS); computer science (MS); electrical engineering (MS); mechanical engineering (MS); space systems (Engr); space systems operations (MS). Program only open to commissioned officers of the United States and friendly nations and selected United States federal civilian employees. Part-time programs available. *Degree requirements:* For master's and Engr, thesis; for doctorate, thesis/dissertation. *Faculty research:* Military applications for space; space reconnaissance and remote sensing; radiation-hardened electronics for space; design, construction and operations of small satellites; satellite communications systems.

Naval Postgraduate School, Departments and Academic Groups, Undersea Warfare Academic Group, Monterey, CA 93943. Offers applied mathematics (MS); applied physics (MS); applied science (MS), including acoustics, operations research, physical oceanography, signal processing; electrical engineering (MS); engineering acoustics (MS, PhD); engineering science (MS), including electrical engineering, mechanical engineering; mechanical engineer (ME); mechanical engineering (MS, MSME); meteorology (MS); operations research (MS); physical oceanography (MS). Program only open to commissioned officers of the United States and friendly nations and selected United States federal civilian employees. Part-time programs available. *Degree requirements:* For master's, thesis. *Faculty research:* Unmanned/autonomous vehicles, sea mines and countermeasures, submarine warfare in the twentieth and twenty-first centuries.

New Jersey Institute of Technology, Newark College of Engineering, Newark, NJ 07102. Offers biomedical engineering (MS, PhD); chemical engineering (MS, PhD); computer engineering (MS, PhD); electrical engineering (MS, PhD); engineering management (MS); healthcare systems management (MS); industrial engineering (MS, PhD); Internet engineering (MS); manufacturing engineering (MS); mechanical engineering (MS, PhD); occupational safety and health engineering (MS); pharmaceutical bioprocessing (MS); pharmaceutical engineering (MS); pharmaceutical systems management (MS); power and energy systems (MS); telecommunications (MS); transportation (MS, PhD). Part-time and evening/weekend programs available. Terminal master's awarded for partial completion of doctoral program. *Degree requirements:* For master's, thesis optional; for doctorate, thesis/dissertation. *Entrance requirements:* For master's, GRE General Test; for doctorate, GRE General Test, minimum graduate GPA of 3.5. Additional exam requirements/recommendations for international students: Required—TOEFL (minimum score 550 paper-based; 79 iBT). Electronic applications accepted.

New Mexico Institute of Mining and Technology, Graduate Studies, Program in Mechanical Engineering, Socorro, NM 87801. Offers explosives engineering (MS); fluid and thermal sciences (MS); mechatronics systems engineering (MS); solid mechanics (MS). *Degree requirements:* For master's, thesis (for some programs). *Entrance requirements:* For master's, GRE General Test. Additional exam requirements/recommendations for international students: Required—TOEFL (minimum score 540 paper-based). *Faculty research:* Vibrations, fluid-structure interactions.

New Mexico State University, College of Engineering, Department of Mechanical Engineering, Las Cruces, NM 88003-8001. Offers MSAE, MSME, PhD. Part-time programs available. Postbaccalaureate distance learning degree programs offered (no on-campus study). *Faculty:* 18 full-time (1 woman), 1 part-time/adjunct (0 women). *Students:* 38 full-time (8 women), 15 part-time (1 woman); includes 12 minority (1 Black or African American, non-Hispanic/Latino; 1 Asian, non-Hispanic/Latino; 9 Hispanic/Latino; 1 Two or more races, non-Hispanic/Latino), 29 international. Average age 27. 89 applicants, 40% accepted, 12 enrolled. In 2014, 10 master's, 3 doctorates awarded. *Degree requirements:* For master's, thesis (for some programs); for doctorate, comprehensive exam, thesis/dissertation, 2 research tools, qualifying exam. *Entrance requirements:* For master's and doctorate, GRE, minimum GPA of 3.0. Additional exam requirements/recommendations for international students: Required—TOEFL (minimum score 550 paper-based; 79 iBT), IELTS (minimum score 6.5). *Application deadline:* For fall admission, 7/1 priority date for domestic students; for spring admission, 11/1 for domestic students. Applications are processed on a rolling basis. Application fee: $40 ($50 for international students). Electronic applications accepted. *Expenses:* Tuition, state resident: full-time $3969; part-time $220.50 per credit hour. Tuition, nonresident: full-time $13,838; part-time $768.80 per credit hour. *Required fees:* $853; $47.40 per credit hour. *Financial support:* In 2014–15, 38 students received support, including 12 research assistantships (averaging $14,176 per year), 21 teaching assistantships (averaging $14,534 per year); career-related internships or fieldwork, Federal Work-Study, scholarships/grants, traineeships, health care benefits, and unspecified assistantships also available. Support available to part-time students. Financial award application deadline: 3/1. *Faculty research:* Computational mechanics and micromechanics; robotics and mechatronics; control, dynamics, and nonlinear vibrations; composites; experimental and computational fluid dynamics; aeroelasticity and flutter. *Total annual research expenditures:* $1.3 million. *Unit head:* Dr. Ian Leslie, Academic Department Head, 575-646-1945, Fax: 575-646-6111, E-mail: ileslie@nmsu.edu. *Application contact:* 575-646-3502, Fax: 575-646-6111.
Website: http://mae.nmsu.edu/.

New York University, Polytechnic School of Engineering, Department of Mechanical and Aerospace Engineering, New York, NY 10012-1019. Offers mechanical engineering (MS, PhD). Part-time and evening/weekend programs available. *Faculty:* 17 full-time (4 women), 7 part-time/adjunct (0 women). *Students:* 74 full-time (10 women), 15 part-time (3 women); includes 12 minority (1 Black or African American, non-Hispanic/Latino; 8 Asian, non-Hispanic/Latino; 2 Hispanic/Latino; 1 Two or more races, non-Hispanic/Latino), 60 international. Average age 25. 369 applicants, 36% accepted, 40 enrolled. In 2014, 35 master's, 4 doctorates awarded. *Degree requirements:* For master's, comprehensive exam (for some programs), thesis (for some programs); for doctorate, comprehensive exam, thesis/dissertation. *Entrance requirements:* Additional exam requirements/recommendations for international students: Required—TOEFL (minimum score 550 paper-based; 80 iBT); Recommended—IELTS (minimum score 6.5). *Application deadline:* For fall admission, 2/15 priority date for domestic and international students; for spring admission, 11/1 priority date for domestic and international students. Applications are processed on a rolling basis. Application fee: $75. Electronic applications accepted. *Financial support:* Career-related internships or fieldwork, institutionally sponsored loans, scholarships/grants, and unspecified assistantships available. Support available to part-time students. Financial award applicants required to submit FAFSA. *Faculty research:* Underwater applications of dynamical systems, systems science approaches to understanding variation in state traffic and alcohol policies, development of ankle instability rehabilitation robot, synthetic osteochondral grafts for knee osteoarthritis. *Total annual research expenditures:* $5.3 million. *Unit head:* Dr. George Vradis, Program Director, 718-260-3875, E-mail: cst262@nyu.edu. *Application contact:* Raymond Lutzky, Director, Graduate Enrollment Management, 718-637-5984, Fax: 718-260-3624, E-mail: rlutzky@poly.edu.

North Carolina Agricultural and Technical State University, School of Graduate Studies, College of Engineering, Department of Mechanical Engineering, Greensboro, NC 27411. Offers MSME, PhD. Part-time programs available. *Degree requirements:* For master's, thesis, qualifying exam, thesis defense; for doctorate, thesis/dissertation. *Entrance requirements:* For master's, BS in mechanical engineering from accredited institution with minimum overall GPA of 3.0; for doctorate, GRE, MS in mechanical engineering or closely-related field with minimum GPA of 3.3. *Faculty research:* Composites, smart materials and sensors, mechanical systems modeling and finite element analysis, computational fluid dynamics and engine research, design and manufacturing.

North Carolina State University, Graduate School, College of Engineering, Department of Mechanical and Aerospace Engineering, Program in Mechanical Engineering, Raleigh, NC 27695. Offers MS, PhD. Part-time programs available. Postbaccalaureate distance learning degree programs offered (no on-campus study). *Degree requirements:* For master's, thesis optional, oral exam; for doctorate, thesis/dissertation, oral and preliminary exams. *Entrance requirements:* For master's and doctorate, GRE General Test. Additional exam requirements/recommendations for international students: Required—TOEFL (minimum score 550 paper-based). Electronic applications accepted. *Faculty research:* Vibration and control, fluid dynamics, thermal sciences, structures and materials, aerodynamics acoustics.

North Dakota State University, College of Graduate and Interdisciplinary Studies, College of Engineering and Architecture, Department of Mechanical Engineering and Applied Mechanics, Fargo, ND 58108. Offers MS, PhD. Part-time programs available. *Degree requirements:* For master's, thesis; for doctorate, comprehensive exam, thesis/dissertation. *Entrance requirements:* For master's and doctorate, minimum GPA of 3.0. Additional exam requirements/recommendations for international students: Required—TOEFL (minimum score 550 paper-based). Electronic applications accepted. *Faculty research:* Thermodynamics, finite element analysis, automotive systems, robotics, nanotechnology.

Northeastern University, College of Engineering, Boston, MA 02115-5096. Offers bioengineering (PhD); chemical engineering (MS, PhD); civil engineering (MS, PhD); computer engineering (PhD); computer systems engineering (MS); electrical and computer engineering (MS); electrical and engineering leadership (MS); electrical engineering (PhD); energy systems (MS); engineering leadership (Certificate); engineering management (MRTP); industrial engineering (MS, PhD); information assurance (PhD); information systems (MS); interdisciplinary (PhD); mechanical engineering (MS, PhD); operations research (MS); telecommunication systems management (MS). Part-time programs available. *Expenses:* Contact institution.

Northern Arizona University, Graduate College, College of Engineering, Forestry and Natural Sciences, Programs in Engineering, Flagstaff, AZ 86011. Offers civil and environmental engineering (M Eng); civil engineering (MSE); computer science (MSE); electrical engineering (M Eng, MSE); engineering (M Eng, MSE); environmental engineering (M Eng, MSE); mechanical engineering (M Eng, MSE). Part-time programs available. Postbaccalaureate distance learning degree programs offered (no on-campus study). *Degree requirements:* For master's, thesis. *Entrance requirements:* For master's, GRE General Test. Additional exam requirements/recommendations for international students: Required—TOEFL (minimum score 550 paper-based; 80 iBT), IELTS (minimum score 7). Electronic applications accepted.

Northern Illinois University, Graduate School, College of Engineering and Engineering Technology, Department of Mechanical Engineering, De Kalb, IL 60115-2854. Offers MS. Part-time programs available. *Faculty:* 9 full-time (0 women). *Students:* 39 full-time (5 women), 40 part-time (4 women); includes 8 minority (1 Black or African American, non-Hispanic/Latino; 5 Asian, non-Hispanic/Latino; 2 Hispanic/Latino), 49 international. Average age 26. 150 applicants, 41% accepted, 23 enrolled. In 2014, 14 master's awarded. *Degree requirements:* For master's, comprehensive exam, thesis optional. *Entrance requirements:* For master's, GRE General Test, minimum GPA of 2.75. Additional exam requirements/recommendations for international students: Required—TOEFL (minimum score 550 paper-based). *Application deadline:* For fall admission, 6/1 for domestic students, 5/1 for international students; for spring admission, 11/1 for domestic students, 10/1 for international students. Applications are processed on a rolling basis. Application fee: $40. Electronic applications accepted. *Financial support:* In 2014–15, 3 research assistantships with full tuition reimbursements, 22 teaching assistantships with full tuition reimbursements were awarded; fellowships with full tuition reimbursements, Federal Work-Study, scholarships/grants, tuition waivers (full), and staff assistantships also available. Support available to part-time students. Financial award applicants required to submit FAFSA. *Faculty research:* Robotics, nonlinear dynamic systems, piezo mechanics, quartz resonators, sheet metal forming. *Unit head:* Dr. Pradip Majumdar, Chair, 815-753-9970, Fax: 815-753-0416, E-mail: pmajumdar@niu.edu. *Application contact:* Graduate School Office, 815-753-0395, E-mail: gradsch@niu.edu.
Website: http://www.niu.edu/me/graduate/.

Northwestern University, McCormick School of Engineering and Applied Science, Department of Mechanical Engineering, Evanston, IL 60208. Offers MS, PhD. MS and PhD offered through the Graduate School. Part-time programs available. *Faculty:* 21 full-time (5 women). *Students:* 135 full-time (27 women), 9 part-time (1 woman); includes 18 minority (4 Black or African American, non-Hispanic/Latino; 10 Asian, non-Hispanic/Latino; 1 Hispanic/Latino; 3 Two or more races, non-Hispanic/Latino), 85 international. Average age 26. 556 applicants, 17% accepted, 36 enrolled. In 2014, 29 master's, 14 doctorates awarded. Terminal master's awarded for partial completion of doctoral program. *Degree requirements:* For master's, thesis optional; for doctorate, comprehensive exam, thesis/dissertation. *Entrance requirements:* For master's and doctorate, GRE General Test. Additional exam requirements/recommendations for international students: Required—TOEFL (minimum score 577 paper-based; 90 iBT) or IELTS (minimum score of 7.0). *Application deadline:* For fall admission, 12/31 for domestic and international students. Application fee: $95. Electronic applications accepted. *Financial support:* Fellowships with full tuition reimbursements, research assistantships with full tuition reimbursements, teaching assistantships with full tuition reimbursements, career-related internships or fieldwork, institutionally sponsored loans, health care benefits, and unspecified assistantships available. Financial award application deadline: 1/15; financial award applicants required to submit FAFSA. *Faculty research:* MEMS/nanotechnology, robotics, virtual design and manufacturing, tribology, microfluidics, computational solid and fluid mechanics, composite materials,

nondestructive materials characterization and structural reliability, neuromechanics, biomimetics. *Total annual research expenditures:* $7.9 million. *Unit head:* Dr. Kevin Lynch, Chair, 847-467-5451, Fax: 847-491-3915, E-mail: kmlynch@northwestern.edu. *Application contact:* Dr. Wei Chen, Director of Graduate Admissions, 847-467-7019, Fax: 847-491-3915, E-mail: weichen@northwestern.edu.
Website: http://www.mech.northwestern.edu/.

Oakland University, Graduate Study and Lifelong Learning, School of Engineering and Computer Science, Department of Mechanical Engineering, Rochester, MI 48309-4401. Offers MS, PhD. Part-time and evening/weekend programs available. *Entrance requirements:* For master's, minimum GPA of 3.0. Additional exam requirements/recommendations for international students: Required—TOEFL (minimum score 550 paper-based). Electronic applications accepted. *Expenses:* Contact institution. *Faculty research:* Root cause analysis and testing of transparent composites.

The Ohio State University, Graduate School, College of Engineering, Department of Mechanical and Aerospace Engineering, Columbus, OH 43210. Offers aerospace engineering (MS, PhD); mechanical engineering (MS, PhD); nuclear engineering (MS, PhD). *Faculty:* 63. *Students:* 312 full-time (47 women), 10 part-time (1 woman); includes 20 minority (3 Black or African American, non-Hispanic/Latino; 1 American Indian or Alaska Native, non-Hispanic/Latino; 10 Asian, non-Hispanic/Latino; 3 Hispanic/Latino; 3 Two or more races, non-Hispanic/Latino), 115 international. Average age 25. In 2014, 122 master's, 33 doctorates awarded. *Degree requirements:* For doctorate, thesis/ dissertation. *Entrance requirements:* For master's and doctorate, GRE. Additional exam requirements/recommendations for international students: Required—TOEFL (minimum score 550 paper-based; 79 iBT), Michigan English Language Assessment Battery (minimum score 82); Recommended—IELTS (minimum score 7). *Application deadline:* For fall admission, 11/30 priority date for domestic and international students; for winter admission, 12/1 for domestic students, 11/1 for international students; for spring admission, 10/1 for domestic and international students. Applications are processed on a rolling basis. Application fee: $60 ($70 for international students). Electronic applications accepted. *Financial support:* Fellowships, research assistantships, teaching assistantships, career-related internships or fieldwork, Federal Work-Study, institutionally sponsored loans, and unspecified assistantships available. Support available to part-time students. *Unit head:* Dr. Ahmet Selamet, Chair, 614-292-4143, E-mail: selamet.1@osu.edu. *Application contact:* Janeen Sands, Graduate Program Administrator, 614-247-6605, Fax: 614-292-3656, E-mail: maegradadmissions@osu.edu.
Website: http://mae.osu.edu/.

Ohio University, Graduate College, Russ College of Engineering and Technology, Department of Mechanical Engineering, Athens, OH 45701-2979. Offers biomedical engineering (MS); mechanical engineering (MS), including CAD/CAM, design, energy, manufacturing, materials, robotics, thermofluids. Part-time programs available. *Degree requirements:* For master's, comprehensive exam (for some programs), thesis. *Entrance requirements:* For master's, GRE, BS in engineering or science, minimum GPA of 2.8. Additional exam requirements/recommendations for international students: Required—TOEFL (minimum score 550 paper-based; 80 iBT) or IELTS (minimum score 6.5). Electronic applications accepted. *Faculty research:* Biomedical, energy and the environment, materials and manufacturing, bioengineering.

Ohio University, Graduate College, Russ College of Engineering and Technology, Program in Mechanical and Systems Engineering, Athens, OH 45701-2979. Offers industrial engineering (PhD); mechanical engineering (PhD). *Degree requirements:* For doctorate, comprehensive exam, thesis/dissertation. *Entrance requirements:* For doctorate, GRE General Test, MS in engineering or related field. Additional exam requirements/recommendations for international students: Required—TOEFL (minimum score 550 paper-based; 80 iBT) or IELTS (minimum score 6.5). Electronic applications accepted. *Faculty research:* Material processing, expert systems, environmental geotechnical manufacturing, thermal systems, robotics.

Oklahoma State University, College of Engineering, Architecture and Technology, School of Mechanical and Aerospace Engineering, Stillwater, OK 74078. Offers mechanical and aerospace engineering (MS, PhD); mechanical engineering (MS, PhD). Postbaccalaureate distance learning degree programs offered. *Faculty:* 25 full-time (0 women), 7 part-time/adjunct (1 woman). *Students:* 34 full-time (5 women), 100 part-time (17 women); includes 11 minority (1 Black or African American, non-Hispanic/Latino; 2 Hispanic/Latino; 8 Two or more races, non-Hispanic/Latino), 72 international. Average age 27. 302 applicants, 16% accepted, 23 enrolled. In 2014, 41 master's, 10 doctorates awarded. *Degree requirements:* For master's, thesis or alternative; for doctorate, comprehensive exam, thesis/dissertation. *Entrance requirements:* For master's and doctorate, GRE or GMAT. Additional exam requirements/recommendations for international students: Required—TOEFL (minimum score 550 paper-based; 79 iBT). *Application deadline:* For fall admission, 3/1 priority date for international students; for spring admission, 8/1 priority date for international students. Applications are processed on a rolling basis. Application fee: $40 ($75 for international students). Electronic applications accepted. *Expenses:* Tuition, state resident: full-time $4488; part-time $187 per credit hour. Tuition, nonresident: full-time $18,360; part-time $765 per credit hour. *Required fees:* $2413; $100.55 per credit hour. Tuition and fees vary according to campus/location. *Financial support:* In 2014–15, 67 research assistantships (averaging $15,734 per year), 53 teaching assistantships (averaging $13,562 per year) were awarded; career-related internships or fieldwork, Federal Work-Study, scholarships/ grants, health care benefits, tuition waivers (partial), and unspecified assistantships also available. Support available to part-time students. Financial award application deadline: 3/1; financial award applicants required to submit FAFSA. *Unit head:* Dr. Daniel E. Fisher, Department Head, 405-744-5900, Fax: 405-744-7873, E-mail: maehead@okstate.edu. *Application contact:* Dr. Charlotte Fore, Manager of Graduate Studies and Research Development, 405-744-5900, Fax: 405-744-7873, E-mail: charlotte.fore@okstate.edu.
Website: http://www.mae.okstate.edu.

Old Dominion University, Frank Batten College of Engineering and Technology, Program in Mechanical Engineering, Norfolk, VA 23529. Offers ME, MS, D Eng, PhD. Part-time and evening/weekend programs available. Postbaccalaureate distance learning degree programs offered (no on-campus study). *Faculty:* 22 full-time (2 women). *Students:* 21 full-time (6 women), 48 part-time (6 women); includes 12 minority (2 Black or African American, non-Hispanic/Latino; 1 Asian, non-Hispanic/Latino; 4 Hispanic/Latino; 5 Two or more races, non-Hispanic/Latino), 29 international. Average age 30. 50 applicants, 76% accepted, 7 enrolled. In 2014, 15 master's, 4 doctorates awarded. *Degree requirements:* For master's, comprehensive exam, thesis optional; for doctorate, thesis/dissertation, candidacy exam. *Entrance requirements:* For master's, GRE, minimum GPA of 3.0; for doctorate, GRE, minimum GPA of 3.5. Additional exam requirements/recommendations for international students: Required—TOEFL (minimum score 550 paper-based). *Application deadline:* For fall admission, 6/1 for domestic students, 2/15 priority date for international students; for spring admission, 11/1 for domestic students, 10/1 for international students. Applications are processed on a rolling basis. Application fee: $50. Electronic applications accepted. *Expenses:* Tuition, state resident: full-time $10,488; part-time $437 per credit. Tuition, nonresident: full-time $26,136; part-time $1089 per credit. *Required fees:* $64 per semester. One-time fee:

$50. *Financial support:* In 2014–15, 12 students received support, including 5 fellowships with partial tuition reimbursements available (averaging $16,000 per year), 11 research assistantships with partial tuition reimbursements available (averaging $15,000 per year), 15 teaching assistantships with partial tuition reimbursements available (averaging $6,400 per year); career-related internships or fieldwork, institutionally sponsored loans, scholarships/grants, and unspecified assistantships also available. Financial award application deadline: 2/15; financial award applicants required to submit FAFSA. *Faculty research:* Computational applied mechanics, manufacturing, experimental stress analysis, systems dynamics and control, mechanical design. *Total annual research expenditures:* $1.8 million. *Unit head:* Dr. Sebastian Bawab, Chair, 757-683-5637, Fax: 757-683-5344, E-mail: sbawab@odu.edu. *Application contact:* Dr. Han Bao, Graduate Program Director, 757-683-4922, Fax: 757-683-3200, E-mail: hbao@aero.odu.edu.
Website: http://eng.odu.edu/mae.

Oregon State University, College of Engineering, Program in Mechanical Engineering, Corvallis, OR 97331. Offers M Eng, MS, PhD. Part-time programs available. *Faculty:* 45 full-time (7 women), 1 part-time/adjunct (0 women). *Students:* 139 full-time (12 women), 16 part-time (1 woman); includes 17 minority (1 Black or African American, non-Hispanic/Latino; 6 Asian, non-Hispanic/Latino; 8 Hispanic/Latino; 2 Two or more races, non-Hispanic/Latino), 59 international. Average age 27. 353 applicants, 36% accepted, 67 enrolled. In 2014, 30 master's, 4 doctorates awarded. *Entrance requirements:* For master's and doctorate, GRE. Additional exam requirements/recommendations for international students: Required—TOEFL (minimum score 80 iBT), IELTS (minimum score 6.5). *Application deadline:* For fall admission, 8/1 for domestic students, 4/1 for international students; for winter admission, 12/1 for domestic students, 7/1 for international students; for spring admission, 2/1 for domestic students, 10/1 for international students; for summer admission, 5/1 for domestic students, 1/1 for international students. Application fee: $60. *Expenses:* Expenses: $15,359 full-time resident tuition and fees; $23,405 non-resident. *Financial support:* Application deadline: 1/15. *Unit head:* Dr. Robert Stone, Professor and School Head, 541-737-3638, Fax: 541-737-2600, E-mail: rob.stone@oregonstate.edu. *Application contact:* Jean Robinson, Mechanical Engineering Advisor, 541-737-9191, E-mail: jean.robinson@oregonstate.edu.
Website: http://mime.oregonstate.edu/academics/grad/me.

Penn State University Park, Graduate School, College of Engineering, Department of Mechanical and Nuclear Engineering, University Park, PA 16802. Offers mechanical engineering (PhD); nuclear engineering (PhD). *Unit head:* Dr. Amr S. Elnashai, Dean, 814-865-7537, Fax: 814-863-4749, E-mail: ase2@psu.edu. *Application contact:* Lori A. Stania, Director, Graduate Student Services, 814-867-5278, Fax: 814-863-4627, E-mail: gswww@psu.edu.
Website: http://www.mne.psu.edu/.

Polytechnic University of Puerto Rico, Graduate School, Hato Rey, PR 00919. Offers business administration (MBA), including computer information systems, general management, management of information systems, management of international enterprises; civil engineering (ME, MS); computer engineering (ME, MS); computer science (MCS, MS); electrical engineering (ME, MS); engineering management (MEM); environmental management (MEM); landscape architecture (M Land Arch); manufacturing competitiveness (MMC, MS); manufacturing engineering (ME, MS); mechanical engineering (M Mech E). Part-time and evening/weekend programs available. *Entrance requirements:* For master's, 3 letters of recommendation.

Portland State University, Graduate Studies, College of Liberal Arts and Sciences, Systems Science Program, Portland, OR 97207-0751. Offers computational intelligence (Certificate); computer modeling and simulation (Certificate); systems science (MS); systems science/anthropology (PhD); systems science/business administration (PhD); systems science/civil engineering (PhD); systems science/economics (PhD); systems science/engineering management (PhD); systems science/general (PhD); systems science/mathematical sciences (PhD); systems science/mechanical engineering (PhD); systems science/psychology (PhD); systems science/sociology (PhD). *Faculty:* 2 full-time (0 women), 1 part-time/adjunct (0 women). *Students:* 6 full-time (2 women), 29 part-time (8 women); includes 6 minority (1 Black or African American, non-Hispanic/Latino; 1 American Indian or Alaska Native, non-Hispanic/Latino; 1 Asian, non-Hispanic/Latino; 3 Hispanic/Latino). Average age 41. 32 applicants, 19% accepted, 6 enrolled. In 2014, 10 master's, 3 doctorates awarded. *Degree requirements:* For master's, comprehensive exam (for some programs), thesis optional; for doctorate, variable foreign language requirement, comprehensive exam (for some programs), thesis/dissertation. *Entrance requirements:* For master's, GRE/GMAT scores are recommended but not required., GPA 3.0 for undergraduate or 3.0 for graduate work, 2 letters of recommendation, and statement of interest; for doctorate, GMAT, GRE General Test, GPA requirement is 3.0 for undergraduate and 3.25 for graduate, 2 letters of recommendation and statement of interest. Additional exam requirements/recommendations for international students: Required—TOEFL (minimum score 550 paper-based; 80 iBT). *Application deadline:* For fall admission, 1/15 for domestic and international students; for spring admission, 11/1 for domestic students. Application fee: $50. Electronic applications accepted. *Expenses:* Tuition, state resident: part-time $222 per credit. Tuition, nonresident: part-time $527 per credit. *Required fees:* $22 per contact hour. $100 per quarter. Tuition and fees vary according to program. *Financial support:* In 2014–15, 1 research assistantship with full and partial tuition reimbursement (averaging $2,358 per year) was awarded; teaching assistantships with full and partial tuition reimbursements, career-related internships or fieldwork, Federal Work-Study, scholarships/grants, and unspecified assistantships also available. Support available to part-time students. Financial award application deadline: 3/1; financial award applicants required to submit FAFSA. *Faculty research:* Systems theory and methodology, artificial intelligence neural networks, information theory, nonlinear dynamics/chaos, modeling and simulation. *Total annual research expenditures:* $137,833. *Unit head:* Prof. Wayne Wakeland, PhD, Chair, 503-725-4975, E-mail: wakeland@pdx.edu.
Website: http://www.pdx.edu/sysc/.

Portland State University, Graduate Studies, Maseeh College of Engineering and Computer Science, Department of Mechanical Engineering, Portland, OR 97207-0751. Offers M Eng, MS, PhD. Part-time and evening/weekend programs available. *Faculty:* 15 full-time (1 woman), 2 part-time/adjunct (0 women). *Students:* 46 full-time (10 women), 32 part-time (2 women); includes 10 minority (1 Black or African American, non-Hispanic/Latino; 4 Asian, non-Hispanic/Latino; 2 Hispanic/Latino; 3 Two or more races, non-Hispanic/Latino), 25 international. Average age 30. 86 applicants, 58% accepted, 32 enrolled. In 2014, 21 master's awarded. *Degree requirements:* For master's, thesis or alternative; for doctorate, one foreign language, thesis/dissertation, oral and written exams. *Entrance requirements:* For master's, minimum GPA of 3.0 in upper-division course work, BS in mechanical engineering or allied field, and 3 letters of recommendation; for doctorate, GRE General Test, GRE Subject Test, minimum GPA of 3.0 in upper-division course work, and 3 letters of recommendation. Additional exam requirements/recommendations for international students: Required—TOEFL (minimum score 550 paper-based; 80 iBT). *Application deadline:* For fall admission, 1/15 priority date for domestic and international students; for winter admission, 9/1 for domestic students, 8/1 for international students; for spring admission, 11/1 for domestic students,

Mechanical Engineering

10/1 for international students. Applications are processed on a rolling basis. Application fee: $50. Electronic applications accepted. *Expenses:* Tuition, state resident: part-time $222 per credit. Tuition, nonresident: part-time $527 per credit. *Required fees:* $22 per contact hour. $100 per quarter. Tuition and fees vary according to program. *Financial support:* In 2014–15, 7 research assistantships with full tuition reimbursements (averaging $13,119 per year), 19 teaching assistantships with full and partial tuition reimbursements (averaging $2,110 per year) were awarded; Federal Work-Study, scholarships/grants, and unspecified assistantships also available. Support available to part-time students. Financial award application deadline: 3/1; financial award applicants required to submit FAFSA. *Faculty research:* Mechanical system modeling, indoor air quality, manufacturing process, computational fluid dynamics, building science. *Total annual research expenditures:* $1.5 million. *Unit head:* Gerald Recktenwald, Chair, 503-725-4290, Fax: 503-725-8255, E-mail: gerry@pdx.edu. *Application contact:* Karen Heine, Student Coordinator, 503-725-4250, Fax: 503-725-8255, E-mail: kheine@pdx.edu.
Website: http://www.pdx.edu/mme/.

Princeton University, Graduate School, School of Engineering and Applied Science, Department of Mechanical and Aerospace Engineering, Princeton, NJ 08544. Offers M Eng, MSE, PhD. Terminal master's awarded for partial completion of doctoral program. *Degree requirements:* For master's, thesis (MSE); for doctorate, thesis/dissertation, general exam. *Entrance requirements:* For master's, GRE General Test, 3 letters of recommendation; for doctorate, GRE General Test, official transcript(s), 3 letters of recommendation, personal statement. Additional exam requirements/recommendations for international students: Required—TOEFL. Electronic applications accepted. *Faculty research:* Bioengineering and bio-mechanics; combustion, energy conversion, and climate; fluid mechanics, dynamics, and control systems; lasers and applied physics; materials and mechanical systems.

Purdue University, College of Engineering, School of Mechanical Engineering, West Lafayette, IN 47907-2088. Offers MS, MSE, MSME, PhD, Certificate. MS and PhD degree programs in biomedical engineering offered jointly with School of Electrical and Computer Engineering and School of Chemical Engineering. Part-time programs available. Postbaccalaureate distance learning degree programs offered (no on-campus study). *Entrance requirements:* For master's and doctorate, GRE General Test, minimum GPA of 3.2. Additional exam requirements/recommendations for international students: Required—TOEFL (minimum score 575 paper-based; 77 iBT); Recommended—TWE. Electronic applications accepted. *Faculty research:* Design, manufacturing, thermal/fluid sciences, mechanics, electromechanical systems.

Purdue University Calumet, Graduate Studies Office, School of Engineering, Mathematics, and Science, Department of Engineering, Hammond, IN 46323-2094. Offers computer engineering (MSE); electrical engineering (MSE); engineering (MS); mechanical engineering (MSE). Evening/weekend programs available. *Entrance requirements:* Additional exam requirements/recommendations for international students: Required—TOEFL.

Queen's University at Kingston, School of Graduate Studies, Faculty of Applied Science, Department of Mechanical and Materials Engineering, Kingston, ON K7L 3N6, Canada. Offers M Eng, M Sc, M Sc Eng, PhD. Part-time programs available. *Degree requirements:* For master's, thesis optional; for doctorate, comprehensive exam, thesis/dissertation. *Entrance requirements:* Additional exam requirements/recommendations for international students: Required—TOEFL. Electronic applications accepted. *Faculty research:* Dynamics and control systems, manufacturing and design, materials and engineering, heat transferring fluid dynamics, energy systems and combustion.

Rensselaer at Hartford, Department of Engineering, Program in Mechanical Engineering, Hartford, CT 06120-2991. Offers ME, MS. Part-time and evening/weekend programs available. *Degree requirements:* For master's, thesis optional. *Entrance requirements:* For master's, GRE. Additional exam requirements/recommendations for international students: Required—TOEFL (minimum score 600 paper-based; 100 iBT).

Rensselaer Polytechnic Institute, Graduate School, School of Engineering, Program in Mechanical Engineering, Troy, NY 12180-3590. Offers M Eng, MS, D Eng, PhD. *Faculty:* 56 full-time (8 women), 5 part-time/adjunct (2 women). *Students:* 89 full-time (15 women), 14 part-time (0 women); includes 11 minority (4 Black or African American, non-Hispanic/Latino; 4 Asian, non-Hispanic/Latino; 1 Hispanic/Latino; 2 Two or more races, non-Hispanic/Latino), 62 international. Average age 27. 235 applicants, 45% accepted, 43 enrolled. In 2014, 18 master's, 14 doctorates awarded. *Degree requirements:* For master's, thesis (for some programs); for doctorate, thesis/dissertation. *Entrance requirements:* For master's and doctorate, GRE. Additional exam requirements/recommendations for international students: Required—TOEFL (minimum score 600 paper-based; 100 iBT), IELTS (minimum score 7), PTE (minimum score 68). *Application deadline:* For fall admission, 1/1 priority date for domestic and international students; for spring admission, 8/15 priority date for domestic and international students. Applications are processed on a rolling basis. Application fee: $75. Electronic applications accepted. *Expenses: Tuition:* Full-time $46,700; part-time $1945 per credit. Tuition and fees vary according to course load. *Financial support:* In 2014–15, 85 students received support, including research assistantships (averaging $18,500 per year), teaching assistantships (averaging $18,500 per year); fellowships also available. Financial award application deadline: 1/1. *Faculty research:* Advanced nuclear materials; aerodynamics; design; dynamics and vibrations, fission systems and radiation transport; fluid mechanics (computational, theoretical, and experimental); heat transfer and energy conversion; manufacturing, medical imaging and health physics; multiscale/computational modeling; nanostructured materials and properties; nuclear physics/nuclear reactor; propulsion. *Total annual research expenditures:* $6.9 million. *Unit head:* Dr. Theo Borca-Tasciuc, Graduate Program Director, 518-276-2627, E-mail: borcat@rpi.edu. *Application contact:* Office of Graduate Admissions, 518-276-6216, E-mail: gradadmissions@rpi.edu.
Website: http://mane.rpi.edu/academics.

Rice University, Graduate Programs, George R. Brown School of Engineering, Department of Mechanical Engineering and Materials Science, Houston, TX 77251-1892. Offers materials science (MMS, MS, PhD); mechanical engineering (MME, MS, PhD); MBA/ME. Part-time programs available. Terminal master's awarded for partial completion of doctoral program. *Degree requirements:* For master's, comprehensive exam, thesis; for doctorate, comprehensive exam, thesis/dissertation. *Entrance requirements:* For master's and doctorate, GRE General Test, minimum GPA of 3.0. Additional exam requirements/recommendations for international students: Required—TOEFL (minimum score 600 paper-based; 90 iBT), IELTS (minimum score 7). Electronic applications accepted. *Faculty research:* Heat transfer, biomedical engineering, fluid dynamics, aero-astronautics, control systems/robotics, materials science.

Rochester Institute of Technology, Graduate Enrollment Services, College of Applied Science and Technology, School of Engineering Technology, MS Program in Manufacturing and Mechanical Systems Integration, Rochester, NY 14623-5604. Offers MS. Part-time and evening/weekend programs available. *Students:* 39 full-time (8 women), 6 part-time (1 woman); includes 1 minority (Asian, non-Hispanic/Latino), 34 international. Average age 24. 62 applicants, 66% accepted, 23 enrolled. In 2014, 10 master's awarded. *Degree requirements:* For master's, thesis (for some programs).

Entrance requirements: For master's, GRE, and TOEFL, IELTS, or PTE for non-native English speakers, Recommended minimum GPA of 3.0. Additional exam requirements/recommendations for international students: Required—PTE (minimum score 58), TOEFL (minimum score 550 paper-based; 79 iBT) or IELTS (minimum score 6.5). *Application deadline:* For fall admission, 2/15 priority date for domestic and international students; for winter admission, 11/1 for domestic and international students; for spring admission, 12/15 priority date for domestic and international students. Applications are processed on a rolling basis. Application fee: $60. Electronic applications accepted. *Expenses:* Expenses: $1,673 per credit hour. *Financial support:* In 2014–15, 18 students received support. Research assistantships with partial tuition reimbursements available, teaching assistantships with partial tuition reimbursements available, career-related internships or fieldwork, Federal Work-Study, institutionally sponsored loans, scholarships/grants, and unspecified assistantships available. Support available to part-time students. Financial award application deadline: 2/15; financial award applicants required to submit FAFSA. *Faculty research:* Product development, electronics packaging, automated manufacturing, quality and systems management. *Unit head:* Dr. S. Manian Ramkumar, Program Chair, 585-475-6081, E-mail: smrmet@rit.edu. *Application contact:* Diane Ellison, Associate Vice President, Graduate Enrollment Services, 585-475-2229, Fax: 585-475-7164, E-mail: gradinfo@rit.edu.
Website: http://www.rit.edu/cast/mmet/graduate-programs/ms-in-manufacturing-and-mechanical-systems-integration.

Rochester Institute of Technology, Graduate Enrollment Services, Kate Gleason College of Engineering, Mechanical Engineering Department, ME Program in Mechanical Engineering, Rochester, NY 14623-5603. Offers ME. Part-time programs available. *Students:* 85 full-time (13 women), 24 part-time (4 women); includes 5 minority (1 Asian, non-Hispanic/Latino; 4 Hispanic/Latino), 72 international. Average age 24. 245 applicants, 67% accepted, 59 enrolled. In 2014, 53 master's awarded. *Degree requirements:* For master's, thesis or alternative. *Entrance requirements:* For master's, TOEFL, IELTS, or PTE for non-native English speakers, Recommended minimum GPA of 3.0. Additional exam requirements/recommendations for international students: Required—PTE (minimum score 58), TOEFL (minimum score 550 paper-based; 79 iBT) or IELTS (minimum score 6.5). *Application deadline:* For fall admission, 2/15 priority date for domestic and international students; for spring admission, 12/15 priority date for domestic and international students. Applications are processed on a rolling basis. Electronic applications accepted. *Expenses:* Expenses: $1,673 per credit hour. *Financial support:* In 2014–15, 95 students received support. Research assistantships with partial tuition reimbursements available, teaching assistantships with partial tuition reimbursements available, career-related internships or fieldwork, Federal Work-Study, institutionally sponsored loans, scholarships/grants, and unspecified assistantships available. Support available to part-time students. Financial award applicants required to submit FAFSA. *Faculty research:* Transportation, aerospace systems, unmanned aircraft design, automotive systems, assistive device technologies, healthcare: artificial organ engineering and biomedical device engineering, nano-science engineering: microscale heat and mass transfer, energy engineering. *Unit head:* Dr. Agamemnon Crassidis, Graduate Director, 585-475-5181, E-mail: alceme@rit.edu. *Application contact:* Diane Ellison, Associate Vice President, Graduate Enrollment Services, 585-475-2229, Fax: 585-475-7164, E-mail: gradinfo@rit.edu.
Website: http://www.rit.edu/kgcoe/mechanical/program/graduate-meng/overview.

Rochester Institute of Technology, Graduate Enrollment Services, Kate Gleason College of Engineering, Mechanical Engineering Department, MS Program in Mechanical Engineering, Rochester, NY 14623-5603. Offers MS. Part-time programs available. *Students:* 12 full-time, 12 part-time (4 women); includes 3 minority (2 Asian, non-Hispanic/Latino; 1 Hispanic/Latino), 12 international. Average age 24. 97 applicants, 5% accepted. In 2014, 11 master's awarded. *Degree requirements:* For master's, thesis. *Entrance requirements:* For master's, GRE and TOEFL, IELTS, or PTE for non-native English speakers, Recommended minimum GPA of 3.0. Additional exam requirements/recommendations for international students: Required—PTE (minimum score 58), TOEFL (minimum score 550 paper-based; 79 iBT) or IELTS (minimum score 6.5). *Application deadline:* For fall admission, 2/15 priority date for domestic and international students; for spring admission, 12/15 priority date for domestic and international students. Applications are processed on a rolling basis. Electronic applications accepted. *Expenses:* Expenses: $1,673 per credit hour. *Financial support:* In 2014–15, 16 students received support. Research assistantships with partial tuition reimbursements available, teaching assistantships with partial tuition reimbursements available, career-related internships or fieldwork, Federal Work-Study, institutionally sponsored loans, scholarships/grants, and unspecified assistantships available. Support available to part-time students. Financial award applicants required to submit FAFSA. *Faculty research:* Transportation, aerospace systems, unmanned aircraft design, automotive systems, assistive device technologies, healthcare: artificial organ engineering and biomedical device engineering, nano-science engineering: microscale heat and mass transfer, energy engineering. *Unit head:* Dr. Agamemnon Crassidis, Graduate Director, 585-475-5181, E-mail: alceme@rit.edu. *Application contact:* Diane Ellison, Associate Vice President, Graduate Enrollment Services, 585-475-2229, Fax: 585-475-7164, E-mail: gradinfo@rit.edu.
Website: http://www.rit.edu/kgcoe/mechanical/program/graduate-ms/overview.

Rose-Hulman Institute of Technology, Faculty of Engineering and Applied Sciences, Department of Mechanical Engineering, Terre Haute, IN 47803-3999. Offers M Eng, MS. Part-time programs available. Postbaccalaureate distance learning degree programs offered (minimal on-campus study). *Faculty:* 28 full-time (3 women). *Students:* 9 full-time (1 woman), 4 part-time (1 woman); includes 2 minority (1 American Indian or Alaska Native, non-Hispanic/Latino; 1 Two or more races, non-Hispanic/Latino), 6 international. Average age 24. 18 applicants, 83% accepted, 7 enrolled. In 2014, 3 master's awarded. *Degree requirements:* For master's, thesis. *Entrance requirements:* For master's, GRE, minimum GPA of 3.0. Additional exam requirements/recommendations for international students: Required—TOEFL (minimum score 580 paper-based; 92 iBT). *Application deadline:* For fall admission, 2/1 priority date for domestic students. Applications are processed on a rolling basis. Application fee: $0. *Expenses: Tuition:* Full-time $40,449. *Financial support:* In 2014–15, 11 students received support. Fellowships with full and partial tuition reimbursements available, research assistantships with full and partial tuition reimbursements available, institutionally sponsored loans, scholarships/grants, and tuition waivers (full and partial) available. *Faculty research:* Finite elements, MEMS, thermodynamics, heat transfer, design methods, noise and vibration analysis. *Total annual research expenditures:* $106,477. *Unit head:* Dr. David J. Purdy, Chairman, 812-877-8320, Fax: 812-877-3198. *Application contact:* Dr. Azad Siahmakoun, Associate Dean of the Faculty, 812-877-8400, Fax: 812-877-8061, E-mail: siahmako@rose-hulman.edu.
Website: http://www.rose-hulman.edu/academics/academic-departments/mechanical-engineering.aspx.

Rowan University, Graduate School, College of Engineering, Department of Mechanical Engineering, Glassboro, NJ 08028-1701. Offers MS. *Faculty:* 5 full-time (2 women). *Students:* 9 full-time (2 women), 7 part-time (1 woman); includes 3 minority (1 Black or African American, non-Hispanic/Latino; 2 Asian, non-Hispanic/Latino). Average age 26. 6 applicants, 100% accepted, 3 enrolled. In 2014, 4 master's awarded. *Application deadline:* For fall admission, 8/1 for domestic students, 5/1 for international students; for spring admission, 11/1 for domestic and international students; for summer admission, 4/1 for domestic students, 2/15 for international students. Applications are processed on a rolling basis. Application fee: $65. Electronic applications accepted. *Expenses: Tuition, area resident:* Part-time $648 per credit. Tuition, state resident: part-time $648 per credit. Tuition, nonresident: part-time $648 per credit. *Required fees:* $145 per credit. Tuition and fees vary according to degree level, campus/location, program and student level. *Unit head:* Dr. Steve Chin, Dean, 856-256-5301. *Application contact:* Dr. Ralph Dusseau, Program Adviser, 856-256-5332.

Royal Military College of Canada, Division of Graduate Studies and Research, Engineering Division, Department of Mechanical Engineering, Kingston, ON K7K 7B4, Canada. Offers M Eng, MA Sc, PhD. *Degree requirements:* For master's, thesis; for doctorate, comprehensive exam, thesis/dissertation. *Entrance requirements:* For master's, honours degree with second-class standing; for doctorate, master's degree. Electronic applications accepted.

Rutgers, The State University of New Jersey, New Brunswick, Graduate School-New Brunswick, Program in Mechanical and Aerospace Engineering, Piscataway, NJ 08854-8097. Offers design and control (MS, PhD); fluid mechanics (MS, PhD); solid mechanics (MS, PhD); thermal sciences (MS, PhD). Part-time and evening/weekend programs available. *Degree requirements:* For master's, thesis (for some programs); for doctorate, thesis/dissertation. *Entrance requirements:* For master's, GRE General Test, BS in mechanical/aerospace engineering or related field; for doctorate, GRE General Test, MS in mechanical/aerospace engineering or related field. Additional exam requirements/recommendations for international students: Required—TOEFL. Electronic applications accepted. *Faculty research:* Combustion, propulsion, thermal transport, crystal plasticity, optimization, fabrication, nanoidentation.

St. Cloud State University, School of Graduate Studies, College of Science and Engineering, Program in Mechanical Engineering, St. Cloud, MN 56301-4498. Offers MS. *Degree requirements:* For master's, thesis or alternative. *Entrance requirements:* For master's, GRE General Test, minimum GPA of 2.75. Additional exam requirements/recommendations for international students: Required—Michigan English Language Assessment Battery; Recommended—TOEFL (minimum score 550 paper-based), IELTS (minimum score 6.5). Electronic applications accepted.

Saint Martin's University, Office of Graduate Studies, Program in Mechanical Engineering, Lacey, WA 98503. Offers MME. Part-time and evening/weekend programs available. *Faculty:* 4 full-time (0 women), 1 part-time/adjunct (0 women). *Students:* 5 part-time (1 woman); includes 1 minority (Asian, non-Hispanic/Latino). Average age 30. 9 applicants, 33% accepted, 2 enrolled. *Degree requirements:* For master's, thesis optional. *Entrance requirements:* For master's, official transcripts from all colleges and universities attended, three letters of recommendation preferably from professors, registered engineers or supervisors. Additional exam requirements/recommendations for international students: Required—TOEFL (minimum score 550 paper-based, 79 iBT) or IELTS (minimum score 6.5). *Application deadline:* For fall admission, 4/1 priority date for domestic and international students; for spring admission, 11/1 priority date for domestic and international students. Applications are processed on a rolling basis. Application fee: $50. Electronic applications accepted. *Expenses: Tuition:* Part-time $1045 per credit. *Financial support:* Unspecified assistantships available. Financial award application deadline: 3/1; financial award applicants required to submit FAFSA. *Unit head:* Dr. A. Jim Witsmeer, Program Director, 360-438-4323, E-mail: awitsmeer@stmartin.edu. *Application contact:* Bailey Craft, Assistant Director for Graduate Recruitment, 360-412-6142, E-mail: gradstudies@stmartin.edu. Website: http://www.stmartin.edu/GradStudies/MME/.

San Diego State University, Graduate and Research Affairs, College of Engineering, Department of Mechanical Engineering, San Diego, CA 92182. Offers engineering sciences and applied mechanics (PhD); manufacture and design (MS); mechanical engineering (MS). PhD offered jointly with University of California, San Diego and Department of Aerospace Engineering and Engineering Mechanics. Evening/weekend programs available. *Degree requirements:* For master's, comprehensive exam (for some programs), thesis (for some programs); for doctorate, thesis/dissertation. *Entrance requirements:* For master's, GRE General Test; for doctorate, GRE, 3 letters of recommendation. Additional exam requirements/recommendations for international students: Required—TOEFL. Electronic applications accepted. *Faculty research:* Energy analysis and diagnosis, seawater pump design, space-related research.

San Jose State University, Graduate Studies and Research, Charles W. Davidson College of Engineering, Department of Mechanical and Aerospace Engineering, Program in Mechanical Engineering, San Jose, CA 95192-0001. Offers MS. Part-time programs available. *Degree requirements:* For master's, thesis optional. *Entrance requirements:* For master's, GRE. Additional exam requirements/recommendations for international students: Required—TOEFL. Electronic applications accepted. *Faculty research:* Gas dynamics, mechanics/vibrations, heat transfer, structural analysis, two-phase fluid flow.

Santa Clara University, School of Engineering, Santa Clara, CA 95053. Offers analog circuit design (Certificate); applied mathematics (MS); ASIC design and test (Certificate); bioengineering (MS); civil engineering (MS); computer science and engineering (MS, PhD); controls (Certificate); digital signal processing (Certificate); dynamics (Certificate); electrical engineering (MS, PhD); engineering (Engineer); engineering management (MS); fundamentals of electrical engineering (Certificate); information assurance (Certificate); materials engineering (Certificate); mechanical design analysis (Certificate); mechanical engineering (MS, PhD); mechatronics systems engineering (Certificate); microwave and antennas (Certificate); networking (Certificate); renewable energy (Certificate); software engineering (Certificate); sustainable energy (MS); technology jump-start (Certificate); thermofluids (Certificate). Part-time and evening/weekend programs available. *Faculty:* 59 full-time (23 women), 80 part-time/adjunct (14 women). *Students:* 584 full-time (239 women), 353 part-time (102 women); includes 224 minority (7 Black or African American, non-Hispanic/Latino; 144 Asian, non-Hispanic/Latino; 50 Hispanic/Latino; 2 Native Hawaiian or other Pacific Islander, non-Hispanic/Latino; 21 Two or more races, non-Hispanic/Latino; 548 international. Average age 27. 1,248 applicants, 51% accepted, 375 enrolled. In 2014, 283 master's, 5 doctorates, 1 other advanced degree awarded. *Degree requirements:* For master's, thesis (for some programs); for doctorate, thesis/dissertation; for other advanced degree, thesis. *Entrance requirements:* For master's, GRE, transcript; for doctorate, GRE, master's degree or equivalent; for other advanced degree, master's degree, published paper. Additional exam requirements/recommendations for international students: Required—TOEFL (minimum score 550 paper-based; 79 iBT). *Application deadline:* For fall admission, 8/1 for domestic students, 7/15 for international students; for winter admission, 10/28 for domestic students, 9/23 for international students; for spring admission, 2/25 for domestic students, 1/21 for international students. Applications are processed on a rolling basis. Application fee: $60. Electronic applications accepted. *Expenses:* Expenses: Contact institution. *Financial support:* In 2014–15, 94 students received support. Fellowships with full and partial tuition reimbursements available, research assistantships with full and partial tuition reimbursements available, teaching assistantships with full tuition reimbursements available, career-related internships or fieldwork, Federal Work-Study, institutionally sponsored loans, and scholarships/grants available. Support available to part-time

students. Financial award application deadline: 3/2; financial award applicants required to submit FAFSA. *Faculty research:* Video encoding, nanostructures, robotics, microfluidics, water resources. *Total annual research expenditures:* $1.6 million. *Unit head:* Dr. Alex Zecevic, Associate Dean for Graduate Studies, 408-554-2394, E-mail: azecevic@scu.edu. *Application contact:* Stacey Tinker, Director of Enrollment Management, 408-554-4748, Fax: 408-554-4323, E-mail: stinker@scu.edu. Website: http://www.scu.edu/engineering/graduate/.

Simon Fraser University, Office of Graduate Studies, Faculty of Applied Sciences, School of Mechatronic Systems Engineering, Burnaby, BC V5A 1S6, Canada. Offers MA Sc, PhD. *Degree requirements:* For master's, one foreign language, thesis; for doctorate, one foreign language, comprehensive exam, thesis/dissertation. *Entrance requirements:* Additional exam requirements/recommendations for international students: Required—TOEFL (minimum score 580 paper-based; 93 iBT), IELTS (minimum score 7), TWE (minimum score 5). Electronic applications accepted. *Faculty research:* Intelligent systems and smart materials, micro-electro mechanical systems (MEMS), biomedical engineering, thermal engineering, alternative energy.

South Carolina State University, College of Graduate and Professional Studies, Department of Civil and Mechanical Engineering Technology, Orangeburg, SC 29117-0001. Offers MS. Part-time and evening/weekend programs available. *Faculty:* 3 full-time (1 woman), 1 part-time/adjunct (0 women). *Students:* 14 full-time (6 women); includes 13 minority (all Black or African American, non-Hispanic/Latino), 1 international. Average age 29. 7 applicants, 100% accepted, 6 enrolled. In 2014, 3 master's awarded. *Degree requirements:* For master's, comprehensive exam, thesis, departmental qualifying exam. *Entrance requirements:* For master's, GRE. Additional exam requirements/recommendations for international students: Recommended—TOEFL. *Application deadline:* For fall admission, 6/15 for domestic and international students; for spring admission, 11/1 for domestic and international students. Application fee: $25. Electronic applications accepted. *Expenses:* Tuition, state resident: full-time $7290; part-time $405 per credit. Tuition, nonresident: full-time $17,058; part-time $948 per credit. *Required fees:* $2798; $155 per credit hour. *Financial support:* Fellowships, research assistantships, career-related internships or fieldwork, Federal Work-Study, institutionally sponsored loans, and unspecified assistantships available. Financial award application deadline: 6/1. *Unit head:* Dr. Ali Akbar Eliadorani, Chair, 803-536-7117, Fax: 803-516-4607, E-mail: aeliadorani@scsu.edu. *Application contact:* Curtis Foskey, Coordinator of Graduate Admission, 803-536-8419, Fax: 803-536-8812, E-mail: cfoskey@scsu.edu. Website: http://www.scsu.edu/schoolofgraduatestudies.aspx.

South Dakota School of Mines and Technology, Graduate Division, Department of Mechanical Engineering, Rapid City, SD 57701-3995. Offers MS, PhD. Part-time programs available. *Faculty:* 17 full-time (2 women). *Students:* 16 full-time (0 women), 9 part-time (0 women); includes 2 minority (1 Black or African American, non-Hispanic/Latino; 1 Asian, non-Hispanic/Latino), 8 international. Average age 28. 34 applicants, 38% accepted, 5 enrolled. *Degree requirements:* For master's, thesis (for some programs); for doctorate, thesis/dissertation. *Entrance requirements:* For master's, GRE General Test. Additional exam requirements/recommendations for international students: Required—TOEFL (minimum score 520 paper-based; 68 iBT), TWE. *Application deadline:* For fall admission, 7/1 priority date for domestic students, 4/1 for international students; for spring admission, 11/1 for domestic students, 9/1 for international students. Applications are processed on a rolling basis. Application fee: $35. Electronic applications accepted. *Expenses:* Tuition, state resident: full-time $5050; part-time $210.40 per credit hour. Tuition, nonresident: full-time $11,290; part-time $470.30 per credit hour. *Required fees:* $4680. *Financial support:* In 2014–15, 1 fellowship (averaging $2,375 per year), 6 research assistantships with partial tuition reimbursements (averaging $11,780 per year), 8 teaching assistantships with partial tuition reimbursements (averaging $8,338 per year) were awarded; Federal Work-Study and institutionally sponsored loans also available. Support available to part-time students. Financial award application deadline: 5/15. *Faculty research:* Advanced composite materials, robotics, computer-integrated manufacturing, enhanced heat transfer, dynamic systems controls. *Total annual research expenditures:* $241,892. *Unit head:* Dr. Michael Langerman, Chair, 605-394-2408, E-mail: michael.langerman@sdsmt.edu. *Application contact:* Rachel Howard, Office of Graduate Education, 605-355-3468, Fax: 605-394-1767, E-mail: rachel.howard@sdsmt.edu.

South Dakota State University, Graduate School, College of Engineering, Department of Mechanical Engineering, Brookings, SD 57007. Offers agricultural, biosystems and mechanical engineering (PhD); engineering (MS). PhD offered jointly with the Department of Agricultural and Biosystems Engineering. Part-time programs available. *Degree requirements:* For master's, thesis (for some programs), oral exam. *Entrance requirements:* Additional exam requirements/recommendations for international students: Required—TOEFL (minimum score 525 paper-based; 71 iBT). *Faculty research:* Thermo-fluid science, solid mechanics and dynamics, industrial and quality control engineering, bioenergy.

Southern Illinois University Carbondale, Graduate School, College of Engineering, Department of Mechanical Engineering and Energy Processes, Carbondale, IL 62901-4701. Offers MS. *Faculty:* 16 full-time (0 women), 1 part-time/adjunct (0 women). *Students:* 30 full-time (6 women), 17 part-time (0 women); includes 3 minority (2 Black or African American, non-Hispanic/Latino; 1 Hispanic/Latino), 26 international. Average age 23. 123 applicants, 20% accepted, 7 enrolled. In 2014, 11 master's awarded. *Degree requirements:* For master's, comprehensive exam, thesis or alternative. *Entrance requirements:* For master's, GRE General Test, minimum GPA of 2.7. Additional exam requirements/recommendations for international students: Required—TOEFL. *Application deadline:* For fall admission, 1/31 for domestic students. Applications are processed on a rolling basis. Application fee: $50. *Expenses:* Tuition, state resident: full-time $10,176; part-time $1153 per credit. Tuition, nonresident: full-time $20,814; part-time $1744 per credit. *Required fees:* $7092; $394 per credit. $2364 per semester. *Financial support:* Fellowships with full tuition reimbursements, research assistantships with full tuition reimbursements, teaching assistantships with full tuition reimbursements, Federal Work-Study, and institutionally sponsored loans available. Support available to part-time students. *Faculty research:* Coal conversion and processing, combustion, materials science and engineering, mechanical system dynamics. *Total annual research expenditures:* $1.4 million. *Unit head:* Dr. Rasit Koc, Chair, 618-536-2396, E-mail: kocr@siu.edu. *Application contact:* Tammy Hopkins, Office Administrator, 618-536-2396, E-mail: tammy@siu.edu.

Southern Illinois University Edwardsville, Graduate School, School of Engineering, Department of Mechanical and Industrial Engineering, Program in Mechanical Engineering, Edwardsville, IL 62026. Offers MS. Part-time and evening/weekend programs available. *Students:* 31 full-time (2 women), 24 part-time (0 women); includes 2 minority (both Black or African American, non-Hispanic/Latino), 38 international. 75 applicants, 64% accepted. In 2014, 14 master's awarded. *Degree requirements:* For master's, comprehensive exam (for some programs), thesis (for some programs). *Entrance requirements:* Additional exam requirements/recommendations for international students: Required—TOEFL (minimum score 550 paper-based; 79 iBT), IELTS (minimum score 6.5). *Application deadline:* For fall admission, 7/24 for domestic students, 7/15 for international students; for spring admission, 12/11 for domestic

students, 11/15 for international students; for summer admission, 4/29 for domestic students, 4/15 for international students. Applications are processed on a rolling basis. Application fee: $30. Electronic applications accepted. *Expenses:* Tuition, state resident: full-time $5026. Tuition, nonresident: full-time $12,566. *International tuition:* $25,136 full-time. *Required fees:* $1682. Tuition and fees vary according to course load, campus/location and program. *Financial support:* In 2014–15, 34 students received support, including 1 fellowship with tuition reimbursement available (averaging $8,370 per year), 15 research assistantships with full tuition reimbursements available, 18 teaching assistantships with full tuition reimbursements available; institutionally sponsored loans, scholarships/grants, and unspecified assistantships also available. Financial award application deadline: 3/1; financial award applicants required to submit FAFSA. *Unit head:* Dr. Mahid Molki, Chair, 618-650-3389, E-mail: mmolki@siue.edu. *Application contact:* Melissa K Mace, Assistant Director of Admissions for Graduate and International Recruitment, 618-650-2756, Fax: 618-650-3618, E-mail: mmace@siue.edu.
Website: http://www.siue.edu/engineering/me.

Southern Methodist University, Bobby B. Lyle School of Engineering, Department of Mechanical Engineering, Dallas, TX 75205. Offers manufacturing systems management (MS); mechanical engineering (MSME, PhD); packaging of electronic and optical devices (MS). Part-time and evening/weekend programs available. Postbaccalaureate distance learning degree programs offered (no on-campus study). Terminal master's awarded for partial completion of doctoral program. *Degree requirements:* For master's, thesis optional; for doctorate, thesis/dissertation, oral and written qualifying exams, oral final exam. *Entrance requirements:* For master's, GRE General Test, minimum GPA of 3.0 in last 2 years; bachelor's degree in engineering, mathematics, or sciences; for doctorate, preliminary counseling exam, minimum graduate GPA of 3.0, bachelor's degree in related field. Additional exam requirements/recommendations for international students: Required—TOEFL. *Faculty research:* Design, systems, and controls; thermal and fluid sciences.

Stanford University, School of Engineering, Department of Mechanical Engineering, Stanford, CA 94305-9991. Offers biomechanical engineering (MS); mechanical engineering (MS, PhD, Eng); product design (MS). *Degree requirements:* For doctorate, thesis/dissertation; for Eng, thesis. *Entrance requirements:* For master's, GRE General Test, undergraduate degree in engineering, math or sciences; for doctorate and Eng, GRE General Test, MS in engineering, math or sciences. Additional exam requirements/recommendations for international students: Required—TOEFL. *Expenses: Tuition:* Full-time $44,184; part-time $982 per credit hour. *Required fees:* $191.

Stevens Institute of Technology, Graduate School, Charles V. Schaefer Jr. School of Engineering, Department of Mechanical Engineering, Hoboken, NJ 07030. Offers advanced manufacturing (Certificate); air pollution technology (Certificate); computational fluid mechanics and heat transfer (Certificate); design and production management (Certificate); integrated product development (M Eng), including armament engineering, computer and electrical engineering, manufacturing technologies, systems reliability and design; mechanical engineering (M Eng, PhD), including manufacturing systems (M Eng), pharmaceutical manufacturing systems (M Eng), product design (M Eng), thermal engineering (M Eng); pharmaceutical manufacturing (M Eng, MS, Certificate); power generation (Certificate); product architecture and engineering (M Eng); robotics and control (Certificate); structural analysis and design (Certificate); vibration and noise control (Certificate). Part-time and evening/weekend programs available. Terminal master's awarded for partial completion of doctoral program. *Degree requirements:* For master's, thesis optional; for doctorate, variable foreign language requirement, thesis/dissertation; for Certificate, project or thesis. *Entrance requirements:* Additional exam requirements/recommendations for international students: Required—TOEFL. Electronic applications accepted. *Faculty research:* Acoustics, incineration, CAD/CAM, computational fluid dynamics and heat transfer, robotics.

Stony Brook University, State University of New York, Graduate School, College of Engineering and Applied Sciences, Department of Mechanical Engineering, Stony Brook, NY 11794. Offers MS, PhD. Evening/weekend programs available. *Faculty:* 23 full-time (2 women), 6 part-time/adjunct (1 woman). *Students:* 173 full-time (22 women), 35 part-time (5 women); includes 27 minority (6 Black or African American, non-Hispanic/Latino; 12 Asian, non-Hispanic/Latino; 8 Hispanic/Latino; 1 Two or more races, non-Hispanic/Latino), 130 international. Average age 25. 370 applicants, 68% accepted, 100 enrolled. In 2014, 67 master's, 4 doctorates awarded. *Degree requirements:* For master's, thesis or alternative; for doctorate, comprehensive exam, thesis/dissertation. *Entrance requirements:* For master's, GRE General Test, minimum GPA of 3.0; for doctorate, GRE General Test, minimum GPA of 3.5. Additional exam requirements/recommendations for international students: Required—TOEFL. *Application deadline:* For fall admission, 1/15 for domestic students; for spring admission, 10/1 for domestic students. Application fee: $100. *Expenses:* Tuition, state resident: full-time $10,370; part-time $432 per credit. Tuition, nonresident: full-time $20,190; part-time $841 per credit. *Required fees:* $1431. *Financial support:* In 2014–15, 20 research assistantships, 13 teaching assistantships were awarded; fellowships also available. *Faculty research:* Atmospheric sciences, thermal fluid sciences, solid mechanics. *Total annual research expenditures:* $943,777. *Unit head:* Dr. Jeffrey Q. Ge, Interim Chairman, 631-632-8310, Fax: 631-632-8544, E-mail: fu-pen.chiang@stonybrook.edu. *Application contact:* Mayra Santiago, Coordinator, 631-632-8340, Fax: 631-632-8544, E-mail: mayra.santiago@stonybrook.edu.
Website: http://me.eng.sunysb.edu/.

Syracuse University, L. C. Smith College of Engineering and Computer Science, Program in Mechanical and Aerospace Engineering, Syracuse, NY 13244. Offers MS, PhD. Part-time programs available. *Students:* 171 full-time (23 women), 22 part-time (2 women); includes 9 minority (4 Black or African American, non-Hispanic/Latino; 2 Asian, non-Hispanic/Latino; 1 Hispanic/Latino; 2 Two or more races, non-Hispanic/Latino), 159 international. Average age 25. 358 applicants, 60% accepted, 74 enrolled. In 2014, 55 master's, 8 doctorates awarded. *Degree requirements:* For master's, project or thesis; for doctorate, comprehensive exam, thesis/dissertation. *Entrance requirements:* For master's and doctorate, GRE General Test. Additional exam requirements/recommendations for international students: Required—TOEFL (minimum score 100 iBT). *Application deadline:* For fall admission, 7/1 priority date for domestic students, 6/1 priority date for international students. Applications are processed on a rolling basis. Application fee: $75. Electronic applications accepted. *Expenses: Tuition:* Part-time $1341 per credit. *Required fees:* $1341 per credit. *Financial support:* Fellowships with full tuition reimbursements, research assistantships with full and partial tuition reimbursements, teaching assistantships with full and partial tuition reimbursements, scholarships/grants, and tuition waivers (partial) available. Financial award application deadline: 1/1. *Faculty research:* Solid mechanics and materials, fluid mechanics, thermal sciences, controls and robotics. *Unit head:* Dr. H. Ezzat Khalifa, Department Chair, 315-443-2341, Fax: 315-443-9099, E-mail: gradinfo@syr.edu. *Application contact:* Kathy Datthyn-Madigan, Information Contact, 315-443-4367, E-mail: kjdatthy@syr.edu.
Website: http://lcs.syr.edu/our-departments/mechanical-and-aerospace-engineering.

Temple University, College of Engineering, Department of Mechanical Engineering, Philadelphia, PA 19122-6096. Offers MSME, PhD. Part-time and evening/weekend programs available. *Faculty:* 18 full-time (2 women), 15 part-time/adjunct (1 woman). *Students:* 9 full-time (1 woman), 3 part-time (0 women); includes 3 minority (all Hispanic/Latino), 4 international. Average age 30. 33 applicants, 64% accepted, 7 enrolled. In 2014, 7 master's awarded. Terminal master's awarded for partial completion of doctoral program. *Degree requirements:* For master's, thesis optional; for doctorate, thesis/dissertation, preliminary exam, dissertation proposal and defense. *Entrance requirements:* For master's, GRE General Test, minimum GPA of 3.0; BS in engineering from ABET-accredited or equivalent institution; resume; goals statement; three letters of reference; official transcripts; for doctorate, GRE General Test, minimum GPA of 3.0; MS in engineering from ABET-accredited or equivalent institution (preferred); resume; goals statement; three letters of reference; official transcripts. Additional exam requirements/recommendations for international students: Required—TOEFL (minimum score 550 paper-based; 79 iBT), IELTS (minimum score 6.5). *Application deadline:* For fall admission, 3/1 priority date for domestic and international students; for spring admission, 11/1 priority date for domestic students, 8/1 priority date for international students. Applications are processed on a rolling basis. Application fee: $60. Electronic applications accepted. *Expenses:* Expenses: $913 per credit hour in-state; $1,210 per credit hour out-of-state. *Financial support:* Fellowships with full and partial tuition reimbursements, research assistantships with full and partial tuition reimbursements, teaching assistantships with full and partial tuition reimbursements, Federal Work-Study, scholarships/grants, health care benefits, and unspecified assistantships available. Financial award application deadline: 3/1; financial award applicants required to submit FAFSA. *Faculty research:* Renewable and alternative energy, advanced materials, nanotechnology, dynamic systems and controls, thin film photovoltaics, thermal and fluid engineering, biomechanics and biofluid mechanics. *Unit head:* Dr. Mohammad Kiani, Chair, 215-204-4644, Fax: 215-204-4956, E-mail: mkiani@temple.edu. *Application contact:* Mojan Arshad, Assistant Coordinator, Graduate Studies, 215-204-7800, Fax: 215-204-6936, E-mail: gradengr@temple.edu.
Website: http://engineering.temple.edu/department/mechanical-engineering.

Tennessee State University, The School of Graduate Studies and Research, College of Engineering, Nashville, TN 37209-1561. Offers biomedical engineering (ME); civil engineering (ME); computer and information systems engineering (MS, PhD); electrical engineering (ME); environmental engineering (ME); manufacturing engineering (ME); mathematical sciences (MS); mechanical engineering (ME). Part-time and evening/weekend programs available. *Degree requirements:* For master's, project; for doctorate, comprehensive exam, thesis/dissertation. *Entrance requirements:* For doctorate, minimum GPA of 3.3. *Faculty research:* Robotics, intelligent systems, human-computer interaction software systems, biomedical engineering, signal/image processing, probabilistic design, intelligent manufacturing, cooperative mobile robots, condition based maintenance, sensor fusion.

Tennessee Technological University, College of Graduate Studies, College of Engineering, Department of Mechanical Engineering, Cookeville, TN 38505. Offers MS. Part-time programs available. *Faculty:* 25 full-time (2 women). *Students:* 30 full-time (2 women), 9 part-time (1 woman); includes 3 minority (2 Asian, non-Hispanic/Latino; 1 Two or more races, non-Hispanic/Latino), 20 international. Average age 28. 115 applicants, 72% accepted, 25 enrolled. In 2014, 5 master's awarded. *Degree requirements:* For master's, thesis. *Entrance requirements:* For master's, GRE. Additional exam requirements/recommendations for international students: Required—TOEFL (minimum score 550 paper-based; 79 iBT), IELTS (minimum score 5.5), PTE (minimum score 53), or TOEIC (Test of English as an International Communication). *Application deadline:* For fall admission, 8/1 for domestic students, 5/1 for international students; for spring admission, 12/1 for domestic students, 10/1 for international students. Applications are processed on a rolling basis. Application fee: $35 ($40 for international students). Electronic applications accepted. *Expenses:* Tuition, state resident: full-time $9783; part-time $492 per credit hour. Tuition, nonresident: full-time $24,071; part-time $1179 per credit hour. *Financial support:* In 2014–15, fellowships (averaging $8,000 per year), 20 research assistantships (averaging $8,190 per year), 8 teaching assistantships (averaging $6,711 per year) were awarded. Financial award application deadline: 4/1. *Faculty research:* Energy-related systems, design, acoustics and acoustical systems. *Unit head:* Dr. Mohan Rao, Chairperson, 931-372-3254, Fax: 931-372-6340, E-mail: mrao@tntech.edu. *Application contact:* Shelia K. Kendrick, Coordinator of Graduate Studies, 931-372-3808, Fax: 931-372-3497, E-mail: skendrick@tntech.edu.

Texas A&M University, College of Engineering, Department of Mechanical Engineering, College Station, TX 77843. Offers M Eng, MS, PhD. *Faculty:* 51. *Students:* 368 full-time (57 women), 60 part-time (11 women); includes 42 minority (5 Black or African American, non-Hispanic/Latino; 3 American Indian or Alaska Native, non-Hispanic/Latino; 12 Asian, non-Hispanic/Latino; 21 Hispanic/Latino; 1 Two or more races, non-Hispanic/Latino), 282 international. Average age 28. 1,151 applicants, 16% accepted, 87 enrolled. In 2014, 65 master's, 38 doctorates awarded. *Degree requirements:* For master's, thesis (for MS); for doctorate, thesis/dissertation. *Entrance requirements:* For master's, GRE General Test, minimum undergraduate GPA of 3.0; for doctorate, GRE General Test, minimum graduate GPA of 3.5. Additional exam requirements/recommendations for international students: Required—TOEFL (minimum score 570 paper-based). *Application deadline:* For fall admission, 2/1 priority date for domestic students; for spring admission, 11/1 for domestic students. Applications are processed on a rolling basis. Application fee: $50 ($90 for international students). Electronic applications accepted. *Expenses:* Tuition, state resident: full-time $4078; part-time $226.55 per credit hour. Tuition, nonresident: full-time $10,594; part-time $577.55 per credit hour. *Required fees:* $2813; $237.70 per credit hour. $278.50 per semester. Tuition and fees vary according to degree level and student level. *Financial support:* In 2014–15, 368 students received support, including 40 fellowships with full and partial tuition reimbursements available (averaging $6,451 per year), 230 research assistantships with full and partial tuition reimbursements available (averaging $7,196 per year), 80 teaching assistantships with full and partial tuition reimbursements available (averaging $5,438 per year); career-related internships or fieldwork, institutionally sponsored loans, scholarships/grants, traineeships, health care benefits, tuition waivers (full and partial), and unspecified assistantships also available. Support available to part-time students. Financial award application deadline: 3/1; financial award applicants required to submit FAFSA. *Faculty research:* Thermal/fluid sciences, materials/manufacturing and controls systems. *Unit head:* Dr. Andreas A. Polycarpou, Department Head, 979-845-5337, E-mail: apolycarpou@tamu.edu. *Application contact:* Dr. Daniel A. McAdams, Graduate Program Director, 979-862-7834, E-mail: dmcadams@tamu.edu.
Website: http://engineering.tamu.edu/mechanical.

Texas A&M University–Kingsville, College of Graduate Studies, College of Engineering, Department of Mechanical and Industrial Engineering, Program in Mechanical Engineering, Kingsville, TX 78363. Offers ME, MS. *Students:* 137 full-time (6 women), 28 part-time (3 women); includes 7 minority (1 Black or African American, non-Hispanic/Latino; 1 Asian, non-Hispanic/Latino; 5 Hispanic/Latino), 153 international. Average age 24. 280 applicants, 83% accepted, 82 enrolled. In 2014, 24 master's awarded. *Degree requirements:* For master's, variable foreign language requirement, comprehensive exam, thesis (for some programs). *Entrance requirements:* For master's, GRE, MAT, GMAT, minimum GPA 2.6, minimum GRE score (Q+V) 950 (old scale). Additional exam requirements/recommendations for international students: Required— TOEFL (minimum score 550 paper-based; 79 iBT). *Application deadline:* For fall admission, 8/15 for domestic students, 6/1 for international students; for spring admission, 12/15 for domestic students, 10/1 for international students; for summer admission, 5/15 for domestic students, 4/1 for international students. Applications are processed on a rolling basis. Application fee: $35 ($50 for international students). Electronic applications accepted. *Financial support:* In 2014–15, 46 students received support, including 6 research assistantships (averaging $1,067 per year), 9 teaching assistantships (averaging $3,080 per year); career-related internships or fieldwork, Federal Work-Study, institutionally sponsored loans, scholarships/grants, health care benefits, tuition waivers (full and partial), and unspecified assistantships also available. Support available to part-time students. Financial award application deadline: 5/15; financial award applicants required to submit FAFSA. *Unit head:* Dr. Larry Peel, Department Chair, 361-593-2003, Fax: 361-593-4026, E-mail: larry.peel@tamuk.edu. *Application contact:* Dr. Mohamed Abdelrahman, Dean of Graduate Studies, 361-593-2809, E-mail: mohamed.abdelrahman@tamuk.edu.

Texas Tech University, Graduate School, Edward E. Whitacre Jr. College of Engineering, Department of Mechanical Engineering, Lubbock, TX 79409. Offers MSME, PhD. Part-time programs available. *Faculty:* 39 full-time (8 women), 3 part-time/adjunct (0 women). *Students:* 114 full-time (11 women), 21 part-time (2 women); includes 16 minority (2 Black or African American, non-Hispanic/Latino; 5 Asian, non-Hispanic/Latino; 8 Hispanic/Latino; 1 Two or more races, non-Hispanic/Latino), 76 international. Average age 29. 237 applicants, 11% accepted, 19 enrolled. In 2014, 20 master's, 10 doctorates awarded. *Degree requirements:* For master's, comprehensive exam, thesis (for some programs); for doctorate, comprehensive exam, thesis/dissertation. *Entrance requirements:* For master's and doctorate, GRE (Verbal and Quantitative). Additional exam requirements/recommendations for international students: Required—TOEFL (minimum score 550 paper-based; 79 iBT). *Application deadline:* For fall admission, 6/1 priority date for domestic students, 1/15 priority date for international students; for spring admission, 9/1 priority date for domestic students, 6/15 priority date for international students. Applications are processed on a rolling basis. Application fee: $60. Electronic applications accepted. *Expenses:* Tuition, state resident: full-time $6310; part-time $262.92 per credit hour. Tuition, nonresident: full-time $14,998; part-time $624.92 per credit hour. *Required fees:* $2701; $36.50 per credit. $912.50 per semester. Tuition and fees vary according to course load. *Financial support:* In 2014–15, 112 students received support, including 108 fellowships (averaging $1,969 per year), 25 research assistantships (averaging $27,088 per year), 51 teaching assistantships (averaging $19,614 per year); scholarships/grants, tuition waivers (partial), and unspecified assistantships also available. Financial award application deadline: 4/15; financial award applicants required to submit FAFSA. *Faculty research:* Biomedical and bio engineering, energetic, high-pressure, nano and bio materials, nonlinear dynamics and control, turbulence and wind energy, microfluidics. *Total annual research expenditures:* $2.7 million. *Unit head:* Dr. Jharna Chaudhuri, Professor and Chair, 806-742-3563, Fax: 806-742-3540, E-mail: jharna.chandhuri@ttu.edu. *Application contact:* Gwen Clymo, Graduate Academic Advisor, 806-834-7711, Fax: 806-742-3540, E-mail: gwen.clymo@ttu.edu.
Website: http://www.depts.ttu.edu/me/.

Tufts University, School of Engineering, Department of Mechanical Engineering, Medford, MA 02155. Offers bioengineering (ME, MS), including bioinformatics, biomechanical systems and devices, signals and systems; bioinformatics (MS); human factors (MS); mechanical engineering (ME, MS, PhD). Part-time programs available. *Faculty:* 15 full-time (1 woman), 7 part-time/adjunct (1 woman). *Students:* 35 full-time (12 women), 23 part-time (11 women); includes 11 minority (3 Black or African American, non-Hispanic/Latino; 1 American Indian or Alaska Native, non-Hispanic/Latino; 3 Asian, non-Hispanic/Latino; 2 Hispanic/Latino; 2 Two or more races, non-Hispanic/Latino), 14 international. Average age 27. 112 applicants, 47% accepted, 16 enrolled. In 2014, 18 master's, 6 doctorates awarded. Terminal master's awarded for partial completion of doctoral program. *Degree requirements:* For master's, thesis; for doctorate, thesis/dissertation. *Entrance requirements:* For master's and doctorate, GRE General Test. Additional exam requirements/recommendations for international students: Required—TOEFL (minimum score 550 paper-based; 80 iBT), IELTS (minimum score 6.5). *Application deadline:* For fall admission, 1/15 priority date for domestic students, 1/15 for international students; for spring admission, 9/15 for domestic and international students. Applications are processed on a rolling basis. Application fee: $75. Electronic applications accepted. *Expenses: Tuition:* Full-time $45,590; part-time $1161 per credit hour. *Required fees:* $782. Full-time tuition and fees vary according to degree level, program and student level. Part-time tuition and fees vary according to course load. *Financial support:* Fellowships with full tuition reimbursements, research assistantships with full and partial tuition reimbursements, teaching assistantships with full and partial tuition reimbursements, Federal Work-Study, scholarships/grants, tuition waivers (partial), and unspecified assistantships available. Financial award application deadline: 5/15; financial award applicants required to submit FAFSA. *Faculty research:* Applied mechanics, biomaterials, controls/robotics, design/systems, human factors. *Unit head:* Dr. Robert C. White, Graduate Program Director. *Application contact:* Office of Graduate Admissions, 617-627-3395, E-mail: gradadmissions@tufts.edu.
Website: http://engineering.tufts.edu/me.

Tuskegee University, Graduate Programs, College of Engineering, Department of Mechanical Engineering, Tuskegee, AL 36088. Offers MSME. *Degree requirements:* For master's, thesis or alternative. *Entrance requirements:* For master's, GRE General Test, GRE Subject Test. Additional exam requirements/recommendations for international students: Required—TOEFL (minimum score 500 paper-based). *Expenses: Tuition:* Full-time $18,560; part-time $1542 per credit hour. *Required fees:* $2910; $1455 per semester. *Faculty research:* Superalloys, fatigue and surface machinery, energy management, solar energy.

Union Graduate College, School of Engineering and Computer Science, Schenectady, NY 12308-3107. Offers computer science (MS); electrical engineering (MS); engineering and management systems (MS); mechanical engineering (MS). Part-time and evening/weekend programs available. *Degree requirements:* For master's, capstone course. *Entrance requirements:* For master's, minimum GPA of 3.0, letters of recommendation. Additional exam requirements/recommendations for international students: Required—TOEFL (minimum score 550 paper-based). Electronic applications accepted. *Expenses:* Contact institution.

Université de Moncton, Faculty of Engineering, Program in Mechanical Engineering, Moncton, NB E1A 3E9, Canada. Offers M Sc A. *Degree requirements:* For master's, thesis, proficiency in French. *Faculty research:* Composite materials, thermal energy systems, control systems, fluid mechanics and heat transfer, CAD/CAM and robotics.

Université de Sherbrooke, Faculty of Engineering, Department of Mechanical Engineering, Sherbrooke, QC J1K 2R1, Canada. Offers M Sc A, PhD. *Degree requirements:* For master's, one foreign language, thesis; for doctorate, comprehensive exam, thesis/dissertation. *Entrance requirements:* For master's, bachelor's degree in engineering or equivalent; for doctorate, master's degree in engineering or equivalent. Electronic applications accepted. *Faculty research:* Acoustics, aerodynamics, vehicle dynamics, composite materials, heat transfer.

Université Laval, Faculty of Sciences and Engineering, Department of Mechanical Engineering, Programs in Mechanical Engineering, Québec, QC G1K 7P4, Canada. Offers M Sc, PhD. Part-time programs available. Terminal master's awarded for partial completion of doctoral program. *Degree requirements:* For master's, thesis; for doctorate, comprehensive exam, thesis/dissertation. *Entrance requirements:* For master's and doctorate, knowledge of French. Electronic applications accepted.

University at Buffalo, the State University of New York, Graduate School, School of Engineering and Applied Sciences, Department of Mechanical and Aerospace Engineering, Buffalo, NY 14260. Offers aerospace engineering (MS, PhD); mechanical engineering (MS, PhD). Part-time programs available. *Faculty:* 35 full-time (5 women), 8 part-time/adjunct (1 woman). *Students:* 212 full-time (32 women), 28 part-time (2 women); includes 10 minority (4 Black or African American, non-Hispanic/Latino; 5 Asian, non-Hispanic/Latino; 1 Hispanic/Latino), 167 international. Average age 25. 1,216 applicants, 14% accepted, 55 enrolled. In 2014, 67 master's, 6 doctorates awarded. Terminal master's awarded for partial completion of doctoral program. *Degree requirements:* For master's, comprehensive exam, project or thesis; for doctorate, thesis/dissertation. *Entrance requirements:* For master's and doctorate, GRE General Test, GRE Subject Test. Additional exam requirements/recommendations for international students: Required—TOEFL (minimum score 79 iBT). *Application deadline:* For fall admission, 2/1 priority date for domestic and international students; for spring admission, 10/1 priority date for domestic and international students. Applications are processed on a rolling basis. Application fee: $75. Electronic applications accepted. *Financial support:* In 2014–15, 85 students received support, including 11 fellowships with full and partial tuition reimbursements available (averaging $30,000 per year), 16 research assistantships with full and partial tuition reimbursements available (averaging $27,660 per year), 32 teaching assistantships with full and partial tuition reimbursements available (averaging $21,775 per year); career-related internships or fieldwork, Federal Work-Study, institutionally sponsored loans, scholarships/grants, health care benefits, tuition waivers (full and partial), and unspecified assistantships also available. Support available to part-time students. Financial award application deadline: 2/1; financial award applicants required to submit FAFSA. *Faculty research:* Fluid and thermal sciences, systems and design, mechanics and materials. *Total annual research expenditures:* $7.8 million. *Unit head:* Dr. Kemper Lewis, Chair, 716-645-2682, Fax: 716-645-2883, E-mail: kelewis@buffalo.edu. *Application contact:* Dr. Pineet Singla, Director of Graduate Studies, 716-645-1429, Fax: 716-645-3875, E-mail: psingla@.buffalo.edu.
Website: http://www.mae.buffalo.edu/.

The University of Akron, Graduate School, College of Engineering, Department of Mechanical Engineering, Akron, OH 44325. Offers engineering (PhD); mechanical engineering (MS). Part-time and evening/weekend programs available. *Faculty:* 26 full-time (1 woman), 11 part-time/adjunct (0 women). *Students:* 87 full-time (10 women), 24 part-time (3 women), 72 international. Average age 28. 100 applicants, 60% accepted, 24 enrolled. In 2014, 15 master's, 5 doctorates awarded. Terminal master's awarded for partial completion of doctoral program. *Degree requirements:* For master's, thesis optional; for doctorate, one foreign language, thesis/dissertation, candidacy exam, qualifying exam. *Entrance requirements:* For master's, GRE, minimum GPA of 2.75, baccalaureate degree in engineering, three letters of recommendation, statement of purpose, resume; for doctorate, GRE, minimum GPA of 3.0 with bachelor's degree, 3.5 with master's degree; three letters of recommendation, statement of purpose, resume. Additional exam requirements/recommendations for international students: Required—TOEFL (minimum score 550 paper-based; 79 iBT), IELTS (minimum score 6.5). *Application deadline:* Applications are processed on a rolling basis. Application fee: $45 ($70 for international students). Electronic applications accepted. *Expenses:* Tuition, state resident: full-time $7578; part-time $421 per credit hour. Tuition, nonresident: full-time $12,977; part-time $721 per credit hour. *Required fees:* $1388; $35 per credit hour. Tuition and fees vary according to course load. *Financial support:* In 2014–15, 37 research assistantships with full tuition reimbursements, 36 teaching assistantships with full tuition reimbursements were awarded. *Faculty research:* Materials science, tribology and lubrication, vibration and dynamic analysis, solid mechanics, micro and nanoelectromechanical systems (MEMS and NEMS), bio-mechanics. *Total annual research expenditures:* $3.7 million. *Unit head:* Dr. Sergio Felicelli, Chair, 330-972-7367, E-mail: sergio@uakron.edu. *Application contact:* Dr. Xiaosheng Gao, Associate Chair for Graduate Programs, 330-972-2415, E-mail: xgao@uakron.edu.
Website: http://www.uakron.edu/engineering/ME/.

The University of Alabama, Graduate School, College of Engineering, Department of Mechanical Engineering, Tuscaloosa, AL 35487. Offers MS, PhD. Part-time programs available. *Faculty:* 23 full-time (2 women). *Students:* 58 full-time (6 women), 10 part-time (1 woman); includes 7 minority (2 Black or African American, non-Hispanic/Latino; 1 Asian, non-Hispanic/Latino; 2 Hispanic/Latino; 2 Two or more races, non-Hispanic/Latino), 29 international. Average age 26. 77 applicants, 64% accepted, 22 enrolled. In 2014, 20 master's, 7 doctorates awarded. Terminal master's awarded for partial completion of doctoral program. *Degree requirements:* For master's, comprehensive exam, thesis (for some programs); for doctorate, comprehensive exam, thesis/dissertation. *Entrance requirements:* For master's, GRE General Test, minimum GPA of 3.0; for doctorate, GRE General Test, minimum GPA of 3.0 with MS, 3.3 without MS. Additional exam requirements/recommendations for international students: Required—TOEFL (minimum score 600 paper-based). *Application deadline:* For fall admission, 7/1 priority date for domestic students, 1/15 priority date for international students; for spring admission, 11/1 priority date for domestic students, 6/1 priority date for international students. Applications are processed on a rolling basis. Application fee: $50 ($60 for international students). Electronic applications accepted. *Expenses:* Tuition, state resident: full-time $9826. Tuition, nonresident: full-time $24,950. *Financial support:* In 2014–15, 32 students received support, including 5 fellowships with full tuition reimbursements available (averaging $18,000 per year), 14 research assistantships with full tuition reimbursements available (averaging $17,500 per year), 13 teaching assistantships with full tuition reimbursements available (averaging $13,000 per year); career-related internships or fieldwork, health care benefits, and unspecified assistantships also available. Financial award application deadline: 3/30. *Faculty research:* Thermal/fluids, robotics, numerical modeling, energy conservation, energy and combustion systems, internal combustion engines, heating, ventilation and air conditioning, medical devices, manufacturing, vehicular systems, controls, acoustics solid mechanics and materials. *Total annual research expenditures:* $1.7 million. *Unit head:* Dr. Kenneth Clark Midkiff, Jr., Professor and Interim Head, 205-348-1645, Fax: 205-348-6419, E-mail: cmidkiff@eng.ua.edu. *Application contact:* Dr. Steve Shepard, Graduate Program Coordinator and Professor, 205-348-1650, Fax: 205-348-6419, E-mail: sshepard@eng.ua.edu.
Website: http://www.me.ua.edu.

The University of Alabama at Birmingham, School of Engineering, Program in Mechanical Engineering, Birmingham, AL 35294. Offers mechanical engineering (MSME); research/design (MSME); technology/engineering management (MSME).

Students: 8 full-time (1 woman), 16 part-time (1 woman); includes 2 minority (1 Black or African American, non-Hispanic/Latino; 1 Asian, non-Hispanic/Latino), 8 international. Average age 27. In 2014, 5 master's awarded. *Degree requirements:* For master's, thesis (for some programs). *Entrance requirements:* For master's, GRE (minimum 50th percentile ranking on Quantitative Reasoning and Verbal Reasoning sections), minimum B-level scholarship overall or over the last 60 semester hours of earned credit. Additional exam requirements/recommendations for international students: Required—TOEFL (minimum score 80 iBT). *Application deadline:* For fall admission, 7/1 for domestic students; for spring admission, 11/1 for domestic students; for summer admission, 4/1 for domestic students. Electronic applications accepted. *Expenses:* Tuition, state resident: full-time $7090; part-time $370 per credit hour. Tuition, nonresident: full-time $16,072; part-time $869 per credit hour. Full-time tuition and fees vary according to course load and program. *Financial support:* Research assistantships available. *Unit head:* Dr. David Littlefield, Graduate Program Director, 205-934-8460, E-mail: littlefield@uab.edu. *Application contact:* Susan Noblitt Banks, Director of Graduate School Operations, 205-934-8227, Fax: 205-934-8413, E-mail: gradschool@uab.edu.
Website: http://www.uab.edu/engineering/home/departments-research/me/graduate.

The University of Alabama in Huntsville, School of Graduate Studies, College of Engineering, Department of Chemical and Materials Engineering, Huntsville, AL 35899. Offers biotechnology science and engineering (PhD); chemical engineering (MSE); materials science (MS, PhD); mechanical engineering (PhD), including chemical engineering. Part-time and evening/weekend programs available. *Degree requirements:* For master's, comprehensive exam, thesis or alternative, oral and written exams; for doctorate, comprehensive exam, thesis/dissertation. *Entrance requirements:* For master's, GRE General Test, appropriate bachelor's degree, minimum GPA of 3.0; for doctorate, GRE General Test, minimum GPA of 3.0. Additional exam requirements/recommendations for international students: Required—TOEFL (minimum score 500 paper-based; 80 iBT), IELTS (minimum score 6.5). Electronic applications accepted. *Faculty research:* Ultrathin films for optical, sensor and biological applications; materials processing including low gravity; hypergolic reactants; computational fluid dynamics; biofuels and renewable resources.

The University of Alabama in Huntsville, School of Graduate Studies, College of Engineering, Department of Mechanical and Aerospace Engineering, Huntsville, AL 35899. Offers aerospace engineering (MSE), including aerospace engineering, missile systems engineering, rotorcraft systems engineering; aerospace systems engineering (MS, PhD); mechanical engineering (MSE, PhD). Part-time and evening/weekend programs available. *Degree requirements:* For master's, comprehensive exam, thesis or alternative, oral and written exams; for doctorate, comprehensive exam, thesis/dissertation, oral and written exams. *Entrance requirements:* For master's, GRE General Test, BSE, minimum GPA of 3.0; for doctorate, GRE General Test, minimum GPA of 3.0. Additional exam requirements/recommendations for international students: Required—TOEFL (minimum score 500 paper-based; 80 iBT), IELTS (minimum score 6.5). Electronic applications accepted. *Faculty research:* Rocket propulsion and plasma engineering, materials engineering and solid mechanics, energy conversion, transport, and storage.

University of Alaska Fairbanks, College of Engineering and Mines, Department of Mechanical Engineering, Fairbanks, AK 99775-5905. Offers MS. Part-time programs available. *Faculty:* 7 full-time (1 woman). *Students:* 6 full-time (0 women), 2 part-time (0 women); includes 1 minority (Hispanic/Latino), 2 international. Average age 27. 10 applicants, 40% accepted, 3 enrolled. In 2014, 7 master's awarded. *Degree requirements:* For master's, comprehensive exam, oral defense of project or thesis. *Entrance requirements:* For master's, GRE General Test, bachelor's degree from accredited institution with minimum cumulative undergraduate and major GPA of 3.0. Additional exam requirements/recommendations for international students: Required—TOEFL (minimum score 550 paper-based; 79 iBT), IELTS (minimum score 6.5). *Application deadline:* For fall admission, 6/1 for domestic students, 3/1 for international students; for spring admission, 10/15 for domestic students, 9/1 for international students. Applications are processed on a rolling basis. Application fee: $60. Electronic applications accepted. *Expenses:* Tuition, state resident: full-time $7614; part-time $423 per credit. Tuition, nonresident: full-time $15,552; part-time $864 per credit. Tuition and fees vary according to course level, course load and reciprocity agreements. *Financial support:* In 2014–15, 1 research assistantship with full tuition reimbursement (averaging $620 per year), 6 teaching assistantships with full tuition reimbursements (averaging $6,679 per year) were awarded; fellowships with full tuition reimbursements, career-related internships or fieldwork, Federal Work-Study, scholarships/grants, health care benefits, and unspecified assistantships also available. Support available to part-time students. Financial award application deadline: 7/1; financial award applicants required to submit FAFSA. *Faculty research:* Cold regions engineering, fluid mechanics, heat transfer, energy systems, indoor air quality. *Unit head:* Dr. Rorik Peterson, Department Chair, 907-474-7136, Fax: 907-474-6141, E-mail: fymech@uaf.edu. *Application contact:* Mary Kreta, Director of Admissions, 907-474-7500, Fax: 907-474-7097, E-mail: admissions@uaf.edu.
Website: http://cem.uaf.edu/me/.

University of Alberta, Faculty of Graduate Studies and Research, Department of Mechanical Engineering, Edmonton, AB T6G 2E1, Canada. Offers engineering management (M Eng); mechanical engineering (M Eng, M Sc, PhD); MBA/M Eng. Part-time programs available. *Degree requirements:* For master's, thesis; for doctorate, thesis/dissertation. *Entrance requirements:* For master's and doctorate, minimum GPA of 7.0 on a 9.0 scale. Additional exam requirements/recommendations for international students: Required—TOEFL (minimum score 580 paper-based). *Faculty research:* Combustion and environmental issues, advanced materials, computational fluid dynamics, biomedical, acoustics and vibrations.

The University of Arizona, College of Engineering, Department of Aerospace and Mechanical Engineering, Program in Mechanical Engineering, Tucson, AZ 85721. Offers MS, PhD. Part-time programs available. *Degree requirements:* For master's, thesis or alternative; for doctorate, one foreign language, thesis/dissertation. *Entrance requirements:* For master's and doctorate, GRE General Test, minimum GPA of 3.25, 3 letters of recommendation, statement of purpose. Additional exam requirements/recommendations for international students: Required—TOEFL (minimum score 550 paper-based; 79 iBT). Electronic applications accepted. *Faculty research:* Fluid mechanics, structures, computer-aided design, stability and control, probabilistic design.

University of Arkansas, Graduate School, College of Engineering, Department of Mechanical Engineering, Fayetteville, AR 72701-1201. Offers MSE, MSME, PhD. Part-time programs available. Postbaccalaureate distance learning degree programs offered. *Degree requirements:* For master's, thesis optional; for doctorate, one foreign language, thesis/dissertation. Electronic applications accepted.

University of Bridgeport, School of Engineering, Department of Mechanical Engineering, Bridgeport, CT 06604. Offers MS. *Degree requirements:* For master's, thesis optional. *Entrance requirements:* Additional exam requirements/recommendations for international students: Recommended—TOEFL (minimum score 550 paper-based; 80 iBT), IELTS (minimum score 6.5). Electronic applications accepted. *Faculty research:* Residual stress in composite material resins, helicopter composite structure and dynamic components, water spray cooling, heat transfer.

The University of British Columbia, Faculty of Applied Science, Mechanical Engineering Department, Vancouver, BC V6P 4T5, Canada. Offers M Eng, MA Sc, PhD. *Degree requirements:* For master's, thesis; for doctorate, comprehensive exam, thesis/dissertation, 33 credits. *Entrance requirements:* For master's, bachelor's degree, minimum B+ average; for doctorate, master's degree, minimum B+ average. Additional exam requirements/recommendations for international students: Required—TOEFL (minimum score 580 paper-based; 93 iBT), IELTS (minimum score 6.5); Recommended—TWE. Electronic applications accepted. *Faculty research:* Applied mechanics, manufacturing, robotics and controls, thermodynamics and combustion, fluid/aerodynamics, acoustics.

University of Calgary, Faculty of Graduate Studies, Schulich School of Engineering, Department of Mechanical and Manufacturing Engineering, Calgary, AB T2N 1N4, Canada. Offers M Eng, M Sc, PhD. Part-time programs available. *Degree requirements:* For master's, thesis (for some programs); for doctorate, thesis/dissertation, candidacy exam. *Entrance requirements:* For master's, minimum GPA of 3.0; for doctorate, minimum GPA of 3.3. Additional exam requirements/recommendations for international students: Required—TOEFL (minimum score 550 paper-based; 80 iBT), IELTS (minimum score 7). *Faculty research:* Thermofluids, solid mechanics, materials, biomechanics, manufacturing.

University of California, Berkeley, Graduate Division, College of Engineering, Department of Mechanical Engineering, Berkeley, CA 94720-1500. Offers M Eng, MS, D Eng, PhD. *Degree requirements:* For master's, comprehensive exam or thesis (MS); for doctorate, thesis/dissertation, preliminary and qualifying exams. *Entrance requirements:* For master's and doctorate, GRE General Test, minimum GPA of 3.0, 3 letters of recommendation. Additional exam requirements/recommendations for international students: Required—TOEFL.

University of California, Davis, College of Engineering, Program in Mechanical and Aeronautical Engineering, Davis, CA 95616. Offers aeronautical engineering (M Engr, MS, D Engr, PhD, Certificate); mechanical engineering (M Engr, MS, D Engr, PhD, Certificate); M Engr/MBA. *Degree requirements:* For master's, comprehensive exam (for some programs), thesis (for some programs); for doctorate, thesis/dissertation. *Entrance requirements:* For master's and doctorate, GRE General Test, minimum GPA of 3.0. Additional exam requirements/recommendations for international students: Required—TOEFL (minimum score 550 paper-based). Electronic applications accepted.

University of California, Irvine, Henry Samueli School of Engineering, Department of Mechanical and Aerospace Engineering, Irvine, CA 92697. Offers MS, PhD. Part-time programs available. *Students:* 164 full-time (32 women), 7 part-time (1 woman); includes 40 minority (1 Black or African American, non-Hispanic/Latino; 1 American Indian or Alaska Native, non-Hispanic/Latino; 18 Asian, non-Hispanic/Latino; 17 Hispanic/Latino; 3 Two or more races, non-Hispanic/Latino), 83 international. Average age 26. 724 applicants, 22% accepted, 75 enrolled. In 2014, 44 master's, 18 doctorates awarded. Terminal master's awarded for partial completion of doctoral program. *Degree requirements:* For doctorate, thesis/dissertation. *Entrance requirements:* For master's and doctorate, GRE General Test, minimum GPA of 3.0, 3 letters of recommendation. Additional exam requirements/recommendations for international students: Required—TOEFL (minimum score 550 paper-based). *Application deadline:* For fall admission, 1/15 priority date for domestic students, 1/15 for international students. Applications are processed on a rolling basis. Application fee: $90 ($110 for international students). Electronic applications accepted. *Financial support:* Fellowships with tuition reimbursements, research assistantships with full tuition reimbursements, teaching assistantships with tuition reimbursements, institutionally sponsored loans, traineeships, health care benefits, and unspecified assistantships available. Financial award application deadline: 3/1; financial award applicants required to submit FAFSA. *Faculty research:* Thermal and fluid sciences, combustion and propulsion, control systems, robotics, lightweight structures. *Unit head:* Prof. Derek Dunn-Rankin, Chair, 949-824-8745, Fax: 949-824-8585, E-mail: ddunnran@uci.edu. *Application contact:* Prof. Timothy Rupert, Graduate Admissions Advisor, 949-824-4937, Fax: 949-824-8585, E-mail: trupert@uci.edu.
Website: http://mae.eng.uci.edu/.

University of California, Los Angeles, Graduate Division, Henry Samueli School of Engineering and Applied Science, Department of Mechanical and Aerospace Engineering, Program in Mechanical Engineering, Los Angeles, CA 90095-1597. Offers MS, PhD. *Faculty:* 31 full-time (2 women), 6 part-time/adjunct (0 women). *Students:* 246 full-time (38 women); includes 69 minority (1 Black or African American, non-Hispanic/Latino; 50 Asian, non-Hispanic/Latino; 13 Hispanic/Latino; 5 Two or more races, non-Hispanic/Latino), 109 international. 750 applicants, 37% accepted, 99 enrolled. In 2014, 75 master's, 24 doctorates awarded. *Degree requirements:* For master's, comprehensive exam or thesis; for doctorate, thesis/dissertation, qualifying exams. *Entrance requirements:* For master's, GRE General Test, minimum GPA of 3.0; for doctorate, GRE General Test, minimum GPA of 3.25. Additional exam requirements/recommendations for international students: Required—TOEFL (minimum score 560 paper-based; 87 iBT), IELTS (minimum score 7). *Application deadline:* For fall admission, 12/15 for domestic and international students; for winter admission, 10/1 for domestic students; for spring admission, 12/31 for domestic students. Application fee: $80 ($100 for international students). Electronic applications accepted. *Financial support:* In 2014–15, 105 fellowships, 194 research assistantships, 89 teaching assistantships were awarded; Federal Work-Study, institutionally sponsored loans, and tuition waivers (full and partial) also available. Financial award application deadline: 1/5; financial award applicants required to submit FAFSA. *Faculty research:* Applied mathematics, applied plasma physics, dynamics, fluid mechanics, heat and mass transfer, design, robotics and manufacturing, nanoelectromechanical/microelectromechanical systems (NEMS/MEMS), structural and solid mechanics, systems and control. *Total annual research expenditures:* $14.4 million. *Unit head:* Dr. Tsu-Chin Tsao, Chair, 310-206-2819, E-mail: ttsao@seas.ucla.edu. *Application contact:* Angie Castillo, Student Affairs Officer, 310-825-7793, Fax: 310-206-4830, E-mail: angie@seas.ucla.edu.
Website: http://www.mae.ucla.edu/.

University of California, Merced, Graduate Division, School of Engineering, Merced, CA 95343. Offers biological engineering and small scale technologies (MS, PhD); electrical engineering and computer science (MS, PhD); environmental systems (MS, PhD); mechanical engineering (MS); mechanical engineering and applied mechanics (PhD). *Faculty:* 38 full-time (6 women), 1 part-time/adjunct (0 women). *Students:* 128 full-time (36 women), 2 part-time (0 women); includes 21 minority (1 Black or African American, non-Hispanic/Latino; 11 Asian, non-Hispanic/Latino; 6 Hispanic/Latino; 3 Two or more races, non-Hispanic/Latino), 72 international. Average age 28. 230 applicants, 39% accepted, 38 enrolled. In 2014, 5 master's, 18 doctorates awarded. *Degree requirements:* For master's, variable foreign language requirement, comprehensive exam, thesis (for some programs); for doctorate, variable foreign language requirement, comprehensive exam, thesis/dissertation. *Entrance requirements:* For master's and doctorate, GRE. Additional exam requirements/recommendations for international students: Required—TOEFL (minimum score 550 paper-based; 68 iBT);

Recommended—IELTS. Application fee: $80 ($100 for international students). *Expenses:* Tuition, state resident: full-time $11,220; part-time $2805 per semester. *Required fees:* $1940; $970 per semester hour. *Financial support:* In 2014–15, 19 fellowships with full and partial tuition reimbursements (averaging $6,683 per year) were awarded; scholarships/grants also available. *Faculty research:* Artificial intelligence, biomedical imaging, thermal science, ecology, nanotechnology. *Unit head:* Dr. Erik Rolland, Interim Dean, 209-228-4296, Fax: 209-228-4047, E-mail: erolland@ucmerced.edu. *Application contact:* Tsu Ya, Graduate Admissions and Academic Services Manager, 209-228-4521, Fax: 209-228-6906, E-mail: tya@ucmerced.edu.

University of California, Riverside, Graduate Division, Department of Mechanical Engineering, Riverside, CA 92521. Offers MS, PhD. Part-time programs available. Terminal master's awarded for partial completion of doctoral program. *Degree requirements:* For master's, comprehensive exam or thesis, seminar in mechanical engineering; for doctorate, comprehensive exam, thesis/dissertation, seminar in mechanical engineering. *Entrance requirements:* Additional exam requirements/recommendations for international students: Required—TOEFL (minimum score 550 paper-based; 80 iBT). *Expenses:* Tuition, state resident: full-time $5399. Tuition, nonresident: full-time $10,433. *Faculty research:* Advanced robotics and machine design, air quality modeling group, computational fluid dynamics, computational mechanics and materials, biomaterials and nanotechnology laboratory.

University of California, San Diego, Graduate Division, Department of Mechanical and Aerospace Engineering, Program in Mechanical Engineering, La Jolla, CA 92093. Offers MS, PhD. *Students:* 122 full-time (22 women), 10 part-time (5 women); includes 27 minority (1 Black or African American, non-Hispanic/Latino; 1 American Indian or Alaska Native, non-Hispanic/Latino; 19 Asian, non-Hispanic/Latino; 6 Hispanic/Latino), 70 international. 646 applicants, 22% accepted, 36 enrolled. In 2014, 33 master's, 12 doctorates awarded. *Degree requirements:* For master's, comprehensive exam or thesis; for doctorate, comprehensive exam, thesis/dissertation. *Entrance requirements:* For master's and doctorate, GRE General Test, minimum GPA of 3.0. Additional exam requirements/recommendations for international students: Required—TOEFL (minimum score 550 paper-based; 80 iBT), IELTS (minimum score 7). *Application deadline:* For fall admission, 12/15 for domestic students, 1/2 for international students. Application fee: $90 ($110 for international students). Electronic applications accepted. *Expenses:* Tuition, state resident: full-time $11,220; part-time $5610 per quarter. Tuition, nonresident: full-time $26,322; part-time $13,161 per quarter. *Required fees:* $570 per quarter. Tuition and fees vary according to program. *Financial support:* Fellowships, research assistantships, teaching assistantships, scholarships/grants, and unspecified assistantships available. Financial award application deadline: 1/2; financial award applicants required to submit FAFSA. *Faculty research:* Mechatronics, sensor integration, robotics, vehicle design in water/land/air, medical devices. *Unit head:* Vitali Nesterenko, Chair, 858-534-0113, E-mail: mae-chair-l@ucsd.edu. *Application contact:* Linda McKamey, Graduate Coordinator, 858-534-4065, E-mail: mae-gradadm-l@ucsd.edu.
Website: http://maeweb.ucsd.edu/.

University of California, Santa Barbara, Graduate Division, College of Engineering, Department of Mechanical Engineering, Santa Barbara, CA 93106-5070. Offers computational science and engineering (MS, PhD); mechanical engineering (MS, PhD); MS/PhD. Terminal master's awarded for partial completion of doctoral program. *Degree requirements:* For master's, thesis; for doctorate, comprehensive exam, thesis/dissertation. *Entrance requirements:* For master's and doctorate, GRE. Additional exam requirements/recommendations for international students: Required—TOEFL (minimum score 550 paper-based; 80 iBT), IELTS (minimum score 7). Electronic applications accepted. *Faculty research:* Micro/nanoscale technology; bioengineering and systems biology; computational science and engineering; dynamics systems, controls and robotics; thermofluid sciences; solid mechanics, materials, and structures.

University of Central Florida, College of Engineering and Computer Science, Department of Mechanical and Aerospace Engineering, Program in Mechanical Engineering, Orlando, FL 32816. Offers MSME, PhD. *Students:* 100 full-time (10 women), 56 part-time (5 women); includes 29 minority (1 Black or African American, non-Hispanic/Latino; 10 Asian, non-Hispanic/Latino; 16 Hispanic/Latino; 2 Two or more races, non-Hispanic/Latino), 56 international. Average age 28. 153 applicants, 64% accepted, 45 enrolled. In 2014, 47 master's, 9 doctorates awarded. *Degree requirements:* For master's, thesis or alternative; for doctorate, thesis/dissertation, candidacy exam, departmental qualifying exam. *Application deadline:* For fall admission, 7/15 priority date for domestic students; for spring admission, 12/1 priority date for domestic students. Electronic applications accepted. *Expenses:* Tuition, state resident: part-time $288.16 per credit hour. Tuition, nonresident: part-time $1073.31 per credit hour. *Financial support:* In 2014–15, 63 students received support, including 18 fellowships with partial tuition reimbursements available (averaging $6,100 per year), 40 research assistantships with partial tuition reimbursements available (averaging $9,700 per year), 27 teaching assistantships with partial tuition reimbursements available (averaging $11,800 per year); career-related internships or fieldwork, institutionally sponsored loans, scholarships/grants, tuition waivers (partial), and unspecified assistantships also available. *Unit head:* Dr. Challapalli Suryanarayana, Interim Chair, 407-823-6662, Fax: 407-823-0208, E-mail: surya@ucf.edu. *Application contact:* Barbara Rodriguez Lamas, Director, Admissions and Student Services, 407-823-2766, Fax: 407-823-6442, E-mail: gradadmissions@ucf.edu.
Website: http://mae.ucf.edu/academics/graduate/.

University of Central Oklahoma, The Jackson College of Graduate Studies, College of Mathematics and Science, Department of Engineering and Physics, Edmond, OK 73034-5209. Offers biomedical engineering (MS); electrical engineering (MS); mechanical systems (MS); physics (MS). Part-time programs available. *Degree requirements:* For master's, thesis optional. *Entrance requirements:* For master's, GRE, 24 hours of course work in physics or equivalent, mathematics through differential equations, minimum GPA of 2.75 overall and 3.0 in last 60 hours attempted. Additional exam requirements/recommendations for international students: Required—TOEFL (minimum score 550 paper-based). Electronic applications accepted.

University of Cincinnati, Graduate School, College of Engineering and Applied Science, Department of Mechanical and Materials Engineering, Program in Mechanical Engineering, Cincinnati, OH 45221. Offers MS, PhD. Evening/weekend programs available. Terminal master's awarded for partial completion of doctoral program. *Degree requirements:* For master's, oral exam or thesis defense; for doctorate, variable foreign language requirement, thesis/dissertation. *Entrance requirements:* For master's and doctorate, GRE General Test. Additional exam requirements/recommendations for international students: Required—TOEFL (minimum score 575 paper-based). Electronic applications accepted. *Faculty research:* Signature analysis, structural analysis, energy, design, robotics.

University of Colorado Boulder, Graduate School, College of Engineering and Applied Science, Department of Mechanical Engineering, Boulder, CO 80309. Offers ME, MS, PhD. *Faculty:* 26 full-time (5 women). *Students:* 166 full-time (32 women), 33 part-time (5 women); includes 21 minority (2 American Indian or Alaska Native, non-Hispanic/Latino; 9 Asian, non-Hispanic/Latino; 7 Hispanic/Latino; 3 Two or more races, non-Hispanic/Latino), 60 international. Average age 26. 381 applicants, 43% accepted, 53 enrolled. In 2014, 59 master's, 17 doctorates awarded. Terminal master's awarded for partial completion of doctoral program. *Degree requirements:* For master's, comprehensive exam, thesis optional; for doctorate, comprehensive exam, thesis/dissertation, final and preliminary exams. *Entrance requirements:* For master's and doctorate, minimum undergraduate GPA of 3.0. Additional exam requirements/recommendations for international students: Required—TOEFL. *Application deadline:* For fall admission, 1/15 for domestic and international students; for spring admission, 10/1 for domestic students, 9/1 for international students. Applications are processed on a rolling basis. Application fee: $50 ($70 for international students). Electronic applications accepted. *Financial support:* In 2014–15, 304 students received support, including 34 fellowships (averaging $9,883 per year), 71 research assistantships with full and partial tuition reimbursements available (averaging $35,824 per year), 27 teaching assistantships with full and partial tuition reimbursements available (averaging $31,942 per year); institutionally sponsored loans, scholarships/grants, health care benefits, and unspecified assistantships also available. Financial award application deadline: 1/15; financial award applicants required to submit FAFSA. *Faculty research:* Mechanical engineering, materials engineering, materials: engineering properties, biomedical engineering. *Total annual research expenditures:* $9 million.
Website: http://www.colorado.edu/mechanical.

University of Colorado Colorado Springs, College of Engineering and Applied Science, Department of Mechanical and Aerospace Engineering, Colorado Springs, CO 80933-7150. Offers mechanical engineering (MS). Part-time and evening/weekend programs available. *Faculty:* 15 full-time (2 women), 4 part-time/adjunct (0 women). *Students:* 6 full-time (0 women), 24 part-time (7 women); includes 6 minority (all Hispanic/Latino), 1 international. Average age 28. 20 applicants, 60% accepted, 4 enrolled. In 2014, 9 master's awarded. *Degree requirements:* For master's, thesis or alternative. *Entrance requirements:* For master's, GRE General Test, bachelor's degree in engineering or related degree, minimum GPA of 3.0. Additional exam requirements/recommendations for international students: Required—TOEFL (minimum score 550 paper-based; 79 iBT). *Application deadline:* For fall admission, 3/1 for domestic and international students; for spring admission, 10/1 for domestic and international students. Applications are processed on a rolling basis. Application fee: $60 ($100 for international students). *Expenses:* Tuition, state resident: full-time $9900; part-time $1892 per course. Tuition, nonresident: full-time $18,792; part-time $3375 per course. One-time fee: $100. Tuition and fees vary according to course load, program and reciprocity agreements. *Financial support:* In 2014–15, 3 students received support, including 2 fellowships (averaging $6,000 per year), 3 research assistantships (averaging $9,000 per year); Federal Work-Study and scholarships/grants also available. Support available to part-time students. Financial award application deadline: 3/1; financial award applicants required to submit FAFSA. *Faculty research:* Advanced propulsion design and testing, rarefied gas dynamics, microfluidics, micropropulsion and spacecraft-thruster interactions, heat transfer and thermodynamics with application to renewable energy, modeling simulation and control of dynamic systems, tethered spacecraft, theoretical and computational fluid dynamics, thermal fluid sciences with a focus on microscale heat transfer and fluid mechanics, flame characterization using advanced diagnostics. *Total annual research expenditures:* $91,458. *Unit head:* Dr. Andrew Ketsdever, Director, 719-255-3573, E-mail: aketsdever@eas.uccs.edu. *Application contact:* Stephanie Vigil, Program Assistant, 719-255-3243, E-mail: svigil5@uccs.edu.
Website: http://eas.uccs.edu/mae/.

University of Colorado Denver, College of Engineering and Applied Science, Department of Bioengineering, Aurora, CO 80045-2560. Offers assistive technology and rehabilitation engineering (MS, PhD); device design and entrepreneurship (MS, PhD); research (MS, PhD); translational bioengineering (MS, PhD). Part-time programs available. *Faculty:* 18 full-time (9 women), 5 part-time/adjunct (1 woman). *Students:* 43 full-time (20 women), 15 part-time (4 women); includes 12 minority (4 Black or African American, non-Hispanic/Latino; 3 Asian, non-Hispanic/Latino; 3 Hispanic/Latino; 2 Two or more races, non-Hispanic/Latino), 4 international. Average age 27. 88 applicants, 55% accepted, 18 enrolled. In 2014, 8 master's, 2 doctorates awarded. Terminal master's awarded for partial completion of doctoral program. *Degree requirements:* For master's, thesis or alternative, 30 credit hours; for doctorate, comprehensive exam, 36 credit hours of classwork (18 core, 18 elective), additional 30 hours of thesis work, three formal examinations, approval of dissertations. *Entrance requirements:* For master's and doctorate, GRE, transcripts, three letters of recommendation, resume, statement of purpose. Additional exam requirements/recommendations for international students: Required—TOEFL (minimum score 550 paper-based; 79 iBT), TOEFL (minimum score 600 paper-based; 100 iBT) for PhD. *Application deadline:* For fall admission, 1/15 priority date for domestic students, 1/1 priority date for international students. Application fee: $50 ($75 for international students). Electronic applications accepted. *Expenses:* Expenses: Contact institution. *Financial support:* In 2014–15, 13 students received support. Fellowships, research assistantships, teaching assistantships, Federal Work-Study, institutionally sponsored loans, scholarships/grants, and traineeships available. Financial award application deadline: 4/1; financial award applicants required to submit FAFSA. *Faculty research:* Imaging and biophotonics, cardiovascular biomechanics and hemodynamics, orthopedic biomechanics, ophthalmology, neuroscience engineering, diabetes, surgery and urological sciences. *Unit head:* Dr. Robin Shandas, Chair, 303-724-4196, E-mail: robin.shandas@ucdenver.edu. *Application contact:* Shawna McMahon, Graduate School Admissions, 303-724-5893, E-mail: shawna.mcmahon@ucdenver.edu.
Website: http://www.ucdenver.edu/academics/colleges/Engineering/Programs/bioengineering/Pages/Bioengineering.aspx.

University of Colorado Denver, College of Engineering and Applied Science, Department of Mechanical Engineering, Denver, CO 80217. Offers mechanical engineering (MS); mechanics (MS); thermal sciences (MS). Part-time and evening/weekend programs available. *Faculty:* 9 full-time (0 women). *Students:* 29 full-time (3 women), 22 part-time (2 women); includes 6 minority (2 Black or African American, non-Hispanic/Latino; 1 Asian, non-Hispanic/Latino; 3 Hispanic/Latino), 22 international. Average age 29. 81 applicants, 41% accepted, 16 enrolled. In 2014, 17 master's awarded. *Degree requirements:* For master's, comprehensive exam, 30 credit hours, project or thesis. *Entrance requirements:* For master's, GRE, three letters of recommendation, personal statement. Additional exam requirements/recommendations for international students: Required—TOEFL (minimum score 537 paper-based; 75 iBT); Recommended—IELTS (minimum score 6.8). *Application deadline:* For fall admission, 5/1 for domestic students, 4/15 for international students; for spring admission, 10/1 for domestic students, 9/15 for international students. Application fee: $50 ($75 for international students). Electronic applications accepted. *Expenses:* Expenses: Contact institution. *Financial support:* In 2014–15, 29 students received support. Fellowships, research assistantships, teaching assistantships, career-related internships or fieldwork, Federal Work-Study, institutionally sponsored loans, scholarships/grants, traineeships, and unspecified assistantships available. Financial award application deadline: 4/1; financial award applicants required to submit FAFSA. *Faculty research:* Applied and computational mechanics, bioengineering, energy systems, tribology, micro/mesofluidics and biomechanics, vehicle dynamics. *Unit head:* Dr. Sam Welch, Chair, 303-556-8488, Fax: 303-556-6371, E-mail: sam.welch@ucdenver.edu. *Application*

Mechanical Engineering

contact: Catherine McCoy, Program Assistant, 303-556-8516, E-mail: catherine.mccoy@ucdenver.edu. Website: http://www.ucdenver.edu/academics/colleges/Engineering/Programs/Mechanical-Engineering/Pages/MechanicalEngineering.aspx.

University of Colorado Denver, College of Engineering and Applied Science, Master of Engineering Program, Denver, CO 80217-3364. Offers civil engineering (M Eng), including civil engineering, geographic information systems, transportation systems; electrical engineering (M Eng); mechanical engineering (M Eng). Part-time programs available. *Students:* 30 full-time (9 women), 20 part-time (7 women); includes 3 minority (1 Black or African American, non-Hispanic/Latino; 2 Hispanic/Latino), 8 international. Average age 34. 35 applicants, 83% accepted, 15 enrolled. In 2014, 14 master's awarded. *Degree requirements:* For master's, comprehensive exam, 27 credit hours of course work, 3 credit hours of report or thesis work. *Entrance requirements:* For master's, GRE (for those with GPA below 2.75), transcripts, references, statement of purpose. Additional exam requirements/recommendations for international students: Required—TOEFL (minimum score 537 paper-based; 75 iBT); Recommended—IELTS (minimum score 6.5). *Application deadline:* For fall admission, 4/1 for domestic students, 3/1 for international students; for spring admission, 10/1 for domestic students, 9/15 for international students. Applications are processed on a rolling basis. Application fee: $50 ($75 for international students). Electronic applications accepted. *Expenses:* Expenses: Contact institution. *Financial support:* In 2014–15, 4 students received support. Fellowships, research assistantships, teaching assistantships, Federal Work-Study, institutionally sponsored loans, scholarships/grants, traineeships, and unspecified assistantships available. Financial award application deadline: 4/1; financial award applicants required to submit FAFSA. *Faculty research:* Civil, electrical and mechanical engineering. *Unit head:* 303-556-2870, Fax: 303-556-2511, E-mail: engineering@ucdenver.edu. *Application contact:* Graduate School Admissions, 303-556-2704, E-mail: admissions@ucdenver.edu. Website: http://www.ucdenver.edu/academics/colleges/Engineering/admissions/Masters/Pages/MastersAdmissions.aspx.

University of Connecticut, Graduate School, School of Engineering, Department of Mechanical Engineering, Storrs, CT 06269. Offers MS, PhD. Terminal master's awarded for partial completion of doctoral program. *Degree requirements:* For master's, comprehensive exam, thesis or alternative; for doctorate, thesis/dissertation. *Entrance requirements:* For master's and doctorate, GRE General Test, GRE Subject Test. Additional exam requirements/recommendations for international students: Required—TOEFL (minimum score 550 paper-based). Electronic applications accepted. *Faculty research:* Design, applied mechanics, dynamics and control, energy and thermal sciences, manufacturing.

University of Dayton, Department of Mechanical and Aerospace Engineering, Dayton, OH 45469. Offers aerospace engineering (MSAE, DE, PhD); mechanical engineering (MSME, DE, PhD); renewable and clean energy (MS). Part-time programs available. Postbaccalaureate distance learning degree programs offered (no on-campus study). *Faculty:* 15 full-time (3 women), 10 part-time/adjunct (1 woman). *Students:* 197 full-time (43 women), 37 part-time (6 women); includes 11 minority (7 Black or African American, non-Hispanic/Latino; 2 Asian, non-Hispanic/Latino; 2 Hispanic/Latino), 156 international. Average age 27. 340 applicants, 44% accepted, 58 enrolled. In 2014, 69 master's, 2 doctorates awarded. Terminal master's awarded for partial completion of doctoral program. *Degree requirements:* For master's, thesis optional; for doctorate, variable foreign language requirement, thesis/dissertation, departmental qualifying exam. *Entrance requirements:* For master's, BS in engineering, math, or physics. Additional exam requirements/recommendations for international students: Required—TOEFL (minimum score 550 paper-based; 80 iBT), IELTS (minimum score 6.5). *Application deadline:* For fall admission, 8/1 priority date for domestic students, 5/1 priority date for international students; for winter admission, 9/1 for international students; for spring admission, 12/1 for domestic students, 9/1 priority date for international students; for summer admission, 4/1 for domestic students, 3/1 priority date for international students. Applications are processed on a rolling basis. Application fee: $0 ($50 for international students). Electronic applications accepted. *Expenses: Tuition:* Full-time $10,176; part-time $848 per credit. *Required fees:* $25; $25 per course. Part-time tuition and fees vary according to course level, course load, degree level and program. *Financial support:* In 2014–15, 3 fellowships with full tuition reimbursements (averaging $25,000 per year), 16 research assistantships with full tuition reimbursements (averaging $12,000 per year), 4 teaching assistantships with full tuition reimbursements (averaging $8,000 per year) were awarded; institutionally sponsored loans, health care benefits, and unspecified assistantships also available. Financial award application deadline: 3/1; financial award applicants required to submit FAFSA. *Faculty research:* Jet engine combustion, surface coating friction and wear, aircraft thermal management, aerospace fuels, energy efficient buildings, energy efficient manufacturing, renewable energy. *Total annual research expenditures:* $1.2 million. *Unit head:* Dr. Kelly Kissock, Chair, 937-229-2999, Fax: 937-229-4766, E-mail: jkissock1@udayton.edu. *Application contact:* Dr. Vinod Jain, Graduate Program Director, 937-229-2992, Fax: 937-229-4766, E-mail: vjain1@udayton.edu. Website: https://www.udayton.edu/engineering/departments/mechanical_and_aerospace/index.php.

University of Delaware, College of Engineering, Department of Mechanical Engineering, Newark, DE 19716. Offers MEM, MSME, PhD. Part-time programs available. Terminal master's awarded for partial completion of doctoral program. *Degree requirements:* For master's, thesis (for some programs); for doctorate, thesis/dissertation. *Entrance requirements:* For master's and doctorate, GRE General Test. Additional exam requirements/recommendations for international students: Required—TOEFL (minimum score 600 paper-based). Electronic applications accepted. *Faculty research:* Biomedical engineering, clean energy, composites and nanotechnology, robotics and controls, fluid mechanics.

University of Denver, Daniel Felix Ritchie School of Engineering and Computer Science, Department of Mechanical and Materials Engineering, Denver, CO 80208. Offers bioengineering (MS); engineering (MS, PhD); engineering/management (MS); materials science (MS, PhD); mechanical engineering (MS, PhD); nanoscale science and engineering (MS, PhD). Part-time programs available. *Faculty:* 10 full-time (1 woman), 1 (woman) part-time/adjunct. *Students:* 4 full-time (2 women), 44 part-time (12 women); includes 6 minority (1 Black or African American, non-Hispanic/Latino; 3 Asian, non-Hispanic/Latino; 1 Hispanic/Latino; 1 Two or more races, non-Hispanic/Latino), 20 international. Average age 29. 67 applicants, 88% accepted, 16 enrolled. In 2014, 7 master's, 1 doctorate awarded. Terminal master's awarded for partial completion of doctoral program. *Degree requirements:* For master's, thesis optional; for doctorate, comprehensive exam, thesis/dissertation. *Entrance requirements:* For master's, GRE General Test, bachelor's degree, transcripts, personal statement, resume or curriculum vitae, two letters of recommendation; for doctorate, GRE General Test, master's degree, transcripts, personal statement, resume or curriculum vitae, two letters of recommendation. Additional exam requirements/recommendations for international students: Required—TOEFL (minimum score 550 paper-based; 80 iBT). *Application deadline:* For fall admission, 2/1 priority date for domestic and international students. Applications are processed on a rolling basis. Application fee: $65. Electronic

applications accepted. *Expenses:* Expenses: $1,199 per credit hour. *Financial support:* In 2014–15, 24 students received support, including 17 research assistantships with full and partial tuition reimbursements available (averaging $12,842 per year), 17 teaching assistantships with full and partial tuition reimbursements available (averaging $9,975 per year); Federal Work-Study, institutionally sponsored loans, scholarships/grants, health care benefits, and unspecified assistantships also available. Financial award application deadline: 2/15; financial award applicants required to submit FAFSA. *Faculty research:* Aerosols, biomechanics, composite materials, photo optics, drug delivery. *Unit head:* Dr. Matt Gordon, Chair, 303-871-3580, Fax: 303-871-4450, E-mail: matthew.gordon@du.edu. *Application contact:* Yvonne Petitt, Assistant to the Chair, 303-871-2107, Fax: 303-871-4450, E-mail: yvonne.petitt@du.edu. Website: http://www.du.edu/rsecs/departments/mme/index.html.

University of Detroit Mercy, College of Engineering and Science, Department of Mechanical Engineering, Detroit, MI 48221. Offers mechanical engineering (ME, DE). Evening/weekend programs available. *Degree requirements:* For doctorate, thesis/dissertation. *Faculty research:* CAD/CAM.

University of Florida, Graduate School, College of Engineering, Department of Mechanical and Aerospace Engineering, Gainesville, FL 32611. Offers aerospace engineering (ME, MS, PhD); mechanical engineering (ME, MS, PhD). Part-time programs available. Postbaccalaureate distance learning degree programs offered. *Faculty:* 50 full-time (4 women), 30 part-time/adjunct (5 women). *Students:* 386 full-time (38 women), 92 part-time (11 women); includes 61 minority (11 Black or African American, non-Hispanic/Latino; 24 Asian, non-Hispanic/Latino; 26 Hispanic/Latino), 259 international. 739 applicants, 59% accepted, 192 enrolled. In 2014, 186 master's, 37 doctorates awarded. *Degree requirements:* For master's, thesis (for some programs); for doctorate, comprehensive exam, thesis/dissertation. *Entrance requirements:* For master's and doctorate, minimum GPA of 3.0. Additional exam requirements/recommendations for international students: Required—TOEFL (minimum score 550 paper-based; 80 iBT), IELTS (minimum score 6). *Application deadline:* Applications are processed on a rolling basis. Application fee: $30. Electronic applications accepted. *Financial support:* Institutionally sponsored loans and unspecified assistantships available. Support available to part-time students. Financial award applicants required to submit FAFSA. *Faculty research:* Thermal sciences, design, controls and robotics, manufacturing, energy transport and utilization. *Unit head:* David W. Hahn, PhD, Chair, 352-392-0807, Fax: 352-392-1071, E-mail: dwhahn@ufl.edu. *Application contact:* David W. Mikolaitis, PhD, Graduate Coordinator, 352-392-7632, Fax: 352-392-7303, E-mail: mollusk@ufl.edu. Website: http://www.mae.ufl.edu/.

University of Hawaii at Manoa, Graduate Division, College of Engineering, Department of Mechanical Engineering, Honolulu, HI 96822. Offers MS, PhD. Part-time programs available. *Degree requirements:* For master's, comprehensive exam, thesis; for doctorate, comprehensive exam, thesis/dissertation. *Entrance requirements:* For master's and doctorate, GRE General Test. Additional exam requirements/recommendations for international students: Required—TOEFL (minimum score 550 paper-based; 79 iBT), IELTS (minimum score 5). *Faculty research:* Materials and manufacturing; mechanics, systems and control; thermal and fluid sciences.

University of Houston, Cullen College of Engineering, Department of Mechanical Engineering, Houston, TX 77204. Offers MME, MSME, PhD. Part-time programs available. Terminal master's awarded for partial completion of doctoral program. *Degree requirements:* For master's, thesis (for some programs); for doctorate, thesis/dissertation, departmental qualifying exam. *Entrance requirements:* For master's and doctorate, GRE General Test. Additional exam requirements/recommendations for international students: Required—TOEFL.

University of Idaho, College of Graduate Studies, College of Engineering, Department of Mechanical Engineering, Moscow, ID 83844-0902. Offers M Engr, MS, PhD. *Faculty:* 12 full-time, 1 part-time/adjunct. *Students:* 18 full-time, 27 part-time. Average age 31. In 2014, 22 master's, 2 doctorates awarded. *Degree requirements:* For master's, thesis or alternative; for doctorate, thesis/dissertation. *Entrance requirements:* For master's, minimum GPA of 2.8; for doctorate, minimum undergraduate GPA of 2.8, 3.0 graduate. Additional exam requirements/recommendations for international students: Required—TOEFL. *Application deadline:* For fall admission, 8/1 for domestic students; for spring admission, 12/15 for domestic students. Applications are processed on a rolling basis. Application fee: $60. Electronic applications accepted. *Expenses:* Tuition, state resident: full-time $4784; part-time $280.50 per credit hour. Tuition, nonresident: full-time $18,314; part-time $957.50 per credit hour. *Required fees:* $2000; $58.50 per credit hour. Tuition and fees vary according to program. *Financial support:* Research assistantships and teaching assistantships available. Financial award applicants required to submit FAFSA. *Faculty research:* Thermodynamics and energy, fluid mechanics and heat transfer, robotics, vibrational characteristics of composite materials, mechanics and materials science. *Unit head:* Dr. John C. Crepeau, Chair, 208-885-6579, E-mail: medept@uidaho.edu. *Application contact:* Sean Scoggin, Graduate Recruitment Coordinator, 208-885-4001, Fax: 208-885-4406, E-mail: graduateadmissions@uidaho.edu. Website: http://www.uidaho.edu/engr/ME.

University of Illinois at Chicago, Graduate College, College of Engineering, Department of Mechanical and Industrial Engineering, Program in Mechanical Engineering, Chicago, IL 60607-7128. Offers fluids engineering (MS, PhD); mechanical analysis and design (MS, PhD); thermomechanical and power engineering (MS, PhD). Part-time programs available. *Students:* 149 full-time (9 women), 19 part-time (2 women); includes 17 minority (1 American Indian or Alaska Native, non-Hispanic/Latino; 9 Asian, non-Hispanic/Latino; 6 Hispanic/Latino; 1 Two or more races, non-Hispanic/Latino), 123 international. Average age 25. 376 applicants, 53% accepted, 62 enrolled. In 2014, 33 master's, 10 doctorates awarded. *Degree requirements:* For master's, thesis. *Entrance requirements:* For master's, GRE General Test, minimum GPA of 2.75. Additional exam requirements/recommendations for international students: Required—TOEFL. *Application deadline:* For fall admission, 5/15 for domestic students, 2/15 for international students; for spring admission, 11/1 for domestic students, 7/15 for international students. Applications are processed on a rolling basis. Application fee: $60. Electronic applications accepted. *Expenses:* Expenses: $17,602 in-state; $29,600 out-of-state. *Financial support:* Fellowships with full tuition reimbursements, research assistantships with full tuition reimbursements, teaching assistantships with full tuition reimbursements, Federal Work-Study, scholarships/grants, traineeships, tuition waivers (full), and unspecified assistantships available. Financial award application deadline: 3/1; financial award applicants required to submit FAFSA. *Faculty research:* Micro/nanoelectromechanical systems (MEMS/NEMS), micro/nanomanipulation, nanoparticle, nanofluidics, microtransducers and micromechanisms, electrospinning, acoustics, dynamics and vibration, medical imaging and diagnostics, biomechanics and computational mechanics, product design, mechatronics and automatic control, multi-body systems and vehicle dynamics, IC engines, combustors, plasma, combustion, heat transfer, turbulence, multi-phase flows, molecular dynamics and air pollution control. *Unit head:* Prof. Farzad Mashayek, Head, 312-996-6122, E-mail: mashayek@uic.edu. Website: http://catalog.uic.edu/gcat/colleges-schools/engineering/me/.

University of Illinois at Urbana–Champaign, Graduate College, College of Engineering, Department of Mechanical Science and Engineering, Champaign, IL 61820. Offers mechanical engineering (MS, PhD); theoretical and applied mechanics (MS, PhD). Terminal master's awarded for partial completion of doctoral program. *Entrance requirements:* Additional exam requirements/recommendations for international students: Required—TOEFL (minimum score 613 paper-based; 103 iBT), IELTS (minimum score 7). *Application deadline:* For fall admission, 1/4 for domestic students; for spring admission, 10/1 for domestic students. Application fee: $70 ($90 for international students). *Financial support:* Application deadline: 12/15. *Unit head:* Placid Mathew Ferreira, Head, 217-333-0639, Fax: 217-244-6534, E-mail: pferreir@illinois.edu. *Application contact:* Katrina Hagler, Assistant Director of Graduate Recruiting and Admissions, 217-244-3416, Fax: 217-244-6534, E-mail: kkappes2@illinois.edu.
Website: http://mechanical.illinois.edu/.

The University of Iowa, Graduate College, College of Engineering, Department of Mechanical Engineering, Iowa City, IA 52242-1316. Offers energy systems (MS, PhD); engineering design (MS, PhD); fluid dynamics (MS, PhD); materials and manufacturing (MS, PhD); wind energy (MS, PhD). *Faculty:* 14 full-time (1 woman). *Students:* 50 full-time (5 women); includes 1 minority (Black or African American, non-Hispanic/Latino), 34 international. Average age 28. 68 applicants, 19% accepted, 4 enrolled. In 2014, 9 master's, 7 doctorates awarded. Terminal master's awarded for partial completion of doctoral program. *Degree requirements:* For master's, oral exam or thesis; for doctorate, comprehensive exam, thesis/dissertation. *Entrance requirements:* For master's and doctorate, GRE. Additional exam requirements/recommendations for international students: Required—TOEFL (minimum score 600 paper-based; 100 iBT). *Application deadline:* For fall admission, 1/15 for domestic and international students; for spring admission, 9/1 for domestic and international students; for summer admission, 1/15 for domestic and international students. Application fee: $60 ($100 for international students). Electronic applications accepted. *Financial support:* In 2014–15, 3 fellowships with partial tuition reimbursements (averaging $19,933 per year), 36 research assistantships with full tuition reimbursements (averaging $20,823 per year), 21 teaching assistantships with full tuition reimbursements (averaging $6,457 per year) were awarded; traineeships and unspecified assistantships also available. Financial award applicants required to submit FAFSA. *Faculty research:* Computer simulation methodology, biomechanics, metal casting, dynamics, laser processing, system reliability, ship hydrodynamics, solid mechanics, fluid dynamics, energy, human modeling and nano technology. *Total annual research expenditures:* $9.8 million. *Unit head:* Dr. Andrew Kusiak, Departmental Executive Officer, 319-335-5934, Fax: 319-335-5669, E-mail: andrew-kusiak@uiowa.edu. *Application contact:* Andrea Flaherty, Academic Program Specialist, 319-335-5939, Fax: 319-335-5669, E-mail: mech_eng@engineering.uiowa.edu.
Website: http://www.engineering.uiowa.edu/mie.

The University of Kansas, Graduate Studies, School of Engineering, Department of Mechanical Engineering, Lawrence, KS 66045. Offers MS, DE, PhD. Part-time programs available. *Faculty:* 19 full-time, 1 part-time/adjunct. *Students:* 49 full-time (8 women), 15 part-time (2 women); includes 7 minority (1 Black or African American, non-Hispanic/Latino; 3 Asian, non-Hispanic/Latino; 1 Hispanic/Latino; 2 Two or more races, non-Hispanic/Latino), 35 international. Average age 26. 88 applicants, 59% accepted, 22 enrolled. In 2014, 11 master's, 2 doctorates awarded. *Degree requirements:* For master's, thesis or alternative, exam; for doctorate, comprehensive exam, thesis/dissertation. *Entrance requirements:* For master's, minimum GPA of 3.0; for doctorate, minimum GPA of 3.5. Additional exam requirements/recommendations for international students: Required—TOEFL. *Application deadline:* For fall admission, 6/1 priority date for domestic students, 3/31 priority date for international students; for spring admission, 11/1 priority date for domestic students, 9/30 priority date for international students. Applications are processed on a rolling basis. Application fee: $55 ($65 for international students). Electronic applications accepted. *Financial support:* Fellowships with full and partial tuition reimbursements, research assistantships with full and partial tuition reimbursements, teaching assistantships with full and partial tuition reimbursements, and career-related internships or fieldwork available. Financial award application deadline: 5/15. *Faculty research:* Heat transfer, energy analysis, computer-aided design, biomedical engineering, computational mathematics. *Unit head:* Theodore Bergman, Chair, 785-864-3181, E-mail: tlbergman@ku.edu. *Application contact:* Kate Maisch, Graduate Admissions Contact, 785-864-3181, E-mail: kume@ku.edu.
Website: http://www.me.engr.ku.edu/.

University of Kentucky, Graduate School, College of Engineering, Program in Mechanical Engineering, Lexington, KY 40506-0032. Offers MSME, PhD. *Degree requirements:* For master's, comprehensive exam, thesis optional; for doctorate, comprehensive exam, thesis/dissertation. *Entrance requirements:* For master's, GRE General Test, minimum undergraduate GPA of 2.75; for doctorate, GRE General Test, minimum undergraduate GPA of 3.0. Additional exam requirements/recommendations for international students: Required—TOEFL (minimum score 550 paper-based). Electronic applications accepted. *Faculty research:* Combustion, computational fluid dynamics, design and systems, manufacturing, thermal and fluid sciences.

University of Louisiana at Lafayette, College of Engineering, Department of Mechanical Engineering, Lafayette, LA 70504. Offers MSE. Evening/weekend programs available. *Degree requirements:* For master's, comprehensive exam, thesis or alternative. *Entrance requirements:* For master's, GRE General Test, BS in mechanical engineering, minimum GPA of 2.85. Additional exam requirements/recommendations for international students: Required—TOEFL (minimum score 550 paper-based). Electronic applications accepted. *Faculty research:* CAD/CAM, machine design and vibration, thermal science.

University of Louisville, J. B. Speed School of Engineering, Department of Mechanical Engineering, Louisville, KY 40292-0001. Offers M Eng, MS, PhD. *Accreditation:* ABET (one or more programs are accredited). Part-time programs available. *Students:* 59 full-time (9 women), 56 part-time (13 women); includes 14 minority (2 Black or African American, non-Hispanic/Latino; 3 Asian, non-Hispanic/Latino; 4 Hispanic/Latino; 5 Two or more races, non-Hispanic/Latino), 12 international. Average age 25. 42 applicants, 50% accepted, 4 enrolled. In 2014, 19 master's, 2 doctorates awarded. Terminal master's awarded for partial completion of doctoral program. *Degree requirements:* For master's, comprehensive exam (for some programs), thesis or alternative; for doctorate, comprehensive exam, thesis/dissertation, minimum GPA of 3.0. *Entrance requirements:* For master's and doctorate, GRE General Test. Additional exam requirements/recommendations for international students: Required—TOEFL (minimum score 550 paper-based; 80 iBT), IELTS (minimum score 6.5). *Application deadline:* For fall admission, 5/1 priority date for domestic and international students; for spring admission, 11/1 priority date for domestic and international students. Applications are processed on a rolling basis. Application fee: $60. Electronic applications accepted. *Expenses:* Tuition, state resident: full-time $11,326; part-time $630 per credit hour. Tuition, nonresident: full-time $23,568; part-time $1311 per credit hour. *Required fees:* $196. Tuition and fees vary according to program and reciprocity agreements. *Financial support:* In 2014–15, 1 fellowship with full tuition reimbursement (averaging $22,000 per year), 4 research assistantships with full tuition reimbursements (averaging $22,500 per year), 11 teaching assistantships with full tuition reimbursements (averaging $20,000 per year) were awarded. Financial award application deadline: 1/25; financial award applicants required to submit FAFSA. *Faculty research:* Aerospace and automotive engineering, air pollution control, biomechanics and rehabilitation engineering, computer-aided design, micro and nanotechnology. *Total annual research expenditures:* $1.3 million. *Unit head:* Dr. Glen Prater, Jr., Chair, 502-852-6331, Fax: 502-852-6053, E-mail: gprater@louisville.edu. *Application contact:* Dr. Michael Day, Associate Dean, 502-852-6195, Fax: 502-852-7294, E-mail: day@louisville.edu.
Website: http://www.louisville.edu/speed/mechanical.

University of Maine, Graduate School, College of Engineering, Department of Mechanical Engineering, Orono, ME 04469. Offers MS, PSM, PhD. *Faculty:* 12 full-time (0 women), 2 part-time/adjunct (1 woman). *Students:* 23 full-time (5 women), 2 part-time (0 women), 13 international. Average age 32. 25 applicants, 56% accepted, 3 enrolled. In 2014, 5 master's, 2 doctorates awarded. *Degree requirements:* For master's, thesis (for some programs); for doctorate, comprehensive exam, thesis/dissertation. *Entrance requirements:* For master's and doctorate, GRE General Test. Additional exam requirements/recommendations for international students: Required—TOEFL. *Application deadline:* For fall admission, 12/1 priority date for domestic students; for spring admission, 6/1 for domestic students; for summer admission, 11/1 for domestic students. Applications are processed on a rolling basis. Application fee: $65. Electronic applications accepted. *Expenses:* Tuition, state resident: part-time $658 per credit hour. Tuition, nonresident: part-time $1550 per credit hour. *Financial support:* In 2014–15, 18 students received support, including 2 fellowships with full tuition reimbursements available (averaging $22,400 per year), 9 research assistantships with full tuition reimbursements available (averaging $14,600 per year), 7 teaching assistantships with full tuition reimbursements available (averaging $14,600 per year); Federal Work-Study and tuition waivers (full and partial) also available. Financial award application deadline: 3/1. *Faculty research:* Renewable energy, robotics, biomechanics, injury reduction and rehabilitation, rock mechanics. *Total annual research expenditures:* $1.1 million. *Unit head:* Dr. Senthil Vel, Chair, 207-581-2777, Fax: 207-581-2379, E-mail: senthil.vel@maine.edu. *Application contact:* Scott G. Delcourt, Assistant Vice President for Graduate Studies and Senior Associate Dean, 207-581-3291, Fax: 207-581-3232, E-mail: graduate@maine.edu.
Website: http://umaine.edu/mecheng/.

The University of Manchester, School of Mechanical, Aerospace and Civil Engineering, Manchester, United Kingdom. Offers advanced manufacturing technology (M Ent); aerospace engineering (M Phil, M Sc, PhD); civil engineering (M Phil, M Sc, PhD); environmental engineering (M Phil, PhD); management of projects (M Phil, M Sc, PhD); mechanical engineering (M Phil, M Sc, PhD); mechanical engineering design (M Ent); nuclear engineering (M Phil, D Eng, PhD).

University of Manitoba, Faculty of Graduate Studies, Faculty of Engineering, Department of Mechanical and Manufacturing Engineering, Winnipeg, MB R3T 2N2, Canada. Offers M Eng, M Sc, PhD. *Degree requirements:* For master's, thesis; for doctorate, thesis/dissertation.

University of Maryland, Baltimore County, The Graduate School, College of Engineering and Information Technology, Department of Mechanical Engineering, Baltimore, MD 21250. Offers computational thermal/fluid dynamics (Postbaccalaureate Certificate); mechanical engineering (MS, PhD); mechatronics (Postbaccalaureate Certificate). Part-time programs available. *Faculty:* 16 full-time (4 women), 3 part-time/adjunct (0 women). *Students:* 55 full-time (8 women), 17 part-time (4 women); includes 17 minority (5 Black or African American, non-Hispanic/Latino; 1 American Indian or Alaska Native, non-Hispanic/Latino; 6 Asian, non-Hispanic/Latino; 5 Hispanic/Latino), 22 international. Average age 29. 80 applicants, 65% accepted, 20 enrolled. In 2014, 7 master's, 6 doctorates awarded. *Degree requirements:* For master's, comprehensive exam (for some programs), thesis (for some programs); for doctorate, comprehensive exam, thesis/dissertation. *Entrance requirements:* Additional exam requirements/recommendations for international students: Required—TOEFL (minimum score 550 paper-based; 80 iBT). *Application deadline:* For fall admission, 6/1 for domestic students, 1/1 for international students; for spring admission, 11/1 for domestic students, 6/1 for international students. Applications are processed on a rolling basis. Application fee: $70. Electronic applications accepted. *Expenses:* Tuition, state resident: part-time $557. Tuition, nonresident: part-time $922. *Required fees:* $122 per semester. One-time fee: $200 part-time. *Financial support:* In 2014–15, 1 fellowship with full tuition reimbursement (averaging $27,000 per year), 15 research assistantships with full tuition reimbursements (averaging $16,000 per year), 19 teaching assistantships with full tuition reimbursements (averaging $14,000 per year) were awarded; career-related internships or fieldwork, Federal Work-Study, scholarships/grants, health care benefits, tuition waivers (partial), and unspecified assistantships also available. Support available to part-time students. Financial award application deadline: 6/30; financial award applicants required to submit FAFSA. *Faculty research:* Solid mechanics and materials sciences, thermal/fluids sciences, design-manufacturing and systems, bio-mechanical engineering, engineering education. *Total annual research expenditures:* $869,338. *Unit head:* Dr. Charles Eggleton, Professor and Acting Chair, 410-455-3334, Fax: 410-455-1052, E-mail: eggleton@umbc.edu. *Application contact:* Dr. Neil Rothman, Professor/Graduate Program Director, 410-455-5507, Fax: 410-455-1052, E-mail: nrothman@umbc.edu.
Website: http://www.me.umbc.edu/.

University of Maryland, College Park, Academic Affairs, A. James Clark School of Engineering, Department of Mechanical Engineering, College Park, MD 20742. Offers electronic packaging and reliability (MS, PhD); manufacturing and design (MS, PhD); mechanics and materials (MS, PhD); reliability engineering (M Eng, MS, PhD); thermal and fluid sciences (MS, PhD). Part-time and evening/weekend programs available. Postbaccalaureate distance learning degree programs offered. *Degree requirements:* For master's, thesis optional; for doctorate, thesis/dissertation, qualifying exam. *Entrance requirements:* For master's, GRE General Test, 3 letters of recommendation; for doctorate, GRE General Test, minimum GPA of 3.0. Additional exam requirements/recommendations for international students: Required—TOEFL. Electronic applications accepted. *Faculty research:* Injection molding, electronic packaging, fluid mechanics, product engineering.

University of Massachusetts Amherst, Graduate School, College of Engineering, Department of Mechanical and Industrial Engineering, Amherst, MA 01003. Offers industrial engineering and operations research (MS, PhD); mechanical engineering (MSME, PhD). Part-time programs available. *Faculty:* 29 full-time (4 women). *Students:* 90 full-time (20 women), 29 part-time (6 women); includes 12 minority (2 Black or African American, non-Hispanic/Latino; 1 American Indian or Alaska Native, non-Hispanic/Latino; 4 Asian, non-Hispanic/Latino; 3 Hispanic/Latino; 2 Two or more races, non-Hispanic/Latino), 65 international. Average age 28. 411 applicants, 31% accepted, 33 enrolled. In 2014, 27 master's, 7 doctorates awarded. Terminal master's awarded for partial completion of doctoral program. *Degree requirements:* For master's, thesis or alternative; for doctorate, comprehensive exam, thesis/dissertation. *Entrance requirements:* For master's and doctorate, GRE General Test. Additional exam requirements/recommendations for international students: Required—TOEFL (minimum score 550 paper-based; 80 iBT), IELTS (minimum score 6.5). *Application deadline:* For

fall admission, 1/15 for domestic and international students; for spring admission, 10/1 for domestic and international students. Applications are processed on a rolling basis. Application fee: $75. Electronic applications accepted. *Expenses:* Tuition, state resident: full-time $1980; part-time $110 per credit. Tuition, nonresident: full-time $14,644; part-time $414 per credit. *Required fees:* $11,417. One-time fee: $357. *Financial support:* Fellowships with full and partial tuition reimbursements, research assistantships with full and partial tuition reimbursements, teaching assistantships with full and partial tuition reimbursements, career-related internships or fieldwork, Federal Work-Study, scholarships/grants, traineeships, health care benefits, tuition waivers (full and partial), and unspecified assistantships available. Support available to part-time students. Financial award application deadline: 1/15. *Unit head:* Dr. David Schmidt, Graduate Program Director, 413-545-3827, Fax: 413-545-1027. *Application contact:* Lindsay DeSantis, Supervisor of Admissions, 413-545-0722, Fax: 413-577-0100, E-mail: gradadm@grad.umass.edu.
Website: http://mie.umass.edu/.

University of Massachusetts Dartmouth, Graduate School, College of Engineering, Department of Mechanical Engineering, North Dartmouth, MA 02747-2300. Offers industrial and systems engineering (MS); mechanical engineering (MS). Part-time programs available. *Faculty:* 11 full-time (1 woman). *Students:* 8 full-time (1 woman), 11 part-time (0 women); includes 1 minority (Asian, non-Hispanic/Latino), 9 international. Average age 26. 30 applicants, 60% accepted, 2 enrolled. In 2014, 10 master's awarded. *Degree requirements:* For master's, comprehensive exam, thesis or project. *Entrance requirements:* For master's, GRE (UMass Dartmouth mechanical engineering bachelor's degree recipients are exempt), statement of purpose (minimum of 300 words), resume, 3 letters of recommendation, official transcripts. Additional exam requirements/recommendations for international students: Required—TOEFL (minimum score 533 paper-based; 72 iBT), IELTS (minimum score 6). *Application deadline:* For fall admission, 2/15 priority date for domestic students, 1/15 priority date for international students; for spring admission, 11/15 priority date for domestic students, 10/15 priority date for international students. Applications are processed on a rolling basis. Application fee: $60. Electronic applications accepted. *Expenses:* Tuition, state resident: full-time $2071; part-time $86.29 per credit. Tuition, nonresident: full-time $8099; part-time $337.46 per credit. *Required fees:* $16,520; $712.33 per credit. Tuition and fees vary according to course load and reciprocity agreements. *Financial support:* In 2014–15, 1 research assistantship with full tuition reimbursement (averaging $5,718 per year), 3 teaching assistantships with full tuition reimbursements (averaging $10,000 per year) were awarded; Federal Work-Study and unspecified assistantships also available. Support available to part-time students. Financial award application deadline: 3/1; financial award applicants required to submit FAFSA. *Faculty research:* Biopreservation, renewable energy, fluid structure interaction, buoyant flows, high performance heat exchanges, mechanics of biomaterials, composite materials, computational mechanics. *Total annual research expenditures:* $1.2 million. *Unit head:* John Rice, Graduate Program Director, 508-999-8498, Fax: 508-999-8881, E-mail: jrice@umassd.edu. *Application contact:* Steven Briggs, Director of Marketing and Recruitment for Graduate Studies, 508-999-8604, Fax: 508-999-8183, E-mail: graduate@umassd.edu.
Website: http://www.umassd.edu/engineering/mne/.

University of Massachusetts Lowell, Francis College of Engineering, Department of Mechanical Engineering, Lowell, MA 01854. Offers MS Eng, D Eng, PhD. Part-time programs available. *Degree requirements:* For master's, thesis or alternative; for doctorate, 2 foreign languages, comprehensive exam, thesis/dissertation. *Entrance requirements:* For master's and doctorate, GRE General Test. Additional exam requirements/recommendations for international students: Required—TOEFL (minimum score 560 paper-based). Electronic applications accepted. *Faculty research:* Composites, heat transfer.

University of Memphis, Graduate School, Herff College of Engineering, Department of Mechanical Engineering, Memphis, TN 38152. Offers industrial engineering (MS); power systems (MS). Part-time programs available. *Faculty:* 5 full-time (0 women). *Students:* 8 full-time (1 woman), 4 part-time (0 women); includes 4 minority (3 Black or African American, non-Hispanic/Latino; 1 Asian, non-Hispanic/Latino), 5 international. Average age 25. 14 applicants, 79% accepted, 4 enrolled. In 2014, 7 master's awarded. Terminal master's awarded for partial completion of doctoral program. *Degree requirements:* For master's, comprehensive exam, thesis; for doctorate, comprehensive exam, thesis/dissertation. *Entrance requirements:* For master's, GRE General Test, BS in mechanical engineering, minimum undergraduate GPA of 3.0. *Application deadline:* For fall admission, 8/1 for domestic students; for spring admission, 12/1 for domestic students. Application fee: $35 ($60 for international students). *Financial support:* In 2014–15, 6 students received support. Fellowships with full tuition reimbursements available, research assistantships with full tuition reimbursements available, teaching assistantships with full tuition reimbursements available, career-related internships or fieldwork, Federal Work-Study, scholarships/grants, and unspecified assistantships available. Financial award application deadline: 2/15; financial award applicants required to submit FAFSA. *Faculty research:* Computational fluid dynamics, computational mechanics, integrated design, nondestructive testing, operations research. *Unit head:* Dr. John I. Hochstein, Chair, 901-678-2173, Fax: 901-678-5459, E-mail: jhochste@memphis.edu. *Application contact:* Dr. Teong Tan, Graduate Studies Coordinator, 901-678-3264, Fax: 901-678-5459, E-mail: ttan@memphis.edu.
Website: http://www.me.memphis.edu/.

University of Miami, Graduate School, College of Engineering, Department of Mechanical and Aerospace Engineering, Coral Gables, FL 33124. Offers MSME, PhD. Part-time programs available. *Degree requirements:* For master's, thesis (for some programs); for doctorate, comprehensive exam, thesis/dissertation. *Entrance requirements:* For master's and doctorate, GRE General Test, minimum GPA of 3.0. Additional exam requirements/recommendations for international students: Required—TOEFL (minimum score 550 paper-based). Electronic applications accepted. *Faculty research:* Internal combustion engines, heat transfer, hydrogen energy, controls, fuel cells.

University of Michigan, College of Engineering, Department of Mechanical Engineering, Ann Arbor, MI 48109. Offers MSE, PhD. Part-time programs available. *Students:* 422 full-time (56 women), 8 part-time (1 woman). 1,511 applicants, 20% accepted, 165 enrolled. In 2014, 95 master's, 56 doctorates awarded. Terminal master's awarded for partial completion of doctoral program. *Degree requirements:* For master's, thesis optional; for doctorate, thesis/dissertation, oral defense of dissertation, preliminary and qualifying exams. *Entrance requirements:* For master's, GRE General Test, undergraduate degree in same or relevant field; for doctorate, GRE General Test. Additional exam requirements/recommendations for international students: Required—TOEFL (minimum score 560 paper-based). *Application deadline:* Applications are processed on a rolling basis. Electronic applications accepted. *Financial support:* Fellowships, research assistantships, teaching assistantships, institutionally sponsored loans, health care benefits, tuition waivers (full), and unspecified assistantships available. *Faculty research:* Design and manufacturing, systems and controls, combustion and heat transfer, materials and solid mechanics, dynamics and vibrations, biosystems, fluid mechanics, microsystems, environmental sustainabilities. *Total annual research expenditures:* $28.3 million. *Unit head:* Kon-Well Wang, Department Chair, 734-764-8464, E-mail: kwwang@umich.edu. *Application contact:* Michele Mahler, Graduate Admissions and Program Coordinator, 734-763-9223, Fax: 734-647-7303, E-mail: me.grad.application@umich.edu.
Website: http://me.engin.umich.edu/.

University of Michigan–Dearborn, College of Engineering and Computer Science, Mechanical Engineering (MSE) Program, Dearborn, MI 48128. Offers MSE. Part-time and evening/weekend programs available. Postbaccalaureate distance learning degree programs offered (no on-campus study). *Faculty:* 23 full-time (3 women), 8 part-time/adjunct (2 women). *Students:* 56 full-time (6 women), 171 part-time (28 women); includes 34 minority (2 Black or African American, non-Hispanic/Latino; 21 Asian, non-Hispanic/Latino; 8 Hispanic/Latino; 3 Two or more races, non-Hispanic/Latino), 110 international. 154 applicants, 71% accepted, 83 enrolled. In 2014, 33 master's awarded. *Degree requirements:* For master's, thesis optional. *Entrance requirements:* For master's, BS in mechanical engineering or equivalent from accredited school with minimum GPA of 3.0. Additional exam requirements/recommendations for international students: Required—TOEFL (minimum score 560 paper-based; 84 iBT), IELTS (minimum score 6.5), or Michigan English Language Assessment Battery. *Application deadline:* For fall admission, 8/1 priority date for domestic students, 5/1 for international students; for winter admission, 12/1 priority date for domestic students, 9/1 for international students; for spring admission, 4/1 priority date for domestic students, 11/1 for international students. Applications are processed on a rolling basis. Application fee: $60. Electronic applications accepted. *Expenses:* Tuition, state resident: full-time $12,202; part-time $707 per credit hour. Tuition, nonresident: full-time $20,980; part-time $1209 per credit hour. *Required fees:* $798; $302 per term. Tuition and fees vary according to course level, course load, degree level and program. *Financial support:* In 2014–15, 78 students received support, including 16 research assistantships with full tuition reimbursements available (averaging $20,488 per year), 2 teaching assistantships with full tuition reimbursements available (averaging $17,073 per year); Federal Work-Study, scholarships/grants, health care benefits, and unspecified assistantships also available. Financial award application deadline: 4/1; financial award applicants required to submit FAFSA. *Faculty research:* Materials processing, magnetohydrodynamics flows for energy generation and storage, nanomaterials for energy and biosystems, energy management for automobiles, biomechanics of soft tissue. *Unit head:* Dr. Ben Q. Li, Chair, 313-593-5241, Fax: 313-593-3851, E-mail: benqli@umich.edu. *Application contact:* Rebekah S. Awood, Graduate Secretary, 313-593-5241, Fax: 313-593-3851, E-mail: rsdew@umd.umich.edu.
Website: http://umdearborn.edu/cecs/ME/grad_prog/index.php.

University of Minnesota, Twin Cities Campus, College of Science and Engineering, Department of Mechanical Engineering, Minneapolis, MN 55455-0213. Offers MSME, PhD. Part-time programs available. *Degree requirements:* For doctorate, thesis/dissertation. *Entrance requirements:* For master's, GRE General Test, minimum GPA of 3.0; for doctorate, GRE General Test. Additional exam requirements/recommendations for international students: Required—TOEFL. Electronic applications accepted. *Faculty research:* Particle technology, solar energy, controls, heat transfer, fluid power, plasmas, medical devices, bioengineering, nanotechnology, intelligent vehicles.

University of Missouri, Office of Research and Graduate Studies, College of Engineering, Department of Mechanical and Aerospace Engineering, Columbia, MO 65211. Offers MS, PhD. *Faculty:* 22 full-time (0 women), 1 part-time/adjunct (0 women). *Students:* 57 full-time (8 women), 45 part-time (8 women); includes 4 minority (1 Black or African American, non-Hispanic/Latino; 1 Asian, non-Hispanic/Latino; 2 Hispanic/Latino), 73 international. Average age 26. 167 applicants, 23% accepted, 22 enrolled. In 2014, 21 master's, 6 doctorates awarded. *Degree requirements:* For master's, thesis; for doctorate, one foreign language, thesis/dissertation. *Entrance requirements:* For master's and doctorate, GRE General Test, minimum GPA of 3.0. Additional exam requirements/recommendations for international students: Required—TOEFL (minimum score 500 paper-based; 61 iBT). *Application deadline:* For fall admission, 5/31 priority date for domestic and international students; for winter admission, 10/31 priority date for domestic and international students; for spring admission, 4/30 priority date for domestic and international students. Applications are processed on a rolling basis. Application fee: $55 ($75 for international students). Electronic applications accepted. *Financial support:* Fellowships, research assistantships, teaching assistantships, institutionally sponsored loans, scholarships/grants, health care benefits, and unspecified assistantships available. Support available to part-time students. *Faculty research:* Dynamics and control, design and manufacturing, materials and solids and thermal and fluid science engineering. *Unit head:* Dr. Yuwen Zhang, Interim Department Chair, 573-882-6936, E-mail: zhangyu@missouri.edu. *Application contact:* Marilyn Nevels, Graduate Administrative Assistant, 573-884-8610, E-mail: nevelsma@missouri.edu.
Website: http://engineering.missouri.edu/mae/degree-programs/.

University of Missouri–Kansas City, School of Computing and Engineering, Kansas City, MO 64110-2499. Offers civil engineering (MS); computer and electrical engineering (PhD); computer science (MS), including bioinformatics, software engineering, telecommunications networking; computer science and informatics (PhD); computing (PhD); electrical engineering (MS); engineering (PhD); engineering and construction management (Graduate Certificate); mechanical engineering (MS); telecommunications and computer networking (PhD). PhD (interdisciplinary) offered through the School of Graduate Studies. Part-time programs available. *Faculty:* 39 full-time (5 women), 26 part-time/adjunct (3 women). *Students:* 500 full-time (143 women), 136 part-time (28 women); includes 18 minority (5 Black or African American, non-Hispanic/Latino; 8 Asian, non-Hispanic/Latino; 4 Hispanic/Latino; 1 Two or more races, non-Hispanic/Latino), 551 international. Average age 24. 1,924 applicants, 39% accepted, 200 enrolled. In 2014, 124 master's, 1 other advanced degree awarded. *Degree requirements:* For doctorate, thesis/dissertation. *Entrance requirements:* For master's, GRE General Test, minimum GPA of 3.0, 3 letters of recommendation from professors; for doctorate, GRE General Test, minimum GPA of 3.5. Additional exam requirements/recommendations for international students: Required—TOEFL (minimum score 550 paper-based; 80 iBT). *Application deadline:* For fall admission, 1/15 priority date for domestic students, 1/15 for international students. Applications are processed on a rolling basis. Application fee: $45 ($50 for international students). *Financial support:* In 2014–15, 34 research assistantships with partial tuition reimbursements (averaging $15,602 per year), 24 teaching assistantships with partial tuition reimbursements (averaging $15,090 per year) were awarded; career-related internships or fieldwork, Federal Work-Study, scholarships/grants, tuition waivers (partial), and unspecified assistantships also available. Support available to part-time students. Financial award application deadline: 3/1; financial award applicants required to submit FAFSA. *Faculty research:* Algorithms, bioinformatics and medical informatics, biomechanics/biomaterials, civil engineering materials, networking and telecommunications, thermal science. *Unit head:* Dr. Kevin Z. Truman, Dean, 816-235-2399, Fax: 816-235-5159. *Application contact:* 816-235-2399, Fax: 816-235-5159.
Website: http://sce.umkc.edu/.

University of Nebraska–Lincoln, Graduate College, College of Engineering, Department of Mechanical and Materials Engineering, Lincoln, NE 68588-0526. Offers biomedical engineering (PhD); engineering mechanics (MS); materials engineering (PhD); mechanical engineering (MS), including materials science engineering, metallurgical engineering; mechanical engineering and applied mechanics (PhD); MS/MS. MS/MS offered with University of Rouen-France. *Degree requirements:* For master's, thesis optional; for doctorate, comprehensive exam, thesis/dissertation. *Entrance requirements:* For master's and doctorate, GRE General Test. Additional exam requirements/recommendations for international students: Required—TOEFL (minimum score 550 paper-based). Electronic applications accepted. *Faculty research:* Medical robotics, rehabilitation dynamics, and design; combustion, fluid mechanics, and heat transfer; nano-materials, manufacturing, and devices; fiber, tissue, bio-polymer, and adaptive composites; blast, impact, fracture, and failure; electro-active and magnetic materials and devices; functional materials, design, and added manufacturing; materials characterization, modeling, and computational simulation.

University of Nevada, Las Vegas, Graduate College, Howard R. Hughes College of Engineering, Department of Mechanical Engineering, Las Vegas, NV 89154-4027. Offers biomedical engineering (MS); materials and nuclear engineering (MS); mechanical engineering (MS); nuclear criticality safety engineering (Certificate). Part-time programs available. *Faculty:* 13 full-time (0 women), 1 (woman) part-time/adjunct. *Students:* 33 full-time (13 women), 13 part-time (3 women); includes 8 minority (1 Asian, non-Hispanic/Latino; 2 Hispanic/Latino; 5 Two or more races, non-Hispanic/Latino), 12 international. Average age 29. 43 applicants, 51% accepted, 11 enrolled. In 2014, 9 master's, 6 doctorates, 3 other advanced degrees awarded. *Degree requirements:* For master's, comprehensive exam, thesis (for some programs), project; for doctorate, comprehensive exam, thesis/dissertation. *Entrance requirements:* For master's, doctorate, and Certificate, GRE General Test. Additional exam requirements/recommendations for international students: Required—TOEFL (minimum score 550 paper-based; 80 iBT), IELTS (minimum score 7). *Application deadline:* For fall admission, 8/1 for domestic students, 5/1 for international students; for spring admission, 12/1 for domestic students, 10/1 for international students. Application fee: $60 ($95 for international students). Electronic applications accepted. *Financial support:* In 2014–15, 33 students received support, including 6 research assistantships with partial tuition reimbursements available (averaging $15,198 per year), 27 teaching assistantships with partial tuition reimbursements available (averaging $14,029 per year); institutionally sponsored loans, scholarships/grants, health care benefits, and unspecified assistantships also available. Financial award application deadline: 3/1. *Faculty research:* Dynamics and control systems; energy systems including renewable and nuclear; computational fluid and solid mechanics; structures, materials and manufacturing; vibrations and acoustics. *Total annual research expenditures:* $1.9 million. *Unit head:* Dr. Brendan O'Toole, Chair/Professor, 702-895-3885, Fax: 702-895-3936, E-mail: brendan.otoole@unlv.edu. *Application contact:* Graduate College Admissions Evaluator, 702-895-3320, Fax: 702-895-4180, E-mail: gradcollege@unlv.edu.
Website: http://me.unlv.edu/.

University of Nevada, Reno, Graduate School, College of Engineering, Department of Mechanical Engineering, Reno, NV 89557. Offers MS, PhD. Terminal master's awarded for partial completion of doctoral program. *Degree requirements:* For master's, thesis optional; for doctorate, thesis/dissertation. *Entrance requirements:* For master's, GRE General Test, minimum GPA of 2.75; for doctorate, GRE General Test, minimum GPA of 3.0. Additional exam requirements/recommendations for international students: Required—TOEFL (minimum score 500 paper-based; 61 iBT), IELTS (minimum score 6). Electronic applications accepted. *Faculty research:* Composite, solid, fluid, thermal, and smart materials.

University of New Brunswick Fredericton, School of Graduate Studies, Faculty of Engineering, Department of Mechanical Engineering, Fredericton, NB E3B 5A3, Canada. Offers applied mechanics (M Eng, M Sc E, PhD); mechanical engineering (M Eng, M Sc E, PhD). Part-time programs available. *Faculty:* 15 full-time (1 woman), 24 part-time/adjunct (4 women). *Students:* 50 full-time (6 women), 6 part-time (0 women). In 2014, 13 master's awarded. *Degree requirements:* For master's, thesis; for doctorate, comprehensive exam, thesis/dissertation, qualifying exam. *Entrance requirements:* For master's, minimum GPA of 3.0; B Sc E; for doctorate, minimum GPA of 3.0; M Sc E. Additional exam requirements/recommendations for international students: Required—TOEFL (minimum score 580 paper-based; 80 iBT), IELTS (minimum score 7), TWE (minimum score 4), Michigan English Language Assessment Battery (minimum score 85) or CanTest (minimum score 4.5). *Application deadline:* For fall admission, 3/1 for domestic students. Applications are processed on a rolling basis. Application fee: $50 Canadian dollars. Electronic applications accepted. *Financial support:* In 2014–15, 8 fellowships, 79 research assistantships, 74 teaching assistantships were awarded. *Faculty research:* Acoustics and vibration, biomedical, manufacturing and materials processing, mechatronics and design, nuclear and threat detection, renewable energy systems, robotics and applied mechanics, thermofluids and aerodynamics. *Unit head:* Dr. Andy Simoneau, Director of Graduate Studies, 506-458-7767, Fax: 506-453-5025, E-mail: simoneau@unb.ca. *Application contact:* Paulette Steever, Graduate Secretary, 506-458-7786, Fax: 506-453-5025, E-mail: psteever@unb.ca.
Website: http://go.unb.ca/gradprograms.

University of New Hampshire, Graduate School, College of Engineering and Physical Sciences, Department of Mechanical Engineering, Durham, NH 03824. Offers M Engr, MS, PhD. Part-time programs available. *Faculty:* 19 full-time (2 women). *Students:* 31 full-time (2 women), 30 part-time (1 woman); includes 3 minority (2 Asian, non-Hispanic/Latino; 1 Two or more races, non-Hispanic/Latino), 19 international. Average age 27. 39 applicants, 56% accepted, 9 enrolled. In 2014, 12 master's awarded. *Degree requirements:* For master's, thesis or alternative; for doctorate, thesis/dissertation. *Entrance requirements:* For master's and doctorate, GRE. Additional exam requirements/recommendations for international students: Required—TOEFL (minimum score 550 paper-based; 80 iBT). *Application deadline:* For fall admission, 4/1 priority date for domestic students, 4/1 for international students; for spring admission, 12/1 for domestic students. Applications are processed on a rolling basis. Application fee: $65. Electronic applications accepted. *Expenses:* Tuition, state resident: full-time $13,500; part-time $750 per credit hour. Tuition, nonresident: full-time $26,460; part-time $1110 per credit hour. *Required fees:* $1788; $447 per semester. *Financial support:* In 2014–15, 34 students received support, including 3 fellowships, 11 research assistantships, 19 teaching assistantships; Federal Work-Study, scholarships/grants, and tuition waivers (full and partial) also available. Support available to part-time students. Financial award application deadline: 2/15. *Faculty research:* Solid mechanics, dynamics, materials science, dynamic systems, automatic control. *Unit head:* Dr. Brad Kinsey, Chairperson, 603-862-1811. *Application contact:* Tracey Harvey, Administrative Assistant, 603-862-1353, E-mail: mechanical.engineering@unh.edu.
Website: http://www.unh.edu/mechanical-engineering/.

University of New Haven, Graduate School, Tagliatela College of Engineering, Program in Mechanical Engineering, West Haven, CT 06516-1916. Offers MS. Part-time and evening/weekend programs available. *Degree requirements:* For master's, thesis or alternative. *Entrance requirements:* Additional exam requirements/recommendations for international students: Required—TOEFL (minimum score 75 iBT), IELTS, PTE (minimum score 50). Electronic applications accepted. Application fee is waived when completed online.

University of New Mexico, Graduate School, School of Engineering, Program in Mechanical Engineering, Albuquerque, NM 87131-2039. Offers MS, PhD. Part-time programs available. *Faculty:* 12 full-time (2 women), 5 part-time/adjunct (0 women). *Students:* 47 full-time (5 women), 42 part-time (4 women); includes 30 minority (1 American Indian or Alaska Native, non-Hispanic/Latino; 1 Asian, non-Hispanic/Latino; 27 Hispanic/Latino; 1 Two or more races, non-Hispanic/Latino), 13 international. Average age 29. 79 applicants, 46% accepted, 29 enrolled. In 2014, 16 master's, 2 doctorates awarded. *Degree requirements:* For master's, thesis optional; for doctorate, comprehensive exam, thesis/dissertation. *Entrance requirements:* For master's and doctorate, GRE. Additional exam requirements/recommendations for international students: Required—TOEFL (minimum score 550 paper-based; 80 iBT). *Application deadline:* For fall admission, 7/30 for domestic students, 3/1 for international students; for spring admission, 11/30 for domestic students, 8/1 for international students. Applications are processed on a rolling basis. Application fee: $50. Electronic applications accepted. *Financial support:* In 2014–15, 49 students received support, including 1 fellowship (averaging $10,000 per year), 33 research assistantships with full and partial tuition reimbursements available (averaging $15,740 per year), 13 teaching assistantships with full and partial tuition reimbursements available (averaging $7,066 per year); scholarships/grants, health care benefits, and unspecified assistantships also available. Financial award application deadline: 3/1; financial award applicants required to submit FAFSA. *Faculty research:* Engineering mechanics and materials (including solid mechanics and materials science), mechanical sciences and engineering (including dynamic systems, controls and robotics), thermal sciences and engineering. *Total annual research expenditures:* $811,981. *Unit head:* Dr. Chris Hall, Chairperson, 505-277-1325, Fax: 505-277-1571, E-mail: cdhall@unm.edu. *Application contact:* Dr. Yu-Lin Shen, Director of Graduate Programs, 505-277-6286, Fax: 505-277-1571, E-mail: shenyl@unm.edu.
Website: http://megrad.unm.edu/.

University of New Orleans, Graduate School, College of Engineering, Concentration in Mechanical Engineering, New Orleans, LA 70148. Offers MS. *Degree requirements:* For master's, thesis optional. *Entrance requirements:* For master's, GRE General Test, minimum GPA of 3.0. Additional exam requirements/recommendations for international students: Required—TOEFL (minimum score 550 paper-based; 79 iBT). Electronic applications accepted. *Faculty research:* Two-phase flow instabilities, thermal-hydrodynamic modeling, solar energy, heat transfer from sprays, boundary integral techniques in mechanics.

The University of North Carolina at Charlotte, The William States Lee College of Engineering, Department of Mechanical Engineering and Engineering Science, Charlotte, NC 28223-0001. Offers engineering (MS); mechanical engineering (MSE, MSME, PhD). Evening/weekend programs available. *Faculty:* 31 full-time (3 women). *Students:* 75 full-time (10 women), 35 part-time (7 women); includes 7 minority (2 Black or African American, non-Hispanic/Latino; 2 Asian, non-Hispanic/Latino; 3 Hispanic/Latino), 70 international. Average age 27. 246 applicants, 53% accepted, 29 enrolled. In 2014, 18 master's, 13 doctorates awarded. Terminal master's awarded for partial completion of doctoral program. *Degree requirements:* For master's, thesis; for doctorate, thesis/dissertation. *Entrance requirements:* For master's, GRE General Test, minimum GPA of 3.0 in undergraduate major, 2.75 overall; for doctorate, GRE General Test, 3 letters of reference from faculty or professionals. Additional exam requirements/recommendations for international students: Required—TOEFL (minimum score 557 paper-based; 83 iBT). *Application deadline:* For fall admission, 5/1 priority date for domestic students, 5/1 for international students; for spring admission, 10/1 for domestic and international students. Applications are processed on a rolling basis. Application fee: $75. Electronic applications accepted. *Expenses:* Tuition, state resident: full-time $4008. Tuition, nonresident: full-time $16,295. *Required fees:* $2755. Tuition and fees vary according to course load and program. *Financial support:* In 2014–15, 84 students received support, including 3 fellowships (averaging $37,674 per year), 48 research assistantships (averaging $10,596 per year), 33 teaching assistantships (averaging $6,742 per year); career-related internships or fieldwork, institutionally sponsored loans, scholarships/grants, and unspecified assistantships also available. Support available to part-time students. Financial award application deadline: 4/1; financial award applicants required to submit FAFSA. *Faculty research:* Precision metrology, bioengineering/cell preservation, computational mechanics/computational modeling, materials processing, precision design. *Total annual research expenditures:* $3 million. *Unit head:* Dr. Scott Smith, Department Chair, 704-687-8350, Fax: 704-687-8345, E-mail: kssmith@uncc.edu. *Application contact:* Kathy B. Giddings, Director of Graduate Admissions, 704-687-5503, Fax: 704-687-1668, E-mail: gradadm@uncc.edu.
Website: http://mees.uncc.edu/.

University of North Dakota, Graduate School, School of Engineering and Mines, Department of Mechanical Engineering, Grand Forks, ND 58202. Offers M Engr, MS. Part-time programs available. *Degree requirements:* For master's, comprehensive exam, thesis or alternative. *Entrance requirements:* For master's, GRE General Test, minimum GPA of 3.0 (MS), 2.5 (M Engr). Additional exam requirements/recommendations for international students: Required—TOEFL (minimum score 550 paper-based; 79 iBT), IELTS (minimum score 6.5). Electronic applications accepted. *Faculty research:* Energy conversion, dynamics, control, manufacturing processes with special emphasis on machining, stress vibration analysis.

University of North Florida, College of Computing, Engineering, and Construction, School of Engineering, Jacksonville, FL 32224. Offers MSCE, MSEE, MSME. Part-time programs available. *Faculty:* 17 full-time (1 woman), 1 part-time/adjunct (0 women). *Students:* 9 full-time (2 women), 22 part-time (7 women); includes 8 minority (1 Black or African American, non-Hispanic/Latino; 4 Asian, non-Hispanic/Latino; 2 Hispanic/Latino; 1 Two or more races, non-Hispanic/Latino), 4 international. Average age 28. 60 applicants, 28% accepted, 8 enrolled. In 2014, 14 master's awarded. *Application deadline:* For fall admission, 7/1 for domestic students, 5/1 for international students; for spring admission, 11/1 for domestic students, 10/1 for international students. Application fee: $30. *Expenses:* Tuition, state resident: full-time $9794; part-time $408.10 per credit hour. Tuition, nonresident: full-time $22,383; part-time $932.61 per credit hour. *Required fees:* $2047; $85.29 per credit hour. Tuition and fees vary according to course load and program. *Financial support:* In 2014–15, 16 students received support, including 2 research assistantships (averaging $2,775 per year); teaching assistantships, Federal Work-Study, scholarships/grants, tuition waivers, and unspecified assistantships also available. Financial award application deadline: 4/1; financial award applicants required to submit FAFSA. *Total annual research expenditures:* $863,034. *Unit head:* Dr. Murat Tiryakioglu, Associate Dean, 904-620-2504, E-mail: m.tiryakioglu@unf.edu. *Application contact:* Dr. Amanda Pascale, Director, The Graduate School, 904-320-1360, Fax: 904-620-1362, E-mail: graduateschool@unf.edu.
Website: http://www.unf.edu/ccec/engineering/.

University of North Texas, Robert B. Toulouse School of Graduate Studies, Denton, TX 76203-5459. Offers accounting (MS); applied anthropology (MA, MS); applied behavior analysis (Certificate); applied geography (MA); applied technology and performance improvement (M Ed, MS); art education (MA); art history (MA); art museum education (Certificate); arts leadership (Certificate); audiology (Au D); behavior analysis

Mechanical Engineering

(MS); behavioral science (PhD); biochemistry and molecular biology (MS); biology (MA, MS); biomedical engineering (MS); business analysis (MS); chemistry (MS); clinical health psychology (PhD); communication studies (MA, MS); computer engineering (MS); computer science (MS); counseling (M Ed, MS), including clinical mental health counseling (MS), college and university counseling, elementary school counseling, secondary school counseling; creative writing (MA); criminal justice (MS); curriculum and instruction (M Ed); decision sciences (MBA); design (MA, MFA), including fashion design (MFA), innovation studies, interior design (MFA); early childhood studies (MS); economics (MS); educational leadership (M Ed, Ed D); educational psychology (MS, PhD), including family studies (MS), gifted and talented (MS), human development (MS), learning and cognition (MS), research, measurement and evaluation (MS); electrical engineering (MS); emergency management (MPA); engineering technology (MS); English (MA); English as a second language (MA); environmental science (MS); finance (MBA, MS); financial management (MPA); French (MA); health services management (MBA); higher education (M Ed, Ed D); history (MA, MS); hospitality management (MS); human resources management (MPA); information science (MS); information systems (PhD); information technologies (MBA); interdisciplinary studies (MA, MS); international studies (MA); international sustainable tourism (MS); jazz studies (MM); journalism (MA, MJ, Graduate Certificate), including interactive and virtual digital communication (Graduate Certificate), narrative journalism (Graduate Certificate), public relations (Graduate Certificate); kinesiology (MS); linguistics (MA); local government management (MPA); logistics (PhD); logistics and supply chain management (MBA); long-term care, senior housing, and aging services (MA); management (PhD); marketing (MBA); mathematics (MA, MS); mechanical and energy engineering (MS, PhD); music (MA), including ethnomusicology, music theory, musicology, performance; music composition (PhD); music education (MM Ed, PhD); nonprofit management (MPA); operations and supply chain management (MBA); performance (MM, DMA); philosophy (MA); political science (MA); professional and technical communication (MA); radio, television and film (MA, MFA); rehabilitation counseling (Certificate); sociology (MA); Spanish (MA); special education (M Ed); speech-language pathology (MA); strategic management (MBA); studio art (MFA); teaching (M Ed); MBA/MS. Part-time and evening/weekend programs available. Postbaccalaureate distance learning degree programs offered. *Faculty:* 651 full-time (215 women), 233 part-time/adjunct (139 women). *Students:* 3,040 full-time (1,598 women), 3,401 part-time (2,097 women); includes 1,740 minority (533 Black or African American, non-Hispanic/Latino; 15 American Indian or Alaska Native, non-Hispanic/Latino; 286 Asian, non-Hispanic/Latino; 746 Hispanic/Latino; 3 Native Hawaiian or other Pacific Islander, non-Hispanic/Latino; 157 Two or more races, non-Hispanic/Latino), 1,145 international. Terminal master's awarded for partial completion of doctoral program. *Degree requirements:* For master's, variable foreign language requirement, comprehensive exam (for some programs), thesis (for some programs); for doctorate, variable foreign language requirement, comprehensive exam (for some programs), thesis/dissertation; for other advanced degree, variable foreign language requirement, comprehensive exam (for some programs). *Entrance requirements:* For master's and doctorate, GRE, GMAT. Additional exam requirements/recommendations for international students: Required—TOEFL (minimum score 550 paper-based; 79 iBT). *Application deadline:* For fall admission, 7/15 for domestic students, 3/15 for international students; for spring admission, 11/15 for domestic students, 9/15 for international students; for summer admission, 5/1 for domestic students. Applications are processed on a rolling basis. Application fee: $60. Electronic applications accepted. *Expenses:* Tuition, state resident: full-time $5450; part-time $3633 per year. Tuition, nonresident: full-time $11,966; part-time $7977 per year. *Required fees:* $1301; $398 per credit hour. $685 per semester. Tuition and fees vary according to program and reciprocity agreements. *Financial support:* Fellowships with partial tuition reimbursements, research assistantships with partial tuition reimbursements, teaching assistantships, career-related internships or fieldwork, Federal Work-Study, institutionally sponsored loans, scholarships/grants, health care benefits, and library assistantships available. Support available to part-time students. Financial award applicants required to submit FAFSA. *Unit head:* Mark Wardell, Dean, 940-565-2383, E-mail: mark.wardell@unt.edu. *Application contact:* Toulouse School of Graduate Studies, 940-565-2383, Fax: 940-565-2141, E-mail: gradsch@unt.edu.
Website: http://tsgs.unt.edu/.

University of Notre Dame, Graduate School, College of Engineering, Department of Aerospace and Mechanical Engineering, Notre Dame, IN 46556. Offers aerospace and mechanical engineering (M Eng, PhD); aerospace engineering (MS Aero E); mechanical engineering (MEME, MSME). Terminal master's awarded for partial completion of doctoral program. *Degree requirements:* For master's, comprehensive exam, thesis or alternative; for doctorate, thesis/dissertation, candidacy exam. *Entrance requirements:* For master's and doctorate, GRE General Test. Additional exam requirements/recommendations for international students: Required—TOEFL (minimum score 600 paper-based; 80 iBT). Electronic applications accepted. *Faculty research:* Aerodynamics/fluid dynamics, design and manufacturing, controls/robotics, solid mechanics or biomechanics/biomaterials.

University of Oklahoma, Gallogly College of Engineering, School of Aerospace and Mechanical Engineering, Program in Mechanical Engineering, Norman, OK 73019. Offers combustion (MS). Part-time programs available. *Students:* 25 full-time (6 women), 18 part-time (0 women); includes 7 minority (1 American Indian or Alaska Native, non-Hispanic/Latino; 2 Hispanic/Latino; 4 Two or more races, non-Hispanic/Latino), 17 international. Average age 28. 39 applicants, 31% accepted, 8 enrolled. In 2014, 17 master's, 4 doctorates awarded. *Degree requirements:* For master's, comprehensive exam (for some programs), thesis (for some programs); for doctorate, comprehensive exam, thesis/dissertation. *Entrance requirements:* For master's and doctorate, GRE, letters of reference, resume, statement of purpose. Additional exam requirements/recommendations for international students: Required—TOEFL (minimum score 79 iBT). *Application deadline:* For fall admission, 1/15 for domestic and international students; for spring admission, 9/1 for domestic and international students. Application fee: $50 ($100 for international students). Electronic applications accepted. *Expenses:* Tuition, state resident: full-time $4394; part-time $183.10 per credit hour. Tuition, nonresident: full-time $16,970; part-time $707.10 per credit hour. *Required fees:* $2892; $109.95 per credit hour. $126.50 per semester. *Financial support:* In 2014–15, 28 students received support. Scholarships/grants and unspecified assistantships available. Financial award application deadline: 6/1; financial award applicants required to submit FAFSA. *Faculty research:* Composite materials, nanomechanics, robotics, biomechanics/soft tissues, multi-phase flows. *Unit head:* Dr. Cengiz Altan, Director, 405-325-1744, Fax: 405-325-1088, E-mail: altan@ou.edu. *Application contact:* Kate O'Brien-Hamoush, Student Services Coordinator, 405-325-5013, Fax: 405-325-1088, E-mail: kobrien@ou.edu.
Website: http://www.ou.edu/content/coe/ame.html.

University of Ottawa, Faculty of Graduate and Postdoctoral Studies, Faculty of Engineering, Ottawa-Carleton Institute for Mechanical and Aerospace Engineering, Ottawa, ON K1N 6N5, Canada. Offers M Eng, MA Sc, PhD. MA Sc, M Eng, PhD offered jointly with Carleton University. *Degree requirements:* For master's, thesis or alternative; for doctorate, thesis/dissertation, seminar series, qualifying exam. *Entrance requirements:* For master's, honors degree or equivalent, minimum B average; for doctorate, master's degree, minimum B+ average. Electronic applications accepted. *Faculty research:* Fluid mechanics-heat transfer, solid mechanics, design, manufacturing and control.

University of Pennsylvania, School of Engineering and Applied Science, Department of Mechanical Engineering and Applied Mechanics, Philadelphia, PA 19104. Offers applied mechanics (MSE, PhD); mechanical engineering (MSE, PhD). Part-time programs available. *Faculty:* 34 full-time (7 women), 13 part-time/adjunct (3 women). *Students:* 154 full-time (33 women), 47 part-time (12 women); includes 22 minority (3 Black or African American, non-Hispanic/Latino; 16 Asian, non-Hispanic/Latino; 2 Hispanic/Latino; 1 Two or more races, non-Hispanic/Latino), 117 international. 875 applicants, 21% accepted, 83 enrolled. In 2014, 84 master's, 9 doctorates awarded. *Degree requirements:* For master's, thesis optional; for doctorate, thesis/dissertation. *Entrance requirements:* Additional exam requirements/recommendations for international students: Required—TOEFL. *Application deadline:* For fall admission, 1/2 priority date for domestic students. Applications are processed on a rolling basis. Application fee: $70. Electronic applications accepted. *Financial support:* Fellowships, research assistantships, teaching assistantships, institutionally sponsored loans, scholarships/grants, traineeships, health care benefits, and unspecified assistantships available. *Faculty research:* Heat transfer, fluid mechanics, energy conversion, solid mechanics, dynamics of mechanisms and robots. *Unit head:* Eduardo D. Glandt, Dean, 215-898-7244, E-mail: seasdean@seas.upenn.edu. *Application contact:* School of Engineering and Applied Science Graduate Admissions, 215-898-4542, E-mail: gradstudies@seas.upenn.edu.
Website: http://www.me.upenn.edu.

University of Pittsburgh, Dietrich School of Arts and Sciences, Program in Computational Modeling and Simulation, Pittsburgh, PA 15260. Offers bioengineering (PhD); biological science (PhD); civil and environmental engineering (PhD); computer science (PhD); economics (PhD); industrial engineering (PhD); mathematics (PhD); mechanical engineering and materials science (PhD); physics and astronomy (PhD); psychology (PhD); statistics (PhD). Part-time programs available. *Faculty:* 4 full-time (0 women). *Students:* 5 full-time (2 women), 1 part-time (0 women), 5 international. Average age 22. 14 applicants, 14% accepted, 2 enrolled. *Degree requirements:* For doctorate, comprehensive exam, thesis/dissertation, preliminary exam. *Entrance requirements:* For doctorate, GRE, statement of purpose, transcripts for all college-level institutions attended, three letters of reference. Additional exam requirements/recommendations for international students: Required—TOEFL (minimum score 90 iBT), IELTS (minimum score 7). *Application deadline:* For fall admission, 2/21 for domestic and international students. Applications are processed on a rolling basis. Application fee: $0 ($50 for international students). Electronic applications accepted. *Expenses:* Tuition, state resident: full-time $20,742; part-time $838 per credit. Tuition, nonresident: full-time $33,960; part-time $1389 per credit. *Required fees:* $800; $205 per term. Tuition and fees vary according to program. *Financial support:* In 2014–15, 5 students received support, including 3 fellowships with tuition reimbursements available (averaging $25,500 per year), 2 research assistantships with tuition reimbursements available (averaging $26,000 per year). *Unit head:* Kathleen Blee, Associate Dean, Graduate Studies and Research, 412-624-3939, Fax: 412-624-6855. *Application contact:* Dave R. Carmen, Administrative Secretary, 412-624-6094, Fax: 412-624-6855, E-mail: drc41@pitt.edu.
Website: http://cmsp.pitt.edu/.

University of Pittsburgh, Swanson School of Engineering, Department of Mechanical Engineering and Materials Science, Pittsburgh, PA 15260. Offers MSME, MSNE, PhD. Part-time programs available. Postbaccalaureate distance learning degree programs offered. *Faculty:* 28 full-time (2 women), 33 part-time/adjunct (0 women). *Students:* 153 full-time (29 women), 131 part-time (16 women); includes 12 minority (4 Black or African American, non-Hispanic/Latino; 3 Asian, non-Hispanic/Latino; 4 Hispanic/Latino; 1 Two or more races, non-Hispanic/Latino), 120 international. 639 applicants, 36% accepted, 71 enrolled. In 2014, 72 master's, 16 doctorates awarded. Terminal master's awarded for partial completion of doctoral program. *Degree requirements:* For master's, thesis optional; for doctorate, comprehensive exam, thesis/dissertation, final oral exams. *Entrance requirements:* For master's and doctorate, minimum GPA of 3.0. Additional exam requirements/recommendations for international students: Required—TOEFL (minimum score 550 paper-based; 80 iBT). *Application deadline:* For fall admission, 3/1 priority date for domestic and international students; for spring admission, 7/1 priority date for domestic and international students. Applications are processed on a rolling basis. Application fee: $50. Electronic applications accepted. *Expenses:* Tuition, state resident: full-time $20,742; part-time $838 per credit. Tuition, nonresident: full-time $33,960; part-time $1389 per credit. *Required fees:* $800; $205 per term. Tuition and fees vary according to program. *Financial support:* In 2014–15, 98 students received support, including 9 fellowships with full tuition reimbursements available (averaging $29,376 per year), 60 research assistantships with full tuition reimbursements available (averaging $24,996 per year), 29 teaching assistantships with full tuition reimbursements available (averaging $25,692 per year); scholarships/grants and tuition waivers (full and partial) also available. Financial award application deadline: 4/15. *Faculty research:* Smart materials and structure solid mechanics, computational fluid dynamics, multiphase bio-fluid dynamics, mechanical vibration analysis. *Total annual research expenditures:* $7.5 million. *Unit head:* Dr. Brian M. Gleeson, Chairman, 412-624-1185, Fax: 412-624-4846, E-mail: bgleeson@pitt.edu. *Application contact:* Dr. Qing-Ming Wang, Graduate Coordinator, 412-624-4885, Fax: 412-624-4846, E-mail: qiw4@pitt.edu.
Website: http://www.engineering.pitt.edu/MEMS/.

University of Portland, School of Engineering, Portland, OR 97203-5798. Offers biomedical engineering (MBME); civil engineering (ME); computer science (ME); electrical engineering (ME); mechanical engineering (ME). Part-time and evening/weekend programs available. *Faculty:* 10 full-time (2 women), 1 part-time/adjunct (0 women). *Students:* 4 full-time (1 woman), 2 part-time (0 women); includes 1 minority (Two or more races, non-Hispanic/Latino), 1 international. Average age 27. In 2014, 2 master's awarded. *Degree requirements:* For master's, thesis optional. *Entrance requirements:* For master's, GRE General Test, minimum GPA of 3.0, 3 letters of recommendation, resume, statement of goals, official transcripts. Additional exam requirements/recommendations for international students: Required—TOEFL (minimum score 550 paper-based; 80 iBT), IELTS (minimum score 7). *Application deadline:* For fall admission, 7/15 priority date for domestic and international students; for spring admission, 12/15 priority date for domestic and international students. Applications are processed on a rolling basis. Application fee: $50. *Expenses:* Expenses: Contact institution. *Financial support:* Career-related internships or fieldwork, Federal Work-Study, and scholarships/grants available. Support available to part-time students. Financial award application deadline: 3/1; financial award applicants required to submit FAFSA. *Unit head:* Dr. Sharon Jones, Dean, 503-943-8169, E-mail: joness@up.edu. *Application contact:* Allison Able, Graduate Program Coordinator, 503-943-7107, Fax: 503-943-7315, E-mail: able@up.edu.
Website: http://engineering.up.edu/default.aspx?cid-6464&pid-2432.

University of Puerto Rico, Mayagüez Campus, Graduate Studies, College of Engineering, Department of Mechanical Engineering, Mayagüez, PR 00681-9000. Offers ME, MS. Part-time programs available. *Faculty:* 20 full-time (3 women). *Students:*

42 full-time (8 women), 11 part-time (0 women). 14 applicants, 100% accepted, 11 enrolled. In 2014, 10 master's awarded. *Degree requirements:* For master's, comprehensive exam, thesis. *Entrance requirements:* For master's, BS in mechanical engineering or the equivalent; minimum GPA of 2.75, 3.0 in field of specialty. Additional exam requirements/recommendations for international students: Required—TOEFL. *Application deadline:* For fall admission, 2/15 for domestic and international students; for spring admission, 9/15 for domestic and international students. Applications are processed on a rolling basis. Application fee: $25. *Expenses: Tuition, area resident:* Full-time $2466; part-time $822 per credit. *International tuition:* $6371 full-time. *Required fees:* $1095; $1095 per year. Tuition and fees vary according to course level, course load and reciprocity agreements. *Financial support:* In 2014–15, 34 students received support, including 15 research assistantships (averaging $7,342 per year), 29 teaching assistantships (averaging $4,142 per year); fellowships with full tuition reimbursements available, Federal Work-Study, institutionally sponsored loans, and unspecified assistantships also available. *Faculty research:* Metallurgy, hybrid vehicles, manufacturing, thermal and fluid sciences, HVAC. *Unit head:* Dr. Nilsa Paris, Director, 787-832-4040 Ext. 3659, E-mail: nilsa.paris@upr.edu. *Application contact:* Yolanda Perez, Graduate Program Secretary, 787-832-4040 Ext. 3659, Fax: 787-265-3817, E-mail: yolanda.perez4@upr.edu.
Website: http://www.me.uprm.edu.

University of Rochester, Hajim School of Engineering and Applied Sciences, Department of Mechanical Engineering, Rochester, NY 14627. Offers MS, PhD. Part-time programs available. *Faculty:* 14 full-time (1 woman). *Students:* 38 full-time (8 women), 2 part-time (0 women); includes 3 minority (all Hispanic/Latino), 19 international. 87 applicants, 45% accepted, 13 enrolled. In 2014, 14 master's, 2 doctorates awarded. Terminal master's awarded for partial completion of doctoral program. *Degree requirements:* For master's, comprehensive exam, thesis optional; for doctorate, thesis/dissertation, preliminary and qualifying exams. *Entrance requirements:* For master's and doctorate, GRE. Additional exam requirements/recommendations for international students: Required—TOEFL. *Application deadline:* For fall admission, 2/1 for domestic students. Application fee: $60. *Expenses: Tuition:* Full-time $46,150; part-time $1442 per credit hour. *Required fees:* $504. *Financial support:* Fellowships, research assistantships, teaching assistantships, and tuition waivers (full and partial) available. Financial award application deadline: 2/1. *Faculty research:* Applied mechanics, biomechanics, fusion/plasma, materials science. *Unit head:* John C. Lambropoulos, Chair, 585-275-4070. *Application contact:* Sarah Ansini, Graduate Program Advisor/Coordinator, 585-275-2849.
Website: http://www.me.rochester.edu/graduate/index.html.

University of Rochester, Hajim School of Engineering and Applied Sciences, Master of Science in Technical Entrepreneurship and Management Program, Rochester, NY 14642. Offers biomedical engineering (MS); chemical engineering (MS); computer science (MS); electrical and computer engineering (MS); energy and the environment (MS); materials science (MS); mechanical engineering (MS); optics (MS). Program offered in collaboration with the Simon School of Business. Part-time programs available. *Students:* 36 full-time (12 women), 7 part-time (1 woman); includes 3 minority (2 Hispanic/Latino; 1 Two or more races, non-Hispanic/Latino), 33 international. Average age 24. 152 applicants, 68% accepted, 27 enrolled. In 2014, 28 master's awarded. *Degree requirements:* For master's, comprehensive exam. *Entrance requirements:* For master's, GRE or GMAT, 3 letters of recommendation; personal statement; official transcript; bachelor's degree (or equivalent for international students) in engineering, science, or mathematics. Additional exam requirements/recommendations for international students: Required—TOEFL or IELTS. *Application deadline:* For fall admission, 2/1 for domestic and international students. Applications are processed on a rolling basis. Application fee: $60. Electronic applications accepted. *Expenses: Tuition:* Full-time $46,150; part-time $1442 per credit hour. *Required fees:* $504. *Financial support:* Career-related internships or fieldwork and scholarships/grants available. Financial award application deadline: 2/1. *Faculty research:* High efficiency solar cells, macromolecular self-assembly, digital signal processing, memory hierarchy management, molecular and physical mechanisms in cell migration, optical imaging systems. *Unit head:* Duncan T. Moore, Vice Provost for Entrepreneurship, 585-275-5248, Fax: 585-473-6745, E-mail: moore@optics.rochester.edu. *Application contact:* Andrea M. Galati, Executive Director, 585-276-3407, Fax: 585-276-2357, E-mail: andrea.galati@rochester.edu.
Website: http://www.rochester.edu/team.

University of St. Thomas, Graduate Studies, School of Engineering, St. Paul, MN 55105-1096. Offers electrical engineering (MS); manufacturing engineering and operations (MS); manufacturing systems (Certificate); mechanical engineering (MS); medical device development (Certificate); regulatory science (MS); software engineering (MS); software management (MS); systems engineering (MS); technology leadership (Certificate); technology management (MS). *Accreditation:* ABET (one or more programs are accredited). *Entrance requirements:* For master's, resume, official transcripts. Additional exam requirements/recommendations for international students: Required—TOEFL (minimum score 550 paper-based). Electronic applications accepted. *Expenses:* Contact institution.

University of Saskatchewan, College of Graduate Studies and Research, College of Engineering, Mechanical Engineering Program, Saskatoon, SK S7N 5A9, Canada. Offers M Eng, M Sc, PhD. Part-time programs available. *Degree requirements:* For master's, thesis (for some programs), 30 credits (for M Eng); thesis and 12 credits (for MS); for doctorate, comprehensive exam, thesis/dissertation, qualifying exam, 18 credits. *Entrance requirements:* For master's and doctorate, GRE. Additional exam requirements/recommendations for international students: Required—TOEFL (minimum iBT score 80), IELTS (6.5), CanTEST (4.5), or PTE (59). Electronic applications accepted. *Faculty research:* Advanced engineering design and manufacturing, advanced materials for clean energy, applied mechanics and machine design, bioengineering, control systems, fluid power, fluid dynamics, material science and metallurgy, robotics, thermal science and energy.

University of South Alabama, College of Engineering, Department of Mechanical Engineering, Mobile, AL 36688. Offers MSME. *Faculty:* 4 full-time (1 woman). *Students:* 16 full-time (1 woman), 1 part-time (0 women); includes 1 minority (Asian, non-Hispanic/Latino), 6 international. Average age 26. 51 applicants, 29% accepted, 6 enrolled. In 2014, 5 master's awarded. *Degree requirements:* For master's, comprehensive exam, project or thesis. *Entrance requirements:* For master's, GRE General Test, BS in engineering, minimum GPA of 3.0. Additional exam requirements/recommendations for international students: Required—TOEFL (minimum score 79 iBT). *Application deadline:* For fall admission, 7/15 priority date for domestic students, 6/15 priority date for international students; for spring admission, 12/1 priority date for domestic students, 11/1 priority date for international students. Applications are processed on a rolling basis. Application fee: $35. Electronic applications accepted. *Expenses:* Expenses: Contact institution. *Financial support:* Fellowships, research assistantships, teaching assistantships, career-related internships or fieldwork, Federal Work-Study, institutionally sponsored loans, scholarships/grants, and unspecified assistantships available. Support available to part-time students. Financial award application deadline: 5/31; financial award applicants required to submit FAFSA. *Faculty research:* Thermal dilution measurement, polymer composite materials, advanced composition systems, bioengineering, multiscale dynamic fracture analysis. *Unit head:* Dr. David Nelson, Department Chair, 251-460-6168, Fax: 251-460-6549, E-mail: danelson@southalabama.edu. *Application contact:* Dr. Thomas G. Thomas, Jr., Graduate Studies, College of Engineering, 251-460-6140, Fax: 251-460-6343, E-mail: engineering@southalabama.edu.
Website: http://www.southalabama.edu/colleges/engineering/me/index.html.

University of South Carolina, The Graduate School, College of Engineering and Computing, Department of Mechanical Engineering, Columbia, SC 29208. Offers ME, MS, PhD. Part-time and evening/weekend programs available. Postbaccalaureate distance learning degree programs offered. *Degree requirements:* For master's, thesis (for some programs); for doctorate, thesis/dissertation. *Entrance requirements:* For master's and doctorate, GRE General Test. Additional exam requirements/recommendations for international students: Required—TOEFL (minimum score 600 paper-based). Electronic applications accepted. *Faculty research:* Heat exchangers, computer vision measurements in solid mechanics and biomechanics, robot dynamics and control.

University of Southern California, Graduate School, Viterbi School of Engineering, Department of Aerospace and Mechanical Engineering, Los Angeles, CA 90089. Offers aerospace and mechanical engineering: computational fluid and solid mechanics (MS); aerospace and mechanical engineering: dynamics and control (MS); aerospace engineering (MS, PhD, Engr), including aerospace engineering (PhD, Engr); green technologies (MS); mechanical engineering (MS, PhD, Engr), including energy conversion (MS), mechanical engineering (PhD, Engr), nuclear power (MS); product development engineering (MS). Part-time and evening/weekend programs available. Postbaccalaureate distance learning degree programs offered (no on-campus study). Terminal master's awarded for partial completion of doctoral program. *Degree requirements:* For master's, thesis optional; for doctorate, thesis/dissertation. *Entrance requirements:* For master's, doctorate, and Engr, GRE General Test. Additional exam requirements/recommendations for international students: Recommended—TOEFL. Electronic applications accepted. *Faculty research:* Mechanics and materials, aerodynamics of air/ground vehicles, gas dynamics, aerosols, astronautics and space science, geophysical and microgravity flows, planetary physics, power MEMs and MEMS vacuum pumps, heat transfer and combustion.

University of South Florida, College of Engineering, Department of Mechanical Engineering, Tampa, FL 33620-9951. Offers MME, MSME, PhD. Part-time programs available. *Faculty:* 15 full-time (2 women). *Students:* 72 full-time (9 women), 23 part-time (4 women); includes 17 minority (1 Black or African American, non-Hispanic/Latino; 4 Asian, non-Hispanic/Latino; 11 Hispanic/Latino; 1 Two or more races, non-Hispanic/Latino), 55 international. Average age 28. 172 applicants, 54% accepted, 23 enrolled. In 2014, 21 master's, 5 doctorates awarded. Terminal master's awarded for partial completion of doctoral program. *Degree requirements:* For master's, comprehensive exam, thesis or alternative; for doctorate, comprehensive exam, thesis/dissertation, 2 tools of research as specified by dissertation committee. *Entrance requirements:* For master's, GRE General Test (minimum preferred scores at or above the 50th percentile for quantitative and verbal), minimum GPA of 3.0 in last two years of undergraduate coursework from ABET-accredited engineering program; statement of research interests (for MSME); for doctorate, GRE General Test (minimum preferred scores at or above the 60th percentile for quantitative and verbal), MS in mechanical engineering or closely-related field (preferred); one-page statement of purpose and research interests. Additional exam requirements/recommendations for international students: Required—TOEFL (minimum score 550 paper-based; 79 iBT) or IELTS (minimum score 6.5). *Application deadline:* For fall admission, 2/15 for domestic students, 1/2 for international students; for spring admission, 10/15 for domestic students, 6/1 for international students. Application fee: $30. Electronic applications accepted. *Financial support:* In 2014–15, 64 students received support, including 42 research assistantships with tuition reimbursements available (averaging $12,819 per year), 22 teaching assistantships with partial tuition reimbursements available (averaging $14,017 per year). Financial award applicants required to submit FAFSA. *Faculty research:* Acoustic transducers, cellular mechanotransduction and biomaterials, computational fluid dynamics and heat transfer, computational methods research and education, environmentally benign design and manufacturing, micro/nano integration, nanochemical testing, Nanotechnology Research and Education Center (NREC), rehabilitation engineering and electromechanical design, rehabilitation robotics, vibrations/dynamic systems. *Total annual research expenditures:* $3.3 million. *Unit head:* Dr. Rajiv Dubey, Professor and Department Chair, 813-974-5619, Fax: 813-974-3539, E-mail: dubey@usf.edu. *Application contact:* Dr. Delcie Durham, Professor and Graduate Program Director, 813-974-5656, Fax: 813-974-3539, E-mail: drdurham@usf.edu.
Website: http://me.eng.usf.edu/.

The University of Tennessee, Graduate School, College of Engineering, Department of Mechanical, Aerospace and Biomedical Engineering, Program in Mechanical Engineering, Knoxville, TN 37996. Offers MS, PhD, MS/MBA. Part-time programs available. Postbaccalaureate distance learning degree programs offered (minimal on-campus study). *Faculty:* 28 full-time (1 woman), 4 part-time/adjunct (0 women). *Students:* 72 full-time (6 women), 25 part-time (1 woman); includes 9 minority (2 Black or African American, non-Hispanic/Latino; 2 American Indian or Alaska Native, non-Hispanic/Latino; 3 Asian, non-Hispanic/Latino; 2 Two or more races, non-Hispanic/Latino), 32 international. Average age 30. 201 applicants, 38% accepted, 38 enrolled. In 2014, 25 master's, 8 doctorates awarded. *Degree requirements:* For master's, thesis or alternative; for doctorate, comprehensive exam, thesis/dissertation. *Entrance requirements:* For master's, GRE General Test (for MS students pursuing research thesis), minimum GPA of 2.7 (for U.S. degree holders), 3.0 (for international degree holders); 3 references; statement of purpose; for doctorate, GRE General Test (for all PhD candidates), minimum GPA of 3.0 on previous graduate course work; 3 references; statement of purpose. Additional exam requirements/recommendations for international students: Required—TOEFL (minimum score 550 paper-based). *Application deadline:* For fall admission, 2/1 priority date for domestic and international students; for spring admission, 6/15 for domestic and international students. Applications are processed on a rolling basis. Application fee: $35. Electronic applications accepted. *Financial support:* In 2014–15, 57 students received support, including 15 research assistantships with full tuition reimbursements available (averaging $20,695 per year), 28 teaching assistantships with full tuition reimbursements available (averaging $18,093 per year); fellowships with full tuition reimbursements available, career-related internships or fieldwork, Federal Work-Study, institutionally sponsored loans, health care benefits, and unspecified assistantships also available. Financial award application deadline: 2/1; financial award applicants required to submit FAFSA. *Faculty research:* Automotive systems and technology; combustion and emissions; alternative fuels; electromechanical actuators; nanomechanics, nanomaterials, and nanotechnology. *Unit head:* Dr. Matthew Mench, Head, 865-974-5115, Fax: 865-974-5274, E-mail: mmench@utk.edu. *Application contact:* Dr. Gary V. Smith, Associate Head, 865-974-5271, Fax: 865-974-5274, E-mail: gvsmith@utk.edu.
Website: http://www.engr.utk.edu/mabe.

Mechanical Engineering

The University of Tennessee, The University of Tennessee Space Institute, Tullahoma, TN 37388. Offers aerospace engineering (MS, PhD); biomedical engineering (MS, PhD); engineering science (MS, PhD); industrial and systems engineering/engineering management (MS, PhD); mechanical engineering (MS, PhD); physics (MS, PhD). Part-time programs available. Postbaccalaureate distance learning degree programs offered. *Faculty:* 19 full-time (3 women), 4 part-time/adjunct. *Students:* 31 full-time (6 women), 82 part-time (11 women); includes 10 minority (6 Black or African American, non-Hispanic/Latino; 1 American Indian or Alaska Native, non-Hispanic/Latino; 2 Asian, non-Hispanic/Latino; 1 Hispanic/Latino), 11 international. 60 applicants, 55% accepted, 22 enrolled. In 2014, 25 master's, 5 doctorates awarded. Terminal master's awarded for partial completion of doctoral program. *Degree requirements:* For doctorate, one foreign language, thesis/dissertation. *Entrance requirements:* Additional exam requirements/recommendations for international students: Required—TOEFL (minimum score 550 paper-based; 80 iBT), IELTS (minimum score 6.5). *Application deadline:* For fall admission, 2/1 for international students; for spring admission, 6/15 for international students. Applications are processed on a rolling basis. Application fee: $60. Electronic applications accepted. *Financial support:* In 2014–15, 6 fellowships with full tuition reimbursements (averaging $2,451 per year), 24 research assistantships with full tuition reimbursements (averaging $20,244 per year) were awarded; career-related internships or fieldwork, Federal Work-Study, institutionally sponsored loans, health care benefits, and unspecified assistantships also available. *Faculty research:* Fluid mechanics/aerodynamics, chemical and electric propulsion and laser diagnostics, computational mechanics and simulations, carbon fiber production and composite materials. *Total annual research expenditures:* $1.8 million. *Unit head:* Dr. Charles Johnson, Associate Executive Director, 931-393-7318, Fax: 931-393-7211, E-mail: cjohnson@utsi.edu. *Application contact:* Dee Merriman, Director, 931-393-7213, Fax: 931-393-7211, E-mail: dmerrima@utsi.edu.
Website: http://www.utsi.edu/.

The University of Tennessee at Chattanooga, Program in Engineering, Chattanooga, TN 37403. Offers chemical engineering (MS Engr); civil engineering (MS Engr); computational engineering (MS Engr); electrical engineering (MS Engr); industrial engineering (MS Engr); mechanical engineering (MS Engr). Part-time and evening/weekend programs available. *Faculty:* 20 full-time (3 women), 3 part-time/adjunct (0 women). *Students:* 42 full-time (7 women), 41 part-time (5 women); includes 6 minority (2 Black or African American, non-Hispanic/Latino; 1 Asian, non-Hispanic/Latino; 2 Hispanic/Latino; 1 Two or more races, non-Hispanic/Latino), 30 international. Average age 29. 96 applicants, 32% accepted, 17 enrolled. In 2014, 29 master's awarded. *Degree requirements:* For master's, comprehensive exam, thesis or alternative, engineering project. *Entrance requirements:* For master's, GRE General Test, minimum undergraduate GPA of 2.5 or 3.0 in last 30 hours of coursework. Additional exam requirements/recommendations for international students: Required—TOEFL (minimum score 550 paper-based; 79 iBT), IELTS (minimum score 6). *Application deadline:* For fall admission, 6/13 priority date for domestic students, 6/1 for international students; for spring admission, 10/15 priority date for domestic students, 10/1 for international students. Applications are processed on a rolling basis. Application fee: $30 ($35 for international students). Electronic applications accepted. *Expenses:* Tuition, state resident: full-time $7708; part-time $428 per credit hour. Tuition, nonresident: full-time $23,826; part-time $1323 per credit hour. *Required fees:* $1708; $252 per credit hour. *Financial support:* In 2014–15, 24 research assistantships with tuition reimbursements (averaging $7,669 per year), 7 teaching assistantships with tuition reimbursements (averaging $5,735 per year) were awarded; career-related internships or fieldwork, scholarships/grants, and unspecified assistantships also available. Support available to part-time students. *Faculty research:* Quality control and reliability engineering, financial management, thermal science, energy conservation, structural analysis. *Total annual research expenditures:* $1.6 million. *Unit head:* Dr. William Sutton, Dean, 423-425-2256, Fax: 423-425-5229, E-mail: will-sutton@utc.edu. *Application contact:* Dr. J. Randy Walker, Interim Dean of Graduate Studies, 423-425-4478, Fax: 423-425-5223, E-mail: randy-walker@utc.edu.
Website: http://www.utc.edu/Departments/engrcs/ms_engr.php.

The University of Texas at Arlington, Graduate School, College of Engineering, Department of Mechanical and Aerospace Engineering, Program in Mechanical Engineering, Arlington, TX 76019. Offers M Engr, MS, PhD. Part-time and evening/weekend programs available. Postbaccalaureate distance learning degree programs offered (minimal on-campus study). Terminal master's awarded for partial completion of doctoral program. *Degree requirements:* For master's, thesis optional; for doctorate, comprehensive exam, thesis/dissertation. *Entrance requirements:* For master's and doctorate, GRE General Test, minimum GPA of 3.0. Additional exam requirements/recommendations for international students: Required—TOEFL (minimum score 550 paper-based).

The University of Texas at Austin, Graduate School, Cockrell School of Engineering, Department of Mechanical Engineering, Austin, TX 78712-1111. Offers mechanical engineering (MS, PhD); operations research and industrial engineering (MS, PhD); MBA/MSE; MP Aff/MSE. *Entrance requirements:* For master's and doctorate, GRE General Test. Additional exam requirements/recommendations for international students: Required—TOEFL.

The University of Texas at Dallas, Erik Jonsson School of Engineering and Computer Science, Department of Mechanical Engineering, Richardson, TX 75080. Offers mechanical engineering (PhD); mechanical systems engineering (MSME); microelectromechanical systems (MSME). Part-time and evening/weekend programs available. *Faculty:* 15 full-time (2 women), 2 part-time/adjunct (0 women). *Students:* 132 full-time (14 women), 18 part-time (4 women); includes 14 minority (2 Black or African American, non-Hispanic/Latino; 4 Asian, non-Hispanic/Latino; 7 Hispanic/Latino; 1 Two or more races, non-Hispanic/Latino), 111 international. Average age 25. 327 applicants, 49% accepted, 76 enrolled. In 2014, 19 master's awarded. *Degree requirements:* For master's, thesis or major design project; for doctorate, comprehensive exam, thesis/dissertation, final exam, research project, qualifying exam. *Entrance requirements:* For master's, GRE General Test, minimum GPA of 3.0 in related bachelor's degree; for doctorate, GRE, essay. Additional exam requirements/recommendations for international students: Required—TOEFL (minimum score 550 paper-based). *Application deadline:* For fall admission, 7/15 for domestic students, 5/1 priority date for international students; for spring admission, 11/15 for domestic students, 9/1 priority date for international students. Applications are processed on a rolling basis. Application fee: $50 ($100 for international students). Electronic applications accepted. *Expenses:* Tuition, state resident: full-time $11,940; part-time $663 per credit. Tuition, nonresident: full-time $22,282; part-time $1238 per credit. *Financial support:* In 2014–15, 59 students received support, including 3 fellowships (averaging $15,000 per year), 25 research assistantships with partial tuition reimbursements available (averaging $16,650 per year), 22 teaching assistantships with partial tuition reimbursements available (averaging $16,650 per year); career-related internships or fieldwork, Federal Work-Study, institutionally sponsored loans, scholarships/grants, and unspecified assistantships also available. Support available to part-time students. Financial award application deadline: 4/30; financial award applicants required to submit FAFSA. *Faculty research:* Nano-materials and nano-electronic devices, biomedical devices, nonlinear systems and controls, semiconductor and oxide surfaces, flexible electronics. *Unit head:*

Dr. Mario Rotea, Department Head, 972-883-2720, Fax: 972-883-2813, E-mail: rotea@utdallas.edu. *Application contact:* Dr. Hongbing Lu, Associate Department Head, 972-883-4647, Fax: 972-883-2813, E-mail: megrad@utdallas.edu.
Website: http://me.utdallas.edu.

The University of Texas at El Paso, Graduate School, College of Engineering, Department of Mechanical Engineering, El Paso, TX 79968-0001. Offers environmental science and engineering (PhD); mechanical engineering (MS). Part-time programs available. *Degree requirements:* For master's, thesis optional; for doctorate, thesis/dissertation. *Entrance requirements:* For master's, GRE, minimum GPA of 3.0, letter of reference; for doctorate, GRE, minimum GPA of 3.5, letters of reference, BS or equivalent. Additional exam requirements/recommendations for international students: Required—TOEFL; Recommended—IELTS. Electronic applications accepted. *Faculty research:* Aerospace, energy, combustion and propulsion, design engineering, high temperature materials.

The University of Texas at San Antonio, College of Engineering, Department of Mechanical Engineering, San Antonio, TX 78249-0617. Offers advanced manufacturing and enterprise engineering (MS); mechanical engineering (MS, PhD). Part-time and evening/weekend programs available. *Faculty:* 19 full-time (2 women), 5 part-time/adjunct (0 women). *Students:* 67 full-time (10 women), 43 part-time (7 women); includes 39 minority (4 Black or African American, non-Hispanic/Latino; 6 Asian, non-Hispanic/Latino; 24 Hispanic/Latino; 5 Two or more races, non-Hispanic/Latino), 44 international. Average age 28. 143 applicants, 73% accepted, 36 enrolled. In 2014, 20 master's, 2 doctorates awarded. Terminal master's awarded for partial completion of doctoral program. *Degree requirements:* For master's, comprehensive exam, thesis; for doctorate, comprehensive exam, thesis/dissertation. *Entrance requirements:* For master's, GRE General Test, bachelor's degree in mechanical engineering or related field from accredited institution of higher education; for doctorate, GRE General Test, master's degree in mechanical engineering or exceptionally outstanding undergraduate record in mechanical engineering or related field, minimum GPA of 3.33. Additional exam requirements/recommendations for international students: Required—TOEFL (minimum score 550 paper-based; 79 iBT), IELTS (minimum score 6.5). *Application deadline:* For fall admission, 7/1 for domestic students, 4/1 for international students; for spring admission, 11/1 for domestic students, 9/1 for international students. Applications are processed on a rolling basis. Application fee: $45 ($80 for international students). Electronic applications accepted. *Expenses:* Expenses: Contact institution. *Financial support:* In 2014–15, 25 students received support, including 10 fellowships with partial tuition reimbursements available (averaging $25,000 per year), 8 research assistantships (averaging $15,665 per year), 27 teaching assistantships (averaging $10,000 per year); career-related internships or fieldwork and unspecified assistantships also available. Financial award application deadline: 10/1. *Faculty research:* Mechanics and materials, advanced manufacturing, wind turbine, computational fluid dynamics, robotics, biomechanics, wind energy. *Total annual research expenditures:* $1.7 million. *Unit head:* Dr. Hai-Chao Han, Department Chair/Professor. *Application contact:* Dr. Frank Chen, Professor/Graduate Advisor of Record, 210-458-5382, E-mail: ff.chen@utsa.edu.
Website: http://engineering.utsa.edu/me/.

The University of Texas at Tyler, College of Engineering and Computer Science, Department of Mechanical Engineering, Tyler, TX 75799-0001. Offers MS. Part-time and evening/weekend programs available. *Degree requirements:* For master's, engineering project. *Entrance requirements:* For master's, GRE or GMAT, bachelor's degree in engineering. *Faculty research:* Mechatronics vibration analysis, fluid dynamics, electronics and instrumentation, manufacturing processes, optics, computational fluid dynamics, signal processing, high voltage related studies, real time systems, semiconductors.

The University of Texas–Pan American, College of Engineering and Computer Science, Department of Mechanical Engineering, Edinburg, TX 78539. Offers MS. *Expenses:* Tuition, state resident: full-time $4187; part-time $232.60 per credit hour. Tuition, nonresident: full-time $10,857; part-time $603.16 per credit hour. *Required fees:* $782; $27.50 per credit hour. $143.35 per semester.

The University of Toledo, College of Graduate Studies, College of Engineering, Department of Mechanical, Industrial, and Manufacturing Engineering, Toledo, OH 43606-3390. Offers industrial engineering (MS, PhD); mechanical engineering (MS, PhD). Part-time programs available. Postbaccalaureate distance learning degree programs offered (minimal on-campus study). *Degree requirements:* For master's, thesis optional; for doctorate, thesis/dissertation, qualifying exam. *Entrance requirements:* For master's, GRE General Test, minimum GPA of 3.0; for doctorate, GRE General Test, minimum GPA of 3.3. Additional exam requirements/recommendations for international students: Required—TOEFL (minimum score 550 paper-based; 80 iBT). Electronic applications accepted. *Faculty research:* Computational and experimental thermal sciences, manufacturing process and systems, mechanics, materials, design, quality and management engineering systems.

University of Toronto, School of Graduate Studies, Faculty of Applied Science and Engineering, Department of Mechanical and Industrial Engineering, Toronto, ON M5S 2J7, Canada. Offers M Eng, MA Sc, PhD. Part-time programs available. *Degree requirements:* For master's, thesis (for some programs), oral exam/thesis defense (MA Sc); for doctorate, thesis/dissertation, thesis defense, qualifying examination. *Entrance requirements:* For master's, GRE (recommended), minimum B+ average in last 2 years of undergraduate study, 2 letters of reference, resume, Canadian citizenship or permanent residency (M Eng); for doctorate, GRE (recommended), minimum B+ average, 2 letters of reference, resume. Additional exam requirements/recommendations for international students: Required—TOEFL (minimum score 580 paper-based), Michigan English Language Assessment Battery (minimum score 85), IELTS (minimum score 7), or COPE (minimum score 4). Electronic applications accepted.

The University of Tulsa, Graduate School, College of Engineering and Natural Sciences, Department of Mechanical Engineering, Tulsa, OK 74104-3189. Offers ME, MSE, PhD. Part-time programs available. *Faculty:* 13 full-time (0 women). *Students:* 36 full-time (6 women), 13 part-time (2 women); includes 1 minority (Hispanic/Latino), 30 international. Average age 28. 52 applicants, 73% accepted, 18 enrolled. In 2014, 8 master's, 2 doctorates awarded. Terminal master's awarded for partial completion of doctoral program. *Degree requirements:* For master's, thesis (MSE); for doctorate, thesis/dissertation. *Entrance requirements:* For master's and doctorate, GRE General Test. Additional exam requirements/recommendations for international students: Required—TOEFL (minimum score 550 paper-based; 80 iBT), IELTS (minimum score 6). *Application deadline:* Applications are processed on a rolling basis. Application fee: $55. Electronic applications accepted. *Expenses:* Tuition: Full-time $20,160; part-time $1120 per credit hour. *Required fees:* $6 per credit hour. Tuition and fees vary according to course level and course load. *Financial support:* In 2014–15, 36 students received support, including 10 fellowships with full and partial tuition reimbursements available (averaging $4,726 per year), 31 research assistantships with full and partial tuition reimbursements available (averaging $12,534 per year), 11 teaching assistantships with full and partial tuition reimbursements available (averaging $10,156 per year); career-related internships or fieldwork, Federal Work-Study, scholarships/grants, health care

benefits, tuition waivers (full and partial), and unspecified assistantships also available. Support available to part-time students. Financial award application deadline: 2/1; financial award applicants required to submit FAFSA. *Faculty research:* Erosion and corrosion, solid mechanics, composite material, computational fluid dynamics, coiled tubing mechanics. *Total annual research expenditures:* $3.4 million. *Unit head:* Dr. John Henshaw, Chairperson, 918-631-3002, Fax: 918-631-2397, E-mail: john-henshaw@utulsa.edu. *Application contact:* Dr. Siamack A. Shirazi, Adviser, 918-631-3001, Fax: 918-631-2397, E-mail: grad@utulsa.edu.
Website: http://engineering.utulsa.edu/academics/mechanical-engineering/.

University of Utah, Graduate School, College of Engineering, Department of Mechanical Engineering, Salt Lake City, UT 84112. Offers MS, PhD, MS/MBA. Part-time programs available. Postbaccalaureate distance learning degree programs offered (no on-campus study). *Faculty:* 27 full-time (5 women), 11 part-time/adjunct (1 woman). *Students:* 98 full-time (14 women), 73 part-time (5 women); includes 17 minority (9 Asian, non-Hispanic/Latino; 5 Hispanic/Latino; 3 Two or more races, non-Hispanic/Latino), 40 international. Average age 30. 211 applicants, 55% accepted, 26 enrolled. In 2014, 44 master's, 6 doctorates awarded. Terminal master's awarded for partial completion of doctoral program. *Degree requirements:* For master's, comprehensive exam (for some programs), thesis (for some programs); for doctorate, comprehensive exam, thesis/dissertation, qualifying exam. *Entrance requirements:* For master's and doctorate, GRE General Test, typical admitted student scores above 80th percentile, minimum GPA of 3.0, statement of purpose, 3 letters of recommendation, curriculum vitae/resume, transcripts. Additional exam requirements/recommendations for international students: Required—TOEFL (minimum score 590 paper-based; 96 iBT). *Application deadline:* For fall admission, 1/1 priority date for domestic students, 12/1 priority date for international students; for spring admission, 10/1 priority date for domestic students; for summer admission, 2/15 priority date for domestic students. Application fee: $10 ($25 for international students). Electronic applications accepted. *Expenses:* Expenses: Contact institution. *Financial support:* In 2014–15, 110 students received support, including 12 fellowships with full tuition reimbursements available (averaging $22,995 per year), 118 research assistantships with full and partial tuition reimbursements available (averaging $19,000 per year), 113 teaching assistantships with full and partial tuition reimbursements available (averaging $13,506 per year); institutionally sponsored loans, traineeships, health care benefits, and unspecified assistantships also available. Financial award application deadline: 1/15; financial award applicants required to submit FAFSA. *Faculty research:* Design, ergonomics, manufacturing and systems; robotics, controls and mechantronics; solid mechanics; thermal fluids and energy systems. *Total annual research expenditures:* $3 million. *Unit head:* Dr. Timothy Ameel, Chair, 801-585-9730, Fax: 801-585-9826, E-mail: ameel@mech.utah.edu. *Application contact:* Dr. A. K. Balaji, Director of Graduate Studies, 801-587-7772, Fax: 801-585-9826, E-mail: balaji@mech.utah.edu.
Website: http://www.mech.utah.edu/.

University of Vermont, Graduate College, College of Engineering and Mathematics, Department of Mechanical Engineering, Burlington, VT 05405. Offers MS, PhD. *Degree requirements:* For master's, thesis; for doctorate, thesis/dissertation. *Entrance requirements:* For master's and doctorate, GRE General Test (for research assistant or teaching assistant funding). Additional exam requirements/recommendations for international students: Required—TOEFL (minimum score 550 paper-based; 80 iBT). Electronic applications accepted.

University of Victoria, Faculty of Graduate Studies, Faculty of Engineering, Department of Mechanical Engineering, Victoria, BC V8W 2Y2, Canada. Offers M Eng, MA Sc, PhD. Part-time programs available. *Degree requirements:* For master's, thesis (for some programs); for doctorate, thesis/dissertation, candidacy exam. *Entrance requirements:* For master's, minimum B average in undergraduate course work. Additional exam requirements/recommendations for international students: Required—TOEFL (minimum score 575 paper-based), IELTS (minimum score 7). Electronic applications accepted. *Faculty research:* CAD/CAM, energy systems, cryofuels, fuel cell technology, computational mechanics.

University of Virginia, School of Engineering and Applied Science, Department of Mechanical and Aerospace Engineering, Charlottesville, VA 22903. Offers ME, MS, PhD. Postbaccalaureate distance learning degree programs offered (no on-campus study). *Faculty:* 24 full-time (3 women). *Students:* 79 full-time (12 women), 7 part-time (1 woman); includes 7 minority (5 Asian, non-Hispanic/Latino; 2 Hispanic/Latino), 36 international. Average age 26. 217 applicants, 22% accepted, 25 enrolled. In 2014, 15 master's, 9 doctorates awarded. *Degree requirements:* For master's, thesis (MS); for doctorate, comprehensive exam, thesis/dissertation. *Entrance requirements:* For master's and doctorate, GRE General Test, 3 letters of recommendation. Additional exam requirements/recommendations for international students: Required—TOEFL (minimum score 650 paper-based; 90 iBT), IELTS (minimum score 7). *Application deadline:* For fall admission, 8/1 for domestic students, 4/1 for international students; for winter admission, 12/1 for domestic students, 8/1 for international students; for spring admission, 5/1 for domestic students, 1/1 for international students. Applications are processed on a rolling basis. Application fee: $60. Electronic applications accepted. *Expenses:* Tuition, state resident: full-time $14,164; part-time $349 per credit hour. Tuition, nonresident: full-time $23,722; part-time $1300 per credit hour. *Required fees:* $2514. *Financial support:* Fellowships, research assistantships, and teaching assistantships available. Financial award application deadline: 1/15; financial award applicants required to submit FAFSA. *Faculty research:* Solid mechanics, dynamical systems and control, thermofluids. *Unit head:* Hossein Haj-Hariri, Chair, 434-924-7424, Fax: 434-982-2037, E-mail: mae-adm@virginia.edu. *Application contact:* Graduate Secretary, 434-924-7425, Fax: 434-982-2037, E-mail: mae-adm@virginia.edu.
Website: http://www.mae.virginia.edu/NewMAE/.

University of Washington, Graduate School, College of Engineering, Department of Mechanical Engineering, Seattle, WA 98195-2600. Offers MSE, MSME, PhD. Part-time programs available. Postbaccalaureate distance learning degree programs offered (minimal on-campus study). *Faculty:* 30 full-time (4 women). *Students:* 183 full-time (39 women), 67 part-time (8 women). Average age 27. 622 applicants, 43% accepted, 87 enrolled. In 2014, 65 master's, 16 doctorates awarded. *Degree requirements:* For master's, thesis optional; for doctorate, comprehensive exam, thesis/dissertation, qualifying, general, and final exams. *Entrance requirements:* For master's, GRE General Test (minimum scores: 150 Verbal, 155 Quantitative, and 4.0 Analytical Writing), minimum GPA of 3.0 (overall undergraduate GPA of 3.3 preferred); letters of recommendation; statement of purpose; for doctorate, GRE General Test (minimum scores: 150 Verbal, 155 Quantitative, and 4.0 Analytical Writing), minimum GPA of 3.0 (overall undergraduate GPA of 3.3, graduate 3.5 preferred); letters of recommendation; statement of purpose. Additional exam requirements/recommendations for international students: Required—TOEFL (minimum score 580 paper-based; 92 iBT). *Application deadline:* For fall admission, 12/15 priority date for domestic students, 12/15 for international students; for winter admission, 11/1 for domestic and international students; for spring admission, 2/1 for domestic and international students; for summer admission, 4/1 for domestic and international students. Applications are processed on a rolling basis. Application fee: $85. Electronic applications accepted. *Expenses:* Expenses: Contact institution. *Financial support:* In 2014–15, 152 students received support, including 51 fellowships with partial tuition reimbursements available, 75 research assistantships with full tuition reimbursements available, 26 teaching assistantships with full tuition reimbursements available; Federal Work-Study and health care benefits also available. Financial award application deadline: 1/15; financial award applicants required to submit FAFSA. *Faculty research:* Environmentally-friendly energy conversion, mechanics and advanced material systems, system and dynamics, bio-health systems. *Total annual research expenditures:* $8.3 million. *Unit head:* Dr. Per Reinhall, Professor/Chair, 206-543-5090, Fax: 206-685-8047, E-mail: reinhall@uw.edu. *Application contact:* Wanwisa Kisalang, Graduate Academic Adviser, 206-543-7963, Fax: 206-685-8047, E-mail: megrad@uw.edu.
Website: http://www.me.washington.edu.

University of Waterloo, Graduate Studies, Faculty of Engineering, Department of Mechanical and Mechatronics Engineering, Waterloo, ON N2L 3G1, Canada. Offers mechanical engineering (M Eng, MA Sc, PhD); mechanical engineering design and manufacturing (M Eng). Part-time and evening/weekend programs available. *Degree requirements:* For master's, research paper or thesis; for doctorate, comprehensive exam, thesis/dissertation. *Entrance requirements:* For master's, honors degree, minimum B average, resume; for doctorate, master's degree, minimum A- average, resumé. Additional exam requirements/recommendations for international students: Required—TOEFL (minimum score 550 paper-based), TWE (minimum score 4). Electronic applications accepted. *Faculty research:* Fluid mechanics, thermal engineering, solid mechanics, automation and control, materials engineering.

The University of Western Ontario, Faculty of Graduate Studies, Physical Sciences Division, Faculty of Engineering, London, ON N6A 5B8, Canada. Offers chemical and biochemical engineering (ME Sc, PhD); civil and environmental engineering (M Eng, ME Sc, PhD); electrical and computer engineering (M Eng, ME Sc, PhD); mechanical and materials engineering (M Eng, ME Sc, PhD). Part-time programs available. Terminal master's awarded for partial completion of doctoral program. *Degree requirements:* For master's, thesis; for doctorate, thesis/dissertation. *Entrance requirements:* For master's, minimum B average; for doctorate, minimum B+ average. *Faculty research:* Wind, geotechnical, chemical reactor engineering, applied electrostatics, biochemical engineering.

University of Windsor, Faculty of Graduate Studies, Faculty of Engineering, Department of Mechanical, Automotive, and Materials Engineering, Windsor, ON N9B 3P4, Canada. Offers engineering materials (M Eng, MA Sc, PhD); mechanical engineering (M Eng, MA Sc, PhD). Part-time programs available. *Degree requirements:* For master's, thesis; for doctorate, comprehensive exam, thesis/dissertation. *Entrance requirements:* For master's, minimum B average; for doctorate, master's degree, minimum B average. Additional exam requirements/recommendations for international students: Required—TOEFL (minimum score 600 paper-based). Electronic applications accepted. *Faculty research:* Thermofluids, applied mechanics, materials engineering.

University of Wisconsin–Madison, Graduate School, College of Engineering, Department of Mechanical Engineering, Madison, WI 53706-1380. Offers mechanical engineering (MS, PhD); polymers (ME). Part-time programs available. Postbaccalaureate distance learning degree programs offered (no on-campus study). *Faculty:* 30 full-time (3 women), 1 part-time/adjunct (0 women). *Students:* 217 full-time (26 women), 31 part-time (0 women); includes 19 minority (1 Black or African American, non-Hispanic/Latino; 1 American Indian or Alaska Native, non-Hispanic/Latino; 9 Asian, non-Hispanic/Latino; 7 Hispanic/Latino; 1 Native Hawaiian or other Pacific Islander, non-Hispanic/Latino). Average age 27. 615 applicants, 19% accepted, 49 enrolled. In 2014, 67 master's, 10 doctorates awarded. Terminal master's awarded for partial completion of doctoral program. *Degree requirements:* For master's, thesis optional; for doctorate, thesis/dissertation, qualifying exam, preliminary exam, final oral defense. *Entrance requirements:* For master's, GRE, BS in mechanical engineering or related field, minimum GPA of 3.0 in last 60 hours of course work; for doctorate, GRE, BS in mechanical engineering or related field, minimum undergraduate GPA of 3.0 in last 60 hours of course work. Additional exam requirements/recommendations for international students: Required—TOEFL (minimum score 550 paper-based; 80 iBT). *Application deadline:* For fall admission, 8/1 for domestic students, 6/1 for international students; for spring admission, 1/1 for domestic students, 11/1 for international students; for summer admission, 5/1 for domestic students, 3/1 for international students. Applications are processed on a rolling basis. Application fee: $56. Electronic applications accepted. *Expenses:* Tuition, state resident: full-time $10,723; part-time $745 per credit. Tuition, nonresident: full-time $24,054; part-time $1578 per credit. *Required fees:* $374 per semester. Tuition and fees vary according to course load, program and reciprocity agreements. *Financial support:* In 2014–15, 150 students received support, including 6 fellowships with full tuition reimbursements available (averaging $45,000 per year), 294 research assistantships with full tuition reimbursements available (averaging $21,000 per year), 97 teaching assistantships with full tuition reimbursements available (averaging $10,500 per year); career-related internships or fieldwork, institutionally sponsored loans, scholarships/grants, traineeships, health care benefits, and unspecified assistantships also available. Financial award application deadline: 5/31. *Faculty research:* Design and manufacturing, materials processing, combustion, energy systems nanotechnology. *Total annual research expenditures:* $16 million. *Unit head:* Jaal B. Ghandhi, Chair, 608-263-1684, E-mail: ghandhi@engr.wisc.edu. *Application contact:* Theresa J. Pillar-Groesbeck, Advisor to Graduate Students, 608-263-3955, Fax: 608-890-2204, E-mail: pillar@wisc.edu.
Website: http://www.engr.wisc.edu/me/.

University of Wisconsin–Milwaukee, Graduate School, College of Engineering and Applied Science, Program in Engineering, Milwaukee, WI 53201-0413. Offers civil engineering (MS); electrical and computer engineering (MS); energy engineering (Certificate); engineering (PhD); engineering management (MS); engineering mechanics (MS); ergonomics (Certificate); industrial and management engineering (MS); manufacturing engineering (MS); materials engineering (MS); mechanical engineering (MS); MUP/MS. Part-time programs available. *Degree requirements:* For master's, comprehensive exam (for some programs), thesis or alternative; for doctorate, comprehensive exam, thesis/dissertation, internship. *Entrance requirements:* For master's, GRE, minimum GPA of 2.75; for doctorate, GRE, minimum GPA of 3.5. Additional exam requirements/recommendations for international students: Required—TOEFL (minimum score 550 paper-based; 79 iBT), IELTS (minimum score 6.5).

University of Wyoming, College of Engineering and Applied Sciences, Department of Mechanical Engineering, Laramie, WY 82071. Offers MS, PhD. Terminal master's awarded for partial completion of doctoral program. *Degree requirements:* For master's, thesis; for doctorate, thesis/dissertation. *Entrance requirements:* For master's, GRE General Test (minimum score 900), minimum GPA of 3.0; for doctorate, GRE General Test (minimum score: 1000), minimum GPA of 3.0. Additional exam requirements/recommendations for international students: Required—TOEFL (minimum score 550 paper-based). Electronic applications accepted. *Faculty research:* Composite materials, thermal and fluid sciences, continuum mechanics, material science.

Utah State University, School of Graduate Studies, College of Engineering, Department of Mechanical and Aerospace Engineering, Logan, UT 84322. Offers aerospace engineering (MS, PhD); mechanical engineering (ME, MS, PhD). Terminal master's awarded for partial completion of doctoral program. *Degree requirements:* For master's, thesis (for some programs); for doctorate, thesis/dissertation. *Entrance requirements:* For master's, GRE General Test, minimum GPA of 3.0; for doctorate, GRE General Test, minimum GPA of 3.3. Additional exam requirements/recommendations for international students: Required—TOEFL. *Faculty research:* In-space instruments, cryogenic cooling, thermal science, space structures, composite materials.

Vanderbilt University, School of Engineering, Department of Mechanical Engineering, Nashville, TN 37240-1001. Offers M Eng, MS, PhD. MS and PhD offered through the Graduate School. Part-time programs available. Terminal master's awarded for partial completion of doctoral program. *Degree requirements:* For master's, comprehensive exam, thesis; for doctorate, comprehensive exam, thesis/dissertation. *Entrance requirements:* For master's and doctorate, GRE General Test. Additional exam requirements/recommendations for international students: Required—TOEFL (minimum score 550 paper-based); Recommended—TWE (minimum score 4). Electronic applications accepted. *Expenses: Tuition:* Full-time $42,768; part-time $1782 per credit hour. *Required fees:* $422. One-time fee: $30 full-time. *Faculty research:* Active noise and vibration control, robotics, mesoscale and microscale energy conversions, laser diagnostics, combustion.

Villanova University, College of Engineering, Department of Electrical and Computer Engineering, Program in Electrical Engineering, Villanova, PA 19085-1699. Offers electric power systems (Certificate); electrical engineering (MSEE); electro mechanical systems (Certificate); high frequency systems (Certificate); intelligent control systems (Certificate); wireless and digital communications (Certificate). Part-time and evening/weekend programs available. *Degree requirements:* For master's, thesis optional. *Entrance requirements:* For master's, GRE General Test (for applicants with degrees from foreign universities), BEE, minimum GPA of 3.0. Additional exam requirements/recommendations for international students: Required—TOEFL (minimum score 600 paper-based; 100 iBT). *Faculty research:* Signal processing, communications, antennas, devices.

Villanova University, College of Engineering, Department of Mechanical Engineering, Villanova, PA 19085-1699. Offers electro-mechanical systems (Certificate); machinery dynamics (Certificate); mechanical engineering (MSME); nonlinear dynamics and control (Certificate); thermofluid systems (Certificate). Part-time and evening/weekend programs available. Postbaccalaureate distance learning degree programs offered (no on-campus study). *Degree requirements:* For master's, thesis optional. *Entrance requirements:* For master's, GRE General Test (for applicants with degrees from foreign universities), BME, minimum GPA of 3.0. Additional exam requirements/recommendations for international students: Required—TOEFL (minimum score 600 paper-based; 100 iBT). Electronic applications accepted. *Faculty research:* Composite materials, power plant systems, fluid mechanics, automated manufacturing, dynamic analysis.

Virginia Commonwealth University, Graduate School, School of Engineering, Department of Mechanical and Nuclear Engineering, Richmond, VA 23284-9005. Offers MS, PhD. *Entrance requirements:* For master's and doctorate, GRE. Additional exam requirements/recommendations for international students: Required—TOEFL (minimum score 600 paper-based; 100 iBT). Electronic applications accepted.

Virginia Polytechnic Institute and State University, Graduate School, College of Engineering, Blacksburg, VA 24061. Offers aerospace engineering (ME, MS, PhD); biological systems engineering (ME, MS, PhD); biomedical engineering (MS, PhD); chemical engineering (ME, MS, PhD); civil engineering (ME, MS, PhD); computer engineering (ME, MS, PhD); computer science (MS, PhD); electrical engineering (ME, PhD); engineering education (PhD); engineering mechanics (ME, MS, PhD); environmental engineering (MS); environmental science and engineering (MS); industrial and systems engineering (ME, MS, PhD); materials science and engineering (ME, MS, PhD); mechanical engineering (ME, MS, PhD); mining and minerals engineering (PhD); mining engineering (ME, MS); nuclear engineering (MS, PhD); ocean engineering (MS); systems engineering (ME, MS). *Accreditation:* ABET (one or more programs are accredited). *Faculty:* 356 full-time (60 women), 3 part-time/adjunct (1 woman). *Students:* 1,700 full-time (398 women), 345 part-time (58 women); includes 213 minority (43 Black or African American, non-Hispanic/Latino; 1 American Indian or Alaska Native, non-Hispanic/Latino; 87 Asian, non-Hispanic/Latino; 58 Hispanic/Latino; 1 Native Hawaiian or other Pacific Islander, non-Hispanic/Latino; 23 Two or more races, non-Hispanic/Latino), 1,079 international. Average age 27. 5,228 applicants, 18% accepted, 471 enrolled. In 2014, 438 master's, 211 doctorates awarded. *Degree requirements:* For master's, comprehensive exam (for some programs), thesis (for some programs); for doctorate, comprehensive exam (for some programs), thesis/dissertation (for some programs). *Entrance requirements:* For master's and doctorate, GRE/GMAT (may vary by department). Additional exam requirements/recommendations for international students: Required—TOEFL (minimum score 550 paper-based). *Application deadline:* For fall admission, 8/1 for domestic students, 4/1 for international students; for spring admission, 1/1 for domestic students, 9/1 for international students. Applications are processed on a rolling basis. Application fee: $75. Electronic applications accepted. *Expenses:* Tuition, state resident: full-time $11,656; part-time $647.50 per credit hour. Tuition, nonresident: full-time $23,351; part-time $1297.25 per credit hour. *Required fees:* $2533; $465.75 per semester. Tuition and fees vary according to course load, campus/location and program. *Financial support:* In 2014–15, 148 fellowships with full tuition reimbursements (averaging $8,031 per year), 855 research assistantships with full tuition reimbursements (averaging $22,855 per year), 288 teaching assistantships with full tuition reimbursements (averaging $20,291 per year) were awarded. Financial award application deadline: 3/1; financial award applicants required to submit FAFSA. *Total annual research expenditures:* $90.5 million. *Unit head:* Dr. Richard C. Benson, Dean, 540-231-9752, Fax: 540-231-3031, E-mail: deaneng@vt.edu. *Application contact:* Linda Perkins, Executive Assistant, 540-231-9752, Fax: 540-231-3031, E-mail: lperkins@vt.edu.
Website: http://www.eng.vt.edu/.

Washington State University, Voiland College of Engineering and Architecture, Engineering and Computer Science Programs, Vancouver Campus, Pullman, WA 99164. Offers MS. *Students:* 32 full-time (4 women), 9 part-time (1 woman); includes 12 minority (1 Black or African American, non-Hispanic/Latino; 10 Asian, non-Hispanic/Latino; 1 Hispanic/Latino), 11 international. Average age 30. 39 applicants, 36% accepted, 13 enrolled. In 2014, 16 master's awarded. *Degree requirements:* For master's, comprehensive exam, thesis optional. *Entrance requirements:* For master's, official transcripts from all colleges and universities attended; one-page statement of purpose; three letters of recommendation. Additional exam requirements/recommendations for international students: Required—TOEFL; Recommended—IELTS. *Application deadline:* For fall admission, 1/10 priority date for domestic and international students; for spring admission, 7/1 priority date for domestic and international students. Application fee: $75. Electronic applications accepted. *Expenses:* Tuition, state resident: full-time $11,768. Tuition, nonresident: full-time $25,200. *Required fees:* $960. Tuition and fees vary according to program. *Financial support:* In 2014–15, 24 students received support, including 2 fellowships, 4 research assistantships (averaging $13,379 per year), 24 teaching assistantships (averaging $13,379 per year); health care benefits, tuition waivers, and unspecified assistantships also available. Financial award application deadline: 3/1; financial award applicants required to submit FAFSA. *Faculty research:* High yield production of bioenergy biofuels and bioproducts, nanomaterials, power systems, microfluidics, atmospheric research. *Total annual research expenditures:* $586,000. *Unit head:* Dr. David Field, Associate Dean, 509-335-8730, Fax: 509-335-7632, E-mail: dfield@wsu.edu. *Application contact:* Graduate School Admissions, 800-GRADWSU, Fax: 509-335-1949, E-mail: gradsch@wsu.edu.

Washington State University, Voiland College of Engineering and Architecture, School of Mechanical and Materials Engineering, Pullman, WA 99164-2920. Offers materials science and engineering (MS, PhD); mechanical engineering (MS, PhD). MS programs also offered at Tri-Cities campus. Part-time programs available. *Faculty:* 29 full-time (4 women), 3 part-time/adjunct (1 woman). *Students:* 79 full-time (12 women), 27 part-time (4 women); includes 5 minority (2 Black or African American, non-Hispanic/Latino; 2 Asian, non-Hispanic/Latino; 1 Hispanic/Latino), 60 international. Average age 29. 169 applicants, 37% accepted, 39 enrolled. In 2014, 23 master's, 7 doctorates awarded. Terminal master's awarded for partial completion of doctoral program. *Degree requirements:* For master's, comprehensive exam, thesis; for doctorate, comprehensive exam, thesis/dissertation, preliminary exam. *Entrance requirements:* For master's, GRE, bachelor's degree, minimum GPA of 3.0, resume, statement of purpose, 3 letters of recommendation, official transcripts, Student Interest Profile form; for doctorate, GRE, bachelor's degree, minimum GPA of 3.4, resume, statement of purpose, 3 letters of recommendation, official transcripts, Student Interest Profile form. Additional exam requirements/recommendations for international students: Required—TOEFL (minimum score 500 paper-based), IELTS. *Application deadline:* For fall admission, 1/10 priority date for domestic and international students; for spring admission, 7/1 priority date for domestic and international students. Applications are processed on a rolling basis. Application fee: $75. Electronic applications accepted. *Expenses:* Tuition, state resident: full-time $11,768. Tuition, nonresident: full-time $25,200. *Required fees:* $960. Tuition and fees vary according to program. *Financial support:* In 2014–15, 94 students received support, including 3 fellowships with full tuition reimbursements available (averaging $38,200 per year), 22 research assistantships with full tuition reimbursements available (averaging $13,883 per year), 32 teaching assistantships with full tuition reimbursements available (averaging $13,862 per year); career-related internships or fieldwork, scholarships/grants, health care benefits, and unspecified assistantships also available. Financial award application deadline: 4/1; financial award applicants required to submit FAFSA. *Faculty research:* Multiscale modeling and characterization of materials; advanced energy; bioengineering; engineering education and curricular innovation; modeling and visualization in the areas of product realization, materials, and processes. *Total annual research expenditures:* $4.4 million. *Unit head:* Dr. Michael Kessler, Director, 509-335-8654, Fax: 509-335-4662, E-mail: michael.kessler@wsu.edu. *Application contact:* Graduate School Admissions, 800-GRADWSU, Fax: 509-335-1949, E-mail: gradsch@wsu.edu.
Website: http://www.mme.wsu.edu/.

Washington University in St. Louis, School of Engineering and Applied Science, Department of Mechanical Engineering and Materials Science, St. Louis, MO 63130-4899. Offers aerospace engineering (MS, PhD); materials science (MS); mechanical engineering (M Eng, MS, PhD). Part-time programs available. Terminal master's awarded for partial completion of doctoral program. *Degree requirements:* For master's, thesis optional; for doctorate, thesis/dissertation optional. *Entrance requirements:* For master's, GRE; for doctorate, GRE General Test, departmental qualifying exam. *Faculty research:* Aerosols science and technology, applied mechanics, biomechanics and biomedical engineering, design, dynamic systems, combustion science, composite materials, materials science.

Wayne State University, College of Engineering, Department of Mechanical Engineering, Detroit, MI 48202. Offers MS, PhD. *Students:* 192 full-time (16 women), 51 part-time (3 women); includes 26 minority (1 Black or African American, non-Hispanic/Latino; 22 Asian, non-Hispanic/Latino; 2 Hispanic/Latino; 1 Two or more races, non-Hispanic/Latino), 183 international. Average age 26. 656 applicants, 46% accepted, 105 enrolled. In 2014, 39 master's, 10 doctorates awarded. *Degree requirements:* For master's, thesis optional; for doctorate, thesis/dissertation. *Entrance requirements:* For master's, GRE (if BS is not from ABET-accredited university), minimum undergraduate GPA of 3.0; for doctorate, GRE, minimum graduate or undergraduate upper-division GPA of 3.5, completed undergraduate major or substantial specialized work in proposed doctoral field. Additional exam requirements/recommendations for international students: Required—TOEFL (minimum score 550 paper-based; 79 iBT), TWE (minimum score 5.5), Michigan English Language Assessment Battery (minimum score 85); Recommended—IELTS (minimum score 6.5). *Application deadline:* For fall admission, 6/1 priority date for domestic students, 5/1 priority date for international students; for winter admission, 10/1 priority date for domestic students, 9/1 priority date for international students; for spring admission, 2/1 priority date for domestic students, 1/1 priority date for international students. Applications are processed on a rolling basis. Application fee: $0. Electronic applications accepted. *Expenses:* Expenses: Contact institution. *Financial support:* In 2014–15, 88 students received support, including 5 fellowships with tuition reimbursements available (averaging $18,474 per year), 11 research assistantships with tuition reimbursements available (averaging $18,722 per year), 7 teaching assistantships with tuition reimbursements available (averaging $18,432 per year); scholarships/grants, health care benefits, and unspecified assistantships also available. Financial award application deadline: 3/31; financial award applicants required to submit FAFSA. *Faculty research:* Acoustics and vibrations/noise control, engine combustion and emission controls, advanced materials and structures, computational fluid mechanics, material processing and manufacturing. *Total annual research expenditures:* $1.2 million. *Unit head:* Dr. Walter Bryzik, Chair, 313-577-5135, E-mail: wbryzik@eng.wayne.edu. *Application contact:* Dr. Trilochan Singh, Associate Chairman, 313-577-5548, E-mail: tsing@eng.wayne.edu.
Website: http://engineering.wayne.edu/me/.

Western Michigan University, Graduate College, College of Engineering and Applied Sciences, Department of Mechanical and Aerospace Engineering, Kalamazoo, MI 49008. Offers mechanical engineering (MSE, PhD). Part-time programs available. *Degree requirements:* For master's, thesis optional; for doctorate, thesis/dissertation. *Application deadline:* For fall admission, 2/15 for domestic students. *Financial support:* Application deadline: 2/15. *Application contact:* Admissions and Orientation, 269-387-2000, Fax: 269-387-2096.

Western New England University, College of Engineering, Department of Mechanical Engineering, Springfield, MA 01119. Offers MSME. Part-time and evening/weekend programs available. *Students:* 19 part-time (2 women); includes 2 minority (both Two or more races, non-Hispanic/Latino), 6 international. Average age 25. In 2014, 2 master's awarded. *Degree requirements:* For master's, comprehensive exam, thesis optional. *Entrance requirements:* For master's, official transcript, bachelor's degree in engineering or related field, two recommendations, resume. Additional exam requirements/recommendations for international students: Required—TOEFL (minimum score 79 iBT). *Application deadline:* Applications are processed on a rolling basis. Application fee: $30. Electronic applications accepted. *Financial support:* Application deadline: 4/15; applicants required to submit FAFSA. *Faculty research:* Low-loss fluid mixing, flow separation delay and alleviation, high-lift airfoils, ejector research, compact heat exchangers. *Unit head:* Dr. Said Dini, Chair, 413-782-1498, E-mail: said.dini@wne.edu. *Application contact:* Matthew Fox, Director of Recruiting and Marketing for Adult Learners, 413-782-1517, Fax: 413-782-1779, E-mail: study@wne.edu. Website: http://www1.wne.edu/engineering/index.cfm?selection-doc.8530.

West Virginia University, College of Engineering and Mineral Resources, Department of Mechanical and Aerospace Engineering, Program in Mechanical Engineering, Morgantown, WV 26506. Offers MSME, PhD. Part-time programs available. Terminal master's awarded for partial completion of doctoral program. *Degree requirements:* For master's, thesis; for doctorate, comprehensive exam, thesis/dissertation, qualifying exam, proposal and defense. *Entrance requirements:* For master's and doctorate, GRE Subject Test, minimum GPA of 3.0, 3 references. Additional exam requirements/recommendations for international students: Required—TOEFL. *Faculty research:* Thermal sciences, material sciences, automatic controls, mechanical/structure design.

Wichita State University, Graduate School, College of Engineering, Department of Mechanical Engineering, Wichita, KS 67260. Offers MS, PhD. Part-time programs available. *Unit head:* Dr. Muhammad M. Rahman, Chair, 316-978-3402, Fax: 316-978-3236, E-mail: muhammad.rahman@wichita.edu. *Application contact:* Jordan Oleson, Admission Coordinator, 316-978-3095, Fax: 316-978-3253, E-mail: jordan.oleson@wichita.edu. Website: http://www.wichita.edu/mechanical.

Widener University, Graduate Programs in Engineering, Program in Mechanical Engineering, Chester, PA 19013-5792. Offers M Eng. Part-time and evening/weekend programs available. *Degree requirements:* For master's, thesis optional. *Faculty research:* Computational fluid mechanics, thermal and solar engineering, energy conversion, composite materials, solid mechanics.

Wilkes University, College of Graduate and Professional Studies, College of Science and Engineering, Department of Mechanical Engineering and Engineering Management, Wilkes-Barre, PA 18766-0002. Offers engineering management (MS); mechanical engineering (MS). *Students:* 14 full-time (0 women), 14 part-time (0 women); includes 4 minority (1 Black or African American, non-Hispanic/Latino; 1 Asian, non-Hispanic/Latino; 1 Hispanic/Latino; 1 Two or more races, non-Hispanic/Latino), 14 international. Average age 31. In 2014, 21 master's awarded. *Unit head:* Dr. Terese Wignot, Interim Dean, 570-408-6000, Fax: 570-408-7860, E-mail: terese.wignot@wilkes.edu. *Application contact:* Joanne Thomas, Director of Graduate Enrollment, 570-408-4234, Fax: 570-408-7846, E-mail: joanne.thomas1@wilkes.edu. Website: http://www.wilkes.edu/academics/colleges/science-and-engineering/mechanical-engineering-engineering-management-applied-and-engineering-sciences/index..

Worcester Polytechnic Institute, Graduate Studies and Research, Department of Mechanical Engineering, Worcester, MA 01609-2280. Offers manufacturing engineering (MS, PhD); materials process engineering (MS); materials science and engineering (MS, PhD); mechanical engineering (MS, PhD, Graduate Certificate). Part-time and evening/weekend programs available. Postbaccalaureate distance learning degree programs offered (minimal on-campus study). *Faculty:* 29 full-time (4 women), 3 part-time/adjunct (1 woman). *Students:* 77 full-time (12 women), 62 part-time (8 women); includes 12 minority (3 Black or African American, non-Hispanic/Latino; 6 Asian, non-Hispanic/Latino; 3 Hispanic/Latino), 38 international. 272 applicants, 56% accepted, 54 enrolled. In 2014, 104 master's, 1 doctorate awarded. *Degree requirements:* For master's, thesis optional; for doctorate, comprehensive exam, thesis/dissertation. *Entrance requirements:* For master's, GRE (recommended), BS in mechanical engineering or related field, 3 letters of recommendation, statement of purpose; for doctorate, GRE (recommended), MS in mechanical engineering or related field, 3 letters of recommendation, statement of purpose. Additional exam requirements/recommendations for international students: Required—TOEFL (minimum score 563 paper-based; 84 iBT), IELTS (minimum score 7). *Application deadline:* For fall admission, 1/1 priority date for domestic and international students; for spring admission, 10/1 priority date for domestic and international students. Applications are processed on a rolling basis. Application fee: $70. Electronic applications accepted. *Financial support:* Research assistantships, teaching assistantships, career-related internships or fieldwork, institutionally sponsored loans, scholarships/grants, and unspecified assistantships available. Financial award application deadline: 1/1; financial award applicants required to submit FAFSA. *Unit head:* Dr. Jamal Yagoobi, Interim Head, 508-831-5556, Fax: 508-831-5680, E-mail: jyagoobi@wpi.edu. *Application contact:* Dr. Mark Richman, Graduate Coordinator, 508-831-5556, Fax: 508-831-5680, E-mail: mrichman@wpi.edu. Website: http://www.wpi.edu/academics/me.

Wright State University, School of Graduate Studies, College of Engineering and Computer Science, Programs in Engineering, Program in Mechanical and Materials Engineering, Dayton, OH 45435. Offers materials science and engineering (MSE); mechanical engineering (MSE). *Degree requirements:* For master's, thesis or course option alternative. *Entrance requirements:* Additional exam requirements/recommendations for international students: Required—TOEFL.

Yale University, Graduate School of Arts and Sciences, School of Engineering and Applied Science, Department of Mechanical Engineering, New Haven, CT 06520. Offers MS, PhD. Terminal master's awarded for partial completion of doctoral program. *Degree requirements:* For doctorate, thesis/dissertation, exam. *Entrance requirements:* For master's and doctorate, GRE General Test. Additional exam requirements/recommendations for international students: Required—TOEFL. *Faculty research:* Mechanics of fluids, mechanics of solids/material science.

Youngstown State University, Graduate School, College of Science, Technology, Engineering and Mathematics, Department of Mechanical Engineering, Youngstown, OH 44555-0001. Offers MSE. Part-time and evening/weekend programs available. *Degree requirements:* For master's, thesis optional. *Entrance requirements:* For master's, minimum GPA of 2.75 in field. Additional exam requirements/recommendations for international students: Required—TOEFL. *Faculty research:* Kinematics and dynamics of machines, computational and experimental heat transfer, machine controls and mechanical design.

Mechanics

Brown University, Graduate School, School of Engineering, Program in Mechanics of Solids and Structures, Providence, RI 02912. Offers Sc M, PhD. *Degree requirements:* For doctorate, thesis/dissertation, preliminary exam.

California Institute of Technology, Division of Engineering and Applied Science, Option in Applied Mechanics, Pasadena, CA 91125-0001. Offers MS, PhD. *Degree requirements:* For doctorate, thesis/dissertation. *Faculty research:* Elasticity, mechanics of quasi-static and dynamic fracture, dynamics and mechanical vibrations, stability and control.

Carnegie Mellon University, Carnegie Institute of Technology, Department of Civil and Environmental Engineering, Pittsburgh, PA 15213. Offers advanced infrastructure systems (MS, PhD); advanced infrastructure systems technology development and application (MS); air quality engineering and science (MS); civil and environmental engineering (MS, PhD); civil and environmental engineering/engineering and public policy (PhD); civil engineering (MS, PhD); computational mechanics (MS, PhD); computational modeling and monitoring for resilient structural and material systems (MS); energy infrastructure systems (MS); environmental engineering (MS, PhD); environmental management and science (MS, PhD); IT-based sustainable global infrastructure and construction management (MS); sustainability and green design (MS); water quality engineering and science (MS). Part-time programs available. *Faculty:* 21 full-time (5 women), 12 part-time/adjunct (3 women). *Students:* 229 full-time (99 women), 31 part-time (11 women); includes 18 minority (4 Black or African American, non-Hispanic/Latino; 13 Asian, non-Hispanic/Latino; 1 Hispanic/Latino), 193 international. Average age 26. 590 applicants, 68% accepted, 124 enrolled. In 2014, 85 master's, 11 doctorates awarded. Terminal master's awarded for partial completion of doctoral program. *Degree requirements:* For master's, thesis optional; for doctorate, comprehensive exam, thesis/dissertation, two-part qualifying exam, public defense of dissertation. *Entrance requirements:* For master's, GRE General Test, BS in engineering, science or mathematics; for doctorate, GRE General Test, BS or MS in engineering, science or mathematics. Additional exam requirements/recommendations for international students: Required—TOEFL (minimum score 84 iBT) or IELTS. *Application deadline:* For fall admission, 1/5 priority date for domestic and international students; for spring admission, 9/15 priority date for domestic and international students. Application fee: $65. Electronic applications accepted. *Financial support:* In 2014–15, 169 students received support. Fellowships with full and partial tuition reimbursements available, research assistantships with full and partial tuition reimbursements available, scholarships/grants, tuition waivers (full and partial), unspecified assistantships, and service assistantships available. Financial award application deadline: 1/5. *Faculty research:* Advanced infrastructure systems; environmental engineering, sustainability, and science; mechanics, materials, and computing. *Total annual research expenditures:* $4.9 million. *Unit head:* Dr. David A. Dzombak, Head, 412-268-2941, Fax: 412-268-7813, E-mail: dzombak@cmu.edu. *Application contact:* Melissa L. Brown, Director of Graduate Admissions & Recruiting, 412-268-8762, Fax: 412-268-7813, E-mail: mlb2@andrew.cmu.edu. Website: http://www.cmu.edu/cee/.

Columbia University, Fu Foundation School of Engineering and Applied Science, Department of Civil Engineering and Engineering Mechanics, New York, NY 10027. Offers civil engineering (MS, Eng Sc D, PhD); construction engineering and management (MS); engineering mechanics (MS, Eng Sc D, PhD). Part-time programs available. Postbaccalaureate distance learning degree programs offered (no on-campus study). *Faculty:* 19 full-time (4 women), 27 part-time/adjunct (2 women). *Students:* 153 full-time (40 women), 100 part-time (27 women); includes 19 minority (1 Black or African American, non-Hispanic/Latino; 11 Asian, non-Hispanic/Latino; 6 Hispanic/Latino; 1 Two or more races, non-Hispanic/Latino), 194 international. 504 applicants, 38% accepted, 110 enrolled. In 2014, 131 master's, 7 doctorates awarded. Terminal master's awarded for partial completion of doctoral program. *Degree requirements:* For doctorate, thesis/dissertation, qualifying exam. *Entrance requirements:* For master's and doctorate, GRE General Test. Additional exam requirements/recommendations for international students: Required—TOEFL, IELTS, PTE. *Application deadline:* For fall admission, 12/15 priority date for domestic and international students; for spring admission, 10/1 priority date for domestic and international students. Application fee: $85. Electronic applications accepted. *Financial support:* In 2014–15, 44 students received support, including 13 fellowships with full tuition reimbursements available (averaging $27,500 per year), 18 research assistantships with full tuition reimbursements available (averaging $32,448 per year), 13 teaching assistantships with full tuition reimbursements available (averaging $32,448 per year); health care benefits also available. Financial award application deadline: 12/15; financial award applicants required to submit FAFSA. *Faculty research:* Structural dynamics, structural health and monitoring, fatigue and fracture mechanics, geo-environmental engineering, multiscale science and engineering. *Unit head:* Dr. George Deodatis, Professor and Chair, Civil Engineering and Engineering Mechanics, 212-854-6267, E-mail: deodatis@civil.columbia.edu. *Application contact:* Scott Kelly, Graduate Admissions and Student Affairs, 212-854-3219, E-mail: kelly@civil.columbia.edu. Website: http://www.civil.columbia.edu/.

Cornell University, Graduate School, Graduate Fields of Engineering, Field of Theoretical and Applied Mechanics, Ithaca, NY 14853-0001. Offers advanced composites and structures (M Eng); dynamics and space mechanics (MS, PhD); fluid mechanics (MS, PhD); mechanics of materials (MS, PhD); solid mechanics (MS, PhD). *Degree requirements:* For master's, thesis (MS); for doctorate, one foreign language, comprehensive exam, thesis/dissertation, teaching experience. *Entrance requirements:* For master's and doctorate, GRE General Test, 3 letters of recommendation. Additional exam requirements/recommendations for international students: Required—TOEFL (minimum score 600 paper-based; 77 iBT). Electronic applications accepted. *Faculty research:* Biomathematics, bio-fluids, animal locomotion; non-linear dynamics, celestial mechanics, control; mechanics of materials, computational mechanics; experimental mechanics; non-linear elasticity, granular materials, phase transitions.

Drexel University, College of Engineering, Department of Mechanical Engineering and Mechanics, Philadelphia, PA 19104-2875. Offers mechanical engineering (MS, PhD). Part-time and evening/weekend programs available. Terminal master's awarded for partial completion of doctoral program. *Degree requirements:* For master's, thesis optional; for doctorate, thesis/dissertation. *Entrance requirements:* For master's, minimum GPA of 3.0, BS in engineering or science; for doctorate, minimum GPA of 3.5, MS in engineering or science. Additional exam requirements/recommendations for international students: Required—TOEFL. Electronic applications accepted. *Faculty research:* Composites, dynamic systems and control, combustion and fuels, biomechanics, mechanics and thermal fluid sciences.

École Polytechnique de Montréal, Graduate Programs, Department of Mechanical Engineering, Montréal, QC H3C 3A7, Canada. Offers aerothermics (M Eng, M Sc A, PhD); applied mechanics (M Eng, M Sc A, PhD); tool design (M Eng, M Sc A, PhD). Part-time and evening/weekend programs available. *Degree requirements:* For master's, one foreign language, thesis; for doctorate, one foreign language, thesis/

Mechanics

dissertation. *Entrance requirements:* For master's, minimum GPA of 2.75; for doctorate, minimum GPA of 3.0. *Faculty research:* Noise control and vibration, fatigue and creep, aerodynamics, composite materials, biomechanics, robotics.

Georgia Institute of Technology, Graduate Studies, College of Engineering, School of Civil and Environmental Engineering, Program in Engineering Science and Mechanics, Atlanta, GA 30332-0001. Offers MS, PhD. *Students:* 3 full-time, 2 international. Average age 25. 12 applicants, 33% accepted, 2 enrolled. In 2014, 3 master's awarded. Terminal master's awarded for partial completion of doctoral program. *Degree requirements:* For master's, thesis optional; for doctorate, comprehensive exam, thesis/dissertation. *Entrance requirements:* For master's and doctorate, GRE, http://www.grad.gatech.edu/esm. Additional exam requirements/recommendations for international students: Required—TOEFL (minimum score 550 paper-based; 79 iBT). *Application deadline:* For fall admission, 12/15 for domestic and international students; for spring admission, 8/31 for domestic and international students. Applications are processed on a rolling basis. Application fee: $75. Electronic applications accepted. *Expenses:* Tuition, state resident: full-time $12,344; part-time $515 per credit hour. Tuition, nonresident: full-time $27,600; part-time $1150 per credit hour. *Required fees:* $1196 per term. Part-time tuition and fees vary according to course load. *Financial support:* Fellowships, research assistantships, teaching assistantships, career-related internships or fieldwork, Federal Work-Study, institutionally sponsored loans, tuition waivers (partial), and unspecified assistantships available. Support available to part-time students. Financial award application deadline: 5/1. *Faculty research:* Bioengineering, structural mechanics, solid mechanics, dynamics. *Unit head:* Jim Mulholland, Director, 404-894-1695, E-mail: james.mulholland@ce.gatech.edu. *Application contact:* Robert Simon, Graduate Coordinator, 404-894-1660, E-mail: robert.simon@gatech.edu. Website: http://www.ce.gatech.edu.

Iowa State University of Science and Technology, Program in Engineering Mechanics, Ames, IA 50011. Offers M Eng, MS, PhD. *Entrance requirements:* For master's and doctorate, GRE. Additional exam requirements/recommendations for international students: Required—TOEFL (minimum score 550 paper-based; 80 iBT), IELTS (minimum score 6.5). Electronic applications accepted.

Johns Hopkins University, G. W. C. Whiting School of Engineering, Master of Science in Engineering Management Program, Baltimore, MD 21218-2699. Offers biomaterials (MSEM); civil engineering (MSEM); communications science (MSEM); computer science (MSEM); environmental systems analysis, economics and public policy (MSEM); fluid mechanics (MSEM); materials science and engineering (MSEM); mechanical engineering (MSEM); mechanics and materials (MSEM); nano-biotechnology (MSEM); nanomaterials and nanotechnology (MSEM); operations research (MSEM); probability and statistics (MSEM); smart product and device design (MSEM). *Entrance requirements:* For master's, GRE, 3 letters of recommendation, resume. Additional exam requirements/recommendations for international students: Required—TOEFL (minimum score 600 paper-based; 100 iBT) or IELTS (minimum score 7). Electronic applications accepted.

Lehigh University, P.C. Rossin College of Engineering and Applied Science, Department of Mechanical Engineering and Mechanics, Bethlehem, PA 18015. Offers computational engineering and mechanics (MS); mechanical engineering (M Eng, PhD); MBA/E. Part-time and evening/weekend programs available. Postbaccalaureate distance learning degree programs offered (no on-campus study). *Faculty:* 27 full-time (1 woman), 2 part-time/adjunct (1 woman). *Students:* 139 full-time (17 women), 29 part-time (4 women); includes 17 minority (3 Black or African American, non-Hispanic/Latino; 8 Asian, non-Hispanic/Latino; 5 Hispanic/Latino; 1 Two or more races, non-Hispanic/Latino), 89 international. Average age 26. 657 applicants, 18% accepted, 51 enrolled. In 2014, 50 master's, 6 doctorates awarded. Terminal master's awarded for partial completion of doctoral program. *Degree requirements:* For master's, thesis (for MS); for doctorate, thesis/dissertation, general exam. *Entrance requirements:* Additional exam requirements/recommendations for international students: Required—TOEFL (minimum score 550 paper-based; 79 iBT). *Application deadline:* For fall admission, 7/15 for domestic and international students; for spring admission, 12/1 for domestic and international students. Application fee: $75. Electronic applications accepted. *Expenses:* Expenses: $1,340 per credit hour. *Financial support:* In 2014–15, 36 students received support, including 5 fellowships with full and partial tuition reimbursements available (averaging $25,787 per year), 47 research assistantships with full and partial tuition reimbursements available (averaging $24,300 per year), 14 teaching assistantships with full and partial tuition reimbursements available (averaging $26,559 per year); unspecified assistantships and dean's doctoral assistantships also available. Financial award application deadline: 1/15. *Faculty research:* Thermofluids, dynamic systems, CAD/CAM, computational mechanics, solid mechanics. *Total annual research expenditures:* $3.1 million. *Unit head:* Dr. D. Gary Harlow, Chairman, 610-758-4102, Fax: 610-758-6224, E-mail: dgh0@lehigh.edu. *Application contact:* Jo Ann M. Casciano, Graduate Coordinator, 610-758-4107, Fax: 610-758-6224, E-mail: jmc4@lehigh.edu. Website: http://www.lehigh.edu/~inmem/.

Louisiana State University and Agricultural & Mechanical College, Graduate School, College of Engineering, Department of Civil and Environmental Engineering, Baton Rouge, LA 70803. Offers environmental engineering (MSCE, PhD); geotechnical engineering (MSCE, PhD); structural engineering and mechanics (MSCE, PhD); transportation engineering (MSCE, PhD); water resources (MSCE, PhD). Part-time programs available. *Faculty:* 26 full-time (1 woman). *Students:* 90 full-time (24 women), 28 part-time (6 women); includes 12 minority (5 Black or African American, non-Hispanic/Latino; 1 American Indian or Alaska Native, non-Hispanic/Latino; 5 Asian, non-Hispanic/Latino; 1 Two or more races, non-Hispanic/Latino), 67 international. Average age 30. 147 applicants, 50% accepted, 23 enrolled. In 2014, 26 master's, 8 doctorates awarded. *Degree requirements:* For master's, thesis optional; for doctorate, one foreign language, thesis/dissertation. *Entrance requirements:* For master's and doctorate, GRE General Test, minimum GPA of 3.0. Additional exam requirements/recommendations for international students: Required—TOEFL (minimum score 550 paper-based; 79 iBT), IELTS (minimum score 6.5), or PTE (minimum score 59). *Application deadline:* For fall admission, 1/1 priority date for domestic students, 5/15 for international students; for spring admission, 10/15 for domestic and international students; for summer admission, 5/15 for domestic and international students. Applications are processed on a rolling basis. Application fee: $50 ($70 for international students). Electronic applications accepted. *Financial support:* In 2014–15, 88 students received support, including 7 fellowships with full and partial tuition reimbursements available (averaging $26,784 per year), 59 research assistantships with full and partial tuition reimbursements available (averaging $16,992 per year), 13 teaching assistantships with full and partial tuition reimbursements available (averaging $16,290 per year); career-related internships or fieldwork, institutionally sponsored loans, scholarships/grants, and health care benefits also available. Financial award application deadline: 3/1; financial award applicants required to submit FAFSA. *Faculty research:* Mechanics and structures, environmental, geotechnical transportation, water resources. *Total annual research expenditures:* $3.2 million. *Unit head:* Dr. George Z. Voyiadjis, Chair/Professor, 225-578-8442, Fax: 225-578-8652, E-mail: voyiadjis@lsu.edu. *Application contact:* Dr. Ayman Ikeli, Professor, 225-578-7048, E-mail: aokeli@lsu.edu. Website: http://www.cee.lsu.edu/.

McGill University, Faculty of Graduate and Postdoctoral Studies, Faculty of Engineering, Department of Civil Engineering and Applied Mechanics, Montréal, QC H3A 2T5, Canada. Offers environmental engineering (M Eng, M Sc, PhD); fluid mechanics (M Sc); fluid mechanics and hydraulic engineering (M Eng, PhD); materials engineering (M Eng, PhD); rehabilitation of urban infrastructure (M Eng, PhD); soil behavior (M Eng, PhD); soil mechanics and foundations (M Eng, PhD); structures and structural mechanics (M Eng, PhD); water resources (M Sc); water resources engineering (M Eng, PhD).

Michigan State University, The Graduate School, College of Engineering, Department of Mechanical Engineering, East Lansing, MI 48824. Offers engineering mechanics (MS, PhD); mechanical engineering (MS, PhD). *Entrance requirements:* For master's, GRE General Test. Additional exam requirements/recommendations for international students: Required—TOEFL. Electronic applications accepted.

Michigan Technological University, Graduate School, College of Engineering, Department of Mechanical Engineering-Engineering Mechanics, Houghton, MI 49931. Offers engineering mechanics (MS); hybrid electric drive vehicle engineering (Graduate Certificate); mechanical engineering (MS); mechanical engineering-engineering mechanics (PhD). Part-time programs available. Postbaccalaureate distance learning degree programs offered (minimal on-campus study). *Faculty:* 63 full-time, 38 part-time/adjunct. *Students:* 243 full-time, 85 part-time; includes 11 minority (3 Black or African American, non-Hispanic/Latino; 4 Asian, non-Hispanic/Latino; 3 Hispanic/Latino; 1 Two or more races, non-Hispanic/Latino), 250 international. Average age 27. 1,421 applicants, 23% accepted, 95 enrolled. In 2014, 106 master's, 16 doctorates, 12 other advanced degrees awarded. Terminal master's awarded for partial completion of doctoral program. *Degree requirements:* For master's, comprehensive exam (for some programs), thesis (for some programs); for doctorate, comprehensive exam, thesis/dissertation. *Entrance requirements:* For master's, GRE (Michigan Tech students exempt - recommended for external funding opportunities), statement of purpose, official transcripts, 2 letters of recommendation, resume/curriculum vitae; for doctorate, GRE (Michigan Tech students exempt - recommended for external funding opportunities), MS (preferred), statement of purpose, official transcripts, 2 letters of recommendation, resume/curriculum vitae; for Graduate Certificate, statement of purpose, official transcripts, BS in engineering. Additional exam requirements/recommendations for international students: Required—TOEFL (minimum score 90 iBT) or IELTS. *Application deadline:* For fall admission, 3/1 priority date for domestic and international students; for spring admission, 8/1 priority date for domestic and international students. Applications are processed on a rolling basis. Electronic applications accepted. *Expenses:* Expenses: Contact institution. *Financial support:* In 2014–15, 182 students received support, including 16 fellowships with full and partial tuition reimbursements available (averaging $13,824 per year), 33 research assistantships with full and partial tuition reimbursements available (averaging $13,824 per year), 28 teaching assistantships with full and partial tuition reimbursements available (averaging $13,824 per year); career-related internships or fieldwork, Federal Work-Study, scholarships/grants, health care benefits, unspecified assistantships, and cooperative program also available. Financial award applicants required to submit FAFSA. *Faculty research:* Design and dynamic systems, energy-thermofluids, manufacturing, solid mechanics, sustainability. *Total annual research expenditures:* $3.7 million. *Unit head:* Dr. William W. Predebon, Chair, 906-487-2551, Fax: 906-487-2822, E-mail: wwpredeb@mtu.edu. *Application contact:* Jillian Isaacson, Office Assistant, 906-487-3611, Fax: 906-487-2822, E-mail: jillian@mtu.edu. Website: http://www.mtu.edu/mechanical/.

Missouri University of Science and Technology, Graduate School, Department of Civil, Architectural, and Environmental Engineering, Rolla, MO 65409. Offers civil engineering (MS, DE, PhD); construction engineering (MS, DE, PhD); environmental engineering (MS); fluid mechanics (MS, DE, PhD); geotechnical engineering (MS, DE, PhD); hydrology and hydraulic engineering (MS, DE, PhD). Part-time and evening/weekend programs available. Terminal master's awarded for partial completion of doctoral program. *Degree requirements:* For master's, thesis optional; for doctorate, comprehensive exam, thesis/dissertation. *Entrance requirements:* For master's, GRE General Test (minimum combined score 1100), minimum GPA of 3.0; for doctorate, GRE General Test (minimum score: verbal and quantitative 400, writing 3.5), minimum GPA of 3.0. Additional exam requirements/recommendations for international students: Required—TOEFL. Electronic applications accepted. *Faculty research:* Earthquake engineering, structural optimization and control systems, structural health monitoring/damage detection, soil-structure interaction, soil mechanics and foundation engineering.

Montana State University, The Graduate School, College of Engineering, Department of Civil Engineering, Bozeman, MT 59717. Offers civil engineering (MS); construction engineering management (MCEM); engineering (PhD), including applied mechanics option, civil engineering option. Part-time programs available. *Degree requirements:* For master's, comprehensive exam, thesis (for some programs); for doctorate, comprehensive exam, thesis/dissertation. *Entrance requirements:* For master's and doctorate, GRE General Test. Additional exam requirements/recommendations for international students: Required—TOEFL (minimum score 550 paper-based). Electronic applications accepted. *Faculty research:* Snow and ice mechanics, biofilm engineering, transportation, structural and geo materials, water resources.

New Mexico Institute of Mining and Technology, Graduate Studies, Program in Mechanical Engineering, Socorro, NM 87801. Offers explosives engineering (MS); fluid and thermal sciences (MS); mechatronics systems engineering (MS); solid mechanics (MS). *Degree requirements:* For master's, thesis (for some programs). *Entrance requirements:* For master's, GRE General Test. Additional exam requirements/recommendations for international students: Required—TOEFL (minimum score 540 paper-based). *Faculty research:* Vibrations, fluid-structure interactions.

North Dakota State University, College of Graduate and Interdisciplinary Studies, College of Engineering and Architecture, Department of Mechanical Engineering and Applied Mechanics, Fargo, ND 58108. Offers MS, PhD. Part-time programs available. *Degree requirements:* For master's, thesis; for doctorate, comprehensive exam, thesis/dissertation. *Entrance requirements:* For master's and doctorate, minimum GPA of 3.0. Additional exam requirements/recommendations for international students: Required—TOEFL (minimum score 550 paper-based). Electronic applications accepted. *Faculty research:* Thermodynamics, finite element analysis, automotive systems, robotics, nanotechnology.

Northwestern University, McCormick School of Engineering and Applied Science, Program in Theoretical and Applied Mechanics, Evanston, IL 60208. Offers MS, PhD. Admissions and degrees offered through The Graduate School. *Faculty:* 27 full-time (4 women). *Students:* 19 full-time (3 women); includes 1 minority (Hispanic/Latino), 16 international. Average age 24. 36 applicants, 25% accepted, 5 enrolled. In 2014, 4 doctorates awarded. Terminal master's awarded for partial completion of doctoral program. *Degree requirements:* For master's, thesis optional; for doctorate, comprehensive exam, thesis/dissertation. *Entrance requirements:* For master's and doctorate, GRE General Test, minimum 2 letters of recommendation, transcripts from all academic institutions attended. Additional exam requirements/recommendations for international students: Required—TOEFL (minimum score 577 paper-based; 90 iBT), IELTS (minimum score 7). *Application deadline:* For fall admission, 12/31 for domestic

and international students. Application fee: $75. Electronic applications accepted. *Financial support:* In 2014–15, 16 students received support. Fellowships with full tuition reimbursements available, research assistantships with full tuition reimbursements available, teaching assistantships with full tuition reimbursements available, career-related internships or fieldwork, institutionally sponsored loans, health care benefits, and unspecified assistantships available. Financial award application deadline: 12/31; financial award applicants required to submit FAFSA. *Faculty research:* Computational mechanics, mechanics in biology and fluids, micro/nanomechanics, multifunctional materials, geomechanics, structural reliability and nondestructive characterization. *Unit head:* Prof. Horacio Espinosa, Director, 847-467-5989, Fax: 847-491-5227, E-mail: espinosa@northwestern.edu. *Application contact:* Dr. Bruce Alan Lindvall, Assistant Dean for Graduate Studies, 847-491-4547, Fax: 847-491-5341, E-mail: b-lindvall@northwestern.edu.
Website: http://www.tam.northwestern.edu/education/index.html.

Ohio University, Graduate College, Russ College of Engineering and Technology, Department of Civil Engineering, Athens, OH 45701-2979. Offers civil engineering (PhD); construction engineering and management (MS); environmental (MS); geotechnical and geoenvironmental (MS); mechanics (MS); structures (MS); transportation (MS); water resources (MS). Part-time programs available. *Degree requirements:* For master's, comprehensive exam (for some programs), thesis or alternative; for doctorate, comprehensive exam, thesis/dissertation. *Entrance requirements:* For master's, GRE General Test, minimum GPA of 3.0, 3 letters of recommendation; for doctorate, GRE General Test. Additional exam requirements/recommendations for international students: Required—TOEFL (minimum score 550 paper-based; 80 iBT) or IELTS (minimum score 6.5). Electronic applications accepted. *Faculty research:* Noise abatement, materials and environment, highway infrastructure, subsurface investigation (pavements, pipes, bridges).

Penn State University Park, Graduate School, College of Engineering, Department of Engineering Science and Mechanics, University Park, PA 16802. Offers engineering mechanics (M Eng); engineering science (M Eng); engineering science and mechanics (MS, PhD). *Unit head:* Dr. Amr S. Elnashai, Dean, 814-865-7537, Fax: 814-863-4749, E-mail: ase2@psu.edu. *Application contact:* Lori A. Stania, Director, Graduate Student Services, 814-867-5278, Fax: 814-863-4627, E-mail: gswww@psu.edu.
Website: http://www.esm.psu.edu/.

Rutgers, The State University of New Jersey, New Brunswick, Graduate School-New Brunswick, Program in Mechanics, Piscataway, NJ 08854-8097. Offers MS, PhD. Part-time programs available. Terminal master's awarded for partial completion of doctoral program. *Degree requirements:* For master's, thesis optional, qualifying exam; for doctorate, thesis/dissertation, qualifying exam. *Entrance requirements:* For master's and doctorate, GRE General Test, GRE Subject Test (recommended). Additional exam requirements/recommendations for international students: Required—TOEFL. Electronic applications accepted. *Faculty research:* Continuum mechanics, constitutive theory, thermodynamics, visolasticity, liquid crystal theory.

San Diego State University, Graduate and Research Affairs, College of Engineering, Department of Aerospace Engineering and Engineering Mechanics, San Diego, CA 92182. Offers aerospace engineering (MS); engineering mechanics (MS); engineering sciences and applied mechanics (PhD); flight dynamics (MS); fluid dynamics (MS). PhD offered jointly with University of California, San Diego and Department of Mechanical Engineering. Terminal master's awarded for partial completion of doctoral program. *Degree requirements:* For master's, comprehensive exam (for some programs), thesis (for some programs); for doctorate, thesis/dissertation. *Entrance requirements:* For master's, GRE General Test; for doctorate, GRE, 3 letters of recommendation. Additional exam requirements/recommendations for international students: Required—TOEFL. Electronic applications accepted. *Faculty research:* Organized structures in post-stall flow over wings/three dimensional separated flow, airfoil growth effect, probabilities, structural mechanics.

Southern Illinois University Carbondale, Graduate School, College of Engineering, Department of Civil and Environmental Engineering, Carbondale, IL 62901-4701. Offers civil engineering (MS). *Faculty:* 10 full-time (1 woman). *Students:* 34 full-time (2 women), 10 part-time (1 woman); includes 3 minority (all Hispanic/Latino), 27 international. Average age 26. 74 applicants, 24% accepted, 8 enrolled. In 2014, 10 master's awarded. *Degree requirements:* For master's, comprehensive exam, thesis. *Entrance requirements:* For master's, minimum GPA of 2.7. Additional exam requirements/recommendations for international students: Required—TOEFL. *Application deadline:* Applications are processed on a rolling basis. Application fee: $50. *Expenses:* Tuition, state resident: full-time $10,176; part-time $1153 per credit. Tuition, nonresident: full-time $20,814; part-time $1744 per credit. *Required fees:* $7092; $394 per credit. $2364 per semester. *Financial support:* In 2014–15, 21 students received support, including 5 research assistantships with full tuition reimbursements available, 9 teaching assistantships with full tuition reimbursements available; fellowships with full tuition reimbursements available, Federal Work-Study, institutionally sponsored loans, and tuition waivers (full) also available. Support available to part-time students. Financial award application deadline: 7/1. *Faculty research:* Composite materials, wastewater treatment, solid waste disposal, slurry transport, geotechnical engineering. *Total annual research expenditures:* $230,856. *Unit head:* Dr. Sanjeev Kumar, Chair, 618-453-7815, E-mail: kumars@ce.siu.edu. *Application contact:* Christine O'Dell, Office Support Specialist, 618-536-2369, E-mail: codell@siu.edu.
Website: http://engineering.siu.edu/civil/.

Stanford University, School of Engineering, Department of Civil and Environmental Engineering, Stanford, CA 94305-9991. Offers atmosphere and energy (MS, PhD); construction (MS), including construction engineering and management, design-construction integration, sustainable design and construction; environmental engineering and science (MS, PhD, Eng); environmental fluid mechanics and hydrology (PhD); geomechanics (MS); structural engineering (MS). Terminal master's awarded for partial completion of doctoral program. *Degree requirements:* For doctorate, thesis/dissertation, qualifying exam; for Eng, thesis. *Entrance requirements:* For master's, doctorate, and Eng, GRE General Test. Additional exam requirements/recommendations for international students: Required—TOEFL. Electronic applications accepted. *Expenses: Tuition:* Full-time $44,184; part-time $982 per credit hour. *Required fees:* $191.

The University of Alabama, Graduate School, College of Engineering, Department of Aerospace Engineering and Mechanics, Tuscaloosa, AL 35487. Offers aerospace engineering (MSAEM); engineering science and mechanics (PhD). Part-time programs available. Postbaccalaureate distance learning degree programs offered (no on-campus study). *Faculty:* 16 full-time (1 woman), 1 part-time/adjunct (0 women). *Students:* 22 full-time (1 woman), 27 part-time (3 women); includes 1 minority (Black or African American, non-Hispanic/Latino), 15 international. Average age 28. 45 applicants, 58% accepted, 11 enrolled. In 2014, 10 master's, 2 doctorates awarded. Terminal master's awarded for partial completion of doctoral program. *Degree requirements:* For master's, comprehensive exam (for some programs), thesis (for some programs); for doctorate, comprehensive exam, thesis/dissertation, 1-year residency. *Entrance requirements:* For master's and doctorate, GRE (minimum score of 300), minimum undergraduate GPA of 3.0. Additional exam requirements/recommendations for international students: Required—TOEFL (minimum score 550 paper-based; 79 iBT). *Application deadline:* For fall admission, 1/1 priority date for domestic students, 5/15 priority date for international students; for spring admission, 1/1 priority date for domestic students, 6/1 priority date for international students. Applications are processed on a rolling basis. Application fee: $50 ($60 for international students). Electronic applications accepted. *Expenses:* Tuition, state resident: full-time $9826. Tuition, nonresident: full-time $24,950. *Financial support:* In 2014–15, 18 students received support, including fellowships with full tuition reimbursements available (averaging $15,000 per year), research assistantships with full tuition reimbursements available (averaging $20,000 per year), teaching assistantships with full tuition reimbursements available (averaging $14,025 per year); Federal Work-Study, institutionally sponsored loans, scholarships/grants, health care benefits, and unspecified assistantships also available. Financial award application deadline: 2/15. *Faculty research:* Aeronautics, astronautics, solid mechanics, fluid mechanics, computational modeling. *Total annual research expenditures:* $1.2 million. *Unit head:* Dr. John Baker, Professor/Department Head, 205-348-4997, Fax: 205-348-7240, E-mail: john.baker@eng.ua.edu. *Application contact:* Dr. James Paul Hubner, Associate Professor, 205-348-1617, Fax: 208-348-7240, E-mail: phubner@eng.ua.edu.
Website: http://aem.eng.ua.edu/.

University of Calgary, Faculty of Graduate Studies, Schulich School of Engineering, Department of Civil Engineering, Calgary, AB T2N 1N4, Canada. Offers avalanche mechanics (M Sc, PhD); civil engineering (M Eng, M Sc, PhD); energy and environment engineering (M Eng, M Sc, PhD); environmental engineering (M Eng, M Sc, PhD); geotechnical engineering (M Eng, M Sc, PhD); materials science (M Eng, M Sc, PhD); project management (M Eng, M Sc, PhD); structures and solid mechanics (M Eng, M Sc, PhD); transportation engineering (M Eng, M Sc, PhD); water resources (M Eng, M Sc, PhD). Part-time programs available. *Degree requirements:* For master's, thesis; for doctorate, thesis/dissertation, written and oral candidacy exam. *Entrance requirements:* For master's, minimum GPA of 3.0; for doctorate, minimum GPA of 3.5. Additional exam requirements/recommendations for international students: Required—TOEFL (minimum score 580 paper-based; 93 iBT), IELTS (minimum score 7). Electronic applications accepted. *Faculty research:* Geotechnical engineering, energy and environment, transportation, project management, structures and solid mechanics.

University of California, Berkeley, Graduate Division, College of Engineering, Department of Civil and Environmental Engineering, Berkeley, CA 94720-1500. Offers engineering and project management (M Eng, MS, D Eng, PhD); environmental engineering (M Eng, MS, D Eng, PhD); geoengineering (M Eng, MS, D Eng, PhD); structural engineering, mechanics and materials (M Eng, MS, D Eng, PhD); transportation engineering (M Eng, MS, D Eng, PhD); M Arch/MS; MCP/MS; MPP/MS. *Degree requirements:* For master's, comprehensive exam or thesis (MS); for doctorate, thesis/dissertation, qualifying exam. *Entrance requirements:* For master's, GRE General Test, minimum GPA of 3.0, 3 letters of recommendation; for doctorate, GRE General Test, minimum GPA of 3.5, 3 letters of recommendation. Additional exam requirements/recommendations for international students: Required—TOEFL (minimum score 570 paper-based). Electronic applications accepted.

University of California, Merced, Graduate Division, School of Engineering, Merced, CA 95343. Offers biological engineering and small scale technologies (MS, PhD); electrical engineering and computer science (MS, PhD); environmental systems (MS, PhD); mechanical engineering (MS); mechanical engineering and applied mechanics (PhD). *Faculty:* 38 full-time (6 women), 1 part-time/adjunct (0 women). *Students:* 128 full-time (36 women), 2 part-time (0 women); includes 21 minority (1 Black or African American, non-Hispanic/Latino; 11 Asian, non-Hispanic/Latino; 6 Hispanic/Latino; 3 Two or more races, non-Hispanic/Latino), 72 international. Average age 28. 230 applicants, 39% accepted, 38 enrolled. In 2014, 5 master's, 18 doctorates awarded. *Degree requirements:* For master's, variable foreign language requirement, comprehensive exam, thesis (for some programs); for doctorate, variable foreign language requirement, comprehensive exam, thesis/dissertation. *Entrance requirements:* For master's and doctorate, GRE. Additional exam requirements/recommendations for international students: Required—TOEFL (minimum score 550 paper-based; 68 iBT); Recommended—IELTS. Application fee: $80 ($100 for international students). *Expenses:* Tuition, state resident: full-time $11,220; part-time $2805 per semester. *Required fees:* $1940; $970 per semester hour. *Financial support:* In 2014–15, 19 fellowships with full and partial tuition reimbursements (averaging $6,683 per year) were awarded; scholarships/grants also available. *Faculty research:* Artificial intelligence, biomedical imaging, thermal science, ecology, nanotechnology. *Unit head:* Dr. Erik Rolland, Interim Dean, 209-228-4296, Fax: 209-228-4047, E-mail: erolland@ucmerced.edu. *Application contact:* Tsu Ya, Graduate Admissions and Academic Services Manager, 209-228-4521, Fax: 209-228-6906, E-mail: tya@ucmerced.edu.

University of California, San Diego, Graduate Division, Department of Mechanical and Aerospace Engineering, Program in Applied Mechanics, La Jolla, CA 92093. Offers MS, PhD. *Students:* 8 full-time (1 woman), all international. 36 applicants, 25% accepted, 1 enrolled. In 2014, 3 master's, 2 doctorates awarded. *Degree requirements:* For master's, comprehensive exam or thesis; for doctorate, comprehensive exam, thesis/dissertation. *Entrance requirements:* For master's and doctorate, GRE General Test, minimum GPA of 3.0. Additional exam requirements/recommendations for international students: Required—TOEFL (minimum score 550 paper-based; 80 iBT), IELTS (minimum score 7). *Application deadline:* For fall admission, 12/15 for domestic students; for spring admission, 1/2 for domestic students. Application fee: $90 ($110 for international students). Electronic applications accepted. *Expenses:* Tuition, state resident: full-time $11,220; part-time $5610 per quarter. Tuition, nonresident: full-time $26,322; part-time $13,161 per quarter. *Required fees:* $570 per quarter. Tuition and fees vary according to program. *Financial support:* Fellowships, research assistantships, teaching assistantships, scholarships/grants, and unspecified assistantships available. Financial award application deadline: 1/2; financial award applicants required to submit FAFSA. *Faculty research:* Interfacial properties, durability, aging, and failure of composites; granular materials, rocks, and centimentious materials; computational methods for materials processing; advanced analytical methods in the theory of elasticity; synthesis, processing, and characterization of advanced ceramics, metals, and composites; shock synthesis and compaction. *Unit head:* Vitali Nesterenko, Chair, 858-534-0113, E-mail: mae-chair-l@ucsd.edu. *Application contact:* Linda McKamey, Graduate Coordinator, 858-534-4065, E-mail: mae-gradadm-l@ucsd.edu.
Website: http://maeweb.ucsd.edu/.

University of Cincinnati, Graduate School, College of Engineering and Applied Science, Department of Aerospace Engineering and Engineering Mechanics, Cincinnati, OH 45221. Offers MS, PhD. Part-time programs available. Terminal master's awarded for partial completion of doctoral program. *Degree requirements:* For master's, project or thesis; for doctorate, thesis/dissertation. *Entrance requirements:* For master's and doctorate, GRE General Test. Additional exam requirements/recommendations for international students: Required—TOEFL (minimum score 550 paper-based). Electronic applications accepted. *Faculty research:* Computational fluid mechanics/propulsion, large space structures, dynamics and guidance of VTOL vehicles.

University of Colorado Denver, College of Engineering and Applied Science, Department of Mechanical Engineering, Denver, CO 80217. Offers mechanical engineering (MS); mechanics (MS); thermal sciences (MS). Part-time and evening/

weekend programs available. *Faculty:* 9 full-time (0 women). *Students:* 29 full-time (3 women), 22 part-time (2 women); includes 6 minority (2 Black or African American, non-Hispanic/Latino; 1 Asian, non-Hispanic/Latino; 3 Hispanic/Latino), 22 international. Average age 29. 81 applicants, 41% accepted, 16 enrolled. In 2014, 17 master's awarded. *Degree requirements:* For master's, comprehensive exam, 30 credit hours, project or thesis. *Entrance requirements:* For master's, GRE, three letters of recommendation, personal statement. Additional exam requirements/recommendations for international students: Required—TOEFL (minimum score 537 paper-based; 75 iBT); Recommended—IELTS (minimum score 6.8). *Application deadline:* For fall admission, 5/1 for domestic students, 4/15 for international students; for spring admission, 10/1 for domestic students, 9/15 for international students. Application fee: $50 ($75 for international students). Electronic applications accepted. *Expenses:* Expenses: Contact institution. *Financial support:* In 2014–15, 29 students received support. Fellowships, research assistantships, teaching assistantships, career-related internships or fieldwork, Federal Work-Study, institutionally sponsored loans, scholarships/grants, traineeships, and unspecified assistantships available. Financial award application deadline: 4/1; financial award applicants required to submit FAFSA. *Faculty research:* Applied and computational mechanics, bioengineering, energy systems, tribology, micro/mesofluidics and biomechanics, vehicle dynamics. *Unit head:* Dr. Sam Welch, Chair, 303-556-8488, Fax: 303-556-6371, E-mail: sam.welch@ucdenver.edu. *Application contact:* Catherine McCoy, Program Assistant, 303-556-8516, E-mail: catherine.mccoy@ucdenver.edu.
Website: http://www.ucdenver.edu/academics/colleges/Engineering/Programs/Mechanical-Engineering/Pages/MechanicalEngineering.aspx.

University of Dayton, Department of Civil and Environmental Engineering and Engineering Mechanics, Dayton, OH 45469. Offers engineering mechanics (MSEM); environmental engineering (MSCE); geotechnical engineering (MSCE); structural engineering (MSCE); transportation engineering (MSCE); water resources engineering (MSCE). Part-time and evening/weekend programs available. *Faculty:* 9 full-time (2 women), 3 part-time/adjunct (1 woman). *Students:* 23 full-time (4 women), 6 part-time (2 women), 22 international. Average age 26. 70 applicants, 39% accepted, 4 enrolled. In 2014, 11 master's awarded. *Degree requirements:* For master's, thesis optional. *Entrance requirements:* For master's, minimum GPA of 3.0 in undergraduate work. Additional exam requirements/recommendations for international students: Required—TOEFL (minimum score 550 paper-based; 80 iBT). *Application deadline:* For fall admission, 8/1 priority date for domestic students, 5/1 priority date for international students; for winter admission, 7/1 priority date for international students; for spring admission, 11/1 priority date for international students. Applications are processed on a rolling basis. Application fee: $0 ($50 for international students). Electronic applications accepted. *Expenses: Tuition:* Full-time $10,176; part-time $848 per credit. *Required fees:* $25; $25 per course. Part-time tuition and fees vary according to course level, course load, degree level and program. *Financial support:* In 2014–15, 3 students received support. Institutionally sponsored loans, scholarships/grants, and department-funded awards (averaging $2448 per year) available. Financial award application deadline: 3/1; financial award applicants required to submit FAFSA. *Faculty research:* Physical modeling of water resource systems, finite element methods, mechanics of composite materials, transportation systems safety, biological treatment processes, fiber reinforced concrete. *Total annual research expenditures:* $250,000. *Unit head:* Dr. Donald V. Chase, Chair, 937-229-3847, Fax: 937-229-3491, E-mail: dchase1@udayton.edu. *Application contact:* 937-229-4462, E-mail: graduateadmission@udayton.edu.
Website: https://www.udayton.edu/engineering/departments/civil/index.php.

University of Illinois at Urbana–Champaign, Graduate College, College of Engineering, Department of Mechanical Science and Engineering, Champaign, IL 61820. Offers mechanical engineering (MS, PhD); theoretical and applied mechanics (MS, PhD). Terminal master's awarded for partial completion of doctoral program. *Entrance requirements:* Additional exam requirements/recommendations for international students: Required—TOEFL (minimum score 613 paper-based; 103 iBT), IELTS (minimum score 7). *Application deadline:* For fall admission, 1/4 for domestic students; for spring admission, 10/1 for domestic students. Application fee: $70 ($90 for international students). *Financial support:* Application deadline: 12/15. *Unit head:* Placid Mathew Ferreira, Head, 217-333-0639, Fax: 217-244-6534, E-mail: pferreir@illinois.edu. *Application contact:* Katrina Hagler, Assistant Director of Graduate Recruiting and Admissions, 217-244-3416, Fax: 217-244-6534, E-mail: kkappes2@illinois.edu.
Website: http://mechanical.illinois.edu/.

University of Maryland, College Park, Academic Affairs, A. James Clark School of Engineering, Department of Mechanical Engineering, College Park, MD 20742. Offers electronic packaging and reliability (MS, PhD); manufacturing and design (MS, PhD); mechanics and materials (MS, PhD); reliability engineering (M Eng, MS, PhD); thermal and fluid sciences (MS, PhD). Part-time and evening/weekend programs available. Postbaccalaureate distance learning degree programs offered. *Degree requirements:* For master's, thesis optional; for doctorate, thesis/dissertation, qualifying exam. *Entrance requirements:* For master's, GRE General Test, 3 letters of recommendation; for doctorate, GRE General Test, minimum GPA of 3.0. Additional exam requirements/recommendations for international students: Required—TOEFL. Electronic applications accepted. *Faculty research:* Injection molding, electronic packaging, fluid mechanics, product engineering.

University of Massachusetts Amherst, Graduate School, College of Engineering, Department of Civil and Environmental Engineering, Amherst, MA 01003. Offers civil engineering (MSCE, PhD); environmental and water resources engineering (MSCE); geotechnical engineering (MSCE); structural engineering and mechanics (MSCE); transportation engineering (MSCE). Part-time programs available. *Faculty:* 32 full-time (8 women). *Students:* 104 full-time (43 women), 15 part-time (7 women); includes 16 minority (3 Black or African American, non-Hispanic/Latino; 4 Asian, non-Hispanic/Latino; 7 Hispanic/Latino; 2 Two or more races, non-Hispanic/Latino), 44 international. Average age 26. 219 applicants, 62% accepted, 40 enrolled. In 2014, 36 master's, 4 doctorates awarded. Terminal master's awarded for partial completion of doctoral program. *Degree requirements:* For master's, thesis or alternative; for doctorate, comprehensive exam, thesis/dissertation. *Entrance requirements:* For master's and doctorate, GRE General Test. Additional exam requirements/recommendations for international students: Required—TOEFL (minimum score 550 paper-based; 80 iBT), IELTS (minimum score 6.5). *Application deadline:* For fall admission, 1/2 for domestic and international students; for spring admission, 10/1 for domestic and international students. Applications are processed on a rolling basis. Application fee: $75. Electronic applications accepted. *Expenses:* Tuition, state resident: full-time $1980; part-time $110 per credit. Tuition, nonresident: full-time $14,644; part-time $414 per credit. *Required fees:* $11,417. One-time fee: $357. *Financial support:* Fellowships with full and partial tuition reimbursements, research assistantships with full and partial tuition reimbursements, teaching assistantships with full and partial tuition reimbursements, career-related internships or fieldwork, Federal Work-Study, scholarships/grants, traineeships, health care benefits, tuition waivers (full and partial), and unspecified assistantships available. Support available to part-time students. Financial award application deadline: 1/2. *Unit head:* Dr. Sanjay Arwade, Graduate Program Director, 413-545-0686, Fax: 413-545-2840. *Application contact:* Lindsay DeSantis, Supervisor of Admissions, 413-545-0722, Fax: 413-577-0100, E-mail: gradadm@grad.umass.edu.
Website: http://cee.umass.edu/.

University of Massachusetts Dartmouth, Graduate School, College of Engineering, Program in Engineering and Applied Science, North Dartmouth, MA 02747-2300. Offers applied mechanics and materials (PhD); computational science and engineering (PhD); computer science and information systems (PhD); industrial and systems engineering (PhD). Part-time programs available. *Students:* 21 full-time (6 women), 1 (woman) part-time; includes 2 minority (1 Black or African American, non-Hispanic/Latino; 1 Two or more races, non-Hispanic/Latino), 12 international. Average age 30. 23 applicants, 65% accepted, 5 enrolled. In 2014, 1 doctorate awarded. *Degree requirements:* For doctorate, comprehensive exam, thesis/dissertation. *Entrance requirements:* For doctorate, GRE, statement of purpose (minimum of 300 words), resume, 3 letters of recommendation, official transcripts. Additional exam requirements/recommendations for international students: Required—TOEFL (minimum score 550 paper-based; 79 iBT). *Application deadline:* For fall admission, 2/15 priority date for domestic students, 1/15 priority date for international students; for spring admission, 11/15 priority date for domestic students, 10/15 priority date for international students. Applications are processed on a rolling basis. Application fee: $60. Electronic applications accepted. *Expenses:* Tuition, state resident: full-time $2071; part-time $86.29 per credit. Tuition, nonresident: full-time $8099; part-time $337.46 per credit. *Required fees:* $16,520; $712.33 per credit. Tuition and fees vary according to course load and reciprocity agreements. *Financial support:* In 2014–15, 8 fellowships with full tuition reimbursements (averaging $16,577 per year), 8 research assistantships with full tuition reimbursements (averaging $13,627 per year), 5 teaching assistantships with full tuition reimbursements (averaging $12,400 per year) were awarded; Federal Work-Study and unspecified assistantships also available. Support available to part-time students. Financial award application deadline: 3/1; financial award applicants required to submit FAFSA. *Faculty research:* Tissue/cell engineering, biotransport sensors/networks, marine systems biomimetic materials, composite/polymeric materials, resilient infrastructure robotics, renewable energy. *Total annual research expenditures:* $1.7 million. *Unit head:* Gaurav Khanna, Graduate Program Director, 508-910-6605, Fax: 508-999-9115, E-mail: gkhanna@umassd.edu. *Application contact:* Steven Briggs, Director of Marketing and Recruitment for Graduate Studies, 508-999-8604, Fax: 508-999-8183, E-mail: graduate@umassd.edu.
Website: http://www.umassd.edu/engineering/graduate/doctoraldegreeprograms/egrandappliedsciencephd/.

University of Minnesota, Twin Cities Campus, College of Science and Engineering, Department of Aerospace Engineering and Mechanics, Minneapolis, MN 55455-0213. Offers MS, PhD. Part-time programs available. *Degree requirements:* For doctorate, thesis/dissertation. *Entrance requirements:* Additional exam requirements/recommendations for international students: Required—TOEFL (minimum score 550 paper-based). Electronic applications accepted. *Faculty research:* Fluid mechanics, solid mechanics and materials, aerospace systems, nanotechnology.

University of Nebraska–Lincoln, Graduate College, College of Engineering, Department of Engineering Mechanics, Lincoln, NE 68588. Offers MS, PhD. *Degree requirements:* For master's, thesis optional; for doctorate, comprehensive exam, thesis/dissertation. *Entrance requirements:* For master's and doctorate, GRE. Additional exam requirements/recommendations for international students: Required—TOEFL (minimum score 550 paper-based). Electronic applications accepted. *Faculty research:* Polymer mechanics, piezoelectric materials, meshless methods, smart materials, fracture mechanics.

University of Nebraska–Lincoln, Graduate College, College of Engineering, Department of Mechanical and Materials Engineering, Lincoln, NE 68588-0526. Offers biomedical engineering (PhD); engineering mechanics (MS); materials engineering (PhD); mechanical engineering (MS), including materials science engineering, metallurgical engineering; mechanical engineering and applied mechanics (PhD); MS/MS. MS/MS offered with University of Rouen-France. *Degree requirements:* For master's, thesis optional; for doctorate, comprehensive exam, thesis/dissertation. *Entrance requirements:* For master's and doctorate, GRE General Test. Additional exam requirements/recommendations for international students: Required—TOEFL (minimum score 550 paper-based). Electronic applications accepted. *Faculty research:* Medical robotics, rehabilitation dynamics, and design; combustion, fluid mechanics, and heat transfer; nano-materials, manufacturing, and devices; fiber, tissue, bio-polymer, and adaptive composites; blast, impact, fracture, and failure; electro-active and magnetic materials and devices; functional materials, design, and added manufacturing; materials characterization, modeling, and computational simulation.

University of New Brunswick Fredericton, School of Graduate Studies, Faculty of Engineering, Department of Mechanical Engineering, Fredericton, NB E3B 5A3, Canada. Offers applied mechanics (M Eng, M Sc E, PhD); mechanical engineering (M Eng, M Sc E, PhD). Part-time programs available. *Faculty:* 15 full-time (1 woman), 24 part-time/adjunct (4 women). *Students:* 50 full-time (6 women), 6 part-time (0 women). In 2014, 13 master's awarded. *Degree requirements:* For master's, thesis; for doctorate, comprehensive exam, thesis/dissertation, qualifying exam. *Entrance requirements:* For master's, minimum GPA of 3.0; B Sc E; for doctorate, minimum GPA of 3.0; M Sc E. Additional exam requirements/recommendations for international students: Required—TOEFL (minimum score 580 paper-based; 80 iBT), IELTS (minimum score 7), TWE (minimum score 4), Michigan English Language Assessment Battery (minimum score 85) or CanTest (minimum score 4.5). *Application deadline:* For fall admission, 3/1 for domestic students. Applications are processed on a rolling basis. Application fee: $50 Canadian dollars. Electronic applications accepted. *Financial support:* In 2014–15, 8 fellowships, 79 research assistantships, 74 teaching assistantships were awarded. *Faculty research:* Acoustics and vibration, biomedical, manufacturing and materials processing, mechatronics and design, nuclear and threat detection, renewable energy systems, robotics and applied mechanics, thermofluids and aerodynamics. *Unit head:* Dr. Andy Simoneau, Director of Graduate Studies, 506-458-7767, Fax: 506-453-5025, E-mail: simoneau@unb.ca. *Application contact:* Paulette Steever, Graduate Secretary, 506-458-7786, Fax: 506-453-5025, E-mail: psteever@unb.ca.
Website: http://go.unb.ca/gradprograms.

University of Pennsylvania, School of Engineering and Applied Science, Department of Mechanical Engineering and Applied Mechanics, Philadelphia, PA 19104. Offers applied mechanics (MSE, PhD); mechanical engineering (MSE, PhD). Part-time programs available. *Faculty:* 34 full-time (7 women), 13 part-time/adjunct (3 women). *Students:* 154 full-time (33 women), 47 part-time (12 women); includes 22 minority (3 Black or African American, non-Hispanic/Latino; 16 Asian, non-Hispanic/Latino; 2 Hispanic/Latino; 1 Two or more races, non-Hispanic/Latino), 117 international. 875 applicants, 21% accepted, 83 enrolled. In 2014, 84 master's, 9 doctorates awarded. *Degree requirements:* For master's, thesis optional; for doctorate, thesis/dissertation. *Entrance requirements:* Additional exam requirements/recommendations for international students: Required—TOEFL. *Application deadline:* For fall admission, 1/2 priority date for domestic students. Applications are processed on a rolling basis. Application fee: $70. Electronic applications accepted. *Financial support:* Fellowships, research assistantships, teaching assistantships, institutionally sponsored loans,

scholarships/grants, traineeships, health care benefits, and unspecified assistantships available. *Faculty research:* Heat transfer, fluid mechanics, energy conversion, solid mechanics, dynamics of mechanisms and robots. *Unit head:* Eduardo D. Glandt, Dean, 215-898-7244, E-mail: seasdean@seas.upenn.edu. *Application contact:* School of Engineering and Applied Science Graduate Admissions, 215-898-4542, E-mail: gradstudies@seas.upenn.edu.
Website: http://www.me.upenn.edu.

University of Southern California, Graduate School, Viterbi School of Engineering, Sonny Astani Department of Civil Engineering, Los Angeles, CA 90089. Offers applied mechanics (MS); civil engineering (MS, PhD); computer-aided engineering (ME, Graduate Certificate); construction management (MCM); engineering technology commercialization (Graduate Certificate); environmental engineering (MS, PhD); environmental quality management (ME); structural design (ME); sustainable cities (Graduate Certificate); transportation systems (MS, Graduate Certificate); water and waste management (MS). Part-time and evening/weekend programs available. Terminal master's awarded for partial completion of doctoral program. *Degree requirements:* For master's, thesis optional; for doctorate, thesis/dissertation. *Entrance requirements:* For master's and doctorate, GRE General Test. Additional exam requirements/recommendations for international students: Recommended—TOEFL. Electronic applications accepted. *Faculty research:* Geotechnical engineering, transportation engineering, structural engineering, construction management, environmental engineering, water resources.

The University of Texas at Austin, Graduate School, Cockrell School of Engineering, Department of Aerospace Engineering and Engineering Mechanics, Program in Engineering Mechanics, Austin, TX 78712-1111. Offers MS, PhD. *Degree requirements:* For doctorate, one foreign language, thesis/dissertation, qualifying exam. *Entrance requirements:* For master's and doctorate, GRE General Test.

University of Wisconsin–Madison, Graduate School, College of Engineering, Department of Engineering Physics, Madison, WI 53706. Offers engineering mechanics (MS, PhD); nuclear engineering and engineering physics (MS, PhD). Part-time programs available. Postbaccalaureate distance learning degree programs offered (minimal on-campus study). *Faculty:* 21 full-time (1 woman), 8 part-time/adjunct (4 women). *Students:* 123 full-time (20 women), 9 part-time (0 women); includes 17 minority (3 Black or African American, non-Hispanic/Latino; 1 American Indian or Alaska Native, non-Hispanic/Latino; 6 Asian, non-Hispanic/Latino; 5 Hispanic/Latino; 2 Two or more races, non-Hispanic/Latino), 25 international. Average age 26. 221 applicants, 47% accepted, 48 enrolled. In 2014, 36 master's, 11 doctorates awarded. Terminal master's awarded for partial completion of doctoral program. *Degree requirements:* For master's, thesis optional; for doctorate, thesis/dissertation. *Entrance requirements:* For master's and doctorate, GRE General Test, minimum GPA of 3.0 in last 60 hours, appropriate bachelor's degree. Additional exam requirements/recommendations for international students: Required—TOEFL (minimum score 600 paper-based). *Application deadline:* For fall admission, 1/1 priority date for domestic and international students. Applications are processed on a rolling basis. Application fee: $56. Electronic applications accepted. *Expenses:* Tuition, state resident: full-time $10,723; part-time $745 per credit. Tuition, nonresident: full-time $24,054; part-time $1578 per credit. *Required fees:* $374 per semester. Tuition and fees vary according to course load, program and reciprocity agreements. *Financial support:* In 2014–15, 74 students received support, including 21 fellowships with full tuition reimbursements available (averaging $25,101 per year), 89 research assistantships with full tuition reimbursements available (averaging $21,224 per year), 16 teaching assistantships with full tuition reimbursements available (averaging $14,326 per year); career-related internships or fieldwork, Federal Work-Study, institutionally sponsored loans, unspecified assistantships, and project assistantships also available. Support available to part-time students. Financial award application deadline: 1/15. *Faculty research:* Fission reactor engineering and safety, plasma physics and fusion technology, plasma processing and ion implantation, nanotechnology, engineering mechanics and

astronautics. *Total annual research expenditures:* $16.3 million. *Unit head:* Dr. Doug Henderson, Chair, 608-263-0391, Fax: 608-263-7451, E-mail: henderson@engr.wisc.edu. *Application contact:* Betsy A. Wood, Graduate Coordinator, 608-263-7038, Fax: 608-263-7451, E-mail: betsy.wood@wisc.edu.
Website: http://www.engr.wisc.edu/ep/.

University of Wisconsin–Milwaukee, Graduate School, College of Engineering and Applied Science, Program in Engineering, Milwaukee, WI 53201-0413. Offers civil engineering (MS); electrical and computer engineering (MS); energy engineering (Certificate); engineering (PhD); engineering management (MS); engineering mechanics (MS); ergonomics (Certificate); industrial and management engineering (MS); manufacturing engineering (MS); materials engineering (MS); mechanical engineering (MS); MUP/MS. Part-time programs available. *Degree requirements:* For master's, comprehensive exam (for some programs), thesis or alternative; for doctorate, comprehensive exam, thesis/dissertation, internship. *Entrance requirements:* For master's, GRE, minimum GPA of 2.75; for doctorate, GRE, minimum GPA of 3.5. Additional exam requirements/recommendations for international students: Required—TOEFL (minimum score 550 paper-based; 79 iBT), IELTS (minimum score 6.5).

Virginia Polytechnic Institute and State University, Graduate School, College of Engineering, Blacksburg, VA 24061. Offers aerospace engineering (ME, MS, PhD); biological systems engineering (ME, MS, PhD); biomedical engineering (MS, PhD); chemical engineering (ME, MS, PhD); civil engineering (ME, MS, PhD); computer engineering (ME, MS, PhD); computer science (MS, PhD); electrical engineering (ME, PhD); engineering education (PhD); engineering mechanics (ME, MS, PhD); environmental engineering (MS); environmental science and engineering (MS); industrial and systems engineering (ME, MS, PhD); materials science and engineering (ME, MS, PhD); mechanical engineering (ME, MS, PhD); mining and minerals engineering (PhD); mining engineering (ME, MS); nuclear engineering (MS, PhD); ocean engineering (MS); systems engineering (ME, MS). *Accreditation:* ABET (one or more programs are accredited). *Faculty:* 356 full-time (60 women), 3 part-time/adjunct (1 woman). *Students:* 1,700 full-time (398 women), 345 part-time (58 women); includes 213 minority (43 Black or African American, non-Hispanic/Latino; 1 American Indian or Alaska Native, non-Hispanic/Latino; 87 Asian, non-Hispanic/Latino; 58 Hispanic/Latino; 1 Native Hawaiian or other Pacific Islander, non-Hispanic/Latino; 23 Two or more races, non-Hispanic/Latino), 1,079 international. Average age 27. 5,228 applicants, 18% accepted, 471 enrolled. In 2014, 438 master's, 211 doctorates awarded. *Degree requirements:* For master's, comprehensive exam (for some programs), thesis (for some programs); for doctorate, comprehensive exam (for some programs), thesis/dissertation (for some programs). *Entrance requirements:* For master's and doctorate, GRE/GMAT (may vary by department). Additional exam requirements/recommendations for international students: Required—TOEFL (minimum score 550 paper-based). *Application deadline:* For fall admission, 8/1 for domestic students, 4/1 for international students; for spring admission, 1/1 for domestic students, 9/1 for international students. Applications are processed on a rolling basis. Application fee: $75. Electronic applications accepted. *Expenses:* Tuition, state resident: full-time $11,656; part-time $647.50 per credit hour. Tuition, nonresident: full-time $23,351; part-time $1297.25 per credit hour. *Required fees:* $2533; $465.75 per semester. Tuition and fees vary according to course load, campus/location and program. *Financial support:* In 2014–15, 148 fellowships with full tuition reimbursements (averaging $8,031 per year), 855 research assistantships with full tuition reimbursements (averaging $22,855 per year), 288 teaching assistantships with full tuition reimbursements (averaging $20,291 per year) were awarded. Financial award application deadline: 3/1; financial award applicants required to submit FAFSA. *Total annual research expenditures:* $90.5 million. *Unit head:* Dr. Richard C. Benson, Dean, 540-231-9752, Fax: 540-231-3031, E-mail: deaneng@vt.edu. *Application contact:* Linda Perkins, Executive Assistant, 540-231-9752, Fax: 540-231-3031, E-mail: lperkins@vt.edu.
Website: http://www.eng.vt.edu/.

Section 18
Ocean Engineering

This section contains a directory of institutions offering graduate work in ocean engineering. Additional information about programs listed in the directory may be obtained by writing directly to the dean of a graduate school or chair of a department at the address given in the directory.

For programs offering related work, see also in this book *Civil and Environmental Engineering* and *Engineering and Applied Sciences.* In the other guides in this series:

Graduate Programs in the Biological/Biomedical Sciences & Health-Related Medical Professions
See *Marine Biology*

Graduate Programs in the Physical Sciences, Mathematics, Agricultural Sciences, the Environment & Natural Resources
See *Environmental Sciences and Management* and *Marine Sciences and Oceanography*

CONTENTS

Program Directory

Ocean Engineering

Florida Atlantic University, College of Engineering and Computer Science, Department of Ocean and Mechanical Engineering, Boca Raton, FL 33431-0991. Offers mechanical engineering (MS, PhD); ocean engineering (MS, PhD). Part-time and evening/weekend programs available. Terminal master's awarded for partial completion of doctoral program. *Degree requirements:* For master's, thesis (for some programs); for doctorate, comprehensive exam, thesis/dissertation, qualifying exam. *Entrance requirements:* For master's and doctorate, GRE General Test, minimum GPA of 3.0. Additional exam requirements/recommendations for international students: Required—TOEFL (minimum score 500 paper-based; 61 iBT), IELTS (minimum score 6). *Expenses:* Tuition, state resident: full-time $7396; part-time $369.82 per credit hour. Tuition, nonresident: full-time $19,392; part-time $1024.81 per credit hour. Tuition and fees vary according to course load. *Faculty research:* Marine materials and corrosion, ocean structures, marine vehicles, acoustics and vibrations, hydrodynamics, coastal engineering.

Florida Institute of Technology, Graduate Programs, College of Engineering, Program in Ocean Engineering, Melbourne, FL 32901-6975. Offers MS, PhD. Part-time programs available. *Students:* 24 full-time (7 women), 6 part-time (2 women), 18 international. Average age 29. 42 applicants, 57% accepted, 9 enrolled. In 2014, 10 master's, 1 doctorate awarded. *Degree requirements:* For master's, comprehensive exam (for some programs), thesis optional, technical paper, thesis or final exam; for doctorate, comprehensive exam, thesis/dissertation, research program and publication. *Entrance requirements:* For master's, GRE General Test, minimum GPA of 3.0, 3 letters of recommendation, resume, transcripts, statement of objectives; for doctorate, GRE General Test, minimum GPA of 3.3, resume, 3 letters of recommendation, statement of objectives, on-campus interview (highly recommended). Additional exam requirements/recommendations for international students: Required—TOEFL (minimum score 550 paper-based; 79 iBT). *Application deadline:* Applications are processed on a rolling basis. Application fee: $0. Electronic applications accepted. *Expenses: Tuition:* Part-time $1179 per credit hour. Tuition and fees vary according to campus/location. *Financial support:* Career-related internships or fieldwork, institutionally sponsored loans, tuition waivers (partial), unspecified assistantships, and tuition remissions available. Support available to part-time students. Financial award application deadline: 3/1; financial award applicants required to submit FAFSA. *Faculty research:* Underwater technology, materials and structures, coastal processes and engineering, marine vehicles and ocean systems, naval architecture. *Unit head:* Dr. Thomas Waite, Department Head, 321-674-8934, Fax: 321-674-7212, E-mail: twaite@fit.edu. *Application contact:* Cheryl A. Brown, Associate Director of Graduate Admission, 321-674-7581, Fax: 321-723-9468, E-mail: cbrown@fit.edu.
Website: http://coe.fit.edu/dmes/.

Massachusetts Institute of Technology, School of Engineering, Department of Mechanical Engineering, Cambridge, MA 02139. Offers manufacturing (M Eng); mechanical engineering (SM, PhD, Sc D, Mech E); naval architecture and marine engineering (SM, PhD, Sc D); naval engineering (Naval E); ocean engineering (SM, PhD, Sc D); oceanographic engineering (SM, PhD, Sc D); SM/MBA. *Faculty:* 70 full-time (8 women). *Students:* 549 full-time (140 women); includes 98 minority (8 Black or African American, non-Hispanic/Latino; 1 American Indian or Alaska Native, non-Hispanic/Latino; 47 Asian, non-Hispanic/Latino; 28 Hispanic/Latino; 14 Two or more races, non-Hispanic/Latino), 252 international. Average age 27. 1,409 applicants, 19% accepted, 200 enrolled. In 2014, 166 master's, 60 doctorates, 9 other advanced degrees awarded. Terminal master's awarded for partial completion of doctoral program. *Degree requirements:* For master's and other advanced degree, thesis; for doctorate, comprehensive exam, thesis/dissertation, a minor program of study in a field different from that of the major. *Entrance requirements:* For master's, doctorate, and other advanced degree, GRE General Test. Additional exam requirements/recommendations for international students: Required—TOEFL (minimum score 577 paper-based; 90 iBT), IELTS (minimum score 7). *Application deadline:* For fall and spring admission, 12/15 for domestic and international students. Application fee: $75. Electronic applications accepted. *Expenses: Tuition:* Full-time $44,720; part-time $699 per unit. *Required fees:* $296. *Financial support:* In 2014–15, 459 students received support, including 102 fellowships (averaging $32,900 per year), 338 research assistantships (averaging $33,600 per year), 50 teaching assistantships (averaging $36,700 per year); Federal Work-Study, institutionally sponsored loans, scholarships/grants, traineeships, health care benefits, and unspecified assistantships also available. Financial award application deadline: 4/15; financial award applicants required to submit FAFSA. *Faculty research:* Mechanics: modeling, experimentation and computation; design, manufacturing, and product development; controls, instrumentation, and robotics; energy science and engineering; ocean science and engineering; bioengineering; micro- and nano-engineering. *Total annual research expenditures:* $64 million. *Unit head:* Gang Chen, Department Head, 617-253-2201, Fax: 617-258-6156, E-mail: mehq@mit.edu. *Application contact:* Graduate Office, 617-253-2291, Fax: 617-258-5802, E-mail: megradoffice@mit.edu.
Website: http://meche.mit.edu/.

Memorial University of Newfoundland, School of Graduate Studies, Faculty of Engineering and Applied Science, St. John's, NL A1C 5S7, Canada. Offers civil engineering (M Eng, PhD); electrical and computer engineering (M Eng, PhD); mechanical engineering (M Eng, PhD); ocean and naval architecture engineering (M Eng, PhD). Part-time programs available. *Degree requirements:* For master's, thesis; for doctorate, comprehensive exam, thesis/dissertation, oral thesis defense. *Entrance requirements:* For master's, 2nd class degree; for doctorate, master's degree in engineering. Electronic applications accepted. *Faculty research:* Engineering analysis, environmental and hydrotechnical studies, manufacturing and robotics, mechanics, structures and materials.

Princeton University, Graduate School, Department of Geosciences, Princeton, NJ 08544-1019. Offers atmospheric and oceanic sciences (PhD); geosciences (PhD); ocean sciences and marine biology (PhD). *Degree requirements:* For doctorate, one foreign language, thesis/dissertation. *Entrance requirements:* For doctorate, GRE General Test. Additional exam requirements/recommendations for international students: Required—TOEFL (minimum score 600 paper-based). Electronic applications accepted. *Faculty research:* Biogeochemistry, climate science, earth history, regional geology and tectonics, solid–earth geophysics.

Stevens Institute of Technology, Graduate School, Charles V. Schaefer Jr. School of Engineering, Department of Civil, Environmental, and Ocean Engineering, Program in Ocean Engineering, Hoboken, NJ 07030. Offers M Eng, PhD. *Degree requirements:* For master's, thesis optional; for doctorate, variable foreign language requirement, thesis/dissertation. *Entrance requirements:* For doctorate, GRE. Additional exam requirements/recommendations for international students: Required—TOEFL. Electronic applications accepted. *Faculty research:* Estuarine oceanography, hydrodynamic and environmental processes, wave/ship interaction.

Texas A&M University, College of Engineering, Zachry Department of Civil Engineering, College Station, TX 77843. Offers civil engineering (M Eng, MS, PhD); ocean engineering (M Eng, MS, PhD). Part-time programs available. *Faculty:* 52. *Students:* 431 full-time (123 women), 58 part-time (15 women); includes 42 minority (5 Black or African American, non-Hispanic/Latino; 2 American Indian or Alaska Native, non-Hispanic/Latino; 15 Asian, non-Hispanic/Latino; 17 Hispanic/Latino; 3 Two or more races, non-Hispanic/Latino), 337 international. Average age 27. 904 applicants, 53% accepted, 176 enrolled. In 2014, 101 master's, 37 doctorates awarded. *Degree requirements:* For master's, thesis (MS); for doctorate, dissertation (PhD), internship (D Eng). *Entrance requirements:* For master's and doctorate, GRE General Test. Additional exam requirements/recommendations for international students: Required—TOEFL. *Application deadline:* Applications are processed on a rolling basis. Application fee: $50 ($90 for international students). Electronic applications accepted. *Expenses:* Tuition, state resident: full-time $4078; part-time $226.55 per credit hour. Tuition, nonresident: full-time $10,594; part-time $577.55 per credit hour. *Required fees:* $2813; $237.70 per credit hour. $278.50 per semester. Tuition and fees vary according to degree level and student level. *Financial support:* In 2014–15, 362 students received support, including 59 fellowships with full and partial tuition reimbursements available (averaging $3,445 per year), 156 research assistantships with full and partial tuition reimbursements available (averaging $6,404 per year), 55 teaching assistantships with full and partial tuition reimbursements available (averaging $4,665 per year); career-related internships or fieldwork, institutionally sponsored loans, scholarships/grants, traineeships, health care benefits, tuition waivers (full and partial), and unspecified assistantships also available. Support available to part-time students. Financial award application deadline: 4/15; financial award applicants required to submit FAFSA. *Unit head:* Dr. Robin Autenrieth, Interim Head, 979-845-2438, E-mail: rautenrieth@civil.tamu.edu. *Application contact:* Laura Byrd, Program Assistant, Graduate Student Services, 979-845-2498, E-mail: lbyrd@civil.tamu.edu.
Website: http://engineering.tamu.edu/civil/.

University of Alaska Anchorage, School of Engineering, Program in Civil Engineering, Anchorage, AK 99508. Offers civil engineering (MCE, MS); coastal, ocean, and port engineering (Certificate). Part-time and evening/weekend programs available. *Degree requirements:* For master's, thesis (for some programs). *Entrance requirements:* For master's, bachelor's degree in engineering. Additional exam requirements/recommendations for international students: Required—TOEFL (minimum score 550 paper-based). *Faculty research:* Structural engineering, engineering education, astronomical observations related to engineering.

University of California, San Diego, Graduate Division, Department of Electrical and Computer Engineering, La Jolla, CA 92093. Offers applied ocean science (MS, PhD); applied physics (MS, PhD); communication theory and systems (MS, PhD); computer engineering (MS, PhD); electronic circuits and systems (MS, PhD); intelligent systems, robotics and control (MS, PhD); medical devices and systems (MS, PhD); nanoscale devices and systems (MS, PhD); photonics (MS, PhD); signal and image processing (MS, PhD). *Students:* 435 full-time (81 women), 43 part-time (8 women); includes 78 minority (2 Black or African American, non-Hispanic/Latino; 1 American Indian or Alaska Native, non-Hispanic/Latino; 69 Asian, non-Hispanic/Latino; 6 Hispanic/Latino), 306 international. 2,710 applicants, 18% accepted, 177 enrolled. In 2014, 109 master's, 50 doctorates awarded. *Degree requirements:* For master's, thesis or written exam; for doctorate, comprehensive exam, thesis/dissertation. *Entrance requirements:* For master's and doctorate, GRE General Test, minimum GPA of 3.0. Additional exam requirements/recommendations for international students: Required—TOEFL (minimum score 550 paper-based; 80 iBT), IELTS. *Application deadline:* For fall admission, 12/15 for domestic students. Application fee: $90 ($110 for international students). Electronic applications accepted. *Expenses:* Tuition, state resident: full-time $11,220; part-time $5610 per quarter. Tuition, nonresident: full-time $26,322; part-time $13,161 per quarter. *Required fees:* $570 per quarter. Tuition and fees vary according to program. *Financial support:* Fellowships, research assistantships, teaching assistantships, scholarships/grants, and unspecified assistantships available. Financial award applicants required to submit FAFSA. *Faculty research:* Applied ocean science; applied physics; communication theory and systems; computer engineering; electronic circuits and systems; intelligent systems, robotics and control; medical devices and systems; nanoscale devices and systems; photonics; signal and image processing. *Unit head:* Truong Nguyen, Chair, 858-822-5554, E-mail: nguyent@ece.ucsd.edu. *Application contact:* Shana Slebioda, Graduate Coordinator, 858-822-2513, E-mail: ecegradapps@ece.ucsd.edu.
Website: http://ece.ucsd.edu/.

University of California, San Diego, Graduate Division, Department of Mechanical and Aerospace Engineering, Program in Applied Ocean Science, La Jolla, CA 92093. Offers MS, PhD. *Students:* 3 full-time (2 women), 1 (woman) part-time; includes 1 minority (Hispanic/Latino), 1 international. 7 applicants, 57% accepted. In 2014, 1 master's awarded. *Degree requirements:* For master's, comprehensive exam or thesis; for doctorate, comprehensive exam, thesis/dissertation. *Entrance requirements:* For master's and doctorate, GRE General Test, minimum GPA of 3.0. Additional exam requirements/recommendations for international students: Required—TOEFL (minimum score 550 paper-based; 80 iBT), IELTS (minimum score 7). *Application deadline:* For fall admission, 12/15 for domestic students, 1/2 for international students. Application fee: $90 ($110 for international students). Electronic applications accepted. *Expenses:* Tuition, state resident: full-time $11,220; part-time $5610 per quarter. Tuition, nonresident: full-time $26,322; part-time $13,161 per quarter. *Required fees:* $570 per quarter. Tuition and fees vary according to program. *Financial support:* Fellowships, research assistantships, teaching assistantships, scholarships/grants, and unspecified assistantships available. Financial award application deadline: 1/2; financial award applicants required to submit FAFSA. *Faculty research:* Water quality in the coastal ocean and subsurface resources; internal waves, gravity currents, wake flows; ocean process modeling. *Unit head:* Vitali Nesterenko, Chair, 858-534-0113, E-mail: mae-chair-l@ucsd.edu. *Application contact:* Linda McKamey, Graduate Coordinator, 858-534-4065, E-mail: mae-gradadm-l@ucsd.edu.
Website: http://maeweb.ucsd.edu/.

University of Delaware, College of Earth, Ocean, and Environment, School of Marine Science and Policy, Newark, DE 19716. Offers marine policy (MMP); marine studies (MS, PhD), including marine biosciences, oceanography, physical ocean science and engineering; oceanography (PhD).

University of Delaware, College of Engineering, Department of Civil and Environmental Engineering, Newark, DE 19716. Offers environmental engineering (MAS, MCE, PhD); geotechnical engineering (MAS, MCE, PhD); ocean engineering (MAS, MCE, PhD); structural engineering (MAS, MCE, PhD); transportation engineering (MAS, MCE, PhD); water resource engineering (MAS, MCE, PhD). Part-time programs available. Terminal master's awarded for partial completion of doctoral program. *Degree requirements:* For master's, thesis; for doctorate, thesis/dissertation. *Entrance requirements:* For master's and doctorate, GRE General Test. Additional exam requirements/recommendations for international students: Required—TOEFL. Electronic applications accepted. *Faculty research:* Structural engineering and mechanics; transportation engineering; ocean engineering; soil mechanics and foundation; water resources and environmental engineering.

University of Florida, Graduate School, College of Engineering, Department of Civil and Coastal Engineering, Gainesville, FL 32611. Offers civil engineering (ME, MS, PhD), including civil engineering; coastal and oceanographic engineering (ME, MS, PhD). Part-time programs available. Postbaccalaureate distance learning degree programs offered (no on-campus study). *Faculty:* 44 full-time (5 women), 22 part-time/adjunct (3 women). *Students:* 140 full-time (27 women), 43 part-time (11 women); includes 26 minority (7 Black or African American, non-Hispanic/Latino; 1 American Indian or Alaska Native, non-Hispanic/Latino; 5 Asian, non-Hispanic/Latino; 13 Hispanic/Latino), 87 international. 418 applicants, 41% accepted, 54 enrolled. In 2014, 145 master's, 17 doctorates awarded. Terminal master's awarded for partial completion of doctoral program. *Degree requirements:* For master's, thesis (for some programs); for doctorate, comprehensive exam, thesis/dissertation. *Entrance requirements:* For master's and doctorate, minimum GPA of 3.0. Additional exam requirements/recommendations for international students: Required—TOEFL (minimum score 550 paper-based; 80 iBT), IELTS (minimum score 6). *Application deadline:* For fall admission, 8/1 priority date for domestic students, 1/31 for international students; for winter admission, 9/30 for international students; for spring admission, 12/1 for domestic students, 1/31 for international students. Applications are processed on a rolling basis. Application fee: $30. Electronic applications accepted. *Financial support:* Unspecified assistantships available. Financial award application deadline: 1/31; financial award applicants required to submit FAFSA. *Faculty research:* Traffic congestion mitigation, wind mitigation, sustainable infrastructure materials, improved sensors for in situ measurements, storm surge modeling. *Unit head:* Kirk Hatfield, PhD, Director, Engineering School of Sustainable Infrastructure and Environment, 352-392-9537 Ext. 1400, Fax: 352-392-3394, E-mail: director@essie.ufl.edu. *Application contact:* Ariel Drescher, Coordinator, Graduate Programs, 352-392-9537 Ext. 1435, Fax: 352-392-3394, E-mail: ariel.drescher@essie.ufl.edu.
Website: http://www.essie.ufl.edu/departments/civil_and_coastal_engineering/cce_grad_student_info/.

University of Hawaii at Manoa, Graduate Division, School of Ocean and Earth Science and Technology, Department of Ocean and Resources Engineering, Honolulu, HI 96822. Offers MS, PhD. *Accreditation:* ABET (one or more programs are accredited). Part-time programs available. *Degree requirements:* For master's, thesis optional, exams; for doctorate, comprehensive exam, thesis/dissertation, exams. *Entrance requirements:* For master's and doctorate, GRE General Test. Additional exam requirements/recommendations for international students: Required—TOEFL (minimum score 560 paper-based; 83 iBT), IELTS (minimum score 5). *Faculty research:* Coastal and harbor engineering, near shore environmental ocean engineering, marine structures/naval architecture.

University of Michigan, College of Engineering, Department of Naval Architecture and Marine Engineering, Ann Arbor, MI 48109. Offers MS, MSE, PhD, Mar Eng, Nav Arch, MBA/MSE. Part-time programs available. *Students:* 79 full-time (12 women), 5 part-time (1 woman). 138 applicants, 43% accepted, 36 enrolled. In 2014, 43 master's, 12 doctorates awarded. Terminal master's awarded for partial completion of doctoral program. *Degree requirements:* For master's, thesis (for some programs); for doctorate, comprehensive exam, thesis/dissertation, oral defense of dissertation, written and oral preliminary exams; for other advanced degree, comprehensive exam, thesis, oral defense of thesis. *Entrance requirements:* For doctorate, GRE General Test, master's degree; for other advanced degree, GRE General Test. Additional exam requirements/recommendations for international students: Required—TOEFL (minimum score 560 paper-based). *Application deadline:* Applications are processed on a rolling basis. Electronic applications accepted. *Financial support:* Fellowships, research assistantships, teaching assistantships, career-related internships or fieldwork, Federal Work-Study, institutionally sponsored loans, scholarships/grants, and unspecified assistantships available. *Faculty research:* System and structural reliability, design and analysis of offshore structures and vehicles, marine systems design, remote sensing of ship wakes and sea surfaces, marine hydrodynamics, nonlinear seakeeping analysis. *Total annual research expenditures:* $12.2 million. *Unit head:* Dr. Steven Ceccio, Department Chair, 734-936-7636, Fax: 734-936-8820, E-mail: ceccio@umich.edu. *Application contact:* Nathalie Fiveland, Graduate Program Coordinator, 734-936-0566, Fax: 734-936-8820, E-mail: fiveland@umich.edu.
Website: http://name.engin.umich.edu/.

University of New Hampshire, Graduate School, College of Engineering and Physical Sciences, Program in Ocean Engineering, Durham, NH 03824. Offers ocean engineering (MS, PhD); ocean mapping (MS). *Students:* 14 full-time (5 women), 5 part-time (1 woman); includes 1 minority (Hispanic/Latino), 10 international. Average age 29. 35 applicants, 60% accepted, 8 enrolled. In 2014, 3 master's, 1 doctorate, 6 other advanced degrees awarded. *Degree requirements:* For master's, thesis. *Entrance requirements:* Additional exam requirements/recommendations for international students: Required—TOEFL (minimum score 550 paper-based; 80 iBT). *Application deadline:* For fall admission, 4/1 priority date for domestic students; for spring admission, 12/1 for domestic students. Applications are processed on a rolling basis. Application fee: $65. Electronic applications accepted. *Expenses:* Tuition, state resident: full-time $13,500; part-time $750 per credit hour. Tuition, nonresident: full-time $26,460; part-time $1110 per credit hour. *Required fees:* $1788; $447 per semester. *Financial support:* In 2014-15, 13 students received support, including 11 research assistantships, 1 teaching assistantship; fellowships, Federal Work-Study, scholarships/grants, and tuition waivers (full and partial) also available. Support available to part-time students. Financial award application deadline: 2/15. *Unit head:* Dr. Kenneth Baldwin, Chairperson, 603-862-1898. *Application contact:* Abby Pagan-Allis, Administrative Assistant, 603-862-3433, E-mail: ocean.engineering@unh.edu.
Website: http://www.unh.edu/oe/.

University of Rhode Island, Graduate School, College of Engineering, Department of Ocean Engineering, Narragansett, RI 02882. Offers MS, PhD. Part-time programs

available. *Faculty:* 10 full-time (2 women), 1 part-time/adjunct (0 women). *Students:* 23 full-time (5 women), 10 part-time (2 women), 7 international. In 2014, 18 master's, 2 doctorates awarded. *Degree requirements:* For master's, comprehensive exam (for some programs), thesis optional; for doctorate, comprehensive exam, thesis/dissertation. *Entrance requirements:* For master's and doctorate, 2 letters of recommendation. Additional exam requirements/recommendations for international students: Required—TOEFL (minimum score 550 paper-based). *Application deadline:* For fall admission, 7/15 for domestic students, 2/1 for international students; for spring admission, 11/15 for domestic students, 7/15 for international students. Application fee: $65. Electronic applications accepted. *Expenses:* Tuition, state resident: full-time $11,532; part-time $641 per credit. Tuition, nonresident: full-time $23,606; part-time $1311 per credit. *Required fees:* $1442; $39 per credit. $35 per semester. One-time fee: $155. *Financial support:* In 2014-15, 2 research assistantships with full and partial tuition reimbursements (averaging $7,922 per year), 2 teaching assistantships with full tuition reimbursements (averaging $7,998 per year) were awarded. Financial award application deadline: 2/1; financial award applicants required to submit FAFSA. *Faculty research:* Tele-presence technology for high bandwidth ship-to-shore link, wave-induced sediment transport, tsunami impact, geohazards, acoustical oceanography, underwater vehicle mechanical and control system design, deep sea drilling. *Total annual research expenditures:* $696,953. *Unit head:* Dr. Christopher H. Baxter, Chairman, 401-874-6575, Fax: 401-874-6837, E-mail: baxter@oce.uri.edu. *Application contact:* Graduate Admission, 401-874-2872, E-mail: gradadm@etal.uri.edu.
Website: http://www.oce.uri.edu/.

Virginia Polytechnic Institute and State University, Graduate School, College of Engineering, Blacksburg, VA 24061. Offers aerospace engineering (ME, MS, PhD); biological systems engineering (ME, MS, PhD); biomedical engineering (MS, PhD); chemical engineering (ME, MS, PhD); civil engineering (ME, MS, PhD); computer engineering (ME, MS, PhD); computer science (MS, PhD); electrical engineering (ME, PhD); engineering education (PhD); engineering mechanics (ME, MS, PhD); environmental engineering (MS); environmental science and engineering (MS); industrial and systems engineering (ME, MS, PhD); materials science and engineering (ME, MS, PhD); mechanical engineering (ME, MS, PhD); mining and minerals engineering (PhD); mining engineering (ME, MS); nuclear engineering (MS, PhD); ocean engineering (MS); systems engineering (ME, MS). *Accreditation:* ABET (one or more programs are accredited). *Faculty:* 356 full-time (60 women), 3 part-time/adjunct (1 woman). *Students:* 1,700 full-time (398 women), 345 part-time (58 women); includes 213 minority (43 Black or African American, non-Hispanic/Latino; 1 American Indian or Alaska Native, non-Hispanic/Latino; 87 Asian, non-Hispanic/Latino; 58 Hispanic/Latino; 1 Native Hawaiian or other Pacific Islander, non-Hispanic/Latino; 23 Two or more races, non-Hispanic/Latino), 1,079 international. Average age 27. 5,228 applicants, 18% accepted, 471 enrolled. In 2014, 438 master's, 211 doctorates awarded. *Degree requirements:* For master's, comprehensive exam (for some programs), thesis (for some programs); for doctorate, comprehensive exam (for some programs), thesis/dissertation (for some programs). *Entrance requirements:* For master's and doctorate, GRE/GMAT (may vary by department). Additional exam requirements/recommendations for international students: Required—TOEFL (minimum score 550 paper-based). *Application deadline:* For fall admission, 8/1 for domestic students, 4/1 for international students; for spring admission, 1/1 for domestic students, 9/1 for international students. Applications are processed on a rolling basis. Application fee: $75. Electronic applications accepted. *Expenses:* Tuition, state resident: full-time $11,656; part-time $647.50 per credit hour. Tuition, nonresident: full-time $23,351; part-time $1297.25 per credit hour. *Required fees:* $2533; $465.75 per semester. Tuition and fees vary according to course load, campus/location and program. *Financial support:* In 2014-15, 148 fellowships with full tuition reimbursements (averaging $8,031 per year), 855 research assistantships with full tuition reimbursements (averaging $22,855 per year), 288 teaching assistantships with full tuition reimbursements (averaging $20,291 per year) were awarded. Financial award application deadline: 3/1; financial award applicants required to submit FAFSA. *Total annual research expenditures:* $90.5 million. *Unit head:* Dr. Richard C. Benson, Dean, 540-231-9752, Fax: 540-231-3031, E-mail: deaneng@vt.edu. *Application contact:* Linda Perkins, Executive Assistant, 540-231-9752, Fax: 540-231-3031, E-mail: lperkins@vt.edu.
Website: http://www.eng.vt.edu/.

Virginia Polytechnic Institute and State University, VT Online, Blacksburg, VA 24061. Offers advanced transportation systems (Certificate); aerospace engineering (MS); agricultural and life sciences (MSLFS); business information systems (Graduate Certificate); career and technical education (MS); civil engineering (MS); computer engineering (M Eng, MS); decision support systems (Graduate Certificate); eLearning leadership (MA); electrical engineering (M Eng, MS); engineering administration (MEA); environmental engineering (Certificate); environmental politics and policy (Graduate Certificate); environmental sciences and engineering (MS); foundations of political analysis (Graduate Certificate); health product risk management (Graduate Certificate); industrial and systems engineering (MS); information policy and society (Graduate Certificate); information security (Graduate Certificate); information technology (MIT); instructional technology (MA); integrative STEM education (MA Ed); liberal arts (Graduate Certificate); life sciences: health product risk management (MS); natural resources (MNR, Graduate Certificate); networking (Graduate Certificate); nonprofit and nongovernmental organization management (Graduate Certificate); ocean engineering (MS); political science (MA); security studies (Graduate Certificate); software development (Graduate Certificate). *Expenses:* Tuition, state resident: full-time $11,656; part-time $647.50 per credit hour. Tuition, nonresident: full-time $23,351; part-time $1297.25 per credit hour. *Required fees:* $2533; $465.75 per semester. Tuition and fees vary according to course load, campus/location and program.

Woods Hole Oceanographic Institution, MIT/WHOI Joint Program in Oceanography/Applied Ocean Science and Engineering, Woods Hole, MA 02543-1541. Offers applied ocean science and engineering (PhD); biological oceanography (PhD); chemical oceanography (PhD); marine geology and geophysics (PhD); physical oceanography (PhD). Program offered jointly with Massachusetts Institute of Technology. *Degree requirements:* For doctorate, thesis/dissertation. *Entrance requirements:* For doctorate, GRE General Test, GRE Subject Test. Additional exam requirements/recommendations for international students: Required—TOEFL. Electronic applications accepted.

Section 19
Paper and Textile Engineering

This section contains a directory of institutions offering graduate work in paper and textile engineering. Additional information about programs listed in the directory may be obtained by writing directly to the dean of a graduate school or chair of a department at the address given in the directory.

For programs offering related work, see also in this book *Engineering and Applied Sciences* and *Materials Sciences and Engineering*. In another guide in this series:

Graduate Programs in the Humanities, Arts & Social Sciences
See *Family and Consumer Sciences (Clothing and Textiles)*

CONTENTS

Program Directories

Paper and Pulp Engineering

North Carolina State University, Graduate School, College of Natural Resources, Department of Wood and Paper Science, Raleigh, NC 27695. Offers MS, MWPS, PhD. Postbaccalaureate distance learning degree programs offered. *Degree requirements:* For master's, thesis optional; for doctorate, thesis/dissertation. *Entrance requirements:* For master's and doctorate, GRE General Test. Additional exam requirements/recommendations for international students: Required—TOEFL. Electronic applications accepted. *Faculty research:* Pulping, bleaching, recycling, papermaking, drying of wood.

State University of New York College of Environmental Science and Forestry, Department of Paper and Bioprocess Engineering, Syracuse, NY 13210-2779. Offers biomaterials engineering (MS, PhD); bioprocess engineering (MPS, MS, PhD); bioprocessing (Advanced Certificate); paper science and engineering (MPS, MS, PhD); sustainable engineering management (MPS). *Degree requirements:* For master's, thesis; for doctorate, comprehensive exam, thesis/dissertation; for Advanced Certificate, 15 credit hours. *Entrance requirements:* For master's and doctorate, GRE General Test, minimum GPA of 3.0; for Advanced Certificate, BS, calculus plus science major. Additional exam requirements/recommendations for international students: Required—TOEFL (minimum score 550 paper-based; 80 iBT), IELTS (minimum score 6). *Faculty research:* Sustainable products and processes, biorefinery, pulping and papermaking, nanocellulose, bioconversions, process control and modeling.

The University of Manchester, School of Materials, Manchester, United Kingdom. Offers advanced aerospace materials engineering (M Sc); advanced metallic systems (PhD); biomedical materials (M Phil, M Sc, PhD); ceramics and glass (M Phil, M Sc, PhD); composite materials (M Sc, PhD); corrosion and protection (M Phil, M Sc, PhD); materials (M Phil, PhD); metallic materials (M Phil, M Sc, PhD); nanostructural materials (M Phil, M Sc, PhD); paper science (M Phil, M Sc, PhD); polymer science and engineering (M Phil, M Sc, PhD); technical textiles (M Sc); textile design, fashion and management (M Phil, M Sc, PhD); textile science and technology (M Phil, M Sc, PhD); textiles (M Phil, PhD); textiles and fashion (M Ent).

University of Minnesota, Twin Cities Campus, Graduate School, College of Food, Agricultural and Natural Resource Sciences, Program in Natural Resources Science and Management, St. Paul, MN 55108. Offers assessment, monitoring, and geospatial analysis (MS, PhD); economics, policy, management, and society (MS, PhD); forest hydrology and watershed management (MS, PhD); forest products (MS, PhD); forests: biology, ecology, conservation, and management (MS, PhD); natural resources science and management (MS, PhD); paper science and engineering (MS, PhD); recreation resources, tourism, and environmental education (MS, PhD); wildlife ecology and management (MS, PhD). Part-time programs available. *Faculty:* 65 full-time, 55 part-time/adjunct. *Students:* 65 full-time (30 women), 37 part-time (12 women); includes 3 minority (1 Black or African American, non-Hispanic/Latino; 1 American Indian or Alaska Native, non-Hispanic/Latino; 1 Asian, non-Hispanic/Latino), 11 international. 90 applicants, 44% accepted, 26 enrolled. In 2014, 17 master's, 5 doctorates awarded. Terminal master's awarded for partial completion of doctoral program. *Degree requirements:* For master's, comprehensive exam, thesis; for doctorate, comprehensive exam, thesis/dissertation. *Entrance requirements:* For master's and doctorate, GRE General Test. Additional exam requirements/recommendations for international students: Required—TOEFL (minimum score 550 paper-based; 79 iBT), IELTS (minimum score 6.5). *Application deadline:* For fall admission, 12/16 priority date for domestic and international students; for spring admission, 10/15 for domestic and international students. Applications are processed on a rolling basis. Application fee: $75 ($95 for international students). Electronic applications accepted. *Financial support:* In 2014–15, fellowships with full tuition reimbursements (averaging $40,000 per year), research assistantships with full tuition reimbursements (averaging $40,000 per year), teaching assistantships with full tuition reimbursements (averaging $40,000 per year) were awarded; scholarships/grants, health care benefits, tuition waivers (full and partial), and unspecified assistantships also available. *Faculty research:* Paper science, forestry, recreation resource management, wildlife ecology, environmental education, hydrology, conservation, tourism, economics, policy, watershed management, GIS, forest products. *Unit head:* Dr. Michael Kilgore, Director of Graduate Studies, 612-624-6298, E-mail: mkilgore@umn.edu. *Application contact:* Jennifer Welsh, Program Coordinator, 612-624-7683, Fax: 612-625-5212, E-mail: jwelsh@umn.edu. Website: http://www.nrsm.umn.edu.

Western Michigan University, Graduate College, College of Engineering and Applied Sciences, Department of Chemical and Paper Engineering, Kalamazoo, MI 49008. Offers MS, MSE, PhD. *Degree requirements:* For master's, thesis optional; for doctorate, one foreign language, comprehensive exam, thesis/dissertation. *Application deadline:* For fall admission, 2/15 for domestic students. *Financial support:* Application deadline: 2/15. *Application contact:* Admissions and Orientation, 269-387-2000, Fax: 269-387-2096.

Textile Sciences and Engineering

Cornell University, Graduate School, Graduate Fields of Human Ecology, Field of Fiber Science and Apparel Design, Ithaca, NY 14853. Offers apparel design (MA, MPS); fiber science (MS, PhD); polymer science (MS, PhD); textile science (MS, PhD). *Degree requirements:* For master's, thesis (MA, MS), project paper (MPS); for doctorate, comprehensive exam, thesis/dissertation. *Entrance requirements:* For master's, GRE General Test, 2 letters of recommendation, portfolio (for functional apparel design); for doctorate, GRE General Test, 2 letters of recommendation. Additional exam requirements/recommendations for international students: Required—TOEFL (minimum score 600 paper-based; 77 iBT). Electronic applications accepted. *Faculty research:* Apparel design, consumption, mass customization, 3-D body scanning.

North Carolina State University, Graduate School, College of Textiles, Department of Textile and Apparel Technology and Management, Raleigh, NC 27695. Offers MS, MT. *Degree requirements:* For master's, thesis optional. *Entrance requirements:* For master's, GRE. Electronic applications accepted. *Faculty research:* Textile and apparel products and processes, management systems, nonwovens, process simulation, structure design and analysis.

North Carolina State University, Graduate School, College of Textiles, Department of Textile Engineering, Chemistry, and Science, Program in Textile Chemistry, Raleigh, NC 27695. Offers MS. *Degree requirements:* For master's, thesis optional. *Entrance requirements:* For master's, GRE. Electronic applications accepted. *Faculty research:* Color science, polymer science, dye chemistry, fiber formation, wet processing technology.

North Carolina State University, Graduate School, College of Textiles, Department of Textile Engineering, Chemistry, and Science, Program in Textile Engineering, Raleigh, NC 27695. Offers MS. *Degree requirements:* For master's, thesis optional. *Entrance requirements:* For master's, GRE. Electronic applications accepted. *Faculty research:* Electro-mechanical design, inventory and supply chain control, textile composites, biomedical textile appliations, pollution prevention.

North Carolina State University, Graduate School, College of Textiles, Program in Fiber and Polymer Science, Raleigh, NC 27695. Offers PhD. *Degree requirements:* For doctorate, one foreign language, thesis/dissertation, cumulative exams. *Entrance requirements:* For doctorate, GRE. Electronic applications accepted. *Faculty research:* Polymer science, fiber mechanics, medical textiles, nanotechnology.

Philadelphia University, School of Engineering and Textiles, PhD Program in Textile Engineering and Sciences, Philadelphia, PA 19144. Offers PhD.

Philadelphia University, School of Engineering and Textiles, Program in Textile Engineering, Philadelphia, PA 19144. Offers MS. Part-time programs available. *Degree requirements:* For master's, thesis. *Entrance requirements:* For master's, GRE, minimum GPA of 2.8. Additional exam requirements/recommendations for international students: Required—TOEFL (minimum score 550 paper-based; 79 iBT). Electronic applications accepted.

University of Massachusetts Dartmouth, Graduate School, College of Engineering, Department of Bioengineering, North Dartmouth, MA 02747-2300. Offers textile chemistry (MS); textile technology (MS). Part-time programs available. *Faculty:* 6 full-time (2 women). In 2014, 1 master's awarded. *Degree requirements:* For master's, thesis. *Entrance requirements:* Additional exam requirements/recommendations for international students: Required—TOEFL (minimum score 533 paper-based; 72 iBT). *Application deadline:* For fall admission, 2/15 for domestic students, 1/15 for international students; for spring admission, 11/15 for domestic students, 10/15 for international students. Applications are processed on a rolling basis. Application fee: $60. Electronic applications accepted. *Expenses:* Tuition, state resident: full-time $2071; part-time $86.29 per credit. Tuition, nonresident: full-time $8099; part-time $337.46 per credit. *Required fees:* $16,520; $712.33 per credit. Tuition and fees vary according to course load and reciprocity agreements. *Financial support:* Federal Work-Study available. Support available to part-time students. Financial award application deadline: 3/1; financial award applicants required to submit FAFSA. *Faculty research:* Regenerative and bioactive materials, bioreactors and waste conversion processes, tissue engineering applications, biocompatibility of hydrogels and synthetic polymers. *Total annual research expenditures:* $3,000. *Unit head:* Dr. Qinguo Fan, Graduate Program Director, 508-999-9147, Fax: 508-999-9139, E-mail: qfan@umassd.edu. *Application contact:* Steven Briggs, Director of Marketing and Recruitment for Graduate Studies, 508-999-8604, Fax: 508-999-8183, E-mail: graduate@umassd.edu. Website: http://www.umassd.edu/engineering/mtx/graduate/msinmaterialsandtextiles/.

The University of Texas at Austin, Graduate School, College of Natural Sciences, School of Human Ecology, Program in Textile and Apparel Technology, Austin, TX 78712-1111. Offers MS.

Section 20
Telecommunications

This section contains a directory of institutions offering graduate work in tele-communications. Additional information about programs listed in the directory may be obtained by writing directly to the dean of a graduate school or chair of a department at the address given in the directory.

For programs offering related work, see also in this book *Computer Science and Information Technology* and *Engineering and Applied Sciences*. In the other guides in this series:

Graduate Programs in the Humanities, Arts & Social Sciences
See *Communication and Media*

Graduate Programs in Business, Education, Information Studies, Law & Social Work
See *Business Administration and Management*

CONTENTS

Program Directories

Telecommunications

Ball State University, Graduate School, College of Communication, Information, and Media, Department of Telecommunications, Muncie, IN 47306-1099. Offers digital storytelling (MA). *Faculty:* 3 full-time (1 woman). *Students:* 12 full-time (3 women), 15 part-time (3 women); includes 2 minority (both Black or African American, non-Hispanic/Latino), 3 international. Average age 25. 17 applicants, 65% accepted, 10 enrolled. In 2014, 4 master's awarded. Application fee: $50. *Financial support:* In 2014–15, 12 students received support, including 10 research assistantships with partial tuition reimbursements available (averaging $7,959 per year), 2 teaching assistantships with partial tuition reimbursements available (averaging $5,817 per year); unspecified assistantships also available. *Unit head:* Timothy Pollard, Chairperson, 765-285-1480, Fax: 765-285-9278, E-mail: tpollard@bsu.edu. *Application contact:* Dr. Robert Morris, Associate Provost for Research and Dean of the Graduate School, 765-285-4723, Fax: 765-285-1328, E-mail: rmorris@bsu.edu.
Website: http://www.bsu.edu/tcom/.

Boston University, Metropolitan College, Department of Computer Science, Boston, MA 02215. Offers computer information systems (MS), including computer networks, database management and business intelligence, health informatics, IT project management, security, Web application development; computer networks (Certificate); digital forensics (Certificate); health informatics (Certificate); information technology project management (Certificate); software engineering in health care systems (Certificate); telecommunications (MS), including security. Part-time and evening/weekend programs available. Postbaccalaureate distance learning degree programs offered (no on-campus study). *Faculty:* 13 full-time (3 women), 43 part-time/adjunct (3 women). *Students:* 76 full-time (22 women), 768 part-time (188 women); includes 251 minority (68 Black or African American, non-Hispanic/Latino; 1 American Indian or Alaska Native, non-Hispanic/Latino; 117 Asian, non-Hispanic/Latino; 57 Hispanic/Latino; 2 Native Hawaiian or other Pacific Islander, non-Hispanic/Latino; 6 Two or more races, non-Hispanic/Latino), 130 international. Average age 34. 463 applicants, 79% accepted, 248 enrolled. In 2014, 222 master's, 25 other advanced degrees awarded. *Degree requirements:* For master's, thesis optional. *Entrance requirements:* For master's and Certificate, official transcripts from regionally-accredited bachelor's degree program, 3 letters of recommendation, professional resume, personal statement. Additional exam requirements/recommendations for international students: Required—TOEFL (minimum score 84 iBT), IELTS. *Application deadline:* For fall admission, 6/1 priority date for international students; for spring admission, 10/1 priority date for international students. Applications are processed on a rolling basis. Application fee: $80. Electronic applications accepted. *Expenses:* Expenses: $800 per credit part-time; student services fees: $60 per semester; technology fee of $60 per credit (for online courses). *Financial support:* In 2014–15, 11 research assistantships (averaging $8,400 per year) were awarded; unspecified assistantships also available. Support available to part-time students. Financial award applicants required to submit FAFSA. *Faculty research:* Medical informatics, Web technologies, telecom and networks, security and forensics, software engineering, programming languages, multimedia and artificial intelligence (AI), information systems and IT project management. *Unit head:* Dr. Anatoly Temkin, Chairman, 617-353-2566, Fax: 617-353-2367, E-mail: csinfo@bu.edu. *Application contact:* Lesley Moreau, Academic Program Coordinator, 617-353-2566, Fax: 617-353-2367, E-mail: metcs@bu.edu.
Website: http://www.bu.edu/csmet/.

California Miramar University, Program in Telecommunications Management, San Diego, CA 92126. Offers MST.

Claremont Graduate University, Graduate Programs, Center for Information Systems and Technology, Claremont, CA 91711-6160. Offers electronic commerce (MS, PhD); health information management (MS); information systems (Certificate); knowledge management (MS, PhD); systems development (MS, PhD); telecommunications and networking (MS, PhD); MBA/MS. Part-time programs available. *Faculty:* 5 full-time (0 women), 2 part-time/adjunct (0 women). *Students:* 60 full-time (21 women), 65 part-time (22 women); includes 26 minority (5 Black or African American, non-Hispanic/Latino; 1 American Indian or Alaska Native, non-Hispanic/Latino; 15 Asian, non-Hispanic/Latino; 4 Hispanic/Latino; 1 Two or more races, non-Hispanic/Latino), 65 international. Average age 36. In 2014, 17 master's, 1 doctorate awarded. *Degree requirements:* For doctorate, comprehensive exam, thesis/dissertation, portfolio. *Entrance requirements:* For master's and doctorate, GMAT, GRE General Test. Additional exam requirements/recommendations for international students: Required—TOEFL (minimum score 550 paper-based; 80 iBT). *Application deadline:* For fall admission, 2/1 priority date for domestic and international students. Applications are processed on a rolling basis. Application fee: $80. Electronic applications accepted. *Expenses:* Tuition: Full-time $41,784; part-time $1741 per credit. *Required fees:* $600; $300 per semester. *Financial support:* Fellowships, research assistantships, teaching assistantships, Federal Work-Study, institutionally sponsored loans, and scholarships/grants available. Support available to part-time students. Financial award application deadline: 2/15; financial award applicants required to submit FAFSA. *Faculty research:* Man-machine interaction, organizational aspects of computing, implementation of information systems, information systems practice. *Unit head:* Tom Horan, Dean, 909-607-9302, Fax: 909-621-8564, E-mail: tom.horan@cgu.edu. *Application contact:* Leah Litwack, Administrative Assistant, 909-621-8209, E-mail: leah.litwack@cgu.edu.
Website: http://www.cgu.edu/pages/153.asp.

Drexel University, College of Engineering, Department of Electrical and Computer Engineering, Program in Telecommunications Engineering, Philadelphia, PA 19104-2875. Offers MSEE. *Entrance requirements:* For master's, BS in electrical engineering or physics, minimum GPA of 3.0. Additional exam requirements/recommendations for international students: Required—TOEFL. Electronic applications accepted.

Fairfield University, School of Engineering, Fairfield, CT 06824. Offers automated manufacturing (CAS); database management (CAS); electrical and computer engineering (MS); information security (CAS); management of technology (MS); mechanical engineering (MS); network technology (CAS); software engineering (MS); Web application development (CAS). Part-time and evening/weekend programs available. *Faculty:* 4 full-time (1 woman), 18 part-time/adjunct (5 women). *Students:* 193 full-time (50 women), 69 part-time (11 women); includes 20 minority (4 Black or African American, non-Hispanic/Latino; 6 Asian, non-Hispanic/Latino; 10 Hispanic/Latino), 199 international. Average age 27. 516 applicants, 64% accepted, 124 enrolled. In 2014, 38 master's awarded. *Degree requirements:* For master's, thesis, capstone course. *Entrance requirements:* For master's, interview, minimum GPA of 2.8, resume, 2 recommendations. Additional exam requirements/recommendations for international students: Required—TOEFL (minimum score 550 paper-based; 80 iBT) or IELTS (minimum score 6.5). *Application deadline:* For fall admission, 5/15 for international students; for spring admission, 10/15 for international students. Applications are processed on a rolling basis. Application fee: $60. Electronic applications accepted. *Expenses:* Expenses: $750 per credit hour. *Financial support:* In 2014–15, 30 students received support. Scholarships/grants and unspecified assistantships available. Financial award applicants required to submit FAFSA. *Faculty research:* Ocean dynamics modeling, thermo fluids, Web/mobile software applications, microwaves/electromagnetics, micro/nano manufacturing. *Unit head:* Dr. Bruce Berdanier, Dean, 203-254-4147, Fax: 203-254-4013, E-mail: bberdanier@fairfield.edu. *Application contact:* Marianne Gumpper, Director of Graduate and Continuing Studies Admission, 203-254-4184, Fax: 203-254-4073, E-mail: gradadmis@fairfield.edu.
Website: http://www.fairfield.edu/academics/schoolscollegescenters/schoolofengineering/graduateprograms/.

Florida International University, College of Engineering and Computing, School of Computing and Information Sciences, Program in Telecommunications and Networking, Miami, FL 33175. Offers MS. Part-time and evening/weekend programs available. *Entrance requirements:* For master's, minimum undergraduate GPA of 3.0 in upper-level coursework. Additional exam requirements/recommendations for international students: Required—TOEFL (minimum score 550 paper-based; 80 iBT). Electronic applications accepted. *Faculty research:* Wireless networks and mobile computing, high-performance routers and switches, network-centric middleware components, distributed systems, networked databases.

Franklin Pierce University, Graduate and Professional Studies, Rindge, NH 03461-0060. Offers curriculum and instruction (M Ed); emerging network technologies (Graduate Certificate); energy and sustainability studies (MBA); health administration (MBA, Graduate Certificate); human resource management (MBA, Graduate Certificate); information technology (MBA); information technology management (MS); leadership (MBA); nursing (MS); physical therapy (DPT); physician assistant studies (MPAS); special education (M Ed); sports management (MBA). *Accreditation:* APTA. Part-time programs available. Postbaccalaureate distance learning degree programs offered (no on-campus study). *Faculty:* 18 full-time (11 women), 96 part-time/adjunct (57 women). *Students:* 357 full-time (207 women), 185 part-time (123 women); includes 31 minority (9 Black or African American, non-Hispanic/Latino; 4 American Indian or Alaska Native, non-Hispanic/Latino; 17 Asian, non-Hispanic/Latino; 1 Native Hawaiian or other Pacific Islander, non-Hispanic/Latino), 19 international. Average age 38. In 2014, 118 master's, 66 doctorates awarded. *Degree requirements:* For master's, concentrated original research projects; student teaching; fieldwork and/or internship; leadership project; PRAXIS I and II (for M Ed); for doctorate, concentrated original research projects, clinical fieldwork and/or internship, leadership project. *Entrance requirements:* For master's, minimum GPA of 2.5, 3 letters of recommendation; competencies in accounting, economics, statistics, and computer skills through life experience or undergraduate coursework (for MBA); certification/e-portfolio, minimum C grade in all education courses (for M Ed); license to practice as RN (for MS in nursing); for doctorate, GRE, BA/BS, 3 letters of recommendation, personal mission statement, interview, writing sample, minimum cumulative GPA of 2.8, master's degree (for DA); 80 hours of observation/work in PT settings, completion of anatomy, chemistry, physics, and statistics, minimum GPA of 3.0 (for DPT). Additional exam requirements/recommendations for international students: Required—TOEFL (minimum score 550 paper-based; 61 iBT). *Application deadline:* Applications are processed on a rolling basis. Application fee: $0. Electronic applications accepted. *Expenses: Tuition:* Part-time $645 per credit. *Required fees:* $100 per term. One-time fee: $200 part-time. Tuition and fees vary according to degree level and program. *Financial support:* In 2014–15, 125 students received support, including 32 teaching assistantships with full and partial tuition reimbursements available (averaging $8,000 per year); career-related internships or fieldwork and unspecified assistantships also available. Support available to part-time students. Financial award applicants required to submit FAFSA. *Faculty research:* Evidence-based practice in sports physical therapy, human resource management in economic crisis, leadership in nursing, innovation in sports facility management, differentiated learning and understanding by design. *Unit head:* Dr. Maria Altobello, Interim Dean of Graduate and Professional Studies, 603-647-3530, Fax: 603-229-4580, E-mail: altobellom@franklinpierce.edu. *Application contact:* Graduate Studies, 800-437-0048, Fax: 603-626-4815, E-mail: cgps@franklinpierce.edu.
Website: http://www.franklinpierce.edu/academics/gradstudies/index.htm.

George Mason University, Volgenau School of Engineering, Department of Electrical and Computer Engineering, Fairfax, VA 22030. Offers computer engineering (MS); computer forensics (MS); electrical and computer engineering (PhD, Certificate); electrical engineering (MS); telecommunications (MS). MS programs offered jointly with Old Dominion University, University of Virginia, Virginia Commonwealth University, and Virginia Polytechnic Institute and State University. *Faculty:* 31 full-time (4 women), 41 part-time/adjunct (5 women). *Students:* 258 full-time (77 women), 275 part-time (51 women); includes 113 minority (33 Black or African American, non-Hispanic/Latino; 54 Asian, non-Hispanic/Latino; 17 Hispanic/Latino; 1 Native Hawaiian or other Pacific Islander, non-Hispanic/Latino; 8 Two or more races, non-Hispanic/Latino), 237 international. Average age 30. 554 applicants, 69% accepted, 158 enrolled. In 2014, 153 master's, 4 doctorates, 24 other advanced degrees awarded. *Degree requirements:* For master's, thesis optional; for doctorate, comprehensive exam, thesis or scholarly paper. *Entrance requirements:* For master's, GRE, personal goals statement; 2 official copies of transcripts; self-evaluation form; 3 letters of recommendation; resume; official bank statement; photocopy of passport; proof of financial support; for doctorate, GRE (waived for GMU electrical and computer engineering master's graduates with minimum GPA of 3.0), personal goals statement; 2 official copies of transcripts; self-evaluation form; 3 letters of recommendation; resume; official bank statement; photocopy of passport; proof of financial support. Additional exam requirements/recommendations for international students: Required—TOEFL (minimum score 575 paper-based; 80 iBT), IELTS (minimum score 6.5), PTE. *Application deadline:* For fall admission, 1/15 priority date for domestic students; for spring admission, 8/15 priority date for domestic students. Applications are processed on a rolling basis. Application fee: $65 ($80 for international students). Electronic applications accepted. *Expenses:* Expenses: Contact institution. *Financial support:* In 2014–15, 68 students received support, including 33 research assistantships with full and partial tuition reimbursements available (averaging $18,359 per year), 38 teaching assistantships with full and partial tuition reimbursements available (averaging $11,521 per year); career-related internships or fieldwork, Federal Work-Study, scholarships/grants, unspecified assistantships, and health care benefits (for full-time research or teaching assistantship recipients) also available. Support available to part-time students. Financial award application deadline: 3/1; financial award applicants required to submit FAFSA. *Faculty research:* Communication networks, signal processing, system failure diagnosis, multiprocessors, material processing using microwave energy. *Total annual research expenditures:* $2.3 million. *Unit head:* Andre Manitius, Chair, 703-993-1570, Fax: 703-993-1601, E-mail: amanitiu@gmu.edu. *Application contact:* Jammie Chang, Academic Program Coordinator, 703-993-1570, Fax: 703-993-1601, E-mail: jchangn@gmu.edu.
Website: http://ece.gmu.edu/.

The George Washington University, School of Engineering and Applied Science, Department of Electrical and Computer Engineering, Washington, DC 20052. Offers electrical engineering (MS, PhD); telecommunication and computers (MS). Part-time and evening/weekend programs available. *Faculty:* 28 full-time (2 women), 18 part-time/adjunct (0 women). *Students:* 126 full-time (31 women), 68 part-time (14 women); includes 19 minority (6 Black or African American, non-Hispanic/Latino; 8 Asian, non-Hispanic/Latino; 5 Hispanic/Latino), 148 international. Average age 27. 536 applicants, 55% accepted, 62 enrolled. In 2014, 98 master's, 7 doctorates, 2 other advanced degrees awarded. *Degree requirements:* For master's, thesis optional; for doctorate, comprehensive exam, thesis/dissertation, dissertation defense, qualifying exam. *Entrance requirements:* For master's, appropriate bachelor's degree, minimum GPA of 3.0; for doctorate, GRE (if highest earned degree is BS), appropriate bachelor's or master's degree, minimum GPA of 3.3; for other advanced degree, appropriate master's degree, minimum GPA of 3.0. Additional exam requirements/recommendations for international students: Required—TOEFL or The George Washington University English as a Foreign Language Test. *Application deadline:* For fall admission, 3/1 priority date for domestic students; for spring admission, 10/1 for domestic students. Applications are processed on a rolling basis. Application fee: $75. *Financial support:* In 2014–15, 39 students received support. Fellowships with tuition reimbursements available, research assistantships, teaching assistantships with tuition reimbursements available, career-related internships or fieldwork, and institutionally sponsored loans available. Financial award application deadline: 3/1; financial award applicants required to submit FAFSA. *Faculty research:* Computer graphics, multimedia systems. *Unit head:* Mona Zaghloul, Chair, 202-994-9380, E-mail: zaghloul@gwu.edu. *Application contact:* Adina Lav, Marketing, Recruiting and Admissions, 202-994-5827, Fax: 202-994-0909, E-mail: engineering@gwu.edu.
Website: http://www.ece.gwu.edu/.

Illinois Institute of Technology, Graduate College, Armour College of Engineering, Department of Electrical and Computer Engineering, Chicago, IL 60616. Offers biomedical imaging and signals (MAS); computer engineering (MS, PhD); electrical engineering (MS, PhD); electricity markets (MAS); network engineering (MAS); power engineering (MAS); telecommunications and software engineering (MAS); vlsi and microelectronics (MAS); MS/MS. Part-time and evening/weekend programs available. Postbaccalaureate distance learning degree programs offered (minimal on-campus study). *Faculty:* 27 full-time (4 women), 3 part-time/adjunct (0 women). *Students:* 439 full-time (84 women), 90 part-time (11 women); includes 13 minority (11 Asian, non-Hispanic/Latino; 2 Hispanic/Latino), 476 international. Average age 26. 2,461 applicants, 39% accepted, 206 enrolled. In 2014, 155 master's, 7 doctorates awarded. Terminal master's awarded for partial completion of doctoral program. *Degree requirements:* For master's, comprehensive exam (for some programs), thesis (for some programs); for doctorate, comprehensive exam, thesis/dissertation. *Entrance requirements:* For master's and doctorate, GRE General Test (minimum score 1100 Quantitative and Verbal, 3.5 Analytical Writing), minimum undergraduate GPA of 3.0. Additional exam requirements/recommendations for international students: Required—TOEFL (minimum score 550 paper-based; 80 iBT); Recommended—IELTS (minimum score 5.5). *Application deadline:* For fall admission, 5/1 for domestic and international students; for spring admission, 10/15 for domestic and international students. Applications are processed on a rolling basis. Application fee: $50. Electronic applications accepted. *Expenses: Tuition:* Full-time $22,500; part-time $1250 per credit hour. *Required fees:* $30 per course. $260 per semester. One-time fee: $235. Tuition and fees vary according to course load and program. *Financial support:* Fellowships with full and partial tuition reimbursements, research assistantships with full and partial tuition reimbursements, teaching assistantships with full and partial tuition reimbursements, career-related internships or fieldwork, Federal Work-Study, institutionally sponsored loans, scholarships/grants, health care benefits, tuition waivers (full), and unspecified assistantships available. Support available to part-time students. Financial award applicants required to submit FAFSA. *Faculty research:* Communication systems, wireless networks, computer systems, computer networks, wireless security, cloud computing and micro-electronics; electromagnetics and electronics; power and control systems; signal and image processing. *Unit head:* Dr. Ashfaq Khokhar, Chair & Professor of Electrical and Computer Engineering, 312-567-5780, Fax: 312-567-8976, E-mail: ashfaq@iit.edu. *Application contact:* Rishab Malhotra, Director, Graduate Admission, 866-472-3448, Fax: 312-567-3138, E-mail: inquiry.grad@iit.edu.
Website: http://www.ece.iit.edu.

Illinois Institute of Technology, Graduate College, College of Science, Department of Computer Science, Chicago, IL 60616. Offers business (MCS); computational intelligence (MCS); computer networking and communications (MCS); computer science (MCS, MS, PhD); cyber-physical systems (MCS); data analytics (MCS); data science (MAS); database systems (MCS); distributed and cloud computing (MCS); education (MCS); finance (MCS); information security and assurance (MCS); software engineering (MCS); telecommunications and software engineering (MAS); MS/MAS. Part-time and evening/weekend programs available. Postbaccalaureate distance learning degree programs offered (no on-campus study). *Faculty:* 29 full-time (5 women), 8 part-time/adjunct (1 woman). *Students:* 432 full-time (108 women), 117 part-time (27 women); includes 11 minority (3 Black or African American, non-Hispanic/Latino; 7 Asian, non-Hispanic/Latino; 1 Two or more races, non-Hispanic/Latino), 495 international. Average age 26. 2,573 applicants, 42% accepted, 244 enrolled. In 2014, 164 master's, 2 doctorates awarded. Terminal master's awarded for partial completion of doctoral program. *Degree requirements:* For master's, thesis optional; for doctorate, comprehensive exam, thesis/dissertation. *Entrance requirements:* For master's, MS GRE General Test (minimum scores: 298 Quantitative and Verbal, 3.0 Analytical Writing); MAS GRE General Test (minimum scores: 292 Quantitative and Verbal, 2.5 Analytical Writing), minimum undergraduate GPA of 3.0; for doctorate, GRE General Test (minimum scores: 304 Quantitative and Verbal, 3.5 Analytical Writing), minimum undergraduate GPA of 3.0. Additional exam requirements/recommendations for international students: Required—TOEFL (minimum score 523 paper-based; 70 iBT). *Application deadline:* For fall admission, 5/1 for domestic and international students; for spring admission, 10/15 for domestic and international students. Applications are processed on a rolling basis. Application fee: $50. Electronic applications accepted. *Expenses: Tuition:* Full-time $22,500; part-time $1250 per credit hour. *Required fees:* $30 per course. $260 per semester. One-time fee: $235. Tuition and fees vary according to course load and program. *Financial support:* Fellowships with partial tuition reimbursements, research assistantships with full and partial tuition reimbursements, teaching assistantships with full and partial tuition reimbursements, career-related internships or fieldwork, Federal Work-Study, institutionally sponsored loans, scholarships/grants, traineeships, health care benefits, tuition waivers (partial), and unspecified assistantships available. Support available to part-time students. Financial award applicants required to submit FAFSA. *Faculty research:* Parallel and distributed processing, high-performance computing, computational linguistics, information retrieval, data mining, grid computing. *Unit head:* Dr. Eunice Santos, Chair/Professor, 312-567-5150, E-mail: eunice.santos@iit.edu. *Application contact:* Rishab Malhotra, Director, Graduate Admission, 866-472-3448, Fax: 312-567-3138, E-mail: inquiry.grad@iit.edu.
Website: http://www.iit.edu/csl/cs/.

Indiana University Bloomington, University Graduate School, College of Arts and Sciences, The Media School, Department of Telecommunications, Program in Telecommunications, Bloomington, IN 47405-7000. Offers MA, MS. *Faculty:* 17 full-time (6 women). *Students:* 20 full-time (12 women), 1 part-time (0 women); includes 1 minority (Hispanic/Latino), 7 international. Average age 28. 37 applicants, 43% accepted, 9 enrolled. In 2014, 13 master's awarded. *Degree requirements:* For master's, comprehensive exam (for some programs), thesis (for some programs). *Entrance requirements:* For master's, GRE General Test, minimum undergraduate GPA of 3.0, 3 letters of recommendation. Additional exam requirements/recommendations for international students: Required—TOEFL (minimum score 600 paper-based; 100 iBT). *Application deadline:* For fall admission, 1/15 priority date for domestic students, 12/1 priority date for international students. Applications are processed on a rolling basis. Application fee: $55 ($65 for international students). Electronic applications accepted. *Financial support:* Application deadline: 1/15. *Faculty research:* Media management, media psychology, media processes and effects, telecommunications law and policy, economics of media and virtual worlds, media design and production (video games, virtual worlds, documentary, multi-media art). *Application contact:* Tamera Theodore, Graduate Program Secretary, 812-855-2017, E-mail: ttheodor@indiana.edu.
Website: http://www.indiana.edu/~telecom/index.shtml.

Instituto Tecnologico de Santo Domingo, Graduate School, Area of Engineering, Santo Domingo, Dominican Republic. Offers construction administration (MS, Certificate); data telecommunications (M Eng, MS, Certificate); industrial engineering (M Eng, Certificate); industrial management (M Mgmt); information technology (Certificate); maintenance engineering (M Eng); occupational hazard prevention (M Mgmt); production management (Certificate); quantitative methods (Certificate); sanitary and environmental engineering (M Eng); structural engineering (M Eng); systems engineering and electronic data processing (Certificate); transportation (Certificate).

Johns Hopkins University, Engineering Program for Professionals, Part-time Program in Computer Science, Baltimore, MD 21218-2699. Offers bioinformatics (MS); computer science (MS, Post-Master's Certificate); telecommunications and networking (MS). Part-time and evening/weekend programs available. Postbaccalaureate distance learning degree programs offered (no on-campus study). Electronic applications accepted.

Michigan State University, The Graduate School, College of Communication Arts and Sciences, Department of Telecommunication, Information Studies, and Media, East Lansing, MI 48824. Offers digital media arts and technology (MA); information and telecommunication management (MA); information, policy and society (MA); serious game design (MA). *Entrance requirements:* Additional exam requirements/recommendations for international students: Required—TOEFL. Electronic applications accepted.

National University, Academic Affairs, School of Engineering and Computing, La Jolla, CA 92037-1011. Offers computer science (MS), including advanced computing, database engineering, software engineering; cyber security and information assurance (MS), including computer forensics, ethical hacking and penetration testing, health information assurance, information assurance and security; data analytics (MS); engineering management (MS), including enterprise architecture, project management, systems engineering, technology management; environmental engineering (MS); homeland security and emergency management (MS); management information systems (MS); project management (Certificate); sustainability management (MS); wireless communications (MS). Part-time and evening/weekend programs available. Postbaccalaureate distance learning degree programs offered (no on-campus study). *Faculty:* 24 full-time (5 women), 21 part-time/adjunct (5 women). *Students:* 275 full-time (72 women), 86 part-time (24 women); includes 147 minority (41 Black or African American, non-Hispanic/Latino; 48 Asian, non-Hispanic/Latino; 37 Hispanic/Latino; 7 Native Hawaiian or other Pacific Islander, non-Hispanic/Latino; 14 Two or more races, non-Hispanic/Latino), 95 international. Average age 33. In 2014, 281 master's awarded. *Degree requirements:* For master's, thesis (for some programs). *Entrance requirements:* For master's, interview, minimum GPA of 2.5. Additional exam requirements/recommendations for international students: Required—TOEFL (minimum score 550 paper-based; 79 iBT), IELTS (minimum score 6). *Application deadline:* Applications are processed on a rolling basis. Application fee: $60 ($65 for international students). Electronic applications accepted. *Expenses: Tuition:* Full-time $14,184; part-time $1773 per course. *Financial support:* Career-related internships or fieldwork, institutionally sponsored loans, scholarships/grants, and tuition waivers (partial) available. Support available to part-time students. Financial award application deadline: 6/30; financial award applicants required to submit FAFSA. *Faculty research:* Educational technology, scholarships in science. *Unit head:* School of Engineering and Computing, 800-628-8648, E-mail: soec@nu.edu. *Application contact:* Frank Rojas, Vice President for Enrollment Services, 800-628-8648, E-mail: advisor@nu.edu.
Website: http://www.nu.edu/OurPrograms/SchoolOfEngineeringAndTechnology.html.

New Jersey Institute of Technology, Newark College of Engineering, Newark, NJ 07102. Offers biomedical engineering (MS, PhD); chemical engineering (MS, PhD); computer engineering (MS, PhD); electrical engineering (MS, PhD); engineering management (MS); healthcare systems management (MS); industrial engineering (MS, PhD); Internet engineering (MS); manufacturing engineering (MS); mechanical engineering (MS, PhD); occupational safety and health engineering (MS); pharmaceutical bioprocessing (MS); pharmaceutical engineering (MS); pharmaceutical systems management (MS); power and energy systems (MS); telecommunications (MS); transportation (MS, PhD). Part-time and evening/weekend programs available. Terminal master's awarded for partial completion of doctoral program. *Degree requirements:* For master's, thesis optional; for doctorate, thesis/dissertation. *Entrance requirements:* For master's, GRE General Test; for doctorate, GRE General Test, minimum graduate GPA of 3.5. Additional exam requirements/recommendations for international students: Required—TOEFL (minimum score 550 paper-based; 79 iBT). Electronic applications accepted.

Northeastern University, College of Engineering, Boston, MA 02115-5096. Offers bioengineering (PhD); chemical engineering (MS, PhD); civil engineering (MS, PhD); computer engineering (PhD); computer systems engineering (MS); electrical and computer engineering (MS); electrical and engineering leadership (MS); electrical engineering (PhD); energy systems (MS); engineering leadership (Certificate); engineering management (MRTP); industrial engineering (MS, PhD); information assurance (PhD); information systems (MS); interdisciplinary (PhD); mechanical engineering (MS, PhD); operations research (MS); telecommunication systems management (MS). Part-time programs available. *Expenses:* Contact institution.

Ohio University, Graduate College, Scripps College of Communication, J. Warren McClure School of Information and Telecommunication Systems, Athens, OH 45701-2979. Offers MCTP. Part-time programs available. *Degree requirements:* For master's, comprehensive exam (for some programs), thesis (for some programs). *Entrance requirements:* For master's, GRE or GMAT, minimum cumulative GPA of 3.0. Additional exam requirements/recommendations for international students: Required—TOEFL (minimum score 550 paper-based; 80 iBT) or IELTS (minimum score 6.5). Electronic applications accepted. *Faculty research:* Voice and data networks, with special emphasis on the interaction of technology and policy issues in the successful design, deployment, and operation of complex networks and information systems.

Pace University, Seidenberg School of Computer Science and Information Systems, New York, NY 10038. Offers computer science (MS); computing science (DPS); information systems (MS); Internet technology (MS); large computing systems (Certificate); network administration (Certificate); security and information assurance (Certificate); software development and engineering (MS, Certificate); telecommunications (Certificate); telecommunications systems and networks (MS). Part-time and evening/weekend programs available. *Faculty:* 26 full-time (7 women), 7 part-time/adjunct (2 women). *Students:* 167 full-time (57 women), 324 part-time (90 women); includes 182 minority (83 Black or African American, non-Hispanic/Latino; 1 American Indian or Alaska Native, non-Hispanic/Latino; 46 Asian, non-Hispanic/Latino; 47 Hispanic/Latino; 5 Two or more races, non-Hispanic/Latino), 132 international. Average age 35. 441 applicants, 84% accepted, 157 enrolled. In 2014, 115 master's, 7 doctorates, 9 other advanced degrees awarded. *Degree requirements:* For master's, thesis or alternative, capstone course; for doctorate, comprehensive exam (for some programs), thesis/dissertation. *Entrance requirements:* For master's, GRE General Test. Additional exam requirements/recommendations for international students: Required—TOEFL. *Application deadline:* For fall admission, 8/1 priority date for domestic students, 6/1 for international students; for spring admission, 12/1 for domestic students, 10/1 for international students. Applications are processed on a rolling basis. Application fee: $70. Electronic applications accepted. *Expenses:* Expenses: Contact institution. *Financial support:* Research assistantships and career-related internships or fieldwork available. Support available to part-time students. Financial award applicants required to submit FAFSA. *Faculty research:* Computer security and forensics, cybersecurity, telehealth, mobile computing, distributed teams, robotics. *Total annual research expenditures:* $685,824. *Unit head:* Dr. Amar Gupta, Dean, Seidenberg School of Computer Science and Information Systems, 914-773-3750, Fax: 914-773-3533, E-mail: agupta@pace.edu. *Application contact:* Susan Ford-Goldschein, Director of Graduate Admissions, 914-422-4283, Fax: 914-422-4287, E-mail: gradwp@pace.edu.
Website: http://www.pace.edu/seidenberg.

Roosevelt University, Graduate Division, College of Arts and Sciences, Department of Computer Science and Telecommunications, Program in Telecommunications, Chicago, IL 60605. Offers MST. Part-time and evening/weekend programs available. *Entrance requirements:* For master's, GRE. *Faculty research:* Coding theory, mathematical models, network design, simulation models.

Saint Mary's University of Minnesota, Schools of Graduate and Professional Programs, Graduate School of Business and Technology, Information Technology Management Program, Winona, MN 55987-1399. Offers MS.

Southern Methodist University, Bobby B. Lyle School of Engineering, Department of Electrical Engineering, Dallas, TX 75275-0338. Offers applied science (MS); electrical engineering (MSEE, PhD); telecommunications (MS). Part-time and evening/weekend programs available. Postbaccalaureate distance learning degree programs offered (no on-campus study). Terminal master's awarded for partial completion of doctoral program. *Degree requirements:* For master's, thesis optional; for doctorate, thesis/dissertation, oral and written qualifying exams, oral final exam. *Entrance requirements:* For master's, GRE General Test, minimum GPA of 3.0 in last 2 years; bachelor's degree in engineering, mathematics, or sciences; for doctorate, preliminary counseling exam, minimum GPA of 3.0, bachelor's degree in related field. Additional exam requirements/recommendations for international students: Required—TOEFL. Electronic applications accepted. *Faculty research:* Mobile communications, optical communications, digital signal processing, photonics.

State University of New York Polytechnic Institute, Program in Telecommunications, Utica, NY 13504-3050. Offers MS. Part-time and evening/weekend programs available. *Degree requirements:* For master's, thesis or project. *Entrance requirements:* For master's, GRE General Test, minimum GPA of 3.0, one letter of reference, bachelor's degree in telecommunications or a related field, resume. Additional exam requirements/recommendations for international students: Required—TOEFL (minimum score 550 paper-based; 79 iBT), IELTS (minimum score 6.5). Electronic applications accepted. *Faculty research:* Cloud security, virtualization, wireless networks, cyber physical system.

Stevens Institute of Technology, Graduate School, Wesley J. Howe School of Technology Management, Program in Telecommunications Management, Hoboken, NJ 07030. Offers business (MS); global innovation management (MS); management of wireless networks (MS); online security, technology and business (MS); project management (MS); technical management (MS); telecommunications management (PhD, Certificate). *Degree requirements:* For master's, thesis optional; for doctorate, thesis/dissertation. *Entrance requirements:* For master's and doctorate, GMAT, GRE General Test. Additional exam requirements/recommendations for international students: Required—TOEFL. Electronic applications accepted.

Stratford University, School of Graduate Studies, Falls Church, VA 22043. Offers accounting (MS); business administration (IMBA, MBA); enterprise business management (MS); entrepreneurial management (MS); information assurance (MS); information systems (MS); software engineering (MS); telecommunications (MS). Part-time and evening/weekend programs available. Postbaccalaureate distance learning degree programs offered (no on-campus study). *Degree requirements:* For master's, comprehensive exam, capstone project. *Entrance requirements:* For master's, GRE or GMAT, baccalaureate degree. Additional exam requirements/recommendations for international students: Required—TOEFL (minimum score 79 iBT) or IELTS (6.5). Electronic applications accepted.

Syracuse University, School of Information Studies, Program in Telecommunications and Network Management, Syracuse, NY 13244. Offers MS, MS/CAS. Part-time and evening/weekend programs available. Postbaccalaureate distance learning degree programs offered (minimal on-campus study). *Students:* 32 full-time (5 women), 15 part-time (2 women); includes 6 minority (2 Black or African American, non-Hispanic/Latino; 2 Asian, non-Hispanic/Latino; 2 Hispanic/Latino), 25 international. Average age 29. 103 applicants, 65% accepted, 14 enrolled. In 2014, 27 master's awarded. *Degree requirements:* For master's, internship or research project. *Entrance requirements:* For master's, GRE General Test. Additional exam requirements/recommendations for international students: Required—TOEFL (minimum score 100 iBT). *Application deadline:* For fall admission, 1/1 priority date for domestic and international students; for spring admission, 10/15 priority date for domestic and international students. Applications are processed on a rolling basis. Application fee: $75. Electronic applications accepted. *Expenses: Tuition:* Part-time $1341 per credit. *Required fees:* $1341 per credit. *Financial support:* Fellowships with full tuition reimbursements, research assistantships with partial tuition reimbursements, teaching assistantships with partial tuition reimbursements, career-related internships or fieldwork, and Federal Work-Study available. Financial award application deadline: 1/1. *Faculty research:* Multimedia, information resources management. *Unit head:* Carsten Oesterlund,, Program Director Carsten Oesterlund, Program Director, 309 Hinds Hall, 315-443-2911,, 315-443-2911, Fax: 315-443-6886, E-mail: igrad@syr.edu. *Application contact:* Susan Corieri, Director of Enrollment Management, 315-443-2575, E-mail: ischool@syr.edu.
Website: http://ischool.syr.edu/.

Universidad del Turabo, Graduate Programs, School of Engineering, Program in Telecommunication and Network Administration, Gurabo, PR 00778-3030. Offers MS.

Université du Québec, Institut National de la Recherche Scientifique, Graduate Programs, Research Center–Energy Materials Telecommunications, Varennes, QC J3X 1S2, Canada. Offers energy and materials science (M Sc, PhD); telecommunications (M Sc, PhD). Part-time programs available. *Faculty:* 39 full-time. *Students:* 177 full-time (50 women), 7 part-time (1 woman), 123 international. Average age 30. 51 applicants, 84% accepted, 33 enrolled. In 2014, 16 master's, 16 doctorates awarded. *Degree requirements:* For master's, thesis (for some programs); for doctorate, thesis/dissertation. *Entrance requirements:* For master's, appropriate bachelor's degree, proficiency in French; for doctorate, appropriate master's degree, proficiency in French. *Application deadline:* For fall admission, 3/30 for domestic and international students; for winter admission, 11/1 for domestic and international students; for spring admission, 3/1 for domestic and international students. Application fee: $45. Electronic applications accepted. *Financial support:* In 2014–15, fellowships (averaging $16,500 per year) were awarded; research assistantships also available. *Faculty research:* New energy sources, plasmas, telecommunications, advanced materials ultrafast photonics. *Unit head:* Federico Rosei, Director, 450-228-6905, E-mail: rosei@emt.inrs.ca. *Application contact:* Sylvie Richard, Registrar, 418-654-2518, Fax: 418-654-3858, E-mail: sylvie.richard@adm.inrs.ca.
Website: http://www.emt.inrs.ca/emt.

University of Alberta, Faculty of Graduate Studies and Research, Department of Electrical and Computer Engineering, Edmonton, AB T6G 2E1, Canada. Offers communications (M Eng, M Sc, PhD); computer engineering (M Eng, M Sc, PhD); electromagnetics (M Eng, M Sc, PhD); nanotechnology and microdevices (M Eng, M Sc, PhD); power/power electronics (M Eng, M Sc, PhD); systems (M Eng, M Sc, PhD). Terminal master's awarded for partial completion of doctoral program. *Degree requirements:* For master's, thesis; for doctorate, thesis/dissertation. *Entrance requirements:* Additional exam requirements/recommendations for international students: Required—TOEFL. Electronic applications accepted. *Faculty research:* Controls, communications, microelectronics, electromagnetics.

University of Arkansas, Graduate School, College of Engineering, Department of Electrical Engineering, Fayetteville, AR 72701-1201. Offers electrical engineering (MSEE, PhD); telecommunications engineering (MS Tc E). *Degree requirements:* For master's, thesis optional; for doctorate, one foreign language, thesis/dissertation. *Entrance requirements:* For master's and doctorate, GRE General Test. Electronic applications accepted.

University of California, San Diego, Graduate Division, Department of Electrical and Computer Engineering, La Jolla, CA 92093. Offers applied ocean science (MS, PhD); applied physics (MS, PhD); communication theory and systems (MS, PhD); computer engineering (MS, PhD); electronic circuits and systems (MS, PhD); intelligent systems, robotics and control (MS, PhD); medical devices and systems (MS, PhD); nanoscale devices and systems (MS, PhD); photonics (MS, PhD); signal and image processing (MS, PhD). *Students:* 435 full-time (81 women), 43 part-time (8 women); includes 78 minority (2 Black or African American, non-Hispanic/Latino; 1 American Indian or Alaska Native, non-Hispanic/Latino; 69 Asian, non-Hispanic/Latino; 6 Hispanic/Latino), 306 international. 2,710 applicants, 18% accepted, 177 enrolled. In 2014, 109 master's, 50 doctorates awarded. *Degree requirements:* For master's, thesis or written exam; for doctorate, comprehensive exam, thesis/dissertation. *Entrance requirements:* For master's and doctorate, GRE General Test, minimum GPA of 3.0. Additional exam requirements/recommendations for international students: Required—TOEFL (minimum score 550 paper-based; 80 iBT), IELTS. *Application deadline:* For fall admission, 12/15 for domestic students. Application fee: $90 ($110 for international students). Electronic applications accepted. *Expenses:* Tuition, state resident: full-time $11,220; part-time $5610 per quarter. Tuition, nonresident: full-time $26,322; part-time $13,161 per quarter. *Required fees:* $570 per quarter. Tuition and fees vary according to program. *Financial support:* Fellowships, research assistantships, teaching assistantships, scholarships/grants, and unspecified assistantships available. Financial award applicants required to submit FAFSA. *Faculty research:* Applied ocean science; applied physics; communication theory and systems; computer engineering; electronic circuits and systems; intelligent systems, robotics and control; medical devices and systems; nanoscale devices and systems; photonics; signal and image processing. *Unit head:* Truong Nguyen, Chair, 858-822-5554, E-mail: nguyent@ece.ucsd.edu. *Application contact:* Shana Slebioda, Graduate Coordinator, 858-822-2513, E-mail: ecegradapps@ece.ucsd.edu.
Website: http://ece.ucsd.edu/.

University of California, San Diego, Graduate Division, Program in Wireless Embedded Systems, La Jolla, CA 92093. Offers MAS. Part-time programs available. *Students:* 53 part-time (6 women); includes 23 minority (2 Black or African American, non-Hispanic/Latino; 16 Asian, non-Hispanic/Latino; 5 Hispanic/Latino), 15 international. 46 applicants, 70% accepted, 23 enrolled. In 2014, 20 master's awarded. *Degree requirements:* For master's, capstone project. *Entrance requirements:* For master's, GRE General Test (only if applicant possesses fewer than 2 years' work experience), 3 letters of recommendation, statement of purpose, resume or curriculum vitae. Additional exam requirements/recommendations for international students: Required—TOEFL (minimum score 550 paper-based; 80 iBT), IELTS (minimum score 7). *Application deadline:* For fall admission, 4/30 priority date for domestic students. Application fee: $90 ($110 for international students). Electronic applications accepted. *Expenses:* Expenses: Contact institution. *Financial support:* Applicants required to submit FAFSA. *Unit head:* George Papen, Chair, 858-822-1728, E-mail: gpapen@ucsd.edu. *Application contact:* Charmaine Samahin-Manns, Graduate Coordinator, 858-534-6547, E-mail: wes-mas@ucsd.edu.
Website: http://maseng.ucsd.edu/wes.

University of California, Santa Cruz, Division of Graduate Studies, Jack Baskin School of Engineering, Program in Computer Engineering, Santa Cruz, CA 95064. Offers computer engineering (MS, PhD); network engineering (MS). Part-time programs available. Terminal master's awarded for partial completion of doctoral program. *Degree requirements:* For master's, thesis; for doctorate, comprehensive exam, thesis/dissertation, oral qualifying exams. *Entrance requirements:* For master's and doctorate, GRE General Test, GRE Subject Test. Additional exam requirements/recommendations for international students: Required—TOEFL (minimum score 570 paper-based; 89 iBT); Recommended—IELTS (minimum score 8). Electronic applications accepted. *Faculty research:* Computer-aided design of digital systems, networks, robotics and control, sensing and interaction.

University of Colorado Boulder, Graduate School, College of Engineering and Applied Science, Interdisciplinary Telecommunications Program, Boulder, CO 80309. Offers MS, JD/MS, MBA/MS. *Students:* 109 full-time (19 women), 28 part-time (5 women); includes 8 minority (3 Black or African American, non-Hispanic/Latino; 3 Asian, non-Hispanic/Latino; 2 Hispanic/Latino), 101 international. Average age 28. 265 applicants,

54% accepted, 56 enrolled. In 2014, 52 master's awarded. Terminal master's awarded for partial completion of doctoral program. *Degree requirements:* For master's, comprehensive exam, thesis or alternative. *Entrance requirements:* For master's, minimum undergraduate GPA of 3.0. *Application deadline:* For fall admission, 6/15 for domestic students, 3/15 for international students; for spring admission, 11/1 for domestic students, 10/1 for international students. Applications are processed on a rolling basis. Application fee: $50 ($70 for international students). Electronic applications accepted. *Financial support:* In 2014–15, 103 students received support, including 19 fellowships (averaging $7,131 per year), 2 research assistantships with full and partial tuition reimbursements available (averaging $38,669 per year); institutionally sponsored loans, scholarships/grants, health care benefits, and unspecified assistantships also available. Financial award applicants required to submit FAFSA. *Faculty research:* Technology, planning, and management of telecommunications systems. *Total annual research expenditures:* $65,711.
Website: http://engineeringanywhere.colorado.edu/itp/.

University of Denver, University College, Denver, CO 80208. Offers geographic information systems (Certificate); global affairs (Certificate), including translation studies, world history and culture; information and communications technology (MCIS), including geographic information systems, information systems security, project management (MCIS, Certificate), software design and programming, technology management, telecommunications technology, Web design and development; leadership and organizations (Certificate), including human capital in organizations, philanthropic leadership, project management (MCIS, Certificate), strategic innovation and change; organizational and professional communication (MPS), including alternative dispute resolution, organizational communication, organizational development and training, public relations and marketing; security management (MAS, Certificate), including emergency planning and response, information security (MAS), organizational security. Part-time and evening/weekend programs available. Postbaccalaureate distance learning degree programs offered (no on-campus study). *Faculty:* 8 full-time (4 women), 133 part-time/adjunct (46 women). *Students:* 54 full-time (21 women), 1,327 part-time (775 women); includes 272 minority (106 Black or African American, non-Hispanic/Latino; 6 American Indian or Alaska Native, non-Hispanic/Latino; 26 Asian, non-Hispanic/Latino; 108 Hispanic/Latino; 1 Native Hawaiian or other Pacific Islander, non-Hispanic/Latino; 25 Two or more races, non-Hispanic/Latino), 116 international. Average age 35. 768 applicants, 95% accepted, 620 enrolled. In 2014, 391 master's, 196 other advanced degrees awarded. *Degree requirements:* For master's, capstone project. *Entrance requirements:* For master's, transcripts, two letters of recommendation, personal statement, resume. Additional exam requirements/recommendations for international students: Required—TOEFL (minimum score 550 paper-based; 80 iBT). *Application deadline:* For fall admission, 6/21 priority date for domestic students, 5/1 priority date for international students; for winter admission, 9/14 priority date for domestic students, 9/19 priority date for international students; for spring admission, 1/11 for domestic students, 12/12 for international students; for summer admission, 3/29 priority date for domestic students, 3/6 priority date for international students. Applications are processed on a rolling basis. Application fee: $75. Electronic applications accepted. *Expenses:* Expenses: $959 per credit hour. *Financial support:* In 2014–15, 19 students received support. Applicants required to submit FAFSA. *Unit head:* Dr. Michael McGuire, Interim Dean, 303-871-3518, E-mail: mmcguire@du.edu. *Application contact:* Information Contact, 303-871-2291, E-mail: ucoladm@du.edu. Website: http://www.universitycollege.du.edu/.

University of Hawaii at Manoa, Graduate Division, College of Social Sciences, School of Communications, Program in Telecommunication and Information Resource Management, Honolulu, HI 96822. Offers Graduate Certificate. Part-time programs available. *Entrance requirements:* Additional exam requirements/recommendations for international students: Required—TOEFL (minimum score 500 paper-based; 61 iBT), IELTS (minimum score 5).

University of Houston, College of Technology, Department of Engineering Technology, Houston, TX 77204. Offers construction management (MS); engineering technology (MS); network communications (M Tech). Part-time programs available. *Degree requirements:* For master's, project or thesis (most programs). *Entrance requirements:* For master's, GRE. Additional exam requirements/recommendations for international students: Required—TOEFL (minimum score 550 paper-based; 79 iBT). Electronic applications accepted.

University of Louisiana at Lafayette, College of Engineering, Department of Electrical and Computer Engineering, Program in Telecommunications, Lafayette, LA 70504. Offers MSTC. *Degree requirements:* For master's, thesis or alternative. *Entrance requirements:* For master's, GRE General Test, minimum GPA of 2.75. Additional exam requirements/recommendations for international students: Required—TOEFL (minimum score 550 paper-based). Electronic applications accepted.

University of Maryland, College Park, Academic Affairs, A. James Clark School of Engineering, Department of Electrical and Computer Engineering, Program in Telecommunications, College Park, MD 20742. Offers MS. Part-time and evening/weekend programs available. *Degree requirements:* For master's, thesis or alternative. *Entrance requirements:* For master's, GRE General Test, minimum GPA of 3.0, professional experience. Additional exam requirements/recommendations for international students: Required—TOEFL. Electronic applications accepted.

University of Massachusetts Dartmouth, Graduate School, College of Engineering, Department of Electrical and Computer Engineering, North Dartmouth, MA 02747-2300. Offers acoustics (Postbaccalaureate Certificate); communications (Postbaccalaureate Certificate); computer engineering (MS, PhD); computer systems engineering (Postbaccalaureate Certificate); digital signal processing (Postbaccalaureate Certificate); electrical engineering (MS, PhD); electrical engineering systems (Postbaccalaureate Certificate). Part-time programs available. *Faculty:* 16 full-time (3 women). *Students:* 47 full-time (15 women), 38 part-time (2 women); includes 8 minority (1 Black or African American, non-Hispanic/Latino; 4 Asian, non-Hispanic/Latino; 2 Hispanic/Latino; 1 Two or more races, non-Hispanic/Latino), 45 international. Average age 27. 127 applicants, 60% accepted, 26 enrolled. In 2014, 9 master's, 4 doctorates, 1 other advanced degree awarded. *Degree requirements:* For master's, thesis or project; for doctorate, comprehensive exam, thesis/dissertation. *Entrance requirements:* For master's, GRE (UMass Dartmouth electrical/computer engineering bachelor's degree recipients are exempt), statement of purpose (minimum of 300 words), resume, 3 letters of recommendation, official transcripts; for doctorate, GRE, statement of purpose (minimum of 300 words), resume, 3 letters of recommendation, official transcripts; for Postbaccalaureate Certificate, statement of purpose (minimum of 300 words), resume, official transcripts. Additional exam requirements/recommendations for international students: Required—TOEFL (minimum score 533 paper-based; 72 iBT), IELTS (minimum score 6). *Application deadline:* For fall admission, 2/15 priority date for domestic students, 1/15 priority date for international students; for spring admission, 11/1 priority date for domestic students, 10/1 priority date for international students. Applications are processed on a rolling basis. Application fee: $60. Electronic applications accepted. *Expenses:* Tuition, state resident: full-time $2071; part-time $86.29 per credit. Tuition, nonresident: full-time $8099; part-time $337.46 per credit. *Required fees:* $16,520; $712.33 per credit. Tuition and fees vary according to course

load and reciprocity agreements. *Financial support:* In 2014–15, 2 fellowships with full and partial tuition reimbursements (averaging $14,337 per year), 13 research assistantships with full and partial tuition reimbursements (averaging $12,775 per year), 11 teaching assistantships with full and partial tuition reimbursements (averaging $12,273 per year) were awarded; Federal Work-Study and unspecified assistantships also available. Support available to part-time students. Financial award application deadline: 3/1; financial award applicants required to submit FAFSA. *Faculty research:* Computer engineering, cyber security, acoustics, signals and systems, electromagnetics, electronics and solid-state devices, marine systems, photonics. *Total annual research expenditures:* $2.5 million. *Unit head:* Dr. Karen Payton, Graduate Program Director, 508-999-8434, Fax: 508-999-8489, E-mail: kpayton@umassd.edu. *Application contact:* Steven Briggs, Director of Marketing and Recruitment for Graduate Studies, 508-999-8604, Fax: 508-999-8183, E-mail: graduate@umassd.edu. Website: http://www.umassd.edu/engineering/ece/.

University of Missouri–Kansas City, School of Computing and Engineering, Kansas City, MO 64110-2499. Offers civil engineering (MS); computer and electrical engineering (PhD); computer science (MS), including bioinformatics, software engineering, telecommunications networking; computer science and informatics (PhD); computing (PhD); electrical engineering (MS); engineering (PhD); engineering and construction management (Graduate Certificate); mechanical engineering (MS); telecommunications and computer networking (PhD). PhD (interdisciplinary) offered through the School of Graduate Studies. Part-time programs available. *Faculty:* 39 full-time (5 women), 26 part-time/adjunct (3 women). *Students:* 500 full-time (143 women), 136 part-time (28 women); includes 18 minority (5 Black or African American, non-Hispanic/Latino; 8 Asian, non-Hispanic/Latino; 4 Hispanic/Latino; 1 Two or more races, non-Hispanic/Latino), 551 international. Average age 24. 1,924 applicants, 39% accepted, 200 enrolled. In 2014, 124 master's, 1 other advanced degree awarded. *Degree requirements:* For doctorate, thesis/dissertation. *Entrance requirements:* For master's, GRE General Test, minimum GPA of 3.0, 3 letters of recommendation from professors; for doctorate, GRE General Test, minimum GPA of 3.5. Additional exam requirements/recommendations for international students: Required—TOEFL (minimum score 550 paper-based; 80 iBT). *Application deadline:* For fall admission, 1/15 priority date for domestic students, 1/15 for international students. Applications are processed on a rolling basis. Application fee: $45 ($50 for international students). *Financial support:* In 2014–15, 34 research assistantships with partial tuition reimbursements (averaging $15,602 per year), 24 teaching assistantships with partial tuition reimbursements (averaging $15,090 per year) were awarded; career-related internships or fieldwork, Federal Work-Study, scholarships/grants, tuition waivers (partial), and unspecified assistantships also available. Support available to part-time students. Financial award application deadline: 3/1; financial award applicants required to submit FAFSA. *Faculty research:* Algorithms, bioinformatics and medical informatics, biomechanics/biomaterials, civil engineering materials, networking and telecommunications, thermal science. *Unit head:* Dr. Kevin Z. Truman, Dean, 816-235-2399, Fax: 816-235-5159. *Application contact:* 816-235-2399, Fax: 816-235-5159. Website: http://sce.umkc.edu/.

The University of North Carolina at Chapel Hill, Graduate School, School of Journalism and Mass Communication, Chapel Hill, NC 27599. Offers mass communication (MA, PhD); technology and communication (MA). *Accreditation:* ACEJMC (one or more programs are accredited). Part-time programs available. Postbaccalaureate distance learning degree programs offered (minimal on-campus study). *Degree requirements:* For master's, comprehensive exam, thesis; for doctorate, comprehensive exam, thesis/dissertation. *Entrance requirements:* For master's and doctorate, GRE General Test, minimum GPA of 3.0. Additional exam requirements/recommendations for international students: Required—TOEFL (minimum score 620 paper-based; 105 iBT); Recommended—IELTS (minimum score 7.5). Electronic applications accepted. *Expenses:* Contact institution. *Faculty research:* Media processes and production, legal and regulatory issues, media effects, media history.

University of Oklahoma, Gallogly College of Engineering, School of Electrical and Computer Engineering, Program in Telecommunications Engineering, Tulsa, OK 74135. Offers MS. Part-time programs available. *Students:* 7 full-time (1 woman), 3 part-time (2 women), 9 international. Average age 26. 21 applicants, 62% accepted, 4 enrolled. In 2014, 6 master's awarded. *Degree requirements:* For master's, thesis. *Entrance requirements:* For master's, GRE. Additional exam requirements/recommendations for international students: Required—TOEFL (minimum score 79 iBT). *Application deadline:* For fall admission, 8/24 for domestic students, 4/1 for international students; for spring admission, 1/12 for domestic students, 9/1 for international students. Application fee: $50 ($100 for international students). Electronic applications accepted. *Expenses:* Tuition, state resident: full-time $4394; part-time $183.10 per credit hour. Tuition, nonresident: full-time $16,970; part-time $707.10 per credit hour. *Required fees:* $2892; $109.95 per credit hour. $126.50 per semester. *Financial support:* In 2014–15, 8 students received support. Unspecified assistantships available. Financial award application deadline: 6/1; financial award applicants required to submit FAFSA. *Faculty research:* Optical networks, wireless networks, network security, quantum cryptography, next generation networks. *Unit head:* Dr. Pramode Verma, Director, 918-660-3236, Fax: 918-660-3238, E-mail: pverma@ou.edu. *Application contact:* Renee Wagenblatt, Administrative Assistant, 918-660-3235, Fax: 918-660-3238, E-mail: rwagenblatt@ou.edu. Website: http://www.ou.edu/coe/tcom.

University of Pennsylvania, School of Engineering and Applied Science, Telecommunications and Networking Program, Philadelphia, PA 19104. Offers MSE. Part-time programs available. *Students:* 2 part-time (0 women), 1 international. In 2014, 38 master's awarded. *Application deadline:* For fall admission, 6/1 for domestic students, 5/1 for international students; for spring admission, 11/1 for domestic students, 10/1 for international students. Application fee: $70. Electronic applications accepted. *Unit head:* Eduardo D. Glandt, Dean, 215-898-7244, E-mail: seasdean@seas.upenn.edu. *Application contact:* School of Engineering and Applied Science Graduate Admissions, 215-898-4542, E-mail: gradstudies@seas.upenn.edu. Website: http://www.seas.upenn.edu.

University of Pittsburgh, School of Information Sciences, Telecommunications and Networking Program, Pittsburgh, PA 15260. Offers information science (PhD), including telecommunications; telecommunications and networking (MST, Certificate). Part-time programs available. *Faculty:* 4 full-time (0 women), 2 part-time/adjunct (0 women). *Students:* 67 full-time (17 women), 7 part-time (1 woman); includes 2 minority (both Asian, non-Hispanic/Latino), 65 international. 132 applicants, 71% accepted, 24 enrolled. In 2014, 31 master's, 4 doctorates, 1 other advanced degree awarded. *Degree requirements:* For master's, thesis optional; for doctorate, comprehensive exam, thesis/dissertation. *Entrance requirements:* For master's, GRE General Test, GMAT, undergraduate degree with minimum GPA of 3.0; previous course work in computer programming, calculus, and probability; for doctorate, GRE, GMAT, master's degree; minimum GPA of 3.3; course work in computer programming (2 languages), differential and integral calculus, and probability and statistics; for Certificate, MSIS, MST from accredited university. Additional exam requirements/recommendations for international students: Required—TOEFL (minimum score 550 paper-based; 80 iBT). *Application*

deadline: For fall admission, 1/15 priority date for domestic and international students; for winter admission, 9/15 priority date for domestic students, 6/15 priority date for international students; for spring admission, 9/15 priority date for domestic students, 6/15 priority date for international students; for summer admission, 1/15 priority date for domestic students, 12/15 priority date for international students. Applications are processed on a rolling basis. Application fee: $50. Electronic applications accepted. *Expenses:* Expenses: $21,810 in-state, $35,710 out-of-state; $889 per credit in-state, $1,470 out-of-state (for summer); mandatory fees: $900. *Financial support:* Fellowships with full and partial tuition reimbursements, research assistantships with full and partial tuition reimbursements, teaching assistantships with full and partial tuition reimbursements, career-related internships or fieldwork, scholarships/grants, health care benefits, tuition waivers (full and partial), and unspecified assistantships available. Financial award application deadline: 1/15; financial award applicants required to submit FAFSA. *Faculty research:* Telecommunications systems, telecommunications policy, network design and management, wireless information systems, network security. *Unit head:* Dr. David Tipper, Program Chair, 412-624-9421, Fax: 412-624-2788, E-mail: tipper@tele.pitt.edu. *Application contact:* Shabana Reza, Enrollment Manager, 412-624-3988, Fax: 412-624-5231, E-mail: teleinq@sis.pitt.edu.
Website: http://www.ischool.pitt.edu/tele/.

University of Southern California, Graduate School, Viterbi School of Engineering, Daniel J. Epstein Department of Industrial and Systems Engineering, Los Angeles, CA 90089. Offers digital supply chain management (MS); engineering management (MS); engineering technology communication (Graduate Certificate); health systems operations (Graduate Certificate); industrial and systems engineering (MS, PhD, Engr); manufacturing engineering (MS); operations research engineering (MS); optimization and supply chain management (Graduate Certificate); product development engineering (MS); safety systems and security (MS); systems architecting and engineering (MS, Graduate Certificate); systems safety and security (Graduate Certificate); transportation systems (Graduate Certificate); MS/MBA. Part-time and evening/weekend programs available. Postbaccalaureate distance learning degree programs offered (no on-campus study). Terminal master's awarded for partial completion of doctoral program. *Degree requirements:* For master's, thesis optional; for doctorate, thesis/dissertation. *Entrance requirements:* For master's and doctorate, GRE General Test. Additional exam requirements/recommendations for international students: Recommended—TOEFL. Electronic applications accepted. *Faculty research:* Health systems, music cognition and retrieval, transportation and logistics, manufacturing and automation, engineering systems design, risk and economic analysis.

University of Southern California, Graduate School, Viterbi School of Engineering, Ming Hsieh Department of Electrical Engineering, Los Angeles, CA 90089. Offers computer engineering (MS, PhD); electric power (MS); electrical engineering (MS, PhD, Engr); engineering technology commercialization (Graduate Certificate); multimedia and creative technologies (MS); telecommunications (MS); VLSI design (MS); wireless health technology (MS). Part-time programs available. Postbaccalaureate distance learning degree programs offered (no on-campus study). Terminal master's awarded for partial completion of doctoral program. *Degree requirements:* For master's, thesis optional; for doctorate, thesis/dissertation. *Entrance requirements:* For master's and doctorate, GRE General Test. Additional exam requirements/recommendations for international students: Recommended—TOEFL. Electronic applications accepted. *Faculty research:* Communications, computer engineering and networks, control systems, integrated circuits and systems, electromagnetics and energy conversion, micro electro-mechanical systems and nanotechnology, photonics and quantum electronics, plasma research, signal and image processing.

The University of Texas at Dallas, Erik Jonsson School of Engineering and Computer Science, Department of Electrical Engineering, Richardson, TX 75080. Offers computer engineering (MS, PhD); electrical engineering (MSEE, PhD); systems engineering and management (MS); telecommunications engineering (MSTE, PhD). Part-time and evening/weekend programs available. *Faculty:* 51 full-time (4 women), 5 part-time/adjunct (1 woman). *Students:* 756 full-time (186 women), 288 part-time (83 women); includes 89 minority (14 Black or African American, non-Hispanic/Latino; 44 Asian, non-Hispanic/Latino; 24 Hispanic/Latino; 7 Two or more races, non-Hispanic/Latino), 870 international. Average age 26. 3,191 applicants, 30% accepted, 363 enrolled. In 2014, 250 master's, 31 doctorates awarded. *Degree requirements:* For master's, thesis or major design project; for doctorate, thesis/dissertation. *Entrance requirements:* For master's, GRE General Test, minimum GPA of 3.0 in related bachelor's degree; for doctorate, GRE General Test, minimum GPA of 3.5. Additional exam requirements/recommendations for international students: Required—TOEFL (minimum score 550 paper-based). *Application deadline:* For fall admission, 7/15 for domestic students, 5/1 priority date for international students; for spring admission, 11/15 for domestic students, 9/1 priority date for international students. Applications are processed on a rolling basis. Application fee: $50 ($100 for international students). Electronic applications accepted. *Expenses:* Tuition, state resident: full-time $11,940; part-time $663 per credit. Tuition, nonresident: full-time $22,282; part-time $1238 per credit. *Financial support:* In 2014–15, 269 students received support, including 13 fellowships with partial tuition reimbursements available (averaging $5,598 per year), 129 research assistantships with partial tuition reimbursements available (averaging $17,609 per year), 80 teaching assistantships with partial tuition reimbursements available (averaging $17,480 per year); Federal Work-Study, institutionally sponsored loans, scholarships/grants, unspecified assistantships, and cooperative positions also available. Support available to part-time students. Financial award application deadline: 4/30; financial award applicants required to submit FAFSA. *Faculty research:* Semiconductor device manufacturing, photonics devices and systems, signal processing and language technology, nano-fabrication, energy efficient digital systems. *Unit head:* Dr. James L. Coleman, Department Head, 972-883-6755, Fax: 972-883-2710, E-mail: james.coleman@utdallas.edu. *Application contact:* Patricia Williams, Degree Plan Evaluator, 972-883-4315, Fax: 972-883-2710, E-mail: gradeeadvisors@utdallas.edu.
Website: http://www.ee.utdallas.edu.

Widener University, Graduate Programs in Engineering, Program in Telecommunications Engineering, Chester, PA 19013-5792. Offers M Eng. Part-time and evening/weekend programs available. *Degree requirements:* For master's, thesis optional. *Faculty research:* Signal and image processing, electromagnetics, telecommunications and computer network.

Telecommunications Management

Alaska Pacific University, Graduate Programs, Business Administration Department, Programs in Information and Communication Technology, Anchorage, AK 99508-4672. Offers MBAICT. Part-time and evening/weekend programs available. *Degree requirements:* For master's, capstone course. *Entrance requirements:* For master's, GMAT or GRE General Test, minimum GPA of 3.0.

Boston University, Metropolitan College, Department of Computer Science, Boston, MA 02215. Offers computer information systems (MS), including computer networks, database management and business intelligence, health informatics, IT project management, security, Web application development; computer networks (Certificate); digital forensics (Certificate); health informatics (Certificate); information technology project management (Certificate); software engineering in health care systems (Certificate); telecommunications (MS), including security. Part-time and evening/weekend programs available. Postbaccalaureate distance learning degree programs offered (no on-campus study). *Faculty:* 13 full-time (3 women), 43 part-time/adjunct (3 women). *Students:* 76 full-time (22 women), 768 part-time (188 women); includes 251 minority (68 Black or African American, non-Hispanic/Latino; 1 American Indian or Alaska Native, non-Hispanic/Latino; 117 Asian, non-Hispanic/Latino; 57 Hispanic/Latino; 2 Native Hawaiian or other Pacific Islander, non-Hispanic/Latino; 6 Two or more races, non-Hispanic/Latino), 130 international. Average age 34. 463 applicants, 79% accepted, 248 enrolled. In 2014, 222 master's, 25 other advanced degrees awarded. *Degree requirements:* For master's, thesis optional. *Entrance requirements:* For master's and Certificate, official transcripts from regionally-accredited bachelor's degree program, 3 letters of recommendation, professional resume, personal statement. Additional exam requirements/recommendations for international students: Required—TOEFL (minimum score 84 iBT), IELTS. *Application deadline:* For fall admission, 6/1 priority date for international students; for spring admission, 10/1 priority date for international students. Applications are processed on a rolling basis. Application fee: $80. Electronic applications accepted. *Expenses:* Expenses: $800 per credit part-time; student services fees: $60 per semester; technology fee of $60 per credit (for online courses). *Financial support:* In 2014–15, 11 research assistantships (averaging $8,400 per year) were awarded; unspecified assistantships also available. Support available to part-time students. Financial award applicants required to submit FAFSA. *Faculty research:* Medical informatics, Web technologies, telecom and networks, security and forensics, software engineering, programming languages, multimedia and artificial intelligence (AI), information systems and IT project management. *Unit head:* Dr. Anatoly Temkin, Chairman, 617-353-2566, Fax: 617-353-2367, E-mail: csinfo@bu.edu. *Application contact:* Lesley Moreau, Academic Program Coordinator, 617-353-2566, Fax: 617-353-2367, E-mail: metcs@bu.edu.
Website: http://www.bu.edu/csmet/.

California Miramar University, Program in Telecommunications Management, San Diego, CA 92126. Offers MST.

Capitol Technology University, Graduate Programs, Laurel, MD 20708-9759. Offers business administration (MBA); computer science (MS); electrical engineering (MS); information and telecommunications systems management (MS); information architecture (MS); network security (MS). Part-time and evening/weekend programs available. Postbaccalaureate distance learning degree programs offered (no on-campus study). *Entrance requirements:* For master's, minimum GPA of 3.0. Electronic applications accepted.

Carnegie Mellon University, Carnegie Institute of Technology, Information Networking Institute, Pittsburgh, PA 15213. Offers information networking (MS); information security (MS); information technology - information security (MS); information technology - mobility (MS); information technology - software management (MS). *Degree requirements:* For master's, thesis optional. *Entrance requirements:* For master's, GRE General Test, bachelor's degree in computer science, computer engineering, or electrical engineering, or related technology degree; programming skills (C/C++ fluency for some programs). Additional exam requirements/recommendations for international students: Required—TOEFL. *Faculty research:* Computer forensics and incident response; dependable systems, embedded systems, mobile systems, and sensor networks; computer and information networks, network and information security, human and socio-economic factors in secure system design; wireless sensor networks, survivable embedded systems, signal processing/compression; strategic management, international strategic management, group dynamics and decision-making structures, simulated competitive environments.

Concordia University, School of Graduate Studies, Faculty of Engineering and Computer Science, Concordia Institute for Information Systems Engineering (CIISE), Montréal, QC H3G 1M8, Canada. Offers 3D graphics and game development (Certificate); information systems security (M Eng, MA Sc); quality systems engineering (M Eng, MA Sc); service engineering and network management (Certificate).

East Carolina University, Graduate School, College of Engineering and Technology, Department of Technology Systems, Greenville, NC 27858-4353. Offers computer network professional (Certificate); information assurance (Certificate); Lean Six Sigma Black Belt (Certificate); network technology (MS), including computer networking management, digital communications technology, information security, Web technologies; occupational safety (MS); technology management (PhD); technology systems (MS), including industrial distribution and logistics, manufacturing systems, performance improvement, quality systems; Website developer (Certificate). *Entrance requirements:* For master's and Certificate, GRE General Test or MAT, minimum GPA of 2.5; for doctorate, GRE General Test, related work experience. *Expenses:* Tuition, state resident: full-time $4223. Tuition, nonresident: full-time $16,540. *Required fees:* $2184.

Instituto Tecnológico y de Estudios Superiores de Monterrey, Campus Ciudad de México, School of Design, Engineering and Architecture, Ciudad de Mexico, Mexico. Offers management (MA); telecommunications (MA). Part-time and evening/weekend programs available. Postbaccalaureate distance learning degree programs offered (minimal on-campus study). *Faculty research:* Telecommunications; informatics; technology development; computer systems.

Instituto Tecnológico y de Estudios Superiores de Monterrey, Campus Ciudad Obregón, Program in Administration of Telecommunications, Ciudad Obregón, Mexico. Offers MAT.

Instituto Tecnológico y de Estudios Superiores de Monterrey, Campus Estado de México, Professional and Graduate Division, Estado de Mexico, Mexico. Offers administration of information technologies (MITA); architecture (M Arch); business administration (GMBA, MBA); computer sciences (MCS, PhD); education (M Ed); educational institution administration (MAD); educational technology and innovation (PhD); electronic commerce (MEC); environmental systems (MS); finance (MAF); humanistic studies (MHS); information sciences and knowledge management (MISKM); information systems (MS); manufacturing systems (MS); marketing (MEM); quality systems and productivity (MS); science and materials engineering (PhD); telecommunications management (MTM). Part-time programs available. Postbaccalaureate distance learning degree programs offered (minimal on-campus study). *Degree requirements:* For master's, one foreign language, thesis (for some programs); for doctorate, one foreign language, thesis/dissertation. *Entrance requirements:* For master's, E-PAEP 500, interview; for doctorate, E-PAEP 500, research proposal. Additional exam requirements/recommendations for international students: Required—TOEFL (minimum score 550 paper-based). *Faculty research:* Surface treatments by plasmas, mechanical properties, robotics, graphical computing, mechatronics security protocols.

Instituto Tecnológico y de Estudios Superiores de Monterrey, Campus Irapuato, Graduate Programs, Irapuato, Mexico. Offers administration (MBA); administration of information technology (MAIT); administration of telecommunications (MAT); architecture (M Arch); computer science (MCS); education (M Ed); educational administration (MEA); educational innovation and technology (DEIT); educational technology (MET); electronic commerce (MBA); environmental administration and planning (MEAP); environmental systems (MES); finances (MBA); humanistic studies (MHS); international management for Latin American executives (MIMLAE); library and information science (MLIS); manufacturing quality management (MMQM); marketing research (MBA).

Murray State University, College of Business and Public Affairs, Program in Telecommunications Systems Management, Murray, KY 42071. Offers MS. *Entrance requirements:* For master's, GMAT or GRE. Additional exam requirements/recommendations for international students: Required—TOEFL. *Faculty research:* Network security, emergency management communications, network economies.

New York University, Polytechnic School of Engineering, Department of Technology Management, New York, NY 10012-1019. Offers construction management (Advanced Certificate); electronic business management (Advanced Certificate); entrepreneurship (Advanced Certificate); human resources management (Advanced Certificate); industrial engineering (MS); information management (Advanced Certificate); management (MS); management of technology (MS); manufacturing engineering (MS); organizational behavior (MS, Advanced Certificate); project management (Advanced Certificate); technology management (MBA, PhD, Advanced Certificate); telecommunications management (Advanced Certificate). Part-time and evening/weekend programs available. *Faculty:* 11 full-time (2 women), 43 part-time/adjunct (1 woman). *Students:* 294 full-time (126 women), 102 part-time (38 women); includes 42 minority (5 Black or African American, non-Hispanic/Latino; 1 American Indian or Alaska Native, non-Hispanic/Latino; 26 Asian, non-Hispanic/Latino; 9 Hispanic/Latino; 1 Two or more races, non-Hispanic/Latino, 301 international. Average age 26. 843 applicants, 48% accepted, 165 enrolled. In 2014, 193 master's awarded. *Degree requirements:* For master's, comprehensive exam (for some programs), thesis (for some programs); for doctorate, comprehensive exam, thesis/dissertation. *Entrance requirements:* For master's, GMAT, minimum B average in undergraduate course work. Additional exam requirements/recommendations for international students: Required—TOEFL (minimum score 550 paper-based; 80 iBT); Recommended—IELTS (minimum score 6.5). *Application deadline:* For fall admission, 2/15 priority date for domestic and international students; for spring admission, 11/1 priority date for domestic and international students. Applications are processed on a rolling basis. Application fee: $75. Electronic applications accepted. *Financial support:* In 2014–15, 1 fellowship (averaging $26,400 per year) was awarded; research assistantships, teaching assistantships, institutionally sponsored loans, scholarships/grants, and unspecified assistantships also available. Support available to part-time students. *Faculty research:* Global innovation and research and development strategy, managing emerging technologies, technology and development, service design and innovation, tech entrepreneurship and commercialization, sustainable and clean-tech innovation, impacts of information technology upon individuals, organizations and society. *Total annual research expenditures:* $271,808. *Unit head:* Prof. Bharadwaj Rao, Head, 718-260-3617, Fax: 718-260-3874, E-mail: bharat.rao@nyu.edu. *Application contact:* Raymond Lutzky, Director of Graduate Enrollment Management, 718-637-5984, Fax: 718-260-3624, E-mail: rlutzky@poly.edu.
Website: http://www.poly.edu/academics/departments/technology/.

Oklahoma State University, Graduate College, Stillwater, OK 74078. Offers aerospace security (Graduate Certificate); bioenergy and sustainable technology (Graduate Certificate); business data mining (Graduate Certificate); business sustainability (Graduate Certificate); environmental science (MS); international studies (MS); non-profit management (Graduate Certificate); teaching English to speakers of other languages (Graduate Certificate); telecommunications management (MS). Programs are interdisciplinary. *Faculty:* 3 full-time (1 woman), 2 part-time/adjunct (1 woman). *Students:* 49 full-time (27 women), 94 part-time (45 women); includes 21 minority (3 Black or African American, non-Hispanic/Latino; 1 American Indian or Alaska Native, non-Hispanic/Latino; 3 Asian, non-Hispanic/Latino; 4 Hispanic/Latino; 10 Two or more races, non-Hispanic/Latino), 36 international. Average age 30. 385 applicants, 76% accepted, 55 enrolled. In 2014, 47 master's, 1 doctorate awarded. *Degree requirements:* For master's, thesis (for some programs); for doctorate, comprehensive exam, thesis/dissertation. *Entrance requirements:* For master's and doctorate, GRE or GMAT. Additional exam requirements/recommendations for international students: Required—TOEFL (minimum score 550 paper-based; 79 iBT). *Application deadline:* For fall admission, 3/1 priority date for international students; for spring admission, 8/1 priority date for international students. Applications are processed on a rolling basis. Application fee: $40 ($75 for international students). Electronic applications accepted. *Expenses:* Tuition, state resident: full-time $4488; part-time $187 per credit hour. Tuition, nonresident: full-time $18,360; part-time $765 per credit hour. *Required fees:* $2413; $100.55 per credit hour. Tuition and fees vary according to campus/location. *Financial support:* In 2014–15, 4 research assistantships (averaging $14,400 per year) were awarded; career-related internships or fieldwork, Federal Work-Study, scholarships/grants, health care benefits, tuition waivers (partial), and unspecified assistantships also available. Support available to part-time students. Financial award application deadline: 3/1; financial award applicants required to submit FAFSA. *Unit head:* Dr. Sheryl Tucker, Dean, 405-744-6368, Fax: 405-744-0355, E-mail: gradi@okstate.edu. *Application contact:* Dr. Susan Mathew, Coordinator of Admissions, 405-744-6368, Fax: 405-744-0355, E-mail: gradi@okstate.edu.
Website: http://gradcollege.okstate.edu/.

Oklahoma State University, Spears School of Business, Department of Management Science and Information Systems, Stillwater, OK 74078. Offers management information systems (MS); management science and information systems (PhD); telecommunications management (MS). Part-time programs available. Postbaccalaureate distance learning degree programs offered. *Faculty:* 18 full-time (2 women), 5 part-time/adjunct (1 woman). *Students:* 121 full-time (25 women), 101 part-time (17 women); includes 13 minority (5 Black or African American, non-Hispanic/Latino; 1 Asian, non-Hispanic/Latino; 3 Hispanic/Latino; 4 Two or more races, non-Hispanic/Latino), 160 international. Average age 28. 883 applicants, 14% accepted, 81 enrolled. In 2014, 131 master's, 2 doctorates awarded. *Degree requirements:* For master's, thesis or alternative; for doctorate, comprehensive exam, thesis/dissertation.

Entrance requirements: For master's and doctorate, GRE or GMAT. Additional exam requirements/recommendations for international students: Required—TOEFL (minimum score 550 paper-based; 79 iBT). *Application deadline:* For fall admission, 3/1 priority date for international students; for spring admission, 8/1 priority date for international students. Applications are processed on a rolling basis. Application fee: $40 ($75 for international students). Electronic applications accepted. *Expenses:* Tuition, state resident: full-time $4488; part-time $187 per credit hour. Tuition, nonresident: full-time $18,360; part-time $765 per credit hour. *Required fees:* $2413; $100.55 per credit hour. Tuition and fees vary according to campus/location. *Financial support:* In 2014–15, 2 research assistantships (averaging $6,000 per year), 22 teaching assistantships (averaging $11,906 per year) were awarded; career-related internships or fieldwork, Federal Work-Study, scholarships/grants, health care benefits, tuition waivers (partial), and unspecified assistantships also available. Support available to part-time students. Financial award application deadline: 3/1; financial award applicants required to submit FAFSA. *Unit head:* Dr. Rick Wilson, Department Head, 405-744-3551, Fax: 405-744-5180, E-mail: rick.wilson@okstate.edu. *Application contact:* Dr. Rathin Sarathy, Graduate Coordinator, 405-744-8646, Fax: 405-744-5180, E-mail: rathin.sarathy@okstate.edu.
Website: http://spears.okstate.edu/msis.

San Diego State University, Graduate and Research Affairs, College of Professional Studies and Fine Arts, School of Communication, San Diego, CA 92182. Offers advertising and public relations (MA); critical-cultural studies (MA); interaction studies (MA); intercultural and international studies (MA); new media studies (MA); news and information studies (MA); telecommunications and media management (MA). *Degree requirements:* For master's, thesis. *Entrance requirements:* For master's, GRE General Test, 3 letters of recommendation. Additional exam requirements/recommendations for international students: Required—TOEFL. Electronic applications accepted.

Stevens Institute of Technology, Graduate School, Wesley J. Howe School of Technology Management, Doctoral Program in Technology Management, Hoboken, NJ 07030. Offers information management (PhD); technology management (PhD); telecommunications management (PhD). Part-time and evening/weekend programs available. Postbaccalaureate distance learning degree programs offered (minimal on-campus study). *Entrance requirements:* Additional exam requirements/recommendations for international students: Required—TOEFL. Electronic applications accepted.

Stevens Institute of Technology, Graduate School, Wesley J. Howe School of Technology Management, Program in Business Administration, Hoboken, NJ 07030. Offers engineering management (MBA); financial engineering (MBA); information management (MBA); information technology in financial services (MBA); information technology in the pharmaceutical industry (MBA); information technology outsourcing (MBA); pharmaceutical management (MBA); project management (MBA); technology management (MBA); telecommunications management (MBA).

Stevens Institute of Technology, Graduate School, Wesley J. Howe School of Technology Management, Program in Information Systems, Hoboken, NJ 07030. Offers computer science (MS); e-commerce (MS); enterprise systems (MS); entrepreneurial information technology (MS); information architecture (MS); information management (MS, Certificate); information security (MS); information technology in financial services industry (MS); information technology in the pharmaceutical industry (MS); information technology outsourcing management (MS); project management (MS, Certificate); software engineering (MS); telecommunications (MS). *Degree requirements:* For master's, thesis optional. *Entrance requirements:* For master's, GMAT, GRE General Test. Additional exam requirements/recommendations for international students: Required—TOEFL. Electronic applications accepted.

Stevens Institute of Technology, Graduate School, Wesley J. Howe School of Technology Management, Program in Telecommunications Management, Hoboken, NJ 07030. Offers business (MS); global innovation management (MS); management of wireless networks (MS); online security, technology and business (MS); project management (MS); technical management (MS); telecommunications management (PhD, Certificate). *Degree requirements:* For master's, thesis optional; for doctorate, thesis/dissertation. *Entrance requirements:* For master's and doctorate, GMAT, GRE General Test. Additional exam requirements/recommendations for international students: Required—TOEFL. Electronic applications accepted.

Strayer University, Graduate Studies, Washington, DC 20005-2603. Offers accounting (MS); acquisition (MBA); business administration (MBA); communications technology (MS); educational management (M Ed); finance (MBA); health services administration (MHSA); hospitality and tourism management (MBA); human resource management (MBA); information systems (MS), including computer security management, decision support system management, enterprise resource management, network management, software engineering management, systems development management; management (MBA); management information systems (MS); marketing (MBA); professional accounting (MS), including accounting information systems, controllership, taxation; public administration (MPA); supply chain management (MBA); technology in education (M Ed). Programs also offered at campus locations in Birmingham, AL; Chamblee, GA; Cobb County, GA; Morrow, GA; White Marsh, MD; Charleston, SC; Columbia, SC; Greensboro, NC; Greenville, SC; Lexington, KY; Louisville, KY; Nashville, TN; North Raleigh, NC; Washington, DC. Part-time and evening/weekend programs available. Postbaccalaureate distance learning degree programs offered (minimal on-campus study). *Degree requirements:* For master's, thesis. *Entrance requirements:* For master's, GMAT, GRE General Test, bachelor's degree from an accredited college or university, minimum undergraduate GPA of 2.75. Electronic applications accepted.

Syracuse University, School of Information Studies, Program in Information Systems and Telecommunications Management, Syracuse, NY 13244. Offers CAS. Part-time and evening/weekend programs available. Postbaccalaureate distance learning degree programs offered. *Students:* 2 part-time (1 woman). Average age 43. 3 applicants. In 2014, 12 CASs awarded. *Entrance requirements:* Additional exam requirements/recommendations for international students: Required—TOEFL (minimum score 100 iBT). *Application deadline:* For fall admission, 1/1 priority date for domestic and international students; for spring admission, 10/15 priority date for domestic and international students. Applications are processed on a rolling basis. Application fee: $75. Electronic applications accepted. *Expenses:* Tuition: Part-time $1341 per credit. *Required fees:* $1341 per credit. *Financial support:* Application deadline: 1/1. *Unit head:* Carsten Oesterlund, Program Director, 315-443-2911, Fax: 315-443-6886, E-mail: igrad@syr.edu. *Application contact:* Susan Corieri, Director of Enrollment Management, 315-443-2575, E-mail: ischool@syr.edu.
Website: http://ischool.syr.edu/.

Syracuse University, School of Information Studies, Program in Telecommunications and Network Management, Syracuse, NY 13244. Offers MS, MS/CAS. Part-time and evening/weekend programs available. Postbaccalaureate distance learning degree programs offered (minimal on-campus study). *Students:* 32 full-time (5 women), 15 part-time (2 women); includes 6 minority (2 Black or African American, non-Hispanic/Latino; 2 Asian, non-Hispanic/Latino; 2 Hispanic/Latino), 25 international. Average age 29. 103 applicants, 65% accepted, 14 enrolled. In 2014, 27 master's awarded. *Degree*

Telecommunications Management

requirements: For master's, internship or research project. *Entrance requirements:* For master's, GRE General Test. Additional exam requirements/recommendations for international students: Required—TOEFL (minimum score 100 iBT). *Application deadline:* For fall admission, 1/1 priority date for domestic and international students; for spring admission, 10/15 priority date for domestic and international students. Applications are processed on a rolling basis. Application fee: $75. Electronic applications accepted. *Expenses: Tuition:* Part-time $1341 per credit. *Required fees:* $1341 per credit. *Financial support:* Fellowships with full tuition reimbursements, research assistantships with partial tuition reimbursements, teaching assistantships with partial tuition reimbursements, career-related internships or fieldwork, and Federal Work-Study available. Financial award application deadline: 1/1. *Faculty research:* Multimedia, information resources management. *Unit head:* Carsten Oesterlund, Program Director, 309 Hinds Hall, 315-443-2911, Fax: 315-443-6886, E-mail: igrad@syr.edu. *Application contact:* Susan Corieri, Director of Enrollment Management, 315-443-2575, E-mail: ischool@syr.edu.
Website: http://ischool.syr.edu/.

University of Colorado Boulder, Graduate School, College of Engineering and Applied Science, Interdisciplinary Telecommunications Program, Boulder, CO 80309. Offers MS, JD/MS, MBA/MS. *Students:* 109 full-time (19 women), 28 part-time (5 women); includes 8 minority (3 Black or African American, non-Hispanic/Latino; 3 Asian, non-Hispanic/Latino; 2 Hispanic/Latino), 101 international. Average age 28. 265 applicants, 54% accepted, 56 enrolled. In 2014, 52 master's awarded. Terminal master's awarded for partial completion of doctoral program. *Degree requirements:* For master's, comprehensive exam, thesis or alternative. *Entrance requirements:* For master's, minimum undergraduate GPA of 3.0. *Application deadline:* For fall admission, 6/15 for domestic students, 3/15 for international students; for spring admission, 11/1 for domestic students, 10/1 for international students. Applications are processed on a rolling basis. Application fee: $50 ($70 for international students). Electronic applications accepted. *Financial support:* In 2014–15, 103 students received support, including 19 fellowships (averaging $7,131 per year), 2 research assistantships with full and partial tuition reimbursements available (averaging $38,669 per year); institutionally sponsored loans, scholarships/grants, health care benefits, and unspecified assistantships also available. Financial award applicants required to submit FAFSA. *Faculty research:* Technology, planning, and management of telecommunications systems. *Total annual research expenditures:* $65,711.
Website: http://engineeringanywhere.colorado.edu/itp/.

University of Pennsylvania, School of Engineering and Applied Science, Telecommunications and Networking Program, Philadelphia, PA 19104. Offers MSE. Part-time programs available. *Students:* 2 part-time (0 women), 1 international. In 2014, 38 master's awarded. *Application deadline:* For fall admission, 6/1 for domestic students, 5/1 for international students; for spring admission, 11/1 for domestic students, 10/1 for international students. Application fee: $70. Electronic applications accepted. *Unit head:* Eduardo D. Glandt, Dean, 215-898-7244, E-mail: seasdean@seas.upenn.edu. *Application contact:* School of Engineering and Applied Science Graduate Admissions, 215-898-4542, E-mail: gradstudies@seas.upenn.edu.
Website: http://www.seas.upenn.edu.

University of South Africa, College of Human Sciences, Pretoria, South Africa. Offers adult education (M Ed); African languages (MA, PhD); African politics (MA, PhD); Afrikaans (MA, PhD); ancient history (MA, PhD); ancient Near Eastern studies (MA, PhD); anthropology (MA, PhD); applied linguistics (MA); Arabic (MA, PhD); archaeology (MA); art history (MA); Biblical archaeology (MA); Biblical studies (M Th, D Th, PhD); Christian spirituality (M Th, D Th); church history (M Th, D Th); classical studies (MA, PhD); clinical psychology (MA); communication (MA, PhD); comparative education (M Ed, Ed D); consulting psychology (D Admin, D Com, PhD); curriculum studies (M Ed, Ed D); development studies (M Admin, MA, D Admin, PhD); didactics (M Ed, Ed D); education (M Tech); education management (M Ed, Ed D); educational psychology (M Ed); English (MA); environmental education (M Ed); French (MA, PhD); German (MA, PhD); Greek (MA); guidance and counseling (M Ed); health studies (MA, PhD), including health sciences education (MA), health services management (MA), medical and surgical nursing science (critical care general) (MA), midwifery and neonatal nursing science (MA), trauma and emergency care (MA); history (MA, PhD); history of education (Ed D); inclusive education (M Ed, Ed D); information and communications technology policy and regulation (MA); information science (MA, MIS, PhD); international politics (MA, PhD); Islamic studies (MA, PhD); Italian (MA, PhD); Judaica (MA, PhD); linguistics (MA, PhD); mathematical education (M Ed); mathematics education (MA); missiology (M Th, D Th); modern Hebrew (MA, PhD); musicology (MA, MMus, D Mus, PhD); natural science education (M Ed); New Testament (M Th, D Th); Old Testament (D Th); pastoral therapy (M Th, D Th); philosophy (MA); philosophy of education (M Ed, Ed D); politics (MA, PhD); Portuguese (MA, PhD); practical theology (M Th, D Th); psychology (MA, MS, PhD); psychology of education (M Ed, Ed D); public health (MA); religious studies (MA, D Th, PhD); Romance languages (MA); Russian (MA, PhD); Semitic languages (MA, PhD); social behavior studies in HIV/AIDS (MA); social science (mental health) (MA); social science in development studies (MA); social science in psychology (MA); social science in social work (MA); social science in sociology (MA); social work (MSW, DSW, PhD); socio-education (M Ed, Ed D); sociolinguistics (MA); sociology (MA); Spanish (MA, PhD); systematic theology (M Th, D Th); TESOL (teaching English to speakers of other languages) (MA); theological ethics (M Th, D Th); theory of literature (MA, PhD); urban ministries (D Th); urban ministry (M Th).

University of Wisconsin–Stout, Graduate School, College of Technology, Engineering, and Management, Program in Information and Communication Technologies, Menomonie, WI 54751. Offers MS. Part-time programs available. Postbaccalaureate distance learning degree programs offered (minimal on-campus study). *Degree requirements:* For master's, thesis. *Entrance requirements:* For master's, minimum GPA of 2.75. Additional exam requirements/recommendations for international students: Required—TOEFL (minimum score 500 paper-based; 61 iBT). Electronic applications accepted.

APPENDIXES

Institutional Changes
Since the 2015 Edition

Following is an alphabetical listing of institutions that have recently closed, merged with other institutions, or changed their names or status. In the case of a name change, the former name appears first, followed by the new name.

Adler School of Professional Psychology (Chicago, IL): *name changed to Adler University*

Ambrose University College (Calgary, AB, Canada): *name changed to Ambrose University*

American InterContinental University South Florida (Weston, FL): *closed*

Baptist Bible College of Pennsylvania (Clarks Summit, PA): *name changed to Summit University*

Bay Path College (Longmeadow, MA): *name changed to Bay Path University*

Bethesda University of California (Anaheim, CA): *name changed to Bethesda University*

Blessed John XXIII National Seminary (Weston, MA): *name changed to Pope St. John XXIII National Seminary*

Capitol College (Laurel, MD): *name changed to Capitol Technology University*

Clearwater Christian College (Clearwater, FL): *closed*

Cold Spring Harbor Laboratory, Watson School of Biological Sciences (Cold Spring Harbor, NY): *institution name changed to Cold Spring Harbor Laboratory*

Delaware Valley College (Doylestown, PA): *name changed to Delaware Valley University*

DeVry University (Daly City, CA): *closed*

DeVry University (Elk Grove, CA): *closed*

DeVry University (Miami, FL): *closed*

DeVry University (Tampa, FL): *closed*

DeVry University (Schaumburg, IL): *closed*

DeVry University (Indianapolis, IN): *closed*

DeVry University (St. Louis, MO): *closed*

DeVry University (Portland, OR): *closed*

DeVry University (Pittsburgh, PA): *closed*

DeVry University (Memphis, TN): *closed*

DeVry University (Houston, TX): *closed*

DeVry University (Richardson, TX): *closed*

DeVry University (Bellevue, WA): *closed*

DeVry University (Federal Way, WA): *closed*

DeVry University (Milwaukee, WI): *closed*

DeVry University (Waukesha, WI): *closed*

Harrington College of Design (Chicago, IL): *closed*

Heritage Baptist College and Heritage Theological Seminary (Cambridge, ON, Canada): *name changed to Heritage College and Seminary*

International Baptist College (Chandler, AZ): *name changed to International Baptist College and Seminary*

John Hancock University (Oakbrook Terrace, IL): *name changed to Ellis University*

Jones International University (Centennial, CO): *closed*

Keck Graduate Institute of Applied Life Sciences (Claremont, CA): *now listed as Keck Graduate Institute*

Luther Rice University (Lithonia, GA): *name changed to Luther Rice College & Seminary*

Monterey Institute of International Studies (Monterey, CA): *name changed to Middlebury Institute of International Studies*

Morrison University (Reno, NV): *closed*

Mount St. Mary's College (Los Angeles, CA): *name changed to Mount Saint Mary's University*

New Life Theological Seminary (Charlotte, NC): *name changed to Charlotte Christian College and Theological Seminary*

Northland International University (Dunbar, WI): *merged into Southern Baptist Theological Seminary (Louisville, KY)*

Pacific Lutheran Theological Seminary (Berkeley, CA): *merged into California Lutheran University (Thousand Oaks, CA)*

Ponce School of Medicine & Health Sciences (Ponce, PR): *name changed to Ponce Health Sciences University*

The Richard Stockton College of New Jersey (Galloway, NJ): *name changed to Stockton University*

Sojourner-Douglass College (Baltimore, MD): *closed*

State University of New York Institute of Technology (Utica, NY): *name changed to State University of New York Polytechnic Institute*

Tennessee Temple University (Chattanooga, TN): *merged into Piedmont International University (Winston-Salem, NC)*

Texas State University–San Marcos (San Marcos, TX): *name changed to Texas State University*

Thomas M. Cooley Law School (Lansing, MI): *name changed to Western Michigan University Cooley Law School*

University of Phoenix–Central Massachusetts Campus (Westborough, MA): *closed*

University of Phoenix–Chattanooga Campus (Chattanooga, TN): *name changed to University of Phoenix–Chattanooga Learning Center and no longer profiled as a campus*

University of Phoenix–Cheyenne Campus (Cheyenne, WY): *closed*

University of Phoenix–Cincinnati Campus (West Chester, OH): *closed*

University of Phoenix–Columbus Ohio Campus (Columbus, OH): *closed*

University of Phoenix–Denver Campus (Lone Tree, CO): *name changed to University of Phoenix–Colorado Campus*

University of Phoenix–Eastern Washington Campus (Spokane, WA): *closed*

University of Phoenix–Louisiana Campus (Metairie, LA): *name changed to University of Phoenix–New Orleans Learning Center and no longer profiled as a campus*

University of Phoenix–Madison Campus (Madison, WI): *closed*

University of Phoenix–Minneapolis/St. Louis Park Campus (St. Louis Park, MN): *name changed to University of Phoenix–Minneapolis/St. Paul Campus*

University of Phoenix–Northwest Arkansas Campus (Rogers, AR): *closed*

University of Phoenix–Omaha Campus (Omaha, NE): *closed*

University of Phoenix–Pittsburgh Campus (Pittsburgh, PA): *closed*

University of Phoenix–Southern Colorado Campus (Colorado Springs, CO): *name changed to University of Phoenix–Colorado Springs Downtown Campus*

University of Phoenix–Springfield Campus (Springfield, MO): *closed*

University of Phoenix–Tulsa Campus (Tulsa, OK): *name changed to University of Phoenix–Tulsa Learning Center and no longer profiled as a campus*

University of Phoenix–West Florida Campus (Temple Terrace, FL): *name changed to University of Phoenix–West Florida Learning Center and no longer profiled as a campus*

University of Phoenix–Wichita Campus (Wichita, KS): *closed*

University of South Florida–St. Petersburg Campus (St. Petersburg, FL): *name changed to University of South Florida, St. Petersburg*

Valley Forge Christian College (Phoenixville, PA): *name changed to University of Valley Forge*

Washington State University Spokane (Spokane, WA): *merged into a single entry for Washington State University (Pullman, WA) by request from the institution*

Washington State University Tri-Cities (Richland, WA): *merged into a single entry for Washington State University (Pullman, WA) by request from the institution*

Washington State University Vancouver (Vancouver, WA): *merged into a single entry for Washington State University (Pullman, WA) by request from the institution*

Abbreviations Used in the Guides

The following list includes abbreviations of degree names used in the profiles in the 2016 edition of the guides. Because some degrees (e.g., Doctor of Education) can be abbreviated in more than one way (e.g., D.Ed. or Ed.D.), and because the abbreviations used in the guides reflect the preferences of the individual colleges and universities, the list may include two or more abbreviations for a single degree.

DEGREES

A Mus D	Doctor of Musical Arts
AC	Advanced Certificate
AD	Artist's Diploma
	Doctor of Arts
ADP	Artist's Diploma
Adv C	Advanced Certificate
AGC	Advanced Graduate Certificate
AGSC	Advanced Graduate Specialist Certificate
ALM	Master of Liberal Arts
AM	Master of Arts
AMBA	Accelerated Master of Business Administration
AMRS	Master of Arts in Religious Studies
APC	Advanced Professional Certificate
APMPH	Advanced Professional Master of Public Health
App Sc	Applied Scientist
App Sc D	Doctor of Applied Science
AstE	Astronautical Engineer
ATC	Advanced Training Certificate
Au D	Doctor of Audiology
B Th	Bachelor of Theology
BN	Bachelor of Naturopathy
CAES	Certificate of Advanced Educational Specialization
CAGS	Certificate of Advanced Graduate Studies
CAL	Certificate in Applied Linguistics
CAPS	Certificate of Advanced Professional Studies
CAS	Certificate of Advanced Studies
CASPA	Certificate of Advanced Study in Public Administration
CASR	Certificate in Advanced Social Research
CATS	Certificate of Achievement in Theological Studies
CBHS	Certificate in Basic Health Sciences
CCJA	Certificate in Criminal Justice Administration
CCTS	Certificate in Clinical and Translational Science
CE	Civil Engineer
CEM	Certificate of Environmental Management
CET	Certificate in Educational Technologies
CGS	Certificate of Graduate Studies
Ch E	Chemical Engineer
Clin Sc D	Doctor of Clinical Science
CM	Certificate in Management
CMH	Certificate in Medical Humanities
CMM	Master of Church Ministries
CMS	Certificate in Ministerial Studies
CNM	Certificate in Nonprofit Management
CPASF	Certificate Program for Advanced Study in Finance
CPC	Certificate in Professional Counseling
	Certificate in Publication and Communication
CPH	Certificate in Public Health
CPM	Certificate in Public Management
CPS	Certificate of Professional Studies
CScD	Doctor of Clinical Science
CSD	Certificate in Spiritual Direction
CSS	Certificate of Special Studies
CTS	Certificate of Theological Studies

CURP	Certificate in Urban and Regional Planning
D Admin	Doctor of Administration
D Arch	Doctor of Architecture
D Be	Doctor in Bioethics
D Com	Doctor of Commerce
D Couns	Doctor of Counseling
D Des	Doctorate of Design
D Div	Doctor of Divinity
D Ed	Doctor of Education
D Ed Min	Doctor of Educational Ministry
D Eng	Doctor of Engineering
D Engr	Doctor of Engineering
D Ent	Doctor of Enterprise
D Env	Doctor of Environment
D Law	Doctor of Law
D Litt	Doctor of Letters
D Med Sc	Doctor of Medical Science
D Min	Doctor of Ministry
D Miss	Doctor of Missiology
D Mus	Doctor of Music
D Mus A	Doctor of Musical Arts
D Phil	Doctor of Philosophy
D Prof	Doctor of Professional Studies
D Ps	Doctor of Psychology
D Sc	Doctor of Science
D Sc D	Doctor of Science in Dentistry
D Sc IS	Doctor of Science in Information Systems
D Sc PA	Doctor of Science in Physician Assistant Studies
D Th	Doctor of Theology
D Th P	Doctor of Practical Theology
DA	Doctor of Accounting
	Doctor of Arts
DAH	Doctor of Arts in Humanities
DAOM	Doctorate in Acupuncture and Oriental Medicine
DAT	Doctorate of Athletic Training
	Professional Doctor of Art Therapy
DBA	Doctor of Business Administration
DBH	Doctor of Behavioral Health
DBL	Doctor of Business Leadership
DC	Doctor of Chiropractic
DCC	Doctor of Computer Science
DCD	Doctor of Communications Design
DCL	Doctor of Civil Law
	Doctor of Comparative Law
DCM	Doctor of Church Music
DCN	Doctor of Clinical Nutrition
DCS	Doctor of Computer Science
DDN	Diplôme du Droit Notarial
DDS	Doctor of Dental Surgery
DE	Doctor of Education
	Doctor of Engineering
DED	Doctor of Economic Development
DEIT	Doctor of Educational Innovation and Technology
DEL	Doctor of Executive Leadership
DEM	Doctor of Educational Ministry
DEPD	Diplôme Études Spécialisées
DES	Doctor of Engineering Science
DESS	Diplôme Études Supérieures Spécialisées
DET	Doctor of Educational Technology
DFA	Doctor of Fine Arts
DGP	Diploma in Graduate and Professional Studies
DH Ed	Doctor of Health Education

DH Sc	Doctor of Health Sciences
DHA	Doctor of Health Administration
DHCE	Doctor of Health Care Ethics
DHL	Doctor of Hebrew Letters
DHPE	Doctorate of Health Professionals Education
DHS	Doctor of Health Science
DHSc	Doctor of Health Science
Dip CS	Diploma in Christian Studies
DIT	Doctor of Industrial Technology
	Doctor of Information Technology
DJS	Doctor of Jewish Studies
DLS	Doctor of Liberal Studies
DM	Doctor of Management
	Doctor of Music
DMA	Doctor of Musical Arts
DMD	Doctor of Dental Medicine
DME	Doctor of Manufacturing Management
	Doctor of Music Education
DMEd	Doctor of Music Education
DMFT	Doctor of Marital and Family Therapy
DMH	Doctor of Medical Humanities
DML	Doctor of Modern Languages
DMP	Doctorate in Medical Physics
DMPNA	Doctor of Management Practice in Nurse Anesthesia
DN Sc	Doctor of Nursing Science
DNAP	Doctor of Nurse Anesthesia Practice
DNP	Doctor of Nursing Practice
DNP-A	Doctor of Nursing Practice - Anesthesia
DNS	Doctor of Nursing Science
DO	Doctor of Osteopathy
DOT	Doctor of Occupational Therapy
DPA	Doctor of Public Administration
DPDS	Doctor of Planning and Development Studies
DPH	Doctor of Public Health
DPM	Doctor of Plant Medicine
	Doctor of Podiatric Medicine
DPPD	Doctor of Policy, Planning, and Development
DPS	Doctor of Professional Studies
DPT	Doctor of Physical Therapy
DPTSc	Doctor of Physical Therapy Science
Dr DES	Doctor of Design
Dr NP	Doctor of Nursing Practice
Dr OT	Doctor of Occupational Therapy
Dr PH	Doctor of Public Health
Dr Sc PT	Doctor of Science in Physical Therapy
DrAP	Doctor of Anesthesia Practice
DRSc	Doctor of Regulatory Science
DS	Doctor of Science
DS Sc	Doctor of Social Science
DSJS	Doctor of Science in Jewish Studies
DSL	Doctor of Strategic Leadership
DSS	Doctor of Strategic Security
DSW	Doctor of Social Work
DTL	Doctor of Talmudic Law
	Doctor of Transformational Leadership
DV Sc	Doctor of Veterinary Science
DVM	Doctor of Veterinary Medicine
DWS	Doctor of Worship Studies
EAA	Engineer in Aeronautics and Astronautics
EASPh D	Engineering and Applied Science Doctor of Philosophy
ECS	Engineer in Computer Science
Ed D	Doctor of Education
Ed DCT	Doctor of Education in College Teaching
Ed L D	Doctor of Education Leadership
Ed M	Master of Education
Ed S	Specialist in Education
Ed Sp	Specialist in Education

EDB	Executive Doctorate in Business
EDBA	Executive Doctor of Business Administration
EDM	Executive Doctorate in Management
EE	Electrical Engineer
EJD	Executive Juris Doctor
EMBA	Executive Master of Business Administration
EMFA	Executive Master of Forensic Accounting
EMHA	Executive Master of Health Administration
EMIB	Executive Master of International Business
EML	Executive Master of Leadership
EMPA	Executive Master of Public Administration
EMPL	Executive Master in Public Leadership
EMS	Executive Master of Science
EMTM	Executive Master of Technology Management
Eng	Engineer
Eng Sc D	Doctor of Engineering Science
Engr	Engineer
Exec M Tax	Executive Master of Taxation
Exec MAC	Executive Master of Accounting
Exec Ed D	Executive Doctor of Education
Exec MBA	Executive Master of Business Administration
Exec MPA	Executive Master of Public Administration
Exec MPH	Executive Master of Public Health
Exec MS	Executive Master of Science
Executive Fellows MBA	Executive Fellows Master of Business Administration
G Dip	Graduate Diploma
GBC	Graduate Business Certificate
GDM	Graduate Diploma in Management
GDPA	Graduate Diploma in Public Administration
GDRE	Graduate Diploma in Religious Education
GEMBA	Global Executive Master of Business Administration
GMBA	Global Master of Business Administration
GP LL M	Global Professional Master of Laws
GPD	Graduate Performance Diploma
GSS	Graduate Special Certificate for Students in Special Situations
IEMBA	International Executive Master of Business Administration
IMA	Interdisciplinary Master of Arts
IMBA	International Master of Business Administration
IMES	International Master's in Environmental Studies
Ingeniero	Engineer
JCD	Doctor of Canon Law
JCL	Licentiate in Canon Law
JD	Juris Doctor
JM	Juris Master
JSD	Doctor of Juridical Science
	Doctor of Jurisprudence
	Doctor of the Science of Law
JSM	Master of the Science of Law
L Th	Licenciate in Theology
LL B	Bachelor of Laws
LL CM	Master of Comparative Law
LL D	Doctor of Laws
LL M	Master of Laws
LL M in Tax	Master of Laws in Taxation
LL M CL	Master of Laws in Common Law
M Ac	Master of Accountancy
	Master of Accounting
	Master of Acupuncture
M Ac OM	Master of Acupuncture and Oriental Medicine
M Acc	Master of Accountancy
	Master of Accounting
M Acct	Master of Accountancy
	Master of Accounting

M Accy	Master of Accountancy
M Actg	Master of Accounting
M Acy	Master of Accountancy
M Ad	Master of Administration
M Ad Ed	Master of Adult Education
M Adm	Master of Administration
M Adm Mgt	Master of Administrative Management
M Admin	Master of Administration
M ADU	Master of Architectural Design and Urbanism
M Adv	Master of Advertising
M AEST	Master of Applied Environmental Science and Technology
M Ag	Master of Agriculture
M Ag Ed	Master of Agricultural Education
M Agr	Master of Agriculture
M Anesth Ed	Master of Anesthesiology Education
M App Comp Sc	Master of Applied Computer Science
M App St	Master of Applied Statistics
M Appl Stat	Master of Applied Statistics
M Aq	Master of Aquaculture
M Arc	Master of Architecture
M Arch	Master of Architecture
M Arch I	Master of Architecture I
M Arch II	Master of Architecture II
M Arch E	Master of Architectural Engineering
M Arch H	Master of Architectural History
M Bioethics	Master in Bioethics
M Biomath	Master of Biomathematics
M Ch E	Master of Chemical Engineering
M Chem	Master of Chemistry
M Cl D	Master of Clinical Dentistry
M Cl Sc	Master of Clinical Science
M Comp	Master of Computing
M Comp Sc	Master of Computer Science
M Coun	Master of Counseling
M Dent	Master of Dentistry
M Dent Sc	Master of Dental Sciences
M Des	Master of Design
M Des S	Master of Design Studies
M Div	Master of Divinity
M E Sci	Master of Earth Science
M Ec	Master of Economics
M Econ	Master of Economics
M Ed	Master of Education
M Ed T	Master of Education in Teaching
M En	Master of Engineering
M En S	Master of Environmental Sciences
M Eng	Master of Engineering
M Eng Mgt	Master of Engineering Management
M Engr	Master of Engineering
M Ent	Master of Enterprise
M Env	Master of Environment
M Env Des	Master of Environmental Design
M Env E	Master of Environmental Engineering
M Env Sc	Master of Environmental Science
M Fin	Master of Finance
M FSc	Master of Fisheries Science
M Geo E	Master of Geological Engineering
M Geoenv E	Master of Geoenvironmental Engineering
M Geog	Master of Geography
M Hum	Master of Humanities
M IDST	Master's in Interdisciplinary Studies
M Kin	Master of Kinesiology
M Land Arch	Master of Landscape Architecture
M Litt	Master of Letters
M Mat SE	Master of Material Science and Engineering
M Math	Master of Mathematics
M Mech E	Master of Mechanical Engineering
M Med Sc	Master of Medical Science
M Mgmt	Master of Management
M Mgt	Master of Management
M Min	Master of Ministries
M Mtl E	Master of Materials Engineering
M Mu	Master of Music
M Mus	Master of Music
M Mus Ed	Master of Music Education
M Music	Master of Music
M Nat Sci	Master of Natural Science
M Pet E	Master of Petroleum Engineering
M Pharm	Master of Pharmacy
M Phil	Master of Philosophy
M Phil F	Master of Philosophical Foundations
M Pl	Master of Planning
M Plan	Master of Planning
M Pol	Master of Political Science
M Pr Met	Master of Professional Meteorology
M Prob S	Master of Probability and Statistics
M Psych	Master of Psychology
M Pub	Master of Publishing
M Rel	Master of Religion
M Sc	Master of Science
M Sc A	Master of Science (Applied)
M Sc AC	Master of Science in Applied Computing
M Sc AHN	Master of Science in Applied Human Nutrition
M Sc BMC	Master of Science in Biomedical Communications
M Sc CS	Master of Science in Computer Science
M Sc E	Master of Science in Engineering
M Sc Eng	Master of Science in Engineering
M Sc Engr	Master of Science in Engineering
M Sc F	Master of Science in Forestry
M Sc FE	Master of Science in Forest Engineering
M Sc Geogr	Master of Science in Geography
M Sc N	Master of Science in Nursing
M Sc OT	Master of Science in Occupational Therapy
M Sc P	Master of Science in Planning
M Sc Pl	Master of Science in Planning
M Sc PT	Master of Science in Physical Therapy
M Sc T	Master of Science in Teaching
M SEM	Master of Sustainable Environmental Management
M Serv Soc	Master of Social Service
M Soc	Master of Sociology
M Sp Ed	Master of Special Education
M St	Master of Studies
M Stat	Master of Statistics
M Sys E	Master of Systems Engineering
M Sys Sc	Master of Systems Science
M Tax	Master of Taxation
M Tech	Master of Technology
M Th	Master of Theology
M Tox	Master of Toxicology
M Trans E	Master of Transportation Engineering
M U Ed	Master of Urban Education
M Urb	Master of Urban Planning
M Vet Sc	Master of Veterinary Science
MA	Master of Accounting
	Master of Administration
	Master of Arts
MA Comm	Master of Arts in Communication
MA Ed	Master of Arts in Education
MA Ed/HD	Master of Arts in Education and Human Development
MA Ext	Master of Agricultural Extension
MA Min	Master of Arts in Ministry
MA Past St	Master of Arts in Pastoral Studies
MA Ph	Master of Arts in Philosophy

MA Psych	Master of Arts in Psychology
MA Sc	Master of Applied Science
MA Sp	Master of Arts (Spirituality)
MA Th	Master of Arts in Theology
MA-R	Master of Arts (Research)
MAA	Master of Administrative Arts
	Master of Applied Anthropology
	Master of Applied Arts
	Master of Arts in Administration
MAAA	Master of Arts in Arts Administration
MAAAP	Master of Arts Administration and Policy
MAAD	Master of Advanced Architectural Design
MAAE	Master of Arts in Art Education
MAAPPS	Master of Arts in Asia Pacific Policy Studies
MAAS	Master of Arts in Aging and Spirituality
MAASJ	Master of Arts in Applied Social Justice
MAAT	Master of Arts in Applied Theology
	Master of Arts in Art Therapy
MAB	Master of Agribusiness
MABC	Master of Arts in Biblical Counseling
MABE	Master of Arts in Bible Exposition
MABL	Master of Arts in Biblical Languages
MABM	Master of Agribusiness Management
MABS	Master of Arts in Biblical Studies
MABT	Master of Arts in Bible Teaching
MAC	Master of Accountancy
	Master of Accounting
	Master of Arts in Communication
	Master of Arts in Counseling
MACC	Master of Arts in Christian Counseling
	Master of Arts in Clinical Counseling
MACCT	Master of Accounting
MACD	Master of Arts in Christian Doctrine
MACE	Master of Arts in Christian Education
MACH	Master of Arts in Church History
MACI	Master of Arts in Curriculum and Instruction
MACIS	Master of Accounting and Information Systems
MACJ	Master of Arts in Criminal Justice
MACL	Master of Arts in Christian Leadership
	Master of Arts in Community Leadership
MACM	Master of Arts in Christian Ministries
	Master of Arts in Christian Ministry
	Master of Arts in Church Music
	Master of Arts in Counseling Ministries
MACN	Master of Arts in Counseling
MACO	Master of Arts in Counseling
MAcOM	Master of Acupuncture and Oriental Medicine
MACP	Master of Arts in Christian Practice
	Master of Arts in Church Planting
	Master of Arts in Counseling Psychology
MACS	Master of Applied Computer Science
	Master of Arts in Catholic Studies
	Master of Arts in Christian Studies
MACSE	Master of Arts in Christian School Education
MACT	Master of Arts in Communications and Technology
MAD	Master in Educational Institution Administration
	Master of Art and Design
MADR	Master of Arts in Dispute Resolution
MADS	Master of Animal and Dairy Science
	Master of Applied Disability Studies
MAE	Master of Aerospace Engineering
	Master of Agricultural Economics
	Master of Agricultural Education
	Master of Applied Economics
	Master of Architectural Engineering
	Master of Art Education

	Master of Arts in Education
	Master of Arts in English
MAEd	Master of Arts Education
MAEL	Master of Arts in Educational Leadership
MAEM	Master of Arts in Educational Ministries
MAEP	Master of Arts in Economic Policy
	Master of Arts in Educational Psychology
MAES	Master of Arts in Environmental Sciences
MAET	Master of Arts in English Teaching
MAF	Master of Arts in Finance
MAFE	Master of Arts in Financial Economics
MAFLL	Master of Arts in Foreign Language and Literature
MAFM	Master of Accounting and Financial Management
MAFS	Master of Arts in Family Studies
MAG	Master of Applied Geography
MAGS	Master of Arts in Global Service
MAGU	Master of Urban Analysis and Management
MAH	Master of Arts in Humanities
MAHA	Master of Arts in Humanitarian Assistance
MAHCM	Master of Arts in Health Care Mission
MAHG	Master of American History and Government
MAHL	Master of Arts in Hebrew Letters
MAHN	Master of Applied Human Nutrition
MAHR	Master of Applied Historical Research
MAHS	Master of Arts in Human Services
MAHSR	Master in Applied Health Services Research
MAIA	Master of Arts in International Administration
	Master of Arts in International Affairs
MAIDM	Master of Arts in Interior Design and Merchandising
MAIH	Master of Arts in Interdisciplinary Humanities
MAIOP	Master of Applied Industrial/Organizational Psychology
MAIPCR	Master of Arts in International Peace and Conflict Management
MAIS	Master of Arts in Intercultural Studies
	Master of Arts in Interdisciplinary Studies
	Master of Arts in International Studies
MAIT	Master of Administration in Information Technology
MAJ	Master of Arts in Journalism
MAJ Ed	Master of Arts in Jewish Education
MAJCS	Master of Arts in Jewish Communal Service
MAJE	Master of Arts in Jewish Education
MAJPS	Master of Arts in Jewish Professional Studies
MAJS	Master of Arts in Jewish Studies
MAL	Master in Agricultural Leadership
MALA	Master of Arts in Liberal Arts
MALD	Master of Arts in Law and Diplomacy
MALER	Master of Arts in Labor and Employment Relations
MALL	Master of Arts in Language Learning
MALP	Master of Arts in Language Pedagogy
MALS	Master of Arts in Liberal Studies
MAM	Master of Acquisition Management
	Master of Agriculture and Management
	Master of Applied Mathematics
	Master of Arts in Management
	Master of Arts in Ministry
	Master of Arts Management
	Master of Avian Medicine
MAMB	Master of Applied Molecular Biology
MAMC	Master of Arts in Mass Communication
	Master of Arts in Ministry and Culture
	Master of Arts in Ministry for a Multicultural Church
	Master of Arts in Missional Christianity
MAME	Master of Arts in Missions/Evangelism

MAMFC	Master of Arts in Marriage and Family Counseling		Master's in Administration of Telecommunications
MAMFT	Master of Arts in Marriage and Family Therapy	Mat E	Materials Engineer
MAMHC	Master of Arts in Mental Health Counseling	MATCM	Master of Acupuncture and Traditional Chinese Medicine
MAMS	Master of Applied Mathematical Sciences	MATDE	Master of Arts in Theology, Development, and Evangelism
	Master of Applied Meditation Studies	MATDR	Master of Territorial Management and Regional Development
	Master of Arts in Ministerial Studies		
	Master of Arts in Ministry and Spirituality	MATE	Master of Arts for the Teaching of English
MAMT	Master of Arts in Mathematics Teaching	MATESL	Master of Arts in Teaching English as a Second Language
MAN	Master of Applied Nutrition		
MANT	Master of Arts in New Testament	MATESOL	Master of Arts in Teaching English to Speakers of Other Languages
MAOL	Master of Arts in Organizational Leadership		
MAOM	Master of Acupuncture and Oriental Medicine	MATF	Master of Arts in Teaching English as a Foreign Language/Intercultural Studies
MAOT	Master of Arts in Old Testament		
MAP	Master of Applied Politics	MATFL	Master of Arts in Teaching Foreign Language
	Master of Applied Psychology	MATH	Master of Arts in Therapy
	Master of Arts in Planning	MATI	Master of Administration of Information Technology
	Master of Psychology		
	Master of Public Administration	MATL	Master of Arts in Teacher Leadership
MAP Min	Master of Arts in Pastoral Ministry		Master of Arts in Teaching of Languages
MAPA	Master of Arts in Public Administration		Master of Arts in Transformational Leadership
MAPC	Master of Arts in Pastoral Counseling	MATM	Master of Arts in Teaching of Mathematics
MAPE	Master of Arts in Physics Education	MATS	Master of Arts in Theological Studies
	Master of Arts in Political Economy		Master of Arts in Transforming Spirituality
MAPM	Master of Arts in Pastoral Ministry	MATSL	Master of Arts in Teaching a Second Language
	Master of Arts in Pastoral Music	MAUA	Master of Arts in Urban Affairs
	Master of Arts in Practical Ministry	MAUD	Master of Arts in Urban Design
MAPP	Master of Arts in Public Policy	MAURP	Master of Arts in Urban and Regional Planning
MAPS	Master of Arts in Pastoral Studies	MAW	Master of Arts in Worship
	Master of Arts in Public Service	MAWSHP	Master of Arts in Worship
MAPT	Master of Practical Theology	MAYM	Master of Arts in Youth Ministry
MAPW	Master of Arts in Professional Writing	MB	Master of Bioinformatics
MAR	Master of Arts in Reading	MBA	Master of Business Administration
	Master of Arts in Religion	MBA-AM	Master of Business Administration in Aviation Management
Mar Eng	Marine Engineer		
MARC	Master of Arts in Rehabilitation Counseling	MBA-EP	Master of Business Administration– Experienced Professionals
MARE	Master of Arts in Religious Education		
MARL	Master of Arts in Religious Leadership	MBAA	Master of Business Administration in Aviation
MARS	Master of Arts in Religious Studies	MBAE	Master of Biological and Agricultural Engineering
MAS	Master of Accounting Science		
	Master of Actuarial Science		Master of Biosystems and Agricultural Engineering
	Master of Administrative Science		
	Master of Advanced Study	MBAH	Master of Business Administration in Health
	Master of Aeronautical Science	MBAi	Master of Business Administration– International
	Master of American Studies		
	Master of Animal Science	MBAICT	Master of Business Administration in Information and Communication Technology
	Master of Applied Science		
	Master of Applied Statistics	MBATM	Master of Business Administration in Technology Management
	Master of Archival Studies		
MASA	Master of Advanced Studies in Architecture	MBC	Master of Building Construction
MASD	Master of Arts in Spiritual Direction	MBE	Master of Bilingual Education
MASE	Master of Arts in Special Education		Master of Bioengineering
MASF	Master of Arts in Spiritual Formation		Master of Bioethics
MASJ	Master of Arts in Systems of Justice		Master of Biomedical Engineering
MASLA	Master of Advanced Studies in Landscape Architecture		Master of Business Economics
			Master of Business Education
MASM	Master of Aging Services Management	MBEE	Master in Biotechnology Enterprise and Entrepreneurship
	Master of Arts in Specialized Ministries		
MASP	Master of Applied Social Psychology	MBET	Master of Business, Entrepreneurship and Technology
	Master of Arts in School Psychology		
MASPAA	Master of Arts in Sports and Athletic Administration	MBID	Master of Biomedical Innovation and Development
		MBIOT	Master of Biotechnology
MASS	Master of Applied Social Science	MBiotech	Master of Biotechnology
	Master of Arts in Social Science	MBL	Master of Business Law
MAST	Master of Arts in Science Teaching		Master of Business Leadership
MAT	Master of Arts in Teaching	MBLE	Master in Business Logistics Engineering
	Master of Arts in Theology	MBME	Master's in Biomedical Engineering
	Master of Athletic Training	MBMSE	Master of Business Management and Software Engineering

MBOE	Master of Business Operational Excellence
MBS	Master of Biblical Studies
	Master of Biological Science
	Master of Biomedical Sciences
	Master of Bioscience
	Master of Building Science
	Master of Business and Science
MBST	Master of Biostatistics
MBT	Master of Biomedical Technology
	Master of Biotechnology
	Master of Business Taxation
MBV	Master of Business for Veterans
MC	Master of Communication
	Master of Counseling
	Master of Cybersecurity
MC Ed	Master of Continuing Education
MC Sc	Master of Computer Science
MCA	Master in Collegiate Athletics
	Master of Commercial Aviation
	Master of Criminology (Applied)
MCAM	Master of Computational and Applied Mathematics
MCC	Master of Computer Science
MCD	Master of Communications Disorders
	Master of Community Development
MCE	Master in Electronic Commerce
	Master of Christian Education
	Master of Civil Engineering
	Master of Control Engineering
MCEM	Master of Construction Engineering Management
MCHE	Master of Chemical Engineering
MCIS	Master of Communication and Information Studies
	Master of Computer and Information Science
	Master of Computer Information Systems
MCIT	Master of Computer and Information Technology
MCJ	Master of Criminal Justice
MCL	Master in Communication Leadership
	Master of Canon Law
	Master of Comparative Law
MCM	Master of Christian Ministry
	Master of Church Music
	Master of City Management
	Master of Communication Management
	Master of Community Medicine
	Master of Construction Management
	Master of Contract Management
MCMin	Master of Christian Ministry
MCMP	Master of City and Metropolitan Planning
MCMS	Master of Clinical Medical Science
MCN	Master of Clinical Nutrition
MCOL	Master of Arts in Community and Organizational Leadership
MCP	Master of City Planning
	Master of Community Planning
	Master of Counseling Psychology
	Master of Cytopathology Practice
	Master of Science in Quality Systems and Productivity
MCPC	Master of Arts in Chaplaincy and Pastoral Care
MCPD	Master of Community Planning and Development
MCR	Master in Clinical Research
MCRP	Master of City and Regional Planning
	Master of Community and Regional Planning
MCRS	Master of City and Regional Studies
MCS	Master of Chemical Sciences
	Master of Christian Studies

	Master of Clinical Science
	Master of Combined Sciences
	Master of Communication Studies
	Master of Computer Science
	Master of Consumer Science
MCSE	Master of Computer Science and Engineering
MCSL	Master of Catholic School Leadership
MCSM	Master of Construction Science and Management
MCTM	Master of Clinical Translation Management
MCTP	Master of Communication Technology and Policy
MCTS	Master of Clinical and Translational Science
MCVS	Master of Cardiovascular Science
MD	Doctor of Medicine
MDA	Master of Dietetic Administration
MDB	Master of Design-Build
MDE	Master of Developmental Economics
	Master of Distance Education
	Master of the Education of the Deaf
MDH	Master of Dental Hygiene
MDM	Master of Design Methods
	Master of Digital Media
MDP	Master in Sustainable Development Practice
	Master of Development Practice
MDR	Master of Dispute Resolution
MDS	Master of Dental Surgery
	Master of Design Studies
	Master of Digital Sciences
ME	Master of Education
	Master of Engineering
	Master of Entrepreneurship
ME Sc	Master of Engineering Science
ME-PD	Master of Education–Professional Development
MEA	Master of Educational Administration
	Master of Engineering Administration
MEAE	Master of Entertainment Arts and Engineering
MEAP	Master of Environmental Administration and Planning
MEB	Master of Energy Business
MEBD	Master in Environmental Building Design
MEBT	Master in Electronic Business Technologies
MEC	Master of Electronic Commerce
Mech E	Mechanical Engineer
MED	Master of Education of the Deaf
MEDS	Master of Environmental Design Studies
MEE	Master in Education
	Master of Electrical Engineering
	Master of Energy Engineering
	Master of Environmental Engineering
MEEM	Master of Environmental Engineering and Management
MEENE	Master of Engineering in Environmental Engineering
MEEP	Master of Environmental and Energy Policy
MEERM	Master of Earth and Environmental Resource Management
MEH	Master in Humanistic Studies
	Master of Environmental Health
	Master of Environmental Horticulture
MEHS	Master of Environmental Health and Safety
MEIM	Master of Entertainment Industry Management
	Master of Equine Industry Management
MEL	Master of Educational Leadership
	Master of English Literature
MELP	Master of Environmental Law and Policy
MEM	Master of Engineering Management
	Master of Environmental Management
	Master of Marketing

MEME	Master of Engineering in Manufacturing Engineering
	Master of Engineering in Mechanical Engineering
MENR	Master of Environment and Natural Resources
MENVEGR	Master of Environmental Engineering
MEP	Master of Engineering Physics
MEPC	Master of Environmental Pollution Control
MEPD	Master of Environmental Planning and Design
MER	Master of Employment Relations
MERE	Master of Entrepreneurial Real Estate
MERL	Master of Energy Regulation and Law
MES	Master of Education and Science
	Master of Engineering Science
	Master of Environment and Sustainability
	Master of Environmental Science
	Master of Environmental Studies
	Master of Environmental Systems
	Master of Special Education
MESM	Master of Environmental Science and Management
MET	Master of Educational Technology
	Master of Engineering Technology
	Master of Entertainment Technology
	Master of Environmental Toxicology
METM	Master of Engineering and Technology Management
MEVE	Master of Environmental Engineering
MF	Master of Finance
	Master of Forestry
MFA	Master of Fine Arts
MFALP	Master of Food and Agriculture Law and Policy
MFAM	Master's of Food Animal Medicine
MFAS	Master of Fisheries and Aquatic Science
MFAW	Master of Fine Arts in Writing
MFC	Master of Forest Conservation
MFCS	Master of Family and Consumer Sciences
MFE	Master of Financial Economics
	Master of Financial Engineering
	Master of Forest Engineering
MFES	Master of Fire and Emergency Services
MFG	Master of Functional Genomics
MFHD	Master of Family and Human Development
MFM	Master of Financial Management
	Master of Financial Mathematics
MFPE	Master of Food Process Engineering
MFR	Master of Forest Resources
MFRC	Master of Forest Resources and Conservation
MFRE	Master of Food and Resource Economics
MFS	Master of Food Science
	Master of Forensic Sciences
	Master of Forest Science
	Master of Forest Studies
	Master of French Studies
MFST	Master of Food Safety and Technology
MFT	Master of Family Therapy
	Master of Food Technology
MFWB	Master of Fishery and Wildlife Biology
MFWCB	Master of Fish, Wildlife and Conservation Biology
MFWS	Master of Fisheries and Wildlife Sciences
MFYCS	Master of Family, Youth and Community Sciences
MG	Master of Genetics
MGA	Master of Global Affairs
	Master of Government Administration
	Master of Governmental Administration
MGC	Master of Genetic Counseling
MGD	Master of Graphic Design

MGE	Master of Geotechnical Engineering
MGEM	Master of Global Entrepreneurship and Management
MGIS	Master of Geographic Information Science
	Master of Geographic Information Systems
MGM	Master of Global Management
MGP	Master of Gestion de Projet
MGPS	Master of Global Policy Studies
MGREM	Master of Global Real Estate Management
MGS	Master of Gerontological Studies
	Master of Global Studies
MGsc	Master of Geoscience
MH	Master of Humanities
MH Sc	Master of Health Sciences
MHA	Master of Health Administration
	Master of Healthcare Administration
	Master of Hospital Administration
	Master of Hospitality Administration
MHB	Master of Human Behavior
MHC	Master of Mental Health Counseling
MHCA	Master of Health Care Administration
MHCD	Master of Health Care Design
MHCI	Master of Human-Computer Interaction
MHCL	Master of Health Care Leadership
MHE	Master of Health Education
	Master of Human Ecology
MHE Ed	Master of Home Economics Education
MHEA	Master of Higher Education Administration
MHHS	Master of Health and Human Services
MHI	Master of Health Informatics
	Master of Healthcare Innovation
MHIHIM	Master of Health Informatics and Health Information Management
MHIIM	Master of Health Informatics and Information Management
MHIS	Master of Health Information Systems
MHK	Master of Human Kinetics
MHM	Master of Healthcare Management
MHMS	Master of Health Management Systems
MHP	Master of Health Physics
	Master of Heritage Preservation
	Master of Historic Preservation
MHPA	Master of Heath Policy and Administration
MHPE	Master of Health Professions Education
MHR	Master of Human Resources
MHRD	Master in Human Resource Development
MHRIR	Master of Human Resources and Industrial Relations
MHRLR	Master of Human Resources and Labor Relations
MHRM	Master of Human Resources Management
MHS	Master of Health Science
	Master of Health Sciences
	Master of Health Studies
	Master of Hispanic Studies
	Master of Human Services
	Master of Humanistic Studies
MHSA	Master of Health Services Administration
MHSE	Master of Health Science Education
MHSM	Master of Health Systems Management
MI	Master of Information
	Master of Instruction
MI Arch	Master of Interior Architecture
MIA	Master of Interior Architecture
	Master of International Affairs
MIAA	Master of International Affairs and Administration
MIAM	Master of International Agribusiness Management

MIAPD	Master of Interior Architecture and Product Design
MIB	Master of International Business
MIBA	Master of International Business Administration
MICM	Master of International Construction Management
MID	Master of Industrial Design
	Master of Industrial Distribution
	Master of Interior Design
	Master of International Development
MIDA	Master of International Development Administration
MIDC	Master of Integrated Design and Construction
MIDP	Master of International Development Policy
MIE	Master of Industrial Engineering
MIHTM	Master of International Hospitality and Tourism Management
MIJ	Master of International Journalism
MILR	Master of Industrial and Labor Relations
MIM	Master in Ministry
	Master of Information Management
	Master of International Management
MIMLAE	Master of International Management for Latin American Executives
MIMS	Master of Information Management and Systems
	Master of Integrated Manufacturing Systems
MIP	Master of Infrastructure Planning
	Master of Intellectual Property
	Master of International Policy
MIPA	Master of International Public Affairs
MIPD	Master of Integrated Product Design
MIPM	Master of International Policy Management
MIPP	Master of International Policy and Practice
	Master of International Public Policy
MIPS	Master of International Planning Studies
MIR	Master of Industrial Relations
	Master of International Relations
MIRHR	Master of Industrial Relations and Human Resources
MIS	Master of Imaging Science
	Master of Industrial Statistics
	Master of Information Science
	Master of Information Systems
	Master of Integrated Science
	Master of Interdisciplinary Studies
	Master of International Service
	Master of International Studies
MISE	Master of Industrial and Systems Engineering
MISKM	Master of Information Sciences and Knowledge Management
MISM	Master of Information Systems Management
MISW	Master of Indigenous Social Work
MIT	Master in Teaching
	Master of Industrial Technology
	Master of Information Technology
	Master of Initial Teaching
	Master of International Trade
	Master of Internet Technology
MITA	Master of Information Technology Administration
MITM	Master of Information Technology and Management
MJ	Master of Journalism
	Master of Jurisprudence
MJ Ed	Master of Jewish Education
MJA	Master of Justice Administration
MJM	Master of Justice Management
MJS	Master of Judicial Studies

	Master of Juridical Studies
MK	Master of Kinesiology
MKM	Master of Knowledge Management
ML	Master of Latin
ML Arch	Master of Landscape Architecture
MLA	Master of Landscape Architecture
	Master of Liberal Arts
MLAS	Master of Laboratory Animal Science
	Master of Liberal Arts and Sciences
MLAUD	Master of Landscape Architecture in Urban Development
MLD	Master of Leadership Development
	Master of Leadership Studies
MLE	Master of Applied Linguistics and Exegesis
MLER	Master of Labor and Employment Relations
MLI Sc	Master of Library and Information Science
MLIS	Master of Library and Information Science
	Master of Library and Information Studies
MLM	Master of Leadership in Ministry
MLPD	Master of Land and Property Development
MLRHR	Master of Labor Relations and Human Resources
MLS	Master of Leadership Studies
	Master of Legal Studies
	Master of Liberal Studies
	Master of Library Science
	Master of Life Sciences
MLSCM	Master of Logistics and Supply Chain Management
MLSP	Master of Law and Social Policy
MLT	Master of Language Technologies
MLTCA	Master of Long Term Care Administration
MLW	Master of Studies in Law
MLWS	Master of Land and Water Systems
MM	Master of Management
	Master of Ministry
	Master of Missiology
	Master of Music
MM Ed	Master of Music Education
MM Sc	Master of Medical Science
MM St	Master of Museum Studies
MMA	Master of Marine Affairs
	Master of Media Arts
	Master of Ministry Administration
	Master of Musical Arts
MMAL	Master of Maritime Administration and Logistics
MMAS	Master of Military Art and Science
MMB	Master of Microbial Biotechnology
MMC	Master of Manufacturing Competitiveness
	Master of Mass Communications
	Master of Music Conducting
MMCM	Master of Music in Church Music
MMCSS	Master of Mathematical Computational and Statistical Sciences
MME	Master of Manufacturing Engineering
	Master of Mathematics Education
	Master of Mathematics for Educators
	Master of Mechanical Engineering
	Master of Mining Engineering
	Master of Music Education
MMF	Master of Mathematical Finance
MMFT	Master of Marriage and Family Therapy
MMH	Master of Management in Hospitality
	Master of Medical Humanities
MMI	Master of Management of Innovation
MMIS	Master of Management Information Systems
MML	Master of Managerial Logistics
MMM	Master of Manufacturing Management

	Master of Marine Management		Master of Physician Assistant
	Master of Medical Management		Master of Professional Accountancy
MMP	Master of Management Practice		Master of Professional Accounting
	Master of Marine Policy		Master of Public Administration
	Master of Medical Physics		Master of Public Affairs
	Master of Music Performance	MPAC	Master of Professional Accounting
MMPA	Master of Management and Professional Accounting	MPAID	Master of Public Administration and International Development
MMQM	Master of Manufacturing Quality Management	MPAP	Master of Physician Assistant Practice
MMR	Master of Marketing Research		Master of Public Administration and Policy
MMRM	Master of Marine Resources Management		Master of Public Affairs and Politics
MMS	Master of Management Science	MPAS	Master of Physician Assistant Science
	Master of Management Studies		Master of Physician Assistant Studies
	Master of Manufacturing Systems	MPC	Master of Professional Communication
	Master of Marine Studies		Master of Professional Counseling
	Master of Materials Science	MPD	Master of Product Development
	Master of Mathematical Sciences		Master of Public Diplomacy
	Master of Medical Science	MPDS	Master of Planning and Development Studies
	Master of Medieval Studies	MPE	Master of Physical Education
MMSE	Master of Manufacturing Systems Engineering	MPEM	Master of Project Engineering and Management
MMSM	Master of Music in Sacred Music		
MMT	Master in Marketing	MPH	Master of Public Health
	Master of Music Teaching	MPHE	Master of Public Health Education
	Master of Music Therapy	MPHM	Master in Plant Health Management
	Master's in Marketing Technology	MPHS	Master of Population Health Sciences
MMus	Master of Music	MPHTM	Master of Public Health and Tropical Medicine
MN	Master of Nursing	MPI	Master of Product Innovation
	Master of Nutrition	MPIA	Master of Public and International Affairs
MN NP	Master of Nursing in Nurse Practitioner	MPM	Master of Pastoral Ministry
MNA	Master of Nonprofit Administration		Master of Pest Management
	Master of Nurse Anesthesia		Master of Policy Management
MNAL	Master of Nonprofit Administration and Leadership		Master of Practical Ministries
			Master of Project Management
MNAS	Master of Natural and Applied Science		Master of Public Management
MNCM	Master of Network and Communications Management	MPNA	Master of Public and Nonprofit Administration
MNE	Master of Nuclear Engineering	MPNL	Master of Philanthropy and Nonprofit Leadership
MNL	Master in International Business for Latin America	MPO	Master of Prosthetics and Orthotics
		MPOD	Master of Positive Organizational Development
MNM	Master of Nonprofit Management	MPP	Master of Public Policy
MNO	Master of Nonprofit Organization	MPPA	Master of Public Policy Administration
MNPL	Master of Not-for-Profit Leadership		Master of Public Policy and Administration
MNpS	Master of Nonprofit Studies	MPPAL	Master of Public Policy, Administration and Law
MNR	Master of Natural Resources	MPPM	Master of Public and Private Management
MNRD	Master of Natural Resources Development		Master of Public Policy and Management
MNRES	Master of Natural Resources and Environmental Studies	MPPPM	Master of Plant Protection and Pest Management
MNRM	Master of Natural Resource Management	MPRTM	Master of Parks, Recreation, and Tourism Management
MNRMG	Master of Natural Resource Management and Geography		
		MPS	Master of Pastoral Studies
MNRS	Master of Natural Resource Stewardship		Master of Perfusion Science
MNS	Master of Natural Science		Master of Planning Studies
MO	Master of Oceanography		Master of Political Science
MOD	Master of Organizational Development		Master of Preservation Studies
MOGS	Master of Oil and Gas Studies		Master of Prevention Science
MOL	Master of Organizational Leadership		Master of Professional Studies
MOM	Master of Organizational Management		Master of Public Service
	Master of Oriental Medicine	MPSA	Master of Public Service Administration
MOR	Master of Operations Research	MPSG	Master of Population and Social Gerontology
MOT	Master of Occupational Therapy	MPSIA	Master of Political Science and International Affairs
MP	Master of Physiology		
	Master of Planning	MPSL	Master of Public Safety Leadership
MP Ac	Master of Professional Accountancy	MPSRE	Master of Professional Studies in Real Estate
MP Acc	Master of Professional Accountancy	MPT	Master of Pastoral Theology
	Master of Professional Accounting		Master of Physical Therapy
	Master of Public Accounting		Master of Practical Theology
MP Aff	Master of Public Affairs	MPVM	Master of Preventive Veterinary Medicine
MP Th	Master of Pastoral Theology	MPW	Master of Professional Writing
MPA	Master of Performing Arts		Master of Public Works

MQM	Master of Quality Management		Master of Science in Agriculture
MQS	Master of Quality Systems		Master of Science in Analytics
MR	Master of Recreation		Master of Science in Anesthesia
	Master of Retailing		Master of Science in Architecture
MRA	Master in Research Administration		Master of Science in Aviation
MRC	Master of Rehabilitation Counseling		Master of Sports Administration
MRCP	Master of Regional and City Planning		Master of Surgical Assisting
	Master of Regional and Community Planning	MSAA	Master of Science in Astronautics and Aeronautics
MRD	Master of Rural Development		
MRE	Master of Real Estate	MSAAE	Master of Science in Aeronautical and Astronautical Engineering
	Master of Religious Education		
MRED	Master of Real Estate Development	MSABE	Master of Science in Agricultural and Biological Engineering
MREM	Master of Resource and Environmental Management		
		MSAC	Master of Science in Acupuncture
MRLS	Master of Resources Law Studies	MSACC	Master of Science in Accounting
MRM	Master of Resources Management	MSACS	Master of Science in Applied Computer Science
MRP	Master of Regional Planning	MSAE	Master of Science in Aeronautical Engineering
MRRD	Master in Recreation Resource Development		Master of Science in Aerospace Engineering
MRS	Master of Religious Studies		Master of Science in Applied Economics
MRSc	Master of Rehabilitation Science		Master of Science in Applied Engineering
MRTP	Master of Rural and Town Planning		Master of Science in Architectural Engineering
MS	Master of Science	MSAEM	Master of Science in Aerospace Engineering and Mechanics
MS Cmp E	Master of Science in Computer Engineering		
MS Kin	Master of Science in Kinesiology	MSAF	Master of Science in Aviation Finance
MS Acct	Master of Science in Accounting	MSAG	Master of Science in Applied Geosciences
MS Accy	Master of Science in Accountancy	MSAH	Master of Science in Allied Health
MS Aero E	Master of Science in Aerospace Engineering	MSAL	Master of Sport Administration and Leadership
MS Ag	Master of Science in Agriculture	MSAM	Master of Science in Applied Mathematics
MS Arch	Master of Science in Architecture	MSANR	Master of Science in Agriculture and Natural Resources
MS Arch St	Master of Science in Architectural Studies		
MS Bio E	Master of Science in Bioengineering	MSAPM	Master of Security Analysis and Portfolio Management
MS Bm E	Master of Science in Biomedical Engineering		
MS Ch E	Master of Science in Chemical Engineering	MSAS	Master of Science in Applied Statistics
MS Cp E	Master of Science in Computer Engineering		Master of Science in Architectural Studies
MS Eco	Master of Science in Economics	MSAT	Master of Science in Accounting and Taxation
MS Econ	Master of Science in Economics		Master of Science in Advanced Technology
MS Ed	Master of Science in Education		Master of Science in Athletic Training
MS El	Master of Science in Educational Leadership and Administration	MSB	Master of Science in Biotechnology
			Master of Sustainable Business
MS En E	Master of Science in Environmental Engineering	MSBA	Master of Science in Business Administration
			Master of Science in Business Analysis
MS Eng	Master of Science in Engineering	MSBAE	Master of Science in Biological and Agricultural Engineering
MS Engr	Master of Science in Engineering		
MS Env E	Master of Science in Environmental Engineering		Master of Science in Biosystems and Agricultural Engineering
		MSBC	Master of Science in Building Construction
MS Exp Surg	Master of Science in Experimental Surgery		Master of Science in Business Communication
MS Mat E	Master of Science in Materials Engineering	MSBCB	Master's in Bioinformatics and Computational Biology
MS Mat SE	Master of Science in Material Science and Engineering		
		MSBE	Master of Science in Biological Engineering
MS Met E	Master of Science in Metallurgical Engineering		Master of Science in Biomedical Engineering
MS Mgt	Master of Science in Management	MSBENG	Master of Science in Bioengineering
MS Min	Master of Science in Mining	MSBH	Master of Science in Behavioral Health
MS Min E	Master of Science in Mining Engineering	MSBIT	Master of Science in Business Information Technology
MS Mt E	Master of Science in Materials Engineering		
MS Otol	Master of Science in Otolaryngology	MSBM	Master of Sport Business Management
MS Pet E	Master of Science in Petroleum Engineering	MSBME	Master of Science in Biomedical Engineering
MS Sc	Master of Social Science	MSBMS	Master of Science in Basic Medical Science
MS Sp Ed	Master of Science in Special Education	MSBS	Master of Science in Biomedical Sciences
MS Stat	Master of Science in Statistics	MSBTM	Master of Science in Biotechnology and Management
MS Surg	Master of Science in Surgery		
MS Tax	Master of Science in Taxation	MSC	Master of Science in Commerce
MS Tc E	Master of Science in Telecommunications Engineering		Master of Science in Communication
			Master of Science in Computers
MS-R	Master of Science (Research)		Master of Science in Counseling
MSA	Master of School Administration		Master of Science in Criminology
	Master of Science in Accountancy		Master of Strategic Communication
	Master of Science in Accounting	MSCC	Master of Science in Community Counseling
	Master of Science in Administration	MSCD	Master of Science in Communication Disorders
	Master of Science in Aeronautics		Master of Science in Community Development

MSCE	Master of Science in Civil Engineering
	Master of Science in Clinical Epidemiology
	Master of Science in Computer Engineering
	Master of Science in Continuing Education
MSCEE	Master of Science in Civil and Environmental Engineering
MSCF	Master of Science in Computational Finance
MSCH	Master of Science in Chemical Engineering
MSChE	Master of Science in Chemical Engineering
MSCI	Master of Science in Clinical Investigation
MSCIS	Master of Science in Computer and Information Science
	Master of Science in Computer and Information Systems
	Master of Science in Computer Information Science
	Master of Science in Computer Information Systems
MSCIT	Master of Science in Computer Information Technology
MSCJ	Master of Science in Criminal Justice
MSCJA	Master of Science in Criminal Justice Administration
MSCJS	Master of Science in Crime and Justice Studies
MSCLS	Master of Science in Clinical Laboratory Studies
MSCM	Master of Science in Church Management
	Master of Science in Conflict Management
	Master of Science in Construction Management
	Master of Supply Chain Management
MSCNU	Master of Science in Clinical Nutrition
MSCP	Master of Science in Clinical Psychology
	Master of Science in Community Psychology
	Master of Science in Computer Engineering
	Master of Science in Counseling Psychology
MSCPE	Master of Science in Computer Engineering
MSCPharm	Master of Science in Pharmacy
MSCR	Master of Science in Clinical Research
MSCRP	Master of Science in City and Regional Planning
	Master of Science in Community and Regional Planning
MSCS	Master of Science in Clinical Science
	Master of Science in Computer Science
	Master of Science in Cyber Security
MSCSD	Master of Science in Communication Sciences and Disorders
MSCSE	Master of Science in Computer Science and Engineering
MSCTE	Master of Science in Career and Technical Education
MSD	Master of Science in Dentistry
	Master of Science in Design
	Master of Science in Dietetics
MSE	Master of Science Education
	Master of Science in Economics
	Master of Science in Education
	Master of Science in Engineering
	Master of Science in Engineering Management
	Master of Software Engineering
	Master of Special Education
	Master of Structural Engineering
MSECE	Master of Science in Electrical and Computer Engineering
MSED	Master of Sustainable Economic Development
MSEE	Master of Science in Electrical Engineering
	Master of Science in Environmental Engineering
MSEH	Master of Science in Environmental Health
MSEL	Master of Science in Educational Leadership
MSEM	Master of Science in Engineering Management
	Master of Science in Engineering Mechanics
	Master of Science in Environmental Management
MSENE	Master of Science in Environmental Engineering
MSEO	Master of Science in Electro-Optics
MSEP	Master of Science in Economic Policy
MSES	Master of Science in Embedded Software Engineering
	Master of Science in Engineering Science
	Master of Science in Environmental Science
	Master of Science in Environmental Studies
	Master of Science in Exercise Science
MSET	Master of Science in Educational Technology
	Master of Science in Engineering Technology
MSEV	Master of Science in Environmental Engineering
MSF	Master of Science in Finance
	Master of Science in Forestry
	Master of Spiritual Formation
MSFA	Master of Science in Financial Analysis
MSFCS	Master of Science in Family and Consumer Science
MSFE	Master of Science in Financial Engineering
MSFM	Master of Sustainable Forest Management
MSFOR	Master of Science in Forestry
MSFP	Master of Science in Financial Planning
MSFS	Master of Science in Financial Sciences
	Master of Science in Forensic Science
MSFSB	Master of Science in Financial Services and Banking
MSFT	Master of Science in Family Therapy
MSGC	Master of Science in Genetic Counseling
MSH	Master of Science in Health
	Master of Science in Hospice
MSHA	Master of Science in Health Administration
MSHCA	Master of Science in Health Care Administration
MSHCI	Master of Science in Human Computer Interaction
MSHCPM	Master of Science in Health Care Policy and Management
MSHE	Master of Science in Health Education
MSHES	Master of Science in Human Environmental Sciences
MSHFID	Master of Science in Human Factors in Information Design
MSHFS	Master of Science in Human Factors and Systems
MSHI	Master of Science in Health Informatics
MSHP	Master of Science in Health Professions
	Master of Science in Health Promotion
MSHR	Master of Science in Human Resources
MSHRL	Master of Science in Human Resource Leadership
MSHRM	Master of Science in Human Resource Management
MSHROD	Master of Science in Human Resources and Organizational Development
MSHS	Master of Science in Health Science
	Master of Science in Health Services
	Master of Science in Homeland Security
MSI	Master of Science in Information
	Master of Science in Instruction
	Master of System Integration
MSIA	Master of Science in Industrial Administration
	Master of Science in Information Assurance
MSIB	Master of Science in International Business
MSIDM	Master of Science in Interior Design and Merchandising
MSIE	Master of Science in Industrial Engineering
	Master of Science in International Economics

MSIEM	Master of Science in Information Engineering and Management
MSIID	Master of Science in Information and Instructional Design
MSIM	Master of Science in Information Management
	Master of Science in International Management
MSIMC	Master of Science in Integrated Marketing Communications
MSIR	Master of Science in Industrial Relations
MSIS	Master of Science in Information Science
	Master of Science in Information Studies
	Master of Science in Information Systems
	Master of Science in Interdisciplinary Studies
MSISE	Master of Science in Infrastructure Systems Engineering
MSISM	Master of Science in Information Systems Management
MSISPM	Master of Science in Information Security Policy and Management
MSIST	Master of Science in Information Systems Technology
MSIT	Master of Science in Industrial Technology
	Master of Science in Information Technology
	Master of Science in Instructional Technology
MSITM	Master of Science in Information Technology Management
MSJ	Master of Science in Journalism
	Master of Science in Jurisprudence
MSJC	Master of Social Justice and Criminology
MSJE	Master of Science in Jewish Education
MSJFP	Master of Science in Juvenile Forensic Psychology
MSJJ	Master of Science in Juvenile Justice
MSJPS	Master of Science in Justice and Public Safety
MSJS	Master of Science in Jewish Studies
MSL	Master of School Leadership
	Master of Science in Leadership
	Master of Science in Limnology
	Master of Strategic Leadership
	Master of Studies in Law
MSLA	Master of Science in Legal Administration
MSLFS	Master of Science in Life Sciences
MSLP	Master of Speech-Language Pathology
MSLS	Master of Science in Library Science
MSLSCM	Master of Science in Logistics and Supply Chain Management
MSLT	Master of Second Language Teaching
MSM	Master of Sacred Ministry
	Master of Sacred Music
	Master of School Mathematics
	Master of Science in Management
	Master of Science in Medicine
	Master of Science in Organization Management
	Master of Security Management
MSMA	Master of Science in Marketing Analysis
MSMAE	Master of Science in Materials Engineering
MSMC	Master of Science in Mass Communications
MSME	Master of Science in Mathematics Education
	Master of Science in Mechanical Engineering
MSMFT	Master of Science in Marriage and Family Therapy
MSMHC	Master of Science in Mental Health Counseling
MSMIS	Master of Science in Management Information Systems
MSMIT	Master of Science in Management and Information Technology
MSMLS	Master of Science in Medical Laboratory Science
MSMOT	Master of Science in Management of Technology
MSMP	Master of Science in Medical Physics

MSMS	Master of Science in Management Science
	Master of Science in Marine Science
	Master of Science in Medical Sciences
MSMSE	Master of Science in Manufacturing Systems Engineering
	Master of Science in Material Science and Engineering
	Master of Science in Mathematics and Science Education
MSMT	Master of Science in Management and Technology
MSMus	Master of Sacred Music
MSN	Master of Science in Nursing
MSNA	Master of Science in Nurse Anesthesia
MSNE	Master of Science in Nuclear Engineering
MSNED	Master of Science in Nurse Education
MSNM	Master of Science in Nonprofit Management
MSNS	Master of Science in Natural Science
	Master of Science in Nutritional Science
MSOD	Master of Science in Organization Development
	Master of Science in Organizational Development
MSOEE	Master of Science in Outdoor and Environmental Education
MSOES	Master of Science in Occupational Ergonomics and Safety
MSOH	Master of Science in Occupational Health
MSOL	Master of Science in Organizational Leadership
MSOM	Master of Science in Operations Management
	Master of Science in Oriental Medicine
MSOR	Master of Science in Operations Research
MSOT	Master of Science in Occupational Technology
	Master of Science in Occupational Therapy
MSP	Master of Science in Pharmacy
	Master of Science in Planning
	Master of Speech Pathology
MSPA	Master of Science in Physician Assistant
	Master of Science in Professional Accountancy
MSPAS	Master of Science in Physician Assistant Studies
MSPC	Master of Science in Professional Communications
MSPE	Master of Science in Petroleum Engineering
MSPH	Master of Science in Public Health
MSPHR	Master of Science in Pharmacy
MSPM	Master of Science in Professional Management
	Master of Science in Project Management
MSPNGE	Master of Science in Petroleum and Natural Gas Engineering
MSPO	Master of Science in Prosthetics and Orthotics
MSPPM	Master of Science in Public Policy and Management
MSPS	Master of Science in Pharmaceutical Science
	Master of Science in Political Science
	Master of Science in Psychological Services
MSPT	Master of Science in Physical Therapy
MSpVM	Master of Specialized Veterinary Medicine
MSR	Master of Science in Radiology
	Master of Science in Reading
MSRA	Master of Science in Recreation Administration
MSRE	Master of Science in Real Estate
	Master of Science in Religious Education
MSRED	Master of Science in Real Estate Development
	Master of Sustainable Real Estate Development
MSRLS	Master of Science in Recreation and Leisure Studies
MSRM	Master of Science in Risk Management
MSRMP	Master of Science in Radiological Medical Physics
MSRS	Master of Science in Radiological Sciences
	Master of Science in Rehabilitation Science

MSS	Master of Security Studies
	Master of Social Science
	Master of Social Services
	Master of Software Systems
	Master of Sports Science
	Master of Strategic Studies
	Master's in Statistical Science
MSSA	Master of Science in Social Administration
MSSCM	Master of Science in Supply Chain Management
MSSD	Master of Arts in Software Driven Systems Design
	Master of Science in Sustainable Design
MSSE	Master of Science in Software Engineering
	Master of Science in Special Education
MSSEM	Master of Science in Systems and Engineering Management
MSSI	Master of Science in Security Informatics
	Master of Science in Strategic Intelligence
MSSL	Master of Science in School Leadership
	Master of Science in Strategic Leadership
MSSLP	Master of Science in Speech-Language Pathology
MSSM	Master of Science in Sports Medicine
MSSP	Master of Science in Social Policy
MSSPA	Master of Science in Student Personnel Administration
MSSS	Master of Science in Safety Science
	Master of Science in Systems Science
MSST	Master of Science in Security Technologies
MSSW	Master of Science in Social Work
MSSWE	Master of Science in Software Engineering
MST	Master of Science and Technology
	Master of Science in Taxation
	Master of Science in Teaching
	Master of Science in Technology
	Master of Science in Telecommunications
	Master of Science Teaching
MSTC	Master of Science in Technical Communication
	Master of Science in Telecommunications
MSTCM	Master of Science in Traditional Chinese Medicine
MSTE	Master of Science in Telecommunications Engineering
	Master of Science in Transportation Engineering
MSTL	Master of Science in Teacher Leadership
MSTM	Master of Science in Technology Management
	Master of Science in Transfusion Medicine
MSTOM	Master of Science in Traditional Oriental Medicine
MSUASE	Master of Science in Unmanned and Autonomous Systems Engineering
MSUD	Master of Science in Urban Design
MSUS	Master of Science in Urban Studies
MSW	Master of Social Work
MSWE	Master of Software Engineering
MSWREE	Master of Science in Water Resources and Environmental Engineering
MT	Master of Taxation
	Master of Teaching
	Master of Technology
	Master of Textiles
MTA	Master of Tax Accounting
	Master of Teaching Arts
	Master of Tourism Administration
MTCM	Master of Traditional Chinese Medicine
MTD	Master of Training and Development
MTE	Master in Educational Technology
MTESOL	Master in Teaching English to Speakers of Other Languages
MTHM	Master of Tourism and Hospitality Management
MTI	Master of Information Technology
MTID	Master of Tangible Interaction Design
MTL	Master of Talmudic Law
MTM	Master of Technology Management
	Master of Telecommunications Management
	Master of the Teaching of Mathematics
MTMH	Master of Tropical Medicine and Hygiene
MTMS	Master in Teaching Mathematics and Science
MTOM	Master of Traditional Oriental Medicine
MTPC	Master of Technical and Professional Communication
MTR	Master of Translational Research
MTS	Master of Theatre Studies
	Master of Theological Studies
MTWM	Master of Trust and Wealth Management
MTX	Master of Taxation
MUA	Master of Urban Affairs
MUCD	Master of Urban and Community Design
MUD	Master of Urban Design
MUDS	Master of Urban Design Studies
MUEP	Master of Urban and Environmental Planning
MUP	Master of Urban Planning
MUPDD	Master of Urban Planning, Design, and Development
MUPP	Master of Urban Planning and Policy
MUPRED	Master of Urban Planning and Real Estate Development
MURP	Master of Urban and Regional Planning
	Master of Urban and Rural Planning
MUS	Master of Urban Studies
MUSA	Master of Urban Spatial Analytics
MVP	Master of Voice Pedagogy
MVPH	Master of Veterinary Public Health
MVS	Master of Visual Studies
MWC	Master of Wildlife Conservation
MWM	Master of Water Management
MWPS	Master of Wood and Paper Science
MWR	Master of Water Resources
MWS	Master of Women's Studies
	Master of Worship Studies
MWSc	Master of Wildlife Science
MZS	Master of Zoological Science
Nav Arch	Naval Architecture
Naval E	Naval Engineer
ND	Doctor of Naturopathic Medicine
NE	Nuclear Engineer
Nuc E	Nuclear Engineer
OD	Doctor of Optometry
OTD	Doctor of Occupational Therapy
PBME	Professional Master of Biomedical Engineering
PC	Performer's Certificate
PD	Professional Diploma
PGC	Post-Graduate Certificate
PGD	Postgraduate Diploma
Ph L	Licentiate of Philosophy
Pharm D	Doctor of Pharmacy
PhD	Doctor of Philosophy
PhD Otol	Doctor of Philosophy in Otolaryngology
PhD Surg	Doctor of Philosophy in Surgery
PhDEE	Doctor of Philosophy in Electrical Engineering
PMBA	Professional Master of Business Administration
PMC	Post Master Certificate
PMD	Post-Master's Diploma
PMS	Professional Master of Science
	Professional Master's
Post-Doctoral MS	Post-Doctoral Master of Science
Post-MSN Certificate	Post-Master of Science in Nursing Certificate
PPDPT	Postprofessional Doctor of Physical Therapy

ABBREVIATIONS USED IN THE GUIDES

Pro-MS	Professional Science Master's
Professional MA	Professional Master of Arts
Professional MBA	Professional Master of Business Administration
Professional MS	Professional Master of Science
PSM	Professional Master of Science
	Professional Science Master's
Psy D	Doctor of Psychology
Psy M	Master of Psychology
Psy S	Specialist in Psychology
Psya D	Doctor of Psychoanalysis
S Psy S	Specialist in Psychological Services
Sc D	Doctor of Science
Sc M	Master of Science
SCCT	Specialist in Community College Teaching
ScDPT	Doctor of Physical Therapy Science
SD	Doctor of Science
	Specialist Degree
SJD	Doctor of Juridical Sciences
SLPD	Doctor of Speech-Language Pathology
SM	Master of Science
SM Arch S	Master of Science in Architectural Studies

SMACT	Master of Science in Art, Culture and Technology
SMBT	Master of Science in Building Technology
SP	Specialist Degree
Sp Ed	Specialist in Education
Sp LIS	Specialist in Library and Information Science
SPA	Specialist in Arts
Spec	Specialist's Certificate
Spec M	Specialist in Music
Spt	Specialist Degree
SSP	Specialist in School Psychology
STB	Bachelor of Sacred Theology
STD	Doctor of Sacred Theology
STL	Licentiate of Sacred Theology
STM	Master of Sacred Theology
TDPT	Transitional Doctor of Physical Therapy
Th D	Doctor of Theology
Th M	Master of Theology
TOTD	Transitional Doctor of Occupational Therapy
VMD	Doctor of Veterinary Medicine
WEMBA	Weekend Executive Master of Business Administration
XMA	Executive Master of Arts

INDEXES

Displays and Close-Ups

Directories and Subject Areas

Following is an alphabetical listing of directories and subject areas. Also listed are cross-references for subject area names not used in the directory structure of the guides, for example, "City and Regional Planning (*see* Urban and Regional Planning)."

Graduate Programs in the Humanities, Arts & Social Sciences

Addictions/Substance Abuse Counseling
Administration (*see* Arts Administration; Public Administration)
African-American Studies
African Languages and Literatures (*see* African Studies)
African Studies
Agribusiness (*see* Agricultural Economics and Agribusiness)
Agricultural Economics and Agribusiness
Alcohol Abuse Counseling (*see* Addictions/Substance Abuse Counseling)
American Indian/Native American Studies
American Studies
Anthropology
Applied Arts and Design—General
Applied Behavior Analysis
Applied Economics
Applied History (*see* Public History)
Applied Psychology
Applied Social Research
Arabic (*see* Near and Middle Eastern Languages)
Arab Studies (*see* Near and Middle Eastern Studies)
Archaeology
Architectural History
Architecture
Archives Administration (*see* Public History)
Area and Cultural Studies (*see* African-American Studies; African Studies; American Indian/Native American Studies; American Studies; Asian-American Studies; Asian Studies; Canadian Studies; Cultural Studies; East European and Russian Studies; Ethnic Studies; Folklore; Gender Studies; Hispanic Studies; Holocaust Studies; Jewish Studies; Latin American Studies; Near and Middle Eastern Studies; Northern Studies; Pacific Area/ Pacific Rim Studies; Western European Studies; Women's Studies)
Art/Fine Arts
Art History
Arts Administration
Arts Journalism
Art Therapy
Asian-American Studies
Asian Languages
Asian Studies
Behavioral Sciences (*see* Psychology)
Bible Studies (*see* Religion; Theology)
Biological Anthropology
Black Studies (*see* African-American Studies)
Broadcasting (*see* Communication; Film, Television, and Video Production)
Broadcast Journalism
Building Science
Canadian Studies
Celtic Languages
Ceramics (*see* Art/Fine Arts)
Child and Family Studies
Child Development
Chinese
Chinese Studies (*see* Asian Languages; Asian Studies)
Christian Studies (*see* Missions and Missiology; Religion; Theology)
Cinema (*see* Film, Television, and Video Production)
City and Regional Planning (*see* Urban and Regional Planning)
Classical Languages and Literatures (*see* Classics)
Classics

Clinical Psychology
Clothing and Textiles
Cognitive Psychology (*see* Psychology—General; Cognitive Sciences)
Cognitive Sciences
Communication—General
Community Affairs (*see* Urban and Regional Planning; Urban Studies)
Community Planning (*see* Architecture; Environmental Design; Urban and Regional Planning; Urban Design; Urban Studies)
Community Psychology (*see* Social Psychology)
Comparative and Interdisciplinary Arts
Comparative Literature
Composition (*see* Music)
Computer Art and Design
Conflict Resolution and Mediation/Peace Studies
Consumer Economics
Corporate and Organizational Communication
Corrections (*see* Criminal Justice and Criminology)
Counseling (*see* Counseling Psychology; Pastoral Ministry and Counseling)
Counseling Psychology
Crafts (*see* Art/Fine Arts)
Creative Arts Therapies (*see* Art Therapy; Therapies—Dance, Drama, and Music)
Criminal Justice and Criminology
Cultural Anthropology
Cultural Studies
Dance
Decorative Arts
Demography and Population Studies
Design (*see* Applied Arts and Design; Architecture; Art/Fine Arts; Environmental Design; Graphic Design; Industrial Design; Interior Design; Textile Design; Urban Design)
Developmental Psychology
Diplomacy (*see* International Affairs)
Disability Studies
Drama Therapy (*see* Therapies—Dance, Drama, and Music)
Dramatic Arts (*see* Theater)
Drawing (*see* Art/Fine Arts)
Drug Abuse Counseling (*see* Addictions/Substance Abuse Counseling)
Drug and Alcohol Abuse Counseling (*see* Addictions/Substance Abuse Counseling)
East Asian Studies (*see* Asian Studies)
East European and Russian Studies
Economic Development
Economics
Educational Theater (*see* Theater; Therapies—Dance, Drama, and Music)
Emergency Management
English
Environmental Design
Ethics
Ethnic Studies
Ethnomusicology (*see* Music)
Experimental Psychology
Family and Consumer Sciences—General
Family Studies (*see* Child and Family Studies)
Family Therapy (*see* Child and Family Studies; Clinical Psychology; Counseling Psychology; Marriage and Family Therapy)
Filmmaking (*see* Film, Television, and Video Production)
Film Studies (*see* Film, Television, and Video Production)
Film, Television, and Video Production
Film, Television, and Video Theory and Criticism
Fine Arts (*see* Art/Fine Arts)
Folklore
Foreign Languages (*see* specific language)
Foreign Service (*see* International Affairs; International Development)
Forensic Psychology
Forensic Sciences
Forensics (*see* Speech and Interpersonal Communication)
French

Gender Studies
General Studies (*see* Liberal Studies)
Genetic Counseling
Geographic Information Systems
Geography
German
Gerontology
Graphic Design
Greek (*see* Classics)
Health Communication
Health Psychology
Hebrew (*see* Near and Middle Eastern Languages)
Hebrew Studies (*see* Jewish Studies)
Hispanic and Latin American Languages
Hispanic Studies
Historic Preservation
History
History of Art (*see* Art History)
History of Medicine
History of Science and Technology
Holocaust and Genocide Studies
Home Economics (*see* Family and Consumer Sciences—General)
Homeland Security
Household Economics, Sciences, and Management (*see* Family and Consumer Sciences—General)
Human Development
Humanities
Illustration
Industrial and Labor Relations
Industrial and Organizational Psychology
Industrial Design
Interdisciplinary Studies
Interior Design
International Affairs
International Development
International Economics
International Service (*see* International Affairs; International Development)
International Trade Policy
Internet and Interactive Multimedia
Interpersonal Communication (*see* Speech and Interpersonal Communication)
Interpretation (*see* Translation and Interpretation)
Islamic Studies (*see* Near and Middle Eastern Studies; Religion)
Italian
Japanese
Japanese Studies (*see* Asian Languages; Asian Studies; Japanese)
Jewelry (*see* Art/Fine Arts)
Jewish Studies
Journalism
Judaic Studies (*see* Jewish Studies; Religion)
Labor Relations (*see* Industrial and Labor Relations)
Landscape Architecture
Latin American Studies
Latin (*see* Classics)
Law Enforcement (*see* Criminal Justice and Criminology)
Liberal Studies
Lighting Design
Linguistics
Literature (*see* Classics; Comparative Literature; specific language)
Marriage and Family Therapy
Mass Communication
Media Studies
Medical Illustration
Medieval and Renaissance Studies
Metalsmithing (*see* Art/Fine Arts)
Middle Eastern Studies (*see* Near and Middle Eastern Studies)
Military and Defense Studies
Mineral Economics
Ministry (*see* Pastoral Ministry and Counseling; Theology)
Missions and Missiology
Motion Pictures (*see* Film, Television, and Video Production)
Museum Studies
Music
Musicology (*see* Music)
Music Therapy (*see* Therapies—Dance, Drama, and Music)

National Security
Native American Studies (*see* American Indian/Native American Studies)
Near and Middle Eastern Languages
Near and Middle Eastern Studies
Near Environment (*see* Family and Consumer Sciences)
Northern Studies
Organizational Psychology (*see* Industrial and Organizational Psychology)
Oriental Languages (*see* Asian Languages)
Oriental Studies (*see* Asian Studies)
Pacific Area/Pacific Rim Studies
Painting (*see* Art/Fine Arts)
Pastoral Ministry and Counseling
Philanthropic Studies
Philosophy
Photography
Playwriting (*see* Theater; Writing)
Policy Studies (*see* Public Policy)
Political Science
Population Studies (*see* Demography and Population Studies)
Portuguese
Printmaking (*see* Art/Fine Arts)
Product Design (*see* Industrial Design)
Psychoanalysis and Psychotherapy
Psychology—General
Public Administration
Public Affairs
Public History
Public Policy
Public Speaking (*see* Mass Communication; Rhetoric; Speech and Interpersonal Communication)
Publishing
Regional Planning (*see* Architecture; Urban and Regional Planning; Urban Design; Urban Studies)
Rehabilitation Counseling
Religion
Renaissance Studies (*see* Medieval and Renaissance Studies)
Rhetoric
Romance Languages
Romance Literatures (*see* Romance Languages)
Rural Planning and Studies
Rural Sociology
Russian
Scandinavian Languages
School Psychology
Sculpture (*see* Art/Fine Arts)
Security Administration (*see* Criminal Justice and Criminology)
Slavic Languages
Slavic Studies (*see* East European and Russian Studies; Slavic Languages)
Social Psychology
Social Sciences
Sociology
Southeast Asian Studies (*see* Asian Studies)
Soviet Studies (*see* East European and Russian Studies; Russian)
Spanish
Speech and Interpersonal Communication
Sport Psychology
Studio Art (*see* Art/Fine Arts)
Substance Abuse Counseling (*see* Addictions/Substance Abuse Counseling)
Survey Methodology
Sustainable Development
Technical Communication
Technical Writing
Telecommunications (*see* Film, Television, and Video Production)
Television (*see* Film, Television, and Video Production)
Textile Design
Textiles (*see* Clothing and Textiles; Textile Design)
Thanatology
Theater
Theater Arts (*see* Theater)
Theology
Therapies—Dance, Drama, and Music
Translation and Interpretation

Transpersonal and Humanistic Psychology
Urban and Regional Planning
Urban Design
Urban Planning (*see* Architecture; Urban and Regional Planning;
    Urban Design; Urban Studies)
Urban Studies
Video (*see* Film, Television, and Video Production)
Visual Arts (*see* Applied Arts and Design; Art/Fine Arts; Film,
    Television, and Video Production; Graphic Design; Illustration;
    Photography)
Western European Studies
Women's Studies
World Wide Web (*see* Internet and Interactive Multimedia)
Writing

Graduate Programs in the Biological/Biomedical Sciences & Health-Related Medical Professions

Acupuncture and Oriental Medicine
Acute Care/Critical Care Nursing Administration (*see* Health Services
    Management and Hospital Administration; Nursing and Healthcare
    Administration; Pharmaceutical Administration)
Adult Nursing
Advanced Practice Nursing (*see* Family Nurse Practitioner Studies)
Allied Health—General
Allied Health Professions (*see* Clinical Laboratory Sciences/Medical
    Technology; Clinical Research; Communication Disorders; Dental
    Hygiene; Emergency Medical Services; Occupational Therapy;
    Physical Therapy; Physician Assistant Studies; Rehabilitation
    Sciences)
Allopathic Medicine
Anatomy
Anesthesiologist Assistant Studies
Animal Behavior
Bacteriology
Behavioral Sciences (*see* Biopsychology; Neuroscience; Zoology)
Biochemistry
Bioethics
Biological and Biomedical Sciences—General Biological Chemistry
    (*see* Biochemistry)
Biological Oceanography (*see* Marine Biology)
Biophysics
Biopsychology
Botany
Breeding (*see* Botany; Plant Biology; Genetics)
Cancer Biology/Oncology
Cardiovascular Sciences
Cell Biology
Cellular Physiology (*see* Cell Biology; Physiology)
Child-Care Nursing (*see* Maternal and Child/Neonatal Nursing)
Chiropractic
Clinical Laboratory Sciences/Medical Technology
Clinical Research
Community Health
Community Health Nursing
Computational Biology
Conservation (*see* Conservation Biology; Environmental Biology)
Conservation Biology
Crop Sciences (*see* Botany; Plant Biology)
Cytology (*see* Cell Biology)
Dental and Oral Surgery (*see* Oral and Dental Sciences)
Dental Assistant Studies (*see* Dental Hygiene)
Dental Hygiene
Dental Services (*see* Dental Hygiene)
Dentistry
Developmental Biology Dietetics (*see* Nutrition)
Ecology
Embryology (*see* Developmental Biology)
Emergency Medical Services
Endocrinology (*see* Physiology)
Entomology

Environmental Biology
Environmental and Occupational Health
Epidemiology
Evolutionary Biology
Family Nurse Practitioner Studies
Foods (*see* Nutrition)
Forensic Nursing
Genetics
Genomic Sciences
Gerontological Nursing
Health Physics/Radiological Health
Health Promotion
Health-Related Professions (*see* individual allied health professions)
Health Services Management and Hospital Administration
Health Services Research
Histology (*see* Anatomy; Cell Biology)
HIV/AIDS Nursing
Hospice Nursing
Hospital Administration (*see* Health Services Management and
    Hospital Administration)
Human Genetics
Immunology
Industrial Hygiene
Infectious Diseases
International Health
Laboratory Medicine (*see* Clinical Laboratory Sciences/Medical
    Technology; Immunology; Microbiology; Pathology)
Life Sciences (*see* Biological and Biomedical Sciences)
Marine Biology
Maternal and Child Health
Maternal and Child/Neonatal Nursing
Medical Imaging
Medical Microbiology
Medical Nursing (*see* Medical/Surgical Nursing)
Medical Physics
Medical/Surgical Nursing
Medical Technology (*see* Clinical Laboratory Sciences/Medical
    Technology)
Medical Sciences (*see* Biological and Biomedical Sciences)
Medical Science Training Programs (*see* Biological and Biomedical
    Sciences)
Medicinal and Pharmaceutical Chemistry
Medicinal Chemistry (*see* Medicinal and Pharmaceutical Chemistry)
Medicine (*see* Allopathic Medicine; Naturopathic Medicine;
    Osteopathic Medicine; Podiatric Medicine)
Microbiology
Midwifery (*see* Nurse Midwifery)
Molecular Biology
Molecular Biophysics
Molecular Genetics
Molecular Medicine
Molecular Pathogenesis
Molecular Pathology
Molecular Pharmacology
Molecular Physiology
Molecular Toxicology
Naturopathic Medicine
Neural Sciences (*see* Biopsychology; Neurobiology; Neuroscience)
Neurobiology
Neuroendocrinology (*see* Biopsychology; Neurobiology; Neuroscience;
    Physiology)
Neuropharmacology (*see* Biopsychology; Neurobiology; Neuroscience;
    Pharmacology)
Neurophysiology (*see* Biopsychology; Neurobiology; Neuroscience;
    Physiology)
Neuroscience
Nuclear Medical Technology (*see* Clinical Laboratory Sciences/
    Medical Technology)
Nurse Anesthesia
Nurse Midwifery
Nurse Practitioner Studies (*see* Family Nurse Practitioner Studies)
Nursing Administration (*see* Nursing and Healthcare Administration)
Nursing and Healthcare Administration
Nursing Education
Nursing—General
Nursing Informatics

Nutrition
Occupational Health (*see* Environmental and Occupational Health; Occupational Health Nursing)
Occupational Health Nursing
Occupational Therapy
Oncology (*see* Cancer Biology/Oncology)
Oncology Nursing
Optometry
Oral and Dental Sciences
Oral Biology (*see* Oral and Dental Sciences)
Oral Pathology (*see* Oral and Dental Sciences)
Organismal Biology (*see* Biological and Biomedical Sciences; Zoology)
Oriental Medicine and Acupuncture (*see* Acupuncture and Oriental Medicine)
Orthodontics (*see* Oral and Dental Sciences)
Osteopathic Medicine
Parasitology
Pathobiology
Pathology
Pediatric Nursing
Pedontics (*see* Oral and Dental Sciences)
Perfusion
Pharmaceutical Administration
Pharmaceutical Chemistry (*see* Medicinal and Pharmaceutical Chemistry)
Pharmaceutical Sciences
Pharmacology
Pharmacy
Photobiology of Cells and Organelles (*see* Botany; Cell Biology; Plant Biology)
Physical Therapy
Physician Assistant Studies
Physiological Optics (*see* Vision Sciences)
Podiatric Medicine
Preventive Medicine (*see* Community Health and Public Health)
Physiological Optics (*see* Physiology)
Physiology
Plant Biology
Plant Molecular Biology
Plant Pathology
Plant Physiology
Pomology (*see* Botany; Plant Biology)
Psychiatric Nursing
Public Health—General
Public Health Nursing (*see* Community Health Nursing)
Psychiatric Nursing
Psychobiology (*see* Biopsychology)
Psychopharmacology (*see* Biopsychology; Neuroscience; Pharmacology)
Radiation Biology
Radiological Health (*see* Health Physics/Radiological Health)
Rehabilitation Nursing
Rehabilitation Sciences
Rehabilitation Therapy (*see* Physical Therapy)
Reproductive Biology
School Nursing
Sociobiology (*see* Evolutionary Biology)
Structural Biology
Surgical Nursing (*see* Medical/Surgical Nursing)
Systems Biology
Teratology
Therapeutics
Theoretical Biology (*see* Biological and Biomedical Sciences)
Therapeutics (*see* Pharmaceutical Sciences; Pharmacology; Pharmacy)
Toxicology
Transcultural Nursing
Translational Biology
Tropical Medicine (*see* Parasitology)
Veterinary Medicine
Veterinary Sciences
Virology
Vision Sciences
Wildlife Biology (*see* Zoology)
Women's Health Nursing
Zoology

Graduate Programs in the Physical Sciences, Mathematics, Agricultural Sciences, the Environment & Natural Resources

Acoustics
Agricultural Sciences
Agronomy and Soil Sciences
Analytical Chemistry
Animal Sciences
Applied Mathematics
Applied Physics
Applied Statistics
Aquaculture
Astronomy
Astrophysical Sciences (*see* Astrophysics; Atmospheric Sciences; Meteorology; Planetary and Space Sciences)
Astrophysics
Atmospheric Sciences
Biological Oceanography (*see* Marine Affairs; Marine Sciences; Oceanography)
Biomathematics
Biometry
Biostatistics
Chemical Physics
Chemistry
Computational Sciences
Condensed Matter Physics
Dairy Science (*see* Animal Sciences)
Earth Sciences (*see* Geosciences)
Environmental Management and Policy
Environmental Sciences
Environmental Studies (*see* Environmental Management and Policy)
Experimental Statistics (*see* Statistics)
Fish, Game, and Wildlife Management
Food Science and Technology
Forestry
General Science (*see* specific topics)
Geochemistry
Geodetic Sciences
Geological Engineering (*see* Geology)
Geological Sciences (*see* Geology)
Geology
Geophysical Fluid Dynamics (*see* Geophysics)
Geophysics
Geosciences
Horticulture
Hydrogeology
Hydrology
Inorganic Chemistry
Limnology
Marine Affairs
Marine Geology
Marine Sciences
Marine Studies (*see* Marine Affairs; Marine Geology; Marine Sciences; Oceanography)
Mathematical and Computational Finance
Mathematical Physics
Mathematical Statistics (*see* Applied Statistics; Statistics)
Mathematics
Meteorology
Mineralogy
Natural Resource Management (*see* Environmental Management and Policy; Natural Resources)
Natural Resources
Nuclear Physics (*see* Physics)
Ocean Engineering (*see* Marine Affairs; Marine Geology; Marine Sciences; Oceanography)
Oceanography
Optical Sciences
Optical Technologies (*see* Optical Sciences)
Optics (*see* Applied Physics; Optical Sciences; Physics)
Organic Chemistry

Paleontology
Paper Chemistry (*see* Chemistry)
Photonics
Physical Chemistry
Physics
Planetary and Space Sciences
Plant Sciences
Plasma Physics
Poultry Science (*see* Animal Sciences)
Radiological Physics (*see* Physics)
Range Management (*see* Range Science)
Range Science
Resource Management (*see* Environmental Management and Policy; Natural Resources)
Solid-Earth Sciences (*see* Geosciences)
Space Sciences (*see* Planetary and Space Sciences)
Statistics
Theoretical Chemistry
Theoretical Physics
Viticulture and Enology
Water Resources

Graduate Programs in Engineering & Applied Sciences

Aeronautical Engineering (*see* Aerospace/Aeronautical Engineering)
Aerospace/Aeronautical Engineering
Aerospace Studies (*see* Aerospace/Aeronautical Engineering)
Agricultural Engineering
Applied Mechanics (*see* Mechanics)
Applied Science and Technology
Architectural Engineering
Artificial Intelligence/Robotics
Astronautical Engineering (*see* Aerospace/Aeronautical Engineering)
Automotive Engineering
Aviation
Biochemical Engineering
Bioengineering
Bioinformatics
Biological Engineering (*see* Bioengineering)
Biomedical Engineering
Biosystems Engineering
Biotechnology
Ceramic Engineering (*see* Ceramic Sciences and Engineering)
Ceramic Sciences and Engineering
Ceramics (*see* Ceramic Sciences and Engineering)
Chemical Engineering
Civil Engineering
Computer and Information Systems Security
Computer Engineering
Computer Science
Computing Technology (*see* Computer Science)
Construction Engineering
Construction Management
Database Systems
Electrical Engineering
Electronic Materials
Electronics Engineering (*see* Electrical Engineering)
Energy and Power Engineering
Energy Management and Policy
Engineering and Applied Sciences
Engineering and Public Affairs (*see* Technology and Public Policy)
Engineering and Public Policy (*see* Energy Management and Policy; Technology and Public Policy)
Engineering Design
Engineering Management
Engineering Mechanics (*see* Mechanics)
Engineering Metallurgy (*see* Metallurgical Engineering and Metallurgy)
Engineering Physics
Environmental Design (*see* Environmental Engineering)
Environmental Engineering
Ergonomics and Human Factors

Financial Engineering
Fire Protection Engineering
Food Engineering (*see* Agricultural Engineering)
Game Design and Development
Gas Engineering (*see* Petroleum Engineering)
Geological Engineering
Geophysics Engineering (*see* Geological Engineering)
Geotechnical Engineering
Hazardous Materials Management
Health Informatics
Health Systems (*see* Safety Engineering; Systems Engineering)
Highway Engineering (*see* Transportation and Highway Engineering)
Human-Computer Interaction
Human Factors (*see* Ergonomics and Human Factors)
Hydraulics
Hydrology (*see* Water Resources Engineering)
Industrial Engineering (*see* Industrial/Management Engineering)
Industrial/Management Engineering
Information Science
Internet Engineering
Macromolecular Science (*see* Polymer Science and Engineering)
Management Engineering (*see* Engineering Management; Industrial/Management Engineering)
Management of Technology
Manufacturing Engineering
Marine Engineering (*see* Civil Engineering)
Materials Engineering
Materials Sciences
Mechanical Engineering
Mechanics
Medical Informatics
Metallurgical Engineering and Metallurgy
Metallurgy (*see* Metallurgical Engineering and Metallurgy)
Mineral/Mining Engineering
Modeling and Simulation
Nanotechnology
Nuclear Engineering
Ocean Engineering
Operations Research
Paper and Pulp Engineering
Petroleum Engineering
Pharmaceutical Engineering
Plastics Engineering (*see* Polymer Science and Engineering)
Polymer Science and Engineering
Public Policy (*see* Energy Management and Policy; Technology and Public Policy)
Reliability Engineering
Robotics (*see* Artificial Intelligence/Robotics)
Safety Engineering
Software Engineering
Solid-State Sciences (*see* Materials Sciences)
Structural Engineering
Surveying Science and Engineering
Systems Analysis (*see* Systems Engineering)
Systems Engineering
Systems Science
Technology and Public Policy
Telecommunications
Telecommunications Management
Textile Sciences and Engineering
Textiles (*see* Textile Sciences and Engineering)
Transportation and Highway Engineering
Urban Systems Engineering (*see* Systems Engineering)
Waste Management (*see* Hazardous Materials Management)
Water Resources Engineering

Graduate Programs in Business, Education, Information Studies, Law & Social Work

Accounting
Actuarial Science

Adult Education
Advertising and Public Relations
Agricultural Education
Alcohol Abuse Counseling (*see* Counselor Education)
Archival Management and Studies
Art Education
Athletics Administration (*see* Kinesiology and Movement Studies)
Athletic Training and Sports Medicine
Audiology (*see* Communication Disorders)
Aviation Management
Banking (*see* Finance and Banking)
Business Administration and Management—General
Business Education
Communication Disorders
Community College Education
Computer Education
Continuing Education (*see* Adult Education)
Counseling (*see* Counselor Education)
Counselor Education
Curriculum and Instruction
Developmental Education
Distance Education Development
Drug Abuse Counseling (*see* Counselor Education)
Early Childhood Education
Educational Leadership and Administration
Educational Measurement and Evaluation
Educational Media/Instructional Technology
Educational Policy
Educational Psychology
Education—General
Education of the Blind (*see* Special Education)
Education of the Deaf (*see* Special Education)
Education of the Gifted
Education of the Hearing Impaired (*see* Special Education)
Education of the Learning Disabled (*see* Special Education)
Education of the Mentally Retarded (*see* Special Education)
Education of the Physically Handicapped (*see* Special Education)
Education of Students with Severe/Multiple Disabilities
Education of the Visually Handicapped (*see* Special Education)
Electronic Commerce
Elementary Education
English as a Second Language
English Education
Entertainment Management
Entrepreneurship
Environmental Education
Environmental Law
Exercise and Sports Science
Exercise Physiology (*see* Kinesiology and Movement Studies)
Facilities and Entertainment Management
Finance and Banking
Food Services Management (*see* Hospitality Management)
Foreign Languages Education
Foundations and Philosophy of Education
Guidance and Counseling (*see* Counselor Education)
Health Education
Health Law
Hearing Sciences (*see* Communication Disorders)
Higher Education
Home Economics Education
Hospitality Management
Hotel Management (*see* Travel and Tourism)
Human Resources Development
Human Resources Management
Human Services
Industrial Administration (*see* Industrial and Manufacturing Management)
Industrial and Manufacturing Management
Industrial Education (*see* Vocational and Technical Education)
Information Studies
Instructional Technology (*see* Educational Media/Instructional Technology)
Insurance
Intellectual Property Law
International and Comparative Education
International Business

International Commerce (*see* International Business)
International Economics (*see* International Business)
International Trade (*see* International Business)
Investment and Securities (*see* Business Administration and Management; Finance and Banking; Investment Management)
Investment Management
Junior College Education (*see* Community College Education)
Kinesiology and Movement Studies
Law
Legal and Justice Studies
Leisure Services (*see* Recreation and Park Management)
Leisure Studies
Library Science
Logistics
Management (*see* Business Administration and Management)
Management Information Systems
Management Strategy and Policy
Marketing
Marketing Research
Mathematics Education
Middle School Education
Movement Studies (*see* Kinesiology and Movement Studies)
Multilingual and Multicultural Education
Museum Education
Music Education
Nonprofit Management
Nursery School Education (*see* Early Childhood Education)
Occupational Education (*see* Vocational and Technical Education)
Organizational Behavior
Organizational Management
Parks Administration (*see* Recreation and Park Management)
Personnel (*see* Human Resources Development; Human Resources Management; Organizational Behavior; Organizational Management; Student Affairs)
Philosophy of Education (*see* Foundations and Philosophy of Education)
Physical Education
Project Management
Public Relations (*see* Advertising and Public Relations)
Quality Management
Quantitative Analysis
Reading Education
Real Estate
Recreation and Park Management
Recreation Therapy (*see* Recreation and Park Management)
Religious Education
Remedial Education (*see* Special Education)
Restaurant Administration (*see* Hospitality Management)
Science Education
Secondary Education
Social Sciences Education
Social Studies Education (*see* Social Sciences Education)
Social Work
Special Education
Speech-Language Pathology and Audiology (*see* Communication Disorders)
Sports Management
Sports Medicine (*see* Athletic Training and Sports Medicine)
Sports Psychology and Sociology (*see* Kinesiology and Movement Studies)
Student Affairs
Substance Abuse Counseling (*see* Counselor Education)
Supply Chain Management
Sustainability Management
Systems Management (*see* Management Information Systems)
Taxation
Teacher Education (*see* specific subject areas)
Teaching English as a Second Language (*see* English as a Second Language)
Technical Education (*see* Vocational and Technical Education)
Transportation Management
Travel and Tourism
Urban Education
Vocational and Technical Education
Vocational Counseling (*see* Counselor Education)

Directories and Subject Areas in this Book

NOTES

NOTES

NOTES